Key to Concordance

Entry Word and Context Line

ART

And snatch a Grace beyond the Reach of Art, ... 1.EOC.155.258

Identifier information

1. Volume of Twickenham edition (Vol. 1).
2. Poem designation (*Essay on Criticism*).
3. Line number (155).
4. Page number in Twickenham edition (258).

Line number for variant:

Versions of line 76 from two other editions

1.EOC.76A.247

1.EOC.76B.247

Lines inserted in another edition

1.EOC.160Z1.258

1.EOC.160Z2.258

Alphabetization of Entry Words

In each alphabetical division the computer arrangement of Entry Words gives precedence to punctuated forms in the following order:

Accented letter (acute, circumflex, diaeresis, grave, and cedilla)

Left angle bracket

Hyphen

Asterisk

Apostrophe

Thus, *Aëtion*, *a-bed*, and *a'ter* precede *Aaron*; *S*z* comes before *S'il*; *D'Urfy* is at the beginning of the D's and *Durfy* near the end.

The computer also makes certain modifications in the entry words themselves, omitting the initial apostrophe (e.g., in *'sdeath*), square brackets, italics, and the ligature form of *ae* and *oe* (but these details are retained in the quoted lines).

For a list of Entry Words, see Alphabetical List of Word Frequencies, I, xxxv. A guide to alternate spellings will be found on page I, xvii.

For other primary aids see:

Note to Users, I, ix

Corrections, Additions, and Explanatory Notes, I, xxv

A Concordance to the Poems
of Alexander Pope

Alexander Pope (1688-1744)

*Portrait by Jonathan Richardson. The Beinecke Rare Book and
Manuscript Library, Yale University.*

A Concordance to the Poems
of Alexander Pope

Compiled by

EMMETT G. BEDFORD, *Literary Editor*

University of Wisconsin-Parkside

and

ROBERT J. DILLIGAN, *Technical Editor*

University of Southern California

in Two Volumes Volume 2, N-Z

Gale Research Company, Book Tower,

Detroit, Michigan 48226

**Library of Congress
Cataloging in Publication Data**

Bedford, Emmett G
    A concordance to the poems of Alexander Pope.

    Based on the Twickenham ed. of the Poems of Alexander Pope.
      1. Pope, Alexander, 1688-1744--Concordances. I. Dilligan,
Robert J., joint author. II. Title.
PR3632.B4   821'.5   74-852
ISBN 0-8103-1008-2

Contents

*Concordance to the Poems
of Alexander Pope*

N-Z

NÔTRE
Jones and Le Nôtre have it not to give. ....3.Ep4.46.141.

NAÏS
His Mother was a *Naïs* of the Flood; ....Il.20.442.413.

NABAL
Abusive *Nabal* ow'd his forfeit Life ....2.ChJM.71.18.

NAEVIUS
Nor lets, like Nævius, ev'ry error pass, ...4.HS2.65.59.

NAIAD
From a fair *Naiad* and *Bucolion* sprung: ....Il.6.28.325.

NAIAD'S
In secret Woods he won the *Naiad's* Grace, ...Il.6.31.325.

NAIADS
The *Naiads* wept in ev'ry Watry Bow'r, ...1.PSu.7.72.
And to the *Naiads* flow'ry garlands brought, ...1.TrFD.18.386.

NAIL'D
But pierc'd his Foot, and nail'd it to the Plain. ....Il.11.482.55.
And nail'd it to the Eugh<Yew>: The wounded Hand ....Il.13.747.140.
From space to space, and nail'd the planks along; ....Od.5.322.187.

NAILS
And some have hammer'd Nails into their Brain, ...2.ChWB.408.77.
'Twere well if she would pare her Nails, ...6.14v(a).5.48.
An ignominious cross, the nails, the spear: ....6.25.6.77.
For not the Desk with silver Nails, ...6.58.9.171.

NAKED
The hollow Winds thro' naked Temples roar; ....1.W-F.68.156.
When Frosts have whiten'd all the naked Groves; ....1.W-F.126.162.
And leave inanimate the naked Wall; ....1.W-F.308.178.
And naked Youths and painted Chiefs admire ....1.W-F.405.192.
While naked Youth and painted Chiefs admire ....1.W-F.405A.192.
Whose naked Youth and painted Chiefs admire ....1.W-F.405B.192.
The *naked Nature* and the *living Grace*, ...1.EOC.294.272.
And on his naked Arm inflicts a Wound. ....1.TrES.114.454.
Here naked Rocks, and empty Wastes were seen, ...2.TemF.15.254.
A naked Lover bound and bleeding lies! ....2.ElAb.100.328.
And there a naked Leda with a Swan. ....3.Ep2.10A.49.
Is there, a naked Leda with a Swan. ....3.Ep2.10.49.
To draw the Naked is your true delight! ....3.Ep2.188.65.
The woods recede around the naked seat, ...3.Ep3.209.110.
Asleep and naked as an Indian lay, ...3.Ep3.361.123.
Me, naked me, to Posts, to Pumps they draw, ...4.HAdv.173.89.
In naked majesty great Dennis stands, ...5.DunA2.271.134.
In naked majesty Oldmixon stands, ...5.DunA2.271B.134.
While naked mourns the Dormitory wall, ...5.DunA3.323.189.
In naked majesty Oldmixon stands, ...5.DunB2.283.309.
But chief her shrine where naked Venus keeps, ...5.DunB4.307.374.
I tell the naked fact without disguise, ...5.DunB4.433.383.
Who ne'er saw naked Sword, or look'd in, *Plato*. ....6.41.44.114.
Whose Limbs unbury'd on the naked Shore, ...Il.1.5.82.
Beheld him mourning on the naked Shores, ...Il.1.472.110.
Th' insidious Foe the naked Town invade. ....Il.8.650.426.
Now soil'd with Dust, and naked to the Sky, ...Il.11.135.41.
And on his naked Arm inflicts a Wound. ....Il.12.468.98.
A naked, wand'ring, melancholy Ghost! ....Il.16.1035.283.
For naked now, despoil'd of Arms he lies; ....Il.17.133.292.
He too may haste the naked Corps to gain; ....Il.17.779.319.
His naked Corps: His Arms are *Hector's* Right. ....Il.18.24.324.
But can'st thou, naked, issue to the Plains? ....Il.18.167.330.

NAKED (CONTINUED)
Far from *Troy* Walls, and on a naked Coast. ....Il.18.302.336.
Must feast the Vultures on the naked Plains. ....Il.22.125.458.
A naked, wandring, melancholy Ghost! ....Il.22.458.474.
Have Dogs dismember'd on the naked Plains, ...Il.24.499.557.
And common turf, lie naked on the plain, ...Od.1.209.42.
And dogs had torn him on the naked plains. ....Od.3.323.102.
With naked strength, and plunge into the wave. ....Od.5.437.193.
All naked now, on heaving billows laid, ...Od.5.478.195.
Naked, defenceless on a foreign land. ....Od.6.214.220.
To cloath the naked, and thy way to guide— ....Od.6.235.221.
With naked force, and shoot along the wave, ...Od.7.361.254.
O'erwatch'd and batter'd in the naked bay. ....Od.9.84.306.
Lest to the<e> naked secret fraud be meant, ...Od.10.359.361.
His cold remains all naked to the sky ....Od.11.67.383.
My naked breast, and shot along the tide. ....Od.14.386.53.
And cloath the naked from th' inclement sky. ....Od.16.84.106.
All naked of their element, and bare, ...Od.22.428.309.

NAM'D
Thy Offspring, *Thames!* the fair *Lodona* nam'd, ...1.W-F.172.165.
E're *Cæsar* was, or *Newton* nam'd, ...4.HOde9.10.159.
I never nam'd—the Town's enquiring yet. ....4.EpS2.21.314.
Then thron'd in glass, and nam'd it CAROLINE: ....5.DunB4.409.382.
The Doctor, and He that's nam'd next to the Devil, ...6.42i.2.116.
And thence from *Simois* nam'd the lovely Boy. ....Il.4.549.247.
The Chiefs you nam'd, already, at his Call, ...Il.10.144.8.
A Chief there was, the brave *Euchenor* nam'd, ...Il.13.833.145.
Now worn with age, *Eurymedusa* nam'd: ....Od.7.10.233.
Ogygia nam'd, in *Ocean's* wat'ry arms: ....Od.7.328.252.
And nam'd *Ulysses* as the destin'd hand. ....Od.9.600.331.
A youth there was, *Elpenor* was he nam'd, ...Od.10.659.375.
Hence nam'd *Erratic* by the Gods above. ....Od.12.74.434.
She nam'd *Arnæus* on his natal day; ....Od.18.8.166.
(*Ctesippus* nam'd) this Lord *Ulysses* ey'd, ...Od.20.357.249.

NAMBY
And Namby Pamby be prefer'd for Wit! ....5.DunA3.322.188.

NAME
A Shepherd's Boy (he seeks no better Name) ....1.PSu.1.71.
That taught the Groves my *Rosalinda's* Name; ....1.PSu.42.75.
And *Delia's* Name and *Doris* fill'd the Grove. ....1.PAu.4.80.
Thro' Rocks and Caves the Name of *Delia* sounds, ...1.PAu.49.83.
Thro' Rocks and Caves the Name of Thyrsis sounds, ...1.PAu.49A.83.
Silent, or only to her Name replies, ...1.PWi.42.92.
Her Name with Pleasure once she taught the Shore, ...1.PWi.43.92.
Her Name alone the mournful *Eccho* sounds, ...1.PWi.42A.92.
Behold us kindly who your Name implore, ...1.PWi.75.94.
Thy Name, thy Honour, and thy Praise shall live! ....1.PWi.84.94.
Our haughty *Norman* boasts that barb'rous Name, ...1.W-F.63.155.
Still bears the Name the hapless Virgin bore, ...1.W-F.207.168.
First the fam'd Authors of his ancient Name, ...1.W-F.339.183.
And justly bear a Critick's noble Name, ...1.EOC.47.244.
Before *his* sacred Name flies ev'ry Fault, ...1.EOC.422.288.
Name a new *Play*, and he's the Poet's Friend, ...1.EOC.620.309.
At length, *Erasmus, that great, injur'd* Name, ...1.EOC.693.318.
Cremona now shall ever boast thy Name, ...1.EOC.707.322.
A lovely youth, and Acis was his name; ....1.TrPA.2.365.
A crystal fountain, and preserv'd his name; ....1.TrPA.164.373.
A flow'ry plant, which still preserves her name. ....1.TrFD.34.387.
Imperfect words, and lisp his mother's name, ...1.TrFD.81.389.
Must then her Name the wretched Writer prove? ....1.TrSP.3.393.
Tho' short my Stature, yet my Name extends ....1.TrSP.39.395.
Encrease of Glory to the *Latian* Name; ....1.TrSt.32.411.
And Crimes that grieve the trembling Gods to name? ....1.TrSt.326.423.
Whose impious Rites disgrace thy mighty Name, ...1.TrSt.387.426.

NAME (CONTINUED)

We to thy Name our Annual Rites will pay, 1.TrSt.592.435.
With *Phœbus'* Name resounds the vaulted Hall. 1.TrSt.651.437.
To bright *Apollo's* awful Name design'd, 1.TrSt.658.438.
Attend thy *Manes,* and preserve thy Name; 1.TrSt.752.441.
What Name you bear, from what high Race you spring? 1.TrSt.791.443.
(Oh gen'rous Prince) my Nation or my name, 1.TrSt.799.443.
Replies—Ah why forbears the Son to Name 1.TrSt.808.443.
Sacred to *Phorcys'* Pow'r, whose Name it bears; 1.TrUl.26.466.
Arriv'st thou here, a Stranger to our Name? 1.TrUl.117.469.
Oft have I heard, in *Crete,* this Island's Name, 1.TrUl.140.470.
To slander Wives, and Wedlock's holy Name. 2.ChJM.223.25.
I loath a Whore, and startle at the Name. 2.ChJM.592.43.
Let such (a God's Name) with fine Wheat be fed, 2.ChWB.48.58.
Mount up, and take a *Salamander's* Name. 2.RL1.60.150.
A watchful Sprite, and *Ariel* is my Name. 2.RL1.106.153.
Which from the neighb'ring *Hampton* takes its Name. 2.RL3.4.169.
So long my Honour, Name, and Praise shall live! 2.RL3.170.182.
And mid'st the Stars inscribe *Belinda's* Name! 2.RL5.150.212.
And the Great Founder of the *Persian* Name: 2.TemF.96.260.
To whom old Fables gave a lasting Name, 2.TemF.130.264.
Who then with Incense shall adore our Name? 2.TemF.367.281.
The Joy let others have, and we the Name, 2.TemF.390.282.
Or if no Basis bear my rising Name, 2.TemF.519.289.
And *Eloisa* yet must kiss the name. 2.ElAb.8.319.
Dear fatal name! rest ever unreveal'd, 2.ElAb.9.319.
Oh write it not, my hand—The name appears 2.ElAb.13.319.
That well-known name awakens all my woes. 2.ElAb.30.321.
Oh name for ever sad! for ever dear! 2.ElAb.31.321.
When Love approach'd me under Friendship's name; 2.ElAb.60.324.
If there be yet another name more free, 2.ElAb.89.327.
May one kind grave unite each hapless name, 2.ElAb.343.347.
So peaceful rests, without a stone, a name, 2.Elegy.69.368.
Cease then, nor ORDER Imperfection name: 3.EOM1.281.49.
Wits, just like fools, at war about a Name, 3.EOM2.85.65.
Exalt their kind, and take some Virtue's name. 3.EOM2.100.67.
Nor Virtue, male or female, can we name, 3.EOM2.193.78.
A *Cheat!* a *Whore!* who starts not at the Name, 3.EOM2.220Z1.82.
Thus States were form'd; the name of King unknown, 3.EOM3.209.114.
Good, Pleasure, Ease, Content! whate'er thy name: 3.EOM4.2.128.
Fame but from death a villain's name can save, 3.EOM4.249.151.
Or ravish'd with the whistling of a Name, 3.EOM4.283.155.
Oh! while along the stream of Time thy name 3.EOM4.383.165.
Why pique all mortals, yet affect a name? 3.Ep2.61.55.
"His race, his form, his name almost unknown?" 3.Ep3.284.116.
Will never mark the marble with his Name: 3.Ep3.286.116.
"Virtue! and Wealth! what are ye but a name!" 3.Ep3.334.120.
A plain good man, and Balaam was his name; 3.Ep3.342.121.
Lull with *Amelia's* liquid Name the Nine, 4.HS1.31.7.
The fewer still you name, you wound the more; 4.HS1.43.9.
A Thing which *Adam* had been pos'd to name; 4.JD4.25.27.
"To crave your sentiment, if—'s your name. 4.JD4.67.31.
Think how Posterity will treat thy name; 4.HS2.108.61.
Whether the Name belong to Pope or Vernon? 4.HS2.166.69.
"I'd never name Queens, Ministers, or Kings; 4.Arbu.76.101.
Preserv'd in *Milton's* or in *Shakespear's* name. 4.Arbu.168.108.
What tho' my Name stood rubric on the walls? 4.Arbu.215.111.
That Fop whose pride affects a Patron's name, 4.Arbu.291.116.
The Fop whose pride affects a Patron's name, 4.Arbu.291A.116.
For food digested takes another name. 4.JD2.34.135.
Shall bless thy name at least some twice a day, 4.HOde1.30C.153.
(Its Name I know not, and it's no great matter) 4.2HE2.45.167.
And virtuous Alfred, a more sacred Name, 4.2HE1.8.195.
Great Friend of LIBERTY! in *Kings* a Name 4.2HE1.25.197.
Renounce our Country, and degrade our Name? 4.1HE6.125.245.
Name a Town Life, and in a trice, 4.HS6.155.259.
And let, a God's-name, ev'ry Fool and Knave 4.EpS1.85.305.
F. Yet none but you by Name the Guilty lash; 4.EpS2.10.313.
Ye Rev'rend Atheists!— *F.* Scandal! name them, Who? 4.EpS2.18.314.
To save a Bishop, may I name a Dean? 4.EpS2.33.314.
And melts to Goodness, need I SCARBROW name? 4.EpS2.65.316.
Call *Verres, Wolsey,* any odious name? 4.EpS2.137.321.
Call *Clodius, Wolsey,* any odious name? 4.EpS2.137A.321.
All gaze with ardour: some, a Poet's name, 5.DunA2.47.102.
"Hear Jove! whose name my bards and I adore, 5.DunA2.75.107.
So shall each hostile name become our own, 5.DunA2.131.113.
Of Genseric! and Attila's dread name! 5.DunA3.84.157.
Lo Bond and Foxton, ev'ry nameless name, 5.DunA3.151.164.
Lo thousand thousand, ev'ry nameless name, 5.DunA3.151A.164.
But pious Needham dropt the name of God; 5.DunB1.324.293.
All gaze with ardour: Some a poet's name, 5.DunB2.51.298.
Hear Jove! whose name my bards and I adore, 5.DunB2.79.299.
So shall each hostile name become our own, 5.DunB2.139.302.
The name of these blind puppies than of those. 5.DunB2.310A.310.
Of Genseric! and Attila's dread name! 5.DunB3.92.324.
Each Songster, Riddler, ev'ry nameless name, 5.DunB3.157.328.
Ænigma Bard, and ev'ry nameless name, 5.DunB3.157A.328.
Milton's on this, on that one Johnston's name. 5.DunB4.112.352.
Rous'd at his name, up rose the bowzy Sire, 5.DunB4.493.390.
First slave to Words, then vassal to a Name, 5.DunB4.501.391.
As Meat digested takes a diff'rent Name; 6.7.12.16.
Silence, the Knave's Repute, the Whore's good Name, 6.8.25.18.
For fear to wrong them with a Name too low; 6.9xi.2.23.
The *Granvilles* write their Name plain *Greenfield,* 6.10.47.26.
Nay, e'en the Parts of Shame by Name would call: 6.14ii.41.44.
full often change its name 6.14v(b).21A.50.
And *Monthausier* was only chang'd in Name: 6.19.70.64.
Rank'd in the Name of *Tom D'Urfy.* 6.30.6.85.
Thy Name De Urfey or D'Urfey. 6.30.6A.85.
That seem'd to fill the Name unworthy 6.30.5B.85.
To the sweet Name of *Tom D'Urfy.* 6.30.12.86.
In the great Name of *Tom D'Urfy.* 6.30.18.86.
A Place in any *British* Name; 6.30.20.86.
To form the Name of Tom: D'Urfey 6.30.12A.86.
In the great Name of *Thomas Durfy.* 6.30.12B.86.
Durfeius his true *Latin* Name; 6.30.37.87.

NAME (CONTINUED)

In the great Name of *Tom Durfy.* 6.30.47.87.
D'urfeius the true *Latin* Name; 6.30.37A.87.
To turn the Name into good *Latin:* 6.30.37B.87.
Part of the Name of stuttering *T—* 6.30.53.88.
We form'd this Name, renown'd in Rhyme; 6.30.56.88.
Unless i' th' Name of *Tom D'Urfy.* 6.30.63.88.
To turn quite backward *D'Urfy's* Name? 6.30.67.88.
Except ith' Name of *Tom D'Urfy.* 6.30.63A.88.
To the great Name of *Tom Durfy.* 6.30.83.89.
Plu—Plutarch, what's his name that writes his life? 6.41.31.114.
So mix'd our studies, and so join'd our name, 6.52.10.156.
Muse! at that name thy sacred sorrows shed, 6.52.47.157.
Thou but preserv'st a Face and I a Name. 6.52.78.158.
Thou but preserv'st a Form and I a Name. 6.52.78A.158.
The Learn'd themselves we Book-Worms name; 6.53.13.161.
Whence deathless *Kit-Cat* took its Name, 6.59.1.177.
From no trim Beau's its Name it boasts, 6.59.5.177.
Some bury'd marble half preserves a name; 6.71.16.203.
That Name the learn'd with fierce disputes pursue, 6.71.17.203.
Thro' climes and ages bears each form and name: 6.71.32.203.
"Paste we this Recreant's Name, 6.79.142.223.
So long her Honour, Name, and Praise shall last! 6.82i.8.229.
Teach me to wooe thee by thy best-lov'd Name! 6.96iv.96.279.
I'd call thee *Houyhnhnm,* that high sounding Name, 6.96iv.107.279.
Wrapt round and sanctify'd with *Shakespear's* Name; 6.98.18.283.
Affronting all, yet fond of a good Name, 6.99.9.287.
No *Gentleman! no man! no-thing! no name!* 6.116iv.2.326.
More, shrunk to *Smith—and* Smith's no name at all. 6.116iv.4.327.
The Name of *Savil* and of *Boyle.* 6.119.16.337.
The *Fop,* whose Pride affects a *Patron's* name, 6.120.1.339.
Whose Private Name all Titles recommend, 6.134.3.364.
Clear from a *Barber's* or a *Benson's* Name. 6.148ii.2.395.
Pure from a Barber or a *Benson's* Name. 6.148ii.2A.395.
Dryas the bold, or *Ceneus'* deathless Name, Il.1.348.105.
From *Thebè* sacred to *Apollo's* Name, Il.1.478.110.
(Whom Gods *Briareus,* Men *Ægeon* name) Il.1.523.113.
Each Prince of Name, or Chief in Arms approv'd, Il.2.225.138.
Nor let those Lips profane the Name of King. Il.2.313.142.
The Strength and Glory of th' *Epean* Name. Il.2.752.161.
Thessalians all, tho' various in their Name, Il.2.835.164.
From *Cyphus, Guneus* was their Leader's Name. Il.2.907.166.
And oh! that still he bore a Brother's Name! Il.3.238.203.
The rest I know, and could in Order name; Il.3.299.207.
And guard from Wrong fair Friendship's holy Name. Il.3.438.213.
When Heav'n no longer hears the Name of *Troy.* Il.4.60.223.
Still to our Name their Hecatombs expire, Il.4.71.224.
Be still thy self; in Arms a mighty Name; Il.4.300.235.
The bounding Steed, in Arms a mighty Name) Il.4.423.240.
Our Glories darken their diminish'd Name. Il.4.465.242.
Old *Priam's* Son, *Democoon* was his Name; Il.4.574.249.
The Race forgotten, and the Name no more. Il.5.203.276.
And boasted Glory of the *Lycian* Name? Il.5.221.278.
And learn to tremble at the Name of Arms. Il.5.438.289.
And only Men in Figure and in Name! Il.5.981.314.
The honour'd Author of my Birth and Name; Il.6.254.339.
In *Jove's* high Name to sprinkle on the Ground, Il.6.323.342.
That caus'd these Woes, deserves a Sister's Name! Il.6.433.348.
To this lov'd Infant *Hector* gave the Name Il.6.500.351.
Attaint the Lustre of my former Name, Il.6.564.354.
A thousand Griefs shall waken at the Name! Il.6.589.355.
The Stone shall tell your vanquish'd Hero's Name, Il.7.103.368.
The mightiest Warrior of th' *Achaian* Name Il.7.135.370.
Attend on *Greece,* and all the *Grecian* Name? Il.7.146.371.
Each Name, each Action, and each Hero's Sire? Il.7.154.372.
And nine, the noblest of the *Grecian* Name, Il.7.196.373.
Then hear me, Princes of the *Trojan* Name! Il.7.436.386.
Th' admiring Chiefs, and all the *Grecian* Name, Il.7.480.388.
The Ruin vanish'd, and the Name no more Il.7.555.392.
And ask'd Destruction to the *Trojan* Name. Il.8.289.411.
(My self will name them) to *Pelides'* Tent: Il.9.220.443.
To me more dear than all that bear the Name. Il.9.264.445.
The Ships, the *Greeks,* and all the *Grecian* Name. Il.9.315.449.
From *Cleopatra* chang'd this Daughter's Name, Il.9.676.468.
And call'd *Alcyone;* a Name to show Il.9.677.468.
Well hast thou spoke; but at the Tyrant's Name, Il.9.759.471.
Dolon his Name, *Eumedes'* only Boy, Il.10.372.19.
Now while on *Rhesus'* Name he calls in vain, Il.10.614.29.
Thou living Glory of the *Grecian* Name! Il.10.641.30.
Æsymnus, Agelaus; all Chiefs of Name; Il.11.393.52.
Oh may this Instant end the *Grecian* Name! Il.12.78.84.
And you whose Ardour hopes an equal Name! Il.12.318.93.
They vow Destruction to the *Grecian* Name, Il.13.65.107.
Shall these, so late who trembled at your Name, Il.13.145.111.
Of *Greece,* and *Argos* be no more a Name. Il.13.1051.155.
O Grace and Glory of th' *Achaian* Name! Il.14.49.160.
Nor lives in *Greece* a Stranger to his Name. Il.14.142.164.
Whom Mortals name the dread *Titanian* Gods. Il.14.316.178.
(*Chalcis* his Name with those of heav'nly Birth, Il.14.329.179.
O *Greeks!* if yet ye can deserve the Name! Il.14.422.183.
Of all the *Grecians,* what immortal Name, Il.14.603.191.
Him *Ajax* honour'd with a Brother's Name, Il.15.379.211.
And save the Reliques of the *Grecian* Name. Il.15.435.214.
(To thee, *Polydamas!* an honour'd Name) Il.15.523.217.
Mycenian Periphes, a mighty Name, Il.15.770.226.
Perhaps yon' Reliques of the *Grecian* Name, Il.16.24.236.
Arm, e'er the *Grecians* be no more a Name; Il.16.159.244.
Then brave *Automedon* (an honour'd Name, Il.16.178.245.
And add new Glories to his mighty Name. Il.16.327.255.
From *Panthus* sprung, *Euphorbus* was his Name; Il.16.973.281.
How vain, without the Merit is the Name? Il.17.158.293.
Be Men (my Friends) in Action as in Name, Il.17.207.295.
The long-succeeding Numbers who can name? Il.17.306.299.
(*Ajax,* to *Peleus'* Son the second Name, Il.17.328.300.
But now *Patroclus* is an empty Name! Il.17.545.309.
Eëtion's Son, and *Podes* was his Name; Il.17.649.313.

NAME (CONTINUED)

What *Grecian* now shall tremble at thy Name? ....Il.17.659.313.
Of martial *Merion: Cœranus* his Name, ...Il.17.691.314.
Thalia, Glauce, (ev'ry wat'ry Name) ....Il.18.47.325.
The bravest far that ever bore the Name; ....Il.18.74.326.
An ever dear, and ever honour'd Name! ....Il.18.462.344.
The bravest sure that ever bore the Name; ....Il.18.510.346.
Then slain by *Phœbus* (*Hector* had the Name) ....Il.18.525.346.
The *Greeks* accept, and shout *Pelides'* Name. ....Il.19.78.375.
Xanthus his Name with those of heavenly Birth, ...Il.20.101.398.
The sacred *Tros,* of whom the *Trojan* Name. ....Il.20.275.405.
(The Son of *Pireus,* an illustrious Name,) ....Il.20.562.417.
Some Pity to a Suppliant's Name afford, ...Il.21.86.425.
His earthly Honours, and immortal Name; ....Il.21.144.427.
And in one Ruin sink the *Trojan* Name. ....Il.21.441.438.
And hopes this day to sink the *Trojan* Name ....Il.21.692.450.
Dearer than all that own a Brother's Name; ....Il.22.300.468.
Is now that Name no more, unhappy Boy! ....Il.22.652.483.
Ye Kings and Princes of th' *Achaian* Name! ....Il.23.294.501.
(*Æthe* her Name) at home to end his Days, ...Il.23.367.504.
Ordain'd to *Amarynces'* mighty Name; ....Il.23.726.519.
And known to Gods by *Percnos'* lofty Name. ....Il.24.390.552.
Polyctor is my Sire, an honour'd Name, ...Il.24.487.556.
The promise of a great, immortal name. ....Od.1.123.38.
Gives to the roll of death his glorious name! ....Od.1.218.43.
Thy name, thy lineage, and paternal land: ....Od.1.220.43.
Mentes my name; I rule the *Taphian* race, ...Od.1.229.43.
Join to that royal youth's, your rival name, ...Od.1.393.51.
But oh! forbear that dear, disastrous name, ...Od.1.437.53.
What, and from whence? his name and lineage shew. ....Od.1.516.57.
Mentes, an ever-honour'd name, of old ....Od.1.527.57.
Tho' *Tyro* nor *Mycene* match her name, ...Od.2.137.67.
What tho' from pole to pole resounds her name? ....Od.2.143.68.
Abhorr'd by all, accurs'd my name would grow, ...Od.2.159.69.
(Oh grace and glory of the *Grecian* name!) ....Od.3.95.90.
Has told the glories of his noble name, ...Od.3.101.91.
A yearling bullock to thy name shall smoke, ...Od.3.490.111.
And lov'd in age, *Eurydicé* her name) ....Od.3.577.116.
Whose age I honour with a parent's name. ....Od.4.216.130.
And mourn the brave *Antilochus,* a name ....Od.4.275.132.
Each noted leader's name you thrice invoke, ...Od.4.379.139.
Proteus, a name tremendous o'er the main, ...Od.4.521.145.
Their wrath aton'd, to *Agamemnon's* name ....Od.4.793.156.
Thus with vile censure taint my spotless name. ....Od.6.330.227.
Alcinous' Queen, *Arete* is her name, ...Od.7.70.237.
Father and Prince of the *Phæacian* name: ....Od.7.80.237.
Then thus *Ulysses;* Happy King, whose name ....Od.8.417.286.
Our self we give, memorial of our name: ....Od.8.466.288.
Say what thy birth, and what the name you bore, ...Od.8.597.294.
Behold *Ulysses!* no ignoble name, ...Od.9.19.301.
Lotos the name, divine, nectareous juice! ....Od.9.106.307.
Its name *Lachæa,* crown'd with many a grove, ...Od.9.135.311.
Atrides' friends, (in arms a mighty name) ....Od.9.314.319.
Declare thy name; not mortal is this juice, ...Od.9.421.323.
And plead my title: *Noman* is my name. ....Od.9.432.323.
And name a chief each party to command; ....Od.10.233.351.
Moly the name, to mortals hard to find, ...Od.10.365.362.
O more than human! tell thy race, thy name. ....Od.10.388.363.
And is the name of *Ithaca* forgot? ....Od.10.561.369.
By the soft tye and sacred name of friend! ....Od.11.82.385.
There high in air, memorial of my name ....Od.11.96.385.
Founders of *Thebes,* and men of mighty name; ....Od.11.320.398.
Name *Clytemnestra,* they will curse the kind. ....Od.11.540.410.
But sure the eye of Time beholds no name ....Od.11.591.412.
We know whate'er the Kings of mighty name ....Od.12.228.443.
Cautious the name of *Scylla* I suppress; ....Od.12.266.445.
Sacred to *Phorcys'* pow'r, whose name it bears: ....Od.13.117.7.
To his high name let twelve black oxen fall. ....Od.13.211.15.
Arriv'st thou here a stranger to our name? ....Od.13.284.19.
Oft have I heard, in *Crete,* this Island's name; ....Od.13.307.21.
For whose curs'd cause, in *Agamemnon's* name, ...Od.14.81.40.
Such thou may'st be. But he whose name you crave ....Od.14.154.43.
That name, for ever dread, yet ever dear, ...Od.14.167.43.
The name of him awakes a thousand woes. ....Od.14.195.45.
Your name, your parents, and your native air? ....Od.14.215.45.
Castor Hylacides (that name he bore) ....Od.14.231.47.
To *Crete* return'd, an honourable name. ....Od.14.271.49.
And he *Amphiaraus,* immortal name! ....Od.15.268.81.
Thy name, thy lineage, and paternal land. ....Od.15.287.82.
And great *Ulysses* (ever honour'd name!) ....Od.15.291.83.
Far hence remote, and *Syria* is the name; ....Od.15.439.90.
She told her name, her race, and all she knew. ....Od.15.465.93.
Deaf to the mighty *Ulyssæan* name. ....Od.16.76.106.
Forbear, he cry'd; for heav'n reserve that name, ...Od.16.222.114.
O'er earth (returns the Prince) resounds thy name, ...Od.16.262.117.
Twice twenty six, all peers of mighty name, ...Od.16.269.118.
Whate'er gives man the envy'd name of Great; ....Od.17.502.157.
Irus, a name expressive of th' employ. ....Od.18.11.167.
O my *Ulysses!* ever honour'd name! ....Od.18.243.178.
Thy name, thy lineage, and thy natal land. ....Od.19.126.198.
Forbear to know my lineage, or my name: ....Od.19.138.199.
Studious of peace; and *Æthon* is my name. ....Od.19.214.203.
With all thy wants the name of poor shall end; ....Od.19.290.209.
Of *Thessaly,* his name I heard renown'd: ....Od.19.310.209.
And distant tongues extoll the patron-name. ....Od.19.386.212.
Autolycus the bold: (a mighty name ....Od.19.466.218.
"And Name the blessing that your pray'rs have won." ....Od.19.476.220.
"The boy shall bear; *Ulysses* be his name! ....Od.19.480.220.
Nor dread to name your self the bowyer's prize: ....Od.19.684.229.
They name the standard of their dearest vow. ....Od.20.46.234.
She thus: O cease that ever-honour'd name ....Od.20.169.241.
And by the name on earth I most revere, ...Od.20.405.252.
Let then to *Phœbus'* name the fatted thighs ....Od.21.282.273.
Base to insult who bears a suppliant's name, ...Od.21.335.276.
And thus posterity upbraid our name. ....Od.21.356.276.
O royal mother! ever-honour'd name! ....Od.21.369.277.
Oh ev'ry sacred name in one! my friend! ....Od.22.226.297.
And base revilers of our house and name? ....Od.22.498.313.
Sunk what was mortal of thy mighty name, ...Od.24.92.352.
And ev'n the best that bears a Woman's name. ....Od.24.231.358.
And old *Laertes* was his father's name. ....Od.24.317.365.
My palace there; *Eperitus* my name. ....Od.24.354.366.
Well-pleas'd you told its nature, and its name, ...Od.24.393.368.
A son and grandson of th' *Arcesian* name ....Od.24.596.376.

NAMELESS

Are *nameless Graces* which no Methods teach, ...1.EOC.144.256.
Has made the father of a nameless race, ...3.Ep1.229.35.
Where nameless somethings in their causes sleep, ...5.DunA1.54.66.
Lo Bond and Foxton, ev'ry nameless name, ...5.DunA3.151.164.
Lo thousand thousand, ev'ry nameless name, ...5.DunA3.151A.164.
Where nameless Somethings in their causes sleep, ...5.DunB1.56.274.
Each Songster, Riddler, ev'ry nameless name, ...5.DunB3.157.328.
Ænigma Bard, and ev'ry nameless name, ...5.DunB3.157A.328.
Let *D[enni]s* write, and nameless numbers rail: ....6.63.4.188.
Beneath a rude and nameless stone he lies, ...6.72.3.208.

NAMES

Nations *unborn* your mighty Names shall sound, ...1.EOC.193.263.
Some judge of Authors' *Names,* not *Works,* and then ....1.EOC.412.287.
Inscriptions here of various Names I view'd, ...2.TemF.31.255.
Criticks I saw, that other Names deface, ...2.TemF.37.256.
There Names inscrib'd unnumber'd Ages past ....2.TemF.49.256.
With *Agis,* not the last of *Spartan* Names: ....2.TemF.175.269.
Your Statues moulder'd, and your Names unknown. ....2.TemF.353.280.
And, all those tender names in one, thy love! ....2.ElAb.154.332.
To this were Trifles, Toys, and empty Names. ....4.JD4.8.27.
He names the *Price* for ev'ry *Office* paid, ...4.JD4.162.39.
"No Names—be calm—learn Prudence of a Friend: ....4.Arbu.102.103.
Unspotted Names! and memorable long, ...4.Arbu.386.126.
Weave Laurel Crowns, and take what Names we please. ....4.2HE2.142.175.
(Tho' but, perhaps, a muster-roll of Names) ....4.2HE1.124.205.
Tells all their names, lays down the law, ...4.HS6.202.263.
Names, which I long have lov'd, nor lov'd in vain, ...4.EpS2.90.318.
Here, Last of *Britons!* let your Names be read; ....4.EpS2.250.327.
Whose names once up, they thought it was not wrong ....4.1740.21.333.
By names of Toasts retails each batter'd jade, ...5.DunA2.126.112.
By names of Toasts retails each batter'd jade; ....5.DunB2.134.301.
Ask ye their names? I could as soon disclose ....5.DunB2.309.310.
The names of these blind puppies as of those. ....5.DunB2.310.310.
Ask ye their names? I sooner could disclose ....5.DunB2.309A.310.
Still changing Names, Religions, Climes, ...6.14v(b).14.50.
Ev'n in those tombs where their proud names survive, ...6.22.16.72.
They print their Names in Letters small, ...6.29.9.83.
N, by whom Names subsist, declar'd, ...6.30.13.86.
Or if in ranging of the Names I judge ill, ...6.40.5.112.
In vain you boast Poetick Names of yore, ...6.43.1A.121.
Unenvy'd Titles grace our mighty Names, ...6.48iv.13.136.
Their Names, their Numbers, and their Chiefs I sing. ....Il.2.585.155.
For this your Names are call'd, before the rest, ...Il.4.396.239.
O Friends! O Heroes! Names for ever dear, ...Il.15.890.231.
Abash'd, she names his own Imperial Spouse; ....Il.21.595.446.
Then your high lineage and your names declare: ....Od.4.72.122.
Speak they their lineage, or their names declare? ....Od.4.186.128.
(For from the natal hour distinctive names, ...Od.8.599.294.
And names a *Van:* there fix it on the plain, ...Od.11.158.389.
The names, and numbers of th' audacious train; ....Od.16.259.117.
Nymphs of this fountain! to whose sacred names ....Od.17.284.146.
Mix'd with her genuine sons, adopted names ....Od.19.198.201.

NAMING

Embitters all thy Woes, by naming me. ....Il.6.587.355.
Imploring all, and naming one by one. ....Il.22.529.478.

NAP

After an hundred and thirty years' nap, ...6.148i.1.395.

NAPE

Full in his Nape infix'd the fatal Spear; ....Il.5.96.271.

NAPKINS

The Napkins white, the Carpet red: ....4.HS6.197.263.

NARCISSA

(Were the last words that poor Narcissa spoke) ....3.Ep1.243.36.

NARCISSA'S

Narcissa's nature, tolerably mild, ...3.Ep2.53.54.

NARCISSUS

Narcissus, prais'd with all a Parson's pow'r, ...5.DunB4.103.351.
Narcissus here a different fate had prov'd, ...6.4ii.7.9.
And pale *Narcissus* on the bank, in vain ....6.14iv.11.47.

NARDAC

If Ducal *Nardac, Lilliputian* Peer, ...6.96iv.103.279.

NARRATION

My long narration of a life of woes. ....Od.14.228.46.

NARRATIVE

And boasting Youth, and Narrative old Age. ....2.TemF.291.277.
Behold this Narrative that's here; ....6.94.15.259.
But Wise thro' Time, and Narrative with Age, ...Il.3.200.200.
The banquet done, the Narrative old man ....Od.3.80.90.
Then gushing tears the narrative confound, ...Od.10.537.369.

NARROW

So *vast* is Art, so *narrow* Human Wit: ....1.EOC.61.246.
Shall *Jove,* for one, extend the narrow Span, ...1.TrES.240.458.
Nor bound thy narrow Views to Things below. ....2.RL1.36.148.

NARROW (CONTINUED)
Which first should issue thro the narrow Vent: 2.TemF.492.287.
Have you not seen at Guild-hall's narrow Pass, 4.2HE2.104.173.
See Nature in some partial narrow shape, 5.DunB4.455.385.
'And give Idea's of a narrow Pass; 6.13.23.39.
A narrow Pass there is, with Houses low; 6.14ii.2.43.
A narrow orb each crouded conquest keeps, 6.71.25.203.
My narrow Genius does the power deny) 6.75.4.211.
Fond of his Hillock Isle, his narrow Mind 6.96v.25.280.
Tho strait be the passage, and narrow the Gate; 6.122.22.342.
Brave *Glaucus* then each narrow Thought resign'd, Il.6.290.340.
There ends thy narrow Span assign'd by Fate, Il.11.566.59.
No Space for Combat in yon' narrow Bounds. Il.12.74.84.
The Soul came issuing at the narrow Vent: Il.13.842.145.
Shall *Jove*, for one, extend the narrow Span, Il.16.543.265.
Haste then; yon' narrow Road before our Sight Il.23.493.510.
This narrow way? Take larger Field (he cry'd) Il.23.508.510.
Such, and so narrow now the Space between Il.23.603.513.
Full thro' the narrow mouths descend the tides: Od.6.314.226.
These gates would seem too narrow for they flight. Od.18.427.189.
Beneath the feastful bow'r. A narrow space Od.19.376.212.
A high and narrow, but the only pass: Od.22.145.294.

NARROW'D
Bounded by Nature, narrow'd still by Art, 5.DunB4.503.392.

NARROW'R
The narrow'r end I sharpen'd to a spire; Od.9.386.322.

NARROWER
Points him two ways, the narrower is the better. 5.DunB4.152.356.

NARSES
Or heal, old Narses, thy obscener ail, 3.Ep3.91.97.

NASH
O Nash! more blest in ev'ry other thing, 6.131i.1.360.

NASO
Nor Motteux talk'd, nor Naso whisper'd more; 5.DunA2.382.147.
Nor Kelsey talk'd, nor Naso whisper'd more; 5.DunA2.382B.147.

NASO'S
Not *Naso's* self more impudently near, 4.JD4.178A.41.

NASSAU
And great Nassau to Kneller's hand decreed 4.2HE1.382.227.

NASTINESS
Such Nastiness and so much Pride 6.14v(a).8.48.

NAT
Yet swinken nat sans Secresie. 6.14i.2.41.
Women, tho' nat sans Leacherie, 6.14i.1A.41.

NAT'RAL
Account for moral as for nat'ral things: 3.EOM1.162.35.
These nat'ral love maintain'd, habitual those: 3.EOM3.140.107.

NATAL
Or in the natal, or the mortal hour. 3.EOM1.288.50.
Who forms the Genius in the natal Hour; 4.2HE2.279.185.
What Stars concurring blest his natal Hour? Il.24.674.565.
Safe with his friends to gain his natal shore: Od.1.8.28.
(Ah men unbless'd!) to touch that natal shore. Od.1.12.29.
Long-lab'ring gains his natal shore at last; Od.3.290.100.
The best of brothers, at his natal home, Od.4.114.125.
Fated to wander from his natal coast! Od.4.248.131.
To bless the natal, and the nuptial hour; Od.4.286.132.
Their state, since last you left your natal land; Od.4.528.146.
Nor sight of natal shore, nor regal dome Od.4.641.149.
So shalt thou view with joy thy natal shore, Od.6.375.230.
Sad from my natal hour my days have ran, Od.8.171.271.
If I am lame, that stain my natal hour Od.8.351.282.
Impos'd by parents in the natal hour? Od.8.598.294.
(For from the natal hour distinctive names, Od.8.599.294.
To reach his natal shore was thy decree; Od.13.154.13.
Restor'd and breathing in his natal place. Od.14.166.43.
To launch thy vessel for thy natal shore: Od.15.18.70.
In spacious *Crete* he drew his natal air: Od.16.62.105.
Such, when *Ulysses* left his natal coast; Od.17.386.150.
She nam'd *Arnæus* on his natal day, Od.18.8.166.
Say, since *Ulysses* left his natal coast, Od.19.9.193.
Thy name, thy lineage, and thy natal land. Od.19.126.198.
The dues of nature to his natal home!— Od.19.193.201.
To waft the Heroe to his natal land. Od.19.334.210.
Ended in man, his mother's natal clime Od.19.485.220.
The Goddess pleas'd, regains her natal skies. Od.20.67.235.

NATION
No more shall Nation against Nation rise, 1.Mes.57.117.
No more shall Nation against Nation rise, 1.Mes.57.117.
Then Unbelieving Priests reform'd the Nation, 1.EOC.546.300.
The *Rules*, a Nation born to serve, obeys, 1.EOC.713.322.
From the dire Nation in its early Times, 1.TrSt.6.409.
Against a Nation thy peculiar Care: 1.TrSt.406.427.
(Oh gen'rous Prince) my Nation or my name, 1.TrSt.799.443.
Towns to one grave, a Nation to the deep? 3.EOM1.144A.33.
And therefore hopes this Nation may be sold: 3.Ep3.126.102.
When the tir'd nation breath'd from civil war. 4.2HE1.273.219.
The veriest Hermit in the Nation 4.HS6.183.261.
Espouse the nation, you [debauched before]. 4.1740.48.334*.
And the hoarse nation croak'd, God save King Log! 5.DunA1.260.95.
And the loud nation croak'd, God save King Log! 5.DunA1.260A.95.
And the hoarse nation croak'd, "God save King Log!" 5.DunB1.330.294.
What Fav'rites gain, and what the Nation owes, 6.8.35.19.

NATION (CONTINUED)
What's Fame with Men, by Custom of the Nation, 6.46.1.127.
What's Fame in Men, by Custom of the Nation, 6.46.1A.127.
In what new Nation shall we fix our Seat? 6.65.6.192.
King, Queen and Nation, staring with Amaze, 6.96iv.72.278.
Lov'd and esteem'd by all the Nation? 6.151.4.399.
The wandring Nation of a Summer's Day, Il.2.553.154.
The same their Nation, and their Chief the same. Il.2.836.164.
Yet leaves his Nation safe, his Children free; Il.15.585.219.
(For *Jove* had turn'd the Nation all to Stone:) Il.24.770.569.
A lawless nation of gygantic foes: Od.6.8.203.
The recreant nation to fair *Scheria* led, Od.6.11.203.
A happy nation, and an happy King. Od.6.238.221.
Perish'd the nation in unrighteous war, Od.7.76.237.
The dusky nation of *Cimmeria* dwells; Od.11.16.380.
Sure fixt on Virtue may your nation stand, Od.13.60.4.
A nation ever to the stranger kind; Od.16.251.117.
From realm to realm a Nation to explore Od.23.285.337.

NATION'S
B. It raises Armies in a Nation's aid, 3.Ep3.33A.88.
It raises Armies in a Nation's aid, 3.Ep3.33.88.
To spoil the nation's last great trade, Quadrille! 3.Ep3.64.92.
To town he comes, completes the nation's hope, 3.Ep3.213.110.
Behold the hand that wrought a Nation's cure, 4.2HE1.225.215.
"Harley, the Nation's great Support,"— 4.1HE7.83.273.
And all I sung should be the *Nation's Sense:* 4.EpS1.78.304.
Vice thus abus'd, demands a Nation's care; 4.EpS1.128.307.
Not *Waller's* Wreath can hide the Nation's Scar, 4.EpS2.230.325.
Lost was the Nation's Sense, nor could be found, 5.DunB4.611.404.
Ripe Politicks the Nation's Barrel fill, 6.48i.3.133*.
Before thy Pen vanish the Nation's Ills, 6.48ii.9.134.
Well spread with Sense, shall be the Nation's Plaister. 6.48ii.12.134.
Say, shall not I one Nation's Fate command, Il.18.429.341.

NATIONS
See barb'rous Nations at thy Gates attend, 1.Mes.91.121.
There mighty Nations shall inquire their Doom, 1.W-F.381.188.
Whole Nations enter with each swelling Tyde, 1.W-F.399.191.
Nations *unborn* your mighty Names shall sound, 1.EOC.193.263.
And give the Nations to the Waste of War. 1.TrSt.341.424.
Of these the Chief the Care of Nations own, 2.RL2.89.165.
With like Confusion different Nations fly, 2.RL3.83.174.
And all the Nations, summon'd at the Call, 2.TemF.278.276.
For thee whole Nations fill'd with Flames and Blood, 2.TemF.346.280.
Towns to one grave, whole nations to the deep? 3.EOM1.144.33.
Towns to one grave, and Nations to the deep? 3.EOM1.144B.33.
Towns to one grave, or Nations to the deep? 3.EOM1.144C.33.
Who taught the nations of the field and wood 3.EOM3.99.101.
Who taught the nations of the field and flood 3.EOM3.99A.101.
And Nations wonder'd while they dropp'd the sword! 4.2HE1.399.229.
And all the nations cover'd in her shade! 5.DunA3.64.155.
And all the nations cover'd in her shade! 5.DunB3.72.323.
And all the Nations summon'd to the Throne. 5.DunB4.72.348.
O sing, and hush the Nations with thy Song! 5.DunB4.626.406.
To the pale Nations of the Dead, 6.11.52.32.
The spoils of nations, and the pomp of wars, 6.32.28.96.
Can Popish Writings do the Nations good? 6.48iii.9.134.
Preserve the Limits of these nations, 6.61.54.183.
God keep the Limits of these nations, 6.61.54A.183.
Imperial wonders rais'd on Nations spoil'd, 6.71.5.202.
In vain a nations zeal a senate's cares 6.130.31.359.
What else to *Troy* th' assembled Nations draws, Il.1.209.96.
Ill fits a Chief who mighty Nations guides, Il.2.27.128.
Ill fits a Chief who mighty Nations guides, Il.2.77.130.
Ill suits a Chief who mighty Nations guides, Il.2.77A.130.
In Tribes and Nations to divide thy Train: Il.2.431.148.
In Tribes and Nations rank'd on either side. Il.2.523.151.
And crowded Nations wait his dread Command. Il.2.696.159.
Nations on Nations fill the dusky Plain, Il.2.979.170.
Nations on Nations fill the dusky Plain, Il.2.979.170.
To Pygmy-Nations Wounds and Death they bring, Il.3.9.188.
And diff'ring Nations part in Leagues of Peace. Il.3.132.196.
The Nations hear, with rising Hopes possest, Il.3.153.198.
The Nations call, thy joyful People wait, Il.3.320.208.
And joyful Nations join in Leagues of Peace. Il.3.401.211.
Say, to new Nations must I cross the Main, Il.3.495.215.
And thro' his Gates the crowding Nations flow. Il.4.26.222.
Assembled Nations, set two Worlds in Arms? Il.4.38.223.
To fright the Nations with a dire Portent, Il.4.102.225.
Such Clamours rose from various Nations round, Il.4.496.244.
The Nations bleed, where-e'er her Steps she turns, Il.4.506.245.
To warn the Nations, and to curb the Great! Il.6.76.327.
And you whom distant Nations send to War! Il.6.136.330.
The warring Nations to suspend their Rage; Il.7.54.365.
O'erwhelms the Nations with new Toils and Woes; Il.7.82.367.
And gives whole Nations to the Waste of Wars. Il.7.254.376.
And joy the Nations whom thy Arm defends; Il.7.359.381.
Monarch of Nations! whose superior Sway Il.9.127.438.
Made Nations tremble, and whole Hosts retire, Il.9.403.452.
What to these Shores th' assembled Nations draws, Il.9.446.454.
The Neighbour Nations thence commencing Foes. Il.9.664.467.
Great King of Nations! (*Ithacus* reply'd) Il.9.794.473.
The Nations meet; there *Pylos, Elis* here. Il.11.873.75.
Their Guardians these, the Nations round confess, Il.13.919.148.
Whole Nations fear'd: but not an *Argive* shook. Il.13.1019.153.
When happy Nations bear the Marks divine! Il.15.577.218.
The warring Nations meet, the Battel roars, Il.15.842.229.
For this in Arms the warring Nations stood, Il.15.858.229.
It flew, and fir'd the Nations as it went. Il.17.98.291.
Of neighb'ring Nations, or of distant Lands! Il.17.261.298.
Contending Nations won and lost the Day; Il.18.310.336.
The King of Nations forc'd his royal Slave: Il.18.518.346.
O King of Nations! whose superiour Sway Il.19.143.377.
Earth echoes, and the Nations rush to Arms. Il.20.66.396.
And Nations breathe, deliver'd from their Fate. Il.21.724.451.

NATIONS (CONTINUED)

The Boast of Nations! the Defence of *Troy!* ... Il.22.557.479.
O King of Nations! all thy *Greeks* proclaim; ... Il.23.1055.533.
And many-languag'd nations has survey'd; ... Od.3.408.106.
But crush the nations with an iron rod, ... Od.5.16.171.
Ev'n from the Chief who men and nations knew, ... Od.7.178.244.
Or nations subject to the western ray. ... Od.8.30.263.
Say whence, ye Gods, contending nations strive ... Od.10.42.341.
To all the Phantome-nations of the dead; ... Od.10.627.374.
To all the Phantom nations of the dead. ... Od.11.44.381.
Be humbled, nations! and your Monarch hear. ... Od.13.207.15.
Who calls, from distant nations to his own, ... Od.17.460.155.
By rival nations courted for their songs; ... Od.17.467.156.
Nations embattel'd to revenge the slain? ... Od.20.54.234.
Fear shook the nations. At the voice divine ... Od.24.616.377.
"And willing nations knew their lawful Lord." ... Od.24.631.378.

NATIVE

'Till in your Native Shades You tune the Lyre: ... 1.PSp.12.61.
Nor fragrant Herbs their native Incense yield. ... 1.PWi.48.92.
"My native Shades—there weep, and murmur there." ... 1.W-F.202.168.
Till the freed *Indians* in their native Groves ... 1.W-F.409.192.
Ev'n he, the terror of his native grove, ... 1.TrPA.17.366.
Frighted, beneath my native deeps I fled; ... 1.TrPA.140.371.
Which lost its native red; and first appear'd ... 1.TrPA.153.372.
Like you, contented with his Native Groves; ... 1.TrVP.86.380.
He strait assum'd his Native Form again; ... 1.TrVP.113.381.
That charm'd me more, with Native Moss o'ergrown, ... 1.TrSP.165.400.
Which charm'd me more, with Native Moss o'ergrown, ... 1.TrSP.165A.400.
Venus for thee shall smooth her native Main. ... 1.TrSP.251.404.
Nor *Bacchus* less his Native Town defend, ... 1.TrSt.408.427.
Had slain his Brother, leaves his Native Land, ... 1.TrSt.556.433.
His native Mountains lessen to his Sight; ... 1.TrSt.643.437.
Jocasta's Son, and *Thebes* my Native Place. ... 1.TrSt.805.443.
The breathless Body to his Native Land. ... 1.TrES.249.459.
Far from the *Lycian* Shores, his happy Native Reign. ... 1.TrES.260.459.
And massie Beams in native Marble shone, ... 1.TrUl.36.467.
The dear Remembrance of his Native Coast; ... 1.TrUl.57.467.
And sought around his Native Realm in vain; ... 1.TrUl.71.468.
And safe restor'd me to my Native Land. ... 1.TrUl.83.468.
For 'twas from *Crete,* my Native Soil, I came; ... 1.TrUl.141.470.
Secure thou seest thy Native Shore at last? ... 1.TrUl.170.471.
Tell me, oh tell, is this my Native Place? ... 1.TrUl.202.472.
Others, long absent from their Native Place, ... 1.TrUl.213.472.
The pleasing Prospect of thy Native Shore! ... 1.TrUl.225.473.
Where slaves once more their native land behold, ... 3.EOM1.107.28.
In Spencer native Muses play; ... 4.HOde9.6.159.
Back to my native Moderation slide, ... 4.1HE1.33.281.
She rul'd, in native Anarchy, the mind. ... 5.DunA1.14.61.
Secure us kindly in our native night. ... 5.DunA1.154.82.
Ascend, and recognize their native place: ... 5.DunA1.224.90.
A cold, long-winded, native of the deep! ... 5.DunA2.288.137.
Imbrown'd with native Bronze, lo Henley stands, ... 5.DunA3.195.173.
She rul'd, in native Anarchy, the mind. ... 5.DunB1.16.270.
Secure us kindly in our native night. ... 5.DunB1.176.283.
Ascend, and recognize their Native Place. ... 5.DunB1.268.290.
A cold, long-winded, native of the deep: ... 5.DunB2.300.310.
Imbrown'd with native bronze, lo! Henly stands, ... 5.DunB3.199.330.
Content to breathe his native air, ... 6.1.3.3.
Contented breaths his Native Air, ... 6.1.3A.3.
Contented breaths his native air, ... 6.1.3B.3.
When wise *Ulysses,* from his native coast ... 6.15.1.51.
Neglect their Native Channel, Neighb'ring Coast, ... 6.17ii.14.56.
Have Humour, Wit, a native Ease and Grace; ... 6.19.27.63.
And view familiar, in its native skies, ... 6.23.10.73.
And view familiar, in her native skies, ... 6.23.10A.73.
Be justly warm'd with your own native rage. ... 6.32.44.97.
Fresnoy's close art, and *Dryden's* native fire: ... 6.52.8.156.
WELCOME, thrice welcome to thy native Place! ... 6.96iv.1.276.
The World's the native City of the Wise; ... 6.96v.21.280.
With native Humour temp'ring virtuous Rage, ... 6.125.3.350.
Safe to the Pleasures of your native Shore. ... Il.1.26.87.
Far from her native Soil, and weeping Sire. ... Il.1.46.88.
And Walls of Rocks, secure my native Reign, ... Il.1.204.96.
My Bark shall waft her to her native Land; ... Il.1.242.98.
Two Ages o'er his native Realm he reign'd, ... Il.1.335.104.
Safe and inglorious, to our native Shore. ... Il.2.170.136.
Behold them weeping for their native Shore! ... Il.2.354.144.
For this, constrain'd to quit his native Place, ... Il.2.803.163.
There in three Tribes divides his native Band, ... Il.2.809.163.
There lies, far distant from his native Plain; ... Il.2.857.165.
In Throngs around his native Bands repair, ... Il.2.990.170.
Thus may the *Greeks* review their native Shore, ... Il.3.107.194.
My Brothers these; the same our native Shore, ... Il.3.305.208.
Adorn'd with Honours in their native Shore, ... Il.3.313.208.
So shall the *Greeks* review their native Shore, ... Il.3.328.208.
Apollo's Altars in his Native Town. ... Il.4.151.228.
In Arms encircled with his native Bands. ... Il.4.237.232.
Before his helpless Friends, and native Bands, ... Il.4.604.250.
And left the Chariots in my Native Land. ... Il.5.257.279.
Æneas' Friend, and in his native Place ... Il.5.661.299.
In sable Ships they left their native Soil, ... Il.5.678.300.
'Till pierc'd at distance from their native Den, ... Il.5.685.300.
My much-lov'd Consort, and my native Shore, ... Il.5.845.305.
In fair *Arisba's* Walls (his native Place) ... Il.6.17.325.
To add new Honours to my native Land, ... Il.6.258.339.
Her pleasing Empire and her native Plain, ... Il.6.541.353.
The pleasing *Arnè* was his native Place. ... Il.7.14.363.
Stretch'd by some *Argive* on his native Shore: ... Il.8.436.418.
Haste to the Joys our native Country yields; ... Il.9.36.433.
To quit these Shores, their native Seats enjoy, ... Il.9.540.460.
Safe to transport him to his native Plains, ... Il.9.809.473.
Far from your Friends, and from your native Shore! ... Il.11.951.77.
That far, far distant from our native Home ... Il.13.296.119.
Ah! never may he see his native Land, ... Il.13.303.119.
Alike divine, and Heav'n their native Place; ... Il.13.446.126.

NATIVE (CONTINUED)

Th' assisting Forces of his native Bands: ... Il.13.617.135.
So joys *Æneas,* and his native Band ... Il.13.626.136.
Thro' filial Love he left his native Shore, ... Il.13.807.143.
He dwelt far distant from his native Place, ... Il.13.872.147.
And sent to *Argos,* and his native Shore. ... Il.15.34.195.
O *Jove!* if ever, on his native Shore, ... Il.15.428.213.
To fight our Wars, he left his native Air. ... Il.15.513.216.
'Tis hostile Ground you tread; your native Lands ... Il.15.900.232.
Or come sad Tidings from our native Land? ... Il.16.18.235.
The breathless Body to his native Land. ... Il.16.554.266.
Far from the *Lycian* Shores, his happy native Reign. ... Il.16.565.266.
First to the Fight his native Troops he warms, ... Il.16.653.270.
Far from *Larissa* lies, his native Air, ... Il.17.346.301.
Greece, in her native Fortitude elate, ... Il.17.372.302.
Far lyes *Patroclus* from his native plain! ... Il.18.127.328.
To *Troy* I sent him! but his native Shore ... Il.18.513.346.
And make me Empress in his native Land. ... Il.19.318.385.
My much lov'd Parents, and my native Shore— ... Il.19.469.391.
That barr such numbers from their native Plain: ... Il.21.69.424.
Far from his Father, Friends, and native Shore; ... Il.21.89.425.
Arm'd with protended Spears, my native Band; ... Il.21.172.428.
Deform'd, dishonour'd, in his native Land! ... Il.22.508.477.
Delightful roll along my native Coast! ... Il.23.179.497.
Thy Altars stand, perfum'd with native Flow'rs! ... Il.23.185.497.
No more *Achilles* sees his native Plain; ... Il.23.187.497.
Prepar'd perchance to leave thy native Land. ... Il.24.470.556.
One Ship convey'd us from our native Place; ... Il.24.486.556.
Pursu'd for Murder, flies his native Clime) ... Il.24.591.561.
Now at their native realms the *Greeks* arriv'd; ... Od.1.15.29.
A hopeless exile from his native home, ... Od.1.97.36.
That wise *Ulysses* to his native land ... Od.1.108.36.
Freighted with Iron from my native land, ... Od.1.233.43.
The great *Ulysses* reach'd his native shore. ... Od.2.389.80.
'Till great *Ulysses* views his native land. ... Od.2.397.80.
It fits to ask ye, what your native shore, ... Od.3.83.90.
Back to thy native Islands might'st thou sail, ... Od.3.143.92.
Safe reach'd the *Mirmydons* their native land, ... Od.3.228.96.
The bard they banish'd from his native soil, ... Od.3.340.103.
Too long a stranger to thy native land; ... Od.3.399.106.
'Till pitying *Jove* my native realm restor'd— ... Od.4.44.122.
Constrain'd me from my native realm to rove: ... Od.4.360.137.
Whate'er thy title in thy native sky, ... Od.4.508.144.
But when, his native shape resum'd, he stands ... Od.4.569.147.
The breathless heroes on their native shore? ... Od.4.660.150.
Before he anchors in his native port, ... Od.4.930.161.
Abandon'd, banish'd from his native reign, ... Od.5.21.172.
The son in safety to his native shore; ... Od.5.35.172.
What mov'd this journey from my native sky, ... Od.5.121.178.
Him, *Jove* now orders to his native lands ... Od.5.143.178.
And inly pining for his native shore; ... Od.5.195.181.
In peace shall land thee at thy native home. ... Od.5.220.182.
Be mortal, and this earth thy native place, ... Od.6.182.218.
"Perhaps a native of some distant shore, ... Od.6.333.227.
But would'st thou soon review thy native plain? ... Od.6.347.228.
'Till great *Ulysses* hail'd his native land. ... Od.6.394.230.
Snatch'd from *Epirus,* her sweet native shore, ... Od.7.12.233.
Far from my native coast, I rove alone, ... Od.7.33.235.
The native Islanders alone their care, ... Od.7.43.235.
But to his native land our charge resign'd, ... Od.7.260.248.
No glorious native of yon azure sky: ... Od.7.284.250.
A speedy voyage to his native shores. ... Od.8.174.271.
And grant him to his spouse and native shores! ... Od.8.446.287.
My native soil is *Ithaca* the fair, ... Od.9.21.302.
Then to my native country had I sail'd; ... Od.9.89.306.
Far from our destin'd course, and native land, ... Od.9.311.319.
Strong were the Rams, with native purple fair, ... Od.9.505.326.
Let not *Ulysses* breathe his native air, ... Od.9.621.332.
The tenth presents our welcome native shore: ... Od.10.31.340.
And drank oblivion of their native coast. ... Od.10.275.356.
Ah hope not yet to breathe thy native air! ... Od.10.578.370.
With promis'd off'rings on thy native shore; ... Od.10.621.374.
Your hopes already touch your native shore: ... Od.10.672.375.
A prosp'rous voyage to his native shores; ... Od.11.127.387.
Nor have these eyes beheld my native shores, ... Od.11.204.391.
To land *Ulysses* on his native shores. ... Od.11.413.404.
And fitter pomp to hail my native shores: ... Od.11.447.406.
Thro' tedious toils to view thy native coast. ... Od.12.177.440.
His native home deep-imag'd in his soul. ... Od.13.38.3.
Then send the stranger to his native shore. ... Od.13.67.4.
And massy beams in native marble shone: ... Od.13.127.8.
And bears triumphant to his native Isle ... Od.13.160.13.
The dear remembrance of his native coast. ... Od.13.224.16.
And sought, around, his native realm in vain: ... Od.13.238.17.
And safe restor'd me to my native land. ... Od.13.250.18.
For 'twas from *Crete* my native soil I came, ... Od.13.308.21.
Secure thou seest thy native shore at last? ... Od.13.337.23.
Tell me, oh tell, is this my native place? ... Od.13.369.25.
Others, long absent from their native place, ... Od.13.380.25.
The pleasing prospect of thy native shore. ... Od.13.392.26.
Else had I seen my native walls in vain, ... Od.13.439.27.
Encircled with a fence of native thorn, ... Od.14.14.35.
To native pastors is their charge assign'd, ... Od.14.127.42.
Again to hail them in their native shore. ... Od.14.164.43.
Your name, your parents, and your native air? ... Od.14.215.45.
Belov'd and honour'd in his native shore; ... Od.14.232.47.
For murder banish'd from his native home. ... Od.14.420.56.
To speed *Ulysses* to his native shore. ... Od.14.471.58.
Ere yet thy footsteps press thy native land. ... Od.15.36.71.
Art come to bless her in thy native land. ... Od.15.50.72.
Snatch'd thee an infant from thy native land! ... Od.15.411.89.
But snatch'd by pyrates from my native place, ... Od.15.468.93.
A wretch in safety to her native shore." ... Od.15.475.93.
'Tis giv'n at length to view my native coast. ... Od.16.227.114.
O'er seas convey'd me to my native reign: ... Od.16.253.117.
Retire we instant to our native reign, ... Od.16.404.125.

NATIVE (CONTINUED)

Thence safe I voyag'd to my native shore. … Od.17.169.139.
The dear remembrance of my native land, … Od.19.189.200.
I liv'd inglorious in my native Isle, … Od.19.213.203.
The vest much envy'd on your native coast, … Od.19.292.209.
Some bid the goblets boast their native gold: … Od.20.191.242.
Ulysses bore not from his native land, … Od.21.38.261.
The lost *Ulysses* to his native reign? … Od.21.202.269.
Thy lost *Ulysses* to his native shores, … Od.23.168.328.
Thence swift re-sailing to my native shores, … Od.23.295.337.
And whirls him groaning from his native shores: … Od.23.342.341.
Detain'd reluctant from my native shores. … Od.23.380.343.
Were all the partners of one native air? … Od.24.133.354.
Far from his friends, and from his native reign, … Od.24.340.365.
Thy town, thy parents, and thy native place? … Od.24.349.365.
Restor'd, and breathing in his native land. … Od.24.378.367.
Inhume the natives in their native plain, … Od.24.479.371.
In the best blood of all his native land. … Od.24.494.372.

NATIVE'S

And bold *Pelasgi* boast a native's due: … Od.19.201.202.

NATIVES

Long-winded both, as natives of the deep! … 5.DunA2.288A.137.
And well her Natives merit at thy Hand! … Il.6.70.327.
Anxious for *Troy,* the Guard the Natives keep; … Il.10.490.25.
Was not. The Natives were content to till … Il.20.258.404.
The coasts they ravage, and the natives kill. … Od.14.293.50.
No want, no famine the glad natives know, … Od.15.446.92.
The country ravage, and the natives kill. … Od.17.514.157.
Inhume the natives in their native plain, … Od.24.479.371.
"Forbear ye natives! your mad hands forbear … Od.24.614.377.

NATUR'D

Well-natur'd *Garth* inflam'd with early praise, … 4.Arbu.137.105.
With Wit well-natur'd, and with Books well-bred; … 6.19.8.62.
We'd be the best, good-natur'd things alive. … 6.41.14.113.

NATURAL

Oft, leaving what is Natural and fit, … 1.EOC.448.290.
To Be, contents his natural desire, … 3.EOM1.109.28.
And brings all natural events to pass, … 4.JD2.49.137.
And brings all Natural Events to pass: … 4.JD2A.55.136.

NATURE

And lavish Nature paints the Purple Year? … 1.PSp.28.63.
All Nature mourns, the Skies relent in Show'rs, … 1.PSp.69.68.
All Nature laughs, the Groves are fresh and fair, … 1.PSp.73.68.
And vanquish'd Nature seems to charm no more. … 1.PSp.76.68.
All Nature laughs, the Groves fresh Honours wear, … 1.PSp.73A.68.
Oh, skill'd in Nature! see the Hearts of Swains, … 1.PAu.11.81.
"Let Nature change, let Heav'n and Earth deplore, … 1.PWi.27.90.
Ah what avail the Beauties Nature wore? … 1.PWi.35.91.
Sharp *Boreas* blows, and Nature feels Decay, … 1.PWi.87.95.
See Nature hasts her earliest Wreaths to bring, … 1.Mes.23.114.
Whom Nature charms, and whom the Muse inspires, … 1.W-F.238.171.
To follow Nature, and regard his End. … 1.W-F.252.172.
Nature affords at least a *glimm'ring Light;* … 1.EOC.21.241.
And some made *Coxcombs* Nature meant but *Fools.* … 1.EOC.27.242.
Nature to all things fix'd the Limits fit, … 1.EOC.52.244.
First follow NATURE, and your Judgment frame … 1.EOC.68.246.
Unerring Nature, still divinely bright, … 1.EOC.70.246.
Are *Nature* still, but *Nature Methodiz'd;* … 1.EOC.89.249.
Are *Nature* still, but *Nature Methodiz'd;* … 1.EOC.89.249.
Nature, like *Liberty,* is but restrain'd … 1.EOC.90.249.
Nature, like *Monarchy,* is but restrain'd … 1.EOC.90A.249.
Nature and *Homer* were, he found, the same: … 1.EOC.135.255.
To copy *Nature* is to copy *Them.* … 1.EOC.140.255.
Whatever Nature has in *Worth* deny'd, … 1.EOC.205.264.
Where *Nature moves,* and *Rapture warms* the Mind; … 1.EOC.236.266.
In Wit, as Nature, what affects our Hearts … 1.EOC.243.267.
The *naked Nature* and the *living Grace,* … 1.EOC.294.272.
True Wit is *Nature* to Advantage drest, … 1.EOC.297.272.
The Face of Nature we no more Survey, … 1.EOC.313.274.
Persians and *Greeks* like *Turns of Nature* found, … 1.EOC.380.283.
And ready Nature waits upon his Hand; … 1.EOC.487.294.
Good-Nature and *Good-Sense* must ever join; … 1.EOC.524.297.
Not only *Nature* did his Laws obey, … 1.EOC.648Z1.312.
Who conquer'd *Nature,* shou'd preside o'er *Wit.* … 1.EOC.652.313.
To them by nature, but to me by love: … 1.TrPA.4.365.
And yields an Off-spring more than Nature gives; … 1.TrVP.14.377.
To me what Nature has in Charms deny'd … 1.TrSP.37.395.
Break all the Bonds of Nature, and prepare … 1.TrSt.116.415.
Of Nature broke; and Royal Perjuries; … 1.TrSt.179.418.
Thro' violated Nature force his way, … 1.TrSt.332.424.
Till Nature quicken'd by th'Inspiring Ray, … 1.TrSt.586.434.
And give to Fame what we to Nature owe; … 1.TrES.50.451.
"Wou'd I vouchsafe to sell what Nature gave, … 2.ChWB.201.66.
Here stood *Ill-nature* like an *ancient Maid,* … 2.RL4.27.185.
Superior Worlds, and look all Nature thro'. … 2.TemF.237.274.
And startled Nature trembled with the Blast. … 2.TemF.417.283.
As Flames by Nature to the Skies ascend, … 2.TemF.428.284.
Still rebel nature holds out half my heart; … 2.ElAb.26.321.
When love is liberty, and nature, law: … 2.ElAb.92.327.
Oh come! oh teach me nature to subdue, … 2.ElAb.203.336.
Then conscience sleeps, and leaving nature free, … 2.ElAb.227.338.
Nature stands check'd; Religion disapproves; … 2.ElAb.259.341.
From these perhaps (ere nature bade her die) … 2.Elegy.23.364.
Yet simple Nature to his hope has giv'n, … 3.EOM1.103.27.
"For me kind Nature wakes her genial pow'r, … 3.EOM1.133.32.
But errs not Nature from this gracious end, … 3.EOM1.141.32.
Then Nature deviates; and can Man do less? … 3.EOM1.150.34.
And Nature deviates; how can Man do less? … 3.EOM1.150A.34.
Nature as much a constant course requires … 3.EOM1.151A.34.
Is kept in Nature, and is kept in Man. … 3.EOM1.172.36.
Nature to these, without profusion kind, … 3.EOM1.179.37.

NATURE (CONTINUED)

Nature to each, without profusion kind, … 3.EOM1.179A.37.
But what his nature and his state can bear. … 3.EOM1.192.38.
If nature thunder'd in his op'ning ears, … 3.EOM1.201.40.
All Nature quick, and bursting into birth. … 3.EOM1.234A.44.
And Nature tremble to the throne of God: … 3.EOM1.256.46.
Whose body Nature is, and God the soul; … 3.EOM1.268.47.
All Nature is but Art, unknown to thee; … 3.EOM1.289.50.
Two Principles in human nature reign; … 3.EOM2.53.62.
Nature its mother, Habit is its nurse; … 3.EOM2.145.72.
Teach us to mourn our Nature, not to mend, … 3.EOM2.153.73.
Strong grows the Virtue with his nature mix'd; … 3.EOM2.178.76.
Thus Nature gives us (let it check our pride) … 3.EOM2.195.78.
Extremes in Nature equal ends produce, … 3.EOM2.205.79.
The learn'd is happy nature to explore, … 3.EOM2.263.87.
The learn'd are happy nature to explore, … 3.EOM2.263A.87.
See plastic Nature working to this end, … 3.EOM3.9.93.
Nature that Tyrant checks; he only knows, … 3.EOM3.51.97.
Sure by quick Nature happiness to gain, … 3.EOM3.91.101.
One in their nature, which are two in ours, … 3.EOM3.96.101.
God, in the nature of each being, founds … 3.EOM3.109.103.
Or pours profuse on earth; one nature feeds … 3.EOM3.117.104.
The state of Nature was the reign of God: … 3.EOM3.148.107.
Who, foe to Nature, hears the gen'ral groan, … 3.EOM3.163.109.
See him from Nature rising slow to Art! … 3.EOM3.169.110.
Thus then to Man the voice of Nature spake— … 3.EOM3.171.110.
"Laws wise as Nature, and as fix'd as Fate. … 3.EOM3.190.112.
Great Nature spoke; observant Men obey'd; … 3.EOM3.199.113.
When Love and Liberty, and Nature Law. … 3.EOM3.208.114.
'Till then by Nature crown'd, each Patriarch sate, … 3.EOM3.215.114.
For Nature knew no right divine in Men, … 3.EOM3.236.116.
The Faith and Moral, Nature gave before; … 3.EOM3.286.121.
Thus God and Nature link'd the gen'ral frame, … 3.EOM3.317.126.
Or God and Nature meant to mere Mankind; … 3.EOM4.78.135.
When Nature sicken'd, and each gale was death? … 3.EOM4.108.138.
There deviates Nature, and here wanders Will. … 3.EOM4.112.138.
Or Change admits, or Nature lets it fall, … 3.EOM4.115.139.
God sends not Ill, 'tis Nature lets it fall … 3.EOM4.113Z1.139.
Say, at what part of nature will they stand? … 3.EOM4.166.143.
But looks thro' Nature, up to Nature's God; … 3.EOM4.332.160.
He sees, why Nature plants in Man alone … 3.EOM4.345.162.
(Nature, whose dictates to no other kind … 3.EOM4.347.162.
Teach me, like thee, in various nature wise, … 3.EOM4.377.165.
Nature well known, no Miracles remain, … 3.Ep1.208A.33.
Know, God and Nature only are the same: … 3.Ep1.154.28.
Judge we by Nature? Habit can efface, … 3.Ep1.168.29.
Thus with each gift of nature and of art, … 3.Ep1.192.31.
Nature well known, no prodigies remain, … 3.Ep1.208.33.
Here honest Nature ends as she begins. … 3.Ep1.227.34.
Narcissa's nature, tolerably mild, … 3.Ep2.53.54.
Why then declare Good-nature is her scorn, … 3.Ep2.59.55.
Nature in her then err'd not, but forgot. … 3.Ep2.158.64.
None see what Parts of Nature it conceals. … 3.Ep2.190.65.
That, Nature gives; and where the lesson taught … 3.Ep2.211.67.
B. What Nature wants, commodious Gold bestows, … 3.Ep3.21A.85.
Opine, that Nature, as in duty bound, … 3.Ep3.9.83.
What Nature wants, commodious Gold bestows, … 3.Ep3.21.85.
What Nature wants (a phrase I much distrust) … 3.Ep3.25.88.
"Extremes in Nature equal good produce, … 3.Ep3.163.106.
Of mad Good-nature, and of mean Self-love. … 3.Ep3.228.111.
In all, let Nature never be forgot. … 3.Ep4.50.142.
Nature shall join you, Time shall make it grow … 3.Ep4.69.143.
The suff'ring eye inverted Nature sees, … 3.Ep4.119.149.
Tim'rous by Nature, of the Rich in awe, … 4.HS1.7.5.
Nature made ev'ry Fop to plague his Brother, … 4.JD4.258.47.
Nothing in Nature is so lewd as *Peg,* … 4.HAdv.31.77.
Hath not indulgent Nature spread a Feast, … 4.HAdv.96.83.
In search of Vanities from Nature strays: … 4.HAdv.99.83.
Has Nature set no bounds to wild Desire? … 4.HAdv.143.87.
And just that White and Red which Nature gave. … 4.HAdv.164.89.
Yet soft by Nature, more a Dupe than Wit, … 4.Arbu.368.123.
By Nature honest, by Experience wise, … 4.Arbu.400.126.
You think 'tis Nature, and a knack to please: … 4.2HE2.177.177.
That God of Nature, who, within us still, … 4.2HE2.280.185.
"Of Shakespear's Nature, and of Cowley's Wit; … 4.2HE1.83.201.
But Times corrupt, and Nature, ill-inclin'd, … 4.2HE1.251.217.
Shall One whom Nature, Learning, Birth, conspir'd … 4.1HE6.40.239.
As Beasts of Nature may we hunt the Squires? … 4.EpS2.31.314.
(Where *Kent* and Nature vye for PELHAM'S LOVE) … 4.EpS2.67.316.
Or those proud fools whom nature, rank, and fate … 4.1740.67.335.
With Shakespear's nature, or with Johnson's art, … 5.DunA2.216.127.
Fam'd for good-nature, B[urnet] and for truth; … 5.DunA3.175.168.
Not touch'd by Nature, and not reach'd by Art." … 5.DunA3.228.176.
Bays, form'd by nature Stage and Town to bless, … 5.DunB1.109.277.
With Shakespear's nature, or with Johnson's art, … 5.DunB2.224.307.
Not touch'd by Nature, and not reach'd by Art." … 5.DunB3.230.331.
See Nature in some partial narrow shape, … 5.DunB4.455.385.
And last, to Nature's Cause thro' Nature led. … 5.DunB4.468.386.
Make Nature still incroach upon his plan; … 5.DunB4.473.387.
That NATURE our Society adores, … 5.DunB4.491.390.
Bounded by Nature, narrow'd still by Art, … 5.DunB4.503.392.
More she had spoke, but yawn'd—All Nature nods: … 5.DunB4.605.403.
More she had said, but yawn'd—All Nature nods: … 5.DunB4.605A.403.
Nature itself is only gay, … 6.4iv.20.11.
Thou wert e'er Nature first began to be, … 6.8.2A.17.
Read something of a diff'rent Nature, … 6.10.5.24.
His easie Art may happy Nature seem, … 6.19.3.62.
By nature yielding, stubborn but for Fame; … 6.19.35.63.
Amidst the wrack of nature undismay'd, … 6.21.9.69.
Informs great nature and directs the whole! … 6.23.4.73.
Go fathom Nature, take the Heights of Art! … 6.27.13.81.
Cease, fond Nature, cease thy strife, … 6.31ii.5.94.
Tyrants no more their savage nature kept, … 6.32.7.96.
There Nature reigns, and Passion void of Art, … 6.33.9.99.
Here Nature reigns, and Passion void of Art, … 6.33.9A.99.
Nature to your undoing arms mankind … 6.38.15.108.

NATURE (CONTINUED)

What awes the World is Envy and ill Nature. ....6.48iii.8.134.
And binding Nature fast in Fate, ...6.50.11.146.
Which nature has imprest? ....6.51ii.10.153.
Why, nature, dost thou soonest fire ....6.51ii.11.153.
Old, and void of all good-nature; ....6.70.7.201.
Good Nature, she declar'd it, was her Scorn, ...6.99.7.286.
Bring me what Nature, Taylor to the *Bear,* ....6.100iii.1.289.
Next in three Books, sunk human *Nature,* ....6.101.10.290.
At once, to nature, history, and you. ....6.107.20.311.
[*Nature!* informer of the poet's art, ...6.107.27.311.
Whose Art was Nature, and whose Pictures thought; ....6.108.2.312.
Living, great Nature fear'd he might outvie ....6.108.7.312.
Living, great Nature fear'd he would outvie ....6.108.7A.312.
Nature, and Nature's Laws lay hid in Night. ....6.111.1.317.
All Nature and her Laws lay hid in Night. ....6.111.1A.317.
All Nature and its Laws lay hid in Night. ....6.111.1B.317.
Patron of Arts, and Judge of Nature, dy'd! ....6.118.2.334.
Yet soft his Nature, tho' severe his Lay, ...6.118.5.334.
But still in her Heart she held *Nature* more *clever.* ....6.124i.4.346.
Severe of Morals, but of Nature mild; ....6.125.1B.349.
Beauty which Nature only can impart, ...6.126ii.5.353.
Approach. Great NATURE studiously behold! ....6.142.7.382.
'Tis Nature's Voice, and Nature we obey. ....Il.2.168.136.
Not blest by Nature with the Charms of Face, ...Il.10.375.20.
And give to Fame what we to Nature owe; ....Il.12.394.96.
And Nature speaks at ev'ry Pause of Art. ....Il.24.905.574.
Ev'n Nature starts, and what ye ask denies. ....Od.2.148.69.
The waste of nature let the feast repair, ...Od.4.71.122.
The wants of nature with repast suffice, ...Od.4.581.147.
Thus spent already, how shall nature bear ....Od.5.602.201.
But still long-weary'd nature wants repair; ....Od.7.294.250.
They eat, they drink, and nature gives the feast; ....Od.9.104.307.
They all their products to free nature owe. ....Od.9.122.310.
And shew'd its nature and its wond'rous pow'r: ....Od.10.363.362.
And all-composing rest my nature craves, ...Od.11.410.404.
Whatever frugal nature needs, is thine, ...Od.15.528.95.
Of nature courteous, and by far the best; ....Od.15.560.96.
The man by nature prone to insolence: ....Od.17.477.156.
The dues of nature to his natal home!— ....Od.19.193.201.
Now, pay the debt to craving nature due, ...Od.20.63.235.
Nature her debt, than disappointed live, ...Od.21.164.267.
My weary nature craves the balm of rest: ....Od.23.173.329.
Well-pleas'd you told its nature, and its name, ...Od.24.393.368.

NATURE'S

'Tis done, and Nature's various Charms decay; ....1.PWi.29.91.
And but from *Nature's Fountains* scorn'd to draw: ....1.EOC.133.254.
Which *out of* Nature's *common Order* rise, ...1.EOC.159.258.
Nature's chief Master-piece is writing well. ....1.EOC.724.323.
Or did from Change, or Nature's Pow'r proceed, ...2.ChJM.427.35.
Eye Nature's walks, shoot Folly as it flies, ...3.EOM1.13.14.
From Nature's chain whatever link you strike, ...3.EOM1.245.45.
A mortal Man unfold all Nature's law, ...3.EOM2.32.60.
Suffice that Reason keep to Nature's road, ...3.EOM2.115.69.
Yes, Nature's road must ever be prefer'd; ....3.EOM2.161.74.
Wild Nature's vigor working at the root. ....3.EOM2.184.77.
Behold the child, by Nature's kindly law, ...3.EOM2.275.88.
Know, Nature's children all divide her care; ....3.EOM3.43.96.
Nor think, in NATURE'S STATE they blindly trod; ....3.EOM3.147.107.
That proud exception to all Nature's laws, ...3.EOM3.243.117.
Take Nature's path, and mad Opinion's leave, ...3.EOM4.29.130.
All Nature's diff'rence keeps all Nature's peace. ....3.EOM4.56.133.
All Nature's diff'rence keeps all Nature's peace. ....3.EOM4.56.133.
But looks thro' Nature, up to Nature's God; ....3.EOM4.332.160.
For Wit's false mirror held up Nature's light; ....3.EOM4.393.166.
Add Nature's, Custom's, Reason's, Passion's strife, ...3.Ep1.21.17.
In Love's, in Nature's spite, the siege they hold ....4.JD2.23.133.
In Nature's spight, the Stubborn Siege they hold ....4.JD2A.27.134.
If one, thro' Nature's Bounty or his Lord's, ...4.EpS2.173.323.
Thence a new world, to Nature's laws unknown, ...5.DunA3.237.177.
Then a new world, to Nature's laws unknown, ...5.DunA3.237A.177.
Thence a new world to Nature's laws unknown, ...5.DunB3.241.332.
Did Nature's pencil ever blend such rays, ...5.DunB4.411.382.
And last, to Nature's Cause thro' Nature led. ....5.DunB4.468.386.
Of untaught nature's humble pride, ...6.6ii.18.15.
Thou wert e'er Nature's self began to be, ...6.8.2.17.
Luxurious Nature's Wealth in Thought surveys, ...6.17iii.20.58.
Such wholsome Foods as Nature's Wants supply, ...6.17iii.26.58.
All Nature's Incence rise! ....6.50.52.148.
In Miniature see *Nature's* Power appear; ....6.96v.1.280.
Nature, and Nature's Laws lay hid in Night. ....6.111.1.317.
From Nature's temp'rate feast rose satisfy'd, ...6.112.9.318.
'Tis Nature's Voice, and Nature we obey. ....Il.2.168.136.
Nor dare to combate her's and Nature's Sire. ....Il.8.519.421.
See'st thou not me, whom Nature's Gifts adorn, ...Il.21.119.426.
When nature's hush'd beneath her brooding shade, ...Od.19.602.225.

NATURES

And Middle natures, how they long to join, ...3.EOM1.227.43.
Natures æthereal, human, angel, man, ...3.EOM1.238.44.
What happier natures shrink at with affright, ...3.EOM2.229.83.
Can those be Sins with Natures God ....6.50.20Z3.147*.
Can those be Crimes to Natures God ....6.50.20Z3A.147.
Which Natures selfe inspires? ....6.50.20Z4.147*.
Nor dare to combate her's and Natures Sire. ....Il.8.499.420.

NAUBOLIDES

Naubolides with grace unequall'd shone, ...Od.8.121.269.

NAUGHTY

Fye, naughty Fop! where e'er you come ....6.135.15.366.
Fye, naughty thing! where e'er you come ....6.135.15A.366.

NAUSEATE

Which nauseate all, and nothing can digest. ....1.EOC.389.284.
I puke, I nauseate,—yet he thrusts in more; ....4.JD4.153.37.

NAUSICAA

A heav'n of charms divine *Nausicaa* lay: ....Od.6.22.204.
They sport, they feast; *Nausicaa* lifts her voice, ...Od.6.115.211.
With equal grace *Nausicaa* trod the plain, ...Od.6.127.212.
Forth from her snowy hand *Nausicaa* threw ....Od.6.133.213.
Now on return her care *Nausicaa* bends, ...Od.6.299.225.
"What stranger this, whom thus *Nausicaa* leads? ....Od.6.331.227.
Nurse of *Nausicaa* from her infant years, ...Od.7.15.234.
Nausicaa blooming as a Goddess stands, ...Od.8.496.289.

NAUSITHOUS

Then great *Nausithous* from *Hyperia* far ....Od.6.9.203.
For know, from Ocean's God *Nausithous* sprung, ...Od.7.72.237.

NAUSTES

Amphimachus and *Naustes* guide the Train, ...Il.2.1060.172.
Naustes the bold, *Amphimachus* the vain, ...Il.2.1061.172.

NAUTES

There *Proreus, Nautes, Eratreus* appear, ...Od.8.117.268.

NAUTILUS

"Learn of the little Nautilus to sail, ...3.EOM3.177.111.

NAVAL

Next, to secure our Camp, and Naval Pow'rs, ...Il.7.406.384.
Then, to secure the Camp and Naval Pow'rs, ...Il.7.520.389.
(Their Naval Station where th' *Ajaces* keep, ...Il.13.854.146.
Ev'n to the last, his Naval Charge defends, ...Il.15.886.231.
So well the Chief his Naval Weapon sped, ...Il.15.906.232.
The Heroes heard, and all the Naval Train ....Il.19.45.373.
And now they reach'd the naval Walls, and found ....Il.24.545.558.
To naval arts inur'd, and stormy toil. ....Od.1.232.43.
(When night advances) bear the naval stores; ....Od.2.328.77.
And stow'd within its womb the naval stores. ....Od.2.439.82.
Amassing gold, and gath'ring naval stores; ....Od.3.385.105.
For I alone sustain their naval cares, ...Od.3.462.109.
For sailing arts and all the naval toil, ...Od.7.137.242.
Studious of freight, in naval trade well skill'd, ...Od.8.181.272.
With speed debarking land the naval stores; ....Od.16.347.123.

NAVEL

Spreads her Fore-Buttocks to the Navel bare. ....4.HAdv.34.79.
And her fore-buttocks to the navel bare. ....5.DunA2.152Z2.120.
Now her Fore Buttocks to the Navel bare. ....6.99.12Z2.287.
And thro' his Navel drove the pointed Death: ....Il.4.607.250.
Chersidamas, beneath the Navel thrust, ...Il.11.533.57.
Forth thro' the Navel burst the thrilling Steel; ....Il.20.481.414.

NAVES

The bossie Naves of solid Silver shone; ....Il.5.896.308.
The Wheel's round Naves appear to brush the Goal. ....Il.23.412.506.

NAVIES

And future Navies on thy Shores appear. ....1.W-F.222.170.
And future Navies on thy Banks appear. ....1.W-F.222A.170.
But future Buildings, future Navies grow: ....3.Ep4.188.155.
And Navies yawn'd for Orders on the Main. ....5.DunB4.618.405.
If to besiege our Navies they prepare, ...Il.10.247.13.
To guard their Navies, and defend the Wall. ....Il.12.158.87.
This Day, preserve our Navies from the Flame, ...Il.15.434.214.
And the toss'd Navies beat the heaving Main. ....Il.20.82.397.
To build proud navies, and command the main; ....Od.7.46.235.
She fills with navies, hosts, and loud alarms ....Od.17.342.148.
When our triumphant navies touch'd your shore; ....Od.24.141.354.

NAVIGABLE

The Town, the Tents, and navigable Seas. ....Il.8.66.398.

NAVY

But *Pallas* knew (thy Friends and Navy lost) ....1.TrUl.220.473.
Such place hath *Deptford,* Navy-building Town, ...6.14ii.46.44.
But raging still amidst his Navy sate ....Il.1.634.118.
The Fields, the Tents, the Navy, and the Bay. ....Il.2.963.169.
The Steeds and Chariot, to the Navy led, ...Il.5.33.267.
Their Steeds and Chariot to the Navy born. ....Il.5.211.277.
Till *Ilion* falls, or till yon' Navy burns. ....Il.7.84.367.
The breathless Carcase to your Navy sent, ...Il.7.97.368.
Till their proud Navy wrapt in Smoak and Fires, ...Il.8.222.407.
Whose distant Ships the guarded Navy bound. ....Il.8.273.410.
The Navy flaming, and thy *Greeks* in Flight, ...Il.8.591.424.
A martial Council near the Navy-Walls, ...Il.8.610.425.
Has he not fenc'd his guarded Navy round, ...Il.9.460.455.
Not till amidst yon' sinking Navy slain, ...Il.9.765.472.
Returns the Chief, or must our Navy fall? ....Il.9.793.473.
Prepare to meet us near the Navy-wall. ....Il.10.145.8.
Whose Ships remote the guarded Navy bound. ....Il.11.12.35.
The Navy shakes, and at the dire Alarms ....Il.11.15.35.
Tydides mounts, and to the Navy speeds. ....Il.11.508.56.
Our bravest Heroes in the Navy groan, ...Il.11.805.72.
And Drifts of Dust the clouded Navy hide: ....Il.12.300.92.
Brave *Greece* victorious, and her Navy free: ....Il.13.134.111.
Safe in their Arms, the Navy fears no Flame; ....Il.13.407.125.
A Princess rap'd transcends a Navy storm'd: ....Il.13.782.142.
Long e'er in Flames our lofty Navy fall, ...Il.13.1028.153.
Now to the Navy born on silent Wings, ...Il.14.407.183.
To flank the Navy, and the Shores defend. ....Il.15.345.210.
And flank the Navy with a brazen Wall; ....Il.15.677.222.
To view the Navy blazing to the Skies; ....Il.15.719.223.
And shew'd the Shores, the Navy, and the Main: ....Il.15.811.228.
And wise *Ulysses,* at the Navy groan ....Il.16.36.236.
How first the Navy blaz'd with *Trojan* Flame? ....Il.16.141.243.

NAVY (CONTINUED)
Clear'd from the Smoke the joyful Navy lies; ... Il.16.350.256.
Forc'd from the Navy, yet the Fight maintains. ... Il.16.363.257.
Safe to the Navy thro' the Storm of War. ... Il.17.519.308.
And the swift Chariot to the Navy flies. ... Il.17.704.315.
Fierce on yon' Navy will we pour our Arms. ... Il.18.354.338.
This Instant from the Navy shall be sent ... Il.19.139.377.
The Corps of *Hector,* at yon' Navy slain. ... Il.24.238.546.
Thro' the mid seas he bids our navy steer, ... Od.3.211.96.
And safe to *Argos'* port his navy brought, ... Od.3.396.105.
While from the shores the winged navy flies: ... Od.8.550.292.
Thro' all-surrounding shade our navy brought; ... Od.9.166.312.
Our sight the whole collected navy chear'd, ... Od.9.637.332.
Snatch'd in the whirl, the hurried navy flew, ... Od.10.52.342.
But two rush'd out, and to the navy flew. ... Od.10.134.347.
Heap'd high his navy with unnumber'd spoils. ... Od.11.654.416.
'Tis thine alone (thy friends and navy lost) ... Od.12.176.440.
But *Pallas* knew (thy friends and navy lost) ... Od.13.387.25.
From *Malea's* gusty cape his navy drove ... Od.19.217.204.

NAVY-BUILDING
Such place hath *Deptford,* Navy-building Town, ... 6.14ii.46.44.

NAVY-WALL
Prepare to meet us near the Navy-wall; ... Il.10.145.8.

NAVY-WALLS
A martial Council near the Navy-Walls: ... Il.8.610.425.

NAVY'S
With Gold and Brass his loaded Navy's sides. ... Il.9.178.441.
With Gold and Brass thy loaded Navy's sides. ... Il.9.365.451.
And spread your Glory with the Navy's Flame. ... Il.15.573.218.

NAY
Nay tell me first, in what more happy Fields ... 1.PSp.89.69.
Conceal his Force, nay seem sometimes to *Fly.* ... 1.EOC.178.261.
Oft *hide* his Force, nay seem sometimes to *Fly.* ... 1.EOC.178A.261.
Nay shou'd great *Homer* lift his awful Head, ... 1.EOC.464.292.
Nay *Wits* had *Pensions,* and *young Lords* had *Wit:* ... 1.EOC.539.298.
Nay show'd his Faults—but when wou'd Poets mend? ... 1.EOC.621.309.
Nay, fly to *Altars; there* they'll talk you dead; ... 1.EOC.624.310.
Nay, run to *Altars; there* they'll talk you dead; ... 1.EOC.624A.310.
Nay, if my Lord affirm'd that Black was White, ... 2.ChJM.160.22.
Nay, were they taken in a strict Embrace, ... 2.ChJM.663.47.
Nay, (quoth the King) dear Madam be not wroth; ... 2.ChJM.700.48.
"But see! I'm all your own—nay hold—for Shame! ... 2.ChWB.203.66.
Nay once by Heav'n he struck me on the Face: ... 2.ChWB.335.73.
Nay oft, in Dreams, Invention we bestow, ... 2.RL2.99.165.
"Plague on't! 'tis past a Jest—nay prithee, Pox! ... 2.RL4.129.194.
Nay, *Poll* sate mute, and *Shock* was most Unkind! ... 2.RL4.164.197.
To patch, nay ogle, might become a Saint, ... 2.RL5.23.201.
Nay, feasts the animal he dooms his feast, ... 3.EOM3.65.98.
Nay, why external for internal giv'n? ... 3.EOM4.161.143.
Belies his features, nay extends his hands; ... 3.Ep3.294.117.
Nay, all that lying Travellers can feign. ... 4.JD4.31.29.
Henley himself I've heard, nay *Budgel* too: ... 4.JD4.51.29.
Nay troth, th' *Apostles,* (tho' perhaps too rough) ... 4.JD4.76.31.
"Oh! Sir, politely well! nay, let me dye, ... 4.JD4.112A.35.
"Oh! Sir, politely so! nay, let me dye, ... 4.JD4.112.35.
Nay hints, 'tis by Connivance of the Court, ... 4.JD4.164.39.
The Dog-star rages! nay 'tis past a doubt, ... 4.Arbu.3.96.
Still *Sapho—"Hold!* nay see you—you'll offend: ... 4.Arbu.101A.103.
Has drunk with *Cibber,* nay has rym'd for *Moor.* ... 4.Arbu.373.123.
Has drank with *Cibber,* nay has rym'd for *Moor.* ... 4.Arbu373A.123.
Nay worse, to ask for Verse at such a time! ... 4.2HE2.31.167.
Nay tho' at Court (perhaps) it may find grace: ... 4.2HE2.162.177.
All Worldly's Hens, nay Partridge, sold to town, ... 4.2HE2.234.181.
All He[athco]te's Hens, nay Partridge, sold to town, ... 4.2HE2.234A.181.
Forgot his Epic, nay Pindaric Art, ... 4.2HE1.77.201.
Nay half in Heav'n—except (what's mighty odd) ... 4.1HE1.187.293.
Some, in their choice of Friends (nay, look not grave) ... 4.EpS2.100.318.
Nay, Mahomet! the Pigeon at thine ear; ... 5.DunB4.364.378.
Nay, Mr. *Wycherly* see *Binfield.* ... 6.10.48.26.
Nay, e'en the Parts of Shame by Name would call: ... 6.14ii.41.44.
Nay, to yourselves alone that knowledge owe. ... 6.27.15.81.
Nay, did all *J[a]c[o]b* breath in thee, ... 6.64.18.190.
Nay, did James Baker breath in thee, ... 6.64.18A.190.
"Nay, mix with Children, as they play'd at Taw; ... 6.96ii.28.271.
Nay, wou'd kind *Jove* my Organs so dispose, ... 6.96iv.105.279.
"Red, Blue, and Green, nay white and black, ... 6.140.19.378.
Nay promis'd (vainly promis'd!) to bestow ... Od.5.173.180.
Nay promis'd, vainly promis'd, to bestow ... Od.7.342.253.
The day shall come; nay, 'tis already near, ... Od.17.296.146.

NE
Ne swinken but with Secrecie: ... 6.14i.2A.41.
She scratched, bit, and spar'd ne Lace ne Band, ... 6.14ii.39.44.
She scratched, bit, and spar'd ne Lace ne Band, ... 6.14ii.39.44.
Ne Village is without, on either side, ... 6.14ii.51.44.
Ne *Richmond's* self, from whose tall Front are ey'd ... 6.14ii.53.44.
044.Ne *Richmond's* self, from whose tall Front is ey'd ... 6.14ii.53A.44.

NE'ER
Against the *Precept,* ne'er transgress its *End,* ... 1.EOC.164.259.
Thinks what ne'er was, nor is, nor e'er shall be. ... 1.EOC.254.268.
So vast a Throng the Stage can ne'er contain. ... 1.EOC.283.271.
The Stage can ne'er so vast a Throng contain. ... 1.EOC.283A.271.
What oft was *Thought,* but ne'er so well *Exprest,* ... 1.EOC.298.273.
What oft was *Thought,* but ne'er before *Exprest,* ... 1.EOC.298A.273.
Some ne'er advance a Judgment of their own, ... 1.EOC.408.287.
And own *stale Nonsense* which they ne'er invent. ... 1.EOC.411.287.
Ah ne'er so *dire* a *Thirst of Glory* boast, ... 1.EOC.522.297.
With mean Complacence ne'er betray your Trust, ... 1.EOC.580.306.
And Things *ne'er known* propos'd as Things *forgot:* ... 1.EOC.575A.306.
And found the springs that ne'er till then deny'd ... 1.TrFD.51.388.

NE'ER (CONTINUED)
You ne'er had us'd these killing Words to me. ... 2.ChJM.775.52.
Jove ne'er spoke Oracle more true than this, ... 2.ChJM.809.54.
And sure the certain Stint was ne'er defin'd. ... 2.ChWB.16.57.
The wasting Moth ne'er spoil'd my best Array; ... 2.ChWB.288.71.
So perish all, whose breast ne'er learn'd to glow ... 2.Elegy.45.366.
But where th'Extreme of Vice, was ne'er agreed: ... 3.EOM2.221.82.
But where the *Point* of Vice, was ne'er agreed: ... 3.EOM2.221A.82.
Say, was it Virtue, more tho' Heav'n ne'er gave, ... 3.EOM4.103.138.
Yet ne'er looks forward farther than his nose. ... 3.EOM4.224.148.
Yet ne'er looks forward further than his nose. ... 3.EOM4.224A.148.
That ne'er shall answer till a Husband cool, ... 3.Ep2.261A.71.
Yet ne'er so sure our passion to create, ... 3.Ep2.51.54.
She, who ne'er answers till a Husband cools, ... 3.Ep2.261.71.
To gain those Riches he can ne'er enjoy: ... 3.Ep4.2.134.
His wealth, to purchase what he ne'er can taste? ... 3.Ep4.4.134.
With Eyes that pry not, Tongue that ne'er repeats, ... 4.HS1.135.19.
All you, who think the *City* ne'er can thrive, ... 4.HAdv.47.79.
And so obliging that he ne'er oblig'd; ... 4.Arbu.208.110.
Yet Wit ne'er tastes, and Beauty ne'er enjoys, ... 4.Arbu.312.118.
Yet Wit ne'er tastes, and Beauty ne'er enjoys, ... 4.Arbu.312.118.
"Let him take Castles who has ne'er a Groat." ... 4.2HE2.51.167.
He ne'er rebels, or plots, like other men: ... 4.2HE1.194.211.
If I ne'er got, or lost a groat, ... 4.HS6.13.251.
Great Ministers ne'er think of these; ... 4.HS6.38.253.
And that they ne'er consider'd yet. ... 4.HS6.42.253.
"You ne'er consider whom you shove, ... 4.HS6.58.253.
The worthy Youth shall ne'er be in a rage: ... 4.EpS1.48.301.
But random Praise—the Task can ne'er be done, ... 4.EpS2.106.319.
What's that to you, who ne'er was out nor in? ... 4.EpS2.163.322.
All shall be darkness, as it ne'er were Day; ... 5.DunA3.337Z2.192.
And ceas'd so soon, he ne'er was Boy, nor Man. ... 5.DunB4.288.372.
(Tho' ne'er so weighty) reach a wondrous height; ... 6.7.16.16.
He ne'er (good Man) bore *Hellen* Grudge, ... 6.10.98.27.
And ne'er reproach him with his Luxury. ... 6.17iii.27.58.
They ne'er gave *Sixpence* for *two Lines,* ... 6.29.23.83.
E shew'd, a *Comma* ne'er could claim ... 6.30.19.86.
He'd ne'er be us'd so like a Beast; ... 6.30.28A.86.
He'd ne'er be serv'd so like a Beast; ... 6.30.28B.86.
Himself could ne'er be *Jupiter;* ... 6.30.39.87.
G swore, by G—d, it ne'er should be; ... 6.30.44.87.
Cou'd ne'er bring in *Psi* and *Xi;* ... 6.30.69.88.
May *Satire* ne'er befool ye, or beknave ye, ... 6.40.9.112.
Those strange examples ne'er were made to fit ye, ... 6.41.41.114.
Who ne'er saw naked Sword, or look'd in, *Plato.* ... 6.41.44.114.
Who ne'er knew Joy, but Friendship might divide, ... 6.85.3.242.
Molly had ne'er a Midwife been, ... 6.94.83.262.
The Richmond Fair ones ne'er will spoil their Looks, ... 6.95.3A.264.
These filthy Sluts, their Jordans ne'er abscond ... 6.96ii.30Z3.271.
Shall I ne'er see thee turn my watches key ... 6.96ii.30Z43.272.
"Shall I ne'er bear thy self and House again? ... 6.96ii.60.273.
Yet ne'er one Sprig of Laurel grac'd those Ribbalds, ... 6.98.13.283.
And so obliging that he ne'er oblig'd: ... 6.98.58.285.
See who ne'er was or will be half read! ... 6.101.1.290.
'Tis ten to one he'll ne'er come back. ... 6.103.4.295.
For *Jammie* ne'er grew *James;* and what they call ... 6.116iv.3.327.
Lies He who ne'er car'd, and still cares not a Pin, ... 6.144.5.386.
Lies one who ne'er car'd, and who cares not a Pin, ... 6.144.5A.386.
Lies one who ne'er car'd, and still cares not a Pin, ... 6.144.5B.386.
Yet ne'er a friend forgetting, till forgot. ... 6.147vii.2.391.
Ne'er to return was then the common Cry, ... Il.2.352.144.
But ne'er 'till now such Numbers charg'd a Field. ... Il.2.969.169.
Our Eyes, till now, that Aspect ne'er beheld, ... Il.6.153.333.
Those Wheels returning ne'er shall mark the Plain; ... Il.12.128.86.
Ne'er did my Soul so strong a Passion prove, ... Il.14.359.180.
Th' immortal Seats should ne'er behold her more; ... Il.19.128.377.
Yet was it ne'er my Fate, from thee to find ... Il.24.968.576.
Raptur'd I stand! for earth ne'er knew to bear ... Od.6.201.219.
The sons of men shall ne'er approach thy shore, ... Od.9.415.323.
The Sun ne'er views th' uncomfortable seats, ... Od.11.17.380.
Who ne'er knew salt, or heard the billows roar, ... Od.11.153.389.
I ne'er discern'd, before this social hour. ... Od.19.406.214.
The day (ne'er brighten'd with a beam of joy!) ... Od.19.598.225.
Who ne'er knew salt, or heard the billows roar, ... Od.23.286.337.
With nobler contest ne'er renown'd a grave. ... Od.24.114.353.

NE'R
F. Alas young Man! your Days can ne'r be long, ... 4.HS1.101.15.
Yet ne'r one sprig of Laurel grac'd these ribalds, ... 4.Arbu.163.108.
I ne'r with Wits or Witlings past my days, ... 4.Arbu.223.112.
I ne'r with Wits and Witlings past my days, ... 4.Arbu.223A.112.
He'd do't; and ne'r stand Shill—I Shall—I, ... 6.44.9.123.
And so obliging, that he ne'r oblig'd: ... 6.49iii.22.143.
but ne'r eats a Dinner, ... 6.68.4.196.
Here lies the Youth who ne'r his Friend deny'd; ... 6.85.3A.242.

NE'RE
All for a Thing you ne're so much as *saw?* ... 4.HAdv.136.87.

NEAERA
From *Phœbus* and the bright *Neæra* sprung; ... Od.12.169.440.

NEAMAS
O'ertaken *Neamas* by *Merion* bleeds; ... Il.16.410.258.

NEAR
I'll stake yon' Lamb that near the Fountain plays, ... 1.PSp.33.63.
I'll stake my Lamb that near the Fountain plays, ... 1.PSp.33A.63.
Near, and more near, the closing Lines invest; ... 1.W-F.108.161.
Near, and more near, the closing Lines invest; ... 1.W-F.108.161.
Consider'd *singly,* or behold too *near,* ... 1.EOC.172.260.
An Elm was near, to whose Embraces led, ... 1.TrVP.59.379.
But lo! I saw, (as near her side I stood) ... 1.TrFD.27.387.
And *Thetis,* near *Ismenos'* swelling Flood, ... 1.TrSt.58.412.
Satyrion near, with hot *Eringo's* stood, ... 2.ChJM.377.32.
'Till Coughs awak'd him near the Morning Light. ... 2.ChJM.421.35.

NEAR (CONTINUED)

Ye Fair draw near, let *May's* Example move .... 2.ChJM.434.35.
Thrice she look'd back, and thrice the Foe drew near. .... 2.RL3.138.178.
For ever sep'rate, yet for ever near! .... 3.EOM1.224.43.
Death still draws nearer, never seeming near. .... 3.EOM3.76.99.
Stays 'till we call, and then not often near; .... 3.EOM3.87.100.
Here rose one little state; another near .... 3.EOM3.201.113.
Which still so near us, yet beyond us lies, ... 3.EOM4.5.128.
Not *Naso's* self more impudently near, ... 4.JD4.178A.41.
Not *Fannius* self more impudently near, ... 4.JD4.178.41.
No Mistress *H[e]ysh[a]m* near, no Lady *B[uc]k!* .... 4.HAdv.176.89.
Bear, like the *Turk,* no brother near the throne, ... 4.Arbu.198.110.
The Whisper that to Greatness still too near, ... 4.Arbu.356.122.
If on a Pillory, or near a Throne, ... 4.Arbu.366.122.
Has Life no sourness, drawn so near its end? .... 4.2HE2.316.187.
"This may be troublesome, is near the Chair; .... 4.1HE6.105.243.
There, leaning near a gentle Brook, ... 4.HS6.129.259.
To a tall house near Lincoln's-Inn: .... 4.HS6.186.261.
But if you'd have me always near— .... 4.1HE7.41.271.
Near fifty, and without a Wife, ... 4.1HE7.73.273.
If any ask you, "Who's the Man, so near .... 4.EpS1.45.301.
Receive, and place for ever near a King! .... 4.EpS1.96.305.
From her black grottos near the Temple-wall, ... 5.DunB2.98.300.
Next bidding all draw near on bended knees, ... 5.DunB4.565.398.
A Brandy and Tobacco Shop is near, ... 6.14ii.12.43.
Lo *I,* his *God!* in all his toils am near: .... 6.21.33.70.
Bear, like the Turk, no Brother near the Throne; .... 6.49iii.12.143.
And *Athens* rising near the pole! .... 6.51i.22.152.
An *Athens* rising near the pole! .... 6.51i.22A.152.
Come near, they trod upon your Toes; .... 6.79.19.218.
Lies down to die, the arrow near his heart; .... 6.81.12C.226.
And ill can bear no living near the Throne. .... 6.82ix(a).2A.234.
To this sad Shrine, who'er thou art, draw near, ... 6.85.1.242.
Bear, like the *Turk,* no Brother near the Throne; .... 6.98.48.284.
To let no noble Slave come near, ... 6.135.75.369.
And near thy *Shakespear* place thy honour'd Bust, ... 6.152.2.400.
Where near his Tents his hollow Vessels lay. .... Il.1.403.107.
Then near the Altar of the darting King, ... Il.1.584.115.
While hov'ring near, with miserable Moan, ... Il.2.380.145.
And *Schœnos, Scolos, Græa* near the Main, ... Il.2.592.156.
From his high Chariot: Him, approaching near, ... Il.3.43.190.
From his proud Chariot: Him, approaching near, ... Il.3.43A.190.
Held by the midst, athwart; and near the Foe .... Il.3.111.195.
And glancing downward, near his Flank descends. .... Il.3.442.213.
'Till from the dying Chief, approaching near, ... Il.4.614.250.
Fierce for Renown the Brother Chiefs draw near, ... Il.5.21.266.
Who near ador'd *Scamander* made Abode, ... Il.5.101.271.
Now near the *Greeks* the black Battalions drew, ... Il.5.750.302.
While near *Tydides* stood th' *Athenian* Maid: .... Il.5.987.314.
She said, and to the Steeds approaching near, ... Il.5.1028.315.
Two Twins were near, bold beautiful and young, ... Il.6.27.325.
Near as they drew, *Tydides* thus began. .... Il.6.151.333.
Near *Priam's* Court and *Hector's* Palace stands .... Il.6.392.346.
The Nurse stood near, in whose Embraces prest .... Il.6.496.351.
Himself had challeng'd, and the Foe drew near. .... Il.7.264.377.
And glancing downwards near his Flank descends. .... Il.7.302.379.
But *Ajax* watchful as his Foe drew near, ... Il.7.311.379.
A martial Council near the Navy-Walls: .... Il.8.610.425.
How near our Fleet approach the *Trojan* Fires? .... Il.9.104.437.
So near, and favour'd by the gloomy Shade. .... Il.10.113.7.
Prepare to meet us near the Navy-wall; .... Il.10.145.8.
Near the Night-Guards, our chosen Council waits. .... Il.10.147.8.
Or favour'd by the Night, approach so near, ... Il.10.245.13.
Near *Ilus'* Tomb, in Order rang'd around, ... Il.11.73.37.
Now near the Beech-tree, and the *Scæan* Gates, ... Il.11.223.45.
Then near the Corselet, at the Monarch's Heart, ... Il.11.301.48.
Aim'd at the King, and near his Elbow strook. .... Il.11.326.49.
Near, and more near, the shady Cohorts prest; .... Il.11.522.57.
Near, and more near, the shady Cohorts prest; .... Il.11.522.57.
Charops, the Son of *Hippasus,* was near; .... Il.11.535.57.
Near as he drew, the Warrior thus began. .... Il.11.539.57.
Distress'd he seems, and no Assistance near: .... Il.11.585.60.
Him, near his Tent, *Meriones* attends; .... Il.13.325.120.
The wary *Cretan,* as his Foe drew near, ... Il.13.489.130.
Antilochus, Deipyrus were near, ... Il.13.604.135.
Valiant as *Mars, Meriones* drew near, ... Il.13.668.137.
The Son of *Asius, Adamas,* drew near, ... Il.13.710.138.
Fir'd with Revenge, *Polydamas* drew near, ... Il.14.525.188.
Near his lov'd Master, as he liv'd, he dy'd. .... Il.15.505.216.
Mark how the Flames approach, how near they fall, ... Il.15.598.219.
Unhappy Glories! for his Fate was near, ... Il.15.736.224.
Stern *Hector* wav'd his Sword; and standing near .... Il.16.142.243.
Which sunk him to the dead: when *Troy,* too near .... Il.16.715.271.
Oppos'd to each, that near the Carcase came, ... Il.17.9.288.
And call'd *Æneas* fighting near his Side. .... Il.17.551.309.
To face the Foe, *Polydamas* drew near .... Il.17.678.314.
To him the King. Belov'd of *Jove!* draw near, ... Il.17.771.318.
Who near him wheeling, drove his Steeds along; .... Il.17.786.319.
Vulcan draw near, 'tis *Thetis* asks your Aid. .... Il.18.460.343.
While near impending from a neighb'ring Height, ... Il.20.3.392.
A Fate so near him, chills his Soul with Fright, ... Il.20.331.407.
Nor tempt too near the Terrors of his Hand. .... Il.20.434.412.
Near as they drew, *Achilles* thus began. .... Il.21.165.428.
And the near Hero rising on his Sight! .... Il.21.616.448.
To the near Goal with doubled Ardor flies. .... Il.22.34.453.
To the near Goal with double Ardor flies. Il.22.34A.453*
At the near Prize each gathers all his Soul, ... Il.23.452.508.
Still edging near, and bears him tow'rd the Steep. .... Il.23.504.510.
No sooner had he spoke, but thund'ring near .... Il.23.579.513.
Behind, *Atrides* urg'd the Race, more near .... Il.23.599.513.
Draw near, but first his certain Fortune know, ... Il.23.776.520.
Alone, for so we will: No *Trojan* near; .... Il.24.183.544.
Alone, for so he wills: No *Trojan* near, ... Il.24.213.546.
Then, as the pensive Pomp advanc'd more near, ... Il.24.872.573.
They came, and near him plac'd the stranger-guest. .... Od.3.529.113.
Impatient Fate his near return attends, ... Od.5.145.178.

NEAR (CONTINUED)

Behold how near *Phæacia's* land he draws! .... Od.5.371.190.
And now, as near approaching as the sound .... Od.5.514.197.
And near, a Forum flank'd with marble shines, ... Od.6.318.226.
When near the fam'd *Phæacian* walls he drew, ... Od.7.23.235.
So near approach we their celestial kind, ... Od.7.277.249.
The land of *Cyclops* lay in prospect near; .... Od.9.192.313.
Near this, a fence of marble from the rock, ... Od.9.215.314.
Near half a forest on his back he bore, ... Od.9.276.318.
Where lies she anchor'd? near, or off the shore? .... Od.9.334.320.
And near the ship came thund'ring on the flood. .... Od.9.568.329.
More near and deep, domestic woes succeed! .... Od.9.628.332.
So near the pastures, and so short the way, ... Od.10.98.345.
Domestick thus the griesly beasts drew near; .... Od.10.250.354.
When near *Anticlea* mov'd, and drank the blood. .... Od.11.187.390.
And near them walk'd, with solemn pace and slow, ... Od.11.397.403.
A friendly pair! near these the * *Pylian* stray'd, ... Od.11.577.412.
The sun descending, and so near the shore? .... Od.12.338.448.
Secure he sits, near great *Atrides* plac'd; .... Od.13.490.29.
Soon as *Ulysses* near th' enclosure drew, ... Od.14.33.36.
Nor near me any of your crew descry'd .... Od.15.479.93.
The Prince's near approach the dogs descry, ... Od.16.5.102.
When near he drew, the Prince breaks forth; Proclaim .... Od.16.482.130.
The day shall come; nay, 'tis already near, ... Od.17.296.146.
Thus, near the gates conferring as they drew, ... Od.17.344.148.
Eumæus took, and plac'd it near his Lord. .... Od.17.407.152.
Fed near the limpid lake with golden grain, ... Od.19.628.227.
Up-rose, and thus divin'd the vengeance near. .... Od.20.422.253.
Full many foes, and fierce, observe us near; .... Od.21.244.271.
There stood a window near, whence looking down .... Od.22.142.293.
So near adjoins, that one may guard the strait. .... Od.22.153.294.
And thus address'd *Ulysses* near his side. .... Od.22.179.296.
And on a column near the roof suspend; .... Od.22.191.296.
Near great *Ulysses;* Four against an host. .... Od.22.220.297.
Near the high top he strain'd it strongly round, ... Od.22.501.313.

NEARER

And lift her Turrets nearer to the Skies; .... 1.W-F.288.175.
Thus *Pegasus,* a nearer way to take, ... 1.EOC.150.257.
A nearer woe, a sister's stranger fate. .... 1.TrFD.6.385.
Death still draws nearer, never seeming near. .... 3.EOM3.76.99.
The nearer to its End, or Purpose, home. .... 6.17i(a).6.55.
The Queen, on nearer view, the guest survey'd .... Od.7.314.251.
Nor nearer than the gate presum'd to draw. .... Od.10.68.342.
In rich *Thesprotia,* and the nearer bound .... Od.19.309.209.

NEAREST

The virtue nearest to our vice ally'd; .... 3.EOM2.196.79.
First in my care, and nearest at my heart: .... 5.DunA1.144.81.
Who sate the nearest, by the words o'ercome .... 5.DunA2.369.145.
Who sate the nearest, by the words o'ercome, ... 5.DunB2.401.316.
Ships thou hast store, and nearest to the Main, ... Il.9.62.434.
And launch what Ships lie nearest to the Main; .... Il.14.82.161.
When to the nearest verge of land we drew, ... Od.9.211.314.

NEARLY

Which now, alas! too nearly threats my Son. .... Il.1.549.114.

NEAT

Who feeds yon Alms-house, neat, but void of state, ... 3.Ep3.265A.115.
He feeds yon Alms-house, neat, but void of state, ... 3.Ep3.265B.115.
Behold yon Alms-house, neat, but void of state, ... 3.Ep3.265.115.
Or, when a tight, neat Girl, will serve the Turn, ... 4.HAdv.151.87.
And cry'd, "I vow you're mighty neat. .... 4.HS6.174.261.

NEATH

But 'neath thy roof, *Argyle,* are bred .... 6.141.5.380.

NEATLY

Of twelve vast *French* Romances, neatly gilt. .... 2.RL2.38.161.

NEATNESS

Neatness itself impertinent in him. .... 4.JD4.253.47.

NEC

Scriptus & in tergo, nec dum finitus Orestes. .... 6.24iii(b).2.76.

NECESSITY

Or strong Necessity, or urgent Fear: .... Il.9.262.445.
For strong *Necessity* our Toils demands, ... Il.10.134.8.
Or say, does high necessity of state .... Od.2.39.62.
Necessity demands our daily bread; .... Od.7.299.250.
In meer necessity of coat and cloak, ... Od.14.516.62.

NECK

Pants on her Neck, and fans her parting Hair. .... 1.W-F.196.168.
Then round your Neck in wanton Wreaths I twine, ... 1.TrSP.149.400.
With shining Ringlets the smooth Iv'ry Neck. .... 2.RL2.22.160.
With shining Ringlets her smooth Iv'ry Neck. .... 2.RL2.22A.160.
This just behind *Belinda's* Neck he spread, ... 2.RL3.133.178.
Once gave new Beauties to the snowie Neck. .... 2.RL4.170.198.
Her great great Grandsire wore about his Neck .... 2.RL5.90.207.
A heavy Chest, thick Neck, or heaving Side. .... 4.HAdv.117.85.
Pearls on her neck, and roses in her hair, ... 5.DunA2.152Z1.120.
Break Priscian's head, the Pegasus's neck; .... 5.DunA3.156.165.
Break Priscian's head, and Pegasus's neck; .... 5.DunB3.162.328.
Forth thrust a white Neck, and red Crest. .... 6.14i.20.42.
Fair *Venus'* Neck, her Eyes that sparkled Fire, ... Il.3.489.215.
Full in the Boaster's Neck the Weapon stood, ... Il.5.816.305.
His Neck o'ershading to his Ancle hung; .... Il.6.145.331.
Full on his Neck, from *Hector's* weighty Hand; .... Il.7.17.363.
It reach'd his Neck, with matchless Strength impell'd; .... Il.7.313.379.
Touch'd where the Neck and hollow Chest unite: .... Il.8.392.416.
Divides the Neck, and cuts the Nerves in two; .... Il.10.525.26.
Full on his Neck, that fell'd him to the Ground. .... Il.11.308.48.
Impatient panted on his Neck behind) .... Il.13.486.130.

NECK (CONTINUED)
The hollow Vein that to the Neck extends ..... Il.13.692.138.
Full on the Juncture of the Neck and Head, ... Il.14.544.189.
Drove thro' the Neck, and hurl'd him to the Plain; ..... Il.14.579.190.
Thro' his fair Neck the thrilling Arrow flies; ..... Il.15.528.217.
Full on the Juncture of the Neck and Head: ..... Il.16.407.258.
The weighty Shock his Neck and Shoulders feel; ..... Il.16.956.280.
Wide thro' the Neck appears the grizly Wound, ... Il.17.51.289.
Pierc'd thro' the Neck: He left him panting there, ... Il.20.527.416.
Full on his Neck the falling Falchion sped, ... Il.20.557.417.
And buried in his Neck the reeking Blade. ..... Il.21.130.427.
Where 'twixt the Neck and Throat the jointed Plate ..... Il.22.408.472.
Their flowing Manes, and sleek their glossy Neck. ..... Il.23.350.503.
Full on his Neck he feels the sultry Breeze, ... Il.23.459.508.
The Buckler's Margin, at the Neck he drove. ..... Il.23.968.527.
A Show'r of Ashes o'er his Neck and Head. ..... Il.24.202.545.
Around his Neck her milk-white Arms she threw, ... Il.24.907.574.
Full on his neck, and cut the nerves in two. ..... Od.3.571.115.
His neck obliquely o'er his shoulder hung, ... Od.9.441.324.
Lux'd the neck joynt—my soul descends to hell. ..... Od.11.80.385.
Hung round his neck, while tears his cheek bedew; ..... Od.16.235.114.
Rains kisses on his neck, his face, his eyes: ..... Od.17.49.135.
Deep in the neck his fangs indent their hold; ..... Od.19.267.208.
His neck with fond embrace infolding fast, ... Od.19.554.223.
Around his neck their longing arms they cast, ... Od.21.234.271.
And pierc'd the neck. He falls, and breathes his last. ..... Od.22.20.287.
Full thro' his neck the weighty faulchion sped: ..... Od.22.365.305.
Hangs round her neck and speaks his joy in tears. ..... Od.23.248.335.

NECKLACE
Or lose her Heart, or Necklace, at a Ball; ..... 2.RL2.109.166.
Pisander bears a necklace, wrought with art; ..... Od.18.347.184.

NECKS
Alike disdain with servile Necks to bear ..... 1.TrSt.186.418.
Must we, alas! our doubtful Necks prepare, ... 1.TrSt.236.420.
Stretch their long Necks, and clap their rustling Wings, ... Il.2.543.153.
Bends their strong Necks, and tears them to the Ground. ..... Il.5.209.276.
Circled their arching Necks, and wav'd in State, ... Il.17.499.307.
Circled their arched Necks, and wav'd in State, ... Il.17.499A.307*.
They cuff, they tear, their cheeks and necks they rend, ... Od.2.179.70.
Six horrid necks she rears, and six terrific heads; ..... Od.12.112.437.

NECTAR
Ye Heav'ns! from high the dewy Nectar pour, ... 1.Mes.13.114.
Our foaming Bowls with gen'rous *Nectar* crown'd, ... 1.TrES.31.450.
Our foaming Bowls with purer *Nectar* crown'd, ... 1.TrES.31A.450.
The double Bowl with sparkling *Nectar* crown'd, ... Il.1.753.123.
When the brisk Nectar overlook'd the Brim. ..... Il.11.779.70.
Our foaming Bowls with purer Nectar crown'd, ... Il.12.375.95.
They hail her Queen; the *Nectar* streams around. ..... Il.15.95.200.
Bid the crown'd Nectar circle round the Hall; ..... Il.15.103.200.
With Nectar sweet, (Refection of the Gods!) ..... Il.19.376.387.
And offer'd from her Hand the Nectar Bowl: ..... Il.24.134.540.
(Ambrosial cates, with Nectar rosie red) ..... Od.5.118.178.
And never shalt thou taste this Nectar more. ..... Od.9.416.323.
A rill of Nectar, streaming from the Gods. ..... Od.9.426.323.
He Nectar quaffs, and *Hebe* crowns his joys. ..... Od.11.746.423.

NECTAR'D
Each to his Lips apply'd the nectar'd Urn. ..... Il.1.769.124.
With nectar'd drops the sick'ning sense restor'd. ..... Od.4.600.148.

NECTAREOUS
"The juice nectareous, and the balmy dew; ..... 3.EOM1.136.32.
Nectareous Drops, and rich Ambrosia showr'd ..... Il.19.40.373.
Lotos the name, divine, nectareous juice! ..... Od.9.106.307.
And luscious as the Bee's nectareous dew: ..... Od.14.94.40.
The tasteful inwards, and nectareous wines. ..... Od.20.325.249.

NED
And sigh'd) "My lands and tenements to Ned." ..... 3.Ep1.257.37.

NEED
Let it be *seldom,* and *compell'd by Need,* ..... 1.EOC.165.259.
But to be *found,* when Need requires, with Ease. ..... 1.EOC.674A.316.
She shall not want an Answer at her Need. ..... 2.ChJM.658.46.
All they shall need is to protest, and swear, ... 2.ChJM.665.47.
They need no more but to protest, and swear, ... 2.ChJM.665A.47.
Lord! When you have enough, what need you care ..... 2.ChWB.134.62.
I levied first a Tax upon his Need, ... 2.ChWB.168.64.
I still have shifts against a Time of Need: ..... 2.ChWB.297.71.
Tears still are mine, and those I need not spare, ... 2.ElAb.45.322.
What Pope or Council can they need beside? ..... 3.EOM3.84.100.
(For what to shun will no great knowledge need, ... 3.Ep3.201.110.
"Right, cries his Lordship, for a Rogue in need ..... 4.HS2.111.63.
Now, in such exigencies not to need, ... 4.1HE6.89.243.
And melts to Goodness, need I Scarbrow name? ..... 4.EpS2.65.316.
None need a guide, by sure Attraction led, ... 5.DunB4.75.348.
And, to excuse it, need but shew the prize; ..... 5.DunB4.434.383.
That carries double when there's need: ..... 6.39.4.110.
That carries double if there's need: ..... 6.39.4A.110.
Yet if a friend a night, or so, should need her, ... 6.41.33.114.
I need but once a Week. ..... 6.47.36.129.
Once (says an Author, where, I need not say) ..... 6.145.1.388.
Thy Aid we need not, and thy Threats defy. ..... Il.1.226.97.
Nor need I to command, nor ought to blame. ..... Il.4.413.240.
The distant Dart be prais'd, tho' here we need ..... Il.5.274.280.
Troy's sacred Walls, nor need a foreign Hand? ..... Il.5.578.296.
Ulysses, Diomed we chiefly need; ..... Il.10.123.7.
What need I more? If any *Greek* there be ..... Il.13.351.122.
Be still your selves, and we shall need no more. ..... Il.14.428.184.
Tho' certain be my news, and great my need. ..... Od.14.179.44.
What need of aids, if favour'd by the skies? ..... Od.16.281.118.
A wretch unhappy, meerly for his need? ..... Od.17.471.156.
Nor will that hand to utmost need afford ..... Od.17.539.158.

NEED (CONTINUED)
But Heav'n that knows what all terrestrials need, ... Od.19.691.229.
(So need compells.) Then all united strive ..... Od.22.89.290.

NEEDFUL
She gives in large Recruits of *needful Pride;* ..... 1.EOC.206.264.
One Caution yet is needful to be told, ... 2.ChJM.99.19.
More pow'rful each as needful to the rest, ... 3.EOM3.299.123.
Something there is more needful than Expence, ... 3.Ep4.41.140.
So let his Friends be nigh, a needful Train ..... Il.23.779.520.
Shall rise spontaneous in the needful hour. ..... Od.3.36.88.
Did not my fate my needful haste constrain, ... Od.4.813.157.
And Prudence sav'd him in the needful hour. ..... Od.5.557.199.
Turn'd mean deserters in the needful hour? ..... Od.16.102.107.
Turn'd mean deserters in the needful hour. ..... Od.16.122.108.

NEEDHAM
But pious Needham dropt the name of God; ..... 5.DunB1.324.293.
The first we find with Needham, Brooks, or Briton. ..... 6.82vi.4.232.

NEEDHAM'S
Not thus at *N[ee]dh[a]m's;* your judicious Eye ..... 4.HAdv.133.87.
To Needham's quick the voice triumphal rode, ... 5.DunB1.323.293.

NEEDLE
And the touch'd Needle trembles to the Pole: ..... 2.TemF.431.284.
And stuck her Needle into *Grildrig's* Bed; ..... 6.96ii.6.270.
Skill'd in the Needle, and the lab'ring Loom; ..... Il.23.330.503.

NEEDLESS
A *needless Alexandrine* ends the Song, ... 1.EOC.356.280.
Else why these needless Cautions, Sir, to me? ..... 2.ChJM.595.43.
This needless Labour, and contend no more, ... 6.7.22.16.
With question needless, or enquiry vain. ..... Od.7.40.235.

NEEDS
Will needs *mistake* an Author *into Vice;* ..... 1.EOC.557.304.
Who, if *once wrong,* will needs be *always so;* ..... 1.EOC.569.305.
That, if *once wrong,* will needs be *always so;* ..... 1.EOC.569A.305.
As, to be hated, needs but to be seen; ..... 3.EOM2.218.82.
And still new needs, new helps, new habits rise, ... 3.EOM3.137.106.
There needs but thinking right, and meaning well; ..... 3.EOM4.32.131.
And if we count among the Needs of life ..... 3.Ep3.27.88.
And needs no Rod but Ripley with a Rule. ..... 3.Ep4.18.137.
And needs no Rod but S[taffor]d with a Rule ..... 3.Ep4.18A.137*.
And needs no Rod but S[heppar]d with a Rule ..... 3.Ep4.18B.137*.
Or if you needs must write, write Cæsar's Praise: ..... 4.HS1.21.7.
We needs will write Epistles to the King; ..... 4.2HE1.369.227.
[Plain Truth, dear Murray, needs no flow'rs of speech, ... 4.1HE6.3.237.
must needs ..... 4.1740.27Z1.333*.
In ancient Sense if any needs will deal, ... 5.DunB4.229.365.
Who needs will back the Muses Cock-horse, ... 6.10.10.24.
Will needs misconstrue what the Poet writ; ..... 6.38.11Z2.108.
Which nothing seeks to show, or needs to hide, ... 6.73.2.209.
Yon Luminary Amputation needs, ... 6.100v.1.289.
What needs, O Monarch, this invidious Praise, ... Il.4.456.242.
What needs he the Defence this Arm can make? ..... Il.9.458.455.
To guide thy Conduct, little Precept needs; ..... Il.23.379.505.
What needs appealing in a Fact so plain? ..... Il.23.658.515.
Small Stock of Iron needs that Man provide; ..... Il.23.987.528.
Whatever frugal nature needs, is thine, ... Od.15.528.95.
(For she needs little) daily bread and wine. ..... Od.15.529.95.

NEEDY
As needy Beggars sing at doors for meat. ..... 4.JD2.26.133.
As needy Beggars sing at Doors for Meat ..... 4.JD2A.30.134.
Have you less Pity for the needy Cheat, ... 4.EpS2.44.315.
The needy Poet sticks to all he meets, ... 5.DunA3.292.184.
The needy Poet sticks to all he meets, ... 5.DunB3.290.334.
When I the needy see ..... 6.50.37Z2.148*.
Me, as some needy peasant, would ye leave, ... Od.3.447.108.
No needy mortals here, with hunger bold, ... Od.9.137.311.
For needy strangers still to flatt'ry fly, ... Od.14.148.42.
A man unknown, a needy wanderer? ..... Od.21.314.274.

NEGLECT
For her, the feather'd Quires neglect their Song; ..... 1.PAu.24.82.
For him, the feather'd Quires neglect their Song; ..... 1.PAu.24A.82.
Th'industrious Bees neglect their Golden Store; ..... 1.PWi.51.92.
Neglect the Rules each *Verbal Critick* lays, ... 1.EOC.261.269.
And here and there disclos'd a brave Neglect. ..... 2.TemF.195.271.
In rev'rend S[utto]n note a *small Neglect,* ..... 4.EpS1.16A.298.
Neglect their Native Channel, Neighb'ring Coast, ... 6.17ii.14.56.
O may the King that one Neglect forgive, ... 6.96iv.91.279.
To mix in combate which your selves neglect? ..... Il.4.393.239.
And spent with Toil neglect the Watch of Night? ..... Il.10.366.19.
And tir'd with Toils, neglect the Watch of Night? ..... Il.10.470.24.
Thy Friend *Sarpedon* proves thy base Neglect: ..... Il.17.166.294.
Neglect that Thought, thy dearer Glory save. ..... Il.22.79.456.
Thro' your neglect if lagging on the Plain ..... Il.23.489.509.
And will Omnipotence neglect to save ..... Od.1.78.35.

NEGLECTED
Now all neglected, he forgets his home, ... 1.TrPA.19.366.
Had stood neglected and a barren shade; ..... 1.TrVP.64.380.
The Lute neglected, and the Lyric Muse; ..... 1.TrSP.6.393.
Whose now neglected Altars, in thy Reign ..... 1.TrUl.230.473.
Left me to see neglected Genius bloom, ... 4.Arbu.257.114.
Neglected die! and tell it on his Tomb; ..... 4.Arbu.258.114.
Unfed, unhous'd, neglected, on the clay, ... 6.15.11.51.
Whole Years neglected for some Months ador'd, ... 6.19.43.63.
Had dropt like fruit, neglected, when it fell. ..... 6.38.14.107.
Neglected on your Chair to lie, ... 6.64.7.189.
Perhaps neglected, on the dang'rous strand ..... 6.96ii.30Z21.271.
His Troops, neglected on the sandy Shore, ... Il.2.939.168.
Stretch'd on the Shore, and thus neglected dies. ..... Il.4.561.248.

NEGLECTED (CONTINUED)

In Vengeance of neglected Sacrifice; ....Il.9.658.467.
Their Pow'rs neglected and no Victim slain, ...Il.12.7.81.
As when the Flocks, neglected by the Swain ....Il.16.420.259.
But whole he lies, neglected in the Tent: ....Il.24.504.557.
Nine Days neglected lay expos'd the Dead; ....Il.24.768.569.
Thy spousal ornament neglected lies; ....Od.6.31.205.
Whose now-neglected altars, in thy reign, ...Od.13.397.26.
Un-hous'd, neglected, in the publick way; ....Od.17.357.149.
If these neglected, faded charms can move? ....Od.21.71.262.
To me, neglected as I am, I know ....Od.21.248.271.
My haste neglected yonder door to bar, ...Od.22.170.295.
Cold and neglected, spread the marble floor. ....Od.24.215.358.
Nothing neglected, but thy self alone. ....Od.24.293.364.

NEGLECTFUL

Of all neglectful, wage a hateful War.) ....Il.19.348.386.
Cease; lest neglectful of high *Jove's* Command ......Il.24.716.567.
Thy absent spouse neglectful of thy charms ....Od.8.335.281.
On fond pursuits neglectful while you roam, ...Od.15.15.70.

NEGLECTING

My Brother next, neglecting Wealth and Fame, ...1.TrSP.75.397.

NEGLECTS

Forgets her Father, and neglects her Fame, ...1.TrSt.698.439.
His Post neglects, or leaves the Fair at large, ...2.RL2.124.167.
Arthur, whose giddy Son neglects the Laws, ...4.Arbu.23.97.
In rev'rend Bishops note some *small Neglects,* ......4.EpS1.16.298.
Sighs for an Otho, and neglects his bride. ....6.71.44.204.
Shakes for his Danger, and neglects his own; ....Il.5.694.301.
Commences courtier, and neglects his charge. ....Od.17.293.146.
Who-e'er neglects to pay distinction due, ...Od.19.370.212.

NEGLIGENCE

Horace still charms with graceful Negligence, ...1.EOC.653.313.

NEGLIGENT

As prone to *Ill,* as negligent of *Good,* ....4.JD4.20.27.

NEGLIGENTLY

His Sword beside him negligently hung, ...Il.3.30.189.

NEICE

She—and my Neice—and one more worthy Wife ....2.ChWB.272.70.

NEIGH

And let each grateful *Houyhnhnm* neigh thy Praise. ..6.96iii.4.274.
And round the Lists the gen'rous Coursers neigh. ...Il.3.408.212.
Loud neigh the Coursers o'er their Heaps of Corn, ...Il.8.707.429.
Just on the Brink, they neigh, and paw the Ground, ...Il.12.59.83.

NEIGH'BRING

A Stone, the Limit of the neigh'bring Land, ...Il.21.469.440.

NEIGH'D

With Voice dissembled to his Loves he neigh'd, ...Il.20.266.405.

NEIGHB'RING

Delights the *Nereids* of the neighb'ring Seas; ....1.TrUl.34.466.
Delights the *Nereids* of the neighb'ring Seas; ....1.TrUl.229.473.
Which from the neighb'ring *Hampton* takes its Name. ..2.RL3.4.169.
On neighb'ring Air a soft Impression make; ....2.TemF.443.284.
While others, timely, to the neighb'ring Fleet ....5.DunB2.427.318.
Neglect their Native Channel, Neighb'ring Coast, ...6.17ii.14.56.
And high *Cerinthus* views the neighb'ring Main. .....Il.2.648.157.
Where *Pheræ* hears the neighb'ring Waters fall, ...Il.2.866.165.
And *Sestos* and *Abydos'* neighb'ring Strands, ...Il.2.1013.171.
Axius, that swells with all his neighb'ring Rills, ...Il.2.1032.171.
The Lambs reply from all the neighb'ring Hills: ......Il.4.495.244.
They cleanse their Bodies in the neighb'ring Main: ..Il.10.674.31.
To join its Summit to the neighb'ring Skies, ...Il.14.326.178.
Of neighb'ring Nations, or of distant Lands! ....Il.17.261.298.
While near impending from a neighb'ring Height, ...Il.20.3.392.
Axius, who swells with all the neighb'ring Rills, ...Il.21.175.428.
From hence: Nor ask the neighb'ring City's Aid, ...Il.23.989.528.
Resort the Nobles from the neighb'ring Isles; ....Il.1.316.48.
The neighb'ring main, and sorrowing treads the shores. ..Od.2.294.76.
And heav'd the fleet into the neighb'ring bay. ....Od.3.379.105.
My ship equip'd within the neighb'ring port, ...Od.4.854.159.
Instant prepare me, on the neighb'ring strand, ...Od.4.894.160.
Then to the neighb'ring forest led the way. ....Od.5.304.185.
No less a terror, from the neighb'ring groves ....Od.6.161.216.
Then took the shelter of the neighb'ring wood. ....Od.7.367.254.
Dance the green *Nereids* of the neighb'ring seas. ....Od.12.378.494.
Delights the *Nereids* of the neighb'ring seas; ....Od.13.125.8.
Delights the *Nereids* of the neighb'ring seas: ....Od.13.396.26.
O'er the fair islands of the neighb'ring main, ...Od.14.118.41.
Each neighb'ring realm conducive to our woe ....Od.16.129.109.
Beneath a neighb'ring tree, the Chief divine ....Od.24.269.362.
Haste then, and ere to neighb'ring *Pyle* he flies, ...Od.24.495.372.

NEIGHBOR

Not one will change his neighbor with himself. ......3.EOM2.262.87.

NEIGHBOUR

Our Neighbour Prince, and Heir of *Calydon:* ....1.TrSt.793.443.
This Clerk, my self, and my good Neighbour *Alce,* ..2.ChWB.281.70.
Propt on some tomb, a neighbour of the dead! ....2.ElAb.304.344.
Propt in some tomb, a neighbour of the dead! ....2.ElAb.304A.344.
But thinks his neighbour farther gone than he. ....3.EOM2.226.82.
Form'd and impell'd its neighbour to embrace, ...3.EOM3.12.93.
Friend, parent, neighbour, first it will embrace, ...3.EOM4.367.164.
Each does but hate his Neighbour as himself: ....3.Ep3.110.100.
It was a Sin to call our Neighbour Fool, ...4.Arbu.383.126.
Prop thine, O Empress! like each neighbour Throne, ..5.DunB4.333.376.

NEIGHBOUR (CONTINUED)

And said to him, Good Neighbour, ...6.94.38.260.
Not touch me! never Neighbour call'd me Slut! ....6.96iv.25.277.
But he's my Neighbour, cries the Peer polite, ...6.143.3.385.
While to his Neighbour each express'd his Thought; ..Il.2.332.143.
The Neighbour Nations thence commencing Foes. ...Il.9.664.467.
Each rules his race, his neighbour not his care, ...Od.9.131.311.
Whilst to his neighbour each express'd his thought, ..Od.10.41.341.
The neighbour town? the town shall force the door, ..Od.22.150.294.

NEIGHBOUR'S

Whence is our Neighbour's Wife so rich and gay? ....2.ChWB.75.60.
To light a Taper at a Neighbour's Fire. ....2.ChWB.139.63.
Gives thee to make thy neighbour's blessing thine. ..3.EOM4.354.162.
Never, ah, never! kiss thy Neighbour's Wife. ....4.HAdv.105.85.
But he, who hurts a harmless neighbour's peace, ...4.Arbu.287.116.
A Neighbour's Madness, or his Spouse's, ...4.HS6.148.259.
Her evening cates before his neighbour's shop,) ....5.DunA2.68.106.
Her evening cates before his neighbour's shop,) ....5.DunB2.72.299.

NEIGHBOURHOOD

Scolds answer foul-mouth'd Scolds; bad Neighbourhood I
ween. ....6.14ii.18.43.

NEIGHBOURING

The neighbouring mountains, and resounding main ..1.TrPA.47.367.
While others timely, to the neighbouring Fleet ....5.DunA2.395.149.
All others timely, to the neighbouring Fleet ....5.DunA2.395A.149.
The wall was stone from neighbouring quarries born, ..Od.14.13.35.

NEIGHBOURS

Around, the Neighbours, and my Clerk too, mourn. ..2.ChWB.314.72.
Or makes his Neighbours glad, if he encrease; ....3.Ep4.182.154.
Curs'd by thy neighbours, thy Trustees, thy self, ...4.HS2.106.61.
The grunting Hogs alarm the Neighbours round, ...6.14ii.26.43.
The Windows open; all the Neighbours rise: ....6.96iv.46.277.
The Neighbours answer, *With the Sorrel Mare.* ....6.96iv.48.277.
Well-pleas'd to give our neighbours due applause, ...6.107.21.311.
A Bishop by his Neighbours hated ....6.151.1.399.
Remote from neighbours, in a forest wide, ...Od.5.631.202.
As our dire neighbours of *Cyclopean* birth ....Od.7.279.249.

NEIGHING

The neighing Coursers their new Fellows greet, ...Il.10.668.31.

NEION

Where waving groves on airy *Neion* grow, ...Od.1.239.44.

NEIS

(*Satnius* the brave, whom beauteous *Neis* bore ....Il.14.519.188.

NEITHER

Some neither can for *Wits* nor *Criticks* pass, ...1.EOC.38.243.
As heavy Mules are neither *Horse* nor *Ass.* ....1.EOC.39.243.
But in such Lays as neither *ebb,* nor *flow,* ....1.EOC.239.267.
They tugg, they sweat, but neither gain, nor yield, ..1.TrES.159.455.
Great Idol of Mankind! we neither claim ....2.TemF.358.281.
All neither wholly false, nor wholly true. ....2.TemF.457.285.
Yet neither *Charles* nor *James* be in a Rage? ....4.HS1.114.15.
And neither leans on this side, nor on that: ....4.HS2.62.59.
And neither leans on this side, or on that: ....4.HS2.62A.59.
If neither Gems adorn, nor Silver tip ....4.HAdv.147.87.
The things, we know, are neither rich nor rare, ...4.Arbu.171.108.
Who neither writes nor pays for what is writ ....4.JD2A.110.142.
But I that sail, am neither less nor bigger. ....4.2HE2.299.185.
I neither strut with ev'ry fav'ring breath, ...4.2HE2.300.185.
Does neither Rage inflame, nor Fear appall? ....4.2HE2.308.187.
How sweet the periods, neither said nor sung! ....5.DunA3.198.174.
How sweet the periods, neither sad, nor sung! ....5.DunB3.202.330.
And neither swell too high, nor sink too low; ....6.17ii.20.56.
Now *Europe's* balanc'd, neither Side prevails, ...6.28.1.82.
And blasted both, that it might neither wound. ....6.69i.4.197.
The *Thing,* we know, is neither rich nor rare, ...6.98.21.284.
All he can say for 't is, he neither made ....6.105vi.3.302.
"That dares tell neither Truth nor Lies, ...6.140.30.379.
Shall neither hear thee sigh, nor see thee weep. ......Il.6.593.355.
They tugg, they sweat; but neither gain, nor yield, ..Il.12.513.100.
Him neither Rocks can crush, nor Steel can wound, ..Il.13.412.126.
Wounded, we wound; and neither side can fail, ...Il.20.298.406.
Thus gazing long, the Silence neither broke, ...Il.24.802.570.
Let neither flatt'ry smooth, nor pity hide. ....Od.3.115.91.
But neither mead nor plain supplies, to feed ....Od.4.825.158.

NELEUS

O Son of *Neleus* (thus the King rejoin'd) ....Il.10.94.6.
Old *Neleus* glory'd in his conqu'ring Son. ....Il.11.827.73.
O son of *Neleus!* awful *Nestor,* tell ....Od.3.308.101.
Where antient *Neleus* sate, a rustic throne; ....Od.3.521.113.
And god-like *Neleus* rul'd the *Pylian* plain: ....Od.11.312.397.
With gifts unnumber'd *Neleus* sought her arms, ...Od.11.343.399.
Neleus his treasures one long year detains; ....Od.15.256.80.
Then (*Neleus* vanquish'd, and consign'd the Fair ..Od.15.262.80.

NELEUS'

There sate the mournful Kings: when *Neleus'* Son, ..Il.10.239.12.
Glory of *Greece,* old *Neleus'* valiant Son! ....Il.11.633.61.
For *Neleus'* Sons *Alcides'* Rage had slain; ....Il.11.832.73.
Before old *Neleus'* venerable walls. ....Od.3.6.86.

NEMEA'S

E're yet adorn'd with *Nemea's* dreadful Spoils. .....1.TrSt.570.434.
Of *Nemea's* Stream the yielding Fair enjoy'd: ....1.TrSt.677.438.

NEMERTES

Nemertes with *Apseudes* lifts the Head: ....Il.18.59.326.

NEOPTOLEMUS

What more, should *Neoptolemus* the brave, ... Il.19.345.386.

NEPENTHE

Lull'd with the sweet *Nepenthe* of a Court; ..... 4.EpS1.98.305.

NEPHEW

"But ho! our Nephew," (crieth one,) ..... 6.14i.11.42.

NEPTUNE

Blue *Neptune* storms, the bellowing Deeps resound; ..... 2.RL5.50.203.
Neptune and *Jove* survey the rapid Race: ..... 2.TemF.217.272.
Neptune shrinks! ..... 6.96i.44.269.
His Strength like *Neptune,* and like *Mars* his Mien, ... Il.2.569.155.
And thus to *Neptune:* Thou! whose Force can make ..... Il.8.242.409.
Neptune with Wrath rejects the rash Design: ..... Il.8.254.409.
To *Neptune,* Ruler of the Seas profound, ... Il.9.239.444.
If mighty *Neptune* send propitious Gales; ..... Il.9.474.456.
Then *Actor's* Sons had dy'd, but *Neptune* shrouds ..... Il.11.884.75.
Then *Neptune* and *Apollo* shook the Shore, ... Il.12.15.81.
But *Neptune,* rising from the Seas profound, ... Il.13.67.108.
Neptune meanwhile the routed *Greeks* inspir'd; ..... Il.13.117.110.
While *Neptune* rising from his azure Main, ... Il.13.442.126.
Neptune in human Form conceal'd his Aid. ..... Il.13.450.127.
By *Neptune* now the hapless Hero dies, ... Il.13.545.132.
Fierce in his Front: but *Neptune* wards the Blow, ... Il.13.712.138.
Now, *Neptune!* now, th' important Hour employ, ... Il.14.411.183.
Neptune, with Zeal encreas'd, renews his Care, ... Il.14.419.183.
The Legions march, and *Neptune* leads the way: ..... Il.14.444.185.
O say, when *Neptune* made proud *Ilion* yield, ... Il.14.601.191.
And to blue *Neptune* thus the Goddess calls. ..... Il.15.195.204.
The Wrath of *Neptune* shall for ever last. ..... Il.15.243.206.
Beneath, stern *Neptune* shakes the solid Ground, ... Il.20.77.397.
Against blue *Neptune,* Monarch of the Main: ..... Il.20.92.398.
Cœrulean *Neptune,* rose, and led the Way. ..... Il.20.173.400.
Here *Neptune,* and the Gods of *Greece* repair, ... Il.20.180.401.
The *Dardan* Prince, O *Neptune,* be thy Care; ..... Il.20.360.410.
Neptune and *Pallas* haste to his Relief, ... Il.21.330.435.
Propitious *Neptune,* and the blue-ey'd Maid. ..... Il.21.335.435.
Neptune and *Jove* on thee conferr'd the Skill, ... Il.23.377.505.
But *Neptune* this, and *Pallas* this denies, ... Il.24.36.536.
Neptune, by pray'r repentant rarely won, ... Od.1.88.35.
Whom *Neptune* ey'd with bloom of beauty blest, ... Od.1.94.36.
Neptune aton'd, his wrath shall now refrain, ... Od.1.100.36.
These rites of *Neptune,* monarch of the deep, ... Od.3.56.89.
There hecatombs of bulls to *Neptune* slain ..... Od.3.217.96.
Sacred to *Neptune* and the pow'rs divine. ..... Od.3.426.107.
By *Neptune* rescu'd from *Minerva's* hate, ... Od.4.671.150.
Stern *Neptune* ey'd him, and contemptuous said: ..... Od.5.479.195.
To thee from *Neptune* and the raging main. ..... Od.5.571.199.
(By *Neptune* aw'd) apparent from the sky: ..... Od.6.392.230.
For angry *Neptune* rouz'd the raging main: ..... Od.7.356.253.
Apollo comes, and *Neptune* comes along, ... Od.8.362.283.
Loud laugh the rest, ev'n *Neptune* laughs aloud, ... Od.8.381.284.
Will *Neptune* (*Vulcan* then) the faithless trust? ..... Od.8.385.284.
When *Neptune* sues, my part is to obey. ..... Od.8.392.285.
How *Neptune* rag'd, and how by his command ..... Od.8.619.295.
Whom angry *Neptune* whelm'd beneath the main; ..... Od.9.340.320.
"To *Jove* or to thy father *Neptune* pray." ..... Od.9.489.326.
As sure, as *Neptune* cannot give thee sight. ..... Od.9.614.332.
Hear me, oh *Neptune!* thou whose arms are hurl'd ..... Od.9.617.332.
And angry *Neptune* heard th' unrighteous pray'r. ..... Od.9.630.332.
I see! I see, thy bark by *Neptune* tost, ... Od.11.130.387.
When late stern *Neptune* points the shaft with death; ..... Od.11.167.389.
For know, thou *Neptune* view'st! and at my nod ..... Od.11.305.397.
Can mighty *Neptune* thus of man complain? ..... Od.13.164.13.
Neptune, tremendous o'er the boundless main! ..... Od.13.165.13.
Stern *Neptune* rag'd; and how by his command ..... Od.13.202.15.
On angry *Neptune* now for mercy call: ..... Od.13.210.15.
Delightful rise, when angry *Neptune* roars, ... Od.23.250.335.
When late stern *Neptune* points the shaft of death; ..... Od.23.300.337.
Or did the rage of stormy *Neptune* sweep ..... Od.24.134.354.

NEPTUNE'S

Not *Neptune's* self from all his Streams receives ..... 1.W-F.223.170.
Not *Neptune's* self from all his Floods receives ..... 1.W-F.223A.170.
Not *Neptune's* self from all her streams receives ..... 1.W-F.223B.170.
Or some fair Isle which *Neptune's* Arms surround? ..... 1.TrUl.115.469.
And Mighty *Neptune's* unrelenting Rage?— ..... 1.TrUl.223.473.
Onchestus, Neptune's celebrated Groves; ..... Il.2.600.156.
'Twas *Neptune's* Charge his Coursers to unbrace, ... Il.8.546.422.
Cteatus' Son, of *Neptune's* boasted Line; ..... Il.13.249.117.
Cteatus' Son, of *Neptune's* forceful Line; ..... Il.13.249A.117*.
(Great *Neptune's* Care preserv'd from hostile Rage ..... Il.13.702.138.
To *Neptune's* Ear soft *Sleep* his Message brings; ..... Il.14.408.183.
The delegate of *Neptune's* watry reign. ..... Od.4.522.145.
To *Neptune's* wrath, stern Tyrant of the Seas, ... Od.5.431.193.
Strip off thy garments; *Neptune's* fury brave ..... Od.5.436.193.
Close to the bay great *Neptune's* fane adjoins: ..... Od.6.317.226.
Who now by *Neptune's* am'rous pow'r compress, ... Od.7.78.237.
Neptune's smooth face, and cleave the yielding deep. ..... Od.9.210.314.
Great *Neptune's* blessing on the watry way: ..... Od.9.606.331.
Or some fair isle which *Neptune's* arms surround? ..... Od.13.282.19.
And mighty *Neptune's* unrelenting rage? ..... Od.13.390.25.

NEPTUNES

Leap'd from his Throne, lest *Neptunes* Arm should lay ..... Il.20.85.397.
At *Neptunes* Shrine on *Helice's* high Shores ..... Il.20.468.414.

NEREIDS

Delights the *Nereids* of the neighb'ring Seas; ..... 1.TrUl.34.466.
Delights the *Nereids* of the neighb'ring Seas; ..... 1.TrUl.229.473.
The circling *Nereids* with their Mistress weep, ... Il.18.45.325.
Ye Sister *Nereids!* to your Deeps descend, ... Il.18.177.331.
Dance the green *Nereids* of the neighb'ring seas. ..... Od.12.378.449.
Delights the *Nereids* of the neighb'ring seas; ..... Od.13.125.8.

NEREIDS (CONTINUED)

Delights the *Nereids* of the neighb'ring seas: ..... Od.13.396.26.

NEREUS

With hoary *Nereus,* and the watry Train, ... Il.18.42.325.

NERICUS

And proud *Nericus* trembled as I storm'd. ..... Od.24.438.369.

NERITOS

Where high *Neritos* shakes his waving Woods, ... Il.2.770.162.

NERITUS

Behold where *Neritus* the Clouds divides, ... 1.TrUl.232.473.
Where high *Neritus* waves his woods in air: ..... Od.9.22.302.
Behold! where *Neritus* the clouds divides, ... Od.13.399.26.
Neritus, Ithacus, Polyctor there ..... Od.17.236.143.

NERO

And Nero reigns a Titus, if he will. ..... 3.EOM2.198.79.

NERO'S

And Nero's Terraces desert their walls: ..... 3.Ep4.72.144.

NERVE

Each Motion guides, and ev'ry Nerve sustains; ..... 1.EOC.78.248.
Tugs with full Force, and ev'ry Nerve applies; ..... 1.TrES.130.454.
Each aking Nerve refuse the Lance to throw, ... Il.2.464.149.
Close to his Breast he strains the Nerve below, ... Il.4.154.228.
Apply'd each Nerve, and swinging round on high, ... Il.7.321.379.
And each immortal Nerve with Horror shake. ..... Il.8.565.423.
Tugs with full force, and ev'ry Nerve applies; ..... Il.12.484.99.
And broke the Nerve my Hands had twin'd with Art, ... Il.15.552.218.
Loose in each Joint; each Nerve with Horror shakes. ..... Il.16.969.281.
Each nerve we stretch, and ev'ry oar we ply. ..... Od.9.574.330.
Each nerve to strain, each bending oar to ply. ..... Od.10.148.347.
Strain ev'ry nerve, and bid the vessel fly. ..... Od.12.255.444.

NERVELESS

There sunk Thalia, nerveless, cold, and dead, ... 5.DunB4.41.345.
There sunk Thalia, nerveless, faint, and dead, ... 5.DunB4.41A.345.
Down dropt he, nerveless, and extended lay. ..... Il.23.801.521.

NERVES

The Nerves unbrac'd no more his Bulk sustain, ... 1.TrES.265.459.
Break all their nerves, and fritter all their sense: ..... 5.DunB4.56.347.
And Nerves to second what thy Soul inspires! ..... Il.4.363.238.
The Nerves unbrac'd support his Limbs no more; ..... Il.4.536.247.
Burst the strong Nerves, and crash'd the solid Bone: ..... Il.4.602.250.
His Nerves confirm'd, his languid Spirits chear'd; ..... Il.5.155.274.
But while my Nerves are strong, my Force entire, ... Il.5.316.281.
But while my Nerves are strung, my Force entire, ... Il.5.316A.281.
Such Nerves I gave him, and such Force in Fight. ..... Il.5.1005.314.
Headlong he tumbles: His slack Nerves unbound ..... Il.7.21.363.
Divides the Neck, and cuts the Nerves in two; ..... Il.10.525.26.
Unstrings my Nerves, and ends my manly Prime; ..... Il.11.815.72.
And took the Joint, and cut the Nerves in twain: ..... Il.14.545.189.
Tore all the Brawn, and rent the Nerves away: ..... Il.16.374.257.
The Nerves unbrac'd no more his Bulk sustain, ... Il.16.570.266.
With all his Nerves he drives it at the Foe; ..... Il.16.893.277.
With Nerves relax'd he tumbles to the Ground: ..... Il.17.342.300.
Ourself will Swiftness to your Nerves impart, ... Il.17.516.308.
Where the knit Nerves the pliant Elbow strung; ..... Il.20.554.417.
The stunning Stroke his stubborn Nerves unbound; ..... Il.21.474.441.
Endu'd his Knees with strength, his Nerves with Pow'r: ..... Il.22.266.466.
And kept the Nerves undry'd, the Flesh entire, ... Il.23.234.499.
The Strength t'evade, and where the Nerves combine, ... Il.23.844.523.
Full on his neck, and cut the nerves in two. ..... Od.3.571.115.
To reach *Phæacia* all thy nerves extend, ... Od.5.438.193.
Or that these wither'd nerves like thine were strung; ..... Od.16.104.107.
Gods! how his nerves a matchless strength proclaim: ..... Od.18.84.170.
These aged nerves with new-born vigor strung, ... Od.20.296.247.
Where to the pastern-bone by nerves combin'd, ... Od.20.367.250.
But you! whom heav'n with better nerves has blest, ... Od.21.143.265.

NERVOUS

Swells their bold Hearts, and strings their nervous Arms; ..... Il.2.531.152.
Breath'd in his Heart, and strung his nervous Arms; ..... Il.10.559.27.
Fix'd in his nervous Thigh the Weapon stood, ... Il.11.710.66.
The nervous Ancles bor'd, his Feet he bound ..... Il.22.497.477.
Amid the Ring each nervous Rival stands, ... Il.23.822.522.
For this, he bids those nervous Artists vie, ... Il.23.981.528.
What nervous arms he boasts! how firm his tread! ..... Od.8.147.270.
Broad spread his shoulders, and his nervous thighs ..... Od.18.76.170.

NESAEA

Nesæa mild, and Silver *Spio* came. ..... Il.18.48.326.

NEST

And turtles taken from their airy nest. ..... 1.TrPA.89.369.
And children sacred held a *Martin's* nest, ... 4.HS2.38.57.
A Nest, a Toad, a Fungus, or a Flow'r. ..... 5.DunB4.400.381.
A *Phœnix* couch'd upon her Fun'ral Nest. ..... 6.9viii.2.22.
When shall we nest thy hallow'd Altars raise, ... 6.65.7.192.
Eight callow Infants fill'd the mossie Nest; ..... Il.2.377.145.
The Mother last, as round the Nest she flew, ... Il.2.382.145.

NESTOR

Experience'd *Nestor,* in Persuasion skill'd, ... Il.1.331.103.
Th' experienc'd *Nestor,* in Persuasion skill'd, ... Il.1.331A.103.
When *Nestor* spoke, they listen'd and obey'd. ..... Il.1.359.105.
Whose Visionary Form like *Nestor* came, ... Il.2.73.130.
He spoke, and sate; when *Nestor* rising said, ... Il.2.99.131.
(*Nestor,* whom *Pylos'* sandy Realms obey'd) ..... Il.2.100.131.
Then *Nestor* thus—These vain Debates forbear, ... Il.2.402.146.
And *Nestor* first, as most advanc'd in Years. ..... Il.2.481.149.

NESTOR (CONTINUED)

The gen'rous *Nestor* thus the Prince addrest. .... Il.2.515.151.
Nestor alone, improv'd by length of Days, ... Il.2.669.158.
Nestor the Sage conducts his chosen Host: .... Il.2.716.160.
There rev'rend *Nestor* ranks his *Pylian* Bands, ... Il.4.336.236.
Old *Nestor* saw, and rowz'd the Warrior's Rage; .... Il.6.83.327.
Grave *Nestor*, then, in graceful Act arose. .... Il.7.144.371.
What then he was, Oh were your *Nestor* now! .... Il.7.189.373.
What then I was, Oh were your *Nestor* now! .... Il.7.189A.373.
Old *Nestor* shook the Casque. By Heav'n inspir'd, ... Il.7.219.375.
Nestor, in each persuasive Art approv'd, ... Il.7.389.383.
Nestor alone amidst the Storm remain'd. .... Il.8.102.402.
Thus said the Chief; and *Nestor*, skill'd in War, ... Il.8.143.404.
To whom *Gerenian Nestor* thus reply'd, ... Il.8.183.406.
Wise *Nestor* then his Rev'rend Figure rear'd; .... Il.9.71.435.
Then *Nestor* spoke, for Wisdom long approv'd, ... Il.9.125.438.
The Monarch thus: the Rev'rend *Nestor* then: .... Il.9.215.443.
Wise *Nestor* turns on each his careful Eye, ... Il.9.233.444.
To seek sage *Nestor* now the Chief resolves, ... Il.10.24.3.
Our self to hoary *Nestor* will repair; .... Il.10.65.5.
To him thus *Nestor*. Trust the Pow'rs above, ... Il.10.114.7.
Lo faithful *Nestor* thy Command obeys; .... Il.10.121.7.
Then none (said *Nestor*) shall his Rule withstand, ... Il.10.148.8.
Then, with his Foot, old *Nestor* gently shakes .... Il.10.178.9.
Nestor with Joy the Wakeful Band survey'd, ... Il.10.223.11.
Old *Nestor* first perceiv'd th' approaching Sound, ... Il.10.624.29.
They greet the Kings; and *Nestor* first demands: .... Il.10.639.30.
There *Nestor* and *Idomeneus* oppose .... Il.11.624.61.
To *Nestor* then *Idomeneus* begun; .... Il.11.632.61.
Old *Nestor* mounts the Seat: Beside him rode .... Il.11.638.62.
Go now to *Nestor*, and from him be taught .... Il.11.748.68.
The cordial Bev'rage rev'rend *Nestor* shares .... Il.11.785.70.
Old *Nestor* rising then, the Hero led .... Il.11.790.71.
As first of Gods, to *Nestor*, of Mankind. .... Il.11.895.75.
What drives thee, *Nestor*, from the Field of Fame? .... Il.14.50.160.
Gerenian Nestor then. So Fate has will'd; .... Il.14.59.160.
Experienc'd *Nestor* chief obtests the Skies, ... Il.15.426.213.
Warms the bold Son of *Nestor* in his Cause. .... Il.15.681.222.
Man Courage breathes in Man; but *Nestor* most .... Il.15.792.226.
In equal Arms two Sons of *Nestor* stand, ... Il.16.376.257.
Meanwhile the Sons of *Nestor*, in the Rear, ... Il.17.436.304.
And skirmish wide: So *Nestor* gave Command, ... Il.17.438.304.
The Sons of *Nestor*, *Phyleus'* valiant Heir, ... Il.19.245.383.
Nestor, *Idomeneus*, *Ulysses* sage, ... Il.19.331.386.
Experienc'd *Nestor* gives his Son the Reins, ... Il.23.371.505.
Experienc'd *Nestor* gives the Son the Reins, ... Il.23.371A.505.
Young *Nestor* leads the Race: *Eumelus* then; .... Il.23.429.507.
While thus young *Nestor* animates his Steeds. .... Il.23.482.509.
Young *Nestor* follows (who by Art, not Force, ... Il.23.597.513.
But youthful *Nestor*, jealous of his Fame, ... Il.23.619.514.
Achilles this to rev'rend *Nestor* bears, ... Il.23.705.517.
Prize after Prize by *Nestor* born away, ... Il.23.736.519.
The Son of *Nestor*, worthy of his Sire. .... Il.23.940.526.
Of *Nestor*, hoary Sage, his doom demand; .... Od.1.370.50.
Where *Nestor* sate with youthful *Thrasymed*. .... Od.3.50.89.
On *Nestor* first, and *Nestor's* royal line; .... Od.3.71.89.
To him experienc'd *Nestor* thus rejoin'd. .... Od.3.125.91.
Ulysses first and *Nestor* dis-agreed: .... Od.3.196.95.
Thus he, and *Nestor* took the word: My son, ... Od.3.258.98.
O son of *Neleus!* awful *Nestor*, tell .... Od.3.308.101.
The rev'rend *Nestor* with his Queen repos'd. .... Od.3.515.112.
Sage *Nestor* fill'd it, and the sceptre sway'd. .... Od.3.523.113.
In youth by *Nestor* lov'd, of spotless fame, ... Od.3.576.116.
On the bright eminence young *Nestor* shone, ... Od.4.29.121.
But silence soon the son of *Nestor* broke, ... Od.4.257.131.
Frequent, O King, was *Nestor* wont to raise .... Od.4.259.131.
In thee renew'd the soul of *Nestor* shines: .... Od.4.282.132.
Such, happy *Nestor!* was thy glorious doom; .... Od.4.289.132.
Whom I with *Nestor* on the *Phrygian* coast .... Od.4.656.150.
Sage *Nestor*, *Periclimenus* the bold, ... Od.11.348.399.
In sleep profound the Son of *Nestor* lies; .... Od.15.7.70.
Rise, son of *Nestor!* for the road prepare, ... Od.15.55.72.
Farewel and prosper, youths! let *Nestor* know .... Od.15.168.76.
Ere yet to *Nestor* I the tale relate: .... Od.15.235.79.
Where *Nestor*, shepherd of his people, reigns. .... Od.17.125.137.
But *Nestor* spoke, they listen'd, and obey'd. .... Od.24.70.351.

NESTOR'S

Nor think your *Nestor's* Years and Wisdom vain. .... Il.1.344.105.
He thus advancing, *Nestor's* valiant Son .... Il.5.693.301.
A broken Rock by *Nestor's* Son was thrown, ... Il.5.711.301.
And *Nestor's* Son laid stern *Ablerus* dead. .... Il.6.38.325.
And *Nestor's* trembling Hand confess'd his Fright. .... Il.8.166.406.
Give me to seize rich *Nestor's* Shield of Gold; .... Il.8.235.408.
Would hardly stile thee *Nestor's* youngest Son. .... Il.9.82.436.
(For *Nestor's* Influence best that Quarter guides; .... Il.10.67.5.
The King to *Nestor's* sable Ship repairs; .... Il.10.81.6.
Bold *Merion* strove, and *Nestor's* valiant Heir; .... Il.10.272.14.
While *Nestor's* Chariot far from Fight retires: .... Il.11.727.67.
Greece, as the Prize of *Nestor's* Wisdom, gave) .... Il.11.767.69.
Last *Nestor's* Son the same bold Ardour takes, ... Il.13.129.110.
Remain the Prize of *Nestor's* youthful Son. .... Il.13.508.130.
Touch'd ev'ry *Greek*, but *Nestor's* Son the most. .... Il.13.528.131.
This Youth, the Joy of *Nestor's* glorious Age) .... Il.13.703.138.
Could charm the Cares of *Nestor's* watchful Soul: .... Il.14.2.156.
Nestor's Approach alarm'd each *Grecian* Breast, ... Il.14.47.160.
Phalces and *Mermer*, *Nestor's* Son o'erthrew. .... Il.14.607.191.
Stood *Nestor's* Son, the Messenger of Woe: .... Il.18.4.322.
While *Nestor's* Son sustains a manlier Part, ... Il.18.37.325.
No more shall *Nestor's* Hand your Food supply, ... Il.23.491.510.
Not without Cause incens'd at *Nestor's* Son, ... Il.23.649.515.
His youthful Equals, *Nestor's* Son the last. .... Il.23.884.524.
On *Nestor* first, and *Nestor's* royal line; .... Od.3.71.89.
And *Nestor's* Youngest stops the vents of breath. .... Od.3.579.116.
Suffic'd, soft-whispering thus to *Nestor's* son, ... Od.4.81.123.
With him at *Nestor's* high command I came, ... Od.4.215.130.

NESTOR'S (CONTINUED)

With *Nestor's* Son, *Telemachus* was lay'd; .... Od.15.6.70.
But *Nestor's* son the chearful silence broke, ... Od.15.186.77.
To *Nestor's* heir *Ulysses'* god-like son: .... Od.15.219.78.
Still at his side is *Nestor's* son survey'd, ... Od.24.27.348.
(From old experience *Nestor's* counsel springs, ... Od.24.71.351.

NESTOREAN

The last fair branch of the *Nestorean* line .... Od.3.593.116.

NET

Wind the shrill Horn, or spread the waving Net. .... 1.W-F.96.159.
Till hov'ring o'er 'em sweeps the swelling Net. .... 1.W-F.104.160.
"Entangle Justice in her net of Law, ... 3.EOM3.192.113.
The Net that held them, and the Wreath that crown'd, ... Il.22.601.481.
A wond'rous Net he labours, to betray .... Od.8.317.281.
With conscious dread they shun the quiv'ring net: .... Od.22.340.304.

NETHER

Oft, as he fish'd her nether realms for wit, ... 5.DunA2.93.108.
Where as he fish'd her nether realms for Wit, ... 5.DunB2.101.300.
Had hurl'd indignant to the nether Sky, ... Il.14.292.176.
Thence on the nether World the Fury fell; .... Il.19.131.377.
Sunk in one Instant to the nether World; .... Il.20.534.416.
To seek *Tiresias* in the nether sky, ... Od.11.201.391.
Or pale and wan beholds these nether skies? .... Od.11.571.411.
Gild the gross vapor of this nether sphere! .... Od.19.41.194.

NETS

Like nets or lime-twigs, for rich Widows hearts? .... 4.JD2.58.137.
Mending old Nets to catch the scaly Fry; .... 6.14ii.16.43.
Sweep with their arching nets the hoary main, ... Od.22.426.308.

NETTLES

His court with nettles, moats with cresses stor'd, ... 3.Ep3.183.109.
His Rump well pluck'd with Nettles stings, ... 6.93.21.257.

NETTS

Like Netts or Limetwiggs for the Ladies Hearts, ... 4.JD2A.62.138.

NEUFGERMAIN

Not thine, Immortal *Neufgermain!* .... 6.30.57.88.

NEUTRAL

Swear, to stand neutral while we cope in fight. .... Od.18.65.169.

NEVER

Which still *presides*, yet never does *Appear;* .... 1.EOC.75A.247.
Cavil you may, but never *Criticize*. .... 1.EOC.123.252.
You may *Confound*, but never *Criticize*. .... 1.EOC.123A.252.
Is *Pride*, the *never-failing Vice of Fools*. .... 1.EOC.204.264.
Sure *some* to *vex*, but never *all* to *please;* .... 1.EOC.505.295.
Seldom at *Council*, never in a *War:* .... 1.EOC.537.298.
And never shock'd, and never turn'd aside, ... 1.EOC.629.310.
And never shock'd, and never turn'd aside, ... 1.EOC.629.310.
To distant Lands *Vertumnus* never roves; .... 1.TrVP.85.380.
The Vows you never will return, receive; .... 1.TrSP.107.398.
(At least to feign was never hard to you.) .... 1.TrSP.112.398.
Not so *Patroclus* never-erring Dart; .... 1.TrES.285.460.
But vainly boast the Joys they never try'd, ... 2.ChJM.35.16.
Vain Fortune's Favours, never at a Stay, ... 2.ChJM.53.17.
A Noble Fool was never in a Fault. .... 2.ChJM.165.23.
Who, wisely, never thinks the Case his own. .... 2.ChJM.507.40.
A wiser Monarch never saw the Sun: .... 2.ChJM.632.45.
I pass, as Gambols never known to you: .... 2.ChJM.745.51.
Paul, knowing One cou'd never serve our Turn, ... 2.ChWB.28.58.
For never was it giv'n to Mortal Man, ... 2.ChWB.70.59.
Can never be a Mouse of any Soul. .... 2.ChWB.299.71.
For better Fruit did never Orchard bear: .... 2.ChWB.398.76.
Oft she rejects, but never once offends. .... 2.RL2.12.160.
(Which never more shall join its parted Hair, ... 2.RL4.134.195.
Which never more its Honours shall renew, ... 2.RL4.135.195.
If *Hampton-Court* these Eyes had never seen! .... 2.RL4.150.196.
Where the gilt *Chariot* never marks the Way, ... 2.RL4.155.196.
Where the gilt *Chariot* never mark'd the Way, ... 2.RL4.155A.196.
Oh may we never love as these have lov'd! .... 2.ElAb.352.348.
Man never Is, but always To be blest: .... 3.EOM1.96.26.
His soul proud Science never taught to stray .... 3.EOM1.101.27.
That never air or ocean felt the wind; .... 3.EOM1.167.36.
That never passion discompos'd the mind: .... 3.EOM1.168.36.
Yet never pass th' insuperable line! .... 3.EOM1.228.44.
Or never feel the rage, or never own; .... 3.EOM2.228.83.
Or never feel the rage, or never own; .... 3.EOM2.228.83.
Death still draws nearer, never seeming near. .... 3.EOM3.76.99.
Sure never to o'er-shoot, but just to hit, ... 3.EOM3.89.101.
This too serves always, Reason never long; .... 3.EOM3.93.101.
And simple Reason never sought but one: .... 3.EOM3.230.115.
'Tis never to be bought, but always free, ... 3.EOM4.17.129.
Esteem and Love were never to be sold. .... 3.EOM4.188.145.
For ever exercis'd, yet never tir'd; .... 3.EOM4.322.159.
Never elated, while one man's oppress'd; .... 3.EOM4.323.159.
Never dejected, while another's bless'd; .... 3.EOM4.324.159.
That never answers till a Husband cools .... 3.Ep2.261B.71.
Who never answers till a Husband cools .... 3.Ep2.261C.71.
Or, if you rule him, never show you rule .... 3.Ep2.262A.71.
Or her, that owns her Faults, but never mends, ... 3.Ep2.103.58.
But never, never, reach'd one gen'rous Thought. .... 3.Ep2.162.64.
But never, never, reach'd one gen'rous Thought. .... 3.Ep2.162.64.
As never yet to love, or to be lov'd. .... 3.Ep2.166.64.
Of all her Dears she never slander'd one, ... 3.Ep2.175.64.
Then never break your heart when Cloe dies. .... 3.Ep2.180.64.
Still out of reach, yet never out of view, ... 3.Ep2.232.68.
Or, if she rules him, never shows she rules; .... 3.Ep2.262.71.
Will never mark the marble with his Name: .... 3.Ep3.286.116.
With tape-typ'd curtains, never meant to draw, ... 3.Ep3.302.118.
That never Coxcomb reach'd Magnificence! .... 3.Ep4.22.139.

NEVER (CONTINUED)

In all, let Nature never be forgot. .... 3.Ep4.50.142.
Soft and Agreeable come never there. .... 3.Ep4.102.147.
With here a Fountain, never to be play'd, ... 3.Ep4.121.149.
Who never mentions Hell to ears polite. .... 3.Ep4.150.152.
They'll never poison you, they'll only cheat. .... 4.HS1.90.13.
With foolish *Pride* my Heart was never fir'd, ... 4.JD4.9.27.
I'd never doubt at Court to make a Friend. .... 4.HS2.44.57.
"I never touch a Dame of Quality. .... 4.HAdv.70.81.
He too can say, "With Wives I never sin." .... 4.HAdv.73.81.
Never, ah, never! kiss thy Neighbour's Wife. .... 4.HAdv.105.85.
Never, ah, never! kiss thy Neighbour's Wife. .... 4.HAdv.105.85.
A War-horse never for the Service chose, ... 4.HAdv.114.85.
"I'd never name Queens, Ministers, or Kings; .... 4.Arbu.76.101.
I never answer'd, I was not in debt: .... 4.Arbu.154.107.
"No, such a Genius never can lye still," .... 4.Arbu.278.115.
And sees at *Cannons* what was never there: .... 4.Arbu.300.117.
Let never honest Man my satire dread, ... 4.Arbu.303A.117.
Laugh'd at the loss of Friends he never had, ... 4.Arbu.346.120.
The Blow unfelt, the Tear he never shed; .... 4.Arbu.349.120.
Here a lean Bard, whose wit could never give .... 4.JD2.13.133.
'Tis such a bounty as was never known, ... 4.JD2.65.139.
Dear *Cibber!* never match'd one Ode of thine. .... 4.2HE2.138.175.
Finds Envy never conquer'd, but by Death. .... 4.2HE1.16.195.
Or say our fathers never broke a rule; .... 4.2HE1.93.203.
To prove, that Luxury could never hold; .... 4.2HE1.167.209.
Who builds a Bridge that never drove a pyle? .... 4.2HE1.185.211.
These Madmen never hurt the Church or State: .... 4.2HE1.190.211.
Flight of Cashiers, or Mobs, he'll never mind; .... 4.2HE1.195.211.
Flight of Cashiers, or Fires, he'll never mind; .... 4.2HE1.195A.211.
How Van wants grace, who never wanted wit! .... 4.2HE1.289.219.
To sing, or cease to sing, we never know; .... 4.2HE1.361.227.
Still, still be getting, never, never rest. .... 4.1HE6.96.243.
Still, still be getting, never, never rest. .... 4.1HE6.96.243.
When twenty Fools I never saw .... 4.HS6.64.255.
Contriving never to oblige ye. .... 4.1HE7.30.271.
You give the things you never care for. .... 4.1HE7.34.271.
You gave the things you never care for. .... 4.1HE7.34A.271.
"And never gallop Pegasus to death; .... 4.1HE1.14.279.
You never change one muscle of your face, ... 4.1HE1.171.291.
The Great man never offer'd you a Groat. .... 4.EpS1.26.299.
And never laugh—for all my life to come? .... 4.EpS1.28.300.
Who never chang'd his Principle, or Wig: .... 4.EpS1.40.301.
I never nam'd—the Town's enquiring yet. .... 4.EpS2.21.314.
Like Royal Harts, be never more run down? .... 4.EpS2.29.314.
I never (to my sorrow I declare) .... 4.EpS2.98.318.
Has never made a Friend in private life, ... 4.EpS2.134.321.
Must never Patriot then declaim at Gin, ... 4.EpS2.191.324.
For born a Goddess, Dulness never dies. .... 5.DunA1.16.62.
With all such reading as was never read; .... 5.DunA1.166.83.
But sad examples never fail to move. .... 5.DunA1.176.84.
Never was dash'd out, at one lucky hit, ... 5.DunA2.43.101.
Hung silent down his never-blushing head; .... 5.DunA2.385.148.
Ev'n Arnall hung the never-blushing head; .... 5.DunA2.385B.148.
No fiercer sons, had Easter never been. .... 5.DunA3.110.159.
And never wash'd, but in Castalia's streams: .... 5.DunA3.144.162.
Tho' stale, not ripe; tho' thin, yet never clear; .... 5.DunA3.164.167.
For ever reading, never to be read. .... 5.DunA3.190.172.
Are ever reading and are never read. .... 5.DunA3.190A.172.
Safe in its heaviness, can never stray, ... 5.DunA3.297.184.
For, born a Goddess, Dulness never dies. .... 5.DunB1.18.270.
The brisk Example never fail'd to move. .... 5.DunB1.194.283.
The sad Example never fail'd to move. .... 5.DunB1.194A.283.
Never was dash'd out, at one lucky hit, ... 5.DunB2.47.298.
Hung silent down his never-blushing head; .... 5.DunB2.417.318.
And never wash'd, but in Castalia's streams. .... 5.DunB3.18.321.
No fiercer sons, had Easter never been. .... 5.DunB3.118.325.
Tho' stale, not ripe; tho' thin, yet never clear; .... 5.DunB3.170.328.
For ever reading, never to be read! .... 5.DunB3.194.329.
His never-blushing head he turn'd aside, ... 5.DunB3.231.331.
Safe in its heaviness, shall never stray, ... 5.DunB3.295.334.
Safe in its heaviness, can never stray, ... 5.DunB3.295A.334.
We never suffer it to stand too wide. .... 5.DunB4.154.356.
His Hat, which never vail'd to human pride, ... 5.DunB4.205.362.
And Alsop never but like Horace joke: .... 5.DunB4.224.365.
Like buoys, that never sink into the flood, ... 5.DunB4.241.366.
With all such reading as was never read: .... 5.DunB4.250.368.
Never by tumbler thro' the hoops was shown .... 5.DunB4.257.369.
A dauntless infant! never scar'd with God. .... 5.DunB4.284.372.
But, sad example! never to escape .... 5.DunB4.527.394.
Thy stream, like his, is never past, ... 6.6ii.7.14.
There learn'd she Speech from Tongues that never cease. .... 6.14ii.32.44.
And the Gay mourn'd who never mourn'd before; .... 6.19.16.62.
And fill the shade with never ceasing lays; .... 6.20.67.68.
Can never fail Cuckolding *Two* or *Three* Spouses. .... 6.36.7.104.
And Beauty's Goddess Childhood never knew, ... 6.37.2.106.
To a good honest Junta that never will teaze you. .... 6.42iii.6.117.
To tell Men things they never *knew at all.* .... 6.48iii.4.134.
The Worm that never dies! .... 6.53.32.162.
Was never such a loving Pair, ... 6.79.39.219.
Never was such a loving Pair, ... 6.79.39A.219.
That never spareth none. .... 6.82viii.4.233.
And what never stands still, ... 6.91.10.253.
In whose Heart, like his Writings, was never found flaw; .... 6.92.2.255.
But *Richmond's* Fair-ones never spoil their Locks, ... 6.95.3.264.
And never will return, or bring him home. .... 6.96ii.30Z28.271.
"And never will return, or bring thee home. .... 6.96ii.38.272.
Did never *Yahoo* tread that Ground before? .... 6.96iii.12.274.
O! may'st thou never want an easy Pad! .... 6.96iii.38.275.
Not touch me! never Neighbour call'd me Slut! .... 6.96iv.25.277.
Never for this can just returns be shown; .... 6.105v.3.302.
An *Author* that cou'd never *write,* .... 6.116ii.3.326.
And sees at *C[a]nons* what was never there; .... 6.120.8.339.
(I promis'd I never would mention Miss Vane.) .... 6.122.14.342.
Lord! never ask who thus could serve ye? .... 6.127.3.355.
What wonder tryumphs never turn'd his brain .... 6.130.7.358.

NEVER (CONTINUED)

One half will never be believ'd, ... 6.133.3.363.
The other never read. .... 6.133.4.363.
Sure *Bounce* is one you never read of. .... 6.135.8.366.
Who never flatter'd Folks like you: .... 6.138.3.376.
But never, never, reach'd one gen'rous Thought. .... 6.139.6.377.
But never, never, reach'd one gen'rous Thought. .... 6.139.6.377.
As never yet to love, or to be lov'd. .... 6.139.10.377.
Of all her Dears she never slander'd one, ... 6.139.19.377.
Then never break your heart when Cloë dies. .... 6.139.24.377.
For never Heart felt Passion more sincere: .... 6.152.4.400.
For never *Briton* more disdain'd a Slave! .... 6.152.6.400.
The distant *Trojans* never injur'd me. .... Il.1.200.96.
Which never more shall Leaves or Blossoms bear, ... Il.1.310.103.
The Triple Dog had never felt his Chain, ... Il.8.447.418.
And solemn swear those Charms were never mine; .... Il.9.172.441.
As never Father gave a Child before. .... Il.9.194.442.
Pluto, the grizly God who never spares, ... Il.9.209.442.
As never Father gave a Child before. .... Il.9.381.451.
Atrides' Daughter never shall be led .... Il.9.510.458.
Never, ah never let me leave thy side! .... Il.9.572.462.
Never, ah never let me leave thy side! .... Il.9.572.462.
Then (never to return) he sought the Shore, ... Il.10.399.21.
A Coward's Weapon never hurts the Brave. .... Il.11.498.56.
Ah! never may he see his native Land, ... Il.13.303.119.
Never, ah never, to behold it more! .... Il.13.808.143.
Never, ah never, to behold it more! .... Il.13.808.143.
May never Rage like thine my Soul enslave, ... Il.16.40.237.
Which never Man had stain'd with ruddy Wine, ... Il.16.274.249.
Not so *Patroclus'* never erring Dart; .... Il.16.590.267.
That Plume, which never stoop'd to Earth before, ... Il.16.961.280.
Still as a Tomb-stone, never to be mov'd, ... Il.17.492.307.
For sadder Tydings never touch'd thy Ear; .... Il.17.772.318.
He never, never must return again. .... Il.18.78.326.
He never, never must return again. .... Il.18.78.326.
An aged Father never see me more! .... Il.18.388.340.
Never, ah never, shall receive him more; .... Il.18.514.346.
Never, ah never, shall receive him more; .... Il.18.514.346.
Burn with a Fury that can never die? .... Il.19.70.374.
Sorrows on Sorrows, never doom'd to end! .... Il.19.308.385.
When round and round with never-weary'd Pain, ... Il.20.579.418.
Such is the Lust of never-dying Fame! .... Il.20.590.418.
Now never to return! and doom'd to go .... Il.21.54.424.
No Thought but Rage, and never-ceasing Strife, ... Il.22.341.470.
Would I had never been!—O thou, the Ghost .... Il.22.616.481.
But this, my Prize, I never shall forego; .... Il.23.633.514.
If, in that Gloom which never Light must know, ... Il.24.740.568.
Never to manly Age that Son shall rise, ... Il.24.914.574.
For thy stern Father never spar'd a Foe: .... Il.24.930.575.
Which never, never could be lost in Air, ... Il.24.938.575.
Which never, never could be lost in Air, ... Il.24.938.575.
The God vindictive doom'd them never more .... Od.1.11.29.
Our eyes, unhappy! never greeted more. .... Od.1.274.46.
But never from this nobler suit we cease; .... Od.2.235.73.
O never, never more! let King be just, ... Od.2.261.74.
O never, never more! let King be just, ... Od.2.261.74.
For never, never, wicked man was wise. .... Od.2.320.76.
For never, never, wicked man was wise. .... Od.2.320.76.
An honest business never blush to tell. .... Od.3.20.87.
And sure he will: For Wisdom never lies. .... Od.3.26.87.
Their fates or fortunes never reach'd my ear. .... Od.3.224.96.
The father's fortune never to return, ... Od.3.256.98.
Never on man did heav'nly favour shine .... Od.3.273.99.
But never, never shall *Calypso* send .... Od.5.179.180.
But never, never shall *Calypso* send .... Od.5.179.180.
Where never science rear'd her lawrel'd head: .... Od.6.12.203.
Never, I never view'd 'till this blest hour .... Od.6.191.218.
Never, I never view'd 'till this blest hour .... Od.6.191.218.
As yet, unbid they never grac'd our feast, ... Od.7.269.249.
(For here affliction never pleads in vain:) .... Od.8.32.263.
And never, never may'st thou want this sword! .... Od.8.450.287.
And never, never may'st thou want this sword! .... Od.8.450.287.
My country's image never was forgot, ... Od.9.36.303.
And never shalt thou taste this Nectar more. .... Od.9.416.323.
Never, alas! thou never shalt return, ... Od.10.317.359.
Never, alas! thou never shalt return, ... Od.10.317.359.
Swear, by the Vow which never can be vain. .... Od.10.410.364.
When sworn that oath which never can be vain? .... Od.10.450.365.
Shall never the dear land in prospect rise, ... Od.10.562.369.
But never have thy eyes astonish'd view'd .... Od.11.519.409.
But my *Orestes* never met these eyes, ... Od.11.559.411.
Truth I revere: For Wisdom never lies. .... Od.11.572.411.
And never, never be to Heav'n resign'd? .... Od.12.146.439.
And never, never be to Heav'n resign'd? .... Od.12.146.439.
Never, I never, scene so dire survey'd! .... Od.12.309.447.
Never, I never, scene so dire survey'd! .... Od.12.309.447.
And publick evil never touch the land! .... Od.13.61.4.
The swain reply'd. It never was our guise .... Od.14.65.38.
So mild a master never shall I find: .... Od.14.160.43.
That, true to honour, never lagg'd behind, ... Od.14.245.48.
Never, I never hop'd to view this day, ... Od.16.25.103.
Never, I never hop'd to view this day, ... Od.16.25.103.
Other *Ulysses* shalt thou never see, ... Od.16.224.114.
Who never, never shall behold him more! .... Od.17.378.150.
Who never, never shall behold him more! .... Od.17.378.150.
Yet if injustice never be secure, ... Od.17.564.160.
Yet never, never from thy dome we move, ... Od.18.333.184.
Yet never, never from thy dome we move, ... Od.18.333.184.
Doom'd to survive, and never to return! .... Od.19.297.209.
He never dar'd defraud the sacred fane, ... Od.19.428.215.
(Who never must review his dear domain; .... Od.20.407.252.
A hope so idle never touch'd his brain: .... Od.21.341.276.
Never did I a sleep so sweet enjoy, ... Od.23.21.319.
O *Troy—may* never tongue pronounce thee more! .... Od.23.24.320.
For never must *Ulysses* view this shore; .... Od.23.69.322.
Never! the lov'd *Ulysses* is no more! .... Od.23.70.322.

NEVER-BLUSHING
Hung silent down his never-blushing head; 5.DunA2.385.148.
Ev'n Arnall hung the never-blushing head; 5.DunA2.385B.148.
Hung silent down his never-blushing head; 5.DunB2.417.318.
His never-blushing head he turn'd aside, 5.DunB3.231.331.

NEVER-CEASING
No Thought but Rage, and never-ceasing Strife, Il.22.341.470.

NEVER-DYING
Such is the Lust of never-dying Fame! Il.20.590.418.

NEVER-ERRING
Not so *Patroclus* never-erring Dart; 1.TrES.285.460.

NEVER-FAILING
Is *Pride,* the *never-failing Vice of Fools.* 1.EOC.204.264.

NEVER-WEARY'D
When round and round with never-weary'd Pain, Il.20.579.418.

NEW
See NEWCASTLE.
If *Sylvia* smiles, new Glories gild the Shore, 1.PSp.75.68.
Swell'd with new Passion, and o'erflows with Tears; 1.PWi.66.93.
And bid new Musick charm th'unfolding Ear. 1.Mes.42.116.
New Falls of Water murm'ring in his Ear: 1.Mes.70.119.
And in the new-shorn Field the Partridge feeds, 1.W-F.98.160.
And add new Lustre to her Silver *Star.* 1.W-F.290.175.
Heav'ns! what new Wounds, and how her old have bled? 1.W-F.322.180.
Their ample Bow, a new *White-Hall* ascend! 1.W-F.380.188.
Led by new Stars, and born by spicy Gales! 1.W-F.392.190.
And the new World launch forth to seek the Old. 1.W-F.402.191.
New, distant Scenes of *endless* Science rise! 1.EOC.224.265.
Then build a New, or act it in a Plain. 1.EOC.284.271.
Alike Fantastick, if *too New,* or *Old;* 1.EOC.334.276.
Be not the *first* by whom the *New* are try'd, 1.EOC.335.276.
Regard not then if Wit be *Old* or *New,* 1.EOC.406.287.
New *Blackmores* and new *Milbourns* must arise; 1.EOC.463.291.
New *Blackmores* and new *Milbourns* must arise; 1.EOC.463.291.
New *S[hadwell]s* and new *M[ilbour]ns* must arise; 1.EOC.463B.291.
New *S[hadwell]s* and new *M[ilbour]ns* must arise; 1.EOC.463B.291.
Reflect new Glories, and augment the Day. 1.EOC.473.292.
Where a *new World* leaps out at his command, 1.EOC.486.294.
Name a new *Play,* and *he's* the Poet's *Friend,* 1.EOC.620.309.
And call new Beauties forth from ev'ry Line! 1.EOC.666.315.
While nice, and anxious in his new disease, 1.TrPA.21.366.
The spring was new, and all the verdant boughs 1.TrFD.22.386.
If this be false, let these new greens decay, 1.TrFD.73.389.
Yet latent life thro' her new branches reign'd, 1.TrFD.102.390.
Ask not the cause that I new Numbers chuse, 1.TrSP.5.393.
New Lords they madly make, then tamely bear, 1.TrSt.228.420.
Madly they make new Lords, then tamely bear, 1.TrSt.228A.420.
Gilds with new Lustre the divine Abodes, 1.TrSt.293.422.
Wakes to new Vigor with the rising Day. 1.TrSt.587.434.
And suck'd new Poisons with his triple Tongue) 1.TrSt.667.438.
His fainting Squadrons to new Fury warms. 1.TrES.144.454.
In what new Region is *Ulysses* tost? 1.TrUl.75.468.
And a new Vigour springs in ev'ry Part. 2.ChJM.130.21.
And a new Palsie seiz'd them when I frown'd. 2.ChWB.67.59.
My Garments always must be new and gay, 2.ChWB.112.62.
And old Impertinence expel by new. 2.RL1.94.152.
While ev'ry Beam new transient Colours flings, 2.RL2.67.163.
Or stain her Honour, or her new Brocade, 2.RL2.107.166.
New Stratagems, the radiant Lock to gain. 2.RL3.120.176.
When each new Night-Dress gives a new Disease. 2.RL4.38.186.
When each new Night-Dress gives a new Disease. 2.RL4.38.186.
Once gave new Beauties to the snowie Neck. 2.RL4.170.198.
Which adds new Glory to the shining Sphere! 2.RL5.142.211.
These ever new, nor subject to Decays, 2.TemF.51.256.
Of old Mismanagements, Taxations new— 2.TemF.456.285.
And all who told it, added something new, 2.TemF.470.286.
Repent old pleasures, and sollicit new: 2.ElAb.186.335.
And still new needs, new helps, new habits rise, 3.EOM3.137.106.
And still new needs, new helps, new habits rise, 3.EOM3.137.106.
And still new needs, new helps, new habits rise, 3.EOM3.137.106.
Re-lum'd her ancient light, not kindled new; 3.EOM3.287.121.
On air or sea new motions be imprest, 3.EOM4.125.139.
New-market-fame, and judgment at a Bett. 3.Ep1.145.27.
Shall parts so various aim at nothing new? 3.Ep1.186.31.
Fix'd Principles, with Fancy ever new; 3.Ep2.279.72.
Erect new wonders, and the old repair, 3.Ep4.192.155.
Had no *new Verses,* or *new Suit* to show; 4.JD4.13.27.
Had no *new Verses,* or *new Suit* to show; 4.JD4.13.27.
He asks, "What *News?"* I tell him of new Plays, 4.JD4.124.35.
New Eunuchs, Harlequins, and Operas. 4.JD4.125.35.
Shall half the new-built Churches round thee fall? 4.HS2.119.63.
And yet no new built Palaces aspire, 4.JD2A.117.142.
Schoolmen new tenements in Hell must make; 4.JD2.42.135.
No young Divine, new-benefic'd, can be 4.JD2.51.137.
So vast, our new Divines, we must confess, 4.JD2.97.141.
We see no new-built Palaces aspire, 4.JD2.111.143.
What tho he swears tis all his own, and new; 4.JD2A.37.134.
Schoolmen new Tenements in Hell must make; 4.JD2A.46.136.
Not Young Divines, new-benefic'd can be 4.JD2A.57.136.
Again? new Tumults in my Breast? 4.HOde1.1.151.
These rais'd new Empires o'er the Earth, 4.HOde9.11.159.
And Those new Heav'ns and Systems fram'd; 4.HOde9.12.159.
He walks, an Object new beneath the Sun! 4.2HE2.119.173.
Or bid the new be *English,* Ages hence, 4.2HE2.169.177.
When works are censur'd, not as bad, but new; 4.2HE1.116.205.
What then was new, what had been ancient now? 4.2HE1.136.207.
New-market's Glory rose, as Britain's fell; 4.2HE1.144.207.
But art thou one, whom new opinions sway, 4.1HE6.63.241.
Or, "Have you nothing new to-day 4.HS6.93.255.
This new Court jargon, or the good old song? 4.1HE1.98.287.

NEW (CONTINUED)
Prefer a new Japanner to their shoes, 4.1HE1.156.291.
Or each new-pension'd Sycophant, pretend 4.EpS2.142.321.
To hatch a new Saturnian age of Lead. 5.DunA1.26.63.
And New-year Odes, and all the Grubstreet race. 5.DunA1.42.65.
How new-born Nonsense first is taught to cry, 5.DunA1.58.67.
And ductile dulness new meanders takes; 5.DunA1.62.67.
The page admires new beauties, not its own. 5.DunA1.120.77.
A past, vamp'd, future, old, reviv'd, new piece, 5.DunA1.238.91.
Imbibes new life, and scours and stinks along, 5.DunA2.98.109.
A second effort brought but new disgrace, 5.DunA2.167.121.
Demand new bodies, and in Calf's array 5.DunA3.21.152.
Old in new state, another yet the same. 5.DunA3.32.154.
And a new Cibber shall the Stage adorn. 5.DunA3.134.161.
Thence a new world, to Nature's laws unknown, 5.DunA3.237.177.
Another Cynthia her new journey runs, 5.DunA3.239.177.
Then a new world, to Nature's laws unknown, 5.DunA3.237A.177.
New wizards rise: here Booth, and Cibber there: 5.DunA3.262.179.
For new Abortions, all ye pregnant Fair! 5.DunA3.312.186.
To hatch a new Saturnian age of Lead. 5.DunB1.28.271.
And New-year Odes, and all the Grub-street race. 5.DunB1.44.274.
How new-born nonsense first is taught to cry, 5.DunB1.60.274.
And ductile dulness new meanders takes; 5.DunB1.64.274.
A past, vamp'd, future, old, reviv'd, new piece, 5.DunB1.284.290.
New edge their dulness, and new bronze their face. 5.DunB2.10.296.
New edge their dulness, and new bronze their face. 5.DunB2.10.296.
New point their dulness, and new bronze their face. 5.DunB2.10A.296.
New point their dulness, and new bronze their face. 5.DunB2.10A.296.
Imbibes new life, and scours and stinks along; 5.DunB2.106.300.
A second effort brought but new disgrace, 5.DunB2.175.304.
Demand new bodies, and in Calf's array, 5.DunB3.29.321.
Old in new state, another yet the same. 5.DunB3.40.322.
And a new Cibber shall the stage adorn. 5.DunB3.142.326.
Thence a new world to Nature's laws unknown, 5.DunB3.241.332.
Another Cynthia her new journey runs, 5.DunB3.243.332.
New wizards rise; I see my Cibber there! 5.DunB3.266.333.
For new abortions, all ye pregnant fair! 5.DunB3.314.335.
See under Ripley rise a new White-hall, 5.DunB3.327.336.
Of dull and venal a new World to mold, 5.DunB4.15.341.
Strong in new Arms, lo! Giant Handel stands, 5.DunB4.65.348.
A new Edition of old Æson gave, 5.DunB4.122.353.
Admire new light thro' holes yourselves have made. 5.DunB4.126.354.
And bring new heav'ns before our eyes; 6.6ii.14.15.
Lac'd in her *Cosins* new appear'd the Bride, 6.9vii.1.22.
Still gain new Titles with new Forms; 6.14v(b).22.50.
Still gain new Titles with new Forms; 6.14v(b).22.50.
Still makes new Conquests, and maintains the past: 6.19.62.64.
New greens shall spring, new flow'rs around me grow, 6.20.68.68.
New greens shall spring, new flow'rs around me grow, 6.20.68.68.
Pray heartily for some new Gift, 6.39.23.111.
These *smart, new Characters* supplyd. 6.44.22.123.
To what new clime, what distant sky 6.51i.13.151.
'Till some new Tyrant lifts his purple hand, 6.51i.23.152.
And each from each contract new strength and light. 6.52.16.156.
New graces yearly, like thy works, display; 6.52.65.158.
See, see, ye great New—le comes, 6.58.43A.172.
In what new Nation shall we fix our Seat? 6.65.6.192.
And so he did—for to *New Court* 6.79.125.222.
With added years if Life bring nothing new, 6.86.5.245.
With added Days if Life give nothing new, 6.86.5B.245.
With added years if Life give nothing new, 6.86.5C.245.
Subservient to *New-market's* annual cheat! 6.96iii.26.275.
O teach me, Dear, new Words to speak my Flame; 6.96iv.95.279.
To see his own Maids serve a new Lord and Master. 6.122.18.342.
Satyr still just with humour ever new; 6.125.1Z4.349.
But for thy Windsor, a New Fabric Raise 6.147ix.5.392.
Prepar'd new Toils and doubled Woes on Woes. Il.2.501.150.
But new to all the Dangers of the Main. Il.2.746.161.
Encreas'd and prosper'd in their new Abodes, Il.2.811.163.
Say, to new Nations must I cross the Main, Il.3.495.215.
Thus with new Ardour he the Brave inspires, Il.4.274.234.
New to the Field, and still a Foe to Fame. Il.5.414.286.
He said: new Courage swell'd each Hero's Heart. Il.5.572.296.
And adds new Horrors to the darken'd Field; Il.5.622.297.
Each *Trojan* Bosom with new Warmth he fires. Il.5.626.298.
Her Speech new Fury to their Hearts convey'd; Il.5.986.314.
To add new Honours to my native Land, Il.6.258.339.
And draw new Spirits from the gen'rous Bowl; Il.6.326.342.
Fair as the new-born Star that gilds the Morn. Il.6.499.351.
O'erwhelms the Nations with new Toils and Woes; Il.7.82.367.
Thro' ev'ry *Argive* Heart new Transport ran, Il.7.259.377.
Ev'n *Hector* paus'd, and with new Doubt opprest Il.7.261.377.
New to the Field, and trembling at the Fight? Il.7.286.378.
Awake thy Squadrons to new Toils of Fight. Il.7.397.383.
Till the new Sun restores the chearful Light: Il.7.447.386.
Nor with new Treaties vex my Peace in vain. Il.9.411.452.
And meditates new Cheats on all his Slaves: Il.9.486.456.
And new to Perils of the direful Field: Il.9.569.462.
Then, for his Spoils, a new Debate arose, Il.9.663.467.
What new Distress, what sudden Cause of Fright Il.10.160.9.
The Wise new Prudence from the Wise acquire, Il.10.267.13.
But him, new Dangers, new Atchievements fire: Il.10.587.28.
But him, new Dangers, new Atchievements fire: Il.10.587.28.
The neighing Coursers their new Fellows greet, Il.10.668.31.
With new-born Day to gladden mortal Sight, Il.11.3.34.
New Force, new Spirit to each Breast returns; Il.11.277.47.
New Force, new Spirit to each Breast returns; Il.11.277.47.
Each takes new Courage at the Hero's Sight; Il.11.724.67.
Honey new-press'd, the sacred Flow'r of Wheat, Il.11.770.69.
To gain new Glories, or augment the old. Il.12.322.93.
His fainting Squadrons to new Fury warms. Il.12.498.99.
New rising Spirits all my Force alarm, Il.13.109.110.
But breathe new Courage as they feel the Pow'r: Il.13.124.110.
New rising Spirits all the Man alarm, Il.13.109A.110.
Come, follow to the Fleet thy new Allies; Il.13.480.130.
What new Alarm, divine *Machaon* say, Il.14.5.157.

NEW (CONTINUED)

In ev'ry *Greek* a new *Achilles* rise? Il.14.58.160.
But lest new Wounds on Wounds o'erpower us quite, Il.14.149.165.
Than new fal'n Snow, and dazling as the Light. Il.14.214.170.
Thick new-born Vi'lets a soft Carpet spread, Il.14.397.182.
Pours new Destruction on her Sons again? Il.15.329.210.
The sportive Wanton, pleas'd with some new Play, Il.15.418.213.
And catch'd new Fury at the Voice divine. Il.15.439.214.
New-ting'd with *Tyrian* Dye: In Dust below, Il.15.634.220.
His manly Breast, and with new Fury burns. Il.15.711.223.
As if new Vigour from new Fights they won, Il.15.846.229.
As if new Vigour from new Fights they won, Il.15.846.229.
Pour a new Deluge on the *Grecian* Band. Il.15.881.230.
And add new Glories to his mighty Name. Il.16.327.255.
Great *Merion* follows, and new Shouts arise: Il.16.764.273.
Then rash *Patroclus* with new Fury glows, Il.16.946.280.
Thus round her new fal'n Young, the Heifer moves, Il.17.5.287.
His manly Breast, and with new Fury burn'd, Il.17.122.292.
She breathes new Vigour in her Hero's Breast, Il.17.639.312.
New Woes, new Sorrows shall create again: Il.18.116.328.
New Woes, new Sorrows shall create again: Il.18.116.328.
Shall take new Courage, and disdain to fly. Il.18.240.333.
Along the Street the new-made Brides are led, Il.18.571.350.
With new-made Wounds; another dragg'd a dead; Il.18.622.352.
The new-ear'd Earth in blacker Ridges roll'd; Il.18.635A.354.
(With new-born mortal Sight, Il.19.3.371.
And pour new Furies on the feebler Foe. Il.19.236.382.
To their new Seats the Female Captives move; Il.19.295.384.
Stung with new Ardor, thus by Heav'n impell'd, Il.21.346.435.
From the pleas'd Crowd new Peals of Thunder rise, Il.23.1042.530.
The new-made Car with solid Beauty shin'd; Il.24.334.550.
Where yet new labours his arrival wait; Od.1.26.30.
And the new friend with courteous air embrac'd. Od.1.160.40.
New to his friends embrace, had breath'd his last! Od.1.304.47.
For my lost Sire, nor add new woe to woe. Od.2.78.64.
And rais'd new discord. Then (so Heav'n decreed) Od.3.195.95.
New from the corse, the scaly frauds diffuse Od.4.597.148.
He said: new thoughts my beating heart employ, Od.4.741.153.
Provoke new sorrow from these grateful eyes. Od.4.750.154.
New to the plow, unpractis'd in the trace. Od.4.861.159.
With new-born day to gladden mortal sight, Od.5.3.170.
New horrors now this destin'd head enclose; Od.5.387.190.
So the rude *Boreas*, o'er the field new shorn, Od.5.470.195.
On what new region is *Ulysses* tost? Od.6.140.214.
New from his nuptials, hapless youth! expir'd. Od.7.83.237.
Call on the *Cicons*, with new fury fir'd; Od.9.52.304.
The new-fall'n young here bleating for their dams; Od.9.259.317.
Thus with new taunts insult the monster's ear. Od.9.586.330.
New wine and milk, with honey temper'd, bring, Od.10.618.374.
New wine, with honey-temper'd milk, we bring, Od.11.31.380.
New to the realms of death, *Elpenor's* shade: Od.11.66.383.
New trains of dangers, and new scenes of woes: Od.11.129.387.
New trains of dangers, and new scenes of woes: Od.11.129.387.
New foes arise, domestic ills attend! Od.11.147.388.
And add new horror to the realms of woe. Od.11.574.411.
New horrors rise! let prudence by thy guide, Od.12.69.433.
Still are new toils and war thy dire delight? Od.12.144.439.
Approach! and learn new wisdom from the wise. Od.12.227.443.
O stay, and learn new wisdom from the wise! Od.12.231.443.
New chains they add, and rapid urge the way, Od.12.236.443.
Still must we restless rove, new seas explore, Od.12.337.448.
Without new treasures let him not remove, Od.13.15.2.
In what new region is *Ulysses* tost? Od.13.242.17.
(With flour imbrown'd) next mingled wine yet new, Od.14.93.40.
New frauds were plotted by the faithless train, Od.14.375.53.
New from his crime, and reeking yet with gore. Od.15.251.80.
My new-accepted guest I haste to find, Od.17.66.135.
To some new channel soon, the changeful tide Od.19.102.197.
New from the birth: and with a mother's hand Od.19.409.214.
Was new disclos'd to birth: the banquet ends, Od.19.472.219.
Soon as the morn, new-rob'd in purple light, Od.19.499.220.
Down her pale cheek new-streaming sorrow flows: Od.19.702.229.
His heart with rage this new dishonour stung, Od.20.13.231.
These aged nerves with new-born vigor strung, Od.20.296.247.
With each new sun to some new hope a prey, Od.21.165.267.
With each new sun to some new hope a prey, Od.21.165.267.
These aged sinews with new vigor strung, Od.21.207.269.
To some new strain when he adapts the lyre, Od.21.442.281.
Wrapt in a new-slain Oxe's ample hide: Od.22.403.307.
New as they were to that infernal shore, Od.24.29.348.
Swell with new joy, and thus his son address. Od.24.583.376.

NEW-ACCEPTED

My new-accepted guest I haste to find, Od.17.66.135.

NEW-BENEFIC'D

No young Divine, new-benefic'd, can be 4.JD2.51.137.
Not Young Divines, new-benefic'd can be 4.JD2A.57.136.

NEW-BORN

How new-born Nonsense first is taught to cry, 5.DunA1.58.67.
How new-born nonsense first is taught to cry, 5.DunB1.60.274.
Fair as the new-born Star that gilds the Morn. Il.6.499.351.
With new-born Day to gladden mortal Sight, Il.11.3.34.
Thick new-born Vi'lets a soft Carpet spread, Il.14.397.182.
(With new-born Day to gladden mortal Sight, Il.19.3.371.
With new-born day to gladden mortal sight, Od.5.3.170.
These aged nerves with new-born vigor strung, Od.20.296.247.

NEW-BUILT

Shall half the new-built Churches round thee fall? 4.HS2.119.63.
We see no new-built Palaces aspire, 4.JD2.111.143.

NEW-EAR'D

The new-ear'd Earth in blacker Ridges roll'd; Il.18.635A.354.

NEW-FALL'N

The new-fall'n young here bleating for their dams; Od.9.259.317.

NEW-MADE

Along the Street the new-made Brides are led, Il.18.571.350.
With new-made Wounds; another dragg'd a dead; Il.18.622.352.
The new-made Car with solid Beauty shin'd; Il.24.334.550.

NEW-MARKET-FAME

New-market-fame, and judgment at a Bett. 3.Ep1.145.27.

NEW-MARKET'S

New-market's Glory rose, as Britain's fell; 4.2HE1.144.207.
Subservient to *New-market's* annual cheat! 6.96iii.26.275.

NEW-PENSION'D

Or each new-pension'd Sycophant, pretend 4.EpS2.142.321.

NEW-PRESS'D

Honey new-press'd, the sacred Flow'r of Wheat, Il.11.770.69.

NEW-ROB'D

Soon as the morn, new-rob'd in purple light, Od.19.499.220.

NEW-SHORN

And in the new-shorn Field the Partridge feeds, 1.W-F.98.160.

NEW-SLAIN

Wrapt in a new-slain Oxe's ample hide: Od.22.403.307.

NEW-STREAMING

Down her pale cheek new-streaming sorrow flows: Od.19.702.229.

NEW-TING'D

New-ting'd with *Tyrian* Dye: In Dust below, Il.15.634.220.

NEW-YEAR

And New-year Odes, and all the Grubstreet race. 5.DunA1.42.65.
And New-year Odes, and all the Grub-street race. 5.DunB1.44.274.

NEWCASTLE

See NEW.
N[ewcastle] laugh, or D[orset] sager [sneer] 4.1740.61.335*.
There, stamp'd with arms, Newcastle shines compleat, 5.DunA1.122.78.
There, stamp'd with arms, Newcastle shines complete: 5.DunB1.142.280.

NEWFOUND

To weep upon Fresh Cod in *Newfound*-land: 6.96ii.76A.273.

NEWFOUND-LAND

To weep upon our Cod in *Newfound*-land: 6.96ii.76.273.

NEWGATE

Ev'n *Guthry* saves half *Newgate* by a Dash. 4.EpS2.11.313.

NEWLY

Milk newly prest, the sacred flow'r of wheat, Od.10.270.355.

NEWS

There various News I heard, of Love and Strife, 2.TemF.448.285.
News travel'd with Increase from Mouth to Mouth; 2.TemF.474.286.
He asks, "What *News?*" I tell him of new Plays, 4.JD4.124.35.
They change their weekly Barber, weekly News, 4.1HE1.155.291.
To end with News—the best I know, 6.10.105.27.
And much good News, and little Spleen as may be; 6.13.12.39.
Toast Church and Queen, explain the News, 6.39.21.111.
Arriv'd Express, with News of Weight, 6.94.7.259.
From office, business, news, and strife: 6.114.10.321.
The Truth or Falshood of the News I tell. Il.10.515.26.
The fatal News— *Atrides* hasts away. Il.17.740.371.
But till the News of my sad Fate invades Il.19.358.387.
But not as yet the fatal News had spread Il.22.562.479.
Fear not, oh Father! no ill News I bear; Il.24.209.545.
Tho' certain be my news, and great my need. Od.14.179.44.
To bring *Penelope* the wish'd-for news, Od.15.48.72.
Unwelcome news, or vex the royal ear; Od.15.401.88.
Haste, to our ambush'd friends the news convey! Od.16.365.124.
There wake her with the news—The matron cry'd; Od.22.468.311.
Struck at the news, thy azure mother came; Od.24.65.350.
If, while the news thro' ev'ry city flies, Od.24.413.369.
To the chast Queen shall we the news convey? Od.24.466.371.
And tells the news. They arm with all their pow'r. Od.24.571.375.

NEWTON

And shew'd a NEWTON as we shew an Ape. 3.EOM2.34.60.
E're Cæsar was, or Newton nam'd, 4.HOde9.10.159.
God said, *Let Newton be!* and All was *Light*. 6.111.2.317.

NEWTON'S

A Newton's Genius, or a Seraph's flame: 5.DunA3.214.175.
A Newton's Genius, or a Milton's flame: 5.DunA3.214A.175.
The source of Newton's Light, of Bacon's Sense! 5.DunA3.216.176.
A Newton's genius, or a Milton's flame: 5.DunB3.216.331.
The source of Newton's Light, of Bacon's Sense! 5.DunB3.218.331.
How Plato's, Bacon's, Newton's looks agree; 6.71.60.204.

NEXT

Next *Ægon* sung, while *Windsor* Groves admir'd; 1.PAu.55.84.
Happy next him who to these Shades retires, 1.W-F.237.171.
Turn'd *Criticks* next, and prov'd plain *Fools* at last; 1.EOC.37.243.
In the next Line, it *whispers thro' the Trees*; 1.EOC.351.279.
This hour she's *idoliz'd*, the next *abus'd*; 1.EOC.433.288.
As next in Place to *Mantua*, next in Fame! 1.EOC.708.322.
As next in Place to *Mantua*, next in Fame! 1.EOC.708.322.
A Fisher next, his trembling Angle bears. 1.TrVP.42.379.
My Brother next, neglecting Wealth and Fame, 1.TrSP.75.397.

NEXT (CONTINUED)

Next a long Order of Inferior Pow'rs 1.TrSt.286.422.
Next to the Bounds of *Nisus'* Realm repairs, 1.TrSt.468.429.
The next more fatal pierc'd *Achilles'* Steed, 1.TrES.269.459.
The next transpierc'd *Achilles'* mortal Steed, 1.TrES.269A.459.
His Treasures next, *Alcinous'* Gifts, they laid 1.TrUl.49.467.
What next ensu'd beseems not me to say; 2.ChJM.383.33.
Next, your own Honour undefil'd maintain; 2.ChJM.560.42.
And witness next what *Roman* Authors tell, 2.ChJM.675.47.
Thus ends our Tale, whose Moral next to make, 2.ChJM.817.54.
I'll take the next good Christian I can find. 2.ChWB.27.58.
With his broad Sabre next, a Chief in Years, 2.RL3.55.172.
A Vial next she fills with fainting Fears, 2.RL4.85.190.
Her infant Grandame's *Whistle* next it grew, 2.RL5.93.207.
When next he looks thro' *Galilæo's* Eyes; 2.RL5.138.211.
Much-suff'ring Heroes next their Honours claim, 2.TemF.168.268.
A Golden Column next in Rank appear'd, 2.TemF.196.271.
Next these the Good and Just, an awful Train, 2.TemF.318.279.
A Troop came next, who Crowns and Armour wore, 2.TemF.342.280.
Next these a youthful Train their Vows exprest, 2.TemF.378.282.
That, in its turn, impels the next above; 2.TemF.445.285.
This hour a slave, the next a deity. 3.EOM1.68.21.
Attract, attracted to, the next in place 3.EOM3.11.93.
See Matter next, with various life endu'd, 3.EOM3.13.93.
Behold it next, with various life endu'd, 3.EOM3.13A.93.
Next his grim idol smear'd with human blood; 3.EOM3.266.119.
Look next on Greatness; say where Greatness lies? 3.EOM4.217.147.
His country next, and next all human race, 3.EOM4.368.164.
His country next, and next all human race, 3.EOM4.368.164.
Next, that he varies from himself no less: 3.Ep1.20.17.
The next a Tradesman, meek, and much a lyar; 3.Ep1.104.22.
Thinks who endures a knave, is next a knave, 3.Ep1.137.26.
The next a Fountain, spouting thro' his Heir, 3.Ep3.176.107.
Next goes his Wool—to clothe our valiant bands, 3.Ep3.211.110.
His Gardens next your admiration call, 3.Ep4.113.148.
Is Vice too high, reserve it for the next: 4.HS1.60.11.
One whom the mob, when next we find or make 4.JD4.34.29.
Why am I ask'd, what next shall see the light? 4.Arbu.271.115.
Madness, I hope is in the next Degre 4.JD2A.71.138.
Next pleas'd his Excellence a Town to batter; 4.2HE2.44.167.
We wake next morning in a raging Fit, 4.2HE1.179.209.
And smiling, whispers to the next, 4.HS6.52.253.
(October next it will be four) 4.HS6.84.255.
When (each Opinion with the next at strife, 4.1HE1.167.291.
That first was *H[er]v[e]y's, F[ox]'s* next, and then 4.EpS1.71.303.
Consid'ring what a Gracious Prince was next. 4.EpS1.108.306.
From him the next receives it, thick or thin, 4.EpS2.175.323.
And write next winter more *Essays on Man.* 4.EpS2.255.327.
And plac'd it next him, a distinction rare! 5.DunA2.92.108.
To seize his papers, Curl, was next thy care; 5.DunA2.105.109.
To seize his papers, *C[url]l,* was next thy care; 5.DunA2.106A.109.
See in the circle next, Eliza plac'd; 5.DunA2.149.119.
Next Smedley div'd; slow circles dimpled o'er 5.DunA2.279.135.
Next *E[usden]* div'd; slow circles dimpled o'er 5.DunA2.279A.135.
H[ill] try'd the next, but hardly snatch'd from sight, 5.DunA2.283A.136.
"Lo next two slip-shod Muses traipse along, 5.DunA3.141.162.
"See next two slip-shod Muses traipse along, 5.DunA3.141A.162.
Next, o'er his Books his eyes began to roll, 5.DunB1.127.278.
And plac'd it next him, a distinction rare! 5.DunB2.96.300.
To seize his papers, Curl, was next thy care; 5.DunB2.113.301.
See in the circle next, Eliza plac'd, 5.DunB2.157.303.
Next Smedley div'd; slow circles dimpled o'er 5.DunB2.291.309.
Next plung'd a feeble, but a desp'rate pack, 5.DunB2.305.310.
Let her thy heart, next Drabs and Dice, engage, 5.DunB3.303.334.
Dunce scorning Dunce beholds the next advance, 5.DunB4.137.354.
Next bidding all draw near on bended knees, 5.DunB4.565.398.
The sun (next those the fairest light) 6.5.3.12.
So swift,—this moment here, the next 'tis gone, 6.9iv.1.21.
Send it, I pray, by the next Post, 6.10.115.28.
What Lawrels *Marlbro'* next shall reap, decree, 6.17iv.5.59.
At the next Bottle, all their Schemes they cease, 6.17iv.7.59.
These Censures o'er, to different Subjects next, 6.17iv.15.59.
To the next Day's Repentance, as they boast, 6.17iv.20.59.
What if the *Hebrew* next should aim 6.30.66.88.
What if the *Hebrew* next should claim 6.30.66A.88.
Howbeit,—likewise—now to my next, 6.39.14.110.
The Doctor, and He that's nam'd next to the Devil, 6.42i.2.116.
Next Lords and Lordings, 'Squires and Knights, 6.58.45A.172.
Of Course resign'd it to the next that writ: 6.60.36.179.
I ever lov'd it—next to Gold. 6.64.14.190.
Where shall we next thy lasting Temples raise, 6.65.7A.192.
Tho' next the Servile drop thee next the Vain, 6.84.31Z4.239.
Tho' next the Servile drop thee next the Vain, 6.84.31Z4.239.
Next in three Books, sunk human *Nature,* 6.101.10.290.
Her charms the *Gallic* muses next inspir'd: 6.107.7.310.
What does she next, but bids the Earth 6.119.11.337.
Oh next him skill'd to draw the tender Tear, 6.152.3.400.
For know, thy Blood, when next thou dar'st invade, Il.1.398.107.
The Host to expiate next the King prepares, Il.1.410.107.
Next on the Shore their Hecatomb they land, Il.1.570.115.
Around him next the Regal Mantle threw, Il.2.54.129.
To rich *Thyestes* next the Prize descends; Il.2.134.134.
If, on thy next Offence, this Hand forbear Il.2.322.142.
Next came *Idomeneus* and *Tydeus'* Son, Il.2.482.149.
The *Phocians* next in forty Barks repair, Il.2.620.157.
Eubæa next her martial Sons prepares, Il.2.641.157.
Next move to War the gen'rous *Argive* Train, Il.2.675.159.
Thoas came next, *Andræmon's* valiant Son, Il.2.775.162.
Next eighty Barks the *Cretan* King commands, Il.2.785.162.
Next thirty Galleys cleave the liquid Plain, Il.2.821.164.
Say next O Muse! of all *Achaia* breeds, Il.2.924.167.
The fierce *Pelasgi* next, in War renown'd, Il.2.1018.171.
Next *Acamas* and *Pyrous* lead their Hosts Il.2.1022.171.
Next all unbuckling the rich Mail they wore, Il.3.157.198.
And next the wisest of the Rev'rend Throng, Il.3.196.200.
Next from the Car descending on the Plain, Il.3.334.209.

NEXT (CONTINUED)

Next to decide by sacred Lots prepare, Il.3.392.211.
And next the Troops of either *Ajax* views: Il.4.311.235.
Then to the next the Gen'ral bends his Course; Il.4.334.236.
From forth his Chariot, mount the next in haste; Il.4.353.237.
And next *Ulysses,* with his Subject Bands. Il.4.383.239.
Next, sent by *Greece* from where *Asopus* flows, Il.4.436.241.
Thy Fate was next, O *Phæstus!* doom'd to feel Il.5.57.269.
Next artful *Phereclus* untimely fell; Il.5.75.269.
Young *Xanthus* next and *Thoon* felt his Rage, Il.5.196.276.
Next rushing to the *Dardan* Spoil, detains Il.5.399.286.
Me next he charg'd, and dares all Heav'n engage: Il.5.558.295.
Next *Oenomaus,* and *Oenops'* Offspring dy'd; Il.5.868.307.
The massy golden Helm she next assumes, Il.5.918.310.
Me next encount'ring, me he dar'd to wound; Il.5.1085.318.
Next *Teuthras'* Son distain'd the Sands with Blood, Il.6.15.323.
And next he lay'd *Opheltius* on the Plain. Il.6.26.325.
Unblest *Adrastus* next at Mercy lies Il.6.45.325.
Next the bold *Amazon's* whole Force defy'd; Il.6.229.337.
And next his Bulk gigantic *Ajax* rear'd: Il.7.200.373.
Next, to secure our Camp, and Naval Pow'rs, Il.7.406.384.
Next let a Truce be ask'd, that *Troy* may burn Il.7.450.386.
Next, O ye Chiefs! we ask a Truce to burn Il.7.470.387.
Th' *Atridæ* first, th' *Ajaces* next succeed: Il.8.316.412.
Euæmon's Son next issues to the Foe, Il.8.319.412.
The Godlike *Lycophon* next press'd the Plain, Il.8.331.413.
The next rich Honorary Gift be thine: Il.8.350.414.
As the next Dawn, the last they shall enjoy, Il.8.671.427.
Next him *Ascalaphus, Iälmen,* stood, Il.9.113.437.
Great *Ajax* next, and *Ithacus* the sage. Il.9.222.443.
Next on his Feet the shining Sandals bound; Il.10.28.3.
The Care is next our other Chiefs to raise: Il.10.122.7.
Next him *Ulysses* took a shining Sword, Il.10.307.16.
The Helmet next by *Merion* was possess'd, Il.10.317.17.
The beaming Cuirass next adorn'd his Breast, Il.11.25.36.
His Buckler's mighty Orb was next display'd, Il.11.43.36.
Two Sons of *Priam* next to Battel move, Il.11.137.41.
Opites next was added to their side, Il.11.390.52.
Next *Ennomus* and *Thoon* sunk to Hell; Il.11.532.57.
On strong *Pandocus* next inflicts a Wound, Il.11.612.61.
Next her white Hand an antique Goblet brings, Il.11.772.69.
Before the next the graceful *Paris* shines, Il.12.105.85.
Next him, the bravest at their Army's Head, Il.12.117.85.
Next *Ormenus* and *Pylon* yield their Breath: Il.12.217.89.
And *Merion* next, th' impulsive Fury found; Il.13.128.110.
Next brave *Deipyrus* in Dust was lay'd; Il.13.727.139.
The former Day; the next, engag'd in War.) Il.13.998.152.
Around her next a heav'nly Mantle flow'd, Il.14.207.170.
Mecistes next, *Polydamas* o'erthrew; Il.15.384.211.
The godlike *Ajax* next his *Greeks* addrest. Il.15.591.219.
Now man the next, receding tow'rd the Main: Il.15.787.226.
Eudorus next; whom *Polymele* the gay, Il.16.216.247.
Headlong he fell. Next *Thoas* was thy Chance, Il.16.370.257.
Next *Erymas* was doom'd his Fate to feel, Il.16.414.259.
Thestor was next; who saw the Chief appear, Il.16.486.262.
Next on *Eryalus* he flies; a Stone Il.16.500.262.
The next transpierc'd *Achilles'* mortal Steed, Il.16.574.266.
Æneas next, and *Hector* he accosts; Il.16.657.270.
Echeclus follows; next young *Megas* bleeds; Il.16.852.276.
Euphorbus next; the third mean Part thy own. Il.16.1025.282.
Next him *Idomeneus,* more slow with Age, Il.17.304.299.
In graceful Stature next, and next in Fame.) Il.17.329.300.
In graceful Stature next, and next in Fame.) Il.17.329.300.
Next thee, *Asteropeus!* in Place and Fame. Il.17.403.303.
Next *Callianira, Callianassa* show Il.18.55.326.
A Field deep-furrow'd, next the God design'd, Il.18.627.352.
Next, rip in yellow Gold, a Vineyard shines, Il.18.651.355.
Next this, the Eye the Art of *Vulcan* leads Il.18.677.356.
Sev'n Captives next a lovely Line compose; Il.19.253.383.
Next, his high Head the Helmet grac'd; behind Il.19.410.389.
Demoleon next, *Antenor's* Offspring, laid Il.20.457.413.
Thy Life *Echeclus!* next the Sword bereaves, Il.20.549.417.
The next, that God whom Men in vain withstand, Il.21.52.424.
Like Lightning next the *Pelian* Jav'lin flies; Il.21.185.429.
Next by *Scamander's* double Source they bound, Il.22.195.463.
Next these a melancholy Band appear, Il.23.164.495.
Next these the melancholy Band appear, Il.23.164A.495*.
Achilles next, oppress with mighty Woe, Il.23.167.496.
Next the white Bones his sad Companions place Il.23.313.502.
Next him *Antilochus* demands the Course, Il.23.369.505.
Next bold *Meriones* was seen to rise, Il.23.425.507.
And next, the Brother of the King of Men: Il.23.430.507.
The next, tho' distant, *Menelas* succeeds; Il.23.481.509.
The golden Talents *Merion* next obtain'd; Il.23.703.517.
The Prizes next are order'd to the Field Il.23.753.520.
Next stands a Goblet, massy, large and round. Il.23.758.520.
The third bold Game *Achilles* next demands, Il.23.814.521.
And next, the Losers Spirits to restore, Il.23.818.521.
Ajax to lift, *Ulysses* next essays, Il.23.848.523.
Ulysses next; and he whose Speed surpast Il.23.883.524.
The next *Ulysses,* meas'ring Pace with Pace; Il.23.888.524.
Next these a Buckler, Spear and Helm, he brings, Il.23.941.526.
Leonteus next a little space surpast, Il.23.997.529.
He next invites the twanging Bow to bend: Il.23.1007.529.
Two Tripods next and twice two Chargers shine, Il.24.285.548.
Next on his Sons his erring Fury falls, Il.24.311.549.
Next with the Gifts (the Price of *Hector* slain) Il.24.341.550.
Next heap'd on high the num'rous Presents bear Il.24.726.568.
The next, to raise his Monument be giv'n; Il.24.836.571.
The mournful Mother next sustains her Part. Il.24.942.575.
Sad *Helen* next in Pomp of Grief appears: Il.24.959.576.
When next the morning warms the purple east, Od.1.354.49.
Next these in worth, and firm those urns be seal'd; Od.2.399.80.
Next, to the court, impatient of delay Od.2.442.82.
Next grant the *Pylian* states their just desires, Od.3.72.89.
Thron'd next the King, a fair attendant brings Od.4.63.122.

NEXT (CONTINUED)

Next, *Æthiopia's* utmost bound explore, ... Od.4.101.124.
When purple light shall next suffuse the skies, ... Od.4.550.146.
With him, the peerage next in pow'r to you: ... Od.4.876.159.
And next, a wedge to drive with sweepy sway: ... Od.5.303.185.
What will ye next ordain, ye Pow'rs on high! ... Od.5.599.201.
He next their princes lofty domes admires, ... Od.7.57.236.
There next his side the god-like hero sate; ... Od.7.228.247.
The table next in regal order spread, ... Od.7.234.247.
He next betakes him to his evening cares, ... Od.9.288.318.
A milky deluge next the giant swill'd; ... Od.9.353.321.
When slumber next should tame the man of blood. ... Od.9.393.322.
Next seiz'd two wretches more, and headlong cast, ... Od.9.404.322.
The next proud *Lamos'* stately tow'rs appear, ... Od.10.92.343.
A vest and tunick o'er me next she threw, ... Od.10.429.365.
Be next thy care the sable sheep to place ... Od.10.628.374.
Next, where the Sirens dwell, you plow the seas; ... Od.12.51.431.
His treasures next, *Alcinous'* gifts, they laid ... Od.13.140.11.
(With flour imbrown'd) next mingled wine yet new, ... Od.14.93.40.
Ere the next moon increase, or this decay, ... Od.14.186.44.
The next chang'd all the colour of my Fate. ... Od.14.318.50.
The beauteous Queen advancing next, display'd ... Od.15.136.75.
Crunus they pass'd, next *Chalcis* roll'd away, ... Od.15.316.84.
Next came *Ulysses,* lowly at the door, ... Od.17.410.152.
In the next month renews her faded wane, ... Od.19.352.211.
Who next the goblet held his holy place: ... Od.21.154.266.
'Till the next dawn this ill-tim'd strife forgoe, ... Od.21.276.273.
Next bold *Amphinomus* his arm extends ... Od.22.105.291.
Fate doom'd thee next, *Eurydamas,* to bear ... Od.22.312.301.
Thy next-belov'd, *Antilochus'* remains. ... Od.24.100.353.
First came the son; the father next succeeds, ... Od.24.183.356.
And next his sons, a long-succeeding train. ... Od.24.447.370.

NEXT-BELOV'D

Thy next-belov'd, *Antilochus'* remains. ... Od.24.100.353.

NIC

And *Nic.* of *Lancastere.* ... 6.79.8.218.
And so down fell Duke *Nic.* ... 6.79.64.220.
Alas, oh *Nic!* Oh *Nic.* alas! ... 6.79.65.220.
Alas, oh *Nic!* Oh *Nic.* alas! ... 6.79.65.220.
And Duke *Nic.* up leap'd he: ... 6.79.98.221.
"The Day I meet him, *Nic.* shall rue ... 6.79.139.222.
"The Day I meet *Nic.* he shall rue ... 6.79.139A.222.
May learn this Lesson from Duke *Nic.* ... 6.79.147.223.

NICE

Our Author, happy in a Judge so nice, ... 1.EOC.273.270.
Curious, not *Knowing,* not *exact,* but *nice,* ... 1.EOC.286.271.
Yet shun their Fault, who, *Scandalously nice,* ... 1.EOC.556.304.
Blunt Truths more Mischief than *nice Falshoods* do; ... 1.EOC.573.306.
While nice, and anxious in his new disease, ... 1.TrPA.21.366.
With nice Exactness weighs her woolly Store) ... 1.TrES.168Z2.455.
His Friends were summon'd, on a Point so nice, ... 2.ChJM.81.18.
To Work by Counsel when Affairs are nice: ... 2.ChJM.152.22.
In that nice Moment, lo! the wondring Knight ... 2.ChJM.748.51.
Whence some infer, whose Conscience is too nice, ... 2.ChWB.11.57.
I, for a few slight Spots, am not so nice. ... 2.ChWB.39.58.
By this nice Conduct and this prudent Course, ... 2.ChWB.162.64.
On one nice *Trick* depends the gen'ral Fate. ... 2.RL3.94.174.
And the nice Conduct of a *clouded Cane)* ... 2.RL4.124.194.
The strong connections, nice dependencies, ... 3.EOM1.30.17.
In the nice bee, what sense so subtly true ... 3.EOM1.219.42.
'Twixt that, and Reason, what a nice barrier; ... 3.EOM1.223.43.
80.Tho' oft so mix'd, the difference is too nice ... 3.EOM2.209A.81.
And oft so mix, the diff'rence is too nice ... 3.EOM2.209.81.
Such happy Spots the nice admirer take, ... 3.Ep2.43A.53.
To her, Calista prov'd her conduct nice, ... 3.Ep2.31.52.
Their happy Spots the nice admirer take, ... 3.Ep2.43.53.
Weakness or Delicacy; all so nice, ... 3.Ep2.205.67.
In that nice Moment, as another Lye ... 4.JD4.174.41.
Most warp'd to Flatt'ry's side; but some, more nice, ... 4.2HE1.259.217.
But *Horace,* Sir, was delicate, was nice; ... 4.EpS1.11.298.
Where in nice balance, truth with gold she weighs, ... 5.DunA1.51.66.
Then his nice taste directs our Operas: ... 5.DunA2.196.124.
Where, in nice balance, truth with gold she weighs, ... 5.DunB1.53.274.
Then his nice taste directs our Operas: ... 5.DunB2.204.305.
Still hoarding up, most scandalously nice, ... 6.41.19.114.
With nice Exactness weighs her woolly Store) ... Il.12.524.101.
And now *Antilochus,* with nice survey, ... Il.23.497.510.

NICELY

From each she nicely culls with curious Toil, ... 2.RL1.131.156.
Thus others Talents having nicely shown, ... 4.JD4.80.31.
Old puns restore, lost blunders nicely seek, ... 5.DunA1.163.82.

NICER

P. Alas! few Verses touch their nicer Ear; ... 4.HS1.33.7.

NICEST

This Lady's Charms the Nicest cou'd not blame, ... 2.ChJM.238.26.
Which writ and folded, with the nicest Art, ... 2.ChJM.398.34.

NICETY

Then let him—'twas a *Nicety* indeed! ... 2.ChWB.169.65.
"Such Nicety, as Lady or Lord *Fanny?*— ... 4.HAdv.92.83.

NICHES

Of *Ægypt's* Priests the gilded Niches grace, ... 2.TemF.110.262.

NICHOLAS

From out the Boot bold *Nicholas* ... 6.79.117.222.

NIECE

See NEICE.

NIGER

Blest in one Niger, till he knows of two." ... 5.DunB4.370.379.

NIGGARD

But what by niggard Fortune was deny'd ... Od.14.242.48.

NIGGARDS

Be Niggards of Advice on no Pretence; ... 1.EOC.578.306.

NIGH

But nigh yon' Mountain let me tune my Lays, ... 1.PSu.37.75.
But nigh that Mountain let me tune my Lays, ... 1.PSu.37A.75.
And singled out a Pear-Tree planted nigh: ... 2.ChJM.602.44.
But cou'd not climb, and had no Servant nigh, ... 2.ChJM.727.49.
Self-love still stronger, as its objects nigh; ... 3.EOM2.71.63.
Self-love yet stronger, as its objects nigh; ... 3.EOM2.71A.63.
Dryden alone (what wonder?) came not nigh, ... 4.Arbu.245.113.
Conspicuous Scene! another yet is nigh, ... 4.1HE6.50.239.
I languish when her charms draw nigh, ... 6.4iv.23.11.
Declare our doom in drawing nigh. ... 6.5.12.12.
And hear a spark, yet think no danger nigh; ... 6.45.4.124.
In Leister fields, in house full nigh, ... 6.61.36.182.
Nigh thy Ear, ... 6.96i.45.269.
In Wants, in Sickness, shall a *Friend* be nigh, ... 6.117.11.333.
A Chief stood nigh who from *Abydos* came, ... Il.4.573.249.
Brave *Pelagon,* his fav'rite Chief, was nigh, ... Il.5.854.307.
And nigh the Fleet a Fun'ral Structure rear: ... Il.7.401.384.
Coon, Antenor's eldest Hope, was nigh: ... Il.11.321.49.
His Steeds too distant, and the Foe too nigh; ... Il.11.440.53.
Stabb'd at the Sight, *Deiphobus* drew nigh, ... Il.13.509.131.
And not her Steeds and flaming Chariot nigh? ... Il.14.340.179.
Troy saw, and thought the dread *Achilles* nigh, ... Il.16.336.255.
Phylides' Dart, (as *Amphiclus* drew nigh) ... Il.16.372.257.
Black Fate hangs o'er thee, and thy Hour draws nigh; ... Il.16.1029.283.
Cymothoe and *Cymodoce* were nigh, ... Il.18.49.326.
But vainly glories, for his Fate is nigh. ... Il.18.170.330.
Thus pond'ring, like a God the *Greek* drew nigh; ... Il.22.173.460.
'Tis so—Heav'n wills it, and my Hour is nigh! ... Il.22.378.471.
So let his Friends be nigh, a needful Train ... Il.23.779.520.
For much I fear, Destruction hovers nigh: ... Il.24.437.554.
Divining of their loves. Attending nigh, ... Od.1.144.39.
'Till coasting nigh the Cape, where *Malea* shrowds ... Od.4.685.151.
Close ambush'd nigh the spacious hall he plac'd. ... Od.4.710.152.
Virgin awake! the marriage hour is nigh, ... Od.6.39.206.
Nigh where a grove, with verdant poplars crown'd ... Od.6.349.229.
His fair ones arms—he thinks her, once, too nigh. ... Od.8.356.282.
'Till now approaching nigh the magic bow'r, ... Od.10.327.360.
Why is she silent, while her Son is nigh? ... Od.11.177.390.
Nigh the curst shore, and listen to the lay; ... Od.12.54.432.
Nigh to the lodge, and now appear'd in view. ... Od.16.12.102.
Nigh in her bright alcove, the pensive Queen ... Od.20.463.256.
Each look'd for arms in vain; no arms were nigh: ... Od.22.30.288.
To *Jove's* inviolable altar nigh, ... Od.22.372.306.

NIGHT

By Night he scorches, as he burns by Day. ... 1.PSu.92.79.
Thus sung the Shepherds till th'Approach of Night, ... 1.PAu.97.87.
By Day o'ersees them, and by Night protects; ... 1.Mes.52.117.
Read them by Day, and meditate by Night, ... 1.EOC.125.253.
Some praise at Morning what they blame at Night; ... 1.EOC.430.288.
My daily Longing, and my Dream by Night: ... 1.TrSP.144.399.
O Night more pleasing than the brightest Day, ... 1.TrSP.145.400.
Night shades the Groves, and all in Silence lye, ... 1.TrSP.175.401.
Led a long Death in everlasting Night; ... 1.TrSt.70.413.
Then self-condemn'd to Shades of endless Night, ... 1.TrSt.99.414.
And dark Dominions of the silent Night; ... 1.TrSt.131.415.
Veil'd her fair Glories in the Shades of Night. ... 1.TrSt.137.415.
How oft the Furies from the deeps of Night ... 1.TrSt.321.423.
His daily Vision, and his Dream by Night; ... 1.TrSt.446.428.
'Twas now the Time when *Phœbus* yields to Night, ... 1.TrSt.474.430.
Streak with long Gleams the scatt'ring Shades of Night; ... 1.TrSt.485.430.
But with a thicker Night black *Auster* shrouds ... 1.TrSt.492.430.
Thro' the brown Horrors of the Night he fled, ... 1.TrSt.516.432.
And seiz'd with Horror, in the Shades of Night, ... 1.TrSt.557.433.
And seiz'd with Horror, 'midst the Shades of Night, ... 1.TrSt.557A.433.
And thus invokes the silent *Queen* of *Night.* ... 1.TrSt.582.434.
A Third dispels the Darkness of the Night, ... 1.TrSt.609.436.
When from the close Apartments of the Night, ... 1.TrSt.623.436.
When Night with sable Wings o'erspreads the Ground, ... 1.TrSt.711.440.
A Night of sultry Clouds involv'd around ... 1.TrSt.742.441.
Relate your Fortunes, while the friendly Night ... 1.TrSt.794.443.
Gloomy as Night, and shakes two shining Spears; ... 1.TrES.200.456.
Unseen I scap'd; and favour'd by the Night, ... 1.TrUl.148.470.
In dead of Night an unknown Port we gain'd, ... 1.TrUl.152.470.
In Bliss all Night, and Innocence all Day: ... 2.ChJM.40.16.
A Night-Invasion, and a Mid-day-Devil. ... 2.ChJM.48.17.
Th' entrancing Raptures of th' approaching Night; ... 2.ChJM.350.31.
As all were nothing he had done by Night; ... 2.ChJM.386.33.
The lumpish Husband snor'd away the Night, ... 2.ChJM.420.35.
Was Captive kept; he watch'd her Night and Day, ... 2.ChJM.488.39.
So just recov'ring from the Shades of Night, ... 2.ChJM.802.54.
And keep an equal Reck'ning ev'ry Night; ... 2.ChWB.53.59.
Doubt not, sufficient will be left at Night. ... 2.ChWB.137.63.
And swore the Rambles that I took by Night, ... 2.ChWB.156.64.
Or Curtain-Lectures made a restless Night. ... 2.ChWB.165.64.
Now all my Conquests, all my Charms good night! ... 2.ChWB.226.67.
It chanc'd my Husband on a Winter's Night ... 2.ChWB.377.75.
Frantic at Night, and in the Morning dead. ... 2.ChWB.406.76.
And half the Night was thus consum'd in vain; ... 2.ChWB.414.77.
A Youth more glitt'ring than a *Birth-night Beau,* ... 2.RL1.23.147.
Pursue the Stars that shoot athwart the Night, ... 2.RL2.82.165.
Hover, and catch the shooting Stars by Night; ... 2.RL2.82A.165.
But what, or where, the Fates have wrapt in Night. ... 2.RL2.104.166.
When each new Night-Dress gives a new Disease. ... 2.RL4.38.186.
Oh! if to dance all Night, and dress all Day, ... 2.RL5.19.200.
And each Majestic Phantom sunk in Night. ... 2.TemF.355.280.

NIGHT (CONTINUED)

Which still unfolded stand, by Night, by Day, ...2.TemF.426.284.
Where awful arches make a noon-day night, ...2.ElAb.143.331.
0 curst, dear horrors of all-conscious night! ....2.ElAb.229.338.
Let this great truth be present night and day; ....3.EOM3.5.92.
Let that great truth be present night and day; ....3.EOM3.5A.92.
Last night, her Lord was all that's good and great, ...3.Ep2.141.62.
So these their merry, miserable Night; ....3.Ep2.240.69.
I nod in Company, I wake at Night, ...4.HS1.13.5.
At night, wou'd swear him dropt out of the moon, ...4.JD4.33.29.
Then ask'd Ten Thousand for a second Night: ....4.HAdv.8.75.
Tir'd with a tedious March, one luckless night, ...4.2HE2.35.167.
See! strow'd with learned dust, his Night-cap on, ...4.2HE2.118.173.
From morn to night, at Senate, Rolls, and Hall, ...4.1HE6.36.239.
So Russel did, but could not eat at night, ...4.1HE6.115.245.
('Twas on the night of a Debate, ...4.HS6.187.261.
Long as the Night to her whose love's away; ....4.1HE1.36.281.
That very night he longs to lye alone. ....4.1HE1.149.291.
Daughter of Chaos and eternal Night: ....5.DunA1.10.61.
Now Night descending, the proud scene was o'er, ...5.DunA1.87.69.
Secure us kindly in our native night. ....5.DunA1.154.82.
In a dun night-gown of his own loose skin, ...5.DunA2.34.100.
Like forms in clouds, or visions of the night! ....5.DunA2.104.109.
Thick as the stars of night, or morning dews, ...5.DunA3.24.152.
Thick as the stars of night, and morning dews, ...5.DunA3.24A.152.
And makes Night hideous—Answer him, ye Owls! ....5.DunA3.160.165.
With Night Primæval, and with Chaos old. ....5.DunA3.338.192.
Art after Art goes out, and all is Night. ....5.DunA3.346.193.
Daughter of Chaos and eternal Night: ....5.DunB1.12.269.
Now Night descending, the proud scene was o'er, ...5.DunB1.89.276.
Secure us kindly in our native night. ....5.DunB1.176.283.
In a dun night-gown of his own loose skin; ....5.DunB2.38.297.
Like forms in clouds, or visions of the night. ....5.DunB2.112.300.
Thick as the stars of night, or morning dews, ...5.DunB3.32.322.
And makes Night hideous—Answer him, ye Owls! ....5.DunB3.166.328.
Indulge, dread Chaos, and eternal Night! ....5.DunB4.2.339.
Then rose the Seed of Chaos, and of Night, ...5.DunB4.13.340.
Of *Night* Primæval, and of *Chaos* old! ....5.DunB4.630.407.
Art after *Art* goes out, and all is Night. ....5.DunB4.640.407.
Sound sleep by night; study and ease ....6.1.13.3.
Repose at night; study and ease ....6.1.13A.3.
No dismal dreams or groaning ghosts by night. ....6.21.12.69.
Yet if a friend a night, or so, should need her, ...6.41.33.114.
That gnaws them Night and Day. ....6.53.28.162.
Himself both Day and Night. ....6.54.8.164.
Hear how a Ghost in dead of Night, ...6.58.13.171.
Hear how a Ghost at dead of Night, ...6.58.13A.171.
"Sir Duke! be here to Night." ....6.79.48.219.
"No not to-morrow, but to night ....6.79.103.221.
When learning, after the long *Gothic* night, ...6.107.1.310.
To night, our home-spun author would be true, ...6.107.19.311.
Nature, and Nature's Laws lay hid in Night. ....6.111.1.317.
All Nature and her Laws lay hid in Night. ....6.111.1A.317.
All Nature and its Laws lay hid in Night. ....6.111.1B.317.
Let him to Night his just Assistance lend, ...6.128.23.356.
Last Night her Lord was all that's good and great; ....6.154.27.403.
Breathing Revenge, a sudden Night he spread, ...Il.1.65.89.
'Twas Night: the Chiefs beside their Vessel lie, ...Il.1.622.117.
And thus commands the *Vision* of the Night. ....Il.2.8.127.
Resolves to Air, and mixes with the Night. ....Il.2.44.129.
Late as I slumber'd in the Shades of Night, ...Il.2.71.130.
Before the Night her gloomy Veil extends, ...Il.2.493.150.
A Night of Vapors round the Mountain-Heads, ...Il.3.16.188.
'Till black as Night the swelling Tempest shows, ...Il.4.318.235.
The soul indignant seeks the Realms of Night. ....Il.5.360.283.
These claim thy Thoughts by Day, thy Watch by Night: ....Il.5.598.297.
His flying Coursers, sunk to endless Night: ....Il.5.710.301.
The Soul disdainful seeks the Caves of Night, ...Il.5.818.305.
And o'er his Eye-balls swum the Shades of Night. ....Il.5.857.307.
But now the Night extends her awful Shade; ....Il.7.341.381.
The Goddess parts you: Be the Night obey'd. ....Il.7.342.381.
Let him demand the Sanction of the Night: ....Il.7.346.381.
Since then the Night extends her gloomy Shade, ...Il.7.356.381.
And Heav'n enjoins it, be the Night obey'd. ....Il.7.357.381.
Guard well the Walls, relieve the Watch of Night, ...Il.7.446.386.
The doubtful Confines of the Day and Night; ....Il.7.517.389.
All Night they feast, the *Greek* and *Trojan* Pow'rs; ....Il.7.570.392.
Enjoy'd the balmy Blessings of the Night. ....Il.7.579.393.
This Night, this glorious Night, the Fleet is ours. ....Il.8.239.409.
This Night, this glorious Night, the Fleet is ours. ....Il.8.239.409.
And drew behind the cloudy Veil of Night: ....Il.8.606.425.
Obey the Night, and use her peaceful Hours ....Il.8.627.425.
Lest in the Silence and the Shades of Night, ...Il.8.635.426.
Suffice, to Night, these Orders to obey; ....Il.8.651.426.
As when the Moon, refulgent Lamp of Night! ....Il.8.687.428.
Thus joyful *Troy* maintain'd the Watch of Night, ...Il.9.1.430.
This Night, refresh and fortify thy Train; ....Il.9.93.437.
What Eye beholds 'em, and can close to night? ....Il.9.106.437.
Thro' the still Night they march, and hear the roar ....Il.9.237.444.
But here this Night let rev'rend *Phœnix* stay: ....Il.9.551.460.
And favour'd by the Night, o'er leap'd the Wall. ....Il.9.597.464.
This Night, let due Repast refresh our Pow'rs; ....Il.9.825.474.
All Night the Chiefs before their Vessels lay, ...Il.10.1.1.
Tir'd with the Toils of Day, and Watch of Night: ....Il.10.111.7.
Near the Night-Guards, our chosen Council waits. ....Il.10.147.8.
Thus leads you wandring in the silent Night? ....Il.10.161.9.
All, all depend on this important Night! ....Il.10.167.9.
Rest seems inglorious, and the Night too long. ....Il.10.181.9.
When Night descending, from his vengeful Hand ....Il.10.235.12.
Or favour'd by the Night, approach so near, ...Il.10.245.13.
And pass unharm'd the Dangers of the Night; ....Il.10.250.13.
But let us haste—Night rolls the Hours away, ...Il.10.295.15.
And let some Deed this signal Night adorn, ...Il.10.333.18.
And spent with Toil neglect the Watch of Night? ....Il.10.366.19.
To roam the silent Fields in dead of Night? ....Il.10.456.24.
And tir'd with Toils, neglect the Watch of Night? ....Il.10.470.24.

NIGHT (CONTINUED)

Where lies encamp'd the *Trojan* Chief to Night? ....Il.10.478.24.
Thro' the still Night they cross the devious Fields, ...Il.10.540.27.
And wond'ring view the Slaughters of the Night. ....Il.10.617.29.
Thro' the dark Clouds, and now in Night retires; ....Il.11.84.38.
The Lion's roaring thro' the mid-night Shade; ....Il.11.228.45.
And sacred Night her awful Shade extend. ....Il.11.252.46.
And sacred Night her awful Shade extend. ....Il.11.268.47.
Opheltius, Orus, sunk to endless Night, ...Il.11.392.52.
There slain, they left them in eternal Night; ....Il.11.419.53.
Pallas, descending in the Shades of Night, ...Il.11.850.74.
Gloomy as Night! and shakes two shiny Spears: ....Il.12.554.102.
Leave these at Anchor till the coming Night: ....Il.14.83.161.
But gentle *Night,* to whom I fled for Aid, ...Il.14.293.176.
Sate *Sleep,* in Likeness of the Bird of Night, ...Il.14.328.178.
On rush'd bold *Hector,* gloomy as the Night, ...Il.15.394.212.
O'er the fierce Armies pours pernicious Night, ...Il.16.696.271.
Then sunk *Pylartes* to eternal Night; ....Il.16.855.276.
Conceals the Warriors' shining Helms in Night: ....Il.17.319.300.
Such o'er *Patroclus* Body hung the Night, ...Il.17.426.303.
The self same Night to both a Being gave, ...Il.18.297.336.
Haste then to *Ilion,* while the fav'ring Night ....Il.18.313.336.
While the long Night extends her sable Reign, ...Il.18.365.339.
Weep all the Night, and murmur all the Day: ....Il.18.400.340.
Troy yet shall dare to camp a second Night? ....Il.19.74.375.
And ye, fell Furies of the Realms of Night, ...Il.19.270.383.
So to Night-wand'ring Sailors, pale with Fears, ...Il.19.404.389.
Enough—When Heav'n ordains, I sink in Night, ...Il.19.470.391.
In gloomy Tempests, and a Night of Clouds: ....Il.20.70.396.
By Night, or Day, by Force or by Design, ...Il.21.123.426.
To him whose Thunders blacken Heav'n with Night? ....Il.21.582.446.
As soon as Night her dusky Veil extends, ...Il.21.661.449.
Thro' the thick Gloom of some tempestuous Night ....Il.22.38.454.
Which, timely follow'd but the former Night, ...Il.22.142.459.
Far-beaming o'er the silver Host of Night, ...Il.22.400.472.
Once more return'st thou from the Realms of Night? ....Il.23.110.492.
This Night my Friend, so late in Battel lost, ...Il.23.126.493.
She watch'd him all the Night, and all the Day, ...Il.23.230.499.
And all the Night the plenteous Flame aspires. ....Il.23.271.500.
All Night, *Achilles* hails *Patroclus* Soul, ...Il.23.272.500.
'Twas when, emerging thro' the Shades of Night, ...Il.23.280.501.
We will not: *Thetis* guards it Night and Day. ....Il.24.94.539.
With Words of Omen like a Bird of Night. ....Il.24.268.547.
Is seal'd in Sleep, thou wander'st thro' the Night? ....Il.24.448.555.
But now the peaceful Hours of sacred Night ....Il.24.753.568.
Inhabitant of deep disastrous Night, ...Od.1.377.50.
Whene'er *Ulysses* roams the realm of Night, ...Od.1.503.56.
Adorn'd the matron-brow of sable Night; ....Od.1.534.57.
Rose anxious from th' inquietudes of Night. ....Od.2.4.59.
By night revers'd the labour of the day. ....Od.2.118.67.
(When night advances) bear the naval stores; ....Od.2.328.77.
And watch'd all night, all day; a faithful guard. ....Od.2.393.80.
For when the fav'ring shades of night arise, ...Od.2.402.80.
When Night descends, embodyed on the strand. ....Od.2.433.82.
Thus all the night they stem the liquid way, ...Od.2.474.84.
Such numbers fell, such Heroes sunk to night: ....Od.3.132.92.
Th' unquiet night strange projects entertain'd; ....Od.3.183.94.
And in their hollow bark to pass the night: ....Od.3.442.108.
There in the vessel shall I pass the night; ....Od.3.466.109.
And pleas'd they sleep (the blessing of the night.) ....Od.3.622.118.
And o'er the shaded landscape rush'd the night. ....Od.3.630.118.
'Till night with grateful shade involv'd the skies, ...Od.4.582.147.
'Till night with silent shade invests the pole; ....Od.4.782.156.
Or lies he wrapt in ever-during night? ....Od.4.1088.168.
The clouds of night, and darkens heav'n with storms) ....Od.5.31.172.
In slumber wore the heavy night away, ...Od.5.199.181.
And rising night her friendly shade extends. ....Od.5.290.185.
Down rush'd the night. East, west, together roar, ...Od.5.379.190.
Here by the stream if I the night out-wear, ...Od.5.601.201.
There, as the night in silence roll'd away, ...Od.6.21.204.
Obedient to the vision of the night. ....Od.6.60.208.
Bright as the lamp of night, or orb of day. ....Od.7.111.240.
Night now approaching, in the palace stand ....Od.7.182.244.
Then from around him drop'd the veil of night; ....Od.7.190.245.
Repair we to the blessings of the night: ....Od.7.249.248.
'Twas night; and cover'd in the foliage deep, ...Od.7.368.254.
All night I slept, oblivious of my pain; ....Od.7.370.254.
Rose instant from the slumbers of the night; ....Od.8.4.261.
The feast or bath by day, and love by night: ....Od.8.286.278.
Be swift to give; that he this night may share ....Od.8.429.287.
And Night rush'd headlong on the shaded deeps. ....Od.9.78.306.
For gloomy Night descended on the main, ...Od.9.167.312.
Thus breaks our slumbers, and disturbs the night? ....Od.9.480.325.
And send thee howling to the realms of night! ....Od.9.613.332.
At night each pair on splendid carpets lay, ...Od.10.11.340.
The shepherd quitting here at night the plain, ...Od.10.94.343.
And joyn the labours of the night and day. ....Od.10.100.345.
With sleep repair'd the long debauch of night: ....Od.10.664.375.
And o'er the shaded billows rush'd the night: ....Od.11.12.379.
Unhappy race! whom endless night invades, ...Od.11.19.380.
To the black palace of eternal Night. ....Od.11.185.390.
Whether the night descends, or day prevails, ...Od.11.220.392.
Thee she by night, and thee by day bewails. ....Od.11.221.392.
But should I all recount, the night would fail, ...Od.11.408.404.
But here this night the royal guest detain, ...Od.11.436.405.
To whom the Prince: This night with joy I stay, ...Od.11.442.406.
And lo! a length of night behind remains, ...Od.11.464.407.
Since yet the early hour of night allows ....Od.11.472.407.
Nor glides a Phantom thro' the realms of night. ....Od.11.568.411.
Touch'd at his sour retreat, thro' deepest night, ...Od.11.693.419.
Gloomy as night he stands, in act to throw ....Od.11.749.423.
A stony image, in eternal night! ....Od.11.788.425.
Lo I this night, your faithful guide, explain ....Od.12.37.431.
Then sable Night ascends, and balmy rest ....Od.12.41.431.
In vain! the dismal dungeon dark as night ....Od.12.276.445.
And lo! the night begins her gloomy reign, ...Od.12.339.448.

NIGHT (CONTINUED)
Oft in the dead of night loud winds arise, ... Od.12.341.448.
Then while the night displays her awful shade, ... Od.12.347.448.
Sweet time of slumber! be the night obey'd! ... Od.12.348.448.
Now far the night advanc'd her gloomy reign, ... Od.12.367.449.
All night it rag'd; when morning rose, to land ... Od.12.375.449.
Night dwells o'er all the deep: and now out flies ... Od.12.477.455.
All night I drove; and at the dawn of day ... Od.12.507.457.
He sate, and ey'd the sun, and wish'd the night; ... Od.13.36.3.
Unseen I 'scap'd; and favour'd by the night ... Od.13.315.21.
In dead of night an unknown port we gain'd, ... Od.13.319.22.
Constant as *Jove* the night and day bestows, ... Od.14.115.41.
And tempt the secret ambush of the night. ... Od.14.254.48.
He hung a night of horrors o'er their head, ... Od.14.335.51.
No more—th' approaching hours of silent night ... Od.14.449.57.
Now came the Night, and darkness cover'd o'er ... Od.14.510.61.
Beneath *Troy* walls by night we took our way: ... Od.14.531.63.
When now was wasted more than half the night, ... Od.14.543.63.
Nor let the night retard thy full career; ... Od.15.40.71.
There pass the night; while he his course pursues ... Od.15.47.72.
To tempt the dangers of forbidding night? ... Od.15.58.72.
Like radiant *Hesper* o'er the gems of night. ... Od.15.123.74.
'Till night descending intercepts the way. ... Od.15.209.78.
With him all night the youthful strangers stay'd, ... Od.15.212.78.
Yet one night more, my friends, indulge your guest; ... Od.15.326.85.
The night; then down to short repose they lay; ... Od.15.533.95.
In tedious cares, and weeps the night away. ... Od.16.38.104.
All night we watch'd, 'till with her orient wheels ... Od.16.380.124.
Of night draws on, go seek the rural bow'r: ... Od.17.677.165.
Oh hide it, death, in everlasting night! ... Od.18.91.171.
Deem not in ambush here to lurk by night, ... Od.19.81.196.
The night still ravell'd, what the day renew'd. ... Od.19.173.200.
Resign'd the skies, and night involv'd the pole. ... Od.19.496.220.
Pierc'd with her golden shafts the rere of night; ... Od.19.500.220.
Tho' night, dissolving grief in grateful ease, ... Od.19.594.225.
The night assists my ever-wakeful woes: ... Od.19.601.225.
Repose to night, and toil to day decreed: ... Od.19.692.229.
Whilst night extends her soft oblivious veil, ... Od.20.99.237.
The night renews the day-distracting theme, ... Od.20.102.237.
In vain the Queen the night-refection prest; ... Od.20.172.241.
But universal night usurps the pole! ... Od.20.430.254.
And still to last, the vision of my night! ... Od.21.80.262.
So end our night: Before the day shall spring, ... Od.21.280.273.
Then to the lute's soft voice prolong the night, ... Od.21.473.283.
There pass thy pleasing night, oh gentle swain! ... Od.22.212.297.
The wheels of night retarding, to detain ... Od.23.261.336.
Whose flaming steeds, emerging thro' the night, ... Od.23.263.336.
But end we here—the night demands repose, ... Od.23.271.336.
That drives the ghosts to realms of night or day, ... Od.24.5.347.
Each following night revers'd the toils of day. ... Od.24.167.356.
Display'd the radiance of the night and day. ... Od.24.174.356.

NIGHT-CAP
See! strow'd with learned dust, his Night-cap on, ... 4.2HE2.118.173.

NIGHT-DRESS
When each new Night-Dress gives a new Disease. ... 2.RL4.38.186.

NIGHT-GOWN
In a dun night-gown of his own loose skin, ... 5.DunA2.34.100.
In a dun night-gown of his own loose skin; ... 5.DunB2.38.297.

NIGHT-GUARDS
Near the Night-Guards, our chosen Council waits. ... Il.10.147.8.

NIGHT-INVASION
A Night-Invasion, and a Mid-day-Devil. ... 2.ChJM.48.17.

NIGHT-REFECTION
In vain the Queen the night-refection prest; ... Od.20.172.241.

NIGHT-WAND'RING
So to Night-wand'ring Sailors, pale with Fears, ... Il.19.404.389.

NIGHT'S
And Night's dark Mantle overspread the Sky. ... 2.ChJM.370.32.
Guideless, alone, through Night's dark Shade to go, ... Il.10.47.4.
And of Night's Empire but a third remains. ... Il.10.298.15.
These to the north and night's dark regions run, ... Od.9.25.303.

NIGHTGOWN
Nor Nightgown without Sleeves, avails ... 6.58.11A.171.

NIGHTINGALE
So when the Nightingale to Rest removes, ... 1.PSp.13.61.

NIGHTINGALES
No more the Nightingales repeat her Lays, ... 1.PWi.55A.93.

NIGHTLY
Soon as the Flocks shook off the nightly Dews, ... 1.PSp.17.62.
When Swains from Sheering seek their nightly Bow'rs; ... 1.PSu.64.76.
And bid *Endymion* nightly tend his Sheep. ... 1.TrSP.100.398.
No nightly Bands in glitt'ring Armour wait ... 1.TrSt.204.419.
Nor nightly Bands in glitt'ring Armour wait ... 1.TrSt.204A.419.
No nightly Bands in glitt'ring Arms did wait ... 1.TrSt.204B.419.
The Birds obscene, that nightly flock'd to Tast, ... 1.TrSt.735.441.
This was his nightly Dream, his daily Care, ... 2.ChJM.15.15.
As thro' the Moon-light shade they nightly stray, ... 2.RL*A*2.177.137.
The daily Anodyne, and nightly Draught, ... 3.Ep2.111.58.
Why shou'd I sing what bards the nightly Muse ... 5.DunA2.389.148.
Why should I sing what bards the nightly Muse ... 5.DunB2.421.318.
The *Trojan* Peers in nightly Council sate: ... Il.7.415.385.
Sev'n were the Leaders of the nightly Bands, ... Il.9.117.437.
And the red Fiends that walk the nightly Round. ... Il.9.686.468.
Whose nightly Joys the beauteous *Iphis* shar'd: ... Il.9.783.472.

NIGHTLY (CONTINUED)
Seek'st thou some Friend, or nightly Centinel? ... Il.10.92.6.
And now the Chiefs approach the nightly Guard; ... Il.10.207.11.
'Tis well, my Sons, your nightly Cares employ, ... Il.10.225.12.
Or nightly Pillager that strips the slain. ... Il.10.408.21.
No certain Guards the nightly Watch partake; ... Il.10.488.25.
So the grim Lion, from his nightly Den, ... Il.10.564.27.
Repuls'd by Numbers from the nightly Stalls, ... Il.11.676.65.
So turns the Lion from the nightly Fold, ... Il.17.741.317.
Reserv'd in bowls, supply'd his nightly feast. ... Od.9.294.318.
To these, the nightly prostitutes to shame, ... Od.22.497.313.
Did nightly thieves, or Pyrates cruel bands, ... Od.24.136.354.

NIGHTS
And wastes the Days in Grief, the Nights in Tears. ... 1.TrUl.219.473.
With store of Pray'rs, for Mornings, Nights, and Noons, ... 2.RL4.29.185.
Sprightly our Nights, polite are all our Days; ... 2.TemF.383.282.
Why, if the Nights seem tedious—take a Wife; ... 4.HS1.16.5.
Meer *Houshold Trash!* of Birth-Nights, Balls and Shows, ... 4.JD4.130.35.
Oh! when rank Widows purchase luscious nights, ... 4.JD2.87A.141.
And when rank Widows purchase luscious nights, ... 4.JD2.87.141.
O charming Noons! and Nights divine! ... 4.HS6.133.259.
In twice ten thousand rhyming nights and days, ... 5.DunB4.172.358.
Wou'd you enjoy soft nights and solid dinners? ... 6.41.23.114.
Laborious Lobster-nights, farewell! ... 6.47.45.130.
Days of ease, and nights of pleasure; ... 6.51ii.43.154.
Recall those Nights that clos'd thy toilsom Days, ... 6.84.15.239.
Still think on those gay Nights of toilsome Days, ... 6.84.15A.239.
And wak'd and wish'd whole Nights for thy Return? ... 6.96iv.4.276.
For nine long Nights, thro' all the dusky Air ... Il.1.71.89.
To waste long Nights in indolent Repose? ... Il.2.30.128.
To waste long Nights in indolent Repose. ... Il.2.80.130.
Long sleepless Nights in heavy Arms I stood, ... Il.9.430.453.
My Spouse alone must bless his lustful Nights: ... Il.9.443.454.
Strong Guards they plac'd, and watch'd nine Nights entire; ... Il.9.594.464.
Full sev'nteen nights he cut the foamy way; ... Od.5.355.189.
And now two nights, and now two days were past, ... Od.5.496.196.
Twice ten tempestuous nights I roll'd, resign'd ... Od.6.205.220.
Two tedious days and two long nights we lay, ... Od.9.83.306.
Six days and nights a doubtful course we steer, ... Od.10.91.343.
Spent and o'erwatch'd. Two days and nights roll'd on, ... Od.10.167.348.
And wastes the days in grief, the nights in tears. ... Od.13.386.25.
Long nights the now-declining year bestows; ... Od.15.426.89.
Six calmy days and six smooth nights we sail, ... Od.15.511.94.
Three days have spent their beams, three nights have run ... Od.17.606.161.
'Till sev'nteen nights and sev'nteen days return'd, ... Od.24.81.352.

NIGRINA
Nigrina black, and Merdamante brown, ... 5.DunA2.310.139.
Nigrina black, and Merdamante brown, ... 5.DunB2.334.314.

NIHIL
Ex nihilo nihil fit. ... 6.116iv.7.327.

NIHILO
Ex nihilo nihil fit. ... 6.116iv.7.327.

NILE
As half-form'd Insects on the Banks of *Nile;* ... 1.EOC.41.243.
And scarce are seen the prostrate Nile or Rhine, ... 6.71.28.203.
And scarce are seen the prostrate Nile and Rhine, ... 6.71.28A.203.
Thro' regions fatten'd with the flows of *Nile.* ... Od.4.100.124.
Who sway'd the sceptre, where prolific *Nile* ... Od.4.317.134.
Fronts the deep roar of disemboguing *Nile:* ... Od.4.480.143.
Once more the *Nile,* who from the secret source ... Od.4.643.149.
We gain the stream of *Jove*-descended Nile: ... Od.4.790.156.

NILE'S
To the soft joys of *Nile's* delightful shore. ... 6.20.10.66.

NILUS
From Heav'n it self tho' sev'nfold *Nilus* flows, ... 1.W-F.359.185.
Let weeping *Nilus* hear the Timbrel sound. ... 1.TrSt.376.425.
The Sun e're got, or slimy *Nilus* bore, ... 4.JD4.29.29.

NILUS'
And swallows roost in Nilus' dusty Urn. ... 3.Ep4.126.149.

NIMBLE
The nimble Juice soon seiz'd his giddy Head, ... 2.ChWB.405.76.
As clocks to weight their nimble motion owe, ... 5.DunA1.179.84.
As clocks to weight their nimble motion owe, ... 5.DunB1.183.283.
So Clocks to Lead their nimble Motions owe, ... 6.17i(b).1.55.
Then mounts again; again their nimble Feet ... Il.10.622.29.
Out-fly the nimble sail, and leave the lagging wind? ... Od.11.74.384.
Ply the strong oar, and catch the nimble gales; ... Od.12.106.436.
Thro' the mid seas the nimble pinnace sails, ... Od.14.329.51.

NIMBLER
But nimbler *W[elste]d* reaches at the ground, ... 5.DunA2.293B.138.
Some other be dispatch'd, of nimbler Feet, ... Il.10.125.7.

NIMBLEST
And bad the nimblest racer seize the prize; ... 5.DunA2.32.99.
And bids the nimblest racer seize the prize; ... 5.DunA2.32A.99.
And bade the nimblest racer seize the prize; ... 5.DunB2.36.297.

NIMBLY
And Songs were sung, and Healths went nimbly round; ... 2.ChJM.354A.31.
The Knights so nimbly o'er the Greensword bound, ... 2.ChJM.621.45.
And pondrous Slugs move nimbly thro' the Sky. ... 6.7.18.16.
Urg'd on all hands it nimbly spins about, ... Od.9.459.325.
Nimbly he rose, and cast his garment down; ... Od.14.565.64.

NIMROD
Proud *Nimrod* first the bloody Chace began, ... 1.W-F.61.155.

NINE
Thou, whom the Nine with *Plautus'* Wit inspire, ... 1.PAu.7.80.
Ye sacred Nine! that all my Soul possess, ... 1.W-F.259.173.
Thee, bold *Longinus!* all the Nine inspire, ... 1.EOC.675.316.
Now by the Nine, those Pow'rs ador'd by me, ... 1.TrSP.121.399.
Each Band the number of the Sacred Nine. .... 2.RL3.30.171.
Beneath, in Order rang'd, the tuneful Nine .... 2.TemF.270.276.
Lull with *Amelia's* liquid Name the Nine, ... 4.HS1.31.7.
This saving counsel, "Keep your Piece nine years." .... 4.Arbu.40.98.
Nine years! cries he, who high in *Drury-lane* .... 4.Arbu.41.99.
And own'd, that nine such Poets made a *Tate.* .... 4.Arbu.190.109.
In Palace-Yard at Nine you'll find me there— .... 4.2HE2.94.171.
Call *Tibbald Shakespear,* and he'll swear the Nine .... 4.2HE2.137.175.
At ninety nine, a Modern, and a Dunce? .... 4.2HE1.60.199.
And if we will recite nine hours in ten, ... 4.2HE1.362.227.
Cast on the prostrate Nine a scornful look, ... 5.DunB4.51.346.
Descend ye Nine! descend and sing; .... 6.11.1.29.
With *Styx* nine times round her, ... 6.11.91.33.
You have the *Nine* in your *Wit,* and *Three* in your *Faces.* .... 6.62i.2.185.
You've the *Nine* in your *Wit,* and the *Three* in your *Face* ..... 6.62i.2A.185.
And own that nine such Poets make a *Tate;* .... 6.98.40.284.
This radiant pile nine rural sisters raise; .... 6.126ii.2.353.
For nine long Nights, thro' all the dusky Air .... Il.1.71.89.
Worn with nine Years of unsuccessful War? .... Il.2.96.131.
Nine sacred Heralds now proclaiming loud .... Il.2.123.133.
Now nine long Years of mighty *Jove* are run, ... Il.2.161.136.
The tedious Length of nine revolving Years. .... Il.2.361.144.
All-knowing *Goddesses!* immortal Nine! .... Il.2.573.155.
Led nine swift Vessels thro' the foamy Seas; .... Il.2.794.163.
For nine long Years have set the World in Arms; .... Il.3.206.201.
Nine Days he feasted, and nine Bulls he slew. .... Il.6.214.336.
Nine Days he feasted, and nine Bulls he slew. .... Il.6.214.336.
For which nine Oxen paid (a vulgar Price) .... Il.6.293.341.
And nine, the noblest of the *Grecian* Name, ... Il.7.196.373.
Strong Guards they plac'd, and watch'd nine Nights entire; ..... Il.9.594.464.
Ye sacred Nine, Celestial Muses! tell, ... Il.11.281.47.
Delug'd the Rampire nine continual Days; .... Il.12.24.82.
Ye all-beholding, all-recording Nine! .... Il.14.600.191.
Nine Years imprison'd in those Tow'rs ye lay? .... Il.18.336.337.
Nine Years kept secret in the dark Abode, ... Il.18.469.344.
And nine sour Dogs compleat the rustic Band. .... Il.18.670.356.
For when *Alcmena's* nine long Months were run, ... Il.19.103.376.
Of nine large Dogs, domestick at his Board, ... Il.23.212.498.
Nine Days are past, since all the Court above .... Il.24.141.541.
And gen'rous *Antiphon:* For yet these nine .... Il.24.315.549.
Nine Cubits long the Traces swept the Ground; .... Il.24.337.550.
Nine Days neglected lay expos'd the Dead; .... Il.24.768.569.
Nine Days to vent our Sorrows I request, ... Il.24.834.571.
These Toils continue nine succeeding Days, ... Il.24.993.577.
At nine green Theatres the *Pylians* stood, ... Od.3.8.86.
At each, nine oxen on the sand lay slain. .... Od.3.10.87.
Nine painful years, on that detested shore .... Od.3.145.92.
The *Greeks,* (whose arms for nine long years employ'd .... Od.5.133.178.
Full nine days floating to the wave and wind. .... Od.7.339.253.
Up rose nine Seniors, chosen to survey .... Od.8.295.279.
Nine days our fleet th' uncertain tempest bore .... Od.9.93.306.
And nine fat goats each vessel bears away: .... Od.9.185.313.
Nine prosp'rous days we ply'd the lab'ring oar; .... Od.10.30.340.
Lo! when nine times the moon renews her horn, ... Od.11.299.396.
The wond'rous youths had scarce nine winters told, ... Od.11.381.401.
Nine ells aloft they rear'd their tow'ring head, ... Od.11.383.401.
And full nine cubits broad their shoulders spread. .... Od.11.384.402.
O'erspreads nine acres of infernal ground; .... Od.11.710.421.
Then nine long days I plow'd the calmer seas, ... Od.12.529.458.
Nine times Commander, or by land or main, ... Od.14.267.49.
Nine years we warr'd; the tenth saw *Ilion* fall; .... Od.14.276.49.
Nine ships I mann'd equip'd with ready stores, ... Od.14.280.49.
For nine long days the billows tilting o'er, ... Od.14.349.51.
Known nine long years, and felt by Heroes dead? .... Od.22.249.298.

NINETEEN
Nineteen one Mother bore—Dead, all are dead! .... Il.24.616.562.

NINETY
At ninety nine, a Modern, and a Dunce? .... 4.2HE1.60.199.
In ninety Sail, from *Pylos'* sandy Coast, ... Il.2.715.160.
And ninety cities crown the sea-born Isle: .... Od.19.197.201.

NINTH
Herself the ninth: The Serpent as he hung, ... Il.2.378.145.
Divided Right; each ninth revolving year .... Od.19.206.202.

NINUS
There *Ninus* shone, who spread th' *Assyrian* Fame, ... 2.TemF.95.260.

NIOBE
Fast by, like Niobe (her children gone) .... 5.DunB2.311.310.
The haughty *Niobe* whose impious pride .... 6.20.56.67.
Not thus did *Niobe,* of Form divine, ... Il.24.757.568.

NIPPLE
But on the *Maiden's Nipple* when you rid, ... 6.96iv.87.278.

NIPT
Poor W[harton] nipt in Folly's broadest bloom, ... 5.DunB4.513.392*.

NIREUS
Three Ships with *Nireus* sought the *Trojan* Shore, ... Il.2.815.163.
Nireus, whom *Aglae* to *Charopus* bore, ... Il.2.816.163.
Nireus, in faultless Shape, and blooming Grace, ... Il.2.817.163.

NISA
Platæa green, and *Nisa* the divine. .... Il.2.603.156.

NISUS'
Next to the Bounds of *Nisus'* Realm repairs, ... 1.TrSt.468.429.
She dearly pays for *Nisus'* injur'd Hair! .... 2.RL3.124.177.

NISYRUS
With them the Youth of *Nisyrus* repair, ... Il.2.823.164.

NOÛS
And much Divinity without a *Noûs.* .... 5.DunB4.244.367.

NOËMON
Alcander, Prytanis, Noëmon fell, ... Il.5.836.305.
Whom young *Noëmon* lowly thus addrest. .... Od.4.853.158.
(*Noëmon* cry'd) the vessel was resign'd. .... Od.4.873.159.

NOËMON'S
Resign'd the Courser to *Noëmon's* Hand, ... Il.23.700.517.

NO
Enjoy the Glory to be Great no more, ... 1.PSp.8.61.
No Lambs or Sheep for Victims I'll impart, ... 1.PSp.51.66.
Feed here my Lambs, I'll seek no distant Field. .... 1.PSp.64.67.
And vanquish'd Nature seems to charm no more. .... 1.PSp.76.68.
A Shepherd's Boy (he seeks no better Name) .... 1.PSu.1.71.
But since those Graces please thy Eyes no more, ... 1.PSu.29.74.
But since those Graces please thy Sight no more, ... 1.PSu.29A.74.
This harmless Grove no lurking Viper hides, ... 1.PSu.67.77.
But your *Alexis* knows no Sweets but you. .... 1.PSu.70.77.
Ye Gods! and is there no Relief for Love? .... 1.PSu.88.79.
No more ye Hills, no more resound my Strains! .... 1.PAu.96.87.
No more ye Hills, no more resound my Strains! .... 1.PAu.96.87.
"Fair *Daphne's* dead, and Love is now no more!" .... 1.PWi.28.91.
Fair *Daphne's* dead, and Beauty is no more! .... 1.PWi.36.91.
Fair *Daphne's* dead, and Beauty's now no more! .... 1.PWi.36A.91.
Now *Daphne's* dead, and Pleasure is no more! .... 1.PWi.44.92.
No grateful Dews descend from Ev'ning Skies, ... 1.PWi.45.92.
No rich Perfumes refresh the fruitful Field, ... 1.PWi.47.92.
Fair *Daphne's* dead, and Sweetness is no more! .... 1.PWi.52.92.
No more the mounting Larks, while *Daphne* sings, ... 1.PWi.53.92.
Eccho no more the rural Song rebounds, ... 1.PWi.41A.92.
No more the Birds shall imitate her Lays, ... 1.PWi.55.93.
No more the Streams their Murmurs shall forbear, ... 1.PWi.57.93.
Fair *Daphne's* dead, and Musick is no more! .... 1.PWi.60.93.
Daphne, our Grief! our Glory now no more! .... 1.PWi.68.93.
No more the Nightingales repeat her Lays, ... 1.PWi.55A.93.
Daphne, our Goddess, and our Grief no more! .... 1.PWi.76.94.
Delight no more—O Thou my Voice inspire .... 1.Mes.5.112.
No Sigh, no Murmur the wide World shall hear, ... 1.Mes.45.117.
No Sigh, no Murmur the wide World shall hear, ... 1.Mes.45.117.
No more shall Nation against Nation rise, ... 1.Mes.57.117.
The Brazen Trumpets kindle Rage no more: .... 1.Mes.60.118.
No more the rising *Sun* shall gild the Morn, ... 1.Mes.99.121.
No wonder Savages or Subjects slain .... 1.W-F.57A.154.
No Seas so rich, so gay no Banks appear, ... 1.W-F.225.170.
No Seas so rich, so gay no Banks appear, ... 1.W-F.225.170.
No Lake so gentle, and no Spring so clear. .... 1.W-F.226.170.
No Lake so gentle, and no Spring so clear. .... 1.W-F.226.170.
No Seas so rich so full no Streams appear, ... 1.W-F.225A.170.
No Seas so rich so full no Streams appear, ... 1.W-F.225A.170.
No more the Forests ring, or Groves rejoice; .... 1.W-F.278.174.
These now no more shall be the Muse's Themes, ... 1.W-F.361.185.
No more my Sons shall dye with *British* Blood .... 1.W-F.367.186.
The shady Empire shall retain no Trace .... 1.W-F.371.186.
Till Conquest cease, and Slav'ry be no more: .... 1.W-F.408.192.
Some Beauties yet, no Precepts can declare, ... 1.EOC.141.255.
Are *nameless Graces* which no Methods teach, ... 1.EOC.144.256.
No single Parts unequally surprize; .... 1.EOC.249.268.
No monstrous Height, or Breadth, or Length appear; .... 1.EOC.251.268.
The Face of Nature we no more Survey, ... 1.EOC.313.274.
'Tis not enough no Harshness gives Offence, ... 1.EOC.364.281.
Our *wiser Sons,* no doubt, will think *us* so. .... 1.EOC.439.288.
No longer now that Golden Age appears, ... 1.EOC.478.293.
No Pardon vile *Obscenity* should find, ... 1.EOC.530.297.
The modest Fan was lifted up no more, ... 1.EOC.542.299.
Be Niggards of Advice on no Pretence; .... 1.EOC.578.306.
Whom, when they *Praise,* the World believes no more, ... 1.EOC.594.307.
No Place so Sacred from such Fops is barr'd, ... 1.EOC.622.310.
(Her Guide now lost) no more attempts to *rise,* .... 1.EOC.737.325.
But finds no shelter from his raging fires. .... 1.TrPA.38.366.
No lightning wounds me but your angry eyes, ... 1.TrPA.117.370.
These thefts, false nymph, thou shalt enjoy no more, ... 1.TrPA.138.371.
No further speech the thundering rock affords, ... 1.TrPA.146.372.
Yet what we cou'd, and what no fates deny'd, ... 1.TrPA.148.372.
The Streams and Fountains, no Delights cou'd yield; .... 1.TrVP.6.377.
No Dart she wielded, but a Hook did bear, ... 1.TrVP.9A.377.
So may no Frost, when early Buds appear, ... 1.TrVP.108.381.
No nymph of all *Oechalia* could compare .... 1.TrFD.7.385.
No more a woman, nor yet quite a tree: .... 1.TrFD.64.388.
No wilful crime this heavy vengeance bred, ... 1.TrFD.71.389.
I can no more; the creeping rind invades .... 1.TrFD.96.390.
No more my Soul a Charm in Musick finds, ... 1.TrSP.13.393.
Soft Scenes of Solitude no more can please, ... 1.TrSP.15.393.
No more the *Lesbian* Dames my Passion move, ... 1.TrSP.17.394.
Nymphs that in Verse no more cou'd rival me, ... 1.TrSP.29.394.
No less Renown attends the moving Lyre, ... 1.TrSP.35.394.
If to no Charms thou wilt thy Heart resign, ... 1.TrSP.45.395.
No Time the dear Remembrance can remove, ... 1.TrSP.51.396.
No more my Robes in waving Purple flow, ... 1.TrSP.81.397.
No more my Locks in Ringlets curl'd diffuse .... 1.TrSP.83.397.
No Tear did you, no parting Kiss receive, ... 1.TrSP.115.398.
No Tear did you, no parting Kiss receive, ... 1.TrSP.115.398.
No Lover's Gift your *Sapho* cou'd confer, ... 1.TrSP.117.398.
No Charge I gave you, and no Charge cou'd give, ... 1.TrSP.119.398.

NO (CONTINUED)

No Charge I gave you, and no Charge cou'd give, 1.TrSP.119.398.
No Gift on thee thy *Sapho* cou'd confer, 1.TrSP.117A.398.
No Sigh to rise, no Tear had pow'r to flow; 1.TrSP.127.399.
No Sigh to rise, no Tear had pow'r to flow; 1.TrSP.127.399.
But, *Phaon* gone, those Shades delight no more. 1.TrSP.168.400.
Alas! the *Muses* now no more inspire, 1.TrSP.228.403.
No more your Groves with my glad Songs shall ring, 1.TrSP.234.404.
No more these Hands shall touch the trembling String: 1.TrSP.235.404.
Gods! can no Pray'rs, no Sighs, no Numbers move 1.TrSP.242.404.
Gods! can no Pray'rs, no Sighs, no Numbers move 1.TrSP.242.404.
Gods! can no Pray'rs, no Sighs, no Numbers move 1.TrSP.242.404.
Tho' *Jove* himself no less content wou'd be, 1.TrSt.41.411.
Yet then no proud aspiring Piles were rais'd, 1.TrSt.200.418.
No fretted Roofs with polish'd Metals blaz'd, 1.TrSt.201.418.
No labour'd Columns in long Order plac'd, 1.TrSt.202.418.
No *Grecian* Stone the pompous Arches grac'd; 1.TrSt.203.418.
No nightly Bands in glitt'ring Armour wait 1.TrSt.204.419.
No Chargers then were wrought in burnish'd Gold, 1.TrSt.206.419.
No nightly Bands in glitt'ring Arms did wait 1.TrSt.204B.419.
Ev'n Fortune rules no more:—Oh servile Land, 1.TrSt.241.420.
No more let Mortals *Juno's* Pow'r invoke, 1.TrSt.370.425.
Her Fanes no more with Eastern Incense smoke, 1.TrSt.371.425.
No less *Dione* might for *Thebes* contend, 1.TrSt.407.427.
No Force can bend me, no Persuasion move. 1.TrSt.414.427.
No Force can bend me, no Persuasion move. 1.TrSt.414.427.
Yet no red Clouds, with golden Borders gay, 1.TrSt.482.430.
No faint Reflections of the distant Light 1.TrSt.484.430.
From no blind Zeal or fond Tradition rise; 1.TrSt.661.438.
For whom, as Man no longer claim'd thy Care, 1.TrSt.765.442.
From Gods above no more Compassion find; 1.TrSt.768.442.
Or pleas'd to find fair *Delos* float no more, 1.TrSt.833.444.
Which claims no less the Fearful than the Brave, 1.TrES.44.451.
The Nerves unbrac'd no more his Bulk sustain, 1.TrES.265.459.
The rugged Soil allows no level Space 1.TrUl.122.470.
No less, than Mortals are surpass'd by thine: 1.TrUl.174.471.
He vow'd to lead this Vicious Life no more. 2.ChJM.10.15.
He vow'd to lead that Vicious Life no more. 2.ChJM.10A.15.
No crafty Widows shall approach my Bed, 2.ChJM.107.19.
Since if I found no Pleasure in my Spouse, 2.ChJM.115.20.
Or such a *Wit* as no Man e'er can rule? 2.ChJM.189.24.
And swear no Mortal's happier in a Wife; 2.ChJM.201.24.
And thought no Mortal cou'd dispute his Choice: 2.ChJM.251.26.
And thought no Mortal cou'd dispute this choice: 2.ChJM.251A.26.
Good Heav'n no doubt the nuptial State approves, 2.ChJM.282.27.
No less in Wedlock than in Liberty. 2.ChJM.332.30.
He look'd, he languish'd, and cou'd take no Rest: 2.ChJM.362.31.
He look'd, he lanquish'd, and cou'd find no Rest: 2.ChJM.362A.31.
But now no longer from our Tale to stray; 2.ChJM.520.40.
And sought no Treasure but thy Heart alone. 2.ChJM.551.41.
From thy dear Side I have no Pow'r to part, 2.ChJM.571.42.
And, what no less you to my Charge commend, 2.ChJM.579.43.
Or die the Death I dread no less than Hell, 2.ChJM.587.43.
And sad Experience leaves no room for Doubt. 2.ChJM.630.45.
The Son of *Sirach* testifies no less. 2.ChJM.640.46.
No impious Wretch shall 'scape unpunish'd long, 2.ChJM.649.46.
By this no more was meant, than to have shown, 2.ChJM.679.47.
They need no more but to protest, and swear, 2.ChJM.665A.47.
But cou'd not climb, and had no Servant nigh, 2.ChJM.727.49.
So help me Fates, as 'tis no perfect Sight, 2.ChJM.776.52.
Come down, and vex your tender Heart no more: 2.ChJM.790.53.
Disturb'd with Doubts and Jealousies no more: 2.ChJM.814.54.
No pious Christian ought to marry twice. 2.ChWB.12.57.
No Precept for Virginity he found: 2.ChWB.33.58.
Sure to be lov'd, I took no Pains to please, 2.ChWB.62.59.
There swims no Goose so gray, but, soon or late, 2.ChWB.98.61.
Sir, I'm no Fool: Nor shall you, by St. *John,* 2.ChWB.126.62.
With empty Hands no Tassels you can lure, 2.ChWB.172.65.
Wine lets no Lover unrewarded go, 2.ChWB.219.67.
So bless the good Man's Soul, I say no more. 2.ChWB.252.69.
To these I made no Scruple to reveal. 2.ChWB.274.70.
But when no End of these vile Tales I found, 2.ChWB.412.77.
What tho' no Credit doubting Wits may give? 2.RL1.39.148.
And tho' she plays no more, o'erlooks the Cards. 2.RL1.54.150.
Wounds, Charms, and *Ardors,* were no sooner read, 2.RL1.119.154.
No cheerful Breeze this sullen Region knows, 2.RL4.19.184.
Or caus'd Suspicion when no Soul was rude, 2.RL4.73.190.
So spoke the Dame, but no Applause ensu'd; 2.RL5.35.201.
No common Weapons in their Hands are found, 2.RL5.43.202.
Who sought no more than on his Foe to die. 2.RL5.78.206.
With such a Prize no Mortal must be blest, 2.RL5.111.208.
Yet Part no Injuries of Heav'n cou'd feel, 2.TemF.45.256.
And *Brutus* his ill Genius meets no more. 2.TemF.177.270.
No less deserv'd a just Return of Praise. 2.TemF.331.280.
In fact, 'tis true, no Nymph we cou'd persuade, 2.TemF.386.282.
Calm, thinking Villains, whom no Faith cou'd fix, 2.TemF.410.283.
Calm, thinking Villains, whom no Faith can fix, 2.TemF.410B.283.
And this or that unmix'd, no Mortal e'er shall find. 2.TemF.496.287.
Or if no Basis bear my rising Name, 2.TemF.519.289.
No happier task these faded eyes pursue, 2.ElAb.47.322.
Too soon they taught me 'twas no sin to love. 2.ElAb.68.324.
No, make me mistress to the man I love; 2.ElAb.88.326.
No craving Void left aking in the breast: 2.ElAb.94.327.
I can no more; by shame, by rage suppress, 2.ElAb.105.328.
Ah no! instruct me other joys to prize, 2.ElAb.125.330.
No weeping orphan saw his father's stores 2.ElAb.135.330.
No silver saints, by dying misers giv'n, 2.ElAb.137.331.
But now no face divine contentment wears, 2.ElAb.147.331.
No more these scenes my meditation aid, 2.ElAb.161.332.
And wait, till 'tis no sin to mix with thine. 2.ElAb.176.334.
I wake—no more I hear, no more I view, 2.ElAb.235.339.
I wake—no more I hear, no more I view, 2.ElAb.235.339.
Alas no more!—methinks we wandring go 2.ElAb.241.339.
No pulse that riots, and no blood that glows. 2.ElAb.252.340.
No pulse that riots, and no blood that glows. 2.ElAb.252.340.
No, fly me, fly me! far as Pole from Pole; 2.ElAb.289.343.

NO (CONTINUED)

Ah no—in sacred vestments may'st thou stand, 2.ElAb.325.346.
It will be then no crime to gaze on me. 2.ElAb.330.346.
And ev'n my *Abelard* be lov'd no more. 2.ElAb.334.346.
And ev'n my *Abelard* belov'd no more. 2.ElAb.334A.346.
When this rebellious heart shall beat no more; 2.ElAb.346.348.
And image charms he must behold no more, 2.ElAb.362.348.
Is there no bright reversion in the sky, 2.Elegy.9.363.
And those love-darting eyes must roll no more. 2.Elegy.34.365.
No friend's complaint, no kind domestic tear 2.Elegy.49.367.
No friend's complaint, no kind domestic tear 2.Elegy.49.367.
What tho' no friends in sable weeds appear, 2.Elegy.55.367.
What tho' no weeping Loves thy ashes grace, 2.Elegy.59.367.
What tho' no sacred earth allow thee room, 2.Elegy.61.367.
The Muse forgot, and thou belov'd no more! 2.Elegy.82.368.
Why form'd no weaker, blinder, and no less! 3.EOM1.38.18.
Why form'd no weaker, blinder, and no less! 3.EOM1.38.18.
Why made no weaker, blinder, and no less! 3.EOM1.38A.18.
Why made no weaker, blinder, and no less! 3.EOM1.38A.18.
No fiends torment, no Christians thirst for gold! 3.EOM1.108.28.
No fiends torment, no Christians thirst for gold! 3.EOM1.108.28.
He asks no Angel's wing, no Seraph's fire; 3.EOM1.110.28.
He asks no Angel's wing, no Seraph's fire; 3.EOM1.110.28.
No fiends torment, nor Christians thirst for gold! 3.EOM1.108A.28.
He asks no Angel's wing, or Seraph's fire; 3.EOM1.110A.28.
He asks no Angel's wing, nor Seraph's fire; 3.EOM1.110B.28.
"No ('tis reply'd) the first Almighty Cause 3.EOM1.145.33.
"No ('tis reply'd) he acts by *gen'ral Laws;* 3.EOM1.146A.33.
No pow'rs of body or of soul to share, 3.EOM1.191.38.
No self-confounding Faculties to share; 3.EOM1.191A.38.
No Senses stronger than his brain can bear. 3.EOM1.192A.38.
Beast, bird, fish, insect! what no eye can see, 3.EOM1.239.44.
No glass can reach! from Infinite to thee, 3.EOM1.240.45.
To him no high, no low, no great, no small; 3.EOM1.279.49.
To him no high, no low, no great, no small; 3.EOM1.279.49.
To him no high, no low, no great, no small; 3.EOM1.279.49.
To him no high, no low, no great, no small; 3.EOM1.279.49.
Man, but for that, no action could attend, 3.EOM2.61.63.
And, but for this, were active to no end; 3.EOM2.62.63.
Have full as oft no meaning, or the same. 3.EOM2.86.65.
Reason is here no guide, but still a guard: 3.EOM2.162.74.
A thousand ways, is there no black or white? 3.EOM2.214.81.
No creature owns it in the first degree, 3.EOM2.225.82.
Which seeks no int'rest, no reward but praise; 3.EOM2.246.85.
Which seeks no int'rest, no reward but praise; 3.EOM2.246.85.
The fool is happy that he knows no more; 3.EOM2.264.87.
Which sees no more the stroke, or feels the pain, 3.EOM3.67.98.
No murder cloath'd him, and no murder fed. 3.EOM3.154.108.
No murder cloath'd him, and no murder fed. 3.EOM3.154.108.
For Nature knew no right divine in Men, 3.EOM3.236.116.
No ill could fear in God; and understood 3.EOM3.237.116.
Then sacred seem'd th'etherial vault no more; 3.EOM3.263.119.
Fix'd to no spot is Happiness sincere, 3.EOM4.15.129.
'Tis no where to be found, or ev'ry where; 3.EOM4.16.129.
Obvious her goods, in no extreme they dwell, 3.EOM4.31.130.
No Bandit fierce, no Tyrant mad with pride, 3.EOM4.41.131.
No Bandit fierce, no Tyrant mad with pride, 3.EOM4.41.131.
No cavern'd Hermit, rests self-satisfy'd. 3.EOM4.42.132.
This cries there is, and that, there is no God. 3.EOM4.140.141.
"No—shall the good want Health, the good want Pow'r?" 3.EOM4.158.143.
"Why bounded Pow'r? why private? why no king?" 3.EOM4.160.143.
No joy, or be destructive of the thing: 3.EOM4.182.144.
Honour and shame from no Condition rise; 3.EOM4.193.145.
No less alike the Politic and Wise, 3.EOM4.225.148.
Oh wealth ill-fated! which no act of fame 3.EOM4.299.156.
And if it lose, attended with no pain: 3.EOM4.316.158.
And where no wants, no wishes can remain, 3.EOM4.325.159.
And where no wants, no wishes can remain, 3.EOM4.325.159.
Slave to no sect, who takes no private road, 3.EOM4.331.160.
Slave to no sect, who takes no private road, 3.EOM4.331.160.
See, that no being any bliss can know, 3.EOM4.335.161.
(Nature, whose dictates to no other kind 3.EOM4.347.162.
(So Darkness fills the eye no less than Light) 3.Ep1.112A.23.
His constant Bounty no one friend has made; 3.Ep1.198A.32.
His constant Bounty no one friend had made; 3.Ep1.198B.32.
His angel Tongue, no mortal can persuade; 3.Ep1.199A.32.
His angel Tongue, no mortal could persuade; 3.Ep1.199B.32.
Nature well known, no Miracles remain, 3.Ep1.208A.33.
You hold him no Philosopher at all. 3.Ep1.8.16.
Next, that he varies from himself no less: 3.Ep1.20.17.
That instant 'tis his Principle no more. 3.Ep1.38.18.
(So Darkness strikes the sense no less than Light) 3.Ep1.112.23.
Save just at dinner—then prefers, no doubt, 3.Ep1.138.26.
Priests, Princes, Women, no dissemblers here. 3.Ep1.177.30.
Grown all to all, from no one vice exempt, 3.Ep1.194.31.
A constant Bounty which no friend has made; 3.Ep1.198.32.
An angel Tongue, which no man can persuade; 3.Ep1.199.32.
Nature well known, no prodigies remain, 3.Ep1.208.33.
Is there no hope? Alas!—then bring the jowl. 3.Ep1.237.35.
"No, let a charming Chintz, and Brussels lace 3.Ep1.244.36.
Cries, "oh! how charming if there's no such place!" 3.Ep2.108A.58.
"Most Women have no Characters at all". 3.Ep2.2.46.
No Ass so meek, no Ass so obstinate: 3.Ep2.102.58.
No Ass so meek, no Ass so obstinate: 3.Ep2.102.58.
Cries, "Ah! how charming if there's no such place!" 3.Ep2.108.58.
For true No-meaning puzzles more than Wit. 3.Ep2.114.59.
No Thought advances, but her Eddy Brain 3.Ep2.121.60.
No Passion gratify'd except her Rage. 3.Ep2.126.61.
Asks no firm hand, and no unerring line; 3.Ep2.152.62.
Asks no firm hand, and no unerring line; 3.Ep2.152.62.
If QUEENSBERRY to strip there's no compelling, 3.Ep2.193.66.
From Peer or Bishop 'tis no easy thing 3.Ep2.195.66.
No thought of Peace or Happiness at home. 3.Ep2.224.68.
Reduc'd to feign it, when they give no more: 3.Ep2.238.69.
Fair to no purpose, artful to no end, 3.Ep2.245.70.
Fair to no purpose, artful to no end, 3.Ep2.245.70.

NO (CONTINUED)

No poor Court-badge, great Scriv'ner! fir'd thy brain, ...3.Ep3.147A.105.
'Twas no Court-badge, great Scriv'ner! fir'd thy brain, ...3.Ep3.147B.105.
No gay Court-badge, great Scriv'ner! Fir'd thy brain, ...3.Ep3.147C.105.
No lordly Luxury, no City Gain: ....3.Ep3.148A.105.
No lordly Luxury, no City Gain: ....3.Ep3.148A.105.
No lordly Luxury, nor City Gain: ....3.Ep3.148B.105.
No selfish motive this profusion draws, ...3.Ep3.205A.110.
B. And what? no monument, inscription, stone? ....3.Ep3.283A.116.
No grace of Heav'n or token of th' Elect; ....3.Ep3.18.84.
No mean Court-badge, great Scriv'ner! fir'd thy brain, ...3.Ep3.147.105.
No, 'twas thy righteous end, asham'd to see ....3.Ep3.149.105.
Than ev'n that Passion, if it has no Aim; ....3.Ep3.158.106.
If Cotta liv'd on pulse, it was no more ....3.Ep3.185.109.
No rafter'd roofs with dance and tabor sound, ...3.Ep3.191.109.
No noontide-bell invites the country round; ....3.Ep3.192.109.
(For what to shun will no great knowledge need, ...3.Ep3.201.110.
Yet no mean motive this profusion draws, ...3.Ep3.205.110.
The Sylvans groan—no matter—for the Fleet: ....3.Ep3.210.110.
Balk'd are the Courts, and contest is no more. ....3.Ep3.272.115.
"And what? no monument, inscription, stone? ....3.Ep3.283.116.
No Wit to flatter, left of all his store! ....3.Ep3.311.119.
No Fool to laugh at, which he valu'd more. ....3.Ep3.312.119.
Think we all these are for himself? no more ....3.Ep4.11.136.
And needs no Rod but Ripley with a Rule. ....3.Ep4.18.137.
And tho' no science, fairly worth the sev'n: ....3.Ep4.44.140.
Enjoy them, you! Villario can no more; ....3.Ep4.86.146.
No pleasing Intricacies intervene, ...3.Ep4.115.148.
No artful wildness to perplex the scene; ....3.Ep4.116.148.
And there a Summer-house, that knows no shade; ....3.Ep4.122.149.
No, 'tis a Temple, and a Hecatomb. ....3.Ep4.156.152.
And swear no Day was ever past so ill. ....3.Ep4.168.153.
And needs no Rod but S[taffor]d with a Rule ....3.Ep4.18A.137*.
And needs no Rod but S[heppar]d with a Rule ....3.Ep4.18B.137*.
No artful Wilderness to perplex the scene; ....3.Ep4.116A.148.
F. I'd write no more. *P.* Not write? but then I *think,* ....4.HS1.11.5.
But touch me, and no Minister so sore. ....4.HS1.76.13.
And no man wonders he's not stung by Pug: ....4.HS1.88.13.
Un-plac'd, un-pension'd, no Man's Heir, or Slave? ....4.HS1.116.17.
Yes, while I live, no rich or noble knave ....4.HS1.119.17.
Know, while I live, no rich or noble knave ....4.HS1.119A.17.
No Pimp of Pleasure, and no Spy of State, ...4.HS1.134.19.
No Pimp of Pleasure, and no Spy of State, ...4.HS1.134.19.
I hop'd for no *Commission* from his Grace; ....4.JD4.11.27.
I bought no *Benefice,* I begg'd no *Place;* ....4.JD4.12.27.
I bought no *Benefice,* I begg'd no *Place;* ....4.JD4.12.27.
Had no *new Verses,* or *new Suit* to show; ....4.JD4.13.27.
Since 'twas no form'd Design of serving God: ....4.JD4.18.27.
"Permit (he cries) no stranger to your fame ....4.JD4.66.31.
"I make no question but the *Tow'r* had stood." ....4.JD4.85.33.
"No Lessons now are taught the *Spartan* way: ....4.JD4.93.33.
Why *Turnpikes* rise, and now no Cit, nor Clown ....4.JD4.144.37.
Shortly no Lad shall *chuck,* or Lady *vole,* ....4.JD4.146.37.
Why *Turnpikes* rose, and why no Cit, nor Clown ....4.JD4.144A.37.
Why *Turnpikes* rose, and now no Cit, nor Clown ....4.JD4.144B.37.
No wonder some Folks bow, and think them *Kings.* ....4.JD4.211.43.
See! where the *British* Youth, engag'd no more ....4.JD4.212.43.
And now the *British* Youth, engag'd no more ....4.JD4.212A.43.
Courts are no match for Wits so weak as mine; ....4.JD4.280A.49.
He finds no relish in the sweetest Meat; ....4.HS2.32.57.
Avidien or his Wife (no matter which, ...4.HS2.49.57.
He'll find no relish in the sweetest Meat; ....4.HS2.31A.57.
He'll find no relish in the sweetest Meat; ....4.HS2.32B.57.
Perhaps, young men! our Fathers had no nose? ....4.HS2.92.61.
Are no rewards for Want, and Infamy! ....4.HS2.104.61.
'Tis true, no Turbots dignify my boards, ...4.HS2.141.67.
Some feel no Flames but at the *Court* or *Ball,* ....4.HAdv.37.79.
"'Tis *Fornicatio simplex,* and no other: ....4.HAdv.42.79.
May no such Praise (cries *J[efferie]s*) e'er be mine! ....4.HAdv.45.79.
To *Palmer's* Bed no Actress comes amiss, ...4.HAdv.71.81.
First, Silks and Diamonds veil no finer Shape, ...4.HAdv.106.85.
No Eagle sharper, every Charm to find, ...4.HAdv.120.85.
And if the Dame says yes, the Dress says no. ....4.HAdv.132.87.
"The Hare once seiz'd the Hunter heeds no more ....4.HAdv.137.87.
Has Nature set no bounds to wild Desire? ....4.HAdv.143.87.
No Sense to guide, no Reason to enquire, ...4.HAdv.144.87.
No Sense to guide, no Reason to enquire, ...4.HAdv.144.87.
Who asks no more (right reasonable Peer) ....4.HAdv.159.89.
No furious Husband thunders at the Door; ....4.HAdv.167.89.
No barking Dog, no Household in a Roar; ....4.HAdv.168.89.
No barking Dog, no Household in a Roar; ....4.HAdv.168.89.
From gleaming Swords no shrieking Women run; ....4.HAdv.169.89.
No wretched Wife cries out, *Undone! Undone!* ....4.HAdv.170.89.
No Mistress *H[e]ysh[a]m* near, no Lady *B[uc]k!* ....4.HAdv.176.89.
No Mistress *H[e]ysh[a]m* near, no Lady *B[uc]k!* ....4.HAdv.176.89.
No place is sacred, not the Church is free, ...4.Arbu.11.96.
Ev'n *Sunday* shines no *Sabbath-day* to me: ....4.Arbu.12.96.
"Informs you Sir, 'twas when he knew no better. ....4.Arbu.52.100.
The Play'rs and I are, luckily, no friends. ....4.Arbu.60.100.
Sir, let me see your works and you no more. ....4.Arbu.68.100.
Cibber and I are, luckily, no friends. ....4.Arbu.60A.100.
No creature smarts so little as a Fool. ....4.Arbu.84.101.
"No Names—be calm—learn Prudence of a Friend: ....4.Arbu.102.103.
I left no Calling for this idle trade, ...4.Arbu.129.105.
No Duty broke, no Father dis-obey'd. ....4.Arbu.130.105.
No Duty broke, no Father dis-obey'd. ....4.Arbu.130.105.
I wag'd no war with *Bedlam* or the *Mint.* ....4.Arbu.156.107.
Bear, like the *Turk,* no brother near the throne, ...4.Arbu.198.110.
I sought no homage from the Race that write; ....4.Arbu.219.111.
No more than Thou, great GEORGE! a Birth-day Song. ....4.Arbu.222.112.
Has Life no Joys for me? or (to be grave) ....4.Arbu.273.115.
Have I no Friend to serve, no Soul to save? ....4.Arbu.274.115.
Have I no Friend to serve, no Soul to save? ....4.Arbu.274.115.
"I found him close with *Swift*"—"*Indeed?* no doubt" ....4.Arbu.275.115.
"No, such a Genius never can lye still," ....4.Arbu.278.115.
A Lash like mine no honest man shall dread, ...4.Arbu.303.117.

NO (CONTINUED)

That harmless Mother thought no Wife a Whore,— ....4.Arbu.384.126.
Born to no Pride, inheriting no Strife, ...4.Arbu.392.126.
Born to no Pride, inheriting no Strife, ...4.Arbu.392.126.
No Courts he saw, no Suits would ever try, ...4.Arbu.396.126.
No Courts he saw, no Suits would ever try, ...4.Arbu.396.126.
Un-learn'd, he knew no Schoolman's subtle Art, ...4.Arbu.398.126.
No Language, but the Language of the Heart. ....4.Arbu.399.126.
Be no unpleasing Melancholy mine: ....4.Arbu.407.127.
No Commentat more dextrously can pass ....4.JD2A.104.140.
And yet no new built Palaces aspire, ...4.JD2A.117.142.
And hopes no captious Fools will wrest my sense ....4.JD2A.132.144.
It brought (no doubt) th' *Excise* and *Army* in: ....4.JD2.8.133.
One sings the Fair; but Songs no longer move, ...4.JD2.21.133.
No Rat is rhym'd to death, nor Maid to love: ....4.JD2.22.133.
'Tis chang'd no doubt from what it was before, ...4.JD2.31.135.
His rank digestion makes it wit no more: ....4.JD2.32.135.
Sense, past thro' him, no longer is the same, ...4.JD2.33.135.
Of whose strange crimes no Canonist can tell ....4.JD2.43.135.
No young Divine, new-benefic'd, can be ....4.JD2.51.137.
No Commentator can more slily pass ....4.JD2.101.141.
We see no new-built Palaces aspire, ...4.JD2.111.143.
No Kitchens emulate the Vestal Fire. ....4.JD2.112.143.
Extremely fine, but what no man will wear. ....4.JD2.124.145.
Let no Court-Sycophant pervert my sense, ...4.JD2.126.145.
No sly Informer watch these words to draw ....4.JD2.127.145.
Like those of Witchcraft now can work no harms: ....4.JD2A.24.134.
His rank Digestion makes it Wit no more. ....4.JD2A.36.134.
And whose strange Sins no Canonist can tell, ...4.JD2A.47.136.
To no more purpose, than when pris'ners swear ....4.JD2A.78.138.
Ah sound no more thy soft alarms, ...4.HOde1.5.151.
Spare me, ah Spare! no more the man ....4.HOde1.3A.151.
Ah sound no more your soft alarms, ...4.HOde1.5A.151.
Ah sound no more the soft alarms, ...4.HOde1.5B.151.
For me, the vernal Garlands bloom no more. ....4.HOde1.32.153.
They had no Poet and they dyd! ....4.HOde9.14.159.
They had no Poet and are dead! ....4.HOde9.16.159.
(Its Name I know not, and it's no great matter) ....4.2HE2.45.167.
Indebted to no Prince or Peer alive, ...4.2HE2.69.169.
No Poets there, but *Stephen,* you, and me. ....4.2HE2.140.175.
But show no mercy to an empty line; ....4.2HE2.175.177.
A worthy Member, no small Fool, a Lord; ....4.2HE2.185.177.
To Rules of Poetry no more confin'd, ...4.2HE2.202.179.
But sure no Statute in his favour says, ...4.2HE2.288.185.
But does no other lord it at this hour, ...4.2HE2.306.187.
Has Life no sourness, drawn so near its end? ....4.2HE2.316.187.
One likes no language but the Faery Queen; ....4.2HE1.39.197.
"Who lasts a Century can have no flaw, ...4.2HE1.55.199.
You'd think no Fools disgrac'd the former Reign, ...4.2HE1.127.205.
No wonder then, when all was Love and Sport, ...4.2HE1.151.209.
And promise our best Friends to ryme no more; ....4.2HE1.178.209.
And knows no losses while the Muse is kind. ....4.2HE1.196.211.
And (tho' no Soldier) useful to the State. ....4.2HE1.204.211.
No whiter page than Addison remains. ....4.2HE1.216.213.
"No Lord's anointed, but a Russian Bear." ....4.2HE1.389.229.
[Plain Truth, dear MURRAY, needs no flow'rs of speech, ...4.1HE6.3.237.
Shall be no more than TULLY, or than HYDE! ....4.1HE6.53.241.
"Send for him up, take no excuse. ....4.HS6.36.253.
No matter where the money's found; ....4.HS6.40.253.
"'Tis now no secret—I protest ....4.HS6.118.257.
I know no more than my Lord Mayor, ...4.HS6.122.257.
Here no man prates of idle things, ...4.HS6.141.259.
Yet to his Guest tho' no way sparing, ...4.HS6.169.261.
No sooner said, but from the Hall ....4.HS6.212.263.
For your damn'd Stucco has no chink) ....4.HS6.219.263.
"The Dog-days are no more the case." ....4.1HE7.15.269.
"No Sir, you'll leave them to the *Hogs.*" ....4.1HE7.28.271.
I'm no such Beast, nor his Relation; ....4.1HE7.60.273.
There dy'd my Father, no man's Debtor, ...4.1HE7.79.273.
Sworn to no Master, of no Sect am I: ....4.1HE1.24.281.
Sworn to no Master, of no Sect am I: ....4.1HE1.24.281.
Which done, the poorest can no wants endure, ...4.1HE1.45.281.
And the first Wisdom, to be Fool no more. ....4.1HE1.66.283.
But to the world, no bugbear is so great, ...4.1HE1.67.283.
True, conscious Honour is to feel no sin, ...4.1HE1.93.285.
"No place on earth (he cry'd) like Greenwich hill!" ....4.1HE1.139.289.
But when no Prelate's Lawn with Hair-shirt lin'd, ...4.1HE1.165.291.
Bubo observes, he lash'd no sort of *Vice:* ....4.EpS1.12.298.
Patriots there are, who wish you'd jest no more— ....4.EpS1.24.299.
Come, come, at all I laugh He laughs, no doubt, ...4.EpS1.35.300.
He thinks one Poet of no venal kind. ....4.EpS1.34A.300.
Come harmless *Characters* that no one hit, ...4.EpS1.65.302.
So—Satire is no more—I feel it die— ....4.EpS1.83.304.
No *Gazeteer* more innocent than I! ....4.EpS1.84.305.
There, where no Passion, Pride, or Shame transport, ...4.EpS1.97.305.
There, where no Father's, Brother's, Friend's Disgrace ....4.EpS1.99.305.
No Cheek is known to blush, no Heart to throb, ...4.EpS1.103.305.
No Cheek is known to blush, no Heart to throb, ...4.EpS1.103.305.
Let *Greatness* own her, and she's mean no more: ....4.EpS1.144.309.
'Tis Av'rice all, Ambition is no more! ....4.EpS1.162.309.
Fr. A Dean, Sir? no: his Fortune is not made, ...4.EpS2.34.314.
Arraign no mightier Thief than wretched *Wild,* ....4.EpS2.39.315.
Speak out, and bid me blame no Rogues at all. ....4.EpS2.53.315.
Still let me say! No Follower, but a Friend. ....4.EpS2.93.318.
No Pow'r the Muse's Friendship can command; ....4.EpS2.118.320.
No Pow'r, when Virtue claims it, can withstand: ....4.EpS2.119.320.
—What are you thinking? *Fr.* Faith, the thought's no Sin, ...4.EpS2.122.320.
Then wisely plead, to me they meant no hurt, ...4.EpS2.144.321.
Sure, if I spare the Minister, no rules ....4.EpS2.146.321.
And must no Egg in *Japhet's* Face be thrown, ...4.EpS2.189.324.
No zealous Pastor blame a failing Spouse, ...4.EpS2.193.324.
Fr. You're strangely proud. *P.* So proud I am no Slave: ....4.EpS2.205.324.
So impudent, I own myself no Knave: ....4.EpS2.206.324.
And damns the market where he takes no gold. ....4.1740.12.332.
No more than of Sir Har[r]y or Sir P[aul]. ....4.1740.20.333*.
Tho' still he travels on no bad pretence, ...4.1740.51.334.

NO (CONTINUED)

Let him no trifler from his school, ...4.1740.87.337.
Affect no conquest, but endure no wrong. ....4.1740.94.337.
Affect no conquest, but endure no wrong. ....4.1740.94.337.
Fierce champion Fortitude, that knows no fears ....5.DunA1.45.65.
Plung'd for his sense, but found no bottom there; ....5.DunA1.113.77.
How Index-learning turns no student pale, ...5.DunA1.233.90.
Safe, where no criticks damn, no duns molest, ...5.DunA1.249.92.
Safe, where no criticks damn, no duns molest, ...5.DunA1.249.92.
I see! I see!—" Then rapt, she spoke no more. ....5.DunA1.255.94.
No meagre, muse-rid mope, adust and thin, ...5.DunA2.33.100.
But such a bulk as no twelve bards could raise, ...5.DunA2.35.100.
No rag, no scrap, of all the beau, or wit, ...5.DunA2.111.110.
No rag, no scrap, of all the beau, or wit, ...5.DunA2.111.110.
(Sure sign, that no spectator shall be drown'd). ....5.DunA2.166.121.
The King of Dykes! than whom, no sluice of mud ....5.DunA2.261.133.
The quaking mud, that clos'd, and ope'd no more. ....5.DunA2.280.136.
He bears no token of the sabler streams, ...5.DunA2.285.137.
No noise, no stir, no motion can'st thou make, ...5.DunA2.291.138.
No noise, no stir, no motion can'st thou make, ...5.DunA2.291.138.
No noise, no stir, no motion can'st thou make, ...5.DunA2.291.138.
No crab more active in the dirty dance, ...5.DunA2.297.139.
Yet silent bow'd to Christ's No kingdom here. ....5.DunA2.368.145.
"Lo Rome herself, proud mistress now no more ....5.DunA3.93.158.
No fiercer sons, had Easter never been. ....5.DunA3.110.159.
Embrace, embrace my Sons! be foes no more! ....5.DunA3.171.167.
And prove, no Miracles can match thy own. ....5.DunA3.210.175.
Till Birch shall blush with noble blood no more, ...5.DunA3.330.191.
Shrinks to her hidden cause, and is no more: ....5.DunA3.350.193.
No more the Monarch could such raptures bear; ....5.DunA3.357A.193.
Fierce champion Fortitude, that knows no fears ....5.DunB1.47.274.
Plung'd for his sense, but found no bottom there, ...5.DunB1.119.278.
Ev'n Ralph repents, and Henly writes no more. ....5.DunB1.216.285.
Ev'n Ralph is lost, and Henly writes no more. ....5.DunB1.216A.285.
No merit now the dear Nonjuror claims, ...5.DunB1.253.289.
How Index-learning turns no student pale, ...5.DunB1.279.290.
Know, Eusden thirsts no more for sack or praise; ....5.DunB1.293.291.
Safe, where no Critics damn, no duns molest, ...5.DunB1.295.291.
Safe, where no Critics damn, no duns molest, ...5.DunB1.295.291.
No meagre, muse-rid mope, adust and thin, ...5.DunB2.37.297.
But such a bulk as no twelve bards could raise, ...5.DunB2.39.298.
No rag, no scrap, of all the beau, or wit, ...5.DunB2.119.301.
No rag, no scrap, of all the beau, or wit, ...5.DunB2.119.301.
(Sure sign, that no spectator shall be drown'd) ....5.DunB2.174.304.
The King of dykes! than whom no sluice of mud ....5.DunB2.273.309.
The quaking mud, that clos'd, and op'd no more. ....5.DunB2.292.310.
He bears no token of the sabler streams, ...5.DunB2.297.310.
No noise, no stir, no motion can'st thou make, ...5.DunB2.303.310.
No noise, no stir, no motion can'st thou make, ...5.DunB2.303.310.
No noise, no stir, no motion can'st thou make, ...5.DunB2.303.310.
"These are, —ah no! these were, the Gazetteers!" ....5.DunB2.314.311.
No crab more active in the dirty dance, ...5.DunB2.319.312.
Yet silent bow'd to Christ's No kingdom here. ....5.DunB2.400.316.
Morgan and Mandevil could prate no more; ....5.DunB2.414.317.
(Once swan of Thames, tho' now he sings no more.) ....5.DunB3.20.321.
"Lo! Rome herself, proud mistress now no more ....5.DunB3.101.324.
No fiercer sons, had Easter never been. ....5.DunB3.118.325.
Embrace, embrace my sons! be foes no more! ....5.DunB3.177.329.
'Till Birch shall blush with noble blood no more, ...5.DunB3.334.336.
Arrest him, Empress; or you sleep no more"— ....5.DunB4.69.348.
Whate'er of mungril no one class admits, ...5.DunB4.89.349.
Nor absent they, no members of her state, ...5.DunB4.91.349.
"What! no respect, he cry'd, for Shakespear's page?" ....5.DunB4.114A.352.
There TALBOT sunk, and was a Wit no more! ....5.DunB4.168.357.
Or Tyber, now no longer Roman, rolls, ...5.DunB4.299.373.
Spoil'd his own language, and acquir'd no more; ....5.DunB4.320.374.
Left his own language, and acquir'd no more; ....5.DunB4.320A.374.
No cause, no Trust, no Duty, and no Friend. ....5.DunB4.340.376.
No cause, no Trust, no Duty, and no Friend. ....5.DunB4.340.376.
No cause, no Trust, no Duty, and no Friend. ....5.DunB4.340.376.
No cause, no Trust, no Duty, and no Friend. ....5.DunB4.340.376.
No Maid cries, charming! and no Youth, divine! ....5.DunB4.414.382.
No Maid cries, charming! and no Youth, divine! ....5.DunB4.414.382.
Dismiss my soul, where no Carnation fades." ....5.DunB4.418.382.
All-seeing in thy mists, we want no guide, ...5.DunB4.469.386.
And strait succeeded, leaving shame no room, ...5.DunB4.531.394.
Which no one looks in with another's eyes: ....5.DunB4.534.394.
No more, alas! the voice of Fame they hear, ...5.DunB4.543.395.
Shrinks to her second cause, and is no more. ....5.DunB4.644.408.
Taught by your hand, can charm no less than he; ....6.3.10.7.
For here no frowns make tender love afraid, ...6.4ii.3.9.
No sweets but *Serenissa's* sighs. ....6.4v.4.11.
And the bright sun admire no more; ....6.6i.2.13.
The god of love himself's no more: ....6.6i.10.14.
What tho' no Bees around your Cradle flew, ...6.7.5.15.
Wit, past thro' thee, no longer is the same, ...6.7.11.16.
Since no Reprizals can be made on thee. ....6.7.14.16.
This needless Labour, and contend no more, ...6.7.22.16.
Faith 'tis not five; no Play's begun; ....6.10.3.24.
No Game at *Ombre* lost or won. ....6.10.4.24.
To *Brocas's* Lays no more you listen ....6.10.21.25.
Beware; your Heart's no *Salamander!* ....6.10.54.26.
You have no Cause to take Offence, Sir, ...6.10.101.27.
Intestine War no more our *Passions* wage, ...6.11.34.31.
Passions no more the Soul engage, ...6.11.34A.31.
No Crime was thine, if 'tis no Crime to love. ....6.11.96.33.
No Crime was thine, if 'tis no Crime to love. ....6.11.96.33.
Of *Orpheus* now no more let Poets tell, ...6.11.131.34.
She wears no Colours (sign of Grace) ....6.14v(a).13.49.
No Pains it takes, and no Offence it gives, ...6.16.5.53.
No Pains it takes, and no Offence it gives, ...6.16.5.53.
As 'tis at last the Cause they write no more; ....6.16.10.53.
Sees no foul Discords at their Banquets bred, ...6.17iii.36.58.
Still with Esteem no less convers'd than read; ....6.19.7.62.
She sighs, and is no *Dutchess* at her Heart. ....6.19.56.63.
No matter for the Rules of Time and Place: ....6.19.28A.63.

NO (CONTINUED)

No chains I felt, but went a glorious ghost, ...6.20.17.66.
No guilt of mine the rage of Heav'n cou'd move; ....6.20.60.67.
I knew no crime, if 'tis no crime to love. ....6.20.61.67.
I knew no crime, if 'tis no crime to love. ....6.20.61.67.
By day no perils shall the just affright, ...6.21.11.69.
No dismal dreams or groaning ghosts by night. ....6.21.12.69.
No harms can reach thee, and no force shall move. ....6.21.22.69.
No harms can reach thee, and no force shall move. ....6.21.22.69.
Believe, believe the treach'rous world no more. ....6.22.2.71.
The world no longer trembles at their pow'r! ....6.22.15.71.
My *Pylades!* what *Juv'nal* says, no Jest is; ....6.24iii(b).1.76.
Look on this marble, and be vain no more! ....6.27.17.81.
Now *Europe's* balanc'd, and no Side prevails, ...6.28.1A.82.
To have no Place in this was hard: ....6.30.14.86.
So hop'd to stand no less than he ....6.30.17.86.
Than be no Part in *Tom D'Urfy.* ....6.30.26.86.
Than be no Part of *Tom* D'Urfey. ....6.30.26A.86.
No less than *Pythagorick Y,* ....6.30.73.88.
Letters, you swear, no more you'l be ....6.30.62A.88.
Must thou no more this Frame inspire? ....6.31i.3.93.
No more a pleasing, chearful Guest? ....6.31i.4.93.
And Wit and Humour are no more! ....6.31i.8.93.
Tyrants no more their savage nature kept, ...6.32.7.96.
No common object to your sight displays, ...6.32.19.96.
No guard but virtue, no redress but tears. ....6.38.18.108.
No guard but virtue, no redress but tears. ....6.38.18.108.
Stern *Cato's* self was no relentless spouse: ....6.41.30.114.
To your Friends who at least have no Cares but to please you .6.42iii.5.117.
One day it will be no disgrace, ...6.42v.5.119.
And cite those Sapphoes wee admire no more; ....6.43.2.120.
But shines himselfe till they are seen no more. ....6.43.12.120.
And shines himselfe till they are seen no more. ....6.43.12A.121.
Was he discouragd? no such matter; ....6.44.3.123.
From *French?* He scornd it; no, from *Greek.* ....6.44.8.123.
And hear a spark, yet think no danger nigh; ....6.45.4.124.
Then gives a smacking buss, and cries—No words! ....6.45.26.125.
Thy Fools no more I'll teize: ....6.47.2.128.
When I no Favour seek? ....6.47.34.129.
When *Barnivelt* no Faction lets alone. ....6.48ii.6.134.
Bear, like the Turk, no Brother near the Throne; ....6.49iii.12.143.
Bear, like the Turk, no Brother on the Throne; ....6.49iii.12A.143.
Bear, like the Turk, no Brother to the Throne; ....6.49iii.12B.143.
Or bid the furious *Gaul* be rude no more? ....6.51i.16.151.
This, from no venal or ungrateful Muse. ....6.52.2.156.
Then view this marble, and be vain no more! ....6.52.54.157.
Some few short Years, no more! ....6.53.38.162.
No wicked Whores shall have such Luck ....6.54.13.165.
Poor *Ovid* finds no Quarter! ....6.58.42.172.
From no trim Beau's its Name it boasts, ...6.59.5.177.
Since some have writ, and shewn no Wit at all. ....6.60.8.178.
We take no Measure of your Fops and Beaus; ....6.60.26.178.
Let no One Fool engross it, or confine: ....6.60.31.179.
Let no One Man engross it, or confine: ....6.60.31A.179.
And Wit and Love no Sin, ...6.61.4.180.
And Love and Wit no Sin, ...6.61.4A.180.
You may meet the *Two Champions* who are no Lord *S[herrar]d* ....6.62v.2.186.
For writing? no,—for writing not. ....6.62vi.2.186.
You may meet your *Two Champions* who are no Lord Sherrards. ....6.62v.2A.186.
No, trust the Sex's sacred Rule; ....6.64.21.190.
Meerly because it is no Plain; ....6.67.16.195.
no Stick to beat him— ....6.68.12.196.
Live well and fear no sudden fate; ....6.69ii.5.199.
'Tis, (no 'tisn't) like Miss *Meadows.* ....6.70.5.201.
Their ruins ruin'd, and their place no more! ....6.71.22.203.
Their ruins perish'd, and their place no more! ....6.71.22A.203.
Can taste no pleasure since his Shield was scour'd; ....6.71.42.204.
"Who broke no promise, serv'd no private end, ...6.71.69.204.
"Who broke no promise, serv'd no private end, ...6.71.69.204.
"Who gain'd no title, and who lost no friend, ...6.71.70.204.
"Who gain'd no title, and who lost no friend, ...6.71.70.204.
And boasts a Warmth that from no Passion flows; ....6.73.4.209.
They'll fit no Man alive. ....6.77.8.214.
They'll serve no Man alive. ....6.77.8A.214.
No Sleep to Toil so easing ....6.78i.7B.215.
This sad Decree, no Joy shall last. ....6.78ii.2.216.
For why? he deem'd no Man his Mate, ...6.79.27.218.
No Vixen Civet-Cat so sweet, ...6.79.31.218.
For why? he thought no Man his Mate, ...6.79.27A.218.
No Vixen Civet-Cat more sweet, ...6.79.31A.218.
And having no Friend left but this, ...6.79.43.219.
Ah no, ah no, the guileless *Guise* ....6.79.49.219.
Ah no, ah no, the guileless *Guise* ....6.79.49.219.
"No *Sheet* is here to save thee: ....6.79.78.220.
"No not to-morrow, but to night ....6.79.103.221.
For you well know, that Wit's of no Religion. ....6.82iii.2.230.
And ill can bear no living near the Throne. ....6.82ix(a).2A.234.
Wit has its Bigotts, who can bear no jest; ....6.82ix(b).1B.234.
They praise no works but what are like their own ....6.82ix(f).4.235.
(No Hireling she, no Prostitute to Praise) ....6.84.36.240.
(No Hireling she, no Prostitute to Praise) ....6.84.36.240.
Ah, no! 'tis vain to strive—It will not be. ....6.85.9Z1.242.
No Grief, that can be told, is felt for 'thee. ....6.85.9Z2.242.
Fair to no Purpose, artful to no End, ...6.86.7A.245.
Fair to no Purpose, artful to no End, ...6.86.7A.245.
"Has she no Faults then (Envy says) Sir?" ....6.89.9.250.
"Has she no Faults then (Envy says)?" ....6.89.9A.250.
Put no water at all; ....6.91.17.253.
Morning from Noon there was no knowing, ...6.93.11.257.
No Doctor like a FERRET. ....6.94.20.259.
No *British* Miss sincerer Grief has known, ...6.96ii.3.270.
She dragg'd the Cruet, but no *Grildrig* found. ....6.96ii.24.270.
"And shall I set thee on my Hand no more, ...6.96ii.61.273.
"No more behold thee turn my Watches Key, ...6.96ii.65.273.

NO (CONTINUED)

Have ye no Griefs at Home, to fix ye there? .... Il.24.297.549.
No, you must feel him too; your selves must fall; .... Il.24.301.549.
From me, no Harm shall touch thy rev'rend Head; .... Il.24.456.555.
Majestical in Death! No Stains are found .... Il.24.511.557.
Thou ow'st thy Guidance to no mortal Hand: .... Il.24.564.559.
No Comfort to my Griefs, no Hopes remain, ... Il.24.612.562.
No Comfort to my Griefs, no Hopes remain, ... Il.24.612.562.
No Race succeeding to imperial Sway: .... Il.24.678.565.
His Corse, and take the Gifts: I ask no more. .... Il.24.700.566.
Move me no more (*Achilles* thus replies .... Il.24.705.566.
No human Hand the weighty Gates unbarr'd, ... Il.24.713.567.
And shake the Purpose of my Soul no more. .... Il.24.719.567.
No less the royal Guest the Hero eyes, ... Il.24.798.570.
This felt no Chains, but went a glorious Ghost .... Il.24.948.575.
No mark of Pain, or Violence of Face; .... Il.24.955.576.
Sad *Helen* has no Friend now thou art gone! .... Il.24.978.576.
To me, no Seer, th' inspiring Gods suggest; .... Od.1.260.45.
No longer live the cankers of my court; .... Od.1.477.55.
Speak him descended of no vulgar race: .... Od.1.518.57.
No more my Sire will glad these longing eyes: .... Od.1.522.57.
Stretch'd on the downy fleece, no rest he knows, ... Od.1.557.58.
No story I unfold of public woes, ... Od.2.49.62.
"Tho' cold in death *Ulysses* breathes no more, ... Od.2.107.66.
For lo! my words no fancy'd woes relate: .... Od.2.197.71.
Then would that busy head no broils suggest, ... Od.2.215.72.
Ah! no such hope (the Prince with sighs replies) .... Od.3.279.99.
Mentor, no more—the mournful thought forbear; .... Od.3.298.100.
For he no more must draw his country's breath, ... Od.3.299.100.
Then Virtue was no more (her guard away) .... Od.3.344.103.
No—long as life this mortal shall inspire, ... Od.3.451.109.
No vulgar manhood, no ignoble age. .... Od.3.483.111.
No vulgar manhood, no ignoble age. .... Od.3.483.111.
No peril in my cause he ceas'd to prove, ... Od.4.137.126.
No fame reveals; but doubtful of his doom, ... Od.4.143.127.
No *Greek* an equal space had e'er possest .... Od.4.231.130.
No vows had we prefer'd, nor victim slain! .... Od.4.475.142.
From the bleak pole no winds inclement blow, ... Od.4.771.155.
Ulysses let no partial favours fall, ... Od.4.920.161.
Let Kings no more with gentle mercy sway, ... Od.5.14.171.
For now the soft Enchantress pleas'd no more: .... Od.5.196.181.
No more in sorrows languish life away: .... Od.5.208.181.
No form'd design, no meditated end .... Od.5.241.183.
No form'd design, no meditated end .... Od.5.241.183.
No, if this sceptre yet commands the main. .... Od.5.374.190.
Where Fate has destin'd he shall toil no more. .... Od.5.495.196.
No port receives me from the angry main, ... Od.5.526.197.
No footing sure affords the faithless sand, ... Od.5.530.198.
He dropt his sinewy arms: his knees no more .... Od.5.581.200.
There no rude winds presume to shake the skies, ... Od.6.51.207.
No rains descend, no snowy vapours rise; .... Od.6.52.207.
No rains descend, no snowy vapours rise; .... Od.6.52.207.
No less a terror, from the neighb'ring groves .... Od.6.161.216.
'Tis mine to bid the wretched grieve no more, ... Od.6.234.221.
To them the King. No longer I detain .... Od.6.257.222.
No bird so light, no thought so swift as they. .... Od.7.48.235.
No bird so light, no thought so swift as they. .... Od.7.48.235.
No son surviv'd; *Arete* heir'd his state, ... Od.7.84.237.
With that the Goddess deign'd no longer stay, ... Od.7.99.238.
To you, the thoughts of no inhuman heart. .... Od.7.247.248.
Let no such thought (with modest grace rejoin'd .... Od.7.281.249.
No glorious native of yon azure sky: .... Od.7.284.250.
Where thy soul rests, and labour is no more. .... Od.7.410.257.
Thus he. No word th' experienc'd man replies, ... Od.7.421.258.
(Retorts *Euryalus:)* He boasts no claim .... Od.8.177.271.
Yet thus by woes impair'd, no more I wa<i>ve .... Od.8.207.273.
To whom appeas'd: No more I urge delay; .... Od.8.391.285.
No helm secures their course, no pilot guides, ... Od.8.605.295.
No helm secures their course, no pilot guides, ... Od.8.605.295.
Behold *Ulysses!* no ignoble name, ... Od.9.19.301.
Or, the charm tasted, had return'd no more. .... Od.9.114.308.
By these no statutes and no rights are known, ... Od.9.127.310.
By these no statutes and no rights are known, ... Od.9.127.310.
No council held, no Monarch fills the throne, ... Od.9.128.310.
No council held, no Monarch fills the throne, ... Od.9.128.310.
No needy mortals here, with hunger bold, ... Od.9.137.311.
For there no vessel with vermilion prore, ... Od.9.145.311.
No mortal forces from the lofty gate .... Od.9.361.321.
"If no man hurt thee, but the hand divine .... Od.9.487.326.
No ease, no pleasure my sad heart receives, ... Od.9.541.328.
No ease, no pleasure my sad heart receives, ... Od.9.541.328.
No sooner freed, and thro' th' enclosure past, ... Od.9.545.328.
'Twas on no coward, no ignoble slave, ... Od.9.559.329.
'Twas on no coward, no ignoble slave, ... Od.9.559.329.
Th' immortal father no less boasts the son. .... Od.9.608.331.
But mourn in vain; no prospect of return. .... Od.10.90.343.
No tracks of beasts, or signs of men we found, ... Od.10.113.346.
No more was seen the human form divine, ... Od.10.278.356.
Swear, in thy soul no latent frauds remain, ... Od.10.409.364.
Divine *Ulysses!* asks no mortal guide. .... Od.10.599.372.
Or if no more her absent Lord she wails, ... Od.11.216.392.
No costly carpets raise his hoary head, ... Od.11.228.393.
No rich embroid'ry shines to grace his bed: .... Od.11.229.393.
No dire disease bereav'd me of my breath; .... Od.11.244.393.
No more the substance of the man remains, ... Od.11.263.394.
Hail happy nymph! no vulgar births are ow'd .... Od.11.297.396.
Is bent, all hell contains no fouler fiend: .... Od.11.532.409.
But sure the eye of Time beholds no name .... Od.11.591.412.
No circumstance the voice of fame relates; .... Od.11.616.414.
To *Troy* no Hero came of nobler line, ... Od.11.637.416.
No more my heart the dismal din sustains, ... Od.11.783.425.
No more that wretch shall view the joys of life, ... Od.12.55.432.
No bird of air, no dove of swiftest wing, ... Od.12.75.435.
No bird of air, no dove of swiftest wing, ... Od.12.75.435.
No more the vessel plow'd the dreadful wave, ... Od.12.244.443.
In vain they call! those arms are stretch'd no more. .... Od.12.299.446.

NO (CONTINUED)

'Till now from sea or flood no succour found, ... Od.12.393.450.
No longer now from shore to shore to roam, ... Od.13.7.2.
Shall then no more, O Sire of Gods! be mine .... Od.13.148.12.
No more unlicens'd thus to brave the main. .... Od.13.175.14.
No more unlicens'd brave the deeps, no more .... Od.13.208.15.
No more unlicens'd brave the deeps, no more .... Od.13.208.15.
The rugged soil allows no level space .... Od.13.289.19.
No less than mortals are surpass'd by thine. .... Od.13.341.24.
But these, no doubt, some oracle explore, ... Od.14.111.41.
That tells, the great *Ulysses* is no more. .... Od.14.112.41.
To Fame no stranger, nor perhaps to me; .... Od.14.143.42.
'Till his return, no title shall I plead, ... Od.14.178.44.
And mark the ruins of no vulgar man. .... Od.14.250.48.
No more—th' approaching hours of silent night .... Od.14.449.57.
Thy lips let fall no idle word or vain: .... Od.14.577.64.
No change of garments to our hinds is known: .... Od.14.582.65.
No—sooner far their riot and their lust .... Od.15.37.71.
No Prince will let *Ulysses'* heir remove .... Od.15.95.73.
No friend in *Ithaca* my place supplies, ... Od.15.102.73.
No pow'rful hands are there, no watchful eyes: .... Od.15.103.73.
No pow'rful hands are there, no watchful eyes: .... Od.15.103.73.
And chose the largest; with no vulgar art .... Od.15.120.74.
No farther from our vessel, I implore, ... Od.15.224.79.
Brooks no repulse, nor cou'dst thou soon depart: .... Od.15.237.79.
Declare sincerely to no foe's demand .... Od.15.286.82.
Stay then: no eye askance beholds thee here; .... Od.15.354.86.
No profit springs beneath usurping pow'rs; .... Od.15.404.89.
No want, no famine the glad natives know, ... Od.15.446.92.
No want, no famine the glad natives know, ... Od.15.446.92.
The sev'nth, the fraudful wretch (no cause descry'd) .... Od.15.513.95.
Torn from thy country to no hapless end, ... Od.15.526.95.
No other roof a stranger shou'd receive, ... Od.15.553.96.
No—let *Eurymachus* receive my guest, ... Od.15.559.96.
No race but thine shall *Ithaca* obey, ... Od.15.575.98.
Ah me! I boast no brother; heav'n's dread King .... Od.16.123.108.
Wild springs the vine, no more the garden blows. .... Od.16.155.110.
Thou art not—no, thou can'st not be my sire. .... Od.16.215.114.
With grace divine; her pow'r admits no bounds: .... Od.16.229.114.
No—by the righteous pow'rs of heav'n I swear, ... Od.16.456.129.
Then fear no mortal arm: If heav'n destroy, ... Od.16.462.129.
No father, with a fonder grasp of joy, ... Od.17.128.138.
No sailors there, no vessels to convey, ... Od.17.166.139.
No sailors there, no vessels to convey, ... Od.17.166.139.
This told *Atrides,* and he told no more. .... Od.17.168.139.
Now let us speed; my friend, no more my guest! .... Od.17.208.141.
To no brave prize aspir'd the worthless swain, ... Od.17.258.144.
(Reply'd the Chief) to no unheedful breast; .... Od.17.333.147.
The bravely-patient to no fortune yields: .... Od.17.336.147.
His bulk and beauty speak no vulgar praise; .... Od.17.370.150.
Him no fell Savage on the plain withstood, ... Od.17.382.150.
To him *Telemachus.* No more incense .... Od.17.476.156.
Nourish'd deep anguish, tho' he shed no tear; .... Od.17.583.161.
Proud as thou art, henceforth no more be proud, ... Od.18.28.168.
Irus alas! shall *Irus* be no more, ... Od.18.82.170.
No more I bathe, since he no longer sees .... Od.18.211.177.
No more I bathe, since he no longer sees .... Od.18.211.177.
O why, my son, why now no more appears .... Od.18.255.179.
Thy riper days no growing worth impart, ... Od.18.257.179.
But now no crime is theirs: this wrong proceeds .... Od.18.275.179.
Ulysses sail'd, then beauty was no more! .... Od.18.294.180.
The Gods decreed these eyes no more should keep .... Od.18.295.180.
No longer durst sustain the sovereign look. .... Od.18.390.186.
Some God no doubt this strange kindly sends; .... Od.18.400.187.
No, thy ill-judging thoughts the brave disgrace; .... Od.18.422.189.
I cheer no lazy vagrants with repast; .... Od.19.31.194.
Receive no stranger-guest, no poor relieve; .... Od.19.158.200.
Receive no stranger-guest, no poor relieve; .... Od.19.158.200.
"Where dead *Ulysses* claims no future part; .... Od.19.163.200.
From nuptial rites they now no more recede, ... Od.19.178.200.
No poor un-father'd product of disgrace. .... Od.19.187.200.
Breathes in no distant clime the vital air: .... Od.19.308.209.
My Lord's return shou'd fate no more retard, ... Od.19.356.211.
No ceas'd discourse (the banquet of the soul) .... Od.19.494.220.
O Queen! no vulgar vision of the sky .... Od.19.641.227.
On this poor breast no dawn of bliss shall beam; .... Od.19.680.229.
Tempest of wrath his soul no longer tost; .... Od.20.30.233.
No truce the warfare of my heart suspends! .... Od.20.101.237.
No conscious blush, no sense of right restrains .... Od.20.213.243.
No conscious blush, no sense of right restrains .... Od.20.213.243.
No vulgar roof protects thy honour'd age; .... Od.20.329.249.
No more ye lewd Compeers, with lawless pow'r .... Od.20.378.251.
No clouds of error dim th' etherial rays, ... Od.20.439.254.
Dear sell the slaves! demand no greater gain. .... Od.20.458.255.
Their first, last pledges! for they met no more. .... Od.21.36.261.
No vulgar task! Ill suits this courtly crew .... Od.21.94.263.
No more excuses then, no more delay; .... Od.21.115.264.
No more excuses then, no more delay; .... Od.21.115.264.
Then if no happy'r Knight the conquest boast, ... Od.21.119.264.
Take it who will, he cries, I strive no more. .... Od.21.160.267.
Tears follow'd tears; no word was in their pow'r, ... Od.21.236.271.
Not so, *Eurymachus:* That no man draws .... Od.21.272.273.
Mov'd by no weak surmize, but sense of shame, ... Od.21.347.276.
Wrong and oppression no renown can raise; .... Od.21.359.277.
Speak him descended from no vulgar race. .... Od.21.362.277.
A son's just right. No *Grecian* Prince but I .... Od.21.371.277.
Each look'd for arms in vain; no arms were nigh: .... Od.22.30.288.
Dogs, ye have had your day; ye fear'd no more .... Od.22.41.288.
And this bold Archer soon shall shoot no more. .... Od.22.151.294.
No so (reply'd *Ulysses)* leave him there, ... Od.22.184.296.
The hour is come, when yon' fierce man no more .... Od.22.272.299.
No help, no flight; but wounded ev'ry way, ... Od.22.341.304.
No help, no flight; but wounded ev'ry way, ... Od.22.341.304.
Whence no contending foot could reach the ground. .... Od.22.502.313.
Ulysses comes! The Suitors are no more! .... Od.23.8.319.
No more they view the golden light of day; .... Od.23.9.319.

NO (CONTINUED)
Ah no! with sighs *Penelope* rejoyn'd, ...Od.23.59.321.
Ah no! some God the Suitors deaths decreed, ...Od.23.63.321.
Never! the lov'd *Ulysses* is no more! ....Od.23.70.322.
Thus speaks the Queen, and no reply attends, ...Od.23.87.323.
Stubborn the breast that with no transport glows, ...Od.23.103.324.
No more.—This day our deepest care requires, ...Od.23.117.326.
Thus they—but nobly chaste she weds no more. ....Od.23.148.328.
Ah no! she cries, a tender heart I bear, ...Od.23.175.329.
A foe to pride: no adamant is there; ....Od.23.176.329.
Since what no eye has seen thy tongue reveal'd, ...Od.23.245.335.
Ajax, and great *Achilles,* are no more! ....Od.24.24.348.
Where dead *Ulysses* claims no more a part, ...Od.24.155.355.
No friend to bathe our wounds! or tears to shed ....Od.24.216.358.
The much-enduring man could bear no more. ....Od.24.274.363.
Thy ancient friend, oh stranger, is no more! ....Od.24.329.365.
Whom heav'n, alas! decreed to meet no more. ....Od.24.366.366.
Their feeble weight no more; his arms alone ....Od.24.403.368.

NO-MEANING
For true No-meaning puzzles more than Wit. ....3.Ep2.114.59.

NO-THING
No *Gentleman!* no *man! no-thing!* no *name!* ....6.116iv.2.326.
For how can no-thing be annihilated? ....6.116iv.6.327.

NOAH
Noah had refus'd it lodging in his Ark, ...4.JD4.26.27.

NOBILITY
For huffing, braggart, puft *Nobility?* ....4.JD4.201.43.

NOBLE
Here noble *Surrey* felt the sacred Rage, ...1.W-F.291.175.
And justly bear a Critick's noble Name, ...1.EOC.47.244.
But if in Noble Minds some Dregs remain, ...1.EOC.526.297.
With Manners gen'rous as his Noble Blood; ....1.EOC.726.324.
Great *Jove* and *Phœbus* grac'd his noble Line; ....1.TrSt.542.433.
Then thus the King: Perhaps, my Noble Guests, ...1.TrSt.656.437.
The noble *Tydeus* stands confess'd, and known ....1.TrSt.792.443.
A Noble Fool was never in a Fault. ....2.ChJM.165.23.
If what I speak my noble Lord offend, ...2.ChJM.214.24.
Hither the Noble Knight wou'd oft repair ....2.ChJM.465.37.
Hither the Noble Lord wou'd oft repair ....2.ChJM.465A.37.
Our noble Knight was urg'd to Am'rous Play: ....2.ChJM.522A.40.
Heav'n rest thy Spirit, noble *Solomon,* ....2.ChJM.631.45.
Who noble ends by noble means obtains, ...3.EOM4.233.148.
Who noble ends by noble means obtains, ...3.EOM4.233.148.
When Cæsar made a noble dame a whore, ...3.Ep1.213.33.
Her Head's untouch'd, that noble Seat of Thought: ....3.Ep2.74.56.
Yet shall (my Lord) your just, your noble rules ....3.Ep4.25.139.
Just as they are, yet shall noble rules ....3.Ep4.25A.139.
Yes, while I live, no rich or noble knave ....4.HS1.119.17.
Know, while I live, no rich or noble knave ....4.HS1.119A.17.
Tremble before a *noble Serving-Man?* ....4.JD4.199.43.
"In me 'tis noble, suits my birth and state, ...4.HS2.113.63.
Nor marrying Discord in a Noble Wife, ...4.Arbu.393.126.
Noble and young, who strikes the heart ....4.HOde1.11.151.
Noble and young, who wins the heart ....4.HOde1.11A.151.
"D'ye think me, noble Gen'ral, such a Sot? ....4.2HE2.50.167.
Effects unhappy! from a Noble Cause. ....4.2HE1.160.209.
Exact Racine, and Corneille's noble fire ....4.2HE1.274.219.
For Fame, for Riches, for a noble Wife? ....4.1HE6.39.239.
A noble superfluity it craves, ...4.1HE6.91.243.
CARLETON's calm Sense, and STANHOPE's noble Flame, ...4.EpS2.80.317.
Secure, thro' her, the noble prize to carry, ...5.DunA2.211.127.
Till Birch shall blush with noble blood no more, ...5.DunA3.330.191.
Secure, thro' her, the noble prize to carry, ...5.DunB2.219.306.
'Till Birch shall blush with noble blood no more, ...5.DunB3.334.336.
But pour them thickest on the noble head. ....5.DunB4.358.378.
To let no noble Slave come near, ...6.135.75.369.
That so a Noble Youth, and true, ...6.135.77A.369.
With Oxford, Cowper, Noble Strafford by: ....6.147ix.4.392.
Those slain he left; and sprung with noble Rage ....Il.5.188.275.
And catch from Breast to Breast the noble Fire! ....Il.5.654.299.
Unnerves the Limbs, and dulls the noble Mind. ....Il.6.331.342.
Each noble Matron, and illustrious Dame. ....Il.6.357.343.
To whom the noble *Hector* thus reply'd: ....Il.6.666.360.
That not a *Grecian* met this noble Foe! ....Il.7.112.369.
All these, alike inspir'd with noble Rage, ...Il.7.205.374.
I steal no Conquest from a noble Foe. ....Il.7.294.378.
Oh first of *Greeks!* (his noble Foe rejoin'd) ....Il.7.349.381.
The noble *Hector* on this Lance reclin'd, ...Il.8.619.425.
and *Lycomed,* of *Creon's* noble Line. ....Il.9.116.437.
Stand but as Slaves before a noble Mind. ....Il.9.495.457.
Where this but lights, some noble Life expires, ...Il.11.501.56.
Who drew from *Hyrtacus* his noble Blood, ...Il.12.110.85.
This on the Helm discharg'd a noble Blow; ....Il.13.769.141.
Already noble Deeds ye have perform'd, ...Il.13.781.142.
This drew from *Phylacus* his noble Line; ....Il.13.869.147.
And who to *Tydeus* owes his noble Line. ....Il.14.38.159.
A noble Mind disdains not to repent. ....Il.15.227.205.
And catch from Breast to Breast the noble Fire. ....Il.15.669.221.
The daring *Lycon* aim'd a noble Blow; ....Il.16.405.258.
A Train of noble Youth the Charge shall bear; ....Il.19.191.379.
Then lift thy Weapon for a noble Blow, ...Il.20.140.400.
It fits us now a noble Stand to make, ...Il.22.297.468.
Jove by these Hands shall shed thy noble Life; ....Il.22.328.469.
Perhaps that noble Heat has cost his Breath, ...Il.22.590.480.
Let others for the noble Task prepare, ...Il.23.353.504.
Your noble Vigour, oh my Friends restrain; ....Il.23.856.523.
Here too great *Merion* hopes the noble Prize; ....Il.23.1050.531.
Those Hands, yet red with *Hector's* noble Gore! ....Il.24.250.547.
Here, youthful Grace and noble Fire engage, ...Il.24.800.570.
Thy noble Corse was dragg'd around the Tomb, ...Il.24.951.576.
Grieve not, oh daring Prince! that noble heart: ....Od.2.341.77.

NOBLE (CONTINUED)
Has told the glories of his noble name, ...Od.3.101.91.
Receiv'd him charg'd with *Ilion's* noble spoil) ....Od.5.53.174.
Howe'er the noble, suff'ring mind, may grieve ....Od.7.297.250.
From that fierce wrath the noble song arose, ...Od.8.71.266.
Pleas'd with the din of war, and noble shout of foes. ....Od.11.316.397.
To raise a bounty noble as thy soul; ....Od.11.445.406.
Wise is thy voice, and noble is thy heart. ....Od.11.455.407.
Thy eyes shall see him burn with noble fire, ...Od.11.557.411.
A prize more worth than *Ilion's* noble spoil. ....Od.13.161.13.
(A noble prize!) and to your ship convey. ....Od.15.490.94.
What noble beast in this abandon'd state ....Od.17.368.150.
Tho' all unknown his clime, or noble race. ....Od.17.449.155.
Ye Peers and rivals in this noble love! ....Od.17.556.159.
And modest worth with noble scorn retires. ....Od.20.168.241.
The eldest born of *Oenops'* noble race, ...Od.21.153.266.
If what I ask your noble minds approve, ...Od.21.292.274.
In clouds of smoke, rais'd by the noble fray, ...Od.24.55.350.

NOBLE'S
In Noble's Titles; Pride and Simony, ...4.JD2A.87.140.

NOBLER
And then a nobler Prize I will resign, ...1.PSp.91.70.
Not proud *Olympus* yields a nobler Sight, ...1.W-F.33.151.
Might change *Olympus* for a nobler Hill. ....1.W-F.234.170.
None taught the Trees a nobler Race to bear, ...1.TrVP.3.377.
Those, that imparted, court a nobler aim, ...3.EOM2.99.66.
But nobler scenes Maria's dreams unfold, ...3.Ep3.131.104.
Wilt thou do nothing for a nobler end, ...4.1HE1.73.283.
So Proteus, hunted in a nobler shape, ...5.DunA2.121.111.
But now for Authors nobler palms remain: ....5.DunA2.183.124.
Pass these to nobler sights lo Henley stands, ...5.DunA3.195A.173.
So Proteus, hunted in a nobler shape, ...5.DunB2.129.301.
But now for Authors nobler palms remain; ....5.DunB2.191.304.
Others import yet nobler arts from France, ...5.DunB4.597.402.
They hid their Knowledge of a nobler Race, ...6.96iii.15.275.
We Country Dogs love nobler Sport, ...6.135.13.366.
Stretch'd forth in honour's nobler bed, ...6.141.7.380.
Beneath a nobler roof, the sky. ....6.141.8.380.
Stretch'd out in honour's nobler bed, ...6.141.7A.380.
To nobler Sentiment to fire the Brave, ...6.152.5.400.
Perhaps their Sword some nobler Quarrel draws, ...Il.3.309.208.
Of full five Years, and of the nobler Kind. ....Il.7.381.382.
A nobler Charge shall rowze the dawning Day. ....Il.8.652.426.
A nobler Care the *Grecians* shall employ, ...Il.9.63.434.
The Gifts of Heav'n are of a nobler kind. ....Il.10.655.31.
(Others in Council fam'd for nobler Skill, ...Il.18.135.329.
Hereafter *Greece* some nobler Work may raise, ...Il.23.308.502.
But never from this nobler suit we cease; ....Od.2.235.73.
Such, and not nobler, in the realms above ....Od.4.89.123.
The nobler portion want, a knowing mind. ....Od.8.196.273.
To *Troy* no Hero came of nobler line, ...Od.11.637.416.
Or if of nobler, *Memnon,* it was thine. ....Od.11.638.416.
I chuse the nobler part, and yield my breath ....Od.16.111.108.
But serv'd a master of a nobler kind, ...Od.17.377.150.
With nobler contest ne'er renown'd a grave. ....Od.24.114.353.

NOBLES
Aw'd by his Nobles, by his Commons curst, ...1.W-F.73.157.
P. Who starves by Nobles, or with Nobles eats? ....3.Ep3.237A.112.
P. Who starves by Nobles, or with Nobles eats? ....3.Ep3.237A.112.
Who starves by Nobles, or with Nobles eats? ....3.Ep3.237.112.
Who starves by Nobles, or with Nobles eats? ....3.Ep3.237.112.
Our Birth-day Nobles splendid Livery: ....4.1HE6.33.239.
See, all our Nobles begging to be Slaves! ....4.EpS1.163.309.
Thy Nobles Sl[ave]s, thy Se[nate]s bought with gold. ....4.1740.81.336*.
Teach Oaths to Gamesters, and to Nobles Wit? ....5.DunB1.204.284.
Teach Oaths to Gamesters, and to Nobles—Wit? ....5.DunB1.204A.284.
And grant, his Nobles all ....6.79.146.223.
Nobles, whom Arms or Arts adorn, ...6.135.65.368.
Resort the Nobles from the neighb'ring Isles; ....Od.1.316.48.
Of nobles, and invite a foreign pow'r? ....Od.4.891.160.
Where in high state the nobles of the land ....Od.6.305.225.
The Nobles gaze, with awful fear opprest; ....Od.7.192.245.
Nobles and Chiefs who rule *Phæacia's* states, ...Od.8.11.262.

NOBLEST
An honest Man's the noblest work of God. ....3.EOM4.248.151.
This with the noblest force of sculpture grac'd, ...6.20.27.66.
There bade the noblest of the *Grecian* Peers; ....Il.2.480.149.
The noblest Spoil from sack'd *Lyrnessus* born, ...Il.2.842.164.
Who bravest fought, or rein'd the noblest Steeds? ....Il.2.925.167.
And nine, the noblest of the *Grecian* Name, ...Il.7.196.373.
The noblest Pow'r that might the World controul ....Il.9.55.434.
The best and noblest of the *Grecian* Train; ....Il.9.647.466.
The boldest Warrior, and the noblest Mind: ....Il.17.355.301.
And twelve, the noblest of the *Trojan* Line, ...Il.18.394.340.
In *Theban* Games the noblest Trophy bore, ...Il.23.786.521.
And with the noblest gifts asserts his claim. ....Od.15.22.71.
The noblest presents that our love can make: ....Od.15.86.73.
And from the Peers select the noblest Lord; ....Od.19.622.226.
And was the noblest the first mark of fate? ....Od.24.40.349.

NOBLIER
Rose in his majesty, and noblier trod; ....Od.11.660.416.

NOBLY
Chast tho' not rich; and tho' not nobly born, ...2.ChJM.260.27.
And nobly wishing Party-rage to cease, ...3.Ep3.151.106.
Or nobly wild, with *Budgell's* Fire and Force, ...4.HS1.27.7.
We nobly take the high Priori Road, ...5.DunB4.471.386.
And nobly conscious, Princes are but things ....5.DunB4.601.403.
A fate so glorious, and so nobly born, ...6.20.34.67.
Where, nobly-pensive, ST. JOHN sate and thought; ....6.142.10.383.
There, nobly-pensive, ST. JOHN sate and thought; ....6.142.10A.383.

NOBLY (CONTINUED)
Here, nobly-pensive, St. John sate and thought; ... 6.142.10B.383.
Or nobly face the horrid Front of War? ... Il.1.300.101.
And to their Owners send them nobly back. ... Il.13.381.123.
And what he greatly thought, he nobly dar'd. ... Od.2.312.76.
Fell before *Troy*, and nobly prest the plain? ... Od.11.463.407.
Or nobly seiz'd thee in the dire alarms ... Od.11.497.408.
Nor nobly seiz'd me in the dire alarms, ... Od.11.503.408.
Swells his bold heart, his bosom nobly glows? ... Od.11.604.413.
With which he nobly may discharge his seat, ... Od.20.363.250.
Thus they—but nobly chaste she weds no more. ... Od.23.148.328.

NOBLY-PENSIVE
Where, nobly-pensive, St. John sate and thought; ... 6.142.10.383.
There, nobly-pensive, St. John sate and thought; ... 6.142.10A.383.
Here, nobly-pensive, St. John sate and thought; ... 6.142.10B.383.

NOCKS
You should be better skill'd in Nocks, ... 6.93.29.257.

NOCTURNAL
Now from nocturnal Sweat, and sanguine Stain, ... Il.10.673.31.
The dews descending, and nocturnal air? ... Od.5.603.201.
Well arm'd, and fenc'd against nocturnal air; ... Od.14.595.66.
Nocturnal with *Eurymachus:* With eyes ... Od.18.373.185.
So in nocturnal solitude forlorn, ... Od.19.611.226.
Whilst to nocturnal joys impure, repair ... Od.20.11.230.
Secur'd him from the keen nocturnal air. ... Od.20.178.241.
Where flock nocturnal bats, and birds obscene; ... Od.24.10.347.

NOD
Serene he look'd, and gave an awful Nod, ... 1.TrSt.282.422.
Heav'n's whole foundations to their centre nod, ... 3.EOM1.255.46.
Imbrown the Slope, and nod on the Parterre, ... 3.Ep4.174.154.
Imbrown thy Slope, and nod on thy Parterre, ... 3.Ep4.174A.154.
I nod in Company, I wake at Night, ... 4.HS1.13.5.
Ev'n mitred *Rochester* would nod the head, ... 4.Arbu.140.105.
To whom to nod, whom take into your Coach, ... 4.1HE6.102.243.
And heavy harvests nod beneath the snow. ... 5.DunA1.76.68.
And now to this side, now to that, they nod, ... 5.DunA2.363.144.
A matchless youth: His nod these worlds controuls, ... 5.DunA3.251.178.
And heavy harvests nod beneath the snow. ... 5.DunB1.78.275.
'Till Senates nod to Lullabies divine, ... 5.DunB1.317.293.
And now to this side, now to that they nod, ... 5.DunB2.395.316.
A matchless Youth! his nod these worlds controuls, ... 5.DunB3.255.332.
Low bow'd the rest" He, kingly, did but nod; ... 5.DunB4.207.363.
On Learning's surface we but lie and nod. ... 5.DunB4.242.366.
A drowzy Watchman in the land of Nod. ... 5.DunB4.444A.384.
This Nod confirms each Privilege your own. ... 5.DunB4.584.400.
Jove with a nod may bid the world to rest, ... 6.4i.13.9.
This Duke did only nod. ... 6.79.36.219.
The Nod that ratifies the Will Divine, ... Il.1.680.119.
Shakes his Ambrosial Curls, and gives the Nod; ... Il.1.684.120.
Thus He who Shakes *Olympus* with his Nod; ... Il.5.1108.320.
Jove, at whose Nod whole Empires rise or fall, ... Il.9.32.433.
The leading Sign, th' irrevocable Nod, ... Il.12.275.91.
Fierce as he past, the lofty Mountains nod, ... Il.13.29.105.
Hush'd are her Mountains, and her Forests nod. ... Il.14.324.178.
I gave, and seal'd it with th' Almighty Nod, ... Il.15.81.199.
There sate th' Eternal; He, whose Nod controuls ... Il.15.172.203.
And lo! the Turrets nod, the Bulwarks fall. ... Il.15.415.213.
If e'er thou sign'st our Wishes with thy Nod; ... Il.15.432.214.
Jove dooms it now on *Hector's* Helm to nod; ... Il.16.964.280.
Then with his sable Brow he gave the Nod, ... Il.17.245.297.
Th' affrighted Hills from their Foundations nod, ... Il.17.672.314.
The Forests wave, the Mountains nod around; ... Il.20.78.397.
Swift at the royal nod th' attending train ... Od.6.85.209.
For know, thou *Neptune* view'st! and at my nod ... Od.11.305.397.
He said: then gave a nod; and at the word ... Od.21.475.283.
And at his nod the damsel train descends; ... Od.23.46.321.
Let all be peace.—He said, and gave the nod ... Od.24.560.375.

NODDED
How, when you nodded, o'er the land and deep, ... 4.2HE1.400.229.
Slept first, the distant nodded to the hum. ... 5.DunA2.370.145.
Slept first; the distant nodded to the hum. ... 5.DunB2.402.316.
Ev'n Palinurus nodded at the Helm: ... 5.DunB4.614.405.
The waving Horse-hair nodded on his Head. ... Il.3.418.212.
Where the black Horse-hair nodded o'er his Crest: ... Il.6.12.323.
Achilles' Helmet nodded o'er his Head. ... Il.16.169.244.
(The sable Plumage nodded o'er his Head) ... Il.17.212.295.
The rev'rend Elders nodded o'er the Case; ... Il.18.586.351.
His dreadful Plumage nodded from on high; ... Il.22.174.460.
His dreadful Plumage nodded as he spoke. ... Il.22.316.469.

NODDING
See nodding Forests on the Mountains dance, ... 1.Mes.26.115.
And nodding tempt the joyful Reaper's Hand, ... 1.W-F.40.152.
Earth shakes her nodding Tow'rs, the Ground gives way; ... 2.RL5.51.203.
And low-brow'd rocks hang nodding o'er the deeps. ... 2.ElAb.244.339.
Or some old temple, nodding to its fall, ... 3.EOM4.129.140.
And then a nodding Beam, or Pig of Lead, ... 4.2HE2.102.171.
Benigner influence on thy nodding head. ... 5.DunB4.346.377.
With nodding arches, broken temples spread! ... 6.71.3.202.
And nodding *Ilion* waits th' impending Fall. ... Il.2.18.128.
And nodding *Ilion* waits th' impending Fall. ... Il.2.40.129.
And nodding *Ilion* waits th' impending Fall. ... Il.2.90.130.
With nodding Plumes and Groves of waving Spears. ... Il.2.182.137.
Scar'd at the dazling Helm, and nodding Crest. ... Il.6.597.356.
With nodding Horse-hair formidably grac'd; ... Il.11.54.37.
Bent with the Weight the nodding Woods are seen, ... Il.12.339.93.
As when an Earthquake stirs the nodding Grove; ... Il.13.184.114.
The Plume dropp'd nodding to the Plain below, ... Il.13.770.141.
His nodding Helm emits a streamy Ray; ... Il.13.1014.153.
With nodding Horsehair formidably grac'd; ... Il.15.567.218.
The nodding Plumage on his Helmet danc'd. ... Il.20.195.402.

NODDING (CONTINUED)
Nodding at ev'ry Step: (*Vulcanian* Frame!) ... Il.22.397.472.
Nodding, his Head hangs down his Shoulder o'er; ... Il.23.810.521.
And nodding cypress form'd a fragrant shade; ... Od.5.83.176.
Crown'd with rough thickets, and a nodding wood. ... Od.9.224.316.
He said; then nodding with the fumes of wine ... Od.9.439.324.
With cliffs, and nodding forests over-hung. ... Od.14.4.34.
Obliquely drops, and nodding knocks his breast; ... Od.18.282.180.
And nodding helm, I tread th' ensanguin'd field, ... Od.18.419.189.
Then, happier thoughts return the nodding scale, ... Od.20.279.246.
He frowns beneath his nodding plume, that play'd ... Od.22.140.293.

NODS
The green Reed trembles, and the Bulrush nods. ... 1.Mes.72.119.
Nor is it *Homer Nods*, but *We* that *Dream*. ... 1.EOC.180.261.
From side to side the trembling Balance nods, ... 1.TrES.168.455.
Nods, groans, and reels, 'till with a crackling Sound ... 1.TrES.290.460.
Nods to the Axe, till with a groaning Sound ... 1.TrES.290A.460.
The doubtful Beam long nods from side to side; ... 2.RL5.73.206.
Grove nods at grove, each Alley has a brother, ... 3.Ep4.117.149.
"Not one but nods, and talks of Johnson's Art, ... 4.2HE1.82.201.
A yawning ruin hangs and nods in air; ... 5.DunA1.28.63.
Great Tibbald nods: The proud Parnassian sneer, ... 5.DunA2.5A.97.
And Shadwell nods the poppy on his brows; ... 5.DunA2.324.141.
Hence, from the straw where Bedlam's Prophet nods, ... 5.DunA3.7.150.
See, the Cirque falls! th' unpillar'd Temple nods! ... 5.DunA3.99.158.
Hence, from the straw where Bedlam's Prophet nods, ... 5.DunB3.7.320.
And Shadwell nods the Poppy on his brows. ... 5.DunB3.22.321.
See, the Cirque falls, th' unpillar'd Temple nods, ... 5.DunB3.107.325.
More she had spoke, but yawn'd—All Nature nods: ... 5.DunB4.605.403.
More she had said, but yawn'd—All Nature nods: ... 5.DunB4.605A.403.
—but here she stops, she yawns, she nods;— ... 5.DunB4.605B.403.
Makes love with nods, and knees beneath a table; ... 6.45.28.125.
The Mountain nods, the Forest shakes, ... 6.78ii.6.216.
Obscures the Glade, and nods his shaggy Brows, ... Il.2.919.167.
Shakes his huge Spear, and nods his Plumy Crest: ... Il.2.989.170.
That dreadful nods with four o'ershading Plumes; ... Il.5.919.310.
At *Thetis'* Suit the partial Thund'rer nods. ... Il.8.450.418.
From side to side the trembling Balance nods, ... Il.12.522.101.
Beneath his Helmet, nods upon his Breast; ... Il.13.687.137.
Imperial *Troy* from her Foundations nods; ... Il.13.972.151.
The panting Thund'rer nods, and sinks to Rest. ... Il.14.406.183.
Waves when he nods, and lightens as he turns: ... Il.15.733.224.
Nods to the Axe, till with a groaning Sound ... Il.16.595.267.
On *Ossa, Pelion* nods with all his wood: ... Od.11.388.403.
See how with nods assent yon princely train! ... Od.18.16.167.

NOEMON
Then to *Noemon* swift she runs, she flies, ... Od.2.434.82.

NOISE
Eurota's Banks remurmur'd to the Noise; ... 1.TrSt.166.417.
To sooth his Cares, and free from Noise and Strife ... 2.ChJM.27.16.
He us'd from Noise and Business to retreat; ... 2.ChJM.470.38.
With ceaseless Noise the ringing Walls resound: ... 2.TemF.423.283.
And learn, my sons, the wond'rous pow'r of Noise. ... 5.DunA2.214.127.
And Noise, and Norton, Brangling, and Breval, ... 5.DunA2.230.128.
Noise, Noncence, *N[orto]n*, Brangling, and B[reval], ... 5.DunA2.230B.128.
No noise, no stir, no motion can'st thou make, ... 5.DunA2.291.138.
And learn, my sons, the wond'rous pow'r of Noise. ... 5.DunB2.222.306.
And Noise and Norton, Brangling and Breval, ... 5.DunB2.238.307.
No noise, no stir, no motion can'st thou make, ... 5.DunB2.303.310.
The Business and the Noise of Towns, ... 6.1.2A.3.
The rage of courts, and noise of towns; ... 6.1.2B.3.
'Till wrangling *Science* taught it Noise and Show, ... 6.8.11.18.
And run precipitant, with Noise and Strife, ... 6.17ii.5.56.
Soft as the Speaking Trumpet's mellow Noise: ... 6.96ii.72.273.
Good without noise, without pretension great. ... 6.109.4.314.
Now light with Noise; with Noise the Field resounds. ... Il.2.545.153.
Now light with Noise; with Noise the Field resounds. ... Il.2.545.153.
With Noise, and Order, thro' the mid-way Sky; ... Il.3.8.188.
Methinks the Noise of tramp'ling Steeds I hear ... Il.10.626.30.
Not with less Noise, with less impetuous force, ... Il.16.464.260.
Not with less Noise, with less tumultuous Rage, ... Il.16.929.279.
Ah follow me! (she cry'd) what plaintive Noise ... Il.22.578.480.
Yet thro' my court the noise of Revel rings, ... Od.2.61.63.
The song is noise, and impious is the feast. ... Od.2.350.78.
Rush'd with dire noise, and dash'd the sides in twain; ... Od.12.497.456.
Arriv'd, with wild tumultuous noise they sate ... Od.16.424.127.
Then swill'd with wine, with noise the crowds obey, ... Od.18.472.191.
And all was riot, noise, and wild uproar. ... Od.21.390.279.

NOISEFUL
From noiseful revel far remote she flies, ... Od.15.557.96.

NOISES
At length the Tumult sinks, the Noises cease, ... Il.2.253.139.

NOISIE
With noisie Care and various Tumult sound. ... 1.TrSt.606.435.
Then pompous *Silence* reigns, and stills the noisie Laws. ... 6.8.33.18.

NOISOME
And od'rous Myrtle to the noisome Weed. ... 1.Mes.76.119.

NOISY
Those of less noisy, and less guilty Fame, ... 2.TemF.169.268.
Much-suff'ring Heroes, of less noisy Fame, ... 2.TemF.169A.268.
Yet softer Honours, and less noisy Fame ... 6.132.9.362.
Th' appointed Heralds still the noisy Bands, ... Il.18.583.351.
What-time the Judge forsakes the noisy bar ... Od.12.519.457.
Then from the hall, and from the noisy crew, ... Od.21.193.269.

NOMAN
And plead my title: *Noman* is my name. ... Od.9.432.323.
Noman shall be the last I will devour. ... Od.9.438.324.

NOMAN (CONTINUED)

Friends, *Noman* kills me; *Noman* in the hour   Od.9.485.326.
Friends, *Noman* kills me; *Noman* in the hour   Od.9.485.326.
(The deed of *Noman* and his wicked train)   Od.9.534.328.
While such a monster as vile *Noman* lives.   Od.9.542.328.

NONCENCE

See NONSENSE
Noise, Noncence, *N[orto]n*, Brangling, and B[reval],   5.DunA2.230B.128.

NONE

'Tis with our *Judgments* as our *Watches*, none   1.EOC.9.239.
Since none can compass more than they *Intend;*   1.EOC.256.268.
It *gilds* all Objects, but it *alters* none.   1.EOC.317.274.
And none had *Sense enough to be Confuted.*   1.EOC.443.289.
None taught the Trees a nobler Race to bear,   1.TrVP.3.377.
By none alas! by none thou can'st be mov'd,   1.TrSP.47.395.
By none alas! by none thou can'st be mov'd,   1.TrSP.47.395.
(For none want Reasons to confirm their Will)   2.ChJM.20.16.
'Tis true, Perfection none must hope to find   2.ChJM.190.24.
Let none oppose th'Election, since on this   2.ChJM.256.27.
The lovely Prize, and share my Bliss with none!   2.ChJM.265.27.
His spacious Garden, made to yield to none,   2.ChJM.448.36.
Here let us walk, he said, observ'd by none,   2.ChJM.543.41.
None shall want Arts to varnish an Offence,   2.ChJM.661.46.
None judge so wrong as those who think amiss.   2.ChJM.810.54.
And none can long be modest that are gay.   2.ChWB.141.63.
All this I said; but Dreams, Sirs, I had none.   2.ChWB.304.71.
Favours to none, to all she Smiles extends,   2.RL2.11.160.
Where none learn *Ombre*, none e'er taste *Bohea!*   2.RL4.156.197.
Where none learn *Ombre*, none e'er taste *Bohea!*   2.RL4.156.197.
Tho' mark'd by none but quick Poetic Eyes: 2.RL5.124.210.
But thank'd by few, rewarded yet by none,   2.TemF.302.278.
Oh grant an honest Fame, or grant me none!   2.TemF.524.289.
Be, or endow'd with all, or pleas'd with none?   3.EOM1.188A.37.
That Vice or Virtue there is none at all.   3.EOM2.212.81.
All fear, none aid you, and few understand.   3.EOM4.266.153.
Others so very close, they're hid from none;   3.Ep1.111.23.
Where none distinguish twixt your Shame and Pride,   3.Ep2.204A.67.
Where none distinguish twixt your Shame or Pride,   3.Ep2.204B.67.
But none of Cloe's shall you ever hear.   3.Ep2.174.64.
None see what Parts of Nature it conceals.   3.Ep2.190.65.
There, none distinguish 'twixt your Shame or Pride,   3.Ep2.204.67.
The Folly's greater to have none at all.   3.Ep3.160.106.
P. Each Mortal has his Pleasure: None deny   4.HS1.45.9.
"None shou'd, by my Advice, learn *Virtue* there."   4.JD4.97.33.
(A Doctrine sage, but truly none of mine)   4.HS2.3.55.
None comes too early, none departs too late;   4.HS2.158.67.
None comes too early, none departs too late;   4.HS2.158.67.
(For none but Lady M[ohun] shows the Rest)   4.HAdv.125.85.
(For none but Lady M—show'd the Rest)   4.HAdv.125A.85.
Beauty that shocks you, Parts that none will trust,   4.Arbu.332.120.
In which none 'ere cou'd surfeit, none could starve   4.JD2A.126.142.
In which none 'ere cou'd surfeit, none could starve   4.JD2A.126.142.
Which tho they're rich, are Things that none will wear   4.JD2A.130.144.
In which none e'er could surfeit, none could starve.   4.JD2.120.143.
In which none e'er could surfeit, none could starve.   4.JD2.120.143.
How match the Bards whom none e'er match'd before?   4.2HE2.115.173.
"But why all this of Av'rice? I have none."   4.2HE2.304.187.
None e'er has risen, and none e'er shall rise.   4.2HE1.30.197.
None e'er has risen, and none e'er shall rise.   4.2HE1.30.197.
All that may make me none of mine.   4.1HE1.64.273.
"Full many a Beast goes in, but none comes out."   4.1HE1.117.287.
Who ought to make me (what he can, or none,)   4.1HE1.179.293.
F. Yet none but you by Name the Guilty lash;   4.EpS2.10.313.
Are none, none living! let me praise the Dead,   4.EpS2.251.327.
Are none, none living? let me praise the Dead,   4.EpS2.251.327.
The Classicks of an Age that heard of none;   5.DunA1.128.79.
Small thanks to France and none to Rome or Greece,   5.DunA1.237.91.
"Oh born to see what none can see awake!"   5.DunA3.35.154.
'None but Thy self can be thy parallel.'   5.DunA3.272.180.
The Classics of an Age that heard of none;   5.DunB1.148.281.
Small thanks to France, and none to Rome or Greece,   5.DunB1.283.290.
"Oh born to see what none can see awake!   5.DunB3.43.322.
And scream thyself as none e'er scream'd before!   5.DunB3.306.335.
None need a guide, by sure Attraction led,   5.DunB4.75.348.
None want a place, for all their Centre found,   5.DunB4.77.349.
Such skill in passing all, and touching none.   5.DunB4.258.369.
Wits have short Memories, and Dunces none)   5.DunB4.620.406.
Wits have short Memories, and Dulness none)   5.DunB4.620A.406.
But none but you can give us Strength to walk;   6.2.29.6.
I hope, you think me none of those   6.10.29.25.
Few write to those, and none can live to these.   6.19.30.63.
Howe're she liv'd none ever dy'd so well.   6.20.16.66.
That none had so much Right to be   6.30.52.88.
But ever writ, as none e'er writ before.   6.34.10.101.
And Climb the dark Stairs to your Friends who have none: 6.42iii.4.117.
Loves all Mankind, but flatters none,   6.47.51.130.
None can like thee its Fermentation still.   6.48i.4.133*.
That never spareth none.   6.82viii.4.233.
None from a page can ever learn the truth.   6.96ii.30Z20.271.
But none hath eyes to trace the passing wind,   6.96ii.30Z29.271.
No, none of these—Heav'n spare his Life!   6.101.33.291.
Which none but you can clear,   6.102.6.294.
None knows which leads, or which is led,   6.105iv.7.301.
None knows which leads, nor which is led,   6.105iv.7A.301.
Has writ such stuff, as none e'er writ before.   6.116i.2.325.
Some Vices were too high but none too low   6.130.10.358.
None but a Peer of Wit and Grace,   6.135.67.369.
But none of Cloë's shall you ever hear.   6.139.18.377.
Poor *Colley*, thy Reas'ning is none of the strongest,   6.149.3.397.
But your reas'ning, God help you! is none of the strongest,   6.149.3A.397.
To Pow'r superior none such Hatred bear: Il.1.230.98.
None match thir Grandeur and exalted Mien: Il.3.224.203.
None stands so dear to *Jove* as sacred *Troy*.   Il.4.68.224.
Before the rest let none too rashly ride;   Il.4.348.237.

NONE (CONTINUED)

Enquiries none they made; the dreadful Day   Il.5.631.298.
None turn their Backs to mean ignoble Flight,   Il.5.862.307.
Thy Pow'r in War with Justice none contest;   Il.6.668.360.
The *Greeks* gave ear, but none the Silence broke,   Il.7.474.388.
Such as himself will chuse, who yield to none,   Il.9.181.441.
Such as thy self shall chuse; who yield to none,   Il.9.368.451.
Belov'd by none but those of *Atreus'* Race?   Il.9.449.454.
Then none (said *Nestor*) shall his Rule withstand,   Il.10.148.8.
By none but *Dolon* shall this Prize be born,   Il.10.391.21.
None stoop'd a Thought to base inglorious Flight;   Il.11.95.39.
Each wounds, each bleeds, but none resign the Day.   Il.11.98.39.
None fears it more, as none promotes it less: Il.12.286.92.
None fears it more, as none promotes it less: Il.12.286.92.
But *Peleus'* Son; and *Peleus'* Son to none   Il.16.276.249.
Or stoop to none but great *Achilles'* Hand.   Il.17.82.291.
Arms I have none, and can I fight unarm'd?   Il.18.226.332.
Yet a short Interval, and none shall dare   Il.19.237.382.
(Guide or Companion, Friends! I ask ye none)   Il.22.532.478.
Prizes which none beside our self could gain,   Il.23.343.503.
By none in Weight or Workmanship excell'd: Il.23.866.524.
Each look'd on other, none the Silence broke,   Il.24.596.561.
None by to weep them, to inhume them none;   Il.24.769.569.
None by to weep them, to inhume them none;   Il.24.769.569.
Death only is the lot which none can miss,   Od.3.293.100.
For lo! none other of the court above,   Od.3.484.111.
Distinguish'd long, and second now to none!   Od.7.290.250.
Let none to strangers honours due disclaim;   Od.8.39.264.
None wield the gauntlet with so dire a sway,   Od.8.101.267.
None in the leap spring with so strong a bound,   Od.8.103.268.
In such heroic games I yield to none,   Od.8.237.275.
And none, ah none so lovely to my sight,   Od.9.29.303.
And none, ah none so lovely to my sight,   Od.9.29.303.
The rest are vanish'd, none repass'd the gate;   Od.10.307.359.
None but *Orion* e'er surpass'd their height: Od.11.380.401.
None but *Pelides* brighter shone in arms.   Od.11.580.412.
None match'd this hero's wealth, of all who reign   Od.14.117.41.
None 'scaped him, bosom'd in the gloomy wood;   Od.17.383.150.
Be calm, replies the Sire; no terms impart,   Od.19.50.195.
None imag'd e'er like thee my master lost.   Od.19.445.216.
Let none to call or issue forth presume,   Od.21.417.280.
When *Agelaus* thus: Has none the sense   Od.22.148.294.
The lot, which all lament, and none can shun!   Od.24.42.350.
To none it yields but great *Ulysses'* hands;   Od.24.199.358.
None now the kindred of th' unjust shall own;   Od.24.554.374.

NONJUROR

No merit now the dear Nonjuror claims,   5.DunB1.253.289.

NONSENSE

See NONCENCE.
And own *stale Nonsense* which they ne'er invent.   1.EOC.411.287.
To *fetch and carry* Nonsense for my Lord.   1.EOC.417.287.
'Twixt Sense and Nonsense daily change their Side.   1.EOC.435.288.
But *ratling Nonsense* in full *Vollies* breaks;   1.EOC.628.310.
And he, who now to sense, now nonsense leaning,   4.Arbu.185.109.
Stop, or turn nonsense at one glance of Thee?   4.HOde1.40.153.
Stop, or turn nonsense at one glance from Thee?   4.HOde1.40A.153.
How new-born Nonsense first is taught to cry,   5.DunA1.58.67.
He grins, and looks broad nonsense with a stare.   5.DunA2.186.124.
All nonsense thus, of old or modern date,   5.DunA3.51.155.
How fluent nonsense trickles from his tongue!   5.DunA3.197.174.
How honey'd nonsense trickles from his tongue!   5.DunA3.197A.174
How new-born nonsense first is taught to cry,   5.DunB1.60.274.
Nonsense precipitate, like running Lead,   5.DunB1.123.278.
Soon to that mass of Nonsense to return,   5.DunB1.241.288.
He grins, and looks broad nonsense with a stare.   5.DunB2.194.305.
All nonsense thus, of old or modern date,   5.DunB3.59.323.
How fluent nonsense trickles from his tongue!   5.DunB3.201.330.
Johnson, who now to Sense, now Nonsense leaning,   6.98.35.284.

NOOK

Yea when she passed by or Lane or Nook,   6.14ii.42.44.
Whene'er she passed by or Lane or Nook,   6.14ii.42A.44.
Far in a lonely nook, beside the sea,   Od.24.177.356.

NOON

At Morn the Plains, at Noon the shady Grove;   1.PSp.78.68.
Nor Plains at Morn, nor Groves at Noon delight.   1.PSp.80.68.
More bright than Noon, yet fresh as early Day,   1.PSp.82.69.
Now, when declining from the Noon of Day,   2.RLA1.83.129.
Mean while declining from the Noon of Day,   2.RL3.19.170.
Is there a Lord, who knows a cheerful noon   3.Ep3.239.112.
The Watch would hardly let him pass at noon,   4.JD4.32.29.
Count the slow clock, and dine exact at noon;   6.45.18.125.
Morning from Noon there was no knowing,   6.93.11.257.
Resplendent as the blaze of summer-noon,   Od.4.55.122.

NOON-DAY

But see, the Shepherds shun the Noon-day Heat,   1.PSu.85.79.
Where awful arches make a noon-day night,   2.ElAb.143.331.
And pays his host with hideous noon-day dreams.   Od.20.454.255.

NOON-TIDE

Alas! not dazzled with their noon-tide ray,   3.EOM4.305.156.
An oily steam, and taints the noon-tide gales.   Od.4.548.146.

NOON'S

Foretell the noon's increasing beams;   6.5.8A.12.

NOONDAY

Thence, e'er the Sun advanc'd his noonday Flame,   Il.11.862.74.

NOONS
With store of Pray'rs, for Mornings, Nights, and Noons, ...2.RL4.29.185.
O charming Noons! and Nights divine! ....4.HS6.133.259.

NOONTIDE
No noontide-bell invites the country round; ....3.Ep3.192.109.
What are these noontide bowers and solemn shades, ...6.81.7B.225.
Alas! not dazled with his Noontide ray, ... 6.130.35.359.

NOONTIDE-BELL
No noontide-bell invites the country round; ....3.Ep3.192.109.

NOOSE
A sliding Noose, and waver'd in the Wind. ....2.ChWB.396.76.

NOR (OMITTED)
987

NORMAN
Our haughty *Norman* boasts that barb'rous Name, ...1.W-F.63.155.

NORTH
And the cold North receives a fainter Day; ....1.TrSt.215.419.
Which the cold North congeals to haily Show'rs. ....1.TrSt.495.431.
Thus flying East and West, and North and South, ...2.TemF.473.286.
Ask where's the North? at York, 'tis on the Tweed; ....3.EOM2.222.82.
The North by myriads pours her mighty sons, ...5.DunA3.81.157.
The North by myriads pours her mighty sons, ...5.DunB3.89.324.
When now the *North* his boist'rous Rage has spent, ...Il.5.643.299.
A double Tempest of the West and North ....Il.9.6.431.
The *Western Spirit,* and the *North* to rise; ....Il.23.259.499.
And south, and north, roll mountains to the shore. ....Od.5.380.190.
And now the south, and now the north, bear sway, ...Od.5.421.192.
These to the north and night's dark regions run, ...Od.9.25.303.
Sharp blew the North; snow whitening all the fields ....Od.14.536.63.
And when the north had ceas'd the stormy roar, ...Od.19.232.204.

NORTHERN
From old *Belerium* to the *Northern* Main, ...1.W-F.316.179.
But ripens Spirits in cold *Northern Climes;* .... 1.EOC.401.286.
Thence Arts o'er all the *Northern World* advance; ....1.EOC.711.322.
In *Northern* Wilds, and freeze beneath the Pole; ....1.TrSt.813.443.
But Mortals enter at the Northern End. ....1.TrUl.44.467.
In some lone Isle, or distant *Northern* Land; ....2.RL4.154.196.
Of *Gothic* Structure was the Northern Side, ...2.TemF.119.263.
Improves the keenness of the Northern wind. ....3.Ep4.112.148.
Howl to the roarings of the Northern deep. ....4.2HE1.329.223.
The *Pleiads, Hyads,* with the Northern Team; ....Il.18.561.349.
There view'd the *Pleiads,* and the northern Team, ...Od.5.347.188.
Strong was the tyde, which by the northern blast ....Od.9.91.306.
The northern winds shall wing thee on thy way. ....Od.10.601.372.
But mortals enter at the northern end. ....Od.13.135.9.
Aloof from *Crete,* before the northern gales: ....Od.14.330.51.

NORTON
She saw in *N[orto]n* all his father shine, ...5.DunA1.101A.71.
And Noise, and Norton, Brangling, and Breval, ...5.DunA2.230.128.
Noise, Noncence, *N[orto]n,* Brangling, and B[reval], ...5.DunA2.230B.128.
Norton, from Daniel and Ostrœa sprung, ...5.DunA2.383.148.
Ev'n *N[orto]n,* gifted with his mother's tongue, ...5.DunA2.383A.148.
And Noise and Norton, Brangling and Breval, ...5.DunB2.238.307.
Norton, from Daniel and Ostrœa sprung, ...5.DunB2.415.317.

NOS
Where all that passes, *inter nos,* .... 4.HS6.99.257.

NOS'D
Goose-rump'd, Hawk-nos'd, Swan-footed, is my Dear? ....4.HAdv.122.85.

NOSE
And the high Dome re-ecchoes to his Nose. ....2.RL5.86.207.
Yet ne'er looks forward farther than his nose. ....3.EOM4.224.148.
Yet ne'er looks forward further than his nose. ....3.EOM4.224A.148.
All eyes may see—a Pimple on her nose. ....3.Ep2.36.53.
The Nose of Hautgout, and the Tip of Taste, ...3.Ep2.80.57.
To Chartres, Vigour; Japhet, Nose and Ears? ....3.Ep3.88.95.
When half his Nose is in his Patron's Ear. ....4.JD4.179.41.
Perhaps, young men! our Fathers had no nose? ....4.HS2.92.61.
Such *Ovid's* nose, and "Sir! you have an *Eye*—" .... 4.Arbu.118.104.
C[ompton] that Roman in his nose alone, ...4.1740.65.335.
High sounds, attempred to the vocal nose. ....5.DunA2.246.129.
High Sound, attemp'red to the vocal nose; ....5.DunB2.256.308.
High Notes, attemp'red to the vocal nose; ....5.DunB2.256A.308.
Look in their Face, they tweak'd your Nose, ...6.79.17.218.
He tweak'd his Nose, trod on his Toes, ...6.79.59.219.
From his Nose ....6.96i.37.269.
Your Eyes, your Nose, Inconstancy betray; ....6.96iv.7.276.
Your Nose you stop, your Eyes you turn away. ....6.96iv.8.276.
To hymn harmonious *Houyhnhnm* thro' the Nose, ...6.96iv.106.279.
And let me tell you, have a Nose ....6.135.29.367.
The Nose and Eye-ball the proud *Lycian* fixt; ....Il.5.354.283.
Nose, Mouth and Front, one undistinguish'd Wound: ....Il.23.476.509.
From mouth and nose the briny torrent ran; ....Od.5.584.200.
Who casts thy mangled ears and nose a prey ....Od.18.98.171.
His nose they shorten'd, and his ears they slit, ...Od.21.321.275.
A stream of gore burst spouting from his nose; ....Od.22.22.287.
The wretch, and shorten'd of his nose and ears; ....Od.22.512.313.

NOSEGAY
As on the Nosegay in her Breast reclin'd, ...2.RL3.141.178.

NOSES
Such waxen Noses, stately, staring things, ...4.JD4.210.43.
Review them, and tell Noses; ....6.58.70.174.
Thy Children's Noses all should twang the same. ....6.96iv.108.279.

NOSTER
So *Luther* thought the *Pater noster* long, ...4.JD2A.111.142.

NOSTRIL
Constrain'd, his nostril eccho'd thro' the crowd. ....Od.17.625.163.

NOSTRILS
That while my Nostrils draw the vital Air, ...2.RL4.137.195.
Just where the Breath of Life his Nostrils drew, ...2.RL5.81.206.
Fierce in the Fight, their Nostrils breath'd a Flame, ...Il.2.930.167.
Her pitchy Nostrils flaky Flames expire; ....Il.6.223.337.
Clouds from their Nostrils the fierce Coursers blow, ...Il.11.361.50.
His Mouth, his Eyes, his Nostrils pour a Flood; ....Il.16.418.259.
Full on my Shoulders let their Nostrils blow, ...Il.17.570.310.
Then in the Nostrils of the Slain she pour'd ....Il.19.39.373.
His Mouth and Nostrils pour the clotted Gore; ....Il.23.811.521.
At length emerging, from his nostrils wide ....Od.5.411.192.
His mouth and nostrils spout a purple flood, ...Od.18.116.172.

NOSTRUM
What *Drop* or *Nostrum* can this Plague remove? ....4.Arbu.29.98.

NOT (OMITTED)
1547

NOTCH
Thrusts your poor Vowell from his Notch: ....6.30.22.86.

NOTCH'D
Then notch'd the shaft, releast, and gave it wing; ....Od.21.460.282.

NOTCHES
To him who notches Sticks at Westminster. ....4.1HE1.84.285.

NOTE
Begin, the Vales shall ev'ry Note rebound. ....1.PSp.44.65.
His drooping Swans on ev'ry Note expire, ...1.W-F.275.174.
To Fifty chosen *Sylphs,* of special Note, ...2.RL2.117.166.
Loves of his own and raptures swell the note: ....3.EOM3.34.95.
"Treat on, treat on," is her eternal Note, ...4.HAdv.13.75.
And quits his Mistress, Money, Ring, and Note! ....4.HAdv.54.79.
That from a Patriot of distinguish'd note, ...4.2HE2.196.179.
On each enervate string they taught the Note ....4.2HE1.153.209.
Such is the shout, the long-applauding note, ...4.2HE1.330.223.
In rev'rend Bishops note some *small Neglects,* .... 4.EpS1.16.298.
In rev'rend S[utto]n note a *small Neglect,* .... 4.EpS1.16A.298.
"God save king Cibber!" mounts in ev'ry note. ....5.DunB1.320.293.
And ev'ry piercing note inflicts a wound. ....Od.1.440.53.
To ev'ry note his tears responsive flow, ...Od.8.587.294.
One care remains, to note the loyal few ....Od.16.328.121.

NOTED
A *noted Dean* much busy'd in the Park, ...4.HAdv.40.79.
Heard, noted, answer'd, as in full Debate: ....4.2HE2.187.177.
Their Manners noted, and their States survey'd. ....Od.1.6.28.
Each noted leader's name you thrice invoke, ...Od.4.379.139.
What customs noted, and what coasts survey'd? ....Od.8.626.296.
Which noted token of the woodland war ....Od.19.545.223.

NOTES
To *Delia's* Ear the tender Notes convey! ....1.PAu.18.82.
To *Thyrsis* Ear the tender Notes convey! ....1.PAu.18A.82.
In Notes more sad than when they sing their own. ....1.PWi.40.92.
In sadder Notes than when they sing their own. ....1.PWi.40A.92.
Oft as the mounting Larks their Notes prepare, ...1.W-F.133.162.
To the same Notes, of Love, and soft Desire: ....1.W-F.296.176.
With *sweeter Notes* each *rising Temple* rung; ....1.EOC.703.320.
Love taught my Tears in sadder Notes to flow, ...1.TrSP.7.393.
Or while my Muse in melting Notes complains, ...1.TrSP.93.397.
The breathing Flute's soft Notes are heard around, ...2.ChJM.318.29.
Hear how the Doves with pensive Notes complain, ...2.ChJM.527.41.
The Notes at first were rather sweet than loud: ....2.TemF.311.279.
Let fuller Notes th' applauding World amaze, ...2.TemF.326.279.
And on the Winds triumphant swell the Notes; ....2.TemF.373.281.
And up the Winds triumphant swell the Notes; ....2.TemF.373A.281.
Notes to dull books, and prologues to dull plays; ....5.DunA1.168.83.
And these to Notes are fritter'd quite away. ....5.DunA1.232.90.
And those to Notes are fritter'd quite away. ....5.DunA1.232A.90.
And these to Notes are fritter'd quite away: ....5.DunB1.278.290.
High Notes, attemp'red to the vocal nose; ....5.DunB2.256A.308.
To the same notes thy sons shall hum, or snore, ...5.DunB4.59.347.
While in more lengthen'd Notes and slow, ...6.11.10.30.
Exulting in Triumph now swell the bold Notes, ...6.11.16.30.
In more lengthen'd Notes and slow, ...6.11.10A.30.
Born on the swelling Notes our Souls aspire, ...6.11.128.34.
There oft' are heard the Notes of Infant Woe, ...6.14ii.5.43.
The scolding Quean to louder Notes doth rise, ...6.14ii.23.43.
And round the orb in lasting notes be read, ...6.71.66.204.
Such were the Notes, thy once-lov'd Poet sung, ...6.84.1.238.
The *Greeks* restor'd the grateful Notes prolong; ....Il.1.620.117.
High notes responsive to the trembling string, ...Od.21.441.281.

NOTHING
Which nauseate all, and nothing can digest. ....1.EOC.389.284.
All was *Believ'd,* but nothing *understood,* .... 1.EOC.689A.317.
As all were nothing he had done by Night; ....2.ChJM.386.33.
Nothing to add, and nothing to abate. ....3.EOM1.184.37.
Nothing to add, and nothing to abate. ....3.EOM1.184.37.
Is Heav'n unkind to nothing but to Man? ....3.EOM1.186A.37.
Be pleas'd with nothing, if not bless'd with all? ....3.EOM1.188.38.
From thee to Nothing!—On superior pow'rs ....3.EOM1.241.45.
Ask your own heart, and nothing is so plain; ....3.EOM2.215.81.
Nothing is foreign: Parts relate to whole; ....3.EOM3.21.94.
All serv'd, all serving! nothing stands alone; ....3.EOM3.25.94.
Each serv'd, and serving! nothing stands alone; ....3.EOM3.25A.94.
All serv'd, and serving! nothing stands alone; ....3.EOM3.25B.94.

NOTHING (CONTINUED)
What nothing earthly gives, or can destroy, 3.EOM4.167.143.
Shall parts so various aim at nothing new? 3.Ep1.186.31.
And wanting nothing but an honest heart; 3.Ep1.193.31.
Nothing so true as what you once let fall, 3.Ep2.1.46.
And die of nothing but a Rage to live. 3.Ep2.100.58.
Then as a licens'd Spy, whom nothing can 4.JD4.158.39.
Nothing in Nature is so lewd as *Peg,* 4.HAdv.31.77.
Nothing so mean for which he can't run mad; 4.HAdv.64.81.
"Tis nothing"—Nothing? if they bite and kick? 4.Arbu.78.101.
"Tis nothing"—Nothing? if they bite and kick? 4.Arbu.78.101.
Steals much, spends little, yet has nothing left: 4.Arbu.184.109.
Heav'ns! was I born for nothing but to write? 4.Arbu.272.115.
D'ye think me good for nothing but to rhime? 4.2HE2.32.167.
The good man heaps up nothing but mere metre, 4.2HE1.198.211.
There's nothing blackens like the ink of fools; 4.2HE1.411.229.
If to live well means nothing but to eat; 4.1HE6.111.245.
Or, "Have you nothing new to-day 4.HS6.93.255.
He brought him Bacon (nothing lean) 4.HS6.165.261.
Wilt thou do nothing for a nobler end, 4.1HE1.73.283.
Nothing, to make Philosophy thy friend? 4.1HE1.74.283.
Alike in nothing but one Lust of Gold, 4.1HE1.124.289.
And when it comes, the Court see nothing in't. 4.EpS1.2.297.
These nothing hurts; they keep their Fashion still, 4.EpS1.43.301.
"Nothing is Sacred now but Villany." 4.EpS1.170.309.
Where the tall Nothing stood, or seem'd to stand; 5.DunA2.102.109.
Where the tall Nothing stood, or seem'd to stand; 5.DunB2.110.300.
With nothing but a Solo in his head; 5.DunB4.324.375.
And nothing left but Homage to a King! 5.DunB4.524.394.
Attends; all flesh is nothing in his sight! 5.DunB4.550.396.
While vows and service nothing gain'd, 6.4iii.9.10.
'Twas one vast Nothing, All, and All slept fast in thee. 6.8.3.17.
You'd at present do nothing but give us a Visit. 6.42i.8.116.
Come these soft lines, with nothing Stiff in 6.61.5.180.
Come these lines, with nothing Stiff in 6.61.5A.180.
At Court thou may'st be lik'd, but nothing gain; 6.66.6.194.
For Shrubs, when nothing else at top is, 6.67.9.195.
Which nothing seeks to show, or needs to hide, 6.73.2.209.
With added years if Life bring nothing new, 6.86.5.245.
With added Days if Life give nothing new, 6.86.5B.245.
With added years if Life give nothing new, 6.86.5C.245.
That's made of nothing but a Lady's *Corn.* 6.96iv.58.278.
Steals much, spends little, yet has nothing left: 6.98.34.284.
Saw nothing to regret, or there to fear; 6.112.8.318.
Saw nothing to regret, Nor there to fear; 6.112.8A.318.
Want nothing else, except your wife. 6.114.12.321.
Yet this, like their old one, for nothing will spare, 6.122.19.342.
"I tell ye, fool, there's nothing in't: 6.140.26.379.
And life itself can nothing more supply 6.147viii.1.392.
Jove to his *Thetis* nothing could deny, Il.1.720.122.
And Hell's Abyss hide nothing from your sight, Il.2.575.155.
Greece, if she conquers, nothing wins from me. Il.5.588.296.
The Day shall come (which nothing can avert) Il.21.121.426.
Then, nothing loth, the enamour'd fair he led, Od.8.337.281.
A cloak and vest—but I am nothing now! Od.14.575.64.
Nothing neglected, but thy self alone. Od.24.293.364.

NOTHING'S
Pleas'd with a Work where nothing's just or fit; 1.EOC.291.272.
For nothing's left in either of the Scales. 6.28.2.82.
Now nothing's left, but wither'd, pale, and shrunk, 6.49i.25.138.

NOTHINGS
Such *labour'd Nothings,* in so *strange* a Style, 1.EOC.326.275.

NOTICE
Yet ev'n this Creature may some Notice claim, 6.98.17.283.

NOTING
And noting, ere we rise in vengeance prove Od.16.330.121.

NOTION
But *catch* the *spreading Notion* of the Town; 1.EOC.409.287.
Fools! who from hence into the notion fall, 3.EOM2.211.81.
And all we gain, some pensive Notion more; 6.86.8B.245.

NOTIONS
Thence form your Judgment, thence your Notions bring, 1.EOC.126A.253.
They talk of *Principles,* but Notions prize, 1.EOC.265.270.
The *truest Notions* in the *easiest way.* 1.EOC.656.314.
Maxims are drawn from Notions, those from Guess. 3.Ep1.14A.16.
Maxims are drawn from Notions, these from Guess. 3.Ep1.14.16.

NOTUS
Thus from his flaggy Wings when *Notus* sheds Il.3.15.188.
Dispells the gather'd Clouds that *Notus* forms; Il.11.396.52.

NOUGHT
Such Wits and Beauties are not prais'd for nought, 4.JD4.234.45.
Of nought so certain as our *Reason* still, 5.DunB4.481.389.
Of nought so doubtful as of *Soul* and *Will.* 5.DunB4.482.389.
And nought was seen, and nought was heard 6.11.51Z3.32.
And nought was seen, and nought was heard 6.11.51Z3.32.
Te-he cry'd Ladies; Clerke nought spake: 6.14i.21.42.
Thus, (nought unsaid) the much-advising Sage Il.23.423.506.
For nought unprosp'rous shall thy ways attend, Od.3.37.88.
This dares a Seer, but nought the Seer prevails, Od.11.357.399.
Thus jovial they; but nought the Prince replies; Od.20.459.255.
Nought else are all that shin'd on earth before; Od.24.23.348.

NOURISH
The common Cares that nourish Life, foregoe. Il.24.756.568.
Then linger life away, and nourish woe! Od.12.416.451.

NOURISH'D
Within her arms, and nourish'd at her breast. 1.TrFD.20.386.
Between her arms, and nourish'd at her breast. 1.TrFD.20A.386.
Nourish'd two Locks, which graceful hung behind 2.RL2.20.160.
Bred by *Ulysses,* nourish'd at his board, Od.17.348.148.
Nourish'd deep anguish, tho' he shed no tear; Od.17.583.161.

NOURISHMENT
They owe their Life and Nourishment to Earth; Il.21.538.444.

NOVEL
For novel lays attract our ravish'd ears; Od.1.447.54.

NOW (OMITTED)
1376

NOW-DECLINING
Long nights the now-declining year bestows; Od.15.426.89.

NOW-NEGLECTED
Whose now-neglected altars, in thy reign, Od.13.397.26.

NOXIOUS
Arise, the Pines a noxious Shade diffuse; 1.PWi.86.95.
But *Phœbus,* ask'd why noxious Fires appear, 1.TrSt.747.441.
Gath'ring like Vapours of a noxious kind Il.18.141.329.
When fed with noxious Herbs his turgid Veins Il.22.132.458.
With fire and sulphur, cure of noxious fumes, Od.22.529.314.

NUM'ROUS
Those half-learn'd Witlings, num'rous in our Isle, 1.EOC.40.243.
Salute the God in num'rous Hymns of Praise. 1.TrSt.655.437.
Her num'rous Off-spring for a fatal Boast. 1.TrSt.850.445.
Our num'rous Herds that range each fruitful Field, 1.TrES.29.450.
Our num'rous Herds that range the fruitful Field, 1.TrES.29A.450.
By Love of *Courts* to num'rous Ills betray'd. 2.RL4.152.196.
And Priests and Party-Zealots, num'rous Bands 2.TemF.464.286.
Fed num'rous Poultry in her Pens, 6.93.3.256.
No daring *Greek* of all the num'rous Band, Il.1.113.92.
Mean time *Atrides* launch'd with num'rous Oars Il.1.404.107.
What Chief, or Soldier, of the num'rous Band, Il.2.434.148.
Thus num'rous and confus'd, extending wide, Il.2.546.153.
Great *Agamemnon* rules the num'rous Band, Il.2.694.159.
Beneath four Chiefs (a num'rous Army) came: Il.2.751.161.
A Fleet he built, and with a num'rous Train Il.2.805.163.
Yet two are wanting of the num'rous Train, Il.3.301.207.
For know, of all the num'rous Towns that rise Il.4.65.224.
Sedate and silent move the num'rous Bands; Il.4.486.243.
As Torrents roll, increas'd by num'rous Rills, Il.4.516.246.
And the brave Prince in num'rous Toils engag'd. Il.6.200.336.
Let num'rous Fires the absent Sun supply; Il.8.632.426.
A warmer Couch with num'rous Carpets spread. Il.9.734.470.
Our num'rous Herds that range the fruitful Field, Il.12.373.95.
And num'rous Flocks, that whiten'd all the Field. Il.14.140.164.
But strive, tho' num'rous, to repulse in vain. Il.15.471.215.
(Where num'rous Oxen, as at ease they feed, Il.15.762.226.
There, in the *Forum* swarm a num'rous Train; Il.18.577.350.
Since You of all our num'rous Race, alone Il.22.303.468.
'Tis more by Art, than Force of num'rous Strokes, Il.23.385.505.
Rejoic'd, of all the num'rous *Greeks,* to see Il.23.747.520.
Surviv'd, sad Relicks of his num'rous Line. Il.24.316.549.
Thro' *Grecian* Foes, so num'rous and so strong? Il.24.450.555.
Next heap'd on high the num'rous Presents bear Il.24.726.568.
My num'rous woes, in silence let them dwell. Od.2.238.73.
Where the bold youth, the num'rous fleets to store, Od.6.319.226.
Graze num'rous herds along the verdant shores; Od.11.135.387.
But now the years a num'rous train have ran; Od.11.555.411.
Against that num'rous, and determin'd band? Od.16.267.117.
The sad survivor of his num'rous train, Od.17.163.139.
What num'rous deaths attend this fatal bow? Od.21.161.267.
With ships he parted and a num'rous train, Od.24.491.371.

NUMA'S
Awful as Pluto's Grove or Numa's grot 6.142.9A.383.

NUMB'D
From his numb'd Hand the Iv'ry-studded Reins Il.5.713.301.
And his numb'd Hand dismiss'd his useless Bow. Il.8.396.416.

NUMB'RING
Numb'ring his flocks and herds, not far remote. Od.4.865.159.

NUMBER
Each Band the number of the Sacred Nine. 2.RL3.30.171.
Not less in Number were the spacious Doors, 2.TemF.424.283.
To *Number five* direct your Doves, 4.HOde1.9.151.
The Number may be hang'd, but not be crown'd. 4.EpS2.111.319.
The gath'ring number, as it moves along, 5.DunB4.81.349.
The honest Number that you left behind. 6.96iv.14.276.
So small their Number, that if Wars were ceas'd, Il.2.155.135.
Not less in Number, than th' embody'd Cranes, Il.2.540.152.
If not—but hear me, while I number o'er Il.9.342.450.
Tho' Bribes were heap'd on Bribes, in Number more Il.9.506.458.
And thrice the Number of unrival'd Steeds, Il.11.824.73.
And call'd to fill the Number of the Dead? Il.16.850.276.
And twice the Number of high-bounding Steeds: Il.19.252.383.
And number all his Days by Miseries! Il.22.87.456.
Their number summ'd, repos'd in sleep profound Od.4.557.146.
Now without number ghost by ghost arose, Od.11.663.417.
They part, and join him; but the number stay'd. Od.24.531.373.

NUMBER'D
The Gold, the Vests, the Tripods number'd o'er; 1.TrUl.95.469.
Rank'd with their Friends, not number'd with their Train; 4.EpS2.91.318.
Then number'd with the puppies in the mud. 5.DunB2.308.310.
Else shall our Fates be number'd with the Dead, Il.5.294.281.

NUMBER'D (CONTINUED)
The Chiefs out-number'd by the *Trojan* Train: ... Il.10.633.30.
What Troops, out-number'd scarce the War maintain? ... Il.13.927.149.
Or number'd in my Father's social train? ... Od.1.224.43.
More wretched you! twice number'd with the dead! ... Od.12.32.431.
The gold, the vests, the tripods, number'd o'er: ... Od.13.262.18.

NUMBERS
And yet my Numbers please the rural Throng, ... 1.PSu.49.75.
Attend the Muse, tho' low her Numbers be, ... 1.PAu.11A.81.
Thames heard the Numbers as he flow'd along, ... 1.PWi.13.89.
There the last Numbers flow'd from *Cowley's* Tongue. ... 1.W-F.272.173.
Make *Windsor* Hills in lofty Numbers rise, ... 1.W-F.287.174.
Some few in *that,* but Numbers err in *this,* ... 1.EOC.5.239.
But most by *Numbers* judge a Poet's Song, ... 1.EOC.337.276.
And the *smooth Stream* in *smoother Numbers* flows; ... 1.EOC.367.282.
But in low Numbers short Excursions tries: ... 1.EOC.738.326.
Ask not the cause that I new Numbers chuse, ... 1.TrSP.5.393.
My languid Numbers have forgot to flow, ... 1.TrSP.230.403.
Gods! can no Pray'rs, no Sighs, no Numbers move ... 1.TrSP.242.404.
The Winds my Pray'rs, my Sighs, my Numbers bear, ... 1.TrSP.244.404.
Such Numbers fell by Pestilential Air! ... 1.TrSt.766.442.
Think not your softest Numbers can display ... 2.ChJM.337.30.
And so do Numbers more, I'll boldly say, ... 2.ChWB.353.74.
Pleas'd with the strange Success, vast Numbers prest ... 2.TemF.394.282.
Yet numbers feel, the want of what he had. ... 3.Ep3.332.120.
I lisp'd in Numbers, for the Numbers came. ... 4.Arbu.128.105.
I lisp'd in Numbers, for the Numbers came. ... 4.Arbu.128.105.
Soft were my Numbers, who could take offence ... 4.Arbu.147.106.
Wit grew polite, and Numbers learn'd to flow. ... 4.2HE1.266.217.
But liv'd, in Settle's numbers, one day more. ... 5.DunA1.88.69.
Yet liv'd, in Settle's numbers, one day more. ... 5.DunA1.88A.69.
And in sweet numbers celebrates the seat. ... 5.DunA1.226.90.
My *Henley's* periods, or my Blackmore's numbers? ... 5.DunA2.338.142.
But liv'd, in Settle's numbers, one day more. ... 5.DunB1.90.276.
"My H—ley's periods, or my Blackmore's numbers; ... 5.DunB2.370.315.
Hark! the Numbers, soft and clear, ... 6.11.12.30.
His Numbers rais'd a Shade from Hell, ... 6.11.133.34.
His Numbers such, as Sanger's self might use. ... 6.12.3.37.
My Numbers too for ever will I vary, ... 6.40.3.112.
Yet should the Muses bid my numbers roll, ... 6.52.73.158.
Let *D[enni]s* write, and nameless numbers rail: ... 6.63.4.188.
And roar in Numbers worthy *Bounce.* ... 6.135.94.370.
Begets no numbers grave or gay. ... 6.141.4.380.
What Scenes of Grief and Numbers of the Slain! ... Il.2.50.129.
Atrides' Speech. The mighty Numbers move. ... Il.2.174.136.
Their Names, their Numbers, and their Chiefs I sing. ... Il.2.585.155.
But ne'er 'till now such Numbers charg'd a Field. ... Il.2.969.169.
What Numbers lost, what Numbers yet remain? ... Il.3.244.204.
What Numbers lost, what Numbers yet remain? ... Il.3.244.204.
And Strength of Numbers, to this *Grecian* Race. ... Il.3.252.204.
On him, amidst the flying Numbers found, ... Il.5.103.271.
There the brave Chief who mighty Numbers sway'd ... Il.5.383.285.
And Numbers more his Sword had sent to Hell: ... Il.5.837.305.
Till *Greece,* provok'd, from all her Numbers show ... Il.7.45.365.
Sprung from such Fathers, who such Numbers sway; ... Il.7.193.373.
What Numbers fell! what Numbers yet shall fall! ... Il.8.430.417.
What Numbers fell! what Numbers yet shall fall! ... Il.8.430.417.
He fought with numbers, and made numbers yield. ... Il.10.344.18.
He fought with numbers, and made numbers yield. ... Il.10.344.18.
And sav'd from Numbers, to his Car conveys. ... Il.11.609.61.
Repuls'd by Numbers from the nightly Stalls, ... Il.11.676.65.
Ev'n the sweet Charms of sacred Numbers tire. ... Il.13.798.143.
Fall mighty Numbers; mighty Numbers run; ... Il.14.616.192.
Fall mighty Numbers; mighty Numbers run; ... Il.14.616.192.
Admiring Numbers follow with their Eyes. ... Il.15.829.228.
To guard his Body *Troy* in Numbers flies; ... Il.16.685.270.
The show'ring Darts, and Numbers sunk to Hell. ... Il.16.941.280.
To boast our Numbers, and the Pomp of War; ... Il.17.263.298.
Vain hope! what Numbers shall the Field o'erspread, ... Il.17.278.298.
The long-succeeding Numbers who can name? ... Il.17.306.299.
By Valour, Numbers, and by Arts of War, ... Il.17.381.302.
With that, he gluts his Rage on Numbers slain: ... Il.20.525.416.
That barr such numbers from their native Plain: ... Il.21.69.424.
And Numbers more his Lance had plung'd to Hell; ... Il.21.228.430.
What gasping Numbers now had bit the Ground? ... Il.22.26.453.
What Numbers had been sav'd by *Hector's* Flight? ... Il.22.143.459.
But won by Numbers, not by Art or Force: ... Il.23.734.519.
Such numbers fell, such Heroes sunk to night: ... Od.3.132.92.
Abash'd, the numbers hear the god-like man, ... Od.8.267.277.
What foes were vanquish'd, and what numbers fell; ... Od.11.634.415.
What gasping numbers then shall press the ground! ... Od.13.450.27.
O'erpow'r'd by numbers, is but brave in vain. ... Od.16.90.106.
Oppress'd by numbers in the glorious strife, ... Od.16.110.108.
The names, and numbers of th' audacious train; ... Od.16.259.117.
Hear then their numbers: From *Dulichium* came ... Od.16.268.117.
Chief of the numbers who the Queen addrest, ... Od.16.412.126.
And numbers leagu'd in impious union dread: ... Od.18.274.179.
What single arm with numbers can contend? ... Od.20.384.251.
And Fate to numbers by a single hand. ... Od.22.18.287.
Led the sad numbers by *Ulysses* slain. ... Od.24.124.354.

NUMBING
His slacken'd Knees receiv'd the numbing Stroke; ... Il.7.324.379.

NUMBRED
For since the Day that numbred with the Dead ... Il.24.806.570.

NUMEROUS
When numerous Wax-lights in bright Order blaze, ... 2.RL3.168.182.
Yet secret go; for numerous are my foes, ... Od.16.142.109.
How could that numerous and outragious band ... Od.23.39.321.

NUN
Demure and chast as any Vestal Nun, ... 2.ChJM.202.24.
Stol'n from a Duel, follow'd by a Nun, ... 5.DunB4.327.375.

NUNQUAM
"But *Tully* has it, *Nunquam minus solus:"* ... 4.JD4.91.33.
"You'll die of Spleen"..Excuse me, *Nunquam minus..* ... 4.JD4.91A.33.

NUPTIAL
Averse from *Venus* and the Nuptial Joy; ... 1.TrVP.18.377.
Now shou'd the Nuptial Pleasures prove so great, ... 2.ChJM.272.27.
Good Heav'n no doubt the nuptial State approves, ... 2.ChJM.282.27.
Bacchus himself, the Nuptial Feast to grace, ... 2.ChJM.326.30.
For gentle Lays, and joyous Nuptial Song; ... 2.ChJM.336.30.
Honest and dull, in Nuptial Bed they lay, ... 2.ChJM.424.35.
With Dance and Song we kept the Nuptial Day. ... 2.ChWB.330.73.
Or dy'd at least before thy Nuptial Rite! ... Il.3.58.192.
False to my Country and my Nuptial Bed, ... Il.3.230.203.
With Torches flaming, to the nuptial Bed; ... Il.18.572.350.
Three Sons renown'd adorn'd his nuptial Bed, ... Il.20.276.406.
And yield his consort to the nuptial bed. ... Od.2.252.73.
To bless his sons and daughters nuptial hour. ... Od.4.6.119.
To bless the natal, and the nuptial hour; ... Od.4.286.132.
An absent heroe's nuptial joys profane! ... Od.4.448.141.
Whom to my nuptial train *Icarius* gave, ... Od.4.973.163.
"In evil hour the nuptial rite intends, ... Od.4.1019.165.
With her own son she joyn'd in nuptial bands, ... Od.11.331.398.
Kills for the feast, to crown the nuptial board. ... Od.11.514.409.
To deck thy bride, and grace thy nuptial day. ... Od.15.141.75.
Or pay due honours to the nuptial bed? ... Od.16.74.106.
An absent Heroe's nuptial joys prophane! ... Od.17.139.138.
When the dear partner of my nuptial joy, ... Od.19.146.199.
From nuptial rites they now no more recede, ... Od.19.178.200.
Shall I my virgin nuptial vow revere; ... Od.19.616.226.
But whilst to learn their lots in nuptial love, ... Od.20.88.237.
The Lord selected to the nuptial joys, ... Od.20.399.251.
Around the tree I rais'd a nuptial bow'r, ... Od.23.195.333.
To the chaste love-rites of the nuptial bed. ... Od.23.318.339.

NUPTIALS
Some greater *Greek* let those high Nuptials grace, ... Il.9.514.458.
To grace those Nuptials, from the bright Abode ... Il.24.80.538.
And public nuptials justify the bride. ... Od.6.346.228.
New from his nuptials, hapless youth! expir'd. ... Od.7.83.237.
And the hop'd nuptials turn to joy or woe. ... Od.15.564.97.
Not the lost nuptials can affect me more, ... Od.21.266.272.

NURS'D
Here stood her Opium, here she nurs'd her Owls, ... 5.DunA1.35.O64.
Here stood her Opium, here she nurs'd her Owls, ... 5.DunB1.271.290.
To Fates averse, and nurs'd for future Woes? ... Il.1.543.114.
Nurs'd the young Stranger with a Mother's Care. ... Il.5.94.271.
So two young Mountain Lions, nurs'd with Blood ... Il.5.681.300.
And nurs'd in *Thrace* where snowy Flocks are fed. ... Il.11.286.48.
"Oh nurs'd with Gall, unknowing how to yield! ... Il.16.244.249.
A child she nurs'd him, and a man attends.) ... Od.1.548.58.
Who gave me life, and nurs'd my infant years? ... Od.2.150.69.
Nurs'd the most wretched King that breathes the air! ... Od.2.395.80.
Those air-bred people, and their goat-nurs'd *Jove:* ... Od.9.330.319.
The soyl that nurs'd us, and that gave us breath: ... Od.10.499.367.
Who nurs'd the children, and now tends the sire: ... Od.24.450.370.

NURSE
Let some kind nurse supply a mother's care: ... 1.TrFD.77.389.
Then must my Nurse be pleas'd, and Fav'rite Maid; ... 2.ChWB.114.62.
Of all the Nurse and all the Priest have taught, ... 2.RL1.30.147.
Nature its mother, Habit is its nurse; ... 3.EOM2.145.72.
The mothers nurse it, and the sires defend; ... 3.EOM3.126.105.
To wholesome Solitude, the Nurse of Sense: ... 4.JD4.185.41.
Great nurse of Goths, of Alans, and of Huns. ... 5.DunA3.82.157.
And suckle Armies, and dry-nurse the land: ... 5.DunB1.316.293.
Great nurse of Goths, of Alans, and of Huns! ... 5.DunB3.90.324.
Of some Dry-Nurse to save her Hen; ... 6.93.18.257.
Of some Dry-Nurse to serve for Hen; ... 6.93.18A.257.
The Nurse attended with her Infant Boy, ... Il.6.486.350.
The Nurse stood near, in whose Embraces prest ... Il.6.496.351.
(Fair Nurse of Fountains, and of Savage Game) ... Il.8.58.398.
(Fair Nurse of Fountains and of savage Game) ... Il.15.171.203.
Nurse of *Nausicaa* from her infant years, ... Od.7.15.234.
The nurse replies: "If *Jove* receives my pray'r, ... Od.17.588.161.
The Nurse with eager rapture speeds her way; ... Od.23.2.316.

NURSE'S
The Babe clung crying to his Nurse's Breast, ... Il.6.596.356.
Sunk soft in Down upon the Nurse's Breast, ... Il.22.649.483.

NURSES
And glad both Babes and Nurses. ... 6.58.56.173.

NURSING
A Nursing-mother, born to rock the throne! ... 5.DunA1.251Z4.93.
And I, a Nursing-mother, rock the throne, ... 5.DunB1.312.293.
I owe the nursing of my tender Years. ... Il.14.346.179.

NURSING-MOTHER
A Nursing-mother, born to rock the throne! ... 5.DunA1.251Z4.93.
And I, a Nursing-mother, rock the throne, ... 5.DunB1.312.293.

NURST
And nurst the Hope of Mischiefs yet to come: ... 1.TrSt.88.413.

NURTURE
That ow'd his Nurture to the blue-ey'd Maid, ... Il.2.658.158.
Say thou, to whom my youth its nurture owes, ... Od.20.161.241.

NUT
Full oft I drain'd the Spicy Nut-brown Bowl; ... 2.ChWB.214.67.
Full oft I drain'd the Spicy Nut-brown Bowl ... 2.ChWB.214A.67.
Then sung, how shown him by the Nut-brown maids ... 5.DunB2.337.314.
And strip white *Ceres* of her nut-brown Coat. ... 6.100vi.3.289.

NUT-BROWN
Full oft I drain'd the Spicy Nut-brown Bowl; ....2.ChWB.214.67.
Full oft I drain'd the Spicy Nut-brown Bowl ....2.ChWB.214A.67.
Then sung, how shown him by the Nut-brown maids ....5.DunB2.337.314.
And strip white *Ceres* of her nut-brown Coat. ....6.100vi.3.289.

NUTATION
So from the mid-most the nutation spreads ....5.DunA2.377.146.
So from the mid-most the nutation spreads ....5.DunB2.409.317.

NUTBROWN
Then sung, how shown him by the nutbrown maids, ...5.DunA2.313.140.

NUTRITION
To draw nutrition, propagate, and rot; ....3.EOM2.64.63.

NUZZLES
Drops to the third who nuzzles close behind; ....4.EpS2.178.323.

NYMPH
Each am'rous Nymph prefers her Gifts in vain, ...1.PSu.53.76.
Come lovely Nymph, and bless the silent Hours, ...1.PSu.63.76.
As some coy Nymph her Lover's warm Address ....1.W-F.19.150.
Above the rest a rural Nymph was fam'd, ...1.W-F.171.165.
Scarce could the Goddess from her Nymph be known, ...1.W-F.175.166.
Now fainting, sinking, pale, the Nymph appears; ....1.W-F.191.167.
Oh! lovely nymph, and more than lilies fair, ...1.TrPA.53.367.
And these, dear nymph, are kept to play with thee: ....1.TrPA.91.369.
These thefts, false nymph, thou shalt enjoy no more, ...1.TrPA.138.371.
What Nymph cou'd e'er attract such Crowds as you? ....1.TrVP.70.380.
The Nymph surveys him, and beholds the Grace ....1.TrVP.120.382.
The Nymph survey'd him and beheld the Grace ....1.TrVP.120A.382.
No nymph of all *Oechalia* could compare ....1.TrFD.7.385.
This nymph compress'd by him who rules the day, ...1.TrFD.11.386.
Lotis the nymph (if rural tales be true) ....1.TrFD.31.387.
And all the nymph was lost within the tree: ....1.TrFD.101.390.
The Nymph, her Father's Anger to evade, ...1.TrSt.680.438.
Each Nymph by turns his wav'ring Mind possest, ...2.ChJM.230.25.
Thus doubting long what Nymph he shou'd obey ....2.ChJM.242.26.
But see! the *Nymph* in Sorrow's Pomp appears, ...2.RL*A*2.59.133.
First, rob'd in White, the Nymph intent adores ....2.RL1.123.155.
This Nymph, to the Destruction of Mankind, ...2.RL2.19.160.
Whether the Nymph shall break *Diana's* Law, ...2.RL2.105.166.
Some, Orb in Orb, around the Nymph extend, ...2.RL2.138.168.
The skilful Nymph reviews her Force with Care; ....2.RL3.45.172.
The Nymph exulting fills with Shouts the Sky, ...2.RL3.99.174.
What Wonder then, fair Nymph! thy Hairs shou'd feel ....2.RL3.177.182.
But anxious Cares the pensive Nymph opprest, ...2.RL4.1.183.
A Nymph there is, that all thy Pow'r disdains, ...2.RL4.65.189.
Sunk in *Thalestris'* Arms the Nymph he found, ...2.RL4.89.191.
Then see! the *Nymph* in beauteous Grief appears, ...2.RL4.143.196.
Silence ensu'd, and thus the Nymph began. ....2.RL5.8.199.
O cruel Nymph! a living Death I bear, ... 2.RL5.61.205.
Then cease, bright Nymph! to mourn thy ravish'd Hair ....2.RL5.141.211.
Then cease, bright Nymph! to mourn the ravish'd Hair ....2.RL5.141A.211.
In fact, 'tis true, no Nymph we cou'd persuade, ...2.TemF.386.282.
How many pictures of one Nymph we view, ...3.Ep2.5.48.
A Nymph of Quality admires our Knight; ....3.Ep3.385.124.
Give me a willing Nymph! 'tis all I care, ...4.HAdv.161.89.
The nymph her graces here express'd may find, ...6.4ii.1.9.
The yielding nymph by these confest, ...6.4v.5.11.
Else might th' ambitious nymph aspire, ...6.5.17.12.
The nymph despis'd, the Rape had been unknown. ....6.38.4.107.
The Nymph whose Tail is all on Flame ....6.53.15.161.
Nymph of the Grot, these sacred Springs I keep, ...6.87.1.248.
The loveliest Nymph of *Priam's* Royal Race) ....Il.3.168.199.
Haste, happy Nymph! for thee thy *Paris* calls, ...Il.3.481.215.
A Nymph in *Caria* or *Meönia* bred, ...Il.4.172.229.
The Nymph descending from the Hills of *Ide,* .... Il.4.546.247.
(Fair *Castianira,* Nymph of Form Divine, ...Il.8.369.415.
Temper'd in this, the Nymph of Form divine ....Il.11.780.70.
(This Nymph, the Fruit of *Priam's* ravish'd Joy, ...Il.13.233.116.
And in his cave the yielding nymph compress. ....Od.1.95.36.
Attend the nymph to *Phthia's* distant reign. ....Od.4.12.121.
Round the descending nymph the waves redounding roar. ....Od.4.578.147.
Then seek the place the sea-born nymph assign'd, ...Od.4.589.147.
Go, to the nymph be these our orders born; ....Od.5.40.172.
Large was the Grot, in which the nymph he found, ...Od.5.72.175.
(The fair-hair'd nymph with ev'ry beauty crown'd) ....Od.5.73.176.
To *Hermes* thus the nymph divine begun. ....Od.5.110.177.
Thus having spoke, the nymph the table spread, ...Od.5.117.177.
The Nymph, obedient to divine command, ...Od.5.191.180.
For him, the Nymph a rich repast ordains, ...Od.5.251.183.
The Nymph just show'd him, and with tears withdrew. ....Od.5.310.186.
The nymph dismist him, (od'rous garments giv'n, ...Od.5.335.188.
The Nymph directed, as he sail'd the deep. ....Od.5.354.189.
The waters waft it, and the nymph receives. ....Od.5.593.201.
Two nymphs the portals guard, each nymph a Grace. ....Od.6.24.204.
Swift fly the mules: nor rode the nymph alone, ...Od.6.97.210.
All but the Nymph: the nymph stood fix'd alone, ...Od.6.167.216.
All but the Nymph: the nymph stood fix'd alone, ...Od.6.167.216.
A plant so stately, or a nymph so fair. ....Od.6.202.219.
To whom the Nymph: O stranger cease thy care, ...Od.6.227.220.
The wond'ring Nymph his glorious port survey'd, ...Od.6.285.224.
(Or Nymph, or Goddess) ecchos from the room? ....Od.10.261.355.
Or Nymph, or Goddess, chaunting to the loom. ....Od.10.300.358.
The golden ew'r a nymph obsequious brings, ...Od.10.433.365.
The nymph, that added lustre to the day: ....Od.10.650.375.
Alas! far otherwise the nymph declares, ...Od.10.673.376.
Hail happy nymph! no vulgar births are ow'd ....Od.11.297.396.
One nymph alone, a miracle of grace. ....Od.11.350.399.
The Goddess aims her shaft, the Nymph expires. ....Od.11.404.404.
I then: O nymph propitious to my pray'r, ...Od.12.139.439.
This nymph, where anchor'd the *Phenician* train ....Od.15.460.93.
The golden ew'r Nymph attendant brings, ...Od.17.104.137.
When in the form of mortal nymph array'd, ...Od.20.37.234.

NYMPH (CONTINUED)
Where the gay blooming Nymph constrain'd his stay, ...Od.23.361.342.

NYMPH'S
The Nymph's seducements, and the magic bow'r. ....Od.5.11.171.
The nymph's fair head a veil transparent grac'd, ...Od.5.295.185.

NYMPHS
Blest Swains, whose Nymphs in ev'ry Grace excell; ....1.PSp.95.70.
Blest Nymphs, whose Swains those Graces sing so well! ....1.PSp.96.70.
The Nymphs forsaking ev'ry Cave and Spring, ...1.PSu.51.76.
Ye *Mantuan* Nymphs, your sacred Succour bring; ....1.PAu.5.80.
Let *Nymphs* and *Sylvans* Cypress Garlands bring; ....1.PWi.22.90.
Ye Nymphs of *Solyma!* begin the Song: ....1.Mes.1.112.
Than the fair Nymphs that gild thy Shore below; ....1.W-F.232A.170.
Than the fair Nymphs that grace thy side below; ....1.W-F.232B.170.
Whose Charms as far all other Nymphs out-shine, ...1.TrVP.53.379.
And first the pardon of the nymphs implor'd, ...1.TrFD.37.387.
Yet first the pardon of the nymphs implor'd, ...1.TrFD.37A.387.
Nymphs that in Verse no more cou'd rival me, ...1.TrSP.29.394.
But ah beware, *Sicilian* Nymphs! nor boast ....1.TrSP.65.396.
I go, ye Nymphs! those Rocks and Seas to prove; ....1.TrSP.201.402.
I go, ye Nymphs! where furious Love inspires: ....1.TrSP.203.402.
The Royal Nymphs approach divinely bright, ...1.TrSt.624.436.
The Royal Nymphs approach'd divinely bright, ...1.TrSt.624A.436.
On which the Labours of the Nymphs were roll'd, ...1.TrUl.37.467.
Hither our Nymphs and Heroes did resort, ...2.RL*A*1.73.129.
And Nymphs prepar'd their *Chocolate* to take; ....2.RL1.16A.145.
And sip with *Nymphs,* their Elemental Tea. ....2.RL1.62.150.
Some Nymphs there are, too conscious of their Face, ...2.RL1.79.151.
Fair Nymphs, and well-drest Youths around her shone, ...2.RL2.5.159.
Of Foreign Tyrants, and of Nymphs at home; ....2.RL3.6.169.
Hither the Heroes and the Nymphs resort, ...2.RL3.9.169.
While Nymphs take Treats, or Assignations give, ...2.RL3.169.182.
There, Youths and Nymphs, in consort gay, ...4.HOde1.29.153.
Smit with his mien, the Mud-nymphs suck'd him in: ....5.DunA2.308.139.
Smit with his mien, the Mud-nymphs suck'd him in: ....5.DunB2.332.313.
When by thy glass,the nymphs were drest, ...6.6ii.19.15.
To treat those Nymphs like yours of *Drury,* ....6.10.51.26.
The Nymphs of *Drury,* not of *Drury*-Lane; ....6.13.18.39.
'But the well-worn Paths of the Nymphs of Drury ....6.13.24.39.
The Nymphs forsake the Fountains ....6.78i.3.215.
While Coffee shall to British Nymphs be dear; ....6.82i.5.229.
To send at a dash all these Nymphs to the Devil? ....6.122.10.341.
Surpass'd the Nymphs of *Troy's* illustrious Race) ....Il.6.315.341.
The Mountain Nymphs the rural Tomb adorn'd, ...Il.6.531.353.
Besides full twenty Nymphs of *Trojan* Race, ...Il.9.179.441.
Besides full twenty Nymphs of *Trojan* Race, ...Il.9.366.451.
Thessalian Nymphs there are, of Form divine, ...Il.9.518.458.
Two nymphs the portals guard, each nymph a Grace. ....Od.6.24.204.
Above the nymphs she treads with stately grace; ....Od.6.124.212.
The voice of nymphs that haunt the sylvan bow'rs? ....Od.6.144.214.
But, nymphs, recede! safe chastity denies ....Od.6.263.222.
The nymphs withdrawn, at once into the tide ....Od.6.265.223.
Rows'd by the woodland nymphs, at early dawn, ...Od.9.178.312.
Nymphs sprung from fountains, or from shady woods, ...Od.10.415.364.
Swift she descends: A train of nymphs divine ....Od.12.25.430.
On which the labours of the nymphs were roll'd, ...Od.13.128.8.
One sacred to the *Nymphs* apart they lay; ....Od.14.484.59.
Beneath, sequester'd to the nymphs, is seen ....Od.17.242.143.
Nymphs of this fountain! to whose sacred names ....Od.17.284.146.
Attendant Nymphs in beauteous order wait ....Od.19.64.195.
To diff'rent tasks their toil the Nymphs addres'd: ....Od.19.73.196.

NYSSA'S
With brandish'd Steel from *Nyssa's* sacred Grove, ...Il.6.164.334.

OÏLEAN
Oïlean Ajax first his Javelin sped, ...Il.14.517.188.
Oïlean Ajax first the Voice obey'd, ...Il.17.302.299.
Oïlean Ajax rises to the Race; ....Il.23.882.524.

OÏLEUS
And brave *Oïleus,* prove your Force in Fight: ....1.TrES.84.453.
Oïleus follow'd, *Idomen* was there, ...Il.7.201.373.
Mages for Strength, *Oïleus* fam'd for Speed. ....Il.10.124.7.
Whose Squire *Oïleus,* with a sudden spring, ...Il.11.129.41.
And brave *Oïleus,* prove your Force in Fight: ....Il.12.438.97.
Strips his bright Arms, *Oïleus* lops his Head: ....Il.13.270.117.
Iphyclus' Son: and that (*Oïleus)* thine: ....Il.13.870.147.
But hapless *Medon* from *Oïleus* came; ....Il.15.378.211.
Old Man! (*Oïleus* rashly thus replies) ....Il.23.556.511.
All start at once; *Oïleus* led the Race; ....Il.23.887.524.

OÏLEUS'
Ajax the less, *Oïleus'* valiant Son; ....Il.2.631.157.
Oïleus' Son whom beauteous *Rhena* bore. ....Il.2.883.165.
Th' inspiring God, *Oïleus'* active Son ....Il.13.97.109.
But stretch'd in heaps before *Oïleus'* Son, ...Il.14.615.192.
Beneath *Oïleus'* Arm, a living Prize; ....Il.16.395.258.

O
Accept, O *Garth,* the Muse's early Lays, ...1.PSu.9.72.
Delight no more—O Thou my Voice inspire ....1.Mes.5.112.
Granville commands: Your Aid O Muses bring! ....1.W-F.5.148.
"Let me, O let me, to the Shades repair, ...1.W-F.201.168.
(The *World's* just Wonder, and ev'n *thine* O *Rome!)* .... 1.EOC.248.268.
A wretch undone: O parents help, and deign ....1.TrPA.142.371.
She stood and cry'd, "O you that love in vain! ....1.TrSP.187.401.
And fix, O Muse! the Barrier of thy Song, ...1.TrSt.20.410.
Exclaim'd—O *Thebes!* for thee what Fates remain, ...1.TrSt.234.420.
Reverse, O *Jove,* thy too severe Decree, ...1.TrSt.396.426.
Propitious hear our Pray'r, O Pow'r Divine! ....1.TrSt.855.445.
What Words are these, O Sov'reign of the Skies? ....1.TrES.238.458.
O grace serene! oh virtue heav'nly fair! ....2.ElAb.297.343.
And Peace, O Virtue! Peace is all thy own. ....3.EOM4.82B.136.
"But the best *Words?"*—*"O* Sir, the *Dictionary."* .... 4.JD4.69.31.

O (CONTINUED)

Hast thou, O *Sun!* beheld an emptier sort, ... 4.JD4.204.43.
But O! with one, immortal One dispense, ... 5.DunA3.215.175.
Hibernian Politicks, O Swift, thy doom, ... 5.DunA3.327.190.
Hibernian Politicks, O Swift, thy fate, ... 5.DunA3.327A.190.
To serve his cause, O Queen! is serving thine. .... 5.DunB1.214.285.
Hibernian Politics, O Swift! thy fate; .... 5.DunB3.331.336.
To sound or sink in *cano,* O or A, ... 5.DunB4.221.364.
Prop thine, O Empress! like each neighbour Throne, ... 5.DunB4.333.376.
Thy stone, O *Sysiphus,* stands still; .... 6.11.66.32.
Wou'd each hope to be *O* in *Thomas;* .... 6.30.71.88.
And cry, O hone! O hone! .... 6.90.13.251.
And cry, O hone! O hone! .... 6.90.13.251.
Where sleeps my Gulliver? *O tell me where?* .... 6.96iv.47.277.
'Tis not for that I grieve; O, 'tis to see .... 6.96iv.59A.278.
Oh born to Arms! O Worth in Youth approv'd! .... 6.113.3.320.
Did MILTON'S Prose, O CHARLES, thy Death defend .... 6.116viii.1.328.
Then mix this Dust with thine—O spotless Ghost! .... 6.123.5.343.
And O! wou'd Fate the Bliss decree .... 6.135.69.369.
Declare, O Muse! in what ill-fated Hour .... Il.1.9.85.
Of all the *Grecian* Woes, O Goddess, sing! .... Il.1.2A.82.
A Prize as small, O Tyrant! match'd with thine, ... Il.1.215.97.
'Tis just, O Goddess! I thy Dictates hear. .... Il.1.288.100.
Leave me, O King! to calm *Achilles'* Rage; .... Il.1.372.106.
If e'er, O Father of the Gods! she said, ... Il.1.652.118.
Ev'n now, O King! 'tis giv'n thee to destroy .... Il.2.35.129.
Ev'n now, O King! 'tis giv'n thee to destroy .... Il.2.85.130.
But now, O Monarch! all thy Chiefs advise: .... Il.2.428.147.
Say next O Muse! of all *Achaia* breeds, ... Il.2.924.167.
My self, O King! have seen that wondrous Man; .... Il.3.266.205.
Arise, O Father of the *Trojan* State! .... Il.3.319.208.
Shall then, O Tyrant of th' Æthereal Reign! .... Il.4.35.222.
Secure of me, O King! exhort the rest: .... Il.4.303.235.
What needs, O Monarch, this invidious Praise, ... Il.4.456.242.
Thy Fate was next, O *Phæstus!* doom'd to feel .... Il.5.57.269.
Thy Father's Skill, O *Phereclus,* was thine, ... Il.5.77.270.
Too late, O Friend! my Rashness I deplore; .... Il.5.258.279.
Not these, O Daughter, are thy proper Cares, ... Il.5.519.293.
Thy Sire, O Prince! o'erturn'd the *Trojan* State, ... Il.5.804.304.
From thee, O Father! all these Ills we bear, ... Il.5.1072.317.
Be this, O Mother, your religious Care; .... Il.6.348.343.
What cause, O Daughter of Almighty *Jove!* .... Il.7.29.364.
You then, O Princes of the *Greeks!* appear, ... Il.7.85.367.
Whither, O *Menelaus!* would'st thou run, ... Il.7.127.369.
How dear, O Kings! this fatal Day has cost, ... Il.7.392.383.
Next, O ye Chiefs! we ask a Truce to burn .... Il.7.470.387.
The Gods, O Chief! from whom our honours spring, ... Il.9.51.434.
But thou, O King, to Council call the old: .... Il.9.96.437.
Regard in time, O Prince divinely brave! .... Il.9.326.450.
The Goddess then: O Son of *Priam* hear! .... Il.11.257.46.
O Friends! O *Greeks!* assert your Honours won; .... Il.11.355.50.
And stand we deedless, O eternal Shame! .... Il.11.407.53.
Thither, O *Hector,* thither urge thy Steeds; .... Il.11.650.62.
What God, O *Grecians!* has your Hearts dismay'd? .... Il.11.714.67.
'Tis yours, O Warriors, all our Hopes to raise; .... Il.13.73.108.
Attend, O *Hector,* what I judge the best. .... Il.13.922.148.
And must I then (said she) O Sire of Floods! .... Il.15.224.205.
(That valu'd Life, O *Phœbus!* was thy Care) .... Il.15.618.220.
O Friends! O Heroes! Names for ever dear, ... Il.15.890.231.
What Words are these, O Sov'reign of the Skies? .... Il.16.541.265.
Is this, O Chief! a Hero's boasted Fame? .... Il.17.157.293.
Vouchsafe, O *Thetis!* at our Board to share .... Il.18.475.344.
Stretch not henceforth, O Prince! thy sov'reign Might, ... Il.19.179.379.
The *Dardan* Prince, O *Neptune,* be thy Care; .... Il.20.360.410.
What Pow'r, O Prince, with Force inferior far, ... Il.20.381.411.
The yellow Flood began: O Son of *Jove!* .... Il.21.249.431.
Have mercy on me, O my Son! Revere .... Il.22.114.457.
What God, O Muse! assisted *Hector's* Force, ... Il.22.263.466.
Too long, O *Hector!* have I born the Sight .... Il.22.295.468.
Then he. O Prince! ally'd in Blood and Fame, ... Il.22.299.468.
Enough, O Son of *Peleus! Troy* has view'd
Would I had never been!—O thou, the Ghost .... Il.22.616.481.
(O King of Men!) it claims thy royal Care, ... Il.23.61.489.
To you O *Grecians!* be my Wrong declar'd: .... Il.23.654.515.
Still may our Souls, O gen'rous Youth! agree, ... Il.23.685.517.
Accept thou this, O sacred Sire! (he said) .... Il.23.707.517.
Assist O Goddess! (thus in Thought he pray'd) .... Il.23.901.525.
Arise! O *Thetis,* from thy Seats below. .... Il.24.116.540.
I mark some Foes Advance: O King! beware; .... Il.24.435.554.
To whom the latent God. O King forbear .... Il.24.529.558.
Nor thou O Father! thus consum'd with Woe, ... Il.24.755.568.
Such Griefs, O King! have other Parents known; .... Il.24.780.569.
To whom the Prince. O thou whose guardian care .... Od.2.394.80.
Then thus the blue-ey'd Maid: O full of days! .... Od.3.423.107.
View'st thou un-mov'd, O ever-honour'd most! .... Od.4.83.123.
Thy voice, O King! with pleas'd attention heard, ... Od.4.213.129.
Frequent, O King, was *Nestor* wont to raise .... Od.4.259.131.
I thus: O thou, whose certain eye foresees .... Od.4.627.149.
He thus; O were the woes you speak the worst! .... Od.4.924.161.
To whom the Nymph: O stranger cease thy care, ... Od.6.227.220.
Then to the Bard aloud: O cease to sing, ... Od.8.93.267.
Then thus *Euryalus:* O Prince, whose sway .... Od.8.435.287.
Thence to the Queen. O partner of our reign, ... Od.8.459.288.
Then to the Bard aloud: O cease to sing, ... Od.8.585.294.
Thy promis'd boon, O *Cyclop!* now I claim, ... Od.9.431.323.
At last with tears—O what relentless doom .... Od.11.493.408.
The Ghost returns: O chief of humankind .... Od.11.499.408.
Delusive hope! O wife, thy deeds disgrace .... Od.11.537.409.
I then: O nymph propitious to my pray'r, ... Od.12.139.439.
Then she: O worn by toils, oh broke in fight, ... Od.12.143.439.
And *Circe* warns! O be their voice obey'd: .... Od.12.327.447.
To whom with grief—O swift to be undone, ... Od.12.353.448.
To whom the thund'ring Pow'r: O source of day! .... Od.12.452.453.
Then thus: O Queen farewell! be still possest .... Od.13.74.4.
Shall then no more, O Sire of Gods! be mine .... Od.13.148.12.
Then why (she said) O favour'd of the skies! .... Od.16.180.112.

O (CONTINUED)

To win thy grace: O save us, pow'r divine! .... Od.16.203.113.
I am thy father. O my son! my son! .... Od.16.206.114.
What ship transported thee, O father say, ... Od.16.246.116.
To whom with stern regards: O insolence, ... Od.18.20.167.
To whom with frowns: O impudent in wrong! .... Od.18.385.186.
To whom incens'd: Should we, O Prince, engage .... Od.18.410.188.
He thus: O Queen! whose far-resounding fame, ... Od.19.127.199.
Then he, with pity touch'd: O Royal Dame! .... Od.19.298.209.
They're doom'd to bleed; O say, cœlestial maid! .... Od.20.52.234.
Instant, O *Jove!* confound the Suitor train, ... Od.20.147.240.
She thus: O cease that ever-honour'd name .... Od.20.169.241.
O Monarch ever dear!—O man of woe!— .... Od.20.259.245.
Antinous then: O miserable guest! .... Od.21.309.274.
O Prince! O Friend! lo here thy *Medon* stands; .... Od.22.407.307.

O'

As e'er cou'd *Dennis,* of the Laws o' th' Stage; .... 1.EOC.270B.270.
Twice-marry'd Dames are Mistresses o' th' Trade: .... 2.ChJM.110.20.
They'l praise her *Elbow, Heel,* or *Tip o' th' Ear.* .... 4.HAdv.123.85.
A Scot will fight for Christ's Kirk o' the Green; .... 4.2HE1.40.197.
The Courtier's Learning, Policy o' th' Gown, ... 6.8.38.19.

O'CLOCK

As, "What's o'clock?" And, "How's the Wind?" .... 4.HS6.89.255.

O'ER

Pour'd o'er the whitening Vale their fleecy Care, ... 1.PSp.19.62.
O'er Golden Sands let rich *Pactolus* flow, ... 1.PSp.61.66.
And the fleet Shades glide o'er the dusky Green. .... 1.PAu.64.85.
Th' Æthereal Spirit o'er its Leaves shall move, ... 1.Mes.11.113.
Peace o'er the World her Olive-Wand extend, ... 1.Mes.19.114.
Nor Fields with gleaming Steel be cover'd o'er; .... 1.Mes.59.118.
Or Fields with gleaming Steel be cover'd o'er; .... 1.Mes.59A.118.
The levell'd Towns with Weeds lie cover'd o'er, ... 1.W-F.67.156.
O'er Heaps of Ruin stalk'd the stately Hind; .... 1.W-F.70.156.
Stretch'd o'er the Poor, and Church, his Iron Rod, ... 1.W-F.75.157.
O'er sandy Wilds were yellow Harvests spread, ... 1.W-F.88.158.
Till hov'ring o'er 'em sweeps the swelling Net. .... 1.W-F.104.160.
Swarm o'er the Lawns, the Forest Walks surround, ... 1.W-F.149.164.
Hang o'er their Coursers Heads with eager Speed, ... 1.W-F.157.164.
Here was she seen o'er Airy Wastes to rove, ... 1.W-F.167.165.
O'er figur'd Worlds now travels with his Eye. .... 1.W-F.246.172.
Consults the Dead, and lives past Ages o'er. .... 1.W-F.248.172.
Here o'er the Martyr-King the Marble weeps, ... 1.W-F.313.179.
His Tresses dropt with Dews, and o'er the Stream .... 1.W-F.331.182.
Project long Shadows o'er the Chrystal Tyde. .... 1.W-F.376.187.
Mount o'er the Vales, and seem to tread the Sky; .... 1.EOC.226.265.
Hills peep o'er Hills, and *Alps* on *Alps* arise! .... 1.EOC.232.265.
Flies o'er th'unbending Corn, and skims along the Main. .... 1.EOC.373.283.
Than when they promise to give *Scribling* o'er. .... 1.EOC.595.307.
Who conquer'd *Nature,* shou'd preside o'er *Wit.* .... 1.EOC.652.313.
A *second* Deluge Learning thus o'er-run, ... 1.EOC.691.317.
Rome's ancient *Genius,* o'er its *Ruins* spread, ... 1.EOC.699.319.
Thence Arts o'er all the *Northern World* advance; .... 1.EOC.711.322.
So great the tale, I scarce can count them o'er; .... 1.TrPA.80.368.
My father o'er your seas presides; and he .... 1.TrPA.112.370.
Roar'd out for rage, and hurried o'er the plain: .... 1.TrPA.133.371.
Oft o'er his Back a crooked Scythe is laid, ... 1.TrVP.33.378.
Spread thy soft Wings, and waft me o'er the Main, ... 1.TrSP.210.403.
O'er the wide Fields the furious Mother flew, ... 1.TrSt.16.410.
O'er the wide Earth, and o'er the watry Main, ... 1.TrSt.44.411.
O'er the wide Earth, and o'er the watry Main, ... 1.TrSt.44.411.
Ye Gods that o'er the gloomy Regions reign .... 1.TrSt.81.413.
While These exalt their Scepters o'er my Urn; .... 1.TrSt.106.414.
Which o'er their Childrens Children shall prevail: .... 1.TrSt.112.414.
Which shall o'er long Posterity prevail: .... 1.TrSt.112A.414.
A Robe obscene was o'er her Shoulders thrown, ... 1.TrSt.154.416.
And o'er the *Theban* Palace spreads her Wings, ... 1.TrSt.170.417.
When banish'd *Cadmus* wandring o'er the Main, ... 1.TrSt.247.420.
High o'er the rowling Heav'ns, a Mansion lyes, ... 1.TrSt.276.421.
Triumphant o'er th'eluded Rage of *Jove!* .... 1.TrSt.303.422.
When all my Glories o'er her Limbs were spread, ... 1.TrSt.362.425.
And draws a radiant Circle o'er the Skies. .... 1.TrSt.442.428.
Then sees *Cythæron* towring o'er the Plain, ... 1.TrSt.466.429.
Wide o'er the World in solemn Pomp she drew .... 1.TrSt.476.430.
And spreads its ancient Poysons o'er the Grounds: .... 1.TrSt.503.431.
That driv'n by Storms, and pouring o'er the Plain, ... 1.TrSt.514.432.
O'er all his Bosom secret Transports reign, ... 1.TrSt.579.434.
O'er all his Bosom sacred Transports reign, ... 1.TrSt.579A.434.
O'er their fair Cheeks the glowing Blushes rise, ... 1.TrSt.630.436.
(Transfix'd as o'er *Castalia's* Streams he hung, ... 1.TrSt.666.438.
With Orbs unroll'd lay stretch'd o'er all the Plain, ... 1.TrSt.665A.438.
So stalks the Lordly Savage o'er the Plain, ... 1.TrES.15.450.
A Show'r of Blood o'er all the fatal Field. .... 1.TrES.257.459.
The Car rowls slowly o'er the dusty Plain. .... 1.TrES.280.460.
Which o'er the Warrior's Shoulder took its Course, ... 1.TrES.283.460.
O'er all his Limbs *Ambrosial* Odours shed, ... 1.TrES.328.461.
So mounts the bounding Vessel o'er the Main: .... 1.TrUl.10.465.
Perpetual Waters o'er the Pavement glide; .... 1.TrUl.41.467.
Cast a long Look o'er all the Coast and Main, ... 1.TrUl.70.468.
The Gold, the Vests, the Tripods number'd o'er; .... 1.TrUl.95.469.
But in due Time, when Sixty Years were o'er, ... 2.ChJM.9.15.
And each bright Image wander'd o'er his Heart. .... 2.ChJM.233.25.
The gliding Shadows o'er the polish'd Glass. .... 2.ChJM.237.26.
That ere the Rites are o'er, you may repent! .... 2.ChJM.281.27.
The Knights so nimbly o'er the Greensword bound, ... 2.ChJM.621.45.
Madam, 'tis past, and my short Anger o'er; .... 2.ChJM.789.53.
He hugg'd her close, and kiss'd her o'er and o'er, ... 2.ChJM.813.54.
He hugg'd her close, and kiss'd her o'er and o'er, ... 2.ChJM.813.54.
If once my Husband's Arm was o'er my Side, ... 2.ChWB.166.64.
The Pit fill'd up, with Turf we cover'd o'er, ... 2.ChWB.251.69.
And Empire o'er his Tongue, and o'er his Hand. .... 2.ChWB.433.78.
And Empire o'er his Tongue, and o'er his Hand. .... 2.ChWB.433.78.
The Morning-Dream that hover'd o'er her Head. .... 2.RL1.22.147.
Hang o'er the *Box,* and hover round the *Ring.* .... 2.RL1.44.149.

O'ER (CONTINUED)

The Sun first rises o'er the purpled Main, ... 2.RL2.2.159.
Soft o'er the Shrouds Aerial Whispers breathe, ... 2.RL2.57.163.
Or o'er the Glebe distill the kindly Rain. .... 2.RL2.86.165.
Others on Earth o'er human Race preside, ... 2.RL2.87.165.
A livid Paleness spreads o'er all her Look; .... 2.RL3.90.174.
Some o'er her Lap their careful Plumes display'd, ... 2.RL3.115.176.
As o'er the fragrant Steams she bends her Head: .... 2.RL3.134.178.
A constant *Vapour* o'er the Palace flies; .... 2.RL4.39.186.
Full o'er their Heads the swelling Bag he rent, ... 2.RL4.91.191.
O'er the wide Prospect as I gaz'd around, ... 2.TemF.21.254.
Rise white in Air, and glitter o'er the Coast; .... 2.TemF.54.256.
O'er-wrought with Ornaments of barb'rous Pride. .... 2.TemF.120.263.
Which o'er each Object casting various Dies, ... 2.TemF.133.264.
Grav'd o'er their Seats the Form of *Time* was found, ... 2.TemF.147.265.
High o'er the rest *Epaminondas* stood; .... 2.TemF.161.267.
Six pompous Columns o'er the rest aspire; .... 2.TemF.179.270.
His Silver Beard wav'd gently o'er his Breast; .... 2.TemF.185.270.
Troy flam'd in burning Gold, and o'er the Throne .... 2.TemF.208.272.
The Youths hang o'er their Chariots as they run; .... 2.TemF.218.272.
Troy flam'd in burnish'd Gold, and o'er the Throne .... 2.TemF.208A.272.
Myrtles and Bays, hung hov'ring o'er his Head. .... 2.TemF.231.274.
O'er which a pompous Dome invades the Skies: .... 2.TemF.245.275.
O'er dusky Fields and shaded Waters fly, ... 2.TemF.285.277.
And spread o'er all the fluid Element. .... 2.TemF.447.285.
The darksom pines that o'er yon' rocks reclin'd .... 2.ElAb.155.332.
But o'er the twilight groves, and dusky caves, ... 2.ElAb.163.332.
I hear thee, view thee, gaze o'er all thy charms, ... 2.ElAb.233.339.
And low-brow'd rocks hang nodding o'er the deeps. .... 2.ElAb.244.339.
Till ev'ry motion, pulse, and breath, be o'er; .... 2.ElAb.333.346.
Then, ages hence, when all my woes are o'er, ... 2.ElAb.345.347.
O'er the pale marble shall they join their heads, ... 2.ElAb.349.348.
Nor hallow'd dirge be mutter'd o'er thy tomb? .... 2.Elegy.62.367.
Life's idle business at one gasp be o'er, ... 2.Elegy.81.368.
Expatiate free o'er all this scene of Man; .... 3.EOM1.5.11.
His fiery course, or drives him o'er the plains; .... 3.EOM1.62.21.
Or touch, if tremblingly alive all o'er, ... 3.EOM1.197.39.
His touch, if tremblingly alive all o'er, ... 3.EOM1.197A.39.
The touch, if tremblingly alive all o'er, ... 3.EOM1.197B.39.
Or touch, so tremblingly alive all o'er, ... 3.EOM1.197C.39.
'Till tir'd he sleeps, and Life's poor play is o'er! .... 3.EOM2.282.88.
Thou too must perish, when thy feast is o'er! .... 3.EOM3.70.99.
Sure never to o'er-shoot, but just to hit, ... 3.EOM3.89.101.
And Reason raise o'er Instinct as you can, ... 3.EOM3.97.101.
"Yet go! and thus o'er all the creatures sway, ... 3.EOM3.195.113.
O'er-look'd, seen double, by the fool, and wise. .... 3.EOM4.6.128.
But grant him Riches, your demand is o'er? .... 3.EOM4.157.142.
Stuck o'er with titles and hung round with strings, ... 3.EOM4.205.146.
That buys your sex a Tyrant o'er itself. .... 3.Ep2.288A.73.
Rufa, whose eye quick-glancing o'er the Park, ... 3.Ep2.21.50.
Which buys your sex a Tyrant o'er itself. .... 3.Ep2.288.73.
A single leaf may waft an Army o'er, ... 3.Ep3.73A.93.
A single leaf can waft an Army o'er, ... 3.Ep3.73B.93.
A single leaf shall waft an Army o'er, ... 3.Ep3.73.93.
Benighted wanderers, the forest o'er, ... 3.Ep3.195.109.
With silver-quiv'ring rills mæander'd o'er— .... 3.Ep4.85.146.
Behold! my Lord advances o'er the Green .... 3.Ep4.127A.149.
Rolls o'er my *Grotto*, and but sooths my Sleep. .... 4.HS1.124.17.
He past it o'er; affects an easy Smile .... 4.JD4.122.35.
He past it o'er; put on an easy Smile .... 4.JD4.122A.35.
And talks *Gazettes* and *Post-Boys* o'er by heart. .... 4.JD4.155.39.
Thou, who since Yesterday, has roll'd o'er all .... 4.JD4.202.43.
And shake all o'er, like a discover'd Spy. .... 4.JD4.279.49.
My Verse, and QUEENSB'RY weeping o'er thy Urn! .... 4.Arbu.260.114.
O'er a learn'd, un-intelligible Place; .... 4.JD2A.105.142.
I pass o'er all those Confessors and Martyrs .... 4.JD2.35.135.
O'er a learn'd, unintelligible place; .... 4.JD2.102.143.
Shall glitter o'er the pendent green, ... 4.HOde1.23.151.
With me, alas! those joys are o'er; .... 4.HOde1.31.153.
With me, alas! these joys are o'er; .... 4.HOde1.31A.153.
These rais'd new Empires o'er the Earth, ... 4.HOde9.11.159.
But let the Fit pass o'er, I'm wise enough, ... 4.2HE2.151.175.
(Like twinkling Stars the Miscellanies o'er) .... 4.2HE1.110.205.
Her Arts victorious triumph'd o'er our Arms: .... 4.2HE1.264.217.
And snatch me, o'er the earth, or thro' the air, ... 4.2HE1.346.225.
T' enroll your triumphs o'er the seas and land; .... 4.2HE1.373.227.
How, when you nodded, o'er the land and deep, ... 4.2HE1.400.229.
Hang their old Trophies o'er the Garden gates, ... 4.1HE1.8.279.
Our Youth, all liv'ry'd o'er with foreign Gold, ... 4.EpS1.155.309.
On Crimes that scape, or triumph o'er the Law: .... 4.EpS1.168.309.
Spin all your Cobwebs o'er the Eye of Day! .... 4.EpS2.222.325.
Blotch thee all o'er, and sink.. .... 4.1740.84.337.
Dulnes o'er all possess'd her antient right, ... 5.DunA1.9.61.
She, tinsel'd o'er in robes of varying hues, ... 5.DunA1.79.69.
Now Night descending, the proud scene was o'er, ... 5.DunA1.87.69.
Ah! still o'er Britain stretch that peaceful wand, ... 5.DunA1.155.82.
And labours, 'till it clouds itself all o'er. .... 5.DunA1.172.84.
O'er head and ears plunge for the plublick weal. .... 5.DunA1.196.86.
Sudden she flies, and whelms it o'er the pyre: .... 5.DunA1.215.89.
The Goddess then o'er his anointed head, ... 5.DunA1.241.91.
The stream, and smoaking, flourish'd o'er his head. .... 5.DunA2.172.122.
Now gentle touches wanton o'er his face, ... 5.DunA2.193.124.
But far o'er all, sonorous Blackmore's strain, ... 5.DunA2.247.129.
Next Smedley div'd; slow circles dimpled o'er .... 5.DunA2.279.135.
Next *E[usden]* div'd; slow circles dimpled o'er .... 5.DunA2.279A.135.
Th' unconscious flood sleeps o'er thee like a lake. .... 5.DunA2.292.138.
If there be man who o'er such works can wake, ... 5.DunA2.340.142.
Then down are roll'd the books; stretch'd o'er 'em lies .... 5.DunA2.371.145.
Round, and more round, o'er all the sea of heads. .... 5.DunA2.378.146.
Boyer the State, and Law the Stage gave o'er, ... 5.DunA2.381.146.
T[raver]s and *T[rapp]* the church and state gave o'er, ... 5.DunA2.381A.146.
As thick as bees o'er vernal blossoms fly, ... 5.DunA3.25.152.
The hand of Bavius drench'd thee o'er and o'er. .... 5.DunA3.38.154.
The hand of Bavius drench'd thee o'er and o'er. .... 5.DunA3.38.154.
Then stretch thy sight o'er all her rising reign, ... 5.DunA3.57.155.
And Her Parnassus glancing o'er at once, ... 5.DunA3.129.161.

O'ER (CONTINUED)

And all Parnassus glancing o'er at once, ... 5.DunA3.129A.161.
Her magic charms o'er all unclassic ground: .... 5.DunA3.254.178.
And pour'd her Spirit o'er the land and deep. .... 5.DunB1.8.269.
Dulness o'er all possess'd her ancient right, ... 5.DunB1.11.269.
Where o'er the gates, by his fam'd father's hand .... 5.DunB1.31.271.
She, tinsel'd o'er in robes of varying hues, ... 5.DunB1.81.275.
Now Night descending, the proud scene was o'er, ... 5.DunB1.89.276.
Next, o'er his Books his eyes began to roll, ... 5.DunB1.127.278.
And suck'd all o'er, like an industrious Bug. .... 5.DunB1.130.279.
O'er head and ears plunge for the Commonweal? .... 5.DunB1.210.285.
And see! thy very Gazetteers give o'er, ... 5.DunB1.215.285.
Now, see thy very Gazetteers give o'er, ... 5.DunB1.215A.285.
Sudden she flies, and whelms it o'er the pyre; .... 5.DunB1.259.289.
The Goddess then, o'er his anointed head, ... 5.DunB1.287.290.
Where the tall may-pole once o'er-look'd the Strand; .... 5.DunB2.28.297.
The stream, and smoking flourish'd o'er his head. .... 5.DunB2.180.304.
Now gentle touches wanton o'er his face, ... 5.DunB2.201.305.
But far o'er all, sonorous Blackmore's strain; .... 5.DunB2.259.308.
Next Smedley div'd; slow circles dimpled o'er .... 5.DunB2.291.309.
Th' unconscious stream sleeps o'er thee like a lake. .... 5.DunB2.304.310.
Here brisker vapours o'er the Temple creep, ... 5.DunB2.345.314.
"If there be man, who o'er such works can wake, ... 5.DunB2.372.315.
Then down are roll'd the books; stretch'd o'er 'em lies .... 5.DunB2.403.316.
Round and more round, o'er all the sea of heads. .... 5.DunB2.410.317.
Boyer the State, and Law the Stage gave o'er, ... 5.DunB2.413.317.
As thick as bees o'er vernal blossoms fly, ... 5.DunB3.33.322.
The hand of Bavius drench'd thee o'er and o'er. .... 5.DunB3.46.322.
The hand of Bavius drench'd thee o'er and o'er. .... 5.DunB3.46.322.
Then stretch thy sight o'er all her rising reign, ... 5.DunB3.65.323.
And her Parnassus glancing o'er at once, ... 5.DunB3.137.326.
Her magic charms o'er all unclassic ground: .... 5.DunB3.258.332.
O'er ev'ry vein a shudd'ring horror runs; .... 5.DunB4.143.355.
There truant WYNDHAM ev'ry Muse gave o'er, ... 5.DunB4.167.357.
While tow'ring o'er your Alphabet, like Saul, ... 5.DunB4.217.363.
Stands our Digamma, and o'er-tops them all. .... 5.DunB4.218.364.
Or chew'd by blind old Scholiasts o'er and o'er. .... 5.DunB4.232.365.
Or chew'd by blind old Scholiasts o'er and o'er. .... 5.DunB4.232.365.
And labours till it clouds itself all o'er. .... 5.DunB4.254.369.
Intrepid then, o'er seas and lands he flew: .... 5.DunB4.293.373.
Or, at one bound o'er-leaping all his laws, ... 5.DunB4.477.388.
Wide, and more wide, it spread o'er all the realm; .... 5.DunB4.613.405.
The Vapour mild o'er each Committee crept; .... 5.DunB4.615.405.
And pours her Spirit o'er the Land and Deep. .... 5.DunB4.627Z2.407.
Mountains of Casuistry heap'd o'er her head! .... 5.DunB4.642.408.
Therefore, dear Friend, at my Advice give o'er .... 6.7.21.16.
O'er all the dreary Coasts! .... 6.11.55.32.
O'er th' *Elysian* Flowers, ... 6.11.73.33.
O'er Death and o'er Hell, ... 6.11.88.33.
O'er Death and o'er Hell, ... 6.11.88.33.
See, wild as the Winds, o'er the Desart he flies; .... 6.11.110.34.
Lo the glad gales o'er all her beauties stray, ... 6.14iii.5.45.
Quite o'er the Banks to their own Ruin force. .... 6.17ii.17.56.
These Censures o'er, to different Subjects next, ... 6.17iv.15.59.
'Till Death scarce felt did o'er his Pleasures creep, ... 6.19.13A.62.
And o'er his breast extend his saving shield: .... 6.21.14.69.
At length, my soul! thy fruitless hopes give o'er, ... 6.22.1.71.
A Damp creeps cold o'er every Part, ... 6.31ii.6Z3.94.
Live o'er each scene, and be what they behold: .... 6.32.4.96.
Or o'er cold coffee trifle with the spoon, ... 6.45.17.125.
Together o'er the *Alps* methinks we fly, ... 6.52.25.157.
Wide o'er th' aerial Vault extends thy sway, ... 6.65.3.192.
And o'er th' infernal Regions void of day, ... 6.65.4.192.
Wide o'er th' Æthereal Walks extends thy sway, ... 6.65.3A.192.
And o'er th' infernal Mansions void of day, ... 6.65.4A.192.
Full gently praunch'd he o'er the Lawn; .... 6.79.109.221.
Long look'd the Field all o'er: .... 6.79.114.221.
Some joy still lost, as each vain year runs o'er, ... 6.86.7.245.
And so the Work was o'er. .... 6.94.68.261.
"From Place to Place o'er *Brobdingnag* I'll roam, ... 6.96ii.37.272.
"To see thee leap the Lines, and traverse o'er .... 6.96ii.62.273.
And all thy Dangers I weep o'er again! .... 6.96iv.86.278.
Fair, o'er the western world, renew'd his light, ... 6.107.2.310.
No Conquests she, but o'er herself desir'd, ... 6.115.3.322.
"O'er his vast heaps in drunkenness of pride .... 6.130.33.359.
(Aye watching o'er his Saints with Eye unseen,) .... 6.137.3.373.
Or any good Creature shall lay o'er my Head; .... 6.144.4.386.
May *Jove* restore you, when your Toils are o'er, ... Il.1.25.86.
Th' Assembly seated, rising o'er the rest, ... Il.1.77.90.
Achilles self conduct her o'er the Main; .... Il.1.190.96.
To Reason yield the Empire o'er his Mind. .... Il.1.276.100.
Two Ages o'er his native Realm he reign'd, ... Il.1.335.104.
And oft look'd back, slow-moving o'er the Strand. .... Il.1.453.109.
O'er the wild Margin of the Deep he hung, ... Il.1.456.109.
O'er all his wide Dominion of the Dead, ... Il.1.537.113.
'Till rosie Morn had purpled o'er the Sky: .... Il.1.623.117.
Who rolls the Thunder o'er the vaulted Skies. .... Il.1.671.119.
Destruction hangs o'er yon' devoted Wall, ... Il.2.17.128.
Descends and hovers o'er *Atrides'* Head; .... Il.2.20.128.
Destruction hangs o'er yon' devoted Wall, ... Il.2.39.129.
The heav'nly *Phantome* hover'd o'er my Head, ... Il.2.75.130.
Destruction hangs o'er yon' devoted Wall, ... Il.2.89.130.
And o'er the Vale descends the living Cloud. .... Il.2.116.133.
Our shatter'd Barks may yet transport us o'er, ... Il.2.169.136.
Thus o'er the Field the moving Host appears, ... Il.2.181.137.
That o'er the Windings of *Cayster's* Springs, ... Il.2.542.153.
With rushing Troops the Plains are cover'd o'er, ... Il.2.548.153.
Tow'rs o'er his Armies, and outshines them all: .... Il.2.565.154.
Jove o'er his Eyes celestial Glories spread, ... Il.2.570.155.
These, o'er the bending Ocean, *Helen's* Cause .... Il.2.709.159.
And bounded there, where o'er the Vallies rose .... Il.2.749.161.
But those who view fair *Elis* o'er the Seas .... Il.2.759.162.
Of willing Exiles wander'd o'er the Main; .... Il.2.806.163.
Yet o'er the silver Surface pure they flow, ... Il.2.912.167.
O'er Fields of Death they whirl the rapid Car, ... Il.2.932.167.
And wand'ring o'er the Camp, requir'd their Lord. .... Il.2.945.168.

O'ER (CONTINUED)
His fiery Coursers thunder o'er the Plains. Il.2.1017.171.
Moves into Ranks, and stretches o'er the Land. Il.3.2.186.
Flow'd o'er his Armour with an easy Pride, Il.3.28.189.
O'er her fair Face a snowy Veil she threw, Il.3.187.200.
The stately Ram thus measures o'er the Ground, Il.3.259.204.
A radiant Baldric, o'er his Shoulder ty'd, Il.3.415.212.
The matchless *Helen* o'er the Walls reclin'd: Il.3.474.214.
At length, ripe Vengeance o'er their Heads impends, Il.4.41.223.
And shake his *Ægis* o'er their guilty Head. Il.4.203.231.
Lo his proud Vessels scatter'd o'er the Main, Il.4.216.231.
Foam o'er the Rocks, and thunder to the Skies. Il.4.483.243.
And Shades Eternal settle o'er his Eyes. Il.4.527.246.
As o'er their Prey rapacious Wolves engage, Il.4.540.247.
Which o'er the Warrior's Shoulder took its Course, Il.5.23.266.
Rapt thro' the Ranks he thunders o'er the Plain, Il.5.113.272.
The purple Current wand'ring o'er his Vest. Il.5.145.274.
Then leaps victorious o'er the lofty Mound. Il.5.181.275.
Such Coursers whirl him o'er the dusty Field, Il.5.232.278.
And two transport *Æneas* o'er the Plain. Il.5.335.283.
O'er the fall'n Trunk his ample Shield display'd, Il.5.365.284.
A sudden Cloud comes swimming o'er his Eyes. Il.5.382.285.
Full o'er your Tow'rs shall fall, and sweep away Il.5.595.297.
Drives o'er the Barn, and whitens all the Hinds. Il.5.616.297.
Mars hovers o'er them with his sable Shield, Il.5.621.297.
And o'er his Eye-balls swum the Shades of Night. Il.5.857.307.
O'er her broad Shoulders hangs his horrid Shield, Il.5.911.309.
O'er all the Gods, superior and alone. Il.5.939.311.
O'er the wide Main extends his boundless Eye, Il.5.961.312.
Whose ample Belt that o'er his Shoulder lay, Il.5.994.314.
The Goddess leaning o'er the bending Yoke, Il.5.996.314.
Black *Orcus'* Helmet o'er her radiant Head. Il.5.1037.316.
High o'er the dusty Whirlwind scales the Heav'n. Il.5.1063.317.
Where the black Horse-hair nodded o'er his Crest: Il.6.12.323.
Wide o'er the Field, resistless as the Wind, Il.6.51.326.
Atrides o'er him shakes the vengeful Steel; Il.6.54.326.
Most priz'd for Art, and labour'd o'er with Gold, Il.6.114.329.
Who o'er the Sons of Men in Beauty shin'd, Il.6.195.335.
Wide o'er th' *Aleian* Field he chose to stray, Il.6.247.338.
O'er these a Range of Marble Structure runs, Il.6.306.341.
Most priz'd for Art, and labour'd o'er with Gold, Il.6.341.343.
His Mane dishevel'd o'er his Shoulders flies; Il.6.657.360.
Prone fell the Giant o'er a Length of Ground. Il.7.188.373.
And pious Children o'er their Ashes weep. Il.7.403.384.
High o'er them all a gen'ral Tomb be rais'd. Il.7.405.384.
Thus they in Heav'n: while, o'er the *Grecian* Train, Il.7.556.392.
Where o'er her pointed Summits proudly rais'd, Il.8.59.398.
O'er Heav'ns clear Azure spread the sacred Light; Il.8.84.399.
The Clouds burst dreadful o'er the *Grecian* Heads Il.8.94.401.
Curl'd o'er the Brow, it stung him to the Brain; Il.8.106.402.
Roll'd the big Thunder o'er the vast Profound: Il.8.162.405.
He said; and hasty, o'er the gasping Throng Il.8.190.406.
High o'er their slighted Trench our Steeds shall bound, Il.8.218.407.
And pass victorious o'er the levell'd Mound. Il.8.219.407.
Furious he said; then, bending o'er the Yoke, Il.8.224.408.
High o'er the wond'ring Hosts he soar'd above, Il.8.299.412.
O'er the broad Ditch impell'd his foaming Horse; Il.8.306.412.
Their Car in Fragments scatter'd o'er the Sky; Il.8.493.420.
Your Car in Fragments scatter'd o'er the Sky; Il.8.515.421.
Soon was your Battel o'er: Proud *Troy* retir'd Il.8.558.423.
Wide o'er the Field, high-blazing to the Sky, Il.8.631.426.
Whose Wrath hung heavy o'er the *Trojan* Tow'rs; Il.8.682.427.
O'er Heav'ns clear Azure spreads her sacred Light, Il.8.688.428.
O'er the dark Trees a yellower Verdure shed, Il.8.693.428.
And shoot a shady Lustre o'er the Field. Il.8.704.428.
O'er Heav'ns clear Azure sheds her sacred Light, Il.8.688A.428.
Loud neigh the Coursers o'er their Heaps of Corn, Il.8.707.429.
Swells o'er the Sea, from *Thracia's* frozen Shore, Il.9.7.431.
They gave Dominion o'er the Seas and Land, Il.9.54.434.
Yet hear me farther: When our Wars are o'er, Il.9.183.441.
He said; *Patroclus* o'er the blazing Fire Il.9.271.446.
If not—but hear me, while I number o'er Il.9.342.450.
Yet hear me farther: When our Wars are o'er, Il.9.370.451.
But now those ancient Enmities are o'er; Il.9.469.455.
(That spreads her Conquest o'er a thousand States, Il.9.502.458.
And favour'd by the Night, o'er leap'd the Wall. Il.9.587.464.
I pass my Watchings o'er thy helpless Years, Il.9.612.464.
Sweeps the wide Earth, and tramples o'er Mankind, Il.9.629.465.
Till Sleep descending o'er the Tents, bestows Il.9.836.474.
Now o'er the Fields, dejected, he surveys Il.10.13.2.
Whose Son, with *Merion,* o'er the Watch presides.) Il.10.68.5.
Hangs o'er the Fleet, and shades our Walls below? Il.10.183.10.
This said, the Hero o'er his Shoulders flung Il.10.202.10.
Then o'er the Trench the following Chieftains led. Il.10.228.12.
A Boar's white Teeth grinn'd horrid o'er his Head. Il.10.312.16.
Thro' Dust, thro' Blood, o'er Arms, and Hills of Slain. Il.10.356.18.
Which willful err'd, and o'er his Shoulder past; Il.10.442.23.
(Enquir'd the Chief) or scatter'd o'er the Plain? Il.10.495.25.
Slipp'ry with Blood, o'er Arms and Heaps of Shields, Il.10.541.27.
The gath'ring Tumult spreads o'er all the Plain; Il.10.615.29.
Then o'er the Trench the bounding Coursers flew; Il.10.664.31.
And, wrapt in Tempests, o'er the Fleet descends. Il.11.8.35.
Like colour'd Rainbows o'er a show'ry Cloud: Il.11.36.36.
A radiant Baldrick, o'er his Shoulder ty'd, Il.11.39.36.
Last o'er his Brows his fourfold Helm he plac'd, Il.11.53.37.
High o'er the Chief they clash'd their Arms in Air, Il.11.59.37.
Red Drops of Blood o'er all the fatal Field; Il.11.70.37.
O'er Heav'ns pure Azure spread the growing Light, Il.11.116.39.
So when a Lion, ranging o'er the Lawns, Il.11.153.42.
And o'er the Forests roll the Flood of Fire, Il.11.202.44.
Wide o'er the Field with guideless Fury rolls, Il.11.209.44.
And o'er the Body spreads his ample Shield. Il.11.334.49.
O'er his dim Sight the misty Vapours rise, Il.11.459.54.
The scatter'd Crowds fly frighted o'er the Field; Il.11.607.61.
Pours from the Mountains o'er the delug'd Plains, Il.11.615.61.
I know him well, distinguish'd o'er the Field Il.11.648.62.

O'ER (CONTINUED)
O'er Heaps of Carcasses, and Hills of Shields. Il.11.657.63.
O'er his broad Back his moony Shield he threw, Il.11.672.65.
On each bright Handle, bending o'er the Brink, Il.11.776.69.
O'er heapy Shields, and o'er the prostrate Throng, Il.11.886.75.
O'er heapy Shields, and o'er the prostrate Throng, Il.11.886.75.
Where o'er the Vales th' *Olenian* Rocks arose; Il.11.889.75.
Press'd by fresh Forces her o'er-labour'd Train Il.11.932.77.
Shine 'twixt the Hills, or wander o'er the Plain. Il.12.36.83.
And first the Mountain Tops are cover'd o'er, Il.12.337.93.
And the white Ruin rises o'er the Plain. Il.12.344.94.
So stalks the lordly Savage o'er the Plain, Il.12.359.94.
Th' enormous Monsters, rolling o'er the Deep, Il.13.43.107.
And pour her Armies o'er our batter'd Wall; Il.13.78.108.
And swarms victorious o'er their yielding Walls: Il.13.120.110.
An Iron Scene gleams dreadful o'er the Fields, Il.13.179.114.
Thus his bright Armour o'er the dazled Throng Il.13.323.120.
And their bright Arms shot Horror o'er the Plain. Il.13.395.124.
Rush like a fiery Torrent o'er the Field, Il.13.421.126.
Then spreads a length of Ruin o'er the Ground. Il.13.496.130.
O'er his safe Head the Javelin idly sung, Il.13.517.131.
Then *Idomen,* insulting o'er the slain; Il.13.558.133.
O'er spacious *Crete,* and her bold Sons I reign, Il.13.568.133.
Lord of a Host, o'er all my Host I shine, Il.13.570.133.
O'er his bent Back the bristly Horrors rise, Il.13.598.134.
Like *Ida's* Flocks proceeding o'er the Plain; Il.13.621.135.
Moves on in Rank, and stretches o'er the Land. Il.13.627.136.
And o'er their Heads unheeded Javelins sing. Il.13.631.136.
His Shield revers'd o'er the fall'n Warrior lies; Il.13.688.137.
And Conquest hovers o'er th' *Achaian* Bands: Il.13.848.146.
O'er their huge Limbs the Foam descends in Snow, Il.13.883.147.
Black Fate hangs o'er thee from th' avenging Gods, Il.13.971.151.
Wide o'er the blasted Fields the Tempest sweeps, Il.13.1001.152.
Far o'er the Plains, in dreadful Order bright, Il.13.1008.153.
Appears a Warrior furrow'd o'er with Age; Il.14.156.165.
But Heav'n forsakes not thee: O'er yonder Sands Il.14.165.165.
Appears a Hero furrow'd o'er with Age; Il.14.156A.165.
Part o'er her Shoulders wav'd like melted Gold. Il.14.206.170.
Then o'er her Head she casts a Veil more white Il.14.213.170.
O'er high *Pieria* thence her Course she bore, Il.14.259.173.
O'er fair *Emathia's* ever pleasing Shore, Il.14.260.173.
O'er *Hæmus'* Hills with Snows eternal crown'd; Il.14.261.173.
She speeds to *Lemnos* o'er the rowling Deep, Il.14.264.173.
Who spread'st thy Empire o'er each God and Man; Il.14.267.175.
O'er other Gods I spread my easy Chain; Il.14.278.175.
And stretch the other o'er the sacred Main. Il.14.308.177.
Then swift as Wind, o'er *Lemnos* smoaky Isle, Il.14.317.178.
O'er Earth and Seas, and thro' th' aerial way, Il.14.350.179.
Celestial Dews, descending o'er the Ground, Il.14.403.183.
Around the Ships: Seas hanging o'er the Shores, Il.14.455.185.
These proud in Arms, those scatter'd o'er the Plain; Il.15.9.194.
As some way-faring Man, who wanders o'er Il.15.86.199.
Dares, tho' the Thunder bursting o'er my Head Il.15.132.201.
O'er the wide Clouds, and o'er the starry Plain, Il.15.214.205.
O'er the wide Clouds, and o'er the starry Plain, Il.15.214.205.
Stood shining o'er him, half unseal'd his Sight: Il.15.279.207.
His Mane dishevel'd o'er his Shoulders flies; Il.15.303.208.
Sate doubtful Conquest hov'ring o'er the Field; Il.15.361.210.
And o'er the Slaughter stalks gigantic Death. Il.15.393.212.
O'er the dread Fosse (a late-impervious Space) Il.15.410.213.
At one proud Bark, high-tow'ring o'er the Fleet Il.15.482.216.
The fourfold Buckler o'er his Shoulder ty'd; Il.15.565.218.
So when a Savage, ranging o'er the Plain, Il.15.702.223.
Howl o'er the Masts, and sing thro' ev'ry Shroud: Il.15.755.225.
At large expatiate o'er the ranker Mead;) Il.15.763.226.
O'er all his Country's Youth conspicuous far, Il.15.776.226.
A sudden Ray shot beaming o'er the Plain, Il.15.810.227.
O'er the high Stern the curling Volumes rise, Il.16.152.243.
Achilles' Helmet nodded o'er his Head. Il.16.169.244.
Far o'er the rest, in glitt'ring Pomp appear, Il.16.264.249.
Fly diverse, scatter'd o'er the distant Plain. Il.16.347.256.
O'er Heav'ns Expanse like one black Cieling spread; Il.16.355.257.
But *Troy* repuls'd, and scatter'd o'er the Plains, Il.16.362.257.
He sinks, with endless Darkness cover'd o'er, Il.16.386.258.
(Or Kids, or Lambs) lie scatter'd o'er the Plain, Il.16.421.259.
O'er his broad Shoulders spread the massy Shield; Il.16.429.259.
Dark o'er the Fields th' ascending Vapour flies, Il.16.436.259.
Scour o'er the Fields, and stretch to reach the Town. Il.16.453.260.
Loud o'er the Rout was heard the Victor's Cry, Il.16.454.260.
High-bounding o'er the Fosse: the whirling Car Il.16.460.260.
A Show'r of Blood o'er all the fatal Field. Il.16.562.266.
The Car rowls slowly o'er the dusty Plain. Il.16.585.267.
Which o'er the Warrior's Shoulder took its course, Il.16.588.267.
But o'er the Dead the fierce *Patroclus* stands, Il.16.679.270.
The Clash of Armour rings o'er all the Plain. Il.16.694.271.
O'er the fierce Armies pours pernicious Night, Il.16.696.271.
His shatter'd Helm, and stretch'd him o'er the Slain. Il.16.708.271.
Wide o'er the Land was stretch'd his large Domain, Il.16.723.272.
The Lance hiss'd harmless o'er his cov'ring Shield, Il.16.741.272.
O'er all his Limbs Ambrosial Odours shed, Il.16.815.274.
Black Fate hangs o'er thee, and thy Hour draws nigh; Il.16.1029.283.
Rapt in the Chariot o'er the distant Plains, Il.16.1047.283.
When o'er the slaughter'd Bull they hear him roar, Il.17.71.290.
O'er all the black Battalions sent his View, Il.17.123.292.
All grim in Arms, and cover'd o'er with Blood, Il.17.126.292.
Dark o'er the fiery Balls, each hanging Eye-brow lowrs. Il.17.150.293.
(The sable Plumage nodded o'er his Head) Il.17.212.295.
Jove, pouring Darkness o'er the mingled Fight, Il.17.318.300.
He drops *Patroclus'* Foot, and o'er him spread Il.17.344.301.
Such o'er *Patroclus* Body hung the Night, Il.17.426.303.
But Death and Darkness o'er the Carcase spread, Il.17.434.304.
Their Knees, their Legs, their Feet are cover'd o'er, Il.17.447.304.
The brawny Curriers stretch; and labour o'er Il.17.452.304.
For yet 'tis giv'n to *Troy,* to ravage o'er Il.17.520.308.
Then o'er their Backs they spread their solid Shields; Il.17.559.310.
And hiss'd innoxious o'er the Hero's Head: Il.17.597.311.

O'ER (CONTINUED)

So looks the Lion o'er a mangled Boar, ... Il.17.608.312.
And o'er his Seat the bloody Trophies hung. ..... Il.17.611.312.
O'er the dark Clouds extends his Purple Bow, ... Il.17.617.312.
So burns the vengeful Hornet (Soul all o'er) ..... Il.17.642.313.
This heard, o'er *Hector* spreads a Cloud of Woe, ... Il.17.666.314.
Confusion, Tumult, Horror, o'er the Throng ..... Il.17.823.320.
Spreads his broad Waters o'er the level Plains, ... Il.17.840.321.
The scorching Ashes o'er his graceful Head; ..... Il.18.28.325.
The Rage of *Hector* o'er the Ranks was born: ..... Il.18.192.331.
Let but *Achilles* o'er yon' Trench appear, ... Il.18.237.333.
Her *Ægis, Pallas* o'er his Shoulders throws; ..... Il.18.242.334.
(Seen from some Island, o'er the Main afar, ... Il.18.247.334.
Pours unavailing Sorrows o'er the Dead. ..... Il.18.278.335.
Wide o'er the World was *Ilion* fam'd of old ..... Il.18.337.337.
And o'er the Vales, and o'er the Forrest bounds; ..... Il.18.375.339.
And o'er the Vales, and o'er the Forrest bounds; ..... Il.18.375.339.
They brought, and plac'd it o'er the rising Flame: ..... Il.18.406.340.
Last o'er the Dead the milkwhite Veil they threw; ..... Il.18.415.340.
Last o'er the Dead the milkwhite Linen threw; ..... Il.18.415A.340.
Last o'er the Dead the milkwhite Mantle threw; ..... Il.18.415B.340.
The rushing Ocean murmur'd o'er my Head. ..... Il.18.472.344.
The rev'rend Elders nodded o'er the Case; ..... Il.18.586.351.
Soon the white Flocks proceeded o'er the Plains, ... Il.18.607.352.
Stretch'd o'er *Patroclus'* Corse; while all the rest ..... Il.19.7.371.
O'er all the Corse: The Flies forbid their Prey, ... Il.19.41.373.
That tend the Ships, or guide them o'er the Main, ... Il.19.46.373.
When the stern Fury of the War is o'er, ... Il.19.199.381.
Pale lyes my Friend, with Wounds disfigur'd o'er, ... Il.19.209.381.
From *Scyros* Isle conduct him o'er the Main, ... Il.19.353.387.
And scatter o'er the Fields of driving Snow; ..... Il.19.381.388.
Full in the midst, high tow'ring o'er the rest, ... Il.19.390.388.
Then o'er his Breast was brac'd the hollow Gold: ..... Il.19.399.388.
Wide o'er the wat'ry Waste, a Light appears, ... Il.19.405.389.
Loud howls the Storm, and drives them o'er the Main. ..... Il.19.409.389.
Wav'd o'er their Backs, and to the Chariot join'd. ..... Il.19.431.389.
High o'er the Host, all terrible he stands, ... Il.19.438.389.
No—could our Swiftness o'er the Winds prevail, ... Il.19.460.391.
Swift o'er *Olympus* hundred Hills she flies, ... Il.20.7.393.
Mars hov'ring o'er his *Troy,* his Terror shrouds ..... Il.20.69.396.
Spread o'er his Breast the fencing Shield he bore, ... Il.20.196.402.
And cours'd the dappled Beauties o'er the Mead: ..... Il.20.267.405.
And o'er him high the riven Targe extends, ... Il.20.328.407.
And casts thick Darkness o'er *Achilles'* Eyes. ..... Il.20.370.410.
While thus *Achilles* glories o'er the Slain. ..... Il.20.448.413.
Then with revengeful Eyes he scan'd him o'er: ..... Il.20.497.415.
The purple Death comes floating o'er his Eyes. ..... Il.20.552.417.
And stretch'd the Servant o'er his dying Lord. ..... Il.20.568.418.
Then o'er the Stubble up the Mountain flies, ... Il.20.571.418.
As with Autumnal Harvests cover'd o'er, ... Il.20.577.418.
Dash'd from their Hoofs while o'er the Dead they fly, ... Il.20.583.418.
High o'er the Scene of Death *Achilles* stood, ... Il.20.587.418.
Part to the Town fly diverse o'er the Plain, ... Il.21.4.421.
Arm'd with his Sword, high-brandish'd o'er the Waves; ..... Il.21.23.422.
Swift o'er the rolling Pebbles, down the Hills ..... Il.21.295.433.
And shine in mazy Wand'rings o'er the Plains. ..... Il.21.298.433.
O'er all th' expanded Plain the Waters spread; ..... Il.21.348.435.
High o'er the surging Tide, by Leaps and Bounds, ... Il.21.352.435.
Wide o'er the Plain he pours the boundless Blaze; ..... Il.21.399.436.
Loud o'er the Fields his ringing Arms resound: ..... Il.21.475.441.
O'er slaughter'd Heroes, and o'er rolling Steeds. ..... Il.21.606.447.
O'er slaughter'd Heroes, and o'er rolling Steeds. ..... Il.21.606.447.
Now o'er the Fields they stretch with lengthen'd Strides, ... Il.21.713.451.
Close to the Walls advancing o'er the Fields, ... Il.22.5.453.
And o'er the feebler Stars exerts his Rays; ..... Il.22.40.454.
Met at an Oak, or journeying o'er a Plain; ..... Il.22.168.460.
Shot trembling Rays that glitter'd o'er the Land; ..... Il.22.176.461.
As thro' the Forest, o'er the Vale and Lawn, ... Il.22.243.465.
He stoop'd, while o'er his Head the flying Spear ..... Il.22.351.470.
Far-beaming o'er the silver Host of Night, ... Il.22.400.472.
Securely cas'd the Warrior's Body o'er. ..... Il.22.406.472.
O'er the dead Hero, thus (unheard) replies. ..... Il.22.460.474.
High o'er the Slain the great *Achilles* stands, ... Il.22.471.475.
O'er the proud Citadel at length should rise, ... Il.22.520.478.
And bending o'er thee, mix'd the tender Show'r! ..... Il.22.547.479.
The bristly Victims hissing o'er the Fire; ..... Il.23.40.488.
The Form familiar hover'd o'er his Head, ... Il.23.82.490.
O'er Hills, o'er Dales, o'er Crags, o'er Rocks, they go: ..... Il.23.141.494.
O'er Hills, o'er Dales, o'er Crags, o'er Rocks, they go: ..... Il.23.141.494.
O'er Hills, o'er Dales, o'er Crags, o'er Rocks, they go: ..... Il.23.141.494.
O'er Hills, o'er Dales, o'er Crags, o'er Rocks, they go: ..... Il.23.141.494.
Jumping high o'er the Shrubs of the rough Ground, ... Il.23.142.495.
O'er all the Corse their scatter'd Locks they throw. ..... Il.23.166.495.
Bends o'er th' extended Body of the Dead. ..... Il.23.169.496.
Thus o'er *Patroclus* while the Hero pray'd, ... Il.23.190.497.
Suspends around, low-bending o'er the Pile. ..... Il.23.209.498.
Celestial *Venus* hover'd o'er his Head, ... Il.23.228.498.
Mourns o'er the Ashes of an only Son, ... Il.23.275.501.
O'er the broad Ocean pour'd the golden Day: ..... Il.23.283.501.
Wide o'er the Pyle the sable Wine they throw, ... Il.23.311.502.
The Urn a Veil of Linen cover'd o'er. ..... Il.23.316.502.
(Each o'er his flying Courser hung in Air) ..... Il.23.448.508.
And hov'ring o'er, their stretching Shadows sees. ..... Il.23.460.508.
The Coursers bounding o'er the dusty Field. ..... Il.23.531.511.
And hear his Shouts victorious o'er the Plain. ..... Il.23.563.512.
High o'er his Head the circling Lash he wields; ..... Il.23.581.513.
O'er-past *Atrides)* second in the Course. ..... Il.23.598.513.
With Plates of Brass the Corselet cover'd o'er, ... Il.23.639.515.
High o'er the Crowd, enormous Bulk! he rose, ... Il.23.768.520.
Nodding, his Head hangs down his Shoulder o'er; ..... Il.23.810.521.
Besmear'd with Filth, and blotted o'er with Clay, ... Il.23.911.525.
High o'er the wond'ring Crowds the whirling Circle flew. ..... Il.23.996.529.
O'er both their Marks it flew; till fiercely flung ..... Il.23.999.529.
The ruddy Morning rises o'er the Waves; ..... Il.24.22.535.
Spread o'er the sacred Corse his golden Shield. ..... Il.24.33.536.
Refulgent gliding o'er the sable Deeps. ..... Il.24.102.539.

O'ER (CONTINUED)

The Deeps dividing, o'er the Coast they rise, ... Il.24.127.540.
A Show'r of Ashes o'er his Neck and Head. ..... Il.24.202.545.
To view that deathful Eye, and wander o'er ..... Il.24.249.547.
O'er the wide Earth, and o'er the boundless Main: ..... Il.24.420.553.
O'er the wide Earth, and o'er the boundless Main: ..... Il.24.420.553.
O'er all the Corse, and clos'd is ev'ry Wound, ... Il.24.512.557.
O'er pathless Forests, or the roaring Main. ..... Il.24.540.558.
And o'er the Trenches led the rolling Cars. ..... Il.24.550.559.
Of Fir the Roof was rais'd, and cover'd o'er ..... Il.24.553.559.
This low on Earth, that gently bending o'er, ... Il.24.640.563.
These unavailing Sorrows o'er the Dead; ..... Il.24.693.566.
Release my Knees, thy suppliant Arts give o'er, ... Il.24.718.567.
The Sire obey'd him, trembling and o'er-aw'd. ..... Il.24.720.567.
This done, the Garments o'er the Corse they spread; ..... Il.24.736.568.
The Pow'r descending hover'd o'er his Head: ..... Il.24.850.572.
Then pour your boundless Sorrows o'er the Dead. ..... Il.24.895.573.
Now hostile Fleets must waft those Infants o'er, ... Il.24.920.574.
Now twice ten Years (unhappy Years) are o'er ..... Il.24.964.576.
Last o'er the Urn the sacred Earth they spread, ... Il.24.1007.577.
O'er earth and ocean wide prepar'd to soar, ... Od.1.128.38.
O'er the full banquet, and the sprightly bowl) ..... Od.1.336.48.
Plant the fair Column o'er the vacant grave, ... Od.1.380.51.
Sole o'er my vassals, and domestic train. ..... Od.1.508.56.
Then sailing o'er the domes and tow'rs they fly, ... Od.2.181.70.
Destruction sure o'er all your heads impends; ..... Od.2.191.71.
A bark to waft me o'er the rolling main; ..... Od.2.242.73.
Plant the fair column o'er the mighty dead, ... Od.2.251.73.
There, as the waters o'er his hands he shed, ... Od.2.295.76.
O'er the wide waves success thy ways attends: ..... Od.2.310.76.
Wide o'er the bay, by vessel vessel rides; ..... Od.2.333.77.
The best I chuse, to waft thee o'er the tides. ..... Od.2.334.77.
The bark, to waft thee o'er the swelling tides. ..... Od.2.346.77.
Mean time, o'er all the dome, they quaff, they feast, ... Od.2.363.78.
Untouch'd they stood, 'till his long labours o'er ..... Od.2.388.80.
High o'er the roaring waves the spreading sails ..... Od.2.466.83.
And wide o'er earth diffus'd his chearing ray, ... Od.3.3.85.
And held the golden goblet foaming o'er; ..... Od.3.52.89.
Now, gentle guests! the genial banquet o'er, ... Od.3.82.90.
Engage your journey o'er the pathless main? ..... Od.3.87.90.
Brown with o'er-arching shades and pendent woods, ... Od.3.97.90.
Far o'er the rest thy mighty father shin'd, ... Od.3.149.93.
The fourth day shone, when all their labours o'er ..... Od.3.219.96.
Then slowly rising, o'er the sandy space ..... Od.3.496.111.
With rosie lustre purpled o'er the lawn; ..... Od.3.517.112.
Brought the full laver, o'er their hands to pour, ... Od.3.558.114.
O'er his fair limbs a flow'ry vest he threw, ... Od.3.596.117.
With rosy lustre purpled o'er the lawn; ..... Od.3.624.118.
And o'er the shaded landscape rush'd the night. ..... Od.3.630.118.
O'er the warm *Libyan* wave to spread my sails: ..... Od.4.104.124.
Diffus'd o'er each resembling line appear, ... Od.4.191.129.
Such wavy ringlets o'er his shoulders flow! ..... Od.4.202.129.
O'er the congenial dust injoin'd to shear ..... Od.4.271.132.
Seam'd o'er with wounds, which his own sabre gave, ... Od.4.335.135.
And o'er soft palls of purple grain unfold ..... Od.4.405.139.
Th' imperial mantle o'er his vest he threw; ..... Od.4.414.140.
This toilsom voyage o'er the surgy main? ..... Od.4.424.140.
High o'er a gulphy sea, the *Pharian* Isle ..... Od.4.479.142.
Propitious winds, to waft us o'er the main: ..... Od.4.490.143.
Proteus, a name tremendous o'er the main, ... Od.4.521.145.
Our cares were lost. When o'er the eastern lawn, ... Od.4.585.147.
To speed a prosp'rous voyage o'er the seas? ..... Od.4.634.149.
The fleet swift tilting o'er the surges flew, ... Od.4.797.156.
"When o'er her son disastrous death impends." ..... Od.4.1020.165.
A sceptred Lord, who o'er the fruitful plain ..... Od.4.1051.167.
O'er the wide earth, and o'er the boundless main. ..... Od.5.59.174.
O'er the wide earth, and o'er the boundless main. ..... Od.5.59.174.
With wings expanded o'er the foaming flood, ... Od.5.65.175.
Thus o'er the world of waters *Hermes* flew, ... Od.5.68.175.
And roll'd his eyes o'er all the restless main, ... Od.5.203.181.
Sublime to bear thee o'er the gloomy deep. ..... Od.5.212.181.
Then o'er the vessel rais'd the taper mast, ... Od.5.324.187.
A mighty wave rush'd o'er him as he spoke, ... Od.5.403.192.
Flew sail and sail-yards ratling o'er the main. ..... Od.5.408.192.
And now the west-wind whirls it o'er the sea. ..... Od.5.423.192.
Burst o'er the float, and thunder'd on his head. ..... Od.5.467.195.
So the rude *Boreas,* o'er the field new shorn, ... Od.5.470.195.
Ah me! when o'er a length of waters tost, ... Od.5.524.197.
And o'er their limbs diffuse ambrosial oil; ..... Od.6.110.211.
O'er the green mead the sporting virgins play: ..... Od.6.112.211.
As when o'er *Erymanth Diana* roves, ... Od.6.117.211.
High o'er the lawn, with more majestic pace, ... Od.6.123.212.
And shone transcendent o'er the beauteous train. ..... Od.6.128.212.
Springs o'er the fence, and dissipates the fold. ..... Od.6.160.216.
Wide o'er the shore with many a piercing cry ..... Od.6.165.216.
But blest o'er all, the youth with heav'nly charms, ... Od.6.189.218.
O'er all his limbs his hands the wave diffuse, ... Od.6.267.223.
And o'er the silver pours the fusile gold. ..... Od.6.278.224.
Far blooming o'er the field: and as she press'd ..... Od.6.301.225.
Where o'er the furrows waves the golden grain: ..... Od.6.310.225.
The silver scourge, it glitter'd o'er the field: ..... Od.6.378.230.
But o'er the world of waters wing'd her way: ..... Od.7.100.239.
Silver the lintels deep-projecting o'er, ... Od.7.116.240.
In pleasing thought he ran the prospect o'er, ... Od.7.180.244.
From lands remote, and o'er a length of sea? ..... Od.7.319.251.
Wide o'er the world *Alcinous'* glory shine! ..... Od.7.425.258.
O'er unknown seas arriv'd from unknown shores. ..... Od.8.14.262.
How o'er the feast they doom the fall of *Troy;* ..... Od.8.73.266.
Start from the goal, and vanish o'er the strand: ..... Od.8.126.269.
O'er whom supreme, imperial pow'r I bear: ..... Od.8.426.286.
He said, and o'er his shoulder flung the blade. ..... Od.8.451.287.
Now o'er the earth ascends the evening shade: ..... Od.8.452.287.
The fuming water bubble o'er the blaze. ..... Od.8.474.288.
Then o'er his limbs a gorgeous robe he spreads, ... Od.8.493.289.
And o'er the banquet every heart be gay: ..... Od.8.590.294.
Ev'n the stern God that o'er the waves presides, ... Od.8.613.295.

O'ER (CONTINUED)

And o'er the foaming bowl the laughing wine. ....Od.9.10.301.
O'er heav'n's pure azure spread the growing light, ...Od.9.64.305.
Wide o'er the waste the rage of *Boreas* sweeps, ...Od.9.77.306.
From hill to hill, o'er all the desart ground. ....Od.9.140.311.
Our sails we gather'd, cast our cables o'er, ...Od.9.172.312.
The mountain goats came bounding o'er the lawn: ....Od.9.179.313.
Now sunk the sun, and darkness cover'd o'er ....Od.9.195.314.
Arising glitter'd o'er the dewy lawn, ...Od.9.198.314.
High, and with dark'ning lawrels cover'd o'er; ....Od.9.213.314.
Brown with o'er-arching pine, and spreading oak. ....Od.9.216.314.
From *Troy's* fam'd fields, sad wand'rers o'er the main, ...Od.9.307.319.
But answer, the good ship that brought ye o'er, ...Od.9.333.320.
Then stretch'd in length o'er half the cavern'd rock, ...Od.9.354.321.
His flocks, obedient, spread o'er all the hills. ....Od.9.375.321.
And held the brimming goblet foaming o'er: ....Od.9.407.322.
His neck obliquely o'er his shoulder hung, ...Od.9.441.324.
As when a shipwright stands his workmen o'er, ...Od.9.457.324.
And search'd each passing sheep, and felt it o'er, ...Od.9.497.326.
When rosy morning glimmer'd o'er the dales, ...Od.9.515.327.
High o'er the billows flew the massy load, ...Od.9.567.329.
Some vessel, not his own, transport him o'er; ....Od.9.626.332.
'Till ruddy morning purpled o'er the east. ....Od.9.653.333.
And smiling calmness silver'd o'er the deep. ....Od.10.108.345.
When evening rose, and darkness cover'd o'er ....Od.10.210.350.
O'er the fair web the rising figures shine, ...Od.10.256.355.
I heard, and instant o'er my shoulders flung ....Od.10.309.359.
My haughty step, I stalk'd the vally o'er. ....Od.10.326.360.
One o'er the couches painted carpets threw, ...Od.10.417.364.
That in the tripod o'er the kindled pyle ....Od.10.423.365.
A vest and tunick o'er me next she threw, ...Od.10.429.365.
Sad, pleasing sight! with tears each eye ran o'er, ...Od.10.471.366.
Poplars and willows trembling o'er the floods: ....Od.10.605.373.
And o'er th' ingredients strow the hallow'd flour: ....Od.10.617.374.
Full o'er the pit, and hell-ward turn their face: ....Od.10.629.374.
Wide o'er the pool thy faulchion wav'd around ....Od.10.638.374.
My limbs, and o'er me cast a silken vest. ....Od.10.648.375.
Already, friends! ye think your toils are o'er, ...Od.10.671.375.
Still heav'd their hearts, and still their eyes ran o'er. ....Od.10.684.376.
And o'er the shaded billows rush'd the night: ....Od.11.12.379.
And hellward bending, o'er the beach descry ....Od.11.23.380.
O'er these was strow'd the consecrated flour, ...Od.11.33.381.
To speed our course, and waft us o'er the floods, ...Od.11.36.381.
These, and a thousand more swarm'd o'er the ground, ...Od.11.53.383.
Now swift I wav'd my faulchion o'er the blood; ....Od.11.61.383.
Yet as I shook my faulchion o'er the blood, ...Od.11.110.386.
But the false woman o'er the wife prevails. ....Od.11.217.392.
O'er proud *Iölcos Pelias* stretch'd his reign, ...Od.11.311.397.
And stretch the Giant-monsters o'er the ground. ....Od.11.394.403.
The hand of Time had silver'd o'er with snow, ...Od.11.429.405.
O'er the full bowl, the traitor stab'd his guest; ....Od.11.508.408.
And o'er the pavement floats the dreadful tyde— ....Od.11.524.409.
This arm that thunder'd o'er the *Phrygian* plain, ...Od.11.611.414.
Now griesly forms, shoot o'er the lawns of hell. ....Od.11.708.420.
Scream o'er the fiend, and riot in his blood, ...Od.11.712.421.
For as o'er *Panopé's* enamel'd plains ....Od.11.715.421.
Swift o'er the waves we fly; the fresh'ning gales ....Od.11.793.426.
Thus o'er the rolling surge the vessel flies, ...Od.12.1.427.
Fierce o'er the Pyre, by fanning breezes spread, ...Od.12.17.430.
To mark distinct thy voyage o'er the main: ....Od.12.68.433.
High o'er the main two Rocks exalt their brow, ...Od.12.71.433.
Plows o'er that roaring surge its desp'rate way; ....Od.12.80.435.
Wing'd her fleet sail, and push'd her o'er the tyde. ....Od.12.86.436.
Here watchful o'er the flocks, in shady bow'rs ....Od.12.170.440.
Hear all! Fate hangs o'er all! on you it lies ....Od.12.192.441.
Thus the sweet charmers warbled o'er the main; ....Od.12.232.443.
Like waters bubbling o'er the fiery blaze; ....Od.12.285.446.
There while the wild winds whistled o'er the main, ...Od.12.379.449.
There o'er my hands the living wave I pour; ....Od.12.397.450.
Then o'er my eyes the Gods soft slumber shed, ...Od.12.401.450.
But should the pow'rs that o'er mankind preside, ...Od.12.413.451.
Strow'd o'er with morsels cut from ev'ry part. ....Od.12.426.451.
Spreads o'er the coast, and scents the tainted gales; ....Od.12.434.452.
Full o'er our heads, and blackens heav'n with storms. ....Od.12.476.455.
Night dwells o'er all the deep: and now out flies ....Od.12.477.455.
Howls o'er the shroud, and rends it from the mast: ....Od.12.480.455.
And o'er the dungeon cast a dreadful shade. ....Od.12.516.457.
So mounts the bounding vessel o'er the main. ....Od.13.101.6.
Perpetual waters o'er the pavement glide; ....Od.13.132.8.
Neptune, tremendous o'er the boundless main! ....Od.13.165.13.
Nor o'er our City hang the dreadful hill. ....Od.13.213.16.
Cast a long look o'er all the coast and main, ...Od.13.237.17.
The gold, the vests, the tripods, number'd o'er: ....Od.13.262.18.
O'er thy smooth skin a bark of wrinkles spread, ...Od.13.457.28.
But lo! an ambush waits his passage o'er; ....Od.13.492.29.
A swift old-age o'er all his members spread; ....Od.13.498.29.
But He, deep-musing, o'er the mountains stray'd, ...Od.14.1.32.
O'er the fair islands of the neighb'ring main, ...Od.14.118.41.
Not with such transport wou'd my eyes run o'er, ...Od.14.163.43.
And tilting o'er the bay the vessels ride: ....Od.14.289.49.
He hung a night of horrors o'er their head, ...Od.14.335.51.
For nine long days the billows tilting o'er, ...Od.14.349.51.
A few revolving months shou'd waft him o'er, ...Od.14.423.56.
Now came the Night, and darkness cover'd o'er ....Od.14.510.61.
His weighty faulchion o'er his shoulder ty'd: ....Od.14.596.66.
Let o'er thy house some chosen maid preside, ...Od.15.29.71.
Then o'er his ample shoulders whirl'd the cloak, ...Od.15.69.72.
And o'er the coals the smoaking fragments lays. ....Od.15.113.74.
Like radiant *Hesper* o'er the gems of night. ....Od.15.123.74.
He said; and bending o'er his chariot, flung ....Od.15.206.78.
But bear, oh bear me o'er yon azure flood; ....Od.15.302.83.
With rapid speed to whirl them o'er the sea. ....Od.15.315.84.
To turn the tasteful viand o'er the flame; ....Od.15.340.86.
While yet she was , tho' clouded o'er with grief, ...Od.15.386.88.
Rude Pyrates seiz'd, and shipp'd thee o'er the main? ....Od.15.419.89.
In grateful banquet o'er the rosy wine. ....Od.15.540.96.

O'ER (CONTINUED)

When o'er the waves you plow'd the desp'rate way. ....Od.16.26.103.
Thick o'er the board the plenteous viands lay, ...Od.16.51.104.
What vessel bore him o'er the wat'ry way? ....Od.16.58.105.
Long doom'd to wander o'er the land and main, ...Od.16.63.105.
Seen or unseen, o'er earth at pleasure move) ....Od.16.175.111.
She said, and o'er him waves her wand of gold; ....Od.16.186.112.
Twice ten sad years o'er earth and ocean tost, ...Od.16.226.114.
She o'er my limbs old age and wrinkles shed; ....Od.16.230.114.
O'er seas convey'd me to my native reign: ....Od.16.253.117.
O'er earth (returns the Prince) resounds thy name, ...Od.16.262.117.
"Then, beaming o'er th' illumin'd wall they shone: ....Od.16.310.120.
Who o'er *Dulichium* stretch'd his spacious reign, ...Od.16.410.126.
Age o'er his limbs, that tremble as he treads. ....Od.16.479.130.
Then like a Lion o'er the threshold bounds; ....Od.17.37.134.
Hangs o'er her son; in his embraces dies; ....Od.17.48.135.
Then o'er their limbs refulgent robes they threw, ...Od.17.102.136.
And the proud steer was o'er the marble spread. ....Od.17.202.141.
Must be my care; and hence transport thee o'er, ...Od.17.298.146.
The voice of Glory call'd him o'er the main. ....Od.17.351.148.
Or trac'd the mazy leveret o'er the lawn. ....Od.17.355.149.
With roving pyrates o'er th' *Ægyptian* main: ....Od.17.510.157.
He now but waits the wind, to waft him o'er ....Od.17.616.162.
Swell o'er his well-strung limbs, and brace his frame! ....Od.18.85.170.
A dreaded tyrant o'er the bestial train! ....Od.18.127.172.
Scornful he spoke, and o'er his shoulder flung ....Od.18.130.172.
A beam of glory o'er thy future day! ....Od.18.148.173.
O'er all her sense, as the couch she prest, ...Od.18.221.177.
And the pure ivory o'er her bosom spreads. ....Od.18.228.178.
A veil translucent o'er her brow display'd, ...Od.18.249.179.
Floats in bright waves redundant o'er the ground. ....Od.18.342.184.
O'er all the palace a fictitious day; ....Od.18.356.184.
A worthless triumph o'er a worthless foe! ....Od.18.435.189.
O'er which the panther's various hide was thrown. ....Od.19.71.196.
O'er all his frame: illustrious on his breast, ...Od.19.263.208.
O'er which a promontory-shoulder spread: ....Od.19.281.208.
Darts o'er the lawn his horizontal beam. ....Od.19.506.221.
Deep o'er his knee inseam'd, remain'd the scar: ....Od.19.544.223.
And *Itylus* sounds warbling o'er the plains; ....Od.19.607.226.
O'er my suspended woe thy words prevail, ...Od.19.689.229.
And o'er her eyes ambrosial slumber shed. ....Od.19.704.229.
Then o'er the chief, *Eurynome* the chaste ....Od.20.5.230.
As o'er her young the mother-mastiff growls, ...Od.20.20.232.
And hov'ring o'er his head in view confess'd, ...Od.20.39.234.
O'er the *Cerulean* Vault, and shake the Pole; ....Od.20.142.240.
For whom o'er-toil'd I grind the golden grain: ....Od.20.148.240.
O'er the protracted feast the Suitors sit, ...Od.20.447.254.
Then o'er the pavement glides with grace divine, ...Od.21.43.261.
I well remember (for I gaz'd him o'er ....Od.21.96.263.
Already in despair he gives it o'er; ....Od.21.159.267.
Spreads o'er an ample board a bullock's hide. ....Od.21.184.268.
With melted lard they soak the weapon o'er, ...Od.21.185.268.
With tear-full eyes o'er all their master gaz'd: ....Od.21.233.271.
The first fair wind transports him o'er the main; ....Od.21.328.275.
Turn'd on all sides, and view'd it o'er and o'er; ....Od.21.428.280.
Turn'd on all sides, and view'd it o'er and o'er; ....Od.21.428.280.
When fierce the Heroe o'er the threshold strode; ....Od.22.1.284.
O'er all the dome they cast a haggard eye, ...Od.22.29.287.
And prone he falls extended o'er the board: ....Od.22.98.291.
O'er the high crest, and cast a dreadful shade. ....Od.22.141.293.
From o'er the porch, appear'd the subject town. ....Od.22.143.294.
Thus laden, o'er the threshold as he stept, ...Od.22.201.297.
And thus *Philætius* gloried o'er the dead. ....Od.22.317.301.
The arm of vengeance o'er their guilty heads; ....Od.22.331.302.
Wide o'er the sands are spread the stiff'ning prey ....Od.22.430.309.
His breast with marks of carnage painted o'er, ...Od.22.442.309.
With thirsty sponge they rub the tables o'er, ...Od.22.488.313.
Stern as the surly lion o'er his prey, ...Od.23.50.321.
That forc'd *Ulysses* o'er the watry way, ...Od.23.74.322.
O'er all the man her eyes she rolls in vain, ...Od.23.97.324.
O'er every limb a show'r of fragrance sheds: ....Od.23.151.328.
Beam o'er the eastern hills with streaming light. ....Od.23.264.336.
Flame from the Ocean o'er the eastern hills: ....Od.23.374.343.
The Suitors stopp'd, and gaz'd the Heroe o'er. ....Od.24.30.348.
Tears flow'd from ev'ry eye, and o'er the dead ....Od.24.63.350.
Thick clouds of dust o'er all the circle rise, ...Od.24.89.352.
Thus they; while *Hermes* o'er the dreary plain ....Od.24.123.354.
O'er the pale corse! the honours of the dead. ....Od.24.217.358.
Gaz'd o'er his Sire, retracing ev'ry line, ...Od.24.270.362.
Nor wail'd his father o'er th' untimely dead, ...Od.24.345.365.
With thousand kisses wander'd o'er his face, ...Od.24.374.367.
Thus having said, they trac'd the garden o'er, ...Od.24.421.369.
And air celestial dawning o'er his face. ....Od.24.430.369.
The rest in ships are wafted o'er the main. ....Od.24.480.371.
As o'er the heaps of death *Ulysses* strode, ...Od.24.510.372.
Who rolls the thunder o'er the vaulted skies) ....Od.24.548.374.
And o'er the past, *Oblivion* stretch her wing. ....Od.24.557.375.
Wide o'er the world their martial fame was spread; ....Od.24.588.376.

O'ER-ARCHING

Brown with o'er-arching shades and pendent woods, ...Od.3.97.90.
Brown with o'er-arching pine, and spreading oak. ....Od.9.216.314.

O'ER-AW'D

The Sire obey'd him, trembling and o'er-aw'd. ....Il.24.720.567.

O'ER-LABOUR'D

Press'd by fresh Forces her o'er-labour'd Train ....Il.11.932.77.

O'ER-LEAPING

Or, at one bound o'er-leaping all his laws, ...5.DunB4.477.388.

O'ER-LOOK'D

O'er-look'd, seen double, by the fool, and wise. ....3.EOM4.6.128.
Where the tall may-pole once o'er-look'd the Strand; ....5.DunB2.28.297.

O'ER-PAST
O'er-past *Atrides)* second in the Course. ....Il.23.598.513.

O'ER-RUN
A *second* Deluge Learning thus o'er-run, ...1.EOC.691.317.

O'ER-SHOOT
Sure never to o'er-shoot, but just to hit, ...3.EOM3.89.101.

O'ER-TOIL'D
For whom o'er-toil'd I grind the golden grain: ....Od.20.148.240.

O'ER-TOPS
Stands our Digamma, and o'er-tops them all. ....5.DunB4.218.364.

O'ER-WROUGHT
O'er-wrought with Ornaments of barb'rous Pride. ....2.TemF.120.263.

O'ERARCH'D
Where screen'd from *Boreas,* high-o'erarch'd, they lay. ....Od.14.601.66.

O'ERAW'D
The Heroe reascends: The Prince o'eraw'd ....Od.16.194.112.

O'ERBURTHEN'D
The earth o'erburthen'd groan'd beneath their weight, ...Od.11.379.401.

O'ERCAME
So when Curll's Stomach the strong Drench o'ercame, ...6.82x.1.236.

O'ERCAST
Thro' School and College, thy kind cloud o'ercast, ...5.DunB4.289.372.
The pomp was darken'd, and the day o'ercast, ...6.32.32.97.
Death's sable Shade at once o'ercast their Eyes, ...Il.4.626.250.
Huge was its Orb, with sev'n thick Folds o'ercast, ...Il.7.267.377.
Thou canst not fair *Thetis,* but with Grief o'ercast, ...Il.24.137.540.
Her hapless death my brighter days o'ercast, ...Od.15.396.88.
Stung to the soul, o'ercast with holy dread, ...Od.18.181.175.
Now, Grief, thou all art mine! the Gods o'ercast ....Od.18.299.181.

O'ERCASTS
And not a Cloud o'ercasts the solemn Scene; ....Il.8.690.428.

O'ERCHARG'D
And thus express'd a Heart o'ercharg'd with Woes. ....Il.3.379.211.

O'ERCHARGE
O'ercharge the Shoulders of the seeming Swain. ....1.TrVP.32.378.

O'ERCOME
Int'rest o'ercome, or Policy take place: ....3.Ep1.169.29.
"This China-Jordan, let the chief o'ercome ....5.DunA2.157.120.
Chetwood, thro' perfect modesty o'ercome, ...5.DunA2.181.124.
Chapman thro' perfect modesty o'ercome. ....5.DunA2.181B.124.
Osborn thro' perfect modesty o'ercome. ....5.DunA2.181C.124.
Who sate the nearest, by the words o'ercome ....5.DunA2.369.145.
"This China Jordan let the chief o'ercome ....5.DunB2.165.303.
Osborne, thro' perfect modesty o'ercome, ...5.DunB2.189.304.
Who sate the nearest, by the words o'ercome, ...5.DunB2.401.316.
T'o'ercome the slave your eyes have doom'd to Death ....6.3.2A.7.
Alas! I hop'd, the toils of war o'ercome, ...Od.11.535.409.

O'ERCOMES
There Sleep at last o'ercomes the Hero's Eyes; ....Il.24.27.536.

O'ERFLEEC'D
Short woolly curls o'erfleec'd his bending head, ...Od.19.280.208.

O'ERFLOW
O'erflow thy Courts: The LIGHT HIMSELF shall shine .....1.Mes.103.122.
Line after line my gushing eyes o'erflow, ...2.ElAb.35.321.
Then raptures high the seat of sense o'erflow, ...5.DunA3.5.150.
Then raptures high the seat of Sense o'erflow, ...5.DunB3.5.320.
Thy Tents are crowded, and thy Chests o'erflow. ....Il.2.280.141.
Heleon and *Hylè,* which the Springs o'erflow; ....Il.2.596.156.
Tears after Tears his mournful Cheeks o'erflow, ...Il.22.516.478.

O'ERFLOWING
Heady, not strong; o'erflowing, tho' not full. ....5.DunB3.172.328.

O'ERFLOWINGS
Wide and more wide, th'o'erflowings of the mind ....3.EOM4.369.164.

O'ERFLOWS
Swell'd with new Passion, and o'erflows with Tears; ....1.PWi.66.93.
Sudden, with starting Tears each Eye o'erflows, ...2.RL5.85.207.
Whose measure full o'erflows on human race ....3.Ep3.231.111.
Here the blue fig with luscious juice o'erflows, ...6.35.7.103.
His Mother's conscious Heart o'erflows with Joy. ....Il.6.615.357.
That the green Banks in Summer's Heat o'erflows, ...Il.22.199.463.
A Show'r of Tears o'erflows her beauteous Eyes, ...Il.24.874.573.
Here the blue fig with luscious juice o'erflows, ...Od.7.148.243.
The tumbling goblet the wide floor o'erflows, ...Od.22.21.287.

O'ERFLY
Which scarce the sea-fowl in a year o'erfly) ....Od.3.412.106.

O'ERGROWN
That charm'd me more, with Native Moss o'ergrown, ...1.TrSP.165.400.
Which charm'd me more, with Native Moss o'ergrown, ...1.TrSP.165A.400.

O'ERHANGS
So some tall Rock o'erhangs the hoary Main, ...Il.15.746.224.
Whose shaggy brow o'erhangs the shady deep, ...Od.3.375.104.
Where the dark rock o'erhangs th' infernal lake, ...Od.10.612.374.

O'ERHEARD
Mummius o'erheard him; Mummius, Fool-renown'd, ...5.DunB4.371.379.

O'ERHUNG
Whose waving Woods o'erhung the Deeps below, ...Il.13.20.105.
But when his Ev'ning Wheels o'erhung the Main, ...Il.16.942.280.
But when his evening wheels o'erhung the main, ...Od.9.67.305.

O'ERJOY'D
O'erjoy'd to see what God had sent. ....6.93.24.257.

O'ERLABOUR'D
Th' o'erlabour'd *Cyclop* from his Task retires; ....1.TrSt.306.423.
Press'd by fresh Forces, her o'erlabour'd Train ....Il.16.62.238.
O'erlabour'd now, with Dust, and Sweat and Gore, ...Il.17.446.304.

O'ERLAY'D
With pomp of various architrave o'erlay'd. ....Od.21.46.261.

O'ERLEAPS
O'erleaps the Fences, and invades the Pen; ....Il.10.565.27.

O'ERLOOK
"(Cou'd you o'erlook but that)—it is, to steal. ....4.2HE2.20.165.

O'ERLOOK'D
As if the *Stagyrite* o'erlook'd each Line. ....1.EOC.138.255.
Where the tall May-pole once o'erlook'd the Strand; ....5.DunA2.24.99.
As from a Brazen Tow'r, o'erlook'd the Field. ....Il.7.266.377.
Of his proud Fleet, o'erlook'd the Fields of Fight; ....Il.11.731.67.
Whose ridge o'erlook'd a shady length of land; ....Od.10.170.349.

O'ERLOOKS
And tho' she plays no more, o'erlooks the Cards. ....2.RL1.54.150.
Half that the Dev'l o'erlooks from Lincoln Town. ....4.2HE2.245.183.
Where *Dios* from her Tow'rs o'erlooks the Plain, ...Il.2.647.157.
Or where fair *Ithaca* o'erlooks the Floods, ...Il.2.769.162.
On yonder Decks, and yet o'erlooks the Plains! ....Il.13.938.149.
O'erlooks th' embattled Host, and hopes the bloody Day. ....Il.19.397.388.
From where high *Ithaca* o'erlooks the floods, ...Od.3.96.90.
By *Phœbus'* altars; thus o'erlooks the ground; ....Od.6.194.219.
Her bosom terribly o'erlooks the tyde. ....Od.12.116.437.

O'ERMATCH
The valiant few o'ermatch an host of foes. ....Od.2.280.74.

O'ERMATCH'D
O'ermatch'd he falls; to two at once a Prey, ...Il.15.656.221.

O'ERPASS'D
These seas o'erpass'd, be wise! but I refrain ....Od.12.67.433.

O'ERPOW'R'D
O'erpow'r'd they fall beneath the Force of Men. ....Il.5.686.300.
Spent and o'erpow'r'd, he barely breathes at most; ....Il.16.136.242.
O'erpow'r'd by numbers, is but brave in vain. ....Od.16.90.106.

O'ERPOW'RING
Thus loudly roaring, and o'erpow'ring all, ...Il.15.444.214.

O'ERPOW'RS
His Aid in vain: The Man o'erpow'rs the God. ....Il.20.344.408.

O'ERPOWER
But lest new Wounds on Wounds o'erpower us quite, ...Il.14.149.165.

O'ERSEES
By Day o'ersees them, and by Night protects; ....1.Mes.52.117.

O'ERSHADE
Where Doves in Flocks the leafless Trees o'ershade, ...1.W-F.127.162.
While Angels with their silver wings o'ershade ....2.Elegy.67.367.

O'ERSHADES
While the spread Fan o'ershades your closing eyes; ....6.45.37.125.
Spreads all the Beach, and wide o'ershades the Plain: ....Il.2.118.133.
For *Jove* o'ershades her with his Arm divine, ...Il.9.804.473.

O'ERSHADING
That dreadful nods with four o'ershading Plumes; ....Il.5.919.310.
His Neck o'ershading to his Ancle hung; ....Il.6.145.331.

O'ERSPENT
O'erspent with Toil, reposing on the Ground; ....Il.5.989.314.

O'ERSPREAD
Once *School-Divines* this zealous Isle o'erspread; ....1.EOC.440.288.
Once *School-Divines* our zealous Isle o'erspread; ....1.EOC.440A.288.
His ample Hat his beamy Locks o'erspread, ...1.TrSt.431.428.
Behold the Market-place with poor o'erspread! ....3.Ep3.263.115.
His Mountain-Shoulders half his Breast o'erspread, ...Il.2.265.140.
His youthful Face a polish'd Helm o'erspread; ....Il.3.417.212.
Ulysses heard; The Hero's Warmth o'erspread ....Il.4.402.240.
Short of its Crest, and with no Plume o'erspread; ....Il.10.304.16.
His following Shield the fallen Chief o'erspread; ....Il.14.489.187.
Vain hope! what Numbers shall the Field o'erspread, ...Il.17.278.298.
Shews every mournful Face with Tears o'erspread, ...Il.23.132.493.
Such Joy the *Spartan's* shining Face o'erspread, ...Il.23.683.517.
(The vestures cleans'd o'erspread the shelly sand, ...Od.6.107.211.
O'erspread the land, when spring descends in show'rs: ....Od.9.56.304.

O'ERSPREADS
When Night with sable Wings o'erspreads the Ground, ...1.TrSt.711.440.
Of all the lands that heav'n o'erspreads with light! ....Od.9.30.303.
O'erspreads nine acres of infernal ground; ....Od.11.710.421.

O'ERTAKE
Shall feel sharp Vengeance soon o'ertake his Sins, ...2.RL2.125.167.
And my swift Soul o'ertake my slaughter'd Friend! ....Il.21.324.434.

O'ERTAKEN
O'ertaken *Neamas* by *Merion* bleeds; ....Il.16.410.258.

O'ERTAKES
O'ertakes the flying boy, and smothers half his words. ....1.TrPA.147.372.
Cold Death o'ertakes them in their blooming Years, ...Il.5.200.276.
Smoaks thro' the Ranks, o'ertakes the flying War, ...Il.16.461.260.
Inevitable Fate o'ertakes the Deed; ....Il.17.338.300.
One Evil yet o'ertakes his latest Day, ...Il.24.677.565.
And, past the limits of the Court, o'ertakes. ....Od.21.196.269.

O'ERTHREW
Ev'n mighty *Pam* that Kings and Queens o'erthrew, ...2.RL3.61.172.
Then, when the Chief the *Theban* Walls o'erthrew, ...Il.2.843.164.
Phalces and *Mermer, Nestor's* Son o'erthrew. ....Il.14.607.191.
Mecistes next, *Polydamas* o'erthrew; ....Il.15.384.211.

O'ERTHROW
Us, and our house if treason must o'erthrow, ...Od.17.92.136.

O'ERTHROWN
The Tale reviv'd, the Lye so oft o'erthrown; ....4.Arbu.350.121.
The Tales of Vengeance; Lyes so oft o'erthrown; ....4.Arbu.350A.121.
See Madam! see, the Arts o'erthrown, ...6.119.19.337.
See Madam! all the Arts O'erthrown, ...6.119.19B.337.
But other Forces have our Hopes o'erthrown, ...Il.2.159.136.
And what the Cause of *Ilion* not o'erthrown? ....Il.2.437.148.
His the first Praise were *Ilion's* Tow'rs o'erthrown, ...Il.4.470.242.
The Heroes slain, the Palaces o'erthrown, ...Il.9.704.469.
Whole Ranks are broken, and whole Troops o'erthrown. ....Il.11.344.49.
The Ranks lie scatter'd, and the Troops o'erthrown) ....Il.11.665.63.
There, *Greece* has strength: but this, this Part o'erthrown, ...Il.13.79.108.
Thy own lov'd boasted Offspring lies o'erthrown, ...Il.15.124.201.
Where Horse and Arms, and Chariots lie o'erthrown, ...Il.16.456.260.
Transfix'd with deep Regret, they view o'erthrown ....Il.16.673.270.
Transfix'd with deep Regret, they view'd o'erthrown ....Il.16.673A.270.
Patroclus thus, so many Chiefs o'erthrown, ...Il.16.999.281.
By Fate and *Phœbus* was I first o'erthrown, ...Il.16.1024.282.
To either Host. *Troy* soon must lye o'erthrown, ...Il.20.37.394.
Now toils the Heroe; trees on trees o'erthrown ....Od.5.311.186.

O'ERTHROWS
A breath revives him, or a breath o'erthrows! ....4.2HE1.301.221.

O'ERTOOK
But *Merion's* Spear o'ertook him as he flew, ...Il.13.717.138.
The Wings of Death o'ertook thee on the Dart, ...Il.14.542.189.
Minerva smiling heard, the Pair o'ertook, ...Il.21.496.442.

O'ERTURN
O'erturn the Strength of *Ajax* on the Ground; ....Il.23.835.522.

O'ERTURN'D
Thy Sire, O Prince! o'erturn'd the *Trojan* State, ...Il.5.804.304.
My Heroes slain, my Bridal Bed o'erturn'd, ...Il.22.88.456.
(O'erturn'd by *Pallas)* where the slipp'ry Shore ....Il.23.907.525.
But if o'erturn'd by rude, ungovern'd hands, ...Od.23.207.333.

O'ERTURNED
Lo statues, temples, theatres o'erturned, ...5.DunA3.97Z1.158.

O'ERTURNS
Proud Tyrants humbles, and whole Hosts o'erturns. ....Il.5.925.310.
Proud Tyrants humbles, and whole Hosts o'erturns. ....Il.8.475.419.
O'erturns, confounds, and scatters all their Bands. ....Il.11.402.52.
Proud Tyrants humbles, and whole hosts o'erturns. ....Od.1.131.38.

O'ERULING
'Twas *Jove's* high Will alone, o'eruling all, ...Il.19.285.384.

O'ERWATCH'D
O'erwatch'd and batter'd in the naked bay. ....Od.9.84.306.
Spent and o'erwatch'd. Two days and nights roll'd on, ...Od.10.167.348.

O'ERWHELM
O'erwhelm me, Earth! and hide a Monarch's Shame. ....Il.4.219.231.
O'erwhelm me Earth! and hide a Warrior's Shame. ....Il.8.182.406.
The Wretch relentless, and o'erwhelm with Shame! ....Il.14.164.165.

O'ERWHELM'D
O'erwhelm'd with Anguish and dissolv'd in Tears; ....Il.5.462.290.
So pierc'd with Sorrows, so o'erwhelm'd as mine? ....Il.18.502.345.
I see his friends o'erwhelm'd beneath the main; ....Od.2.204.71.
His ship o'erwhelm'd: but frowning on the floods, ...Od.4.673.151.
I see thy friends o'erwhelm'd in liquid graves! ....Od.11.143.387.
O'erwhelm'd it sinks: while round a smoke expires, ...Od.12.81.435.

O'ERWHELMS
In Heaps on Heaps; one Fate o'erwhelms them all. ....2.RL3.86.174.
O'erwhelms the Bridge, and bursts the lofty Bounds; ....Il.5.119.273.
O'erwhelms the Nations with new Toils and Woes; ....Il.7.82.367.
Fierce *Ajax* thus o'erwhelms the yielding Throng, ...Il.11.618.61.
And lifts his Billows, and o'erwhelms his Shores. ....Il.21.357.435.
Death hastes amain: one hour o'erwhelms them all! ....Od.2.322.76.
The rock o'erwhelms us, and we 'scap'd in vain. ....Od.9.584.330.

O'ERWROUGHT
For their fair Handles now, o'erwrought with Flow'rs, ...Il.18.445.342.

OAK
Then, as the Mountain Oak, or Poplar tall, ...1.TrES.288A.460.
Link Towns to Towns with Avenues of Oak, ...4.2HE2.260.183.

OAK (CONTINUED)
As when the Mountain Oak, or Poplar tall, ...Il.13.493.130.
Fixt as some Column, or deep-rooted Oak, ...Il.13.549.132.
The Mountain-Oak in flaming Ruin lies, ...Il.14.483.187.
Then, as the Mountain Oak, or Poplar tall, ...Il.16.593.267.
Met at an Oak, or journeying o'er a Plain; ....Il.22.168.460.
Of some once-stately Oak the last Remains, ...Il.23.401.506.
Brown with o'er-arching pine, and spreading oak. ....Od.9.216.314.
Swift from the oak they strip the shady pride; ....Od.12.421.451.
Of stubborn labour hewn from heart of oak; ....Od.14.16.35.
A weighty ax, and cleft the solid oak; ....Od.14.464.58.
The pyre to build, the stubborn oak to rend; ....Od.15.339.86.
(With polish'd oak the level pavements shine) ....Od.21.44.261.

OAK'S
Beneath an ample Oak's expanded Shade. ....Il.18.648.355.

OAKS
Let opening Roses knotted Oaks adorn, ...1.PAu.37.83.
While by our Oaks the precious Loads are born, ...1.W-F.31.151.
Where tow'ring Oaks their growing Honours rear, ...1.W-F.221.170.
Where tow'ring Oaks their spreading Honours rear, ...1.W-F.221A.170.
Ask of thy mother earth, why oaks are made ....3.EOM1.39.18.
And Pines and Oaks, from their Foundations torn, ...Il.11.616.61.
As two tall Oaks, before the Wall they rise; ....Il.12.145.86.
Who hear, from rustling Oaks, thy dark Decrees; ....Il.16.290.253.
Who hear, from rustling Oaks, their dark Decrees; ....Il.16.290A.253.
The broad Oaks crackle, and the *Sylvans* groan; ....Il.16.926.279.
On all sides round the Forest hurles her Oaks ....Il.23.147.495.
The dext'rous Woodman shapes the stubborn Oaks; ....Il.23.386.505.
Some wield the sounding ax; the dodder'd oaks ....Od.20.200.243.

OAR
"Spread the thin oar, and catch the driving gale. ....3.EOM3.178.111.
Taylor, their better Charon, lends an oar, ...5.DunB3.19.321.
And brush the dangerous deep with strawy Oar? ....6.96ii.30Z14.271.
"Thy Bark a Bean-shell, and a Straw thy Oar? ....6.96ii.58.273.
That long had heav'd the weary Oar in vain, ...Il.7.6.363.
Must view his billows white beneath thy oar, ...Od.4.645.150.
Shape the broad sail, or smooth the taper oar; ....Od.6.320.226.
Launch the tall bark, and order ev'ry oar, ...Od.8.35.263.
We furl'd the sail, we ply'd the lab'ring oar, ...Od.9.81.306.
Each nerve we stretch, and ev'ry oar we ply. ....Od.9.574.330.
Nine prosp'rous days we ply'd the lab'ring oar; ....Od.10.30.340.
Each nerve to strain, each bending oar to ply. ....Od.10.148.347.
Fix the smooth oar, and bid me live to fame. ....Od.11.97.385.
Bear on thy back an *Oar:* with strange amaze ....Od.11.156.389.
A shepherd meeting thee, the *Oar* surveys, ...Od.11.157.389.
And high above it rose the tapering oar. ....Od.12.22.430.
Ply the strong oar, and catch the nimble gales; ....Od.12.106.436.
Now every sail we furl, each oar we ply; ....Od.12.206.441.
Each drop'd his oar: But swift from man to man ....Od.12.246.444.
Hoise ev'ry sail, and ev'ry oar prepare. ....Od.15.245.80.
With level oar along the glassy deep. ....Od.15.510.94.
An Oar my hand must bear; a shepherd eyes ....Od.23.289.337.

OAR'D
And oar'd with lab'ring arms along the flood. ....Od.12.526.458.
And what blest hands have oar'd thee on the way? ....Od.16.247.116.

OARS
At once they bend, and strike their equal Oars, ...1.TrUl.3.465.
And tugg'd their Oars, and measur'd back the Main. ....1.TrUl.52.467.
Resum'd their Oars, and measur'd back the Main. ....1.TrUl.52A.467.
With chosen Pilots, and with lab'ring Oars. ....Il.1.184.96.
Mean time *Atrides* launch'd with num'rous Oars ....Il.1.404.107.
Fly, *Grecians* fly, your Sails and Oars employ, ...Il.2.171.136.
With equal Oars, the hoarse-resounding Deep. ....Il.2.619.157.
Spread all your Canvas, all your Oars employ, ...Il.9.37.433.
And hear with Oars the *Hellespont* resound. ....Il.9.472.455.
Beneath his Oars the whitening Billows fly. ....Il.9.801.473.
Us too he bids our Oars and Sails employ, ...Il.9.802.473.
Yet where the Oars are plac'd, he stands to wait ....Il.15.884.231.
Full fifty Vessels, mann'd with fifty Oars: ....Il.16.207.247.
And now they ship their oars, and crown with wine ....Od.2.470.83.
For *Tenedos* we spread our eager oars, ...Od.3.191.95.
With shatter'd vessels, and disabled oars: ....Od.3.381.105.
Rang'd on the banks, beneath our equal oars ....Od.4.787.156.
Nor oars to cut th' immeasurable way. ....Od.5.25.172.
What oars to cut the long laborious way? ....Od.5.182.180.
And snatch their oars, and rush into the deep. ....Od.9.554.328.
The sailors catch the word, their oars they seize, ...Od.10.149.347.
Our oars we shipp'd: all day the swelling sails ....Od.11.9.379.
My mates ascend the ship; they strike their oars; ....Od.11.791.426.
Here fills her sails and spreads her oars in vain; ....Od.12.122.437.
Then bending to the stroke, their oars they drew ....Od.12.182.441.
We drop our oars: at ease the pilot guides; ....Od.12.186.441.
Plunge all at once their oars, and cleave the main. ....Od.12.217.442.
Attend my words! your oars incessant ply; ....Od.12.254.444.
While yet I speak, at once their oars they seize, ...Od.12.264.445.
At once they bend, and strike their equal oars, ...Od.13.94.5.
Resum'd their oars, and measur'd back the main. ....Od.13.143.12.
And plac'd in order, spread their equal oars. ....Od.15.592.98.
With gather'd sails they stood, and lifted oars. ....Od.16.369.124.
Nor oars to cut th' immeasurable way— ....Od.17.167.139.

OATH
(That dreadful Oath which binds the Thunderer) ....1.TrSt.412.427.
I yield it up; but since I gave my Oath, ...2.ChJM.701.48.
Whose Air cries Arm! whose very Look's an Oath: ....4.JD4.261.47.
Nor dar'd an Oath, nor hazarded a Lye: ....4.Arbu.397.126.
Has sworn by *Sticks* (the Poet's Oath, ...6.135.91.370.
Has sworn by Styx (the Poet's Oath, ...6.135.91A.370.
(Tremendous Oath! inviolate to Kings) ....Il.1.316.103.
Styx pours them forth, the dreadful Oath of Gods! ....Il.2.915.167.
By ev'ry Oath that Pow'rs immortal ties, ...Il.15.41.195.

OATH (CONTINUED)

Saturnia ask'd an Oath, to vouch the Truth, ... Il.19.109.376.
Then bids *Saturnius* bear his Oath in mind; ... Il.19.119.376.
Grief seiz'd the Thund'rer, by his Oath engag'd; ... Il.19.123.377.
The dread, th' irrevocable Oath he swore, ... Il.19.127.377.
Hear then my solemn Oath, to yield to Fate ... Il.21.438.438.
Now plight thy mutual Oath, I ask no more. ... Il.22.332.470.
Nor Oath nor Pact *Achilles* plights with thee: ... Il.22.336.470.
And vindicate by Oath th' ill-gotten Prize. ... Il.23.660.515.
(A sacred oath) each proud oppressor slain ... Od.1.485.55.
(A sacred oath) if heav'n the pow'r supply, ... Od.2.169.70.
A solemn oath impos'd the secret seal'd, ... Od.4.986.163.
Swear, by the solemn oath that binds the Gods. ... Od.5.232.182.
Or swear that oath by which the Gods are ty'd, ... Od.10.408.364.
When sworn that oath which never can be vain? ... Od.10.450.365.
Doubt you my oath? yet more my faith to try, ... Od.14.433.56.

OATHS

Thy oaths I quit, thy memory resign, ... 2.ElAb.293.343.
Teach Oaths to Gamesters, and to Nobles Wit? ... 5.DunB1.204.284.
Teach Oaths to Gamesters, and to Nobles—Wit? ... 5.DunB1.204A.284.
Support his front, and Oaths bring up the rear: ... 5.DunB1.308.292.
Tydcombe take Oaths on the Communion; ... 6.10.46.26.
False oaths, false tears, deceits, disguises, ... 6.51ii.38A.154.
Those Hands we plighted, and those Oaths we swore, ... Il.4.193.230.
Talk not of Oaths (the dreadful Chief replies, ... Il.22.333.470.
But swear her first by those dread oaths that tie ... Od.10.357.361.

OATS

Sullen you turn from both, and call for *Oats.* ... 6.96iv.54.277.
Sullen you turn'd from both, and call'd for *Oats.* ... 6.96iv.54A.277.

OBDURATE

Obdurate to reject the stranger-guest; ... Od.4.40.122.

OBEDIENCE

So geese to gander prone obedience keep, ... 4.1740.35.334.
And prompt Obedience to the Queen of Air; ... Il.15.177.203.
My prompt obedience bows. But deign to say, ... Od.4.653.150.
Demand obedience, for your words are wise. ... Od.11.431.405.
Her prompt obedience on his order waits; ... Od.21.419.280.

OBEDIENT

And teach th'obedient Branches where to spring. ... 1.TrVP.12.377.
The rest move on, obedient to the Rein; ... 1.TrES.279.460.
Forth came the Priest, and bade th'obedient Wife ... 2.ChJM.311.29.
'Obedient slumbers that can wake and weep'; ... 2.ElAb.212.337.
And roll obedient Rivers thro' the Land; ... 3.Ep4.202.156.
Up starts a Palace, lo! th' obedient base ... 4.1HE1.140.289.
What gen'rous *Greek* obedient to thy Word, ... Il.1.197.96.
But sheath, Obedient, thy revenging Steel. ... Il.1.280.100.
Hector obedient heard; and, with a Bound, ... Il.6.125.330.
Desist, obedient to his high Command; ... Il.8.510.421.
The rest move on, obedient to the Rein; ... Il.16.584.267.
Self-mov'd, obedient to the Beck of Gods: ... Il.18.444.342.
Achilles to the Strand obedient went; ... Il.19.43.373.
He hears, obedient to the God of Light, ... Il.20.435.412.
Infest a God: Th' obedient Flame withdraws: ... Il.21.445.438.
I go, ye Gods! obedient to your Call: ... Il.24.275.547.
Th' obedient Tears, melodious in their Woe. ... Il.24.903.574.
Must speed, obedient to their high command. ... Od.1.109.36.
The bolt, obedient to the silken cord, ... Od.1.553.58.
The Chief his orders gives; th' obedient band ... Od.2.462.83.
Who bound, obedient to superior force, ... Od.4.525.145.
Then she. Obedient to my rule, attend: ... Od.4.538.146.
The Nymph, obedient to divine command, ... Od.5.191.180.
And order mules obedient to the rein; ... Od.6.42.207.
Obedient to the vision of the night. ... Od.6.60.208.
Obedient to the call, the chief they guide ... Od.6.251.222.
Swift at the word, obedient to the King ... Od.8.293.278.
Th' assenting Peers, obedient to the King, ... Od.8.433.287.
His flocks, obedient, spread o'er all the hills. ... Od.9.375.321.
She said. Obedient to her high command ... Od.10.481.366.
The luscious wine th' obedient herald brought; ... Od.13.68.4.
The chief his orders gives: th' obedient band ... Od.15.310.84.
All with obedient haste forsake the shores, ... Od.15.591.98.
Obedient handmaids with assistant toil ... Od.17.100.136.
The Prince obedient to the same command, ... Od.19.17.193.
Divide, obedient to the forceful strokes. ... Od.20.201.243.
The bolt, obedient to the silken string, ... Od.21.47.261.
His ardour strait th' obedient Prince suppress, ... Od.21.137.265.
She hears, and at the word obedient flies. ... Od.22.528.314.

OBEISANCE

See OBEYSANCE.

OBELISKS

Between the Statues Obelisks were plac'd, ... 2.TemF.117.262.

OBEY

Time conquers All, and We must Time obey. ... 1.PWi.88.95.
Not only *Nature* did his Laws obey, ... 1.EOC.648Z1.312.
Which monsters wild, and savages obey! ... 1.TrPA.14.366.
Whom *Delphi* and the *Delian* isle obey, ... 1.TrFD.12.386.
Of Kings impos'd, and grudgingly obey, ... 1.TrSt.231.420.
Bid Hell's black Monarch my Commands obey, ... 1.TrSt.417.427.
His train obey; while all the Courts around ... 1.TrSt.605.435.
Thus doubting long what Nymph he shou'd obey ... 2.ChJM.242.26.
"One of us two must rule, and one obey, ... 2.ChWB.192.65.
Here Thou, Great *Anna!* whom three Realms obey, ... 2.RL3.7.169.
Sad proof how well a lover can obey! ... 2.ElAb.172.334.
In this weak queen, some fav'rite still obey. ... 3.EOM2.150.73.
"Thus let the wiser make the rest obey, ... 3.EOM3.196.113.
Yet have your humour most, when you obey ... 3.Ep2.264A.71.
Those, only fix'd, they first or last obey, ... 3.Ep2.209.67.
Schools, courts, and senates shall my laws obey, ... 5.DunA1.251Z5.93.

OBEY (CONTINUED)

T' enjoy, is to obey. ... 6.50.20.146.
Command thy Passions, and the Gods obey. ... Il.1.286.100.
Him must our Hosts, our Chiefs, our Self obey? ... Il.1.382.106.
Goddess (he cry'd) be patient and obey. ... Il.1.755.123.
The gath'ring Hosts the Monarch's Word obey; ... Il.2.63.130.
This hear Observant, and the Gods obey! ... Il.2.91.130.
Then let us haste, obey the God's Alarms, ... Il.2.105.132.
Dissolve the Council, and their Chief obey: ... Il.2.108.132.
'Tis Nature's Voice, and Nature we obey. ... Il.2.168.136.
His are the Laws, and Him let all obey. ... Il.2.244.139.
Obey, ye *Grecians!* with Submission wait, ... Il.2.398.145.
'Till great *Alcides* made the Realms obey: ... Il.2.826.164.
Leonteus leads, and forty Ships obey. ... Il.2.905.166.
From these the congregated Troops obey ... Il.2.1006.170.
O first and greatest Pow'r! whom all obey, ... Il.3.346.209.
Obey the Pow'r from whom thy Glories rise: ... Il.3.514.216.
So some fell Lion whom the Woods obey, ... Il.3.561.218.
So shall the Gods our joint Decrees obey, ... Il.4.89.224.
Those only heard; with Awe the rest obey, ... Il.4.488.243.
He said; *Saturnia,* ardent to obey, ... Il.5.956.312.
Thy Voice we hear, and thy Behests obey: ... Il.5.1077.318.
If first he ask it, I content obey, ... Il.7.347.381.
Yet *Ægæ, Helicè,* thy Pow'r obey, ... Il.8.246.409.
Obey the Night, and use her peaceful Hours ... Il.8.627.425.
Suffice, to Night, these Orders to obey; ... Il.8.651.426.
Thus spoke the hoary Sage: the rest obey, ... Il.9.109.437.
Assembled States, and Lords of Earth obey, ... Il.9.128.438.
Him *Enope,* and *Phæræ* him obey, ... Il.9.196.442.
Great tho' he be, it fits him to obey; ... Il.9.213.443.
Thee *Enope,* and *Phærae* thee obey, ... Il.9.383.451.
These reconciling Goddesses obey: ... Il.9.638.466.
Some God within commands, and I obey. ... Il.10.262.13.
Whate'er thy Will, *Patroclus* shall obey. ... Il.11.741.68.
Such gentle Force the fiercest Minds obey; ... Il.11.923.76.
Hear then ye Warriors! and obey with speed; ... Il.12.87.84.
And all obey their sev'ral Chief's Commands. ... Il.12.100.85.
But tends to raise that Pow'r which I obey. ... Il.12.252.90.
While I the Dictates of high Heav'n obey. ... Il.12.282.92.
Calls on his Host; his Host obey the Call; ... Il.12.296.92.
The Mass of Waters will no Wind obey; ... Il.14.25.158.
The banded Legions of all *Greece* obey? ... Il.14.105.162.
Young tho' he be, disdain not to obey: ... Il.14.123.163.
He added not: The list'ning Kings obey, ... Il.14.153.165.
Hear, and obey the Mistress of the Skies, ... Il.14.301.177.
Then soon the haughty Sea-God shall obey, ... Il.15.55.196.
Your Vassal Godheads grudgingly obey; ... Il.15.117.201.
Submiss, Immortals! all he wills, obey; ... Il.15.120.201.
Thus then, Immortals! thus shall *Mars* obey; ... Il.15.128.201.
Then *Juno* call'd (*Jove's* Orders to obey) ... Il.15.162.202.
The Warrior spoke, the list'ning *Greeks* obey, ... Il.15.338.210.
Drives four fair Coursers, practis'd to obey, ... Il.15.824.228.
Five chosen Leaders the fierce Bands obey, ... Il.16.208.247.
Th' impetuous Torrents from their Hills obey, ... Il.16.472.261.
If *Greece* must perish, we thy Will obey, ... Il.17.731.316.
And *Vulcan's* Joy, and Duty, to obey, ... Il.18.498.345.
(Returns *Achilles)* all our Hosts obey! ... Il.19.144.377.
Whate'er this Heart can prompt, or Hand obey; ... Il.20.411.412.
O sacred Stream! thy Word we shall obey; ... Il.21.241.431.
But stronger Love impell'd, and I obey. ... Il.22.308.468.
He spoke; they hear him, and the Word obey; ... Il.23.67.489.
The *Greeks* obey; where yet the Embers glow, ... Il.23.310.502.
And yield the Glory yours—The Steeds obey; ... Il.23.527.511.
The Hero's Words the willing Chiefs obey, ... Il.23.860.523.
His pious Sons the King's Command obey. ... Il.24.228.546.
The sorrowing Friends his frantick Rage obey. ... Il.24.310.549.
Our slaught'ring Arm, and bid the Hosts obey. ... Il.24.827.571.
Obey that sweet compulsion, nor profane ... Od.1.471.55.
With joyous pride the summons I'd obey. ... Od.1.502.56.
To council calls the Peers: the Peers obey. ... Od.2.10.60.
"Guard thou his age, and his behests obey.] ... Od.2.258.74.
The sons obey, and join them to the yoke. ... Od.3.607.117.
The wealthy tribes of *Pharian Thebes* obey) ... Od.4.170.128.
Or bless a people willing to obey, ... Od.5.15.171.
'Tis mine, with joy and duty to obey. ... Od.5.114.177.
And now the east the foamy floods obey, ... Od.5.422.192.
Observe my orders, and with heed obey, ... Od.5.444.194.
The Goddess answer'd. Father, I obey, ... Od.7.35.235.
Thus spoke the Prince: th' attending Peers obey, ... Od.8.43.264.
Thus spoke the King; th' attending Peers obey: ... Od.8.105.268.
When *Neptune* sues, my part is to obey. ... Od.8.392.285.
Rules this blest realm, repentant I obey! ... Od.8.436.287.
As first in virtue, these thy realms obey! ... Od.9.2.298.
His word alone the list'ning storms obey, ... Od.10.23.340.
In vain essay'd, nor would his tongue obey, ... Od.10.289.357.
The laws of Fate compell, and I obey. ... Od.10.324.360.
With ready speed the joyful crew obey: ... Od.10.507.368.
To gen'rous acts; our part is to obey. ... Od.11.433.405.
Hear and obey: If freedom I demand, ... Od.12.198.441.
Pilot, attentive listen and obey! ... Od.12.259.445.
The wide-extended continents obey: ... Od.14.120.41.
The steer-man governs, and the ships obey. ... Od.14.287.49.
Swift as the word his willing mates obey, ... Od.15.246.80.
Minerva calls; the ready gales obey ... Od.15.314.84.
Let those whom sleep invites, the call obey, ... Od.15.430.89.
But both in constant peace one Prince obey, ... Od.15.454.92.
No race but thine shall *Ithaca* obey, ... Od.15.575.98.
To this *Peiræus;* Joyful I obey, ... Od.15.585.98.
The Prince reply'd; *Eumæus,* I obey; ... Od.16.31.103.
To whom the swain. I hear, and I obey: ... Od.16.144.109.
Slaves to a boy, go, flatter and obey. ... Od.16.403.125.
Imperious hunger bids, and I obey: ... Od.18.63.169.
Force I forbear, and without force obey. ... Od.18.457.190.
Then swill'd with wine, with noise the crowds obey, ... Od.18.472.191.
Whose pious rule a warlike race obey! ... Od.19.130.199.
Your sovereign Will my duty bids obey. ... Od.19.195.201.

OBEY (CONTINUED)
Thesprotian tribes, a duteous race, obey: ....Od.19.330.210.
What maids dishonour us, and what obey? ....Od.22.457.310.
Nor me nor chast *Penelope* obey; ....Od.22.463.311.
Then *Euryclea;* Joyful I obey, ...Od.22.523.314.
For Wisdom all is thine! lo I obey, ...Od.23.125.326.
This spoke the King: Th' observant train obey, ...Od.23.139.327.
Words seal'd with sacred truth, and truth obey: ....Od.23.190.332.
To whom the Queen. Thy word we shall obey, ...Od.23.273.336.
To arms! aloud he cries: His friends obey, ...Od.23.395.343.
But when, arising in his wrath t'obey ....Od.24.191.356.
Offend not *Jove:* Obey, and give the peace. ....Od.24.627.377.

OBEY'D
What could be free, when lawless Beasts obey'd, ...1.W-F.51.153.
She said, the World obey'd, and all was *Peace!* ....1.W-F.328.181.
Admir'd as Heroes, and as Gods obey'd? ....1.TrES.34.451.
Th'obliging Dames obey'd with one Consent; ....2.ChJM.410.34.
To haste before; the gentle Squire obey'd: ....2.ChJM.536.41.
Great Nature spoke; observant Men obey'd; ....3.EOM3.199.113.
The same which in a Sire the Sons obey'd, ...3.EOM3.213.114.
With Authors, Stationers obey'd the call, ...5.DunA2.27.99.
With Authors, Stationers obey'd the call, ...5.DunB2.31.297.
She bow'd, obey'd him, and cut Paper. ....6.119.8.336.
When *Nestor* spoke, they listen'd and obey'd. ....Il.1.359.105.
(*Nestor,* whom *Pylos'* sandy Realms obey'd) ....Il.2.100.131.
Ulysses heard, nor uninspir'd obey'd. ....Il.2.220.138.
At this, the Fairest of her Sex obey'd, ...Il.3.521.216.
No longer now a *Trojan* Lord obey'd. ....Il.5.402.286.
Whose hard Commands *Bellerophon* obey'd. ....Il.6.198.336.
The Goddess parts you: Be the Night obey'd. ....Il.7.342.381.
And Heav'n enjoins it, be the Night obey'd. ....Il.7.357.381.
These late obey'd *Æneas'* guiding Rein; ....Il.8.137.404.
Be the fierce Impulse of his Rage obey'd: ....Il.9.820.474.
In haste he mounted, and her Word obey'd; ....Il.10.599.29.
He spoke, and *Iris* at his Word obey'd; ....Il.11.253.46.
The Hero said, His Friend obey'd with haste, ...Il.11.754.68.
Divine *Sarpedon* the last Band obey'd, ...Il.12.115.85.
Th' Advice of wise *Polydamas* obey'd; ....Il.12.124.85.
Admir'd as Heroes, and as Gods obey'd? ....Il.12.378.95.
He spoke, and all as with one Soul obey'd; ....Il.13.614.135.
Speak her Request, and deem her Will obey'd. ....Il.14.224.172.
Obey'd the Sister and the Wife of *Jove:* ....Il.14.244.172.
His Will divine the Son of *Jove* obey'd. ....Il.15.265.207.
The Friend with Ardour and with Joy obey'd. ....Il.16.161.244.
Oïlean Ajax first the Voice obey'd, ...Il.17.302.299.
Swift as the Word was giv'n, the Youths obey'd; ....Il.19.249.383.
Proclaim, his Counsels are obey'd too late, ...Il.22.141.459.
Obey'd; and rested, on his Lance reclin'd. ....Il.22.290.468.
The Troops obey'd; and thrice in order led ....Il.23.15.486.
(Which late obey'd the *Dardan* Chief's Command, ...Il.23.361.504.
Howe'er be Heav'ns almighty Sire obey'd— ....Il.24.121.540.
Nor Augur, Priest, or Seer had been obey'd. ....Il.24.272.547.
The Sire obey'd him, trembling and o'er-aw'd. ....Il.24.720.567.
"When he, whom living mighty realms obey'd, ...Od.2.113.67.
But half the people with respect obey'd ....Od.3.187.95.
And his stern rule the groaning land obey'd; ....Od.3.389.105.
The sober train attended and obey'd. ....Od.3.432.108.
Be the kind dictates of thy heart obey'd, ...Od.3.457.109.
Jealous, to see their high behests obey'd, ...Od.4.477.142.
He either had obey'd my fond desire, ...Od.4.970.163.
My train obey'd me and the ship unty'd. ....Od.9.208.314.
While yet he spoke, the Prophet I obey'd, ...Od.11.122.387.
For wealthy Kings are loyally obey'd! ....Od.11.449.406.
And *Circe* warns! O be their voice obey'd: ....Od.12.327.447.
Sweet time of slumber! be the night obey'd! ....Od.12.348.448.
Mild I obey'd, for who shall war with thee? ....Od.13.155.13.
The Monarch spoke: they trembled and obey'd, ...Od.13.214.16.
'Tis *Jove's* high will, and be his will obey'd! ....Od.19.99.197.
The ready swains obey'd with joyful haste, ...Od.22.193.296.
But *Nestor* spoke, they listen'd, and obey'd. ....Od.24.70.351.
The King obey'd. The Virgin-seed of *Jove* ....Od.24.629.377.

OBEYS
The *Rules,* a Nation born to serve, obeys, ...1.EOC.713.322.
The God obeys, and to his Feet applies ....1.TrSt.429.428.
Her heart still dictates, and her hand obeys. ....2.ElAb.16.320.
The hog, that plows not nor obeys thy call, ...3.EOM3.41.96.
Yet has her humour most, when she obeys; ....3.Ep2.264.71.
Resistless falls: The Muse obeys the Pow'r. ....5.DunB4.628.407.
Pallas obeys, and from *Olympus'* Height ....Il.2.203.137.
Or bravely fights, or ill obeys Command, ...Il.2.435.148.
Lo faithful *Nestor* thy Command obeys; ....Il.10.121.7.
The gen'rous Impulse ev'ry *Greek* obeys; ....Il.12.315.93.
Obeys each Motion of the Master's Mind, ...Il.13.707.138.
Such was our Word, and Fate the Word obeys. ....Il.15.83.199.
How *Hector* calls, and *Troy* obeys his Call! ....Il.15.599.219.
The *Greek* obeys him, and with Awe retires. ....Il.16.868.277.
The Pow'r Ignipotent her Word obeys: ....Il.21.398.436.
The Wretch obeys, retiring with a Tear. ....Il.22.641.483.
The God obeys, his golden Pinions binds, ...Il.24.417.553.
That stranger-guest the *Taphian* realm obeys, ...Od.1.525.57.
His sage advice the list'ning King obeys; ....Od.7.224.247.
Thee in *Telemachus* thy realm obeys; ....Od.11.222.392.
The menial Fair obeys with duteous haste; ....Od.19.121.198.
The fleecy pile obeys the whisp'ring gales, ...Od.19.240.205.
Her equal pow'r each faithful sense obeys. ....Od.20.440.254.
With speed *Telemachus* obeys, and flies ....Od.22.126.292.
The aged Governess with speed obeys: ....Od.22.435.309.

OBEYSANCE
They bow'd, and made Obeysance as she pass'd, ...Il.15.93.200.
His sons around him mild obeysance pay, ...Od.3.524.113.
He made obeysance, and thus spoke aloud. ....Od.8.156.271.
Pay low obeysance as he moves along: ....Od.8.516.290.

OBJECT
Fair *Geraldine,* bright Object of his Vow, ...1.W-F.297.176.
Which o'er each Object casting various Dies, ...2.TemF.133.264.
How the dear object from the crime remove, ...2.ElAb.193.335.
But greedy that its object would devour, ...3.EOM2.89.65.
Good, from each object, from each place acquir'd, ...3.EOM4.321.159.
Mistake, confound, object, at all he spoke. ....4.JD4.117.35.
He walks, an Object new beneath the Sun! ....4.2HE2.119.173.
Yet by some object ev'ry brain is stirr'd; ....5.DunB4.445.384.
Congenial object in the Cockle-kind; ....5.DunB4.448A.384.
THOU art my God, sole object of my love; ....6.25.1.77.
No common object to your sight displays, ...6.32.19.96.
Call round her tomb each object of desire, ...6.52.49.157.
In yonder Walls that Object let me shun, ...Il.3.382.211.
Deplor'd *Amphimachus,* sad Object! lies; ....Il.13.263.117.
Some low in Dust (a mournful Object) lay, ...Il.13.959.151.
Too soon her Eyes the killing Object found, ...Il.22.596.480.
Sad Object as I am for heav'nly Sight! ....Il.24.119.540.
Am I the only Object of Despair? ....Il.24.298.549.
Behold an Object to thy Charge consign'd, ...Il.24.413.552.
Why, dearest object of my duteous love, ...Od.1.441.53.
With ease can save each object of his love; ....Od.3.286.100.
The darling object of your royal care ....Od.4.928.161.
The piteous object of a prostrate Queen. ....Od.4.953.162.
The dear, tho' mortal, object of my love, ...Od.5.278.185.
From the loath'd object ev'ry sight shall turn, ...Od.13.463.28.
Object uncouth! a man of miseries! ....Od.13.509.30.
Nor less the darling object of her love. ....Od.15.395.88.
And views that object which she wants the most! ....Od.19.245.206.
The royal object of your dearest care, ...Od.19.307.209.
The darling object of your royal love, ...Od.19.339.210.
Soon as her eyes the welcome object met, ...Od.22.444.309.
(Their light and dearest object long ago) ....Od.24.251.361.

OBJECTED
The mist objected, and condens'd the skies) ....Od.7.54.236.

OBJECTIONS
'Till, what with Proofs, Objections, and Replies, ...2.ChJM.143.21.

OBJECTS
In *Prospects,* thus, some *Objects* please our Eyes, ...1.EOC.158.258.
It *gilds* all Objects, but it *alters* none. ....1.EOC.317.274.
The sun all objects views beneath the sky, ...1.TrPA.110.370.
Once the dear Objects of my guilty Love; ....1.TrSP.18.394.
Themes of my Verse, and Objects of my Flames, ...1.TrSP.233.404.
Imperfect Objects may your Sense beguile: ....2.ChJM.798.53.
Self-love still stronger, as its objects nigh; ....3.EOM2.71.63.
Self-love yet stronger, as its objects nigh; ....3.EOM2.71A.63.
On diff'rent senses diff'rent objects strike; ....3.EOM2.128.70.
The optics seeing, as the objects seen. ....3.Ep1.24.17.
In town, what Objects could I meet? ....4.1HE7.7.269.
And leaves such Objects as distract the Fair. ....Il.11.504.56.
But when the Gods these objects of their hate ....Od.3.338.103.
Objects uncouth! to check the genial joy. ....Od.17.453.155.

OBLATIONS
Hear, Goddess, hear, by those oblations won; ....Od.4.1009.164.

OBLIG'D
Not ev'ry Man's oblig'd to sell his Store, ...2.ChWB.42.58.
Oblig'd by hunger and Request of friends: ....4.Arbu.44.99.
And so obliging that he ne'er oblig'd; ....4.Arbu.208.110.
How Church and State should be oblig'd to thee! ....6.8.29.18.
And so obliging, that he ne'r oblig'd: ....6.49iii.22.143.
Tho' distanc't one by one th' Oblig'd desert, ...6.84.31Z5.239.
And all th' Oblig'd desert, and all the Vain; ....6.84.32.240.
When all th'Oblig'd desert, and all the Vain; ....6.84.32A.240.
And so obliging that he ne'er oblig'd: ....6.98.58.285.
Oblig'd the Wealthy, and reliev'd the Poor. ....Il.6.20.325.

OBLIGE
Oblige her, and she'll hate you while you live: ....3.Ep2.138.62.
And from the moment we oblige the town, ...4.2HE1.370.227.
Contriving never to oblige ye. ....4.1HE7.30.271.
Would he oblige me? let me only find, ...4.EpS1.33.300.
Phryne had Talents to oblige Mankind, ...6.14v(b).1A.49.
Oblige her, and she'll hate you while you live. ....6.154.24.403.

OBLIGING
Th'obliging Dames obey'd with one Consent; ....2.ChJM.410.34.
"Obliging Sir! I love you, I profess, ...4.JD4.86A.33.
"Obliging Sir! for Courts you sure were made: ....4.JD4.86.33.
Go on, obliging Creatures, make me see ....4.Arbu.119.104.
And so obliging that he ne'er oblig'd; ....4.Arbu.208.110.
To all obliging she'd appear: ....6.14v(b).10.49.
And so obliging, that he ne'r oblig'd: ....6.49iii.22.143.
And so obliging that he ne'er oblig'd: ....6.98.58.285.
How skill'd he was in each obliging Art; ....Il.17.755.318.

OBLIGINGLY
And then for mine obligingly mistakes ....4.Arbu.279.115.

OBLIQUE
Oblique his Tusks, erect his Bristles stood, ...1.TrSt.573.434.
Ere Wit oblique had broke that steddy light, ...3.EOM3.231.115.
And dark thro' Paths oblique their Progress take. ....Il.10.320.17.
Wide with distorted Legs, oblique he goes, ...Il.18.480.345.
With well-taught Feet: Now shape, in oblique ways, ...Il.18.691.357.
Nor 'till oblique he slop'd his evening ray, ...Od.7.372.254.
His tusks oblique he aim'd the knee to goar; ....Od.19.525.221.

OBLIQUELY
The Sun obliquely shoots his burning Ray; ....2.RL3.20.170.
Obliquely wadling to the mark in view. ....5.DunA1.150.82.
Obliquely wadling to the mark in view: ....5.DunB1.172.282.

OBLIQUELY (CONTINUED)
Raz'd the smooth Cone, and thence obliquely glanc'd. ....Il.11.454.54.
And pierc'd, obliquely, King *Hypsenor's* Breast: ....Il.13.520.131.
Obliquely wheeling thro' th' aerial Way; ....Il.22.186.463.
His neck obliquely o'er his shoulder hung, ...Od.9.441.324.
The sun obliquely shot his dewy ray. ....Od.17.688.165.
Obliquely drops, and nodding knocks his breast; ....Od.18.282.180.

OBLIVION
(*Lodona's* Fate, in long Oblivion cast, ...1.W-F.173.165.
Be all your Acts in dark Oblivion drown'd; ....2.TemF.351.280.
Be all your Acts in dark Oblivion crown'd; ....2.TemF.351A.280.
Divine oblivion of low-thoughted care! ....2.ElAb.298.343.
When what t'oblivion better were resign'd, ...3.EOM4.251.151.
And there in sweet oblivion drown ....4.HS6.131.259.
Shall, raz'd and lost, in long Oblivion sleep. ....Il.7.540.391.
And long oblivion of the bridal bed. ....Od.3.278.99.
Each drinks a full oblivion of his cares, ...Od.3.508.112.
A blank oblivion, and untimely grave? ....Od.4.943.162.
Each drinks a full oblivion of his cares, ...Od.7.309.251.
And drank oblivion of their native coast: ....Od.10.275.356.
In sweet oblivion let my sorrow sleep! ....Od.19.140.199.
Stretch'd in a long oblivion of their lust. ....Od.22.481.312.
And o'er the past, *Oblivion* stretch her wing. ....Od.24.557.375.

OBLIVIOUS
Behold the wonders of th' Oblivious Lake. ....5.DunA3.36.154.
Behold the wonders of th' oblivious Lake. ....5.DunB3.44.322.
All night I slept, oblivious of my pain; ....Od.7.370.254.
The rest repell'd, a train oblivious fly. ....Od.11.183.390.
'Till soft oblivious shade *Minerva* spread, ...Od.19.703.229.
Whilst night extends her soft oblivious veil, ...Od.20.99.237.

OBLOQUY
Dwelt *Obloquy,* who in her early Days ....6.14ii.29.44.
Mean Intercourse of Obloquy and Pride! ....Il.20.502.415.

OBSCENE
The Fox obscene to gaping Tombs retires, ...1.W-F.71.156.
A Robe obscene was o'er her Shoulders thrown, ...1.TrSt.154.416.
The Birds obscene, that nightly flock'd to Tast, ...1.TrSt.735.441.
He, from the taste obscene reclaims our Youth, ...4.2HE1.217.213.
Obscene with filth the Miscreant lies bewray'd, ...5.DunA2.71.106.
Obscene with filth the varlet lies bewray'd, ...5.DunA2.71A.106.
Obscene with filth the miscreant lies bewray'd, ...5.DunB2.75.299.
Of link-boys vile, and watermen obscene; ....5.DunB2.100.300.
And by his Hand obscene the Porter took, ...6.14ii.44.44.
First Grubs obscene, then wriggling Worms, ...6.14v(b).23.50.
From the Grub Obscene, & wriggling Worm ....6.14v(b).23A.50.
Shall Flies and Worms obscene, pollute the Dead? ....Il.19.30.372.
Obscene to sight, the ruefull Racer lay; ....Il.23.912.525.
Won by destructive Lust (Reward obscene) ....Il.24.40.537.
But fowls obscene dismember'd his remains, ...Od.3.322.102.
Her parts obscene the raging billows hide; ....Od.12.115.437.
Late worn with years in weeds obscene you trod, ...Od.16.220.114.
Obscene with reptiles, took his sordid bed. ....Od.17.359.149.
Obscene with smoke, their beamy lustre lost, ...Od.19.10.193.
Like thee, in rags obscene decreed to roam! ....Od.20.262.246.
Where flock nocturnal bats, and birds obscene; ....Od.24.10.347.

OBSCENER
Or heal, old Narses, thy obscener ail, ...3.Ep3.91.97.
A Boar's obscener shape the God belies: ....Od.4.618.149.

OBSCENITY
No Pardon vile *Obscenity* should find, ...1.EOC.530.297.
But *Dulness* with *Obscenity* must prove ....1.EOC.532.297.

OBSCUR'D
And their brown Arms obscur'd the dusky Fields. ....Il.4.325.236.
This, tho' surrounding Shades obscur'd their View, ...Il.10.323.17.

OBSCURE
See gloomy Clouds obscure the chearful Day! ....1.PWi.30.91.
(Obscure the Place, and uninscrib'd the Stone) ....1.W-F.320.180.
It draws up Vapours which obscure its Rays; ....1.EOC.471.292.
Yet ev'n in those obscure Abodes to live, ...1.TrSt.691.439.
Obscure by Birth, renown'd by Crimes, ...6.14v(b).13.50.
The thronging Troops obscure the dusky Fields, ...Il.7.69.366.
Or chase thro' Woods obscure the trembling Hinde; ....Il.10.428.23.
Obscure in Smoak, his Forges flaming round, ...Il.18.436.341.
Mountains on mountains, and obscure the pole. ....Od.3.369.104.
Where waving shades obscure the mazy streams. ....Od.6.250.222.
The ship we moor on these obscure abodes; ....Od.11.21.380.
Eternal mists obscure th' aereal plain, ...Od.12.286.446.
Thus cautious, in th' obscure he hop'd to fly ....Od.19.458.217.

OBSCURER
Yet I can pardon those obscurer Rapes, ...1.TrSt.358.425.

OBSCURES
Obscures my Glories, and resumes my Prize. ....Il.1.467.110.
Obscures the Glade, and nods his shaggy Brows, ...Il.2.919.167.

OBSEQUIES
Give all his rites, and all his obsequies! ....6.20.38.67.
Dry pomps and Obsequies without a sigh. ....6.130.26.358.
Ah save his Arms, secure his Obsequies! ....Il.15.497.216.
On the bare Beach, depriv'd of Obsequies. ....Il.24.698.566.
Nor *Grecian* virgins shriek'd his obsequies, ...Od.3.321.102.

OBSEQUIOUS
Damian alone, the Knight's obsequious Squire, ...2.ChJM.359.31.
Thither th'obsequious Squire address'd his Pace, ...2.ChJM.605.44.
To where the Seine, obsequious as she runs, ...5.DunB4.297.373.
If e'er obsequious to thy *Juno's* Will, ...Il.14.268.175.

OBSEQUIOUS (CONTINUED)
The golden ew'r a maid obsequious brings, ...Od.1.179.41.
Fast by the Throne obsequious *Fame* resides, ...Od.1.497.56.
Th' obsequious Herald guides each princely guest: ....Od.4.408.140.
Instant the God obsequious will disclose ....Od.4.529.146.
The golden ew'r a nymph obsequious brings, ...Od.10.433.365.
His bright alcove th' obsequious youth ascends: ....Od.19.59.195.
Reveal, obsequious to my first demand, ...Od.19.125.198.
Instant obsequious to the mild-command, ...Od.19.420.214.
Accept the bath from this obsequious hand. ....Od.19.441.216.
He said: obsequious with redoubl'd pace, ...Od.19.587.224.

OBSERV'D
And have observ'd this useful Maxim still, ...2.ChJM.158.22.
Here let us walk, he said, observ'd by none, ...2.ChJM.543.41.
Who from *Æsetes'* Tomb observ'd the Foes; ....Il.2.961.169.
Observ'd each other, and had mark'd for War. ....Il.6.150.333.
Observ'd the Thund'rer, nor observ'd in vain. ....Il.13.18.104.
Observ'd the Thund'rer, nor observ'd in vain. ....Il.13.18.104.
His Time observ'd; for clos'd by Foes around, ...Il.13.698.138.
Thoas with Grief observ'd his dreadful Course, ...Il.15.318.209.
Observ'd the Storm of Darts the *Grecians* pour, ...Il.16.430.259.
Observ'd her ent'ring; her soft Hand she press'd, ...Il.18.451.343.
Observ'd the Fury of his flying Spear; ....Il.20.120.399.
He well observ'd the Chief who led the way, ...Il.23.535.511.
Observ'd, nor heedful of the setting light, ...Od.3.170.94.
Conceal'd he wept: the King observ'd alone ....Od.8.91.267.
Conceal'd he griev'd: the King observ'd alone ....Od.8.583.294.
Observ'd *Eumæus* ent'ring in the hall; ....Od.17.401.152.

OBSERVANCE
Will ask Observance, and exact her Dues. ....2.ChJM.213.24.
With due observance wait the chief's command; ....Od.2.463.83.
With due observance wait the chief's command: ....Od.15.311.84.

OBSERVANT
Great Nature spoke; observant Men obey'd; ....3.EOM3.199.113.
Ev'n now, observant of the parting Ray, ...6.84.37.240.
He said, observant of the blue-ey'd Maid; ....Il.1.291.100.
This hear Observant, and the Gods obey! ....Il.2.91.130.
And solemn swear, (observant of the Rite) ....Il.19.174.378.
Wand'ring from clime to clime, observant stray'd, ...Od.1.5.28.
Luxurious then they feast. Observant round ....Od.1.193.42.
Observant of the Gods, and sternly just, ...Od.1.342.49.
The ribs and limbs, observant of the rite: ....Od.3.583.116.
Observant of his word. The word scarce spoke, ...Od.3.606.117.
Observant of her word, he turn'd aside ....Od.5.590.200.
His fav'rite Isle! Observant *Mars* descries ....Od.8.327.281.
Instant the Queen, observant of the King, ...Od.8.469.288.
Observant of the Gods, begins the rite; ....Od.14.468.58.
To town, observant of our Lord's behest, ...Od.17.207.141.
Observant of his voice, *Eumæus* sate ....Od.17.682.165.
Observant of the Prince's high behest, ...Od.20.349.249.
The son observant not a moment stays: ....Od.22.434.309.
This spoke the King: Th' observant train obey, ...Od.23.139.327.

OBSERVATION
Nor will Life's stream for Observation stay, ...3.Ep1.31A.18.
Life's stream for Observation will not stay, ...3.Ep1.31.18.

OBSERVATIONS
To Observations which ourselves we make, ...3.Ep1.11.16.

OBSERVATOR
Than *Ev'ning Post,* or *Observator;* .... 6.10.6.24.

OBSERVE
T'observe a Mean, be to himself a Friend, ...1.W-F.251.172.
Made him observe the *Subject* and the *Plot,* .... 1.EOC.275.270.
Observe how system into system runs, ...3.EOM1.25.16.
P. But how unequal it bestows, observe, ...3.Ep3.23A.88.
But how unequal it bestows, observe, ...3.Ep3.23.88.
Pretty! in Amber to observe the forms ....4.Arbu.169.108.
And all mankind wou'd that blest Mean observe ....4.JD2A.125.142.
And all mankind might that just mean observe, ...4.JD2.119.143.
"Observe his Shape how clean! his Locks how curl'd! ....4.2HE2.5.165.
Observe how seldom ev'n the best succeed: ....4.2HE1.286.219.
Learn but to trifle; or, who most observe, ...5.DunB4.457.385.
Pretty, in Amber to observe the forms ....6.98.19.284.
Observe my Father's Steeds, renown'd in Fight, ...Il.5.279.280.
Observe my Father's Steeds, renown'd in War. ....Il.5.279A.280.
Observe the Steeds of *Tros,* renown'd in War, ...Il.8.134.404.
Observe, and in the truths I speak confide: ....Od.4.518.145.
Observe my orders, and with heed obey, ...Od.5.444.194.
Pious observe our hospitable laws, ...Od.7.252.248.
Observe the warnings of a pow'r divine: ....Od.15.32.71.
Full many foes, and fierce, observe us near; ....Od.21.244.271.
Observe what vigour Gratitude can lend, ...Od.22.255.299.

OBSERVER
In vain th' observer eyes the builder's toil, ...3.Ep1.220.34.

OBSERVER'S
We grow more partial for th' observer's sake; ....3.Ep1.12.16.

OBSERVES
Observes how much a Chintz exceeds Mohair. ....3.Ep2.170.64.
Some Wag observes me thus perplext, ...4.HS6.51.253.
Bubo observes, he lash'd no sort of *Vice:* .... 4.EpS1.12.298.
Observes how much a Chintz exceeds Mohair. ....6.139.14.377.
Observes the Compass of the hollow way. ....Il.23.498.510.
The King observes them: he the hall forsakes, ...Od.21.195.269.

OBSERVING
Observing, cry'd, "You scape not so, ...4.1HE7.57.271.
Observing *Hector* to the Rescue flew; ....Il.15.700.222.

OBSERVING (CONTINUED)
Observing still the foremost on the Plain. ....Il.23.398.506.
Go, guard the Sire; th' observing Foe prevent, ...Il.24.415.552.
With longing eyes, observing, to survey ....Od.5.560.199.
Th' observing Augur took the Prince aside, ...Od.15.571.98.

OBSOLETE
Spenser himself affects the obsolete, ...4.2HE1.97.203.
Who now that obsolete Example fears? ....4.EpS2.56.315.

OBSTACLES
Dangers on Dangers! obstacles by dozens! ....4.HAdv.128.85.

OBSTETRIC
And Douglas lend his soft, obstetric hand." ....5.DunB4.394.380.

OBSTINACY
From spleen, from obstinacy, hate, or fear! ....3.EOM2.186.77.

OBSTINATE
Thus obstinate to Death, they fight, they fall; ....1.TrES.161.455.
No Ass so meek, no Ass so obstinate: ....3.Ep2.102.58.
Thus obstinate to Death, they fight, they fall; ....Il.12.515.100.
Restive they stood, and obstinate in Woe: ....Il.17.491.307.
On me, confirm'd, and obstinate in woe. ....Od.19.388.212.

OBSTINATELY
With pow'rs united, obstinately bold ....Od.4.561.147.
Tho' tempted chaste, and obstinately just? ....Od.11.215.392.

OBSTREP'ROUS
With din obstrep'rous, and ungrateful cries. ....Od.14.456.57.

OBSTRUCT
Stays will obstruct above, and Hoops below, ...4.HAdv.131.87.
Obstruct Achilles, or commence the Fight, ...Il.20.167.400.

OBSTRUCTED
'Tis he th'obstructed Paths of Sound shall clear, ...1.Mes.41.116.

OBTAIN
Soon to obtain, and long possess the Prize: ....2.RL2.44.162.
Each has his share; and who would more obtain, ...3.EOM4.47.132.
In who obtain defence, or who defend, ...3.EOM4.59.134.
But these less taste them, as they worse obtain. ......3.EOM4.84.136.
Shall heav'n so soon the prize obtain? ....6.4iii.4.10.
Can Book, or Man, more Praise obtain? ....6.64.15.190.
Repuls'd he yields; the Victor Greeks obtain ....Il.13.259.117.
What Honour, and what Love shall I obtain, ...Il.14.239.172.
This half-recover'd Day shall Troy obtain'd ....Il.14.423.184.
(So Jove decreed!) At length the Greeks obtain .....Il.16.805.274.
Oh! were Patroclus ours, we might obtain ....Il.17.179.294.
While shielded from the Darts, the Greeks obtain ...Il.18.273.335.
Who hopes the Palm of Swiftness to obtain, ...Il.23.879.524.
Forsake these Ramparts, and with Gifts obtain ....Il.24.237.546.
The royal car at early dawn obtain, ...Od.6.41.207.
And may his child the royal car obtain? ....Od.6.70.208.
Then grant, what here all sons of woe obtain, ...Od.8.31.263.
Not undeserving, some support obtain. ....Od.15.335.85.

OBTAIN'D
The Lock, obtain'd with Guilt, and kept with Pain. ....2.RL5.109.208.
Which, were you woman, had obtain'd; ....6.4iii.10.10.
The Peace rejected, but the Truce obtain'd ....Il.7.493.388.
Nor Priam, nor his Sons obtain'd their Grace; ....Il.8.683.427.
My Sire three hundred chosen Sheep obtain'd. ....Il.11.835.73.
The first great Ancestor obtain'd his Grace, ...Il.20.351.408.
One Length, one Moment had the Race obtain'd. ....Il.23.606.513.
The Praise of Wisdom, in thy Youth obtain'd, ...Il.23.651.515.
The golden Talents Merion next obtain'd; ....Il.23.703.517.
A previous pledge of sacred faith obtain'd, ...Od.4.347.136.

OBTAINS
Who noble ends by noble means obtains, ...3.EOM4.233.148.
In Britain's Senate he a seat obtains, ...3.Ep3.393.124.
Still happy Impudence obtains the prize. ....5.DunA2.178.123.
Still happy Impudence obtains the prize. ....5.DunB2.186.304.
It is not Strength, but Art, obtains the Prize, ...Il.23.383.505.

OBTEND
And to his shafts obtend these ample boards, ...Od.22.88.290.

OBTESTING
And thus, obtesting Heav'n I mourn'd aloud. ....Od.12.436.452.
His hands obtesting, and this pray'r conceiv'd. ....Od.17.281.145.

OBTESTS
Experienc'd Nestor chief obtests the Skies, ...Il.15.426.213.
He lifts his wither'd Arms; obtests the Skies; ....Il.22.45.454.

OBTRUDE
Hence! Nor obtrude your Anguish on my Eyes. ....Il.24.296.549.
On God or mortal to obtrude a lye ....Od.14.427.56.

OBTRUDING
Obtruding on my choice a second Lord, ...Od.19.154.200.

OBVIOUS
Obvious her goods, in no extreme they dwell, ...3.EOM4.31.130.
When Man's whole frame is obvious to a Flea. ....5.DunB4.238.366.
Amidst the Heap, and obvious to the Eye, ...Il.23.299.501.
Like the full Moon, stood obvious to the Sight. ....Il.23.539.511.

OCALEA
And Medeon lofty, and Ocalea low; ....Il.2.597.156.

OCCASION
But with th' Occasion and the Place comply, ...1.EOC.177.261.
Yet he shall find, wou'd time th'occasion shew, ...1.TrPA.124.370.
Yet hoping Time th'Occasion might betray, ...2.ChJM.396.34.
When kind Occasion prompts their warm Desires, ...2.RL1.75.151.
On just occasion, coute qui coute. ....4.HS6.164.261.
T'administer on this Occasion, ...6.10.114.28.
Now seize th' Occasion, now the Troops survey, ...Il.2.518.151.
Then seize th' Occasion, dare the mighty Deed, ...Il.4.129.226.
O Hector! say, what great Occasion calls ....Il.6.318.341.
Or weigh the great Occasion, and be more. ....Il.16.682.270.
Thee, welcome Goddess! what Occasion calls, ...Il.18.495.345.
Presents th' occasion, could we use it right. ....Il.23.494.510.
He took th' occasion as they stood intent, ...Od.15.499.94.

OCCASIONS
To please a Wife when her Occasions call, ...2.ChJM.210.24.

OCEAN
To the cool Ocean, where his Journey ends; ....1.PSu.90.79.
As on the Land while here the Ocean gains, ...1.EOC.54.245.
And the black Ocean foams and roars below. ....1.TrUl.12.465.
By him, who made the Ocean, Earth, and Air, ...2.ChJM.209.24.
Who heaves old Ocean, and who wings the storms, ...3.EOM1.158.35.
That never air or ocean felt the wind; ....3.EOM1.167.36.
See, thro' this air, this ocean, and this earth, ...3.EOM1.233.44.
On life's vast ocean diversely we sail, ...3.EOM2.107.67.
That Pow'r who bids the Ocean ebb and flow, ...3.Ep3.166.107.
His pond an Ocean, his parterre a Down: ....3.Ep4.106.147.
Realms shift their place, and Ocean turns to land. ....5.DunA1.70.68.
Realms shift their place, and Ocean turns to land. ....5.DunB1.72.275.
Thus from the ocean first did rise. ....6.5.4.12.
Where aged Ocean holds his wat'ry Reign, ...Il.1.469.110.
The parted Ocean foams and roars below: ....Il.1.627.117.
Murmuring they move, as when old Ocean roars, ...Il.2.249.139.
These, o'er the bending Ocean, Helen's Cause ......Il.2.709.159.
And bath'd in Ocean, shoots a keener Light. ....Il.5.10.266.
The Waves scarce heave, the Face of Ocean sleeps, ...Il.7.73.366.
Strong God of Ocean! Thou, whose Rage can make ...Il.7.544.391.
I heave the Gods, the Ocean, and the Land, ...Il.8.30.397.
Now deep in Ocean sunk the Lamp of Light, ...Il.8.605.425.
A sudden Storm the purple Ocean sweeps, ...Il.11.385.51.
The God of Ocean, marching stern before, ...Il.12.29.82.
Such, and so swift, the Pow'r of Ocean flew; ....Il.13.95.109.
The God of Ocean, fir'd with stern Disdain, ...Il.13.273.117.
With Shouts incessant Earth and Ocean rung, ...Il.13.1057.155.
The God of Ocean (to inflame their Rage) ....Il.14.155.165.
Ocean and Tethys their old Empire keep, ...Il.14.231.172.
The Sire of all, old Ocean, owns my Reign, ...Il.14.279.175.
The rev'rend Ocean and grey Tethys reign, ...Il.14.343.179.
Deep under Seas, where hoary Ocean dwells. ....Il.14.354.180.
Both Armies join: Earth thunders, Ocean roars. ....Il.14.456.185.
(The King of Ocean thus, incens'd, replies) ....Il.15.207.204.
The Horses thunder, Earth and Ocean roar! ....Il.15.405.212.
The glowing Ocean reddens with the Fires. ....Il.16.157.244.
The boiling Ocean works from Side to Side, ...Il.17.313.299.
All these, and all that deep in Ocean held ....Il.18.65.326.
Soon as the Sun in Ocean hides his Rays, ...Il.18.249.334.
The rushing Ocean murmur'd o'er my Head. ....Il.18.472.344.
There Earth, there Heav'n, there Ocean he design'd; ...Il.18.558.349.
With his last Hand, and pour'd the Ocean round; .....Il.18.702.357.
All but old Ocean, hoary Sire! who keeps ....Il.20.15.393.
The King of Ocean to the Fight descends, ...Il.20.367.410.
And Ocean listens to the grateful Sound. ....Il.20.470.414.
Th' Eternal Ocean, from whose Fountains flow ....Il.21.213.430.
The Pow'r of Ocean first. Forbear thy Fear, ...Il.21.332.435.
These from old Ocean at my Word shall blow, ...Il.21.390.436.
The God of Ocean dares the God of Light. ....Il.21.507.442.
To sacred Ocean, and the Floods below: ....Il.23.253.499.
O'er the broad Ocean pour'd the golden Day: ....Il.23.283.501.
Meteorous the Face of Ocean sweeps, ...Il.24.101.539.
O'er earth and ocean wide prepar'd to soar, ...Od.1.128.38.
Thro' the wide Ocean first to sandy Pyle, ...Od.1.369.50.
(A length of Ocean and unbounded sky, ...Od.3.411.106.
The flocks of Ocean to the strand repair: ....Od.4.604.148.
White curl the waves, and the vex'd ocean roars. ....Od.4.788.156.
Such length of ocean and unmeasur'd deep? ....Od.5.126.178.
Alone, abandon'd, in mid ocean tost, ...Od.5.169.180.
In the black ocean, or the wat'ry war, ...Od.5.284.185.
To curl old Ocean, and to warm the skies. ....Od.5.342.188.
The King of Ocean saw, and seeing burn'd, ...Od.5.363.190.
Then prone on Ocean in a moment flung, ...Od.5.476.195.
Safe in the love of heav'n, an ocean flows ....Od.6.243.221.
And Ocean whitens in long tracts below. ....Od.7.420.258.
Dire is the Ocean, dread in all its forms! ....Od.8.151.271.
Far in wide ocean, and from sight of shore. ....Od.9.94.306.
Old Ocean shook, and back his surges flew. ....Od.9.582.330.
The gushing tempest sweeps the Ocean round; ......Od.10.51.342.
The Ocean widen'd, and the shores withdrew. ....Od.10.53.342.
The man from Troy, who wander'd Ocean round; ....Od.10.393.363.
And back to Ocean glance with rev'rend awe. ....Od.10.631.374.
Where on Trinacrian rocks the Ocean roars, ...Od.11.134.387.
A bull, a ram, a boar; and hail the Ocean-King. ......Od.11.161.389.
Where rouls yon smoke, yon tumbling ocean raves; ...Od.12.261.445.
She dreins the ocean with the refluent tides: ....Od.12.289.446.
Air thunders, rolls the ocean, groans the ground. ....Od.12.374.449.
Or deep in Ocean plunge the burning ray. ....Od.12.449.452.
Beeves, slain by heaps, along the ocean bleed. ....Od.12.463.453.
And all above is sky, and ocean all around! ....Od.12.474.454.
And the black Ocean foams and roars below. ....Od.13.103.6.
The King of Ocean all the tribes implore; ....Od.13.218.16.
Thro' the wild ocean plow the dang'rous way, ...Od.13.482.29.
(The shaded Ocean blacken'd as it spread) ....Od.14.336.51.
Twice ten sad years o'er earth and ocean tost, ...Od.16.226.114.
Took in the ocean with a broad survey: ....Od.16.383.124.
Me with his whelming wave let Ocean shroud! ....Od.20.77.236.

OCEAN (CONTINUED)
Flame from the Ocean o'er the eastern hills: ....Od.23.374.343.

OCEAN-KING
A bull, a ram, a boar; and hail the Ocean-King. ....Od.11.161.389.

OCEAN'S
As when old Ocean's silent Surface sleeps, ...Il.14.21.157.
In Ocean's Waves th' unwilling Light of Day ....Il.18.284.335.
But Ocean's God, whose Earthquakes rock the Ground, ...Il.20.339.408.
And yields to Ocean's hoary Sire, the Prize? ....Il.21.548.444.
(A Race unrival'd, which from Ocean's God ....Il.23.345.503.
(Old Ocean's Daughter, silver-footed Dame) ....Il.24.710.567.
Of Ocean's King she then implores the grace. ....Od.3.68.89.
For know, from Ocean's God *Nausithous* sprung, ...Od.7.72.237.
Ogygia nam'd, in *Ocean's* wat'ry arms: ....Od.7.328.252.
Her mother *Persè,* of old Ocean's strain, ...Od.10.159.348.
Soon shalt thou reach old Ocean's utmost ends, ...Od.10.602.372.
When lo! we reach'd old Ocean's utmost bounds, ...Od.11.13.379.
Nor yet forgot old Ocean's dread Supreme ....Od.13.144.12.
Twelve herds, twelve flocks, on Ocean's margin feed, ...Od.14.122.41.
What time the sun, from ocean's peaceful stream, ...Od.19.505.221.
And *Leucas'* rock, and *Ocean's* utmost streams, ...Od.24.17.347.

OCEANS
And Oceans join whom they did first divide; ....1.W-F.400A.191.
Where Mountains rise, and circling Oceans flow; ....2.TemF.14.254.
Rise *Alps* between us! and whole oceans roll! ....2.ElAb.290.343.
Tho' mountains rise between, and oceans roar. ....Od.6.376.230.
To coasts unknown, and oceans yet untry'd. ....Od.9.118.308.
And round the coast circumfluent oceans rise. ....Od.16.60.105.
On rolling oceans, and in fighting fields, ...Od.17.337.148.

OCT
Witness Ann. prim. of Henry Oct. ....6.67.14.195.

OCTAVIUS
In *Rome's* proud *Forum* young *Octavius* plac'd, ...6.20.28.66.

OCTAVO'S
Quarto's, Octavo's, shape the less'ning pyre, ...5.DunA1.141.81.

OCTAVOS
Quartos, octavos, shape the less'ning pyre; ....5.DunB1.161.282.

OCTOBER
(October next it will be four) ....4.HS6.84.255.
October, store, and best *Virginia,* ....6.39.5.110.
October, store, the best *Virginia,* ....6.39.5A.110.

OCYALUS
The prize *Ocyalus* and *Prymneus* claim, ...Od.8.115.268.

OD'ROUS
And od'rous Myrtle to the noisome Weed. ....1.Mes.76.119.
With od'rous Spices they perfum'd the Place, ...2.ChJM.355.31.
And od'rous fumes from loaded altars roll'd. ....Od.3.349.103.
Cedar and frankincense, an od'rous pile, ...Od.5.76.176.
The nymph dismist him, (od'rous garments giv'n, ...Od.5.335.188.

ODD
Could not but think, to pay his *Fine* was odd, ...4.JD4.17.27.
The *Presence* seems, with things so richly odd, ...4.JD4.238.45.
All this may be; the People's Voice is odd, ...4.2HE1.89.201.
Nay half in Heav'n—except (what's mighty odd) ....4.1HE1.187.293.
A Joke on JEKYL, or some odd *Old Whig,* ....4.EpS1.39.300.
So odd, my Country's Ruin makes me grave. ....4.EpS2.207.324.
But some odd Graces and fine Flights she had, ...6.99.3.286.
Pallas grew vap'rish once and odd, ...6.119.1.336.
Here lies a round Woman, who thought *mighty odd* ....6.124i.1.346.

ODDLY
Yet dye thou can'st not, Phantom, oddly fated: ....6.116iv.5.327.

ODDS
I will not cope against such odds, ...6.79.99.221.
On Valor's side the Odds of Combate lie, ...Il.5.655.299.
On Valour's side the odds of Combate lie, ...Il.15.670.221.
And gain'd at length the glorious Odds of Fate. ....Il.17.383.302.

ODE
Dear *Cibber!* never match'd one Ode of thine. ....4.2HE2.138.175.
Much future Ode, and abdicated Play; ....5.DunB1.122.278.
A twisted Birth-day Ode completes the spire. ....5.DunB1.162.282.
And all be sleep, as at an Ode of thine." ....5.DunB1.318.293.

ODES
(Like Journals, Odes, and such forgotten things ....4.2HE1.416.231.
And New-year Odes, and all the Grubstreet race. ....5.DunA1.42.65.
And New-year Odes, and all the Grub-street race. ....5.DunB1.44.274.
When Laureates make Odes, do you ask of what sort? ....6.153.1.402.

ODIN
And *Odin* here in mimick Trances dies. ....2.TemF.124.264.

ODIOUS
"Odious! in woollen! 'twould a Saint provoke, ...3.Ep1.242.36.
All bath'd in tears—"Oh odious, odious Trees!" ....3.Ep2.40.53.
All bath'd in tears—"Oh odious, odious Trees!" ....3.Ep2.40.53.
Call *Verres, Wolsey,* any odious name? ....4.EpS2.137.321.
Call *Clodius, Wolsey,* any odious name? ....4.EpS2.137A.321.
I've no red Hair to breathe an odious Fume; ....6.96iv.27.277.
Anxious to thee, and odious to thy Lord. ....Il.1.729.122.
An odious Conquest and a Captive Wife, ...Il.3.500.215.
Thou most unjust, most odious in our Eyes! ....Il.5.1097.319.
At length are odious to th' all-seeing Mind; ....Il.20.354.408.

ODIOUS (CONTINUED)
They form a deed more odious and accurst; ....Od.4.925.161.

ODIUS
Whom *Odius* and *Epistrophus* command, ...Il.2.1043.172.
First *Odius* falls, and bites the bloody Sand, ...Il.5.51.269.

ODLY
Her Tongue bewitch'd as odly as her Eyes, ...3.Ep2.47.54.
Are odly join'd by Fate: ....6.14v(a).9.48.

ODORS
And burn rich Odors in *Minerva's* Fane. ....Il.6.339.343.
Where treasur'd Odors breath'd a costly Scent. ....Il.6.359.343.
With liquid odors, and embroider'd vests. ....Od.4.60.122.
And glowing violets threw odors round. ....Od.5.94.176.
Sulphureous odors rose, and smould'ring smoke. ....Od.12.492.456.

ODOUR
Odour divine! whose soft refreshing streams ....Od.6.93.209.
When lo! an odour from the feast exhales, ...Od.12.433.451.

ODOURS
Nor Morning Odours from the Flow'rs arise. ....1.PWi.46.92.
While Plants their Shade, or Flow'rs their Odours give, ...1.PWi.83.94.
O'er all his Limbs *Ambrosial* Odours shed, ...1.TrES.328.461.
At ev'ry Breath were balmy Odours shed, ...2.TemF.314.279.
In Hues as gay, and Odours as divine, ...4.JD4.216.45.
Colours as gay, and Odours as divine, ...4.JD4.216A.45.
And waft their grateful Odours to the Skies. ....Il.1.417.107.
Fair as a God with Odours round him spread ....Il.3.483.215.
His Fane breath'd Odours, and his Altar blaz'd: ....Il.8.60.398.
O'er all his Limbs Ambrosial Odours shed, ...Il.16.815.274.
And breathing odours scent the balmy skies. ....Od.8.398.285.

OECHALIA
No nymph of all *Oechalia* could compare ....1.TrFD.7.385.

OECHALIAN
Th' *Oechalian* Race, in those high Tow'rs contain'd, ...Il.2.884.166.

OECONOMY
Join with Oeconomy, Magnificence; ....3.Ep3.224.111.

OEDIPUS
At *Oedipus—from* his Disasters trace ....1.TrSt.21.410.
Now wretched *Oedipus,* depriv'd of Sight, ...1.TrSt.69.413.
Assist, if *Oedipus* deserve thy Care! ....1.TrSt.86.413.
Thy Curse, oh *Oedipus,* just Heav'n alarms, ...1.TrSt.338.424.
All these the Woes of *Oedipus* have known, ...1.TrSt.818.444.
(The Games ordain'd dead *Oedipus* to grace) ....Il.23.787.521.

OENEUS
For now the Sons of *Oeneus* were no more! ....Il.2.780.162.
Oeneus the strong, *Bellerophon* the bold: ....Il.6.268.340.
Oeneus a Belt of matchless Work bestow'd, ...Il.6.273.340.
His suppliant Father, aged *Oeneus,* came; ....Il.9.695.468.
Then rest in Courage) *Oeneus* was the last. ....Il.14.133.164.

OENEUS'
On *Oeneus'* Fields she sent a monstrous Boar, ...Il.9.659.467.

OENIDES'
Oenides' manly Shoulders overspread, ...1.TrSt.572.434.
Hear then in me the great *Oenides'* Son, ...Il.14.126.163.

OENOMÄUS
Of fierce *Oenomäus,* defil'd with Blood; ....1.TrSt.389.426.

OENOMAS
But *Oenomas* receiv'd the *Cretan's* stroke, ...Il.13.640.136.

OENOMAUS
Next *Oenomaus,* and *Oenops'* Offspring dy'd; ....Il.5.868.307.
And *Oenomaus* and *Thoon* close the Rear; ....Il.12.154.87.

OENOPS'
Next *Oenomaus,* and *Oenops'* Offspring dy'd; ....Il.5.868.307.
The eldest born of *Oenops'* noble race, ...Od.21.153.266.

OETE
Oete, with high *Parnassus,* heard the Voice; ....1.TrSt.165.417.

OETYLOS'
And those whom *Œtylos'* low Walls contain, ...Il.2.707.159.

OF (OMITTED)
8073

OFF
Soon as the Flocks shook off the nightly Dews, ...1.PSp.17.62.
From ev'ry Face he wipes off ev'ry Tear. ....1.Mes.46.117.
So modest Plainness sets off sprightly Wit: ....1.EOC.302.273.
Not yet purg'd off, of Spleen and sow'r Disdain, ...1.EOC.527.297.
And drove those *Holy Vandals* off the Stage. ....1.EOC.696.319.
Shakes off the *Dust,* and rears his rev'rend Head! ....1.EOC.700.319.
Death with his Scythe cut off the fatal Thread, ...1.TrSt.745.441.
He said, and leap'd from off his lofty Car; ....1.TrES.217.457.
He spake; and speaking, leaps from off the Car; ....1.TrES.217A.457.
Led off two captive Trumps, and swept the Board. ....2.RL3.50.172.
First strip off all her equipage of Pride, ...3.EOM2.44.61.
Strike off his Pension, by the setting sun, ...3.Ep1.160.29.
Dip in the Rainbow, trick her off in Air, ...3.Ep2.18.50.
Or ship off Senates to some distant Shore; ....3.Ep3.74A.93.
Or ship off Senates to a distant Shore; ....3.Ep3.74.93.
And I not strip the Gilding off a Knave, ...4.HS1.115.17.

OFF (CONTINUED)
But ey'd him round, and stript off all the Cloaths; .... 4.HAdv.115.85.
May Dunce by Dunce be whistled off my hands! .... 4.Arbu.254.114.
Walk sober off; before a sprightlier Age .... 4.2HE2.324.187.
He marches off, his Grace's Secretary. .... 5.DunA2.212.127.
And mounts far off, among the swans of Thames. .... 5.DunA2.286.137.
And carry'd off in some Dog's tail at last. .... 5.DunA3.294A.184.
The sick'ning Stars fade off th' æthereal plain; .... 5.DunA3.342.192.
He marches off, his Grace's Secretary. .... 5.DunB2.220.306.
And mounts far off among the Swans of Thames. .... 5.DunB2.298.310.
And carry'd off in some Dog's tail at last. .... 5.DunB3.292.334.
To lug the pond'rous volume off in state.] .... 5.DunB4.118.353.
And hew the Block off, and get out the Man. .... 5.DunB4.270.370.
And titt'ring push'd the Pedants off the place: .... 5.DunB4.276.371.
And shove him off as far as e'er we can: .... 5.DunB4.474.387.
The vulgar herd turn off to roll with Hogs, ... 5.DunB4.525.394.
The sick'ning stars fade off th'ethereal plain; .... 5.DunB4.636.407.
And take off Ladies Limitations. .... 6.61.55.183.
But take off Ladies Limitations. .... 6.61.55A.183.
And Jove with Joy puts off the *Bear*. .... 6.80.4.224.
When Int'rest calls off all her sneaking Train, ... 6.84.31.239.
Tho' Int'rest calls off all her sneaking Train, ... 6.84.31Z3.239.
So skimming the fat off, ... 6.91.27.254.
Say Grace, with your hat off .... 6.91.28.254.
Then skimming the fat off, ... 6.91.27A.254.
Yet thence to think I'd bite your Head off! .... 6.135.7.366.
But thence to think I'le bite your Head off! .... 6.135.7A.366.
To keep off Flatt'rers, Spies, and Panders, ... 6.135.74.369.
Ascends in Clouds from off the heapy Corn; .... Il.5.614.297.
Cut off, and exil'd from th' Æthereal Race. .... Il.8.569.423.
Stand off, approach not, but thy Purpose tell. .... Il.10.93.6.
Drag off the Car where *Rhesus* Armour lay, ... Il.10.590.28.
The Spoils contested, and bear off the slain. .... Il.13.260.117.
His tir'd, slow Steps, he drags from off the Field. .... Il.13.653.136.
The Helm fell off, and roll'd amid the Throng: .... Il.13.730.139.
Tore off his Arms, and loud-exulting said. .... Il.13.778.141.
In slow Procession bore from off the Plain. .... Il.13.822.144.
He spake; and speaking, leaps from off the Car; .... Il.16.520.263.
From off the ringing Orb, it struck the Ground. .... Il.22.372.471.
And cast, far off, the regal Veils away. .... Il.22.513.477.
To heave the batter'd Carcase off the Plain. .... Il.23.780.520.
He said; and straining, heav'd him off the Ground .... Il.23.842.523.
With Force conjoin'd heave off the weighty Prize. .... Il.23.1005.529.
Strip off thy garments; *Neptune's* fury brave .... Od.5.436.193.
Cast it far off, and turn thy eyes away. .... Od.5.445.194.
'Till the huge surge roll'd off. Then backward sweep .... Od.5.548.198.
The three we sent, from off th' inchanting ground .... Od.9.111.308.
Consult our safety, and put off to sea. .... Od.9.267.317.
Where lies she anchor'd? near, or off the shore? .... Od.9.334.320.
Now off at sea, and from the shallows clear, ... Od.9.555.328.
Again I shov'd her off; our fate to fly, ... Od.9.573.330.
And with desponding hearts put off to sea. .... Od.10.88.343.
Fragments they rend from off the craggy brow, ... Od.10.139.347.
This *Hermes* gave, then gliding off the glade .... Od.10.367.362.
Fall off, miraculous effect of art: .... Od.10.466.366.
'Till dying off, the distant sounds decay: .... Od.12.237.443.
Let wit cast off the sullen yoke of sense. .... Od.14.525.62.
Instant, the racer vanish'd off the ground; .... Od.14.566.64.
Or we perhaps might take him off thy hands. .... Od.17.261.144.

OFF-SPRING
And yields an Off-spring more than Nature gives; .... 1.TrVP.14.377.
Th'illustrious Off-spring of the God was born. .... 1.TrSt.679.438.
Her num'rous Off-spring for a fatal Boast. .... 1.TrSt.850.445.
To shield his Off-spring, and avert his Fate. .... 1.TrES.140.454.
Or to his Doom my bravest Off-spring yield, ... 1.TrES.235.458.
To shield his Off-spring, and avert his Fate. .... Il.12.494.99.
Of *Maia's* off-spring and the martial Maid. .... Od.11.772.424.

OFF'RING
(A pleasing Off'ring when 'tis made by you;) .... 1.TrVP.97.381.
The sacred Off'ring of the salted Cake; .... Il.1.587.116.
And burns the Off'ring with his holy Hands, ... Il.1.607.117.
The sacred Off'ring of the salted Cake: .... Il.2.487.150.
Ungrateful Off'ring to th' immortal Pow'rs, ... Il.8.681.427.
Poor as it is, some Off'ring to thy Shade. .... Il.17.607.312.
He crops, and off'ring meditates his Vow. .... Il.19.262.383.
Turns the burnt-off'ring with his holy hands, ... Od.3.587.116.
Prepar'd for rest, and off'ring to the * God .... Od.7.184.244.
An off'ring sacred to th' immortal pow'rs: .... Od.8.558.292.
A threefold off'ring to his Altar bring, ... Od.11.160.389.

OFF'RINGS
And grateful Off'rings on your Altars laid .... 1.TrUl.247.474.
The various Off'rings of the World appear; .... 2.RL1.130.155.
With feasts, and off'rings, and a thankful strain: .... 4.2HE1.244.215.
Bears Pisa's off'rings to his Arethuse) .... 5.DunB2.342.314.
My tears the want of off'rings had supply'd; .... 6.20.41.67.
The first fat Off'rings, to th' Immortals due, ... Il.9.287.448.
Are mov'd by Off'rings, Vows, and Sacrifice; .... Il.9.621.465.
Nor rais'd in Off'rings to the Pow'rs divine, ... Il.16.275.249.
Had rais'd in Off'rings, but to *Jove* alone. .... Il.16.277.249.
Still on our Shrines his grateful Off'rings lay, ... Il.24.89.539.
To raise in off'rings to almighty *Jove*, ... Od.8.467.288.
With promis'd off'rings on thy native shore; .... Od.10.621.374.
These solemn vows and holy off'rings paid .... Od.10.626.374.
And grateful off'rings on your altars laid. .... Od.13.414.26.
The choicest off'rings let *Melanthius* bring; .... Od.21.281.273.

OFFENCE
But, of the two, less dang'rous is th' Offence, ... 1.EOC.3.239.
'Tis not enough no Harshness gives Offence, ... 1.EOC.364.281.
At ev'ry Trifle scorn to take Offence, ... 1.EOC.386.284.
Art shall be theirs to varnish an Offence, ... 2.ChJM.661.46.
None shall want Arts to varnish an Offence, ... 2.ChJM.661A.46.
What dire Offence from am'rous Causes springs, ... 2.RL1.1.144.

OFFENCE (CONTINUED)
Now turn'd to heav'n, I weep my past offence, ... 2.ElAb.187.335.
And love th' offender, yet detest th' offence? .... 2.ElAb.192.335.
Soft were my Numbers, who could take offence .... 4.Arbu.147.106.
Thus much I've said, I trust without Offence; .... 4.JD2A.131.144.
One, one man only breeds my just offence; .... 4.JD2.45.137.
Thus much I've said, I trust without offence; .... 4.JD2.125.145.
Tis *Coscus* only breeds my just Offence, ... 4.JD2A.51.136.
Then might I sing without the least Offence, ... 4.EpS1.77.304.
Some Dæmon stole my pen (forgive th' offence) .... 5.DunB1.187.283.
You have no Cause to take Offence, Sir, ... 6.10.101.27.
No Pains it takes, and no Offence it gives, ... 6.16.5.53.
And, for the King's Offence, the People dy'd. .... Il.1.14.86.
If, on thy next Offence, this Hand forbear .... Il.2.322.142.
What high Offence has fir'd the Wife of *Jove*, ... Il.4.49.223.
Howe'er th' Offence by other Gods be past, ... Il.15.242.206.
Superior as thou art, forgive th' Offence, ... Il.23.669.516.
Respecting him, my Soul abjures th' Offence; .... Il.24.535.558.
Not only flies the guilt, but shuns th' offence: .... Od.6.342.228.
Warm are thy words, but warm without offence; .... Od.8.271.278.
The Gods and men the dire offence detest, ... Od.11.333.398.
Due pains shall punish then this slave's offence, ... Od.17.290.146.
Peace wretch! and eat thy bread without offence, ... Od.17.568.160.
Indecently to rail without offence! .... Od.18.21.167.
Know, to *Telemachus* I tell th' offence: .... Od.18.387.186.
Th' offence was great, the punishment was just. .... Od.24.527.373.

OFFENCES
When *Israel's* Daughters mourn'd their past Offences, ... 6.95.1.264.

OFFEND
Great Wits sometimes may *gloriously offend*, ... 1.EOC.152.257.
Moderns, beware! Or if you must offend .... 1.EOC.163.259.
Form *short Ideas*; and offend in *Arts* .... 1.EOC.287.271.
Averse alike to *Flatter*, or *Offend*, ... 1.EOC.743.326.
Two Races now, ally'd to *Jove*, offend; .... 1.TrSt.315.423.
If what I speak my noble Lord offend, ... 2.ChJM.214.24.
How soft is Silia! fearful to offend, ... 3.Ep2.29.52.
Offend her, and she knows not to forgive; .... 3.Ep2.137.62.
Still *Sapho*—*"Hold!* for God-sake—you'll offend: .... 4.Arbu.101.103.
Still *Sapho*—*"Hold!* nay see you—you'll offend: .... 4.Arbu.101A.103.
And how did, pray, the Florid Youth offend. .... 4.EpS2.166.323.
Offend her, and she knows not to forgive, ... 6.154.23.403.
'Tis hers t'offend; and ev'n offending share .... Il.5.1078.318.
Distast the People, or offend the King. .... Il.9.86.436.
Forbids t' offend, instructs them to apply: .... Il.9.234.444.
Grant that our Chief offend thro' Rage or Lust .... Il.13.153.111.
Thy warm Impatience makes thy Tongue offend. .... Il.13.976.152.
Much would ye blame, should others thus offend: .... Il.23.577.512.
Thus spake the Youth, nor did his Words offend; .... Il.23.635.515.
For ah! how few, who should like thee offend, ... Il.23.691.517.
But fearful to offend, by wisdom sway'd, ... Od.6.173.216.
If that low race offend thy pow'r divine, ... Od.13.168.13.
Offend not *Jove:* Obey, and give the peace. .... Od.24.627.377.

OFFENDED
And those offended sylvan pow'rs ador'd: .... 1.TrFD.38.387.
When not his Lust offended, but his Pride: .... 4.HAdv.84.83.
Sprung the fierce Strife, from what offended Pow'r? .... Il.1.10.85.
Is Heav'n offended, and a Priest profan'd, ... Il.1.138.93.
And all th' offended synod of the skies; .... Od.4.636.149.
To the stern sanction of th' offended sky .... Od.4.652.150.
Of royal grace th' offended Queen may guide; .... Od.19.103.197.

OFFENDER
And love th' offender, yet detest th' offence? .... 2.ElAb.192.335.
Since cold in death th' offender lies; oh spare .... Od.22.66.290.

OFFENDERS
Must great Offenders, once escap'd the Crown, ... 4.EpS2.28.314.
Such just Examples on Offenders shown, ... Il.2.338.143.
To dash th' offenders in the whelming tyde. .... Od.12.457.453.
And whelms th' offenders in the roaring tydes: .... Od.23.358.342.

OFFENDING
When love would strike th' offending fair, ... 6.4v.1.11.
'Tis hers t'offend; and ev'n offending share .... Il.5.1078.318.
Trembling afar th' offending Pow'rs appear'd, ... Il.8.554.423.
Offending Man their high Compassion wins, ... Il.9.622.465.
Or terrifies th' offending World with Wars: .... Il.13.320.120.
To whom offending men are made a prey .... Od.14.105.41.
Dooms to full vengeance all th' offending train) .... Od.17.437.154.
If yet there live of all th' offending kind. .... Od.22.422.308.
Th' offending females to that task we doom, ... Od.22.474.312.

OFFENDS
Oft she rejects, but never once offends. .... 2.RL2.12.160.
Who-e'er offends, at some unlucky Time .... 4.HS1.77.13.
The Zeal of Fools offends at any time, ... 4.2HE1.406.229.
Well, if our author in the Wife offends, ... 6.41.25.114.
Each Office hurts him, and each Face offends. .... Il.24.294.549.
True are his words, and he whom truth offends .... Od.18.460.190.

OFFENSIVE
Thy Realm disarm'd of each offensive Tool, ... 6.131i.3.360.
Let fall th' offensive truncheon from his hand. .... Od.14.36.37.
Avaunt, she cry'd, offensive to my sight! .... Od.19.80.196.
Here, vagrant still! offensive to my Lords! .... Od.20.225.244.

OFFER
Than what more humble Mountains offer here, ... 1.W-F.35.151.
For thee shall bear their fruits, and offer all to thee! .... 1.TrPA.77.368.
And offer Annual Honours, Feasts, and Praise; .... 1.TrSt.787.443.
And offer Country, Parent, Wife, or Son! .... 4.EpS1.158.309.
Nor what they offer, thou thy self despise. .... Il.2.429.148.
Or offer Heav'n's great Sire polluted Praise. .... Il.6.337.343.

OFFER (CONTINUED)
And giving thousands, offer thousands more; ....Il.22.440.473.
With Gifts to sue; and offer to his Hands ....Il.24.153.541.
May offer all thy Treasures yet contain, ...Il.24.856.572.
To spare thy Age; and offer all in vain! ....Il.24.857.572.
And offer hecatombs to thund'ring *Jove?* .... Od.12.408.450.
'Tis you that offer, and I scorn them all: ....Od.22.76.290.

OFFER'D
The Match was offer'd, the Proposals made: ....2.ChJM.300.28.
The Great man never offer'd you a Groat. ....4.EpS1.26.299.
With offer'd Gifts to make the God relent; ....Il.1.505.112.
With offer'd Vows, in *Ilion's* topmost Tow'r. ....Il.6.112.329.
Lo, sev'n are offer'd, and of equal Charms. ....Il.9.752.471.
One *Greek* enrich'd thy Shrine with offer'd Gore; ....Il.15.429.214.
Shall *Hector's* Head be offer'd to thy Shade; ....Il.18.392.340.
To all those Insults thou hast offer'd here, ...Il.20.306.407.
Twelve *Trojan* Heroes offer'd to thy Shade; ....Il.23.223.498.
And offer'd from her Hand the Nectar Bowl: ....Il.24.134.540.
The thighs thus offer'd, and the entrails drest, ...Od.12.429.451.
Then pour'd of offer'd wine the sable wave: ....Od.14.499.60.
If offer'd, vainly should for mercy call; ....Od.22.75.290.

OFFERING
With smoaking thighs, and offering to the God. ....Od.3.12.87.
Dis-bark the sheep, an offering to the Gods; ....Od.11.22.380.

OFFERINGS
Bears Pisa's offerings to his Arethuse) ....5.DunA2.318.140.

OFFERS
That in my Presence offers such a Wrong. ....2.ChJM.650.46.
When Offers are disdain'd, and Love deny'd. ....2.RL1.82.151.
This, humbly offers me his Case— ....4.HS6.67.255.
Whose spoils this paper offers to your eye, ...5.DunB4.435.383.
What *Lintott* offers to your Hand, ...6.29.7Z3.83.
Then offers Vows with Hecatombs to crown ....Il.4.150.228.
Such are thy Offers as a Prince may take, ...Il.9.217.443.
Should all these offers for my Friendship call; ....Il.9.508.458.
'Tis he that offers, and I scorn them all. ....Il.9.509.458.
Our Offers now, illustrious Prince! receive; ....Il.13.475.130.

OFFICE
Thou, *Abelard!* the last sad office pay, ...2.ElAb.321.345.
He names the *Price* for ev'ry *Office* paid, ...4.JD4.162.39.
Me, let the tender Office long engage ....4.Arbu.408.127.
His *Office* keeps your Parchment-Fates entire, ...4.JD2.71.139.
To save thee in th' infectious office *dies.* .... 4.1740.76.336.
In office here fair Cloacina stands, ...5.DunA2.89.108.
In office here fair Cloacina stands, ...5.DunB2.93.300.
Unfinish'd Treaties in each Office slept; ....5.DunB4.616.405.
From office, business, news, and strife: ....6.114.10.321.
Vulcan with awkward Grace his Office plies, ...Il.1.770.124.
By me that holy Office were prophan'd; ....Il.6.334.342.
Yet knows no Office, nor has felt the Flame: ....Il.9.160.440.
Yet knows no Office, nor has felt the Flame: ....Il.9.347.450.
To Birth, or Office, no respect be paid; ....Il.10.280.14.
That Office paid, he issu'd from his Tent, ...Il.13.284.119.
Th' attending Heralds, as by Office bound, ...Il.23.49.489.
Oh more than Brother! Think each Office paid, ...Il.23.111.492.
Each Office hurts him, and each Face offends. ....Il.24.294.549.
We check'd our haste, by pious office bound, ...Od.3.362.104.
Perform'd their office, or his weight upheld: ....Od.5.582.200.
Soon as warm life its wonted office found, ...Od.5.588.200.
For any office could the slave be good, ...Od.17.262.145.

OFFICES
The honors, and the offices of men: ....Od.14.573.64.

OFFICIOUS
Officious, bold Disturbances they grow, ... 6.17iii.4.57.
A weak officious Friend becomes a Foe. ....6.116viii.4.328.
The Maids officious round their Mistress wait, ...Il.3.526.216.
No more officious, with endearing Charms, ...Il.17.243.297.
Officious with the Cincture girds him round; ....Il.23.791.521.
What make ye here? Officious Crowds? (he cries) ....Il.24.295.549.
While these officious tend the rites divine, ...Od.3.592.116.
He bathes: the damsels with officious toil, ...Od.8.491.289.
The ill-tim'd efforts of officious love; ....Od.15.78.72.
Rise, *Euryclea!* with officious care ....Od.19.414.214.

OFFSPRING
Thy Offspring, *Thames!* the fair *Lodona* nam'd, ...1.W-F.172.165.
T'admit your offspring in your watry reign! ....1.TrPA.143.371.
(My self the offspring of a second bride.) ....1.TrFD.10.386.
On thy own Offspring hast thou fix'd this Fate, ...1.TrSt.245.420.
As Berecynthia, while her offspring vye ....5.DunA3.123.160.
As Berecynthia, while her offspring vye ....5.DunB3.131.326.
With thund'ring Offspring all around, ...6.135.46.368.
The mighty Offspring of the foodful Earth. ....Il.2.660.158.
Antenor's Offspring from a foreign Bed, ...Il.5.92.270.
And guards her Offspring with a Mother's Care. ....Il.5.388.285.
And dropt her Offspring from her weak Embrace. ....Il.5.428.289.
Alcides' Offspring meets the Son of *Jove.* .... Il.5.779.303.
Next *Oenomaus,* and *Oenops'* Offspring dy'd; ....Il.5.868.307.
The vig'rous Offspring of a stol'n Embrace, ...Il.8.344.414.
This Offspring added to King *Priam's* Line) ....Il.8.370.415.
The double Offspring of the Warrior-God. ....Il.9.114.437.
The wounded Offspring of the healing God. ....Il.11.639.62.
The youthful Offspring of the God of War, ...Il.13.605.135.
And unreveng'd, deplor'd his Offspring dead. ....Il.13.826.145.
(His valiant Offspring) hasten'd to the Field; ....Il.14.14.157.
Thy own lov'd boasted Offspring lies o'erthrown, ...Il.15.124.201.
If that lov'd boasted Offspring be thy own, ...Il.15.125.201.
Her secret Offspring to her Sire she bare; ....Il.16.228.248.
Laerces' valiant Offspring led the last. ....Il.16.235.248.

OFFSPRING (CONTINUED)
Or to his Doom my bravest Offspring yield, ...Il.16.538.265.
Nor *Jove* vouchsaf'd his hapless Offspring Aid. ....Il.16.642.269.
(The lawless Offspring of King *Priam's* Bed,) ....Il.16.896.277.
Her mournful Offspring, to his Sighs reply'd; ....Il.18.92.327.
For soon alas! that wretched Offspring slain, ...Il.18.115.328.
I vow'd his much-lov'd Offspring to restore, ...Il.18.381.339.
(My only Offspring) sink into the Grave? ....Il.19.346.386.
If yet that Offspring lives, (I distant far, ...Il.19.347.386.
Thetis' this Day, or *Venus'* Offspring dies, ...Il.20.248.404.
Demoleon next, *Antenor's* Offspring, laid ....Il.20.457.413.
(*Antenor's* Offspring, haughty, bold and brave) ....Il.21.644.449.
Wretch that I am! my bravest Offspring slain, ...Il.24.319.549.
He seem'd, fair Offspring of some princely Line! ....Il.24.426.553.
The teeming Ewes a triple offspring bear; ....Od.4.106.125.
Around thee full of years, thy offspring bloom, ...Od.4.290.132.
(The monarch's offspring, and his best belov'd) ....Od.7.227.247.
How we their offspring dignify our race. ....Od.8.280.278.
Or the fair offspring of the sacred floods. ....Od.10.416.364.
His blooming offspring, or his beauteous wife! ....Od.12.56.432.
For know, to *Sparta* thy lov'd offspring came, ...Od.13.477.29.
Torn from his offspring in the eve of life, ...Od.15.378.87.
And more, the infant offspring of the King. ....Od.15.488.94.
An unblest offspring of a sire unblest! ....Od.16.128.108.
Offspring of Kings, and more than woman wise! ....Od.18.330.183.
Yet by another sign thy offspring know; ....Od.24.388.368.

OFFSPRING'S
Cease then thy Offspring's Death unjust to call; ....Il.15.156.202.

OFSPRING
Sigh, with his Captive for his ofspring lost ....6.130.22.358.

OFT
Beneath yon Poplar oft we past the Day: ....1.PAu.66.85.
Oft on the Rind I carv'd her Am'rous Vows, ...1.PAu.67.85.
To thee, bright Goddess, oft a Lamb shall bleed, ...1.PWi.81.94.
Oft, as in Airy Rings they skim the Heath, ...1.W-F.131.162.
Oft as the mounting Larks their Notes prepare, ...1.W-F.133.162.
In her chast Current oft the Goddess laves, ...1.W-F.209.169.
Oft in her Glass the musing Shepherd spies ....1.W-F.211.169.
But oft in *those,* confin'd to *single Parts.* ....1.EOC.63.246.
Those oft are *Stratagems* which *Errors* seem, ...1.EOC.179.261.
Oft *hide* his Force, nay seem sometimes to *Fly.* ....1.EOC.178A.261.
As Men of Breeding, oft the Men of Wit, ...1.EOC.259A.269.
What oft was *Thought,* but ne'er so well *Exprest,* .... 1.EOC.298.273.
What oft was *Thought,* but ne'er before *Exprest,* .... 1.EOC.298A.273.
Tho' oft the Ear the *open Vowels* tire, ...1.EOC.345.278.
And ten low Words oft creep in one dull Line, ...1.EOC.347.278.
As oft the *Learn'd* by being *Singular;* .... 1.EOC.425.288.
Oft, leaving what is Natural and fit, ...1.EOC.448.290.
How oft the *Satyrs* and the wanton *Fawns,* .... 1.TrVP.21.378.
Oft o'er his Back a crooked Scythe is laid, ...1.TrVP.33.378.
Oft in his harden'd Hand a Goad he bears, ...1.TrVP.35.378.
Where oft entwin'd in am'rous Folds we lay; ....1.TrSP.170.401.
Tisiphone! that oft hast heard my Pray'r, ...1.TrSt.85.413.
How oft the Furies from the deeps of Night ....1.TrSt.321.423.
Oft have I heard, in *Crete,* this Island's Name, ...1.TrUl.140.470.
One only Doubt remains; Full oft I've heard ....2.ChJM.268.27.
Hither the Noble Knight wou'd oft repair ....2.ChJM.465.37.
Hither the Noble Lord wou'd oft repair ....2.ChJM.465A.37.
Full oft in Tears did hapless *May* complain, ...2.ChJM.490.39.
And sigh'd full oft, but sigh'd and wept in vain; ....2.ChJM.491.39.
Why to her House do'st thou so oft repair? ....2.ChWB.78.60.
I tax'd them oft with Wenching and Amours, ...2.ChWB.154.64.
Yet with Embraces, Curses oft I mixt, ...2.ChWB.176.65.
"Of *Job's* great Patience since so oft you preach, ...2.ChWB.186.65.
Full oft I drain'd the Spicy Nut-brown Bowl; ....2.ChWB.214.67.
Full oft I drain'd the Spicy Nut-brown Bowl ....2.ChWB.214A.67.
Oft, when his Shoe the most severely wrung, ...2.ChWB.239.68.
Oft has he blush'd from Ear to Ear for Shame, ...2.ChWB.275.70.
That oft a Day I to this Gossip went; ....2.ChWB.278.70.
But oft repented, and repent it still; ....2.ChWB.333.73.
Oft wou'd he say, Who builds his House on Sands, ...2.ChWB.347.74.
A certain Treatise oft at Evening read, ...2.ChWB.356.74.
How oft she scolded in a Day, he knew, ...2.ChWB.389.76.
Oft when the World imagine Women stray, ...2.RL1.91.152.
Oft she rejects, but never once offends. ....2.RL2.12.160.
With *Flavia's* Busk that oft had rapp'd his own: ....2.RL2.39Z2.161.
Nay oft, in Dreams, Invention we bestow, ...2.RL2.99.165.
Oft have we known that sev'nfold Fence to fail, ...2.RL2.119.167.
Here *Britain's* Statesmen oft the Fall foredoom ....2.RL3.5.169.
And now, (as oft in some distemper'd State) ....2.RL3.93.174.
But see how oft Ambitious Aims are cross'd, ...2.RL5.107.208.
There, at one Passage, oft you might survey ....2.TemF.489.287.
Have full as oft no meaning, or the same. ....3.EOM2.86.65.
Or (oft more strong than all) the love of ease; ....3.EOM2.170.75.
80.Tho' oft so mix'd, the difference is too nice ....3.EOM2.209A.81.
And oft so mix, the diff'rence is too nice ....3.EOM2.209.81.
Yet seen too oft, familiar with her face, ...3.EOM2.219.82.
But seen too oft, familiar with her face, ...3.EOM2.219A.82.
How oft by these at sixty are undone ....3.EOM4.183.144.
How each for other oft is wholly lost; ....3.EOM4.272.153.
Oft in the Passions' wild rotation tost, ...3.Ep1.41.18.
Oft have you hinted to your brother Peer, ...3.Ep4.39.140.
Remembers oft the School-boy's simple fare, ...4.HS2.73.59.
The Tale reviv'd, the Lye so oft o'erthrown; ....4.Arbu.350.121.
The Tales of Vengeance; Lyes so oft o'erthrown; ....4.Arbu.350A.121.
I, who so oft renounce the Muses, lye, ...4.2HE1.175.209.
Your Country's Peace, how oft, how dearly bought! ....4.2HE1.397.229.
And kept you up so oft till one; ....4.1HE7.48.271.
Oft in the clear, still Mirrour of Retreat, ...4.EpS2.78.317.
Oft, as he fish'd her nether realms for wit, ...5.DunA2.93.108.
Thus oft they rear, and oft the head decline, ...5.DunA2.361.143.
Thus oft they rear, and oft the head decline, ...5.DunA2.361.143.
Oft had the Goddess heard her servant's call, ...5.DunB2.97.300.

OFT (CONTINUED)

She oft had favour'd him, and favours yet. ....5.DunB2.102.300.
Thus oft they rear, and oft the head decline, ...5.DunB2.393.316.
Thus oft they rear, and oft the head decline, ...5.DunB2.393.316.
Oft to her heart sad Tragedy addrest ....5.DunB4.37A.344.
Oft her gay Sister's life and spirit fled; ....5.DunB4.39Z1.344.
Yet have we oft discover'd in their stead, ...6.7.7.15.
But Rebel Wit deserts thee oft in vain; ....6.8.13.18.
(Tho' Dinners oft they want and Suppers too) ....6.17iv.24.60.
Oft in an *Aldus,* or a *Plantin,* .... 6.29.17.83.
For him, thou oft hast bid the World attend, ...6.84.7.238.
And oft look'd back, slow-moving o'er the Strand. ....Il.1.453.109.
Oft hast thou triumph'd in the glorious Boast, ...Il.1.514.112.
While vainly fond, in Fancy oft he hears ....Il.2.713.160.
How oft, my Brother, thy Reproach I bear, ...Il.12.245.90.
Fly we at length from *Troy's* oft-conquer'd Bands, ...Il.13.139.111.
Groans to the oft-heav'd Axe, with many a Wound, ...Il.13.495.130.
Which oft, in Cities storm'd, and Battels won, ...Il.15.630.220.
And oft prevents the meditated Blow. ....Il.18.40.325.
Unpitying Pow'rs! how oft each holy Fane ....Il.24.44.537.
Oft have these Eyes that godlike *Hector* view'd ....Il.24.479.556.
How oft, alas! has wretched *Priam* bled? ....Il.24.617.562.
Fix'd in my Heart, and oft repeated there! ....Il.24.939.575.
Oft, *Jove's* ætherial rays (resistless fire) ....Od.1.443.53.
Which in my wand'rings oft reliev'd my woe: ....Od.4.42.122.
And oft in bitterness of soul deplor'd ....Od.4.361.137.
With rapture oft the verge of *Greece* reviews, ...Od.4.697.152.
Have not your fathers oft my Lord defin'd, ...Od.4.916.161.
Oft with some favour'd traveller they stray, ...Od.7.273.249.
Full oft the Monarch urg'd me to relate ....Od.10.15.340.
Full oft I told: at length for parting mov'd; ....Od.10.17.340.
Oft in the dead of night loud winds arise, ...Od.12.341.448.
Oft have I heard, in *Crete,* this Island's name; ....Od.13.307.21.
And want too oft betrays the tongue to lye. ....Od.14.149.42.
While here I sojourn'd, oft I heard the fame ....Od.14.355.51.
Full oft has *Phidon,* whilst he pour'd the wine, ...Od.14.367.53.
For oft in others freely I reprove ....Od.15.77.72.
"Oft ready swords in luckless hour incite ....Od.16.316.121.
They (curious oft of mortal actions) deign ....Od.17.578.160.
Alas, the brave too oft is doom'd to bear ....Od.18.149.173.
Great without vice, that oft attends the great: ....Od.18.154.173.
But oft revolve the vision in thy heart: ....Od.19.51.195.
There oft implor'd his tutelary pow'r, ...Od.19.430.215.
(In woes bewilder'd, oft the wisest errs.) ....Od.20.166.241.
Full oft was check'd th' injustice of the rest: ....Od.22.352.304.
Where oft *Laertes* holy vows had paid, ...Od.22.373.306.
And oft *Ulysses* smoking victims laid. ....Od.22.374.306.
Oft have I seen with solemn fun'ral games ....Od.24.111.353.
(Oft warn'd by *Mentor* and my self in vain) ....Od.24.523.373.

OFT-CONQUER'D

Fly we at length from *Troy's* oft-conquer'd Bands, ...Il.13.139.111.

OFT-HEAV'D

Groans to the oft-heav'd Axe, with many a Wound, ...Il.13.495.130.

OFT'

And to his mother let him oft' be led, ...1.TrFD.78.389.
Yet to his mother let him oft' be led, ...1.TrFD.78A.389.
How oft', when press'd to marriage, have I said, ...2.ElAb.73.325.
There oft' are heard the Notes of Infant Woe, ...6.14ii.5.43.
Oft' bend to *Auster's* blasts, or *Boreas'* Rage, ...6.26i.3.79.
How oft' in pleasing tasks we wear the day, ...6.52.17.156.
How oft' our slowly-growing works impart, ...6.52.19.156.
How oft' review; each finding like a friend ....6.52.21.156.
Oft' roll'd his Eyes around, ...6.79.110.221.
Assembled Armies oft' have I beheld; ....Il.2.968.169.
The Boaster *Paris* oft' desir'd the Day ....Il.3.537.217.
And oft' afflicts his Brutal Breast with Woes. ....Il.5.955.312.
Unwilling parts, and oft' reverts her Eye ....Il.6.641.358.
So oft' has steep'd the strength'ning Grain in Wine. ....Il.8.233.408.
Thus oft' the *Grecians* turn'd, but still they flew; ....Il.8.411.417.
And oft' that partial Pow'r has lent his Aid. ....Il.11.468.54.
Now wants that Succour which so oft' he lent. ....Il.11.971.78.
Oft' had the Father told his early Doom, ...Il.13.837.145.
As oft' th' *Ajaces* his Assault sustain; ....Il.18.195.331.
And oft' the Victor triumphs, but to fall. ....Il.18.360.338.
The Dogs (oft' chear'd in vain) desert the Prey, ...Il.18.675.356.
Full oft' the God his Son's hard Toils bemoan'd, ...Il.19.133.377.
Oft' stay'd *Achilles* rushing to the War. ....Il.19.338A.386.
Oft' as he turn'd the Torrent to oppose, ...Il.21.303.433.
So oft' the Surge, in wat'ry Mountains spread, ...Il.21.305.433.
Oft' as to reach the *Dardan* Gates he bends, ...Il.22.251.466.
So oft' *Achilles* turns him to the Plain: ....Il.22.255.466.

OFTEN

For *Wit* and *Judgment* often are at strife, ...1.EOC.82.248.
How often must it love, how often hate! ....2.ElAb.198.336.
How often must it love, how often hate! ....2.ElAb.198.336.
How often, hope, despair, resent, regret, ...2.ElAb.199.336.
Stays 'till we call, and then not often near; ....3.EOM3.87.100.
I've often wish'd that I had clear ....4.HS6.1.251.
I often wish'd that I had clear ....4.HS6.1A.251.
Such tattle often entertains ....4.HS6.95.257.
Be brib'd as often, and as often lie? ....4.EpS1.118.306.
Be brib'd as often, and as often lie? ....4.EpS1.118.306.
full often change its name ....6.14v(b).21A.50.
O friends! Oh often try'd in adverse storms! ....Od.12.248.444.

OGILBY

Here swells the shelf with Ogilby the great: ....5.DunA1.121.78.
(As sings thy great fore-father, Ogilby,) ....5.DunA1.258.94.
Here swells the shelf with Ogilby the great; ....5.DunB1.141.280.
(As sings thy great forefather Ogilby) ....5.DunB1.328.294.

OGLE

To patch, nay ogle, might become a Saint, ...2.RL5.23.201.

OGLETHORP

Shall fly, like *Oglethorp,* from Pole to Pole: ....4.2HE2.277.185.

OGLING

With singing, laughing, ogling, and all that. ....2.RL3.18.170.

OGYGIA

Ogygia nam'd, in *Ocean's* wat'ry arms: ....Od.7.328.252.
Of fair *Ogygia,* and *Calypso's* bow'rs; ....Od.23.360.342.

OGYGIAN

Heav'n drove my wreck th' *Ogygian* Isle to find, ...Od.7.338.253.
Weary and wet th' *Ogygian* shores I gain, ...Od.12.531.458.

OH

Oh deign to visit our forsaken Seats, ...1.PSu.71.77.
Oh! how I long with you to pass my Days, ...1.PSu.77.78.
Oh, skill'd in Nature! see the Hearts of Swains, ...1.PAu.11.81.
Oh mighty Love, what Magick is like thee! ....1.PAu.84A.86.
Oh sing of *Daphne's* Fate, and *Daphne's* Praise! ....1.PWi.8.89.
Oh spring to Light, Auspicious Babe, be born! ....1.Mes.22.114.
Bear me, oh bear me to sequester'd Scenes, ...1.W-F.261.173.
Oh wou'dst thou sing what Heroes *Windsor* bore, ...1.W-F.299.176.
Oh Fact accurst! What Tears has *Albion* shed, ...1.W-F.321.180.
Oh stretch thy Reign, fair *Peace!* from Shore to Shore, ...1.W-F.407.192.
Oh may some Spark of *your* Cœlestial Fire ....1.EOC.195.263.
Oh! lovely nymph, and more than lilies fair, ...1.TrPA.53.367.
Oh! yeild at last, nor still remain severe; ....1.TrPA.114.370.
For oh! I burn, nor you my flames asswage; ....1.TrPA.130.371.
Acis too run, and help, oh help! he said, ...1.TrPA.141.371.
Oh crown so constant and so pure a Fire! ....1.TrVP.105.381.
Oh, let him fly the crystal lakes and floods, ...1.TrFD.85.389.
For oh! how vast a Memory has Love? ....1.TrSP.52.396.
Or coldly thus, *Farewel oh* Lesbian *Maid!* ....1.TrSP.114.398.
Oh when, alas! shall more auspicious Gales ....1.TrSP.246.404.
Oh bless thy *Rome* with an Eternal Reign, ...1.TrSt.33.411.
Oh hear, and aid the Vengeance I require; ....1.TrSt.101.414.
What Joys, oh Tyrant! swell'd thy Soul that Day, ...1.TrSt.220.419.
Ev'n Fortune rules no more:—Oh servile Land, ...1.TrSt.241.420.
Oh wretched we, a vile submissive Train, ...1.TrSt.263.421.
Oh Race confed'rate into Crimes, that prove ....1.TrSt.302.422.
Thy Curse, oh *Oedipus,* just Heav'n alarms, ...1.TrSt.338.424.
Oh thou who freest me from my doubtful State, ...1.TrSt.588.434.
Be present still, oh Goddess! in our Aid; ....1.TrSt.590.435.
(Oh gen'rous Prince) my Nation or my name, ...1.TrSt.799.443.
Oh Father *Phœbus!* whether *Lycia's* Coast ....1.TrSt.829.444.
Oh Stain to Honour! oh Disgrace of Arms! ....1.TrES.212.457.
Oh Stain to Honour! oh Disgrace of Arms! ....1.TrES.212.457.
Oh Stain to Honour! oh Disgrace to Arms! ....1.TrES.212A.457.
Oh Stain to Honour! oh Disgrace to Arms! ....1.TrES.212A.457.
Oh righteous Gods! of all the Great, how few ....1.TrUl.86.468.
Tell me, oh tell, is this my Native Place? ....1.TrUl.202.472.
For oh, 'twas fix'd, she must possess or die! ....2.ChJM.493.39.
This was his Song; Oh kind and constant be, ...2.ChJM.714.49.
She stopp'd, and sighing, Oh good Gods, she cry'd, ...2.ChJM.720.49.
But oh good Gods! whene'er a Thought I cast ....2.ChWB.221.67.
And Husband-Bull—Oh monstrous! fie, for Shame! ....2.ChWB.386.76.
Where grows this Plant (reply'd the Friend) oh where? ....2.ChWB.397.76.
Oh thou hast slain me for my Wealth (I cry'd) ....2.ChWB.420.77.
Oh had the Youth but been content to seize ....2.RL*A*2.19.132.
Oh say what stranger Cause, yet unexplor'd, ...2.RL1.9.145.
Oh blind to Truth! the *Sylphs* contrive it all. ....2.RL1.104.153.
Warn'd by thy *Sylph,* oh Pious Maid beware! ....2.RL1.112.154.
Warn'd by the *Sylph,* oh Pious Maid beware! ....2.RL1.112A.154.
And wins (oh shameful Chance!) the *Queen* of *Hearts.* .... 2.RL3.88.174.
Oh thoughtless Mortals! ever blind to Fate, ...2.RL3.101.175.
But oh! if e'er thy *Gnome* could spoil a Grace, ...2.RL4.67.189.
Oh had I rather un-admir'd remain'd ....2.RL4.153.196.
Oh hadst thou, Cruel! been content to seize ....2.RL4.175.198.
Oh! if to dance all Night, and dress all Day, ...2.RL5.19.200.
Oh! if the Muse must flatter lawless Sway, ...2.TemF.517.289.
Oh grant an honest Fame, or grant me none! ....2.TemF.524.289.
Oh write it not, my hand—The name appears ....2.ElAb.13.319.
Oh name for ever sad! for ever dear! ....2.ElAb.31.321.
Yet write, oh write me all, that I may join ....2.ElAb.41.322.
Oh happy state! when souls each other draw, ...2.ElAb.91.327.
(Oh pious fraud of am'rous charity!) ....2.ElAb.150.331.
Oh come! oh teach me nature to subdue, ...2.ElAb.203.336.
Oh come! oh teach me nature to subdue, ...2.ElAb.203.336.
O grace serene! oh virtue heav'nly fair! ....2.ElAb.297.343.
Oh may we never love as these have lov'd! ....2.ElAb.352.348.
Oh ever beauteous, ever friendly! tell, ...2.Elegy.5.362.
What can atone (oh ever-injur'd shade!) ....2.Elegy.47.366.
Oh blindness to the future! kindly giv'n, ...3.EOM1.85.24.
Vile worm!—oh Madness, Pride, Impiety! ....3.EOM1.258.46.
Oh Happiness! our being's end and aim! ....3.EOM4.1.128.
Oh sons of earth! attempt ye still to rise, ...3.EOM4.73.135.
And Peace, oh Virtue! Peace is all thy own. ....3.EOM4.82.136.
Oh blind to truth, and God's whole scheme below, ...3.EOM4.93.137.
Oh blameless Bethel! to relieve thy breast? ....3.EOM4.126.140.
Oh fool! to think God hates the worthy mind, ...3.EOM4.189.145.
Oh wealth ill-fated! which no act of fame ....3.EOM4.299.156.
Oh master of the poet, and the song! ....3.EOM4.374.164.
Oh! while along the stream of Time thy name ....3.EOM4.383.165.
"Oh, save my Country, Heav'n!" shall be your last. ....3.Ep1.265.38.
Cries, "oh! how charming if there's no such place!" ....3.Ep2.108A.58.
All bath'd in tears—"Oh odious, odious Trees!" ....3.Ep2.40.53.
Oh! blest with Temper, whose unclouded ray ....3.Ep2.257.71.
Oh! that such bulky Bribes as all might see, ...3.Ep3.35.88.
Oh filthy check on all industrious skill, ...3.Ep3.63.92.
Oh teach us, BATHURST! yet unspoil'd by wealth! ....3.Ep3.226.111.
Where-e'er he shines, oh Fortune, gild the scene, ...3.Ep3.245.113.
"Oh say, what sums that gen'rous hand supply? ....3.Ep3.277.116.

OH (CONTINUED)

"Oh! Sir, politely well! nay, let me dye, 4.JD4.112A.35.
"Oh 'tis the sweetest of all earthly things 4.JD4.100.33.
"Oh! Sir, politely so! nay, let me dye, 4.JD4.112.35.
But oh! what Terrors must distract a Soul 4.JD4.244B.47.
Bear me, some God! oh quickly bear me hence 4.JD4.184.41.
But oh! what Terrors must distract the Soul, 4.JD4.244.47.
Oh blast it, South-winds! till a stench exhale, 4.HS2.27.55.
Oh Impudence of wealth! with all thy store, 4.HS2.117.63.
Oh Love! be deep Tranquility my Luck! 4.HAdv.175.89.
Oh let me live my own! and die so too! 4.Arbu.261.114.
Oh keep me what I am! not Fortune's fool 4.Arbu.334A.120.
Oh grant me thus to live, and thus to die! 4.Arbu.404.127.
Oh! when rank Widows purchase luscious nights, 4.JD2.87A.141.
But oh, those Works are out of Fashion now: 4.JD2A.128.144.
But oh! these works are not in fashion now: 4.JD2.122.145.
"Oh but a Wit can study in the Streets, 4.2HE2.98.171.
Oh! could I mount on the Mæonian wing, 4.2HE1.394.229.
As thus, "Vouchsafe, oh gracious Maker! 4.HS6.17.251.
Oh, could I see my Country Seat! 4.HS6.128.259.
Oh All-accomplish'd St. JOHN! deck thy Shrine? 4.EpS2.139.321.
"And oh! (he cry'd) what street, what lane, but knows 5.DunA2.145.119.
"Oh born to see what none can see awake! 5.DunA3.35.154.
Oh glorious ruin! and *Apelles* burn'd. 5.DunA3.97Z2.158.
Oh spread thy Influence, but restrain thy Rage! 5.DunA3.114.160.
Oh great Restorer of the good old Stage, 5.DunA3.201.175.
Oh worthy thou of Ægypt's wise abodes, 5.DunA3.203.175.
"Yet oh my sons! a father's words attend: 5.DunA3.211.175.
But oh! what scenes, what miracles behind? 5.DunA3.201Z1.175.
"And oh! (he cry'd) what street, what lane but knows, 5.DunB2.153.303.
"Oh born to see what none can see awake! 5.DunB3.43.322.
Oh spread thy influence, but restrain thy Rage. 5.DunB3.122.325.
Oh great Restorer of the good old Stage, 5.DunB3.205.330.
Oh worthy thou of Ægypt's wise abodes, 5.DunB3.207.330.
"Yet oh, my sons! a father's words attend: 5.DunB3.213.330.
But oh! with One, immortal one dispense, 5.DunB3.217.331.
"Oh (cry'd the Goddess) for some pedant Reign! 5.DunB4.175.358.
Oh punish him, or to th' Elysian shades 5.DunB4.417.382.
Oh hide the God still more! and make us see 5.DunB4.483.389.
Oh hide the God still more! or make us see 5.DunB4.483A.389.
Then take them all, oh take them to thy breast! 5.DunB4.515.393.
Speak, Gracious Lord, oh speak; thy Servant hears: 6.2.1.5.
Speak, gracious Lord, oh speak; thy Servant hears. 6.2.18.6.
Then oh! she cries, what Slaves I round me see? 6.9vii.4.22.
And oh! she cries, what Slaves I round me see? 6.9x.4A.22.
But oh! she cries, what Slaves I round me see? 6.9x.4B.22.
Oh take the Husband, or return the Wife! 6.11.82.33.
Oh unperforming, false mortality! 6.22.12.71.
Oh teach the mind t' ætherial heights to rise, 6.23.9.73.
Oh quicken this dull mass of mortal clay; 6.23.13.73.
Quit, oh quit this mortal frame: 6.31ii.2.94.
Oh the pain, the bliss of dying! 6.31ii.4.94.
Where mighty Death! Oh where's thy Sting? 6.31ii.6Z6.94.
Oh! may all *gentle* Bards together place ye, 6.40.7.112.
Oh had I been Ambassador created, 6.48iv.5.136.
Who's here? cries *Umbra:* "Only *Johnson*"—Oh! 6.49ii.3.140.
If I am right, oh teach my heart 6.50.29.147.
If I am wrong, Oh reach my heart 6.50.31B.147.
Oh heav'n-born sisters! source of art! 6.51i.9.151.
Oh curs'd effects of civil hate, 6.51i.29.152.
OH tyrant Love! hast thou possest 6.51ii.1.152.
Oh source of ev'ry social tye, 6.51ii.25.153.
Oh lasting as those colours may they shine, 6.52.63.158.
Where many a Damsel cries oh lack. 6.61.13.181.
Oh when shall Britain, conscious of her claim, 6.71.53.204.
So would I draw (but oh, 'tis vain to try 6.75.3.211.
Oh, thus it was. He lov'd him dear, 6.79.41.219.
Oh Kingly *Kensington!* 6.79.56.219.
Alas, oh *Nic!* Oh *Nic.* alas! 6.79.65.220.
Alas, oh *Nic!* Oh *Nic.* alas! 6.79.65.220.
Up didst thou look, oh woeful Duke! 6.79.73.220.
Oh just beheld, and lost! admir'd, and mourn'd! 6.84.3.238.
Oh let thy once-lov'd Friend inscribe thy Stone, 6.85.7.242.
Oh be thou blest with all that Heav'n can send, 6.86.1.244.
And, oh! when Death shall that fair Face destroy, 6.86.17B.245.
Oh born to Arms! O Worth in Youth approv'd! 6.113.3.320.
Oh! save the Salary, and drink the Sack! 6.116v.6.327.
Who reach that High place oh their joy shall be great! 6.122.21A.342.
Who climbs these High Seats oh his joy shall be great! 6.122.21.342.
Oh doe but silence Cibber, and the Bells. 6.131i.6.360.
Oh next him skill'd to draw the tender Tear, 6.152.3.400.
But oh! relieve a wretched Parent's Pain, Il.1.27.87.
Oh might a Parent's careful Wish prevail, Il.1.546.114.
Avenge this Wrong, oh ever just and wise! Il.1.658.118.
Or oh declare, of all the Pow'rs above Il.1.668.119.
Then thus the God: Oh restless Fate of Pride, Il.1.726.122.
Oh *Atreus'* Son! canst thou indulge thy Rest? Il.2.26.128.
And, Dost thou sleep, Oh *Atreus'* Son? (he said) Il.2.76.130.
Oh lasting Shame in ev'ry future Age! Il.2.152.135.
Shall then the *Grecians* fly? Oh dire Disgrace! Il.2.193.137.
Oh Women of *Achaia!* Men no more! Il.2.293.141.
But vanquish'd! baffled! oh eternal Shame! Il.2.363.144.
Oh would the Gods, in Love to *Greece,* decree Il.2.442.148.
Oh Thou! whose Thunder rends the clouded Air, Il.2.489.150.
Oh say what Heroes, fir'd by Thirst of Fame, Il.2.578.155.
Oh had'st thou dy'd when first thou saw'st the Light, Il.3.57.192.
Yet hence oh Heav'n! convey that fatal Face, Il.3.209.201.
And oh! that still he bore a Brother's Name! Il.3.238.203.
Oh give that Author of the War to Fate, Il.3.399.211.
Oh hadst thou dy'd beneath the righteous Sword Il.3.535.217.
Oh lasting Rancour! oh insatiate Hate Il.4.47.223.
Oh lasting Rancour! oh insatiate Hate Il.4.47.223.
Oh dear as Life! did I for this agree Il.4.186.230.
Oh! e're that dire Disgrace shall blast my Fame, Il.4.218.231.
Oh! had'st thou Strength to match thy brave Desires, Il.4.362.238.
What once thou wert, oh ever might'st thou be. Il.4.366.238.

OH (CONTINUED)

Oh great in Action, and in Council wise! Il.4.411.240.
Oh Son of *Tydeus!* (He, whose Strength could tame Il.4.422.240.
Oh give my Lance to reach the *Trojan* Knight, Il.5.150.274.
Oh pierce that Mortal, if we Mortal call Il.5.222.278.
(Which oh avert from our unhappy State! Il.5.226.278.
Oh suffer not the Foe to bear away Il.5.842.305.
Oh Sight accurst! Shall faithless *Troy* prevail, Il.5.876.308.
Oh spare my Youth, and for the Life I owe Il.6.57.326.
And furious, thus. Oh impotent of Mind! Il.6.67.327.
Oh would kind Earth the hateful Wretch embrace, Il.6.352.343.
Oh awful Goddess! ever-dreadful Maid, Il.6.378.344.
(Oh Wretch ill-fated, and thy Country's Foe!) Il.6.407.347.
Yet charge my Absence less, oh gen'rous Chief! Il.6.420.347.
Oh gen'rous Brother! if the guilty Dame Il.6.432.348.
Oh grant me Gods! e're *Hector* meets his Doom, Il.6.518.351.
Oh prove a Husband's and a Father's Care! Il.6.549.354.
Women of Greece! Oh Scandal of your Race, Il.7.109.369.
Oh *Peleus,* old in Arms, in Wisdom old! Il.7.150.372.
Oh would to tell th' immortal Pow'rs above, Il.7.159.372.
What then he was, Oh were your *Nestor* now! Il.7.189.373.
What then I was, Oh were your *Nestor* now! Il.7.189A.373.
Oh first of *Greeks!* (his noble Foe rejoin'd) Il.7.349.381.
(Oh had he perish'd e'er they touch'd our Shore) Il.7.465.387.
Oh take not, Friends! defrauded of your Fame, Il.7.476.388.
Or far, oh far from steep *Olympus* thrown, Il.8.15.395.
Oh First and Greatest! God by Gods ador'd! Il.8.39.397.
Whither, oh whither does *Ulysses* run? Il.8.117.403.
Oh Flight unworthy great *Laertes'* Son! Il.8.118.403.
Oh turn and save from *Hector's* direful Rage Il.8.121.403.
Oh *Argives!* Shame of human Race; he cry'd, Il.8.274.410.
Oh mighty *Jove!* oh Sire of the distress'd! Il.8.282.410.
Oh mighty *Jove!* oh Sire of the distress'd! Il.8.282.410.
Oh Daughter of that God, whose Arm can wield Il.8.423.417.
Oh had my Wisdom known this dire Event, Il.8.445.418.
What hast thou said, Oh Tyrant of the Skies! Il.8.575.424.
To Morrow's Light (oh haste the glorious Morn!) Il.8.663.427.
Certain as this, oh might my Days endure, Il.8.667.427.
Return, *Achilles!* oh return, tho' late, Il.9.320.449.
Oh let not headlong Passion bear the Sway; Il.9.637.466.
Oh Soul of Battels, and thy People's Guide! Il.9.757.471.
So now be present, Oh celestial Maid! Il.10.345.18.
Oh speed our Labours, and direct our ways! Il.10.535.27.
Or oh! perhaps those Heroes are no more. Il.10.635.30.
Oh spare our Youth, and for the Life we owe, Il.11.171.43.
Oh worthy better Fate! oh early slain! Il.11.311.49.
Oh worthy better Fate! oh early slain! Il.11.311.49.
Oh, turn to Arms; 'tis *Ajax* claims your Aid. Il.11.715.67.
Oh! had I still that Strength my Youth possess'd, Il.11.816.72.
Oh thou! bold Leader of our *Trojan* Bands, Il.12.69.84.
Oh may this Instant end the *Grecian* Name! Il.12.78.84.
Oh thou! brave Leader of our *Trojan* Bands, Il.12.69A.84.
Oh recollect your ancient Worth and Praise! Il.13.74.108.
Oh lasting Infamy, oh dire Disgrace Il.13.131.110.
Oh lasting Infamy, oh dire Disgrace Il.13.131.110.
Wills us to fall, inglorious! Oh my Friend! Il.13.297.119.
Oh were thy Sway the Curse of meaner Pow'rs, Il.14.92.162.
Indignant thus—Oh once of martial Fame! Il.14.421.183.
Oh yet, if Glory any Bosom warms, Il.14.429.184.
Oh! all of *Trojan,* all of *Lycian* Race! Il.15.494.216.
Then *Ajax* thus—Oh *Greeks!* respect your Fame, Il.15.666.221.
Than thou hast mine! Oh tell me, to what end Il.16.15.235.
Oh! would to all th' immortal Pow'rs above, Il.16.122.241.
"Oh nurs'd with Gall, unknowing how to yield! Il.16.244.249.
Oh thou Supreme! high-thron'd, all Height above! Il.16.284.250.
Oh Great! *Pelasgic, Dodonæan Jove!* Il.16.285.250.
Oh! be his Guard thy providential Care, Il.16.298.254.
Oh Warriors, Part'ners of *Achilles'* Praise! Il.16.324.255.
Oh Stain to Honour! oh Disgrace to Arms! Il.16.515.263.
Oh hear me! God of ev'ry healing Art! Il.16.636.269.
Oh too forgetful of the Friends of *Troy!* Il.16.660.270.
Oh save from hostile Rage his lov'd Remains: Il.16.668.270.
Oh gen'rous *Greek!* when with full Vigour thrown Il.16.713.271.
Oh valiant Leader of the *Dardan* Host! Il.16.749.273.
To him the King. Oh *Ajax,* oh my Friend! Il.17.129.292.
To him the King. Oh *Ajax,* oh my Friend! Il.17.129.292.
Oh! were *Patroclus* ours, we might obtain Il.17.179.294.
Oh Chiefs! oh Princes! to whose Hand is giv'n Il.17.294.299.
Oh Chiefs! oh Princes! to whose Hand is giv'n Il.17.294.299.
Thus He—what Methods yet, oh Chief! remain, Il.17.378.302.
Oh lasting Shame! to our own Fears a Prey, Il.17.390.302.
Oh keep the foaming Coursers close behind! Il.17.569.310.
O Chief, Oh Father! (*Atreus'* Son replies) Il.17.630.312.
Oh Prince (he cry'd) oh foremost once in Fame! Il.17.658.313.
Oh Prince (he cry'd) oh foremost once in Fame! Il.17.658.313.
Oh King! oh Father! hear my humble Pray'r: Il.17.728.315.
Oh King! oh Father! hear my humble Pray'r: Il.17.728.315.
Oh guard these Relicks to your Charge consign'd, Il.17.753.318.
Oh had'st thou still, a Sister of the Main, Il.18.109.328.
Let me—But oh! ye gracious Pow'rs above! Il.18.137.329.
Oh *Vulcan!* say, was ever Breast divine Il.18.501.345.
Oh Monarch! better far had been the Fate Il.19.57.374.
Prevent, oh *Jove!* this ignominious Date, Il.21.315.434.
Oh! had I dy'd in Fields of Battel warm, Il.21.321.434.
Oh how unworthy of the Brave and Great! Il.21.326.434.
O *Vulcan,* oh! what Pow'r resists thy Might? Il.21.418.437.
Oh if in yonder hostile Camp they live, Il.22.66.455.
Oh lov'd of *Jove!* this Day our Labours cease, Il.22.279.467.
Oh had thy gentle Spirit past in Peace, Il.22.544.479.
Oh more than Brother! Think each Office paid, Il.23.111.492.
Oh! had I now that Force I felt of yore, Il.23.723.519.
Your noble Vigour, oh my Friends restrain; Il.23.856.523.
Fear not, oh Father! no ill News I bear; Il.24.209.545.
(Oh Heart of Steel!) the Murd'rer of thy Race! Il.24.248.546.
Oh! in his dearest Blood might I allay Il.24.261.547.
Oh send me, Gods! e'er that sad Day shall come, Il.24.307.549.

OH (CONTINUED)

Oh First, and Greatest! Heav'ns Imperial Lord! ....Il.24.377.551.
Ah tell me truly, where, oh where are laid ....Il.24.497.557.
But thou, oh gen'rous Youth! this Goblet take, ...Il.24.525.558.
Oh hear the Wretched, and the Gods revere! ....Il.24.625.563.
To whom the King. Oh favour'd of the Skies! ....Il.24.696.566.
Oh give me *Hector!* to my Eyes restore ....Il.24.699.566.
And oh my *Hector!* oh my Lord! she cries, ...Il.24.908.574.
And oh my *Hector!* oh my Lord! she cries, ...Il.24.908.574.
Oh thou, the best, the dearest to my Heart! ....Il.24.943.575.
(Oh had I perish'd, e'er that Form divine ....Il.24.966.576.
Long exercis'd in woes, oh Muse! resound. ....Od.1.2.25.
Oh snatch some portion of these acts from fate, ...Od.1.13.29.
Oh true descendent of a scepter'd line! ....Od.1.286.46.
Oh! in that portal shou'd the Chief appear, ...Od.1.331.48.
But oh! forbear that dear, disastrous name, ...Od.1.437.53.
Oh son of *Polybus!* the Prince replies, ...Od.1.521.57.
But you oh Peers! and thou oh Prince! give ear: ....Od.2.127.67.
But you oh Peers! and thou oh Prince! give ear: ....Od.2.127.67.
Hear all! but chiefly you, oh Rivals! hear. ....Od.2.190.71.
Ulysses lies: oh wert thou lay'd as low! ....Od.2.214.72.
Threat on, oh Prince! elude the bridal day, ...Od.2.231.72.
Hear from thy heav'ns above, oh warrior-maid! ....Od.2.301.76.
Grieve not, oh daring Prince! that noble heart: ....Od.2.341.77.
Tremble ye not, oh friends! and coward fly, ...Od.2.366.78.
Oh whither, whither flies my son? she cry'd, ...Od.2.408.80.
Oh beat those storms, and roll the seas in vain! ....Od.2.415.81.
Oh tell me *Mentor!* tell me faithful guide, ...Od.3.27.87.
Thee first it fits, oh stranger! to prepare ....Od.3.57.89.
Oh thou! whose arms this ample globe embrace, ...Od.3.69.89.
(Oh grace and glory of the *Grecian* name!) ....Od.3.95.90.
And oh! what'er heav'n destin'd to betide ....Od.3.114.91.
Oh then, if ever thro' the ten years war ....Od.3.118.91.
And calm *Minerva's* wrath. Oh blind to fate! ....Od.3.177.94.
The prudent youth reply'd. Oh thou, the grace ....Od.3.246.97.
Oh! had the Gods so large a boon deny'd, ...Od.4.123.126.
But oh! *Ulysses—deeper* than the rest ....Od.4.131.126.
But prostrate I implore, oh King! relate ....Od.4.435.140.
With patient ear, oh royal youth, attend ....Od.4.467.142.
I've heard with pain, but oh! the tale pursue; ....Od.4.746.153.
But oh belov'd by heav'n! reserv'd to thee ....Od.4.761.155.
But hear, oh earth, and hear ye sacred skies! ....Od.5.238.182.
And thou oh *Styx!* whose formidable floods ....Od.5.239.183.
Oh sprung from Gods! in wisdom more than man. ....Od.5.258.184.
Lov'd and ador'd, oh Goddess, as thou art, ...Od.5.275.184.
Oh! had I dy'd before that well-fought wall, ...Od.5.395.191.
Oh indolent! to waste thy hours away! ....Od.6.29.205.
For Misery, oh Queen, before thee stands! ....Od.6.204.220.
Oh let soft pity touch thy gen'rous mind! ....Od.6.212.220.
A suppliant bends: oh pity human woe! ....Od.7.198.245.
Oh sight (he cry'd) dishonest and unjust! ....Od.7.214.247.
But finish, oh ye Peers! what you propose, ...Od.7.301.250.
Hard is the task, oh Princess! you impose: ....Od.7.322.251.
This is the truth: And oh ye pow'rs on high! ....Od.7.382.255.
O *Jove!* oh father! what the King accords ....Od.7.423.258.
O *Jove,* he cry'd, oh all ye pow'rs above, ...Od.8.347.282.
Wou'dst thou enchain'd like *Mars,* oh *Hermes,* lye, ...Od.8.375.284.
And free, he cries, oh *Vulcan!* free from shame ....Od.8.383.284.
Crown, oh ye heav'ns, with joy his peaceful hours, ...Od.8.445.287.
And oh, what first, what last shall I relate, ...Od.9.15.301.
But oh! thus furious, thirsting thus for gore, ...Od.9.414.323.
Oh! didst thou feel for thy afflicted Lord, ...Od.9.535.328.
Hear me, oh *Cyclop!* hear ungracious host! ....Od.9.558.329.
Oh heav'ns! oh faith of ancient prophecies! ....Od.9.594.330.
Oh heav'ns! oh faith of ancient prophecies! ....Od.9.594.330.
Hear me, oh *Neptune!* thou whose arms are hurl'd ....Od.9.617.332.
Rare gift! but oh, what gift to fools avails! ....Od.10.29.340.
They said: and (oh curs'd fate!) the thongs unbound; ....Od.10.50.341.
But grant, oh grant our loss we may retrieve: ....Od.10.79.343.
Ulysses? oh! thy threat'ning fury cease, ...Od.10.395.363.
Oh much-enduring, much-experienc'd man! ....Od.10.476.366.
To whom with tears: These rites, oh mournful shade, ...Od.11.98.385.
Unerring truths, oh man, my lips relate; ....Od.11.170.390.
The latent cause, oh sacred Seer, reveal! ....Od.11.178.390.
Oh most inur'd to grief of all mankind! ....Od.11.260.394.
Turn then, oh peaceful turn, thy wrath controul, ...Od.11.689.418.
Oh if thy vessel plow the direful waves ....Od.12.133.438.
Then she: O worn by toils, oh broke in fight, ...Od.12.143.439.
O friends, oh ever partners of my woes, ...Od.12.190.441.
O stay, oh pride of *Greece! Ulysses* stay! ....Od.12.222.442.
O friends! Oh often try'd in adverse storms! ....Od.12.248.444.
O friends! oh ever exercis'd in care! ....Od.12.324.447.
Oh should the fierce south-west his rage display, ...Od.12.343.448.
Oh all ye blissful pow'rs that reign above! ....Od.12.438.452.
My following fates to thee oh King, are known, ...Od.12.535.459.
Scorn'd ev'n by man, and (oh severe disgrace) ....Od.13.150.12.
Oh certain faith of ancient prophecies! ....Od.13.197.15.
Oh righteous Gods! of all the great, how few ....Od.13.253.18.
Tell me, oh tell, is this my native place? ....Od.13.369.25.
To this *Ulysses.* Oh celestial maid! ....Od.13.437.27.
Must he too suffer? he, oh Goddess! bear ....Od.13.480.29.
Why would'st not thou, oh all-enlighten'd mind! ....Od.13.484.29.
And, oh ye Gods! with all your blessings grace ....Od.14.63.38.
Oh had he left me to that happier doom, ...Od.14.303.50.
Oh! had he perisht on some well-fought day, ...Od.14.401.55.
And why, oh swain of unbelieving mind! ....Od.14.431.56.
Doubtless, oh guest! great laud and praise were mine ....Od.14.443.57.
Oh be thou dear (*Ulysses* cry'd) to *Jove,* .... Od.14.490.59.
And die asham'd (oh wisest of mankind) ....Od.14.549.63.
Oh were my strength as then, as then my age! ....Od.14.570.64.
When, Oh *Telemachus!* (the Goddess said) ....Od.15.11.70.
And oh! return'd might we *Ulysses* meet! ....Od.15.174.76.
Oh! if this promis'd bliss by thund'ring *Jove,* .... Od.15.202.78.
But bear, oh bear me o'er yon azure flood; .... Od.15.302.83.
To him the Man of woes. Oh gracious *Jove!* .... Od.15.360.86.
And, oh *Eumæus!* thou (he cries) hast felt ....Od.15.409.89.

OH (CONTINUED)

Enter, oh seldom seen! for lawless pow'rs ....Od.16.29.103.
And cries aloud, Thy son, oh Queen returns: ....Od.16.355.123.
Oh dearest, most rever'd of womankind! ....Od.17.56.135.
Oh suff'ring consort of the suff'ring man! ....Od.17.173.140.
Oh be some God his convoy to our shore! ....Od.17.289.146.
Oh! that as surely great *Apollo's* dart, ...Od.17.300.146.
Just is, oh friend, thy caution, and addrest ....Od.17.332.147.
Oh had you seen him, vig'rous, bold and young, ...Od.17.380.150.
Oh hide it, death, in everlasting night! ....Od.18.91.171.
And Oh! (he mildly cries) may heav'n display ....Od.18.147.173.
Oh talk not, talk not of vain beauty's care! ....Od.18.210.177.
Oh were it giv'n to yield this transient breath, ...Od.18.239.178.
Send, oh *Diana,* send the sleep of death! ....Od.18.240.178.
He grasp'd my hand, and oh my spouse! I leave ....Od.18.303.181.
Oh whither wanders thy distemper'd brain, ...Od.18.375.185.
Oh thou, of mortals most inur'd to woes! ....Od.20.41.234.
Oh impotence of faith! *Minerva* cries, ...Od.20.55.234.
Attest, oh *Jove,* the truth I now relate! ....Od.20.286.247.
Oh lay the cause on youth yet immature! ....Od.21.139.265.
Philætius thus. Oh were thy word not vain? ....Od.21.205.269.
I mourn the common cause; for, oh my friends! ....Od.21.264.272.
Retire oh Queen! thy houshold task resume, ...Od.21.377.277.
Oh! could the vigor of this arm as well ....Od.21.403.279.
Since cold in death th' offender lies; oh spare ....Od.22.66.290.
Oh curst event! and oh unlook'd-for aid! ....Od.22.164.295.
Oh curst event! and oh unlook'd-for aid! ....Od.22.164.295.
Oh my dear son!—The father with a sigh: ....Od.22.166.295.
There pass thy pleasing night, oh gentle swain! ....Od.22.212.297.
Oh ev'ry sacred name in one! my friend! ....Od.22.226.297.
Oh sharp in scandal, voluble and vain! ....Od.22.319.301.
Oh spare an Augur's consecrated head, ...Od.22.355.304.
Oh mix not, Father, with those impious dead ....Od.22.395.307.
But thou sincere! Oh *Euryclea,* say, ...Od.22.456.310.
At length *Telemachus—Oh* who can find ....Od.23.99.324.
And oh my Queen! he cries; what pow'r above ....Od.23.165.328.
Canst thou, oh cruel, unconcern'd survey ....Od.23.169.328.
'Tis thine, oh Queen, to say: And now impart, ...Od.23.209.333.
The tears pour'd down amain: And oh, she cries, ...Od.23.215.333.
'Twas caution, oh my Lord! not want of love: ....Od.23.230.334.
Oh! better hadst thou sunk in *Trojan* ground, ...Od.24.43.350.
And such thy honours, oh belov'd of heaven! ....Od.24.116.353.
Son of *Melanthus!* (he began) Oh say! ....Od.24.129.354.
Oh blest *Ulysses* (thus the King exprest ....Od.24.218.358.
Not such, oh *Tyndarus!* thy daughter's deed, ...Od.24.226.358.
Great is thy skill, oh father! great thy toil, ...Od.24.287.363.
But chief oh tell me (what I question most) ....Od.24.304.364.
Thy ancient friend, oh stranger, is no more! ....Od.24.329.365.
I, I am he; oh father rise! behold ....Od.24.375.367.
These floods of sorrow, oh my Sire, restrain! ....Od.24.379.367.
Oh! would to all the deathless pow'rs on high, ...Od.24.433.369.
Then thus broke out. Oh long, oh daily mourn'd! ....Od.24.460.370.
Then thus broke out. Oh long, oh daily mourn'd! ....Od.24.460.370.
Who knows thy blest, thy wish'd return? oh say, ...Od.24.465.371.
Great deeds, oh friends! this wond'rous man has wrought, ...Od.24.489.371.
Oh Pow'r supreme, oh ruler of the whole! ....Od.24.543.374.
Oh Pow'r supreme, oh ruler of the whole! ....Od.24.543.374.

OICLEUS

The first begot *Oicleus* great in fame, ...Od.15.267.81.

OIL

"Sir, Spain has sent a thousand jars of oil; ....3.Ep3.44.89.
Their Joints they supple with dissolving Oil, ...Il.10.676.32.
Then Jars of Honey, and of fragrant Oil ....Il.23.208.498.
To wash the Body, and anoint with Oil; ....Il.24.731.568.
Here jars of oil breath'd forth a rich perfume; ....Od.2.384.79.
To bathe the Prince, and pour the fragrant oil. ....Od.3.595.117.
Unsavoury stench of oil, and brackish ooze: ....Od.4.598.148.
And o'er their limbs diffuse ambrosial oil; ....Od.6.110.211.
The balmy oil, a fragrant show'r, he sheds, ...Od.6.269.223.
Shed sweets shed unguents, in a show'r of oil: ....Od.8.492.289.
Supply the limpid wave, and fragrant oil: ....Od.17.101.136.
In the warm bath foment with fragrant oil. ....Od.19.367.212.
With plenteous unction of ambrosial oil. ....Od.19.590.225.

OIL'D

As oil'd with magic juices for the course, ...5.DunA2.96.109.
As oil'd with magic juices for the course, ...5.DunB2.104.300.
With Essence oil'd his Hair; ....6.79.30.218.

OILEAN

On *Gyræ,* safe *Oilean Ajax* sate, ...Od.4.672.151.

OILS

Soft Oils of Fragrance, and ambrosial Show'rs: ....Il.14.198.168.
Fresh from the bath with fragrant oils renew'd, ...Od.4.344.136.
And bath'd in fragrant oils that breath'd of heav'n) ....Od.5.336.188.
With oils and honey blaze th' augmented fires, ...Od.24.85.352.

OILY

An oily steam, and taints the noon-tide gales. ....Od.4.548.146.

OLD

The Young, the Old, one Instant makes our Prize, ...1.W-F.109A.161.
Let old *Arcadia* boast her ample Plain, ...1.W-F.159.164.
Let old *Arcadia* boast her spacious Plain, ...1.W-F.159A.164.
Here too, 'tis sung, of old *Diana* stray'd, ...1.W-F.165.165.
Here, as old Bards have sung, *Diana* stray'd, ...1.W-F.165A.165.
Or raise old Warriors whose ador'd Remains ....1.W-F.301.177.
From old *Belerium* to the *Northern* Main, ...1.W-F.316.179.
From old *Belerium* to the *German* Main ....1.W-F.316A.179.
Heav'ns! what new Wounds, and how her old have bled? ....1.W-F.322.180.
Old Father *Thames* advanc'd his rev'rend Head. ....1.W-F.330.181.
And the new World launch forth to seek the Old. ....1.W-F.402.191.
Those RULES of old *discover'd,* not *devis'd,* .... 1.EOC.88.249.

OLD (CONTINUED)

Some by *Old Words* to Fame have made Pretence; ... 1.EOC.324.275.
Alike Fantastick, if *too New,* or *Old;* ... 1.EOC.334.276.
Nor yet the *last* to lay the *Old* aside. ... 1.EOC.336.276.
Regard not then if Wit be *Old* or *New,* ... 1.EOC.406.287.
Of old, those met *Rewards* who cou'd *excel,* ... 1.EOC.510.295.
Of old, those found *Rewards* who cou'd *excel,* ... 1.EOC.510A.295.
Like some *fierce Tyrant* in *Old Tapestry!* ... 1.EOC.587.307.
In *Sounds* and jingling *Syllables* grown old, ... 1.EOC.605.308.
Still humming on, their old dull Course they keep, ... 1.EOC.600A.308.
We still defy'd the *Romans,* as *of old.* ... 1.EOC.718.323.
And old *Silenus,* youthful in Decay, ... 1.TrVP.24.378.
My Sons their old, unhappy Sire despise, ... 1.TrSt.103.414.
Tho' there the Brazen Tow'r was storm'd of old, ... 1.TrSt.356.425.
Old Limbs of Trees from crackling Forests torn, ... 1.TrSt.506.431.
Which *Danaus* us'd in sacred Rites of old, ... 1.TrSt.635.436.
Great was the Cause; our old Solemnities ... 1.TrSt.660.438.
And enters old *Crotopus'* humble Courts. ... 1.TrSt.669.438.
And enter'd old *Crotopus'* humble Court. ... 1.TrSt.669A.438.
In Days of old, a wise and worthy Knight; ... 2.ChJM.2.15.
Heroick *Judeth,* as old *Hebrews* show, ... 2.ChJM.73.18.
To guide your Choice; This Wife must not be old: ... 2.ChJM.100.19.
Old Fish at Table, but young Flesh in Bed. ... 2.ChJM.102.19.
Old as I am, my lusty Limbs appear ... 2.ChJM.135.21.
To heathnish Authors, Proverbs, and old Saws. ... 2.ChJM.219.25.
Old Wives there are, of Judgment most acute, ... 2.ChJM.295.28.
The Old have Int'rest ever in their Eye: ... 2.ChJM.302.28.
Full many an Age old *Hymen* had not spy'd ... 2.ChJM.333.30.
Whose Use old Bards describe in luscious Rhymes, ... 2.ChJM.379.33.
The good old Knight mov'd slowly by her Side. ... 2.ChJM.403.34.
Old as I am, and now depriv'd of Sight, ... 2.ChJM.552.42.
But since he's blind and old, (a helpless Case) ... 2.ChJM.645.46.
Old as he was, and void of Eye-sight too, ... 2.ChJM.728.49.
The three were Old, but rich and fond beside, ... 2.ChWB.58.59.
They made their Court, like *Jupiter* of old. ... 2.ChWB.65.59.
Hark old Sir *Paul* ('twas thus I us'd to say) ... 2.ChWB.74.60.
For Gold we love the Impotent and Old, ... 2.ChWB.174.65.
What Sums from these old Spouses I cou'd raise, ... 2.ChWB.207.66.
And old Examples set before my Eyes; ... 2.ChWB.342.73.
When old, and past the Relish of Delight, ... 2.ChWB.373.75.
As now your own, our Beings were of old, ... 2.RL1.47.149.
And old Impertinence expel by new. ... 2.RL1.94.152.
Charm'd the Small-pox, or chas'd old Age away; ... 2.RL5.20.200.
Or Worthys old, whom Arms or Arts adorn, ... 2.TemF.70.257.
To whom old Fables gave a lasting Name, ... 2.TemF.130.264.
And boasting Youth, and Narrative old Age. ... 2.TemF.291.277.
Of old Mismanagements, Taxations new— ... 2.TemF.456.285.
Repent old pleasures, and sollicit new: ... 2.ElAb.186.335.
Who heaves old Ocean, and who wings the storms, ... 3.EOM1.158.35.
Correct old Time, and regulate the Sun; ... 3.EOM2.22.57.
Correct old Time, and teach the Sun his way; ... 3.EOM2.22A.57.
Or some old temple, nodding to its fall, ... 3.EOM4.129.140.
Old Politicians chew on wisdom past, ... 3.Ep1.248.37.
"I give and I devise, (old Euclio said, ... 3.Ep1.256.37.
Beauties, like Tyrants, old and friendless grown, ... 3.Ep2.227.68.
A Youth of frolicks, an old Age of Cards, ... 3.Ep2.244.70.
Young without Lovers, old without a Friend, ... 3.Ep2.246.70.
Still, as of old, incumber'd Villainy! ... 3.Ep3.36.88.
"Old Cato is as great a Rogue as you." ... 3.Ep3.68.93.
Or heal, old Narses, thy obscener ail, ... 3.Ep3.91.97.
Old Cotta sham'd his fortune and his birth, ... 3.Ep3.179.108.
Like some lone Chartreux stands the good old Hall, ... 3.Ep3.189.109.
The young who labour, and the old who rest. ... 3.Ep3.268.115.
And long'd to tempt him like good Job of old: ... 3.Ep3.350.122.
My good old Lady catch'd a cold, and dy'd. ... 3.Ep3.384.124.
Load some vain Church with old Theatric state, ... 3.Ep4.29.140.
Erect new wonders, and the old repair, ... 3.Ep4.192.155.
As downright *Shippen,* or as old *Montagne.* ... 4.HS1.52.9.
Whether old Age, with faint, but chearful Ray, ... 4.HS1.93.13.
As *Herod's* Hang-dogs in old Tapestry, ... 4.JD4.267.47.
Thus much is left of old Simplicity! ... 4.HS2.36.57.
At such a feast old vinegar to spare, ... 4.HS2.57.59.
And more, the Sickness of long Life, Old-age: ... 4.HS2.88.61.
From yon old wallnut-tree a show'r shall fall; ... 4.HS2.145.67.
Spies, Guardians, Guests, old Women, Aunts, and Cozens& ... 4.HAdv.129.85.
The good old Landlords hospitable Door? ... 4.JD2A.120.142.
Out-cant old Esdras, or out-drink his Heir, ... 4.JD2.37.135.
The good old Landlord's hospitable door? ... 4.JD2.114.143.
Like rich old Wardrobes, things extremely rare, ... 4.JD2.123.145.
In ANNA's Wars, a Soldier poor and old, ... 4.2HE2.33.167.
Command old words that long have slept, to wake, ... 4.2HE2.167.177.
Authors, like Coins, grow dear as they grow old; ... 4.2HE1.35.197.
Ben, old and poor, as little seem'd to heed ... 4.2HE1.73.199.
"What Boy but hears the sayings of old Ben? ... 4.2HE1.80.201.
Extols old Bards, or Merlin's Prophecy, ... 4.2HE1.132.207.
Old Edward's Armour beams on Cibber's breast! ... 4.2HE1.319.223.
Which made old Ben, and surly Dennis swear, ... 4.2HE1.388.229.
Our old Friend Swift will tell his Story. ... 4.1HE7.82.273.
Hang their old Trophies o'er the Garden gates, ... 4.1HE1.8.279.
This new Court jargon, or the good old song? ... 4.1HE1.98.287.
A Joke on JEKYL, or some odd *Old Whig,* ... 4.EpS1.39.300.
And wear their strange old Virtue as they will. ... 4.EpS1.44.301.
Old *England's* Genius, rough with many a Scar, ... 4.EpS1.152.309.
Before her dance, behind her crawl the Old! ... 4.EpS1.156.309.
Still her old empire to confirm, she tries, ... 5.DunA1.15.61.
She saw old Pryn in restless Daniel shine, ... 5.DunA1.101.71.
Old Bodies of Philosophy appear. ... 5.DunA1.132.80.
Dulness! whose good old cause I yet defend, ... 5.DunA1.145.81.
Old puns restore, lost blunders nicely seek, ... 5.DunA1.163.82.
Now flames old Memnon, now Rodrigo burns, ... 5.DunA1.208.87.
Rowz'd by the light, old Dulness heav'd the head, ... 5.DunA1.213.89.
A past, vamp'd, future, old, reviv'd, new piece, ... 5.DunA1.238.91.
On Codrus' old, or Dunton's modern bed; ... 5.DunA2.136.117.
Old James himself unfinish'd left his tale, ... 5.DunA2.380.146.
Old Bavius sits, to dip poetic souls, ... 5.DunA3.16.151.
Old in new state, another yet the same. ... 5.DunA3.32.154.

OLD (CONTINUED)

How many stages thro' old Monks she rid? ... 5.DunA3.44.154.
All nonsense thus, of old or modern date, ... 5.DunA3.51.155.
Old scenes of glory, times long cast behind, ... 5.DunA3.55.155.
Oh great Restorer of the good old Stage, ... 5.DunA3.201.175.
In Lud's old walls, tho' long I rul'd renown'd, ... 5.DunA3.275.183.
With Night Primæval, and with Chaos old. ... 5.DunA3.338.192.
See sculking Truth in her old cavern lye, ... 5.DunA3.347.193.
Still her old Empire to restore she tries, ... 5.DunB1.17.270.
She saw old Pryn in restless Daniel shine, ... 5.DunB1.103.276.
Dulness! whose good old cause I yet defend, ... 5.DunB1.165.282.
Moliere's old stubble in a moment flames. ... 5.DunB1.254.289.
Rowz'd by the light, old Dulness heav'd the head; ... 5.DunB1.257.289.
A past, vamp'd, future, old, reviv'd, new piece, ... 5.DunB1.284.290.
On Codrus' old, or Dunton's modern bed; ... 5.DunB2.144.302.
Old Bavius sits, to dip poetic souls, ... 5.DunB3.24.321.
Old in new state, another yet the same. ... 5.DunB3.40.322.
How many stages thro' old Monks she rid? ... 5.DunB3.52.323.
All nonsense thus, of old or modern date, ... 5.DunB3.59.323.
Old scenes of glory, times long cast behind ... 5.DunB3.63.323.
Oh great Restorer of the good old Stage, ... 5.DunB3.205.330.
In Lud's old walls tho' long I rul'd, renown'd ... 5.DunB3.277.333.
The young, the old, who feel her inward sway, ... 5.DunB4.73.348.
A new Edition of old Æson gave, ... 5.DunB4.122.353.
Or chew'd by blind old Scholiasts o'er and o'er. ... 5.DunB4.232.365.
With that, a WIZARD OLD his *Cup* extends; ... 5.DunB4.517.393.
Of *Night* Primæval, and of *Chaos* old! ... 5.DunB4.630.407.
See skulking *Truth* to her old Cavern fled, ... 5.DunB4.641.407.
The silent wood, of old, a poet drew ... 6.3.11A.7.
Which yet not much that Old Bard's Anger rais'd, ... 6.12.6A.37.
Mending old Nets to catch the scaly Fry; ... 6.14ii.16.43.
Arriv'd at last, poor, old, disguis'd, alone, ... 6.15.3.51.
Like an old servant now cashier'd, he lay; ... 6.15.12.51.
And some esteem *Old*-Elzevir; ... 6.29.4.83.
Grown old in Rhyme, 'twere barbarous to discard ... 6.34.1.101.
Tho' Plays for Honour in old Time he made, ... 6.34.17.101.
How *Pallas* talk'd when she was Seven Years old. ... 6.37.10.106.
In days of old they pardon'd breach of vows, ... 6.41.29.114.
And all his old Friends would rebuke ... 6.42iv.9.118.
Old-fashion'd halls, dull aunts, and croaking rooks, ... 6.45.12.125.
Of old *Cats* and young *Kits.* ... 6.59.8.177.
But spare old *England,* lest you hurt a Friend. ... 6.60.22.178.
Old, and void of all good-nature; ... 6.70.7.201.
And give to Titus old Vespasian's due. ... 6.71.18.203.
Since my old Friend is grown so great, ... 6.74.1.211.
Fate plays her old Dog Trick! ... 6.79.62.220.
Fate shews an old Dog Trick! ... 6.79.62A.220.
A Youth of Frolicks, an Old-Age of Cards; ... 6.86.6A.245.
Young without Lovers, old without a Friend; ... 6.86.8A.245.
Bards of old ... 6.96i.11.268.
What Wonders there the Man grown old, did! ... 6.101.15.290.
In merry old England it once was a rule, ... 6.105vii.1.302.
On one so old your sword you scorn to draw. ... 6.116vii.6.328.
Yet this, like their old one, for nothing will spare, ... 6.122.19.342.
But pities *Belisarius,* Old and Blind? ... 6.128.6.355.
And be the Critick's, *Briton's,* Old-man's Friend. ... 6.128.24.356.
Roast beef, tho' old, proclaims him stout, ... 6.150.13.399.
Yet if it be the old Man's Case, ... 6.151.5.399.
With these of old to Toils of Battel bred, ... Il.1.351.105.
The Thund'rer sate, where old *Olympus* shrouds ... Il.1.648.118.
Murmuring they move, as when old *Ocean* roars, ... Il.2.249.139.
The shaded Tomb of old *Æpytus* stood; ... Il.2.732.161.
Alcides' Uncle, old *Lycimnius,* slew; ... Il.2.802.163.
Prothous the swift, of old *Tenthredon's* Blood; ... Il.2.917.167.
The Old consulting, and the Youths around. ... Il.2.959.169.
Old *Merops* Sons; whom skill'd in Fates to come ... Il.2.1008.170.
(Old *Priam's* Chiefs, and most in *Priam's* Grace) ... Il.3.192.200.
The good old *Priam* welcom'd her, and cry'd, ... Il.3.211.201.
The solemn Council best becomes the Old: ... Il.4.377.239.
Old *Priam's* Son, *Democoon* was his Name; ... Il.4.574.249.
Sons of *Eurydamas,* who wise and old, ... Il.5.190.275.
The good old Warrior bade me trust to these, ... Il.5.248.279.
Lo the brave Heir of old *Lycaon's* Line, ... Il.5.304.281.
His faithful Servant, old *Calesius* dy'd. ... Il.6.24.325.
Old *Nestor* saw, and rowz'd the Warrior's Rage; ... Il.6.83.327.
Know, Chief, our Grandsires have been Guests of old; ... Il.6.267.339.
Oh *Peleus,* old in Arms, in Wisdom old! ... Il.7.150.372.
Oh *Peleus,* old in Arms, in Wisdom old! ... Il.7.150.372.
But when old Age had dim'd *Lycurgus* Eyes, ... Il.7.179.372.
Old *Nestor* shook the Casque. By Heav'n inspir'd, ... Il.7.219.375.
Old Man, if void of Fallacy or Art ... Il.7.432.386.
While old *Laömedon's* divine Abodes, ... Il.7.538.391.
But thou, O King, to Council call the old: ... Il.9.96.437.
That young and old may in thy Praise combine, ... Il.9.336.450.
When *Greece* of old beheld my youthful Flames, ... Il.9.576.462.
Old as he was, ador'd a Stranger's Charms. ... Il.9.579.462.
A great Example drawn from Times of old; ... Il.9.650.467.
That old in Arms, disdain'd the Peace of Age. ... Il.10.87.6.
Then, with his Foot, old *Nestor* gently shakes ... Il.10.178.9.
Wond'rous old Man! whose Soul no Respite knows, ... Il.10.186.10.
Old *Nestor* first perceiv'd th' approaching Sound, ... Il.10.624.29.
Old as I am, to Age I scorn to yield, ... Il.10.646.30.
In blazing heaps the Grove's old Honours fall, ... Il.11.203.44.
Glory of *Greece,* old *Neleus'* valiant Son! ... Il.11.633.61.
Old *Nestor* mounts the Seat: Beside him rode ... Il.11.638.62.
Old *Nestor* rising then, the Hero led ... Il.11.790.71.
Old *Neleus* glory'd in his conqu'ring Son. ... Il.11.827.73.
In their old Bounds the Rivers roll again, ... Il.12.35.83.
To gain new Glories, or augment the old. ... Il.12.322.93.
He fresh in Youth, and I in Arms grown old. ... Il.13.611.135.
Polydus' Son, a Seer of old Renown. ... Il.13.836.145.
As when old Ocean's silent Surface sleeps, ... Il.14.21.157.
Glad I submit, whoe'er, or young or old, ... Il.14.118.163.
"The old, yet still successful, Cheat of Love"; ... Il.14.188.168.
Ocean and *Tethys* their old Empire keep, ... Il.14.231.172.
What-time old *Saturn,* from *Olympus* cast, ... Il.14.234.172.

OLD (CONTINUED)

The Sire of all, old *Ocean,* owns my Reign, ...Il.14.279.175.
And all the Gods that round old *Saturn* dwell, ...Il.15.254.207.
Chief of the Foot, of old *Antenor's* Race. ....Il.15.613.220.
Sprung from the Race of old *Laomedon,* .... Il.15.623.220.
Ah yet be mindful of your old Renown, ...Il.15.892.231.
Old *Chiron* rent, and shap'd it for his Sire; ....Il.16.175.245.
Hear, as of old! Thou gav'st, at *Thetis* Pray'r, ...Il.16.292.253.
(A Herald in *Anchises'* Love grown old, ...Il.17.376.302.
Wide o'er the World was *Ilion* fam'd of old ....Il.18.337.337.
Of old, she stalk'd 'amid the bright Abodes, ...Il.19.99.376.
But old Experience and calm Wisdom, mine. ....Il.19.218.382.
Old *Chiron* fell'd, and shap'd it for his Sire; ....Il.19.423.389.
All but old Ocean, hoary Sire! who keeps ....Il.20.15.393.
From him *Tithonus,* now in Cares grown old, ...Il.20.284.406.
Part plunge into the Stream: Old *Xanthus* roars, ...Il.21.9.421.
(Old *Altes'* Daughter, and *Lelegia's* Heir, ...Il.21.97.425.
These from old Ocean at my Word shall blow, ...Il.21.390.436.
Where, in old *Zephyr's* open Courts on high, ...Il.23.246.499.
(Some Tomb perhaps of old, the Dead to grace; ....Il.23.405.506.
And sends before old *Phœnix* to the Place, ...Il.23.435.507.
The old Man's Fury rises, and ye die. ....Il.23.492.510.
Old Man! (*Oïleus* rashly thus replies) ....Il.23.556.511.
(A green old Age unconscious of Decays, ...Il.23.929.526.
The Sword, *Asteropeus* possest of old, ...Il.23.951.527.
Or, old and helpless, at his Feet to fall, ...Il.24.439.554.
Thy self not young, a weak old Man thy Guide. ....Il.24.454.555.
Old like thy self, and not unknown to Fame; ....Il.24.488.556.
See him in me, as helpless and as old! ....Il.24.627.563.
The Old Man's Cheek he gently turn'd away. ....Il.24.637.563.
Thou too, Old Man, hast happier Days beheld; ....Il.24.683.565.
A weak old Man to see the Light and live! ....Il.24.704.566.
(Old *Ocean's* Daughter, silver-footed Dame) ....Il.24.710.567.
The Old Man's Fears, and turn'd within the Tent; .....Il.24.841.572.
An old hereditary Guest I come: ....Od.1.242.44.
Magnificence of old, (the Prince reply'd,) ....Od.1.295.47.
(For so of old my father's court he grac'd, ...Od.1.334.48.
Phemius! let acts of Gods, and Heroes old, ...Od.1.433.53.
But old, the mind with inattention hears. ....Od.1.448.54.
Mentes, an ever-honour'd name, of old ....Od.1.527.57.
Ye young, ye old, the weighty cause disclose: ....Od.2.37.62.
Rev'rend old man! lo here confest he stands ....Od.2.47.62.
Before old *Neleus'* venerable walls. ....Od.3.6.86.
The banquet done, the Narrative old man ....Od.3.80.90.
And laid our old companion in the ground. ....Od.3.363.104.
Belov'd old man! benevolent as wise. ....Od.3.456.109.
A debt, contracted in the days of old. ....Od.3.469.109.
The old man early rose, walk'd forth, and sate ....Od.3.518.112.
(The first-born she, of old *Clymenus'* line; ....Od.3.575.116.
His good old Sire with sorrow to the tomb ....Od.4.144.127.
To *Sparta's* Queen of old the radiant vase ....Od.4.167.128.
And Isles remote enlarge his old domain. ....Od.4.998.164.
The patient man shall view his old abodes, ...Od.5.42.172.
This shows thee, friend, by old experience taught, ...Od.5.235.182.
To curl old Ocean, and to warm the skies. ....Od.5.342.188.
(*Eurymedon's* last hope, who rul'd of old ....Od.7.74.237.
Thither of old, Earth's * Giant-son to view, ...Od.7.413.257.
Old Ocean shook, and back his surges flew. ....Od.9.582.330.
(The mighty Seer who on these hills grew old; ....Od.9.596.331.
Her mother *Persè,* of old Ocean's strain, ...Od.10.159.348.
Soon shalt thou reach old Ocean's utmost ends, ...Od.10.602.372.
When lo! we reach'd old Ocean's utmost bounds, ...Od.11.13.379.
Say if my sire, good old *Laertes,* lives? ....Od.11.210.392.
Or weak and old, my youthful arm demands, ...Od.11.607.413.
Nor yet forgot old Ocean's dread Supreme ....Od.13.144.12.
A swift old-age o'er all his members spread; ....Od.13.498.29.
Ulysses, friend! shall view his old abodes, ...Od.14.173.43.
Not old *Laertes,* broken with despair; ....Od.14.198.45.
Old age untimely posting ere his day. ....Od.15.381.88.
But old *Laertes* weeps his life away, ...Od.16.145.109.
Wretched old man! (with tears the Prince returns) ...Od.16.158.110.
She o'er my limbs old age and wrinkles shed; ....Od.16.230.114.
Propt on a staff, a beggar old and bare, ...Od.17.228.143.
The good old proverb how this pair fulfill! ....Od.17.250.143.
A figure despicable, old, and poor, ...Od.17.411.152.
Old as I am, should once my fury burn, ...Od.18.30.168.
Thus old with woes my fancy paints him now! ....Od.19.418.214.
Old *Euryclea* calling then aside, ...Od.21.411.279.
Which old *Laertes* wont in youth to wield, ...Od.22.198.297.
Old *Euryclea* to the death-ful hall: ....Od.22.433.309.
The good old man, to wasting woes a prey, ...Od.23.387.343.
(From old experience *Nestor's* counsel springs, ...Od.24.71.351.
(The vase to *Thetis Bacchus* gave of old, ...Od.24.95.352.
At an old swineherd's rural lodge he lay. ....Od.24.178.356.
Scorn'd by the young, forgotten by the old, ...Od.24.188.356.
And one *Sicilian* matron, old and sage, ...Od.24.242.360.
If yet I share the old man's memory? ....Od.24.249.361.
His buskins old, in former service torn, ...Od.24.265.361.
And old *Laertes* was his father's name. ....Od.24.317.365.
Thy son, with twenty winters now grown old; ....Od.24.376.367.
To old *Autolycus's* realms I went. ....Od.24.387.367.
The hoary King his old *Sicilian* maid ....Od.24.425.369.
Call'd by the careful old *Sicilian* dame, ...Od.24.449.370.
Their loves in vain; old *Dolius* spreads his hands, ...Od.24.457.370.
In vain old *Mentor's* form the God bely'd, ...Od.24.514.372.
Old *Dolius* too his rusted arms put on; ....Od.24.574.375.
And, still more old, in arms *Laertes* shone. ....Od.24.575.375.
Good old *Laertes* heard with panting joy; ....Od.24.593.376.

OLD-AGE

And more, the Sickness of long Life, Old-age: ....4.HS2.88.61.
A Youth of Frolicks, an Old-Age of Cards; ....6.86.6A.245.
A swift old-age o'er all his members spread; ....Od.13.498.29.

OLD-FASHION'D

Old-fashion'd halls, dull aunts, and croaking rooks, ...6.45.12.125.

OLD-MAN'S

And be the Critick's, *Briton's,* Old-man's Friend. ......6.128.24.356.

OLDFIELD

Oldfield, with more than Harpy throat endu'd, ...4.HS2.25.55.
Lament dear charming *Oldfield,* dead and gone! ......4.HAdv.4.75.
Engaging *Oldfield!* who, with Grace and Ease, ...4.HAdv.5.75.
When Oldfield loves, what Dartineuf detests. ....4.2HE2.87.171.

OLDFIELD'S

At Quin's high plume, or Oldfield's petticoat, ...4.2HE1.331.223.

OLDMIXON

And *Oldmixon* and *Burnet* both out-lie. ....4.JD4.61.31.
But Oldmixon the Poet's healing balm ....5.DunA2.199.125.
Unlucky Oldmixon! thy lordly master ....5.DunA2.201.126.
In naked majesty Oldmixon stands, ...5.DunA2.271B.134.
In naked majesty Oldmixon stands, ...5.DunB2.283.309.

OLDMIXONS

Not from the *Burnets, Oldmixons,* and *Cooks.* ...... 4.Arbu.146.106.

OLENIAN

Th' *Olenian* Rock; and where *Alisium* flows; ....Il.2.750.161.
And rough *Pylenè,* and th' *Olenian* Steep ....Il.2.777.162.
Where o'er the Vales th' *Olenian* Rocks arose; ....Il.11.889.75.

OLIM

Haec olim meminisse juvabit. ....6.42iv.18.118.

OLIVE

Peace o'er the World her Olive-Wand extend, ...1.Mes.19.114.
High at the Head a branching Olive grows, ...1.TrUl.31.466.
As the young Olive, in some Sylvan Scene, ...Il.17.57.290.
Like some fair Olive, by my careful Hand ....Il.18.75.326.
Green looks the olive, the pomegranate glows, ...Od.11.728.421.
High at the head a branching Olive grows, ...Od.13.122.7.
This hand the wonder fram'd; An olive spread ....Od.23.191.332.
Or still inviolate the olive stands, ...Od.23.208.333.
The olive green, blue fig, and pendent pear; ....Od.24.290.363.

OLIVE-WAND

Peace o'er the World her Olive-Wand extend, ...1.Mes.19.114.

OLIVE'S

In the wild Olive's unfrequented Shade; ....1.TrUl.50.467.
(An Olive's cloudy Grain the Handle made, ...Il.13.767.141.
Wrought of the clouded olive's easy grain; ....Od.5.302.185.
In the wild olive's unfrequented shade, ...Od.13.141.11.
Now seated in the Olive's sacred shade ....Od.13.425.26.

OLIVES

Where Peace descending bids her Olives spring, ...1.W-F.429.194.
With Rocky Mountains, and with Olives crown'd! .....1.TrUl.227.473.
Cheap eggs, and herbs, and olives still we see, ...4.HS2.35.57.
And verdant olives flourish round the year. ....6.35.10.103.
There grew two Olives, closest of the grove, ...Od.5.616.201.
And verdant olives flourish round the year. ....Od.7.151.243.
With rocky mountains, and with olives crown'd. ....Od.13.394.26.

OLOÖSSON'S

And *Oloösson's* chalky Cliffs arise. ....Il.2.899.166.

OLYMPIAN

The Gods had summon'd to th' *Olympian* Height. ....Il.1.641.118.
Troy yet found Grace before th' *Olympian* Sire, ...Il.8.401.416.
From *Ida's* Summits to th' *Olympian* Height. ....Il.8.543.422.
Rang'd in bright Order on th' *Olympian* Hill; ....Il.11.104.39.
High-thron'd amidst the great *Olympian* Hall, ...Il.13.661.137.
To ask Consent, I leave th' *Olympian* Bow'r; ....Il.14.352.179.
Headlong I hurl'd them from th' *Olympian* Hall, ...Il.15.27.195.
To yon' bright Synod on th' *Olympian* Hill; ....Il.15.58.196.
And one vast Ruin whelm th' *Olympian* State. ....Il.15.155.202.
No Deed perform'd, to our *Olympian* Sire? ....Il.21.511.443.
While thus they commun'd, from th' *Olympian* Bow'rs ....Il.24.177.543.
Those who inhabit the *Olympian* Bow'r ....Il.24.521.558.
Since all who in th' *Olympian* bow'r reside ....Od.1.103.36.
But if descended from th' *Olympian* bow'r, ...Od.7.265.248.
Dwells there a God on all th' *Olympian* brow ....Od.8.369.283.
Whom glory circles in th' *Olympian* bow'rs. ....Od.13.71.4.
Descended *Pallas* from th' *Olympian* hill. ....Od.24.563.375.

OLYMPUS

Not proud *Olympus* yields a nobler Sight, ...1.W-F.33.151.
Might change *Olympus* for a nobler Hill. ....1.W-F.234.170.
And all *Olympus* rings with loud Alarms. ....2.RL5.48.203.
The Goddess swift to high *Olympus* flies, ...Il.1.293.100.
To great *Olympus* crown'd with fleecy Snow. ....Il.1.551.114.
The Thund'rer sate, where old *Olympus* shrouds ......Il.1.648.118.
And all *Olympus* to the Centre shook. ....Il.1.687.120.
Thus He who Shakes *Olympus* with his Nod; ....Il.5.1108.320.
From vast *Olympus* to the gleaming Plain ....Il.7.24.364.
Or far, oh far from steep *Olympus* thrown, ...Il.8.15.395.
And wide beneath him, all *Olympus* shakes. ....Il.8.553.422.
What-time old *Saturn,* from *Olympus* cast, ...Il.14.234.172.
Whilst from *Olympus* pleas'd *Saturnia* flew. ....Il.14.258.173.
Daughters of *Jove!* that on *Olympus* shine, ...Il.14.599.191.
Olympus, and this Earth, in common lie; ....Il.15.218.205.
Olympus trembled, and the Godhead said. ....Il.17.230.296.
Where vast *Olympus* starry Summits shine: ....Il.18.180.331.
From bright *Olympus* and the starry Heav'n: ....Il.19.130.377.
Swift o'er *Olympus* hundred Hills she flies, ...Il.20.7.393.
Back to *Olympus,* from the War's Alarms, ...Il.21.601.447.

OLYMPUS (CONTINUED)
And in a Moment to *Olympus* flew. ... Il.24.865.572.
Of high *Olympus, Jove* conven'd the Gods: ... Od.1.36.31.
From high *Olympus* prone her flight she bends, ... Od.1.132.38.
Shot to *Olympus* from the woodland shade. ... Od.10.368.362.
Heav'd on *Olympus* tott'ring *Ossa* stood; ... Od.11.387.402.

OLYMPUS'
And from *Olympus'* lofty Tops descends. ... Il.1.62.89.
To high *Olympus'* shining Court ascend, ... Il.1.511.112.
Pallas obeys, and from *Olympus'* Height ... Il.2.203.137.
And *Eleon,* shelter'd by *Olympus'* Shades, ... Il.2.897.166.
And now *Olympus'* shining Gates unfold; ... Il.4.1.220.
And shot like Light'ning from *Olympus'* Height. ... Il.4.100.225.
Confus'd, *Olympus'* hundred Heads arise; ... Il.5.937.311.
Where high *Olympus'* cloudy Tops arise. ... Il.8.4.395.
I fix the Chain to great *Olympus'* Height, ... Il.8.31.397.
To great *Olympus'* shining Gates she flies, ... Il.8.504.420.
Meantime *Saturnia* from *Olympus'* Brow, ... Il.14.179.165.
Swift from *Olympus'* snowy Summit flies, ... Il.18.711.357.
The joyful Goddess, from *Olympus'* Height, ... Il.19.113.376.
And from *Olympus'* snowy Tops descends. ... Il.24.156.542.

OLYUMPUS'
Far on *Olyumpus'* Top in secret State ... Il.20.33.394.

OLYZON'S
Olyzon's Rocks, or *Mœlibæa's* Fields, ... Il.2.873.165.

OMBRE
And Love of *Ombre,* after Death survive. ... 2.RL1.56.150.
At *Ombre* singly to decide their Doom; ... 2.RL3.27.171.
Where none learn *Ombre,* none e'er taste *Bohea!* ... 2.RL4.156.197.
No Game at *Ombre* lost or won. ... 6.10.4.24.

OMEGA
Omicron and *Omega* from us ... 6.30.70.88.

OMEN
Trust in his Omen, and support the War. ... Il.2.387.145.
Hail'd the glad Omen, and address'd the Maid. ... Il.10.326.17.
A signal Omen stopp'd the passing Host, ... Il.12.231.89.
For sure to warn us *Jove* his Omen sent, ... Il.12.255.90.
And asks no Omen but his Country's Cause. ... Il.12.284.92.
To *Jove's* glad Omen all the *Grecians* rise, ... Il.13.1040.154.
Far be the Omen which my Thoughts suggest! ... Il.22.584.480.
With Words of Omen like a Bird of Night. ... Il.24.268.547.
Embrac'd the omen, and majestic rose: ... Od.2.44.62.
Succeed the Omen, Gods! (the youth rejoin'd) ... Od.15.577.98.
The smiling Queen the happy omen blest: ... Od.17.626.163.
This said, the pleasing feather'd omen ceas'd. ... Od.19.646.227.
Let one a blissful omen here disclose: ... Od.20.123.239.
Sinister to their hope! This omen ey'd ... Od.20.304.247.
And Omen of our death! In vain we drew ... Od.24.197.358.

OMEN'D
First rais'd our Walls on that ill-omen'd Plain ... 1.TrSt.251.421.
Or omen'd Voice (the messenger of *Jove)* ... Od.1.367.50.
An omen'd Voice invades his ravish'd ear. ... Od.20.131.240.
What words ill-omen'd from thy lips have fled? ... Od.21.176.268.

OMENS
Proceed, and firm those Omens thou hast made! ... 1.TrSt.591.435.
This Day, black Omens threat the brightest Fair ... 2.RL2.101.166.
'Twas this, the Morning *Omens* seem'd to tell; ... 2.RL4.161.197.
'Twas this, the Morning *Omens* did fortel; ... 2.RL4.161A.197.
Theirs are his Omens, and his Thunder theirs. ... Il.9.310.449.
To judge the winged Omens of the sky. ... Od.1.262.45.
Born with good omens, and with heav'n thy friend. ... Od.3.38.88.
And learn'd in all wing'd omens of the air) ... Od.9.598.331.
With happiest omens, thy desires approve! ... Od.15.127.75.
Say if to us the Gods these Omens send, ... Od.15.188.77.
Succeed those omens Heav'n! (the Queen rejoin'd) ... Od.17.186.140.
And all the wing'd good omens of the skies. ... Od.24.364.366.

OMICRON
Omicron and *Omega* from us ... 6.30.70.88.

OMINOUS
Rose ominous, nor flies without a God: ... Od.15.574.98.

OMIT
And if unwatch'd is sure t' omit Ses Heires: ... 4.JD2A.103.140.
He the least point shoud shorten or omit ... 4.JD2A.109.142.

OMITS
The Deeds, and dextrously omits, *ses Heires:* ... 4.JD2.100.141.

OMITTED
And Vows omitted forfeited the Prize. ... Il.23.626.514.

OMNIPOTENCE
Omnipotence I bound ... 6.50.22A.147.
Omnipotence we bound ... 6.50.22B.147.
Durst threat with Chains th' Omnipotence of Heav'n. ... Il.1.521.113.
In vain resists th' Omnipotence of *Jove.* ... Il.1.735.122.
Join all, and try th' Omnipotence of *Jove:* ... Il.8.24.396.
Strength and Omnipotence invest thy Throne; ... Il.8.576.424.
If Heav'ns Omnipotence descend in Arms? ... Il.15.187.203.
If Heav'ns Omnipotence descend in Arms? ... Il.15.203.204.
And will Omnipotence neglect to save ... Od.1.78.35.
Thron'd in omnipotence, supremest *Jove* ... Od.4.325.134.

OMNIPOTENT
The Will it self, Omnipotent, fulfills. ... Od.14.497.60.

ON (OMITTED)
2592

ON'T
"Plague on't! 'tis past a Jest—nay prithee, Pox! ... 2.RL4.129.194.
Then clap four slices of Pilaster on't, ... 3.Ep4.33.140.

ONCE
Once I was skill'd in ev'ry Herb that grew, ... 1.PSu.31.74.
Her Name with Pleasure once she taught the Shore, ... 1.PWi.43.92.
Waste sandy Vallies, once perplex'd with Thorn, ... 1.Mes.73.119.
At once the Monarch's and the Muse's Seats, ... 1.W-F.2.148.
At once the Chaser and at once the Prey. ... 1.W-F.82.158.
At once the Chaser and at once the Prey. ... 1.W-F.82.158.
Such was the Life great *Scipio* once admir'd, ... 1.W-F.257.172.
And fast beside him, once-fear'd *Edward* sleeps: ... 1.W-F.314.179.
Once more to bend before a *British* QUEEN. ... 1.W-F.384.189.
Peru once more a Race of Kings behold, ... 1.W-F.411.192.
A *Fool* might once *himself* alone expose, ... 1.EOC.7.239.
At once the *Source,* and *End,* and *Test* of *Art.* ... 1.EOC.73.247.
Without all these at once before your Eyes, ... 1.EOC.122.252.
The *Heart,* and all its End *at once* attains. ... 1.EOC.157.258.
If once right Reason drives *that Cloud* away, ... 1.EOC.211.264.
The *Whole* at once is *Bold,* and *Regular.* ... 1.EOC.252.268.
Once on a time, *La Mancha's* Knight, they say, ... 1.EOC.267.270.
But let a *Lord* once own the *happy Lines,* ... 1.EOC.420.287.
Once *School-Divines* this zealous Isle o'erspread; ... 1.EOC.440.288.
Once *School-Divines* our zealous Isle o'erspread; ... 1.EOC.440A.288.
Might he return, and bless once more our Eyes, ... 1.EOC.462.291.
Who, if *once wrong,* will needs be *always so;* ... 1.EOC.569.305.
That, if *once wrong,* will needs be *always so;* ... 1.EOC.569A.305.
Such once were *Criticks,* such the Happy *Few,* ... 1.EOC.643.311.
She ceas'd at once to speak, and ceas'd to be; ... 1.TrFD.100.390.
Once the dear Objects of my guilty Love; ... 1.TrSP.18.394.
Yet once thy *Sapho* cou'd thy Cares employ, ... 1.TrSP.49.395.
Once in her Arms you center'd all your Joy: ... 1.TrSP.50.395.
As if once more forsaken, I complain, ... 1.TrSP.157.400.
I view the *Grotto,* once the Scene of Love, ... 1.TrSP.163.400.
I kiss that Earth which once was prest by you, ... 1.TrSP.171.401.
"Deucalion once with hopeless Fury burn'd, ... 1.TrSP.193.402.
This Breast which once, in vain! you lik'd so well; ... 1.TrSP.226.403.
Once more invades the guilty Dome, and shrouds ... 1.TrSt.171.417.
Whence, far below, the Gods at once survey ... 1.TrSt.277.421.
And stain the sacred Womb where once he lay? ... 1.TrSt.333.424.
Where once his Steeds their savage Banquet found, ... 1.TrSt.390.426.
At once the rushing Winds with roaring Sound ... 1.TrSt.488.430.
Such once employ'd *Alcides'* youthful Toils, ... 1.TrSt.569.434.
The King once more the solemn Rites requires, ... 1.TrSt.603.435.
Once more resound the Great *Apollo's* Praise. ... 1.TrSt.828.444.
At once bold *Teucer* draws the twanging Bow, ... 1.TrES.135.454.
At once they bend, and strike their equal Oars, ... 1.TrUl.3.465.
Till I beheld thy radiant Form once more, ... 1.TrUl.199.472.
Once more 'twas giv'n thee to behold thy Coast: ... 1.TrUl.221.473.
To you once more your own *Ulysses* bows, ... 1.TrUl.242.473.
Once, ere he dy'd, to taste the blissful Life ... 2.ChJM.17.15.
Secure at once himself and Heav'n to please; ... 2.ChJM.38.16.
Once more in haste he summon'd ev'ry Friend, ... 2.ChJM.252.26.
At once with carnal and devout Intent: ... 2.ChJM.310.29.
The Foe once gone, our Knight prepar'd t'undress, ... 2.ChJM.373.32.
The Foe once gone, our Knight wou'd strait undress, ... 2.ChJM.373A.32.
It happ'd, that once upon a Summer's Day, ... 2.ChJM.521.40.
For who that once possest those Heav'nly Charms, ... 2.ChJM.573.43.
Or once renounce the Honour of my Race. ... 2.ChJM.590.43.
Help dearest Lord, and save at once the Life ... 2.ChJM.724.49.
And think, for once, a Woman tells you true. ... 2.ChWB.4.57.
Christ saw a Wedding once, the Scripture says, ... 2.ChWB.9.57.
But once grown sleek, will from her Corner run, ... 2.ChWB.144.63.
If once my Husband's Arm was o'er my Side, ... 2.ChWB.166.64.
This wicked World was once my dear Delight; ... 2.ChWB.225.67.
A Conjurer once that deeply cou'd divine, ... 2.ChWB.321.72.
Nay once by Heav'n he struck me on the Face: ... 2.ChWB.335.73.
At once they gratifie their Smell and Taste, ... 2.RL*A*1.95.130.
And once inclos'd in Woman's beauteous Mold; ... 2.RL1.48.149.
That all her Vanities at once are dead: ... 2.RL1.52.149.
Unnumber'd Treasures ope at once, and here ... 2.RL1.129.155.
Oft she rejects, but never once offends. ... 2.RL2.12.160.
At once they gratify their Scent and Taste, ... 2.RL3.111.176.
Like that where once *Ulysses* held the Winds; ... 2.RL4.82.190.
Clipt from the lovely Head where once it grew) ... 2.RL4.136A.195.
Once gave new Beauties to the snowie Neck. ... 2.RL4.170.198.
And tempts once more thy sacrilegious Hands. ... 2.RL4.174.198.
And Poets once had promis'd they should last. ... 2.TemF.34.255.
Druids and *Bards* (their once loud Harps unstrung) ... 2.TemF.127.264.
Not all at once, as Thunder breaks the Cloud; ... 2.TemF.310.279.
And once the lot of *Abelard* and me. ... 2.ElAb.98.327.
But let heav'n seize it, all at once 'tis fir'd, ... 2.ElAb.201.336.
To dream once more I close my willing eyes; ... 2.ElAb.239.339.
Ah come not, write not, think not once of me, ... 2.ElAb.291.343.
Once like thy self, I trembled, wept, and pray'd, ... 2.ElAb.311.344.
Teach me at once, and learn of me to die. ... 2.ElAb.328.346.
Ah then, thy once-lov'd *Eloisa* see! ... 2.ElAb.329.346.
Most souls, 'tis true, but peep out once an age, ... 2.Elegy.17.363.
What once had beauty, titles, wealth, and fame. ... 2.Elegy.70.368.
How lov'd, how honour'd once, avails thee not, ... 2.Elegy.71.368.
Where slaves once more their native land behold, ... 3.EOM1.107.28.
At once extend the int'rest, and the love; ... 3.EOM3.134.106.
Yet make at once their circle round the Sun: ... 3.EOM3.314.126.
You'll find, if once the monarch acts the monk, ... 3.EOM4.201.146.
At once his own bright prospect to be blest, ... 3.EOM4.351.162.
His Principle of action once explore, ... 3.Ep1.37.18.
Must then at once (the character to save) ... 3.Ep1.77.21.
That gay Free-thinker, a fine talker once, ... 3.Ep1.162.29.
This clue once found, unravels all the rest, ... 3.Ep1.178.30.
'Twas thus Calypso once our hearts alarm'd, ... 3.Ep2.45A.53.
Nothing so true as what you once let fall, ... 3.Ep2.1.46.
'Twas thus Calypso once each heart alarm'd, ... 3.Ep2.45.53.

ONCE (CONTINUED)

And paid a Tradesman once to make him stare, ... 3.Ep2.56.55.
Th' Address, the Delicacy—stoops at once, ... 3.Ep2.85.57.
Scarce once herself, by turns all Womankind! .... 3.Ep2.116.60.
Once, we confess, beneath the Patriot's cloak, ... 3.Ep3.65.92.
On once a flock-bed, but repair'd with straw, ... 3.Ep3.301.118.
"Where once I went to church, I'll now go twice— .... 3.Ep3.367.123.
And pompous buildings once were things of Use. .... 3.Ep4.24.139.
Who *live* at *Court,* for going once that Way! .... 4.JD4.23.27.
Had once a pretty Gift of Tongues enough. .... 4.JD4.77.31.
If once he catch you at your *Jesu! Jesu!* .... 4.JD4.257.47.
And is at once their vinegar and wine. .... 4.HS2.54.59.
And Hemsley once proud Buckingham's delight, ... 4.HS2.177.69.
"The Hare once seiz'd the Hunter heeds no more .... 4.HAdv.137.87.
The truth once told, (and wherefore shou'd we lie?) .... 4.Arbu.81.101.
Full ten years slander'd, did he once reply? .... 4.Arbu.374.123.
"Once, (and but once) I caught him in a Lye, ... 4.2HE2.17.165.
"Once, (and but once) I caught him in a Lye, ... 4.2HE2.17.165.
Or damn to all Eternity at once, ... 4.2HE1.59.199.
And, having once been wrong, will be so still. .... 4.2HE1.130.207.
Farce once the taste of Mobs, but now of Lords; .... 4.2HE1.311.221.
Let me for once presume t'instruct the times, ... 4.2HE1.340.225.
As once for LOUIS, Boileau and Racine. .... 4.2HE1.375.227.
As once a week we travel down .... 4.HS6.97.257.
Once on a time (so runs the Fable) .... 4.HS6.157.259.
A Weasel once made shift to slink .... 4.1HE7.51.271.
Adieu to Virtue if you're once a Slave: .... 4.1HE1.118.287.
They hire their Sculler, and when once aboard, ... 4.1HE1.159.291.
Nor once to Chanc'ry, nor to Hales apply; .... 4.1HE1.173.291.
You grow *correct* that once with Rapture writ, ... 4.EpS1.3.297.
The *S[ena]te's,* and then *H[er]v[e]y's* once agen. .... 4.EpS1.72.303.
Once break their Rest, or stir them from their Place; .... 4.EpS1.100.305.
Must great Offenders, once escap'd the Crown, ... 4.EpS2.28.314.
You make men desp'rate if they once are bad: .... 4.EpS2.59.315.
Thus SOMMERS once, and HALIFAX were mine. .... 4.EpS2.77.317.
It anger'd TURENNE, once upon a day. .... 4.EpS2.150.322.
Whose names once up, they thought it was not wrong .... 4.1740.21.333.
And free at once the Senate and the Throne; .... 4.1740.90.337.
What City-Swans once sung within the walls; .... 5.DunA1.94.70.
And crucify poor Shakespear once a week. .... 5.DunA1.164.83.
Take up th' Attorney's (once my better) Guide? .... 5.DunA1.190.85.
Where the tall May-pole once o'erlook'd the Strand; .... 5.DunA2.24.99.
That once so flutter'd, and that once so writ. .... 5.DunA2.112.110.
That once so flutter'd, and that once so writ. .... 5.DunA2.112.110.
"Here strip my children! here at once leap in! .... 5.DunA2.263.133.
And "Take (he said) these robes which once were mine, ... 5.DunA2.327.141.
That once was Britain—Happy! had she seen .... 5.DunA3.109.159.
And Her Parnassus glancing o'er at once, ... 5.DunA3.129.161.
And all Parnassus glancing o'er at once, ... 5.DunA3.129A.161.
Preacher at once, and Zany of thy Age! .... 5.DunA3.202.175.
What City Swans once sung within the walls; .... 5.DunB1.96.276.
Remembring she herself was Pertness once. .... 5.DunB1.112.277.
And once betray'd me into common sense: .... 5.DunB1.188.283.
Take up the Bible, once my better guide? .... 5.DunB1.200.284.
At once the Bear and Fiddle of the town. .... 5.DunB1.224.286.
Or peaceably forgot, at once be blest .... 5.DunB1.239.287.
Where the tall may-pole once o'er-look'd the Strand; .... 5.DunB2.28.297.
That once so flutter'd, and that once so writ. .... 5.DunB2.120.301.
That once so flutter'd, and that once so writ. .... 5.DunB2.120.301.
"Here strip, my children! here at once leap in, ... 5.DunB2.275.309.
"Receive (he said) those robes which once were mine, ... 5.DunB2.351.314.
(Once swan of Thames, tho' now he sings no more.) .... 5.DunB3.20.321.
That once was Britain—Happy! had she seen .... 5.DunB3.117.325.
And her Parnassus glancing o'er at once, ... 5.DunB3.137.326.
Preacher at once, and Zany of thy age! .... 5.DunB3.206.330.
Then take at once the Poet and the Song. .... 5.DunB4.8.340.
Full in the midst of Euclid dip at once, ... 5.DunB4.263.369.
In flow'd at once a gay embroider'd race, ... 5.DunB4.275.371.
Rememb'ring she herself was Pertness once. .... 5.DunB4.280Z2.371.
Thence bursting glorious, all at once let down, ... 5.DunB4.291.373.
Once brightest shin'd this child of Heat and Air. .... 5.DunB4.424.383.
"O! would the Sons of Men once think their Eyes .... 5.DunB4.453.385.
Beeves, at his touch, at once to jelly turn, ... 5.DunB4.551.396.
Which winds and lightning both at once assail. .... 6.3.4.7.
Had he but once this fairer shade descry'd, ... 6.4ii.9.9.
Her bashful beauties once descry'd, ... 6.4iv.4.10.
So spicy gales at once betray .... 6.4v.7.11.
Thy streams were once th' impartial test .... 6.6ii.17.15.
And the same Stream at once both cools and burns. .... 6.9v.4.21.
To get, by once more murd'ring *Caius,* .... 6.10.73.26.
(As once you said of you know who) .... 6.10.94.27.
Where *Daphne,* now a tree as once a maid, ... 6.14iv.23.47.
The stream at once preserves her virgin leaves, ... 6.14iv.27.48.
At once a shelter from her boughs receives, ... 6.14iv.28.48.
At once their Motion, Sweetness, and their Use; .... 6.17ii.10.56.
And, if it can, at once both Please and Preach: .... 6.19.24.62.
All is but *dust,* when once their breath is fled; .... 6.22.13.71.
At once our great original and end, ... 6.23.18.73.
At once our means, our end, our guide, our way, ... 6.23.19.73.
At once our Strength, our Aid, our guide, our way, ... 6.23.19A.73.
Rage strait Collects his Venom all at once, ... 6.26i.14.79.
How things are priz'd, which once belong'd to you: .... 6.38.2.107.
With Gay, who Petition'd you once on a time, ... 6.42i.3.116.
That your Lordship would once let your Cares all alone .... 6.42iii.3.117.
I need but once a Week. .... 6.47.36.129.
Sufficient Sap, at once to bear and rot. .... 6.49i.12.137.
And men, once ignorant, are slaves. .... 6.51i.28.152.
With thee repose, where *Tully* once was laid, ... 6.52.29.157.
For he lives twice, who can at once employ .... 6.55.10.167.
All hail! once pleasing, once inspiring Shade, ... 6.66.1.194.
All hail! once pleasing, once inspiring Shade, ... 6.66.1.194.
Was *DRYDEN* once: The rest who does not know? .... 6.83.2.237.
Such were the Notes, thy once-lov'd Poet sung, ... 6.84.1.238.
Oh let thy once-lov'd Friend inscribe thy Stone, ... 6.85.7.242.
Let then thy once-lov'd Friend inscribe thy Stone, ... 6.85.7A.242.
Yet let thy once-lov'd Friend inscribe thy Stone, ... 6.85.7B.242.

ONCE (CONTINUED)

Once in danger of Death, once in danger of Law. .... 6.92.4.255.
Once in danger of Death, once in danger of Law. .... 6.92.4.255.
Once *thou* didst cleave, and *I* could cleave for Life. .... 6.96iv.10.276.
Were once my Present; *Love* that Armour gave. .... 6.96iv.76.278.
Then took his Muse at once, and dipt her .... 6.101.13.290.
Whom once a *Lobster* kill'd, and now a *Log.* .... 6.105i.2.300.
In merry old England it once was a rule, ... 6.105vii.1.302.
At once can teach, delight, and lash the age, ... 6.106iv.2.307.
At once, to nature, history, and you. .... 6.107.20.311.
Once in his Life M[OOR]E judges right: .... 6.116ii.1.326.
Shou'd D[enni]s print how once you robb'd your Brother, ... 6.116vii.1.328.
Pallas grew vap'rish once and odd, ... 6.119.1.336.
Who by six such fair Maidens at once is possest. .... 6.122.4.341.
Yet ah! how once we lov'd, remember still, ... 6.123.3.343.
Form'd to delight at once and lash the age; .... 6.125.4.350.
Here shunning idleness at once and praise, ... 6.126ii.1.353.
Tho, once my Tail in wanton play, ... 6.135.3.366.
Once chance to hurt your Lap dog ship .... 6.135.6A.366.
Once (says an Author, where, I need not say) .... 6.145.1.388.
Scarce once herself, by Turns all Womankind? .... 6.154.2.402.
Or doom'd to deck the Bed she once enjoy'd. .... Il.1.44.88.
A Godlike Race of Heroes once I knew, ... Il.1.345.105.
Once more attend! avert the wastful Woe, ... Il.1.596.116.
Once in your Cause I felt his matchless Might, ... Il.1.760.123.
Once great in Arms, the common Scorn we grow, ... Il.2.153.135.
Once more refulgent shine in Brazen Arms. .... Il.2.200.137.
Once all their Voice, but ah! forgotten now: .... Il.2.351.144.
Superior once of all the tuneful Race, ... Il.2.722.160.
Where once *Eurytus* in proud Triumph reign'd, ... Il.2.885.166.
Her Country, Parents, all that once were dear, ... Il.3.185.200.
Panthus, and *Hicetäon,* once the strong, ... Il.3.195.200.
My Brother once, before my Days of Shame; .... Il.3.237.203.
In *Phrygia* once were gallant Armies known, ... Il.3.245.204.
This said, once more he view'd the Warrior-Train: .... Il.3.253.204.
This said, once more he view'd the martial Train: .... Il.3.253A.204.
Great as a God! I saw him once before, ... Il.3.297.207.
Then, as once more he lifts the deadly Dart, ... Il.3.465.214.
Of that brave Man whom once I call'd my Lord! .... Il.3.536.217.
Go now, once more thy Rival's Rage excite, ... Il.3.539.217.
Once more they glitter in refulgent Arms, ... Il.4.254.233.
Once more the Fields are fill'd with dire Alarms. .... Il.4.255.233.
The Charge once made, no Warrior turn the Rein, ... Il.4.350.237.
What once thou wert, oh ever might'st thou be. .... Il.4.366.238.
That Strength which once in boiling Youth I knew; .... Il.4.371.238.
But Heav'n its Gifts not all at once bestows, ... Il.4.374.239.
I saw him once, when gath'ring martial Pow'rs .... Il.4.430.240.
Death's sable Shade at once o'ercast their Eyes, ... Il.4.626.250.
These Shafts, once fatal, carry Death no more. .... Il.5.259.279.
The Race of those which once the thund'ring God .... Il.5.328.282.
Once from the Walls your tim'rous Foes engag'd, ... Il.5.982.314.
Alone, unguarded, once he dar'd to go, ... Il.5.1002.314.
Once from their Walls your tim'rous Foes engag'd, ... Il.5.982A.314.
Once more will perish if my *Hector* fall. .... Il.6.547.354.
Once more impetuous dost thou bend thy way, ... Il.7.31.364.
War with a fiercer Tide once more returns, ... Il.7.83.367.
But all at once, thy Fury to compose, ... Il.7.123.369.
Once with what Joy the gen'rous Prince would hear .... Il.7.151.372.
And give this Arm the Spring which once it knew: .... Il.7.162.372.
That done, once more the Fate of War be try'd, ... Il.7.452.387.
That done, once more the Fate of War be try'd, ... Il.7.472.387.
No Trace remain where once the Glory grew. .... Il.7.551.392.
Thy once-proud Hopes, presumptuous Prince! are fled; .... Il.8.202.407.
There arm once more the bold *Titanian* Band; .... Il.8.603.425.
At once my present Judgment, and my past; .... Il.9.140.439.
Deceiv'd for once, I trust not Kings again. .... Il.9.455.455.
He try'd it once, and scarce was sav'd by Fate. .... Il.9.468.455.
For once deceiv'd, was his; but twice, were mine. .... Il.9.491.456.
Or *Troy* once held, in Peace and Pride of Sway, ... Il.9.526.459.
Once fought th' *Ætolian* and *Curetian* Bands; .... Il.9.654.467.
Or *Troy* once more must be the Seat of War? .... Il.10.248.13.
No—once a Traytor, thou betray'st no more. .... Il.10.521.26.
The same which once King *Cinyras* possest: .... Il.11.26.36.
These on the Mountains once *Achilles* found, ... Il.11.143.42.
The daring Wretch who once in Council stood .... Il.11.181.43.
At once, his weighty Sword discharg'd a Wound .... Il.11.307.48.
At once a Virgin, and at once a Bride! .... Il.11.314.49.
At once a Virgin, and at once a Bride! .... Il.11.314.49.
Once more thank *Phœbus* for thy forfeit Breath, ... Il.11.465.54.
And end at once the great *Hippasian* Race, ... Il.11.544.58.
Once taught *Achilles,* and *Achilles* thee. .... Il.11.967.78.
No Fragment tells where once the Wonder stood; .... Il.12.34.83.
So *Jove* once more may drive their routed Train, ... Il.12.327.93.
At once bold *Teucer* draws the twanging Bow, ... Il.12.489.99.
Once foremost in the Fight, still prone to lend .... Il.13.298.119.
He once, of *Ilion's* Youth, the loveliest Boy, ... Il.13.543.132.
At once the Tent and Ligature supply'd. .... Il.13.752.141.
Such *Tydeus* was, the foremost once in Fame! .... Il.14.141.164.
Once more their Minds in mutual Ties engage, ... Il.14.241.172.
Nor once her flying Foot approach'd the Ground. .... Il.14.262.173.
Indignant thus—Oh once of martial Fame! .... Il.14.421.183.
To Earth at once the Head and Helmet fly: .... Il.14.583.190.
To rise afresh, and once more wake the War, ... Il.15.64.197.
They fly: at once the Chasers and the Prey. .... Il.15.313.209.
Once more bold *Teucer,* in his Country's Cause, ... Il.15.536.217.
If once your Vessels catch the *Trojan* Fire? .... Il.15.597.219.
O'ermatch'd he falls; to two at once a Prey, ... Il.15.656.221.
Till *Greece* at once, and all her Glory end; .... Il.15.660.221.
Once Sons of *Mars,* and Thunderbolts of War! .... Il.15.891.231.
Thy self a *Greek;* and, once, of *Greeks* the best! .... Il.16.32.236.
The Fleet once sav'd, desist from farther chace, ... Il.16.116.241.
(Once great *Aëtion's,* now *Achilles'* Pride) .... Il.16.187.246.
At once they see, they tremble, and they fly. .... Il.16.337.255.
At once his Country's Pillar, and their own; .... Il.16.674.270.
At once bold *Hector* leaping from his Car, ... Il.16.913.279.
Wounded at once, *Patroclus* yields to fear, ... Il.16.984.281.

ONCE (CONTINUED)

Thy Pride once promis'd, of subverting *Troy;* ... Il.16.1004.282.
Forgive me, *Greece,* if once I quit the Field; ... Il.17.107.291.
But Words are vain—Let *Ajax* once appear, ... Il.17.183.294.
I deem'd thee once the wisest of thy Kind, ... Il.17.191.294.
Which once the greatest of Mankind had worn. ... Il.17.238.297.
Once more at *Ajax, Hector's* Jav'lin flies; ... Il.17.350.301.
Oh Prince (he cry'd) oh foremost once in Fame! ... Il.17.658.313.
A Chief, once thought no Terror of the Field; ... Il.17.661.313.
Grasps his once formidable Lance in vain. ... Il.17.682.314.
Thetis once more ascends the blest Abodes, ... Il.18.183.331.
At once resigns his Armour, Life, and Fame. ... Il.18.526.347.
Resounding breath'd: At once the Blast expires, ... Il.18.541.348.
And twenty Forges catch at once the Fires; ... Il.18.542.348.
A figur'd Dance succeeds: Such once was seen ... Il.18.681.356.
Now all at once they rise, at once descend, ... Il.18.690.357.
Now all at once they rise, at once descend, ... Il.18.690.357.
Now forth at once, too swift for sight, they spring, ... Il.18.693.357.
And all at once on haughty *Troy* descend. ... Il.19.242.382.
Once tender Friend of my distracted Mind! ... Il.19.304.385.
Once spread th' inviting Banquet in our Tents; ... Il.19.336.386.
Once stay'd *Achilles,* rushing to the War. ... Il.19.338.386.
Once (as I think) you saw this brandish'd Spear ... Il.20.228.403.
Defrauded of my Conquest once before, ... Il.20.236.403.
The richest, once, of *Asia's* wealthy Kings; ... Il.20.261.404.
Content for once, with all his Gods, to fly. ... Il.20.400.412.
Wretch! Thou hast scap'd again. Once more thy Flight ... Il.20.519.416.
Then, as once more he plung'd amid the Flood, ... Il.21.40.423.
Once more *Lycaon* trembles at thy Knee; ... Il.21.85.425.
Once more *Lycaon* trembling at thy Knee; ... Il.21.85A.425.
At once *Asteropeus* discharg'd each Lance, ... Il.21.180.429.
At once consumes the dead, and dries the Soil; ... Il.21.400.436.
Propitious once, and kind! Then welcome Fate! ... Il.22.385.471.
An only Child, once Comfort of my Pains, ... Il.22.620.482.
When once we pass, the Soul returns no more. ... Il.23.94.491.
When once the last Funereal Flames ascend, ... Il.23.95.491.
Once more return'st thou from the Realms of Night? ... Il.23.110.492.
Once more afresh the *Grecian* Sorrows flow: ... Il.23.192.497.
Of some once-stately Oak the last Remains, ... Il.23.401.506.
At once the Coursers from the Barrier bound; ... Il.23.437.507.
The lifted Scourges all at once resound; ... Il.23.438.507.
Such once I was! Now to these Tasks succeeds ... Il.23.739.519.
Tho' once the foremost Hero of the Field. ... Il.23.742.519.
All start at once; *Oïleus* led the Race; ... Il.23.887.524.
Thro' *Phrygia* once, and foreign Regions known, ... Il.24.245.546.
(The Pledge of Treaties once with friendly *Thrace)*<:> ... Il.24.288.548.
In Riches once, in Children once excell'd; ... Il.24.684.565.
In Riches once, in Children once excell'd; ... Il.24.684.565.
Provok'd to Passion, once more rouze to Ire ... Il.24.733.568.
A Parent once, whose Sorrows equal'd thine: ... Il.24.758.569.
An only Son, once Comfort of our Pains, ... Il.24.912.574.
Vanish'd at once! unheard of, and unknown! ... Od.1.311.47.
Why here once more in solemn council sit? ... Od.2.36.62.
Thus she: at once the gen'rous train complies, ... Od.2.115.67.
Descend once more, propitious to my aid. ... Od.2.302.76.
To the strong stroke at once the rowers bend. ... Od.2.459.83.
There too my son—ah once my best delight, ... Od.3.135.92.
Once swift of foot, and terrible in fight, ... Od.3.136.92.
Confest, is thine, as once thy father's aid. ... Od.3.487.111.
And the pale mariner at once deplores ... Od.4.491.143.
Once more the *Nile,* who from the secret source ... Od.4.643.149.
At once the face of earth and sea deforms, ... Od.5.377.190.
(Herself a mortal once, of *Cadmus'* strain, ... Od.5.426.193.
Once more I view the face of humankind: ... Od.6.211.220.
The nymphs withdrawn, at once into the tide ... Od.6.265.223.
At once the seats they fill: and every eye ... Od.8.17.262.
At once the sailors to their charge arise: ... Od.8.46.264.
Should a whole host at once discharge the bow, ... Od.8.249.276.
When storms and hunger both at once assail. ... Od.8.266.277.
Light-bounding from the earth, at once they rise, ... Od.8.303.279.
But yet I trust, this once ev'n *Mars* would fly ... Od.8.355.282.
His fair ones arms—he thinks her, once, too nigh. ... Od.8.356.282.
Once more harmonious strike the sounding string, ... Od.8.539.291.
Once more I raise my voice; my friends afraid ... Od.9.577.330.
But all at once my interposing train ... Od.10.521.368.
As from a lethargy at once they rise, ... Od.10.558.369.
At once the mast we rear, at once unbind ... Od.11.3.377.
At once the mast we rear, at once unbind ... Od.11.3.377.
His shafts *Apollo* aim'd; at once they sound, ... Od.11.393.403.
At once we fix our haulsers on the land, ... Od.12.7.430.
At once descend, and press the desart sand; ... Od.12.8.430.
At once six mouths expands, at once six men devours. ... Od.12.124.437.
At once six mouths expands, at once six men devours. ... Od.12.124.437.
Sunk were at once the winds; the air above, ... Od.12.202.441.
And waves below, at once forgot to move! ... Od.12.203.441.
Plunge all at once their oars, and cleave the main. ... Od.12.217.442.
Now all at once tremendous scenes unfold; ... Od.12.240.443.
While yet I speak, at once their oars they seize, ... Od.12.264.445.
Better to rush at once to shades below, ... Od.12.415.451.
Tears up the deck; then all at once descends: ... Od.12.482.455.
At once into the main the crew it shook: ... Od.12.491.456.
Once more undaunted on the ruin rode, ... Od.12.525.458.
At once they bend, and strike their equal oars, ... Od.13.94.5.
'Till I beheld thy radiant form once more, ... Od.13.366.25.
Once more 'twas giv'n thee to behold thy coast: ... Od.13.388.25.
To you once more your own *Ulysses* bows; ... Od.13.409.26.
As lov'd *Ulysses* once more to embrace, ... Od.14.165.43.
To end at once the great *Arcesian* line. ... Od.14.211.45.
And Misery demands me once again. ... Od.14.376.53.
Once I was strong (wou'd heav'n restore those days) ... Od.14.526.62.
Was once my Sire: tho' now for ever lost ... Od.15.292.83.
Where once thy parents dwelt? or did they keep ... Od.15.416.89.
At once to pity and resent thy wrong. ... Od.16.94.107.
At once with grace divine his frame improves; ... Od.16.188.112.
At once with majesty enlarg'd he moves: ... Od.16.189.112.
Once more attend: When *she whose pow'r inspires ... Od.16.302.120.

ONCE (CONTINUED)

At once his vestures change; at once she sheds ... Od.16.478.130.
At once his vestures change; at once she sheds ... Od.16.478.130.
Once I enjoy'd in luxury of state ... Od.17.501.157.
Old as I am, should once my fury burn, ... Od.18.30.168.
Might see the sable field at once arise! ... Od.18.417.189.
Reduc'd to crave the good I once could give: ... Od.19.93.197.
But, Prince! for once at least believe a friend, ... Od.20.455.255.
Re-enter then, not all at once, but stay ... Od.21.246.271.
What once I was, whom wretched you despise; ... Od.21.303.274.
That ancient vigor, once my pride and boast. ... Od.21.468.283.
At once in brazen Panoply they shone, ... Od.22.130.293.
At once each servant brac'd his armour on; ... Od.22.131.293.
That courage, once the *Trojans* daily dread, ... Od.22.248.298.
Let each at once discharge the deadly dart, ... Od.22.276.300.
Then all at once their mingled lances threw, ... Od.22.280.300.
'Tis now (brave friends) our turn, at once to throw ... Od.22.288.300.
He spoke: at once their fiery lances flew: ... Od.22.292.300.
Once more the palace set in fair array, ... Od.22.491.313.
And burst at once in vengeance on the foes. ... Od.23.34.320.
Say, once more say, is my *Ulysses* here? ... Od.23.38.321.
At once they bathe, and dress in proud array; ... Od.23.140.327.
Once more *Ulysses* my belov'd in thee! ... Od.23.178.329.
And gulph'd in crouds at once the sailors dye, ... Od.23.252.335.
Your lives at once, and whelm beneath the deep? ... Od.24.135.354.
And pour at once the torrent of his soul? ... Od.24.278.363.
Sunk is the glory of this once-fam'd shore! ... Od.24.328.365.
Grief seiz'd at once, and wrapt up all the man; ... Od.24.368.366.
My strength were still, as once in better days; ... Od.24.436.369.
Or sink at once forgotten with the dead. ... Od.24.501.372.
At once the present and the future knew) ... Od.24.519.373.
The opening gates at once their war display: ... Od.24.578.375.

ONCE-FAM'D

Sunk is the glory of this once-fam'd shore! ... Od.24.328.365.

ONCE-FEAR'D

And fast beside him, once-fear'd *Edward* sleeps: ... 1.W-F.314.179.

ONCE-LOV'D

Ah then, thy once-lov'd *Eloisa* see! ... 2.ElAb.329.346.
Such were the Notes, thy once-lov'd Poet sung, ... 6.84.1.238.
Oh let thy once-lov'd Friend inscribe thy Stone, ... 6.85.7.242.
Let then thy once-lov'd Friend inscribe thy Stone, ... 6.85.7A.242.
Yet let thy once-lov'd Friend inscribe thy Stone, ... 6.85.7B.242.

ONCE-PROUD

Thy once-proud Hopes, presumptuous Prince! are fled; ... Il.8.202.407.

ONCE-STATELY

Of some once-stately Oak the last Remains, ... Il.23.401.506.

ONCHESTUS

Onchestus, Neptune's celebrated Groves; ... Il.2.600.156.

ONE

And in one Garland all their Beauties join; ... 1.PSu.56.76.
In whom all Beauties are compriz'd in One. ... 1.PSu.58.76.
While one his Mistress mourns, and one his Friend: ... 1.PAu.4A.80.
While one his Mistress mourns, and one his Friend: ... 1.PAu.4A.80.
One Leap from yonder Cliff shall end my Pains. ... 1.PAu.95.87.
The Steer and Lion at one Crib shall meet; ... 1.Mes.79.119.
One Tyde of Glory, one unclouded Blaze, ... 1.Mes.102.122.
One Tyde of Glory, one unclouded Blaze, ... 1.Mes.102.122.
The Young, the Old, one Instant makes our Prize, ... 1.W-F.109A.161.
The captive Race, one Instant makes our Prize, ... 1.W-F.109B.161.
Ten Censure wrong for one who Writes amiss; ... 1.EOC.6.239.
Now *One* in *Verse* makes many more in *Prose.* ... 1.EOC.8.239.
Unfinish'd Things, one knows not what to call, ... 1.EOC.42.243.
Or *one vain Wit's,* that might a hundred tire. ... 1.EOC.45.244.
Or *one vain Wit's,* that wou'd a hundred tire. ... 1.EOC.45A.244.
One *Science* only will one *Genius* fit; ... 1.EOC.60.245.
One *Science* only will one *Genius* fit; ... 1.EOC.60.245.
One *clear, unchang'd,* and *Universal* Light, ... 1.EOC.71.247.
That shunning Faults, one quiet *Tenour* keep; ... 1.EOC.241.267.
And All to one lov'd Folly Sacrifice. ... 1.EOC.266.270.
One *glaring Chaos* and *wild Heap* of *Wit:* ... 1.EOC.292.272.
And ten low Words oft creep in one dull Line, ... 1.EOC.347.278.
To *one small Sect,* and All are *damn'd beside.)* ... 1.EOC.397.285.
With one large eye my ample front is grac'd, ... 1.TrPA.108.370.
Like one who late unyok'd the sweating Steers. ... 1.TrVP.36.378.
And one whose tender Care if far above ... 1.TrVP.79.380.
One *Daphne* warm'd, and one the *Cretan* Dame; ... 1.TrSP.28.394.
One *Daphne* warm'd, and one the *Cretan* Dame; ... 1.TrSP.28.394.
Shall Fortune still in one sad Tenor run, ... 1.TrSP.71.397.
Sure 'twas not much to bid one kind Adieu, ... 1.TrSP.111.398.
One savage Heart, or teach it how to love? ... 1.TrSP.243.404.
And one of those who groan beneath the Sway ... 1.TrSt.230.420.
And live out all in one triumphant Day. ... 1.TrSt.452.429.
This rural Prince one only Daughter blest, ... 1.TrSt.670.438.
This *Argive* Prince one only Daughter blest, ... 1.TrSt.670A.438.
One Foot, one Inch, of the contended Field: ... 1.TrES.160.455.
One Foot, one Inch, of the contended Field: ... 1.TrES.160.455.
Shall *Jove,* for one, extend the narrow Span, ... 1.TrES.240.458.
One solid Comfort, our Eternal Wife, ... 2.ChJM.55.17.
And many Heads are wiser still than one; ... 2.ChJM.96.19.
One Caution yet is needful to be told, ... 2.ChJM.99.19.
Still one by one, in swift Succession, pass ... 2.ChJM.236.25.
Still one by one, in swift Succession, pass ... 2.ChJM.236.25.
And one had Grace, that wanted all the rest. ... 2.ChJM.241.26.
And one had Grace, yet wanted all the rest. ... 2.ChJM.241A.26.
One only Doubt remains; Full oft I've heard ... 2.ChJM.268.27.
One, that may do your Business to a Hair; ... 2.ChJM.286.28.
Th'obliging Dames obey'd with one Consent; ... 2.ChJM.410.34.
Cou'd live one Moment, absent from thy Arms? ... 2.ChJM.574.43.
Ere I my Fame by one lewd Act disgrace, ... 2.ChJM.589.43.

ONE (CONTINUED)

One only just, and righteous, hope to find: 2.ChJM.636.45.
Yet one good Woman is not to be found. 2.ChJM.638.46.
Yet one good Woman were not to be found. 2.ChJM.638A.46.
Call'd Women Fools, and knew full many a one? 2.ChJM.670.47.
Who only *Is*, and is but only *One*. 2.ChJM.681.47.
And one, whose Faith has ever sacred been. 2.ChJM.704.48.
As one whose Thoughts were on his Spouse intent; 2.ChJM.751.51.
And saw but one, 'tis thought, in all his Days; 2.ChWB.10.57.
More Wives than One by *Solomon* were try'd, 2.ChWB.21.57.
Paul, knowing One cou'd never serve our Turn, 2.ChWB.28.58.
One proper Gift, another grants to those: 2.ChWB.41.58.
One you shall quit—in spight of both your Eyes— 2.ChWB.128.62.
For not one Word in Man's Arrears am I. 2.ChWB.179.65.
"One of us two must rule, and one obey, 2.ChWB.192.65.
"One of us two must rule, and one obey, 2.ChWB.192.65.
For not one Word in their Arrears am I. 2.ChWB.179A.65.
A trusty Gossip, one dame *Alison*. 2.ChWB.266.69.
She—and my Neice—and one more worthy Wife 2.ChWB.272.70.
The Mouse that always trusts to one poor Hole, 2.ChWB.298.71.
For all their Lies) were in one Volume bound. 2.ChWB.358.74.
That not one Woman keeps her Marriage Vow. 2.ChWB.375.75.
Thro' Hatred one, and one thro' too much Love; 2.ChWB.402.76.
Thro' Hatred one, and one thro' too much Love; 2.ChWB.402.76.
And with one Buffet fell'd him on the Floor. 2.ChWB.416.77.
One fatal stroke the sacred Hair does sever 2.RL*A*1.117.130.
If e'er one Vision touch'd thy infant Thought, 2.RL1.29.147.
If e'er one Vision touch thy infant Thought, 2.RL1.29A.147.
To one Man's Treat, but for another's Ball? 2.RL1.96.152.
One speaks the Glory of the *British Queen*, 2.RL3.13.170.
And one describes a charming *Indian Screen*; 2.RL3.14.170.
Gain'd but one Trump and one *Plebeian* Card. 2.RL3.54.172.
Gain'd but one Trump and one *Plebeian* Card. 2.RL3.54.172.
Puts forth one manly Leg, to sight reveal'd; 2.RL3.57.172.
In Heaps on Heaps; one Fate o'erwhelms them all. 2.RL3.86.174.
On one nice *Trick* depends the gen'ral Fate. 2.RL3.94.174.
Here living *Teapots* stand, one Arm held out, 2.RL4.49.188.
One bent; the Handle this, and that the Spout: 2.RL4.50.188.
Or who would learn one earthly Thing of Use? 2.RL5.22.200.
One dy'd in *Metaphor*, and one in *Song*. 2.RL5.60.204.
One dy'd in *Metaphor*, and one in *Song*. 2.RL5.60.204.
She with one Finger and a Thumb subdu'd: 2.RL5.80.206.
There, at one Passage, oft you might survey 2.TemF.489.287.
One came, methought, and whisper'd in my Ear; 2.TemF.498.287.
And, all those tender names in one, thy love! 2.ElAb.154.332.
One thought of thee puts all the pomp to flight, 2.ElAb.273.342.
Come, with one glance of those deluding eyes, 2.ElAb.283.343.
Nor share one pang of all I felt for thee. 2.ElAb.292.343.
May one kind grave unite each hapless name, 2.ElAb.343.347.
One human tear shall drop, and be forgiv'n. 2.ElAb.358.348.
Nor left one virtue to redeem her Race. 2.Elegy.28.365.
Life's idle business at one gasp be o'er, 2.Elegy.81.368.
See worlds on worlds compose one universe, 3.EOM1.24.16.
A thousand movements scarce one purpose gain; 3.EOM1.54.20.
In God's, one single can its end produce; 3.EOM1.55.20.
Towns to one grave, whole nations to the deep? 3.EOM1.144.33.
Towns to one grave, a Nation to the deep? 3.EOM1.144A.33.
Towns to one grave, and Nations to the deep? 3.EOM1.144B.33.
Towns to one grave, or Nations to the deep? 3.EOM1.144C.33.
Is not thy Reason all these pow'rs in one? 3.EOM1.232.44.
Is not thy Reason all those pow'rs in one? 3.EOM1.232A.44.
Where, one step broken, the great scale's destroy'd: 3.EOM1.244.45.
The least confusion but in one, not all 3.EOM1.249.46.
All are but parts of one stupendous whole, 3.EOM1.267.47.
Safe in the hand of one disposing Pow'r, 3.EOM1.287.50.
One truth is clear, "Whatever IS, is RIGHT." 3.EOM1.294.51.
Describe or fix one movement of his Mind? 3.EOM2.36.60.
Describe or fix one movement of the Soul? 3.EOM2.36A.60.
Describe or fix one movement of his Mind? 3.EOM2.36B.60.
Self-love and Reason to one end aspire, 3.EOM2.87.65.
And hence one master Passion in the breast, 3.EOM2.131.70.
And in one interest body acts with mind. 3.EOM2.180.76.
But HEAV'N's great view is One, and that the Whole: 3.EOM2.238.84.
'Till one Man's weakness grows the strength of all. 3.EOM2.252.85.
Not one will change his neighbor with himself. 3.EOM2.262.87.
One prospect lost, another still we gain; 3.EOM2.289.89.
See! and confess, one comfort still must rise, 3.EOM2.293.90.
"Acts to one end, but acts by various laws." 3.EOM3.2.92.
Press to one centre still, the gen'ral Good. 3.EOM3.14.93.
See, lifeless Matter moving to one End 3.EOM3.9A.93.
One all-extending, all-preserving Soul 3.EOM3.22.94.
Who thinks all made for one, not one for all. 3.EOM3.48.97.
Who thinks all made for one, not one for all. 3.EOM3.48.97.
All feed on one vain Patron, and enjoy 3.EOM3.61.98.
One must go right, the other may go wrong. 3.EOM3.94.101.
One in their nature, which are two in ours, 3.EOM3.96.101.
Or pours profuse on earth; one nature feeds 3.EOM3.117.104.
Each sex desires alike, 'till two are one. 3.EOM3.122.104.
Still as one brood, and as another rose, 3.EOM3.139.107.
Thus as one brood, and as another rose, 3.EOM3.139A.107.
Here rose one little state; another near 3.EOM3.201.113.
'Till common int'rest plac'd the sway in one. 3.EOM3.210.114.
One great first father, and that first ador'd. 3.EOM3.226.115.
And simple Reason never sought but one: 3.EOM3.230.115.
Th' enormous faith of many made for one; 3.EOM3.242.117.
To one Man's pow'r, ambition, lucre, lust: 3.EOM3.270.120.
For, what one likes if others like as well, 3.EOM3.273.120.
What serves one will, when many wills rebel? 3.EOM3.274.120.
That touching one must strike the other too; 3.EOM3.292.122.
Draw to one point, and to one centre bring 3.EOM3.301.123.
Draw to one point, and to one centre bring 3.EOM3.301.123.
All must be false that thwart this One great End, 3.EOM3.309.125.
And one regards Itself, and one the Whole. 3.EOM3.316.126.
And one regards Itself, and one the Whole. 3.EOM3.316.126.
One grants his Pleasure is but Rest from pain, 3.EOM4.28Z1.130.
One doubts of All, one owns ev'n Virtue vain. 3.EOM4.28Z2.130.

ONE (CONTINUED)

One doubts of All, one owns ev'n Virtue vain. 3.EOM4.28Z2.130.
Subsist not in the good of one, but all. 3.EOM4.38.131.
One common blessing, as one common soul. 3.EOM4.62.134.
One common blessing, as one common soul. 3.EOM4.62.134.
One they must want, which is, to pass for good. 3.EOM4.92.137.
One thinks on Calvin Heav'n's own spirit fell, 3.EOM4.137.141.
What shocks one part will edify the rest, 3.EOM4.141.141.
Nor with one system can they all be blest. 3.EOM4.142.141.
One flaunts in rags, one flutters in brocade, 3.EOM4.196.145.
One flaunts in rags, one flutters in brocade, 3.EOM4.196.145.
Not one looks backward, onward still be goes, 3.EOM4.223.148.
One self-approving hour whole years out-weighs 3.EOM4.255.152.
Never elated, while one man's oppress'd; 3.EOM4.323.159.
In one close system of Benevolence: 3.EOM4.358.163.
That REASON, PASSION, answer one great aim; 3.EOM4.395.166.
While one there is that charms us with his Spleen. 3.Ep1.121A.24.
His constant Bounty no one friend has made; 3.Ep1.198A.32.
His constant Bounty no one friend had made; 3.Ep1.198B.32.
To ease the Soul of one oppressive weight, 3.Ep1.57.19.
One action Conduct; one, heroic Love. 3.Ep1.86.21.
One action Conduct; one, heroic Love. 3.Ep1.86.21.
While one there is who charms us with his Spleen. 3.Ep1.121.24.
Grown all to all, from no one vice exempt, 3.Ep1.194.31.
In this one Passion man can strength enjoy, 3.Ep1.222.34.
For one puff more, and in that puff expires. 3.Ep1.241.36.
"One would not, sure, be frightful when one's dead— 3.Ep1.246.36.
How many pictures of one Nymph we view, 3.Ep2.5.48.
Let then the Fair one beautifully cry, 3.Ep2.11.49.
Finds all her life one warfare upon earth: 3.Ep2.118.60.
By Wealth of Follow'rs! without one distress 3.Ep2.145.62.
But never, never, reach'd one gen'rous Thought. 3.Ep2.162.64.
Of all her Dears she never slander'd one, 3.Ep2.175.64.
One certain Portrait may (I grant) be seen, 3.Ep2.181.64.
Nor leave one sigh behind them when they die. 3.Ep2.230.68.
Poor Avarice one torment more would find; 3.Ep3.47.90.
Congenial souls! whose life one Av'rice joins, 3.Ep3.133.104.
And one fate buries in th' Asturian Mines. 3.Ep3.134.104.
Ask we what makes one keep, and one bestow? 3.Ep3.165.107.
Ask we what makes one keep, and one bestow? 3.Ep3.165.107.
One solid dish his week-day meal affords, 3.Ep3.345.122.
In one abundant show'r of Cent. per Cent., 3.Ep3.372.123.
There (so the Dev'l ordain'd) one Christmas-tide 3.Ep3.383.124.
And one more Pensioner St. Stephen gains. 3.Ep3.394.124.
And of one beauty many blunders make; 3.Ep4.28.140.
One boundless Green, or flourish'd Carpet views, 3.Ep4.95.146.
Bond is but one, but *Harpax* is a Score. 4.HS1.44.9.
Like in all else, as one Egg to another. 4.HS1.50.9.
One whom the mob, when next we find or make 4.JD4.34.29.
The suit, if by the fashion one might guess, 4.JD4.40.29.
He forms one Tongue exotic and refin'd. 4.JD4.49.29.
And (all those Plagues in one) the bawling Bar; 4.JD4.55.29.
"I have but one, I hope the Fellow's clean." 4.JD4.111.35.
As one of *Woodward's* Patients, sick and sore, 4.JD4.152.37.
Run out as fast, as one that pays his Bail, 4.JD4.182A.41.
One of our Giant *Statutes* ope its Jaw! 4.JD4.173.41.
Ran out as fast, as one that pays his Bail, 4.JD4.182.41.
Or should one Pound of Powder less bespread 4.JD4.246.47.
Just as one Beauty mortifies another. 4.JD4.259.47.
Hear Bethel's Sermon, one not vers'd in schools, 4.HS2.9.55.
To one that was, or would have been a Peer. 4.HS2.40.57.
About one Vice, and fall into the other: 4.HS2.46.57.
One half-pint bottle serves them both to dine, 4.HS2.53.59.
Nor stops, for one bad Cork, his Butler's pay, 4.HS2.63.59.
And all the Man is one intestine war) 4.HS2.72.59.
Thou hast at least bestow'd one penny well. 4.HS2.110.63.
How dar'st thou let one worthy man be poor? 4.HS2.118.63.
Well, if the Use be mine, can it concern one 4.HS2.165.69.
And thirsts and hungers only at one End: 4.HAdv.24.77.
And one is fired by Heads, and one by Tails; 4.HAdv.36.79.
And one is fired by Heads, and one by Tails; 4.HAdv.36.79.
One bleeds in Person, and one bleeds in Purse; 4.HAdv.58.81.
One bleeds in Person, and one bleeds in Purse; 4.HAdv.58.81.
Who shames a Scribler? break one cobweb thro', 4.Arbu.89.102.
Does not one Table *Bavius* still admit? 4.Arbu.99.102.
Still to one Bishop *Philips* seem a Wit? 4.Arbu.100.102.
Scriblers like Spiders, break one cobweb thro', 4.Arbu.89A.102.
Does not one Table Arnall still admit? 4.Arbu.99A.102.
"But Foes like these!"—One Flatt'rer's worse than all; 4.Arbu.104.103.
One dedicates, in high Heroic prose, 4.Arbu.109.103.
One from all *Grubstreet* will my fame defend, 4.Arbu.111.103.
"But all these foes!"—One Flatt'rer's worse than all; 4.Arbu.104A.103.
Ammon's great Son one shoulder had too high, 4.Arbu.117.104.
With open arms receiv'd one Poet more. 4.Arbu.142.106.
Yet ne'r one sprig of Laurel grac'd these ribalds, 4.Arbu.163.108.
Peace to all such! but were there One whose fires 4.Arbu.193.109.
That tends to make one worthy Man my foe, 4.Arbu.284.116.
And he himself one vile Antithesis. 4.Arbu.325.119.
Not proud, nor servile, be one Poet's praise 4.Arbu.336.120.
Nor proud, nor servile, be one Poet's praise 4.Arbu.336A.120.
To please a *Mistress*, One aspers'd his life; 4.Arbu.376.124.
And keep a while one Parent from the Sky! 4.Arbu.413.127.
One supreme State, so excellently ill; 4.JD2A.4.132.
One the most meagre of the hungry Train 4.JD2A.13.132.
One Giant-Vice, so excellently ill, 4.JD2.4.133.
That all beside one pities, not abhors; 4.JD2.5.133.
One sings the Fair; but Songs no longer move, 4.JD2.21.133.
One, one man only breeds my just offence; 4.JD2.45.137.
One, one man only breeds my just offence; 4.JD2.45.137.
That all beneath one pities, not abhors; 4.JD2.5A.133.
One wou'd move Love; by Rhymes; but Verses charms 4.JD2A.23.134.
Stop, or turn nonsense at one glance of Thee? 4.HOde1.40.153.
Stop, or turn nonsense at one glance from Thee? 4.HOde1.40A.153.
Tir'd with a tedious March, one luckless night, 4.2HE2.35.167.
In one our Frolicks, one Amusements end, 4.2HE2.74.171.
In one our Frolicks, one Amusements end, 4.2HE2.74.171.

ONE (CONTINUED)

In one a Mistress drops, in one a Friend: 4.2HE2.75.171.
In one a Mistress drops, in one a Friend: 4.2HE2.75.171.
One likes the Pheasant's wing, and one the leg; 4.2HE2.84.171.
One likes the Pheasant's wing, and one the leg; 4.2HE2.84.171.
There's a Rehearsal, Sir, exact at One.— 4.2HE2.97.171.
Not quite so well however as one ought; 4.2HE2.100.171.
One lull'd th' *Exchequer*, and one stunn'd the *Rolls;* 4.2HE2.130.173.
One lull'd th' *Exchequer*, and one stunn'd the *Rolls;* 4.2HE2.130.173.
Dear *Cibber!* never match'd one Ode of thine. 4.2HE2.138.175.
Say, can you find out one such Lodger there? 4.2HE2.223.181.
Why, of two Brothers, rich and restless one 4.2HE2.270.183.
Why one like *Bu—* with Pay and Scorn content, 4.2HE2.274.185.
One, driv'n by strong Benevolence of Soul, 4.2HE2.276.185.
'Tis one thing madly to disperse my store, 4.2HE2.292.185.
When, of a hundred thorns, you pull out one? 4.2HE2.321.187.
Just in one instance, be it yet confest 4.2HE1.31.197.
One likes no language but the Faery Queen; 4.2HE1.39.197.
"Not one but nods, and talks of Johnson's Art, 4.2HE1.82.201.
One Simile, that solitary shines 4.2HE1.111.205.
One Tragic sentence if I dare deride 4.2HE1.121.205.
Now Times are chang'd, and one Poetick Itch 4.2HE1.169.209.
One knighted Blackmore, and one pension'd Quarles; 4.2HE1.387.227.
One knighted Blackmore, and one pension'd Quarles; 4.2HE1.387.227.
Thus good, or bad, to one extreme betray 4.1HE6.24.239.
Shall One whom Nature, Learning, Birth, conspir'd 4.1HE6.40.239.
But art thou one, whom new opinions sway, 4.1HE6.63.241.
One, who believes as Tindal leads the way, 4.1HE6.64.241.
Add one round hundred, and (if that's not fair) 4.1HE6.75.241.
Or if your life be one continu'd Treat, 4.1HE6.110.245.
Or if our life be one continu'd Treat, 4.1HE6.110A.245.
And, Mr. Dean, one word from you— 4.HS6.82.255.
'Tis one to me—"Then tell us, pray, 4.HS6.119.257.
"As sweet a Cave as one shall see! 4.HS6.175.261.
And not to every one that comes, 4.1HE7.23.269.
And kept you up so oft till one; 4.1HE7.48.271.
Which one belonging to the House 4.1HE7.55.271.
Nor one that Temperance advance, 4.1HE7.61.273.
('Tis Reason's voice, which sometimes one can hear) 4.1HE1.12.279.
Alike in nothing but one Lust of Gold, 4.1HE1.124.289.
But show me one, who has it in his pow'r 4.1HE1.136.289.
(They know not whither) in a Chaise and one; 4.1HE1.158.291.
One ebb and flow of follies all my Life) 4.1HE1.168.291.
You never change one muscle of your face, 4.1HE1.171.291.
He thinks one Poet of no venal kind. 4.EpS1.34A.300.
Come harmless *Characters* that no one hit, 4.EpS1.65.302.
Show there was one who held it in disdain. 4.EpS1.172.309.
Ye Statesmen, Priests, of one Religion all! 4.EpS2.16.314.
To *Cato, Virgil* pay'd one honest line; 4.EpS2.120.320.
Knew one a Man of Honour, one a Knave; 4.EpS2.153.322.
Knew one a Man of Honour, one a Knave; 4.EpS2.153.322.
If one, thro' Nature's Bounty or his Lord's, 4.EpS2.173.323.
Whose wit and equally provoke one, 4.1740.27.333.
Amaz'd that one can read, that one can write: 4.1740.34.333.
Amaz'd that one can read, that one can write: 4.1740.34.333.
The wisdom of the one and other chair, 4.1740.60.335.
Alas! on one alone our all relies, 4.1740.85.337.
And one man's honesty redeem the land. 4.1740.98.337.
Here in one bed two shiv'ring sisters lye, 5.DunA1.31.63.
Here one poor Word a hundred clenches makes, 5.DunA1.61.67.
But liv'd, in Settle's numbers, one day more. 5.DunA1.88.69.
Yet liv'd, in Settle's numbers, one day more. 5.DunA1.88A.69.
One clasp'd in wood, and one in strong cow-hide. 5.DunA1.130.80.
One clasp'd in wood, and one in strong cow-hide. 5.DunA1.130.80.
Nor sleeps one error in its father's grave, 5.DunA1.162.82.
In one quick flash see Proserpine expire, 5.DunA1.209.87.
Never was dash'd out, at one lucky hit, 5.DunA2.43.101.
(Tho' one his son dissuades, and one his wife) 5.DunA2.160.121.
(Tho' one his son dissuades, and one his wife) 5.DunA2.160.121.
Now thousand tongues are heard in one loud din: 5.DunA2.227.128.
Then mount the clerks; and in one lazy tone, 5.DunA2.355.143.
One circle first, and then a second makes, 5.DunA2.374.146.
Like motion, from one circle to the rest; 5.DunA2.376.146.
One man immortal all that pride confounds, 5.DunA3.67.156.
And one bright blaze turns Learning into air. 5.DunA3.70.156.
One god-like Monarch all that pride confounds, 5.DunA3.67A.156.
See Christians, Jews, one heavy sabbath keep; 5.DunA3.91.157.
But O! with one, immortal One dispense, 5.DunA3.215.175.
But O! with one, immortal One dispense, 5.DunA3.215.175.
Till one wide Conflagration swallows all. 5.DunA3.236.177.
Lo! one vast Egg produces human race. 5.DunA3.244.177.
As one by one, at dread Medæa's strain, 5.DunA3.341.192.
As one by one, at dread Medæa's strain, 5.DunA3.341.192.
Clos'd one by one to everlasting rest; 5.DunA3.344.192.
Clos'd one by one to everlasting rest; 5.DunA3.344.192.
One Cell there is, conceal'd from vulgar eye, 5.DunB1.33.271.
Here one poor word an hundred clenches makes, 5.DunB1.63.274.
But liv'd, in Settle's numbers, one day more. 5.DunB1.90.276.
One clasp'd in wood, and one in strong cow-hide; 5.DunB1.150.281.
One clasp'd in wood, and one in strong cow-hide; 5.DunB1.150.281.
Never was dash'd out, at one lucky hit, 5.DunB2.47.298.
One on his manly confidence relies, 5.DunB2.169.304.
One on his vigour and superior size. 5.DunB2.170.304.
Now thousand tongues are heard in one loud din: 5.DunB2.235.307.
With holy envy gave one Layman place. 5.DunB2.324.313.
Then mount the Clerks, and in one lazy tone 5.DunB2.387.316.
One circle first, and then a second makes; 5.DunB2.406.317.
Like motion from one circle to the rest; 5.DunB2.408.317.
One god-like Monarch all that pride confounds, 5.DunB3.75.324.
And one bright blaze turns Learning into air. 5.DunB3.78.324.
See Christians, Jews, one heavy sabbath keep, 5.DunB3.99.324.
But oh! with One, immortal one dispense, 5.DunB3.217.331.
But oh! with One, immortal one dispense, 5.DunB3.217.331.
'Till one wide conflagration swallows all. 5.DunB3.240.332.
Lo! one vast Egg produces human race. 5.DunB3.248.332.
Yet, yet a moment, one dim Ray of Light 5.DunB4.1.339.

ONE (CONTINUED)

One Trill shall harmonize joy, grief, and rage, 5.DunB4.57.347.
One instinct seizes, and transports away. 5.DunB4.74.348.
Whate'er of mungril no one class admits, 5.DunB4.89.349.
Milton's on this, on that one Johnston's name. 5.DunB4.112.352.
We hang one jingling padlock on the mind: 5.DunB4.162.357.
O! if my sons may learn one earthly thing, 5.DunB4.183.360.
Teach but that one, sufficient for a King; 5.DunB4.184.360.
Nor has one Atterbury spoil'd the flock. 5.DunB4.246.367.
We bring to one dead level ev'ry mind. 5.DunB4.268.370.
The Sire saw, one by one, his Virtues wake: 5.DunB4.285.372.
The Sire saw, one by one, his Virtues wake: 5.DunB4.285.372.
This glorious Youth, and add one Venus more. 5.DunB4.330.375.
Blest in one Niger, till he knows of two." 5.DunB4.370.379.
Such vary'd light in one promiscuous blaze? 5.DunB4.412.382.
Or, at one bound o'er-leaping all his laws, 5.DunB4.477.388.
Sire, Ancestors, Himself. One casts his eyes 5.DunB4.519.394.
Which no one looks in with another's eyes: 5.DunB4.534.394.
Another (for in all what one can shine?) 5.DunB4.555.397.
To three essential Partriges in one? 5.DunB4.562.397.
Nor past the meanest unregarded, one 5.DunB4.575.399.
Rose a Gregorian, one a Gormogon. 5.DunB4.576.399.
Proud to my list to add one Monarch more; 5.DunB4.600.403.
And make one Mighty Dunciad of the Land " 5.DunB4.604.403.
Strive to my list to add one Monarch more; 5.DunB4.600A.403.
As one by one, at dread Medea's strain, 5.DunB4.635.407.
As one by one, at dread Medea's strain, 5.DunB4.635.407.
Clos'd one by one to everlasting rest; 5.DunB4.638.407.
Clos'd one by one to everlasting rest; 5.DunB4.638.407.
So from one cloud soft show'rs we view, 6.5.9.12.
'Twas one vast Nothing, All, and All slept fast in thee. 6.8.3.17.
In one more various Animal combin'd, 6.8.8.17.
Since your Acquaintance with one *Brocas,* 6.10.9.24.
(For so one sure may call that Head, 6.10.27.25.
I but lug out to one or two 6.10.31.25.
When was it known one Bard did follow 6.10.39.25.
And one may say of *Dryden* too, 6.10.93.27.
One of our Dogs is dead and gone, 6.10.111.27.
"But ho! our Nephew," (crieth one,) 6.14i.11.42.
But sets up One, a greater, in their Place; 6.19.38.63.
The monarch dies—one moment's turn destroys 6.22.10.71.
Fix'd to one side, but mod'rate to the rest; 6.27.4.81.
All these were join'd in one, yet fail'd to save 6.27.7.81.
Chim'd in so smoothly, one by one, 6.30.11.86.
Chim'd in so smoothly, one by one, 6.30.11.86.
To run so smoothly, one by one 6.30.11A.86.
To run so smoothly, one by one 6.30.11A.86.
For only one in *Tom Durfeius.* 6.30.33.87.
The People one, and one supplies the King. 6.35.34.104.
The People one, and one supplies the King. 6.35.34.104.
Prodigious this! the Frail one of our Play 6.41.1.113.
As Spiritual one, as the other is Carnal), 6.42i.6.116.
One day it will be no disgrace, 6.42v.5.119.
Yet takes one kiss before she parts for ever: 6.45.6.124.
Then give one flirt, and all the vision flies. 6.45.38.125.
Part you with one, and I'll renounce the other. 6.46.4.127.
If you'l but give up one, I'll give up tother. 6.46.4A.127.
And not one Muse of all he fed, 6.47.27.129.
Whose fragrant Wit revives, as one may say, 6.48ii.3.134.
But were there One whom better Stars conspire 6.49iii.7.142.
But should there One whose better Stars conspire 6.49iii.7A.142.
Should such a One, too fond to Reign alone, 6.49iii.11A.142.
Should such a One, resolv'd to Reign alone, 6.49iii.11C.142.
Who but must Grieve if such a One there be? 6.49iii.29B.143.
If I condemn one Sect or part 6.50.29A.147.
One Chorus let all Being raise! 6.50.51.148.
And burn for ever one; 6.51ii.22.153.
What various joys on one attend, 6.51ii.27.153.
One dip the pencil, and one string the lyre. 6.52.70.158.
One dip the pencil, and one string the lyre. 6.52.70.158.
Finds not one moment he cou'd wish away, 6.55.6.166.
Fix'd to one side, but mod'rate to the rest; 6.57.4.169.
Read this, e'er you translate one Bit 6.58.3.170.
Read this ere ye translate one Bit 6.58.3A.170.
John Dunton, Steel, or any one. 6.58.52.173.
Shall join with *F[rowde]* in one Accord, 6.58.63.173*.
Let no One Fool engross it, or confine: 6.60.31.179.
Let no One Man engross it, or confine: 6.60.31A.179.
To one fair Lady out of court 6.61.1.180.
One that should be a Saint, 6.68.1.196.
and one that's a Sinner, 6.68.2.196.
And one that pays reckning 6.68.3.196.
In one short view subjected to your eye 6.71.33.203.
To gain Pescennius one employs his schemes, 6.71.39.203.
In one short view subjected to our eye 6.71.33A.203.
One grasps a Cecrops in ecstatic dreams; 6.71.40.204.
One grateful woman to thy fame supplies 6.72.7.208.
One Grateful woman to thy fame supply'd 6.72.7A.208.
Who to be savd by one, must damn the rest. 6.82ix(b).2.234.
As one Hog lives on what another sh—. 6.82ix(e).2.235.
Tho' distanc't one by one th' Oblig'd desert, 6.84.31Z5.239.
Tho' distanc't one by one th' Oblig'd desert, 6.84.31Z5.239.
Thro' Fortune's Cloud One truly Great can see, 6.84.39.240.
One truly Great thro' Fortune's Cloud can see, 6.84.31Z11.240.
One day I mean to Fill Sir Godfry's tomb, 6.88.1.249.
Yes she has one, I must aver: 6.89.10.250.
The Muse this one Verse to learn'd Pigot addresses, 6.92.1.255.
The Simile yet one thing shocks, 6.93.27Z5.257.
Better two Heads than one; 6.94.86.262.
O may the King that one Neglect forgive, 6.96iv.91.279.
Yet ne'er one Sprig of Laurel grac'd those Ribbalds, 6.98.13.283.
Peace to all such! but were there one, whose Fires 6.98.43.284.
Maul'd human *Wit* in one thick Satyr, 6.101.9.290.
'Tis ten to one he'll ne'er come back. 6.103.4.295.
If *France* excel him in one free-born thought, 6.107.25.311.
Go, where to love and to enjoy are one! 6.109.16.314.

ONE (CONTINUED)

Has but one way to teaze—by *Law*. ... 6.116ii.5.326.
Let's rather wait one year for better luck; ... 6.116v.3.327.
One year may make a singing Swan of *Duck*. ... 6.116v.4.327.
Of one so poor you cannot take the law; ... 6.116vii.5.328.
On one so old your sword you scorn to draw. ... 6.116vii.6.328.
The Sense and Taste of one that bears ... 6.119.15.337.
Alas! one bad Example shown, ... 6.119.17.337.
The wit & sense of one who bears ... 6.119.15A.337.
Alas! one ill Example shown, ... 6.119.17C.337.
Yet this, like their old one, for nothing will spare, ... 6.122.19.342.
'*she*. Yes, we have liv'd— one pang, and then we part! ... 6.123.1.343.
Is there on earth one Care, one Wish beside? ... 6.123.7.344.
Is there on earth one Care, one Wish beside? ... 6.123.7.344.
One equal course how Guilt and Greatness ran, ... 6.130.3.358.
Alas what *wealth,* which no one act of fame ... 6.130.13.358.
Or add one Patriot to a sinking state; ... 6.132.4.362.
One half will never be believ'd, ... 6.133.3.363.
Sure *Bounce* is one you never read of. ... 6.135.8.366.
A hundred Sons! and not one *Fop*. ... 6.135.48.368.
Not one true *Bounce* will be a Thief; ... 6.135.50.368.
Not one without Permission feed, ... 6.135.51.368.
One ushers Friends to *Bathurst's* Door; ... 6.135.63.368.
One fawns, at *Oxford's,* on the Poor. ... 6.135.64.368.
Nor one without Permission feed, ... 6.135.51A.368.
In peace let one poor Poet sleep, ... 6.138.2.376.
But never, never, reach'd one gen'rous Thought. ... 6.139.6.377.
Of all her Dears she never slander'd one, ... 6.139.19.377.
Lies one who ne'er car'd, and who cares not a Pin, ... 6.144.5A.386.
Lies one who ne'er car'd, and still cares not a Pin, ... 6.144.5B.386.
With not one sin but poetry, ... 6.150.2.398.
(Without a blot) to eighty one. ... 6.150.4.398.
Finds all her Life one Warfare upon Earth; ... 6.154.4.402.
By Wealth, of Followers; without one Distress, ... 6.154.31.403.
worship of one ... 6.155.8Z5.404*.
Suppliant the Goddess stood: One Hand she plac'd ... Il.1.650.118.
Beneath his Beard, and one his Knees embrac'd. ... Il.1.651.118.
Nor let one Sail be hoisted on the Main. ... Il.2.202.137.
To One sole Monarch *Jove* commits the Sway; ... Il.2.243.139.
One Eye was blinking, and one Leg was lame: ... Il.2.264.140.
One Eye was blinking, and one Leg was lame: ... Il.2.264.140.
And, one short Month, endure the Wintry Main? ... Il.2.357.144.
One was *Amphimachus,* and *Thalpius* one; ... Il.2.755.161.
One was *Amphimachus,* and *Thalpius* one; ... Il.2.755.161.
Troy yet may wake, and one avenging Blow ... Il.3.83.193.
As one unskill'd or dumb, he seem'd to stand, ... Il.3.281.207.
One bold on Foot, and one renown'd for Horse. ... Il.3.304.208.
One bold on Foot, and one renown'd for Horse. ... Il.3.304.208.
One House contain'd us, as one Mother bore. ... Il.3.306.208.
One House contain'd us, as one Mother bore. ... Il.3.306.208.
Sprung, with thy self, from one Cělestial Sire, ... Il.4.84.224.
One from a hundred feather'd Deaths he chose, ... Il.4.148.228.
And one prodigious Ruin swallow All. ... Il.4.199.230.
In one firm Orb the Bands were rang'd around, ... Il.4.312.235.
He spar'd but one to bear the dreadful Tale. ... Il.4.449.241.
Thus fell two Heroes; one the Pride of *Thrace,* ... Il.4.624.250.
And one the Leader of th' *Epeian* Race; ... Il.4.625.250.
And flatted Vineyards, one sad Waste appear; ... Il.5.121.273.
Two Sons of *Priam* in one Chariot ride, ... Il.5.204.276.
One Chief at least beneath this Arm shall die; ... Il.5.320.282.
That both shall fall by one victorious Hand; ... Il.5.323.282.
Ye scape not both; One, headlong from his Car, ... Il.5.349.283.
Or one vast Burst of all-involving Fate ... Il.5.594.296.
Beneath one Foot the yet-warm Corps he prest, ... Il.5.768.303.
Add one more Ghost to *Pluto's* gloomy Reign. ... Il.5.813.305.
Not one of all the Race, not Sex, nor Age, ... Il.6.71.327.
Not one of all the Race, nor Sex, nor Age, ... Il.6.71A.327.
One Hour demands me in the *Trojan* Wall, ... Il.6.139.330.
With two brave Sons and one fair Daughter bless'd; ... Il.6.242.338.
She, with one Maid of all her Menial Train, ... Il.6.465.349.
So shall my Days in one sad Tenor run, ... Il.6.520.352.
In one sad Day beheld the Gates of Hell; ... Il.6.535.353.
And trembling all before one hostile Hand; ... Il.7.156.372.
And sends thee One, a Sample of her Host. ... Il.7.280.378.
Here, where on one promiscuous Pile they blaz'd, ... Il.7.404.384.
All *Greece,* encompass'd, in one Blaze expires. ... Il.8.223.408.
But who to meet one martial Man is found, ... Il.8.280.410.
Gods! shall one raging Hand thus level All? ... Il.8.429.417.
Who dares think one thing, and another tell, ... Il.9.412.452.
Nor did my fair one less Distinction claim; ... Il.9.452.454.
One only valu'd Gift your Tyrant gave, ... Il.9.481.456.
One Stratagem has fail'd, and others will ... Il.9.548.460.
Yet hear one word, and lodge it in thy Heart, ... Il.9.721.470.
Burns with one Love, with one Resentment glows; ... Il.9.726.470.
Burns with one Love, with one Resentment glows; ... Il.9.726.470.
One should our Int'rests, and our Passions be; ... Il.9.727.470.
One Woman-Slave was ravish'd from thy Arms: ... Il.9.751.471.
By fits one Flash succeeds, as one expires, ... Il.10.9.2.
By fits one Flash succeeds, as one expires, ... Il.10.9.2.
In one great Day, by one great Arm atchiev'd, ... Il.10.56.4.
In one great Day, by one great Arm atchiev'd, ... Il.10.56.4.
And one brave Hero fans another's Fire. ... Il.10.268.13.
One Instant snatch'd his trembling Soul to Hell, ... Il.10.526.26.
The Product one of Marriage, one of Love; ... Il.11.138.41.
The Product one of Marriage, one of Love; ... Il.11.138.41.
And one refulgent Ruin levells all. ... Il.11.204.44.
Tow'ring they rode in one refulgent Car: ... Il.11.426.53.
Not so this Dart, which thou may'st one day feel; ... Il.11.499.56.
And add one Spectre to the Realms below! ... Il.11.557.58.
Strong as he is; yet, one oppos'd to all, ... Il.11.586.60.
And one great Day destroy, and bury all! ... Il.12.80.84.
In one promiscuous Carnage crush'd and bruis'd, ... Il.12.84.84.
And one bright Waste hides all the Works of Men: ... Il.12.340.93.
One Foot, one Inch, of the contended Field: ... Il.12.514.100.
One Foot, one Inch, of the contended Field: ... Il.12.514.100.
And one black Day clouds all her former Fame. ... Il.13.136.111.

ONE (CONTINUED)

Gods of one Source, of one ethereal Race, ... Il.13.445.126.
Gods of one Source, of one ethereal Race, ... Il.13.445.126.
See! on one *Greek* three *Trojan* Ghosts attend, ... Il.13.560.133.
One Table fed you, and one Roof contain'd. ... Il.13.587.134.
One Table fed you, and one Roof contain'd. ... Il.13.587.134.
He spoke, and all as with one Soul obey'd; ... Il.13.614.135.
Join'd to one Yoke, the stubborn Earth they tear, ... Il.13.881.147.
And one devouring Vengeance swallow all. ... Il.13.974.152.
Jove sends one Gust, and bids them roll away. ... Il.14.26.158.
Against your King, nor will one Chief engage? ... Il.14.56.160.
For know, thy lov'd one shall be ever thine, ... Il.14.303.177.
Let the great Parent Earth one Hand sustain, ... Il.14.307.177.
That she, my lov'd one, shall be ever mine, ... Il.14.311.177.
One Hero's Loss too tamely you deplore, ... Il.14.427.184.
(One brac'd his Shield, and one sustain'd his Sword.) ... Il.14.468.186.
(One brac'd his Shield, and one sustain'd his Sword.) ... Il.14.468.186.
Nor one of all the heav'nly Host engage ... Il.15.79.199.
And one vast Ruin whelm th' *Olympian* State. ... Il.15.155.202.
One to the bold *Bœotians* ever dear, ... Il.15.374.211.
And one *Menestheus'* Friend, and fam'd Compeer. ... Il.15.375.211.
Stretch'd on one Heap, the Victors spoil the slain. ... Il.15.389.212.
One *Greek* enrich'd thy Shrine with offer'd Gore; ... Il.15.429.214.
At one proud Bark, high-tow'ring o'er the Fleet ... Il.15.482.216.
For one bright Prize the matchless Chiefs contend; ... Il.15.484.216.
One kept the Shore, and one the Vessel trod; ... Il.15.486.216.
One kept the Shore, and one the Vessel trod; ... Il.15.486.216.
And better far, in one decisive Strife, ... Il.15.604.220.
One Day should end our Labour, or our Life; ... Il.15.605.220.
In one sad Sepulchre, one common Fall. ... Il.15.663.221.
In one sad Sepulchre, one common Fall. ... Il.15.663.221.
And cast the Blaze of both the Hosts on one. ... Il.15.735.224.
All *Greece* in Heaps; but one he seiz'd, and slew. ... Il.15.769.226.
Wedg'd in one Body at the Tents they stand, ... Il.15.788.226.
The Gods their Fates on this one Action lay, ... Il.15.804.227.
He shifts his Seat, and vaults from one to one; ... Il.15.827.228.
He shifts his Seat, and vaults from one to one; ... Il.15.827.228.
That not one *Trojan* might be left alive, ... Il.16.124.242.
Float in one Sea, and wave before the Wind. ... Il.16.263.249.
Two Friends, two Bodies with one Soul inspir'd. ... Il.16.267.249.
O'er Heav'ns Expanse like one black Cieling spread; ... Il.16.355.257.
Wedg'd in the Trench, in one vast Carnage bruis'd. ... Il.16.443.260.
Shall *Jove,* for one, extend the narrow Span, ... Il.16.543.265.
His Front, Brows, Eyes, one undistinguish'd Wound, ... Il.16.897.278.
And the whole Forest in one Crash descends. ... Il.16.928.279.
Impel one *Trojan* Hand, or *Trojan* Heart; ... Il.17.174.294.
One instant saw, one Instant overtook ... Il.17.214.295.
One instant saw, one Instant overtook ... Il.17.214.295.
Yet live! I give thee one illustrious Day, ... Il.17.239.297.
In one thick Darkness all the Fight was lost; ... Il.17.422.303.
Thus they. While with one Voice the *Trojans* said, ... Il.17.480.306.
High on the splendid Car: One glorious Prize ... Il.17.514.308.
High on the Chariot at one Bound he sprung, ... Il.17.610.312.
At one Regard of his all-seeing Eye, ... Il.17.674.314.
The sad *Achilles* how his lov'd one fell: ... Il.17.778.318.
Wedg'd in one Body like a Flight of Cranes, ... Il.17.846.321.
And mourn my lov'd one with a Mother's Heart. ... Il.18.84.327.
Greece from one Glance of that tremendous Eye ... Il.18.239.333.
One wise in Council, one in Action brave.) ... Il.18.298.336.
One wise in Council, one in Action brave.) ... Il.18.298.336.
If there be one whose Riches cost him Care, ... Il.18.349.338.
One Fate the Warrior and the Friend shall strike, ... Il.18.385.339.
Say, shall not I one Nation's Fate command, ... Il.18.429.341.
Not wreak my Vengeance on one guilty Land? ... Il.18.430.341.
The Image one of Peace, and one of War. ... Il.18.568.350.
The Image one of Peace, and one of War. ... Il.18.568.350.
One pleads the Fine discharg'd, which one deny'd, ... Il.18.579.350.
One pleads the Fine discharg'd, which one deny'd, ... Il.18.579.350.
And one would pillage, one wou'd burn the Place. ... Il.18.594.351.
And one would pillage, one wou'd burn the Place. ... Il.18.594.351.
One rear'd a Dagger at a Captive's Breast, ... Il.18.620.352.
One held a living Foe, that freshly bled ... Il.18.621.352.
To this, one Pathway gently winding leads, ... Il.18.657.355.
One Chief with Patience to the Grave resign'd, ... Il.19.231.382.
My three brave Brothers in one mournful Day ... Il.19.311.385.
To Grief and Anguish one abstemious Day. ... Il.19.328.386.
Mix in one Stream, reflecting Blaze on Blaze: ... Il.19.387.388.
And swift ascended at one active Bound. ... Il.19.433.389.
Not one was absent; not a Rural Pow'r ... Il.20.11.393.
To one that fears thee, some unwarlike Boy: ... Il.20.241.404.
Or save one Member of the sinking State; ... Il.20.364.410.
To one that dreads thee, some unwarlike Boy: ... Il.20.500.415.
Both in one Instant from the Chariot hurl'd, ... Il.20.533.416.
Sunk in one Instant to the nether World; ... Il.20.534.416.
That one the Spear destroy'd, and one the Sword. ... Il.20.536.416.
That one the Spear destroy'd, and one the Sword. ... Il.20.536.416.
One Hand embrac'd them close, one stopt the Dart; ... Il.21.82.425.
One Hand embrac'd them close, one stopt the Dart; ... Il.21.82.425.
For ah! one Spear shall drink each Brother's Gore, ... Il.21.101.426.
One struck, but pierc'd not the *Vulcanian* Shield; ... Il.21.182.429.
One raz'd *Achilles* Hand; the spouting Blood ... Il.21.183.429.
Corses and Arms to one bright Ruin turn, ... Il.21.392.436.
And in one Ruin sink the *Trojan* Name. ... Il.21.441.438.
One only Soul informs that dreadful Frame: ... Il.21.673.450.
Beneath one Roof of well-compacted Shields ... Il.22.6.453.
Mean Fame, alas! for one of heav'nly Strain, ... Il.22.29.453.
Two from one Mother sprung, my *Polydore,* ... Il.22.64.455.
One urg'd by Fury, one by Fear impell'd; ... Il.22.190.463.
One urg'd by Fury, one by Fear impell'd; ... Il.22.190.463.
By these they past, one chasing, one in Flight, ... Il.22.205.464.
By these they past, one chasing, one in Flight, ... Il.22.205.464.
Shall he prolong one *Trojan's* forfeit Breath! ... Il.22.235.465.
One to pursue, and one to lead the Chace, ... Il.22.258.466.
One to pursue, and one to lead the Chace, ... Il.22.258.466.
To such I call the Gods! One constant state ... Il.22.339.470.
One place at length he spies, to let in Fate, ... Il.22.407.472.

ONE (CONTINUED)

Drain their whole Realm to buy one fun'ral Flame; ... Il.22.442.474.
Nor rob the Vultures of one Limb of thee. ... Il.22.444.474.
And the whole City wears one Face of Woe. ... Il.22.517.478.
Imploring all, and naming one by one. ... Il.22.529.478.
Imploring all, and naming one by one. ... Il.22.529.478.
One, not exempt from Age and Misery, ... Il.22.537.478.
O fatal Change! become in one sad Day ... Il.22.560.479.
Born with one Fate, to one unhappy Life! ... Il.22.609.481.
Born with one Fate, to one unhappy Life! ... Il.22.609.481.
For sure one Star its baneful Beam display'd ... Il.22.610.481.
In one promiscuous Stream, the reeking Blood. ... Il.23.44.488.
One House receiv'd us, and one Table fed; ... Il.23.106.491.
One House receiv'd us, and one Table fed; ... Il.23.106.491.
May mix our Ashes in one common Grave. ... Il.23.108.491.
But grant one last Embrace, unhappy Boy! ... Il.23.113.492.
Involves, and joins them in one common Blaze. ... Il.23.217.498.
Nose, Mouth and Front, one undistinguish'd Wound: ... Il.23.476.509.
Here, where but one could pass, to shun the Throng ... Il.23.501.510.
One Length, one Moment had the Race obtain'd. ... Il.23.606.513.
One Length, one Moment had the Race obtain'd. ... Il.23.606.513.
One lash'd the Coursers, while one rul'd the Reins. ... Il.23.738.519.
One lash'd the Coursers, while one rul'd the Reins. ... Il.23.738.519.
Not one but honours sacred Age and me: ... Il.23.748.520.
If he be one, enrich'd with large Domain ... Il.23.985.528.
Still for one Loss he rages unresign'd, ... Il.24.58.538.
His Age, nor touch one venerable Hair, ... Il.24.192.544.
Thy Age, nor touch one venerable Hair, ... Il.24.222.546.
One cold Embrace at least may be allow'd, ... Il.24.279.548.
For one last Look to buy him back to *Troy!* ... Il.24.290.548.
One Ship convey'd us from our native Place; ... Il.24.486.556.
Yet still one Comfort in his Soul may rise; ... Il.24.608.562.
Nineteen one Mother bore—Dead, all are dead! ... Il.24.616.562.
Still One was left, their Loss to recompense; ... Il.24.618.562.
A Father one, and one a Son, deplore: ... Il.24.641.563.
A Father one, and one a Son, deplore: ... Il.24.641.563.
One universal, solemn Show'r began; ... Il.24.645.563.
The Source of Evil one, and one of Good; ... Il.24.664.565.
The Source of Evil one, and one of Good; ... Il.24.664.565.
One Evil yet o'ertakes his latest Day, ... Il.24.677.565.
One only Son! and he (alas!) ordain'd ... Il.24.679A.565.
In one sad Day beheld the *Stygian* Shades; ... Il.24.760.569.
And *Troy* sends forth one universal Groan. ... Il.24.885.573.
Dumb ye all stand, and not one tongue affords ... Od.2.273.74.
Death hastes amain: one hour o'erwhelms them all! ... Od.2.322.76.
And kills us all in one tremendous draught? ... Od.2.371.78.
Thy Sire and I were one; nor vary'd aught ... Od.3.155.93.
Howe'er, my friend, indulge one labour more, ... Od.3.405.106.
Let one, dispatchful, bid some swain to lead ... Od.3.534.113.
One seek the harbour where the vessels moor, ... Od.3.536.113.
O shame to manhood! shall one daring boy ... Od.4.888.159.
Whilst one most jovial thus accosts the board; ... Od.4.1017.165.
Nor break the transport with one thought of me. ... Od.5.262.184.
With water one, and one with sable wine; ... Od.5.338.188.
With water one, and one with sable wine; ... Od.5.338.188.
In one man's favour? while a distant guest ... Od.5.369.190.
With sister-fruits; one fertile, one was wild. ... Od.5.619.201.
With sister-fruits; one fertile, one was wild. ... Od.5.619.201.
The People one, and one supplies the King. ... Od.7.175.244.
The People one, and one supplies the King. ... Od.7.175.244.
Such as thou art, thy thought and mine were one, ... Od.7.399.256.
Steal from corroding care one transient day, ... Od.8.163.271.
Nor can one word be chang'd but for a worse; ... Od.8.192.272.
One common right, the great and lowly claims:) ... Od.8.600.294.
(An herald one) the dubious coast to view, ... Od.9.100.307.
To cool one cup suffic'd: the goblet crown'd ... Od.9.244.317.
Not one, or male or female, stay'd behind; ... Od.9.398.322.
From all their dens the one-ey'd race repair, ... Od.9.475.325.
'Till one resolve my varying counsel ends. ... Od.9.504.326.
One ram remain'd, the leader of the flock; ... Od.9.511.327.
But one, the vengeance fated from above ... Od.9.561.329.
One for his food the raging glutton slew, ... Od.10.133.347.
I led the one, and of the other side ... Od.10.234.352.
One o'er the couches painted carpets threw, ... Od.10.417.364.
This with one voice declar'd, the rising train ... Od.10.527.368.
For fate decreed one wretched man to fall. ... Od.10.658.375.
One nymph alone, a miracle of grace. ... Od.11.350.399.
And should Posterity one virtuous find, ... Od.11.539.409.
Without one look the murther'd father dies; ... Od.11.560.411.
Safe he return'd, without one hostile scar; ... Od.11.656.416.
One only month my wife enjoy'd my stay; ... Od.14.278.49.
By one *Etolian* robb'd of all belief, ... Od.14.418.56.
One sacred to the *Nymphs* apart they lay; ... Od.14.484.59.
For here one vest suffices ev'ry swain; ... Od.14.581.65.
Of one lost joy, I lose what yet remain. ... Od.15.107.73.
Neleus his treasures one long year detains; ... Od.15.256.80.
Yet one night more, my friends, indulge your guest; ... Od.15.326.85.
One roof contain'd us, and one table fed. ... Od.15.389.88.
One roof contain'd us, and one table fed. ... Od.15.389.88.
But both in constant peace one Prince obey, ... Od.15.454.92.
But one choice blessing (such is *Jove's* high will) ... Od.15.524.95.
One scene of woe; to endless cares consign'd, ... Od.16.208.114.
One care remains, to note the loyal few ... Od.16.328.121.
Medon the herald (one who pleas'd them best, ... Od.17.196.141.
One rogue is usher to another still. ... Od.17.251.143.
"Not one survives to breath<e> to-morrow's air." ... Od.17.589.161.
To him, to me, one common lot was giv'n, ... Od.17.644.164.
To fell the Giant at one vengeful blow, ... Od.18.105.172.
Of iv'ry one; whence flit to mock the brain, ... Od.19.658.228.
As one who long with pale-ey'd famine pin'd, ... Od.20.32.233.
Let one a blissful omen here disclose: ... Od.20.123.239.
One maid, unequal to the task assign'd, ... Od.20.138.240.
Cries one, with scornful leer and mimic voice, ... Od.20.449.255.
One loss was private, one a publick debt: ... Od.21.20.259.
One loss was private, one a publick debt: ... Od.21.20.259.
Trust it one moment to my hands to-day: ... Od.21.301.274.

ONE (CONTINUED)

Boundless the *Centaur* rag'd; 'till one and all ... Od.21.319.275.
And drew with ease. One hand aloft display'd ... Od.21.446.281.
The bending horns, and one the string essay'd. ... Od.21.447.281.
One vent'rous game this hand has won to-day, ... Od.22.7.286.
So near adjoins, that one may guard the strait. ... Od.22.153.294.
One hand sustain'd a helm, and one the shield ... Od.22.197.296.
One hand sustain'd a helm, and one the shield ... Od.22.197.296.
Oh ev'ry sacred name in one! my friend! ... Od.22.226.297.
And aiding this one hour, repay it all. ... Od.22.230.298.
One sure of six shall reach *Ulysses'* heart: ... Od.22.277.300.
Thus shall one stroke the glory lost regain: ... Od.22.278.300.
And thirsty all of one man's blood they flew; ... Od.22.281.300.
With deaden'd sound, one on the threshold falls, ... Od.22.284.300.
One strikes the gate, one rings against the walls; ... Od.22.285.300.
One strikes the gate, one rings against the walls; ... Od.22.285.300.
One common crime one common fate requires. ... Od.22.362.304.
One common crime one common fate requires. ... Od.22.362.304.
Not one! compleat the bloody tale he found, ... Od.22.423.308.
By one be slain, tho' by an Heroe's hand? ... Od.23.40.321.
If one man's blood, tho' mean, distain our hands, ... Od.23.119.326.
If one more happy, while the tempest raves ... Od.23.253.335.
Say, could one city yield a troop so fair? ... Od.24.132.354.
Were all the partners of one native air? ... Od.24.133.354.
And one *Sicilian* matron, old and sage, ... Od.24.242.360.
And not one empty spot escapes thy care. ... Od.24.291.363.
A friend I seek, a wise one and a brave, ... Od.24.312.364.

ONE-EY'D

From all their dens the one-ey'd race repair, ... Od.9.475.325.

ONE'S

"One would not, sure, be frightful when one's dead— ... 3.Ep1.246.36.
The Frail one's advocate, and weak one's friend: ... 3.Ep2.30A.52.
The Frail one's advocate, and weak one's friend: ... 3.Ep2.30A.52.
The Frail one's advocate, the Weak one's friend: ... 3.Ep2.30.52.
The Frail one's advocate, the Weak one's friend: ... 3.Ep2.30.52.
And Curio, restless by the Fair-one's side, ... 6.71.43.204.
The Fair one's Grief, and sees her falling Tears. ... Il.2.714.160.

ONES

The Fair-ones feel such Maladies as these, ... 2.RL4.37.186.
To kill those foes to Fair ones, Time and Thought. ... 3.Ep2.112.59.
Ye Fair ones that are able! ... 6.58.68Z2.173.
The Great Ones are thought mad, the Small Ones Fools: ... 6.60.2.178.
The Great Ones are thought mad, the Small Ones Fools: ... 6.60.2.178.
But *Richmond's* Fair-ones never spoil their Locks, ... 6.95.3.264.
The Richmond Fair ones ne'er will spoil their Looks, ... 6.95.3A.264.
When other Fair ones to the Shades go down, ... 6.110.1A.316.
And tho' no Doctors, Whig or Tory ones, ... 6.135.83.369.
His fair ones arms—he thinks her, once, too nigh. ... Od.8.356.282.

ONEUS

Oneus himself, and *Meleager* dead; ... Il.2.782.162.

ONLY

Silent, or only to her Name replies, ... 1.PWi.42.92.
One *Science* only will one *Genius* fit; ... 1.EOC.60.245.
Not only bounded to *peculiar Arts,* ... 1.EOC.62.246.
Then, at the *last,* and *only* Couplet fraught ... 1.EOC.354.279.
The *Ancients* only, or the *Moderns* prize: ... 1.EOC.395.285.
Tho' *Triumphs* were to *Gen'rals* only due, ... 1.EOC.512.296.
That only makes *Superior* Sense *belov'd.* ... 1.EOC.577.306.
Not only *Nature* did his Laws obey, ... 1.EOC.648Z1.312.
His only pleasure, and his early care. ... 1.TrPA.6.365.
Nor boast we only common dainties here, ... 1.TrPA.86.369.
You, only you, can move the God's Desire: ... 1.TrVP.104.381.
Her tender mother's only hope and pride, ... 1.TrFD.9.386.
And as she struggles, only moves above; ... 1.TrFD.42.387.
All other Loves are lost in only thine, ... 1.TrSP.19.394.
He's gone, whom only she desir'd to please! ... 1.TrSP.88.397.
This rural Prince one only Daughter blest, ... 1.TrSt.670.438.
This *Argive* Prince one only Daughter blest, ... 1.TrSt.670A.438.
And not for Pleasure only, or for Love. ... 2.ChJM.122.20.
One only Doubt remains; Full oft I've heard ... 2.ChJM.268.27.
The Loss of thee is what I only fear. ... 2.ChJM.556.42.
The only Strain a Wife must hope to hear. ... 2.ChJM.598.44.
One only just, and righteous, hope to find: ... 2.ChJM.636.45.
Who only *Is,* and is but only *One.* ... 2.ChJM.681.47.
Who only *Is,* and is but only *One.* ... 2.ChJM.681.47.
How sore I gall'd him, only Heav'n cou'd know, ... 2.ChWB.241.68.
That he, and only he, shou'd serve my Turn. ... 2.ChWB.295.71.
And of all Monarchs only grasps the Globe? ... 2.RL3.74.173.
Not grace, or zeal, love only was my call, ... 2.ElAb.117.329.
And only vocal with the Maker's praise. ... 2.ElAb.140.331.
Death, only death, can break the lasting chain; ... 2.ElAb.173.334.
O death all-eloquent! you only prove ... 2.ElAb.335.346.
'Tis ours to trace him only in our own. ... 3.EOM1.22.15.
Is only this, if God has plac'd him wrong? ... 3.EOM1.50.19.
That system only, but the whole must fall. ... 3.EOM1.250.46.
The only Science of Mankind is Man. ... 3.EOM2.2A.53.
Nature that Tyrant checks; he only knows, ... 3.EOM3.51.97.
Its only thinking thing this turn of mind. ... 3.EOM3.78.99.
'Twas VIRTUE ONLY (or in arts or arms, ... 3.EOM3.211.114.
Then VIRTUE ONLY (or in arts or arms, ... 3.EOM3.211A.114.
Count me those only who were good and great. ... 3.EOM4.210.147.
The only point where human bliss stands still, ... 3.EOM4.311.157.
Where only Merit constant pay receives, ... 3.EOM4.313.158.
That VIRTUE only makes our Bliss below; ... 3.EOM4.397.166.
Shall only Man be taken in the gross? ... 3.Ep1.17.17.
Know, God and Nature only are the same: ... 3.Ep1.154.28.
Those, only fix'd, they first or last obey, ... 3.Ep2.209.67.
His only daughter in a stranger's pow'r, ... 3.Ep3.325.120.
Only to show, how many Tastes he wanted. ... 3.Ep4.14.137.
Good Sense, which only is the gift of Heav'n, ... 3.Ep4.43.140.
I only wear it in a Land of Hectors, ... 4.HS1.71.11.

ONLY (CONTINUED)

They'll never poison you, they'll only cheat. 4.HS1.90.13.
To VIRTUE ONLY and HER friends, A FRIEND, 4.HS1.121.17.
"Your only wearing is your *Padua-soy.*" 4.JD4.113.35.
"Not Sir, my only—I have better still, 4.JD4.114.35.
You only make the Matter worse and worse. 4.JD4.121.35.
Of hollow Gewgaws, only Dress and Face, 4.JD4.209.43.
And grapes, long-lingring on my only wall, 4.HS2.146.67.
"Why, you'll enjoy it only all your life."— 4.HS2.164.69.
And thirsts and hungers only at one End: 4.HAdv.24.77.
Were he a Dupe of only common Sense. 4.HAdv.68.81.
The only danger is, when they *repent.* 4.Arbu.108B.103.
One, one man only breeds my just offence; 4.JD2.45.137.
'Twas only Suretyship that brought 'em there. 4.JD2.70.139.
Tis *Coscus* only breeds my just Offence, 4.JD2A.51.136.
That only suertyship has brought them there: 4.JD2A.79.138.
"My only Son, I'd have him see the World: 4.2HE2.6.165.
When this Heroicks only deigns to praise, 4.2HE2.82.171.
"Men only feel the Smart, but not the Vice." 4.2HE2.217.179.
Bestow a Garland only on a Bier. 4.2HE1.68.199.
"These, only these, support to the crouded stage, 4.2HE1.87.201.
Roscommon only boasts unspotted Bays; 4.2HE1.214.213.
But only what my Station fits, 4.HS6.21.251.
And where's the Glory? 'twill be only thought 4.EpS1.25.299.
Would he oblige me? let me only find, 4.EpS1.33.300.
The only diff'rence is, I dare laugh out. 4.EpS1.36.300.
Ev'n *Peter* trembles only for his Ears. 4.EpS2.57.315.
Yet think not Friendship only prompts my Lays; 4.EpS2.94.318.
P. I only call those Knaves who are so now. 4.EpS2.127.320.
How hurt he you? he only stain'd the Gown. 4.EpS2.165.323.
That counts your Beauties only by your Stains, 4.EpS2.221.325.
To touch Achilles' only tender part; 5.DunA2.210.127.
This only merit pleading for the prize, 5.DuhA2.289A.137.
Which only heads, refin'd from reason, know. 5.DunA3.6.150.
(His only suit) for twice three years before: 5.DunA3.30.154.
Wits, who like Owls see only in the dark, 5.DunA3.188.172.
To touch Achilles' only tender part; 5.DunB2.218.306.
Which only heads refin'd from Reason know. 5.DunB3.6.320.
(His only suit) for twice three years before: 5.DunB3.38.322.
Wits, who like owls, see only in the dark, 5.DunB3.192.329.
Pity! the charm works only in our wall, 5.DunB4.165.357.
We only furnish what he cannot use, 5.DunB4.261.369.
Thou, only thou, directing all our way! 5.DunB4.296.373.
She pity'd! but her Pity only shed 5.DunB4.345.377.
I meddle, Goddess! only in my sphere. 5.DunB4.432.383.
For *Sol's* is now the only ray. 6.4iv.12.10.
Nature itself is only gay, 6.4iv.20.11.
The only Honour of the wishing Dame; 6.8.26.18.
Good Humour only teaches Charms to last, 6.19.61.64.
The willing Heart, and only holds it long. 6.19.68.64.
And *Monthausier* was only chang'd in Name: 6.19.70.64.
Those tears, which only cou'd have eas'd my breast. 6.20.32.67.
The only wretch beneath thy happy reign! 6.20.51.67.
For only one in *Tom Durfeius.* 6.30.33.87.
Others opine you only chose ill, 6.44.17.123.
Is call'd in Women only Reputation: 6.46.2.127.
Who's here? cries *Umbra:* "Only *Johnson*"—Oh! 6.49ii.3.140.
Our Fate thou only can'st adjourn 6.53.37.162.
Thou only can'st our Fates adjourn 6.53.37A.162.
For Fools are only laugh'd at, Wits are hated. 6.60.4.178.
By the bare Outside only knew, 6.64.2.189.
Can only constitute a Coppice. 6.67.10.195.
This Duke did only nod. 6.79.36.219.
Or only take a Fee. 6.79.124.222.
And only dwells where WORTLEY casts her eyes. 6.81.6.225.
Beholds thee glorious only in thy Fall. 6.84.20.239.
My *only* Token was a Cup like Horn, 6.96iv.57.278.
Go then, where only bliss sincere is known! 6.109.15.314.
Convinc'd, that Virtue only is our own. 6.115.6.322.
Beauty which Nature only can impart, 6.126ii.5.353.
The only way to save 'em from our A[sse]s. 6.131ii.2.360.
Thou see'st that Island's Wealth, where only free, 6.142.6Z1.382.
You see that Island's Wealth, where only free, 6.142.6Z1A.382.
Let such, such only, tread this sacred Floor, 6.142.13.383.
The treasures of a land, where, only free, 6.142.8Z1.383.
Such only such shall tread the sacred Floor, 6.142.13A.383.
Such only such may tread this sacred Floor, 6.142.13B.383.
Let such, such only, tread this Poet's Floor, 6.142.13C.383.
Let such, such only, tread the Poet's Floor, 6.142.13D.383.
Let such, such only, tread their Poet's Floor, 6.142.13E.383.
Let such, such only, tread the sacred Floor, 6.142.13F.383.
To take the only way to be forgiven. 6.146.8.389.
The only proof that C[aroline] had bowels. 6.147ii.2.390.
Our Cares are only for the Publick Weal: Il.1.146.94.
Yet if our Chief for Plunder only fight, Il.1.163.95.
Thersites only clamour'd in the Throng, Il.2.255.139.
Pelides only match'd his early Charms; Il.2.819.164.
Eager of Fight, and only wait Command: Il.3.24.189.
So fairly form'd, and only to deceive! Il.3.56.192.
False to them all, to *Paris* only kind! Il.3.232.203.
Heav'n only knows, for Heav'n disposes all. Il.3.385.211.
And only mourn, without my Share of Praise? Il.4.207.231.
Those only heard; with Awe the rest obey, Il.4.488.243.
Whom *Borus* sent (his Son and only Joy) Il.5.59.269.
Vast was his Wealth, and these the only Heirs Il.5.198.276.
And only Men in Figure and in Name! Il.5.981.314.
And *Venus* only found Resistance here. Il.5.1015.315.
His only Hope hung smiling at her Breast, Il.6.497.351.
Patroclus only of the Royal Train, Il.9.251.445.
And solemn swear those Charms were only thine; Il.9.359.451.
And only triumphs to deserve thy Hands. Il.9.405.452.
I only must refund, of all his Train; Il.9.440.454.
One only valu'd Gift your Tyrant gave, Il.9.481.456.
The Gods (the only great, and only wise) Il.9.620.465.
The Gods (the only great, and only wise) Il.9.620.465.
And Woes, that only with his Life shall end! Il.10.99.7.

ONLY (CONTINUED)

In this great Enterprize, is only thine. Il.10.278.14.
Dolon his Name, *Eumedes'* only Boy, Il.10.372.19.
A Wretch, whose Swiftness was his only Fame, Il.10.661.31.
Peleus said only this,—"My Son! be brave". Il.11.915.76.
Gods! shall two Warriors only guard their Gates, Il.12.195.88.
Ilioneus, his Father's only Care: Il.14.574.190.
Might only we the vast Destruction shun, Il.16.126.242.
And only we destroy th' accursed Town! Il.16.127.242.
The only Hope of *Chalcon's* trembling Age: Il.16.722.272.
Man only vaunts his Force, and vaunts in vain. Il.17.24.288.
Only alas! to share in mortal Woe? Il.17.507.308.
Is only mine: th' Event belongs to *Jove.* Il.17.583.311.
For *Thetis* only such a Weight of Care? Il.18.504.346.
I, only I, of all the wat'ry Race, Il.18.505.346.
(My only Offspring) sink into the Grave? Il.19.346.386.
A Spear which stern *Achilles* only wields, Il.19.424.389.
His Eyes around, for *Hector* only burn'd; Il.20.106.398.
This Diff'rence only their sad Fates afford, Il.20.535.416.
Me, only me, with all his wastfull Rage? Il.21.433.438.
One only Soul informs that dreadful Frame: Il.21.673.450.
I, only I, will issue from your Walls, Il.22.531.478.
An only Child, once Comfort of my Pains, Il.22.620.482.
Mourns o'er the Ashes of an only Son, Il.23.275.501.
Achilles only boasts a swifter Pace: Il.23.932.526.
But *Hector* only boasts a mortal Claim, Il.24.74.538.
(The only Honours Men to Gods can pay) Il.24.90.539.
Am I the only Object of Despair? Il.24.298.549.
They, only they are blest, and only free. Il.24.662.564.
They, only they are blest, and only free. Il.24.662.564.
An only Son! and he (alas!) ordain'd Il.24.679.565.
One only Son! and he (alas!) ordain'd Il.24.679A.565.
My only Food my Sorrows and my Sighs! Il.24.809.570.
Industrious *Hermes* only was awake, Il.24.847.572.
An only Son, once Comfort of our Pains, Il.24.912.574.
Nor for a dear, lost Father only flow Od.1.313.47.
Move not the brave, or only move their hate. Od.2.230.72.
Death only is the lot which none can miss, Od.3.293.100.
(Leave only two the gally to attend) Od.3.538.113.
His labours equal'd only by my love: Od.4.138.127.
His only son, their ambush'd fraud employ, Od.5.27.172.
And love, the only sweet of life, destroy. Od.5.152.178.
Spares only to inflict some mightier woe! Od.6.208.220.
Not only flies the guilt, but shuns th' offence: Od.6.342.228.
Perish'd the Prince, and left this only heir.) Od.7.77.237.
Me, only me, the hand of fortune bore Od.7.332.253.
Fear only fools, secure in men of sense: Od.8.272.278.
With only twelve, the boldest and the best, Od.9.227.316.
And only his, of all the Gods on high. Od.9.610.331.
And only rich in barren fame return. Od.10.47.341.
I only in the bay refus'd to moor, Od.10.109.345.
And all around it only seas and skies! Od.10.226.351.
I only wait behind, of all the train; Od.10.305.359.
One only month my wife enjoy'd my stay; Od.14.278.49.
The only fool who left his cloak behind. Od.14.550.63.
And only ask your counsel, and a guide: Od.15.329.85.
From foreign climes an only son receives, Od.16.18.102.
I must behold it, and can only grieve. Od.16.88.106.
Gives from our stock an only branch to spring: Od.16.124.108.
Heav'n such illusion only can impose, Od.16.216.114.
I tell thee all, my child, my only joy! Od.16.249.117.
When thus the Queen. My son! my only friend! Od.17.116.137.
But *Jove,* all-governing whose only will Od.17.507.157.
He only asks a more propitious hour, Od.17.660.164.
Her beauty seems, and only seems, to shade: Od.18.250.179.
Their wonted grace, but only serve to weep. Od.18.296.180.
You, only you, make her ye love your prey. Od.18.324.182.
Is bounded only by the starry frame: Od.19.128.199.
He, only he of all the Suitor-throng, Od.21.155.266.
Those only now remain'd; but those confest Od.21.191.269.
A high and narrow, but the only pass: Od.22.145.294.
Thus, and thus only, shalt thou join thy friend. Od.22.243.298.

ONSET

They stand to Arms: the *Greeks* their Onset dare, Il.11.275.47.
Stand the First Onset, and provoke the Storm: Il.15.335.210.
And thrice three Heroes at each Onset slew. Il.16.949.280.
A furious onset with the sound of war. Od.4.612.148.

ONSLOW

"And perfect *Speaker?*"—"Onslow, past dispute." 4.JD4.71.31.
This Truth, let *L[iddel], J[effer]ys, O[nslo]w* tell. 4.HAdv.178.89.
How! what can O[nslo]w, what can D[e la Warr] 4.1740.59.335.

ONWARD

Not one looks backward, onward still be goes, 3.EOM4.223.148.
Onward she drives him, furious to engage, Il.5.13.266.
March'd onward, bending with the Gifts they bore. Il.19.292.384.
And sees (and labours onward as he sees) Od.5.512.197.

OOZE

And each ferocious feature grim with ooze. 5.DunA2.304.139.
And each ferocious feature grim with ooze. 5.DunB2.328.313.
Unsavoury stench of oil, and brackish ooze: Od.4.598.148.
The brackish ooze his manly grace deforms. Od.6.164.216.
And from his locks compress the weedy ooze; Od.6.268.223.
All pale, with ooze deform'd, he views the strand, Od.23.255.335.

OOZY

In that blest Moment, from his Oozy Bed 1.W-F.329.181.
His oozy limbs. Emerging from the wave, Od.4.543.146.

OP'D

But gracious Heav'n has op'd my Eyes at last, 2.ChJM.91.19.
The Silver Key that op'd the Garden Door. 2.ChJM.468A.37.
And op'd those Eyes which brighter shine than they; 2.RL1.14A.145.

OP'D (CONTINUED)

And op'd those Eyes that must eclipse the Day; .....2.RL1.14.146.
The quaking mud, that clos'd, and op'd no more. .....5.DunB2.292.310.
The ruthless Falchion op'd his tender Side; .....Il.20.544.417.
As a light quiver's lid is op'd and clos'd. .....Od.9.373.321.

OP'NER
His Son's fine Taste an op'ner Vista loves, ...3.Ep4.93.146.

OP'NING
If nature thunder'd in his op'ning ears, ...3.EOM1.201.40.
Fair op'ning to some Court's propitious shine, ...3.EOM4.9.128.
The op'ning clouds disclose each work by turns, ...5.DunB1.249.288.
While op'ning Hell spouts wild-fire at your head. .....5.DunB3.316.335.
By the French horn, or by the op'ning hound. .....5.DunB4.278.371.
In op'ning prospects of ideal joy, ...Od.20.281.246.

OP'RA
She went from Op'ra, park, assembly, play, ...6.45.13.125.

OP'RA'S
To Op'ra's, Theatres, Rehearsals throng, ...4.2HE1.173A.209.
His royal Sense, of Op'ra's or the Fair; .....5.DunB4.314.374.

OPAKE
But all about was so opake, ...6.94.55.261.

OPE
Unnumber'd Treasures ope at once, and here .....2.RL1.129.155.
One of our Giant *Statutes* ope its Jaw! .....4.JD4.173.41.
Thy Politicks should ope the Eyes of *Spain,* .....6.48iv.7.136.
Thy Mouth yet durst not ope, ...6.79.74.220.
Now first her Legs are ope, ...6.94.50.260.

OPE'D
The quaking mud, that clos'd, and ope'd no more. .....5.DunA2.280.136.

OPE'S
And ope's the Temple of Eternity; .....4.EpS2.235.326.

OPEN
Unlock your Springs, and open all your Shades. .....1.W-F.4.148.
Tho' oft the Ear the *open* Vowels tire, ...1.EOC.345.278.
And to fair *Argos'* open Court succeeds. .....1.TrSt.562.434.
The Breach lyes open, but your Chief in vain .....1.TrES.147.455.
Shook high her flaming Torch, in open Sight, ...2.ChJM.329.30.
And set the Strumpet here in open View, ...2.ChJM.653.46.
And all the Woman glares in open Day. .....2.ChWB.105.61.
The whole Creation open to my Eyes: .....2.TemF.12.254.
And Thousand open Eyes, and Thousand list'ning Ears. .....2.TemF.269.276.
Pervious to Winds, and open ev'ry way. .....2.TemF.427.284.
Try what the open, what the covert yield; .....3.EOM1.10.13.
Tom struts a Soldier, open, bold, and brave; .....3.Ep1.105.22.
True, some are open, and to all men known; .....3.Ep1.110.23.
Your Virtues open fairest in the shade. .....3.Ep2.202.67.
Bid Harbors open, public Ways extend, ...3.Ep4.197.156.
Like batt'ring Rams, beats open ev'ry Door; .....4.JD4.265.47.
With open arms receiv'd one Poet more. .....4.Arbu.142.106.
The balanc'd World, and open all the Main; .....4.2HE1.2.195.
To some fam'd round-house, ever open gate! .....5.DunA2.392.148.
Now stretch thy view, and open all thy mind. .....5.DunA3.201Z2.175.
To some fam'd round-house, ever open gate! .....5.DunB2.424.318.
They teach the Misteries thou dost open lay; .....6.2.26.6.
Open she was, and unconfin'd, ...6.14v(b).2.49.
To him reveal my joys, and open all my skies. .....6.21.42.70.
With aspect open, shall erect his head, ...6.71.65.204.
His long Jaws open, and his Colour fly; .....6.82x.4.236.
The Windows open; all the Neighbours rise: .....6.96iv.46.277.
Between both Armies thus, in open Sight, ...Il.4.107.225.
Heav'n Gates spontaneous open to the Pow'rs, ...Il.5.928.310.
Fast by the Road, his ever-open Door .....Il.6.19.325.
But open be our Fight, and bold each Blow; .....Il.7.293.378.
Heav'n-Gates spontaneous open to the Pow'rs, ...Il.8.478.419.
Mix purer Wine, and open ev'ry Soul. .....Il.9.268.445.
The Breach lies open, but your Chief in vain .....Il.12.501.99.
(The Winds collected at each open Door) .....Il.13.740.140.
Troy's scatt'ring Orders open to the Show'r. .....Il.13.902.148.
As thus he spoke, behold in open View, ...Il.13.1038.154.
The rest in Sunshine fought, and open Light: .....Il.17.427.303.
His dark Dominions open to the Day, ...Il.20.86.397.
Mark with what Insolence, in open Field .....Il.21.494.442.
With open Beak and shrilling Cries he springs, ...Il.22.187.463.
Where, in old *Zephyr's* open Courts on high, ...Il.23.246.499.
And open all the wounds of *Greece* anew? .....Od.3.128.92.
When thronging thick to bask in open air, ...Od.4.603.148.
Where the ports open, or the shores descend, ...Od.5.535.198.
Met by the Goddess there with open arms, ...Od.7.340.253.
Alas! must open all my wounds anew. .....Od.9.14.301.
Tho' bold in open field, they yet surround .....Od.11.321.398.
With open mouths the furious mastives flew; .....Od.14.34.36.
With open look, and thus bespoke his guest. .....Od.14.96.40.
My gate, an emblem of my open soul, ...Od.19.96.197.
Let him in open air behold the day. .....Od.20.436.254.
From blood and carnage to yon open court: .....Od.22.416.308.

OPEN'D
And now the Palace Gates are open'd wide, ...2.ChJM.315.29.
Thy Eyes first open'd on a *Billet-doux;* .....2.RL1.118.154.
He first the Snuff-box open'd, then the Case, ...2.RL4.126.194.
And ampler *Vista's* open'd to my View, ...2.TemF.263.276.
And Paradise was open'd in the Wild. .....2.ElAb.134.330.
When those blue eyes first open'd on the sphere; .....3.Ep2.284.73.
Smooth'd ev'ry brow, and open'd ev'ry soul: .....4.2HE1.248.217.
The first thus open'd: "Hear thy suppliant's call, ...5.DunB4.403.381.
The most recluse, discreetly open'd, find .....5.DunB4.447.384.
The Gates half-open'd to receive the last. .....Il.12.136.86.

OPEN'D (CONTINUED)
Soon as the Prospect open'd to his View, ...Il.14.17.157.
His open'd Mouth receiv'd the *Cretan* Steel: .....Il.16.415.259.
His Belly open'd with a ghastly Wound, ...Il.21.195.429.
From forth his open'd Stores, this said, he drew .....Il.24.281.548.
Approaching sudden to our open'd Tent, ...Il.24.820.571.
Radiant she came; the portals open'd wide: .....Od.10.302.358.
Here open'd Hell, all Hell I here implor'd, ...Od.11.27.380.
A trench he open'd; in a line he plac'd .....Od.21.125.264.

OPENING
While opening Blooms diffuse their Sweets around. .....1.PSp.100.70.
Let opening Roses knotted Oaks adorn, ...1.PAu.37.83.
There, interspers'd in Lawns and opening Glades, ...1.W-F.21.150.
Rowze the fleet Hart, and chear the opening Hound. .....1.W-F.150.164.
And bring the Scenes of opening Fate to Light. .....1.W-F.426.194.
His Purple Pinions opening to the Sun, ...2.RL2.71.164.
When opening Buds salute the welcome Day, ...2.TemF.3.253.
And mild as opening gleams of promis'd heav'n. .....2.ElAb.256.340.
And dawning grace is opening on my soul: .....2.ElAb.280.342.
From opening skies may streaming glories shine, ...2.ElAb.341.347.
Calls in the Country, catches opening glades, ...3.Ep4.61.142.
And yours my friends? thro' whose free-opening gate .....4.HS2.157.67.
The Scene, the Master, opening to my view, ...4.EpS2.68.316.
The opening clouds disclose each work by turns, ...5.DunA1.207.87.
While opening Hell spouts wild-fire at your head. .....5.DunA3.314.186.
Where opening *Roses* breathing sweets diffuse, ...6.14iv.3.47.
And ev'ry opening Virtue blooming round, ...6.132.2.362.
His opening Hand in Death forsakes the Rein; .....Il.8.153.405.
The Council opening, in these Words begun. .....Il.10.240.12.
The Scene wide-opening to the Blaze of Light. .....Il.15.813.228.
Attend her Way. Wide-opening part the Tides, ...Il.18.87.327.
The opening Folds; the sounding Hinges rung. .....Il.21.628.448.
The beauteous city opening to his view, ...Od.7.24.235.
With opening streets and shining structures spread, ...Od.7.104.239.
Youth smil'd celestial, with each opening grace. .....Od.10.332.360.
The opening gates at once their war display: .....Od.24.578.375.

OPENINGS
Full in the openings of the spacious main .....Od.2.440.82.

OPENNESS
Whence this unguarded openness of soul, ...Od.18.454.190.

OPENS
As the mind opens, and its functions spread, ...3.EOM2.142.72.
And opens still, and opens on his soul, ...3.EOM4.342.161.
And opens still, and opens on his soul, ...3.EOM4.342.161.
As Fancy opens the quick springs of Sense, ...5.DunB4.156.357.
Heav'n opens on my eyes! my ears .....6.31ii.14.94.
Takes, opens, swallows it, before their Sight. .....6.145.8.388.
Lifts up her Light, and opens Day above. .....Il.2.60.130.
The smiling Scene wide opens to the Sight, ...Il.16.360.257.
And opens all the Floodgates of the Skies: .....Il.16.471.261.
Glows in our veins, and opens ev'ry soul, ...Od.11.522.409.
The brass-cheek'd helmet opens to the wound; .....Od.24.606.376.

OPERA
"A perfect Genius at an Opera-Song— .....4.2HE2.11.165.
Already, Opera prepares the way, ...5.DunA3.303.185.
Already Opera prepares the way, ...5.DunB3.301.334.

OPERA-SONG
"A perfect Genius at an Opera-Song— .....4.2HE2.11.165.

OPERAS
New Eunuchs, Harlequins, and Operas, ...4.JD4.125.35.
Then his nice taste directs our Operas: .....5.DunA2.196.124.
Then his nice taste directs our Operas: .....5.DunB2.204.305.

OPERATES
Spreads undivided, operates unspent, ...3.EOM1.274.48.

OPERATION
And to their proper operation still, ...3.EOM2.57.62.

OPERATOR
Hail, dear Collegiate, Fellow-Operator, ...6.48ii.1.134.

OPES
Welsted his mouth with Classic flatt'ry opes, ...5.DunA2.197.124.
Bentley his mouth with Classic flatt'ry opes, ...5.DunA2.197D.124.
Bentley his mouth with classic flatt'ry opes, ...5.DunB2.205.305.
And opes his cloudy Magazine of Storms; .....Il.12.332.93.

OPHELESTES
With *Chromius, Dætor, Ophelestes* slain: .....Il.8.332.413.

OPHELTIUS
And next he lay'd *Opheltius* on the Plain. .....Il.6.26.325.
Opheltius, Orus, sunk to endless Night, ...Il.11.392.52.

OPHYR'S
And Seeds of Gold in *Ophyr's* Mountains glow. .....1.Mes.96.121.

OPIATE
Then all for Death, that Opiate of the soul! .....3.Ep2.91.57.
Thus Dulness, the safe Opiate of the Mind, ...6.16.1.53.

OPIATES
What help from J[ekyll]s opiates canst thou draw .....4.1740.63.335*.

OPINE
Opine, that Nature, as in duty bound, ...3.Ep3.9.83.
Others opine you only chose ill, ...6.44.17.123.

OPINION
But always think the *last* Opinion *right.* ... 1.EOC.431.288.
Each, in his own Opinion, went his Way; ... 2.ChJM.225.25.
Weigh thy Opinion against Providence; ... 3.EOM1.114.29.
Mean-while Opinion gilds with varying rays ... 3.EOM2.283.89.
'Till then, Opinion gilds with varying rays ... 3.EOM2.283A.89.
When (each Opinion with the next at strife, ... 4.1HE1.167.291.
Sir, you're so stiff in your Opinion, ... 6.10.79.27.

OPINION'S
Take Nature's path, and mad Opinion's leave, ... 3.EOM4.29.130.
And all Opinion's colours cast on life. ... 3.Ep1.22.17.

OPINIONS
Ask men's Opinions: J[ohnsto]n now shall tell ... 3.Ep1.158A.28.
Ask men's Opinions: Jaunssen now shall tell ... 3.Ep1.158B.28.
Ask men's Opinions: Scoto now shall tell ... 3.Ep1.158.28.
Opinions? they still take a wider range: ... 3.Ep1.172.29.
But art thou one, whom new opinions sway, ... 4.1HE6.63.241.

OPITES
Opites next was added to their side, ... Il.11.390.52.

OPIUM
Of Mirth and Opium, Ratafie and Tears, ... 3.Ep2.110.58.
Here stood her Opium, here she nurs'd her Owls, ... 5.DunA1.35.O64.
With mystic words, the sacred Opium shed; ... 5.DunA1.242.91.
Here stood her Opium, here she nurs'd her Owls, ... 5.DunB1.271.290.
With mystic words, the sacred Opium shed. ... 5.DunB1.288.290.

OPPONENT
And springs impetuous with opponent speed: ... Od.19.524.221.

OPPONENTS
Can such Opponents stand, when we assail? ... Il.17.556.310.

OPPOS'D
With his broad Shield oppos'd, he forc'd his way ... 1.TrSt.528.432.
Oppos'd in Combate on the dusty Shore. ... 1.TrES.80.452.
The Warriors thus oppos'd in Arms engage, ... 1.TrES.223.458.
Her ponyard, had oppos'd the dire command. ... 2.ElAb.102.328.
Or till'd their Fields along the Coast oppos'd; ... Il.2.768.162.
To Armour Armour, Lance to Lance oppos'd, ... Il.4.509.245.
Pallas oppos'd her Hand, and caus'd to glance ... Il.5.1046.316.
Oppos'd to those, where *Priam's* Daughters sate: ... Il.6.309.341.
To Lances, Lances, Shields to Shields oppos'd, ... Il.8.76.399.
I first oppos'd, and faithful durst dissuade; ... Il.9.142.439.
Himself, oppos'd t' *Ulysses* full in sight, ... Il.9.285.448.
Strong as he is; yet, one oppos'd to all, ... Il.11.586.60.
Oppos'd their Breasts, and stood themselves the War. ... Il.12.162.87.
Oppos'd in Combat on the dusty Shore. ... Il.12.424.97.
His left Arm high oppos'd the shining Shield; ... Il.13.765.141.
And all the raging Gods oppos'd in vain? ... Il.15.26.195.
The Warriors thus oppos'd in Arms, engage ... Il.16.526.264.
Oppos'd me fairly, they had sunk in Fight: ... Il.16.1023.282.
Oppos'd to each, that near the Carcase came, ... Il.17.9.288.
Oppos'd to *Pallas,* War's triumphant Maid. ... Il.20.94.398.
Oppos'd in Arms not long they idly stood, ... Il.23.963.527.
T'explore the fraud: with guile oppos'd to guile, ... Od.4.377.139.
Oppos'd to the *Cyclopean* coasts, there lay ... Od.9.133.311.
The gate oppos'd pellucid valves adorn, ... Od.19.660.228.
Six beams, oppos'd to six in equal space: ... Od.19.671.228.
And foes how weak, oppos'd against a friend! ... Od.22.256.299.
Oppos'd, before the shining Fire she sate. ... Od.23.92.323.
Nor ceas'd the strife, 'till *Jove* himself oppos'd, ... Od.24.58.350.

OPPOSE
Let none oppose th'Election, since on this ... 2.ChJM.256.27.
Whom, in our Right, I must, and will oppose. ... 2.ChJM.699.48.
Oppose thy self to heav'n; dispute my heart; ... 2.ElAb.282.343.
In vain the Youths oppose, the Mastives bay ... Il.3.39A.190.
Trojans be bold, and Force with Force oppose; ... Il.4.587.249.
With Force incessant the brave *Greeks* oppose; ... Il.5.599.297.
Haste, let us arm, and Force with Force oppose! ... Il.5.883.308.
Now Hosts oppose thee, and thou must be slain! ... Il.6.517.351.
If I oppose thee, Prince! thy Wrath with-hold, ... Il.9.45.434.
There *Nestor* and *Idomeneus* oppose ... Il.11.624.61.
Nor long the Trench or lofty Walls oppose; ... Il.12.5.81.
T' oppose thy Bosom where the foremost fight. ... Il.13.377.123.
Against his Wisdom to oppose her Charms, ... Il.14.189.168.
Arms his proud Host, and dares oppose a God: ... Il.14.450.185.
Thessalia there, and *Greece,* oppose their Arms. ... Il.16.692.271.
And crowd to spoil the Dead: The *Greeks* oppose: ... Il.16.731.272.
Oft' as he turn'd the Torrent to oppose, ... Il.21.303.433.
Whose Force with rival Forces to oppose, ... Il.23.993.529.
Yet would your pow'rs in vain our strength oppose; ... Od.2.279.74.
With ire-full taunts each other they oppose, ... Od.3.179.94.
Here lakes profound, there floods oppose their waves, ... Od.11.194.391.
Ill, said the King, shou'd I thy wish oppose; ... Od.15.76.72.

OPPOSES
Th' Award opposes, and asserts his Claim. ... Il.23.620.514.

OPPOSING
Th' *opposing Body's* Grossness, not its *own.* ... 1.EOC.469.292.

OPPOSITE
Full opposite he sate, and listen'd long ... Il.9.253.445.
Full opposite, before the folding gate, ... Od.17.110.137.

OPPRESS
These younger Champions will oppress thy Might. ... Il.8.130.404.
But should they turn, and here oppress our Train, ... Il.12.81.84.
From the high Turrets might oppress the Foe.) ... Il.22.254.466.
Oppress, destroy, and be the scourge of God; ... Od.2.264.74.
With homicidal rage the King oppress! ... Od.4.718.152.

OPPRESS (CONTINUED)
Of sleep, oppress thee, or by fraud or pow'r? ... Od.9.482.325.

OPPRESS'D
The *Greeks* oppress'd, their utmost Force unite, ... 1.TrES.93.453.
Never elated, while one man's oppress'd; ... 3.EOM4.323.159.
To ease th' oppress'd, and raise the sinking heart? ... 3.Ep3.244.113.
Oppress'd we fell the Beam directly beat, ... 4.2HE1.21.195.
Rich ev'n when plunder'd, honour'd while oppress'd, ... 4.1HE1.182.293.
Oppress'd with Argumental Tyranny, ... 6.8.17.18.
Oppress'd with gen'rous Grief the Heroe stood, ... Il.2.207.138.
Oppress'd had sunk to Death's Eternal Shade, ... Il.5.384.285.
She mounts the Seat oppress'd with silent Woe, ... Il.5.455.290.
Woes heap'd on Woes oppress'd his wasted Heart; ... Il.6.249A.339.
Was ever King like me, like me oppress'd? ... Il.8.283.410.
Oppress'd by Multitudes, the best may fall. ... Il.11.587.60.
When this bold Arm th' *Epeian* Pow'rs oppress'd, ... Il.11.817.72.
Oppress'd, we arm'd; and now, this Conquest gain'd, ... Il.11.834.73.
The *Greeks,* oppress'd, their utmost Force unite, ... Il.12.447.97.
The Kings, tho' wounded, and oppress'd with Pain, ... Il.14.439.184.
But when oppress'd, his Country claim'd his Care, ... Il.15.648.221.
Or darling son oppress'd by ruffian-force ... Od.4.311.134.
Has fate oppress'd thee in the roaring waves, ... Od.11.496.408.
Has Fate oppress'd me on the roaring waves! ... Od.11.502.408.
For still th' oppress'd are his peculiar care. ... Od.13.258.18.
Oppress'd by numbers in the glorious strife, ... Od.16.110.108.
Thy autumns bend with copious fruit oppress'd: ... Od.19.132.199.

OPPRESSES
Of sleep, oppresses me with fraudful pow'r. ... Od.9.486.326.

OPPRESSION
Experience, this; by Man's oppression curst, ... 3.Ep2.213.67.
Your drooping eyes with soft oppression seize; ... Od.19.595.225.
Wrong and oppression no renown can raise; ... Od.21.359.277.

OPPRESSION'S
Heav'ns! could a stranger feel oppression's hand ... Od.18.263.179.

OPPRESSIVE
To ease the Soul of one oppressive weight, ... 3.Ep1.57.19.
Since here resolv'd oppressive these reside, ... Od.20.275.246.
Th' oppressive Suitors from my walls expell! ... Od.21.404.279.

OPPRESSOR
Th' Oppressor rul'd Tyrannick where he *durst,* ... 1.W-F.74.157.
And blended lie th' Oppressor and th' Opprest! ... 1.W-F.318.179.
(A sacred oath) each proud oppressor slain ... Od.1.485.55.
In blood and dust each proud oppressor mourn, ... Od.14.188.45.

OPPRESSORS
The proud Oppressors fly the vengeful sword. ... Od.1.154.40.
And all your wrongs the proud oppressors rue! ... Od.1.330.48.

OPPREST
And blended lie th' Oppressor and th' Opprest! ... 1.W-F.318.179.
Pensive and slow, with sudden Grief opprest, ... 1.TrUl.68.468.
For still th'Opprest are his peculiar Care: ... 1.TrUl.91.469.
But anxious Cares the pensive Squire opprest, ... 2.ChJM.392.33.
All but the *Sylph—With* careful Thoughts opprest, ... 2.RL2.53.163.
But anxious Cares the pensive Nymph opprest, ... 2.RL4.1.183.
To sink opprest with aromatic pain? ... 3.EOM1.200A.40.
As Argus' eyes, by Hermes' wand opprest, ... 5.DunA3.343.192.
As Argus' eyes by Hermes' wand opprest, ... 5.DunB4.637.407.
Achilles heard, with Grief and Rage opprest, ... Il.1.251.98.
Canst thou, with all a Monarch's Cares opprest, ... Il.2.25.128.
When ah! opprest by Life-consuming Woe, ... Il.6.542.353.
Ev'n *Hector* paus'd, and with new Doubt opprest ... Il.7.261.377.
See'st thou the *Greeks* by Fates unjust opprest, ... Il.8.244.409.
Strook thro' the Back the *Phrygian* fell opprest; ... Il.8.311.412.
With more than vulgar Grief he stood opprest; ... Il.9.21.432.
All but the King; with various Thoughts opprest, ... Il.10.3.1.
Tho' sore of Battel, tho' with Wounds opprest, ... Il.14.145.164.
At length with Love and Sleep's soft Pow'r opprest, ... Il.14.405.183.
For this he griev'd; and till the *Greeks* opprest ... Il.18.519.346.
Tho' god-like Thou art by no Toils opprest, ... Il.19.155.378.
E'er Thirst and Want his Forces have opprest, ... Il.19.368.387.
Else had I sunk opprest in fatal Fight, ... Il.20.125.399.
Achilles next, opprest with mighty Woe, ... Il.23.167.496.
For brave *Ulysses,* still by fate opprest. ... Od.1.62.33.
Deem not unjustly by my doom opprest ... Od.1.86.35.
The wondring Rivals gaze with cares opprest, ... Od.2.183.71.
Drowzy they rose, with heavy fumes opprest, ... Od.2.446.82.
Of this to learn, opprest with tender fears ... Od.3.110.91.
The wand'ring Chief, with toils on toils opprest, ... Od.5.424.192.
To heal divisions, to relieve th' opprest; ... Od.7.95.238.
The Nobles gaze, with awful fear opprest; ... Od.7.192.245.
Alas, a mortal! most opprest of those ... Od.7.287.250.
Then first my eyes, by watchful toils opprest, ... Od.10.34.341.
Then pale and pensive stand, with cares opprest, ... Od.11.5.379.
With cautious fears opprest, I thus begun. ... Od.12.323.447.
Pensive and slow, with sudden grief opprest ... Od.13.235.17.
A man opprest, dependant, yet a man: ... Od.14.70.39.
Was yet to save th' opprest and innocent. ... Od.14.346.51.
Restless he griev'd, with various fears opprest, ... Od.15.9.70.
Whilst yet the Monarch paus'd, with doubts opprest, ... Od.15.190.77.
"So may these impious fall, by fate opprest!" ... Od.17.627.163.
Whose loose head tottering as with wine opprest, ... Od.18.281.180.
Their drooping eyes the slumb'rous shade opprest, ... Od.19.497.220.
The Heroe stands opprest with mighty woe, ... Od.22.162.295.
He faints, he sinks, with mighty joys opprest: ... Od.24.405.368.

OPPROBRIOUS
And inly groaning, thus opprobrious spoke. ... Il.7.108.369.
Opprobrious, thus, th' impatient Chief reprov'd. ... Il.13.964.151.
Should I not punish that opprobrious tongue; ... Od.18.431.189.

OPS

(Daughter of Ops, the just *Pisenor's* son, ...Od.1.541.57.
Euryclea, who, great *Ops!* thy lineage shar'd, ...Od.2.392.80.

OPTICS

Say what the use, were finer optics giv'n, ...3.EOM1.195.39.
The optics seeing, as the objects seen. ....3.Ep1.24.17.

OPUNTIA'S

Charg'd with rich Spoils, to fair *Opuntia's* Shore! ....Il.18.382.339.

OPUS

Opus, Calliarus, and *Scarphe's* Bands; ....Il.2.636.157.

OR (OMITTED)

2339

ORAC'LOUS

Some, over each Orac'lous Glass, fore-doom ....6.17iv.3.59.

ORACLE

The World's great Oracle in Times to come; ....1.W-F.382.188.
The King th'accomplish'd Oracle surveys, ...1.TrSt.576.434.
Jove ne'er spoke Oracle more true than this, ...2.ChJM.809.54.
Their law his eye, their oracle his tongue. ....3.EOM3.218.114.
If some dire Oracle his Breast alarm, ...Il.11.926.77.
If some dire Oracle thy Breast alarm, ...Il.16.54.237.
Mov'd by some Oracle, or voice divine? ....Od.3.264.98.
In early bloom an Oracle of age. ....Od.4.284.132.
But these, no doubt, some oracle explore, ...Od.14.111.41.

ORACLES

Who deem'd each other Oracles of Law; ....4.2HE2.128.173.
As Heav'n's own Oracles from Altars heard. ....4.2HE1.28.197.
He hears loud Oracles, and talks with Gods. ....5.DunA3.8.150.
He hears loud Oracles, and talks with Gods: ....5.DunB3.8.320.
And whose blest Oracles thy Lips declare; ....Il.1.111.92.
For this are *Phœbus'* Oracles explor'd, ...Il.1.135.93.
And heav'nly Oracles believ'd in vain. ....Il.2.142.135.
Our Fanes frequent, our Oracles implore, ...Il.7.531.391.
And heav'nly Oracles believ'd in vain; ....Il.9.26.433.
Nor Words from *Jove,* nor *Oracles* he hears; ....Il.16.69.238.
Those, my sole Oracles, inspire my Rage: ....Il.16.73.238.
Of all Heav'ns Oracles believ'd in vain, ...Il.21.317.434.
Or to be learn'd from *Oracles* alone? ....Od.2.246.73.
Or priests in fabled Oracles advise? ....Od.16.100.107.
Nor priests in fabled oracles advise; ....Od.16.120.108.
And the sure oracles of righteous *Jove.* ....Od.16.419.126.

ORACULOUS

Th' oraculous Seer frequents the *Pharian* coast, ...Od.4.519.145.
Let him, Oraculous, the end, the way ....Od.10.642.374.

ORANGE

With Handkerchief and Orange at my side: ....4.Arbu.228.112.
Here *Orange-* trees with blooms and pendants shine, ...6.14iv.17.47.
Here, where the fragrant Orange groves arise, ...6.20.70.68.

ORANGE-TREES

Here *Orange-* trees with blooms and pendants shine, ...6.14iv.17.47.

ORANGES

Not wrap up Oranges, to pelt your sire! ....5.DunB1.236.287.

ORATOR

And the puff'd Orator bursts out in tropes. ....5.DunA2.198.125.
And the puff'd orator bursts out in tropes. ....5.DunB2.206.306.
When thus th' attendant Orator begun. ....5.DunB4.281.372.

ORATORY

Come *Henley's* Oratory, *Osborn's* Wit! ....4.EpS1.66.302.

ORB

But as around his rowling orb he cast, ...1.TrPA.136.371.
Such Light does *Phœbe's* bloody Orb bestow, ...1.TrSt.147A.416.
Now, e'er ten Moons their Orb with Light adorn, ...1.TrSt.678.438.
And e'er ten Moons their Orb with Light adorn, ...1.TrSt.678A.438.
Within whose Orb the thick Bull-hides were roll'd, ...1.TrSt.9.450.
Some, Orb in Orb, around the Nymph extend, ...2.RL2.138.168.
Some, Orb in Orb, around the Nymph extend, ...2.RL2.138.168.
And unobserv'd the glaring Orb declines. ....3.Ep2.256.70.
Not closer, orb in orb, conglob'd are seen ....5.DunB4.79.349.
Not closer, orb in orb, conglob'd are seen ....5.DunB4.79.349.
A narrow orb each crouded conquest keeps, ...6.71.25.203.
And round the orb in lasting notes be read, ...6.71.66.204.
And, un-observed, the glaring Orb declines. ....6.106i.7A.306.
Round the vast Orb an hundred Serpents roll'd, ...Il.2.528.151.
Eternal *Jove!* and you bright Orb that roll ....Il.3.348.209.
His figur'd Shield, a shining Orb, he takes, ...Il.3.419.212.
Nor pierc'd the brazen Orb, but with a Bound ....Il.3.429.212.
In one firm Orb the Bands were rang'd around, ...Il.4.312.235.
When fresh he rears his radiant Orb to Sight, ...Il.5.9.266.
Pierc'd the tough Orb, and in his Cuirass hung. ....Il.5.344.283.
And the dire Orb Portentous *Gorgon* crown'd. ....Il.5.917.310.
The Shield's large Orb behind his Shoulder cast, ...Il.6.144.331.
Huge was its Orb, with sev'n thick Folds o'ercast, ...Il.7.267.377.
Then close beneath the sev'nfold Orb withdrew. ....Il.8.324.413.
His Buckler's mighty Orb was next display'd, ...Il.11.43.36.
Whose ample Orb a brazen Charger grac'd: ....Il.11.769.69.
Within whose Orb the thick Bull-Hides were roll'd, ...Il.12.353.94.
On the rais'd Orb to distance bore the Spear: ....Il.13.220.116.
His fervid Orb thro' half the Vault of Heav'n; ....Il.16.939.280.
And in an Orb, contracts the crowded War, ...Il.17.411.303.
Quench<'d> his red Orb, at *Juno's* high Command, ...Il.18.285.335.
Sacred to *Jove,* and yon' bright Orb of Day. ....Il.19.196.379.
From off the ringing Orb, it struck the Ground. ....Il.22.372.471.

ORB (CONTINUED)

Refulgent Orb! Above his four-fold Cone ....Il.22.395.472.
Whose visual orb *Ulysses* robb'd of light; ....Od.1.90.36.
While with the purple orb the spindle glows. ....Od.6.370.229.
Bright as the lamp of night, or orb of day. ....Od.7.111.240.
Again the restless orb his toil renews, ...Od.11.739.422.
Nor gives the Sun his golden orb to rowl, ...Od.20.429.254.

ORBIT

Let Earth unbalanc'd from her orbit fly, ...3.EOM1.251.46.
In the broad orbit of his monstrous eye ....Od.9.391.322.

ORBITS

Thick with Bull-hides, and brazen Orbits bound, ...Il.13.514.131.
Thick with Bull-hides, with brazen Orbits bound, ...Il.13.514A.131.

ORBS

Now marks the Course of rolling Orbs on high; ....1.W-F.245.171.
Those empty Orbs, from whence he tore his Eyes, ...1.TrSt.78.413.
Forc'd from these Orbs the bleeding Balls of Sight. ....1.TrSt.100.414.
Tore from these Orbs the bleeding Balls of Sight. ....1.TrSt.100A.414.
With Orbs unroll'd lay covering all the Plain, ...1.TrSt.665.438.
With Orbs unroll'd lay o'er all the Plain, ...1.TrSt.665A.438.
Some guide the Course of wandring Orbs on high, ...2.RL2.79.164.
Instruct the planets in what orbs to run, ...3.EOM2.21.56.
Roll'd the large Orbs of her majestic Eyes, ...Il.1.713.121.
(Far as from hence these aged Orbs can see) ....Il.3.220.203.
Forc'd from their ghastly Orbs, and spouting Gore, ...Il.13.775.141.

ORCADES

In Scotland, at the Orcades; and there, ...3.EOM2.223.82.

ORCAS'

Loud as the Wolves on Orcas' stormy steep, ...4.2HE1.328.223.

ORCHARD

Nor Winds, when first your florid Orchard blows, ...1.TrVP.110.381.
For better Fruit did never Orchard bear: ....2.ChWB.398.76.
Their orchard-bounds to strengthen and adorn. ....Od.24.260.361.
Haste to the cottage by this orchard side, ...Od.24.417.369.

ORCHARD-BOUNDS

Their orchard-bounds to strengthen and adorn. ....Od.24.260.361.

ORCHARDS

Her private Orchards wall'd on ev'ry side, ...1.TrVP.19.377.
To him your Orchards early Fruits are due, ...1.TrVP.96.381.

ORCHOMENIAN

Who plow the spacious *Orchomenian* Plain. ....Il.2.611.156.
The *Phenean* Fields, and *Orchomenian* Downs, ...Il.2.734.161.
The many-peopled *Orchomenian* Town; ....Il.9.499.457.

ORCHOMENOS

Great in *Orchomenos,* in *Pylos* great, ...Od.11.345.399.
In rich *Orchomenos,* or *Sparta's* court? ....Od.11.566.411.

ORCUS

To people *Orcus,* and the burning coasts! ....Od.20.428.254.

ORCUS'

Black *Orcus'* Helmet o'er her radiant Head. ....Il.5.1037.316.

ORDAIN

For thus did the Predicting God ordain. ....1.TrSt.554.433.
The Hour draws on; the Destinies ordain, ...1.TrES.227.458.
For thee the fates, severely kind, ordain ....2.ElAb.249.339.
But now, so ANNE and Piety ordain, ...5.DunA2.25.99.
But now (so ANNE and Piety ordain) ....5.DunB2.29.297.
O would the Stars, to ease my Bonds, ordain, ...6.96iii.33.275.
Or, if our Royal Pleasure shall ordain, ...Il.1.189.96.
They breathe or perish, as the Fates ordain. ....Il.8.531.422.
Ev'n till the Day, when certain Fates ordain ....Il.8.592.424.
Audacious *Hector,* if the Gods ordain ....Il.10.118.7.
Iris! descend, and what we here ordain ....Il.15.180.203.
The Hour draws on; the Destinies ordain, ...Il.16.530.264.
Against what Fate and pow'rful *Jove* ordain, ...Il.16.841.276.
To save your *Troy,* tho' Heav'n its Fall ordain? ....Il.17.339.302.
To *Troy* I sent him; but the Fates ordain, ...Il.18.77.326.
Or (if the Gods ordain it) meet my End. ....Il.18.146.329.
Die thou the first! When *Jove* and Heav'n ordain, ...Il.22.461.474.
To the pale Shade funereal rites ordain, ...Od.1.379.51.
Go then he may (he must, if He ordain) ....Od.5.177.180.
What will ye next ordain, ye Pow'rs on high! ....Od.5.599.201.
These did the Ruler of the deep ordain ....Od.7.45.235.
Then must he suffer what the Fates ordain; ....Od.7.262.248.
Pleas'd will I suffer all the Gods ordain, ...Od.7.303.250.
Now Fortune changes (so the fates ordain) ....Od.9.59.304.
And if the Gods ordain a safe return, ...Od.12.411.451.

ORDAIN'D

By the same Laws which first *herself* ordain'd. ....1.EOC.91.249.
Licence repress'd, and *useful Laws* ordain'd; ....1.EOC.682.316.
For so the Gods ordain'd, to keep unseen ....1.TrUl.60.468.
What if the foot, ordain'd the dust to tread, ...3.EOM1.259.46.
There (so the Dev'l ordain'd) one Christmas-tide ....3.Ep3.383.124.
So Time, that changes all things, had ordain'd! ....4.JD4.43.29.
Those *Spectacles,* ordain'd thine Eyes to save, ...6.96iv.75.278.
Ordain'd the first to whirl the weighty Lance. ....Il.3.405.212.
Ordain'd the first to whirl the mighty Lance. ....Il.3.405A.212.
The Monarch's Daughter there (so *Jove* ordain'd) ....Il.14.136.164.
Exempted from the Race ordain'd to die? ....Il.15.159.202.
Such, *Jove* to honour the great Dead ordain'd. ....Il.17.461.305.
Ordain'd, to sink me with the Weight of Woe? ....Il.18.12.323.
Ordain'd with Man's contentious Race to dwell. ....Il.19.132.377.
Ordain'd to *Amarynces'* mighty Name; ....Il.23.726.519.

ORDAIN'D (CONTINUED)
(The Games ordain'd dead *Oedipus* to grace) .... Il.23.787.521.
And now succeed the Gifts, ordain'd to grace .... Il.23.863.524.
An only Son! and he (alas!) ordain'd .... Il.24.679.565.
One only Son! and he (alas!) ordain'd .... Il.24.679A.565.
(So *Jove*, that urg'd us to our fate, ordain'd.) .... Od.3.184.95.
Such were the glories which the Gods ordain'd .... Od.7.176.244.
Hear then the woes, which mighty *Jove* ordain'd .... Od.9.39.303.
Blest is the man ordain'd our voice to hear, ... Od.12.224.442.
For so the Gods ordain'd, to keep unseen .... Od.13.227.17.
Ordain'd for lawless rioters to bleed; .... Od.14.48.38.
Who (so the Gods, and so the Fates ordain'd) .... Od.14.144.42.
To better fate the blameless Chief ordain'd, ... Od.19.317.209.
And have the Fates thy babling age ordain'd .... Od.19.563.224.

ORDAINS
The great directing MIND of ALL ordains. .... 3.EOM1.266.47.
And Heav'n ordains him by thy Lance to bleed. .... Il.16.884.277.
Enough—When Heav'n ordains, I sink in Night, ... Il.19.470.391.
For him, the Nymph a rich repast ordains, ... Od.5.251.183.
(If *Jove* ordains it) mix with happier men. .... Od.5.483.195.
Ordains the fleecy couch, and cov'ring vest; .... Od.7.428.258.
What heav'n ordains the wise with courage bear. .... Od.11.173.390.
And know, whatever heav'n ordains, is best. .... Od.13.487.29.
At distance follow, as their King ordains. .... Od.21.259.272.

ORDER
Where twelve fair Signs in beauteous Order lye? .... 1.PSp.40.64.
Where twelve bright Signs in beauteous Order lye? .... 1.PSp.40A.64.
Where Order in Variety we see, ... 1.W-F.15.149.
Which *out of* Nature's *common Order* rise, ... 1.EOC.159.258.
All rang'd in *Order*, and dispos'd with *Grace*, ... 1.EOC.672.315.
No labour'd Columns in long Order plac'd, ... 1.TrSt.202.418.
Next a long Order of Inferior Pow'rs .... 1.TrSt.286.422.
Now plac'd in order, the *Phæacian* Train .... 1.TrUl.1A.465.
The Guests appear in Order, Side by Side, ... 2.ChJM.316.29.
Each Silver Vase in mystic Order laid. .... 2.RL1.122.155.
When numerous Wax-lights in bright Order blaze, ... 2.RL3.168.182.
A Train of Phantoms in wild Order rose, ... 2.TemF.9.253.
The Walls in venerable Order grace: .... 2.TemF.72.258.
Beneath, in Order rang'd, the tuneful Nine .... 2.TemF.270.276.
Of ORDER, sins against th' Eternal Cause. .... 3.EOM1.130.31.
The gen'ral ORDER, since the whole began, ... 3.EOM1.171.36.
All this dread ORDER break—for whom? for thee? .... 3.EOM1.257.46.
All this dread ORDER shall it break? for thee? .... 3.EOM1.257A.46.
Cease then, nor ORDER Imperfection name: .... 3.EOM1.281.49.
So from the first eternal ORDER ran, ... 3.EOM3.113.103.
From Order, Union, full Consent of things! .... 3.EOM3.296.123.
From Union, Order, full Consent of things! .... 3.EOM3.296A.123.
ORDER is Heav'n's first law; and this confest, ... 3.EOM4.49.132.
ORDER is Heav'n's great law; and this confest, ... 3.EOM4.49A.132.
Pageants on pageants, in long order drawn, ... 4.2HE1.316.223.
To blot out Order, and extinguish Light, ... 5.DunB4.14.340.
In beauteous order terminate the scene. .... 6.35.27.103.
Leads the long Order of Ætherial Pow'rs. .... Il.1.643.118.
Soon as the Throngs in Order rang'd appear, ... Il.2.125.133.
These rang'd in Order on the floating Tide, ... Il.2.628.157.
A hundred Vessels in long Order stand, ... Il.2.695.159.
Beneath their Chiefs in martial Order here, ... Il.2.986.170.
With Noise, and Order, thro' the mid-way Sky; .... Il.3.8.188.
The rest I know, and could in Order name; .... Il.3.299.207.
With strictest Order sets his Train in Arms, ... Il.4.338.236.
The Billows float in order to the Shore, ... Il.4.480.243.
Eight brazen Spokes in radiant Order flame; .... Il.5.892.308.
Held out in Order to the *Grecian* Peers. .... Il.7.222.375.
A Senate void of Order as of Choice, ... Il.7.416.385.
Attend his Order, and their Prince surround. .... Il.8.614.425.
The Troops exulting sate in order round, ... Il.8.685.428.
Soft Wool within; without, in order spread, ... Il.10.311.16.
Their Arms in order on the Ground reclin'd, ... Il.10.546.27.
Near *Ilus'* Tomb, in Order rang'd around, ... Il.11.73.37.
Rang'd in bright Order on th' *Olympian* Hill; .... Il.11.104.39.
So close their Order, so dispos'd their Fight, ... Il.13.173.113.
In order follow all th' embody'd Train; .... Il.13.620.135.
Far o'er the Plains, in dreadful Order bright, ... Il.13.1008.153.
The trembling Queen (th' Almighty Order giv'n) .... Il.15.84.199.
Shields touching Shields in order blaze above, ... Il.15.678.222.
Directs their Order, and the War commands. .... Il.16.205.247.
Greece, in close Order and collected Might, ... Il.17.418.303.
And stills the Bellows, and (in order laid) .... Il.18.481.345.
And curl'd on silver Props, in order glow: .... Il.18.654.355.
In order rank'd let all our Gifts appear, ... Il.19.193.379.
But, with his Chariot each in order led, ... Il.23.11.486.
The Troops obey'd; and thrice in order led .... Il.23.15.486.
These in fair Order rang'd upon the Plain, ... Il.23.339.503.
They stand in order, an impatient Train; .... Il.23.433.507.
Each stood in order: First *Epæus* threw; .... Il.23.995.529.
Where seemly rang'd in peaceful order stood .... Od.1.169.40.
They wash. The tables in fair order spread, ... Od.1.183.41.
Marshal'd in order due, to each a Sew'r .... Od.1.191.42.
In comely order to the regal dome. .... Od.3.499.112.
(In order told, we make the sum compleat.) .... Od.4.608.148.
And order mules obedient to the rein; .... Od.6.42.207.
In beauteous order terminate the scene. .... Od.7.168.244.
The table next in regal order spread, ... Od.7.234.247.
Launch the tall bark, and order ev'ry oar, ... Od.8.35.263.
Her self the chest prepares: in order roll'd .... Od.8.475.288.
Now plac'd in order, on their banks they sweep .... Od.9.115.308.
In order seated on their banks, they sweep .... Od.9.209.314.
In order rang'd, our admiration drew: .... Od.9.255.317.
Now rang'd in order on our banks, we sweep .... Od.9.656.333.
I wash'd. The table in fair order spread, ... Od.10.437.365.
The time would fail should I in order tell .... Od.11.633.415.
Now plac'd in order, the *Phæacian* train .... Od.13.92.5.
They wash. The tables in fair order spread, ... Od.15.152.76.
And plac'd in order, spread their equal oars. .... Od.15.592.98.

ORDER (CONTINUED)
But thou attentive, what we order heed; .... Od.17.10.133.
They wash: the table, in fair order spread, ... Od.17.108.137.
In order due, the steward of the feast, ... Od.17.405.152.
With purple juice, and bore in order round; .... Od.18.469.191.
Attendant Nymphs in beauteous order wait .... Od.19.64.195.
Of perfect Hecatombs in order slain: .... Od.19.429.215.
The seats with purple cloathe in order due; .... Od.20.188.242.
Dis-roab'd, their vests apart in order lay, ... Od.20.312.248.
By Heralds rank'd, in marshal'd order move .... Od.20.342.249.
"From right to left, in order take the bow; .... Od.21.150.266.
In order circling to the peers around. .... Od.21.289.274.
Her prompt obedience on his order waits; .... Od.21.419.280.
To ev'ry plant in order as we came, ... Od.24.392.368.
On chairs and beds in order seated round, ... Od.24.452.370.

ORDER'D
As the Stars order'd, such my Life has been: .... 2.ChWB.323.72.
Here order'd vines in equal ranks appear .... 6.35.17.103.
He order'd then his Coach and Four; .... 6.94.29.260.
He ceas'd; then order'd for the Sage's Bed .... Il.9.733.470.
Had call'd the Chiefs, and order'd all the War, ... Il.16.237.248.
The Prizes next are order'd to the Field .... Il.23.753.520.
(So *Pallas* order'd, *Pallas* to their eyes .... Od.7.53.236.
Here order'd vines in equal ranks appear, ... Od.7.158.244.

ORDERS
These pleasing Orders to the Tyrant's Ear; .... 1.TrSt.422.427.
And proud his mistress' orders to perform, ... 5.DunA3.259.179.
And proud his Mistress' orders to perform, ... 5.DunB3.263.333.
And Navies yawn'd for Orders on the Main. .... 5.DunB4.618.405.
These shall perform th' almighty orders given, ... 6.21.27.69.
From Rank to Rank he moves, and orders all. .... Il.3.258.204.
Thus in thick Orders settling wide around, ... Il.7.75.366.
Suffice, to Night, these Orders to obey; .... Il.8.651.426.
Himself his Orders to the Heralds bears, ... Il.9.13.431.
Each Portion parts, and orders ev'ry Rite. .... Il.9.286.448.
To whom the *Spartan:* These thy Orders born, ... Il.10.69.5.
Plies all the Troops, and orders all the Field. .... Il.11.82.38.
Thro' broken Orders, swifter than the Wind, ... Il.11.441.53.
By Orders strict the Charioteers enjoin'd, ... Il.12.97.84.
Troy's scatt'ring Orders open to the Show'r. .... Il.13.902.148.
Then *Juno* call'd (*Jove's* Orders to obey) .... Il.15.162.202.
The God who gives, resumes, and orders all, ... Il.16.845.276.
Jove orders *Iris* to the *Trojan* Tow'rs. .... Il.24.178.543.
To ask our Counsel or our Orders take, ... Il.24.819.571.
The Chief his orders gives; th' obedient band .... Od.2.462.83.
Thy ship and sailors but for orders stay; .... Od.3.414.106.
I to the ship, to give the orders due, ... Od.3.460.109.
And duteous take the orders of the day. .... Od.3.525.113.
Go, to the nymph be these our orders born; .... Od.5.40.172.
Him, *Jove* now orders to his native lands .... Od.5.143.178.
Observe my orders, and with heed obey, ... Od.5.444.194.
The chief his orders gives: th' obedient band .... Od.15.310.84.

ORDURE'S
Renew'd by ordure's sympathetic force. .... 5.DunA2.95.108.
Renew'd by ordure's sympathetic force, ... 5.DunB2.103.300.

ORE
And *Phœbus* warm the ripening Ore to Gold. .... 1.W-F.396.190.
On the cast ore, another Pollio, shine; .... 6.71.64.204.
And scatter ore the Fields the driving Snow, ... 6.82v.2.231.
In Molds prepar'd, the glowing Ore he pours. .... Il.18.446.342.
Of beauteous Handmaids, Steeds, and shining Ore, ... Il.23.630.514.
Two lavers from the richest ore refin'd, ... Od.4.173.128.
Of brass, of vestures, and resplendent Ore; .... Od.5.51.174.
The polish'd Ore, reflecting ev'ry ray, ... Od.7.130.241.
Of brass, rich garments, and refulgent ore: .... Od.13.159.13.
Of steel elab'rate, and refulgent ore, ... Od.14.360.51.
There shone high-heap'd the labour'd brass and ore, ... Od.21.13.259.
To him sev'n talents of pure ore I told, ... Od.24.320.365.

ORESBIUS
Oresbius last fell groaning at their side: .... Il.5.869.308.
Oresbius, in his painted Mitre gay, ... Il.5.870.308.

ORESTES
Scriptus & in tergo, nec dum finitus Orestes. .... 6.24iii(b).2.76.
Teuthras the great, *Orestes* the renown'd .... Il.5.866.307.
Orestes, Acamas in Front appear, ... Il.12.153.87.
Iamenus, Orestes, Menon, bled; .... Il.12.223.89.
Whom young *Orestes* to the dreary coast .... Od.1.39.31.
To warn the wretch, that young *Orestes* grown .... Od.1.51.33.
Hast thou not heard how young *Orestes* fir'd .... Od.1.387.51.
And be, what brave *Orestes* was before! .... Od.3.245.97.
Orestes brandish'd the revenging sword, ... Od.3.391.105.
Unless with filial rage *Orestes* glow, ... Od.4.737.153.
But my *Orestes* never met these eyes, ... Od.11.559.411.

ORESTES'
And with *Orestes'* self divide my Care. .... Il.9.186.441.
And with *Orestes'* self divide his Care. .... Il.9.373.451.

ORGAN
Thus as the pipes of some carv'd Organ move, ... 4.JD2.17.133.
You bless the Powers who made that Organ .... 6.10.25.25.
When the full Organ joins the tuneful Quire, ... 6.11.126.34.

ORGANS
And swelling organs lift the rising soul; .... 2.ElAb.272.342.
The proper organs, proper pow'rs assign'd; .... 3.EOM1.180.37.
As strong or weak, the organs of the frame; .... 3.EOM2.130.70.
In Organs thus the mounting Puppetts move .... 4.JD2A.19.134.
The deep, majestick, solemn Organs blow. .... 6.11.11.30.
Nay, wou'd kind *Jove* my Organs so dispose, ... 6.96iv.105.279.

ORIENT

And orient Science at a birth begun. ....5.DunA3.66.156.
and orient Science their bright course begun: ....5.DunB3.74.323.
And orient Science first their course begun: ....5.DunB3.74A.323.
But when the tenth bright Morning Orient glow'd, ...Il.6.215.336.
The red'ning Orient shows the coming Day, ...Il.10.296.15.
Soon as the Morn the purple Orient warms ....Il.18.353.338.
Soon as the Morn the rosie Orient warms ....Il.18.353B.338.
Soon as Aurora heav'd her orient Head ....Il.19.1.371.
Aurora streaks the sky with orient light, ...Od.4.268.132.
Soon as the morn, in orient purple drest, ...Od.4.411.140.
When to his realm I plow'd the orient wave. ....Od.4.838.155.
The dawn, and all the orient flam'd with red. ....Od.6.58.208.
And all the ruddy Orient flames with day: ....Od.8.2.260.
So speaking, from the ruddy orient shone ....Od.10.645.375.
But soon as morning from her orient bed ....Od.15.214.78.
All night we watch'd, 'till with her orient wheels ....Od.16.380.124.

ORIGINAL

At once our great original and end, ...6.23.18.73.

ORIGINALL

Who decreed to restore . . . originall hight ....6.155.8Z2.404*.

ORIGINE

Hear how the glorious Origine we prove ....Il.20.254.404.

ORION

But see, Orion sheds unwholsome Dews, ...1.PWi.85.95.
See pale Orion sheds unwholsome Dews, ...1.PWi.85A.95.
None but Orion e'er surpass'd their height: ....Od.11.380.401.
There huge Orion of portentous size, ...Od.11.703.419.

ORION'S

And great Orion's more refulgent Beam; ....Il.18.562.349.
Orion's Dog (the Year when Autumn weighs) ....Il.22.39.454.
So when Aurora sought Orion's love, ...Od.5.155.179.
And great Orion's more refulgent beam, ...Od.5.348.188.

ORIS

Hannoniae qui primus ab oris. ....6.42iv.6.118.

ORISONS

For them, thy daily orisons were paid: ....Od.22.360.304.

ORMENIAN

The bold Ormenian and Asterian Bands ....Il.2.892.166.

ORMENUS

Orsilochus; then fell Ormenus dead: ....Il.8.330.413.
Next Ormenus and Pylon yield their Breath: ....Il.12.217.89.

ORMENUS'

This from Amyntor, rich Ormenus' Son, ...Il.10.313.16.

ORNAMENT

Ev'n in an ornament its place remark, ...3.Ep4.77.144.
Thy spousal ornament neglected lies; ....Od.6.31.205.
"A pall of state, the ornament of death. ....Od.19.167.200.

ORNAMENTS

And hide with Ornaments their Want of Art. ....1.EOC.296.272.
O'er-wrought with Ornaments of barb'rous Pride. ....2.TemF.120.263.
Reverse your Ornaments, and hang them all ....3.Ep4.31.140.
(Late their proud Ornaments, but now their Chains.) ....Il.21.37.423.
Her Hair's fair Ornaments, the Braids that bound, ...Il.22.600.480.
"A task of grief, his ornaments of death. ....Od.2.110.66.
And safe to sail with ornaments of love. ....Od.16.80.106.
A task of grief, his ornaments of death: ....Od.24.159.356.

ORNIA'S

Fair Arethyrea, Ornia's fruitful Plain, ...Il.2.688.159.

ORPHAN

No weeping orphan saw his father's stores ....2.ElAb.135.330.
"A Virgin Tragedy, an Orphan Muse." ....4.Arbu.56.100.
A Widow I, an helpless Orphan He! ....Il.6.513.351.
My tender Orphan with a Parent's Care, ...Il.19.352.387.
Robs the sad Orphan of his Father's Friends: ....Il.22.629.482.
Nor in the helpless Orphan dread a foe. ....Od.2.66.64.
Whatever ill the friendless orphan bears, ...Od.4.219.130.
So Pandarus, thy hopes, three orphan fair ....Od.20.78.236.

ORPHANS

Him portion'd maids, apprentic'd orphans blest, ...3.Ep3.267.115.
Its Touch makes Orphans, bathes the cheeks of Sires, ...Il.11.502.56.

ORPHEUS

Here Orpheus sings; Trees moving to the Sound ....2.TemF.83.259.
Orpheus could charm the trees, but thus a tree ....6.3.9.7.
When you, like Orpheus, strike the warbling Lyre, ...6.7.9.15.
Sad Orpheus sought his Consort lost; ....6.11.51Z1.32.
Of Orpheus now no more let Poets tell, ...6.11.131.34.
Thus Orpheus travell'd to reform his Kind, ...6.96iii.19.275.

ORPHEUS'

But wou'd you sing, and rival Orpheus' Strain, ...1.PSu.81.78.

ORRERY

When thou had'st Meat enough, and Orrery? ....6.156.2.405.

ORSILOCHUS

Whose Son, the swift Orsilochus, I slew, ...1.TrUl.145.470.
In Dust Orsilochus and Crethon laid, ...Il.5.670.300.
He got Orsilochus, Diöcleus He, ...Il.5.675.300.
Orsilochus; then fell Ormenus dead: ....Il.8.330.413.

ORSILOCHUS (CONTINUED)

Whose son, the swift Orsilochus, I slew: ....Od.13.312.21.
Beneath Orsilochus his roof they met; ....Od.21.19.259.

ORTHÈ

Girtonè's Warriors; and where Orthè lies, ...Il.2.898.166.

ORTHAEUS

Cebrion, Phalces, stern Orthæus stood, ...Il.13.994.152.

ORTHIAN

With Horror sounds the loud Orthian Song: ....Il.11.14.35.

ORTOLANS

Cramm'd to the throat with Ortolans: ....4.1HE7.62.273.

ORTYGIA

'Till in Ortygia, Dian's winged dart ....Od.5.157.179.
Above Ortygia lies an Isle of fame, ...Od.15.438.90.

ORUS

Opheltius, Orus, sunk to endless Night, ...Il.11.392.52.

ORYTHIA

These Orythia, Clymene, attend, ...Il.18.61.326.

OSBORN

Osborn and Curl accept the glorious strife, ...5.DunA2.159C.121.
First Osborn, lean'd against his letter'd post; ....5.DunA2.163C.121.
Osborn thro' perfect modesty o'ercome. ....5.DunA2.181C.124.

OSBORN'S

Come Henley's Oratory, Osborn's Wit! ....4.EpS1.66.302.

OSBORNE

Osborne and Curl accept the glorious strife, ...5.DunB2.167.303.
First Osborne lean'd against his letter'd post; ....5.DunB2.171.304.
Osborne, thro' perfect modesty o'ercome, ...5.DunB2.189.304.
Sits Mother Osborne, stupify'd to stone! ....5.DunB2.312.311.

OSIER

These, three and three, with osier bands we ty'd, ...Od.9.507.326.

OSIERS

Let Vernal Airs thro' trembling Osiers play, ...1.PSp.5.60.
And captive led, with pliant Osiers bound; ....Il.11.144.42.
(With yielding osiers fenc'd, to break the force ....Od.5.327.187.
With twining osiers which the bank supply'd. ....Od.10.193.349.
And bids the rural throne with osiers rise. ....Od.16.48.104.

OSSA

Heav'd on Olympus tott'ring Ossa stood; ....Od.11.387.402.
On Ossa, Pelion nods with all his wood: ....Od.11.388.403.

OSTENT

Whoe'er from heav'n has gain'd this rare Ostent, ...Od.20.143.240.

OSTROEA

Norton, from Daniel and Ostrœa sprung, ...5.DunA2.383.148.
Norton, from Daniel and Ostrœa sprung, ...5.DunB2.415.317.

OSTROGOTHS

See, the gold Ostrogoths on Latium fall; ....5.DunA3.85.157.
See the bold Ostrogoths on Latium fall; ....5.DunB3.93.324.

OSYRIS

Or great Osyris, who first taught the Swain ....1.TrSt.859.446.

OTHELLO

Not fierce Othello in so loud a Strain ....2.RL5.105.208.

OTHER

Let other Swains attend the Rural Care, ...1.PSu.35.74.
And learn of Man each other to undo.) ....1.W-F.124.162.
And other Mexico's be roof'd with Gold. ....1.W-F.412.192.
In other Parts it leaves wide sandy Plains; ....1.EOC.55.245.
When we but praise Our selves in Other Men. ....1.EOC.455.290.
The Owner's Wife, that other Men enjoy, ...1.EOC.501.294.
Whose Charms as far all other Nymphs out-shine, ...1.TrVP.53.379.
As other Gardens are excell'd by thine! ....1.TrVP.54.379.
All other Loves are lost in only thine, ...1.TrSP.19.394.
All other Goods by Fortune's Hand are giv'n, ...2.ChJM.51.17.
'Till both were conscious what each other meant. ....2.ChJM.499.39.
Each other Loss with Patience I can bear, ...2.ChJM.555.42.
With other Gossips, from Jerusalem, ...2.ChWB.244.68.
Thou by some other shalt be laid as low. ....2.RL5.98.207.
Criticks I saw, that other Names deface, ...2.TemF.37.256.
Oh happy state! when souls each other draw, ...2.ElAb.91.327.
Ah no! instruct me other joys to prize, ...2.ElAb.125.330.
With other beauties charm my partial eyes, ...2.ElAb.126.330.
Far other dreams my erring soul employ, ...2.ElAb.223.338.
Far other raptures, of unholy joy: ....2.ElAb.224.338.
And drink the falling tears each other sheds, ...2.ElAb.350.348.
What other planets circle other suns, ...3.EOM1.26.16.
What other planets circle other suns, ...3.EOM1.26.16.
What other planets and what other suns, ...3.EOM1.26A.16.
What other planets and what other suns, ...3.EOM1.26A.16.
Yet serves to second too some other use. ....3.EOM1.56.20.
Submit—In this, or any other sphere, ...3.EOM1.285.50.
Like varying winds, by other passions tost, ...3.EOM2.167.75.
Heav'n forming each on other to depend, ...3.EOM2.249.85.
Bids each on other for assistance call, ...3.EOM2.251.85.
The single atoms each to other tend, ...3.EOM3.10.93.

OTHER (CONTINUED)

All forms that perish other forms supply, ... 3.EOM3.17.93.
One must go right, the other may go wrong. ... 3.EOM3.94.101.
That touching one must strike the other too; ... 3.EOM3.292.122.
How much of other each is sure to cost; ... 3.EOM4.271.153.
How each for other oft is wholly lost; ... 3.EOM4.272.153.
(Nature, whose dictates to no other kind ... 3.EOM4.347.162.
That each from other differs, first confess; ... 3.Ep1.19.17.
All how unlike each other, all how true! ... 3.Ep2.6.48.
Say, for such worth are other worlds prepar'd? ... 3.Ep3.335.120.
Sir Balaam now, he lives like other folks, ... 3.Ep3.357.122.
"And am so clear too of all other vice." ... 3.Ep3.368.123.
And half the platform just reflects the other. ... 3.Ep4.118.149.
Because God made these large, the other less. ... 4.HS2.24.55.
About one Vice, and fall into the other: ... 4.HS2.46.57.
"'Tis *Fornicatio simplex*, and no other: ... 4.HAdv.42.79.
Yet each declares the other, fool or knave. ... 4.Arbu.114Z2.104.
As who knows Sapho, smiles at other whores. ... 4.JD2.6.133.
Who deem'd each other Oracles of Law; ... 4.2HE2.128.173.
The other slights, for Women, Sports, and Wines, ... 4.2HE2.272.185.
But does no other lord it at this hour, ... 4.2HE2.306.187.
He ne'er rebels, or plots, like other men: ... 4.2HE1.194.211.
Not but there are, who merit other palms; ... 4.2HE1.229.215.
You lose your patience, just like other men. ... 4.2HE1.363.227.
And not like forty other Fools: ... 4.HS6.16.251.
"To grant me this and t' other Acre: ... 4.HS6.18.251.
A hundred other Men's affairs ... 4.HS6.69.255.
There other *Trophies* deck the truly Brave, ... 4.EpS2.236.326.
Far other *Stars* than *and** wear, ... 4.EpS2.238.326.
Made just for him, as other fools for Kings; ... 4.1740.6.332.
The wisdom of the one and other chair, ... 4.1740.60.335.
And other planets circle other suns: ... 5.DunA3.240.177.
And other planets circle other suns: ... 5.DunA3.240.177.
Or serve (like other Fools) to fill a room; ... 5.DunB1.136.280.
And other planets circle other suns. ... 5.DunB3.244.332.
And other planets circle other suns. ... 5.DunB3.244.332.
See other Cæsars, other Homers rise; ... 5.DunB4.360.378.
See other Cæsars, other Homers rise; ... 5.DunB4.360.378.
(T'other day) my little eyes, ... 6.18.2.61.
Damnation follows Death in other Men, ... 6.24i.1.75.
Jove call'd before him t'other Day ... 6.30.1.85.
To other Letters cou'd I say? ... 6.30.65A.88.
Damnation follows Death in other Men, ... 6.34.3.101.
The Comick *Tom* abounds in other Treasure. ... 6.34.24.101.
As Spiritual one, as the other is Carnal), ... 6.42i.6.116.
Part you with one, and I'll renounce the other. ... 6.46.4.127.
Thus *Churchill's* race shall other hearts surprize, ... 6.52.59.157.
And other Beauties envy *Worsley's* eyes, ... 6.52.60.158.
And other Beauties envy *Wortley's* eyes, ... 6.52.60A.158.
And when all other Dukes did bow, ... 6.79.35.219.
Now wits gain praise by copying other wits ... 6.82ix(e).1.235.
With other Herbs muckle; ... 6.91.8.253.
Was there no other Way to set him free? ... 6.96iv.93.279.
Yet, if he writes, is dull as other folks? ... 6.105iii.2.301.
But when he writes, he's dull as other folks? ... 6.105iii.2A.301.
When other Ladies to the Groves go down, ... 6.110.1.316.
When other Fair ones to the Shades go down, ... 6.110.1A.316.
When other Ladies to the Shades go down, ... 6.110.1B.316.
Where other Buckhursts, other Dorsets shine, ... 6.118.13.335.
Where other Buckhursts, other Dorsets shine, ... 6.118.13.335.
Upon something or other, she found better *Fun*. ... 6.124i.6.346.
And now she's in t'other, she thinks it but *Queer*. ... 6.124i.10.347.
O Nash! more blest in ev'ry other thing, ... 6.131i.1.360.
Thy happy Reign all other Discord quells; ... 6.131i.5.360.
The other never read. ... 6.133.4.363.
But let him give the other half to court. ... 6.147vi.2.391.
This Hand shall seize some other Captive Dame. ... Il.1.176.96.
But other Forces have our Hopes o'erthrown, ... Il.2.159.136.
What other *Paris* is thy Darling now? ... Il.3.498.215.
Observ'd each other, and had mark'd for War. ... Il.6.150.333.
Some other Sun may see the happier Hour, ... Il.8.173.406.
That other Shaft with erring Fury flew, ... Il.8.376.415.
(Heav'ns awful Empress, *Saturn's* other Heir) ... Il.8.465.419.
When Morning dawns: if other he decree, ... Il.9.810.473.
The Care is next our other Chiefs to raise: ... Il.10.122.7.
Some other be dispatch'd, of nimbler Feet, ... Il.10.125.7.
But let some other chosen Warrior join, ... Il.10.263.13.
Far other Rulers those proud Steeds demand, ... Il.10.473.24.
Their other Princes? tell what Watch they keep? ... Il.10.480.25.
These other Spoils from conquer'd *Dolon* came, ... Il.10.660.31.
Far other Task! than when they wont to keep ... Il.11.141.41.
And join each other in the Realms below. ... Il.11.340.49.
On other Works tho' *Troy* with Fury fall, ... Il.13.77.108.
In other Battels I deserv'd thy Blame, ... Il.13.977.152.
O'er other Gods I spread my easy Chain; ... Il.14.278.175.
And stretch the other o'er the sacred Main. ... Il.14.308.177.
Howe'er th' Offence by other Gods be past, ... Il.15.242.206.
In vain their Javelins at each other flew, ... Il.16.402.258.
What other Methods may preserve thy *Troy?* ... Il.17.160.293.
Vulcanian Arms: What other can I wield? ... Il.18.229.332.
Vulcanian Arms: What other should I wield? ... Il.18.229A.332.
Turn from each other in the Walks of War— ... Il.20.496.415.
On other Gods his dreadful Arm employ, ... Il.21.434.438.
Nor other Lance, nor other Hope remain; ... Il.22.374.471.
Nor other Lance, nor other Hope remain; ... Il.22.374.471.
And other Steeds, than lately led the Way? ... Il.23.543.511.
Rise then some other, and inform my Sight, ... Il.23.552.511.
Each look'd on other, none the Silence broke, ... Il.24.596.561.
Such Griefs, O King! have other Parents known; ... Il.24.780.569.
While all my other Sons in barb'rous Bands ... Il.24.946.575.
Some other *Greeks* a fairer claim may plead; ... Od.1.505.56.
If she must wed, from other hands require ... Od.2.59.63.
With ire-full taunts each other they oppose, ... Od.3.179.94.
Pass we to other subjects; and engage ... Od.3.301.100.
And measur'd tracts unknown to other ships, ... Od.3.409.106.
For lo! none other of the court above, ... Od.3.484.111.

OTHER (CONTINUED)

Our other column of the state is born: ... Od.4.963.163.
Some other motive, Goddess! sways thy mind, ... Od.5.223.182.
But other Gods intend me other woes? ... Od.5.453.194.
But other Gods intend me other woes? ... Od.5.453.194.
Go, learn'd in woes, and other woes essay! ... Od.5.480.195.
Beyond these tracts, and under other skies, ... Od.7.327.252.
Let other realms the deathful gauntlet wield, ... Od.8.281.278.
Nor other home nor other care intends, ... Od.9.109.308.
Nor other home nor other care intends, ... Od.9.109.308.
And what rich liquors other climates boast. ... Od.9.411.323.
I led the one, and of the other side ... Od.10.234.352.
What other joy can equal thy return? ... Od.10.497.367.
Far other journey first demands thy care; ... Od.10.579.370.
Far other journey first demands our cares. ... Od.10.674.376.
Me into other realms my cares convey, ... Od.13.475.29.
To other regions is his virtue known. ... Od.13.489.29.
And far from ken of any other coast, ... Od.14.332.51.
But other counsels pleas'd the sailors mind: ... Od.14.374.53.
No other roof a stranger shou'd receive, ... Od.15.553.96.
Nor other hands than ours the welcome give. ... Od.15.554.96.
Far other vests thy limbs majestic grace, ... Od.16.198.113.
Far other glories lighten from thy face! ... Od.16.199.113.
Other *Ulysses* shalt thou never see, ... Od.16.224.114.
Far other cares its dwellers now imploy; ... Od.17.320.147.
Want brings enough of other ills along! ... Od.17.563.160.
From ev'ry other hand redress he found, ... Od.17.594.161.
Thy other wants her subjects shall supply. ... Od.17.641.163.
Your other task, ye menial train, forbear; ... Od.19.362.211.
Of other wretches care the torture ends: ... Od.20.100.237.
That other feeds on planetary schemes, ... Od.20.453.255.
But *Iphitus* employ'd on other cares, ... Od.21.25.260.
Enough—on other cares your thought imploy, ... Od.21.242.271.
Some other like it sure the man must know, ... Od.21.432.281.
Lo hence I run for other arms to wield, ... Od.22.118.292.
But other methods of defence remain, ... Od.22.154.294.
Me other work requires—With tim'rous awe ... Od.22.417.308.

OTHER'S

Tho' meant each other's Aid, like *Man* and *Wife*. ... 1.EOC.83.248.
Thro' dreary wastes, and weep each other's woe; ... 2.ElAb.242.339.
Tho' each by turns the other's bound invade, ... 3.EOM2.207.80.
Now this, now that the other's bound invades ... 3.EOM2.207A.80.
Or other's wants with Scorn deride ... 6.50.35B.148.
For pow'rs celestial to each other's view ... Od.5.100.177.
Or if each other's wrongs ye still support, ... Od.20.382.251.

OTHERS

Thin Trees arise that shun each others Shades. ... 1.W-F.22.150.
Let such teach others who themselves excell, ... 1.EOC.15.240.
Those hate as *Rivals* all that write; and others ... 1.EOC.30A.242.
Some hate as *Rivals* all that write; and others ... 1.EOC.30B.242.
Others for *Language* all their Care express, ... 1.EOC.305.274.
Employ their Pains to spurn some others down; ... 1.EOC.515.296.
If thou all others didst despise and scorn: ... 1.TrPA.119.370.
The Life which others pay, let Us bestow, ... 1.TrES.49.451.
Others, long absent from their Native Place, ... 1.TrUl.213.472.
How merrily soever others fare? ... 2.ChWB.135.63.
Some fold the Sleeve, whilst others plait the Gown; ... 2.RL1.147.158.
Some fold the Sleeve, while others plait the Gown; ... 2.RL1.147A.158.
Others on Earth o'er human Race preside, ... 2.RL2.87.165.
Make some take Physick, others scribble Plays; ... 2.RL4.62.189.
Their own like others soon their Place resign'd, ... 2.TemF.39.256.
Enlarges some, and others multiplies. ... 2.TemF.134.264.
The Joy let others have, and we the Name, ... 2.TemF.390.282.
Destroying others, by himself destroy'd. ... 3.EOM2.66.63.
The scale to measure others wants by thine. ... 3.EOM2.292.90.
For, what one likes if others like as well, ... 3.EOM3.273.120.
Abstract what others feel, what others think, ... 3.EOM4.45.132.
Abstract what others feel, what others think, ... 3.EOM4.45.132.
Not that themselves are wise, but others weak. ... 3.EOM4.228.148.
Nor that themselves are wise, but others weak. ... 3.EOM4.228A.148.
What's Fame? a fancy'd life in others breath, ... 3.EOM4.237.149.
What's Fame? that fancy'd life in others breath, ... 3.EOM4.237A.149.
To see all others faults, and feel our own: ... 3.EOM4.262.153.
Some plunge in bus'ness, others shave their crowns: ... 3.Ep1.56.19.
Others so very close, they're hid from none; ... 3.Ep1.111.23.
Who, with herself, and others, from her birth ... 3.Ep2.117A.60.
Who, with herself, or others, from her birth ... 3.Ep2.117.60.
Thus others Talents having nicely shown, ... 4.JD4.80.31.
And others hunt white Aprons in the *Mall*. ... 4.HAdv.38.79.
"Or others Spouses, like my Lord of— ... 4.HAdv.44.79.
And others roar aloud, "Subscribe, subscribe." ... 4.Arbu.114.103.
Were others angry? I excus'd them too; ... 4.Arbu.173.108.
And others (harder still) he pay'd in kind. ... 4.Arbu.244.113.
Is he who makes his meal on others wit: ... 4.JD2.30.135.
Is He who makes his Meals of Others Wit; ... 4.JD2A.34.134.
I, who at some times spend, at others spare, ... 4.2HE2.290.185.
Who says in verse what others say in prose; ... 4.2HE1.202.211.
But pray, when others praise him, do I blame? ... 4.EpS2.136.321.
Others, a sword-knot and lac'd suit inflame. ... 5.DunA2.48.103.
Let others aim: 'Tis yours to shake the soul ... 5.DunA2.217.127.
While others timely, to the neighbouring Fleet ... 5.DunA2.395.149.
All others timely, to the neighbouring Fleet ... 5.DunA2.395A.149.
Grave mummers! sleeveless some, and shirtless others. ... 5.DunA3.108.159.
Others a sword-knot and lac'd suit inflame. ... 5.DunB2.52.298.
Let others aim: 'Tis yours to shake the soul ... 5.DunB2.225.307.
While others, timely, to the neighb'ring Fleet ... 5.DunB2.427.318.
Grave Mummers! sleeveless some, and shirtless others. ... 5.DunB3.116.325.
Let others creep by timid steps, and slow, ... 5.DunB4.465.386.
On others Int'rest her gay liv'ry flings, ... 5.DunB4.537.395.
Others the Syren Sisters warble round, ... 5.DunB4.541.395.
Others the Syren Sisters compass round, ... 5.DunB4.541A.395.
Others import yet nobler arts from France, ... 5.DunB4.597.402.
Which in all others they themselves destroy? ... 6.4i.8.9.
Or waste, for others Use, their restless Years ... 6.17ii.3.56.

OTHERS (CONTINUED)

Or others Ease and theirs alike destroy, 6.17ii.7.56.
Others with *Aldus* would besot us; 6.29.5.83.
Others account 'em but so so; 6.29.2.82.
Let others screw their Hypocritick Face, 6.33.7.99.
Let others screw a Hypocritick Face, 6.33.7A.99.
Others to tread the liquid harvest join, 6.35.21.103.
Others opine you only chose ill, 6.44.17.123.
Saw others happy, and with sighs withdrew; 6.45.8.124.
Solicitous for others Ends, 6.47.41.130.
To bawd for others, and go Shares with Punk. 6.49i.26.138.
That Mercy I to others show, 6.50.39.148.
As I to others mercy show, 6.50.39A.148.
Others bring Goods and Treasure to their Houses, 6.96iv.55.278.
Are others angry? I excuse them too, 6.98.23.284.
To help us thus to read the works of others: 6.105v.2.302.
Who with herself, and others from her Birth, 6.154.3.402.
Let others in the Field their Arms employ, Il.6.558.354.
Some line the Trench, and others man the Wall. Il.9.120.438.
And all his Rapine cou'd from others wrest; Il.9.497.457.
One Stratagem has fail'd, and others will: Il.9.548.460.
While others sleep, thus range the Camp alone? Il.10.91.6.
The Life which others pay, let us bestow, Il.12.393.96.
While these fly trembling, others pant for Breath, Il.15.392.212.
Nor fights like others, fix'd to certain Stands, Il.15.818.228.
Wounded, they wound; and seek each others Hearts Il.15.862.230.
(Others in Council fam'd for nobler Skill, Il.18.135.329.
Our Care devolves on others left behind. Il.19.232.382.
Hence sprung twelve others of unrival'd Kind, Il.20.268.405.
Now then let others bleed—This said, aloud Il.20.401.412.
Like others fly, and be like others slain? Il.21.652.449.
Like others fly, and be like others slain? Il.21.652.449.
Let others for the noble Task prepare, Il.23.353.504.
A Joy to others, a Reproach to me. Il.23.416.506.
Much would ye blame, should others thus offend: Il.23.577.512.
Others 'tis own'd, in Fields of Battle shine, Il.23.773.520.
Ye both have won: Let others who excell Il.23.858.523.
When others curst the Auth'ress of their Woe, Il.24.970.576.
Others apart, the spacious hall prepare, Od.1.146.40.
And others, dictated by heav'nly pow'r, Od.3.35.87.
The lives of others, vent'rous of their own. Od.3.89.90.
In virtue rich; in blessing others, blest. Od.7.96.238.
Others to tread the liquid harvest join, Od.7.162.244.
While others beauteous as th' æthereal kind, Od.8.195.273.
Heedless of others, to his own severe. Od.9.132.311.
The lives of others, and expose your own? Od.9.302.318.
Each others face, and each his story told: Od.10.536.369.
Others, long absent from their native place, Od.13.380.25.
For oft in others freely I reprove Od.15.77.72.
For others good, and melt at others woe: Od.18.270.179.
For others good, and melt at others woe: Od.18.270.179.
Mark then what others can—He ended there, Od.21.181.268.

OTHERS'

How vain that second Life in others' Breath, 2.TemF.505.288.
See how the force of others' pray'rs I try, 2.ElAb.149.331.
But why should I on others' pray'rs depend? 2.ElAb.151.332.
For others' good, or melt at others' woe. 2.Elegy.46.366.
For others' good, or melt at others' woe. 2.Elegy.46.366.

OTHERWISE

Alas! far otherwise the nymph declares, Od.10.673.376.

OTHO

Otho a warrior, Cromwell a buffoon? 3.Ep1.147.27.
Lord of an Otho, if I vouch it true; 5.DunB4.369.379.
Sighs for an Otho, and neglects his bride. 6.71.44.204.

OTHRYONEUS

First by his Hand *Othryoneus* was slain, Il.13.457.128.
And great *Othryoneus,* so fear'd of late? Il.13.970.151.

OTREUS'

In ancient Time, when *Otreus'* fill'd the Throne, Il.3.246.204.

OTRYNTEUS

From great *Otrynteus* he deriv'd his Blood, Il.20.441.413.

OTRYNTIDES

Lye there *Otryntides!* the *Trojan* Earth Il.20.449.413.

OTUS

Otus and *Ephialtes* held the Chain: Il.5.478.291.
Polydamas laid *Otus* on the Sand, Il.15.614.220.
Hence *Ephialtes,* hence stern *Otus* sprung, Od.11.377.401.

OTWAY

"And you shall rise up *Otway* for your pains." 4.2HE2.146.175.
And full in Shakespear, fair in Otway shone: 4.2HE1.277.219.
But Otway fail'd to polish or refine, 4.2HE1.278.219.

OUGHT

LEARN then what MORALS Criticks ought to show, 1.EOC.560.304.
Excuse me, Dear, if ought amiss was said, 2.ChJM.791.53.
No pious Christian ought to marry twice. 2.ChWB.12.57.
Who seek in love for ought but love alone. 2.ElAb.84.326.
I ought to grieve, but cannot what I ought; 2.ElAb.183.335.
I ought to grieve, but cannot what I ought; 2.ElAb.183.335.
Say rather, Man's as perfect as he ought; 3.EOM1.70.22.
We ought to blame the culture, not the soil: 3.EOM4.14.129.
She speaks, behaves, and acts just as she ought; 3.Ep2.161.64.
It ought to bring all Courtiers on their backs. 4.JD4.207.43.
And always thinks the very thing he ought: 4.HS2.130.65.
Not quite so well however as one ought; 4.2HE2.100.171.
Say with what eyes we ought at Courts to gaze, 4.1HE6.16.237.
Whether we ought to chuse our Friends, 4.HS6.149.259.

OUGHT (CONTINUED)

This, He who loves me, and who ought to mend? 4.1HE1.178.293.
Who ought to make me (what he can, or none,) 4.1HE1.179.293.
Grieve not at ought our sister realm acquires: 5.DunA1.24.62.
Mourn not, my SWIFT, at ought our Realm acquires, 5.DunB1.26.271.
At ought thy Wisdom has deny'd, 6.50.35.148.
Or ought thy Goodness lent. 6.50.36.148.
for ought that thou hast given 6.50.34A.148.
"If thou hast ought to speak, speak out." 6.79.81.220.
"If thou hast ought to say, now speak." 6.79.81A.220.
And sure if ought below the Seats Divine 6.84.21.239.
Yet sure if ought below the Seats Divine 6.84.21A.239.
If ought within we may descry 6.94.51.260.
She speaks, behaves, and acts just as she ought; 6.139.5.377.
No Force can shake: What *is,* that *ought* to be. Il.1.731.122.
And durst he, as he ought, resent that Wrong, Il.2.300.142.
He spoke no more than just the Thing he ought. Il.3.278.206.
Nor need I to command, nor ought to blame. Il.4.413.240.
Not *Mars* himself, nor ought Immortal fear. Il.5.1021.315.
Lives there a Chief whom *Ajax* ought to dread, Il.7.235.376.
If ought of use thy waking Thoughts suggest, Il.10.106.7.
If ought from Heav'n with-hold his saving Arm; Il.11.927.77.
If ought disturb the Tenour of his Breast, Il.13.370.123.
In such Distress if Counsel profit ought; Il.14.68.160.
Ought, more conducive to our Weal, unfold. Il.14.119.163.
If ought from *Jove,* or *Thetis,* stop thy Arm, Il.16.55.237.
Nor ought a Mother's Caution can suggest; Il.16.70.238.
Shall ought avail him, if our Rage unite: Il.21.369.436.
Detested as thou art, and ought to be, Il.22.335.470.
Or why reflects my Mind on ought but thee Il.22.482.476.
The Mare, or ought thou ask'st, be freely thine, Il.23.674.516.
But say with speed, if ought thy Desire Il.24.824.571.
To slight the poor, or ought humane despise. Od.14.66.39.
Nor garment shalt thou want, nor ought beside, Od.14.578.64.
The Stranger then. Nor shall I ought conceal, Od.15.296.83.
Thus he: nor ought *Telemachus* reply'd, Od.17.31.134.
Nor ought remits the work, while thus he said. Od.24.286.363.

OUR (OMITTED)
1327

OURS

'Tis ours, the Dignity They give, to grace; 1.TrES.37.451.
Ours is the Place at Banquets, Balls and Plays; 2.TemF.382.282.
'Tis ours to trace him only in our own. 3.EOM1.22.15.
Were we to press, inferior might on ours: 3.EOM1.242.45.
One in their nature, which are two in ours, 3.EOM3.96.101.
And gently pressd my hand, and said, Be Ours!— 6.66.4.194.
'Tis ours, the Chance of fighting Fields to try, Il.1.301.101.
Be that their Care; to fight like Men be ours. Il.2.315.142.
With ours, thy Care and Ardour are the same, Il.4.412.240.
'Tis ours, to labour in the glorious Fight. Il.4.473.242.
Let Conquest make them ours: Fate shakes their Wall, Il.7.478.388.
This Night, this glorious Night, the Fleet is ours. Il.8.239.409.
'Tis thine to punish; ours to grieve alone. Il.8.577.424.
What for our selves we can, is always ours; Il.9.824.474.
Lo *Jove* himself declares the Conquest ours! Il.11.372.51.
And ours was all the Plunder of the Plains: Il.11.821.73.
'Tis ours, the Dignity they give, to grace; Il.12.381.95.
But ours, the bravest have confess'd in Fight. Il.13.312.120.
To conquer *Troy,* with ours thy Forces join, Il.13.477.130.
But 'tis not ours, with Forces not our own Il.13.989.152.
And thou the Shame of any Host but ours! Il.14.93.162.
Shall find its Match—No more: 'Tis ours to fight. Il.15.563.218.
Such is the Fate of *Greece,* and such is ours: Il.15.580.218.
Oh! were *Patroclus* ours, we might obtain Il.17.179.294.
Nor ours the Fault, but God decrees thy Doom. Il.19.455.391.
The pious Care be ours, the Dead to burn— Il.23.198.497.
'Tis ours this son of sorrow to relieve, Od.6.245.222.
Nor other hands than ours the welcome give. Od.15.554.96.
'Tis ours, with good the scanty round to grace. Od.19.378.212.

OURSELF

What then remains? Ourself. Still, still remain 5.DunB1.217.286.
"This Eve at Whisk ourself will play, 6.79.47.219.
Ourself in Arms shall tear her from his Heart. Il.1.425.108.
Ourself will Swiftness to your Nerves impart, Il.17.516.308.
Ourself with rising Spirits swell your Heart. Il.17.517.308.
Ourself will sit, and see the Hand of Fate Il.20.34.394.

OURSELVES

And all our Knowledge is, OURSELVES TO KNOW. 3.EOM4.398.166.
To Observations which ourselves we make, 3.Ep1.11.16.
Our spring of action to ourselves is lost: 3.Ep1.42.18.
Refine ourselves to Spirit, for your Sake. 6.82vi.2.232.
But shall not we, ourselves, the Truth maintain? Il.23.657.515.

OUT

And pointed out those arduous Paths they trod, 1.EOC.95.250.
Which *out of* Nature's *common Order* rise, 1.EOC.159.258.
Were but a *Combate in the Lists* left out. 1.EOC.278.271.
What! Leave the Combate out? Exclaims the Knight; 1.EOC.279.271.
And glitt'ring Thoughts struck out at ev'ry Line; 1.EOC.290.271.
Now *Sighs* steal out, and *Tears begin to flow:* 1.EOC.379.283.
Where a *new World* leaps out at his command, 1.EOC.486.294.
Strain out the last, dull droppings of their Sense, 1.EOC.608.308.
Bursts out, resistless, with a thundring Tyde! 1.EOC.630.310.
Roar'd out for rage, and hurried o'er the plain: 1.TrPA.133.371.
Whose Charms as far all other Nymphs out-shine, 1.TrVP.53.379.
And live out all in one triumphant Day. 1.TrSt.452.429.
From the wide Wound gush'd out a Stream of Blood, 1.TrES.320.461.
And singled out a Pear-Tree planted nigh: 2.ChJM.602.44.
A thousand Authors have this Truth made out, 2.ChJM.629.45.
Look'd out, and stood restor'd to sudden Sight. 2.ChJM.749.51.
When their weak Legs scarce dragg'd 'em out of Doors; 2.ChWB.155.64.
(My Husband, thank my Stars, was out of Town) 2.ChWB.279.70.

OUT (CONTINUED)

With some grave Sentence out of Holy Writ. ....2.ChWB.346.74.
Here living *Teapots* stand, one Arm held out, ...2.RL4.49.188.
And thus broke out—"My Lord, why, what the Devil? ....2.RL4.127.194.
Loud Laughs burst out, and bitter Scoffs fly round, ...2.TemF.403.282.
Fame sits aloft, and points them out their Course, ...2.TemF.483.286.
At last agreed, together out they fly, ...2.TemF.493.287.
Already written—wash it out, my tears! ....2.ElAb.14.320.
Still rebel nature holds out half my heart; ....2.ElAb.26.321.
Excuse the blush, and pour out all the heart, ...2.ElAb.56.323.
Blot out each bright Idea of the skies. ....2.ElAb.284.343.
Most souls, 'tis true, but peep out once an age, ...2.Elegy.17.363.
"Suckles each herb, and spreads out ev'ry flow'r; ....3.EOM1.134.32.
"Suckles each herb, and swells out ev'ry flow'r; ....3.EOM1.134A.32.
The doctor fancies he has driv'n them out. ....3.EOM2.160.74.
One self-approving hour whole years out-weighs ....3.EOM4.255.152.
"In pow'r your Servant, out of pow'r your Friend." ....3.Ep1.161Z2.29.
Alone, in company; in place, or out; ....3.Ep1.131.25.
As weak, as earnest, and as gravely out, ...3.Ep1.250.37.
Just brought out this, when scarce his tongue could stir, ...3.Ep1.254.37.
So much the Fury still out-ran the Wit, ...3.Ep2.127.61.
Which Heav'n has varnish'd out, and made a *Queen:* ....3.Ep2.182.64.
Worn out in public, weary ev'ry eye, ...3.Ep2.229.68.
Still out of reach, yet never out of view, ...3.Ep2.232.68.
Still out of reach, yet never out of view, ...3.Ep2.232.68.
Where all cry out, "What sums are thrown away!" ....3.Ep4.100.147.
I love to pour out all myself, as plain ....4.HS1.51.9.
Chiefs, out of War, and Statesmen, out of Place. ....4.HS1.126.17.
Chiefs, out of War, and Statesmen, out of Place. ....4.HS1.126.17.
At night, wou'd swear him dropt out of the moon, ...4.JD4.33.29.
And *Oldmixon* and *Burnet* both out-lie. ....4.JD4.61.31.
He spies me out. I whisper, gracious God! ....4.JD4.62.31.
Till I cry'd out, "You prove yourself so able, ...4.JD4.82.33.
Whose Place is *quarter'd out,* three Parts in four, ...4.JD4.136.37.
Run out as fast, as one that pays his Bail, ...4.JD4.182A.41.
Ran out as fast, as one that pays his Bail, ...4.JD4.182.41.
But ancient friends, (tho' poor, or out of play) ....4.HS2.139.65.
Himself shut out, and *Jacob Hall* let in. ....4.HAdv.86.83.
No wretched Wife cries out, *Undone! Undone!* ....4.HAdv.170.89.
All *Bedlam,* or *Parnassus,* is let out: ....4.Arbu.4.96.
Out with it, *Dunciad!* let the secret pass, ...4.Arbu.79.101.
(Cries prating *Balbus*) "something will come out." ....4.Arbu.276.115.
Who writes a Libel, or who copies out: ....4.Arbu.290.116.
Nor disputant, in vouching Texts, leave out ....4.JD2A.106.142.
But oh, those Works are out of Fashion now: ....4.JD2A.128.144.
Out-cant old Esdras, or out-drink his Heir, ...4.JD2.37.135.
Out-cant old Esdras, or out-drink his Heir, ...4.JD2.37.135.
Out-usure Jews, or Irishmen out-swear; ....4.JD2.38.135.
Out-usure Jews, or Irishmen out-swear; ....4.JD2.38.135.
Or court a Wife, spread out his wily parts, ...4.JD2.57.137.
Or, in Quotation, shrewd Divines leave out ....4.JD2.103.143.
T' out doe Italians, and out usure Jews; ....4.JD2A.42.136.
T' out doe Italians, and out usure Jews; ....4.JD2A.42.136.
Out drink the Sea and that bold Wretch outswear, ...4.JD2A.43.136.
When out of twenty I can please not two; ....4.2HE2.81.171.
Say, can you find out one such Lodger there? ....4.2HE2.223.181.
When, of a hundred thorns, you pull out one? ....4.2HE2.321.187.
I pluck out year by year, as hair by hair, ...4.2HE1.64.199.
For vulgar eyes, and point out ev'ry line. ....4.2HE1.367.227.
Prevent the greedy, and out-bid the bold: ....4.1HE6.72.241.
Go dine with Chartres, in each Vice out-do ....4.1HE6.120.245.
Of Land, set out to plant a Wood. ....4.HS6.6.251.
Hold out some months 'twixt Sun and Fire, ...4.1HE7.18.269.
Cou'd not get out as he got in: ....4.1HE7.54.271.
"Full many a Beast goes in, but none comes out." ....4.1HE1.117.287.
The only diff'rence is, I dare laugh out. ....4.EpS1.36.300.
Swear like a Lord? or a *Rich* out-whore a Duke? ....4.EpS1.116.306.
Out-do *Landaffe,* in Doctrine—yea, in Life; ....4.EpS1.134.308.
Speak out, and bid me blame no Rogues at all. ....4.EpS2.53.315.
And love him, court him, praise him, in or out. ....4.EpS2.103.319.
I think your Friends are out, and would be in. ....4.EpS2.123.320.
P. If merely to come in, Sir, they go out, ...4.EpS2.124.320.
[In Pow'r a Servant, out of Pow'r a Friend.] ....4.EpS2.161.322.
What's that to you, who ne'er was out nor in? ....4.EpS2.163.322.
Drag out with all its dirt and all its weight, ...4.1740.71.336.
Here pleas'd behold her mighty wings out-spread, ...5.DunA1.25.63.
And Eusden eke out Blackmore's endless line; ....5.DunA1.102.72.
Never was dash'd out, at one lucky hit, ...5.DunA2.43.101.
He left huge Lintot, and out-stript the wind. ....5.DunA2.58.105.
And the puff'd Orator bursts out in tropes. ....5.DunA2.198.125.
Then [Aaron] essay'd: scarce vanish'd out of sight ....5.DunA2.283B.136.
Suck the thread in, then yield it out again: ....5.DunA3.50.155.
Breaks out refulgent, with a heav'n its own: ....5.DunA3.238.177.
Art after Art goes out, and all is Night. ....5.DunA3.346.193.
Here pleas'd behold her mighty wings out-spread ....5.DunB1.27.271.
And Eusden eke out Blackmore's endless line; ....5.DunB1.104.276.
High on a gorgeous seat, that far out-shone ....5.DunB2.1.296.
Never was dash'd out, at one lucky hit, ...5.DunB2.47.298.
He left huge Lintot, and out-strip'd the wind. ....5.DunB2.62.298.
And the puff'd orator bursts out in tropes. ....5.DunB2.206.306.
Then * essay'd; scarce vanish'd out of sight, ...5.DunB2.295.310.
Suck the thread in, then yield it out again: ....5.DunB3.58.323.
Breaks out refulgent, with a heav'n its own: ....5.DunB3.242.332.
To blot out Order, and extinguish Light, ...5.DunB4.14.340.
His stretch'd-out arm display'd a Volume fair; ....5.DunB4.106.351.
And hew the Block off, and get out the Man. ....5.DunB4.270.370.
And shook from out his Pipe the seeds of fire; ....5.DunB4.494.391.
Mark'd out for Honours, honour'd for their Birth, ...5.DunB4.507.392.
And Chiefless Armies doz'd out the Campaign; ....5.DunB4.617.405.
Art after *Art* goes out, and all is Night. ....5.DunB4.640.407.
If light breaks out or goes away, ...6.4iv.11.10.
I but lug out to one or two ....6.10.31.25.
Take out your Box of right *Brasil,* ....6.10.64.26.
And stoppen, and lough, and callen out,— ....6.14i.13.42.
Now all her various States worn out ....6.14v(b).13A.50.
Still out of reach, tho' ever in their view. ....6.22.6.71.

OUT (CONTINUED)

The *honest Fellow out at Heels* ....6.44.23.123.
And in a borrow'd Play, out-did poor *Cr[own].* ....6.49i.8.137.
I'll answer Dennis, when he's out of debt: ....6.49iii.4B.142.
Whether thy hand strike out some free design, ...6.52.3.156.
Sees his past days safe out of fortune's pow'r, ...6.55.3.166.
He sees past days safe out of fortune's pow'r, ...6.55.3A.166.
And from the Key-Hole bolted out, ...6.58.31.172.
And at the Key-Hole bolted out, ...6.58.31A.172.
To one fair Lady out of court ....6.61.1.180.
and shut out Miles Davies. ....6.68.16.197.
First struck out this, and then that Thought; ....6.77.2.214.
Thrust out his Lady dear, ...6.79.58.219.
"If thou hast ought to speak, speak out." ....6.79.81.220.
From out the Boot bold *Nicholas* ....6.79.117.222.
As pointing out the gloomy Glade ....6.79.119.222.
With silver sounds, and sweetly tune out time. ....6.82xii.2.237.
Peaceful sleep out the Sabbath of the Tomb, ...6.86.19.246.
Sternhold himself he *out-Sternholded,* ....6.101.16.290.
Enjoys the *Jest,* and copies *Scandal* out: ....6.120.6.339.
Sapho enrag'd crys out your Back is round, ...6.129.3.357.
Stretch'd out in honour's nobler bed, ...6.141.7A.380.
So much the Fury still out-ran the Wit, ...6.154.13.403.
Have singled out, is *Ithacus* the Wise: ....Il.3.262.204.
'Till the bright Point look'd out beneath the Chin. ....Il.5.356.283.
His panting Steeds, remov'd from out the War, ...Il.5.397.286.
Held out in Order to the *Grecian* Peers. ....Il.7.222.375.
Some future Day shall lengthen out the Strife, ...Il.7.354.381.
The Chiefs out-number'd by the *Trojan* Train: ....Il.10.633.30.
Breaking their Ranks, and crushing out their Souls; ....Il.11.210.44.
Till some wide Wound lets out their mighty Soul. ....Il.12.168.87.
The stately Car, and labours out his Breath. ....Il.13.506.130.
While Life's red Torrent gush'd from out the Wound. ....Il.13.820.144.
What Troops, out-number'd scarce the War maintain? ....Il.13.927.149.
He singles out; arrests, and lays him dead. ....Il.15.767.226.
The Hills shine out, the Rocks in Prospect rise, ...Il.16.358.257.
He sobs his Soul out in the Gush of Blood. ....Il.16.419.259.
From the wide Wound gush'd out a Stream of Blood, ...Il.16.625.268.
Breathe their brave Souls out, in another's War. ....Il.16.662.270.
When Men distrest hang out the Sign of War) ....Il.18.248.334.
And the whole War came out, and met the Eye; ....Il.18.625.352.
Courage may prompt; but, ebbing out his Strength, ...Il.19.163.378.
Work out our Will. Celestial Pow'rs! descend, ...Il.20.35.394.
Far on his out-stretch'd Arm, *Pelides* held ....Il.20.310.407.
The trampling Steers beat out th' unnumber'd Grain. ....Il.20.580.418.
Tread down whole Ranks, and crush out Hero's Souls. ....Il.20.582.418.
Lock fast the brazen Bars, and shut out Death. ....Il.21.626.448.
But reach *Atrides!* Shall his Mare out-go ....Il.23.487.509.
Nor weary out your gen'rous Strength in vain. ....Il.23.857.523.
And here had sigh'd and sorrow'd out the Day; ....Il.24.891.573.
(Already dry'd.) These pointing out to view, ...Od.5.309.186.
Some bark's broad bottom to out-ride the storms, ...Od.5.320.187.
Thus, thus find out the destin'd shore, and then ....Od.5.482.195.
Here by the stream if I the night out-wear, ...Od.5.601.201.
High at its head, from out the cavern'd rock ....Od.9.161.312.
The grain deep-piercing till it scoops it out: ....Od.9.460.325.
But two rush'd out, and to the navy flew. ....Od.10.134.347.
And send out spies the dubious coast to view. ....Od.10.180.349.
Unwieldy, out They rush'd, with gen'ral cry, ...Od.10.461.366.
Out-fly the nimble sail, and leave the lagging wind? ....Od.11.74.384.
Stretch'd out her snowy hand, and thus she spoke: ....Od.11.417.405.
Pours out deep groans; (with groans all hell resounds) ....Od.11.720.421.
They call, and aid with out-stretch'd arms implore: ....Od.12.298.446.
Night dwells o'er all the deep: and now out flies ....Od.12.477.455.
And many a long-repented word bring out. ....Od.14.523.62.
Whilst *Eteoneus* portions out the shares, ...Od.15.156.76.
Pin'd out her bloom, and vanish'd to a ghost. ....Od.15.383.88.
And thus burst out, imposthumate with pride. ....Od.20.358.249.
Stript of his rags, he blaz'd out like a God. ....Od.22.2.284.
Ev'n then to drain it lengthen'd out his breath; ....Od.22.15.287.
Pour out my soul, and dye within thy arms! ....Od.23.226.333.
Out-lives the tumult of conflicting waves, ...Od.23.254.335.
Points out the long, uncomfortable way. ....Od.24.6.347.
Then thus broke out. Oh long, oh daily mourn'd! ....Od.24.460.370.
Each faithful youth, and breathes out ardent vows: ....Od.24.471.371.

OUT-BID

Prevent the greedy, and out-bid the bold: ....4.1HE6.72.241.

OUT-CANT

Out-cant old Esdras, or out-drink his Heir, ...4.JD2.37.135.

OUT-CAST

He dies, sad out-cast of each church and state, ...3.Ep1.204.32.

OUT-DID

And in a borrow'd Play, out-did poor *Cr[own].* ....6.49i.8.137.

OUT-DO

Go dine with Chartres, in each Vice out-do ....4.1HE6.120.245.
Out-do *Landaffe,* in Doctrine—yea, in Life; ....4.EpS1.134.308.

OUT-DRINK

Out-cant old Esdras, or out-drink his Heir, ...4.JD2.37.135.

OUT-FLY

Out-fly the nimble sail, and leave the lagging wind? ....Od.11.74.384.

OUT-GO

But reach *Atrides!* Shall his Mare out-go ....Il.23.487.509.

OUT-LIE

And *Oldmixon* and *Burnet* both out-lie. ....4.JD4.61.31.

OUT-LIVES
Out-lives the tumult of conflicting waves, ...Od.23.254.335.

OUT-NUMBER'D
The Chiefs out-number'd by the *Trojan* Train: ....Il.10.633.30.
What Troops, out-number'd scarce the War maintain? ....Il.13.927.149.

OUT-RAN
So much the Fury still out-ran the Wit, ...3.Ep2.127.61.
So much the Fury still out-ran the Wit, ...6.154.13.403.

OUT-RIDE
Some bark's broad bottom to out-ride the storms, ...Od.5.320.187.

OUT-SHINE
Whose Charms as far all other Nymphs out-shine, ...1.TrVP.53.379.

OUT-SHONE
High on a gorgeous seat, that far out-shone ....5.DunB2.1.296.

OUT-SIDE
The rest on Out-side merit but presume, ...5.DunB1.135.280.

OUT-SPREAD
Here pleas'd behold her mighty wings out-spread, ...5.DunA1.25.63.
Here pleas'd behold her mighty wings out-spread ....5.DunB1.27.271.

OUT-STERNHOLDED
Sternhold himself he *out-Sternholded,* ....6.101.16.290.

OUT-STRETCH'D
Far on his out-stretch'd Arm, *Pelides* held ....Il.20.310.407.
They call, and aid with out-stretch'd arms implore: ....Od.12.298.446.

OUT-STRIP'D
He left huge Lintot, and out-strip'd the wind. ....5.DunB2.62.298.

OUT-STRIPT
He left huge Lintot, and out-stript the wind. ....5.DunA2.58.105.

OUT-SWEAR
Out-usure Jews, or Irishmen out-swear; ....4.JD2.38.135.

OUT-USURE
Out-usure Jews, or Irishmen out-swear; ....4.JD2.38.135.

OUT-WEAR
Here by the stream if I the night out-wear, ...Od.5.601.201.

OUT-WEIGHS
One self-approving hour whole years out-weighs ....3.EOM4.255.152.

OUT-WHORE
Swear like a Lord? or a *Rich* out-whore a Duke? ....4.EpS1.116.306.

OUTCAST
He, wretched Outcast of Mankind! appears ....Il.22.630.482.
He wanders, Outcast both of Earth and Heav'n. ....Il.24.670.565.
A man, an outcast to the storm and wave, ...Od.5.165.179.
Outcast I rove, familiar with the storms! ....Od.6.210.220.

OUTCASTS
Outcasts of earth, to breathe an unknown sky? ....Od.16.395.125.

OUTLAST
A Work t'outlast Immortal *Rome* design'd, ...1.EOC.131.254.

OUTLASTING
A Work outlasting Monumental Brass. ....2.TemF.227.273.

OUTLET
To guard the outlet, plac'd *Eumæus* there: ....Od.22.147.294.
Melanthius then: That outlet to the gate ....Od.22.152.294.

OUTRAG'D
And outrag'd by the wrongs of base mankind. ....Od.16.209.114.
If outrag'd, cease that outrage to repel, ...Od.16.296.119.

OUTRAGE
If outrag'd, cease that outrage to repel, ...Od.16.296.119.
I bear their outrage, tho' my soul rebell: ....Od.18.272.179.

OUTRAGES
Perhaps, these outrages from *Irus* flow, ...Od.18.434.189.

OUTRAGIOUS
How could that numerous and outragious band ....Od.23.39.321.

OUTSHIN'D
All *Pelias'* Race *Alcestè* far outshin'd, ...Il.2.870.165.
And * both her warlike Lords outshin'd in *Helen's* Eyes? ......Il.3.72.193.
A Host of Heroes, and outshin'd them all. ....Il.16.676.270.

OUTSHINES
Tow'rs o'er his Armies, and outshines them all: ....Il.2.565.154.

OUTSHONE
High on a gorgeous seat, that far outshone ....5.DunA2.1.96.
He forg'd; the Cuirass that outshone the Fires; ....Il.18.706.357.

OUTSIDE
By the bare Outside only knew, ...6.64.2.189.

OUTSPREAD
Here dulness reigns, with mighty wings outspread, ...6.106iv.11.307.
Steep'd in their Blood, and in the Dust outspread, ...Il.24.767.569.

OUTSPREAD (CONTINUED)
With sails outspread we fly th' unequal strife, ...Od.9.71.305.

OUTSTRETCH'D
The Peers transported, as outstretch'd he lies, ...Od.18.118.172.

OUTSTRIP
So two wild Boars outstrip the following Hounds, ...Il.11.421.53.

OUTSTRIPS
Or thank that Swiftness which outstrips the Death. ....Il.11.466.54.

OUTSWEAR
Out drink the Sea and that bold Wretch outswear, ...4.JD2A.43.136.

OUTVIE
Living, great Nature fear'd he might outvie ....6.108.7.312.
Living, great Nature fear'd he would outvie ....6.108.7A.312.

OUTWARD
In Ranks adorn'd the Temple's outward Face; ....2.TemF.131.264.
Pride, Pomp, and State but reach her outward Part, ...6.19.55.63.
Soft moving Speech, and pleasing outward Show, ...Il.3.95.194.
Compos'd the Shield; of Brass each outward Fold, ...Il.20.319.407.
In outward show heav'n gives thee to excell, ...Od.8.197.273.
(The males were penn'd in outward courts behind) ....Od.9.283.318.
The midmost bore a man; the outward two ....Od.9.509.327.

OUTWORKS
To pass our Outworks, or elude the Guard. ....Il.24.715.567.

OVER
Nor over-dress, nor leave her wholly bare; ....3.Ep4.52.142.
Shall stretch thy Conquests over half the kind: ....4.HOde1.16.151.
Shall stretch his Conquest over half the kind: ....4.HOde1.16A.151.
Shall spread thy Conquests over half the kind: ....4.HOde1.16B.151.
See Ward by batter'd Beaus invited over, ...4.1HE6.56.241.
Rather than so, see Ward invited over, ...4.1HE6.56A.241.
Her boundless Empire over seas and lands. ....5.DunA3.60.155.
Her boundless empire over seas and lands. ....5.DunB3.68.323.
Some, over each Orac'lous Glass, fore-doom ....6.17iv.3.59.
A close over clap on; ....6.91.20.253.
Over Woods, ...6.96i.19.268.
Over Floods. ....6.96i.20.268.
Or any good Christian lays over my Head; ....6.144.4A.386.
With cliffs, and nodding forests over-hung. ....Od.14.4.34.

OVER-DRESS
Nor over-dress, nor leave her wholly bare; ....3.Ep4.52.142.

OVER-HUNG
With cliffs, and nodding forests over-hung. ....Od.14.4.34.

OVERCAST
A Cloud of Sorrow overcast his Sight, ...Il.20.487.415.

OVERCHARG'D
As full blown Poppies overcharg'd with Rain ....Il.8.371.415.

OVERCOME
She said; the Cloud-Compeller overcome, ...1.TrES.254.459.
She said; the Cloud-compeller overcome, ...Il.16.559.266.

OVERHANG
Of whelming mountains overhang their head! ....Od.13.183.15.

OVERHANGS
As on a Rock that overhangs the Main, ...Il.16.494.262.
As from some rock that overhangs the flood, ...Od.12.300.446.

OVERHUNG
A spreading Elm, that overhung the Flood; ....Il.21.268.431.

OVERLAID
E'er sixteen passing years had overlaid ....1.TrPA.7.365.

OVERLOOK'D
When the brisk Nectar overlook'd the Brim. ....Il.11.779.70.

OVERLOOKS
Where the high Watch-tow'r overlooks the Plain; ....Il.22.192.463.
The lofty palace overlooks the town, ...Od.6.363.229.

OVERSHADES
Rolls the black troop, and overshades the street, ...5.DunB2.360.315.

OVERSIGHT
Not so his Son, he mark'd this oversight, ...3.Ep3.199.109.

OVERSPREAD
Oenides' manly Shoulders overspread, ...1.TrSt.572.434.
And Night's dark Mantle overspread the Sky. ....2.ChJM.370.32.

OVERTAKE
Nor this can fly, nor that can overtake. ....Il.22.260.466.

OVERTHROW
'Tis hers to rectify, not overthrow, ...3.EOM2.163.74.
Nor could the Strength of *Ajax* overthrow ....Il.23.836.522.
And much thy betters wine can overthrow: ....Od.21.316.274.

OVERTHROWN
Triumph! All Arts are overthrown, ...6.119.19A.337.
Thy present Vigour Age has overthrown, ...Il.23.715.518.
Now all confus'd, distracted, overthrown! ....Il.24.246.546.

OVERTON
Between *John Overton* and *You.* .... 6.119.20.337.
Betwixt *John Overton* and *You.* .... 6.119.20A.337.

OVERTOOK
One instant saw, one Instant overtook .... Il.17.214.295.

OVERTOPS
Tho' great *Atrides* overtops his Head. .... Il.3.256.204.

OVERTURN
Overturn .... 6.96i.26.268.

OVERWATCH'D
Was overwatch'd, for all his hundred Eyes: .... 2.ChJM.505.40.

OVID
Well sung sweet *Ovid,* in the Days of yore, ... 2.ChJM.514.40.
"Let me be *Horace,* and be *Ovid* you. .... 4.2HE2.144.175.
How sweet an Ovid, MURRAY was our boast! .... 5.DunB4.169.357.
Tho' *Ovid* lay without. .... 6.58.28.171.
Poor *Ovid* finds no Quarter! .... 6.58.42.172.
For to poor *Ovid* shall befal .... 6.58.71.174.
"To what, (quoth 'Squire) shall *Ovid* change?" .... 6.58.75.174.
"To what,(quoth Sam) shall *Ovid* change?" .... 6.58.75A.174.

OVID'S
Chrysippus and *Tertullian; Ovid's* Art; .... 2.ChWB.360.74.
Such *Ovid's* nose, and "Sir! you have an *Eye*—" .... 4.Arbu.118.104.

OW'D
Thy Monster's Death to me was ow'd alone, ... 1.TrSt.761.442.
Jove ow'd the Glory of the destin'd Fight. .... 1.TrES.174.456.
His Life is ow'd to fierce *Patroclus'* Hands. .... 1.TrES.230.458.
Abusive *Nabal* ow'd his forfeit Life .... 2.ChJM.71.18.
Honour and Fame at least the Thund'rer ow'd, ... Il.1.464.110.
Urge all the Ties to former Service ow'd, ... Il.1.512.112.
That ow'd his Nurture to the blue-ey'd Maid, ... Il.2.658.158.
And those are ow'd to gen'rous Wine and Food) .... Il.9.827.474.
Was ow'd the Glory of the destin'd Fight. .... Il.12.200.88.
And what my Youth has ow'd, repay their Age. .... Il.14.242.172.
A Victim ow'd to my brave Brother's Death. .... Il.14.566.190.
His Life is ow'd to fierce *Patroclus'* Hands. .... Il.16.533.264.
To Heav'n is ow'd whate'er your own you call, ... Il.16.1020.282.
To whom her Safety and her Fame she ow'd, ... Il.22.558.479.
Why was my Birth to great *Aëtion* ow'd, ... Il.22.614.481.
Hail happy nymph! no vulgar births are ow'd .... Od.11.297.396.
O deem thy fall not ow'd to man's decree, ... Od.11.687.418.
To whom whate'er his slave enjoys is ow'd, ... Od.14.75.39.
To him, whatever to a guest is ow'd .... Od.24.318.365.

OW'ST
Propt on that Spear to which thou ow'st thy Fall, ... Il.14.533.189.
Thou ow'st thy Guidance to no mortal Hand: .... Il.24.564.559.
To me thou ow'st, to me, the vital air. .... Od.8.502.289.

OWE
And give to Fame what we to Nature owe; .... 1.TrES.50.451.
To these we owe true friendship, love sincere, ... 3.EOM2.255.86.
'Tis to their Changes half their charms we owe; .... 3.Ep2.42A.53.
'Tis to their Changes that their charms they owe; .... 3.Ep2.42.53.
We owe to models of an humble kind. .... 3.Ep2.192.65.
Yet to their Lord owe more than to the soil; .... 3.Ep4.184.154.
As clocks to weight their nimble motion owe, ... 5.DunA1.179.84.
As clocks to weight their nimble motion owe, ... 5.DunB1.183.283.
So Clocks to Lead their nimble Motions owe, ... 6.17i(b).1.55.
Nay, to yourselves alone that knowledge owe. .... 6.27.15.81.
And pay in Glory what in Life you owe. .... Il.1.655.118.
Divine *Idomeneus!* what Thanks we owe .... Il.4.292.235.
Oh spare my Youth, and for the Life I owe .... Il.6.57.326.
What must not *Greece* to her Deliv'rer owe? .... Il.10.254.13.
O spare my Youth, and for the Breath I owe, ... Il.10.449.23.
Oh spare our Youth, and for the Life we owe, ... Il.11.171.43.
To great *Achilles* this Respect I owe; .... Il.11.794.71.
And give to Fame what we to Nature owe; .... Il.12.394.96.
This Deed to fierce *Idomeneus* we owe; .... Il.13.588.134.
And owe Destruction to a Prince like thee. .... Il.14.113.163.
I owe the nursing of my tender Years. .... Il.14.346.179.
This Death deplor'd to *Hector's* Rage we owe; .... Il.15.514.217.
They owe their Life and Nourishment to Earth; .... Il.21.538.444.
And to what ship I owe the friendly freight? .... Od.1.222.43.
Regardful of the friendly dues I owe, ... Od.4.128.126.
And owe thy country and thy friends to her. .... Od.7.98.238.
'Tis what the happy to th' unhappy owe. .... Od.7.199.245.
They all their products to free nature owe. .... Od.9.122.310.
'Tis what the happy to th' unhappy owe: .... Od.9.320.319.
The Ghost reply'd: To Hell my doom I owe, ... Od.11.75.384.
A gen'ral tribute, which the State shall owe. .... Od.13.18.2.
And to what ship I owe the friendly freight? .... Od.14.217.45.
Our freedom to thy prowess'd arm we owe .... Od.18.139.173.
This gift acquits the dear respect I owe; .... Od.20.362.250.
To copious wine this insolence we owe, ... Od.21.315.274.

OWES
What Fav'rites gain, and what the Nation owes, ... 6.8.35.19.
What Fav'rites gain, and what th'Exchequer owes, ... 6.8.35A.19.
Which nor to Guilt, nor Fear, its Caution owes, ... 6.73.3.209.
And much to both he owes; .... 6.102.10.294.
To whom its Safety a whole People owes, ... Il.2.29.128.
To whom its Safety a whole People owes; .... Il.2.79.130.
Heav'n owes *Ulysses* yet a longer Date. .... Il.11.567.59.
And gives to Passion what to *Greece* he owes. .... Il.11.899.75.
And who to *Tydeus* owes his noble Line. .... Il.14.38.159.
Fate owes thee sure a miserable end! .... Od.15.347.86.
By that regard a son his father owes; .... Od.16.323.121.
Say thou, to whom my youth its nurture owes, ... Od.20.161.241.

OWING
His Fame in Arms, not owing all to me. .... Il.16.301.254.

OWL
Something betwixt a H[eidegger] and Owl) .... 5.DunA1.244.92.
Something betwixt a Heideggre and owl,) .... 5.DunB1.290.290.
Sick was the Sun, the Owl forsook his bow'r, ... 5.DunB4.11.340.
Which Chalcis Gods, and mortals call an Owl, ... 5.DunB4.362.378.

OWL'S
Mix'd the Owl's ivy with the Poet's bays? .... 5.DunA3.46.154.
Mix'd the Owl's ivy with the Poet's bays? .... 5.DunB3.54.323.

OWLERS
By running Goods, these graceless Owlers gain, ... 6.60.11.178.

OWLS
Here stood her Opium, here she nurs'd her Owls, ... 5.DunA1.35.O64.
She ceas'd: her owls responsive clap the wings, ... 5.DunA1.255A.94.
And makes Night hideous—Answer him ye Owls! .... 5.DunA3.160.165.
Wits, who like Owls see only in the dark, ... 5.DunA3.188.172.
Here stood her Opium, here she nurs'd her Owls, ... 5.DunB1.271.290.
And makes Night hideous—Answer him, ye Owls! .... 5.DunB3.166.328.
Wits, who like owls, see only in the dark, ... 5.DunB3.192.329.

OWN
In Notes more sad than when they sing their own. .... 1.PWi.40.92.
In sadder Notes than when they sing their own. .... 1.PWi.40A.92.
A sweeter Musick than their own to hear, ... 1.PWi.58.93.
Thy *Realm* for ever lasts! thy own *Messiah* reigns! .... 1.Mes.108.122.
Reap their own Fruits, and woo their Sable Loves, ... 1.W-F.410.192.
There hateful *Envy* her own Snakes shall feel, ... 1.W-F.419.193.
Go just *alike,* yet each believes his own. .... 1.EOC.10.240.
And then turn Criticks in their own Defence. .... 1.EOC.29.242.
Be sure *your self* and your own *Reach* to know, ... 1.EOC.48.244.
Against the Poets *their own Arms* they turn'd, ... 1.EOC.106.251.
T' *admire* Superior Sense, and *doubt* their own! .... 1.EOC.200.263.
Leave such to tune their own dull Rhimes, and know .... 1.EOC.358.280.
Some *foreign* Writers, some our *own* despise; .... 1.EOC.394.285.
Some the *French* Writers, some our *own* despise; .... 1.EOC.394A.285.
Some ne'er advance a Judgment of their own, ... 1.EOC.408.287.
And own *stale Nonsense* which they ne'er invent. .... 1.EOC.411.287.
But let a *Lord* once own the *happy Lines,* .... 1.EOC.420.287.
But let his Lordship own the *happy Lines,* .... 1.EOC.420A.287.
Some valuing those of their own *Side,* or *Mind,* .... 1.EOC.452.290.
Th' *opposing Body's* Grossness, not its *own.* .... 1.EOC.469.292.
But you, with Pleasure own your Errors past, ... 1.EOC.570.305.
With his own Tongue still edifies his Ears, ... 1.EOC.614.309.
Garth did not write his own *Dispensary.* .... 1.EOC.619.309.
Whose *own Example* strengthens all his Laws, ... 1.EOC.679.316.
And ev'ry Author's *Merit,* but his own. .... 1.EOC.728.325.
For his firm Faith I dare ingage my own, ... 1.TrVP.83.380.
And kindly sigh for sorrows not your own; .... 1.TrFD.4.385.
Love enters there, and I'm my own Disease: .... 1.TrSP.16.394.
Pleas'd to behold unbounded Pow'r thy own, ... 1.TrSt.222.419.
On thy own Offspring hast thou fix'd this Fate, ... 1.TrSt.245.420.
Thy own *Arcadians* there the Thunder claim, ... 1.TrSt.386.426.
With Transport views the airy Rule his own, ... 1.TrSt.449.428.
Enjoys an airy Empire, all his own, ... 1.TrSt.449A.428.
And conscious Virtue, still its own Reward, ... 1.TrSt.758.442.
Be mine the Vengeance, as the Crime my own. .... 1.TrSt.779.442.
You seek to share in Sorrows not your own; .... 1.TrSt.803.443.
To you once more your own *Ulysses* bows, ... 1.TrUl.242.473.
As still I hold your own Advice the best. .... 2.ChJM.155.22.
Each, in his own Opinion, went his Way; .... 2.ChJM.225.25.
Who, wisely, never thinks the Case his own. .... 2.ChJM.507.40.
When Un-endow'd, I took thee for my own, ... 2.ChJM.550.41.
While thou art faithful to thy own true Knight, ... 2.ChJM.553.42.
Next, your own Honour undefil'd maintain; .... 2.ChJM.560.42.
Make your own Terms; and ere to-morrow's Sun .... 2.ChJM.563.42.
And join'd to them, my own unequal Age; .... 2.ChJM.570.42.
Whilst thou art faithful to thy own true Knight, ... 2.ChJM.553A.42.
And joined to that, my own unequal Age; .... 2.ChJM.570A.42.
But jealous Men on their own Crimes reflect, ... 2.ChJM.593.43.
Now, by my own dread Majesty I swear, ... 2.ChJM.647.46.
David, the Monarch after Heav'ns' own Mind, ... 2.ChJM.692.48.
"But see! I'm all your own—nay hold—for Shame! .... 2.ChWB.203.66.
I follow'd always my own Inclination. .... 2.ChWB.328.72.
Brought her own Spouse and all his Race to Woe; .... 2.ChWB.380.75.
Hear and believe! thy own Importance know, ... 2.RL1.35.148.
As now your own, our Beings were of old, ... 2.RL1.47.149.
And *Betty's* prais'd for Labours not her own. .... 2.RL1.148.158.
With *Flavia's* Busk that oft had rapp'd his own: .... 2.RL2.39Z2.161.
Of these the Chief the Care of Nations own, ... 2.RL2.89.165.
My hands shall rend what ev'n thy own did spare. .... 2.RL4.168A.197.
And in its Fellow's Fate foresees its own; .... 2.RL4.172.198.
And in its Fellow's Fate foresees it own; .... 2.RL4.172A.198.
And fix their own with Labour in their place: .... 2.TemF.38.256.
Their own like others soon their Place resign'd, ... 2.TemF.39.256.
Cæsar, the World's great Master, and his own; .... 2.TemF.156.266.
His own strict Judge, and Patron of Mankind. .... 2.TemF.167.268.
Those Ills we dar'd thy Inspiration own, ... 2.TemF.348.280.
I tremble too where-e'er my own I find, ... 2.ElAb.33.321.
And close confin'd to their own palace sleep. .... 2.Elegy.22.364.
And close confin'd in their own palace sleep. .... 2.Elegy.22A.364.
'Tis ours to trace him only in our own. .... 3.EOM1.22.15.
Each beast, each insect, happy in its own; .... 3.EOM1.185.37.
Know thy own point: This kind, this due degree .... 3.EOM1.283.49.
Know thy own point: This just, this kind degree .... 3.EOM1.283A.49.
Explain his own beginning, or his end? .... 3.EOM2.38.60.
But when his own great work is but begun, ... 3.EOM2.41.60.
And Reason bids us for our own provide; .... 3.EOM2.96.66.
Ask your own heart, and nothing is so plain; .... 3.EOM2.215.81.
Or never feel the rage, or never own; .... 3.EOM2.228.83.
View thy own World; behold the chain of Love .... 3.EOM3.7A.92.
Loves of his own and raptures swell the note: .... 3.EOM3.34.95.

OWN (CONTINUED)

Heav'ns not his own, and worlds unknown before? .... 3.EOM3.106.102.
Murders their species, and betrays his own. .... 3.EOM3.164.109.
And ev'ry death its own avenger breeds; .... 3.EOM3.166.109.
With Heav'n's own thunders shook the world below, ... 3.EOM3.267.119.
On their own Axis as the Planets run, ... 3.EOM3.313.126.
And Peace, oh Virtue! Peace is all thy own. .... 3.EOM4.82.136.
And Peace, fair Virtue! Peace is all thy own. .... 3.EOM4.82A.136.
And Peace, O Virtue! Peace is all thy own. .... 3.EOM4.82B.136.
One thinks on Calvin Heav'n's own spirit fell, ... 3.EOM4.137.141.
His own Contentment, or another's Trust? .... 3.EOM4.186A.144.
Nor own, your fathers have been fools so long. .... 3.EOM4.214.147.
Not own, your fathers have been fools so long. .... 3.EOM4.214A.147.
The same (my Lord) if Tully's or your own. .... 3.EOM4.240.150.
To see all others faults, and feel our own: .... 3.EOM4.262.153.
At once his own bright prospect to be blest, ... 3.EOM4.351.162.
By his own Sons that pass him by unbless'd: .... 3.Ep1.231A.35.
All Manners take a tincture from our own, ... 3.Ep1.25.17.
By his own son, that passes by unbless'd: .... 3.Ep1.231.35.
She, who can own a Sister's charms, or hears .... 3.Ep2.259B.71.
Here Fannia, leering on her own good man, ... 3.Ep2.9.49.
Asham'd to own they gave delight before, ... 3.Ep2.237.69.
B. Who suffer thus, mere Charity should own, ... 3.Ep3.113A.101.
Who suffer thus, mere Charity should own, ... 3.Ep3.113.101.
That live-long wig which Gorgon's self might own, ... 3.Ep3.295.117.
Or are they both, in this their own reward? .... 3.Ep3.336.120.
Wife, son, and daughter, Satan, are thy own, ... 3.Ep3.399.124.
Envy must own, I live among the Great, ... 4.HS1.133.19.
He came by sure Transition to his own: .... 4.JD4.81.31.
He came by soft Transition to his own: .... 4.JD4.81A.31.
'Tis yet in vain, I own, to keep a pother .... 4.HS2.45.57.
Thence comes your mutton, and these chicks my own: .... 4.HS2.144.67.
I'll hire another's, is not that my own, ... 4.HS2.156.67.
"I wish to God this house had been your own: .... 4.HS2.162.67.
Who cries, my father's damn'd, and all's my own. .... 4.HS2.174.69.
Let Us be fix'd, and our own Masters still. .... 4.HS2.180.69.
That cries, my father's damn'd, and all's my own .... 4.HS2.174A.69.
Yet starves herself, so little her own Friend, ... 4.HAdv.23.77.
Who judg'd themselves, and saw with their own Eyes) .... 4.HAdv.113.85.
Her Shape her own, whatever Shape she have, ... 4.HAdv.163.89.
Dipt me in Ink, my Parents', or my own? .... 4.Arbu.126.104.
And sit attentive to his own applause; .... 4.Arbu.210.111.
Oh let me live my own! and die so too! .... 4.Arbu.261.114.
There let me live my own, and die so too, ... 4.Arbu.263A.114.
Th' imputed Trash, and Dulness not his own; .... 4.Arbu.351.121.
The imputed Trash, the Dulness not his own; .... 4.Arbu.351A.121.
He gain his Prince's Ear, or lose his own. .... 4.Arbu.367.122.
Each Parent sprung—"What Fortune, pray?"— Their own, ... 4.Arbu.390.126.
Each Parent sprung—"What Fortune, pray?"— their own, ... 4.Arbu.390A.126.
If Peter deigns to help you to your *own:* .... 4.JD2.66.139.
What tho he swears tis all his own, and new; .... 4.JD2A.37.134.
To have been mine, the Excrement's his own .... 4.JD2A.40.136.
All these their Hell in their own Bosom find, ... 4.JD2A.49.136.
If Coscus deigns to help you to your *own:* .... 4.JD2.66A.139.
With Laws, to which you gave your own assent? .... 4.2HE2.30.167.
Ev'n to their own S[ir]r[e]v[ere]nce in a Carr? .... 4.2HE2.107.173.
Their own strict Judges, not a word they spare .... 4.2HE2.159.175.
His Ven'son too, a Guinea makes your own: .... 4.2HE2.235.181.
Yet these are Wights, who fondly call their own .... 4.2HE2.244.183.
Ready, by force, or of your own accord, ... 4.2HE2.250.183.
As Heav'n's own Oracles from Altars heard. .... 4.2HE1.28.197.
Foes to all living worth except your own, ... 4.2HE1.33.197.
And grew Immortal in his own despight. .... 4.2HE1.72.199.
But let them own, that greater faults than we .... 4.2HE1.95.203.
I lose my patience, and I own it too, ... 4.2HE1.115.205.
And in our own (excuse some Courtly stains) .... 4.2HE1.215.213.
And in our own (excuse some Courtly strains) .... 4.2HE1.215A.213.
Not but the Tragic spirit was our own, ... 4.2HE1.276.219.
Till Earth's extremes your mediation own, ... 4.2HE1.402.229.
Then turn about, and laugh at your own Jest. .... 4.1HE6.109.245.
If, after all, we must with Wilmot own, ... 4.1HE6.126.245.
I own, I'm pleas'd with this rebuke, ... 4.HS6.60.253.
For their own Worth, or our own Ends? .... 4.HS6.150.259.
For their own Worth, or our own Ends? .... 4.HS6.150.259.
Of all these ways, if each pursues his own, ... 4.1HE1.134.289.
That Man divine whom Wisdom calls her own; .... 4.1HE1.180.293.
And own, the *Spaniard* did a *waggish thing,* .... 4.EpS1.17.298.
Let *Greatness* own her, and she's mean no more: .... 4.EpS1.144.309.
Pleas'd let me own, in *Esher's* peaceful Grove .... 4.EpS2.66.316.
The Master of our Passions, and his own. .... 4.EpS2.89.318.
Because the Deed he forg'd was not my own? .... 4.EpS2.190.324.
So impudent, I own myself no Knave: .... 4.EpS2.206.324.
C[arteret], his own proud dupe, thinks Monarchs things .... 4.1740.5.332.
Who hears all causes, B[ritain], but thy own, ... 4.1740.66.335.
Europe's just balance and our own may stand, ... 4.1740.97.337.
The clubs of Quidnunc's, or her own Guild-hall. .... 5.DunA1.34.O64.
And with her own fool's colours gilds them all. .... 5.DunA1.82.69.
The page admires new beauties, not its own. .... 5.DunA1.120.77.
And last, his own cold Æschylus took fire. .... 5.DunA1.210.88.
'Till each fam'd Theatre my empire own, ... 5.DunA1.253.93.
I see a Monarch proud my race to own! .... 5.DunA1.251Z3.93.
In a dun night-gown of his own loose skin, ... 5.DunA2.34.100.
Three wicked imps of her own Grubstreet Choir .... 5.DunA2.115.110.
So shall each hostile name become our own, ... 5.DunA2.131.113.
For straining more, it flies in his own face; .... 5.DunA2.168.122.
Thus visit not thy own! on this blest age .... 5.DunA3.113.160.
And prove, no Miracles can match thy own. .... 5.DunA3.210.175.
Breaks out refulgent, with a heav'n its own: .... 5.DunA3.238.177.
Refulgent rises, with a heav'n its own: .... 5.DunA3.238A.177.
A godlike youth: See *Jove's* own bolt he flings .... 5.DunA3.251A.178.
Unknown to thee? These wonders are thy own. .... 5.DunA3.270.180.
Tho' my own Aldermen conferr'd my bays, ... 5.DunA3.277.183.
Reduc'd at last to hiss in my own dragon. .... 5.DunA3.288.184.
And with her own fools-colours gilds them all. .... 5.DunB1.84.275.
And Quarles is sav'd by Beauties not his own. .... 5.DunB1.140.280.
The clubs of Quidnuncs, or her own Guild-hall: .... 5.DunB1.270.290.

OWN (CONTINUED)

"O! when shall rise a Monarch all our own, ... 5.DunB1.311.292.
In a dun night-gown of his own loose skin; .... 5.DunB2.38.297.
Three wicked imps, of her own Grubstreet choir, ... 5.DunB2.123.301.
So shall each hostile name become our own, ... 5.DunB2.139.302.
Thus visit not thy own! on this blest age .... 5.DunB3.121.325.
Breaks out refulgent, with a heav'n its own: .... 5.DunB3.242.332.
Unknown to thee? These wonders are thy own. .... 5.DunB3.274.333.
Tho' my own Aldermen confer'd the bays, ... 5.DunB3.279.333.
Reduc'd at last to hiss in my own dragon. .... 5.DunB3.286.334.
See, see, our own true Phœbus wears the bays! .... 5.DunB3.323.335.
Another Phœbus, thy own Phœbus reigns, ... 5.DunB4.61.347.
And Jove's own Thunders follow Mars's Drums. .... 5.DunB4.68.348.
Not those alone who passive own her laws, ... 5.DunB4.85.349.
A Page, a Grave, that they can call their own; .... 5.DunB4.128.354.
See! still thy own, the heavy Canon roll, ... 5.DunB4.247.367.
The Sire saw, smiling, his own Virtues wake: .... 5.DunB4.285A.372.
Spoil'd his own language, and acquir'd no more; .... 5.DunB4.320.374.
Left his own language, and acquir'd no more; .... 5.DunB4.320A.374.
And make a long Posterity thy own." .... 5.DunB4.334.376.
Honour a Syrian Prince above his own; .... 5.DunB4.368.378.
Down his own throat he risqu'd the Grecian gold; .... 5.DunB4.382.380.
This Nod confirms each Privilege your own. .... 5.DunB4.584.400.
In his own ground. .... 6.1.4.3.
Not for his own, but hers, the youth had dy'd. .... 6.4ii.10.9.
As pale as her own lovers are. .... 6.4iii.6.10.
How much her sweets their own excel. .... 6.4iv.9.10.
(That Simile is not my own, ... 6.10.17.25.
As e'er he did his own dear Lady. .... 6.10.100.27.
In his own Palace forc'd to ask his bread, ... 6.15.7.51.
Forgot of all his own domestic crew; .... 6.15.9.51.
Their own Destruction by their Industry. .... 6.17ii.8.56.
Quite o'er the Banks to their own Ruin force. .... 6.17ii.17.56.
Like his own Person, large and fair. .... 6.29.8.83.
Be justly warm'd with your own native rage. .... 6.32.44.97.
Who in your own *Despite* has strove to please ye. .... 6.34.8.101.
From her own sex should mercy find to day! .... 6.41.2.113.
Fights and subdues in quarrells not her own. .... 6.43.8.120.
Howe're, the *Coxcomb's* thy own Merit, ... 6.44.29.123.
Yet 'tis a Praise that few their own can call, ... 6.48iii.3.134.
With borrow'd Pins, and Patches not her own; .... 6.49i.22.138.
And sits attentive to his own Applause; .... 6.49iii.26.143.
She first convers'd with her own Kind, ... 6.53.11.161.
Who follow their own Wills, ... 6.54.14.165.
Let him that takes it, wear it as his own. .... 6.60.38.179.
Sent his own lightning, and the Victims seiz'd. .... 6.69i.6.198.
How Rome her own sad Sepulchre appears, ... 6.71.2.202.
Perhaps, by its own ruins sav'd from flame, ... 6.71.15.203.
They praise no works but what are like their own .... 6.82ix(f).4.235.
And with a Father's Sorrows mix his own! .... 6.85.8.242.
For England hath its own. .... 6.90.14.251.
But since you hatch, pray own your Chicks: .... 6.93.28.257.
To make us Capons own your Chicks. .... 6.93.27Z2.257.
He still might shew his own. .... 6.94.88.262.
And by their wiser Morals mend your own. .... 6.96iii.18.275.
Be kind at least to these, they are thy own: .... 6.96iv.12.276.
Be kind at least to these, they are thy own. .... 6.96iv.18.276.
But still, with partial Love, extol his own. .... 6.96v.14.280.
And own that nine such Poets make a *Tate;* .... 6.98.40.284.
And sits attentive to his own Applause; .... 6.98.62.285.
But judg'd *Roboam* his own Son. .... 6.101.20.290.
A modest man may like what's not his own. .... 6.105ii.4.300.
For who will help us e'er to teach thy own? .... 6.105v.4.302.
Britain, by juster title, makes her own. .... 6.107.10.310.
Convinc'd, that Virtue only is our own. .... 6.115.6.322.
Another's Age, shall hasten on my own; .... 6.117.8.333.
To see his own Maids serve a new Lord and Master. .... 6.122.18.342.
And shook the Stage with Thunders all his own! .... 6.128.16.356.
Judged for themselves, and saw with their own eyes. .... 6.147i.2.390.
That holds their Ashes and expects her own. .... 6.152.14.400.
To her own *Chrysa* send the black-ey'd Maid. .... Il.1.124.93.
Ulysses' Spoils, or ev'n thy own be mine. .... Il.1.178.96.
As thy own Actions if compar'd to mine. .... Il.1.216.97.
Rule thy own Realms with arbitrary Sway: .... Il.1.236.98.
And *Troy* prevails by Armies not her own. .... Il.2.160.136.
Thus to their Country bear their own Disgrace, ... Il.2.211.138.
Your own resistless Eloquence employ, ... Il.2.217.138.
But safer Plunder thy own Host supplies; .... Il.2.287.141.
This Deed, thy Foes Delight, thy own Disgrace, ... Il.3.73.193.
The golden Web her own sad Story crown'd, ... Il.3.170.199.
Let *Argive Helen* own her lawful Lord, ... Il.3.572.219.
And, if we fail, the chief Disgrace his own. .... Il.4.471.242.
Nor saw his Country's Peril, nor his own. .... Il.5.84.270.
These, were the rich immortal Prize our own, ... Il.5.336.283.
Go, let thy own soft Sex employ thy Care, ... Il.5.435.289.
Pierc'd in his own Dominions of the Dead; .... Il.5.488.291.
Shakes for his Danger, and neglects his own; .... Il.5.694.301.
Shall raise my Glory when thy own is lost: .... Il.5.811.305.
I own thy Presence, and confess thy Aid. .... Il.5.1011.315.
Well may we deem the wond'rous Birth thy own. .... Il.5.1081.318.
He gave his own, of Gold divinely wrought, ... Il.6.294.341.
And guard my Father's Glories, and my own. .... Il.6.569.354.
Sought her own Palace, and indulg'd her Woe. .... Il.6.643.358.
His Country's Fame, his own immortal Praise. .... Il.7.210.374.
The Lots produc'd, each Hero signs his own, ... Il.7.211.374.
Till Godlike *Ajax* finds the Lot his own; .... Il.7.224.375.
Each sounds your Praise, and War is all your own. .... Il.7.340.381.
And *Argive Helen* own her ancient Lord. .... Il.7.423.385.
We own thy Might, our Father and our Lord! .... Il.8.40.397.
Your great Forefathers Glories, and your own. .... Il.8.213.407.
Fears like his own to ev'ry *Grecian* Breast? .... Il.9.58.434.
And Millions own the Care of thee and Heav'n. .... Il.9.130.438.
A Prince's Faults, and I with Reason own. .... Il.9.148.439.
Hear thy own Glory, and the Voice of Fame: .... Il.9.401.452.
On her own Son to wreak her Brother's Death: .... Il.9.684.468.
Consume your Vessels, and approach my own; .... Il.9.768.472.

OWN (CONTINUED)
What *Dolon* knows, his faithful Tongue shall own. ....Il.10.485.25.
Your great Forefathers Virtues, and your own. ....Il.11.370.51.
And questions thus his own unconquer'd Soul. ....Il.11.512.56.
These, in the Warrior, their own Fate inclose; ....Il.11.523.57.
Amaz'd he stood, with Terrors not his own. ....Il.11.671.65.
Wedg'd in the Trench, by our own Troops confus'd, ...Il.12.83.84.
Trust thy own Cowardice to 'scape their Fire. ....Il.12.288.92.
And *Hector's* Force, and *Jove's* own Aid, be vain. ....Il.13.86.109.
Strength, not their own, the Touch divine imparts, ...Il.13.89.109.
His own bright evidence reveals a God. ....Il.13.104.109.
He liv'd, belov'd and honour'd as his own. ....Il.13.238.116.
Arms are her Trade, and War is all her own. ....Il.13.292.119.
And ev'ry Art of dang'rous War thy own. ....Il.13.373.123.
And ev'ry Art of glorious War thy own; ....Il.13.910.148.
But 'tis not ours, with Forces not our own ....Il.13.989.152.
Prest in his own, the Gen'ral's Hand he took, ...Il.14.157.165.
And own the Terrors of th' Almighty Hand! ....Il.14.486.187.
By his own Ardour, his own Pity sway'd ....Il.15.49.196.
By his own Ardour, his own Pity sway'd ....Il.15.49.196.
Thy own lov'd boasted Offspring lies o'erthrown, ...Il.15.124.201.
If that lov'd boasted Offspring be thy own, ...Il.15.125.201.
Bid him from Fight to his own Deeps repair, ...Il.15.182.203.
To thy own Deeps, or to the Fields of Air. ....Il.15.199.204.
Seeks his own Seas, and trembles at our Rage! ....Il.15.251.206.
His own brave Friends shall glory in his Fate; ....Il.15.587.219.
To your own Hands are trusted all your Fates: ....Il.15.603.220.
Your great Forefathers Virtues, and your own. ....Il.15.893.231.
More for their Country's Wounds, than for their own. ....Il.16.37.236.
Do her own Work, and leave the rest to Fate. ....Il.16.121.241.
At once his Country's Pillar, and their own; ....Il.16.674.270.
So many Lives effus'd, expires his own. ....Il.16.1000.281.
Thy own *Achilles* cannot lend thee Aid; ....Il.16.1010.282.
To Heav'n is ow'd whate'er your own you call, ...Il.16.1020.282.
Euphorbus next; the third mean Part thy own. ....Il.16.1025.282.
When Mortals boast of Prowess not their own? ....Il.17.20.288.
Come, for my Brother's Blood repay thy own. ....Il.17.38.289.
And thus explor'd his own unconquer'd Mind. ....Il.17.100.291.
There his own Mail unbrac'd, the Field bestrow'd; ....Il.17.217.296.
Oh lasting Shame! to our own Fears a Prey, ...Il.17.390.302.
And *Jove's* own Glories blaze around his Head. ....Il.17.637.312.
'Tis our own Vigour must the Dead regain; ....Il.17.798.319.
(Won by his own, or by *Patroclus'* Arms) ....Il.18.34.325.
Thy Friend's Disgrace, thy own eternal Shame! ....Il.18.218.332.
With her own Shout *Minerva* swells the Sound; ....Il.18.257.334.
On their own Spears, by their own Chariots crush'd: ....Il.18.272.335.
On their own Spears, by their own Chariots crush'd: ....Il.18.272.335.
To their own Sense condemn'd! and left to chuse ....Il.18.363.339.
Their Sov'reign's Sorrows in their own exprest. ....Il.19.8.371.
My martial Troops , my Treasures , are thy own: ....Il.19.138.377.
Nor mourn'd *Patroclus'* Fortunes, but their own. ....Il.19.322.385.
In Care of human Race; ev'n *Jove's* own Eye ....Il.20.31.394.
Why shou'd cœlestial Pow'rs exert their own? ....Il.20.163.400.
With guiltless Blood, for Vices not his own? ....Il.20.346.408.
Secure, no *Grecian* Force transcends thy own. ....Il.20.388.411.
To spare a Form, an Age so like thy own! ....Il.20.540.417.
How far *Minerva's* Force transcends thy own? ....Il.21.479.441.
(Forgetful of my Wrongs, and of thy own) ....Il.21.515.443.
To their own Hands commit the frantick Scene, ...Il.21.541.444.
Abash'd, she names his own Imperial Spouse; ....Il.21.595.446.
(Their Grandsire's Wealth, by right of Birth their own, ...Il.22.68.455.
Like *Jove's* own Lightning, or the rising Sun. ....Il.22.178.461.
Dearer than all that own a Brother's Name; ....Il.22.300.468.
Defend my Life regardless of your own. ....Il.22.304.468.
Or what must prove my Fortune or thy own. ....Il.22.360.470.
By thy own Soul! by those who gave thee Breath! ....Il.22.426.473.
Ev'n from his own paternal Roof expell'd, ...Il.22.626.482.
Compare those Rivals Judgment, and thy own: ....Il.23.382.505.
Suffice thy Father's Merits, and thy own: ....Il.23.694.517.
But left the Glory of the past thy own. ....Il.23.716.518.
Achilles of your own Ætherial Race ....Il.24.76.538.
Born to his own, and to his Parents Woe! ....Il.24.258.547.
The Coursers fly with Spirit not their own. ....Il.24.544.558.
Some God impells with Courage not thy own: ....Il.24.712.567.
Who match'd her own with bright *Latona's* Line; ....Il.24.764.569.
She stands her own sad Monument of Woe; ....Il.24.778.569.
Remember theirs, and mitigate thy own. ....Il.24.781.569.
All who deserv'd his choice, he made his own, ...Od.1.225.43.
To their own districts drive the Suitor-crowd: ....Od.1.353.49.
And in the publick woe forget your own; ....Od.1.451.54.
Search, for some thoughts, thy own suggesting mind; ....Od.3.34.87.
The lives of others, vent'rous of their own. ....Od.3.89.90.
Envy will own, the purchase dearly paid. ....Od.4.96.124.
Seam'd o'er with wounds, which his own sabre gave, ...Od.4.335.135.
To his own prowess all the glory gave, ...Od.4.675.151.
Far from his own domain salutes the soil; ....Od.4.696.152.
Seek for his father's fate, but find his own. ....Od.4.899.160.
I own me conscious of th' unpleasing deed: ....Od.4.983.163.
Still to your own æthereal race the worst! ....Od.5.150.178.
By *Pallas* arm'd with boldness not her own. ....Od.6.168.216.
Rob'd in the garments her own hands had made; ....Od.7.315.251.
Or urg'd by *Jove*, or her own changeful heart. ....Od.7.349.253.
Base to his friend, to his own interest blind: ....Od.8.244.275.
Heedless of others, to his own severe. ....Od.9.132.311.
The lives of others, and expose your own? ....Od.9.302.318.
For his I am, and I the lineage own; ....Od.9.607.331.
Some vessel, not his own, transport him o'er; ....Od.9.626.332.
And their own voice affrights them when they groan. ....Od.10.281.356.
Transform'd to beasts, with accents not their own. ....Od.10.402.364.
Leave to repentance and his own sad heart, ...Od.10.524.368.
With her own son she joyn'd in nuptial bands, ...Od.11.331.398.
To you once more your own *Ulysses* bows; ....Od.13.409.26.
Estrange thee from thy own, thy son, thy wife; ....Od.13.462.28.
His own industrious hands had rais'd the pile) ....Od.14.12.35.
Enough my master's sorrows, and my own. ....Od.14.46.38.
To seek his father's fate, and find his own! ....Od.14.209.45.

OWN (CONTINUED)
(Stripp'd of my own) and to the vessel bound. ....Od.14.380.53.
From God's own hand descend our joys and woes; ....Od.14.494.60.
And joyn'd me with them, ('twas their own command) ....Od.14.529.62.
Fool that I was! I left behind my own; ....Od.14.540.63.
Hence therefore, while thy stores thy own remain; ....Od.15.23.71.
Her own fair hands embroider'd ev'ry part: ....Od.15.121.74.
By all the lives of these; thy own dear head, ...Od.15.285.82.
Of my own tribe an *Argive* wretch I slew; ....Od.15.298.83.
Array'd in garments her own hands had wove, ...Od.15.394.88.
Thy father's fate, and tell me all thy own. ....Od.17.55.135.
Of his own fortunes, and *Ulysses'* fame, ...Od.17.82.136.
Kind to *Ulysses'* race as to his own; ....Od.17.127.138.
Mankind, to seek their own similitude. ....Od.17.253.143.
Who calls, from distant nations to his own, ...Od.17.460.155.
Shameless they give, who give what's not their own. ....Od.17.536.158.
From his own roof with meditated blows ....Od.18.12.167.
Thy finish'd charms, all *Greece* would own thy sway, ...Od.18.288.180.
Befriended by my own domestic spies, ...Od.19.176.200.
Ulysses view'd an image of his own. ....Od.19.283.208.
My own experience shall their doom decide; ....Od.19.584.224.
Ulysses speaks his own return decreed; ....Od.19.652.227.
With their own blood, and intercept the shame; ....Od.20.16.232.
Imported in a shallop not his own: ....Od.20.237.244.
With her own art *Penelope* inspires: ....Od.21.2.257.
Your own *Ulysses!* twice ten years detain'd ....Od.21.213.270.
To thy own dogs a prey thou shalt be made; ....Od.21.395.279.
Before your rapines, join'd with all your own, ...Od.22.74.290.
And their own darts shall pierce the Prince and King. ....Od.22.157.294.
Falshood is folly, and 'tis just to own ....Od.22.168.295.
From thy own hand, of this detested deed? ....Od.22.183.296.
Ulysses lives, thy own *Ulysses* reigns: ....Od.23.28.320.
Haste, daughter haste, thy own *Ulysses* calls! ....Od.23.54.321.
I yield, I yield! my own *Ulysses* lives! ....Od.23.240.335.
Could work this wonder: welcome to thy own! ....Od.24.463.370.
The ills ye mourn; your own the guilty deed. ....Od.24.521.373.
Is not thy thought my own? (the God replies ....Od.24.547.374.
None now the kindred of th' unjust shall own; ....Od.24.554.374.

OWN'D
But *Fancy's* boundless Empire own'd his Sway. ....1.EOC.648Z2.312.
Like these, *Vertumnus* own'd his faithful Flame, ...1.TrVP.27.378.
The same Apostle too has elsewhere own'd ....2.ChWB.32.58.
And own'd a Father when he own'd a God. ....3.EOM3.234.116.
And own'd a Father when he own'd a God. ....3.EOM3.234.116.
And own'd, that nine such Poets made a *Tate*. ....4.Arbu.190.109.
Own'd his returning Lord, look'd up, and dy'd! ....6.15.18.52.
Which own'd, would all their Sires and Sons disgrace. ....6.96iii.16.275.
These own'd as Chief *Protesilas* the brave, ...Il.2.853.164.
In secret own'd resistless Beauty's Pow'r: ....Il.3.204.201.
Proud of his Boy, he own'd the gen'rous Flame, ...Il.8.345.414.
The strong *Dolopians* thenceforth own'd my Reign, ...Il.9.602.464.
The God of War had own'd a just Surprize. ....Il.13.176.113.
Great *Ajax* saw, and own'd the Hand divine, ...Il.16.148.243.
Others 'tis own'd, in Fields of Battle shine, ...Il.23.773.520.
Extended *Phrygia* own'd thy ample Reign, ...Il.24.685.565.
'Till great *Alcinous* rising own'd the sign. ....Od.13.195.15.

OWNER
And whither, whither its sad Owner flie? ....1.TrUl.79.468.
For dark in Death the godlike Owner lies! ....Il.13.732.139.
And whither, whither its sad owner fly? ....Od.13.246.18.
Heav'n bless its owner with a better mind! ....Od.17.482.156.
Its owner absent, and untry'd so long. ....Od.21.430.281.

OWNER'S
The *Owner's Wife,* that *other Men* enjoy, ...1.EOC.501.294.

OWNERS
And to their Owners send them nobly back. ....Il.13.381.123.

OWNING
Both fairly owning, Riches in effect ....3.Ep3.17.84.
And owning her *Ulysses,* thus she speaks. ....Od.11.189.390.

OWNS
Reveres *Apollo's* vocal Caves, and owns ....1.TrSt.577.434.
And the Great Father of his Country owns. ....2.TemF.243.274.
No creature owns it in the first degree, ...3.EOM2.225.82.
One doubts of All, one owns ev'n Virtue vain. ....3.EOM4.28Z2.130.
Or her, that owns her Faults, but never mends, ...3.Ep2.103.58.
Each shudd'ring owns the Genius of the Schools; ....5.DunB4.146A.355.
Marcus with blushes owns he loves, ...6.51ii.7.152.
Varius with blushes owns he loves, ...6.51ii.7A.152.
He owns their learning, but disdains their laws. ....6.107.22.311.
And owns no Help but from thy saving Hands: ....Il.9.304.449.
Exults, and owns the Monarch of the Main; ....Il.13.47.107.
The Sire of all, old *Ocean,* owns my Reign, ...Il.14.279.175.
And owns th' Assistance of immortal Hands. ....Il.16.652.269.

OX
When the dull Ox, why now he breaks the clod, ...3.EOM1.63.21.
Whose gentle progress makes a Calf an Ox, ...4.JD2.48.137.
That plodding on must make a Calf an Ox ....4.JD2A.54.136.
"With cow-like-udders, and with ox-like eyes. ....5.DunA2.156.120.
"With cow-like udders, and with ox-like eyes. ....5.DunB2.164.303.
Great *D[enni]s* roar'd, like Ox at Slaughter. ....6.10.62.26.
The Victim-Ox the sturdy Youth prepare; ....Il.18.649.355.
The huge Ox bellowing falls; with feebler cries ....Il.23.41.488.
A well-fed Ox was for the second plac'd; ....Il.23.876.524.
Between the mule and ox, from plow to plow; ....Od.8.130.270.
To low the ox, to bleat the woolly train. ....Od.12.319.447.
Devour the grazing ox and browzing goat, ...Od.17.620.162.

OX-LIKE

"With cow-like-udders, and with ox-like eyes. ....5.DunA2.156.120.
"With cow-like udders, and with ox-like eyes. ....5.DunB2.164.303.

OXE

Some Brass or Iron, some an Oxe, or Slave. ....Il.7.569.392.
Lay panting. Thus an Oxe, in Fetters ty'd, ...Il.13.721.139.
The stately Oxe, and bleeds within the stalls. ....Od.11.510.408.
A victim Oxe beneath the sacred hand ....Od.13.27.2.

OXE'S

Wrapt in a new-slain Oxe's ample hide: ....Od.22.403.307.

OXEN

While yon slow Oxen turn the furrow'd Plain. ....1.PSp.30.63.
While lab'ring Oxen, spent with Toil and Heat, ...1.PAu.61.84.
Blush'd with the Blood of Sheep and Oxen slain. ....1.TrUl.231.473.
"A hundred oxen at your levee roar." ....3.Ep3.46.89.
His oxen perish in his country's cause; ....3.Ep3.206.110.
Or fed the Flames with Fat of Oxen slain; ....Il.1.58.88.
Ador'd with Sacrifice and Oxen slain; ....Il.2.662.158.
For which nine Oxen paid (a vulgar Price) ....Il.6.293.341.
Strait from the Town be Sheep and Oxen sought, ...Il.8.629.426.
Fat Sheep and Oxen from the Town are led, ...Il.8.677.427.
There Heifers graze, and lab'ring Oxen toil; ....Il.9.203.442.
There Heifers graze, and lab'ring Oxen toil; ....Il.9.390.452.
And Hides of Oxen on the Floor display'd: ....Il.11.979.79.
So flies a Herd of Oxen, scatter'd wide, ...Il.15.366.211.
Fed his large Oxen on Percote's Plain; ....Il.15.647.221.
(Where num'rous Oxen, as at ease they feed, ...Il.15.762.226.
If Sheep or Oxen seek the winding Stream. ....Il.18.606.352.
The bellowing Oxen the Besiegers hear; ....Il.18.615.352.
Here, Herds of Oxen march, erect and bold, ...Il.18.665.355.
A hundred Oxen were his Price that Day, ...Il.21.90.425.
And well-fed Sheep, and sable Oxen slay: ....Il.23.205.498.
A Train of Oxen, Mules, and stately Steeds, ...Il.23.324.503.
Of twice six Oxen its reputed Price; ....Il.23.817.521.
Their Mules and Oxen harness to the Wain, ...Il.24.990.577.
At each, nine oxen on the sand lay slain. ....Od.3.10.87.
Whose oxen long have torn the furrow'd soil, ...Od.13.40.3.
To his high name let twelve black oxen fall. ....Od.13.211.15.
Forth on the sands the victim oxen led: ....Od.13.215.16.
Blush'd with the blood of sheep and oxen slain. ....Od.13.398.26.
The bellowing oxen, and the bleating sheep, ...Od.15.443.92.
Two hundred oxen ev'ry Prince shall pay: ....Od.22.69.290.
Like oxen madden'd by the breeze's sting, ...Od.22.335.302.
The oxen sacred to the God of day, ...Od.23.356.342.
And fatted sheep and sable oxen slay; ....Od.24.84.352.

OXFORD

Of Oxford he, a most egregious Clerk: ....2.ChWB.264.69.
Perhaps forgets that OXFORD e r was Great; ....6.84.18.239.
The Lord of Oxford knows. ....6.102.12.294.
With Oxford, Cowper, Noble Strafford by: ....6.147ix.4.392.

OXFORD'S

Who copies Your's, or OXFORD's better part, ...3.Ep3.243.112.
One fawns, at Oxford's, on the Poor. ....6.135.64.368.

OYL

Oyl, tho' it stink, they drop by drop impart, ...4.HS2.59.59.
Embalm the Wounds, anoint the Limbs with Oyl; ....Il.18.412.340.

OYSTER

Cod, Whiting, Oyster, Mackrel, Sprat, or Plaice: ....6.14ii.31.44.
Two Trav'lers found an Oyster in their Way; ....6.145.2.388.
'Twas a fat Oyster——Live in Peace——Adieu. ....6.145.12.388.

OYSTERS

Let me extoll a Cat on Oysters fed, ...4.HS2.41.57.

OZEL'S

And Ozel's with Lord Hervey's: ....6.58.58.173.

OZELL

Can make a Cibber, Johnson, or Ozell. ....5.DunA1.240.91.
Can make a Cibber, Tibbald, or Ozell. ....5.DunB1.286.290.
Ozell, at Sanger's Call, invok'd his Muse, ...6.12.1.37.
For those were slander'd most whom Ozell prais'd: ....6.12.7.37.
Since those were slander'd most whom Ozell praised: ....6.12.7A.37.
And that this Piece was meant for Ozell. ....6.44.18.123.

OZIER

We made the ozier-fringed bank our bed. ....Od.14.533.63.

OZIER-FRINGED

We made the ozier-fringed bank our bed. ....Od.14.533.63.

P

See PISS.
See POX.
See POPE.
Meat, Fire, and Cloaths. B. What more? P. Meat, Cloaths, and
    Fire. ....3.Ep3.82A.94.
She bears a Coronet and P—x for life. ....3.Ep3.392.124.
F. I'd write no more. P. Not write? but then I think, ...4.HS1.11.5.
Ev'n those you touch not, hate you. P. What should ail'em? ....4.HS1.41.9.
With all a Woman's Virtues but the P—x, ...4.HAdv.17.75.
My Friends? he cry'd, p—x take you for your care! ....4.2HE2.195.179.
And P—x and P* both in town! ....4.1HE7.14.269.
Go see Sir ROBERT !— hum ....4.EpS1.27.299.
Go see Sir ROBERT !— P. See Sir Robert !— hum
The pois'ning Dame— Fr. You mean— P. I don't.— Fr. You
    do. ....4.EpS2.22.314.
Fr. stop! stop! P. Must Satire then, nor rise, nor fall ....4.EpS2.52.315.
Fr. Strange spleen to S[elkir]k! P. Do I wrong the Man? ....4.EpS2.62.316.
Fr. Then why so few commended? P. Not so fierce& ....4.EpS2.104.319.

P (CONTINUED)

Quite turns my Stomach— P. So does Flatt'ry mine; ....4.EpS2.182.323.
Fr. You're strangely proud. P. So proud I am no Slave: ....4.EpS2.205.324.
X and Z cry'd, P—x and Z—s ....6.30.43.87.
To f—t and p—ss about the Room, ...6.135.16.366.

PA-GOD

The Mosque of Mahound, or some queer Pa-god. ....4.JD4.239.45.

PAC'D

And forth she pac'd, majestically sad. ....Il.24.124.540.
To seek Ulysses, pac'd along the sand. ....Od.5.192.180.

PACE

As from the God she flew with furious Pace, ...1.W-F.189.167.
As after Stumbling, Jades will mend their Pace. ....1.EOC.603.308.
Of matchless Swiftness, but of silent Pace, ...1.TrES.345.462.
Strait seek their Home, and fly with eager Pace, ...1.TrUl.214.472.
Thither th'obsequious Squire address'd his Pace, ...2.ChJM.605.44.
He springs to Vengeance with an eager pace, ...2.RL3.97.174.
And seem'd to emulate great Jacob's pace. ....5.DunA2.64.105.
Attending each with stately Pace, ...6.135.72.369.
Each walking with Majestick pace ....6.135.72A.369.
The gen'rous Greeks recede with tardy Pace, ...Il.5.860.307.
He moves to Combate with majestic Pace; ....Il.7.251.376.
With beating Bosom, and with eager Pace, ...Il.8.408.417.
Then rush behind him, and prevent his Pace. ....Il.10.410.21.
The Coursers past me with so swift a Pace. ....Il.11.753.68.
Weak was his Pace, but dauntless was his Heart. ....Il.11.945.77.
Fierce as the God of Battels, urg'd his Pace. ....Il.13.419.126.
Thus issuing radiant, with majestic Pace, ...Il.14.216.170.
Of matchless Swiftness, but of silent Pace, ...Il.16.832.275.
Swift was his Pace, and ready was his Aid; ....Il.17.303.299.
The big round Drops cours'd down with silent pace, ...Il.17.497.307.
With weary'd Limbs, but with unwilling Pace: ....Il.17.750.317.
With weary Limbs, but with unwilling Pace: ....Il.17.750A.317*.
He, like the warlike Eagle speeds his Pace, ...Il.21.281.432.
No Stop, no Check, no Aid! With feeble pace, ...Il.21.617.448.
As Men in Slumbers seem with speedy pace, ...Il.22.257.466.
She spoke; and furious, with distracted Pace, ...Il.22.592.480.
Minerva's Spirit drives his matchless Pace, ...Il.23.479.509.
And the fierce Coursers urg'd their rapid Pace ....Il.23.587.513.
The next Ulysses, meas'ring Pace with Pace; ....Il.23.888.524.
The next Ulysses, meas'ring Pace with Pace. ....Il.23.888.524.
Achilles only boasts a swifter Pace: ....Il.23.932.526.
With solemn Pace thro' various Rooms he went, ...Il.24.578.560.
Swift as she spoke, with rapid pace she leads. ....Od.2.452.83.
Their equal pace, and smoak'd along the field. ....Od.3.615.117.
High o'er the lawn, with more majestic pace, ...Od.6.123.212.
Now far the last, with pensive pace and slow ....Od.9.531.328.
They saw, they knew me, and with eager pace ....Od.10.469.366.
And near them walk'd, with solemn pace and slow, ...Od.11.397.403.
Strait seek their home, and fly with eager pace ....Od.13.381.25.
But when the softly-stealing pace of time ....Od.15.390.88.
She saw, she wept, she ran with eager pace, ...Od.17.41.134.
He said: obsequious with redoubl'd pace, ...Od.19.587.224.
Then, with a manly pace, he took his stand; ....Od.21.129.264.
Again the matron springs with eager pace, ...Od.22.531.314.
And trod thy footsteps with unequal pace: ....Od.24.391.368.

PACES

Show all his paces, not a step advance. ....5.DunB4.266.370.

PACIFIC

Their full-fed Heroes, their pacific May'rs, ...5.DunA3.279.183.
Their full-fed Heroes, their pacific May'rs, ...5.DunB3.281.334.
He paus'd, and these pacific Words ensue. ....Il.7.443.386.
Pacific now prolong the jovial feast; ....Od.1.473.55.

PACIFICK

Of modest wisdom, and pacifick truth: ....6.109.2.313.
Of modest Reason, and pacifick truth: ....6.109.2A.313.

PACING

Slow-pacing thrice around th' insidious pile; ....Od.4.378.139.

PACK

"And mighty Dukes pack cards for half a crown. ....3.Ep3.144.105.
Next plung'd a feeble, but a desp'rate pack, ...5.DunB2.305.310.
But from this Pell-mell-Pack of Toasts, ...6.59.7.177.
The pack impatient snuff the tainted gale; ....Od.19.507.221.

PACKET

Bless me! a Packet.—"'Tis a stranger sues, ...4.Arbu.55.100.

PACKHORSE

Can the light packhorse, or the heavy steer, ...4.1740.69.336.

PACT

Nor Oath nor Pact Achilles plights with thee: ....Il.22.336.470.

PACTOLUS

O'er Golden Sands let rich Pactolus flow, ...1.PSp.61.66.

PACTS

Such Pacts, as Lambs and rabid Wolves combine, ...Il.22.337.470.

PAD

O! may'st thou never want an easy Pad! ....6.96iii.38.275.

PADLOCK

We hang one jingling padlock on the mind: ....5.DunB4.162.357.

PADUA

"Your only wearing is your Padua-soy." ....4.JD4.113.35.
Padua with sighs beholds her Livy burn; ....5.DunA3.97.158.

PADUA (CONTINUED)
Padua, with sighs, beholds her Livy burn, ... 5.DunB3.105.325.

PADUA-SOY
"Your only wearing is your *Padua-soy.*" ... 4.JD4.113.35.

PAEËON
See PAEON, POEON'S.

PAEANS
Hear, in *all Tongues* consenting Pæans ring! ... 1.EOC.186.262.
Hear, in *all Tongues* Triumphant *Pæans* ring! ... 1.EOC.186A.262.
The *Pæans* lengthen'd 'till the Sun descends: ... Il.1.619.117.
The Corps of *Hector,* and your *Pæans* sing. ... Il.22.492.476.

PAEON
See POEON'S.
Where *Pæon* sprinkling heav'nly Balm around, ... Il.5.489.291.
From *Pæon* sprung, their patron-god imparts ... Od.4.321.134.

PAEONIA'S
From rich *Pæonia's* Vales the Warrior came, ... Il.17.402.303.
From rich *Pæonia's* Vallies I command ... Il.21.171.428.

PAEONIAN
The far-fam'd Hero of Pæonian Strain; ... Il.11.438.53.
The great *Pæonian,* bold *Pyrechmes,* stood; ... Il.16.342.256.

PAEONIANS
Th' amaz'd *Pæonians* scour along the Plain: ... Il.21.224.430.

PAEONS
The *Pæons,* dreadful with their bended Bows, ... Il.10.497.25.

PAGAN
And Pan to Moses lends his Pagan horn; ... 5.DunA3.102.159.
And Pan to Moses lends his pagan horn; ... 5.DunB3.110.325.

PAGE
With *Edward's* Acts adorn the shining Page, ... 1.W-F.303.177.
His *Fable, Subject, Scope* in ev'ry Page, ... 1.EOC.120.252.
All but the page prescrib'd, their present state; ... 3.EOM1.78.23.
Hard Words or Hanging, if your Judge be *Page* ... 4.HS1.82.13.
Or lengthen'd Thought that gleams thro' many a page, ... 4.2HE1.113.205.
No whiter page than Addison remains. ... 4.2HE1.216.213.
Or *P[a]ge* pour'd forth the Torrent of his Wit? ... 4.EpS2.159.322.
She saw slow Philips creep like Tate's poor page, ... 5.DunA1.103.72.
The page admires new beauties, not its own. ... 5.DunA1.120.77.
Thro' the long, heavy, painful page, drawl on; ... 5.DunA2.356.143.
She saw slow Philips creep like Tate's poor page, ... 5.DunB1.105.277.
Or where the pictures for the page attone, ... 5.DunB1.139.280.
Thro' the long, heavy, painful page drawl on; ... 5.DunB2.388.316.
And dies, when Dulness gives her Page the word. ... 5.DunB4.30.343.
Withdrew his hand, and clos'd the pompous page. ... 5.DunB4.114.352.
"What! no respect, he cry'd, for Shakespear's page?" ... 5.DunB4.114A.352.
A Page, a Grave, that they can call their own; ... 5.DunB4.128.354.
A Page is blotted, or Leaf wanting: ... 6.29.18.83.
None from a page can ever learn the truth. ... 6.96ii.30Z20.271.
"Who from a *Page* can ever learn the Truth? ... 6.96ii.32.272.

PAGEANT
The gaze of fools, and pageant of a day! ... 2.Elegy.44.366.

PAGEANTRY
The Pomp, the Pageantry, the Proud Array. ... 2.ChJM.308.29.

PAGEANTS
Pageants on pageants, in long order drawn, ... 4.2HE1.316.223.
Pageants on pageants, in long order drawn, ... 4.2HE1.316.223.

PAGES
And view with scorn *Two Pages* and a *Chair.* ... 2.RL1.46.149.
Wicked as Pages, who in early years ... 4.JD2.39.135.

PAGOD
See thronging Millions to the Pagod run, ... 4.EpS1.157.309.

PAID
Those Honours paid, his sacred Corps bequeath ... 1.TrES.330.461.
To you shall Rites Divine be ever paid, ... 1.TrUl.246.474.
Each paid his Thanks, and decently retir'd. ... 2.ChJM.372.32.
And endless Treats, and endless Visits paid, ... 2.ChWB.115.62.
But all that Score I paid—As how? you'll say, ... 2.ChWB.231.68.
Visits to ev'ry Church we daily paid, ... 2.ChWB.283.70.
Who gave the *Ball,* or paid the *Visit* last: ... 2.RL3.12.170.
Who gave a *Ball,* or paid the *Visit* last; ... 2.RL3.12A.170.
While *Visits* shall be paid on solemn Days, ... 2.RL3.167.181.
And paid a Tradesman once to make him stare, ... 3.Ep2.56.55.
And paid for all my Satires, all my Rhymes: ... 4.JD4.6.27.
He names the *Price* for ev'ry *Office* paid, ... 4.JD4.162.39.
You pay a Penny, and he paid a Pound. ... 4.2HE2.239.181.
My tears eternal tribute shou'd be paid: ... 6.20.40.67.
If all your Debts to *Greece* and *Rome* were paid. ... 6.34.14.101.
'Tis now for better Reasons——to be paid. ... 6.34.18.101.
Let Altars smoke, and Hecatombs be paid. ... Il.1.88.91.
'Till the great King, without a Ransom paid, ... Il.1.123.93.
First let the just Equivalent be paid; ... Il.1.172.95.
And Bulls and Goats to *Phœbus'* Altars paid. ... Il.1.415.107.
There *Lycia's* Monarch paid him Honours due; ... Il.6.213.336.
For which nine Oxen paid (a vulgar Price) ... Il.6.293.341.
Who paid their Vows to *Panomphæan Jove;* ... Il.8.300.412.
All these, to buy his Friendship, shall be paid, ... Il.9.169.441.
All these, to buy thy Friendship, shall be paid, ... Il.9.356.451.
Some Present too to ev'ry Prince was paid; ... Il.9.438.454.
Were these not paid thee by the Terms we bring, ... Il.9.641.466.

PAID (CONTINUED)
To Birth, or Office, no respect be paid; ... Il.10.280.14.
There first to *Jove* our solemn Rites were paid; ... Il.11.864.74.
That Office paid, he issu'd from his Tent, ... Il.13.284.119.
Till Death for Death be paid, and Blow for Blow. ... Il.13.988.152.
We paid the fattest Firstlings of the Fold; ... Il.15.431.214.
Thus have I sooth'd my Griefs, and thus have paid ... Il.17.606.311.
And the full Price of injur'd Honour paid. ... Il.19.178.379.
To all the Gods his constant Vows were paid; ... Il.20.347.408.
Breathless in Dust, the Price of Rashness paid. ... Il.20.458.413.
And the short Absence of *Achilles* paid. ... Il.21.150.427.
Yet let the Sacrifice at least be paid, ... Il.22.660.484.
And bid the Forests fall: (Such Rites are paid ... Il.23.63.489.
Oh more than Brother! Think each Office paid, ... Il.23.111.492.
Behold, *Achilles'* Promise fully paid, ... Il.23.222.498.
With Joy *Pelides* saw the Honour paid, ... Il.23.1052.533.
Such Honours *Ilion* to her Hero paid, ... Il.24.1015.577.
Thus she; and having paid the rite divine, ... Od.3.76.90.
Envy will own, the purchase dearly paid. ... Od.4.96.124.
All *Greece* had paid my solemn fun'rals then, ... Od.5.399.192.
These solemn vows and holy off'rings paid ... Od.10.626.374.
Thus solemn rites and holy vows we paid ... Od.11.43.381.
Due to thy Ghost, shall to thy Ghost be paid. ... Od.11.99.385.
Nor paid too dearly for unequal'd charms; ... Od.11.344.399.
Then by my realms due homage would be paid; ... Od.11.448.406.
O fatal slumber, paid with lasting woes! ... Od.12.440.452.
To you shall rites divine be ever paid, ... Od.13.413.26.
By that dread pow'r to whom thy vows are paid; ... Od.15.284.82.
With pious deed, and pure devotion, paid? ... Od.19.427.215.
Partook the sacred feast, and ritual honours paid. ... Od.20.346.249.
For them, thy daily orisons were paid: ... Od.22.360.304.
Where oft *Laertes* holy vows had paid, ... Od.22.373.306.
I paid, and hospitable gifts bestow'd; ... Od.24.319.365.
'Tis so—the Suitors for their wrongs have paid— ... Od.24.411.369.

PAIL
"A Dish of Tea like Milk-Pail on thy Head? ... 6.96ii.68.273.
From Pail to Pail with busie Murmur run ... Il.2.556.154.
From Pail to Pail with büsie Murmur run ... Il.2.556.154.
But ev'ry season fills the foaming pail. ... Od.4.112.125.

PAILS
The Pails high-foaming with a milky Flood, ... Il.16.780.273.
Full pails, and vessels of the milking trade. ... Od.9.263.317.

PAIN
Not balmy Sleep to Lab'rers faint with Pain, ... 1.PAu.44.83.
This said, he rose, and frantick with his pain, ... 1.TrPA.132.371.
Where guilty Spirits feel Eternal Pain; ... 1.TrSt.82.413.
Yet not ungrateful to the Peasant's Pain, ... 1.TrUl.124.470.
But, by th' Immortal Pow'rs, I feel the Pain, ... 2.ChJM.204.24.
Sad in the midst of Triumphs, sigh'd for Pain; ... 2.ChJM.358.31.
To visit *Damian,* and divert his Pain. ... 2.ChJM.409.34.
By secret Writing to disclose his Pain, ... 2.ChJM.497.39.
And in soft Murmurs tell the Trees their Pain; ... 2.ChJM.528.41.
I'd spend my dearest Blood to ease thy Pain. ... 2.ChJM.737.50.
Pain at her Side, and *Megrim* at her Head. ... 2.RL4.24.185.
Pain at her Side, and *Languor* at her Head. ... 2.RL4.24A.185.
Roar'd for the Handkerchief that caus'd his Pain. ... 2.RL5.106.208.
The Lock, obtain'd with Guilt, and kept with Pain. ... 2.RL5.109.208.
Then share thy pain, allow that sad relief; ... 2.ElAb.49.323.
The crime was common, common be the pain. ... 2.ElAb.104.328.
A cool suspense from pleasure and from pain; ... 2.ElAb.250.339.
In human works, tho' labour'd on with pain, ... 3.EOM1.53.19.
Die of a rose in aromatic pain? ... 3.EOM1.200.40.
To sink oppress with aromatic pain? ... 3.EOM1.200A.40.
Mere curious pleasure, or ingenious pain: ... 3.EOM2.48.61.
Pain their aversion, Pleasure their desire; ... 3.EOM2.88.65.
Hate, Fear, and Grief, the family of pain; ... 3.EOM2.118.69.
'Tis to mistake them, costs the time and pain. ... 3.EOM2.216.81.
Which sees no more the stroke, or feels the pain, ... 3.EOM3.67.98.
Not less foresees the stroke, or feels the pain. ... 3.EOM3.67A.98*.
Some sunk to Beasts, find pleasure end in pain; ... 3.EOM4.23.130.
One grants his Pleasure is but Rest from pain, ... 3.EOM4.28Z1.130.
Shall find, the pleasure pays not half the pain. ... 3.EOM4.48.132.
And if it lose, attended with no pain: ... 3.EOM4.316.158.
You purchase Pain with all that Joy can give, ... 3.Ep2.99A.58.
Who purchase Pain with all that Joy can give, ... 3.Ep2.99.58.
And pity Men of Pleasure still in Pain! ... 4.HAdv.50.79.
While thus each hand promotes the pleasing pain, ... 5.DunA2.203.126.
While thus each hand promotes the pleasing pain, ... 5.DunB2.211.306.
It fled, I follow'd; now in hope, now pain; ... 5.DunB4.427.383.
Musick can soften Pain to Ease, ... 6.11.120.34.
Make Life a Scene of Pain, and constant Toil, ... 6.17iii.6.57.
Pleasures sincere, and unallay'd with Pain, ... 6.17iii.10.58.
I share his griefs, and feel my self his pain: ... 6.21.36.70.
Then *Jove* thus spake: With Care and Pain ... 6.30.55.88.
Then *Jove* spake thus with Care and Pain ... 6.30.55A.88.
Oh the pain, the bliss of dying! ... 6.31ii.4.94.
Of anxious love's alternate joy and pain, ... 6.56.2.168.
This more than pays whole years of thankless pain; ... 6.63.5.188.
Above all Pain, all Passion, and all Pride, ... 6.84.24.239.
Above all Pain, all Anger, and all Pride, ... 6.84.24A.239.
Without a Pain, a Trouble, or a Fear; ... 6.86.16.245.
The Piteous Images renew my Pain, ... 6.96iv.85.278.
But oh! relieve a wretched Parent's Pain, ... Il.1.27.87.
There groan'd the Chief in agonizing Pain; ... Il.2.880.165.
Wild with Delay, and more enrag'd by Pain. ... Il.5.173.275.
Great *Juno's* self has born her Weight of Pain, ... Il.5.481.291.
The smoaking Steel, *Mars* bellows with the Pain: ... Il.5.1053.316.
Wild with his Pain, he sought the bright Abodes, ... Il.5.1064.317.
Condemn'd to Pain, tho' fated not to die. ... Il.5.1091.318.
And scarce my Heart support its Load of Pain. ... Il.10.101.7.
Stung with the Smart, all panting with the Pain, ... Il.11.351.50.
And Pain augmented, thus exhorts the Throng. ... Il.11.354.50.
Achilles heeds not, but derides our Pain; ... Il.11.809.72.

PAIN (CONTINUED)
He drops the Weight, disabled with the Pain, Il.13.670.137.
The Kings, tho' wounded, and oppress'd with Pain, Il.14.439.184.
Their Pain, soft Arts of Pharmacy can ease, Il.16.38.237.
Lo! stiff with clotted Blood, and Pierc'd with Pain, Il.16.637.269.
Pierc'd thro' the Wrist; and raging with the Pain Il.17.681.314.
When round and round with never-weary'd Pain, Il.20.579.418.
Slowly he rises, scarcely breathes with Pain, Il.21.488.441.
Brought back the grateful Day that crown'd our Pain; Il.21.524.443.
Tho' strook, tho' wounded, scarce perceives the Pain, Il.21.681.450.
Great *Jove* has plac'd, sad Spectacle of Pain! Il.22.84.456.
My Heart partakes the gen'rous *Hector's* Pain; Il.22.223.464.
Each burns with double Hope, with double Pain, Il.23.453.508.
The Fraud celestial *Pallas* sees with Pain, Il.23.467.509.
Sooths weary Life, and softens human Pain. Il.24.166.542.
Lo! the sad Father, frantick with his Pain, Il.24.291.548.
No mark of Pain, or Violence of Face; Il.24.955.576.
Thy gentle Accents soften'd all my Pain. Il.24.974.576.
My heart bleeds fresh with agonizing pain; Od.4.133.126.
He ceas'd: heart-wounded with afflictive pain, Od.4.649.150.
I've heard with pain, but oh! the tale pursue; Od.4.746.153.
Joys ever-young, unmix'd with pain or fear, Od.4.767.155.
Or if a dungeon be the pain decreed, Od.4.982.163.
Fixt by some Dæmon to his bed of pain, Od.5.509.196.
To raise the blush, or pain the modest eyes. Od.6.264.223.
For Fate has wove the thread of life with pain, Od.7.263.248.
All night I slept, oblivious of my pain; Od.7.370.254.
Our hour was come, to taste our share of pain. Od.9.60.304.
And the soul saddens by the use of pain. Od.10.551.369.
Unknown to pain, in age resign thy breath, Od.11.166.389.
Yet not ungrateful to the peasant's pain, Od.13.291.19.
On all their weary ways wait Care and Pain, Od.15.366.87.
For too much rest itself becomes a pain. Od.15.429.89.
And void of pain, the silent arrows kill. Od.15.451.92.
For heav'n has wove his thread of life with pain. Od.16.64.105.
The pain of anger punishes the fault: Od.17.17.133.
Death ill exchang'd for bondage and for pain! Od.17.523.158.
Breath'd from the Gods to soften human pain) Od.17.611.161.
Some light, and sooth her soul's eternal pain. Od.17.637.163.
On earth he rush'd with agonizing pain; Od.19.531.221.
Poor suff'ring heart! he cry'd, support the pain Od.20.23.232.
The bow inflexible resists their pain. Od.21.188.268.
Unknown to pain in age resign my breath, Od.23.299.337.
The ground himself had purchas'd with his pain, Od.24.236.360.

PAINFUL
Painful preheminence! yourself to view 3.EOM4.267.153.
Virtue she finds too painful an endeavour, 3.Ep2.163.64.
While pensive Poets painful vigils keep, 5.DunA1.91.70.
But pensive Poets painful vigils keep, 5.DunA1.91A.70.
Thro' the long, heavy, painful page, drawl on; 5.DunA2.356.143.
While pensive Poets painful vigils keep, 5.DunB1.93.276.
Thro' the long, heavy, painful page drawl on; 5.DunB2.388.316.
Virtue she finds too painful an endeavour, 6.139.7.377.
Large painful Drops from all his Members run, Il.11.941.77.
In airy Circles wings his painful way, Il.12.238.90.
And painful Sweat from all his Members flows. Il.16.135.242.
His painful Arm, yet useless with the Smart Il.16.629.269.
And painful Sweat from all their Members flows. Il.23.797.521.
(Painful vicissitude!) his bosom tear. Od.1.151.40.
Nine painful years, on that detested shore Od.3.145.92.
But now let sleep the painful waste repair Od.4.399.139.
And take the painful sense of toil away. Od.10.428.365.
Thus cares on cares his painful days consume, Od.11.238.393.
In painful dungeons, and coercive chains; Od.11.360.400.

PAINS
Their artless Passions, and their tender Pains. 1.PAu.12.81.
One Leap from yonder Cliff shall end my Pains. 1.PAu.95.87.
Whose Fame with *Pains* we guard, but lose with *Ease,* 1.EOC.504.295.
Maintain'd with *Pains,* but forfeited with *Ease;* 1.EOC.504A.295.
The Fame with Pains we gain, but lose with ease; 1.EOC.504B.295.
Employ their Pains to spurn some others down; 1.EOC.515.296.
While to his reeds he sung his amorous pains, 1.TrPA.51.367.
Have pity, *Venus,* on your Poet's Pains! 1.TrSP.70.396.
That knew my Pleasures, cou'd relieve my Pains. 1.TrSP.162.400.
Augments his Joys, or mitigates his Pains. 2.ChJM.42.17.
And told them all, their Pains were at an End. 2.ChJM.253.26.
Sure to be lov'd, I took no Pains to please, 2.ChWB.62.59.
Free Gifts we scorn, and love what costs us Pains: 2.ChWB.260.69.
How vain are all these Glories, all our Pains, 2.RL5.15.200.
Repentant sighs, and voluntary pains: 2.ElAb.18.320.
Just as absurd, to mourn the tasks or pains 3.EOM1.265.47.
Pains, reading, study, are their just pretence, 4.Arbu.159.108.
"And you shall rise up *Otway* for your pains." 4.2HE2.146.175.
If such the Plague and pains to write by rule, 4.2HE2.180.177.
Some doubt, if equal pains or equal fire 4.2HE1.282.219.
'Tis He, who gives my breast a thousand pains, 4.2HE1.342.225.
Be Virtuous, and be happy for your pains. 4.1HE6.62.241.
See him, with pains of body, pangs of soul, 4.1HE1.71.283.
And begg'd, he'd take the pains to kick the rest. 4.EpS2.155.322.
There, thy good Scholiasts with unweary'd pains 5.DunA1.159.82.
And *Wit* dreads Exile, Penalties and Pains. 5.DunB4.22.342.
Thy mighty Scholiast, whose unweary'd pains 5.DunB4.211.363.
The Pains and Penalties of Idleness. 5.DunB4.344.377.
No Pains it takes, and no Offence it gives, 6.16.5.53.
Not for the fear of endless pains below, 6.25.3.77.
Nor for the fears of endless pains below, 6.25.3A.77.
And finish'd more thro' happiness than pains! 6.52.68.158.
He'll lose his Pains and Verses too; 6.77.6.214.
Whose Wife, a clean, pains-taking Woman, 6.93.2.256.
Said, to reward your Pains, 6.94.70.261.
Pains, Reading, Study, are their just Pretence, 6.98.9.283.
Sunk on his Knees and stagg'ring with his Pains, Il.5.379.285.
My early Youth was bred to martial Pains, Il.6.566.354.
Of all my Dangers, all my glorious Pains, Il.9.422.453.

PAINS (CONTINUED)
Ulysses thus, unconquer'd by his Pains, Il.11.604.61.
Jove thinking of his Pains, they past away. Il.15.274.207.
Before him scatt'ring, they prevent his pains, Il.21.297.433.
An only Child, once Comfort of my Pains, Il.22.620.482.
Sprung to their Car; and with united Pains Il.23.737.519.
Box was the Yoke, embost with costly Pains, Il.24.335.550.
An only Son, once Comfort of our Pains, Il.24.912.574.
Pains the sage ear, and hurts the sober eye. Od.1.294.47.
Nor came my fate by ling'ring pains and slow, Od.11.242.393.
Due pains shall punish then this slave's offence, Od.17.290.146.
The stubborn horn resisted all his pains: Od.21.158.267.

PAINS-TAKING
Whose Wife, a clean, pains-taking Woman, 6.93.2.256.

PAINT
Fresh rising Blushes paint the watry Glass, 1.PSu.28.74.
Now blushing Berries paint the yellow Grove; 1.PAu.75.85.
Now blushing Berries paint the fertile Grove; 1.PAu.75A.85.
And floating Forests paint the Waves with Green. 1.W-F.216.169.
To paint anew the flow'ry Sylvan Scenes, 1.W-F.285.174.
And with fresh Blushes paint the conscious Morn. 1.TrSP.98.398.
To glad the Glebe, and paint the flow'ry Fields. 2.ChJM.612.44.
Nor could it sure be such a Sin to paint. 2.RL5.24.201.
He best can paint'em, who shall feel'em most. 2.ElAb.366.349.
When Folly grows romantic, we must paint it. 3.Ep2.16A.49.
If Folly grows romantic, must I paint it? 3.Ep2.16B.49.
If Folly grow romantic, I must paint it. 3.Ep2.16C.49.
If Folly grows romantic, I must paint it. 3.Ep2.16.49.
Chameleons who can paint in white and black? 3.Ep2.156.63.
'Tis well—but, Artists! who can paint or write, 3.Ep2.187.65.
Paint Angels trembling round his *falling Horse?* 4.HS1.28.7.
Paint, Marble, Gems, and Robes of *Persian* Dye, 4.2HE2.265.183.
We build, we paint, we sing, we dance as well, 4.2HE1.46.197.
So well in paint and stone they judg'd of merit: 4.2HE1.384.227.
Feign what I will, and paint it e'er so strong, 4.EpS2.8.313.
But as the Flatt'rer or Dependant paint, 5.DunB4.535.395.
Let *Jervas* paint them, and let *Pope* commend. 6.38.28.108.
Let Kneller paint them, and let *Pope* commend. 6.38.28A.108.
Let *Jervase* gratis paint, and *Frowd* 6.47.11.128.
Yet still her charms in breathing paint engage; 6.52.55.157.
Nor work, nor play, nor paint, nor sing. 6.119.4.336.
Not work, nor play nor paint, nor sing. 6.119.4A.336.

PAINTED
His painted Wings, and Breast that flames with Gold? 1.W-F.118.161.
A painted Quiver on her Shoulder sounds, 1.W-F.179.166.
And naked Youths and painted Chiefs admire 1.W-F.405.192.
While naked Youth and painted Chiefs admire 1.W-F.405A.192.
Whose naked Youth and painted Chiefs admire 1.W-F.405B.192.
A *Raphael* painted, and a *Vida* sung! 1.EOC.704.320.
A painted Mitre shades his furrow'd Brows. 1.TrVP.49.379.
And painted Sandals on her Feet she wore: 1.TrUl.107.469.
Of painted Meadows, and of purling Springs. 2.ChJM.455.37.
O painted Monster form'd Mankind to cheat 2.ChJM.479.38.
But now secure the painted Vessel glides, 2.RL2.47.162.
Or dip their Pinions in the painted Bow, 2.RL2.84.165.
In glittring Dust and painted Fragments lie! 2.RL3.160.180.
Since painted, or not painted, all shall fade, 2.RL5.27.201.
Since painted, or not painted, all shall fade, 2.RL5.27.201.
Those painted clouds that beautify our days; 3.EOM2.284.89.
For what has Virro painted, built, and planted? 3.Ep4.13.137.
On painted Cielings you devoutly stare, 3.Ep4.145.151.
Such painted Puppets, such a varnish'd Race 4.JD4.208.43.
Painted for sight, and essenc'd for the smell, 4.JD4.226.45.
A painted Mistress, or a purling Stream. 4.Arbu.150.107.
This painted Child of Dirt that stinks and stings; 4.Arbu.310.118.
There painted vallies of eternal green, 5.DunA1.74.68.
There painted vallies of eternal green, 5.DunB1.76.275.
Each painted flouret in the lake below 6.14iv.9.47.
Then painted Butterflies. 6.14v(b).24.50.
The Fops are painted Butterflies, 6.53.17.161.
With door all painted green, 6.61.37.182.
When KNELLER painted These? 6.76.2.212.
And painted Crystals break the sparkling Rill, 6.142.4C.382.
When *Greece* beheld thy painted Canvas flow, Il.3.67.192.
To whom the Goddess of the painted Bow; Il.3.173.199.
Driv'n by the Goddess of the painted Bow. Il.5.456.290.
Oresbius, in his painted Mitre gay, Il.5.870.308.
He heard, return'd, and took his painted Shield: Il.10.168.9.
High on the painted Stern *Ulysses* laid, Il.10.671.31.
The various Goddess of the painted Bow, Il.18.205A.331.
She shone amidst them, on her painted Bow: Il.23.248.499.
Then thus the Goddess of the painted Bow. Il.24.115.540.
One o'er the couches painted carpets threw, Od.10.417.364.
A painted wonder flying on the main. Od.11.155.389.
Beneath the seats, soft painted robes they spread, Od.13.88.5.
And painted Sandals on her Feet she wore. Od.13.274.19.
His breast with marks of carnage painted o'er, Od.22.442.309.
A painted wonder, flying on the main. Od.23.288.337.

PAINTER
To painter *K[en]t* presents his *coin;* 6.121.2.340.
To painter Kent gave all this *Coin;* 6.121.2A.340.

PAINTER'S
The living image in the Painter's breast? 6.52.42.157.

PAINTERS
Poets like Painters, thus, unskill'd to trace 1.EOC.293.272.
Poets heap Virtues, Painters Gems at will, 3.Ep2.185.65.

PAINTING
To closer Shades the painting Flocks remove, 1.PSu.87.79.
Shines, in exposing Knaves, and painting Fools, 3.Ep2.119.60.

PAINTING (CONTINUED)
Shines in exposing Knaves and painting Fools, ...6.154.5.403.

PAINTS
And lavish Nature paints the Purple Year? ....1.PSp.28.63.
Here blushing *Flora* paints th'enamel'd Ground, ...1.W-F.38.151.
Paints the green Forests and the flow'ry Plains, ...1.W-F.428.194.
Paints as you plant, and, as you work, designs. ....3.Ep4.64.143.
But soon as Morning paints the Fields of Air, ...Il.8.658.427.
She paints the Horrors of a conquer'd Town, ...Il.9.703.469.
Your Eyes shall view, when Morning paints the Sky ....Il.9.800.473.
And soon as Morning paints the Eastern Skies, ...Il.24.751.568.
And soon as morning paints the fields of light, ...Od.3.467.109.
Thus old with woes my fancy paints him now! ....Od.19.418.214.
How scarce himself surviv'd: He paints the bow'r, ...Od.23.345.341.

PAIR
Such was the Discord of the Royal Pair, ...1.TrSt.190.418.
But as he march'd, good Gods! he show'd a Pair ....2.ChWB.315.72.
There lay three Garters, half a Pair of Gloves; ....2.RL2.39.161.
A Fan, a Garter, half a Pair of Gloves; ....2.RL2.39Z3.161.
"Behold yon Pair, in strict embraces join'd; ....5.DunA3.173.168.
"Behold yon Pair, in strict embraces join'd; ....5.DunB3.179.329.
A pair so faithful could expire; ....6.69ii.2.199.
Was never such a loving Pair, ...6.79.39.219.
Never was such a loving Pair, ...6.79.39A.219.
Thanks, dirty Pair! you teach me what to say, ...6.129.5.357.
Th' afflicted Pair, their Sorrows to proclaim, ...Il.9.675.468.
Forth from the Portals rush'd th' intrepid Pair, ...Il.12.161.87.
Which held so long that ancient Pair in Peace. ....Il.14.238.172.
Which held so long this ancient Pair in Peace. ....Il.14.348.179.
There golden Clouds conceal the heav'nly Pair, ...Il.14.401.183.
He said, and touch'd his Heart. The raging Pair ....Il.17.135.293.
Clytius and *Lampus*, ever-honour'd Pair; ....Il.20.286.406.
Minerva smiling heard, the Pair o'ertook, ...Il.21.496.442.
Now, now, my gen'rous Pair, exert your Force; ....Il.23.483.509.
Along the shore th' illustrious pair he led, ...Od.3.49.89.
Slew the dire pair, and gave to fun'ral flame ....Od.3.392.105.
Then to the dome the friendly pair invite, ...Od.4.53.122.
Who grace our palace now, that friendly pair, ...Od.4.185.128.
To the close grot the lonely pair remove, ...Od.5.291.185.
At night each pair on splendid carpets lay, ...Od.10.11.340.
A friendly pair! near these the * *Pylian* stray'd, ...Od.11.577.412.
The good old proverb how this pair fulfill! ....Od.17.250.143.
The royal pair; she guides them, and retires. ....Od.23.316.338.

PAIR'D
And glossy Jett is pair'd with shining White. ....1.TrSP.44.395.
Figures ill-pair'd, and Similes unlike. ....5.DunA1.64.67.
Figures ill pair'd, and Similies unlike. ....5.DunB1.66.275.
Pair'd with his Fellow-Charioteer the Sun; ....5.DunB4.588.401.
From those the well-pair'd mules we shall receive, ...Od.15.98.73.

PALACE
And o'er the *Theban* Palace spreads her Wings, ...1.TrSt.170.417.
And at the *Theban* Palace did alight, ...1.TrSt.170A.417.
And to the Regal Palace bent his way; ....1.TrSt.536.432.
And now the Palace Gates are open'd wide, ...2.ChJM.315.29.
A constant *Vapour* o'er the Palace flies; ....2.RL4.39.186.
And close confin'd to their own palace sleep. ....2.Elegy.22.364.
And close confin'd in their own palace sleep. ....2.Elegy.22A.364.
In Palace-Yard at Nine you'll find me there— ....4.2HE2.94.171.
That less admires the Palace than the Park; ....4.1HE1.113.287.
Up starts a Palace, lo! th' obedient base ....4.1HE1.140.289.
The Stews and Palace equally explor'd, ...5.DunB4.315.374.
In his own Palace forc'd to ask his bread, ...6.15.7.51.
While that in pipes beneath the palace flows, ...6.35.31.104.
In whose Bright Palace every Guest, ...6.135.61Z1.368.
Be *Priam's* Palace sunk in *Grecian* Fires, ...Il.2.495.150.
Her in the Palace, at her Loom she found; ....Il.3.169.199.
Arriv'd, and enter'd at the Palace Gate, ...Il.3.525.216.
To *Jove's* high Palace for a Cure he fled, ...Il.5.487.291.
Near *Priam's* Court and *Hector's* Palace stands ....Il.6.392.346.
Sought her own Palace, and indulg'd her Woe. ....Il.6.643.358.
Forth issues *Paris* from the Palace Wall. ....Il.6.649.358.
Meanwhile, conven'd at *Priam's* Palace Gate, ...Il.7.414.385.
Far in the Bay his shining Palace stands, ...Il.13.34.106.
The lofty Palace, and the large Domain. ....Il.19.355.387.
No—pent in this sad Palace let us give ....Il.24.255.547.
Wide as appears some Palace Gate display'd, ...Il.24.391.552.
First to the Palace let the Car proceed, ...Il.24.894.573.
Ev'n to the Palace the sad Pomp they wait: ....Il.24.898.573.
To see the smoke from his lov'd palace rise, ...Od.1.75.34.
Who crowd his palace, and with lawless pow'r ....Od.1.116.37.
On hides of Beeves, before the palace gate, ...Od.1.140.39.
There rule, from palace-cares remote and free, ...Od.1.457.54.
A tow'ring structure to the palace join'd; ....Od.1.537.57.
"My friend (he cry'd) my palace be thy care; ....Od.2.256.74.
The royal Palace to the Queen convey, ...Od.2.378.79.
Reel'd from the palace, and retir'd to rest. ....Od.2.447.82.
Thy Palace fill with insults and alarms? ....Od.3.261.98.
While lawless feasters in thy palace sway; ....Od.3.401.106.
He to thy palace shall thy steps pursue; ....Od.3.459.109.
On polish'd stone before his Palace gate: ....Od.3.519.112.
'Twas then that issuing thro' the palace gate ....Od.4.27.121.
Above, beneath, around the Palace shines ....Od.4.85.123.
With a sack'd Palace, and barbaric spoils. ....Od.4.122.126.
Who grace our palace now, that friendly pair, ...Od.4.185.128.
Fair in the plan the future palace rose, ...Od.4.236.130.
To his high palace thro' the fields of air ....Od.6.19.204.
Lo, to the Palace I direct thy way: ....Od.6.304.225.
And to the lofty palace bend thy way: ....Od.6.362.229.
The lofty palace overlooks the town, ...Od.6.363.229.
The turning wheel before the Palace stays. ....Od.7.4.233.
Well known to me the palace you enquire, ...Od.7.37.235.
At length the kingly palace gates he view'd: ....Od.7.61.236.

PALACE (CONTINUED)
Mean-while *Ulysses* at the Palace waits, ...Od.7.107.239.
While that in pipes beneath the palace flows, ...Od.7.172.244.
Night now approaching, in the palace stand ....Od.7.182.244.
A Palace stor'd with treasures shou'd be thine. ....Od.7.402.256.
Swift to the palace, all ye Peers ascend: ....Od.8.38.264.
Then to the palace move: A gath'ring throng, ...Od.8.49.264.
High on a column in the palace hung: ....Od.8.108.268.
But, herald, to the palace swift repair, ...Od.8.291.278.
The well-fill'd palace, the perpetual feast, ...Od.9.5.301.
In pomps or joys, the palace or the grott, ...Od.9.35.303.
Of *Circe's* Palace bosom'd in the grove. ....Od.10.176.349.
The Palace in a woody vale they found, ...Od.10.240.352.
A Palace in a woody vale we found ....Od.10.297.358.
Of *Circe's* Palace, where *Ulysses* leads. ....Od.10.526.368.
Or the lov'd palace glitter in our eyes? ....Od.10.563.369.
So in our palace, at our safe return ....Od.11.39.381.
To the black palace of eternal Night. ....Od.11.185.390.
And in his palace like a brother plac'd, ...Od.14.353.51.
Thy stately palace, and thy wide domain. ....Od.15.143.75.
And soon he reach'd the Palace of his Sire. ....Od.15.243.80.
There form'd his empire; there his palace rose. ....Od.15.265.81.
What-time it chanc'd the palace entertain'd ....Od.15.458.92.
An artist to my father's palace came, ...Od.15.495.94.
Strait to the Queen and Palace shall I fly, ...Od.15.549.96.
And give the Palace to the Queen a dow'r, ...Od.16.400.125.
And rising instant to the Palace mov'd. ....Od.16.423.127.
Stabb'd in his Palace if your Prince must fall, ...Od.17.91.136.
Strait to the feast-full palace he repair'd, ...Od.17.306.146.
Well may this Palace admiration claim, ...Od.17.314.147.
Till propp'd reclining on the palace walls; ....Od.18.123.172.
But to the palace measur'd back the way. ....Od.18.134.172.
O'er all the palace a fictitious day; ....Od.18.356.184.
A Palace, wealth, and slaves, I late possess'd, ...Od.19.94.197.
But thou on whom my palace-cares depend, ...Od.19.117.198.
Beneath thy palace-roof forget thy care; ....Od.20.43.234.
Fast by my palace shall your domes ascend, ...Od.21.223.270.
Suffic'd it not within the palace plac'd ....Od.21.311.274.
Clos'd in an instant were the Palace gates. ....Od.21.420.280.
In thy spoil'd Palace, and exhausted land; ....Od.22.60.289.
Within the stricture of this palace wall ....Od.22.186.296.
Drive to yon' court, without the Palace wall, ...Od.22.478.312.
Once more the palace set in fair array, ...Od.22.491.313.
To purge the palace: then the Queen attend, ...Od.22.519.314.
Heap'd lie the dead without the Palace walls,— ....Od.23.53.321.
And rule our Palace with an equal sway: ....Od.23.382.343.
Thou with thy Maids within the Palace stay, ...Od.23.391.343.
My palace there; *Eperitus* my name. ....Od.24.354.366.
Stretch'd in our palace, by these hands lie slain. ....Od.24.381.367.
In throngs they rise, and to the palace crowd; ....Od.24.476.371.
When from the Palace to the wond'ring throng ....Od.24.504.372.

PALACE-CARES
There rule, from palace-cares remote and free, ...Od.1.457.54.
But thou on whom my palace-cares depend, ...Od.19.117.198.

PALACE-ROOF
Beneath thy palace-roof forget thy care; ....Od.20.43.234.

PALACE-YARD
In Palace-Yard at Nine you'll find me there— ....4.2HE2.94.171.

PALACES
Then Palaces shall rise; the joyful Son ....1.Mes.63.118.
And yet no new built Palaces aspire, ...4.JD2A.117.142.
We see no new-built Palaces aspire, ...4.JD2.111.143.
Thus Honey-combs seem Palaces to Bees; ....6.96v.29.281.
Stretch'd on the spoils of plunder'd palaces ....6.130.12.358.
Unfinish'd his proud Palaces remain, ...Il.2.858.165.
Thro' Streets of Palaces and Walks of State; ....Il.6.490.350.
The Heroes slain, the Palaces o'erthrown, ...Il.9.704.469.
Then to the Palaces of heav'n she sails, ...Od.6.47.207.

PALAEMON
And press'd *Palæmon* closer in her Arms. ....1.TrSt.168.417.

PALANCES
Reflects her bord'ring Palances and Bow'rs. ....Il.2.1041.172.

PALATE
Hard Task! to hit the Palate of such Guests, ...4.2HE2.86.171.
Let not my Palate know the Taste of Food, ...Il.19.207.381.

PALATES
Woud you your writings to some Palates fit ....6.82ix(f).1.235.

PALE
See pale *Orion* sheds unwholsome Dews, ...1.PWi.85A.95.
Now fainting, sinking, pale, the Nymph appears; ....1.W-F.191.167.
Gigantick *Pride*, pale *Terror*, gloomy *Care*, ...1.W-F.415.193.
Like some sad Statue, speechless, pale, I stood; ....1.TrSP.125.399.
And the pale Spectres trembled at her View: ....1.TrSt.133.415.
Let the pale Sire revisit *Thebes*, and bear ....1.TrSt.421.427.
Pale ev'n in Joy, nor yet forget to fear. ....1.TrSt.732.440.
And, pale in Death, lay groaning on the Shore. ....1.TrES.295.460.
Now livid pale her Cheeks, now glowing red; ....2.RL*A*2.61.133.
Some less refin'd, beneath the Moon's pale Light ....2.RL2.81.165.
Pale Spectres, gaping Tombs, and Purple Fires: ....2.RL4.44.187.
And the pale Ghosts start at the Flash of Day! ....2.RL5.52.203.
Pale Suns, unfelt, at distance roll away, ...2.TemF.55.256.
With Studies pale, with Midnight Vigils blind; ....2.TemF.301.278.
At the dread Sound, pale Mortals stood aghast, ...2.TemF.416.283.
Shrines! where their vigils pale-ey'd virgins keep, ...2.ElAb.21.320.
The shrines all trembled, and the lamps grew pale: ....2.ElAb.112.329.
Where round some mould'ring tow'r pale ivy creeps, ...2.ElAb.243.339.
O'er the pale marble shall they join their heads, ...2.ElAb.349.348.

PALE (CONTINUED)

Pleas'd thy pale ghost, or grac'd thy mournful bier; ... 2.Elegy.50.367.
Who sees pale Mammon pine amidst his store, ... 3.Ep3.173.107.
How pale, each Worshipful and rev'rend Guest ... 4.HS2.75.59.
Scar'd at the spectre of pale Poverty! ... 4.1HE1.70.283.
And sees pale Virtue carted in her stead! ... 4.EpS1.150.309.
How Index-learning turns no student pale, ... 5.DunA1.233.90.
How proud! how pale! how earnest all appear! ... 5.DunA3.152Z1.164.
Tears gush'd again, as from pale Priam's eyes ... 5.DunB1.255.289.
How Index-learning turns no student pale, ... 5.DunB1.279.290.
The pale Boy-Senator yet tingling stands, ... 5.DunB4.147.355.
And keep them in the pale of Words till death. ... 5.DunB4.160.357.
As pale as her own lovers are. ... 6.4iii.6.10.
To the pale Nations of the Dead, ... 6.11.52.32.
And the pale Spectres dance! ... 6.11.68.32.
And pale *Narcissus* on the bank, in vain ... 6.14iv.11.47.
Now nothing's left, but wither'd, pale, and shrunk, ... 6.49i.25.138.
With sharpen'd sight pale Antiquaries pore, ... 6.71.35.203.
Trembling and pale, he starts with wild Affright, ... Il.3.49.191.
All pale with Rage, and shake the threat'ning Lance. ... Il.3.426.212.
Pale *Flight* around, and dreadful *Terror* reign; ... Il.4.500.244.
Pale was her Cheek, and livid look'd the Wound. ... Il.5.444.289.
To stretch thee pale and gasping on the Ground; ... Il.5.500.292.
Humbled they stood; pale Horror seiz'd on all, ... Il.7.574.393.
All pale and breathless on the sanguin Field. ... Il.8.384.416.
Expiring, pale, and terrible no more, ... Il.8.462.419.
While Fear, pale Comrade of inglorious Flight, ... Il.9.2.430.
Then thus pale *Dolon* with a fearful Look, ... Il.10.461.24.
And the pale Features now deform'd with Blood. ... Il.11.324.49.
They, pale with Terror, mark its Spires unroll'd, ... Il.12.241.90.
Who breathless, pale, with length of Labours tir'd, ... Il.13.118.110.
Which to pale Man the Wrath of Heav'n declares, ... Il.13.319.120.
No Force, no Firmness, the pale Coward shows; ... Il.13.359.123.
Pale Mortals tremble, and confess their Fears. ... Il.14.448.185.
Stiff with Amaze the pale Beholders stand, ... Il.14.485.187.
And the pale Matron in our Triumphs mourn. ... Il.14.594.191.
Pale, trembling, tir'd, the Sailors freeze with Fears; ... Il.15.756.225.
So pale the *Greeks* the Eyes of *Hector* meet, ... Il.15.758.225.
And pale in Death, lay groaning on the Shore. ... Il.16.600.267.
Lies pale in Death, extended on the Field. ... Il.16.684.270.
On the pale Carcase thus address'd the dead. ... Il.16.1037.283.
All pale with Fear, at distance scatter'd round, ... Il.17.73.290.
Now pale and dead, shall succour *Greece* no more. ... Il.17.776.318.
All pale they tremble, and forsake the Field. ... Il.17.820.320.
So shall *Achilles* fall! stretch'd pale and dead, ... Il.18.151.329.
(Unhappy Change!) now senseless, pale, he found, ... Il.18.281.335.
Cleanse the pale Corse, and wash each honour'd Wound. ... Il.18.404.340.
Pale lyes my Friend, with Wounds disfigur'd o'er, ... Il.19.209.381.
So to Night-wand'ring Sailors, pale with Fears, ... Il.19.404.389.
Pale *Troy* beheld, and seem'd already lost; ... Il.20.60.396.
Then Tumult rose; fierce Rage and pale Affright ... Il.20.64.396.
Thus while he spake, the *Trojan* pale with Fears ... Il.21.74.424.
And the pale Crescent fades upon her Brows. ... Il.21.596.446.
The Pale Inhabitants, some fall, some fly; ... Il.21.609.447.
Pale *Troy* against *Achilles* shuts her Gate; ... Il.21.723.451.
All pale they wander on the *Stygian* Coast; ... Il.22.71.455.
Let my pale Corse the Rites of Burial know, ... Il.23.87.490.
And glares on the pale Visage of the Dead. ... Il.23.133.493.
Lye pale and breathless round the Fields of *Troy!* ... Il.24.206.545.
Pale grew his Face, and upright stood his Hair; ... Il.24.442.554.
Just gains some Frontier, breathless, pale! amaz'd! ... Il.24.592.561.
Kiss his pale Cheek, and rend their scatter'd Hair: ... Il.24.889.573.
To the pale Shade funereal rites ordain, ... Od.1.379.51.
Or the pale radiance of the midnight moon. ... Od.4.56.122.
Extended pale, by swarthy *Memnon* slain! ... Od.4.256.131.
And the pale mariner at once deplores ... Od.4.491.143.
With famine pale, and ask thy care in vain? ... Od.4.506.144.
'Till the twelfth moon had wheel'd her pale career; ... Od.4.704.152.
As ghastly pale he groans, and faints, and dies; ... Od.8.574.293.
Then pale and pensive stand, with cares opprest, ... Od.11.5.379.
And wither'd Elders, pale and wrinkled shades: ... Od.11.50.383.
Back started the pale throngs, and trembling stood. ... Od.11.62.383.
All pale ascends my royal mother's shade: ... Od.11.105.385.
Deep are his sighs, his visage pale, his dress ... Od.11.232.393.
Then tho' pale death froze cold in ev'ry vein, ... Od.11.527.409.
Or pale and wan beholds these nether skies? ... Od.11.571.411.
Throng'd with pale ghosts, familiar with the dead? ... Od.11.586.412.
From the pale ghosts, and hell's tremendous shade. ... Od.12.24.430.
Pensive and pale from grove to grove I stray'd, ... Od.12.395.450.
Pale hunger wastes the manly strength away. ... Od.12.406.450.
Pensive and pale he wanders half a ghost. ... Od.16.157.110.
Pale grief destroy what time a while forbears. ... Od.16.353.123.
With clouded looks, a pale assembly sate. ... Od.16.361.123.
Then pale with fears, and sick'ning at the sight, ... Od.18.86.170.
When the pale Empress of yon' starry train ... Od.19.351.211.
Down her pale cheek new-streaming sorrow flows: ... Od.19.702.229.
As one who long with pale-ey'd famine pin'd, ... Od.20.32.233.
Sunk was each heart, and pale was ev'ry face. ... Od.21.451.282.
From their pale cheeks recedes the flying blood; ... Od.22.54.289.
'Till pale as yonder wretch each Suitor lies. ... Od.22.78.290.
With guilty fears the pale assembly shook. ... Od.22.82.290.
The damsel train turn'd pale at every wound, ... Od.23.43.321.
And the pale silver glows with fusile gold: ... Od.23.160.328.
All pale, with ooze deform'd, he views the strand, ... Od.23.255.335.
All he unfolds: His list'ning spouse turns pale ... Od.23.331.340.
His royal mother, pale *Anticlea's* shade; ... Od.23.350.341.
O'er the pale corse! the honours of the dead. ... Od.24.217.358.

PALE-EY'D

Shrines! where their vigils pale-ey'd virgins keep, ... 2.ElAb.21.320.
As one who long with pale-ey'd famine pin'd, ... Od.20.32.233.

PALENESS

A livid Paleness spreads o'er all her Look; ... 2.RL3.90.174.

PALER

And, ev'n in Gold, turns paler as she dies. ... 1.TrSt.639.437.

PALES

And Pales of glitt'ring Tin th' Enclosure grace. ... Il.18.656.355.
And strong with pales, by many a weary stroke ... Od.14.15.35.

PALINURUS

Ev'n Palinurus nodded at the Helm: ... 5.DunB4.614.405.

PALISADES

And, fenc'd with Palisades, a Hall of State, ... Il.24.555.559.

PALL

They pall *Moliere's* and *Lopez* sprightly strain, ... 6.60.15.178.
To spread the pall beneath the regal chair ... Od.4.163.128.
"A pall of state, the ornament of death. ... Od.19.167.200.

PALLADIAN

Conscious they act a true Palladian part, ... 3.Ep4.37.140.
Palladian walls, Venetian doors, ... 4.HS6.193.263.
At *Burlington's* Palladian Gates: ... 6.135.60.368.
And awful reach the high *Palladian* Dome, ... Il.6.371.344.
As when a Shipwright, with *Palladian* Art, ... Il.15.474.215.

PALLADIO

Jones and Palladio to themselves restore, ... 3.Ep4.193.155.

PALLAS

Celestial *Pallas,* stood before his Eyes; ... 1.TrUl.101.469.
The more shall *Pallas* aid thy just Desires, ... 1.TrUl.211.472.
But *Pallas* knew (thy Friends and Navy lost) ... 1.TrUl.220.473.
If *Jove* prolong my Days, and *Pallas* crown ... 1.TrUl.244.473.
'Gainst *Pallas, Mars; Latona, Hermes* arms; ... 2.RL5.47.202.
E'er Pallas issued from the Thund'rer's head, ... 5.DunA1.8.61.
E'er Pallas issu'd from the Thund'rer's head, ... 5.DunB1.10.269.
Pallas they say Sprung from the Head of *Jove,* ... 6.37.3.106.
Venus and *Pallas* both had Children been. ... 6.37.6.106.
How *Pallas* talk'd when she was Seven Years old. ... 6.37.10.106.
Pallas grew vap'rish once and odd, ... 6.119.1.336.
Pallas, you give yourself strange Airs; ... 6.119.13.337.
Pallas obeys, and from *Olympus'* Height ... Il.2.203.137.
The blue-ey'd *Pallas,* his Celestial Friend, ... Il.2.342.143.
Him *Pallas* plac'd amidst her wealthy Fane, ... Il.2.661.158.
See ready *Pallas* waits thy high Commands, ... Il.4.91.224.
They said, while *Pallas* thro' the *Trojan* Throng ... Il.4.115.226.
Pallas assists, and (weaken'd in its Force) ... Il.4.160.228.
For *Pallas* strung his Arm, and edg'd his Sword. ... Il.4.443.241.
By *Pallas* guarded thro' the dreadful Field, ... Il.4.631.251.
But *Pallas* now *Tydides* Soul inspires, ... Il.5.1.263.
Such Glories *Pallas* on the Chief bestow'd, ... Il.5.11.266.
For lov'd by *Pallas, Pallas* did impart ... Il.5.79.270.
For lov'd by *Pallas, Pallas* did impart ... Il.5.79.270.
Her shalt thou wound: So *Pallas* gives Command. ... Il.5.169.275.
So *Pallas* tells me, and forbids to fly. ... Il.5.321.282.
Which driv'n by *Pallas,* pierc'd a vital Part; ... Il.5.352.283.
Like *Pallas* dreadful with her sable Shield, ... Il.5.410.286.
But thou (tho' *Pallas* urg'd thy frantic Deed) ... Il.5.493.291.
Juno and *Pallas* with a Smile survey'd, ... Il.5.507.292.
To *Mars* and *Pallas* leave the Deeds of Arms. ... Il.5.522.293.
Pallas disrobes; Her radiant Veil unty'd, ... Il.5.904.309.
Pallas commands, and *Pallas* lends thee Force. ... Il.5.1023.315.
Pallas commands, and *Pallas* lends thee Force. ... Il.5.1023.315.
Pallas oppos'd her Hand, and caus'd to glance ... Il.5.1046.316.
Juno and *Pallas* mount the blest Abodes, ... Il.5.1120.321.
Troy's strong Defence, unconquer'd *Pallas,* aid! ... Il.6.379.345.
When *Juno's* self, and *Pallas* shall appear, ... Il.8.459.419.
Pallas, meanwhile, her various Veil unbound, ... Il.8.466.419.
Pallas and *Juno!* say, why heave your Hearts? ... Il.8.557.423.
Juno and *Pallas* grieving hear the Doom, ... Il.8.570.423.
Like *Pallas* worship'd, like the Sun renown'd; ... Il.8.670.427.
And vy'd with *Pallas* in the Works of Art. ... Il.9.513.458.
Daughter of *Jove,* unconquer'd *Pallas!* hear. ... Il.10.336.18.
The Heroes pray'd, and *Pallas* from the Skies, ... Il.10.351.18.
(Inspir'd by *Pallas)* in his Bosom wrought, ... Il.10.436.23.
To fav'ring *Pallas* dedicates the Prize. ... Il.10.531.26.
Pallas (this said) her Hero's Bosom warms, ... Il.10.558.27.
Pallas appears, and thus her Chief commands. ... Il.10.593.28.
And first to *Pallas* the Libations pour: ... Il.10.678.32.
Pallas, descending in the Shades of Night, ... Il.11.850.74.
Till *Pallas* stopp'd us where *Alisium* flows. ... Il.11.890.75.
Pallas assists, and lofty *Ilion* burns. ... Il.15.77.199.
But *Pallas* springing thro' the bright Abode, ... Il.15.140.202.
To *Hermes, Pallas,* and the Queen of Heav'n; ... Il.15.237.206.
Due to stern *Pallas,* and *Pelides'* Spear: ... Il.15.737.224.
Apollo, Pallas, and almighty *Jove!* ... Il.16.123.242.
Her *Ægis, Pallas* o'er his Shoulders throws; ... Il.18.242.334.
So *Pallas* robb'd the Many of their Mind, ... Il.18.362.339.
They march; by *Pallas* and by *Mars* made bold; ... Il.18.599.351.
Oppos'd to *Pallas,* War's triumphant Maid. ... Il.20.94.398.
Those, *Pallas, Jove,* and We, in Ruins laid: ... Il.20.233.403.
Pallas and I, by all that Gods can bind, ... Il.20.361.410.
Neptune and *Pallas* haste to his Relief, ... Il.21.330.435.
While *Pallas* fills him with immortal Force. ... Il.21.355.435.
She moves: Let *Pallas,* if she dares, pursue. ... Il.21.495.442.
Then *Pallas* thus: Shall he whose Vengeance forms ... Il.22.233.465.
'Tis *Pallas, Pallas* gives thee to my Lance. ... Il.22.346.470.
'Tis *Pallas, Pallas* gives thee to my Lance. ... Il.22.346.470.
A God deceiv'd me; *Pallas,* 'twas thy Deed. ... Il.22.381.471.
The Fraud celestial *Pallas* sees with Pain, ... Il.23.467.509.
The panting Chief to *Pallas* lifts his Soul: ... Il.23.900.525.
(O'erturn'd by *Pallas)* where the slipp'ry Shore ... Il.23.907.525.
And *Pallas,* not *Ulysses* won the Day. ... Il.23.920.525.
But *Neptune* this, and *Pallas* this denies, ... Il.24.36.536.
'Till *Pallas,* piteous of her plaintive cries, ... Od.1.463.54.
Pallas with grace divine his form improves, ... Od.2.15.61.

PALLAS (CONTINUED)
The Youth, whom *Pallas* destin'd to be wise, ... Od.3.92.90.
Then *Discord*, sent by *Pallas* from above, ... Od.3.165.93.
Pallas herself, the War-triumphant Maid, ... Od.3.486.111.
To *Pallas* high the foaming bowl he crown'd, ... Od.3.506.112.
To *Pallas*, first of Gods, prepare the feast, ... Od.3.532.113.
So wrought, as *Pallas* might with pride behold. ... Od.3.556.114.
As *Pallas* will'd, along the sable skies ... Od.4.1053.167.
Pallas, to these, deplores th' unequal fates ... Od.5.8.171.
Jove's daughter *Pallas* watch'd the fav'ring hour. ... Od.5.489.195.
But instant *Pallas* enter'd in his soul. ... Od.5.545.198.
But all-subduing *Pallas* lent her pow'r, ... Od.5.556.199.
'Till *Pallas* pour'd soft slumbers on his eyes; ... Od.5.635.202.
His woes forgot! But *Pallas* now addrest ... Od.6.131.213.
By *Pallas* arm'd with boldness not her own. ... Od.6.168.216.
By *Pallas* taught, he frames the wond'rous mold, ... Od.6.277.224.
So *Pallas* his heroic frame improves ... Od.6.279.224.
To *Pallas* sacred, shades the holy ground, ... Od.6.350.229.
To *Pallas* thus the pensive Heroe pray'd. ... Od.6.384.230.
Propitious *Pallas*, to secure her care, ... Od.7.19.234.
(So *Pallas* order'd, *Pallas* to their eyes ... Od.7.53.236.
(So *Pallas* order'd, *Pallas* to their eyes ... Od.7.53.236.
Pallas to these her double gifts imparts, ... Od.7.140.242.
And would to *Phœbus*, *Pallas*, and to *Jove*, ... Od.7.398.256.
Pallas with grace divine his form improves, ... Od.8.19.262.
That instant *Pallas*, bursting from a cloud, ... Od.8.219.274.
Th' *Epæan* fabric, fram'd by *Pallas*, sing: ... Od.8.540.291.
He fights, subdues: for *Pallas* strings his arms. ... Od.8.568.293.
I thought, devis'd, and *Pallas* heard my prayer. ... Od.9.377.321.
And *Pallas*, by the *Trojans* judg'd the cause. ... Od.11.670.417.
Celestial *Pallas*, stood before his eyes; ... Od.13.268.18.
The more shall *Pallas* aid thy just desires, ... Od.13.378.25.
But *Pallas* knew (thy friends and navy lost) ... Od.13.387.25.
If *Jove* prolong my days, and *Pallas* crown ... Od.13.411.26.
Hundreds shall fall, if *Pallas* aid my hand. ... Od.13.446.27.
While *Pallas*, cleaving the wide fields of air, ... Od.13.510.30.
Me *Pallas* gave to lead the martial storm, ... Od.14.251.48.
Pallas, unconquer'd maid, my frame surrounds ... Od.16.228.114.
So *Pallas* wills—but thou my son, explain ... Od.16.258.117.
By mighty *Pallas*, and by thund'ring *Jove*. ... Od.16.283.118.
Nor ceas'd, 'till *Pallas* bid her sorrows fly, ... Od.16.468.130.
Pallas his form with grace divine improves: ... Od.17.74.136.
For *Pallas* seals his doom: All sad he turns ... Od.18.185.175.
And *Pallas* taught the texture of the loom. ... Od.20.87.237.
Whom *Pallas* with unpard'ning fury fir'd, ... Od.20.351.249.
But *Pallas* clouds with intellectual gloom ... Od.20.413.252.
But vengeful *Pallas* with preventing speed ... Od.20.467.256.
And *Pallas* now, to raise the rivals fires, ... Od.21.1.257.
'Till gentle *Pallas*, piteous of her cries, ... Od.21.387.279.
Jove's daughter *Pallas*, War's triumphant maid: ... Od.22.222.297.
Of *Pallas* latent in the friendly form. ... Od.22.232.298.
Some, turn'd by *Pallas*, on the threshold fall, ... Od.22.302.301.
Now *Pallas* shines confess'd; aloft she spreads ... Od.22.330.302.
By *Pallas* taught, he frames the wond'rous mold, ... Od.23.159.328.
So *Pallas* his heroic form improves ... Od.23.161.328.
But *Pallas* backward held the rising day, ... Od.23.260.335.
Now flames the rosy dawn, but *Pallas* shrouds ... Od.23.398.343.
Pallas attending gives his frame to shine ... Od.24.427.369.
Pallas, and *Jove*, and him who gilds the sky! ... Od.24.434.369.
Descended *Pallas* from th' *Olympian* hill. ... Od.24.563.375.
So *Pallas* spoke: The mandate from above ... Od.24.628.377.

PALLAS'
This Day the Foe prevail'd by *Pallas'* Pow'r; ... Il.3.545.217.
As *Pallas'* Priestess, and unbars the Gates. ... Il.6.373.344.
By *Pallas'* Care, the Spear, tho' deep infix'd, ... Il.11.549.58.
As *Pallas'* self might view with fixt Delight; ... Il.13.174.113.
That rich with *Pallas'* labour'd Colours glow'd; ... Il.14.208.170.
Not *Pallas'* self, her Breast when Fury warms, ... Il.17.458.305.
Then parts the Lance: But *Pallas'* heav'nly Breath, ... Il.20.507.415.
Corrects thy Folly thus by *Pallas'* Hand; ... Il.21.481.441.
Doubt you the Gods? Lo *Pallas'* self descends, ... Od.20.57.235.

PALLID
Can they, in gems bid pallid Hippia glow, ... 3.Ep3.89.96.

PALLS
The golden Vase in purple Palls they roll'd, ... Il.24.1005.577.
And o'er soft palls of purple grain unfold ... Od.4.405.139.
With splendid palls the downy fleece adorn: ... Od.19.364.212.
With splendid palls, and canopies of state: ... Od.19.394.213.

PALM
Strives to extract from his soft, giving palm; ... 5.DunA2.200.126.
Strives to extract from his soft, giving palm; ... 5.DunB2.208.306.
Beneath her Palm here sad Judæa weeps, ... 6.71.26.203.
My spacious palm in Stature scarce a Span ... 6.96ii.30Z41.272.
"My spacious Palm? Of Stature scarce a Span, ... 6.96ii.63.273.
Let sage Advice, the Palm of Age, be mine. ... Il.4.379.239.
This said, she wip'd from *Venus'* wounded Palm ... Il.5.505.292.
Assists great *Hector*, and our Palm denies. ... Il.8.172.406.
On whom *Apollo* shall the Palm bestow, ... Il.23.763.520.
Who hopes the Palm of Swiftness to obtain, ... Il.23.879.524.
Thus seems the Palm with stately honours crown'd ... Od.6.193.218.

PALMER'S
To *Palmer's* Bed no Actress comes amiss, ... 4.HAdv.71.81.

PALMERS
"Behold yon' Isle, by Palmers, Pilgrims trod, ... 5.DunA3.105.159.
"See'st thou an Isle, by Palmers, Pilgrims trod, ... 5.DunA3.105A.159.
"Behold yon' Isle, by Palmers, Pilgrims trod, ... 5.DunB3.113.325.

PALMS
To leaf-less Shrubs the flow'ring Palms succeed, ... 1.Mes.75.119.
And Palms Eternal flourish round his Urn. ... 1.W-F.312.179.

PALMS (CONTINUED)
Celestial palms, and ever-blooming flow'rs. ... 2.ElAb.318.345.
With simp'ring Angels, Palms, and Harps divine; ... 3.Ep2.14.49.
Not but there are, who merit other palms; ... 4.2HE1.229.215.
But now for Authors nobler palms remain: ... 5.DunA2.183.124.
But now for Authors nobler palms remain; ... 5.DunB2.191.304.
And sixteen Palms his Brows large Honours spread: ... Il.4.141.227.

PALMUS
Palmus, with *Polyphetes* the divine, ... Il.13.995.152.

PALMY
See, where the Morning gilds the palmy shore, ... 5.DunA3.87.157.
See, where the morning gilds the palmy shore ... 5.DunB3.95.324.

PALPABLE
Fast by in darkness palpable inshrin'd ... 5.DunA3.187A.172.

PALSIE
And a new Palsie seiz'd them when I frown'd. ... 2.ChWB.67.59.

PALSY
A sudden Palsy seiz'd his turning Head; ... Il.10.445.23.

PALTRY
Paltry and proud, as drabs in Drury-lane. ... 4.JD2.64.139.
This subtle Thief of Life, this paltry Time, ... 4.2HE2.76.171.
Is it for *Bond* or *Peter* (paltry Things!) ... 4.EpS1.121.307.
Is it for *W[a]rd* or *Peter* (paltry Things!) ... 4.EpS1.121A.307.

PAM
Ev'n mighty *Pam* that Kings and Queens o'erthrew, ... 2.RL3.61.172.

PAMBY
And Namby Pamby be prefer'd for Wit! ... 5.DunA3.322.188.

PAMELA
The Gods, to curse *Pamela* with her Pray'rs, ... 6.19.49.63.

PAMMON
Hippothous, Pammon, Helenus the Seer, ... Il.24.314.549.

PAMPER'D
"See man for mine!" replies a pamper'd goose; ... 3.EOM3.46.96.
Not to say worse in pamper'd Churchmens Lives ... 4.JD2A.88.140.
When pamper'd *Cupids*, bestly *Veni's*, ... 6.135.39.367.
Pamper'd and proud, he seeks the wonted Tides, ... Il.6.654.359.
As when the pamper'd Steed, with Reins unbound, ... Il.15.298.208.
To pamper'd insolence devoted fall ... Od.4.431.140.
With care domestic pamper'd at the floor. ... Od.15.181.77.
But pamper'd luxury) *Melanthius* came; ... Od.17.247.143.

PAMPHLETS
For writing pamphlets, and for burning Popes; ... 5.DunA3.282.183.
For writing pamphlets, and for roasting Popes; ... 5.DunA3.282A.183.
For writing Pamphlets, and for roasting Popes; ... 5.DunB3.284.334.

PAMS
As knavish *Pams*, and fawning *Trays*; ... 6.135.38.367.

PAN
Rough *Satyrs* dance, and *Pan* applauds the Song: ... 1.PSu.50.75.
Pan came, and ask'd, what Magick caus'd my Smart, ... 1.PAu.81.86.
See *Pan* with Flocks, with Fruits *Pomona* crown'd, ... 1.W-F.37.151.
Pan saw and lov'd, and burning with Desire ... 1.W-F.183.166.
Pan saw and lov'd, and furious with Desire ... 1.W-F.183A.166.
And Pan to Moses lends his Pagan horn; ... 5.DunA3.102.159.
And Pan to Moses lends his pagan horn; ... 5.DunB3.110.325.
In a Stewing pan put it. ... 6.91.4.253.

PANDARUS
Were led by *Pandarus*, of Royal Blood. ... Il.2.1001.170.
The warlike *Pandarus*, for strength renown'd; ... Il.4.120.226.
Exploring *Pandarus* with careful Eyes. ... Il.5.215.277.
Where, *Pandarus*, are all thy Honours now, ... Il.5.218.278.
So *Pandarus*, thy hopes, three orphan fair ... Od.20.78.236.

PANDERS
To keep off Flatt'rers, Spies, and Panders, ... 6.135.74.369.
Instead of Spyes, & Pimps, & Panders, ... 6.135.74A.369.

PANDION
Whose fatal Bow the strong *Pandion* bore. ... 1.TrES.90.453.
Whose fatal Bow the strong *Pandion* bore. ... Il.12.444.97.

PANDOCUS
On strong *Pandocus* next inflicts a Wound, ... Il.11.612.61.

PANE
Lull'd by soft Zephyrs thro' the broken Pane, ... 4.Arbu.42.99.

PANEGYRIC
And I'm not us'd to Panegyric strains: ... 4.2HE1.405.229.

PANG
Nor share one pang of all I felt for thee. ... 2.ElAb.292.343.
And the last pang shall tear thee from his heart, ... 2.Elegy.80.368.
'*she*. Yes, we have liv'd— one pang, and then we part! ... 6.123.1.343.
Forth flows the Blood; an eager Pang succeeds; ... Il.11.507.56.
Where sharp the Pang, and mortal is the Wound. ... Il.13.719.138.

PANGS
Not fiercer Pangs distract the mournful Dame, ... 1.TrSP.133.399.
What Pangs, what sudden Shoots distend my Side? ... 2.ChJM.721.49.
In trance extatic may thy pangs be drown'd, ... 2.ElAb.339.347.
Survey the Pangs they bear, the Risques they run, ... 4.HAdv.51.79.

PANGS (CONTINUED)
See him, with pains of body, pangs of soul, ... 4.1HE1.71.283.
Asswag'd the glowing Pangs, and clos'd the Wound. .... Il.5.490.291.
Yet long th' inflicted Pangs thou shalt not mourn, ... Il.5.1104.320.
While Death's strong Pangs distend his lab'ring Side, ... Il.13.722.139.
The Eels lie twisting in the Pangs of Death: .... Il.21.413.437.
Rack'd with convulsive pangs in dust I roul; .... Od.4.726.153.
What pangs for thee this wretched bosom bears! .... Od.19.425.215.
And cure the pangs of this convulsive heart. .... Od.20.73.236.

PANICK
Thus to their Bulwarks, smit with Panick, Fear, ... Il.22.1.452.

PANOMPHAEAN
Who paid their Vows to *Panomphæan Jove;* .... Il.8.300.412.

PANOPÉ'S
For as o'er *Panopé's* enamel'd plains .... Od.11.715.421.

PANOPËA
From *Panopëa, Chrysa* the Divine, ... Il.2.624.157.

PANOPE
In little *Panope* for Strength renown'd, ... Il.17.356.301.
Then *Proto, Doris, Panope* appear; .... Il.18.52.326.

PANOPLY
Celestial *Panoply,* to grace a God! .... Il.10.511.26.
In heav'nly Panoply divinely bright .... Il.17.233.297.
In radiant Panoply his limbs incas'd; .... Od.1.333.48.
At once in brazen Panoply they shone, ... Od.22.130.293.
And brazen Panoply invests the band. .... Od.24.577.375.

PANT
And heave, and pant, and kiss, and cling, for Gold. .... 2.ChWB.175.65.
Pant on thy lip, and to thy heart be prest; .... 2.ElAb.123.330.
The dying gales that pant upon the trees, ... 2.ElAb.159.332.
Th' inspiring Bellows lie and pant below. .... 4.JD2.20.133.
Th' inspiring Bellows lie and pant below. .... 4.JD2A.22.134.
To pant, or tremble thro' an Eunuch's throat. .... 4.2HE1.154.209.
Pant for the Fight, and threat the Fleet with Fire: .... Il.12.102.85.
Pant in the Ships; while *Troy* to Conquest calls, ... Il.13.119.110.
While these fly trembling, others pant for Breath, ... Il.15.392.212.
But round the Corps, the Heroes pant for Breath, ... Il.17.444.304.
Her bravest Heroes pant with inward Fear, ... Il.20.61.396.
Or pant and heave beneath the floating Waves. .... Il.21.33.422.
Shall pant, and tremble at our Arms again; .... Il.21.244.431.
Her routed Squadrons pant behind their Wall: .... Il.21.341.435.
Now glow the Waves, the Fishes pant for Breath, ... Il.21.412.437.
No less the lab'ring Heroes pant and strain; .... Il.22.261.466.
They pant, they stretch, they shout along the Plain. .... Il.23.450.508.
So pant the wretches, struggling in the sky, ... Od.12.305.447.
They pant, and struggle in the moving gold. .... Od.19.268.208.
The fishes pant, and gasp in thinner air; .... Od.22.429.309.

PANTALOON
With Whiskers, Band, and Pantaloon, ... 6.58.33.172.

PANTED
While *Procris* panted in the secret shade; .... 6.14iii.2.45.
Impatient panted on his Neck behind) .... Il.13.486.130.
Then stopp'd, and panted, where the Chariots lie; .... Il.15.3.193.
Shook with her Sighs, and panted on her Breast. .... Il.21.592.446.

PANTHER
Nor Panther braves his spotted Foe in Fight, ... Il.17.22.288.
So from some deep grown Wood a Panther starts, ... Il.21.677.450.

PANTHER'S
In Form a God! the Panther's speckled Hyde .... Il.3.27.189.
O'er which the panther's various hide was thrown. .... Od.19.71.196.

PANTHUS
Panthus, and *Hicetäon,* once the strong, ... Il.3.195.200.
And thus their Arms the Race of *Panthus* wield: .... Il.14.530.189.
From *Panthus* sprung, *Euphorbus* was his Name; .... Il.16.973.281.
The Son of *Panthus,* skill'd the Dart to send, ... Il.17.11.288.
These Sons of *Panthus* vent their haughty Mind. .... Il.17.26.288.
The Son of *Panthus,* thus exprest his Fears; .... Il.18.295.336.

PANTHUS'
To *Panthus'* Son, at *Hector's* high Command, ... Il.13.951.151.

PANTING
Panting with Hope, he tries the furrow'd Grounds, ... 1.W-F.100.160.
Flutters in Blood, and panting beats the Ground. .... 1.W-F.114.161.
The Fair sate panting at a *Courtier's Play,* .... 1.EOC.540.299.
And print warm kisses on the panting rind, ... 1.TrFD.60.388.
Whose panting Vitals, warm with Life, she draws, ... 1.TrSt.721.440.
He foams, he roars, he rends the panting Prey. .... 1.TrES.20.450.
Then drew the Weapon from his panting Heart, ... 1.TrES.318.461.
His panting Heart exulted in his Breast: .... 1.TrUl.135.470.
Diffusing languor in the panting gales: .... 5.DunB4.304.374.
The Lordly Savage rends the panting Prey .... Il.3.40A.190.
Rais'd from the Field the panting Youth she led, ... Il.3.469.214.
Confus'd and panting, thus, the hunted Deer .... Il.4.280.234.
His panting Steeds, remov'd from out the War, ... Il.5.397.286.
The King beside his panting Steeds she found, ... Il.5.988.314.
Then pressing with his Foot his panting Heart, ... Il.6.81.327.
The *Hours* unloos'd them, panting as they stood, ... Il.8.536.422.
Now, like two Lions panting for the Prey, ... Il.10.353.18.
The panting Warriors seize him as He stands, ... Il.10.447.23.
The yet-warm *Thracians* panting on the Coast; .... Il.10.612.29.
All drown'd in Sweat the panting Mother flies, ... Il.11.159.42.
Stung with the Smart, all panting with the Pain, ... Il.11.351.50.
And held its Passage thro' the panting Heart. .... Il.11.561.59.

PANTING (CONTINUED)
The panting Steeds *Eurymedon* unbound. .... Il.11.757.69.
The panting Steeds impatient Fury breathe, ... Il.12.57.83.
He foams, he roars, he rends the panting Prey. .... Il.12.364.94.
Lay panting. Thus an Oxe, in Fetters ty'd, ... Il.13.721.139.
The panting Thund'rer nods, and sinks to Rest. .... Il.14.406.183.
Ejecting Blood, and panting yet for Breath, ... Il.15.13.194.
Which held its Passage thro' the panting Heart, ... Il.15.639.221.
Some mighty Fish draws panting to the Shore; .... Il.16.496.262.
Then drew the Weapon from his panting Heart, ... Il.16.623.268.
His panting Coursers, in his Breast debates, ... Il.16.870.277.
In strong Convulsions panting on the Sands .... Il.17.366.301.
The frighted *Trojans* (panting from the War, ... Il.18.287.335.
With Words like these the panting Chief address'd. .... Il.20.380.411.
The panting *Trojan* rivets to the Ground. .... Il.20.466.413.
Pierc'd thro' the Neck: He left him panting there, ... Il.20.527.416.
The panting Liver pours a Flood of Gore, ... Il.20.545.417.
As trembling, panting, from the Stream he fled, ... Il.21.60.424.
Prone fell the Youth; and panting on the Land, ... Il.21.131.427.
Beneath the Hero's Feet he panting lies, ... Il.21.197.429.
And thus short-panting, to the God he said. .... Il.21.417.437.
And gasping, panting, fainting, labour on .... Il.21.635.448.
Thus at the panting Dove a Falcon flies, ... Il.22.183.463.
The panting Coursers swiftly turn the Goal, ... Il.22.215.464.
The Chief himself unyokes the panting Steeds. .... Il.23.596.513.
Lies panting: Not less batter'd with his Wound, ... Il.23.804.521.
The panting Chief to *Pallas* lifts his Soul: .... Il.23.900.525.
And hourly panting in the arms of death. .... Od.5.499.196.
Clasp'd the gay panting Goddess in his arms, ... Od.8.310.281.
Stretch'd forth, and panting in the sunny ray. .... Od.10.186.349.
His panting heart exulted in his breast; .... Od.13.302.21.
And lash'd his panting coursers to the strand. .... Od.15.231.79.
The Monarch savage rends the panting prey: .... Od.17.145.138.
Good old *Laertes* heard with panting joy; .... Od.24.593.376.

PANTINGS
And in short Pantings sobb'd his Soul away; .... Il.13.818.144.
His Breath, in quick, short Pantings, comes, and goes; .... Il.16.134.242.

PANTS
Pants on the Leaves, and dies upon the Trees. .... 1.PWi.80.94.
Th'impatient Courser pants in ev'ry Vein, ... 1.W-F.151.164.
Pants on her Neck, and fans her parting Hair. .... 1.W-F.196.168.
She, while her Lover pants upon her breast, ... 3.Ep2.167.64.
Who pants for glory finds but short repose, ... 4.2HE1.300.221.
When the brisk Minor pants for twenty-one; .... 4.1HE1.38.281.
Bleeds drop by drop, and pants his life away. .... 6.81.14.226.
Inly she bleeds, and pants her Soul away. .... 6.81.14A.226.
Inly he bleeds, and pants his Soul away. .... 6.81.14B.226.
At ev'ry Danger pants thy Consort's Breast, ... 6.96iv.65.278.
See, in the Tube he pants, and sprawling lies, ... 6.96v.7.280.
She, while her Lover pants upon her breast, ... 6.139.11.377.
The Foe rush'd furious as he pants for Breath, ... Il.4.606.250.
Pierc'd by *Antilochus,* he pants beneath .... Il.13.505.130.
And ev'ry kindling Bosom pants for Fame. .... Il.15.609.220.
The groaning Warrior pants upon the Ground. .... Il.16.345.256.
The Scales of *Jove,* and pants with Awe divine. .... Il.16.800.274.
Descends, and pants in *Apisaon's* Breast: .... Il.17.401.303.
That drowns his Bosom, till he pants no more. .... Il.20.546.417.
The bleeding Hero pants upon the Ground. .... Il.23.805.521.
Pants for the battle, and the war demands; .... Od.11.648.416.

PANURGE
Good common Linguists, and so *Panurge* was: .... 4.JD4.75.31.
As home, as ever did *Panurge:* .... 6.10.92.27.

PAP
Deep in his Breast above the Pap it went, ... Il.4.611.250.

PAPAL
And Papal piety, and Gothic fire. .... 6.71.14.203.

PAPER
For this your Locks in Paper-Durance bound, ... 2.RL4.99.191.
Blest paper-credit! that advanc'd so high! .... 3.Ep3.69A.93.
Blest paper-credit! last and best supply! .... 3.Ep3.69.93.
Is there, who lock'd from Ink and Paper, scrawls .... 4.Arbu.19.97.
Is there, who lock'd from pen and Paper, scrawls .... 4.Arbu.19A.97.
Mid snows of paper, and fierce hail of pease; .... 5.DunA3.258.179.
'Mid snows of paper, and fierce hail of pease; .... 5.DunB3.262.332.
On passive paper, or on solid brick. .... 5.DunB4.130.354.
Soft on the paper ruff its leaves I spread, ... 5.DunB4.407.382.
Whose spoils this paper offers to your eye, ... 5.DunB4.435.383.
First lay this Paper under, then, ... 6.10.65.26.
Quoth *Sandys: To Waste-Paper.* .... 6.58.76.174.
Quoth Sand's *To Waste-Paper.* .... 6.58.76A.174.
Quoth *Sandys: Into Waste*-Paper. .... 6.58.76B.174.
She bow'd, obey'd him, and cut Paper. .... 6.119.8.336.

PAPER-CREDIT
Blest paper-credit! last and best supply! .... 3.Ep3.69.93.

PAPER-DURANCE
For this your Locks in Paper-Durance bound, ... 2.RL4.99.191.

PAPERS
Fire in each eye, and Papers in each hand, ... 4.Arbu.5.96.
Fire in their eye, and Papers in their hand, ... 4.Arbu.5A.96.
"Or do the Prints and Papers lye? .... 4.HS6.115.257.
To seize his papers, Curl, was next thy care; .... 5.DunA2.105.109.
His papers light, fly diverse, tost in air: .... 5.DunA2.106.109.
To seize his papers, *C[url]l,* was next thy care; .... 5.DunA2.106A.109.
His papers all, the sportive winds up-lift .... 5.DunA2.107A.109.
To seize his papers, Curl, was next thy care; .... 5.DunB2.113.301.
His papers light, fly diverse, tost in air; .... 5.DunB2.114.301.
Stealing the Papers thence she put .... 6.94.79.261.

PAPHIAN
Then thus, incens'd, the *Paphian* Queen replies; ....Il.3.513.216.

PAPHLAGONIAN
Him on his Car the *Paphlagonian* Train ....Il.13.821.144.
And lov'd of all the *Paphlagonian* Race! ....Il.13.830.145.

PAPHLAGONIANS
The *Paphlagonians Pylæmenes* rules, ...Il.2.1034.171.
Who sheath'd in Brass the *Paphlagonians* led. ....Il.5.706.301.

PAPHOS
To visit *Paphos* and her blooming groves, ...Od.8.396.285.

PAPILLIA
Papillia, wedded to her am'rous spark ....3.Ep2.37A.53.
Papillia, wedded to her doating spark, ...3.Ep2.37.53.

PAPIST
Papist or Protestant, or both between, ...4.HS1.65.11.
Convict a Papist He, and I a Poet. ....4.2HE2.67.169.
A Papist wear the Lawrel! is it fit? ....6.48iii.11.135.
The Papist masques his Treason in a Joke; ....6.48iv.2.135.

PAPISTS
Peace, Fools! or *Gonson* will for Papists seize you, ...4.JD4.256.47.
Like that of Papists, now not worth their Hate ....4.JD2A.12.132.
Yet like the Papists is the Poets state, ...4.JD2.11.133.
Hopes after Hopes of pious Papists fail'd, ...4.2HE2.62.169.

PARACLETE'S
To *Paraclete's* white walls, and silver springs, ...2.ElAb.348.348.

PARADISE
Alone, and ev'n in Paradise, unblest, ...2.ChJM.60.17.
And Paradise was open'd in the Wild. ....2.ElAb.134.330.
And bring all Paradise before your eye. ....3.Ep4.148.151.
Hence the Fool's paradise, the Statesman's scheme, ...5.DunA3.9.150.
Hence the Fool's Paradise, the Statesman's Scheme, ...5.DunB3.9.320.
And turn a bird of paradise, ...6.6i.4.13.
A Type of Paradise, the Rural Scene! ....6.17iii.39.58.
To fix the ground where paradise was plac'd. ....6.126i.2.353.

PARALLEL
'None but Thy self can be thy parallel.' ....5.DunA3.272.180.

PARALLELS
Who made the spider parallels design, ...3.EOM3.103.102.

PARAMOUNT
Stood Paramount in Pride; ....6.79.22.218.

PARCH'D
They parch'd with Heat, and I inflam'd by thee. ....1.PSu.20.73.
As the parch'd Earth drinks Rain (but grace afford) ....6.2.11.6.
Choak the parch'd Earth, and blacken all the Skies; ....Il.5.1061.317.
Thither, all parch'd with Thirst, a heartless Train, ...Il.21.633.448.

PARCHMENT
His *Office* keeps your Parchment-Fates entire, ...4.JD2.71.139.
On Parchment long Assurances he draws: ....4.JD2A.97.140.
On parchment scraps y-fed, and Wormius hight. ....5.DunA3.184.171.
On parchment scraps y-fed, and Wormius hight. ....5.DunB3.188.329.

PARCHMENT-FATES
His *Office* keeps your Parchment-Fates entire, ...4.JD2.71.139.

PARCHT
And the parcht borders of th' *Arabian* shore: ....Od.4.102.124.

PARD
Sudden, our bands a spotted Pard restrain: ....Od.4.616.148.

PARDON
No Pardon vile *Obscenity* should find, ...1.EOC.530.297.
And first the pardon of the nymphs implor'd, ...1.TrFD.37.387.
Yet first the pardon of the nymphs implor'd, ...1.TrFD.37A.387.
Yet I can pardon those obscurer Rapes, ...1.TrSt.358.425.
Ev'n those I pardon, for whose sinful sake ....4.JD2.41.135.
Ev'n those I pardon, For whose sinful Sake ....4.JD2A.45.136.
These fools demand not Pardon, but Applause. ....4.2HE1.118.205.
And pardon me a little Fooling, ...6.10.7.24.
And pardon her the Fault by which I live! ....6.96iv.92.279.
The Priest may pardon, and the God may spare. ....Il.1.126.93.

PARDON'D
In days of old they pardon'd breach of vows, ...6.41.29.114.

PARE
'Twere well if she would pare her Nails, ...6.14v(a).5.48.

PARENT
Within this plant my hapless parent lies: ....1.TrFD.83.389.
King, priest, and parent of his growing state; ....3.EOM3.216.114.
Lent Heav'n a parent to the poor and me? ....3.EOM4.110.138.
Friend, parent, neighbour, first it will embrace, ...3.EOM4.367.164.
Each Parent sprung—"What Fortune, pray?"— Their own, ...4.Arbu.390.126.
Each Parent sprung—"What Fortune, pray?"— their own, ...4.Arbu.390A.126.
And keep a while one Parent from the Sky! ....4.Arbu.413.127.
And offer Country, Parent, Wife, or Son! ....4.EpS1.158.309.
The childless Parent and the widow'd Wife ....6.152.12.400.
On the bare Mountains left its Parent Tree ....Il.1.312.103.
O Parent Goddess! since in early Bloom ....Il.1.460.110.
To these his Skill their * Parent-God imparts, ...Il.2.890.166.
No Parent now remains, my Griefs to share, ...Il.6.522.352.
With secret Pleasure each fond Parent smil'd, ...Il.6.598.356.

PARENT (CONTINUED)
Let the great Parent Earth one Hand sustain, ...Il.14.307.177.
Dear as a Parent, with a Parent's Care, ...Il.15.512.216.
A Parent once, whose Sorrows equal'd thine: ....Il.24.758.569.
Though on the blazing pile his parent lay, ...Od.4.309.134.
The people's parent, he protected all: ....Od.4.921.161.
By fate impos'd; such me my parent bore: ....Od.8.352.282.
Regardless of her son the Parent stood. ....Od.11.111.386.
Thus I, and thus the parent shade returns. ....Od.11.218.392.
Or parent vulture, mourns her ravish'd young; ....Od.16.239.116.
But from this dome my Parent-Queen to chase!— ....Od.20.411.252.

PARENT-GOD
To these his Skill their * Parent-God imparts, ...Il.2.890.166.

PARENT-QUEEN
But from this dome my Parent-Queen to chase!— ....Od.20.411.252.

PARENT'S
My Parent's Ashes drank my early Tears. ....1.TrSP.74.397.
Go, and a Parent's heavy Curses bear; ....1.TrSt.115.415.
The murd'ring Son ascend his Parent's Bed, ...1.TrSt.331.424.
What Passions in a Parent's Breast debate! ....1.TrES.231.458.
With lenient Arts prolong a Parent's Breath, ...6.117.5.333.
Could save a Parent's justest Pride from fate, ...6.132.3A.362.
But oh! relieve a wretched Parent's Pain, ...Il.1.27.87.
Reveal the Cause, and trust a Parent's Care. ....Il.1.475.110.
Oh might a Parent's careful Wish prevail, ...Il.1.546.114.
Far more than Heirs of all our Parent's Fame, ...Il.4.464.242.
Who charm'd her Parent's and her Husband's Heart, ...Il.13.541.132.
Dear as a Parent, with a Parent's Care, ...Il.15.512.216.
Her Sire caress'd him with a Parent's Care. ....Il.16.229.248.
What Passions in a Parent's Breast debate! ....Il.16.534.264.
To sooth a Consort's and a Parent's Woe. ....Il.17.42.289.
And ill requites his Parent's tender Care. ....Il.17.347.301.
Reveal the Cause, and trust a Parent's Care. ....Il.18.98.327.
My tender Orphan with a Parent's Care, ...Il.19.352.387.
The Words of Age; attend a Parent's Pray'r! ....Il.22.115.457.
Who search the Sorrows of a Parent's Heart, ...Il.24.474.556.
Whose age I honour with a parent's name. ....Od.4.216.130.
And anxious hope, to hear my parent's doom, ...Od.4.427.140.
And give soft transport to a parent's heart. ....Od.6.34.206.
Their parent's pride, and pleasure of their reign. ....Od.10.8.339.
With the strong raptures of a parent's joy. ....Od.16.211.114.
Her son's return, and ease a parent's heart; ....Od.16.351.123.

PARENTS
His parents joy, who did a comfort prove ....1.TrPA.3.365.
A wretch undone: O parents help, and deign ....1.TrPA.142.371.
By both his Parents of Descent divine, ...1.TrSt.541.433.
Of honest Parents, and may serve my Turn. ....2.ChJM.261.27.
The Parents, you may think, wou'd soon comply; ....2.ChJM.301.28.
Parents of Vapors and of Female Wit, ...2.RL4.59.189.
Averted half your Parents simple Pray'r, ...3.Ep2.286.73.
Or their fond Parents drest in red and gold; ....5.DunB1.138.280.
Her Country, Parents, all that once were dear, ...Il.3.185.200.
To seek her Parents on his flow'ry Side, ...Il.4.547.247.
Alas! my Parents, Brothers, Kindred, all, ...Il.6.546.354.
Where the great Parents (sacred Source of Gods!) ....Il.14.230.172.
Where the great Parents of the deathless Gods, ...Il.14.342.179.
And by their Parents, by themselves, implores. ....Il.15.795.226.
Your Wives, your Infants, and your Parents share: ....Il.15.799.227.
Of trembling Parents on the Turrets stand. ....Il.18.598.351.
My much lov'd Parents, and my native Shore— ....Il.19.469.391.
Parents and Children our just Arms employ, ...Il.21.695.450.
While both thy Parents wept thy fatal Hour, ...Il.22.546.479.
O *Hector,* late thy Parents Pride and Joy, ...Il.22.556.479.
From diff'rent Parents, diff'rent Climes we came, ...Il.22.612.481.
Both Parents still, nor feel what he has lost, ...Il.22.639.483.
Born to his own, and to his Parents Woe! ....Il.24.258.547.
Such Griefs, O King! have other Parents known; ....Il.24.780.569.
Thence, many Evils his sad Parents bore, ...Il.24.932.575.
His Parents many, but his Consort more. ....Il.24.933.575.
For vulgar parents cannot strip their race ....Od.4.75.123.
Bereav'd of parents in his infant years, ...Od.4.220.130.
The same her parents, and her pow'r the same. ....Od.7.71.237.
Impos'd by parents in the natal hour? ....Od.8.598.294.
My absent parents rose before my sight, ...Od.9.37.303.
'Tis what my parents call me, and my peers. ....Od.9.434.324.
Less dear the parents whom I left behind, ...Od.14.161.43.
Your name, your parents, and your native air? ....Od.14.215.45.
Snatch'd from thy parents arms, thy parents eyes, ...Od.15.412.89.
Snatch'd from thy parents arms, thy parents eyes, ...Od.15.412.89.
Where once thy parents dwelt? or did they keep ....Od.15.416.89.
Such as in fondness parents ask of heav'n. ....Od.18.208.177.
My anxious parents urge a speedy choice, ...Od.19.180.200.
Young *Itylus,* his parents darling joy! ....Od.19.608.226.
Thy town, thy parents, and thy native place? ....Od.24.349.365.

PARENTS'
Devours young Babes before their Parents' Eyes, ...1.TrSt.712.440.
If on the Sons the Parents' Crimes descend, ...1.TrSt.820.444.
Dipt me in Ink, my Parents', or my own? ....4.Arbu.126.104.
And, in his Parents' Sight, now dragg'd along! ....Il.22.510.477.
Far from thy Parents' and thy Consort's Care, ...Il.22.655.483.

PARIAN
Than *Phrygian* Marble or the *Parian* Stone. ....1.TrSP.166.400.
The wond'rous Rock like *Parian* Marble shone, ...2.TemF.29.255.
Eternal buckle takes in Parian stone. ....3.Ep3.296.117.
And gaze on Parian Charms with learned eyes: ....4.1HE6.31.239.

PARIDEL
Thee too, my Paridel! she mark'd thee there, ...5.DunB4.341.376.

PARING 82 PART

PARING
He eat himself the Rind and paring. ....4.HS6.170.261.

PARIS
Nor envy'd *Paris* with the *Spartan* Bride: ....2.ChJM.348.31.
Let *Paris* tremble—"What? that Thing of silk, ...4.Arbu.305A.117.
"Paris, that mere white Curd of Ass's milk? ....4.Arbu.306A.117.
(Whence hapless Monsieur much complains at Paris ....5.DunA2.127.112.
As taught by Venus, Paris learnt the art ....5.DunA2.209.127.
(Whence hapless Monsieur much complains at Paris ....5.DunB2.135.301.
As taught by Venus, Paris learnt the art ....5.DunB2.217.306.
Whom *Troy* sent forth, the beauteous *Paris* came: ....Il.3.26.189.
Unhappy *Paris!* but to Women brave, ...Il.3.55.192.
His Silence here, with Blushes, *Paris* breaks; ....Il.3.85.193.
By *Paris* there the *Spartan* King be fought, ...Il.3.101.194.
What *Paris,* Author of the War, demands. ....Il.3.124.196.
Me *Paris* injur'd; all the War be mine. ....Il.3.138.197.
Paris alone and *Sparta's* King advance, ...Il.3.179.199.
False to them all, to *Paris* only kind! ....Il.3.232.203.
Paris thy Son, and *Sparta's* King advance, ...Il.3.322.208.
Hear, and be Witness. If, by *Paris* slain, ...Il.3.354.210.
Then *Paris,* thine leap'd forth, by fatal Chance ....Il.3.404.211.
Haste, happy Nymph! for thee thy *Paris* calls, ...Il.3.481.215.
What other *Paris* is thy Darling now? ....Il.3.498.215.
Hence let me sail: And if thy *Paris* bear ....Il.3.501.215.
The Boaster *Paris* oft' desir'd the Day ....Il.3.537.217.
Paris he seeks, impatient to destroy, ...Il.3.563.219.
What Gifts from *Troy,* for *Paris* wou'd'st thou gain, ...Il.4.127.226.
Beneath his Hand the Fleet of *Paris* rose, ...Il.5.81.270.
I go to rowze soft *Paris* to the War; ....Il.6.349.343.
Whom from soft *Sidon* youthful *Paris* bore, ...Il.6.362.344.
Paris and *Greece* against us both conspire; ....Il.6.408.347.
Or go, and *Paris* shall not lag behind. ....Il.6.429.347.
Bore all, and *Paris* of those Ills the worst. ....Il.6.441.348.
Forth issues *Paris* from the Palace Wall. ....Il.6.649.358.
The graceful *Paris* first excus'd his Stay. ....Il.6.665.360.
Or Godlike *Paris* live a Woman's Slave! ....Il.6.671.360.
Him *Paris* follow'd to the dire Alarms; ....Il.7.3.363.
Bold *Paris* first the Work of Death begun, ...Il.7.11.363.
What *Paris,* Author of the War, declares. ....Il.7.463.387.
Him, while he triumph'd, *Paris* ey'd from far, ...Il.11.473.55.
Before the next the graceful *Paris* shines, ...Il.12.105.85.
Paris, Deïphobus, Agenor join; ....Il.13.618.135.
Paris from far the moving Sight beheld, ...Il.13.827.145.
The graceful *Paris;* whom, with Fury mov'd, ...Il.13.963.151.
Ill-fated *Paris!* Slave to Womankind, ...Il.13.965.151.
When *Paris* thus: My Brother and my Friend, ...Il.13.975.152.
By *Paris, Deiochus* inglorious dies, ...Il.15.386.211.
Phœbus and *Paris* shall avenge my Fate, ...Il.22.451.474.
What time young *Paris,* simple Shepherd Boy, ...Il.24.39.537.
Polites, Paris, Agathon, he calls, ...Il.24.312.549.
Since *Paris* brought me to the *Trojan* Shore; ....Il.24.965.576.

PARIS'
Thro' *Paris'* Shield the forceful Weapon went, ...Il.3.440.213.
Full in her *Paris'* Sight the Queen of Love ....Il.3.529.216.
Her Act has rescu'd *Paris'* forfeit Life, ...Il.4.17.221.
Hector to *Paris'* lofty Dome repairs. ....Il.6.389.345.
With Toils, sustain'd for *Paris'* sake and mine: ....Il.6.445.348.
Unwilling he remain'd, for *Paris'* Dart ....Il.8.103.402.
And voted *Helen's* Stay, for *Paris'* Gold. ....Il.11.164.42.
From *Paris'* Bow a vengeful Arrow fled. ....Il.11.709.66.

PARISH
Better than e'er our Parish Priest cou'd do. ....2.ChWB.268.69.

PARK
Sooner shall Grass in *Hide*-Park Circus *grow,* ....2.RL4.117.193.
Rufa, whose eye quick-glancing o'er the Park, ...3.Ep2.21.50.
Sighs for the shades—"How charming is a Park!" ....3.Ep2.38.53.
A Park is purchas'd, but the Fair he sees ....3.Ep2.39.53.
A *noted Dean* much busy'd in the Park, ...4.HAdv.40.79.
Thoughts, which at Hyde-Park-Corner I forgot, ...4.2HE2.208.179.
Whether you call them Villa, Park, or Chace) ....4.2HE2.255.183.
That less admires the Palace than the Park; ....4.1HE1.113.287.
She went from Op'ra, park, assembly, play, ...6.45.13.125.
Back in the Dark, by *Brompton* Park, ...6.79.129.222.

PARKER
Great C[owper], H[arcourt], P[arker], R[aymond], K[ing], ...5.DunB4.545.395.

PARLEY
A Parley *Hector* asks, a Message bears; ....Il.3.117.195.

PARLIAMENT
And gets an Act of Parliament to rob? ....4.JD4.143.37.
Bows and votes on, in Court and Parliament; ....4.2HE2.275.185.

PARLY
Approach unarm'd, and parly with the Foe, ...Il.22.155.459.

PARNASS'
On *Parnass'* top I chac'd the tusky boar. ....Od.21.229.270.

PARNASSIAN
Twin'd with the wreaths Parnassian lawrels yield, ...3.EOM4.11.129.
Lost the arch'd eye-brown, or *Parnassian* sneer? ....4.Arbu.96.102.
Great Tibbald sate: The proud Parnassian sneer, ...5.DunA2.5.97.
Great Tibbald nods: The proud Parnassian sneer, ...5.DunA2.5A.97.
Great Cibber sate: the proud Parnassian sneer, ...5.DunB2.5.296.
To breath the Sweets of pure Parnassian *Air,* ....6.26ii.2.79.

PARNASSUS
Who haunt *Parnassus* but to please their Ear, ...1.EOC.341.277.
Oete, with high *Parnassus,* heard the Voice; ....1.TrSt.165.417.
All *Bedlam,* or *Parnassus,* is let out: ....4.Arbu.4.96.

PARNASSUS (CONTINUED)
And Her Parnassus glancing o'er at once, ...5.DunA3.129.161.
And all Parnassus glancing o'er at once, ...5.DunA3.129A.161.
And her Parnassus glancing o'er at once, ...5.DunB3.137.326.
This on *Parnassus* combating the boar, ...Od.19.462.218.
Parnassus, thick perplex'd with horrid shades, ...Od.19.503.220.

PARNASSUS'
High on *Parnassus'* Top her Sons she show'd, ...1.EOC.94.250.
Now, they who reach *Parnassus'* lofty Crown, ...1.EOC.514.296.
Now, those that reach *Parnassus'* lofty Crown, ...1.EOC.514A.296.
But fir'd with Rage, from cleft *Parnassus'* Brow ....1.TrSt.739.441.

PARNEL
"From Pope, from Parnel, or from Gay? ....4.HS6.94.255.

PARNELL
And Parnell, that would, if he had but a Rhyme. ....6.42i.4.116.
(That Gay the poor Sec: and that arch Chaplain Parnell, ...6.42i.5.116.
The Doctor and Dean, Pope, Parnell and Gay ....6.42iii.1.117.
And Parnell who saw you not since ....6.68.9.196.
Still hear thy *Parnell* in his living Lays: ....6.84.16.239.

PARRHASIA
Parrhasia, on her snowy Cliffs reclin'd, ...Il.2.737.161.

PARROTS
Men, Monkies, Lap-dogs, Parrots, perish all! ....2.RL4.120.193.

PARSON
The cobler apron'd, and the parson gown'd, ...3.EOM4.197.145.
Or, cobler-like, the parson will be drunk, ...3.EOM4.202.146.
From honest Mah'met, or plain Parson Hale. ....3.Ep2.198.66.
Is there a Parson, much be-mus'd in Beer, ...4.Arbu.15.97.
Parson, these Things in thy possessing ....6.39.1.110.

PARSON'S
Narcissus, prais'd with all a Parson's pow'r, ...5.DunB4.103.351.
The Parson's Cant, the Lawyer's Sophistry, ...6.8.40.19.

PARSONS
In various Shapes of *Parsons, Criticks, Beaus;* .... 1.EOC.459.291.

PART
And part admit and part exclude the Day; ....1.W-F.18.150.
And part admit and part exclude the Day; ....1.W-F.18.150.
By *Doctor's Bills* to play the *Doctor's Part,* .... 1.EOC.109.251.
But when t'examine ev'ry Part he came, ... 1.EOC.134.254.
From *vulgar Bounds* with *brave Disorder* part, ... 1.EOC.154.257.
Still make the *Whole* depend upon a *Part,* .... 1.EOC.264.269.
With *Gold* and *Jewels* cover ev'ry Part, ... 1.EOC.295.272.
And force *that Sun* but on a *Part* to Shine; ....1.EOC.399.286.
To part his Throne and share his Heav'n with thee; ....1.TrSt.42.411.
Aim'd at his Breast, it pierc'd the mortal Part ....1.TrES.286.460.
And a new Vigour springs in ev'ry Part. ....2.ChJM.130.21.
While Fancy pictur'd ev'ry lively Part, ...2.ChJM.232.25.
Fair without Spot, whose ev'ry charming Part ....2.ChJM.531.41.
From thy dear Side I have no Pow'r to part, ...2.ChJM.571.42.
In all these Trials I have born a Part; ....2.ChWB.5.57.
"Why take me Love! take all and ev'ry part! ....2.ChWB.199.66.
To find in Pleasures I have had my Part, ...2.ChWB.223.67.
Valerius, whole; and of St. *Jerome,* Part; ....2.ChWB.359.74.
With varying Vanities, from ev'ry Part, ...2.RL1.99.152.
The greater Part by hostile Time subdu'd; ....2.TemF.32.255.
Yet Part no Injuries of Heav'n cou'd feel, ...2.TemF.45.256.
Motion and Life did ev'ry Part inspire, ...2.TemF.192.271.
Finish'd the whole, and labour'd ev'ry Part, ...2.TemF.198.271.
All is not Heav'n's while *Abelard* has part, ...2.ElAb.25.321.
Heav'n claims me all in vain, while he has part, ...2.ElAb.25A.321.
Ev'n thought meets thought ere from the lips it part, ...2.ElAb.95.327.
To act a Lover's or a *Roman's* part? ....2.Elegy.8.363.
Then from his closing eyes thy form shall part, ...2.Elegy.79.368.
Look'd thro'? or can a part contain the whole? ....3.EOM1.32.17.
'Tis but a part we see, and not a whole. ....3.EOM1.60.20.
Just as absurd for any part to claim ....3.EOM1.263.47.
Breathes in our soul, informs our mortal part, ...3.EOM1.275.48.
To deem himself a Part of God, or Beast; ....3.EOM2.8A.55.
Alas what wonder! Man's superior part ....3.EOM2.39.60.
And pours it all upon the peccant part. ....3.EOM2.144.72.
Part pays, and justly, the deserving steer: ....3.EOM3.40.96.
To copy Instinct then was Reason's part; ....3.EOM3.170.110.
What shocks one part will edify the rest, ...3.EOM4.141.141.
Say, at what part of nature will they stand? ....3.EOM4.166.143.
Act well your part, there all the honour lies. ....3.EOM4.194.145.
Extend it, let thy enemies have part: ....3.EOM4.356.163.
"Not that,—I cannot part with that"—and dy'd. ....3.Ep1.261.37.
A very Heathen in the carnal part, ...3.Ep2.67.55.
"With ev'ry pleasing, ev'ry prudent part, ...3.Ep2.159.64.
Perhaps you think the Poor might have their part? ....3.Ep3.101.98.
Who copies Your's, or OXFORD's better part, ...3.Ep3.243.112.
Conscious they act a true Palladian part, ...3.Ep4.37.140.
Trims *Europe's* Balance, tops the Statesman's part, ...4.JD4.154.39.
Suppose that honest Part that rules us all, ...4.HAdv.87.83.
Amphibious Thing! that acting either Part, ...4.Arbu.326.119.
Did ever Smock-face act so vile a Part? ....4.Arbu.326A.119.
Of gentle Blood (part shed in Honour's Cause, ...4.Arbu.388.126.
With every sprightly, every decent part; ....4.HOde1.12.151.
"But Sir, to you, with what wou'd I not part? ....4.2HE2.15.165.
Shall I, in *London,* act this idle part? ....4.2HE2.125.173.
A part I will enjoy, as well as keep. ....4.2HE2.285.185.
"In all debates where Criticks bear a part, ...4.2HE1.81.201.
But not this part of the poetic state ....4.2HE1.348.225.
To touch Achilles' only tender part; ....5.DunA2.210.127.
To touch Achilles' only tender part; ....5.DunB2.218.306.
Of Souls the greater Part, Heav'ns common make, ...5.DunB4.441A.383.
On any Part except her Face; ....6.14v(a).14.49.

PART (CONTINUED)

Pride, Pomp, and State but reach her outward Part, … 6.19.55.63.
I, for my part, admire *Lintottus.*—— … 6.29.6.83.
Sooner I'd quit my Part in thee, … 6.30.25.86.
Than be no Part in *Tom D'Urfy.* … 6.30.26.86.
Sooner we'd quit our Part in thee, … 6.30.25A.86.
Who'd sooner quit our Part in thee, … 6.30.25B.86.
Than be no Part of *Tom* D'Urfey. … 6.30.26A.86.
Part of the Name of stuttering *T*— … 6.30.53.88.
A Damp creeps cold o'er every Part, … 6.31ii.6Z3.94.
Then come and take part in … 6.42iv.13.118.
Come then, my lord, and take your part in … 6.42v.7.119.
Part you with one, and I'll renounce the other. … 6.46.4.127.
If I condemn one Sect or part … 6.50.29A.147.
The verse and sculpture bore an equal part, … 6.71.51.204.
Each play'd a Lion's Part. … 6.79.12.218.
So the struck deer in some sequester'd part … 6.81.11.226.
So the struck doe in some sequester'd part … 6.81.11A.226.
Lo! the struck deer in some sequester'd part … 6.81.11B.226.
And ev'n the Grateful are but last to part; … 6.84.31Z6.239.
When scaling Armies climb'd up ev'ry Part, … 6.96iv.69.278.
And the meer Heathen in her carnal Part. … 6.99.19.287.
Not parted long, and now to part no more! … 6.109.14.314.
'*she.* Yes, we have liv'd— one pang, and then we part! … 6.123.1.343.
"With ev'ry pleasing, ev'ry prudent part, … 6.139.3.377.
Submit he must; or if they will not part, … Il.1.424.108.
The choicest Morsels lay from ev'ry Part. … Il.1.605.117.
Th' Assistants part, transfix, and roast the rest: … Il.1.611.117.
Then part, where stretch'd along the winding Bay … Il.1.632.118.
But part in Peace, secure thy Pray'r is sped: … Il.1.678.119.
The choicest Morsels lie from ev'ry Part. … Il.2.507.150.
Th' Assistants part, transfix, and roast the rest; … Il.2.511.151.
And diff'ring Nations part in Leagues of Peace. … Il.3.132.196.
The Heralds part it, and the Princes share; … Il.3.343.209.
Can *Peteus'* Son forget a Warrior's Part, … Il.4.390.239.
Which driv'n by *Pallas,* pierc'd a vital Part; … Il.5.352.283.
Haste all, and take the gen'rous Warrior's Part. … Il.5.571.296.
(His Friends, each busy'd in his sev'ral Part, … Il.5.826.305.
Sidonian Maids embroider'd ev'ry Part, … Il.6.361.343.
Himself the Mansion rais'd, from ev'ry Part … Il.6.390.345.
To seek his Spouse, his Soul's far dearer Part; … Il.6.463.349.
And Woes, of which so large a Part was thine! … Il.6.581.355.
Andromache! my Soul's far better Part, … Il.6.624.357.
The Squadrons part; th' expecting *Trojans* stand. … Il.7.62.366.
And sage *Idæus* on the Part of *Troy,* … Il.7.334.380.
Had pierc'd his Courser in a mortal Part; … Il.8.104.402.
And heav'n-bred Horror, on the *Grecian* part, … Il.9.3.430.
No Time shall part us, an no Fate divide. … Il.9.573.462.
No more molest me on *Atrides'* Part: … Il.9.722.470.
Do this, my *Phœnix,* 'tis a gen'rous Part, … Il.9.729.470.
Greece to preserve, is now no easy part, … Il.10.51.4.
Preventing ev'ry Part perform'd by you; … Il.10.133.8.
When now few Furrows part th' approaching Ploughs. … Il.10.422.22.
The thrilling Steel transpierc'd the brawny Part, … Il.11.327.49.
Atrides, marking an ungarded Part, … Il.11.335.49.
Unskill'd in Arms to act a manly Part! … Il.11.494.56.
And knowing this, I know a Soldier's Part. … Il.11.520.57.
By these, by those, on ev'ry Part is ply'd; … Il.11.529.57.
But partial *Jove,* espousing *Hector's* Part, … Il.11.668.63.
But thou, *Patroclus!* act a friendly Part, … Il.11.962.78.
The Forces part in five distinguish'd Bands, … Il.12.99.84.
My Javelin can revenge so base a Part, … Il.12.293.92.
Behold a Day when each may act his Part! … Il.12.320.93.
There, *Greece* has strength: but this, this Part o'erthrown, … Il.13.79.108.
A dropping Sweat creeps cold on ev'ry Part; … Il.13.361.123.
There hear what *Greece* has on her Part to say. … Il.13.481.130.
Part on her Head in shining Ringlets roll'd, … Il.14.205.170.
Part o'er her Shoulders wav'd like melted Gold. … Il.14.206.170.
Smooths the rough Wood, and levels ev'ry Part; … Il.15.475.215.
Aim'd at his Breast, it pierc'd the mortal Part … Il.16.591.267.
He drew the Dolours from the wounded Part, … Il.16.649.269.
Euphorbus next; the third mean Part thy own. … Il.16.1025.282.
Lies slain the great *Achilles'* dearer Part: … Il.17.236.297.
With *Hector* part the Spoil, and share the Fame. … Il.17.273.298.
While *Nestor's* Son sustains a manlier Part, … Il.18.37.325.
I go at least to bear a tender part, … Il.18.83.327.
Attend her Way. Wide-opening part the Tides, … Il.18.87.327.
Another Part (a Prospect differing far) … Il.18.591.351.
Part to the Town fly diverse o'er the Plain, … Il.21.4.421.
Part plunge into the Stream: Old *Xanthus* roars, … Il.21.9.421.
With him the mournful Mother bears a Part; … Il.22.110.457.
Gave entrance: Thro' that penetrable Part … Il.22.409.472.
Then, when his earthly Part shall mount in Fire, … Il.23.65.489.
Part of himself; th' immortal Mind remains: … Il.23.123.492.
The mournful Mother next sustains her Part. … Il.24.942.575.
But since to part, for sweet refection due … Od.1.403.51.
Ill suits gay youth the stern, heroic part. … Od.2.342.77.
They draw, they part, and celebrate the feast. … Od.3.79.90.
Part, the storm urges on the coast of *Creet,* … Od.3.371.104.
Soon as due vows on ev'ry part were pay'd, … Od.3.568.115.
The choicest morsels lay from ev'ry part. … Od.3.585.116.
Th' assistants part, transfix, and broil the rest. … Od.3.591.116.
Part led the coursers, from the car enlarg'd, … Od.4.49.122.
Part in a portico, profusely grac'd … Od.4.51.122.
Part live; the rest, a lamentable train! … Od.4.665.150.
Thus wilt thou leave me, are we thus to part? … Od.5.260.184.
Part twist the threads, and part the wool dispose, … Od.6.369.229.
Part twist the threads, and part the wool dispose, … Od.6.369.229.
The eighth, she voluntary moves to part, … Od.7.348.253.
Inur'd a melancholy part to bear, … Od.8.205.273.
Who takes the kind, and pays th' ungrateful part; … Od.8.242.275.
When *Neptune* sues, my part is to obey. … Od.8.392.285.
Delicious food, an honorary part; … Od.8.520.290.
Various the *Trojans* counsell'd; part consign'd … Od.8.554.292.
The monster to the sword, part sentence gave … Od.8.555.292.
Or bled some friend? who bore a brother's part, … Od.8.635.297.

PART (CONTINUED)

Strait in three squadrons all our crew we part, … Od.9.182.313.
Then first my hands did from the rudder part, … Od.10.36.341.
Those hairs of late that bristled ev'ry part, … Od.10.465.366.
Felt pity enter, and sustain'd her part. … Od.10.474.366.
To gen'rous acts; our part is to obey. … Od.11.433.405.
Thy better soul abhors the liar's part, … Od.11.454.406.
Strow'd o'er with morsels cut from ev'ry part. … Od.12.426.451.
In my respect he bears a Prince's part, … Od.14.169.43.
The choicest morsels lay from ev'ry part. … Od.14.477.59.
Her own fair hands embroider'd ev'ry part: … Od.15.121.74.
A part we consecrate to soft repose, … Od.15.427.89.
A part in pleasing talk we entertain; … Od.15.428.89.
They part; while less'ning from the Hero's view, … Od.15.595.99.
I chuse the nobler part, and yield my breath … Od.16.111.108.
Who sav'd thy father with a friendly part? … Od.16.443.128.
My gen'rous soul abhors th' ungrateful part, … Od.16.460.129.
A yearling boar, and gave the Gods their part, … Od.16.473.130.
In haste the Prince arose, prepar'd to part; … Od.17.3.132.
"Where dead *Ulysses* claims no future part; … Od.19.163.200.
A sabre, when the warrior press'd to part, … Od.19.273.208.
I part reluctant from the pleasing tale. … Od.19.690.229.
He gave the bow; and on *Ulysses'* part … Od.21.33.261.
In arms attend us, and their part sustain. … Od.22.121.292.
And like a God adorn'd, thy earthly part expires. … Od.24.86.352.
Where dead *Ulysses* claims no more a part, … Od.24.155.355.
They part, and join him; but the number stay'd. … Od.24.531.373.

PART'NER

Ulysses following, as his Part'ner slew, … Il.10.570.28.
In Peace his Friend, and Part'ner of the War) … Il.16.180.245.

PART'NERS

Ease of their toil and part'ners of their care: … 4.2HE1.246.215.
Oh Warriors, Part'ners of *Achilles'* Praise! … Il.16.324.255.
Whilst we, the wretched part'ners of his toils, … Od.10.45.341.

PARTAKE

O let us still the secret Joy partake, … 2.TemF.364.281.
Pursue the triumph, and partake the gale? … 3.EOM4.386.165.
Calm Temperance, whose blessings those partake … 5.DunA1.47.65.
Calm Temperance, whose blessings those partake … 5.DunB1.49.274.
Ye Sons of *Mars,* partake your Leader's Care, … Il.2.139.135.
The Men who *Glaphyra's* fair Soil partake, … Il.2.864.165.
Mestles and *Antiphus* the Charge partake; … Il.2.1054.172.
Ye Sons of *Greece!* partake your Leader's Care, … Il.9.23.432.
No certain Guards the nightly Watch partake; … Il.10.488.25.
To call some Hero to partake the Deed. … Il.13.575.133.
And here, as Brothers, equal Fates partake. … Il.22.298.468.
The Various Goddess to partake the Rites. … Il.23.251.499.
Suffice, we know and we partake thy Cares: … Il.24.139.540.
Partake the Troubles of thy Husband's Breast: … Il.24.234.546.
Now Gods and Men the Gifts of Sleep partake; … Il.24.846.572.
Wash, and partake serene the friendly feast. … Od.4.294.133.
Alternate all partake the grateful springs: … Od.4.298.133.
Partake his councils, and assist his reign? … Od.19.618.226.
Partake my guest, he cry'd, without controul … Od.20.326.249.

PARTAKER

Tho' not Partaker, Witness of the War. … Il.14.148.164.

PARTAKES

Who now partakes the Secrets of the Skies? … Il.1.699.121.
My Heart partakes the gen'rous *Hector's* Pain; … Il.22.223.464.
Now each partakes the feast, the wine prepares, … Od.8.513.290.

PARTAKING

Partaking free, my sole-invited guest; … Od.19.369.212.

PARTED

Back to the Stern the parted Billows flow, … 1.TrUl.11.465.
(Which never more shall join its parted Hair, … 2.RL4.134.195.
Not parted long, and now to part no more! … 6.109.14.314.
The parted Ocean foams and roars below: … Il.1.627.117.
Not like a Warrior parted from the Foe, … Il.3.485.215.
This said, each parted to his sev'ral Cares; … Il.10.80.6.
And Shares were parted to each *Pylian* Lord. … Il.11.829.73.
The kindling Chariot thro' the parted War: … Il.17.527.308.
My Spear, that parted on the Wings of Wind, … Il.20.394.411.
The parted Visage falls on equal Sides: … Il.20.446.413.
He wades, and mounts; the parted Wave resounds. … Il.21.353.435.
Where two fam'd Fountains burst the parted Ground; … Il.22.196.463.
A-down the Main-mast fell the parted String, … Il.23.1026.530.
Down plung'd the Maid; (the parted Waves resound) … Il.24.105.539.
Just to his realms, he parted grounds from grounds, … Od.6.15.204.
With that, she parted: In her potent hand … Od.10.457.366.
If but a moment parted from thy eyes, … Od.10.574.370.
Back to the stern the parted billows flow, … Od.13.102.6.
With ships he parted and a num'rous train, … Od.24.491.371.

PARTERRE

His pond an Ocean, his parterre a Down: … 3.Ep4.106.147.
Imbrown the Slope, and nod on the Parterre, … 3.Ep4.174.154.
Imbrown thy Slope, and nod on thy Parterre, … 3.Ep4.174A.154.
What are the gay parterre, the chequer'd shade, … 6.81.7.225.

PARTERRES

The vast Parterres a thousand hands shall make, … 3.Ep4.73.144.
Tir'd of the scene Parterres and Fountains yield, … 3.Ep4.87.146.
Whose wide Parterres are not asham'd to feed … 3.Ep4.185A.154.

PARTHENIA

Or sees the blush of soft *Parthenia* rise, … 6.45.46.126.

PARTHENISSA
Or sees the blush of *Parthenissa* rise, ...6.45.46A.126.

PARTHENIUS
And where *Parthenius,* roll'd thro' Banks of Flow'rs, ...Il.2.1040.172.

PARTIAL
Authors are partial to their *Wit,* 'tis true, ...1.EOC.17.241.
And murm'ring Pow'rs condemn their partial *Jove.* .... 1.TrES.245.459.
With other beauties charm my partial eyes, ...2.ElAb.126.330.
"Acts not by partial, but by gen'ral laws; ....3.EOM1.146.33.
All partial Evil, universal Good: ....3.EOM1.292.51.
Gods partial, changeful, passionate, unjust, ...3.EOM3.257.118.
"Acts not by partial, but by gen'ral laws;" ....3.EOM4.36.131.
Or partial Ill is universal Good, ...3.EOM4.114.139.
We grow more partial for th' observer's sake; ....3.Ep1.12.16.
Your People, Sir, are partial in the rest. ....4.2HE1.32.197.
See Nature in some partial narrow shape, ...5.DunB4.455.385.
But still, with partial Love, extol his own. ....6.96v.14.280.
Yet who his Countrey's partial Love can blame? ....6.96v.19.280.
While I, too partial, aid the *Trojan* Arms? ....Il.1.675.119.
Of partial *Jove* with Justice I complain, ...Il.2.141.135.
Thus wak'd the Fury of his partial Queen. ....Il.4.8.221.
Not all the Gods are partial and unjust. ....Il.4.44.223.
So boundless she, and thou so partial grown, ...Il.5.1080.318.
At *Thetis'* Suit the partial Thund'rer nods. ....Il.8.450.418.
Of partial *Jove* too justly we complain, ...Il.9.25.432.
And each accus'd the partial Will of *Jove.* .... Il.11.106.39.
And oft' that partial Pow'r has lent his Aid. ....Il.11.468.54.
But partial *Jove,* espousing *Hector's* Part, ...Il.11.668.63.
Thy Will is partial, not thy Reason wrong: ....Il.12.270.91.
Where he, inces'd at partial *Priam,* stands, ...Il.13.578.133.
And murm'ring Pow'rs condemn their partial *Jove.* .... Il.16.548.265.
Sure where such partial Favour Heav'n bestow'd, ...Il.17.105.291.
His partial Favour, and assists your Wars, ...Il.17.385.302.
For this, or that, the partial People stand: ....Il.18.582.351.
The partial Monarch may refuse the Prize; ....Il.20.219.403.
Has sav'd thee, and the partial God of Light. ....Il.20.520.416.
And partial Aid to *Troy's* perfidious Race. ....Il.21.483.441.
The Chief incens'd—Too partial God of Day! ....Il.22.23.453.
No Gods indignant blame their partial *Jove?* .... Il.22.238.465.
If equal Honours by the partial Skies ....Il.24.70.538.
Ulysses let no partial favours fall, ...Od.4.920.161.
With partial hands the Gods their gifts dispense; ....Od.8.185.272.

PARTICIPATE
Participate their Fame, and pleas'd enquire ....Il.7.153.372.

PARTICLE
What heav'nly Particle inspires the clay? ....4.HS2.78.59.

PARTICOLOUR'D
And Particolour'd Troops, a shining Train, ...2.RL3.43.172.

PARTIES
Parties in *Wit* attend on those of *State,* .... 1.EOC.456.290.
The Time approach'd, to Church the Parties went, ...2.ChJM.309.29.
All side in Parties, and begin th' Attack; ....2.RL5.39.202.
(Diff'rent our parties, but with equal grace ....5.DunA3.283.183.
Why should I stay? Both Parties rage; ....6.47.21.129.

PARTING
Pants on her Neck, and fans her parting Hair. ....1.W-F.196.168.
My son, thy mother's parting kiss receive, ...1.TrFD.94.390.
No Tear did you, no parting Kiss receive, ...1.TrSP.115.398.
And Fun'ral Flames, that parting wide in Air, ...1.TrSt.53.412.
Thus, thro' the parting Clouds the Son of *May* .... 1.TrSt.437.428.
Shall hail the rising, close the parting day. ....4.HOde1.30.153.
Salute the coming, close the parting day. ....4.HOde1.30A.153.
Salute the rising, close the parting day. ....4.HOde1.30B.153.
Ev'n now, observant of the parting Ray, ...6.84.37.240.
The parting Heroes mutual Presents left; ....Il.6.271.340.
Demands a parting Word, a tender Tear: ....Il.6.459.348.
Her parting Step? If to the Fane she went, ...Il.6.475.350.
His parting Son, these Accents were his last. ....Il.9.329.450.
Then shall you see our parting Vessels crown'd, ...Il.9.471.455.
The parting Waves before his Coursers fly; ....Il.13.48.107.
I mark'd his parting, and the Steps he trod, ...Il.13.103.109.
And, fir'd with Hate, a parting Javelin cast: ....Il.13.655.136.
Mine is the Glory, his thy parting Ghost. ....Il.16.756.273.
Tho much at parting that great Chief might say, ...Il.16.1011.282.
Sees, thro' its parting Plates, the upper Air, ...Il.20.329.407.
Then parting from the Pyle he ceas'd to weep, ...Il.23.288.501.
Then gave his Hand at parting, to prevent ....Il.24.840.572.
But parting then for that detested shore, ...Od.1.273.46.
The crooked keel the parting surge divides, ...Od.2.468.83.
Atrides, parting for the *Trojan* war, ...Od.3.334.102.
Between the parting rocks at length he spy'd ....Od.5.562.199.
Now parting from the stream, *Ulysses* found ....Od.5.594.201.
Full oft I told: at length for parting mov'd; ....Od.10.17.340.
Thus he; then parting prints the sandy shore ....Od.13.80.5.
Welcome the coming, speed the parting guest. ....Od.15.84.73.
A limpid fount; that spread in parting rills ....Od.17.233.143.
And parting, to the Suitor pow'rs descends: ....Od.17.669.164.
Swift as the word the parting arrow sings, ...Od.22.11.287.
Ulysses parting thro' the sable flood; ....Od.24.362.366.

PARTIOT
There partiot sighs from Wyndham's bosom stole ....6.142.11B.383.

PARTITION
The just Partition, and due Victims pay'd. ....Il.11.841.73.
Who in partition seek his realm to share; ....Od.20.273.246.

PARTITIONS
What thin partitions Sense from Thought divide: ....3.EOM1.226.43.

PARTLY
Whose Heads she partly, whose completely blest; ....5.DunB4.622.406.
Attend (tho' partly thou hast guest) the truth. ....Od.3.317.102.

PARTNER
When the bright Partner of his awful Reign, ...Il.1.518.113.
Go, lest the haughty Partner of my Sway ....Il.1.676.119.
In vain the Partner of Imperial State. ....Il.1.701.121.
Th' imperial Partner of the heav'nly Reign; ....Il.5.482.291.
The first, the dearest Partner of his Love, ...Il.19.316.385.
Guard of his Life, and Partner of his Way. ....Il.24.190.544.
Guard of thy Life, and Partner of thy Way. ....Il.24.220.546.
Guard of thy Life, and Partner of thy Way. ....Il.24.538.558.
And the chaste partner of his bed and throne, ...Od.4.147.127.
Thence to the Queen. O partner of our reign, ...Od.8.459.288.
The royal partner of fam'd *Cretheus'* bed. ....Od.11.282.395.
Sad *Ariadne,* partner of their woe; ....Od.11.398.403.
And the bright partner of thy royal throne. ....Od.12.536.459.
When the dear partner of my nuptial joy, ...Od.19.146.199.
Ardent the partner of his arms to find; ....Od.19.222.204.

PARTNERS
The partners of his fame and toils at *Troy,* .... Od.4.721.152.
O friends, oh ever partners of my woes, ...Od.12.190.441.
(The partners of her cares) the silver wool; ....Od.18.362.185.
When the brave partners of thy ten years toil ....Od.20.26.233.
Were all the partners of one native air? ....Od.24.133.354.

PARTOOK
He spoke; each Leader in his Grief partook, ...Il.16.671.270.
Hermes the hospitable rite partook, ...Od.5.119.178.
Partook the sacred feast, and ritual honours paid. ....Od.20.346.249.

PARTRIDGE
And in the new-shorn Field the Partridge feeds, ...1.W-F.98.160.
This *Partridge* soon shall view in cloudless Skies, ...2.RL5.137.211.
All Worldly's Hens, nay Partridge, sold to town, ...4.2HE2.234.181.
All He[athco]te's Hens, nay Partridge, sold to town, ...4.2HE2.234A.181.
All as a partridge plump, full-fed, and fair, ...5.DunA2.37.100.
All as a partridge plump, full-fed, and fair, ...5.DunB2.41.298.

PARTRIDGES
Sell their presented Partridges, and Fruits, ...4.HS2.51.59.

PARTRIGES
To three essential Partriges in one? ....5.DunB4.562.397.

PARTS
In *other Parts* it leaves wide sandy Plains; ....1.EOC.55.245.
But oft in *those,* confin'd to *single Parts.* .... 1.EOC.63.246.
But ev'n in *those,* confin'd to *single Parts.* .... 1.EOC.63A.246.
Is not th' Exactness of peculiar Parts; ....1.EOC.244.267.
No single Parts unequally surprize; ....1.EOC.249.268.
They talk of *Principles,* but Parts they prize, ...1.EOC.265A.270.
(As most in *Manners)* by a *Love to Parts.* .... 1.EOC.288.271.
Passes the Strait that parts the foaming Seas, ...1.TrSt.472.430.
These, where two Ways in equal Parts divide, ...1.TrSt.718.440.
He said; the rest in diff'rent Parts divide, ...2.ChJM.139.21.
All are but parts of one stupendous whole, ...3.EOM1.267.47.
Expunge the whole, or lop th'excrescent parts ....3.EOM2.49.61.
Parts it may ravage, but preserves the whole. ....3.EOM2.106.67.
'Tis but by parts we follow good or ill, ...3.EOM2.235.83.
Nothing is foreign: Parts relate to whole; ....3.EOM3.21.94.
In Parts superior what advantage lies? ....3.EOM4.259.152.
If Parts allure thee, think how Bacon shin'd, ...3.EOM4.281.154.
If Parts allure thee, think how Wh[arton] shin'd, ...3.EOM4.281A.154.
God loves from Whole to Parts: but human soul ....3.EOM4.361.163.
Shall parts so various aim at nothing new? ....3.Ep1.186.31.
None see what Parts of Nature it conceals. ....3.Ep2.190.65.
Whose Cause-way parts the vale with shady rows? ....3.Ep3.259.114.
Ascribes his gettings to his parts and merit, ...3.Ep3.376.123.
Parts answ'ring parts shall slide into a whole, ...3.Ep4.66.143.
Parts answ'ring parts shall slide into a whole, ...3.Ep4.66.143.
The Wood supports the Plain, the parts unite, ...3.Ep4.81.145.
Whose Place is *quarter'd out,* three Parts in four, ...4.JD4.136.37.
Beauty that shocks you, Parts that none will trust, ...4.Arbu.332.120.
Or court a Wife, spread out his wily parts, ...4.JD2.57.137.
To court a Wife, and spread his wily parts, ...4.JD2.57A.137.
To court a Wife, or spread his wily parts, ...4.JD2.57B.137.
Displays his Titles, lays forth all his Parts, ...4.JD2A.61.138.
Has Age but melted the rough parts away, ...4.2HE2.318.187.
Decay of Parts, alas! we all must feel— ....4.EpS1.5.297.
All Parts perform'd, and *all* her Children blest! ....4.EpS1.82.304.
All Parts perform'd, and all her Children blest! ....4.EpS1.82A.304.
How parts relate to parts, or they to whole, ...5.DunB4.235.366.
How parts relate to parts, or they to whole, ...5.DunB4.235.366.
"My sons! (she answer'd) both have done your parts: ....5.DunB4.437.383.
Who shew their Parts as *Pentlow* does, ...6.10.30.25.
Nay, e'en the Parts of Shame by Name would call: ....6.14ii.41.44.
The *Polygott—three Parts,—my Text,* .... 6.39.13.110.
Three Parts—the Polyglott,—my *Text,* .... 6.39.13A.110.
Yet takes one kiss before she parts for ever: ....6.45.6.124.
I knew their Persons, and admir'd their Parts, ...Il.3.271.205.
Thus toil'd the Chiefs in diff'ring Parts engag'd, ...Il.5.110.272.
Thus toil'd the Chiefs in diff'rent Parts engag'd, ...Il.5.110A.272.
Sudden the Fluids fix, the Parts combin'd; ....Il.5.1114.321.
His Princess parts with a prophetick Sigh, ...Il.6.640.358.
Unwilling parts, and oft' reverts her Eye ....Il.6.641.358.
The Goddess parts you: Be the Night obey'd. ....Il.7.342.381.
The Parts transfixes, and with Skill divides. ....Il.9.276.447.
Each Portion parts, and orders ev'ry Rite. ....Il.9.286.448.
Hazard and Fame all Parts alike attend. ....Il.13.399.125.
From diff'rent parts, and mingle in the Skies. ....Il.15.355.210.

PARTS (CONTINUED)
So from the Fold th' unwilling Lion parts, ... Il.17.117.292.
So parts the Chief; from Rank to Rank he flew, ... Il.17.759.318.
On adverse Parts the warring Gods engage. ... Il.20.44.395.
Then parts the Lance: But *Pallas'* heav'nly Breath, ... Il.20.507.415.
With Skill prepare them, and in Parts divide: ... Il.24.789.570.
In equal parts I strait divide my band, ... Od.10.232.351.
Her parts obscene the raging billows hide; ... Od.12.115.437.
On all parts round, and heaps on heaps lie dead. ... Od.14.300.50.
On all parts round, and heaps on heaps lay dead. ... Od.17.521.157.
In haste the matron parts: The King proceeds. ... Od.22.471.311.

PARTY
And Priests and Party-Zealots, num'rous Bands ... 2.TemF.464.286.
And nobly wishing Party-rage to cease, ... 3.Ep3.151.106.
I'll have a Party at the *Bedford Head,* ... 4.HS2.42.57.
Tho' long my Party built on me their hopes, ... 5.DunA3.281.183.
Or bidst thou rather Party to embrace? ... 5.DunB1.205.284.
(A friend to Party thou, and all her race; ... 5.DunB1.206.285.
Tho' long my Party built on me their hopes, ... 5.DunB3.283.334.
Then dupe to Party; child and man the same; ... 5.DunB4.502.391.
Int'rest, that waves on Party-colour'd wings: ... 5.DunB4.538.395.
Whose Publick Virtue knew no Party rage: ... 6.134.2.364.
In Circle close each heav'nly Party sate, ... Il.20.184.401.
And name a chief each party to command; ... Od.10.233.351.

PARTY-COLOUR'D
Int'rest, that waves on Party-colour'd wings: ... 5.DunB4.538.395.

PARTY-RAGE
And nobly wishing Party-rage to cease, ... 3.Ep3.151.106.

PARTY-ZEALOTS
And Priests and Party-Zealots, num'rous Bands ... 2.TemF.464.286.

PASIPHAE
Virgil, when call'd *Pasiphae Virgo* ... 6.10.89.27.

PASITHEA
The youngest *Grace, Pasithea* the divine. ... Il.14.304.177.
The youngest *Grace, Pasithea* the divine. ... Il.14.312.178.

PASQUIN
Shall this a Pasquin, that a Grumbler write; ... 5.DunA3.178.170.
Shall this a Pasquin, that a Grumbler write; ... 5.DunB3.182.329.

PASS
Oh! how I long with you to pass my Days, ... 1.PSu.77.78.
Ev'n I more sweetly pass my careless Days, ... 1.W-F.431.194.
Some neither can for *Wits* nor *Criticks* pass, ... 1.EOC.38.243.
To pass the Fences, and surprize the Fair? ... 1.TrVP.26.378.
Attempts alone the guarded Pass to gain: ... 1.TrES.148.455.
And pass his inoffensive Hours away, ... 2.ChJM.39.16.
Like empty Shadows, pass, and glide away; ... 2.ChJM.54.17.
Like flitting Shadows, pass, and glide away; ... 2.ChJM.54A.17.
To pass their Judgment, and to give Advice; ... 2.ChJM.82.18.
Still one by one, in swift Succession, pass ... 2.ChJM.236.25.
To pass my Age in Sanctity and Ease: ... 2.ChJM.263.27.
I pass each previous Settlement and Deed, ... 2.ChJM.305.28.
I pass, as Gambols never known to you: ... 2.ChJM.745.51.
Who pass, repass, advance, and glide away; ... 2.TemF.460.285.
Nor pass these lips in holy silence seal'd. ... 2.ElAb.10.319.
Thus unlamented pass the proud away, ... 2.Elegy.43.366.
Yet never pass th' insuperable line! ... 3.EOM1.228.44.
To welcome death, and calmly pass away. ... 3.EOM2.260.86.
One they must want, which is, to pass for good. ... 3.EOM4.92.137.
By his own Sons that pass him by unbless'd: ... 3.Ep1.231A.35.
His word would pass for more than he was worth. ... 3.Ep3.344.122.
At Timon's Villa let us pass a day, ... 3.Ep4.99.146.
The Watch would hardly let him pass at noon, ... 4.JD4.32.29.
"Why yes, 'tis granted, these indeed may pass ... 4.JD4.74.31.
In time to come, may pass for *Holy Writ.* ... 4.JD4.287.49.
Nor lets, like Nævius, ev'ry error pass, ... 4.HS2.65.59.
Out with it, *Dunciad!* let the secret pass, ... 4.Arbu.79.101.
No Commentatr more dextrously can pass ... 4.JD2A.104.140.
I pass o'er all those Confessors and Martyrs ... 4.JD2.35.135.
And brings all natural events to pass, ... 4.JD2.49.137.
No Commentator can more slily pass ... 4.JD2.101.141.
Well let Them pass and so may those that use ... 4.JD2A.41.136.
And brings all Natural Events to pass: ... 4.JD2A.55.136.
Have you not seen at Guild-hall's narrow Pass, ... 4.2HE2.104.173.
But let the Fit pass o'er, I'm wise enough, ... 4.2HE2.151.175.
How free, or frugal, I shall pass my days: ... 4.2HE2.289.185.
The Greatest can but blaze, and pass away. ... 4.1HE6.47.239.
Pass these to nobler sights lo Henley stands, ... 5.DunA3.195A.173.
Sent with a Pass, and vagrant thro' the land; ... 5.DunB1.232.287.
O! pass more innocent, in infant state, ... 5.DunB1.237.287.
Whose tuneful whistling makes the waters pass: ... 5.DunB3.156.327.
And as you please their Doom to pass on, ... 6.10.34.25.
And as you please to pass their Doom. ... 6.10.34A.25.
'And give Idea's of a narrow Pass; ... 6.13.23.39.
A narrow Pass there is, with Houses low; ... 6.14ii.2.43.
He that has these, may pass his Life, ... 6.39.17.111.
The Play may pass—but that strange creature, *Shore,* ... 6.41.5.113.
To pass her time 'twixt reading and Bohea, ... 6.45.15.125.
Before you pass th' imaginary sights ... 6.45.35.125.
That Pass *Tydides, Ajax* strive to gain, ... Il.6.554.354.
And pass victorious o'er the levell'd Mound. ... Il.8.219.407.
And Godlike *Idomen,* now pass the Mound; ... Il.8.318A.412.
His Son was first to pass the lofty Mound, ... Il.9.111.437.
Thither the Spoils of this long War shall pass, ... Il.9.477.456.
I pass my Watchings o'er thy helpless Years, ... Il.9.612.464.
No Hour must pass, no Moment must be lost; ... Il.10.195.10.
And pass unharm'd the Dangers of the Night; ... Il.10.250.13.
Wisdom like his might pass thro' Flames of Fire. ... Il.10.290.15.
Safe may we pass beneath the gloomy Shade, ... Il.10.331.17.

PASS (CONTINUED)
Yet let him pass, and win a little Space; ... Il.10.409.21.
And try the Pass impervious to the Horse. ... Il.12.66.83.
No Pass thro' those, without a thousand Wounds, ... Il.12.73.84.
The dreadful Pass, and round them heap the slain. ... Il.12.212.88.
Attempts alone the guarded Pass to gain: ... Il.12.502.100.
Or quit the Fleet, and pass unhurt away, ... Il.13.933.149.
But there no Pass the crossing Belts afford, ... Il.14.467.186.
Now in swift Flight they pass the Trench profound, ... Il.15.1.193.
Now Steeds, and Men, and Cars, tumultuous pass. ... Il.15.411.213.
When once we pass, the Soul returns no more. ... Il.23.94.491.
So shalt thou pass the Goal, secure of Mind, ... Il.23.417.506.
Here, where but one could pass, to shun the Throng ... Il.23.501.510.
A furious Pass the Spear of *Ajax* made ... Il.23.965.527.
Singly to pass thro' Hosts of Foes! to face ... Il.24.247.546.
To pass thro' Foes, and thus undaunted face ... Il.24.655.564.
To pass our Outworks, or elude the Guard. ... Il.24.715.567.
To pass the Ramparts, and the Watch to blind. ... Il.24.849.572.
A private voyager I pass the main. ... Od.2.358.78.
Pass we to other subjects; and engage ... Od.3.301.100.
And in their hollow bark to pass the night: ... Od.3.442.108.
There in the vessel shall I pass the night; ... Od.3.466.109.
On a slight Raft to pass the swelling sea ... Od.5.226.182.
Advance at distance, while I pass the plain ... Od.6.309.225.
Attend, and speedy thou shalt pass the main: ... Od.6.348.229.
Safe as they pass, and safe repass the tides, ... Od.8.614.295.
A Queen, to *Troy* she saw our legions pass; ... Od.11.106.386.
To whom with sighs: I pass these dreadful gates ... Od.11.587.412.
Alive to pass thro' hell's eternal gates! ... Od.12.30.431.
With ev'ry stranger pass from shore to shore; ... Od.13.209.15.
There pass the night; while he his course pursues ... Od.15.47.72.
He ended, and (receiving as they pass ... Od.16.39.104.
The court's main gate: To guard that pass be thine. ... Od.21.257.272.
To force the pass: the god-like man defends. ... Od.22.106.291.
Driv'n from the gate, th' important pass be lost. ... Od.22.125.292.
A high and narrow, but the only pass: ... Od.22.145.294.
There pass thy pleasing night, oh gentle swain! ... Od.22.212.297.
And pass the City-gate; *Ulysses* leads the way. ... Od.23.397.343.
Where all, from age to age who pass the coast, ... Od.24.105.353.

PASS'D
He pass'd the Gates which then unguarded lay, ... 1.TrSt.535.432.
And pass'd the Groin of valiant *Thrasymed,* ... 1.TrES.264.459.
Thro' both he pass'd, and bow'd from side to side: ... 5.DunB4.108.352.
The World's great Victor pass'd unheeded by; ... 6.32.34.97.
(In Shape a Mortal) pass'd disguis'd along. ... Il.4.116.226.
Pass'd the broad Belt, and thro' the Corslet drove; ... Il.4.167.228.
He said, and pass'd where great *Tydides* lay, ... Il.4.418.240.
Where twenty Days in Genial Rites he pass'd. ... Il.6.270.340.
Hither great *Hector* pass'd, nor pass'd unseen ... Il.6.312.341.
Hither great *Hector* pass'd, nor pass'd unseen ... Il.6.312.341.
And Godlike *Idomen,* now pass'd the Mound; ... Il.8.318.412.
When flying they had pass'd the Trench profound, ... Il.8.413.417.
Pass'd thro the Hosts, and reach'd the Royal Tent. ... Il.9.787.472.
Scarce had he pass'd the Steeds and *Trojan* Throng, ... Il.10.401.21.
(As *Dolon* pass'd) behind a Heap of dead: ... Il.10.416.21.
Where e'er he pass'd, a purple Stream pursu'd; ... Il.10.560.27.
Not unobserv'd they pass'd: the God of Light ... Il.10.602.29.
The *Trojan* stoop'd, the Javelin pass'd in Air. ... Il.11.300.48.
The Stream they pass'd, and pitch'd their Tents below. ... Il.11.849.74.
They bow'd, and made Obeysance as she pass'd, ... Il.15.93.200.
And pass'd the Groin of valiant *Thrasymed,* ... Il.16.569.266.
Which pass'd the Shield of *Aretus* the young; ... Il.17.585.311.
Pass'd this, and that way, thro' the Ranks of Fight: ... Il.17.768.318.
What if they pass'd me to the *Trojan* Wall, ... Il.21.656.449.
Daughter! what words have pass'd thy lips unweigh'd? ... Od.1.84.35.
The foe deceiv'd, he pass'd the tented plain, ... Od.4.337.136.
He felt their fleeces as they pass'd along, ... Od.9.520.328.
Scarce the fam'd *Argo* pass'd these raging floods, ... Od.12.83.435.
Unseen I pass'd by *Scylla's* dire abodes: ... Od.12.527.458.
And now, when thro' the royal dóme they pass'd, ... Od.15.146.75.
Crunus they pass'd, next *Chalcis* roll'd away. ... Od.15.316.84.
Now pass'd the rugged road, they journey down ... Od.17.230.143.
What words, my son, have pass'd thy lips severe? ... Od.19.576.224.
And tim'rous pass'd, and awfully withdrew. ... Od.24.126.354.

PASSAGE
Expects its Passage to the farther Strand: ... 1.TrSt.420.427.
The bearded Shaft the destin'd Passage found, ... 1.TrES.113.454.
Full in the Passage of each spacious Gate ... 2.TemF.145.265.
There, at one Passage, oft you might survey ... 2.TemF.489.287.
And smooth my passage to the realms of day: ... 2.ElAb.322.345.
A bird of passage! lost as soon as found, ... 3.Ep1.156A.28.
A bird of passage! gone as soon as found, ... 3.Ep1.156.28.
And hail her passage to the Realms of Rest, ... 4.EpS1.81.304.
His rapid waters in their passage burn. ... 5.DunA2.176.123.
His rapid waters in their passage burn. ... 5.DunB2.184.304.
Tho strait be the passage, and narrow the Gate; ... 6.122.22.342.
To bar his Passage fifty Warriors lay; ... Il.4.445.241.
If chance a swelling Brook his Passage stay, ... Il.5.736.302.
Forth rush a Tide of *Greeks,* the Passage freed; ... Il.8.315.412.
And held its Passage thro' the panting Heart. ... Il.11.561.59.
The bearded Shaft the destin'd Passage found, ... Il.12.467.98.
Which held its Passage thro' the panting Heart, ... Il.15.639.221.
Beneath the Brain the Point a Passage tore, ... Il.16.416.259.
My Spear, the destin'd Passage had it found, ... Il.16.747.273.
Thro' his broad Belt the Spear a Passage found, ... Il.17.652.313.
Thro' two strong Plates the Point is Passage held, ... Il.20.316.407.
And for the Soul an ample Passage made. ... Il.20.530.416.
The young *Lycaon* in his Passage stood; ... Il.21.41.423.
Soon as he clears whate'er their passage staid, ... Il.21.293.433.
The ruffled Seas beneath their Passage roar. ... Il.23.287.501.
Quite thro' and thro' the Point its Passage found, ... Il.23.1036.530.
The brazen Portal in his Passage rung. ... Il.24.398.552.
That car. be fate's, a speedy passage thine. ... Od.4.734.153.
At length he took the passage to the Wood, ... Od.5.613.201.

PASSAGE (CONTINUED)
To wait my passage from the *Trojan* land. ... Od.9.40.303.
To thwart thy passage, and repel thy fleet? ... Od.10.72.342.
I speed my passage to th' enchanted dome: ... Od.10.370.362.
The dolesome passage to th' infernal sky. ... Od.11.24.380.
And guard thy various passage thro' the tyde. ... Od.12.70.433.
And the dire passage down to hell descends. ... Od.12.104.436.
But lo! an ambush waits his passage o'er; ... Od.13.492.29.
To smooth thy passage, and supply thy sails: ... Od.15.42.71.
The brazen portals in their passage rung. ... Od.15.217.78.
Where images of truth for passage wait, ... Od.19.662.228.
Thence thro' his breast its bloody passage tore; ... Od.22.109.292.

PASSED
Yea when she passed by or Lane or Nook, ... 6.14ii.42.44.
Whene'er she passed by or Lane or Nook, ... 6.14ii.42A.44.

PASSEN
Right then, there passen by the Way, ... 6.14i.7.41.

PASSENGER
Tho' many a passenger he rightly call, ... 3.Ep1.7.16.
What is't to me (a Passenger God wot) ... 4.2HE2.296.185.

PASSENGERS
There passengers shall stand, and pointing say, ... 2.Elegy.39.365.
The snappish Cur, (the Passengers annoy) ... 6.14ii.19.43.
That hence th' eluded passengers may say, ... Od.23.135.327.

PASSERAN
And so may'st Thou, Illustrious *Passeran!* ... 4.EpS1.124.307.

PASSES
Passes the Strait that parts the foaming Seas, ... 1.TrSt.472.430.
By his own son, that passes by unbless'd: ... 3.Ep1.231.35.
Where all that passes, *inter nos,* ... 4.HS6.99.257.
What passes in the dark third row ... 6.61.8.181.

PASSING
Which, without passing thro' the *Judgment,* gains ... 1.EOC.156.258.
E'er sixteen passing years had overlaid ... 1.TrPA.7.365.
Such skill in passing all, and touching none. ... 5.DunB4.258.369.
To sigh unheard in, to the passing winds? ... 6.81.10.225.
To sigh unseen into the passing Wind? ... 6.81.10A.225.
But none hath eyes to trace the passing wind, ... 6.96ii.30Z29.271.
"But who hath Eyes to trace the passing Wind, ... 6.96ii.39.272.
And Crowds stood wond'ring at the passing Show; ... Il.3.68.192.
And now the Warriors passing on the way, ... Il.6.664.360.
For passing Chariots, and a Trench profound. ... Il.7.409.385.
For passing Chariots; and a Trench profound, ... Il.7.523.390.
Hears in the passing Wind their Music blow, ... Il.10.15.2.
Each Step of passing Feet increas'd th' Affright; ... Il.10.221.11.
A signal Omen stopp'd the passing Host, ... Il.12.231.89.
Approach'd him passing, and submissive said; ... Od.6.68.208.
And search'd each passing sheep, and felt it o'er, ... Od.9.497.326.
Immur'd we sate, and catch'd each passing sound; ... Od.23.44.321.

PASSION
Swell'd with new Passion, and o'erflows with Tears; ... 1.PWi.66.93.
Where *Jove,* subdu'd by mortal Passion still, ... 1.W-F.233.170.
Nor knew I then which passion greater prov'd, ... 1.TrPA.11.365.
With greater Passion, but with like Success; ... 1.TrVP.28A.378.
A sudden Passion in her Breast did move, ... 1.TrVP.122A.382.
No more the *Lesbian* Dames my Passion move, ... 1.TrSP.17.394.
But when its way th'impetuous Passion found, ... 1.TrSP.129.399.
Reflect what Truth was in my Passion shown, ... 2.ChJM.549.41.
The wise Man's Passion, and the vain Man's Toast? ... 2.RL5.10.199.
Before true passion all those views remove, ... 2.ElAb.79.326.
Unequal task! a passion to resign, ... 2.ElAb.195.336.
That never passion discompos'd the mind: ... 3.EOM1.168.36.
Chaos of Thought and Passion, all confus'd; ... 3.EOM2.13.55.
What Reason weaves, by Passion is undone. ... 3.EOM2.42.60.
Reason the card, but Passion is the gale; ... 3.EOM2.108.68.
And hence one master Passion in the breast, ... 3.EOM2.131.70.
The Mind's disease, its ruling Passion came; ... 3.EOM2.138.71.
The ruling Passion, be it what it will, ... 3.EOM2.148Z1.72.
The ruling Passion conquers Reason still. ... 3.EOM2.148Z2.72.
And treat this passion more as friend than foe: ... 3.EOM2.164.74.
Grafts on this Passion our best principle: ... 3.EOM2.176.76.
Whate'er the Passion, knowledge, fame, or pelf, ... 3.EOM2.261.86.
See some fit Passion ev'ry age supply, ... 3.EOM2.273.87.
Each Virtue in each Passion takes its turn; ... 3.EOM3.136.106.
Is yellow dirt the passion of thy life? ... 3.EOM4.279.154.
That REASON, PASSION, answer one great aim; ... 3.EOM4.395.166.
'Tis in the Ruling Passion: There, alone, ... 3.Ep1.174A.30.
Search then the Ruling Passion: There, alone, ... 3.Ep1.174.30.
Whose ruling Passion was the Lust of Praise; ... 3.Ep1.181.30.
His Passion still, to covet gen'ral praise, ... 3.Ep1.196.32.
In this one Passion man can strength enjoy, ... 3.Ep1.222.34.
Shall feel your ruling passion strong in death: ... 3.Ep1.263.38.
Yet ne'er so sure our passion to create, ... 3.Ep2.51.54.
Now Conscience chills her, and now Passion burns; ... 3.Ep2.65.55.
On the soft Passion, and the Taste refin'd, ... 3.Ep2.84.57.
For ever in a Passion, or a Pray'r: ... 3.Ep2.106.58.
No Passion gratify'd except her Rage. ... 3.Ep2.126.61.
To that each Passion turns, or soon or late; ... 3.Ep2.133.61.
A Fop their Passion, but their Prize a Sot, ... 3.Ep2.247.70.
"The ruling Passion, be it what it will, ... 3.Ep3.155.106.
"The ruling Passion conquers Reason still." ... 3.Ep3.156.106.
Than ev'n that Passion, if it has no Aim; ... 3.Ep3.158.106.
Hear then the truth: "'Tis Heav'n each Passion sends, ... 3.Ep3.161.106.
Can make me feel each Passion that he feigns, ... 4.2HE1.343.225.
Is Wealth thy passion? Hence! from Pole to Pole, ... 4.1HE6.69.241.
But if to Pow'r and Place your Passion lye, ... 4.1HE6.97.243.
There, where no Passion, Pride, or Shame transport, ... 4.EpS1.97.305.
Thro' Clouds of Passion P[ulteney]'s views are clear, ... 4.1740.9.332.

PASSION (CONTINUED)
D[uckit] for pious passion to the youth. ... 5.DunA3.176.169.
The third mad passion of thy doting age. ... 5.DunB3.304.334.
T'approve our passion and forbid our fears. ... 6.4ii.6.9.
There Nature reigns, and Passion void of Art, ... 6.33.9.99.
Here Nature reigns, and Passion void of Art, ... 6.33.9A.99.
And boasts a Warmth that from no Passion flows; ... 6.73.4.209.
Above all Pain, all Passion, and all Pride, ... 6.84.24.239.
A Fop their Passion, but their Prize a Sot; ... 6.86.9A.245.
Not warp'd by Passion, aw'd by Rumour, ... 6.89.5.250.
Thou art his guide; each passion, every line, ... 6.107.29.311.
Passion and Pride were to her soul unknown, ... 6.115.5.322.
To Wyndham's breast the patriot passion stole ... 6.142.11H.383.
For never Heart felt Passion more sincere: ... 6.152.4.400.
No Passion gratify'd except her Rage; ... 6.154.12.403.
To that each Passion turns or soon or late, ... 6.154.19.403.
To calm their Passion with the Words of Age, ... Il.1.329.103.
The raging Chief in frantick Passion lost, ... Il.1.446.109.
But *Juno,* impotent of Passion, broke ... Il.4.33.222.
Suppress thy Passion, and the King revere: ... Il.4.467.242.
As late she try'd with Passion to inflame ... Il.5.511.292.
The Wife whom Choice and Passion doth approve, ... Il.9.450.454.
Oh let not headlong Passion bear the Sway; ... Il.9.637.466.
On whom his Passion, lavish of his Store, ... Il.11.317.49.
And gives to Passion what to *Greece* he owes. ... Il.11.899.75.
Ne'er did my Soul so strong a Passion prove, ... Il.14.359.180.
By what wild Passion, Furious! art thou tost? ... Il.15.146.202.
From her lov'd Breast, with fonder Passion weeps; ... Il.16.12.235.
If, (e'er the Day when by mad Passion sway'd, ... Il.19.59.374.
He said: and *Ajax* by mad Passion born, ... Il.23.572.512.
He said; and pleas'd his Passion to command, ... Il.23.699.517.
Provok'd to Passion, once more rouze to Ire ... Il.24.733.568.
Will guide her passion, and reward the choice ... Od.1.362.50.
Will guide her passion, and reward her choice, ... Od.2.225.72.
From the brave youth the streaming passion broke: ... Od.4.150.127.
His hand the King with tender passion press'd, ... Od.4.829.158.
Then thus her anguish and her passion broke. ... Od.5.148.178.
Saw stately *Ceres* to her passion yield, ... Od.5.160.179.
Is then thy home the passion of thy heart? ... Od.5.259.184.
When hush'd their passion, thus the Goddess cries: ... Od.10.539.369.
Nor turn the passion into groundless joy ... Od.14.399.55.
Thy passion, Prince, belies thy knowing mind. ... Od.17.459.155.

PASSION'S
Add Nature's, Custom's, Reason's, Passion's strife, ... 3.Ep1.21.17.

PASSIONATE
Gods partial, changeful, passionate, unjust, ... 3.EOM3.257.118.

PASSIONS
Their artless Passions, and their tender Pains. ... 1.PAu.12.81.
The *Manners, Passions, Unities,* what not? ... 1.EOC.276.271.
And bid Alternate Passions fall and rise! ... 1.EOC.375.283.
In her soft Breast consenting Passions move, ... 1.TrVP.122.382.
What Passions in a Parent's Breast debate! ... 1.TrES.231.458.
"Their tender Husbands, and their Passions cool'd. ... 2.ChWB.196.66.
And secret Passions labour'd in her Breast. ... 2.RL4.2.183.
Sighs, Sobs, and Passions, and the War of Tongues. ... 2.RL4.84.190.
And heav'nly Breasts with human Passions rage; ... 2.RL5.46.202.
There dy'd the best of passions, Love and Fame. ... 2.ElAb.40.322.
Those restless passions in revenge inspires; ... 2.ElAb.82.326.
And Passions are the elements of Life. ... 3.EOM1.170.36.
Modes of Self-love the Passions we may call; ... 3.EOM2.93.66.
Passions, tho' selfish, if their means be fair, ... 3.EOM2.97.66.
Passions, like Elements, tho' born to fight, ... 3.EOM2.111.68.
Hence diff'rent Passions more or less inflame, ... 3.EOM2.129.70.
She but removes weak passions for the strong: ... 3.EOM2.158.74.
Like varying winds, by other passions tost, ... 3.EOM2.167.75.
The surest Virtues thus from Passions shoot, ... 3.EOM2.183.77.
Wants, frailties, passions, closer still ally ... 3.EOM2.253.85.
The Fury-passions from that blood began, ... 3.EOM3.167.110.
To Man's low passions, or their glorious ends, ... 3.EOM4.376.164.
Or come discolour'd thro' our Passions shown. ... 3.Ep1.26.17.
By Passions? these Dissimulation hides: ... 3.Ep1.171.29.
In sev'ral Men we sev'ral Passions find, ... 3.Ep2.207A.67.
In Men, we various Ruling Passions find, ... 3.Ep2.207.67.
"But, for the Passions, Southern sure and Rowe. ... 4.2HE1.86.201.
And sets the Passions on the side of Truth; ... 4.2HE1.218.213.
The Master of our Passions, and his own. ... 4.EpS2.89.318.
Intestine War no more our *Passions* wage, ... 6.11.34.31.
Passions no more the Soul engage, ... 6.11.34A.31.
What tender passions take their turns, ... 6.51ii.33.154.
Command thy Passions, and the Gods obey. ... Il.1.286.100.
And all her Passions kindled into Flame. ... Il.1.697.120.
To tender Passions all his mighty Mind: ... Il.6.505.351.
Such various Passions urg'd the troubled Host. ... Il.9.10.431.
To calm thy Passions, and subdue thy Rage: ... Il.9.333.450.
One should our Int'rests, and our Passions be; ... Il.9.727.470.
What Passions in a Parent's Breast debate! ... Il.16.534.264.
But great *Achilles* diff'rent Passions rend, ... Il.24.642.563.

PASSIONS'
His actions', passions', being's, use and end; ... 3.EOM1.66.21.
Oft in the Passions' wild rotation tost, ... 3.Ep1.41.18.

PASSIVE
Not those alone who passive own her laws, ... 5.DunB4.85.349.
On passive paper, or on solid brick. ... 5.DunB4.130.354.
Thro' each vain passive form constrain his flight. ... Od.4.568.147.

PAST
Beneath yon Poplar oft we past the Day: ... 1.PAu.66.85.
Not thus the Land appear'd in Ages past, ... 1.W-F.43.152.
Consults the Dead, and lives past Ages o'er. ... 1.W-F.248.172.
Some have at first for *Wits,* then *Poets* past, ... 1.EOC.36.243.
Th' Eternal Snows appear already past, ... 1.EOC.227.265.

PAST (CONTINUED)
Which from the first has shone on *Ages past,* 1.EOC.402.286.
But *Sense* surviv'd, when *merry Jests* were past; 1.EOC.460.291.
But you, with Pleasure own your Errors past, 1.EOC.570.305.
Their *ancient Bounds* the banish'd Muses past; 1.EOC.710.322.
Swift as she past, the flitting Ghosts withdrew, 1.TrSt.132.415.
Suffic'd it not, that thy long Labours past 1.TrUl.169.471.
To hope the future, or esteem the past; 2.ChJM.34.16.
With due Regret I view my Vices past, 2.ChJM.92.19.
Who past all Pleasure, damn the Joys of Sense, 2.ChJM.174.23.
Heav'n put it past your Doubt whene'er you wed, 2.ChJM.279.27.
The Winter's past, the Clouds and Tempests fly, 2.ChJM.529.41.
Where *Damian* kneeling, worshipp'd as she past. 2.ChJM.600.44.
Where *Damian* kneeling, rev'renc'd as she past. 2.ChJM.600A.44.
Madam, 'tis past, and my short Anger o'er; 2.ChJM.789.53.
Thus with my first three Lords I past my Life; 2.ChWB.205.66.
Tho' past my Bloom, not yet decay'd was I, 2.ChWB.209.66.
On all the Joys of Youth and Beauty past, 2.ChWB.222.67.
Thus Day by Day, and Month by Month we past; 2.ChWB.307.71.
But to my Tale: A Month scarce past away, 2.ChWB.329.72.
When old, and past the Relish of Delight, 2.ChWB.373.75.
But after many a hearty Struggle past, 2.ChWB.425.77.
In various Talk the chearful hours they past, 2.RL*A* 1.75.129.
In various Talk th' instructive hours they past, 2.RL3.11.169.
Safe past the *Gnome* thro' this fantastick Band, 2.RL4.55.188.
"Plague on't! 'tis past a Jest—nay prithee, Pox! 2.RL4.129.194.
Yet wide was spread their Fame in Ages past, 2.TemF.33.255.
There Names inscrib'd unnumber'd Ages past 2.TemF.49.256.
Now turn'd to heav'n, I weep my past offence, 2.ElAb.187.335.
Which serv'd the past, and must the times to come! 3.EOM2.52.62.
(Tho' past the recollection of the thought) 3.Ep1.47.18.
Old Politicians chew on wisdom past, 3.Ep1.248.37.
Such in those moments as in all the past, 3.Ep1.264.38.
Like Doctors thus, when much dispute has past, 3.Ep3.15.84.
Alas! 'tis more than (all his Visions past) 3.Ep3.85.94.
And swear no Day was ever past so ill. 3.Ep4.168.153.
"And perfect *Speaker?"*—"Onslow, past dispute." 4.JD4.71.31.
He past it o'er; affects an easy Smile 4.JD4.122.35.
He past it o'er; put on an easy Smile 4.JD4.122A.35.
The Dog-star rages! nay 'tis past a doubt, 4.Arbu.3.96.
I ne'r with Wits or Witlings past my days, 4.Arbu.223.112.
I ne'r with Wits and Witlings past my days, 4.Arbu.223A.112.
Welcome for thee, fair Virtue! all the past: 4.Arbu.358.122.
His Life, tho' Long, to sickness past unknown, 4.Arbu.402.126.
Sense, past thro' him, no longer is the same, 4.JD2.33.135.
The great Alcides, ev'ry Labour past, 4.2HE1.17.195.
St John, whose love indulg'd my labours past 4.1HE1.1.279.
But past the Sense of human Miseries, 4.EpS1.101.305.
Grave, righteous S[andys] joggs on till, past belief, 4.1740.13.332*.
A past, vamp'd, future, old, reviv'd, new piece, 5.DunA1.238.91.
This labour past, by Bridewell all descend, 5.DunA2.257.132.
Judge of all present, past, and future wit, 5.DunA2.344.142.
And let the past and future fire thy brain. 5.DunA3.58.155.
As thou preserv'st the dulness of the past! 5.DunA3.186.172.
A past, vamp'd, future, old, reviv'd, new piece, 5.DunB1.284.290.
This labour past, by Bridewell all descend, 5.DunB2.269.308.
"Judge of all present, past, and future wit; 5.DunB2.376.315.
And let the past and future fire thy brain. 5.DunB3.66.323.
As thou preserv'st the dulness of the past! 5.DunB3.190.329.
Safe and unseen the young Æneas past: 5.DunB4.290.373.
Nor past the meanest unregarded, one 5.DunB4.575.399.
Thy stream, like his, is never past, 6.6ii.7.14.
Wit, past thro' thee, no longer is the same, 6.7.11.16.
Past Services of Friends, good Deeds of Foes, 6.8.34.19.
Decry'd each past, to raise each present Writer 6.17iv.13.59.
So to mine Host, the greatest Jest, they past, 6.17iv.17.59.
Still makes new Conquests, and maintains the past: 6.19.62.64.
As her dead Father's rev'rend image past, 6.32.31.97.
Sees his past days safe out of fortune's pow'r, 6.55.3.166.
He sees past days safe out of fortune's pow'r, 6.55.3A.166.
The present well, and ev'n the past enjoy. 6.55.11.167.
Wretched Lovers, Fate, has past 6.78ii.1.216.
When *Israel's* Daughters mourn'd their past Offences, 6.95.1.264.
'Tis all my Pleasure thy past Toil to know, 6.96iv.63.278.
No joy no pleasure from successes past 6.130.19.358.
While, Scale in Hand, Dame *Justice* past along. 6.145.4.388.
You will have the *last word,* after all that is past? 6.149.1A.397*.
The past, the present, and the future knew. Il.1.94.91.
For tho' we deem the short-liv'd Fury past, Il.1.105.92.
Who lost to Sense of gen'rous Freedom past Il.1.307.102.
Two Generations now had past away, Il.1.333.103.
The Gods command me to forgive the past; Il.1.396.107.
Unskill'd to judge the Future by the Past, Il.1.448.109.
Past silent, as the Heralds held her Hand, Il.1.452.109.
In Silence past along the winding Strand Il.1.453A.109.
Twelve Days were past, and now the dawning Light Il.1.640.118.
The Vision spoke, and past in Air away. Il.2.92.131.
What past at *Aulis, Greece* can witness bear, Il.2.366.145.
Your Leagues concluded, your Engagements past? Il.2.405.147.
Where many Seas, and many Suff'rings past, Il.2.807.163.
Between the Bladder and the Bone it past: Il.5.88.270.
Confus'd he stops, a Length of Country past, Il.5.738.302.
This said, with ample Strides the Hero past; Il.6.143.331.
So flourish these, when those are past away. Il.6.186.335.
He said, and past with sad presaging Heart Il.6.462.349.
The Thoughts of Glory past, and present Shame, Il.6.588.355.
At once my present Judgment, and my past; Il.9.140.439.
His steely Lance, that lighten'd as he past. Il.10.155.8.
The Trenches past, th' assembl'd Kings around Il.10.231.12.
Now *Dolon* list'ning, heard them as they past; Il.10.423.22.
Which willful err'd, and o'er his Shoulder past; Il.10.442.23.
Now past the Tomb where ancient *Ilus* lay, Il.11.217.45.
Shouts, as he past, the crystal Regions rend, Il.11.445.54.
The Coursers past me with so swift a Pace. Il.11.753.68.
Thro' intermingled Ships and Tents, he past; Il.11.755.68.
Three Days were past, when *Elis* rose to War, Il.11.842.73.

PAST (CONTINUED)
Swift thro' the Wall their Horse and Chariots past, Il.12.135.86.
Fierce as he past, the lofty Mountains nod, Il.13.29.105.
Deiphobus beheld him as he past, Il.13.654.136.
And sprinkling, as he past, the Sands with Gore. Il.13.681.137.
Not *Jove* himself, upon the Past has pow'r. Il.14.62.160.
Past are the Days when happier *Greece* was blest, Il.14.77.161.
He past to *Argos*, and in Exile dwell'd; Il.14.135.164.
In their kind Arms my tender years were past; Il.14.233.172.
Howe'er th' Offence by other Gods be past, Il.15.242.206.
Jove thinking of his Pains, they past away. Il.15.274.207.
But bear we this—The Wrongs I grieve, are past; Il.16.82.238.
Had caus'd such Sorrows past, and Woes to come. Il.18.114.328.
'Tis past—I quell it; I resign to Fate. Il.18.144.329.
She spoke, and past in Air. The Hero rose; Il.18.241.333.
Skill'd to discern the Future by the past, Il.18.294.336.
Is past, forgotten, and resign'd to Fate: Il.19.68.374.
Slow as she past, beheld with sad survey Il.19.297.384.
Ten Days were past, since in his Father's Reign Il.21.50.424.
He spoke; and past: *Latona,* stooping low, Il.21.585.446.
Vain thy past Labour, and thy present vain: Il.22.20.453.
By these they past, one chasing, one in Flight, Il.22.205.464.
Oh had thy gentle Spirit past in Peace, Il.22.544.479.
But slow, and past their Vigour, are my Steeds. Il.23.380.505.
O'er-past *Atrides)* second in the Course. Il.23.598.513.
But left the Glory of the past thy own. Il.23.716.518.
So past them all the rapid Circle flies: Il.23.1003.529.
All past before him in Remembrance dear, Il.24.15.535.
So past the Goddess thro' the closing Wave, Il.24.109.539.
Nine Days are past, since all the Court above Il.24.141.541.
Then past the Monarch to his Bridal-Room, Il.24.229.546.
With Hands uplifted, eye him as he past, Il.24.405.552.
Or safe return'd, the race of glory past, Od.1.303.47.
Now twice ten years are past, and now he comes! Od.2.206.71.
We past the wide, immeasurable main. Od.3.22.87.
Happier his lot, who, many sorrows past, Od.3.289.100.
Secure of storms, your royal brother past: Od.4.684.151.
'Tis past—and *Jove* decrees he shall remove; Od.5.175.180.
Four days were past, and now the work compleat Od.5.333.188.
And now two nights, and now two days were past, Od.5.496.196.
Tho' fenc'd from cold, and tho' my toil be past, Od.5.608.201.
She past, delighted with the well-known seats; Od.7.105.239.
With torches blazing in their hands they past, Od.7.431.258.
The song recals past horrours to my eyes, Od.8.537.291.
Him while he past the monster blind bespoke: Od.9.525.328.
No sooner freed, and thro' th' enclosure past, Od.9.545.328.
The scenes of life recur, and actions past; Od.11.181.390.
These ills are past; now hear thy future woes. Od.12.48.431.
Past sight of shore, along the surge we bound, Od.12.473.454.
Whatever toils the great *Ulysses* past, Od.13.5.1.
Suffic'd it not, that thy long labours past Od.13.336.23.
Soon past beyond their sight, I left the flood, Od.14.387.53.
Their love is always with the lover past; Od.15.27.71.
The banquet past, and satiate ev'ry man, Od.15.324.85.
The melancholy joy of evils past: Od.15.435.90.
Your vessel loaded, and your traffic past, Od.15.485.93.
While I, so many wand'rings past and woes, Od.15.530.95.
So past in pleasing dialogue away Od.15.532.95.
Arm'd with his lance the Prince then past the gate; Od.17.72.136.
Past on, and sate by faithful *Mentor's* side; Od.17.79.136.
Storms have I past, and many a stern debate; Od.17.338.148.
The pleasure past supplies a copious theme Od.19.681.229.
Long, long the scene of all my past delight, Od.21.79.262.
And, past the limits of the Court, o'ertakes. Od.21.196.269.
Full thro' his throat *Ulysses'* weapon past, Od.22.19.287.
Full thro' his liver past the mortal wound, Od.22.101.291.
Behind the felon unperceiv'd they past, Od.22.194.296.
The storm past innocent. The god-like man Od.22.286.300.
That impious race to all their past mis-deeds Od.22.290.300.
When twice ten years are past of mighty woes: Od.23.104.324.
Then how unharm'd he past the *Siren*-coasts, Od.23.352.341.
Icarius' daughter, glory of the past, Od.24.222.358.
Past to *Laertes'* cultivated land. Od.24.235.360.
This past on earth, while in the realms above Od.24.540.373.
And o'er the past, *Oblivion* stretch her wing. Od.24.557.375.

PASTE
"Paste we this Recreant's Name, 6.79.142.223.

PASTERN
Where to the pastern-bone by nerves combin'd, Od.20.367.250.

PASTERN-BONE
Where to the pastern-bone by nerves combin'd, Od.20.367.250.

PASTIME
Thy joy, thy pastime, thy attire, thy food? 3.EOM3.28.95.
Ah why th' ill-suiting pastime must I try? Od.8.168.271.

PASTIMES
Stand forth ye wrestlers who these pastimes grace! Od.8.235.275.
And the soft Lyre to grace our pastimes bear. Od.8.292.278.

PASTOR
No zealous Pastor blame a failing Spouse, 4.EpS2.193.324.
His People's Pastor, good *Hypenor,* dy'd; Il.5.185.275.
His People's Pastor, *Hyperenor* fell; Il.14.612.192.

PASTORA
Is there, Pastora by a fountain side: 3.Ep2.8.49.

PASTORALS
The Bard whom pilf'red Pastorals renown, 4.Arbu.179.109.
The Wretch whom pilfer'd Pastorals renown, 6.98.29.284.

PASTORELLA
There, *Pastorella* by a fountain side: ....3.Ep2.8A.49.

PASTORS
To native pastors is their charge assign'd, ...Od.14.127.42.

PASTRY
Some say from *Pastry Cook* it came, ...6.59.3.177.

PASTURE
Seeks freshest Pasture and the purest Air, ...1.Mes.50.117.
Where the fat Herds in plenteous Pasture rove; ....II.2.735.161.
From *Practius'* Stream, *Percoté's* Pasture Lands, ...II.2.1012.171.
Half Pasture green, and half with Vin'yards crown'd.) ....II.9.694.468.
He drove to pasture all the lusty males: ....Od.9.516.327.
And forth to pasture send the bristly care. ....Od.16.4.102.

PASTURES
To beasts his pastures, and to fish his floods; ....3.EOM3.58.98.
Like some proud Bull that round the Pastures leads ....II.2.566.154.
Æpea fair, the Pastures *Hyra* yields, ...II.9.199.442.
Æpea fair, the Pastures *Hyra* yields, ...II.9.386.451.
In fair *Pedæus'* verdant Pastures bred, ...II.13.230.116.
Three thousand Mares his spacious Pastures bred, ...II.20.262.405.
(Whose stately steeds luxuriant pastures bless) ....Od.3.327.102.
So near the pastures, and so short the way, ...Od.10.98.345.
As from fresh pastures and the dewy field ....Od.10.485.366.
Of these fair pastures: If ye touch, ye die. ....Od.12.382.449.

PASTY
Not quite a Mad-man, tho' a Pasty fell, ...4.2HE2.190.179.

PAT
See how they pat thee with their pretty Paws: ....6.96iv.15.276.

PATCH
Thrice from my trembling hand the *Patch-box* fell; ....2.RL4.162.197.
To patch, nay ogle, might become a Saint, ...2.RL5.23.201.
In patch-work flutt'ring, and her head aside ....5.DunB4.48.346.

PATCH-BOX
Thrice from my trembling hand the *Patch-box* fell; ....2.RL4.162.197.

PATCH-WORK
In patch-work flutt'ring, and her head aside ....5.DunB4.48.346.

PATCH'D
On some patch'd dog-hole ek'd with ends of wall, ...3.Ep4.32.140.
Peel'd, patch'd, and pyebald, linsey-woolsey brothers, ...5.DunA3.107.159.
Peel'd, patch'd, and pyebald, linsey-wolsey brothers, ...5.DunB3.115.325.
Wide-patch'd, and knotted to a twisted thong. ....Od.13.507.30.
Wide patch'd, and fasten'd by a twisted thong. ....Od.17.221.142.
The broad-patch'd scrip; the scrip in tatters hung ....Od.18.131.172.

PATCHES
Puffs, Powders, Patches, Bibles, Billet-doux. ....2.RL1.138.156.
With borrow'd Pins, and Patches not her own; ....6.49i.22.138.

PATE
As that which in the Hero's Pate ....6.10.77.26.
You beat your Pate, and fancy Wit will come: ....6.124iii.1.348.

PATENT
That of his Grace he'd make a Patent ....6.30.36A.87.

PATER
So *Luther* thought the *Pater noster* long, ...4.JD2A.111.142.

PATERNAL
This, long revolv'd in his Paternal Breast, ...1.TrSt.549.433.
Depriv'd us soon of our Paternal Cell; ....4.2HE2.59.169.
Shrink back to my Paternal Cell, ...4.1HE7.76.273.
Each hurries back to his paternal ground, ...4.1740.39.334.
A few paternal acres bound, ...6.1.2.3.
Wake each Paternal Virtue in thy Soul: ....II.5.161.274.
And glad his Eyes with his paternal Reign, ...II.19.354.387.
And now he shakes his great paternal Spear, ...II.19.420.389.
Ev'n from his own paternal Roof expell'd, ...II.22.626.482.
An exile from his dear paternal coast, ...Od.1.19.30.
Thy name, thy lineage, and paternal land: ....Od.1.220.43.
To great *Icarius,* whose paternal care ....Od.1.361.50.
To great *Icarius,* whose paternal care ....Od.2.224.72.
But since thy veins paternal virtue fires, ...Od.2.317.76.
Dismay'd, heart-wounded with paternal woes, ...Od.4.205.129.
Ægisthus govern'd in paternal state. ....Od.4.692.151.
Thus leaving careless thy paternal right ....Od.15.13.70.
For all the proofs of his paternal care, ...Od.15.170.76.
Thy name, thy lineage, and paternal land. ....Od.15.287.82.
(Child of his age) with strong paternal joy ....Od.16.19.103.
Soon will he grace this dear paternal dome. ....Od.19.346.211.
That form'd for empire with paternal care, ...Od.19.432.215.
His lineage and paternal clime declare: ....Od.20.242.244.
Whilst in paternal pomp, with plenty blest, ...Od.20.401.251.

PATERNOSTER
So Luther thought the Paternoster long, ...4.JD2.105.143.

PATH
Nor knows, amaz'd, what doubtful Path to tread, ...1.TrSt.517.432.
Self-love forsook the path it first pursu'd, ...3.EOM3.281.121.
Take Nature's path, and mad Opinion's leave, ...3.EOM4.29.130.
Or tread the path by vent'rous Heroes trod, ...5.DunB1.201.284.
Direct each step, and smooth the path to Heaven. ....6.21.28.70.
The Patriot's plain, but untrod path pursue; ....6.73.16.210.
My Muse attending strews thy path with Bays, ...6.84.31Z7.239.
And trod the Path his Feet must tread no more. ....II.10.400.21.

PATH (CONTINUED)
Along the Path the Spy unwary flew; ....II.10.417.21.
That Path they take, and speed to reach the Town. ....II.11.220.45.
And chose the certain, glorious Path to Death. ....II.13.840.145.
While I decline to yonder Path, that leads ....II.21.657.449.
By great *Ulysses* taught the path to fame; ....Od.2.24.61.
He took the path that winded to the cave. ....Od.5.71.175.
All, soon or late, are doom'd that path to tread; ....Od.12.31.431.
Know Friend! that Virtue is the path to praise. ....Od.21.360.277.

PATHETIC
Implore your help in these pathetic strains: ....4.2HE1.232.215.
While thus pathetic to the Prince he spoke, ...Od.4.149.127.
Whilst with pathetic warmth his hand he press'd. ....Od.20.248.245.

PATHLESS
Seek the clear Spring, or haunt the pathless Grove; ....1.W-F.168.165.
O'er pathless Forests, or the roaring Main. ....II.24.540.558.
Engage your journey o'er the pathless main? ....Od.3.87.90.
Where savage goats thro' pathless thickets rove: ....Od.9.136.311.

PATHOS
Alike to them, by Pathos or by Pun. ....4.2HE1.295.221.

PATHS
'Tis he th'obstructed Paths of Sound shall clear, ...1.Mes.41.116.
And pointed out those arduous Paths they trod, ...1.EOC.95.250.
Back thro' the paths of pleasing sense I ran, ...2.ElAb.69.324.
To Virtue, in the paths of Pleasure, trod, ...3.EOM3.233.116.
'But the well-worn Paths of the Nymphs of Drury ....6.13.24.39.
And strove to tempt him from the Paths of Fame. ....II.6.202.336.
The Paths so many, and the Camp so wide. ....II.10.73.5.
And dark thro' Paths oblique their Progress take. ....II.10.320.17.
With equal steps the paths of glory trace; ....Od.1.392.51.
To tread th' uncomfortable paths beneath, ...Od.10.580.371.
To tread th' uncomfortable paths beneath, ...Od.10.675.376.
The paths of Gods what mortal can survey? ....Od.10.689.376.
To point them to the arduous paths of fame; ....Od.11.302.397.
He trod so fatally the paths of Fame. ....Od.14.82.40.
The paths of death, by Man or by a God. ....Od.23.86.323.

PATHWAY
To this, one Pathway gently winding leads, ...II.18.657.355.

PATIENCE
To tire our *Patience,* than mis-lead our *Sense:* ....1.EOC.4.239.
Each other Loss with Patience I can bear, ...2.ChJM.555.42.
Now prove your Patience, gentle Ladies all, ...2.ChJM.740.50.
I thought your Patience had been better try'd: ....2.ChJM.759.51.
"Of *Job's* great Patience since so oft you preach, ...2.ChWB.186.65.
Wild to get loose, his Patience I provoke, ...4.JD4.116.35.
I lose my patience, and I own it too, ...4.2HE1.115.205.
You lose your patience, just like other men. ....4.2HE1.363.227.
Dione then. Thy Wrongs with Patience bear, ...II.5.471.290.
One Chief with Patience to the Grave resign'd, ...II.19.231.382.
If yet he lives, with patience I forbear ....Od.2.247.73.
Not more thy patience, than her constant mind. ....Od.24.221.358.

PATIENT
The patient Fisher takes his silent Stand ....1.W-F.137.163.
Patient of Right, familiar in the Throne? ....1.TrSt.261.421.
With patient Touches of unweary'd Art: ....2.TemF.199.271.
Patient of labour when the end was rest, ...4.2HE1.242.215.
All that we ask is but a patient Ear. ....4.1HE1.64.283.
Not to his patient touch, or happy flame, ...6.107.23.311.
The Patient Chief, who lab'ring long, arriv'd ....6.155.1.404.
Goddess (he cry'd) be patient and obey. ....II.1.755.123.
The patient Animal maintains his Ground, ...II.11.687.65.
Patient of Horrors, to behold thy Death? ....II.22.555.479.
Patient permit the sadly-pleasing strain; ....Od.1.449.54.
Wise to resolve, and patient to perform. ....Od.4.372.137.
With patient ear, oh royal youth, attend ....Od.4.467.142.
Patient of conquest, and your cause demands; ....Od.4.570.147.
Thy patient ear hath heard me long relate ....Od.4.799.156.
To bid thee patient his return attend. ....Od.4.1084.168.
The patient man shall view his old abodes, ...Od.5.42.172.
This store, with joy the patient Heroe found, ...Od.5.628.202.
The patient, heav'nly man thy suppliant pray'd ....Od.7.1.232.
For active courage, and a patient mind; ....Od.11.500.408.
The Master of his grief, the man of patient mind. ....Od.14.172.43.
Patient to roam the street, by hunger led, ...Od.15.330.85.
The bravely-patient to no fortune yields: ....Od.17.336.147.
Fair truth alone (the patient man reply'd) ....Od.17.642.163.
By patient prudence, from the death decreed. ....Od.20.28.233.
Be patient, Peers! at length *Antinous* cries; ....Od.20.336.249.
The patient body and the constant mind? ....Od.22.247.298.
That stranger, patient of the Suitors wrongs, ...Od.23.29.320.
Patient he suffer'd with a constant mind. ....Od.24.190.356.
The suff'ring Heroe felt his patient breast ....Od.24.582.376.

PATIENTLY
Who took it patiently, and wip'd his Head; ....2.ChWB.391.76.

PATIENTS
As one of *Woodward's* Patients, sick and sore, ...4.JD4.152.37.

PATRIARCH
When *Patriarch-Wits* surviv'd a *thousand Years;* ....1.EOC.479.293.
'Till then by Nature crown'd, each Patriarch sate, ...3.EOM3.215.114.

PATRIARCH-WITS
When *Patriarch-Wits* surviv'd a *thousand Years;* ....1.EOC.479.293.

PATRICIAN
What he prefers to the *Patrician* Board: ....6.17iii.25.58.

PATRICIANS
Say great Patricians! (since your selves inspire 5.DunA1.3.61.

PATRIMONIAL
Some Stranger plows his patrimonial Field. Il.22.627.482.
Your patrimonial stores in peace possess; Od.1.511.56.
Your patrimonial wealth, a prudent heir. Od.19.26.193.

PATRIMONIES
Whose luxury whole patrimonies sweeps, Od.17.541.158.

PATRIOT
And make a patriot as it makes a knave. 3.EOM2.202.79.
Poet or Patriot, rose but to restore 3.EOM3.285.121.
"Statesman and Patriot ply alike the stocks, 3.Ep3.141.105.
That from a Patriot of distinguish'd note, 4.2HE2.196.179.
Sometimes a Patriot, active in debate, 4.1HE1.27.281.
A Patriot is a Fool in ev'ry age, 4.EpS1.41.301.
In Soldier, Churchman, Patriot, Man in Pow'r, 4.EpS1.161.309.
Must never Patriot then declaim at Gin, 4.EpS2.191.324.
And see what succour from the Patriot Race. 4.1740.4.332.
He foams a Patriot to subside a Peer; 4.1740.10.332.
Thee shall the Patriot, thee the Courtier taste, 5.DunB3.297.334.
Beholds himself a Patriot, Chief, or Saint. 5.DunB4.536.395.
An honest Courtier, and a Patriot too; 6.27.5.81.
An honest Courtier, yet a Patriot too, 6.57.5.169.
An honest Courtier, and a Patriot too, 6.57.5A.169.
Or add one Patriot to a sinking state; 6.132.4.362.
Here patriot sighs from Wyndham's bosom stole, 6.142.11A.383.
To Wyndham's breast the patriot passion stole 6.142.11H.383.
Inspire some Patriot, and demand debate! Od.2.40.62.

PATRIOT'S
Once, we confess, beneath the Patriot's cloak, 3.Ep3.65.92.
Here, rising bold, the Patriot's honest face; 6.71.57.204.
The Patriot's plain, but untrod path pursue; 6.73.16.210.

PATRIOTS
In vain may Heroes fight, and Patriots rave; 3.Ep3.37.88.
Senates degen'rate, Patriots disagree, 3.Ep3.150.105.
Britain, that pays her Patriots with her Spoils? 3.Ep3.216.111.
Patriots there are, who wish you'd jest no more— 4.EpS1.24.299.
Courtiers and Patriots in two ranks divide, 5.DunB4.107.352.
Such tears, as Patriots shed for dying Laws: 6.32.14.96.
And Patriots still, or Poets, deck the Line. 6.118.14.335.
Such flames, as high in patriots burn, 6.141.9.381.

PATRITIO'S
Who would not praise Patritio's high desert, 3.Ep1.140.26.

PATROCLUS
Patroclus lights, and sternly waits the War. 1.TrES.218.457.
Not so *Patroclus* never-erring Dart; 1.TrES.285.460.
Achilles with *Patroclus* took his Way, Il.1.402.107.
Patroclus haste, the fair *Briseïs* bring; Il.1.438.108.
Patroclus now th'unwilling Beauty brought; Il.1.450.109.
That stern *Achilles* (his *Patroclus* slain) Il.8.593.424.
Patroclus only of the Royal Train, Il.9.251.445.
Then thus— *Patroclus,* crown a larger Bowl, Il.9.267.445.
He said; *Patroclus* o'er the blazing Fire Il.9.271.446.
Mean while *Patroclus* sweats the Fire to raise; Il.9.277.447.
Amidst the greedy Flames *Patroclus* threw; Il.9.288.448.
Last, for *Patroclus* was the Couch prepar'd, Il.9.782.472.
Graceful as *Mars, Patroclus* quits his Tent, Il.11.737.68.
Whate'er thy Will, *Patroclus* shall obey. Il.11.741.68.
Mean time *Patroclus,* by *Achilles* sent, Il.11.788.71.
But thou, *Patroclus!* act a friendly Part, Il.11.962.78.
Patroclus cut the forky Steel away. Il.11.981.79.
Shall send *Patroclus,* but shall send in vain. Il.15.70.199.
Still in the Tent *Patroclus* sate, to tend Il.15.452.215.
Meantime *Patroclus* to *Achilles* flies; Il.16.3.233.
Patroclus, say, what Grief thy Bosom bears, Il.16.9.235.
Another follow'd, and *Patroclus* spoke. Il.16.30.236.
Patroclus! thy *Achilles* knows no Fears; Il.16.68.238.
Go then *Patroclus!* court fair Honour's Charms Il.16.87.238.
Yet now, *Patroclus,* issue to the Plain; Il.16.105.240.
Arm, arm, *Patroclus!* Lo, the Blaze aspires! Il.16.156.244.
Or if a surer, great *Patroclus!* thine. Il.16.233.248.
There, bold *Automedon; Patroclus* here; Il.16.265.249.
Patroclus gone, I stay but half behind. Il.16.297.254.
Then first thy Spear, divine *Patroclus!* flew, Il.16.338.255.
But still the foremost bold *Patroclus* flew: Il.16.365.257.
Fierce on the Rear, with Shouts, *Patroclus* flies; Il.16.448.260.
Patroclus shakes his Lance; but Fate denies. Il.16.463.260.
All grim in Dust and Blood, *Patroclus* stands, Il.16.482.262.
Patroclus mark'd him as he shunn'd the War, Il.16.490.262.
Patroclus lights, and sternly waits the War. Il.16.521.263.
But o'er the Dead the fierce *Patroclus* stands, Il.16.679.270.
Fierce to the Van of Flight *Patroclus* came; Il.16.709.271.
This said, *Patroclus* to the Battel flies; Il.16.763.273.
The radiant Arms are by *Patroclus* born, Il.16.807.274.
Meanwhile *Patroclus* pours along the Plains, Il.16.837.276.
Thrice at the Battlements *Patroclus* strook, Il.16.859.276.
Patroclus! cease: This Heav'n-defended Wall Il.16.863.277.
Patroclus lights, impatient for the Fight; Il.16.891.277.
To spoil the Carcase fierce *Patroclus* flies: Il.16.908.279.
And by the Foot *Patroclus* drags the Dead. Il.16.920.279.
Then rash *Patroclus* with new Fury glows, Il.16.946.280.
Wounded at once, *Patroclus* yields to fear, Il.16.984.281.
Patroclus thus, so many Chiefs o'erthrown, Il.16.999.281.
Lie there *Patroclus!* and with thee, the Joy Il.16.1003.282.
He spoke, *Patroclus* march'd, and thus he sped. Il.16.1015.282.
On the cold Earth divine *Patroclus* spread, Il.17.1.286.
This Hand, *Atrides,* laid *Patroclus* low; Il.17.13.288.
Then shall I quit *Patroclus* on the Plain, Il.17.101.291.
Of his and our *Patroclus—This,* no more, Il.17.113.292.

PATROCLUS (CONTINUED)
Oh! were *Patroclus* ours, we might obtain Il.17.179.294.
Whatever Hand shall win *Patroclus* slain, Il.17.270.298.
And save *Patroclus* from the Dogs of *Troy.* Il.17.301.299.
Such o'er *Patroclus* Body hung the Night, Il.17.426.303.
We lost *Patroclus,* and our Glory lost. Il.17.479.306.
Patroclus, while he liv'd, their Rage cou'd tame, Il.17.544.309.
But now *Patroclus* is an empty Name! Il.17.545.309.
Accept, *Patroclus!* this mean sacrifice. Il.17.605.311.
His Friend, his lov'd *Patroclus,* is no more. Il.17.724.315.
The Foe, he fear'd, might yet *Patroclus* gain, Il.17.751.317.
This is not all: *Patroclus* on the Shore, Il.17.775.318.
Himself returns to his *Patroclus* slain. Il.17.792.319.
Fal'n is the Warrior, and *Patroclus* he! Il.18.16.323.
Dead is *Patroclus!* For his Corps they fight; Il.18.23.324.
Patroclus—Ah!—Say Goddess can I boast Il.18.101.328.
Patroclus, lov'd of all my martial Train, Il.18.103.328.
Patroclus dead, *Achilles* hates to live. Il.18.118.328.
Far lyes *Patroclus* from his native plain! Il.18.127.328.
Ev'n yet, *Patroclus* had he born away, Il.18.201.331.
Assist the Combate, and *Patroclus* save: Il.18.210.332.
Around *Patroclus* mourn'd the *Grecian* Train. Il.18.366.339.
Yet, my *Patroclus!* yet a space I stay, Il.18.389.340.
Where gash'd with cruel Wounds, *Patroclus* lay. Il.19.298.384.
Thou too, *Patroclus!* (thus his Heart he vents) Il.19.335.386.
I hop'd *Patroclus* might survive, to rear Il.19.351.387.
Nor, as ye left *Patroclus,* leave your Lord. Il.19.445.390.
Fell thy *Patroclus,* but by heav'nly Force. Il.19.457.391.
Patroclus dead, whoever meets me, dies: Il.21.112.426.
The great, the good *Patroclus* is no more! Il.21.116.426.
Thus is aton'd *Patroclus* honour'd Shade, Il.21.149.427.
But the rich Mail *Patroclus* lately wore, Il.22.405.472.
Who fear'd no Vengeance for *Patroclus* slain: Il.22.416.472.
Divine *Patroclus!* Death has seal'd his Eyes; Il.22.483.476.
Perform due Honours to *Patroclus* dead. Il.23.12.486.
All hail *Patroclus!* let thy honour'd Ghost Il.23.25.488.
Of sad *Patroclus* rose, or seem'd to rise; Il.23.79.490.
Sleeps my *Achilles,* his *Patroclus* dead? Il.23.84.490.
Amidst, lay dead *Patroclus* on the Bier: Il.23.165.495.
Patroclus decent, on th' appointed Ground Il.23.170.496.
Patroclus bears them to the Shades below. Il.23.189.497.
Thus o'er *Patroclus* while the Hero pray'd, Il.23.190.497.
All hail, *Patroclus!* let thy vengeful Ghost Il.23.220.498.
Nor yet the Pile where dead *Patroclus* lies, Il.23.236.499.
All Night, *Achilles* hails *Patroclus* Soul, Il.23.272.500.
Lost in *Patroclus* now, that wont to deck Il.23.349.503.
In dear Memorial of *Patroclus* dead; Il.23.708.517.
Dead, and for ever lost *Patroclus* lies, Il.23.709.518.
To brave *Patroclus* gave the rich Reward. Il.23.873.524.
And great *Patroclus* in short Triumph bore. Il.23.944.526.
And all his Soul on his *Patroclus* fed: Il.24.10.535.
And thrice *Patroclus!* round thy Monument Il.24.25.536.
There wise *Patroclus,* fill an early grave: Od.3.134.92.
And lov'd *Patroclus* still attends his shade. Od.24.28.348.
With dear *Patroclus,* the departed friend: Od.24.98.353.

PATROCLUS'
His Life is ow'd to fierce *Patroclus'* Hands. 1.TrES.230.458.
From strong *Patroclus'* Hand the Jav'lin fled, 1.TrES.263.459.
Here *Hector* glorious from *Patroclus'* Fall, 2.TemF.190.271.
Divine Compassion touch'd *Patroclus'* Breast, Il.11.946.77.
Meanwhile the Troops beneath *Patroclus'* Care, Il.16.312.254.
Their rising Rage *Patroclus'* Breath inspires, Il.16.322.255.
Patroclus' Arm forbids the spreading Fires, Il.16.348.256.
His Life is ow'd to fierce *Patroclus'* Hands. Il.16.533.264.
From strong *Patroclus'* Hand the Javelin fled, Il.16.568.266.
Not so *Patroclus'* never erring Dart; Il.16.590.267.
Stretch'd by *Patroclus'* Arm on yonder Plains, Il.16.667.270.
The Force of *Hector* to *Patroclus'* Fall, Il.16.788.274.
Patroclus' Ships the glorious Spoils adorn. Il.16.808.274.
And in *Patroclus'* Blood efface thy Shame. Il.16.882.277.
Nor tho' disarm'd, *Patroclus'* Fury stood: Il.16.980.281.
Haste, and *Patroclus'* lov'd Remains defend: Il.17.130.292.
He drops *Patroclus'* Foot, and o'er him spread Il.17.344.301.
He, yet unconscious of *Patroclus'* Fall, Il.17.464.305.
(Won by his own, or by *Patroclus'* Arms) Il.18.34.325.
Nor yet their Chiefs *Patroclus'* Body bore Il.18.187.331.
Stretch'd o'er *Patroclus'* Corse; while all the rest Il.19.7.371.
Nor mourn'd *Patroclus'* Fortunes, but their own. Il.19.322.385.
Sad Victims! destin'd to *Patroclus'* Shade. Il.21.39.423.
With his, who wrought thy lov'd *Patroclus'* Death. Il.21.108.426.
Shall view *Patroclus'* and *Achilles'* Tomb. Il.23.157.495.
Let on *Patroclus'* Pile your Blast be driv'n, Il.23.260.499.
(The self-same Place beside *Patroclus'* Pyre, Il.23.909.525.
He groans, and calls on lov'd *Patroclus'* Shade. Il.24.739.568.
Advanc'd *Achilles'* and *Patroclus'* ghost, Od.11.576.411.

PATRON
As his mistaken Patron to advise, 2.ChJM.163.23.
His own strict Judge, and Patron of Mankind. 2.TemF.167.268.
All feed on one vain Patron, and enjoy 3.EOM3.61.98.
"I want a Patron; ask him for a Place." 4.Arbu.50.100.
May some choice Patron bless each gray goose quill! 4.Arbu.249.114.
Above a Patron, tho' I condescend 4.Arbu.265.114.
While You, great Patron of Mankind, sustain 4.2HE1.1.195.
"He wins this Patron who can tickle best." 5.DunA2.188.124.
"He wins this Patron, who can tickle best." 5.DunB2.196.305.
Would his best Patron let his Pen 6.102.3.294.
What Patron this, a doubt must be 6.102.5.294.
Patron of Arts, and Judge of Nature, dy'd! 6.118.2.334.
This done, the Patron of the Silver Bow Il.5.545.294.
To *Phœbus,* Patron of the Shaft and Bow. Il.23.1023.529.
Then hear, ye Gods! the Patron of the Bow. Il.24.73.538.
From *Pæon* sprung, their patron-god imparts Od.4.321.134.
Patron of industry and manual arts: Od.15.337.86.
Beneath *Eurymachus,* his patron lord, Od.17.308.146.

PATRON (CONTINUED)
And distant tongues extoll the patron-name. ...Od.19.386.212.
Hermes his Patron-god those gifts bestow'd, ...Od.19.468.219.
So shall the patron of these arts bestow ...Od.21.284.273.

PATRON-GOD
From *Pæon* sprung, their patron-god imparts ...Od.4.321.134.
Hermes his Patron-god those gifts bestow'd, ...Od.19.468.219.

PATRON-NAME
And distant tongues extoll the patron-name. ...Od.19.386.212.

PATRON'S
When half his Nose is in his Patron's Ear. ...4.JD4.179.41.
That Fop whose pride affects a Patron's name, ...4.Arbu.291.116.
The Fop whose pride affects a Patron's name, ...4.Arbu.291A.116.
For which thy Patron's weekly thank'd: ...6.39.8.110.
The *Fop*, whose Pride affects a *Patron's* name, ...6.120.1.339.

PATRONIZ'D
Who rhym'd for hire, and patroniz'd for pride. ...5.DunB4.102.351.

PATRONS
Patrons, who sneak from living worth to dead, ...5.DunB4.95.350.

PATS
Gay pats my shoulder, and you vanish quite; ...6.45.47.126.

PATTERN
O Fairest Pattern to a failing Age! ...6.134.1.364.
Consummate pattern of imperial sway, ...Od.19.129.199.

PATTY
—But why? ah PATTY, still too dear! ...4.HOde1.37C.153.

PAUL
Paul, knowing One cou'd never serve our Turn, ...2.ChWB.28.58.
For so said *Paul*, and *Paul's* a sound Divine. ...2.ChWB.55.59.
Hark old Sir *Paul* ('twas thus I us'd to say) ...2.ChWB.74.60.
"Why,—if I must—(then wept) I give it Paul." ...3.Ep1.259.37.
Should rise, and say—"Sir *Robert!* or Sir *Paul!* ...4.HAdv.88.83.
Sometimes, with Aristippus, or St. Paul, ...4.1HE1.31.281.
From low St. James's up to high St. Paul; ...4.1HE1.82.285.
No more than Sir Har[r]y or Sir P[aul]. ...4.1740.20.333*.
Lo here the *Septuagint,—and Paul,* ...6.39.15.110.

PAUL'S
Nor is *Paul's Church* more safe than *Paul's Church-yard:* ...1.EOC.623.310.
Nor is *Paul's Church* more safe than *Paul's Church-yard:* ...1.EOC.623.310.
For so said *Paul,* and *Paul's* a sound Divine. ...2.ChWB.55.59.
There, all from Paul's to Aldgate drink and sleep. ...5.DunB2.346.314.

PAULO'S
Paulo's free stroke, and *Titian's* warmth divine. ...6.52.38.157.

PAUNCH
(Reply'd soft Annius) this our paunch before ...5.DunB4.388.380.
With Paunch distended, and with lolling Tongue, ...Il.16.199.247.

PAUS'D
Tydides paus'd amidst his full Carrier; ...Il.5.732.302.
Now paus'd the Battel, (Godlike *Hector* gone) ...Il.6.147.331.
Ev'n *Hector* paus'd, and with new Doubt opprest ...Il.7.261.377.
He paus'd, and these pacific Words ensue. ...Il.7.443.386.
Here paus'd a moment, while the gentle Gale ...Il.11.760.69.
Ev'n *Ajax* paus'd (so thick the Javelins fly) ...Il.15.882.231.
Here paus'd the God, and pensive thus replies ...Od.1.55.3.
But when the music paus'd, he ceas'd to shed ...Od.8.83.267.
Whilst yet the Monarch paus'd, with doubts opprest, ...Od.15.190.77.
The Heroe paus'd, and ponder'd this request, ...Od.15.228.79.
Graceful a-while he paus'd, then mildly said. ...Od.16.415.126.

PAUSE
Snuff, or the *Fan,* supply each Pause of Chat, ...2.RL3.17.170.
As breathe, or pause, by fits, the airs divine: ...5.DunA2.362.143.
As breathe, or pause, by fits, the airs divine. ...5.DunB2.394.316.
No Pause of Words admits, no dull Delay; ...Il.5.632.298.
And Nature speaks at ev'ry Pause of Art. ...Il.24.905.574.
Words to her dumb complaint a pause supplies, ...Od.4.954.162.
A pause of silence hush'd the shady rooms: ...Od.13.3.1.
A pause inspiriting her languish'd pow'rs, ...Od.19.287.209.
A gloomy pause ensu'd of dumb despair; ...Od.20.70.235.

PAUSES
The musing Monarch pauses at the door: ...Od.17.395.151.

PAUSING
Then deeply thoughtful, pausing e'er he spoke, ...Il.2.346.143.
Then *Hector* pausing, as his Eyes he fed ...Il.16.1036.283.

PAV'D
Streets pav'd with Heroes, Tyber choak'd with Gods! ...5.DunA3.100.158.
Streets pav'd with Heroes, Tyber choak'd with Gods: ...5.DunB3.108.325.

PAVEMENT
Perpetual Waters o'er the Pavement glide; ...1.TrUl.41.467.
With various-colour'd Light the Pavement shone, ...2.TemF.254.275.
And on the broken Pavement here and there, ...6.14ii.10.43.
Flows on the Pavement of the Court of *Jove.* ...Il.5.907.309.
And stain the Pavement of my regal Hall; ...Il.22.95.456.
The rocky Pavement glitter'd with the Show. ...Il.23.249.499.
On the mid Pavement pours the rosy Wine, ...Il.24.375.551.
(A purple carpet spread the pavement wide) ...Od.1.173.40.
The pavement swims with brains and mingled gore. ...Od.9.345.320.
His batter'd brains shou'd on the pavement smoke. ...Od.9.540.328.
The vaulted roofs and solid pavement rung. ...Od.10.255.355.

PAVEMENT (CONTINUED)
And o'er the pavement floats the dreadful tyde— ...Od.11.524.409.
Perpetual waters o'er the pavement glide; ...Od.13.132.8.
The marble pavement with his step resounds: ...Od.17.38.134.
Or greet the pavement with his worthless head? ...Od.17.277.145.
Then o'er the pavement glides with grace divine, ...Od.21.43.261.
And spreads the pavement with a mingled flood ...Od.22.25.287.
And down reluctant on the pavement threw. ...Od.22.204.297.
Drop harmless, on the pavement sounding dead. ...Od.22.305.301.
Along the pavement roll'd the mutt'ring head. ...Od.22.366.305.

PAVEMENTS
How wide the pavements float with guilty gore! ...Od.13.452.28.
(With polish'd oak the level pavements shine) ...Od.21.44.261.

PAVILION
Strait to *Tydides'* high Pavilion born, ...Il.10.666.31.
In his pavilion there to sleep repairs; ...Od.1.539.57.
The warm pavilion of a dreadful boar. ...Od.19.516.221.

PAVILION'D
Abides, pavilion'd on the grassy plain. ...Od.4.560.147.
As thus pavilion'd in the porch he lay, ...Od.20.9.230.

PAVILIONS
Its bright Pavilions in a Veil of Clouds. ...1.TrSt.172.417.

PAVILLIONS
The rich Pavillions of his fifty Sons, ...Il.6.307.341.

PAW
"Trembling, I've seen thee dare the Kitten's Paw; ...6.96ii.27.271.
Paw with his Hoofs aloft, and lash the Air. ...Il.8.108.403.
Just on the Brink, they neigh, and paw the Ground, ...Il.12.59.83.

PAW'D
Rowl'd in the bloody Dust, and paw'd the slipp'ry Ground. ...1.TrES.272.459.
Rowl'd in the bloody dust, and paw'd the slip'ry ground. ...Il.16.577.267.

PAWING
And pawing, seems to beat the distant Plain, ...1.W-F.152.164.

PAWN'D
I pawn'd my Honour and ingag'd my Vow, ...2.ChWB.293.71.
Who, having lost his Credit, pawn'd his Rent, ...4.JD4.138.37.

PAWS
So lyes a Bull beneath the Lion's Paws, ...1.TrES.296.460.
See how they pat thee with their pretty Paws: ...6.96iv.15.276.
So lies a Bull beneath the Lion's Paws, ...Il.16.601.267.

PAXTON
Fr. Tis all a Libel— *Paxton* (Sir) will say. ...4.EpS2.1.313.
When *Paxton* gives him double Pots and Pay, ...4.EpS2.141.321.

PAY
With Heads declin'd, ye Cedars, Homage pay; ...1.Mes.35.116.
We to thy Name our Annual Rites will pay, ...1.TrSt.592.435.
But sav'd from Death, our *Argives* yearly pay ...1.TrSt.662.438.
The Life which others pay, let Us bestow, ...1.TrES.49.451.
Let my good Spouse pay Tribute, do me Right, ...2.ChWB.52.59.
To pay due Visits, and address the Fair: ...2.TemF.385.282.
Thou, *Abelard!* the last sad office pay, ...2.ElAb.321.345.
Where only Merit constant pay receives, ...3.EOM4.313.158.
For very want; he could not pay a dow'r. ...3.Ep3.326.120.
Could not but think, to pay his *Fine* was odd, ...4.JD4.17.27.
As deep in *Debt,* without a thought to pay, ...4.JD4.21.27.
Pay their last Duty to the *Court,* and come ...4.JD4.214.45.
Nor stops, for one bad Cork, his Butler's pay, ...4.HS2.63.59.
Than not to wait too long, nor pay too dear. ...4.HAdv.160.89.
There are, who to my Person pay their court, ...4.Arbu.115.104.
I pay my Debts, believe, and say my Pray'rs, ...4.Arbu.268.114.
I pay my Debts, believe, and go to Pray'rs, ...4.Arbu.268A.114.
You pay a Penny, and he paid a Pound. ...4.2HE2.239.181.
Why one like *Bu*— with Pay and Scorn content, ...4.2HE2.274.185.
And pay the Great our homage of Amaze? ...4.1HE6.17.237.
"When are the Troops to have their pay? ...4.HS6.120.257.
To pay their Debts or keep their Faith like Kings? ...4.EpS1.122.307.
When *Paxton* gives him double Pots and Pay, ...4.EpS2.141.321.
To see a Footman kick'd that took his pay: ...4.EpS2.151.322.
G[owe]r, C[obha]m, B[athurs]t, pay thee due regards, ...4.1740.23.333.
From dreams of millions, and three groats to pay! ...5.DunA2.242.129.
From dreams of millions, and three groats to pay. ...5.DunB2.252.307.
Who pay her homage in her sons, the Great; ...5.DunB4.92.349.
Last to *yourself* my best Respects I pay, ...6.13.29.40.
Aukward and supple, each Devoir to pay, ...6.49i.17.138.
Is this the Pay our Blood and Toils deserve, ...Il.1.211.97.
Or barren Praises pay the Wounds of War. ...Il.1.220.97.
And pay in Glory what in Life you owe. ...Il.1.655.118.
Th' appointed Fine let *Ilion* justly pay, ...Il.3.360.210.
Th' appointed Fine let *Ilion* justly pay, ...Il.3.573.219.
And swear the Firstlings of thy Flock to pay ...Il.4.133.226.
And pay due Vows to all the Gods around. ...Il.6.324.240.
No, die, and pay the Forfeit of your Race. ...Il.11.184.43.
Whole Hecatombs of *Trojan* Ghosts shall pay. ...Il.11.472.55.
The Life which others pay, let us bestow. ...Il.12.393.96.
Pay the large Debt of last revolving Sun; ...Il.13.936.149.
Yet *Jove* deferr'd the Death he was to pay, ...Il.15.738.224.
And pay the Forfeit of their haughty Lord? ...Il.16.26.236.
And pay the Forfeit of their guilty Sire. ...Il.16.393.258.
For such Desert what Service can I pay? ...Il.18.474.344.
Enough, when Death demands the Brave, to pay ...Il.19.229.382.
Till yonder Sun descend, ah let me pay ...Il.19.327.386.
Whole Hecatombs of *Trojan* Ghosts shall pay. ...Il.20.524.416.
But not till *Troy* the destin'd Vengeance pay, ...Il.21.242.431.
Will learn their Rashness, when they pay the Price. ...Il.23.571.512.

PAY (CONTINUED)
Fortune denies, but Justice bids us pay .... Il.23.614.514.
Those due distinctions thou so well can't pay, ... Il.23.749.520.
Shall pay the Stroke, and grace the Striker's Side: .... Il.23.953.527.
(The only Honours Men to Gods can pay) .... Il.24.90.539.
Ere long shall pay—their forfeit lives the price. .... Od.2.270.74.
The sacred rites and hecatombs to pay, ... Od.3.176.94.
There land, and pay due victims to the pow'rs: .... Od.3.192.95.
To pay whose honours to the Shades of hell .... Od.3.361.104.
His sons around him mild obeysance pay, ... Od.3.524.113.
I'll pay my brother's ghost a warrior's due, ... Od.4.274.132.
Due ritual honours to the Gods I pay: .... Od.4.588.147.
Pay due devotions to the *martial maid, ... Od.4.991.163.
But to *Jove's* will submission we must pay; .... Od.5.129.178.
Let first the herald due libation pay .... Od.7.220.247.
Let all around the due libation pay .... Od.7.240.248.
Must pay the penalty for lawless charms. .... Od.8.372.284.
Pay low obeysance as he moves along: .... Od.8.516.290.
His double toils may claim a double pay, ... Od.10.99.345.
To worth in misery a rev'rence pay, ... Od.11.424.405.
Expect me with the morn, to pay the skies .... Od.15.545.96.
Well pleas'd the hospitable rites to pay. .... Od.15.586.98.
Or pay due honours to the nuptial bed? .... Od.16.74.106.
Thy head shall pay the forfeit of thy tongue! .... Od.19.116.198.
Who-e'er neglects to pay distinction due, ... Od.19.370.212.
Now, pay the debt to craving nature due, ... Od.20.63.235.
And pay the menials for the master's treat. .... Od.20.364.250.
Two hundred oxen ev'ry Prince shall pay: .... Od.22.69.290.
To Gods alone, and god-like worth, we pay. .... Od.22.386.307.
And let thy son attest, nor sordid pay .... Od.22.391.307.
Condemn'd to pay the great arrear so soon, ... Od.24.41.349.

PAY'D
The Gallant too, to whom she pay'd it down, ... 4.HAdv.9.75.
He pay'd some Bards with Port, and some with Praise, ... 4.Arbu.242.113.
And others (harder still) he pay'd in kind. .... 4.Arbu.244.113.
To *Cato, Virgil* pay'd one honest line; .... 4.EpS2.120.320.
For God is pay'd when Man receives, ... 6.50.19.146.
For Heav'n is pay'd when Man receives, ... 6.50.19A.146.
The just Partition, and due Victims pay'd. .... Il.11.841.73.
And how the Murd'rer pay'd his forfeit breath; .... Od.3.236.97.
Soon as due vows on ev'ry part were pay'd, ... Od.3.568.115.
Yet as we fled, our fellows rites we pay'd, ... Od.9.73.305.
Soon as the morn restor'd the day, we pay'd .... Od.12.11.430.
Where constant vows by travellers are pay'd, ... Od.17.244.143.
Justly the price of worthlessness they pay'd, ... Od.22.454.310.

PAYS
And pays in hollow Rocks his awful Vows, ... 1.TrSt.862.446.
She dearly pays for *Nisus'* injur'd Hair! .... 2.RL3.124.177.
Shall shortly want the gen'rous tear he pays; .... 2.Elegy.78.368.
Part pays, and justly, the deserving steer: .... 3.EOM3.40.96.
Shall find, the pleasure pays not half the pain. .... 3.EOM4.48.132.
When universal homage Umbra pays, ... 3.Ep1.118.24.
Britain, that pays her Patriots with her Spoils? .... 3.Ep3.216.111.
Run out as fast, as one that pays his Bail, ... 4.JD4.182A.41.
Ran out as fast, as one that pays his Bail, ... 4.JD4.182.41.
Who neither writes nor pays for what is writ .... 4.JD2A.110.142.
To Thee, the World its present homage pays, ... 4.2HE1.23.195.
And pays prodigious dear for—Sense. .... 6.29.26.83.
This more than pays whole years of thankless pain; .... 6.63.5.188.
And one that pays reckning .... 6.68.3.196.
Pays the last Tribute of a Saint to Heav'n. .... 6.132.14.362.
And ill he pays the Promise of a God; .... Il.1.465.110.
Then each to Heav'n the due Libations pays; .... Il.9.835.474.
He pays due Vengeance to his Kinsman's Shade. .... Il.16.704.271.
Who, sinking now with Age, and Sorrow, pays .... Il.18.507.346.
Blest is the Man who pays the Gods above .... Il.24.519.557.
When, for the dear delight, another pays. .... Od.1.206.42.
Who takes the kind, and pays th' ungrateful part; .... Od.8.242.275.
In sacred groves celestial rites he pays, ... Od.11.223.392.
So pays the wretch, whom fact constrains to roam, ... Od.19.192.201.
And pays his host with hideous noon-day dreams. .... Od.20.454.255.

PEA
Except on *Pea-Chicks*, at the *Bedford-head?* .... 4.HAdv.150.87.

PEA-CHICKS
Except on *Pea-Chicks*, at the *Bedford-head?* .... 4.HAdv.150.87.

PEACE
Peace o'er the World her Olive-Wand extend, ... 1.Mes.19.114.
And Peace and Plenty tell, a STUART reigns. .... 1.W-F.42.152.
She said, the World obey'd, and all was *Peace!* .... 1.W-F.328.181.
Hail Sacred *Peace!* hail long-expected Days, ... 1.W-F.355.185.
And Temples rise, the beauteous Works of Peace. .... 1.W-F.378.187.
Oh stretch thy Reign, fair *Peace!* from Shore to Shore, ... 1.W-F.407.192.
Where Peace descending bids her Olives spring, ... 1.W-F.429.194.
Scotists and *Thomists*, now, in Peace remain, ... 1.EOC.444.289.
And sacred Silence reigns, and universal Peace. .... 1.TrSt.291.422.
Blest with calm Peace in his declining Days, ... 1.TrSt.540.433.
Sleep fled his Eyes, and Peace forsook his Breast; .... 2.ChJM.393.34.
Well, I may make my Will in Peace, and die, ... 2.ChWB.178.65.
When Merchants from th' *Exchange* return in Peace, ... 2.RL*A*1.87.129.
While her rackt Soul Repose and Peace requires, ... 2.RL*A*2.11.132.
The Merchant from th' *Exchange* returns in Peace, ... 2.RL3.23.170.
Nor ever Silence, Rest or Peace is here. .... 2.TemF.435.284.
Of Peace and War, Health, Sickness, Death, and Life; .... 2.TemF.449.285.
The joy, the peace, the glory of Mankind. .... 3.EOM2.248.85.
All Nature's diff'rence keeps all Nature's peace. .... 3.EOM4.56.133.
Lie in three words, Health, Peace, and Competence. .... 3.EOM4.80.136.
And Peace, oh Virtue! Peace is all thy own. .... 3.EOM4.82.136.
And Peace, oh Virtue! Peace is all thy own. .... 3.EOM4.82.136.
And Peace, fair Virtue! Peace is all thy own. .... 3.EOM4.82A.136.
And Peace, fair Virtue! Peace is all thy own. .... 3.EOM4.82A.136.
And Peace, O Virtue! Peace is all thy own. .... 3.EOM4.82B.136.

PEACE (CONTINUED)
And Peace, O Virtue! Peace is all thy own. .... 3.EOM4.82B.136.
No thought of Peace or Happiness at home. .... 3.Ep2.224.68.
To buy both sides, and give thy Country peace. .... 3.Ep3.152.106.
His Father's Acres who enjoys in peace, ... 3.Ep4.181.154.
These Honours, Peace to happy Britain brings, ... 3.Ep4.203.156.
Peace is my dear Delight—not *Fleury's* more: .... 4.HS1.75.11.
Shall walk in peace and credit to the grave. .... 4.HS1.120A.17.
Shall walk in peace, and credit, to his grave. .... 4.HS1.120C.17.
Secure of Peace at least beyond the Grave. .... 4.JD4.4.27.
Peace, Fools! or *Gonson* will for Papists seize you, ... 4.JD4.256.47.
In Peace provides fit arms against a War? .... 4.HS2.128.65.
Peace to all such! but were there One whose fires .... 4.Arbu.193.109.
But he, who hurts a harmless neighbour's peace, ... 4.Arbu.287.116.
He stuck to Poverty with Peace of Mind; .... 4.2HE2.65.169.
Much do I suffer, much, to keep in peace .... 4.2HE2.147.175.
Verse prays for Peace, or sings down Pope and Turk. .... 4.2HE1.236.215.
Your Country's Peace, how oft, how dearly bought! .... 4.2HE1.397.229.
Peace stole her wing, and wrapt the world in sleep; .... 4.2HE1.401.229.
In peace, great Goddess! ever be ador'd; .... 5.DunA3.111.160.
In peace, great Goddess, ever be ador'd; .... 5.DunB3.119.325.
In health of body, peace of mind, ... 6.1.11.3.
All rest in Peace at last, and sleep eternally. .... 6.8.42.19.
To talk of War, and live in Peace; .... 6.10.42.25.
And soften'd Mortals learn'd the Arts of Peace. .... 6.11.35Z2.31.
With *Envy*, (spitting Cat,) dread Foe to Peace: .... 6.14ii.34.44.
That interrupt our Peace, and work our Woe: .... 6.17iii.5.57.
Beholds them cheary eat the Bread of Peace: .... 6.17iii.35.58.
Content at last to leave the World in Peace. .... 6.17iv.8.59.
This Year in Peace, ye Critics, dwell, ... 6.47.3.128.
This day, be Bread and Peace my Lot; .... 6.50.45.148.
In health of body, and in peace of mind: .... 6.55.1Z4.167.
A love to peace, and hate of tyranny; .... 6.57.10.169.
Peace to thy gentle shade, and endless Rest! .... 6.72.5.208.
Peace to all such! but were there one, whose Fires .... 6.98.43.284.
Lover of peace, and friend of human kind: .... 6.109.8.314.
Content with Science in the Vale of Peace. .... 6.112.6.318.
Content with Science in the arms of Peace. .... 6.112.6A.318.
In peace let one poor Poet sleep, ... 6.138.2.376.
'Twas a fat Oyster——Live in Peace——Adieu. .... 6.145.12.388.
Peace, blubbring Bishop! peace thou flattring Dean! .... 6.147iii.3.390.
Peace, blubbring Bishop! peace thou flattring Dean! .... 6.147iii.3.390.
Peace to thy gentle Shade, and endless Rest! .... 6.152.7.400.
But part in Peace, secure thy Pray'r is sped: .... Il.1.678.119.
Peace at his Heart, and Pleasure his Design, ... Il.1.740.122.
We, in eternal Peace and constant Joy. .... Il.1.745.123.
In Peace enjoy the Fruits of broken Vows? .... Il.2.196.137.
And a still Silence lulls the Camp to Peace. .... Il.2.254.139.
Peace, factious Monster, born to vex the State, ... Il.2.306.142.
And *Troy* possess her fertile Fields in Peace; .... Il.3.106.194.
And diff'ring Nations part in Leagues of Peace. .... Il.3.132.196.
And *Troy* possess her fertile Fields in Peace; .... Il.3.327.208.
And joyful Nations join in Leagues of Peace. .... Il.3.401.211.
Shall Heav'n by Peace the bleeding Kingdoms spare, ... Il.4.21.222.
So let it be, and *Jove* his Peace enjoy, ... Il.4.59.223.
And the proud *Trojans* first infringe the Peace. .... Il.4.94.225.
Jove, the great Arbiter of Peace and Wars! .... Il.4.114.226.
The Peace infring'd, nor heard the Sounds of War; .... Il.4.385.239.
My Treasures too, for Peace, I will resign; .... Il.7.438.386.
Of added *Trojan* Wealth to buy the Peace. .... Il.7.467.387.
Then thus the King of Kings rejects the Peace: .... Il.7.482.388.
The Peace rejected, but the Truce obtain'd. .... Il.7.493.388.
Nor with new Treaties vex my Peace in vain. .... Il.9.411.452.
Your mighty Monarch these in Peace possest; .... Il.9.436.454.
Or *Troy* once held, in Peace and Pride of Sway, ... Il.9.526.459.
But found no Peace from fierce *Althæa's* Hate: .... Il.9.680.468.
That old in Arms, disdain'd the Peace of Age. .... Il.10.87.6.
Peace was his Charge; receiv'd with peaceful Show, ... Il.10.341.18.
Regard thy Safety, and depart in Peace; .... Il.10.595.28.
The Gods in peace their golden Mansions fill, ... Il.11.103.39.
For proffer'd Peace! And sues his Seed for Grace? .... Il.11.183.43.
In Peace and War, in Council, and in Fight; .... Il.12.250.90.
Which held so long that ancient Pair in Peace. .... Il.14.238.172.
Which held so long this ancient Pair in Peace. .... Il.14.348.179.
In Peace, in War, for ever at his side, ... Il.15.504.216.
In ev'ry Virtue, or of Peace or War: .... Il.15.777.226.
In Peace his Friend, and Part'ner of the War) .... Il.16.180.245.
The Image one of Peace, and one of War. .... Il.18.568.350.
And treat on Terms of Peace to save the Town: .... Il.22.157.459.
May share our Wealth, and leave our Walls in Peace. .... Il.22.163.459.
Wash'd their fair Garments in the Days of Peace. .... Il.22.204.464.
Oh had thy gentle Spirit past in Peace, ... Il.22.544.479.
In peace and joy, the people's rightful Lord; .... Od.1.153.40.
Your patrimonial stores in peace possess; .... Od.1.511.56.
Peace the blest land, and joys incessant crown; .... Od.2.51.62.
The wanton youth inglorious peace enjoy'd; .... Od.3.325.102.
Brothers in peace, not rivals in command, ... Od.4.243.130.
To know, what known will violate thy peace: .... Od.4.662.150.
In peace shall land thee at thy native home. .... Od.5.220.182.
The seat of Gods, the regions mild of peace, ... Od.6.49.207.
To thy calm hours continu'd peace afford, ... Od.8.449.287.
Hear the sweet song, and taste the feast in peace. .... Od.8.464.288.
Sheath thy bright sword, and join our hands in peace; .... Od.10.396.363.
My consort blameless, and my friends in peace. .... Od.13.55.4.
The foes of peace, and scourges of mankind, ... Od.14.104.41.
But works of peace my soul disdain'd to bear, ... Od.14.259.48.
In *Egypt* thus with peace and plenty blest, ... Od.14.315.50.
But both in constant peace one Prince obey, ... Od.15.454.92.
And here at least I may in peace repose. .... Od.16.143.109.
Peace wretch! and eat thy bread without offence, ... Od.17.568.160.
Shall her pleas'd ear receive my words in peace. .... Od.17.655.164.
In peace away! lest if persuasions fail, ... Od.18.18.167.
Studious of peace; and *Æthon* is my name. .... Od.19.214.203.
Lest arms avenge the violated peace. .... Od.20.333.249.
Give heav'n this day, and rest the bow in peace. .... Od.21.297.274.
Thou, with the heav'n-taught bard, in peace resort .... Od.22.415.308.

PEACE (CONTINUED)

Be deck'd the couch! and peace a-while, my woes! ....Od.23.272.336.
Then heav'n decrees in peace to end my days, ...Od.23.297.337.
Let all be peace.—He said, and gave the nod ....Od.24.560.375.
"From mutual slaughter: *Peace* descends to spare." ....Od.24.615.377.
Offend not *Jove:* Obey, and give the peace. ....Od.24.627.377.

PEACEABLY

Or peaceably forgot, at once be blest ....5.DunB1.239.287.

PEACEFUL

Nor saw displeas'd the peaceful Cottage rise. ....1.W-F.86.158.
Be mine the Blessings of a peaceful Reign. ....1.W-F.366.186.
Musick has Charms alone for peaceful Minds: ....1.TrSP.14.393.
Ere such a soul regains its peaceful state, ...2.ElAb.197.336.
So peaceful rests, without a stone, a name, ...2.Elegy.69.368.
As the small pebble stirs the peaceful lake; ....3.EOM4.364.164.
Pleas'd let me own, in *Esher's* peaceful Grove ....4.EpS2.66.316.
Ah! still o'er Britain stretch that peaceful wand, ...5.DunA1.155.82.
Peaceful sleep out the Sabbath of the Tomb, ...6.86.19.246.
Few Leagues remov'd, we wish our peaceful Seat, ...Il.2.358.144.
And rules them peaceful in a foreign Land; ....Il.2.810.163.
And peaceful Prospects dawn in ev'ry Breast. ....Il.3.154.198.
The *Phrygian* Monarch to the Peaceful Rite, ...Il.3.162.198.
Still *Priam's* Walls in peaceful Honours grow, ...Il.4.25.222.
A peaceful Guest, he sought *Mycenæ's* Tow'rs; ....Il.4.431.241.
And peaceful sleeps the liquid Element, ...Il.5.644.299.
Between the Swords their peaceful Sceptres rear'd; ....Il.7.335.380.
Obey the Night, and use her peaceful Hours ....Il.8.627.425.
A peaceful Death in *Pthia's* friendly Land. ....Il.9.553.460.
Peace was his Charge; receiv'd with peaceful Show, ...Il.10.341.18.
Peaceful He sleeps, with all our Rites adorn'd, ...Il.22.421.472.
Expells him helpless from his peaceful State; ....Il.24.605.562.
But now the peaceful Hours of sacred Night ....Il.24.753.568.
And peaceful slept the mighty *Hector's* Shade. ....Il.24.1016.577.
Where seemly rang'd in peaceful order stood ....Od.1.169.40.
And peaceful slumbers close my mother's eyes, ...Od.2.403.80.
Nor peaceful port was there, nor winding bay, ...Od.5.518.197.
And peaceful slumbers calm'd his anxious breast; ....Od.6.2.203.
Crown, oh ye heav'ns, with joy his peaceful hours, ...Od.8.445.287.
How sweet the products of a peaceful reign? ....Od.9.3.298.
Some God directing, to this peaceful bay ....Od.10.165.348.
And the possession of a peaceful grave. ....Od.11.90.385.
So peaceful shalt thou end thy blissful days, ...Od.11.164.389.
Turn then, oh peaceful turn, thy wrath controul, ...Od.11.689.418.
And grant me peaceful to my realms again. ....Od.12.400.450.
With him, rest peaceful in the rural cell, ...Od.13.473.29.
Than when two friends, alone, in peaceful place ....Od.14.222.46.
Suggest, that *Jove* the peaceful thought inspir'd, ...Od.19.13.193.
What time the sun, from ocean's peaceful stream, ...Od.19.505.221.
Thus anchor'd safe on reason's peaceful coast, ...Od.20.29.233.
Because the Priest is born a peaceful slave. ....Od.21.180.268.
Or peaceful amity, or stern debate? ....Od.24.545.374.

PEACH'S

"Or sunk within the Peach's Down, repose? ....6.96ii.46.273.

PEAL

Booth enters—hark! the Universal Peal! ....4.2HE1.334.223.

PEAL'D

There Webster! peal'd thy voice, and Whitfield! thine. ....5.DunB2.258.308.

PEALS

Let Peals of Laughter, *Codrus!* round thee break, ...4.Arbu.85.101.
In Peals of Thunder now she roars, and now ....6.96ii.9.270.
Like Peals of Thunder now she roars, and now ....6.96ii.9A.270.
On all sides thick, the Peals of Arms resound. ....Il.13.699.138.
And Peals of Thunder shook the Firmament, ...Il.15.437.214.
But now in Peals of Thunder calls to Arms; ....Il.15.877.230.
And Peals on Peals redoubled rend the Poles. ....Il.20.76.397.
And Peals on Peals redoubled rend the Poles. ....Il.20.76.397.
From the pleas'd Crowd new Peals of Thunder rise, ...Il.23.1042.530.

PEAR

And singled out a Pear-Tree planted nigh: ....2.ChJM.602.44.
By easier Steps, to where the Pear-Tree grew: ....2.ChJM.717.49.
The branch here bends beneath the weighty pear, ...6.35.9.103.
Each dropping pear a following pear supplies, ...6.35.13.103.
Each dropping pear a following pear supplies, ...6.35.13.103.
The branch here bends beneath the weighty pear, ...Od.7.150.243.
Each dropping pear a following pear supplies, ...Od.7.154.243.
Each dropping pear a following pear supplies, ...Od.7.154.243.
The olive green, blue fig, and pendent pear; ....Od.24.290.363.
Twelve pear-trees bowing with their pendent load, ...Od.24.395.368.

PEAR-TREE

And singled out a Pear-Tree planted nigh: ....2.ChJM.602.44.
By easier Steps, to where the Pear-Tree grew: ....2.ChJM.717.49.

PEAR-TREES

Twelve pear-trees bowing with their pendent load, ...Od.24.395.368.

PEARLS

Now hung with Pearls the dropping Trees appear, ...1.PWi.31.91.
Thy branches hung with humid pearls appear, ...1.TrFD.65.388.
In flow'rs and pearls by bounteous Kirkall dress'd. ....5.DunA2.152.120.
Pearls on her neck, and roses in her hair, ...5.DunA2.152Z1.120.
In flow'rs and pearls by bounteous Kirkall dress'd. ....5.DunB2.160.303.
In Di'monds, Pearls, and rich Brocades, ...6.14v(b).16.50.

PEARLY

The Pearly Shell its lucid Glove infold, ...1.W-F.395.190.
Her airy Chariot, hung with Pearly Dew; ....1.TrSt.477.430.
Bright *Galatea* quits her pearly Bed: ....Il.18.60.326.

PEARS

And hung with dangling Pears was ev'ry Bough. ....2.ChJM.604.44.
There dangling pears exalted scents unfold, ...Od.11.729.421.

PEASANT

"An't please your Honour, quoth the Peasant, ...4.HS6.220.263.
"Now please your Honour, quoth the Peasant, ...4.HS6.220A.263.
So when a Peasant to his Garden brings ....Il.21.289.432.
Me, as some needy peasant, would ye leave, ...Od.3.447.108.
As some poor peasant, fated to reside ....Od.5.630.202.

PEASANT'S

Yet not ungrateful to the Peasant's Pain, ...1.TrUl.124.470.
Yet not ungrateful to the peasant's pain, ...Od.13.291.19.

PEASANTS

Peasants in vain with threatning cries pursue, ...Od.15.182.77.

PEASE

Mid snows of paper, and fierce hail of pease; ....5.DunA3.258.179.
'Mid snows of paper, and fierce hail of pease; ....5.DunB3.262.332.
The Season of green Pease is fled, ...6.10.107.27.
For Sallads, Tarts, and Pease! ....6.47.48.130.

PEBBLE

As the small pebble stirs the peaceful lake; ....3.EOM4.364.164.
Or whirl the sounding Pebble from the Sling, ...Il.13.894.148.

PEBBLES

Swift o'er the rolling Pebbles, down the Hills ....Il.21.295.433.

PECCANT

And pours it all upon the peccant part. ....3.EOM2.144.72.

PECK

"A peck of coals a-piece shall glad the rest." ....5.DunA2.270.134.
"A peck of coals a-piece shall glad the rest." ....5.DunB2.282.309.

PECULIAR

Not only bounded *peculiar* Arts, ...1.EOC.62.246.
Is not th' Exactness of peculiar Parts; ....1.EOC.244.267.
Against a Nation thy peculiar Care: ....1.TrSt.406.427.
For still th'Opprest are his peculiar Care: ....1.TrUl.91.469.
A Wife is the peculiar Gift of Heav'n: ....2.ChJM.52.17.
(His Scene of Pleasure, and peculiar Care) ....2.ChJM.466.37.
Heav'n gave to woman the peculiar Grace ....2.ChWB.160.64.
Himself *alone*, high Heav'ns peculiar care; ....3.EOM1.108Z3.28.
Fix'd like a plant on his peculiar spot, ...3.EOM2.63.63.
The good must merit God's peculiar care; ....3.EOM4.135.140.
There's some Peculiar in each leaf and grain, ...3.Ep1.15.17.
Lo Horneck's fierce, and Roome's peculiar face; ....5.DunA3.146C.162.
Lo Horneck's fierce, and Roome's peculiar face; ....5.DunA3.146D.162.
Sure to charm all was his peculiar Fate, ...6.19.5.62.
The Muse asserts as her peculiar care. ....6.38.6.107.
Th' insulted Sire (his God's peculiar Care) ....Il.1.494.111.
Be godlike *Hector* thy peculiar Care, ...Il.15.260.207.
But mine, and ev'ry God's peculiar Grace ....Il.24.87.539.
This grace peculiar will the Gods afford ....Od.4.775.155.
He, as my guest, is my peculiar care, ...Od.11.422.405.
For still th' oppress'd are his peculiar care. ....Od.13.258.18.
Or fates peculiar to thy self portend? ....Od.15.189.77.

PEDAEUS

From *Meges'* Force the swift *Pedæus* fled, ...Il.5.91.270.

PEDAEUS'

In fair *Pedæus'* verdant Pastures bred, ...Il.13.230.116.

PEDANT

A Pedant makes; the Storm of *Gonson's* Lungs, ...4.JD4.53.29.
"Oh (cry'd the Goddess) for some pedant Reign! ....5.DunB4.175.358.

PEDANTS

And titt'ring push'd the Pedants off the place: ....5.DunB4.276.371.

PEDASUS

The gen'rous *Pedasus*, of *Theban* Breed; ....1.TrES.270.459.
Who held in *Pedasus* his proud Abode, ...Il.6.41.325.
And sacred *Pedasus*, for Vines renown'd; ....Il.9.198.442.
And sacred *Pedasus*, for Vines renown'd; ....Il.9.385.451.
Swift *Pedasus* was added to their side, ...Il.16.186.245.
The gen'rous *Pedasus*, of *Theban* Breed; ....Il.16.575.267.
Lyrnessus, Pedasus in Ashes lay; ....Il.20.123.399.
Who held in *Pedasus* his fam'd Abode, ...Il.21.98.425.

PEDESTAL

Stept from its Pedestal to take the Air. ....4.2HE2.122.173.

PEDESTALS

Refulgent pedestals the walls surround, ...Od.7.128.241.

PEDIGREE

Who proud of Pedigree, is poor of Purse) ....4.1HE6.84.243.

PEEL'D

Peel'd, patch'd, and pyebald, linsey-woolsey brothers, ...5.DunA3.107.159.
Peel'd, patch'd, and pyebald, linsey-wolsey brothers, ...5.DunB3.115.325.

PEEP

Hills peep o'er Hills, and *Alps* on *Alps* arise! ....1.EOC.232.265.
Most souls, 'tis true, but peep out once an age, ...2.Elegy.17.363.

PEEP'D

Peep'd in your fans, been serious, thus, and cry'd, ...6.41.4.113.

PEEPS 93 PELEUS

PEEPS
Still sits at squat, and peeps not from its hole. ....3.Ep1.115.24.

PEER
The Peer now spreads the glitt'ring *Forfex* wide, ...2.RL3.147.179.
It grieves me much (reply'd the Peer again) ....2.RL4.131.194.
From Peer or Bishop 'tis no easy thing ....3.Ep2.195.66.
Oft have you hinted to your brother Peer, ...3.Ep4.39.140.
To one that was, or would have been a Peer. ....4.HS2.40.57.
Who asks no more (right reasonable Peer) ....4.HAdv.159.89.
A maudlin Poetess, a ryming Peer, ...4.Arbu.16.97.
Whom have I hurt? has Poet yet, or Peer, ...4.Arbu.95.102.
A hireling Scribler, or a hireling Peer, ...4.Arbu.364.122.
Indebted to no Prince or Peer alive, ...4.2HE2.69.169.
Indue a Peer with Honour, Truth, and Grace, ...4.2HE2.221.181.
And at a Peer, or Peeress shall I fret, ...4.EpS1.111.306.
He foams a Patriot to subside a Peer; ....4.1740.10.332.
Or thy dread truncheon M[arlborough]'s mighty peer? ....4.1740.62.335.
The sowzing Prelate, or the sweating Peer, ...4.1740.70.336.
This polish'd Hardness, that reflects the Peer; ....5.DunB1.220.286.
The Sire is made a Peer, the Son a Fool. ....5.DunB4.548.396.
If Ducal *Nardac, Lilliputian* Peer, ...6.96iv.103.279.
All hail, arch-poet without peer! ....6.106v.1.308.
Blest Peer! his great Forefathers ev'ry Grace ....6.118.11.335.
None but a Peer of Wit and Grace, ...6.135.67.369.
But he's my Neighbour, cries the Peer polite, ...6.143.3.385.
Let him espouse her to the Peer she loves: ....Od.2.130.67.
From Peer to Peer, and thus incessant cries. ....Od.8.10.262.
From Peer to Peer, and thus incessant cries. ....Od.8.10.262.
Each peer a tripod, each a vase bestow, ...Od.13.17.2.
Sends forth her peers, and every peer a foe: ....Od.16.130.109.
And ev'ry Peer, expressive of his heart, ...Od.18.348.184.
Peer against Peer; and what the weighty cause? ....Od.18.449.190.
Peer against Peer; and what the weighty cause? ....Od.18.449.190.
Each Peer successive his libation pours ....Od.18.470.191.
A *Samian* Peer, more studious than the rest ....Od.20.353.249.
Each destin'd Peer impending Fates invade: ....Od.20.424.253.

PEERAGE
Convoke the Peerage, and the Gods attest; ....Od.1.355.49.
With him, the peerage next in pow'r to you: ....Od.4.876.159.
While thus the Peerage in the games contends, ...Od.8.141.270.
From council strait th' assenting peerage ceas'd, ...Od.20.310.247.
By us, in heaps th' illustrious peerage falls, ...Od.23.121.326.

PEERESS
Proud as a Peeress, prouder as a Punk; ....3.Ep2.70.56.
"Peeress and Butler share alike the Box, ...3.Ep3.142.105.
And at a Peer, or Peeress shall I fret, ...4.EpS1.111.306.

PEERLESS
Fair ev'n in death! this peerless *Butterfly."* .... 5.DunB4.436.383.

PEERS
While Peers and Dukes, and all their sweeping Train, ...2.RL1.84.152.
And laugh at Peers that put their Trust in *Peter.* .... 4.HS1.40.9.
Scriblers or Peers, alike are *Mob* to me. ....4.HS1.140.19.
And Peers give way, exalted as they are, ...4.2HE2.106.173.
Then Peers grew proud in Horsemanship t' excell, ...4.2HE1.143.207.
Peers, Heralds, Bishops, Ermin, Gold, and Lawn; ....4.2HE1.317.223.
The modern language of corrupted Peers, ...4.1HE1.99.287.
Thy dragons Magistrates and Peers shall taste, ...5.DunA3.299.184.
His Peers shine round him with reflected grace, ...5.DunB2.9.296.
By singing Peers up-held on either hand, ...5.DunB4.49.346.
Wits, Witlings, Prigs, and Peers; ....6.58.46.172.
Tho' now of Mighty Peers he sings ....6.135.89A.370.
"You'll bring a House (I mean of Peers) ....6.140.18.378.
There calls a Senate of the Peers around. ....Il.2.66.130.
There bade the noblest of the *Grecian* Peers; ....Il.2.480.149.
Alive, unharm'd, with all his Peers around, ...Il.5.629.298.
Held out in Order to the *Grecian* Peers. ....Il.7.222.375.
The *Trojan* Peers in nightly Council sate: ....Il.7.415.385.
To bid to Council all the *Grecian* Peers, ...Il.9.14.431.
The Peers and Leaders of th' *Achaian* Bands ....Il.9.789.472.
This could be learn, and to our Peers recite, ...Il.10.249.13.
Th' assembled Peers their lofty Chief inclos'd; ....Il.10.359.19.
Hector, the Peers assembling in his Tent, ...Il.10.486.25.
Bespeaking thus the *Grecian* Peers around. ....Il.10.625.30.
Before the *Grecian* Peers renounce thine Ire: ....Il.19.36.373.
In sage debates, surrounded with his Peers, ...Od.1.113.37.
I, to the Peers assembled, shall propose ....Od.1.475.55.
The peers of *Ithaca* wou'd arm in aid. ....Od.1.514.56.
To council calls the Peers: the Peers obey. ....Od.2.10.60.
To council calls the Peers: the Peers obey. ....Od.2.10.60.
The hoary Peers, and Aged Wisdom bow'd. ....Od.2.18.61.
Say then, ye Peers! by whose commands we meet? ....Od.2.35.62.
Rise then ye Peers! with virtuous anger rise! ....Od.2.71.64.
But you oh Peers! and thou oh Prince! give ear: ....Od.2.127.67.
Above th' assembled Peers they wheel on high, ...Od.2.175.70.
He ceas'd; and while abash'd the Peers attend, ...Od.2.253.73.
(His people's Father with his Peers around) ....Od.3.599.117.
Where circled with his Peers *Atrides* sate: ....Od.4.62.122.
Sustain those Peers, the reliques of our host, ...Od.4.655.150.
Antinous first th' assembled Peers addrest, ...Od.4.886.159.
Mean-time *Phæacia's* peers in council sate; ....Od.6.65.208.
Befits a Monarch. Lo! the Peers around ....Od.7.217.247.
Princes and Peers, attend! while we impart ....Od.7.246.248.
But finish, oh ye Peers! what you propose, ...Od.7.301.250.
Th' assembled Peers with gen'ral praise approv'd ....Od.7.307.251.
Swift to the palace, all ye Peers ascend: ....Od.8.38.264.
Thus spoke the Prince: th' attending Peers obey, ...Od.8.43.264.
Thus spoke the King; th' attending Peers obey: ....Od.8.105.268.
Who suppliant to the King and Peers, implores ....Od.8.173.271.
And thus benevolent accosts the Peers. ....Od.8.422.286.
Th' assenting Peers, obedient to the King, ...Od.8.433.287.
And to the court th' embody'd Peers repair. ....Od.8.454.288.

PEERS (CONTINUED)
The Peers encircling form an awful round. ....Od.8.518.290.
'Tis what my parents call me, and my peers. ....Od.9.434.324.
He first was seen of all the Peers to rise, ...Od.11.625.414.
And you the Peers and Princes of the land! ....Od.13.48.3.
The best our Lords consume; those thoughtless Peers, ...Od.14.99.40.
Sends forth her peers, and every peer a foe: ....Od.16.130.109.
Twice twenty six, all peers of mighty name, ...Od.16.269.118.
Ye Peers and rivals in this noble love! ....Od.17.556.159.
Sure of defeat, before the Peers engage; ....Od.18.38.168.
The Peers assent: when strait his sacred head ....Od.18.66.170.
The Peers transported, as outstretch'd he lies, ...Od.18.118.172.
The Peers with smiles addrest their unknown King: ....Od.18.136.173.
To joyn the Peers, resumes his throne, and mourns. ....Od.18.186.175.
Radiant before the gazing Peers she stands; ....Od.18.248.178.
The Peers dispatch their heralds to convey ....Od.18.335.184.
'Till mutual thus the Peers indignant cry; ....Od.18.445.190.
The Peers assent; the goblet *Mulius* crown'd ....Od.18.468.191.
Peers from the distant *Samian* shore retort; ....Od.19.150.199.
"Ye Peers, I cry, who press to gain a heart, ...Od.19.162.200.
Beeves for his train the *Cnossian* Peers assign, ...Od.19.228.204.
And from the Peers select the noblest Lord; ....Od.19.622.226.
And let the Peers consummate the disgrace? ....Od.20.18.232.
O Peers! the sanguinary scheme suspend: ....Od.20.307.247.
Be patient, Peers! at length *Antinous* cries; ....Od.20.336.249.
The sentence I propose, ye Peers, attend: ....Od.20.359.249.
A just reproof, ye Peers! Your rage restrain ....Od.20.389.251.
The Peers reproach the sure Divine of Fate; ....Od.20.432.254.
The rival peers the ringlets and the bow. ....Od.21.82.263.
In order circling to the peers around. ....Od.21.289.274.
Ye peers and rivals in the royal love! ....Od.21.293.274.
Ill I deserv'd these haughty Peers disdain; ....Od.21.469.283.
Thetis herself to all our peers proclaims ....Od.24.107.353.
Ye Peers (she cry'd) who press to gain my heart ....Od.24.154.355.
Hear me, ye Peers and Elders of the land, ...Od.24.508.372.

PEEVISH
In peevish Fits to have you say, ...6.64.9.189.

PEEVISHNESS
At all my Peevishness, and turns his Style. ....4.JD4.123.35.
At all my Peevishness, and chang'd his Style. ....4.JD4.123A.35.

PEG
Nothing in Nature is so lewd as *Peg,* .... 4.HAdv.31.77.

PEGASAEAN
Fly Pegasæan *Steed, thy Rider bear,* .... 6.26ii.1.79.

PEGASUS
Thus *Pegasus,* a nearer way to take, ...1.EOC.150.257.
"And never gallop Pegasus to death; ....4.1HE1.14.279.

PEGASUS'S
Break Priscian's head, the Pegasus's neck; ....5.DunA3.156.165.
Break Priscian's head, and Pegasus's neck; ....5.DunB3.162.328.

PEICES
See PIECES.
In a few peices cut it, ...6.91.3.253.

PEIRAEUS
Then to *Peiræus—Thou* whom time has prov'd ....Od.15.581.98.
To this *Peiræus;* Joyful I obey, ...Od.15.585.98.

PELAGON
Bias the good, and *Pelagon* the great. ....Il.4.341.237.
Brave *Pelagon,* his fav'rite Chief, was nigh, ...Il.5.854.307.
The Son of *Pelagon,* whose lofty Line ....Il.21.157.428.

PELASGI
The fierce *Pelasgi* next, in War renown'd, ...Il.2.1018.171.
And bold *Pelasgi* boast a native's due: ....Od.19.201.202.

PELASGIAN
The *Carians, Caucons,* the *Pelasgian* Host, ...Il.10.498.25.

PELASGIC
Now Muse recount *Pelasgic Argos'* Pow'rs, ...Il.2.829.164.
Oh Great! *Pelasgic, Dodonæan Jove!* .... Il.16.285.250.

PELASGUS'
The Son of *Lethus,* brave *Pelasgus'* Heir, ...Il.17.334.300.

PELEUS
Oh *Peleus,* old in Arms, in Wisdom old! ....Il.7.150.372.
When *Peleus* in his aged Arms embrac'd ....Il.9.328.450.
The rev'rend *Peleus* shall elect my Wife; ....Il.9.517.458.
The Son of *Peleus* ceas'd: The Chiefs around ....Il.9.556.460.
The Royal *Peleus,* when from *Pthia's* Coast ....Il.9.566.461.
Peleus said only this,—"My Son! be brave". ....Il.11.915.76.
And hoary *Peleus* yet extends his Days; ....Il.16.21.236.
"Stern Son of *Peleus* (thus ye us'd to say, ...Il.16.242.248.
No Stop, no Check, the Steeds of *Peleus* knew; ....Il.16.458.260.
To *Peleus,* and the silver-footed Dame; ....Il.16.702.271.
By aged *Peleus* to *Achilles* given, ...Il.17.221.296.
As first to *Peleus* by the Court of Heav'n: ....Il.17.222.296.
Sad Tydings, Son of *Peleus!* thou must hear; ....Il.18.21.324.
On *Peleus; Hector* bears the glorious Load. ....Il.18.106.328.
And happier *Peleus,* less ambitious, led ....Il.18.111.328.
Rise, Son of *Peleus!* rise divinely brave! ....Il.18.209.332.
The Son of *Peleus* thus: And thus replies ....Il.19.153.378.
What more, if hoary *Peleus* were deceast? ....Il.19.342.386.
For *Peleus* breaths no more the vital Air; ....Il.19.356.387.
The Son of *Peleus* sees, with Joy possest, ...Il.20.491.415.
O Son of *Peleus!* what avails to trace ....Il.21.169.428.

PELEUS (CONTINUED)
Of *Peleus, Æacus,* and *Jove,* am I; ... Il.21.206.430.
O Son of *Peleus!* Lo thy Gods appear! ... Il.21.333.435.
Enough, O Son of *Peleus! Troy* has view'd ... Il.22.317.469.
Peleus receiv'd, and on his Son bestow'd.) ... Il.23.346.503.
O *Peleus* Son! the Mare so justly mine. ... Il.23.622.514.
(A Goddess by our self to *Peleus* giv'n, ... Il.24.78.538.
Who more than *Peleus* shone in Wealth and Pow'r? ... Il.24.673.565.
Say if my sire, the rev'rend *Peleus* reigns ... Od.11.605.413.
O son of *Peleus!* greater than mankind! ... Od.24.51.350.

PELEUS'
To read in Greek, the Wrath of Peleus' Son. ... 4.2HE2.53.169.
The Wrath of *Peleus'* Son the direful Spring ... Il.1.1A.82.
And enter'd *Peleus'* hospitable Court. ... Il.11.905.76.
To crown with Glory *Peleus'* godlike Son, ... Il.13.439.126.
But *Peleus'* Son; and *Peleus'* Son to none ... Il.16.276.249.
But *Peleus'* Son; and *Peleus'* Son to none ... Il.16.276.249.
(*Ajax,* to *Peleus'* Son the second Name, ... Il.17.328.300.
At last thy Will prevails: Great *Peleus'* Son ... Il.18.419.341.
Nor dread the Vaunts of *Peleus'* haughty Son; ... Il.20.418.412.
And what (he cries) has *Peleus'* Son in view, ... Il.22.15.453.
But *Peleus'* Son intreats, with Sacrifice, ... Il.23.258.499.
To Dogs, to Vultures, and to *Peleus'* Son! ... Il.24.260.547.
Illustrious shade, (I cry'd) of *Peleus'* fates ... Od.11.615.414.

PELF
Whate'er the Passion, knowledge, fame, or pelf, ... 3.EOM2.261.86.
And gave you Beauty, but deny'd the Pelf ... 3.Ep2.287.73.
Yet, to be just to these poor men of pelf, ... 3.Ep3.109.100.
When Luxury has lick'd up all thy pelf, ... 4.HS2.105.61.

PELHAM
See first the merry P[elham] comes ... 6.58.43.172.

PELHAM'S
(Where *Kent* and Nature vye for PELHAM'S LOVE) ... 4.EpS2.67.316.

PELIAN
Thro' the thin Verge the *Pelian* Weapon glides, ... Il.20.325.407.
His Back scarce turn'd, the *Pelian* Jav'lin gor'd; ... Il.20.567.418.
Like Lightning next the *Pelian* Jav'lin flies; ... Il.21.185.429.
The *Pelian* Jav'lin, in his better Hand, ... Il.22.175.460.

PELIAS
O'er proud *Iölcos Pelias* stretch'd his reign, ... Od.11.311.397.

PELIAS'
All *Pelias'* Race *Alcestè* far outshin'd, ... Il.2.870.165.

PELIDES
To whom *Pelides.* From thy inmost Soul ... Il.1.107.92.
At this, *Pelides* frowning stern, reply'd: ... Il.1.193.96.
To her *Pelides.* With regardful Ear ... Il.1.287.100.
Pelides only match'd his early Charms; ... Il.2.819.164.
Pelides grasp'd their Hands, and thus begun. ... Il.9.260.445.
That bear *Pelides* thro' the Ranks of War. ... Il.10.382.20.
O first of Friends! (*Pelides* thus reply'd) ... Il.11.742.68.
Divine *Pelides,* with Compassion mov'd, ... Il.16.7.234.
I come, *Pelides!* from the Queen of *Jove,* ... Il.18.221.332.
I dread *Pelides* now: his Rage of Mind ... Il.18.307.336.
Stern in superior Grief *Pelides* stood; ... Il.18.367.339.
Thus round *Pelides* breathing War and Blood, ... Il.20.1.392.
To meet *Pelides* you persuade in vain: ... Il.20.118.399.
Against *Pelides* he directs his Course, ... Il.20.148.400.
Not so *Pelides;* furious to engage, ... Il.20.198.402.
Far on his out-stretch'd Arm, *Pelides* held ... Il.20.310.407.
Thrice struck *Pelides* with indignant Heart, ... Il.20.515.416.
Then from his side the Sword *Pelides* drew, ... Il.21.189.429.
Or let him bear, by stern *Pelides* slain, ... Il.22.231.465.
To stern *Pelides,* and triumphing, cries. ... Il.22.278.467.
But chief, *Pelides:* thick succeeding Sighs ... Il.23.21.487.
But great *Pelides,* stretch'd along the Shore ... Il.23.70.489.
Pelides points the Barrier on the Plain, ... Il.23.434.507.
Pelides points the Barrier with his Hand; ... Il.23.886.524.
Th' Effect succeeds the Speech. *Pelides* cries, ... Il.23.935.526.
With Joy *Pelides* saw the Honour paid, ... Il.23.1052.533.
Thee *Hermes* to *Pelides* shall convey, ... Il.24.219.546.
The stern *Pelides;* and nor sacred Age ... Il.24.734.568.
None but *Pelides* brighter shone in arms. ... Od.11.580.412.
O mighty chief! (*Pelides* thus began) ... Od.24.35.348.

PELIDES'
When from *Pelides'* Tent you forc'd the Maid, ... Il.9.141.439.
(My self will name them) to *Pelides'* Tent: ... Il.9.220.443.
Due to stern *Pallas,* and *Pelides'* Spear: ... Il.15.737.224.
Alone, untouch'd, *Pelides'* Javelin stands, ... Il.16.172.244.
Not to be pois'd but by *Pelides'* Hands: ... Il.16.173.244.
From thy tir'd Limbs unbrace *Pelides'* Arms! ... Il.17.244.297.
The mournful Message to *Pelides'* Ear; ... Il.17.722.315.
The *Greeks* accept, and shout *Pelides'* Name. ... Il.19.78.375.
No more shall *Hector's* and *Pelides'* Spear ... Il.20.495.415.
The Flood impell'd him, on *Pelides'* Head ... Il.21.163.428.
If then thou art of stern *Pelides'* Train, ... Il.24.495.557.
Safe to *Pelides'* Tent conduct my way. ... Il.24.528.558.
And now approach'd *Pelides'* lofty Tent. ... Il.24.552.559.

PELION
Descend from *Pelion* to the Main. ... 6.11.41.31.
Who dwell where *Pelion* crown'd with Piny Boughs ... Il.2.918.167.
On *Ossa, Pelion* nods with all his wood: ... Od.11.388.403.

PELION'S
(That Day, when hurl'd from *Pelion's* cloudy Head, ... Il.2.902.166.
From *Pelion's* shady Brow the Plant entire ... Il.16.174.245.
From *Pelion's* cloudy Top an Ash entire ... Il.19.422.389.

PELL
You *B[ala]n[di]ne, G[ri]ff[i]n,* and little *La P[e]ll,* ... 6.62iii.1.185.

PELL-MELL
But from this Pell-mell-Pack of Toasts, ... 6.59.7.177.

PELL-MELL-PACK
But from this Pell-mell-Pack of Toasts, ... 6.59.7.177.

PELLENÈ
And where *Pellenè* yields her fleecy Store, ... Il.2.691.159.

PELLUCID
The gate oppos'd pellucid valves adorn, ... Od.19.660.228.

PELOPS
To *Pelops* He th' immortal Gift resign'd; ... Il.2.131.133.
Th' immortal Gift great *Pelops* left behind, ... Il.2.132.133.

PELT
Not wrap up Oranges, to pelt your sire! ... 5.DunB1.236.287.

PEMBROKE
For Pembroke Statues, dirty Gods, and Coins; ... 3.Ep4.8.134.
For Fountain Statues, and for Pembroke Coins ... 3.Ep4.8B.134.

PEN
Matchless his Pen, victorious was his Lance; ... 1.W-F.293.175.
And use that Weapon which they have, their Pen; ... 2.ChWB.372.75.
P. What? arm'd for *Virtue* when I point the Pen, ... 4.HS1.105.15.
Is there, who lock'd from pen and Paper, scrawls ... 4.Arbu.19A.97.
And call for Pen and Ink to show our Wit. ... 4.2HE1.180.211.
Allow him but his Play-thing of a Pen, ... 4.2HE1.193.211.
Yes, the last Pen for Freedom let me draw, ... 4.EpS2.248.327.
Not that my pen to Critiques was confin'd, ... 5.DunA1.173A.84.
Yes, to my Country I my pen consign, ... 5.DunA1.193.86.
Then gnaw'd his pen, then dash'd it on the ground, ... 5.DunB1.117.278.
Some Dæmon stole my pen (forgive th' offence) ... 5.DunB1.187.283.
Before thy Pen vanish the Nation's Ills, ... 6.48ii.9.134.
Tho' with a Golden Pen you scrawl, ... 6.58.7.171.
Tho' with a Golden Pen ye scrawl, ... 6.58.7A.171.
This 'Squire he dropp'd his Pen full soon, ... 6.58.35.172.
Ye *Ladies* too draw forth your Pen, ... 6.58.65.173.
Would his best Patron let his Pen ... 6.102.3.294.
His Sword and Pen not worth a Straw, ... 6.116ii.2.326.
"A standish, steel and golden pen; ... 6.140.14.378.
O'erleaps the Fences, and invades the Pen; ... Il.10.565.27.

PEN'D
These flocks are mine, and more are pen'd at home, ... 1.TrPA.78.368.

PENAL
Thy captives; I ensure the penal claim. ... Od.8.384.284.

PENALTIES
And *Wit* dreads Exile, Penalties and Pains. ... 5.DunB4.22.342.
The Pains and Penalties of Idleness. ... 5.DunB4.344.377.

PENALTY
Must pay the penalty for lawless charms. ... Od.8.372.284.

PENANCE
Marry, do Penance, and dismiss your Fear. ... 2.ChJM.298.28.
Too hard a Penance for defeated Sin, ... 4.HAdv.85.83.

PENCE
"I'll now give six-pence where I gave a groat, ... 3.Ep3.366.123.
In shillings and in pence at first they deal, ... 4.JD2.83.141.
Save Three-pence, and his Soul. ... 6.47.12.128.
For Six-pence, I'd have giv'n a thousand Pound. ... 6.96iv.80.278.

PENCIL
So when the faithful *Pencil* has design'd ... 1.EOC.484.293.
Did Nature's pencil ever blend such rays, ... 5.DunB4.411.382.
One dip the pencil, and one string the lyre. ... 6.52.70.158.
What God, what Genius did the Pencil move ... 6.76.1.212.

PENDANT
The watry Landskip of the pendant Woods, ... 1.W-F.213.169.
What are the falling Rills, the pendant Shades, ... 6.81.7A.225.

PENDANTS
Some hang upon the Pendants of her Ear; ... 2.RL2.140.168.
Here *Orange-* trees with blooms and pendants shine, ... 6.14iv.17.47.
Far-beaming Pendants tremble in her Ear, ... Il.14.211.170.
Chains, Bracelets, Pendants, all their Toys I wrought. ... Il.18.468.344.

PENDENT
Shall glitter o'er the pendent green, ... 4.HOde1.23.151.
(His House thy Fane) shall deck the pendent Green ... 4.HOde1.23A.151.
Along fair *Ida's* Vales, and pendent Groves. ... Il.21.522.443.
Brown with o'er-arching shades and pendent woods, ... Od.3.97.90.
And pendent round it clasps his leathern wings. ... Od.12.514.457.
The olive green, blue fig, and pendent pear; ... Od.24.290.363.
Twelve pear-trees bowing with their pendent load, ... Od.24.395.368.

PENELEUS
Peneleus, Leitus, Prothoënor led: ... Il.2.587.155.
Then stern *Peneleus* rises to the Fight; ... Il.13.126.110.
But touch'd the Breast of bold *Peneleus* most: ... Il.14.570.190.
Swift his broad Faulchion fierce *Peneleus* spread, ... Il.14.581.190.
Lycon the brave, and fierce *Peneleus* came; ... Il.16.401.258.
The Sword broke short; but his, *Peneleus* sped ... Il.16.406.258.
Then trembled *Greece:* The Flight *Peneleus* led; ... Il.17.676.314.

PENELOPE

And all *Penelope* thy soul inspires, Od.2.318.76.
O why, *Penelope*, this causeless fear, Od.4.1059.167.
And chaste *Penelope*, extends his care. Od.13.468.28.
To bring *Penelope* the wish'd-for news, Od.15.48.72.
Severely chaste *Penelope* remains, Od.16.36.104.
The man, who calls *Penelope* his friend. Od.17.189.140.
This both *Penelope* and I afford. Od.17.484.156.
Thus spoke *Penelope*. *Eumæus* flies Od.17.632.163.
Thy soul, *Penelope*, from heav'n inspires; Od.18.188.175.
With her own art *Penelope* inspires: Od.21.2.257.
How long in vain *Penelope* we sought? Od.21.167.267.
Nor me nor chast *Penelope* obey; Od.22.463.311.
Ah no! with sighs *Penelope* rejoyn'd, Od.23.59.321.
A woman like *Penelope* unkind? Od.23.100.324.
Canst thou, *Penelope*, when heav'n restores Od.23.167.328.
Intent he hears *Penelope* disclose Od.23.323.339.
Shall learn from me *Penelope* was chast. Od.24.591.376.

PENELOPE'S

To chaste *Penelope's* increase decree. Od.1.288.47.

PENETRABLE

Gave entrance: Thro' that penetrable Part Il.22.409.472.

PENETRATE

Born where Heav'n's influence scarce can penetrate: 3.Ep1.94.22.

PENEUS

And into *Peneus* rolls his easy Tides; Il.2.911.167.
Or where thro' flow'ry *Tempè Peneus* stray'd, Il.2.920.167.

PENITENCE

Or how distinguish penitence from love? 2.ElAb.194.335.
Take back my fruitless penitence and pray'rs, 2.ElAb.286.343.
But thou, atton'd by Penitence and Pray'r, Il.6.384.345.

PENN'D

Come with Petitions fairly penn'd, 4.HS6.65.255.
(The males were penn'd in outward courts behind) Od.9.283.318.

PENNEL

There's Captain *Pennel*, absent half his Life, 6.96iv.21.276.

PENNELL'S

Yet *Pennell's* Wife is brown, compar'd to me; 6.96iv.23.276.

PENNY

Thou hast at least bestow'd one penny well. 4.HS2.110.63.
You pay a Penny, and he paid a Pound. 4.2HE2.239.181.
Their Copy cost 'em not a Penny. 6.29.21.83.

PENS

Who pens a Stanza when he should *engross?* 4.Arbu.18.97.
But Pens can forge, my Friend, that cannot write. 4.EpS2.188.324.
Fed num'rous Poultry in her Pens, 6.93.3.256.

PENSION

Strike off his Pension, by the setting sun, 3.Ep1.160.29.
Who sins with whom? who got his Pension *Rug*, 4.JD4.134.37.
Expect a Place, or Pension from the Crown; 4.2HE1.371.227.
A Pension, or such Harness for a slave 4.1HE1.87.285.
With-hold the pension, and set up the head; 5.DunB4.96.350.
All melted down, in Pension, or in Punk! 5.DunB4.510.392.

PENSION'D

Could pension'd *Boileau* lash in honest Strain 4.HS1.111.15.
One knighted Blackmore, and one pension'd Quarles; 4.2HE1.387.227.
Or each new-pension'd Sycophant, pretend 4.EpS2.142.321.

PENSIONER

And one more Pensioner St. Stephen gains. 3.Ep3.394.124.

PENSIONS

Nay *Wits* had *Pensions*, and *young Lords* had *Wit:* 1.EOC.539.298.

PENSIVE

Pensive and slow, with sudden Grief opprest, 1.TrUl.68.468.
But anxious Cares the pensive Squire opprest, 2.ChJM.392.33.
Hear how the Doves with pensive Notes complain, 2.ChJM.527.41.
But anxious Cares the pensive Nymph opprest, 2.RL4.1.183.
She sighs for ever on her pensive Bed, 2.RL4.23.185.
Where heav'nly-pensive, contemplation dwells, 2.ElAb.2.319.
The well-sung woes will sooth my pensive ghost; 2.ElAb.365.348.
The well-sung woes shall sooth my pensive ghost; 2.ElAb.365A.348.
Nor pensive Cowley's moral Lay. 4.HOde9.8.159.
Meet and rejoin me, in the pensive Grott. 4.2HE2.209.179.
Meet and rejoin me, in my pensive Grott. 4.2HE2.209A.179.
While pensive Poets painful vigils keep, 5.DunA1.91.70.
But pensive Poets painful vigils keep, 5.DunA1.91A.70.
While pensive Poets painful vigils keep, 5.DunB1.93.276.
In pensive thought recall the fancy'd scene, 6.45.33.125.
And all we gain, some pensive Notion more; 6.86.8B.245.
Pensive hast follow'd to the silent tomb, 6.109.12.314.
Striking their pensive bosoms— *Here* lies GAY. 6.125.12.350.
Where, nobly-pensive, ST. JOHN sate and thought; 6.142.10.383.
There, nobly-pensive, ST. JOHN sate and thought; 6.142.10A.383.
Here, nobly-pensive, ST. JOHN sate and thought; 6.142.10B.383.
Pensive they walk along the barren Sands: Il.1.427.108.
She, in soft Sorrows, and in pensive Thought, Il.1.451.109.
Pensive she stood on *Ilion's* Tow'ry Height, Il.6.468.349.
Then pensive thus, to War's triumphant Maid. Il.8.422.417.
The pensive Goddesses, abash'd, controul'd, Il.8.540.422.
A pensive Scene! 'till *Tydeus'* warlike Son Il.9.41.433.
His pensive Brow the gen'rous Care exprest Il.13.279.119.
The pensive Father, Father now no more! Il.13.823.144.

PENSIVE (CONTINUED)

Pensive he said; then pressing as he lay Il.16.1042.283.
The pensive Steeds of great *Achilles* stood; Il.17.485.306.
Pensive he sate; for all that Fate design'd, Il.18.7.323.
He reach'd the Throne where pensive *Thetis* sate; Il.18.492.345.
Pensive she ply'd the melancholy Loom; Il.22.567.479.
Thus humbled in the Dust, the pensive Train Il.23.1.485.
From his dead Friend the pensive Warrior went, Il.23.47.488.
Pensive he muses with uplifted Hands. Il.23.121.492.
Stood at my side, a pensive, plaintive Ghost; Il.23.127.493.
Pensive she sate, revolving Fates to come, Il.24.113.539.
The Goddess seats her by her pensive Son, Il.24.161.542.
From Room to Room his pensive Daughters roam; Il.24.203.545.
Then, as the pensive Pomp advanc'd more near, Il.24.872.573.
Here paus'd the God, and pensive thus replies Od.1.55.33.
Pensive, the rules the Goddess gave, he weigh'd; Od.1.556.58.
Or glides in *Stygian* gloom a pensive ghost, Od.4.142.127.
While pensive in the silent slumb'rous shade, Od.4.1045.166.
To whom the Queen, (whilst yet her pensive mind Od.4.1065.167.
Him pensive on the lonely beach he found, Od.5.193.180.
To *Pallas* thus the pensive Heroe pray'd. Od.6.384.230.
Again *Ulysses* veil'd his pensive head, Od.8.89.267.
Now far the last, with pensive pace and slow Od.9.531.328.
Blind to the future, pensive with our fears, Od.9.658.333.
Pensive they march, and pensive we remain. Od.10.239.352.
Pensive they march, and pensive we remain. Od.10.239.352.
Eurylochus with pensive steps and slow, Od.10.286.357.
Pensive I sate; my tears bedew'd the bed; Od.10.589.372.
Then pale and pensive stand, with cares opprest, Od.11.5.379.
Fair, pensive youths, and soft-enamour'd maids, Od.11.49.383.
O son of woe, the pensive shade rejoyn'd, Od.11.259.394.
Pensive and sad I stand, at length accost, Od.11.677.418.
When rising sad and slow, with pensive look, Od.12.188.441.
Pensive and pale from grove to grove I stray'd, Od.12.395.450.
Pensive and slow, with sudden grief opprest Od.13.235.17.
While pensive in this solitary den, Od.14.409.55.
In *Stygian* gloom he glides a pensive ghost! Od.15.293.83.
Pensive and pale he wanders half a ghost. Od.16.157.110.
Chasten'd with coy *Diana's* pensive air) Od.17.47.134.
The pensive mother sits in humble state; Od.17.111.137.
He ceas'd; nor made the pensive Queen reply, Od.17.170.139.
Let for a space the pensive Queen attend, Od.17.650.164.
While fix'd in thought the pensive Heroe sate, Od.18.1.166.
The pensive Queen perchance desires to know Od.19.56.195.
Chasten'd with coy *Diana's* pensive air. Od.19.67.196.
Whom thus with pensive air the Queen address. Od.19.593.225.
Amuse my pensive hours. The bird of *Jove* Od.19.629.227.
In *Stygian* gloom he glides a pensive ghost! Od.20.264.246.
Nigh in her bright alcove, the pensive Queen Od.20.463.256.
And pensive sate, and tears began to flow. Od.21.58.262.
To the proud Suitors bears in pensive state Od.21.61.262.
His head, that bow'd with many a pensive care, Od.24.263.361.

PENT

And long 'twas doubtful, both so closely pent, 2.TemF.491.287.
So pent by Hills, the wild Winds roar aloud Il.16.923.279.
No—pent in this sad Palace let us give Il.24.255.547.

PENTHEUS'

And *Pentheus'* Blood enrich'd the rising Ground, 1.TrSt.465.429.

PENTLOW

Who shew their Parts as *Pentlow* does, 6.10.30.25.

PENURY

And Pine and Penury, a meagre train. Od.15.367.87.
With penury, contempt, repulse, and care, Od.20.255.245.

PEOPLE

And Feather'd People crowd my wealthy Side, 1.W-F.404.191.
And People Heav'n with *Roman* Deities. 1.TrSt.46.411.
Adrastus here his happy People sways, 1.TrSt.539.433.
His Friends and People, to his future Praise, 1.TrES.250.459.
A Prince the Father of a People made. 3.EOM3.214.114.
Taught Pow'r's due use to People and to Kings, 3.EOM3.289.121.
Now save a People, and now save a Groat. 3.Ep1.145Z4.27.
The Boys flock round him, and the People stare: 4.2HE2.120.173.
Your People, Sir, are partial in the rest. 4.2HE1.32.197.
For Farce the people true delight affords, 4.2HE1.310A.221.
The people, sure, the people are the sight! 4.2HE1.323.223.
The people, sure, the people are the sight! 4.2HE1.323.223.
"What shook the stage, and made the people stare?" 4.2HE1.336.225.
"I wonder what some people mean," 4.HS6.104.257.
The People are a many-headed Beast: 4.1HE1.121.287.
Alas! the people curse, the carman swears, 4.1740.73.336.
The Clergy perjur'd, thy whole People sold. 4.1740.82.336.
'Twixt Prince and People close the Curtain draw, 5.DunB1.313.293.
The People one, and one supplies the King. 6.35.34.104.
Tho very chaste people, to die of a Clap. 6.69iii.2.201.
I half could wish this people might be sav'd. 6.146.4.389.
I half could wish this people should be sav'd. 6.146.4A.389.
And, for the King's Offence, the People dy'd. Il.1.14.86.
And suffer, rather than my People fall. Il.1.148.94.
Scourge of thy People, violent and base! Il.1.305.101.
And glut his Vengeance with my People slain! Il.1.725.122.
To whom its Safety a whole People owes, Il.2.29.128.
To whom its Safety a whole People owes, Il.2.79.130.
The Nations call, thy joyful People wait, Il.3.320.208.
The People pray with elevated Hands, Il.3.394.211.
And unreveng'd see *Priam's* People die? Il.5.566.295.
A Prince and People studious of their Gain. Il.5.873.308.
And shall our Promise to our People fail? Il.5.877.308.
The People pray with lifted Eyes and Hands, Il.7.213.374.
What *Greeks* are perish'd! what a People lost! Il.7.393.383.
To *Jason*, Shepherd of his People, bore) Il.7.565.392.
My Glory ravish'd, and my People slain! Il.8.285.410.

PEOPLE (CONTINUED)
And gives the People to their Monarch's Pray'rs. .... Il.8.296.411.
Our Wealth, our People, and our Glory lost. .... Il.9.30.433.
Distast the People, or offend the King. .... Il.9.86.436.
The rest the People shar'd; my self survey'd .... Il.11.840.73.
His Friends and People, to his future Praise, ... Il.16.555.266.
Who guarded Right, and kept his People free; .... Il.16.665.270.
For this, or that, the partial People stand: .... Il.18.582.351.
Dismiss the People then, and give command, ... Il.19.169.378.
I feel my Folly in my People slain. .... Il.22.145.459.
Scarce the whole People stop his desp'rate Course, ... Il.22.524.478.
He said: The People to their Ships return: .... Il.23.199.497.
On his slow Wheels the following People wait, ... Il.24.403.552.
The Waves of People at his Word divide, ... Il.24.896.573.
A duteous people, and industrious Isle, ... Od.1.231.43.
But half the people with respect obey'd .... Od.3.187.95.
Or leagu'd against thee, do thy people join, ... Od.3.263.98.
Or bless a people willing to obey, ... Od.5.15.171.
Produc'd a Monarch that his people blest, ... Od.7.79.237.
The People one, and one supplies the King. .... Od.7.175.244.
Your people blessing, by your people blest! .... Od.7.205.246.
Your people blessing, by your people blest! .... Od.7.205.246.
A land rejoycing, and a people blest. .... Od.9.6.301.
Those air-bred people, and their goat-nurs'd *Jove:* .... Od.9.330.319.
And all my vessels, all my people, lost! .... Od.9.648.333.
The people were? who monarch of the place? .... Od.10.124.346.
That done, a people far from Sea, explore, ... Od.11.152.388.
Thy people blessing, by thy people blest! .... Od.11.169.390.
Thy people blessing, by thy people blest! .... Od.11.169.390.
To thee, to thine, the people, and the King! .... Od.13.79.5.
The swarming people hail their ship to land, ... Od.13.179.14.
Where *Nestor,* shepherd of his people, reigns. .... Od.17.125.137.
To people *Orcus,* and the burning coasts! .... Od.20.428.254.
Thy suppliant people, and receive their pray'r! .... Od.22.67.290.
My people blessing, by my people blest. .... Od.23.302.337.
My people blessing, by my people blest. .... Od.23.302.337.
His people blessing, by his people blest. .... Od.24.559.375.
His people blessing, by his people blest. .... Od.24.559.375.

PEOPLE'S
These now controul a wretched People's Fate, ... 1.TrSt.239.420.
But with their Toils their People's Safety bought: .... 2.TemF.160.267.
The People's Fable, and the Scorn of all. .... 2.TemF.401.282.
"Learn each small People's genius, policies, ... 3.EOM3.183.111.
All this may be; the People's Voice is odd, ... 4.2HE1.89.201.
His People's Pastor, good *Hypenor,* dy'd; .... Il.5.185.275.
The Chief, to perish at his People's Head. .... Il.5.763.303.
Oh Soul of Battels, and thy People's Guide! .... Il.9.757.471.
And all my People's Miseries are mine. .... Il.10.105.7.
And slew *Bienor* at his People's Head: .... Il.11.128.41.
The Chief, his People's Guardian now no more! .... Il.13.522.131.
His People's Pastor, *Hyperenor* fell; .... Il.14.612.192.
Am I become my People's common Show, ... Il.24.299.549.
In peace and joy, the people's rightful Lord; .... Od.1.153.40.
(His people's Father with his Peers around) .... Od.3.599.117.
The people's parent, he protected all: .... Od.4.921.161.
Pleas'd with his people's fame the Monarch hears, ... Od.8.421.286.
O Monarch, care of heav'n! thy people's pride! .... Od.15.101.73.
The people's Saviour, and divinely wise, ... Od.15.269.81.

PEOPLED
From the green myriads in the peopled grass: .... 3.EOM1.210.41.
To the green myriads in the peopled grass: .... 3.EOM1.210A.41.
Serve peopled Towns, and stately Cities grace; .... 6.17ii.24.56.
The many-peopled *Orchomenian* Town; .... Il.9.499.457.
Tho' all in Arms the peopled City rise, ... Il.20.201.402.
To want like mine, the peopled town can yield .... Od.17.22.133.

PEOPLES
What vary'd being peoples ev'ry star, ... 3.EOM1.27.16.

PEPPER
Salt, pepper and mace .... 6.91.5.253.
"While Pepper-Water-Worms thy Bait supply'd; .... 6.96ii.20.270.

PEPPER-WATER-WORMS
"While Pepper-Water-Worms thy Bait supply'd; .... 6.96ii.20.270.

PER
In one abundant show'r of Cent. per Cent., ... 3.Ep3.372.123.
As M**o's was, but not at five *per Cent.* .... 4.HS2.122.63.
For Int'rest, ten *per Cent.* her constant Rate is; .... 4.HAdv.19.77.
With rhymes of this *per Cent.* and that *per Year?* .... 4.JD2.56.137.
With rhymes of this *per Cent.* and that *per Year?* .... 4.JD2.56.137.
While with the silent growth of ten per Cent, ... 4.1HE1.132.289.

PERAULT
Reviving *Perault,* murd'ring *Boileau,* he .... 6.12.4.37.

PERCEIV'D
Perceiv'd a colder and a harder breast, ... 1.TrFD.50.388.
Perceiv'd, and thus with Accent mild began. .... Il.1.433.108.
No Voice succeeding, he perceiv'd the Foe. .... Il.10.426.22.
Old *Nestor* first perceiv'd th' approaching Sound, ... Il.10.624.29.
Perceiv'd the first, and thus to *Telamon.* .... Il.13.98.109.

PERCEIVE
A Light, which in yourself you must perceive; .... 3.Ep4.45.141.
And steal so little, few perceive they steal; .... 4.JD2.84.141.

PERCEIVES
Glad Earth perceives, and from her Bosom pours .... Il.14.395.181.
And at his Back perceives the quiv'ring Spear: .... Il.20.330.407.
Tho' strook, tho' wounded, scarce perceives the Pain, ... Il.21.681.450.

PERCH
The bright-ey'd Perch with Fins of *Tyrian* Dye, ... 1.W-F.142.163.

PERCH'D
Full fairly perch'd among the Boughs above. .... 2.ChJM.719.49.
First *Ariel* perch'd upon a *Matadore,* .... 2.RL3.33.171.
Perch'd on his crown. "All hail! and hail again, ... 5.DunA1.245.92.
Perch'd on his crown. "All hail! and hail again, ... 5.DunB1.291.291.
From his Ambrosial Head, where perch'd she sate, ... Il.19.125.377.
Perch'd on the battlements he thus began, ... Od.19.639.227.
Perch'd like a swallow on a rafter's height, ... Od.22.262.299.

PERCHANCE
Perchance the Reins forsook the Driver's Hand, ... Il.23.548.511.
Prepar'd perchance to leave thy native Land. .... Il.24.470.556.
Perchance behold thee, and our Grace prevent. .... Il.24.821.571.
Arrive, (or is perchance already come) .... Od.15.200.78.
The pensive Queen perchance desires to know .... Od.19.56.195.

PERCNOS'
And known to Gods by *Percnos'* lofty Name. .... Il.24.390.552.

PERCOPE'S
With twelve black Ships he reach'd *Percope's* Strand, ... Il.11.295.48.

PERCOTÈ'S
From *Practius'* Stream, *Percotè's* Pasture Lands, ... Il.2.1012.171.

PERCOTE'S
Fed his large Oxen on *Percote's* Plain; .... Il.15.647.221.

PERFECT
A perfect Judge will *read* each Work of Wit .... 1.EOC.233.266.
So help me Fates, as 'tis no perfect Sight, ... 2.ChJM.776.52.
Think fit to live in perfect Chastity, ... 2.ChWB.37.58.
Such as are perfect, may, I can't deny; .... 2.ChWB.44.58.
Say rather, Man's as perfect as he ought; .... 3.EOM1.70.22.
If to be perfect in a certain sphere, ... 3.EOM1.73.22.
26.If to be perfect in a certain State, ... 3.EOM1.73A.22.
Alone made perfect here, immortal there: .... 3.EOM1.120.30.
"And what created perfect?"—Why then Man? .... 3.EOM1.148.34.
As full, as perfect, in a hair as heart; .... 3.EOM1.276.48.
As full, as perfect, in vile Man that mourns, ... 3.EOM1.277.48.
To the first good, first perfect, and first fair; .... 3.EOM2.24.58.
The last, scarce ripen'd into perfect Man, ... 3.EOM3.141.107.
"And perfect *Speaker?*"—'Onslow, past dispute." .... 4.JD4.71.31.
That perfect hate to that, now makes me more .... 4.JD2A.5.132.
"A perfect Genius at an Opera-Song— .... 4.2HE2.11.165.
And then—a perfect Hermit in his Diet. .... 4.2HE1.200.211.
Chetwood, thro' perfect modesty o'ercome, ... 5.DunA2.181.124.
Chapman thro' perfect modesty o'ercome. .... 5.DunA2.181B.124.
Osborn thro' perfect modesty o'ercome. .... 5.DunA2.181C.124.
Osborne, thro' perfect modesty o'ercome, ... 5.DunB2.189.304.
Yet making here a perfect Botch, ... 6.30.21.86.
Do thou make perfect! sacred be his words! .... Od.7.424.258.
And still his words live perfect in my mind. .... Od.17.137.138.
In body perfect, and compleat in mind! .... Od.18.292.180.
Of perfect Hecatombs in order slain: .... Od.19.429.215.
(His perfect skill the wond'ring gazers ey'd, ... Od.21.127.264.

PERFECTED
For strong the God, and perfected in guile. .... Od.4.554.146.
Thus the fam'd Heroe, perfected in wiles, ... Od.19.234.204.

PERFECTION
When mellowing Years their full Perfection give, ... 1.EOC.490.294.
When mellowing Time does full Perfection give, ... 1.EOC.490A.294.
'Tis true, Perfection none must hope to find .... 2.ChJM.190.24.
When thus ripe Lyes are to perfection sprung, ... 2.TemF.479.286.
Who clasps the bright perfection in his arms! .... Od.6.190.218.
Sev'n golden talents to perfection wrought, ... Od.9.236.316.

PERFECTLY
In short, I'm perfectly content, ... 4.HS6.29.251.
But should be perfectly content, ... 4.HS6.29A.251.
See now, half-cur'd, and perfectly well-bred, ... 5.DunB4.323.375.

PERFECTS
Then urg'd, she perfects her illustrious toils; .... Od.2.125.67.

PERFIDIOUS
Whor'd by my Slave—Perfidious Wretch! may Hell .... 2.ChJM.770.52.
And leave unpunish'd this perfidious Race? .... Il.2.194.137.
To me, Perfidious! this lamenting Strain? .... Il.5.1094.318.
Well hast thou known proud *Troy's* perfidious Land, ... Il.6.69.327.
O Race perfidious, who delight in War! .... Il.13.780.142.
To favour *Ilion,* that perfidious Place, ... Il.15.238.206.
And partial Aid to *Troy's* perfidious Race. .... Il.21.483.441.
But absent now, perfidious and ingrate! .... Od.4.922.161.
To liberty restor'd, perfidious fly, ... Od.8.388.285.
The mulct I bear, if, *Mars* perfidious flies. .... Od.8.390.285.

PERFORM
And will perform, by this—my Dear, and this.— .... 2.ChJM.566.42.
And proud his mistress' orders to perform, ... 5.DunA3.259.179.
And proud his Mistress' orders to perform, ... 5.DunB3.263.333.
Thy *Magus,* Goddess! shall perform the rest." .... 5.DunB4.516.393.
These shall perform th' almighty orders given, ... 6.21.27.69.
But this the Gods in later Times perform; .... Il.12.37.83.
Or Arms, or Counsels; now perform thy best, ... Il.13.299.119.
Swift to perform Heav'n's fatal Will it fled, ... Il.14.543.189.
Perform the Promise of a gracious God! .... Il.15.433.214.
Perform due Honours to *Patroclus* dead. .... Il.23.12.486.
Perform, ye *Trojans!* what the Rites require, ... Il.24.985.576.
Wise to resolve, and patient to perform. .... Od.4.372.137.
What I suggest thy wisdom will perform; .... Od.5.434.193.

PERFORM'D
We soon perform'd, and Acis deify'd, ...1.TrPA.149.372.
His Task perform'd, he sadly went his Way, ...2.ChJM.363.31.
In this fair Garden he perform'd and sped. ....2.ChJM.474A.38.
A solemn Sacrifice, perform'd in state, ...3.Ep4.157.152.
All Parts perform'd, and *all* her Children blest! ....4.EpS1.82.304.
All Parts perform'd, and all her Children blest! ....4.EpS1.82A.304.
Or wise *Ulysses* see perform'd our Will, ...Il.1.188.96.
Incens'd he threaten'd, and his Threats perform'd: ....Il.1.503.112.
Their Pray'rs perform'd, the Chiefs the Rite pursue, ...Il.2.502.150.
Their Task perform'd, and mix among the Gods. ....Il.5.1121.321.
The Rite perform'd, the Chiefs their Thirst allay, ...Il.9.231.444.
Preventing ev'ry Part perform'd by you; ....Il.10.133.8.
Already noble Deeds ye have perform'd, ...Il.13.781.142.
No Deed perform'd, to our *Olympian* Sire? ....Il.21.511.443.
Perform'd their office, or his weight upheld: ....Od.5.582.200.
In vain! I view perform'd the direful deed, ...Od.12.462.453.

PERFORMS
And thus performs *Minerva's* high commands. ....Od.4.1058.167.

PERFUM'D
With od'rous Spices they perfum'd the Place, ...2.ChJM.355.31.
Or soft Adonis, so perfum'd and fine, ...3.Ep3.61.91.
The Winds perfum'd, the balmy Gale Convey ....Il.14.199.169.
Thy Altars stand, perfum'd with native Flow'rs! ....Il.23.185.497.
Flam'd on the hearth, and wide perfum'd the Isle; ....Od.5.77.176.
Perfum'd and wash'd, and gorgeously array'd. ....Od.24.426.369.

PERFUME
Perfume to you, to me is Excrement. ....4.EpS2.184.324.
And with fresh sweets perfume the air, ...6.4iv.14.11.
Perfume the Mount, and breathe *Ambrosia* round. ....Il.14.404.183.
Where Cedar-Beams the lofty Roofs perfume, ...Il.24.230.546.
Here jars of oil breath'd forth a rich perfume; ....Od.2.384.79.
Before her breath'd a gale of rich perfume. ....Od.4.158.128.
Where treasur'd garments cast a rich perfume; ....Od.21.54.261.

PERFUMES
No rich Perfumes refresh the fruitful Field, ...1.PWi.47.92.
And *Carmel's* flow'ry Top perfumes the Skies! ....1.Mes.28.115.
And with the Perfumes of sweet *Ambrosial* Dews, ...1.TrES.342.462.
And wings of Seraphs shed divine perfumes; ....2.ElAb.218.338.
And all the Dome perfumes with Heav'nly Dews. ....Il.3.472.214.
That shed Perfumes, and whisp'ring thus addrest. ....Il.3.480.215.
And with Perfumes of sweet Ambrosial Dews, ...Il.16.829.275.

PERHAPS
Perhaps he seem'd *above* the Critick's Law, ...1.EOC.132.254.
Then thus the King: Perhaps, my Noble Guests, ...1.TrSt.656.437.
Some juster Prince perhaps had entertain'd, ...1.TrUl.82.468.
Seek, and perhaps you'll find, among the Fair, ...2.ChJM.285.28.
From these perhaps (ere nature bade her die) ....2.Elegy.23.364.
Grieve for an hour, perhaps, then mourn a year, ...2.Elegy.56.367.
Perhaps acts second to some sphere unknown, ...3.EOM1.58.20.
Perhaps acts second to a sphere unknown ....3.EOM1.58A.20.
Better for Us, perhaps, it might appear, ...3.EOM1.165.35.
As Man, perhaps, the moment of his breath, ...3.EOM2.133.71.
Is thus, perhaps, the cause of all we do. ....3.Ep1.50A.18.
Is thus, perhaps, the cause of half we do. ....3.Ep1.50B.18.
Cæsar perhaps had told you he was beat. ....3.Ep1.82A.21.
Is thus, perhaps, the cause of most we do. ....3.Ep1.50.18.
Perhaps Prosperity becalm'd his breast, ...3.Ep1.63.20.
Perhaps the Wind just shifted from the east: ....3.Ep1.64.20.
Perhaps was sick, in love, or had not din'd. ....3.Ep1.80.21.
Cæsar perhaps might answer he was drunk. ....3.Ep1.84.21.
Now in the Moon perhaps, now under ground. ....3.Ep1.157.28.
Shov'd from the wall perhaps, or rudely press'd ....3.Ep1.230.35.
Perhaps you think the Poor might have their part? ....3.Ep3.101.98.
What but a want, which you perhaps think mad, ...3.Ep3.331.120.
A Work to wonder at—perhaps a STOW. ....3.Ep4.70.143.
Nay troth, th' *Apostles,* (tho' perhaps too rough) ....4.JD4.76.31.
Perhaps, young men! our Fathers had no nose? ....4.HS2.92.61.
Whose Word is *If, Perhaps,* and *By-and-By,* ....4.HAdv.156.87.
Perhaps, yet vibrates on his SOVEREIGN'S Ear— ....4.Arbu.357.122.
Nay tho' at Court (perhaps) it may find grace: ....4.2HE2.162.177.
Who dy'd, perhaps, an hundred years ago? ....4.2HE1.52.199.
(Tho' but, perhaps, a muster-roll of Names) ....4.2HE1.124.205.
Perhaps may waken to a Humming-bird; ....5.DunB4.446A.384.
Perhaps more high some daring son may soar, ...5.DunB4.599.402.
Perhaps — * * * * ....5.DunB4.601B.403.
Some Squire, perhaps, you take delight to rack; ....6.45.23.125.
Perhaps ev'n *Britain's* utmost shore ....6.51i.19.151.
Perhaps in time you'll leave High Diet, ...6.61.33.182.
Perhaps at last you'll leave High Diet, ...6.61.33A.182.
Perhaps, by its own ruins sav'd from flame, ...6.71.15.203.
Perhaps forgets that OXFORD e r was Great; ....6.84.18.239.
Perhaps all Maim'd lye grovelling on the ground? ....6.96ii.30Z10.271.
Perhaps neglected, on the dang'rous strand ....6.96ii.30Z21.271.
"Perhaps all maim'd, lie grov'ling on the Ground? ....6.96ii.44.272.
The rest God knows—perhaps the Devil. ....6.104ii.2.297.
The rest Gods knows, perhaps the Devil. ....6.104i.2A.297.
Perhaps, with added Sacrifice and Pray'r, ...Il.1.125.93.
Perhaps in *Grecian* Blood to drench the Plain, ...Il.1.724.122.
Perhaps the Chiefs, from warlike Toils at ease, ...Il.3.307.208.
Perhaps their Sword some nobler Quarrel draws, ...Il.3.309.208.
Perhaps had perish'd; had not *Hermes'* Care ....Il.5.479.291.
This Day (perhaps the last that sees me here) ....Il.6.458.348.
Some future Day, perhaps he may be mov'd ....Il.8.453.418.
Some Spy perhaps, to lurk beside the Main; ....Il.10.407.21.
Perhaps some Horses of the *Trojan* Breed ....Il.10.628.30.
Perhaps, ev'n now pursu'd, they seek the Shore; ....Il.10.634.30.
Or oh! perhaps those Heroes are no more. ....Il.10.635.30.
Perhaps great *Hector* then had found his Fate, ...Il.11.213.45.
Anetor's Brother, or perhaps his Son. ....Il.14.556.190.
Perhaps some fav'ring God his Soul may bend; ....Il.15.466.215.

PERHAPS (CONTINUED)
Perhaps yon' Reliques of the *Grecian* Name, ...Il.16.24.236.
Perhaps *Apollo* shall thy Arms succeed, ...Il.16.883.277.
"Return not, my brave Friend (perhaps he said) ....Il.16.1013.282.
On thee, on me, perhaps (my Friend) on all. ....Il.17.287.299.
Perhaps to Him: This *Thetis* had reveal'd; ....Il.17.470.305.
(Who now, perhaps, in *Pthia* dreads to hear ....Il.19.343.386.
Ev'n this, perhaps, will hardly prove thy Lot: ....Il.20.226.403.
Perhaps excel us in this wordy War; ....Il.20.301.406.
Ev'n now perhaps, e'er yet I turn the Wall, ...Il.21.665.449.
And lov'd *Lycaon;* now perhaps no more! ....Il.22.65.455.
These I have yet to see, perhaps yet more! ....Il.22.91.456.
Perhaps ev'n I, reserv'd by angry Fate ....Il.22.92.456.
My Grief perhaps his Pity may engage; ....Il.22.534.478.
Perhaps at least he may respect my Age. ....Il.22.535.478.
Perhaps that noble Heat has cost his Breath, ...Il.22.590.480.
(Some Tomb perhaps of old, the Dead to grace; ....Il.23.405.506.
(For these dim Eyes, perhaps, discern not right) ....Il.23.553.511.
Perhaps he sought not Heav'n by Sacrifice, ...Il.23.625.514.
Rash Heat perhaps a Moment might controul, ...Il.23.687.517.
Yet now perhaps, some Turn of human Fate ....Il.24.604.562.
Condemn'd perhaps some foreign shore to tread; ....Od.3.314.101.
Perhaps may seize thy realm, and share the spoil; ....Od.3.402.106.
Perhaps I yet may fall a bloody prey ....Od.5.610.201.
"Perhaps a native of some distant shore, ...Od.6.333.227.
Perhaps from realms that view the rising day, ...Od.8.29.263.
Destroys perhaps the strength that time wou'd spare: ....Od.8.150.271.
Pyrates perhaps, who seek thro' seas unknown ....Od.9.301.318.
Some juster Prince perhaps had entertain'd, ...Od.13.249.18.
Perhaps supported at another's board, ...Od.14.49.38.
To Fame no stranger, nor perhaps to me; ....Od.14.143.42.
So left perhaps to tend the fleecy train, ...Od.15.418.89.
Perhaps she weds regardless of her fame, ...Od.16.75.106.
Or we perhaps might take him off thy hands. ....Od.17.261.144.
Wander, perhaps, some inmate of the skies; ....Od.17.577.160.
Thy arms, (he cry'd) perhaps to find a grave: ....Od.18.304.181.
Perhaps by righteous heav'n that I must bleed! ....Od.18.310.181.
Perhaps, these outrages from *Irus* flow, ...Od.18.434.189.
Too like *Ulysses,* and perhaps the same! ....Od.19.417.214.
Perhaps, like thee, poor guest! in wanton pride ....Od.19.436.216.
Inroll'd, perhaps, in *Pluto's* dreary train.) ....Od.20.408.252.
Perhaps he makes them, or perhaps he steals.— ....Od.21.434.281.
Perhaps he makes them, or perhaps he steals.— ....Od.21.434.281.

PERIBAEA
And *Peribæa,* beautiful and young: ....Od.7.73.237.

PERIBAEA'S
(Fair *Peribæa's* Love the God had crown'd, ...Il.21.159.428.

PERIBOEA
See PERIBAEA.

PERICLIMENUS
Sage *Nestor, Periclimenus* the bold, ...Od.11.348.399.

PERIGORD
Thy Treufles, Perigord! thy Hams, Bayonne! ....5.DunB4.558.397.

PERIL
Nor saw his Country's Peril, nor his own. ....Il.5.84.270.
No peril in my cause he ceas'd to prove, ...Od.4.137.126.

PERILOUS
For perilous th' assay, unheard the toil, ...Od.4.535.146.

PERILS
And will you run to Perils, Sword, and Law, ...4.HAdv.135.87.
By day no perils shall the just affright, ...6.21.11.69.
Great Perils, Father! wait th' unequal Fight; ....Il.8.129.404.
Long Toils, long Perils in their Cause I bore, ...Il.9.416.453.
And new to Perils of the direful Field: ....Il.9.569.462.
And 'scap'd the perils of the gulfy Main. ....Od.1.17.30.
(Doom'd to repeat the perils of the main, ...Od.4.650.150.
Enur'd to perils, to the worst resign'd. ....Od.5.286.185.
On the black sea what perils shou'd ensue. ....Od.5.386.190.
Thro' various seas by various perils tost, ...Od.9.309.319.
In storms by sea, in perils on the shore; ....Od.10.543.369.
But what those perils heav'n decrees, impart; ....Od.23.277.336.

PERIMEDES
Eurylochus and *Perimedes* bore. ....Od.11.26.380.

PERIOD
Say, from what Period then has *Jove* design'd ....1.TrSt.381.425.
"Who puts a Period to Domestick Strife! ....2.ChWB.191.65.
"And *Ho[adl]y* for a Period of a Mile." ....4.JD4.73.31.
Still must I mourn the Period of thy Days, ...Il.4.206.231.
And this the Period of our Wars and Fame? ....Il.11.955.78.
Without the Gods, how short a Period stands ....Il.12.9.81.

PERIODS
Labour and rest, that equal periods keep; ....2.ElAb.211.337.
My *Henley's* periods, or my Blackmore's numbers? ....5.DunA2.338.142.
How sweet the periods, neither said nor sung! ....5.DunA3.198.174.
"My H—ley's periods, or my Blackmore's numbers; ....5.DunB2.370.315.
How sweet the periods, neither sad, nor sung! ....5.DunB3.202.330.
At diff'rent Periods, yet our Fate the same! ....Il.22.613.481.

PERIPHAETES
Strong *Periphætes* and *Prothoön* bled, ...Il.14.609.192.

PERIPHAS
Just then Gigantic *Periphas* lay slain, ...Il.5.1038.316.
He seem'd like aged *Periphas* to Sight. ....Il.17.375.302.

PERIPHES

Mycenian Periphes, a mighty Name, ...Il.15.770.226.

PERISH

Dye ev'ry Flow'r, and perish All, but She. ....1.PAu.34.82.
Dye ev'ry Flow'r, and perish All, but He. ....1.PAu.34A.82.
As *Bodies* perish through Excess of *Blood.* ....1.EOC.304.274.
Men, Monkies, Lap-dogs, Parrots, perish all! ....2.RL4.120.193.
Some to remain, and some to perish soon, ...2.TemF.485.287.
So perish all, whose breast ne'er learn'd to glow ....2.Elegy.45.366.
A hero perish, or a sparrow fall, ...3.EOM1.88.25.
All forms that perish other forms supply, ...3.EOM3.17.93.
Thou too must perish, when thy feast is o'er! ....3.EOM3.70.99.
His oxen perish in his country's cause; ....3.Ep3.206.110.
In Flow'r of Age you perish for a Song! ....4.HS1.102.15.
I will, or perish in the gen'rous Cause. ....4.HS1.117.17.
Heav'ns! what a pyle! whole ages perish there: ....5.DunA3.69.156.
Heav'ns! what a pile! whole ages perish there, ...5.DunB3.77.324.
Gods! let me perish on this hateful Shore. ....Il.2.320.142.
The Chief, to perish at his People's Head. ....Il.5.763.303.
Ilion shall perish whole, and bury All; ....Il.6.73.327.
Once more will perish if my *Hector* fall. ....Il.6.547.354.
Or all must perish in the Wrath of *Jove.* ....Il.8.46.398.
They breathe or perish, as the Fates ordain. ....Il.8.531.422.
Lest all should perish in the Rage of *Jove.* ....Il.8.583.424.
But now to perish by *Atrides'* Sword: ....Il.11.146.42.
Thus must ye perish on a barb'rous Coast? ....Il.11.949.77.
All *Troy* must perish, if their Arms prevail, ...Il.12.85.84.
Fools! will ye perish for your Leader's Vice? ....Il.13.149.111.
Resolv'd to perish in his Country's Cause, ...Il.13.534.132.
Than perish in the Danger we may shun. ....Il.14.87.162.
So may he perish, so may *Jove* disclaim ....Il.14.163.165.
But *Hector* was not doom'd to perish then: ....Il.15.540.217.
What Victims perish round the mighty Dead? ....Il.17.279.298.
First perish all, e'er haughty *Troy* shall boast ....Il.17.478.306.
If *Greece* must perish, we thy Will obey, ...Il.17.731.316.
But let us perish in the Face of Day! ....Il.17.732.317.
Now perish *Troy!* He said, and rush'd to Fight. ....Il.19.471.391.
So perish *Troy,* and all the *Trojan* Line! ....Il.21.141.427.
Or if I perish, let her see me fall ....Il.22.152.459.
'Tis true I perish, yet I perish great: ....Il.22.386.471.
'Tis true I perish, yet I perish great: ....Il.22.386.471.
All, all must perish, and by fraud you die! ....Od.2.413.81.
Is mark'd to perish in a deathful snare: ....Od.4.929.161.
Perish those arms which by the Gods decree ....Od.11.681.418.
Ye perish all! tho' he who rules the main ....Od.12.135.438.
To live, or perish! to be safe, be wise! ....Od.12.193.441.
Ah perish *Helen!* perish all her kind! ....Od.14.80.40.
Ah perish *Helen!* perish all her kind! ....Od.14.80.40.
To perish in the rough *Trinacrian* sea. ....Od.19.316.209.
The rest must perish, their great leader slain. ....Od.22.279.300.

PERISH'D

A *Beau* and *Witling* perish'd in the Throng, ...2.RL5.59.204.
Cut from the root my perish'd joys I see, ...2.ElAb.258Z1.340.
Their ruins perish'd, and their place no more! ....6.71.22A.203.
They rush'd to War, and perish'd on the Plain. ....Il.2.1011.170.
Perhaps had perish'd; had not *Hermes'* Care ....Il.5.479.291.
What *Greeks* are perish'd! what a People lost! ....Il.7.393.383.
(Oh! had we perish'd e'er they touch'd our Shore! ....Il.7.465.387.
They rush'd to Fight, and perish'd on the Plain! ....Il.11.430.53.
No *Greek* shall e'er his perish'd Relicks grace, ...Il.21.375.436.
Well have they perish'd, for in Fight they fell. ....Il.22.99.456.
(Oh had I perish'd, e'er that Form divine ....Il.24.966.576.
You weep not for a perish'd Lord, alone. ....Od.1.452.54.
And now had perish'd, whelm'd beneath the main, ...Od.5.554.199.
Perish'd the nation in unrighteous war, ...Od.7.76.237.
Perish'd the Prince, and left this only heir.) ....Od.7.77.237.
Swept from the earth, he perish'd in his prime; ....Od.8.258.276.
So perish'd he: and left (for ever lost) ....Od.14.158.43.
Long, long since perish'd on a distant shore! ....Od.17.379.150.
Or haply perish'd on some distant coast, ...Od.20.263.246.
The sad remembrance of a perish'd man. ....Od.21.90.263.

PERISHABLE

(Who thrice has seen the perishable kind ....Od.3.303.101.

PERISHES

Some *Athens* perishes, some *Tully* bleeds. ....6.51i.32.152.
Some *Athens* perishes, or some *Tully* bleeds. ....6.51i.32A.152.

PERISHT

Oh! had he perisht on some well-fought day, ...Od.14.401.55.

PERITHOUS

Whence rose *Perithous* like the Gods in Fame. ....Il.14.362.180.

PERITHOUS'

This *Polypætes,* great *Perithous'* Heir, ...Il.12.143.86.
The god-like *Theseus,* and *Perithous'* shade; ....Od.11.778.425.
Perithous' roofs with frantick riot rung; ....Od.21.318.274.

PERIWIG

E'er since Sir Fopling's Periwig was Praise, ...5.DunB1.167.282.

PERJUR'D

Of perjur'd *Doris,* dying I complain: ....1.PAu.58.84.
Of perjur'd *Doris,* dying I'll complain: ....1.PAu.58A.84.
A perjur'd Prince a leaden Saint revere, ...3.Ep1.148.28.
The Clergy perjur'd, thy whole People sold. ....4.1740.82.336.
For perjur'd Kings, and all who falsely swear! ....Il.3.353.209.
And Faith is scorn'd by all the perjur'd Line. ....Il.4.191.230.
Such mighty Woes on perjur'd Princes wait; ....Il.4.204.231.
Whose Crimes sit heavy on her perjur'd Head; ....Il.4.271.234.
Whose perjur'd Monarch well deserv'd his Fate; ....Il.5.805.304.
For perjur'd Kings, and all who falsely swear! ....Il.19.272.383.

PERJUR'D (CONTINUED)

Not till within her Tow'rs the perjur'd Train ....Il.21.243.431.
And destin'd Vengeance on the perjur'd King. ....Il.21.530.443.
But by the pow'rs that hate the perjur'd, swear, ...Od.2.418.81.
The perjur'd sex, and blacken all the race; ....Od.11.538.409.

PERJURIES

Of Nature broke; and Royal Perjuries; ....1.TrSt.179.418.
The Field shall prove how Perjuries succeed, ...Il.4.308.235.

PERJURY

Add Perjury to Fraud, and make it thine.— ....Il.23.522.510.
The due reward of fraud and perjury. ....Od.14.442.57.

PERKS

When ev'ry Coxcomb perks them in my face? ....4.Arbu.74.101.
That *Edward's* Miss thus perks it in your face, ...6.41.46.114.

PERMISSION

Not one without Permission feed, ...6.135.51.368.
Nor one without Permission feed, ...6.135.51A.368.

PERMIT

Let me (if tears and grief permit) relate ....1.TrFD.5.385.
Mean while permit that my preluding Muse ....1.TrSt.49.411.
Did but for *David's* Righteous Sake permit; ....2.ChJM.691.48.
"Permit (he cries) no stranger to your fame ....4.JD4.66.31.
Permit thy Daughter, gracious *Jove!* to tell ....Il.5.509.292.
Some Space at least permit the War to breathe, ...Il.7.398.383.
But ah! permit to pity human State; ....Il.8.41.397.
Permit not these to sue, and sue in vain! ....Il.9.648.466.
Permit the mourning Legions to retire, ...Il.23.196.497.
Permit me now, belov'd of *Jove!* to steep ....Il.24.804.570.
If then thy Will permit (the Monarch said) ....Il.24.828.571.
Patient permit the sadly-pleasing strain; ....Od.1.449.54.
But now to *Pyle* permit my destin'd way, ...Od.4.817.157.
Since audience mild is deign'd, permit my tongue ....Od.16.93.107.
A few hours space permit me here to stay; ....Od.17.28.133.
Gracious permit this pray'r, imperial Dame! ....Od.19.137.199.
If, stranger! I permit that mean attire, ...Od.19.375.212.
Wou'd *Jove* permit the meditated blow, ...Od.20.338.249.
Permit me (cries *Telemachus*) to claim ....Od.21.370.277.
If yet he breathes, permit thy son to give ....Od.22.399.307.
Permit me first thy royal robes to bring: ....Od.22.525.314.

PERMITS

Yet unreveng'd permits to press the Field; ....Il.8.156.405.
If Heav'n permits them then to enter *Troy.* ....Il.18.318.337.
In vain—He arms not, but permits his Friend ....Il.18.522.346.
And then permits their udder to the lambs. ....Od.9.403.322.

PERMITTED

Shuns the permitted, the forbid pursues! ....4.HAdv.101.83.

PERNICIOUS

Pernicious, wild, regardless of the Right. ....Il.5.1075.318.
Inflaming Wine, pernicious to Mankind, ...Il.6.330.342.
Learn hence, betimes to curb pernicious Ire, ...Il.9.709.469.
O'er the fierce Armies pours pernicious Night, ...Il.16.696.271.

PERO

Kings on their thrones for lovely *Pero* burn, ...Od.11.351.399.
For lovely *Pero* rack'd his lab'ring mind! ....Od.15.259.80.

PEROLLA

Now flames the Cid, and now Perolla burns; ....5.DunB1.250.288.

PERPETUAL

Perpetual Waters o'er the Pavement glide; ....1.TrUl.41.467.
His Soul, I hope, enjoys perpetual Glory, ...2.ChWB.237A.68.
The well-fill'd palace, the perpetual feast, ...Od.9.5.301.
Perpetual waters o'er the pavement glide; ....Od.13.132.8.

PERPETUITY

Abhor, a *Perpetuity* should stand: ....4.2HE2.247.183.

PERPLEX

Unknown, with Wonder may perplex your Mind. ....1.TrSt.659.438.
No artful wildness to perplex the scene; ....3.Ep4.116.148.
No artful Wilderness to perplex the scene; ....3.Ep4.116A.148.

PERPLEX'D

Waste sandy Vallies, once perplex'd with Thorn, ...1.Mes.73.119.
O ever gracious to perplex'd mankind! ....5.DunA1.151.82.
O! ever gracious to perplex'd mankind, ...5.DunB1.173.283.
Parnassus, thick perplex'd with horrid shades, ...Od.19.503.220.

PERPLEXT

Some Wag observes me thus perplext, ...4.HS6.51.253.

PERRHEBIANS

In twenty Sail the bold *Perrhebians* came ....Il.2.906.166.

PERSÈ

Her mother *Persè,* of old Ocean's strain, ...Od.10.159.348.

PERSECUTE

Plague with Dispute, or persecute with Rhyme. ....5.DunB4.260.369.

PERSECUTING

At *Hester's* Suit, the Persecuting Sword ....2.ChJM.75.18.

PERSECUTION

And *Persecution* mourn her broken Wheel: ....1.W-F.420.193.

PERSEPHONE
To whom *Persephone,* entire and whole, ...Od.10.584.371.

PERSEUS
Inspir'd young *Perseus* with a gen'rous Flame, ...1.TrSP.42.395.
From God-like *Perseus* those of *Argive* Race. ....1.TrSt.318.423.
Here to the Clouds victorious *Perseus* flies; ....1.TrSt.637.437.
And *Perseus* dreadful with *Minerva's* Shield: ....2.TemF.80.258.
Stream into Life, whence *Perseus* brave and bold. ......II.14.364.180.
Then *Perseus, Aretus,* and *Thrasymed;* ....Od.3.527.113.
In act to strike: Before him *Perseus* stood, ...Od.3.562.115.

PERSEVERANCE
If perseverance gain the Diver's prize, ...5.DunA2.289.137.
If perseverance gain the Diver's prize, ...5.DunB2.301.310.

PERSEVERING
The buzzing Flies, a persevering Train, ...II.16.781.273.

PERSIAN
Or *Mitra,* to whose Beams the *Persian* bows, ...1.TrSt.861.446.
E're look'd so lovely on her *Persian* King: ....2.ChJM.344.30.
And the Great Founder of the *Persian* Name: ....2.TemF.96.260.
Who turns a *Persian* Tale for half a crown, ...4.Arbu.180.109.
Paint, Marble, Gems, and Robes of *Persian* Dye, ...4.2HE2.265.183.
They shall like *Persian* Tales be read, ...6.58.55.173.
Who turns a *Persian* Tale for half a Crown, ...6.98.30.284.

PERSIANS
Persians and *Greeks* like *Turns of Nature* found, ...1.EOC.380.283.

PERSIST
Persist, by all divine in Man un-aw'd, ...5.DunA3.221.176.
Persist, by all divine in Man unaw'd, ...5.DunB3.223.331.
But if thou still persist to search my Birth, ...II.6.187.335.

PERSISTING
Some positive persisting Fops we know, ...1.EOC.568.305.

PERSON
His Royal Person from his Friends and Queen, ...1.TrUl.61.468.
Conceal thy Person, thy Designs direct, ...1.TrUl.180.471.
To give your Person than your Goods away: ....2.ChJM.183.23.
One bleeds in Person, and one bleeds in Purse; ....4.HAdv.58.81.
This, or that Person, what avails to shun? ....4.HAdv.77.81.
Could you directly to her Person go, ...4.HAdv.130.87.
(*Midas,* a sacred Person and a King) ....4.Arbu.70.100.
There are, who to my Person pay their court, ...4.Arbu.115.104.
The libel'd Person, and the pictur'd Shape; ....4.Arbu.353.121.
Spare then the Person, and expose the Vice. ....4.EpS2.12.314.
And thrusts his person full into your face. ....5.DunA3.132.161.
And thrusts his person full into your face ....5.DunB3.140.326.
Like his own Person, large and fair. ....6.29.8.83.
Without thy Person *Greece* shall win the Day, ...II.16.60.237.
Which, flowing long, her graceful Person clad; ....II.24.123.540.
These serv'd his Person at the royal Feast, ...II.24.582.561.
His trembling Limbs, his helpless Person, see! ....II.24.602.562.
Should such report thy honour'd Person here, ...II.24.822.571.
His royal person from his friends and Queen; ....Od.13.228.17.
Conceal thy person, thy designs direct, ...Od.13.347.24.
Bright in his person, brighter in his mind. ....Od.14.205.45.

PERSONAE
He courts the whole *Personæ Dramatis:* ....4.HAdv.72.81.

PERSONAGE
(The same, his ancient Personage to deck, ...2.RL5.89.207.

PERSONS
I knew their Persons, and admir'd their Parts, ...II.3.271.205.

PERSU
See PERSUES, PURSUE.
This more than Heaven persu ....6.50.16A.146.

PERSUADE
See PERSWADE.
Who taught thee Arts, *Alcinous* to persuade, ...1.TrUl.177.471.
In fact, 'tis true, no Nymph we cou'd persuade, ...2.TemF.386.282.
Or from a judge turn pleader, to persuade ....3.EOM2.155.73.
His angel Tongue, no mortal can persuade; ....3.Ep1.199A.32.
His angel Tongue, no mortal could persuade; ....3.Ep1.199B.32.
An angel Tongue, which no man can persuade; ....3.Ep1.199.32.
To meet *Pelides* you persuade in vain: ....II.20.118.399.
And let thy words *Telemachus* persuade: ....Od.3.458.109.
Who taught thee arts, *Alcinous* to persuade, ...Od.13.344.24.
His mod'rate words some better minds persuade: ....Od.24.530.373.

PERSUADED
Half-forc'd, and half-persuaded to the Fight. ....II.20.112.398.

PERSUADES
Alone *Eurylochus* persuades their stay. ....Od.10.508.368.

PERSUADING
A mighty sum of ill-persuading gold: ....Od.4.702.152.

PERSUASION
No Force can bend me, no Persuasion move. ....1.TrSt.414.427.
Experience'd *Nestor,* in Persuasion skill'd, ...II.1.331.103.
Th' experienc'd *Nestor,* in Persuasion skill'd, ...II.1.331A.103.
He fir'd with Praise and with Persuasion mov'd. ....II.2.226.138.
He, from whose Lips divine Persuasion flows, ...II.7.143.371.
The Azure Queen; let her Persuasion move ....II.24.96.539.
Kind the persuasion, and sincere my aim; ....Od.5.243.183.
And mild persuasion flow'd in eloquence. ....Od.7.213.247.

PERSUASIONS
In peace away! lest if persuasions fail, ...Od.18.18.167.

PERSUASIVE
Yet these with soft, persuasive Arts I sway'd, ...II.1.358.105.
And Steel well-temper'd, and persuasive Gold. ....II.6.62.326.
Go forth persuasive, and a while engage ....II.7.53.365.
Nestor, in each persuasive Art approv'd, ...II.7.389.383.
And steel well-temper'd, and persuasive Gold. ....II.11.176.43.
Persuasive Speech, and more persuasive Sighs, ...II.14.251.173.
Persuasive Speech, and more persuasive Sighs, ...II.14.251.173.
So Fathers speak (persuasive speech and mild!) ....Od.1.401.51.
Persuasive, thus, with accent soft began. ....Od.22.378.306.

PERSUES
See PERSU, PURSUE.
Dreaded in life, the mutter'd curse persues; ....Od.19.380.212.

PERSWADE
See PERSUADE.
Mentor beware, nor let that tongue perswade ....Od.22.235.298.

PERT
More pert, more proud, more positive than he. ....4.JD2.52.137.
More pert, more proud, more positive than he. ....4.JD2A.58.136.
What pert low Dialogue has Farqu'ar writ! ....4.2HE1.288.219.
With pert flat eyes she window'd well its head, ...5.DunA2.39.100.
Three Cambridge Sophs and three pert Templars came, ...5.DunA2.347.143.
With pert flat eyes she window'd well its head; ....5.DunB2.43.298.
Intoxicates the pert, and lulls the grave: ....5.DunB2.344.314.
Three College Sophs, and three pert Templars came, ...5.DunB2.379.315.
Serves but to keep fools pert, and knaves awake: ......5.DunB4.442.383.
More pert than witty, more a Wit than wise. ....6.99.6.286.

PERTNESS
Remembring she herself was Pertness once. ....5.DunB1.112.277.
Rememb'ring she herself was Pertness once. ....5.DunB4.280Z2.371.

PERU
Peru once more a Race of Kings behold, ...1.W-F.411.192.

PERUSE
Still with *It self compar'd,* his *Text* peruse; ....1.EOC.128.253.
Sleep, or peruse some ancient Book, ...4.HS6.130.259.
The brightest Eyes of *Britain* now peruse, ...6.19.78.64.

PERUSING
The bow perusing with exactest eye. ....Od.21.439.281.

PERUVIAN
For Indian spices, for Peruvian gold, ...4.1HE6.71.241.

PERVADE
And now pervade the dusky land of *Dreams,* ....Od.24.18.348.

PERVADING
Gradations just, has thy pervading soul ....3.EOM1.31.17.
And Centres just, has thy pervading soul ....3.EOM1.31A.17.

PERVERSE
But Man corrupt, perverse in all his ways, ...4.HAdv.98.83.
Perverse Mankind! whose Wills, created free, ...Od.1.41.31.

PERVERT
Let no Court-Sycophant pervert my sense, ...4.JD2.126.145.

PERVIOUS
Pervious to Winds, and open ev'ry way. ....2.TemF.427.284.
The bolted Valves are pervious to her flight. ....Od.4.1056.167.

PESCENNIUS
To gain Pescennius one employs his schemes, ...6.71.39.203.

PEST
The Pest a Virgin's Face and Bosom bears; ....1.TrSt.707.439.
But He, our Chief, provok'd the raging Pest, ...II.1.119.92.
The God propitiate, and the Pest asswage. ....II.1.192.96.
Thy direful Darts inflict the raging Pest; ....II.1.595.116.
This Pest he slaughter'd (for he read the Skies, ...II.6.225.337.
That Pest of *Troy,* that Ruin of our Race! ....II.6.353.343.
Begot this Pest of me, and all my Race.) ....II.22.539.478.
Tremendous pest! abhorr'd by man and Gods! ....Od.12.108.436.
Deathless the pest! impenetrably strong! ....Od.12.148.439.
This dreadful Pest! To her direct thy pray'r, ...Od.12.157.439.
The hideous pest, my labouring eyes I roll'd; ....Od.12.275.445.
Art thou foredoom'd my pest? the Heroe cry'd: ....Od.19.561.224.

PESTILENCE
Spreads the red Rod of angry Pestilence, ...6.137.4.373.
Shakes down Diseases, Pestilence and War; ....II.19.413.389.

PESTILENTIAL
Such Numbers fell by Pestilential Air! ....1.TrSt.766.442.

PESTLE
Thy Pestle braining all the Sons of *Rome.* ....6.48ii.8.134.

PET
If Dennis rails, and raves in furious Pet, ...6.49iii.3A.142.
If Dennis writes, and rails in furious Pet, ...6.49iii.3B.142.

PETEON
Those who in *Peteon* or *Ilesion* dwell, ...II.2.594.156.

PETER

Wise Peter sees the World's respect for Gold, ...3.Ep3.125.102.
Glorious Ambition! Peter, swell thy store, ...3.Ep3.127.102.
Scarce to wise *Peter* complaisant enough, ...4.HS1.3.5.
And laugh at Peers that put their Trust in *Peter*. ....4.HS1.40.9.
From you to me, from me to Peter Walter, ...4.HS2.168.69.
If Peter deigns to help you to your *own:* ....4.JD2.66.139.
What thanks, what praise, if Peter but supplies! ....4.JD2.67.139.
For not in Chariots Peter puts his trust; ....4.JD2.74.139.
To cheat a Friend, or Ward, he leaves to Peter; ....4.2HE1.197.211.
"To laugh at Fools who put their trust in *Peter*." ....4.EpS1.10.297.
"Laugh at those Fools who put their trust in *Peter*." ....4.EpS1.10A.297.
Is it for *Bond* or *Peter* (paltry Things!) ....4.EpS1.121.307.
Is it for *W[a]rd* or *Peter* (paltry Things!) ....4.EpS1.121A.307.
Ev'n *Peter* trembles once for his Ears. ....4.EpS2.57.315.
Fr. What always *Peter? Peter* thinks you mad, ...4.EpS2.58.315.
Fr. What always *Peter? Peter* thinks you mad, ...4.EpS2.58.315.
Peter complains, that God has given ....6.124iv.1.348.
Consider *Peter*, he's in Heaven; ....6.124iv.3.348.

PETER'S

Till Peter's Keys some christen'd Jove adorn, ...5.DunA3.101.159.
'Till Peter's keys some christ'ned Jove adorn, ...5.DunB3.109.325.

PETEUS'

Can *Peteus'* Son forget a Warrior's Part, ...Il.4.390.239.
Your Aid (said *Thoos*) *Peteus'* Son demands, ...Il.12.426.97.

PETEUS'S

Your Aid (said *Thoos*) *Peteus's* Son demands, ...1.TrES.80Z2.452.

PETITION'D

With Gay, who Petition'd you once on a time, ...6.42i.3.116.

PETITIONS

Come with Petitions fairly penn'd, ...4.HS6.65.255.
All vain petitions, mounting to the sky, ...5.DunA2.85.108.
Whose vain petitions, mounting to the sky, ...5.DunA2.85A.108.
All vain petitions, sent by winds on high, ...5.DunA2.85B.108.
All vain petitions, mounting to the sky, ...5.DunB2.89.300.

PETRIFY

And petrify a Genius to a Dunce: ....5.DunB4.264.370.

PETRONIUS

Fancy and Art in gay *Petronius* please, ...1.EOC.667.315.
Fancy and Art in gay *Petronius* meet, ...1.EOC.667A.315.

PETT

And send the Godly in a Pett, to pray. ....2.RL4.64.189.

PETTICOAT

We trust th'important Charge, the *Petticoat:* ....2.RL2.118.167.
At Quin's high plume, or Oldfield's petticoat, ...4.2HE1.331.223.

PETTICOATS

Or rumpled Petticoats, or tumbled Beds, ...2.RL4.72.190.

PETTY

Marriage may all those petty Tyrants chace, ...6.19.37.63.

PEWS

How could Devotion touch the country pews, ...4.2HE1.233.215.
The rest, some farm the Poor-box, some the Pews; ....4.1HE1.128.289.
Talk with Church-Wardens about Pews, ...6.39.22.111.

PHAËTON

So like a *Phaëton* appears, ...6.5.14.12.

PHAEA'S

The silver *Phæa's* glitt'ring Rills they lost, ...Od.15.318.85.

PHAEACIA

To reach *Phæacia* all thy nerves extend, ...Od.5.438.193.
Swift to *Phæacia* wing'd her rapid flight. ....Od.6.4.203.
"This realm, she flies: *Phæacia* is her scorn. ....Od.6.340.227.
Fierce to *Phæacia* crost the vast profound. ....Od.13.185.15.

PHAEACIA'S

Ah why forsake *Phæacia's* happy Shore? ....1.TrUl.81.468.
And this the Faith *Phæacia's* Rulers boast? ....1.TrUl.85.468.
And this the Faith *Phæacia's* Princes boast? ....1.TrUl.85A.468.
And heard thy Counsels on *Phæacia's* Shore. ....1.TrUl.200.472.
Then swell'd to sight *Phæacia's* dusky coast, ...Od.5.357.189.
Behold how near *Phæacia's* land he draws! ....Od.5.371.190.
Mean-time *Phæacia's* peers in council sate; ....Od.6.65.208.
Nobles and Chiefs who rule *Phæacia's* states, ...Od.8.11.262.
Than what *Phæacia's* sons discharg'd in air. ....Od.8.212.274.
Ah why forsake *Phæacia's* happy shore? ....Od.13.248.18.
And this the faith *Phæacia's* rulers boast? ....Od.13.252.18.
And heard thy counsels on *Phæacia's* shore. ....Od.13.367.25.
How sav'd from storms *Phæacia's* coast he trod, ...Od.23.365.342.

PHAEACIAN

The Sun descending, the *Phæacian* Train ....1.TrUl.1.465.
Now plac'd in order, the *Phæacian* Train ....1.TrUl.1A.465.
In elder times the soft *Phæacian* train ....Od.6.5.203.
Where their fair vests *Phæacian* virgins lave. ....Od.6.44.207.
They seek the cisterns where *Phæacian* dames ....Od.6.99.210.
Know, the *Phæacian* tribes this land divide; ....Od.6.236.221.
The captive dame *Phæacian* rovers bore, ...Od.7.11.233.
When near the fam'd *Phæacian* walls he drew, ...Od.7.23.235.
Unseen of all the rude *Phæacian* race. ....Od.7.52.236.
Father and Prince of the *Phæacian* name: ....Od.7.80.237.
In distant regions the *Phæacian* fame: ....Od.8.100.267.
Now plac'd in order, the *Phæacian* train ....Od.13.92.5.

PHAEACIAN (CONTINUED)

He landed on the fair *Phæacian* coast. ....Od.19.320.209.

PHAEACIANS

The bold *Phæacians,* there, whose haughty line ....Od.5.46.173.
Rise ye *Phæacians,* try your force, he cry'd; ....Od.8.230.275.
By soft *Phæacians,* my degen'rate race! ....Od.13.151.13.
Phæacians bore me to the port assign'd, ...Od.16.250.117.

PHAEBUS

Aurora dawn'd, and *Phæbus* shin'd in vain, ...Od.7.371.254.
And would to *Phæbus, Pallas,* and to *Jove,* ....Od.7.398.256.

PHAEBUS'

The first, by *Phæbus'* burning arrows fir'd, ...Od.7.82.237.

PHAEDRA

There mournful *Phædra* with sad *Procris* moves, ...Od.11.395.403.

PHAENICIAN

In a *Phænician* Vessel took my Flight; ....1.TrUl.149.470.
In a *Phænician* vessel took my flight, ...Od.13.316.22.
A false *Phænician* of insidious mind, ...Od.14.319.50.

PHAERAE

See PHERAE.
Him *Enope,* and *Phæræ* him obey, ...Il.9.196.442.
Thee *Enope,* and *Phæræ* thee obey, ...Il.9.383.451.
To *Diocles,* at *Phæræ,* they repair, ...Od.15.210.78.

PHAESTAN

Thus sav'd from death they gain'd the *Phæstan* shores, ...Od.3.380.105.

PHAESTUS

Thy Fate was next, O *Phæstus!* doom'd to feel ....Il.5.57.269.

PHAETHUSA

Lampetie fair, and *Phaethusa* young, ...Od.12.168.440.

PHALANX

Who forms the phalanx, and who points the way? ....3.EOM3.108.103.
With whom the firm *Athenian* Phalanx stands; ....Il.4.382.239.
Pierc'd the black *Phalanx,* and let in the Light. ......Il.11.126.41.
Broke the dark *Phalanx,* and let in the Light. ....Il.11.663.63.
A chosen Phalanx, firm, resolv'd as Fate, ...Il.13.177.113.
The *Grecian* Phalanx moveless as a Tow'r, ...Il.15.744.224.

PHALCES

Cebrion, Phalces, stern *Orthæus* stood, ...Il.13.994.152.
Phalces and *Mermer, Nestor's* Son o'erthrew. ....Il.14.607.191.

PHANTOM

And each Majestic Phantom sunk in Night. ....2.TemF.355.280.
And round thy phantom glue my clasping arms. ....2.ElAb.234.339.
The phantom flies me, as unkind as you. ....2.ElAb.236.339.
A wit it was, and call'd the phantom, More. ....5.DunA2.46.101.
A Wit it was, and call'd the phantom More. ....5.DunB2.50.298.
Yet dye thou can'st not, Phantom, oddly fated: ......6.116iv.5.327.
A Phantom rais'd, the same in Shape and Show ....Il.5.546.294.
And sleeps *Achilles,* (thus the Phantom said) ....Il.23.83.490.
To calm the Queen the Phantom-sister flies. ....Od.4.1054.167.
Enquire not of his doom, the Phantom cries, ...Od.4.1089.168.
To all the Phantom nations of the dead. ....Od.11.44.381.
Still as I spoke, the Phantom seem'd to moan, ...Od.11.100.385.
The phantom Prophet ceas'd, and sunk from sight ....Od.11.184.390.
Imperial Phantom, bow'd thee to the tomb? ....Od.11.494.408.
Nor glides a Phantom thro' the realms of night. .....Od.11.568.411.
Not to this troop, I fear, that phantom soar'd, ...Od.19.664.228.
The adverse host the phantom warrior ey'd, ...Od.22.233.298.

PHANTOM-SISTER

To calm the Queen the Phantom-sister flies. ....Od.4.1054.167.

PHANTOME

Then bids an empty Phantome rise to sight, ...Il.2.7.127.
The *Phantome* said; then, vanish'd from his sight, ...Il.2.43.129.
The heav'nly *Phantome* hover'd o'er my Head, ...Il.2.75.130.
To all the Phantome-nations of the dead; ....Od.10.627.374.

PHANTOME-NATIONS

To all the Phantome-nations of the dead; ....Od.10.627.374.

PHANTOMS

Strange Phantoms dance around, and skim before your Sight. .2.ChJM.804.54.
Strange Phantoms rising as the Mists arise; ....2.RL4.40.186.
A Train of Phantoms in wild Order rose, ...2.TemF.9.253.
Hosts rais'd by Fear, and Phantoms of a Day. ......2.TemF.461.285.
Two portals firm the various phantoms keep: ....Od.19.657.228.
Conferr'd the mournful Phantoms of the dead. .....Od.24.233.360.

PHAON

Phaon to *Ætna's* scorching Fields retires, ...1.TrSP.11.393.
A brighter *Phœbus, Phaon* might appear; ....1.TrSP.24.394.
Not *Bacchus'* self with *Phaon* cou'd compare: ....1.TrSP.26.394.
Phaon alone by *Phaon* must be lov'd! ....1.TrSP.48.395.
Phaon alone by *Phaon* must be lov'd! ....1.TrSP.48.395.
But, *Phaon* gone, those Shades delight no more. ...1.TrSP.168.400.
Of *Tereus* she, of *Phaon* I complain. ....1.TrSP.178.401.
(Wretch that I am, to call that *Phaon* mine!) ......1.TrSP.237.404.
Poor *Sapho* dies while careless *Phaon* stays. ....1.TrSP.249.404.
If not from *Phaon* I must hope for Ease, ...1.TrSP.256.404.
Since *Phaon* fled, I all those Joys resign, ...1.TrSP.236A.404.

PHAON'S

Can *Phaon's* Eyes forget his *Sapho's* Hand? .....1.TrSP.2.393.
For those might *Cynthia* lengthen *Phaon's* Sleep. ...1.TrSP.99.398.

PHAON'S (CONTINUED)
To Rocks and Seas I fly from *Phaon's* Hate, ...1.TrSP.205.402.
My *Phaon's* fled, and I those Arts resign, ...1.TrSP.236.404.

PHARAOH
Moses he serv'd as *Moses Pharaoh*, ...6.101.21.290.

PHARES
Phares and *Brysia's* valiant Troops, and those ....Il.2.703.159.

PHARIAN
In *Pharian* Fields to sow the Golden Grain; ....1.TrSt.860.446.
The wealthy tribes of *Pharian Thebes* obey) ....Od.4.170.128.
To all the *Pharian* race his healing arts. ....Od.4.322.134.
High o'er a gulphy sea, the *Pharian* Isle ....Od.4.479.142.
Th' oraculous Seer frequents the *Pharian* coast, ...Od.4.519.145.
Then steering backward from the *Pharian* Isle, ...Od.4.789.156.

PHARMACY
Such as sage *Chiron*, Sire of *Pharmacy*, ...Il.11.966.78.
Their Pain, soft Arts of Pharmacy can ease, ...Il.16.38.237.

PHEA'S
I led my Troops to *Phea's* trembling Wall, ...Il.7.164.372.

PHEASANT
See! from the Brake the whirring Pheasant springs, ...1.W-F.111.161.
Will chuse a *Pheasant* still before a *Hen*; ....4.HS2.18.55.
You would have sworn this Hen a Pheasant. ....6.93.8.256.

PHEASANT'S
One likes the Pheasant's wing, and one the leg; ....4.2HE2.84.171.

PHEDON
Phedon the fact affirm'd, whose sov'reign sway ....Od.19.329.210.

PHEGEUS
And first bold *Phegeus* cast his sounding Spear, ...Il.5.22.266.

PHELUS
This sprung from *Phelus*, and th' *Athenians* led; ....Il.15.377.211.

PHEMIUS
To *Phemius* was consign'd the chorded Lyre, ...Od.1.197.42.
Phemius, whose voice divine cou'd sweetest sing ....Od.1.199.42.
Phemius! let acts of Gods, and Heroes old, ...Od.1.433.53.
Medon, and *Phemius* skill'd in heav'nly song. ....Od.16.273.118.
(For *Phemius* to the Lyre attun'd the strain.) ....Od.17.312.147.
Phemius alone the hand of vengeance spar'd, ...Od.22.367.305.
Phemius the sweet, the heav'n-instructed bard. ....Od.22.368.305.
Sage *Medon* came, and *Phemius* came along; ....Od.24.505.372.

PHENEAN
The *Phenean* Fields, and *Orchomenian* Downs, ...Il.2.734.161.

PHENICIAN
This nymph, where anchor'd the *Phenician* train ....Od.15.460.93.

PHENOMENON
See PHOENOMENON.

PHERAE
See PHAERAE.
Where *Pheræ* hears the neighb'ring Waters fall, ...Il.2.866.165.
In well-built *Pheræ* held his lofty Seat: ....Il.5.672.300.
To *Pheræ* now, *Diocleus'* stately seat, ...Od.3.619.117.

PHERECLUS
Next artful *Phereclus* untimely fell; ....Il.5.75.269.
Thy Father's Skill, O *Phereclus*, was thine, ...Il.5.77.270.

PHERES
She gallant *Pheres* and fam'd *Æson* bred: ....Od.11.314.397.

PHERETIAN
As Eagles fleet, and of *Pheretian* Race; ....Il.2.927.167.
First flew *Eumelus* on *Pheretian* Steeds; ....Il.23.455.508.

PHERUSA
Thoa, Pherusa, Doto, Melita; ....Il.18.53.326.

PHIDAS
The Flow'r of *Athens, Stichius, Phidas* led, ...Il.13.863.147.

PHIDIAS
Or Phidias broken, and Apelles burn'd. ....5.DunA3.104.159.
Or Phidias broken, and Apelles burn'd. ....5.DunB3.112.325.

PHIDIPPUS
These *Antiphus* and bold *Phidippus* bring, ...Il.2.827.164.

PHIDON
Full oft has *Phidon*, whilst he pour'd the wine, ...Od.14.367.53.

PHILAETIUS
Philætius late arriv'd, a faithful swain. ....Od.20.234.244.
High canisters of bread *Philætius* plac'd; ....Od.20.320.248.
Philætius too relents, but secret shed ....Od.21.85.263.
Philætius thus. Oh were thy word not vain? ....Od.21.205.269.
To thy strict charge, *Philætius!* we consign ....Od.21.256.272.
In the same moment forth *Philætius* flies, ...Od.21.421.280.
And thus *Philætius* gloried o'er the dead. ....Od.22.317.301.

PHILEMON
And there, the groaning shelves Philemon bends. ....5.DunA1.134.80.
And here, the groaning shelves Philemon bends. ....5.DunA1.134A.80.

PHILEMON (CONTINUED)
And here the groaning shelves Philemon bends. ....5.DunB1.154.281.

PHILETOR'S
And stopp'd *Demuchus*, great *Philetor's* Heir, ...Il.20.528.416.

PHILIP
Charles to the Convent, Philip to the Field. ....3.Ep1.60.19.

PHILIP'S
If Justice *Philip's* costive Head ....6.58.53.173.

PHILIPS
Con. Philips cries, "A sneaking Dog I hate." ....4.HAdv.11.75.
Still to one Bishop *Philips* seem a Wit? ....4.Arbu.100.102.
As Eusden, Philips, Settle, writ of Kings) ....4.2HE1.417.231.
She saw slow Philips creep like Tate's poor page, ...5.DunA1.103.72.
And *Ambrose Philips* be prefer'd for Wit! ....5.DunA3.322B.188.
She saw slow Philips creep like Tate's poor page, ...5.DunB1.105.277.
Lo! Ambrose Philips is prefer'd for Wit! ....5.DunB3.326.336.
Of *gentle Philips* will I ever sing, ...6.40.1.112.
With *gentle Philips* shall the Vallies ring. ....6.40.2.112.
Lean *Philips*, and fat *Johnson*. ....6.47.20.129.
When Am[brose] Ph[ilip]s, now of high Renown, ...6.49i.1A.137.
When Ambrose Philips was preferr'd for Wit! ....6.106iii.3.307.

PHILIPS'S
Was *Philips's* beyond Dispute. ....6.44.26.123.

PHILOCTETES
With *Philoctetes* sail'd, whose matchless Art ....Il.2.874.165.
Brave *Philoctetes*, taught to wing the dart; ....Od.3.231.97.
Great *Philoctetes* taught the shaft to fly. ....Od.8.252.276.

PHILOMED
So Philomed"e, lect'ring all mankind ....3.Ep2.83.57.

PHILOMEDA'S
Sprung from the fair *Philomeda's* Embrace, ...Il.7.13.363.

PHILOMEL
When warbling *Philomel* salutes the Spring? ....1.PSp.26.63.
All, but the mournful *Philomel* and I: ....1.TrSP.176.401.
With mournful *Philomel* I join my Strain, ...1.TrSP.177.401.
And sung as sweet as Evening *Philomel*. ....2.ChWB.212.67.
Sad *Philomel*, in bow'ry shades unseen, ...Od.19.605.225.

PHILOMELA
Or hears the hawk when Philomela sings? ....3.EOM3.56.97.

PHILOMELA'S
Such Silence waits on *Philomela's* Strains, ...1.PWi.78.94.

PHILOMELIDES
His prowess *Philomelides* confess'd, ...Od.4.463.142.
His prowess *Philomelides* confest, ...Od.17.154.139.

PHILOSOPHER
Thou wert my guide, philosopher, and friend? ....3.EOM4.390.166.
You hold him no Philosopher at all. ....3.Ep1.8.16. ·
So *B[athurs]t* cries, Philosopher and Rake! ....4.HAdv.158.89.
Is this my Guide, Philosopher, and Friend? ....4.1HE1.177.293.

PHILOSOPHIC
There are, my Friend! whose philosophic eyes ....4.1HE6.7.237.

PHILOSOPHY
Deriv'd his high Philosophy from Those; ....2.ChJM.443.36.
Deriv'd this high Philosophy from Those; ....2.ChJM.443A.36.
Ev'n av'rice, prudence; sloth, philosophy; ....3.EOM2.188.77.
Turns you from sound Philosophy aside; ....4.HS2.6.55.
Nothing, to make Philosophy thy friend? ....4.1HE1.74.283.
Old Bodies of Philosophy appear. ....5.DunA1.132.80.
And proud *Philosophy* with breeches tore, ...5.DunA3.191z3.172.
While proud Philosophy repines to show ....5.DunA3.193.173.
Philosophy, that touch'd the Heavens before, ...5.DunA3.349.193.
While proud Philosophy repines to show, ...5.DunB3.197.330.
Philosophy, that lean'd on Heav'n before, ...5.DunB4.643.408.

PHILTRE
And this for Lust an am'rous Philtre bought, ...2.ChWB.404.76.

PHLEGETON
Which flaming *Phlegeton* surrounds, ...6.11.50.32.

PHLEGETON'S
Where *Phlegeton's* loud torrents rushing down, ...Od.10.608.374.

PHLEGIAS'
In *Phlegias'* Doom thy just Revenge appears, ...1.TrSt.851.445.

PHLEGM
Where Bile, and wind, and phlegm, and acid jar, ...4.HS2.71.59.

PHLEGN
When Bile, and wind, and Phlegn, and acid jar, ...4.HS2.71A.59.

PHLEGYANS
Of warring *Phlegyans*, and *Ephyrian* Arms; ....Il.13.391.124.

PHOCAE
The *Phocæ* swift surround his rocky cave, ...Od.4.544.146.
Of four vast *Phocæ* takes, to veil her wiles; ....Od.4.594.148.

PHOCIAN
Where the three Roads the *Phocian* Fields divide: ... 1.TrSt.92.414.
By *Hector* here the *Phocian Schedius* dy'd; ... Il.15.611.220.
Schedius the brave, of all the *Phocian* Kind ... Il.17.354.301.

PHOCIANS
The *Phocians* next in forty Barks repair, ... Il.2.620.157.

PHOCION
Here his Abode the martyr'd *Phocion* claims, ... 2.TemF.174.269.

PHOEBÈ'S
His beauteous Daughter fell by *Phœbè's* Dart; ... Il.6.250.339.

PHOEBE
To headless Phœbe his fair bride postpone, ... 5.DunB4.367.378.
Latona there and *Phœbe* heal'd the Wound, ... Il.5.543.294.
Nor glimmer'd *Phœbe* in th' ethereal plain: ... Od.9.168.312.

PHOEBE'S
Such Rays from *Phœbe's* bloody Circle flow, ... 1.TrSt.147.416.
Such Light does *Phœbe's* bloody Orb bestow, ... 1.TrSt.147A.416.

PHOEBUS
Inspire me *Phœbus,* in my *Delia's* Praise, ... 1.PSp.45.65.
Now setting *Phœbus* shone serenely bright, ... 1.PAu.13.81.
And *Phœbus* warm the ripening Ore to Gold. ... 1.W-F.396.190.
Ere warning *Phœbus* touch'd his trembling Ears, ... 1.EOC.131A.254.
The Harp and Bow wou'd you like *Phœbus* bear, ... 1.TrSP.23.394.
A brighter *Phœbus, Phaon* might appear; ... 1.TrSP.24.394.
Yet *Phœbus* lov'd, and *Bacchus* felt the Flame, ... 1.TrSP.27.394.
On *Phœbus* Shrine my Harp I'll then bestow, ... 1.TrSP.212.403.
"*Sapho* to *Phœbus* consecrates her Lyre, ... 1.TrSP.215.403.
"What suits with *Sapho, Phœbus,* suits with thee; ... 1.TrSP.216.403.
And *Phœbus* self is less a God to me. ... 1.TrSP.221.403.
Tho' *Phœbus* longs to mix his Rays with thine, ... 1.TrSt.39.411.
Not All bright *Phœbus* views in early Morn, ... 1.TrSt.212.419.
'Twas now the Time when *Phœbus* yields to Night, ... 1.TrSt.474.430.
Great *Jove* and *Phœbus* grac'd his noble Line; ... 1.TrSt.542.433.
Of awful *Phœbus:* I confess the Gods! ... 1.TrSt.597.435.
But *Phœbus* lov'd, and on the Flow'ry Side ... 1.TrSt.676.438.
Avenging *Phœbus* bent his deadly Bow, ... 1.TrSt.740.441.
But *Phœbus,* ask'd why noxious Fires appear, ... 1.TrSt.747.441.
Nor shalt thou, *Phœbus,* find a Suppliant here: ... 1.TrSt.760.442.
Unwelcome Life relenting *Phœbus* gives; ... 1.TrSt.781.442.
These solemn Feasts propitious *Phœbus* please, ... 1.TrSt.788.443.
Oh Father *Phœbus!* whether *Lycia's* Coast ... 1.TrSt.829.444.
Then thus to *Phœbus,* in the Realms above, ... 1.TrES.322.461.
Descend my *Phœbus,* on the *Phrygian* Plain, ... 1.TrES.324.461.
Clear was the Day, and *Phœbus* rising bright, ... 2.ChJM.613.44.
For this, ere *Phœbus* rose, he had implor'd ... 2.RL2.35.161.
This Phœbus promis'd (I forget the year) ... 3.Ep2.283.73.
Ascendant Phœbus watch'd that hour with care, ... 3.Ep2.285.73.
A youth unknown to Phœbus, in despair, ... 5.DunA2.205.127.
A youth unknown to Phœbus, in despair, ... 5.DunB2.213.306.
See, see, our own true Phœbus wears the bays! ... 5.DunB3.323.335.
Another Phœbus, thy own Phœbus reigns, ... 5.DunB4.61.347.
Another Phœbus, thy own Phœbus reigns, ... 5.DunB4.61.347.
Who false to Phœbus, bow the knee to Baal; ... 5.DunB4.93.350.
Rare Imp of *Phœbus,* hopeful Youth! ... 6.58.17.171.
Sheffield approves, consenting *Phœbus* bends, ... 6.63.7.188.
Twas Friendship—warm as *Phœbus,* kind as Love, ... 6.76.3.212.
And dread avenging *Phœbus,* Son of *Jove.* ... Il.1.30.87.
And *Phœbus* dart his burning Shafts no more. ... Il.1.90.91.
Why angry *Phœbus* bends his fatal Bow? ... Il.1.98.91.
The Priest of *Phœbus* sought by Gifts to gain ... Il.1.484.111.
To *Phœbus* pray'd, and *Phœbus* heard the Pray'r: ... Il.1.495.111.
To *Phœbus* pray'd, and *Phœbus* heard the Pray'r: ... Il.1.495.111.
Ulysses led to *Phœbus* sacred Fane; ... Il.1.573.115.
Supply'd by *Phœbus,* fill the swelling Sails; ... Il.1.625.117.
To *Lycian Phœbus* with the Silver Bow, ... Il.4.132.226.
But *Phœbus* now from *Ilion's* tow'ring Height ... Il.4.585.249.
Or *Phœbus* urg'd me to these Fields in vain. ... Il.5.137.273.
Him *Phœbus* took: He casts a Cloud around ... Il.5.429.289.
Then *Phœbus* bore the Chief of *Venus'* Race ... Il.5.541.294.
Venus, and *Phœbus* with the dreadful Bow, ... Il.5.946.311.
Minerva, Phœbus, and Almighty *Jove!* ... Il.7.160.372.
(From *Hector Phœbus* turn'd the flying Wound) ... Il.8.377.415.
While *Phœbus* shines, or Men have tongues to praise? ... Il.10.252.13.
Once more thank *Phœbus* for thy forfeit Breath, ... Il.11.465.54.
These, turn'd by *Phœbus* from their wonted ways, ... Il.12.23.82.
While *Phœbus* hastes, great *Hector* to prepare ... Il.15.63.197.
As *Phœbus* shooting from th' *Idæan* Brow, ... Il.15.268.207.
Behold! thy *Phœbus* shall his Arms employ, ... Il.15.290.208.
Phœbus, propitious still to thee, and *Troy.* ... Il.15.291.208.
Phœbus himself the rushing Battel led; ... Il.15.348.210.
As long as *Phœbus* bore unmov'd the Shield, ... Il.15.360.210.
Impending *Phœbus* pours around 'em Fear, ... Il.15.370.211.
And where the Bow, which *Phœbus* taught to bend? ... Il.15.517.217.
(That valu'd Life, O *Phœbus!* was thy Care) ... Il.15.618.220.
Some God, like *Phœbus,* ever kind to *Troy.* ... Il.16.119.241.
To *Phœbus* then ('twas all he could) he pray'd. ... Il.16.632.269.
Then thus to *Phœbus,* in the Realms above, ... Il.16.809.274.
Descend, my *Phœbus!* on the *Phrygian* Plain, ... Il.16.811.274.
But flaming *Phœbus* kept the sacred Tow'r. ... Il.16.858.276.
Thus while he thought, beside him *Phœbus* stood, ... Il.16.873.277.
By Fate and *Phœbus* was I first o'erthrown, ... Il.16.1024.282.
But *Phœbus* urg'd *Æneas* to the Fight; ... Il.17.374.302.
Then slain by *Phœbus* (*Hector* had the Name) ... Il.18.525.346.
Not brighter, *Phœbus* in th' Æthereal Way, ... Il.19.436.389.
In aid of *Troy, Latona, Phœbus* came, ... Il.20.51.396.
First silver-shafted *Phœbus* took the Plain ... Il.20.91.398.
Phœbus impells, and *Phœbus* gives him Force. ... Il.20.149.400.
Phœbus impells, and *Phœbus* gives him Force. ... Il.20.149.400.
By *Phœbus* urg'd; but *Phœbus* has bestow'd ... Il.20.343.408.
By *Phœbus* urg'd; but *Phœbus* has bestow'd ... Il.20.343.408.

PHOEBUS (CONTINUED)
But *Phœbus* warns him from high Heav'n, to shun ... Il.20.431.412.
Full and express? that *Phœbus* should employ ... Il.21.251.431.
And is it thus the youthful *Phœbus* flies, ... Il.21.547.444.
Phœbus rush'd forth, the flying Bands to meet, ... Il.21.629.448.
Phœbus it was; who, in his latest Hour, ... Il.22.265.466.
Then *Phœbus* left him. Fierce *Minerva* flies ... Il.22.277.467.
Phœbus and *Paris* shall avenge my Fate, ... Il.22.451.474.
Nor sacred *Phœbus* less employ'd his Care; ... Il.23.232.499.
But angry *Phœbus* to *Tydides* flies , ... Il.23.462.508.
To *Phœbus,* Patron of the Shaft and Bow. ... Il.23.1023.529.
For *Phœbus* watch'd it with superior Care, ... Il.24.30.536.
Or *Phœbus* animates with all his fires: ... Od.8.532.291.
For who by *Phœbus* uniform'd, could know ... Od.8.533.291.
(The Priest of *Phœbus* at th' *Ismarian* shrine) ... Od.9.231.316.
'Till evening *Phœbus* roll'd away the light: ... Od.9.651.333.
Here *Phœbus* rising in th' etherial way, ... Od.12.5.430.
'Till *Phœbus* downward plung'd his burning ray; ... Od.12.40.431.
From *Phœbus* and the bright *Neæra* sprung; ... Od.12.169.440.
To *Phœbus* shrines shall rise, and altars burn. ... Od.12.412.451.
And *Polyphides* on whom *Phœbus* shone ... Od.15.274.82.
With riper beams when *Phœbus* warms the day. ... Od.17.30.133.
While the broad beams of *Phœbus* are display'd, ... Od.17.214.142.
'Till *Phœbus* wheeling to the western goal ... Od.19.495.220.
Sacred to *Phœbus* is the solemn day, ... Od.21.274.273.
And to his hand if *Phœbus* give the day, ... Od.21.364.277.
If heav'n and *Phœbus* lend the Suitors aid. ... Od.21.396.279.
Phœbus assist! nor be the labour vain. ... Od.22.10.286.

PHOEBUS'
Defence from *Phœbus',* not from *Cupid's* Beams; ... 1.PSu.14.72.
Now *Cancer* glows with *Phœbus'* fiery Car; ... 1.W-F.147.163.
For this, I suffer'd *Phœbus'* Steeds to stray, ... 1.TrSt.308.423.
With *Phœbus'* Name resounds the vaulted Hall. ... 1.TrSt.651.437.
For this are *Phœbus'* Oracles explor'd, ... Il.1.135.93.
And Bulls and Goats to *Phœbus'* Altars paid. ... Il.1.415.107.
Hail Rev'rend Priest! to Phœbus' awful Dome ... Il.1.576.115.
Be calm, nor *Phœbus'* honour'd Gift disgrace. ... Il.5.273.280.
On *Phœbus'* Temple I'll his Arms bestow: ... Il.7.96.367.
Safe in his Helm (the Gift of *Phœbus'* Hands) ... Il.11.455.54.
By *Phœbus'* Darts she prophesy'd my Fall, ... Il.21.319.434.
Rosy and fair! as *Phœbus'* silver Bow ... Il.24.956.576.
By *Phœbus'* altars; thus o'erlooks the ground; ... Od.6.194.219.
Were doom'd by *Jove,* and *Phœbus'* just decree, ... Od.19.315.209.
Let then to *Phœbus'* name the fatted thighs ... Od.21.282.273.

PHOENICIAN
From *Cyprus* to the far *Phœnician* coast, ... Od.4.98.124.

PHOENIX
A *Phœnix* couch'd upon her Fun'ral Nest. ... 6.9viii.2.22.
Let *Phœnix* lead, rever'd for hoary Age, ... Il.9.221.443.
That done, to *Phœnix Ajax* gave the Sign; ... Il.9.291.448.
But here this Night let rev'rend *Phœnix* stay: ... Il.9.551.460.
Attend the stern Reply. Then *Phœnix* rose; ... Il.9.558.460.
How shall thy Friend, thy *Phœnix,* stay behind? ... Il.9.565.461.
Or at my Knee, by *Phœnix* wouldst thou stand; ... Il.9.610.464.
And *Phœnix* felt a Father's Joys in thee: ... Il.9.615.464.
Do this, my *Phœnix,* 'tis a gen'rous Part, ... Il.9.729.470.
In Slumbers sweet the rev'rend *Phœnix* lay. ... Il.9.778.472.
But *Phœnix* in his Tent the Chief retains, ... Il.9.808.473.
And *Phœnix;* strive to calm his Grief and Rage ... Il.19.332.386.
And sends before old *Phœnix* to the Place, ... Il.23.435.507.

PHOENIX'
No Food was grateful but from *Phœnix'* Hand. ... Il.9.611.464.
Not *Phœnix'* Daughter, beautiful and young, ... Il.14.367.180.
The fourth by *Phœnix'* grave Command was grac'd; ... Il.16.234.248.
Assuming *Phœnix'* Shape, on Earth she falls ... Il.17.624.312.

PHOENOMENON
Of that *Phœnomenon.* ... 6.94.28.260.

PHOENOPS
The Joy and Hope of *Phœnops* feeble Age, ... Il.5.197.276.
Like *Phœnops, Asius'* Son, appear'd the God; ... Il.17.655.313.

PHOESTUS
Or where by *Phœstus* silver *Jardan* runs; ... Il.2.789.162.

PHORBAS
(*Phorbas* the rich, of all the *Trojan* Train ... Il.14.575.190.

PHORCYS
Behold the Port of *Phorcys* fenc'd around ... 1.TrUl.226.473.
Phorcys and brave *Ascanius* here unite ... Il.2.1050.172.
Now *Phorcys, Chromius,* and *Hippothous* fires; ... Il.17.256.297.
Phorcys, as slain *Hippothous* he defends, ... Il.17.362.301.
Of *Phorcys,* dreaded in the sounds and seas:) ... Od.1.93.36.
Behold the port of *Phorcys!* fenc'd around ... Od.13.393.26.

PHORCYS'
Sacred to *Phorcys'* Pow'r, whose Name it bears; ... 1.TrUl.26.466.
Sacred to *Phorcys'* pow'r, whose name it bears: ... Od.13.117.7.

PHORONEUS'
Must I whose Cares *Phoroneus'* Tow'rs defend, ... 1.TrSt.350.424.

PHOSPHOR
Why sit we sad, when *Phosphor* shines so clear, ... 1.PSp.27.63.

PHRADMON
Young *Ageläus* (*Phradmon* was his Sire) ... Il.8.309.412.

PHRASE

Ancients in *Phrase,* meer Moderns in their *Sense!* .... 1.EOC.325.275.
'Tis Truth I tell, tho' not in Phrase refin'd; ....2.ChJM.742.51.
'Tis phrase absurd to call a Villain Great: ....3.EOM4.230.148.
What Nature wants (a phrase I much distrust) ....3.Ep3.25.88.
Of whose best Phrase and courtly Accent join'd, ...4.JD4.48.29.
"And coarse of Phrase—your *English* all are so. ....4.JD4.109.35.
Mark where a bold expressive Phrase appears, ...4.2HE2.165.177.
For Attic Phrase in Plato let them seek, ...5.DunB4.227.365.

PHRENSY

See FRENSIE, FRENZY, PHRENZY.
What pleasing Phrensy steals away my Soul? ....6.106ii.1.307.

PHRENZY

See FRENSIE, FRENZY, PHRENSY.
And from access of phrenzy lock'd the brain. ....Od.12.213.442.
A mirthful phrenzy seiz'd the fated crowd; ....Od.20.415.252.
With pleasing phrenzy has posses'd my mind; ....Od.21.106.264.

PHRONTES

Atrides' pilot, *Phrontes,* there expir'd; ....Od.3.354.103.
(*Phrontes,* of all the sons of men admir'd ....Od.3.355.103.

PHRYGIA

In *Phrygia* once were gallant Armies known, ...Il.3.245.204.
Thro' *Phrygia* once, and foreign Regions known, ...Il.24.245.546.
I see your Blood the Fields of *Phrygia* drown, ...Il.24.305.549.
Extended *Phrygia* own'd thy ample Reign, ...Il.24.685.565.

PHRYGIA'S

To *Phrygia's* Monarch, and the *Phrygian* State! ....Il.4.48.223.
And *Phrygia's* Horse, by *Thymbras'* ancient Wall; ....Il.10.502.26.

PHRYGIAN

Than *Phrygian* Marble or the *Parian* Stone. ....1.TrSP.166.400.
On golden Wings, the *Phrygian* to the Stars; ....1.TrSt.641.437.
Thy Rage the *Phrygian* felt, who durst aspire ....1.TrSt.845.445.
My God-like Son shall press the *Phrygian* Plain: ....1.TrES.228.458.
Descend my *Phœbus,* on the *Phrygian* Plain, ...1.TrES.324.461.
Jove was alike to *Latian* and to *Phrygian,* ....6.82iii.1.230.
Jove was alike to Trojan and to *Phrygian,* ....6.82iii.1A.230.
In Loves and Pleasures on the *Phrygian* Shore. ....Il.2.295.141.
And all who live to breathe this *Phrygian* Air. ....Il.2.367.145.
'Till ev'ry Soldier grasp a *Phrygian* Wife, ...Il.2.421.147.
Beneath his Conduct sought the *Phrygian* Shores. ....Il.2.774.162.
And dy'd a *Phrygian* Lance with *Grecian* Gore: ....Il.2.856.165.
Th' unwelcome Message to the *Phrygian* King. ....Il.2.965.169.
The *Phrygian* Monarch to the Peaceful Rite; ....Il.3.162.198.
And keen Reproach, from ev'ry *Phrygian* Dame: ....Il.3.510.216.
Thus having spoke, th' enamour'd *Phrygian* Boy ....Il.3.555.218.
To *Phrygia's* Monarch, and the *Phrygian* State! ....Il.4.48.223.
To raise in Arms the *Greek* and *Phrygian* Bands; ....Il.4.92.224.
To him the Goddess: *Phrygian!* can'st thou hear ....Il.4.123.226.
They fell with Glory on the *Phrygian* Plain. ....Il.5.680.300.
The *Phrygian* Queen to her rich Wardrobe went, ...Il.6.358.343.
And all the *Phrygian* Glories at an end. ....Il.6.417.347.
This seeks the *Grecian,* that the *Phrygian* Train. ....Il.7.371.382.
Not ev'n a *Phrygian* Dame, who dreads the Sword ....Il.8.188.406.
To lead in Exile the fair *Phrygian* Dames, ...Il.8.201.407.
Strook thro' the Back the *Phrygian* fell opprest; ....Il.8.311.412.
Till ev'ry Shaft in *Phrygian* Blood be dy'd. ....Il.8.358.414.
Some lasting Token of the *Phrygian* Foe, ...Il.8.640.426.
And such the Contract of the *Phrygian* King! ....Il.13.474.129.
My godlike Son shall press the *Phrygian* Plain: ....Il.16.531.264.
Descend, my *Phœbus!* on the *Phrygian* Plain, ...Il.16.811.274.
What skilful Divers are our *Phrygian* Foes! ....Il.16.904.278.
To *Grecian* Gods such let the *Phrygian* be, ...Il.21.502.442.
These *Phrygian* Fields, and press a foreign Shore. ....Il.21.698.450.
Must he, whose altars on the *Phrygian* shore ....Od.1.80.35.
Since great Ulysses sought the *Phrygian* plains, ...Od.2.33.61.
When great *Ulysses* sought the *Phrygian* shores ....Od.2.199.71.
Thy martial *Brother; on the *Phrygian* plain ....Od.4.255.131.
If *Phrygian* camps the friendly toils attest, ...Od.4.443.141.
Whom I with *Nestor* on the *Phrygian* coast ....Od.4.656.150.
Some dear-lov'd brother press'd the *Phrygian* plain? ....Od.8.634.297.
Com'st thou a wand'rer from the *Phrygian* shores? ....Od.11.197.391.
This arm that thunder'd o'er the *Phrygian* plain, ...Od.11.611.414.
He wing'd his voyage to the *Phrygian* shore. ....Od.19.233.204.

PHRYGIAN'S

Gods! can thy Courage fear the *Phrygian's* Pride? ....Il.8.184.406.

PHRYGIANS

Th' *Ascanian Phrygians,* eager for the Fight. ....Il.2.1051.172.
This if the *Phrygians* shall refuse to yield, ...Il.3.362.210.
The *Phrygians* now her scatter'd spoils enjoy, ...Il.18.341.338.

PHRYNE

Ask you why Phryne the whole Auction buys? ....3.Ep3.121.101.
Phryne foresees a general Excise. ....3.Ep3.122.101.
Phryne had Talents for Mankind, ...6.14v(b).1.49.
Phryne had Talents to oblige Mankind, ...6.14v(b).1A.49.

PHTHIA'S

See PTHIA'S.
Attend the nymph to *Phthia's* distant reign. ....Od.4.12.121.

PHYLACÈ

To these the Youth of *Phylacè* succeed, ...Il.2.847.164.

PHYLACE

A banish'd Man, in *Phylace* he dwell'd, ...Il.15.381.211.

PHYLACIAN

Whose arm should ravish from *Phylacian* fields ....Od.11.354.399.

PHYLACUS

And *Phylacus* from *Leitus* flies in vain. ....Il.6.44.325.
This drew from *Phylacus* his noble Line; ....Il.13.869.147.
As long, he groan'd in *Phylacus* his chains: ....Od.15.257.80.

PHYLEUS

Begot by *Phyleus,* the Belov'd of *Jove.* ....Il.2.762.162.
Phyleus and *Polydorus,* with the Spear. ....Il.23.732.519.

PHYLEUS'

But *Meges, Phyleus'* ample Breastplate wore, ...Il.15.626.220.
The Sons of *Nestor, Phyleus'* valiant Heir, ...Il.19.245.383.

PHYLIDES'

Phylides' Dart, (as *Amphiclus* drew nigh) ....Il.16.372.257.

PHYLO

In her soft hands the beauteous *Phylo* brought: ....Od.4.166.128.
Which heap'd with wool the beauteous *Phylo* brought: ....Od.4.180.128.

PHYSIC

"Learn from the beasts the physic of the field; ....3.EOM3.174.110.
See Physic beg the Stagyrite's defence! ....5.DunA3.351.193.
And lick up all their Physic of the Soul. ....5.DunB3.82.324.
Physic of *Metaphysic* begs defence, ...5.DunB4.645.408.

PHYSICAL

What makes all physical or moral ill? ....3.EOM4.111.138.

PHYSICIAN

And trembling *Greece* for her Physician fear'd. ....Il.11.631.61.
A wise Physician, skill'd our Wounds to heal, ...Il.11.636.62.

PHYSICIANS

Which grave Physicians scruple not to give; ....2.ChJM.376.32.
And Death-watches Physicians. ....6.53.24.162.

PHYSICK

And of their fragrant Physick spoils the Fields: ....1.W-F.242.171.
Make some take Physick, others scribble Plays; ....2.RL4.62.189.
And lick up all their Physick of the Soul. ....5.DunA3.74.156.

PICK

Go drench a Pick-pocket, and join the Mob. ....4.EpS2.41.315.
Can stoop to pick up *Strings* and *Sticks.* ....6.135.12.366.
May wear a Pick-lock at his Side; ....6.135.34.367.

PICK-LOCK

May wear a Pick-lock at his Side; ....6.135.34.367.

PICK-POCKET

Go drench a Pick-pocket, and join the Mob. ....4.EpS2.41.315.

PICK'D

Forth from the heap she pick'd her Vot'ry's pray'r. ....5.DunA2.91.108.
Forth from the heap she pick'd her Vot'ry's pray'r, ...5.DunB2.95.300.

PICKENBURG

See BUCKENBURG.
Tell P[ickenbur]g how slim she's grown ....6.61.24.181.
Tell P[ickenbur]g how thin she's grown ....6.61.24A.181.

PICKLE

Poor *Umbra,* left in this abandon'd Pickle, ...6.49ii.13.140.
The plenteous Pickle shall preserve the Fish, ...6.96ii.77.274.

PICKS

Picks from each sex, to make the Fav'rite blest, ...3.Ep2.273A.72.
Picks from each sex, to make its Fav'rite blest, ...3.Ep2.273.72.
And, in the Happy Minute, picks your Fob: ....4.HAdv.22.77.

PICQUETTE

He thanks you not, his pride was in Picquette, ...3.Ep1.144A.27.
He thanks you not, his pride is in Picquette, ...3.Ep1.144.27.

PICTUR'D

While Fancy pictur'd ev'ry lively Part, ...2.ChJM.232.25.
The libel'd Person, and the pictur'd Shape; ....4.Arbu.353.121.
While pictur'd to thy mind appear'd in view ....Od.4.254.131.

PICTURE

As, in some well-wrought picture, light and shade, ...3.EOM2.208.81.
And by this picture learn to dress her mind; ....6.4ii.2.9.
Strike in the sketch, or in the picture glow; ....6.52.44.157.

PICTURES

How many pictures of one Nymph we view, ...3.Ep2.5.48.
Pictures like these, dear Madam, to design, ...3.Ep2.151.62.
Artists must chuse his Pictures, Music, Meats: ....3.Ep4.6.134.
"Tho' in his Pictures Lust be full display'd, ...4.JD4.94.33.
Much they extoll'd his Pictures, much his Seat, ...4.Arbu.239.113.
Much they extoll'd the Pictures, much the Seat, ...4.Arbu.239A.113.
Or where the pictures for the page attone, ...5.DunB1.139.280.
Divert her eyes with pictures in the fire, ...6.45.19.125.
Whose Art was Nature, and whose Pictures thought; ....6.108.2.312.

PIDDLE

Content with little, I can piddle here ....4.HS2.137.65.

PIDLING

From slashing *Bentley* down to pidling *Tibalds.* ....4.Arbu.164.108.
From daring Bentley down to pidling *Tibalds.* ....4.Arbu.164B.108.
From slashing *B[entle]y* down to pidling *T[ibbald]s:* ....6.98.14.283.

PIDLING 104 PIETY

PIDLING (CONTINUED)
From sanguine *Sew[ell]* down to pidling *T[ibbald]s:* .... 6.98.14A.283.

PIDYTES
Ulysses' Spear *Pidytes* sent to Hell; .... Il.6.36.325.

PIECE
Whoever thinks a faultless Piece to see, ... 1.EOC.253.268.
Nature's chief Master-piece is writing well. .... 1.EOC.724.323.
This saving counsel, "Keep your Piece nine years." .... 4.Arbu.40.98.
"The Piece you think is incorrect: why take it, ... 4.Arbu.45.99.
Such piece-meal Critics some regard may claim, ... 4.Arbu.167A.108.
A past, vamp'd, future, old, reviv'd, new piece, ... 5.DunA1.238.91.
A past, vamp'd, future, old, reviv'd, new piece, ... 5.DunB1.284.290.
And South beheld that Master-piece of Man." .... 5.DunB4.174.358.
Fore-piece and Buttons all-to-brest, ... 6.14i.19.42.
He was a Piece of Emperor, ... 6.30.29.87.
To see a piece of failing flesh and blood, ... 6.41.47.114.
And that this Piece was meant for *Ozell.* .... 6.44.18.123.
Each heav'nly piece unweary'd we compare, ... 6.52.35.157.
A small Euphrates thro' the piece is roll'd, ... 6.71.29.203.

PIECE-MEAL
Such piece-meal Critics some regard may claim, ... 4.Arbu.167A.108.

PIECEMEAL
Piecemeal they win this Acre first, then that, ... 4.JD2.91.141.
Piecemeal he gains this Acre first, then that, ... 4.JD2A.94.140.

PIECES
See PEICES.
(Tho' cut in pieces e'er my Lord can eat) .... 4.HS2.22.55.
In small pieces cut it, ... 6.91.3A.253.
And first in Pieces cut it; .... 6.94.42.260.

PIERC'D
Their Manly Breasts are pierc'd with many a Wound, ... 1.TrES.163.455.
The next more fatal pierc'd *Achilles'* Steed, ... 1.TrES.269.459.
Aim'd at his Breast, it pierc'd the mortal Part .... 1.TrES.286.460.
He pierc'd the glitt'ring Clouds with golden Streams, ... 2.ChJM.615.44.
The pierc'd Battalions dis-united fall, ... 2.RL3.85.174.
For hearts so touch'd, so pierc'd, so lost as mine. .... 2.ElAb.196.336.
And He, whose Lightning pierc'd th' *Iberian* Lines, ... 4.HS1.129.17.
Strongest of Men, they pierc'd the Mountain Boar, ... Il.1.355.105.
Nor can the Depths of Fate be pierc'd by thee. .... Il.1.707.121.
Nor pierc'd the brazen Orb, but with a Bound .... Il.3.429.212.
Who pierc'd long since beneath his Arrows bled; .... Il.4.139.227.
The Folds it pierc'd, the plaited Linen tore, ... Il.4.168.229.
Pierc'd with a winged Shaft (the Deed of *Troy)* .... Il.4.232.232.
Pierc'd by some *Lycian* or *Dardanian* Bow, ... Il.4.240.232.
Thus pierc'd by *Ajax, Simoïsius* lies .... Il.4.560.248.
But pierc'd his Breast, and stretch'd him on the Plain. .... Il.5.26.266.
And pierc'd his Shoulder as he mounts his Car; .... Il.5.62.269.
Deep in his Shoulder pierc'd, and drank the Gore: .... Il.5.131.273.
Pierc'd the tough Orb, and in his Cuirass hung. .... Il.5.344.283.
Which driv'n by *Pallas,* pierc'd a vital Part; .... Il.5.352.283.
Pierc'd in his own Dominions of the Dead; .... Il.5.488.291.
'Till pierc'd at distance from their native Den, ... Il.5.685.300.
Pierc'd by my Spear to endless Darkness go! .... Il.5.800.304.
The gloomy Volumes, pierc'd with Light, divide. .... Il.5.935.311.
It pierc'd the God: His Groin receiv'd the Wound. .... Il.5.1051.316.
Or pierc'd with *Grecian* Darts, for Ages lie, ... Il.5.1090.318.
Had pierc'd his Courser in a mortal Part; .... Il.8.104.402.
Pierc'd in the Back, a vile, dishonest Wound? .... Il.8.120.403.
Pierc'd the deep Ranks; their strongest Battel tore; .... Il.8.307.412.
He miss'd the Mark; but pierc'd *Gorgythio's* Heart, ... Il.8.367.414.
Pierc'd the black *Phalanx,* and let in the Light. .... Il.11.126.41.
Which pierc'd his Brain, & stretch'd him on the Ground: .... Il.11.132.41.
Pierc'd in the Breast the base-born *Isus* bleeds; .... Il.11.147.42.
And pierc'd his Breast: supine he breath'd his last. .... Il.11.186.43.
While pierc'd with Grief the much-lov'd Youth he view'd, ... Il.11.323.49.
But pierc'd his Foot, and nail'd it to the Plain. .... Il.11.482.55.
Pierc'd thro' the Shoulder, first *Deiopis* fell; .... Il.11.531.57.
He said, and forceful pierc'd his spacious Shield; .... Il.11.546.58.
But pierc'd by this, to endless Darkness go, ... Il.11.556.58.
Between his Shoulders pierc'd the following Dart, ... Il.11.560.59.
Had pierc'd *Machaon* with a distant Wound: .... Il.11.629.61.
Lie pierc'd with Wounds and bleeding in the Fleet. .... Il.11.961.78.
Pierc'd thro' his Helmet's brazen Vizor, fell; .... Il.12.214.88.
Their manly Breasts are pierc'd with many a Wound, ... Il.12.517.100.
The glitt'ring Javelin pierc'd the tough Bull-hide: .... Il.13.216.116.
But pierc'd not thro: Unfaithful to his Hand, ... Il.13.217.116.
Him *Teucer* pierc'd between the Throat and Ear; .... Il.13.239.116.
Sung on, and pierc'd *Amphimachus* his Heart, ... Il.13.248.117.
And pierc'd with Sorrow for his * Grandson slain, ... Il.13.274.117.
Pierc'd by *Antilochus,* he pants beneath .... Il.13.505.130.
And pierc'd, obliquely, King *Hypsenor's* Breast: .... Il.13.520.131.
And pierc'd *Ascalaphus,* the brave and young: .... Il.13.657.137.
He pierc'd his Throat; the bending Head deprest .... Il.13.686.137.
Pierc'd with his Lance the Hand that grasp'd the Bow, ... Il.13.746.140.
Nor pierc'd *Pisander* thro' *Atrides'* Shield; .... Il.13.759.141.
For these were pierc'd with many a ghastly Wound, ... Il.13.957.151.
Pierc'd by whose Point, the Son of *Enops* bled; .... Il.14.518.188.
He pierc'd his Heart—Such Fate attends you all, ... Il.14.561.190.
Pierc'd in the Flank by *Menelaus'* Steel, ... Il.14.611.192.
Pierc'd thro' the Shoulder as he basely flies. .... Il.15.387.212.
But pierc'd by *Telamon's* huge Lance expires; .... Il.15.490.216.
There pierc'd by *Ajax,* sunk *Laodamas,* .... Il.15.612.220.
He pierc'd the Centre of his sounding Shield: .... Il.15.625.220.
Lies pierc'd with Wounds, and bleeding in his Tent. .... Il.16.34.236.
Pierc'd in the Flank, lamented Youth! he lies. .... Il.16.379.257.
Pierc'd thro' the Shoulder as he mounts his Steeds; .... Il.16.411.259.
Which pierc'd below the Shield his valiant Heart. .... Il.16.485.262.
Aim'd at his Breast, it pierc'd the mortal Part .... Il.16.591.267.
Lo! stiff with clotted Blood, and Pierc'd with Pain, ... Il.16.637.269.
Pierc'd thro' the Bosom with a sudden Wound, ... Il.16.727.272.

PIERC'D (CONTINUED)
Pierc'd thro' the dauntless Heart, then tumbles slain; .... Il.16.911.279.
Lies pierc'd with Wounds among the vulgar Dead. .... Il.17.2.286.
It pierc'd his Throat, and bent him to the Plain; .... Il.17.50.289.
It pierc'd his Belt, emboss'd with curious Art; .... Il.17.586.311.
Pierc'd thro' the Wrist; and raging with the Pain .... Il.17.681.314.
So pierc'd with Sorrows, so o'erwhelm'd as mine? .... Il.18.502.345.
And pierc'd the *Dardan* Shield's extremest Bound, ... Il.20.323.407.
Pierc'd thro' the Neck: He left him panting there, ... Il.20.527.416.
One struck, but pierc'd not the *Vulcanian* Shield; .... Il.21.182.429.
Nor pierc'd the Windpipe yet, nor took the Pow'r .... Il.22.411.472.
The conscious Monarch pierc'd the coy disguise, ... Od.4.153.127.
Or seen his mother pierc'd with grief expire. .... Od.4.971.163.
Had pierc'd the hapless hunter to the heart. .... Od.5.158.179.
With those he pierc'd 'em, and with clinchers bound. .... Od.5.318.187.
From the pierc'd pupil spouts the boiling blood; .... Od.9.462.325.
Pierc'd with her golden shafts the rere of night; .... Od.19.500.220.
Pierc'd thro' and thro', the solid gate resounds. .... Od.21.464.282.
And pierc'd the neck. He falls, and breathes his last. .... Od.22.20.287.
Pierc'd thro' the breast the rude *Ctesippus* bled, ... Od.22.316.301.

PIERCE
Can pierce the Darkness, and abhors the Day; .... 1.TrSt.72.413.
But who can pierce into the Depths of Fate?) .... 1.TrSt.546.433.
He, who thro' vast immensity can pierce, ... 3.EOM1.23.15.
They pierce my Thickets, thro' my Grot they glide, ... 4.Arbu.8.96.
Pierce the soft lab'rinth of a Lady's ear .... 4.JD2.55.137.
The dagger wont to pierce the Tyrant's breast; .... 5.DunB4.38.344.
Force thro' the *Greeks,* and pierce their haughty Lord; .... Il.1.256.99.
Incessant fly, and pierce the *Grecian* Hearts: .... Il.1.497.112.
Pierce the tough Cors'lets and the brazen Shields. .... Il.2.652.158.
Oh pierce that Mortal, if we Mortal call .... Il.5.222.278.
Like Arrows pierce me, for thy Words are wise. .... Il.14.115.163.
Pierce the thick Battel, and provoke the War. .... Il.17.136.293.
Thy certain Arrows pierce the savage Race? .... Il.21.562.445.
Whose eye can pierce the dark recess of fate. .... Od.4.472.142.
Stun my scar'd ears, and pierce hell's utmost bounds. .... Od.11.782.425.
Whose eye can pierce the dark recess of fate. .... Od.17.161.139.
Or some brave Suitor's sword, might pierce the heart .... Od.17.301.146.
Nor solar ray, cou'd pierce the shadowy bow'r, ... Od.19.514.221.
And their own darts shall pierce the Prince and King. .... Od.22.157.294.

PIERCES
His Cors'let pierces, and his Garment rends, ... Il.3.441.213.

PIERCING
The browzing cattel, or the piercing steel. .... 1.TrFD.91.390.
The Balls are wounded with the piercing Ray, ... 2.ChJM.800.53.
The Balls seem wounded with the piercing Ray, ... 2.ChJM.800A.53.
His piercing Eyes, erect, appear to view .... 2.TemF.236.274.
By *Laurels* shielded from the piercing Day: .... 6.14iv.22.47.
As when the piercing blasts of Boreas blow, ... 6.82v.1A.231.
With Eyes so piercing, yet so pleasant, ... 6.93.7.256.
Use, use (quoth Jove) those piercing eyes, ... 6.119.5A.336.
With piercing Frosts, or thick-descending Rain, ... Il.3.6.188.
With piercing Shrieks the Youth resigns his Breath, ... Il.4.577.249.
Thy angry Lance; which piercing to the Bone .... Il.5.821.305.
With piercing Cries, and supplicating Tears: .... Il.9.702.469.
Heart-piercing Anguish, at his haughty Boast, ... Il.13.527.131.
His piercing Eyes thro' all the Battel stray, ... Il.13.1015.153.
At the fierce Foe he launch'd his piercing Steel; .... Il.14.538.189.
Heart-piercing Anguish struck the *Grecian* Host, ... Il.14.569.190.
With Anguish *Ajax* views the piercing Sight, ... Il.15.508.216.
Ev'n yet, the *Greeks* with piercing Shouts inspires, ... Il.15.888.231.
Sharp in his Thigh he felt the piercing Wound; .... Il.16.367.257.
And round on all sides sent his piercing View. .... Il.17.760.318.
As when the piercing Blasts of *Boreas* blow, ... Il.19.380.387.
And on his Knees with piercing Shrieks he fell; .... Il.20.482.414.
The wretched Matron feels thy piercing Dart; .... Il.21.559.445.
With piercing Shrieks his bitter Fate she moans, ... Il.22.514.477.
Amid the Clouds the piercing Arrow feels; .... Il.23.1035.530.
The hoary Monarch thus. Her piercing Cries .... Il.24.241.546.
(*Atlas* her sire, to whose far-piercing eye .... Od.1.67.33.
And ev'ry piercing note inflicts a wound. .... Od.1.440.53.
'Till haply piercing thro' the dark disguise .... Od.4.340.136.
Hard toil! the prophet's piercing eye to shun; .... Od.4.596.148.
Nor wind sharp-piercing, nor the rushing show'r; .... Od.5.621.201.
Wide o'er the shore with many a piercing cry .... Od.6.165.216.
The grain deep-piercing till it scoops it out: .... Od.9.460.325.
His eye how piercing, and his scent how true, ... Od.17.384.150.

PIERIA
O'er high *Pieria* thence her Course she bore, ... Il.14.259.173.
Fam'd thro' *Pieria* for the fleetest Breed, ... Il.23.357.504.

PIERIA'S
Bred where *Pieria's* fruitful Fountains flow, ... Il.2.928.167.
Then shoots from heav'n to high *Pieria's* steep, ... Od.5.62.174.

PIERIAN
Drink deep, or taste not the *Pierian* Spring: .... 1.EOC.216.264.

PIES
Redeem'd from tapers and defrauded pies, ... 5.DunB1.156.282.

PIETY
With Piety, the Soul's securest Guard, ... 1.TrSt.757.442.
But such plain roofs as piety could raise, ... 2.ElAb.139.331.
Sprung it from piety, or from despair? .... 2.ElAb.180.334.
Faithless thro' Piety, and dup'd thro' Wit? .... 3.Ep1.151.28.
But now, so ANNE and Piety ordain, ... 5.DunA2.25.99.
But now (so ANNE and Piety ordain) .... 5.DunB2.29.297.
And Papal piety, and Gothic fire. .... 6.71.14.203.
These rites to piety and grief discharg'd, ... Od.4.795.156.
The swain, whom acts of piety delight, ... Od.14.467.58.
To whom *Ulysses'* piety preferr'd .... Od.17.286.146.

PIG

And then a nodding Beam, or Pig of Lead, ...4.2HE2.102.171.
"A pig of lead to him who dives the best. ....5.DunA2.269.134.
"A pig of lead to him who dives the best; ....5.DunB2.281.309.
Tythe-Pig, and mortuary *Guinea:* ....6.39.6.110.

PIGEON

Nay, Mahomet! the Pigeon at thine ear; ....5.DunB4.364.378.

PIGEONS

Turns Hares to Larks, and Pigeons into Toads. ....5.DunB4.554.397.

PIGMY

Their Pigmy King, and little Fairy Queen, ...2.ChJM.461.37.
Thy Pigmy Island and thy tiny Spouse ....6.96ii.30Z33.272.
"Thy Pigmy Children, and thy tiny Spouse, ...6.96ii.53.273.
Of Laws and Manners in his Pigmy State. ....6.96v.10.280.
Not this weak pigmy-wretch, of mean design, ...Od.9.603.331.

PIGMY-WRETCH

Not this weak pigmy-wretch, of mean design, ...Od.9.603.331.

PIGOT

The Muse this one Verse to learn'd Pigot addresses, ...6.92.1.255.

PIKES

Swords, Pikes, and Guns, with everlasting Rust! ....4.HS1.74.11.

PIL'D

Here Loaves in Canisters are pil'd on high, ...1.TrSt.611.436.
By mountains pil'd on mountains, to the skies? ....3.EOM4.74.135.
And the pil'd Victims round the Body spread. ....Il.23.207.498.
This on the earth he pil'd; a boar full fed ....Od.14.465.58.
Is pil'd with viands and the strength of bread. ....Od.17.109.137.
And the bright basket pil'd with loaves of bread. ....Od.17.409.152.
Where pil'd on heaps the royal armour lies; ....Od.22.127.292.

PILASTER

Then clap four slices of Pilaster on't, ...3.Ep4.33.140.

PILE

Then gazing up, a glorious Pile beheld, ...2.TemF.25.255.
As *Atlas* fix'd, each hoary Pile appears, ...2.TemF.59.256.
Stupendous Pile! not rear'd by mortal Hands. ....2.TemF.62.256.
But quite mistakes the scaffold for the pile. ....3.Ep1.221.34.
Founds the whole pile, of all his works the base: ....5.DunB1.160.282.
Heav'ns! what a pile! whole ages perish there, ...5.DunB3.77.324.
On the same pile the faithful fair expire; ....6.69i.2.197.
On the same pile their faithful fair expire; ....6.69i.2A.197.
This radiant pile nine rural sisters raise; ....6.126ii.2.353.
Here, where on one promiscuous Pile they blaz'd, ...Il.7.404.384.
And decent on the Pile dispose the dead; ....Il.7.513.389.
And round the Pile a gen'ral Tomb they rear'd. ....Il.7.519.389.
The bloody Pile great *Melanippus* crown'd. ....Il.8.334.413.
Full fifty Guards each flaming Pile attend, ...Il.8.705.429.
Their *Hector* on the Pile they should not see, ...Il.22.443.474.
That *Greece* the Warrior's fun'ral Pile prepare, ...Il.23.62.489.
To load the Timber and the Pile to rear, ...Il.23.136.493.
They place, and heap the Sylvan Pile around. ....Il.23.171.496.
Suspends around, low-bending o'er the Pile. ....Il.23.209.498.
Nor yet the Pile where dead *Patroclus* lies, ...Il.23.236.499.
Let on *Patroclus'* Pile your Blast be driv'n, ...Il.23.260.499.
Forth to the Pile was born the Man divine, ...Il.24.996.577.
Thence to the bath, a beauteous pile, descend; ....Od.4.58.122.
Though on the blazing pile his parent lay, ...Od.4.309.134.
Slow-pacing thrice around th' insidious pile; ....Od.4.378.139.
Cedar and frankincense, an od'rous pile, ...Od.5.76.176.
His own industrious hands had rais'd the pile) ....Od.14.12.35.
Of five years age, before the pile was led: ....Od.14.466.58.
The fleecy pile obeys the whisp'ring gales, ...Od.19.240.205.
Beneath a pile that close the dome adjoin'd, ...Od.20.132.240.

PILES

Yet then no proud aspiring Piles were rais'd, ...1.TrSt.200.418.
But when the *Trojan* Piles in Ashes lay, ...1.TrUl.195.472.
While fancy brings the vanish'd piles to view, ...6.52.31.157.
The Bodies decent on the Piles were plac'd: ....Il.7.509.389.
Strong Piles infix'd stood adverse to the Foe. ....Il.7.525.390.
The flaming Piles with plenteous Fuel raise, ...Il.8.633.426.
A thousand Piles the dusky Horrors gild, ...Il.8.703.428.
With Piles, with Ramparts, and a Trench profound? ....Il.9.461.455.
Vast Stones and Piles from their Foundation heaves, ...Il.12.31.82.
Upheave the Piles that prop the solid Wall; ....Il.12.307.92.
But when the *Trojan* piles in ashes lay, ...Od.13.362.24.

PILF'RED

The Bard whom pilf'red Pastorals renown, ...4.Arbu.179.109.

PILF'RING

Your pilf'ring Lord, with simple Pride, ...6.135.33.367.

PILFER

Hemm'd round with Glories, pilfer Cloth or Bread, ...3.Ep1.145Z2.27.

PILFER'D

The Wretch whom pilfer'd Pastorals renown, ...6.98.29.284.

PILGRIM

Then bad *Eumæus* call the Pilgrim in. ....Od.17.597.161.

PILGRIM'S

And harmless Serpents lick the Pilgrim's Feet. ....1.Mes.80.120.

PILGRIMAGE

He dy'd when last from Pilgrimage I came, ...2.ChWB.243.68.
Thy pilgrimage to come, and remnant of thy day. ....Od.10.644.374.

PILGRIMS

Or lets his Wife abroad with Pilgrims roam, ...2.ChWB.349.74.
"Behold yon' Isle, by Palmers, Pilgrims trod, ...5.DunA3.105.159.
"See'st thou an Isle, by Palmers, Pilgrims trod, ...5.DunA3.105A.159.
"Behold yon' Isle, by Palmers, Pilgrims trod, ...5.DunB3.113.325.

PILLAG'D

Drench with your blood your pillag'd country's sands? ....Od.24.137.354.

PILLAGE

And one would pillage, one wou'd burn the Place. ....Il.18.594.351.

PILLAGER

Or nightly Pillager that strips the slain. ....Il.10.408.21.

PILLAR

The Wars of *Troy* were round the Pillar seen: ....2.TemF.188.271.
The polish'd Pillar diff'rent Sculptures grace; ....2.TemF.226.273.
At once his Country's Pillar, and their own; ....Il.16.674.270.
Spurn'd, but not mov'd: He, like a pillar stood, ...Od.17.274.145.
Against a cypress pillar lean'd his weight; ....Od.17.415.152.

PILLAR'D

He props his spear against the pillar'd wall; ....Od.17.36.134.

PILLARS

On Doric Pillars of white Marble rear'd, ...2.TemF.76.258.
Rais'd on a thousand Pillars, wreath'd around ....2.TemF.139.264.
The pillars silver, on a brazen base; ....Od.7.115.240.

PILLORY

If on a Pillory, or near a Throne, ...4.Arbu.366.122.
As thick as eggs at Ward in Pillory. ....5.DunA3.26.152.
As thick as eggs at Ward in Pillory. ....5.DunB3.34.322.

PILLORY'D

Earless on high, stood pillory'd *D[efoe]*, ...5.DunA2.139A.117.

PILLOW

Belinda still her downy Pillow prest, ...2.RL1.19.147.
Or the small Pillow grace a Lady's Bed, ...2.RL3.166.181.
On that soft pillow, from that envy'd height ....Od.22.213.297.

PILLS

As all Diseases fly before thy Pills. ....6.48ii.10.134.
With *Mercury* and *Pills.* ....6.54.16.165.

PILOSOPHICK

Thus, with a Pilosophick Frown, began. ....2.ChJM.177.23.

PILOT

By Art, the Pilot thro' the boiling Deep ....Il.23.387.505.
Atrides' pilot, *Phrontes,* there expir'd; ....Od.3.354.103.
And *Asteris* th' advancing Pilot knew: ....Od.4.1104.169.
No helm secures their course, no pilot guides, ...Od.8.605.295.
We sit, and trust the pilot and the wind. ....Od.9.88.306.
Full from the guiding pilot catch'd the gales. ....Od.11.10.379.
We drop our oars: at ease the pilot guides; ....Od.12.186.441.
Pilot, attentive listen and obey! ....Od.12.259.445.
The pilot by the tumbling ruin slain, ...Od.12.483.455.

PILOT'S

If to the right to urge the pilot's toil, ...Od.3.205.95.

PILOTS

With chosen Pilots, and with lab'ring Oars. ....Il.1.184.96.
Pilots their course: For when the glimm'ring ray ....Od.4.880.159.

PIMP

Un-elbow'd by a Gamester, Pimp, or Play'r? ....3.Ep3.242.112.
Could Laureate *Dryden* Pimp and Fry'r engage, ...4.HS1.113.15.
No Pimp of Pleasure, and no Spy of State, ...4.HS1.134.19.
Or have a Pimp or Flaterer in the Wind, ...6.129.2.357.

PIMPLE

Or raise a Pimple on a beauteous Face, ...2.RL4.68.189.
All eyes may see—a Pimple on her nose. ....3.Ep2.36.53.

PIMPS

Pimps, Poets, Wits , Lord *Fanny's,* Lady *Mary's,* ....4.HAdv.2.75.
So Pimps grow rich, while Gallants are undone. ....6.24ii.2.75.
As Pimps grow rich, while Gallants are undone. ....6.34.22.101.
Instead of Spyes, & Pimps, & Panders, ...6.135.74A.369.

PIN

All upright as a Pin, ...6.58.32.172.
Lies He who ne'er car'd, and still cares not a Pin, ...6.144.5.386.
Lies one who ne'er car'd, and who cares not a Pin, ...6.144.5A.386.
Lies one who ne'er car'd, and still cares not a Pin, ...6.144.5B.386.

PIN'D

And pin'd, unconscious of his rising fate; ....5.DunA1.110.76.
What-time, with hunger pin'd, my absent mates ....Od.4.497.144.
For ever sad with proud disdain he pin'd, ...Od.11.667.417.
Pin'd out her bloom, and vanish'd to a ghost. ....Od.15.383.88.
As one who long with pale-ey'd famine pin'd, ...Od.20.32.233.

PINCH

May pinch ev'n there—why lay it on a King. ....4.EpS2.51.315.

PINCHES

The winter pinches, and with cold I die, ...Od.14.548.63.

PINDAR

Here, like some furious Prophet, *Pindar* rode, ...2.TemF.212.272.
And a true *Pindar* stood without a head) ....4.Arbu.236.112.

PINDAR'S
To sweeter Sounds, and temper'd *Pindar's* Fire: ....2.TemF.223.273.

PINDARIC
Sharp Satire that, and that Pindaric lays? ....4.2HE2.83.171.
Forgot his Epic, nay Pindaric Art, ...4.2HE1.77.201.

PINDARS
The Pindars, and the Miltons, of a Curl. ....5.DunA3.158.165.
The Pindars, and the Miltons, of a Curl. ....5.DunB3.164.328.

PINDUS
The Dreams of *Pindus* and th' *Aonian* Maids, ...1.Mes.4.112.
In all the Courts of *Pindus* guiltless quite; ....4.EpS2.187.324.

PINE
A pine which ships might challenge for a mast: ....1.TrPA.44.367.
Then as the stately Pine, or Poplar tall, ...1.TrES.288.460.
Or Pine (fit Mast for some great Admiral) ....1.TrES.289A.460.
Who sees pale Mammon pine amidst his store, ...3.Ep3.173.107.
Or Pine, fit Mast for some great Admiral, ...Il.13.494.130.
Or Pine (fit Mast for some great Admiral) ....Il.16.594.267.
A solid Pine-tree barr'd of wond'rous Length; ....Il.24.558.559.
Brown with o'er-arching pine, and spreading oak. ....Od.9.216.314.
And Pine and Penury, a meagre train. ....Od.15.367.87.

PINE-TREE
A solid Pine-tree barr'd of wond'rous Length; ....Il.24.558.559.

PINES
While your *Alexis* pines in hopeless Love? ....1.PSu.24.73.
Arise, the Pines a noxious Shade diffuse; ....1.PWi.86.95.
The darksom pines that o'er yon' rocks reclin'd ....2.ElAb.155.332.
As to soft gales top-heavy pines bow low ....5.DunA2.359.143.
As to soft gales top-heavy pines bow low ....5.DunB2.391.316.
And Pines and Oaks, from their Foundations torn, ...Il.11.616.61.
Of poplars, pines, and firs, a lofty wood, ...Od.5.306.185.
And pines with thirst amidst a sea of waves: ....Od.11.722.421.

PINING
There hid in Shades, and pining Day by Day, ...6.81.13B.226.
Hear him in accents of a pining Ghost ....6.130.21.358.
And inly pining for his native shore. ....Od.5.195.181.
Then Envy grieves, with inly-pining Hate; ....Od.6.225.220.
Spent with fatigue, and shrunk with pining fast, ...Od.7.295.250.

PINION
Milton's strong pinion now not Heav'n can bound, ...4.2HE1.99.203.
And feels a Pinion lifting ev'ry Limb. ....Il.19.419.389.
And feels a Pinion lifting ev'ry Limb. ....Il.23.904.525.

PINION'D
Seen with both Eyes, and pinion'd on the Place, ...2.ChJM.664.47.
Some Slave of mine be pinion'd to their side." ....5.DunB4.134.354.

PINIONS
There spreads her dusky Pinions to the Skies. ....1.TrSt.135.415.
Stoop with their sounding Pinions to the Fight; ....1.TrES.220.458.
Stoop with re-sounding Pinions to the Fight; ....1.TrES.220A.458.
His Purple Pinions opening to the Sun, ...2.RL2.71.164.
Or dip their Pinions in the painted Bow, ...2.RL2.84.165.
Swift on his sooty Pinions flitts the *Gnome*, ...2.RL4.17.184.
His Scythe revers'd, and both his Pinions bound. ....2.TemF.148.265.
With Heads advanc'd, and Pinions stretch'd for Flight; ....2.TemF.211.272.
Hope humbly then; with trembling pinions soar; ....3.EOM1.91.25.
Then mounting on the Pinions of the Wind, ...Il.8.524.421.
Jove's Bird on sounding Pinions beat the Skies; ....Il.12.233.89.
Stoop with re-sounding Pinions to the Fight; ....Il.16.523.264.
High on pois'd Pinions, threats their callow Young. ....Il.17.848.321.
Or beat the Pinions of the Western Gale, ...Il.19.461.391.
A Moment hung, and spread her Pinions free, ...Il.23.1040.530.
So broad, his Pinions stretch'd their ample Shade, ...Il.24.392.552.
So broad, his Pinions stretch their ample Shade, ...Il.24.392A.552.
The God obeys, his golden Pinions binds, ...Il.24.417.553.
Fast to his feet his golden pinions binds, ...Od.5.57.174.
Now dip their pinions in the briny deep. ....Od.5.67.175.
And clang their pinions with terrific sound; ....Od.11.748.423.

PINKS
For Pinks and Daisies search'd the flow'ry Plain; ....2.ChJM.624.45.

PINKY
To make poor Pinky eat with vast applause! ....4.2HE1.293.221.

PINN'D
Not *Cynthia* when her *Manteau's* pinn'd awry, ...2.RL4.8.183.

PINNACE
And dropt their Anchors, and the Pinnace ty'd. ....Il.1.569.115.
The winged Pinnace shot along the sea. ....Od.13.187.15.
Thro' the mid seas the nimble pinnace sails, ...Od.14.329.51.

PINS
Here Files of Pins extend their shining Rows, ...2.RL1.137.156.
Be stopt in *Vials*, or transfixt with *Pins*; ....2.RL2.126.167.
With borrow'd Pins, and Patches not her own; ....6.49i.22.138.

PINT
He takes his chirping pint, he cracks his jokes: ....3.Ep3.358A.123.
He takes his chirping pint, and cracks his jokes: ....3.Ep3.358.123.
One half-pint bottle serves them both to dine, ...4.HS2.53.59.

PINY
And *Mycalessia's* ample Piny Plain. ....Il.2.593.156.
Who dwell where *Pelion* crown'd with Piny Boughs ....Il.2.918.167.

PIOUS
No pious Christian ought to marry twice. ....2.ChWB.12.57.
Than that *Mausolus'* Pious Widow plac'd, ...2.ChWB.248.69.
Warn'd by thy *Sylph*, oh Pious Maid beware! ....2.RL1.112.154.
Warn'd by the *Sylph*, oh Pious Maid beware! ....2.RL1.112A.154.
(Oh pious fraud of am'rous charity!) ....2.ElAb.150.331.
Hopes after Hopes of pious Papists fail'd, ...4.2HE2.62.169.
What force have pious vows! the Queen of Love ....5.DunA2.207.127.
D[uckit] for pious passion to the youth. ....5.DunA3.176.169.
But pious Needham dropt the name of God; ....5.DunB1.324.293.
What force have pious vows! The Queen of Love ....5.DunB2.215.306.
So he; but pious, whisper'd first his pray'r. ....5.DunB4.354.377.
Receiv'd each Demi-God, with pious care, ...5.DunB4.383.380.
Whose pious hope aspires to see the day ....5.DunB4.461.385.
The pious Son, fond Husband, faithful Friend: ....6.134.4.364.
Wash'd by the briny Wave, the pious Train ....Il.1.412.107.
Around him flock'd, all press'd with pious Care ....Il.6.300.341.
The pious Maids their mingled Sorrows shed, ...Il.6.646.358.
And pious Children o'er their Ashes weep. ....Il.7.403.384.
The Wounds they wash'd, their pious Tears they shed, ...Il.7.506.389.
Nor less the *Greeks* their pious Sorrows shed, ...Il.7.512.389.
Their loyal Thoughts and pious Loves conspire ....Il.10.192.10.
(So may, ye Gods! my pious Hopes succeed) ....Il.10.629.30.
His Brother's Corps the pious *Trojan* draws, ...Il.11.331.49.
With pious Care, great *Ajax* joins the Band: ....Il.11.723.67.
While thus the Hero's pious Cares attend ....Il.12.1.80.
Griev'd as he was, his pious Arms attend ....Il.13.529.131.
Now, *Trojan* Prince, employ thy pious Arms, ...Il.13.582.134.
Around his Waste his pious Arms he threw, ...Il.13.676.137.
The pious Warrior of *Anchises'* Line, ...Il.14.500.188.
The Body then they bathe with pious Toil, ...Il.18.411.340.
Far from our pious Rites, those dear Remains ....Il.22.124.458.
Some Ease at least those pious Rites may give, ...Il.23.57.489.
The pious Care be ours, the Dead to burn— ....Il.23.198.497.
Meantime erect the Tomb with pious Hands, ...Il.23.306.501.
His pious Sons the King's Command obey. ....Il.24.228.546.
See him, in *Troy*, the pious Care decline ....Il.24.681.565.
Assembled there, from pious Toil they rest, ...Il.24.1013.577.
Homeward with pious speed repass the main, ...Od.1.378.50.
Was then the martial brother's pious care? ....Od.3.313.101.
We check'd our haste, by pious office bound, ...Od.3.362.104.
The rest may here the pious duty share, ...Od.3.542.114.
Her pious speed a female train attends: ....Od.4.1002.164.
And for the pious sire preserve the son: ....Od.4.1010.164.
Who pious, following his great father's fame, ...Od.5.28.172.
As pious children joy with vast delight ....Od.5.506.196.
Pious observe our hospitable laws, ...Od.7.252.248.
The friends and guardians of our pious race. ....Od.7.276.249.
With pious mind to Heav'n I consecrate. ....Od.9.644.333.
There pious on my cold remains attend, ...Od.11.87.385.
And down my cheek the pious sorrows flow. ....Od.11.109.386.
Pious! to guard the hospitable rite, ...Od.14.313.50.
If heav'n be thy abode, with pious care ....Od.16.200.113.
Whose pious rule a warlike race obey! ....Od.19.130.199.
With pious deed, and pure devotion, paid? ....Od.19.427.215.
O destin'd head! The pious vows are lost; ....Od.19.434.215.
When thus the Prince with pious rage inflam'd: ....Od.20.372.250.

PIOUSLY
"The wretch he starves"—and piously denies: ....3.Ep3.106.100.

PIPE
He said; *Alexis*, take this Pipe, the same ....1.PSu.41.75.
To clear my Quail-pipe, and refresh my Soul, ...2.ChWB.213.67.
Stands known; *Divinity* with box and pipe, ...5.DunA3.191z2.172.
So swells each wind-pipe, Ass intones to Ass, ...5.DunB2.253.307.
Hist'ry her Pot, Divinity his Pipe, ...5.DunB3.196.330.
Hist'ry her Pot, Divinity her Pipe, ...5.DunB3.196A.330.
And shook from out his Pipe the seeds of fire; ....5.DunB4.494.391.

PIPES
Thus as the pipes of some carv'd Organ move, ...4.JD2.17.133.
And her full Pipes those shrilling Cries confound: ....6.14ii.24.43.
To her full Pipes the grunting Hog replies; ....6.14ii.25.43.
While that in pipes beneath the palace flows, ...6.35.31.104.
While that in pipes beneath the palace flows, ...Od.7.172.244.

PIPING
Behind them, piping on their Reeds, they go, ...Il.18.609.352.

PIPKIN
A Pipkin there like *Homer's Tripod* walks; ....2.RL4.51.188.

PIQU'D
The Dev'l was piqu'd such saintship to behold, ...3.Ep3.349.122.

PIQUE
Why pique all mortals, yet affect a name? ....3.Ep2.61.55.
Not Verse, to that he had a Pique— ....6.44.7.123.

PIRAEUS
Much ask'd the Seniors; till *Piræus* came. ....Od.17.83.136.
He, (when *Piræus* ask'd for slaves to bring ....Od.17.86.136.
This said, to sage *Piræus* sped the Seer, ...Od.20.445.254.

PIRAEUS'
Now to *Piræus'* honour'd charge consign'd. ....Od.17.67.135.

PIREUS
(The Son of *Pireus*, an illustrious Name,) ....Il.20.562.417.

PIRITHOUS
Sprung from *Pirithous* of immortal Race, ...Il.2.900.166.

PIRITHOUS'
Lives there a Chief to match *Pirithous'* Fame, ...Il.1.347.105.

PIRUS
A broken Rock the Force of *Pirus* threw, ...Il.4.599.250.

PISA'S
Bears Pisa's offerings to his Arethuse) ....5.DunA2.318.140.
Bears Pisa's off'rings to his Arethuse) ....5.DunB2.342.314.

PISANDER
This said, *Pisander* from the Car he cast, ...Il.11.185.43.
Behold! *Pisander*, urg'd by Fate's Decree, ...Il.13.753.141.
Nor pierc'd *Pisander* thro' *Atrides'* Shield; ....Il.13.759.141.
Pisander follow'd; matchless in his Art ....Il.16.230.248.
Pisander bears a necklace, wrought with art; ....Od.18.347.184.
With these, *Pisander* great *Polyctor's* son, ...Od.22.266.299.

PISANDER'S
Pisander's Spear fell shiver'd on the Field. ....Il.13.760.141.
The Goatherd's quiver'd in *Pisander's* heart; ....Od.22.295.300.

PISENOR'S
Clytus, *Pisenor's* Son, renown'd in Fame, ...Il.15.522.217.
(Daughter of Ops, the just *Pisenor's* son, ...Od.1.541.57.

PISISTRATUS
Pisistratus was first, to grasp their hands, ...Od.3.47.88.
Fast by his side *Pisistratus* lay spread, ...Od.3.512.112.
The last *Pisistratus* arose from rest: ....Od.3.528.113.
His faithful guide *Pisistratus* attends: ....Od.3.611.117.
See there confess'd, *Pisistratus* replies, ...Od.4.209.129.
Thy cheeks, *Pisistratus*, the tears bedew, ...Od.4.253.131.
Mean-while *Pisistratus* he gently shakes, ...Od.15.53.72.
Let not *Pisistratus* in vain be prest, ...Od.15.220.78.

PISS
See P.
"And piss against the same. ....6.79.144.223.
To them a piss–pot, but to thee a pond. ....6.96ii.30Z4.271.

PISSER
"So that each Pisser-by shall read, ...6.79.143.223.

PISSER-BY
"So that each Pisser-by shall read, ...6.79.143.223.

PISSING
"Mean Time on every Pissing-Post ....6.79.141.223.

PISSING-POST
"Mean Time on every Pissing-Post ....6.79.141.223.

PISSPOTS
How many Pisspots on the Sage she threw; ....2.ChWB.390.76.

PIST
Had but my Husband Pist against a Wall, ...2.ChWB.270.70.
By worthier Footmen pist upon and whipt! ....4.HAdv.56.81.

PIT
The Pit fill'd up, with Turf we cover'd o'er, ...2.ChWB.251.69.
Pit, Box and Gall'ry in convulsions hurl'd, ...4.Arbu.87.101.
The many-headed Monster of the Pit; ....4.2HE1.305.221.
And all the Thunder of the Pit ascends! ....4.2HE1.327.223.
Full o'er the pit, and hell-ward turn their face: ....Od.10.629.374.

PITCH
And at an humbler pitch prefer ....6.6i.7.14.
Woolwich and *Wapping*, smelling strong of Pitch; ....6.14ii.47.44.
And pitch your Lances in the yielding Plain. ....Il.3.126.196.
Thrice to its pitch his lofty Voice he rears; ....Il.11.580.60.

PITCH'D
The Stream they pass'd, and pitch'd their Tents below. ....Il.11.849.74.

PITCHY
Her pitchy Nostrils flaky Flames expire; ....Il.6.223.337.

PITEOUS
With that she gave him (piteous of his case, ...5.DunA2.133.115.
With that the Goddess (piteous of his case, ...5.DunA2.133A.115.
With that she gave him (piteous of his case, ...5.DunB2.141.302.
The Piteous Images renew my Pain, ...6.96iv.85.278.
'Till *Pallas*, piteous of her plaintive cries, ...Od.1.463.54.
O, piteous of my fate, vouchsafe to shew, ...Od.4.513.144.
The piteous object of a prostrate Queen. ....Od.4.953.162.
Piteous, regard a wretch consum'd with care! ....Od.20.146.240.
'Till gentle *Pallas*, piteous of her cries, ...Od.21.387.279.

PITEOUSLY
And toil'd most piteously to please their Bride: ....2.ChWB.59.59.

PITHOLEON
Pitholeon sends to me: "You know his Grace, ...4.Arbu.49.99.
Pitholeon greets me thus: "You know his Grace, ...4.Arbu.49A.99.
Pitholeon libell'd me—"but here's a Letter ....4.Arbu.51.100.

PITIES
That all beside one pities, not abhors; ....4.JD2.5.133.
That all beneath one pities, not abhors; ....4.JD2.5A.133.
And pities *Procris*, while her lover dies. ....6.14iii.14.46.
But pities *Belisarius*, Old and Blind? ....6.128.6.355.
Heav'n hears and pities hapless men like me, ...Od.5.572.199.
Some pow'r divine who pities human woe ....Od.10.182.349.

PITY
If in your breasts or love or pity dwell, ...1.TrFD.89.390.
Have pity, *Venus*, on your Poet's Pains! ....1.TrSP.70.396.
Or Men, whose Bosom tender Pity warms? ....1.TrUl.77.468.
The Maker saw, took pity, and bestow'd ....2.ChJM.63.17.
Your gentle Minds to pity those who love! ....2.ChJM.435.36.
Then sadly say, with mutual pity mov'd, ...3.ElAb.351.348.
We first endure, then pity, then embrace. ....3.EOM2.220.82.
Pity mistakes for some poor tradesman craz'd). ....3.Ep3.52.90.
"Pity! you was not Druggerman at *Babel:* ....4.JD4.83.33.
And the free Soul looks down to pity Kings. ....4.JD4.187.41.
"Pity! to build, without a son or wife: ....4.HS2.163.67.
And pity Men of Pleasure still in Pain! ....4.HAdv.50.79.
Pity the rest, than I abhorrd before ....4.JD2A.6.132.
With Pity, and with Terror, tear my heart; ....4.2HE1.345.225.
Have you less Pity for the needy Cheat, ...4.EpS2.44.315.
Pity! the charm works only in our wall, ...5.DunB4.165.357.
She pity'd! but her Pity only shed ....5.DunB4.345.377.
At last in pity, for our sake, ...6.4iii.11.10.
If Heav'n, to pity human woes inclin'd, ...6.20.45.67.
What pity, Heav'n! if such a Man there be? ....6.49iii.29.143.
'Tis pity that two Squires so Gent— ....6.94.39.260.
Yes, Thousands. But in Pity to their Kind, ...6.96iii.13.274.
What Pity, Heav'n! if such a Man there be. ....6.98.65.285.
As show'd, Vice had his Hate and Pity too. ....6.118.8.334.
Preserv'd the Son, in Pity to the Sire. ....Il.5.32.267.
As Pity pleaded for his vanquish'd Prize, ...Il.6.65.327.
What Pity, Sloath should seize a Soul so brave, ...Il.6.670.360.
But ah! permit to pity human State; ....Il.8.41.397.
A transient Pity touch'd his vengeful Breast. ....Il.11.735.68.
To tender Pity all his manly Mind; ....Il.13.591.134.
With Pity soften'd, and with Fury swell'd: ....Il.13.828.145.
By his own Ardour, his own Pity sway'd ....Il.15.49.196.
He, not untouch'd with Pity, to the Plain ....Il.15.69.199.
Or may some meaner Cause thy Pity claim? ....Il.16.23.236.
Let *Greece* at length with Pity touch thy Breast, ...Il.16.31.236.
Pity! that all their Practice is by Land. ....Il.16.906.279.
Beheld with Pity; as apart he sate, ...Il.17.227.296.
The rest, in pity to her Son, conceal'd. ....Il.17.471.305.
But thou, in Pity, by my Pray'r be won; ....Il.18.527.347.
And thus, with Pity, to his blue-ey'd Maid. ....Il.19.363.387.
Some Pity to a Suppliant's Name afford, ...Il.21.86.425.
If ever yet soft Pity touch'd thy mind, ...Il.21.105.426.
Pity, while yet I live, these silver Hairs; ....Il.22.80.456.
My Grief perhaps his Pity may engage; ....Il.22.534.478.
If ever Pity touch'd thee for Mankind, ...Il.24.414.552.
You tempt me, Father, and with Pity touch: ....Il.24.477.556.
Whatever Pity that stern Heart can know. ....Il.24.573.560.
Think of thy Father's Age, and pity mine! ....Il.24.599.562.
These Words soft Pity in the Chief inspire, ...Il.24.634.563.
So shall thy Pity and Forbearance give ....Il.24.703.566.
Thy Pity check'd my Sorrows in their Flow: ....Il.24.971.576.
With tender pity touch'd, the Goddess cry'd: ....Od.1.327.48.
Let neither flatt'ry smooth, nor pity hide. ....Od.3.115.91.
And melting with fraternal pity spoke. ....Od.4.258.131.
Recite them! nor in erring pity fear ....Od.4.439.140.
Proteus her sire divine. With pity press'd, ...Od.4.495.144.
It was my crime to pity, and to save; ....Od.5.166.180.
But giv'n the sense, to pity, and to feel. ....Od.5.246.183.
Leucothea saw, and pity touch'd her breast: ....Od.5.425.193.
Or men, whose bosom tender pity warms? ....Od.6.142.214.
Oh let soft pity touch thy gen'rous mind! ....Od.6.212.220.
A suppliant bends: oh pity human woe! ....Od.7.198.245.
Or men, whose bosom tender pity warms? ....Od.8.628.296.
Or such who harbour pity in their breast, ...Od.9.205.314.
Thus I with art to move their pity try'd, ...Od.10.81.343.
By justice sway'd, by tender pity prest: ....Od.10.452.365.
Felt pity enter, and sustain'd her part. ....Od.10.474.366.
Or Men, whose bosom tender pity warms? ....Od.13.244.17.
At once to pity and resent thy wrong. ....Od.16.94.107.
Soft pity touch'd the mighty master's soul; ....Od.17.364.149.
The proud feel pity, and relief bestow, ...Od.17.440.155.
And melting pity soften'd ev'ry face; ....Od.17.593.161.
Then he, with pity touch'd: O Royal Dame! ....Od.19.298.209.

PITY'D
She pity'd! but her Pity only shed ....5.DunB4.345.377.
To her I su'd; she pity'd my distress; ....Od.7.376.254.
My state he pity'd, and my tears he dry'd, ...Od.14.310.50.

PITYEA'S
High *Teree's* Summits, and *Pityea's* Bow'rs; ....Il.2.1005.170.

PITYING
Not louder Shrieks to pitying Heav'n are cast, ...2.RL3.157.180.
She said: the pitying Audience melt in Tears, ...2.RL5.1.199.
And pitying saints, whose statues learn to weep! ....2.ElAb.22.320.
Fate snatch'd her early to the pitying sky. ....3.Elegy.24.364.
In pitying love we but our weakness show, ...6.32.11.96.
Here pitying heav'n that virtue mutual found, ...6.69i.3.197.
And 'tis a wise design on pitying heav'n, ...6.146.6.389.
Great *Menelaus* views with pitying Eyes, ...Il.5.689.300.
The God beheld him with a pitying Look, ...Il.15.15.194.
Nor *Jove* disdain'd to cast a pitying Look, ...Il.17.502.308.
And hopes th' Assistance of his pitying Friends, ...Il.22.252.466.
Achilles saw, and pitying thus begun. ....Il.23.611.514.
But not deserted by the pitying Skies. ....Il.24.29.536.
The Synod griev'd, and gave a pitying sigh, ...Od.2.92.65.
'Till pitying *Jove* my native realm restor'd— ....Od.4.44.122.
Lenient of grief, the pitying God began.— ....Od.4.731.153.
But pitying *Jove* avert the dire designs! ....Od.4.927.161.
Her heroe's danger touch'd the pitying Pow'r, ...Od.5.10.171.
Bid the Great hear, and pitying heal my woes. ....Od.6.390.330.
Cyclop! if any, pitying thus disgrace, ...Od.9.587.330.
The pitying Gods themselves my chains unbind. ....Od.14.384.53.
My pitying eyes effus'd a plenteous stream, ...Od.19.633.227.

PITYING (CONTINUED)

The pitying God his guardian aid avows. ....Od.20.127.239.
Some pitying God (*Ulysses* sad reply'd) ....Od.20.211.243.

PLAC'D

Round like a shield, and in the middle plac'd: ....1.TrPA.109.370.
Then plac'd beside her on the flow'ry Ground, ...1.TrVP.57.379.
And this Inscription shall be plac'd below. ....1.TrSP.213.403.
No labour'd Columns in long Order plac'd, ...1.TrSt.202.418.
Now plac'd in order, the *Phæacian* Train ....1.TrUl.1A.465.
And gently plac'd him on the Rocky Shore: ....1.TrUl.48.467.
Nor those, that plac'd beneath his utmost Reign, ...1.TrUl.120.470.
And, plac'd in State, the Bridegroom and the Bride. ....2.ChJM.317.29.
Than that *Mausolus'* Pious Widow plac'd, ...2.ChWB.248.69.
Superior by the Head, was *Ariel* plac'd; ....2.RL2.70.164.
Between the Statues Obelisks were plac'd, ...2.TemF.117.262.
Is only this, if God has plac'd him wrong? ....3.EOM1.50.19.
Plac'd on this isthmus of a middle state, ...3.EOM2.3.53.
'Till common int'rest plac'd the sway in one. ....3.EOM3.210.114.
While those are plac'd in Hope, and these in Fear: ....3.EOM4.70.135.
In Pow'r, Wit, Figure, Virtue, Fortune, plac'd ....4.2HE2.302.187.
A Poet's form she plac'd before their eyes, ...5.DunA2.31.99.
And plac'd it next him, a distinction rare! ....5.DunA2.92.108.
See in the circle next, Eliza plac'd; ....5.DunA2.149.119.
But Fate with Butchers plac'd thy priestly Stall, ...5.DunA3.205.175.
A Poet's form she plac'd before their eyes, ...5.DunB2.35.297.
And plac'd it next him, a distinction rare! ....5.DunB2.96.300.
See in the circle next, Eliza plac'd, ...5.DunB2.157.303.
But fate with butchers plac'd thy priestly stall, ...5.DunB3.209.330.
Plac'd at the door of Learning, youth to guide, ...5.DunB4.153.356.
In *Rome's* proud *Forum* young *Octavius* plac'd, ...6.20.28.66.
To fix the ground where paradise was plac'd. ....6.126i.2.353.
High on the Deck was fair *Chruseïs* plac'd, ...Il.1.406.107.
Suppliant the Goddess stood: One Hand she plac'd ....Il.1.650.118.
Th' Assembly plac'd, the King of Men exprest ....Il.2.67.130.
Then wise *Ulysses* in his Rank was plac'd; ....Il.2.484.150.
Him *Pallas* plac'd amidst her wealthy Fane, ...Il.2.661.158.
Had plac'd the beauteous Progeny of *Jove;* ....Il.3.530.216.
Plac'd on *Minerva's* Knees, and thus she prays. ....Il.6.377.344.
And plac'd the beaming Helmet on the Ground. ....Il.6.601.356.
Before great *Ajax* plac'd the mighty Chine. ....Il.7.387.383.
The Bodies decent on the Piles were plac'd: ....Il.7.509.389.
High on the cloudy Point his Seat he plac'd. ....Il.8.64.398.
Plac'd in his Tent, attends the lofty Strain: ....Il.9.252.445.
And plac'd in Seats with purple Carpets spread. ....Il.9.266.445.
Strong Guards they plac'd, and watch'd nine Nights entire; ....Il.9.594.464.
High on a spreading Tamarisk he plac'd; ....Il.10.537.27.
Plac'd as a Sign to Man amid the Skies.) ....Il.11.38.36.
Last o'er his Brows his fourfold Helm he plac'd, ...Il.11.53.37.
Behind the Column plac'd, he bent his Bow. ....Il.11.477.55.
A Table first with azure Feet she plac'd; ....Il.11.768.69.
But plac'd aloft, on *Ida's* shady Height ....Il.14.183.168.
Plac'd on the Margin of the flow'ry Ground. ....Il.14.510.188.
There sate the Pow'rs in awful Synod plac'd; ....Il.15.92.200.
On his brave Head a crested Helm he plac'd, ...Il.15.566.218.
Yet where the Oars are plac'd, he stands to wait ....Il.15.884.231.
Plac'd on the Hero's Grave. Along their Face, ...Il.17.496.307.
They brought, and plac'd it o'er the rising Flame: ....Il.18.406.340.
That plac'd on living Wheels of massy Gold, ...Il.18.441.342.
And various Artifice, the Queen she plac'd; ....Il.18.458.343.
There plac'd beside her on the shining Frame, ...Il.18.493.345.
These on the sacred Seats of Council plac'd, ...Il.19.53.374.
Great *Jove* has plac'd, sad Spectacle of Pain! ....Il.22.84.456.
There plac'd 'em round: Then from the Ships proceeds ....Il.23.323.503.
Two golden Talents for the fourth were plac'd; ....Il.23.337.503.
The Herald plac'd the Sceptre in his Hands, ...Il.23.647.515.
He said, and plac'd the Goblet at his side; ....Il.23.717.518.
A well-fed Ox was for the second plac'd; ....Il.23.876.524.
A Massy Spear amid the Circle plac'd, ...Il.23.1045.531.
There plac'd amidst her melancholy Train ....Il.24.111.539.
The Chief himself to each his Portion plac'd, ...Il.24.794.570.
And plac'd aloft: while all, with streaming Eyes, ...Il.24.997.577.
There in the portal plac'd, the heav'n-born maid ....Od.1.138.39.
The spear receiving from her hand, he plac'd ....Od.1.167.40.
Hath plac'd beneath the storms which toss the great! ....Od.1.280.46.
There then arriv'd, on thrones around him plac'd, ...Od.3.500.112.
They came, and near him plac'd the stranger-guest. ....Od.3.529.113.
All plac'd at ease the holy banquet join, ...Od.3.600.117.
With rich magnificence, the chariot plac'd: ....Od.4.52.122.
Close ambush'd nigh the spacious hall he plac'd. ....Od.4.710.152.
Before herself were plac'd the cates divine, ...Od.5.253.184.
Plac'd at the helm he sate, and mark'd the skies, ...Od.5.345.188.
Now plac'd in order, on their banks they sweep ....Od.9.115.308.
Plac'd at her loom within, the Goddess sung; ....Od.10.254.354.
With semblance fair th' unhappy men she plac'd. ....Od.10.269.355.
White linnen lay beneath. Another plac'd ....Od.10.419.364.
Then led and plac'd me on the sov'reign seat, ...Od.10.431.365.
They bore the treasures, and in safety plac'd. ....Od.13.24.2.
Thy lyre divine, *Demodocus!* was plac'd. ....Od.13.34.3.
Now plac'd in order, the *Phæacian* train ....Od.13.92.5.
And gently plac'd him on the rocky shore. ....Od.13.139.11.
Nor those that plac'd beneath his utmost reign ....Od.13.287.19.
Secure he sits, near great *Atrides* plac'd; ....Od.13.490.29.
He heard, he sav'd, he plac'd me at his side; ....Od.14.309.50.
Plac'd on the mast (the last recourse of life) ....Od.14.347.51.
And in his palace like a brother plac'd, ...Od.14.353.51.
In great *Ulysses'* hand he plac'd the bowl, ...Od.14.500.60.
High on a throne the King each stranger plac'd. ....Od.15.147.75.
And by his side the guest accepted plac'd. ....Od.15.309.84.
And plac'd in order, spread their equal oars. ....Od.15.592.98.
There stood an empty seat, where late was plac'd ....Od.17.404.152.
Eumæus took, and plac'd it near his Lord. ....Od.17.407.152.
By fam'd *Icmalius* wrought, the menials plac'd: ....Od.19.69.196.
A seat adorn'd with furry spoils she plac'd: ....Od.19.122.198.
The fleece and carpet in the dome he plac'd; ....Od.20.117.238.
High canisters of bread *Philætius* plac'd; ....Od.20.320.248.

PLAC'D (CONTINUED)

He said; and of the steer before him plac'd, ...Od.20.365.250.
A trench he open'd; in a line he plac'd ....Od.21.125.264.
Thus speaking, on the floor the bow he plac'd, ...Od.21.171.267.
Suffic'd it not within the palace plac'd ....Od.21.311.274.
Revolv'd his words, and plac'd them in her heart. ....Od.21.384.278.
To guard the outlet, plac'd *Eumæus* there: ....Od.22.147.294.

PLACE

(Obscure the Place, and uninscrib'd the Stone) ....1.W-F.320.180.
Which, but *proportion'd* to their *Light*, or *Place*, ...1.EOC.173.260.
But with th' *Occasion* and the *Place* comply, ...1.EOC.177.261.
Its gawdy Colours spreads on *ev'ry place;* ....1.EOC.312.274.
No Place so Sacred from such Fops is barr'd, ...1.EOC.622.310.
Thus *useful Arms* in Magazines we place, ...1.EOC.671.315.
As next in Place to *Mantua*, next in Fame! ....1.EOC.708.322.
Watch'd by the Sylvan *Genius* of the Place. ....1.TrSP.184.401.
And crowd their shining Ranks to yield thee place; ....1.TrSt.36.411.
Place on their Heads that Crown distain'd with Gore, ...1.TrSt.113.414.
Jocasta's Son, and *Thebes* my Native Place. ....1.TrSt.805.443.
The first in Valour, as the first in Place: ....1.TrES.38.451.
A Tide of *Trojans* flows, and fills the Place; ....1.TrES.206.457.
Thou art, that wander'st in this desart Place, ...1.TrUl.109.469.
Tell me, oh tell, is this my Native Place? ....1.TrUl.202.472.
Others, long absent from their Native Place, ...1.TrUl.213.472.
The King with Joy confess'd his Place of Birth, ...1.TrUl.236.473.
(So Poets sing) was present on the Place; ....2.ChJM.327.30.
With od'rous Spices they perfum'd the Place, ...2.ChJM.355.31.
(Tho' God of Gardens) of this charming Place: ....2.ChJM.451.36.
A Place to tire the rambling Wits of *France* ....2.ChJM.452.36.
To this sweet Place, in Summer's sultry Heat, ...2.ChJM.469.37.
Which in due Place and Season, you may hear. ....2.ChJM.513.40.
And climbing, in the Summit took his Place: ....2.ChJM.606.44.
Seen with both Eyes, and pinion'd on the Place, ...2.ChJM.664.47.
Seen with both Eyes, and seiz'd upon the Place, ...2.ChJM.664A.47.
Are, as when Women, wondrous fond of Place. ....2.RL3.36.171.
Two Handmaids wait the Throne: Alike in Place, ...2.RL4.25.185.
In ev'ry place is sought, but sought in vain: ....2.RL5.110.208.
And fix their own with Labour in their place: ....2.TemF.38.256.
Their own like others soon their Place resign'd, ...2.TemF.39.256.
Ours is the Place at Banquets, Balls and Plays; ....2.TemF.382.282.
Hither, as to their proper Place, arise ....2.TemF.432.284.
Each talk'd aloud, or in some secret Place, ...2.TemF.466.286.
Thy place is here, sad sister come away! ....2.ElAb.310.344.
So flew the soul to its congenial place, ...2.Elegy.27.365.
His knowledge measur'd to his state and place, ...3.EOM1.71.22.
His Being measur'd to his state and place, ...3.EOM1.71A.22.
Attract, attracted to, the next in place ....3.EOM3.11.93.
Some place the bliss in action, some in ease, ...3.EOM4.21.129.
God in Externals could not place Content. ....3.EOM4.66.134.
Good, from each object, from each place acquir'd, ...3.EOM4.321.159.
Alone, in company; in place, or out; ....3.Ep1.131.25.
Int'rest o'ercome, or Policy take place: ....3.Ep1.169.29.
Cries, "oh! how charming if there's no such place!" ....3.Ep2.108A.58.
Cries, "Ah! how charming if there's no such place!" ....3.Ep2.108.58.
Behold the Market-place with poor o'erspread! ....3.Ep3.263.115.
Despairing Quacks with curses fled the place, ...3.Ep3.273.115.
Consult the Genius of the Place in all; ....3.Ep4.57.142.
Ev'n in an ornament its place remark, ...3.Ep4.77.144.
Chiefs, out of War, and Statesmen, out of Place. ....4.HS1.126.17.
I bought no *Benefice*, I begg'd no *Place;* ....4.JD4.12.27.
Whose Place is *quarter'd out*, three Parts in four, ...4.JD4.136.37.
Swears every *Place entail'd* for Years to come, ...4.JD4.160.39.
Then chearful healths (your Mistress shall have place) ....4.HS2.149.67.
No place is sacred, not the Church is free, ...4.Arbu.11.96.
"I want a Patron; ask him for a Place." ....4.Arbu.50.100.
While pure Description held the place of Sense? ....4.Arbu.148.106.
Who first his Judgment ask'd, and then a Place: ....4.Arbu.238.113.
O'er a learn'd, un-intelligible Place; ....4.JD2A.105.142.
O'er a learn'd, unintelligible place; ....4.JD2.102.143.
Again to rhime, can *London* be the Place? ....4.2HE2.89.171.
Howe'er unwillingly it quits its place, ...4.2HE2.161.177.
When servile Chaplains cry, that Birth and Place ....4.2HE2.220.181.
A man so poor wou'd live without a *Place:* ....4.2HE2.287.185.
And place, on good Security, his Gold. ....4.2HE1.168.209.
What's long or short, each accent where to place, ...4.2HE1.207.213.
Expect a Place, or Pension from the Crown; ....4.2HE1.371.227.
Fit to bestow the Laureat's weighty place. ....4.2HE1.379.227.
But if to Pow'r and Place your Passion lye, ...4.1HE6.97.243.
That, begs my int'rest for a Place— ....4.HS6.68.255.
Behold the place, where if a Poet ....4.HS6.189.261.
And what a dust in ev'ry place! ....4.1HE7.11.269.
"Get Place and Wealth, if possible, with Grace; ....4.1HE1.103.287.
"If not, by any means get Wealth and Place." ....4.1HE1.104.287.
"No place on earth (he cry'd) like Greenwich hill!" ....4.1HE1.139.289.
F. Why so? if Satire know its Time and Place, ...4.EpS1.87.305.
Receive, and place for ever near a King! ....4.EpS1.96.305.
Once break their Rest, or stir them from their Place; ....4.EpS1.100.305.
Turn, turn they eyes from wicked men in place, ...4.1740.3.332.
Realms shift their place, and Ocean turns to land. ....5.DunA1.70.68.
That altar crowns: A folio Common-place ....5.DunA1.139.81.
Her ample presence fills up all the place; ....5.DunA1.217.89.
Ascend, and recognize their native place: ....5.DunA1.224.90.
A place there is, betwixt earth, air and seas, ...5.DunA2.79.107.
"Mark first the youth who takes the foremost place, ...5.DunA3.131.161.
"Mark first that youth who takes the foremost place, ...5.DunA3.131A.161.
And place it here! here all ye Heroes bow! ....5.DunA3.316.186.
Realms shift their place, and Ocean turns to land. ....5.DunB1.72.275.
That altar crowns: A folio Common-place ....5.DunB1.159.282.
Her ample presence fills up all the place; ....5.DunB1.261.289.
Ascend, and recognize their Native Place. ....5.DunB1.268.290.
A place there is, betwixt earth, air, and seas, ...5.DunB2.83.299.
With holy envy gave one Layman place. ....5.DunB2.324.313.
"Mark first that Youth who takes the foremost place, ...5.DunB3.139.326.
And place it here! here all ye Heroes bow! ....5.DunB3.318.335.
None want a place, for all their Centre found, ...5.DunB4.77.349.

PLACE (CONTINUED)

Shrink, and confess the Genius of the place: ..... 5.DunB4.146.355.
And titt'ring push'd the Pedants off the place: ..... 5.DunB4.276.371.
Thrust some Mechanic Cause into his place; ..... 5.DunB4.475.387.
Worthy to fill Pythagoras's place: ..... 5.DunB4.572.399.
Ten Miles from Town, t' a Place call'd *Epsom*, ... 6.10.50.26.
Such place hath *Deptford*, Navy-building Town, ... 6.14ii.46.44.
Tho' not too strictly bound to Time and Place: ..... 6.19.28.63.
But sets up One, a greater, in their Place; ..... 6.19.38.63.
No matter for the Rules of Time and Place: ..... 6.19.28A.63.
To have no Place in this was hard: ..... 6.30.14.86.
A Place in any *British* Name; ..... 6.30.20.86.
To have a Place in *Tom D'Urfy*. ..... 6.30.74.88.
She shews her Grief in a sincerer Place; ..... 6.33.8.99.
Oh! may all *gentle* Bards together place ye, ... 6.40.7.112.
In scribbler to have had a place. ..... 6.42v.6.119.
Holds not the highest Place! ..... 6.50.32A.147.
Yet should the Graces all thy figures place, ... 6.52.71.158.
Their ruins ruin'd, and their place no more! ..... 6.71.22.203.
Their ruins perish'd, and their place no more! ..... 6.71.22A.203.
And sacred, place by *Dryden's* awful dust: ..... 6.72.2.208.
Then what's join'd to a place, ... 6.91.7.253.
Veal-Cutlets in their Place. ..... 6.94.80.261.
"From Place to Place o'er *Brobdingnag* I'll roam, ... 6.96ii.37.272.
"From Place to Place o'er *Brobdingnag* I'll roam, ... 6.96ii.37.272.
WELCOME, thrice welcome to thy native Place! ..... 6.96iv.1.276.
Who reach that High place oh their joy shall be great! ..... 6.122.21A.342.
And who of his court, to the place will not go, ... 6.122.23A.342.
And who now of his Court, to this place would not go, ... 6.122.23.342.
Here, here's the place, where these bright angels walk. ..... 6.126i.4.353.
He stands the Guardian of the Place ..... 6.135.58Z2.368.
I'll lay my Life, I know the Place: ..... 6.151.6.399.
And near thy *Shakespear* place thy honour'd Bust, ... 6.152.2.400.
For this, constrain'd to quit his native Place, ... Il.2.803.163.
Now here, now there, he darts from Place to Place, ... Il.5.114.272.
Now here, now there, he darts from Place to Place, ... Il.5.114.272.
With tender Shrieks the Goddess fill'd the Place, ... Il.5.427.289.
To *Troy's* high Fane, and to his Holy Place; ..... Il.5.542.294.
Æneas' Friend, and in his native Place ..... Il.5.661.299.
In fair *Arisba's* Walls (his native Place) ..... Il.6.17.325.
Before my Eyes my mighty Sires to place, ... Il.6.259.339.
Where Heroes war, the foremost Place I claim, ... Il.6.636.358.
The pleasing *Arnè* was his native Place. ..... Il.7.14.363.
Till to supply his Place and rule the Car, ... Il.8.157.405.
On this our Hill no more shall hold his Place, ... Il.8.568.423.
A Place there was, yet undefil'd with Gore, ... Il.10.233.12.
The *Spartan* wish'd the second Place to gain, ... Il.10.273.14.
To guide their Footsteps to the Place again. ..... Il.10.539.27.
The wounded Monarch at his Tent they place. ..... Il.11.364.51.
The first in Valour, as the first in Place. ..... Il.12.382.95.
A Tyde of *Trojans* flows, and fills the Place; ..... Il.12.560.102.
He shifts his Place, his Colour comes and goes; ..... Il.13.360.123.
He said; and *Merion* to th' appointed Place, ... Il.13.418.126.
Alike divine, and Heav'n their native Place; ..... Il.13.446.126.
He dwelt far distant from his native Place, ... Il.13.872.147.
Sends forth his active Mind from Place to Place, ... Il.15.88.200.
Sends forth his active Mind from Place to Place, ... Il.15.88.200.
The Goddess said, and sullen took her Place; ..... Il.15.108.200.
To favour *Ilion*, that perfidious Place, ... Il.15.238.206.
For this, in *Priam's* Court he held his Place, ... Il.15.650.221.
His Eyes on Heaven, his Feet upon the Place ..... Il.16.281.250.
With ample Strides he stalks from Place to Place. ..... Il.16.655.270.
With ample Strides he stalks from Place to Place. ..... Il.16.655.270.
Next thee, *Asteropeus!* in Place and Fame. ..... Il.17.403.303.
So mov'd *Atrides* from his dang'rous Place ..... Il.17.749.317.
And marks the Place to fix his Head on high. ..... Il.18.216.332.
From Place to Place, around the blest Abodes, ... Il.18.443.342.
From Place to Place, around the blest Abodes, ... Il.18.443.342.
On Seats of Stone, within the sacred Place, ... Il.18.585.351.
And one would pillage, one wou'd burn the Place. ..... Il.18.594.351.
A Place for Ambush fit, they found, and stood ..... Il.18.603.352.
A darker Metal mixt, intrench'd the Place, ... Il.18.655.355.
Such pond'rous Ruin shall confound the Place, ... Il.21.374.436.
Drop round, and idly mark the dusty Place. ..... Il.21.572.446.
One place at length he spies, to let in Fate, ... Il.22.407.472.
Till on the Pyre I place thee; till I rear ..... Il.23.55.489.
Till then, the Spirit finds no resting place, ... Il.23.89.490.
Circling around the Place, where Times to come ..... Il.23.156.495.
They place, and heap the Sylvan Pile around. ..... Il.23.171.496.
Next the white Bones his sad Companions place ..... Il.23.313.502.
They mount their Seats; the Lots their Place dispose; ..... Il.23.427.507.
And sends before old *Phœnix* to the Place, ... Il.23.435.507.
The Hero said, and starting from his Place ..... Il.23.881.524.
(The self-same Place beside *Patroclus'* Pyre, ... Il.23.909.525.
(*Minerva* rising, gave the Mourner place) ..... Il.24.132.540.
Except, to place the Dead with decent Care, ... Il.24.184.544.
Except to place the Dead with decent Care, ... Il.24.214.546.
And last a large well-labour'd Bowl had place, ... Il.24.287.548.
One Ship convey'd us from our native Place; ..... Il.24.486.556.
And place the Couches, and the Cov'rings lay. ..... Il.24.815.571.
They weep, and place him on the Bed of State. ..... Il.24.899.573.
The snowy Bones his Friends and Brothers place ..... Il.24.1003.577.
Their unknown guests, and at the banquet place. ..... Od.3.46.88.
Nor lost in time, nor circumscrib'd by place. ..... Od.3.288.100.
Then seek the place the sea-born nymph assign'd, ... Od.4.589.147.
And swift transport him to his place of rest. ..... Od.5.49.174.
Be mortal, and this earth thy native place, ... Od.6.182.218.
And humbled in the ashes took his place. ..... Od.7.207.246.
And seat him fair in some distinguish'd place. ..... Od.7.219.247.
Arriv'd, his sinewy arms incessant place ..... Od.8.315.281.
We boldly landed on the hostile place, ... Od.9.43.304.
And learn what habitants possest the place? ..... Od.9.101.307.
The people were? who monarch of the place? ..... Od.10.124.346.
I quit the place, and hasten to the strand. ..... Od.10.482.366.
Be next thy care the sable sheep to place ..... Od.10.628.374.
Forth issuing then, from place to place I flew; ..... Od.10.653.375.

PLACE (CONTINUED)

Forth issuing then, from place to place I flew; ..... Od.10.653.375.
The first in glory, as the first in place. ..... Od.11.441.406.
Fast by the roarings of the main we place; ..... Od.12.20.430.
Thou art, that wander'st in this desart place! ..... Od.13.276.19.
Tell me, oh tell, is this my native place? ..... Od.13.369.25.
Others, long absent from their native place, ... Od.13.380.25.
The King with joy confess'd his place of birth, ... Od.13.403.26.
Restor'd and breathing in his natal place. ..... Od.14.166.43.
Than when two friends, alone, in peaceful place ..... Od.14.222.46.
'Tis sweet to play the fool in time and place, ... Od.14.519.62.
No friend in *Ithaca* my place supplies, ... Od.15.102.73.
But snatch'd by pyrates from my native place, ... Od.15.468.93.
But in my absence riot fills the place, ... Od.15.555.96.
For me, this house shall find an humbler place: ..... Od.16.44.104.
He took his place, and Plenty heap'd the board. ..... Od.17.309.146.
As on the listed field he us'd to place ..... Od.19.670.228.
Who next the goblet held his holy place: ..... Od.21.154.266.
A double strength of valves secur'd the place, ... Od.22.144.294.
And spreads her Lord's return from place to place. ..... Od.22.532.314.
And spreads her Lord's return from place to place. ..... Od.22.532.314.
We then collect thy snowy bones, and place ..... Od.24.93.352.
Thy town, thy parents, and thy native place? ..... Od.24.349.365.
Then all beneath their father take their place, ... Od.24.472.371.

PLACEBO

Placebo This was call'd, and *Justin* That. ..... 2.ChJM.146.21.
First to the Knight *Placebo* thus begun, ... 2.ChJM.147.21.
What does my Friend, my dear *Placebo* say? ..... 2.ChJM.221.25.

PLACES

And haunt the places where their Honour dy'd. ..... 3.Ep2.242.69.
He tells what Strumpet Places sells for Life, ... 4.JD4.148.37.
While Fools have places purely for their Zeal. ..... 6.82ix(d).2.235.
And haunt the Places where their Honour dy'd. ..... 6.110.4.316.

PLACING

In Moderation placing all my Glory, ... 4.HS1.67.11.

PLAGIARY

To prove himself no Plagiary, MOORE, ... 6.116i.1.325.
To prove himself no Plagiary, a *M[00]re*, ... 6.116i.1A.325.

PLAGU'D

(Not plagu'd with headachs, or the want of rhime) ..... 6.45.42.125.
Plagu'd with his Pride, or punish'd for his Lust. ..... Il.2.292.141.
What God has plagu'd us with this gormaund guest? ..... Od.17.529.158.

PLAGUE

The dear-bought Curse and lawful Plague of Life: ..... 2.ChJM.46.17.
Or some devouring Plague consume you all, ... 2.ChJM.642.46.
"Plague on't! 'tis past a Jest—nay prithee, Pox! ..... 2.RL4.129.194.
Some War, some Plague, some Famine they foresee, ... 3.Ep3.115A.101.
Some War, some Plague, or Famine they foresee, ... 3.Ep3.115.101.
So when you plague a Fool, 'tis still the Curse, ... 4.JD4.120.35.
Nature made ev'ry Fop to plague his Brother, ... 4.JD4.258.47.
But here's the *Captain*, that will plague them both, ... 4.JD4.260.47.
But here's the *Captain*, that will plague you both, ... 4.JD4.260A.47.
What *Drop* or *Nostrum* can this Plague remove? ..... 4.Arbu.29.98.
A Plague, whose strange Infection men are sure, ... 4.JD2A.9.132.
Catch'd like the plague, or love, the Lord knows how, ... 4.JD2.9.133.
If such the Plague and pains to write by rule, ... 4.2HE2.180.177.
The plague is on thee, Britain, and who tries ..... 4.1740.75.336.
Plague with Dispute, or persecute with Rhyme. ..... 5.DunB4.260.369.
He sent him War, or Plague, or Famine sore. ..... 6.137.10.373.
The Plague destroying whom the Sword would spare, ... Il.1.81.90.
A dreadful Plague ensues; Th' avenging Darts ..... Il.1.496.112.
What tho' by *Jove* the female Plague design'd, ... Il.21.557.445.
The double plague of luxury and love! ..... Od.4.911.161.

PLAGUES

Famine and Drought proceed, and Plagues, and Death: ..... 1.TrSt.153.416.
Thy Plagues, and curse 'em with such Sons as those. ..... 1.TrSt.399.426.
Of Fires and Plagues, and Stars with blazing Hair, ... 2.TemF.453.285.
If plagues or earthquakes break not Heav'n's design, ... 3.EOM1.155.34.
And (all those Plagues in one) the bawling Bar; ..... 4.JD4.55.29.
But Plagues shall spread, and Fun'ral Fires increase, ... Il.1.122.93.
Prophet of Plagues, for ever boding Ill! ..... Il.1.132.93.
Pregnant with Plagues, and shedding Seeds of Death, ... Il.5.1059.317.
Taints the red Air with Fevers, Plagues, and Death. ..... Il.22.42.454.
Thence to her son the choicest plagues she brings, ... Od.11.339.398.

PLAICE

Cod, Whiting, Oyster, Mackrel, Sprat, or Plaice: ..... 6.14ii.31.44.

PLAIN

While yon slow Oxen turn the furrow'd Plain. ..... 1.PSp.30.63.
Me gentle *Delia* beckons from the Plain, ... 1.PSp.53.66.
More fell than Tygers on the *Lybian* Plain; ..... 1.PAu.90A.86.
That call'd the list'ning *Dryads* to the Plain? ..... 1.PWi.12.89.
The trembling Trees, in ev'ry Plain and Wood, ... 1.PWi.63.93.
Here Hills and Vales, the Woodland and the Plain, ... 1.W-F.11.149.
And pawing, seems to beat the distant Plain, ... 1.W-F.152.164.
Let old *Arcadia* boast her ample Plain, ... 1.W-F.159.164.
Let old *Arcadia* boast her spacious Plain, ... 1.W-F.159A.164.
Turn'd *Criticks* next, and prov'd plain *Fools* at last; ..... 1.EOC.37.243.
Some dryly plain, without Invention's Aid, ... 1.EOC.114.252.
Then build a New, or act it in a Plain. ..... 1.EOC.284.271.
Not so, when swift *Camilla* scours the Plain, ... 1.EOC.372.282.
So Schismatics the *plain Believers* quit, ... 1.EOC.428.288.
With heavy steps he sinks the sandy plain; ..... 1.TrPA.36.366.
Roar'd out for rage, and hurried o'er the plain: ..... 1.TrPA.133.371.
O launch thy Bark, nor fear the watry Plain, ... 1.TrSP.250.404.
First rais'd our Walls on that ill-omen'd Plain ..... 1.TrSt.251.421.
Then sees *Cythæron* towring o'er the Plain, ... 1.TrSt.466.429.
That driv'n by Storms, and pouring o'er the Plain, ... 1.TrSt.514.432.

PLAIN (CONTINUED)

With Orbs unroll'd lay covering all the Plain, ... 1.TrSt.665.438.
With Orbs unroll'd lay stretch'd o'er all the Plain, ... 1.TrSt.665A.438.
To fix the Fortune of the fatal Plain, ... 1.TrES.2.449.
So stalks the Lordly Savage o'er the Plain, ... 1.TrES.15.450.
Where *Xanthus'* Streams enrich the *Lycian* Plain? ... 1.TrES.28.450.
Cou'd heave th'unwieldy Burthen from the Plain: ... 1.TrES.102.453.
Forsake, inglorious, the contended Plain; ... 1.TrES.213.457.
My God-like Son shall press the *Phrygian* Plain: ... 1.TrES.228.458.
The God, his Eyes averting from the Plain, ... 1.TrES.258.459.
He falls, and falling, bites the bloody Plain. ... 1.TrES.266.459.
The Car rowls slowly o'er the dusty Plain. ... 1.TrES.280.460.
Descend my *Phœbus,* on the *Phrygian* Plain, ... 1.TrES.324.461.
Toss their high Heads, and scour along the Plain; ... 1.TrUl.9.465.
For Pinks and Daisies search'd the flow'ry Plain; ... 2.ChJM.624.45.
For, by th'Immortal Pow'rs, it *seem'd* too plain— ... 2.ChJM.779.52.
Not with more Glories, in th' Etherial Plain, ... 2.RL2.1.159.
Draw forth to Combat on the Velvet Plain. ... 2.RL3.44.172.
Plain was their Dress, and modest was their Mein. ... 2.TemF.357.281.
Fill all the wat'ry Plain, and to the Margin dance. ... 2.TemF.441.284.
But such plain roofs as piety could raise, ... 2.ElAb.139.331.
Then, in the scale of reas'ning life, 'tis plain ... 3.EOM1.47.19.
Then, in the scale of Life and Sence, 'tis plain ... 3.EOM1.47A.19.
For this plain reason, Man is not a Fly. ... 3.EOM1.194.39.
For this plain reason, Man is not a Mite. ... 3.EOM1.194A.39.
Ask your own heart, and nothing is so plain; ... 3.EOM2.215.81.
Is thine alone the seed that strews the plain? ... 3.EOM3.37.96.
Or plain tradition that this All begun, ... 3.EOM3.227.115.
A plain rough Hero turn a crafty Knave? ... 3.Ep1.78A.21.
Comets are regular, and *Clodio* plain. ... 3.Ep1.209A.33.
The plain rough Hero turn a crafty Knave? ... 3.Ep1.78.21.
But these plain Characters we rarely find; ... 3.Ep1.122.25.
Comets are regular, and Wharton plain. ... 3.Ep1.209.33.
Yet on plain Pudding deign'd at-home to eat; ... 3.Ep2.82.57.
From honest Mah'met, or plain Parson Hale. ... 3.Ep2.198.66.
Then in plain prose, were made two sorts of Men, ... 3.Ep3.13A.84.
But clear and artless, pouring thro' the plain ... 3.Ep3.257.114.
A plain good man, and Balaam was his name; ... 3.Ep3.342.121.
Or cut wide views thro' Mountains to the Plain, ... 3.Ep4.75.144.
The Wood supports the Plain, the parts unite, ... 3.Ep4.81.145.
I love to pour out all myself, as plain ... 4.HS1.51.9.
Or tames the Genius of the stubborn Plain, ... 4.HS1.131.19.
First turn plain rash, then vanish quite away. ... 4.JD4.45.29.
"So much *alone,* (to speak plain Truth between us) ... 4.JD4.90A.33.
If then plain Bread and milk will do the feat, ... 4.HS2.15.55.
Plain, but not sordid, tho' not splendid, clean. ... 4.HS2.48.57.
I'm a plain Man, whose Maxim is profest, ... 4.HAdv.153.87.
Well, on the whole, *plain* Prose must be my fate: ... 4.2HE2.198.179.
[Plain Truth, dear MURRAY, needs no flow'rs of speech, ... 4.1HE6.3.237.
The sick'ning Stars fade off th' æthereal plain; ... 5.DunA3.342.192.
On plain Experience lay foundations low, ... 5.DunB4.466.386.
The sick'ning stars fade off th'ethereal plain; ... 5.DunB4.636.407.
Fattens the flocks, and cloaths the plain; ... 6.6ii.2.14.
His Eye-Balls burn, he wounds the smoaking Plain, ... 6.9ix.1.22.
And for plain *Spanish* quit *Brasil;* ... 6.10.44.25.
The *Granvilles* write their Name plain *Greenfield,* ... 6.10.47.26.
Who the *Plain-dealer* damns, and prints the *Biter.* ... 6.12.11.37.
This in our Tale is plain y-fond, ... 6.14i.3A.41.
And tho' ev'n then expiring on the Plain, ... 6.15.12Z1.51.
Damn'd the *Plain-dealer,* and admir'd the *Biter.* ... 6.17iv.14.59.
When thunder roars, and lightning blasts the plain, ... 6.21.8.69.
For drizling Damps descend adown the Plain ... 6.42vi.3.120.
Tis plain, tis very plain, was *Cary.* ... 6.44.28.123.
Tis plain, tis very plain, was *Cary.* ... 6.44.28.123.
She went, to plain-work, and to purling brooks, ... 6.45.11.125.
Meerly because it is no Plain; ... 6.67.16.195.
The Patriot's plain, but untrod path pursue; ... 6.73.16.210.
Blest with plain Reason and with sober Sense; ... 6.115.2.322.
In Manners plain, in Sense alone refind, ... 6.134.5.364.
Left by *Achilles* on the *Trojan* Plain, ... Il.1.223.97.
Perhaps in *Grecian* Blood to drench the Plain, ... Il.1.724.122.
Lead all his *Grecians* to the dusty Plain. ... Il.2.12.127.
Lead all thy *Grecians* to the dusty Plain; ... Il.2.34.129.
And lead the *Grecians* to the dusty Plain; ... Il.2.84.130.
Spreads all the Beach, and wide o'ershades the Plain: ... Il.2.118.133.
Ev'n then the *Greeks* had left the hostile Plain, ... Il.2.189.137.
Lie unreveng'd on yon' detested Plain? ... Il.2.198.137.
Desert the Ships, and pour upon the Plain. ... Il.2.248.139.
Collects his Flock from Thousands on the Plain. ... Il.2.563.154.
Collects his Flock from Millions on the Plain. ... Il.2.563A.154.
And *Mycalessia's* ample Piny Plain. ... Il.2.593.156.
Who plow the spacious *Orchomenian* Plain. ... Il.2.611.156.
Where *Dios* from her Tow'rs o'erlooks the Plain, ... Il.2.647.157.
Led by *Menestheus* thro' the liquid Plain, ... Il.2.656.158.
From high *Trœzenè,* and *Maseta's* Plain, ... Il.2.676.159.
Fair *Arethyrea, Ornia's* fruitful Plain, ... Il.2.688.159.
The first to battel on th' appointed Plain, ... Il.2.745.161.
Where mighty Towns in Ruins spread the Plain, ... Il.2.799.163.
Next thirty Galleys cleave the liquid Plain, ... Il.2.821.164.
There lies, far distant from his native Plain; ... Il.2.857.165.
Nations on Nations fill the dusky Plain, ... Il.2.979.170.
Amidst the Plain in sight of *Ilion* stands ... Il.2.982.170.
They rush'd to War, and perish'd on the Plain. ... Il.2.1011.170.
So when inclement Winters vex the Plain ... Il.3.5.188.
A moving Cloud, swept on, and hid the Plain. ... Il.3.22.189.
He boldly stalk'd, the foremost on the Plain, ... Il.3.34.189.
With falling Woods to strow the wasted Plain. ... Il.3.92.194.
And pitch your Lances in the yielding Plain. ... Il.3.126.196.
See on the Plain thy *Grecian* Spouse appears, ... Il.3.213.202.
What's He, whose Arms lie scatter'd on the Plain? ... Il.3.254.204.
Just was his Sense, and his Expression plain, ... Il.3.276.205.
Next from the Car descending on the Plain, ... Il.3.334.209.
Great *Menelaus* press the fatal Plain; ... Il.3.355.210.
Or carry Wars to some soft *Asian* Plain? ... Il.3.496.215.
(A fatal Sign to Armies on the Plain, ... Il.4.103.225.
Why stand ye gazing round the dreadful Plain, ... Il.4.278.234.

PLAIN (CONTINUED)

Beneath this Arm fell prostrate on the Plain. ... Il.4.373.239.
And *Discord* raging bathes the purple Plain: ... Il.4.501.244.
Rush to the Vales, and pour'd along the Plain, ... Il.4.518.246.
And scorch'd by Suns, it withers on the Plain. ... Il.4.559.248.
And sinks a breathless Carcass on the Plain. ... Il.4.566.248.
The Corps now breathless on the bloody Plain, ... Il.4.618.250.
These from their Steeds, *Tydides* on the Plain. ... Il.5.20.266.
But pierc'd his Breast, and stretch'd him on the Plain. ... Il.5.26.266.
Rapt thro' the Ranks he thunders o'er the Plain, ... Il.5.113.272.
These see thou shun, thro' all th' embattled Plain, ... Il.5.166.275.
With tenfold Ardor now invades the Plain, ... Il.5.172.275.
The Youths return'd not from the doubtful Plain, ... Il.5.192.276.
If e'er with Life I quit the *Trojan* Plain, ... Il.5.268.280.
And two transport *Æneas* o'er the Plain. ... Il.5.335.283.
And follow'd where *Tydides* swept the Plain. ... Il.5.406.286.
Thus they in Heav'n: While on the Plain below ... Il.5.523.294.
The God of Battel issues on the Plain, ... Il.5.561.295.
From Troop to Troop he toils thro' all the Plain. ... Il.5.650.299.
They fell with Glory on the *Phrygian* Plain. ... Il.5.680.300.
He left the Town a wide, deserted Plain. ... Il.5.795.304.
Alastor, Chromius, Halius strow'd the Plain, ... Il.5.835.305.
Where Lakes surround low *Hylè's* watry Plain; ... Il.5.872.308.
What lawless Rage on yon' forbidden Plain, ... Il.5.944.311.
Now issuing fearless they possess the Plain, ... Il.5.984.314.
Else had'st thou seen me sink on yonder Plain, ... Il.5.1088.318.
While *Troy's* fam'd <*> Streams that bound the deathful Plain ... Il.6.5.322.
And next he lay'd *Opheltius* on the Plain. ... Il.6.26.325.
In Combate on the *Solymæan* Plain. ... Il.6.252.339.
Her pleasing Empire and her native Plain, ... Il.6.541.353.
He snuffs the Females in the distant Plain, ... Il.6.658.360.
From vast *Olympus* to the gleaming Plain ... Il.7.24.364.
To mortal Combate on the listed Plain. ... Il.7.56.365.
(Soft *Zephyr* curling the wide wat'ry Plain) ... Il.7.72.366.
Then with majestic Grace they quit the Plain; ... Il.7.370.382.
Go search your slaughter'd Chiefs on yonder Plain, ... Il.7.486.388.
Some search the Plain, some fell the sounding Grove: ... Il.7.495.389.
Thro' Heaps of Carnage search'd the mournful Plain. ... Il.7.503.389.
Squadrons on Squadrons cloud the dusky Plain: ... Il.8.72.399.
The Steeds fly back: He falls, and spurns the Plain. ... Il.8.154.405.
The Godlike *Lycophon* next press'd the Plain, ... Il.8.331.413.
Decline the Head, and drooping kiss the Plain; ... Il.8.372.415.
Quits his bright Car, and issues on the Plain. ... Il.8.386.416.
What Heaps of *Argives* then shall load the Plain, ... Il.8.588.424.
Shall rise in Vengeance, and lay waste the Plain. ... Il.8.594.424.
Go thou inglorious! from th' embattel'd Plain; ... Il.9.61.434.
The whole Extent to *Pylos'* sandy Plain ... Il.9.201.442.
The whole Extent to *Pylos'* sandy Plain ... Il.9.388.452.
And twelve lay smoaking on the *Trojan* Plain: ... Il.9.433.453.
The World's great Empress on th' *Ægyptian* Plain, ... Il.9.501.458.
And Steeds unrival'd on the dusty Plain; ... Il.9.529.459.
Great *Meleager* stretch'd along the Plain. ... Il.9.662.467.
(The Plain beside with mangled Corps was spread, ... Il.10.237.12.
Thro' the black Horrors of th' ensanguin'd Plain ... Il.10.355.18.
But the rash Youth prepares to scour the Plain: ... Il.10.394.21.
This Javelin else shall fix thee to the Plain. ... Il.10.440.23.
(Enquir'd the Chief) or scatter'd o'er the Plain? ... Il.10.495.25.
Then heap'd with Reeds and gathr'd Boughs the Plain, ... Il.10.538.27.
The gath'ring Tumult spreads o'er all the Plain; ... Il.10.615.29.
Swells the red Horrors of this direful Plain: ... Il.11.102.39.
Atrides spoil'd, and left them on the Plain; ... Il.11.133.41.
Horse trod by Horse, lay foaming on the Plain. ... Il.11.194.44.
Mean-while on ev'ry side, around the Plain, ... Il.11.225.45.
Unwept, uncover'd, on the Plain he lay, ... Il.11.319.49.
Stern *Hector's* Conquests in the middle Plain ... Il.11.423.53.
They rush'd to Fight, and perish'd on the Plain! ... Il.11.430.53.
But yet so stunn'd, that stagg'ring on the Plain, ... Il.11.457.54.
But pierc'd his Foot, and nail'd it to the Plain. ... Il.11.482.55.
What shame, inglorious if I quit the Plain; ... Il.11.514.57.
Fam'd Son of *Hippasus!* there press the Plain; ... Il.11.565.59.
Loud Groans proclaim his Progress thro' the Plain, ... Il.11.622.61.
Trojans on *Trojans* yonder load the Plain. ... Il.11.645.62.
Crops the tall Harvest, and lays waste the Plain; ... Il.11.685.65.
And many a Javelin, guiltless on the Plain, ... Il.11.700.66.
His feasted Eyes beheld around the Plain ... Il.11.732.67.
Along fair *Arene's* delightful Plain, ... Il.11.858.74.
Two Chiefs from each, fell breathless to the Plain. ... Il.11.883.75.
Shine 'twixt the Hills, or wander o'er the Plain. ... Il.12.36.83.
Each quits his Car, and issues on the Plain. ... Il.12.96.84.
Those Wheels returning ne'er shall mark the Plain; ... Il.12.128.86.
Fierce to the left he drives, where from the Plain ... Il.12.133.86.
A Snowy Inundation hides the Plain; ... Il.12.334.93.
And the white Ruin rises o'er the Plain. ... Il.12.344.94.
So stalks the lordly Savage o'er the Plain, ... Il.12.359.94.
Where *Xanthus'* Streams enrich the *Lycian* Plain, ... Il.12.372.95.
Could heave th' unwieldy Burthen from the Plain. ... Il.12.456.98.
The Sea subsiding spreads a level Plain, ... Il.13.46.107.
Not born to Glories of the dusty Plain; ... Il.13.142.111.
Whirls, leaps, and thunders down, impetuous to the Plain: ... Il.13.198.115.
Together let us battel on the Plain; ... Il.13.309.119.
So *Mars* Armipotent invades the Plain, ... Il.13.384.123.
And their bright Arms shot Horror o'er the Plain. ... Il.13.395.124.
From diff'rent Quarters sweep the sandy Plain; ... Il.13.425.126.
Before his Chariot warring on the Plain; ... Il.13.484.130.
Like *Ida's* Flocks proceeding o'er the Plain; ... Il.13.621.135.
Stretch'd on the Plain, he sobs away his Breath, ... Il.13.644.136.
The hollow Helmet rings against the Plain. ... Il.13.671.137.
The Plume dropp'd nodding to the Plain below, ... Il.13.770.141.
In slow Procession bore from off the Plain. ... Il.13.822.144.
But round the Battlements, and round the Plain, ... Il.13.953.151.
The time shall come, when chas'd along the Plain, ... Il.13.1032.153.
With answ'ring Thunders fill'd the echoing Plain; ... Il.13.1059.155.
And wilt thou thus desert the *Trojan* Plain? ... Il.14.98.162.
What-time, deserting *Ilion's* wasted Plain, ... Il.14.285.176.
Loud Shouts of Triumph fill the crowded Plain; ... Il.14.493.188.

PLAIN (CONTINUED)
The dropping Head first tumbled to the Plain. ......Il.14.546.189.
Say, is this Chief, extended on the Plain, ...Il.14.551.189.
Drove thro' the Neck, and hurl'd him to the Plain; ......Il.14.579.190.
Thou first, great *Ajax!* on th' ensanguin'd Plain ......Il.14.605.191.
These proud in Arms, those scatter'd o'er the Plain; ......Il.15.9.194.
Steeps *Troy* in Blood, and ranges round the Plain; ......Il.15.48.196.
Let her descend, and from th' embattel'd Plain ......Il.15.61.196.
Steeps *Troy* in Blood, and rages round the Plain; ......Il.15.48A.196.
He, not untouch'd with Pity, to the Plain ......Il.15.69.199.
Descending first to yon' forbidden Plain, ...Il.15.130.201.
O'er the wide Clouds, and o'er the starry Plain, ...Il.15.214.205.
Lay yon' proud Structures level with the Plain, ...Il.15.241.206.
Glides down the Mountain to the Plain below. ......Il.15.269.207.
He snuffs the Females in the well known Plain, ...Il.15.304.208.
Polites' Arm laid *Echius* on the Plain; ......Il.15.388.212.
Indulgent *Jove!* how plain thy Favours shine, ...Il.15.576.218.
Fed his large Oxen on *Percote's* Plain; ......Il.15.647.221.
So when a Savage, ranging o'er the Plain, ...Il.15.702.223.
Amidst the Plain of some wide-water'd Fen, ...Il.15.761.225.
A sudden Ray shot beaming o'er the Plain, ...Il.15.810.227.
Yet now, *Patroclus*, issue to the Plain; ......Il.16.105.240.
The brazen Head falls sounding on the Plain. ......Il.16.147.243.
Fly diverse, scatter'd o'er the distant Plain. ......Il.16.347.256.
(Or Kids, or Lambs) lie scatter'd o'er the Plain, ...Il.16.421.259.
So from the Ships, along the dusky Plain, ...Il.16.438.259.
Forsake, inglorious, the contended Plain; ......Il.16.516.263.
My godlike Son shall press the *Phrygian* Plain: ......Il.16.531.264.
The God, his Eyes averting from the Plain, ...Il.16.563.266.
He falls, and falling bites the bloody Plain. ......Il.16.571.266.
The Car rowls slowly o'er the dusty Plain. ......Il.16.585.267.
The Clash of Armour rings o'er all the Plain. ......Il.16.694.271.
With conqu'ring Shouts the *Trojans* shake the Plain, ...Il.16.730.272.
There yet scarce spent, it quivers on the Plain, ...Il.16.743.272.
Descend, my *Phœbus!* on the *Phrygian* Plain, ...Il.16.811.274.
Who last, beneath thy Vengeance, press'd the Plain; ......Il.16.848.276.
Struck from the Car, falls headlong on the Plain. ......Il.16.900.278.
Nor thus the Boar (those Terrors of the Plain) ......Il.17.23.288.
It pierc'd his Throat, and bent him to the Plain; ......Il.17.50.289.
Then shall I quit *Patroclus* on the Plain, ...Il.17.101.291.
Swift thro' the spacious Plain he sent a Look; ......Il.17.213.295.
Condemn'd to Vulturs on the *Trojan* Plain; ......Il.17.285.298.
The shatter'd Crest, and Horse-hair, strow the Plain: ......Il.17.341.300.
Dispers'd around the Plain, by fits they fight, ...Il.17.432.304.
Expects him glorious from the conquer'd Plain, ...Il.17.466.305.
Of Geese, that scream, and scatter round the Plain. ......Il.17.529.309.
By *Hector* wounded, *Leitus* quits the Plain, ...Il.17.680.314.
Prone from the Seat he tumbles to the Plain; ......Il.17.699.314.
In vain I charg'd him soon to quit the Plain, ...Il.18.17.323.
Far lyes *Patroclus* from his native plain! ......Il.18.127.328.
Or fetch a thousand Circles round the Plain, ...Il.18.329.337.
Still shines exalted on th' ætherial Plain, ...Il.18.565.349.
Studious to see that Terror of the Plain, ...Il.19.49.373.
Tho' vast the Heaps that strow the crimson Plain, ...Il.19.221.382.
Thy friendly Hand uprear'd me from the Plain, ...Il.19.313.385.
And like a Deluge pour'd upon the Plain. ......Il.19.379.387.
While great *Achilles*, (Terror of the Plain) ......Il.20.57.396.
Troy's Turrets totter on the rocking Plain; ......Il.20.81.397.
First silver-shafted *Phœbus* took the Plain ......Il.20.91.398.
Th' Immortals guard him thro' the dreadful Plain, ...Il.20.130.399.
Swept the wide Shore, and drove him to the Plain. ......Il.20.179.401.
These lightly skimming, when they swept the Plain, ...Il.20.270.405.
With loud-resounding Arms he strikes the Plain; ......Il.20.447.413.
To vaunt his Swiftness, wheels around the Plain, ...Il.20.477.414.
Then *Dryops* tumbled to th' ensanguin'd Plain, ...Il.20.526.416.
Part to the Town fly diverse o'er the Plain, ...Il.21.4.421.
That barr such numbers from their native Plain: ......Il.21.69.424.
Bent as he stands, he tumbles to the Plain; ......Il.21.194.429.
Th' amaz'd *Pæonians* scour along the Plain: ......Il.21.224.430.
O'er all th' expanded Plain the Waters spread; ......Il.21.348.435.
Wide o'er the Plain he pours the boundless Blaze; ......Il.21.399.436.
And propt on her fair Arm, forsakes the Plain. ......Il.21.489.441.
Hoary with Dust, they beat the hollow Plain; ......Il.21.634.448.
What, shall I fly this Terror of the Plain? ......Il.21.651.449.
What boots thee now, that *Troy* forsook the Plain? ......Il.22.19.453.
And stretch'd beneath that Fury of the Plain. ......Il.22.54.455.
Met at an Oak, or journeying o'er a Plain; ......Il.22.168.460.
Where the high Watch-tow'r overlooks the Plain; ......Il.22.192.463.
So oft' *Achilles* turns him to the Plain: ......Il.22.255.466.
At last is *Hector* stretch'd upon the Plain, ...Il.22.415.472.
His graceful Head was trail'd along the Plain. ......Il.22.500.477.
Confronts *Achilles;* chas'd along the Plain, ...Il.22.586.480.
Then Clouds of Foot that smoak along the Plain; ......Il.23.163.495.
No more *Achilles* sees his native Plain; ......Il.23.187.497.
Heap with a rising Pyramid the Plain. ......Il.23.201.497.
These in fair Order rang'd upon the Plain, ...Il.23.339.503.
Should our immortal Coursers take the Plain; ......Il.23.344.503.
Observing still the foremost on the Plain. ......Il.23.398.506.
Pelides points the Barrier on the Plain, ...Il.23.434.507.
They pant, they stretch, they shout along the Plain. ......Il.23.450.508.
His matchless Horses <'> labour on the Plain. ......Il.23.464.508.
Thro' your neglect if lagging on the Plain ......Il.23.489.509.
The flound'ring Coursers rolling on the Plain, ...Il.23.517.510.
For since the Goal they doubled, round the Plain ......Il.23.546.511.
And hear his Shouts victorious o'er the Plain. ......Il.23.563.512.
What needs appealing in a Fact so plain? ......Il.23.658.515.
Lifts the green Ear above the springing Plain, ...Il.23.680.516.
To heave the batter'd Carcase off the Plain. ......Il.23.780.520.
Stand forth, and bear these Prizes from the Plain. ......Il.23.880.524.
Unhappy *Ajax* stumbles on the Plain; ......Il.23.906.525.
Cast on the Plain the brazen Burthen rings: ......Il.23.942.526.
Great *Jove* beheld him as he crost the Plain, ...Il.24.409.552.
Those, *Cynthia's* Arrows stretch'd upon the Plain. ......Il.24.762.569.
Shall sink, a smoaking Ruin on the Plain. ......Il.24.917.574.
Or else some *Greek* whose Father prest the Plain, ...Il.24.926.575.
And common turf, lie naked on the plain, ...Od.1.209.42.

PLAIN (CONTINUED)
Better the Chief, on *Ilion's* hostile plain ......Od.1.301.47.
And those whom *Idomen* from *Ilion's* plain ......Od.3.232.97.
Where winding round the rich *Cydonian* plain, ...Od.3.372.104.
Thy martial *Brother; on the *Phrygian* plain ......Od.4.255.131.
Of vegetable venom, taints the plain; ......Od.4.320.134.
The foe deceiv'd, he pass'd the tented plain, ...Od.4.337.136.
Abides, pavilion'd on the grassy plain. ......Od.4.560.147.
But neither mead nor plain supplies, to feed ......Od.4.825.158.
A sceptred Lord, who o'er the fruitful plain ......Od.4.1051.167.
Mean-time the Suitors plow the wat'ry plain, ...Od.4.1099.169.
And double-edg'd; the handle smooth and plain, ...Od.5.301.185.
Sudden, full twenty on the plain are strow'd, ...Od.5.313.186.
Who shines exalted on th' etherial plain, ...Od.5.351.188.
Prest in *Atrides'* cause the *Trojan* plain: ......Od.5.394.191.
Then glassy smooth lay all the liquid plain, ...Od.5.501.196.
In ease possest the wide *Hyperian* plain; ......Od.6.6.203.
Or crop the verdant herbage of the plain. ......Od.6.104.211.
With equal grace *Nausicaa* trod the plain, ...Od.6.127.212.
Advance at distance, while I pass the plain ......Od.6.309.225.
But would'st thou soon review thy native plain? ......Od.6.347.228.
With these gay *Hermes* trod the starry plain; ......Od.8.363.283.
Some dear-lov'd brother press'd the *Phrygian* plain? ......Od.8.634.297.
And fountains streaming down the fruitful plain. ......Od.9.156.312.
Nor glimmer'd *Phœbe* in th' ethereal plain: ......Od.9.168.312.
A fathom's length, to shape it and to plain; ......Od.9.385.321.
A larger rock then heaving from the plain, ...Od.9.631.332.
Mean-while our vessels plough the liquid plain, ...Od.10.58.342.
The shepherd quitting here at night the plain, ...Od.10.94.343.
Or saw gay vessel stem the wat'ry plain, ...Od.11.154.389.
And names a *Van:* there fix it on the plain, ...Od.11.158.389.
He added not, but mounting spurn'd the plain, ...Od.11.307.397.
And god-like *Neleus* rul'd the *Pylian* plain: ......Od.11.312.397.
And *Castor* glorious on th' embattled plain ......Od.11.369.401.
There *Ephimedia* trod the gloomy plain, ...Od.11.375.401.
'Till the sun flames along th' etherial plain; ......Od.11.437.405.
Fell before *Troy*, and nobly prest the plain? ......Od.11.463.407.
And high above the rest, *Atrides* prest the plain. ......Od.11.484.408.
This arm that thunder'd o'er the *Phrygian* plain, ...Od.11.611.414.
The swiftest racer of the azure plain ......Od.12.121.437.
Two sister Goddesses possess the plain, ...Od.12.166.440.
Then to my mates I measur'd back the plain, ...Od.12.180.441.
Eternal mists obscure th' aereal plain, ...Od.12.286.446.
Tho' Gods descend from heav'n's aereal plain ......Od.12.345.448.
And setting stars roll'd down the azure plain; ......Od.12.368.449.
Low thro' the grove, or range the flow'ry plain: ......Od.12.390.450.
Toss their high heads, and scour along the plain; ......Od.13.100.6.
Before the Græcians touch'd the *Trojan* plain, ...Od.14.266.49.
But thou, when morn salutes th' aerial plain, ...Od.16.290.119.
Him no fell Savage on the plain withstood, ...Od.17.382.150.
(Smooth'd by the workman to a polish'd plain) ......Od.17.416.152.
With flocks and herds each grassy plain is stor'd; ......Od.19.133.199.
View'd his enormous bulk extended on the plain. ......Od.19.533.221.
And all wide *Elis'* courser-breeding plain, ...Od.21.374.277.
Nor saw gay vessel stem the surgy plain, ...Od.23.287.337.
And calls a Corn-van: This upon the plain ......Od.23.291.337.
Cicons on *Cicons* swell th' ensanguin'd plain; ......Od.23.334.340.
Thrice happy thou! to press the martial plain ......Od.24.53.350.
Thus they; while *Hermes* o'er the dreary plain ......Od.24.123.354.
And labour made the rugged soil a plain. ......Od.24.237.360.
Inhume the natives in their native plain, ...Od.24.479.371.
Before the city, in an ample plain, ...Od.24.536.373.

PLAIN-DEALER
Who the *Plain-dealer* damns, and prints the *Biter.* ...... 6.12.11.37.
Damn'd the *Plain-dealer,* and admir'd the *Biter.* ...... 6.17iv.14.59.

PLAIN-WORK
She went, to plain-work, and to purling brooks, ...6.45.11.125.

PLAINLY
As plainly proves, Experience dwells with Years: ......2.ChJM.150.21.
And *Pyramus* and *Thisbe* plainly show ......2.ChJM.516.40.
Full plainly doth appear, ...6.79.6.218.

PLAINNESS
So modest Plainness sets off sprightly Wit: ......1.EOC.302.273.

PLAINS
Nor blush to sport on *Windsor's* blissful Plains: ......1.PSp.2.59.
At Morn the Plains, at Noon the shady Grove; ......1.PSp.78.68.
Nor Plains at Morn, nor Groves at Noon delight. ......1.PSp.80.68.
The sultry *Sirius* burns the thirsty Plains, ...1.PSu.21.73.
I'll fly from Shepherds, Flocks, and flow'ry Plains.— ......1.PAu.86.86.
From Shepherds, Flocks, and Plains, I may remove, ...1.PAu.87.86.
Here in full Light the russet Plains extend; ......1.W-F.23.150.
Rich Industry sits smiling on the Plains, ...1.W-F.41.152.
To Plains with well-breath'd Beagles we repair, ...1.W-F.121.161.
To Plains with well-bred Beagles we repair, ...1.W-F.121A.161.
And Pykes, the Tyrants of the watry Plains. ......1.W-F.146.163.
Paints the green Forests and the flow'ry Plains, ...1.W-F.428.194.
In *other Parts* it leaves wide sandy Plains; ......1.EOC.55.245.
And you that rule *Sicilia's* happy Plains, ...1.TrSP.69.396.
Thro' lonely Plains, and thro' the silent Grove, ...1.TrSP.160.400.
As if the silent Grove, and lonely Plains ......1.TrSP.161.400.
Ascend from Hills, and Plains, and shady Bow'rs; ......1.TrSt.287.422.
His fiery course, or drives him o'er the plains; ......3.EOM1.62.21.
Hence on thy Life, and fly these hostile Plains, ...Il.1.35.87.
We launch a Bark to plow the watry Plains, ...Il.1.182.96.
Or milk-white Swans in *Asius'* watry Plains, ...Il.2.541.152.
With rushing Troops the Plains are cover'd o'er, ...Il.2.548.153.
His fiery Coursers thunder o'er the Plains. ......Il.2.1017.171.
Three Towns are *Juno's* on the *Grecian* Plains, ...Il.4.75.224.
And her dead Warriors strow the mournful Plains. ......Il.4.273.234.
Rush fearless to the Plains, and uncontroul'd ......Il.5.683.300.
Dropt in the Dust are trail'd along the Plains. ......Il.5.714.301.

PLAINS 112 PLANTS

PLAINS (CONTINUED)
A hundred Armies on a hundred Plains. ....Il.5.921.310.
Not Fear, thou know'st, withholds me from the Plains, ...Il.5.1012.315.
My Soul impells me to th' embattel'd Plains; ....Il.6.567.354.
Safe to transport him to his native Plains, ...Il.9.809.473.
The Stars shine fainter on th' Ætherial Plains, ...Il.10.297.15.
Pours from the Mountains o'er the delug'd Plains, ...Il.11.615.61.
And ours was all the Plunder of the Plains: ....Il.11.821.73.
Her hardy Heroes from the well-fought Plains ....Il.13.293.119.
The Plains resounded as the Boaster fell. ....Il.13.470.128.
On yonder Decks, and yet o'erlooks the Plains! ....Il.13.938.149.
Far o'er the Plains, in dreadful Order bright, ...Il.13.1008.153.
Drove thro' the thickest of th' embattel'd Plains ....Il.15.524.217.
Not faster, trickling to the Plains below, ...Il.16.5.234.
But *Troy* repuls'd, and scatter'd o'er the Plains, ...Il.16.362.257.
Stretch'd by *Patroclus'* Arm on yonder Plains, ...Il.16.667.270.
Meanwhile *Patroclus* pours along the Plains, ...Il.16.837.276.
But where the rising Whirlwind clouds the Plains, ...Il.16.935.279.
Rapt in the Chariot o'er the distant Plains, ...Il.16.1047.283.
Still would we turn, still battle on the Plains, ...Il.17.111.292.
Spreads his broad Waters o'er the level Plains, ...Il.17.840.321.
The *Greeks,* late Victors, now to quit the Plains? ....Il.18.10.323.
But can'st thou, naked, issue to the Plains? ....Il.18.167.330.
Soon the white Flocks proceeded o'er the Plains, ...Il.18.607.352.
Whole Flocks and Herds lye bleeding on the Plains, ...Il.18.613.352.
And shine in mazy Wand'rings o'er the Plains. ....Il.21.298.433.
Must feast the Vultures on the naked Plains. ....Il.22.125.458.
Have gather'd half the Poisons of the Plains; ....Il.22.133.458.
And leads amidst a wide Extent of Plains; ....Il.23.322.503.
Why roam thy Mules and Steeds the Plains along, ...Il.24.449.555.
But say, convey'st thou thro' the lonely Plains ....Il.24.467.556.
Have Dogs dismember'd on the naked Plains, ...Il.24.499.557.
In thronging Crowds they issue to the Plains, ...Il.24.882.573.
Since great Ulysses sought the *Phrygian* plains, ...Od.2.33.61.
And dogs had torn him on the naked plains. ....Od.3.323.102.
Elysium shall be thine; the blissful plains ....Od.4.765.155.
Shine in her hand: Along the sounding plains ....Od.6.96.210.
Commands the prospect of the plains below: ....Od.10.112.346.
The evening stars still mount th' ethereal plains. ....Od.11.465.407.
For as o'er *Panopé's* enamel'd plains ....Od.11.715.421.
Sev'n herds, sev'n flocks enrich the sacred plains, ...Od.12.162.440.
Now had *Minerva* reach'd those ample plains, ...Od.15.1.67.
Soon as the Morning blush'd along the plains, ...Od.16.1.100.
To her the youth. We reach'd the *Pylian* plains, ...Od.17.124.137.
And *Itylus* sounds warbling o'er the plains; ....Od.19.607.226.
Since the just Gods who tread the starry plains ....Od.23.275.336.

PLAINT
Thus she began her plaint. Immortal *Jove!* .... Od.5.12.171.

PLAINTIFF
In such a Cause the Plaintiff will be hiss'd, ...4.HS1.155.21.

PLAINTIVE
With answering Sighs return'd the plaintive Sound. ....Il.4.185.230.
And plaintive glides along the dreary Coast, ...Il.22.457.474.
Ah follow me! (she cry'd) what plaintive Noise ....Il.22.578.480.
Stood at my side, a pensive, plaintive Ghost; ....Il.23.127.493.
With plaintive Sighs, and Musick's solemn Sound: ....Il.24.901.573.
'Till *Pallas,* piteous of her plaintive cries, ...Od.1.463.54.
With speaking eyes, and voice of plaintive sound, ...Od.17.438.154.
Trembling the Spectres glide, and plaintive vent ....Od.24.7.347.

PLAINTS
Thus pour'd his Plaints before th' immortal Throne. ....Il.5.1067.317.

PLAINY
As with these Eyes I plainy saw thee whor'd; ....2.ChJM.769.52.

PLAIST
'Twas *S'il vous plaist, Monsieur.* .... 6.14v(b).12.49.
& *S'il vous plaist, Monsieur.* .... 6.14v(b).12A.49.

PLAISTER
The floors of plaister, and the walls of dung, ...3.Ep3.300.118.
Well spread with Sense, shall be the Nation's Plaister. ....6.48ii.12.134.
Can smell a Plaister, or an Issue. ....6.135.32.367.

PLAISTER'D
With all th' embroid'ry plaister'd at thy tail? ....3.Ep3.92.97.
Or plaister'd posts, with Claps in capitals? ....4.Arbu.216.111.

PLAIT
Some fold the Sleeve, whilst others plait the Gown; ....2.RL1.147.158.
Some fold the Sleeve, while others plait the Gown; ....2.RL1.147A.158.

PLAITED
The Folds it pierc'd, the plaited Linen tore, ...Il.4.168.229.

PLAN
A mighty maze! but not without a plan; ....3.EOM1.6.11.
A mighty maze! of walks without a plan; ....3.EOM1.6A.11.
Be call'd to Court, to plan some work divine, ...4.2HE1.374.227.
Make Nature still incroach upon his plan; ....5.DunB4.473.387.
Than just to plan our projects, and to die. ....6.147viii.2.392.
Fair in the plan the future palace rose, ...Od.4.236.130.
And plan with all thy arts the scene of fate. ....Od.13.442.27.
And plan the scene of death, I bend my way: ....Od.16.257.117.
They plan our future ruin, and resort ....Od.24.181.356.

PLANE
('Twas where the Plane-tree spread its Shades around) ....Il.2.370.145.

PLANE-TREE
('Twas where the Plane-tree spread its Shades around) ....Il.2.370.145.

PLANES
More strait than alders, taller than the planes; ....1.TrPA.60.367.

PLANET
Could he, who taught each Planet where to roll, ...3.EOM2.35A.60.
The Morning Planet told th' approach of Light; ....Il.23.281.501.

PLANETARY
And careful watch'd the Planetary Hour. ....2.TemF.106.261.
That other feeds on planetary schemes, ...Od.20.453.255.

PLANETS
Or roll the Planets thro' the boundless Sky. ....2.RL2.80.165.
What other planets circle other suns, ...3.EOM1.26.16.
What other planets and what other suns, ...3.EOM1.26A.16.
Planets and Suns run lawless thro' the sky, ...3.EOM1.252.46.
Planets and Suns rush lawless thro' the sky, ...3.EOM1.252A.46.
Instruct the planets in what orbs to run, ...3.EOM2.21.56.
Shew by what Laws the wand'ring Planets stray ....3.EOM2.21A.56.
On their own Axis as the Planets run, ...3.EOM3.313.126.
And other planets circle other suns: ....5.DunA3.240.177.
And other planets circle other suns. ....5.DunB3.244.332.
Around her Throne the vivid Planets roll, ...Il.8.691.428.

PLANK
Sole on a plank, on boiling surges tost, ...Od.7.337.253.
His arms and legs, and fix a plank behind; ....Od.22.189.296.

PLANKS
Then thundring thro' the Planks, with forceful Sway, ...1.TrES.195.456.
Then thund'ring thro' the Planks, with forceful Sway, ...Il.12.549.101.
From space to space, and nail'd the planks along; ....Od.5.322.187.
Thus then I judge: while yet the planks sustain ....Od.5.458.194.
Planks, Beams, dis-parted fly: the scatter'd wood ....Od.5.468.195.

PLANN'D
Deep Harvests bury all his pride has plann'd, ...3.Ep4.175.154.
Deep Harvests bury all thy pride has plann'd, ...3.Ep4.175A.154.
And here she plann'd th' Imperial seat of Fools. ....5.DunB1.272.290.

PLANS
And form sure plans to save the sinking state. ....Od.1.357.49.
The plans of war against the town prepar'd. ....Od.4.350.136.
Secret revolves; and plans the vengeance due. ....Od.17.183.140.
Whilst, forming plans of death, *Ulysses* stay'd, ...Od.19.62.195.

PLANT
And ev'ry Plant that drinks the Morning Dew; ....1.PSu.32.74.
The Sick and Weak the healing Plant shall aid; ....1.Mes.15.114.
A flow'ry plant, which still preserves her name. ....1.TrFD.34.387.
Prostrate, with tears their kindred plant bedew, ...1.TrFD.61.388.
Within this plant my hapless parent lies: ....1.TrFD.83.389.
Protect your plant, nor let my branches feel ....1.TrFD.90.390.
And long the plant a human heat retain'd. ....1.TrFD.103.390.
Where grows this Plant (reply'd the Friend) oh where? ....2.ChWB.397.76.
Fix'd like a plant on his peculiar spot, ...3.EOM2.63.63.
Plant of celestial seed! if dropt below, ...3.EOM4.7.128.
To build, to plant, whatever you intend, ...3.Ep4.47.141.
Paints as you plant, and, as you work, designs. ....3.Ep4.64.143.
Of Land, set out to plant a Wood. ....4.HS6.6.251.
I plant, root up, I build, and then confound, ...4.1HE1.169.291.
At last it fix'd, 'twas on what plant it pleas'd, ...5.DunB4.429.383.
Visits each plant, and waters all the ground: ....6.35.30.103.
Darts on the consecrated Plant of *Jove,* .... Il.14.482.187.
From *Pelion's* shady Brow the Plant entire ....Il.16.174.245.
The tender Plant, and withers all its Shades; ....Il.17.62.290.
Like some fair Plant beneath my careful Hand ....Il.18.511.346.
The Plant uprooted to his Weight gave way, ...Il.21.270.432.
Plant the fair Column o'er the vacant grave, ...Od.1.380.51.
Plant the fair column o'er the mighty dead, ...Od.2.251.73.
A plant so stately, or a nymph so fair. ....Od.6.202.219.
Visits each plant, and waters all the ground: ....Od.7.171.244.
Untaught to plant, to turn the glebe and sow, ...Od.9.121.310.
The plant I give thro' all the direful bow'r ....Od.10.343.360.
Thus while he spoke, the sovereign plant he drew, ...Od.10.361.361.
Like some fair plant set by a heav'nly hand, ...Od.14.202.45.
And clear'd a Plant, encumber'd with its wood. ....Od.24.268.362.
Who digging round the plant still hangs his head, ...Od.24.285.363.
On ev'ry plant and tree thy cares are shown, ...Od.24.292.364.
To ev'ry plant in order as we came, ...Od.24.392.368.

PLANTATIONS
Let his plantations stretch from down to down, ...3.Ep4.189.155.

PLANTED
And singled out a Pear-Tree planted nigh: ....2.ChJM.602.44.
And in my Garden planted shall it be! ....2.ChWB.400.76.
If e'er with airy Horns I planted Heads, ...2.RL4.71.189.
For what has Virro painted, built, and planted? ....3.Ep4.13.137.
In Forest planted by a Father's hand, ...4.HS2.135.65.
Apollo, planted at the Trench's Bound, ...Il.15.406.213.
Below, their planted Feet at distance fixt: ....Il.23.825.522.

PLANTER'S
As fruits ungrateful to the planter's care ....3.EOM2.181.76.

PLANTIN
Oft in an *Aldus,* or a *Plantin,* .... 6.29.17.83.
Some *Plantin* to the rest prefer, ...6.29.3.82.

PLANTS
While Plants their Shade, or Flow'rs their Odours give, ...1.PWi.83.94.
Let *India* boast her Plants, nor envy we ....1.W-F.29.151.
Now sliding Streams the thirsty Plants renew, ...1.TrVP.15.377.
Plants of thy hand, and children of thy pray'r. ....2.ElAb.130.330.
He sees, why Nature plants in Man alone ....3.EOM4.345.162.

PLANTS (CONTINUED)
- The thriving plants ignoble broomsticks made, 3.Ep4.97.146.
- Who plants like BATHURST, or who builds like BOYLE. 3.Ep4.178.154.
- And feed with pregnant Streams the Plants and Flow'rs; Il.21.292.433.
- Yet here all products and all plants abound, Od.9.151.311.

PLASH
- Fal'n in the plash his wickedness had lay'd; 5.DunA2.72.107.
- Fal'n in the plash his wickedness had laid: 5.DunB2.76.299.

PLASTIC
- See plastic Nature working to this end, 3.EOM3.9.93.
- So watchful Bruin forms with plastic care 5.DunA1.99.71.
- So watchful Bruin forms, with plastic care, 5.DunB1.101.276.

PLATAEA
- *Platæa* green, and *Nisa* the divine. Il.2.603.156.

PLATE
- Not when from Plate to Plate your eyeballs roll, 4.HS2.7.55.
- Not when from Plate to Plate your eyeballs roll, 4.HS2.7.55.
- Of beaming diamonds, and reflected plate; 4.1HE6.29.239.
- And golden Rings the double Back-plate join'd: Il.20.480.414.
- Where 'twixt the Neck and Throat the jointed Plate Il.22.408.472.

PLATED
- But harmless bounded from the plated Steel. Il.13.738.139.

PLATES
- Rich silver Plates his shining Car infold; Il.10.508.26.
- But the broad Belt, with Plates of Silver bound, Il.11.303.48.
- Five ample Plates the broad Expanse compose, Il.18.555.348.
- Thro' two strong Plates the Point is Passage held, Il.20.316.407.
- Five Plates of various Metal, various Mold, Il.20.318.407.
- Sees, thro' its parting Plates, the upper Air, Il.20.329.407.
- With Plates of Brass the Corselet cover'd o'er, Il.23.639.515.
- Rich plates of gold the folding doors incase; Od.7.114.240.

PLATFORM
- And half the platform just reflects the other. 3.Ep4.118.149.

PLATO
- Go, soar with Plato to th' empyreal sphere, 3.EOM2.23.57.
- For Attic Phrase in Plato let them seek, 5.DunB4.227.365.
- What *Plato* thought, and godlike *Cato* was: 6.32.18.96.
- Who ne'er saw naked Sword, or look'd in, *Plato.* 6.41.44.114.
- Where heav'nly visions *Plato* fir'd, 6.51i.3.151.

PLATO'S
- How Plato's, Bacon's, Newton's looks agree; 6.71.60.204.

PLATONIC
- Z—ds! let some Eunuch or Platonic take— 4.HAdv.157.87.

PLAUSIBLE
- And veiling Truth in plausible Disguise; 1.TrUl.137.470.
- And veiling truth in plausible disguise, Od.13.304.21.
- Thus veil the truth in plausible disguise. Od.16.307.120.

PLAUTUS
- 'Twixt Plautus, Fletcher, Congreve, and Corneille, 5.DunA1.239.91.
- 'Twixt Plautus, Fletcher, Shakespear, and Corneille, 5.DunB1.285.290.

PLAUTUS'
- Thou, whom the Nine with *Plautus'* Wit inspire, 1.PAu.7.80.

PLAY
- Let Vernal Airs thro' trembling Osiers play, 1.PSp.5.60.
- And with their forky Tongue shall innocently play. 1.Mes.84.120.
- And with their forky Tongue, and pointless Sting shall play. 1.Mes.84A.120.
- Where Beams of warm *Imagination* play, 1.EOC.58.245.
- By *Doctor's Bills* to play the *Doctor's Part,* 1.EOC.109.251.
- Produc'd his Play, and beg'd the Knight's Advice, 1.EOC.274.270.
- Unlucky, as *Fungoso* in the Play , 1.EOC.328.275.
- The Fair sate panting at a *Courtier's Play,* 1.EOC.540.299.
- Name a new *Play,* and *he's* the Poet's *Friend,* 1.EOC.620.309.
- And these, dear nymph, are kept to play with thee: 1.TrPA.91.369.
- Where late was Dust, now rapid Torrents play, 1.TrSt.504.431.
- He kiss'd his balmy Spouse, with wanton Play, 2.ChJM.388.33.
- Our rev'rend Knight was urg'd to Am'rous Play: 2.ChJM.522.40.
- Our noble Knight was urg'd to Am'rous Play: 2.ChJM.522A.40.
- Those play the Scholars who can't play the Men; 2.ChWB.371.75.
- Those play the Scholars who can't play the Men; 2.ChWB.371.75.
- Smooth flow the Waves, the Zephyrs gently play, 2.RL2.51.162.
- Some in the Fields of purest *Æther* play, 2.RL2.77.164.
- And on th' impassive Ice the Lightnings play: 2.TemF.56.256.
- Had he thy Reason, would he skip and play? 3.EOM1.82.24.
- Some livelier play-thing gives his youth delight, 3.EOM2.277.88.
- 'Till tir'd he sleeps, and Life's poor play is o'er! 3.EOM2.282.88.
- And Gold but sent to keep the fools in play, 3.Ep3.5.83.
- My Lady falls to play; so bad her chance, 3.Ep3.395.124.
- But ancient friends, (tho' poor, or out of play) 4.HS2.139.65.
- A Self-Tormentor, worse than (in the Play) 4.HAdv.25.77.
- In Spencer native Muses play; 4.HOde9.6.159.
- Better (say I) be pleas'd, and play the fool; 4.2HE2.181.177.
- But Britain, changeful as a Child at play, 4.2HE1.155.209.
- Allow him but his Play-thing of a Pen, 4.2HE1.193.211.
- Farewel the stage! if just as thrives the Play, 4.2HE1.302.221.
- The Play stands still; damn action and discourse, 4.2HE1.314.223.
- Or if three Ladies like a luckless Play, 4.1HE6.87.243.
- Call forth each mass, a poem or a play 5.DunA1.56.67.
- Till Thames see Eton's sons for ever play, 5.DunA3.331.191.
- Call forth each mass, a Poem, or a Play: 5.DunB1.58.274.
- Now (shame to Fortune!) an ill Run at Play 5.DunB1.113.277.
- Much future Ode, and abdicated Play; 5.DunB1.122.278.
- 'Till Thames see Eaton's sons for ever play, 5.DunB3.335.336.

PLAY (CONTINUED)
- Some play, some eat, some cack against the Wall, 6.14ii.8.43.
- Breathe on her lips, and in her bosom play! 6.14iii.6.45.
- There in bright drops the crystal Fountains play, 6.14iv.21.47.
- And fires around him innocently play. 6.21.16.69.
- I hear around soft Musick play, 6.31ii.6Z7.95.
- Prodigious this! the Frail one of our Play 6.41.1.113.
- The Play may pass—but that strange creature, *Shore,* 6.41.5.113.
- She went from Op'ra, park, assembly, play, 6.45.13.125.
- And in a borrow'd Play, out-did poor *Cr[own].* 6.49i.8.137.
- By all their winding Play; 6.53.26.162.
- Condemn a Play of theirs, and they evade it, 6.60.9.178.
- The play full smiles around the dimpled mouth 6.75.1.211.
- "This Eve at Whisk ourself will play, 6.79.47.219.
- "Or rent him Limb from Limb in cruel Play, 6.96ii.35.272.
- And the babes play-things that adorn thy house. 6.96ii.30Z34.272.
- "The Baby Play-things that adorn thy House, 6.96ii.54.273.
- Nor work, nor play, nor paint, nor sing. 6.119.4.336.
- Not work, nor play nor paint, nor sing. 6.119.4A.336.
- Tho, once my Tail in wanton play, 6.135.3.366.
- My Tail indeed 'twas but in play 6.135.3A.366.
- Or Leaves the Trees; or thick as Insects play, Il.2.552.153.
- And Swords around him innocently play, Il.4.633.251.
- High on his Helm Celestial Lightnings play, Il.5.5.265.
- And heavy Whales in aukward Measures play: Il.13.45.107.
- The sportive Wanton, pleas'd with some new Play, Il.15.418.213.
- As Wasps, provok'd by Children in their Play, Il.16.314.254.
- Aghast they see the living Light'nings play, Il.18.267.335.
- Swift was the Course; No vulgar Prize they play, Il.22.207.464.
- O'er the green mead the sporting virgins play: Od.6.112.211.
- With strength the future prize of fame to play, Od.8.23.263.
- The herald bears the Lyre: Intent to play, Od.8.299.279.
- The glancing splendors as their sandals play. Od.8.306.279.
- The careless lovers in their wanton play: Od.8.340.282.
- Not the fleet bark when prosp'rous breezes play, Od.12.79.435.
- In flow'ry meads the sportive *Sirens* play, Od.12.194.441.
- Then where a fountain's gurgling waters play, Od.12.361.448.
- 'Tis sweet to play the fool in time and place, Od.14.519.62.
- The bounding shafts upon the harness play, Od.15.208.78.
- His steps I hear; the dogs familiar play. Od.16.10.102.
- To bid the banquet interrupts their play. Od.17.198.141.
- Another, Princes! yet remains to play; Od.22.8.286.

PLAY-HOUSE
- Shakespear, (whom you and ev'ry Play-house bill 4.2HE1.69.199.

PLAY-THING
- Some livelier play-thing gives his youth delight, 3.EOM2.277.88.
- Allow him but his Play-thing of a Pen, 4.2HE1.193.211.

PLAY-THINGS
- "The Baby Play-things that adorn thy House, 6.96ii.54.273.

PLAY'D
- Where dancing Sun-beams on the Waters play'd, 1.PSu.3.71.
- Where the *Loves* play'd, and where the *Muses* dwell.— 1.TrSP.227.403.
- And play'd the God an engine on his foe. 3.EOM3.268.120.
- With here a Fountain, never to be play'd, 3.Ep4.121.149.
- You've play'd, and lov'd, and eat, and drank your fill: 4.2HE2.323.187.
- If *Blount* dispatch'd himself, he play'd the man, 4.EpS1.123.307.
- If *Blount* destroy'd himself, he play'd the man, 4.EpS1.123A.307.
- Strong Drink was drunk, and Gambolls play'd, 6.13.6.39.
- Chearful, he play'd the Trifle, Life, away, 6.19.12.62.
- Each play'd a Lion's Part. 6.79.12.218.
- "Nay, mix with Children, as they play'd at Taw; 6.96ii.28.271.
- And dawning Conquest play'd around his Head. Il.2.571.155.
- Poplars and alders ever quiv'ring play'd, Od.5.82.176.
- Yet innocent they play'd, and guiltless of a wound. Od.11.658.416.
- Thy last of games unhappy hast thou play'd; Od.22.32.288.
- He frowns beneath his nodding plume, that play'd Od.22.140.293.

PLAY'R
- Un-elbow'd by a Gamester, Pimp, or Play'r? 3.Ep3.242.112.

PLAY'RS
- The Tribe of Templars, Play'rs, Apothecaries, 4.HAdv.1.75.
- The Play'rs and I are, luckily, no friends. 4.Arbu.60.100.

PLAY'S
- Faith 'tis not five; no Play's begun; 6.10.3.24.

PLAYERS
- And why not Players strut in Courtiers Cloaths? 4.JD4.222.45.
- He says, poor Poets lost, while Players won, 6.34.21.101.

PLAYS
- I'll stake yon' Lamb that near the Fountain plays, 1.PSp.33.63.
- I'll stake my Lamb that near the Fountain plays, 1.PSp.33A.63.
- And tho' she plays no more, o'erlooks the Cards. 2.RL1.54.150.
- Make some take Physick, others scribble Plays; 2.RL4.62.189.
- Ours is the Place at Banquets, Balls and Plays; 2.TemF.382.282.
- Plays round the head, but comes not to the heart: 3.EOM4.254.152.
- He asks, "What *News?*" I tell him of new Plays, 4.JD4.124.35.
- Our Wives read Milton, and our Daughters Plays, 4.2HE1.172.209.
- Notes to dull books, and prologues to dull plays; 5.DunA1.168.83.
- Cibber preside Lord-Chancellor of Plays, 5.DunA3.320.187.
- Our Midas sits Lord Chancellor of Plays! 5.DunB3.324.335.
- Which must be heav'nly when an angel plays; 6.3.6.7.
- Such Plays alone should please a *British* ear, 6.32.45.97.
- Such plays alone should win a *British* ear, 6.32.45A.97.
- Tho' Plays for Honour in old Time he made, 6.34.17.101.
- Yet plays the fool before she dies. 6.70.9.201.
- Fate plays her old Dog Trick! 6.79.62.220.
- The price of prologues and of plays, 6.150.16.399.
- And plays and dances to the gentle Air; Il.17.60.290.
- His glowing Breath upon his Shoulders plays; Il.23.895.524.

PLEA

This is my Plea, on this I rest my Cause— ....4.HS1.141.19.
F. Your Plea is good. But still I say, beware! ....4.HS1.143.19.
My valour was my plea, a gallant mind ....Od.14.244.48.
Such be the plea, and by the plea deceive: ....Od.16.318.121.
Such be the plea, and by the plea deceive: ....Od.16.318.121.

PLEAD

And have, at least, *Their Precedent* to plead. ....1.EOC.166.259.
Stick to the Bar and barefac'd plead the Cause ....4.JD2A.83.140.
Plead much, read more, dine late, or not at all. ....4.1HE6.37.239.
Then wisely plead, to me they meant no hurt, ...4.EpS2.144.321.
And Pray'rs, and Tears, and Bribes shall plead in vain; ....Il.1.40.87.
And Service, Faith, and Justice plead in vain. ....Il.1.509.112.
To *Troy* he came, to plead the *Grecian* Cause; ....Il.3.268.205.
If Honour, and if Int'rest plead in vain; ....Il.9.397.452.
Thy Friend to plead against so just a Rage. ....Il.9.644.466.
To plead Indulgence and thy Fault attone, ...Il.23.693.517.
Some other *Greeks* a fairer claim may plead; ....Od.1.505.56.
And plead my title: *Noman* is my name. ....Od.9.432.323.
For mercy pleaded, nor could plead in vain. ....Od.10.522.368.
But if unheard, in vain compassion plead, ...Od.11.91.385.
Still as they plead, the fatal lots he rowls, ...Od.11.701.419.
'Till his return, no title shall I plead, ...Od.14.178.44.

PLEADED

As Pity pleaded for his vanquish'd Prize, ...Il.6.65.327.
She seems attentive to their pleaded vows, ...Od.1.321.48.
Thy pleaded reason, but consult with mine: ....Od.5.455.194.
His pleaded reason, and the suit he mov'd. ....Od.7.308.251.
For mercy pleaded, nor could plead in vain. ....Od.10.522.368.

PLEADER

Or from a judge turn pleader, to persuade ....3.EOM2.155.73.

PLEADING

This only merit pleading for the prize, ...5.DunA2.289A.137.

PLEADS

Bankrupt, at Court in vain he pleads his cause, ...3.Ep3.217A.111.
Alas, at Court he vainly pleads his cause, ...3.Ep3.217B.111.
In vain at Court the Bankrupt pleads his cause, ...3.Ep3.217.111.
For whom thus rudely pleads my loud-tongu'd Gate, ...6.100i.1.288.
Before her each with Clamour pleads the Laws, ...6.145.5.388.
One pleads the Fine discharg'd, which one deny'd, ...Il.18.579.350.
In vain his Youth, in vain his Beauty pleads: ....Il.20.538.416.
(For here affliction never pleads in vain:) ....Od.8.32.263.

PLEAS

Their Pleas were diff'rent, their Request the same; .....2.TemF.292.278.
And wooe in language of the Pleas and Bench? ....4.JD2.60.139.
And woes in Language of the Pleas and Bench ....4.JD2A.64.138.

PLEAS'D

Pleas'd, the green Lustre of the Scales survey, ...1.Mes.83.120.
Pleas'd, in the Gen'ral's Sight, the Host lye down ......1.W-F.107A.161.
Pleas'd in the silent Shade with empty Praise; ....1.W-F.432.194.
So pleas'd at first, the towring *Alps* we try, ...1.EOC.225.265.
Pleas'd with a Work where nothing's just or fit; ....1.EOC.291.272.
Who still are pleas'd *too little,* or *too much.* ......1.EOC.385.284.
Which lives as long as *Fools* are pleas'd to *Laugh.* ..1.EOC.451.290.
Still *pleas'd* to *teach,* and yet not *proud* to *know?* ..1.EOC.632.311.
Still pleas'd to *praise,* yet not afraid to *blame.* ....1.EOC.742.326.
That pleas'd a God, succeeded to her arms. ....1.TrFD.14.386.
In all I pleas'd, but most in what was best, ...1.TrSP.57.396.
Pleas'd to behold unbounded Pow'r thy own, ...1.TrSt.222.419.
Or pleas'd to find fair *Delos* float no more, ...1.TrSt.833.444.
The Knight should marry, when and where he pleas'd. ..2.ChJM.227.25.
Pleas'd her best Servant wou'd his Courage try, ...2.ChJM.331.30.
Both, pleas'd and blest, renew'd their mutual Vows, ..2.ChJM.815.54.
Treated, caress'd, where-e'er she's pleas'd to roam— ..2.ChWB.76.60.
Then must my Nurse be pleas'd, and Fav'rite Maid; ..2.ChWB.114.62.
It pleas'd the Lord to take my Spouse at last! ....2.ChWB.308.71.
But what most pleas'd him was the *Cretan* Dame, ..2.ChWB.385.76.
I condescended to be pleas'd at last. ....2.ChWB.426.77.
And pleas'd pursue its Progress thro' the Skies. ....2.RL5.132.211.
Pleas'd with *Alcæus'* manly Rage t'infuse ....2.TemF.224.273.
Pleas'd with the strange Success, vast Numbers prest ..2.TemF.394.282.
Pleas'd thy pale ghost, or grac'd thy mournful bier; ..2.Elegy.50.367.
Pleas'd to the last, he crops the flow'ry food, ...3.EOM1.83.24.
Be, or endow'd with all, or pleas'd with none? ....3.EOM1.188A.37.
Be pleas'd with nothing, if not bless'd with all? ....3.EOM1.188.38.
Pleas'd with a rattle, tickled with a straw; ....3.EOM2.276.88.
Pleas'd with this bauble still, as that before; ....3.EOM2.281.88.
That pleas'd can see a younger charm, or hear ....3.Ep2.259A.71.
Pleas'd *Vaga* echoes thro' her winding bounds, ...3.Ep3.251.114.
Thro' his young Woods how pleas'd *Sabinus* stray'd, ..3.Ep4.89.146.
The Lines are weak, another's pleas'd to say, ...4.HS1.5.5.
For I am pleas'd to learn, and you to teach; ....4.JD4.67A.31.
More pleas'd to keep it till their friends could come, ..4.HS2.95.61.
More pleas'd to keep it till their friends should come, ..4.HS2.95B.61.
That, if he pleas'd, he pleas'd by manly ways; ....4.Arbu.337.120.
That, if he pleas'd, he pleas'd by manly ways; ....4.Arbu.337.120.
And write whate'er he pleas'd, except his *Will;* ....4.Arbu.379.125.
Next pleas'd his Excellence a Town to batter; ....4.2HE2.44.167.
Better (say I) be pleas'd, and play the fool; ....4.2HE2.181.177.
And pleas'd, if sordid Want be far away. ....4.2HE2.295.185.
Pleas'd to look forward, pleas'd to look behind, ...4.2HE2.314.187.
Pleas'd to look forward, pleas'd to look behind, ...4.2HE2.314.187.
If not so pleas'd, at Council-board rejoyce ....4.1HE6.34.239.
I own, I'm pleas'd with this rebuke, ...4.HS6.60.253.
Each willing to be pleas'd, and please, ...4.HS6.139.259.
Pudding, that might have pleas'd a Dean; ....4.HS6.166.261.
Pleas'd let me own, in *Esher's* peaceful Grove ......4.EpS2.66.316.
Here pleas'd behold her mighty wings out-spread ...5.DunA1.25.63.
Pleas'd with the Madness of the mazy dance: ....5.DunA1.66.67.

PLEAS'D (CONTINUED)

Well-pleas'd he enter'd, and confess'd his Home: ......5.DunA1.222.90.
And the pleas'd dame soft-smiling leads away. ....5.DunA2.180.123.
And the pleas'd dame soft-smiling lead'st away. ....5.DunA2.180A.123.
Here pleas'd behold her mighty wings out-spread ....5.DunB1.27.271.
Pleas'd with the madness of the mazy dance: ....5.DunB1.68.275.
Well-pleas'd he enter'd, and confess'd his home. .....5.DunB1.266.289.
And the pleas'd dame, soft-smiling, lead'st away. ....5.DunB2.188.304.
(Not half so pleas'd when Goodman prophesy'd) .....5.DunB3.232.331.
Pleas'd, she accepts the Hero, and the Dame, ...5.DunB4.335.376.
At last it fix'd, 'twas on what plant it pleas'd, ...5.DunB4.429.383.
And pleas'd, look downward to the skies. ....6.6ii.16.15.
Who without Flatt'ry pleas'd the Fair and Great; .....6.19.6.62.
Pleas'd while with Smiles his happy Lines you view, ..6.19.75.64.
Were you all pleas'd, yet what I pray, ...6.30.64.88.
Pleas'd in these lines, *Belinda,* you may view ....6.38.1.107.
Or pleas'd to wound, and yet afraid to strike, ...6.49iii.17.143.
Or pleas'd to wound, but yet afraid to strike, ...6.49iii.17C.143.
Pleas'd with the series of each happy day. ....6.55.7.166.
Hearts so sincere th' Almighty saw well pleas'd, ...6.69i.5.198.
Victims so pure Heav'n saw well pleas'd ....6.69ii.3.199.
These pleas'd the Fathers of poetic rage; ....6.71.50.204.
Europa pleas'd accepts the *Bull,* ....6.80.3.224.
And pleas'd to 'scape from Flattery to Wit. ....6.84.12.239.
For pleas'd Remembrance builds Delight on Woe. ...6.96iv.64.278.
A softer wonder my pleas'd soul surveys, ...6.106i.2.306.
Well-pleas'd to give our neighbours due applause, ...6.107.21.311.
And pleas'd, dispense the flowing Bowls around. ....Il.1.617.117.
The gracious Pow'r is willing to be pleas'd. ....Il.1.751.123.
He heard, and madly at the Motion pleas'd, ...Il.4.135.226.
Pleas'd with his Charge, and ardent to fulfill ....Il.5.623.297.
Silent the Warrior smil'd, and pleas'd resign'd ....Il.6.504.351.
While pleas'd amidst the gen'ral Shouts of *Troy,* ...Il.6.614.357.
Participate their Fame, and pleas'd enquire ....Il.7.153.372.
Pleas'd may ye hear (so Heav'n succeed my Pray'rs) ..Il.7.462.387.
Pleas'd *Hector* braves the Warrior as he flies. ......Il.8.195.407.
Pleas'd with the solemn Harp's harmonious Sound. ..Il.9.246.444.
An untam'd Heifer pleas'd the blue-ey'd Maid, ...Il.11.865.74.
This Counsel pleas'd: the God-like *Hector* sprung ..Il.12.93.84.
The Counsel pleas'd; and *Hector,* with a Bound, ..Il.13.939.149.
Whilst from *Olympus* pleas'd *Saturnia* flew. .....Il.14.258.173.
Well-pleas'd the Thund'rer saw their earnest care, ..Il.15.176.203.
The sportive Wanton, pleas'd with some new Play, ..Il.15.418.213.
Pleas'd in their Age to hear their Children's Praise. ..Il.16.22.236.
That pleas'd a God, succeeded to her Arms; ....Il.16.225.248.
For, pleas'd at length the *Grecian* Arms to aid, ...Il.17.614.312.
Pleas'd to be first of all the Pow'rs addrest, ...Il.17.638.312.
Swift at the Mandate pleas'd *Tritonia* flies, ...Il.22.241.465.
Pleas'd with the well-turn'd Flattery of a Friend, ...Il.23.636.515.
He said; and pleas'd his Passion to command, ...Il.23.699.517.
While pleas'd I take the Gift thy Hands present, ...Il.23.745.519.
From the pleas'd Crowd new Peals of Thunder rise, ..Il.23.1042.530.
Pleas'd from the Hero's Lips his Praise to hear, ...Il.23.1060.533.
(Well-pleas'd to share the Feast,) amid the Quire ....Il.24.82.538.
Thee, far as *Argos,* pleas'd I could convey; ....Il.24.537.558.
But since the God his Hand has pleas'd to turn, ...Il.24.688.565.
Such the pleas'd ear will drink with silent joy. ....Od.1.436.53.
Pleas'd with their Hecatomb's ascending fires; ......Od.3.73.89.
And pleas'd they sleep (the blessing of the night.) ..Od.3.622.118.
Thy voice, O King! with pleas'd attention heard, ...Od.4.213.129.
But my pleas'd bosom glow'd with secret joy: ....Od.4.356.136.
Pleas'd with the false review, secure he lies, ...Od.4.609.148.
For now the soft Enchantress pleas'd no more: ......Od.5.196.181.
Now pleas'd and satiate from the social rite ....Od.7.248.248.
Pleas'd will I suffer all the Gods ordain, ...Od.7.303.250.
Enough the feast has pleas'd, enough the pow'r .....Od.8.95.267.
That pleas'd th' admiring stranger may proclaim ....Od.8.99.267.
Pleas'd with his people's fame the Monarch hears, ..Od.8.421.286.
Then pleas'd and whistling, drives his flock before; ..Od.9.370.321.
Pleas'd with th' effect of conduct and of art. ....Od.9.492.326.
Pleas'd with the din of war, and noble shout of foes. ..Od.11.316.397.
War was his joy, and pleas'd with loud alarms, ...Od.11.579.412.
But hear with pleas'd attention the renown ....Od.11.617.414.
This sentence pleas'd: Then all their steps addrest ..Od.13.19.2.
But other counsels pleas'd the sailors mind: ....Od.14.374.53.
Well pleas'd, and pleasing, in our cottage rest, ...Od.15.356.86.
And pleas'd remembrance builds delight on woe. ...Od.15.437.90.
Well pleas'd the hospitable rites to pay. ....Od.15.586.98.
The Prince well pleas'd to disappoint their wiles, ...Od.16.496.131.
Medon the herald (one who pleas'd them best, ...Od.17.196.141.
Shall her pleas'd ear receive my words in peace. ....Od.17.655.164.
Why urge we not to blows? Well-pleas'd they spring ..Od.18.48.169.
While pleas'd he hears, *Antinous* bears the food, ..Od.18.143.173.
Well-pleas'd *Ulysses* hears his Queen deceive ....Od.18.325.182.
In happy hour, (Pleas'd *Euryclea* cries) ....Od.19.23.193.
The fiction pleas'd; their loves I long elude; ....Od.19.172.200.
Pleas'd with his wise reply, the Queen rejoin'd: ....Od.19.403.214.
The Goddess pleas'd, regains her natal skies. ....Od.20.67.235.
Thy wish produc'd in act, with pleas'd survey, ...Od.20.290.247.
The city-tribes, to pleas'd *Apollo's* grove: ....Od.20.343.249.
They heard well pleas'd: the ready heralds bring ...Od.21.286.273.
Active and pleas'd, the zealous swains fulfil ....Od.22.205.297.
Pleas'd with her virtuous fears, the King replies, ...Od.23.113.325.
The fiction pleas'd: our gen'rous train complies, ...Od.24.164.356.
Well-pleas'd you told its nature, and its name, ...Od.24.393.368.

PLEASANT

And taught more *Pleasant* Methods of Salvation; ..1.EOC.547.302.
"This same Dessert is not so pleasant: ....4.HS6.221.263.
She shall bring forth most Pleasant Fruit, ...6.54.9.164.
With Eyes so piercing, yet so pleasant, ...6.93.7.256.

PLEASANTRY

And with a tender pleasantry reproves: ....Od.24.284.363.

PLEASE

But since those Graces please thy Eyes no more, ... 1.PSu.29.74.
But since those Graces please thy Sight no more, ... 1.PSu.29A.74.
And yet my Numbers please the rural Throng, ... 1.PSu.49.75.
Whom humbler Joys of home-felt Quiet please, ... 1.W-F.239.171.
In *Prospects*, thus, some *Objects* please our Eyes, ... 1.EOC.158.258.
Who haunt *Parnassus* but to please their Ear, ... 1.EOC.341.277.
Sure *some* to *vex*, but never *all* to *please;* .... 1.EOC.505.295.
Such without *Wit* are Poets when they please, ... 1.EOC.590.307.
Fancy and Art in gay *Petronius* please, ... 1.EOC.667.315.
But less to please the Eye, than arm the Hand, ... 1.EOC.673.316.
Nor thus alone the Curious Eye to please, ... 1.EOC.673A.316.
He vainly studies every art to please: .... 1.TrPA.22.366.
Two little bears, I found them, and did please .... 1.TrPA.92.369.
Well, he may please himself, and you may share .... 1.TrPA.122.370.
And tries all Forms, that may *Pomona* please. .... 1.TrVP.93.381.
Of these she crop'd, to please her infant son; .... 1.TrFD.25.387.
Soft Scenes of Solitude no more can please, ... 1.TrSP.15.393.
He's gone, whom only she desir'd to please! .... 1.TrSP.88.397.
Yet while I blush, confess how much they please! .... 1.TrSP.154.400.
Say, can those Honours please? and canst thou love .... 1.TrSt.392.426.
Unless our Desart Cities please thy Sight, ... 1.TrSt.774.442.
These solemn Feasts propitious *Phœbus* please, ... 1.TrSt.788.443.
Whether the Style of *Titan* please thee more, ... 1.TrSt.857.445.
Secure at once himself and Heav'n to please; .... 2.ChJM.38.16.
We form like Wax, and mold them as we please. .... 2.ChJM.112.20.
To please a Wife when her Occasions call, ... 2.ChJM.210.24.
Her will I wed, if gracious Heav'n so please; .... 2.ChJM.262.27.
Nor please too lavishly your gentle Mate. .... 2.ChJM.294.28.
And toil'd most piteously to please their Bride: .... 2.ChWB.59.59.
Sure to be lov'd, I took no Pains to please, ... 2.ChWB.62.59.
Assume what Sexes and what Shapes they please. .... 2.RL1.70.151.
Long have we sought t'instruct and please Mankind, ... 2.TemF.300.278.
What you (she cry'd) unlearn'd in Arts to please, ... 2.TemF.396.282.
Let pow'r or knowledge, gold or glory, please, ... 3.EOM2.169.75.
And mourn our various portions as we please, ... 3.EOM4.33.131.
Intent to reason, or polite to please. .... 3.EOM4.382.165.
They please as Beauties, here as Wonders strike. .... 3.Ep1.96.22.
Wise Fool! with Pleasures too refin'd to please, ... 3.Ep2.95A.57.
Wise Wretch! of Pleasures too refin'd to please, ... 3.Ep2.95B.57.
Is but to please can Pleasure seem a fault? .... 3.Ep2.212A.67.
Please by receiving, by submitting sway .... 3.Ep2.263A.71.
Wise Wretch! with Pleasures too refin'd to please, ... 3.Ep2.95.57.
Is still to please, can Pleasure seem a fault? .... 3.Ep2.212.67.
Leaves the dull Cits, and joins (to please the fair) .... 3.Ep3.387.124.
Preach as I please, I doubt our curious men .... 4.HS2.17.55.
Could joyn the Arts, to ruin, and to please. .... 4.HAdv.6.75.
Blest with each Talent and each Art to please, ... 4.Arbu.195.109.
And see what friends, and read what books I please. .... 4.Arbu.264.114.
To see what Friends, or read what Books I please; .... 4.Arbu.262A.114.
To please a *Mistress*, One aspers'd his life; .... 4.Arbu.376.124.
"Your Barber, Cook, Upholst'rer, what you please. .... 4.2HE2.10.165.
When out of twenty I can please not two; .... 4.2HE2.81.171.
Weave Laurel Crowns, and take what Names we please. .... 4.2HE2.142.175.
You think 'tis Nature, and a knack to please: .... 4.2HE2.177.177.
Whom Folly pleases, and whose Follies please. .... 4.2HE2.327.187.
Those Suns of Glory please not till they set. .... 4.2HE1.22.195.
To please a lewd, or un-believing Court. .... 4.2HE1.212.213.
The Poets learn'd to please, and not to wound: .... 4.2HE1.258.217.
There, all Men may be cur'd, whene'er they please. .... 4.1HE6.59.241.
"You may for certain, if you please; .... 4.HS6.80.255.
Each willing to be pleas'd, and please, ... 4.HS6.139.259.
"An't please your Honour, quoth the Peasant, ... 4.HS6.220.263.
"Now please your Honour, quoth the Peasant, ... 4.HS6.220A.263.
South-sea Subscriptions take who please, ... 4.1HE7.65.273.
Could please at Court, and make AUGUSTUS smile: .... 4.EpS1.20.299.
Could please at Court, and made AUGUSTUS smile: .... 4.EpS1.20A.299.
A Horse-laugh, if you please, at *Honesty;* .... 4.EpS1.38.300.
P. I fain wou'd please you, if I knew with what: .... 4.EpS2.26.314.
O thou! whatever Title please thine ear, ... 5.DunA1.17.62.
O Thou! whatever title please thine ear, ... 5.DunB1.19.270.
So upright Quakers please both Man and God. .... 5.DunB4.208.363.
And innocence, which most does please, ... 6.1.15.3.
Dear Mr. Cromwell, May it please ye! .... 6.10.1.24.
And as you please their Doom to pass on, ... 6.10.34.25.
And as you please to pass their Doom. .... 6.10.34A.25.
And make Despair and Madness please: .... 6.11.121.34.
Make Entertainments please us as they shou'd; .... 6.17iv.29.60.
And, if it can, at once both Please and Preach: .... 6.19.24.62.
Criticks in Wit, or Life, are hard to please, ... 6.19.29.63.
Nor let false Shows, or empty Titles please: .... 6.19.47.63.
And, all that in us lies, please each; .... 6.30.78.89.
Such Plays alone should please a *British* ear, ... 6.32.45.97.
Who strives to please the Fair *against her Will:* .... 6.34.6.101.
Who in your own *Despite* has strove to please ye. .... 6.34.8.101.
To your Friends who at least have no Cares but to please you .6.42iii.5.117.
Who born with Talents, bred in Arts to please, ... 6.49iii.9.142.
Blest with each Talent, and each Art to please .... 6.49iii.9A.142.
To Please her shall her Husband strive .... 6.54.5.164.
(Studious in ev'ry Thing to please thy Taste) .... 6.96iv.50.277.
Whether the Style of *Grildrig* please thee most, ... 6.96iv.97.279.
Blest with each Talent, and each Art to please, ... 6.98.45.284.
Attend whatever title please thine ear, ... 6.106iv.7.307.
Whate'er he draws to please, must all be thine. .... 6.107.30.311.
You please to see, on Twit'nam green, ... 6.114.7.321.
Blest Courtier! who could King and Country please, ... 6.118.9.334.
Khock as you please, there's no body at home. .... 6.124iii.2.348.
My Words cou'd please thee, or my Actions aid; .... Il.1.653.118.
Shall waste the Form whose Crime it was to please! .... Il.3.234.203.
His be the Chariot that shall please him most, ... Il.10.367.19.
When Wine and Feasts thy golden Humours please. .... Il.14.275.175.
Is bent to please him; this Request forbear: .... Il.19.326.386.
And please a Soul, desirous to bestow,) .... Il.23.628.514.
For wealth and beauty less than virtue please. .... Od.2.236.73.
He there, tho' late, to please the Monarch, stay'd. .... Od.3.198.95.
High-flaming please the monarch of the main. .... Od.3.218.96.

PLEASE (CONTINUED)

And ev'n these slighted charms might learn to please. .... Od.5.266.184.
Taught by the Gods to please, when high he sings .... Od.8.41.264.
Who most shall please, who most our Hero give? .... Od.10.43.341.
Me wou'dst thou please? for them thy cares imploy, ... Od.10.455.365.
If heav'n thou please; and how to please attend! .... Od.11.133.387.
If heav'n thou please; and how to please attend! .... Od.11.133.387.
Their song is death, and makes destruction please. .... Od.12.52.432.
Then if a wider course shall rather please .... Od.15.91.73.
But ah! not fated long to please his Lord! .... Od.17.349.148.
Those charms, for whom alone I wish'd to please. .... Od.18.212.177.
Careless to please, with insolence ye wooe! .... Od.18.320.182.
And if *Eurymachus* the motion please; .... Od.21.296.274.
What? hopes the fool to please so many lords? .... Od.21.400.279.
To this *Ulysses.* As the Gods shall please .... Od.24.415.369.

PLEASES

Whom Folly pleases, and whose Follies please. .... 4.2HE2.327.187.
Who now reads Cowley? if he pleases yet, ... 4.2HE1.75.201.
His moral pleases, not his pointed wit; .... 4.2HE1.76.201.
A double Jest still pleases sweet Sir Harry— .... 6.82vi.12.232.

PLEASING

For her, the Lymes their pleasing Shades deny; .... 1.PAu.25.82.
For him, the Lymes their pleasing Shades deny; .... 1.PAu.25A.82.
Ye Pow'rs, what pleasing Frensie sooths my Mind! .... 1.PAu.51.83.
The Woods and Fields their pleasing Toils deny. .... 1.W-F.120.161.
If *Chrystal Streams with pleasing Murmurs creep,* .... 1.EOC.352.279.
O far more pleasing than the flow'ry field! .... 1.TrPA.57.367.
And prais'd the Beauty of the pleasing Sight. .... 1.TrVP.62.380.
(A pleasing Off'ring when 'tis made by you;) .... 1.TrVP.97.381.
Her smiling babe (a pleasing charge) she prest .... 1.TrFD.19.386.
O Night more pleasing than the brightest Day, ... 1.TrSP.145.400.
These pleasing Orders to the Tyrant's Ear; .... 1.TrSt.422.427.
And stately *Corinth's* pleasing Site surveys. .... 1.TrSt.473.430.
And waits 'till pleasing Slumbers seal his Eyes. .... 1.TrSt.538.433.
To Woods and Wilds the pleasing Burden bears, ... 1.TrSt.682.439.
And pleasing Slumbers steal upon his Eyes. .... 1.TrUl.6.465.
Wrapt in a pleasing, deep, and death-like Rest. .... 1.TrUl.20.466.
While in th'Embrace of pleasing Sleep I lay, ... 1.TrUl.155.471.
With pleasing Smiles to view the God-like Man; .... 1.TrUl.161.471.
The pleasing Prospect of thy Native Shore! .... 1.TrUl.225.473.
(Mild were his Looks, and pleasing was his Tone) .... 2.ChJM.148.21.
Pleasing to God, and shou'd be so to Man; .... 2.ChJM.169.23.
With pleasing Poison, and with soft Deceit! .... 2.ChJM.480.38.
Not a less pleasing, tho' less glorious Care. .... 2.RL2.92.165.
Courts we frequent, where 'tis our pleasing Care .... 2.TemF.384.282.
Back thro' the paths of pleasing sense I ran, ... 2.ElAb.69.324.
Less pleasing far than Virtue's very tears. .... 3.EOM4.320.159.
"With ev'ry pleasing, ev'ry prudent part, ... 3.Ep2.159.64.
No pleasing Intricacies intervene, ... 3.Ep4.115.148.
He spins the slight, self-pleasing thread anew; .... 4.Arbu.90.102.
Still spin the slight, self-pleasing thread anew; .... 4.Arbu.90A.102.
Turn, turn to willing Hearts your pleasing fires. .... 4.HOde1.8A.151.
With growing years the pleasing Licence grew, ... 4.2HE1.249.217.
How pleasing ATTERBURY'S softer hour! .... 4.EpS2.82.317.
Now May'rs and Shrieves in pleasing slumbers lay, ... 5.DunA1.89A.70.
While thus each hand promotes the pleasing pain, ... 5.DunA2.203.126.
In pleasing memory of all he stole, ... 5.DunB1.128.279.
While thus each hand promotes the pleasing pain, ... 5.DunB2.211.306.
In a sadly-pleasing Strain .... 6.11.5.30.
No more a pleasing, chearful Guest? .... 6.31i.4.93.
How oft' in pleasing tasks we wear the day, ... 6.52.17.156.
Each pleasing *Blount* shall endless smiles bestow, ... 6.52.61.158.
A pleasing form, a firm, yet cautious mind, ... 6.57.1.169.
All hail! once pleasing, once inspiring Shade, ... 6.66.1.194.
Not Showers to Larks so pleasing, ... 6.78i.5.215.
Each pretty Carecter with pleasing Smart .... 6.82iv.1.231.
Soon as *Glumdalclitch* mist her pleasing Care, ... 6.96ii.1.270.
What pleasing Phrensy steals away my Soul? .... 6.106ii.1.307.
Words ever pleasing, yet sincerely true, ... 6.125.1Z3.349.
"With ev'ry pleasing, ev'ry prudent part, ... 6.139.3.377.
Now pleasing *Sleep* had seal'd each mortal Eye, ... Il.2.1.126.
And those who dwell where pleasing *Augia* stands, ... Il.2.637.157.
And fair *Mantinea's* ever-pleasing Site; .... Il.2.739.161.
Or where the pleasing *Titaresius* glides, ... Il.2.910.167.
Soft moving Speech, and pleasing outward Show, ... Il.3.95.194.
With pleasing Sweets his fainting Sense renews, ... Il.3.471.214.
Her pleasing Empire and her native Plain, ... Il.6.541.353.
Restor'd the pleasing Burden to her Arms; .... Il.6.617.357.
The pleasing *Arnè* was his native Place. .... Il.7.14.363.
Still in my Arms (an ever-pleasing Load) .... Il.9.609.464.
And pleasing Conference beguiles the Day. .... Il.11.787.71.
And grizly War appears a pleasing Sight. .... Il.14.178.165.
Sacred to Dress, and Beauty's pleasing Cares: .... Il.14.192.168.
O'er fair *Emathia's* ever pleasing Shore, ... Il.14.260.173.
Sweet pleasing Sleep! (*Saturnia* thus began) .... Il.14.266.174.
As now my Veins receive the pleasing Fire. .... Il.14.372.180.
For *Juno's* Love, and *Somnus'* pleasing Ties, ... Il.14.415.183.
In Stature, Voice, and pleasing Look, the same. .... Il.23.81.490.
And pleasing Slumbers quiet all their Care. .... Il.24.4.534.
The Form so pleasing, and the Heart so kind, ... Il.24.11.535.
Mindless of Food, or Love whose pleasing Reign .... Il.24.165.542.
Shou'd second love a pleasing flame inspire, ... Od.1.358.49.
Patient permit the sadly-pleasing strain; .... Od.1.449.54.
Thus mild, the pleasing conference began. .... Od.3.81.90.
Sweet *Polycaste,* took the pleasing toil .... Od.3.594.116.
Still in short intervals of pleasing woe, ... Od.4.127.126.
And pleasing thus her sceptred Lord address'd. .... Od.4.184.128.
The pleasing sounds each latent warrior warm'd, ... Od.4.381.139.
Then lose the cares of life in pleasing rest.— .... Od.4.783.156.
Close to her head the pleasing vision stands, ... Od.4.1057.167.
Unwilling, have I trod this pleasing land; .... Od.5.124.178.
Forsaking *Scheria's* ever-pleasing shore, ... Od.7.101.239.
In pleasing thought he ran the prospect o'er, ... Od.7.180.244.
In sev'nteen days appear'd your pleasing coast, ... Od.7.353.253.

PLEASING (CONTINUED)
Then gently waft thee to the pleasing shore, ... Od.7.409.257.
To my dear country's ever-pleasing coast, ... Od.8.508.289.
The rest in haste forsook the pleasing shore, ... Od.9.113.308.
With wonder seiz'd, we view the pleasing ground, ... Od.9.176.312.
Sad, pleasing sight! with tears each eye ran o'er, ... Od.10.471.366.
The pleasing transport, and compleats his loves. ... Od.11.294.396.
He ceas'd; but left so pleasing on their ear ... Od.13.1.1.
And pleasing slumbers steal upon his eyes. ... Od.13.97.5.
Wrapt in a pleasing, deep, and death-like rest. ... Od.13.111.6.
While in th' embrace of pleasing sleep I lay, ... Od.13.322.23.
With pleasing smiles to view the god-like man. ... Od.13.328.23.
The pleasing prospect of thy native shore. ... Od.13.392.26.
Well pleas'd, and pleasing, in our cottage rest, ... Od.15.356.86.
Her pleasing converse minister'd relief; ... Od.15.387.88.
A part in pleasing talk we entertain; ... Od.15.428.89.
So past in pleasing dialogue away ... Od.15.532.95.
She pours a pleasing, deep, and deathlike rest, ... Od.18.222.177.
So, melted with the pleasing tale he told, ... Od.19.242.206.
Truth forms my tale; to pleasing truth attend. ... Od.19.306.209.
Smiles dew'd with tears the pleasing strife exprest ... Od.19.550.223.
The bath renew'd, she ends the pleasing toil ... Od.19.589.225.
Awhile, reluctant to her pleasing force, ... Od.19.596.225.
This said, the pleasing feather'd omen ceas'd. ... Od.19.646.227.
In all thy speech what pleasing force I find! ... Od.19.688.229.
I part reluctant from the pleasing tale. ... Od.19.690.229.
With pleasing phrenzy has posses'd my mind; ... Od.21.106.264.
There pass thy pleasing night, oh gentle swain! ... Od.22.212.297.
Thus he; but pleasing hopes his bosom warm ... Od.22.231.298.
To whom *Ulysses* with a pleasing eye: ... Od.22.411.307.
And servitude with pleasing tasks deceive; ... Od.22.461.310.
With pleasing horror at the dreadful tale, ... Od.23.332.340.

PLEASINGLY
He gains all points, who pleasingly confounds, ... 3.Ep4.55.142.

PLEASURE
Her Name with Pleasure once she taught the Shore, ... 1.PWi.43.92.
Now *Daphne's* dead, and Pleasure is no more! ... 1.PWi.44.92.
The *gen'rous Pleasure* to be charm'd with Wit. ... 1.EOC.238.267.
In the fat Age of Pleasure, Wealth, and Ease, ... 1.EOC.534.297.
But you, with Pleasure own your Errors past, ... 1.EOC.570.305.
His only pleasure, and his early care. ... 1.TrPA.6.365.
Since if I found no Pleasure in my Spouse, ... 2.ChJM.115.20.
And not for Pleasure only, or for Love. ... 2.ChJM.122.20.
Who past all Pleasure, damn the Joys of Sense, ... 2.ChJM.174.23.
And Mirth and Pleasure shone in ev'ry Face. ... 2.ChJM.356.31.
Pleasure the Sov'reign Bliss of Humankind: ... 2.ChJM.441.36.
(His Scene of Pleasure, and peculiar Care) ... 2.ChJM.466.37.
And pray, to crown the Pleasure of their Lives, ... 2.ChJM.819.54.
Yet had more Pleasure far then they had Ease. ... 2.ChWB.63.59.
Ease, Pleasure, Virtue, All, our Sex resign. ... 2.RL4.106.192.
The Men of Pleasure, Dress, and Gallantry: ... 2.TemF.381.282.
And what we want in Pleasure, grant in Fame. ... 2.TemF.391.282.
A cool suspense from pleasure and from pain; ... 2.ElAb.250.339.
Mere curious pleasure, or ingenious pain: ... 3.EOM2.48.61.
Pain their aversion, Pleasure their desire; ... 3.EOM2.88.65.
Pleasure, or wrong or rightly understood, ... 3.EOM2.91.65.
Shares with his lord the pleasure and the pride: ... 3.EOM3.36.95.
For more his pleasure, yet for more his pride: ... 3.EOM3.60.98.
Nor ends the pleasure with the fierce embrace; ... 3.EOM3.123.104.
While pleasure, gratitude, and hope, combin'd, ... 3.EOM3.145.107.
To Virtue, in the paths of Pleasure, trod, ... 3.EOM3.233.116.
Good, Pleasure, Ease, Content! whate'er thy name: ... 3.EOM4.2.128.
Those call it Pleasure, and Contentment these; ... 3.EOM4.22.129.
Some sunk to Beasts, find pleasure end in pain; ... 3.EOM4.23.130.
One grants his Pleasure is but Rest from pain, ... 3.EOM4.28Z1.130.
Shall find, the pleasure pays not half the pain. ... 3.EOM4.48.132.
Reason's whole pleasure, all the joys of Sense, ... 3.EOM4.79.136.
Content, or Pleasure, but the Good and Just? ... 3.EOM4.186.145.
A fool to Pleasure, yet a slave to Fame: ... 3.Ep2.62A.55.
Is but to please can Pleasure seem a fault? ... 3.Ep2.212A.67.
A fool to Pleasure, and a slave to Fame: ... 3.Ep2.62.55.
The Pleasure miss'd her, and the Scandal hit. ... 3.Ep2.128.61.
The Love of Pleasure, and the Love of Sway. ... 3.Ep2.210.67.
Is still to please, can Pleasure seem a fault? ... 3.Ep2.212.67.
Men, some to Bus'ness, some to Pleasure take; ... 3.Ep2.215.67.
Your love of Pleasure, our desire of Rest, ... 3.Ep2.274.72.
That life of pleasure, and that soul of whim! ... 3.Ep3.306.118.
Smit with the mighty pleasure, to be seen: ... 3.Ep4.128.149.
P. Each Mortal has his Pleasure: None deny ... 4.HS1.45.9.
No Pimp of Pleasure, and no Spy of State, ... 4.HS1.134.19.
The pleasure lies in *you,* and not the meat. ... 4.HS2.16.55.
The pleasure lies in *you,* not in the meat. ... 4.HS2.16A.55.
And pity Men of Pleasure still in Pain! ... 4.HAdv.50.79.
How'ere some pleasure 'tis, this Fool to see ... 4.JD2A.69.138.
Now all for Pleasure, now for Church and State; ... 4.2HE1.158.209.
If weak the pleasure that from these can spring, ... 4.1HE6.18.237.
"Or if it be thy Will and Pleasure ... 4.HS6.19.251.
Of Social Pleasure, ill-exchang'd for Pow'r; ... 4.EpS1.30.300.
Yon stars, yon suns, he rears at pleasure higher, ... 5.DunA3.255.179.
Yon stars, yon suns, he rears at pleasure higher, ... 5.DunB3.259.332.
Your Pleasure is a Vice, but not your Pride; ... 6.19.34.63.
A Morning's Pleasure, and at Evening torn: ... 6.19.66.64.
Then wake with pleasure at the Sound! ... 6.31ii.6Z12A.95.
But what with pleasure heav'n itself surveys; ... 6.32.20.96.
Tho' *Tom* the Poet writ with Ease and Pleasure, ... 6.34.23.101.
Days of ease, and nights of pleasure; ... 6.51ii.43.154.
And Pleasure about Town; ... 6.58.2.170.
Can taste no pleasure since his Shield was scour'd; ... 6.71.42.204.
She still with pleasure eyes thy Evening Ray, ... 6.84.31Z9.240.
Long Health, long Youth, long Pleasure, and a Friend: ... 6.86.2.244.
Long Life, long Health, long Pleasure, and a Friend: ... 6.86.2A.244.
Long Life, long Youth, long Pleasure, and a Friend: ... 6.86.2B.244.
But like a Sieve let ev'ry Pleasure thro', ... 6.86.6B.245.
For 'tis a Pleasure to support a Friend. ... 6.96iii.36.275.

PLEASURE (CONTINUED)
'Tis all my Pleasure thy past Toil to know, ... 6.96iv.63.278.
A Fool to Pleasure, yet a Slave to Fame; ... 6.99.10.287.
Men, some to Business, some to Pleasure take. ... 6.99.15.287.
A Fool to Pleasure, and a Slave to Fame; ... 6.99.10A.287.
No joy no pleasure from successes past ... 6.130.19.358.
The Pleasure miss'd her, and the Scandal hit; ... 6.154.14.403.
Or, if our Royal Pleasure shall ordain, ... Il.1.189.96.
Peace at his Heart, and Pleasure his Design, ... Il.1.740.122.
Then is it still thy Pleasure to deceive? ... Il.3.493.215.
With secret Pleasure each fond Parent smil'd, ... Il.6.598.356.
The troubled Pleasure soon chastis'd by Fear, ... Il.6.620.357.
His Pleasure guides me, and his Will confines: ... Il.9.718.470.
A Pleasure now? Revenge itself is lost: ... Il.18.102.328.
Takes a sad Pleasure the last Bones to burn, ... Il.23.276.501.
A secret pleasure touch'd *Athena's* soul, ... Od.3.65.89.
He rose with pleasure, and retir'd to rest. ... Od.7.434.258.
No ease, no pleasure my sad heart receives, ... Od.9.541.328.
Their parent's pride, and pleasure of their reign. ... Od.10.8.339.
You share the pleasure,—then in bounty share; ... Od.11.423.405.
And more, the pleasure to relieve the poor. ... Od.15.399.88.
Shut from the walks of men, to pleasure lost, ... Od.16.156.110.
Seen or unseen, o'er earth at pleasure move) ... Od.16.175.111.
And the sooth'd heart with secret pleasure fills. ... Od.17.605.161.
The pleasure past supplies a copious theme ... Od.19.681.229.

PLEASURE'S
Love, Hope, and Joy, fair pleasure's smiling train, ... 3.EOM2.117.69.

PLEASURES
His pleasures too (tho' that I scarce can bear) ... 1.TrPA.123.370.
Your Rural Cares, and Pleasures, are the same. ... 1.TrVP.95.381.
That knew my Pleasures, cou'd relieve my Pains. ... 1.TrSP.162.400.
And try the Pleasures of a lawful Bed. ... 2.ChJM.14.15.
Now shou'd the Nuptial Pleasures prove so great, ... 2.ChJM.272.27.
Nor in your Pleasures all your Might imploy, ... 2.ChJM.292.28.
Abridg'd her Pleasures, and confin'd her Sway. ... 2.ChJM.489.39.
Come, and in mutual Pleasures let's engage, ... 2.ChJM.533.41.
Conscious of Pleasures to the World unknown: ... 2.ChJM.544.41.
To find in Pleasures I have had my Part, ... 2.ChWB.223.67.
Pleasures above, for Tortures felt below: ... 2.ChWB.437.78.
To taste awhile the Pleasures of a Court; ... 2.RL3.10.169.
Repent old pleasures, and sollicit new: ... 2.ElAb.186.335.
Pleasures are ever in our hands or eyes, ... 3.EOM2.123.70.
All pleasures sicken, and all glories sink; ... 3.EOM4.46.132.
All Reason's pleasures, all the joys of Sense, ... 3.EOM4.79A.136.
Wise Fool! with Pleasures too refin'd to please, ... 3.Ep2.95A.57.
Wise Wretch! of Pleasures too refin'd to please, ... 3.Ep2.95B.57.
Wise Wretch! with Pleasures too refin'd to please, ... 3.Ep2.95.57.
Pleasures the sex, as children Birds, pursue, ... 3.Ep2.231.68.
Pleasures sincere, and unallay'd with Pain, ... 6.17iii.10.58.
'Till Death scarce felt did o'er his Pleasures creep, ... 6.19.13A.62.
Not that their pleasures caus'd her discontent, ... 6.45.9.124.
What pleasures thy free Bounty gives, ... 6.50.17A.146.
Safe to the Pleasures of your native Shore. ... Il.1.26.87.
In Loves and Pleasures on the *Phrygian* Shore. ... Il.2.295.141.
The Queen of Pleasures shares the Toils of Fight, ... Il.4.14.221.
To share the Pleasures of the Genial Feast: ... Il.4.397.239.
And thy soft Pleasures serv'd with captive Dames! ... Il.16.1006.282.
Pursu'd the Pleasures of the wat'ry Reign; ... Il.18.110.328.
And crown'd with love the pleasures of the day. ... Od.10.12.340.
And share the pleasures of this genial hour. ... Od.10.545.369.
Nor stain with grief the pleasures of the day; ... Od.21.88.263.

PLEBEIAN
Gain'd but one Trump and one *Plebeian* Card. ... 2.RL3.54.172.
But if a clam'rous vile *Plebeian* rose, ... Il.2.235.138.

PLEDG'D
He pledg'd it to the knight; the knight had wit, ... 3.Ep3.363.123.

PLEDGE
(This from his Pledge I learn'd, which safely stor'd ... Il.6.275.340.
Molus receiv'd, the Pledge of social Ties; ... Il.10.316.17.
(Pledge of Benevolence, and kind Intent) ... Il.23.746.519.
(The Pledge of Treaties once with friendly *Thrace*)<:> ... Il.24.288.548.
A Pledge of Gratitude for *Hector's* sake; ... Il.24.526.558.
The Pledge of many a lov'd, and loving Dame; ... Il.24.615.562.
And the rich pledge of plighted faith receive, ... Od.1.405.52.
I shall revisit; and that pledge receive, ... Od.1.411.52.
Alcandra gave, a pledge of royal grace: ... Od.4.168.128.
A previous pledge of sacred faith obtain'd, ... Od.4.347.136.
A pledge and monument of sacred love. ... Od.4.810.156.
A pledge the sceptred pow'r of *Sidon* gave, ... Od.4.837.158.
Bring gold, a pledge of love, a talent bring, ... Od.8.427.286.
A pledge of love! 'tis all a wretch can give. ... Od.8.522.290.
Without some pledge, some monument of love; ... Od.15.96.73.

PLEDGES
They slight the pledges of their former vows; ... Od.15.26.71.
Their first, last pledges! for they met no more. ... Od.21.36.261.

PLEIADS
And from the *Pleiads* fruitful Show'rs descend. ... 1.PSp.102.70.
The *Pleiads, Hyads,* with the Northern Team; ... Il.18.561.349.
There view'd the *Pleiads,* and the northern Team, ... Od.5.347.188.

PLENTEOUS
Our plenteous Streams a various Race supply; ... 1.W-F.141.163.
Expensive Dainties load the plenteous Boards, ... 2.ChJM.317Z1.29.
Two plenteous fountains the whole prospect crown'd, ... 6.35.28.103.
The plenteous Pickle shall preserve the Fish, ... 6.96ii.77.274.
Where the fat Herds in plenteous Pasture rove; ... Il.2.735.161.
Sprung from *Alpheus,* plenteous Stream! that yields ... Il.5.673.300.
Then with a plenteous Draught refresh thy Soul, ... Il.6.325.342.
And well the plenteous Freight supply'd the Host: ... Il.7.567.392.

PLENTEOUS (CONTINUED)

For this, high fed in plenteous Stalls ye stand, ...Il.8.230.408.
The flaming Piles with plenteous Fuel raise, ...Il.8.633.426.
And plenteous *Hermus* swells with Tides of Gold, ...Il.20.452.413.
And all the Night the plenteous Flame aspires. ....Il.23.271.500.
His vessels loaded with a plenteous store ....Od.5.50.174.
Two plenteous fountains the whole prospect crown'd; ....Od.7.169.244.
The plenteous board high-heap'd with cates divine, ...Od.9.9.301.
As plenteous cates and flowing bowls invite; ....Od.9.650.333.
Thick o'er the board the plenteous viands lay, ...Od.16.51.104.
But when the storm was spent in plenteous show'rs, ...Od.19.286.209.
With plenteous unction of ambrosial oil. ....Od.19.590.225.
My pitying eyes effus'd a plenteous stream, ...Od.19.633.227.
A plenteous board: Hence! seek another host! ....Od.20.230.244.

PLENTIFUL

Bears *Rabbits,—Gad!* so plentiful, ...6.94.11.259.

PLENTY

And Peace and Plenty tell, a STUART reigns. ....1.W-F.42.152.
Some thoughtless Town, with Ease and Plenty blest, ...1.W-F.107.161.
Thus many a Day, with Ease and Plenty blest, ...2.ChJM.474Z1.38.
The rich is happy in the plenty giv'n, ...3.EOM2.265.87.
The rich are happy in the plenty giv'n ....3.EOM2.265A.87.
Nor is his claim to plenty, but content. ....3.EOM4.156.142.
With Splendor, Charity; with Plenty, Health; ....3.Ep3.225.111.
In plenty starving, tantaliz'd in state, ...3.Ep4.163.153.
Tho' gen'rous Plenty crown thy loaded Boards, ...Il.9.297.449.
With teeming plenty to reward their toil, ...Od.4.240.130.
In *Egypt* thus with peace and plenty blest, ...Od.14.315.50.
A land of plenty, blest with every grain: ....Od.16.411.126.
He took his place, and Plenty heap'd the board. ....Od.17.309.146.
And let yon' mendicant our plenty share: ....Od.17.419.152.
Whilst in paternal pomp, with plenty blest, ...Od.20.401.251.

PLEURON'S

From *Pleuron's* Walls and chalky *Calydon*, ...Il.2.776.162.
And *Pleuron's* chalky Cliffs emblaze the Skies. ....Il.13.288.119.
Who *Pleuron's* Walls and *Calydon* possest: ....Il.14.131.164.

PLIANT

And captive led, with pliant Osiers bound; ....Il.11.144.42.
Now high, now low, their pliant Limbs they bend, ...Il.18.699.357.
Where the knit Nerves the pliant Elbow strung; ....Il.20.554.417.
A mossy bank with pliant rushes crown'd; ....Od.5.595.201.
An ell in length the pliant wisp I weav'd, ...Od.10.194.350.

PLIES

Imagination plies her dang'rous art, ...3.EOM2.143.72.
That plies the Tongue, and wags the Tail, ...6.14v(a).23.49.
Vulcan with awkward Grace his Office plies, ...Il.1.770.124.
Plies all the Troops, and orders all the Field. ....Il.11.82.38.
Victorious *Ajax* plies the routed Crew; ....Il.11.610.61.
Now plies the Lash, and sooths and threats in vain; ....Il.17.489.307.
Now plies the Jav'lin, now directs the Reins; ....Il.17.533.309.
Graceful in Motion thus, his Foe he plies, ...Il.23.893.524.

PLIGHT

First give thy Faith, and plight a Prince's Word ....Il.1.99.91.
Their Hands they join, their mutual Faith they plight, ...Il.6.289.340.
Now plight thy mutual Oath, I ask no more. ....Il.22.332.470.

PLIGHTED

Those Hands we plighted, and those Oaths we swore, ...Il.4.193.230.
And the rich pledge of plighted faith receive, ...Od.1.405.52.

PLIGHTS

Nor Oath nor Pact *Achilles* plights with thee: ....Il.22.336.470.

PLINY

For me, what Virgil, Pliny may deny, ...5.DunB4.225.365.

PLODDING

That plodding on must make a Calf an Ox ....4.JD2A.54.136.

PLOT

Made him observe the *Subject* and the *Plot*, ...1.EOC.275.270.
A Popish plot, shall for a Jesuit take; ....4.JD4.35.29.
Or shall *Eliza* lay a Plot, ...6.101.29.291.
Convene the tribes, the murd'rous plot reveal, ...Od.4.978.163.

PLOTS

He ne'er rebels, or plots, like other men: ....4.2HE1.194.211.
Theirs are the Rules of *France,* the Plots of *Spain:* ....6.60.12.178.

PLOTTED

New frauds were plotted by the faithless train, ...Od.14.375.53.

PLOUGH

Mean-while our vessels plough the liquid plain, ...Od.10.58.342.

PLOUGH'D

Plough'd half his thigh; I saw, I saw the scar, ...Od.23.76.322.

PLOUGHS

Ploughs, burns, manures, and toils from Sun to Sun; ....4.2HE2.271.185.
When now few Furrows part th' approaching Ploughs. ....Il.10.422.22.
Smoaks in the Dust, and ploughs into the Ground. ....Il.14.480.187.
Ploughs thro' the boiling Surge his desp'rate Way. ....Il.21.256.431.

PLOVERS

The clam'rous Plovers feel the Leaden Death: ....1.W-F.132A.162.

PLOW

And the broad Faulchion in a Plow-share end. ....1.Mes.62.118.
"Learn of the mole to plow, the worm to weave; ....3.EOM3.176.111.

PLOW (CONTINUED)

"Direct my Plow to find a Treasure:" ....4.HS6.20.251.
We launch a Bark to plow the watry Plains, ...Il.1.182.96.
Who plow the spacious *Orchomenian* Plain. ....Il.2.611.156.
In fourscore Barks they plow the watry Way. ....Il.2.685.159.
And *Greece* returning plow the watry Deep. ....Il.3.357.210.
Then back the turning Plow-shares cleave the Soil: ....Od.2.323.76.
And lo, with speed we plow the watry way; ....Od.2.323.76.
Or the strait course to rocky *Chios* plow, ...Od.3.207.95.
New to the plow, unpractis'd in the trace. ....Od.4.861.159.
Mean-time the Suitors plow the wat'ry plain, ...Od.4.1099.169.
Between the mule and ox, from plow to plow; ....Od.8.130.270.
Between the mule and ox, from plow to plow; ....Od.8.130.270.
Or thro' cærulean billows plow the way: ....Od.8.284.278.
Like man intelligent, they plow the tides, ...Od.8.606.295.
Spread your broad sails, and plow the liquid way: ....Od.12.36.431.
Next, where the Sirens dwell, you plow the seas; ....Od.12.51.431.
Oh if thy vessel plow the direful waves ....Od.12.133.438.
Bear wide thy course, nor plow those angry waves ....Od.12.260.445.
Thro' the wild ocean plow the dang'rous way, ...Od.13.482.29.
Soon as remote from shore they plow the wave, ...Od.14.377.53.

PLOW-SHARE

And the broad Faulchion in a Plow-share end. ....1.Mes.62.118.

PLOW-SHARES

Then back the turning Plow-shares cleave the Soil: ....Il.18.634.354.

PLOW'D

And, bound for *Greece,* we plow'd the Watry way; ....1.TrUl.196.472.
Plow'd was his front with many a deep Remark: ....5.DunB4.204.362.
Big with the Fate of *Ilion,* plow'd the Main, ...Il.2.417.147.
Who plow'd, with Fates averse, the wat'ry way; ....Il.8.655.427.
Plow'd half his side, and bar'd it to the Bone. ....Il.11.548.58.
His conqu'ring Son, *Alcides,* plow'd the Main: ....Il.14.286.176.
When to his realm I plow'd the orient wave. ....Od.4.838.158.
No more the vessel plow'd the dreadful wave, ...Od.12.244.443.
Then nine long days I plow'd the calmer seas, ...Od.12.529.458.
And bound for *Greece* we plow'd the wat'ry way; ....Od.13.363.24.
Six days consum'd; the sev'nth we plow'd the main. ....Od.14.283.49.
When o'er the waves you plow'd the desp'rate way. ....Od.16.26.103.
That you to *Pylos* plow'd the wat'ry way, ...Od.16.153.110.

PLOWMAN

As weary plowman spent with stubborn toil, ...Od.13.39.3.

PLOWMEN

As stubborn Steers by brawny Plowmen broke, ...1.TrSt.184.418.
The shining Shares full many Plowmen guide, ...Il.18.629.354.

PLOWS

The hog, that plows not nor obeys thy call, ...3.EOM3.41.96.
Some Stranger plows his patrimonial Field. ....Il.22.627.482.
Plows o'er that roaring surge its desp'rate way; ....Od.12.80.435.

PLOWSHARE

Force the bright Plowshare thro' the fallow Soil, ...Il.13.880.147.
Or should we labour while the plowshare wounds ....Od.18.414.189.

PLOWSHARES

For Plowshares, Wheels, and all the rural Trade. ....Il.23.990.529.

PLU

Plu—Plutarch, what's his name that writes his life? ....6.41.31.114.

PLUBLICK

O'er head and ears plunge for the plublick weal. ....5.DunA1.196.86.

PLUCK

I pluck out year by year, as hair by hair, ...4.2HE1.64.199.

PLUCK'D

His Rump well pluck'd with Nettles stings, ...6.93.21.257.

PLUM

The chestnut, wilding, plum, and every tree, ...1.TrPA.76.368.
Alas! they fear a man will cost a plum. ....3.Ep3.124.102.

PLUM'D

All the plum'd Beau-monde round her gathers; ....6.93.9.256.
While the plum'd Beau–monde round her gathers; ....6.93.9A.256.
On the plum'd Crest of his *Bœotian* Foe, ...Il.16.404.258.
The *Dorians,* plum'd amid the files of war, ...Od.19.202.202.

PLUMAGE

Smit with her varying plumage, spare the dove? ....3.EOM3.54.97.
Nor miss'd its Aim, but where the Plumage danc'd, ...Il.11.453.54.
(The sable Plumage nodded o'er his Head) ....Il.17.212.295.
The nodding Plumage on his Helmet danc'd. ....Il.20.195.402.
His dreadful Plumage nodded from on high; ....Il.22.174.460.
His dreadful Plumage nodded as he spoke. ....Il.22.316.469.
Thick plumage, mingled with a sanguine show'r. ....Od.15.570.98.

PLUMBS

Just as a Scotsman does his Plumbs. ....4.1HE7.24.269.
Or mow from racy plumbs the savo'ry blew, ...6.96ii.30Z47.272.

PLUME

She said; then raging to Sir Plume repairs, ...2.RL4.121.194.
(*Sir Plume,* of *Amber Snuff-box* justly vain, ...2.RL4.123.194.
When bold Sir *Plume* had drawn *Clarissa* down, ...2.RL5.67.206.
As bold Sir *Plume* had drawn *Clarissa* down, ...2.RL5.67A.206.
At Quin's high plume, or Oldfield's petticoat, ...4.2HE1.331.223.
We know him by the various Plume he wears, ...Il.3.118.195.
But shakes his Plume, and fierce to Combate flies, ...Il.5.849.306.
Short of its Crest, and with no Plume o'erspread; ....Il.10.304.16.

PLUME (CONTINUED)
The Plume dropp'd nodding to the Plain below, ...Il.13.770.141.
Achilles' Plume is stain'd with Dust and Gore; ...Il.16.960.280.
That Plume, which never stoop'd to Earth before, ...Il.16.961.280.
He frowns beneath his nodding plume, that play'd ...Od.22.140.293.

PLUMES
The vivid Green his shining Plumes unfold; ...1.W-F.117.161.
Some o'er her Lap their careful Plumes display'd, ...2.RL3.115.176.
And from soak'd Plumes disperse a briny Show'r, ...6.26i.7.79.
With nodding Plumes and Groves of waving Spears. ...Il.2.182.137.
That dreadful nods with four o'ershading Plumes; ...Il.5.919.310.
His Tow'ry Helmet, black with shading Plumes. ...Il.6.639.358.
The floating Plumes unnumber'd wave above, ...Il.13.183.114.
Shakes his white Plumes that to the Breezes flow, ...Il.13.947.150.
Where the high Plumes above the Helmet dance, ...Il.15.633.220.
Thick, undistinguish'd Plumes, together join'd, ...Il.16.262.249.
Trembled the sparkling Plumes, and the loose Glories shed ...Il.19.415.389.
Fledg'd with Ambrosial plumes, and rich with gold, ...Od.1.125.38.
Stretch their broad plumes, and float upon the wind. ...Od.2.174.70.
And from their plumes huge drops of blood descend. ...Od.2.180.70.

PLUMP
All as a partridge plump, full-fed, and'fair, ...5.DunA2.37.100.
All as a partridge plump, full-fed, and fair, ...5.DunB2.41.298.

PLUMPER
Or plumper Thigh, than lurk in humble Crape: ...4.HAdv.107.85.

PLUMPS
As what a Dutchman plumps into the lakes, ...5.DunA2.373.145.
At what a Dutchman plumps into the lakes, ...5.DunA2.373A.145.
As what a Dutchman plumps into the lakes, ...5.DunB2.405.316.

PLUMS
Plums, and Directors, *Shylock* and his Wife, ...4.HS1.103.15.
To tax Directors, who (thank God) have Plums; ...4.EpS2.49.315.

PLUMY
With fleeces sheep, and birds with plumy trains; ...1.TrPA.105.370.
Shakes his huge Spear, and nods his Plumy Crest: ...Il.2.989.170.
To spoil his glitt'ring Arms, and Plumy Pride. ...Il.5.771.303.
The Bow, the Quiver, and its plumy Pride. ...Il.21.568.445.
Let the strong Sov'reign of the plumy Race ...Il.24.363.551.
Let the strong Sov'reign of the plumy Race ...Il.24.383.552.
As thus the plumy sov'reign of the air ...Od.15.194.78.
The plumy-crested helms, and pointed spears, ...Od.19.36.194.
View in this plumy form thy victor Lord; ...Od.19.643.227.

PLUMY-CRESTED
The plumy-crested helms, and pointed spears, ...Od.19.36.194.

PLUNDER
As meanly plunder as they bravely fought, ...3.Ep1.145Z3.27.
Or cross, to plunder Provinces, the Main: ...4.1HE1.127.289.
But Sense must sure thy safest Plunder be, ...6.7.13.16.
Lost, like the common Plunder of the Grave! ...6.27.9.81.
Yet if our Chief for Plunder only fight, ...Il.1.163.95.
But safer Plunder thy own Host supplies; ...Il.2.287.141.
Of all the Plunder of the vanquish'd Host; ...Il.10.368.19.
Or art some Wretch by hopes of Plunder led, ...Il.10.459.24.
And ours was all the Plunder of the Plains: ...Il.11.821.73.
Forbids to plunder, animates the Fight, ...Il.15.395.212.
Who stops to plunder, in this signal Hour, ...Il.15.400.212.
Than left the Plunder of our Country's Foes. ...Il.18.352.338.

PLUNDER'D
Or infamous for plunder'd provinces. ...3.EOM4.298.156.
Plunder'd by Thieves, or Lawyers which is worse, ...4.HAdv.57.81.
Rich ev'n when plunder'd, honour'd while oppress'd, ...4.1HE1.182.293.
How here he sipp'd, how there he plunder'd snug ...5.DunB1.129.279.
Stretch'd on the spoils of plunder'd palaces ...6.130.12.358.

PLUNDERERS
Suits Tyrants, Plunderers, but suits not me. ...4.JD4.195.43.

PLUNG'D
"But when from hence he plung'd into the Main, ...1.TrSP.195.402.
Sprung from the Rocks, and plung'd into the Main. ...1.TrSt.18.410.
Deep in her Breast he plung'd his shining Sword, ...1.TrSt.725.440.
Deep in his Breast he plung'd the pointed Steel, ...1.TrES.124.454.
Sow'd in a Sack, and plung'd into a Well: ...2.ChJM.588.43.
Or plung'd in Lakes of bitter *Washes* lie, ...2.RL2.127.168.
Plung'd for his sense, but found no bottom there; ...5.DunA1.113.77.
Shot to the black abyss and plung'd down-right. ...5.DunA2.276.135.
Plung'd for his sense, but found no bottom there, ...5.DunB1.119.278.
Shot to the black abyss, and plung'd down-right. ...5.DunB2.288.309.
Next plung'd a feeble, but a desp'rate pack, ...5.DunB2.305.310.
Then down the Deep she plung'd from whence she rose, ...Il.1.563.115.
In *Hector's* Breast be plung'd this shining Sword, ...Il.2.496.150.
There mourn'd *Achilles,* plung'd in Depth of Care, ...Il.2.845.164.
And plung'd amid the thickest *Trojans* lies. ...Il.3.52.191.
But plung'd in *Eniopeus'* Bosom lay. ...Il.8.152.405.
Plung'd in the Rear, or blazing in the Van; ...Il.11.86.38.
Then plung'd amidst the thickest Ranks of Fight. ...Il.11.420.53.
Deep in his Breast he plung'd the pointed Steel; ...Il.12.478.99.
His Dream of Glory lost, he plung'd to Hell; ...Il.13.469.128.
And plung'd into the Bosom of the Flood. ...Il.15.245.206.
And plung'd the pointed Javelin in his Breast. ...Il.15.783.226.
Plung'd in his Throat the smoaking Weapon lies; ...Il.16.398.258.
And plung'd amidst the Tumult of the Fight. ...Il.16.886.277.
Plung'd in his Throat, the Weapon drank his Blood, ...Il.17.358.301.
And plung'd within the Ranks, awaits the Fight. ...Il.20.436.413.
Thrice in impassive Air he plung'd the Dart: ...Il.20.516.416.
So plung'd in *Xanthus* by *Achilles'* Force, ...Il.21.18.422.
Then, as once more he plung'd amid the Flood, ...Il.21.40.423.

PLUNG'D (CONTINUED)
And Numbers more his Lance had plung'd to Hell; ...Il.21.228.430.
Down plung'd the Maid; (the parted Waves resound) ...Il.24.105.539.
She plung'd, and instant shot the dark Profound. ...Il.24.106.539.
He plung'd into the gulf which Heav'n foretold. ...Od.1.54.33.
Jove plung'd my senses in the death of sleep. ...Od.7.369.254.
And in the scabbard plung'd the glitt'ring blade: ...Od.11.123.387.
Then plung'd into the chambers of the main. ...Od.11.308.397.
And such was mine! who basely plung'd her sword ...Od.11.533.409.
'Till *Phœbus* downward plung'd his burning ray; ...Od.12.40.431.
If Monarchs by the Gods are plung'd in woe, ...Od.20.245.244.

PLUNGE
Some plunge in bus'ness, others shave their crowns: ...3.Ep1.56.19.
The surge, and plunge his Father in the deep; ...3.Ep3.354.122.
O'er head and ears plunge for the plublick weal. ...5.DunA1.196.86.
O'er head and ears plunge for the Commonweal? ...5.DunB1.210.285.
And plunge the *Greeks* in all the Woes of War: ...Il.2.6.127.
To plunge the Ponyard in my Father's Breast: ...Il.9.589.463.
The brass-hoof'd Steeds tumultuous plunge and bound, ...Il.11.197.44.
To plunge the *Grecians* headlong in the Main, ...Il.12.139.86.
Your Swords must plunge them to the Shades of Hell. ...Il.16.760.273.
The Sea-green Sisters plunge beneath the Wave: ...Il.18.182.331.
Part plunge into the Stream: Old *Xanthus* roars, ...Il.21.9.421.
With naked strength, and plunge into the wave. ...Od.5.437.193.
The refluent tydes, and plunge him in the deep. ...Od.5.549.198.
And plunge the vestures in the cleansing wave: ...Od.6.106.211.
To plunge it headlong in the whelming wave; ...Od.8.556.292.
To plunge the brand, and twirl the pointed wood; ...Od.9.392.322.
If still to live, or desp'rate plunge to Fate: ...Od.10.55.342.
Plunge all at once their oars, and cleave the main. ...Od.12.217.442.
Decree to plunge us in the whelming tide, ...Od.12.414.451.
Or deep in Ocean plunge the burning ray. ...Od.12.449.452.

PLUNGES
But *Jove* forbids, who plunges those he hates ...Il.2.446.148.
Now down he plunges, now he whirls it round, ...Il.21.24.422.

PLUNGING
In seas of flame my plunging soul is drown'd, ...2.ElAb.275.342.
The plunging Prelate, and his pond'rous Grace, ...5.DunB2.323.312.
Behold me plunging in the thickest Fight. ...Il.4.407.240.
Here *Hector* plunging thro' the thickest Fight ...Il.11.662.63.
He ceas'd, and plunging in the vast profound, ...Od.4.777.155.
Thus in his eyeball hiss'd the plunging stake. ...Od.9.468.325.
And plunging forth with transport grasps the land. ...Od.23.256.335.

PLUTARCH
Plu—Plutarch, what's his name that writes his life? ...6.41.31.114.

PLUTO
Pluto with Cato thou for her shalt join, ...5.DunA3.307.185.
Pluto with Cato thou for this shalt join, ...5.DunB3.309.335.
Pluto, the grizly God who never spares, ...Il.9.209.442.
Infernal *Pluto* sways the Shades below; ...Il.15.213.205.
Of *Pluto* sent, a blood-polluted Ghost. ...Od.1.40.31.
To griesly *Pluto,* and his gloomy bride. ...Od.10.637.374.
To griesly *Pluto,* and his gloomy bride. ...Od.11.60.383.

PLUTO'S
Awful as Pluto's Grove or Numa's grot ...6.142.9A.383.
That Wrath which hurl'd to *Pluto's* gloomy Reign ...Il.1.3.82.
Add one more Ghost to *Pluto's* gloomy Reign. ...Il.5.813.305.
When to grim *Pluto's* gloomy Gates he went; ...Il.8.446.418.
Go, guide thy darksome Steps, to *Pluto's* dreary Hall! ...Il.14.534.189.
Not unappeas'd, He enters *Pluto's* Gate, ...Il.14.567.190.
This Instant sends thee down to *Pluto's* Coast, ...Il.16.755.273.
And pour in Light on *Pluto's* dear Abodes, ...Il.20.87.397.
Hear, and rejoice on *Pluto's* dreary Coast; ...Il.23.26.488.
Hear, and exult on *Pluto's* dreary Coast. ...Il.23.221.498.
A willing Ghost to *Pluto's* dreary Dome! ...Il.24.308.549.
Sent many a shade to *Pluto's* dreary coast. ...Od.4.354.136.
Range the dark bounds of *Pluto's* dreary reign. ...Od.4.666.150.
To glide with ghosts thro' *Pluto's* gloomy gate. ...Od.10.201.350.
The dreadful scenes of *Pluto's* dreary state. ...Od.12.44.431.
Inroll'd, perhaps, in *Pluto's* dreary train.) ...Od.20.408.252.
Cyllenius now to *Pluto's* dreary reign ...Od.24.1.345.

PLY
"Statesman and Patriot ply alike the stocks, ...3.Ep3.141.105.
With what a shifting gale your course you ply; ...4.2HE1.298.221.
We ply the Memory, we load the brain, ...5.DunB4.157.357.
The Coursers ply, and thunder tow'rds the Fleet. ...Il.10.623.29.
There ply the early feast, and late carouse. ...Od.1.480.55.
There ply the early feast, and late carouse. ...Od.2.164.70.
Some ply the loom; their busy fingers move ...Od.7.134.241.
Each nerve we stretch, and ev'ry oar we ply. ...Od.9.574.330.
Each nerve to strain, each bending oar to ply. ...Od.10.148.347.
Ply the strong oar, and catch the nimble gales; ...Od.12.106.436.
Now every sail we furl, each oar we ply; ...Od.12.206.441.
Attend my words! your oars incessant ply; ...Od.12.254.444.

PLY'D
The Tempter saw his time; the work he ply'd; ...3.Ep3.369.123.
And with an Air divine her *Colmar* ply'd. ...6.9vii.3.22.
By these, by those, on ev'ry Part is ply'd; ...Il.11.529.57.
Where furious *Ajax* ply'd his Ashen Spear, ...Il.16.143.243.
Nor ply'd the Grass, nor bent the tender Grain; ...Il.20.271.405.
Pensive she ply'd the melancholy Loom; ...Il.22.567.479.
The well-ply'd Whip is hung athwart the Beam; ...Il.23.592.513.
The work she ply'd; but studious of delay, ...Od.2.117.67.
We furl'd the sail, we ply'd the lab'ring oar, ...Od.9.81.306.
Nine prosp'rous days we ply'd the lab'ring oar; ...Od.10.30.340.
We ply'd the banquet and the bowl we crown'd, ...Od.10.554.369.
The work she ply'd; but studious of delay, ...Od.24.166.356.

PLYE

Who plye the wimble, some huge beam to bore; ....Od.9.458.324.

PO

And Trees weep Amber on the Banks of *Po;* ....1.PSp.62.67.
Nor *Po* so swells the fabling Poet's Lays, ...1.W-F.227.170.
Not fabled *Po* more swells the Poets Lays, ...1.W-F.227A.170.

POACH

I poach in Suidas for unlicens'd Greek. ....5.DunB4.228.365.

POCKET

May pocket States, or fetch or carry Kings; ....3.Ep3.72A.93.
Can pocket States, or fetch or carry Kings; ....3.Ep3.72B.93.
Can pocket States, can fetch or carry Kings; ....3.Ep3.72.93.
"Eat some, and pocket up the rest—" ....4.1HE7.26.269.
Or *Japhet* pocket, like his Grace, a Will? ....4.EpS1.120.306.
Go drench a Pick-pocket, and join the Mob. ....4.EpS2.41.315.

PODALIRIUS

Which *Podalirius* and *Machaon* guide. ....Il.2.889.166.
Of two fam'd Surgeons, *Podalirius* stands ....Il.11.968.78.

PODARCES

His Troops in forty Ships *Podarces* led, ...Il.2.860.165.
And brave *Podarces,* active in the Fight. ....Il.13.868.147.

PODARGE

Whom the wing'd *Harpye,* swift *Podarge,* bore, ...Il.16.184.245.

PODARGES'

Xanthus and *Balius!* of *Podarges'* Strain, ...Il.19.440.390.

PODARGUS

And thou, *Podargus!* prove thy gen'rous Race: ....Il.8.227.408.
Then *Menelaus* his *Podargus* brings, ...Il.23.363.504.

PODES

Eëtion's Son, and *Podes* was his Name; ....Il.17.649.313.
By the same Arm illustrious *Podes* bled, ...Il.17.664.313.

POEM

Can sleep without a Poem in my head, ...4.Arbu.269.115.
Call forth each mass, a poem or a play ....5.DunA1.56.67.
Call forth each mass, a Poem, or a Play: ....5.DunB1.58.274.

POEMS

Write dull *Receits* how Poems may be made: ....1.EOC.115.252.
Poems I heeded (now be-rym'd so long) ....4.Arbu.221.111.
Has sanctify'd whole Poems for an age. ....4.2HE1.114.205.

POEON'S

See PAEON.
Then gave to *Pœon's* Care the bleeding God. ....Il.5.1109.320.

POEONIAN

Pyrechmes the *Pœonian* Troops attend, ...Il.2.1028.171.

POESY

And smit with love of Poesy and Prate. ....5.DunA2.350.143.
And smit with love of Poesy and Prate. ....5.DunB2.382.316.
The genuine seeds of Poesy are sown; ....Od.22.384.307.

POET

The Doves that round the Infant Poet spread ....2.TemF.230.274.
Supremely blest, the poet in his muse. ....3.EOM2.270.87.
Poet or Patriot, rose but to restore ....3.EOM3.285.121.
Oh master of the poet, and the song! ....3.EOM4.374.164.
To you gave Sense, Good-humour, and a Poet. ....3.Ep2.292.74.
How coming to the Poet ev'ry Muse? ....4.HS2.84.61.
And, what's more rare, a Poet shall say *Grace.* ....4.HS2.150.67.
And, what's more rare, the Poet shall say *Grace.* ....4.HS2.150A.67.
Whom have I hurt? has Poet yet, or Peer, ...4.Arbu.95.102.
With open arms receiv'd one Poet more. ....4.Arbu.142.106.
They had no Poet and they dyd! ....4.HOde9.14.159.
They had no Poet and are dead! ....4.HOde9.16.159.
Convict a Papist He, and I a Poet. ....4.2HE2.67.169.
A Poet begs me, I will hear him read: ....4.2HE2.93.171.
Go, lofty Poet! and in such a Croud, ...4.2HE2.108.173.
Say at what age a Poet grows divine? ....4.2HE1.50.199.
The Rights a Court attack'd, a Poet sav'd. ....4.2HE1.224.215.
Ah luckless Poet! stretch thy lungs and roar, ...4.2HE1.324.223.
To know the Poet from the Man of Rymes: ....4.2HE1.341.225.
Ah think, what Poet best may make them known? ....4.2HE1.377.227.
Behold the place, where if a Poet ....4.HS6.189.261.
He thinks one Poet of no venal kind. ....4.EpS1.34A.300.
Dare they to hope a Poet for their Friend? ....4.EpS2.115.319.
Truth guards the Poet, sanctifies the line, ...4.EpS2.246.327.
The needy Poet sticks to all he meets, ...5.DunA3.292.184.
The needy Poet sticks to all he meets, ...5.DunB3.290.334.
Then take at once the Poet and the Song. ....5.DunB4.8.340.
A Poet the first day, he dips his quill, ...5.DunB4.163.357.
And what the last? a very Poet still. ....5.DunB4.164.357.
A poet made the silent wood pursue; ....6.3.11.7.
This vocal wood had drawn the poet too. ....6.3.12.7.
The silent wood, of old, a poet drew ....6.3.11A.7.
Love, strong as Death, the poet led ....6.11.51.32.
But your damn'd Poet lives and writes agen. ....6.24i.2.75.
But your damn'd Poet lives and writes again. ....6.34.4.101.
Tho' *Tom* the Poet writ with Ease and Pleasure, ...6.34.23.101.
Will needs misconstrue what the Poet writ; ....6.38.11Z2.108.
Such were the Notes, thy once-lov'd Poet sung, ...6.84.1.238.
Lofty Poet! touch the Sky. ....6.96i.50.269.

POET (CONTINUED)

The King had his Poet, and also his Fool: ....6.105vii.2.302.
That *Cibber* can serve both for Fool and for Poet. ....6.105vii.4.302.
All hail, arch-poet without peer! ....6.106v.1.308.
The man, as well as poet, is in fault. ....6.107.26.311.
A Poet, blest beyond a Poet's fate, ...6.112.3.318.
A Poet, blest beyond a Poet's fate, ...6.112.3A.318.
Your friend, your poet, and your host; ....6.114.8.321.
That every Poet is a Fool: ....6.124ii.2.347.
That every Fool is not a Poet. ....6.124ii.4.347.
But in thy Poet wretched as a King! ....6.131i.2.360.
In peace let one poor Poet sleep, ...6.138.2.376.
Kind *Boyle* before his poet lays ....6.150.5.398.
My Countrys Poet, to record her Fame. ....6.155.8.404.
The heav'n-taught Poet, and enchanting strain: ....Od.9.4.301.
As when some heav'n-taught Poet charms the ear, ...Od.17.609.161.
Save then the Poet, and thy self reward; ....Od.22.387.307.
(Their great reward) a Poet in her praise. ....Od.24.225.358.

POET'S

Nor *Po* so swells the fabling Poet's Lays, ...1.W-F.227.170.
The gen'rous Critick fann'd the *Poet's Fire,* ....1.EOC.100.250.
But most by *Numbers* judge a Poet's Song, ...1.EOC.337.276.
Name a new *Play,* and *he's* the Poet's *Friend,* ....1.EOC.620.309.
And bless *their* Critick with a *Poet's Fire.* ....1.EOC.676.316.
And blest *their* Critick with a *Poet's Fire.* ....1.EOC.676A.316.
The Poet's *Bays* and Critick's *Ivy* grow: ....1.EOC.706.320.
Have pity, *Venus,* on your Poet's Pains! ....1.TrSP.70.396.
Absent from thee, the Poet's Flame expires, ...1.TrSP.240.404.
And justly CÆSAR scorns the Poet's Lays, ...4.HS1.35.7.
The Poet's Hell, its Tortures, Fiends and Flames, ...4.JD4.7.27.
Maintain a Poet's Dignity and Ease, ...4.Arbu.263.114.
Not proud, nor servile, be one Poet's praise ....4.Arbu.336.120.
Not proud, nor servile, be one Poet's praise ....4.Arbu.336A.120.
The Life to come, in ev'ry Poet's Creed. ....4.2HE1.74.201.
The Life to come, that makes a Poet's Creed ....4.2HE1.74A.201.
Yet let me show, a Poet's of some weight, ...4.2HE1.203.211.
But fill their purse, our Poet's work is done, ...4.2HE1.294.221.
We Poets are (upon a Poet's word) ....4.2HE1.358.225.
Takes the whole House upon the Poet's day. ....4.1HE6.88.243.
A Poet's form she plac'd before their eyes, ...5.DunA2.31.99.
A Poet's form she sets before their eyes, ...5.DunA2.31A.99.
All gaze with ardour: some, a Poet's name, ...5.DunA2.47.102.
But Oldmixon the Poet's healing balm ....5.DunA2.199.125.
But Welsted most the Poet's healing balm ....5.DunA2.199B.125.
And Poet's vision of eternal fame. ....5.DunA3.12.150.
Mix'd the Owl's ivy with the Poet's bays? ....5.DunA3.46.154.
A Poet's form she plac'd before their eyes, ...5.DunB2.35.297.
All gaze with ardour: Some a poet's name, ...5.DunB2.51.298.
But Welsted most the Poet's healing balm ....5.DunB2.207.306.
And Poet's vision of eternal Fame. ....5.DunB3.12.319.
Mix'd the Owl's ivy with the Poet's bays? ....5.DunB3.54.323.
That lies within a Poet's Head, ...6.10.76.26.
To hear the Poet's Pray'r; ....6.11.84.33.
First sought a Poet's Fortune in the Town: ....6.49i.2.137.
And crown'd your Infant Poet's Head, ...6.82vii.7.233.
[*Nature!* informer of the poet's art, ...6.107.27.311.
A Poet, blest beyond the Poet's fate, ...6.112.3.318.
A Poet, blest beyond a Poet's fate, ...6.112.3A.318.
Has sworn by *Sticks* (the Poet's Oath, ...6.135.91.370.
Has sworn by Styx (the Poet's Oath, ...6.135.91A.370.
Let such, such only, tread this Poet's Floor, ...6.142.13C.383.
Let such, such only, tread the Poet's Floor, ...6.142.13D.383.
Let such, such only, tread their Poet's Floor, ...6.142.13E.383.
To cheer the grave, and warm the Poet's rage) ....Od.13.12.2.
And spare the Poet's ever-gentle kind. ....Od.22.380.306.

POETESS

A maudlin Poetess, a ryming Peer, ...4.Arbu.16.97.

POETIC

Who give th' *Hysteric* or *Poetic* Fit, ...2.RL4.60.189.
Tho' mark'd by none but quick Poetic Eyes: ....2.RL5.124.210.
Thus we dispose of all poetic Merit, ...4.2HE1.135.175.
But not this part of the poetic state ....4.2HE1.348.225.
Poetic Justice, with her lifted scale; ....5.DunA1.50.66.
And learn to crawl upon poetic feet. ....5.DunA1.60.67.
Old Bavius sits, to dip poetic souls, ...5.DunA3.16.151.
With tresses staring from poetic dreams, ...5.DunA3.143.162.
Poetic Justice, with her lifted scale, ...5.DunB1.52.274.
And learn to crawl upon poetic feet. ....5.DunB1.62.274.
Her tresses staring from poetic dreams, ...5.DunB3.17.321.
Old Bavius sits, to dip poetic souls, ...5.DunB3.24.321.
While thro' Poetic scenes the Genius roves, ...5.DunB4.489.390.
These pleas'd the Fathers of poetic rage; ....6.71.50.204.

POETICK

Now Times are chang'd, and one Poetick Itch ....4.2HE1.169.209.
In vain you boast Poetick Dames of yore, ...6.43.1.120.
In vain you boast Poetick Names of yore, ...6.43.1A.121.
With no poetick ardors fir'd, ...6.141.1.380.

POETRY

Musick resembles *Poetry,* in each ....1.EOC.143.256.
But Care in Poetry must still be had, ...1.EOC.160Z1.258.
And curses Wit, and Poetry, and *Pope.* ....4.Arbu.26.97.
It is not Poetry, but Prose run mad: ....4.Arbu.188.109.
But sick of Fops, and Poetry, and Prate, ...4.Arbu.229.112.
Ev'n Poetry, tho tis indeed a Sin ....4.JD2A.7.132.
Possest with Muse, and sick with Poetry; ....4.JD2A.70.138.
To Rules of Poetry no more confin'd, ...4.2HE2.202.179.
The cave of Poverty and Poetry. ....5.DunA1.32.O64.
The Cave of Poverty and Poetry. ....5.DunB1.34.272.
This, prose on stilts; that, poetry fall'n lame. ....5.DunB1.190.283.
Ah! why did he write Poetry, ...6.58.21.171.
It is not Poetry, but Prose run mad: ....6.98.38.284.

POETRY (CONTINUED)
With not one sin but poetry, 6.150.2.398.

POETRY'S
I grant that Poetry's a crying sin; 4.JD2.7.133.

POETS
Not fabled *Po* more swells the Poets Lays, 1.W-F.227A.170.
By God-like Poets Venerable made: 1.W-F.270.173.
In *Poets* as true *Genius* is but rare, 1.EOC.11.240.
Some have at first for *Wits,* then *Poets* past, 1.EOC.36.243.
Against the Poets *their own Arms* they turn'd, 1.EOC.106.251.
Poets like Painters, thus, unskill'd to trace 1.EOC.293.272.
Such without *Wit* are Poets when they please, 1.EOC.590.307.
Still *run on* Poets in a raging Vein, 1.EOC.606.308.
Still *run on* Poets in a frantick Vein, 1.EOC.606A.308.
Nay show'd his Faults—but when wou'd Poets mend? 1.EOC.621.309.
Poets, a *Race* long unconfin'd and free, 1.EOC.649.313.
Grave Authors say, and witty Poets sing, 2.ChJM.21.16.
(So Poets sing) was present on the Place; 2.ChJM.327.30.
The weary Sun, as Learned Poets write, 2.ChJM.367.32.
And Poets once had promis'd they should last. 2.TemF.34.255.
And Youths that dy'd to be by Poets sung. 2.TemF.128.264.
Poets themselves must fall, like those they sung; 2.Elegy.75.368.
She sins with Poets thro' pure Love of Wit. 3.Ep2.76.56.
Poets heap Virtues, Painters Gems at will, 3.Ep2.185.65.
Pimps, Poets, Wits , Lord *Fanny's,* Lady *Mary's,* 4.HAdv.2.75.
And own'd, that nine such Poets made a *Tate.* 4.Arbu.190.109.
His Library, (where Busts of Poets dead 4.Arbu.235.112.
Yet like the Papists is the Poets state, 4.JD2.11.133.
No Poets there, but *Stephen,* you, and me. 4.2HE2.140.175.
There is a time when Poets will grow dull: 4.2HE2.200.179.
The Poets learn'd to please, and not to wound: 4.2HE1.258.217.
We Poets are (upon a Poet's word) 4.2HE1.358.225.
(More silent far) where Kings and Poets lye; 4.1HE6.51.239.
While pensive Poets painful vigils keep, 5.DunA1.91.70.
But pensive Poets painful vigils keep, 5.DunA1.91A.70.
Then first (if Poets aught of truth declare) 5.DunA2.73.107.
And stretch'd on bulks, as usual, Poets lay. 5.DunA2.388.148.
Nor glad vile Poets with true Criticks' gore. 5.DunA3.172.168.
While pensive Poets painful vigils keep, 5.DunB1.93.276.
Then first (if Poets aught of truth declare) 5.DunB2.77.299.
And stretch'd on bulks, as usual, Poets lay. 5.DunB2.420.318.
Nor glad vile Poets with true Critic's gore. 5.DunB3.178.329.
The melancholy poets theme, 6.6ii.3.14.
Of *Orpheus* now no more let Poets tell, 6.11.131.34.
Our Friends the Wits and Poets to advise, 6.17iv.23.60.
He says, poor Poets lost, while Players won, 6.34.21.101.
Wit's Queen, (if what the Poets sing be true) 6.37.1.106.
Poets make Characters, as *Salesmen* Cloaths, 6.60.25.178.
But Poets in all Ages, had the Care 6.60.33.179.
And own that nine such Poets make a *Tate;* 6.98.40.284.
Lies crown'd with Princes Honours, Poets Lays, 6.108.5.312.
Rests crown'd with Princes Honours, Poets Lays, 6.108.5A.312.
And Patriots still, or Poets, deck the Line. 6.118.14.335.
And Dread of Dogs and Poets both) 6.135.92.370.
The Dread of Dogs and Poets both) 6.135.92A.370.
But chief to Poets such respect belongs, Od.17.466.155.

POETS'
On Poets' Tombs see Benson's titles writ! 5.DunB3.325.336.

POINT
And mark *that Point* where Sense and Dullness *meet.* 1.EOC.51.244.
Here point your Thunder, and exhaust your Rage! 1.EOC.555.304.
His Friends were summon'd, on a Point so nice, 2.ChJM.81.18.
The knotty Point was urg'd on either Side; 2.ChJM.140.21.
The knotty Point was urg'd on ev'ry Side; 2.ChJM.140A.21.
But when my Point was gain'd, then thus I spoke, 2.ChWB.182.65.
His time a moment, and a point his space. 3.EOM1.72.22.
Know thy own point: This kind, this due degree 3.EOM1.283.49.
Know thy own point: This just, this kind degree 3.EOM1.283A.49.
But where the *Point* of Vice, was ne'er agreed: 3.EOM2.221A.82.
Draw to one point, and to one centre bring 3.EOM3.301.123.
The only point where human bliss stands still, 3.EOM4.311.157.
That knotty point, my Lord, shall I discuss, 3.Ep3.337A.120.
A knotty point! to which we now proceed. 3.Ep3.337B.120.
A knotty point! to which we now proceed. 3.Ep3.337.120.
Or rather truly, if your Point be Rest, 4.HS1.17.5.
P. What? arm'd for *Virtue* when I point the Pen, 4.HS1.105.15.
And 'twas their point, I ween, to make it last: 4.HS2.94.61.
To Hounslow-heath I point, and Bansted-down, 4.HS2.143.67.
But here's his point; A Wench (he cries) for me! 4.HAdv.69.81.
He the least point shoud shorten or omit 4.JD2A.109.142.
Loose on the point of ev'ry wav'ring Hour; 4.2HE2.249.183.
Produc'd the point that left a sting behind; 4.2HE1.252.217.
For vulgar eyes, and point out ev'ry line. 4.2HE1.367.227.
Point she to Priest or Elder, Whig or Tory, 4.EpS2.96.318.
"Ascend this hill, whose cloudy point commands 5.DunA3.59.155.
Heav'ns twinkling Sparks draw light, and point their horns. 5.DunB2.12.296.
New point their dulness, and new bronze their face. 5.DunB2.10A.296.
Heav'ns Starry Sparks draw light, and point their horns. 5.DunB2.12A.296.
"Ascend this hill, whose cloudy point commands 5.DunB3.67.323.
Well argu'd, Faith! Your Point you urge 6.10.91.27.
Now coy and studious in no Point to fall, 6.99.11.287.
And beaten Gold each taper Point adorns. Il.4.143.227.
'Till the barb'd Point approach the circling Bow; Il.4.155.228.
Where to the steely Point the Reed was join'd, Il.4.246.232.
Whose forky Point the hollow Breastplate tore, Il.5.130.273.
'Till the bright Point look'd out beneath the Chin. Il.5.356.283.
To meet whose Point was strong *Deicoon's* Chance; Il.5.660.299.
Far as a shepherd, from some Point on high, Il.5.960.312.
The steely Point with golden Ringlets join'd, Il.6.396.346.
The blunted Point against the Buckler bends. Il.7.310.379.
High on the cloudy Point his Seat he plac'd. Il.8.64.398.
The Point was Brass, refulgent to behold, Il.8.617.425.

POINT (CONTINUED)
The Point was Steel, refulgent to behold, Il.8.617A.425.
And point at ev'ry Ship their vengeful Flame! Il.9.308.449.
The Point rebated, and repell'd the Wound. Il.11.304.48.
Fix'd was the Point, but broken was the Wood. Il.11.711.66.
The Point broke short, and sparkled in the Sand. Il.13.218.116.
Beneath the Chin the Point was seen to glide, Il.13.491.130.
Beneath the Bone the glancing Point descends, Il.13.815.144.
And light on *Lectos,* on the Point of *Ide.* Il.14.320.178.
Pierc'd by whose Point, the Son of *Enops* bled; Il.14.518.188.
But bathes its Point within a *Grecian* Heart. Il.14.532.189.
Nor dare to act, but when we point the way. Il.15.56.196.
Thus point your Arms; and when such Foes appear, Il.15.336.210.
A Dart, whose Point with Brass refulgent shines, Il.15.568.218.
Beneath the Brain the Point a Passage tore, Il.16.416.259.
The brittle Point before his Corselet yields; Il.17.685.314.
Thro' two strong Plates the Point is Passage held, Il.20.316.407.
Longing to dip its thirsty Point in Blood; Il.21.81.425.
So shone the Point of great *Achilles'* Spear. Il.22.402.472.
Quite thro' and thro' the Point its Passage found, Il.23.1036.530.
And reach *Gerestus* at the point of day. Od.3.216.96.
But when to *Sunium's* sacred point we came, Od.3.352.103.
A child may point the way. With earnest gait Od.6.365.229.
And point the wand'ring traveler his way: Od.7.36.235.
I left my vessel at the point of land, Od.9.225.316.
Whose point we harden'd with the force of fire, Od.9.387.322.
From thence we climb'd a point, whose airy brow Od.10.111.346.
From the high point I mark'd, in distant view, Od.10.173.349.
To point them to the arduous paths of fame; Od.11.302.397.
Shall prompt our speed, and point the ready way. Od.15.60.72.
Who met the point, and forc'd it in his breast: Od.22.96.291.
At ev'ry point their master's rigid will: Od.22.206.297.
May point *Achilles'* tomb, and hail the mighty ghost. Od.24.106.353.

POINT'S
Heroes are much the same, the point's agreed, 3.EOM4.219.147.

POINTED
And pointed out those arduous Paths they trod, 1.EOC.95.250.
And while two pointed Jav'lins arm his Hands, 1.TrES.11.450.
Deep in his Breast he plung'd the pointed Steel, 1.TrES.124.454.
Pointed above, and rough and gross below: 1.TrES.184.456.
And crowns the pointed Cliffs with shady Boughs. 1.TrUl.32.466.
His Hands a Bow and pointed Jav'lin hold, 2.TemF.115.262.
That pointed back to youth, this on to age; 3.EOM3.144.107.
His moral pleases, not his pointed wit; 4.2HE1.76.201.
And takes a Shelter from his pointed Fires. 6.17iii.31.58.
And pointed Crystals break the sparkling Rill, 6.142.4.382.
Whilst pointed Crystals break the sparkling Rill, 6.142.4D.382.
Two pointed Spears he shook with gallant Grace, Il.3.31.189.
Who first shall launce his pointed Spear in Air. Il.3.393.211.
And in his Hand a pointed Jav'lin shakes. Il.3.420.212.
The pointed Lance with erring Fury flew, Il.4.563.248.
And thro' his Navel drove the pointed Death: Il.4.607.250.
So took my Bow and pointed Darts in hand, Il.5.256.279.
Full on the Bone the pointed Marble lights; Il.5.376.285.
Where o'er her pointed Summits proudly rais'd, Il.8.59.398.
His warlike Hand a pointed Javelin held. Il.10.30.3.
The shining Helmet, and the pointed Spears: Il.10.85.6.
And in his Hand a pointed Javelin shin'd. Il.10.398.21.
A pointed Lance, and speeds from Band to Band; Il.11.272.47.
And while two pointed Javelins arm his Hands, Il.12.355.94.
Deep in his Breast he plung'd the pointed Steel; Il.12.478.99.
Pointed above, and rough and gross below: Il.12.538.101.
Beneath his Ear the pointed Arrow went; Il.13.841.145.
The pointed Death arrests him from behind: Il.15.527.217.
And plung'd the pointed Javelin in his Breast. Il.15.783.226.
The brazen-pointed Spear, with Vigour thrown, Il.16.368.257.
Still, pointed at his Breast, his Javelin flam'd: Il.16.427.259.
Pointed above, and rough and gross below: Il.16.894.277.
And his cold Feet are pointed to the Door. Il.19.210.381.
Broad-glitt'ring Breastplates, Spears with pointed Rays Il.19.386.388.
Of pointed Arrows, and the silver Bow! Il.21.550.444.
Beneath the pointed Steel; but safe from Harms Il.21.701.450.
And rocky *Imbrus* lifts its pointed Heads, Il.24.104.539.
The youth of *Pylos,* some on pointed wood Od.3.43.88.
To plunge the brand, and twirl the pointed wood; Od.9.392.322.
The pointed torment on his visual ball. Od.9.454.324.
From the tall hill he rends a pointed rock; Od.9.566.329.
And crowns the pointed cliffs with shady boughs. Od.13.123.7.
Pois'd in his hand the pointed jav'lin shakes. Od.15.594.99.
The javelin, pointed with a star of brass) Od.16.40.104.
A pointed javelin, and a fenceful shield. Od.16.321.121.
His hand impatient grasps the pointed dart; Od.17.4.132.
The plumy-crested helms, and pointed spears, Od.19.36.194.
Receiv'd a pointed sword and missile dart: Od.21.34.261.

POINTING
There passengers shall stand, and pointing say, 2.Elegy.39.365.
P. Where London's column, pointing at the skies 3.Ep3.339A.121.
Where London's column, pointing at the skies 3.Ep3.339.121.
As pointing out the gloomy Glade 6.79.119.222.
And level'd at the Skies with pointing Rays, Il.13.185.114.
And thus inflam'd him, pointing to the Dead. Il.15.653.221.
(Already dry'd.) These pointing out to view, Od.5.309.186.
Edg'd round with cliffs, high-pointing to the skies; Od.10.102.345.

POINTLESS
And with their forky Tongue, and pointless Sting shall play. 1.Mes.84A.120.
His pointless Spear the Warrior shakes in vain; Il.16.146.243.
And aim to wound the Prince with pointless wit: Od.20.448.255.

POINTS
The meeting Points the sacred Hair dissever 2.RL3.153.179.
Fame sits aloft, and points them out their Course, 2.TemF.483.286.
Invites my step, and points to yonder glade? 2.Elegy.2.362.

POINTS (CONTINUED)

Who mark'd their Points, to rise, and to descend ....3.EOM2.37B.60.
Who forms the phalanx, and who points the way? ....3.EOM3.108.103.
He gains all points, who pleasingly confounds, ...3.Ep4.55.142.
Comma's and points they set exactly right, ...4.Arbu.161.108.
But knottier Points we knew not half so well, ...4.2HE2.58.169.
All arm'd with points, antitheses and puns! ....5.DunA1.251Z2.93.
Light-arm'd with Points, Antitheses, and Puns. ....5.DunB1.306.292.
Points him two ways, the narrower is the better. ....5.DunB4.152.356.
The whistling darts shall turn their points away, ...6.21.15.69.
Just when his fancy points your sprightly eyes, ...6.45.45.125.
Comma's and *Points* they set exactly right; ....6.98.11.283.
And points the Crime, and thence derives the Woes: ....II.1.499.112.
Might Darts be bid to turn their Points away, ...II.4.632.251.
Tydeus' and *Atreus'* Sons their Points have found, ...II.5.260.279.
There *Agamemnon* points his dreadful Host, ...II.6.553.354.
And eight bold Heroes by their Points lie dead: ....II.8.362.414.
Shot from their flashing Points a quiv'ring Light. ....II.10.175.9.
And points to *Diomed* the tempting Prize. ....II.10.551.27.
Points to the Fleet: For by the Gods, who flies, ...II.15.396.212.
He points his Ardour, and exerts his Might. ....II.15.743.224.
The *Bear* revolving, points his golden Eye, ...II.18.564.349.
Pelides points the Barrier on the Plain, ...II.23.434.507.
Pelides points the Barrier with his Hand; ....II.23.886.524.
The Bear revolving, points his golden eye; ....Od.5.350.188.
When late stern *Neptune* points the shaft with death; ....Od.11.167.389.
To rouze *Ulysses*, points the Suitors' tongues: ....Od.18.396.187.
The level axes, and the points made fast. ....Od.21.126.264.
And scatter'd short, or wide, the points of death; ....Od.22.283.300.
When late stern *Neptune* points the shaft of death; ....Od.23.300.337.
Points out the long, uncomfortable way. ....Od.24.6.347.

POIS'D

See POIZ'D.
Each heav'd the Shield, and pois'd the lifted Spear: ....1.TrES.262.459.
Of *Greece* and *Troy*, and pois'd the mighty Weight. ....II.8.90.401.
Till pois'd aloft, the resting Beam suspends ....II.12.525.101.
Not to be pois'd but by *Pelides'* Hands: ....II.16.173.244.
Each heav'd the Shield, and pois'd the lifted Spear: ....II.16.567.266.
High on pois'd Pinions, threats their callow Young. ....II.17.848.321.
Erect with Ardour, pois'd upon the Rein, ...II.23.449.508.
Pois'd in his hand the pointed jav'lin shakes. ....Od.15.594.99.
Each pois'd his shield, and each advanc'd his spear; ....Od.16.493.131.
And level pois'd the wings of Victory: ....Od.22.260.299.

POIS'NING

The pois'ning Dame— *Fr.* You mean— *P.* I don't.— *Fr.* You
    do. ....4.EpS2.22.314.

POIS'NOUS

See POYS'NOUS.
On this side *Lerna's* pois'nous Water lies, ...1.TrSt.533.432.
The pois'nous Vapor blots the purple Skies, ...2.TemF.340.280.
From pois'nous herbs extracts the healing dew: ....3.EOM1.220.42.
A pois'nous *Hydra* gave the burning Wound, ...II.2.879.165.

POISES

His arms he poises, and his Motions tries; ....II.19.417.389.
And poises high in Air his Iron Hands; ....II.23.794.521.
And poises high in air his adverse hands. ....Od.18.103.172.

POISING

Poising his lifted lance in act to throw: ....Od.19.522.221.

POISON

With pleasing Poison, and with soft Deceit! ....2.ChJM.480.38.
Still drink delicious poison from thy eye, ...2.ElAb.122.329.
To shun their poison, and to chuse their food? ....3.EOM3.100.101.
Is hung on high, to poison half mankind. ....3.EOM4.252.151.
As Poison heals, in just proportion us'd: ....3.Ep3.234.111.
They'll never poison you, they'll only cheat. ....4.HS1.90.13.
Spread their cold Poison thro' our Soldiers' Breasts, ...II.12.292.92.
The poison mantled in the golden bowl. ....Od.10.378.362.

POISONS

Blue steaming Poisons, and a Length of Flame; ....1.TrSt.151.416.
And suck'd new Poisons with his triple Tongue) ....1.TrSt.667.438.
Have gather'd half the Poisons of the Plains; ....II.22.133.458.
Or comes from *Ephyré* with poisons fraught, ...Od.2.370.78.

POITIERS

Or what was spoke at CRESSY and POITIERS? ....4.1HE1.100.287.

POIZ'D

See POIS'D.
He poiz'd, and swung it round; then tost on high, ...1.TrES.103.453.
'Till poiz'd aloft, the resting Beam suspends ....1.TrES.169.455.
Poiz'd with a tail, may steer on Wilkins' wings. ....5.DunB4.542.384.
He said, and poiz'd in Air the Jav'lin sent, ...II.3.439.213.
He poiz'd, and swung it round; then toss'd on high, ...II.12.457.98.
There, poiz'd a while above the bounding tydes, ...Od.5.473.195.
His cornel javelin poiz'd, with regal port, ...Od.20.179.241.

POIZE

The Poize of Dulness to the heavy Skull, ...6.17(a).1.55.
The pond'rous Ballance keeps its Poize the same, ...6.17(b).3.55.
No room to poize the Lance, or bend the Bow; ....II.15.860.229.

POKE

Who poke at me, can make no Brags; ....6.135.22.367.
That poke at me, can make no Brags; ....6.135.22A.367.

POLAND

The Crown of Poland, venal twice an age, ...3.Ep3.129.103.

POLAND'S

Shows *Poland's* Int'rests, takes the *Primate's* ....4.JD4.154A.39.

POLE

Where clearer Flames glow round the frozen Pole; ....1.W-F.390.189.
And stretch'd his Empire to the frozen Pole; ....1.TrSt.28.411.
From Pole to Pole the Thunder roars aloud, ...1.TrSt.496.431.
From Pole to Pole the Thunder roars aloud, ...1.TrSt.496.431.
In *Northern* Wilds, and freeze beneath the Pole; ....1.TrSt.813.443.
From Pole to Pole the Winds diffuse the Sound, ...2.TemF.308.279.
From Pole to Pole the Winds diffuse the Sound, ...2.TemF.308.279.
And the touch'd Needle trembles to the Pole: ....2.TemF.431.284.
And waft a sigh from *Indus* to the *Pole*. ....2.ElAb.58.323.
No, fly me, fly me! far as Pole from Pole; ....2.ElAb.289.343.
No, fly me, fly me! far as Pole from Pole; ....2.ElAb.289.343.
Shall fly, like *Oglethorp*, from Pole to Pole: ....4.2HE2.277.185.
Shall fly, like *Oglethorp*, from Pole to Pole: ....4.2HE2.277.185.
Is Wealth thy passion? Hence! from Pole to Pole, ...4.1HE6.69.241.
Is Wealth thy passion? Hence! from Pole to Pole, ...4.1HE6.69.241.
Burn through the Tropic, freeze beneath the Pole! ....4.1HE1.72.283.
Where the tall May-pole once o'erlook'd the Strand, ...5.DunA2.24.99.
Where the tall may-pole once o'er-look'd the Strand; ....5.DunB2.28.297.
And Metaphysic smokes involve the Pole. ....5.DunB4.248.368.
And *Athens* rising near the pole! ....6.51i.22.152.
An *Athens* rising near the pole! ....6.51i.22A.152.
From East to West, and view from Pole to Pole! ....II.3.349.209.
From East to West, and view from Pole to Pole! ....II.3.349.209.
I see the God, already, from the Pole ....II.4.200.230.
She shook her Throne that shook the starry Pole: ....II.8.241.409.
Not all the Gods that crown the starry Pole. ....II.8.563.423.
And Stars unnumber'd gild the glowing Pole, ...II.8.692.428.
From Pole to Pole the Trail of Glory flies. ....II.13.322.120.
From Pole to Pole the Trail of Glory flies. ....II.13.322.120.
His right, beneath, the cover'd Pole-Axe held; ....II.13.766.141.
And awe the younger Brothers of the Pole; ....II.15.221.205.
These to the Chariots polish'd Pole they bound, ...II.24.338.550.
What tho' from pole to pole resounds her name? ....Od.2.143.68.
What tho' from pole to pole resounds her name? ....Od.2.143.68.
Mountains on mountains, and obscure the pole. ....Od.3.369.104.
From the bleak pole no winds inclement blow, ...Od.4.771.155.
'Till night with silent shade invests the pole; ....Od.4.782.156.
The keen-edg'd pole-axe, or the shining sword, ...Od.9.466.325.
And forky lightnings flash from pole to pole; ....Od.12.486.456.
And forky lightnings flash from pole to pole; ....Od.12.486.456.
He lanch'd the fiery bolt; from pole to pole ....Od.14.337.51.
He lanch'd the fiery bolt; from pole to pole ....Od.14.337.51.
Resign'd the skies, and night involv'd the pole. ....Od.19.496.220.
O'er the *Cerulean* Vault, and shake the Pole; ....Od.20.142.240.
But universal night usurps the pole! ....Od.20.430.254.

POLE-AXE

His right, beneath, the cover'd Pole-Axe held; ....II.13.766.141.
The keen-edg'd pole-axe, or the shining sword, ...Od.9.466.325.

POLEMIC

Each staunch Polemic, stubborn as a rock, ...5.DunB4.195.361.

POLES

See round the Poles where keener spangles shine, ...5.DunA3.61.155.
See, round the Poles where keener spangles shine, ...5.DunB3.69.323.
Between th' extended Earth and starry Poles. ....II.5.959.312.
Shakes all the Thrones of Heav'n, and bends the Poles. ....II.15.119.201.
The trembling World, and shakes the steady Poles. ....II.15.173.203.
Wraps the vast Mountains, and involves the Poles. ....II.15.729.224.
And Sheets of Smoak mount heavy to the Poles. ....II.17.830.321.
And Peals on Peals redoubled rend the Poles. ....II.20.76.397.

POLICIES

"Learn each small People's genius, policies, ...3.EOM3.183.111.

POLICY

True faith, true policy, united ran, ...3.EOM3.239.116.
Suppress them, or miscall them Policy? ....3.Ep1.76A.21.
The Dull, flat Falshood serves for policy, ...3.Ep1.126A.25.
Suppress them, half, or call them Policy? ....3.Ep1.76.21.
Or Falshood serves the dull for policy, ...3.Ep1.126.25.
Int'rest o'ercome, or Policy take place: ....3.Ep1.169.29.
The Courtier's Learning, Policy o' th' Gown, ...6.8.38.19.

POLISH

Heav'n, when it strives to polish all it can ....3.Ep2.271.72.
Then polish all, with so much life and ease, ...4.2HE2.176.177.
But Otway fail'd to polish or refine, ...4.2HE1.278.219.
And such a polish as disgraces Art; ....6.126ii.6.353.
And such a polish as disgraceth Art; ....6.126ii.6A.353.
Smooth as the polish of the mirrour rise ....Od.12.97.436.

POLISH'D

No fretted Roofs with polish'd Metals blaz'd, ...1.TrSt.201.418.
Whose fretted Roofs with polish'd Metals blaz'd, ...1.TrSt.201A.418.
The gliding Shadows o'er the polish'd Glass. ....2.ChJM.237.26.
The polish'd Pillar diff'rent Sculptures grace; ....2.TemF.226.273.
Nor polish'd marble emulate thy face? ....2.Elegy.60.367.
(In polish'd Verse) the Manners and the Mind. ....4.2HE1.393.229.
This polish'd Hardness, that reflects the Peer; ....5.DunB1.220.286.
This small, well-polish'd gem, the work of years! ....6.52.40.157.
So from the polish'd Arms, and brazen Shields, ...II.2.538.152.
His youthful Face a polish'd Helm o'erspread; ....II.3.417.212.
The *Greeks* with Smiles the polish'd Trophy view. ....II.3.464.214.
His polish'd Bow with hasty Rashness seiz'd. ....II.4.136.226.
Or press'd the Car with polish'd Brass inlay'd, ...II.4.261.233.
Ten polish'd Chariots I possess'd at home, ...II.5.244.279.
Of sounding Brass; the polish'd Axle Steel. ....II.5.891.308.
Of equal Beauty, and of polish'd Stone. ....II.6.311.341.
Of polish'd Silver with its costly Frame) ....II.9.248.445.
Then in the polish'd Bath, refresh'd from Toil, ...II.10.675.32.

POLISH'D (CONTINUED)

And polish'd Arms emblaz'd the Flaming Fields: ....Il.13.433.126.
Whose polish'd Bed receives the falling Rills; ....Il.22.202.464.
There, for the Gifts, a polish'd Casket lay: ....Il.24.227.546.
These to the Chariots polish'd Pole they bound, ...Il.24.338.550.
(Great *Hector's* Ransome) from the polish'd Car. ....Il.24.727.568.
There polish'd chests embroider'd vestures grac'd; ....Od.2.383.79.
On polish'd stone before his Palace gate: ....Od.3.519.112.
Three sprightly coursers, and a polish'd car: ....Od.4.806.156.
A polish'd Urn the seeming Virgin bore, ...Od.7.26.235.
The polish'd Ore, reflecting ev'ry ray, ...Od.7.130.241.
Whose polish'd vase with copious streams supplies ....Od.7.232.247.
Before his seat a polish'd table shines, ...Od.8.65.265.
A polish'd chest and stately robes to bear, ...Od.8.461.288.
The horses join, the polish'd car ascend. ....Od.15.161.76.
Fair on his feet the polish'd sandals shine, ...Od.17.5.132.
(Smooth'd by the workman to a polish'd plain) ....Od.17.416.152.
From stains of luxury the polish'd board: ....Od.19.75.196.
And columns fair incas'd with polish'd horn: ....Od.19.661.228.
With steel and polish'd elephant adorn'd: ....Od.21.10.259.
(With polish'd oak the level pavements shine) ....Od.21.44.261.
Behind, her train the polish'd coffer brings, ...Od.21.63.262.
Against the polish'd quiver propt the dart. ....Od.21.146.265.
And the fair dome with polish'd marble shines. ....Od.23.198.333.
A bowl, that rich with polish'd silver flames, ...Od.24.322.365.

POLISHED

And polished Crystals break the sparkling Rill, ...6.142.4A.382.

POLISHING

Bright'ning the Shield, and polishing the Bow. ....Il.6.401.346.
Then polishing the whole, the finish'd mold ....Od.23.205.333.

POLISHT

With unguents smooth, of polisht marble wrought; ....Od.17.99.136.

POLITE

Sprightly our Nights, polite are all our Days; ....2.TemF.383.282.
Intent to reason, or polite to please. ....3.EOM4.382.165.
He marries, bows at Court, and grows polite: ....3.Ep3.386.124.
Who never mentions Hell to ears polite. ....3.Ep4.150.152.
But why then publish? *Granville* the polite, ...4.Arbu.135.105.
Wit grew polite, and Numbers learn'd to flow. ....4.2HE1.266.217.
His sly, polite, insinuating stile ....4.EpS1.19.298.
Equal in wit, and equally polite, ...5.DunA3.177.170.
Equal in wit, and equally polite, ...5.DunB3.181.329.
Was very learn'd, but not polite— ....6.10.96.27.
But he's my Neighbour, cries the Peer polite, ...6.143.3.385.

POLITELY

"Oh! Sir, politely well! nay, let me dye, ...4.JD4.112A.35.
"Oh! Sir, politely so! nay, let me dye, ...4.JD4.112.35.

POLITES

His wounded Brother good *Polites* tends; ....Il.13.675.137.
Polites, Paris, Agathon, he calls, ...Il.24.312.549.
Polites to the rest the question mov'd, ...Od.10.258.355.

POLITES'

Polites' Shape, the Monarch's Son, she chose, ...Il.2.960.169.
Polites' Arm laid *Echius* on the Plain; ....Il.15.388.212.

POLITIC

No less alike the Politic and Wise, ...3.EOM4.225.148.

POLITICIAN

Coffee, (which makes the Politician wise, ...2.RL3.117.176.

POLITICIANS

Old Politicians chew on wisdom past, ...3.Ep1.248.37.

POLITICK

My Lord, forsake your Politick Utopians, ...6.42ii.1.117.

POLITICKS

Of crooked Counsels and dark Politicks; ....2.TemF.411.283.
In Puns, or Politicks, or Tales, or Lyes, ...4.Arbu.321.119.
Hibernian Politicks, O Swift, thy doom, ...5.DunA3.327.190.
Hibernian Politicks, O Swift, thy fate, ...5.DunA3.327A.190.
Ripe Politicks the Nation's Barrel fill, ...6.48i.3.133*.
Thy Politicks should ope the Eyes of *Spain*, ...6.48iv.7.136.

POLITICS

Hibernian Politics, O Swift! thy fate; ....5.DunB3.331.336.

POLL

Nay, *Poll* sate mute, and *Shock* was most Unkind! ....2.RL4.164.197.

POLLIO

Came, cramm'd with capon, from where Pollio dines. ....5.DunB4.350.377.
Bid me with Pollio sup, as well as dine: ....5.DunB4.392.380.
So back to Pollio, hand in hand, they went. ....5.DunB4.396.381.
On the cast ore, another Pollio, shine; ....6.71.64.204.

POLLUTE

Shall Flies and Worms obscene, pollute the Dead? ....Il.19.30.372.

POLLUTED

Or offer Heav'n's great Sire polluted Praise. ....Il.6.337.343.
Of *Pluto* sent, a blood-polluted Ghost. ....Od.1.40.31.
The ground polluted floats with human gore, ...Od.12.59.432.
Her Queen endures, polluted joys she shares ....Od.18.372.185.
He purg'd the walls and blood-polluted rooms. ....Od.22.530.314.

POLLUTES

"Who flings most filth, and wide pollutes around ....5.DunA2.267.134.
"Who flings most mud, and wide pollutes around ....5.DunA2.267A.134.
"Who flings most filth, and wide pollutes around ....5.DunB2.279.309.
His baneful suit pollutes these bless'd abodes, ...Od.10.85.343.

POLLUTION

The foul pollution of the briny wave: ....Od.6.260.222.
"From the pollution of the fuming fires; ....Od.16.313.121.

POLLUX

Castor and *Pollux,* first in martial Force, ...Il.3.303.207.
Hence *Pollux* sprung who wields with furious sway ....Od.11.367.400.

POLWARTH

COBHAM'S a Coward, POLWARTH is a Slave, ...4.EpS2.130.320.
Good M[arch]m[on]t's fate tore P[olwar]th from thy side, ...4.1740.79.336.

POLYÏDUS

Abas, and *Polyïdus* to engage; ....Il.5.189.275.

POLYBUS

If leaving *Polybus,* I took my Way ....1.TrSt.89.413.
Bold *Polybus, Agenor* the divine; ....Il.11.77.38.
Oh son of *Polybus!* the Prince replies, ...Od.1.521.57.
For *Polybus* her Lord, (whose sov'reign sway ....Od.4.169.128.
(The work of *Polybus,* divinely wrought) ....Od.8.408.285.
Sage *Polybus,* and stern *Amphimedon,* ....Od.22.267.299.
And *Polybus* renown'd the faithful swain. ....Od.22.315.301.

POLYCASTE

Sweet *Polycaste,* took the pleasing toil ....Od.3.594.116.

POLYCTOR

Polyctor is my Sire, an honour'd Name, ...Il.24.487.556.
Neritus, Ithacus, Polyctor there ....Od.17.236.143.

POLYCTOR'S

With these, *Pisander* great *Polyctor's* son, ...Od.22.266.299.

POLYDAMAS

There wise *Polydamas* and *Hector* stood; ....Il.11.75.38.
This saw *Polydamas;* who, wisely brave, ...Il.12.67.83.
Polydamas, and brave *Cebriones.* ....Il.12.104.85.
Th' Advice of wise *Polydamas* obey'd; ....Il.12.124.85.
Bold *Hector* and *Polydamas* pursue; ....Il.12.226.89.
Then first *Polydamas* the Silence broke, ...Il.12.243.90.
But sage *Polydamas,* discreetly brave, ...Il.13.905.148.
Around *Polydamas,* distain'd with Blood, ...Il.13.993.152.
Polydamas, Agenor the divine, ...Il.14.499.188.
Fir'd with Revenge, *Polydamas* drew near, ...Il.14.525.188.
Here, proud *Polydamas,* here turn thy Eyes! ....Il.14.549.189.
Mecistes next, *Polydamas* o'erthrew; ....Il.15.384.211.
(To thee, *Polydamas!* an honour'd Name) ....Il.15.523.217.
Till sad *Polydamas* the Steeds restrain'd, ...Il.15.532.217.
Polydamas laid *Otus* on the Sand, ...Il.15.614.220.
Now fires *Agenor,* now *Polydamas;* ....Il.16.656.270.
To face the Foe, *Polydamas* drew near ....Il.17.678.314.
Silent they stood: *Polydamas* at last, ...Il.18.293.336.
Shall proud *Polydamas* before the Gate ....Il.22.140.459.

POLYDORE

Then fell on *Polydore* his vengeful Rage, ...Il.20.471.414.
Thus sadly slain, th' unhappy *Polydore;* ....Il.20.486.414.
And I succeed to slaughter'd *Polydore.* ....Il.21.102.426.
Two from one Mother sprung, my *Polydore,* ....Il.22.64.455.

POLYDORUS

Phyleus and *Polydorus,* with the Spear. ....Il.23.732.519.

POLYDUS'

Polydus' Son, a Seer of old Renown. ....Il.13.836.145.

POLYGLOTT

Three Parts—the Polyglott,—my *Text,* ....6.39.13A.110.

POLYGOTT

The *Polygott—*three Parts,—my *Text,* ....6.39.13.110.

POLYMELE

Eudorus next; whom *Polymele* the gay, ...Il.16.216.247.

POLYMELUS

Ipheas, Evippus, Polymelus, die; ....Il.16.507.262.

POLYNEUS'

And fam'd *Amphialus, Polyneus'* heir: ....Od.8.118.268.

POLYNICES

Mean time the banish'd *Polynices* roves ....1.TrSt.443.428.

POLYPAETES

See POLYPOETES.
With *Polypætes* join'd in equal Sway ....Il.2.904.166.
Astyalus by *Polypætes* fell; ....Il.6.35.325.
This *Polypætes,* great *Perithous'* Heir, ...Il.12.143.86.
From *Polypætes* Arm, the *Discus* sung: ....Il.23.1000.529.

POLYPEMON'S

Of *Polypemon's* royal line I spring. ....Od.24.356.366.

POLYPHEME

Teach thou the warb'ling Polypheme to roar, ...5.DunB3.305.334.
Behold the Monster, *Polypheme.* ....6.78ii.4.216.
Great *Polypheme,* of more than mortal might! ....Od.1.91.36.
What hurts thee, *Polypheme?* what strange affright ....Od.9.479.325.

POLYPHEME (CONTINUED)
The vengeance vow'd for eyeless *Polypheme.* .... Od.13.145.12.
Dire *Polypheme* devour'd: I then was freed .... Od.20.27.233.

POLYPHEMUS
Acis I lov'd, and Polyphemus too .... 1.TrPA.9.365.
Thy force the barb'rous Polyphemus try'd, ... 1.TrPA.15.366.
Or *Polyphemus,* like the Gods in Fight? .... Il.1.350.105.

POLYPHETES
Palmus, with *Polyphetes* the divine, ... Il.13.995.152.

POLYPHIDES
And *Polyphides* on whom *Phœbus* shone .... Od.15.274.82.

POLYPOETES
See POLYPAETES.
Thy Troops, *Argissa, Polypœtes* leads, ... Il.2.896.166.
Stern *Polypœtes* stept before the Throng, ... Il.23.991.529.

POLYPOETES'
First *Damasus,* by *Polypœtes'* Steel, ... Il.12.213.88.

POLYPUS
As when the *Polypus* from forth his cave .... Od.5.550.198.

POLYXENUS
And great *Polyxenus,* of Force divine. .... Il.2.758.162.

POMATUMS
Combs, Bodkins, Leads, Pomatums, to prepare? .... 2.RL*A*2.16.132.
Gums and *Pomatums* shall his Flight restrain, ... 2.RL2.129.168.

POMEGRANATE
With deeper red the full pomegranate glows, ... 6.35.8.103.
With deeper red the full pomegranate glows, ... Od.7.149.243.
Green looks the olive, the pomegranate glows, ... Od.11.728.421.

POMONA
See *Pan* with Flocks, with Fruits *Pomona* crown'd, ... 1.W-F.37.151.
The fair *Pomona* flourish'd in his Reign; .... 1.TrVP.1.377.
And tries all Forms, that may *Pomona* please. .... 1.TrVP.93.381.

POMP
When the sad Pomp along his Banks was led? .... 1.W-F.274.174.
Works *without Show,* and *without Pomp* presides: .... 1.EOC.75.247.
Wide o'er the World in solemn Pomp she drew .... 1.TrSt.476.430.
The Pomp, the Pageantry, the Proud Array. .... 2.ChJM.308.29.
Of lavish Pomp, and proud Magnificence: .... 2.ChJM.445.36.
But see! the *Nymph* in Sorrow's Pomp appears, ... 2.RL*A*2.59.133.
One thought of thee puts all the pomp to flight, ... 2.ElAb.273.342.
And swell the pomp of dreadful sacrifice, ... 2.ElAb.354.348.
If in the Pomp of Life consist the Joy; .... 4.1HE6.98.243.
Here stopt the Goddess; and in pomp proclaims .... 5.DunB2.365.315.
And all their Spight on active Pomp display. .... 6.17iii.15.58.
Pride, Pomp, and State but reach her outward Part, ... 6.19.55.63.
To grace his conquests and his pomp adorn? .... 6.20.8.66.
The spoils of nations, and the pomp of wars, ... 6.32.28.96.
The pomp was darken'd, and the day o'ercast, ... 6.32.32.97.
In silent Pomp he moves along the Main. .... Il.2.700.159.
Attends the mournful Pomp along the Shore, ... Il.13.824.145.
Far o'er the rest, in glitt'ring Pomp appear, ... Il.16.264.249.
To boast our Numbers, and the Pomp of War; .... Il.17.263.298.
While the long Pomp the silver Wave divides. .... Il.18.88.327.
And to the Field in martial Pomp restore, ... Il.18.529.347.
Here sacred Pomp, and genial Feast delight, ... Il.18.569.350.
How vain that martial Pomp, and dreadful Show, ... Il.21.549.444.
(Dire Pomp of sov'reign Wretchedness!) must fall, ... Il.22.94.456.
High on their Cars, in all the Pomp of War; .... Il.23.159.495.
Then, as the pensive Pomp advanc'd more near, ... Il.24.872.573.
Ev'n to the Palace the sad Pomp they wait: .... Il.24.898.573.
Sad *Helen* next in Pomp of Grief appears: .... Il.24.959.576.
With Hecatombs and pray'r in pomp prefer'd, ... Od.1.34.31.
On whom a radiant pomp of Graces wait, ... Od.4.19.121.
Grave *Eteoneus* saw the pomp appear, ... Od.4.31.121.
Of man, who dares in pomp with *Jove* contest, ... Od.4.93.124.
With art illustrious, for the pomp of Kings. .... Od.4.162.128.
Then mingling in the mournful pomp with you, ... Od.4.273.132.
Then will the Gods, with holy pomp ador'd, ... Od.4.647.150.
Where late in regal pomp *Thyestes* reign'd; .... Od.4.690.151.
In pomp ride forth: for pomp becomes the great, ... Od.6.45.207.
In pomp ride forth: for pomp becomes the great, ... Od.6.45.207.
Then drest in pomp magnificently treads. .... Od.6.270.223.
From ev'ry dome by pomp superior known; .... Od.6.364.229.
Aloft, the King in pomp Imperial sate. .... Od.8.458.288.
And fitter pomp to hail my native shores: .... Od.11.447.406.
To come in pomp, or bear a secret sail? .... Od.14.366.53.
I swell'd in pomp, and arrogance of state; .... Od.18.166.174.
Demands the pomp of centuries to waste! .... Od.19.338.210.
With pomp and joy have wing'd my youthful hours!) .... Od.19.679.229.
Mean-while the pomp of festival increas'd: .... Od.20.341.249.
Whilst in paternal pomp, with plenty blest, ... Od.20.401.251.
With pomp of various architrave o'erlay'd. .... Od.21.46.261.
Thence all descend in pomp and proud array, ... Od.23.131.327.
Then drest in pomp, magnificent he treads. .... Od.23.152.328.
Of great *Atrides:* Him in pomp pursu'd .... Od.24.32.348.

POMPOUS
Where *Windsor-Domes* and pompous Turrets rise, ... 1.W-F.352.184.
A vile Conceit in pompous Words exprest, ... 1.EOC.320.275.
A vile Conceit in pompous Style exprest, ... 1.EOC.320A.275.
No *Grecian* Stone the pompous Arches grac'd; .... 1.TrSt.203.418.
Nor *Grecian* Stone the pompous Arches grac'd; .... 1.TrSt.203A.418.
That long behind he trails his pompous Robe, ... 2.RL3.73.173.
Six pompous Columns o'er the rest aspire; .... 2.TemF.179.270.
O'er which a pompous Dome invades the Skies: .... 2.TemF.245.275.

POMPOUS (CONTINUED)
And haunt their slumbers in the pompous shade. .... 3.EOM4.304.156.
And pompous buildings once were things of Use. .... 3.Ep4.24.139.
Withdrew his hand, and clos'd the pompous page. .... 5.DunB4.114.352.
Then pompous *Silence* reigns, and stills the noisie Laws. .... 6.8.33.18.
The fierce, the pompous majesty lyes dead! .... 6.22.14.71.
Rome's pompous glories rising to our thought! .... 6.52.24.156.
And haunt his slumbers in the pompous Shade. .... 6.130.18.358.
The pompous Structure, and the Town commands, ... Il.6.393.346.
With song and dance the pompous revel end. .... Od.1.204.42.
And slept beneath the pompous Colonnade; .... Od.3.511.112.
A pompous wretch! accurs'd upon a throne. .... Od.11.336.398.
There end thy pompous vaunts, and high disdain; .... Od.22.318.301.

POMPOUSLY
The bounding steed you pompously bestride, ... 3.EOM3.35.95.

POMPS
(Pomps without guilt, of bloodless swords and maces, ... 5.DunA1.85.69.
(Pomps without guilt, of bloodless swords and maces, ... 5.DunB1.87.275.
Dry pomps and Obsequies without a sigh. .... 6.130.26.358.
In pomps or joys, the palace or the grott, ... Od.9.35.303.

POND
His pond an Ocean, his parterre a Down: .... 3.Ep4.106.147.
To them a piss–pot, but to thee a pond. .... 6.96ii.30Z4.271.

POND'RING
Thus pond'ring, like a God the *Greek* drew nigh; .... Il.22.173.460.
Schemes of revenge his pond'ring breast elate, ... Od.17.33.134.

POND'ROUS
Which as more pond'rous makes their aim more true, ... 5.DunA1.149.82.
And pond'rous slugs cut swiftly thro' the sky; .... 5.DunA1.178.84.
The pond'rous books two gentle readers bring; .... 5.DunA2.351.143.
Which, as more pond'rous, made its aim more true, ... 5.DunB1.171.282.
And pond'rous slugs cut swiftly thro the sky; .... 5.DunB1.182.283.
The plunging Prelate, and his pond'rous Grace, ... 5.DunB2.323.312.
The pond'rous books two gentle readers bring; .... 5.DunB2.383.316.
To lug the pond'rous volume off in state.] .... 5.DunB4.118.353.
Which, as more pond'rous, makes its Aim more true, ... 6.17i(a).3.55.
The pond'rous Ballance keeps its Poize the same, ... 6.17i(b).3.55.
Pond'rous he falls: his clanging Arms resound; .... Il.4.579.249.
Full on his Ankle dropt the pond'rous Stone, ... Il.4.601.250.
Discharg'd the pond'rous Ruin at the Foe. .... Il.5.374.285.
Pond'rous and huge; that when her Fury burns, ... Il.5.924.310.
Beneath his pond'rous Shield his Sinews bend, ... Il.5.993.314.
His pond'rous Buckler thunders on the Ground. .... Il.8.314.412.
Huge, pond'rous, strong! that when her Fury burns, ... Il.8.474.419.
Then seiz'd his pond'rous Lance, and strode along. .... Il.10.204.10.
By the long Lance, the Sword, or pond'rous Stone, ... Il.11.343.49.
Pond'rous with Brass, and bound with ductile Gold: .... Il.12.354.94.
The pond'rous Ruin crush'd his batter'd Crown. .... Il.12.460.98.
It shakes; the pond'rous Stones disjointed yield; .... Il.12.485.99.
A pond'rous Stone bold *Hector* heav'd to throw, ... Il.12.537.101.
Precipitate the pond'rous Mass descends: .... Il.13.194.115.
Before the pond'rous Stroke his Corselet yields, ... Il.13.551.132.
That shook the pond'rous Lance, in Act to throw, ... Il.13.735.139.
The pond'rous Targe be wielded by the strong. .... Il.14.434.184.
A pond'rous Stone up-heaving from the Sand, ... Il.14.472.186.
And quit the Quiver for the pond'rous Shield. .... Il.15.557.218.
A pond'rous Mace, with Studs of Iron crown'd, ... Il.15.816.228.
Full on his Crown the pond'rous Fragment flew, ... Il.16.502.262.
As when the pond'rous Axe descending full, ... Il.17.588.311.
And pond'rous as he falls, his Arms resound. .... Il.17.653.313.
The pond'rous Hammer loads his better Hand, ... Il.18.548.348.
Bent with the pond'rous Harvest of its Vines; .... Il.18.652.355.
Pond'rous and huge! which not a *Greek* could rear. .... Il.19.421.389.
Deep thro' the Front the pond'rous Falchion cleaves; .... Il.20.550.417.
Deep thro' his Front the pond'rous Falchion cleaves; .... Il.20.550A.417.
Such pond'rous Ruin shall confound the Place, ... Il.21.374.436.
The Quoit to toss, the pond'rous Mace to wield, ... Il.23.713.518.
Beneath that pond'rous Arm's resistless Sway .... Il.23.800.521.
Pond'rous and vast; which when her fury burns .... Od.1.130.38.
Bright in his hand a pond'rous javelin shin'd; .... Od.2.13.60.
With gifts of price and pond'rous treasure fraught. .... Od.3.397.105.
His pond'rous hammer, and his anvil sound, ... Od.3.550.114.
The pond'rous engine rais'd to crush us all, ... Od.4.892.160.
By far more pond'rous and more huge by far, ... Od.8.211.273.
And cast the pond'rous burden at the door. .... Od.9.277.318.
A pond'rous mace of brass with direful sway .... Od.11.705.420.
His pond'rous footstool, shook it at his lord. .... Od.17.493.156.
Some weak, or pond'rous with the brazen head, ... Od.22.304.301.

PONDER
Absent I ponder, and absorpt in care: .... Od.10.442.365.

PONDER'D
Maturely ponder'd in his riper Age; .... 2.ChJM.78.18.
The Heroe paus'd, and ponder'd this request, ... Od.15.228.79.

PONDROUS
Before his feet his pondrous staff he cast; .... 1.TrPA.43.367.
Pondrous with Brass, and bound with ductile Gold; .... 1.TrES.10.450.
The pondrous Ruin crush'd his batter'd Crown. .... 1.TrES.106.453.
It shakes; the pondrous Stones disjoynted yield; .... 1.TrES.131.454.
A pondrous Stone bold *Hector* heav'd to throw, ... 1.TrES.183.456.
There Heroes' Wits are kept in pondrous Vases, ... 2.RL5.115.208.
And pondrous Slugs move nimbly thro' the Sky. .... 6.7.18.16.
His Cutlace sheath'd beside his pondrous Sword. .... Il.3.341.209.
He said, then shook the pondrous Lance and flung, ... Il.5.342.283.
He groans in Death, and pondrous sinks to Ground: .... Il.5.716.301.
The Bowstring burst beneath the pondrous Blow, ... Il.8.395.416.
The Tendon burst beneath the pondrous Blow, ... Il.8.395A.416.
Swift at the Word, his pondrous Javelin fled; .... Il.11.452.54.
(By the long Lance, the Sword, or pondrous Stone, ... Il.11.664.63.

PONTEUS
Anchialus and *Ponteus,* chiefs of fame: .... Od.8.116.268.

PONTIFIC
Not with more glee, by hands Pontific crown'd, ... 5.DunA2.9.97.
Not with more glee, by hands Pontific crown'd, ... 5.DunB2.13.297.
The Bishop stow (Pontific Luxury!) .... 5.DunB4.593.402.

PONTONOUS
He said. *Pontonous* heard the King's command; .... Od.7.242.248.
To rapturous sounds, at hand *Pontonous* hung: .... Od.8.64.265.
The Monarch to *Pontonous* gave the sign, ... Od.13.64.4.

PONYARD
Her ponyard, had oppos'd the dire command. .... 2.ElAb.102.328.
The *Spaniard* hides his Ponyard in his Cloke, ... 6.48iv.1.135.
To plunge the Ponyard in my Father's Breast: .... Il.9.589.463.
But sheath thy ponyard, while my tongue relates .... Od.11.120.386.

POOL
Wide o'er the pool thy faulchion wav'd around .... Od.10.638.374.

POOP
From the high Poop he tumbles on the Sand, ... Il.15.506.216.
Rise on the poop, and fully stretch the sails. .... Od.4.484.143.
There, while within the poop with care he stor'd .... Od.15.232.79.

POOR
Stretch'd o'er the Poor, and Church, his Iron Rod, ... 1.W-F.75.157.
Poor *Sapho* dies while careless *Phaon* stays. .... 1.TrSP.249.404.
(While some laborious Matron, just and poor, ... 1.TrES.168Z1.455.
The poor Adorer sure had hang'd, or drown'd: .... 2.ChJM.437.36.
Of thy poor Infant, and thy longing Wife! .... 2.ChJM.725.49.
And give up all his Substance to the Poor; .... 2.ChWB.43.58.
If poor (you say) she drains her Husband's Purse; .... 2.ChWB.86.60.
The Mouse that always trusts to one poor Hole, ... 2.ChWB.298.71.
See the poor Remnants of these slighted Hairs! .... 2.RL4.167.197.
See the poor Remnants of this slighted Hair! .... 2.RL4.167A.197.
The Poor, the Rich, the Valiant, and the Sage, ... 2.TemF.290.277.
Be envy'd, wretched, and be flatter'd, poor; .... 2.TemF.510.288.
Lo! the poor Indian, whose untutor'd mind .... 3.EOM1.99.27.
The poor contents him with the care of Heav'n. .... 3.EOM2.266.87.
The poor contented with the care of Heav'n. .... 3.EOM2.266A.87.
'Till tir'd he sleeps, and Life's poor play is o'er! .... 3.EOM2.282.88.
Lent Heav'n a parent to the poor and me? .... 3.EOM4.110.138.
Yet poor with fortune, and with learning blind, ... 3.EOM4.329.160.
(Were the last words that poor Narcissa spoke) .... 3.Ep1.243.36.
Or wanders, Heav'n-directed, to the Poor. .... 3.Ep2.150.62.
No poor Court-badge, great Scriv'ner! fir'd thy brain, ... 3.Ep3.147A.105.
Poor Avarice one torment more would find; .... 3.Ep3.47.90.
Pity mistakes for some poor tradesman craz'd). .... 3.Ep3.52.90.
Perhaps you think the Poor might have their part? .... 3.Ep3.101.98.
Bond damns the Poor, and hates them from his heart: .... 3.Ep3.102.98.
Yet, to be just to these poor men of pelf, ... 3.Ep3.109.100.
Sees but a backward steward for the Poor; .... 3.Ep3.174.107.
And who would take the Poor from Providence? .... 3.Ep3.188.109.
Behold the Market-place with poor o'erspread! .... 3.Ep3.263.115.
Of rich and poor makes all the history; .... 3.Ep3.288.116.
His givings rare, save farthings to the poor. .... 3.Ep3.348.122.
And tempts by making rich, not making poor. .... 3.Ep3.352.122.
Yet hence the Poor are cloath'd, the Hungry fed; .... 3.Ep4.169.153.
Yet these were all *poor Gentlemen!* I dare .... 4.JD4.78.31.
And cheats th'unknowing Widow, and the Poor? .... 4.JD4.141.37.
And the rich feast concludes extremely poor: .... 4.HS2.34.57.
How dar'st thou let one worthy man be poor? .... 4.HS2.118.63.
But ancient friends, (tho' poor, or out of play) .... 4.HS2.139.65.
What push'd poor *Ellis* on th' Imperial Whore? .... 4.HAdv.81.83.
When the poor Suff'rer humbly mourn'd his Case, ... 4.HAdv.94.83.
Poor *Cornus* sees his frantic Wife elope, ... 4.Arbu.25.97.
Poor guiltless I! and can I chuse but smile, ... 4.Arbu.281.116.
"But why insult the Poor, affront the Great?" .... 4.Arbu.360.122.
Yet poor, disarm'd and helpless is their State .... 4.JD2A.11.132.
Where are those Troops of Poor that throng'd before .... 4.JD2A.119.142.
Poor and disarm'd, and hardly worth your hate. .... 4.JD2.12.133.
Where are those Troops of poor, that throng'd of yore .... 4.JD2.113.143.
In ANNA's Wars, a Soldier poor and old, ... 4.2HE2.33.167.
He slept, poor Dog! and lost it, to a doit. .... 4.2HE2.36.167.
A man so poor wou'd live without a *Place:* .... 4.2HE2.287.185.
Ben, old and poor, as little seem'd to heed .... 4.2HE1.73.199.
Has seiz'd the Court and City, Poor and Rich: .... 4.2HE1.170.209.
Ward try'd on Puppies, and the Poor, his Drop; .... 4.2HE1.182.211.
Stretch'd to relieve the Idiot and the Poor, ... 4.2HE1.226.215.
To make poor Pinky eat with vast applause! .... 4.2HE1.293.221.
Who proud of Pedigree, is poor of Purse) .... 4.1HE6.84.243.
And envy'd Thirst and Hunger to the Poor. .... 4.1HE6.117.245.
And which not done, the richest must be poor. .... 4.1HE1.46.281.
The rest, some farm the Poor-box, some the Pews; .... 4.1HE1.128.289.
"Well, but the Poor"—the Poor have the same itch: .... 4.1HE1.154.291.
"Well, but the Poor"—the Poor have the same itch: .... 4.1HE1.154.291.
The poor and friendless Villain, than the Great? .... 4.EpS2.45.315.
Here one poor Word a hundred clenches makes, ... 5.DunA1.61.67.
She saw slow Philips creep like Tate's poor page, ... 5.DunA1.103.72.
And crucify poor Shakespear once a week. .... 5.DunA1.164.83.
Here one poor word an hundred clenches makes, ... 5.DunB1.63.274.
She saw slow Philips creep like Tate's poor page, ... 5.DunB1.105.277.
Here lay poor Fletcher's half-eat scenes, and here .... 5.DunB1.131.279.
Poor W[harton] nipt in Folly's broadest bloom, ... 5.DunB4.513.392*.
From *Rights* of *Subjects,* and the *Poor Man's Cause;* .... 6.8.32.18.
Arriv'd at last, poor, old, disguis'd, alone, ... 6.15.3.51.
Thrusts your poor Vowell from his Notch: .... 6.30.22.86.
He says, poor Poets lost, while Players won, ... 6.34.21.101.
(That Gay the poor Sec: and that arch Chaplain Parnell, ... 6.42i.5.116.
Poor *Y[ounge]r's* sold for Fifty Pound, ... 6.47.31.129.
And in a borrow'd Play, out-did poor *Cr[own].* .... 6.49i.8.137.
Poor *Umbra,* left in this abandon'd Pickle, ... 6.49ii.13.140.
Poor *Ovid* finds no Quarter! .... 6.58.42.172.

POOR (CONTINUED)
For to poor *Ovid* shall befal .... 6.58.71.174.
Here lye two poor Lovers, who had the mishap .... 6.69iii.1.201.
Poor Vadius, long with learned spleen devour'd, ... 6.71.41.204.
And if poor *Pope* is cl–pt, the Fault is yours. .... 6.82vi.16.232.
Well then, poor *G[ay]* lies under ground! .... 6.103.1.295.
Alas! poor *Æschylus!* unlucky Dog! .... 6.105i.1.300.
Of one so poor you cannot take the law; .... 6.116vii.5.328.
To his poor Babe a Life so short: .... 6.124iv.2.348.
I answer thus—poor Sapho you grow grey, ... 6.129.7.357.
One fawns, at *Oxford's,* on the Poor. .... 6.135.64.368.
In peace let one poor Poet sleep, ... 6.138.2.376.
"Of those that sing of these poor eyes." .... 6.140.32.379.
Who dare to love their Country, and be poor. .... 6.142.14.383.
Who dare to serve their Country, and be poor. .... 6.142.14A.383.
Poor *Colley,* thy Reas'ning is none of the strongest, ... 6.149.3.397.
Or wanders, Heaven directed, to the Poor. .... 6.154.36.403.
Oblig'd the Wealthy, and reliev'd the Poor. .... Il.6.20.325.
Can bribe the poor Possession of a Day! .... Il.9.527.459.
(While some laborious Matron, just and poor, ... Il.12.523.101.
Poor as it is, some Off'ring to thy Shade. .... Il.17.607.312.
The long, long Views of poor, designing Man! .... Il.18.384.339.
As a poor Father helpless and undone, ... Il.23.274.501.
As some poor peasant, fated to reside .... Od.5.630.202.
By *Jove* the stranger and the poor are sent, ... Od.6.247.222.
Respect us, human, and relieve us, poor. .... Od.9.318.319.
The poor and stranger are their constant care; .... Od.9.322.319.
There call to mind thy poor departed friend. .... Od.11.88.385.
A slave to some poor hind that toils for bread; .... Od.11.599.412.
To slight the poor, or ought humane despise. .... Od.14.66.39.
'Tis *Jove* that sends the stranger and the poor. .... Od.14.68.39.
And more, the pleasure to relieve the poor. .... Od.15.399.88.
A figure despicable, old, and poor, ... Od.17.411.152.
The poor, distinguish'd by their wants alone? .... Od.17.461.155.
If fiends revenge, and Gods assert the poor, ... Od.17.565.160.
Ill fits the stranger and the poor to wound. .... Od.17.575.160.
But mercy to the poor and stranger show, ... Od.18.128.172.
These poor but honest rags, enkindle rage? .... Od.19.89.196.
Embrac'd the poor, and dealt a bounteous dole. .... Od.19.97.197.
Receive no stranger-guest, no poor relieve; .... Od.19.158.200.
No poor un-father'd product of disgrace. .... Od.19.187.200.
With all thy wants the name of poor shall end; .... Od.19.290.209.
For the poor friend the cleansing bath prepare: .... Od.19.415.214.
Perhaps, like thee, poor guest! in wanton pride .... Od.19.436.216.
On this poor breast no dawn of bliss shall beam; .... Od.19.680.229.
Poor suff'ring heart! he cry'd, support the pain .... Od.20.23.232.
Like thee, poor stranger guest, deny'd his home! .... Od.20.261.246.
To this poor, tim'rous, toil-detesting drone? .... Od.20.452.255.

POOR-BOX
The rest, some farm the Poor-box, some the Pews; .... 4.1HE1.128.289.

POOR'S
Let Clarke make half his life the poor's support, ... 6.147vi.1.391.

POOREST
The poorest shepherd best may tell his store. .... 1.TrPA.81.368.
Which done, the poorest can no wants endure, ... 4.1HE1.45.281.

POPE
See P.
Ev'n tho' the Pope himself had sate at Table. .... 2.ChWB.181.65.
What Pope or Council can they need beside? .... 3.EOM3.84.100.
And heads the bold Train-bands, and burns a Pope. .... 3.Ep3.214.110.
Whether the Name belong to Pope or Vernon? .... 4.HS2.166.69.
"Better than lust for Boys, with *Pope* and *Turk,* .... 4.HAdv.43.79.
And curses Wit, and Poetry, and *Pope.* .... 4.Arbu.26.97.
Verse prays for Peace, or sings down Pope and Turk. .... 4.2HE1.236.215.
"From Pope, from Parnel, or from Gay? .... 4.HS6.94.255.
"Friend Pope! be prudent, let your Muse take breath, ... 4.1HE1.13.279.
And made up half a Pope at least. .... 6.30.30.87.
Let *Jervas* paint them, and let *Pope* commend. .... 6.38.28.108.
Let Kneller paint them, and let *Pope* commend. .... 6.38.28A.108.
The Doctor and Dean, Pope, Parnell and Gay .... 6.42iii.1.117.
Revenge our Wits and Statesmen on a *Pope.* .... 6.48iii.16.135.
Not long, *Pope* enters, and to *Pope* he flies. .... 6.49ii.6.140.
Not long, *Pope* enters, and to *Pope* he flies. .... 6.49ii.6.140.
Pope to the Closet steps aside with *Rowe.* .... 6.49ii.12.140.
And *P[o]pe* translate with *Jervis.* .... 6.58.60.173.
Who think the Turk and Pope a sport .... 6.61.3.180.
Who think both Turk and Pope a sport .... 6.61.3A.180.
In short Pope and Gay (as .... 6.68.5.196.
That *Craggs* will be asham'd of *Pope.* .... 6.74.4.211.
'Tis *Pope* must be asham'd of *Craggs.* .... 6.74.8.211.
And if poor *Pope* is cl–pt, the Fault is yours. .... 6.82vi.16.232.
If *Pope* must tell what *HARCOURT* cannot speak? .... 6.85.6.242.
When *Pope* must tell what *HARCOURT* cannot speak? .... 6.85.6A.242.
Whom Pope prov'd his Friend in his two chief distresses, ... 6.92.3.255.
They say, on Pope would fall .... 6.102.2.294.
Pope is a little Elf, ... 6.105vi.2A.302.
Maul the *French* Tyrant, or pull down the Pope! .... 6.128.18.356.
Yet Master *Pope,* whom Truth and Sense .... 6.135.87.369.
Yet Master P[ope] Whom Witt and Sense .... 6.135.87A.369.
My L[or]d complains, that *P[ope]* (stark mad with Gardens) .... 6.143.1.385.
Is room for all Pope's Works—and Pope himself: .... 6.147ix.2.392.
Quoth *Cibber* to *Pope,* tho' in Verse you foreclose, ... 6.149.1.397.

POPE'S
Down with the Bible, up with the Pope's Arms." .... 5.DunA2.78.107.
And Pope's, translating three whole years with Broome. .... 5.DunA3.328.191.
And Pope's whole years to comment and translate. .... 5.DunA3.328A.191.
Down with the Bible, up with the Pope's Arms. .... 5.DunB2.82.299.
And Pope's, ten years to comment and translate. .... 5.DunB3.332.336.
Suppose, that *Pope's* an Elf; .... 6.105vi.2.302.
Is room for all Pope's Works—and Pope himself: .... 6.147ix.2.392.

POPES 125 PORTENTS

POPES
For writing pamphlets, and for burning Popes; ....5.DunA3.282.183.
For writing pamphlets, and for roasting Popes; ....5.DunA3.282A.183.
For writing Pamphlets, and for roasting Popes; ....5.DunB3.284.334.

POPISH
A Popish plot, shall for a Jesuit take; ....4.JD4.35.29.
Can Popish Writings do the Nations good? ....6.48iii.9.134.

POPLAR
Beneath yon Poplar oft we past the Day: ....1.PAu.66.85.
Then as the stately Pine, or Poplar tall, ...1.TrES.288.460.
Then, as the Mountain Oak, or Poplar tall, ...1.TrES.288A.460.
So falls a Poplar, that in watry Ground ....Il.4.552.247.
As when the Mountain Oak, or Poplar tall, ...Il.13.493.130.
Then, as the Mountain Oak, or Poplar tall, ...Il.16.593.267.
Like poplar-leaves when *Zephyr* fans the grove. ....Od.7.135.241.

POPLAR-LEAVES
Like poplar-leaves when *Zephyr* fans the grove. ....Od.7.135.241.

POPLARS
Poplars and alders ever quiv'ring play'd, ...Od.5.82.176.
Of poplars, pines, and firs, a lofty wood, ...Od.5.306.185.
Nigh where a grove, with verdant poplars crown'd ....Od.6.349.229.
Poplars and willows trembling o'er the floods: ....Od.10.605.373.

POPP'D
Forth popp'd the *Sprite* so thin; ....6.58.30.172.

POPPIES
As full blown Poppies overcharg'd with Rain ....Il.8.371.415.

POPPLE'S
Lo P[op]ple's brow, tremendous to the town, ...5.DunB3.151.327.

POPPY
And Shadwell nods the poppy on his brows; ....5.DunA2.324.141.
"Now Bavius, take the poppy from thy brow, ...5.DunA3.315.186.
And Shadwell nods the Poppy on his brows. ....5.DunB3.22.321.
"Now Bavius take the poppy from thy brow, ...5.DunB3.317.335.

POPULACE
The swarming Populace the Chief detains, ...Il.23.321.502.
Now swarms the populace; a countless throng, ...Od.8.111.268.

POPULARITY
Or Popularity, or Stars and Strings? ....4.1HE6.14.237.

POPULARLY
Yet who, before, more popularly bow'd, ...1.TrSt.259.421.

PORCH
In *Priam's* Porch the *Trojan* Chiefs she found, ...Il.2.958.169.
But in the Porch the King and Herald rest, ...Il.24.844.572.
Of the high porch, *Ulysses* sleeps profound: ....Od.7.436.258.
Three golden goblets in the porch she found, ...Od.15.503.94.
As thus pavilion'd in the porch he lay, ...Od.20.9.230.
From o'er the porch, appear'd the subject town. ....Od.22.143.294.
The porch, depos'd the ghastly heaps of death. ....Od.22.485.312.

PORCHES
The Roofs and Porches flam'd with constant Fire. ....Il.9.595.464.
Stand in their Porches, and enjoy the Show. ....Il.18.576.350.

PORE
To smart and agonize at ev'ry pore? ....3.EOM1.198.40.
With sharpen'd sight pale Antiquaries pore, ...6.71.35.203.
The humid Sweat from ev'ry Pore descends; ....Il.23.831.522.
Chafe ev'ry knot, and supple ev'ry pore. ....Od.21.186.268.

POREING
"There, dim in clouds, the poreing Scholiasts mark, ...5.DunA3.187.172.

PORES
See hairs and pores, examines bit by bit: ....5.DunB4.234.366.

PORING
W[att]s, B[ake]r, M[ilbour]n, all the poring kind, ...5.DunA3.188A.172.
"There, dim in clouds, the poring Scholiasts mark, ...5.DunB3.191.329.

PORKERS
Where the fat porkers slept beneath the sun; ....Od.14.86.40.
Then sheep and goats and bristly porkers bled, ...Od.17.201.141.
Three porkers for the feast, all brawny chin'd, ...Od.20.204.243.
With sheep and shaggy goats the porkers bled, ...Od.20.314.248.

PORKET
Which Flesh of Porket, Sheep, and Goat contains: ....Il.9.274.447.

PORT
Far from the Town, a spacious Port appears, ...1.TrUl.25.466.
Another Port appear'd, another Shore, ...1.TrUl.65.468.
In dead of Night an unknown Port we gain'd, ...1.TrUl.152.470.
Behold the Port of *Phorcys* fenc'd around ....1.TrUl.226.473.
That *Spain* robs on, and *Dunkirk's* still a Port. ....4.JD4.165.39.
He pay'd some Bards with Port, and some with Praise, ...4.Arbu.242.113.
See Alaric's stern port, the martial frame ....5.DunA3.83.157.
And Alma Mater Lye dissolv'd in Port! ....5.DunA3.334.191.
And Alma Mater all dissolv'd in Port! ....5.DunA3.334A.191.
See Alaric's stern port! the martial frame ....5.DunB3.91.324.
And Alma mater lie dissolv'd in Port!" ....5.DunB3.338.336.
In troubled waters, but now sleeps in Port. ....5.DunB4.202.362.
Like some free Port of Trade: ....6.14v(b).3.49.
As some free Port of Trade: ....6.14v(b).3A.49.
In *Chrysa's* Port now sage *Ulysses* rode; ....Il.1.566.115.

PORT (CONTINUED)
The Bloom I boasted, and the Port I bore, ...Il.9.575.462.
I, and *Ulysses,* touch'd at *Pthia's* Port, ...Il.11.904.76.
Mark well his Port! his Figure and his Face ....Il.14.553.189.
His Port majestick, and his ample Size: ....Il.15.815.228.
And gave to *Thoas* at the *Lemnian* Port: ....Il.23.870.524.
Appear'd he now with such heroic port, ...Od.1.346.49.
And let me now regain the *Reithrian* port: ....Od.1.409.52.
Full for the port the *Ithacensians* stand, ...Od.3.13.87.
And safe to *Argos'* port his navy brought, ...Od.3.396.105.
When thus the King with hospitable port:— ....Od.4.69.122.
His port, his features, and his shape the same: ....Od.4.200.129.
With joy impetuous, to the port I speed: ....Od.4.580.147.
My ship equip'd within the neighb'ring port, ...Od.4.854.159.
Before he anchors in his native port, ...Od.4.930.161.
An ample port the rocks projected form, ...Od.4.1105.169.
Nor peaceful port was there, nor winding bay, ...Od.5.518.197.
No port receives me from the angry main, ...Od.5.526.197.
To this calm port the glad *Ulysses* prest, ...Od.5.566.199.
The wond'ring Nymph his glorious port survey'd, ...Od.6.285.224.
Father, arise! for thee thy port proclaims ....Od.8.159.271.
A port there is, inclos'd on either side, ...Od.9.157.312.
This happy port affords our wand'ring fleet ....Od.10.13.340.
And bound within the port their crowded fleet: ....Od.10.106.345.
Whilst in the port each wretch encumber'd dies. ....Od.10.152.347.
Stalk'd with majestic port, a martial train: ....Od.11.52.383.
With graceful port advancing now I spy'd ....Od.11.365.400.
His comely port, his ample frame express ....Od.11.420.405.
But say, resides my son in royal port, ...Od.11.565.411.
With martial port he strode, and stern delight; ....Od.11.630.414.
To the fair port: A herald march'd before, ...Od.13.81.5.
Far from the town a spacious port appears, ...Od.13.116.7.
Full in their port a shady hill shall rise, ...Od.13.176.14.
Another port appear'd, another shore, ...Od.13.232.17.
In dead of night an unknown port we gain'd, ...Od.13.319.22.
Behold the port of *Phorcys!* fenc'd around ....Od.13.393.26.
A ship of *Sidon* anchor'd in our port; ....Od.15.457.92.
While in the port of *Ithaca,* the band ....Od.15.535.96.
Phæacians bore me to the port assign'd, ...Od.16.250.117.
See to the port secure the vessel fly! ....Od.16.371.124.
Where to the port a bark high bounding flew; ....Od.16.491.130.
My Lords! this stranger of gigantic port ....Od.17.446.155.
Thy Port asserts thee of distinguish'd race; ....Od.19.186.200.
His vessels moor'd, (an incommodious port!) ....Od.19.220.204.
That anchor'd in his port the vessels stand, ...Od.19.333.210.
His cornel javelin poiz'd, with regal port, ...Od.20.179.241.
The port, the strength, the grandeur of the man! ....Od.21.99.263.
The stature of our guest, his port, his face, ...Od.21.361.277.
And safe conveyance to his port of rest. ....Od.21.368.277.
What port receiv'd thy vessel from the main? ....Od.24.351.365.
With awful port, and majesty divine; ....Od.24.428.369.

PORTAL
From each wide Portal issuing to the Wars) ....Il.9.505.458.
The brazen Portal in his Passage rung. ....Il.24.398.552.
There in the portal plac'd, the heav'n-born maid ....Od.1.138.39.
Oh! in that portal shou'd the Chief appear, ...Od.1.331.48.
There from the portal, with her mild command ....Od.1.431.53.
Unbarr'd the portal of the roseate east ....Od.4.412.140.
And the wide portal echoes to the sound. ....Od.15.163.76.
His steps impetuous to the portal press'd; ....Od.20.159.241.
Full in the portal the chaste Queen appears, ...Od.21.65.262.
At ev'ry portal let some matron wait, ...Od.21.252.272.
At ev'ry portal let some matron wait, ...Od.21.413.280.

PORTALS
See Heav'n its sparkling Portals wide display, ...1.Mes.97.121.
The Sun's bright Portals and the Skies command, ...Il.5.931.311.
The Sun's bright Portals and the Skies command; ....Il.8.481.420.
Forth from the Portals rush'd th' intrepid Pair, ...Il.12.161.87.
For thee, tho' Hell's black Portals stand display'd, ...Il.13.525.131.
Set wide your Portals to the flying Throng. ....Il.21.622.448.
Thro' Heav'ns eternal, brazen portals blaz'd; ....Od.3.2.85.
Thro' the thick gloom the shining portals blaze; ....Od.6.23.204.
Two nymphs the portals guard, each nymph a Grace. ....Od.6.24.204.
And wide unfold the portals of the hall. ....Od.10.263.355.
Radiant she came; the portals open'd wide: ....Od.10.302.358.
And here thro' sev'n wide portals rush'd the war. ....Od.11.324.398.
Thro' heav'n's bright portals pours the beamy day. ....Od.12.6.430.
Still may thy beams thro' heav'n's bright portals rise, ...Od.12.454.453.
The brazen portals in their passage rung. ....Od.15.217.78.
Two portals firm the various phantoms keep: ....Od.19.657.228.
The sounding portals instant they display; ....Od.22.436.309.

PORTEND
Or fates peculiar to thy self portend? ....Od.15.189.77.
Portend the Suitors fated to my sword. ....Od.19.645.227.

PORTENT
A mighty Dragon shot, of dire Portent; ....Il.2.372.145.
To fright the Nations with a dire Portent, ...Il.4.102.225.
A Fawn his Talons truss'd (divine Portent) ....Il.8.298.412.
And *Jove's* Portent with beating Hearts behold. ....Il.12.242.90.
Gods! what Portent (he cry'd) these Eyes invades? ....Il.15.324.209.

PORTENTOUS
With that, a Tear (portentous sign of Grace!) ....5.DunB1.243.288.
And the dire Orb Portentous *Gorgon* crown'd. ....Il.5.917.310.
Portentous shone, and shaded all the Field, ...Il.15.351.210.
Eternal Silence, and portentous spoke. ....Il.19.451.391.
There huge *Orion* of portentous size, ...Od.11.703.419.
Floating in gore, portentous to survey! ....Od.20.417.253.

PORTENTS
Of Prodigies, and Portents seen in Air, ...2.TemF.452.285.
Portents and Prodigies are lost on me. ....Il.19.467.391.

PORTER
A Fav'rite's *Porter* with his Master vie, ... 4.EpS1.117.306.
And by his Hand obscene the Porter took, ... 6.14ii.44.44.

PORTIA
How *Arria, Portia,* and *Lucretia* fell. ... 2.ChJM.676.47.
Brutus for absent *Portia* sighs, ... 6.51ii.15.153.

PORTICO
And from the sounding portico they flew. ... Od.3.626.118.
Part in a portico, profusely grac'd ... Od.4.51.122.
Beneath an ample Portico, they spread ... Od.4.403.139.
A rural Portico of rugged stone: ... Od.14.10.35.
Beneath the royal Portico display'd, ... Od.15.5.69.
A hide beneath the portico was spread, ... Od.20.175.241.

PORTION
Become the portion of a booby Lord; ... 4.HS2.176.69.
Are now the portion of a booby Lord; ... 4.HS2.176A.69.
"How little, mark! that portion of the ball, ... 5.DunA3.75.156.
"How little, see! that portion of the ball, ... 5.DunA3.75A.156.
"How little, mark! that portion of the ball, ... 5.DunB3.83.324.
Each seiz'd a Portion of the Kingly Feast, ... Il.9.123.438.
Each Portion parts, and orders ev'ry Rite. ... Il.9.286.448.
The Chief himself to each his Portion plac'd, ... Il.24.794.570.
Oh snatch some portion of these acts from fate, ... Od.1.13.29.
To each a portion of the Feast he bore, ... Od.3.51.89.
The royal portion of the choicest chines ... Od.4.78.123.
And portion to his tribes the wide domain. ... Od.4.238.130.
The nobler portion want, a knowing mind. ... Od.8.196.273.
Portions the food, and each his portion shares. ... Od.8.514.290.
And honour'd with a portion of their feast) ... Od.17.197.141.
This said, the portion from his son convey'd ... Od.17.428.153.
The smallest portion of a wasteful board, ... Od.17.540.158.
The choicest portion who subdues his foe; ... Od.18.53.169.

PORTION'D
Him portion'd maids, apprentic'd orphans blest, ... 3.Ep3.267.115.
Rule as he will his portion'd Realms on high; ... Il.15.208.204.
And each was portion'd as the lots decide. ... Od.14.239.48.
The victim portion'd and the goblet crown'd. ... Od.24.424.369.

PORTIONS
And mourn our various portions as we please, ... 3.EOM4.33.131.
Portions the food, and each his portion shares. ... Od.8.514.290.
In sev'n just portions, pure of hand and heart. ... Od.14.483.59.
Whilst *Eteoneus* portions out the shares, ... Od.15.156.76.
Portions like mine if ev'ry Suitor gave, ... Od.17.490.156.

PORTRAIT
One certain Portrait may (I grant) be seen, ... 3.Ep2.181.64.

PORTRAITURE
Instructive work! whose wry-mouth'd portraiture ... 5.DunA2.137.117.
Instructive work! whose wry-mouth'd portraiture ... 5.DunB2.145.302.

PORTS
Where the ports open, or the shores descend, ... Od.5.535.198.
When thro' the ports of heav'n I pour the day, ... Od.12.448.452.

POS'D
A Thing which *Adam* had been pos'd to name; ... 4.JD4.25.27.

POSITIVE
Some positive persisting Fops we know, ... 1.EOC.568.305.
Each wondrous positive, and wondrous wise; ... 2.ChJM.144.21.
More pert, more proud, more positive than he. ... 4.JD2.52.137.
More pert, more proud, more positive than he. ... 4.JD2A.58.136.

POSSES'D
With pleasing phrenzy has posses'd my mind; ... Od.21.106.264.

POSSESS
Ye sacred Nine! that all my Soul possess, ... 1.W-F.259.173.
And thank the Pow'rs, I may possess alone ... 2.ChJM.264.27.
So keen he was, and eager to possess: ... 2.ChJM.374.32.
For oh, 'twas fix'd, she must possess or die! ... 2.ChJM.493.39.
Vapours and Pride by turns possess her Brain: ... 2.ChWB.89.61.
Soon to obtain, and long possess the Prize: ... 2.RL2.44.162.
Such praise is yours—and such shall you possess, ... 6.38.23.108.
And *Troy* possess her fertile Fields in Peace; ... Il.3.106.194.
And *Troy* possess her fertile Fields in Peace; ... Il.3.327.208.
Possess his Soul, which thus the *Spartan* chears: ... Il.4.221.231.
Now issuing fearless they possess the Plain, ... Il.5.984.314.
Allow'd to seize, but not possess the Prize; ... Il.12.260.90.
Your patrimonial stores in peace possess; ... Od.1.511.56.
The prudent *Greek)* possess the royal mind. ... Od.7.282.249.
Two sister Goddesses possess the plain, ... Od.12.166.440.
Better a friend possess them, than a foe: ... Od.17.93.136.
But blest in her, possess these arms alone, ... Od.21.121.264.
For godless men, and rude, possess the coast: ... Od.24.327.365.

POSSESS'D
All I possess'd I gave to his Command, ... 2.ChWB.331.73.
Dulnes o'er all possess'd her antient right, ... 5.DunA1.9.61.
Dulness o'er all possess'd her ancient right, ... 5.DunB1.11.269.
Ten polish'd Chariots I possess'd at home, ... Il.5.244.279.
Amphius Apæsus' happy Soil possess'd, ... Il.5.760.303.
There long the Chief his happy Lot possess'd, ... Il.6.241.338.
The Helmet next by *Merion* was possess'd, ... Il.10.317.17.
The *Trojan* Lines possess'd the rising Ground. ... Il.11.74.38.
Oh! had I still that Strength my Youth possess'd, ... Il.11.816.72.
These riches are possess'd, but not enjoy'd! ... Od.4.118.125.
(So much the love of home possess'd my heart) ... Od.10.37.341.
With speed to learn what men possess'd the land. ... Od.10.116.346.
Possess'd by wild Barbarians, fierce in arms? ... Od.13.243.17.

POSSESS'D (CONTINUED)
Ev'n these, when of their ill-got spoils possess'd, ... Od.14.107.41.
A Palace, wealth, and slaves, I late possess'd, ... Od.19.94.197.

POSSESSES
Sinks deep within him, and possesses whole, ... 3.Ep3.373.123.

POSSESSING
All then is full, possessing, and possest, ... 2.ElAb.93.327.
Parson, these Things in thy possessing ... 6.39.1.110.

POSSESSION
But be this bright Possession ever mine. ... Il.7.439.386.
Can bribe the poor Possession of a Day! ... Il.9.527.459.
And the possession of a peaceful grave. ... Od.11.90.385.

POSSESSIONS
All vast Possessions (just the same the case ... 4.2HE2.254.183.
With Gifts enrich'd, and with Possessions bless'd. ... Il.9.601.464.
Their wives made captive, their possessions shar'd, ... Od.9.45.304.
Late with such affluence and possessions blest, ... Od.14.140.42.
With large possessions and with faithful wives; ... Od.21.222.270.

POSSEST
Strait with the Rage of all their Race possest, ... 1.TrSt.173.417.
That all the Charms of blooming Youth possest; ... 1.TrSt.671.438.
Possest by wild Barbarians fierce in Arms? ... 1.TrUl.76.468.
At this, the Chief with Transport was possest, ... 1.TrUl.134.470.
Our Grandsire *Adam,* ere of *Eve* possest, ... 2.ChJM.59.17.
Each Nymph by turns his wav'ring Mind possest, ... 2.ChJM.230.25.
His lovely Mistress all his Soul possest, ... 2.ChJM.361.31.
Our gen'rous Knight his gentle Dame possest: ... 2.ChJM.474Z2.38.
For who that once possest those Heav'nly Charms, ... 2.ChJM.573.43.
All then is full, possessing, and possest, ... 2.ElAb.93.327.
But Fortune's gifts if each alike possest, ... 3.EOM4.63.134.
This man possest—five hundred pounds a year. ... 3.Ep3.280.116.
Possest with Muse, and sick with Poetry; ... 4.JD2A.70.138.
OH tyrant Love! hast thou possest ... 6.51ii.1.152.
Some think you mad, some think you are possest ... 6.96iv.35.277.
Who by six such fair Maidens at once is possest. ... 6.122.4.341.
With tame Content, and Thou possest of thine? ... Il.1.168.95.
Spleen to Mankind his envious Heart possest, ... Il.2.267.140.
The topmost Branch a Mother-Bird possest; ... Il.2.376.145.
Cos, where *Eurypylus* possest the Sway, ... Il.2.825.164.
The Nations hear, with rising Hopes possest, ... Il.3.153.198.
In ancient Time the happy Walls possest, ... Il.6.192.335.
Your mighty Monarch these in Peace possest; ... Il.9.436.454.
Not tho' he proffer'd all himself possest; ... Il.9.496.457.
The same which once King *Cinyras* possest: ... Il.11.26.36.
Who *Pleuron's* Walls and *Calydon* possest: ... Il.14.131.164.
The Son of *Peleus* sees, with Joy possest, ... Il.20.491.415.
The Sword, *Asteropeus* possest of old, ... Il.23.951.527.
For Virtue's image yet possest her mind, ... Od.3.332.102.
No *Greek* an equal space had e'er possest ... Od.4.231.130.
In ease possest the wide *Hyperian* plain; ... Od.6.6.203.
Possest by wild barbarians fierce in arms, ... Od.6.141.214.
Possest by wild barbarians fierce in arms, ... Od.8.627.296.
And learn what habitants possest the place? ... Od.9.101.307.
Then thus: O Queen farewell! be still possest ... Od.13.74.4.
At this, the chief with transport was possest, ... Od.13.301.20.
Her ancient * Lord an equal joy possest; ... Od.19.488.220.
You reign, of this imperial dome possest. ... Od.20.402.251.

POSSIBLE
Of Systems possible, if 'tis confest ... 3.EOM1.43.18.
"Get Place and Wealth, if possible, with Grace; ... 4.1HE1.103.287.
And all is possible to heav'n, but this. ... Od.3.294.100.

POST
For me, I'll keep the Post assign'd by Heav'n, ... 2.ChWB.50.59.
His Post neglects, or leaves the Fair at large, ... 2.RL2.124.167.
And talks *Gazettes* and *Post-Boys* o'er by heart. ... 4.JD4.155.39.
Knight of the Post corrupt, or of the Shire, ... 4.Arbu.365.122.
Of Curl's chaste press, and Lintot's rubric post, ... 5.DunA1.38.O64.
First Chetwood lean'd against his letter'd post; ... 5.DunA2.163.121.
First Chapman, lean'd against his letter'd post; ... 5.DunA2.163B.121.
First Osborn, lean'd against his letter'd post; ... 5.DunA2.163C.121.
Of Curl's chaste press, and Lintot's rubric post: ... 5.DunB1.40.273.
First Osborne lean'd against his letter'd post: ... 5.DunB2.171.304.
Than *Ev'ning Post,* or *Observator;* ... 6.10.6.24.
Send it, I pray, by the next Post, ... 6.10.115.28.
Yet they'd resign that Post so high, ... 6.30.40.87.
"Mean Time on every Pissing-Post ... 6.79.141.223.
Thou, from this Tow'r defend th' important Post; ... Il.6.552.354.
The Chief reply'd: That Post shall be my Care, ... Il.6.560.354.
(Each at his Post in Arms) a short Repaste. ... Il.7.455.387.
Fix'd at his Post was each bold *Ajax* found, ... Il.13.171.112.
Each godlike *Ajax* makes that Post his Care, ... Il.13.402.125.
To guard this Post (he cry'd) thy Art employ, ... Il.13.942.150.
Yet scarce an Army stirs him from his Post: ... Il.16.137.243.
Nor yields a Step, nor from his Post retires: ... Il.18.198.331.
To raise our Camp: Too dang'rous here our Post, ... Il.18.301.336.
A post of honour with the sons of Fame: ... Od.8.202.273.
Full many a post have those broad shoulders worn, ... Od.17.256.143.
The bold invader from his post to drive; ... Od.22.90.290.
Each, breathing death, resum'd his dang'rous post ... Od.22.219.297.

POST-BOYS
And talks *Gazettes* and *Post-Boys* o'er by heart. ... 4.JD4.155.39.

POSTERIOR
And now had Fame's posterior Trumpet blown, ... 5.DunB4.71.348.

POSTERITY
Which shall o'er long Posterity prevail: ... 1.TrSt.112A.414.
Think how Posterity will treat thy name; ... 4.HS2.108.61.

POSTERITY (CONTINUED)
And make a long Posterity thy own." ....5.DunB4.334.376.
And late Posterity enjoy the Deed! ....Il.15.589.219.
And sad Posterity repeat the Tale. ....Il.19.66.374.
And late Posterity record our Praise. ....Il.23.309.502.
Heav'n gives Posterity, t'avenge the deed. ....Od.3.241.97.
Shall long posterity resound the praise. ....Od.3.249.97.
To shew posterity *Elpenor* was. ....Od.11.95.385.
And should Posterity one virtuous find, ...Od.11.539.409.
And thus posterity upbraid our name. ....Od.21.356.276.
Then lop thy whole posterity away; ....Od.22.240.298.

POSTING
Old age untimely posting ere his day. ....Od.15.381.88.

POSTPONE
To headless Phœbe his fair bride postpone, ...5.DunB4.367.378.

POSTS
Me, naked me, to Posts, to Pumps they draw, ...4.HAdv.173.89.
Or plaister'd posts, with Claps in capitals? ....4.Arbu.216.111.
Deny'd all Posts of Profit or of Trust: ....4.2HE2.61.169.
And sees superior Posts in meaner Hands. ....Il.13.579.134.
Let the leagu'd Squadrons to their Posts retire. ....Il.23.66.489.
Then posts, capacious of the frame, I raise, ...Od.23.201.333.

POSTURE
Compos'd his Posture, and his Look sedate; ....2.TemF.201.271.
The fallen Chief in suppliant Posture press'd ....Il.6.55.326.

POSTURES
The Champions in distorted Postures threat, ...2.TemF.220.272.

POT
Hist'ry her Pot, Divinity his Pipe, ...5.DunA3.192.173.
Hist'ry her Pot, Divinity his Pipe, ...5.DunB3.196.330.
Hist'ry her Pot, Divinity her Pipe, ...5.DunB3.196A.330.
Put this pot of Wood's mettle ....6.91.21.254.
Put your pot of Wood's mettle ....6.91.21A.254.
To them a piss-pot, but to thee a pond. ....6.96ii.30Z4.271.

POTENT
The silenc'd Preacher yields to potent strain, ...4.2HE1.237.215.
By potent Arthur, knock'd his chin and breast. ....5.DunA2.366.144.
By potent Arthur, knock'd his chin and breast. ....5.DunB2.398.316.
Now drain this goblet, potent to digest: ....Od.9.409.323.
With that, she parted: In her potent hand ....Od.10.457.366.
So rich, so potent, whom you stile your Lord? ....Od.14.139.42.
Potent to punish what he cannot praise. ....Od.19.108.197.

POTHECARIES
So modern *Pothecaries,* taught the Art ....1.EOC.108.251.

POTHER
'Tis yet in vain, I own, to keep a pother ....4.HS2.45.57.
About them both why keep we such a pother? ....6.46.3.127.
About them both why make we such a pother? ....6.46.3A.127.
Thinks he's the Hen, clocks, keeps a Pother, ...6.93.25.257.

POTION
And some have drench'd them with a deadly Potion; ....2.ChWB.409.77.
Pours a large Potion of the *Pramnian* Wine; ....Il.11.781.70.
She mixt the potion, fraudulent of soul; ....Od.10.377.362.

POTS
When *Paxton* gives him double Pots and Pay, ...4.EpS2.141.321.

POULT'RERS
Ye Poult'rers eke, destroy the Breed, ...6.94.47.260.

POULTRY
Fed num'rous Poultry in her Pens, ...6.93.3.256.

POUNC'D
Each fav'rite fowl he pounc'd with deathful sway, ...Od.19.631.227.

POUNCE
Truss'd with his sinewy pounce a trembling dove; ....Od.20.303.247.

POUNCES
His deathful pounces tore a trembling dove; ....Od.15.567.97.

POUND
He thinks a Loaf will rise to fifty pound. ....3.Ep3.118.101.
'Twas very want that sold them for two pound. ....3.Ep3.328.120.
Or should one Pound of Powder less bespread ....4.JD4.246.47.
My Friendship, and a Prologue, and ten Pound. ....4.Arbu.48.99.
"Sir, he's your Slave, for twenty pound a year. ....4.2HE2.8.165.
You pay a Penny, and he paid a Pound. ....4.2HE2.239.181.
Or let it cost five hundred pound, ...4.HS6.39.253.
And find his Honour in a Pound, ...4.HS6.47.253.
Content but for five shillings in the pound, ...4.1740.40.334.
With *Two* or *Three* thousand Pound lost at their Houses, ...6.36.6.104.
Poor *Y[ounge]r's* sold for Fifty Pound, ...6.47.31.129.
For Six-pence, I'd have giv'n a thousand Pound. ....6.96iv.80.278.
Mash all his Bones, and all his Body pound: ....Il.23.778.520.

POUNDS
Because he wants a thousand pounds a year. ....3.EOM4.192.145.
This man possest—five hundred pounds a year. ....3.Ep3.280.116.
Ask'd for a groat, he gives a hundred pounds; ....4.1HE6.86.243.
For life, six hundred pounds a year, ...4.HS6.2.251.
"Pray then what wants he?" fourscore thousand pounds, ...4.1HE1.86.285.
With *Two* or *Three* hundred Pounds lost at their Houses, ...6.36.6A.105.

POUR
Ye Heav'ns! from high the dewy Nectar pour, ...1.Mes.13.114.
And on the sightless Eye-ball pour the Day. ....1.Mes.40.116.
Then foaming pour along, and rush into the *Thames.* ....1.W-F.218.169.
Now pour the Wine; and in your tuneful Lays, ...1.TrSt.827.444.
Excuse the blush, and pour out all the heart, ...2.ElAb.56.323.
Stocks and Subscriptions pour on ev'ry side, ...3.Ep3.370.123.
I love to pour out all myself, as plain ....4.HS1.51.9.
Pour the full Tide of Eloquence along, ...4.2HE2.171.177.
But pour them thickest on the noble head. ....5.DunB4.358.378.
Must want a *Trojan* Slave to pour the Wine. ....Il.2.158.136.
Desert the Ships, and pour upon the Plain. ....Il.2.248.139.
Crete's hundred Cities pour forth all her Sons. ....Il.2.790.162.
The Gates unfolding pour forth all their Train, ...Il.2.978.170.
While round his dauntless Head the *Grecians* pour ....Il.3.113.195.
Pour the full Urn; Then draws the *Grecian* Lord ....Il.3.340.209.
Pour the full Urn; Then drew the *Grecian* Lord ....Il.3.340A.209.
Or pour his Vengeance on the *Lycian* Crew. ....Il.5.831.305.
The Gates unfolding pour forth all their Train; ....Il.8.71.399.
They pour forth Vows their Embassy to bless, ...Il.9.241.444.
And first to *Pallas* the Libations pour: ....Il.10.678.32.
Now at my Knees the *Greeks* shall pour their Moan, ...Il.11.746.68.
So fast the Darts on either Army pour, ...Il.12.179.87.
And pour her Armies o'er our batter'd Wall; ....Il.13.78.108.
Their Force embody'd, in a Tyde they pour; ....Il.13.422.126.
The mingled Tempest on the Foes they pour; ....Il.13.901.148.
Less Loud the Woods, when Flames in Torrents pour, ...Il.14.461.186.
Pour a new Deluge on the *Grecian* Band. ....Il.15.881.230.
Warn'd, he retreats. Then swift from all sides pour ....Il.16.150.243.
Pour from their Mansions by the broad High-way, ...Il.16.315.255.
His Mouth, his Eyes, his Nostrils pour a Flood; ....Il.16.418.259.
Observ'd the Storm of Darts the *Grecians* pour, ...Il.16.430.259.
Thus on retreating *Greece* the *Trojans* pour, ...Il.17.817.320.
Fierce on yon' Navy will we pour our Arms. ....Il.18.354.338.
In its wide Womb they pour the rushing Stream; ....Il.18.409.340.
And pour new Furies on the feebler Foe. ....Il.19.236.382.
And pour in Light on *Pluto's* dear Abodes, ...Il.20.87.397.
The reeking Entrails pour upon the Ground. ....Il.21.196.429.
Charge the black Surge, and pour it on his Head. ....Il.21.365.435.
Pour the red Torrent on the wat'ry Foe, ...Il.21.391.436.
And pour on Heaps into the Walls of *Troy.* ....Il.21.718.451.
And pour to Dogs the Life-blood scarcely warm; ....Il.22.105.457.
Pour forth their Lives, and on the Pyre are thrown. ....Il.23.211.498.
And pour in Tears, e'er yet they close the Urn. ....Il.23.277.501.
His Mouth and Nostrils pour the clotted Gore; ....Il.23.811.521.
Take this, and pour to *Jove:* that safe from Harms, ...Il.24.355.551.
Then pour your boundless Sorrows o'er the Dead. ....Il.24.895.573.
Pour thro' the Gates, and, fell'd from *Ida's* Crown, ...Il.24.991.577.
And pour, above, the consecrated stream. ....Od.3.438.108.
Brought the full laver, o'er their hands to pour, ...Od.3.558.114.
To bathe the Prince, and pour the fragrant oil. ....Od.3.595.117.
And bad the herald pour the rosy wine. ....Od.7.239.248.
Youth, and white age, tumultuous pour along: ....Od.8.50.264.
Spontaneous wines from weighty clusters pour, ...Od.9.125.310.
Before him march, and pour into the rock: ....Od.9.397.322.
To all the shades around libations pour, ...Od.10.616.374.
'Twas mine on *Troy* to pour th' imprison'd war: ....Od.11.642.416.
There o'er my hands the living wave I pour; ....Od.12.397.450.
When thro' the ports of heav'n I pour the day, ...Od.12.448.452.
To pour his wrath on yon luxurious prey; ....Od.15.197.78.
Between the Heroe and the Vessel pour ....Od.15.569.98.
Pour out my soul, and dye within thy arms! ....Od.23.226.333.
And pour at once the torrent of his soul? ....Od.24.278.363.

POUR'D
Pour'd o'er the whitening Vale their fleecy Care, ...1.PSp.19.62.
Or *P[a]ge* pour'd forth the Torrent of his Wit? ....4.EpS2.159.322.
And pour'd her Spirit o'er the land and deep. ....5.DunB1.8.269.
Pour'd forth by Thousands, darkens all the Coast. ....Il.2.110.132.
Pour'd forth in Millions, darkens all the Coast. ....Il.2.110A.132.
Rush to the Vales, and pour'd along the Plain, ...Il.4.518.246.
Thus pour'd his Plaints before th' immortal Throne. ....Il.5.1067.317.
With gentle Hand the Balm he pour'd around, ...Il.5.1110.320.
Each pour'd to *Jove* before the Bowl was crown'd, ...Il.7.576.393.
Pour'd to the Tumult on his whirling Car. ....Il.8.112.403.
And down their Summits pour'd a hundred Rills: ....Il.11.238.46.
And pour'd Libations on the flaming Thighs. ....Il.11.907.76.
Then *Ida's* Summits pour'd their wat'ry Store; ....Il.12.16.82.
Of Sacrifice, the purple Draught he pour'd ....Il.16.282.250.
And pour'd swift Spirits thro' each *Trojan* Breast. ....Il.16.890.277.
The golden Sun pour'd forth a stronger Ray, ...Il.17.430.304.
Pour'd on the Rear, and thunder'd close behind; ....Il.18.190.331.
With his last Hand, and pour'd the Ocean round: ....Il.18.702.357.
Then in the Nostrils of the Slain she pour'd ....Il.19.39.373.
And pour'd divine Ambrosia in his Breast, ...Il.19.375.387.
And like a Deluge pour'd upon the Plain. ....Il.19.379.387.
The rushing Entrails pour'd upon the Ground ....Il.20.483.414.
He pour'd around a Veil of gather'd Air, ...Il.23.233.499.
O'er the broad Ocean pour'd the golden Day: ....Il.23.283.501.
He pour'd his latest Blood in manly Fight, ...Il.24.265.547.
Pour'd the full urns; the youths the goblets crown'd: ....Od.3.434.108.
Pour'd the big sorrows of his swelling heart; ....Od.5.104.177.
'Till *Pallas* pour'd soft slumbers on his eyes; ....Od.5.635.202.
He pour'd a pure libation to the ground. ....Od.8.86.267.
Thrice drain'd, and pour'd the deluge on his soul. ....Od.9.428.323.
And from his eyes pour'd down the tender dew; ....Od.11.486.408.
And pour'd prophanely as the victim burns. ....Od.12.428.451.
Full oft has *Phidon,* whilst he pour'd the wine, ...Od.14.367.53.
Then pour'd of offer'd wine the sable wave: ....Od.14.499.60.
Nor less the father pour'd a social flood; ....Od.16.236.114.
In every sorrowing soul I pour'd delight, ...Od.17.505.157.
The tears pour'd down amain: And oh, she cries, ...Od.23.215.333.
Pour'd forth the darts, that thirsted for our blood, ...Od.24.204.358.
With dreadful shouts *Ulysses* pour'd along, ...Od.24.620.377.

POURING
That driv'n by Storms, and pouring o'er the Plain, ...1.TrSt.514.432.
Then pouring after, thro' the gaping Space ....1.TrES.205.457.
But clear and artless, pouring thro' the plain ....3.Ep3.257.114.
Now Foes on Foes came pouring on the Fields, ...Il.5.772.303.
The *Greeks* all fled, the Trojans pouring on: ....Il.11.510.56.
Then pouring after thro' the gaping Space, ...Il.12.559.102.
Jove, pouring Darkness o'er the mingled Fight, ...Il.17.318.300.
He heard, he took, and pouring down his throat ....Od.9.417.323.
And pouring down the mountains, crowd the shore. ....Od.10.138.347.

POURS
From whose dark Womb a ratling Tempest pours, ...1.TrSt.494.431.
Then down on Earth a ratling Tempest pours, ...1.TrSt.494A.431.
The *Baron* now his *Diamonds* pours apace; ....2.RL3.75.173.
Pours fierce Ambition in a Cæsar's mind, ...3.EOM1.159.35.
And pours it all upon the peccant part. ....3.EOM2.144.72.
Is it for thee the linnet pours his throat? ....3.EOM3.33.95.
Or pours profuse on earth; one nature feeds ....3.EOM3.117.104.
It pours the bliss that fills up all the mind. ....3.EOM4.344.162.
And pours each human Virtue in the heart. ....4.2HE1.220.213.
Or that, where on her Curlls the Public pours ....5.DunA2.3.97.
Pours forth, and leaves unpeopled half the land; ....5.DunA2.16.98.
Thro' half the heav'ns he pours th' exalted urn; ....5.DunA2.175.122.
Pours into Thames: Each city-bowl is full ....5.DunA2.319.140.
The North by myriads pours her mighty sons, ...5.DunA3.81.157.
Or that where on her Curls the Public pours, ...5.DunB2.3.296.
Pours forth, and leaves unpeopled half the land. ....5.DunB2.20.297.
Thro' half the heav'ns he pours th' exalted urn; ....5.DunB2.183.304.
Pours into Thames: and hence the mingled wave ....5.DunB2.343.314.
The North by myriads pours her mighty sons, ...5.DunB3.89.324.
Pours at great Bourbon's feet her silken sons; ....5.DunB4.298.373.
And pours her Spirit o'er the Land and Deep. ....5.DunB4.627Z2.407.
Pours Balm into the bleeding *Lover's* Wounds: ....6.11.29.30.
Pours Balm into the *Lover's* Wounds: ....6.11.29A.30.
Pours the black Wine, and sees the Flames aspire; ....Il.1.608.117.
Styx pours them forth, the dreadful Oath of Gods! ....Il.2.915.167.
Pours on the Rear, or lightens in their Face. ....Il.5.115.272.
Pours on the *Greeks:* The *Trojan* Troops pursue: ....Il.5.723.302.
The Storm of hissing Javelins pours behind. ....Il.8.193.406.
And pours her Heroes thro' a hundred Gates, ...Il.9.503.458.
On the black Body of the Foes he pours: ....Il.11.383.51.
Pours from the Mountains o'er the delug'd Plains, ...Il.11.615.61.
Pours a large Potion of the *Pramnian* Wine; ....Il.11.781.70.
Incessant Cataracts the Thund'rer pours, ...Il.12.27.82.
Then pours the silent Tempest, thick, and deep: ....Il.12.336.93.
The Blood pours back, and fortifies my Heart: ....Il.13.112.110.
Here first she bathes; and round her Body pours ....Il.14.197.168.
Glad Earth perceives, and from her Bosom pours ....Il.14.395.181.
Breaks from his Stall, and pours along the Ground; ....Il.15.299.208.
Pours new Destruction on her Sons again? ....Il.15.329.210.
Impending *Phœbus* pours around 'em Fear, ...Il.15.370.211.
Than when in Autumn *Jove* his Fury pours, ...Il.16.466.260.
O'er the fierce Armies pours pernicious Night, ...Il.16.696.271.
Meanwhile *Patroclus* pours along the Plains, ...Il.16.837.276.
And breathing Slaughter, pours amid the Foes. ....Il.16.947.280.
Troy pours along, and this way rolls our Fate. ....Il.17.800.319.
Pours unavailing Sorrows o'er the Dead. ....Il.18.278.335.
In Molds prepar'd, the glowing Ore he pours. ....Il.18.446.342.
Now thro' each *Trojan* Heart he Fury pours ....Il.20.71.396.
The panting Liver pours a Flood of Gore, ...Il.20.545.417.
Around him wide, immense Destruction pours, ...Il.20.575.418.
Wide o'er the Plain he pours the boundless Blaze; ....Il.21.399.436.
On the mid Pavement pours the rosy Wine, ...Il.24.375.551.
And pours deep Slumber on their watchful Eyes: ....Il.24.548.559.
Thro' Desarts wild now pours a weeping Rill; ....Il.24.774.569.
And pours the wine, and bids the flames aspire: ....Od.3.588.116.
And ev'ry fountain pours a sev'ral rill, ...Od.5.91.176.
And o'er the silver pours the fusile gold. ....Od.6.278.224.
Here a rich juice the royal vineyard pours; ....Od.6.355.229.
The water pours; the bubling waters boil: ....Od.10.424.365.
He pours his wat'ry store, the Virgin burns; ....Od.11.284.396.
Pours out deep groans; (with groans all hell resounds) ....Od.11.720.421.
Thro' heav'n's bright portals pours the beamy day. ....Od.12.6.430.
Each from his seat to each Immortal pours, ...Od.13.70.4.
Eumæus pours on high the purple tide; ....Od.14.135.42.
The driving storm the wat'ry west-wind pours, ...Od.14.512.62.
Then to the Gods the rosy juice he pours, ...Od.18.179.175.
She pours a pleasing, deep, and deathlike rest, ...Od.18.222.177.
Each Peer successive his libation pours ....Od.18.470.191.

POVERTY
And all is *splendid Poverty* at best. ....4.JD4.225.45.
He stuck to Poverty with Peace of Mind; ....4.2HE2.65.169.
Scar'd at the spectre of pale Poverty! ....4.1HE1.70.283.
The cave of Poverty and Poetry. ....5.DunA1.32.O64.
The Cave of Poverty and Poetry. ....5.DunB1.34.272.
Live but on what thy poverty bestows. ....Od.15.531.95.
And Poverty look'd smiling in my sight. ....Od.17.506.157.
The gripes of poverty, and stings of care. ....Od.18.150.173.
This garb of Poverty belies the King; ....Od.23.116.325.

POW'R
You, that too wise for Pride, too Good for Pow'r, ...1.PSp.7.61.
O were I made by some transforming Pow'r, ...1.PSu.45.75.
What Eyes but hers, alas, have Pow'r to move! ....1.PAu.83.86.
What Eyes but hers, alas, have Pow'r on me! ....1.PAu.83A.86.
But fix'd *His* Word, *His* saving Pow'r remains: ....1.Mes.107.122.
The solid Pow'r of *Understanding* fails; ....1.EOC.57.245.
The Pow'r of Musick all our Hearts allow; ....1.EOC.382.284.
No Sigh to rise, no Tear had pow'r to flow; ....1.TrSP.127.399.
While Discord waits upon divided Pow'r. ....1.TrSt.183.418.
Pleas'd to behold unbounded Pow'r thy own, ...1.TrSt.222.419.
No more let Mortals *Juno's* Pow'r invoke, ...1.TrSt.370.425.
By turns on each Celestial Pow'r they call; ....1.TrSt.650.437.
For not the vengeful Pow'r, that glow'd with Rage, ...1.TrSt.782.442.

POW'R (CONTINUED)
Propitious hear our Pray'r, O Pow'r Divine! ....1.TrSt.855.445.
Sacred to *Phorcys'* Pow'r, whose Name it bears; ....1.TrUl.26.466.
But He the Pow'r, to whose All-seeing Eyes ....1.TrUl.88.469.
Restless he sate, invoking ev'ry Pow'r ....2.ChJM.351.31.
Or did from Change, or Nature's Pow'r proceed, ...2.ChJM.427.35.
From thy dear Side I have no Pow'r to part, ...2.ChJM.571.42.
Did I for this the Pow'r of Magick prove? ....2.ChJM.764.52.
Propitious Heav'n, and ev'ry Pow'r ador'd, ...2.RL2.36.161.
Th' expressive Emblem of their softer Pow'r; ....2.RL3.40.171.
Amaz'd, confus'd, he found his Pow'r expir'd, ...2.RL3.145.179.
Then thus addrest the Pow'r—Hail wayward Queen! ....2.RL4.57.188.
A Nymph there is, that all thy Pow'r disdains, ...2.RL4.65.189.
What then remains, but well our Pow'r to use, ...2.RL5.29.201.
Of *Talismans* and *Sigils* knew the Pow'r, ...2.TemF.105.261.
With boundless Pow'r unbounded Virtue join'd, ...2.TemF.166.268.
This having heard and seen, some Pow'r unknown ....2.TemF.418.283.
Nor foes nor fortune take this pow'r away. ....2.ElAb.43.322.
"For me kind Nature wakes her genial pow'r, ...3.EOM1.133.32.
Safe in the hand of one disposing Pow'r, ...3.EOM1.287.50.
Reason itself but gives it edge and pow'r; ....3.EOM2.147.72.
A mightier Pow'r the strong direction sends, ...3.EOM2.165.74.
Let pow'r or knowledge, gold or glory, please, ...3.EOM2.169.75.
Know, all enjoy that pow'r which suits them best; ....3.EOM3.80.100.
To Pow'r unseen, and mightier far than they: ....3.EOM3.252.118.
To one Man's pow'r, ambition, lucre, lust: ....3.EOM3.270.120.
"No—shall the good want Health, the good want Pow'r?" ....3.EOM4.158.143.
Add Health and Pow'r, and ev'ry earthly thing; ....3.EOM4.159.143.
"Why bounded Pow'r? why private? why no king?" ....3.EOM4.160.143.
Immense that pow'r, immense were the demand; ....3.EOM4.165.143.
"In pow'r your Servant, out of pow'r your Friend." ....3.Ep1.161Z2.29.
"In pow'r your Servant, out of pow'r your Friend." ....3.Ep1.161Z2.29.
We prize the stronger effort of his pow'r, ...3.Ep1.99.22.
Is he a Churchman? then he's fond of pow'r: ....3.Ep1.107.23.
By Spirit robb'd of Pow'r, by Warmth of Friends, ...3.Ep2.144.62.
Pow'r all their end, but Beauty all the means. ....3.Ep2.220.68.
That POW'R who bids the Ocean ebb and flow, ...3.Ep3.166.107.
"What all so wish, but want the pow'r to do! ....3.Ep3.276.116.
His only daughter in a stranger's pow'r, ...3.Ep3.325.120.
Its proper Pow'r to hurt, each Creature feels, ...4.HS1.85.13.
Seiz'd in the Fact, and in her Cuckold's Pow'r, ...4.HAdv.171.89.
And to be grave, exceeds all Pow'r of Face. ....4.Arbu.36.98.
Adds to Christ's prayer, the *Pow'r and Glory* clause. ....4.JD2.108.143.
Estates have wings, and hang in Fortune's pow'r ....4.2HE2.248.183.
Is known alone to that Directing Pow'r, ...4.2HE2.278.185.
In Pow'r, Wit, Figure, Virtue, Fortune, plac'd ....4.2HE2.302.187.
As wild and mad? the Avarice of Pow'r? ....4.2HE2.307.187.
Grac'd as thou art, with all the Pow'r of Words, ...4.1HE6.48.239.
But if to Pow'r and Place your Passion lye, ...4.1HE6.97.243.
But show me one, who has it in his pow'r ....4.1HE1.136.289.
Of Social Pleasure, ill-exchang'd for Pow'r; ....4.EpS1.30.300.
In Soldier, Churchman, Patriot, Man in Pow'r, ...4.EpS1.161.309.
No Pow'r the Muse's Friendship can command; ....4.EpS2.118.320.
No Pow'r, when Virtue claims it, can withstand: ....4.EpS2.119.320.
[*In Pow'r a Servant, out of Pow'r a Friend.*] ....4.EpS2.161.322.
[*In Pow'r a Servant, out of Pow'r a Friend.*] ....4.EpS2.161.322.
And antedates the hatred due to Pow'r. ....4.1740.8.332.
From thy Bæotia tho' Her Pow'r retires, ...5.DunA1.23.62.
And learn, my sons, the wond'rous pow'r of Noise. ....5.DunA2.214.127.
Sleep's all-subduing pow'r who dares defy, ...5.DunA2.341A.142.
"What pow'r," he cries, "what pow'r these wonders wrought?" .5.DunA3.246.178.
"What pow'r," he cries, "what pow'r these wonders wrought?" .5.DunA3.246.178.
She comes! the Cloud-compelling Pow'r, behold! ....5.DunA3.337.192.
Let there be darkness! (the dread pow'r shall say) ....5.DunA3.337Z1.192.
From thy Bœotia tho' her Pow'r retires, ...5.DunB1.25.271.
And learn, my sons, the wond'rous pow'r of Noise. ....5.DunB2.222.306.
"What pow'r, he cries, what pow'r these wonders wrought' ....5.DunB3.250.332.
"What pow'r, he cries, what pow'r these wonders wrought' ....5.DunB3.250.332.
Roll in her Vortex, and her pow'r confess. ....5.DunB4.84.349.
Narcissus, prais'd with all a Parson's pow'r, ...5.DunB4.103.351.
Each with some wond'rous gift approach'd the Pow'r, ...5.DunB4.399.381.
Resistless falls: The Muse obeys the Pow'r. ....5.DunB4.628.407.
To bright *Cecilia* greater Pow'r is giv'n; ....6.11.132.34.
And boundless pow'r with boundless virtue join'd; ....6.20.47.67.
The world no longer trembles at their pow'r! ....6.22.15.71.
Still, when the lust of tyrant pow'r succeeds, ...6.51i.31.152.
Sees his past days safe out of fortune's pow'r, ...6.55.3.166.
He sees past days safe out of fortune's pow'r, ...6.55.3A.166.
The Rage of Pow'r, the Blast of publick Breath, ...6.84.25.239.
Say first what Cause? That Pow'r here 6.155.8Z1.404*
Sprung the fierce Strife, from what offended Pow'r? ....Il.1.10.85.
Thou Guardian Pow'r of *Cilla* the Divine, ...Il.1.54.88.
Thus *Chryses* pray'd: the fav'ring Pow'r attends, ...Il.1.61.88.
Of sure Protection by thy Pow'r and Sword. ....Il.1.100.92.
Fond of the Pow'r, but fonder of the Prize! ....Il.1.156.95.
To Pow'r superior none such Hatred bear: ....Il.1.230.98.
Thou stood'st a Rival of Imperial Pow'r; ....Il.1.248.98.
For I pronounce (and trust a heav'nly Pow'r) ....Il.1.281.100.
From whom the Pow'r of Laws and Justice springs: ....Il.1.315.103.
Let Kings be just, and Sov'reign Pow'r preside. ....Il.1.365.105.
T'avert the Vengeance of the Pow'r Divine; ....Il.1.501.112.
But dread the Pow'r of this avenging Hand; ....Il.1.733.122.
The gracious Pow'r is willing to be pleas'd. ....Il.1.751.123.
And scarce ensure the wretched Pow'r to fly. ....Il.2.164.136.
That Wretch, too mean to fall by martial Pow'r, ...Il.2.468.149.
In secret own'd resistless Beauty's Pow'r: ....Il.3.204.201.
O first and greatest Pow'r! whom all obey, ...Il.3.346.209.
Obey the Pow'r from whom thy Glories rise: ....Il.3.514.216.
This Day the Foe prevail'd by *Pallas'* Pow'r; ....Il.3.545.217.
Of Pow'r superior why should I complain? ....Il.4.81.224.
The Pow'r descending, and the Heav'ns on Fire! ....Il.4.110.225.
The Gods forget not, nor thy Guardian Pow'r. ....Il.4.159.228.
Inclos'd by both, nor left the Pow'r to fly: ....Il.4.345.237.
Discord! dire Sister of the slaught'ring Pow'r, ...Il.4.502.244.
Stern Pow'r of War! by whom the Mighty fall, ...Il.5.39.267.
When thus the King his Guardian Pow'r addrest, ...Il.5.144.274.

POW'R (CONTINUED)

Ev'n Hell's grim King *Alcides;* Pow'r confest, ... Il.5.485.291.
Know thou, whoe'er with heav'nly Pow'r contends, ... Il.5.495.291.
Stern Pow'r of Arms! by whom the Mighty fall, ... Il.5.553.295.
Mad, furious Pow'r! whose unrelenting Mind ..... Il.5.948.312.
The vig'rous Pow'r the trembling Car ascends, ... Il.5.1030.315.
In vain our Threats, in vain our Pow'r we use; ..... Il.5.1102.319.
Unbar the sacred Gates; and seek the Pow'r ..... Il.6.111.329.
If so the Pow'r, atton'd by fervent Pray'r, ... Il.6.117.329.
Now blest by ev'ry Pow'r who guards the Good, ... Il.6.211.336.
Com'st thou to supplicate th' Almighty Pow'r, ... Il.6.320.342.
So may the Pow'r, atton'd by fervent Pray'r, ... Il.6.344.343.
While these appear before the Pow'r with Pray'rs, ... Il.6.388.345.
Thy Pow'r in War with Justice none contest; ..... Il.6.668.360.
What Mortals henceforth shall our Pow'r adore, ... Il.7.530.391.
Thy Pow'r is honour'd, and thy Fame shall last. ..... Il.7.549.392.
At length his Best-belov'd, the Pow'r of *Wisdom,* spoke. ..... Il.8.38.397.
When *Greece* shall conquer by his heav'nly Pow'r. ..... Il.8.174.406.
Yet *Ægæ, Helicè,* thy Pow'r obey, ... Il.8.246.409.
Ungrateful Prospect to the sullen Pow'r! ..... Il.8.253.409.
With Pow'r immense, with Justice arm'd in vain; ..... Il.8.284.410.
What Pow'r Divine shall *Hector's* Wrath asswage? ..... Il.8.431.417.
The vig'rous Pow'r the trembling Car ascends; ..... Il.8.472.419.
But know, whoe'er Almighty Pow'r withstand! ..... Il.8.560.423.
What Pow'r soe'er provokes our lifted Hand, ... Il.8.567.423.
The noblest Pow'r that might the World controul ..... Il.9.55.434.
There shall he reign with Pow'r and Justice crown'd, ... Il.9.205.442.
There shalt thou reign with Pow'r and Justice crown'd, ... Il.9.392.452.
As when by Light'nings *Jove's* Ætherial Pow'r ..... Il.10.5.2.
Swift to the *Trojan* Camp descends the Pow'r, ... Il.10.606.29.
And oft' that partial Pow'r has lent his Aid. ..... Il.11.468.54.
Her hosts shall sink, nor his the Pow'r to aid? ..... Il.11.901.75.
So *Greece* shall stoop before our conqu'ring Pow'r, ... Il.12.91.84.
What Man could doubt but Troy's victorious Pow'r ..... Il.12.187.88.
But tends to raise that Pow'r which I obey. ..... Il.12.252.90.
And rouze, with Flame divine, the *Grecian* Pow'r. ..... Il.12.314.93.
If yet some heav'nly Pow'r your Breast excite, ... Il.13.83.108.
Such, and so swift, the Pow'r of Ocean flew; ..... Il.13.95.109.
Short as he turn'd, I saw the Pow'r appear: ..... Il.13.102.109.
But breathe new Courage as they feel the Pow'r: ..... Il.13.124.110.
Stand, and my Spear shall rout their scatt'ring Pow'r, ... Il.13.207.115.
Cassandra's Love he sought with Boasts of Pow'r, ... Il.13.461.128.
Not *Jove* himself, upon the Past has pow'r. ..... Il.14.62.160.
At length she trusts her Pow'r; resolv'd to prove ..... Il.14.187.168.
Safe from Access of each intruding Pow'r. ..... Il.14.194.168.
That Pow'r, which Mortals and Immortals warms, ... Il.14.226.172.
O Pow'r of Slumbers! hear, and favour still. ..... Il.14.269.175.
Imperial Dame (the balmy Pow'r replies) ..... Il.14.276.175.
Wait under *Ide:* Of thy superior Pow'r ..... Il.14.351.179.
At length with Love and Sleep's soft Pow'r oppress, ... Il.14.405.183.
Thus having said, the Pow'r of Slumber flew, ... Il.14.417.183.
Clad in his Might th' Earth-shaking Pow'r appears; ..... Il.14.447.185.
Our Pow'r immense, and brave th' Almighty Hand? ..... Il.15.22.194.
Fierce in the Majesty of Pow'r controuls, ... Il.15.118.201.
Strives he with me, by whom his Pow'r was giv'n, ... Il.15.188.203.
Striv'st thou with him, by whom all Pow'r is giv'n? ..... Il.15.204.204.
Ev'n Pow'r immense had found such Battel hard. ..... Il.15.257.207.
On all sides batter'd, yet resists his Pow'r: ..... Il.15.745.224.
I made him Tyrant; gave him Pow'r to wrong ..... Il.16.74.238.
Now *Troy* had stoop'd beneath his matchless Pow'r, ... Il.16.857.276.
The Pow'r conceal'd, and thus to *Hector* cries. ..... Il.17.389.302.
And shall not I, the second Pow'r above, ... Il.18.427.341.
To right with Justice, whom with Pow'r they wrong'd. ..... Il.19.182.379.
Witness thou First! thou greatest Pow'r above! ..... Il.19.267.383.
Not one was absent; not a Rural Pow'r ..... Il.20.11.393.
'Tis true (the Cloud-compelling Pow'r replies) ..... Il.20.29.394.
In Voice and Aspect, seem'd the Pow'r divine; ..... Il.20.114.398.
Were God my Aid, this Arm should check his Pow'r, ... Il.20.132.399.
Our favour'd Hero, let some Pow'r descend. ..... Il.20.151.400.
He, Source of Pow'r and Might! with boundless Sway, ... Il.20.292.406.
What Pow'r, O Prince, with Force inferior far, ... Il.20.381.411.
If any Pow'r assist *Achilles'* Hand. ..... Il.20.522.416.
What Means divine may yet the Pow'r employ, ... Il.21.153.427.
No Pow'r t'avert his miserable End? ..... Il.21.314.434.
The Pow'r of Ocean first. Forbear thy Fear, ... Il.21.332.435.
Go, mighty in thy Rage! display thy Pow'r, ... Il.21.394.436.
The Pow'r Ignipotent her Word obeys: ..... Il.21.398.436.
O *Vulcan,* oh! what Pow'r resists thy Might? ..... Il.21.418.437.
The Pow'r of Battels lifts his brazen Spear, ... Il.21.456.440.
And from the Senior Pow'r, submiss retires; ..... Il.21.544.444.
Thy Force can match the great Earth-shaking Pow'r. ..... Il.21.552.444.
(The Pow'r confest in all his Glory burns) ..... Il.22.14.453.
Endu'd his Knees with strength, his Nerves with Pow'r: ..... Il.22.266.466.
Collect thy Soul, and call forth all thy Pow'r. ..... Il.22.344.470.
Nor pierc'd the Windpipe yet, nor took the Pow'r ..... Il.22.411.472.
While cast to all the Rage of hostile Pow'r, ... Il.22.423.473.
Thee first in Virtue, as in Pow'r supreme, ... Il.23.1054.533.
O snatch the Moments yet within thy Pow'r, ... Il.24.167.542.
Your sole Defence, your guardian Pow'r is gone! ..... Il.24.304.549.
(Libation destin'd to the Pow'r divine) ..... Il.24.352.550.
Uplifts his Eyes, and calls the Pow'r divine. ..... Il.24.376.551.
The Pow'r that mediates between Gods and Men) ..... Il.24.502.557.
My Son forgot not, in exalted Pow'r; ..... Il.24.522.558.
This *Hermes* (such the Pow'r of Gods) set wide; ..... Il.24.561.559.
Who more than *Peleus* shone in Wealth and Pow'r? ..... Il.24.673.565.
The Pow'r descending hover'd o'er his Head: ..... Il.24.850.572.
The source of pow'r on earth deriv'd to Kings! ..... Od.1.58.33.
With frequent rites, and pure, avow'd thy pow'r, ... Od.1.81.35.
Who crowd his palace, and with lawless pow'r ..... Od.1.116.37.
But still the frown of some cælestial pow'r ..... Od.1.253.45.
Shou'd factious pow'r dispute my lineal right, ... Od.1.504.56.
Your private right shou'd impious pow'r invade, ... Od.1.513.56.
Or having pow'r to wrong, betray'd the will; ..... Od.2.80.64.
(A sacred oath) if heav'n the pow'r supply, ... Od.2.169.70.
Be mild in pow'r, or faithful to his trust! ..... Od.2.262.74.
My pow'r shall guard thee, and my hand convey: ..... Od.2.324.77.

POW'R (CONTINUED)

Not first, the Pow'r of Wisdom march'd before, ... Od.3.16.87.
And others, dictated by heav'nly pow'r, ... Od.3.35.87.
We sought direction of the pow'r divine: ..... Od.3.209.96.
Forgetful youth! but know, the Pow'r above ..... Od.3.285.100.
In honour's limits (such the pow'r of Song) ..... Od.3.337.103.
The King himself initiates to the Pow'r; ..... Od.3.564.115.
With double vows invoking *Hymen's* pow'r, ... Od.4.5.119.
Nor sleep's soft pow'r can close my streaming eyes, ... Od.4.135.126.
Affianc'd in your friendly pow'r alone, ... Od.4.223.130.
Some envious pow'r the blissful scene destroys; ..... Od.4.245.131.
With pow'r congenial join'd, propitious aid ..... Od.4.459.142.
Some heav'nly pow'r averse my stay constrains: ..... Od.4.512.144.
What pow'r becalms th' innavigable seas? ..... Od.4.515.145.
But the bright sea-maid's gentle pow'r implor'd, ... Od.4.599.148.
Vain efforts! with superior pow'r compress'd, ... Od.4.623.149.
What vows repentant will the Pow'r appease, ... Od.4.633.149.
The pow'r defrauding who vouchsaf'd to save. ..... Od.4.676.151.
A pledge the sceptred pow'r of *Sidon* gave, ... Od.4.837.158.
With him, the peerage next in pow'r to you: ..... Od.4.876.159.
Of nobles, and invite a foreign pow'r? ..... Od.4.891.160.
Or in their tyrant-Minions vest the pow'r: ..... Od.4.919.161.
And to their pow'r to save his race appeal. ..... Od.4.979.163.
His wish'd return with happy pow'r befriend, ... Od.4.1011.164.
Her heroe's danger touch'd the pitying Pow'r, ... Od.5.10.171.
What words are these (reply'd the Pow'r who forms ..... Od.5.30.172.
What pow'r so great, to dare to disobey? ..... Od.5.130.178.
With conquest proud, inces'd *Minerva's* pow'r: ..... Od.5.136.178.
To her, the Pow'r who bears the charming rod. ..... Od.5.185.180.
(Unequal contest) not his rage and pow'r, ... Od.5.432.193.
Now, scarce withdrawn the fierce Earth-shaking pow'r, ... Od.5.488.195.
But all-subduing *Pallas* lent her pow'r, ... Od.5.556.199.
Nor here the sun's meridian rays had pow'r, ... Od.5.620.201.
The same her parents, and her pow'r the same. ..... Od.7.71.237.
Who now by *Neptune's* am'rous pow'r comprest, ... Od.7.78.237.
And still to live, beyond the pow'r of years. ..... Od.7.123.240.
Gracious approach us some immortal pow'r; ..... Od.7.266.248.
Enough the feast has pleas'd, enough the pow'r ..... Od.8.95.267.
(Inextricably firm) the pow'r to fly: ..... Od.8.342.282.
But there remain, ye guilty, in my pow'r, ... Od.8.357.282.
Where to the pow'r an hundred altars rise, ... Od.8.397.285.
O'er whom supreme, imperial pow'r I bear: ..... Od.8.426.286.
Of some fell monster, fierce with barb'rous pow'r, ... Od.9.249.317.
And learn, our pow'r proceeds with thee and thine, ... Od.9.331.320.
When all thy wretched crew have felt my pow'r, ... Od.9.437.324.
Of sleep, oppress thee, or by fraud or pow'r? ..... Od.9.482.325.
Of sleep, oppresses me with fraudful pow'r. ..... Od.9.486.326.
And wou'd but Fate the pow'r of speech afford! ..... Od.9.536.328.
His pow'r can heal me, and re-light my eye; ..... Od.9.609.331.
Some pow'r divine who pities human woe ..... Od.10.182.349.
Where dwelt th' enchantress skill'd in herbs of pow'r; ..... Od.10.328.360.
And shew'd its nature and its wond'rous pow'r: ..... Od.10.363.362.
Forget whatever was in Fortune's pow'r, ... Od.10.544.369.
Thy fated road (the magic Pow'r reply'd) ..... Od.10.598.372.
A freshning breeze the * Magic pow'r supply'd, ... Od.11.7.379.
The victims, vow'd to each *Tartarean* pow'r, ... Od.11.25.380.
O say what angry pow'r *Elpenor* led ..... Od.11.71.383.
But home return'd, to each ætherial pow'r ..... Od.11.162.389.
O worthy of the pow'r the Gods assign'd, ... Od.11.470.407.
In act to speak the * Pow'r of magic stands, ... Od.12.27.430.
O Prince attend! some fav'ring pow'r be kind, ... Od.12.49.431.
Goddess divine, my guardian pow'r, declare, ... Od.12.140.439.
To whom the thund'ring Pow'r: O source of day! ..... Od.12.452.453.
To *Jove* th' Eternal, (pow'r above all pow'rs! ..... Od.13.29.2.
Sacred to *Phorcys'* pow'r, whose name it bears: ..... Od.13.117.7.
The rights and honours of a pow'r divine? ..... Od.13.149.12.
If that low race offend thy pow'r divine, ... Od.13.168.13.
But he, the Pow'r to whose all-seeing eyes ..... Od.13.255.18.
And witness ev'ry houshold pow'r that waits ..... Od.14.184.44.
Now turn thy thought, and joys within our pow'r. ..... Od.14.193.45.
And witness every pow'r that rules the sky! ..... Od.14.435.56.
And suppliant stands, invoking every pow'r ..... Od.14.470.58.
All pow'r is his, and whatsoe'er he wills ..... Od.14.496.60.
Observe the warnings of a pow'r divine: ..... Od.15.32.71.
By that dread pow'r to whom thy vows are paid; ..... Od.15.284.82.
Lives, but implores of ev'ry pow'r to lay ..... Od.15.376.87.
Live to base insolence of pow'r a slave. ..... Od.16.96.107.
Or are thy brothers, who should aid thy pow'r, ... Od.16.101.107.
Nor are my brothers who should aid my pow'r ..... Od.16.121.108.
The Queen averse to love, yet aw'd by pow'r, ... Od.16.135.109.
Of pow'r divine, and howling, trembling fled. ..... Od.16.177.112.
To combat by thy side, thy guardian pow'r. ..... Od.16.185.112.
To win thy grace: O save us, pow'r divine! ..... Od.16.203.113.
With grace divine; her pow'r admits no bounds: ..... Od.16.229.114.
Once more attend: When *she whose pow'r inspires ..... Od.16.302.120.
My will may covet, but my pow'r denies. ..... Od.17.15.133.
With pow'r congenial joyn'd, propitious aid ..... Od.17.150.139.
In lasting safety from the father's pow'r. ..... Od.17.303.146.
To-day with pow'r elate, in strength he blooms; ..... Od.18.159.174.
The haughty creature on that pow'r presumes: ..... Od.18.160.174.
Proud of the pow'r that to high birth belongs; ..... Od.18.167.174.
And us'd that pow'r to justify my wrongs. ..... Od.18.168.175.
O may'st thou, favour'd by some guardian pow'r, ... Od.18.175.175.
And bless the Pow'r that still delights to bless. ..... Od.19.136.199.
This art, instinct by some cœlestial pow'r, ... Od.19.160.200.
High schemes of pow'r in just succession roul.) ..... Od.19.326.210.
By *Jove,* the source of good, supreme in pow'r! ..... Od.19.347.211.
There oft implor'd his tutelary pow'r, ... Od.19.430.215.
Upbraids thy pow'r, thy wisdom, or thy will: ..... Od.20.258.245.
This sacred truth attest each genial pow'r, ... Od.20.287.247.
No more ye lewd Compeers, with lawless pow'r ..... Od.20.378.251.
Her equal pow'r each faithful sense obeys. ..... Od.20.440.254.
Each pow'r above, with wishes for his Lord. ..... Od.21.210.270.
Tears follow'd tears; no word was in their pow'r, ... Od.21.236.271.
Has pow'r this bow to grant, or to deny. ..... Od.21.372.277.
Again made frustrate by the virgin pow'r. ..... Od.22.301.301.

POW'R (CONTINUED)
And oh my Queen! he cries; what pow'r above ... Od.23.165.328.
The spells of *Circe,* and her magic pow'r; ... Od.23.346.341.
Oh Pow'r supreme, oh ruler of the whole! ... Od.24.543.374.
And tells the news. They arm with all their pow'r. ... Od.24.571.375.

POW'R'S
Taught Pow'r's due use to People and to Kings, ... 3.EOM3.289.121.

POW'RFUL
The moving Mountains hear the pow'rful Call, ... 1.PSu.83.79.
Thy Charms than those may far more pow'rful be, ... 1.TrSP.220.403.
The Force of pow'rful Union conquers All. ... 1.TrES.150.455.
By Vertue of this pow'rful Constellation, ... 2.ChWB.327.72.
Men prove with Child, as pow'rful Fancy works, ... 2.RL4.53.188.
Grant that the pow'rful still the weak controul, ... 3.EOM3.49.97.
More pow'rful each as needful to the rest, ... 3.EOM3.299.123.
Must act on Reasons pow'rful, tho' unknown: ... 3.Ep3.114A.101.
Must act on motives pow'rful, tho' unknown: ... 3.Ep3.114.101.
Now seek some skilful Hand whose pow'rful Art ... Il.4.228.232.
Greece in our Cause shall arm some pow'rful Hand. ... Il.7.134.370.
The Force of pow'rful Union conquers all. ... Il.12.504.100.
'Tis Heav'n, alas! and *Jove's* all-pow'rful Doom, ... Il.13.295.119.
The pow'rful *Cestus* to her snowy Breast. ... Il.14.256.173.
Warn'd by the Words, to pow'rful *Jove* I yield, ... Il.15.232.206.
He comes not, *Jove!* without thy pow'rful Will; ... Il.15.330.210.
The Voice is pow'rful of a faithful Friend. ... Il.15.467.215.
Pow'rful alike to ease the Wretche's Smart; ... Il.16.635.269.
Against what Fate and pow'rful *Jove* ordain, ... Il.16.841.276.
Pow'rful of Godhead, and of Fraud Divine: ... Il.22.28.453.
Since now at length the pow'rful Will of Heav'n ... Il.22.475.475.
Think from some pow'rful Foe thou see'st him fly, ... Il.24.606.562.
Our foes are pow'rful, and your sons the foes: ... Od.2.56.63.
More pow'rful advocates than vain complaints. ... Od.2.68.64.
By *Hermes* pow'rful with the wand of gold) ... Od.10.392.363.
She spake, then touch'd him with her pow'rful wand: ... Od.13.496.29.
No pow'rful hands are there, no watchful eyes: ... Od.15.103.73.
Whose pow'rful friends the luckless deed pursue ... Od.15.299.83.
Pow'rful of charms, bid ev'ry grace attend; ... Od.18.204.176.
Him, if this arm be pow'rful, shall I slay? ... Od.22.181.296.

POW'RLESS
For should'st thou suffer, pow'rless to relieve ... Od.16.87.106.
Pow'rless to move, his stagg'ring feet deny ... Od.18.283.180.
Pow'rless to speak, I scarce uplift my eyes, ... Od.23.109.325.

POW'RS
And Winds shall waft it to the Pow'rs above. ... 1.PSu.80.78.
Ye Pow'rs, what pleasing Frensie sooths my Mind! ... 1.PAu.51.83.
With Chymic Art exalts the Min'ral Pow'rs, ... 1.W-F.243.171.
His Pow'rs in *equal Ranks,* and *fair Array,* ... 1.EOC.176.260.
And those offended sylvan pow'rs ador'd: ... 1.TrFD.38.387.
I swear by all th'unpitying pow'rs of heav'n, ... 1.TrFD.70.389.
Now by the Nine, those Pow'rs ador'd by me, ... 1.TrSP.121.399.
Next a long Order of Inferior Pow'rs ... 1.TrSt.286.422.
And Vindicate the bounteous Pow'rs above: ... 1.TrES.36.451.
High on the Walls appear'd the *Lycian* Pow'rs, ... 1.TrES.91.453.
Nor cou'd the *Greeks* repell the *Lycian* Pow'rs, ... 1.TrES.155.455.
And murm'ring Pow'rs condemn their partial *Jove.* ... 1.TrES.245.459.
To me, whose Wit exceeds the Pow'rs Divine, ... 1.TrUl.173.471.
When the bold *Argives* led their warring Pow'rs ... 1.TrUl.191.472.
And to the Heav'nly Pow'rs his constant Pray'r, ... 2.ChJM.16.15.
To raise up Seed to bless the Pow'rs above, ... 2.ChJM.121.20.
To raise up Seed t'adore the Pow'rs above, ... 2.ChJM.121A.20.
But, by th' Immortal Pow'rs, I feel the Pain, ... 2.ChJM.204.24.
And thank the Pow'rs, I may possess alone ... 2.ChJM.264.27.
Then pray'd the Pow'rs the fruitful Bed to bless, ... 2.ChJM.313.29.
For, by th'Immortal Pow'rs, it *seem'd* too plain— ... 2.ChJM.779.52.
By all those Pow'rs, some Frenzy seiz'd your Mind, ... 2.ChJM.780.52.
Or Virgins visited by Angel-Pow'rs, ... 2.RL1.33.148.
With Head uncover'd, the *Cosmetic* Pow'rs. ... 2.RL1.124.155.
The Pow'rs gave Ear, and granted half his Pray'r, ... 2.RL2.45.162.
And his refulgent *Queen,* with Pow'rs combin'd, ... 2.RL3.77.173.
Why bade ye else, ye Pow'rs! her soul aspire ... 2.Elegy.11.363.
Say what their use, had he the pow'rs of all? ... 3.EOM1.178.36.
The proper organs, proper pow'rs assign'd; ... 3.EOM1.180.37.
No pow'rs of body or of soul to share, ... 3.EOM1.191.38.
The scale of sensual, mental pow'rs ascends: ... 3.EOM1.208.41.
The pow'rs of all subdu'd by thee alone, ... 3.EOM1.231.44.
Is not thy Reason all these pow'rs in one? ... 3.EOM1.232.44.
Is not thy Reason all those pow'rs in one? ... 3.EOM1.232A.44.
From thee to Nothing!—On superior pow'rs ... 3.EOM1.241.45.
See then the acting and comparing pow'rs ... 3.EOM3.95.101.
To him we grant our amplest pow'rs to sit ... 5.DunA2.343.142.
To him we grant our ample pow'rs to sit ... 5.DunA2.343A.142.
"To him we grant our amplest pow'rs to sit ... 5.DunB2.375.315.
Ye Pow'rs! whose Mysteries restor'd I sing, ... 5.DunB4.5.339.
Th' Immortal Pow'rs incline their Ear; ... 6.11.127.34.
Whene'er, by *Jove's* Decree, our conqu'ring Pow'rs ... Il.1.165.95.
The Pow'rs of Earth, and sceptred Sons of *Jove.* ... Il.1.369.105.
Twelve Days the Pow'rs indulge the Genial Rite, ... Il.1.558.115.
Leads the long Order of Ætherial Pow'rs. ... Il.1.643.118.
Or oh declare, of all the Pow'rs above ... Il.1.668.119.
Nor doubt the Vision of the Pow'rs Divine; ... Il.2.102.131.
Say shall we march with our unconquer'd Pow'rs, ... Il.2.283.141.
For our Return we trust the heav'nly Pow'rs; ... Il.2.314.142.
And trembling sought the Pow'rs with Sacrifice, ... Il.2.389.145.
No wonder *Troy* so long resists our Pow'rs. ... Il.2.409.147.
The proud *Mycenè* arms her martial Pow'rs, ... Il.2.686.159.
Now Muse recount *Pelasgic Argos'* Pow'rs, ... Il.2.829.164.
Amidst yon' Circle of his *Cretan* Pow'rs, ... Il.3.296.207.
And add Libations to the Pow'rs Divine. ... Il.3.369.211.
While the full Bowls flow round, the Pow'rs employ ... Il.4.5.221.
Two Pow'rs Divine the Son of *Atreus* aid, ... Il.4.9.221.
Then say ye Pow'rs! what signal Issue waits ... Il.4.19.222.
Can wretched Mortals harm the Pow'rs above, ... Il.4.50.223.

POW'RS (CONTINUED)
When *Priam's* Pow'rs and *Priam's* self shall fall, ... Il.4.198.230.
I saw him once, when gath'ring martial Pow'rs ... Il.4.430.240.
Array'd in Terrors, rowz'd the *Trojan* Pow'rs: ... Il.4.594.249.
And share those Griefs inferior Pow'rs must share; ... Il.5.472.290.
Distance immense! between the Pow'rs that shine ... Il.5.535.294.
Condense their Pow'rs, and wait the growing War. ... Il.5.610.297.
Heav'n Gates spontaneous open to the Pow'rs, ... Il.5.928.310.
For mortal Men Celestial Pow'rs engage, ... Il.5.1070.317.
And all ye deathless Pow'rs! protect my Son! ... Il.6.605.356.
At this agreed, the Heav'nly Pow'rs withdrew; ... Il.7.47.365.
The solemn Silence, and their Pow'rs bespoke. ... Il.7.78.366.
Oh would to tell th' immortal Pow'rs above, ... Il.7.159.372.
Next, to secure our Camp, and Naval Pow'rs, ... Il.7.406.384.
Then, to secure the Camp and Naval Pow'rs, ... Il.7.520.389.
All Night they feast, the *Greek* and *Trojan* Pow'rs; ... Il.7.570.392.
Thou Fate! fulfill it; and ye Pow'rs! approve. ... Il.8.10.395.
League all your Forces then, ye Pow'rs above, ... Il.8.23.396.
Th' Almighty spoke, nor durst the Pow'rs reply, ... Il.8.35.397.
These if we gain, then Victory, ye Pow'rs! ... Il.8.238.409.
Now hear a Monarchs Vow: If Heav'ns high Pow'rs ... Il.8.347.414.
Heav'n-Gates spontaneous open to the Pow'rs, ... Il.8.478.419.
Trembling afar th' offending Pow'rs appear'd, ... Il.8.554.423.
Our Steeds to forage, and refresh our Pow'rs. ... Il.8.628.425.
Firm be the Guard, while distant lie our Pow'rs, ... Il.8.647.426.
Ungrateful Off'ring to th' immortal Pow'rs, ... Il.8.681.427.
These instant shall be his; and if the Pow'rs ... Il.9.175.441.
These instant shall be thine; and if the Pow'rs ... Il.9.362.451.
She beat the Ground, and call'd the Pow'rs beneath ... Il.9.683.468.
This Night, let due Repast refresh our Pow'rs; ... Il.9.825.474.
To try yon' Camp, and watch the *Trojan* Pow'rs? ... Il.10.44.4.
To him thus *Nestor.* Trust the Pow'rs above, ... Il.10.114.7.
When on *Æsopus'* Banks the banded Pow'rs ... Il.10.339.18.
To whom the Spy: Their Pow'rs they thus dispose: ... Il.10.496.25.
Condense their Pow'rs, and wait the coming War. ... Il.11.276.47.
(The Pow'rs that cause the teeming Matron's Throes, ... Il.11.349.50.
Behold, the Gen'ral flies! deserts his Pow'rs! ... Il.11.371.51.
Fix'd as the Bar between two warring Pow'rs, ... Il.11.696.66.
When this bold Arm th' *Epeian* Pow'rs oppress'd, ... Il.11.817.72.
Their Pow'rs neglected and no Victim slain, ... Il.12.7.81.
The Strokes yet echo'd of contending Pow'rs; ... Il.12.39.83.
His Pow'rs untam'd their bold Assault defy, ... Il.12.51.83.
Fierce was the Fight, while yet the *Grecian* Pow'rs ... Il.12.171.87.
In Pow'rs immortal who shall now believe? ... Il.12.185.88.
Their Ardour kindles all the *Grecian* Pow'rs; ... Il.12.329.93.
And vindicate the bount'ous Pow'rs above. ... Il.12.380.95.
High on the Walls appear'd the *Lycian* Pow'rs, ... Il.12.445.97.
Nor could the *Greeks* repell the *Lycian* Pow'rs, ... Il.12.509.100.
While his high Law suspends the Pow'rs of Heav'n. ... Il.13.16.104.
Will'd not Destruction to the *Grecian* Pow'rs, ... Il.13.440.126.
These Pow'rs infold the *Greek* and *Trojan* Train ... Il.13.451.127.
These Pow'rs inclose the *Greek* and *Trojan* Train ... Il.13.451A.127.
To some the Pow'rs of bloody War belong, ... Il.13.915.148.
Oh were thy Sway the Curse of meaner Pow'rs, ... Il.14.92.162.
Invokes the sable Subtartarean Pow'rs, ... Il.14.314.178.
By ev'ry Oath that Pow'rs immortal ties, ... Il.15.41.195.
There sate the Pow'rs in awful Synod plac'd; ... Il.15.92.200.
Thus she proceeds—Attend ye Pow'rs above! ... Il.15.114.201.
Confus'd, and weary all the Pow'rs with Pray'r; ... Il.15.423.213.
Behold, ye Warriors, and exert your Pow'rs. ... Il.15.581.218.
Oh! would to all th' immortal Pow'rs above, ... Il.16.122.241.
Nor rais'd in Off'rings to the Pow'rs divine, ... Il.16.275.249.
And murm'ring Pow'rs condemn their partial *Jove.* ... Il.16.548.265.
Vain Boaster! cease, and know the Pow'rs divine; ... Il.16.1018.282.
Elate her Heart, and rowzing all her Pow'rs, ... Il.17.149.293.
Have forc'd the Pow'rs to spare a sinking State, ... Il.17.382.302.
Pleas'd to be first of all the Pow'rs addrest, ... Il.17.638.312.
Curs'd be that Day, when all the Pow'rs above ... Il.18.107.328.
Let me—But oh! ye gracious Pow'rs above! ... Il.18.137.329.
When Morning dawns, our well-appointed Pow'rs ... Il.18.325.337.
Thetis (reply'd the God) our Pow'rs may claim, ... Il.18.461.343.
(The Work of *Vulcan)* sate the Pow'rs around. ... Il.20.18.393.
Work out our Will. Celestial Pow'rs! descend, ... Il.20.35.394.
But when the Pow'rs descending swell'd the Fight, ... Il.20.63.396.
And thus, assembling all the Pow'rs, she said. ... Il.20.145.400.
Give him to know, what Pow'rs assist this Day: ... Il.20.157.400.
Why shou'd cœlestial Pow'rs exert their own? ... Il.20.163.400.
The adverse Pow'rs, around *Apollo* laid, ... Il.20.182.401.
Saw the Distress, and mov'd the Pow'rs around. ... Il.20.340.408.
But Pow'rs cœlestial sure this Foe defend. ... Il.20.398.411.
And bravely try if all the Pow'rs were Foes; ... Il.21.304.433.
Ring with conflicting Pow'rs, and Heav'n returns the Sound? ... Il.21.509.443.
How dares thy Rashness on the Pow'rs divine ... Il.21.563.445.
March, bending on, the *Greeks* embodied Pow'rs, ... Il.22.7.453.
Consult, ye Pow'rs! ('tis worthy your Debate) ... Il.22.229.465.
Let Heav'ns high Pow'rs be call'd to arbitrate ... Il.22.323.469.
Is not *Troy* fall'n already? Haste, ye Pow'rs! ... Il.22.477.475.
He call'd th' Aerial Pow'rs, along the Skies ... Il.23.242.499.
Unpitying Pow'rs! how oft each holy Fane ... Il.24.44.537.
If in yon' Camp your Pow'rs have doom'd my Fall, ... Il.24.276.547.
Ah think, thou favour'd of the Pow'rs Divine! ... Il.24.598.561.
At length their rage the hostile Pow'rs restrain, ... Od.1.27.30.
The Sanction of th' assembled pow'rs report: ... Od.1.107.36.
Be future vengeance to the pow'rs divine. ... Od.1.351.49.
By all the deathless pow'rs that reign above, ... Od.2.73.64.
Join all your pow'rs! in arms ye *Greeks* arise! ... Od.2.278.74.
Yet would your pow'rs in vain our strength oppose; ... Od.2.279.74.
But by the pow'rs that hate the perjur'd, swear, ... Od.2.418.81.
The holy Goblet to the pow'rs divine: ... Od.2.471.84.
He too, I deem, implores the pow'rs divine: ... Od.3.61.89.
There land, and pay due victims to the pow'rs: ... Od.3.192.95.
Sacred to *Neptune* and the pow'rs divine. ... Od.3.426.107.
With pow'rs united, obstinately bold ... Od.4.561.147.
'Tis impious to surmize, the pow'rs divine ... Od.4.995.164.
Sleep's gentle pow'rs her drooping eyes invade; ... Od.4.1046.166.
For pow'rs celestial to each other's view ... Od.5.100.177.

POW'RS (CONTINUED)

And is it now my turn, ye mighty pow'rs! ....Od.5.163.179.
Heav'ns! how uncertain are the Pow'rs on high? ....Od.5.367.190.
What will ye next ordain, ye pow'rs on high! ....Od.5.599.201.
High on a throne, amid the *Scherian* pow'rs, ...Od.6.371.229.
This is the truth: And oh ye pow'rs on high! ....Od.7.382.255.
And faithful say, to you the pow'rs belong ....Od.8.289.278.
O *Jove*, he cry'd, oh all ye pow'rs above, ...Od.8.347.282.
An off'ring sacred to th' immortal pow'rs: ....Od.8.558.292.
Goddess, and Queen, to whom the pow'rs belong ....Od.10.163.348.
The pow'rs below, the blessed in the sky; ....Od.10.358.361.
For well I know that soon the heav'nly pow'rs ....Od.11.85.385.
Is it, ye pow'rs that smile at human harms! ....Od.11.255.394.
In you I trust, and in the heav'nly pow'rs, ...Od.11.412.404.
Why cease ye then t' implore the pow'rs above, ...Od.12.407.450.
But should the pow'rs that o'er mankind preside, ...Od.12.413.451.
Oh all ye blissful pow'rs that reign above! ....Od.12.438.452.
Vengeance, ye Pow'rs, (he cries) and thou whose hand ....Od.12.445.452.
To *Jove* th' Eternal, (pow'r above all pow'rs! ....Od.13.29.2.
To whom the Father of th' immortal pow'rs, ...Od.13.162.13.
To me, whose wit exceeds the pow'rs divine, ...Od.13.340.24.
When the bold *Argives* led their warring pow'rs, ...Od.13.358.24.
Attesting solemn all the pow'rs divine, ...Od.14.368.53.
(Libation destin'd to the Pow'rs divine) ....Od.15.165.76.
No profit springs beneath usurping pow'rs; ....Od.15.404.89.
Enter, oh seldom seen! for lawless pow'rs ....Od.16.29.103.
Escap'd *Telemachus:* (the pow'rs above ....Od.16.174.111.
Then what assistant pow'rs you boast, relate, ...Od.16.278.118.
Against the banded pow'rs of all mankind: ....Od.16.285.118.
Yet safe he sails! the pow'rs cœlestial give ....Od.16.384.124.
Consult we first th' all-seeing pow'rs above, ...Od.16.418.126.
Sudden before the rival pow'rs she stands: ....Od.16.431.128.
Lawless he ravag'd with his martial pow'rs ....Od.16.444.128.
No—by the righteous pow'rs of heav'n I swear, ...Od.16.456.129.
With all thy handmaids thank th' immortal Pow'rs; ....Od.17.61.135.
And parting, to the Suitor pow'rs descends: ....Od.17.669.164.
Our life to heav'n's immortal pow'rs we trust, ...Od.17.680.165.
Stranger, may *Jove* aid all th' aereal pow'rs, ...Od.18.137.173.
The flowing goblet to the pow'rs divine; ....Od.18.465.190.
A pause inspiriting her languish'd pow'rs, ...Od.19.287.209.
By death dis-rob'd of all their savage pow'rs, ...Od.19.381.212.
Torn from these walls (where long the kinder pow'rs ....Od.19.678.229.
Her faded pow'rs with balmy rest renew. ....Od.20.64.235.
The righteous pow'rs who tread the starry skies, ...Od.23.13.319.
The good they hated, and the Pow'rs defy'd; ....Od.23.67.321.
While yet he speaks, her pow'rs of life decay, ...Od.23.211.333.
The righteous pow'rs that mortal lots dispose, ...Od.23.219.333.
Due victims slay to all th' æthereal pow'rs. ....Od.23.296.337.
Such future scenes th' all-righteous pow'rs display, ...Od.23.303.337.
Thou, for thy Lord; while me th' immortal pow'rs ....Od.23.379.343.
Select the largest to the pow'rs divine. ....Od.24.247.360.
Oh! would to all the deathless pow'rs on high, ...Od.24.433.369.

POWDER

To save the Powder from too rude a Gale, ...2.RL2.93.165.
Or should one Pound of Powder less bespread ....4.JD4.246.47.
My Wig all powder, and all snuff my Band; ....4.1HE1.162.291.
Vain is thy Art, thy Powder vain, ...6.53.35.162.
They use white Powder, and wear Holland-Smocks. ....6.95.4.264.

POWDERS

Puffs, Powders, Patches, Bibles, Billet-doux. ....2.RL1.138.156.

POWER

Or Alom- *Stypticks* with contracting Power ....2.RL2.131.168.
Adds to Christs Prayer the *Power* and *Glory Clause.* ....4.JD2A.114.142.
Lov'd without youth, and follow'd without power, ...4.1HE1.183.293.
My narrow Genius does the power deny) ....6.75.4.211.
In Miniature see *Nature's* Power appear; ....6.96v.1.280.
By Spirit, robb'd of Power; by Warmth, of Friends; ....6.154.30.403.
Whose Power encircles *Cilla* the Divine, ...Il.1.591.116.
And shuns (who wou'd not?) wicked men in power; ....Od.17.661.164.

POWERFUL

When first that Sun too powerful Beams displays, ...1.EOC.470.292.

POWERS

You bless the Powers who made that Organ ....6.10.25.25.

POWR'S

Then gave his Bill, and brib'd the Powr's Divine ....2.ChJM.416.35.

POWRS

Mean-while, in *Ithaca,* the Suitor-powrs ....Od.4.845.158.

POX

See P.
"Plague on't! 'tis past a Jest—nay prithee, Pox! ....2.RL4.129.194.
Charm'd the Small-pox, or chas'd old Age away; ....2.RL5.20.200.
Spleen, Vapours, or Small-pox, above them all, ...3.Ep2.267.72.
As in the Pox, some give it, to get free; ....4.JD4.171.39.
Now pox on those who shew a *Court in Wax!* ....4.JD4.206.43.
Time, that at last matures a Clap to Pox, ...4.JD2.47.137.
Whom ripening Time, that Turns a Clap to Pox ....4.JD2A.53.136.
A Pox of all Senders ....6.42iv.1.118.
A pox on all Senders ....6.42iv.1A.118.
Small-Pox is rife, and *Gay* in dreadful fear— ....6.82vi.13.232.

POYS'NOUS

See POIS'NOUS.
That for her Husband mix'd a Poys'nous Draught; ....2.ChWB.403.76.

POYSON

With livid Poyson and our Children's Blood. ....1.TrSt.730.440.
With livid Poyson and our Infant's Blood. ....1.TrSt.730A.440.
Slander or Poyson, dread from *Delia's* Rage, ...4.HS1.81.13.

POYSON'D

Sooth'd the frail Queen, and poyson'd all her heart. ....Od.3.329.102.

POYSONS

And spreads its ancient Poysons o'er the Grounds: ....1.TrSt.503.431.
For temper'd drugs and poysons shall be vain. ....Od.10.348.360.
Amazing strength, these poysons to sustain! ....Od.10.389.363.

PRACTICE

Bold in the Practice of *mistaken Rules,* ....1.EOC.110.251.
Such was the Muse, whose Rules and Practice tell, ...1.EOC.723.323.
To Practice now from Theory repair. ....5.DunB4.580.399.
Pity! that all their Practice is by Land. ....Il.16.906.279.
The same my practice, were my fate the same. ....Od.5.244.183.
Thous know'st the practice of the female train, ...Od.15.24.71.

PRACTIS'D

Practis'd to Lisp, and hang the Head aside, ...2.RL4.33.186.
Practis'd alike to turn, to stop, to chace, ...Il.5.280.280.
The Horses practis'd to their Lord's Command, ...Il.5.290.281.
Practis'd alike to turn, to stop, to chace, ...Il.8.135.404.
Drives four fair Coursers, practis'd to obey, ...Il.15.824.228.
The chief I challeng'd; he, whose practis'd wit ....Od.4.341.136.
Practis'd, the common messenger to fly, ...Od.18.10.167.

PRACTISE

"Well shou'd you practise, who so well can teach. ....2.ChWB.187.65.
Nor dare to practise till they've learn'd to dance. ....4.2HE1.184.211.
You give the Practise, they but give the Talk. ....6.2.30.6.
As this Advice ye practise, or reject, ...Il.7.426.385.

PRACTISES

He views and practises a milder look. ....1.TrPA.26.366.

PRACTIUS'

From *Practius'* Stream, *Percotè's* Pasture Lands, ...Il.2.1012.171.

PRAETUS

Then mighty *Prætus Argos'* Sceptres sway'd, ...Il.6.197.336.
Fir'd at his Scorn the Queen to *Prætus* fled, ...Il.6.205.336.

PRAIS'D

And such were *Prais'd* who but *endeavour'd well:* ....1.EOC.511.295.
And such were *Prais'd* as but *endeavour'd well:* ....1.EOC.511A.295.
And prais'd the Beauty of the pleasing Sight. ....1.TrVP.62.380.
Some prais'd with Wit, and some with Reason blam'd. ....2.ChJM.142.21.
Be sure my fine Complexion must be prais'd: ....2.ChWB.111.62.
And *Betty's* prais'd for Labours not her own. ....2.RL1.148.158.
Say, why are Beauties prais'd and honour'd most, ...2.RL5.9.199.
Deaf the prais'd ear, and mute the tuneful tongue. ....2.Elegy.76.368.
Such Wits and Beauties are not prais'd for nought, ...4.JD4.234.45.
Our Fathers prais'd rank Ven'son. You suppose ....4.HS2.91.61.
Each prais'd within, is happy all day long. ....4.2HE2.156.175.
Who prais'd my Modesty, and smil'd. ....4.1HE7.68.273.
Narcissus, prais'd with all a Parson's pow'r, ...5.DunB4.103.351.
For those were slander'd most whom *Ozell* prais'd: ....6.12.7.37.
"And prais'd, unenvy'd, by the Muse he lov'd." ....6.71.72.204.
"Know'st thou not me, who (God be prais'd) ....6.79.85.220.
Prais'd, wept, and honour'd, by the Muse he lov'd. ....6.97.6.282.
And prais'd unenvy'd, by the Muse he lov'd. ....6.97.6A.282.
Prais'd great *Eliza* in God's anger, ...6.101.3.290.
'Twas thus the gen'ral Voice the Heroe prais'd, ...Il.2.340.143.
The distant Dart be prais'd, tho' here we need ....Il.5.274.280.
Prais'd be thy counsel, and thy timely aid: ....Od.13.438.27.

PRAISD

Tho' Heav'n be praisd, that ever since I knew ....4.JD2A.1.132.

PRAISE

Inspire me *Phœbus,* in my *Delia's* Praise, ...1.PSp.45.65.
Invoke the Muses, and resound your Praise; ....1.PSu.78.78.
Your Praise the Birds shall chant in ev'ry Grove, ...1.PSu.79.78.
Oh sing of *Daphne's* Fate, and *Daphne's* Praise! ....1.PWi.8.89.
Thy Name, thy Honour, and thy Praise shall live! ....1.PWi.84.94.
She scorn'd the Praise of Beauty, and the Care; ....1.W-F.177.166.
Pleas'd in the silent Shade with empty Praise; ....1.W-F.432.194.
In Praise so just, let ev'ry Voice be join'd, ...1.EOC.187.262.
Immortal Heirs of *Universal* Praise! ....1.EOC.190.262.
For *not* to know some Trifles, is a Praise. ....1.EOC.262.269.
Their Praise is still— *The Stile is excellent:* ....1.EOC.307.274.
And praise the *Easie Vigor* of a Line, ...1.EOC.360.280.
Nor praise nor blame the *Writings,* but the *Men.* ....1.EOC.413.287.
Nor praise nor damn the *Writings,* but the *Men.* ....1.EOC.413A.287.
Some praise at Morning what they blame at Night; ....1.EOC.430.288.
When we but praise *Our selves* in *Other Men.* ....1.EOC.455.290.
His Praise is lost, who stays till *All* commend; ....1.EOC.475.292.
In *Youth* alone its empty Praise we boast, ...1.EOC.496.294.
Are Mortals urg'd thro' *Sacred Lust of Praise.* ....1.EOC.521.296.
Are Mortals urg'd by *Sacred Lust of Praise?* ....1.EOC.521A.296.
Those best can *bear Reproof,* who *merit Praise.* ....1.EOC.583.306.
Whom, when they *Praise,* the World believes no more, ...1.EOC.594.307.
And gladly praise the Merit of a *Foe?* ....1.EOC.638.311.
And *Love to Praise,* with *Reason* on his Side? ....1.EOC.642.311.
This humble Praise, lamented *Shade!* receive, ...1.EOC.733.325.
This Praise at least a grateful Muse may give! ....1.EOC.734.325.
Still pleas'd to *praise,* yet not afraid to *blame,* ....1.EOC.742.326.
And the wide World resounds with *Sapho's* Praise. ....1.TrSP.32.394.
Salute the God in num'rous Hymns of Praise. ....1.TrSt.655.437.
And offer Annual Honours, Feasts, and Praise; ....1.TrSt.787.443.
Once more resound the Great *Apollo's* Praise. ....1.TrSt.828.444.
His Friends and People, to his future Praise, ...1.TrES.250.459.
At least, your Courage all the World must praise, ...2.ChJM.170.23.
Slight is the Subject, but not so the Praise, ...2.RL1.5.144.
So long my Honour, Name, and Praise shall live! ....2.RL3.170.182.
Not more by Envy than Excess of Praise. ....2.TemF.44.256.
The Golden Trumpet of eternal Praise: ....2.TemF.307.278.

PRAISE (CONTINUED)

And the loud Clarion labour in your Praise. ....2.TemF.327.279.
No less deserv'd a just Return of Praise. ....2.TemF.331.280.
The Praise of Merit, nor aspire to Fame; ....2.TemF.359.281.
Wou'd you usurp the Lover's dear-bought Praise? ....2.TemF.399.282.
Art thou, fond Youth, a Candidate for Praise? ....2.TemF.500.287.
Drive from my Breast that wretched Lust of Praise; ....2.TemF.522.289.
And only vocal with the Maker's praise. ....2.ElAb.140.331.
Which seeks no int'rest, no reward but praise; ....3.EOM2.246.85.
All see 'tis Vice, and itch of vulgar praise. ....3.Ep1.119.24.
Who would not praise Patritio's high desert, ...3.Ep1.140.26.
Whose ruling Passion was the Lust of Praise; ....3.Ep1.181.30.
His Passion still, to covet gen'ral praise, ...3.Ep1.196.32.
Had aim'd, like him, by Chastity at praise. ....3.Ep1.217.34.
Yet sure, of qualities deserving praise, ...3.Ep3.202Z1.110.
Or if you needs must write, write CÆSAR's Praise: ....4.HS1.21.7.
It is to *History* he trusts for Praise. ....4.HS1.36.7.
May no such Praise (cries *J[efferie]s)* e'er be mine! ....4.HAdv.45.79.
They'l praise her *Elbow, Heel,* or *Tip o' th' Ear.* ....4.HAdv.123.85.
Time, Praise, or Money, is the least they crave, ...4.Arbu.114Z1.104.
Well-natur'd *Garth* inflam'd with early praise, ...4.Arbu.137.105.
Damn with faint praise, assent with civil leer, ...4.Arbu.201.110.
And wonder with a follish face of praise. ....4.Arbu.212.111.
To spread about the Itch of Verse and Praise; ....4.Arbu.224.112.
He pay'd some Bards with Port, and some with Praise, ...4.Arbu.242.113.
Not proud, nor servile, be one Poet's praise ....4.Arbu.336.120.
Nor proud, nor servile, be one Poet's praise ....4.Arbu.336A.120.
What thanks, what praise, if Peter but supplies! ....4.JD2.67.139.
What thanks, what praise, If Coscus but supplies! ....4.JD2.67A.139.
Gave him much Praise, and some Reward beside. ....4.2HE2.43.167.
When this Heroicks only deigns to praise, ...4.2HE2.82.171.
The Harvest early, but mature the Praise: ....4.2HE1.24.197.
And yet deny the Careless Husband praise, ...4.2HE1.92.203.
Unless he praise some monster of a King, ...4.2HE1.210.213.
On Fame's mad voyage by the wind of Praise; ....4.2HE1.297.221.
Or praise malignly Arts I cannot reach, ...4.2HE1.339.225.
That when I aim at praise, they say I bite. ....4.2HE1.409.229.
"Praise undeserv'd is scandal in disguise:" ....4.2HE1.413.229.
Now sick alike of Envy and of Praise. ....4.1HE1.4.279.
"With Praise or Infamy, leave that to fate; ....4.1HE1.102.287.
Chaste Matrons praise her, and grave Bishops bless: ....4.EpS1.146.309.
God knows, I praise a Courtier where I can. ....4.EpS2.63.316.
I follow *Virtue,* where she shines, I praise, ...4.EpS2.95.318.
And love him, court him, praise him, in or out. ....4.EpS2.103.319.
But random Praise—the Task can ne'er be done, ...4.EpS2.106.319.
Praise cannot stoop, like Satire, to the Ground; ....4.EpS2.110.319.
To 'scape my Censure, not expect my Praise: ....4.EpS2.113.319.
But pray, when others praise him, do I blame? ....4.EpS2.136.321.
Are none, none living? let me praise the Dead, ...4.EpS2.251.327.
Or praise the Court, or magnify Mankind, ...5.DunA1.21.62.
And solid pudding against empty praise. ....5.DunA1.52.66.
Much she revolves their arts, their ancient praise, ...5.DunA1.95.70.
Know, Settle, cloy'd with custard and with praise, ...5.DunA1.247.92.
And bade thee live, to crown Britannia's praise, ...5.DunA3.207.175.
Alike their labours, and alike their praise. ....5.DunA3.268.180.
To me committing their eternal praise, ...5.DunA3.278.183.
Or praise the Court, or magnify Mankind, ...5.DunB1.23.271.
And solid pudding against empty praise. ....5.DunB1.54.274.
Much she revolves their arts, their ancient praise, ...5.DunB1.97.276.
E'er since Sir Fopling's Periwig was Praise, ...5.DunB1.167.282.
Know, Eusden thirsts no more for sack or praise; ....5.DunB1.293.291.
And bade thee live, to crown Britannia's praise, ...5.DunB3.211.330.
Alike their labours, and alike their praise. ....5.DunB3.272.333.
To me committing their eternal praise, ...5.DunB3.280.333.
Else sure some Bard, to our eternal praise, ...5.DunB4.171.357.
And to her Maker's Praise confin'd the Sound. ....6.11.125.34.
And meditates her Charms, and sings her Praise. ....6.17iii.21.58.
Revive the honours of *Rome's* ancient praise; ....6.20.44.67.
Him will I heap with honours, and with praise, ...6.21.39.70.
Some *Colinæus* praise, some *Bleau,* ....6.29.1.82.
To blast his Fame, and to detract your Praise. ....6.38.11Z4.108.
Such praise is yours—and such shall you possess, ...6.38.23.108.
To write their Praise you but in vain essay, ...6.43.9.120.
Ev'n while you write, you take that praise away, ...6.43.10.120.
Yet 'tis a Praise that few their own can call, ...6.48iii.3.134.
Damn with faint praise, assent with civil Leer, ...6.49iii.15.143.
And wonder with a foolish Face of Praise: ....6.49iii.28.143.
The kindred arts shall in their praise conspire, ...6.52.69.158.
Can Book, or Man, more Praise obtain? ....6.64.15.190.
And Quires of Virgins celebrate thy praise? ....6.65.8.192.
Argyle his Praise, when *Southerne* wrote, ...6.77.1.214.
So long her Honour, Name, and Praise shall last! ....6.82i.8.229.
Now wits gain praise by copying other wits ....6.82ix(e).1.235.
They praise no works but what are like their own ....6.82ix(f).4.235.
(No Hireling she, no Prostitute to Praise) ....6.84.36.240.
(A Virgin Muse, not prostitute to praise). ....6.84.31Z8.240.
When all the World conspires to praise her, ...6.89.11.250.
When all the World conspires her praise, ...6.89.11A.250.
Swell with Praise ....6.96i.6.268.
And let each grateful *Houyhnhnm* neigh thy Praise. ....6.96iii.4.274.
Damn with faint Praise, assent with civil Leer, ...6.98.51.284.
And wonder with a foolish Face of Praise. ....6.98.64.285.
Tho' sprightly Sappho force our love and praise, ...6.106i.1.306.
Praise courts, and monarchs, or extol mankind, ...6.106iv.5.307.
Due to his Merit, and brave Thirst of Praise. ....6.108.6.312.
Foe to loud Praise, and Friend to learned Ease, ...6.112.5.318.
Shall Royal praise be rhym'd by such a ribald, ...6.116v.1.327.
Here shunning idleness at once and praise, ...6.126ii.1.353.
And all Mankind, but Cibber, sing thy praise. ....6.131i.8.360.
And There Triumphant Sing Thy Soverain's Praise. ....6.147ix.6.392.
He fir'd with Praise or with Persuasion mov'd. ....Il.2.226.138.
Of long, long Labours, but Eternal Praise. ....Il.2.393.145.
And all the Tribes resound the Goddess' Praise.) ....Il.2.664.158.
For martial Conduct bore an equal Praise. ....Il.2.670.158.
'Till vain of Mortal's empty Praise, he strove ....Il.2.723.160.
Thy gifts I praise, nor thou despise the Charms ....Il.3.93.194.

PRAISE (CONTINUED)

What Praise were thine, cou'd'st thou direct thy Dart ....Il.4.125.226.
And only mourn, without my Share of Praise? ....Il.4.207.231.
To Worth like thine? what Praise shall we bestow? ....Il.4.293.235.
What needs, O Monarch, this invidious Praise, ...Il.4.456.242.
His the first Praise were *Ilion's* Tow'rs o'erthrown, ...Il.4.470.242.
And crown her Hero with distinguish'd Praise. ....Il.5.4.265.
Or offer Heav'n's great Sire polluted Praise. ....Il.6.337.343.
His Country's Fame, his own immortal Praise. ....Il.7.210.374.
The Praise and Conquest of this doubtful Day. ....Il.7.246.376.
Each sounds your Praise, and War is all your own. ....Il.7.340.381.
To this the Chief: With Praise the rest inspire, ...Il.8.355.414.
And Voice to Voice resounds *Tydides'* Praise. ....Il.9.70.435.
And blame ev'n Kings with Praise, because with Truth. ....Il.9.80.436.
That young and old may in thy Praise combine, ...Il.9.336.450.
If I return, I quit immortal Praise ....Il.9.536.460.
Hear what our Fathers were, and what their Praise, ...Il.9.651.467.
Urge by their Father's Fame, their future Praise. ....Il.10.75.6.
While *Phœbus* shines, or Men have tongues to praise? ....Il.10.252.13.
(Reply'd the Sage) to praise me, or to blame: ....Il.10.292.15.
Praise from a Friend, or Censure from a Foe, ...Il.10.293.15.
Thee first of all the heav'nly Host we praise; ....Il.10.534.27.
Threats urge the fearful, and the valiant, Praise. ....Il.12.316.93.
Oh recollect your ancient Worth and Praise! ....Il.13.74.108.
Pleas'd in their Age to hear their Children's Praise. ....Il.16.22.236.
Oh Warriors, Part'ners of *Achilles'* Praise! ....Il.16.324.255.
His Friends and People, to his future Praise, ...Il.16.555.266.
To crown *Achilles'* valiant Friend with Praise ....Il.16.793.274.
'Tis the chief Praise that e'er to Kings belong'd, ...Il.19.181.379.
Thy Praise it is in dreadful Camps to shine, ...Il.19.217.381.
Then had the *Greeks* Eternal Praise acquir'd, ...Il.21.639.448.
And late Posterity record our Praise. ....Il.23.309.502.
Base Wealth preferring to eternal Praise. ....Il.23.368.505.
And *Greece* shall praise thy gen'rous Thirst to give. ....Il.23.632.514.
The Praise of Wisdom, in thy Youth obtain'd, ...Il.23.651.515.
Achilles heard him, prouder of the Praise. ....Il.23.752.520.
Thy artful Praise deserves a better Prize. ....Il.23.936.526.
Pleas'd from the Hero's Lips his Praise to hear, ...Il.23.1060.533.
Historic Marbles, to record his praise; ....Od.1.306.47.
His praise, eternal on the faithful stone, ...Od.1.307.47.
With great revenge, immortal praise acquir'd? ....Od.1.388.51.
My praise the precept is, be thine the deed. ....Od.1.398.51.
Vain were my hopes: few sons attain the praise ....Od.2.315.76.
Shall long posterity resound the praise. ....Od.3.249.97.
And charm attention, with thy copious praise: ....Od.4.260.131.
The matchless merit of the chief you praise: ....Od.4.366.137.
Thy conduct ill deserves the praise of wise: ....Od.4.502.144.
Were ye not tutor'd with *Ulysses'* praise? ....Od.4.915.161.
So when with praise amid the dance they shine, ...Od.6.77.208.
By these my cares adorn'd, that praise is mine. ....Od.6.78.208.
The tongues of all with transport sound her praise, ...Od.7.92.238.
Th' assembled Peers with gen'ral praise approv'd ....Od.7.307.251.
But heav'n denies the praise of thinking well. ....Od.8.198.273.
From all the sons of earth unrival'd praise ....Od.8.253.276.
How lov'd of *Jove* he crown'd our sires with praise, ...Od.8.279.278.
Thy praise was just; their skill transcends thy praise. ....Od.8.420.286.
Thy praise was just; their skill transcends thy praise. ....Od.8.420.286.
Not fond of flattery , nor unpleas'd with praise. ....Od.8.528.291.
In ev'ry land, thy monument of praise. ....Od.8.546.292.
The mighty dead that live in endless praise, ...Od.11.776.424.
Great in the praise, rich in the spoils of war: ....Od.14.269.49.
Historic marbles, to record his praise: ....Od.14.404.55.
His praise, eternal on the faithful stone, ...Od.14.405.55.
Doubtless, oh guest! great laud and praise were mine ....Od.14.443.57.
And with my betters claim'd a share of praise. ....Od.14.527.62.
How will each gift indulge us in thy praise? ....Od.15.177.77.
His bulk and beauty speak no vulgar praise; ....Od.17.370.150.
And I shall praise thee thro' the boundless earth. ....Od.17.500.157.
And hospitality was then my praise: ....Od.17.504.157.
And crown the mother and the wife with praise. ....Od.18.192.176.
Potent to punish what he cannot praise. ....Od.19.108.197.
My drooping verdure, and extend my praise! ....Od.19.149.199.
In silent wonder sigh'd unwilling praise. ....Od.19.272.208.
And vainly to the praise of Queen aspire, ...Od.19.374.212.
Relates the chace, and early praise atchiev'd. ....Od.19.543.223.
Thy charity we praise, but not thy choice; ....Od.20.450.255.
Fit for the praise of ev'ry tongue but mine. ....Od.21.114.264.
Know Friend! that Virtue is the path to praise. ....Od.21.360.277.
Heedless alike of infamy or praise, ...Od.22.49.288.
Historic marbles to record thy praise: ....Od.24.46.350.
Thy praise eternal on the faithful stone ....Od.24.47.350.
(Their great reward) a Poet in her praise. ....Od.24.225.358.
(Reply'd the King elated with his praise) ....Od.24.435.369.

PRAISED

Since those were slander'd most whom *Ozell* praised: ....6.12.7A.37.

PRAISES

And, spight of all its Praises, must declare, ...2.ChJM.196.24.
Beware what lavish Praises you confer ....2.ChJM.688.48.
But all our praises why should Lords engross? ....3.Ep3.249.113.
Who praises now? his Chaplain on his Tomb. ....5.DunB4.514.393.
And since my Tongue is in thy praises slow, ...6.2.4.5.
For if these Praises fit not you, ...6.77.7.214.
Or barren Praises pay the Wounds of War. ....Il.1.220.97.
Say thou, whose Praises all our Host proclaim, ...Il.10.640.30.
Exhort their Men, with Praises, Threats, Commands; ....Il.15.424.213.

PRAMNIAN

Pours a large Potion of the *Pramnian* Wine; ....Il.11.781.70.
And honey fresh, and *Pramnian* wines the treat: ....Od.10.271.355.

PRANCE

Or set on Metaphysic ground to prance, ...5.DunB4.265.370.

PRANKS
And scorn the Pranks of Dogs at Court. 6.135.14.366.

PRATE
They march, to prate their Hour before the Fair, 4.JD4.249.47.
But sick of Fops, and Poetry, and Prate, 4.Arbu.229.112.
And smit with love of Poesy and Prate. 5.DunA2.350.143.
And smit with love of Poesy and Prate. 5.DunB2.382.316.
Morgan and Mandevil could prate no more; 5.DunB2.414.317.
Smit with his Countrey's Love, I've heard him prate 6.96v.9.280.

PRATES
Here no man prates of idle things, 4.HS6.141.259.
Who prates like his Grand mere 6.42iv.8.118.

PRATING
(Cries prating *Balbus*) "something will come out." 4.Arbu.276.115.
A prating Thing, a Magpy height, 6.14v(a).20.49.

PRAUNC'D
Full gently praunc'd he on the Lawn; 6.79.109A.221.

PRAUNCH'D
Full gently praunch'd he o'er the Lawn; 6.79.109.221.

PRAY
'Till the Bell toll'd, and All arose to Pray. 2.ChJM.425.35.
Pray Heav'n, this Magick work the proper Way: 2.ChJM.773.52.
And pray, to crown the Pleasure of their Lives, 2.ChJM.819.54.
And send the Godly in a Pett, to pray. 2.RL4.64.189.
But most be present, if we preach or pray. 3.EOM3.6.92.
But most be present, if thou preach or pray. 3.EOM3.6A.92.
She taught the weak to bend, the proud to pray, 3.EOM3.251.118.
Flavia's a Wit, has too much sense to Pray, 3.Ep2.87.57.
"Pray heav'n it last! (cries Swift) as you go on; 4.HS2.161.67.
Each Parent sprung—"What Fortune, pray?"— Their own, 4.Arbu.390.126.
Each Parent sprung—"What Fortune, pray?"— their own, 4.Arbu.390A.126.
And if I pray by Reason's rules, 4.HS6.15.251.
'Tis one to me—"Then tell us, pray, 4.HS6.119.257.
"Pray dip your Whiskers and your Tail in". 4.HS6.205.263.
"Pray take them, Sir,—Enough's a Feast: 4.1HE7.25.269.
A word, pray, in your Honour's ear. 4.1HE7.42.271.
"Pray then what wants he?" fourscore thousand pounds, 4.1HE1.86.285.
The matter's weighty, pray consider twice: 4.EpS2.43.315.
But pray, when others praise him, do I blame? 4.EpS2.136.321.
And how did, pray, the Florid Youth offend. 4.EpS2.166.323.
Fr. Alas! alas! pray end what you began, 4.EpS2.254.327.
Sit still a Moment; pray be easy— 6.10.2.24.
What mov'd you, pray, without compelling, 6.10.83.27.
Send it, I pray, by the next Post, 6.10.115.28.
To *Baker* first my Service, pray; 6.13.26.40.
—Now, dreadful Critic! tell me pray, 6.24iii(a).4.75.
Were you all pleas'd, yet what I pray, 6.30.64.88.
Pray heartily for some new Gift, 6.39.23.111.
But pray which of you all would take her back? 6.41.36.114.
In manner submissive most humbly do pray, 6.42iii.2.117.
Pray between Friends, was not that *Steel's?* 6.44.24.123.
There starve and pray, for that's the way to heav'n. 6.45.22.125.
I pray where can the Hurt lie? 6.58.66.173.
Pray grant Us Admittance, 6.68.15.197.
But since you hatch, pray own your Chicks: 6.93.28.257.
Pray Heav'n, 'twas all a wanton Maiden did! 6.96iv.88.279.
Pray tell me Sir, whose Dog are you? 6.136.2.372.
With hasty Feasts they sacrifice, and pray Il.2.476.149.
The People pray with elevated Hands, Il.3.394.211.
The People pray with lifted Eyes and Hands, Il.7.213.374.
But pray in secret, lest the Foes should hear, Il.7.231.376.
Now pray to *Jove* to grant what *Greece* demands; Il.9.225.444.
Pray, in deep Silence, and with purest Hands. Il.9.226.444.
Pray to that God, who high on *Ida's* Brow Il.24.359.551.
Suppliant to her, since first he chose to pray, Od.7.386.255.
"To *Jove* or to thy father *Neptune* pray." Od.9.489.326.
But come, accept our gifts, and join to pray Od.9.605.331.

PRAY'D
Faint, breathless, thus she pray'd, nor pray'd in vain; 1.W-F.199.168.
Faint, breathless, thus she pray'd, nor pray'd in vain; 1.W-F.199.168.
Thus, seiz'd with Sacred Fear, the Monarch pray'd; 1.TrSt.598.435.
Then pray'd the Pow'rs the fruitful Bed to bless, 2.ChJM.313.29.
Who pray'd his Spouse, attended by her Train, 2.ChJM.408.34.
Once like thy self, I trembled, wept, and pray'd, 2.ElAb.311.344.
Thus *Chryses* pray'd: the fav'ring Pow'r attends, Il.1.61.88.
To *Phœbus* pray'd, and *Phœbus* heard the Pray'r: Il.1.495.111.
So *Chryses* pray'd, *Apollo* heard his Pray'r: Il.1.598.116.
Thus pray'd the Chief: His unavailing Pray'r Il.2.498.150.
Thus pray'd *Tydides,* and *Minerva* heard, Il.5.154.274.
So pray'd the Priestess in her holy Fane; Il.6.386.345.
Thus pray'd the King, and Heav'ns great Father heard Il.8.293.411.
As from the Right she soar'd, *Ulysses* pray'd, Il.10.325.17.
The Heroes pray'd, and *Pallas* from the Skies, Il.10.351.18.
Thus pray'd the Sage: Th' Eternal gave consent, Il.15.436.214.
To *Phœbus* then ('twas all he could) he pray'd. Il.16.632.269.
Thus o'er *Patroclus* while the Hero pray'd, Il.23.190.497.
Assist O Goddess! (thus in Thought he pray'd) Il.23.901.525.
The royal suppliant to *Minerva* pray'd. Od.2.296.76.
Suppliant he pray'd. And now the victims drest Od.3.78.90.
He pray'd, and strait the gentle stream subsides, Od.5.576.200.
To *Pallas* thus the pensive Heroe pray'd. Od.6.384.230.
The patient, heav'nly man thus suppliant pray'd Od.7.1.232.

PRAY'R
Tisiphone! that oft hast heard my Pray'r, 1.TrSt.85.413.
Thus, in Reproach and Pray'r, the Queen exprest 1.TrSt.400.426.
Propitious hear our Pray'r, O Pow'r Divine! 1.TrSt.855.445.
Thus to the Sea-green Sisters sends his Pray'r. 1.TrUl.239.473.
And to the Heav'nly Pow'rs his constant Pray'r, 2.ChJM.16.15.

PRAY'R (CONTINUED)
The Pow'rs gave Ear, and granted half his Pray'r, 2.RL2.45.162.
Seems to reject him, tho' she grants his Pray'r. 2.RL4.80.190.
Plants of thy hand, and children of thy pray'r. 2.ElAb.130.330.
Assist me heav'n! but whence arose that pray'r? 2.ElAb.179.334.
Each pray'r accepted, and each wish resign'd; 2.ElAb.210.337.
And beads and pray'r-books are the toys of age: 3.EOM2.280.88.
But most be present, if thou preach or pray. 3.EOM3.6A.92.
Has ev'n been prov'd to grant a Lover's pray'r, 3.Ep2.55.55.
For ever in a Passion, or a Pray'r: 3.Ep2.106.58.
Atossa, curs'd with ev'ry granted pray'r, 3.Ep2.147.62.
Averted half your Parents simple Pray'r, 3.Ep2.286.73.
That summons you to all the Pride of Pray'r: 3.Ep4.142.151.
And feels that grace his pray'r besought in vain, 4.2HE1.238.215.
Forth from the heap she pick'd her Vot'ry's pray'r. 5.DunA2.91.108.
Puts his last refuge all in Heav'n and Pray'r. 5.DunA2.206.127.
Puts his last refuge all in Heav'n in Pray'r. 5.DunA2.206A.127.
(As morning-pray'r and flagellation end.) 5.DunA2.258.133.
The caitiff Vaticide conceiv'd a pray'r. 5.DunB2.78.299.
Forth from the heap she pick'd her Vot'ry's pray'r, 5.DunB2.95.300.
Puts his last refuge all in heav'n and pray'r. 5.DunB2.214.306.
(As morning pray'r, and flagellation end) 5.DunB2.270.308.
So he; but pious, whisper'd first his pray'r. 5.DunB4.354.377.
To hear the Poet's Pray'r; 6.11.84.33.
If so, our *Dean* shall drive him forth by Pray'r. 6.96iv.34.277.
Perhaps, with added Sacrifice and Pray'r, Il.1.125.93.
To *Phœbus* pray'd, and *Phœbus* heard the Pray'r: Il.1.495.111.
And solemn Voice, the Priest directs his Pray'r. Il.1.589.116.
So *Chryses* pray'd, *Apollo* heard his Pray'r: Il.1.598.116.
But part in Peace, secure thy Pray'r is sped: Il.1.678.119.
When thus the King prefers his solemn Pray'r. Il.2.488.150.
Thus pray'd the Chief: His unavailing Pray'r Il.2.498.150.
Whoe'er he be, propitiate *Jove* with Pray'r; Il.5.228.278.
The Victor's Knees, and thus his Pray'r addressed. Il.6.56.326.
If so the Pow'r, atton'd by fervent Pray'r, Il.6.117.329.
So may the Pow'r, atton'd by fervent Pray'r, Il.6.344.343.
But thou, atton'd by Penitence and Pray'r, Il.6.384.345.
Thus to the Gods prefer'd a Father's Pray'r. Il.6.603.356.
For *Jove,* averse, our humble Pray'r denies, Il.10.53.4.
Then Godlike *Diomed* prefer'd his Pray'r: Il.10.335.18.
Confus'd, and weary all the Pow'rs with Pray'r; Il.15.423.213.
The Sire of Gods, confirming *Thetis'* Pray'r, Il.15.714.223.
Hear, as of old! Thou gav'st, at *Thetis* Pray'r, Il.16.292.253.
To free the Fleet was granted to his Pray'r; Il.16.308.254.
Oh King! oh Father! hear my humble Pray'r: Il.17.728.315.
With Tears the Hero spoke, and at his Pray'r Il.17.733.317.
But thou, in Pity, by my Pray'r be won; Il.18.527.347.
But thou! appeas'd, propitious to our pray'r, Il.19.141.377.
Unhappy Boy! no Pray'r, no moving Art Il.20.541.417.
The burning River sends his earnest Pray'r. Il.21.431.438.
Hast thou forgot, how at the Monarch's Pray'r, Il.21.517.443.
The Words of Age; attend a Parent's Pray'r! Il.22.115.457.
Again the Goddess. Much my Father's Pray'r, Il.22.305.468.
By all the sacred Prevalence of Pray'r; Il.22.427.473.
Nor all the sacred Prevalence of Pray'r. Il.22.436.473.
But great *Achilles* stands apart in Pray'r, Il.23.172.496.
But fast beside *Achilles* stood in Pray'r, Il.23.238.499.
But yield to Ransom and the Father's Pray'r. Il.24.151.541.
Jove heard his Pray'r, and from the Throne on high Il.24.387.552.
Lo! to thy Pray'r restor'd, thy breathless Son: Il.24.749.568.
With Hecatombs and pray'r in pomp prefer'd, Od.1.34.31.
Neptune, by pray'r repentant rarely won, Od.1.88.35.
Indulgent to his pray'r, the Goddess took Od.2.305.76.
To bless our safe return we join in pray'r, Od.3.193.95.
And sooth the vanquish'd with a victor's pray'r. Od.4.572.147.
But vain his pray'r, his arts are vain to move Od.4.757.154.
The fav'ring Goddess present to the pray'r: Od.4.1014.165.
Or prostrate at her knee address the pray'r. Od.6.172.216.
"Won by her pray'r, th' aereal bridegroom flies. Od.6.336.227.
And angry *Neptune* heard th' unrighteous pray'r. Od.9.630.332.
I then: O nymph propitious to my pray'r, Od.12.139.439.
This dreadful Pest! To her direct thy pray'r, Od.12.157.439.
With pray'r they now address th' æthereal train, Od.12.423.451.
Thus to the sea-green sisters sends his pray'r. Od.13.406.26.
With pure libations, and with solemn pray'r; Od.15.283.82.
Yet strive by pray'r and counsel to restrain Od.16.298.120.
His hands obtesting, and this pray'r conceiv'd. Od.17.281.145.
The nurse replies: "If *Jove* receives my pray'r, Od.17.588.161.
Gracious permit this pray'r, imperial Dame! Od.19.137.199.
Then thus her fate invok'd, with fervent pray'r. Od.20.71.235.
And thus the Gods invok'd, with ardent pray'r. Od.20.119.238.
Soon, with consummate joy to crown his pray'r, Od.20.130.240.
In this blest moment of accepted pray'r Od.20.145.240.
Assents *Eumæus* to the pray'r addrest; Od.20.298.247.
Thy suppliant people, and receive their pray'r! Od.22.67.290.
Jove and *Jove's* daughter first implore in pray'r, Od.24.600.376.

PRAY'R-BOOKS
And beads and pray'r-books are the toys of age: 3.EOM2.280.88.

PRAY'RS
Gods! can no Pray'rs, no Sighs, no Numbers move 1.TrSP.242.404.
The Winds my Pray'rs, my Sighs, my Numbers bear, 1.TrSP.244.404.
And to my fervent Pray'rs so far consent, 2.ChJM.280.27.
Forget her Pray'rs, or miss a Masquerade, 2.RL2.108.166.
With store of Pray'rs, for Mornings, Nights, and Noons, 2.RL4.29.185.
O had I stay'd, and said my Pray'rs at home! 2.RL4.160.197.
The Courtier's Promises, and Sick Man's Pray'rs, 2.RL5.119.209.
Nor pray'rs nor fasts its stubborn pulse restrain, 2.ElAb.27.321.
See how the force of others' pray'rs I try, 2.ElAb.149.331.
But why should I on others' pray'rs depend? 2.ElAb.151.332.
Take back my fruitless penitence and pray'rs, 2.ElAb.286.343.
I pay my Debts, believe, and say my Pray'rs, 4.Arbu.268.114.
I pay my Debts, believe, and go to Pray'rs, 4.Arbu.268A.114.
The Gods, to curse *Pamela* with her Pray'rs, 6.19.49.63.
Had fate decreed, propitious to your pray'rs, 6.38.11.107.

PRAY'RS (CONTINUED)

To morning walks, and pray'rs three hours a day; ....6.45.14.125.
And Pray'rs, and Tears, and Bribes shall plead in vain; ....II.1.40.87.
With pure Lustrations, and with solemn Pray'rs. ....II.1.411.107.
Their Pray'rs perform'd, the Chiefs the Rite pursue, ...II.2.502.150.
While thus their Pray'rs united mount the Sky; ....II.3.370.211.
In Act to throw, but first prefers his Pray'rs. ....II.3.432.212.
While these appear before the Pow'r with Pray'rs, ...II.6.388.345.
And deem your Pray'rs the mean Effect of Fear. ....II.7.232.376.
Pleas'd may ye hear (so Heav'n succeed my Pray'rs) ......II.7.462.387.
And gives the People to their Monarch's Pray'rs. ....II.8.296.411.
With Pray'rs to move him, or with Gifts to bend. ....II.9.146.439.
Who feels no Mercy, and who hears no Pray'rs, ...II.9.210.443.
If thou wilt yield to great *Atrides'* Pray'rs, ...II.9.340.450.
With Pray'rs entreat me, and with Force detain. ....II.9.591.464.
And daily Pray'rs attone for daily Sins. ....II.9.623.465.
Pray'rs are *Jove's* Daughters, of celestial Race, ...II.9.624.465.
While *Pray'rs,* to heal her Wrongs, move slow behind. ....II.9.630.465.
Their Pray'rs were urgent, and their Proffers great; ....II.9.692.468.
Or strive with Pray'rs his haughty Soul to bend? ....II.9.817.474.
And Pray'rs will burst that swelling Heart with Pride. ......II.9.819.474.
Well be Apollo are thy Pray'rs repaid,' ....II.11.467.54.
Still succour Mortals, and attend their Pray'rs; ....II.24.412.552.
Now fearless enter, and prefer thy Pray'rs; ....II.24.570.560.
Then, mix'd with pray'rs, he utters these commands. ....Od.15.167.76.
The seeming beggar answers with his pray's. ....Od.17.425.153.
"And Name the blessing that your pray'rs have won." ....Od.19.476.220.
Ev'n in their wishes, and their pray'rs, forgot! ....Od.21.218.270.

PRAYER

And to the Goddess thus prefer their Prayer: ....2.TemF.299.278.
While bashful *Jenny,* ev'n at Morning-Prayer, ...4.HAdv.33.79.
Adds to Christs Prayer the *Power* and *Glory Clause.* ....4.JD2A.114.142.
Adds to Christ's prayer, the *Pow'r and Glory* clause. ....4.JD2.108.143.
The caitiff Vaticide conceiv'd a prayer. ....5.DunA2.74.107.
Atossa's curs'd with ev'ry granted Prayer, ...6.154.33.403.
The due libation and the solemn prayer. ....Od.3.58.89.
For his return with sacrifice and prayer. ....Od.9.273.318.
I thought, devis'd, and *Pallas* heard my prayer. ....Od.9.377.321.

PRAYING

While praying, trembling, in the dust I roll, ...2.ElAb.279.342.
The frugal Crone, whom praying priests attend, ...3.Ep1.238.35.

PRAYS

In vain lost *Eloisa* weeps and prays, ...2.ElAb.15.320.
Verse prays for Peace, or sings down Pope and Turk. ....4.2HE1.236.215.
'Till, safe at distance, to his God he prays, ...II.1.51.88.
Plac'd on *Minerva's* Knees, and thus she prays. ....II.6.377.344.
And teach him Mercy when a Father prays. ....II.24.380.551.

PRE-EXISTENT

What mortal knows his pre-existent state? ....5.DunA3.40.154.
What mortal knows his pre-existent state? ....5.DunB3.48.322.

PRE-ORDAIN'D

A Man, a Mortal, pre-ordain'd to Death! ....II.22.236.465.

PREACH

Then preach till Midnight in your easie Chair; ....2.ChWB.83.60.
"Of *Job's* great Patience since so oft you preach, ...2.ChWB.186.65.
But most be present, if we preach or pray. ....3.EOM3.6.92.
But most be present, if thou preach or pray. ....3.EOM3.6A.92.
So first to preach a white-glov'd Chaplain goes, ...4.JD4.250.47.
Preach as I please, I doubt our curious men ....4.HS2.17.55.
You go to Church to hear these Flatt'rers preach. ....4.2HE2.225.181.
While K[ennet], B[ramston], W[arren], preach in vain. ......5.DunA3.200.174*.
While Kennet, Hare, and Gibson preach in vain. ....5.DunA3.200B.174.
While Sherlock, Hare, and Gibson preach in vain. ....5.DunB3.204.330.
While Kennett, Hare, and Gibson preach in vain. ....5.DunB3.204A.330.
Or impious, preach his Word without a call. ....5.DunB4.94.350.
May you, may Cam, and Isis preach it long! ....5.DunB4.187.360.
They preach the Doctrine, but thou mak'st us do't; ....6.2.25.6.
And, if it can, at once both Please and Preach. ....6.19.24.62.
On Sundays preach, and eat, his Fill; ....6.39.19.111.
Thrice as long as you preach. ....6.91.26.254.

PREACH'D

This, this the saving doctrine, preach'd to all, ...4.1HE1.81.285.
(St. James's first, for leaden Gilbert preach'd) ....5.DunB4.608.404.

PREACHER

The silenc'd Preacher yields to potent strain, ...4.2HE1.237.215.
Preacher at once, and Zany of thy Age! ....5.DunA3.202.175.
Preacher at once, and Zany of thy age! ....5.DunB3.206.330.

PREACHES

All his Grace preaches, all his Lordship sings, ...4.EpS2.224.325.

PREACHING

Ten Metropolitans in preaching well; ....4.EpS1.132.307.

PRECARIOUS

Alike on alms we both precarious live: ....Od.18.24.168.

PRECARIOUSLY

Our scene precariously subsists too long ....6.32.41.97.
Your scene precariously subsists too long ....6.32.41A.97.

PRECEDE

Six huntsmen with a shout precede his chair; ....5.DunA2.185.124.
Six huntsmen with a shout precede his chair; ....5.DunB2.193.305.
To your pretence their title wou'd precede. ....Od.1.506.56.
And sudden sighs precede approaching woe. ....Od.20.420.253.
Unmanly shrieks precede each dying groan, ...Od.22.345.304.
Ignoble cries precede the dying groans; ....Od.24.210.358.

PRECEDENT

And have, at least, *Their Precedent* to plead. ....1.EOC.166.259.
They reason and conclude by *Precedent,* ....1.EOC.410.287.

PRECEDENTS

From various precedents, and various laws. ....Od.3.307.101.

PRECEDES

Thus affable and mild, the Prince precedes, ...Od.1.165.40.
Precedes the father, follow'd by his race, ...Od.3.497.112.
With friendly step precedes his unknown guest, ...Od.14.58.38.
The King precedes; a bowl with fragrant wine ....Od.15.164.76.

PRECEDING

(Her Priest preceding) thro' the gates of Lud. ....5.DunA2.332.142.
The Mules preceding draw the loaded Wain, ...II.24.399.552.

PRECEPT

Against the *Precept,* ne'er transgress its *End,* ....1.EOC.164.259.
And as the Precept of the Church decrees, ...2.ChJM.93.19.
No Precept for Virginity he found: ....2.ChWB.33.58.
From lips like those what precept fail'd to move? ....2.ElAb.67.324.
Yet still how faint by precept is exprest ....6.52.41.157.
To guide thy Conduct, little Precept needs; ....II.23.379.505.
My praise the precept is, be thine the deed. ....Od.1.398.51.
By the sure precept of the sylvan shrine, ...Od.19.341.210.

PRECEPTS

Just *Precepts* thus from great *Examples* giv'n, ...1.EOC.98.250.
First Learned *Greece* just Precepts did indite, ...1.EOC.92A.250.
Some Beauties yet, no Precepts can declare, ...1.EOC.141.255.
His *Precepts* teach but what his *Works* inspire. ....1.EOC.660.314.
Unaw'd by Precepts, Human or Divine, ...2.ChJM.31.16.
Or better Precepts if you can impart, ...4.1HE6.132.246.
So gravest precepts may successless prove, ...5.DunA1.175.84.
So written precepts may successless prove, ...5.DunA1.175A.84.
So graver precepts may successless prove, ...5.DunA1.175B.84.
Their Precepts raz'd the Prejudice of Youth, ...6.96iii.9.274.
Your ancient Fathers gen'rous Precepts gave; ....II.11.914.76.
Urg'd by the precepts by the Goddess giv'n, ...Od.3.90.90.

PRECIOUS

While by our Oaks the precious Loads are born, ...1.W-F.31.151.
And bids her *Beau* demand the precious Hairs: ....2.RL4.122.194.
Who censure most, more precious hairs would lose, ...6.38.29.108.
What yet most precious of thy Store remains, ...II.24.468.556.
The precious gifts th' illustrious heralds bear, ...Od.8.453.287.
Then took a goatskin fill'd with precious wine, ...Od.9.229.316.
We to thy shore the precious freight shall bear, ...Od.9.412.323.
To thee we now consign the precious load, ...Od.15.132.75.
By precious gifts the vow sincere display: ....Od.18.323.182.
Enough her precious tears already flow— ....Od.21.91.263.

PRECIPICE

The shapeless *Rock,* or hanging *Precipice.* ....1.EOC.160.258.
Fast by the Road a Precipice was worn: ....II.23.500.510.
Hurl me from yon dread precipice on high; ....Od.14.441.57.

PRECIPITANT

And run precipitant, with Noise and Strife, ...6.17ii.5.56.
Precipitant in fear, wou'd wing their flight, ...Od.1.213.43.

PRECIPITATE

Whom Fury drove precipitate to War. ....1.TrSt.191.418.
Nonsense precipitate, like running Lead, ...5.DunB1.123.278.
His headlong Steeds, precipitate in Flight, ...II.6.48.325.
Precipitate the pond'rous Mass descends: ....II.13.194.115.

PRECIPITATELY

Furious he sinks; precipitately dull. ....5.DunA2.294.139.
Furious he dives, precipitately dull. ....5.DunB2.316.312.

PRECIPITATES

Swift to the Field precipitates his Flight; ....1.TrES.337.462.
Swift to the Ships precipitates her Flight; ....II.2.204.138.
And all confus'd, precipitates his Flight. ....II.3.50.191.
Swift to the Field precipitates his Flight; ....II.16.824.275.

PRECISE

End all dispute; and fix the year precise ....4.2HE1.53.199.

PRECLUDES

A witness-judge precludes a long appeal: ....Od.19.585.224.

PREDESTIN'D

Laments his Son, predestin'd to be slain, ...1.TrES.259.459.
For Life predestin'd to the *Gnomes'* Embrace. ....2.RL1.80.151.
For *Trojan* Vulturs a predestin'd Prey. ....II.8.656.427.
And gives great *Hector* the predestin'd Day. ....II.12.302.92.
Laments his Son, predestin'd to be slain, ...II.16.564.266.
The day predestin'd to reward his woes. ....Od.1.24.30.
Behold the long-predestin'd day! (he cries) ....Od.13.196.15.

PREDICTING

For thus did the Predicting God ordain. ....1.TrSt.554.433.

PREEMINENCE

See PREHEMINENCE.

PREF'RENCE

To see the pref'rence due to sacred age ....Od.3.66.89.

PREFACE

With artful preface to his host he spoke. ....Od.14.517.62.

PREFACES
How Prologues into Prefaces decay, ... 5.DunA1.231.90.
How Prologues into Prefaces decay, ... 5.DunB1.277.290.

PREFER
And to the Goddess thus prefer their Prayer: ... 2.TemF.299.278.
In doubt his Mind or Body to prefer, ... 3.EOM2.9.55.
Of *Carps* and *Mullets* why prefer the *great,* ... 4.HS2.21.55.
Prefer a new Japanner to their shoes, ... 4.1HE1.156.291.
And at an humbler pitch prefer ... 6.6i.7.14.
Some *Stephens* to the rest prefer, ... 6.29.3A.82.
Some *Plantin* to the rest prefer, ... 6.29.3.82.
And heav'nly Charms prefer to proffer'd Gold? ... Il.1.140.93.
Now fearless enter, and prefer thy Pray'rs; ... Il.24.570.560.
First to the Queen prefer a suppliant's claim, ... Od.7.69.237.
Go then secure, thy humble suit prefer, ... Od.7.97.238.

PREFER'D
Prefer'd the same Request, and lowly bow'd, ... 2.TemF.329.280.
Yes, Nature's road must ever be prefer'd; ... 3.EOM2.161.74.
And Namby Pamby be prefer'd for Wit! ... 5.DunA3.322.188.
And *Ambrose Philips* be prefer'd for Wit! ... 5.DunA3.322B.188.
Lo! Ambrose Philips is prefer'd for Wit! ... 5.DunB3.326.336.
Thus to the Gods prefer'd a Father's Pray'r. ... Il.6.603.356.
Then Godlike *Diomed* prefer'd his Pray'r: ... Il.10.335.18.
With Hecatombs and pray'r in pomp prefer'd, ... Od.1.34.31.
No vows had we prefer'd, nor victim slain! ... Od.4.475.142.
If e'er *Ulysses* to thy fane prefer'd ... Od.4.1007.164.

PREFERR'D
The *Groom* and *Sorrel Mare* preferr'd to me! ... 6.96iv.60.278.
When Ambrose Philips was preferr'd for Wit! ... 6.106iii.3.307.
His Vows, in Bitterness of Soul preferr'd; ... Il.8.294.411.
Why mourns my Son? thy late-preferr'd Request ... Il.18.95.327.
Nor is my Pride preferr'd before my Friend. ... Il.23.698.517.
He spake, and to her hand preferr'd the bowl: ... Od.3.64.89.
Submissive thus the hoary Sire preferr'd ... Od.3.494.111.
All to the suitors wastful board preferr'd. ... Od.14.130.42.
Yet like my self I wish'd thee here preferr'd, ... Od.17.209.141.
To whom *Ulysses'* piety preferr'd ... Od.17.286.146.
Spontaneous to the Suitors' feast preferr'd: ... Od.20.220.244.
His kind protecting hand my youth preferr'd, ... Od.20.267.246.

PREFERR'ST
Preferr'st thou *Litter* to the Marriage Bed? ... 6.96iv.32.277.

PREFERRING
Base Wealth preferring to eternal Praise. ... Il.23.368.505.

PREFERS
Each am'rous Nymph prefers her Gifts in vain, ... 1.PSu.53.76.
Save just at dinner—then prefers, no doubt, ... 3.Ep1.138.26.
What he prefers to the *Patrician* Board: ... 6.17iii.25.58.
When thus the King prefers his solemn Pray'r. ... Il.2.488.150.
In Act to throw, but first prefers his Pray'rs. ... Il.3.432.212.
To the gay Court a rural shed prefers, ... Od.1.246.44.
Prefers his barb'rous *Sintians* to thy arms! ... Od.8.336.281.
But idly thus thy soul prefers to live, ... Od.18.408.188.

PREGNANT
Pregnant with thousands flits the Scrap unseen, ... 3.Ep3.77.93.
For new Abortions, all ye pregnant Fair! ... 5.DunA3.312.186.
For new abortions, all ye pregnant fair! ... 5.DunB3.314.335.
Pregnant with Plagues, and shedding Seeds of Death, ... Il.5.1059.317.
By *Zephyr* pregnant on the breezy Shore. ... Il.16.185.245.
And feed with pregnant Streams the Plants and Flow'rs; ... Il.21.292.433.
Full fifty pregnant females each contain'd; ... Od.14.19.35.

PREHEMINENCE
Painful preheminence! yourself to view ... 3.EOM4.267.153.
See what Preheminence our Merits gain! ... Il.9.441.454.

PREJUDICE
P. Dear Sir, forgive the Prejudice of Youth: ... 4.EpS1.63.302.
Their Precepts raz'd the Prejudice of Youth, ... 6.96iii.9.274.

PRELATE
And goad the Prelate slumb'ring in his Stall. ... 4.EpS2.219.325.
The sowzing Prelate, or the sweating Peer, ... 4.1740.70.336.
The plunging Prelate, and his pond'rous Grace, ... 5.DunB2.323.312.

PRELATE'S
But when no Prelate's Lawn with Hair-shirt lin'd, ... 4.1HE1.165.291.

PRELUDING
Mean while permit that my preluding Muse ... 1.TrSt.49.411.
More fierce intents, preluding to the fray; ... Od.18.41.169.

PRENTICE
What? can your Prentice raise your Jealousie? ... 2.ChWB.119.62.
I'd scorn your Prentice, shou'd you die to-morrow. ... 2.ChWB.123.62.
What? can our Prentice raise your Jealousie? ... 2.ChWB.119A.62.
Much less the 'Prentice who to morrow may. ... 4.EpS2.37.314.

PRENTICESHIP
He serv'd a 'Prenticeship, who sets up shop; ... 4.2HE1.181.211.

PREPAR'D
Force he prepar'd, but check'd the rash Design; ... 1.TrVP.118.382.
Prepar'd to labour in th'unequal Fight; ... 1.TrES.94.453.
The Foe once gone, our Knight prepar'd t'undress, ... 2.ChJM.373.32.
And Nymphs prepar'd their *Chocolate* to take; ... 2.RL1.16A.145.
Say, for such worth are other worlds prepar'd? ... 3.Ep3.335.120.
Resign'd to live, prepar'd to die, ... 6.150.1.398.
Prepar'd new Toils and doubled Woes on Woes. ... Il.2.501.150.
Prepar'd for Flight, but doom'd to fly in vain? ... Il.4.279.234.

PREPAR'D (CONTINUED)
Prepar'd for Combate, e're the Lance he tost, ... Il.5.782.303.
Meantime *Achilles'* Slaves prepar'd a Bed, ... Il.9.775.472.
Last, for *Patroclus* was the Couch prepar'd, ... Il.9.782.472.
A wakeful Squadron, each in Arms prepar'd: ... Il.10.208.11.
What glorious Man, for high Attempts prepar'd, ... Il.10.361.19.
Sternly he spoke, and as the Wretch prepar'd ... Il.10.522.26.
Prepar'd to labour in th' unequal Fight; ... Il.12.448.97.
This said; the tow'ring Chief, prepar'd to go, ... Il.13.946A.150.
The Steeds, prepar'd my Chariot to convey ... Il.14.349.179.
In Molds prepar'd, the glowing Ore he pours. ... Il.18.446.342.
Achilles rais'd the Spear, prepar'd to wound; ... Il.21.78.424.
The Wood the *Grecians* cleave, prepar'd to burn; ... Il.23.150.495.
Prepar'd perchance to leave thy native Land. ... Il.24.470.556.
O'er earth and ocean wide prepar'd to soar, ... Od.1.128.38.
To tread the walks of death he stood prepar'd, ... Od.2.311.76.
Prepar'd, ere yet descends the evening hour. ... Od.2.401.80.
She bids the Mariners prepar'd to stand, ... Od.2.432.81.
Lo! on the seas prepar'd the vessel stands; ... Od.2.450.83.
Transfix'd the fragments, some prepar'd the food. ... Od.3.44.88.
Prepar'd I stand: he was but born to try ... Od.3.116.91.
For his abode a Capital prepar'd; ... Od.4.234.130.
The beverage now prepar'd t'inspire the feast, ... Od.4.323.134.
The plans of war against the town prepar'd. ... Od.4.350.136.
Prepar'd for rest, and off'ring to the * God ... Od.7.184.244.
With heav'n's high will prepar'd to suffer more. ... Od.7.292.250.
Be chosen youths prepar'd, expert to try ... Od.8.33.263.
And in the bath prepar'd my limbs I lave; ... Od.10.426.365.
Prepar'd to whirl the whizzing spear I stay, ... Od.12.272.445.
The sailors waiting, and the ships prepar'd. ... Od.14.370.53.
He charg'd the houshold cates to be prepar'd. ... Od.15.109.74.
Prepar'd to launch the freighted vessel rides; ... Od.15.508.94.
And now a short repast prepar'd, they fed, ... Od.16.498.131.
In haste the Prince arose, prepar'd to part; ... Od.17.3.132.
And in the dome prepar'd the genial feast. ... Od.20.311.248.
With fire prepar'd they deal the morsels round, ... Od.20.316.248.
But the rich banquet in the dome prepar'd, ... Od.20.347.249.

PREPAR'ST
And lo! already, thou prepar'st to fly. ... Il.17.186.294.

PREPARD
Prepard for the Devil and his Angells also? ... 6.122.24.342.

PREPARE
Prepare the Way! a God, a God appears. ... 1.Mes.30.116.
Oft as the mounting Larks their Notes prepare, ... 1.W-F.133.162.
Break all the Bonds of Nature, and prepare ... 1.TrSt.116.415.
Must we, alas! our doubtful Necks prepare, ... 1.TrSt.236.420.
The dire, tho' just, Revenge which I prepare ... 1.TrSt.405.427.
Combs, Bodkins, Leads, Pomatums, to prepare? ... 2.RL*A*2.16.132.
Strait the three Bands prepare in Arms to join, ... 2.RL3.29.171.
The *Bodkin, Comb,* and *Essence* to prepare; ... 2.RL4.98.191.
I come, I come! prepare your roseate bow'rs, ... 2.ElAb.317.345.
I come, ye ghosts! prepare your roseate bow'rs, ... 2.ElAb.317A.345.
Come then, the colours and the ground prepare! ... 3.Ep2.17.49.
Another Æschylus appears! prepare ... 5.DunA3.311.185.
Another Æschylus appears! prepare ... 5.DunB3.313.335.
Th' Allies to bomb *Toulon* prepare; ... 6.10.109.27.
But then prepare, Imperious Prince! prepare, ... Il.1.243.98.
But then prepare, Imperious Prince! prepare, ... Il.1.243.98.
Accept the Hecatomb the *Greeks* prepare; ... Il.1.579.115.
And now the *Greeks* their Hecatomb prepare; ... Il.1.599.116.
Then spread the Tables, the Repast prepare, ... Il.1.612.117.
Then spread the Tables, the Repast prepare, ... Il.2.512.151.
Prepare ye *Trojans!* while a third we bring ... Il.3.143.197.
With Grief he heard, and bade the Chiefs prepare ... Il.3.330.209.
Who rule the Dead, and horrid Woes prepare ... Il.3.352.209.
Next to decide by sacred Lots prepare, ... Il.3.392.211.
But should this Arm prepare to wreak our Hate ... Il.4.61.223.
Then spread the Tables, the Repast prepare, ... Il.7.384.382.
Prepare to meet us near the Navy-wall; ... Il.10.145.8.
If to besiege our Navies they prepare, ... Il.10.247.13.
What with this Arm I can, prepare to know, ... Il.13.987.152.
Let *Hecamede* the strength'ning Bath prepare, ... Il.14.10.157.
While *Phœbus* hastes, great *Hector* to prepare ... Il.15.63.197.
Now then to conquer or to die prepare, ... Il.17.268.298.
Of all the Goddesses, did *Jove* prepare ... Il.18.503.345.
A secret Ambush on the Foe prepare: ... Il.18.596.351.
The Victim-Ox the sturdy Youth prepare; ... Il.18.649.355.
Each due Atonement gladly I prepare; ... Il.19.185.379.
Who rule the Dead, and horrid Woes prepare ... Il.19.271.383.
Automedon and *Alcimus* prepare ... Il.19.426.389.
That *Greece* the Warrior's fun'ral Pile prepare, ... Il.23.62.489.
These wrapt in double Cauls of Fat, prepare; ... Il.23.302.501.
Let others for the noble Task prepare, ... Il.23.353.504.
The mournful Father *Iris* shall prepare, ... Il.24.152.541.
His Friends prepare the Victim, and dispose ... Il.24.159.542.
She spoke, and vanish'd. *Priam* bids prepare ... Il.24.225.546.
With Skill prepare them, and in Parts divide: ... Il.24.789.570.
With that, *Achilles* bad prepare the Bed, ... Il.24.812.571.
Others apart, the spacious hall prepare, ... Od.1.146.40.
Instant, to foreign realms prepare to sail, ... Od.1.365.50.
Bid instant to prepare the bridal train, ... Od.2.131.67.
The winged vessel studious I prepare, ... Od.2.325.77.
Thee first it fits, oh stranger! to prepare ... Od.3.57.89.
Prepare thy chariot at the dawn of day, ... Od.3.472.110.
To *Pallas,* first of Gods, prepare the feast, ... Od.3.532.113.
And bid the handmaids for the feast prepare, ... Od.3.543.114.
And for the promis'd journey bids prepare ... Od.3.604.117.
At *Helen's* beck prepare the room of state: ... Od.4.402.139.
Rushing impetuous forth, we strait prepare ... Od.4.611.148.
Then bids prepare the hospitable treat: ... Od.4.711.152.
Mean-time my train the friendly gifts prepare, ... Od.4.805.156.
The menial train the regal feast prepare: ... Od.4.840.158.
Instant prepare me, on the neighb'ring strand, ... Od.4.894.160.

PREPARE (CONTINUED)
Arise, prepare the bridal train, arise! Od.6.32.205.
The car prepare, the mules incessant rein. Od.6.86.209.
The train prepare a cruise of curious mold, Od.6.91.209.
Bids her fair train the purple quilts prepare, Od.7.429.258.
And healing waters for the bath prepare: Od.8.462.288.
Then first a fire we kindle, and prepare Od.9.272.318.
Four faithful handmaids the soft rites prepare; Od.10.414.364.
To whom unmov'd; If this the Gods prepare, Od.11.172.390.
Prepare to hear of murther and of blood; Od.11.476.407.
They roast the fragments, and prepare the feast. Od.12.430.451.
Take with free welcome what our hands prepare, Od.14.97.40.
Then doom'd high *Jove* due vengeance to prepare. Od.14.334.51.
Rise, son of *Nestor!* for the road prepare, Od.15.55.72.
Some choice domestic viands to prepare; Od.15.88.73.
Hoise ev'ry sail, and ev'ry oar prepare. Od.15.245.80.
O thou! that dost thy happy course prepare Od.15.282.82.
Prepare then, said *Telemachus,* to know Od.15.288.83.
Awake the sleeping fires, their meal prepare, Od.16.3.100.
Lo! I the ready sacrifice prepare: Od.16.201.113.
A seat soft spread with furry spoils prepare, Od.19.119.198.
Now wash the stranger, and the bed prepare; Od.19.363.211.
For the poor friend the cleansing bath prepare: Od.19.415.214.
Instant he bade prepare the genial feast: Od.19.489.220.
Sated at length they rise, and bid prepare Od.20.465.256.
And bade *Melanthius* a vast pyle prepare; Od.21.182.268.
And sage *Eurynomè,* the couch prepare: Od.23.310.338.

PREPARES
To trim his beard, th'unweildy scythe prepares; 1.TrPA.23.366.
The raging God prepares t'avenge her Fate. 1.TrSt.704.439.
For her the Spouse prepares the bridal ring, 2.ElAb.219.338.
Prepares a dreadful Jest for all mankind! 4.HS2.124.65.
Already, Opera prepares the way, 5.DunA3.303.185.
Already Opera prepares the way, 5.DunB3.301.334.
The Host to expiate next the King prepares, Il.1.410.107.
To grudge the Conquests mighty *Jove* prepares, Il.2.414.147.
Eubæa next her martial Sons prepares, Il.2.641.157.
Atrides then his massy Lance prepares, Il.3.431.212.
Jove seals the League, or bloodier Scenes prepares; Il.4.113.225.
Jove but prepares to strike the fiercer Blow. Il.4.195.230.
When *Jove* to punish faithless Men prepares, Il.7.253.376.
Gifts worthy thee, his Royal Hand prepares; Il.9.341.450.
But the rash Youth prepares to scour the Plain: Il.10.394.21.
The Draught prescrib'd, fair *Hecamede* prepares, Il.11.764.69.
This for the wounded Prince the Dame prepares; Il.11.784.70.
This said; the tow'ring Chief, prepares to go, Il.13.946.150.
And for his wish'd Return prepares in vain; Il.17.467.305.
His lifted Arm prepares the fatal Blow; Il.21.704.450.
Nor less *Achilles* his fierce Soul prepares; Il.22.393.471.
Then studious she prepares the choicest flour, Od.2.426.81.
Her self the chest prepares: in order roll'd Od.8.475.288.
Now each partakes the feast, the wine prepares, Od.8.513.290.
And sitting down, to milk his flocks prepares; Od.9.289.318.
Atrides' son the purple draught prepares. Od.15.157.76.
Then girding his strong loins, the King prepares Od.18.74.170.
Such were his words; and *Hymen* now prepares Od.18.315.182.

PREPARING
The Bath preparing for her Lord's Return: Il.22.571.480.

PREPOSSESSION
Which home-bred Prepossession had confin'd; 6.96v.12.280.

PREPOSSEST
Not *dully prepossest,* nor *blindly right;* 1.EOC.634.311.

PREPOSSET
Not *dully prepposset,* or *blindly right;* 1.EOC.634A.311.

PREROGATIVE
And Man's prerogative to rule, but spare. 3.EOM3.160.109.
Now for Prerogative, and now for Laws; 4.2HE1.159.209.
Guard my Prerogative, assert my Throne: 5.DunB4.583.400.
Enjoy the dear Prerogative of Life. Il.9.523.458.
'Tis right; 'tis man's prerogative to give, Od.18.331.183.

PRESAGE
And yet no dire Presage so wounds my Mind, Il.6.574.355.
A sure presage from ev'ry wing that flew. Od.2.188.71.
But my prophetic fears, alas! presage, Od.19.358.211.

PRESAGES
The flight of birds, and thence presages drew, 1.TrPA.30.366.

PRESAGING
He said, and past with sad presaging Heart Il.6.462.349.
Presaging tears apace began to rain; Od.10.230.351.
Amphinomus, who thus presaging cry'd. Od.20.305.247.

PRESBYTERIAN
A Quaker? sly: A Presbyterian? sow'r: 3.Ep1.108.23.

PRESCIENCE
T'elude the prescience of a God by guile. Od.4.536.146.

PRESCIENT
Prescient, the tides or tempests to withstand, 3.EOM3.101.102.
Prescient he view'd th' aerial tracts, and drew Od.2.187.71.
The prescient Godhead to reveal the rest. Od.4.744.153.
To fly these shores the prescient *Theban* Shade Od.12.326.447.

PRESCRIB'D
Prescrib'd her Heights, and prun'd her tender Wing, 1.EOC.736.325.
Short is the Date prescrib'd to Mortal Man; 1.TrES.239.458.
All but the page prescrib'd, their present state; 3.EOM1.78.23.

PRESCRIB'D (CONTINUED)
The Draught prescrib'd, fair *Hecamede* prepares, Il.11.764.69.
Short is the Date prescrib'd to mortal Man; Il.16.542.265.

PRESCRIBE
Prescribe, apply, and call their *Masters Fools.* 1.EOC.111.251.
Prescribe directions, and confirm the crew. Od.3.461.109.
Unerring will prescribe your destin'd course. Od.4.526.146.
Your couch to fashion as your self prescribe. Od.19.698.229.

PRESCRIBES
Their Date determines, and prescribes their Force: 2.TemF.484.287.
Prescribes, attends, the med'cine makes, and gives. 3.Ep3.270.115.

PRESENCE
And snowy Mountains thy bright Presence boast; 1.TrSt.830.444.
Thy sacred Presence from that Hour I lost; 1.TrUl.198.472.
That in my Presence offers such a Wrong. 2.ChJM.650.46.
Her gloomy presence saddens all the scene, 2.ElAb.167.333.
The *Presence* seems, with things so richly odd, 4.JD4.238.45.
Her ample presence fills up all the place; 5.DunA1.217.89.
Her ample presence fills up all the place; 5.DunB1.261.289.
And whose bright Presence gilds thy *Chrysa's* Shores. Il.1.56.88.
Before thy Presence, Father, I appear Il.3.227.203.
Struck with her Presence, strait the livly Red Il.3.491.215.
I own thy Presence, and confess thy Aid. Il.5.1011.315.
Our ancient Seat his honour'd Presence grac'd, Il.6.269.340.
Confus'd, unnerv'd in *Hector's* Presence grown, Il.11.670.65.
(Thus arm'd) not *Hector* shall our Presence stay; Il.14.435.184.
There in the Father's awful Presence stand, Il.15.166.203.
Or sacred *Ilion,* thy bright Presence boast, Il.16.634.269.
Now since her Presence glads our Mansion, say, Il.18.473.344.
A Ray divine her heav'nly Presence shed, Il.19.9.371.
Thy Presence here shou'd stern *Atrides* see, Il.24.854.572.
Vouchsaf'd thy presence to my wond'ring eyes, Od.2.298.76.
Without thy presence vain is thy command; Od.2.303.76.
Thy sacred presence from that hour I lost: Od.13.365.24.
The presence of thy guest shall best reward Od.15.587.98.
With his bright presence deigns the dome to grace. Od.19.49.195.
To sit distinguish'd, with our presence grac'd, Od.21.312.274.
Doubt we his presence, when he now appears? Od.23.72.322.

PRESENT
Invite my Lays. Be present, Sylvan Maids! 1.W-F.3.148.
Enlights the *present,* and shall warm the *last:* 1.EOC.403.286.
Be present still, oh Goddess! in our Aid; 1.TrSt.590.435.
But *Jove* was present in the dire Debate, 1.TrES.139.454.
Nor know to make the present Blessing last, 2.ChJM.33.16.
(So Poets sing) was present on the Place; 2.ChJM.327.30.
Present the Spear, and arm him for the Fight. 2.RL3.130.177.
Present their Spear, and arm him for the Fight. 2.RL3.130A.177.
Present the Cross before my lifted eye, 2.ElAb.327.346.
All but the page prescrib'd, their present state; 3.EOM1.78.23.
That sees immediate good by present sense; 3.EOM2.73.64.
Present to grasp, and future still to find, 3.EOM2.125.70.
Let this great truth be present night and day; 3.EOM3.5.92.
But most be present, if we preach or pray. 3.EOM3.6.92.
Let that great truth be present night and day; 3.EOM3.5A.92.
But most be present, if thou preach or pray. 3.EOM3.6A.92.
Not present good or ill, the joy or curse, 3.EOM4.71.135.
Wise is her present; she connects in this 3.EOM4.349.162.
Wise is the present; she connects in this 3.EOM4.349A.162.
Publish the present Age, but where my Text 4.HS1.59.11.
To Thee, the World its present homage pays, 4.2HE1.23.195.
Matures my present, and shall bound my last! 4.1HE1.2.279.
Which not at present having time to do— 4.EpS2.156.322.
Baffled, yet present ev'n amidst despair, 5.DunA2.105A.109.
Judge of all present, past, and future wit, 5.DunA2.344.142.
"Judge of all present, past, and future wit; 5.DunB2.376.315.
Each eager to present the first Address. 5.DunB4.136.354.
A second sun thou dost present, 6.6ii.13.15.
Decry'd each past, to raise each present Writer 6.17iv.13.59.
Long future prospects, and short present joys: 6.22.11.71.
You'd at present do nothing but give us a Visit. 6.42i.8.116.
The present well, and ev'n the past enjoy. 6.55.11.167.
Were once my Present; *Love* that Armour gave. 6.96iv.76.278.
The past, the present, and the future knew. Il.1.94.91.
Some trivial Present to my Ships I bear, Il.1.219.97.
Grac'd with the Present of his Shafts and Bow. Il.2.1003.170.
No Crime of thine our present Suff'rings draws, Il.3.215.202.
I make this Present to the Shades below. Il.5.801.304.
But *Jove* was present, and forbad the Death. Il.5.823.305.
Our present Woe, and Infamy to come: Il.6.447.348.
The Thoughts of Glory past, and present Shame, Il.6.588.355.
Their present Triumph, as their late Despair. Il.7.377.382.
At once my present Judgment, and my past; Il.9.140.439.
Some Present too to ev'ry Prince was paid; Il.9.438.454.
0 thou! for ever present in my way, Il.10.329.17.
So now be present, Oh celestial Maid! Il.10.345.18.
The Spoil of Foes, or Present of a God? Il.10.643.30.
But *Jove* was present in the dire Debate, Il.12.493.99.
Let softer Cares the present Hour employ, Il.14.357.180.
(Imperial *Jove)* his present Death withstands; Il.15.542.217.
The Work and Present of celestial Hands; Il.17.220.296.
To save our present, and our future Race. Il.17.265.298.
And bears the blazing Present through the Skies. Il.18.712.357.
But present to his Aid, *Apollo* shrouds Il.20.513.416.
Like us, their present, future Sons destroy, Il.21.533.444.
Vain thy past Labour, and thy present vain: Il.22.20.453.
The Kindest but his present Wants allay, Il.22.636.482.
An ample Present let him thence receive, Il.23.631.514.
Thy present Vigour Age has overthrown, Il.23.715.518.
While pleas'd I take the Gift thy Hands present, Il.23.745.519.
And present at his Thought, descends the Maid. Il.23.902.525.
His Friend's dear Image present to his Mind, Il.24.6.534.
Your selves were present; where this Minstrel-God Il.24.81.538.

PRESENT 137 PRESS

PRESENT (CONTINUED)

A present Goddess brought the high command, ... Il.24.273.547.
The present Synod speaks its author wise; .... Od.2.41.62.
I take the present of the promis'd Vase; .... Od.4.820.157.
The fav'ring Goddess present to the pray'r: .... Od.4.1014.165.
Death, present death on ev'ry side appears. .... Od.5.392.191.
Whose well-taught mind the present age surpast, ... Od.7.210.247.
Your present aid this godlike stranger craves, ... Od.8.27.263.
Just to the tale, as present at the fray, ... Od.8.535.291.
Urg'd by some present God, they swift let fall .... Od.9.453.324.
Then, then be present, and my soul inspire .... Od.13.443.27.
(Reply'd *Eumæus:)* To the present hour .... Od.14.192.45.
Lost in the children of the present spouse .... Od.15.25.71.
To me this present, of *Vulcanian* frame, ... Od.15.130.75.
The Prince the variegated present took. .... Od.15.145.75.
My present labours food and drink procure, ... Od.15.398.88.
And is this present, swineherd! of thy hand? .... Od.17.450.155.
Of decent robes a present has design'd; .... Od.17.639.163.
A present Deity the Prince confess'd, ... Od.19.42.195.
She to her present Lord laments him lost, ... Od.19.244.206.
And from the present bliss abstracts her thought. .... Od.19.559.223.
And give the present hour to genial joy. .... Od.20.309.247.
In sweet repaste the present hour imploy, ... Od.21.471.283.
Enjoy the present good, and former woe; .... Od.23.56.321.
(My father's present in the spousal hour, ... Od.23.243.335.
These eyes, these eyes beheld a present God, ... Od.24.511.372.
At once the present and the future knew) .... Od.24.519.373.

PRESENTED

Sell their presented Partridges, and Fruits, ... 4.HS2.51.59.

PRESENTING

The bowl presenting to *Arete's* hands; .... Od.13.73.4.

PRESENTLY

Then presently he falls to teize, ... 4.HS6.79.255.

PRESENTS

And see my presents, nor the gifts despise. .... 1.TrPA.95.369.
The clear, reflecting Mind, presents his Sin .... 1.TrSt.73.413.
To count these *Presents,* and from thence to prove .... 1.TrUl.92.469.
Presents flow'd in apace: With Show'rs of Gold, ... 2.ChWB.64.59.
A Frenchman comes, presents you with his Boy, ... 4.2HE2.3.165.
Prudence, whose glass presents th' approaching jayl: .... 5.DunA1.49.66.
Prudence, whose glass presents th' approaching jayl: .... 5.DunB1.51.274.
Who visits with a gun, presents you birds, ... 6.45.25.125.
To painter *K[en]t* presents his *coin;* .... 6.121.2.340.
Presents her harp still to his fingers, ... 6.150.8.398.
If Mercy fail, yet my Presents move, ... Il.1.29.87.
The parting Heroes mutual Presents left; .... Il.6.271.340.
I ask no Presents, no Reward for Love. .... Il.9.192.442.
The proffer'd Presents, an exhaustless Store. .... Il.9.343.450.
He asks no Presents, no Reward for Love. .... Il.9.379.451.
Accept the Presents; draw thy conqu'ring Sword; .... Il.9.711.469.
No more with Presents her Embraces meet, ... Il.11.315.49.
Fair *Themis* first presents the golden Bowl, ... Il.15.96.200.
(The Presents of the silver-footed Dame) .... Il.16.272.249.
To keep, or send the Presents, be thy Care; .... Il.19.145.377.
But let the Presents, to *Achilles* made, ... Il.19.171.378.
Till from the Fleet our Presents be convey'd, ... Il.19.189.379.
To bear the Presents from the royal Tent. .... Il.19.244.383.
Presents th' occasion, could we use it right. .... Il.23.494.510.
Next heap'd on high the num'rous Presents bear .... Il.24.726.568.
Presents, to bathe his hands, a radiant ew'r. .... Od.1.192.42.
With rev'rent hand the King presents the gold, ... Od.3.554.114.
And presents, such as suit the state of Kings. .... Od.3.609.117.
And costly presents in return he gave; .... Od.9.235.316.
The tenth presents our welcome native shore: .... Od.10.31.340.
To count these presents, and from thence to prove .... Od.13.259.18.
Shall bid farewel, and bounteous presents bring; .... Od.15.62.72.
The noblest presents that our love can make: .... Od.15.86.73.
To him thy presents show, thy words repeat: .... Od.15.175.77.
The regal presents of the *Spartan* Lord; .... Od.15.233.79.
And trust the presents to his friendly care. .... Od.16.349.123.
Eurymachus presents: and ear-rings bright, ... Od.18.345.184.

PRESERV'D

Who lost my Heart while I preserv'd my Sheep. .... 1.PAu.80.86.
A crystal fountain, and preserv'd the name. .... 1.TrPA.164.373.
Preserv'd the *Jews,* and slew th' *Assyrian* Foe: .... 2.ChJM.74.18.
Still spread the int'rest, and preserv'd the kind. .... 3.EOM3.146.107.
And teach, the Being you preserv'd, to bear. .... 4.Arbu.134.105.
Preserv'd in *Milton's* or in *Shakespear's* name. .... 4.Arbu.168.108.
Preserv'd the freedom, and forbore the vice. .... 4.2HE1.260.217.
Thus Britain lov'd me; and preserv'd my Fame, ... 6.148ii.1.395.
Thus rul'd their Ardour, thus preserv'd their Force, ... Il.4.357.238.
Preserv'd the Son, in Pity to the Sire. .... Il.5.32.267.
His radiant Arms preserv'd from hostile Spoil, ... Il.6.528.353.
(Great *Neptune's* Care preserv'd from hostile Rage .... Il.13.702.138.
Preserv'd their Line, and equal kept the War. .... Il.15.479.216.
Preserv'd from gaping Wounds, and tainting Air; .... Il.24.31.536.
True to his charge, the Bard preserv'd her long .... Od.3.336.103.

PRESERV'ST

As thou preserv'st the dulness of the past! .... 5.DunA3.186.172.
As thou preserv'st the dulness of the past! .... 5.DunB3.190.329.
Thou but preserv'st a Face and I a Name. .... 6.52.78.158.
Thou but preserv'st a Form and I a Name. .... 6.52.78A.158.

PRESERVE

Attend thy *Manes,* and preserve thy Name; .... 1.TrSt.752.441.
So Heav'n preserve the Sight it has restor'd, ... 2.ChJM.768.52.
You tell me, to preserve your Wife's good Grace, ... 2.ChWB.106.61.
Unless good Sense preserve what Beauty gains: .... 2.RL5.16.200.
"Mark what unvary'd laws preserve each state, ... 3.EOM3.189.112.
"Mark what unvary'd laws preserve their state, ... 3.EOM3.189A.112.

PRESERVE (CONTINUED)

May Heav'n, to bless those days, preserve my Friend, ... 4.Arbu.415.127.
Preserve him social, chearful, and serene, ... 4.Arbu.416.127.
Preserve, Almighty Providence! .... 4.HS6.23.251.
To keep these limbs, and to preserve these eyes. .... 4.1HE1.52.283.
(So may the fates preserve the ears you lend) .... 5.DunA3.212.175.
(So may the fates preserve the ears ye lend). .... 5.DunA3.212A.175.
(So may the fates preserve the ears you lend) .... 5.DunB3.214.331.
Did you for death's preserve your charms; .... 6.4iii.2.10.
Preserve the Limits of these nations, ... 6.61.54.183.
Now God preserve our gracious King! .... 6.79.145.223.
The plenteous Pickle shall preserve the Fish, ... 6.96ii.77.274.
Haste, Warrior, haste! preserve thy threaten'd State; .... Il.5.593.296.
Greece to preserve, is now no easy part, ... Il.10.51.4.
This Day, preserve our Navies from the Flame, ... Il.15.434.214.
Preserve his Arms, preserve his social Train, ... Il.16.304.254.
Preserve his Arms, preserve his social Train, ... Il.16.304.254.
What other Methods may preserve thy *Troy?* .... Il.17.160.293.
More useful to preserve, than I to kill) .... Il.18.136.329.
And for the pious sire preserve the son: .... Od.4.1010.164.

PRESERVER

The *Greeks* Preserver, great *Machaon* bore. .... Il.11.729.67.
(The sage Preserver of the *Grecian* Host) .... Il.15.793.226.

PRESERVERING

Your preservering, unexhausted Bard: .... 6.34.2.101.

PRESERVES

A flow'ry plant, which still preserves her name. .... 1.TrFD.34.387.
Parts it may ravage, but preserves the whole. .... 3.EOM2.106.67.
The stream at once preserves her virgin leaves, ... 6.14iv.27.48.
Some bury'd marble half preserves a name; .... 6.71.16.203.
Lov'd for that Valour which preserves Mankind. .... Il.6.196.335.
(For *Fate* preserves them) from the Hunter's Threat .... Il.15.311A.209.
Some Hand divine, preserves him ever fair: .... Il.24.514.557.
In embers heap'd, preserves the seeds of fire: .... Od.5.633.202.

PRESERVING

One all-extending, all-preserving Soul .... 3.EOM3.22.94.

PRESIDE

Who conquer'd *Nature,* shou'd preside o'er *Wit.* .... 1.EOC.652.313.
Others on Earth o'er human Race preside, ... 2.RL2.87.165.
Cibber preside Lord-Chancellor of Plays, ... 5.DunA3.320.187.
Let Kings be just, and Sov'reign Pow'r preside. .... Il.1.365.105.
Preside on bleak *Dodona's* vocal Hill: .... Il.16.287.252.
But should the pow'rs that o'er mankind preside, ... Od.12.413.451.
Let o'er thy house some chosen maid preside, ... Od.15.29.71.

PRESIDENT

Censor of Tories, President of Satyr, ... 6.48ii.2.134.

PRESIDES

Works *without Show,* and *without Pomp* presides: .... 1.EOC.75.247.
Which still *presides,* yet never does *Appear;* .... 1.EOC.75A.247.
My father o'er your seas presides; and he .... 1.TrPA.112.370.
Directs in Council, and in War presides, ... Il.2.28.128.
Directs in Council and in War presides, ... Il.2.78.130.
Achilles at the genial Feast presides, ... Il.9.275.447.
Whose Son, with *Merion,* o'er the Watch presides.) .... Il.10.68.5.
But hear, tho' wisdom in thy soul presides, ... Od.6.307.225.
Ev'n the stern God that o'er the waves presides, ... Od.8.613.295.

PRESIDING

Eternal Reason! whose presiding soul .... 6.23.3.73.

PRESS

And the Press groan'd with Licenc'd *Blasphemies—* .... 1.EOC.553.304.
My God-like Son shall press the *Phrygian* Plain: .... 1.TrES.228.458.
While thro' the Press enrag'd *Thalestris* flies, ... 2.RL5.57.203.
Were we to press, inferior might on ours: .... 3.EOM1.242.45.
Press to one centre still, the gen'ral Good. .... 3.EOM3.14.93.
"But rudely press before a Duke. .... 4.HS6.59.253.
All, all but Truth, drops dead-born from the Press, ... 4.EpS2.226.325.
Of Curl's chaste press, and Lintot's rubric post, ... 5.DunA1.38.O64.
Of Curl's chaste press, and Lintot's rubric post: .... 5.DunB1.40.273.
Now crowds on crowds around the Goddess press, ... 5.DunB4.135.354.
Alone I press; in Dreams I call my Dear, ... 6.96iv.41.277.
I press the bed where *Wilmot* lay: .... 6.141.2.380.
Great *Menelaus* press the fatal Plain; .... Il.3.355.210.
The *Greeks* with Shouts press on, and spoil the Dead, ... Il.4.584.249.
I loath in lazy Fights to press the Car, ... Il.5.314A.281.
Yet unreveng'd permits to press the Field; .... Il.8.156.405.
Or thou beneath this Lance must press the Field— .... Il.11.545.58.
Fam'd Son of *Hippasus!* there press the Plain; .... Il.11.565.59.
My godlike Son shall press the *Phrygian* Plain: .... Il.16.531.264.
Thrice on the Press like *Mars* himself he flew, ... Il.16.948.280.
These *Phrygian* Fields, and press a foreign Shore. .... Il.21.698.450.
Dubious to press the tender theme, or wait .... Od.4.155.127.
To quit the steed we both impatient press, ... Od.4.383.139.
And leaden slumbers press his drooping eyes. .... Od.4.610.148.
Press not too far, reply'd the God; but cease .... Od.4.661.150.
Or firmer, in the wrestling, press the ground. .... Od.8.104.268.
With earnest haste my frighted sailors press, ... Od.10.153.347.
We press to hear what sadly he relates. .... Od.10.294.357.
Tho' hunger press, yet fly the dang'rous prey, ... Od.11.136.387.
At once descend, and press the desart sand; .... Od.12.8.430.
All press to speak, all question with their eyes. .... Od.13.191.15.
What gasping numbers then shall press the ground! .... Od.13.450.27.
Ere yet thy footsteps press thy native land. .... Od.15.36.71.
They press the *Hymenæan* rite abhorr'd. .... Od.19.155.200.
"Ye Peers, I cry, who press to gain a heart, ... Od.19.162.200.
Now press the sovereign dame with warm desire .... Od.20.397.251.
Now thro' the press the bow *Eumæus* bore, ... Od.21.389.279.
Thrice happy thou! to press the martial plain .... Od.24.53.350.

PRESS (CONTINUED)
Ye Peers (she cry'd) who press to gain my heart ......Od.24.154.355.

PRESS'D
His body press'd beneath the stone, the blood ......1.TrPA.151.372.
And press'd *Palæmon* closer in her Arms. ......1.TrSt.168.417.
And the press'd Watch return'd a silver Sound. ......2.RL1.18.146.
How oft', when press'd to marriage, have I said, ...2.ElAb.73.325.
Crawl thro' the Street, shov'd on, or rudely press'd ......3.Ep1.230A.35.
Shov'd from the wall perhaps, or rudely press'd ......3.Ep1.230.35.
Or when the Soul is press'd with Cares ......6.11.26.30.
Or press'd the Car with polish'd Brass inlay'd, ...Il.4.261.233.
For manag'd Steeds, and *Trechus* press'd the Ground; ......Il.5.867.307.
Foremost he press'd, in glorious Toils to share, ...Il.5.1000.314.
The fallen Chief in suppliant Posture press'd ......Il.6.55.326.
Press'd as we are, and sore of former Fight, ...Il.6.105.328.
Around him flock'd, all press'd with pious Care ......Il.6.300.341.
And press'd his Hand, and tender thus begun. ......Il.6.317.341.
Press'd with a Load of Monumental Clay! ......Il.6.591.355.
Ev'n He their Chief, great *Agamemnon* press'd ......Il.7.125.369.
Press'd with its Load the *Grecian* Balance lies ......Il.8.91.401.
The Godlike *Lycophon* next press'd the Plain, ...Il.8.331.413.
By stern *Eurystheus* with long Labours press'd? ......Il.8.442.418.
And now *Ulysses'* thoughtful Temples press'd. ......Il.10.318.17.
Still press'd the Rout, and still the hindmost slew; ......Il.11.232.45.
Then to her Ships shall flying *Greece* be press'd, ...Il.11.250.46.
Honey new-press'd, the sacred Flow'r of Wheat, ...Il.11.770.69.
Press'd by fresh Forces her o'er-labour'd Train ......Il.11.932.77.
So press'd with Hunger, from the Mountain's Brow ......Il.12.357.94.
With equal Steps bold *Teucer* press'd the Shore, ...Il.12.443.97.
Then press'd her Hand, and thus with Transport spoke. ......Il.14.338.179.
Not when I press'd *Ixion's* matchless Dame, ...Il.14.361.180.
Press'd by the Vengeance of an angry Wife; ......Il.15.382.211.
Still press'd, and press'd by such inglorious Hands. ......Il.15.607.220.
Still press'd, and press'd by such inglorious Hands. ......Il.15.607.220.
Press'd by fresh Forces, her o'erlabour'd Train ......Il.16.62.238.
Press'd by his single Force, let *Hector* see, ...Il.16.300.254.
Who last, beneath thy Vengeance, press'd the Plain; ......Il.16.848.276.
Observ'd her ent'ring; her soft Hand she press'd, ...Il.18.451.343.
Then many a Hero had not press'd the Shore, ...Il.19.63.374.
The Leaders press'd the Chief on ev'ry side; ......Il.19.323.386.
Those direful Hands his Kisses press'd, embru'd ......Il.24.588.561.
The sovereign seat then *Jove*-born Helen *press'd,* ...... Od.4.183.128.
Instant to young *Telemachus* he press'd, ...Od.4.419.140.
Proteus her sire divine. With pity press'd, ...Od.4.495.144.
His hand the King with tender passion press'd, ...Od.4.829.158.
And press'd unwilling in *Calypso's* arms. ......Od.5.23.172.
Long press'd he heav'd beneath the weighty wave, ...Od.5.409.192.
The bank he press'd, and gently kiss'd the ground. ......Od.5.596.201.
Far blooming o'er the field: and as she press'd ......Od.6.301.225.
Some dear-lov'd brother press'd the *Phrygian* plain? ......Od.8.634.297.
So round me press'd exulting at my sight, ...Od.10.491.367.
The sovereign seat with graceful air she press'd; ......Od.19.72.196.
A sabre, when the warrior press'd to part, ...Od.19.273.208.
His steps impetuous to the portal press'd; ......Od.20.159.241.
Whilst with pathetic warmth his hand he press'd. ......Od.20.248.245.

PRESSD
And gently pressd my hand, and said, Be Ours!— ......6.66.4.194.

PRESSES
The groaning presses foam with floods of wine. ......6.35.22.103.
Distracted, presses to the *Dardan* Gate. ......Il.22.523.478.
The groaning presses foam with floods of wine. ......Od.7.163.244.

PRESSING
By pressing Youth attack'd on ev'ry side. ......2.ChWB.93.61.
Then pressing with his Foot his panting Heart, ...Il.6.81.327.
Throng'd in bright Arms, a pressing Fight maintain; ......Il.13.898.148.
Full on the Front the pressing *Trojans* bear, ...Il.15.346.210.
Pensive he said; then pressing as he lay ......Il.16.1042.283.

PREST
Her smiling babe (a pleasing charge) she prest ......1.TrFD.19.386.
The child *Amphisus,* to her bosom prest, ...1.TrFD.49.388.
Here the prest Herbs with bending Tops betray ......1.TrSP.169.401.
I kiss that Earth which once was prest by you, ...1.TrSP.171.401.
Dash'd on these Rocks, than to thy Bosom prest? ......1.TrSP.225.403.
Dash'd on sharp Rocks, than to thy Bosom prest? ......1.TrSP.225A.403.
Dash'd on those Rocks, than to thy Bosom prest? ......1.TrSP.225B.403.
So prest with Hunger, from the Mountain's Brow, ...1.TrES.13.450.
With equal Steps bold *Teucer* prest the Shore, ...1.TrES.89.453.
Belinda still her downy Pillow prest, ...2.RL1.19.147.
Pleas'd with the strange Success, vast Numbers prest ......2.TemF.394.282.
Pant on thy lip, and to thy heart be prest; ......2.ElAb.123.330.
Cares not for service, or but serves when prest, ...3.EOM3.86.100.
When prest by Want and Weakness, *Dennis* lies; ......6.128.10.356.
Not so repuls'd, the Goddess closer prest, ...Il.1.664.118.
Where *Typhon,* prest beneath the burning Load, ...Il.2.954.169.
Prest by bold Youths and baying Dogs in vain. ......Il.3.40.190.
Idæus' Arms the golden Goblets prest, ...Il.3.317.208.
The *Thracian* Bands against the Victor prest; ......Il.4.620.250.
When by the blood-stain'd Hand *Minerva* prest ......Il.5.37.267.
Beneath one Foot the yet-warm Corps he prest, ...Il.5.768.303.
As when the Fig's prest Juice, infus'd in Cream, ...Il.5.1112.320.
The *Trojan* Bands, by hostile Fury prest, ...Il.6.451.348.
The Nurse stood near, in whose Embraces prest ......Il.6.496.351.
These Words scarce spoke, with gen'rous Ardour prest, ...Il.7.119.369.
Meanwhile his Brother, prest with equal Woes, ...Il.10.31.4.
Thus having spoke, with gen'rous Ardour prest, ...Il.10.299.15.
Then to her Ships shall flying *Greece* be prest, ...Il.11.266.47.
Near, and more near, the shady Cohorts prest; ......Il.11.522.57.
Prest in his own, the Gen'ral's Hand he took, ...Il.14.157.165.
With Smiles she took the Charm; and smiling prest ......Il.14.255.173.
On the fall'n Chief th' invading *Trojan* prest, ...Il.15.782.226.
Close, and more close, the list'ning Cohorts prest; ......Il.16.253.249.

PREST (CONTINUED)
Thus let me lie till then! thus, closely prest, ...Il.18.397.340.
Thro' the thick Troops th' embolden'd Hero prest: ......Il.20.143.400.
If ever thee in these fond Arms I prest, ...Il.22.116.457.
And much my Mother's, prest me to forbear: ......Il.22.306.468.
She prest his Hand, and tender thus begun. ......Il.24.162.542.
Or else some *Greek* whose Father prest the Plain, ...Il.24.926.575.
Who prest with heart-corroding grief and years, ...Od.1.245.44.
Arriv'd, his hand the gay *Antinous* prest, ...Od.2.339.77.
Telemachus already prest the shore; ......Od.3.15.87.
Here, on his musing mood the Goddess prest, ...Od.5.205.181.
Prest in *Atrides'* cause the *Trojan* plain: ......Od.5.394.191.
To this calm port the glad *Ulysses* prest, ...Od.5.566.199.
The work of matrons: These the Princes prest, ...Od.7.126.241.
Gay blooming in full charms: her hand he prest ......Od.8.331.281.
The bending shelves with loads of cheeses prest, ...Od.9.256.317.
Half the white stream to hard'ning cheese he prest, ...Od.9.292.318.
Prest with the weight of sleep that tames the strong: ......Od.9.442.324.
Up-bore my load, and prest the sinking sands ......Od.10.197.350.
Milk newly prest, the sacred flow'r of wheat, ...Od.10.270.355.
By justice sway'd, by tender pity prest: ......Od.10.452.365.
And as he spoke her tender hand he prest. ......Od.11.296.396.
Fell before *Troy,* and nobly prest the plain? ......Od.11.463.407.
And high above the rest, *Atrides* prest the plain. ......Od.11.484.408.
Thy infant son her fragrant bosom prest, ...Od.11.553.411.
Not more, when great *Achilles* prest the ground, ...Od.11.685.418.
He climb'd the lofty stern; then gently prest ......Od.13.90.5.
Let not *Pisistratus* in vain be prest, ...Od.15.220.78.
Telemachus: whom as to heav'n he prest ......Od.15.280.82.
And prest unwilling in *Calypso's* arms. ......Od.17.165.139.
O'er all her sense, as the couch she prest, ...Od.18.221.177.
In vain the Queen the night-refection prest; ......Od.20.172.241.

PRESUM'D
Of those who *less presum'd,* and *better knew,* ...... 1.EOC.720.323.
Nor nearer than the gate presum'd to draw. ......Od.10.68.342.

PRESUME
The Venture's greater, I'll presume to say, ...2.ChJM.182.23.
What then he did, I'll not presume to tell, ...2.ChJM.422.35.
What then he did, I not presume to tell, ...2.ChJM.422A.35.
Know then thyself, presume not God to scan; ......3.EOM2.1.53.
Let me for once presume t'instruct the times, ...4.2HE1.340.225.
The rest on Out-side merit but presume, ...5.DunB1.135.280.
Presume Thy Bolts to throw, ...6.50.26.147.
Presume not thou the lifted Bolt to stay, ...Il.4.63.224.
Of courts, presume to weigh their private cares? ......Od.4.875.159.
There no rude winds presume to shake the skies, ...Od.6.51.207.
Let none to call or issue forth presume, ...Od.21.417.280.
May I presume to search thy secret soul? ......Od.24.542.374.

PRESUMES
The haughty creature on that pow'r presumes: ......Od.18.160.174.

PRESUMPTION
To kings presumption, and to crowds belief, ...3.EOM2.244.84.

PRESUMPTOUS
Presumptous Youth! like his shall be thy Doom, ...Il.17.33.289.

PRESUMPTUOUS
I know there are, to whose presumptuous Thoughts ......1.EOC.169.259.
Presumptuous *Crete,* that boasts the Tomb of *Jove?* ...... 1.TrSt.393.426.
Presumptuous Man! the reason wouldst thou find, ...3.EOM1.35.17.
Nor ask, Presumptuous, what the King detains; ......Il.1.36.87.
Vain is the Search, presumptuous and abhorr'd, ...Il.1.728.122.
Thy once-proud Hopes, presumptuous Prince! are fled; ......Il.8.202.407.
Presumptuous *Troy* mistook th' accepting Sign, ...Il.15.438.214.
Who strive presumptuous with the Sons of *Jove.* ...... Il.21.202.429.
To thee (presumptuous as thou art) unknown, ...Il.22.359.470.
Ev'n with presumptuous hope her bed t'ascend, ...Od.1.319.48.
Presumptuous are the vaunts, and vain the pride ......Od.4.92.124.
Their love presumptuous shall with life atone. ......Od.4.466.142.
Their love presumptuous shall by death atone. ......Od.17.157.139.
And *Ithaca,* presumptuous boast their loves: ......Od.19.153.199.
Ev'n to our bed presumptuous you aspir'd: ......Od.22.46.288.

PRETENCE
Some by *Old Words* to Fame have made Pretence; ......1.EOC.324.275.
Be Niggards of Advice on no Pretence; ......1.EOC.578.306.
Pains, reading, study, are their just pretence, ...4.Arbu.159.108.
Mine, as a Foe profess'd to false Pretence, ...4.EpS2.201.324.
Tho' still he travels on no bad pretence, ...4.1740.51.334.
Or, if to Wit a coxcomb make pretence, ...5.DunB1.177.283.
—And if each writing Author's best pretence, ...6.16.7.53.
Pains, Reading, Study, are their just Pretence, ...6.98.9.283.
Here rests a Woman, good without pretence, ...6.115.1.322.
To your pretence their title wou'd precede. ......Od.1.506.56.
Or is it but a vain pretence, you love? ......Od.21.72.262.

PRETEND
Who most to shun or hate Mankind pretend, ...3.EOM4.43.132.
Go! and pretend your family is young; ......3.EOM4.213.147.
Shall then this verse to future age pretend ......3.EOM4.389.165.
And shall this verse to future age pretend ......3.EOM4.389A.165.
It grows their Age's prudence to pretend; ......3.Ep2.236A.69.
'Tis half their Age's prudence to pretend; ......3.Ep2.236.69.
But if to Charms more latent you pretend, ...4.HAdv.126.85.
Are they not rich? what more can they pretend? ......4.EpS2.114.319.
Or each new-pension'd Sycophant, pretend ......4.EpS2.142.321.
So Wit, which most to scorn it does pretend, ...6.16.11.53.
The Lords of *Ithaca* their right pretend. ......Od.1.320.48.
"Behold what wretches to the bed pretend ......Od.21.351.276.

PRETENDER'S
Stood up to dash each vain Pretender's Hope, 6.128.17.356.

PRETENDERS
To just Contempt, ye vain Pretenders, fall, 2.TemF.400.282.
For any Pretenders 6.42iv.2.118.

PRETENDING
And wisely curb'd proud Man's pretending Wit: 1.EOC.53.245.

PRETENSION
Good without noise, without pretension great. 6.109.4.314.

PRETTY
Beauties in vain their pretty Eyes may roll; 2.RL5.33.201.
Had once a pretty Gift of Tongues enough. 4.JD4.77.31.
Pretty! in Amber to observe the forms 4.Arbu.169.108.
"A pretty kind of savage Scene! 4.HS6.177.261.
What rob your Boys? those pretty rogues!— 4.1HE7.27.271.
She tripp'd and laugh'd, too pretty much to stand; 5.DunB4.50.346.
G—d save the pretty Lady's there! 6.10.110.27.
And from those pretty Things you speak have told, 6.37.9.106.
You might have held the pretty head aside, 6.41.3.113.
Each pretty Carecter with pleasing Smart 6.82iv.1.231.
Not as the World its pretty Slaves rewards, 6.86.5A.245.
See how they pat thee with their pretty Paws: 6.96iv.15.276.
Something to deck their pretty Babes and Spouses; 6.96iv.56.278.
Pretty, in Amber to observe the forms 6.98.19.284.

PREVAIL
Which o'er their Childrens Children shall prevail: 1.TrSt.112.414.
Which shall o'er long Posterity prevail: 1.TrSt.112A.414.
And trust me, Dear! good Humour can prevail, 2.RL5.31.201.
Thus Song could prevail 6.11.87.33.
But, gentle COLLEY, should thy verse prevail, 6.116vi.3.327.
Oh might a Parent's careful Wish prevail, Il.1.546.114.
Oh Sight accurst! Shall faithless *Troy* prevail, Il.5.876.308.
All *Troy* must perish, if their Arms prevail, Il.12.85.84.
Unite thy Force, my Friend, and we prevail. Il.17.557.310.
Then, while we hop'd our Armies might prevail, Il.18.305.336.
No—could our Swiftness o'er the Winds prevail, Il.19.460.391.
Then let this dictate of my love prevail: Od.1.364.50.
Unheard, unseen, three years her arts prevail; Od.2.121.67.
Th' unwise prevail, they lodge it in the walls, Od.8.559.292.
On dark reserve what better can prevail, Od.14.220.46.
This arm with blows more eloquent prevail. Od.18.19.167.
O'er my suspended woe thy words prevail, Od.19.689.229.
Light mounts despair, alternate hopes prevail; Od.20.280.246.
Unheard, unseen, three years her arts prevail; Od.24.168.356.
Nor rush to ruin. Justice will prevail. Od.24.529.373.

PREVAIL'D
I still prevail'd, and wou'd be in the right, 2.ChWB.164.64.
While mighty WILLIAM's thundring Arm prevail'd. 4.2HE2.63.169.
This Day the Foe prevail'd by *Pallas'* Pow'r; Il.3.545.217.
While *Meleager's* thund'ring Arm prevail'd. Il.9.666.467.
But, the cape doubled, adverse winds prevail'd. Od.9.90.306.
Whilst hope prevail'd to see your Sire restor'd, Od.20.393.251.

PREVAILING
With Fates prevailing, turn'd the Scale of Fight. 1.TrES.171Z2.455.
The Foe prevailing, and his Friends pursu'd, Il.5.213.277.
With Fates prevailing, turn'd the Scale of Fight. Il.12.528.101.
But lifts to Glory *Troy's* prevailing Bands, Il.15.716.223.
With the prevailing eloquence of woes: Od.6.374.230.

PREVAILS
Thus in the *Soul* while *Memory* prevails, 1.EOC.56.245.
But diff'rent Taste in diff'rent Men prevails, 4.HAdv.35.79.
I weigh what author's heaviness prevails, 5.DunA2.336.142.
"I weigh what author's heaviness prevails; 5.DunB2.368.315.
Now *Europe's* balanc'd, neither Side prevails, 6.28.1.82.
Now *Europe's* balanc'd, and no Side prevails, 6.28.1A.82.
And *Troy* prevails by Armies not her own. Il.2.160.136.
At last thy Will prevails: Great *Peleus'* Son Il.18.419.341.
And the good suffers, while the bad prevails: Od.6.230.221.
But the false woman o'er the wife prevails. Od.11.217.392.
Whether the night descends, or day prevails, Od.11.220.392.
This dares a Seer, but nought the Seer prevails, Od.11.357.399.

PREVALENCE
By all the sacred Prevalence of Pray'r; Il.22.427.473.
Nor all the sacred Prevalence of Pray'r. Il.22.436.473.

PREVENT
Prevent the greedy, and out-bid the bold: 4.1HE6.72.241.
What God, what mortal, shall prevent thy fall? 4.1740.2.332.
Haste gen'rous *Ithacus!* prevent the Shame, Il.2.215.138.
If Gods above prevent, or Men below? Il.2.439.148.
To win the Damsel, and prevent my Sire. Il.9.581.462.
But now our Ills industrious to prevent, Il.10.142.8.
Then rush behind him, and prevent his Pace. Il.10.410.21.
Prevent this Evil, and your Country save: Il.13.155.111.
Lo! ev'ry Chief that might her Fate prevent, Il.16.33.236.
Rise, and prevent (if yet thou think of Fame) Il.18.217.332.
Before him scatt'ring, they prevent his pains, Il.21.297.433.
Prevent, oh *Jove!* this ignominious Date, Il.21.315.434.
Go, guard the Sire; th' observing Foe prevent, Il.24.415.552.
Perchance behold thee, and our Grace prevent. Il.24.821.571.
Then gave his Hand at parting, to prevent Il.24.840.572.
And swift prevent the meditated blow: Od.4.738.153.
Prevent the rage of him who reigns above, Od.5.187.180.
The brave prevent misfortune; then be brave, Od.16.396.125.

PREVENTED
His Blow prevented, and transpierc'd his Thigh, Il.16.373.257.

PREVENTING
Their ready Guilt preventing thy Commands: 1.TrSt.121.415.
Or blest with little, whose preventing care 4.HS2.127.65.
Or whose wise forecast and preventing care 4.HS2.127A.65.
Preventing ev'ry Part perform'd by you; Il.10.133.8.
Preventing *Dian* had dispatch'd her Dart, Il.19.61.374.
But vengeful *Pallas* with preventing speed Od.20.467.256.
The cautious King, with all-preventing care, Od.22.146.294.

PREVENTS
Some God prevents our destin'd Enterprize: Il.15.549.217.
But godlike *Thrasimed* prevents his Rage, Il.16.383.258.
But godly *Thrasimed* prevents his Rage, Il.16.383A.258*.
And oft prevents the meditated Blow. Il.18.40.325.
My well-aim'd shaft with death prevents the foe: Od.8.250.276.
Thy spear, *Telemachus!* prevents th' attack, Od.22.107.291.

PREVIOUS
I pass each previous Settlement and Deed, 2.ChJM.305.28.
And something previous ev'n to Taste—'tis Sense: 3.Ep4.42.140.
A previous pledge of sacred faith obtain'd, Od.4.347.136.

PREY
On me Love's fiercer Flames for ever prey, 1.PSu.91.79.
The Shepherds cry, "Thy Flocks are left a Prey—" 1.PAu.78.85.
To Savage Beasts and Savage Laws a Prey, 1.W-F.45.153.
A mighty Hunter, and his Prey was Man. 1.W-F.62.155.
At once the Chaser and at once the Prey. 1.W-F.82.158.
Couch'd close he lyes, and meditates the Prey; 1.W-F.102.160.
Some on the Leaves of ancient Authors prey, 1.EOC.112.251.
The *God* whose Ensign scares the Birds of Prey, 1.TrVP.23.378.
And crackling flames on all my honours prey. 1.TrFD.75.389.
Thro' thickest Woods, and rouz'd the Beasts of Prey. 1.TrSt.529.432.
He foams, he roars, he rends the panting Prey. 1.TrES.20.450.
(With Brutal Force he seiz'd my *Trojan* Prey, 1.TrUl.146.470.
Slight Lines of Hair surprize the Finny Prey, 2.RL2.26.161.
Great lord of all things, yet a prey to all; 3.EOM2.16.55.
Go drive the Deer, and drag the finny-prey; 4.1HE6.113.245.
Th' embroider'd Suit, at least, he deem'd his prey; 5.DunA2.109.110.
Th'embroider'd suit at least he deem'd his prey; 5.DunB2.117.301.
Those Cankers that on busie Honour prey, 6.17iii.14.58.
"Go wallow Harpyes and your prey divide" 6.130.34.359.
Woul'st thou the *Greeks* their lawful Prey shou'd yield, Il.1.157.95.
Thine in each Conquest is the wealthy Prey, Il.1.217.97.
The Lordly Savage rends the panting Prey Il.3.40A.190.
Roars thro' the Desart, and demands his Prey. Il.3.562.218.
As o'er their Prey rapacious Wolves engage, Il.4.540.247.
But trembling leaves the scatt'ring Flocks a Prey. Il.5.179.275.
As the grim Lyon stalks around his Prey. Il.5.364.284.
Sons, Sires, and Wives, an undistinguish'd Prey. Il.5.596.297.
My helpless Corps, an unassisted Prey. Il.5.843.305.
To stern *Tydides* now he falls a Prey, Il.6.21.325.
Then let the Prey before his Altar fall; Il.8.301.412.
For *Trojan* Vulturs a predestin'd Prey. Il.8.656.427.
In Search of Prey she wings the spacious Air, Il.9.426.453.
And all that rests of my unravish'd Prey. Il.9.480.456.
Now, like two Lions panting for the Prey, Il.10.353.18.
And from the Herd still turn the flying Prey: Il.10.430.23.
He falls, and foaming rends the guardless Prey. Il.10.567.27.
Not rabid Wolves more fierce contest their Prey; Il.11.97.39.
And hov'ring Vulturs scream around their Prey. Il.11.571.59.
The Lordly Savage vindicates his Prey. Il.11.603.61.
Mad with the Smart, he drops the fatal Prey, Il.12.237.90.
He foams, he roars, he rends the panting Prey. Il.12.364.94.
A Prey to every Savage of the Wood; Il.13.144.111.
But falls transfix'd, an unresisting Prey: Il.13.504.130.
Swift as a Vultur leaping on his Prey, Il.13.672.137.
They fly: at once the Chasers and the Prey. Il.15.313.209.
O'ermatch'd he falls; to two at once a Prey, Il.15.656.221.
And rend the trembling, unresisting Prey. Il.16.423.259.
Stung with fierce Hunger, each the Prey invades, Il.16.917.279.
But thou a Prey to Vulturs shalt be made! Il.16.1009.282.
And in the Victor's Hands the shining Prey. Il.17.94.291.
And each from *Ajax* hopes the glorious Prey: Il.17.277.298.
Oh lasting Shame! to our own Fears a Prey, Il.17.390.302.
A Prey to Dogs beneath the *Trojan* Wall? Il.17.627.312.
Sow'r he departs, and quits th' untasted Prey. Il.17.748.317.
A Prey to Dogs he dooms the Corse to lye, Il.18.215.332.
The Dogs (oft' chear'd in vain) desert the Prey, Il.18.675.356.
O'er all the Corse: The Flies forbid their Prey, Il.19.41.373.
When from *Achilles'* Arms I forc'd the Prey. Il.19.90.375.
Just when he holds or thinks he holds his Prey, Il.22.185.463.
Now to devouring Flames be these a Prey, Il.22.658.484.
And drove the Bloodhounds from their destin'd Prey. Il.23.231.499.
Vain toils! their impious folly dar'd to prey Od.1.9.28.
The wealth of Kings, and made my youth a prey. Od.2.352.78.
What toils by sea! where dark in quest of prey Od.3.129.92.
She fell, to lust a voluntary prey. Od.3.345.103.
The monarch-savage rends the trembling prey. Od.4.454.141.
My darling son is fled! an easy prey Od.4.1075.168.
Unhappy man! to wasting woes a prey, Od.5.207.181.
Perhaps I yet may fall a bloody prey Od.5.610.201.
Majestically fierce, to seize his prey; Od.6.158.216.
The bounteous Gods afford a copious prey, Od.9.184.313.
To wreak his hunger on the destin'd prey; Od.10.132.347.
Balk'd of his prey, the yelling monster flies, Od.10.135.347.
Tho' hunger press, yet fly the dang'rous prey, Od.11.136.387.
Aloft he whirls, to crush the savage prey; Od.11.706.420.
She makes the huge Leviathan her prey, Od.12.119.437.
Again the fury vindicates her prey, Od.12.154.439.
'Till the fell fiend arise to seize her prey, Od.12.273.445.
When lo! fierce *Scylla* stoop'd to seize her prey, Od.12.294.446.
So the foul monster lifts her prey on high, Od.12.304.447.

PREY (CONTINUED)

By *Circe* giv'n, and fly the dang'rous prey. ....Od.12.358.448.
Then fail'd our food; then fish we make our prey, ...Od.12.391.450.
Why seize ye not yon beeves, and fleecy prey? ....Od.12.409.450.
When swift to ruin they invade the prey. ....Od.12.418.451.
(With brutal force he seiz'd my *Trojan* prey, ...Od.13.313.21.
And leave his fortunes and his house a prey? ....Od.13.483.29.
To whom offending men are made a prey, ...Od.14.105.41.
The robbers prize, the prey to lawless might. ....Od.15.14.70.
To pour his wrath on yon luxurious prey; ....Od.15.197.78.
Might he return, I yield my life a prey ....Od.16.107.108.
They cry, they scream, their unfledg'd brood a prey ....Od.16.240.116.
Lest a sad prey to ever-musing cares, ...Od.16.352.123.
The Monarch savage rends the panting prey: ....Od.17.145.138.
Like some vile swine's, that greedy of his prey ....Od.18.35.168.
Who casts thy mangled ears and nose a prey ....Od.18.98.171.
Who make their Queen and all her wealth a prey: ....Od.18.173.175.
You, only you, make her ye love your prey. ....Od.18.324.182.
But inward on my soul let sorrow prey; ....Od.19.194.201.
His sacrilegious train, who dar'd to prey ....Od.19.313.209.
Then, licens'd rage her hateful prey devours. ....Od.19.382.212.
And to the Furies bore a grateful prey. ....Od.20.93.237.
With each new sun to some new hope a prey, ...Od.21.165.267.
To thy own dogs a prey thou shalt be made; ....Od.21.395.279.
His destin'd prey, and wraps them all in shades. ....Od.22.38.288.
While to your lust and spoil a guardless prey, ...Od.22.43.288.
Headlong they drop: the fowlers seize the prey, ...Od.22.342.304.
Wide o'er the sands are spread the stiff'ning prey ....Od.22.430.309.
When Death had seiz'd her prey, thy son attends, ...Od.23.45.321.
Stern as the surly lion o'er his prey, ...Od.23.50.321.
Our easy faith, and make the sex their prey: ....Od.23.228.334.
The good old man, to wasting woes a prey, ...Od.23.387.343.
He lies a prey to monsters of the main, ...Od.24.341.365.

PREYS

Swift on the sedgy Reeds the Ruin preys; ....Il.21.406.437.
On these the Rage of Fire victorious preys, ...Il.23.216.498.

PRIAM

Shall *Troy*, shall *Priam*, and th' Adult'rous Spouse, ...Il.2.195.137.
Let rev'rend *Priam* in the Truce engage, ...Il.3.145.197.
The good old *Priam* welcom'd her, and cry'd, ...Il.3.211.201.
With Wonder *Priam* view'd the Godlike Man, ...Il.3.239.203.
The Rites now finish'd, rev'rend *Priam* rose, ...Il.3.378.211.
Let *Priam* bleed! If yet thou thirst for more, ...Il.4.55.223.
Than Godlike *Priam*, or than *Priam's* Race. ....Il.4.70.224.
Two Sons of *Priam* in one Chariot ride, ...Il.5.204.276.
How long, ye Sons of *Priam!* will ye fly, ...Il.5.565.295.
The Son of *Priam*, glorying in his Might, ...Il.6.662.360.
O Son of *Priam!* let thy faithful Ear ....Il.7.51.365.
Slow from his Seat the rev'rend *Priam* rose. ....Il.7.441.386.
Sage *Priam* check'd their Grief: With silent Haste ....Il.7.508.389.
Nor *Priam*, nor his Sons obtain'd their Grace; ....Il.8.683.427.
Two Sons of *Priam* next to Battel move, ...Il.11.137.41.
The Goddess then: O Son of *Priam* hear! ....Il.11.257.46.
The Sons of *Priam* with the third appear, ...Il.12.107.85.
Where he, inces'd at partial *Priam*, stands, ...Il.13.578.133.
The Son of *Priam* whirl'd the missive Wood; ....Il.17.688.314.
In hope the Realms of *Priam* to enjoy, ...Il.20.216.403.
And *Priam*, (blest with *Hector*, brave and bold: ....Il.20.285.406.
For *Priam* now, and *Priam's* faithless Kind, ...Il.20.353.408.
The Son of *Priam*, whom the Hero's Hand ....Il.21.42.423.
I sprung from *Priam*, and *Laothöe* fair, ...Il.21.96.425.
High on a Turret hoary *Priam* stands, ...Il.21.613.447.
The careful Eyes of *Priam* first beheld. ....Il.22.36.454.
Of all that *Hecuba* to *Priam* bore, ...Il.22.301.468.
Should *Dardan Priam*, and his weeping Dame ....Il.22.441.473.
Should *Dardan Priam*, and the weeping Dame ....Il.22.441A.473.
Her furious Son from *Priam* to receive ....Il.24.97.539.
She spoke, and vanish'd. *Priam* bids prepare ....Il.24.225.546.
'Tis just (said *Priam*) to the Sire above ....Il.24.369.551.
A Man's approach, and thus to *Priam* cries. ....Il.24.434.554.
Thus *Priam* spoke, and *Hermes* thus reply'd. ....Il.24.476.556.
Thus spoke to *Priam* the cœlestial Guide, ...Il.24.517.557.
How oft, alas! has wretched *Priam* bled? ....Il.24.617.562.
Apart from *Priam*, lest th' unhappy Sire ....Il.24.732.568.
Where full before him rev'rend *Priam* sate: ....Il.24.747.568.
But god-like *Priam* from the Chariot rose: ....Il.24.892.573.
But *Priam* check'd the Torrent as it rose. ....Il.24.984.576.
Back to the Court of *Priam* bent your course. ....Od.4.394.139.

PRIAM'S

Tears gush'd again, as from pale Priam's eyes ....5.DunB1.255.289.
And Fame eternal leave to *Priam's* Race? ....Il.2.212.138.
Such Wisdom soon should *Priam's* Force destroy, ...Il.2.444.148.
Be *Priam's* Palace sunk in *Grecian* Fires, ...Il.2.495.150.
In *Priam's* Porch the *Trojan* Chiefs she found, ...Il.2.958.169.
The loveliest Nymph of *Priam's* Royal Race ....Il.3.168.199.
(Old *Priam's* Chiefs, and most in *Priam's* Grace) ....Il.3.192.200.
(Old *Priam's* Chiefs, and most in *Priam's* Grace) ....Il.3.192.200.
Still *Priam's* Walls in peaceful Honours grow, ...Il.4.25.222.
Than Godlike *Priam*, or than *Priam's* Race. ....Il.4.70.224.
When *Priam's* Pow'rs and *Priam's* self shall fall, ...Il.4.198.230.
When *Priam's* Pow'rs and *Priam's* self shall fall, ...Il.4.198.230.
Old *Priam's* Son, *Democoon* was his Name; ....Il.4.574.249.
And unreveng'd see *Priam's* People die? ....Il.5.566.295.
That propt alone by *Priam's* Race should stand ....Il.5.577.296.
Honour'd and lov'd like *Priam's* Royal Race: ....Il.5.662.299.
Beneath his Arms that *Priam's* Tow'rs should fall; ....Il.5.880.308.
And now to *Priam's* stately Courts he came, ...Il.6.304.341.
Oppos'd to those, where *Priam's* Daughters sate: ....Il.6.309.341.
Near *Priam's* Court and *Hector's* Palace stands ....Il.6.392.346.
He said, nor answer'd *Priam's* warlike Son; ....Il.6.430.347.
Not *Priam's* hoary Hairs defil'd with Gore, ...Il.6.576.355.
Meanwhile, conven'd at *Priam's* Palace Gate, ...Il.7.414.385.
This Offspring added to King *Priam's* Line) ....Il.8.370.415.

PRIAM'S (CONTINUED)

Repell the Rage of *Priam's* single Son? ....Il.9.463.455.
And first *Doryclus, Priam's* Son, he slew, ...Il.11.611.61.
(This Nymph, the Fruit of *Priam's* ravish'd Joy, ...Il.13.233.116.
With *Priam's* Sons, a Guardian of the Throne, ...Il.13.237.116.
For this, in *Priam's* Court he held his Place, ...Il.15.650.221.
Belov'd no less than *Priam's* Royal Race. ....Il.15.651.221.
(The lawless Offspring of King *Priam's* Bed,) ....Il.16.896.277.
For not by you shall *Priam's* Son be born ....Il.17.513.308.
For *Priam* now, and *Priam's* faithless Kind, ...Il.20.353.408.
The youngest Hope of *Priam's* stooping Age: ....Il.20.472.414.
But least, the Sons of *Priam's* hateful Race! ....Il.21.114.426.
On *Priam's* Roof, and *Hippoplacia's* Shade. ....Il.22.611.481.
And swift at *Priam's* mournful Court arrives; ....Il.24.196.545.
You, the Disgrace of *Priam's* House, remain! ....Il.24.320.549.
All *Troy* then moves to *Priam's* Court again, ...Il.24.1011.577.
Of *Priam's* race, and lay'd proud *Troy* in dust? ....Od.22.251.299.

PRIAPUS

Priapus cou'd not half describe the Grace ....2.ChJM.450.36.

PRIAPUS'

As from *Priapus'* lawless lust she flew, ...1.TrFD.32.387.

PRICE

But if the Purchase costs so dear a Price, ...2.TemF.515.289.
That, Vice may merit; 'tis the price of toil; ....3.EOM4.151.142.
He names the *Price* for ev'ry *Office* paid, ...4.JD4.162.39.
Lintot, dull rogue! will think your price too much. ....4.Arbu.63.100.
The price of prologues and of plays, ...6.150.16.399.
For *Troy* to ransom at a Price too dear? ....Il.2.286.141.
Large Gifts of Price my Father shall bestow; ....Il.6.58.326.
For which nine Oxen paid (a vulgar Price) ....Il.6.293.341.
The Price of Blood discharg'd, the Murd'rer lives: ....Il.9.746.471.
Large Gifts of Price my Father shall bestow: ....Il.10.450.23.
The Purchase Infamy, and Life the Price! ....Il.13.150.111.
With Gifts of Price he sought and won the Dame; ....Il.16.227.248.
And the full Price of injur'd Honour paid. ....Il.19.178.379.
Breathless in Dust, the Price of Rashness paid. ....Il.20.458.413.
Where *Jason's* Son the Price demanded gave; ....Il.21.47.424.
A hundred Oxen were his Price that Day, ...Il.21.90.425.
Will learn their Rashness, when they pay the Price. ....Il.23.571.512.
(Price of his Ruin:) For who dares deny ....Il.23.771.520.
Of twice six Oxen its reputed Price; ....Il.23.817.521.
Next with the Gifts (the Price of *Hector* slain) ....Il.24.341.550.
With wealthy dow'r, and bridal gifts of price. ....Od.1.363.50.
With wealthy dow'r, and bridal gifts of price. ....Od.2.226.72.
Ere long shall pay—their forfeit lives the price. ....Od.2.270.74.
With gifts of price and pond'rous treasure fraught. ....Od.3.397.105.
Selected from my stores, of matchless price ....Od.4.833.158.
(A richer price than if his joyful Isle ....Od.5.52.174.
With gifts of price and gorgeous garments grac'd. ....Od.14.354.51.
When slave! to sell thee at a price too dear ....Od.17.297.146.
Welcom'd with gifts of price, a sumless store! ....Od.19.312.209.
"With gifts of price shall send him joyous home." ....Od.19.483.220.
Justly the price of worthlessness they pay'd, ...Od.22.454.310.

PRICK

"Keep close to Ears, and those let Asses prick, ...4.Arbu.77.101.
Prick all their ears up, and forget to graze; ....5.DunA2.250.130.
Prick all their ears up, and forget to graze; ....5.DunB2.262.308.
(Such Honour did them prick) ....6.79.14.218.

PRICK'D

But his high Courage prick'd him forth to wed, ...2.ChJM.13.15.

PRICKS

Pricks his blind Horse across the Fallow Lands, ...2.ChWB.348.74.

PRIDE

You, that too wise for Pride, too Good for Pow'r, ...1.PSp.7.61.
With joyful Pride survey'st our lofty Woods, ...1.W-F.220.169.
With joyful Pride survey our lofty Woods, ...1.W-F.220A.169.
Gigantick *Pride*, pale *Terror*, gloomy *Care*, ...1.W-F.415.193.
Is *Pride*, the never-failing Vice of Fools. ....1.EOC.204.264.
She gives in large Recruits of *needful Pride*; ....1.EOC.206.264.
Pride, where Wit fails, steps in to our Defence, ...1.EOC.209.264.
That always shows *Great Pride*, or *Little Sense*; ....1.EOC.387.284.
Pride, Malice, Folly, against *Dryden* rose, ...1.EOC.458.290.
Gen'rous Converse; a *Soul* exempt from *Pride*; ....1.EOC.641.311.
Her tender mother's only hope and pride, ...1.TrFD.9.386.
Pride of thy Age, and Glory of thy Race, ...1.TrSP.105.398.
These Sons, ye Gods! who with flagitious Pride ....1.TrSt.107.414.
That, from his exil'd Brother, swell'd with Pride ....1.TrSt.423.427.
Alive, the Pride and Terror of the Wood. ....1.TrSt.574.434.
The Pride of Fools, and Slaves insulting Scorn. ....1.TrUl.183.471.
But she, your Sexe's Mirrour, free from Pride, ...2.ChJM.438.36.
Vapours and Pride by turns possess her Brain: ....2.ChWB.89.61.
Some secret Truths from Learned Pride conceal'd, ...2.RL1.37.148.
For when the Fair in all their Pride expire, ...2.RL1.57.150.
These swell their Prospects and exalt their Pride, ...2.RL1.81.151.
Who swell their Prospects and exalt their Pride, ...2.RL1.81A.151.
Trembling, begins the sacred Rites of Pride. ....2.RL1.128.155.
Yet graceful Ease, and Sweetness void of Pride, ...2.RL2.15.160.
Where *Thames* with Pride surveys his rising Tow'rs, ...2.RL3.2.169.
Spite of his haughty Mien, and barb'rous Pride: ....2.RL3.70.173.
Steel cou'd the Works of mortal Pride confound, ...2.RL3.175.182.
Faints into Airs, and languishes with Pride; ....2.RL4.34.186.
O'er-wrought with Ornaments of barb'rous Pride. ....2.TemF.120.263.
Great without Pride, in modest Majesty. ....2.TemF.203.271.
But Mortals! know, 'tis still our greatest Pride, ...2.TemF.368.281.
To low ambition, and the pride of Kings. ....3.EOM1.2.11.
Then shall Man's pride and dulness comprehend ....3.EOM1.65.21.
In Pride, in reas'ning Pride, our error lies; ....3.EOM1.123.30.
In Pride, in reas'ning Pride, our error lies; ....3.EOM1.123.30.
Pride still is aiming at the blest abodes, ...3.EOM1.125.30.

PRIDE (CONTINUED)

In *Pride* (my Friend) in *Pride,* our error lies; 3.EOM1.123A.30.
In *Pride* (my Friend) in *Pride,* our error lies; 3.EOM1.123A.30.
In reas'ning *Pride* (my Friend), our error lies; 3.EOM1.123B.30.
Earth for whose use? Pride answers, "'Tis for mine: 3.EOM1.132.31.
From pride, from pride, our very reas'ning springs; 3.EOM1.161.35.
From pride, from pride, our very reas'ning springs; 3.EOM1.161.35.
The bliss of Man (could Pride that blessing find) 3.EOM1.189.38.
Vile worm!—oh Madness, Pride, Impiety! 3.EOM1.258.46.
And, spite of Pride, in erring Reason's spite, 3.EOM1.293.51.
And, spite of Pride, and in thy Reason's spite, 3.EOM1.293A.51.
With too much weakness for the Stoic's pride, 3.EOM2.6.53.
With too much weakness for a Stoic's pride, 3.EOM2.6A.53.
First strip off all her equipage of Pride, 3.EOM2.44.61.
The monk's humility, the hero's pride, 3.EOM2.173.75.
But what will grow on Pride, or grow on Shame. 3.EOM2.194.78.
Thus Nature gives us (let it check our pride) 3.EOM2.195.78.
But what or grows on Pride, or grows on Shame. 3.EOM2.194A.78.
Shame to the virgin, to the matron pride, 3.EOM2.242.84.
And Pride bestow'd on all, a common friend; 3.EOM2.272.87.
And each vacuity of sense by Pride: 3.EOM2.286.89.
The trim of pride, the impudence of wealth, 3.EOM3.4.92.
Shares with his lord the pleasure and the pride: 3.EOM3.36.95.
For more his pleasure, yet for more his pride: 3.EOM3.60.98.
Pride then was not; nor Arts, that Pride to aid; 3.EOM3.151.108.
Pride then was not; nor Arts, that Pride to aid; 3.EOM3.151.108.
And hell was built on spite, and heav'n on pride. 3.EOM3.262.119.
No Bandit fierce, no Tyrant mad with pride, 3.EOM4.41.131.
Shew'd erring Pride, WHATEVER IS, IS RIGHT; 3.EOM4.394.166.
He thanks you not, his pride was in Picquette, 3.Ep1.144A.27.
Pride guides his steps, and bids him shun the great: 3.Ep1.66.20.
His pride in Reas'ning, not in Acting lies. 3.Ep1.70.20.
He thanks you not, his pride is in Picquette, 3.Ep1.144.27.
Where none distinguish twixt your Shame and Pride, 3.Ep2.204A.67.
Where none distinguish twixt your Shame or Pride, 3.Ep2.204B.67.
Arcadia's Countess, here, in ermin'd pride, 3.Ep2.7.48.
There, none distinguish 'twixt your Shame or Pride, 3.Ep2.204.67.
Courage with Softness, Modesty with Pride, 3.Ep2.278.72.
See! sportive fate, to punish aukward pride, 3.Ep4.19.138.
That summons you to all the Pride of Pray'r: 3.Ep4.142.151.
Sick of his civil Pride from Morn to Eve; 3.Ep4.166.153.
Deep Harvests bury all his pride has plann'd, 3.Ep4.175.154.
Whose rising Forests, not for pride or show, 3.Ep4.187.155.
Deep Harvests bury all thy pride has plann'd, 3.Ep4.175A.154.
With foolish *Pride* my Heart was never fir'd, 4.JD4.9.27.
Not when a gilt Buffet's reflected pride 4.HS2.5.55.
When not his Lust offended, but his Pride: 4.HAdv.84.83.
What solid Happiness, what empty Pride? 4.HAdv.145.87.
In errant Pride continue stiff, and burn? 4.HAdv.152.87.
That Casting-weight Pride adds to Emptiness, 4.Arbu.177.109.
Or simple Pride for Flatt'ry makes demands; 4.Arbu.253.114.
That Fop whose pride affects a Patron's name, 4.Arbu.291.116.
The Fop whose pride affects a Patron's name, 4.Arbu.291A.116.
Wit that can creep, and Pride that licks the dust. 4.Arbu.333.120.
Foe to his Pride, but Friend to his Distress: 4.Arbu.371.123.
Born to no Pride, inheriting no Strife, 4.Arbu.392.126.
In Noble's Titles; Pride and Simony, 4.JD2A.87.140.
Vain was the chief's and sage's pride 4.HOde9.13.159.
Where MURRAY (long enough his Country's pride) 4.1HE6.52.241.
Nor puff'd by Pride, nor sunk by Spleen. 4.HS6.28.251.
Will cure the arrant'st Puppy of his Pride. 4.1HE1.60.283.
As, tho' the Pride of *Middleton* and *Bland,* 4.EpS1.75.304.
There, where no Passion, Pride, or Shame transport, 4.EpS1.97.305.
As Pride in Slaves, and Avarice in Kings, 4.EpS1.110.306.
One man immortal all that pride confounds, 5.DunA3.67.156.
One god-like Monarch all that pride confounds, 5.DunA3.67A.156.
One god-like Monarch all that pride confounds, 5.DunB3.75.324.
Foreign her air, her robe's discordant pride 5.DunB4.47.345.
Who rhym'd for hire, and patroniz'd for pride. 5.DunB4.102.351.
His Hat, which never vail'd to human pride, 5.DunB4.205.362.
Mother of Arrogance, and Source of Pride! 5.DunB4.470.386.
The vanquish'd roses lose their pride, 6.4iv.5.10.
Of untaught nature's humble pride, 6.6ii.18.15.
Vales, Spires, meandring Streams, and *Windsor's* tow'ry Pride. 6.14ii.54.44.
Such Nastiness and so much Pride 6.14v(a).8.48.
All Flutter, Pride, and Talk. 6.14v(a).24.49.
And flutters in her Pride. 6.14v(b).18.50.
Life is, in Courts, and gawdy Pride, mis-spent. 6.17iii.23.58.
Your Pleasure is a Vice, but not your Pride; 6.19.34.63.
Pride, Pomp, and State but reach her outward Part, 6.19.55.63.
And dead as living, 'tis our Author's Pride, 6.19.79.64.
The haughty *Niobe* whose impious pride 6.20.56.67.
But while her Pride forbids her Tears to flow, 6.33.3.99.
But tho' her Pride forbad her Eyes to flow, 6.33.3A.99.
Although her Pride forbade her Tears to flow, 6.33.3B.99.
Save me alike from foolish Pride, 6.50.33.148.
If 'ere my foolish breast knew Pride 6.50.33A.148.
Fanes, which admiring Gods with pride survey, 6.71.9.203.
A soul as full of Worth, as void of Pride, 6.73.1.209.
That Pride will have a Fall. 6.79.4.217.
Stood Paramount in Pride; 6.79.22.218.
That *Pride will have a Fall.* 6.79.148.223.
Above all Pain, all Passion, and all Pride, 6.84.24.239.
Above all Pain, all Anger, and all Pride, 6.84.24A.239.
Not grave thro' Pride, or gay thro' Folly, 6.89.6.250.
Not grave thro' Pride, nor gay thro' Folly, 6.89.6A.250.
Or sway'd by Envy, or through Pride of Mind, 6.96iii.14.275.
How foam, how fret beneath a Load of Pride! 6.96iii.30.275.
When Pride in such contemptuous Beings lies, 6.96v.31.281.
That casting Weight, Pride adds to Emptiness; 6.98.27.284.
What foreign theatres with pride have shewn, 6.107.9.310.
Passion and Pride were to her soul unknown, 6.115.5.322.
Dorset, the Grace of Courts, the Muses Pride, 6.118.1.334.
The Scourge of Pride, tho' sanctify'd or great, 6.118.3.334.
The *Fop,* whose Pride affects a *Patron's* name, 6.120.1.339.
Hence see him modest free from pride or shew 6.130.9.358.

PRIDE (CONTINUED)

"O'er his vast heaps in drunkenness of pride 6.130.33.359.
Could save a Mother's justest Pride from fate, 6.132.3.362.
Could save a Parent's justest Pride from fate, 6.132.3A.362.
Your pilf'ring Lord, with simple Pride, 6.135.33.367.
Yea all to break the Pride of lustful Kings, 6.137.6.373.
Unpolish'd Gemms no Ray on Pride bestow, 6.142.5.382.
Alas! what room for Flattry, or for Pride! 6.147iii.1.390.
Not so *Atrides:* He, with Kingly Pride, Il.1.33.87.
And still thy Priestly Pride provoke thy King? Il.1.134.93.
O Tyrant, arm'd with Insolence and Pride! Il.1.194.96.
Nor thou, *Achilles,* treat our Prince with Pride; Il.1.364.105.
The Pride of *Greece,* and Bulwark of our Host. Il.1.375.106.
Before his Pride must his Superiors fall, Il.1.380.106.
Not so *Atrides:* He, with wonted Pride, Il.1.492.111.
With Giant-Pride at *Jove's* high Throne he stands, Il.1.526.113.
Then thus the God: Oh restless Fate of Pride, Il.1.726.122.
Plagu'd with his Pride, or punish'd for his Lust. Il.2.292.141.
Too daring Bard! whose unsuccessful Pride Il.2.725.160.
Flow'd o'er his Armour with an easy Pride, Il.3.28.189.
In former Days, in all thy gallant Pride, Il.3.65.192.
He seems a Monarch, and his Country's Pride. Il.3.225.203.
Himself a Host: the *Grecian* Strength and Pride. Il.3.294.207.
Himself an Host: the *Grecian* Strength and Pride. Il.3.294A.207.
Thus fell two Heroes; one the Pride of *Thrace,* Il.4.624.250.
He bleeds! The Pride of *Greece!* (the Boaster cries) Il.5.345.283.
To spoil his glitt'ring Arms, and Plumy Pride. Il.5.771.303.
With base Reproaches and unmanly Pride. Il.5.809.304.
Say, mighty Father! Shall we scourge his Pride, Il.5.950.312.
O Son of *Telamon,* thy Country's Pride! Il.7.283.378.
Gods! can thy Courage fear the *Phrygian's* Pride? Il.8.184.406.
Or *Troy* once held, in Peace and Pride of Sway, Il.9.526.459.
Fixt is his Wrath, unconquer'd is his Pride; Il.9.795.473.
And Pray'rs will burst that swelling Heart with Pride. Il.9.819.474.
Pride of the *Greeks,* and Glory of thy Kind! Il.10.95.6.
Each burns for Fame, and swells with martial Pride; Il.11.852.74.
But you, the Pride, the Flow'r of all our Host, Il.13.159.112.
The Pride of haughty Warriors to confound, Il.13.388.124.
Who glories in unutterable Pride! Il.14.162.165.
Who glories in inutterable Pride! Il.14.162A.165.
Thus while she breath'd of Heav'n, with decent Pride Il.14.203.169.
Supreme he sits; and sees, in Pride of Sway, Il.15.116.201.
The Tyrant's Pride lies rooted in my Breast. Il.16.71.238.
(Once great *Aëtion's,* now *Achilles'* Pride) Il.16.187.246.
Thy Pride once promis'd, of subverting *Troy;* Il.16.1004.282.
Vain was his Vigour, and as vain his Pride. Il.17.30.289.
Stalks careless on, with unregarding Pride; Il.20.202.402.
Sons he has many, those thy Pride may quell; Il.20.220.403.
With mean Reproaches, and unmanly Pride: Il.20.243.404.
Mean Intercourse of Obloquy and Pride! Il.20.502.415.
Thy Pride to face the Majesty of Heav'n? Il.21.556.445.
The Bow, the Quiver, and its plumy Pride. Il.21.568.445.
O *Hector,* late thy Parents Pride and Joy, Il.22.556.479.
The last in Merit, as the first in Pride. Il.23.567.512.
Nor is my Pride preferr'd before my Friend. Il.23.698.517.
In Strength of Rage and Impotence of Pride, Il.24.53.538.
Mindful of those, who, late their Pride and Joy, Il.24.205.545.
So was her Pride chastiz'd by Wrath divine, Il.24.763.569.
With joyous pride the summons I'd obey. Od.1.502.56.
A royal robe he wore with graceful pride, Od.2.5.60.
His pride of words, and thy wild dream of fate, Od.2.229.72.
O pride of words, and arrogance of mind! Od.2.276.74.
And turn th' event, confounding human pride: Od.3.162.93.
At first with worthy shame and decent pride, Od.3.330.102.
So wrought, as *Pallas* might with pride behold. Od.3.556.114.
Presumptuous are the vaunts, and vain the pride Od.4.92.124.
The pride of *Delos.* (By the *Delian* coast Od.6.195.219.
Than works of female skill their women's pride, Od.7.138.242.
Nor blame her faultless, nor suspect of pride: Od.7.390.255.
Then thus aloud, (elate with decent pride) Od.8.229.274.
With decent pride refutes a public wrong: Od.8.270.278.
Whose ivory sheath inwrought with curious pride, Od.8.439.287.
Their parent's pride, and pleasure of their reign. Od.10.8.339.
A sable ram, the pride of all thy breed. Od.10.625.374.
Smooth flows the gentle stream with wanton pride, Od.11.285.396.
With him the strength of war, the soldiers pride, Od.11.673.417.
O stay, oh pride of *Greece! Ulysses* stay! Od.12.222.442.
Swift from the oak they strip the shady pride; Od.12.421.451.
Slain are those herds which I with pride survey, Od.12.447.452.
The pride of fools, and slaves insulting scorn. Od.13.350.24.
O Monarch, care of heav'n! thy people's pride! Od.15.101.73.
The pride of Kings, and labour of a God. Od.15.133.75.
Yet short his date of life! by female pride he dies. Od.15.271.81.
Where two fair cities rise with equal pride, Od.15.453.92.
'Midst the swill'd insolence of lust and pride? Od.16.72.106.
And twelve our country's pride; to these belong Od.16.272.118.
And her lov'd Lord unplume thy tow'ring pride. Od.19.104.197.
Perhaps, like thee, poor guest! in wanton pride Od.19.436.216.
With vollied vengeance blast their tow'ring pride! Od.20.212.243.
And goats he brought, the pride of all their race; Od.20.236.244.
By lordly pride and keen reproach inspir'd. Od.20.352.249.
And thus burst out, imposthumate with pride. Od.20.358.249.
That ancient vigor, once my pride and boast. Od.21.468.283.
How weak is mortal pride! To heav'n alone Od.22.320.301.
Yet more, ev'n to our bed thy pride aspires: Od.22.361.304.
A foe to pride: no adamant is there; Od.23.176.329.
Her coy reserve, and prudence mixt with pride, Od.24.148.355.
The bold *Antinous* was his age's pride, Od.24.485.371.

PRIDE'S

And curse their cumbrous pride's unwieldy weight. Od.1.214.43.

PRIEST

Forth came the Priest, and bade th'obedient Wife 2.ChJM.311.29.
If rich, she keeps her Priest, or something worse; 2.ChWB.87.61.
Better than e'er our Parish Priest cou'd do. 2.ChWB.268.69.

PRIEST 142 PRINCE

PRIEST (CONTINUED)
Of all the Nurse and all the Priest have taught, ...2.RL1.30.147.
Unbrib'd, unbloody, stood the blameless priest: ....3.EOM3.158.109.
King, priest, and parent of his growing state; ....3.EOM3.216.114.
Point she to Priest or Elder, Whig or Tory, ...4.EpS2.96.318.
The Priest whose Flattery be-dropt the Crown, ...4.EpS2.164.322.
(Her Priest preceding) thro' the gates of Lud. ....5.DunA2.332.142.
And to mere mortals seem'd a Priest in drink? ....5.DunA2.394.149.
A decent Priest, where monkeys were the Gods! ....5.DunA3.204.175.
And to mere mortals seem'd a Priest in drink: ....5.DunB2.426.318.
A decent priest, where monkeys were the gods! ....5.DunB3.208.330.
Then thus. "From Priest-craft happily set free, ...5.DunB4.499.391.
On some, a Priest succinct in amice white ....5.DunB4.549.396.
The King of Men his Rev'rend Priest defy'd, ...Il.1.13.86.
The Priest to rev'rence, and release the Fair. ....Il.1.32.87.
Mine is thy Daughter, Priest, and shall remain; ....Il.1.39.87.
The trembling Priest along the Shore return'd, ...Il.1.47.88.
Calchas the wise, the *Grecian* Priest and Guide, ...Il.1.92.91.
Against his Priest shall lift an impious Hand: ....Il.1.114.92.
Encourag'd thus, the blameless Priest replies: ....Il.1.117A.92.
Apollo's Vengeance for his injur'd Priest. ....Il.1.120.93.
The Priest may pardon, and the God may spare. ....Il.1.126.93.
Is Heav'n offended, and a Priest profan'd, ...Il.1.138.93.
The Priest of *Phœbus* sought by Gifts to gain ....Il.1.484.111.
The Priest to rev'rence, and release the Fair; ....Il.1.491.111.
Hail Rev'rend Priest! to Phœbus' awful Dome ....Il.1.576.115.
And solemn Voice, the Priest directs his Pray'r. ....Il.1.589.116.
The Priest himself before his Altar stands, ...Il.1.606.117.
A wealthy Priest, but rich without a Fault; ....Il.5.16.266.
Priest of the Stream, and honour'd as a God. ....Il.5.102.271.
Down sunk the Priest: the Purple Hand of Death ....Il.5.108.272.
The Priest of *Jove,* and honour'd like his God. ....Il.16.736.272.
Nor Augur, Priest, or Seer had been obey'd. ....Il.24.272.547.
(The Priest of *Phœbus* at th' *Ismarian* shrine) ....Od.9.231.316.
As priest himself, the blameless rustick rose; ....Od.14.481.59.
And first *Leiodes,* blameless priest, appear'd: ....Od.21.152.266.
Because the Priest is born a peaceful slave. ....Od.21.180.268.
Priest as thou art! for that detested band ....Od.22.357.304.

PRIEST-CRAFT
Then thus. "From Priest-craft happily set free, ...5.DunB4.499.391.

PRIESTESS
Th'inferior Priestess, at her Altar's side, ...2.RL1.127.155.
Her Priestess Muse forbids the Good to dye, ...4.EpS2.234.326*.
As *Pallas'* Priestess, and unbars the Gates. ....Il.6.373.344.
The Priestess then the shining Veil displays, ...Il.6.376.344.
So pray'd the Priestess in her holy Fane; ....Il.6.386.345.

PRIESTHOOD
(The *Glory* of the Priesthood, and the *Shame!*) ....1.EOC.694.318.
Cry, by your Priesthood tell me what you are? ....4.JD4.37.29.

PRIESTLY
But Fate with Butchers plac'd thy priestly Stall, ...5.DunA3.205.175.
But fate with butchers plac'd thy priestly stall, ...5.DunB3.209.330.
And still thy Priestly Pride provoke thy King? ....Il.1.134.93.

PRIESTS
Then Unbelieving Priests reform'd the Nation, ...1.EOC.546.300.
For long ago, let Priests say what they cou'd, ...2.ChJM.7.15.
Of *Ægypt's* Priests the gilded Niches grace, ...2.TemF.110.262.
And Priests and Party-Zealots, num'rous Bands ....2.TemF.464.286.
Priests, Tapers, Temples, swim before my sight: ....2.ElAb.274.342.
As Eastern priests in giddy circles run, ...3.EOM2.27.58.
Priests, Princes, Women, no dissemblers here. ....3.Ep1.177.30.
The frugal Crone, whom praying priests attend, ...3.Ep1.238.35.
Ye Statesmen, Priests, of one Religion all! ....4.EpS2.16.314.
Toland and Tindal, prompt at Priests to jeer, ...5.DunA2.367.144.
C[ollin]s and *Toland* prompt at Priests to jeer, ...5.DunA2.367B.144.
Toland and Tindal, prompt at priests to jeer, ...5.DunB2.399.316.
That which my Priests, and mine alone, maintain, ...5.DunB4.185.360.
The good Priests whisper—Where's the Chevalier? ....6.82vi.14.232.
If, fir'd to Vengeance at thy Priests request, ...Il.1.594.116.
Priests of the Gods, and Elders of the Land; ....Il.9.690.468.
Or priests in fabled Oracles advise? ....Od.16.100.107.
Nor priests in fabled oracles advise; ....Od.16.120.108.

PRIGS
Wits, Witlings, Prigs, and Peers; ....6.58.46.172.

PRIM
Edwardi Sext. or *prim. & quint. Eliz:* ....4.HS1.148.19.
Witness Ann. prim. of Henry Oct. ....6.67.14.195.

PRIMAEVAL
With Night Primæval, and with Chaos old. ....5.DunA3.338.192.
Of *Night* Primæval, and of *Chaos* old! ....5.DunB4.630.407.

PRIMATE'S
Shows *Poland's* Int'rests, takes the *Primate's* ....4.JD4.154A.39.

PRIME
Unstrings my Nerves, and ends my manly Prime; ....Il.11.815.72.
In rosy prime with charms attractive grac'd, ...Od.1.543.58.
Prime of the flock, and choicest of the stall: ....Od.4.432.140.
The fields are florid with unfading prime: ....Od.4.770.155.
Swept from the earth, he perish'd in his prime; ....Od.8.258.276.
Crept on from childhood into youthful prime, ...Od.15.391.88.
Nor think thy self exempt: that rosy prime ....Od.19.100.197.
Lur'd with the promis'd boon, when youthful prime ....Od.19.484.220.

PRIMO
There liv'd, *in primo Georgii* (they record) ....4.2HE2.184.177.

PRIMUS
Hannoniae qui primus ab oris. ....6.42iv.6.118.

PRINCE
While that Prince Threatens, and while this Commands. ....1.TrSt.272.421.
The Prince with Wonder did the Waste behold, ...1.TrSt.510A.431.
This rural Prince one only Daughter blest, ...1.TrSt.670.438.
This *Argive* Prince one only Daughter blest, ...1.TrSt.670A.438.
Our Neighbour Prince, and Heir of *Calydon:* ....1.TrSt.793.443.
(Oh gen'rous Prince) my Nation or my name, ...1.TrSt.799.443.
What Prince from those his Lineage can defend? ....1.TrSt.821.444.
The Prince gave back; not meditating Flight, ...1.TrES.141.454.
The prostrate Prince, and on his Bosom trod; ....1.TrES.317.461.
Some juster Prince perhaps had entertain'd, ...1.TrUl.82.468.
For, like a Prince, he bore the vast Expence ....2.ChJM.444.36.
The Rebel- *Knave,* who dares his Prince engage, ...2.RL3.59.172.
The Rebel- *Knave,* that dares his Prince engage, ...2.RL3.59A.172.
A Prince the Father of a People made. ....3.EOM3.214.114.
Think we, like some weak Prince, th'Eternal Cause, ...3.EOM4.121.139.
A perjur'd Prince a leaden Saint revere, ...3.Ep1.148.28.
'Tis the dear Prince (Sir John) that crowns thy cup, ...3.Ep3.207A.110.
Rouz'd by the Prince of Air, the whirlwinds sweep ....3.Ep3.353.122.
Indebted to no Prince or Peer alive, ...4.2HE2.69.169.
(Believe me, many a German Prince is worse, ...4.1HE6.83.243.
"His Prince, that writes in Verse, and has his Ear? ....4.EpS1.46.301.
Consid'ring what a Gracious Prince was next. ....4.EpS1.108.306.
P. As *S[elkir]k,* if he lives, will love the 'prince. ....4.EpS2.61.316.
'Twixt Prince and People close the Curtain draw, ...5.DunB1.313.293.
Honour a Syrian Prince above his own; ....5.DunB4.368.378.
Just to his Prince, and to his Country true: ....6.27.6.81.
Sermons to *Charles* the First, when Prince; ....6.39.10.110.
Just to his Prince, yet to his Country true; ....6.57.6.169.
He treateth them all, like a Prince of the Air. ....6.122.20A.342.
And treateth them all, like a Prince of the Air. ....6.122.20.342.
Have made Tremendous as a Prince ....6.135.88A.369.
Nor unrewarded let your Prince complain, ...Il.1.153.94.
And some deputed Prince the Charge attend; ....Il.1.186.96.
'Tis mine to threaten, Prince, and thine to fear. ....Il.1.240.98.
But then prepare, Imperious Prince! prepare, ...Il.1.243.98.
Nor thou, *Achilles,* treat our Prince with Pride; ....Il.1.364.105.
But first, and loudest, to your Prince declare, ...Il.1.442.108.
In his black Ship the *Pylian* Prince he found, ...Il.2.65.130.
Each Prince of Name, or Chief in Arms approv'd, ...Il.2.225.138.
The gen'rous *Nestor* thus the Prince addrest. ....Il.2.515.151.
As Godlike *Hector* sees the Prince retreat, ...Il.3.53.191.
Extoll'd the happy Prince, and thus began. ....Il.3.240.203.
Whose Arms shall conquer, and what Prince shall fall, ...Il.3.384.211.
But *Venus* trembl'd for the Prince of Troy: ....Il.3.460.214.
The Queen and Goddess to the Prince ascend. ....Il.3.528.216.
The Prince replies; Ah cease, divinely fair, ...Il.3.543.217.
While round the Prince the *Greeks* employ their Care, ...Il.4.252.232.
Thus to th' experienc'd Prince *Atrides* cry'd; ....Il.4.368.238.
Still first in Front the matchless Prince appear'd: ....Il.4.427.240.
O Prince (*Lycaon's* valiant Son reply'd) ....Il.5.288.281.
Prince, thou art met. Tho' late in vain assail'd, ...Il.5.340.283.
From his proud Car the Prince impetuous springs; ....Il.5.603.297.
Thy Sire, O Prince! o'erturn'd the *Trojan* State, ...Il.5.804.304.
A Prince and People studious of their Gain. ....Il.5.873.308.
Degen'rate Prince! and not of *Tydeus'* Kind, ...Il.5.998.314.
And the brave Prince in num'rous Toils engag'd. ....Il.6.200.336.
Then friendly, thus, the *Lycian* Prince addrest. ....Il.6.263.339.
The Prince beheld, and high-resenting spoke. ....Il.6.405.346.
Too daring Prince! ah whither dost thou run? ....Il.6.510.351.
Once with what Joy the gen'rous Prince would hear ....Il.7.151.372.
(To *Ajax* thus the *Trojan* Prince reply'd) ....Il.7.284.378.
O rev'rend Prince! (*Tydides* thus replies) ....Il.8.177.406.
Thy once-proud Hopes, presumptuous Prince! are fled; ....Il.8.202.407.
Attend his Order, and their Prince surround. ....Il.8.614.425.
If I oppose thee, Prince! thy Wrath with-hold, ...Il.9.45.434.
Thee, Prince! it fits alike to speak and hear, ...Il.9.133.438.
Such are thy Offers as a Prince may take, ...Il.9.217.443.
Regard in time, O Prince divinely brave! ....Il.9.326.450.
Some Present too to ev'ry Prince was paid; ....Il.9.438.454.
And ev'ry Prince enjoys the Gift he made; ....Il.9.439.454.
No—let the stupid Prince, whom *Jove* deprives ....Il.9.492.456.
This said, each Prince a double Goblet crown'd, ...Il.9.771.472.
There call great *Ajax,* and the Prince of *Crete.* ....Il.10.64.5.
This for the wounded Prince the Dame prepares; ....Il.11.784.70.
The Prince gave back, not meditating Flight ....Il.12.495.99.
O Prince! (*Meriones* replies) whose Care ....Il.13.333.121.
Our Offers now, illustrious Prince! receive; ....Il.13.475.130.
Deucalion, blameless Prince! was *Minos'* Heir; ....Il.13.566.133.
Now, *Trojan* Prince, employ thy pious Arms, ...Il.13.582.134.
And owe Destruction to a Prince like thee. ....Il.14.113.163.
The prostrate Prince, and on his Bosom trod; ....Il.16.622.268.
Oh Prince (he cry'd) oh foremost once in Fame! ....Il.17.658.313.
Stretch not henceforth, O Prince! thy sov'reign Might, ...Il.19.179.379.
The *Dardan* Prince, O *Neptune,* be thy Care; ....Il.20.360.410.
The *Dardan* Prince, and bore him thro' the Sky, ...Il.20.374.410.
What Pow'r, O Prince, with Force inferior far, ...Il.20.381.411.
The ransom'd Prince to fair *Arisbe* bore. ....Il.21.49.424.
If Earth at length this active Prince can seize, ...Il.21.72.424.
Then he. O Prince! ally'd in Blood and Fame, ...Il.22.299.468.
Prince! you have mist. My Fate depends on Heav'n. ....Il.22.358.470.
Then Prince! you should have fear'd, what now you feel; ....Il.22.417.472.
Contentious Prince! of all the *Greeks* beside ....Il.23.566.512.
To serve our Prince, it fell on me, the last. ....Il.24.490.556.
And thus, reveal'd—Hear Prince! and understand ....Il.24.563.559.
Unhappy Prince! thus guardless and alone ....Il.24.654.564.
Thus affable and mild, the Prince precedes, ...Od.1.165.40.
His indignation thus the Prince exprest. ....Od.1.202.42.
To prove a genuine birth (the Prince replies) ....Od.1.275.46.
Magnificence of old, (the Prince reply'd,) ....Od.1.295.47.
(Reply'd the Prince) will you the Bard reprove? ....Od.1.442.53.
Aw'd by the Prince, thus haughty, bold, and young, ...Od.1.487.55.
Oh son of *Polybus!* the Prince replies, ...Od.1.521.57.

PRINCE (CONTINUED)

To this his steps the thoughtful Prince inclin'd; ....Od.1.538.57.
Whilst to his couch himself the Prince addrest, ...Od.1.549.58.
But you oh Peers! and thou oh Prince! give ear: ....Od.2.127.67.
The Prince of Augurs, *Halitherses,* rose: ....Od.2.186.71.
And both the Prince and Augur threat in vain: ....Od.2.228.72.
Threat on, oh Prince! elude the bridal day, ...Od.2.231.72.
His injur'd Prince the little aid of words. ....Od.2.274.74.
The royal dome; while sad the Prince explores ....Od.2.293.75.
O Prince, in early youth divinely wise, ...Od.2.307.76.
She spoke: to his high dome the Prince returns, ...Od.2.335.77.
Grieve not, oh daring Prince! that noble heart: ....Od.2.341.77.
Is this (returns the Prince) for mirth a time? ....Od.2.347.78.
Meantime the lofty rooms the Prince surveys, ...Od.2.380.79.
To whom the Prince. O thou whose guardian care ....Od.2.394.80.
Far hence (reply'd the Prince) thy fears be driv'n: ....Od.2.416.81.
While to the rival train the Prince returns, ...Od.2.428.81.
The Prince and Goddess to the stern ascend; ....Od.2.458.83.
Ah! no such hope (the Prince with sighs replies) ....Od.3.279.99.
Deep in a rich Alcove the Prince was laid, ...Od.3.510.112.
To bathe the Prince, and pour the fragrant oil. ....Od.3.595.117.
While thus pathetic to the Prince he spoke, ...Od.4.149.127.
(Replies the Prince) inflam'd with filial love, ...Od.4.426.140.
And thus indignant to the Prince reply'd: ....Od.4.446.141.
And now, young Prince, indulge my fond request; ....Od.4.801.156.
The Prince, departing for the *Pylian* court, ...Od.4.855.159.
The Prince in rural bow'r they fondly thought, ...Od.4.864.159.
When spread the Prince his sail for distant *Pyle?* ....Od.4.867.159.
Perish'd the Prince, and left this only heir.) ....Od.7.77.237.
Father and Prince of the *Phæacian* name: ....Od.7.80.237.
A Prince of grace divine your aid implores, ...Od.8.13.262.
Thus spoke the Prince: th' attending Peers obey, ...Od.8.43.264.
Then thus *Euryalus:* O Prince, whose sway ....Od.8.435.287.
Leave here the man who dares his Prince desert, ...Od.10.523.368.
To whom the Prince: This night with joy I stay, ...Od.11.442.406.
O Prince attend! some fav'ring pow'r be kind, ...Od.12.49.431.
Some juster Prince perhaps had entertain'd, ...Od.13.249.18.
Small is the faith, the Prince and Queen ascribe ....Od.14.146.42.
No Prince will let *Ulysses'* heir remove ....Od.15.95.73.
A bowl; the Prince a silver beaker chose. ....Od.15.117.74.
The Prince the variegated present took. ....Od.15.145.75.
Ah! doubt not our report (the Prince rejoin'd) ....Od.15.172.76.
Scarce ended thus the Prince, when on the right ....Od.15.178.77.
(The Prince reply'd) stand fixt in fate above; ....Od.15.203.78.
Mean-time the Prince with sacrifice adores ....Od.15.248.80.
Stranger (reply'd the Prince) securely rest ....Od.15.304.83.
But both in constant peace one Prince obey, ...Od.15.454.92.
When thus the Prince: Now each his course pursue; ....Od.15.541.96.
The Prince return'd. Renown'd in days of yore ....Od.15.551.96.
Th' observing Augur took the Prince aside, ...Od.15.571.98.
A faithful servant, by thy Prince belov'd! ....Od.15.582.98.
Then from the deck the Prince his sandals takes; ....Od.15.593.99.
While yet he spoke, the Prince advancing drew ....Od.16.11.102.
The Prince reply'd; *Eumæus,* I obey; ....Od.16.31.103.
His seat *Ulysses* to the Prince resign'd. ....Od.16.42.104.
Not so—(exclaims the Prince with decent grace) ....Od.16.43.104.
There sate the Prince: the feast *Eumæus* spread; ....Od.16.49.104.
Such honours as befit a Prince to give; ....Od.16.78.106.
But tell me, dost thou Prince, dost thou behold ....Od.16.97.107.
Wretched old man! (with tears the Prince returns) ....Od.16.158.110.
The Heroe reascends: The Prince o'eraw'd ....Od.16.194.112.
Ah me! (exclaims the Prince with fond desire) ....Od.16.214.114.
He spoke and sate. The Prince with transport flew, ...Od.16.234.114.
The Prince thus interrupts the solemn woe. ....Od.16.245.116.
O'er earth (returns the Prince) resounds thy name, ...Od.16.262.117.
Who loves his Prince; for sure you merit love. ....Od.16.331.121.
Th' associates of the Prince repass'd the bay; ....Od.16.345.122.
To some blest Prince, the Prince decreed by Heav'n. ....Od.16.407.126.
To some blest Prince, the Prince decreed by Heav'n. ....Od.16.407.126.
Wretch! to destroy a Prince that friendship gives, ...Od.16.438.128.
When near he drew, the Prince breaks forth; Proclaim ....Od.16.482.130.
The Prince well pleas'd to disappoint their wiles, ...Od.16.496.131.
In haste the Prince arose, prepar'd to part; ....Od.17.3.132.
To this *Ulysses.* What the Prince requires ....Od.17.20.133.
(Reply'd the Prince) nor be our fates deplor'd, ...Od.17.58.135.
Arm'd with his lance the Prince then past the gate; ....Od.17.72.136.
Stabb'd in his Palace if your Prince must fall, ...Od.17.91.136.
The Prince and stranger shar'd the genial feast, ...Od.17.114.137.
Thy passion, Prince, belies thy knowing mind. ....Od.17.459.155.
Then, Prince! be bounteous of *Ulysses'* board. ....Od.17.485.156.
Of all the *Greeks,* but Prince-like and the first. ....Od.17.498.157.
To whom with filial awe, the Prince returns: ....Od.18.267.179.
To whom incens'd: Should we, O Prince, engage ....Od.18.410.188.
The Prince obedient to the same command, ...Od.19.17.193.
A present Deity the Prince confess'd, ...Od.19.42.195.
Sweet blooms the Prince beneath *Apollo's* care; ....Od.19.106.197.
Prince! he cries, renew'd by your command, ...Od.19.188.200.
Forth-issuing from the dome the Prince repair'd: ....Od.20.181.242.
The Gods from force and fraud the Prince defend; ....Od.20.306.247.
The Prince appoints; but to his Sire assigns ....Od.20.324.248.
Aw'd by the Prince, so haughty, brave, and young, ...Od.20.334.249.
When thus the Prince with pious rage inflam'd: ....Od.20.372.250.
And Prince! to stop the source of future ill, ...Od.20.391.251.
And aim to wound the Prince with pointless wit: ....Od.20.448.255.
But, Prince! for once at least believe a friend, ...Od.20.455.255.
Thus jovial they; but nought the Prince replies; ....Od.20.459.255.
And to the youthful Prince to urge the laws, ...Od.21.23.260.
His ardour strait th' obedient Prince suppress, ...Od.21.137.265.
'Tis impious, Prince! to harm the stranger-guest, ...Od.21.334.276.
A son's just right. No *Grecian* Prince but I ....Od.21.371.277.
Then to the Prince. Nor have I wrought thee shame; ....Od.21.465.282.
Two hundred oxen ev'ry Prince shall pay: ....Od.22.69.290.
(Who-e'er he be) 'till ev'ry Prince lie dead. ....Od.22.86.290.
And their own darts shall pierce the Prince and King. ....Od.22.157.294.
Sprung to the Prince, embrac'd his knee with tears, ...Od.22.405.307.
O Prince! O Friend! lo here thy *Medon* stands; ....Od.22.407.307.
The matron moves, the Prince directs the way. ....Od.22.437.309.
Then thus the Prince. To these shall we afford ....Od.22.495.313.

PRINCE-LIKE

Of all the *Greeks,* but Prince-like and the first. ....Od.17.498.157.

PRINCE'S

He gain his Prince's Ear, or lose his own. ....4.Arbu.367.122.
And worthy of the *prince's ear.* ....6.106v.3.308.
And worthy of thy *prince's ear.* ....6.106v.3A.308.
First give thy Faith, and plight a Prince's Word ....Il.1.99.91.
A Prince's Faults, and I with Reason own. ....Il.9.148.439.
But can I, absent from my Prince's Sight, ...Il.24.531.558.
Like years, like tempers, and their Prince's love. ....Od.3.465.109.
In her sad breast the Prince's fortunes roul, ...Od.4.1039.166.
In my respect he bears a Prince's part, ...Od.14.169.43.
Doom'd a fair prize to grace some Prince's board, ...Od.15.420.89.
The Prince's near approach the dogs descry, ...Od.16.5.102.
Mean-time the Suitors urge the Prince's fate, ...Od.20.300.247.
Observant of the Prince's high behest, ...Od.20.349.249.
Since due regard must wait the Prince's friend, ...Od.20.360.249.
Young as I am, thy Prince's vengeful hand ....Od.21.401.279.
Euryades receiv'd the Prince's dart; ....Od.22.294.300.
The Prince's jav'lin tore its bloody way ....Od.22.327.302.

PRINCELY

A lofty Couch receives each Princely Guest; ....1.TrSt.615.436.
Who seem'd descended from some Princely Line: ....1.TrUl.103.469.
And still they grace *Lycaon's* Princely Dome: ....Il.5.245.279.
He seem'd, fair Offspring of some princely Line! ....Il.24.426.553.
Th' obsequious Herald guides each princely guest: ....Od.4.408.140.
Tell then whence art thou? whence that Princely air? ....Od.7.320.251.
Who seem'd descended from some princely line. ....Od.13.270.19.
Take that, ere yet thou quit this princely throng: ....Od.17.545.159.
May what I speak your princely minds approve, ...Od.17.555.159.
See how with nods assent yon princely train! ....Od.18.16.167.
Thou bold intruder on a princely train? ....Od.18.376.185.
I read a Monarch in that princely air, ...Od.24.298.364.

PRINCES

Hither the *Lycian* Princes bend their Course, ...1.TrES.71.452.
Thither the *Lycian* Princes bend their Course, ...1.TrES.80Z5.452.
And this the Faith *Phæacia's* Princes boast? ....1.TrUl.85A.468.
Priests, Princes, Women, no dissemblers here. ....3.Ep1.177.30.
"To gaze on Princes, and to talk of Kings!" ....4.JD4.101.33.
Now calls in Princes, and now turns away. ....4.2HE1.156.209.
Speak the loud language Princes.. ....4.1740.45.334.
Lift up your gates, ye Princes, see him come! ....5.DunB1.301.291.
"Speak'st thou of Syrian Princes? Traitor base! ....5.DunB4.375.379.
Contending Princes mount them in their Coach. ....5.DunB4.564.398.
Contending Princes take them in their Coach. ....5.DunB4.564A.398.
And nobly conscious, Princes are but things ....5.DunB4.601.403.
Blind with Ambition! to think Princes things ....5.DunB4.603A.403.
Lies crown'd with Princes Honours, Poets Lays, ...6.108.5.312.
Rests crown'd with Princes Honours, Poets Lays, ...6.108.5A.312.
(For both the Princes claim'd her equal Care) ....Il.1.263.99.
Princes of *Greece,* your faithful Ears incline, ...Il.2.101.131.
Expell the Council where our Princes meet, ...Il.2.324.142.
The Heralds part it, and the Princes share; ....Il.3.343.209.
Such mighty Woes on perjur'd Princes wait; ....Il.4.204.231.
You then, O Princes of the *Greeks!* appear, ...Il.7.85.367.
Then hear me, Princes of the *Trojan* Name! ....Il.7.436.386.
To sacred *Troy,* where all her Princes lay ....Il.7.490.388.
Fellows in Arms, and Princes of the War! ....Il.9.24.432.
Conven'd the Princes in his ample Tent; ....Il.9.122.438.
Princes all hail! whatever brought ye here, ...Il.9.261A.445.
Princes all hail! whatever brought you here, ...Il.9.261.445.
(For these the Princes to their Council join'd) ....Il.10.230.12.
Their other Princes? tell what Watch they keep? ....Il.10.480.25.
Hither the *Lycian* Princes bend their Course, ...Il.12.415.96.
Thither the *Lycian* Princes bend their Course, ...Il.12.429.97.
Him, in his March, the wounded Princes meet, ...Il.14.35.159.
Oh Chiefs! oh Princes! to whose Hand is giv'n ....Il.17.294.299.
Princes and Leaders! Countrymen and Friends! ....Il.22.474.475.
With Princes sported, and on Dainties fed, ...Il.22.647.483.
Ye Kings and Princes of th' *Achaian* Name! ....Il.23.294.501.
Nor let a race of Princes wait in vain. ....Od.2.132.67.
Joyful they see applauding Princes gaze, ...Od.6.187.218.
He next their princes lofty domes admires, ...Od.7.57.236.
The work of matrons: These the Princes prest, ...Od.7.126.241.
Princes and Peers, attend! while we impart ....Od.7.246.248.
Twelve Princes in our realm dominion share, ...Od.8.425.286.
The deathful scene, Princes on Princes roll'd! ....Od.11.151.388.
The deathful scene, Princes on Princes roll'd! ....Od.11.151.388.
But hear me, Princes! whom these walls inclose, ...Od.13.9.2.
And you the Peers and Princes of the land! ....Od.13.48.3.
The wrath of Princes ever is severe. ....Od.17.212.142.
"And prove your sev'ral strengths"—The Princes heard, ...Od.21.151.266.
Admitted here with Princes to confer, ...Od.21.313.274.
"And did what all those Princes could not do." ....Od.21.354.276.
Another, Princes! yet remains to play; ....Od.22.8.286.
Aim'st thou at Princes? (all amaz'd they said) ....Od.22.31.288.
With bleeding Princes shall bestrow the floor: ....Od.22.273.300.

PRINCESS

And makes a Princess whom he found a Whore. ....4.HAdv.66.81.
Free, and a Princess, to the *Stygian* coast. ....6.20.18.66.
The mournful image of a Princess dead. ....6.20.22.66.
His beauteous Princess cast a mournful Look, ...Il.6.506.351.
His Princess parts with a prophetick Sigh, ...Il.6.640.358.
A Princess rap'd transcends a Navy storm'd: ....Il.13.782.142.
(A mourning Princess, and a Train in Tears) ....Il.22.553.479.
Hard is the task, oh Princess! you impose: ....Od.7.322.251.
O prudent Princess! bid thy soul confide. ....Od.16.453.129.
Princess, he cry'd, in vain your bounties flow ....Od.19.387.212.

PRINCESS (CONTINUED)
Who wrongs his Princess with a thought so mean. ... Od.21.344.276.

PRINCESS'
Serv'd with pure Wheat, and by a Princess' Hand; ... Il.8.231.408.

PRINCESSE
And the whole Princesse in my work should shine. ... 6.75.10.212.

PRINCIPAL
So Man, who here seems principal alone, ... 3.EOM1.57.20.

PRINCIPLE
Most strength the moving principle requires; ... 3.EOM2.67.63.
Receives the lurking principle of death; ... 3.EOM2.134.71.
Grafts on this Passion our best principle: ... 3.EOM2.176.76.
His Principle of action once explore, ... 3.Ep1.37.18.
That instant 'tis his Principle no more. ... 3.Ep1.38.18.
Who never chang'd his Principle, or Wig: ... 4.EpS1.40.301.
As much Estate, and Principle, and Wit, ... 5.DunB4.325.375.
Extracts his brain, and Principle is fled, ... 5.DunB4.522.394.
Honour unchang'd; a Principle profest; ... 6.27.3.81.
Honour unchang'd, a principle profest, ... 6.57.3.169.
Heav'n with a secret principle indu'd ... Od.17.252.143.

PRINCIPLES
They talk of *Principles,* but Notions prize, ... 1.EOC.265.270.
They talk of *Principles,* but Parts they prize, ... 1.EOC.265A.270.
To those of gen'rous Principles, and just. ... 2.ChJM.181.23.
Two Principles in human nature reign; ... 3.EOM2.53.62.
Tenets with Books, and Principles with Times. ... 3.Ep1.167.29.
Fix'd Principles, with Fancy ever new; ... 3.Ep2.279.72.

PRINT
And print warm kisses on the panting rind, ... 1.TrFD.60.388.
Like *Lee* or *Budgell,* I will Rhyme and Print. ... 4.HS1.100.15.
Fir'd that the House reject him, "'Sdeath I'll print it ... 4.Arbu.61.100.
If want provok'd, or madness made them print, ... 4.Arbu.155.107.
Hunger provok'd, or madness made them print; ... 4.Arbu.155A.107.
Fr. Not twice a twelvemonth you appear in Print, ... 4.EpS1.1.297.
And for that very cause I print to day. ... 4.EpS2.3.313.
They print their Names in Letters small, ... 6.29.9.83.
Hunger, not Malice, makes such Authors print, ... 6.49iii.5.142.
'Tis Hunger and not Malice makes them Print ... 6.49iii.5A.142.
'Tis Hunger, and not Malice, makes them print, ... 6.98.5.283.
The jest is lost, unless you print his Face. ... 6.105iii.4A.301.
Shou'd D[enni]s print how once you robb'd your Brother, ... 6.116vii.1.328.
"In Dryden's Virgil see the print. ... 6.140.28.379.
And print th' important story on thy mind! ... Od.12.50.431.

PRINTED
These Aldus printed, those Du Suëil has bound. ... 3.Ep4.136.150.
Those printed unknown Tongues, 'tis said, ... 6.29.7Z1.83.

PRINTER
But shall a *Printer,* weary of his life, ... 4.EpS1.125.307.
And sure a *Printer* is his Match, ... 6.116ii.8.326.

PRINTING
To court applause by printing what I write: ... 4.2HE2.150.175.
To seek applause by printing what I write: ... 4.2HE2.150A.175.

PRINTS
Rymes e'er he wakes, and prints before *Term* ends, ... 4.Arbu.43.99.
This prints my Letters, that expects a Bribe, ... 4.Arbu.113.103.
"Or do the Prints and Papers lye? ... 4.HS6.115.257.
Who the *Plain-dealer* damns, and prints the *Biter.* ... 6.12.11.37.
Stephens prints *Heathen Greek,* 'tis said, ... 6.29.13.83.
The jest is lost, unless he prints his Face. ... 6.105iii.4.301.
Prints the dry Dust, and thirsts for Blood in vain. ... Il.11.701B.66.
But prints her lofty Footsteps on the Heads ... Il.19.96.376.
Thus he; then parting prints the sandy shore ... Od.13.80.5.
His length of carcass trailing prints the ground; ... Od.18.121.172.

PRIOR
Our Friend Dan *Prior* told, (you know) ... 4.HS6.153.259.
She deck'd like Congreve, Addison, and Prior; ... 5.DunA2.116.110.
Cook shall be Prior, and Concanen, Swift; ... 5.DunA2.130.112.
She deck'd like Congreve, Addison, and Prior; ... 5.DunB2.124.301.
Cook shall be Prior, and Concanen, Swift: ... 5.DunB2.138.301.
'Tis known, a Cook-maid roasted *Prior,* ... 6.10.59.26.

PRIORI
We nobly take the high Priori Road, ... 5.DunB4.471.386.

PRIS'NERS
Dull sullen pris'ners in the body's cage: ... 2.Elegy.18.364.
Grave, as when Pris'ners shake the head, and swear ... 4.JD2.69.139.
To no more purpose, than when pris'ners swear ... 4.JD2A.78.138.

PRISCA'S
Act Sins which Prisca's Confessor scarce hears: ... 4.JD2.40.135.

PRISCIAN'S
Break Priscian's head, the Pegasus's neck; ... 5.DunA3.156.165.
Break Priscian's head, and Pegasus's neck; ... 5.DunB3.162.328.

PRISMATIC
False Eloquence, like the *Prismatic Glass,* ... 1.EOC.311.274.

PRISON
Set *Bacchus* from his glassy Prison free, ... 6.100vi.2.289.
How, the loud storms in prison bound, he sails ... Od.23.339.341.

PRITHEE
"Plague on't! 'tis past a Jest—nay prithee, Pox! ... 2.RL4.129.194.

PRIVACY
To him, with humble Privacy content, ... 6.17iii.22.58.
The wooden Guardian of our Privacy ... 6.100ii.1.288.

PRIVATE
And publick Faction doubles private Hate. ... 1.EOC.457.290.
Her private Orchards wall'd on ev'ry side, ... 1.TrVP.19.377.
Heav'n knows, I shed full many a private Tear, ... 2.ChJM.198.24.
He kept, 'twas thought, a private Miss or two: ... 2.ChWB.230.68.
From private Sparkles raise the gen'ral Flame, ... 3.EOM3.138Z1.106.
And found the private in the public good. ... 3.EOM3.282.121.
"Why bounded Pow'r? why private? why no king?" ... 3.EOM4.160.143.
Slave to no sect, who takes no private road, ... 3.EOM4.331.160.
A Woman's seen in Private life alone: ... 3.Ep2.200.67.
Triumphant Malice rag'd thro' private life. ... 4.2HE1.254.217.
Has never made a Friend in private life, ... 4.EpS2.134.321.
Nor *public* Flame, nor *private,* dares to shine; ... 5.DunB4.651.409.
With thee in private modest *Dulness* lies, ... 6.8.19.18.
Thus *either Men in private useless Ease* ... 6.17ii.1.56.
"Who broke no promise, serv'd no private end, ... 6.71.69.204.
Who broke no promise, serv'd no private end, ... 6.97.3.282.
Who broke no promise, sought no private end, ... 6.97.3A.282.
Whose Private Name all Titles recommend, ... 6.134.3.364.
My private Loss let grateful *Greece* repair; ... Il.1.152.94.
T'avenge a private, not a publick Wrong: ... Il.1.208.96.
Unfit for publick Rule, or private Care; ... Il.9.89.437.
Curs'd be the Man (ev'n private *Greeks* would say) ... Il.17.474.306.
Your private right shou'd impious pow'r invade, ... Od.1.513.56.
A private voyager I pass the main. ... Od.2.358.78.
A private sorrow, not a publick cause. ... Od.3.99.91.
In publick sentence, or in private thought; ... Od.3.156.93.
Of courts, presume to weigh their private cares? ... Od.4.875.159.
Six blooming youths, in private grandeur bred, ... Od.10.5.339.
A private audience if thy grace impart, ... Od.17.602.161.
One loss was private, one a publick debt: ... Od.21.20.259.
Careful he treasur'd in a private room: ... Od.24.194.356.

PRIVILEGE
Full, and eternal privilege of tongue." ... 5.DunA2.346.142.
"Full and eternal privilege of tongue." ... 5.DunB2.378.315.
This Nod confirms each Privilege your own. ... 5.DunB4.584.400.
Has foul Reproach a Privilege from Heav'n? ... Il.1.385.106.
The coward wretch the privilege to fly. ... Od.18.284.180.

PRIVY
"Still of the Council Privy. ... 6.79.92.221.

PRIZ'D
If this is priz'd for *sweetness,* that for *stink?* ... 4.HS2.30.57.
How things are priz'd, which once belong'd to you: ... 6.38.2.107.
Most priz'd for Art, and labour'd o'er with Gold, ... Il.6.114.329.
Most priz'd for Art, and labour'd o'er with Gold, ... Il.6.341.343.
Too dear I priz'd a fair enchanting face: ... Od.8.359.283.
Some care his Age deserves: Or was he priz'd ... Od.17.372.150.

PRIZE
O Love! for *Sylvia* let me gain the Prize, ... 1.PSp.49.65.
Tell me but this, and I'll disclaim the Prize, ... 1.PSp.87.69.
And then a nobler Prize I will resign, ... 1.PSp.91.70.
Sudden they seize th'amaz'd, defenceless Prize, ... 1.W-F.109.161.
The Young, the Old, one Instant makes our Prize, ... 1.W-F.109A.161.
The captive Race, one Instant makes our Prize, ... 1.W-F.109B.161.
Held from afar, aloft, th' Immortal Prize, ... 1.EOC.96.250.
They talk of *Principles,* but Notions prize, ... 1.EOC.265.270.
They talk of *Principles,* but Parts they prize, ... 1.EOC.265A.270.
The *Ancients* only, or the *Moderns* prize: ... 1.EOC.395.285.
Were all those Realms the guilty Victor's Prize! ... 1.TrSt.217.419.
The lovely Prize, and share my Bliss with none! ... 2.ChJM.265.27.
He saw, he wish'd, and to the Prize aspir'd: ... 2.RL2.30.161.
Soon to obtain, and long possess the Prize: ... 2.RL2.44.162.
(The Victory cry'd) the glorious Prize is mine! ... 2.RL3.162.180.
And shall this Prize, th' inestimable Prize, ... 2.RL4.113.193.
And shall this Prize, th' inestimable Prize, ... 2.RL4.113.193.
And Chiefs contend 'till all the Prize is lost! ... 2.RL5.108.208.
With such a Prize no Mortal must be blest, ... 2.RL5.111.208.
On Wit and Learning the just Prize bestow, ... 2.TemF.304.278.
Ah no! instruct me other joys to prize, ... 2.ElAb.125.330.
Is Virtue's prize: A better would you fix? ... 3.EOM4.169.143.
We prize the stronger effort of his pow'r, ... 3.Ep1.99.22.
A Fop their Passion, but their Prize a Sot, ... 3.Ep2.247.70.
Wife, son, and daughter, Satan, are thy prize, ... 3.Ep3.399A.124.
The Devil and the King divide the prize, ... 3.Ep3.401.125.
So weak a Vessel, and so rich a Prize! ... 4.JD4.229.45.
And bad the nimblest racer seize the prize; ... 5.DunA2.32.99.
And bids the nimblest racer seize the prize; ... 5.DunA2.32A.99.
"This prize is mine; who tempt it, are my foes: ... 5.DunA2.50.103.
Still happy Impudence obtains the prize. ... 5.DunA2.178.123.
Secure, thro' her, the noble prize to carry, ... 5.DunA2.211.127.
If perseverance gain the Diver's prize, ... 5.DunA2.289.137.
This only merit pleading for the prize, ... 5.DunA2.289A.137.
And bade the nimblest racer seize the prize; ... 5.DunB2.36.297.
"This prize is mine; who tempt it are my foes; ... 5.DunB2.54.298.
Still happy Impudence obtains the prize. ... 5.DunB2.186.304.
Secure, thro' her, the noble prize to carry, ... 5.DunB2.219.306.
If perseverance gain the Diver's prize, ... 5.DunB2.301.310.
And, to excuse it, need but shew the prize; ... 5.DunB4.434.383.
Fair charmer cease, nor make your voice's prize ... 6.3.1.7.
Shall heav'n so soon the prize obtain? ... 6.4iii.4.10.
And *Cytheræa* now does prize ... 6.4v.3.11.
Yet what more than all we prize ... 6.18.8.61.
But what more than all we prize ... 6.18.8A.61.
A Fop their Passion, but their Prize a Sot; ... 6.86.9A.245.
Because my Prize, my beauteous Maid I hold, ... Il.1.139.93.

PRIZE (CONTINUED)
The Prize, the beauteous Prize I will resign, ... Il.1.149.94.
The Prize, the beauteous Prize I will resign, ... Il.1.149.94.
Fond of the Pow'r, but fonder of the Prize! ..... Il.1.156.95.
Then thus the King. Shall I my Prize resign ..... Il.1.167.95.
The mighty *Ajax* shall his Prize resign, ... Il.1.177.96.
And dar'st thou threat to snatch my Prize away, ... Il.1.213.97.
A Prize as small, O Tyrant! match'd with thine, ... Il.1.215.97.
I heed thee not, but prize at equal rate ..... Il.1.237.98.
Ev'n in thy Tent I'll seize the blooming Prize, ... Il.1.245.98.
That Prize the *Greeks* by common Suffrage gave: ..... Il.1.363.105.
My Prize of War, yet tamely see resumed; ..... Il.1.393.106.
Thence bear *Briseïs* as our Royal Prize: ..... Il.1.423.108.
Obscures my Glories, and resumes my Prize. ..... Il.1.467.110.
But bright *Chruseïs*, heav'nly Prize! was led ..... Il.1.482.111.
And of my Valour's Prize defrauds my Arms, ... Il.1.507.112.
To rich *Thyestes* next the Prize descends; ..... Il.2.134.134.
Say would'st thou seize some valiant Leader's Prize? ..... Il.2.288.141.
From him he forc'd the Prize we jointly gave, ... Il.2.298.142.
The valiant Victor seiz'd the golden Prize. ..... Il.2.1067.172.
Or Mountain Goat, his bulky Prize, appear; ..... Il.3.38.190.
Thus from her Realm convey'd the beauteous Prize, ... Il.3.71.192.
The *Trojan* Wars she weav'd (herself the Prize) ..... Il.3.171.199.
Thy Love the Motive, and thy Charms the Prize. ..... Il.3.182.199.
Now the bright Prize for which Mankind engage, ... Il.3.519.216.
My forc'd, my willing Heav'nly Prize I bore, ... Il.3.552.218.
In sullen Fury slowly quits the Prize. ..... Il.4.623.250.
And these, the Victor's Prize, in Triumph led. ..... Il.5.295.281.
These, were the rich immortal Prize our own, ... Il.5.336.283.
Behold at distance, but forbear the Prize. ..... Il.5.368.284.
And bears the Prize in Triumph to the Fleet. ..... Il.5.721.301.
The God who slew him, leaves his prostrate Prize ..... Il.5.1040.316.
Beneath the *Spartan* Spear, a living Prize. ..... Il.6.46.325.
As Pity pleaded for his vanquish'd Prize, ... Il.6.65.327.
To *Ereuthalion* he consign'd the Prize. ..... Il.7.180.373.
The Wretch and Hero find their Prize the same; ..... Il.9.419.453.
Who honour Worth, and prize thy Valour most. ..... Il.9.756.471.
And gave *Amphydamas;* from him the Prize ..... Il.10.315.17.
And swear to grant me the demanded Prize; ..... Il.10.380.20.
By none but *Dolon* shall this Prize be born, ... Il.10.391.21.
Bold was thy Aim, and glorious was the Prize, ... Il.10.471.24.
To fav'ring *Pallas* dedicates the Prize. ..... Il.10.531.26.
And points to *Diomed* the tempting Prize. ..... Il.10.551.27.
Return'd triumphant with this Prize of War. ..... Il.10.631.30.
Some God, I deem, conferr'd the glorious Prize, ... Il.10.650.30.
And rich *Hippodamus* becomes his Prize. ..... Il.11.434.53.
Greece, as the Prize of *Nestor's* Wisdom, gave) ..... Il.11.767.69.
For Prize defrauded, and insulted Fame, ... Il.11.837.73.
Allow'd to seize, but not possess the Prize; ..... Il.12.260.90.
And just had fastned on the dazling Prize, ... Il.13.254.117.
Imbrius remains the fierce *Ajaces'* Prize. ..... Il.13.264.117.
Remain the Prize of *Nestor's* youthful Son. ..... Il.13.508.130.
And from his Temples rends the glitt'ring Prize; ..... Il.13.667.137.
There, for some luckier *Greek* it rests a Prize, ... Il.13.731.139.
Thou giv'st the Foe: all *Greece* becomes their Prize. ..... Il.14.109.163.
Nor for the Deed expect a vulgar Prize. ..... Il.14.302.177.
For one bright Prize the matchless Chiefs contend; ..... Il.15.484.216.
The Victor leaps upon his prostrate Prize; ..... Il.15.696.222.
Burn at each Foe, and single ev'ry Prize; ..... Il.15.741.224.
Beneath *Oïleus'* Arm, a living Prize; ..... Il.16.395.258.
A living Prize not long the *Trojan* stood; ..... Il.16.396.258.
'Tis half the Glory to maintain our Prize. ..... Il.16.686.270.
And skill'd in Dancing to dispute the Prize, ... Il.16.746.272.
The Prize contested, and despoil the Slain. ..... Il.16.806.274.
Then rushing sudden on his prostrate Prize, ... Il.16.907.279.
Proud of his Deed, and glorious in the Prize, ... Il.17.67.290.
And urg'd great *Hector* to dispute the Prize, ... Il.17.76.291.
And *Hector* glories in the dazling Prize. ..... Il.17.134.293.
High on the splendid Car: One glorious Prize ..... Il.17.514.308.
'Tis *Hector* comes; and when he seeks the Prize, ... Il.17.572.311.
Yet singly, now, the long disputed Prize ..... Il.17.662.313.
Robb'd of the Prize the *Grecian* Suffrage gave, ... Il.18.517.346.
The Prize of him who best adjudg'd the Right. ..... Il.18.590.351.
The partial Monarch may refuse the Prize; ..... Il.20.219.403.
Our latent Godhead, and the Prize deny'd: ..... Il.21.526.443.
And yields to Ocean's hoary Sire, the Prize? ..... Il.21.548.444.
And boast my Conquest, while I yield the Prize. ..... Il.21.584.446.
So the proud Courser, victor of the prize, ... Il.22.33.453.
Swift was the Course; No vulgar Prize they play, ... Il.22.207.464.
The Prize contended was great *Hector's* Life. ..... Il.22.210.464.
But far the first, *Eumelus* hopes the Prize, ... Il.23.356.504.
It is not Strength, but Art, obtains the Prize, ... Il.23.383.505.
The last, but not least ardent for the Prize. ..... Il.23.426.507.
At the near Prize each gathers all his Soul, ... Il.23.452.508.
Then had he lost, or left a doubtful Prize; ..... Il.23.461.508.
Go, but expect not I'll the Prize resign; ..... Il.23.521.510.
Be swift, be vig'rous, and regain the Prize! ..... Il.23.524.510.
Thy Tongue too hastily confers the Prize. ..... Il.23.557.511.
With Joy brave *Sthenelus* receives the Prize, ... Il.23.593.513.
And then *Eumelus* had receiv'd the Prize, ... Il.23.618.514.
And Vows omitted forfeited the Prize. ..... Il.23.626.514.
But this, my Prize, I never shall forego; ..... Il.23.633.514.
And vindicate by Oath th' ill-gotten Prize. ..... Il.23.660.515.
The Prize I quit, if thou thy Wrath resign; ..... Il.23.673.516.
The Sons of *Actor* won the Prize of Horse, ... Il.23.733.519.
Prize after Prize by *Nestor* born away, ... Il.23.736.519.
Prize after Prize by *Nestor* born away, ... Il.23.736.519.
When great *Achilles* thus divides the Prize. ..... Il.23.855.523.
Whence *Tyrian* Sailors did the Prize transport, ... Il.23.869.524.
It stands the Prize of Swiftness in the Race. ..... Il.23.875.524.
All fierce, and ready now the Prize to gain, ... Il.23.905.525.
The well-fed Bull (the second Prize) he shar'd, ... Il.23.913.525.
Takes the last Prize, and takes it with a Jest. ..... Il.23.924.525.
Ye see, to *Ajax* I must yield the Prize; ..... Il.23.927.526.
Thy artful Praise deserves a better Prize. ..... Il.23.936.526.
Whoever dares deserve so rich a Prize! ..... Il.23.946.526.

PRIZE (CONTINUED)
Who farthest hurls it, take it as his Prize: ..... Il.23.984.528.
With Force conjoin'd heave off the weighty Prize. ..... Il.23.1005.529.
And to the Ships brave *Merion* bears the Prize. ..... Il.23.1043.530.
Here too great *Merion* hopes the noble Prize; ..... Il.23.1050.531.
Take then the Prize, but let brave *Merion* bear ..... Il.23.1058.533.
(A grateful prize) and in her bloom bestow'd ..... Od.7.13.233.
With strength the future prize of fame to play, ... Od.8.23.263.
The games begin: Ambitious of the prize, ... Od.8.113.268.
The prize *Ocyalus* and *Prymneus* claim, ... Od.8.115.268.
We drain'd, the prize of our *Ciconian* wars. ..... Od.9.191.313.
What sum, what prize from *Æolus* I brought? ..... Od.10.40.341.
To him alone the beauteous prize he yields, ... Od.11.353.399.
And tow'rds his *Athens* bears the lovely prize; ..... Od.11.402.403.
With fraudful care he waits the finny prize, ... Od.12.302.447.
A prize more worth than *Ilion's* noble spoil. ..... Od.13.161.13.
Their prize escap'd the faithless pyrates mourn'd; ..... Od.14.389.53.
Be then my prize a tunic and a vest; ..... Od.14.437.56.
The robbers prize, the prey to lawless might. ..... Od.15.14.70.
Doom'd a fair prize to grace some Prince's board, ... Od.15.420.89.
(A noble prize!) and to your ship convey. ..... Od.15.490.94.
To no brave prize aspir'd the worthless swain, ... Od.17.258.144.
In rival crouds contest the glorious prize, ... Od.18.289.180.
Nor dread to name your self the bowyer's prize: ..... Od.19.684.229.
Far hence will lead the long-contended prize: ..... Od.20.400.251.
If I the prize, if me you seek to wife, ... Od.21.73.262.
And his proud hopes already win the prize. ..... Od.21.101.263.
Come then ye Suitors! and dispute a prize ..... Od.21.109.264.
Accept the tryal, and the prize contest. ..... Od.21.144.265.
To-morrow let your arms dispute the prize, ... Od.21.298.274.
Your blood is my demand, your lives the prize, ... Od.22.77.290.

PRIZES
Heroic prizes, and advent'rous Games; ..... 5.DunA2.14A.98.
The Prizes purchas'd by their winged Speed) ..... Il.9.164.440.
The Prizes purchas'd by their winged Speed) ..... Il.9.351.450.
Let each reflect, who prizes Fame or Breath, ... Il.13.163.112.
First stood the Prizes to reward the Force ..... Il.23.327.503.
Behold the Prizes, valiant *Greeks!* decreed ..... Il.23.341.503.
Prizes which none beside our self could gain, ... Il.23.343.503.
The Prizes next are order'd to the Field ..... Il.23.753.520.
Stand forth, and bear these Prizes from the Plain. ..... Il.23.880.524.
Heroic prizes and exequial games; ..... Od.24.108.353.

PROBATUM
Lettuce and Cowslip Wine; *Probatum est.* ..... 4.HS1.18.5.

PROBITY
By justice, truth, and probity of mind; ..... Od.7.278.249.

PROCEED
Famine and Drought proceed, and Plagues, and Death: ..... 1.TrSt.153.416.
Proceed, and firm those Omens thou hast made! ..... 1.TrSt.591.435.
Or did from Change, or Nature's Pow'r proceed, ... 2.ChJM.427.35.
A knotty point! to which we now proceed. ..... 3.Ep3.337B.120.
A knotty point! to which we now proceed. ..... 3.Ep3.337.120.
You too proceed! make falling Arts your care, ... 3.Ep4.191.155.
Yet thou proceed; be fallen Arts thy care, ... 3.Ep4.191A.155.
The Case is alter'd—you may then proceed. ..... 4.HS1.154.21.
"Proceed (he cry'd) proceed, my Reverend Brother, ... 4.HAdv.41.79.
"Proceed (he cry'd) proceed, my Reverend Brother, ... 4.HAdv.41.79.
But how severely with themselves proceed ..... 4.2HE2.157.175.
"Proceed great days! till Learning fly the shore, ... 5.DunA3.329.191.
"Proceed, great days! 'till Learning fly the shore, ... 5.DunB3.333.336.
Proceed—a Minister, but still a Man; ..... 6.73.13.210.
Slow they proceed: The sage *Ulysses* then ..... Il.3.336.209.
Swift to *Æneas'* empty Seat proceed, ... Il.5.326.282.
Proceed, and finish what this Arm begun: ..... Il.11.356.50.
Proceed on Foot, and *Hector* lead the way. ..... Il.12.90.84.
Against his Rage if singly thou proceed, ... Il.22.120.458.
The Chariots first proceed, a shining Train; ..... Il.23.162.495.
Bear close to this, and warily proceed, ... Il.23.407.506.
First to the Palace let the Car proceed, ... Il.24.894.573.
Thou, heedful of advice, secure proceed; ..... Od.1.397.51.
Proceed my son! this youthful shame expel; ..... Od.3.19.87.
Just are the ways of heav'n: From heav'n proceed ..... Od.8.631.297.
Proceed *Ulysses* and the faithful swain: ..... Od.17.205.141.
Proceed false slave, and slight their empty words; ..... Od.21.399.279.
Me too ye fathers hear! from you proceed ..... Od.24.520.373.

PROCEEDED
Soon the white Flocks proceeded o'er the Plains, ... Il.18.607.352.

PROCEEDING
Like *Ida's* Flocks proceeding o'er the Plain; ..... Il.13.621.135.

PROCEEDS
The Critick else proceeds without Remorse, ... 1.EOC.167.259.
The Train majestically slow proceeds. ..... Il.6.369.344.
Unseen the *Grecian* Embassy proceeds ..... Il.9.255.445.
Still slaught'ring on, the King of Men proceeds; ..... Il.11.199.44.
Thus she proceeds—Attend ye Pow'rs above! ..... Il.15.114.201.
Such Horror *Jove* imprest! Yet still proceeds ..... Il.17.853.321.
Thro' Blood, thro' Death, *Achilles* still proceeds, ... Il.21.605.447.
There plac'd 'em round: Then from the Ships proceeds ..... Il.23.323.503.
The knowing Racer to his End proceeds; ..... Il.23.394.506.
And learn, our pow'r proceeds with thee and thine, ... Od.9.331.320.
But say, if in my steps my son proceeds, ... Od.11.601.413.
She then proceeds: Now let our compact made ..... Od.15.477.93.
But now no crime is theirs: this wrong proceeds ..... Od.18.275.179.
Proceeds this boldness from a turn of soul, ... Od.18.379.186.
Would add our blood. Injustice still proceeds. ..... Od.22.291.300.
In haste the matron parts: The King proceeds. ..... Od.22.471.311.

PROCESS
Now in the time's full process forth she brings ....Od.11.309.397.

PROCESSION
And bad'st the years in long procession run: ....6.23.6.73.
He bids the Train in long Procession go, ...Il.6.302.341.
Herself with this the long Procession leads; ....Il.6.368.344.
In slow Procession bore from off the Plain. ....Il.13.822.144.
These shining on, in long Procession come ....Il.20.9.393.
The sad Procession of her hoary Sire, ...Il.24.871.572.
(A long procession) timely marching home ....Od.3.498.112.

PROCLAIM
The Rocks proclaim th'approaching Deity. ....1.Mes.32.116.
My Woes, thy Crimes, I to the World proclaim; ....1.TrSP.141.399.
The direful Banquet why shou'd I proclaim ....1.TrSt.325.423.
Before these Altars how shall I proclaim ....1.TrSt.798.443.
Hear her black Trumpet thro' the Land proclaim, ...4.EpS1.159.309.
That of his Grace he would proclaim ....6.30.36.87.
But witness, Heralds, and proclaim my Vow, ...Il.1.440.108.
His Figure such as might his Soul proclaim; ....Il.2.263.140.
Proclaim their Motions, and provoke the War: ....Il.3.4.188.
Before their Ships, proclaim my Son's Intent: ....Il.7.449.386.
Hear how with Shouts their Conquest they proclaim, ...Il.9.307.449.
Th' afflicted Pair, their Sorrows to proclaim, ...Il.9.675.468.
Say thou, whose Praises all our Host proclaim, ...Il.10.640.30.
Loud Groans proclaim his Progress thro' the Plain, ...Il.11.622.61.
If Truth inspires thy Tongue, proclaim our Will ....Il.15.57.196.
Your godlike Master let your Acts proclaim, ...Il.16.326.255.
Proclaim, his Counsels are obey'd too late, ...Il.22.141.459.
O King of Nations! all thy Greeks proclaim; ....Il.23.1055.533.
Nor herald sworn, the session to proclaim) ....Od.3.171.94.
That pleas'd th' admiring stranger may proclaim ....Od.8.99.267.
O forward to proclaim thy soul unwise! ....Od.8.184.272.
When near he drew, the Prince breaks forth; Proclaim ....Od.16.482.130.
Gods! how his nerves a matchless strength proclaim: ....Od.18.84.170.

PROCLAIM'D
Might be proclaim'd at Charing-Cross. ....4.HS6.100.257.
Proclaim'd so loudly by the Voice of Fame, ...Il.20.245.404.

PROCLAIMING
Nine sacred Heralds now proclaiming loud ....Il.2.123.133.

PROCLAIMS
Or well-mouth'd Booth with emphasis proclaims, ...4.2HE1.123.205.
To grace this honour'd day, the Queen proclaims ....5.DunA2.13.98.
Now herald hawker's rusty voice proclaims ....5.DunA2.13A.98.
Her Criticks there she summons, and proclaims ....5.DunA2.333.142.
And now the Queen, to glad her sons, proclaims ....5.DunB2.17.297.
To grace her dauntless Son, she now proclaims ....5.DunB2.17A.297.
Here stopt the Goddess; and in pomp proclaims ....5.DunB2.365.315.
Roast beef, tho' old, proclaims him stout, ...6.150.13.399.
Roast beef tho' cold, proclaims him stout, ...6.150.13A.399.
Commands your Slaughter, or proclaims your Death. ....Il.16.104.239.
Proclaims you from the sage Ulysses sprung. ....Od.4.832.158.
Father, arise! for thee thy port proclaims ....Od.8.159.271.
Whose fate proclaims him hateful to the Gods. ....Od.10.86.343.
Mistaking fame proclaims thy generous mind; ....Od.16.436.128.
Thetis herself to all our peers proclaims ....Od.24.107.353.

PROCRIS
While Procris panted in the secret shade; ....6.14iii.2.45.
And pities Procris, while her lover dies. ....6.14iii.14.46.
There mournful Phædra with sad Procris moves, ...Od.11.395.403.

PROCULUS
To Proculus alone confess'd in view.) ....2.RL5.126.210.

PROCUR'D
Procur'd the Key her Knight was wont to bear; ....2.ChJM.509.40.
Procur'd young Husbands in my riper Days. ....2.ChWB.208.66.

PROCURE
If you, my Friends, this Virgin can procure, ...2.ChJM.266.27.
Procure a Taste to double the surprize, ...4.1HE6.30.239.
Procure her beauty, make that beauty chaste, ...4.1HE6.79.243.
Let their large Gifts procure an Urn at least, ...Il.22.431.473.
My present labours food and drink procure, ...Od.15.398.88.
Or sacred Elis, to procure supplies; ....Od.24.496.372.

PROCURES
Or else her Wit some Fool-Gallant procures, ...2.ChWB.95.61.

PRODIGAL
Insatiate of the Fight, and prodigal of Blood. ....1.TrES.62.452.
Of Fight insatiate, prodigal of Blood. ....1.TrES.62A.452.
To cram the Rich was prodigal expence, ...3.Ep3.187.109.
Is it less strange, the Prodigal should waste ....3.Ep4.3.134.
Bold as thou art, too prodigal of Breath, ...Il.6.177.334.
Of Fight insatiate, prodigal of Blood. ....Il.12.406.96.
He climb'd his Vessel, prodigal of Breath, ...Il.13.839.145.

PRODIGIES
Of Prodigies, and Portents seen in Air, ...2.TemF.452.285.
Nature well known, no prodigies remain, ...3.Ep1.208.33.
And trusted Heav'ns informing Prodigies) ....Il.6.226.337.
By Heav'n alarm'd, by Prodigies amaz'd: ....Il.12.230.89.
Portents and Prodigies are lost on me. ....Il.19.467.391.
These prodigies of art, and wond'rous cost? ....Od.4.84.123.

PRODIGIOUS
And sing, with Horror, his prodigious End. ....1.TrSt.68.413.
Prodigious! how the Things Protest, Protest: ....4.JD4.255.47.
"Prodigious well!" his great Commander cry'd, ...4.2HE2.42.167.
And pays prodigious dear for—Sense. ....6.29.26.83.

PRODIGIOUS (CONTINUED)
Prodigious this! the Frail one of our Play ....6.41.1.113.
And one prodigious Ruin swallow All. ....Il.4.199.230.

PRODIGY
A lasting Prodigy on Aulis' Sands. ....Il.2.385.145.
Heav'ns! what a prodigy these Eyes survey, ...Il.13.137.111.

PRODUC'D
Produc'd his Play, and beg'd the Knight's Advice, ...1.EOC.274.270.
Produc'd the point that left a sting behind; ....4.2HE1.252.217.
Produc'd Æneas to the shouting Train; ....Il.5.628.298.
The Lots produc'd, each Hero signs his own, ...Il.7.211.374.
And raging Seas produc'd thee in a Storm, ...Il.16.51.237.
Fam'd in the graceful Dance, produc'd to Day. ....Il.16.217.247.
The Witness is produc'd on either Hand; ....Il.18.581.350.
Produc'd a Monarch that his people blest, ...Od.7.79.237.
Thy wish produc'd in act, with pleas'd survey, ...Od.20.290.247.

PRODUCE
The loaded Trees their various Fruits produce, ...1.TrUl.126.470.
Who would not scorn what Huswife's Cares produce, ...2.RL5.21.200.
In God's, one single can its end produce; ....3.EOM1.55.20.
Extremes in Nature equal ends produce, ...3.EOM2.205.79.
"Extremes in Nature equal good produce, ...3.Ep3.163.106.
Such as the Heav'ns produce: and round the Gold ....Il.5.894.308.
Let gen'rous Food Supplies of Strength produce, ...Il.19.233.382.
Which Troy shall, sworn, produce; that injur'd Greece ....Il.22.162.459.
Forgive his Anger, and produce the Car. ....Il.24.332.550.
The trees around them all their food produce, ...Od.9.105.307.
Such as th' unblest Cyclopean climes produce, ...Od.9.422.323.
The loaded trees their various fruits produce, ...Od.13.293.19.
Or from the fluent tongue produce the tale, ...Od.14.221.46.
A future vintage! when the Hours produce ....Od.24.399.368.

PRODUCES
Shakes all together, and produces—You. ....3.Ep2.280.73.
Lo! one vast Egg produces human race. ....5.DunA3.244.177.
Lo! one vast Egg produces human race. ....5.DunB3.248.332.

PRODUCT
The Product one of Marriage, one of Love; ....Il.11.138.41.
The purple Product of th' Autumnal Year. ....Il.18.660.355.
Sad Product now of hapless Love, remains! ....Il.22.621.482.
Sad Product now of hapless Love, remains! ....Il.24.913.574.
The purest product of the chrystal springs; ....Od.4.64.122.
No poor un-father'd product of disgrace. ....Od.19.187.200.
When the first product of Laertes' bed ....Od.19.471.219.

PRODUCTIVE
Productive as the Sun. ....6.51ii.24.153.

PRODUCTS
And heap'd with Products of Sabæan Springs! ....1.Mes.94.121.
For this, our Wealth, our Products you enjoy, ...Il.17.266.298.
How sweet the products of a peaceful reign? ....Od.9.3.298.
They all their products to free nature owe. ....Od.9.122.310.
Yet here all products and all plants abound, ...Od.9.151.311.

PROETUS
See PRAETUS.

PROFAN'D
Is Heav'n offended, and a Priest profan'd, ...Il.1.138.93.
Her snowie Hand the razing Steel profan'd, ...Il.5.419.287.
Sincere from royal blood, and faith profan'd; ....Od.1.50.33.

PROFANE
See PROPHANE.
Nor let a Lover's Death the guiltless Flood profane! ....1.TrSP.211.403.
E'er I recount the Sins of these Profane, ...1.TrSt.327.424.
The jealous God, when we profane his fires, ...2.ElAb.81.326.
Nor let those Lips profane the Name of King. ....Il.2.313.142.
Obey that sweet compulsion, nor profane ....Od.1.471.55.
An absent heroe's nuptial joys profane! ....Od.4.448.141.
E're second vows my bridal faith profane. ....Od.20.97.237.
With rapes and riot to profane my court; ....Od.20.383.251.

PROFESS
But most Vertumnus did his Love profess, ...1.TrVP.27A.378.
"Obliging Sir! I love you, I profess, ...4.JD4.86A.33.
Yet for small Turbots such esteem profess? ....4.HS2.23.55.
Impale a Glow-worm, or Vertù profess, ...5.DunB4.569.398.
Ten times more like him, I profess, ...6.10.103.27.
I like this Colour, I profess! ....6.64.12.189.

PROFESS'D
Mine, as a Foe profess'd to false Pretence, ...4.EpS2.201.324.

PROFESSORS
Divine Professors of the Healing Arts. ....Il.2.891.166.

PROFEST
All luckless Wits their Enemies profest, ...2.TemF.511.288.
I'm a plain Man, whose Maxim is profest, ...4.HAdv.153.87.
Honour unchang'd; a principle profest; ....6.27.3.81.
Honour unchang'd; a principle profest, ...6.57.3.169.
Wit is like faith by such warm Fools profest ....6.82ix(b).1.234.
Wit like religion is with spleen profest; ....6.82ix(b).1A.234.
Wit like religion by such Fools profest. ....6.82ix(b).1C.234.

PROFFER
I seiz'd the proffer (ever fond to roam) ....Od.14.322.50.

PROFFER'D 147 PROMIS'D

PROFFER'D
And heav'nly Charms prefer to proffer'd Gold? ....Il.1.140.93.
This Deed recalls thee to the proffer'd Fight; ....Il.3.75.193.
Yet, wou'd'st thou have the proffer'd Combate stand, ...Il.3.97.194.
Their proffer'd Wealth, nor ev'n the *Spartan* Dame. ....Il.7.477.388.
The proffer'd Presents, an exhaustless Store. ....Il.9.343.450.
Not tho' he proffer'd all himself possest; ....Il.9.496.457.
For proffer'd Peace! And sues his Seed for Grace? ....Il.11.183.43.
And promis'd Conquest was the proffer'd Dow'r. ....Il.13.462.128.
The proffer'd Ransom, and the Corps to leave. ....Il.24.98.539.
Nor shun the blessing proffer'd to thy arms, ...Od.10.353.361.
I dread his proffer'd kindness, urg'd in vain. ....Od.15.227.79.

PROFFERS
He proffers injur'd *Greece;* with large Encrease ....Il.7.466.387.
Such are the Proffers which this Day we bring, ...Il.9.394.452.
Wrong'd in my Love, all Proffers I disdain; ....Il.9.454.454.
Their Pray'rs were urgent, and their Proffers great: ....Il.9.692.468.

PROFIT
Say, in pursuit of profit or delight, ...3.EOM4.85.136.
Deny'd all Posts of Profit or of Trust: ....4.2HE2.61.169.
Thou without them may'st speak and profit too; ....6.2.23.6.
In such Distress if Counsel profit ought; ....Il.14.68.160.
Great is the Profit (thus the God rejoin'd) ....Il.15.230.206.
No profit springs beneath usurping pow'rs; ....Od.15.404.89.

PROFITABLE
Hermes, of profitable Arts the Sire, ...Il.20.47.396.

PROFOUND
Draw forth the monsters of th'abyss profound, ...3.EOM3.221.115.
They treat themselves with most profound respect; ....4.2HE2.154.175.
Sinking from thought to thought, a vast profound! ....5.DunA1.112.77.
Sinking from thought to thought, a vast profound! ....5.DunB1.118.278.
Swift to the Seas profound the Goddess flies, ...Il.1.688.120.
But when *Ulysses* rose, in Thought profound, ...Il.3.279.207.
For passing Chariots, and a Trench profound. ....Il.7.409.385.
For passing Chariots; and a Trench profound, ...Il.7.523.390.
Roll'd the big Thunder o'er the vast Profound: ....Il.8.162.405.
When flying they had pass'd the Trench profound, ...Il.8.413.417.
To *Neptune,* Ruler of the Seas profound, ...Il.9.239.444.
With Piles, with Ramparts, and a Trench profound? ....Il.9.461.455.
Hell heard her Curses from the Realms profound, ...Il.9.685.468.
Amidst, lay *Rhesus,* stretch'd in Sleep profound, ...Il.10.548.27.
But *Neptune,* rising from the Seas profound, ...Il.13.67.108.
When stormy Winds disclose the dark Profound; ....Il.14.458.186.
Now in swift Flight they pass the Trench profound, ...Il.15.1.193.
Burn'd to the bottom of the Seas profound; ....Il.15.253.206.
Burn'd to the bottom of his Seas profound; ....Il.15.253A.206.
But from the Bottom of his Gulphs profound, ...Il.21.229.430.
She plung'd, and instant shot the dark Profound. ....Il.24.106.539.
Their number summ'd, repos'd in sleep profound ....Od.4.557.146.
He ceas'd, and plunging in the vast profound, ...Od.4.777.155.
Roar the wild waves; beneath, is sea profound! ....Od.5.529.198.
Of the high porch, *Ulysses* sleeps profound: ....Od.7.436.258.
The vast profound, and bid the vessel fly: ....Od.8.34.263.
Here lakes profound, there floods oppose their waves, ...Od.11.194.391.
Fierce to *Phæacia* crost the vast profound. ....Od.13.185.15.
In sleep profound the Son of *Nestor* lies; ....Od.15.7.70.

PROFUSE
Some, to whom Heav'n in Wit has been profuse, ...1.EOC.80.248.
Or pours profuse on earth; one nature feeds ....3.EOM3.117.104.
You show us, Rome was glorious, not profuse, ...3.Ep4.23.139.

PROFUSELY
And unavailing Tears profusely shed, ...Il.13.825.145.
Part in a portico, profusely grac'd ....Od.4.51.122.

PROFUSION
Nature to these, without profusion kind, ...3.EOM1.179.37.
Nature to each, without profusion kind, ...3.EOM1.179A.37.
No selfish motive this profusion draws, ...3.Ep3.205A.110.
Nor could Profusion squander all in kind. ....3.Ep3.48.90.
Yet no mean motive this profusion draws, ...3.Ep3.205.110.
Nor wonder I, at such profusion shown; ....Od.17.535.158.
Why such profusion of indulgence shown ....Od.20.451.255.

PROGENY
See all her progeny, illustrious sight! ....5.DunA3.121.160.
My better and more christian progeny! ....5.DunB1.228.286.
See all her progeny, illustrious sight! ....5.DunB3.129.325.
Or views his smiling progeny; ....6.51ii.32.153.
Forbear! (the Progeny of *Jove* replies) ....Il.1.273.100.
Had plac'd the beauteous Progeny of *Jove;* ....Il.3.530.216.
O Progeny of *Jove!* unconquer'd Maid! ....Il.5.146.274.
To whom the Progeny of *Jove* replies. ....Il.7.39.364.
Assert their waxen Domes, and buzzing Progeny. ....Il.16.319.255.
Xanthus, Immortal Progeny of *Jove.* ....Il.21.2.420.
How durst thou vaunt thy wat'ry Progeny? ....Il.21.205.430.
(*Xanthus,* immortal Progeny of *Jove)* ....Il.24.863.572.
But chief, the blue-ey'd Progeny of *Jove.* ....Od.2.473.84.

PROGRESS
He chides the lazy Progress of the Sun, ...1.TrSt.453.429.
Might stop the Progress of his warlike Host, ...1.TrES.116.454.
His Heav'nly Progress thro' the *Twins* had run; ....2.ChJM.610.44.
And pleas'd pursue its Progress thro' the Skies. ....2.RL5.132.211.
Whose gentle progress makes a Calf an Ox, ...4.JD2.48.137.
In the Dog's tail his progress ends at last. ....5.DunA3.294.184.
Thus wings thy Progress from the Realms above? ....Il.7.30.364.
Restrains their Progress from the bright Abodes, ...Il.8.506.420.
And all his Progress mark'd by Heaps of dead.) ....Il.10.238.12.
And dark thro' Paths oblique their Progress take. ....Il.10.320.17.
Loud Groans proclaim his Progress thro' the Plain, ...Il.11.622.61.

PROGRESS (CONTINUED)
Might stop the Progress of his warlike Host, ...Il.12.470.98.
And hail, with Shouts, his Progress thro' the Skies: ....Il.13.1041.154.
And mark'd their Progress thro' the Ranks in Blood, ...Il.15.315.209.
Back to the Ships his destin'd Progress held, ...Il.16.477.261.
Her lofty Walls not long our Progress stay'd; ....Il.20.232.403.
Our second progress to my royal friend; ....Od.10.64.342.

PROGRESSIVE
Above, how high progressive life may go! ....3.EOM1.235.44.

PROJECT
Project long Shadows o'er the Chrystal Tyde. ....1.W-F.376.187.

PROJECTED
The Mole projected break the roaring Main; ....3.Ep4.200.156.
With long-projected Beams the Seas are bright, ...Il.18.251.334.
An ample port the rocks projected form, ...Od.4.1105.169.

PROJECTING
Two craggy Rocks, projecting to the Main, ...1.TrUl.27.466.
Silver the lintels deep-projecting o'er, ...Od.7.116.240.
Two craggy rocks projecting to the main, ...Od.13.118.7.

PROJECTORS
Projectors, Quacks, and Lawyers not a few; ....2.TemF.463.286.

PROJECTS
The Falls of Fav'rites, Projects of the Great, ...2.TemF.455.285.
Than just to plan our projects, and to die. ....6.147viii.2.392.
Th' unquiet night strange projects entertain'd; ....Od.3.183.94.

PROLIFIC
Who sway'd the sceptre, where prolific *Nile* ....Od.4.317.134.
And *Jove* descends in each prolific show'r. ....Od.9.126.310.
To the prolific raptures of a God: ....Od.11.298.396.

PROLIX
Woods are (not to be too prolix) ....6.67.5.195.

PROLOGUE
My Friendship, and a Prologue, and ten Pound. ....4.Arbu.48.99.

PROLOGUES
Notes to dull books, and prologues to dull plays; ....5.DunA1.168.83.
How Prologues into Prefaces decay, ...5.DunA1.231.90.
How Prologues into Prefaces decay, ...5.DunB1.277.290.
The price of prologues and of plays, ...6.150.16.399.

PROLONG
If *Jove* prolong my Days, and *Pallas* crown ....1.TrUl.244.473.
And frequent Cups prolong the rich Repast. ....2.RL3.112.176.
While frequent Cups prolong the rich Repast. ....2.RL3.112A.176.
Friend to my Life, (which did not you prolong, ...4.Arbu.27.98.
Friend thro' my Life, (which did'st not thou prolong, ...4.Arbu.27A.98.
With lenient Arts prolong a Parent's Breath, ...6.117.5.333.
Who now his fame or fortune shall prolong ....6.130.27.358.
The *Greeks* restor'd the grateful Notes prolong; ....Il.1.620.117.
Thus the blest Gods the Genial Day prolong, ...Il.1.772.124.
Shall he prolong one *Trojan's* forfeit Breath! ....Il.22.235.465.
Pacific now prolong the jovial feast; ....Od.1.473.55.
Nor fits it to prolong the heav'nly feast ....Od.3.429.107.
Who stay'd to revel, and prolong the feast: ....Od.9.48.304.
The flames ascend: 'Till evening they prolong ....Od.13.31.2.
If *Jove* prolong my days, and *Pallas* crown ....Od.13.411.26.
Beneath the sun prolong they yet their breath, ...Od.15.372.87.
Then to the lute's soft voice prolong the night, ...Od.21.473.283.
Her shall the Muse to infamy prolong, ...Od.24.228.358.

PROLONG'D
Her Guardian *Sylph* prolong'd the balmy Rest. ....2.RL1.20.147.
But *Jove* and Destiny prolong'd his Date. ....Il.11.214.45.
'Twas now no Season for prolong'd Debate; ....Il.18.291.336.
Ah why has Heav'n prolong'd this hated Breath, ...Il.22.554.479.
Prolong'd the feast, and quaff'd the rosy wine: ....Od.10.565.369.

PROMACHUS
As *Promachus* his slaughter'd Brother draws, ...Il.14.560.190.
Behold your *Promachus* depriv'd of Breath, ...Il.14.565.190.
Such, as the House of *Promachus* must know; ....Il.14.590.191.

PROMACHUS'
Such, as to *Promachus'* sad Spouse we bear; ....Il.14.592.191.

PROMETHEAN
Bring forth some Remnant of *Promethean* theft, ...6.100iv.1.289.

PROMIS'D
The promis'd Father of the future Age. ....1.Mes.56.117.
Adorn'd with blossoms, promis'd fruits that vie ....1.TrFD.23.386.
Taught by thy self to win the promis'd Reign: ....1.TrSt.94.414.
The promis'd Empire, and Alternate Reign: ....1.TrSt.426.427.
Rush to the Foe, and claim the promis'd Fight. ....1.TrES.56.451.
Flam'd in the Front of Heav'n, and promis'd Day, ...1.TrUl.22.466.
Is this the promis'd, long expected Coast; ....1.TrUl.84.468.
And Poets once had promis'd they should last. ....2.TemF.34.255.
And mild as opening gleams of promis'd heav'n. ....2.ElAb.256.340.
This Phœbus promis'd (I forget the year) ....3.Ep2.283.73.
My son! the promis'd land expects thy reign. ....5.DunA1.246.92.
My son! the promis'd land expects thy reign. ....5.DunB1.292.291.
And promis'd Vengeance on a barb'rous age. ....5.DunB4.40.345.
(I promis'd I never would mention Miss Vane.) ....6.122.14.342.
A safe Return was promis'd to our Toils, ...Il.2.143.135.
Thy Figure promis'd with a martial Air, ...Il.3.63.192.
His beating Bosom claims the promis'd Fight. ....Il.5.157.274.
A safe Return was promis'd to our toils, ...Il.9.27.433.

PROMIS'D 148 PRONOUS

PROMIS'D (CONTINUED)
And promis'd Comfort to my silver Hairs. ....Il.9.617.464.
In happy Thunders promis'd *Greece* their Aid; ....Il.11.58.37.
Bestow'd so much, and vainly promis'd more! ....Il.11.318.49.
Rush to the Foe, and claim the promis'd Fight. ....Il.12.400.96.
And promis'd Conquest was the proffer'd Dow'r. ....Il.13.462.128.
Thy Pride once promis'd, of subverting *Troy;* ....Il.16.1004.282.
Whate'er *Ulysses* promis'd at thy Tent: ....Il.19.140.377.
Achilles' Care you promis'd I shou'd prove, ...Il.19.315.385.
And Victims promis'd, and Libations cast, ...Il.23.240.499.
Defer the promis'd boon, (the Goddess cries, ...Od.1.407.52.
And for the promis'd journey bids prepare ....Od.3.604.117.
I take the present of the promis'd Vase; ....Od.4.820.157.
Nay promis'd (vainly promis'd!) to bestow ....Od.5.173.180.
Nay promis'd (vainly promis'd!) to bestow ....Od.5.173.180.
Nay promis'd, vainly promis'd, to bestow ....Od.7.342.253.
Nay promis'd, vainly promis'd, to bestow ....Od.7.342.253.
Thy promis'd boon, O *Cyclop!* now I claim, ...Od.9.431.323.
The Giant then. Our promis'd grace receive, ...Od.9.435.324.
With promis'd off'rings on thy native shore; ....Od.10.621.374.
Flam'd in the front of heav'n, and promis'd day; ....Od.13.113.6.
Is this the promis'd, long-expected coast, ...Od.13.251.18.
Oh! if this promis'd bliss by thund'ring *Jove,* ....Od.15.202.78.
Lur'd with the promis'd boon, when youthful prime ....Od.19.484.220.
With deeds consummate soon the promis'd joys! ....Od.20.295.247.
And promis'd, vainly promis'd, to bestow ....Od.23.363.342.
And promis'd, vainly promis'd, to bestow ....Od.23.363.342.

PROMISCUOUS
With Throngs promiscuous strow the level Green. ....2.RL3.80.173.
Sudden I heard a wild promiscuous Sound, ...2.TemF.22.255.
In various Garbs promiscuous Throngs appear'd; ....2.TemF.281.277.
A Wild, where weeds and flow'rs promiscuous shoot, ...3.EOM1.7.13.
Or Wild, where weeds and flow'rs promiscuous shoot, ...3.EOM1.7A.13.
Such vary'd light in one promiscuous blaze? ....5.DunB4.412.382.
May all their Consorts serve promiscuous Lust, ...Il.3.374.211.
Victors and Vanquish'd join promiscuous Cries, ...Il.4.512.246.
Here, where on one promiscuous Pile they blaz'd, ...Il.7.404.384.
Victors and Vanquish'd join promiscuous Cries, ...Il.8.79.399.
In one promiscuous Carnage crush'd and bruis'd, ...Il.12.84.84.
With Cries promiscuous all the Banks resound, ...Il.21.11.421.
In one promiscuous Stream, the reeking Blood. ....Il.23.44.488.
Promiscuous, steeds, and immolated Men) ....Il.23.301.501.
Promiscuous every guest to every bay. ....Od.8.616.295.
Promiscuous death the form of war confounds, ...Od.9.65.305.
Graze the fair herds, the flocks promiscuous stray; ....Od.12.317.447.
Promiscuous ev'ry guest to ev'ry bay, ...Od.13.201.15.
Promiscuous grace on all the Queen confers; ....Od.20.165.241.

PROMISCUOUSLY
Like Birds and Beasts, promiscuously they join: ....2.ChJM.32.16.

PROMISE
Than when they promise to give *Scribling* o'er. ....1.EOC.595.307.
Destroy the Promise of the youthful Year; ....1.TrVP.109.381.
Promise the Skies the bright Return of Day; ....1.TrSt.483.430.
Are just to Heav'n, and to their Promise true! ....1.TrUl.87.468.
And promise our best Friends to ryme no more; ....4.2HE1.178.209.
Exceed their promise in the ripen'd store, ...6.14iv.19.47.
Yet in the rising blossom promise more. ....6.14iv.20.47.
"Who broke no promise, serv'd no private end, ...6.71.69.204.
Who broke no promise, serv'd no private end, ...6.97.3.282.
Who broke no promise, sought no private end, ...6.97.3A.282.
And ill he pays the Promise of a God; ....Il.1.465.110.
Fame is at least by Heav'nly Promise due ....Il.1.656.118.
And shall our Promise to our People fail? ....Il.5.877.308.
Large Promise makes, and breaks the Promise made; ....Il.5.1026.315.
Large Promise makes, and breaks the Promise made; ....Il.5.1026.315.
Much did he promise, rashly I believ'd: ....Il.10.464.24.
And thus (he cries) behold thy Promise sped! ....Il.13.472.129.
In aid of *Greece.* The Promise of a God ....Il.15.80.199.
If yet, forgetful of his Promise giv'n ....Il.15.236.206.
Perform the Promise of a gracious God! ....Il.15.433.214.
In what vain Promise, Gods! did I engage? ....Il.18.379.339.
Large Gifts they promise, and their Elders send; ....Il.18.521.346.
And claims thy Promise to be King of Kings. ....Il.19.122.377.
Behold! *Achilles'* Promise is compleat; ....Il.23.27.488.
Behold, *Achilles'* Promise fully paid, ...Il.23.222.498.
The promise of a great, immortal name. ....Od.1.123.38.
Be mindful, Goddess, of thy promise made; ....Od.10.570.370.
To bristle on the chin, and promise man, ...Od.11.392.403.
Are just to heav'n, and to their promise true! ....Od.13.254.18.
And promise, yet elude the bridal day. ....Od.18.328.183.

PROMISES
The Courtier's Promises, and Sick Man's Pray'rs, ...2.RL5.119.209.

PROMONTORY
Far in the main a promontory grows, ...1.TrPA.39.367.
O'er which a promontory-shoulder spread: ....Od.19.281.208.

PROMONTORY-SHOULDER
O'er which a promontory-shoulder spread: ....Od.19.281.208.

PROMONTORY'S
Thus from the lofty Promontory's Brow ....Il.4.314.235.
Alas! from yonder Promontory's brow, ...Od.10.221.351.

PROMOTE
(Since Rules were made but to promote their End) ....1.EOC.147.256.
Live happy both, and long promote our arts. ....5.DunB4.438.383.

PROMOTES
While thus each hand promotes the pleasing pain, ...5.DunA2.203.126.
While thus each hand promotes the pleasing pain, ...5.DunB2.211.306.
None fears it more, as none promotes it less: ....Il.12.286.92.

PROMOTING
For ever studious in promoting Ill! ....Il.15.18.194.

PROMPT
And whisp'ring Angels prompt her golden dreams. ....2.ElAb.216.337.
May prompt and save His Life who cannot read: ....4.JD2A.16.132.
Each prompt to query, answer, and debate, ...5.DunA2.349.143.
Toland and Tindal, prompt at Priests to jeer, ...5.DunA2.367.144.
C[ollin]s and *Toland* prompt at Priests to jeer, ...5.DunA2.367B.144.
Prompt or to guard or stab, to saint or damn, ...5.DunB2.357.315.
Each prompt to query, answer, and debate, ...5.DunB2.381.316.
Toland and Tindal, prompt at priests to jeer, ...5.DunB2.399.316.
Prompt at the call, around the Goddess roll ....5.DunB4.189.360.
Prompt to impose, and fond to dogmatize:) ....5.DunB4.464.386.
Such thoughts, as prompt the brave to lie, ...6.141.6.380.
And prompt Obedience to the Queen of Air; ....Il.15.177.203.
Whether to urge their prompt Effect, and call ....Il.16.787.274.
Stood prompt to move, the Azure Goddess came: ....Il.18.448.342.
Courage may prompt; but, ebbing out his Strength, ...Il.19.163.378.
Whate'er this Heart can prompt, or Hand obey; ....Il.20.411.412.
My prompt obedience bows. But deign to say, ...Od.4.653.150.
Thus he: and thus (with prompt invention bold) ....Od.14.218.46.
Shall prompt our speed, and point the ready way. ....Od.15.60.72.
Her prompt obedience on his order waits; ....Od.21.419.280.
And prompt to execute th' eternal will, ...Od.24.562.375.

PROMPTED
By *Hector* prompted, or thy daring Mind, ...Il.10.458.24.
Stranger, if prompted to chastize the wrong ....Od.18.68.170.

PROMPTER
And, as the Prompter breathes, the Puppet squeaks; ....4.Arbu.318.118.

PROMPTS
When kind Occasion prompts their warm Desires, ...2.RL1.75.151.
Active its task, it prompts, impels, inspires. ....3.EOM2.68.63.
For some his Int'rest prompts him to provide, ...3.EOM3.59.98.
That something still which prompts th'eternal sigh, ...3.EOM4.3.128.
So prompts, and saves a Rogue who cannot read. ....4.JD2.16.133.
So prompts, and saves some Rogue who cannot read. ....4.JD2.16A.133.
Yet think not Friendship only prompts my Lays; ....4.EpS2.94.318.
Each Art he prompts, each Charm he can create, ...5.DunA3.219.176.
Each Art he prompts, each Charm he can create, ...5.DunB3.221.331.
That prompts his Hand to draw the deadly Sword, ...Il.1.255.98.
What my Soul prompts, and what some God commands. ....Il.7.80.367.
So God-like *Hector* prompts his Troops to dare, ...Il.11.381.51.
Nor prompts alone, but leads himself the War. ....Il.11.382.51.
Prompts their light limbs, and swells their daring hearts. ....Il.13.90.109.
Minerva prompts the Man of mighty woes ....Od.17.433.153.

PRONE
Still prone to change, tho' still the Slaves of State, ...1.TrSt.226.420.
How prone to Doubt, how cautious are the Wise? ....1.TrUl.208.472.
Prone for his fav'rites to reverse his laws? ....3.EOM4.122.139.
As prone to *Ill,* as negligent of *Good,* ....4.JD4.20.27.
So geese to gander prone obedience keep, ...4.1740.35.334.
Prone on his Knees he falls with fruitless Cries, ...Il.5.89.270.
Prone on his Face he sinks beside the Wheel; ....Il.6.53.326.
Prone on the Dust before the *Trojan* Wall. ....Il.6.381.345.
Prone fell the Giant o'er a Length of Ground. ....Il.7.188.373.
Prone down the Steep of Heav'n their Course they guide. ....Il.8.485.420.
Prone on his Brother's bleeding Breast he lay, ...Il.11.337.49.
Falls prone to Earth, and grasps the bloody Dust. ....Il.11.534.57.
Prone down the rocky Steep, he rush'd along; ....Il.13.28.105.
Once foremost in the Fight, still prone to lend ....Il.13.298.119.
Fast-flowing from its Source, as prone he lay, ...Il.13.556.133.
Prone to the Ground the breathless Warrior fell, ...Il.16.504.262.
Prone sinks the Warrior, and his Arms resound. ....Il.17.52.289.
(Forth welling from the Wound, as prone he lay) ....Il.17.93.291.
And prone to Earth was hung their languid Head: ....Il.17.501.308.
Prone from the Seat he tumbles to the Plain; ....Il.17.699.314.
Prone on the Body fell the heav'nly Fair, ...Il.19.299.384.
Prone from his Car the thund'ring Chief descends, ...Il.20.564.418.
Prone fell the Youth; and panting on the Land, ...Il.21.131.427.
Prone on the Field the bleeding Warrior lies, ...Il.22.413.472.
Prone on the Dust. The *Myrmidons* around ....Il.23.35.488.
Prone on the Dust th' unhappy Master fell; ....Il.23.474.509.
And now supine, now prone, the Hero lay, ...Il.24.17.535.
From high *Olympus* prone her flight she bends, ...Od.1.132.38.
Beneath the finny spoils extended prone, ...Od.4.595.148.
How prone to doubt, how cautious are the wise? ....Od.5.237.182.
Then prone on Ocean in a moment flung, ...Od.5.476.195.
Lest malice, prone the virtuous to defame, ...Od.6.329.227.
Not prone to ill, nor strange to foreign guest, ...Od.9.103.307.
Now prone, and groveling on unsav'ry ground, ...Od.10.285.357.
Fall prone their equal: First thy danger know, ...Od.10.341.360.
How prone to doubt, how cautious are the wise! ....Od.13.375.25.
The man by nature prone to insolence: ....Od.17.477.156.
And prone he falls extended o'er the board: ....Od.22.98.291.
Thro' all his bowels: down he tumbles prone, ...Od.22.328.302.

PRONOUNC'D
Had not sage *Rowe* pronounc'd it *Entertaining.* .... 6.12.9.37.
And artful thus pronounc'd the Speech design'd. ....Il.2.138.134.
Pronounc'd those solemn Words that bind a God. ....Il.19.112.376.

PRONOUNCE
Pronounce HE acts too little, or too much ....3.EOM1.116A.29.
For I pronounce (and trust a heav'nly Pow'r) ....Il.1.281.100.
Pronounce with Judgment, with Regard give ear, ...Il.9.134.438.
Ev'n in his absence I pronounce with fear; ....Od.14.168.43.
O *Troy—may* never tongue pronounce thee more! ....Od.23.24.320.

PRONOUS
First *Pronous* dy'd beneath his fiery Dart, ...Il.16.484.262.

PROOF

Sad proof how well a lover can obey! ....2.ElAb.172.334.
Of solid proof, impenetrably dull. ....5.DunA3.18.151.
Of solid proof, impenetrably dull: ....5.DunB3.26.321.
The only proof that C[aroline] had bowels. ....6.147ii.2.390.
So firmly Proof to all the Shocks of Fate? ....Il.3.88.194.
Proof to the wintry Winds and howling Storms, ...Il.23.827.522.
The last, the wretched proof of filial love. ....Od.15.295.83.
Ulysses grac'd, confirm by faithful proof: ....Od.19.254.207.

PROOFS

'Till, what with Proofs, Objections, and Replies, ...2.ChJM.143.21.
For all the proofs of his paternal care, ...Od.15.170.76.

PROP

Till the bright Mountains prop th' incumbent Sky: ....2.TemF.58.256.
Prop thine, O Empress! like each neighbour Throne, ...5.DunB4.333.376.
Upheave the Piles that prop the solid Wall; ....Il.12.307.92.
Or serv'd to ballast, or to prop the Fleet) ....Il.14.474.186.
Rash as thou art to prop the *Trojan* Throne, ...Il.21.514.443.
End in the starry vault, and prop the sphears.) ....Od.1.70.34.

PROP'D

Prop'd on his Staff, and stooping as he goes, ...1.TrVP.48.379.
The Wretch stood prop'd, and quiver'd as he stood; ....Il.10.444.23.

PROPAGATE

To draw nutrition, propagate, and rot; ....3.EOM2.64.63.

PROPER

Know well each Ancient's proper *Character,* .... 1.EOC.119.252.
Pray Heav'n, this Magick work the proper Way: ....2.ChJM.773.52.
One proper Gift, another grants to those: ....2.ChWB.41.58.
His proper Body is not his, but mine; ....2.ChWB.54.59.
Down to the Central Earth, his proper Scene, ...2.RL4.15.184.
Hither, as to their proper Place, arise ....2.TemF.432.284.
The proper organs, proper pow'rs assign'd; ....3.EOM1.180.37.
The proper organs, proper pow'rs assign'd; ....3.EOM1.180.37.
Our proper bliss depends on what we blame. ....3.EOM1.282.49.
The proper study of Mankind is Man. ....3.EOM2.2.53.
And to their proper operation still, ...3.EOM2.57.62.
Its proper bliss, and sets its proper bounds: ....3.EOM3.110.103.
Its proper bliss, and sets its proper bounds: ....3.EOM3.110.103.
Its proper Pow'r to hurt, each Creature feels, ...4.HS1.85.13.
Unless the Gods bestow'd a proper Muse? ....4.2HE1.234.215.
Unless the Gods bestow'd the proper Muse? ....4.2HE1.234A.215.
Not these, O Daughter, are thy proper Cares, ...Il.5.519.293.
The rest they purchas'd at their proper Cost, ...Il.7.566.392.
With proper Instruments they take the Road, ...Il.23.138.493.
Then join'd in council, proper means explore ....Od.7.254.248.
(*Eumæus'* proper treasure bought this slave, ...Od.14.503.60.

PROPERTIES

"Their sep'rate cells and properties maintain. ....3.EOM3.188.112.

PROPERTY

What's *Property?* dear Swift! you see it alter ....4.HS2.167.69.
A *Property,* that's yours on which you live. ....4.2HE2.231.181.
The Gaul subdu'd, or Property secur'd, ...4.2HE1.10.195.
An *English Letter's* Property, ...6.30.46.87.
Unworthy Property, unworthy Light, ...Il.9.88.436.

PROPHAN'D

By me that holy Office were prophan'd; ....Il.6.334.342.
Our Joys prophan'd by each familiar Eye; ....Il.14.377.180.

PROPHANE

See PROFANE.
An absent Heroe's nuptial joys prophane! ....Od.17.139.138.

PROPHANELY

And pour'd prophanely as the victim burns. ....Od.12.428.451.

PROPHECIES

Oh heav'ns! oh faith of ancient prophecies! ....Od.9.594.330.
Oh certain faith of ancient prophecies! ....Od.13.197.15.
Thy lying prophecies deceiv'd the land: ....Od.22.358.304.

PROPHECY

Thus scorning prophecy, and warn'd in vain, ...1.TrPA.35.366.
Extols old Bards, or Merlin's Prophecy, ...4.2HE1.132.207.
Let not my fatal Prophecy be true, ...Il.18.319.337.
Go prophecy at home; thy sons advise: ....Od.2.209.72.
Approach yon walls, I prophecy thy fare: ....Od.17.269.145.

PROPHECY'D

The Sire forewarn'd, and prophecy'd their Doom: ....Il.2.1009.170.

PROPHESY

Such fate I prophesy our guest attends, ...Od.21.325.275.

PROPHESY'D

(Not half so pleas'd when Goodman prophesy'd) ....5.DunB3.232.331.
By *Phœbus'* Darts she prophesy'd my Fall, ...Il.21.319.434.

PROPHET

Here, like some furious Prophet, *Pindar* rode, ...2.TemF.212.272.
Hence, from the straw where Bedlam's Prophet nods, ...5.DunA3.7.150.
His conqu'ring tribes th' Arabian prophet draws, ...5.DunA3.89.157.
Hence, from the straw where Bedlam's Prophet nods, ...5.DunB3.7.320.
His conqu'ring tribes th' Arabian prophet draws, ...5.DunB3.97.324.
The moon-struck Prophet felt the madding hour: ....5.DunB4.12.340.
But let some Prophet, or some sacred Sage, ...Il.1.83.90.
The Prophet spoke; when with a gloomy Frown, ...Il.1.127.93.
Prophet of Plagues, for ever boding Ill! ....Il.1.132.93.
A prophet then, inspir'd by Heav'n arose, ...Il.1.498.112.

PROPHET (CONTINUED)

Thus spoke the Prophet, thus the Fates succeed. ....Il.2.397.145.
Or *Harma* where *Apollo's* Prophet fell; ....Il.2.595.156.
While yet he spoke, the Prophet I obey'd, ...Od.11.122.387.
The phantom Prophet ceas'd, and sunk from sight ....Od.11.184.390.

PROPHET'S

The Rage of *Tydeus,* or the Prophet's Fate? ....1.TrSt.62.412.
The Rage of *Tydeus,* or the Prophet's Fate? ....1.TrSt.63.412.
The raging *Tydeus,* or the Prophet's Fate? ....1.TrSt.62A.412.
The Father's Care and Prophet's Art were vain, ...1.TrSt.553.433.
Hard toil! the prophet's piercing eye to shun; ....Od.4.596.148.

PROPHETIC

In deep Prophetic Arts their Father skill'd, ...Il.11.427.53.
Nor skill'd, nor studious, with prophetic eye ....Od.1.261.45.
Who strait propitious, in prophetic strain ....Od.4.575.147.
Within, irradiate with prophetic light; ....Od.10.583.371.
Won by prophetic knowledge, to fulfill ....Od.11.363.400.
Seiz'd by the hand, and thus prophetic cry'd. ....Od.15.572.98.
But my prophetic fears, alas! presage, ...Od.19.358.211.
I come, prophetic of approaching joy: ....Od.19.642.227.
Of rage, or folly, my prophetic mind, ...Od.20.438.254.

PROPHETICK

It chanc'd prophetick Telemus, who knew ....1.TrPA.29.366.
His Princess parts with a prophetick Sigh, ...Il.6.640.358.

PROPHETS

But without thee, what could the Prophets do? ....6.2.24.6.

PROPITIATE

The God propitiate, and the Pest asswage. ....Il.1.192.96.
Whoe'er he be, propitiate *Jove* with Pray'r; ....Il.5.228.278.
And heav'n propitiate in the stranger's cause: ....Od.7.253.248.

PROPITIOUS

Who more propitious to the suppliant Crowd, ...1.TrSt.260.421.
These solemn Feasts propitious *Phœbus* please, ...1.TrSt.788.443.
Yet if propitious to a Wretch unknown, ...1.TrSt.802.443.
Propitious hear our Pray'r, O Pow'r Divine! ....1.TrSt.855.445.
Propitious Heav'n, and ev'ry Pow'r ador'd, ...2.RL2.36.161.
And hail with Musick its propitious Ray. ....2.RL5.134.211.
Fair op'ning to some Court's propitious shine, ...3.EOM4.9.128.
Benlowes, propitious still to blockheads, bows; ....5.DunB3.21.321.
Had fate decreed, propitious to your pray'rs, ...6.38.11.107.
And smile propitious, and unbend thy Bow. ....Il.1.597.116.
If mighty *Neptune* send propitious Gales; ....Il.9.474.456.
Phœbus, propitious still to thee, and *Troy.* ....Il.15.291.208.
Some God, propitious to the *Trojan* Foe, ...Il.15.550.218.
But thou! appeas'd, propitious to our pray'r, ...Il.19.141.377.
Propitious *Neptune,* and the blue-ey'd Maid. ....Il.21.335.435.
Propitious once, and kind! Then welcome Fate! ....Il.22.385.471.
Propitious to the search. Direct your toil ....Od.1.368.50.
Descend once more, propitious to my aid. ....Od.2.302.76.
Great *Jove* propitious, and our conquest crown'd. ....Od.3.148.92.
The God propitious gave the guiding sign; ....Od.3.210.96.
So guide me, Goddess! so propitious shine ....Od.3.488.111.
With pow'r congenial join'd, propitious aid ....Od.4.459.142.
Propitious winds, to waft us o'er the main: ....Od.4.490.143.
Dictate propitious to my duteous ear, ...Od.4.533.146.
Who strait propitious, in prophetic strain ....Od.4.575.147.
What fate propitious, or what dire dismay ....Od.4.654.150.
Thy son, the Gods propitious will restore, ...Od.4.1063.167.
Propitious to my wants, a Vest supply ....Od.6.215.220.
Propitious *Pallas,* to secure her care, ...Od.7.19.234.
Rob not the God, and so propitious gales ....Od.11.140.387.
I then: O nymph propitious to my pray'r, ...Od.12.139.439.
Rob not the God! and so propitious gales ....Od.12.172.440.
With pow'r congenial joyn'd, propitious aid ....Od.17.150.139.
He only asks a more propitious hour, ...Od.17.660.164.
And to confirm my faith, propitious *Jove!* .... Od.20.124.239.

PROPORTION

All in exact proportion to the state; ....3.EOM1.183.37.
All in exact proportion to their state; ....3.EOM1.183A.37.
And, in proportion as it blesses, blest, ...3.EOM3.300.123.
As Poison heals, in just proportion us'd: ....3.Ep3.234.111.
Such with their shelves as due proportion hold, ...5.DunB1.137.280.
And fair Proportion match'd th' etherial Race. ....Il.11.80.38.
A just proportion of refulgent Brass. ....Od.1.236.44.
'Till all the form in full proportion rise, ...Od.10.467.366.

PROPORTION'D

Which, but *proportion'd* to their *Light,* or *Place,* .... 1.EOC.173.260.
Thus when we view some well-proportion'd Dome, ...1.EOC.247.268.
Cou'dst thou some great, proportion'd Mischief frame, ...1.TrSt.122.415.
So justly all proportion'd to each state; ....3.EOM1.183B.37.
And find the means proportion'd to their end. ....3.EOM3.82.100.
Of all Beau-kind the best proportion'd Fools! ....4.JD4.241.45.
Each, in exchange, proportion'd Treasures gave; ....Il.7.568.392.
Large Gifts, proportion'd to thy Wrath, I bear; ....Il.24.624.563.
A Strength proportion'd to the Woes you feel. ....Il.24.658.564.
A feast proportion'd to their crimes decreed; ....Od.20.468.256.

PROPOS

A Tale extreamly *a propos:* .... 4.HS6.154.259.

PROPOS'D

Th' Intent propos'd, *that Licence* is a *Rule.* .... 1.EOC.149.256.
And Things *unknown* propos'd as Things *forgot:* .... 1.EOC.575.306.
And Things *ne'er known* propos'd as Things *forgot:* .... 1.EOC.575A.306.
And each alternate, Life or Fame propos'd: ....Il.9.533.460.
Who thus the Counsels of his Breast propos'd. ....Il.10.360.19.
Has *Troy* propos'd some spacious Tract of Land? ....Il.20.223.403.
Achilles smil'd: The Gift propos'd (he cry'd) ....Il.23.637.515.

PROPOS'D (CONTINUED)
Propos'd, who first the vent'rous deed should try? ....Od.9.390.322.

PROPOSAL
The bold proposal how shall I fulfill? ....Od.5.229.182.

PROPOSALS
The Match was offer'd, the Proposals made: ....2.ChJM.300.28.
He slights thy Friendship, thy Proposals scorns, ...Il.9.796.473.

PROPOSE
Attend the trial we propose to make: ....5.DunA2.339.142.
"Attend the trial we propose to make: ....5.DunB2.371.315.
Scarce did the Chief the vig'rous Strife propose, ...Il.23.820.522.
I, to the Peers assembled, shall propose ....Od.1.475.55.
Propose departure from the finish'd rite, ...Od.3.441.108.
But finish, oh ye Peers! what you propose, ...Od.7.301.250.
Followers and friends! attend what I propose: ....Od.10.214.350.
Propose the sportive lot, the Chief replies, ...Od.19.683.229.
The sentence I propose, ye Peers, attend: ....Od.20.359.249.
Then, to her Suitors bade his Queen propose ....Od.24.195.357.

PROPP'D
Till propp'd reclining on the palace walls; ....Od.18.123.172.

PROPS
His hundred Heads in Heav'n, and props the Clouds. ....Il.1.649.118.
He shakes the feeble Props of human Trust, ...Il.2.149.135.
Who shakes the feeble Props of human Trust, ...Il.9.33.433.
And curl'd on silver Props, in order glow: ....Il.18.654.355.
He props his spear against the pillar'd wall; ....Od.17.36.134.

PROPT
Propt on their Bodkin Spears, the Sprights survey ....2.RL5.55.203.
Propt on some tomb, a neighbour of the dead! ....2.ElAb.304.344.
Propt in some tomb, a neighbour of the dead! ....2.ElAb.304A.344.
On two unequal crutches propt he came, ...5.DunB4.111.352.
Propt the Skies: ....6.9i.15.268.
That propt alone by *Priam's* Race should stand ....Il.5.577.296.
The Chariot propt against the Crystal Walls. ....Il.8.539.422.
Propt on that Spear to which thou ow'st thy Fall, ...Il.14.533.189.
And propt on her fair Arm, forsakes the Plain. ....Il.21.489.441.
Propt on a staff, a beggar old and bare, ...Od.17.228.143.
Propt on a staff, and trembling as he went. ....Od.17.413.152.
Against the polish'd quiver propt the dart. ....Od.21.146.265.
Propt on a staff, deform'd with age and care, ...Od.24.185.356.

PRORE
For there no vessel with vermilion prore, ...Od.9.145.311.

PRORES
These in twelve Galleys with Vermillion Prores, ...Il.2.773.162.
Then swift invades the Ships, whose beaky Prores ......Il.15.834.229.
Thick beats the Combate on the sounding Prores. ....Il.15.843.229.

PROREUS
There *Proreus, Nautes, Eratreus* appear, ...Od.8.117.268.

PROSE
Now *One* in *Verse* makes many more in *Prose.* ....1.EOC.8.239.
Then in plain prose, were made two sorts of Men, ...3.Ep3.13A.84.
Verse-man or Prose-man, term me which you will, ...4.HS1.64.11.
One dedicates, in high Heroic prose, ...4.Arbu.109.103.
It is not Poetry, but Prose run mad: ....4.Arbu.188.109.
And thought a Lye in Verse or Prose the same: ....4.Arbu.339.120.
Well, on the whole, *plain* Prose must be my fate: ....4.2HE2.198.179.
Well, on the whole, then Prose must be my fate: ....4.2HE2.198A.179.
Now serpent-like, in prose he sweeps the ground, ...4.2HE1.100.203.
Who says in verse what others say in prose; ....4.2HE1.202.211.
Something in Verse as true as Prose; ....4.HS6.26.251.
Prose swell'd to verse, Verse loitring into prose; ....5.DunA1.228.90.
Prose swell'd to verse, Verse loitring into prose; ....5.DunA1.228.90.
As verse, or prose, infuse the drowzy God. ....5.DunA2.364.144.
Else all my Prose and Verse were much the same; .....5.DunB1.189.283.
This, prose on stilts; that, poetry fall'n lame. ....5.DunB1.190.283.
Prose swell'd to verse, verse loit'ring into prose: ......5.DunB1.274.290.
Prose swell'd to verse, verse loit'ring into prose: ......5.DunB1.274.290.
As verse, or prose, infuse the drowzy God. ....5.DunB2.396.316.
Critics like me shall make it Prose again. ....5.DunB4.214.363.
He'd write in Prose—To the *Spectator.* ....6.44.4.152.
It is not Poetry, but Prose run mad: ....6.98.38.284.
Did Milton's Prose, O Charles, thy Death defend ......6.116viii.1.328.
I'll have the last Word, for by G—d I'll write Prose. ....6.149.2.397.

PROSE-MAN
Verse-man or Prose-man, term me which you will, ...4.HS1.64.11.

PROSECUTE
Faith, in such case, if you should prosecute, ...4.2HE2.23.165.

PROSERPINE
In one quick flash see Proserpine expire, ...5.DunA1.209.87.
And link the Mourning-Bride to Proserpine. ....5.DunA3.308.185.
And link the Mourning-Bride to Proserpine. ....5.DunB3.310.335.
Stern *Proserpine* relented, ...6.11.85.33.
And ruthless *Proserpine,* confirm'd his Vow. ....Il.9.585.463.
Now summon'd *Proserpine* to hell's black hall ....Od.11.480.408.

PROSERPINE'S
The barren trees of *Proserpine's* black woods, ...Od.10.604.373.

PROSP'ROUS
O launch thy Bark, secure of prosp'rous Gales, ...1.TrSP.252.404.
Count all th'advantage prosp'rous Vice attains, ...3.EOM4.89.136.
Jove, on the Right, a prosp'rous Signal sent, ...Il.2.418.147.
O blest *Atrides!* born to prosp'rous Fate, ...Il.3.241.204.

PROSP'ROUS (CONTINUED)
Heav'n to my fleet refus'd a prosp'rous wind: ....Od.4.474.142.
To speed a prosp'rous voyage o'er the seas? ....Od.4.634.149.
Thy guilt absolv'd, a prosp'rous voyage gain. ....Od.4.638.149.
And prosp'rous gales to waft thee on thy way. ....Od.5.216.182.
And now, rejoycing in the prosp'rous gales, ...Od.5.343.188.
Nine prosp'rous days we ply'd the lab'ring oar; ....Od.10.30.340.
A prosp'rous voyage to his native shores; ....Od.11.127.387.
Not the fleet bark when prosp'rous breezes play, ...Od.12.79.435.
Full dexter to the car: the prosp'rous sight ....Od.15.184.77.
Too high when prosp'rous, when distrest too low. ...Od.18.164.174.
From friendly *Æolus* with prosp'rous gales; ....Od.23.340.341.
Prosp'rous he sail'd, with dexter Auguries, ...Od.24.363.366.

PROSPECT
Here *Ceres'* Gifts in waving Prospect stand, ...1.W-F.39.152.
Th' *increasing* Prospect *tires* our wandring Eyes, ...1.EOC.231.265.
Now all the Land another Prospect bore, ...1.TrUl.64.468.
The pleasing Prospect of thy Native Shore! ....1.TrUl.225.473.
So spake the Goddess, and the Prospect clear'd, ...1.TrUl.234.473.
O'er the wide Prospect as I gaz'd around, ...2.TemF.21.254.
I shriek, start up, the same sad prospect find, ...2.ElAb.247.339.
Reason's at distance, and in prospect lie: ....3.EOM2.72.64.
And when in act they cease, in prospect rise; ....3.EOM2.124.70.
One prospect lost, another still we gain; ....3.EOM2.289.89.
At once his own bright prospect to be blest, ...3.EOM4.351.162.
The prospect clears and *Clodio* stands confest. .....3.Ep1.179A.30.
The prospect clears, and Wharton stands confest. ..3.Ep1.179.30.
Two plenteous fountains the whole prospect crown'd, ..6.35.28.103.
The Ships and Tents in mingled Prospect lay. ......Il.1.633.118.
High on the Mound, from whence in Prospect lay ...Il.2.962.169.
Ungrateful Prospect to the sullen Pow'r! ....Il.8.253.409.
Then shine the Vales, the Rocks in Prospect rise, ..Il.8.695.428.
Eager they view'd the Prospect dark and deep, ...Il.12.61.83.
Soon as the Prospect open'd to his View, ...Il.14.17.157.
The Hills shine out, the Rocks in Prospect rise, ...Il.16.358.257.
Rose in sad Prospect to his boding Mind. ....Il.18.8.323.
Another Part (a Prospect differing far) ....Il.18.591.351.
Now three times turn'd in prospect of the Goal, ...Il.23.899.525.
While the dear isle in distant prospect lyes, ...Od.1.76.34.
Two plenteous fountains the whole prospect crown'd; ..Od.7.169.244.
In pleasing thought he ran the prospect o'er, ...Od.7.180.244.
The land of *Cyclops* lay in prospect near; ....Od.9.192.313.
But mourn in vain; no prospect of return. ....Od.10.90.343.
Commands the prospect of the plains below: ....Od.10.112.346.
Shall never the dear land in prospect rise, ...Od.10.562.369.
Now all the land another prospect bore, ...Od.13.231.17.
The pleasing prospect of thy native shore. ....Od.13.392.26.
So spake the Goddess, and the prospect clear'd, ..Od.13.401.26.

PROSPECTS
In *Prospects,* thus, some *Objects* please our Eyes, ...1.EOC.158.258.
These swell their Prospects and exalt their Pride, ..2.RL1.81.151.
Who swell their Prospects and exalt their Pride, ...2.RL1.81A.151.
Long future prospects, and short present joys: ....6.22.11.71.
And peaceful Prospects dawn in ev'ry Breast. ....Il.3.154.198.
And glows with Prospects of th' approaching Day. ..Il.13.332.121.
In op'ning prospects of ideal joy, ...Od.20.281.246.

PROSPER
But if you'll prosper, mark what I advise, ...1.TrVP.77.380.
All things wou'd prosper, all the World grow wise. ..2.ChJM.68.18.
Ev'n so all Things shall prosper well, ...6.54.11.164.
Farewel and prosper, youths! let *Nestor* know .....Od.15.168.76.

PROSPER'D
Encreas'd and prosper'd in their new Abodes, ...Il.2.811.163.

PROSPERITY
Perhaps Prosperity becalm'd his breast, ...3.Ep1.63.20.
That spreads and swells in puff'd Prosperity, ...4.HS2.126.65.

PROSTITUTE
(No Hireling she, no Prostitute to Praise) ....6.84.36.240.
(A Virgin Muse, not prostitute to praise). ....6.84.31Z8.240.

PROSTITUTED
And Trafficks in the prostituted Laws: ....4.JD2A.73.138.
With wanton glee, the prostituted fair. ....Od.20.12.230.

PROSTITUTES
To these, the nightly prostitutes to shame, ...Od.22.497.313.

PROSTRATE
See thy bright Altars throng'd with prostrate Kings, ..1.Mes.93.121.
Prostrate, with tears their kindred plant bedew, ...1.TrFD.61.388.
The prostrate Prince, and on his Bosom trod; ....1.TrES.317.461.
Then prostrate falls, and begs with ardent Eyes ....2.RL2.43.162.
And falls like Thunder on the prostrate *Ace.* ....2.RL3.98.174.
While prostrate here in humble grief I lie, ...2.ElAb.277.342.
See god-like Turenne prostrate on the dust! ....3.EOM4.100.137.
Cast on the prostrate Nine a scornful look, ...5.DunB4.51.346.
Now prostrate! dead! behold that Caroline: ....5.DunB4.413.382.
Whom prostrate Kings beheld unrival'd shine, ...6.20.11.66.
And scarce are seen the prostrate Nile or Rhine, ..6.71.28.203.
And scarce are seen the prostrate Nile and Rhine, ..6.71.28A.203.
Tho' prostrate *Greece* should bleed at ev'ry Vein: ...Il.1.445.108.
Beneath this Arm fell prostrate on the Plain. ....Il.4.373.239.
Prostrate on Earth their beauteous Bodies lay, ...Il.5.687.300.
The God who slew him, leaves his prostrate Prize ...Il.5.1040.316.
The quiv'ring Steeds fell prostrate at the Sight; ....Il.8.165.406.
And prostrate Heroes bleed around their Lord. .....Il.8.666.427.
Rang'd in three Lines they view the prostrate Band; ..Il.10.544.27.
But not till half the prostrate Forests lay ....Il.11.123.41.
Just as their Jaws his prostrate Limbs invade, ...Il.11.600.61.
O'er heapy Shields, and o'er the prostrate Throng, ..Il.11.886.75.

PROSTRATE (CONTINUED)

Prostrate he falls; his clanging Arms resound, ... Il.13.251.117.
So lies great *Hector* prostrate on the Shore; .... Il.14.487.187.
The Victor leaps upon his prostrate Prize; .... Il.15.696.222.
The prostrate Prince, and on his Bosom trod; .... Il.16.622.268.
Then rushing sudden on his prostrate Prize, ... Il.16.907.279.
His prostrate Master, rein'd the Steeds around; .... Il.20.566.418.
And glorying thus, the prostrate God reviles. .... Il.21.477.441.
Around the Hero's prostrate Body flow'd .... Il.23.43.488.
And prostrate now before *Achilles* laid, ... Il.24.585.561.
For him thus prostrate at thy Feet I lay; .... Il.24.623.562.
Then with his Hand (as prostrate still he lay) .... Il.24.636.563.
But prostrate I implore, oh King! relate .... Od.4.435.140.
The piteous object of a prostrate Queen. .... Od.4.953.162.
Or prostrate at her knee address the pray'r. .... Od.6.172.216.
And prostrate fell before th' Imperial dame. .... Od.7.189.245.
Thus doubting, prostrate on the deck I lay, ... Od.10.56.342.
He, prostrate falling, with both hands embrac'd .... Od.10.313.359.
And prostrate to my sword the Suitor-train; .... Od.19.572.224.
Shall prostrate to thy sword the Suitor-crowd, ... Od.19.580.224.
In prostrate heaps the wretches beat the ground, ... Od.22.344.304.
Then prostrate stretch'd before the dreadful man, ... Od.22.377.306.

PROSYMNA'S

On that, *Prosymna's* Grove and Temple rise: .... 1.TrSt.534.432.

PROTECT

Protect your plant, nor let my branches feel .... 1.TrFD.90.390.
And now appear, thy Treasures to protect, ... 1.TrUl.179.471.
And all ye deathless Pow'rs! protect my Son! .... Il.6.605.356.
Forbid the Tempest, and protect the Ground; .... Od.12.148.87.
And now appear, thy treasures to protect, ... Od.13.346.24.
Inform him certain, and protect him, kind? .... Od.13.485.29.

PROTECTED

Nor hope the Fall of Heav'n-protected *Troy;* .... Il.9.803.473.
With Toil protected from the prowling Train; .... Il.10.212.11.
He lies protected, and without a Wound. .... Il.14.498.188.
The people's parent, he protected all: .... Od.4.921.161.
From the protected guest, and menial train: .... Od.20.390.251.

PROTECTING

I see protecting Myriads round thee fly, ... 6.21.23.69.
In the protecting care of heav'n confide: .... Od.4.1080.168.
Screen'd by protecting Gods from hostile eyes, ... Od.14.391.54.
My Lord's protecting hand alone wou'd raise .... Od.19.148.199.
His kind protecting hand my youth preferr'd, ... Od.20.267.246.

PROTECTION

Thou know'st those Regions my Protection claim, ... 1.TrSt.352.424.
Of these am I, who thy Protection claim, ... 2.RL1.105.153.
Of sure Protection by thy Pow'r and Sword. .... Il.1.100.92.
War be thy Province, thy Protection mine; .... Il.5.159.274.
Safe thro' the Foe by our Protection led: .... Il.24.188.544.
Safe thro' the Foe by his Protection led: .... Il.24.218.546.
And beg Protection with a feeble Cry, ... Il.24.607.562.
Mean-time, protection to thy stranger-friend? .... Od.15.548.96.
I gave him my protection, grant him thine. .... Od.16.68.105.
And with the royal herd protection buy: .... Od.20.278.246.

PROTECTOR

The sage Protector of the *Greeks* he found .... Il.10.82.6.
To the bright altars of Protector *Jove.* .... Od.22.420.308.

PROTECTS

By Day o'ersees them, and by Night protects; .... 1.Mes.52.117.
Whose Care, like hers, protects the Sylvan Reign, ... 1.W-F.163.165.
Involv'd in Clouds, protects him in the Fray, ... Il.5.326.284.
Watchful he wheels, protects it ev'ry way, ... Il.5.363.284.
Dead, he protects him with superior Care, ... Il.17.322.300.
Who now protects her Wives with guardian Care? .... Il.24.918.574.
Safe in their care, for heav'n protects the just. .... Od.17.681.165.
No vulgar roof protects thy honour'd age; .... Od.20.329.249.

PROTEND

They join, they thicken, they protend their Spears; .... Il.17.275.298.

PROTENDED

But with protended Spears in fighting Fields, ... Il.2.651.158.
The great *Idomeneus'* protended Steel; .... Il.5.58.269.
But swift withdrew the long-protended Wood, ... Il.16.981.281.
Arm'd with protended Spears, my native Band; .... Il.21.172.428.

PROTENDS

Now shakes his Spear, now lifts, and now protends, ... Il.15.887.231.

PROTESILAS

These own'd as Chief *Protesilas* the brave, ... Il.2.853.164.

PROTESILAUS

The same which dead *Protesilaus* bore, ... Il.15.856.229.
Unblest *Protesilaus* to *Ilion's* Shore, ... Il.16.341.256.

PROTEST

But, with the Wiseman's Leave, I must protest, ... 2.ChJM.153.22.
All they shall need is to protest, and swear, ... 2.ChJM.665.47.
They need no more but to protest, and swear, ... 2.ChJM.665A.47.
Prodigious! how the Things *Protest, Protest:* .... 4.JD4.255.47.
Prodigious! how the Things *Protest, Protest:* .... 4.JD4.255.47.
Instructed thus, you bow, embrace, protest, ... 4.1HE6.107.245.
"'Tis now no secret—I protest .... 4.HS6.118.257.
With—I protest, and I'll assure ye;— .... 6.10.52.26.

PROTESTANT

Papist or Protestant, or both between, ... 4.HS1.65.11.

PROTESTED

P protested, puff'd, and swore, ... 6.30.27.86.

PROTEUS

Did ever Proteus, Merlin, any Witch, ... 4.1HE1.152.291.
So Proteus, hunted in a nobler shape, ... 5.DunA2.121.111.
Hence Bards, like Proteus long in vain ty'd down, ... 5.DunB1.37.272.
So Proteus, hunted in a nobler shape, ... 5.DunB2.129.301.
Proteus her sire divine. With pity press'd, ... Od.4.495.144.
Proteus, a name tremendous o'er the main, ... Od.4.521.145.
Then *Proteus* mounting from the hoary deep, ... Od.4.606.148.

PROTHOËNOR

Peneleus, Leitus, Prothoënor led: .... Il.2.587.155.

PROTHOÖN

Strong *Periphætes* and *Prothoön* bled, ... Il.14.609.192.

PROTHOENOR

And at *Prothœnor* shook the trembling Spear; .... Il.14.526.189.
A worthy Vengeance for *Prothœnor* slain? .... Il.14.552.189.

PROTHOUS

Last under *Prothous* the *Magnesians* stood, ... Il.2.916.167.
Prothous the swift, of old *Tenthredon's* Blood, ... Il.2.917.167.
With three bold Sons was gen'rous *Prothous* blest, ... Il.14.130.164.

PROTO

Then *Proto, Doris, Panope* appear; .... Il.18.52.326.

PROTRACT

Not ev'n an Instant to protract their Fate, ... Il.20.363.410.
Long to protract the sad sepulchral hour; .... Od.19.431.215.

PROTRACTED

Was sent to crown the long-protracted joy, ... Od.4.9.120.
O'er the protracted feast the Suitors sit, ... Od.20.447.254.

PROUD

Not proud *Olympus* yields a nobler Sight, ... 1.W-F.33.151.
Proud *Nimrod* first the bloody Chace began, ... 1.W-F.61.155.
And wisely curb'd proud Man's pretending Wit: .... 1.EOC.53.245.
That in *proud Dulness* joins with *Quality,* .... 1.EOC.415.287.
Still *pleas'd* to *teach,* and yet not *proud* to *know?* .... 1.EOC.632.311.
Still fond and proud of *Savage Liberty,* .... 1.EOC.650.313.
The proud despiser of all heav'n beside; .... 1.TrPA.16.366.
How twice he tam'd proud *Ister's* rapid Flood, ... 1.TrSt.25.410.
Yet then no proud aspiring Piles were rais'd, ... 1.TrSt.200.418.
Decrees to proud *Etheocles* the Crown; .... 1.TrSt.219.419.
Or chuse thy Seat in *Ilion's* proud Abodes, ... 1.TrSt.835.444.
Before proud *Ilion* must resign their Breath! .... 1.TrES.243.458.
Till the proud Suitors, for their Crimes, afford .... 1.TrUl.62.468.
Against proud *Ilion's* well-defended Tow'rs, ... 1.TrUl.192.472.
But when proud *Ilion's* Tow'rs in Ashes lay, ... 1.TrUl.195A.472.
Whether she's chast or rampant, proud or civil; .... 2.ChJM.186.23.
The Pomp, the Pageantry, the Proud Array. .... 2.ChJM.308.29.
Of lavish Pomp, and proud Magnificence: .... 2.ChJM.445.36.
Who cause the Proud their Visits to delay, ... 2.RL4.63.189.
He spoke, and speaking, in proud Triumph spread .... 2.RL4.139.195.
Whate'er proud *Rome,* or artful *Greece* beheld, ... 2.TemF.63.256.
Full in the midst, proud *Fame's* Imperial Seat .... 2.TemF.243.256.
And proud Defiance in their Looks they bore: .... 2.TemF.343.280.
Thus unlamented pass the proud away, ... 2.Elegy.43.366.
'Tis all thou art, and all the proud shall be! .... 2.Elegy.74.368.
When the proud steed shall know why Man restrains .... 3.EOM1.61.21.
His soul proud Science never taught to stray .... 3.EOM1.101.27.
Proud of an easy conquest all along, ... 3.EOM2.157.74.
Proud of imagin'd Conquests all along, ... 3.EOM2.157A.74.
That proud exception to all Nature's laws, ... 3.EOM3.243.117.
She taught the weak to bend, the proud to pray, ... 3.EOM3.251.118.
From dirt and sea-weed as proud Venice rose; .... 3.EOM4.292.155.
Proud as a Peeress, prouder as a Punk; .... 3.Ep2.70.56.
Or in proud falls magnificently lost, ... 3.Ep3.256.114.
Blush, Grandeur, blush! proud Courts, withdraw your blaze! ...3.Ep3.281.116.
Gallant and gay, in Cliveden's proud alcove, ... 3.Ep3.307.118.
Proud to catch cold at a Venetian door; .... 3.Ep4.36.140.
Without it, proud Versailles! thy glory fails; .... 3.Ep4.71.144.
So proud, so grand, of that stupendous air, ... 3.Ep4.101.147.
Proud to accomplish what such hands design'd, ... 3.Ep4.196.156.
Dash the proud Gamester in his gilded Car, ... 4.HS1.107.15.
So was I punish'd, as if full as *proud,* .... 4.JD4.19.27.
Such was my Fate; whom Heav'n adjudg'd as *proud,* .... 4.JD4.19A.27.
And Hemsley once proud Buckingham's delight, ... 4.HS2.177.69.
For well they knew, proud Trappings serve to hide .... 4.HAdv.116.85.
Proud of a vast Extent of flimzy lines. .... 4.Arbu.94.102.
Proud, as *Apollo* on his forked hill, ... 4.Arbu.231.112.
Not proud, nor servile, be one Poet's praise .... 4.Arbu.336.120.
The dull, the proud, the wicked, and the mad; .... 4.Arbu.347.120.
Nor proud, nor servile, be one Poet's praise .... 4.Arbu.336A.120.
More pert, more proud, more positive than he. .... 4.JD2.52.137.
Paltry and proud, as drabs in Drury-lane. .... 4.JD2.64.139.
More pert, more proud, more positive than he. .... 4.JD2A.58.137.
Then Peers grew proud in Horsemanship t' excell, ... 4.2HE1.143.207.
Proud Vice to brand, or injur'd Worth adorn, ... 4.2HE1.227.215.
Proud Vice to lash, or injur'd Worth adorn, ... 4.2HE1.227A.215.
Who to disturb their betters mighty proud, ... 4.2HE1.307.221.
Who proud of Pedigree, is poor of Purse) .... 4.1HE6.84.243.
"I thought the Dean had been too proud, ... 4.HS6.53.253.
Proud Fortune, and look shallow Greatness thro': .... 4.1HE1.108.287.
Down, down, proud Satire! tho' a Realm be spoil'd, ... 4.EpS2.38.315.
Down, down, proud Satire! tho' a Land be spoil'd, ... 4.EpS2.38A.315.
And if yet higher the proud List should end, ... 4.EpS2.92.318.
Fr. You're strangely proud. *P.* So proud I am no Slave: ...4.EpS2.205.324.
Fr. You're strangely proud. *P.* So proud I am no Slave: ...4.EpS2.205.324.
Yes, I am proud; I must be proud to see .... 4.EpS2.208.324.
Yes, I am proud; I must be proud to see .... 4.EpS2.208.324.

PROUD (CONTINUED)

C[arteret], his own proud dupe, thinks Monarchs things .... 4.1740.5.332.
Or those proud fools whom nature, rank, and fate .... 4.1740.67.335.
Now Night descending, the proud scene was o'er, ... 5.DunA1.87.69.
I see a Monarch proud my race to own! .... 5.DunA1.251Z3.93.
Great Tibbald sate: The proud Parnassian sneer, ... 5.DunA2.5.97.
Great Tibbald nods: The proud Parnassian sneer, ... 5.DunA2.5A.97.
"Lo Rome herself, proud mistress now no more .... 5.DunA3.93.158.
How proud! how pale! how earnest all appear! .... 5.DunA3.152Z1.164.
And proud *Philosophy* with breeches tore, ... 5.DunA3.191z3.172.
While proud Philosophy repines to show .... 5.DunA3.193.173.
And proud his mistress' orders to perform, ... 5.DunA3.259.179.
Now Night descending, the proud scene was o'er, ... 5.DunB1.89.276.
Great Cibber sate: the proud Parnassian sneer, ... 5.DunB2.5.296.
"Lo! Rome herself, proud mistress now no more .... 5.DunB3.101.324.
While proud Philosophy repines to show, ... 5.DunB3.197.330.
And proud his Mistress' orders to perform, ... 5.DunB3.263.333.
My Sons! be proud, be selfish, and be dull. .... 5.DunB4.582.400.
Proud to my list to add one Monarch more; .... 5.DunB4.600.403.
Again grown proud, the spreading rose .... 6.4iv.16.11.
Proud grief sits swelling in her eyes: .... 6.5.2.12.
Dauntless her Look, her Gesture proud, ... 6.14v(a).16.49.
In *Rome's* proud *Forum* young *Octavius* plac'd, ... 6.20.28.66.
Ev'n in those tombs where their proud names survive, ... 6.22.16.72.
Those four proud Syllables alone .... 6.30.9.86.
Ev'n when proud *Cæsar* 'midst triumphal cars, ... 6.32.27.96.
Proud Reptile, Vile, and vain .... 6.53.6A.161.
Vile reptile, Proud, and vain .... 6.53.6B.161.
Here scantier limits the proud Arch confine, ... 6.71.27.203.
Now scantier limits the proud Arch confine, ... 6.71.27A.203.
To Lordings proud I tune my Lay, ... 6.79.1.217.
To Lordings proud I tune my Song, ... 6.79.1A.217.
Whom Heav'n kept sacred from the Proud and Great. .... 6.112.4.318.
From dirt and sea-weed as proud Venice rose; .... 6.130.2.358.
And *Troy's* proud Walls lie level with the Ground. .... Il.1.24.86.
But know, proud Monarch, I'm thy Slave no more; .... Il.1.221.97.
When the proud Monarch shall thy Arms implore, ... Il.1.283.100.
To *Troy's* proud Monarch, and the Friends of *Troy!* .... Il.1.340.105.
If yon proud Monarch thus thy Son defies, ... Il.1.466.110.
'Till the proud King, and all th' *Achaian* Race .... Il.1.660.118.
'Till *Troy's* proud Structures shou'd in Ashes lie. .... Il.2.353.144.
And *Troy's* proud Matrons render Tear for Tear. .... Il.2.423.147.
Like some proud Bull that round the Pastures leads .... Il.2.566.154.
The proud *Mycœnè* arms her martial Pow'rs, ... Il.2.686.159.
Proud of his Host, unrival'd in his Reign, ... Il.2.699.159.
Unfinish'd his proud Palaces remain, ... Il.2.858.165.
Or proud *Iölcus* lifts her Airy Wall: .... Il.2.867.165.
Where once *Eurytus* in proud Triumph reign'd, ... Il.2.885.166.
And proud *Miletus;* came the *Carian* Throngs, ... Il.2.1058.172.
As thus with glorious Air and proud Disdain, ... Il.3.33.189.
From his proud Chariot: Him, approaching near, ... Il.3.43A.190.
And the proud *Trojans* first infringe the Peace. .... Il.4.94.225.
Which *Troy's* proud Glories in the Dust shall lay, ... Il.4.197.230.
While some proud *Trojan* thus insulting cries, ... Il.4.212.231.
Lo his proud Vessels scatter'd o'er the Main, ... Il.4.216.231.
And *Troy's* proud Walls lie smoaking on the Ground. .... Il.4.333.236.
And Earth's proud Tyrants low in Ashes laid. .... Il.4.359.238.
While the proud Archer thus exulting cry'd. .... Il.5.133.273.
The Nose and Eye-ball the proud *Lycian* fixt; .... Il.5.354.283.
These in proud Triumph to the Fleet convey'd, ... Il.5.401.286.
And the proud Vaunt in just Derision ends. .... Il.5.580.296.
From his proud Car the Prince impetuous springs; .... Il.5.603.297.
Troy felt his Arm, and yon' proud Ramparts stand .... Il.5.792.304.
Proud Tyrants humbles, and whole Hosts o'erturns. .... Il.5.925.310.
Who held in *Pedasus* his proud Abode, ... Il.6.41.325.
Well hast thou known proud *Troy's* perfidious Land, ... Il.6.69.327.
And *Troy's* proud Dames whose Garments sweep the Ground, .Il.6.563.354.
Pamper'd and proud, he seeks the wonted Tides, ... Il.6.654.359.
While the proud Foe his frustrate Triumphs mourns, ... Il.6.678.361.
Proud, *Areïthous'* dreadful Arms to wield; .... Il.7.168.372.
If the proud *Grecians* thus successful boast .... Il.7.532.391.
But yon' proud Work no future Age shall view, ... Il.7.550.392.
Thy once-proud Hopes, presumptuous Prince! are fled; .... Il.8.202.407.
Till their proud Navy wrapt in Smoak and Fires, ... Il.8.222.407.
Encourag'd his proud Steeds, while thus he spoke. .... Il.8.225.408.
Proud of his Boy, he own'd the gen'rous Flame, ... Il.8.345.414.
Proud Tyrants humbles, and whole Hosts o'erturns. .... Il.8.475.419.
Soon was your Battel o'er: Proud *Troy* retir'd .... Il.8.558.423.
Proud *Troy* they hated, and her guilty Race. .... Il.8.684.427.
So many Flames before proud *Ilion* blaze, ... Il.8.699.428.
Give to our Arms proud *Ilion's* hostile Tow'rs, ... Il.9.176.441.
Give to our Arms proud *Ilion's* hostile Tow'rs, ... Il.9.363.451.
Proud *Hector,* now, th' unequal Fight demands, ... Il.9.404.452.
Not all proud *Thebes'* unrival'd Walls contain, ... Il.9.500.457.
Proud as he is, that Iron-heart retains .... Il.9.741.471.
Why shou'd we Gifts to proud *Achilles* send, ... Il.9.816.474.
Nor think proud *Hector's* Hopes confirm'd by *Jove:* .... Il.10.115.7.
Far other Rulers those proud Steeds demand, ... Il.10.473.24.
I saw his Coursers in proud Triumph go, ... Il.10.506.26.
Whole Squadrons vanish, and proud Heads lie low. .... Il.11.206.44.
While the proud Victor bore his Arms away. .... Il.11.320.49.
And from his Car the proud *Thymbræus* fell: .... Il.11.416.53.
Of his proud Fleet, o'erlook'd the Fields of Fight; .... Il.11.731.67.
And proud *Atrides* tremble on his Throne. .... Il.11.747.68.
When the proud *Elians* first commenc'd the War. .... Il.11.831.73.
Proud *Troy* may tremble, and desist from War; .... Il.11.931.77.
Proud of the Favours mighty *Jove* has shown, ... Il.12.75.84.
Such their proud Hopes, but all their Hopes were vain! .... Il.12.140.86.
Tho' these proud Bulwarks tumble at our Feet, ... Il.12.262.90.
Of *Greece* victorious, and proud *Ilion* lost? .... Il.13.290.119.
Proud of himself, and of th' imagin'd Bride, ... Il.13.465.128.
So sunk proud *Asius* in that dreadful Day, ... Il.13.497.130.
So sunk proud *Asius* in that deathful Day, ... Il.13.497A.130.
Not unattended (the proud *Trojan* cries) .... Il.13.523.131.
Stalks the proud Ram, the Father of the Fold: .... Il.13.623.135.
The proud *Ionians* with their sweeping Trains, ... Il.13.860.146.

PROUD (CONTINUED)

Shall then proud *Hector* see his Boast fulfill'd, ... Il.14.51.160.
Fly diverse; while proud Kings, and Chiefs renown'd .... Il.14.167.165.
Arms his proud Host, and dares oppose a God: .... Il.14.450.185.
Here, proud *Polydamas,* here turn thy Eyes! .... Il.14.549.189.
Proud *Argives!* destin'd by our Arms to fall. .... Il.14.562.190.
At the proud Boaster he directs his Course; .... Il.14.571.190.
O say, when *Neptune* made proud *Ilion* yield, ... Il.14.601.191.
These proud in Arms, those scatter'd o'er the Plain; .... Il.15.9.194.
Lay yon' proud Structures level with the Plain, ... Il.15.241.206.
At one proud Bark, high-tow'ring o'er the Fleet .... Il.15.482.216.
From the proud Archer strike his vaunted Bow. .... Il.15.575.218.
Troy in proud Hopes already view'd the Main .... Il.15.850.229.
Proud *Troy* shall tremble, and desert the War: .... Il.16.59.237.
And humble the proud Monarch whom you save. .... Il.16.329.255.
And from the half-burn'd Ship proud *Troy* retires: .... Il.16.349.256.
Before proud *Ilion,* must resign their Breath! .... Il.16.546.265.
While the proud Victor thus his Fall derides, ... Il.16.902.278.
Which ev'n the Graces might be proud to wear, ... Il.17.54.289.
Proud of his Deed, and glorious in the Prize, ... Il.17.67.290.
Hector in proud *Achilles'* Arms shall shine, ... Il.17.209.295.
Him, proud in Triumph glitt'ring from afar, ... Il.17.225.296.
Tho' well he knew, to make proud *Ilion* bend, ... Il.17.468.305.
Now sink in gloomy Clouds the proud Abodes; .... Il.17.827.321.
Let me revenge it on proud *Hector's* Heart, ... Il.18.119.328.
Proud *Troy* shall tremble, and consent to fear; .... Il.18.238.333.
And proud *Mæonia* wasts the Fruits of *Troy.* .... Il.18.342.338.
When my proud Mother hurl'd me from the Sky, ... Il.18.463.344.
(Late their proud Ornaments, but now their Chains.) .... Il.21.37.423.
While the proud Victor thus triumphing said, ... Il.21.199.429.
Not till proud *Hector,* Guardian of her Wall, ... Il.21.245.431.
And guard the Race of proud *Laomedon!* .... Il.21.516.443.
And yon' proud Bulwarks grew beneath my Hands: .... Il.21.520.443.
Dost thou, for this, afford proud *Ilion* Grace, ... Il.21.531.443.
Some proud in Triumph, some with Rage on fire; .... Il.21.603.447.
How proud *Achilles* glories in his Fame! .... Il.21.691.450.
So the proud Courser, victor of the prize, ... Il.22.33.453.
Shall proud *Polydamas* before the Gate .... Il.22.140.459.
Proud on his Car th' insulting Victor stood, ... Il.22.501.477.
O'er the proud Citadel at length should rise, ... Il.22.520.478.
That whirl'd the Car of proud *Laomedon.* .... Il.23.422.506.
Proud of the Gift, thus spake the Full of Days: .... Il.23.751.520.
Stood proud to Hymn, and tune his youthful Lyre. .... Il.24.83.538.
If some proud Brother ey'd me with Disdain, ... Il.24.972.576.
Proud Tyrants humbles, and whole hosts o'erturns. .... Od.1.131.38.
The proud Oppressors fly the vengeful sword. .... Od.1.154.40.
And all your wrongs the proud oppressors rue! .... Od.1.330.48.
(A sacred oath) each proud oppressor slain .... Od.1.485.55.
Nor great *Alcmena,* (the proud boasts of Fame) .... Od.2.138.67.
To shake with war proud *Ilion's* lofty tow'rs, ... Od.2.200.71.
Long time with thee before proud *Ilion's* wall .... Od.3.104.91.
But when (by wisdom won) proud *Ilion* burn'd, ... Od.3.159.93.
And the proud Suitors shall its force confess: .... Od.3.251.97.
And now proud *Sparta* with their wheels resounds, ... Od.4.1.119.
With conquest proud, inces'd *Minerva's* pow'r: .... Od.5.136.178.
A proud, unpolish'd race—To me belongs .... Od.6.327.227.
Thro' the proud street she moves, the publick gaze; .... Od.7.3.232.
To build proud navies, and command the main; .... Od.7.46.235.
The race of Giants, impious, proud and bold; .... Od.7.75.237.
Thence, where proud *Athens* rears her tow'ry head, ... Od.7.103.239.
And bids proud *Ilion* from her ashes rise. .... Od.8.538.291.
And by the Gods decree proud *Ilion* falls; .... Od.8.560.292.
Should bury these proud tow'rs beneath the ground. .... Od.8.622.296.
Who taught proud *Troy* and all her sons to bow; .... Od.9.315.319.
The next proud *Lamos'* stately tow'rs appear, ... Od.10.92.343.
Or (since to dust proud *Troy* submits her tow'rs) .... Od.11.196.391.
Since in the dust proud *Troy* submits her tow'rs. .... Od.11.205.391.
O'er proud *Iölcos Pelias* stretch'd his reign, ... Od.11.311.397.
Curbs the proud steed, reluctant to the rein: .... Od.11.370.401.
Proud of their strength and more than mortal size, ... Od.11.385.402.
Crush the proud rebel, and assert his claim. .... Od.11.614.414.
When *Troy's* proud bulwarks smok'd upon the ground, ... Od.11.652.416.
For ever sad with proud disdain he pin'd, ... Od.11.667.417.
Till the proud suitors for their crimes afford .... Od.13.229.17.
Against proud *Ilion's* well-defended tow'rs; .... Od.13.359.24.
And proud addresses to the matchless Queen. .... Od.13.432.27.
In blood and dust each proud oppressor mourn, ... Od.14.188.45.
Nor dare to question where the proud command: .... Od.15.403.88.
Proud are the lords, and wretched are the swains. .... Od.15.407.89.
The court proud *Samos* and *Dulichium* fills, ... Od.16.131.109.
Exalt the lowly, or the proud debase. .... Od.16.233.114.
While the proud foes, industrious to destroy .... Od.16.338.122.
And the proud steer was o'er the marble spread. .... Od.17.202.141.
Of the proud son; as that we stand this hour .... Od.17.302.146.
Turn'd his proud step, and left them on their way. .... Od.17.305.146.
The proud feel pity, and relief bestow, ... Od.17.440.155.
Death shall lay low the proud aggressor's head, ... Od.17.566.160.
Proud as thou art, henceforth no more be proud, ... Od.18.28.168.
Proud as thou art, henceforth no more be proud, ... Od.18.28.168.
Proud of the pow'r that to high birth belongs; .... Od.18.167.174.
Then let not man be proud: but firm of mind, ... Od.18.169.175.
That yon' proud Suitors, who licentious tread .... Od.18.279.180.
Proud, to seem brave among a coward train! .... Od.18.424.189.
My King returns; the proud Usurpers dye. .... Od.20.282.247.
And the proud steer was on the marble spread. .... Od.20.315.248.
To the proud Suitors bears in pensive state .... Od.21.61.262.
And his proud hopes already win the prize. .... Od.21.101.263.
Than all proud *Argos,* or *Mycæna* knows, ... Od.21.111.264.
To the proud Suitors, or your ancient Lord? .... Od.21.204.269.
Of *Priam's* race, and lay'd proud *Troy* in dust? .... Od.22.251.299.
Thence all descend in pomp and proud array, ... Od.23.131.327.
At once they bathe, and dress in proud array; .... Od.23.140.327.
And proud *Nericus* trembled as I storm'd. .... Od.24.438.369.

PROUDER
Why art thou prouder and more hard than they? ... 1.PSu.18.73.
Proud as a Peeress, prouder as a Punk; ... 3.Ep2.70.56.
Who prouder march'd, with magistrates in state, ... 5.DunA2.391.148.
Or prouder march'd with magistrates in state, ... 5.DunA2.391A.148.
Who prouder march'd, with magistrates in state, ... 5.DunB2.423.318.
Achilles heard him, prouder of the Praise. ... Il.23.752.520.

PROUDEST
The proudest Monument of mortal Hands! ... Il.12.10.81.

PROUDLY
Where o'er her pointed Summits proudly rais'd, ... Il.8.59.398.
Who proudly stalking, leaves the herds at large, ... Od.17.292.146.

PROV'D
Turn'd *Criticks* next, and prov'd plain *Fools* at last; ... 1.EOC.37.243.
Then Criticism the Muse's Handmaid prov'd, ... 1.EOC.102.251.
Nor knew I then which passion greater prov'd, ... 1.TrPA.11.365.
Happy! and happy still She might have prov'd, ... 1.TrSt.674.438.
He prov'd a Rebel to my Sov'reign Will: ... 2.ChWB.334.73.
Bold was the Work, and prov'd the Master's Fire; ... 2.TemF.193.271.
To her, Calista prov'd her conduct nice, ... 3.Ep2.31.52.
Has ev'n been prov'd to grant a Lover's pray'r, ... 3.Ep2.55.55.
Prov'd, by the ends of being, to have been. ... 3.Ep3.290.116.
Cou'd you complain, my Friend, he prov'd so bad? ... 4.2HE2.22.165.
Narcissus here a different fate had prov'd, ... 6.4ii.7.9.
Whom Pope prov'd his Friend in his two chief distresses, ... 6.92.3.255.
My Life, alas! I fear prov'd Death to Thee! ... 6.96iv.94.279.
A well-prov'd Casque with Leather Braces bound ... Il.10.309.16.
So prov'd my Valour for my Country's Good. ... Il.11.897.75.
There stops—So *Hector:* Their whole Force he prov'd, ... Il.13.199.115.
Have prov'd thy Valour and unconquer'd Might; ... Il.13.354.122.
Wisely and well, my Son, thy Words have prov'd ... Il.23.719.518.
Now prove that Prowess you have prov'd so well. ... Il.23.859.523.
Then to *Peiræus—Thou* whom time has prov'd ... Od.15.581.98.
Nor prov'd the toil too hard; nor have I lost ... Od.21.467.282.

PROVE
But *Dulness* with *Obscenity* must prove ... 1.EOC.532.297.
Nor be so *Civil* as to prove *Unjust;* ... 1.EOC.581.306.
His parents joy, who did a comfort prove ... 1.TrPA.3.365.
Must then her Name the wretched Writer prove? ... 1.TrSP.3.393.
I go, ye Nymphs! those Rocks and Seas to prove; ... 1.TrSP.201.402.
They'd prove the Father from whose Loins they came. ... 1.TrSt.123.415.
Oh Race confed'rate into Crimes, that prove ... 1.TrSt.302.422.
Curs'd *Thebes* the Vengeance it deserves, may prove,— ... 1.TrSt.364.425.
Unless great Acts superior Merit prove, ... 1.TrES.35.451.
And brave *Oïleus,* prove your Force in Fight: ... 1.TrES.84.453.
To count these *Presents,* and from thence to prove ... 1.TrUl.92.469.
Not thus *Ulysses;* he decrees to prove ... 1.TrUl.216.473.
But if her Virtues prove the larger Share, ... 2.ChJM.192.24.
Now shou'd the Nuptial Pleasures prove so great, ... 2.ChJM.272.27.
But prove the Scourge to lash you on your Way: ... 2.ChJM.288.28.
Was much too meek to prove a Homicide. ... 2.ChJM.439.36.
Constant and kind I'll ever prove to thee. ... 2.ChJM.715.49.
Now prove your Patience, gentle Ladies all, ... 2.ChJM.740.50.
Did I for this the Pow'r of Magick prove? ... 2.ChJM.764.52.
Then how two Wives their Lord's Destruction prove, ... 2.ChWB.401.76.
Men prove with Child, as pow'rful Fancy works, ... 2.RL4.53.188.
Not *Cæsar's* empress wou'd I deign to prove; ... 2.ElAb.87.326.
O death all-eloquent! you only prove ... 2.ElAb.335.346.
But, sage historians! 'tis your task to prove ... 3.Ep1.85.21.
Will prove at least the Medium must be clear. ... 4.HS1.56.11.
Till I cry'd out, "You prove yourself so able, ... 4.JD4.82.33.
Or, in a mortgage, prove a Lawyer's share, ... 4.HS2.169.69.
Or, in a mortgage, prove the Lawyer's share, ... 4.HS2.169A.69.
To prove, that Luxury could never hold; ... 4.2HE1.167.209.
So gravest precepts may successless prove, ... 5.DunA1.175.84.
So written precepts may successless prove, ... 5.DunA1.175A.84.
So graver precepts may successless prove, ... 5.DunA1.175B.84.
"Here prove who best can dash thro' thick and thin, ... 5.DunA2.264.133.
And prove, no Miracles can match thy own. ... 5.DunA3.210.175.
Did the dead Letter unsuccessful prove? ... 5.DunB1.193.283.
"Here prove who best can dash thro' thick and thin, ... 5.DunB2.276.309.
To prove me, Goddess! clear of all design, ... 5.DunB4.391.380.
To prove a dull *Succession* to be true, ... 6.7.23.16.
Shou'd it so prove, yet who'd admire? ... 6.10.58.26.
Or prove Reviver of a Schism, ... 6.10.81.27.
Both gifts destructive to the givers prove; ... 6.14iii.9.46.
To prove himself no Plagiary, MOORE, ... 6.116i.1.325.
Who shew'd his breech, to prove 'twas not besh— ... 6.116i.4.325.
To prove himself no Plagiary, a *M[00]re,* ... 6.116i.1A.325.
Hence shalt thou prove my Might, and curse the Hour, ... Il.1.247.98.
This Sceptre, form'd by temper'd Steel to prove ... Il.1.313.103.
The Field shall prove how Perjuries succeed, ... Il.4.308.235.
Burns with Desire *Sarpedon's* Strength to prove; ... Il.5.778.303.
Now change we Arms, and prove to either Host ... Il.6.286.340.
Oh prove a Husband's and a Father's Care! ... Il.6.549.354.
This Task let *Ajax* or *Tydides* prove, ... Il.7.217.375.
Such as I am, I come to prove thy Might; ... Il.7.281.378.
Forbear, my Sons! your farther Force to prove, ... Il.7.337.380.
And thou, *Podargus!* prove thy gen'rous Race: ... Il.8.227.408.
Then, then shall *Hector* and *Tydides* prove, ... Il.8.661.427.
Not Titles here, but Works, must prove our Worth. ... Il.10.77.6.
Unless great Acts superior Merit prove, ... Il.12.379.95.
And brave *Oïleus,* prove your Force in Fight: ... Il.12.438.97.
To where the *Mysians* prove their martial Force, ... Il.13.7.104.
At length she trusts her Pow'r; resolv'd to prove ... Il.14.187.168.
Ne'er did my Soul so strong a Passion prove, ... Il.14.359.180.
Lest Arts and Blandishments successless prove, ... Il.15.37.195.
'Tis mine to prove the rash Assertion vain; ... Il.17.194.295.
Yet mighty as they are, my Force to prove, ... Il.17.582.311.
Achilles' Care you promis'd I shou'd prove, ... Il.19.315.385.
And prove his Merits to the Throne of *Troy?* ... Il.20.217.403.
Ev'n this, perhaps, will hardly prove thy Lot: ... Il.20.226.403.

PROVE (CONTINUED)
Hear how the glorious Origine we prove ... Il.20.254.404.
Is not to question, but to prove our Might. ... Il.20.305.407.
So ends thy Glory! Such the Fate they prove ... Il.21.201.429.
Come, prove thy Arm! for first the War to wage, ... Il.21.512.443.
Or what must prove my Fortune or thy own. ... Il.22.360.470.
Prove we our Force, and *Jove* the rest decree. ... Il.23.841.523.
Now prove that Prowess you have prov'd so well. ... Il.23.859.523.
For these he bids the Heroes prove their Art ... Il.23.1048.531.
Successless all her soft caresses prove, ... Od.1.73.34.
Be doom'd the worst of human ills to prove, ... Od.1.82.35.
To prove a genuine birth (the Prince replies) ... Od.1.275.46.
To learn your Father's fortunes: Fame may prove ... Od.1.366.50.
Two youths approach, whose semblant features prove ... Od.4.33.121.
No peril in my cause he ceas'd to prove, ... Od.4.137.126.
(Form'd for libation to the Gods,) shall prove ... Od.4.809.156.
Heav'n grant this festival may prove their last! ... Od.4.909.161.
But all her blandishments successless prove, ... Od.7.344.253.
To prove the heroe.—Slander stings the brave. ... Od.8.208.273.
To count these presents, and from thence to prove ... Od.13.259.18.
Not thus *Ulysses;* he decrees to prove ... Od.13.383.25.
I then explor'd my thought, what course to prove? ... Od.14.301.50.
Sandals, a sword, and robes, respect to prove, ... Od.16.79.106.
And noting, ere we rise in vengeance prove ... Od.16.330.121.
Dispers'd the youth resides; their faith to prove ... Od.16.342.122.
Should he return, what'er my beauties prove, ... Od.18.297.181.
When time shall prove the storied blessing true: ... Od.19.355.211.
"And prove your sev'ral strengths"—The Princes heard, ... Od.21.151.266.
Fain would I prove, before your judging eyes, ... Od.21.302.274.
At ev'ry step debates, her Lord to prove? ... Od.23.89.323.
These boding thoughts, and what he is, to prove! ... Od.23.112.325.
Prove that we live, by vengeance on his head, ... Od.24.500.372.

PROVERB
Why has the Proverb falsly said ... 6.94.85.262.
The good old proverb how this pair fulfill! ... Od.17.250.143.

PROVERBS
To heathnish Authors, Proverbs, and old Saws. ... 2.ChJM.219.25.
Solomon's Proverbs, *Eloïsa's* Loves; ... 2.ChWB.361.74.

PROVES
The *current Folly* proves the *ready Wit,* ... 1.EOC.449.290.
The *current Folly* proves our *ready Wit,* ... 1.EOC.449A.290.
But like a Shadow, proves the *Substance* true; ... 1.EOC.467.292.
But like a Shadow, proves the *Substance* too; ... 1.EOC.467A.292.
As plainly proves, Experience dwells with Years: ... 2.ChJM.150.21.
Proves the just Victim of his Royal Rage. ... 2.RL3.60.172.
And last (which proves him wiser still than all) ... 4.JD4.150.37.
But the last Tyrant ever proves the worst. ... 6.19.40.63.
Proves but what either shou'd conceal, ... 6.116iii.3.326.
A furious Foe unconscious proves a Friend. ... 6.116viii.2.328.
Thy free Remonstrance proves thy Worth and Truth: ... Il.6.419.347.
To die, or conquer, proves a Hero's Heart; ... Il.11.519.57.
Thy Friend *Sarpedon* proves thy base Neglect: ... Il.17.166.294.
That proves the Hero born in better Days!) ... Il.23.930.526.
Distinguish'd excellence the Goddess proves; ... Od.6.125.212.
Thus in surrounding floods conceal'd he proves ... Od.11.293.396.

PROVIDE
And Reason bids us for our own provide; ... 3.EOM2.96.66.
For some his Int'rest prompts him to provide, ... 3.EOM3.59.98.
Yet, would the Gods for human Good provide, ... Il.4.23.222.
A sable Ewe each Leader should provide, ... Il.10.255.13.
Antilochus! we shall our self provide. ... Il.23.638.515.
Small Stock of Iron needs that Man provide; ... Il.23.987.528.
For what Defence alas! couldst thou provide? ... Il.24.453.555.
Soon may kind heav'n a sure relief provide, ... Od.1.328.48.
Thus he, unskill'd of what the fates provide! ... Od.4.1021.165.
But haste, the viands and the bowl provide— ... Od.6.295.225.
'Till our consenting sires a spouse provide ... Od.6.345.228.
Enjoyment of the good the Gods provide. ... Od.14.493.60.
Meet, for the wand'ring suppliant to provide. ... Od.14.579.64.
To-morrow for my self I must provide, ... Od.15.328.85.
While thus the copious banquet they provide; ... Od.17.203.141.
But who the lighted taper will provide, ... Od.19.27.193.
And take the banquet which our cares provide: ... Od.24.418.369.

PROVIDED
Provided still, you moderate your Joy, ... 2.ChJM.291.28.

PROVIDENCE
Weigh thy Opinion against Providence; ... 3.EOM1.114.29.
Who finds not Providence all good and wise, ... 3.EOM1.205.40.
On him, their second Providence, they hung, ... 3.EOM3.217.114.
And who would take the Poor from Providence? ... 3.Ep3.188.109.
And God's good Providence, a lucky Hit. ... 3.Ep3.378.123.
Preserve, Almighty Providence! ... 4.HS6.23.251.
(It was by Providence, they think, ... 4.HS6.218.263.
Cost studious Providence more Time. ... 6.30.58B.88.
Shall as it blazeth, break; while Providence ... 6.137.2.373.
Live, and enjoy the providence of heav'n. ... Od.10.203.350.
And ride aloft, to Providence resign'd, ... Od.12.501.456.
Yet Providence deserts me not at last; ... Od.15.397.88.

PROVIDENCE'S
Admits, and leaves them, Providence's care. ... 3.Ep3.108.100.

PROVIDENTIAL
Oh! be his Guard thy providential Care, ... Il.16.298.254.

PROVIDES
Art from that Fund each *just Supply* provides, ... 1.EOC.74.247.
Provides a Consort worthy of my Bed; ... 2.ChJM.255.26.
In Peace provides fit arms against a War? ... 4.HS2.128.65.
Concludes from both, and best provides for all. ... Il.3.152.198.

PROVIDES 154 PRUNELLA

PROVIDES (CONTINUED)
Studious to ease thy grief, our care provides ....Od.2.345.77.

PROVINCE
Each might his *sev'ral Province* well command, ...1.EOC.66.246.
And a whole Province in his Triumph led. ....1.TrSt.746.441.
Our humbler Province is to tend the Fair, ...2.RL2.91.165.
Words are Man's province, Words we teach alone. ....5.DunB4.150.356.
Be mine; and yours the Province to detain. ....Il.2.98.131.
War be thy Province, thy Protection mine; ....Il.5.159.274.

PROVINCES
Or infamous for plunder'd provinces. ....3.EOM4.298.156.
Or cross, to plunder Provinces, the Main: ....4.1HE1.127.289.

PROVISION
A glutted Market makes Provision cheap. ....2.ChWB.262.69.
With fresh provision hence our fleet to store ....Od.9.264.317.

PROVISIONS
Of ev'ry kind provisions heav'd aboard, ...Od.5.339.188.
And brought another with provisions stor'd: ....Od.9.247.317.

PROVOCATION
Ask you what Provocation I have had? ....4.EpS2.197.324.

PROVOK'D
Provok'd to Vengeance, three large Leaves I tore, ...2.ChWB.415.77.
If want provok'd, or madness made them print, ...4.Arbu.155.107.
Hunger provok'd, or madness made them print; ....4.Arbu.155A.107.
But He, our Chief, provok'd the raging Pest, ...Il.1.119.92.
By me provok'd; a Captive Maid the Cause: ....Il.2.449.149.
Till *Greece*, provok'd, from all her Numbers show ....Il.7.45.365.
Let him, who first provok'd our Chiefs to fight, ...Il.7.345.381.
As Wasps, provok'd by Children in their Play, ...Il.16.314.254.
Provok'd to Passion, once more rouze to Ire ....Il.24.733.568.

PROVOKE
Restrain his Fury, than provoke his Speed; ....1.EOC.85.249.
"Odious! in woollen! 'twould a Saint provoke, ...3.Ep1.242.36.
Or whiten'd Wall provoke the Skew'r to write, ...4.HS1.98.13.
Wild to get loose, his Patience I provoke, ...4.JD4.116.35.
To Virtue's Work provoke the tardy Hall, ...4.EpS2.218.325.
Whose wit and equally provoke one, ...4.1740.27.333.
Glory, and gain, th' industrious tribe provoke; ....5.DunA2.29.99.
Glory, and gain, th'industrious tribe provoke; ....5.DunB2.33.297.
And still thy Priestly Pride provoke thy King? ....Il.1.134.93.
Th' unwary *Greeks* his Fury may provoke; ....Il.2.231.138.
Then well may this long Stay provoke their Tears, ...Il.2.360.144.
Proclaim their Motions, and provoke the War: ....Il.3.4.188.
When Crimes provoke us, Heav'n Success denies; ....Il.3.453.213.
Cease to provoke me, lest I make thee more ....Il.3.517.216.
Provoke *Atrides* and renew the Fight: ....Il.3.540.217.
Content with Jav'lins to provoke the War. ....Il.4.355.238.
Serves not to slaughter, but provoke the Foe. ....Il.5.263.279.
The God but urg'd him to provoke his Fate. ....Il.5.692.301.
Our impious Battels the just Gods provoke. ....Il.7.425.385.
Stand the First Onset, and provoke the Storm: ....Il.15.335.210.
Pierce the thick Battel, and provoke the War. ....Il.17.136.293.
These boastful Words provoke the raging God; ....Il.21.151.427.
Who dares his Foe with lifted Arms provoke, ...Il.23.761.520.
And sheath'd in Steel, provoke his Foe to fight. ....Il.23.948.526.
Provoke new sorrow from these grateful eyes. ....Od.4.750.154.
These words the *Cyclops'* burning rage provoke: ....Od.9.565.329.
What boots the god-less Giant to provoke? ....Od.9.579.330.
Injurious minds just answers but provoke— ....Od.17.478.156.

PROVOKES
Say, wretched Rivals! what provokes your Rage? ....1.TrSt.210.419.
Who breaks with her, provokes Revenge from Hell, ...3.Ep2.129.61.
But when our Country's Cause provokes to Arms, ...6.11.36.31.
Our laughter, *R[oom]e*, whene'er he speaks, provokes; ....6.105iii.1A.301.
Who breaks with her, provokes Revenge from Hell, ...6.154.15.403.
What Pow'r soe'er provokes our lifted Hand, ...Il.8.567.423.
With Voice and Hand provokes their doubting Heart, ...Il.11.379.51.
Defends the Body, and provokes the War. ....Il.16.914.279.
What God provokes thee, rashly thus to dare, ...Il.17.536.309.
What guilt provokes him, and what vows appease? ....Od.4.516.145.

PROVOKING
Discharge that Rage on more Provoking Crimes, ...1.EOC.528.297.
Provoking Dæmons all restraint remove, ...2.ElAb.231.339.

PROW
(The sea-ward prow invites the tardy gales) ....Od.4.1034.166.

PROWESS
And with th' *Arcadian* Spears my Prowess try'd, ...Il.7.165.372.
When *Hector's* Prowess no such Wonders wrought; ....Il.9.465.455.
Who fac'd him first, and by his Prowess fell? ....Il.11.282.47.
And try the Prowess of the Seed of *Jove*. ....Il.13.563.133.
And fam'd for Prowess in a well-fought Field; ....Il.15.624.220.
To me the Spoils my Prowess won, resign; ....Il.17.15.288.
When Mortals boast of Prowess not their own? ....Il.17.20.288.
Now prove that Prowess you have prov'd so well. ....Il.23.859.523.
Some God this arm with equal prowess bless! ....Od.3.250.97.
His prowess *Philomelides* confess'd, ...Od.4.463.142.
To his own prowess all the glory gave, ...Od.4.675.151.
His prowess *Philomelides* confest, ...Od.17.154.139.
What single arm hath prowess to subdue? ....Od.20.50.234.

PROWESS'D
Our freedom to thy prowess'd arm we owe ....Od.18.139.173.

PROWLING
With Toil protected from the prowling Train; ....Il.10.212.11.
To prowling bears, or lions in their way. ....Od.5.611.201.

PRUDE
The graver Prude sinks downward to a *Gnome*, ...2.RL1.63.150.
Or discompos'd the Head-dress of a Prude, ...2.RL4.74.190.
Belinda frown'd, *Thalestris* call'd her Prude. ....2.RL5.36.201.

PRUDENCE
Such Prudence, Sir, in all your Words appears, ...2.ChJM.149.21.
Much in his Prudence did our Knight rejoice, ...2.ChJM.250.26.
Ev'n av'rice, prudence; sloth, philosophy; ....3.EOM2.188.77.
It grows their Age's prudence to pretend; ....3.Ep2.236A.69.
'Tis half their Age's prudence to pretend; ....3.Ep2.236.69.
"No Names—be calm—learn Prudence of a Friend: ....4.Arbu.102.103.
Wit makes you foes, learn Prudence of a Friend ....4.Arbu.102A.103.
Prudence, whose glass presents th' approaching jayl: ....5.DunA1.49.66.
Prudence, whose glass presents th' approaching jayl: ....5.DunB1.51.274.
Thy prudence, Moore, is like that Irish Wit, ...6.116i.3.325.
Thus spoke the Prudence and the Fears of Age. ....Il.1.96.91.
Which *Jove* in Prudence from his Consort hides? ....Il.1.703.121.
And tempt a Fate which Prudence bids thee shun? ....Il.7.128.369.
The Wise new Prudence from the Wise acquire, ...Il.10.267.13.
Rever'd for Prudence, and with Prudence, bold.) ....Il.17.377.302.
Rever'd for Prudence, and with Prudence, bold.) ....Il.17.377.302.
What human Strength and Prudence can supply; ....Il.17.716.315.
And where the Prudence now that aw'd Mankind, ...Il.24.244.546.
A length of days his soul with prudence crown'd, ...Od.2.21.61.
In wit, in prudence, and in force of mind. ....Od.3.150.93.
And Prudence sav'd him in the needful hour. ....Od.5.557.199.
New horrors rise! let prudence by thy guide, ...Od.12.69.433.
To whom the Youth for prudence fam'd, reply'd. ....Od.15.100.73.
Of matchless prudence, and a duteous mind; ....Od.19.411.214.
By patient prudence, from the death decreed. ....Od.20.28.233.
Her coy reserve, and prudence mixt with pride, ...Od.24.148.355.

PRUDENT
A prudent Chief not always must display ....1.EOC.175.260.
To the wise Conduct of a prudent Wife: ....2.ChJM.72.18.
By this nice Conduct and this prudent Course, ...2.ChWB.162.64.
"Great is the Blessing of a prudent Wife, ...2.ChWB.190.65.
"With ev'ry pleasing, ev'ry prudent part, ...3.Ep2.159.64.
Cloe is prudent—would you too be wise? ....3.Ep2.179.64.
"Friend Pope! be prudent, let your Muse take breath, ...4.1HE1.13.279.
The prudent Gen'ral turn'd it to a jest, ...4.EpS2.154.322.
Sincere, tho' prudent; constant, yet resign'd; ....6.27.2.81.
The prudent, learn'd, and virtuous breast? ....6.51ii.2.152.
In prudent ease; still chearful, still resign'd ....6.55.1Z3.167.
Sincere, tho' prudent, constant, yet resign'd; ....6.57.2.169.
Our prudent Dame bethought her then ....6.93.17.257.
"With ev'ry pleasing, ev'ry prudent part, ...6.139.3.377.
Cloë is prudent—would you too be wise? ....6.139.23.377.
For prudent Counsel like the Gods renown'd: ....Il.2.206.138.
His Silence thus the prudent Hero broke. ....Il.2.347.143.
The prudent Goddess yet her Wrath suppress, ...Il.4.32.222.
Our great Fore-fathers held this prudent Course, ...Il.4.356.238.
In Words like these his prudent Thought exprest. ....Il.7.391.383.
The prudent Goddess yet her Wrath repress, ...Il.8.573.424.
Kings thou canst blame; a bold, but prudent Youth; ....Il.9.79.436.
O prudent Chief! (the *Pylian* Sage reply'd) ....Il.10.162.9.
The prudent Chief in sore Distress they found, ...Il.11.592.60.
And *Dracius* prudent, and *Amphion* bold; ....Il.13.866.147.
When Ministers are blest with prudent Mind: ....Il.15.231.206.
But ill this Insult suits a prudent Mind. ....Il.17.192.294.
The prudent Son with unattending Ears. ....Il.23.374.505.
The prudent Chief with calm Attention heard; ....Il.23.667.516.
What time this dome rever'd her prudent Lord; ....Od.1.298.47.
(The Youth with prudent modesty reply'd) ....Od.3.28.87.
(Not all were prudent, and not all were just) ....Od.3.164.93.
The prudent youth reply'd. Oh thou, the grace ....Od.3.246.97.
Thus check'd, reply'd *Ulysses'* prudent heir: ....Od.3.297.100.
Expert of arms, and prudent in debate; ....Od.4.291.132.
An urn shall recompence your prudent choice: ....Od.4.834.158.
Alas! for this (the prudent man replies) ....Od.5.273.184.
He stretch'd his hand the prudent chief to raise, ...Od.7.225.247.
The prudent *Greek)* possess the royal mind. ....Od.7.282.249.
O prudent Princess! bid thy soul confide. ....Od.16.453.129.
Just thy advice, (the prudent Chief rejoin'd) ....Od.17.216.142.
Amidst her maids thus spoke the prudent Queen, ...Od.17.596.161.
Who'er this guest (the prudent Queen replies) ....Od.17.664.164.
Your patrimonial wealth, a prudent heir. ....Od.19.26.193.
The prudent Queen the lofty stair ascends, ...Od.21.7.258.

PRUDENTLY
Suspecting fraud, more prudently remain'd. ....Od.10.267.355.

PRUDERY
What is Prudery? 'Tis a Beldam, ...6.70.1.201.

PRUDISH
But shou'd you catch the Prudish itch, ...6.61.43.182.

PRUDISHLY
[Tho' Christ-church long kept prudishly away.] ....5.DunB4.194.361.

PRUN'D
Prescrib'd her Heights, and prun'd her tender Wing, ...1.EOC.736.325.

PRUNE
Prune the luxuriant, the uncouth refine, ...4.2HE2.174.177.

PRUNELLA
The rest is all but leather or prunella. ....3.EOM4.204.146.

PRUNES

Where Contemplation prunes her ruffled Wings, ...4.JD4.186.41.
Here Contemplation prunes her ruffled Wings, ...4.JD4.186A.41.
There Contemplation prunes her ruffled Wings, ...4.JD4.186B.41.

PRUNING

Sometimes his Pruning-hook corrects the Vines, ...1.TrVP.37.378.

PRUNING-HOOK

Sometimes his Pruning-hook corrects the Vines, ...1.TrVP.37.378.

PRY

With Eyes that pry not, Tongue that ne'er repeats, ...4.HS1.135.19.
Into the woman-state asquint to pry; ......Od.19.82.196.

PRYING

Walk round and round, now prying here, now there; ......5.DunB4.353.377.

PRYMNEUS

The prize *Ocyalus* and *Prymneus* claim, ...Od.8.115.268.

PRYN

She saw old Pryn in restless Daniel shine, ...5.DunA1.101.71.
She saw old Pryn in restless Daniel shine, ...5.DunB1.103.276.

PRYTANIS

Alcander, Prytanis, Noëmon fell, ...Il.5.836.305.

PSALMS

Hopkins and Sternhold glad the heart with Psalms; ......4.2HE1.230.215.

PSI

Cou'd ne'er bring in *Psi* and *Xi;* ......6.30.69.88.

PSYRIAN

(The safer road) beside the *Psyrian* isle; ......Od.3.206.95.

PTELEON

Where *Æpy* high, and little *Pteleon* stand; ......Il.2.718.160.
And grassy *Pteleon* deck'd with chearful Greens, ...Il.2.849.164.

PTHIA

The third Day hence, shall *Pthia* greet our Sails, ...Il.9.473.455.
Pthia to her *Achilles* shall restore ......Il.9.475.456.
(Who now, perhaps, in *Pthia* dreads to hear ......Il.19.343.386.
Great in his *Pthia,* and his throne maintains; ......Od.11.606.413.

PTHIA'S

See PHTHIA'S.
To *Pthia's* Realms no hostile Troops they led; ......Il.1.201.96.
From *Pthia's* spacious Vales, and *Hella,* blest ......Il.2.831.164.
A peaceful Death in *Pthia's* friendly Land. ......Il.9.553.460.
The Royal *Peleus,* when from *Pthia's* Coast ......Il.9.566.461.
In *Pthia's* Court at last my Labours end. ......Il.9.599.464.
I, and *Ulysses,* touch'd at *Pthia's* Port, ...Il.11.904.76.

PTHIANS

Locrians and *Pthians,* and th' *Epæan* Force; ......Il.13.861.146.
The *Pthians Medon,* fam'd for martial Might, ...Il.13.867.147.
These rule the *Pthians,* and their Arms employ ......Il.13.875.147.

PUBLIC

And found the private in the public good. ......3.EOM3.282.121.
Or Public Spirit its great cure, a Crown. ......3.EOM4.172.144.
But grant, in Public Men sometimes are shown, ...3.Ep2.199.66.
Bred to disguise, in Public 'tis you hide; ......3.Ep2.203.67.
Men, some to Quiet, some to public Strife; ......3.Ep2.217.68.
Worn out in public, weary ev'ry care, ...3.Ep2.229.68.
Bid Harbors open, public Ways extend, ...3.Ep4.197.156.
Esteem the public love his best supply, ...4.1740.91.337.
His public virtue makes his title good. ......4.1740.96.337.
Or that, where on her Curlls the Public pours ......5.DunA2.3.97.
Or that where on her Curls the Public pours, ...5.DunB2.3.296.
Nor *public* Flame, nor *private,* dares to shine; ......5.DunB4.651.409.
Now make the wand'ring *Greek* their public care, ...Od.1.104.36.
No story I unfold of public woes, ...Od.2.49.62.
Do public or domestic cares constrain ......Od.4.423.140.
And public nuptials justify the bride. ......Od.6.346.228.
In public more than mortal he appears, ...Od.8.193.272.
With decent pride refutes a public wrong: ......Od.8.270.278.
A public treat, with jars of gen'rous wine. ......Od.19.229.204.
You join your suffrage to the public vote; ......Od.19.448.216.
Say, for the public did ye greatly fall? ......Od.24.139.354.

PUBLICK

And publick Faction doubles private Hate. ......1.EOC.457.290.
And feeds and thrives on Publick Miseries. ......1.TrSt.713.440.
Thus, in some publick *Forum* fix'd on high, ...2.ChJM.234.25.
To midnight dances, and the publick show? ......2.Elegy.58.367.
In publick Stations Men sometimes are shown, ...3.Ep2.199A.66.
An hour, and not defraud the Publick Weal? ......4.2HE1.6.195.
In ev'ry publick Virtue we excell, ...4.2HE1.45.197.
Why then I say, the Publick is a fool. ......4.2HE1.94.203.
And speak in publick with some sort of grace. ......4.2HE1.208.213.
Publick too long, ah let me hide my Age! ......4.1HE1.5.279.
To rowze the Watchmen of the Publick Weal, ...4.EpS2.217.325.
When black Ambition stains a Publick Cause, ...4.EpS2.228.325.
In busie Tumults, and in publick Cares, ...6.17ii.4.56.
And ev'ry Curse that loads a publick Life, ...6.17iii.17.58.
The Rage of Pow'r, the Blast of publick Breath, ...6.84.25.239.
Whose Publick Virtue knew no Party rage: ......6.134.2.364.
Our Cares are only for the Publick Weal: ......Il.1.146.94.
T'avenge a private, not a publick Wrong: ......Il.1.208.96.
Ulysses, first in publick Cares, she found, ...Il.2.205.138.
But some gay Dancer in the publick Show. ......Il.3.486.215.
Then, the sad Victim of the Publick Rage. ......Il.3.520.216.

PUBLICK (CONTINUED)

Unfit for publick Rule, or private Care; ......Il.9.89.437.
The King of Men, on publick Counsels bent, ...Il.9.121.438.
And ratify the best, for publick Good. ......Il.9.136.438.
Is more than Armies to the publick Weal. ......Il.11.637.62.
When *Elis'* Monarch at the publick Course ......Il.11.838.73.
When *Elis'* Monarch at the publick Course ......Il.11.838A.73.
There to high *Jove* were publick Thanks assign'd ......Il.11.894.75.
The publick Mart and Courts of Justice stand, ...Il.11.937.77.
To some great City thro' the publick way; ......Il.15.825.228.
And bade the Publick and the Laws decide: ......Il.18.580.350.
The King of Men shall rise in publick Sight, ...Il.19.173.378.
The rest in publick View the Chiefs dispose, ...Il.19.257.383.
Here, and in publick view, to meet my Fate. ......Il.21.670.450.
And in the publick woe forget your own; ......Od.1.451.54.
A private sorrow, not a publick cause. ......Od.3.99.91.
In publick sentence, or in private thought; ......Od.3.156.93.
Thro' the proud street she moves, the publick gaze; ......Od.7.3.232.
(The publick wonder, and the publick love) ......Od.7.91.238.
(The publick wonder, and the publick love) ......Od.7.91.238.
Large, and expressive of the publick love: ......Od.13.16.2.
For in the midst, with publick honours grac'd, ...Od.13.33.3.
And publick evil never touch the land! ......Od.13.61.4.
By publick bounty let him there be fed, ...Od.17.12.133.
Un-hous'd, neglected, in the publick way; ......Od.17.357.149.
Who publick structures raise, or who design; ......Od.17.463.155.
Scourge thro' the publick street, and cast thee there, ...Od.17.570.160.
One loss was private, one a publick debt: ......Od.21.20.259.

PUBLISH

Publish the present Age, but where my Text ......4.HS1.59.11.
But why then publish? *Granville* the polite, ...4.Arbu.135.105.
Should Dennis publish, you had stabb'd your Brother, ...6.116vii.1A.328.

PUBLISHER

Who's but a *Publisher* himself. ......6.116ii.9.326.

PUDDEN

And for his judgment lo a pudden! ......6.150.12.398.

PUDDING

Yet on plain Pudding deign'd at-home to eat; ......3.Ep2.82.57.
An added pudding solemniz'd the Lord's: ......3.Ep3.346.122.
Pudding, that might have pleas'd a Dean; ......4.HS6.166.261.
And solid pudding against empty praise. ......5.DunA1.52.66.
And solid pudding against empty praise. ......5.DunB1.54.274.

PUDDINGS

And lo! two puddings smoak'd upon the board. ......3.Ep3.360.123.

PUFF

For one puff more, and in that puff expires. ......3.Ep1.241.36.
For one puff more, and in that puff expires. ......3.Ep1.241.36.
Close on *Eumelus'* Back they puff the Wind, ...Il.23.457.508.

PUFF'D

That spreads and swells in puff'd Prosperity, ...4.HS2.126.65.
Sate full-blown *Bufo,* puff'd by ev'ry quill; ......4.Arbu.232.112.
Nor puff'd by Pride, nor sunk by Spleen. ......4.HS6.28.251.
And the puff'd Orator bursts out in tropes. ......5.DunA2.198.125.
And the puff'd orator bursts out in tropes. ......5.DunB2.206.306.
P protested, puff'd, and swore, ...6.30.27.86.

PUFFING

And puffing loud, the roaring Bellows blew. ......Il.18.438.341.

PUFFS

Puffs, Powders, Patches, Bibles, Billet-doux. ......2.RL1.138.156.

PUFT

For huffing, braggart, puft *Nobility?* ......4.JD4.201.43.

PUG

And no man wonders he's not stung by Pug: ......4.HS1.88.13.

PUKE

I puke, I nauseate,—yet he thrusts in more; ......4.JD4.153.37.

PULL

When, of a hundred thorns, you pull out one? ......4.2HE2.321.187.
Maul the *French* Tyrant, or pull down the Pope! ......6.128.18.356.
Nor pull th' unwilling Vengeance on thy Head, ...Il.15.36.195.
And pull descending vengeance from on high. ......Od.15.349.86.

PULL'D

The silver ring she pull'd, the door re-clos'd; ......Od.1.552.58.

PULLET

Buy every Pullet they afford to eat. ......4.2HE2.243.183.

PULLS

He pulls ripe Apples from the bending Boughs. ......1.TrVP.40.378.
Forsakes the staple as she pulls the ring; ......Od.21.48.261.

PULPIT

The gracious Dew of Pulpit Eloquence; ......4.EpS1.69.303.
Safe from the Bar, the Pulpit, and the Throne, ...4.EpS2.210.325.

PULPITS

Pulpits their *Sacred Satire* learn'd to spare, ...1.EOC.550.302.

PULSE

Where, as she try'd his Pulse, he softly drew ......2.ChJM.414.35.
Nor pray'rs nor fasts its stubborn pulse restrain, ...2.ElAb.27.321.
No pulse that riots, and no blood that glows. ......2.ElAb.252.340.
Till ev'ry motion, pulse, and breath, be o'er; ......2.ElAb.333.346.

PULSE (CONTINUED)

If Cotta liv'd on pulse, it was no more ....3.Ep3.185.109.
"Or when my pulse beat highest, ask for any ....4.HAdv.91.83.
Nor moves my Pulse, nor heaves my Heart, ...6.31ii.6Z4.94.
A Pulse unusual flutters at my Heart. ....II.22.581.480.

PULSES

Again his Pulses beat, his Spirits rise; ....II.15.272.207.
And his breath lengthens, and his pulses beat; ....Od.24.408.368.

PULT'NEY

How can I PULT'NEY, CHESTERFIELD forget, ...4.EpS2.84.317.
How many Martials were in PULT'NEY lost! ....5.DunB4.170.357.

PULTENEY

Inflam'd by P[ulteney], or by P[ulteney] dropt; ....4.1740.32.333.
Inflam'd by P[ulteney], or by P[ulteney] dropt; ....4.1740.32.333.
The first firm P[ultene]y soon resign'd his breath, ...4.1740.77.336.

PULTENEY'S

Thro' Clouds of Passion P[ulteney]'s views are clear, ...4.1740.9.332.

PUMPINGS

Our purgings, pumpings, blanketings and blows? ....5.DunA2.146.119.
Our purgings, pumpings, blankettings, and blows? ....5.DunB2.154.303.

PUMPS

Me, naked me, to Posts, to Pumps they draw, ...4.HAdv.173.89.
With Staff and Pumps the Marquis lead the Race; ....5.DunB4.586.400.

PUN

Alike to them, by Pathos or by Pun. ....4.2HE1.295.221.
Alas, like Shutz I cannot pun ....6.61.22.181.

PUNCTUAL

Religious, punctual, frugal, and so forth; ....3.Ep3.343.122.

PUNGENT

The pungent Grains of titillating Dust. ....2.RL5.84.207.

PUNISH

To punish these, see *Jove* himself descend! ....1.TrSt.316.423.
And what rewards your Virtue, punish mine. ....3.EOM4.144.141.
See! sportive fate, to punish aukward pride, ...3.Ep4.19.138.
Then, lest Repentence punish such a Life, ...4.HAdv.104.83.
Oh punish him, or to th' Elysian shades ....5.DunB4.417.382.
Give me, great *Jove!* to punish lawless Lust, ...II.3.433.212.
Loth as thou art to punish lawless Lust, ...II.4.43.223.
To punish *Troy* for slighted Sacrifice; ....II.5.225.278.
When *Jove* to punish faithless Men prepares, ...II.7.253.376.
'Tis thine to punish; ours to grieve alone. ....II.8.577.424.
Descends, to punish unrelenting Men. ....II.9.636.466.
And punish us unkindly by his death? ....Od.2.375.78.
Due pains shall punish then this slave's offence, ...Od.17.290.146.
Sent me (to punish my pursuit of gain) ....Od.17.509.157.
To curb wild riot and to punish wrong? ....Od.17.623.162.
Should I not punish that opprobrious tongue; ....Od.18.431.189.
Potent to punish what he cannot praise. ....Od.19.108.197.

PUNISH'D

So was I punish'd, as if full as *proud,* ....4.JD4.19.27.
And punish'd him that put it in his way. ....4.2HE2.26.167.
Plagu'd with his Pride, and punish'd for his Lust. ....II.2.292.141.
Jove hated *Greece,* and punish'd *Greece* in thee! ....Od.11.688.418.

PUNISHES

The pain of anger punishes the fault: ....Od.17.17.133.

PUNISHMENT

What Punishment all this must follow? ....6.101.25.290.
Th' offence was great, the punishment was just. ....Od.24.527.373.

PUNK

The mighty *Czar* what mov'd to wed a Punk? ....3.Ep1.83A.21.
Why risk the world's great empire for a Punk? ....3.Ep1.83.21.
And now the Punk applaud, and now the Fryer. ....3.Ep1.191.31.
Proud as a Peéress, prouder as a Punk; ....3.Ep2.70.56.
Or for a Titled Punk, or Foreign Flame, ...4.1HE6.124.245.
Slave to a Wife or Vassal to a Punk, ...4.1HE1.62.283.
All melted down, in Pension, or in Punk! ....5.DunB4.510.392.
To bawd for others, and go Shares with Punk. ....6.49i.26.138.

PUNS

In Puns, or Politicks, or Tales, or Lyes, ...4.Arbu.321.119.
Old puns restore, lost blunders nicely seek, ...5.DunA1.163.82.
To lands, that flow with clenches and with puns: ....5.DunA1.252.93.
All arm'd with points, antitheses and puns! ....5.DunA1.251Z2.93.
Light-arm'd with Points, Antitheses, and Puns. ....5.DunB1.306.292.
Their Quibbles routed, and defy'd their Puns; ....6.128.12.356.

PUNTS

Or when a Duke to Jansen punts at White's, ...4.JD2.88.141.

PUNY

A puny insect, shiv'ring at a breeze! ....3.Ep4.108.148.

PUPIL

Whore, Pupil, and lac'd Governor from France. ....5.DunB4.272.370.
From the pierc'd pupil spouts the boiling blood; ....Od.9.462.325.

PUPILS'

Till Isis' Elders reel, their Pupils' sport; ....5.DunA3.333.191.
'Till Isis' Elders reel, their pupils' sport, ...5.DunB3.337.336.

PUPPET

And, as the Prompter breathes, the Puppet squeaks; ....4.Arbu.318.118.

PUPPETS

Such painted Puppets, such a varnish'd Race ....4.JD4.208.43.
The gilded Puppets dance and mount above, ...4.JD2.18.133.

PUPPETTS

In Organs thus the mounting Puppetts move ....4.JD2A.19.134.

PUPPIES

Ward try'd on Puppies, and the Poor, his Drop; ....4.2HE1.182.211.
Then number'd with the puppies in the mud. ....5.DunB2.308.310.
The names of these blind puppies as of those. ....5.DunB2.310.310.
The name of these blind puppies than of those. ....5.DunB2.310A.310.

PUPPY

Nor like a Puppy daggled thro' the Town, ...4.Arbu.225.112.
Will cure the arrant'st Puppy of his Pride. ....4.1HE1.60.283.
Became when seiz'd, a Puppy, or an Ape. ....5.DunA2.122.111.
Became, when seiz'd, a puppy, or an ape. ....5.DunB2.130.301.
Like Puppy tame that uses ....6.58.18.171.
Court Puppy tame that uses ....6.58.18A.171.
Can hope a Puppy of my Race. ....6.135.68.369.

PUPPYES

Before my Puppyes set your Beef, ...6.135.49A.368.

PURCHAS'D

A Park is purchas'd, but the Fair he sees ....3.Ep2.39.53.
The rest they purchas'd at their proper Cost, ...II.7.566.392.
The Prizes purchas'd by their winged Speed) ....II.9.164.440.
The Prizes purchas'd by their winged Speed) ....II.9.351.450.
And thus due Honours purchas'd to his Shade. ....II.17.182.294.
The ground himself had purchas'd with his pain, ...Od.24.236.360.

PURCHASE

But if the Purchase costs so dear a Price, ...2.TemF.515.289.
You purchase Pain with all that Joy can give, ...3.Ep2.99A.58.
Who purchase Pain with all that Joy can give, ...3.Ep2.99.58.
His wealth, to purchase what he ne'er can taste? ....3.Ep4.4.134.
Oh! when rank Widows purchase luscious nights, ...4.JD2.87A.141.
And when rank Widows purchase luscious nights, ...4.JD2.87.141.
You purchase as you want, and bit by bit; ....4.2HE2.237.181.
An easie Purchase, but an ample Gain! ....6.17iii.11.58.
A hundred Beeves the shining Purchase bought. ....II.6.295.341.
Grant him, like me, to purchase just Renown, ...II.6.606.356.
The Purchase Infamy, and Life the Price! ....II.13.150.111.
Envy will own, the purchase dearly paid. ....Od.4.96.124.
The worthy purchase of a foreign lord. ....Od.15.421.89.

PURCHASES

But when he purchases, it were not fit ....4.JD2A.108.142.

PURE

Oh crown so constant and so pure a Fire! ....1.TrVP.105.381.
Whether pure Holiness inspir'd his Mind, ...2.ChJM.11.15.
But what so pure, which envious Tongues will spare? ....2.ChJM.43.17.
Pure let them be, and free from Taint of Vice; ....2.ChWB.38.58.
In pure good Will I took this jovial Spark, ...2.ChWB.263.69.
Boast the pure blood of an illustrious race, ...3.EOM4.207.146.
She sins with Poets thro' pure Love of Wit. ....3.Ep2.76.56.
Or in pure Equity (the Case not clear) ....4.HS2.171.69.
While pure Description held the place of Sense? ....4.Arbu.148.106.
"His French is pure; his Voice too—you shall hear— ....4.2HE2.7.165.
Serenely pure, and yet divinely strong, ...4.2HE2.172.177.
As pure a Mess almost as it came in; ....4.EpS2.176.323.
An hecatomb of pure, unsully'd lays ....5.DunA1.138.81.
An hecatomb of pure, unsully'd lays ....5.DunB1.158.282.
Now to pure Space lifts her extatic state, ...5.DunB4.33.343.
To breath the Sweets of pure Parnassian Air, ...6.26ii.2.79.
With that pure Stuff from whence we rose, ...6.53.12Z3.161.
For why? the Pure and Cleanly Maids ....6.54.17.165.
Victims so pure Heav'n saw well pleas'd ....6.69ii.3.199.
Ev'n Cart'ret and Meadows, so pure of desires, ...6.122.15.342.
Pure from a Barber or a *Benson's* Name. ....6.148ii.2A.395.
With pure Lustrations, and with solemn Pray'rs. ....II.1.411.107.
With pure Libations they conclude the Feast; ....II.1.615.117.
Yet o'er the silver Surface pure they flow, ...II.2.912.167.
Stains the pure Iv'ry with a lively Red; ....II.4.173.229.
Pure Emanation! uncorrupted Flood; ....II.5.423.288.
To the pure Skies these horrid Hands to raise, ...II.6.336.343.
Serv'd with pure Wheat, and by a Princess' Hand; ....II.8.231.408.
Pure from my Arms, and guiltless of my Loves, ...II.9.174.441.
Pure from his Arms, and guiltless of his Loves. ....II.9.361.451.
O'er Heav'ns pure Azure spread the growing Light, ...II.11.116.39.
Pure from his Arms, and guiltless of his Loves. ....II.19.176.379.
Pure and unconscious of my manly Loves. ....II.19.274.383.
The pure Libation, and the holy Feast. ....II.24.92.539.
With ten pure Talents from the richest Mine; ....II.24.286.548.
With frequent rites, and pure, avow'd thy pow'r, ...Od.1.81.35.
(Pure flav'rous wine, by Gods in bounty giv'n, ...Od.2.386.80.
He pour'd a pure libation to the ground. ....Od.8.86.267.
O'er heav'n's pure azure spread the growing light, ...Od.9.64.305.
Com'st thou alive from pure, ætherial day? ....Od.11.192.391.
In sev'n just portions, pure of hand and heart. ....Od.14.483.59.
To the pure regions of eternal light. ....Od.15.52.72.
With pure libations, and with solemn pray'r; ....Od.15.283.82.
Replenish'd from the pure, translucent springs; ....Od.17.105.137.
And the pure ivory o'er her bosom spreads. ....Od.18.228.178.
Some visitant of pure etherial race, ...Od.19.48.195.
(While pure libations crown'd the genial feast) ....Od.19.332.210.
With pious deed, and pure devotion, paid? ....Od.19.427.215.
From the pure flour (the growth and strength of man) ....Od.20.135.240.
And copious waters pure for bathing bear: ....Od.20.193.242.
A fate so pure, as by the martial sword? ....Od.22.496.313.

PURE (CONTINUED)
To him sev'n talents of pure ore I told, ... Od.24.320.365.

PURELY
While Fools have places purely for their Zeal. .... 6.82ix(d).2.235.

PURER
And purer Spirits swell the sprightly Flood, ... 1.W-F.94.159.
Our foaming Bowls with purer *Nectar* crown'd, ... 1.TrES.31A.450.
Sees by Degrees a purer Blush arise, ... 2.RL1.143.157.
While purer Slumbers spread their golden Wings) .... 2.TemF.8.253.
As into air the purer spirits flow, ... 2.Elegy.25.364.
And there the streams in purer rills descend? .... 3.EOM3.204.113.
Why drew Marseille's good bishop purer breath, ... 3.EOM4.107.138.
Exalted Souls, inform'd with purer Fire! .... 6.27.11.81.
To bless, whom Titan touch'd with purer Fire, ... 6.49iii.8.142.
Love's purer flames the Gods approve; .... 6.51ii.13.153.
Each purer frame inform'd with purer fire: .... 6.52.50.157.
Each purer frame inform'd with purer fire: .... 6.52.50.157.
Mix purer Wine, and open ev'ry Soul. .... Il.9.268.445.
Our foaming Bowls with purer Nectar crown'd, ... Il.12.375.95.
Strait from the direful coast to purer air .... Od.11.789.425.

PUREST
Seeks freshest Pasture and the purest Air, ... 1.Mes.50.117.
Some in the Fields of purest *Æther* play, ... 2.RL2.77.164.
On which a Shrine of purest Gold was rear'd; .... 2.TemF.197.271.
And ministers to Jove with purest hands; .... 5.DunA2.90.108.
And ministers to Jove with purest hands. .... 5.DunB2.94.300.
Purest love's unwasting treasure, ... 6.51ii.41.154.
Heav'n, as its purest Gold, by Tortures try'd; .... 6.115.9.323.
Ten weighty Talents of the purest Gold, ... Il.9.157.440.
Pray, in deep Silence, and with purest Hands. .... Il.9.226.444.
Ten weighty Talents of the purest Gold, ... Il.9.344.450.
Receive a Talent of the purest Gold. .... Il.23.938.526.
The purest Water of the living Spring; .... Il.24.372.551.
The purest product of the chrystal springs; .... Od.4.64.122.
Long flowing robes of purest white array .... Od.10.649.375.
He said: replenish'd from the purest springs, ... Od.19.450.216.

PURG'D
Not yet purg'd off, of Spleen and sow'r Disdain, ... 1.EOC.527.297.
They bled, they cupp'd, they purg'd; in short, they cur'd: .... 4.2HE2.193.179.
Have bled and purg'd me to a simple *Vote*. .... 4.2HE2.197.179.
Well-purg'd, and worthy Withers, Quarles, and Blome. .... 5.DunA1.126.78.
Well-purg'd, and worthy *W[esle]y, W[att]s,* and *Bl[ome]* .... 5.DunA1.126A.78.
Well-purg'd, *W[att]s, Q[uarle]s,* and *Bl[ome].* .... 5.DunA1.126B.78.
Well purg'd, and worthy Settle, Banks, and Broome. .... 5.DunB1.146.280.
But Purg'd shall be to Skin and Bone, ... 6.54.15.165.
O happy *Yahoo,* purg'd from human Crimes, ... 6.96iii.5.274.
He purg'd; and wash'd it in the running Stream. .... Il.16.279.249.
Wash'd with th' effusive wave, are purg'd of gore. .... Od.22.490.313.
He purg'd the walls and blood-polluted rooms. .... Od.22.530.314.

PURGATORY
For here on Earth I was his Purgatory. .... 2.ChWB.238.68.
I've had my *Purgatory* here betimes, ... 4.JD4.5.27.

PURGE
He from thick Films shall purge the visual Ray, ... 1.Mes.39.116.
To purge and let thee blood, with fire and sword, ... 4.1740.15.332.
Purge all your verses from the sin of wit .... 6.82ix(f).2.235.
Smiles on the Vomit, and enjoys the Purge. .... 6.82x.6.236.
Yet more, from mortal Mists I purge thy Eyes, ... Il.5.164.274.
To purge the palace: then the Queen attend, ... Od.22.519.314.

PURGES
The dome he purges, now the flame aspires; .... Od.23.52.321.

PURGINGS
Our purgings, pumpings, blanketings and blows? .... 5.DunA2.146.119.
Our purgings, pumpings, blankettings, and blows? .... 5.DunB2.154.303.

PURIFY
With Water purify their Hands, and take .... Il.1.586.116.
To wash, to scent, and purify the room. .... Od.22.475.312.

PURIFY'D
Go, purify'd by flames ascend the sky, ... 5.DunB1.227.286.

PURITY
What guards the Purity of melting Maids, ... 2.RL1.71.151.
Then from the rites of purity repair, ... Od.4.299.133.
The friendly rite of purity declin'd; .... Od.19.439.216.

PURL
Louder and louder purl the falling Rills, ... Il.21.296.433.

PURLING
Of painted Meadows, and of purling Springs. .... 2.ChJM.455.37.
The whisp'ring Zephyr, and the purling rill? .... 3.EOM1.204.40.
A painted Mistress, or a purling Stream. .... 4.Arbu.150.107.
She went, to plain-work, and to purling brooks, ... 6.45.11.125.

PURPLE
And lavish Nature paints the Purple Year? .... 1.PSp.28.63.
And fleecy Clouds were streak'd with Purple Light; .... 1.PAu.14.81.
Ev'n the wild Heath displays her Purple Dies, ... 1.W-F.25.150.
His Purple Crest, and Scarlet-circled Eyes, ... 1.W-F.116.161.
She saw her Sons with purple Deaths expire, ... 1.W-F.323.180.
There purple *Vengeance* bath'd in Gore retires, ... 1.W-F.417.193.
Is like a Clown in regal Purple drest; .... 1.EOC.321.275.
These bright, like gold, and those with purple shine; .... 1.TrPA.72.368.
No more my Robes in waving Purple flow, ... 1.TrSP.81.397.
Where treach'rous *Scylla* cut the Purple Hairs: .... 1.TrSt.469.429.
Embroider'd Purple cloaths the Golden Beds; .... 1.TrSt.607.435.

PURPLE (CONTINUED)
Whose Purple Rays th' *Achæmenes* adore; .... 1.TrSt.858.446.
And Hills where Vines their Purple Harvest yield? .... 1.TrES.30.450.
And the Soul issu'd in the Purple Flood. .... 1.TrES.321.461.
Their Webs Divine of Purple mix'd with Gold. .... 1.TrUl.38.467.
His Purple Pinions opening to the Sun, ... 2.RL2.71.164.
Pale Spectres, gaping Tombs, and Purple Fires: .... 2.RL4.44.187.
The pois'nous Vapor blots the purple Skies, ... 2.TemF.340.280.
And swam to Empire thro' the purple Flood. .... 2.TemF.347.280.
Where slumber Abbots, purple as their wines: .... 5.DunB4.302.373.
And there in autumn's richest purple dy'd. .... 6.35.25.103.
'Till some new Tyrant lifts his purple hand, ... 6.51i.23.152.
And *Arnè* rich, with purple Harvests crown'd; .... Il.2.606.156.
And *Sangar's* Stream ran purple with their Blood. .... Il.3.250.204.
The Purple Cuishes clasp his Thighs around, ... Il.3.411.212.
The golden Goblet crowns with Purple Wine: .... Il.4.4.221.
And raz'd the Skin and drew the Purple Gore. .... Il.4.169.229.
And *Discord* raging bathes the purple Plain: .... Il.4.501.244.
Down sunk the Priest: the Purple Hand of Death .... Il.5.108.272.
The purple Current wand'ring o'er his Vest. .... Il.5.145.274.
And dyes the Ground with Purple as he goes. .... Il.5.851.306.
And dyes the Ground in Purple as he goes. .... Il.5.851A.306.
On either side run purple to the Main. .... Il.6.6.322.
A radiant Belt that rich with Purple glow'd. .... Il.7.369.382.
And tipt the Mountains with a purple Ray. .... Il.7.501.389.
His Purple Robe, bright Ensign of Command. .... Il.8.269.410.
Till the bright Morn her purple Beam displays: .... Il.8.634.426.
And plac'd in Seats with purple Carpets spread. .... Il.9.266.445.
His purple Mantle golden Buckles join'd, ... Il.10.152.8.
Where e'er he pass'd, a purple Stream pursu'd; .... Il.10.560.27.
This, while yet warm, distill'd the purple Flood; .... Il.11.345.50.
A sudden Storm the purple Ocean sweeps, ... Il.11.385.51.
Steeps Earth in purple, gluts the Birds of Air, ... Il.11.503.56.
And dashing purple all the Car before, ... Il.11.659.63.
And Hills where Vines their purple Harvest yield, ... Il.12.374.95.
Life's purple Tyde, impetuous, gush'd away. .... Il.13.557.133.
The Waves just heaving on the purple Deeps; .... Il.14.22.158.
With Clouds of Gold and Purple circled round. .... Il.15.175.203.
Shorn from the Crest, the purple Honours glow. .... Il.15.635.220.
Of Sacrifice, the purple Draught he pour'd .... Il.16.282.250.
And the Soul issu'd in the purple Flood. .... Il.16.626.268.
O'er the dark Clouds extends his Purple Bow, ... Il.17.617.312.
His purple Garments, and his golden Hairs, ... Il.18.29.325.
Soon as the Morn the purple Orient warms .... Il.18.353.338.
(With purple Fillets round her braided Hair) .... Il.18.450.342.
The purple Product of th' Autumnal Year. .... Il.18.660.355.
The purple Death comes floating o'er his Eyes. .... Il.20.552.417.
And the warm Purple circled on the Tyde. .... Il.21.27.422.
The gushing Purple dy'd the thirsty Sand: .... Il.21.132.427.
And a Foam whitens on the purple Waves. .... Il.21.381.436.
And the red Vapours purple all the Sky. .... Il.21.610.447.
Purple the Ground, and streak the sable Sand; .... Il.22.507.477.
With Purple soft, and shaggy Carpets spread; .... Il.24.813.571.
The golden Vase in purple Palls they roll'd, ... Il.24.1005.577.
(A purple carpet spread the pavement wide) .... Od.1.173.40.
The gold gave lustre to the purple draught. .... Od.1.188.42.
With purple robes inwrought, and still with gold, ... Od.1.212.43.
When next the morning warms the purple east, ... Od.1.354.49.
The duteous dame receiv'd the purple vest: .... Od.1.550.58.
The purple vest with decent care dispos'd, ... Od.1.551.58.
In solid gold the purple vintage flows, ... Od.4.67.122.
His face he shrowded with his purple vest: .... Od.4.152.127.
His purple garment veil'd the falling tear. .... Od.4.208.129.
His limbs in military purple dress'd; .... Od.4.345.136.
And o'er soft palls of purple grain unfold .... Od.4.405.139.
Soon as the morn, in orient purple drest, ... Od.4.411.140.
When purple light shall next suffuse the skies, ... Od.4.550.146.
With purple clusters blushing thro' the green. .... Od.5.89.176.
Behind him far, upon the purple waves .... Od.5.592.201.
While with the purple orb the spindle glows. .... Od.6.370.229.
And there in autumn's richest purple dy'd. .... Od.7.166.244.
Bids her fair train the purple quilts prepare, ... Od.7.429.258.
Before his eyes the purple vest he drew, ... Od.8.81.267.
Strong were the Rams, with native purple fair, ... Od.9.505.326.
Whose purple lustre glow'd against the view: .... Od.10.418.364.
Then dy'd the sheep; a purple torrent flow'd, ... Od.11.45.381.
Nor bounds the blood along the purple veins; .... Od.11.264.394.
There figs sky-dy'd, a purple hue disclose, ... Od.11.727.421.
Around the mansion flow'd the purple draught: .... Od.13.69.4.
Their webs divine of purple mix'd with gold. .... Od.13.129.8.
Eumæus pours on high the purple tide; .... Od.14.135.42.
Atrides' son the purple draught prepares. .... Od.15.157.76.
Or foam the goblet with a purple stream. .... Od.15.341.86.
His mouth and nostrils spout a purple flood, ... Od.18.116.172.
With purple juice, and bore in order round; .... Od.18.469.191.
A robe of military purple flow'd .... Od.19.262.207.
A mantle purple-ting'd, and radiant vest, ... Od.19.275.208.
Up-rising early with the purple morn, ... Od.19.365.212.
Soon as the morn, new-rob'd in purple light, ... Od.19.499.220.
His further flank with streaming purple dy'd: .... Od.19.530.221.
So, when the sun restores the purple day, ... Od.19.674.229.
Thus, whilst *Aurora* mounts her purple throne, ... Od.20.110.238.
A radiant sabre grac'd his purple zone, ... Od.20.157.241.
The seats with purple cloathe in order due; .... Od.20.188.242.
By sage *Eumæus* born: the purple tide .... Od.20.318.248.
And cast his purple garment on the ground. .... Od.21.124.264.
Thongs of tough hides, that boast a purple dye; .... Od.23.204.333.
Full fifty purple figs; and many a row .... Od.24.397.368.

PURPLE-TING'D
A mantle purple-ting'd, and radiant vest, ... Od.19.275.208.

PURPLED
The Sun first rises o'er the purpled Main, ... 2.RL2.2.159.
The purpled Shore with Mountains of the Dead, ... Il.1.320.103.
'Till rosie Morn had purpled o'er the Sky: .... Il.1.623.117.

PURPLED 158 PURSUIT

PURPLED (CONTINUED)
With rosie lustre purpled o'er the lawn; ....Od.3.517.112.
With rosy lustre purpled o'er the lawn; ....Od.3.624.118.
The snowy fleece, or twist the purpled wool. ....Od.6.64.208.
'Till ruddy morning purpled o'er the east. ....Od.9.653.333.

PURPOS'D
From me the purpos'd voyage to conceal: ....Od.4.967.163.
So may the God reverse his purpos'd will, ...Od.13.212.15.
The purpos'd deed, and guards the bolted doors: ....Od.19.34.194.

PURPOSE
(This by the Way, but to my Purpose now.) ....2.ChWB.376.75.
A thousand movements scarce one purpose gain; ....3.EOM1.54.20.
The whole strange purpose of their lives, to find ....3.EOM4.221.148.
The first, last purpose of the human soul; ....3.EOM4.338.161.
Fair to no purpose, artful to no end, ...3.Ep2.245.70.
To no more purpose, than when pris'ners swear ....4.JD2A.78.138.
'Tis to small purpose that you hold your tongue, ...4.2HE2.155.175.
The nearer to its End, or Purpose, home. ....6.17i(a).6.55.
Fair to no Purpose, artful to no End, ...6.86.7A.245.
Thy Words express the Purpose of thy Heart, ...Il.7.433.386.
Let *Greece* then know, my Purpose I retain, ...Il.9.410.452.
Its stubborn Purpose, and his Friends disdains. ....Il.9.742.471.
Stand off, approach not, but thy Purpose tell. ....Il.10.93.6.
Or if the Purpose of thy Heart thou vent, ...Il.12.271.91.
Severely bent his Purpose to fulfill, ...Il.15.100.200.
But fix'd remains the Purpose of his Soul: ....Il.22.127.458.
And the stern purpose of his Mind unfolds. ....Il.23.8.486.
And thus the purpose of his Gift declares. ....Il.23.706.517.
And shake the Purpose of my Soul no more. ....Il.24.719.567.
And then the purpose of thy soul declare. ....Od.1.164.40.
As suits the purpose of th' eternal will. ....Od.8.624.296.
Heav'n's stedfast purpose, and thy future fates. ....Od.11.121.387.
The stedfast purpose of th' Almighty will. ....Od.11.364.400.
His purpose when the gen'rous warrior heard, ...Od.15.108.74.
The last I purpose in your walls to rest: ....Od.15.327.85.
Who smooth of tongue, in purpose insincere, ...Od.18.199.176.
To thee the purpose of my soul I told, ...Od.19.111.198.
Declare thy purpose; for thy will is Fate. ....Od.24.546.374.

PURPOSELY
By *Chance* go right, they *purposely* go wrong; ....1.EOC.427.288.

PURSE
If poor (you say) she drains her Husband's Purse; ....2.ChWB.86.60.
Want with a full, or with an empty purse? ....3.Ep3.320.120.
One bleeds in Person, and one bleeds in Purse; ....4.HAdv.58.81.
Had dearly earn'd a little purse of Gold: ....4.2HE2.34.167.
But fill their purse, our Poet's work is done, ...4.2HE1.294.221.
Who proud of Pedigree, is poor of Purse) ....4.1HE6.84.243.
He chinks his purse, and takes his seat of state: ....5.DunA2.189.124.
He chinks his purse, and takes his seat of state: ....5.DunB2.197.305.
May 'these put Money in your Purse, ...6.147v.1.391.

PURSU'D
Pursu'd her Flight; her Flight increas'd his Fire. ....1.W-F.184.167.
He sate, pursu'd by all his flocks of sheep. ....1.TrPA.42.367.
The Spear, pursu'd by gushing Streams of Gore; ....1.TrES.126.454.
In bloody Fields pursu'd Renown in Arms. ....2.TemF.150.265.
Self-love forsook the path it first pursu'd, ...3.EOM3.281.121.
Her ev'ry turn with Violence pursu'd, ...3.Ep2.131.61.
Not meanly, nor ambitiously pursu'd, ...3.Ep3.221.111.
There sober Thought pursu'd th'amusing theme ....4.JD4.188.41.
"The little Scut he so pursu'd before, ...4.HAdv.138.87.
Her ev'ry Turn with Violence pursu'd, ...6.154.17.403.
The Foe prevailing, and his Friends pursu'd, ...Il.5.213.277.
And undissembled Gore pursu'd the Wound. ....Il.5.261.279.
Flush'd with Celestial Blood pursu'd his way, ...Il.5.525.294.
And dry'd the falling Drops, and thus pursu'd. ....Il.6.623.357.
Where e'er he pass'd, a purple Stream pursu'd; ....Il.10.560.27.
Perhaps, ev'n now pursu'd, they seek the Shore; ....Il.10.634.30.
As swift *Atrides,* with loud Shouts pursu'd, ...Il.11.221.45.
Molion, the Charioteer, pursu'd his Lord, ...Il.11.417.53.
The Dart a Tyde of spouting Gore pursu'd, ...Il.11.576.60.
In some wide Field by Troops of Boys pursu'd, ...Il.11.683.65.
The Faulchion strook, and Fate pursu'd the Stroke; ....Il.12.222.89.
The Spear, pursu'd by gushing Streams of Gore; ....Il.12.480.99.
Like frighted Fawns from Hill to Hill pursu'd, ...Il.13.143.111.
So *Greece,* that late in conq'ring Troops pursu'd. ....Il.15.314.209.
The God pursu'd her, urg'd, and crown'd his Fire. ....Il.16.221.248.
Pursu'd the Pleasures of the wat'ry Reign; ....Il.18.110.328.
Then swift pursu'd her to the blest Abode, ...Il.21.589.446.
Then swift pursu'd her to her blest Abode, ...Il.21.589A.446*
(The Mighty fled, pursu'd by stronger Might) ....Il.22.206.464.
Her Walls thrice circled, and her Chief pursu'd. ....Il.22.318.469.
Merion pursu'd, at greater Distance still, ...Il.23.607.514.
Pursu'd for Murder, flies his native Clime) ....Il.24.591.561.
Pursu'd by Wrongs, by meagre Famine driv'n, ...Il.24.669.565.
As swift, the youth pursu'd the way she led; ....Od.3.40.88.
With storms pursu'd them thro' the liquid world. ....Od.5.138.178.
Thro' hell's black bounds I had pursu'd his flight, ...Od.11.694.419.
She strait pursu'd, and seiz'd my willing arm; ....Od.15.501.94.
The stranger-guest pursu'd him close behind; ....Od.17.84.136.
With him the youth pursu'd the goat or fawn, ...Od.17.354.149.
Of great *Atrides:* Him in pomp pursu'd ....Od.24.32.348.
With rival loves pursu'd his royal Dame; ....Od.24.147.355.
Heedless he whistled, and pursu'd his way. ....Od.24.309.364.
Five years have circled since these eyes pursu'd ....Od.24.361.366.

PURSUE
See PERSU, PERSUES.
(Beasts, urg'd by us, their Fellow Beasts pursue, ...1.W-F.123.162.
(Beasts, taught by us, their Fellow Beasts pursue, ...1.W-F.123A.162.
As did the God with equal Speed pursue. ....1.W-F.190A.167.
Envy will *Merit* as its *Shade* pursue, ...1.EOC.466.292.

PURSUE (CONTINUED)
With equal ardour did my love pursue; ....1.TrPA.10.365.
The Troops pursue their Leaders with Delight, ...1.TrES.55.451.
Yet you pursue sage *Solomon's* Advice, ...2.ChJM.151.21.
The dapper Elves their Moonlight Sports pursue; ....2.ChJM.460.37.
Where let us leave them, and our Tale pursue. ....2.ChJM.608.44.
Thro' all the giddy Circle they pursue, ...2.RL1.93.152.
Pursue the Stars that shoot athwart the Night, ...2.RL2.82.165.
And pleas'd pursue its Progress thro' the Skies. ....2.RL5.132.211.
No happier task these faded eyes pursue, ...2.ElAb.47.322.
The dear Ideas, where I fly, pursue, ...2.ElAb.264.341.
Pursue the triumph, and partake the gale? ....3.EOM4.386.165.
Pleasures the sex, as children Birds, pursue, ...3.Ep2.231.68.
B. Thrice happy man! enabled to pursue ....3.Ep3.275A.116.
"Thrice happy man! enabled to pursue ....3.Ep3.275.116.
Free as young Lyttelton, her cause pursue, ...4.1HE1.29.281.
Can they direct what measures to pursue, ...4.1HE1.122.287.
A poet made the silent wood pursue; ....6.3.11.7.
As children birds, so men their bliss pursue, ...6.22.5.71.
That, more than Heav'n pursue. ....6.50.16.146.
That Name the learn'd with fierce disputes pursue, ...6.71.17.203.
The Patriot's plain, but untrod path pursue; ....6.73.16.210.
Fame, and the Muse, pursue thee to the Shade. ....6.84.28B.239.
How quickly all the Sex pursue! ....6.119.18.337.
Calm to resolve, and constant to pursue. ....6.134.8.364.
Their Pray'rs perform'd, the Chiefs the Rite pursue, ...Il.2.502.150.
The mighty Labour dauntless I pursue: ....Il.2.583.155.
Meantime the *Greeks* the *Trojan* Race pursue, ...Il.5.49.268.
Pours on the *Greeks:* The *Trojan* Troops pursue: ....Il.5.723.302.
Doubtful if *Jove's* great Son he should pursue, ...Il.5.830.305.
Now swift pursue, now thunder uncontroll'd; ....Il.8.234.408.
Ev'n to the Royal Tent pursue my way, ...Il.10.385.21.
Soft, at just distance, both the Chiefs pursue. ....Il.10.418.21.
So close, so constant, the bold *Greeks* pursue. ....Il.10.432.23.
The joyful *Greeks* with loud Acclaim pursue. ....Il.10.665.31.
The King's Example all his *Greeks* pursue. ....Il.11.192.44.
Bold *Hector* and *Polydamas* pursue; ....Il.12.226.89.
The Troops pursue their Leaders with Delight, ...Il.12.399.96.
Themselves abandon'd, shall the Fight pursue, ...Il.14.111.163.
There saw the *Trojans* fly, the *Greeks* pursue, ...Il.15.8.194.
Full of the God; and all his Hosts pursue. ....Il.15.307.209.
So strong to fight, so active to pursue? ....Il.15.683.222.
So fears the Youth; all *Troy* with Shouts pursue, ...Il.15.708.223.
Thy melting Sorrows thus pursue thy Friend? ....Il.16.16.235.
Him, bold with Youth, and eager to pursue ....Il.16.725.272.
The bold Example all his Hosts pursue. ....Il.17.395.302.
And now to Conquest with like Speed pursue; ....Il.17.531.309.
Then swift pursue thee on the darksome way. ....Il.18.390.340.
She moves: Let *Pallas,* if she dares, pursue. ....Il.21.495.442.
With mortal Speed a Godhead to pursue? ....Il.22.16.453.
One to pursue, and one to lead the Chace, ...Il.22.258.466.
No vile Dishonour shall thy Corse pursue; ....Il.22.329.470.
Flies thro' the Dome, (the Maids her Steps pursue) ....Il.22.594.480.
And can ye still his cold Remains pursue? ....Il.24.46.537.
Boldly pursue the Journey mark'd by *Jove;* ....Il.24.366.551.
Fearless pursue the Journey mark'd by *Jove.* ....Il.24.386.552.
These, who with endless Hate thy Race pursue? ....Il.24.452.555.
He to thy palace shall thy steps pursue; ....Od.3.459.109.
With equal haste a menial train pursue: ....Od.4.48.122.
I've heard with pain, but oh! the tale pursue; ....Od.4.746.153.
Pursue their flight, but leave them safe to bound ....Od.9.139.311.
To *Sol's* bright Isle our voyage we pursue, ...Od.12.314.447.
Sheds her bright beam, pursue the destin'd way. ....Od.12.350.448.
Peasants in vain with threatning cries pursue, ...Od.15.182.77.
Whose pow'rful friends the luckless deed pursue ....Od.15.299.83.
When thus the Prince: Now each his course pursue; ....Od.15.541.96.
Of these, twice six pursue their wicked way, ...Od.22.462.310.

PURSUER
While a kind Glance at her Pursuer flies, ...1.PSp.59.66.

PURSUES
(That on weak Wings, from far, pursues your Flights; ....1.EOC.197.263.
(That with weak Wings, from far, pursues your Flights; ....1.EOC.197A.263.
Regardless, furious he pursues his way; ....1.TrES.19.450.
Pursues that Chain which links th'immense design, ...3.EOM4.333.161.
How easy ev'ry labour it pursues? ....4.HS2.83.61.
Shuns the permitted, the forbid pursues! ....4.HAdv.101.83.
Of all these ways, if each pursues his own, ...4.1HE1.134.289.
Charm'd with this Heat, the King his Course pursues, ...Il.4.310.235.
She gives th' Example, and her Son pursues. ....Il.5.1103.320.
The *Greek* pursues him, and exults aloud. ....Il.11.464.54.
Ev'n to the Ships victorious *Troy* pursues, ...Il.11.958.78.
Regardless, furious, he pursues his way; ....Il.12.363.94.
The Father of the Floods pursues his way; ....Il.13.58.107.
Lo! still he lives, pursues, and conquers still! ....Il.15.331.210.
Not long—For Fate pursues him, and the God. ....Il.16.965.280.
Breaks thro' the Ranks, and his Retreat pursues: ....Il.16.988.281.
The God pursues, a huger Billow throws, ...Il.21.278.432.
The certain Hound his various Maze pursues. ....Il.22.248.465.
While that but flies, and this pursues, in vain. ....Il.22.262.466.
Since Wisdom's sacred guidance he pursues, ...Od.8.423.286.
Thro' both, *Eurymachus* pursues the dame, ...Od.15.21.70.
There pass the night; while he his course pursues ....Od.15.47.72.
Forbear those acts which Infamy pursues; ....Od.21.358.277.

PURSUING
Swift as the wind before pursuing love; ....1.TrPA.65.368.
The track of friendship, not pursuing, sins. ....Od.24.333.365.

PURSUIT
Say, in pursuit of profit or delight, ...3.EOM4.85.136.
Swift in Pursuit, and active in the Fight. ....Il.2.633.157.
Skill'd in Pursuit, and swiftest in the Chace. ....Il.14.618.192.
Too long amus'd with a Pursuit so vain, ...Il.17.83.291.
Safe from Pursuit, and shut from mortal View, ...Il.21.707.451.

PURSUIT (CONTINUED)
Tempts his Pursuit, and wheels about the Shore. ....Il.21.716.451.
Some mean sea-farer in pursuit of gain; ....Od.8.180.272.
Sent me (to punish my pursuit of gain) ....Od.17.509.157.
Or if a merchant in pursuit of gain, ...Od.24.350.365.

PURSUITS
And all our Days in fresh Pursuits embroil. ....6.17iii.7.57.
On fond pursuits neglectful while you roam, ...Od.15.15.70.

PUSH'D
Self-love thus push'd to social, to divine, ...3.EOM4.353.162.
What push'd poor *Ellis* on th' Imperial Whore? ....4.HAdv.81.83.
And titt'ring push'd the Pedants off the place; ....5.DunB4.276.371.
Push'd at the Bank: Down sunk th' enormous Mound: ......Il.15.407.213.
She push'd her ling'ring Infant into Life: ....Il.19.116.376.
Wing'd her fleet sail, and push'd her o'er the tyde. ..Od.12.86.436.
Our floors with death, and push'd the slaughter on; ...Od.24.442.370.

PUT
Heav'n put it past your Doubt whene'er you wed, ...2.ChJM.279.27.
He put on careless Airs, and sat and sung. ....2.ChWB.240.68.
She bids her Footman put it in her head. ....3.Ep2.178.64.
And laugh at Peers that put their Trust in *Peter.* ....4.HS1.40.9.
He past it o'er; put on an easy Smile ....4.JD4.122A.35.
And punish'd him that put it in his way. ....4.2HE2.26.167.
This put the Man in such a desp'rate Mind, ...4.2HE2.37.167.
"Put my Lord Bolingbroke in mind, ...4.HS6.75.255.
Late as it is, I put my self to school, ...4.1HE1.47.281.
"To laugh at Fools who put their trust in *Peter.*" ...4.EpS1.10.297.
"Laugh at those Fools who put their trust in *Peter.*" .4.EpS1.10A.297.
But well may put some Statesmen in a fury. ....4.EpS1.52.302.
In this church he has put ....6.90.8.251.
In a Stewing pan put it. ....6.91.4.253.
Put no water at all; ....6.91.17.253.
Put this pot of Wood's mettle ....6.91.21.254.
Put your pot of Wood's mettle ....6.91.21A.254.
As far as Man could put it. ....6.94.44.260.
Stealing the Papers thence she put ....6.94.79.261.
She bids her Footman put it in her head. ....6.139.22.377.
May 'these put Money in your Purse, ...6.147v.1.391.
Consult our safety, and put off to sea. ....Od.9.267.317.
And with desponding hearts put off to sea. ....Od.10.88.343.
Old *Dolius* too his rusted arms put on; ....Od.24.574.375.

PUTRIFIE
So Waters putrifie with Rest, and lose ....6.17ii.9.56.

PUTS
Seizes your Fame, and puts his Laws in force. ....1.EOC.168.259.
"Who puts a Period to Domestick Strife! ....2.ChWB.191.65.
Now awful Beauty puts on all its Arms; ....2.RL1.139.156.
Puts forth one manly Leg, to sight reveal'd; ....2.RL3.57.172.
One thought of thee puts all the pomp to flight, ...2.ElAb.273.342.
The rising tempest puts in act the soul, ...3.EOM2.105.67.
For not in Chariots Peter puts his trust; ....4.JD2.74.139.
For not in Chariots Coscus puts his trust; ....4.JD2.74A.139.
Who fairly puts all Characters to bed: ....4.2HE1.291.221.
Puts his last refuge all in Heav'n and Pray'r. ....5.DunA2.206.127.
Puts his last refuge all in Heav'n in Pray'r. ....5.DunA2.206A.127.
Puts his last refuge all in heav'n and pray'r. ....5.DunB2.214.306.
And Jove with Joy puts off the *Bear.* ....6.80.4.224.
Why puts my Brother his bright Armour on? ....Il.10.42.4.

PUZZLES
For true No-meaning puzzles more than Wit. ....3.Ep2.114.59.

PUZZLING
Here puzzling Contraries confound the whole, ...3.Ep1.124A.25.
Or puzzling Contraries confound the whole, ...3.Ep1.124.25.

PYE
Wanton and wild, and chatter'd like a Pye. ....2.ChWB.210.66.
Here sighs a Jar, and there a Goose-pye talks; ....2.RL4.52.188.
Scarsdale his Bottle, *Darty* his Ham-Pye; ....4.HS1.46.9.
Who has not learn'd, fresh Sturgeon and Ham-pye ......4.HS2.103.61.
Who has not learn'd, fresh Sturgeon or Ham-pye ....4.HS2.103A.61.
An hundred Souls of Turkeys in a pye; ....5.DunB4.594.402.

PYEBALD
Peel'd, patch'd, and pyebald, linsey-woolsey brothers, ..5.DunA3.107.159.
Peel'd, patch'd, and pyebald, linsey-wolsey brothers, ...5.DunB3.115.325.

PYES
E're Coxcomb-pyes or Coxcombs were on earth? ....4.HS2.98.61.
Redeem'd from tapers and defrauded pyes, ...5.DunA1.136.80.

PYGMAEAN
Where, or the *Crane,* Foe to *Pygmæan* Race, ...6.26i.5.79.

PYGMY
To Pygmy-Nations Wounds and Death they bring, ...Il.3.9.188.

PYGMY-NATIONS
To Pygmy-Nations Wounds and Death they bring, ...Il.3.9.188.

PYKES
And Pykes, the Tyrants of the watry Plains. ....1.W-F.146.163.

PYLADES
My *Pylades!* what *Juv'nal* says, no Jest is; ....6.24iii(b).1.76.

PYLAEMENES
The *Paphlagonians Pylæmenes* rules, ...Il.2.1034.171.
First *Pylæmenes,* great in Battel, bled, ...Il.5.705.301.
And the bold Son of *Pylæmenes* slew. ....Il.13.804.143.

PYLARTES
Then sunk *Pylartes* to eternal Night; ....Il.16.855.276.

PYLE
For *Pyle* or *Elis* bound; but Tempests tost, ...1.TrUl.150.470.
Who builds a Bridge that never drove a pyle? ....4.2HE1.185.211.
Founds the whole pyle, of all his works the base; ....5.DunA1.140.81.
Heav'ns! what a pyle! whole ages perish there: ....5.DunA3.69.156.
And lay'd him decent on the Fun'ral Pyle; ....Il.6.529.353.
The State of *Pyle* was sunk to last Despair, ...Il.11.830.73.
Then back to *Pyle* triumphant take my way. ....Il.11.893.75.
Till on the Pyle the gather'd Tempest falls. ....Il.23.269.500.
Then sunk the Blaze, the Pyle no longer burn'd, ...Il.23.284.501.
Then parting from the Pyle he ceas'd to weep, ...Il.23.288.501.
Wide o'er the Pyle the sable Wine they throw, ...Il.23.311.502.
Of sandy *Pyle,* the royal Youth shall haste. ....Od.1.119.38.
Thro' the wide Ocean first to sandy *Pyle,* ....Od.1.369.50.
The realms of *Pyle* and *Sparta* to explore, ...Od.2.243.73.
Here, or in *Pyle.*—in *Pyle* or here, your foe. .....Od.2.356.78.
Here, or in *Pyle.*—in *Pyle* or here, your foe. .....Od.2.356.78.
To *Pyle* or *Sparta* to demand supplies. ....Od.2.368.78.
Now on the coast of *Pyle* the vessel falls, ...Od.3.5.86.
But now to *Pyle* permit my destin'd way, ...Od.4.817.157.
Unknowing of the course to *Pyle* design'd, ...Od.4.862.159.
When spread the Prince his sail for distant *Pyle?* ..Od.4.867.159.
From *Pyle* re-sailing and the *Spartan* court, ...Od.4.931.162.
His labour done, he fir'd the pyle that gave ....Od.9.295.318.
That in the tripod o'er the kindled pyle ....Od.10.423.365.
And, heap'd with various wealth, a blazing pyle: .....Od.10.623.374.
Rich with unnumber'd gifts the Pyle shall burn; ......Od.11.40.381.
Or say in *Pyle?* for yet he views the light, ...Od.11.567.411.
And the huge pyle along the shore ascends. ....Od.12.14.430.
For *Pyle* or *Elis* bound: but tempest tost ....Od.13.317.22.
And bade *Melanthius* a vast pyle prepare; ....Od.21.182.268.
Unnumber'd warriors round the burning pyle ....Od.24.87.352.
Thither his son from sandy *Pyle* repairs, ...Od.24.179.356.
Haste then, and ere to neighb'ring *Pyle* he flies, ..Od.24.495.372.

PYLENÈ
And rough *Pylenè,* and th' *Olenian* Steep ....Il.2.777.162.

PYLEUS
Hippothous bold, and *Pyleus* the Divine. ....Il.2.1021.171.

PYLIAN
Slow from his Seat arose the *Pylian* Sage; ....Il.1.330.103.
Cloath'd in the Figure of the *Pylian* Sage, ...Il.2.21.128.
In his black Ship the *Pylian* Prince he found, ...Il.2.65.130.
There rev'rend *Nestor* ranks his *Pylian* Bands, ...Il.4.336.236.
Encrease of Harvests to the *Pylian* Fields: ....Il.5.674.300.
Demand the Fight, To whom the *Pylian* Sage: ....Il.7.206.374.
The hoary Monarch of the *Pylian* Band, ...Il.8.114.403.
The Glory of the *Greeks,* the *Pylian* Sage. ....Il.8.122.404.
O prudent Chief! (the *Pylian* Sage reply'd) ....Il.10.162.9.
A Goblet sacred to the *Pylian* Kings, ...Il.11.773.69.
And Shares were parted to each *Pylian* Lord. ....Il.11.829.73.
Our utmost Frontier on the *Pylian* Lands, ...Il.11.847.74.
There, Horse and Foot, the *Pylian* Troops unite, ...Il.11.860.74.
And bear with haste the *Pylian* King's Reply: ....Il.11.975.78.
Fluctuates, in doubtful Thought, the *Pylian* Sage; ..Il.14.28.158.
When from the Ships he sent the *Pylian* Band. ....Il.17.439.304.
(Tho' sore distrest) to aid the *Pylian* Bands; ......Il.17.790.319.
With beating Heart, and chears his *Pylian* Horse. ...Il.23.370.505.
Known thro' *Buprasium* and the *Pylian* Shore! ......Il.23.724.519.
Next grant the *Pylian* states their just desires, ...Od.3.72.89.
The Prince, departing for the *Pylian* court, ...Od.4.855.159.
And god-like *Neleus* rul'd the *Pylian* plain: ......Od.11.312.397.
A friendly pair! near these the * *Pylian* stray'd, ..Od.11.577.412.
That thou safe sailing from the *Pylian* strand ......Od.15.49.72.
In words alone, the *Pylian* Monarch kind. ....Od.15.239.79.
To her the youth. We reach'd the *Pylian* plains, ...Od.17.124.137.

PYLIANS
Alarms the *Pylians,* and commands the Fight. ....Il.11.851.74.
Ætolians, Pylians, all resign'd the Day. ....Il.23.728.519.
At nine green Theatres the *Pylians* stood, ...Od.3.8.86.

PYLON
Next *Ormenus* and *Pylon* yield their Breath: ....Il.12.217.89.

PYLOS
The Nations meet; there *Pylos, Elis* here. ....Il.11.873.75.
The youth of *Pylos,* some on pointed wood ....Od.3.43.88.
But I to *Pylos* scud before the gales, ...Od.3.221.96.
The tow'rs of *Pylos* sink, its views decay, ...Od.3.616.117.
To sacred *Pylos* and to *Sparta* came. ....Od.5.29.172.
Great in *Orchomenos,* in *Pylos* great, ...Od.11.345.399.
To distant *Pylos* hapless is he gone, ...Od.14.208.45.
To *Pylos* soon they came; when thus begun ....Od.15.218.78.
(*Melampus,* who in *Pylos* flourish'd long, ...Od.15.253.80.
To *Pylos* drove the lowing herds along: ....Od.15.261.80.
That you to *Pylos* plow'd the wat'ry way, ...Od.16.153.110.
Has heav'n from *Pylos* brought my lovely boy? ....Od.17.53.135.

PYLOS'
(*Nestor,* whom *Pylos'* sandy Realms obey'd) ....Il.2.100.131.
In ninety Sail, from *Pylos'* sandy Coast, ...Il.2.715.160.
The whole Extent to *Pylos'* sandy Plain ....Il.9.201.442.
The whole Extent to *Pylos'* sandy Plain ....Il.9.388.452.

PYNE
"Bette is to pyne on Coals and Chalke, ...6.14i.25.42.

PYRAMID
A Marble Tomb and Pyramid shall raise, ...1.TrES.251.459.
His Friends a Tomb and Pyramid shall rear; ....1.TrES.333.461.

PYRAMID (CONTINUED)
A marble Tomb and Pyramid shall raise, ...Il.16.556.266.
His Friends a Tomb and Pyramid shall rear; ....Il.16.820.275.
Heap with a rising Pyramid the Plain. ....Il.23.201.497.

PYRAMIDS
There mingled Farms and Pyramids appear, ...4.2HE2.259.183.

PYRAMUS
And *Pyramus* and *Thisbe* plainly show ....2.ChJM.516.40.

PYRATE
P. But lures the Pyrate, and corrupts the Friend: ....3.Ep3.32A.88.
But lures the Pyrate, and corrupts the Friend: ....3.Ep3.32.88.
Sail in the *Ladies:* How each Pyrate eyes ....4.JD4.228.45.

PYRATES
Where savage Pyrates seek thro' seas unknown ....Od.3.88.90.
Pyrates perhaps, who seek thro' seas unknown ....Od.9.301.318.
Pyrates and conquerors, of harden'd mind, ...Od.14.103.41.
Their prize escap'd the faithless pyrates mourn'd; ....Od.14.389.53.
Rude Pyrates seiz'd, and shipp'd thee o'er the main? ....Od.15.419.89.
But snatch'd by pyrates from my native place, ...Od.15.468.93.
The *Taphian* pyrates on *Thesprotia's* shores; ....Od.16.445.128.
With roving pyrates o'er th' *Ægyptian* main: ....Od.17.510.157.
Did nightly thieves, or Pyrates cruel bands, ...Od.24.136.354.

PYRE
With tender *Billet-doux* he lights the Pyre, ...2.RL2.41.162.
Eliza stretch'd upon the fun'ral Pyre, ...2.TemF.206.272.
Quarto's, Octavo's, shape the less'ning pyre, ...5.DunA1.141.81.
Sudden she flies, and whelms it o'er the pyre: ....5.DunA1.215.89.
Quartos, octavos, shape the less'ning pyre; ....5.DunB1.161.282.
Sudden she flies, and whelms it o'er the pyre; ....5.DunB1.259.289.
No friendly Hand his fun'ral Pyre compose. ....Il.15.399.212.
Their Lives effus'd around thy flaming Pyre. ....Il.18.396.340.
Their Lives effus'd around thy fun'ral Pyre. ....Il.23.32.488.
Till on the Pyre I place thee; till I rear ....Il.23.55.489.
And let the Chiefs alone attend the Pyre; ....Il.23.197.497.
Pour forth their Lives, and on the Pyre are thrown. ....Il.23.211.498.
And cast the deep Foundations round the Pyre; ....Il.23.318.502.
(The self-same Place beside *Patroclus'* Pyre, ...Il.23.909.525.
And fell the Forests for a fun'ral Pyre. ....Il.24.986.576.
Again the mournful Crowds surround the Pyre, ...Il.24.1001.577.
Fierce o'er the Pyre, by fanning breezes spread, ...Od.12.17.430.
The pyre to build, the stubborn oak to rend; ....Od.15.339.86.

PYRECHMES
Pyrechmes the *Pæonian* Troops attend, ...Il.2.1028.171.
The great *Pæonian,* bold *Pyrechmes,* stood; ....Il.16.342.256.

PYRES
The Pyres thick-flaming shot a dismal Glare. ....Il.1.72.90.
And last, *Tlepolemus* and *Pyres* bleed. ....Il.16.509.262.

PYROUS
Next *Acamas* and *Pyrous* lead their Hosts ....Il.2.1022.171.

PYRRHA
"In vain he lov'd, relentless *Pyrrha* scorn'd; ....1.TrSP.194.402.
"*Deucalion* scorn'd, and *Pyrrha* lov'd in vain. ....1.TrSP.196.402.

PYRRHASUS
Sweet *Pyrrhasus,* with blooming Flourets crown'd, ...Il.2.851.164.

PYTHAGORAS'S
Worthy to fill Pythagoras's place: ....5.DunB4.572.399.

PYTHAGOREANS
Except the Sect of *Pythagoreans,* ....6.135.84.369.

PYTHAGORICK
No less than *Pythagorick Y,* ....6.30.73.88.

PYTHIAN
Not all *Apollo's* Pythian Treasures hold, ...Il.9.525.459.
Latona journey'd to the *Pythian* fanes, ...Od.11.716.421.

PYTHO
Where *Pytho, Daulis, Cyparissus* stood, ...Il.2.626.157.

PYTHON
When by a thousand Darts the *Python* slain ....1.TrSt.664.438.
Thy Hand slew *Python;* and the Dame who lost ....1.TrSt.849.445.

Q
And *Q* maintain'd 'twas but his Due ....6.30.15.86.

QUAAKE
Miss star'd; and gray Ducke crieth *Quaake.* ....6.14i.22.42.

QUACKS
Projectors, Quacks, and Lawyers not a few; ....2.TemF.463.286.
Despairing Quacks with curses fled the place, ...3.Ep3.273.115.

QUADRILLE
To spoil the nation's last great trade, Quadrille! ....3.Ep3.64.92.
Than ridicule all *Taste,* blaspheme *Quadrille,* ....4.HS1.38.7.

QUAE
Quaedam quae attinent ad Scriblerum, ...6.42v.3.119.

QUAEDAM
Quaedam quae attinent ad Scriblerum, ...6.42v.3.119.

QUAFF
Mean time, o'er all the dome, they quaff, they feast, ...Od.2.363.78.
To quaff thy bowls, or riot in thy feasts. ....Od.10.454.365.
They feed; they quaff; and now (their hunger fled) ....Od.12.363.448.

QUAFF'D
His quiv'ring limbs, and quaff'd his spouting gore. ....Od.2.26.61.
I took, and quaff'd it, confident in heav'n: ....Od.10.379.363.
Prolong'd the feast, and quaff'd the rosy wine: ....Od.10.565.369.
Eager he quaff'd the gore, and then exprest ....Od.11.124.387.
He quaff'd the gore: and strait his soldier knew, ...Od.11.485.408.
(Not unreveng'd) and quaff'd the spouting gore; ....Od.23.338.341.

QUAFFS
He Nectar quaffs, and *Hebe* crowns his joys. ....Od.11.746.423.

QUAIL
To clear my Quail-pipe, and refresh my Soul, ...2.ChWB.213.67.

QUAIL-PIPE
To clear my Quail-pipe, and refresh my Soul, ...2.ChWB.213.67.

QUAINT
Nor will with quaint Impertinence display ....2.ChJM.307.29.
How quaint an Appetite in Women reigns! ....2.ChWB.259.69.
Then thus in quaint Recitativo spoke. ....5.DunB4.52.346.

QUAK'D
I quak'd at heart; and still afraid to see ....4.JD4.180.41.

QUAKE
Armies quake, ...6.96i.24.268.

QUAKER
A Quaker? sly: A Presbyterian? sow'r: ....3.Ep1.108.23.
A simple Quaker, or a Quaker's Wife, ...4.EpS1.133.308.

QUAKER'S
A simple Quaker, or a Quaker's Wife, ...4.EpS1.133.308.
Or round a Quaker's Beaver cast a Glory. ....4.EpS2.97.318.

QUAKERS
So upright Quakers please both Man and God. ....5.DunB4.208.363.

QUAKING
The quaking mud, that clos'd, and ope'd no more. ....5.DunA2.280.136.
The quaking mud, that clos'd, and op'd no more. ....5.DunB2.292.310.

QUALITIES
First learn your Lady's Qualities at least: ....2.ChJM.185.23.
If second qualities for first they take. ....3.Ep1.211.33.
Yet sure, of qualities deserving praise, ...3.Ep3.202Z1.110.

QUALITY
That in *proud Dulness* joins with *Quality,* ....1.EOC.415.287.
That Robe of Quality so struts and swells, ...3.Ep2.189.65.
A Nymph of Quality admires our Knight; ....3.Ep3.385.124.
"I never touch a Dame of Quality." ....4.HAdv.70.81.
With Fool of Quality compleats the quire. ....5.DunB1.298.291.

QUARLES
One knighted Blackmore, and one pension'd Quarles; ....4.2HE1.387.227.
Well-purg'd, and worthy Withers, Quarles, and Blome. ....5.DunA1.126.78.
Well-purg'd, W[att]s, Q[uarle]s, and B[lome]. ....5.DunA1.126B.78.
And Quarles is sav'd by Beauties not his own. ....5.DunB1.140.280.

QUARREL
With equal Rage their airy Quarrel try, ...1.TrSt.490.430.
Glad of a quarrel, strait I clap the door, ...4.Arbu.67.100.
Glad of a quarrel, strait I clapt the door, ...4.Arbu.67A.100.
"We shall not quarrel for a year or two; ....4.2HE1.61.199.
A single verse, we quarrel with a friend; ....4.2HE1.365.227.
The drivers quarrel, and the master stares. ....4.1740.74.336.
Quarrel with *Dryden* for a Strumpet, ...6.10.85.27.
Should the *Greek* quarrel too, by *Styx,* I ....6.30.68.88.
And bravest Chiefs, in *Helen's* Quarrel slain, ...Il.2.197.137.
Perhaps their Sword some nobler Quarrel draws, ...Il.3.309.208.
But what's the Quarrel then of *Greece* to *Troy?* ....Il.9.445.454.
If when the sword our country's quarrel draws, ...Od.17.558.159.
Midst heaps of heroes in thy quarrel slain: ....Od.24.54.350.

QUARREL'D
"Have brawl'd, and quarrel'd more, ...6.79.86.220.
"Have bawl'd, and quarrel'd more, ...6.79.86A.220.

QUARRELLS
Fights and subdues in quarrells not her own. ....6.43.8.120.

QUARRELS
What mighty Quarrels rise from trivial Things, ...2.RL1.2A.144.
The wretched Quarrels of the mortal State ....Il.1.742.123.

QUARRIES
The wall was stone from neighbouring quarries born, ...Od.14.13.35.

QUARRY
The whole, a labour'd Quarry above ground. ....3.Ep4.110.148.
The stately Quarry on the Cliffs lay dead, ...Il.4.140.227.
Her Quarry seen, impetuous at the Sight, ...Il.13.92.109.

QUART
Consult the Statute: *quart.* I think it is, ...4.HS1.147.19.
See Anno quart. of Edward, third. ....6.67.12.195.

QUARTER 161 QUEEN

QUARTER
The Fool whose Wife elopes some thrice a quarter, ...4.1HE1.150.291.
Poor *Ovid* finds no Quarter! ....6.58.42.172.
In ev'ry Quarter fierce *Tydides* rag'd, ...Il.5.111.272.
That Quarter most the skillful *Greeks* annoy, ...Il.6.550.354.
The Beast they quarter, and the Joints divide, ...Il.7.383.382.
(For *Nestor's* Influence best that Quarter guides; ....Il.10.67.5.
Where stand his Coursers? In what Quarter sleep ....Il.10.479.25.
To watch this Quarter my Adventure falls, ...Il.24.491.556.
Or to what quarter now we turn our eyes, ...Od.10.217.350.
And guard each quarter as the tempest blow. ....Od.14.591.65.

QUARTER'D
Whose Place is *quarter'd out,* three Parts in four, ...4.JD4.136.37.
These quarter'd, sing'd, and fix'd on forks of wood, ...Od.14.88.40.

QUARTERS
Salute the diff'rent Quarters of the Sky. ....2.TemF.68.257.
From diff'rent Quarters fill the crowded Hall: ....2.TemF.279.277.
From diff'rent Quarters sweep the sandy Plain; ....Il.13.425.126.

QUARTO'S
Quarto's, Octavo's, shape the less'ning pyre, ...5.DunA1.141.81.

QUARTOS
Quartos, octavos, shape the less'ning pyre; ....5.DunB1.161.282.

QUAV'RING
With quav'ring cries the vaulted roofs resound: ....Od.20.222.244.

QUE
" *Que ça est bon! Ah goutez ça!* .... 4.HS6.203.263.

QUEAN
The scolding Quean to louder Notes doth rise, ...6.14ii.23.43.

QUEEN
As bright a Goddess, and as chast a Queen; ....1.W-F.162.164.
Once more to bend before a *British* QUEEN. ....1.W-F.384.189.
Great queen of love! how boundless is thy sway; ....1.TrPA.13.366.
Ulysses' Queen, nor *Helen's* fatal Charms. ....1.TrVP.72.380.
He said; and thus the Queen of Heav'n return'd; ....1.TrSt.348.424.
Yet since thou wilt thy Sister-Queen controul, ...1.TrSt.366.425.
Thus, in Reproach and Pray'r, the Queen exprest ....1.TrSt.400.426.
And thus invokes the silent *Queen* of *Night.* .... 1.TrSt.582.434.
He thus bespoke his Sister and his Queen. ....1.TrES.226.458.
His Royal Person from his Friends and Queen, ...1.TrUl.61.468.
Their Pigmy King, and little Fairy Queen, ...2.ChJM.461.37.
Thus, with a Frown, the King bespoke his Queen. ....2.ChJM.626.45.
And will you so, reply'd the Queen, indeed? ....2.ChJM.656.46.
And so has mine, (she said)—I am a Queen! ....2.ChJM.705.48.
Help, for the Love of Heav'ns' immortal Queen! ....2.ChJM.723.49.
This speaks the Glory of the *British Queen,* .... 2.RL*A* 1.77.129.
One speaks the Glory of the *British Queen,* .... 2.RL3.13.170.
And his refulgent *Queen,* with Pow'rs combin'd, ...2.RL3.77.173.
And wins (oh shameful Chance!) the *Queen* of *Hearts.* .... 2.RL3.88.174.
Lurk'd in her Hand, and mourn'd his captive *Queen.* .... 2.RL3.96.174.
Then thus addrest the Pow'r—Hail wayward Queen! ....2.RL4.57.188.
Here fierce *Tydides* wounds the *Cyprian* Queen; ....2.TemF.189.271.
Ambitious Fools! (the Queen reply'd, and frown'd) ....2.TemF.350.280.
The Queen assents, the Trumpet rends the Skies, ...2.TemF.392.282.
In this weak queen, some fav'rite still obey. ....3.EOM2.150.73.
When Flatt'ry glares, all hate it in a Queen, ...3.Ep1.120.24.
Which Heav'n has varnish'd out, and made a *Queen:* .... 3.Ep2.182.64.
But ev'ry Lady would be Queen for life. ....3.Ep2.218.68.
And silent sells a King, or buys a Queen. ....3.Ep3.78.93.
Was velvet in the youth of good Queen *Bess,* .... 4.JD4.41.29.
"The King would smile on you—at least the Queen?" ....4.JD4.89.33.
When the *Queen* frown'd, or smil'd, he knows; and what ....4.JD4.132.37.
(Some say his Queen) was forc'd to speak, or burst. ....4.Arbu.72.100.
The Queen of *Midas* slept, and so may I. ....4.Arbu.82.101.
And just as rich as when he serv'd a QUEEN! ....4.Arbu.417.127.
As in the gentle Reign of My Queen *Anne.* .... 4.HOde1.4.151.
As in the glorious Reign of My Queen *Anne.* .... 4.HOde1.4A.151.
150.As in the glorious Reign of good Queen *Anne.* .... 4.HOde1.4B.151.
One likes no language but the Faery Queen; ....4.2HE1.39.197.
All these and more, the cloud-compelling Queen ....5.DunA1.77.68.
Much to the mindful Queen the feast recalls, ...5.DunA1.93.70.
To grace this honour'd day, the Queen proclaims ....5.DunA2.13.98.
Dulness, good Queen, repeats the jest again. ....5.DunA2.114.110.
What force have pious vows! The Queen of Love ....5.DunA2.207.127.
"Hold (cry'd the Queen) A Catcall each shall win, ...5.DunA2.233.129.
"Hold (cry'd the Queen) ye all alike shall win, ...5.DunA2.233A.129.
For this, our Queen unfolds to vision true ....5.DunA3.53.155.
All these, and more, the cloud-compelling Queen ....5.DunB1.79.275.
Much to the mindful Queen the feast recalls ....5.DunB1.95.276.
To serve his cause, O Queen! is serving thine. ....5.DunB1.214.285.
And now the Queen, to glad her sons, proclaims ....5.DunB2.17.297.
Dulness, good Queen, repeats the jest again. ....5.DunB2.122.301.
What force have pious vows! The Queen of Love ....5.DunB2.215.306.
"Hold (cry'd the Queen) a Cat-call each shall win; ....5.DunB2.243.307.
For this, our Queen unfolds to vision true ....5.DunB3.61.323.
The buzzing Bees about their dusky Queen. ....5.DunB4.80.349.
As if he saw St. James's and the Queen. ....5.DunB4.280.371.
Great Queen, and common Mother of us all! ....5.DunB4.404.381.
Th' Accus'd stood forth, and thus address'd the Queen. ....5.DunB4.420.382.
Smiling on all, and smil'd on by a Queen. ....5.DunB4.506.392.
The Queen confers her *Titles* and *Degrees.* .... 5.DunB4.566.398.
To all his friends, and ev'n his Queen, unknown, ...6.15.4.51.
What, shou'd a *Queen,* so long the boast of fame, ...6.20.5.66.
Let not a suppliant Queen entreat in vain, ...6.20.50.67.
Wit's Queen, (if what the Poets sing be true) ....6.37.1.106.
Full grown, and from the Sea the Queen of Love; ....6.37.4.106.
Toast Church and Queen, explain the News, ...6.39.21.111.
King, Queen and Nation, staring with Amaze, ...6.96iv.72.278.
Yes, I beheld th' Athenian Queen ....6.140.1.378.

QUEEN (CONTINUED)
" *Athenian Queen!* and *sober charms!* .... 6.140.25.379.
This single Crayon, Madam, saints the Queen. ....6.147iii.4.390.
All, but the God's Imperious Queen alone: ....Il.1.695.120.
In close Consult, the Silver-footed Queen. ....Il.1.719.122.
The Thund'rer spoke, nor durst the Queen reply; ....Il.1.736.122.
Which, with a Smile, the white-arm'd Queen receiv'd. ....Il.1.767.124.
But *Jove's* Imperial Queen their Flight survey'd, ...Il.2.191.137.
(A Mortal mixing with the Queen of Love) ....Il.2.995.170.
You met th' Approaches of the *Spartan* Queen, ...Il.3.70.192.
These, when the *Spartan* Queen approach'd the Tow'r, ...Il.3.203.201.
She moves a Goddess, and she looks a Queen! ....Il.3.208.201.
Ajax the great (the beauteous Queen reply'd) ....Il.3.293.207.
The Queen of Love her favour'd Champion shrouds ....Il.3.467.214.
And Breast, reveal'd the Queen of soft Desire. ....Il.3.490.215.
Then thus, incens'd, the *Paphian* Queen replies; ....Il.3.513.216.
The Queen and Goddess to the Prince ascend. ....Il.3.528.216.
Full in her *Paris'* Sight the Queen of Love ....Il.3.529.216.
Thus wak'd the Fury of his partial Queen. ....Il.4.8.221.
The Queen of Pleasures shares the Toils of Fight, ...Il.4.14.221.
Thus while he spoke, the Queen of Heav'n enrag'd ....Il.4.27.222.
And Queen of War, in close Consult engag'd. ....Il.4.28.222.
'Till vast Destruction glut the Queen of Heav'n! ....Il.4.58.223.
The Queen of Love with faded Charms she found, ...Il.5.443.289.
Stern *Mars* attentive hears the Queen complain, ...Il.5.453.289.
Before her Mother Love's bright Queen appears, ...Il.5.461.290.
How this Mischance the *Cyprian* Queen befell. ....Il.5.510.292.
By *Jove's* great Daughter and the Queen of Heav'n, ...Il.5.879.308.
There with her snowy Hand the Queen restrains ....Il.5.940.311.
Direct the Queen to lead th' assembled Train ....Il.6.109.329.
Fir'd at his Scorn the Queen to *Prætus* fled, ...Il.6.205.336.
Of Royal *Hecuba,* his Mother Queen. ....Il.6.313.341.
The *Phrygian* Queen to her rich Wardrobe went, ...Il.6.358.343.
Here as the Queen revolv'd with careful Eyes ....Il.6.364.344.
The Queen of *Hippoplacia's* Sylvan Lands: ....Il.6.539.353.
What Rage, what Madness, furious Queen! is thine? ....Il.8.255.409.
Great Queen of Arms, whose Favour *Tydeus* won, ...Il.10.337.18.
Great Queen of Arms! receive this hostile Spoil, ...Il.10.532.27.
Then grant me (said the Queen) those conqu'ring Charms, ...Il.14.225.172.
She said. With Awe divine the Queen of Love ....Il.14.243.172.
Vain are thy Fears (the Queen of Heav'n replies, ...Il.14.297.177.
The Queen assents, and from th' infernal Bow'rs ....Il.14.313.178.
The trembling Queen (th' Almighty Order giv'n) ....Il.15.84.199.
They hail her Queen; the *Nectar* streams around. ....Il.15.95.200.
And prompt Obedience to the Queen of Air; ....Il.15.177.203.
To *Hermes, Pallas,* and the Queen of Heav'n; ....Il.15.237.206.
He thus bespoke his Sister and his Queen. ....Il.16.529.264.
I come, *Pelides!* from the Queen of *Jove,* ....Il.18.221.332.
Heav'ns Queen, and Consort of the thund'ring *Jove,* ....Il.18.428.341.
And smiling, thus the wat'ry Queen address'd. ....Il.18.452.343.
And various Artifice, the Queen she plac'd; ....Il.18.458.343.
In lofty *Gnossus,* for the *Cretan* Queen, ...Il.18.682.356.
Briseis, radiant as the Queen of Love, ...Il.19.296.384.
Heav'ns awful Queen; and He whose azure Round ....Il.20.45.396.
His vent'rous Act the white-arm'd Queen survey'd, ...Il.20.144.400.
Fear touch'd the Queen of Heav'n: She saw dismay'd, ...Il.21.384.436.
To *Juno* then, Imperial Queen of Air, ...Il.21.430.438.
And first assaults the radiant Queen of War ....Il.21.457.440.
The *Smiles* and *Love's* unconquerable Queen! ....Il.21.493.441.
Silent, he heard the Queen of Woods upbraid: ....Il.21.553.444.
Their Charms rejected for the *Cyprian* Queen. ....Il.24.41.537.
The Azure Queen; let her Persuasion move ....Il.24.96.539.
His Word the silver-footed Queen attends, ...Il.24.155.541.
Then call'd his Queen, and thus began to say. ....Il.24.232.546.
Then took the golden Cup his Queen had fill'd, ...Il.24.374.551.
But two the Goddess, twelve the Queen enjoy'd; ....Il.24.765.569.
Deplor'd his absent Queen, and Empire lost. ....Od.1.20.30.
At Chess they vie, to captivate the Queen, ...Od.1.143.39.
To tempt the spouseless Queen with am'rous wiles, ...Od.1.315.47.
And the chaste Queen connubial rites require; ....Od.1.359.49.
For the chaste Queen select an equal Lord. ....Od.1.383.51.
Reflecting to the Queen the silver sounds. ....Od.1.426.53.
Mature beyond his years the Queen admires ....Od.1.459.54.
Hither, unwelcome, to the Queen they come; ....Od.2.57.63.
Thus spoke th' inventive Queen, with artful sighs. ....Od.2.106.66.
Dismiss the Queen; and if her sire approves, ...Od.2.129.67.
Telemachus may bid the Queen repair ....Od.2.223.72.
The royal Palace to the Queen convey, ...Od.2.378.79.
Sooth'd the frail Queen, and poyson'd all her heart. ....Od.3.329.102.
The rev'rend *Nestor* with his Queen repos'd. ....Od.3.515.112.
Nor scorn'd the Queen the holy Choir to join, ...Od.3.574.116.
To *Sparta's* Queen of old the radiant vase ....Od.4.167.128.
The circle thus the beauteous Queen address'd. ....Od.4.324.134.
Which kindled by th' imperious Queen of love, ...Od.4.359.137.
Swift to the Queen the Herald *Medon* ran, ...Od.4.902.160.
The piteous object of a prostrate Queen. ....Od.4.953.162.
The Queen her speech with calm attention hears, ...Od.4.999.164.
And thus the Queen invokes *Minerva's* aid. ....Od.4.1004.164.
"Too late the Queen selects a second lord: ....Od.4.1018.165.
Mean-time the Queen without refection due, ...Od.4.1037.166.
To calm the Queen the Phantom-sister flies. ....Od.4.1054.167.
To whom the Queen, (whilst yet her pensive mind ....Od.4.1065.167.
The Queen replies: If in the blest abodes, ...Od.4.1085.168.
The Queen awakes, deliver'd of her woes; ....Od.4.1095.169.
The Queen she sought: the Queen her hours bestow'd ....Od.6.61.208.
The Queen she sought: the Queen her hours bestow'd ....Od.6.61.208.
The Queen, assiduous, to her train assigns ....Od.6.89.209.
A sylvan train the huntress Queen surrounds, ...Od.6.119.212.
For Misery, oh Queen, before thee stands! ....Od.6.204.220.
Seek thou the Queen along the rooms of state; ....Od.6.366.229.
But to the Queen thy mournful tale disclose, ...Od.6.373.229.
First to the Queen prefer a suppliant's claim, ...Od.7.69.237.
Alcinous' Queen, *Arete* is her name, ...Od.7.70.237.
This Queen he graces, and divides the throne; ....Od.7.87.238.
The Queen, on nearer view, the guest survey'd ....Od.7.314.251.
He glows, he burns: The fair-hair'd Queen of love ....Od.8.329.281.

QUEEN (CONTINUED)
See the lewd dalliance of the Queen of Love! .... Od.8.348.282.
Before the Queen *Alcinous'* sons unfold .... Od.8.455.288.
Thence to the Queen. O partner of our reign, ... Od.8.459.288.
Instant the Queen, observant of the King, ... Od.8.469.288.
They went; but as they ent'ring saw the Queen .... Od.10.127.347.
Goddess, and Queen, to whom the pow'rs belong .... Od.10.163.348.
Ministrant to their Queen, with busy care .... Od.10.413.364.
The Queen beheld me, and these words addrest. .... Od.10.444.365.
Son of *Laertes!* (then the Queen began) .... Od.10.475.366.
A Queen, to *Troy* she saw our legions pass; .... Od.11.106.386.
Nor bent the silver-shafted Queen her bow; .... Od.11.243.393.
Or has hell's Queen an empty Image sent, ... Od.11.257.394.
'Tis not the Queen of Hell who thee deceives: .... Od.11.261.394.
Jocasta frown'd, th' incestuous *Theban* Queen; .... Od.11.330.398.
Ev'n to thy Queen disguis'd, unknown, return; .... Od.11.562.411.
Then thus: O Queen farewell! be still possest .... Od.13.74.4.
His royal person from his friends and Queen; .... Od.13.228.17.
And proud addresses to the matchless Queen. .... Od.13.432.27.
Small is the faith, the Prince and Queen ascribe .... Od.14.146.42.
But when the constant Queen commands my care; .... Od.14.412.56.
The beauteous Queen revolv'd with careful eyes .... Od.15.118.74.
The beauteous Queen advancing next, display'd .... Od.15.136.75.
The beauteous Queen reliev'd his lab'ring breast. .... Od.15.191.77.
Small is the comfort from the Queen to hear .... Od.15.400.88.
Strait to the Queen and Palace shall I fly, ... Od.15.549.96.
Nor bears the modest Queen a stranger's face, ... Od.15.556.96.
He wooes the Queen with more respectful flame, ... Od.15.561.97.
But say, if in the court the Queen reside .... Od.16.33.103.
Ev'n I unsafe: The Queen in doubt to wed, ... Od.16.73.106.
The Queen averse to love, yet aw'd by pow'r, ... Od.16.135.109.
But go, *Eumæus!* to the Queen impart .... Od.16.140.109.
But to the Queen with speed dispatchful bear .... Od.16.162.110.
Swift to the Queen a herald flies, t'impart .... Od.16.350.123.
And cries aloud, Thy son, oh Queen returns: .... Od.16.355.123.
And give the Palace to the Queen a dow'r, ... Od.16.400.125.
Then wed whom choice approves: the Queen be giv'n .... Od.16.406.125.
Chief of the numbers who the Queen addrest, ... Od.16.412.126.
The murd'rous council to the Queen relates. .... Od.16.427.128.
Afflict his Queen? and with a murd'rous hand .... Od.16.450.129.
Then sorrowing, with sad step the Queen retir'd, ... Od.16.465.129.
Lest to the Queen the swain with transport fly, ... Od.16.480.130.
When thus the Queen. My son! my only friend! .... Od.17.116.137.
He ceas'd; nor made the pensive Queen reply, ... Od.17.170.139.
Succeed those omens Heav'n! (the Queen rejoin'd) .... Od.17.186.140.
(Replies the Queen) the stranger beg'd their grace, ... Od.17.592.161.
Amidst her maids thus spoke the prudent Queen, ... Od.17.596.161.
To this the Queen. The wand'rer let me hear, ... Od.17.618.162.
The smiling Queen the happy omen blest: .... Od.17.626.163.
The Queen invites thee, venerable guest! .... Od.17.634.163.
Let for a space the pensive Queen attend, ... Od.17.650.164.
Swift to the Queen returns the gentle swain: .... Od.17.656.164.
Who'er this guest (the prudent Queen replies) .... Od.17.664.164.
Who make their Queen and all her wealth a prey: .... Od.18.173.175.
Ah me! forbear, returns the Queen, forbear; .... Od.18.209.177.
And to the Queen the damsel train descends: .... Od.18.234.178.
Then to the Queen *Eurymachus* replies: .... Od.18.285.180.
Ah me! returns the Queen, when from this shore .... Od.18.293.180.
Well-pleas'd *Ulysses* hears his Queen deceive .... Od.18.325.182.
A gift bestows: This done, the Queen ascends, ... Od.18.349.184.
Go, with the Queen the spindle guide, or cull .... Od.18.361.185.
Who with the Queen her years an infant led, ... Od.18.369.185.
Her Queen endures, polluted joys she shares .... Od.18.372.185.
The pensive Queen perchance desires to know .... Od.19.56.195.
The Queen, descending from her bow'r of state. .... Od.19.65.195.
Of royal grace th' offended Queen may guide; .... Od.19.103.197.
He thus: O Queen! whose far-resounding fame, ... Od.19.127.199.
Their gifts the Gods resum'd (the Queen rejoin'd.) .... Od.19.144.199.
'Till thus the Queen the tender theme renews. .... Od.19.252.207.
What thanks! what boon! reply'd the Queen, are due, ... Od.19.354.211.
And vainly to the praise of Queen aspire, ... Od.19.374.212.
Pleas'd with his wise reply, the Queen rejoin'd: .... Od.19.403.214.
When *Euryclea* from the Queen descends, ... Od.19.473.219.
Full on the Queen her raptur'd eyes she cast, ... Od.19.555.223.
Whom thus with pensive air the Queen addrest. .... Od.19.593.225.
O Queen! no vulgar vision of the sky .... Od.19.641.227.
Hard is the task, and rare, the Queen rejoin'd, ... Od.19.654.227.
To whom with grace serene the Queen rejoin'd: .... Od.19.687.229.
Thus affable, her bow'r the Queen ascends; .... Od.19.699.229.
Blest in thy Queen! blest in thy blooming heir! .... Od.20.44.234.
Not so the Queen; The downy bands of sleep .... Od.20.68.235.
He thinks the Queen is rushing to his arms. .... Od.20.115.238.
Promiscuous grace on all the Queen confers; .... Od.20.165.241.
In vain the Queen the night-refection prest; .... Od.20.172.241.
And urg'd, for title to a consort Queen, ... Od.20.355.249.
Nor shou'd thy Sire a Queen his daughter boast, ... Od.20.376.251.
Of right the Queen refus'd a second Lord: .... Od.20.394.251.
But from this dome my Parent-Queen to chase!— .... Od.20.411.252.
Nigh in her bright alcove, the pensive Queen .... Od.20.463.256.
The prudent Queen the lofty stair ascends, ... Od.21.7.258.
Full in the portal the chaste Queen appears, ... Od.21.65.262.
To this the Queen her just dislike exprest: .... Od.21.333.276.
Shall I, a Queen, by rival chiefs ador'd, ... Od.21.339.276.
To whom the Queen. If Fame ingage your views, ... Od.21.357.276.
Retire oh Queen! thy houshold task resume, ... Od.21.377.277.
Mature beyond his years, the Queen admir'd .... Od.21.381.278.
What for thy country now, thy Queen, thy son? .... Od.22.253.299.
To purge the palace: then the Queen attend, ... Od.22.519.314.
Then to the Queen, as in repose she lay, ... Od.23.1.316.
Touch'd at her words, the mournful Queen rejoyn'd, ... Od.23.11.319.
While yet she spoke, the Queen in transport sprung .... Od.23.35.320.
To whom with dubious joy the Queen replies, ... Od.23.81.322.
Thus speaks the Queen, and no reply attends, ... Od.23.87.323.
Curious to hear his Queen the silence break: .... Od.23.95.324.
O my *Telemachus!* the Queen rejoin'd, ... Od.23.107.325.
Lo! the Queen weds! we hear the spousal lay! .... Od.23.136.327.

QUEEN (CONTINUED)
Lo! the Queen weds! we hear the spousal lay! .... Od.23.146.328.
And oh my Queen! he cries; what pow'r above .... Od.23.165.328.
Thus speaks the Queen, still dubious, with disguise; .... Od.23.183.330.
'Tis thine, oh Queen, to say: And now impart, ... Od.23.209.333.
The ravish'd Queen with equal rapture glows, ... Od.23.257.335.
To whom the Queen. Thy word we shall obey, ... Od.23.273.336.
And to the Queen *Eurynomè* descends; .... Od.23.314.338.
My Queen, my consort! thro' a length of years, ... Od.23.377.343.
Now, blest again by heav'n, the Queen display, ... Od.23.381.343.
Then, to her Suitors bade his Queen propose .... Od.24.195.357.
To the chast Queen shall we the news convey? .... Od.24.466.371.

QUEEN'S
His Subjects Faith, and Queen's suspected Love, ... 1.TrUl.217.473.
The Queen's fond hope inventive rumour cheers, ... Od.1.523.57.
And finish'd all their Queen's command with haste: .... Od.7.432.258.
His subjects faith, and Queen's suspected love; .... Od.13.384.25.
The Queen's attentive ear: dissolv'd in woe, ... Od.19.236.205.
My will concurring with my Queen's command, ... Od.19.440.216.

QUEENIES
The Motley Race of Hervey queenies .... 6.135.39Z1.367.

QUEENS
And four fair *Queens* whose hands sustain a Flow'r, ... 2.RL3.39.171.
Ev'n mighty *Pam* that Kings and Queens o'erthrew, ... 2.RL3.61.172.
In hearts of Kings, or arms of Queens who lay, ... 3.EOM4.289.155.
Yet mark the fate of a whole Sex of Queens! .... 3.Ep2.219.68.
Toasts live a scorn, and Queens may die a jest. .... 3.Ep2.282.73.
"I'd never name Queens, Ministers, or Kings; .... 4.Arbu.76.101.
All that makes Saints of Queens, and Gods of Kings, ... 4.EpS2.225.325.

QUEENSB'RY
My Verse, and QUEENSB'RY weeping o'er thy Urn! .... 4.Arbu.260.114.

QUEENSBERRY
If QUEENSBERRY to strip there's no compelling, ... 3.Ep2.193.66.

QUEER
The Mosque of *Mahound,* or some queer *Pa-god.* .... 4.JD4.239.45.
And now she's in t'other, she thinks it but *Queer.* .... 6.124i.10.347.

QUELL
'Tis past—I quell it; I resign to Fate. .... Il.18.144.329.
Sons he has many, those thy Pride may quell; .... Il.20.220.403.
Short was that doubt; to quell his rage inur'd, ... Od.17.278.145.

QUELL'D
I quell'd *Clytomedes* in Fights of Hand, ... Il.23.729.519.
The rage of hunger quell'd, they all advance, ... Od.1.195.42.

QUELLS
Thy happy Reign all other Discord quells; .... 6.131i.5.360.
No Bound, no Law thy fiery Temper quells, ... Il.5.1100.319.

QUENCH<'D
Quench<'d> his red Orb, at *Juno's* high Command, ... Il.18.285.335.

QUENCH
And had a wond'rous Gift to quench a Flame. .... 2.ChWB.320.72.
In lavish streams to quench a Country's thirst, ... 3.Ep3.177.108.
First let us quench the yet-remaining Flame .... Il.23.295.501.
And quench with Wine the yet remaining Fire. .... Il.24.1002.577.
Such was the wine: to quench whose fervent stream, ... Od.9.242.316.
Or, instant should he quench the guilty flame .... Od.20.15.232.

QUENCH'D
There stern religion quench'd th' unwilling flame, ... 2.ElAb.39.322.
But when thy Torrent quench'd the dreadful Blaze, ... 6.96iv.71.278.
The *Grecian* Ardour quench'd in deep Despair; .... Il.15.715.223.
Till her last Flame be quench'd with her last Gore, ... Il.20.365.410.
Now quench'd for ever in the Arms of Death. .... Il.22.591.480.
The lamp of day is quench'd beneath the deep, ... Od.3.427.107.
With clouds of darkness quench'd his visual ray, ... Od.8.59.265.

QUERNO
Rome in her Capitol saw Querno sit, ... 5.DunA2.11.97.
Rome in her Capitol saw Querno sit, ... 5.DunB2.15.297.

QUERY
Each prompt to query, answer, and debate, ... 5.DunA2.349.143.
Each prompt to query, answer, and debate, ... 5.DunB2.381.316.

QUEST
What toils by sea! where dark in quest of prey .... Od.3.129.92.
While yet they spoke, in quest of arms again .... Od.22.176.296.
As round the room in quest of arms he goes: .... Od.22.195.296.

QUESTION
And all the question (wrangle e'er so long) .... 3.EOM1.49.19.
"I make no question but the *Tow'r* had stood." .... 4.JD4.85.33.
And question me of this and that; .... 4.HS6.88.255.
Save when they lose a Question, or a Job. .... 4.EpS1.104.305.
Is not to question, but to prove our Might. .... Il.20.305.407.
All mute, yet seem'd to question with their Eyes: .... Il.24.595.561.
To question wisely men of riper years. .... Od.3.32.87.
With question needless, or enquiry vain. .... Od.7.40.235.
Polites to the rest the question mov'd, ... Od.10.258.355.
All press to speak, all question with their eyes. .... Od.13.191.15.
Nor dare to question where the proud command: .... Od.15.403.88.
Now what you question of my ancient friend, ... Od.17.158.139.
While thus they gaze and question with their eyes, ... Od.17.444.155.
By turns to question, and by turns to hear. .... Od.17.663.164.
Nor dare to question: doubts on doubts arise. .... Od.23.110.325.
Of question distant, and of soft essay, ... Od.24.280.363.

QUESTION (CONTINUED)
But chief oh tell me (what I question most) ....Od.24.304.364.

QUESTION'D
And question'd thus the Sire of Men and Gods. ....Il.20.22.393.
He stood, and question'd thus his mighty Mind. ....Il.22.137.458.
And question'd thus his yet-unconquer'd mind. ....Od.5.382.190.

QUESTIONS
Who solve these Questions beyond all Dispute; ....2.ChJM.296.28.
I ask these sober questions of my Heart. ....4.2HE2.211.179.
And questions thus his own unconquer'd Soul. ....Il.11.512.56.
Whom thus he questions: Ever best of Friends! ....Il.13.326.121.
He stops, and questions thus his mighty Soul. ....Il.21.650.449.
And if my questions meet a true reply, ...Od.17.629.163.

QUI
On just occasion, *coute qui coute*. ....4.HS6.164.261.
Hannoniae qui primus ab oris. ....6.42iv.6.118.

QUIBBLE
Lord's Quibble, Critick's Jest; all end in thee, ...6.8.41.19.

QUIBBLES
In Quibbles, Angel and Archangel join, ...4.2HE1.101.203.
Or H[ardwic]k[e]'s quibbles voted into law? ....4.1740.64.335.
Their Quibbles routed, and defy'd their Puns; ....6.128.12.356.

QUICK
By quick degrees, and cover all below: ....1.TrFD.44.387.
Touch'd to the Quick, and tickl'd at the Soul. ....2.ChJM.277.27.
Quick as her Eyes, and as unfix'd as those: ....2.RL2.10.160.
Tho' mark'd by none but quick Poetic Eyes: ....2.RL5.124.210.
Or quick effluvia darting thro' the brain, ...3.EOM1.199.40.
Or quick effluvia darting thro' his brain, ...3.EOM1.199B.40.
All matter quick, and bursting into birth. ....3.EOM1.234.44.
All Nature quick, and bursting into birth. ....3.EOM1.234A.44.
Sure by quick Nature happiness to gain, ...3.EOM3.91.101.
Quick whirls, and shifting eddies, of our minds? ....3.Ep1.30.17.
Tho' strong the bend, yet quick the turns of mind: ....3.Ep1.123.25.
Too quick for Thought, for Action too refin'd: ....3.Ep1.201.32.
Rufa, whose eye quick-glancing o'er the Park, ...3.Ep2.21.50.
So quick retires each flying course, you'd swear ....3.Ep4.159.153.
Loth to enrich me with too quick Replies, ...4.JD4.128.35.
And quick to swallow me, methought I saw ....4.JD4.172.39.
How Hints, like spawn, scarce quick in embryo lie, ...5.DunA1.57.67.
In one quick flash see Proserpine expire, ...5.DunA1.209.87.
And quick sensations skip from vein to vein, ...5.DunA2.204.126.
How hints, like spawn, scarce quick in embryo lie, ...5.DunB1.59.274.
To Needham's quick the voice triumphal rode, ...5.DunB1.323.293.
And quick sensations skip from vein to vein; ....5.DunB2.212.306.
And Major, Minor, and Conclusion quick. ....5.DunB2.242.307.
As Fancy opens the quick springs of Sense, ...5.DunB4.156.357.
How quick Ambition hastes to ridicule! ....5.DunB4.547.396.
Quick on its Axle turn.— ....6.100ii.2.288.
Quick to expand th' inclement Air congeal'd ....6.100iv.2.289.
"That Head so quick, those Hands so taper; ....6.119.6B.336.
His Breath, in quick, short Pantings, comes, and goes; ....Il.16.134.242.
Catch the quick Beams, and brighten all the Fields; ....Il.19.385.388.
Such regards his sparkling eyes bestow; ....Od.4.201.129.
My quick return, young *Ithacus* rejoin'd, ...Od.4.811.156.
Bid *Dolius* quick attend, the faithful slave ....Od.4.972.163.
(Thus quick reply'd the wisest of mankind) ....Od.14.432.56.
Your deeds with quick impartial eye surveys; ....Od.19.107.197.
Quick thro' the father's heart these accents ran; ....Od.24.367.366.

QUICK-GLANCING
Rufa, whose eye quick-glancing o'er the Park, ...3.Ep2.21.50.

QUICK'NING
With gath'ring Force the quick'ning Flames advance; ....2.TemF.476.286.
Whate'er of life all-quick'ning æther keeps, ...3.EOM3.115.103.

QUICKEN
And keener Lightnings quicken in her Eyes. ....2.RL1.144.157.
Oh quicken this dull mass of mortal clay; ....6.23.13.73.

QUICKEN'D
Till Nature quicken'd by th'Inspiring Ray, ...1.TrSt.586.434.
Or quicken'd a Reversion by a *Drug?* ....4.JD4.135.37.
Since quicken'd by thy Breath, ...6.50.42.148.

QUICKER
With quicker Steps the sounding Champain beat. ....Il.23.496.510.

QUICKLY
Almost as quickly, as he conquer'd *Spain*. ....4.HS1.132.19.
Bear me, some God! oh quickly bear me hence ....4.JD4.184.41.
"To get my Warrant quickly sign'd: ....4.HS6.76.255.
You'd quickly find him in Lord *Fanny's* case. ....4.EpS1.50.301.
(The Coach was quickly got 'em) ....6.94.30.260.
How quickly all the Sex pursue! ....6.119.18.337.
Another *Ægypt*, shalt thou quickly find. ....Od.17.532.158.

QUICKNESS
With too much Quickness ever to be taught, ...3.Ep2.97.58.
Not with less Quickness, his exerted Sight ....Il.17.767.318.

QUIDNUNC'S
The clubs of Quidnunc's, or her own Guild-hall. ....5.DunA1.34.O64.

QUIDNUNCS
The clubs of Quidnuncs, or her own Guild-hall: ....5.DunB1.270.290.

QUIET
Whom humbler Joys of home-felt Quiet please, ...1.W-F.239.171.
That shunning Faults, one quiet *Tenour* keep; ....1.EOC.241.267.
Depends my Quiet, and my future Bliss. ....2.ChJM.257.27.
Sedate and quiet the comparing lies, ...3.EOM2.69.63.
In quiet flow from Lucrece to Lucrece; ....3.EOM4.208.146.
Men, some to Quiet, some to public Strife; ....3.Ep2.217.68.
Shall walk the World in quiet to his grave. ....4.HS1.120B.17.
Enjoys his Garden and his Book in quiet; ....4.2HE1.199.211.
The Venal quiet, and intrance the Dull; ....5.DunB4.624.406.
Quiet by day, ...6.1.12.3.
But all is quiet, jocund, and serene, ...6.17iii.38.58.
And Sup with us on Mirth or Quiet, ...6.61.34.182.
And Sup with us on Mirth on Quiet, ...6.61.34A.182.
And Sup with us on Mirth and Quiet, ...6.61.34B.182.
And Sup with us on Milk and Quiet, ...6.61.34C.182.
Steer'd the same course to the same quiet shore, ...6.109.13.314.
Took the same course to the same quiet shore, ...6.109.13A.314.
"Come, if you'll be a quiet soul, ...6.140.29.379.
And sunk to Quiet in th' Embrace of Sleep, ...Il.23.289.501.
And pleasing Slumbers quiet all their Care. ....Il.24.4.534.
To meet soft quiet and repose at home; ....Od.11.536.409.

QUILL
My Head and Heart thus flowing thro' my Quill, ...4.HS1.63.11.
Yet then did *Gildon* draw his venal quill; ....4.Arbu.151.107.
Sate full-blown *Bufo*, puff'd by ev'ry quill; ....4.Arbu.232.112.
May some choice Patron bless each gray goose quill! ....4.Arbu.249.114.
Let *Budgel* charge low *Grubstreet* on his quill, ...4.Arbu.378.124.
Not that my quill to Critiques was confin'd, ...5.DunA1.173.84.
A Poet the first day, he dips his quill; ....5.DunB4.163.357.
Yourself for Goose reject Crow Quill; ....6.10.43.25.
If meagre Gildon draws his venal quill, ...6.49iii.1.142.
If meaner Gildon draws his venal quill, ...6.49iii.1A.142.
If meagre Gildon draws his meaner quill, ...6.49iii.1C.142.
Forthwith he drench'd his desp'rate Quill; ....6.79.45.219.
If meagre *Gildon* draws his venal Quill, ...6.98.1.283.

QUILLS
From him whose quills stand quiver'd at his ear, ...4.1HE1.83.285.
With ready quills the dedicators wait; ....5.DunA2.190.124.
With ready quills the Dedicators wait; ....5.DunB2.198.305.

QUILT
On the rich Quilt sinks with becoming Woe, ...2.RL4.35.186.

QUILTS
Bids her fair train the purple quilts prepare, ...Od.7.429.258.

QUIN'S
At Quin's high plume, or Oldfield's petticoat, ...4.2HE1.331.223.

QUINBUS
Or *Quinbus Flestrin* more Endearment brings, ...6.96iv.101.279.

QUINCUNX
His Quincunx darkens, his Espaliers meet, ...3.Ep4.80.145.
Now, forms my Quincunx, and now ranks my Vines, ...4.HS1.130.17.

QUINT
Edwardi Sext. or *prim. & quint. Eliz:* ....4.HS1.148.19.

QUINTILIAN'S
In grave *Quintilian's* copious Work we find ....1.EOC.669.315.

QUIRE
But in the Centre of the hallow'd Quire ....2.TemF.178.270.
From the full quire when loud *Hosanna's* rise, ...2.ElAb.353.348.
Impatient waits, till ** grace the quire. ....5.DunA1.250Z2.92.
With Fool of Quality compleats the quire. ....5.DunB1.298.291.
Impatient waits 'till H[erv]y grace the quire. ....5.DunB1.298A.291.
When the full Organ joins the tuneful Quire, ...6.11.126.34.
To her high Chamber, from *Diana's* Quire, ...Il.16.220.248.
(Well-pleas'd to share the Feast,) amid the Quire ....Il.24.82.538.
Our swift approach the *Siren* quire descries; ....Od.12.219.442.

QUIRES
For her, the feather'd Quires neglect their Song; ....1.PAu.24.82.
For him, the feather'd Quires neglect their Song; ....1.PAu.24A.82.
And savage Howlings fill the sacred Quires. ....1.W-F.72.156.
And Wolves with Howling fill the sacred Quires. ....1.W-F.72A.156.
And Quires of Virgins celebrate thy praise? ....6.65.8.192.

QUIRKS
Light quirks of Musick, broken and uneven, ...3.Ep4.143.151.

QUIT
When weary Reapers quit the sultry Field, ...1.PSu.65.77.
So Schismatics the *plain Believers* quit, ...1.EOC.428.288.
So Schismatics the *dull Believers* quit, ...1.EOC.428A.288.
Quit all his State, descend, and serve again? ....1.TrSt.258.421.
Disabl'd *Glaucus* slowly quit the Field; ....1.TrES.120.454.
But clear they wrinkled Brown, and quit thy Sorrow, ...2.ChWB.52.60.
One you shall quit—in spight of both your Eyes— ....2.ChWB.128.62.
And make my soul quit *Abelard* for God. ....2.ElAb.128.330.
Thy oaths I quit, thy memory resign, ...2.ElAb.293.343.
All quit their sphere, and rush into the skies. ....3.EOM1.124.30.
The throne a Bigot keep, a Genius quit, ...3.Ep1.150.28.
Well, if it be my time to quit the Stage, ...4.JD4.1.27.
O my fair Mistress, *Truth!* Shall I quit thee, ...4.JD4.200.43.
Frighted, I quit the Room, but leave it so, ...4.JD4.272.49.
As many quit the streams that murm'ring fall ....5.DunB4.199.362.
And for plain *Spanish* quit Brasil; ....6.10.44.25.
Ah quit not the free Innocence of Life! ....6.19.45.63.
Sooner I'd quit my Part in thee, ...6.30.25.86.
Sooner we'd quit our Part in thee, ...6.30.25A.86.

QUIT (CONTINUED)

Who'd sooner quit our Part in thee, ...6.30.25B.86.
Quit, oh quit this mortal frame: ....6.31ii.2.94.
Quit, oh quit this mortal frame: ....6.31ii.2.94.
Dost thou quit this mortal Frame? ....6.31ii.2A.94.
Wretched Lovers, quit your Dream, ...6.78ii.3.216.
Dextrous, the craving, fawning Crowd to quit, ...6.84.11.238.
These, for some Moments when you deign to quit, ..6.96iv.61.278.
For this, constrain'd to quit his native Place, ...II.2.803.163.
If e'er with Life I quit the *Trojan* Plain, ...II.5.268.280.
To quit her Country for some Youth of *Troy;* .....II.5.514.293.
Should *Hector* basely quit the Field of Fame? .....II.6.565.354.
Then with majestic Grace they quit the Plain; ......II.7.370.382.
Haste then, for ever quit these fatal Fields, ...II.9.35.433.
If I return, I quit immortal Praise ....II.9.536.460.
To quit these Shores, their native Seats enjoy, ...II.9.540.460.
What shame, inglorious if I quit the Plain; ....II.11.514.57.
Disabl'd *Glaucus* slowly quit the Field; ....II.12.474.99.
Or quit the Fleet, and pass unhurt away, ...II.13.933.149.
I force not *Greece* to quit this hateful Coast. .....II.14.117.163.
And quit, tho' angry, the contended Field. ....II.15.233.206.
And quit the Quiver for the pond'rous Shield. ......II.15.557.218.
Shall quit the Ships, and *Greece* respire again. ....II.16.63.238.
Then shall I quit *Patroclus* on the Plain, ...II.17.101.291.
Forgive me, *Greece,* if once I quit the Field; ......II.17.107.291.
The *Greeks,* late Victors, now to quit the Plains? ..II.18.10.323.
In vain I charg'd him soon to quit the Plain, ...II.18.17.323.
Our bravest Heroes else shall quit the Fight, ...II.21.360.435.
Or quit the dearest, to converse alone. ....II.23.98.491.
The Prize I quit, if thou thy Wrath resign; ....II.23.673.516.
The mirthful train dispersing quit the court, ...Od.1.535.57.
First *Echephron* and *Stratius* their bed; ....Od.3.546.113.
To quit the steed we both impatient press, ...Od.4.383.139.
There quit the ships, and on the destin'd shore .....Od.4.791.156.
The Suitors quit, and all to council came: ....Od.4.885.159.
Ride the wild waves, and quit the safer shore? .....Od.4.941.162.
In all her tackle trim, to quit the shore. ....Od.4.1032.166.
The rest escape in haste, and quit the coast. ....Od.9.70.305.
My friends advise me, and to quit the shore; ......Od.9.265.317.
I quit the place, and hasten to the strand. ....Od.10.482.366.
Our journey calls us; haste, and quit the land. .....Od.10.656.375.
Much doubting, yet compell'd, I quit the strand. ...Od.14.328.51.
Take that, ere yet thou quit this princely throng: ..Od.17.545.159.
Before thou quit the dome (nor long delay) ....Od.20.289.247.

QUITE

Nor quite indulges, nor can quite repress. ....1.W-F.20.150.
Nor quite indulges, nor can quite repress. ....1.W-F.20.150.
And those explain the Meaning quite away. ....1.EOC.117.252.
And those explain'd the Meaning quite away ......1.EOC.117A.252.
No more a woman, nor yet quite a tree: ....1.TrFD.64.388.
A little louder, but as empty quite: ....3.EOM2.278.88.
But as to Man, mistook the Matter quite; ....3.EOM3.46Z4.96.
There Affectations quite reverse the soul. ....3.Ep1.125A.25.
Or Affectations quite reverse the soul. ....3.Ep1.125.25.
But quite mistakes the scaffold for the pile. ....3.Ep1.221.34.
First turn plain rash, then vanish quite away. ......4.JD4.45.29.
A Fool quite angry is quite innocent; ....4.Arbu.107.103.
A Fool quite angry is quite innocent; ....4.Arbu.107.103.
A Wit quite angry is quite innocent; ....4.Arbu.107A.103.
A Wit quite angry is quite innocent; ....4.Arbu.107A.103.
Not quite so well however as one ought; ....4.2HE2.100.171.
Not quite a Mad-man, tho' a Pasty fell, ...4.2HE2.190.179.
And quite a scandal not to learn: ....4.HS6.146.259.
"I'm quite asham'd—'tis mighty rude ....4.HS6.208.263.
Far from a Lynx, and not a Giant quite, ...4.1HE1.50.283.
Quite turns my Stomach— *P.* So does Flatt'ry mine; .4.EpS2.182.323.
In all the Courts of *Pindus* guiltless quite; ....4.EpS2.187.324.
And each Blasphemer quite escape the Rod, ...4.EpS2.195.324.
And these to Notes are fritter'd quite away. ....5.DunA1.232.90.
And those to Notes are fritter'd quite away. ....5.DunA1.232A.90.
Or quite unravel all the reas'ning thread, ...5.DunB1.179.283.
And these to Notes are fritter'd quite away: ....5.DunB1.278.290.
When Moral Evidence shall quite decay, ...5.DunB4.462.386.
Here *Argus* soon might weep himself quite blind, ..6.9x.2.22.
Before my Sorrow be quite lost. ....6.10.116.28.
Quite o'er the Banks to their own Ruin force. .....6.17ii.17.56.
To turn quite backward *D'Urfy's* Name? ....6.30.67.88.
What is this absorbs me quite? ....6.31ii.9.94.
Gay pats my shoulder, and you vanish quite; .....6.45.47.126.
Then hiss'd from Earth, grew Heav'nly quite; .....6.101.7.290.
But lest new Wounds on Wounds o'erpower us quite, ..II.14.149.165.
Quite thro' and thro' the Point its Passage found, ..II.23.1036.530.
Is common sense quite banish'd from thy breast? ..Od.21.310.274.

QUITS

Hope travels thro', nor quits us when we die. ......3.EOM2.274.88.
This quits an Empire, that embroils a State; ....3.Ep1.58.19.
And quits his Mistress, Money, Ring, and Note! ...4.HAdv.54.79.
Howe'er unwillingly it quits its place, ...4.2HE2.161.177.
In sullen Fury slowly quits the Prize. ....II.4.623.250.
Or God incens'd, who quits the distant Skies ......II.5.224.278.
Forc'd he gives way, and sternly quits the Ground. .II.5.775.303.
Headlong he quits the Car; his Arms resound; .....II.8.313.412.
Quits his bright Car, and issues on the Plain. .....II.8.386.416.
Graceful as *Mars, Patroclus* quits his Tent, ...II.11.737.68.
Each quits his Car, and issues on the Plain. ....II.12.96.84.
Slow he recedes, and sighing, quits the Dead. .....II.17.116.292.
By *Hector* wounded, *Leitus* quits the Plain, ...II.17.680.314.
Sow'r he departs, and quits th' untasted Prey. .....II.17.748.317.
Bright *Galatea* quits her pearly Bed: ....II.18.60.326.
Fast as he could, he sighing quits the Walls, ...II.21.619.448.
Quits his bright Car, and springs upon the Sands; ..II.23.590.513.
But quits his house, his country, and his friends: ..Od.9.110.308.

QUITTING

And quitting sense call imitating God; ....3.EOM2.26.58.
The shepherd quitting here at night the plain, ...Od.10.94.343.

QUIV'RING

And verdant Alders form'd a quiv'ring Shade. ....1.PSu.4.71.
In genial Spring, beneath the quiv'ring Shade ....1.W-F.135.162.
With silver-quiv'ring rills mæander'd o'er— ......3.Ep4.85.146.
And thrice he dropt it from his quiv'ring hand: ...5.DunA1.204.87.
And thrice he dropt it from his quiv'ring hand: ...5.DunB1.246.288.
And left the Members quiv'ring on the Ground. ...II.3.367.210.
Sounds the tough Horn, and twangs the quiv'ring String. ..II.4.157.228.
And quiv'ring in his heaving Bosom stood: ....II.4.613.250.
The Head stood fix'd, the quiv'ring Legs in Air: ..II.5.718.301.
His massy Javelin quiv'ring in his Hand, ...II.7.257.377.
The quiv'ring Steeds fell prostrate at the Sight; ..II.8.165.406.
Shot from their flashing Points a quiv'ring Light. ..II.10.175.9.
And grinds the quiv'ring Flesh with bloody Jaws; ..II.11.156.42.
Its Surface bristled with a quiv'ring Wood, ...II.11.699.66.
Against his Bosom beats his quiv'ring Heart, ...II.13.362.123.
Then stoops, and sowsing on the quiv'ring Hare, ..II.17.765.318.
And at his Back perceives the quiv'ring Spear: ....II.20.330.407.
Stoops from the Clouds to truss the quiv'ring Hare. ..II.22.392.471.
His quiv'ring limbs, and quaff'd his spouting gore. ..Od.2.26.61.
Scatters with quiv'ring hand the sacred flour, ...Od.3.565.115.
Poplars and alders ever quiv'ring play'd, ...Od.5.82.176.
With conscious dread they shun the quiv'ring net: ..Od.22.340.304.
They beat the air with quiv'ring feet below: ....Od.22.504.313.

QUIVER

A painted Quiver on her Shoulder sounds, ...1.W-F.179.166.
The lakes that quiver to the curling breeze; ....2.ElAb.160.332.
And seiz'd the Quiver where it idly hung. ....II.5.265.280.
A Bow and Quiver, with bright Arrows stor'd: ....II.10.308.16.
The well-stor'd Quiver on his Shoulders hung: .....II.15.520.217.
And quit the Quiver for the pond'rous Shield. .....II.15.557.218.
The Bow, the Quiver, and its plumy Pride. ....II.21.568.445.
Her ratling quiver from her shoulder sounds: ......Od.6.120.212.
Their feet half-viewless quiver in the skies: ....Od.8.304.279.
And there the quiver, where now guiltless slept ....Od.21.15.259.
Against the polish'd quiver propt the dart. ....Od.21.146.265.

QUIVER'D

From him whose quills stand quiver'd at his ear, ..4.1HE1.83.285.
The Wretch stood prop'd, and quiver'd as he stood; ..II.10.444.23.
Stuck deep in Earth, and quiver'd where it stood. ..II.13.639.136.
The quiver'd *Dian,* Sister of the Day, ...II.20.96.398.
Ev'n to the middle earth'd; and quiver'd there. ...II.21.188.429.
The quiver'd Huntress of the *Sylvan* Shades. .....II.21.546.444.
And quiver'd deaths, a formidable store; ....Od.22.4.286.
The Goatherd's quiver'd in *Pisander's* heart; .....Od.22.295.300.

QUIVER'S

As a light quiver's lid is op'd and clos'd. ....Od.9.373.321.

QUIVERING

I turn, and view them quivering in the skies; ......Od.12.297.446.
And sudden lifts it quivering to the skies: ....Od.12.303.447.
His feet extended, quivering beat the ground, ...Od.18.115.172.

QUIVERS

And free the Soul that quivers in thy Heart. ......II.12.294.92.
There yet scarce spent, it quivers on the Plain, ...II.16.743.272.

QUIXOTISM

By modern Wits call'd *Quixotism.* ....6.10.82.27.

QUOIT

The Quoit to toss, the pond'rous Mace to wield, ..II.23.713.518.
This mighty Quoit *Aëtion* wont to rear, ...II.23.977.528.

QUOITS

For Quoits, both *Temple-Bar* and *Charing-Cross.* ..4.JD4.277.49.

QUORUM

Or water all the Quorum ten miles round? ....3.Ep3.42.89.

QUOTATION

Or, in Quotation, shrewd Divines leave out ....4.JD2.103.143.

QUOTATIONS

By *Wits,* then *Criticks* in as wrong *Quotations.* ..1.EOC.664.314.

QUOTE

And beastly Skelton Heads of Houses quote: ......4.2HE1.38.197.
I knew Ardelia could not quote the best, ...6.43.6.120.

QUOTH

I say, quoth he, by Heav'n the Man's to blame, ...2.ChJM.222.25.
Nay, (quoth the King) dear Madam be not wroth; ..2.ChJM.700.48.
'Tis Strugling with a Vengeance, (quoth the Knight:) ..2.ChJM.767.52.
What I have said, quoth he, I must maintain; ......2.ChJM.778.52.
"An't please your Honour, quoth the Peasant, ...4.HS6.220.263.
"Now please your Honour, quoth the Peasant, ...4.HS6.220A.263.
"Ho!" quoth another, "Cozen *John!*" ....6.14i.12.42.
"O Moder, Moder," (quoth the Daughter,) ....6.14i.23.42.
Ho! Master *Sam,* quoth *Sandys'* Sprite, ...6.58.37.172.
"To what, (quoth 'Squire) shall *Ovid* change?" ...6.58.75.174.
Quoth *Sandys: To Waste-Paper.* ....6.58.76.174.
"To what,(quoth Sam) shall *Ovid* change?" ......6.58.75A.174.
Quoth Sand's *To Waste–Paper.* ....6.58.76A.174.
Quoth *Sandys: Into Waste-*Paper. ....6.58.76B.174.
A wood? quoth Lewis; and with that, ...6.67.1.195.
"Lye there, thou Caitiff vile! quoth *Guise,* ....6.79.77.220.
"(Quoth *Guise)* I'll fight with thee." ....6.79.104.221.
These Eyes, quoth He, beheld them clear: ....6.94.13.259.

QUOTH (CONTINUED)

Use, use (quoth Jove) those piercing eyes, 6.119.5A.336.
Quoth *Cibber* to *Pope*, tho' in Verse you foreclose, 6.149.1.397.

R

There kick'd and cudgel'd R— might ye view; 5.DunA2.141A.118.
And *R*—, and railing, Brangling, and B[reval], 5.DunA2.230A.128.
Shine in the dignity of F.R.S. 5.DunB4.570.398.
Like R— run to sermons, 6.61.25A.181.

RAB'LAIS'

Or laugh and shake in Rab'lais' easy Chair, 5.DunA1.20.62.
Or laugh and shake in Rab'lais' easy chair, 5.DunB1.22.270.
Or laugh and shake in Rab'lais' easy chair, 6.106iv.4.307.

RABBINS

Eve's Tempter thus the Rabbins have exprest, 4.Arbu.330.119.

RABBIT

The Surgeon with a *Rabbit* came, 6.94.41.260.
You dress not such a *Rabbit,* 6.94.46.260.

RABBIT'S

Rank as the ripeness of a Rabbit's tail. 4.HS2.28.57.
Could *Molly* hide this *Rabbit's* Head, 6.94.87.262.

RABBITS

And humbly live on rabbits and on roots: 4.HS2.52.59.
Bears *Rabbits,—Gad!* so plentiful, 6.94.11.259.
Could they these *Rabbits* smother; 6.94.82.262.

RABBLE

Shou'd chance to make the well-drest Rabble stare; 4.1HE1.111.287.
"Mistress! dismiss that rabble from your throne: 5.DunB4.209.363.

RABID

Not rabid Wolves more fierce contest their Prey; Il.11.97.39.
Such Pacts, as Lambs and rabid Wolves combine, Il.22.337.470.

RACE

Their Vines a Shadow to their Race shall yield; 1.Mes.65.118.
See, a long Race thy spatious Courts adorn; 1.Mes.87.121.
The captive Race, one Instant makes our Prize, 1.W-F.109B.161.
Our plenteous Streams a various Race supply; 1.W-F.141.163.
Peru once more a Race of Kings behold, 1.W-F.411.192.
False Steps but help them to renew the Race, 1.EOC.602.308.
Poets, a *Race* long unconfin'd and free, 1.EOC.649.313.
None taught the Trees a nobler Race to bear, 1.TrVP.3.377.
Pride of thy Age, and Glory of thy Race, 1.TrSP.105.398.
The long Confusions of his guilty Race. 1.TrSt.22.410.
Strait with the Rage of all their Race possest, 1.TrSt.173.417.
Oh Race confed'rate into Crimes, that prove 1.TrSt.302.422.
From God-like *Perseus* those of *Argive* Race. 1.TrSt.318.423.
I from the Root thy guilty Race will tear, 1.TrSt.340.424.
Nor doom to War a Race deriv'd from thee; 1.TrSt.397.426.
Acestis calls, the Guardian of his Race, 1.TrSt.618.436.
Acestis calls, the Tutress of his Race, 1.TrSt.618A.436.
Ah how unworthy those of Race divine? 1.TrSt.685.439.
But if th'abandon'd Race of Human-kind 1.TrSt.767.442.
What Name you bear, from what high Race you spring? 1.TrSt.791.443.
Know then, from *Cadmus* I derive my Race, 1.TrSt.804.443.
And by thy self the Honour of thy Race. 1.TrSt.824.444.
Whose Bounds were fix'd before his Race began? 1.TrES.241.458.
Then *Sleep* and *Death,* two Twins of winged Race, 1.TrES.344.462.
As fiery Coursers in the rapid Race, 1.TrUl.7.465.
To whom the King: Whoe'er of Human Race 1.TrUl.108.469.
For flying Chariots, or the rapid Race; 1.TrUl.123.470.
But by th'Almighty Author of thy Race, 1.TrUl.201.472.
Of gentle Manners, as of gen'rous Race, 2.ChJM.3.15.
That 'tis too much for Human Race to know 2.ChJM.270.27.
Or once renounce the Honour of my Race. 2.ChJM.590.43.
To spin, to weep, and cully Human Race. 2.ChWB.161.64.
"The Wives of all my Race have ever rul'd 2.ChWB.195A.66.
Brought her own Spouse and all his Race to Woe; 2.ChWB.380.75.
Fair Tresses Man's Imperial Race insnare, 2.RL2.27.161.
Others on Earth o'er human Race preside, 2.RL2.87.165.
For *Sylphs,* yet mindful of their ancient Race, 2.RL3.35.171.
Who Cities rais'd, or tam'd a monstrous Race; 2.TemF.71.257.
But on the South a long Majestic Race 2.TemF.109.261.
Neptune and *Jove* survey the rapid Race: 2.TemF.217.272.
Nor left one virtue to redeem her Race. 2.Elegy.28.365.
Mark how it mounts, to Man's imperial race, 3.EOM1.209.41.
Vast Range of Sense! from Man's imperial race 3.EOM1.209A.41.
They love themselves, a third time, in their race. 3.EOM3.124.105.
Another love succeeds, another race. 3.EOM3.130.105.
All love themselves, a third time, in their race. 3.EOM3.124A.105.
Boast the pure blood of an illustrious race, 3.EOM4.207.146.
His country next, and next all human race, 3.EOM4.368.164.
Has made the father of a nameless race, 3.Ep1.229.35.
Whose measure full o'erflows on human race 3.Ep3.231.111.
And vile Attornies, now an useless race. 3.Ep3.274.116.
"His race, his form, his name almost unknown?" 3.Ep3.284.116.
Where all the Race of *Reptiles* might embark: 4.JD4.27.27.
Such painted Puppets, such a varnish'd Race 4.JD4.208.43.
I sought no homage from the Race that write; 4.Arbu.219.111.
Receiv'd of Wits an undistinguish'd race, 4.Arbu.237.112.
This jealous, waspish, wrong-head, rhiming Race; 4.2HE2.148.175.
And see what succour from the Patriot Race. 4.1740.4.332.
And New-year Odes, and all the Grubstreet race. 5.DunA1.42.65.
How Farce and Epic get a jumbled race; 5.DunA1.68.68.
So spirits ending their terrestrial race, 5.DunA1.223.90.
I see a Monarch proud my race to own! 5.DunA1.251Z3.93.
"The race by vigor, not by vaunts is won; 5.DunA2.55.105.
With legs expanded Bernard urg'd the race, 5.DunA2.63.105.
With steps unequal L[into]t urg'd the race, 5.DunA2.63A.105.
Re-passes Lintot, vindicates the race, 5.DunA2.99.109.

RACE (CONTINUED)

Haywood, Centlivre, Glories of their race! 5.DunA3.145.162.
H[aywood] and T[homas], Glories of their race! 5.DunA3.145A.162*.
Lo! one vast Egg produces human race. 5.DunA3.244.177.
The Goddess smiles on Whig and Tory race, 5.DunA3.284.183.
Our Goddess smiles on Whig and Tory race, 5.DunA3.284A.183.
And New-year Odes, and all the Grub-street race. 5.DunB1.44.274.
How Farce and Epic get a jumbled race; 5.DunB1.70.275.
(A friend to Party thou, and all her race; 5.DunB1.206.285.
So Spirits ending their terrestrial race, 5.DunB1.267.290.
They summon all her Race: An endless band 5.DunB2.19.297.
"The race by vigour, not by vaunts is won; 5.DunB2.59.298.
Re-passes Lintot, vindicates the race, 5.DunB2.107.300.
Each Cygnet sweet of Bath and Tunbridge race, 5.DunB3.155.327.
Lo! one vast Egg produces human race. 5.DunB3.248.332.
All Flesh is humbled, Westminster's bold race 5.DunB4.145.355.
In flow'd at once a gay embroider'd race, 5.DunB4.275.371.
Mine, Goddess! mine is all the horned race. 5.DunB4.376.380.
"Of all th' enamel'd race, whose silv'ry wing 5.DunB4.421.383.
Some, deep Free-Masons, join the silent race 5.DunB4.571.398.
With Staff and Pumps the Marquis lead the Race; 5.DunB4.586.400.
And fram'd the clam'rous Race of busie Human-kind. 6.8.9.17.
But more diffusive in its wand'ring Race; 6.17ii.23.56.
Who wert, e're time his rapid race begun, 6.23.5.73.
Where, or the *Crane,* Foe to *Pygmæan* Race, 6.26i.5.79.
Thus *Churchill's* race shall other hearts surprize, 6.52.59.157.
All Humane Race are Worms. 6.53.4A.161.
All Human Race are Worms. 6.53.4B.161.
And from the goal again renews the race; 6.55.9.167.
To Mountain-wolves and all the Savage race, 6.65.2.192.
To Mountain Bores and all the Savage race, 6.65.2A.192.
The savage Race withdrew, nor dar'd 6.82vii.3.233.
Not with those Toys the Female Race admire, 6.86.3B.244.
They hid their Knowledge of a nobler Race, 6.96iii.15.275.
Reflecting, and reflected in his Race; 6.118.12.335.
In whom a Race, for Courage fam'd and Art, 6.132.11.362.
The Motley Race of Hervey queenies 6.135.39Z1.367.
But whatsoe'er the Father's Race, 6.135.53.368.
Can hope a Puppy of my Race. 6.135.68.369.
The Brother-Kings, of *Atreus'* Royal Race. Il.1.22.86.
Rich in her Fruits, and in her martial Race. Il.1.206.96.
Sent in *Jove's* Anger on a slavish Race, Il.1.306.101.
A Godlike Race of Heroes once I knew, Il.1.345.105.
Sure, to so short a Race of Glory born, Il.1.462.110.
The Brother Kings of *Atreus'* Royal Race: Il.1.489.111.
The boldest Warrior of the *Grecian* Race. Il.1.539.113.
The Feasts of *Æthiopia's* blameless Race: Il.1.557.115.
'Till the proud King, and all th' *Achaian* Race Il.1.660.118.
And leave unpunish'd this perfidious Race? Il.2.194.137.
And Fame eternal leave to *Priam's* Race? Il.2.212.138.
And bring the Race of Royal Bastards here, Il.2.285.141.
Unhappy Monarch! whom the *Grecian* Race Il.2.348.143.
Superior once of all the tuneful Race, Il.2.722.160.
The Glories of the mighty Race were fled! Il.2.781.162.
And shun the Vengeance of th' *Herculean* Race, Il.2.804.163.
The loveliest Youth of all the *Grecian* Race; Il.2.818.164.
All *Pelias'* Race *Alcestè* far outshin'd, Il.2.870.165.
Th' *Oechalian* Race, in those high Tow'rs contain'd, Il.2.884.166.
Sprung from *Pirithous* of immortal Race, Il.2.900.166.
As Eagles fleet, and of *Pheretian* Race; Il.2.927.167.
And his, th' unrival'd Race of Heav'nly Steeds) Il.2.937.168.
Divine *Æneas* brings the *Dardan* Race, Il.2.992.170.
And dar'd the Bravest of the *Grecian* Race. Il.3.32.189.
Thy Father's Grief, and Ruin of thy Race; Il.3.74.193.
The loveliest Nymph of *Priam's* Royal Race) Il.3.168.199.
There sate the Seniors of the *Trojan* Race, Il.3.191.200.
A bloodless Race, that send a feeble Voice. Il.3.202.201.
And from Destruction save the *Trojan* Race. Il.3.210.201.
And Strength of Numbers, to this *Grecian* Race. Il.3.252.204.
And all their Race be scatter'd as the Dust! Il.3.375.211.
But *Jove* himself the faithless Race defends: Il.4.42.223.
That *Troy,* and *Troy's* whole Race thou wou'dst confound, Il.4.51.223.
Than Godlike *Priam,* or than *Priam's* Race. Il.4.70.224.
The Race of *Trojans* in thy Ruin join, Il.4.190.230.
To save a trembling, heartless, dastard Race? Il.4.285.234.
But wasting Years that wither human Race, Il.4.364.238.
And one the Leader of th' *Epeian* Race; Il.4.625.250.
Meantime the *Greeks* the *Trojan* Race pursue, Il.5.49.268.
In Woods and Wilds to wound the Savage Race; Il.5.66.269.
The Race forgotten, and the Name no more. Il.5.203.276.
To whom the Chief of *Venus'* Race begun. Il.5.217.278.
To whom the Leader of the *Dardan* Race: Il.5.272.280.
To dare the Shock, or urge the rapid Race: Il.5.281.280.
And great *Æneas,* sprung from Race Divine! Il.5.305.281.
The Race of those which once the thund'ring God Il.5.328.282.
Four of this Race his ample Stalls contain, Il.5.334.282.
And stern *Lycaon's* warlike Race begun. Il.5.339.283.
Then *Phœbus* bore the Chief of *Venus'* Race Il.5.541.294.
That propt alone by *Priam's* Race should stand Il.5.577.296.
Honour'd and lov'd like *Priam's* Royal Race: Il.5.662.299.
How far unlike those Chiefs of Race divine, Il.5.788.304.
But you, unworthy the high Race you boast, Il.5.810.305.
Inglorious *Argives!* to your Race a Shame, Il.5.980.313.
He held his Seat; a Friend to Human Race. Il.6.18.325.
Not one of all the Race, not Sex, nor Age, Il.6.71.327.
Not one of all the Race, nor Sex, nor Age, Il.6.71A.327.
What art thou, boldest of the Race of Man? Il.6.152.333.
Like Leaves on Trees the Race of Man is found, Il.6.181.334.
Another Race the following Spring supplies, Il.6.183.335.
And emulate the Glories of our Race. Il.6.260.339.
Nor stain the sacred Friendship of our Race. Il.6.266.339.
Surpass'd the Nymphs of *Troy's* illustrious Race) Il.6.315.341.
That Pest of *Troy,* that Ruin of our Race! Il.6.353.343.
Fix'd is the Term to all the Race of Earth, Il.6.628.358.
Women of Greece! Oh Scandal of your Race, Il.7.109.369.
Their Sons degen'rate, and their Race a Scorn? Il.7.148.371.

RACE (CONTINUED)

Ulysses, and his brave maternal race ......Od.19.501.220.
The geese (a glutton race) by thee deplor'd, ...Od.19.644.227.
Snatch me, ye whirlwinds! far from humane race, ...Od.20.74.236.
Of human race now rising from repose, ...Od.20.122.239.
The wretch unfriendly to the race of man. ......Od.20.224.244.
And goats he brought, the pride of all their race; ......Od.20.236.244.
Unpiteous of the race thy will began, ...Od.20.253.245.
O race to death devote! with *Stygian* shade ......Od.20.423.253.
The eldest born of *Oenops'* noble race, ...Od.21.153.266.
Hence with long war the double race was curst, ...Od.21.323.275.
Speak him descended from no vulgar race. ......Od.21.362.277.
A gen'ral horror ran thro' all the race, ...Od.21.450.282.
Of *Priam's* race, and lay'd proud *Troy* in dust? ......Od.22.251.299.
That impious race to all their past mis-deeds ......Od.22.290.300.
Stoop from the mountains on the feather'd race, ...Od.22.338.303.
But tell me, who thou art? and what thy race? ......Od.24.348.365.
And six were all the sons of *Dolius'* race: ......Od.24.573.375.
The rebel race, and death had swallow'd all; ......Od.24.611.377.

RACER

And bad the nimblest racer seize the prize; ......5.DunA2.32.99.
And bids the nimblest racer seize the prize; ......5.DunA2.32A.99.
And bade the nimblest racer seize the prize; ......5.DunB2.36.297.
(The swiftest Racer of the liquid Skies) ......Il.22.184.463.
The knowing Racer to his End proceeds; ......Il.23.394.506.
Obscene to sight, the ruefull Racer lay; ......Il.23.912.525.
The swiftest racer of the azure plain ......Od.12.121.437.
Instant, the racer vanish'd off the ground; ......Od.14.566.64.

RACER'S

Urge the fleet courser's or the racer's toil; ......Od.24.88.352.

RACERS

Of rapid Racers in the dusty Course. ......Il.23.328.503.
Fir'd at his Word, the Rival Racers rise; ......Il.23.355.504.
To mark the Racers, and to judge the Race. ......Il.23.436.507.
Rang'd in a Line the ready Racers stand; ......Il.23.885.524.
Rang'd in a line the ready racers stand, ...Od.8.125.269.
Or you, the swiftest racers of the field! ......Od.8.234.275.

RACES

Two Races now, ally'd to *Jove,* offend; ......1.TrSt.315.423.
(Such as in Races crown the speedy Strife) ......Il.22.209.464.

RACINE

Exact Racine, and Corneille's noble fire ......4.2HE1.274.219.
As once for Louis, Boileau and Racine. ......4.2HE1.375.227.

RACING

To the brave Rulers of the racing Steed; ......Il.23.342.503.

RACK

Stretch'd on the rack of a too easy chair, ...5.DunB4.342.377.
Some Squire, perhaps, you take delight to rack; ......6.45.23.125.
Rack your Inventions some, and some *in time* translate. ......6.48iii.14.135.

RACK'D

Rack'd with Sciatics, martyr'd with the Stone, ...4.1HE6.54.241.
Rack'd with convulsive pangs in dust I roul; ......Od.4.726.153.
For lovely *Pero* rack'd his lab'ring mind! ......Od.15.259.80.

RACKS

Some strain in rhyme; the Muses, on their racks, ...5.DunA3.153.164.
Some strain in rhyme; the Muses, on their racks, ...5.DunB3.159.328.
My Racks and tortures soon shall drive them hence, ...5.DunB4.55A.347.
And the full Racks are heap'd with gen'rous Wheat. ......Il.10.669.31.

RACKT

While her rackt Soul Repose and Peace requires, ...2.RLA2.11.132.

RACY

Or mow from racy plumbs the savo'ry blew, ...6.96ii.30Z47.272.
Of social welcome, mix'd the racy wine, ...Od.3.503.112.

RADCLIFF'S

Ev'n Radcliff's Doctors travel first to France, ...4.2HE1.183.211.

RADIANCE

Arms, that reflect a Radiance thro' the Skies. ......Il.15.137.202.
Or the pale radiance of the midnight moon. ......Od.4.56.122.
Display'd the radiance of the night and day. ......Od.24.174.356.

RADIANT

And what is That, which binds the Radiant Sky, ...1.PSp.39.64.
And rising gild the radiant East again. ......1.TrSt.329.424.
And draws a radiant Circle o'er the Skies. ......1.TrSt.442.428.
Then thus the Goddess with the radiant Eyes: ......1.TrES.237.458.
Whose radiant Fires foretell the blushing Morn, ...1.TrUl.22A.466.
Till I beheld thy radiant Form once more, ...1.TrUl.199.472.
Awake my Love, disclose thy radiant Eyes; ......2.ChJM.525.40.
New Stratagems, the radiant Lock to gain. ......2.RL3.120.176.
And drew behind a radiant *Trial of Hair.* ......2.RL5.128.210.
His Sacred Head a radiant Zodiack crown'd, ...2.TemF.234.274.
The radiant Heav'ns, and Earth, and ambient main! ......6.23.2.73.
They, from the Sweetness of that Radiant Look, ...6.37.7.106.
This radiant pile nine rural sisters raise; ......6.126ii.2.353.
"Secure the radiant weapons wield; ......6.140.5.378.
Thy lov'd *Briseïs* with the radiant Eyes. ......Il.1.246.98.
Meantime the radiant Sun, to mortal Sight ......Il.1.776.124.
In radiant Arms, and thirst for *Trojan* Blood. ......Il.2.559.154.
A radiant Baldric, o'er his Shoulder ty'd, ...Il.3.415.212.
At this the Goddess roll'd her radiant Eyes, ...Il.4.73.224.
When fresh he rears his radiant Orb to Sight, ...Il.5.124.273.
And such in Fight the radiant Arms he wore. ......Il.5.548.295.
Eight brazen Spokes in radiant Order flame; ......Il.5.892.308.

RADIANT (CONTINUED)

Pallas disrobes; Her radiant Veil unty'd, ...Il.5.904.309.
Black *Orcus'* Helmet o'er her radiant Head. ......Il.5.1037.316.
His radiant Arms preserv'd from hostile Spoil, ...Il.6.528.353.
Radiant they met, beneath the Beechen Shade; ......Il.7.27.364.
A radiant Belt that rich with Purple glow'd. ......Il.7.369.382.
Those radiant Structures rais'd by lab'ring Gods, ...Il.7.539.391.
There, from his radiant Car, the sacred Sire ......Il.8.61.398.
The radiant Robe her sacred Fingers wove, ...Il.8.468.419.
Those radiant Eyes shall view, and view in vain. ......Il.8.589.424.
These radiant Eyes shall view, and view in vain. ......Il.8.589A.424.
Not those fair Steeds so radiant and so gay, ...Il.10.644.30.
His mighty Limbs in radiant Armour drest. ......Il.11.22.35.
A radiant Baldrick, o'er his Shoulder ty'd, ...Il.11.39.36.
Her artful Hands the radiant Tresses ty'd; ......Il.14.204.170.
Thus issuing radiant, with majestic Pace, ...Il.14.216.170.
A Veil of Clouds involv'd his radiant Head: ......Il.15.349.210.
His radiant Arms triumphant *Meges* bore. ......Il.15.621.220.
The radiant Helmet on his Temples burns, ...Il.15.732.224.
Then thus the Goddess with the radiant Eyes: ......Il.16.540.265.
The radiant Arms are by *Patroclus* born, ...Il.16.807.274.
They draw the conquer'd Corpse, and radiant Arms. ......Il.16.945.280.
His Train to *Troy* the radiant Armour bear, ...Il.17.141.293.
The radiant Spoils to sacred *Ilion* bore. ......Il.17.216.295.
Thy radiant Arms the *Trojan* Foe detains, ...Il.18.168.330.
Two Cities radiant on the Shield appear, ...Il.18.567.350.
Gold were the Gods, their radiant Garments Gold, ...Il.18.600.351.
Then drops the radiant Burden on the Ground; ......Il.19.15.372.
He turns the radiant Gift; and feeds his Mind ......Il.19.23.372.
Briseïs, radiant as the Queen of Love, ...Il.19.296.384.
Th' immortal Coursers, and the radiant Car, ...Il.19.427.389.
Th' Imperial Goddess with the radiant Eyes. ......Il.20.358.410.
His radiant Armour tearing from the Dead: ......Il.21.200.429.
And first assaults the radiant Queen of War ......Il.21.457.440.
As radiant *Hesper* shines with keener Light, ...Il.22.399.472.
The Tripod-Vase, and Dame with radiant Eyes: ......Il.23.594.513.
Presents, to bathe his hands, a radiant ew'r: ......Od.1.192.42.
In radiant Panoply his limbs incas'd; ......Od.1.333.48.
On whom a radiant pomp of Graces wait, ...Od.4.19.121.
To *Sparta's* Queen of old the radiant vase ......Od.4.167.128.
And twenty youths in radiant mail incas'd, ...Od.4.709.152.
Her swelling loins a radiant Zone embrac'd ......Od.5.296.185.
Far on the left those radiant fires to keep ......Od.5.353.189.
All radiant on the Raft the Goddess stood: ......Od.5.429.193.
Attend my royal sire, a radiant band. ......Od.6.306.225.
The front appear'd with radiant splendors gay, ...Od.7.110.240.
High on a radiant throne sublime in state, ...Od.8.61.265.
Then to the radiant thrones they move in state: ......Od.8.457.288.
Radiant she came; the portals open'd wide: ......Od.10.302.358.
Radiant with starry studs, a silver seat ......Od.10.375.362.
The Goddess with a radiant tunick drest ......Od.10.647.375.
When radiant he advances, or retreats: ......Od.11.18.380.
Radiant in arms the blooming Heroe came: ......Od.11.620.414.
Here the gay Morn resides in radiant bow'rs, ...Od.12.3.427.
There sacred to the radiant God of day ......Od.12.316.447.
That God who spreads the radiant beams of light, ...Od.12.385.449.
Whose radiant lamp adorns the azure way, ...Od.12.453.453.
'Till I beheld thy radiant form once more, ...Od.13.366.25.
The radiant helmet from my brows unlac'd, ...Od.14.305.50.
Like radiant *Hesper* o'er the gems of night. ......Od.15.123.74.
'Till radiant rose the messenger of day. ......Od.15.534.95.
Radiant before the gazing Peers she stands; ......Od.18.248.178.
Distinct in rows the radiant columns rise: ......Od.19.45.195.
A mantle purple-ting'd, and radiant vest, ...Od.19.275.208.
A radiant sabre grac'd his purple zone, ...Od.20.157.241.
Radiant before his gazing Consort sate. ......Od.23.164.328.

RAFT

And form a Raft, and build the rising ship, ...Od.5.211.181.
On a slight Raft to pass the swelling sea ......Od.5.226.182.
So large he built the Raft: then ribb'd it strong ......Od.5.321.187.
The Raft it cover'd, and the mast it broke; ......Od.5.404.192.
He seis'd the Raft, and leapt into his seat, ...Od.5.414.192.
All radiant on the Raft the Goddess stood: ......Od.5.429.193.
A Raft was form'd to cross the surging sea; ......Od.7.350.253.
The splitting Raft the furious tempest tore; ......Od.7.358.254.

RAFTER'D

No rafter'd roofs with dance and tabor sound, ...3.Ep3.191.109.

RAFTER'S

Perch'd like a swallow on a rafter's height, ...Od.22.262.299.

RAFTERS

Like two strong Rafters which the Builder forms ......Il.23.826.522.

RAG

Where wave the tatter'd ensigns of Rag-Fair, ...5.DunA1.27.63.
No rag, no scrap, of all the beau, or wit, ...5.DunA2.111.110.
No rag, no scrap, of all the beau, or wit, ...5.DunB2.119.301.
He lap't it in a Linnen Rag, ...6.94.73.261.

RAG-FAIR

Where wave the tatter'd ensigns of Rag-Fair, ...5.DunA1.27.63.

RAG'D

But Flames consum'd, and Billows rag'd in vain. ......1.TrSt.314.423.
He cry'd, he roar'd, he rag'd, he tore his Hair: ......2.ChJM.756A.51.
While *Anna* begg'd and *Dido* rag'd in vain. ......2.RL5.6.199.
Triumphant Malice rag'd thro' private life. ......4.2HE1.254.217.
Like him his Barons rag'd and roar'd, ...6.79.11.218.
Atrides still with deep Resentment rag'd. ......Il.1.419.107.
In ev'ry Quarter fierce *Tydides* rag'd, ...Il.5.111.272.
So rag'd *Tydides,* boundless in his Ire, ...Il.5.124.273.
Now storm'd before him, and now rag'd behind. ......Il.5.731.302.
While fierce in War divine *Achilles* rag'd; ......Il.5.983.314.

RAG'D (CONTINUED)

With direful Jealousy the Monarch rag'd, ...Il.6.199.336.
Rag'd on the left, and rul'd the Tyde of War: ....Il.11.621.61.
Thus rag'd both Armies like conflicting Fires, ...Il.11.726.67.
This stood, while *Hector* and *Achilles* rag'd, ...Il.12.11.81.
Resistless when he rag'd, and when he stop'd, unmov'd. ....Il.13.200.115.
And all the Thunder of the Battel rag'd) ....Il.13.858.146.
While thus the Thunder of the Battel rag'd, ...Il.15.450.215.
Where the War rag'd, and where the Tumult grew. ....Il.16.339.256.
Still rag'd the Conflict round the Hero dead, ...Il.17.472.306.
In mutual Feuds, her King and Hero rag'd; ....Il.18.304.336.
Stung to the Soul, he sorrow'd, and he rag'd. ....Il.19.124.377.
So rag'd *Achilles*: Death and dire Dismay, ...Il.21.611.447.
Tho' *Boreas* rag'd along th' inclement sky. ....Od.5.627.202.
Eager he fed, for keen his hunger rag'd, ...Od.6.297.225.
Stern God! who rag'd with vengeance unrestrain'd, ...Od.6.393.230.
How *Neptune* rag'd, and how by his command ....Od.8.619.295.
All night it rag'd; when morning rose, to land ....Od.12.375.449.
Stern *Neptune* rag'd; and how by his command ....Od.13.202.15.
Boundless the *Centaur* rag'd; 'till one and all ....Od.21.319.275.

RAGE

The Brazen Trumpets kindle Rage no more: ....1.Mes.60.118.
Here noble *Surrey* felt the sacred Rage, ...1.W-F.291.175.
Secure from *Flames*, from *Envy's* fiercer Rage, ...1.EOC.183.261.
Not so by Heav'n (he answers in a Rage) ....1.EOC.281.271.
Discharge that Rage on more Provoking Crimes, ...1.EOC.528.297.
Here point your Thunder, and exhaust your Rage! ....1.EOC.555.304.
And Rhyme with all the *Rage of Impotence!* ....1.EOC.609.308.
And love disdain'd revives with fiercer rage. ....1.TrPA.131.371.
Roar'd out for rage, and hurried o'er the plain: ....1.TrPA.133.371.
And strikes with bolder Rage the sounding Strings, ...1.TrSP.34.394.
Now swell to Rage, now melt in Tears again. ....1.TrSP.132.399.
Fraternal Rage, the guilty *Thebes* Alarms, ...1.TrSt.1.409.
Whose fatal Rage th'unhappy Monarch found; ....1.TrSt.14.410.
The Rage of *Tydeus*, or the Prophet's Fate? ....1.TrSt.62.412.
The Rage of *Tydeus*, or the Prophet's Fate? ....1.TrSt.63.412.
Strait with the Rage of all their Race possest, ...1.TrSt.173.417.
Say, wretched Rivals! what provokes your Rage? ....1.TrSt.210.419.
Here all their Rage, and ev'n their Murmurs cease, ...1.TrSt.290.422.
Triumphant o'er th'eluded Rage of *Jove!* ....1.TrSt.303.422.
Ah why shou'd *Argos* feel the Rage of *Jove?* ....1.TrSt.365.425.
Derive Incitements to renew thy Rage; ....1.TrSt.380.425.
The Rage and Grief contending in her Breast; ....1.TrSt.401.426.
With equal Rage their airy Quarrel try, ...1.TrSt.490.430.
Inflames his Heart with Rage, and wings his Feet with Fears. .1.TrSt.519.432.
But gen'rous Rage the bold *Chorœbus* warms, ...1.TrSt.714.440.
And weary all the wild Efforts of Rage. ....1.TrSt.734.441.
But fir'd with Rage, from cleft *Parnassus'* Brow ....1.TrSt.739.441.
For not the vengeful Pow'r, that glow'd with Rage, ...1.TrSt.782.442.
Thy Rage the *Phrygian* felt, who durst aspire ....1.TrSt.845.445.
With gen'rous Rage, that drives him on the Foes. ....1.TrES.22.450.
With equal Valour, and with equal Rage. ....1.TrES.224.458.
With equal Clamours, and with equal Rage. ....1.TrES.224A.458.
The starting Coursers, and restrain their Rage, ...1.TrES.276.460.
The roaring Winds tempestuous Rage restrain; ....1.TrUl.28.466.
And Mighty *Neptune's* unrelenting Rage?— ....1.TrUl.223.473.
Cou'd swell the Soul to Rage, and fire the Martial Train. ....2.ChJM.325.30.
The Joys are such as far transcend your Rage, ...2.ChJM.339.30.
The Rage of Jealousie then seiz'd his Mind, ...2.ChJM.485.39.
His Rage was such, as cannot be exprest: ....2.ChJM.753.51.
Lord! how you swell, and rage like any Fiend! ....2.ChWB.81.60.
With burning Rage, and frantic Jealousie. ....2.ChWB.236.68.
And in soft Bosoms dwells such mighty Rage? ....2.RL1.12.145.
And dwells such Rage in softest Bosoms then? ....2.RL1.11A.145.
Proves the just Victim of his Royal Rage. ....2.RL3.60.172.
E'er felt such Rage, Resentment and Despair, ...2.RL4.9.183.
And heav'nly Breasts with human Passions rage; ....2.RL5.46.202.
Pleas'd with *Alcæus'* manly Rage t'infuse ....2.TemF.224.273.
I can no more; by shame, by rage suppress, ...2.ElAb.105.328.
Here brib'd the rage of ill-requited heav'n: ....2.ElAb.138.331.
Or never feel the rage, or never own; ....3.EOM2.228.83.
Whose attributes were Rage, Revenge, or Lust; ....3.EOM3.258.118.
And die of nothing but a Rage to live. ....3.Ep2.100.58.
No Passion gratify'd except her Rage. ....3.Ep2.126.61.
In Youth they conquer, with so wild a rage, ...3.Ep2.221.68.
And nobly wishing Party-rage to cease, ...3.Ep3.151.106.
But who, my friend, has reason in his rage? ....3.Ep3.154.106.
Slander or Poyson, dread from *Delia's* Rage, ...4.HS1.81.13.
Yet neither *Charles* nor *James* be in a Rage? ....4.HS1.114.15.
Whose *Satyr's sacred*, and whose Rage *secure*. ....4.JD4.283.49.
If I dislike it, "Furies, death and rage!" ....4.Arbu.57.100.
Well might they rage; I gave them but their due. ....4.Arbu.174.109.
Stranger to Civil and Religious Rage, ...4.Arbu.394.126.
Does neither Rage inflame, nor Fear appall? ....4.2HE2.308.187.
How will our Fathers rise up in a rage, ...4.2HE1.125.205.
How barb'rous rage subsided at your word, ...4.2HE1.398.229.
The worthy Youth shall ne'er be in a rage: ....4.EpS1.48.301.
And all the Mighty Mad in Dennis rage. ....5.DunA1.104.72.
And furious *D[unto]n* foam in *Wh[atley]'s* rage ....5.DunA1.104A.72*.
And furious *D[enni]s* foam in *W[elsted]'s* rage. ....5.DunA1.104B.72*.
And furious *D[enni]s* foam in *W[harton]'s* rage. ....5.DunA1.104C.72*.
And furious *D[enni]s* foam in *W[histon]'s* rage. ....5.DunA1.104D.72*.
And furious *D[enni]s* foam in *W[esley]'s* rage. ....5.DunA1.104E.72*.
Oh spread thy Influence, but restrain thy Rage! ....5.DunA3.114.160.
"Ah Dennis! Gildon ah! what ill-starr'd rage ....5.DunA3.167.167.
Gods, imps, and monsters, music, rage, and mirth, ...5.DunA3.234.177.
And all the mighty Mad in Dennis rage. ....5.DunB1.106.277.
Oh spread thy influence, but restrain thy Rage. ....5.DunB3.122.325.
"Ah Dennis! Gildon ah! what ill-starr'd rage ....5.DunB3.173.328.
Gods, imps, and monsters, music, rage, and mirth, ...5.DunB3.238.332.
But sober History restrain'd her rage, ...5.DunB4.39.344.
One Trill shall harmonize joy, grief, and rage, ...5.DunB4.57.347.
The decent Knight retir'd with sober rage, ...5.DunB4.113.352.
The rage of courts, and noise of towns; ....6.1.2B.3.
And giddy *Factions* hear away their Rage. ....6.11.35.31.

RAGE (CONTINUED)

Ev'n giddy *Factions* hear away their Rage. ....6.11.35A.31.
And *Factions* hear away their Rage. ....6.11.35B.31.
And Fate's severest Rage disarm: ....6.11.119.34.
Vex'd with vain rage, and impotently great, ...6.20.20.66.
No guilt of mine the rage of Heav'n cou'd move; ....6.20.60.67.
When he the rage of sinners shall sustain, ...6.21.35.70.
Oft' bend to *Auster's* blasts, or *Boreas'* Rage, ...6.26i.3.79.
Rage strait Collects his Venom all at once, ...6.26i.14.79.
Be justly warm'd with your own native rage, ...6.32.44.97.
Such rage without betrays the fire within; ....6.41.17.114.
Why should I stay? Both Parties rage; ....6.47.21.129.
So just thy skill, so regular my rage. ....6.52.12.156.
Some hostile fury, some religious rage; ....6.71.12.203.
These pleas'd the Fathers of poetic rage; ....6.71.50.204.
The Rage of Pow'r, the Blast of publick Breath, ...6.84.25.239.
Well may they rage; I give them *but* their Due. ....6.98.24.284.
Well may they rage; I gave them *but* their Due. ....6.98.24A.284.
And thou! whose sense, whose humour, and whose rage, ...6.106iv.1.307.
Amidst corruption, luxury, and rage, ...6.113.9.320.
Uncag'd then let the harmless Monster rage, ...6.116vii.7.328.
With native Humour temp'ring virtuous Rage, ...6.125.3.350.
If there's a Critick of distinguish'd Rage; ....6.128.21.356.
Whose Publick Virtue knew no Party rage: ....6.134.2.364.
No Passion gratify'd except her Rage; ....6.154.12.403.
Explore the Cause of great *Apollo's* Rage; ....Il.1.84.90.
And rage he may, but he shall rage in vain. ....Il.1.180.96.
And rage he may, but he shall rage in vain. ....Il.1.180.96.
Let fierce *Achilles*, dreadful in his Rage, ...Il.1.191.96.
Achilles heard, with Grief and Rage opprest, ...Il.1.251.98.
Nor yet the Rage his boiling Breast forsook, ...Il.1.295.101.
Then rage in Bitterness of Soul, to know ....Il.1.323.103.
Leave me, O King! to calm *Achilles'* Rage; ....Il.1.372.106.
When now the Rage of Hunger was represt, ...Il.1.614.117.
In foreign Contests, and domestic Rage, ...Il.1.673.119.
Lest, rouz'd to Rage, he shake the blest Abodes, ...Il.1.748.123.
Soon as the Rage of Hunger was supprest, ...Il.2.514.151.
But silent, breathing Rage, resolv'd, and skill'd ....Il.3.11.188.
All pale with Rage, and shake the threat'ning Lance. ....Il.3.426.212.
Then, the sad Victim of the Publick Rage. ....Il.3.520.216.
Go now, once more thy Rival's Rage excite, ...Il.3.539.217.
His high Concern may well excuse this Rage, ...Il.4.468.242.
With Rage impetuous down their ecchoing Hills; ....Il.4.517.246.
Man dies on Man, and all is Blood and Rage. ....Il.4.541.247.
Where the Fight burns, and where the thickest rage. ....Il.5.14.266.
Those slain he left; and sprung with noble Rage ....Il.5.188.275.
Young *Xanthus* next and *Thoon* felt his Rage, ...Il.5.196.276.
Dreadful they come, and bend their Rage on thee: ....Il.5.303.281.
First rosie *Venus* felt his brutal Rage; ....Il.5.557.295.
Like trembling Hounds before the Lion's Rage. ....Il.5.582.296.
When now the *North* his boist'rous Rage has spent, ...Il.5.643.299.
This swells the Tumult and the Rage of Fight; ....Il.5.728.302.
What lawless Rage on yon' forbidden Plain, ...Il.5.944.311.
Beneath the Rage of burning *Sirius* rise, ...Il.5.1060.317.
And Gods on Gods exert Eternal Rage. ....Il.5.1071.317.
The Waste of Slaughter, and the Rage of Fight, ...Il.5.1099.319.
Shall save a *Trojan* from our boundless Rage ....Il.6.72.327.
Old *Nestor* saw, and rowz'd the Warrior's Rage; ....Il.6.83.327.
In Rage unbounded, and unmatch'd in Might. ....Il.6.124.330.
With Rage recruited the bold *Trojans* glow, ...Il.6.129.330.
Now breathe thy Rage, and hush the stern Debate: ....Il.7.34.364.
The warring Nations to suspend their Rage; ....Il.7.54.365.
He stoop'd to Reason, and his Rage resign'd. ....Il.7.140.370.
All these, alike inspir'd with noble Rage, ...Il.7.205.374.
When now the Rage of Hunger was remov'd; ....Il.7.388.383.
Strong God of Ocean! Thou, whose Rage can make ....Il.7.544.391.
Oh turn and save from *Hector's* direful Rage ....Il.8.121.403.
What Rage, what Madness, furious Queen! is thine? ....Il.8.255.409.
Still swells the Slaughter, and still grows the Rage! ....Il.8.432.418.
What Frenzy, Goddesses! what Rage can move ....Il.8.508.420.
She flew; and *Juno* thus her Rage resign'd. ....Il.8.525.421.
But *Juno*, impotent of Rage, replies. ....Il.8.574.424.
Lest all should perish in the Rage of *Jove*. ....Il.8.583.424.
Nor shall great *Hector* cease the Rage of Fight, ...Il.8.590.424.
With all thy Rage, with all thy Rebel Force. ....Il.8.596.424.
And the fir'd Fleet behold the Battel rage. ....Il.8.660.427.
Fain wou'd my Heart, which err'd thro' frantic Rage, ...Il.9.153.439.
And calm the Rage of stern *Æacides*. ....Il.9.242.444.
Lest Fate accomplish all his Rage design'd. ....Il.9.317.449.
To calm thy Passions, and subdue thy Rage: ....Il.9.333.450.
Repell the Rage of *Priam's* single Son? ....Il.9.463.455.
Now by thy Rage, thy fatal Rage, resign'd; ....Il.9.618.464.
Now by thy Rage, thy fatal Rage, resign'd. ....Il.9.618.464.
Were Rage still harbour'd in the haughty King, ...Il.9.642.466.
Thy Friend to plead against so just a Rage. ....Il.9.644.466.
Till Rage at length inflam'd his lofty Breast, ...Il.9.667.467.
(For Rage invades the wisest and the best.) ....Il.9.668.467.
The haughtiest Hearts at length their Rage resign, ...Il.9.747.471.
My Rage rekindles, and my Soul's on flame, ...Il.9.760.472.
Be the fierce Impulse of his Rage obey'd; ....Il.9.820.474.
The dreadful Weapons of the Warrior's Rage, ...Il.10.86.6.
That great *Achilles* rise and rage again, ...Il.10.119.7.
The Spot, where *Hector* stop'd his Rage before, ...Il.10.234.12.
Ev'n great *Achilles* scarce their Rage can tame, ...Il.10.475.24.
The Victor's Rage, the dying, and the dead. ....Il.11.114.39.
Before *Atrides'* Rage so sinks the Foe, ...Il.11.205.44.
And Rage, and Death, and Carnage, load the Field. ....Il.11.234.46.
Tho' Rage impells him, and tho' Hunger calls, ...Il.11.677.65.
This Hour he stands the Mark of hostile Rage, ...Il.11.716.67.
For *Neleus'* Sons *Alcides'* Rage had slain; ....Il.11.832.73.
Those Chiefs, that us'd her utmost Rage to meet, ...Il.11.960.78.
And mutual Deaths are dealt with mutual Rage. ....Il.12.4.80.
With equal Rage encompass'd *Hector* glows; ....Il.12.55.83.
With gen'rous Rage that drives him on the Foes. ....Il.12.366.94.
While Tears of Rage stand burning in their Eye. ....Il.13.122.110.
Grant that our Chief offend thro' Rage or Lust ....Il.13.153.111.

RAGE (CONTINUED)
Meanwhile with rising Rage the Battel glows, ...Il.13.225.116.
These can the Rage of haughty *Hector* tame; ....Il.13.406.125.
Thus by Despair, Hope, Rage, together driv'n, ...Il.13.428.126.
Then rising in his Rage, he burns to fight: ....Il.13.592.134.
But most his Hunters rouze his mighty Rage. ....Il.13.601.135.
And from the Rage of Combate gently drew: ....Il.13.677.137.
(Great *Neptune's* Care preserv'd from hostile Rage ....Il.13.702.138.
Then fierce they mingle where the thickest rage. ....Il.13.992.152.
Is ev'ry Heart inflam'd with equal Rage ....Il.14.55.160.
The God of Ocean (to inflame their Rage) ....Il.14.155.165.
With such a Rage the meeting Hosts are driv'n, ...Il.14.463.186.
Not till that Day shall *Jove* relax his Rage, ...Il.15.78.199.
The Skies would yield an ampler Scene of Rage, ...Il.15.153.202.
Seeks his own Seas, and trembles at our Rage! ....Il.15.251.206.
Far from the Hunter's Rage secure they lie, ...Il.15.310.209.
This Death deplor'd to *Hector's* Rage we owe; ....Il.15.514.217.
Rage edg'd his Sword, and strengthen'd ev'ry Blow. ....Il.15.535.217.
It calls to Death, and all the Rage of Fights. ....Il.15.601.220.
Not with more Rage a Conflagration rolls, ...Il.15.728.224.
Thus from the Rage of *Jove*-like Hector, *flew* ....Il.15.768.226.
May never Rage like thine my Soul enslave, ...Il.16.40.237.
Those, my sole Oracles, inspire my Rage: ....Il.16.73.238.
Rage uncontroul'd thro' all the hostile Crew, ...Il.16.112.240.
"Whose Rage defrauds us of so fam'd a Field. ....Il.16.245.249.
Whet all their Stings, and call forth all their Rage; ....Il.16.317.255.
Their rising Rage *Patroclus'* Breath inspires, ...Il.16.322.255.
But godlike *Thrasimed* prevents his Rage, ...Il.16.383.258.
But godly *Thrasimed* prevents his Rage, ...Il.16.383A.258*.
With equal Clamours, and with equal Rage, ...Il.16.527.264.
The starting Coursers, and restrain their Rage, ...Il.16.581.267.
Inflaming thus the Rage of all their Hosts. ....Il.16.658.270.
Oh save from hostile Rage his lov'd Remains: ....Il.16.668.270.
Then *Bathyclæus* fell beneath his Rage, ...Il.16.721.272.
Thus for some slaughter'd Hind, with equal Rage, ...Il.16.915.279.
While all around, Confusion, Rage, and Fright ....Il.16.921.279.
Not with less Noise, with less tumultuous Rage, ...Il.16.929.279.
Far from his Rage th' immortal Coursers drove; ....Il.16.1048.283.
Come all! Let gen'rous Rage your Arms employ, ...Il.17.300.299.
And *Merion,* burning with a Hero's Rage. ....Il.17.305.299.
By the swift Rage of *Ajax Telamon.* ....Il.17.327.300.
Could blame this Scene; such Rage, such Horror reign'd; ....Il.17.460.305.
Patroclus, while he liv'd, their Rage cou'd tame, ...Il.17.544.309.
The Force of *Hector,* and *Æneas'* Rage: ....Il.17.581.311.
All grim with Rage, and horrible with Gore: ....Il.17.609.312.
Or from the Rage of Man, destructive War) ....Il.17.619.312.
But *Hector,* like the Rage of Fire, we dread, ...Il.17.636.312.
Desire of Blood, and Rage, and Lust of Fight. ....Il.17.641.312.
Rage lifts his Lance, and drives him on the Foe. ....Il.17.667.314.
Tho' fierce his Rage, unbounded be his Woe, ...Il.17.795.319.
With Rage insatiate and with Thirst of Blood, ...Il.17.812.320.
Æneas storms, and *Hector* foams with Rage: ....Il.17.844.321.
Thus like the Rage of Fire the Combat burns, ...Il.18.1.322.
The Rage of *Hector* o'er the Ranks was born: ....Il.18.192.331.
Nor with his Death the Rage of *Hector* ends: ....Il.18.214.332.
I dread *Pelides* now: his Rage of Mind ....Il.18.307.336.
So may his Rage be tir'd, and labour'd down; ....Il.18.331.337.
Suppress (my Son) this Rage of Grief, and know ....Il.19.11.371.
And feels with Rage divine his Bosom glow: ....Il.19.20.372.
And Heav'n with Strength supply the mighty Rage! ....Il.19.38.373.
What can the Errors of my Rage attone? ....Il.19.137.377.
Till my insatiate Rage be cloy'd with Blood: ....Il.19.208.381.
Not else *Atrides* could our Rage inflame, ...Il.19.283.384.
And *Phœnix;* strive to calm his Grief and Rage ....Il.19.332.386.
His Rage they calm not , nor his Grief controul; ....Il.19.333.386.
Thy rage in safety thro' the Files of War: ....Il.19.453.391.
With unabated Rage—So let it be! ....Il.19.466.391.
What can they now, if in his Rage he rise? ....Il.20.40.394.
He said, and fir'd their heav'nly Breasts with Rage: ....Il.20.43.395.
Then Tumult rose; fierce Rage and pale Affright ....Il.20.64.396.
Achilles glow'd with more than mortal Rage: ....Il.20.104.398.
He rush'd impetuous. Such the Lion's Rage, ...Il.20.199.402.
He calls up all his Rage; he grinds his Teeth, ...Il.20.208.402.
Nor *Mars* himself, nor great *Minerva's* Rage. ....Il.20.408.412.
Thus, breathing Rage thro' all the Hero said; ....Il.20.427.412.
Then fell on *Polydore* his vengeful Rage, ...Il.20.471.414.
With that, he gluts his Rage on Numbers slain: ....Il.20.525.416.
Yet still insatiate, still with Rage on flame; ....Il.20.589.418.
'Tis not on me thy Rage should heap the Dead. ....Il.21.234.430.
Then rising in his Rage above the Shores, ...Il.21.257.431.
With equal Rage, indignant *Xanthus* roars, ...Il.21.356.435.
Shall ought avail him, if our Rage unite: ....Il.21.369.436.
Go, mighty in thy Rage! display thy Pow'r, ...Il.21.394.436.
Me, only me, with all his wastfull Rage? ....Il.21.433.438.
She bade th' Ignipotent his Rage forbear, ...Il.21.443.438.
Re-kindling Rage each heavenly Breast alarms; ....Il.21.450.439.
She said, and seiz'd her Wrists with eager Rage; ....Il.21.566.445.
Some proud in Triumph, some with Rage on fire; ....Il.21.603.447.
While here thy frantick Rage attacks a God. ....Il.22.22.453.
Yet curst with Sense! a Wretch, whom in his Rage ....Il.22.82.456.
But when the Fates, in Fulness of their Rage, ...Il.22.102.456.
Against his Rage if singly thou proceed, ...Il.22.120.458.
No Thought but Rage, and never-ceasing Strife, ...Il.22.341.470.
Till Death extinguish Rage, and Thought, and Life. ....Il.22.342.470.
While cast to all the Rage of hostile Pow'r, ...Il.22.423.473.
Thy Rage, Implacable! too well I knew: ....Il.22.446.474.
Giv'n to the Rage of an insulting Throng! ....Il.22.509.477.
No less, than if the Rage of hostile Fires ....Il.22.518.478.
Some Rites remain, to glut our Rage of Grief. ....Il.23.14.486.
The Rage of Hunger and of Thirst allay, ...Il.23.68.489.
On these the Rage of Fire victorious preys, ...Il.23.216.498.
Rage fills his Eye with Anguish, to survey ....Il.23.465.508.
Weak are its Counsels, headlong is its Rage. ....Il.23.672.516.
Again they rage, again to Combat rise; ....Il.23.854.523.
In Strength of Rage and Impotence of Pride, ...Il.24.53.538.
Lo how his Rage dishonest drags along ....Il.24.66.538.

RAGE (CONTINUED)
So brave! so many fall'n! To calm his Rage ....Il.24.253.547.
My Rage, and these Barbarities repay! ....Il.24.262.547.
The sorrowing Friends his frantick Rage obey. ....Il.24.310.549.
And scarce their Rulers check their martial Rage. ....Il.24.494.556.
And scarce their Rulers check the martial Rage. ....Il.24.494A.556.
Him too thy Rage has slain! beneath thy Steel ....Il.24.620.562.
Nor *Jove's* Command, should check the rising Rage. ....Il.24.735.568.
When now the Rage of Hunger was represt, ...Il.24.796.570.
Who saves her Infants from the Rage of War? ....Il.24.919.574.
At length their rage the hostile Pow'rs restrain, ...Od.1.27.30.
But grief and rage alternate wound my breast ....Od.1.61.33.
The rage of hunger quell'd, they all advance, ...Od.1.195.42.
Intemp'rate rage a wordy war began; ....Od.1.467.55.
Rage gnaw'd the lip, and wonder chain'd the tongue. ....Od.1.488.55.
Nor let *Antinous* rage, if strong desire ....Od.1.499.56.
And bid the voice of lawless riot rage. ....Od.2.82.64.
While thus he spoke, with rage and grief he frown'd, ...Od.2.89.65.
With haughty rage, and sternly thus returns. ....Od.2.94.65.
Nor fire to rage *Telemachus* his breast. ....Od.2.216.72.
Mis-lead fallacious into idle rage, ...Od.2.220.72.
That flash'd with rage; and as he spoke, he frown'd. ....Od.2.260.74.
The rage of thirst and hunger now suppress, ...Od.3.602.117.
The boiling bosom of tumultuous Rage; ....Od.4.304.134.
With homicidal rage the King oppress! ....Od.4.718.152.
But when superior to the rage of woe, ...Od.4.729.153.
Unless with filial rage *Orestes* glow, ...Od.4.737.153.
Arriv'd, the rage of hunger we controll, ...Od.4.781.156.
Rage sparkling in his eyes, and burning in his breast. ....Od.4.887.159.
Some Kings with arbitrary rage devour, ...Od.4.918.161.
May timely intercept their ruffian rage, ...Od.4.977.163.
With grief and rage the mother-lion stung, ...Od.4.1043.166.
A favour'd mortal, and not feel your rage? ....Od.5.154.179.
Prevent the rage of him who reigns above, ...Od.5.187.180.
(Unequal contest) not his rage and pow'r, ...Od.5.432.193.
Soon as their rage subsides, the seas I brave ....Od.7.360.254.
And now the rage of craving hunger fled. ....Od.8.68.265.
Ere yet he loos'd the rage of war on *Troy.* ....Od.8.78.266.
Arrive'd, he sees, he grieves, with rage he burns; ....Od.8.345.282.
When now the rage of hunger was allay'd, ...Od.8.529.291.
Tho' tempests rage, tho' rolls the swelling main, ...Od.8.611.295.
The seas may roll, the tempests rage in vain. ....Od.8.612.295.
Wide o'er the waste the rage of *Boreas* sweeps, ...Od.9.77.306.
These words the *Cyclops'* burning rage provoke: ....Od.9.565.329.
There *Bacchus* with fierce rage *Diana* fires, ...Od.11.403.404.
Still burns thy rage? and can brave souls resent ....Od.11.679.418.
O fly her rage! thy conquest is thy flight. ....Od.12.152.439.
Oh should the fierce south-west his rage display, ...Od.12.343.448.
And kindles into rage the God of day: ....Od.12.444.452.
To cheer the grave, and warm the Poet's rage) ....Od.13.12.2.
The roaring wind's tempestuous rage restrain; ....Od.13.119.7.
And mighty *Neptune's* unrelenting rage? ....Od.13.390.25.
Restrain'd the rage the vengeful foe exprest, ...Od.14.311.50.
And now the rage of hunger was represt, ...Od.14.508.61.
Some friend would fence me from the winter's rage. ....Od.14.571.64.
And the short rage of thirst and hunger ceast) ....Od.15.159.76.
Mean-time, what anguish and what rage combin'd, ...Od.15.258.80.
With unrelenting rage, and force from home ....Od.15.300.83.
Sunk the fair City by the rage of war, ...Od.15.415.89.
And now, the rage of thirst and hunger fled, ...Od.16.55.105.
Bear it my son! repress thy rising rage: ....Od.16.295.119.
Or chuse ye vagrant from their rage to fly ....Od.16.394.125.
'Till the keen rage of craving hunger fled: ....Od.16.499.131.
'Till now the rage of thirst and hunger ceast. ....Od.17.115.137.
Short was that doubt; to quell his rage inur'd, ...Od.17.278.145.
To whom *Antinous* thus his rage exprest. ....Od.17.528.158.
In rival tasks beneath the burning rage ....Od.18.411.188.
Whirl'd from his arm with erring rage it flew; ....Od.18.437.189.
These poor but honest rags, enkindle rage? ....Od.19.89.196.
Yet him, my guest, thy venom'd rage hath stung; ....Od.19.115.198.
From the devouring rage of grief reclaim. ....Od.19.300.209.
The wounds of Destiny's relentless rage ....Od.19.359.211.
Then, licens'd rage her hateful prey devours. ....Od.19.382.212.
With glancing rage the tusky savage tore. ....Od.19.463.218.
Shall bleed a victim to vindictive rage. ....Od.19.574.224.
But whilst with grief and rage my bosom burn'd, ...Od.19.637.227.
His heart with rage this new dishonour stung, ...Od.20.13.231.
Of wounded honour, and thy rage restrain. ....Od.20.24.233.
Restless his body rolls, to rage resign'd: ....Od.20.31.233.
Unbless'd, abandon'd to the rage of fate! ....Od.20.174.241.
Dread not the railer's laugh, nor ruffian's rage; ....Od.20.328.249.
Rage gnaw'd the lip, amazement chain'd the tongue. ....Od.20.335.249.
When thus the Prince with pious rage inflam'd: ....Od.20.372.250.
A just reproof, ye Peers! Your rage restrain ....Od.20.389.251.
Of rage, or folly, my prophetic mind, ...Od.20.438.254.
Rage flash'd in lightning from the Suitors eyes, ...Od.21.307.274.
With dying rage his forehead beats the ground, ...Od.22.102.291.
Be gone: another might have felt our rage, ...Od.23.25.320.
Or did the rage of stormy *Neptune* sweep ....Od.24.134.354.
And second all *Eupithes'* rage inspir'd. ....Od.24.533.373.
The rage of hunger and of thirst represt: ....Od.24.565.375.
They drop their jav'lins, and their rage resign, ...Od.24.617.377.

RAGERIE
Women ben full of Ragerie, ...6.14i.1.41.

RAGES
The Dog-star rages! nay 'tis past a doubt, ...4.Arbu.3.96.
The stern *Atrides* rages round the Field: ....Il.3.560.218.
Here rages Force, here tremble Flight and Fear, ...Il.5.915.310.
When the Fight rages, and the Flames surround? ....Il.8.281.410.
The vengeful Victor rages round the Fields ....Il.11.341.49.
Here *Hector* rages like the Force of Fire, ...Il.13.81.108.
Steeps *Troy* in Blood, and rages round the Plain; ....Il.15.48A.196.
Behind them rages all the Storm of War; ....Il.17.822.320.
Still for one Loss he rages unresign'd, ...Il.24.58.538.

RAGES 170 RAIS'D

RAGES (CONTINUED)
Whilst thus their fury rages at the bay, ...Od.10.145.347.

RAGGED
See good Sir *George* of ragged Livery stript, ...4.HAdv.55.81.
His ragged claws are stuck with stones and sands; ....Od.5.552.199.
Adieu! but since this ragged garb can bear ....Od.17.26.133.
His ragged vest then drawn aside disclos'd ....Od.21.230.270.

RAGING
I know thee Love! wild as the raging Main, ...1.PAu.89A.86.
Still *run on* Poets in a raging Vein, ...1.EOC.606.308.
But finds no shelter from his raging fires. ....1.TrPA.38.366.
Ah let me seek it from the raging Seas: ....1.TrSP.257.404.
To raging Seas unpity'd I'll remove, ...1.TrSP.258.404.
Ah! let me seek it from the raging Seas: ....1.TrSP.257B.404.
The raging *Tydeus*, or the Prophet's Fate? ....1.TrSt.62A.412.
The raging God prepares t'avenge her Fate. ....1.TrSt.704.439.
And raging *Sirius* blasts the sickly Year, ...1.TrSt.748.441.
And raging Billows drove us on your Coast: ....1.TrUl.151.470.
The raging Flames that in his Bosome dwell, ...2.ChJM.394.34.
She said; then raging to *Sir Plume* repairs, ...2.RL4.121.194.
We wake next morning in a raging Fit, ...4.2HE1.179.209.
And Fevers raging up and down, ...4.1HE7.13.269.
When gath'ring tempests swell the raging main, ...6.21.7.69.
But He, our Chief, provok'd the raging Pest, ...Il.1.119.92.
The raging King return'd his Frowns again. ....Il.1.328.103.
The raging Chief in frantick Passion lost, ...Il.1.446.109.
Thy direful Darts inflict the raging Pest; ....Il.1.595.116.
But raging still amidst his Navy sate ....Il.1.634.118.
But he lay raging on the *Lemnian* Ground, ...Il.2.878.165.
The raging Warrior to the spacious Skies ....Il.3.449.213.
And *Discord* raging bathes the purple Plain: ....Il.4.501.244.
The raging Chief in chace of *Venus* flies: ....Il.5.408.286.
And calling *Mars*, thus urg'd the raging God. ....Il.5.552.295.
Great *Hector* saw, and raging at the View ....Il.5.722.302.
With Slaughter red, and raging round the Field. ....Il.5.1019.315.
Against th' Immortals lifts his raging Hand: ....Il.5.1083.318.
His Eldest-born by raging *Mars* was slain, ...Il.6.251.339.
Another Shaft the raging Archer drew; ....Il.8.375.415.
Gods! shall one raging Hand thus level All? ....Il.8.429.417.
See! Heav'n and Earth the raging Chief defies; ....Il.9.312.449.
As when the Winds with raging Flames conspire, ...Il.11.201.44.
Thus raging *Hector*, with resistless Hands, ...Il.11.401.52.
Then raging with intolerable Smart, ...Il.11.574.59.
Chief after Chief the raging Foe destroys; ....Il.11.812.72.
Resists she yet the raging *Hector's* Hand! ....Il.11.953.77.
With healing Balms the raging Smart allay, ...Il.11.965.78.
Of raging *Asius*, and his furious Band. ....Il.12.152.87.
With raging Grief great *Menelaus* burns, ...Il.13.733.139.
And all the raging Gods oppos'd in vain? ....Il.15.26.195.
Still raging *Hector* with his ample Hand ....Il.15.868.230.
Raging he spoke; nor farther wastes his Breath, ...Il.15.902.232.
And raging Seas produc'd thee in a Storm, ...Il.16.51.237.
While restless, raging, in your Ships you lay) ....Il.16.243.248.
Swift as thou art (the raging Hero cries) ....Il.16.745.272.
He said, and touch'd his Heart. The raging Pair ....Il.17.135.293.
Pierc'd thro' the Wrist; and raging with the Pain ....Il.17.681.314.
While raging *Hector* heap'd our Camps with Dead. ....Il.19.136.377.
These boastful Words provoke the raging God; ....Il.21.151.427.
In all the raging Impotence of Woe. ....Il.22.527.478.
By whose commands the raging deeps I trace ....Od.2.299.76.
This heard the raging Ruler of the main; ....Od.4.677.151.
The raging Monarch shook his azure head, ...Od.5.365.190.
What raging winds? what roaring waters round? ....Od.5.390.191.
The raging God a wat'ry mountain roll'd; ....Od.5.465.195.
To thee from *Neptune* and the raging main. ....Od.5.571.199.
For angry *Neptune* rouz'd the raging main: ....Od.7.356.253.
Mean-time the *Cyclop* raging with his wound, ...Od.9.493.326.
Thus I: while raging he repeats his cries, ...Od.9.615.332.
One for his food the raging glutton slew, ...Od.10.133.347.
And calm the raging tempest of thy soul. ....Od.11.690.418.
Scarce the fam'd *Argo* pass'd these raging floods, ...Od.12.83.435.
Her parts obscene the raging billows hide; ....Od.12.115.437.
And raging billows drove us on your coast. ....Od.13.318.22.

RAGS
One flaunts in rags, one flutters in brocade, ...3.EOM4.196.145.
In silks, in crapes, in garters, and in rags; ....5.DunA2.18.98.
In silks, in crapes, in Garters, and in rags, ...5.DunB2.22.297.
That sturdy Vagrants, Rogues in Rags, ...6.135.21.366.
That Sturdy Beggars, Rogues in Rags, ...6.135.21A.366.
That idle Gypsies, Rogues in Rags, ...6.135.21B.366.
In rags dishonest flutters with the air: ....Od.13.503.30.
Then with these tatter'd rags they wrapt me round, ...Od.14.379.53.
In rags dishonest flut'ring with the air! ....Od.17.229.143.
These poor but honest rags, enkindle rage? ....Od.19.89.196.
Like thee, in rags obscene decreed to roam! ....Od.20.262.246.
Stript of his rags, he blaz'd out like a God. ....Od.22.2.284.
But cast those mean dishonest rags away; ....Od.22.524.314.
And hung with rags, that flutter'd in the air. ....Od.24.186.356.

RAIL
For who can *rail* so long as they can *write?* ....1.EOC.599.308.
Why rail they then, if but a Wreath of mine ....4.EpS2.138.321.
That virtuous ladies envy while they rail; ....6.41.16.113.
To hear 'em rail at honest Sunderland ....6.61.19.181.
To hear you rail at honest S[underlan]d ....6.61.19A.181.
To hear them rail at honest Sunderland ....6.61.19B.181.
Let *D[enni]s* write, and nameless numbers rail: ....6.63.4.188.
For, ev'ry Man has equal Strength to rail: ....Il.20.299.406.
Indecently to rail without offence! ....Od.18.21.167.

RAIL'D
Then kist again, and chid and rail'd betwixt. ....2.ChWB.177.65.

RAILER'S
Dread not the railer's laugh, nor ruffian's rage; ....Od.20.328.249.

RAILING
And *R—*, and railing, Brangling, and B[reval], ...5.DunA2.230A.128.
Railing at Men of Sense, to show their Wit; ....6.17iv.10.59.
Such railing eloquence, and war of words. ....Od.2.96.65.

RAILLERY
But let me die, all raillery apart, ...6.41.11.113.
Farewell *Arbuthnot's* Raillery ....6.47.13.129.

RAILLY
Yet lest you think I railly more than teach, ...4.2HE1.338.225.

RAILS
Who from his study rails at human kind; ....3.Ep1.2.15.
Befringe the rails of Bedlam and Sohoe. ....4.2HE1.419.231.
If Dennis rails, and raves in furious Pet, ...6.49iii.3A.142.
If Dennis writes, and rails in furious Pet, ...6.49iii.3B.142.
That rails at dear *Lepell* and You. ....6.70.11.201.
That rails at dear *Lepell* and *How.* ....6.70.10A.201.

RAIN
Rain follows Thunder, that was all he said. ....2.ChWB.392.76.
Or o'er the Glebe distill the kindly Rain. ....2.RL2.86.165.
Or on the Glebe distill the kindly Rain. ....2.RL2.86A.165.
Thro' reconcil'd extremes of drought and rain, ...3.Ep3.168.107.
For you, he walks the streets thro' rain or dust, ...4.JD2.73.139.
As the parch'd Earth drinks Rain (but grace afford) ....6.2.11.6.
And seem a thicker Dew, or thinner Rain; ....6.42vi.4.120.
Yet Dew or Rain may wett us to the Shift, ...6.42vi.5.120.
When from the Thatch drips fast a Show'r of Rain. ....6.96ii.14.270.
With piercing Frosts, or thick-descending Rain, ...Il.3.6.188.
There left a Subject to the Wind and Rain ....Il.4.558.248.
While *Jove* descends in sluicy Sheets of Rain, ...Il.5.122.273.
As full blown Poppies overcharg'd with Rain ....Il.8.371.415.
Tho' round his Sides a wooden Tempest rain, ...Il.11.684.65.
And hissing Javelins rain an Iron Storm: ....Il.12.50.83.
Whence hissing Darts, incessant, rain below. ....Il.12.312.93.
So from each side increas'd the stony Rain, ...Il.12.343.94.
Not so our Spears: incessant tho' they rain, ...Il.17.713.315.
Presaging tears apace began to rain; ....Od.10.230.351.
To earth they fell; the tears began to rain; ....Od.10.681.376.

RAIN-BOW
The various Goddess of the Rain-bow flies: ....Il.3.166.199.

RAIN-BOWS
And all its varying Rain-bows die away. ....5.DunB4.632.407.
And all her varying Rain-bows die away. ....5.DunB4.632A.407.

RAIN'D
Around his Head an Iron Tempest rain'd; ....Il.5.766.303.
So thick, the Darts an Iron Tempest rain'd: ....Il.16.131.242.
Tho' spears in iron tempests rain'd around, ...Od.11.657.416.
The tears rain'd copious in a show'r of joy. ....Od.16.16.102.

RAINBOW
And forms a Rainbow of alternate Rays. ....2.TemF.257.275.
Dip in the Rainbow, trick her off in Air, ...3.Ep2.18.50.

RAINBOWS
To steal from Rainbows ere they drop in Show'rs ....2.RL2.96.165.
Like colour'd Rainbows o'er a show'ry Cloud: ....Il.11.36.36.

RAINS
So may kind Rains their vital Moisture yield, ...1.PWi.15.89.
Soft Rains and kindly Dews refresh the Field, ...1.TrUl.130.470.
As when a Torrent, swell'd with wintry Rains, ...Il.11.614.61.
Thus when a River swell'd with sudden Rains ....Il.17.839.321.
Or hardy Fir, unperish'd with the Rains. ....Il.23.402.506.
No rains descend, no snowy vapours rise; ....Od.6.52.207.
Soft rains and kindly dews refresh the field, ...Od.13.297.20.
Rains kisses on his neck, his face, his eyes: ....Od.17.49.135.

RAINY
Like some vile Swain, whom, on a rainy Day, ...Il.21.327.434.

RAIS'D
Yet then no proud aspiring Piles were rais'd, ...1.TrSt.200.418.
First rais'd our Walls on that ill-omen'd Plain ....1.TrSt.251.421.
The shining Structures rais'd by lab'ring Gods! ....1.TrSt.836.444.
Then rais'd with Hope, and fir'd with Glory's Charms, ...1.TrES.143.454.
He rais'd his Spouse ere Matin Bell was rung, ...2.ChJM.523.40.
If, by strange Chance, a modest Blush be rais'd, ...2.ChWB.110.62.
He rais'd his Azure Wand, and thus begun. ....2.RL2.72.164.
Which, with a Sigh, she rais'd; and thus she said. ....2.RL4.146.196.
Who Cities rais'd, or tam'd a monstrous Race; ....2.TemF.71.257.
Rais'd on a thousand Pillars, wreath'd around ....2.TemF.139.264.
Till to the Roof her tow'ring Front she rais'd. ....2.TemF.261.276.
Hosts rais'd by Fear, and Phantoms of a Day. ....2.TemF.461.285.
You rais'd these hallow'd walls; the desert smil'd, ...2.ElAb.133.330.
And licks the hand just rais'd to shed his blood. ....3.EOM1.84.24.
And all that rais'd the Hero, sunk the Man. ....3.EOM4.294.155.
Not sunk by sloth, nor rais'd by servitude; ....3.Ep3.222.111.
These rais'd new Empires o'er the Earth, ...4.HOde9.11.159.
As when Belinda rais'd my Strain. ....4.1HE7.50.271.
Till rais'd from Booths to Theatre, to Court, ...5.DunA3.301.185.
'Till rais'd from booths, to Theatre, to Court, ...5.DunB3.299.334.
High on the Stern the *Thracian* rais'd his Strain, ...6.11.39.31.
The *Thracian* rais'd his Strain, ...6.11.39A.31.
His Numbers rais'd a Shade from Hell, ...6.11.133.34.
Not that it much that Author's Anger rais'd, ...6.12.6.37.
Which yet not much that Old Bard's Anger rais'd, ...6.12.6A.37.

RAIS'D (CONTINUED)

Love, rais'd on Beauty, will like That decay, 6.19.63.64.
Was rais'd to fame by all the wits of *Greece*. 6.38.10.107.
Imperial wonders rais'd on Nations spoil'd, 6.71.5.202.
This ' *sheffield* rais'd. The sacred Dust below 6.83.1.237.
He rais'd and level'd right, 6.94.54.261.
And all that rais'd the Hero sunk the Man. 6.130.4.358.
While thus with Arms devoutly rais'd in Air, Il.1.588.116.
The *Sinthians* rais'd me on the *Lemnian* Coast. Il.1.765.124.
The King of Kings his awful Figure rais'd; Il.2.127.133.
Who rising, high th' Imperial Sceptre rais'd: Il.2.341.143.
Beside a Fountain's sacred Brink we rais'd Il.2.368.145.
And I, to join them, rais'd the *Trojan* Force: Il.3.248.204.
Nor rais'd his Head, nor stretch'd his sceptred Hand; Il.3.282.207.
Rais'd his upbraiding Voice, and angry Eyes: Il.3.450.213.
Rais'd from the Field the panting Youth she led, Il.3.469.214.
Which Gods have rais'd, or Earth-born Men enjoy; Il.4.67.224.
Rais'd high the Head, with stately Branches crown'd, Il.4.553.248.
She rais'd her in her Arms, beheld her bleed, Il.5.463.290.
A Phantom rais'd, the same in Shape and Show Il.5.546.294.
Rais'd on the Ruins of his vengeful Hand: Il.5.793.304.
Rais'd on arch'd Columns of stupendous Frame; Il.6.305.341.
Himself the Mansion rais'd, from ev'ry Part Il.6.390.345.
Then rais'd a Mountain where his Bones were burn'd, Il.6.530.353.
High o'er them all a gen'ral Tomb be rais'd. Il.7.405.384.
He rais'd his Voice: The Hosts stood list'ning round. Il.7.459.387.
They rais'd embattel'd Walls with lofty Tow'rs: Il.7.521.390.
Those radiant Structures rais'd by lab'ring Gods, Il.7.539.391.
Where o'er her pointed Summits proudly rais'd, Il.8.59.398.
The hoary Monarch rais'd his Eyes, and said. Il.10.89.6.
He sigh'd; but sighing, rais'd his vengeful Steel, Il.11.415.53.
The Walls were rais'd, the Trenches sunk in vain. Il.12.8.81.
Then rais'd with Hope, and fir'd with Glory's Charms, Il.12.497.99.
Eternal Frame! not rais'd by mortal Hands: Il.13.35.106.
On the rais'd Orb to distance bore the Spear: Il.13.220.116.
On his rais'd Arm by two strong Braces stay'd) Il.13.515.131.
Rais'd on his Knees, he now ejects the Gore; Il.14.511.188.
Nor rais'd in Off'rings to the Pow'rs divine, Il.16.275.249.
Had rais'd in Off'rings, but to *Jove* alone. Il.16.277.249.
The Warrior rais'd his Voice, and wide around Il.17.292.299.
High on the Rampart rais'd his Voice aloud; Il.18.256.334.
Thrice from the Trench his dreadful Voice he rais'd; Il.18.269.335.
Dardania's Walls he rais'd; for *Ilion,* then, Il.20.256.404.
Achilles rais'd the Spear, prepar'd to wound; Il.21.78.424.
On this his Weight, and rais'd upon his Hand, Il.21.275.432.
Troy Walls I rais'd (for such were *Jove's* Commands) Il.21.519.443.
And with them turns the rais'd Spectator's Soul. Il.22.216.464.
Whose glitt'ring Margins rais'd with Silver shine; Il.23.641.515.
Of Fir the Roof was rais'd, and cover'd o'er Il.24.553.559.
The rev'rend Monarch by the Hand he rais'd; Il.24.649.563.
And rais'd his Friend: The God before him goes, Il.24.859.572.
And rais'd the Tomb, Memorial of the Dead. Il.24.1008.577.
The sacred Sun, above the waters rais'd, Od.3.1.85.
And rais'd new discord. Then (so Heav'n decreed) Od.3.195.95.
The pond'rous engine rais'd to crush us all, Od.4.892.160.
Then o'er the vessel rais'd the taper mast, Od.5.324.187.
There round his tribes a strength of wall he rais'd, Od.6.13.204.
Fair thrones within from space to space were rais'd, Od.7.124.240.
The flowing tear, and rais'd his drooping head: Od.8.84.267.
Full of the God he rais'd his lofty strain, Od.8.547.292.
A floating Isle! High-rais'd by toil divine, Od.10.3.335.
High rais'd of stone; a shaded space around: Od.10.241.352.
His own industrious hands had rais'd the pile) Od.14.12.35.
Before the rest I rais'd my ready steel; Od.14.257.48.
Rais'd on his feet, again he reels, he falls, Od.18.122.172.
Around the tree I rais'd a nuptial bow'r, Od.23.195.333.
In clouds of smoke, rais'd by the noble fray, Od.24.55.350.

RAISE

Or raise old Warriors whose ador'd Remains 1.W-F.301.177.
That *Thames's* Glory to the Stars shall raise! 1.W-F.356.185.
Which *Thames's* Glory to the Stars shall raise! 1.W-F.356A.185.
Fear not the Anger of the Wise to raise; 1.EOC.582.306.
Who raise thy Temples where the Chariot stood 1.TrSt.388.426.
Thence we these Altars in his Temple raise, 1.TrSt.786.443.
Raise scaling Engines, and ascend the Wall: 1.TrES.180.456.
Not two strong Men th'enormous Weight cou'd raise, 1.TrES.185.456.
They cuff, they tear, they raise a screaming Cry; 1.TrES.221.458.
A Marble Tomb and Pyramid shall raise, 1.TrES.251.459.
To raise his Wonder, and ingage his Aid? 1.TrUl.178.471.
To raise up Seed to bless the Pow'rs above, 2.ChJM.121.20.
To raise up Seed t'adore the Pow'rs above, 2.ChJM.121A.20.
What? can your Prentice raise your Jealousie? 2.ChWB.119.62.
What? can our Prentice raise your Jealousie? 2.ChWB.119A.62.
What Sums from these old Spouses I cou'd raise, 2.ChWB.207.66.
What Sums from these first Spouses I cou'd raise, 2.ChWB.207A.66.
And knew full well to raise my Voice on high; 2.ChWB.338.73.
And breathes three am'rous Sighs to raise the Fire. 2.RL2.42.162.
On shining Altars of *Japan* they raise 2.RL3.107.175.
Or raise a Pimple on a beauteous Face, 2.RL4.68.189.
Wings raise her Arms, and Wings her Feet infold; 2.TemF.267.276.
For Fame they raise the Voice, and tune the String. 2.TemF.273.276.
The Goddess heard, and bade the Muses raise 2.TemF.306.278.
What cou'd thus high thy rash Ambition raise? 2.TemF.499.287.
But such plain roofs as piety could raise, 2.ElAb.139.331.
That Virtue's ends from Vanity can raise, 3.EOM2.245.85.
And Reason raise o'er Instinct as you can, 3.EOM3.97.101.
From private Sparkles raise the gen'ral Flame, 3.EOM3.138Z1.106.
And buries madmen in the heaps they raise. 3.EOM4.76.135.
To raise the Thought and touch the Heart, be thine! 3.Ep2.250.70.
Why she and Lesbia raise that monstrous sum? 3.Ep3.123A.102.
More go to ruin Fortunes, than to raise. 3.Ep3.202Z2.110.
Why she and Sappho raise that monstrous sum? 3.Ep3.123.102.
To ease th' oppress'd, and raise the sinking heart? 3.Ep3.244.113.
First shade a Country, and then raise a Town. 3.Ep4.190.155.
While Wits and Templers ev'ry sentence raise, 4.Arbu.211.111.

RAISE (CONTINUED)

"And raise his Mind above the Mob he meets." 4.2HE2.99.171.
Inspir'd he seizes: These an altar raise: 5.DunA1.137.80.
But such a bulk as no twelve bards could raise, 5.DunA2.35.100.
To move, to raise, to ravish ev'ry heart, 5.DunA2.215.127.
Contending Theatres our empire raise, 5.DunA3.267.179.
Inspir'd he seizes: These an altar raise: 5.DunB1.157.282.
But such a bulk as no twelve bards could raise, 5.DunB2.39.298.
To move, to raise, to ravish ev'ry heart, 5.DunB2.223.306.
Contending Theatres our empire raise, 5.DunB3.271.333.
To raise *Tiberius Gracchus* Ghost; 6.10.72.26.
Decry'd each past, to raise each present Writer 6.17iv.13.59.
Raise in their arms, and waft thee on their wing, 6.21.26.69.
To raise the genius, and to mend the heart; 6.32.2.96.
Deem it but Scandal which the jealous raise, 6.38.11Z3.108.
To form a Bard, and raise his Genius higher; 6.49iii.8A.142.
To form a Bard, or raise his Genius higher; 6.49iii.8B.142.
To form a Bard, and raise a Genius higher; 6.49iii.8C.142.
While Fops and Templars ev'ry Sentence raise, 6.49iii.27.143.
Whilst Wits and Templars ev'ry Sentence raise, 6.49iii.27A.143.
While Wits and Templars ev'ry Sentence raise, 6.49iii.27B.143.
One Chorus let all Being raise! 6.50.51.148.
Nor raise a Thought, nor draw an Eye; 6.64.8.189.
When shall we nest thy hallow'd Altars raise, 6.65.7.192.
Where shall we next thy lasting Temples raise, 6.65.7A.192.
Nor wish to lose a Foe these Virtues raise; 6.73.11.210.
While Wits and Templars ev'ry Sentence raise, 6.98.63.285.
Whose force alone can raise or melt the heart, 6.107.28.311.
This radiant pile nine rural sisters raise; 6.126ii.2.353.
Apollo's genuine Sons thy fame shall raise 6.131i.7.360.
But for thy Windsor, a New Fabric Raise 6.147ix.5.392.
May Tom, whom heav'n sent down to raise 6.150.15.399.
To raise in Arms the *Greek* and *Phrygian* Bands; Il.4.92.224.
Restore our Blood, and raise the Warrior's Souls, Il.4.297.235.
(Exclaim'd the King) who raise your eager Bands Il.4.328.236.
Our selves to lessen, while our Sires you raise? Il.4.457.242.
Above the *Greeks* his deathless Fame to raise, Il.5.3.263.
Not two strong Men th' enormous Weight could raise, Il.5.371.284.
Shall raise my Glory when thy own is lost: Il.5.811.305.
To the pure Skies these horrid Hands to raise, Il.6.336.343.
Greece on the Shore shall raise a Monument; Il.7.98.368.
Whom Heav'n shall chuse, be his the Chance to raise Il.7.209.374.
Raise an embattel'd Wall, with lofty Tow'rs; Il.7.407.385.
The flaming Piles with plenteous Fuel raise, Il.8.633.426.
He ceas'd: the *Greeks* loud Acclamations raise, Il.9.69.435.
Mean while *Patroclus* sweats the Fire to raise; Il.9.277.447.
Shouts of Acclaim the list'ning Heroes raise, Il.9.834.474.
Still, with your Voice, the sloathful Soldiers raise, Il.10.74.5.
The Care is next our other Chiefs to raise: Il.10.122.7.
To raise my Hopes, and second my Design. Il.10.264.13.
To raise each Act to Life, and sing with Fire! Il.12.206.88.
But tends to raise that Pow'r which I obey. Il.12.252.90.
Raise scaling Engines, and ascend the Wall: Il.12.534.101.
Not two strong Men th' enormous Weight could raise, Il.12.539.101.
'Tis yours, O Warriors, all our Hopes to raise; Il.13.73.108.
And whose blest Trophies, will ye raise to Fame? Il.14.604.191.
Achilles' Glory to the Stars to raise; Il.15.82.199.
They cuff, they tear, they raise a screaming Cry; Il.16.524.264.
A marble Tomb and Pyramid shall raise, Il.16.556.266.
To raise our Camp: Too dang'rous here our Post, Il.18.301.336.
They raise a Tempest, or they gently blow. Il.18.544.348.
No two of Earth's degen'rate Sons could raise. Il.20.338.407.
To raise her sinking with assistant Hands. Il.22.605.481.
Hereafter *Greece* some nobler Work may raise, Il.23.308.502.
He barely stirr'd him, but he could not raise: Il.23.849.523.
Th' admiring *Greeks* loud Acclamations raise, Il.23.896.524.
To raise our Hands, for who so good as *Jove?* Il.24.370.551.
The next, to raise his Monument be giv'n; Il.24.836.571.
And high in Air a Sylvan Structure raise. Il.24.994.577.
Then grateful *Greece* with streaming eyes wou'd raise Od.1.305.47.
And raise all *Ithaca* to aid our cause: Od.2.86.65.
Frequent, O King, was *Nestor* wont to raise Od.4.259.131.
A Cenotaph I raise of deathless fame. Od.4.794.156.
In the young soul illustrious thought to raise, Od.4.914.161.
Whate'er thy Fate, the ills our wrath could raise Od.5.484.195.
To raise the blush, or pain the modest eyes. Od.6.264.223.
To raise the lowly suppliant from the ground Od.7.216.247.
He stretch'd his hand the prudent chief to raise, Od.7.225.247.
But gave him skill to raise the lofty lay. Od.8.60.265.
To raise in off'rings to almighty *Jove,* Od.8.467.288.
And mine shall be the task, henceforth to raise Od.8.545.291.
Once more I raise my voice; my friends afraid Od.9.577.330.
A tomb along the wat'ry margin raise, Od.11.93.385.
No costly carpets raise his hoary head, Od.11.228.393.
To raise a bounty noble as thy soul; Od.11.445.406.
They toss, they foam, a wild confusion raise, Od.12.284.446.
To raise his wonder, and engage his aid: Od.13.345.24.
To raise the mast, the missile dart to wing, Od.14.261.49.
That grateful *Greece* with streaming eyes might raise Od.14.403.55.
How will each speech his grateful wonder raise? Od.15.176.77.
To thee, as to some God, I'll temples raise, Od.15.204.78.
The Gods with ease frail man depress, or raise, Od.16.232.114.
If this raise anger in the stranger's thought, Od.17.16.133.
But much to raise my master's wrath I fear; Od.17.211.141.
Who publick structures raise, or who design; Od.17.463.155.
To love *Ulysses* is to raise thy hate. Od.17.473.156.
They feast, they dance, and raise the mirthful song. Od.17.686.165.
Thy husband's wonder, and thy son's to raise, Od.18.191.175.
The Suitor-train, and raise a thirst to give; Od.18.326.183.
My Lord's protecting hand alone wou'd raise Od.19.148.199.
And *Pallas* now, to raise the rivals fires, Od.21.1.257.
Wrong and oppression no renown can raise; Od.21.359.277.
Depress or raise, enlarge or take away: Od.23.16.319.
Then posts, capacious of the frame, I raise, Od.23.201.333.
Then grateful *Greece* with streaming eyes might raise Od.24.45.350.
High on the shore the growing hill we raise, Od.24.103.353.

RAISE (CONTINUED)
The Gods, to honour her fair fame, shall raise ..... Od.24.224.358.

RAISES
The tender Lambs he raises in his Arms, ... 1.Mes.53.117.
B. It raises Armies in a Nation's aid, ... 3.Ep3.33A.88.
It raises Armies in a Nation's aid, ... 3.Ep3.33.88.
He raises *Hector* to the Work design'd, ... Il.15.723.223.
And now he raises, as the day-light fades, ... Od.18.353.184.

RAKE
But ev'ry Woman is at heart a Rake: ..... 3.Ep2.216.68.
So *B[athurs]t* cries, Philosopher and Rake! ..... 4.HAdv.158.89.
The Mother begg'd the blessing of a Rake. ..... 5.DunB4.286.372.
Most thinking Rake alive. ..... 6.47.40.129.
But ev'ry Woman's in her Soul a Rake. ..... 6.99.16.287.

RAKES
And combs with rakes, his rough, disorder'd hairs: ..... 1.TrPA.24.366.

RALEIGH
Words, that wise *Bacon,* or brave *Raleigh* spake; ..... 4.2HE2.168.177.
Such as wise *Bacon,* or brave *Raleigh* spake; ..... 4.2HE2.168A.177.

RALLIES
The Hero rallies, and renews the Fight. ..... Il.11.725.67.

RALLY
Then fierce they rally, to Revenge led on ..... Il.17.326.300.

RALLYING
'Till rallying all, the Feast became the Text; ..... 6.17iv.16.59.
Since rallying from our Wall we forc'd the Foe, ... Il.8.359.414.

RALPH
"Silence, ye Wolves! while Ralph to Cynthia howls, ... 5.DunA3.159.165.
Ev'n Ralph repents, and Henly writes no more. ..... 5.DunB1.216.285.
Ev'n Ralph is lost, and Henly writes no more. ..... 5.DunB1.216A.285.
"Silence, ye Wolves! while Ralph to Cynthia howls, ... 5.DunB3.165.328.

RAM
The stately Ram thus measures o'er the Ground, ... Il.3.259.204.
Stalks the proud Ram, the Father of the Fold: ..... Il.13.623.135.
One ram remain'd, the leader of the flock; ..... Od.9.511.327.
The master Ram at last approach'd the gate, ... Od.9.523.328.
What makes my ram the lag of all the flock? ..... Od.9.526.328.
Dismiss'd the Ram, the father of the flock. ..... Od.9.544.328.
The master Ram was voted mine by all: ..... Od.9.642.333.
A sable ram, the pride of all thy breed. ..... Od.10.625.374.
The sable ewe, and ram, together bound. ..... Od.10.686.376.
So shall a Ram, the largest of the breed, ... Od.11.41.381.
A bull, a ram, a boar; and hail the Ocean-King. ..... Od.11.161.389.
Of victims vow'd, a ram, a bull, a boar: ..... Od.23.294.337.

RAMBLED
From House to House we rambled up and down, ... 2.ChWB.280.70.

RAMBLER
As true a Rambler as I was before, ... 2.ChWB.339.73.

RAMBLES
And swore the Rambles that I took by Night, ... 2.ChWB.156.64.

RAMBLING
A Place to tire the rambling Wits of *France* ..... 2.ChJM.452.36.

RAMBOÜILLET
And finds a fairer *Ramboüillet* in you. ..... 6.19.76.64.

RAMM'D
When in the *Marrow-Bone* I see thee ramm'd; ..... 6.96iv.83.278.

RAMPANT
Whether she's chast or rampant, proud or civil; ..... 2.ChJM.186.23.

RAMPART
Greece on her Rampart stands the fierce Alarms; ..... Il.12.309.93.
And that the Rampart, late our surest Trust, ... Il.14.73.161.
High on the Rampart rais'd his Voice aloud; ..... Il.18.256.334.
While the sad Father on the Rampart stands, ... Il.22.49.454.

RAMPARTS
To force the Ramparts, and the Gates to rend; ..... 1.TrES.2A.449.
The lofty Ramparts, through the Warlike Throng, ... 1.TrES.78.452.
The lofty Ramparts, through the martial Throng, ... 1.TrES.78A.452.
While to the Ramparts daring *Glaucus* drew, ... 1.TrES.111.453.
And the high Ramparts drop with Human Gore. ..... 1.TrES.166.455.
Troy felt his Arm, and yon' proud Ramparts stand ..... Il.5.792.304.
With Piles, with Ramparts, and a Trench profound? ..... Il.9.461.455.
To force the Ramparts, and the Gates to rend; ..... Il.12.346.94.
The lofty Ramparts, through the martial Throng; ..... Il.12.422.97.
While to the Ramparts daring *Glaucus* drew, ... Il.12.465.98.
And the high Ramparts drop with human Gore. ..... Il.12.520.100.
But since yon' Ramparts by thy Arms lay low, ... Il.13.979.152.
Fled to her Ramparts, and resign'd the Field; ..... Il.17.371.302.
We seek our Ramparts, and desert the Day. ..... Il.17.391.302.
Alone, the *Ilian* Ramparts let him leave, ... Il.24.181.543.
Forsake these Ramparts, and with Gifts obtain ..... Il.24.237.546.
To pass the Ramparts, and the Watch to blind. ..... Il.24.849.572.
Here ramparts stood, there tow'rs rose high in air, ... Od.11.323.398.

RAMPIRE
Delug'd the Rampire nine continual Days; ..... Il.12.24.82.

RAMPIRES
So down the Rampires rolls the rocky Show'r; ..... Il.12.180.87.
Where lay the Fleets, and where the Rampires rose, ... Il.16.481.262.

RAMS
Like batt'ring Rams, beats open ev'ry Door; ..... 4.JD4.265.47.
On fat of Rams, black Bulls, and brawny Swine, ... Il.9.592.464.
Full fifty Rams to bleed in Sacrifice, ... Il.23.182.497.
Strong were the Rams, with native purple fair, ... Od.9.505.326.

RAN
How twice the Mountains ran with *Dacian* Blood, ... 1.TrSt.25A.410.
And starving Wolves, ran howling to the Wood. ..... 1.TrSt.738.441.
With starving Wolves, ran howling to the Wood. ..... 1.TrSt.738A.441.
And scornful Hisses ran thro all the Croud. ..... 2.TemF.405A.283.
Back thro' the paths of pleasing sense I ran, ... 2.ElAb.69.324.
So from the first eternal ORDER ran, ... 3.EOM3.113.103.
True faith, true policy, united ran, ... 3.EOM3.239.116.
In each how guilt and greatness equal ran, ... 3.EOM4.293.155.
So much the Fury still out-ran the Wit, ... 3.Ep2.127.61.
Ran out as fast, as one that pays his Bail, ... 4.JD4.182.41.
One equal course how Guilt and Greatness ran, ... 6.130.3.358.
So much the Fury still out-ran the Wit, ... 6.154.13.403.
And *Sangar's* Stream ran purple with their Blood. ..... Il.3.250.204.
Swift to his Succour thro' the Ranks he ran: ..... Il.4.243.232.
Thro' all her Train the soft Infection ran, ... Il.6.645.358.
Thro' ev'ry *Argive* Heart new Transport ran, ... Il.7.259.377.
As all on Glory ran his ardent Mind, ... Il.15.526.217.
Then ran, the mournful Message to impart, ... Il.17.787.319.
Along the Coast their mingled Clamours ran, ... Il.18.93.327.
Th' infectious Softness thro' the Heroes ran; ..... Il.24.644.563.
And tears ran trickling from her aged eyes. ..... Od.2.407.80.
Swift to the Queen the Herald *Medon* ran, ... Od.4.902.160.
From mouth and nose the briny torrent ran; ..... Od.5.584.200.
In pleasing thought he ran the prospect o'er, ... Od.7.180.244.
Sad from my natal hour my days have ran, ... Od.8.171.271.
Sad, pleasing sight! with tears each eye ran o'er, ... Od.10.471.366.
Still heav'd their hearts, and still their eyes ran o'er. ..... Od.10.684.376.
And a cold fear ran shivering thro' my blood; ..... Od.11.56.383.
But now the years a num'rous train have ran; ..... Od.11.555.411.
While yet I spoke, a sudden sorrow ran ..... Od.12.330.447.
When lo! a wretch ran breathless to the shore, ... Od.15.250.80.
She saw, she wept, she ran with eager pace, ... Od.17.41.134.
A gen'ral horror ran thro' all the race, ... Od.21.450.282.
Quick thro' the father's heart these accents ran; ..... Od.24.367.366.
He ran, he seiz'd him with a strict embrace, ... Od.24.373.367.
Down his wan cheek the trickling torrent ran, ... Od.24.487.371.

RANCOUR
Oh lasting Rancour! oh insatiate Hate ..... Il.4.47.223.
Of lashing Rancour and eternal Hate: ..... Il.22.340.470.
Each burns with rancour to the adverse side. ..... Od.3.182.94.

RANDOM
His flocks at random round the forest roam: ..... 1.TrPA.20.366.
But Wives, a random Choice, untry'd they take; ..... 2.ChWB.102.61.
Who random drawings from your sheets shall take, ... 3.Ep4.27.140.
But random Praise—the Task can ne'er be done, ... 4.EpS2.106.319.
How random Thoughts now meaning chance to find, ... 5.DunA1.229.90.
How random thoughts now meaning chance to find, ... 5.DunB1.275.290.
At random wounds, nor knows the wound she gives: ..... 6.14iii.12.46.
For Want of you, we spend our random Wit on ..... 6.82vi.3.232.

RANG'D
And bathes the Forest where she rang'd before. ..... 1.W-F.208.168.
All rang'd in *Order,* and dispos'd with *Grace,* ..... 1.EOC.672.315.
Then on the Sands he rang'd his wealthy Store, ... 1.TrUl.94.469.
Late, as I rang'd the Crystal Wilds of Air, ... 2.RL1.107.153.
Beneath, in Order rang'd, the tuneful Nine ..... 2.TemF.270.276.
Rang'd the wild Desarts red with Monsters Gore, ... Il.1.356.105.
Soon as the Throngs in Order rang'd appear, ... Il.2.125.133.
These rang'd in Order on the floating Tide, ... Il.2.628.157.
In one firm Orb the Bands were rang'd around, ... Il.4.312.235.
The Foot (the Strength of War) he rang'd behind; ..... Il.4.343.237.
With close-rang'd Chariots, and with thicken'd Shields. ..... Il.8.261.409.
Rang'd at the Ships let all our Squadrons shine, ... Il.9.830.474.
Rang'd in three Lines they view the prostrate Band; ..... Il.10.544.27.
Near *Ilus'* Tomb, in Order rang'd around, ... Il.11.73.37.
Rang'd in two Bands, their crooked Weapons wield, ... Il.11.90.38.
Rang'd in bright Order on th' *Olympian* Hill; ..... Il.11.104.39.
With well-rang'd Squadrons strongly circled round: ..... Il.13.172.113.
While all before, the Billows rang'd on high ..... Il.21.261.431.
These in fair Order rang'd upon the Plain, ... Il.23.339.503.
Rang'd in a Line the ready Racers stand; ..... Il.23.885.524.
Where seemly rang'd in peaceful order stood ..... Od.1.169.40.
Rang'd on the banks, beneath our equal oars ..... Od.4.787.156.
Rang'd in a line the ready racers stand, ... Od.8.125.269.
The robes the vests are rang'd, and heaps of gold: ..... Od.8.476.288.
In order rang'd, our admiration drew: ..... Od.9.255.317.
Now rang'd in order on our banks, we sweep ..... Od.9.656.333.
The King himself the vases rang'd with care; ..... Od.13.25.2.
Then on the sands he rang'd his wealthy store, ... Od.13.261.18.

RANGE
Now range the Hills, the gameful Woods beset, ... 1.W-F.95.159.
Now range the Hills, the thickest Woods beset, ... 1.W-F.95A.159.
Range in the woods, and in the vallies roam: ..... 1.TrPA.79.368.
Our num'rous Herds that range each fruitful Field, ... 1.TrES.29.450.
Our num'rous Herds that range the fruitful Field, ... 1.TrES.29A.450.
Far as Creation's ample range extends, ... 3.EOM1.207.41.
Vast Range of Sense! from Man's imperial race ..... 3.EOM1.209A.41.
Affections? they still take a wider range: ..... 3.Ep1.172A.29.
Opinions? they still take a wider range: ..... 3.Ep1.172.29.
Around in sweet Meanders wildly range, ... 6.17ii.25.56.
To range the Camp, and summon all the Bands: ..... Il.2.62.130.

RANGE (CONTINUED)
Where grazing Heifers range the lonely Wood, ...Il.5.207.276.
O'er these a Range of Marble Structure runs, ...Il.6.306.341.
While others sleep, thus range the Camp alone? ....Il.10.91.6.
Our num'rous Herds that range the fruitful Field, ...Il.12.373.95.
The busy Chiefs their banded Legions range. ....Il.14.438.184.
The seats to range, the fragrant wood to bring, ...Od.3.544.114.
Sparta, whose walls a range of hills surrounds: ....Od.4.2.119.
Range the dark bounds of *Pluto's* dreary reign. ....Od.4.666.150.
The mules unharness'd range beside the main, ...Od.6.103.210.
Where happy as the Gods that range the sky, ...Od.8.489.289.
Low thro' the grove, or range the flow'ry plain: ....Od.12.390.450.
Or range the house of darkness and of death? ....Od.15.373.87.

RANGES
Steeps *Troy* in Blood, and ranges round the Plain; ....Il.15.48.196.

RANGING
Or if in ranging of the Names I judge ill, ...6.40.5.112.
So when a Lion, ranging o'er the Lawns, ...Il.11.153.42.
So when a Savage, ranging o'er the Plain, ...Il.15.702.223.

RANK
Sprung the rank Weed, and thriv'd with large Increase; ....1.EOC.535.297.
On a rank Leacher, and Idolater, ...2.ChJM.689.48.
Then each, according to the Rank they bore; ....2.RL3.34.171.
A Golden Column next in Rank appear'd, ...2.TemF.196.271.
There must be, somewhere, such a rank as Man; ....3.EOM1.48.19.
Rank as the ripeness of a Rabbit's tail. ....4.HS2.28.57.
Our Fathers prais'd rank Ven'son. You suppose ....4.HS2.91.61.
Oh! when rank Widows purchase luscious nights, ...4.JD2.87A.141.
His rank digestion makes it wit no more: ....4.JD2.32.135.
And when rank Widows purchase luscious nights, ...4.JD2.87.141.
His rank Digestion makes it Wit no more. ....4.JD2A.36.134.
Or those proud fools whom nature, rank, and fate ....4.1740.67.335.
Dispos'd in Rank their Hecatomb they bring: ....Il.1.585.115.
Then wise *Ulysses* in his Rank was plac'd; ....Il.2.484.150.
From Rank to Rank she darts her ardent Eyes: ....Il.2.525.151.
From Rank to Rank she darts her ardent Eyes: ....Il.2.525.151.
From Rank to Rank he moves, and orders all. ....Il.3.258.204.
From Rank to Rank he moves, and orders all. ....Il.3.258.204.
Moves on in Rank, and stretches o'er the Land. ....Il.13.627.136.
Thus Rank on Rank the thick Battalions throng, ...Il.13.1006.153.
Thus Rank on Rank the thick Battalions throng, ...Il.13.1006.153.
Rank above Rank, the crowded Ships they moor; ....Il.14.43.160.
Rank above Rank, the crowded Ships they moor; ....Il.14.43.160.
Rank within Rank, on Buckler Buckler spread, ...Il.17.407.303.
Rank within Rank, on Buckler Buckler spread, ...Il.17.407.303.
So parts the Chief; from Rank to Rank he flew, ...Il.17.759.318.
So parts the Chief; from Rank to Rank he flew, ...Il.17.759.318.
O *Greeks* (he cries, and every Rank alarms) ....Il.20.403.412.

RANK'D
Rank'd with their Friends, not number'd with their Train; ....4.EpS2.91.318.
Rank'd in the Name of *Tom D'Urfy.* ....6.30.6.85.
All rank'd by Tens; whole Decads when they dine ....Il.2.157.136.
In Tribes and Nations rank'd on either side. ....Il.2.523.151.
Lay rank'd contiguous on the bending Shores. ....Il.15.835.229.
In order rank'd let all our Gifts appear, ...Il.19.193.379.
Rank'd with his slaves, on earth the Monarch lies: ....Od.11.231.393.
By Heralds rank'd, in marshal'd order move ....Od.20.342.249.
Rank'd by their ages, and the banquet grace. ....Od.24.473.371.

RANKER
At large expatiate o'er the ranker Mead;) ....Il.15.763.226.

RANKS
In crowding Ranks on ev'ry Side arise, ...1.Mes.89.121.
His Pow'rs in *equal Ranks,* and *fair Array,* ....1.EOC.176.260.
And the loose Straglers to their Ranks confines. ....1.TrVP.38.378.
And crowd their shining Ranks to yield thee place; ....1.TrSt.36.411.
In Ranks adorn'd the Temple's outward Face; ....2.TemF.131.264.
That happy frailties to all ranks apply'd, ...3.EOM2.241.84.
Now, forms my Quincunx, and now ranks my Vines, ...4.HS1.130.17.
Courtiers and Patriots in two ranks divide, ...5.DunB4.107.352.
Here order'd vines in equal ranks appear ....6.35.17.103.
And break the Ranks, and thunder thro' the War. ....Il.2.933.167.
Moves into Ranks, and stretches o'er the Land. ....Il.3.2.186.
Amidst the Ranks *Lycaön's* Son she found, ...Il.4.119.226.
Swift to his Succour thro' the Ranks he ran: ....Il.4.243.232.
On Foot thro' all the martial Ranks he moves, ...Il.4.264.233.
There rev'rend *Nestor* ranks his *Pylian* Bands, ...Il.4.336.236.
Nor cause Confusion, nor the Ranks exceed; ....Il.4.347.237.
Nor cause Confusion, or the Ranks exceed; ....Il.4.347A.237.
Who view'd him lab'ring thro' the Ranks of Fight! ....Il.4.429.240.
Rapt thro' the Ranks he thunders o'er the Plain, ...Il.5.113.272.
And thro' the Ranks of Death triumphant ride. ....Il.5.251.279.
Thro' breaking Ranks his furious Course he bends, ...Il.5.415.286.
Stirs all the Ranks, and fires the *Trojan* Train; ....Il.5.562.295.
Rush'd terrible amidst the Ranks of Fight. ....Il.5.839.305.
Broke the thick Ranks, and turn'd the doubtful Day. ....Il.6.8.323.
Pierc'd the deep Ranks; their strongest Battel tore; ....Il.8.307.412.
The Ranks grow thinner as his Arrows fly, ...Il.8.338.413.
With Coursers dreadful in the Ranks of War; ....Il.8.352.414.
Haste, launch thy Chariot, thro' yon Ranks to ride; ....Il.8.455.418.
That bear *Pelides* thro' the Ranks of War. ....Il.10.382.20.
And those swift Steeds that sweep the Ranks of War, ...Il.10.466.24.
Like these, conspicuous thro' the Ranks of Fight. ....Il.10.649.30.
Thus thro' the Ranks appear'd the Godlike Man, ...Il.11.85.38.
And falling Ranks are strow'd on ev'ry side. ....Il.11.94.38.
Breaking their Ranks, and crushing out their Souls; ....Il.11.210.44.
While *Agamemnon* wastes the Ranks around, ...Il.11.243.46.
The Chief she found amidst the Ranks of War, ...Il.11.255.46.
While *Agamemnon* wastes the Ranks around, ...Il.11.259.47.
Now fierce for Fame, before the Ranks he springs. ....Il.11.297.48.
Whole Ranks are broken, and whole Troops o'erthrown. ....Il.11.344.49.

RANKS (CONTINUED)
Now on yon' Ranks impell your foaming Steeds; ....Il.11.373.51.
Then plung'd amidst the thickest Ranks of Fight. ....Il.11.420.53.
His Sword deforms the beauteous Ranks of Fight. ....Il.11.627.61.
Swift thro' the Ranks the rapid Chariot bounds; ....Il.11.655.63.
The Ranks lie scatter'd, and the Troops o'erthrown) ....Il.11.665.63.
Compell the Coursers to their Ranks behind. ....Il.12.98.84.
Antiphates, as thro' the Ranks he broke, ...Il.12.221.89.
Springs thro' the Ranks to fall, and fall by thee, ...Il.13.754.141.
Inspire the Ranks, and rule the distant War. ....Il.14.152.165.
And tow'ring in the foremost Ranks of War, ...Il.14.420.183.
Rose in huge Ranks, and form'd a watry Wall ....Il.14.454.185.
And mark'd their Progress thro' the Ranks in Blood, ...Il.15.315.209.
Thick'ning their Ranks, and form a deep Array. ....Il.15.339.210.
Brave Deeds of Arms thro' all the Ranks were try'd, ...Il.15.480.216.
In the first Ranks indulge thy Thirst of Fame, ...Il.15.558.218.
Beyond the foremost Ranks; his Lance he threw, ...Il.15.688.222.
But enter'd in the *Grecian* Ranks, he turns ....Il.15.710.223.
Still at the closest Ranks, the thickest Fight, ...Il.15.742.224.
Ranks wedg'd in Ranks; of Arms a steely Ring ....Il.16.254.249.
Ranks wedg'd in Ranks; of Arms a steely Ring ....Il.16.254.249.
Amid the Ranks, with mutual Thirst of Fame, ...Il.16.400.258.
Smoaks thro' the Ranks, o'ertakes the flying War, ...Il.16.461.260.
And forc'd the routed Ranks to stand the Day. ....Il.16.479.261.
Breaks thro' the Ranks, and his Retreat pursues: ....Il.16.988.281.
Sheath'd in bright Arms, thro' cleaving Ranks he flies, ...Il.17.95.291.
Now enter'd in the *Spartan* Ranks, he turn'd ....Il.17.121.292.
With headlong Force the foremost Ranks he tore; ....Il.17.330.300.
Close in their Ranks commands to fight or fall, ...Il.17.412.303.
Pass'd this, and that way, thro' the Ranks of Fight: ....Il.17.768.318.
The Rage of *Hector* o'er the Ranks was born: ....Il.18.192.331.
Here stretch'd in Ranks the level'd Swarths are found, ...Il.18.639.354.
The *Trojan* Ranks, and deal Destruction round, ...Il.19.150.377.
And burst like Light'ning thro' the Ranks, and vow'd ....Il.20.107.398.
Why comes *Æneas* thro' the Ranks so far? ....Il.20.214.402.
And plung'd within the Ranks, awaits the Fight. ....Il.20.436.413.
Tread down whole Ranks, and crush out Hero's Souls. ....Il.20.582.418.
Mestor the brave, renown'd in Ranks of War, ...Il.24.321.549.
Here order'd vines in equal ranks appear, ...Od.7.158.244.
And the fair ranks of battle to deform: ....Od.14.252.48.

RANSOM
'Till the great King, without a Ransom paid, ...Il.1.123.93.
For *Troy* to ransom at a Price too dear? ....Il.2.286.141.
Talk not of Life, or Ransom, (he replies) ....Il.21.111.426.
The proffer'd Ransom, and the Corps to leave. ....Il.24.98.539.
But yield to Ransom and the Father's Pray'r. ....Il.24.151.541.
But yield to Ransom, and restore the Slain. ....Il.24.174.543.
To whom *Achilles:* Be the Ransom giv'n, ...Il.24.175.543.
The King of Men the Ransom might defer. ....Il.24.823.571.

RANSOM'D
The ransom'd Prince to fair *Arisbe* bore. ....Il.21.49.424.

RANSOME
Large Heaps of Brass in Ransome shall be told, ...Il.11.175.43.
(Great *Hector's* Ransome) from the polish'd Car. ....Il.24.727.568.

RANTING
Wake the dull Church, and lull the ranting Stage; ....5.DunB4.58.347.

RAP'D
A Princess rap'd transcends a Navy storm'd: ....Il.13.782.142.
In vision rap'd <rapt>; the * *Hyperesian* Seer ....Od.20.421.253.

RAPACIOUS
On that Rapacious Hand for ever blaze? ....2.RL4.116.193.
As o'er their Prey rapacious Wolves engage, ...Il.4.540.247.

RAPE
Europa's Rape, *Agenor's* stern Decree, ...1.TrSt.7.409.
The nymph despis'd, the Rape had been unknown. ....6.38.4.107.
Thus *Helens* Rape and *Menelaus'* wrong ....6.38.7.107.
To have the *Rape* recorded by His Muse. ....6.38.30.108.
Instant he wears, elusive of the rape, ...Od.4.563.147.

RAPES
Yet I can pardon those obscurer Rapes, ...1.TrSt.358.425.
With rapes and riot to profane my court; ....Od.20.383.251.

RAPHAEL
A *Raphael* painted, and a *Vida* sung! ....1.EOC.704.320.

RAPHAEL'S
With thee, on *Raphael's* Monument I mourn, ...6.52.27.157.
Match *Raphael's* grace, with thy lov'd *Guido's* air, ...6.52.36.157.

RAPID
Be smooth ye Rocks, ye rapid Floods give way! ....1.Mes.36.116.
How twice he tam'd proud *Ister's* rapid Flood, ...1.TrSt.25.410.
And trembling *Ister* check'd his rapid Flood; ....1.TrSt.26A.410.
Wings on the whistling Winds his rapid way, ...1.TrSt.438.428.
Where late was Dust, now rapid Torrents play, ...1.TrSt.504.431.
As fiery Coursers in the rapid Race, ...1.TrUl.7.465.
For flying Chariots, or the rapid Race; ....1.TrUl.123.470.
Neptune and *Jove* survey the rapid Race: ....2.TemF.217.272.
With rapid Motion turn'd the Mansion round; ....2.TemF.422.283.
Could he, whose rules the rapid Comet bind, ...3.EOM2.35.60.
And rapid Severn hoarse applause resounds. ....3.Ep3.252.114.
His rapid waters in their passage burn. ....5.DunA2.176.123.
His rapid waters in their passage burn. ....5.DunB2.184.304.
To whom Time bears me on his rapid wing, ...5.DunB4.6.339.
Who wert, e're time his rapid race begun, ...6.23.5.73.
Tost all the Day in rapid Circles round; ....Il.1.762.123.
Descending swift, roll'd down the rapid Light. ....Il.1.777.124.
O'er Fields of Death they whirl the rapid Car, ...Il.2.932.167.

RAPID (CONTINUED)
Swift march the *Greeks:* the rapid Dust around ......Il.3.13.188.
Nor join'd swift Horses to the rapid Car. ......Il.5.243.279.
To dare the Shock, or urge the rapid Race: ......Il.5.281.280.
The Lash resounds, the rapid Chariot flies, ...Il.5.457.290.
Where *Celadon* rolls down his rapid Tide. ......Il.7.166.372.
To dare the Fight, or urge the rapid Race; ......Il.8.136.404.
Swift thro' the Ranks the rapid Chariot bounds; ......Il.11.655.63.
And mangled Carnage clogs the rapid Wheels. ......Il.11.661.63.
To join his rapid Coursers for the Fight: ......Il.15.135.202.
And to the Ships impell thy rapid Horse: ......Il.15.293.208.
Thick Drifts of Dust involve their rapid Flight, ...Il.16.450.260.
He bids *Cebrion* drive the rapid Car; ......Il.16.887.277.
Automedon your rapid Flight shall bear ......Il.17.518.308.
A rapid Torrent thro' the Rushes roars: ......Il.18.668.356.
And rapid as it runs, the single Spokes are lost. ......Il.18.696.357.
The Mountain shook, the rapid Stream stood still. ......Il.20.74.397.
Then like a God, the rapid Billows braves, ...Il.21.22.422.
Not all his Speed escapes the rapid Floods; ......Il.21.301.433.
No less fore-right the rapid Chace they held, ...Il.22.189.463.
He smites the Steeds; the rapid Chariot flies; ......Il.22.503.477.
Of rapid Racers in the dusty Course. ......Il.23.328.503.
The smoaking Chariots, rapid as they bound, ...Il.23.445.508.
Since great *Minerva* wings their rapid Way, ...Il.23.485.509.
And the fierce Coursers urg'd their rapid Pace ......Il.23.587.513.
The Youths contending in the rapid Race. ......Il.23.864.524.
She urg'd her Fav'rite on the rapid Way, ...Il.23.919.525.
So past them all the rapid Circle flies: ......Il.23.1003.529.
Why teach ye not my rapid Wheels to run, ...Il.24.329.550.
By *Jove's* command direct their rapid flight; ......Od.2.172.70.
With rapid step the Goddess urg'd her way; ......Od.2.443.82.
Swift as she spoke, with rapid pace she leads. ......Od.2.452.83.
With rapid swiftness cut the liquid way, ...Od.3.215.96.
The smooth-hair'd horses, and the rapid car, ...Od.3.605.117.
At the fair dome their rapid labour ends; ......Od.4.3.119.
In battel calm he guides the rapid storm, ...Od.4.371.137.
To stem too rapid, and too deep to stand. ......Od.5.531.198.
Swift to *Phæacia* wing'd her rapid flight. ......Od.6.4.203.
Clytonius sprung: he wing'd the rapid way, ...Od.8.131.270.
While to the shore the rapid vessel flies, ...Od.12.218.442.
New chains they add, and rapid urge the way, ...Od.12.236.443.
Now from the rocks the rapid vessel flies, ...Od.12.312.447.
As fiery coursers in the rapid race ......Od.13.98.5.
What hands unseen the rapid bark restrain! ......Od.13.192.15.
For flying chariots or the rapid race; ......Od.13.290.19.
With rapid speed to whirl them o'er the sea. ......Od.15.315.84.
For farther search, his rapid steeds transport ......Od.17.132.138.
Or if dismounted, from the rapid cloud, ...Od.20.76.236.

RAPINE
My hands shall rend what ev'n thy Rapine spares: ......2.RL4.168.197.
When Catiline by rapine swell'd his store, ...3.Ep1.212.33.
And all his Rapine cou'd from others wrest; ......Il.9.497.457.
Autolycus by fraudful Rapine won, ...Il.10.314.17.
Still breathing Rapine, Violence, and Lust! ......Il.13.794.142.
The hand of Rapine make our bounty vain. ......Od.8.482.288.
Their rapine strengthens, and their riots rise: ......Od.14.114.41.
Ev'n now, the hand of Rapine sacks the dome. ......Od.15.16.70.

RAPINES
Before your rapines, join'd with all your own, ...Od.22.74.290.

RAPP'D
With *Flavia's* Busk that oft had rapp'd his own: ......2.RL2.39Z2.161.
"Give her the Hair"—he spoke, and rapp'd his Box. ......2.RL4.130.194.

RAPT
Rapt into future Times, the Bard begun; ......1.Mes.7.113.
Venus for those had rapt thee to the Skies, ...1.TrSP.101.398.
Not touch'd, but rapt; not waken'd, but inspir'd! ......2.ElAb.202.336.
As the rapt Seraph that adores and burns; ......3.EOM1.278.49.
As the rapt Seraphim that sings and burns; ......3.EOM1.278A.49.
I see! I see!—" Then rapt, she spoke no more. ......5.DunA1.255.94.
Rapt thro' the Ranks he thunders o'er the Plain, ...Il.5.113.272.
Rapt by th' Æthereal Steeds the Chariot roll'd; ......Il.8.51.398.
Rapt from the less'ning Thunder of the War; ......Il.13.679.137.
Rapt in the Chariot o'er the distant Plains, ...Il.16.1047.283.
With wonder rapt, on yonder cheek I trace ......Od.4.189.129.
High rapt in wonder of the future deed, ...Od.4.579.147.
And rapt with ecstacy the Sire address'd. ......Od.19.43.195.
In contemplation rapt. This hostile crew ......Od.20.49.234.
In vision rap'd <rapt>; the * *Hyperesian* Seer ......Od.20.421.253.

RAPTUR'D
Raptur'd, he gazes round the dear retreat, ...5.DunA1.225.90.
"Enough! enough!" the raptur'd Monarch cries; ......5.DunA3.357.193.
"Enough! enough!" the raptur'd Monarch cries; ......5.DunB3.339.336.
Which Theocles in raptur'd vision saw, ...5.DunB4.488.389.
The chanter's soul and raptur'd song inspire; ......Od.1.444.54.
Damps the warm wishes of my raptur'd mind: ......Od.4.812.157.
Raptur'd I stood, and as this hour amaz'd, ...Od.6.199.219.
Raptur'd I stand! for earth ne'er knew to bear ......Od.6.201.219.
Full on the Queen her raptur'd eyes she cast, ...Od.19.555.223.
O *Jove* supreme, the raptur'd swain replies, ...Od.20.294.247.

RAPTURE
Whose Judgment sways us, and whose Rapture warms! ......1.PAu.10A.81.
Where *Nature moves,* and *Rapture warms* the Mind; ......1.EOC.236.266.
Yet let not each gay *Turn* thy Rapture move, ...1.EOC.390.284.
You grow *correct* that once with Rapture writ, ...4.EpS1.3.297.
O then, with what rapture ......6.91.29.254.
And then, with what rapture ......6.91.29A.254.
While these to Love's delicious Rapture yield, ...Il.3.559.218.
With rapture oft the verge of *Greece* reviews, ...Od.4.697.152.
Th' unwonted scene surprize and rapture drew; ......Od.7.179.244.
The Nurse with eager rapture speeds her way; ......Od.23.2.316.

RAPTURE (CONTINUED)
Thus slow, to fly with rapture to his arms? ......Od.23.102.324.
While the sweet Lyrist airs of rapture sings, ...Od.23.133.327.
Touch'd to the soul the King with rapture hears, ...Od.23.247.335.
The ravish'd Queen with equal rapture glows, ...Od.23.257.335.
His sudden rapture) in thy Consort blest! ......Od.24.219.358.

RAPTURED
And in his raptured soul the Vision glows. ......Od.1.558.58.

RAPTURES
Whose Raptures fire me, and whose Visions bless, ...1.W-F.260.173.
And in tumultuous Raptures dy'd away. ......1.TrSP.62.396.
Th' entrancing Raptures of th' approaching Night; ......2.ChJM.350.31.
Far other raptures, of unholy joy: ......2.ElAb.224.338.
Loves of his own and raptures swell the note: ......3.EOM3.34.95.
Then raptures high the seat of sense o'erflow, ...5.DunA3.5.150.
No more the Monarch could such raptures bear; ......5.DunA3.357A.193.
Then raptures high the seat of Sense o'erflow, ...5.DunB3.5.320.
What home-felt raptures move! ......6.51ii.34.154.
And wake to Raptures in a Life to come. ......6.86.20.246.
To the prolific raptures of a God: ......Od.11.298.396.
Thy tale with raptures I could hear thee tell, ...Od.11.466.407.
Approach! thy soul shall into raptures rise! ......Od.12.226.443.
With the strong raptures of a parent's joy. ......Od.16.211.114.
Such raptures in my beating bosom rise, ...Od.20.108.238.

RAPTUROUS
To rapturous sounds, at hand *Pontonous* hung: ......Od.8.64.265.

RARE
In *Poets* as true *Genius* is but rare, ...1.EOC.11.240.
Bless the kind Fates, and think your Fortune rare. ......2.ChJM.193.24.
Short and but rare, 'till Man improv'd it all. ......3.EOM4.116.139.
That secret rare, between th' extremes to move ......3.Ep3.227.111.
His givings rare, save farthings to the poor. ......3.Ep3.348.122.
Rare monkish Manuscripts for Hearne alone, ...3.Ep4.9.135.
And, what's more rare, a Poet shall say *Grace.* ......4.HS2.150.67.
And, what's more rare, the Poet shall say *Grace.* ......4.HS2.150A.67.
The things, we know, are neither rich nor rare, ...4.Arbu.171.108.
Not that the things are either rich or rare, ...4.Arbu.171A.108.
Like rich old Wardrobes, things extremely rare, ...4.JD2.123.145.
And plac'd it next him, a distinction rare! ......5.DunA2.92.108.
And plac'd it next him, a distinction rare! ......5.DunB2.96.300.
(Which curious *Germans* hold so rare,) ......6.14v(b).20.50.
Rare Imp of *Phœbus,* hopeful Youth! ......6.58.17.171.
The *Thing,* we know, is neither rich nor rare, ...6.98.21.284.
In youth and beauty wisdom is but rare! ......Od.7.379.254.
Rare gift! but oh, what gift to fools avails! ......Od.10.29.340.
What rare device those vessels might enclose? ......Od.10.39.341.
Rare on the mind those images are trac'd, ...Od.19.259.207.
Hard is the task, and rare, the Queen rejoin'd, ...Od.19.654.227.
Whoe'er from heav'n has gain'd this rare Ostent, ...Od.20.143.240.

RARELY
Much *Fruit* of *Sense* beneath is rarely found. ......1.EOC.310.274.
But these plain Characters we rarely find; ......3.Ep1.122.25.
And rarely Av'rice taints the tuneful mind. ......4.2HE1.192.211.
The Cause of Strife remov'd so rarely well, ...6.145.9.388.
Neptune, by pray'r repentant rarely won, ...Od.1.88.35.
Nor trust the sex that is so rarely wise; ......Od.11.546.410.
But rarely seen, or seen with weeping eyes. ......Od.15.558.96.

RARITIES
And Books for Mead, and Rarities for Sloane. ......3.Ep4.10A.136.

RASCAL
And scorn a rascal and a coach! ......6.150.20.399.
And scorn a rascal in a coach! ......6.150.20A.399.

RASE
Go, rase my *Samos,* let *Mycenè* fall, ...1.TrSt.368.425.

RASH
Force he prepar'd, but check'd the rash Design; ......1.TrVP.118.382.
And I my self the same rash act had done, ...1.TrFD.26.387.
Ah cease rash Youth! desist ere 'tis too late, ...2.RL3.121.176.
What cou'd thus high thy rash Ambition raise? ......2.TemF.499.287.
With all the rash dexterity of Wit: ......3.EOM2.84.65.
Too rash for Thought, for Action too refin'd: ......3.Ep1.201A.32.
First turn plain rash, then vanish quite away. ......4.JD4.45.29.
Rash, impious Man! to stain the blest Abodes, ...Il.5.491.291.
What rash Destruction! and what Heroes slain? ......Il.5.945.311.
Rash, furious, blind, from these to those he flies, ...Il.5.1024.315.
Griev'd tho' thou art, forbear the rash Design; ......Il.7.129.369.
Neptune with Wrath rejects the rash Design: ......Il.8.254.409.
But the rash Youth prepares to scour the Plain: ......Il.10.394.21.
Correct it yet, and change thy rash Intent; ......Il.15.226.205.
Then rash *Patroclus* with new Fury glows, ...Il.16.946.280.
'Tis mine to prove the rash Assertion vain; ......Il.17.194.295.
Rash we contended for the black-ey'd Maid) ......Il.19.60.374.
And let your rash, injurious Clamours end: ......Il.19.84.375.
Rash as thou art to prop the *Trojan* Throne, ...Il.21.514.443.
On my rash Courage charge the Chance of War, ...Il.22.148.459.
An Act so rash (*Antilochus)* has stain'd. ......Il.23.652.515.
Rash Heat perhaps a Moment might controul, ...Il.23.687.517.
Lest rash suspicion might alarm thy mind: ......Od.7.393.256.
A deed so rash had finish'd all our fate, ...Od.9.360.321.
And ah, thy self the rash attempt forbear! ......Od.10.316.359.

RASHLY
Then Sir be cautious, nor too rashly deem; ......2.ChJM.805.54.
And rashly blame the realm of Blunderland. ......6.61.20.181.
and rashly scorn the realm of Blunderland. ......6.61.20B.181.
Curb that impetuous Tongue, nor rashly vain ......Il.2.308.142.
Before the rest let none too rashly ride; ......Il.4.348.237.

RASHLY (CONTINUED)

Nor rashly strive where human Force is vain. ....Il.5.167.275.
Much did he promise, rashly I believ'd: ....Il.10.464.24.
On certain Dangers we too rashly run: ....Il.12.76.84.
Against our Arm which rashly he defy'd, ...Il.17.29.289.
He rashly boasts; the rest our Will denies. ....Il.17.515.308.
What God provokes thee, rashly thus to dare, ...Il.17.536.309.
Old Man! (*Oïleus* rashly thus replies) ....Il.23.556.511.
Why rashly wou'd my son his fate explore, ...Od.4.940.162.
Their wholsome counsel rashly I declin'd, ...Od.9.268.318.
Nor speak I rashly but with faith averr'd, ...Od.14.175.44.

RASHNESS

Fear to the statesman, rashness to the chief, ...3.EOM2.243.84.
His polish'd Bow with hasty Rashness seiz'd. ....Il.4.136.226.
Too late, O Friend! my Rashness I deplore; ....Il.5.258.279.
How shall his Rashness stand the dire Alarms, ...Il.15.186.203.
How shall thy Rashness stand the dire Alarms, ...Il.15.202.204.
Some adverse God thy Rashness may destroy; ....Il.16.118.241.
Breathless in Dust, the Price of Rashness paid. ....Il.20.458.413.
How dares thy Rashness on the Pow'rs divine ....Il.21.563.445.
And wonders at the Rashness of his Foe. ....Il.23.506.510.
Will learn their Rashness, when they pay the Price. ....Il.23.571.512.
He soon his rashness shall with life atone, ...Od.4.898.160.
The leader's rashness made the soldiers bleed. ....Od.10.516.368.

RAT

No Rat is rhym'd to death, nor Maid to love: ....4.JD2.22.133.
"A Rat, a Rat! clap to the door— ....4.HS6.214.263.
"A Rat, a Rat! clap to the door— ....4.HS6.214.263.

RAT'LING

Swift as the rat'ling Hail, or fleecy Snows ....Il.15.192.204.
The Car revers'd came rat'ling on the Field; ....Il.23.472.509.

RATAFIE

Of Mirth and Opium, Ratafie and Tears, ...3.Ep2.110.58.

RATE

But by your father's worth if yours you rate, ...3.EOM4.209.147.
Court-virtues bear, like Gems, the highest rate, ...3.Ep1.93.22.
For th'rest, ten *per Cent.* her constant Rate is; ....4.HAdv.19.77.
Who trades in Frigates of the second Rate? ....4.HAdv.62.81.
Whether my Vessel be first-rate or not? ....4.2HE2.297.185.
I heed thee not, but prize at equal rate ....Il.1.237.98.
The Mast, which late a first-rate Galley bore, ...Il.23.1010.529.

RATHER

Ah! canst thou rather see this tender Breast ....1.TrSP.224.403.
And rather wou'd I chuse, by Heav'n above, ...2.ChJM.547.41.
Oh had I rather un-admir'd remain'd ....2.RL4.153.196.
Rather than so, ah let me still survive, ...2.RL5.101.207.
The Notes at first were rather sweet than loud: ....2.TemF.311.279.
Say rather, Man's as perfect as he ought; ....3.EOM1.70.22.
Or rather truly, if your Point be Rest, ...4.HS1.17.5.
If I would scribble, rather than repose. ....4.2HE2.71.169.
Rather than so, see Ward invited over, ...4.1HE6.56A.241.
Or bidst thou rather Party to embrace? ....5.DunB1.205.284.
Rather with Samuel I beseech with tears ....6.2.17.6.
Rather to starve, as they are us'd to do, ...6.17iv.25.60.
Rather than Letters longer be, ...6.30.62.88.
Let's rather wait one year for better luck; ....6.116v.3.327.
And suffer, rather than my People fall. ....Il.1.148.94.
"Or rather, some descendant of the skies; ....Od.6.335.227.
Rather I chuse laboriously to bear ....Od.11.597.412.
Here wait we rather, till approaching day ....Od.15.59.72.
Then if a wider course shall rather please ....Od.15.91.73.
Rather than bear dishonour worse than death, ...Od.16.112.108.

RATIFIE

I ratifie my speech; before the sun ....Od.19.349.211.

RATIFIES

Assents to Fate, and ratifies the Doom. ....1.TrES.255.459.
The Nod that ratifies the Will Divine, ...Il.1.680.119.
Assents to Fate, and ratifies the Doom. ....Il.16.560.266.

RATIFY

And ratify the best, for publick Good. ....Il.9.136.438.
That Rites divine should ratify the Band, ...Il.19.317.385.
A solemn compact let us ratify, ...Od.14.434.56.

RATIONAL

'Tis but a just and rational Desire, ...2.ChWB.138.63.
Shall he alone, whom rational we call, ...3.EOM1.187.37.

RATLING

But *ratling* Nonsense in full *Vollies* breaks; ....1.EOC.628.310.
From whose dark Womb a ratling Tempest pours, ...1.TrSt.494.431.
Then down on Earth a ratling Tempest pours, ...1.TrSt.494A.431.
Loud Strokes are heard, and ratling Arms resound, ...1.TrES.164.455.
And all for Combate fit the ratling Car. ....Il.2.457.149.
Foretells the ratling Hail, or weighty Show'r, ...Il.10.6.2.
Loud Strokes are heard, and ratling Arms resound, ...Il.12.518.100.
Flew sail and sail-yards ratling o'er the main. ....Od.5.408.192.
Her ratling quiver from her shoulder sounds: ....Od.6.120.212.
Before his feet the ratling show'r he threw, ...Od.22.5.286.
'Till *Jove* in wrath the ratling Tempest guides, ...Od.23.357.342.

RATT'LING

Fierce on his ratt'ling Chariot *Hector* came; ....Il.8.417.417.
This way and that, the ratt'ling Thicket bends, ...Il.16.927.279.

RATTL'D

Lord! Lord! how rattl'd then thy Stones, ...6.79.55.219.

RATTLE

Pleas'd with a rattle, tickled with a straw: ....3.EOM2.276.88.
The Faulchions ring, Shields rattle, Axes sound, ...Il.15.864.230.
Shields, Helmets rattle, as the Warriors close; ....Il.16.765.273.
Rattle the clatt'ring Cars, and the shockt Axles bound. ....Il.23.143.495.

RATTLED

His Arms around him rattled as he fell. ....Il.5.668.300.

RATTLES

The rhymes and rattles of the Man or Boy: ....4.1HE1.18.279.
And the deaf Eccho rattles round the Fields. ....Il.12.182.87.

RATTLING

Rattling an ancient Sistrum at his head. ....5.DunB4.374.379.
The scatt'ring Arrows rattling from the Case, ...Il.21.571.446.
The rattling Ruin of the clashing Cars, ...Il.23.516.510.
Shouts of Applause run rattling thro the Skies. ....Il.23.867.523.
And all the rattling shrouds in fragments torn. ....Od.9.80.306.

RAV'NOUS

Two rav'nous vultures furious for their food ....Od.11.711.421.

RAVAG'D

Lawless he ravag'd with his martial pow'rs ....Od.16.444.128.

RAVAGE

Parts it may ravage, but preserves the whole. ....3.EOM2.106.67.
For yet 'tis giv'n to *Troy,* to ravage o'er ....Il.17.520.308.
His stores ye ravage and usurp his state. ....Od.4.923.161.
The coasts they ravage, and the natives kill. ....Od.14.293.50.
The country ravage, and the natives kill. ....Od.17.514.157.

RAVE

I rave, then weep, I curse, and then complain, ...1.TrSP.131.399.
In vain may Heroes fight, and Patriots rave; ....3.Ep3.37.88.
They rave, recite, and madden round the land. ....4.Arbu.6.96.
Yet then did *Dennis* rave in furious fret; ....4.Arbu.153.107.
In vain! they gaze, turn giddy, rave, and die. ....5.DunA3.354.193.
In vain! they gaze, turn giddy, rave, and die. ....5.DunB4.648.409.
Stay, and the furious Flood shall cease to rave; ....Il.21.336.435.

RAVELL'D

The night still ravell'd, what the day renew'd. ....Od.19.173.200.

RAVENOUS

And ravenous Dogs, allur'd by scented Blood, ...1.TrSt.737.441.
Or Ravenous *Corm'rants* shake their flabby Wings, ...6.26i.6.79.

RAVES

At half mankind when gen'rous Manly raves, ...3.Ep1.116.24.
Sudden, she storms! she raves! You tip the wink, ...3.Ep2.33.52.
If D[enni]s rhymes, and raves in furious Fret, ...6.49iii.3.142.
If Dennis rails, and raves in furious Pet, ...6.49iii.3A.142.
If dreadful *Dennis* raves in furious Fret, ...6.98.3.283.
Thus, when a Mountain-Billow foams and raves, ...Il.17.310.299.
He groans, he raves, he sorrows from his Soul. ....Il.19.334.386.
Then murm'ring from his Beds, he boils, he raves, ...Il.21.380.436.
There as the solitary Mourner raves, ...Il.24.21.535.
There the wide sea with all his billows raves! ....Od.11.195.391.
Say while the sea, and while the tempest raves, ...Od.11.495.408.
Nor while the sea, nor while the tempest raves, ...Od.11.501.408.
Where rouls yon smoke, yon tumbling ocean raves; ....Od.12.261.445.
For on the rocks it bore where *Scylla* raves, ...Od.12.505.457.
If one more happy, while the tempest raves ....Od.23.253.335.
The justling rocks where fierce *Charybdis* raves, ...Od.23.353.341.

RAVISH

By Force to ravish, or by Fraud betray; ....2.RL2.32.161.
What War could ravish, Commerce could bestow, ...3.EOM3.205.113.
To move, to raise, to ravish ev'ry heart, ...5.DunA2.215.127.
To move, to raise, to ravish ev'ry heart, ...5.DunB2.223.306.
Whose arm should ravish from *Phylacian* fields ....Od.11.354.399.

RAVISH'D

The Fields are ravish'd from th'industrious Swains, ...1.W-F.65.155.
Since you a servant's ravish'd form bemoan, ...1.TrFD.3.385.
My ravish'd Breast, and All the Muse inspires. ....1.TrSt.4.409.
As Thou, sad Virgin! for thy ravish'd Hair. ....2.RL4.10.183.
Then cease, bright Nymph! to mourn thy ravish'd Hair ....2.RL5.141.211.
Then cease, bright Nymph! to mourn the ravish'd Hair ....2.RL5.141A.211.
Or ravish'd with the whistling of a Name, ...3.EOM4.283.155.
As Hylas fair was ravish'd long ago. ....5.DunA2.312.140.
As Hylas fair was ravish'd long ago. ....5.DunB2.336.314.
(My God) speak comfort to my ravish'd Ears; ....6.2.32.6.
And wills, that *Helen* and the ravish'd Spoil ....Il.3.129.196.
For ravish'd *Ganymede* on *Tros* bestow'd, ...Il.5.329.282.
Meanwhile (his Conquest ravish'd from his Eyes) ....Il.5.407.286.
My Glory ravish'd, and my People slain! ....Il.8.285.410.
The Matrons ravish'd, the whole Race enslav'd: ....Il.9.705.469.
One Woman-Slave was ravish'd from thy Arms: ....Il.9.751.471.
(This Nymph, the Fruit of *Priam's* ravish'd Joy, ...Il.13.233.116.
The violated Rites, the ravish'd Dame, ...Il.13.785.142.
Seem'd as extinct: Day ravish'd from their Eyes, ...Il.17.424.303.
My Daughters ravish'd, and my City burn'd, ...Il.22.89.456.
The thoughts which rowl within my ravish'd breast, ...Od.1.259.45.
For novel lays attract our ravish'd ears; ....Od.1.447.54.
Or parent vulture, mourns her ravish'd young; ....Od.16.239.116.
An omen'd Voice invades his ravish'd ear. ....Od.20.131.240.
The ravish'd Queen with equal rapture glows, ...Od.23.257.335.

RAVISHER

Gods! shall the Ravisher display this Hair, ...2.RL4.21.132.
Gods! shall the Ravisher display your Hair, ...2.RL4.103.192.

RAVISHT
Was ravisht from the tender vine; ... 6.6ii.22.15.

RAW
Crept the raw hides, and with a bellowing sound ... Od.12.465.453.

RAWLINSON
Ev'n *Ra[wlin]son* might understand. ... 6.29.16.83.
Even *R[awlinson]* may understand: ... 6.29.7Z4.83.

RAY
He from thick Films shall purge the visual Ray, ... 1.Mes.39.116.
And thence exerting his refulgent Ray, ... 1.TrVP.116.381.
But while he dwells where not a chearful Ray ... 1.TrSt.71.413.
When the South glows with his Meridian Ray, ... 1.TrSt.214.419.
Heav'n seems improv'd with a superior Ray, ... 1.TrSt.294.422.
Till Nature quicken'd by th'Inspiring Ray, ... 1.TrSt.586.434.
But when the morning Star with early Ray ... 1.TrUl.21.466.
The Balls are wounded with the piercing Ray, ... 2.ChJM.800.53.
The Balls seem wounded with the piercing Ray, ... 2.ChJM.800A.53.
Sol thro' white Curtains shot a tim'rous Ray, ... 2.RL1.13.145.
The Sun obliquely shoots his burning Ray; ... 2.RL3.20.170.
And hail with Musick its propitious Ray. ... 2.RL5.134.211.
And Earth relenting feels the Genial Ray; ... 2.TemF.4.253.
Those smiling eyes, attemp'ring ev'ry ray, ... 2.ElAb.63.324.
Thy eyes diffus'd a reconciling ray, ... 2.ElAb.145.331.
Alas! not dazzled with their noon-tide ray, ... 3.EOM4.305.156.
Oh! blest with Temper, whose unclouded ray ... 3.Ep2.257.71.
Whether old Age, with faint, but chearful Ray, ... 4.HS1.93.13.
Then, like the Sun, let Bounty spread her ray, ... 4.HS2.115.63.
Now shown by Cynthia's silver Ray, ... 4.HOde1.47.153.
Sure fate of all, beneath whose rising ray ... 4.2HE1.19.195.
And stretch the Ray to Ages yet unborn. ... 4.2HE1.228.215.
Thus he, for then a ray of Reason stole ... 5.DunA3.223.176.
Thus he, for then a ray of Reason stole ... 5.DunB3.225.331.
Yet, yet a moment, one dim Ray of Light ... 5.DunB4.1.339.
Now flam'd the Dog-star's unpropitious ray, ... 5.DunB4.9.340.
'Twas when the Dog-star's unpropitious ray, ... 5.DunB4.9A.340.
For *Sol's* is now the only ray. ... 6.4iv.12.10.
Ev'n now, observant of the parting Ray, ... 6.84.37.240.
She still with pleasure eyes thy Evening Ray, ... 6.84.31Z9.240.
Alas! not dazled with his Noontide ray, ... 6.130.35.359.
Unpolish'd Gemms no Ray on Pride bestow, ... 6.142.5.382.
His beamy Shield emits a living Ray; ... Il.5.6.266.
In Brazen Arms that cast a gleamy Ray, ... Il.6.650.359.
And tipt the Mountains with a purple Ray. ... Il.7.501.389.
Strikes the blue Mountains with her golden Ray, ... Il.9.829.474.
Soon as the Sun, with all-revealing Ray ... Il.11.870.74.
His nodding Helm emits a streamy Ray; ... Il.13.1014.153.
A sudden Ray shot beaming o'er the Plain, ... Il.15.810.227.
Sudden, the Thund'rer, with a flashing Ray, ... Il.16.356.257.
The golden Sun pour'd forth a stronger Ray, ... Il.17.430.304.
Forth burst the Sun with all-enlight'ning Ray; ... Il.17.735.317.
And turn their Eye-balls from the flashing Ray. ... Il.18.268.335.
A Ray divine her heav'nly Presence shed, ... Il.19.9.371.
And fast behind, *Aurora's* warmer Ray ... Il.23.282.501.
Now shed *Aurora* round her Saffron Ray, ... Il.24.866.572.
Now red'ning from the dawn, the Morning ray ... Od.2.1.59.
And end their voyage with the morning ray. ... Od.2.475.84.
And wide o'er earth diffus'd his chearing ray, ... Od.3.3.85.
And studded amber darts a golden ray: ... Od.4.88.123.
Pilots their course: For when the glimm'ring ray ... Od.4.880.159.
When the gay morn unveils her smiling ray: ... Od.6.36.206.
And while the robes imbibe the solar ray, ... Od.6.111.211.
Shot thro' the western clouds a dewy ray; ... Od.6.382.230.
The polish'd Ore, reflecting ev'ry ray, ... Od.7.130.241.
Nor 'till oblique he slop'd his evening ray, ... Od.7.372.254.
And ships shall wait thee with the morning ray. ... Od.7.405.256.
Now fair *Aurora* lifts her golden ray, ... Od.8.1.260.
Or nations subject to the western ray. ... Od.8.30.263.
With clouds of darkness quench'd his visual ray, ... Od.8.59.265.
Ev'n he who sightless wants his visual ray, ... Od.8.221.274.
That lies beneath the sun's all-seeing ray; ... Od.8.608.295.
Stretch'd forth, and panting in the sunny ray. ... Od.10.186.349.
And when the morn unveils her safron ray, ... Od.12.35.431.
'Till *Phœbus* downward plung'd his burning ray; ... Od.12.40.431.
Glows with th' autumnal or the summer ray, ... Od.12.92.436.
She ceas'd: And now arose the morning ray; ... Od.12.178.440.
The wax dissolv'd beneath the burning ray; ... Od.12.211.442.
Haste ye to land! and when the morning ray ... Od.12.349.448.
Or deep in Ocean plunge the burning ray. ... Od.12.449.452.
Sees with delight the sun's declining ray, ... Od.13.41.3.
But when the morning star with early ray ... Od.13.112.6.
The sun obliquely shot his dewy ray. ... Od.17.688.165.
That shot effulgence like the solar ray, ... Od.18.344.184.
It aids our torch-light, and reflects the ray. ... Od.18.402.187.
Nor solar ray, cou'd pierce the shadowy bow'r, ... Od.19.514.221.
Nor had they ended till the morning ray: ... Od.23.259.335.
The mingled web, whose gold and silver ray ... Od.24.173.356.

RAYMENT
So food and rayment constant will I give: ... Od.18.407.188.
With change of rayment, brass, and heaps of gold. ... Od.23.368.343.

RAYMOND
Great C[owper], H[arcourt], P[arker], R[aymond], K[ing], ... 5.DunB4.545.395.

RAYS
But soon the Sun with milder Rays descends ... 1.PSu.89.79.
But lost, dissolv'd in thy superior Rays; ... 1.Mes.101.122.
It draws up Vapours which obscure its Rays; ... 1.EOC.471.292.
Tho' *Phœbus* longs to mix his Rays with thine, ... 1.TrSt.39.411.
Such Rays from *Phœbe's* bloody Circle flow, ... 1.TrSt.147.416.
Impervious Clouds conceal'd thy sullen Rays; ... 1.TrSt.764.442.
Whose Purple Rays th' *Achæmenes* adore; ... 1.TrSt.858.446.
And heighten'd by the Diamond's circling Rays, ... 2.RL4.115.193.

RAYS (CONTINUED)
With equal Rays immortal *Tully* shone, ... 2.TemF.238.274.
Bright azure Rays from lively Saphirs stream, ... 2.TemF.252.275.
And forms a Rainbow of alternate Rays. ... 2.TemF.257.275.
Mean-while Opinion gilds with varying rays ... 3.EOM2.283.89.
'Till then, Opinion gilds with varying rays ... 3.EOM2.283A.89.
Tho' the same Sun with all-diffusive rays ... 3.Ep1.97.22.
Ye little Stars! hide your diminish'd rays. ... 3.Ep3.282.116.
And Splendor borrows all her rays from Sense. ... 3.Ep4.180.154.
For Splendor borrows all her rays from Sense. ... 3.Ep4.180A.154.
Not so, when diadem'd with Rays divine, ... 4.EpS2.232.326.
Mix on his look. All eyes direct their rays ... 5.DunA2.7.97.
Mix on his look: All eyes direct their rays ... 5.DunB2.7.296.
Did Nature's pencil ever blend such rays, ... 5.DunB4.411.382.
And *Winter's* Coolness spite of *Summer's* rays. ... 6.14iv.30.48.
The God who darts around the World his Rays. ... Il.1.52.88.
And gilds fair *Chrysa* with distinguish'd Rays! ... Il.1.593.116.
Where-e'er the Sun's refulgent Rays are cast, ... Il.7.548.392.
There stood the Chariot beaming forth its Rays, ... Il.8.548.422.
And lighten glimm'ring *Xanthus* with their Rays. ... Il.8.700.428.
And level'd at the Skies with pointing Rays, ... Il.13.185.114.
Not ev'n the Sun, who darts thro' Heav'n his Rays, ... Il.14.391.181.
Soon as the Sun in Ocean hides his Rays, ... Il.18.249.334.
Broad-glitt'ring Breastplates, Spears with pointed Rays ... Il.19.386.388.
Blaz'd with long Rays, and gleam'd athwart the Field. ... Il.19.403.388.
And o'er the feebler Stars exerts his Rays; ... Il.22.40.454.
Shot trembling Rays that glitter'd o'er the Land; ... Il.22.176.461.
(A race divided, whom with sloping rays ... Od.1.31.31.
Oft, *Jove's* ætherial rays (resistless fire) ... Od.1.443.53.
With rays so strong, distinguish'd, and divine, ... Od.3.274.99.
Nor here the sun's meridian rays had pow'r, ... Od.5.620.201.
With fullest rays, *Amphiaraus* now gone; ... Od.15.275.82.
And sprightly damsels trim the rays by turns. ... Od.18.358.184.
His shoulders intercept th' unfriendly rays. ... Od.19.457.217.
Dim thro' th' eclipse of fate, the rays divine ... Od.20.243.244.
No clouds of error dim th' etherial rays, ... Od.20.439.254.

RAZ'D
Their Precepts raz'd the Prejudice of Youth, ... 6.96iii.9.274.
The Spoils of Cities raz'd, and Warriors slain, ... Il.1.159.95.
And raz'd the Skin and drew the Purple Gore. ... Il.4.169.229.
Raz'd his high Crest, and thro' his Helmet drives, ... Il.4.525.246.
Raz'd her soft Hand with this lamented Wound. ... Il.5.516.293.
Shall, raz'd and lost, in long Oblivion sleep. ... Il.7.540.391.
Raz'd the smooth Cone, and thence obliquely glanc'd. ... Il.11.454.54.
On the raz'd Shield the falling Ruin rings: ... Il.14.476.187.
And raz'd his Shoulder with a shorten'd Spear: ... Il.17.679.314.
One raz'd *Achilles* Hand; the spouting Blood ... Il.21.183.429.
Of sacred *Troy,* and raz'd her heav'n-built wall, ... Od.1.4.28.
Thy hand, *Telemachus,* it lightly raz'd; ... Od.22.307.301.

RAZE
These thou may'st raze, nor I forbid their Fall: ... Il.4.78.224.
To raze her Walls, tho' built by Hands Divine. ... Il.7.38.364.
Give me to raze *Troy's* long-defended Tow'rs; ... Il.8.348.414.

RAZING
Her snowie Hand the razing Steel profan'd, ... Il.5.419.287.

RE-APPEAR
See! the dull stars roll round and re-appear. ... 5.DunA3.336.192.
When the dull stars roll round and re-appear. ... 5.DunA3.336A.192.
See! the dull stars roll round and re-appear. ... 5.DunB3.322.335.

RE-ASCEND
Alone I re-ascend—With airy mounds ... Od.6.311.225.

RE-ASSERT
To manly years shou'd re-assert the throne. ... Od.1.52.33.
Ulysses soon shall re-assert his claim. ... Od.4.456.141.
Shall great *Ulysses* re-assert his claim. ... Od.17.147.138.

RE-ASSUME
And laughing Ceres re-assume the land. ... 3.Ep4.176.154.

RE-CLOS'D
The silver ring she pull'd, the door re-clos'd; ... Od.1.552.58.

RE-CONSIDER
But re-consider, since the wisest err, ... Od.16.334.122.

RE-ECCHO'D
And sobs of joy re-eccho'd thro' the bow'r: ... Od.10.472.366.

RE-ECCHOES
And the high Dome re-ecchoes to his Nose. ... 2.RL5.86.207.
And Hungerford re-ecchoes, bawl for bawl. ... 5.DunA2.254.131.
And a loud groan re-ecchoes from the main. ... Od.12.16.430.

RE-ECHO
The Heav'ns re-echo, and the Shores reply; ... Il.13.64.107.

RE-ECHO'D
The Field re-echo'd the distressful Sound. ... Il.17.293.299.
The dome re-echo'd to their mingled moan. ... Od.20.238.244.

RE-ECHOE
Their crackling Jaws re-echoe to the Blows, ... Il.23.796.521.

RE-ECHOES
And Hungerford re-echoes bawl for bawl. ... 5.DunB2.266.308.

RE-ECHOING
Blows following Blows are heard re-echoing wide, ... Il.16.769.273.

RE-ENTER
Re-enter then, not all at once, but stay ....Od.21.246.271.

RE-FIT
Staid but a season to re-fit his fleet; ....Od.14.422.56.

RE-INSPIRES
His lab'ring Bosom re-inspires with Breath, ...Il.15.65.197.

RE-JUDGE
Re-judge his justice, be the GOD of GOD! ....3.EOM1.122.30.
Re-judge his Acts, and dignify Disgrace. ....6.84.30.239.

RE-KINDLING
Re-kindling Rage each heavenly Breast alarms; ....Il.21.450.439.

RE-LIGHT
His pow'r can heal me, and re-light my eye; ....Od.9.609.331.

RE-LUM'D
Re-lum'd her ancient light, not kindled new; ....3.EOM3.287.121.

RE-MURMUR
And soft re-murmur in their wonted Bed. ....Il.21.447.438.

RE-MURMUR'D
Our groans the rocks re-murmur'd to the main. ....Od.10.60.342.

RE-PASSES
Re-passes Lintot, vindicates the race, ...5.DunA2.99.109.
Re-passes Lintot, vindicates the race, ...5.DunB2.107.300.

RE-SAILING
From *Pyle* re-sailing and the *Spartan* court, ...Od.4.931.162.
Thence swift re-sailing to my native shores, ...Od.23.295.337.

RE-SOUNDING
Stoop with re-sounding Pinions to the Fight; ....1.TrES.220A.458.
Stoop with re-sounding Pinions to the Fight; ....Il.16.523.264.

RE-TURNS
Turns, and re-turns her, with a Mother's Care. ....Il.17.8.288.

RE-VISIT
Thence to re-visit your imperial dome, ...Od.1.241.44.

REACH
Be sure *your self* and your own *Reach* to know, ...1.EOC.48.244.
And which a *Master-Hand* alone can reach. ....1.EOC.145.256.
And *snatch* a *Grace* beyond the Reach of Art, ...1.EOC.155.258.
Above the reach of *Sacrilegious* Hands, ...1.EOC.182.261.
Now, they who reach *Parnassus'* lofty Crown, ...1.EOC.514.296.
Now, those that reach *Parnassus'* lofty Crown, ...1.EOC.514A.296.
No glass can reach! from Infinite to thee, ...3.EOM1.240.45.
All states can reach it, and all heads conceive; ....3.EOM4.30.130.
Still out of reach, yet never out of view, ...3.Ep2.232.68.
Wants reach all States; they beg but better drest, ...4.JD4.224.45.
In the vast reach of our huge Statute Law ....4.JD2A.134.144.
Within the reach of Treason, or the Law. ....4.JD2.128.145.
Above the reach of vulgar Song; ....4.HOde9.4.159.
Or praise malignly Arts I cannot reach, ...4.2HE1.339.225.
(Tho' ne'er so weighty) reach a wondrous height; ....6.7.16.16.
In vain he strains to reach your Ear, ...6.10.23.25.
Pride, Pomp, and State but reach her outward Part, ...6.19.55.63.
No harms can reach thee, and no force shall move. ....6.21.22.69.
Still out of reach, tho' ever in their view. ....6.22.6.71.
And with my Head Sublime *can reach the Sky.* ....6.26ii.4.79.
If I am wrong, Oh reach my heart ....6.50.31B.147.
Reach thy Size? ....6.96i.4.268.
"Within thy Reach I set the Vinegar? ....6.96ii.18.270.
"Within the reach I set the Vinegar? ....6.96ii.18A.270.
Who reach that High place oh their joy shall be great! ....6.122.21A.342.
Oh give my Lance to reach the *Trojan* Knight, ...Il.5.150.274.
And awful reach the high *Palladian* Dome, ...Il.6.371.344.
This Arm shall reach thy Heart, and stretch thee dead. ....Il.8.203.407.
Flame thro' the Vast of Air, and reach the Sky. ....Il.8.545.422.
That Path they take, and speed to reach the Town. ....Il.11.220.45.
Scour o'er the Fields, and stretch to reach the Town. ....Il.16.453.260.
Did but the Voice of *Ajax* reach my Ear: ....Il.17.110.292.
Forbid by Fate to reach his Father's Years. ....Il.17.224.296.
All, whom this well-known Voice shall reach from far, ...Il.17.298.299.
So may I reach, conceal'd, the cooling Flood, ...Il.21.659.449.
Stand I to doubt, within the reach of Fate? ....Il.21.664.449.
Oft' as to reach the *Dardan* Gates he bends, ...Il.22.251.466.
Now from the Walls the Clamours reach her Ear, ...Il.22.574.480.
Nor reach the Goblet, nor divide the Bread: ....Il.22.635.482.
But reach *Atrides!* Shall his Mare out-go ....Il.23.487.509.
And reach *Gerestus* at the point of day. ....Od.3.216.96.
To reach *Phæacia* all thy nerves extend, ...Od.5.438.193.
And reach high *Ægæ* and the tow'ry dome. ....Od.5.487.195.
The grove they reach, where from the sacred shade ....Od.6.383.230.
To reach this Isle: but there my hopes were lost, ...Od.7.362.254.
So shalt thou instant reach the realm assign'd, ...Od.8.603.294.
And reach our vessel on the winding shore. ....Od.9.548.328.
As far as human voice cou'd reach the ear; ....Od.9.556.329.
Soon shalt thou reach old Ocean's utmost ends, ...Od.10.602.372.
Sent with full force, cou'd reach the depth below. ....Od.12.102.436.
To reach his natal shore was thy decree; ....Od.13.154.13.
One sure of six shall reach *Ulysses'* heart: ....Od.22.277.300.
Whence no contending foot could reach the ground. ....Od.22.502.313.

REACH'D
And now his Shadow reach'd her as she run, ...1.W-F.193.168.
And in a Moment reach'd the *Lycian* Land; ....1.TrES.347.462.
And in a Vapour reach'd the dismal Dome. ....2.RL4.18.184.
But never, never, reach'd one gen'rous Thought. ....3.Ep2.162.64.

REACH'D (CONTINUED)
That never Coxcomb reach'd Magnificence! ....3.Ep4.22.139.
Not touch'd by Nature, and not reach'd by Art." ....5.DunA3.228.176.
Not touch'd by Nature, and not reach'd by Art." ....5.DunB3.230.331.
Had reach'd the Work, the All that mortal can; ....5.DunB4.173.358.
Churches and Chapels instantly it reach'd; ....5.DunB4.607.403.
Then reach'd as high as e'er He cou'd, ...6.94.59.261.
But never, never, reach'd one gen'rous Thought. ....6.139.6.377.
The Fleet he reach'd, and lowly bending down, ...Il.1.486.111.
Agenor's Jav'lin reach'd the Hero's Heart. ....Il.4.533.247.
The *Cretan* Javelin reach'd him from afar, ...Il.5.61.269.
Troy now they reach'd, and touch'd those Banks Divine ....Il.5.964.312.
It reach'd his Neck, with matchless Strength impell'd; ....Il.7.313.379.
To *Ajax* and *Achilles* reach'd the Sound, ...Il.8.272.410.
Pass'd thro the Hosts, and reach'd the Royal Tent. ....Il.9.787.472.
Had reach'd that Monarch on the *Cyprian* Coast; ....Il.11.28.36.
With twelve black Ships he reach'd *Percope's* Strand, ...Il.11.295.48.
Ulysses reach'd him with the fatal Spear; ....Il.11.536.57.
This having reach'd, his brass-hoof'd Steeds he reins, ...Il.13.36.105.
(Who reach'd fair *Ilion,* from *Ascania* far, ...Il.13.997.152.
And in a Moment reach'd the *Lycian* Land; ....Il.16.834.275.
Reach'd the *Vulcanian* Dome, Eternal Frame! ....Il.18.432.341.
He reach'd the Throne where pensive *Thetis* sate; ....Il.18.492.345.
Nor, till he reach'd *Lyrnessus,* turn'd his Head. ....Il.20.231.403.
And now they reach'd the naval Walls, and found ....Il.24.545.558.
The great *Ulysses* reach'd his native shore. ....Od.2.389.80.
Their fates or fortunes never reach'd my ear. ....Od.3.224.96.
Safe reach'd the *Mirmydons* their native land, ...Od.3.228.96.
Secure to seize us ere we reach'd the door. ....Od.9.498.326.
At length we reach'd *Æolia's* sea-girt shore, ...Od.10.1.335.
When lo! we reach'd old Ocean's utmost bounds, ...Od.11.13.379.
And menac'd vengeance, ere he reach'd his shore; ....Od.13.153.13.
Now had *Minerva* reach'd those ample plains, ...Od.15.1.67.
And soon he reach'd the Palace of his Sire. ....Od.15.243.80.
And reach'd the mansion of his faithful swain. ....Od.15.598.99.
They reach'd the dome; the dome with marble shin'd. ....Od.16.41.104.
And reach'd her master with a long embrace. ....Od.17.42.134.
To her the youth. We reach'd the *Pylian* plains, ...Od.17.124.137.
Her keen reproach had reach'd the Sov'reign's ear; ....Od.19.109.197.
Reach'd, in its splendid case, the bow unstrung: ....Od.21.56.262.
What words (the matron cries) have reach'd my ears? ....Od.23.71.322.
How struggling thro' the surge, he reach'd the shores ....Od.23.359.342.
And now they reach'd the *Earth's* remotest ends, ...Od.24.15.347.

REACHES
But nimbler *W[elste]d* reaches at the ground, ...5.DunA2.293B.138.
This *Merion* reaches, bending from the Car, ...Il.17.701.315.
Then cautious thro' the rocky reaches wind, ...Od.15.320.85.

REACHING
Clung to her Knees, and reaching at her Arms, ...Il.16.14.235.

READ
Read them by Day, and meditate by Night, ...1.EOC.125.253.
A perfect Judge will *read* each Work of Wit ....1.EOC.233.266.
Who knew most *Sentences* was *deepest read;* ....1.EOC.441.288.
The Bookful Blockhead, ignorantly read, ...1.EOC.612.309.
Too long for me to write, or you to read; ....2.ChJM.306.29.
But let them read, and solve me, if they can, ...2.ChWB.13.57.
A certain Treatise oft at Evening read, ...2.ChWB.356.74.
Read in this Book, aloud, with strange Delight, ...2.ChWB.378.75.
He read how *Arius* to his Friend complain'd ....2.ChWB.393.76.
All this he read, and read with great Devotion. ....2.ChWB.410.77.
All this he read, and read with great Devotion. ....2.ChWB.410.77.
When still he read, and laugh'd, and read again, ...2.ChWB.413.77.
When still he read, and laugh'd, and read again, ...2.ChWB.413.77.
Wounds, Charms, and *Ardors,* were no sooner read, ...2.RL1.119.154.
As long as *Atalantis* shall be read, ...2.RL3.165.181.
To read and weep is all they now can do. ....2.ElAb.48.323.
Men may be read, as well as Books too much. ....3.Ep1.10.16.
See *Libels, Satires—here* you have it—read. ....4.HS1.149.19.
See *Libels, Satires—there* you have it—read. ....4.Hs1.149A.19.
Such as a *King* might read, a *Bishop* write, ...4.HS1.152.21.
If Foes, they write, if Friends, they read me dead. ....4.Arbu.32.98.
I sit with sad Civility, I read ....4.Arbu.37.98.
My Foes will write, my Friends will read me dead ....4.Arbu.32A.98.
The Courtly *Talbot, Somers, Sheffield* read, ...4.Arbu.139.105.
And see what friends, and read what books I please. ....4.Arbu.264.114.
To see what Friends, or read what Books I please; ....4.Arbu.262A.114.
May prompt and save His Life who cannot read: ....4.JD2A.16.132.
So prompts, and saves a Rogue who cannot read. ....4.JD2.16.133.
So prompts, and saves some Rogue who cannot read. ....4.JD2.16A.133.
To read in Greek, the Wrath of Peleus' Son. ....4.2HE2.53.169.
A Poet begs me, I will hear him read: ....4.2HE2.93.171.
The Men, who write such Verse as we can read? ....4.2HE2.158.175.
At Court, who hates whate'er he read at School. ....4.2HE1.106.203.
Or what remain'd, so worthy to be read ....4.2HE1.137.207.
Our Wives read Milton, and our Daughters Plays, ...4.2HE1.172.209.
Plead much, read more, dine late, or not at all. ....4.1HE6.37.239.
Or gravely try to read the lines ....4.HS6.91.255.
But you may read it, I stop short. ....4.1HE7.84.273.
All Boys may read, and Girls may understand! ....4.EpS1.76.304.
Writ not, and *Chartres* scarce could write or read, ...4.EpS2.186.324.
Here, Last of *Britons!* let your Names be read; ....4.EpS2.250.327.
Amaz'd that one can read, that one can write: ....4.1740.34.333.
In eldest time, e'er mortals writ or read, ...5.DunA1.7.61.
With all such reading as was never read; ....5.DunA1.166.83.
Let all give way—and Durgen may be read. ....5.DunA3.162.165.
Let all give way—and Morris may be read. ....5.DunA3.162A.165.
For ever reading, never to be read. ....5.DunA3.190.172.
Are ever reading and are never read. ....5.DunA3.190A.172.
In eldest time, e'er mortals writ or read, ...5.DunB1.9.269.
Let all give way—and Morris may be read. ....5.DunB3.168.328.
For ever reading, never to be read! ....5.DunB3.194.329.
With all such reading as was never read: ....5.DunB4.250.368.
Read something of a diff'rent Nature, ...6.10.5.24.

READ (CONTINUED)
Which does not Look, but Read Men dead.) .... 6.10.28.25.
Such, who read *Heinsius* and *Masson,* .... 6.10.33.25.
Snuff just three Times, and read again.) .... 6.10.66.26.
Still with Esteem no less convers'd than read; .... 6.19.7.62.
Which some can't construe, some can't read: .... 6.29.14.83.
All fair, and not so much as read. .... 6.29.20.83.
For some Folks read, but all Folks sh—. .... 6.29.30.83.
Which some can't construe, most can't read; .... 6.29.7Z2.83.
Read these instructive leaves, in which conspire .... 6.52.7.156.
Read this, e'er you translate one Bit .... 6.58.3.170.
Read this ere ye translate one Bit .... 6.58.3A.170.
They shall like *Persian* Tales be read, ... 6.58.55.173.
And round the orb in lasting notes be read, ... 6.71.66.204.
"So that each Pisser-by shall read, ... 6.79.143.223.
O reader, if that thou canst read, ... 6.82viii.1.233.
See who ne'er was or will be half read! .... 6.101.1.290.
No Mortal read his *Salomon,* .... 6.101.19.290.
Thus *Amphisbœna* (I have read) .... 6.105iv.5.301.
So *Amphisb na,* we have read .... 6.105iv.5A.301.
To help us thus to read the works of others: .... 6.105v.2.302.
For who will help us e'er to read thy own? .... 6.105v.4.302.
The other never read. .... 6.133.4.363.
Sure *Bounce* is one you never read of. .... 6.135.8.366.
For I assure you, I've read worse. .... 6.147v.2.391.
This Pest he slaughter'd (for he read the Skies, ... Il.6.225.337.
For thus a skilful Seer would read the Skies. .... Il.12.266.91.
Here thou art sage in vain—I better read the skies. .... Od.2.210.72.
To read this sign, and mystick sense of heav'n. .... Od.15.193.77.
Live, an example for the world to read, ... Od.22.413.307.
I read a Monarch in that princely air, ... Od.24.298.364.

READER
O reader, if that thou canst read, ... 6.82viii.1.233.
Made ev'ry Reader curse the *Light;* .... 6.101.8.290.

READER'S
The Reader's threaten'd (not in vain) with *Sleep.* .... 1.EOC.353.279.
More on a Reader's sense, than Gazer's eye. .... 4.2HE1.351.225.

READERS
Sleepless themselves to give their readers sleep. .... 5.DunA1.92.70.
The pond'rous books two gentle readers bring; .... 5.DunA2.351.143.
Sleepless themselves, to give their readers sleep. .... 5.DunB1.94.276.
The pond'rous books two gentle readers bring; .... 5.DunB2.383.316.

READIEST
Nor youngest, yet the readiest to decide. .... Il.23.559.511.

READING
Pains, reading, study, are their just pretence, ... 4.Arbu.159.108.
With all such reading as was never read; .... 5.DunA1.166.83.
How, with less reading than makes felons 'scape, ... 5.DunA1.235.90.
For ever reading, never to be read. .... 5.DunA3.190.172.
Are ever reading and are never read. .... 5.DunA3.190A.172.
How, with less reading than makes felons scape, ... 5.DunB1.281.290.
For ever reading, never to be read! .... 5.DunB3.194.329.
With all such reading as was never read: .... 5.DunB4.250.368.
To pass her time 'twixt reading and Bohea, ... 6.45.15.125.
And reading wish, like theirs, our fate and fame, ... 6.52.9.156.
Pains, Reading, Study, are their just Pretence, ... 6.98.9.283.

READS
Glows while he *reads,* but *trembles* as he *writes)* .... 1.EOC.198.263.
All Books he reads, and all he reads assails, ... 1.EOC.616.309.
All Books he reads, and all he reads assails, ... 1.EOC.616.309.
Each Wight who reads not, and but scans and spells, ... 4.Arbu.165.108.
The Wight who reads not, and but scans and spells, ... 4.Arbu.165A.108.
Each Wight who reads not, but who scans and spells, ... 4.Arbu.165B.108.
Who reads but with a Lust to mis-apply, ... 4.Arbu.301.117.
Who now reads Cowley? if he pleases yet, ... 4.2HE1.75.201.
Amus'd he reads, and then returns the bills .... 5.DunA2.87.108.
Amus'd he reads, and then returns the bills .... 5.DunB2.91.300.
Reads *Malbranche, Boyle,* and *Locke:* .... 6.14v(a).3.48.
Who thinks he *reads* when he but *scans* and *spells,* .... 6.98.15.283.
He reads, and laughs, you think, at what he writes: .... 6.105ii.2A.300.

READY
Before his Lord the ready Spaniel bounds, ... 1.W-F.99.160.
The *current Folly* proves the *ready Wit,* .... 1.EOC.449.290.
The *current Folly* proves our *ready Wit,* .... 1.EOC.449A.290.
And ready Nature waits upon his Hand; .... 1.EOC.487.294.
Still fit for Use, and ready at Command. .... 1.EOC.674.316.
Their ready Guilt preventing thy Commands: .... 1.TrSt.121.415.
Discharge thy Shafts, this ready Bosom rend, ... 1.TrSt.776.442.
His ready Tale th'inventive Hero told. .... 1.TrUl.139.470.
The Servants round stood ready at their Call. .... 2.ChJM.405.34.
The ready Tears apace began to flow, ... 2.ChJM.784.52.
Ready to cast, I yawn, I sigh, and sweat: .... 4.JD4.157.39.
Ready to cast, I yawn, I sigh, I sweat: .... 4.JD4.157A.39.
But Fools are ready Chaps, agog to buy, ... 4.HAdv.118.85.
Ready, by force, or of your own accord, ... 4.2HE2.250.183.
Be mighty ready to do good; .... 4.1HE7.36.271.
Extremely ready to resign .... 4.1HE7.63.273.
With ready quills the dedicators wait; .... 5.DunA2.190.124.
With ready quills the Dedicators wait; .... 5.DunB2.198.305.
See ready *Pallas* waits thy high Commands, ... Il.4.91.224.
The fainting Soul stood ready wing'd for Flight, ... Il.5.856.307.
Herself, impatient, to the ready Car .... Il.5.902.309.
Troy and her aids for ready Vengeance call; .... Il.9.305.449.
This ready Arm, unthinking, shakes the Dart; .... Il.13.111.110.
Then to the Left our ready Arms apply, ... Il.13.416.126.
Swift was his Pace, and ready was his Aid; .... Il.17.303.299.
The glorious Steeds our ready Arms invite, ... Il.17.554.309.
But the brave Squire the ready Coursers brought, ... Il.17.695.314.
A ready Banquet on the Turf is laid, ... Il.18.647.354.

READY (CONTINUED)
Rang'd in a Line the ready Racers stand; .... Il.23.885.524.
All fierce, and ready now the Prize to gain, ... Il.23.905.525.
(Her ready Hands the Ew'er and Bason held) .... Il.24.373.551.
The ready vessel rides, the sailors ready stand. .... Od.2.455.83.
The ready vessel rides, the sailors ready stand. .... Od.2.455.83.
Then bread and wine a ready handmaid brings, ... Od.3.608.117.
With ready love her brothers gath'ring round, ... Od.7.5.233.
Rang'd in a line the ready racers stand, ... Od.8.125.269.
The soil untill'd a ready harvest yields, ... Od.9.123.310.
With ready speed the joyful crew obey: .... Od.10.507.368.
The ready victims at our bark we found, ... Od.10.685.376.
His ready tale th' inventive hero told. .... Od.13.306.21.
The ready meal before *Ulysses* lay'd. .... Od.14.92.40.
The cautious Chief his ready story told. .... Od.14.219.46.
Before the rest I rais'd my ready steel; .... Od.14.257.48.
Nine ships I mann'd equip'd with ready stores, ... Od.14.280.49.
With ready hands they rush to seize their slave; .... Od.14.378.53.
Shall prompt our speed, and point the ready way. .... Od.15.60.72.
At length resolv'd, he turn'd his ready hand, ... Od.15.230.79.
Minerva calls; the ready gales obey .... Od.15.314.84.
Swift as she ask'd, the ready sailors swore. .... Od.15.476.93.
(For watchful Age is ready to surmize) .... Od.15.482.93.
Their stores compleat, and ready now to weigh, ... Od.15.493.94.
Lo! I the ready sacrifice prepare: .... Od.16.201.113.
"Oft ready swords in luckless hour incite .... Od.16.316.121.
See ready for the fight, and hand to hand, ... Od.18.46.169.
Large gifts confer, a ready sail command, ... Od.19.323.210.
They heard well pleas'd: the ready heralds bring .... Od.21.286.273.
The ready swains obey'd with joyful haste, ... Od.22.193.296.

REAL
'Tis real good, or seeming, moves them all; .... 3.EOM2.94.66.
To View a thousand real Blessings rise; .... 6.17iii.9.58.
Or bound in formal, or in real Chains; .... 6.19.42.63.
"Mimick the Actions of a real Man? .... 6.96ii.64.273.
For real suff'rings since I grieve sincere, ... Od.14.397.55.
In real fame, when most humane my deed: .... Od.19.373.212.

REALM
Thy *Realm* for ever lasts! thy own *Messiah* reigns! .... 1.Mes.108.122.
Next to the Bounds of *Nisus'* Realm repairs, ... 1.TrSt.468.429.
About the Realm she walks her dreadful Round, ... 1.TrSt.710.440.
And sought around his Native Realm in vain; .... 1.TrUl.71.468.
"The Ant's republic, and the realm of Bees; .... 3.EOM3.184.112.
Down, down, proud Satire! tho' a Realm be spoil'd, ... 4.EpS2.38.315.
Grieve not at ought our sister realm acquires: .... 5.DunA1.24.62.
Mourn not, my SWIFT, at ought our Realm acquires, ... 5.DunB1.26.271.
Wide, and more wide, it spread o'er all the realm; .... 5.DunB4.613.405.
And rashly blame the realm of Blunderland. .... 6.61.20.181.
and rashly scorn the realm of Blunderland. .... 6.61.20B.181.
On thy third Realm *look down;* unfold our Fate, ... 6.65.5A.192.
Thy Realm disarm'd of each offensive Tool, ... 6.131i.3.360.
Two Ages o'er his native Realm he reign'd, ... Il.1.335.104.
(*Aëtion's* Realm) our conqu'ring Army came, ... Il.1.479.111.
Thus from her Realm convey'd the beauteous Prize, ... Il.3.71.192.
To boundless Vengeance the wide Realm be giv'n, ... Il.4.57.223.
From Realm to Realm three ample Strides he took, ... Il.13.32.106.
From Realm to Realm three ample Strides he took, ... Il.13.32.106.
Drain their whole Realm to buy one fun'ral Flame; .... Il.22.442.474.
To the dark Realm the Spirit wings its Way, ... Il.22.455.474.
The Scourge and Ruin of my Realm and Race; .... Il.24.631.563.
A Realm, a Goddess, to his Wishes giv'n, ... Il.24.675.565.
That from his realm retards his god-like Sire: .... Od.1.121.38.
And in the realm of *Ithaca* descends. .... Od.1.133.38.
Whene'er *Ulysses* roams the realm of Night, ... Od.1.503.56.
That stranger-guest the *Taphian* realm obeys, ... Od.1.525.57.
A realm defended with incircling seas: .... Od.1.526.57.
Of all this happy realm, I grieve alone. .... Od.2.52.62.
The eighth, from *Athens* to his realm restor'd, ... Od.3.390.105.
Perhaps may seize thy realm, and share the spoil; .... Od.3.402.106.
'Till pitying *Jove* my native realm restor'd— .... Od.4.44.122.
Constrain'd me from my native realm to rove: .... Od.4.360.137.
When to his realm I plow'd the orient wave. .... Od.4.838.158.
How in a realm so distant shou'd you know .... Od.4.1069.167.
Say, breathes my Lord the blissful realm of light, ... Od.4.1087.168.
Around our realm, a barrier from the foes; .... Od.6.244.221.
Far from this realm, the fav'rite Isle of heav'n: .... Od.6.290.224.
"This realm, she flies: *Phæacia* is her scorn. .... Od.6.340.227.
Twelve Princes in our realm dominion share, ... Od.8.425.286.
Rules this blest realm, repentant I obey! .... Od.8.436.287.
So shalt thou instant reach the realm assign'd, ... Od.8.603.294.
Thee in *Telemachus* thy realm obeys; .... Od.11.222.392.
For since kind heav'n with wealth our realm has blest, ... Od.11.426.405.
And sought, around, his native realm in vain: .... Od.13.238.17.
'Till urg'd by wrongs a foreign realm he chose, ... Od.15.254.80.
Each neighb'ring realm conducive to our woe .... Od.16.129.109.
His realm might recognize an equal heir. .... Od.19.433.215.
Which spoke *Ulysses* to his realm restor'd: .... Od.19.665.228.
Who in partition seek his realm to share; .... Od.20.273.246.
From realm to realm a Nation to explore .... Od.23.285.337.
From realm to realm a Nation to explore .... Od.23.285.337.

REALMS
And Realms commanded which those Trees adorn. .... 1.W-F.32.151.
And Harvests on a hundred Realms bestows; .... 1.W-F.360.185.
And sleeps thy Thunder in the Realms above? .... 1.TrSt.110.414.
For Crimes like these, not all those Realms suffice, ... 1.TrSt.216.419.
Were all those Realms the guilty Victor's Prize! .... 1.TrSt.217.419.
Not all those Realms cou'd for such Crimes suffice, ... 1.TrSt.216A.419.
The Realms of rising and declining Day, ... 1.TrSt.278.421.
The guilty Realms of *Tantalus* shall bleed; .... 1.TrSt.345.424.
On Impious Realms, and barb'rous Kings, impose .... 1.TrSt.398.426.
And give up *Laius* to the Realms of Day, ... 1.TrSt.418.427.
While future Realms his wandring Thoughts delight, ... 1.TrSt.445.428.
T' *Adrastus'* Realms and Hospital Court, ... 1.TrSt.564.434.

REALMS (CONTINUED)

To *Argos'* Realms the Victor God resorts, ... 1.TrSt.668.438.
The Victor God did to these Realms resort, ... 1.TrSt.668A.438.
Then thus to *Phœbus,* in the Realms above, ... 1.TrES.322.461.
Here Thou, Great *Anna!* whom three Realms obey, ... 2.RL3.7.169.
And smooth my passage to the realms of day: .... 2.ElAb.322.345.
Who first taught souls enslav'd, and realms undone, ... 3.EOM3.241.116.
Hereditary Realms, and worlds of Gold. .... 3.Ep3.132.104.
And hail her passage to the Realms of Rest, ... 4.EpS1.81.304.
Realms shift their place, and Ocean turns to land. .... 5.DunA1.70.68.
Oft, as he fish'd her nether realms for wit, ... 5.DunA2.93.108.
Realms shift their place, and Ocean turns to land. .... 5.DunB1.72.275.
Where as he fish'd her nether realms for Wit, ... 5.DunB2.101.300.
The Fate of Realms, and Conquests yet to come; .... 6.17iv.4.59.
And vanquish'd realms supply recording gold? .... 6.71.56.204.
To *Pthia's* Realms no hostile Troops they led; .... Il.1.201.96.
Rule thy own Realms with arbitrary Sway: .... Il.1.236.98.
When bold Rebellion shook the Realms above, ... Il.1.516.113.
(*Nestor,* whom *Pylos'* sandy Realms obey'd) .... Il.2.100.131.
'Till great *Alcides* made the Realms obey: .... Il.2.826.164.
Round the bleak Realms where *Hellespontus* roars, ... Il.2.1024.171.
Of those who round *Mœonia's* Realms reside, ... Il.2.1052.172.
On thy lov'd Realms whose Guilt demands their Fate, ... Il.4.62.224.
A Goddess born to share the Realms above, ... Il.4.85.224.
Bold *Merion* sent him to the Realms of Hell. .... Il.5.76.270.
The soul indignant seeks the Realms of Night. .... Il.5.360.283.
Thou gav'st that Fury to the Realms of Light, ... Il.5.1074.318.
Thus wings thy Progress from the Realms above? .... Il.7.30.364.
The meanest Subject of our Realms above? .... Il.7.547.391.
And rule the tributary Realms around. .... Il.9.206.442.
And rule the tributary Realms around. .... Il.9.393.452.
If Heav'n restore me to my Realms with Life, ... Il.9.516.458.
Hell heard her Curses from the Realms profound, ... Il.9.685.468.
And share my Realms, my Honours, and my Heart. .... Il.9.730.470.
And join each other in the Realms below. .... Il.11.340.49.
And add one Spectre to the Realms below! .... Il.11.557.58.
Me chief he sought, and from the Realms on high .... Il.14.291.176.
Thro' the drear Realms of gliding Ghosts below: .... Il.15.44.196.
Thro' the dear Realms of gliding Ghosts below: Il.15.44A.196*
Rule as he will his portion'd Realms on high; .... Il.15.208.204.
Of Realms accurs'd, deserted, reprobate! .... Il.15.579.218.
Then thus to *Phœbus,* in the Realms above, ... Il.16.809.274.
He held his Seat, and rul'd the Realms around. .... Il.17.357.301.
And now *Minerva,* from the Realms of Air .... Il.17.612.312.
Had not high *Juno,* from the Realms of Air, ... Il.18.203.331.
Th' immortal Empress of the Realms above; .... Il.18.222.332.
Meanwhile to *Juno,* in the Realms above, ... Il.18.417.341.
And ye, fell Furies of the Realms of Night, ... Il.19.270.383.
In hope the Realms of *Priam* to enjoy, ... Il.20.216.403.
Thou to the dismal Realms for ever gone! .... Il.22.618.481.
And give me Entrance in the Realms below: .... Il.23.88.490.
Once more return'st thou from the Realms of Night? .... Il.23.110.492.
Surveys thy desolated Realms below, ... Il.24.360.551.
Thou to the dismal Realms for ever gone! .... Il.24.910.574.
Now at their native realms the *Greeks* arriv'd; .... Od.1.15.29.
Instant, to foreign realms prepare to sail, ... Od.1.365.50.
"When he, whom living mighty realms obey'd, ... Od.2.113.67.
The realms of *Pyle* and *Sparta* to explore, ... Od.2.243.73.
Thro' seas and realms companion of thy care. .... Od.2.326.77.
To realms, that rocks and roaring seas divide? .... Od.2.409.80.
Such, and not nobler, in the realms above .... Od.4.89.123.
If studious of your realms, you then demand .... Od.4.527.146.
To sea-surrounded realms the Gods assign .... Od.4.827.158.
Just to his realms, he parted grounds from grounds, ... Od.6.15.204.
Perhaps from realms that view the rising day, ... Od.8.29.263.
Chiefly the man, in foreign realms confin'd, ... Od.8.243.275.
In distant realms our glorious deeds display, ... Od.8.275.278.
Let other realms the deathful gauntlet wield, ... Od.8.281.278.
As first in virtue, these thy realms obey! .... Od.9.2.298.
And send thee howling to the realms of night! .... Od.9.613.332.
And view the realms of darkness and of death. .... Od.10.581.371.
Can living eyes behold the realms below? .... Od.10.596.372.
The dreary realms of darkness and of death: .... Od.10.676.376.
New to the realms of death, *Elpenor's* shade: .... Od.11.66.383.
How could thy soul, by realms and seas disjoyn'd, ... Od.11.73.383.
Com'st thou, my son, alive, to realms beneath, ... Od.11.190.391.
The dolesom realms of darkness and of death: .... Od.11.191.391.
Then by my realms due homage would be paid; .... Od.11.448.406.
Nor glides a Phantom thro' the realms of night. .... Od.11.568.411.
If yet he breathes in realms of chearful day; .... Od.11.570.411.
And add new horror to the realms of woe. .... Od.11.574.411.
And grant me peaceful to my realms again. .... Od.12.400.450.
Me into other realms my cares convey, ... Od.13.475.29.
His ancient realms *Ulysses* shall survey, ... Od.14.187.45.
Thro' spacious *Argos,* and the Realms of *Greece,* .... Od.15.92.73.
Or glide a spectre in the realms beneath? .... Od.17.131.138.
Dispeopling realms to gaze upon thy eyes: .... Od.18.290.180.
O had this stranger sunk to realms beneath, ... Od.18.446.190.
To the black realms of darkness and of death, ... Od.18.447.190.
Their affluent joys the grateful realms confess; .... Od.19.135.199.
"Have aw'd the realms around with dire alarms: .... Od.19.478.220.
His dreadful journey to the realms beneath, ... Od.23.347.341.
That drives the ghosts to realms of night or day, ... Od.24.5.347.
The shades thou seest, from yon' fair realms above. .... Od.24.213.358.
To old *Autolycus's* realms I went. .... Od.24.387.367.
This past on earth, while in the realms above .... Od.24.540.373.

REAMS

With reams abundant this abode supply; .... 5.DunA2.86.108.
With reams abundant this abode supply; .... 5.DunB2.90.300.

REAP

And the same Hand that sow'd, shall reap the Field. .... 1.Mes.66.118.
Shall tend the Flocks, or reap the bearded Grain; .... 1.W-F.370.186.
Reap their own Fruits, and woo their Sable Loves, ... 1.W-F.410.192.
What Lawrels *Marlbro'* next shall reap, decree, ... 6.17iv.5.59.

REAP (CONTINUED)

And reap what Glory Life's short Harvest yields. .... Il.18.154.330.
And edge thy sword to reap the glorious field. .... Od.20.62.235.

REAP'D

And reap'd an Iron Harvest of his Toil; .... 1.TrSt.10.409.
Or reap'd in iron harvests of the field? .... 3.EOM4.12.129.
Where Fame is reap'd amid th' embattel'd Field; .... Il.6.154.333.

REAPER

And first a Reaper from the Field appears, ... 1.TrVP.30.378.
With bended Sickles stand the Reaper-Train: .... Il.18.638.354.

REAPER-TRAIN

With bended Sickles stand the Reaper-Train: .... Il.18.638.354.

REAPER'S

And nodding tempt the joyful Reaper's Hand, ... 1.W-F.40.152.
The Reaper's due Repast, the Women's Care. .... Il.18.650.355.

REAPERS

When weary Reapers quit the sultry Field, ... 1.PSu.65.77.
As sweating Reapers in some wealthy Field, ... Il.11.89.38.

REAPS

But *Troy* for ever reaps a dire Delight .... Il.13.799.143.

REAR

See RERE.
Where tow'ring Oaks their growing Honours rear, ... 1.W-F.221.170.
Where tow'ring Oaks their spreading Honours rear, ... 1.W-F.221A.170.
A Serpent from her left was seen to rear .... 1.TrSt.158.416.
A curling Serpent from her left did rear .... 1.TrSt.158A.416.
His Friends a Tomb and Pyramid shall rear; .... 1.TrES.333.461.
To rear the Column, or the Arch to bend, ... 3.Ep4.48.141.
Thus oft they rear, and oft the head decline, ... 5.DunA2.361.143.
Support his front, and Oaths bring up the rear: .... 5.DunB1.308.292.
Thus oft they rear, and oft the head decline, ... 5.DunB2.393.316.
Lo how their heads the lillies rear, ... 6.4iv.13.11.
And hatch'd more Chicks than she could rear. .... 6.93.16.257.
And bold *Meriones* excite the Rear. .... Il.4.289.234.
How vain those Cares! when *Meges* in the Rear .... Il.5.95.271.
Pours on the Rear, or lightens in their Face. .... Il.5.115.272.
And nigh the Fleet a Fun'ral Structure rear: .... Il.7.401.384.
Mad with his Anguish, he begins to rear, ... Il.8.107.403.
Plung'd in the Rear, or blazing in the Van; .... Il.11.86.38.
When his tir'd Arms refuse the Axe to rear, ... Il.11.121.41.
Ev'n there, the hindmost of their Rear I slay, ... Il.11.891.75.
And *Oenomaus* and *Thoon* close the Rear; .... Il.12.154.87.
Far in the Rear the *Locrian* Archers lie, ... Il.13.899.148.
And *Troy* and *Hector* thunder in the Rear. .... Il.15.371.211.
Fierce on the Rear, with Shouts, *Patroclus* flies; .... Il.16.448.260.
His Friends a Tomb and Pyramid shall rear; .... Il.16.820.275.
Meanwhile the Sons of *Nestor,* in the Rear, ... Il.17.436.304.
Ah would *Minerva* send me Strength to rear .... Il.17.634.312.
With *Merion's* Aid, the weighty Corse to rear; .... Il.17.802.319.
Still close they follow, close the Rear engage; .... Il.17.843.321.
Their Locks *Actæa* and *Limnoria* rear, ... Il.18.51.326.
Pour'd on the Rear, and thunder'd close behind; .... Il.18.190.331.
Rear high their Horns, and seem to lowe in Gold, ... Il.18.666.356.
And the fair Train of Captives close the Rear: .... Il.19.194.379.
I hop'd *Patroclus* might survive, to rear .... Il.19.351.387.
Pond'rous and huge! which not a *Greek* could rear. .... Il.19.421.389.
Where the slow *Caucons* close the Rear of Fight. .... Il.20.378.410.
Till on the Pyre I place thee; till I rear .... Il.23.55.489.
To load the Timber and the Pile to rear, ... Il.23.136.493.
To rear his fallen Foe, the Victor lends .... Il.23.806.521.
This mighty Quoit *Aëtion* wont to rear, ... Il.23.977.528.
With speed the mast they rear, with speed unbind .... Od.2.464.83.
From earth they rear him, struggling now with death; .... Od.3.578.116.
But the tall mast above the vessel rear, ... Od.6.323.226.
We rear the masts, we spread the canvas wings; .... Od.9.86.306.
Rear but the mast, the spacious sail display, ... Od.10.600.372.
At once the mast we rear, at once unbind .... Od.11.3.377.
With speed the mast they rear, with speed unbind .... Od.15.312.84.
Haste, rear the mast, the swelling shroud display; .... Od.16.364.124.

REAR'D

Fair to be seen, and rear'd of honest Wood. .... 2.ChWB.246.68.
Stupendous Pile! not rear'd by mortal Hands. .... 2.TemF.62.256.
On Doric Pillars of white Marble rear'd, ... 2.TemF.76.258.
On which a Shrine of purest Gold was rear'd; .... 2.TemF.197.271.
Fair from its humble bed I rear'd this Flow'r, ... 5.DunB4.405.381.
And next his Bulk gigantic *Ajax* rear'd: .... Il.7.200.373.
Between the Swords their peaceful Sceptres rear'd; .... Il.7.335.380.
He said, and rear'd his Sceptre to the Sky. .... Il.7.489.388.
And round the Pile a gen'ral Tomb they rear'd. .... Il.7.519.389.
Wise *Nestor* then his Rev'rend Figure rear'd; .... Il.9.71.435.
But soon as *Ajax* rear'd his tow'rlike Shield, ... Il.17.139.293.
So high his brazen Voice the Hero rear'd: .... Il.18.263.335.
One rear'd a Dagger at a Captive's Breast, ... Il.18.620.352.
Th' infernal Monarch rear'd his horrid Head, ... Il.20.84.397.
At length the River rear'd his languid Head, ... Il.21.416.437.
When the vast fabric of the Steed we rear'd! .... Od.4.374.137.
Where never science rear'd her lawrel'd head: .... Od.6.12.203.
Nine ells aloft they rear'd their tow'ring head, ... Od.11.383.401.
Frequent and thick. Within the space, were rear'd .... Od.14.17.35.
As many stalls for shaggy goats are rear'd; .... Od.14.123.42.
High in his hands he rear'd the golden bowl; .... Od.22.14.287.

REARS

Fair *Liberty, Britannia's* Goddess, rears .... 1.W-F.91.159.
The gulphy *Lee* his sedgy Tresses rears: .... 1.W-F.346.184.
Shakes off the *Dust,* and rears his rev'rend Head! .... 1.EOC.700.319.
To that she bends, to that her Eyes she rears; .... 2.RL1.126.155.
Yon stars, yon suns, he rears at pleasure higher, ... 5.DunA3.255.179.

REARS (CONTINUED)
Yon stars, yon suns, he rears at pleasure higher, ... 5.DunB3.259.332.
Or where her humbler Turrets *Trica* rears, ... Il.2.886.166.
When fresh he rears his radiant Orb to Sight, ... Il.5.9.266.
The various-colour'd Scarf, the Shield he rears, ... Il.10.84.6.
Now to the Skies the foaming Billows rears, ... Il.11.399.52.
Thrice to its pitch his lofty Voice he rears; ... Il.11.580.60.
Th' eternal columns which on earth he rears ... Od.1.69.34.
And last, sublime his stately growth he rears, ... Od.4.621.149.
'Tis *Jove* himself the swelling tempest rears; ... Od.5.391.191.
Thence, where proud *Athens* rears her tow'ry head, ... Od.7.103.239.
Six horrid necks she rears, and six terrific heads; ... Od.12.112.437.
Lifts to the sound his ear, and rears his head. ... Od.17.347.148.
Venus in tender delicacy rears ... Od.20.82.236.

REAS'NING
Then, in the scale of reas'ning life, 'tis plain ... 3.EOM1.47.19.
In Pride, in reas'ning Pride, our error lies; ... 3.EOM1.123.30.
In reas'ning *Pride* (my Friend), our error lies; ... 3.EOM1.123B.30.
From pride, from pride, our very reas'ning springs; ... 3.EOM1.161.35.
Compar'd, half-reas'ning elephant, with thine: ... 3.EOM1.222.43.
Compar'd with thine, half-reas'ning Elephant! ... 3.EOM1.222A.43.
Born but to die, and reas'ning but to err; ... 3.EOM2.10.55.
His pride in Reas'ning, not in Acting lies. ... 3.Ep1.70.20.
In short, that reas'ning, high, immortal Thing, ... 4.1HE1.185.293.
Or quite unravel all the reas'ning thread, ... 5.DunB1.179.283.
Thus fell a reas'ning, not a running. ... 6.67.4.195.
Poor *Colley*, thy Reas'ning is none of the strongest, ... 6.149.3.397.
But your reas'ning, God help you! is none of the strongest, ... 6.149.3A.397.

REASCENDS
The Heroe reascends: The Prince o'eraw'd ... Od.16.194.112.

REASON
And taught the World, *with Reason* to *Admire*. ... 1.EOC.101.250.
If once right Reason drives *that Cloud* away, ... 1.EOC.211.264.
They reason and conclude by *Precedent*, ... 1.EOC.410.287.
And *Love to Praise*, with *Reason* on his Side? ... 1.EOC.642.311.
Some prais'd with Wit, and some with Reason blam'd. ... 2.ChJM.142.21.
And he that smarts has Reason to complain. ... 2.ChJM.205.24.
Consult your Reason, and you soon shall find, ... 2.ChJM.807.54.
"And since in Man right Reason bears the Sway, ... 2.ChWB.193.65.
What can we reason, but from what we know? ... 3.EOM1.18.14.
From which to reason, or to which refer? ... 3.EOM1.20.14.
Presumptuous Man! the reason wouldst thou find, ... 3.EOM1.35.17.
First, if thou canst, the harder reason guess, ... 3.EOM1.37.18.
Had he thy Reason, would he skip and play? ... 3.EOM1.82.24.
In both, to reason right is to submit. ... 3.EOM1.164.35.
For this plain reason, Man is not a Fly. ... 3.EOM1.194.39.
For this plain reason, Man is not a Mite. ... 3.EOM1.194A.39.
'Twixt that, and Reason, what a nice barrier; ... 3.EOM1.223.43.
Is not thy Reason all these pow'rs in one? ... 3.EOM1.232.44.
Is not thy Reason all those pow'rs in one? ... 3.EOM1.232A.44.
Alike in ignorance, his reason such, ... 3.EOM2.11.55.
What Reason weaves, by Passion is undone. ... 3.EOM2.42.60.
Self-love, to urge, and Reason, to restrain; ... 3.EOM2.54.62.
Reason, the future and the consequence. ... 3.EOM2.74.64.
Reason still use, to Reason still attend: ... 3.EOM2.78.64.
Reason still use, to Reason still attend: ... 3.EOM2.78.64.
Each strengthens Reason, and Self-love restrains. ... 3.EOM2.80.64.
And Grace and Virtue, Sense and Reason split, ... 3.EOM2.83.64.
Self-love and Reason to one end aspire, ... 3.EOM2.87.65.
And Reason bids us for our own provide; ... 3.EOM2.96.66.
List under Reason, and deserve her care; ... 3.EOM2.98.66.
Reason the card, but Passion is the gale; ... 3.EOM2.108.68.
Suffice that Reason keep to Nature's road, ... 3.EOM2.115.69.
Reason itself but gives it edge and pow'r; ... 3.EOM2.147.72.
The ruling Passion conquers Reason still. ... 3.EOM2.148Z2.72.
Reason is here no guide, but still a guard: ... 3.EOM2.162.74.
All, all alike, find Reason on their side. ... 3.EOM2.174.75.
And all alike, find Reason on their side. ... 3.EOM2.174A.75.
Reason the byass turns to good from ill, ... 3.EOM2.197.79.
Taught half by Reason, half by mere decay, ... 3.EOM2.259.86.
And just as short of Reason he must fall, ... 3.EOM3.47.96.
And just as short of Reason Man will fall, ... 3.EOM3.47A.96.
Whether with Reason, or with Instinct blest, ... 3.EOM3.79.99.
Reason, however able, cool at best, ... 3.EOM3.85.100.
Which heavier Reason labours at in vain. ... 3.EOM3.92.101.
This too serves always, Reason never long; ... 3.EOM3.93.101.
And Reason raise o'er Instinct as you can, ... 3.EOM3.97.101.
Reflection, Reason, still the ties improve, ... 3.EOM3.133.106.
"And hence let Reason, late, instruct Mankind: ... 3.EOM3.180.111.
"In vain thy Reason finer webs shall draw, ... 3.EOM3.191.112.
And simple Reason never sought but one: ... 3.EOM3.230.115.
Who ask and reason thus, will scarce conceive ... 3.EOM4.163.143.
Grasp the whole worlds of Reason, Life, and Sense, ... 3.EOM4.357.163.
Intent to reason, or polite to please. ... 3.EOM4.382.165.
That REASON, PASSION, answer one great aim; ... 3.EOM4.395.166.
On human actions reason tho' you can, ... 3.Ep1.35.18.
It may be reason, but it is not man: ... 3.Ep1.36.18.
But who, my friend, has reason in his rage? ... 3.Ep3.154.106.
"The ruling Passion conquers Reason still." ... 3.Ep3.156.106.
Resolve me, Reason, which of these is worse, ... 3.Ep3.319.120.
The Feast of Reason and the Flow of Soul: ... 4.HS1.128.17.
No Sense to guide, no Reason to enquire, ... 4.HAdv.144.87.
With Terrors round can Reason hold her throne, ... 4.2HE2.310.187.
Without a staring Reason on his Brows? ... 4.EpS2.194.324.
Which only heads, refin'd from reason, know. ... 5.DunA3.6.150.
Some free from rhyme or reason, rule or check, ... 5.DunA3.155.164.
Blockheads with reason wicked wits abhor, ... 5.DunA3.169.167.
Thus he, for then a ray of Reason stole ... 5.DunA3.223.176.
Which only heads refin'd from Reason know. ... 5.DunB3.6.320.
Some free from rhyme or reason, rule or check, ... 5.DunB3.161.328.
Blockheads with reason wicked wits abhor, ... 5.DunB3.175.329.
Thus he, for then a ray of Reason stole ... 5.DunB3.225.331.
When Reason doubtful, like the Samian letter, ... 5.DunB4.151.356.

REASON (CONTINUED)
And Reason giv'n them but to study *Flies!* ... 5.DunB4.454.385.
And reason downward, till we doubt of God: ... 5.DunB4.472.387.
Of nought so certain as our *Reason* still, ... 5.DunB4.481.389.
And routed *Reason* finds a safe Retreat in thee. ... 6.8.18.18.
'Till having drown'd their Reason, they think f ... 6.17iv.9.59.
Eternal Reason! whose presiding soul ... 6.23.3.73.
Blockheads with Reason Men of Sense abhor; ... 6.60.5.178.
How vain is Reason, Eloquence how weak, ... 6.85.5.242.
Reason, you found, and Virtue were the same. ... 6.96iii.8.274.
Of modest Reason, and pacifick truth: ... 6.109.2A.313.
Blest with plain Reason and with sober Sense; ... 6.115.2.322.
Now fir'd by Wrath, and now by Reason cool'd: ... Il.1.254.98.
To Reason yield the Empire o'er his Mind. ... Il.1.276.100.
He stoop'd to Reason, and his Rage resign'd. ... Il.7.140.370.
A Prince's Faults, and I with Reason own. ... Il.9.148.439.
Thy Will is partial, not thy Reason wrong: ... Il.12.270.91.
What Force of Thought and Reason can supply; ... Il.18.322.337.
Beyond the Bounds of Reason and of Right; ... Il.19.180.379.
Then hear my Counsel, and to Reason yield, ... Il.19.219.382.
Brave tho' he be, yet by no Reason aw'd, ... Il.24.68.538.
Rise then: Let Reason mitigate our Care: ... Il.24.659.564.
Thy pleaded reason, but consult with mine: ... Od.5.455.194.
His pleaded reason, and the suit he mov'd. ... Od.7.308.251.
To sooth their fears a specious reason feign: ... Od.19.8.193.
To ev'ry sense is lost, to reason blind: ... Od.20.434.254.

REASON'D
As far as Goose could judge, he reason'd right, ... 3.EOM3.46Z3.96.

REASON'S
Let Reason's Rule your strong Desires abate, ... 2.ChJM.293.28.
And, spite of Pride, in erring Reason's spite, ... 3.EOM1.293.51.
And, spite of Pride, and in thy Reason's spite, ... 3.EOM1.293A.51.
Reason's comparing balance rules the whole. ... 3.EOM2.60.63.
Reason's at distance, and in prospect lie: ... 3.EOM2.72.64.
To copy Instinct then was Reason's part; ... 3.EOM3.170.110.
Reason's whole pleasure, all the joys of Sense, ... 3.EOM4.79.136.
All Reason's pleasures, all the joys of Sense, ... 3.EOM4.79A.136.
Add Nature's, Custom's, Reason's, Passion's strife, ... 3.Ep1.21.17.
While if our Elders break all Reason's laws, ... 4.2HE1.117.205.
And if I pray by Reason's rules, ... 4.HS6.15.251.
('Tis Reason's voice, which sometimes one can hear) ... 4.1HE1.12.279.
Yes, we are slaves—but yet, by Reason's Force, ... 6.96iii.31.275.
To Reason's equal dictates ever true, ... 6.134.7.364.
Thus anchor'd safe on reason's peaceful coast, ... Od.20.29.233.

REASONABLE
Shall Man, shall reasonable Man, alone, ... 3.EOM1.187A.37.
So very reasonable, so unmov'd, ... 3.Ep2.165.64.
Who asks no more (right reasonable Peer) ... 4.HAdv.159.89.
I know a Reasonable Woman, ... 6.89.3.250.
So very reasonable, so unmov'd, ... 6.139.9.377.

REASONS
These Thoughts he fortify'd with Reasons still, ... 2.ChJM.19.16.
(For none want Reasons to confirm their Will) ... 2.ChJM.20.16.
Who reasons wisely is not therefore wise, ... 3.Ep1.69.20.
Must act on Reasons pow'rful, tho' unknown: ... 3.Ep3.114A.101.
'Tis now for better Reasons——to be paid. ... 6.34.18.101.

REASSUME
While thus my fraudful speech I reassume. ... Od.9.430.323.

REASSUMES
She waves her golden wand, and reassumes ... Od.16.476.130.

REBATE
"Rebate your loves, each rival suit suspend, ... Od.19.164.200.

REBATED
The Point rebated, and repell'd the Wound. ... Il.11.304.48.

REBECCA
Like *Sarah* or *Rebecca* lead her Life: ... 2.ChJM.312.29.
Like *Sarah* and *Rebecca* lead her Life: ... 2.ChJM.312A.29.

REBECCA'S
Twas by *Rebecca's* Aid that *Jacob* won ... 2.ChJM.69.18.

REBEL
He prov'd a Rebel to my Sov'reign Will: ... 2.ChWB.334.73.
The Rebel- *Knave*, who dares his Prince engage, ... 2.RL3.59.172.
The Rebel- *Knave*, that dares his Prince engage, ... 2.RL3.59A.172.
Still rebel nature holds out half my heart; ... 2.ElAb.26.321.
Aspiring to be Angels, Men rebel; ... 3.EOM1.128.31.
What serves one will, when many wills rebel? ... 3.EOM3.274.120.
A Rebel to the very king he loves; ... 3.Ep1.203.32.
Say, does thy blood rebel, thy bosom move ... 4.1HE1.55.283.
Where rebel to thy throne if Science rise, ... 5.DunA1.157.82.
Where 'gainst thy throne if rebel Science rise, ... 5.DunA1.157A.82.
Bind rebel Wit, and double chain on chain, ... 5.DunB4.158.357.
But Rebel Wit deserts thee oft in vain; ... 6.8.13.18.
Can *Mars* rebel, and does no Thunder roll? ... Il.5.943.311.
With all thy Rage, with all thy Rebel Force. ... Il.8.596.424.
Desists at length his Rebel-war to wage, ... Il.15.250.206.
Crush the proud rebel, and assert his claim. ... Od.11.614.414.
Bear it my son! howe'er thy heart rebel. ... Od.16.297.120.
The rebel race, and death had swallow'd all; ... Od.24.611.377.

REBEL-KNAVE
The Rebel- *Knave*, who dares his Prince engage, ... 2.RL3.59.172.
The Rebel- *Knave*, that dares his Prince engage, ... 2.RL3.59A.172.

REBEL-WAR
Desists at length his Rebel-war to wage, ...Il.15.250.206.

REBEL'S
My flying faulchion at the rebel's head. ....Od.10.518.368.

REBELL
I bear their outrage, tho' my soul rebell: ....Od.18.272.179.

REBELL'D
While his swoln Heart at ev'ry Step rebell'd, ...Il.11.681.65.

REBELLING
Smote his rebelling Breast, and fierce begun. ....Il.15.127.201.

REBELLION
There *Faction* roar, *Rebellion* bite her Chain, ...1.W-F.421.193.
But soon, ah soon Rebellion will commence, ...5.DunB4.63.347.
When bold Rebellion shook the Realms above, ...Il.1.516.113.
His Light'ning your Rebellion shall confound, ...Il.8.512.421.
And now had *Jove,* by bold Rebellion driv'n, ...Il.15.138.202.

REBELLIOUS
When this rebellious heart shall beat no more; ....2.ElAb.346.348.
There foam'd rebellious *Logic,* gagg'd and bound, ...5.DunB4.23.342.
To thee the most rebellious things on earth: ....5.DunB4.508.392.
My Light'ning these Rebellious shall confound, ...Il.8.494.420.
Juno, whom thou rebellious dar'st withstand, ...Il.21.480.441.

REBELLOW
Deep Groans and hollow Roars rebellow thro' the Wood. ....1.TrES.299.460.
And Earth and Heav'n rebellow to the Sound. ....Il.5.1057.317.
Deep groans, and hollow roars, rebellow thro' the Wood. ....Il.16.604.267.
And echoing Roars rebellow thro' the Shades. ....Il.16.918.279.
And distant Rocks rebellow to the Roar. ....Il.17.315.300.
The Victim Bull; the Rocks rebellow round, ...Il.20.469.414.

REBELLOWS
The rock rebellows with a thund'ring sound; ....Od.12.290.446.

REBELS
And all thy Mother in thy Soul rebells. ....Il.5.1101.319.
Untaught to bear, 'gainst heav'n the wretch rebells. ....Od.18.162.174.

REBELS
He ne'er rebels, or plots, like other men: ....4.2HE1.194.211.
But who, weak rebels, more advance her cause. ....5.DunB4.86.349.

REBOUND
Begin, the Vales shall ev'ry Note rebound. ....1.PSp.44.65.
The dreadful Signal all the Rocks rebound, ...1.TrSt.163.417.
Restore the Lock! the vaulted Roofs rebound. ....2.RL5.104.208.
The shrill Ecchos rebound: ....6.11.9.30.
And Seas, and Rocks, and Skies rebound ....6.11.47.32.
Darts rebound. ....6.96i.36.269.
The Rocks remurmur, and the Deeps rebound. ....Il.2.252.139.
The hollow Ships each deaf'ning Shout rebound. ....Il.4.401.145.
So mix both Hosts, and so their Cries rebound. ....Il.4.521.246.
Troy starts astonish'd, and the Shores rebound. ....Il.18.258.334.
And thick, strong Strokes, the doubling Vaults rebound. ....Il.18.550.348.
Along the court the fiery steeds rebound, ...Od.15.162.76.

REBOUNDING
Loud sounds the Axe, rebounding Strokes on Strokes; ....Il.23.146A.495.

REBOUNDS
Delia, each Cave and ecchoing Rock rebounds. ....1.PAu.50.83.
Thyrsis, each Cave and ecchoing Rock rebounds. ....1.PAu.50A.83.
Eccho no more the rural Song rebounds, ...1.PWi.41A.92.
The shrilling airs the vaulted roof rebounds, ...Od.1.425.53.
Of thronging multitudes the shore rebounds; ....Od.8.16.262.
With springing hope the Heroe's heart rebounds. ....Od.20.129.240.
Ascends the roof; the vaulted roof rebounds; ....Od.23.144.328.

REBUK'D
The Seneshal rebuk'd in haste withdrew; ....Od.4.47.122.

REBUKE
This just Rebuke inflam'd the *Lycian* Crew, ...1.TrES.151.455.
I own, I'm pleas'd with this rebuke, ...4.HS6.60.253.
Ye Gods! shall *Cibber's* Son, without rebuke ....4.EpS1.115.306.
And all his old Friends would rebuke ....6.42iv.9.118.
Let not the whigs our tory club rebuke; ....6.42v.1.119.
This just Rebuke inflam'd the *Lycian* Crew, ...Il.12.505.100.
But with severe rebuke *Antinous* cry'd. ....Od.4.1022.165.
With conscious shame they hear the stern rebuke, ...Od.18.389.186.
Silent, abash'd, they hear the stern rebuke, ...Od.18.458.190.

REBUKES
From such alone the Great Rebukes endure, ...4.JD4.282.49.
Thy just Rebukes, yet learn to spare them now. ....Il.10.137.8.

RECALL
Forget to thunder, and recall her fires? ....3.EOM4.124.139.
In pensive thought recall the fancy'd scene, ...6.45.33.125.
Recall those Nights that clos'd thy toilsom Days, ...6.84.15.239.
Recall; and me, with Britains Glory fir'd, ...6.155.5.404.
Recall your Armies, and your Chiefs reclaim. ....Il.2.216.138.
Recall the Flame, nor in a mortal cause ....Il.21.444.438.
Honour and Shame th' ungen'rous Thought recall: ....Il.22.139.459.
Nor to the royal heart recall in vain ....Od.21.89.263.
Or good, or grateful, now to mind recall, ...Od.22.229.297.

RECALL'D
Shall first recall'd, rush forward to thy mind; ....5.DunA3.56.155.
Shall first recall'd run forward to thy mind; ....5.DunA3.56A.155.

RECALL'D (CONTINUED)
Shall, first recall'd, rush forward to thy mind: ....5.DunB3.64.323.
Recall'd his Spirit from the Gates of Death. ....Il.5.859.307.
His Form recall'd *Machaon* to my Mind; ....Il.11.751.68.
Scarce from the Verge of Death recall'd, again ....Il.22.606.481.
And stand majestic, and recall'd to men. ....Od.10.464.366.

RECALLS
Much to the mindful Queen the feast recalls, ...5.DunA1.93.70.
Much to her mind the soleum feast recalls, ...5.DunA1.93A.70.
Much to the mindful Queen the feast recalls ....5.DunB1.95.276.
This Deed recalls thee to the proffer'd Fight; ....Il.3.75.193.
And stript, their Features to his Mind recalls. ....Il.11.150.42.
O Friend! my Memory recalls the Day, ...Il.11.902.75.

RECALS
The song recals past horrours to my eyes, ...Od.8.537.291.

RECEDE
The woods recede around the naked seat, ...3.Ep3.209.110.
The gen'rous *Greeks* recede with tardy Pace, ...Il.5.860.307.
The Troops of *Troy* recede with sudden Fear, ...Il.15.690.222.
Struck at the Sight, recede the *Trojan* Train: ....Il.17.368.301.
But, nymphs, recede! safe chastity denies ....Od.6.263.222.
From nuptial rites they now no more recede, ...Od.19.178.200.

RECEDED
Scar'd we receded. Forth, with frantic hand ....Od.9.471.325.

RECEDES
The world recedes; it disappears! ....6.31ii.13.94.
All *Greece* recedes, and 'midst her Triumph fears. ....Il.6.132.330.
Forc'd he recedes, and loudly calls for Aid. ....Il.11.579.60.
Now stiff recedes, yet hardly seems to fly, ...Il.11.694.66.
Slow he recedes, and sighing, quits the Dead. ....Il.17.116.292.
And *Hector* trembles and recedes with Fear; ....Il.17.184.294.
Struck by some God, he fears, recedes, and flies. ....Il.22.180.461.
From their pale cheeks recedes the flying blood; ....Od.22.54.289.

RECEDING
Now man the next, receding tow'rd the Main: ....Il.15.787.226.
The fields receding as the chariot roll'd: ....Od.3.628.118.

RECEIT
In which Commandments large Receit they dwell. ....4.JD2A.48.136.

RECEITS
Write dull *Receits* how Poems may be made: ....1.EOC.115.252.

RECEIV'D
Receiv'd his Laws, and stood convinc'd 'twas fit ....1.EOC.651.313.
Receiv'd his Rules, and stood convinc'd 'twas fit ....1.EOC.651A.313.
If you receiv'd me from *Jocasta's* Womb, ...1.TrSt.87.413.
Receiv'd *Sarpedon,* at the God's Command, ...1.TrES.346.462.
('Twas *June,* and *Cancer* had receiv'd the Sun) ....2.ChJM.401.34.
Receiv'd th'Impressions of the Love-sick Squire, ...2.ChJM.432.35.
Receiv'd the Reins of Absolute Command, ...2.ChWB.431.78.
With open arms receiv'd one Poet more. ....4.Arbu.142.106.
Receiv'd of Wits an undistinguish'd race, ...4.Arbu.237.112.
Receiv'd a Town Mouse at his Board, ...4.HS6.159.259.
Receiv'd each Demi-God, with pious care, ...5.DunB4.383.380.
Receiv'd the weapons of the sky; ....6.140.10.378.
Which, with a Smile, the white-arm'd Queen receiv'd. ....Il.1.767.124.
Receiv'd th' Imperial Sceptre of Command, ...Il.2.222.135.
His bended Arm receiv'd the falling Stone, ...Il.5.712.301.
It pierc'd the God: His Groin receiv'd the Wound. ....Il.5.1051.316.
And *Thetis'* Arms receiv'd the trembling God. ....Il.6.168.334.
His slacken'd Knees receiv'd the numbing Stroke; ....Il.7.324.379.
Your Sire receiv'd me, as his Son caress'd, ...Il.9.600.464.
Molus receiv'd, the Pledge of social Ties; ....Il.10.316.17.
Peace was his Charge; receiv'd with peaceful Show, ...Il.10.341.18.
He stung the Bird, whose Throat receiv'd the Wound: ....Il.12.236.90.
(While the Winds sleep) his Breast receiv'd the Stroke. ....Il.13.550.132.
But *Oenomas* receiv'd the *Cretan's* stroke, ...Il.13.640.136.
The bloody Armour, which his Train receiv'd: ....Il.13.802.143.
But young *Ilioneus* receiv'd the Spear, ...Il.14.573.190.
Thy Breast, unarm'd, receiv'd the *Spartan* Lance. ....Il.16.371.257.
His open'd Mouth receiv'd the *Cretan* Steel: ....Il.16.415.259.
Receiv'd *Sarpedon,* at the God's Command, ...Il.16.833.275.
Thus fell the Youth; the Air his Soul receiv'd, ...Il.17.592.311.
And soft receiv'd me on their silver Breast, ...Il.18.466.344.
Whose grateful Fumes the Gods receiv'd with Joy, ...Il.22.225.464.
One House receiv'd us, and one Table fed; ....Il.23.106.491.
Peleus receiv'd, and on his Son bestow'd.) ....Il.23.346.503.
And then *Eumelus* had receiv'd the Prize, ...Il.23.618.514.
Himself receiv'd and harness'd to his Car: ....Il.24.346.550.
And why receiv'd not I thy last Command? ....Il.24.935.575.
The duteous dame receiv'd the purple vest: ....Od.1.550.58.
But this thy guest, receiv'd with friendly care, ...Od.3.470.110.
Receiv'd him charg'd with *Ilion's* noble spoil) ....Od.5.53.174.
Receiv'd the friendless, and the hungry fed; ....Od.5.172.180.
Receiv'd the vestures, and the mules unbound. ....Od.7.6.233.
Receiv'd my limbs; a footstool eas'd my feet. ....Od.10.376.362.
When *Ilion* in the horse receiv'd her doom, ...Od.11.639.416.
The Sire with hospitable rites receiv'd, ...Od.14.352.51.
In marble urns receiv'd it from above, ...Od.17.238.143.
His shoulder-blade receiv'd th' ungentle shock; ....Od.17.548.159.
By *Jove* receiv'd, in council to confer. ....Od.19.207.203.
My honour'd roof receiv'd the royal guest: ....Od.19.227.204.
When my lov'd *Crete* receiv'd my final view, ...Od.19.389.213.
To light receiv'd the Lord of my desires, ...Od.19.408.214.
Amphithea's arms receiv'd the royal heir: ....Od.19.487.220.
He, safe at *Ithaca* with joy receiv'd, ...Od.19.542.223.
His former seat receiv'd the stranger-guest; ....Od.19.592.225.
Receiv'd a pointed sword and missile dart: ....Od.21.34.261.
Euryades receiv'd the Prince's dart; ....Od.22.294.300.

RECEIV'D (CONTINUED)
What port receiv'd thy vessel from the main? .... Od.24.351.365.
Lo here the wound (he cries) receiv'd of yore, ... Od.24.384.367.

RECEIVE
This humble Praise, lamented *Shade!* receive, ... 1.EOC.733.325.
My son, thy mother's parting kiss receive, ... 1.TrFD.94.390.
The Vows you never will return, receive; .... 1.TrSP.107.398.
No Tear did you, no parting Kiss receive, ... 1.TrSP.115.398.
These unavailing Rites he may receive, ... 1.TrES.334.462.
These unvailing Rites he may receive, ... 1.TrES.334A.462.
What Honours Mortals after Death receive, ... 1.TrES.334B.462.
Attend his Transports, and receive his Vows. .... 1.TrUl.243.473.
But first thought fit th' Assistance to receive, ... 2.ChJM.375.32.
Or some frail *China* Jar receive a Flaw, ... 2.RL2.106.166.
Receive, and wrap me in eternal rest! .... 2.ElAb.302.344.
"Thy arts of building from the bee receive; .... 3.EOM3.175.111.
Receive, and place for ever near a King! .... 4.EpS1.96.305.
"Receive (he said) those robes which once were mine, ... 5.DunB2.351.314.
"Receive, great Empress! thy accomplish'd Son: .... 5.DunB4.282.372.
Her too receive (for her my soul adores) .... 5.DunB4.331.375.
With such a Gust will I receive thy word. .... 6.2.12.6.
Thy heav'nly word by Moses to receive, ... 6.2.14.6.
Or China's Earth receive the sable Tyde; .... 6.82i.4.229.
These little rites, a Stone, a Verse, receive, ... 6.109.19.314.
These little rites, a Stone and Verse, receive, ... 6.109.19A.314.
Unransom'd here receive the spotless Fair; .... Il.1.578.115.
Receive my Words, and credit what you hear. .... Il.2.70.130.
Receive my Words; thy Friend and Brother hear! .... Il.7.52.365.
Great Queen of Arms! receive this hostile Spoil, ... Il.10.532.27.
The Gates half-open'd to receive the last. .... Il.12.136.86.
To whom the *Cretan:* Enter, and receive .... Il.13.337.121.
Our Offers now, illustrious Prince! receive; .... Il.13.475.130.
As now my Veins receive the pleasing Fire. .... Il.14.372.180.
Receive, and execute his dread Command. .... Il.15.167.203.
What Honours Mortals after Death receive, ... Il.16.821.275.
Never, ah never, shall receive him more; .... Il.18.514.346.
Receive this Answer: 'Tis my flying Spear. .... Il.20.307.407.
Come, and receive thy Fate! He spake no more. .... Il.20.498.415.
Till *Troy* receive her flying Sons , till all .... Il.21.340.435.
An ample Present let him thence receive, ... Il.23.631.514.
His Friends receive the Bowl, too dearly bought. .... Il.23.813.521.
Receive a Talent of the purest Gold. .... Il.23.938.526.
Her furious Son from *Priam* to receive .... Il.24.97.539.
And bear what stern *Achilles* may receive: .... Il.24.182.544.
And bear what stern *Achilles* may receive: .... Il.24.212.545.
And hung with Ringlets to receive the Reins; .... Il.24.336.550.
And the rich pledge of plighted faith receive, ... Od.1.405.52.
I shall revisit; and that pledge receive, ... Od.1.411.52.
The vase extending to receive the blood. .... Od.3.563.115.
My child, my darling joy, the car receive; .... Od.6.83.209.
This, let the Master of the Lyre receive, ... Od.8.521.290.
Receive the stranger as a brother's blood. .... Od.8.594.294.
The Giant then. Our promis'd grace receive, ... Od.9.435.324.
Rejoycing round, some morsel to receive, ... Od.10.248.354.
Attend his transports, and receive his vows! .... Od.13.410.26.
From those the well-pair'd mules we shall receive, ... Od.15.98.73.
Receive the suppliant! spare my destin'd blood! .... Od.15.303.83.
No other roof a stranger shou'd receive, ... Od.15.553.96.
No—let *Eurymachus* receive my guest, ... Od.15.559.96.
However, stranger! from our grace receive .... Od.16.77.106.
Shall her pleas'd ear receive my words in peace. .... Od.17.655.164.
And custom bids thee without shame receive; .... Od.18.332.183.
Receive no stranger-guest, no poor relieve; .... Od.19.158.200.
But what I can, receive.—In ample mode, ... Od.19.261.207.
Receive him joyous to their blest abodes: .... Od.19.322.210.
"Receive, she cries, your royal daughter's son; .... Od.19.475.219.
Thy suppliant people, and receive their pray'r! .... Od.22.67.290.
Or drive him hither, to receive the meed .... Od.22.182.296.

RECEIVES
And I those Kisses he receives, enjoy. .... 1.PSu.48.75.
Lo Earth receives him from the bending Skies! .... 1.Mes.33.116.
Not *Neptune's* self from all his Streams receives .... 1.W-F.223.170.
Not *Neptune's* self from all his Floods receives .... 1.W-F.223A.170.
Not *Neptune's* self from all her streams receives .... 1.W-F.223B.170.
Now the cleft Rind inserted Graffs receives, ... 1.TrVP.13.377.
And the cold North receives a fainter Day; .... 1.TrSt.215.419.
A lofty Couch receives each Princely Guest; .... 1.TrSt.615.436.
While *China's* Earth receives the smoking Tyde. .... 2.RL3.110.176.
And *China's* Earth receives the smoking Tyde. .... 2.RL3.110A.176.
What Time wou'd spare, from Steel receives its date, ... 2.RL3.171.182.
Receives the lurking principle of death; .... 3.EOM2.134.71.
Where only Merit constant pay receives, ... 3.EOM4.313.158.
Well may he blush, who gives it, or receives; .... 4.2HE1.414.231.
From him the next receives it, thick or thin, ... 4.EpS2.175.323.
At once a shelter from her boughs receives, ... 6.14iv.28.48.
For God is pay'd when Man receives, ... 6.50.19.146.
For Heav'n is pay'd when Man receives, ... 6.50.19A.146.
Each takes his Seat, and each receives his Share. .... Il.1.613.117.
Each takes his Seat, and each receives his Share. .... Il.2.513.151.
Astynous' Breast the deadly Lance receives, ... Il.5.186.275.
Each takes his Seat, and each receives his Share. .... Il.7.385.383.
His Shoulder-blade receives the fatal Wound; .... Il.16.344.256.
Receives thee dead, tho' *Gygæ* boast thy Birth; .... Il.20.450.413.
Whose polish'd Bed receives the falling Rills; .... Il.22.202.464.
Heavy with Death it sinks, and Hell receives the Weight. .... Il.22.276.467.
With Joy brave *Sthenelus* receives the Prize, ... Il.23.593.513.
My gloomy soul receives a gleam of joy. .... Od.4.742.153.
No port receives me from the angry main, ... Od.5.526.197.
And soft receives him from the rowling sea. .... Od.5.579.200.
The waters waft it, and the nymph receives. .... Od.5.593.201.
No ease, no pleasure my sad heart receives, ... Od.9.541.328.
To hogs transforms 'em, and the Sty receives. .... Od.10.277.356.
An ample vase receives the smoking wave, ... Od.10.425.365.
From foreign climes an only son receives, ... Od.16.18.102.

RECEIVES (CONTINUED)
His black'ning chin receives a deeper shade: .... Od.16.192.112.
While in his guest his murd'rer he receives: .... Od.16.439.128.
The nurse replies: "If *Jove* receives my pray'r, ... Od.17.588.161.

RECEIVING
Please by receiving, by submitting sway .... 3.Ep2.263A.71.
The spear receiving from her hand, he plac'd .... Od.1.167.40.
He ended, and (receiving as they pass .... Od.16.39.104.
With smiles receiving, on his scrip he lay'd. .... Od.17.429.153.

RECENT
All Heav'n beholds me recent from thy Arms? .... Il.14.382.181.
Urg'd on by want, and recent from the storms; .... Od.6.163.216.
And robes like these, so recent and so fair? .... Od.7.321.251.

RECEPTION
Is due reception deign'd, or must they bend .... Od.4.35.121.
A month's reception, and a safe retreat. .... Od.10.14.340.
So just reception from a heart so kind: .... Od.14.62.38.

RECESS
Beneath, a gloomy *Grotto's* cool Recess .... 1.TrUl.33.466.
Behold the gloomy *Grot,* whose cool Recess .... 1.TrUl.228.473.
Keen, hollow winds howl thro' the bleak recess, ... 5.DunA1.29.63.
But in her Temple's last recess inclos'd, ... 5.DunA3.1.150.
Keen, hollow winds howl thro' the bleak recess, ... 5.DunB1.35.272.
But in her Temple's last recess inclos'd .... 5.DunB3.1.320.
If such thy Will, to that Recess retire, ... Il.14.385.181.
He, stretch'd at ease in *Argos'* calm recess, ... Od.3.326.102.
Threat'ning to answer from the dark recess. .... Od.4.384.139.
Whose eye can pierce the dark recess of fate. .... Od.4.472.142.
To that recess, commodious for surprize, ... Od.4.549.146.
The troop forth issuing from the dark recess, ... Od.4.717.152.
That safe recess they gain with happy speed, ... Od.4.1107.169.
His wish'd recess, and to the Goddess flies; .... Od.8.328.281.
Within a long recess a bay there lies, ... Od.10.101.345.
Indignant in the dark recess he stands, ... Od.11.647.416.
Where in a beauteous Grotto's cool recess .... Od.12.377.449.
Beneath, a gloomy Grotto's cool recess .... Od.13.124.7.
Behold the gloomy grot! whose cool recess .... Od.13.395.26.
Whose eye can pierce the dark recess of fate. .... Od.17.161.139.

RECESSES
Far in the bright Recesses of the Skies, ... 1.TrSt.275.421.
The close Recesses of the Virgin's Thought; .... 2.RL3.140.178.
But soft recesses of uneasy minds, ... 6.81.9.225.
But soft recesses for th' uneasy Mind, ... 6.81.9A.225.
Far in the deep Recesses of the Main, ... Il.1.468.110.
Deep in the close Recesses of my Soul. .... Il.1.711.121.
In deep Recesses of the gloomy Wood, ... Il.5.682.300.
Far in the close Recesses of the Dome, ... Il.22.566.479.
And sought the deep recesses of the den. .... Od.9.279.318.
Deep in the close recesses of the cave: .... Od.13.418.26.
Deep in the rough recesses of the wood, ... Od.19.511.221.

RECITATIVO
Then thus in quaint Recitativo spoke. .... 5.DunB4.52.346.

RECITE
The Thoughts of Gods let *Granville's* Verse recite, ... 1.W-F.425.193.
They rave, recite, and madden round the land. .... 4.Arbu.6.96.
And if we will recite nine hours in ten, ... 4.2HE1.362.227.
And both with Mouth and Hand recite; .... 6.10.12.24.
What glorious Toils, what Wonders they recite, ... Il.4.428.240.
This could be learn, and to our Peers recite, ... Il.10.249.13.
But say, be faithful, and the Truth recite! .... Il.10.477.24.
Sincere, from whence began thy course, recite, ... Od.1.221.43.
Recite them! nor in erring pity fear .... Od.4.439.140.

RECITES
M[oo]re always smiles whenever he recites; .... 6.105ii.1.300.
M[oore] always laughs whenever he recites; .... 6.105ii.1A.300.

RECITING
To him the King. Reciting thus thy cares, ... Od.15.522.95.

RECK'NING
And keep an equal Reck'ning ev'ry Night; .... 2.ChWB.53.59.

RECKNING
And one that pays reckning .... 6.68.3.196.

RECLAIM
Wisdom and wit in vain reclaim, ... 6.51ii.3.152.
Recall your Armies, and your Chiefs reclaim. .... Il.2.216.138.
Let this Example future Times reclaim, ... Il.3.437.213.
Scorch all the Banks! and (till our Voice reclaim) .... Il.21.396.436.
'Till righteous heav'n reclaim her stubborn breast. .... Od.2.142.68.
If e'er *Ulysses,* to reclaim your right, ... Od.4.441.140.
From the devouring rage of grief reclaim. .... Od.19.300.209.
Nor threats, thy bold intrusion will reclaim. .... Od.20.228.244.

RECLAIMS
He, from the taste obscene reclaims our Youth, ... 4.2HE1.217.213.

RECLIN'D
High in the midst, upon his Urn reclin'd, ... 1.W-F.349.184.
While on a Bank reclin'd of rising Green, ... 2.ChJM.625.45.
As on the Nosegay in her Breast reclin'd, ... 2.RL3.141.178.
The darksom pines that o'er yon' rocks reclin'd .... 2.ElAb.155.332.
With gloomy Aspect, on his Arm reclin'd. .... Il.1.429.108.
Jove on his Couch reclin'd his awful Head, ... Il.1.780.125.
On this bright Sceptre now the King reclin'd, ... Il.2.137.134.
Parrhasia, on her snowy Cliffs reclin'd, ... Il.2.737.161.
The matchless *Helen* o'er the Walls reclin'd: .... Il.3.474.214.

RECLIN'D (CONTINUED)

The noble *Hector* on this Lance reclin'd, ...Il.8.619.425.
Their Arms in order on the Ground reclin'd, ...Il.10.546.27.
Beneath a Turret, on his Shield reclin'd, ...Il.22.136.458.
Obey'd; and rested, on his Lance reclin'd. ....Il.22.290.468.
Loose on their Shoulders the long Manes reclin'd, ...Il.23.443.508.
His head reclin'd, young *Ithacus* begun. ....Od.4.82.123.
Refresh'd, and careless on the deck reclin'd, ...Od.9.87.306.
In shelter thick of horrid shade reclin'd; ....Od.9.219.314.

RECLINE

Now tir'd with Toils, thy fainting Limbs recline, ...Il.6.444.348.

RECLINES

Soft on her lap her Laureat son reclines. ....5.DunB4.20.341.
Soft he reclines along the murm'ring seas, ...Od.6.283.224.

RECLINING

His Head reclining on his bossy Shield. ....Il.10.173.9.
The Foe reclining, shunn'd the flying Death; ....Il.14.539.181.
Till propp'd reclining on the palace walls; ....Od.18.123.172.
The vase reclining floats the floor around! ....Od.19.549.223.

RECLUSE

The most recluse, discreetly open'd, find ....5.DunB4.447.384.

RECOGNIS'D

Then first he recognis'd th' Ætherial guest; ....Od.1.415.52.
In all he told she recognis'd her Lord: ....Od.19.285.208.

RECOGNIZE

Ascend, and recognize their native place: ....5.DunA1.224.90.
Ascend, and recognize their Native Place. ....5.DunB1.268.290.
His realm might recognize an equal heir. ....Od.19.433.215.

RECOILING

Recoiling, on his head is sure to fall. ....Od.4.893.160.
Recoiling, mutter'd thunder in his breast. ....Od.20.22.232.

RECOLLECT

Oh recollect your ancient Worth and Praise! ....Il.13.74.108.

RECOLLECTION

(Tho' past the recollection of the thought) ....3.Ep1.47.18.

RECOMMEND

As Shades more sweetly recommend the Light, ...1.EOC.301.273.
Or ev'n to crack live *Crawfish* recommend, ...4.HS2.43.57.
He'd recommend her, as a special breeder. ....6.41.34.114.
Whose Private Name all Titles recommend, ...6.134.3.364.

RECOMMENDS

But hear a Mother, when she recommends ....5.DunB4.439.383.
Succeeds, and ev'n a stranger recommends. ....Od.7.68.237.

RECOMPENCE

Shall recompence the Warrior's Toils with Love. ....Il.8.354.414.
An urn shall recompence your prudent choice: ....Od.4.834.158.
Full recompence thy bounty else had born; ....Od.24.330.365.

RECOMPENSE

Still One was left, their Loss to recompense; ....Il.24.618.562.

RECONCIL'D

Thro' reconcil'd extremes of drought and rain, ...3.Ep3.168.107.

RECONCILES

Due Distance *reconciles* to Form and Grace. ....1.EOC.174.260.

RECONCILING

Thy eyes diffus'd a reconciling ray, ...2.ElAb.145.331.
These reconciling Goddesses obey: ....Il.9.638.466.

RECORD

It stands on record, that in *Richard's* Times ....4.HS1.145.19.
It stands on record, that in ancient Times ....4.HS1.145A.19.
There liv'd, *in primo Georgii* (they record) ....4.2HE2.184.177.
And Monumental Brass this record bears, ...5.DunB2.313.311.
My Countrys Poet, to record her Fame. ....6.155.8.404.
And ev'ry Age record the signal Day. ....Il.3.361.210.
And age to Age record the signal Day. ....Il.3.361A.210.
And Age to Age record this signal Day. ....Il.3.574.219.
And late Posterity record our Praise. ....Il.23.309.502.
Historic Marbles, to record his praise; ....Od.1.306.47.
If faithful thou record the tale of fame, ...Od.8.543.291.
Nor better could the Muse record thy woes. ....Od.11.459.407.
Historic marbles, to record his praise: ....Od.14.404.55.
The sacred act of friendship shall record. ....Od.15.64.72.
To sooth my grief, he haply may record: ....Od.19.114.198.
His form, his habit, and his train record. ....Od.19.256.207.
'Tis thine to merit, mine is to record. ....Od.22.388.307.
Historic marbles to record thy praise: ....Od.24.46.350.

RECORDED

To have the *Rape* recorded by his Muse. ....6.38.30.108.
Recorded eminent in deathless fame? ....Od.4.74.123.
To you, your fathers have recorded long: ....Od.4.120.126.

RECORDING

And vanquish'd realms supply recording gold? ....6.71.56.204.
Ye all-beholding, all-recording Nine! ....Il.14.600.191.
Just and unjust recording in their mind, ...Od.17.580.160.

RECORDS

And from the long Records of distant Age ....1.TrSt.379.425.
And trac'd the long Records of Lunar Years. ....2.TemF.112.262.

RECOUNT

E'er I recount the Sins of these Profane, ...1.TrSt.327.424.
Now Muse recount *Pelasgic Argos'* Pow'rs, ...Il.2.829.164.
But should I all recount, the night would fail, ...Od.11.408.404.

RECOUNTS

Her race recounts, and their illustrious deeds. ....Od.11.280.395.

RECOURSE

Plac'd on the mast (the last recourse of life) ....Od.14.347.51.

RECOV'RING

So just recov'ring from the Shades of Night, ...2.ChJM.802.54.
At length recov'ring, to his arms she flew, ...Od.23.213.333.

RECOVER'D

While *Hector* rose, recover'd from the Trance, ...Il.11.462.54.
This half-recover'd Day shall *Troy* obtain? ....Il.14.423.184.
At length, with heart recover'd, I began. ....Od.9.306.319.

RECOVERS

She faints, or but recovers to complain. ....Il.22.607.481.

RECREANT

The recreant Warrior, hateful as the Grave. ....Il.3.566.219.
The recreant Warrior hear the Voice of Fame. ....Il.6.351.343.
The recreant nation to fair *Scheria* led, ...Od.6.11.203.
But hear me, wretch! if recreant in the fray, ...Od.18.94.171.

RECREANT'S

"Paste we this Recreant's Name, ...6.79.142.223.

RECREATION

Together mix'd; sweet recreation, ...6.1.14.3.

RECRUIT

With *Thracian* Wines recruit thy honour'd Guests, ...Il.9.99.437.

RECRUITED

With Rage recruited the bold *Trojans* glow, ...Il.6.129.330.
Divine refection! then recruited, spoke. ....Od.5.120.178.

RECRUITS

She gives in large Recruits of *needful Pride*; ....1.EOC.206.264.

RECTIFY

'Tis hers to rectify, not overthrow, ...3.EOM2.163.74.

RECUMBENT

Recumbent on the shining thrones of state. ....Od.16.425.127.
And fed recumbent on a chair of state. ....Od.17.683.165.

RECUR

The scenes of life recur, and actions past; ....Od.11.181.390.

RED

Red *Iber's* Sands, or *Ister's* foaming Flood; ....1.W-F.368.186.
Which lost its native red; and first appear'd ....1.TrPA.153.372.
With that ripe red th'Autumnal Sun bestows, ...1.TrVP.101.381.
Yet no red Clouds, with golden Borders gay, ...1.TrSt.482.430.
Now livid pale her Cheeks, now glowing red; ....2.RLA2.61.133.
"And—Betty—give this Cheek a little Red." ....3.Ep1.247.36.
Where tawdry yellow strove with dirty red, ...3.Ep3.304.118.
And with a Face as red, and as awry, ...4.JD4.266.47.
The *Robin-red-breast* till of late had rest, ...4.HS2.37.57.
And just that White and Red which Nature gave. ....4.HAdv.164.89.
The Napkins white, the Carpet red: ....4.HS6.197.263.
Wings the red lightning, and the thunder rolls. ....5.DunA3.252.178.
Or their fond Parents drest in red and gold; ....5.DunB1.138.280.
Wings the red lightning, and the thunder rolls. ....5.DunB3.256.332.
Forth thrust a white Neck, and red Crest. ....6.14i.20.42.
With deeper red the full pomegranate glows, ...6.35.8.103.
To wear red Stockings, and to dine with *St[eel]* ....6.49i.4.137.
That Red is charming all will hold, ...6.64.13.190.
What? throw away a *Fool in Red:* ....6.64.20.190.
I've no red Hair to breathe an odious Fume; ....6.96iv.27.277.
Spreads the red Rod of angry Pestilence, ...6.137.4.373.
"Red, Blue, and Green, nay white and black, ...6.140.19.378.
Rang'd the wild Desarts red with Monsters Gore, ...Il.1.356.105.
Launch the red Lightning, and dethrone the Gods. ....Il.1.749.123.
Struck with her Presence, strait the lively Red. ....Il.3.491.215.
As the red Comet from *Saturnius* sent ....Il.4.101.225.
Stains the pure Iv'ry with a lively Red; ....Il.4.173.229.
Bare his red Arm, and bid the Thunder roll; ....Il.4.201.230.
With copious Slaughter all the Fields are red, ...Il.4.628.250.
Like the red Star that fires th' Autumnal Skies, ...Il.5.8.266.
Mars, red with Slaughter, aids our hated Foes: ....Il.5.882.308.
With Slaughter red, and raging round the Field. ....Il.5.1019.315.
From the red Field their scatter'd Bodies bear, ...Il.7.400.384.
And shot red Light'nings thro' the gloomy Shade: ....Il.7.573.393.
And dy'd his Javelin red with *Trojan* Gore. ....Il.8.308.412.
And the red Fiends that walk the nightly Round. ....Il.9.686.468.
Thro' the red Skies her bloody Sign extends, ...Il.11.7.35.
Red Drops of Blood o'er all the fatal Field; ....Il.11.70.37.
As the red Star now shows his sanguine Fires ....Il.11.83.38.
Swells the red Horrors of this direful Plain: ....Il.11.102.39.
And the red Slaughter spreads on ev'ry side. ....Il.11.530.57.
From his torn Liver the red Current flow'd, ...Il.11.706.66.
While Life's red Torrent gush'd from out the Wound. ....Il.13.820.144.
Glows with celestial Red, and thus replies. ....Il.14.374.180.
As when the Bolt, red-hissing from above, ...Il.14.481.187.
Like fiery Meteors his red Eyeballs glow: ....Il.15.731.224.
Bright with the Blaze, and red with Heroes slain: ....Il.15.851.229.
And the red Terrors of the blazing Brands: ....Il.17.746.317.
Quench<'d> his red Orb, at *Juno's* high Command, ...Il.18.285.335.
With his huge Scepter grac'd, and red Attire, ...Il.18.485.345.

RED (CONTINUED)

Above the Waves that blush'd with early Red, ...Il.19.2.371.
Like the red Star, that from his flaming Hair ....Il.19.412.389.
Pour the red Torrent on the wat'ry Foe, ...Il.21.391.436.
And the red Vapours purple all the Sky. ....Il.21.610.447.
Taints the red Air with Fevers, Plagues, and Death. ....Il.22.42.454.
And his red Eye-balls glare with living Fire. ....Il.22.135.458.
His slaught'ring Hands, yet red with Blood, he laid ....Il.23.23.488.
Those Hands, yet red with *Hector's* noble Gore! ....Il.24.250.547.
(Ambrosial cates, with Nectar rosie red) ....Od.5.118.178.
The dawn, and all the orient flam'd with red. ....Od.6.58.208.
With deeper red the full pomegranate glows, ...Od.7.149.243.
Launch'd his red lightning at our scatter'd ships: ....Od.7.335.253.
(Green as it was) and sparkled fiery red. ....Od.9.450.324.
The red-hot metal hisses in the lake, ...Od.9.467.325.
And vengeful murther red with human blood. ....Od.11.756.423.
Aims the red bolt, and hurls the writhen brand! ....Od.12.446.452.
Lo! my red arm I bare, my thunders guide, ...Od.12.456.453.
Red with uncommon wrath, and wrapt in flames: ....Od.12.488.456.
Had ting'd the mountains with her earliest red, ...Od.15.215.78.
And a red deluge floats the reeking stone. ....Od.22.346.304.
And ten, that red with blushing apples glow'd; ....Od.24.396.368.
But *Jove's* red arm the burning thunder aims; ....Od.24.622.377.

RED-HISSING

As when the Bolt, red-hissing from above, ...Il.14.481.187.

RED-HOT

The red-hot metal hisses in the lake, ...Od.9.467.325.

RED'NING

With annual joy the red'ning shoots to greet, ...3.Ep4.91.146.
The red'ning apple ripens here to gold, ...6.35.6.103.
Now, e're the Morn had streak'd with red'ning Light ....Il.7.516.389.
The red'ning Orient shows the coming Day, ...Il.10.296.15.
Repeated Wounds the red'ning River dy'd, ...Il.21.26.422.
Now red'ning from the dawn, the Morning ray ....Od.2.1.59.
The red'ning apple ripens here to gold, ...Od.7.147.243.
The red'ning dawn reveals the circling fields ....Od.14.296.50.
Youth flush'd his red'ning cheek, and from his brows ....Od.16.190.112.

REDCOAT

Here a bright *Redcoat,* there a smart *Toupee.* ....6.9vii.5.22.

REDDEN

The Coral redden, and the Ruby glow, ...1.W-F.394.190.
The blazing Altars redden all the shore. ....Od.13.219.16.
My grape shall redden, and my harvest grow. ....Od.20.381.251.

REDDENS

But *Appius* reddens at each Word you speak, ...1.EOC.585.306.
A fiery Gleam, and reddens all the Sky. ....1.TrSt.149.416.
The glowing Ocean reddens with the Fires. ....Il.16.157.244.
And the sky reddens with the rising day. ....Od.11.469.407.

REDEEM

Nor left one virtue to redeem her Race. ....2.Elegy.28.365.
And one man's honesty redeem the land. ....4.1740.98.337.
Rise to redeem; ah yet, to conquer, rise! ....Il.9.323.449.
Shot down to save her, and redeem her Fame. ....Il.21.642.448.
And urge her Monarch to redeem his Son; ....Il.24.180.543.
And speed my Journey to redeem my Son? ....Il.24.330.550.
And thou, *Euryalus,* redeem thy wrong: ....Od.8.431.287.

REDEEM'D

Redeem'd from tapers and defrauded pyes, ...5.DunA1.136.80.
Redeem'd from tapers and defrauded pies, ...5.DunB1.156.282.
Redeem'd too late, she scarce beheld again ....Il.6.540.353.
The Son redeem'd the Honours of the Race, ...Il.15.774.226.
Let *Greece,* redeem'd from this destructive Strait, ...Il.16.120.241.
When scarce a God redeem'd him from his Hand) ....Il.23.362.504.

REDEEMER

To thee, Redeemer! mercy's sacred spring! ....6.25.15.77.

REDEMPTION

And of *Redemption* made damn'd Work. ....6.101.12.290.

REDNING

The redning dawn reveals the hostile fields ....Od.17.517.157.

REDOUBL'D

Soon with redoubl'd force the wound repay'd; ....Od.19.528.221.
He said: obsequious with redoubl'd pace, ...Od.19.587.224.

REDOUBLED

And fires *Typhœus* with redoubled Blows, ...Il.2.953.169.
The Strokes redoubled on his Buckler rung; ....Il.11.691.66.
And Peals on Peals redoubled rend the Poles. ....Il.20.76.397.
Yet still retentive, with redoubled might ....Od.4.567.147.

REDOUBLES

And the loud shriek redoubles from the main. ....Od.6.136.213.

REDOUBLING

Which thus redoubling on *Atrides* broke. ....Il.1.296.101.
Which thus redoubling on the Monarch broke. ....Il.1.296A.101.
Redoubling Clamours thunder in the Skies. ....Il.12.298.92.
Loud sounds the Axe, redoubling Strokes on Strokes; ....Il.23.146.495.

REDOUND

The mingled fluids from the vase redound; ....Od.19.548.223.

REDOUNDING

Round the descending nymph the waves redounding roar. ....Od.4.578.147.

REDRESS

Than all the Sons of *Adam* cou'd redress. ....2.ChWB.368.75.
Then all the Sons of *Adam* can redress. ....2.ChWB.368A.75.
No guard but virtue, no redress but tears. ....6.38.18.108.
Yet some Redress to suppliant *Greece* afford, ...Il.9.398.452.
Tho' yet thy State require Redress (he cries) ....Il.15.460.215.
What Friend, what Man, from thee shall hope redress? ....Il.16.43.237.
Then might we hope redress from juster laws, ...Od.2.85.65.
And but augment the wrongs thou would'st redress. ....Od.2.222.72.
To heav'n, and all the *Greeks,* redress belongs. ....Od.2.240.73.
Teach me to seek redress for all my woe, ...Od.2.355.78.
For counsel and redress, he sues to you. ....Od.4.218.130.
From ev'ry other hand redress he found, ...Od.17.594.161.
Tears but indulge the sorrow, not redress. ....Od.18.206.177.

REDREST

Had not sage *Helenus* her State redrest, ...Il.6.91.328.
She, and *Eurynome,* my Griefs redrest, ...Il.18.465.344.

REDRIFF

What *Redriff* Wife so long hath kept her Vows? ....6.96iv.6.276.

REDUC'D

Reduc'd to feign it, when they give no more: ....3.Ep2.238.69.
Reduc'd at last to hiss in my own dragon. ....5.DunA3.288.184.
Reduc'd at last to hiss in my own dragon. ....5.DunB3.286.334.
Reduc'd to crave the good I once could give: ....Od.19.93.197.

REDUNDANT

Floats in bright waves redundant o'er the ground. ....Od.18.342.184.

REED

O let my Muse her slender Reed inspire, ...1.PSp.11.61.
The green Reed trembles, and the Bulrush nods. ....1.Mes.72.119.
And eyes the dancing Cork and Bending Reed. ....1.W-F.140.163.
Where to the steely Point the Reed was join'd, ...Il.4.246.232.
Who thro' the rings directs the feather'd reed. ....Od.19.677.229.
Of *Byblos'* reed, a ship from *Egypt* brought) ....Od.21.424.280.

REEDS

But now the Reeds shall hang on yonder Tree, ...1.PSu.43.75.
Yet soon the Reeds shall hang on yonder Tree, ...1.PSu.43A.75.
But tell the Reeds, and tell the vocal Shore, ...1.PWi.59.93.
His whistle (which a hundred reeds compose) ....1.TrPA.45.367.
While to his reeds he sung his amorous pains, ...1.TrPA.51.367.
Long reeds sprung up as on a fountain's brink: ....1.TrPA.156.372.
So on *Mæotis'* Marsh, (where Reeds and Rushes ....6.26i.1.79.
Then heap'd with Reeds and gathr'd Boughs the Plain, ...Il.10.538.27.
Behind them, piping on their Reeds, they go, ...Il.18.609.352.
Swift on the sedgy Reeds the Ruin preys; ....Il.21.406.437.
With Reeds collected from the marshy Shore; ....Il.24.554.559.

REEDY

Whose horned temples reedy wreaths inclose; ....1.TrPA.160.373.

REEK'D

Altars grew marble then, and reek'd with gore: ....3.EOM3.264.119.

REEKING

And mix thy waters with his reeking blood! ....1.TrPA.129.371.
The reeking Fibres clinging to the Dart; ....1.TrES.319.461.
Shall stream in Vengeance on my reeking Blade. ....Il.1.399.107.
Forth from the slain he tugg'd the reeking Dart. ....Il.6.82.327.
Of Heroes slain he bears the reeking Spoils, ...Il.6.611.357.
Doubtful he stood, or with his reeking Blade ....Il.10.588.28.
Their Bones he cracks, their reeking Vitals draws, ...Il.11.155.42.
The reeking Javelin, and rejoin'd his Friends. ....Il.13.674.137.
The thirsty Faulchion drank his reeking Blood: ....Il.16.397.258.
The reeking Fibres clinging to the Dart; ....Il.16.624.268.
And upwards cast the Corps: The reeking Spear ....Il.16.1044.283.
A sanguine Torrent steeps the reeking Ground; ....Il.17.415.303.
As when a slaughter'd Bull's yet reeking Hyde, ...Il.17.450.304.
And buried in his Neck the reeking Blade. ....Il.21.130.427.
The reeking Entrails pour upon the Ground. ....Il.21.196.429.
The reeking Jav'lin, cast it on the Ground. ....Il.22.464.474.
In one promiscuous Stream, the reeking Blood. ....Il.23.44.488.
And kiss those Hands yet reeking with their Gore! ....Il.24.633.563.
The Limbs they sever from the reeking Hyde, ...Il.24.788.570.
I then approach'd him reeking with their gore, ...Od.9.406.322.
New from his crime, and reeking yet with gore. ....Od.15.251.80.
And a red deluge floats the reeking stone. ....Od.22.346.304.

REEL

But you reel home, a drunken beastly Bear, ...2.ChWB.82.60.
Till Isis' Elders reel, their Pupils' sport; ....5.DunA3.333.191.
The sons of *Isis* reel! the towns-mens sport; 5.DunA3.333A.191
'Till Isis' Elders reel, their pupils' sport, ...5.DunB3.337.336.
His Eyes flash Sparkles, his stunn'd Senses reel ....Il.16.957.280.
And rushing forth tumultuous reel away. ....Od.18.473.191.

REEL'D

Fix'd in the Shoulder's Joint, he reel'd around; ....1.TrES.271.459.
Fix'd in the Shoulders Joint, he reel'd around; ....Il.16.576.267.
Reel'd from the palace, and retir'd to rest. ....Od.2.447.82.
Stagg'ring I reel'd, and as I reel'd I fell, ...Od.11.79.385.
Stagg'ring I reel'd, and as I reel'd I fell, ...Od.11.79.385.
Tost and retost, it reel'd beneath the blow; ....Od.12.490.456.

REELING

Now here, now there, the reeling Vessel throw: ....1.TrSt.268.421.
As faintly reeling he confess'd the Smart; ....Il.11.944.77.
Whose Arms support him, reeling thro' the Throng, ...Il.23.808.521.
Sour with debauch, a reeling tribe, they came. ....Od.3.172.94.

REELS

Nods, groans, and reels, 'till with a crackling Sound ....1.TrES.290.460.
Rais'd on his feet, again he reels, he falls, ...Od.18.122.172.
He shrieks, he reels, he falls, and breathless lies. ....Od.18.443.190.

REFECTION

With Nectar sweet, (Refection of the Gods!) ....Il.19.376.387.
Demand Refection, and to Rest invite: ....Il.24.754.568.
But since to part, for sweet refection due ....Od.1.403.51.
Mean-time the Queen without refection due, ...Od.4.1037.166.
Divine refection! then recruited, spoke. ....Od.5.120.178.
Ye Gods! since this worn frame refection knew, ...Od.6.261.222.
First claim refection, then to rest invite; ....Od.14.450.57. ·
He sate, and sweet refection cheer'd his soul. ....Od.14.501.60.
Was care for due refection, and repose, ...Od.20.162.241.
In vain the Queen the night-refection prest; ....Od.20.172.241.
For due refection to the bow'r they came, ...Od.24.448.370.

REFER

From which to reason, or to which refer? ....3.EOM1.20.14.
Refer the choice to fill the vacant Throne. ....Od.1.510.56.

REFIN'D

In useful Craft successfully refin'd; ....1.TrUl.167.471.
'Tis Truth I tell, tho' not in Phrase refin'd; ....2.ChJM.742.51.
Some less refin'd, beneath the Moon's pale Light ....2.RL2.81.165.
Where flames refin'd in breasts seraphic glow. ....2.ElAb.320.345.
The dross cements what else were too refin'd, ...3.EOM2.179.76.
Lust, thro' some certain strainers well refin'd, ...3.EOM2.189.77.
Too rash for Thought, for Action too refin'd: ....3.Ep1.201A.32.
Too quick for Thought, for Action too refin'd: ....3.Ep1.201.32.
Wise Fool! with Pleasures too refin'd to please, ...3.Ep2.95A.57.
Wise Wretch! of Pleasures too refin'd to please, ...3.Ep2.95B.57.
On the soft Passion, and the Taste refin'd, ...3.Ep2.84.57.
Wise Wretch! with Pleasures too refin'd to please, ...3.Ep2.95.57.
He forms one Tongue exotic and refin'd. ....4.JD4.49.29.
He, with a hundred Arts refin'd, ...4.HOde1.15.151.
He, with a thousand Arts refin'd, ...4.HOde1.15A.151.
Which only heads, refin'd from reason, know. ....5.DunA3.6.150.
Which only heads refin'd from Reason know. ....5.DunB3.6.320.
So firm yet soft, so strong yet so refin'd, ...6.115.8.323.
By ten long years refin'd, and rosy-bright.) ....Od.3.505.112.
Two lavers from the richest ore refin'd, ...Od.4.173.128.
O exercis'd in grief! by arts refin'd! ....Od.11.761.424.
In useful craft successfully refin'd! ....Od.13.334.23.
Musick, the banquet's most refin'd delight. ....Od.21.474.283.

REFIND

In Manners plain, in Sense alone refind, ...6.134.5.364.

REFINE

See *Dionysius Homer's* Thoughts refine, ...1.EOC.665.314.
Prune the luxuriant, the uncouth refine, ...4.2HE2.174.177.
But Otway fail'd to polish or refine, ...4.2HE1.278.219.
Refine ourselves to Spirit, for your Sake. ....6.82vi.2.232.

REFINEMENTS

Britain to soft refinements less a foe, ...4.2HE1.265.217.

REFINES

How the *Wit brightens!* How the *Style refines!* ....1.EOC.421.288.
That gen'rous God, who Wit and Gold refines, ...3.Ep2.289A.73.
The gen'rous God, who Wit and Gold refines, ...3.Ep2.289.73.
From those far Regions where the Sun refines ....Il.2.1044.172.

REFITS

Or the dumb lute refits with vocal wire, ...Od.21.443.281.

REFLECT

Reflect new Glories, and augment the Day. ....1.EOC.473.292.
The Learn'd reflect on what before they knew: ....1.EOC.740.326.
The shelving Walls reflect a glancing Light; ....1.TrSt.531.432.
Our Fun'ral Flames reflect a grateful Light. ....1.TrSt.775.442.
And Fun'ral Flames reflect a grateful Light. ....1.TrSt.775.A.442.
Or Fun'ral Flames reflect a grateful Light. ....1.TrSt.775B.442.
Reflect what Truth was in my Passion shown, ...2.ChJM.549.41.
But jealous Men on their own Crimes reflect, ...2.ChJM.593.43.
Yet Sir, reflect, the mischief is not great; ....4.2HE1.189.211.
While images reflect from art to art? ....6.52.20.156.
Let each reflect, who prizes Fame or Breath, ...Il.13.163.112.
The brazen Arms reflect a beamy Light. ....Il.13.1009.153.
Arms, that reflect a Radiance thro' the Skies. ....Il.15.137.202.
And bade the Chief reflect, how late with Scorn ....Il.20.115.398.

REFLECTED

Some wand'ring touches some reflected light, ...3.Ep2.153A.63.
Some wand'ring touch, or some reflected light, ...3.Ep2.153.63.
Not when a gilt Buffet's reflected pride ....4.HS2.5.55.
Of beaming diamonds, and reflected plate. ....4.1HE6.29.239.
His Peers shine round him with reflected grace, ...5.DunB2.9.296.
And Art reflected images to Art. ....6.71.52.204.
Reflecting, and reflected in his Race; ....6.118.12.335.
Reflected various Light, and arching bow'd, ...Il.11.35.36.

REFLECTING

The clear, reflecting Mind, presents his Sin ....1.TrSt.73.413.
Reflecting, and reflected in his Race; ....6.118.12.335.
Was there a gen'rous, a reflecting Mind, ...6.128.5.355.
Reflecting Blaze on Blaze, against the Skies. ....Il.18.254.334.
Mix in one Stream, reflecting Blaze on Blaze: ....Il.19.387.388.
Reflecting to the Queen the silver sounds. ....Od.1.426.53.
The polish'd Ore, reflecting ev'ry ray, ...Od.7.130.241.

REFLECTION

Remembrance and Reflection how ally'd; ....3.EOM1.225.43.
Reflection, Reason, still the ties improve, ...3.EOM3.133.106.

REFLECTION (CONTINUED)

Here still Reflection led on sober Thought, ...4.JD4.188A.41.
And all we gain, some sad Reflection more; ....6.86.8.245.
If modest Youth, with cool Reflection crown'd, ...6.132.1.362.
Of sad reflection, and corroding care. ....Od.4.400.139.
The day reflection, and the midnight dream! ....Od.4.1062.167.
From sad reflection let my soul repose; ....Od.14.194.45.

REFLECTIONS

No faint Reflections of the distant Light ....1.TrSt.484.430.
In vain sedate reflections we would make, ...3.Ep1.33.18.
The long Reflections of the distant Fires ....Il.8.701.428.

REFLECTIVE

My mind reflective, in a thorny maze ....Od.19.613.226.

REFLECTS

And the bright Arch reflects a double Day. ....1.TrSt.295.422.
The Dome's high Arch reflects the mingled Blaze, ..2.TemF.256.275.
And half the platform just reflects the other. ....3.Ep4.118.149.
Where Thames reflects the visionary Scene. ....4.HOde1.24.153.
Whilst Thames reflects the visionary Scene. ....4.HOde1.24A.153.
The silver Thames reflects its marble face. ....4.1HE1.142.289.
This polish'd Hardness, that reflects the Peer, ...5.DunB1.220.286.
In vain fair Thames reflects the double scenes .....6.81.3.225.
Reflects her bord'ring Palances and Bow'rs. ....Il.2.1041.172.
And Heav'n's high Arch reflects the ruddy Light; ..Il.18.252.334.
Or why reflects my Mind on ought but thee ....Il.22.482.476.
It aids our torch-light, and reflects the ray. ....Od.18.402.187.

REFLUENT

With all his refluent Waters circled round) ....Il.21.160.428.
The refluent tydes, and plunge him in the deep. ...Od.5.549.198.
The whole sea shook, and refluent beat the shore. ..Od.9.570.330.
Shake at the weight, and refluent beat the shore. ..Od.9.634.332.
She dreins the ocean with the refluent tides: ....Od.12.289.446.
The mast refunded on her refluent waves. ....Od.12.522.458.

REFORM

But if thou must reform the stubborn Times, ...1.TrSt.377.425.
Thus *Orpheus* travell'd to reform his Kind, ...6.96iii.19.275.

REFORM'D

Then Unbelieving Priests reform'd the Nation, ...1.EOC.546.300.
Or Laws establish'd, and the World reform'd; ......4.2HE1.12.195.

REFORMING

But, as the Fool, that in reforming Days ....4.JD4.15.27.

REFRAIN

Watch'd as she was, yet cou'd He not refrain ....2.ChJM.496.39.
Watch'd as she was, yet cou'd not He refrain ......2.ChJM.496A.39.
From Fields forbidden we submit refrain, ...Il.8.43.397.
From Fields forbidden we submiss refrain, ...Il.8.580.424.
Neptune aton'd, his wrath shall now refrain, ...Od.1.100.36.
Familiar now with grief, your tears refrain, ...Od.1.450.54.
Th' allotted labours of the day refrain, ...Od.4.907.161.
Touch'd at the sight from tears I scarce refrain, ...Od.11.675.417.
These seas o'erpass'd, be wise! but I refrain ......Od.12.67.433.
But honouring age, in mercy I refrain; ....Od.18.17.167.

REFRAIN'D

And scarce refrain'd when I forbad the War. ......Il.5.1001.314.

REFRESH

No rich Perfumes refresh the fruitful Field, ...1.PWi.47.92.
Soft Rains and kindly Dews refresh the Field, ...1.TrUl.130.470.
To clear my Quail-pipe, and refresh my Soul, ...2.ChWB.213.67.
And breath the Zephyrs that refresh thy Grove ....6.106ii.4.307.
Then with a plenteous Draught refresh thy Soul, ..Il.6.325.342.
No chearful Gales refresh the lazy Air: ....Il.8.602.425.
Our Steeds to forage, and refresh our Pow'rs. ....Il.8.628.425.
This Night, refresh and fortify thy Train, ...Il.9.93.437.
This Night, let due Repast refresh our Pow'rs; ....Il.9.825.474.
Refresh thy Wound, and cleanse the clotted Gore; ..Il.14.11.157.
Soft rains and kindly dews refresh the field, ...Od.13.297.20.
But first refresh: and at the dawn of day ....Od.17.678.165.
Let some refresh the vase's sullied mold; ....Od.20.190.242.

REFRESH'D

And, well refresh'd, to bloody Conflict haste. .....Il.2.453.149.
Then late refresh'd with Sleep from Toils of Fight, ..Il.7.578.393.
Then in the polish'd Bath, refresh'd from Toil, ...Il.10.675.32.
Refresh'd, they wait them to the bow'r of state, ...Od.4.61.122.
Refresh'd, and careless on the deck reclin'd, ...Od.9.87.306.
Refresh'd I lay, and Joy beguil'd the hours. ....Od.12.534.459.

REFRESHES

Warms in the sun, refreshes in the breeze, ...3.EOM1.271.48.

REFRESHING

These to the birds refreshing streams may yield; ..6.20.65.67.
Odour divine! whose soft refreshing streams ....Od.6.93.209.
Refreshing meads along the murm'ring main, ...Od.9.155.312.

REFRESHMENT

Now take Refreshment as the Hour demands: ......Il.7.445.386.
Take due Refreshment, and the Watch attend. .....Il.18.348.338.
Ev'n in the circling floods refreshment craves, ...Od.11.721.421.

REFUGE

Puts his last refuge all in Heav'n and Pray'r. .....5.DunA2.206.127.
Puts his last refuge all in Heav'n in Pray'r. ......5.DunA2.206A.127.
Puts his last refuge all in heav'n and pray'r. .....5.DunB2.214.306.
The last kind Refuge weary Wit can find, ...6.16.2.53.
Heav'n is thy hope: thy refuge fix'd above; ....6.21.21.69.

REFUGE (CONTINUED)

How few in *Ilion* else had Refuge found? ....Il.22.25.453.
No Refuge now, no Succour from above; ....Il.22.383.471.
This dome a refuge to thy wrongs shall be, ...Od.20.330.249.

REFULGENT

And thence exerting his refulgent Ray, ...1.TrVP.116.381.
And his refulgent *Queen*, with Pow'rs combin'd, ...2.RL3.77.173.
Breaks out refulgent, with a heav'n its own: ....5.DunA3.238.177.
Refulgent rises, with a heav'n its own: ....5.DunA3.238A.177.
Breaks out refulgent, with a heav'n its own: ....5.DunB3.242.332.
Once more refulgent shine in Brazen Arms. ....Il.2.200.137.
And his refulgent Arms in Triumph wears; ....Il.2.698.159.
Once more they glitter in refulgent Arms, ...Il.4.254.233.
That rich with *Tyrian* Dye refulgent glow'd. ....Il.6.274.340.
And glow'd refulgent as the Morning Star. ....Il.6.367.344.
In Arms refulgent as the God of Day, ...Il.6.661.360.
Where-e'er the Sun's refulgent Rays are cast, ...Il.7.548.392.
Refulgent, flash'd intolerable Day. ....Il.8.54.398.
The Point was Brass, refulgent to behold, ...Il.8.617.425.
The Point was Steel, refulgent to behold, ...Il.8.617A.425.
As when the Moon, refulgent Lamp of Night! ....Il.8.687.428.
And twice ten Vases of refulgent Mold; ....Il.9.158.440.
And twice ten Vases of refulgent Mold; ....Il.9.345.450.
Whose taper tops refulgent Gold adorns. ....Il.10.350.18.
And Steel well temper'd, and refulgent Gold. ....Il.10.452.23.
His solid Arms, refulgent, flame with Gold; ....Il.10.509.26.
Now rose refulgent from *Tithonus*' Bed; ....Il.11.2.34.
And one refulgent Ruin levells all. ....Il.11.204.44.
Tow'ring they rode in one refulgent Car: ....Il.11.426.53.
Shield touching Shield, a long-refulgent Row; ....Il.12.311.93.
Refulgent Arms his mighty Limbs infold, ...Il.13.38.106.
A Dart, whose Point with Brass refulgent shines, ...Il.15.568.218.
With Brass refulgent the broad Surface shin'd, ...Il.17.560.310.
Charg'd with refulgent Arms (a glorious Load) ....Il.18.173.330.
He sent refulgent to the Field of War, ...Il.18.280.335.
And great *Orion's* more refulgent Beam; ....Il.18.562.349.
Glow'd with refulgent Arms, and horrid War. ....Il.18.592.351.
And like the Moon, the broad refulgent Shield ....Il.19.402.388.
When Heav'ns refulgent Host appear in Arms? ....Il.20.159.400.
Refulgent Orb! Above his four-fold Cone ....Il.22.395.472.
Each in refulgent Arms his Limbs attires, ...Il.23.160.495.
Refulgent thro' the Cloud, no Eye could find ....Il.23.585.513.
Clad in refulgent Steel on either hand, ...Il.23.959.527.
Refulgent gliding o'er the sable Deeps. ....Il.24.102.539.
Twelve costly Carpets of refulgent Hue, ...Il.24.282.548.
A just proportion of refulgent Brass. ....Od.1.236.44.
Here ruddy brass and gold refulgent blaz'd; ....Od.2.382.79.
Ten equal talents of refulgent gold. ....Od.4.176.128.
Now rose refulgent from *Tithonus*' bed; ....Od.5.2.170.
And great *Orion's* more refulgent beam, ...Od.5.348.188.
Refulgent pedestals the walls surround, ...Od.7.128.241.
Draw forth and brandish thy refulgent sword, ...Od.10.350.361.
Rich in refulgent robes, and dropping balmy dews: ...Od.10.534.369.
Of brass, rich garments, and refulgent ore: ....Od.13.159.13.
Of steel elab'rate, and refulgent ore, ...Od.14.360.51.
Then o'er their limbs refulgent robes they threw, ...Od.17.102.136.
His royal hands; Each torch refulgent burns ....Od.18.392.186.
Four brazen helmets, eight refulgent spears, ...Od.22.128.292.

REFUND

Is to refund the Medals with the meat. ....5.DunB4.390.380.
I only must refund, of all his Train; ....Il.9.440.454.
Shall I, by waste undone, refund the dow'r? ....Od.2.154.69.

REFUNDED

The mast refunded on her refluent waves. ....Od.12.522.458.
The waste of years refunded in a day. ....Od.22.70.290.

REFUNDS

'Till *Jove* refunds his shameless daughter's dow'r. ...Od.8.358.282.
Thrice in dire thunders she refunds the tyde. ....Od.12.132.438.

REFUS'D

Not ancient Ladies when refus'd a Kiss, ...2.RL4.6.183.
Noah had refus'd it lodging in his Ark, ...4.JD4.26.27.
Great *Jove* refus'd, and tost in empty Air: ....Il.2.499.150.
For distant *Troy* refus'd to sail the Seas: ....Il.3.308.208.
Which *Jove* refus'd, and mingled with the Wind. ....Il.3.377.211.
To his high Seat; the Chief refus'd, and said. ....Il.11.791.71.
The King consented, but the Fates refus'd. ....Il.13.464.128.
This if refus'd, he bids thee timely weigh ....Il.15.200.204.
They urg'd in vain; the Chief refus'd, and swore. ....Il.23.52.489.
Ilus refus'd t'impart the baneful trust: ....Od.1.343.49.
Heav'n to my fleet refus'd a prosp'rous wind: ....Od.4.474.142.
I only in the bay refus'd to moor, ...Od.10.109.345.
Nor food nor wine refus'd: but since the day ....Od.16.152.110.
His *Ithaca* refus'd from fav'ring Fate, ...Od.19.327.210.
Of right the Queen refus'd a second Lord: ....Od.20.394.251.

REFUSE

For her, the Flocks refuse their verdant Food, ...1.PWi.37.91.
What Muse for *Granville* can refuse to sing? ....1.W-F.6.148.
Liv'd to refuse that Mistress half a Crown. ....4.HAdv.10.75.
"Dare you refuse him? *Curl* invites to dine, ...4.Arbu.53.100.
Nor cou'd'st thou, CHESTERFIELD! a tear refuse, ...5.DunB4.43.345.
For who to sing for *Sanger* could refuse? ....6.12.2.37.
This verse be thine, my friend, nor thou refuse ....6.52.1.156.
Refuse, or grant; for what has *Jove* to fear? ....Il.1.667.119.
Each aking Nerve refuse the Lance to throw, ...Il.2.464.149.
This if the *Phrygians* shall refuse to yield, ...Il.3.362.210.
Blush'd to refuse, and to accept it fear'd. ....Il.7.106.368.
When his tir'd Arms refuse the Axe to rear, ...Il.11.121.41.
If he refuse, then let him timely weigh ....Il.15.184.203.
The worst advice, the better to refuse. ....Il.18.364.339.
The worse advice, the better to refuse. ....Il.18.364A.339.

REFUSE (CONTINUED)

The partial Monarch may refuse the Prize; ....Il.20.219.403.

REFUTE

Our Ears refute the Censure of our Eyes. ....Il.3.288.207.

REFUTES

With decent pride refutes a public wrong: ....Od.8.270.278.

REGAIN

Lost Herds and Treasures, we by Arms regain, ...Il.9.528.459.
Tydides follow'd to regain his Lance; ....Il.11.461.54.
'Tis our own Vigour must the Dead regain; ....Il.17.798.319.
Be swift, be vig'rous, and regain the Prize! ....Il.23.524.510.
Like thee, have Talents to regain the Friend? ....Il.23.692.517.
And let me now regain the *Reithrian* port: ....Od.1.409.52.
And soon the known *Æolian* coast regain: ....Od.10.59.342.
Mean-time may'st thou with happiest speed regain ..Od.15.142.75.
Its wonted lustre let the floor regain; ....Od.20.187.242.
By arms avow'd *Ulysses* shall regain, ...Od.20.292.247.
Thus shall one stroke the glory lost regain: ....Od.22.278.300.

REGAIN'D

Leap'd from the Chanel, and regain'd the Land. ......Il.21.276.432.
So soon swift *Æthe* her lost Ground regain'd, ...Il.23.605.513.
'Till he the lines and *Argive* fleet regain'd ....Od.4.348.136.
A floating fragment of the wreck regain'd, ...Od.19.318.209.
The tides of life regain'd their azure course. ....Od.19.537.222.

REGAINS

Ere such a soul regains its peaceful state, ...2.ElAb.197.336.
The Goddess pleas'd, regains her natal skies. ....Od.20.67.235.
Soon as returning life regains its seat, ...Od.24.407.368.

REGAL

The Lillies blazing on the Regal Shield. ....1.W-F.306.178.
Is like a Clown in regal Purple drest; ....1.EOC.321.275.
And to the Regal Palace bent his way; ....1.TrSt.536.432.
Sublime in Regal State, *Adrastus* shone, ...1.TrSt.613.436.
What boots the Regal Circle on his Head, ...2.RL3.71.173.
Around him next the Regal Mantle threw, ...Il.2.54.129.
That, *Agamemnon's* regal Tent affords; ....Il.9.298.449.
And stain the Pavement of my regal Hall; ....Il.22.95.456.
And cast, far off, the regal Veils away. ....Il.22.513.477.
With Steps unwilling, to the regal Tent. ....Il.23.48.489.
Whose bones, defrauded of a regal tomb ....Od.1.208.42.
And soon restore him to his regal seat. ....Od.1.266.45.
In comely order to the regal dome. ....Od.3.499.112.
Hermione, t'extend the regal line; ....Od.4.18.121.
The splendid car roll'd slow in regal state: ....Od.4.28.121.
To spread the pall beneath the regal chair ....Od.4.163.128.
While to his regal bow'r the King ascends, ...Od.4.409.140.
Nor sight of natal shore, nor regal dome ....Od.4.641.149.
Where late in regal pomp *Thyestes* reign'd, ...Od.4.690.151.
The menial train the regal feast prepare; ....Od.4.840.158.
Swift on the regal dome descending right, ...Od.4.1055.167.
And wise *Alcinous* held the regal sway. ....Od.6.18.204.
The table next in regal order spread, ...Od.7.234.247.
Ulysses in the regal walls alone ....Od.7.311.251.
And brass high-heap'd amidst the regal dome; ....Od.14.361.51.
The regal presents of the *Spartan* Lord. ....Od.15.233.79.
Th' imperial scepter, and the regal bed: ....Od.16.134.109.
And regal robe with figur'd gold embost, ...Od.19.293.209.
'Till copious wealth might guard his regal state. ......Od.19.328.210.
His cornel javelin poiz'd, with regal port, ...Od.20.179.241.
When, moving slow, the regal form they view'd ......Od.24.31.348.

REGARD

To follow Nature, and regard his End. ....1.W-F.252.172.
In ev'ry Work regard the *Writer's End*, ...1.EOC.255.268.
Regard not then if Wit be *Old* or *New*, ...1.EOC.406.287.
Let not the Wise these slandrous Words regard, ...2.ChJM.49.17.
And therefore, Sir, as you regard your Rest, ...2.ChJM.184.23.
Ev'n such small Critics some regard may claim, ...4.Arbu.167.108.
Such piece-meal Critics some regard may claim, ...4.Arbu.167A.108.
Thee they regard alone; to thee they tend; ....6.23.17.73.
Thee we regard alone, to thee we tend; ....6.23.17A.73.
Nor blush, these studies thy regard engage; ....6.71.49.204.
Warm'd with some Virtue, some regard of Fame! ....Il.6.443.348.
Pronounce with Judgment, with Regard give ear, ...Il.9.134.438.
Regard in time, O Prince divinely brave! ....Il.9.326.450.
If no Regard thy suff'ring Country claim, ...Il.9.400.452.
Yet if my Years thy kind Regard engage, ...Il.10.198.10.
Regard thy Safety, and depart in Peace; ....Il.10.595.28.
At one Regard of his all-seeing Eye, ...Il.17.674.314.
And Heav'n regard me as I justly swear! ....Il.19.186.379.
A Life so grateful, still regard him dead. ....Il.24.516.557.
To *Jove*, (with stern regard the God replies,) ....Od.4.635.149.
She sheds celestial bloom, regard to draw, ...Od.8.21.263.
To bid me rev'rence or regard the Gods. ....Od.9.328.319.
By that regard a son his father owes; ....Od.16.323.121.
Eurynomè, regard the stranger friend: ....Od.19.118.198.
Piteous, regard a wretch consum'd with care! ....Od.20.146.240.
Since due regard must wait the Prince's friend, ...Od.20.360.249.
Regard thy self, the living, and the dead. ....Od.24.589.376.

REGARDED

Regarded ever by the just and sage. ....Od.3.67.89.

REGARDFUL

To her *Pelides*. With regardful Ear ....Il.1.287.100.
Regardful of the friendly dues I owe, ...Od.4.128.126.
Will my dread Sire his ear regardful deign, ...Od.6.69.208.

REGARDLESS
Regardless, furious he pursues his way; 1.TrES.19.450.
Regardless of our merit or default. 5.DunB4.486.389.
Dead, by regardless Vet'rans born on high 6.130.25.358.
Pernicious, wild, regardless of the Right. Il.5.1075.318.
Regardless, furious, he pursues his way; Il.12.363.94.
What Thoughts, regardless Chief! thy Breast employ? Il.16.659.270.
Defend my Life regardless of your own. Il.22.304.468.
Regardless of her son the Parent stood. Od.11.111.386.
Regardless of his years, abroad he lies, Od.11.236.393.
Perhaps she weds regardless of her fame, Od.16.75.106.
Chiefly derides: regardless of the cares Od.18.371.185.
I live regardless of my state-affairs: Od.19.157.200.

REGARDS
Succeeding Vanities she still regards, 2.RL1.53.149.
And one regards Itself, and one the Whole. 3.EOM3.316.126.
G[owe]r, C[obha]m, B[athurs]t, pay thee due regards, 4.1740.23.333.
Such quick regards his sparkling eyes bestow; Od.4.201.129.
To whom with stern regards: O insolence, Od.18.20.167.

REGENT
A godless Regent tremble at a Star? 3.Ep1.149.28.
So spoke th' imperial Regent of the Skies; Il.8.433.418.
Assist him, *Jove!* thou regent of the skies! Od.2.42.62.
The regent of his *Cephalenian* herd: Od.20.268.246.

REGICIDE
Urge the bold traitor to the Regicide? Od.1.48.32.

REGION
Survey the Region, and confess her Home! 1.W-F.256.172.
In what new Region is *Ulysses* tost? 1.TrUl.75.468.
No cheerful Breeze this sullen Region knows, 2.RL4.19.184.
The dire Report thro' ev'ry Region flies: 2.TemF.335.280.
And say what Region is our destin'd Seat? 6.65.6A.192.
Along the Region runs a deaf'ning Sound; Il.2.119.133.
(The Region stretch'd beneath his mighty Shade) Il.2.921.167.
And wide around the floated Region fills. Il.2.1033.171.
A gen'ral Shout that all the Region rends. Il.4.491.244.
And loud Acclaim the starry Region rends. Il.16.353.256.
And wide around the floated Region fills, Il.21.176.428.
On what new region is *Ulysses* tost? Od.6.140.214.
His giant voice the ecchoing region fills: Od.9.374.321.
Thither to haste, the region to explore, Od.10.177.349.
I view'd the coast, a region flat and low; Od.10.222.351.
Dire is the region, dismal is the way! Od.11.193.391.
Th' aereal region now grew warm with day, Od.12.210.442.
In what new region is *Ulysses* tost? Od.13.242.17.

REGIONS
But see the Man who spacious Regions gave 1.W-F.79.157.
But see the Man whose spacious Regions gave 1.W-F.79A.157.
To the bright Regions of the rising Day; 1.W-F.388.189.
And Seas but join the Regions they divide; 1.W-F.400.191.
Ye Gods that o'er the gloomy Regions reign 1.TrSt.81.413.
Thou know'st those Regions my Protection claim, 1.TrSt.352.424.
And o'er th' infernal Regions void of day, 6.65.4.192.
Yet will he boast of many Regions known, 6.96v.13.280.
Since Earth's wide Regions, Heav'n's unmeasur'd Height, Il.2.574.155.
From those rich Regions where *Cephisus* leads Il.2.622.157.
From those far Regions where the Sun refines Il.2.1044.172.
Shouts, as he past, the crystal Regions rend, Il.11.445.54.
Deep in the liquid Regions lies a Cave, Il.13.50.107.
Deep in the dismal Regions of the Dead, Il.20.83.397.
Or the fam'd Race thro' all the Regions known, Il.23.421.506.
Thro' *Phrygia* once, and foreign Regions known, Il.24.245.546.
Thro' regions fatten'd with the flows of *Nile.* Od.4.100.124.
The seat of Gods, the regions mild of peace, Od.6.49.207.
In distant regions the *Phæacian* fame: Od.8.100.267.
Say from what city, from what regions tost, Od.8.601.294.
And what inhabitants those regions boast? Od.8.602.294.
But say thro' what waste regions hast thou stray'd, Od.8.625.296.
These to the north and night's dark regions run, Od.9.25.303.
Black as these regions, to *Tiresias* bleed. Od.11.42.381.
What angry Gods to these dark regions led Od.11.118.386.
Fly the dire regions, and revere the Gods! Od.12.329.447.
To other regions is his virtue known. Od.13.489.29.
To the pure regions of eternal light. Od.15.52.72.
When milder regions breathe a vernal breeze, Od.19.239.205.
Thus in the regions of eternal shade Od.24.232.359.

REGISTERS
The registers of fate expanded lie) Od.20.91.237.

REGRET
But still the *Worst* with most Regret commend, 1.EOC.518.296.
Divine *Sarpedon* with Regret beheld 1.TrES.119.454.
With due Regret I view my Vices past, 2.ChJM.92.19.
How often, hope, despair, resent, regret, 2.ElAb.199.336.
To covet flying, and regret when lost: 3.Ep2.234.69.
Saw nothing to regret, or there to fear; 6.112.8.318.
Saw nothing to regret, Nor there to fear; 6.112.8A.318.
Divine *Sarpedon* with Regret beheld Il.12.473.99.
Transfix'd with deep Regret, they view o'erthrown Il.16.673.270.
Transfix'd with deep Regret, they view'd o'erthrown Il.16.673A.270.
Sees with Regret unhappy Mortals die. Il.20.32.394.

REGRETS
Nor here regrets the Hell she left below. 1.TrSt.143A.415.
Nor here regrets the Hell she late forsook. 1.TrSt.143.416.

REGRETTED
Alike regretted in the Dust he lies, Il.9.420.453.

REGULAR
The *Whole* at once is *Bold,* and *Regular.* 1.EOC.252.268.
Men, Women, Clergy, Regular and Lay. 2.ChWB.354.74.
Comets are regular, and *Clodio* plain. 3.Ep1.209A.33.
Comets are regular, and Wharton plain. 3.Ep1.209.33.
But soft—by regular approach—not yet— 3.Ep4.129.149.
And more Diverting still than Regular, 6.19.26.63.
So just thy skill, so regular my rage. 6.52.12.156.
Confus'dly regular, the moving Maze: Il.18.692.357.
And bore it, regular from space to space: Od.23.202.333.

REGULARLY
Correctly cold, and *regularly low,* 1.EOC.240.267.

REGULATE
Correct old Time, and regulate the Sun; 3.EOM2.22.57.

REHEARSAL
To some a dry Rehearsal was assign'd, 4.Arbu.243.113.
There's a Rehearsal, Sir, exact at One.— 4.2HE2.97.171.

REHEARSALS
Nor at Rehearsals sweat, and mouth'd, and cry'd, 4.Arbu.227.112.
To Theatres, and to Rehearsals throng, 4.2HE1.173.209.
To Op'ra's, Theatres, Rehearsals throng, 4.2HE1.173A.209.

REHEARSE
Rehearse, ye Muses, what your selves inspir'd. 1.PAu.56.84.
Who slow, and leisurely rehearse, 6.10.13.24.

REIGN
Were equal Crimes in a Despotick Reign; 1.W-F.58.154.
Whose Care, like hers, protects the Sylvan Reign, 1.W-F.163.165.
Be mine the Blessings of a peaceful Reign. 1.W-F.366.186.
Oh stretch thy Reign, fair *Peace!* from Shore to Shore, 1.W-F.407.192.
The following Licence of a Foreign Reign 1.EOC.544.300.
T'admit your offspring in your watry reign! 1.TrPA.143.371.
The fair *Pomona* flourish'd in his Reign; 1.TrVP.1.377.
Th'Alternate Reign destroy'd by Impious Arms, 1.TrSt.2.409.
Oh bless thy *Rome* with an Eternal Reign, 1.TrSt.33.411.
Yet stay, great *Cæsar!* and vouchsafe to reign 1.TrSt.43.411.
Ye Gods that o'er the gloomy Regions reign 1.TrSt.81.413.
Taught by thy self to win the promis'd Reign: 1.TrSt.94.414.
And impotent Desire to Reign alone, 1.TrSt.180.418.
But scarce subsisted to the Second Reign. 1.TrSt.199.418.
What Woes attend this inauspicious Reign? 1.TrSt.235.420.
Can this Imperious Lord forget to Reign, 1.TrSt.257.421.
Fortune's tame Fools, and Slaves in ev'ry Reign! 1.TrSt.264.421.
For this, my Brother of the watry Reign 1.TrSt.312.423.
The promis'd Empire, and Alternate Reign: 1.TrSt.426.427.
O'er all his Bosom secret Transports reign, 1.TrSt.579.434.
Goddess of Shades, beneath whose gloomy Reign 1.TrSt.583.434.
O'er all his Bosom sacred Transports reign, 1.TrSt.579A.434.
Why boast we, *Glaucus,* our extended Reign, 1.TrES.27.450.
Far from the *Lycian* Shores, his happy Native Reign. 1.TrES.260.459.
Nor those, that plac'd beneath his utmost Reign, 1.TrUl.120.470.
Whose now neglected Altars, in thy Reign 1.TrUl.230.473.
Whose Reign Indulgent God, says Holy Writ, 2.ChJM.690.48.
Two Principles in human nature reign; 3.EOM2.53.62.
The state of Nature was the reign of God: 3.EOM3.148.107.
"And these for ever, tho' a Monarch reign, 3.EOM3.187.112.
Like good Aurelius let him reign, or bleed 3.EOM4.235.148.
Flatt'rers and Bigots ev'n in *Louis'* Reign? 4.HS1.112.15.
As in the gentle Reign of My Queen *Anne.* 4.HOde1.4.151.
As in the glorious Reign of My Queen *Anne.* 4.HOde1.4A.151.
150.As in the glorious Reign of good Queen *Anne.* 4.HOde1.4B.151.
You'd think no Fools disgrac'd the former Reign, 4.2HE1.127.205.
My son! the promis'd land expects thy reign. 5.DunA1.246.92.
Then stretch thy sight o'er all her rising reign, 5.DunA3.57.155.
This fav'rite Isle, long sever'd from her reign, 5.DunA3.117.160.
These, Fate reserv'd to grace thy reign divine, 5.DunA3.273.183.
Beneath his reign, shall Eusden wear the bays, 5.DunA3.319.186.
Lo! the great Anarch's ancient reign restor'd, 5.DunA3.339.192.
My son! the promis'd land expects thy reign. 5.DunB1.292.291.
Then stretch thy sight o'er all her rising reign, 5.DunB3.65.323.
This fav'rite Isle, long sever'd from her reign, 5.DunB3.125.325.
These Fate reserv'd to grace thy reign divine, 5.DunB3.275.333.
Joy to great Chaos! let Division reign: 5.DunB4.54.346.
"Oh (cry'd the Goddess) for some pedant Reign! 5.DunB4.175.358.
Which as it dies, or lives, we fall, or reign: 5.DunB4.186.360.
And seeks a surer State, and courts thy gentle Reign. 6.8.15.18.
And Artichoaks reign in their Stead. 6.10.108.27.
Deny'd to reign, I stood resolv'd to die, 6.20.13.66.
The only wretch beneath thy happy reign! 6.20.51.67.
Should such a One, too fond to Reign alone, 6.49iii.11A.142.
Should such a man, too fond to Reign alone, 6.49iii.11B.142.
Should such a One, resolv'd to Reign alone, 6.49iii.11C.142.
Should such a man, be fond to Reign alone, 6.49iii.11D.142.
On thy third Reign look down; disclose our Fate, 6.65.5.192.
But our Great Turks in wit must reign alone 6.82ix(a).1.234.
Where reign our Sires! There, to thy Countrey's Shame, 6.96iii.7.274.
In [george]'s Reign these fruitless lines were writ, 6.106iii.2.307.
Thy happy Reign all other Discord quells; 6.131i.5.360.
That Wrath which hurl'd to *Pluto's* gloomy Reign Il.1.3.82.
And Walls of Rocks, secure my native Reign, Il.1.204.96.
Where aged *Ocean* holds his wat'ry Reign, Il.1.469.110.
When the bright Partner of his awful Reign, Il.1.518.113.
And now the Mark of *Agamemnon's* Reign, Il.2.135.134.
Amidst the Glories of so bright a Reign, Il.2.275.140.
And singly mad, asperse the Sov'reign Reign. Il.2.309.142.
And *Ægion,* and *Adrastus'* ancient Reign; Il.2.689.159.
Proud of his Host, unrival'd in his Reign, Il.2.699.159.
Shall then, O Tyrant of th' Æthereal Reign! Il.4.35.222.
Pale *Flight* around, and dreadful *Terror* reign; Il.4.500.244.
Th' imperial Partner of the heav'nly Reign; Il.5.482.291.
Add one more Ghost to *Pluto's* gloomy Reign. Il.5.813.305.

REIGN (CONTINUED)
With half the Honours of his ample Reign. ... Il.6.238.337.
For such I reign, unbounded and above; ... Il.8.33.397.
There shall he reign with Pow'r and Justice crown'd, ... Il.9.205.442.
There shalt thou reign with Pow'r and Justice crown'd, ... Il.9.392.452.
The strong *Dolopians* thenceforth own'd my Reign, ... Il.9.602.464.
In Winter's bleak, uncomfortable Reign, ... Il.12.333.93.
Why boast we, *Glaucus!* our extended Reign, ... Il.12.371.95.
As warring Winds, in *Sirius'* sultry Reign, ... Il.13.424.126.
O'er spacious *Crete,* and her bold Sons I reign, ... Il.13.568.133.
By his fierce Stepdame from his Father's Reign ... Il.13.873.147.
Of upper Heav'n to *Jove* resign'd the Reign, ... Il.14.235.172.
The Sire of all, old *Ocean,* owns my Reign, ... Il.14.279.175.
The rev'rend *Ocean* and grey *Tethys* reign, ... Il.14.343.179.
Command the Sea-God to his watry Reign: ... Il.15.62.197.
Due to my Conquest of her Father's Reign; ... Il.16.78.238.
Far from the *Lycian* Shores, his happy native Reign. ... Il.16.565.266.
(*Asius* the Great, who held his wealthy Reign ... Il.17.656.313.
Pursu'd the Pleasures of the wat'ry Reign; ... Il.18.110.328.
While the long Night extends her sable Reign, ... Il.18.365.339.
And glad his Eyes with his paternal Reign, ... Il.19.354.387.
Ev'n * He whose Trident sways the watry Reign, ... Il.20.19.393.
On great *Æneas* shall devolve the Reign, ... Il.20.355.408.
Ten Days were past, since in his Father's Reign ... Il.21.50.424.
Mindless of Food, or Love whose pleasing Reign ... Il.24.165.542.
Extended *Phrygia* own'd thy ample Reign, ... Il.24.685.565.
Dulichium, and *Zacynthus'* sylvan reign: ... Od.1.318.48.
May *Jove* delay thy reign, and cumber late ... Od.1.493.56.
At least, the sceptre lost, I still shou'd reign ... Od.1.507.56.
By all the deathless pow'rs that reign above, ... Od.2.73.64.
Since he who like a father held his reign, ... Od.2.265.74.
Imploring all the Gods that reign above, ... Od.2.472.84.
Attend the nymph to *Phthia's* distant reign. ... Od.4.12.121.
Where my *Ulysses* and his race might reign, ... Od.4.237.130.
The delegate of *Neptune's* watry reign. ... Od.4.522.145.
Range the dark bounds of *Pluto's* dreary reign. ... Od.4.666.150.
Long shall the race of just *Arcesius* reign, ... Od.4.997.164.
Of *Thessaly* wide stretch'd his ample reign:) ... Od.4.1052.167.
Abandon'd, banish'd from his native reign, ... Od.5.21.172.
To all that share the blessings of your reign, ... Od.7.197.245.
So reign for ever on your country's breast, ... Od.7.204.246.
Remote from Gods or men she holds her reign, ... Od.7.330.252.
Thence to the Queen. O partner of our reign, ... Od.8.459.288.
How sweet the products of a peaceful reign? ... Od.9.3.298.
Their parent's pride, and pleasure of their reign. ... Od.10.8.339.
To calm the God that holds the wat'ry reign; ... Od.11.159.389.
O'er proud *Iölcos Pelias* stretch'd his reign, ... Od.11.311.397.
Reign the Twin-gods, the fav'rite sons of *Jove.* ... Od.11.374.401.
Than reign the scepter'd monarch of the dead. ... Od.11.600.413.
Beneath, *Charybdis* holds her boist'rous reign ... Od.12.129.438.
And lo! the night begins her gloomy reign, ... Od.12.339.448.
Now far the night advanc'd her gloomy reign, ... Od.12.367.449.
Oh all ye blissful pow'rs that reign above! ... Od.12.438.452.
Nor those that plac'd beneath his utmost reign ... Od.13.287.19.
Whose now-neglected altars, in thy reign, ... Od.13.397.26.
None match'd this hero's wealth, of all who reign ... Od.14.117.41.
O'er seas convey'd me to my native reign: ... Od.16.253.117.
Retire we instant to our native reign, ... Od.16.404.125.
Who o'er *Dulichium* stretch'd his spacious reign, ... Od.16.410.126.
There terrible, affright the dogs, and reign ... Od.18.126.172.
Ulysses will assert his rightful reign. ... Od.19.353.211.
Partake his councils, and assist his reign? ... Od.19.618.226.
Thy wond'ring eyes shall view: his rightful reign ... Od.20.291.247.
You reign, of this imperial dome possest. ... Od.20.402.251.
The lost *Ulysses* to his native reign? ... Od.21.202.269.
Cyllenius now to *Pluto's* dreary reign ... Od.24.1.345.
Far from his friends, and from his native reign, ... Od.24.340.365.

REIGN'D
Thus long succeeding Criticks justly reign'd, ... 1.EOC.681.316.
Yet latent life thro' her new branches reign'd, ... 1.TrFD.102.390.
And reign'd the short-liv'd Tyrant of his Breast; ... 2.ChJM.231.25.
When *Richard Cœur de Lyon* reign'd, ... 6.79.9.218.
Two Ages o'er his native Realm he reign'd, ... Il.1.335.104.
Where once *Eurytus* in proud Triumph reign'd, ... Il.2.885.166.
He won, and flourish'd where *Adrastus* reign'd: ... Il.14.137.164.
In *Asius'* Shape, who reign'd by *Sangar's* Flood; ... Il.16.874.277.
Could blame this Scene; such Rage, such Horror reign'd; ... Il.17.460.305.
Where late in regal pomp *Thyestes* reign'd; ... Od.4.690.151.
Thro' the fond bosom where she reign'd ador'd! ... Od.11.534.409.
Alone *Laertes* reign'd *Arcesius'* heir, ... Od.16.125.108.

REIGNS
While in thy Heart Eternal Winter reigns. ... 1.PSu.22.73.
Thy *Realm* for ever lasts! thy own *Messiah* reigns! ... 1.Mes.108.122.
And Peace and Plenty tell, a STUART reigns. ... 1.W-F.42.152.
And sacred Silence reigns, and universal Peace. ... 1.TrSt.291.422.
How quaint an Appetite in Women reigns! ... 2.ChWB.259.69.
Thus her blind Sister, fickle *Fortune* reigns, ... 2.TemF.296.278.
And ever-musing melancholy reigns; ... 2.ElAb.3.319.
And Nero reigns a Titus, if he will. ... 3.EOM2.198.79.
Still Dunce the second reigns like Dunce the first? ... 5.DunA1.6.61.
Still Dunce the second reigns like Dunce the first; ... 5.DunB1.6.269.
Another Phœbus, thy own Phœbus reigns, ... 5.DunB4.61.347.
Then pompous *Silence* reigns, and stills the noisie Laws. ... 6.8.33.18.
There Nature reigns, and Passion void of Art, ... 6.33.9.99.
Here Nature reigns, and Passion void of Art, ... 6.33.9A.99.
Here dulness reigns, with mighty wings outspread, ... 6.106iv.11.307.
Within these walls inglorious silence reigns. ... Od.2.34.62.
Of utmost earth, where *Rhadamanthus* reigns. ... Od.4.766.155.
Prevent the rage of him who reigns above, ... Od.5.187.180.
Far from the rest, and solitary reigns, ... Od.9.218.314.
Say if my sire, the rev'rend *Peleus* reigns ... Od.11.605.413.
Fam'd for the dance, where *Menelaus* reigns; ... Od.15.2.67.
Nor harbours Charity where Riot reigns: ... Od.15.406.89.
Where *Nestor,* shepherd of his people, reigns. ... Od.17.125.137.

REIGNS (CONTINUED)
Or dwells humanity where riot reigns? ... Od.17.391.150.
Eurynome! to go where riot reigns ... Od.18.195.176.
Ulysses lives, thy own *Ulysses* reigns: ... Od.23.28.320.
Restore thee safe, since my *Ulysses* reigns. ... Od.23.276.336.

REIN
The rest move on, obedient to the Rein; ... 1.TrES.279.460.
That gentle *Gulliver* might guide my Rein! ... 6.96iii.34.275.
The Charge once made, no Warrior turn the Rein, ... Il.4.350.237.
Haste, seize the Whip, and snatch the guiding Rein; ... Il.5.284.280.
Shall hear the Rein, and answer to thy Hand. ... Il.5.291.281.
Fix'd to the Chariot by the straiten'd Rein; ... Il.5.325.282.
Then mounting on his Car, resum'd the Rein, ... Il.5.405.286.
And to her Hand commits the golden Rein: ... Il.5.454.290.
These late obey'd *Æneas'* guiding Rein; ... Il.8.137.404.
His opening Hand in Death forsakes the Rein; ... Il.8.153.405.
Then bids *Cebriones* direct the Rein, ... Il.8.385.416.
They shook with Fear, and drop'd the silken Rein; ... Il.11.168.42.
He mounts the Car, and gives his Squire the Rein: ... Il.11.352.50.
The rest move on, obedient to the Rein; ... Il.16.584.267.
The Charioteer, while yet he held the Rein, ... Il.16.899.278.
In vain *Automedon* now shakes the Rein, ... Il.17.488.307.
His dying Hand forgets the falling Rein: ... Il.17.700.314.
And now contracts, or now extends the Rein, ... Il.23.397.506.
Erect with Ardour, pois'd upon the Rein, ... Il.23.449.508.
He flies more fast, and throws up all the Rein. ... Il.23.510.510.
I well discern him, as he shakes the Rein, ... Il.23.562.511.
Charg'd with the Gifts; *Idæus* holds the Rein, ... Il.24.400.552.
When to his lust *Ægysthus* gave the rein, ... Od.1.45.31.
And order mules obedient to the rein; ... Od.6.42.207.
The car prepare, the mules incessant rein. ... Od.6.86.209.
With skill the virgin guides th' embroider'd rein, ... Od.6.379.230.
Curbs the proud steed, reluctant to the rein: ... Od.11.370.401.
Ye gave your sons, your lawless sons the rein, ... Od.24.522.373.

REIN'D
Who bravest fought, or rein'd the noblest Steeds? ... Il.2.925.167.
And, rein'd with Gold, his foaming Steeds before. ... Il.5.448.289.
She ceas'd, and *Juno* rein'd the Steeds with Care; ... Il.8.464.419.
She ceas'd, and *Juno* rein'd her Steeds with Care; ... Il.8.464A.419.
His prostrate Master, rein'd the Steeds around; ... Il.20.566.418.
Rein'd the rough storms, and calm'd the tossing floods: ... Od.12.470.454.

REINS
But rend the Reins, and bound a diff'rent way, ... 1.TrSt.188.418.
Receiv'd the Reins of Absolute Command, ... 2.ChWB.431.78.
High on his Car he shakes the flowing Reins, ... Il.2.1016.171.
Then seiz'd the Reins his gentle Steeds to guide, ... Il.3.388.211.
But left *Eurymedon* the Reins to guide; ... Il.4.262.233.
From his numb'd Hand the Iv'ry-studded Reins ... Il.5.713.301.
And golden Reins th' immortal Coursers hold. ... Il.5.901.309.
She snatch'd the Reins, she lash'd with all her Force, ... Il.5.1034.316.
The wanton Courser thus, with Reins unbound, ... Il.6.652.359.
Scarce had his Falchion cut the Reins, and freed ... Il.8.109.403.
He drop'd the Reins; and shook with sacred Dread, ... Il.8.167.406.
And leads them, fasten'd by the silver Reins; ... Il.10.583.28.
This having reach'd, his brass-hoof'd Steeds he reins, ... Il.13.36.106.
As when the pamper'd Steed, with Reins unbound, ... Il.15.298.208.
The startling Steeds, and shook his eager Reins. ... Il.15.525.217.
And dropp'd the flowing Reins. Him 'twixt the Jaws ... Il.16.492.262.
With foaming Coursers, and with loosen'd Reins. ... Il.16.838.276.
And stretch'd in Death, forgets the guiding Reins! ... Il.16.937.279.
But swift *Automedon* with loosned Reins ... Il.16.1046.283.
Now plies the Jav'lin, now directs the Reins: ... Il.17.533.309.
Or holds their Fury in suspended Reins: ... Il.17.543.309.
Snatches the Reins, and vaults into the Seat. ... Il.17.549.309.
The Iv'ry studded Reins, return'd behind, ... Il.19.430.389.
Experienc'd *Nestor* gives his Son the Reins, ... Il.23.371.505.
Experienc'd *Nestor* gives the Son the Reins, ... Il.23.371A.505.
But urge the Right, and give him all the Reins; ... Il.23.409.506.
Perchance the Reins forsook the Driver's Hand, ... Il.23.548.511.
One lash'd the Coursers, while one rul'd the Reins. ... Il.23.738.519.
And hung with Ringlets to receive the Reins; ... Il.24.336.550.
Then fix'd a Ring the running Reins to guide, ... Il.24.339.550.
And snatch'd the Reins, and whirl'd the Lash around: ... Il.24.542.558.
With hasty hand the ruling reins he drew: ... Od.3.612.117.
Now mounting the gay seat, the silken reins ... Od.6.95.209.
A stag's torn hide is lapt around his reins: ... Od.13.504.30.

REITHRIAN
And let me now regain the *Reithrian* port: ... Od.1.409.52.

REITHRUS
At *Reithrus,* and secure at anchor rides;. ... Od.1.238.44.

REJECT
Fix on *Vertumnus,* and reject the rest. ... 1.TrVP.82.380.
Cou'd make a gentle *Belle* reject a *Lord?* ... 2.RL1.10.145.
Seems to reject him, tho' she grants his Pray'r. ... 2.RL4.80.190.
Fir'd that the House reject him, "'Sdeath I'll print it ... 4.Arbu.61.100.
In vain, bad Rhimers all mankind reject, ... 4.2HE2.153.175.
Yourself for Goose reject Crow Quill, ... 6.10.43.25.
Who Heaven's Lore reject for brutish Sense; ... 6.137.7.373.
As this Advice ye practise, or reject, ... Il.7.426.385.
Suppress thy Impulse, nor reject Advice. ... Il.24.368.551.
Obdurate to reject the stranger-guest; ... Od.4.40.122.

REJECTED
Like these, rejected by the scornful Dame. ... 1.TrVP.28.378.
The Peace rejected, but the Truce obtain'd. ... Il.7.493.388.
That wise Advice rejected with Disdain, ... Il.22.144.459.
Their Charms rejected for the *Cyprian* Queen. ... Il.24.41.537.
The Sire denies, and Kings rejected mourn. ... Od.11.352.399.

REJECTS
Rejects Mankind, is by some *Sylph* embrac'd: ....2.RL1.68.151.
Oft she rejects, but never once offends. ....2.RL2.12.160.
Then thus the King of Kings rejects the Peace: ....Il.7.482.388.
Neptune with Wrath rejects the rash Design: ....Il.8.254.409.
When Man rejects the humble Suit they make, ...Il.9.633.465.
He stands relentless, and rejects 'em all. ....Il.9.698.468.

REJOIC'D
Rejoic'd, of all the num'rous *Greeks,* to see ....Il.23.747.520.

REJOICE
No more the Forests ring, or Groves rejoice; ....1.W-F.278.174.
But hark! the Groves rejoice, the Forest rings! ....1.W-F.281.174.
Much in his Prudence did our Knight rejoice, ...2.ChJM.250.26.
In Summer-Days like Grashoppers rejoice, ...Il.3.201.200.
Hear, and rejoice on *Pluto's* dreary Coast; ....Il.23.26.488.
Blind they rejoice, tho' now, ev'n now they fall; ....Od.2.321.76.
And warbling sweet, makes earth and heav'n rejoice. ....Od.6.116.211.

REJOICING
The *Gnome* rejoicing bears her Gifts away, ...2.RL4.87.190.
Surveys th' Inscription with rejoicing Eyes, ...Il.7.225.375.
The *Greeks* rejoicing bless the friendly Shade. ....Il.8.608.425.
The conscious Swains, rejoicing in the Sight, ...Il.8.697.428.
They sit, rejoicing in her Aid divine, ...Il.10.679.32.

REJOIN
Meet and rejoin me, in the pensive Grott. ....4.2HE2.209.179.
Meet and rejoin me, in my pensive Grott. ....4.2HE2.209A.179.

REJOIN'D
O still the same *Ulysses!* she rejoin'd, ...1.TrUl.166.471.
Far hence be *Bacchus'* Gifts (the Chief rejoin'd) ....Il.6.329.342.
Oh first of *Greeks!* (his noble Foe rejoin'd) ....Il.7.349.381.
O Son of *Neleus* (thus the King rejoin'd) ....Il.10.94.6.
Then thus (the Godlike *Diomed* rejoin'd) ....Il.10.283.14.
Father! not so, (sage *Ithacus* rejoin'd) ....Il.10.654.31.
The reeking Javelin, and rejoin'd his Friends. ....Il.13.674.137.
Great is the Profit (thus the God rejoin'd) ....Il.15.230.206.
O first of *Greeks* (*Ulysses* thus rejoin'd) ....Il.19.215.381.
Thus he. *Idomeneus* incens'd rejoin'd: ....Il.23.564.512.
Are true, my Son! (the godlike Sire rejoin'd) ....Il.24.460.555.
(The mournful Monarch thus rejoin'd again) ....Il.24.496.557.
The counsel of my friend (the Youth rejoin'd) ....Od.1.399.51.
To him experienc'd *Nestor* thus rejoin'd. ....Od.3.125.91.
That chief (rejoin'd the God) his race derives ....Od.4.751.154.
My quick return, young *Ithacus* rejoin'd, ...Od.4.811.156.
Let no such thought (with modest grace rejoin'd ....Od.7.281.249.
O envy'd youth! (the smiling Youth rejoin'd,) ....Od.8.377.284.
O! could this arm (I thus aloud rejoin'd) ....Od.9.611.332.
O still the same *Ulysses!* she rejoin'd, ...Od.13.333.23.
Thus spoke the faithful swain, and thus rejoin'd ....Od.14.171.43.
(Thus good *Eumæus* with a sigh rejoin'd) ....Od.14.396.54.
Well hast thou spoke (rejoin'd th' attentive swain) ....Od.14.576.64.
Ah! doubt not our report (the Prince rejoin'd) ....Od.15.172.76.
Alas! (*Eumæus* with a sigh rejoin'd) ....Od.15.344.86.
Succeed the Omen, Gods! (the youth rejoin'd) ....Od.15.577.98.
Sufficient they (*Telemachus* rejoin'd) ....Od.16.284.118.
My cause of coming told, he thus rejoin'd; ....Od.17.136.138.
Succeed those omens Heav'n! (the Queen rejoin'd) ....Od.17.186.140.
Just thy advice, (the prudent Chief rejoin'd) ....Od.17.216.142.
Not *Argus* so (*Eumæus* thus rejoin'd) ....Od.17.376.150.
To whom the hospitable swain rejoin'd: ....Od.17.458.155.
Shame suits but ill. *Eumæus* thus rejoin'd: ....Od.17.659.164.
Their gifts the Gods resum'd (the Queen rejoin'd.) ....Od.19.144.199.
Pleas'd with his wise reply, the Queen rejoin'd: ....Od.19.403.214.
Then thus rejoin'd the dame, devoid of fear: ....Od.19.575.224.
Hard is the task, and rare, the Queen rejoin'd, ...Od.19.654.227.
To whom with grace serene the Queen rejoin'd: ....Od.19.687.229.
Just is thy kind reproach (the chief rejoin'd) ....Od.20.47.234.
Tax not, (the heav'n-illumin'd Seer rejoin'd) ....Od.20.437.254.
(Respectful thus *Eurymachus* rejoin'd) ....Od.21.346.276.
O my *Telemachus!* the Queen rejoin'd, ...Od.23.107.325.
(Thus *Agamemnon's* kingly shade rejoin'd) ....Od.24.52.350.

REJOIND
Can then the Sons of *Greece* (the Sage rejoind) ....Il.11.800.71.

REJOINDER
Rejoinder to the churl the King disdain'd, ...Od.20.231.244.

REJOINS
Mean time the Lyre rejoins the sprightly lay; ....Od.1.531.57.
Young and mature! the Monarch thus rejoins, ...Od.4.281.132.
What mutters he? (*Melanthius* sharp rejoins) ....Od.17.294.146.

REJOYCE
If not so pleas'd, at Council-board rejoyce, ...4.1HE6.34.239.

REJOYCING
And now, rejoycing in the prosp'rous gales, ...Od.5.343.188.
A land rejoycing, and a people blest. ....Od.9.6.301.
Rejoycing round, some morsel to receive, ...Od.10.248.354.

REJOYN
rejoyn Ye Kindred Souls, and flame on high, ...6.109.16Z1.314.
And how, dread *Circe!* (furious I rejoyn) ....Od.10.399.363.

REJOYN'D
While yet he spoke, *Leocritus* rejoyn'd: ....Od.2.275.74.
To whom the martial Goddess thus rejoyn'd. ....Od.3.33.87.
O son of woe, the pensive shade rejoyn'd, ...Od.11.259.394.
Touch'd at her words, the mournful Queen rejoyn'd, ...Od.23.11.319.
Ah no! with sighs *Penelope* rejoyn'd, ...Od.23.59.321.

REKINDL'D
Mean-time rekindl'd at the royal charms, ...Od.1.465.54.

REKINDLED
His Soul rekindled, and awak'd his Worth. ....Il.11.406.53.
O might the lamp of life rekindled burn, ...Od.11.609.413.

REKINDLES
My Rage rekindles, and my Soul's on flame, ...Il.9.760.472.

RELAPSE
But grant I may relapse, for want of Grace, ...4.2HE2.88.171.

RELATE
Let me (if tears and grief permit) relate ....1.TrFD.5.385.
I saw, unhappy! what I now relate, ...1.TrFD.53.388.
What Hero, *Clio!* wilt thou first relate? ....1.TrSt.61.412.
To him *Apollo* (wondrous to relate!) ....1.TrSt.545.433.
Relate your Fortunes, while the friendly Night ....1.TrSt.794.443.
Nothing is foreign: Parts relate to whole; ....3.EOM3.21.94.
How parts relate to parts, or they to whole, ...5.DunB4.235.366.
O Muse! relate (for you can tell alone, ...5.DunB4.619.405.
Relate, who first, who last resign'd to rest; ....5.DunB4.621.406.
Lik'd or not lik'd, his Words we must relate, ...Il.9.739.471.
Celestial Muse! and to our world relate. ....Od.1.14.29.
Where the free guest, unnoted, might relate ....Od.1.177.41.
Your Father's friend. *Laertes* can relate ....Od.1.243.44.
The sorrows of your inmost soul relate; ....Od.1.356.49.
For lo! my words no fancy'd woes relate: ....Od.2.197.71.
Relate, if business, or the thirst of gain ....Od.3.86.90.
Antilochus—what more can I relate? ....Od.3.139.92.
Curious to know, and willing to relate. ....Od.3.227.96.
By what strange fraud *Ægysthus* wrought, relate, ...Od.3.310.101.
But prostrate I implore, oh King! relate ....Od.4.435.140.
Learn what I heard the sea-born Seer relate, ...Od.4.471.142.
Thy patient ear hath heard me long relate ....Od.4.799.156.
Relate, *Antinous* cries, devoid of guile, ...Od.4.866.159.
The long, the mournful series to relate, ...Od.7.324.251.
And oh, what first, what last shall I relate, ...Od.9.15.301.
Full oft the Monarch urg'd me to relate ....Od.10.15.340.
But ah! relate our lost companions death. ....Od.10.500.367.
Unerring truths, oh man, my lips relate; ....Od.11.170.390.
Then curious she commands me to relate ....Od.12.43.431.
Sincere from whence begun your course relate, ...Od.14.216.45.
Ere yet to *Nestor* I the tale relate: ....Od.15.235.79.
There in *Ulysses'* roof I may relate ....Od.15.332.85.
Relate the farther fortunes of your Lord; ....Od.15.369.87.
Then what assistant pow'rs you boast, relate, ...Od.16.278.118.
Learn what I heard the *sea-born Seer relate, ...Od.17.160.139.
Divide discourse, in turn thy birth relate: ....Od.19.185.200.
A visionary thought I'll now relate, ...Od.19.625.226.
Attest, oh *Jove,* the truth I now relate! ....Od.20.286.247.
O King of men! I faithful shall relate ....Od.24.144.355.

RELATED
To whom related, or by whom begot; ....2.Elegy.72.368.

RELATES
First he relates, how sinking to the chin, ...5.DunA2.307.139.
First he relates, how sinking to the chin, ...5.DunB2.331.313.
(How my Heart trembles while my Tongue relates!) ....Il.6.571.354.
Of wise *Ulysses,* and his toils relates; ....Od.5.9.171.
We press to hear what sadly he relates. ....Od.10.294.357.
But sheath thy ponyard, while my tongue relates ....Od.11.120.386.
No circumstance the voice of fame relates; ....Od.11.616.414.
The murd'rous council to the Queen relates. ....Od.16.427.128.
Relates the chace, and early praise atchiev'd. ....Od.19.543.223.
The King alternate a dire tale relates, ...Od.23.329.340.

RELATION
I'm no such Beast, nor his Relation; ....4.1HE7.60.273.
Find Virtue local, all Relation scorn, ...5.DunB4.479.389.

RELATIVE
May, must be right, as relative to all. ....3.EOM1.52.19.

RELAX
Not till that Day shall *Jove* relax his Rage, ...Il.15.78.199.
Tire'd by the Tides, his Knees relax with Toil; ....Il.21.309.433.

RELAX'D
And roll'd, with Limbs relax'd, along the Land. ....Il.7.18.363.
With Nerves relax'd he tumbles to the Ground: ....Il.17.342.300.
The bands relax'd, implore the Seer to say ....Od.4.573.147.
By grief relax'd, she wak'd again to weep: ....Od.20.69.235.

RELAXES
Relaxes, strains, and draws them to and fro; ....Od.21.444.281.

RELEAS'D
Releas'd th'impetuous Sluices of the Main,— ....1.TrSt.313.423.
Releas'd from Sleep; and round him might survey ....1.TrUl.54.467.
C vow'd, he'd frankly have releas'd ....6.30.31.87.
C cried, he'd frankly have releas'd ....6.30.31A.87.
Of Gods and Men releas'd the Steeds of Fire: ....Il.8.62.398.
Within, releas'd from cares *Alcinous* lies; ....Od.7.437.258.
Releas'd from sleep, and round him might survey ....Od.13.221.16.
Down dropp'd the leg, from her slack hand releas'd! ....Od.19.547.223.
When from the downy bands of sleep releas'd, ...Od.19.647.227.
So roar'd the lock when it releas'd the spring. ....Od.21.52.261.
Sudden his eyes releas'd their wat'ry store; ....Od.24.273.363.

RELEASE
Release my eyes, and let them freely flow; ....6.20.54.67.
The Priest to rev'rence, and release the Fair. ....Il.1.32.87.
The Priest to rev'rence, and release the Fair; ....Il.1.491.111.

RELEASE (CONTINUED)

Release your smoaking Coursers from the Car;   Il.23.10.486.
Release my Knees, thy suppliant Arts give o'er,   Il.24.718.567.
First I release my self, my fellows last: Od.9.546.328.
And death release me from the silent urn!   Od.11.610.413.
From slaughter'd gluttons to release the dome.   Od.15.201.78.
While heav'n a kind release from ills foreshows,   Od.23.307.337.

RELEAST

Strait be the coursers from the car releast,   Od.4.45.122.
Then notch'd the shaft, releast, and gave it wing;   Od.21.460.282.

RELENT

All Nature mourns, the Skies relent in Show'rs,   1.PSp.69.68.
Hear and relent! hark, how thy Children moan;   6.96iv.11.276.
With offer'd Gifts to make the God relent;   Il.1.505.112.
'Tis time our Fury should relent at last: Il.16.83.238.
Ev'n after death? relent, great Shade, relent!   Od.11.680.418.
Ev'n after death? relent, great Shade, relent!   Od.11.680.418.

RELENTED

Stern *Proserpine* relented,   6.11.85.33.

RELENTING

Inscribe a Verse on this relenting Stone: 1.PWi.26.90.
Unwelcome Life relenting *Phœbus* gives;   1.TrSt.781.442.
There let him lye, 'till his relenting Dame   2.ChJM.365.32.
There let him lye, 'till his relenting Dame   2.ChJM.365A.32.
And Earth relenting feels the Genial Ray;   2.TemF.4.253.
Amid that scene, if some relenting eye   2.ElAb.355.348.
While thus relenting to the Steeds he spoke.   Il.17.503.308.
The God relenting, clear'd the clouded Air;   Il.17.734.317.
The Gods themselves at length relenting, gave   Il.24.771.569.

RELENTLESS

Since Fate relentless stop'd their Heav'nly Voice,   1.W-F.277.174.
"In vain he lov'd, relentless *Pyrrha* scorn'd;   1.TrSP.194.402.
But why alas, relentless Youth! ah why   1.TrSP.218.403.
Relentless walls! whose darksom round contains   2.ElAb.17.320.
Stern *Cato's* self was no relentless spouse: 6.41.30.114.
In vain she tempted the relentless Youth,   Il.6.203.336.
And drain the Dregs of Heav'ns relentless Hate?   Il.8.428.417.
But if all this relentless thou disdain,   Il.9.396.452.
He stands relentless, and rejects 'em all.   Il.9.698.468.
Invok'd by both, relentless they dispose   Il.13.392.124.
The Wretch relentless, and o'erwhelm with Shame!   Il.14.164.165.
No, Wretch accurst! Relentless he replies,   Il.22.433.473.
The Furies that relentless Breast have steel'd,   Il.22.447.474.
All those relentless *Mars* untimely slew,   Il.24.325.550.
But sure relentless folly steels thy breast,   Od.4.39.122.
And hate relentless of my heav'nly foe.   Od.5.541.198.
Relentless mocks her violence of woe,   Od.8.578.293.
At last with tears—O what relentless doom   Od.11.493.408.
Some mighty woe relentless heav'n forbodes: Od.12.328.447.
Of horn the stiff relentless balls appear,   Od.19.248.206.
The wounds of Destiny's relentless rage   Od.19.359.211.

RELENTS

My Heart relents, and answers to my Strains.   1.TrSP.94A.398.
Philætius too relents, but secret shed   Od.21.85.263.

RELICK

The last sad Relick of my ruin'd State,   Il.22.93.456.

RELICKS

The Relicks of a former Sacrifice.   1.TrSt.602.435.
Repriev'd the Relicks of the *Grecian* Band: Il.10.236.12.
Desert the Arms, the Relicks of my Friend?   Il.17.103.291.
And glean the Relicks of exhausted *Troy*.   Il.17.267.298.
Oh guard these Relicks to your Charge consign'd,   Il.17.753.318.
E'er thy dear Relicks in the Grave are laid,   Il.18.391.340.
But ah! the Relicks of my slaughter'd Friend!   Il.19.28.372.
No *Greek* shall e'er his perish'd Relicks grace,   Il.21.375.436.
Dishonour'd Relicks of *Diana's* War.   Il.21.588.446.
The sacred Relicks to the Tent they bore;   Il.23.315.502.
Detain the Relicks of great *Hector* dead;   Il.24.172.543.
Surviv'd, sad Relicks of his num'rous Line.   Il.24.316.549.
My Son's dear Relicks? what befalls him dead?   Od.9.308.319.
Behold the relicks of the *Grecian* train!   Od.9.308.319.
There we thy relicks, great *Achilles!* blend   Od.24.97.352.

RELIEF

Ye Gods! and is there no Relief for Love?   1.PSu.88.79.
And calls on Death, the Wretch's last Relief.   2.ChJM.484.38.
Then share thy pain, allow that sad relief,   2.ElAb.49.323.
Not with such Majesty, such bold relief,   4.2HE1.390.229.
Yet take these tears, Mortality's relief,   6.109.17.314.
With Joy *Sarpedon* view'd the wish'd Relief,   Il.5.840.305.
But thy Distress this Instant claims Relief.   Il.11.976.78.
Not ev'n the Thund'rers Favour brings Relief.   Il.18.100.328.
Neptune and *Pallas* haste to his Relief,   Il.21.330.435.
Some Comfort that had been, some sad Relief,   Il.22.548.479.
E'er yet from Rest or Food wę seek Relief,   Il.23.13.486.
Enough, *Atrides!* give the Troops Relief: Il.23.195.497.
Soon may kind heav'n a sure relief provide,   Od.1.328.48.
Her pleasing converse minister'd relief;   Od.15.387.88.
The proud feel pity, and relief bestow,   Od.17.440.155.

RELĬES

Alas! on one alone our all relies,   4.1740.85.337.
This on his manly confidence relies,   5.DunA2.161.121.
One on his manly confidence relies,   5.DunB2.169.304.
On Female truth assenting faith relies;   Od.1.276.46.
If man on frail unknowing man relies,   Od.20.56.235.

RELIEV'D

Oblig'd the Wealthy, and reliev'd the Poor.   Il.6.20.325.
So *Troy* reliev'd from that wide-wasting Hand   Il.11.487.56.
Which in my wand'rings oft reliev'd my woe: Od.4.42.122.
She gave me life, reliev'd with just supplies   Od.7.380.235.
The Monarch's son a shipwrackt wretch reliev'd,   Od.14.351.51.
The beauteous Queen reliev'd his lab'ring breast.   Od.15.191.77.
His age not honour'd, nor his wants reliev'd?   Od.20.164.241.
Reliev'd our weary'd vessel from the sea.   Od.24.360.366.

RELIEVE

That knew my Pleasures, cou'd relieve my Pains.   1.TrSP.162.400.
Come! with thy looks, thy words, relieve my woe;   2.ElAb.119.329.
Oh blameless Bethel! to relieve thy breast?   3.EOM4.126.140.
Stretch'd to relieve the Idiot and the Poor,   4.2HE1.226.215.
Who flies the tyrant to relieve the slave?   6.4i.6.9.
Still, tho' a rock, can thus relieve my woe,   6.20.58.67.
But oh! relieve a wretched Parent's Pain,   Il.1.27.87.
Thence, to relieve the fainting *Argive* Throng,   Il.5.970.312.
And *Hector* hasted to relieve his Child,   Il.6.599.356.
Guard well the Walls, relieve the Watch of Night,   Il.7.446.386.
To ease a Sov'reign, and relieve a Sire.   Il.10.193.10.
Whom heav'n denies the blessing to relieve?   Od.3.448.108.
Then with a short repast relieve their toil,   Od.6.109.211.
'Tis ours this son of sorrow to relieve,   Od.6.245.222.
To heal divisions, to relieve th' opprest;   Od.7.95.238.
Nor weigh the labour, but relieve the woe)   Od.7.257.248.
Respect us, human, and relieve us, poor.)   Od.9.318.319.
Who knows the son of sorrow to relieve,   Od.15.362.86.
And more, the pleasure to relieve the poor.   Od.15.399.88.
For should'st thou suffer, pow'rless to relieve   Od.16.87.106.
And canst thou envy, when the great relieve?   Od.18.25.168.
Receive no stranger-guest, no poor relieve;   Od.19.158.200.

RELIEVES

Merit distress'd impartial Heav'n relieves;   1.TrSt.780.442.
Is any sick? the MAN of Ross relieves,   3.Ep3.269.115.
The wretched he relieves diffuse his fame,   Od.19.385.212.

RELIGION

Religion, Country, Genius of his *Age*:   1.EOC.121.252.
We their *Religion* had, and they our *Gold*:   1.EOC.545Z2.300.
There stern religion quench'd th' unwilling flame,   2.ElAb.39.322.
Nature stands check'd; Religion disapproves;   2.ElAb.259.341.
And Atheism and Religion take their turns;   3.Ep2.66.55.
Or Virtue, or Religion turn to sport,   4.2HE1.211.213.
Ye Statesmen, Priests, of one Religion all!   4.EpS2.16.314.
Whatever his religion or his blood,   4.1740.95.337.
Religion blushing veils her sacred fires,   5.DunB4.649.409.
The Country Wit, Religion of the Town,   6.8.37.19.
For you well know, that Wit's of no Religion.   6.82iii.2.230.
Wit like religion is with spleen profest;   6.82ix(b).1A.234.
Wit like religion by such Fools profest.   6.82ix(b).1C.234.

RELIGIONS

Still changing Names, Religions, Climes,   6.14v(b).14.50.

RELIGIOUS

Religious, punctual, frugal, and so forth;   3.Ep3.343.122.
Stranger to Civil and Religious Rage,   4.Arbu.394.126.
Yea, moral Ebor, or religious Winton.   4.1740.58.335.
Some hostile fury, some religious rage;   6.71.12.203.
Some who grow dull religious strait commence   6.82ix(c).1.234.
Be this, O Mother, your religious Care;   Il.6.348.343.

RELIQUES

Glance on the stone where our cold reliques lie,   2.ElAb.356.348.
The ground, now sacred by thy reliques made.   2.Elegy.68.368.
Thy reliques, *Rowe*, to this fair urn we trust,   6.72.1.208.
To Rowes dear Reliques be this Marble just   6.72.1A.208.
Thy reliques, *Rowe*, to this fair shrine we trust,   6.72.1B.208.
Thy reliques, *Rowe*, to this fair tomb we trust,   6.72.1C.208.
Thy Reliques, *Rowe!* to this sad Shrine we trust,   6.152.1.400.
And save the Reliques of the *Grecian* Land!   Il.8.292.411.
And save the Reliques of the *Grecian* Name.   Il.15.435.214.
Perhaps yon' Reliques of the *Grecian* Name,   Il.16.24.236.
See the thin Reliques of their baffled Band,   Il.16.91.239.
To guard the Reliques of my slaughter'd Friend.   Il.16.644.269.
Sustain those Peers, the reliques of our host,   Od.4.655.150.
Or food for fish, or dogs, his reliques lye,   Od.14.156.43.
Or savage beasts his mangled reliques tear,   Od.24.342.365.

RELISH

When old, and past the Relish of Delight,   2.ChWB.373.75.
He finds no relish in the sweetest Meat;   4.HS2.32.57.
He'll find no relish in the sweetest Meat;   4.HS2.31A.57.
He'll find no relish in the sweetest Meat;   4.HS2.32B.57.

RELISH'D

And but more relish'd as the more distress'd: 3.EOM4.318.158.

RELUCTANCE

With what Reluctance do we Lawyers bear,   6.96iii.27.275.
Me with reluctance thus the Seer address'd.   Od.4.624.149.

RELUCTANT

And join'd reluctant to the galling Yoke,   1.TrSt.185.418.
Retir'd reluctant from th'unfinish'd Fight.   1.TrES.118.454.
Retir'd reluctant from th' unfinish'd Fight.   Il.12.472.98.
Till late, reluctant, at the Dawn of Day   Il.17.747.317.
Howe'er, reluctant as I am, I stay,   Il.23.59.489.
With sweet, reluctant, amorous delay: Od.1.22.30.
Whose hand reluctant touch'd the warbling wire: Od.1.198.42.
He lives reluctant on a foreign coast.   Od.4.760.155.
With willing duty, not reluctant mind,   Od.4.872.159.
For now, reluctant, and constrain'd by charms,   Od.5.197.181.

RELUCTANT (CONTINUED)
Torn with full force, reluctant beats the wave, ... Od.5.551.199.
I stay reluctant sev'n continu'd years, ... Od.7.346.253.
But if reluctant, who shall force thy stay? ... Od.7.403.256.
With sweet, reluctant, amorous delay; ... Od.9.32.303.
We dragg'd reluctant, and by force we bound: ... Od.9.112.308.
While the impassive soul reluctant flies ... Od.11.267.394.
Curbs the proud steed, reluctant to the rein: ... Od.11.370.401.
Compell'd, reluctant, to their sev'ral styes, ... Od.14.455.57.
Some wretch reluctant views aerial light, ... Od.19.401.214.
Awhile, reluctant to her pleasing force, ... Od.19.596.225.
Shall I, reluctant! to his will accord; ... Od.19.621.226.
I part reluctant from the pleasing tale. ... Od.19.690.229.
And down reluctant on the pavement threw. ... Od.22.204.297.
This hand reluctant touch'd the warbling wire: ... Od.22.390.307.
With sweet reluctant amorous delay; ... Od.23.362.342.
Detain'd reluctant from my native shores. ... Od.23.380.343.

RELUCTANTLY
In Youth's first Bloom reluctantly he dies. ... Il.15.529.217.

RELY
Think of those Authors, Sir, who would rely ... 4.2HE1.350.225.
O Goddess! on thy aid my hopes rely: ... Od.4.532.146.
Be bold, on friendship and my son rely; ... Od.22.412.307.

REMAIN
The wanton Victims of his *Sport* remain. ... 1.W-F.78.157.
Scotists and *Thomists*, now, in Peace remain, ... 1.EOC.444.289.
But if in Noble Minds some Dregs remain, ... 1.EOC.526.297.
And there what kids of equal age remain. ... 1.TrPA.85.369.
Oh! yeild at last, nor still remain severe; ... 1.TrPA.114.370.
Exclaim'd—O *Thebes!* for thee what Fates remain, ... 1.TrSt.234.420.
Not half so fixt the *Trojan* cou'd remain, ... 2.RL5.5.199.
Some to remain, and some to perish soon, ... 2.TemF.485.287.
And here ev'n then, shall my cold dust remain, ... 2.ElAb.174.334.
And where no wants, no wishes can remain, ... 3.EOM4.325.159.
Nature well known, no Miracles remain, ... 3.Ep1.208A.33.
Nature well known, no prodigies remain, ... 3.Ep1.208.33.
Did not some grave Examples yet remain, ... 4.2HE1.128.205.
And splay-foot verse, remain'd, and will remain. ... 4.2HE1.271.219.
Yet may this Verse (if such a Verse remain) ... 4.EpS1.171.309.
But now for Authors nobler palms remain: ... 5.DunA2.183.124.
What then remains? Ourself. Still, still remain ... 5.DunB1.217.286.
But now for Authors nobler palms remain; ... 5.DunB2.191.304.
On earth a while with mortals to remain, ... 6.4i.2.9.
And so remain, for ever and for ay, ... 6.13.30.40.
There, Mordaunt, Fitzwilliams, & c. remain; ... 6.122.13.342.
But when I saw such Charity remain, ... 6.146.3.389.
Mine is thy Daughter, Priest, and shall remain; ... Il.1.39.87.
Unmov'd as Death *Achilles* shall remain, ... Il.1.444.108.
What mighty Toils to either Host remain, ... Il.2.49.129.
Shall beauteous *Helen* still remain unfreed, ... Il.2.213.138.
So many Years the Toils of *Greece* remain; ... Il.2.395.145.
Unfinish'd his proud Palaces remain, ... Il.2.858.165.
What Numbers lost, what Numbers yet remain? ... Il.3.244.204.
Now win the Shores, and scarce the Seas remain. ... Il.5.985.314.
Be his my Spoil, and his these Arms remain; ... Il.7.90.367.
No Trace remain where once the Glory grew. ... Il.7.551.392.
Between the Trench and Wall, let Guards remain: ... Il.9.94.437.
But whether he remain, or sail with me, ... Il.9.554.460.
What Toils attend thee, and what Woes remain? ... Il.10.120.7.
Then thus aloud: Whoe'er thou art, remain; ... Il.10.439.23.
What farther Subterfuge, what Hopes remain? ... Il.11.513.57.
Of twelve bold Brothers, I alone remain! ... Il.11.833.73.
What Hopes, what Methods of Retreat remain? ... Il.12.82.84.
Remain the Prize of *Nestor's* youthful Son. ... Il.13.508.130.
Of all those Heroes, two alone remain; ... Il.13.982.152.
What Hopes remain, what Methods to retire, ... Il.15.596.219.
Thus He—what Methods yet, oh Chief! remain, ... Il.17.378.302.
'Tis in our Hands alone our Hopes remain, ... Il.17.797.319.
Whole Years untouch'd, uninjur'd shall remain ... Il.19.33.373.
Immers'd remain this Terror of the World. ... Il.21.373.436.
A thousand Woes, a thousand Toils remain. ... Il.21.694.450.
Nor other Lance, nor other Hope remain; ... Il.22.374.471.
Some Rites remain, to glut our Rage of Grief. ... Il.23.14.486.
You, the Disgrace of *Priam's* House, remain! ... Il.24.320.549.
No Comfort to my Griefs, no Hopes remain, ... Il.24.612.562.
'Till she retires, determin'd we remain, ... Od.2.227.72.
The wild waves fury, here I fix'd remain: ... Od.5.459.195.
But there remain, ye guilty, in my pow'r, ... Od.8.357.282.
These sons their sisters wed, and all remain ... Od.10.7.339.
If any counsel, any hope remain. ... Od.10.220.351.
Pensive they march, and pensive we remain. ... Od.10.239.352.
I answer'd stern. Inglorious then remain, ... Od.10.321.359.
Swear, in thy soul no latent frauds remain, ... Od.10.409.364.
Can yet a doubt, or any dread remain, ... Od.10.449.365.
The cause remov'd, habitual griefs remain, ... Od.10.550.369.
The sky for ever low'rs, for ever clouds remain. ... Od.12.94.436.
Hence therefore, while thy stores thy own remain; ... Od.15.23.71.
Of one lost joy, I lose what yet remain. ... Od.15.107.73.
Seek thou repose; whilst here I sole remain, ... Od.19.54.195.
But other methods of defence remain, ... Od.22.154.294.
The four remain, but four against an host. ... Od.22.275.300.
Then she. In these thy kingly walls remain ... Od.22.458.310.
If fears remain, or doubts distract thy heart? ... Od.23.210.333.

REMAIN'D
The face was all that now remain'd of thee; ... 1.TrFD.63.388.
Unmov'd remain'd the Ruler of the Sky, ... 1.TrSt.402.426.
Oh had I rather un-admir'd remain'd ... 2.RL4.153.196.
Or what remain'd, so worthy to be read ... 4.2HE1.137.207.
And splay-foot verse, remain'd, and will remain. ... 4.2HE1.271.219.
And now th' Example of the third remain'd. ... Il.1.336.104.
Remain'd unheedful of his Lord's Commands: ... Il.5.396.285.
Nestor alone amidst the Storm remain'd. ... Il.8.102.402.

REMAIN'D (CONTINUED)
Unwilling he remain'd, for *Paris'* Dart ... Il.8.103.402.
But in the Centre *Hector* fix'd remain'd, ... Il.13.851.146.
The fifth Reward, the double Bowl, remain'd. ... Il.23.704.517.
Hermes I sent, while yet his soul remain'd ... Od.1.49.32.
Three sons remain'd: To climb with haughty fires ... Od.2.27.61.
Unmov'd the mind of *Ithacus* remain'd, ... Od.4.385.139.
Remain'd: Beside him, on a splendid throne, ... Od.7.312.251.
One ram remain'd, the leader of the flock; ... Od.9.511.327.
Suspecting fraud, more prudently remain'd. ... Od.10.267.355.
The males without (a smaller race) remain'd; ... Od.14.20.35.
An helpless infant I remain'd behind; ... Od.15.518.95.
Deep o'er his knee inseam'd, remain'd the scar: ... Od.19.544.223.
Those only now remain'd; but those confest ... Od.21.191.269.

REMAINED
But mere tuff-taffety what now remained; ... 4.JD4.42.29.

REMAINING
Then see how little the remaining sum, ... 3.EOM2.51.62.
The two remaining Sons the Line divide: ... Il.20.282.406.
And add half *Ilion's* yet remaining Store, ... Il.22.161.459.
First let us quench the yet-remaining Flame ... Il.23.295.501.
And quench with Wine the yet remaining Fire. ... Il.24.1002.577.

REMAINS
But fix'd *His* Word, *His* saving Pow'r remains: ... 1.Mes.107.122.
Or raise old Warriors whose ador'd Remains ... 1.W-F.301.177.
It self unseen, but in th' *Effects*, remains. ... 1.EOC.79.248.
That still the best and dearest Gift remains. ... 1.TrVP.99.381.
And strait a voice, while yet a voice remains, ... 1.TrFD.67.388.
Tho' Fortune change, his constant Spouse remains, ... 2.ChJM.41.17.
One only Doubt remains; Full oft I've heard ... 2.ChJM.268.27.
What then remains, but well our Pow'r to use, ... 2.RL5.29.201.
A heap of dust alone remains of thee; ... 2.Elegy.73.368.
For fainting Age what cordial drop remains, ... 4.HS2.89.61.
No whiter page than Addison remains. ... 4.2HE1.216.213.
There still remains to mortify a Wit, ... 4.2HE1.304.221.
What then remains? Ourself. Still, still remain ... 5.DunB1.217.286.
Still in Constraint your suff'ring Sex remains, ... 6.19.41.63.
'Tis time to save the few Remains of War. ... Il.1.82.90.
But this when Time requires—It now remains ... Il.1.181.96.
Thy boundless Will, for me, remains in Force, ... Il.1.716.122.
To touch the Booty, while a Foe remains. ... Il.6.86.327.
These Straits demand our last Remains of Might. ... Il.6.106.328.
No Parent now remains, my Griefs to share, ... Il.6.522.352.
For what remains; let Fun'ral Flames be fed ... Il.7.484.388.
With melting Hearts the cold Remains they burn'd; ... Il.7.510.389.
The cold Remains consume with equal Care; ... Il.7.514.389.
Then let me add what yet remains behind, ... Il.9.83.436.
A Life of Labours, lo! what Fruit remains. ... Il.9.423.453.
Ye have my Answer—what remains to do, ... Il.9.456.455.
What yet remains to save th' afflicted State. ... Il.10.26.3.
And of Night's Empire but a third remains. ... Il.10.298.15.
To him the Chief. What then remains to do? ... Il.11.972.78.
Imbrius remains the fierce *Ajaces'* Prize. ... Il.13.264.117.
Come, and the Warrior's lov'd Remains defend. ... Il.13.585.134.
But he impervious and untouch'd remains. ... Il.13.701.138.
There join'd, the whole *Bœotian* Strength remains, ... Il.13.859.146.
Achilles, great *Achilles*, yet remains ... Il.13.937.149.
Oh save from hostile Rage his lov'd Remains: ... Il.16.668.270.
Sunk in soft Dust the mighty Chief remains, ... Il.16.936.279.
And give *Achilles* all that yet remains ... Il.17.112.292.
Haste, and *Patroclus'* lov'd Remains defend: ... Il.17.130.292.
Sole in the Seat the Charioteer remains, ... Il.17.532.309.
The Fight, our glorious Work remains undone. ... Il.19.148.377.
Far from our pious Rites, those dear Remains ... Il.22.124.458.
But fix'd remains the Purpose of his Soul: ... Il.22.127.458.
Sad Product now of hapless Love, remains! ... Il.22.621.482.
Part of himself; th' immortal Mind remains: ... Il.23.123.492.
Of some once-stately Oak the last Remains, ... Il.23.401.506.
With him the Sword and studded Belt remains. ... Il.23.972.528.
And can ye still his cold Remains pursue? ... Il.24.46.537.
What yet most precious of thy Store remains, ... Il.24.468.556.
Or yet unmangled rest his cold Remains? ... Il.24.500.557.
Remains unask'd; what Time the Rites require ... Il.24.825.571.
Nor Man, nor Woman, in the Walls remains. ... Il.24.883.573.
Sad Product now of hapless Love, remains! ... Il.24.913.574.
But fowls obscene dismember'd his remains, ... Od.3.322.102.
Deem not, that here of choice my fleet remains; ... Od.4.511.144.
Hath journey'd half, and half remains to run; ... Od.4.540.146.
Nor entrails, flesh, nor solid bone remains. ... Od.9.349.320.
Still curst with sense, their mind remains alone, ... Od.10.280.356.
With what remains, from certain ruin fly, ... Od.10.319.359.
His cold remains all naked to the sky ... Od.11.67.383.
There pious on my cold remains attend, ... Od.11.87.385.
No more the substance of the man remains, ... Od.11.263.394.
And lo! a length of night behind remains, ... Od.11.464.407.
Severely chaste *Penelope* remains, ... Od.16.36.104.
One care remains, to note the loyal few ... Od.16.328.121.
Some joy remains: To thee a son is giv'n, ... Od.18.207.177.
Another, Princes! yet remains to play; ... Od.22.8.286.
Thy house, for me, remains; by me repress'd ... Od.22.351.304.
Now to dispose the dead, the care remains ... Od.22.472.311.
At labour long, and hard, remains behind; ... Od.23.267.336.
Thy next-belov'd, *Antilochus'* remains. ... Od.24.100.353.

REMARK
Ev'n in an ornament its place remark, ... 3.Ep4.77.144.
My Lord of L[ondo]n, chancing to remark ... 4.HAdv.39.79.
Plow'd was his front with many a deep Remark: ... 5.DunB4.204.362.

REMARKS
Whom honour with your hand: to make remarks, ... 4.1HE6.103.243.

REMEMB'RING

Rememb'ring she herself was Pertness once. ....5.DunB4.280Z2.371.

REMEMBER

Remember, Man, "the Universal Cause ....3.EOM4.35.131.
Don't you remember what Reply he gave? ....4.2HE2.49.167.
(For I remember you were fond of those,) ....6.96iv.52.277.
Yet ah! how once we lov'd, remember still, ...6.123.3.343.
Remember *Troy,* and give the Vengeance way. ......Il.4.64.224.
Hear this, remember, and our Fury dread, ...Il.15.35.195.
Remember theirs, and mitigate thy own. ....Il.24.781.569.
Remember *Cyclops,* and his bloody deed; ....Od.10.515.368.
I well remember (for I gaz'd him o'er ....Od.21.96.263.

REMEMBER'D

(For I remember'd you were fond of those,) ....6.96iv.52A.277.
Shall last remember'd in thy best of days. ....Od.5.485.195.

REMEMBERS

Remembers oft the School-boy's simple fare, ...4.HS2.73.59.

REMEMBRANCE

To thy Remembrance lost, as to thy Love! ....1.TrSP.4.393.
No Time the dear Remembrance can remove, ...1.TrSP.51.396.
Still all those Joys to my Remembrance move, ...1.TrSP.51A.396.
The dear Remembrance of his Native Coast; ....1.TrUl.57.467.
Remembrance and Reflection how ally'd; ....3.EOM1.225.43.
For pleas'd Remembrance builds Delight on Woe. .....6.96iv.64.278.
This, Goddess, this to his Remembrance call, ...Il.1.530.113.
This stern Remembrance to his Troops he gave: ......Il.16.238.248.
All past before him in Remembrance dear, ...Il.24.15.535.
Touch'd with the dear Remembrance of his Sire. .....Il.24.635.563.
In dear remembrance of his royal grace, ...Od.4.819.157.
This ever grateful in remembrance bear, ...Od.8.501.289.
Remembrance sad, whose image to review ....Od.9.13.301.
Of dear remembrance, blessing still and blest! .....Od.13.75.4.
The dear remembrance of his native coast. ....Od.13.224.16.
To dear remembrance makes his image rise, ...Od.14.152.43.
And pleas'd remembrance builds delight on woe. .....Od.15.437.90.
Touch'd with the dear remembrance of her Lord; .....Od.16.467.129.
The dear remembrance of my native land, ...Od.19.189.200.
The sad remembrance of a perish'd man. ....Od.21.90.263.
Time shall the truth to sure remembrance bring: ....Od.23.115.325.

REMEMBRING

Fix'd is their Doom; this all-remembring Breast ....1.TrSt.346.424.
Remembring she herself was Pertness once. ....5.DunB1.112.277.

REMISS

He seems remiss, but bears a valiant Mind; ....Il.10.139.8.

REMISSIVE

Whene'er he breath'd, remissive of his Might, ...Il.13.887.147.

REMIT

On just Attonement, we remit the Deed; ....Il.9.744.471.

REMITS

Nor ought remits the work, while thus he said. .....Od.24.286.363.

REMNANT

Bring forth some Remnant of *Promethean* theft, ...6.100iv.1.289.
The last, black Remnant of so bright a Line. ....Il.16.951.280.
Thy pilgrimage to come, and remnant of thy day. ....Od.10.644.374.
Delusive semblance!—But my remnant life ....Od.19.666.228.

REMNANTS

See the poor Remnants of these slighted Hairs! .....2.RL4.167.197.
See the poor Remnants of this slighted Hair! ....2.RL4.167A.197.
The frugal remnants of the former day. ....Od.16.52.104.
(The remnants of the spoil the suitor-crowd ....Od.20.3.230.

REMONSTRANCE

Thy free Remonstrance proves thy Worth and Truth: ..Il.6.419.347.

REMORSE

The Critick else proceeds without Remorse, ...1.EOC.167.259.
Signs of Remorse, while thus his Spouse he chear'd: .2.ChJM.788.53.
For then with dire remorse, and conscious shame, ...Od.4.357.136.

REMORSELESS

But these, ev'n these, remorseless *Rome* deny'd! ..6.20.42.67.
Mean-time return'd, with dire remorseless sway .....Od.4.453.141.
Mean-time returning, with remorseless sway ....Od.17.144.138.

REMOTE

From what far Clime (said she) remote from Fame, ...1.TrUl.116.469.
Dim and remote the joys of saints I see, ...2.ElAb.71.325.
The hour conceal'd, and so remote the fear, ...3.EOM3.75.99.
Till, by degrees, remote and small, ...6.11.18.30.
And thou, from Camps remote, the Danger shun, ...Il.1.548.114.
Remote their Forces lay, nor knew so far ....Il.4.384.239.
Can'st thou, remote, the mingling Hosts descry .....Il.4.424.240.
To *Mars,* who sate remote, they bent their way; ...Il.5.445.289.
Remote they stand, while Alien Troops engage, ...Il.5.581.296.
Whose Ships remote the guarded Navy bound. ....Il.11.12.35.
The youth had dwelt; remote from War's alarms, ...Il.13.231.116.
For lo! I haste to those remote Abodes, ...Il.14.229.172.
Then she—I haste to those remote Abodes, ...Il.14.341.179.
Unknown to him who sits remote on high, ...Il.18.223.332.
But now the God, remote, a heav'nly guest ....Od.1.29.30.
There rule, from palace-cares remote and free, ...Od.1.457.54.
On themes remote the venerable Sage, ...Od.3.302.101.
The fix'd event of fate's remote decrees; ....Od.4.628.149.
Numb'ring his flocks and herds, not far remote. ....Od.4.865.159.
And Isles remote enlarge his old domain. ....Od.4.998.164.

REMOTE (CONTINUED)

Remote from neighbours, in a forest wide, ...Od.5.631.202.
From lands remote, and o'er a length of sea? ....Od.7.319.251.
Remote from Gods or men she holds her reign, ...Od.7.330.252.
From what far clime (said she) remote from fame, ...Od.13.283.19.
But when remote her chalky cliffs we lost, ...Od.14.331.51.
Soon as remote from shore they plow the wave, ...Od.14.377.53.
Far hence remote, and *Syria* see the land; ....Od.15.439.90.
From noiseful revel far remote she flies, ...Od.15.557.96.
Minerva fix'd her mind on views remote, ...Od.19.558.223.

REMOTEST

To Heav'n it self, and Earth's remotest Ends. ......1.TrSP.40.395.
Their Fame shall fill the World's remotest Ends, ...Il.7.536.391.
Fly, if thou wilt, to Earth's remotest Bound, ...Il.8.597.424.
To those tall Ships, remotest of the Fleet, ...Il.10.126.7.
For him, in *Troy's* remotest Lines, he sought, ...Il.13.577.133.
And now they reach'd the *Earth's* remotest ends, ..Od.24.15.347.

REMOUNT

I know to shift my Ground, remount the Car, ...Il.7.289.378.

REMOUNTS

Remounts his Car, and herds amidst the Crowd; ......Il.11.463.54.

REMOV'D

Then, nor 'till then, the Veil's remov'd away, ...2.ChWB.104.61.
Remov'd from all th' ambitious Scene, ...4.HS6.27.251.
Alone, remov'd from Grandeur and from Strife, ...6.17iii.16.58.
Such this man was; who now, from earth remov'd, ...6.57.11.169.
The Cause of Strife remov'd so rarely well, ...6.145.9.388.
And blest, that timely from our Scene remov'd ......6.152.9.400.
Far hence remov'd, the hoarse-resounding Main ......Il.1.203.96.
Few Leagues remov'd, we wish our peaceful Seat, ...Il.2.358.144.
Remov'd from Fight, on *Xanthus* flow'ry Bounds ....Il.5.47.268.
His panting Steeds, remov'd from out the War, ...Il.5.397.286.
When now the Rage of Hunger was remov'd; ....Il.7.388.383.
Then heav'd the massy Gates, remov'd the Bars, ...Il.24.549.559.
And from his seat *Laodamas* remov'd, ...Od.7.226.247.
The cause remov'd, habitual griefs remain, ...Od.10.550.369.
Far hence is by unequal Gods remov'd ....Od.14.73.39.
From earth remov'd him to the shades below, ...Od.14.237.48.

REMOVAL

Of swift removal, seconds my desires. ....Od.17.21.133.

REMOVE

To closer Shades the painting Flocks remove, ...1.PSu.87.79.
Ye Trees that fade when Autumn-Heats remove, ...1.PAu.29.82.
From Shepherds, Flocks, and Plains, I may remove, ..1.PAu.87.86.
And what alone must all my hopes remove, ...1.TrPA.64.368.
Remove your hands, the bark shall soon suffice .....1.TrFD.98.390.
No Time the dear Remembrance can remove, ...1.TrSP.51.396.
To raging Seas unpity'd I'll remove, ...1.TrSP.258.404.
From thee to those, unpity'd, I'll remove, ...1.TrSP.258A.404.
Before true passion all those views remove, ...2.ElAb.79.326.
How the dear object from the crime remove, ...2.ElAb.193.335.
Provoking Dæmons all restraint remove, ...2.ElAb.231.339.
What *Drop* or *Nostrum* can this Plague remove? ...4.Arbu.29.98.
(And little sure imported to remove, ...4.2HE2.56.169.
Silent and soft, as Saints remove to Heav'n, ...4.EpS1.93.305.
But does the Court a worthy Man remove? ....4.EpS2.74.317.
In some soft Dream may thy mild Soul remove, ...6.86.19A.246.
Or let thy soul in some soft dream remove, ...6.86.19B.246.
Let the mild soul in some soft dream remove, ...6.86.19C.246.
WITHERS adieu! yet not with thee remove ....6.113.7.320.
Or learn the wastful Vengeance to remove, ...Il.1.85.90.
'Tis not in me the Vengeance to remove; ....Il.4.79.224.
Wrath and Revenge from Men and Gods remove: ....Il.18.138.329.
Then rise, and to the feastful hall remove: ....Od.4.901.160.
Or if they still must live, from me remove ....Od.4.910.161.
If from your thoughts *Ulysses* you remove, ...Od.5.18.171.
'Tis past—and *Jove* decrees he shall remove; .....Od.5.175.180.
To the close grot the lonely pair remove, ...Od.5.291.185.
Without new treasures let him not remove, ...Od.13.15.2.
No Prince will let *Ulysses'* heir remove, ...Od.15.95.73.
These to remove th'expiring embers came, ...Od.19.76.196.
O deign he, if *Ulysses,* to remove ....Od.23.111.325.
The Suitors death unknown, 'till we remove ....Od.23.137.327.

REMOVES

So when the Nightingale to Rest removes, ...1.PSp.13.61.
She but removes weak passions for the strong: ......3.EOM2.158.74.
Untouch'd she stay'd, uninjur'd she removes, ...Il.9.173.441.
Untouch'd she stay'd, uninjur'd she removes, ...Il.9.360.451.
That spotless as she came, the Maid removes, ...Il.19.175.379.
The black-ey'd Maid inviolate removes, ...Il.19.273.383.
Removes the rocky mountain from the door, ...Od.9.371.321.

REMOVING

At last, the stone removing from the gate, ...Od.9.495.326.

REMURMUR

Her Fate remurmur to the silver Flood; ....1.PWi.64.93.
The Rocks remurmur, and the Deeps rebound. ....Il.2.252.139.

REMURMUR'D

Eurota's Banks remurmur'd to the Noise; ....1.TrSt.166.417.
And a low Groan remurmur'd thro' the Shore. ....Il.10.563.27.

REND

To rend her hair; her hand is fill'd with leaves; ..1.TrFD.46.387.
I rend my Tresses, and my Breast I wound, ...1.TrSP.130.399.
But rend the Reins, and bound a diff'rent way, ...1.TrSt.188.418.
Burst from th' *Æolian* Caves, and rend the Ground, .1.TrSt.489.430.
Discharge thy Shafts, this ready Bosom rend, ...1.TrSt.776.442.

REND (CONTINUED)
To force the Ramparts, and the Gates to rend; ..... 1.TrES.2A.449.
First may the yawning Earth her Bosome rend, ... 2.ChJM.585.43.
With louder Clamours rend the vaulted Skie: ..... 2.ChJM.755.51.
With such loud Clamours rend the vaulted Skie: ..... 2.ChJM.755A.51.
And Screams of Horror rend th' affrighted Skies. ..... 2.RL3.156.180.
My hands shall rend what ev'n thy Rapine spares: ..... 2.RL4.168.197.
My hands shall rend what ev'n thy own did spare. ..... 2.RL4.168A.197.
Rend with tremendous Sound your ears asunder, ... 4.HS1.25.7.
Rend with tremendous Sound our ears asunder, ... 4.HS1.25A.7.
Sound forth, my Brayers, and the welkin rend." ..... 5.DunA2.236.129.
Sound forth my Brayers, and the welkin rend." ..... 5.DunB2.246.307.
'Till the last Trumpet rend the Ground; ..... 6.31ii.6Z11.95.
Then grinding Tortures his strong Bosom rend, ... Il.11.347.50.
Shouts, as he past, the crystal Regions rend, ... Il.11.445.54.
His following Host with Clamours rend the Skies: ..... Il.12.138.86.
While these they undermine, and those they rend; ..... Il.12.306.92.
To force the Ramparts, and the Gates to rend; ..... Il.12.346.94.
Its Womb they deluge, and its Ribs they rend: ..... Il.15.443.214.
And rend the trembling, unresisting Prey. ..... Il.16.423.259.
And Peals on Peals redoubled rend the Poles. ..... Il.20.76.397.
Such War th' Immortals wage: Such Horrors rend ..... Il.20.89.397.
Might *Hector's* Spear this dauntless Bosom rend, ... Il.21.323.434.
Sav'd from the Flames, for hungry Dogs to rend. ..... Il.23.225.498.
But great *Achilles* diff'rent Passions rend, ... Il.24.642.563.
Kiss his pale Cheek, and rend their scatter'd Hair: ..... Il.24.889.573.
They cuff, they tear, their cheeks and necks they rend, ... Od.2.179.70.
And loud applauses rend the vaulted sky. ..... Od.8.404.285.
Fragments they rend from off the craggy brow, ... Od.10.139.347.
The Gods with all their furies rend his breast: ..... Od.11.334.398.
The pyre to build, the stubborn oak to rend; ..... Od.15.339.86.
With bursts of laughter rend the vaulted skies: ..... Od.18.119.172.

RENDER
Whom Age and long Experience render wise, ... 1.TrVP.78.380.
And *Troy's* proud Matrons render Tear for Tear. ..... Il.2.423.147.
Shall render back the beauteous Maid he lost: ..... Il.16.111.240.
That gift our barren rocks will render vain: ..... Od.4.822.157.
To render sleep's soft blessing unsincere? ..... Od.4.1060.167.

RENDERS
He falls, and renders all their Cares in vain! ..... Il.4.551.247.
Strikes from his Hand the Scourge, and renders vain ..... Il.23.463.508.
The savage renders vain the wound decreed, ... Od.19.523.221.

RENDEZVOUS
Hence, to the vagrant's rendezvous repair; ..... Od.18.377.185.

RENDING
She, from the rending earth and bursting skies, ... 3.EOM3.253.118.
And wide beneath them groans the rending Ground. ..... Il.21.453.439.

RENDS
And beats her Breast, and rends her flowing Hair; ..... 1.TrSt.700.439.
He foams, he roars, he rends the panting Prey. ..... 1.TrES.20.450.
The Shore is heap'd with Death, and Tumult rends the Sky. ..... 1.TrES.208.457.
Loud as the Burst of Cannon rends the Skies, ... 2.TemF.334.280.
The Queen assents, the Trumpet rends the Skies, ... 2.TemF.392.282.
Till the Trumpet rends the Ground; ..... 6.31ii.6Z11A.95.
Oh Thou! whose Thunder rends the clouded Air, ... Il.2.489.150.
The Lordly Savage rends the panting Prey ..... Il.3.40A.190.
His Cors'let pierces, and his Garment rends, ... Il.3.441.213.
A gen'ral Shout that all the Region rends. ..... Il.4.491.244.
Implore the God whose Thunder rends the Skies. ..... Il.7.240.376.
His Corslet enters, and his Garment rends, ... Il.7.301.379.
He rends his Hairs, in sacrifice to *Jove*, ... Il.10.19.2.
He falls, and foaming rends the guardless Prey. ..... Il.10.567.27.
The Savage seizes, draws, and rends the last: ..... Il.11.230.45.
Floats on the Winds, and rends the Heav'ns with Cries: ..... Il.12.239.90.
He foams, he roars, he rends the panting Prey. ..... Il.12.364.94.
The Shore is heap'd with Death, and Tumult rends the Sky. ..... Il.12.562.102.
(Which from the stubborn Stone a Torrent rends) ..... Il.13.193.115.
And from his Temples rends the glitt'ring Prize; ..... Il.13.667.137.
Along the Chine, his eager Javelin rends: ..... Il.13.693.138.
And driving down, the swelling Bladder rends: ..... Il.13.816.144.
Of him, whose Trident rends the solid Ground. ..... Il.14.176.165.
And rends his side, fresh-bleeding with the Dart ..... Il.15.698.222.
And loud Acclaim the starry Region rends. ..... Il.16.353.256.
The God, whose Thunder rends the troubled Air, ... Il.17.226.296.
The *Telamonian* Lance his Belly rends; ..... Il.17.363.301.
Succeeds to Fate: The Spear his Belly rends; ..... Il.20.563.417.
The monarch-savage rends the trembling prey. ..... Od.4.454.141.
With forceful strength a branch the Heroe rends; ..... Od.6.150.214.
From the tall hill he rends a pointed rock; ..... Od.9.566.329.
But the great God, whose thunder rends the skies, ... Od.9.645.333.
Howls o'er the shroud, and rends it from the mast: ..... Od.12.480.455.
The Monarch savage rends the panting prey: ..... Od.17.145.138.

RENEW
False Steps but help them to renew the Race, ... 1.EOC.602.308.
Now sliding Streams the thirsty Plants renew, ... 1.TrVP.15.377.
Derive Incitements to renew thy Rage; ..... 1.TrSt.380.425.
And bids renew the Feasts, and wake the Fires. ..... 1.TrSt.604.435.
And bids renew the Feasts, and wake the sleeping Fires. ..... 1.TrSt.604A.435.
They join, they thicken, and th'Assault renew; ..... 1.TrES.152.455.
Which never more its Honours shall renew, ... 2.RL4.135.195.
Thick as the Bees, that with the Spring renew ..... 2.TemF.282.277.
"Annual for me, the grape, the rose renew ..... 3.EOM1.135.32.
By land, by water, they renew the charge, ... 4.Arbu.9.96.
The Piteous Images renew my Pain, ... 6.96iv.85.278.
Provoke *Atrides* and renew the Fight: ..... Il.3.540.217.
Well might I wish, could Mortal Wish renew ..... Il.4.370.238.
Then mix in Combate and their Toils renew. ..... Il.5.704.301.
Years might again roll back, my Youth renew, ... Il.7.161.372.
Then close impetuous, and the Charge renew: ..... Il.7.306.379.
They join, they thicken, and th' Assault renew; ..... Il.12.506.100.

RENEW (CONTINUED)
Loud shout the *Trojans*, and renew the Fight. ..... Il.17.810.320.
That done, their Sorrows and their Sighs renew. ..... Il.18.416.341.
And thrice their Sorrows and Laments renew; ..... Il.23.17.487.
The Fields their Vegetable Life renew, ... Il.23.681.516.
The genial viands let my train renew; ..... Od.1.404.52.
Again they mount, their journey to renew, ... Od.3.625.118.
Thus while he sung, *Ulysses'* griefs renew, ... Od.8.569.293.
Her faded pow'rs with balmy rest renew. ..... Od.20.64.235.
And let th' abstersive sponge the board renew: ..... Od.20.189.242.

RENEW'D
And with full Lust those horrid Joys renew'd: ..... 1.TrSt.98.414.
These Honours, still renew'd, his antient Wrath appease. ..... 1.TrSt.789.443.
But ere the Rosie Morn renew'd the Day, ... 1.TrUl.154.471.
Both, pleas'd and blest, renew'd their mutual Vows, ... 2.ChJM.815.54.
The still-believing, still-renew'd desire; ..... 4.HOde1.34.153.
Renew'd by ordure's sympathetic force. ..... 5.DunA2.95.108.
Renew'd by ordure's sympathetic force, ... 5.DunB2.103.300.
Fair, o'er the western world, renew'd his light, ... 6.107.2.310.
The Fight renew'd with fiercer Fury burns: ..... Il.11.278.47.
Renew'd by Art divine, the Hero stands, ... Il.16.651.269.
But thrice they clos'd, and thrice the Charge renew'd. ..... Il.23.964.527.
With grief renew'd the weeping fair descends; ..... Od.1.427.53.
In thee renew'd the soul of *Nestor* shines: ..... Od.4.282.132.
Fresh from the bath with fragrant oils renew'd, ... Od.4.344.136.
There stopp'd the Goddess, and her speech renew'd. ..... Od.7.62.236.
But ere the rosy morn renew'd the day, ... Od.13.321.23.
Renew'd th' attack, incontinent of spleen: ..... Od.19.79.196.
The night still ravell'd, what the day renew'd. ..... Od.19.173.200.
Prince! he cries, renew'd by your command, ... Od.19.188.200.
The bath renew'd, she ends the pleasing toil ..... Od.19.589.225.
Then to the King this friendly speech renew'd: ..... Od.20.207.243.
By gentler *Agelaus* thus renew'd. ..... Od.20.388.251.

RENEWS
The War renews, mix'd Shouts and Groans arise; ..... 1.TrES.95A.453.
Restores his Freshness, and his Form renews. ..... 1.TrES.343.462.
And from the goal again renews the race; ..... 6.55.9.167.
With pleasing Sweets his fainting Sense renews, ... Il.3.471.214.
The War renews, the Warriors bleed again; ..... Il.4.539.247.
The Hero rallies, and renews the Fight. ..... Il.11.725.67.
Her Force encreasing, as her Toil renews. ..... Il.11.959.78.
The War renews, mix'd Shouts and Groans arise; ..... Il.12.449.98.
Neptune, with Zeal encreas'd, renews his Care, ... Il.14.419.183.
Restores his Freshness, and his Form renews. ..... Il.16.830.275.
Descends impetuous, and renews the War; ..... Il.17.613.312.
The hearty Draught rewards, renews their Toil; ..... Il.18.633.354.
Sad *Hecuba* renews, and then replies. ..... Il.24.242.546.
The bath, the feast, their fainting soul renews; ..... Od.10.533.369.
Too faithful memory renews your woe; ..... Od.10.549.369.
Lo! when nine times the moon renews her horn, ... Od.11.299.396.
Again the restless orb his toil renews, ... Od.11.739.422.
The tear she wipes, and thus renews her woes. ..... Od.18.236.178.
'Till thus the Queen the tender theme renews. ..... Od.19.252.207.
In the next month renews her faded wane, ... Od.19.352.211.
The night renews the day-distracting theme, ... Od.20.102.237.

RENOUNC'D
Since Battel is renounc'd, thy Thoughts employ ..... Il.17.159.293.

RENOUNCE
Yes, or we must renounce the *Stagyrite*. ..... 1.EOC.280.271.
Or once renounce the Honour of my Race. ..... 2.ChJM.590.43.
Renounce my love, my life, my self—and you. ..... 2.ElAb.204.336.
Forget, renounce me, hate whate'er was mine. ..... 2.ElAb.294.343.
I, who so oft renounce the Muses, lye, ... 4.2HE1.175.209.
Renounce our Country, and degrade our Name? ..... 4.1HE6.125.245.
Part you with one, and I'll renounce the other. ..... 6.46.4.127.
Man and his Works he'll soon renounce, ... 6.135.93.370.
His Lords and Laydes He'le renounce ..... 6.135.93A.370.
Renounce the Glories of thy Heav'nly State, ... Il.3.504.215.
Taught by this Stroke, renounce the War's Alarms, ... Il.5.437.289.
When Kings advise us to renounce our Fame, ... Il.9.43.433.
Before the *Grecian* Peers renounce thine Ire: ..... Il.19.36.373.

RENOWN
No less Renown attends the moving Lyre, ... 1.TrSP.35.394.
In bloody Fields pursu'd Renown in Arms. ..... 2.TemF.150.265.
The Bard whom pilf'red Pastorals renown, ... 4.Arbu.179.109.
When simple *Macer*, now of high Renown, ... 6.49i.1.137.
When Am[brose] Ph[ilip]s, now of high Renown, ... 6.49i.1A.137.
Of Books of high Renown. ..... 6.58.4.170.
The Wretch whom pilfer'd Pastorals renown, ... 6.98.29.284.
Ajax in Arms the first Renown acquir'd, ... Il.2.934.167.
Fierce for Renown the Brother Chiefs draw near, ... Il.5.21.266.
By his Instructions learn to win Renown, ... Il.6.256.339.
Grant him, like me, to purchase just Renown, ... Il.6.606.356.
Short is my Date, but deathless my Renown; ..... Il.9.535.460.
Polydus' Son, a Seer of old Renown. ..... Il.13.836.145.
Ah yet be mindful of your old Renown, ... Il.15.892.231.
Let him with Conquest and Renown retire; ..... Il.16.303.254.
To guard his Life, and add to his Renown, ... Il.20.152.400.
Drunk with Renown, insatiable of War, ... Il.22.282.467.
But hear with pleas'd attention the renown ..... Od.11.617.414.
Chiefs of renown! loud echoing shrieks arise; ..... Od.12.296.446.
To Fame I sent him, to acquire renown: ..... Od.13.488.29.
Wrong and oppression no renown can raise; ..... Od.21.359.277.

RENOWN'D
The *Kennet* swift, for silver Eels renown'd; ..... 1.W-F.341.183.
For her, thro' *Ægypt's* fruitful Clime renown'd, ... 1.TrSt.375.425.
Ev'n to those Shores is *Ithaca* renown'd, ... 1.TrUl.132.470.
Ye Bards! renown'd among the tuneful Throng ..... 2.ChJM.335.30.
Some fresh ingrav'd appear'd of Wits renown'd; ..... 2.TemF.35.255.
(Said Fame) but high above Desert renown'd: ..... 2.TemF.325.279.

RENOWN'D (CONTINUED)
Coscus renown'd for matchless Insolence; .... 4.JD2A.52.136.
In Lud's old walls, tho' long I rul'd renown'd, ... 5.DunA3.275.183.
In Lud's old walls tho' long I rul'd, renown'd .... 5.DunB3.277.333.
Mummius o'erheard him; Mummius, Fool-renown'd, ... 5.DunB4.371.379.
Obscure by Birth, renown'd by Crimes, ... 6.14v(b).13.50.
We form'd this Name, renown'd in Rhyme; .... 6.30.56.88.
Too bright your Form, and too renown'd his Song, ... 6.38.11Z5.108.
Renown'd for Wisdom, and rever'd for Age; .... Il.2.22.128.
Renown'd, triumphant, and enrich'd with Spoils. .... Il.2.144.135.
For prudent Counsel like the Gods renown'd: .... Il.2.206.138.
Th' *Isteian* Fields for gen'rous Vines renown'd, ... Il.2.645.157.
Or *Messè's* Tow'rs for silver Doves renown'd, ... Il.2.705.159.
The fierce *Pelasgi* next, in War renown'd, ... Il.2.1018.171.
One bold on Foot, and one renown'd for Horse. .... Il.3.304.208.
The warlike *Pandarus*, for strength renown'd; .... Il.4.120.226.
Observe my Father's Steeds, renown'd in Fight, ... Il.5.279.280.
Observe my Father's Steeds, renown'd in War. .... Il.5.279A.280.
Not Godlike *Hector* more in Arms renown'd: .... Il.5.570.296.
In ev'ry Art of glorious War renown'd) .... Il.5.753.303.
Teuthras the great, *Orestes* the renown'd .... Il.5.866.307.
(*Argos* the fair for warlike Steeds renown'd) .... Il.6.190.335.
How would the Sons of *Troy*, in Arms renown'd, ... Il.6.562.354.
Observe the Steeds of *Tros*, renown'd in War, ... Il.8.134.404.
Meriones, like *Mars* in Arms renown'd, ... Il.8.317.412.
Like *Pallas* worship'd, like the Sun renown'd; .... Il.8.670.427.
The gen'rous *Thrasymed*, in Arms renown'd: .... Il.9.112.437.
And sacred *Pedasus*, for Vines renown'd; .... Il.9.198.442.
And sacred *Pedasus*, for Vines renown'd; .... Il.9.385.451.
Renown'd for Justice and for length of Days, ... Il.13.10.104.
Thoas, *Deïpyrus*, in Arms renown'd, ... Il.13.127.110.
Merion, and *Aphareus*, in Field renown'd: .... Il.13.606.135.
Fly diverse; while proud Kings, and Chiefs renown'd .... Il.14.167.165.
Clytus, *Pisenor's* Son, renown'd in Fame, ... Il.15.522.217.
Thy Fall, great *Trojan!* had renown'd that Day. .... Il.15.539.217.
And *Ennomus*, in Augury renown'd. .... Il.17.259.297.
In little *Panope* for Strength renown'd, ... Il.17.356.301.
Since here, for brutal Courage far renown'd, ... Il.18.133.329.
Girds the vast Globe; the Maid in Arms renown'd; .... Il.20.46.396.
Three Sons renown'd adorn'd his nuptial Bed, ... Il.20.276.406.
The great *Ætolian* Chief, renown'd in War. .... Il.23.555.511.
(The same renown'd *Asteropæus* wore) .... Il.23.640.515.
Nor could *Ulysses*, for his Art renown'd, ... Il.23.834.522.
Mestor the brave, renown'd in Ranks of War, ... Il.24.321.549.
The Man, for Wisdom's various arts renown'd, ... Od.1.1.25.
From great *Anchialus*, renown'd and wise: .... Od.1.228.43.
In wond'rous arts than woman more renown'd, ... Od.2.135.67.
Meet then the Senior, far renown'd for sense, ... Od.3.23.87.
For martial deeds, and depth of thought renown'd; .... Od.4.368.137.
Two, foremost in the roll of *Mars* renown'd, ... Od.4.667.150.
And twenty chiefs renown'd for valour chose: .... Od.4.1028.165.
Had some distinguish'd day renown'd my fall; .... Od.5.396.191.
Not more renown'd the men of *Scheria's* Isle, ... Od.7.136.241.
Ulysses, far in fighting fields renown'd, ... Od.9.591.330.
The man, for Wisdom's various arts renown'd. .... Od.10.394.363.
Ev'n to those shores is *Ithaca* renown'd, ... Od.13.299.20.
The Prince return'd. Renown'd in days of yore .... Od.15.551.96.
Renown'd for wisdom, by th' abuse accurst! .... Od.16.435.128.
'Till then in ev'ry sylvan chace renown'd, ... Od.17.352.148.
Was ever Chief for wars like these renown'd? .... Od.17.574.160.
(His father's guest) for *Minos'* birth renown'd. .... Od.17.615.162.
Of *Thessaly*, his name I heard renown'd: .... Od.19.310.209.
And *Polybus* renown'd the faithful swain. .... Od.22.315.301.
With nobler contest ne'er renown'd a grave. .... Od.24.114.353.

RENT
Rent from the Walls, a Rocky Fragment lay; .... 1.TrES.100.453.
Full o'er their Heads the swelling Bag he rent, ... 2.RL4.91.191.
Who, having lost his Credit, pawn'd his Rent, ... 4.JD4.138.37.
So bought an Annual Rent or two. .... 4.1HE7.71.273.
Dishonest sight! his breeches rent below; .... 5.DunA3.194.173.
Dishonest sight! his breeches rent below; .... 5.DunB3.198.330.
"Or rent him Limb from Limb in cruel Play, ... 6.96ii.35.272.
From the rent Skin the Warrior tuggs again .... Il.5.1052.316.
Rent from the Walls a rocky Fragment lay; .... Il.12.454.98.
From his torn Arm the *Grecian* rent away .... Il.13.673.137.
Old *Chiron* rent, and shap'd it for his Sire; .... Il.16.175.245.
Tore all the Brawn, and rent the Nerves away: .... Il.16.374.257.
The Teeth it shatter'd, and the Tongue it rent. .... Il.17.698.314.
Rent from his Head the silver Locks away. .... Il.22.109.457.
She rent her Tresses, venerably grey, ... Il.22.512.477.
Nor Dogs nor Vultures have thy *Hector* rent, ... Il.24.503.557.
When he who thunders rent his bark in twain, ... Od.5.167.180.
While by the howling tempest rent in twain .... Od.5.407.192.
In squalid vests with many a gaping rent, ... Od.17.412.152.
Constrain'd! a rent-charge on the rich I live; .... Od.19.92.197.

RENT-CHARGE
Constrain'd! a rent-charge on the rich I live; .... Od.19.92.197.

RENTED
Than in five acres now of rented land. .... 4.HS2.136.65.

RENTS
The Chanc'ry takes your rents for twenty year: .... 4.HS2.172.69.

REPAID
Well be Apollo are thy Pray'rs repaid, ... Il.11.467.54.
Greece with *Achilles'* Friend shou'd be repaid, ... Il.17.181.294.
How fav'ring heav'n repaid my glorious toils .... Od.4.121.126.

REPAIR
To Plains with well-breath'd Beagles we repair, ... 1.W-F.121.161.
To Plains with well-bred Beagles we repair, ... 1.W-F.121A.161.
"Let me, O let me, to the Shades repair, ... 1.W-F.201.168.
Not mend their Minds; as some to *Church* repair, ... 1.EOC.342.277.

REPAIR (CONTINUED)
Go mount the Winds, and to the Shades repair; .... 1.TrSt.416.427.
And bad his Daughters to the Rites repair. .... 1.TrSt.622A.436.
Whether to sweet *Castalia* thou repair, ... 1.TrSt.831.444.
Hither the Noble Knight wou'd oft repair .... 2.ChJM.465.37.
Hither the Noble Lord wou'd oft repair .... 2.ChJM.465A.37.
Why to her House do'st thou so oft repair? .... 2.ChWB.78.60.
Thence, by a soft Transition, we repair .... 2.RL1.49.149.
The light Coquettes in *Sylphs* aloft repair, ... 2.RL1.65.150.
The lucid Squadrons round the Sails repair: .... 2.RL2.56.163.
Haste then ye Spirits! to your Charge repair; .... 2.RL2.111.166.
Swift to the Lock a thousand Sprights repair, ... 2.RL3.135.178.
He must repair it; takes a bribe from France; .... 3.Ep3.396.124.
Erect new wonders, and the old repair, ... 3.Ep4.192.155.
Make Keys, build Bridges, or repair White-hall: .... 4.HS2.120.63.
To Practice now from Theory repair. .... 5.DunB4.580.399.
Far hence to *Egypt* you'll repair, ... 6.30.60.88.
From hence to *Egypt* you'll repair, ... 6.30.60A.88.
WE, willing to repair this Breach, ... 6.30.77.89.
Then why to court should I repair .... 6.61.15.181.
My private Loss let grateful *Greece* repair; .... Il.1.152.94.
To *Agamemnon's* ample Tent repair. .... Il.2.10.127.
The *Phocians* next in forty Barks repair, ... Il.2.620.157.
With them the Youth of *Nisyrus* repair, ... Il.2.823.164.
In Throngs around his native Bands repair, ... Il.2.990.170.
Then thus: *Machaön*, to the King repair, ... Il.4.238.232.
And slowly, sadly, to their Fleet repair. .... Il.7.515.389.
Our self to hoary *Nestor* will repair; .... Il.10.65.5.
And feel a Loss not Ages can repair. .... Il.11.589.60.
Bid him from Fight to his own Deeps repair, ... Il.15.182.203.
He bids thee from forbidden Wars repair .... Il.15.198.204.
These to the Fleet repair with instant Flight, ... Il.20.49.396.
Here *Neptune*, and the Gods of *Greece* repair, ... Il.20.180.401.
All to *Achilles'* sable Ship repair, ... Il.23.37.488.
Then thro' the World of Waters, they repair .... Il.24.125.540.
Let *Hermes* to th' *Atlantic* isle <*> repair; .... Od.1.105.36.
Dismiss'd with honour let her hence repair .... Od.1.360.49.
Telemachus may bid the Queen repair .... Od.2.223.72.
But hence retreating to your domes repair; .... Od.2.285.75.
The waste of nature let the feast repair, ... Od.4.71.122.
Then from the rites of purity repair, ... Od.4.299.133.
But now let sleep the painful waste repair .... Od.4.399.139.
With me repair; and from thy warrior band .... Od.4.551.146.
The flocks of Ocean to the strand repair: .... Od.4.604.148.
Repair we to the blessings of the night: .... Od.7.249.248.
But still long-weary'd nature wants repair; .... Od.7.294.250.
But, herald, to the palace swift repair, ... Od.8.291.278.
And to the court th' embody'd Peers repair. .... Od.8.454.288.
In haste our fellows to the ships repair, ... Od.9.180.313.
Each drooping spirit with bold words repair, ... Od.9.447.324.
From all their dens the one-ey'd race repair, ... Od.9.475.325.
Reviving sweets repair the mind's decay, ... Od.10.427.365.
I speed my flight, and to my mates repair. .... Od.11.790.426.
Then bade his followers to the feast repair. .... Od.13.26.2.
I linger life; nor to the court repair, ... Od.14.411.55.
To *Diocles*, at *Phæræ*, they repair, ... Od.15.210.78.
Our safe return, and back with speed repair: .... Od.16.163.110.
While to th' assembled council I repair; .... Od.17.64.135.
The time, my Lord, invites me to repair .... Od.17.672.165.
Hence, to the vagrant's rendezvous repair; .... Od.18.377.185.
Whilst to nocturnal joys impure, repair .... Od.20.11.230.
Some to the spring, with each a jar, repair, ... Od.20.192.242.
Of twenty virgins to the spring repair: .... Od.20.197.243.
Cease the gay dance, and to their rest repair; .... Od.23.320.339.

REPAIR'D
Repair'd to search the gloomy Cave of *Spleen*. .... 2.RL4.16.184.
On once a flock-bed, but repair'd with straw, ... 3.Ep3.301.118.
With sleep repair'd the long debauch of night: .... Od.10.664.375.
Strait to the feast-full palace he repair'd, ... Od.17.306.146.
Forth-issuing from the dome the Prince repair'd: .... Od.20.181.242.
But well repair'd; and gloves against the thorn. .... Od.24.266.361.

REPAIRS
Next to the Bounds of *Nisus'* Realm repairs, ... 1.TrSt.468.429.
Repairs her Smiles, awakens ev'ry Grace, ... 2.RL1.141.157.
Repairs to search the gloomy Cave of *Spleen*. .... 2.RL4.16A.184.
She said; then raging to *Sir Plume* repairs, ... 2.RL4.121.194.
Hector to *Paris'* lofty Dome repairs. .... Il.6.389.345.
The King to *Nestor's* sable Ship repairs; .... Il.10.81.6.
Swift to her bright Apartment she repairs, ... Il.14.191.168.
And silent, to the joyous hall repairs. .... Od.1.430.53.
In his pavilion there to sleep repairs; .... Od.1.539.57.
And to the gifts of balmy sleep repairs. .... Od.3.509.112.
And to the gifts of balmy sleep repairs. .... Od.7.310.251.
Majestic to the lists of Fame repairs. .... Od.8.110.268.
A gen'rous heart repairs a sland'rous tongue. .... Od.8.432.287.
And social joys, the late-transform'd repairs: .... Od.10.532.369.
Thither his son from sandy *Pyle* repairs, ... Od.24.179.356.

REPASS
Who pass, repass, advance, and glide away; .... 2.TemF.460.285.
Homeward with pious speed repass the main, ... Od.1.378.50.
Will teach you to repass th' unmeasur'd main. .... Od.4.576.147.
Safe as they pass, and safe repass the tides, ... Od.8.614.295.

REPASS'D
Repass'd, and viewless mix'd with common air. .... Od.4.1094.169.
The rest are vanish'd, none repass'd the gate; .... Od.10.307.359.
Th' associates of the Prince repass'd the bay; .... Od.16.345.122.

REPAST
With hollow Screeches fled the dire Repast; .... 1.TrSt.736.441.
And frequent Cups prolong the rich Repast. .... 2.RL3.112.176.
While frequent Cups prolong the rich Repast. .... 2.RL3.112A.176.
Not so: a Buck was then a week's repast, ... 4.HS2.93.61.

REPAST (CONTINUED)

Then spread the Tables, the Repast prepare, ...Il.1.612.117.
But now, ye Warriors, take a short Repast; ....Il.2.452.149.
Then spread the Tables, the Repast prepare, ...Il.2.512.151.
Then spread the Tables, the Repast prepare, ...Il.7.384.382.
This Night, let due Repast refresh our Pow'rs; ....Il.9.825.474.
In due Repast indulge the genial Hour, ...Il.10.677.32.
The Reaper's due Repast, the Women's Care. ....Il.18.650.355.
At least our Armies claim Repast and Rest: ....Il.19.156.378.
With strong Repast to hearten' ev'ry Band; ....Il.19.170.378.
Repast unheeded, while he vents his Woes. ....Il.24.160.542.
And each indulging shar'd in sweet Repast. ....Il.24.795.570.
Of choicest sort and savour, rich repast! ....Od.1.186.42.
They share the honours of the rich repast. ....Od.4.80.123.
The wants of nature with repast suffice, ...Od.4.581.147.
For them to form some exquisite repast? ....Od.4.908.161.
Then take repast, 'till *Hesperus* display'd ....Od.4.1035.166.
For him, the Nymph a rich repast ordains, ...Od.5.251.183.
Then with a short repast relieve their toil, ...Od.6.109.211.
Of choicest sort and savour, rich repast! ....Od.7.237.247.
The loaden shelves afford us full repast; ....Od.9.274.318.
Brain'd on the rock; his second dire repast. ....Od.9.405.322.
Content, and innocent repast display, ...Od.12.357.448.
To take repast, and stills the wordy war; ....Od.12.520.457.
Of choicest sort and favour, rich repast! ....Od.15.155.76.
Holy repast! That instant from the skies ....Od.16.474.130.
And now a short repast prepar'd, they fed, ...Od.16.498.131.
I cheer no lazy vagrants with repast; ....Od.19.31.194.
Incessant turns, impatient for repast: ....Od.20.34.234.
And eager all devour the rich repast. ....Od.20.321.248.
And eve-repast, with equal cost and care: ....Od.20.466.256.

REPASTE

(Each at his Post in Arms) a short Repaste. ....Il.7.455.387.
Now had the *Grecians* snatch'd a short Repaste, ...Il.8.67.398.
My craving bowels still require repaste. ....Od.7.296.250.
Of choicest sort and savour, rich repaste! ....Od.10.440.365.
To late repaste, (the day's hard labour done:) ....Od.13.43.3.
Swell the fat herd; luxuriant, large repaste! ....Od.13.472.29.
They sought repaste; while to th' unhappy kind, ...Od.14.383.53.
Now did the hour of sweet repaste arrive, ...Od.17.194.141.
In sweet repaste the present hour imploy, ...Od.21.471.283.

REPASTING

The Guards repasting, while the Bowls go round; ....Il.24.546.558.

REPASTS

The Fires they light, to short Repasts they fall, ...Il.9.119.438.
Insatiate riots in the sweet repasts, ...Od.9.108.308.

REPAY

And all your Masters well-spent Care repay. ....Il.8.229.408.
And what my Youth has ow'd, repay their Age. ....Il.14.242.172.
Come, for my Brother's Blood repay thy own. ....Il.17.38.289.
Now Sums immense thy Mercy shall repay. ....Il.21.91.425.
This Mule his dauntless Labours shall repay; ....Il.23.765.520.
My Rage, and these Barbarities repay! ....Il.24.262.547.
Thus, shall I thus repay a mother's cares, ...Od.2.149.69.
And wou'dst thou evil for his good repay? ....Od.16.448.128.
"That base, inhospitable blow repay!" ....Od.17.587.161.
And aiding this one hour, repay it all. ....Od.22.230.298.

REPAY'D

By Love to thee his Bounties I repay'd, ...Il.9.604.464.
Soon with redoubl'd force the wound repay'd; ....Od.19.528.221.

REPAYS

Repays not half that *Envy* which it brings. ....1.EOC.495A.294.
And the brave Son repays his Cares with Fame. ....Il.8.346.414.

REPEAT

No more the Nightingales repeat her Lays, ...1.PWi.55A.93.
Repeat unask'd; lament, the Wit's too fine ....4.2HE1.366.227.
And sad Posterity repeat the Tale. ....Il.19.66.374.
(Doom'd to repeat the perils of the main, ...Od.4.650.150.
Repeat them frequent in the genial day; ....Od.8.276.278.
To him thy presents show, thy words repeat: ....Od.15.175.77.
And tears repeat their long-forgotten course! ....Od.19.191.201.

REPEATED

And fires his Host with loud repeated Cries: ....1.TrES.176.456.
And fires his Host with loud repeated Cries. ....Il.12.530.101.
But with repeated Shouts his Army fires. ....Il.13.204.115.
Repeated Wounds the red'ning River dy'd, ...Il.21.26.422.
Forc'd by repeated Insults to return, ...Il.22.644.483.
Fix'd in my Heart, and oft repeated there! ....Il.24.939.575.

REPEATS

With Eyes that pry not, Tongue that ne'er repeats, ...4.HS1.135.19.
Dulness, good Queen, repeats the jest again. ....5.DunA2.114.110.
Dulness, good Queen, repeats the jest again. ....5.DunB2.122.301.
Thus I: while raging he repeats his cries, ...Od.9.615.332.

REPEL

To share the Danger, and repel the Foe. ....1.TrES.76.452.
Vain was his Breastplate to repel the Wound: ....Il.13.468.128.
But join'd, repel not *Hector's* fiery Course. ....Il.13.862.147.
But by our Walls secur'd, repel the Foe. ....Il.22.119.458.
To thwart thy passage, and repel thy fleet? ....Od.10.72.342.
If outrag'd, cease that outrage to repel, ...Od.16.296.119.
But impotent these riots to repel, ...Od.18.271.179.
Retort an insult, or repel a foe? ....Od.21.142.265.

REPELL

To share the Danger, and repell the Foe. ....1.TrES.80Z10.452.
Nor cou'd the *Greeks* repell the *Lycian* Pow'rs, ...1.TrES.155.455.

REPELL (CONTINUED)

Repell the Rage of *Priam's* single Son? ....Il.9.463.455.
And couching close, repell invading Sleep. ....Il.10.210.11.
Repell an Army, and defraud the Fates? ....Il.12.196.88.
To share the Danger, and repell the Foe. ....Il.12.420.97.
To share the Danger, and repell the Foe. ....Il.12.434.97.
Nor could the *Greeks* repell the *Lycian* Pow'rs, ...Il.12.509.100.
Not empty Boasts the Sons of *Troy* repell, ...Il.16.759.273.
Or with these Hands the cruel Stroke repell, ...Il.18.534.347.

REPELL'D

Hippomedon repell'd the hostile Tyde? ....1.TrSt.64.413.
'Till by this Arm the Foe shall be repell'd; ....1.TrES.86.453.
My vary'd Belt repell'd the flying Wound. ....Il.4.225.232.
The Point rebated, and repell'd the Wound. ....Il.11.304.48.
So turn'd stern *Ajax*, by whole Hosts repell'd, ...Il.11.680.65.
Till by this Arm the Foe shall be repell'd; ....Il.12.440.97.
Till faint with Labour, and by Foes repell'd, ...Il.13.652.136.
Repell'd to distance flies the bounding Dart. ....Il.13.744.140.
And now the Chief (the foremost Troops repell'd) ....Il.16.476.261.
But stopp'd, and rested, by the third repell'd; ....Il.20.317.407.
Unerring, but the heav'nly Shield repell'd ....Il.22.370.471.
The rest repell'd, a train oblivious fly. ....Od.11.183.390.

REPENT

That ere the Rites are o'er, you may repent! ....2.ChJM.281.27.
But oft repented, and repent it still; ....2.ChWB.333.73.
Repent old pleasures, and sollicit new: ....2.ElAb.186.335.
Alas! 'tis ten times worse when they *repent*. ....4.Arbu.108.103.
Trust me, 'tis ten times worse when they *repent*. ....4.Arbu.108A.103.
The only danger is, when they *repent*. ....4.Arbu.108B.103.
As decent to *repent* in, as to *sin* in. ....6.95.6.264.
In Blood and Slaughter shall repent at last. ....Il.1.449.109.
A noble Mind disdains not to repent. ....Il.15.227.205.
Lest dragg'd in vengeance, thou repent thy stay; ....Od.18.15.167.

REPENTANCE

Let my Repentance your Forgiveness draw, ...2.ChJM.793.53.
To the next Day's Repentance, as they boast, ...6.17iv.20.59.
Such the Repentance of a suppliant King, ...Il.9.395.452.
Leave to repentance and his own sad heart, ...Od.10.524.368.

REPENTANT

Repentant sighs, and voluntary pains: ....2.ElAb.18.320.
Then turns repentant, and his God adores ....3.Ep1.188.31.
At length the Monarch with repentant Grief ....Il.6.235.337.
Neptune, by pray'r repentant rarely won, ...Od.1.88.35.
What vows repentant will the Pow'r appease, ...Od.4.633.149.
Rules this blest realm, repentant I obey! ....Od.8.436.287.

REPENTED

But oft repented, and repent it still; ....2.ChWB.333.73.
And many a long-repented word bring out. ....Od.14.523.62.

REPENTENCE

Then, lest Repentence punish such a Life, ...4.HAdv.104.83.

REPENTS

Ev'n Ralph repents, and Henly writes no more. ....5.DunB1.216.285.

REPIN'D

What if the head, the eye, or ear repin'd ....3.EOM1.261.46.

REPINE

In vain the gloomy Thund'rer might repine: ....Il.8.249.409.
Nor, tho' a meaner give Advice, repine, ...Il.9.137.438.

REPINES

While proud Philosophy repines to show ....5.DunA3.193.173.
While proud Philosophy repines to show, ...5.DunB3.197.330.
To cheat a Mortal, who repines in vain. ....Il.22.30.453.

REPINING

Their tortur'd Minds repining Envy tears, ...1.TrSt.176.417.

REPLENISH

"Replenish, not ingloriously, at home." ....5.DunA2.158.120.
"Replenish, not ingloriously, at home." ....5.DunB2.166.303.

REPLENISH'D

So clouds replenish'd from some bog below, ...5.DunB2.363.315.
Replenish'd from the cool, translucent springs; ....Od.1.180.41.
Replenish'd from the cool translucent springs, ...Od.7.231.247.
Replenish'd from the cool, translucent springs, ...Od.10.434.365.
Replenish'd from the pure, translucent springs; ....Od.17.105.137.
He said: replenish'd from the purest springs, ...Od.19.450.216.

REPLETE

Replete with mail, and military store, ...Od.4.1031.166.
Replete with water from the chrystal springs; ....Od.15.149.75.

REPLIES

Silent, or only to her Name replies, ...1.PWi.42.92.
When the fair Consort of her son replies. ....1.TrFD.2.385.
Confus'd, and sadly thus at length replies: ....1.TrSt.797.443.
Replies—Ah why forbears the Son to Name ....1.TrSt.808.443.
Goddess of Wisdom! (*Ithacus* replies) ....1.TrUl.188.472.
Thus he: The blue-ey'd Goddess thus replies; ....1.TrUl.207.472.
'Till, what with Proofs, Objections, and Replies, ...2.ChJM.143.21.
'Tis well, 'tis wondrous well, the Knight replies, ...2.ChJM.216.25.
"See man for mine!" replies a pamper'd goose; ....3.EOM3.46.96.
The Man of Ross, each lisping babe replies. ....3.Ep3.262.115.
Squeaks like a high-stretch'd Lutestring, and replies: ....4.JD4.99.33.
Loth to enrich me with too quick Replies, ...4.JD4.128.35.
"God save king Colley!" Drury-lane replies: ....5.DunB1.322.293.
"Be that my task (replies a gloomy Clerk, ...5.DunB4.459.385.

REPLIES (CONTINUED)

To her full Pipes the grunting Hog replies; ....6.14ii.25.43.
Encourag'd thus, the blameless Man replies: ....Il.1.117.92.
Encourag'd thus, the blameless Priest replies: ....Il.1.117A.92.
Insatiate King (*Achilles* thus replies) ....Il.1.155.94.
Forbear! (the Progeny of *Jove* replies) ....Il.1.273.100.
This said, he ceas'd: The King of Men replies; ....Il.1.376.106.
Unhappy Son! (fair *Thetis* thus replies, ...Il.1.540.113.
She said, and sighing thus the God replies ....Il.1.670.119.
He views the Wretch, and sternly thus replies. ....Il.2.305.142.
Then thus, incens'd, the *Paphian* Queen replies; ....Il.3.513.216.
The Prince replies; Ah cease, divinely fair, ...Il.3.543.217.
Sighs from his inmost Soul, and thus replies; ....Il.4.46.223.
Then on the Thund'rer fix'd them, and replies. ....Il.4.74.224.
Struck with his gen'rous Wrath, the King replies; ....Il.4.410.240.
He said, nor *Hector* to the Chief replies, ...Il.5.848.306.
To whom the Progeny of *Jove* replies. ....Il.7.39.364.
Th' Almighty Thund'rer with a Frown replies, ...Il.7.542.391.
O rev'rend Prince! (*Tydides* thus replies) ....Il.8.177.406.
But *Juno,* impotent of Rage, replies. ....Il.8.574.424.
The Goddess thus: and thus the God replies ....Il.8.584.424.
(*Ulysses,* with a scornful Smile, replies) ....Il.10.472.24.
Eurypylus replies: No more (my Friend) ....Il.11.956.78.
O Prince! (*Meriones* replies) whose Care ....Il.13.333.121.
Thus he. The sage *Ulysses* thus replies, ...Il.14.88.162.
Thy just Reproofs (*Atrides* calm replies) ....Il.14.114.163.
Imperial Dame (the balmy Pow'r replies) ....Il.14.276.175.
Vain are thy Fears (the Queen of Heav'n replies, ...Il.14.297.177.
Glows with celestial Red, and thus replies. ....Il.14.374.180.
(Th' immortal Father with a Smile replies!) ....Il.15.54.196.
To whom the white-arm'd Goddess thus replies: ....Il.15.98.200.
(The King of Ocean thus, incens'd, replies) ....Il.15.207.204.
With faint, expiring Breath, the Chief replies. ....Il.16.1017.282.
In happy time (the Charioteer replies) ....Il.17.540.309.
O Chief, Oh Father! (*Atreus'* Son replies) ....Il.17.630.312.
Achilles thus. And *Iris* thus replies. ....Il.18.220.332.
What Words are these (th' Imperial Dame replies, ...Il.18.423.341.
To whom the mournful Mother thus replies, ...Il.18.499.345.
The Son of *Peleus* thus: And thus replies ....Il.19.153.378.
For this (the stern *Æacides* replies) ....Il.19.197.379.
'Tis true (the Cloud-compelling Pow'r replies) ....Il.20.29.394.
The great Earth-shaker thus: To whom replies ....Il.20.357.410.
Talk not of Life, or Ransom, (he replies) ....Il.21.111.426.
The River thus; and thus the Chief replies. ....Il.21.240.430.
Talk not of Oaths (the dreadful Chief replies, ...Il.22.333.470.
No, Wretch accurst! Relentless he replies, ...Il.22.433.473.
O'er the dead Hero, thus (unheard) replies. ....Il.22.460.474.
Old Man! (*Oïleus* rashly thus replies) ....Il.23.556.511.
Are doom'd both Heroes, (*Juno* thus replies) ....Il.24.71.538.
'Tis *Jove* that calls. And why (the Dame replies) ....Il.24.117.540.
Sad *Hecuba* renews, and then replies. ....Il.24.242.546.
Move me no more (*Achilles* thus replies ....Il.24.705.566.
Here paus'd the God, and pensive thus replies ....Od.1.55.33.
To prove a genuine birth (the Prince replies) ....Od.1.275.46.
Those toils (*Telemachus* serene replies) ....Od.1.495.56.
Oh son of *Polybus!* the Prince replies, ...Od.1.521.57.
While yet he speaks, *Telemachus* replies. ....Od.2.147.68.
Or who can say (his gamesome mate replies) ....Od.2.372.78.
Urge him with truth to frame his fair replies; ....Od.3.25.87.
And fam'd among the sons of men, replies. ....Od.3.93.90.
Ah! no such hope (the Prince with sighs replies) ....Od.3.279.99.
Urge him with truth to frame his free replies. ....Od.3.419.107.
Well hast thou spoke (the blue-ey'd maid replies) ....Od.3.455.109.
Insensate! with a sigh the King replies, ...Od.4.37.121.
See there confess'd, *Pisistratus* replies, ...Od.4.209.129.
Inclement fate! *Telemachus* replies, ...Od.4.395.139.
(Replies the Prince) inflam'd with filial love, ...Od.4.426.140.
To *Jove,* (with stern regard the God replies,) ....Od.4.635.149.
The Queen replies: If in the blest abodes, ...Od.4.1085.168.
Alas! for this (the prudent man replies) ....Od.5.273.184.
Thus he. No word th' experienc'd man replies, ...Od.7.421.258.
Well hast thou spoke, (*Euryalus* replies) ....Od.8.153.271.
Inces'd *Ulysses* with a frown replies, ...Od.8.183.272.
Fools that ye are! (the Savage thus replies, ...Od.9.325.319.
Thus they: the *Cyclop* from his den replies ....Od.9.484.325.
Th' astonisht Savage with a roar replies: ....Od.9.593.330.
Nor this, replies the Seer, will I conceal. ....Od.11.179.390.
(*Ulysses* thus replies) a King in mind! ....Od.11.471.407.
Warn'd by my ills beware, the Shade replies, ...Od.11.545.410.
He said: the Shaker of the earth replies. ....Od.13.171.13.
If such thy will—We will it, *Jove* replies. ....Od.13.177.14.
Goddess of Wisdom! *Ithacus* replies, ...Od.13.355.24.
Thus he. The blue-ey'd Goddess thus replies. ....Od.13.374.25.
With warmth replies the man of mighty woes. ....Od.16.92.106.
Mark well my voice, *Ulysses* strait replies: ....Od.16.280.118.
The bold *Melanthius* to their thought replies. ....Od.17.445.155.
The nurse replies: "If *Jove* receives my pray'r, ...Od.17.588.161.
(Replies the Queen) the stranger beg'd their grace, ...Od.17.592.161.
Who'er this guest (the prudent Queen replies) ....Od.17.664.164.
To whom with thought mature the King replies: ....Od.18.151.173.
Then to the Queen *Eurymachus* replies: ....Od.18.285.180.
That speak disdain, the wanton thus replies. ....Od.18.374.185.
While yet he speaks, *Eurymachus* replies, ...Od.18.428.189.
Be calm, replies the Sire; to none impart, ...Od.19.50.195.
And thus impassion'd to herself replies. ....Od.19.423.215.
With cool composure feign'd, the Chief replies: ....Od.19.447.216.
The vision self-explain'd (the Chief replies.) ....Od.19.650.227.
Propose the sportive lot, the Chief replies, ...Od.19.683.229.
O *Jove* supreme, the raptur'd swain replies, ...Od.20.294.247.
Sage and serene *Telemachus* replies; ....Od.20.403.251.
Thus jovial they; but nought the Prince replies; ....Od.20.459.255.
To whom with dubious joy the Queen replies, ...Od.23.81.322.
Pleas'd with her virtuous fears, the King replies, ...Od.23.113.325.
Be that thy care, *Telemachus* replies, ...Od.23.123.326.
Touch'd at her words, the King with warmth replies, ...Od.23.184.332.
At length *Ulysses* with a sigh replies: ....Od.23.265.336.

REPLIES (CONTINUED)

Is not thy thought my own? (the God replies ....Od.24.547.374.

REPLY

A God, a God! the vocal Hills reply, ...1.Mes.31.116.
And from his Throne return'd this stern Reply. ....1.TrSt.403.426.
The Desart ecchoes, and the Rocks reply: ....1.TrES.222.458.
The Walls, the Woods, and long Canals reply. ....2.RL3.100.174.
Full ten years slander'd, did he once reply? ....4.Arbu.374.123.
Don't you remember what Reply he gave? ....4.2HE2.49.167.
Demurely did reply, ...6.79.50.219.
Too dull for laughter, for reply too mad? ....6.116vii.4.328.
The Thund'rer spoke, nor durst the Queen reply; ....Il.1.736.122.
The Lambs reply from all the neighb'ring Hills: ....Il.4.495.244.
Th' Almighty spoke, nor durst the Pow'rs reply, ...Il.8.35.397.
Attend the stern Reply. Then *Phœnix* rose; ....Il.9.558.460.
Attend the stern Reply. *Tydides* broke ....Il.9.814.473.
To whom *Ulysses* made this wise Reply; ....Il.10.453.23.
The vengeful Monarch gave this stern Reply; ....Il.11.179.43.
And bear with haste the *Pylian* King's Reply: ....Il.11.975.78.
The Heav'ns re-echo, and the Shores reply; ....Il.13.64.107.
Since Heav'n commands it (*Ajax* made reply) ....Il.15.554.218.
Thy Friend return'd; and with it, this Reply. ....Il.16.67.238.
The Desert echoes, and the Rocks reply: ....Il.16.525.264.
And let me fall! (*Achilles* made reply) ....Il.18.126.328.
My Son (Cœrulean *Thetis* made reply, ...Il.18.163.330.
And the round Bulwarks, and thick Tow'rs reply: ....Il.18.262.335.
Gives the loud signal, and the Heav'ns reply. ....Il.20.187.401.
His sage reply, and with her train retires. ....Od.1.460.54.
Struck with the kind reproach, I strait reply; ....Od.4.507.144.
She ceas'd, and suppliant thus I made reply; ....Od.4.531.146.
To whom with sighs *Ulysses* gave reply: ....Od.8.167.271.
They, seal'd with truth return the sure reply, ...Od.11.182.390.
And forc'd the stubborn spectre to reply; ....Od.11.695.419.
Thus he, nor deign'd for our reply to stay, ...Od.11.773.424.
Sincere the youthful Heroe made reply. ....Od.16.118.108.
Few are my days, *Ulysses* made reply, ...Od.16.204.113.
All, all (*Ulysses* instant made reply) ....Od.16.248.117.
He ceas'd; nor made the pensive Queen reply, ...Od.17.170.139.
And sow'rly smiling, this reply returns. ....Od.17.544.154.
And if my questions meet a true reply, ...Od.17.629.163.
Pleas'd with his wise reply, the Queen rejoin'd: ....Od.19.403.214.
Without reply vouchsaf'd, *Antinous* ceas'd: ....Od.20.340.249.
His sage reply, and with her train retir'd: ....Od.21.382.278.
Heedless he heard them; but disdain'd reply; ....Od.21.438.281.
Haste and return (*Ulysses* made reply) ....Od.22.122.292.
Then ceas'd; the filial virtue made reply. ....Od.22.167.295.
Thus speaks the Queen, and no reply attends, ...Od.23.87.323.

REPLY'D

Thus *Daphnis* spoke, and *Strephon* thus reply'd. ....1.PSp.22.62.
He ceas'd, and *May* with modest Grace reply'd; ....2.ChJM.575.43.
He ceas'd, and *May* with sober Grace reply'd; ....2.ChJM.575A.43.
And will you so, reply'd the Queen, indeed? ....2.ChJM.656.46.
With all my Soul, he thus reply'd again; ....2.ChJM.736.50.
What ails my Lord? the trembling Dame reply'd; ....2.ChJM.758.51.
(Reply'd the Dame:) Are these the Thanks I find? ....2.ChJM.781.52.
Where grows this Plant (reply'd the Friend) oh where? ....2.ChWB.397.76.
And *Hampton's* Ecchoes, wretched Maid! reply'd? ....2.RLA2.14.132.
(While *Hampton's* Ecchos, wretched Maid! reply'd) ....2.RL4.96.191.
It grieves me much (reply'd the Peer again) ....2.RL4.131.194.
Ambitious Fools! (the Queen reply'd, and frown'd) ....2.TemF.350.280.
"No ('tis reply'd) the first Almighty Cause ....3.EOM1.145.33.
"No ('tis reply'd) he acts by *gen'ral Laws;* ....3.EOM1.146A.33.
As well his Grace reply'd, "Like you, Sir John? ....3.Ep3.317.119.
(Reply'd soft Annius) this our paunch before ....5.DunB4.388.380.
Is it full grown? The Squire reply'd, ...6.94.63.261.
Repuls'd the sacred Sire, and thus reply'd. ....Il.1.34.87.
He said and sate: when *Calchas* thus reply'd, ...Il.1.91.91.
At this, *Pelides* frowning stern, reply'd: ....Il.1.193.96.
Each Army stood: The *Spartan* Chief reply'd. ....Il.3.134.196.
Thus ceas'd the King, and thus the Fair reply'd. ....Il.3.226.203.
Ajax the great (the beauteous Queen reply'd) ....Il.3.293.207.
He shook his hoary Locks, and thus reply'd. ....Il.4.369.238.
O Prince (*Lycaon's* valiant Son reply'd) ....Il.5.288.281.
Mistaken Vaunter! *Diomed* reply'd; ....Il.5.347.283.
Thus haughty spoke. The *Lycian* King reply'd. ....Il.5.803.304.
(Reply'd the Chief) can *Tydeus'* Son enquire? ....Il.6.180.334.
Brother, 'tis just (reply'd the beauteous Youth) ....Il.6.418.347.
The Chief reply'd: This Time forbids to rest: ....Il.6.450.348.
Not to the Court (reply'd th' Attendant Train) ....Il.6.478.350.
The Chief reply'd: That Post shall be my Care, ...Il.6.560.354.
To whom the noble *Hector* thus reply'd: ....Il.6.666.360.
(To *Ajax* thus the *Trojan* Prince reply'd) ....Il.7.284.378.
The Senior spoke, and sate. To whom reply'd ....Il.7.428.385.
To whom *Gerenian Nestor* thus reply'd, ...Il.8.183.406.
(The hollow Vessels to his Voice reply'd) ....Il.8.275.410.
Thus he: The stern *Achilles* thus reply'd. ....Il.9.713.469.
(To *Ajax* thus the first of *Greeks* reply'd) ....Il.9.758.471.
Great King of Nations! (*Ithacus* reply'd) ....Il.9.794.473.
There shalt thou stay (the King of Men reply'd ....Il.10.71.5.
O prudent Chief! (the *Pylian* Sage reply'd) ....Il.10.162.9.
(Reply'd the Sage) to praise me, or to blame: ....Il.10.292.15.
The Warrior thus, and thus the Friend reply'd. ....Il.11.410.53.
O first of Friends! (*Pelides* thus reply'd) ....Il.11.742.68.
Not in the Centre, (*Idomen* reply'd) ....Il.13.400.125.
They ceas'd; and thus the Chief of *Troy* reply'd. ....Il.13.1043.154.
The *Lycian* Leader, and sedate reply'd. ....Il.17.188.294.
Her mournful Offspring, to his Sighs reply'd. ....Il.18.92.327.
Thetis (reply'd the God) our Pow'rs may claim, ...Il.18.461.343.
(The Azure Goddess to her Son reply'd) ....Il.19.32.373.
His fate-ful Voice. Th' intrepid Chief reply'd ....Il.19.465.391.
(Reply'd the Warrior) our illustrious Race? ....Il.21.170.428.
Not so, (the Dame reply'd) I haste to go ....Il.23.252.499.
Stern had reply'd; fierce Scorn inhancing Scorn ....Il.23.573.512.
With Joy, the venerable King reply'd. ....Il.23.718.518.

REPLY'D (CONTINUED)

(Reply'd unmov'd the venerable Man) ....Il.24.269.547.
(The sacred Messenger of Heav'n reply'd) ....Il.24.466.556.
Thus *Priam* spoke, and *Hermes* thus reply'd. ....Il.24.476.556.
And joyful thus the royal Sire reply'd. ....Il.24.518.557.
This thy Request (reply'd the Chief) enjoy: ....Il.24.838.572.
(Reply'd the Thund'rer to the Martial Maid) ....Od.1.85.35.
Magnificence of old, (the Prince reply'd,) ....Od.1.295.47.
(Reply'd the Prince) will you the Bard reprove? ....Od.1.442.53.
Far hence (reply'd the Prince) thy fears be driv'n: ....Od.2.416.81.
(The Youth with prudent modesty reply'd) ....Od.3.28.87.
The prudent youth reply'd. Oh thou, the grace ....Od.3.246.97.
Thus check'd, reply'd *Ulysses*' prudent heir: ....Od.3.297.100.
The Monarch took the word, and grave reply'd. ....Od.4.91.123.
Right well, reply'd the King, your speech displays ....Od.4.365.137.
And thus indignant to the Prince reply'd: ....Od.4.446.141.
Press not too far, reply'd the God; but cease ....Od.4.661.150.
'Tis not, reply'd the Sage, to *Medon* giv'n ....Od.4.944.162.
Courage resume, the shadowy form reply'd, ...Od.4.1079.168.
What words are these (reply'd the Pow'r who forms ......Od.5.30.172.
And gently grasp'd his hand, and thus reply'd. ....Od.5.234.182.
Heroe and King! (*Ulysses* thus reply'd) ....Od.7.389.255.
And touch'd the Youths; but their stern Sire reply'd, ...Od.10.82.343.
Thy fated road (the magic Pow'r reply'd) ....Od.10.598.372.
The Ghost reply'd: To Hell my doom I owe, ...Od.11.75.384.
Of flowing tears, and thus with sighs reply'd. ....Od.11.252.394.
While life informs these limbs, (the King reply'd) ....Od.11.434.405.
The swain reply'd. It never was our guise ....Od.14.65.38.
(Reply'd *Eumæus*) to the wand'ring tribe. ....Od.14.147.42.
(Reply'd *Eumæus:*) To the present hour ....Od.14.192.45.
(Thus quick reply'd the wisest of mankind) ....Od.14.432.56.
(Reply'd the swain for spotless faith divine) ....Od.14.444.57.
Be then thy thanks, (the bounteous swain reply'd) ....Od.14.492.60.
To whom the Youth for prudence fam'd, reply'd. ....Od.15.100.73.
(The Prince reply'd) stand fixt in fate above; ....Od.15.203.78.
Stranger (reply'd the Prince) securely rest ....Od.15.304.83.
Haste then (the false designing youth reply'd) ....Od.15.470.93.
The Prince reply'd; *Eumæus*, I obey; ....Od.16.31.103.
Far hence those fears, (*Eurymachus* reply'd) ....Od.16.452.129.
Thus he: nor ought *Telemachus* reply'd, ...Od.17.31.134.
(Reply'd the Prince) nor be our fates deplor'd, ...Od.17.58.135.
(Reply'd the Chief) to no unheedful breast; ....Od.17.333.147.
Fair truth alone (the patient man reply'd) ....Od.17.642.163.
Mere woman-glutton! (thus the churl reply'd) ....Od.18.32.168.
(Reply'd the sagest of the royal train) ....Od.18.202.176.
What thanks! what boon! reply'd the Queen, are due, ..Od.19.354.211.
Thy aid avails me not, the Chief reply'd; ....Od.19.583.224.
Some pitying God (*Ulysses* sad reply'd) ....Od.20.211.243.
Our weakness scorn? *Antinous* thus reply'd. ....Od.21.271.272.
Alone the bold *Eurymachus* reply'd. ....Od.22.56.289.
No so (reply'd *Ulysses*) leave him there, ...Od.22.184.296.
Not so (*Ulysses* more sedate reply'd) ....Od.22.469.311.
(Reply'd *Amphimedon*) our hapless fate. ....Od.24.145.355.
(Reply'd the King elated with his praise) ....Od.24.435.369.
Already it is known (the King reply'd, ...Od.24.469.371.

REPORT

'Twas then *Belinda!* if Report say true, ...2.RL1.117.154.
The dire Report thro' ev'ry Region flies: ....2.TemF.335.280.
There flies about a strange report ....4.HS6.109.257.
Go then, to *Greece* report our fixt Design; ....Il.9.544.460.
This to report, my hasty Course I bend; ....Il.11.798.71.
Report to yon' mad Tyrant of the Main. ....Il.15.181.203.
Should such report thy honour'd Person here, ...Il.24.822.571.
The Sanction of th' assembled pow'rs report: ....Od.1.107.36.
Say, royal youth, sincere of soul report ....Od.4.421.140.
With terror wing'd conveys the dread report. ....Od.4.706.152.
Ah! doubt not our report (the Prince rejoin'd) ....Od.15.172.76.
Now flying Fame the swift report had spread ....Od.24.474.371.

REPORTED

For so reported the first man I view'd, ...Od.24.306.364.

REPOS'D

On Dulness lap th' Anointed head repos'd. ....5.DunA3.2.150.
On Dulness' lap th' Anointed head repos'd. ....5.DunB3.2.320.
The rev'rend *Nestor* with his Queen repos'd. ....Od.3.515.112.
Their number summ'd, repos'd in sleep profound ....Od.4.557.146.
Where safe repos'd the royal treasures lay; ....Od.21.12.259.

REPOSE

While her rackt Soul Repose and Peace requires, ...2.RLA2.11.132.
A death-like silence, and a dread repose: ....2.ElAb.166.333.
Thy life a long, dead calm of fix'd repose; ....2.ElAb.251.339.
When statesmen, heroes, kings, in dust repose, ...3.EOM4.387.165.
Yet hate Repose, and dread to be alone, ...3.Ep2.228A.68.
Whose Seats the weary Traveller repose? ....3.Ep3.260.114.
If I would scribble, rather than repose. ....4.2HE2.71.169.
Who pants for glory finds but short repose, ...4.2HE1.300.221.
Your Arms, your Actions, your Repose to sing! ......4.2HE1.395.229.
Thence to the banks where rev'rend Bards repose, ...5.DunB2.347.314.
Repose at night; study and ease ....6.1.13A.3.
Let her whom fear denies repose to take, ...6.4i.9.9.
Fly the forgetful World, and in thy Arms repose. .....6.8.36.19.
In Safety, Innocence, and full Repose, ...6.17iii.18.58.
Tho' fond of dear Repose; ....6.47.42.130.
With thee repose, where *Tully* once was laid, ...6.52.29.157.
"Or sunk within the Peach's Down, repose? ....6.96ii.46.273.
To waste long Nights in indolent Repose? ....Il.2.30.128.
To waste long Nights in indolent Repose. ....Il.2.80.130.
Hush'd to Repose, and with a Smile survey'd. ......Il.6.619.357.
The grateful Blessings of desir'd Repose. ....Il.9.837.474.
Alike deny'd the Gifts of soft Repose, ...Il.10.32.4.
Tho' Years and Honours bid thee seek Repose. .....Il.10.187.10.
Shall 'scape with Transport, and with Joy repose. ..Il.19.76.375.
Allow'd their Mules and Steeds a short Repose. ....Il.24.432.554.

REPOSE (CONTINUED)

Why did you fear to trouble my repose? ....Od.4.969.163.
And golden dreams (the gift of sweet repose) ....Od.5.636.202.
But on immortal thrones the blest repose: ....Od.6.53.208.
Come, to repose the genial bed invites: ....Od.8.334.281.
Time for discourse, and time for soft repose, ...Od.11.473.407.
To meet soft quiet and repose at home; ....Od.11.536.409.
And cruel, enviest thou a short repose? ....Od.12.336.448.
Why were my cares beguil'd in short repose? ....Od.12.439.452.
From sad reflection let my soul repose; ....Od.14.194.45.
A part we consecrate to soft repose, ...Od.15.427.89.
The night; then down to short repose they lay; ....Od.15.533.95.
And here at least I may in peace repose. ....Od.16.143.109.
Then to repose withdrawn, apart they lay, ...Od.16.500.131.
Seek thou repose; whilst here I sole remain, ...Od.19.54.195.
And, unattended by sincere repose, ...Od.19.600.225.
Repose to night, and toil to day decreed: ....Od.19.692.229.
And ruminating wrath, he scorns repose. ....Od.20.8.230.
Why rowl those eyes unfriended of repose? ....Od.20.42.234.
Of human race now rising from repose, ...Od.20.122.239.
Now early to repose the rest withdrew; ....Od.20.137.240.
Was care for due refection, and repose, ...Od.20.162.241.
Nor wou'd he court repose in downy state, ...Od.20.173.241.
Then to the Queen, as in repose she lay, ...Od.23.1.316.
Yet Fate, yet cruel Fate repose denies; ....Od.23.266.336.
But end we here—the night demands repose, ...Od.23.271.336.
Then to repose her steps the Matron bends, ...Od.23.313.338.

REPOSING

To rock the Cradle of reposing Age, ...4.Arbu.409.127.
To rock the Cradle of reposing Age, ...6.117.4.333.
O'erspent with Toil, reposing on the Ground; ....Il.5.989.314.

REPOSSESS

Nor shall my father repossess the land: ....Od.3.255.98.

REPRESENTS

Et cæt'ra represents ye all: ....6.30.80.89.
Et cæt'ra represents you all: ....6.30.80A.89.

REPRESS

Nor quite indulges, nor can quite repress. ....1.W-F.20.150.
When to repress, and when indulge our Flights: ......1.EOC.93.250.
Vengeance deserv'd thy malice shall repress, ...Od.2.221.72.
Bear it my son! repress thy rising rage: ....Od.16.295.119.

REPRESS'D

Licence repress'd, and *useful Laws* ordain'd; ....1.EOC.682.316.
Our thirst and hunger hastily repress'd; ....Od.10.62.342.
Thy house, for me, remains; by me repress'd ....Od.22.351.304.

REPREST

When now the Rage of Hunger was represt, ...Il.1.614.117.
The prudent Goddess yet her Wrath represt, ...Il.8.573.424.
His Thirst and Hunger soberly represt. ....Il.9.290.448.
When now the Rage of Hunger was represt, ...Il.24.796.570.
Studious to veil the grief, in vain represt, ...Od.4.151.127.
Their hunger satiate, and their thirst represt, ...Od.5.255.184.
And now the rage of hunger was represt, ...Od.14.508.61.
The wary Chief the rushing foe represt, ...Od.22.95.291.
The rage of hunger and of thirst represt: ....Od.24.565.375.

REPRIEV'D

Repriev'd the Relicks of the *Grecian* Band: ....Il.10.236.12.

REPRIZAL

(That large Reprizal he might justly claim, ...Il.11.836.73.

REPRIZALS

Since no Reprizals can be made on thee. ....6.7.14.16.

REPROACH

Thus, in Reproach and Pray'r, the Queen exprest .....1.TrSt.400.426.
With this Reproach his flying Host he warms, ...1.TrES.211.457.
In vain *Thalestris* with Reproach assails, ...2.RL5.3.199.
Gone ev'ry blush, and silent all reproach, ...5.DunB4.563.398.
And ne'er reproach him with his Luxury. ....6.17iii.27.58.
Walk to his grave without reproach, ...6.150.19.399.
Has foul Reproach a Privilege from Heav'n? ....Il.1.385.106.
And keen Reproach, from ev'ry *Phrygian* Dame: .....Il.3.510.216.
Take back th' unjust Reproach! Behold we stand .....Il.4.404.240.
To whom with stern Reproach the Monarch cry'd. ....Il.4.421.240.
Nor from a Friend th' unkind Reproach appear'd, ...Il.9.49.434.
How oft, my Brother, thy Reproach I bear, ...Il.12.245.90.
Think what Reproach these Ears endur'd so long, ...Il.16.241.248.
With this Reproach his flying Host he warms, ...Il.16.514.263.
Reproach is infinite, and knows no end, ...Il.20.295.406.
A Joy to others, a Reproach to me. ....Il.23.416.506.
To vile Reproach what Answer can we make? ....Il.23.568.512.
Struck with the kind reproach, I strait reply; ....Od.4.507.144.
And thus with just reproach address'd the slave. ......Od.18.125.172.
Her keen reproach had reach'd the Sov'reign's ear; ...Od.19.109.197.
"With just reproach were licens'd to defame; ....Od.19.169.200.
Just is thy kind reproach (the chief rejoin'd) ....Od.20.47.234.
By lordly pride and keen reproach inspir'd. ....Od.20.352.249.
The Peers reproach the sure Divine of Fate; ....Od.20.432.254.

REPROACH'D

Reproach'd by want, our fruitless labours mourn, ...Od.10.46.341.

REPROACHES

The Force of keen Reproaches let him feel, ...Il.1.279.100.
In Scandal busie, in Reproaches bold: ....Il.2.258.140.
Nor add Reproaches to the Wounds I bear, ...Il.3.544.217.
Or thus the fearful with Reproaches fires. ....Il.4.275.234.
With base Reproaches and unmanly Pride. ....Il.5.809.304.

REPROACHES (CONTINUED)
With mean Reproaches, and unmanly Pride: ....Il.20.243.404.

REPROACHFUL
Then smile Belinda at reproachful tongues, ...6.38.25.108.
Forbear ye Chiefs! reproachful to contend; ....Il.23.576.512.

REPROBATE
Of Realms accurs'd, deserted, reprobate! ....Il.15.579.218.

REPROOF
Those best can *bear Reproof,* who *merit Praise.* ....1.EOC.583.306.
Him with Reproof he check'd, or tam'd with Blows. ....Il.2.236.138.
But just Reproof with decent Silence bears. ....Il.5.602.297.
A just reproof, ye Peers! Your rage restrain ....Od.20.389.251.

REPROOFS
His warm Reproofs the list'ning Kings inflame, ...Il.7.195.373.
Thy just Reproofs (*Atrides* calm replies) ....Il.14.114.163.

REPROV'D
With hasty Ardour thus the Chiefs reprov'd. ....Il.4.389.239.
Opprobrious, thus, th' impatient Chief reprov'd. ....Il.13.964.151.
All, ev'n the worst, condemn'd; and some reprov'd. ....Od.17.573.160.

REPROVE
(Reply'd the Prince) will you the Bard reprove? ....Od.1.442.53.
Why this first visit to reprove my fear? ....Od.4.1068.167.
For oft in others freely I reprove ....Od.15.77.72.
I not the fondness of your soul reprove ....Od.19.301.209.

REPROVES
And *Brutus* tenderly reproves. ....6.51ii.8.152.
And these encourages, and those reproves. ....Il.4.265.234.
And with a tender pleasantry reproves: ....Od.24.284.363.

REPTILE
A Cherub's face, a Reptile all the rest; ....4.Arbu.331.120.
Vile Reptile, weak, and vain! ....6.53.6.161.
Proud Reptile, Vile, and vain ....6.53.6A.161.
Vile reptile, Proud, and vain ....6.53.6B.161.
A short-liv'd Reptile in the Dust of Earth. ....Il.5.538.294.

REPTILES
Where all the Race of *Reptiles* might embark: ....4.JD4.27.27.
Shall we, like Reptiles, glory in Conceit? ....6.96v.33.281.
Obscene with reptiles, took his sordid bed. ....Od.17.359.149.

REPUBLIC
"The Ant's republic, and the realm of Bees; ....3.EOM3.184.112.

REPUGNANT
Repugnant to the Lot of all Mankind; ....Il.24.59.538.

REPULS'D
Repuls'd the sacred Sire, and thus reply'd. ....Il.1.34.87.
Not so repuls'd, the Goddess closer prest, ...Il.1.664.118.
Repuls'd and baffled by a feeble Foe. ....Il.2.154.135.
The *Greeks,* repuls'd, retreat behind their Wall, ...Il.8.403.416.
Repuls'd by Numbers from the nightly Stalls, ...Il.11.676.65.
With Shame repuls'd, with Grief and Fury driv'n, ...Il.12.183.87.
Repuls'd he stands; nor from his Stand retires; ....Il.13.203.115.
Repuls'd he yields; the Victor *Greeks* obtain ....Il.13.259.117.
But *Troy* repuls'd, and scatter'd o'er the Plains, ...Il.16.362.257.
Repuls'd, they yield; the *Trojans* seize the slain: ....Il.17.325.300.
Repuls'd in vain, and thirsty still of Gore; ....Il.17.643.313.
But check'd, he turns; repuls'd, attacks again. ....Il.18.196.331.
From ev'ry great man's gate repuls'd with scorn? ....Od.17.257.144.

REPULSE
But strive, tho' num'rous, to repulse in vain. ....Il.15.471.215.
Brooks no repulse, nor cou'dst thou soon depart: ....Od.15.237.79.
With penury, contempt, repulse, and care, ...Od.20.255.245.

REPULSIVE
Repulsive of his Might the Weapon stood: ....Il.21.192.429.

REPUTATION
And Authors think their Reputation safe, ...1.EOC.450.290.
At ev'ry Word a Reputation dies. ....2.RL3.16.170.
Is call'd in Women only Reputation: ....6.46.2.127.

REPUTE
To whom can Riches give Repute, or Trust, ...3.EOM4.185.144.
Silence, the Knave's Repute, the Whore's good Name, ...6.8.25.18.

REPUTED
Of twice six Oxen its reputed Price; ....Il.23.817.521.

REQUEST
Their Pleas were diff'rent, their Request the same; ....2.TemF.292.278.
Prefer'd the same Request, and lowly bow'd, ...2.TemF.329.280.
Around the Shrine, and made the same Request: ....2.TemF.395.282.
Oblig'd by hunger and Request of friends: ....4.Arbu.44.99.
"Consider, 'tis my first request.— ....4.HS6.77.255.
Sure just and modest this request appears, ...6.20.52.67.
Let Ease, his last Request, be of your giving, ...6.34.27.101.
If, fir'd to Vengeance at thy Priests request, ...Il.1.594.116.
Still grasp'd his Knees, and urg'd the dear Request. ....Il.1.665.118.
(Great *Menelaus* urg'd the same Request) ....Il.3.269.205.
Speak her Request, and deem her Will obey'd. ....Il.14.224.172.
Great *Jove* consents to half the Chief's Request, ...Il.16.306.254.
Why mourns my Son? thy late-preferr'd Request ....Il.18.95.327.
Is bent to please him; this Request forbear: ....Il.19.326.386.
Nine Days to vent our Sorrows I request, ...Il.24.834.571.
This thy Request (reply'd the Chief) enjoy: ....Il.24.838.572.

REQUEST (CONTINUED)
Answer'd evasive of the sly request. ....Od.1.530.57.
To the sire's merit give the son's request. ....Od.4.444.141.
And now, young Prince, indulge my fond request; ....Od.4.801.156.
He said, and seconding the kind request, ...Od.14.57.38.
Nor unconsenting hear his friend's request; ....Od.15.221.79.
The Heroe paus'd, and ponder'd this request, ...Od.15.228.79.

REQUESTED
Requested for his speed; but, courteous, say ....Od.4.856.159.

REQUESTS
This *Greece* demands, and *Troy* requests in vain. ....Il.7.469.387.

REQUIR'D
And still the more we *give,* the more *requir'd;* ....1.EOC.503.295.
The more we *give,* the more is still *requir'd:* ....1.EOC.503B.295.
Then rose the Guests; and as the time requir'd, ...2.ChJM.371.32.
And wand'ring o'er the Camp, requir'd their Lord. ....Il.2.945.168.
The helping Hand of *Sthenelus* requir'd; ....Il.5.141.273.
Requir'd his Arm, he sorrow'd unredrest. ....Il.18.520.346.
(For so the common care of *Greece* requir'd) ....Od.4.390.139.

REQUIRE
To tell 'em, wou'd a *hundred Tongues* require, ...1.EOC.44.244.
These *Equal Syllables* alone require, ...1.EOC.344.277.
Oh hear, and aid the Vengeance I require; ....1.TrSt.101.414.
The humbler Muse of Comedy require? ....4.2HE1.283.219.
These wond'rous works; so Jove and Fate require) ....5.DunA1.4.61.
Yet some Distinction *Juno* might require, ...Il.4.83.224.
And teach our Mother what the Gods require: ....Il.6.108.329.
Demand their *Hector,* and his Arm require; ....Il.6.452.348.
Blest in his Conduct, I no Aid require, ...Il.10.289.14.
Tho' yet thy State require Redress (he cries) ....Il.15.460.215.
But go, *Achilles,* (as Affairs require) ....Il.19.35.373.
Remains unask'd; what Time the Rites require ....Il.24.825.571.
Perform, ye *Trojans!* what the Rites require, ...Il.24.985.576.
And the chaste Queen connubial rites require; ....Od.1.359.49.
Did he some loan of antient right require, ...Od.1.519.57.
If she must wed, from other hands require ....Od.2.59.63.
For all mankind alike require their grace, ...Od.3.62.89.
Studious to save what human wants require, ...Od.5.632.202.
My craving bowels still require repaste. ....Od.7.296.250.
'Tis what the Gods require: Those Gods revere, ...Od.9.321.319.
A gift in season which his wants require, ...Od.17.631.163.
Then in such robes as suppliants may require, ...Od.17.652.164.

REQUIRES
But to be *found,* when Need requires, with Ease. ....1.EOC.674A.316.
The King once more the solemn Rites requires, ...1.TrSt.603.435.
While her rackt Soul Repose and Peace requires, ...2.RLA2.11.132.
As much that end a constant course requires ....3.EOM1.151.34.
Nature as much a constant course requires ....3.EOM1.151A.34.
Most strength the moving principle requires; ....3.EOM2.67.63.
Shall burning Ætna, if a sage requires, ...3.EOM4.123.139.
Useful, we grant, it serves what life requires, ...3.Ep3.29A.88.
Useful, I grant, it serves what life requires, ...3.Ep3.29.88.
Admit your Law to spare the Knight requires; ....4.EpS2.30.314.
But this when Time requires—It now remains ....Il.1.181.96.
And I but move what ev'ry God requires, ...Il.7.421.385.
This done, whate'er a Warrior's Use requires ....Il.18.705.357.
Rise to the War! th' insulting Flood requires ....Il.21.386.436.
From him some bribe thy venal tongue requires, ...Od.2.217.72.
To this *Ulysses.* What the Prince requires ....Od.17.20.133.
Such servant as your humble choice requires, ...Od.19.407.214.
One common crime one common fate requires. ....Od.22.362.304.
Me other work requires—With tim'rous awe ....Od.22.417.308.
No more.—This day our deepest care requires, ...Od.23.117.326.

REQUITE
Those Acts of Goodness, which themselves requite. ....2.TemF.363.281.
And cast how to requite him: ....6.79.42.219.
The Spoils of *Ilion* shall thy Loss requite, ...Il.1.164.95.
Say, is it thus those Honours you requite? ....Il.4.400.239.

REQUITED
Here brib'd the rage of ill-requited heav'n; ....2.ElAb.138.331.

REQUITES
And ill requites his Parent's tender Care. ....Il.17.347.301.

RERE
See REAR.
Pierc'd with her golden shafts the rere of night; ....Od.19.500.220.

RESCU'D
Her Act has rescu'd *Paris'* forfeit Life, ...Il.4.17.221.
Triumphant *Greece* her rescu'd Decks ascends, ...Il.16.352.256.
Who tremble yet, scarce rescu'd from their Fates, ...Il.17.719.315.
By *Neptune* rescu'd from *Minerva's* hate, ...Od.4.671.150.

RESCUE
But bold *Tydides* to the Rescue goes, ...Il.8.125.404.
Traverse the Files, and to the Rescue flies; ....Il.11.444.54.
The Warrior rescue, and your Country save. ....Il.11.719.67.
Observing *Hector* to the Rescue flew; ....Il.15.700.222.
To check *Achilles,* and to rescue *Troy?* ....Il.21.154.428.
The City rouz'd shall to our rescue haste, ...Od.22.91.290.

RESEMBLANCE
Whose bright resemblance by himself was lov'd; ....6.4ii.8.9.

RESEMBLES
That *Art* is best which most resembles *Her;* ....1.EOC.74A.247.
Musick resembles *Poetry,* in each ....1.EOC.143.256.

RESEMBLING

Resembling *Venus* in attractive state. ... Od.4.20.121.
Diffus'd o'er each resembling line appear, ... Od.4.191.129.

RESENT

How often, hope, despair, resent, regret, ... 2.ElAb.199.336.
And durst he, as he ought, resent that Wrong, ... Il.2.300.142.
Resent I may, but must resent in vain. ... Il.4.82.224.
Resent I may, but must resent in vain. ... Il.4.82.224.
Still burns thy rage? and can brave souls resent ... Od.11.679.418.
At once to pity and resent thy wrong. ... Od.16.94.107.

RESENTFUL

(Not but his soul, resentful as humane, ... Od.17.436.154.

RESENTING

The Prince beheld, and high-resenting spoke. ... Il.6.405.346.
To grace her gloomy, fierce, resenting Son, ... Il.8.451.418.

RESENTMENT

E'er felt such Rage, Resentment and Despair, ... 2.RL4.9.183.
Touch'd with resentment of ungrateful Man, ... 6.15.13.51.
Atrides still with deep Resentment rag'd. ... Il.1.419.107.
In wild Resentment for the Fair he lost. ... Il.1.565.115.
O Sire! can no Resentment touch thy Soul? ... Il.5.942.311.
Thy close Resentment, and their vengeful Ire. ... Il.6.409.347.
Burns with one Love, with one Resentment glows; ... Il.9.726.470.
'Tis just Resentment, and becomes the brave; ... Il.9.761.472.
The *Trojan* Chief with fixt Resentment ey'd ... Il.17.187.294.
The haughty Suitor with resentment burns, ... Od.17.543.159.
That gen'rous soul with just resentment burns, ... Od.18.268.179.

RESENTS

He tries our Courage, but resents our Fears. ... Il.2.230.138.
And, youth, my gen'rous soul resents the wrong: ... Od.8.200.273.

RESERV'D

Crowns were reserv'd to grace the *Soldiers* too. ... 1.EOC.513.296.
Woman, the last, the best reserv'd of God. ... 2.ChJM.64.17.
Alike reserv'd to blame, or to commend, ... 4.Arbu.205.110.
These, Fate reserv'd to grace thy reign divine, ... 5.DunA3.273.183.
These Fate reserv'd to grace thy reign divine, ... 5.DunB3.275.333.
This was reserv'd, Great *Barnivelt,* for Thee, ... 6.48iii.5.134.
Alike reserv'd to blame or to commend, ... 6.49iii.19.143.
Alike reserv'd to Censure, or commend, ... 6.49iii.19A.143.
Alike reserv'd to blame, or to commend, ... 6.98.55.285.
Perhaps ev'n I, reserv'd by angry Fate ... Il.22.92.456.
Has *Jove* reserv'd, unheard of, and unknown; ... Od.3.107.91.
But oh belov'd by heav'n! reserv'd to thee ... Od.4.761.155.
Reserv'd in bowls, supply'd his nightly feast. ... Od.9.294.318.

RESERV'DLY

He speaks reserv'dly, but he speaks with force, ... Od.8.191.272.

RESERVE

Woman, the last, the best Reserve of God. ... 2.ChJM.64A.17.
For Chartres' head reserve the hanging wall? ... 3.EOM4.130.140.
Reserve with Frankness, Art with Truth ally'd, ... 3.Ep2.277.72.
Is Vice too high, reserve it for the next: ... 4.HS1.60.11.
But still the Great have kindness in reserve, ... 4.Arbu.247.113.
Amidst their virtues, a reserve of vice. ... 6.41.20.114.
On dark reserve what better can prevail, ... Od.14.220.46.
Forbear, he cry'd; for heav'n reserve that name, ... Od.16.222.114.
Reserve, the treasure of thy inmost mind: ... Od.19.570.224.
Her coy reserve, and prudence mixt with pride, ... Od.24.148.355.

RESERVOIR

This year a Reservoir, to keep and spare, ... 3.Ep3.175.107.

RESIDE

Those Ghosts of Beauty ling'ring here reside, ... 6.110.3.316.
Those Ghosts of Beauty wandring here reside, ... 6.110.3A.316.
Or in fair *Tarphe's* Sylvan Seats reside; ... Il.2.639.157.
Of those who round *Mæonia's* Realms reside, ... Il.2.1052.172.
Since all who in th' *Olympian* bow'r reside ... Od.1.103.36.
Beneath our roof with Virtue cou'd reside; ... Od.1.296.47.
As some poor peasant, fated to reside ... Od.5.630.202.
But say, if in the court the Queen reside ... Od.16.33.103.
Can strangers safely in the court reside, ... Od.16.71.106.
Since here resolv'd oppressive these reside, ... Od.20.275.246.

RESIDES

He who beneath thy shelt'ring wing resides, ... 6.21.1.69.
My Eldest-born resides not far, ... 6.135.57.368.
Far from your Capital my ship resides ... Od.1.237.44.
Fast by the Throne obsequious *Fame* resides, ... Od.1.497.56.
A man, he says, a man resides with thee, ... Od.5.131.178.
But say, resides my son in royal port, ... Od.11.565.411.
Himself resides, a God among the Gods; ... Od.11.744.423.
Here the gay Morn resides in radiant bow'rs, ... Od.12.3.427.
At the *Coracian* rock he now resides, ... Od.13.469.28.
Dispers'd the youth resides; their faith to prove ... Od.16.342.122.

RESIGN

And then a nobler Prize I will resign, ... 1.PSp.91.70.
If to no Charms thou wilt thy Heart resign, ... 1.TrSP.45.395.
My *Phaon's* fled, and I those Arts resign, ... 1.TrSP.236.404.
Since *Phaon* fled, I all those Joys resign, ... 1.TrSP.236A.404.
Resign to *Jove* his Empire of the Skies, ... 1.TrSt.45.411.
Before proud *Ilion* must resign their Breath! ... 1.TrES.243.458.
We, Sirs, are Fools; and must resign the Cause ... 2.ChJM.218.25.
The rest, without much Loss, I cou'd resign. ... 2.ChWB.61.59.
Ease, Pleasure, Virtue, All, our Sex resign. ... 2.RL4.106.192.
Ease, Health, and Life, for this they must resign, ... 2.TemF.507.288.
Ease, Health, and Life, for this we must resign, ... 2.TemF.507A.288.
Here all its frailties, all its flames resign, ... 2.ElAb.175.334.

RESIGN (CONTINUED)

Unequal task! a passion to resign, ... 2.ElAb.195.336.
Thy oaths I quit, thy memory resign, ... 2.ElAb.293.343.
Those joys, those loves, those int'rests to resign: ... 3.EOM2.258.86.
Extremely ready to resign ... 4.1HE7.63.273.
Yet they'd resign that Post so high, ... 6.30.40.87.
Wherefore thy claim resign, allow his right; ... 6.116vi.5.327.
The Prize, the beauteous Prize I will resign, ... Il.1.149.94.
Then thus the King. Shall I my Prize resign ... Il.1.167.95.
The mighty *Ajax* shall his Prize resign, ... Il.1.177.96.
Suppose some Hero should his Spoils resign, ... Il.2.318.142.
To me the Labour of the Field resign; ... Il.3.137.197.
To you the glorious Conflict I resign, ... Il.4.378.239.
My Treasures too, for Peace, I will resign; ... Il.7.438.386.
With all her Charms, *Briseis* I resign, ... Il.9.171.441.
With all her Charms, *Briseis* he'll resign, ... Il.9.358.451.
The haughtiest Hearts at length their Rage resign, ... Il.9.747.471.
Each wounds, each bleeds, but none resign the Day. ... Il.11.98.39.
Before proud *Ilion,* must resign their Breath! ... Il.16.546.265.
To me the Spoils my Prowess won, resign; ... Il.17.15.288.
To thee I yield the Seat, to thee resign ... Il.17.546.309.
'Tis past—I quell it; I resign to Fate. ... Il.18.144.329.
To her the Artist-God. Thy Griefs resign, ... Il.18.531.347.
Fate wills not this; not thus can *Jove* resign ... Il.20.349.408.
While these by *Juno's* Will the Strife resign, ... Il.21.448.439.
No—to the Dogs that Carcase I resign. ... Il.22.438.473.
Lo! to the Dogs his Carcass I resign; ... Il.23.29.488.
Go, but expect not I'll the Prize resign; ... Il.23.521.510.
Think not (he cries) I tamely will resign ... Il.23.621.514.
The Prize I quit, if thou thy Wrath resign; ... Il.23.673.516.
But of his wish'd return the care resign; ... Od.1.350.49.
To fate's supreme dispose the dead resign, ... Od.4.733.153.
Stiff are my weary joints; and I resign ... Od.8.264.277.
"Inflict disease, it fits thee to resign: ... Od.9.488.326.
Unknown to pain, in age resign thy breath, ... Od.11.166.389.
To thee my son the suppliant I resign, ... Od.16.67.105.
But if submissive you resign the sway, ... Od.16.402.125.
We must resign; for Man is born to die. ... Od.16.463.129.
Resign, and happy be thy bridal day! ... Od.18.314.182.
Unknown to pain in age resign my breath, ... Od.23.299.337.
They drop their jav'lins, and their rage resign, ... Od.24.617.377.

RESIGN'D

Witness the Martyrs, who resign'd their Breath, ... 2.ChJM.673.47.
"Thou should'st be always thus, resign'd and meek! ... 2.ChWB.185.65.
Resign'd to Fate, and with a Sigh retir'd, ... 2.RL3.146.179.
Their own like others soon their Place resign'd, ... 2.TemF.39.256.
Each pray'r accepted, and each wish resign'd; ... 2.ElAb.210.337.
When what t'oblivion better were resign'd, ... 3.EOM4.251.151.
The first firm P[ultene]y soon resign'd his breath, ... 4.1740.77.336.
Relate, who first, who last resign'd to rest; ... 5.DunB4.621.406.
A heart resign'd the conquest of your eyes: ... 6.3.2.7.
Think not unwilling I resign'd my breath. ... 6.20.4.66.
Sincere, tho' prudent; constant, yet resign'd; ... 6.27.2.81.
In prudent ease; still chearful, still resign'd ... 6.55.1Z3.167.
Here both contented and resign'd, I lye; ... 6.56.5.168.
Sincere, tho' prudent, constant, yet resign'd; ... 6.57.2.169.
Of Course resign'd it to the next that writ: ... 6.60.36.179.
Who living, or dying, still resign'd, and still free, ... 6.144.7A.386.
But who living and dying, resign'd still and free, ... 6.144.7B.386.
Resign'd to live, prepar'd to die, ... 6.150.1.398.
Let great *Achilles,* to the Gods resign'd, ... Il.1.275.100.
To *Pelops* He th' immortal Gift resign'd; ... Il.2.131.133.
A Mountain Goat resign'd the shining Spoil, ... Il.4.138.227.
Brave *Glaucus* then each narrow Thought resign'd, ... Il.6.290.340.
Silent the Warrior smil'd, and pleas'd resign'd ... Il.6.504.351.
He stoop'd to Reason, and his Rage resign'd. ... Il.7.140.370.
She flew; and *Juno* thus her Rage resign'd. ... Il.8.525.421.
Now by thy Rage, thy fatal Rage, resign'd; ... Il.9.618.464.
Æneas heard, and for a Space resign'd ... Il.13.590.134.
Of upper Heav'n to *Jove* resign'd the Reign, ... Il.14.235.172.
Then brave *Laogonus* resign'd his Breath, ... Il.16.733.272.
Fled to her Ramparts, and resign'd the Field; ... Il.17.371.302.
To *Juno's* Hate at length resign'd his Breath, ... Il.18.149.329.
Is past, forgotten, and resign'd to Fate: ... Il.19.68.374.
One Chief with Patience to the Grave resign'd, ... Il.19.231.382.
But now alas! to Death's cold Arms resign'd, ... Il.19.339.386.
Now see him flying! to his Fears resign'd, ... Il.22.227.465.
Resign'd the Courser to *Noëmon's* Hand, ... Il.23.700.517.
Ætolians, Pylians, all resign'd the Day. ... Il.23.728.519.
Not so *Achilles:* He, to Grief resign'd, ... Il.24.5.534.
She tasted, and resign'd it: Then began ... Il.24.135.540.
That day, to great *Achilles'* son resign'd ... Od.4.7.120.
To them my vassals had resign'd a soil, ... Od.4.239.130.
(*Noëmon* cry'd) the vessel was resign'd. ... Od.4.873.159.
Enur'd to perils, to the worst resign'd, ... Od.5.286.185.
Then shook the Heroe, to despair resign'd, ... Od.5.381.190.
Twice ten tempestuous nights I roll'd, resign'd ... Od.6.205.220.
Bear, with a soul resign'd, the will of *Jove;* ... Od.6.231.221.
But to his native land our charge resign'd, ... Od.7.260.248.
Touch'd at the song, *Ulysses* strait resign'd ... Od.8.79.266.
Mov'd at the sight, I for a space resign'd ... Od.11.491.408.
And never, never be to Heav'n resign'd? ... Od.12.146.439.
And ride aloft, to Providence resign'd, ... Od.12.501.456.
Now cold he lies, to death's embrace resign'd: ... Od.14.79.40.
His seat *Ulysses* to the Prince resign'd. ... Od.16.42.104.
Instant thou sail'st, to *Echetus* resign'd, ... Od.18.96.171.
Bear the best humbly, and the worst resign'd; ... Od.18.170.175.
These tatter'd weeds (my decent robe resign'd.) ... Od.19.391.213.
Resign'd the skies, and night involv'd the pole. ... Od.19.496.220.
Restless his body rolls, to rage resign'd: ... Od.20.31.233.
King of a hundred Kings! to whom resign'd ... Od.24.37.349.
Ill-us'd by all! to ev'ry wrong resign'd, ... Od.24.189.356.

RESIGN'D'ST
For me in tortures thou resign'd'st thy breath, ...6.25.9.77.

RESIGNS
Struck blind by thee, resigns his Days to Grief, ...2.ChJM.483.38.
She kneels, she weeps, and worse! resigns her Dow'r. ....4.HAdv.172.89.
With piercing Shrieks the Youth resigns his Breath, ...Il.4.577.249.
And the torn Boar resigns his Thirst and Life. ....Il.16.998.281.
At once resigns his Armour, Life, and Fame. ....Il.18.526.347.

RESIST
What Mortal can resist the Yawn of Gods? ....5.DunB4.606.403.
But leave the few that dare resist thy Laws, ...Il.2.412.147.
No Force can then resist, no Flight can save, ...Il.6.630.358.
This choice is left ye, to resist or die; ....Od.22.80.290.

RESISTANCE
And *Venus* only found Resistance here. ....Il.5.1015.315.

RESISTED
The stubborn horn resisted all his pains: ....Od.21.158.267.

RESISTLESS
Truth breaks upon us with *resistless Day;* ....1.EOC.212.264.
Bursts out, resistless, with a thundring Tyde! ....1.EOC.630.310.
Feels all the Fury of resistless Fate, ...1.TrSt.270.421.
He moves a God, resistless in his Course, ...1.TrES.203.457.
Resistless falls: the Muse obeys the Pow'r. ....5.DunB4.628.407.
Trust not too much your now resistless Charms, ...6.19.59.63.
So *Jove* decrees, resistless Lord of All! ....Il.2.147.135.
Your own resistless Eloquence employ, ...Il.2.217.138.
In secret own'd resistless Beauty's Pow'r: ....Il.3.204.201.
But Fate resistless from his Country led ....Il.5.762.303.
Wide o'er the Field, resistless as the Wind, ...Il.6.51.326.
Not thus resistless rul'd the Stream of Fight, ...Il.6.123.330.
On Sheep or Goats, resistless in his way, ...Il.10.566.27.
Thus raging *Hector,* with resistless Hands, ...Il.11.401.52.
He moves a God, resistless in his Course, ...Il.12.557.102.
Resistless when he rag'd, and when he stop'd, unmov'd. ...Il.13.200.115.
His winged Lance, resistless as the Wind, ...Il.13.706.138.
'Twas thou, bold *Hector!* whose resistless Hand ....Il.15.854.229.
Bore down half *Troy,* in his resistless way, ...Il.16.478.261.
Resistless drove the batter'd Skull before, ...Il.20.461.413.
Whose Son encounters our resistless Ire. ....Il.21.168.428.
Mark how resistless thro' the Floods he goes, ...Il.21.366.436.
Beneath that pond'rous Arm's resistless Sway ....Il.23.800.521.
Oft, *Jove's* ætherial rays (resistless fire) ....Od.1.443.53.

RESISTS
In vain resists th' Omnipotence of *Jove.* ....Il.1.735.122.
No wonder *Troy* so long resists our Pow'rs. ....Il.2.409.147.
If Fate resists, or if our Arms are slow, ...Il.2.438.148.
Resists she yet the raging *Hector's* Hand! ....Il.11.953.77.
On all sides batter'd, yet resists his Pow'r: ....Il.15.745.224.
O *Vulcan,* oh! what Pow'r resists thy Might? ....Il.21.418.437.
The bow inflexible resists their pain. ....Od.21.188.268.

RESOLUTION
I hope it is your Resolution ....4.1HE7.43.271.

RESOLV'D
Resolv'd alike, Divine *Sarpedon* glows ....1.TrES.21.450.
But fix'd before, and well resolv'd was he, ...2.ChJM.83.18.
Resolv'd to win, he meditates the way, ...2.RL2.31.161.
For which, I had resolv'd almost, ...6.10.71.26.
Deny'd to reign, I stood resolv'd to die, ...6.20.13.66.
Should such a One, resolv'd to Reign alone, ...6.49iii.11C.142.
Resolv'd this *Secret* to explore, ...6.94.31.260.
But silent, breathing Rage, resolv'd, and skill'd ....Il.3.11.188.
Both breathing Slaughter, both resolv'd in Arms. ....Il.7.4.363.
Resolv'd alike, divine *Sarpedon* glows ....Il.12.365.94.
A chosen Phalanx, firm, resolv'd as Fate, ...Il.13.177.113.
Resolv'd to perish in his Country's Cause, ...Il.13.534.132.
At length she trusts her Pow'r; resolv'd to prove ....Il.14.187.168.
Nor less resolv'd, the Firm *Achaian* Band ....Il.17.316.300.
Resolv'd on Vengeance, or resolv'd on Death. ....Il.20.209.402.
Resolv'd on Vengeance, or resolv'd on Death. ....Il.20.209.402.
Not less resolv'd, *Antenor's* valiant Heir ....Il.21.685.450.
The Son, resolv'd *Achilles'* Force to dare, ...Il.22.47.454.
Resolv'd he stands, and with a fiery Glance ....Il.22.128.458.
And bade him guide the way, resolv'd to go. ....Od.10.312.359.
I heard inces'd, and first resolv'd to speed ....Od.10.517.368.
Resolv'd I stand! and haply had survey'd ....Od.11.777.425.
At length resolv'd, he turn'd his ready hand, ...Od.15.230.79.
Vengeance resolv'd 'tis dang'rous to deferr. ....Od.16.335.122.
In self-debate the Suitors doom resolv'd. ....Od.20.36.234.
Since here resolv'd oppressive these reside, ...Od.20.275.246.

RESOLVE
Resolve me, Reason, which of these is worse, ...3.Ep3.319.120.
Calm to resolve, and constant to pursue. ....6.134.8.364.
Go then! resolve to Earth from whence ye grew, ...Il.7.113.369.
The firm resolve I here in few disclose. ....Od.1.476.55.
Wise to resolve, and patient to perform. ....Od.4.372.137.
'Till one resolve my varying counsel ends. ....Od.9.504.326.

RESOLVES
The Hero then resolves his Course to bend ....1.TrSt.457.429.
The Heart resolves this matter in a trice, ...4.2HE2.216.179.
That strives to learn what Heav'n resolves to hide; ....Il.1.727.122.
Resolves to Air, and mixes with the Night. ....Il.2.44.129.
Where now are all your high Resolves at last, ...Il.2.404.147.
Then thus in short my fixt Resolves attend, ...Il.9.414.452.
Achilles' high Resolves declare to all; ....Il.9.792.473.
To seek sage *Nestor* now the Chief resolves, ...Il.10.24.3.
What Watch they keep, and what Resolves they take: ....Il.10.364.19.

RESOLVES (CONTINUED)
To learn what Counsels, what Resolves you take, ...Il.10.468.24.
Close up the vent'rous Youth resolves to keep, ...Il.23.503.510.
Since fix'd are thy resolves, may thund'ring *Jove* ....Od.15.126.75.
The King resolves, for mercy sways the brave. ....Od.18.107.172.

RESOLVING
Incens'd he heard, resolving on his Fate; ....Il.6.207.336.

RESORT
When thus the Chiefs from diff'rent Lands resort ....1.TrSt.563.434.
The Victor God did to these Realms resort, ...1.TrSt.668A.438.
Hither our Nymphs and Heroes did resort, ...2.RLA.1.73.129.
Hither the Heroes and the Nymphs resort, ...2.RL3.9.169.
Where late the mourning Matrons made Resort; ....Il.6.476.350.
Resort the Nobles from the neighb'ring Isles; ....Od.1.316.48.
All to your several states with speed resort; ....Od.1.478.55.
And to their several domes to Rest resort. ....Od.1.536.57.
Aside, sequester'd from the vast resort. ....Od.4.849.158.
There foul adult'rers to thy bride resort, ...Od.11.148.388.
And let some handmaid of her train resort ....Od.16.164.110.
(Scene of their insolence) the Lords resort; ....Od.17.191.140.
Thou, with the heav'n-taught bard, in peace resort ....Od.22.415.308.
They plan our future ruin, and resort ....Od.24.181.356.

RESORTS
To *Argos'* Realms the Victor God resorts, ...1.TrSt.668.438.

RESOUND
And *Albion's* Cliffs resound the Rural Lay. ....1.PSp.6.61.
Invoke the Muses, and resound your Praise; ....1.PSu.78.78.
Resound ye Hills, resound my mournful Strain! ....1.PAu.57.84.
Resound ye Hills, resound my mournful Strain! ....1.PAu.57.84.
Resound ye Hills, resound my mournful Lay! ....1.PAu.65.85.
Resound ye Hills, resound my mournful Lay! ....1.PAu.65.85.
Resound ye Hills, resound my mournful Strain! ....1.PAu.71.85.
Resound ye Hills, resound my mournful Strain! ....1.PAu.71.85.
Resound ye Hills, resound my mournful Lay! ....1.PAu.77.85.
Resound ye Hills, resound my mournful Lay! ....1.PAu.77.85.
Resound ye Hills, resound my mournful Strains! ....1.PAu.85.86.
Resound ye Hills, resound my mournful Strains! ....1.PAu.85.86.
Resound ye Hills, resound my mournful Lay! ....1.PAu.93.87.
Resound ye Hills, resound my mournful Lay! ....1.PAu.93.87.
No more ye Hills, no more resound my Strains! ....1.PAu.96.87.
Or shall I *Juno's* Hate to *Thebes* resound, ...1.TrSt.13.409.
Once more resound the Great *Apollo's* Praise. ....1.TrSt.828.444.
The Gates resound, the Brazen Hinges fly, ...1.TrES.65.452.
The brazen Hinges fly, the Walls resound, ...1.TrES.65A.452.
Loud Strokes are heard, and ratling Arms resound, ...1.TrES.164.455.
And striking Watches the tenth Hour resound. ....2.RL1.18A.145.
Blue *Neptune* storms, the bellowing Deeps resound; ....2.RL5.50.203.
With ceaseless Noise the ringing Walls resound: ....2.TemF.423.283.
Far, as loud Bow's stupendous bells resound; ....5.DunA3.276.183.
Far as loud Bow's stupendous bells resound; ....5.DunB3.278.333.
Fierce as he mov'd, his Silver Shafts resound. ....Il.1.64.89.
And all the Tribes resound the Goddess' Praise.) ....Il.2.664.158.
The Tumult thickens, and the Skies resound. ....Il.2.981.170.
Sprung from his Car; his ringing Arms resound. ....Il.4.475.242.
Pond'rous he falls: his clanging Arms resound; ....Il.4.579.249.
Down sinks the Chief: his clanging Arms resound. ....Il.4.579A.249.
His Arms resound, the Spirit wings its way. ....Il.5.56.269.
Earth groans beneath him, and his Arms resound; ....Il.5.358.283.
The Tumult thickens, and the Skies resound. ....Il.8.74.399.
Headlong he quits the Car; his Arms resound; ....Il.8.313.412.
Where on her utmost Verge the Seas resound; ....Il.8.598.424.
Shouts of Applause along the Shores resound. ....Il.8.674.427.
And hear with Oars the *Hellespont* resound. ....Il.9.472.455.
Thick on his Hide the hollow Blows resound, ...Il.11.686.65.
And the Turf trembles, and the Skies resound. ....Il.12.60.83.
Heavy, and thick, resound the batter'd Shields, ...Il.12.181.87.
The brazen Hinges fly, the Walls resound, ...Il.12.409.96.
Loud Strokes are heard, and ratling Arms resound, ...Il.12.518.100.
So falls the Youth; his Arms the Fall resound. ....Il.13.244.116.
Prostrate he falls; his clanging Arms resound, ...Il.13.251.117.
Heaps fall on Heaps, and Heav'n and Earth resound. ....Il.13.683.137.
On all sides thick, the Peals of Arms resound. ....Il.13.699.138.
Swift as he leap'd, his clanging Arms resound. ....Il.13.941.149.
Not half so loud the bellowing Deeps resound, ...Il.14.457.185.
Let his high Roofs resound with frantic Woe, ...Il.14.589.190.
Thund'ring he falls; his falling Arms resound, ...Il.15.694.222.
And hears the gath'ring Multitude resound, ...Il.15.705.223.
From Shore to Shore the doubling Shouts resound, ...Il.16.332.255.
He fell, and falling, made the Fields resound. ....Il.16.728.272.
The Labours of the Woodman's Axe resound; ....Il.16.768.273.
He falls, Earth thunders, and his Arms resound. ....Il.16.990.281.
Prone sinks the Warrior, and his Arms resound. ....Il.17.52.289.
They shout incessant, and the Vales resound. ....Il.17.74.291.
And pond'rous as he falls, his Arms resound. ....Il.17.653.313.
Lash'd by his Tail his heaving sides resound; ....Il.20.207.402.
With Cries promiscuous all the Banks resound, ...Il.21.11.421.
Loud o'er the Fields his ringing Arms resound: ....Il.21.475.441.
The lifted Scourges all at once resound; ....Il.23.438.507.
Their Bones resound with Blows: Sides, Shoulders, Thighs ...Il.23.832.522.
Seas, Shores, and Skies with loud Applause resound, ...Il.23.1028.530.
Down plung'd the Maid; (the parted Waves resound) ....Il.24.105.539.
Long exercis'd in woes, oh Muse! resound. ....Od.1.2.25.
Shall long posterity resound the praise. ....Od.3.249.97.
With festival and mirth the roofs resound: ....Od.4.22.121.
Let not your roof with echoing grief resound, ...Od.4.265.131.
She sate and sung; the rocks resound her lays: ....Od.5.74.176.
Thro' all their inmost-winding caves resound. ....Od.9.470.325.
And joy and music thro' the Isle resound. ....Od.10.10.340.
And with their sobs the vaulted roofs resound. ....Od.10.538.369.
With quav'ring cries the vaulted roofs resound? ....Od.20.222.244.
The roofs resound with causeless laughter loud: ....Od.20.416.253.
The bars fall back; the flying valves resound; ....Od.21.50.261.

RESOUND (CONTINUED)
And bid the dome resound the mirthful lay; ...Od.23.132.327.
First bleeds *Antinous:* thick the shafts resound; ...Od.24.206.358.
They share the gladsome board; the roofs resound. ...Od.24.453.370.
He falls, earth thunders, and his arms resound. ...Od.24.607.376.

RESOUNDED
The hollow Brass resounded with the Shock. ...Il.7.319.379.
The Plains resounded as the Boaster fell. ...Il.13.470.128.
The Fields resounded with his weighty Fall. ...Il.17.361.301.
The Shores resounded with the Voice he sent. ...Il.19.44.373.
(A Tale resounded thro' the spacious Earth) ...Il.20.253.404.
Loud grief resounded thro' the tow'rs of *Troy,* ...Od.4.355.136.

RESOUNDING
The neighbouring mountains, and resounding main ...1.TrPA.47.367.
Leap the resounding Bars, the flying Hinges roar. ...1.TrES.198.456.
To the deaf Rocks, and hoarse-resounding Main. ...1.TrUl.99.469.
In the same temple, the resounding wood, ...3.EOM3.155.108.
The varying verse, the full resounding line, ...4.2HE1.268.217.
Love-whisp'ring woods, and lute-resounding waves. ...5.DunB4.306.374.
Far hence remov'd, the hoarse-resounding Main ...Il.1.203.96.
With long-resounding Cries they urge the Train, ...Il.2.185.137.
With equal Oars, the hoarse-resounding Deep. ...Il.2.619.157.
And *Boreas* beats the hoarse-resounding Shores. ...Il.2.1025.171.
Wash'd by broad *Hellespont's* resounding Seas, ...Il.7.100.368.
Leap the resounding Bars, the flying Hinges roar. ...Il.12.552.101.
Are heard resounding with a hundred Rills) ...Il.14.322.178.
Resounding breath'd: At once the Blast expires, ...Il.18.541.348.
With loud-resounding Arms he strikes the Plain; ...Il.20.447.413.
Roars the resounding Surge with Men and Horse. ...Il.21.19.422.
He spoke, and smote the loud-resounding Shield, ...Il.21.464.440.
Lyes on broad *Hellespont's* resounding Shore: ...Il.23.4.486.
As stooping dexter with resounding Wings ...Il.24.393.552.
And stoops on *Hellespont's* resounding Sea. ...Il.24.424.553.
Impatient on the hoarse-resounding shore. ...Od.1.396.51.
Or wide *Täygetus'* resounding groves; ...Od.6.118.212.
With hasty strokes the hoarse-resounding deep; ...Od.9.657.333.
And heard a voice resounding thro' the wood: ...Od.10.253.354.
To the deaf rocks, and hoarse-resounding main. ...Od.13.266.18.
Heard his resounding step, and instant said: ...Od.16.8.102.
He thus: O Queen! whose far-resounding fame, ...Od.19.127.199.

RESOUNDS
And the wide World resounds with *Sapho's* Praise. ...1.TrSP.32.394.
With *Phœbus'* Name resounds the vaulted Hall. ...1.TrSt.651.437.
And rapid Severn hoarse applause resounds. ...3.Ep3.252.114.
Smedley in vain resounds thro' all the coast. ...5.DunA2.282.136.
E[usden] in vain resounds thro' all the coast. ...5.DunA2.282A.136.
Smedley in vain resounds thro' all the coast. ...5.DunB2.294.310.
Hark! *Hæmus* resounds with the *Bacchanals'* Cries— ...6.11.111.34.
Now light with Noise; with Noise the Field resounds. ...Il.2.545.153.
Thro' ruin'd Moles the rushing Wave resounds, ...Il.5.118.273.
The Lash resounds, the rapid Chariot flies, ...Il.5.457.290.
And Voice to Voice resounds *Tydides'* Praise. ...Il.9.70.435.
Thus having spoke, the Driver's Lash resounds; ...Il.11.654.63.
At ev'ry Shock the crackling Wood resounds; ...Il.13.196.115.
Furious he said; the smarting Scourge resounds; ...Il.15.402.212.
The Lash resounds; the Coursers rush to War. ...Il.16.888.277.
His clam'rous Grief the bellowing Wood resounds. ...Il.18.376.339.
He wades, and mounts; the parted Wave resounds. ...Il.21.353.435.
With echoing grief afresh the dome resounds; ...Od.1.462.54.
What tho' from pole to pole resounds her name? ...Od.2.143.68.
And now proud *Sparta* with their wheels resounds, ...Od.4.1.119.
And with the hunter's cry the grove resounds; ...Od.4.1042.166.
Pours out deep groans; (with groans all hell resounds) ...Od.11.720.421.
O'er earth (returns the Prince) resounds thy name, ...Od.16.262.117.
The marble pavement with his step resounds: ...Od.17.38.134.
Pierc'd thro' and thro', the solid gate resounds. ...Od.21.464.282.

RESPECT
Wise Peter sees the World's respect for Gold, ...3.Ep3.125.102.
Walk with respect behind, while we at ease ...4.2HE2.141.175.
They treat themselves with most profound respect; ...4.2HE2.154.175.
"What! no respect, he cry'd, for Shakespear's page?" ...5.DunB4.114A.352.
In respect to his grandsire; ...6.90.11.251.
No Laws can limit, no Respect controul. ...Il.1.379.106.
Thus grac'd, Attention and Respect to gain, ...Il.2.223.138.
Aw'd by no Shame, by no Respect controul'd, ...Il.2.257.140.
To Birth, or Office, no respect be paid; ...Il.10.280.14.
To great *Achilles* this Respect I owe; ...Il.11.794.71.
Attend, and in the Son, respect the Sire. ...Il.14.144.164.
Then *Ajax* thus—Oh *Greeks!* respect your Fame, ...Il.15.666.221.
Respect your selves, and learn an honest Shame: ...Il.15.667.221.
Perhaps at least he may respect my Age. ...Il.22.535.478.
The constant Tribute of Respect and Love: ...Il.24.520.557.
But half the people with respect obey'd ...Od.3.187.95.
Respect us, human, and relieve us, poor. ...Od.9.318.319.
In my respect he bears a Prince's part, ...Od.14.169.43.
But dear respect to *Jove,* and charity. ...Od.14.430.56.
Sandals, a sword, and robes, respect to prove, ...Od.16.79.106.
But chief to Poets such respect belongs, ...Od.17.466.155.
This gift acquits the dear respect I owe; ...Od.20.362.250.
Or share the feast with due respect, or go ...Od.21.92.263.
And some respect *Telemachus* may claim. ...Od.21.336.276.

RESPECTFUL
But heard respectful, and in secret burn'd: ...Il.4.453.241.
Rose to the Monarch and respectful said. ...Il.23.1053.533.
Respectful met the Monarch, and bespoke. ...Od.15.70.72.
He wooes the Queen with more respectful flame, ...Od.15.561.97.
(Respectful thus *Eurymachus* rejoin'd) ...Od.21.346.276.

RESPECTING
Respecting Man, whatever wrong we call, ...3.EOM1.51.19.
Respecting him, my Soul abjures th' Offence; ...Il.24.535.558.

RESPECTS
Last to *yourself* my best Respects I pay, ...6.13.29.40.

RESPIR'D
Stood check'd a while, and *Greece* respir'd again. ...Il.11.424.53.

RESPIRE
And see! the tortur'd Ghosts respire, ...6.11.64.32.
Shall seek their Walls, and *Greece* respire again. ...Il.11.933.77.
Shall quit the Ships, and *Greece* respire again. ...Il.16.63.238.

RESPITE
No Rest, no Respite, 'till the Shades descend; ...Il.2.459.149.
Wond'rous old Man! whose Soul no Respite knows, ...Il.10.186.10.
And claim a Respite from the Sylvan War; ...Il.11.122.41.
So shall thy tedious toils a respite find, ...Od.10.355.361.

RESPITED
Scarce respited from Woes I yet appear, ...Il.21.92.425.

RESPLENDENT
Their fiery Mouths resplendent Bridles ty'd, ...Il.19.429.389.
Resplendent Brass, and more resplendent Dames. ...Il.23.326.503.
Resplendent Brass, and more resplendent Dames. ...Il.23.326.503.
Resplendent as the blaze of summer-noon, ...Od.4.55.122.
Of brass, of vestures, and resplendent Ore; ...Od.5.51.174.

RESPONDENT
Great, and respondent to the master's fame! ...Od.17.315.147.
The wards respondent to the key turn round; ...Od.21.49.261.

RESPONSIVE
She ceas'd: her owls responsive clap the wings, ...5.DunA1.255A.94.
Just as responsive to his Thought, the Frame ...Il.18.447.342.
High strains, responsive to the vocal string. ...Od.1.200.42.
The vocal lay responsive to the strings. ...Od.8.42.264.
To ev'ry note his tears responsive flow, ...Od.8.587.294.
The cavern ecchoes with responsive cries. ...Od.9.261.317.
High notes responsive to the trembling string, ...Od.21.441.281.
And forms the dance responsive to the strings. ...Od.23.134.327.

REST
So when the Nightingale to Rest removes, ...1.PSp.13.61.
There, while You rest in *Amaranthine* Bow'rs, ...1.PWi.73.94.
Above the rest a rural Nymph was fam'd, ...1.W-F.171.165.
The Grave unites; where ev'n the Great find Rest, ...1.W-F.317.179.
And urg'd the rest by equal Steps to rise; ...1.EOC.97.250.
Fix on *Vertumnus,* and reject the rest. ...1.TrVP.82.380.
Besides, he's lovely far above the rest, ...1.TrVP.90.381.
And the last Joy was dearer than the rest. ...1.TrSP.58.396.
Stung to the Soul, the Brothers start from Rest, ...1.TrSt.174.417.
The rest, succeeding Times shall ripen into Fate. ...1.TrSt.428.427.
Sate heavy on his Heart, and broke his Rest; ...1.TrSt.550.433.
Around, at awful Distance, wait the rest. ...1.TrSt.616.436.
Then, on their Father's rev'rend Features rest. ...1.TrSt.632.436.
The Courtly Train, the Strangers, and the rest, ...1.TrSt.652.437.
Let the sad Tale for ever rest untold! ...1.TrSt.801.443.
The rest move on, obedient to the Rein; ...1.TrES.279.460.
Wrapt in a pleasing, deep, and death-like Rest. ...1.TrUl.20.466.
Their Faith, is mine; the rest belongs to *Jove.* ...1.TrUl.93.469.
He said; the rest in diff'rent Parts divide, ...2.ChJM.139.21.
So may my Soul arrive at Ease and Rest, ...2.ChJM.154.22.
And therefore, Sir, as you regard your Rest, ...2.ChJM.184.23.
And one had Grace, that wanted all the rest. ...2.ChJM.241.26.
And one had Grace, yet wanted all the rest. ...2.ChJM.241A.26.
He look'd, he languish'd, and cou'd take no Rest: ...2.ChJM.362.31.
He look'd, he languish'd, and cou'd find no Rest: ...2.ChJM.362A.31.
For ev'ry Labour must have Rest at last. ...2.ChJM.391.33.
Heav'n rest thy Spirit, noble *Solomon,* ...2.ChJM.631.45.
Do you but stoop, and leave the rest to me. ...2.ChJM.735.50.
The rest, without much Loss, I cou'd resign. ...2.ChWB.61.59.
(Kind Heav'n afford him everlasting Rest) ...2.ChWB.254.69.
That Rest they wish'd for, grant them in the Grave, ...2.ChWB.438.78.
Her Guardian *Sylph* prolong'd the balmy Rest. ...2.RL1.20.147.
The rest, the Winds dispers'd in empty Air. ...2.RL2.46.162.
The rest his many-colour'd Robe conceal'd. ...2.RL3.58.172.
As balmy Sleep had charm'd my Cares to Rest, ...2.TemF.5.253.
High o'er the rest *Epaminondas* stood; ...2.TemF.161.267.
Six pompous Columns o'er the rest aspire; ...2.TemF.179.270.
Nor ever Silence, Rest or Peace is here. ...2.TemF.435.284.
Dear fatal name! rest ever unreveal'd, ...2.ElAb.9.319.
Let tears, and burning blushes speak the rest. ...2.ElAb.106.328.
Give all thou canst—and let me dream the rest. ...2.ElAb.124.330.
Or lull to rest the visionary maid: ...2.ElAb.162.332.
Labour and rest, that equal periods keep; ...2.ElAb.211.337.
Receive, and wrap me in eternal rest! ...2.ElAb.302.344.
Thither, where sinners may have rest, I go, ...2.ElAb.319.345.
He hangs between; in doubt to act, or rest, ...3.EOM2.7.53.
But strength of mind is Exercise, not Rest: ...3.EOM2.104.67.
Like Aaron's serpent, swallows up the rest. ...3.EOM2.132.71.
Here then we rest: "The Universal Cause ...3.EOM3.1.92.
"Thus let the wiser make the rest obey, ...3.EOM3.196.113.
More pow'rful each as needful to the rest, ...3.EOM3.299.123.
One grants his Pleasure is but Rest from pain, ...3.EOM4.28Z1.130.
Some are, and must be, greater than the rest, ...3.EOM4.50.133.
Some are, and must be, mightier than the rest, ...3.EOM4.50A.133.
What shocks one part will edify the rest, ...3.EOM4.141.141.
The rest is all but leather or prunella. ...3.EOM4.204.146.
And strongest motive to assist the rest. ...3.EOM4.352.162.
This clue once found, unravels all the rest, ...3.Ep1.178.30.
Yet hate to rest, and dread to be alone, ...3.Ep2.228.68.
Your love of Pleasure, our desire of Rest, ...3.Ep2.274.72.
The young who labour, and the old who rest. ...3.Ep3.268.115.
Lo some are Vellom, and the rest as good ...3.Ep4.137.150.
To rest, the Cushion and soft Dean invite, ...3.Ep4.149.151.
Or rather truly, if your Point be Rest, ...4.HS1.17.5.

REST (CONTINUED)

This is my Plea, on this I rest my Cause— ... 4.HS1.141.19.
The *Robin-red-breast* till of late had rest, ... 4.HS2.37.57.
And hides in sacred Sluttishness the rest. ... 4.HAdv.111.85.
(For none but Lady M[ohun] shows the Rest) ... 4.HAdv.125.85.
(For none but Lady M—show'd the Rest) ... 4.HAdv.125A.85.
And without sneering, teach the rest to sneer; ... 4.Arbu.202.110.
A Cherub's face, a Reptile all the rest; ... 4.Arbu.331.120.
Thus far was right, the rest belongs to Heav'n. ... 4.Arbu.419.127.
Pity the rest, than I abhorrd before ... 4.JD2A.6.132.
Ah spare me, Venus! let me, let me rest! ... 4.HOde1.2.151.
O spare me, Venus! let me, let me rest ... 4.HOde1.2A.151.
O long a stranger, Venus! let me rest ... 4.HOde1.2B.151.
Your People, Sir, are partial in the rest. ... 4.2HE1.32.197.
Patient of labour when the end was rest, ... 4.2HE1.242.215.
Still, still be getting, never, never rest. ... 4.1HE6.96.243.
"Eat some, and pocket up the rest—" ... 4.1HE7.26.269.
The rest, some farm the Poor-box, some the Pews; ... 4.1HE1.128.289.
Sets half the World, God knows, against the rest; ... 4.EpS1.58.302.
And hail her passage to the Realms of Rest, ... 4.EpS1.81.304.
Once break their Rest, or stir them from their Place; ... 4.EpS1.100.305.
And begg'd, he'd take the pains to kick the rest. ... 4.EpS2.155.322.
As for the rest, each winter up they run, ... 4.1740.29.333.
Where Gildon, Banks, and high-born Howard rest. ... 5.DunA1.250.92.
Where wretched *Withers, Banks,* and *Gildon* rest. ... 5.DunA1.250B.92.
"A peck of coals a-piece shall glad the rest." ... 5.DunA2.270.134.
While Milbourn there, deputed by the rest, ... 5.DunA2.325.141.
Like motion, from one circle to the rest; ... 5.DunA2.376.146.
Clos'd one by one to everlasting rest; ... 5.DunA3.344.192.
The rest on Out-side merit but presume, ... 5.DunB1.135.280.
In Shadwell's bosom with eternal Rest! ... 5.DunB1.240.287.
Where wretched Withers, Ward, and Gildon rest, ... 5.DunB1.296.291.
"A peck of coals a-piece shall glad the rest." ... 5.DunB2.282.309.
And Milbourn chief, deputed by the rest, ... 5.DunB2.349.314.
Like motion from one circle to the rest; ... 5.DunB2.408.317.
Low bow'd the rest" He, kingly, did but nod; ... 5.DunB4.207.363.
And breaks our rest, to tell us what's a clock. ... 5.DunB4.444.384.
Thy *Magus,* Goddess! shall perform the rest." ... 5.DunB4.516.393.
Relate, who first, who last resign'd to rest; ... 5.DunB4.621.406.
Clos'd one by one to everlasting rest; ... 5.DunB4.638.407.
Or should those eyes alone that rest enjoy, ... 6.4i.7.9.
Jove with a nod may bid the world to rest, ... 6.4i.13.9.
And 'tis in thee at last that *Wisdom* seeks for Rest. ... 6.8.24.18.
All rest in Peace at last, and sleep eternally. ... 6.8.42.19.
So Waters putrifie with Rest, and lose ... 6.17ii.9.56.
As smiling Infants sport themselves to Rest: ... 6.19.14.62.
Aim not at Joy, but rest content with Ease. ... 6.19.48.63.
Rouze the huge Dragon, with a spurn, from rest, ... 6.21.31.70.
When foes conspiring rise against his rest, ... 6.21.37.70.
Calm rest, and soft serenity of mind; ... 6.23.16.73.
Fix'd to one side, but mod'rate to the rest; ... 6.27.4.81.
Some *Stephens* to the rest prefer, ... 6.29.3A.82.
Some *Plantin* to the rest prefer, ... 6.29.3.82.
In short, the rest were all in Fray, ... 6.30.48.87.
Calm, as forgiven Hermites rest, ... 6.31ii.6Z9.95.
In all the rest so impudently good: ... 6.41.48.114.
And without sneering, teach the rest to sneer; ... 6.49iii.16.143.
Fix'd to one side, but mod'rate to the rest; ... 6.57.4.169.
Peace to thy gentle shade, and endless Rest! ... 6.72.5.208.
The rest is told you in a Line or two. ... 6.82vi.10.232.
Who to be savd by one, must damn the rest. ... 6.82ix(b).2.234.
Was *DRYDEN* once: The rest who does not know? ... 6.83.2.237.
And gaping Infants squawle to hear the rest. ... 6.96iv.66.278.
And without sneering, teach the rest to sneer; ... 6.98.52.284.
The rest God knows—so does the Devil. ... 6.104i.2.297.
The rest God knows—perhaps the Devil. ... 6.104ii.2.297.
The rest Gods knows, perhaps the Devil. ... 6.104i.2A.297.
Here WITHERS rest! thou bravest, gentlest mind, ... 6.113.1.320.
For three whole days you here may rest ... 6.114.9.321.
Thus far, is right; the rest belongs to Heav'n. ... 6.117.14.333.
Are lump'd with the rest of these charming Hell fires. ... 6.122.16.342.
Peace to thy gentle Shade, and endless Rest, ... 6.152.7.400.
Th' Assembly seated, rising o'er the rest, ... Il.1.77.90.
A sable Cloud conceal'd her from the rest. ... Il.1.266.99.
Th' Assistants part, transfix, and roast the rest: ... Il.1.611.117.
There, far apart, and high above the rest, ... Il.1.647.118.
Then to the rest he fill'd; and, in his Turn, ... Il.1.768.124.
Oh *Atreus'* Son! canst thou indulge thy Rest? ... Il.2.26.128.
By brave Examples should confirm the rest. ... Il.2.228.138.
No Rest, no Respite, 'till the Shades descend; ... Il.2.459.149.
Th' Assistants part, transfix, and roast the rest; ... Il.2.511.151.
(In *Actor's* Court as she retir'd to Rest, ... Il.2.616.157.
With Female Beauty far beyond the rest. ... Il.2.832.164.
The Godlike *Hector,* high above the rest, ... Il.2.988.170.
And live the rest secure of future Harms. ... Il.3.140.197.
Now rest their Spears, or lean upon their Shields; ... Il.3.177.199.
And lofty Stature far exceed the rest? ... Il.3.292.207.
The rest I know, and could in Order name; ... Il.3.299.207.
Tho' all the rest with stated Rules we bound, ... Il.4.298.235.
Secure of me, O King! exhort the rest: ... Il.4.303.235.
Ah would the Gods but breathe in all the rest ... Il.4.330.236.
Before the rest let none too rashly ride; ... Il.4.348.237.
Why stand you distant, and the rest expect ... Il.4.392.239.
For this your Names are call'd, before the rest, ... Il.4.396.239.
Those only heard; with Awe the rest obey, ... Il.4.488.243.
Slow he gave way, the rest tumultuous fled; ... Il.4.583.249.
Rest on the Summits of the shaded Hill; ... Il.5.646.299.
The Chief reply'd: This Time forbids to rest: ... Il.6.450.348.
Up-started fierce: But far before the rest ... Il.7.197.373.
The Sage whose Counsels long had sway'd the rest, ... Il.7.390.383.
The rest they purchas'd at their proper Cost, ... Il.7.566.393.
Go, mighty Hero! grac'd above the rest ... Il.8.196.407.
To this the Chief: With Praise the rest inspire, ... Il.8.355.414.
There ty'd, they rest in high Celestial Stalls; ... Il.8.538.422.
Great *Agamemnon* griev'd above the rest; ... Il.9.11.431.
Thus spoke the hoary Sage: the rest obey; ... Il.9.109.437.

REST (CONTINUED)

Some few my Soldiers had, himself the rest. ... Il.9.437.454.
Rest undetermin'd till the dawning Day. ... Il.9.732.470.
(Since Cares, like mine, deprive thy Soul of Rest) ... Il.10.107.7.
Long e'er the rest, he rose, and sought my Tent. ... Il.10.143.8.
Rest seems inglorious, and the Night too long. ... Il.10.181.9.
Succeed to these my Cares, and rouze the rest; ... Il.10.200.10.
His the fair Steeds that all the rest excell, ... Il.10.369.19.
Himself first rose, himself before the rest ... Il.11.21.35.
The rest were vulgar Deaths, unknown to Fame. ... Il.11.394.52.
His Friend *Machaon* singled from the rest, ... Il.11.734.67.
The rest the People shar'd; my self survey'd ... Il.11.840.73.
Urg'd with Desire of Fame, beyond the rest, ... Il.13.212.116.
And what thou canst not singly, urge the rest. ... Il.13.300.119.
The rest lies rooted in a *Trojan* Shield. ... Il.13.336.121.
In that sharp Service, singled from the rest, ... Il.13.357.122.
'Tis but the Wish to strike before the rest. ... Il.13.371.123.
Above the rest, two tow'ring Chiefs appear, ... Il.13.632.136.
Then rest in Courage) *Oeneus* was the last. ... Il.14.133.164.
Let each go forth, and animate the rest, ... Il.14.146.164.
The panting Thund'rer nods, and sinks to Rest. ... Il.14.406.183.
The Soul of *Ajax* burn'd above the rest. ... Il.14.536.189.
Thy brave Example shall the rest enflame. ... Il.15.559.218.
Some lordly Bull (the rest despers'd and fled) ... Il.15.766.226.
Do her own Work, and leave the rest to Fate. ... Il.16.121.241.
Far o'er the rest, in glitt'ring Pomp appear, ... Il.16.264.249.
But Heav'ns eternal Doom denies the rest; ... Il.16.307.254.
The rest move on, obedient to the Rein; ... Il.16.584.267.
Till *Glaucus'* turning, all the rest inspir'd. ... Il.16.720.272.
The rest dispersing, trust their Fates to Flight. ... Il.16.856.276.
The rest in Sunshine fought, and open Light: ... Il.17.427.303.
The rest, in pity to her Son, conceal'd. ... Il.17.471.305.
He rashly boasts; the rest our Will denies. ... Il.17.515.308.
Stretch'd o'er *Patroclus'* Corse; while all the rest ... Il.19.7.371.
At least our Armies claim Repast and Rest: ... Il.19.156.378.
The rest in publick View the Chiefs dispose, ... Il.19.257.383.
Full in the midst, high tow'ring o'er the rest, ... Il.19.390.388.
Rest here: My self will lead the *Trojan* on, ... Il.22.287.468.
The rest to *Greece* uninjur'd I'll restore: ... Il.22.331.470.
And *Hector's* Ashes in his Country rest. ... Il.22.432.473.
And when still Ev'ning gave him up to Rest, ... Il.22.648.483.
E'er yet from Rest or Food we seek Relief, ... Il.23.13.486.
Ah suffer that my Bones may rest with thine! ... Il.23.104.491.
Whate'er can rest a discontented Shade; ... Il.23.112.492.
The rest around the Margins will be seen, ... Il.23.300.501.
There let them rest, with decent Honour laid, ... Il.23.304.501.
Prove we our Force, and *Jove* the rest decree. ... Il.23.841.523.
Antilochus, more hum'rous than the rest, ... Il.23.923.525.
Or yet unmangled rest his cold Remains? ... Il.24.500.557.
Around, at awful distance, stood the rest. ... Il.24.583.561.
Demand Refection, and to Rest invite: ... Il.24.754.568.
But in the Porch the King and Herald rest, ... Il.24.844.572.
Assembled there, from pious Toil they rest, ... Il.24.1013.577.
Stranger! whoe'er thou art, securely rest ... Od.1.161.40.
With humble affluence, and domestic rest! ... Od.1.282.46.
And to their several domes to Rest resort. ... Od.1.536.57.
Stretch'd on the downy fleece, no rest he knows, ... Od.1.557.58.
The rest with duteous love his griefs asswage, ... Od.2.29.61.
Reel'd from the palace, and retir'd to rest. ... Od.2.447.82.
Far o'er the rest thy mighty father shin'd, ... Od.3.149.93.
Timeless, indecent, but retire to rest. ... Od.3.430.107.
All Youths the rest, whom to this journey move ... Od.3.464.109.
The last *Pisistratus* arose from rest: ... Od.3.528.113.
The rest may here the pious duty share, ... Od.3.542.114.
Th' assistants part, transfix, and broil the rest. ... Od.3.591.116.
But oh! *Ulysses—deeper* than the rest ... Od.4.131.126.
Then thro' th' illumin'd dome, to balmy rest ... Od.4.407.140.
Part live; the rest, a lamentable train! ... Od.4.665.150.
The prescient Godhead to reveal the rest. ... Od.4.744.153.
Then lose the cares of life in pleasing rest.— ... Od.4.783.156.
And high descent, superior to the rest; ... Od.4.852.158.
And rest affianc'd in her guardian aid. ... Od.4.992.163.
And swift transport him to his place of rest. ... Od.5.49.174.
When rosy morning call'd them from their rest, ... Od.5.293.185.
Let then thy waters give the weary rest, ... Od.5.574.200.
While thus the weary Wand'rer sunk to rest, ... Od.6.1.203.
To break the banks of all-composing rest. ... Od.6.132.213.
Prepar'd for rest, and off'ring to the * God ... Od.7.184.244.
Mean-time *Arete,* for the hour of rest ... Od.7.427.258.
He rose with pleasure, and retir'd to rest. ... Od.7.434.258.
Before the rest, what space the hinds allow ... Od.8.129.269.
Loud laugh the rest, ev'n *Neptune* laughs aloud, ... Od.8.381.284.
I then advis'd to fly: not so the rest, ... Od.9.47.304.
The rest escape in haste, and quit the coast. ... Od.9.70.305.
The rest in haste forsook the pleasing shore, ... Od.9.113.308.
Where ships may rest, unanchor'd and unty'd; ... Od.9.158.312.
My dear associates, here indulge your rest: ... Od.9.200.314.
Far from the rest, and solitary reigns, ... Od.9.218.314.
I seek th' adventure, and forsake the rest. ... Od.9.228.316.
The folded flocks each sep'rate from the rest, ... Od.9.257.317.
And high in wicker baskets heap'd: the rest ... Od.9.293.318.
Stretch'd on the shore in careless ease we rest, ... Od.9.652.333.
Comply'd to take the balmy gifts of rest; ... Od.10.35.341.
Polites to the rest the question mov'd, ... Od.10.258.355.
The rest are vanish'd, none repass'd the gate; ... Od.10.307.359.
He fear'd my threats, and follow'd with the rest. ... Od.10.530.369.
Tir'd with long toil, we willing sunk to rest. ... Od.10.553.369.
The rest are forms of empty *Æther* made, ... Od.10.586.372.
And my tost limbs now weary'd into rest, ... Od.10.593.372.
These to the rest; but to the *Seer* must bleed ... Od.10.624.374.
The rest crowd round me with an eager look; ... Od.10.669.375.
To the dark grave retiring as to rest, ... Od.11.168.390.
The rest repell'd, a train oblivious fly. ... Od.11.183.390.
And all-composing rest my nature craves, ... Od.11.410.404.
And high above the rest, *Atrides* prest the plain. ... Od.11.484.408.
Unfold some trifle, but conceal the rest. ... Od.11.548.410.

REST (CONTINUED)
Then sable Night ascends, and balmy rest Od.12.41.431.
To sep'rate mansions, and retir'd to rest. Od.13.20.2.
Then instant, to *Alcinous* and the rest, Od.13.45.3.
The swelling couch, and lay compos'd to rest. Od.13.91.5.
Wrapt in a pleasing, deep, and death-like rest. Od.13.111.6.
Their faith, is mine: the rest belongs to *Jove.* Od.13.260.18.
Dismiss those cares, and leave to heav'n the rest. Od.13.416.26.
With him, rest peaceful in the rural cell, Od.13.473.29.
To this *Minerva.* Be thy soul at rest; Od.13.486.29.
And now in honor's glorious bed at rest. Od.14.141.42.
Before the rest I rais'd my ready steel; Od.14.257.48.
If here *Ulysses* from his labours rest, Od.14.436.56.
First claim refection, then to rest invite; Od.14.450.57.
The rural tribe in common share the rest, Od.14.486.59.
And each betakes him to his couch to rest. Od.14.509.61.
Studious of rest and warmth, *Ulysses* lies, Od.14.514.62.
Lay cover'd by their ample shields at rest. Od.14.539.63.
There lay the King, and all the rest supine; Od.14.592.66.
Beneath the rest it lay divinely bright, Od.15.122.74.
Stranger (reply'd the Prince) securely rest Od.15.304.83.
Mean-time the King, *Eumæus,* and the rest, Od.15.322.85.
The last I purpose in your walls to rest: Od.15.327.85.
Well pleas'd, and pleasing, in our cottage rest, Od.15.356.86.
For too much rest itself becomes a pain. Od.15.429.89.
At rest, or wand'ring in his country's shade, Od.17.181.140.
The rest with equal hand conferr'd the bread; Od.17.494.156.
She pours a pleasing, deep, and deathlike rest, Od.18.222.177.
Sated they rose, and all retir'd to rest. Od.19.498.220.
Establish'd use enjoins; to rest and joy Od.19.695.229.
Her faded pow'rs with balmy rest renew. Od.20.64.235.
Now early to repose the rest withdrew; Od.20.137.240.
With varied toils the rest adorn the dome. Od.20.198.243.
A *Samian* Peer, more studious than the rest Od.20.353.249.
The bold *Antinous* to the rest begun. Od.21.148.265.
Give heav'n this day, and rest the bow in peace. Od.21.297.274.
And safe conveyance to his port of rest. Od.21.368.277.
(Fast by, the rest lay sleeping in the sheath, Od.21.456.282.
The rest must perish, their great leader slain. Od.22.279.300.
The rest retreat: the victors now advance, Od.22.298.300.
Full oft was check'd th' injustice of the rest: Od.22.352.304.
My weary nature craves the balm of rest: Od.23.173.329.
To the dark grave retiring as to rest; Od.23.301.337.
Cease the gay dance, and to their rest repair; Od.23.320.339.
And rest at last, where souls unbodied dwell Od.24.19.348.
Yet still a master ghost, the rest he aw'd, Od.24.25.348.
The rest ador'd him, tow'ring as he trod; Od.24.26.348.
Took their laborious rest, and homely fare; Od.24.241.360.
Be all the rest; and set thy soul at ease. Od.24.416.369.
The rest in ships are wafted o'er the main. Od.24.480.371.
Long shall *Ulysses* in his empire rest, Od.24.558.375.

RESTED
Glad Conquest rested on the *Grecian* Train. Il.16.943.280.
No Vapour rested on the Mountain's Head, Il.17.429.304.
But stopp'd, and rested, by the third repell'd; Il.20.317.407.
Obey'd; and rested, on his Lance reclin'd. Il.22.290.468.
This the twelfth Evening since he rested there, Il.24.505.557.
There as he rested, gathering in a ring Od.18.135.172.

RESTFUL
Suspend the restful hour with sweet discourse. Od.19.597.225.

RESTING
'Till poiz'd aloft, the resting Beam suspends 1.TrES.169.455.
Till pois'd aloft, the resting Beam suspends Il.12.525.101.
Till then, the Spirit finds no resting place, Il.23.89.490.
Then, resting on the threshold of the gate, Od.17.414.152.

RESTIVE
Restive they stood, and obstinate in Woe: Il.17.491.307.

RESTLESS
Restless he sate, invoking ev'ry Pow'r 2.ChJM.351.31.
Or Curtain-Lectures made a restless Night. 2.ChWB.165.64.
Those restless passions in revenge inspires; 2.ElAb.82.326.
Why, of two Brothers, rich and restless one 4.2HE2.270.183.
She saw old Pryn in restless Daniel shine, 5.DunA1.101.71.
She saw old Pryn in restless Daniel shine, 5.DunB1.103.276.
Or waste, for others Use, their restless Years 6.17ii.3.56.
And Curio, restless by the Fair-one's side, 6.71.43.204.
Strife and Debate thy restless Soul employ, Il.1.231.98.
Then thus the God: Oh restless Fate of Pride, Il.1.726.122.
While streamy Sparkles, restless as he flies, Il.11.87.38.
Restless it flies, impatient to be free, Il.13.708.138.
While restless, raging, in your Ships you lay) Il.16.243.248.
Restless he roll'd around his weary Bed, Il.24.9.535.
Then by his Heralds, restless of delay, Od.2.9.60.
And roll'd his eyes around the restless deep; Od.5.106.177.
And roll'd his eyes o'er all the restless main, Od.5.203.181.
Again the restless orb his toil renews, Od.11.739.422.
Still must we restless rove, new seas explore, Od.12.337.448.
Restless he griev'd, with various fears opprest, Od.15.9.70.
Restless his body rolls, to rage resign'd: Od.20.31.233.
(Restless and early sleep's soft bands they broke) Od.24.506.372.

RESTOR'D
And here *restor'd* Wit's *Fundamental Laws.* 1.EOC.722.323.
And Hell's dire Monster back to Hell restor'd. 1.TrSt.726.440.
And safe restor'd me to my Native Land. 1.TrUl.83.468.
Look'd out, and stood restor'd to sudden Sight. 2.ChJM.749.51.
So Heav'n preserve the Sight it has restor'd, 2.ChJM.768.52.
Was sheath'd, and *Luxury* with *Charles* restor'd; 4.2HE1.140.207.
Lo! the great Anarch's ancient reign restor'd, 5.DunA3.339.192.
Ye Pow'rs! whose Mysteries restor'd I sing, 5.DunB4.5.339.
Lo! thy dread Empire, CHAOS! is restor'd; 5.DunB4.653.409.

RESTOR'D (CONTINUED)
The *Greeks* restor'd the grateful Notes prolong; Il.1.620.117.
Be therefore now the *Spartan* Wealth restor'd, Il.3.571.219.
Restor'd the groaning God to upper Air. Il.5.480.291.
Glorious he sate, in Majesty restor'd, Il.5.1118.321.
Restor'd the pleasing Burden to her Arms; Il.6.617.357.
Confirm'd his Sinews, and restor'd to Fight. Il.7.328.380.
Let *Sparta's* Treasures be this Hour restor'd, Il.7.422.385.
There, till the sacred Morn restor'd the Day, Il.9.777.472.
Then to their Sire for ample Sums restor'd; Il.11.145.42.
Thus *Elis* forc'd, her long Arrears restor'd, Il.11.828.73.
Lo, to my Sight beyond our Hope restor'd, Il.17.552.309.
The Mare contested to the King restor'd. Il.23.678.516.
Lo! to thy Pray'r restor'd, thy breathless Son: Il.24.749.568.
Now dost thou sleep, when *Hector* is restor'd? Il.24.852.572.
Now, imag'd in his mind, he sees restor'd Od.1.152.40.
To the strong staple's inmost depth restor'd, Od.1.554.58.
The eighth, from *Athens* to his realm restor'd, Od.3.390.105.
(Late from the mellowing cask restor'd to light, Od.3.504.112.
'Till pitying *Jove* my native realm restor'd— Od.4.44.122.
With nectar'd drops the sick'ning sense restor'd. Od.4.600.148.
I stood restor'd, and tears had ceas'd to flow; Od.4.730.153.
To liberty restor'd, perfidious fly, Od.8.388.285.
Soon as the morn restor'd the day, we pay'd Od.12.11.430.
And safe restor'd me to my native land. Od.13.250.18.
Like great *Atrides,* just restor'd and slain. Od.13.440.27.
Restor'd and breathing in his natal place. Od.14.166.43.
Enter, my child! beyond my hopes restor'd, Od.16.27.103.
From death and treason to thy arms restor'd. Od.17.59.135.
The golden goblets some, and some restor'd Od.19.74.196.
His speech the tempest of her grief restor'd; Od.19.284.208.
Ardent to speak the Monarch safe restor'd: Od.19.556.223.
Which spoke *Ulysses* to his realm restor'd: Od.19.665.228.
Whilst hope prevail'd to see your Sire restor'd, Od.20.393.251.
Restor'd, and breathing in his native land. Od.24.378.367.

RESTORE
To these fond Eyes restore thy welcome Sails? 1.TrSP.247.404.
Now lift thy longing Eyes, while I restore 1.TrUl.224.473.
And, in the very Act, restore his Sight: 2.ChJM.652.46.
Restore the Lock! she cries; and all around 2.RL5.103.208.
Restore the Lock! the vaulted Roofs rebound. 2.RL5.104.208.
Poet or Patriot, rose but to restore 3.EOM3.285.121.
Jones and Palladio to themselves restore, 3.Ep4.193.155.
Old puns restore, lost blunders nicely seek, 5.DunA1.163.82.
Still her old Empire to restore she tries, 5.DunB1.17.270.
See, to my country happy I restore 5.DunB4.329.375.
Restore, restore *Eurydice* to Life; 6.11.81.33.
Restore, restore *Eurydice* to Life; 6.11.81.33.
Light to the Stars the Sun does thus restore, 6.43.11.120.
Who decreed to restore . . . originall hight 6.155.8Z2.404*.
May *Jove* restore you, when your Toils are o'er, Il.1.25.86.
So Heav'n aton'd shall dying *Greece* restore, Il.1.89.91.
At thy Demand shall I restore the Maid? Il.1.171.95.
Restore our Blood, and raise the Warrior's Souls, Il.4.297.235.
Their Treasures I'll restore, but not the Dame; Il.7.437.386.
But to restore the beauteous Bride again, Il.7.468.387.
Pthia to her *Achilles* shall restore Il.9.475.456.
If Heav'n restore me to my Realms with Life, Il.9.516.458.
Not tho' the God that breath'd my Life, restore Il.9.574.462.
Restore their Master to the Gates of *Troy!* Il.12.130.86.
For thou, tho' distant, can'st restore my Might, Il.16.645.269.
The Body to *Achilles* to restore, Il.17.131.292.
Dispel this Cloud, the Light of Heav'n restore; Il.17.729.315.
I vow'd his much-lov'd Offspring to restore, Il.18.381.339.
And to the Field in martial Pomp restore, Il.18.529.347.
What then I lost, the Gods this Day restore. Il.20.237.403.
With honourable Justice to restore; Il.22.160.459.
The rest to *Greece* uninjur'd I'll restore: Il.22.331.470.
And next, the Losers Spirits to restore, Il.23.818.521.
We will, thy Son himself the Corse restore, Il.24.145.541.
But yield to Ransom, and restore the Slain. Il.24.174.543.
His Grace restore thee to our Roof, and Arms, Il.24.356.551.
Oh give me *Hector!* to my Eyes restore Il.24.699.566.
And soon restore him to his regal seat. Od.1.266.45.
'Till the fleet hours restore the circling year. Od.1.375.50.
'Till the fleet hours restore the circling year; Od.2.248.73.
Such to our wish the warrior soon restore, Od.4.461.142.
Thy son, the Gods propitious will restore, Od.4.1063.167.
What cannot Wisdom do? Thou may'st restore Od.5.34.172.
'Till heav'n by miracle his life restore) Od.5.510.197.
Restore me safe thro' weary wand'rings tost, Od.8.507.289.
And them to me restore, and me to joy. Od.10.456.365.
Now lift thy longing eyes, while I restore Od.13.391.25.
But guard him Gods! and to these arms restore! Od.14.196.45.
Once I was strong (wou'd heav'n restore those days) Od.14.526.62.
"Swear first (she cry'd) ye sailors! to restore Od.15.474.93.
Such to our wish the warrior soon restore, Od.17.152.139.
Succeed my wish; your votary restore: Od.17.288.146.
Say, shou'd some fav'ring God restore again Od.21.201.269.
Wou'd mighty *Jove* restore that man again! Od.21.206.269.
Restore thee safe, since my *Ulysses* reigns. Od.23.276.336.

RESTORER
Oh great Restorer of the good old Stage, 5.DunA3.201.175.
Oh great Restorer of the good old Stage, 5.DunB3.205.330.

RESTORES
Restores my fair Deserter to my Arms! 1.TrSP.148.400.
Restores his Freshness, and his Form renews. 1.TrES.343.462.
Fancy restores what vengeance snatch'd away, 2.ElAb.226.338.
Till the new Sun restores the chearful Light: Il.7.447.386.
What God restores him to the frighted Field; Il.15.327.209.
Restores his Freshness, and his Form renews. Il.16.830.275.
Flames from his Chariot, and restores the Day. Il.19.437.389.
'Till heav'n's revolving lamp restores the day. Od.4.296.133.

RESTORES (CONTINUED)
Hail god-like stranger! and when heav'n restores ......Od.8.499.289.
And the drein'd goblet to the Chief restores. ......Od.18.180.175.
So, when the sun restores the purple day, ...Od.19.674.229.
Canst thou, *Penelope*, when heav'n restores ......Od.23.167.328.

RESTORING
For routing *Triplets*, and restoring *ed*. ......6.98.12Z2.283.
She clear'd, restoring all the War to view; ......Il.15.809.227.
(Restoring *Hector*) Heav'ns unquestion'd Will. ......Il.24.743.568.

RESTRAIN
Restrain his Fury, than provoke his Speed; ......1.EOC.85.249.
'Tis best sometimes your Censure to restrain, ...1.EOC.596.308.
Thus did the League their impious Arms restrain, ...1.TrSt.198.418.
Thus did this League their impious Arms restrain, ...1.TrSt.198A.418.
The starting Coursers, and restrain their Rage, ...1.TrES.276.460.
The roaring Winds tempestuous Rage restrain; ......1.TrUl.28.466.
Gums and *Pomatums* shall his Flight restrain, ...2.RL2.129.168.
Nor pray'rs nor fasts its stubborn pulse restrain, ...2.ElAb.27.321.
Barbarian stay! that bloody stroke restrain; ......2.ElAb.103.328.
Barbarian stay! that bloody hand restrain; ......2.ElAb.103A.328.
Self-love, to urge, and Reason, to restrain; ......3.EOM2.54.62.
His safety must his liberty restrain: ......3.EOM3.277.120.
Oh spread thy Influence, but restrain thy Rage! ......5.DunA3.114.160.
Oh spread thy influence, but restrain thy Rage. ......5.DunB3.122.325.
Begone ye Criticks, and restrain your Spite, ...6.7.1.15.
Young as ye are, this youthful Heat restrain, ...Il.1.343.105.
Young as you are, this youthful Heat restrain, ...Il.1.343A.105.
Your shining Swords within the Sheath restrain, ...Il.3.125.196.
Their headstrong Horse unable to restrain, ...Il.11.167.42.
Shall not the Thund'rer's dread Command restrain, ...Il.15.148.202.
Now save the Ships, the rising Fires restrain, ...Il.16.106.240.
The starting Coursers, and restrain their Rage, ...Il.16.581.267.
Restrain his bold Career, at least, t'attend ......Il.20.150.400.
Your noble Vigour, oh my Friends restrain; ......Il.23.856.523.
At length their rage the hostile Pow'rs restrain, ...Od.1.27.30.
To save the state; and timely to restrain ......Od.1.114.37.
Though Adamantine bonds the chief restrain, ...Od.1.264.45.
For this the Gods each fav'ring gale restrain: ......Od.4.476.142.
Sudden, our bands a spotted Pard restrain: ......Od.4.616.148.
Her eyes restrain the silver-streaming tears: ......Od.4.1000.164.
The roaring wind's tempestuous rage restrain; ......Od.13.119.7.
What hands unseen the rapid bark restrain! ......Od.13.192.15.
Yet strive by pray'r and counsel to restrain ......Od.16.298.120.
Of wounded honour, and thy rage restrain. ......Od.20.24.233.
A just reproof, ye Peers! Your rage restrain ......Od.20.389.251.
These floods of sorrow, oh my Sire, restrain! ......Od.24.379.367.

RESTRAIN'D
Nature, like *Liberty*, is but restrain'd ......1.EOC.90.249.
Nature, like *Monarchy*, is but restrain'd ......1.EOC.90A.249.
But sober History restrain'd her rage, ...5.DunB4.39.344.
Then with his Spear restrain'd the Youth of *Troy*, ...Il.3.110.195.
But Hospitable Laws restrain'd his Hate: ......Il.6.208.336.
Then with his Spear restrain'd the Youth of *Troy*, ...Il.7.60.365.
The Squires restrain'd: The Foot, with those who wield ......Il.11.63.37.
Restrain'd great *Hector*, and this Counsel gave. ......Il.12.68.84.
Till sad *Polydamas* the Steeds restrain'd, ...Il.15.532.217.
His heav'nly Hand restrain'd the Flux of Blood; ......Il.16.648.269.
And wrapt in Clouds, restrain'd the Hand of Fate. ......Il.21.646.449.
Thus she: but blushes ill-restrain'd betray ......Od.6.79.208.
Restrain'd the rage the vengeful foe exprest, ...Od.14.311.50.
But shook his head, and rising wrath restrain'd. ......Od.20.232.244.

RESTRAINED
And the vain ardors of our love restrained: ......Od.4.386.139.

RESTRAINS
When the proud steed shall know why Man restrains ......3.EOM1.61.21.
Each strengthens Reason, and Self-love restrains. ......3.EOM2.80.64.
Of what restrains him, Government and Laws. ......3.EOM3.272.120.
There with her snowy Hand the Queen restrains ......Il.5.940.311.
Nor Sloth hath seiz'd me, but thy Word restrains: ......Il.5.1013.315.
Restrains their Progress from the bright Abodes, ...Il.8.506.420.
No *Greek* like him, the heav'nly Steeds restrains, ...Il.17.542.309.
And scarce restrains the Torrent in her Eyes: ......Il.21.574.446.
Directs his Judgment, and his Heat restrains; ......Il.23.372.505.
While thy strict Hand his Fellows Head restrains, ...Il.23.410.506.
The master gone, the servants what restrains? ......Od.17.390.150.
No conscious blush, no sense of right restrains ......Od.20.213.243.

RESTRAINT
Provoking Dæmons all restraint remove, ...2.ElAb.231.339.
The dire restraint his wisdom will defeat, ...Od.1.265.45.
Above restraint the tide of sorrow rose: ......Od.4.206.129.

RESTS
Rests on his Club, and holds th' *Hesperian* Spoil. ......2.TemF.82.259.
So peaceful rests, without a stone, a name, ...2.Elegy.69.368.
Rests and expatiates in a life to come. ......3.EOM1.98.26.
No cavern'd Hermit, rests self-satisfy'd. ......3.EOM4.42.132.
Ixion rests upon his Wheel, ...6.11.67.32.
Rests crown'd with Princes Honours, Poets Lays, ...6.108.5A.312.
Here rests a Woman, good without pretence, ...6.115.1.322.
And all that rests of my unravish'd Prey. ......Il.9.480.456.
There, for some luckier *Greek* it rests a Prize, ...Il.13.731.139.
While *Jove* yet rests, while yet my Vapours shed ......Il.14.413.183.
Untouch'd it rests, and sacred from Decay. ......Il.19.42.373.
Where thy soul rests, and labour is no more. ......Od.7.410.257.

RESULT
But the joint Force and full *Result* of *all*. ......1.EOC.246.268.

RESULTING
Light leaps the golden grain, resulting from the ground: ......Il.13.742.140.
The mortal Dart; resulting with a Bound ......Il.22.371.471.
The huge round stone, resulting with a bound, ...Od.11.737.422.

RESUM'D
Resum'd their Oars, and measur'd back the Main. ......1.TrUl.52A.467.
Then mounting on his Car, resum'd the Rein, ...Il.5.405.286.
And that resum'd; the fair *Lyrnessian* Slave. ......Il.9.482.456.
But when, his native shape resum'd, he stands ......Od.4.569.147.
Resum'd their oars, and measur'd back the main. ......Od.13.143.12.
Thus spoke the Goddess, and resum'd her flight ......Od.15.51.72.
Their gifts the Gods resum'd (the Queen rejoin'd.) ......Od.19.144.199.
Each, breathing death, resum'd his dang'rous post ......Od.22.219.297.
And strait resum'd his seat) while round him bows ......Od.24.470.371.

RESUME
But to resume whate'er thy Av'rice craves, ...Il.1.161.95.
Resume thy Arms, and shine again in War. ......Il.19.142.377.
Forget the brother, and resume the man: ......Od.4.732.153.
Courage resume, the shadowy form reply'd, ...Od.4.1079.168.
Retire oh Queen! thy houshold task resume, ...Od.21.377.277.

RESUMED
My Prize of War, yet tamely see resumed; ......Il.1.393.106.

RESUMES
My Mind resumes the thread it dropt before; ......4.2HE2.207.179.
Obscures my Glories, and resumes my Prize. ......Il.1.467.110.
Thus having said, the glorious Chief resumes ......Il.6.638.358.
Sure Heav'n resumes the little Sense it lent. ......Il.12.272.91.
The God who gives, resumes, and orders all, ...Il.16.845.276.
His various arts he soon resumes in aid: ......Od.4.614.148.
The robes resumes, the glittering car ascends, ...Od.6.300.225.
The grateful conf'rence then the King resumes. ......Od.13.4.1.
To joyn the Peers, resumes his throne, and mourns. ......Od.18.186.175.
Each from the dead resumes his bloody lance. ......Od.22.299.300.

RESUMING
Their cares resuming with the dawning day: ......Od.15.431.90.
Resuming then his seat, *Eupitheus'* son ......Od.21.147.265.

RETAILS
By names of Toasts retails each batter'd jade, ...5.DunA2.126.112.
By names of Toasts retails each batter'd jade; ......5.DunB2.134.301.

RETAIN
The shady Empire shall retain no Trace ......1.W-F.371.186.
Let *Greece* then know, my Purpose I retain, ...Il.9.410.452.
Are left unman'd; or if they yet retain ......Il.22.479.475.
Or fly'st thou now? What Hopes can *Troy* retain? ......Il.24.471.556.
The coursers for the champian sports, retain; ......Od.4.821.157.
Gave to retain th' unseparated soul: ......Od.10.585.372.
The secret that thy father lives, retain ......Od.16.324.121.
'Till then, retain the gifts.—The Heroe said, ...Od.17.96.136.
And still (all infant as I was) retain ......Od.21.98.263.
If yet this arm its ancient force retain; ......Od.21.304.274.

RETAIN'D
And long the plant a human heat retain'd. ......1.TrFD.103.390.
He chang'd his Country, but retain'd his Love. ......6.96iv.20.276.

RETAINS
In words like these, which still my mind retains. ......1.TrPA.52.367.
Proud as he is, that Iron-heart retains ......Il.9.741.471.
But *Phœnix* in his Tent the Chief retains, ...Il.9.808.473.
'Tis true, 'tis certain; Man, tho' dead, retains ......Il.23.122.492.
Too faithfully my heart retains the day ......Od.18.301.181.

RETARD
Nor I, a Goddess, can retard the Blow! ......Il.18.516.346.
Nor let the night retard thy full career; ......Od.15.40.71.
My Lord's return shou'd fate no more retard, ...Od.19.356.211.

RETARDING
The wheels of night retarding, to detain ......Od.23.261.336.

RETARDS
Retards our Host, and fills our Hearts with Fright, ...Il.12.258.90.
That from his realm retards his god-like Sire: ......Od.1.121.38.
With envious joy retards the blissful hour. ......Od.1.254.45.

RETENTIVE
Long Chanc'ry-lane retentive rolls the sound, ...5.DunA2.251.130.
Long Chanc'ry-lane retentive rolls the sound, ...5.DunB2.263.308.
Yet still retentive, with redoubled might ......Od.4.567.147.

RETINUE
His House was stately, his Retinue gay, ...2.ChJM.446.36.
Without retinue, to that friendly shore ......Od.19.311.209.

RETIR'D
Daphnis and *Strephon* to the Shades retir'd, ...1.PSp.17z1.62.
Thus *Atticus*, and *Trumbal* thus retir'd. ......1.W-F.258.172.
And from the wondring God th'unwilling Youth retir'd. ......1.TrSt.785.443.
Retir'd reluctant from th'unfinish'd Fight. ......1.TrES.118.454.
Each paid his Thanks, and decently retir'd. ......2.ChJM.372.32.
Resign'd to Fate, and with a Sigh retir'd. ......2.RL3.146.179.
Our Gen'rals now, retir'd to their Estates, ...4.1HE1.7.279.
The decent Knight retir'd with sober rage, ...5.DunB4.113.352.
The Chiefs in sullen Majesty retir'd. ......Il.1.401.107.
(In *Actor's* Court as she retir'd to Rest, ...Il.2.616.157.
While stern *Achilles* in his Wrath retir'd: ......Il.2.935.167.
The wounded Chief behind his Car retir'd, ...Il.5.140.273.
The *Greeks* with slain *Tlepolemus* retir'd; ......Il.5.828.305.
And frighted *Troy* within her Walls retir'd; ......Il.6.90.328.

RETIR'D (CONTINUED)
Had thence retir'd; and with her second Joy, ...Il.6.466.349.
Soon was your Battel o'er: Proud *Troy* retir'd ....Il.8.558.423.
To her the Chief retir'd from stern Debate, ...Il.9.679.468.
No sooner *Hector* saw the King retir'd, ...Il.11.365.51.
Back to the Lines the wounded *Greek* retir'd, ...Il.11.712.66.
Retir'd reluctant from th' unfinish'd Fight. ....Il.12.472.98.
And the gall'd *Ilians* to their Walls retir'd; ....Il.13.904.148.
He said, and backward to the Lines retir'd; ....Il.15.686.222.
So far the *Trojans* from their Lines retir'd; ....Il.16.719.272.
And *Troy* inglorious to her Walls retir'd; ....Il.21.640.448.
Reel'd from the palace, and retir'd to rest. ....Od.2.447.82.
Then ceas'd the Youth, and from the court retir'd. ....Od.4.883.159.
The Sage retir'd: Unable to controul ....Od.4.950.162.
He rose with pleasure, and retir'd to rest. ....Od.7.434.258.
Mean-time the *Cicons,* to their holds retir'd, ...Od.9.51.304.
For here retir'd the sinking billows sleep, ...Od.10.107.345.
To sep'rate mansions, and retir'd to rest. ....Od.13.20.2.
Then sorrowing, with sad step the Queen retir'd, ...Od.16.465.129.
(The female train retir'd) your toils to guide? ....Od.19.28.193.
Sated they rose, and all retir'd to rest. ....Od.19.498.220.
His sage reply, and with her train retir'd: ....Od.21.382.278.
Then stopt the Goddess, trembled, and retir'd. ....Od.24.625.377.

RETIRE
To their first Elements their Souls retire: ....2.RL1.58.150.
To their first Elements the Souls retire: ....2.RL1.58A.150.
Then southward let your Bard retire, ...4.1HE7.17.269.
Here all his suff'ring brotherhood retire, ...5.DunA1.123.78.
Here all his suff'ring brotherhood retire, ...5.DunB1.143.280.
Hence then: to *Argos* shall the Maid retire; ....Il.1.45.88.
Still must ye wait the Foes, and still retire, ...Il.4.282.234.
While we from interdicted Fields retire, ...Il.5.43.268.
Drove Armies back, and made all *Troy* retire. ....Il.5.125.273.
From Fields of Death when late he shall retire, ...Il.5.497.291.
Retire then Warriors, but sedate and slow; ....Il.5.746.302.
Retire, but with your Faces to the Foe. ....Il.5.747.302.
Meanwhile, thou *Hector* to the Town retire, ...Il.6.107.328.
That mows whole Troops, and makes all *Troy* retire. ....Il.6.120.330.
Who mows whole Troops and makes all *Troy* retire. ....Il.6.347.343.
Before his Wrath the trembling Hosts retire; ....Il.8.97.402.
Retire advis'd, and urge the Chariot hence. ....Il.8.170.406.
Here *Greece* shall stay; or if all *Greece* retire, ...Il.9.65.434.
Made Nations tremble, and whole Hosts retire, ...Il.9.403.452.
Divine *Achilles!* wilt thou then retire, ...Il.9.562.461.
Then gave his Friend the Signal to retire; ....Il.10.586.28.
If such thy Will, to that Recess retire, ...Il.14.385.181.
What Hopes remain, what Methods to retire, ...Il.15.596.219.
Let him with Conquest and Renown retire; ....Il.16.303.254.
The village Curs, and trembling Swains retire; ....Il.17.70.290.
Nor from yon' Boaster shall your Chief retire, ...Il.20.423.412.
As the scorch'd Locusts from their Fields retire, ...Il.21.14.421.
Shall ignominious We with shame retire, ...Il.21.510.443.
Let the leagu'd Squadrons to their Posts retire. ....Il.23.66.489.
Permit the mourning Legions to retire, ...Il.23.196.497.
Timeless, indecent, but retire to rest. ....Od.3.430.107.
Your friendly care: retire, ye virgin train! ....Od.6.258.222.
Retire, while from my weary'd limbs I lave ....Od.6.259.222.
Retire we instant to our native reign, ...Od.16.404.125.
Grac'd with a decent robe he shall retire, ...Od.17.630.163.
Retire we hence! but crown with rosy wine ....Od.18.464.190.
Retire oh Queen! thy houshold task resume, ...Od.21.377.277.

RETIREMENT
Great in his Triumphs, in Retirement great. ....2.TemF.164.267.

RETIRES
The Fox obscene to gaping Tombs retires, ...1.W-F.71.156.
Happy next him who to these Shades retires, ...1.W-F.237.171.
There purple *Vengeance* bath'd in Gore retires, ...1.W-F.417.193.
Then weary grown, to shady grotts retires, ...1.TrPA.37.366.
Phaon to *Ætna's* scorching Fields retires, ...1.TrSP.11.393.
Th' o'erlabour'd *Cyclop* from his Task retires; ....1.TrSt.306.423.
Retires from *Argos* to the Sylvan Shade, ...1.TrSt.681.439.
And murm'ring from the Corps th'unwilling Soul retires. ....1.TrES.110.453.
And murm'ring to the Shades the Soul retires. ....1.TrES.110A.453.
Ev'n here, where frozen chastity retires, ...2.ElAb.181.334.
Collects her breath, as ebbing life retires, ...3.Ep1.240.36.
So quick retires each flying course, you'd swear ....3.Ep4.159.153.
From thy Bæotia tho' Her Pow'r retires, ...5.DunA1.23.62.
Where from Ambrosia, Jove retires for ease. ....5.DunA2.80.107.
From thy Bœotia tho' her Pow'r retires, ...5.DunB1.25.271.
Where, from Ambrosia, Jove retires for ease. ....5.DunB2.84.299.
See! She retires: Nor can we say ....6.4iv.10.10.
Basks in the Sun, then to the Shades retires, ...6.17iii.30.58.
From thy Bœotia, lo! the fog retires, ...6.106iv.9.307.
Smit with a conscious Sense, retires behind, ...Il.3.45.190.
He dreads his Fury, and some Steps retires. ....Il.5.540.294.
Soon as from Fight the blue-ey'd Maid retires, ...Il.5.625.297.
Retires for Safety to the Mother's Arms. ....Il.8.326.413.
Thro' the dark Clouds, and now in Night retires; ....Il.11.84.38.
Then sow'rly slow th' indignant Beast retires. ....Il.11.679.65.
While *Nestor's* Chariot far from Fight retires: ....Il.11.727.67.
And murm'ring to the Shades the Soul retires. ....Il.12.464.98.
Repuls'd he stands; nor from his Stand retires; ....Il.13.203.115.
While stern *Achilles* in his Wrath retires. ....Il.14.426.184.
And from the half-burn'd Ship proud *Troy* retires: ....Il.16.349.256.
The *Greek* obeys him, and with Awe retires. ....Il.16.868.277.
Retires for Succour to his social Train, ...Il.16.985.281.
Nor yields a Step, nor from his Post retires: ....Il.18.198.331.
To the black Labours of his Forge retires. ....Il.18.538.348.
And from the Senior Pow'r, submiss retires; ....Il.21.544.444.
His sage reply, and with her train retires. ....Od.1.460.54.
'Till she retires, determin'd we remain, ...Od.2.227.72.
And modest worth with noble scorn retires. ....Od.20.168.241.
The royal pair; she guides them, and retires. ....Od.23.316.338.

RETIRING
Contracted all, retiring to the breast; ....3.EOM2.103.67.
But sad retiring to the sounding Shore, ...Il.1.455.109.
Enrag'd, to *Troy's* retiring Chiefs he cry'd. ....Il.5.564.295.
The Wretch obeys, retiring with a Tear. ....Il.22.641.483.
Thus wretched, thus retiring all in Tears, ...Il.22.642.483.
To the dark grave retiring as to rest, ...Od.11.168.390.
The Chief retiring. Souls, like that in thee, ...Od.17.537.158.
To the dark grave retiring as to rest; ....Od.23.301.337.

RETORT
Peers from the distant *Samian* shore retort; ....Od.19.150.199.
Retort an insult, or repel a foe? ....Od.21.142.265.

RETORTED
And threats his Followers with retorted Eye. ....Il.11.695.66.
With Heart indignant and retorted Eyes. ....Il.17.120.292.
(Returns *Antinous* with retorted eye) ....Od.17.452.155.

RETORTS
(Insulted *Merion* thus retorts the Boast) ....Il.16.750.273.
(Retorts *Euryalus:)* He boasts no claim ....Od.8.177.271.

RETOST
Tost, and retost, the ball incessant flies. ....Od.6.114.211.
Tost and retost, it reel'd beneath the blow; ....Od.12.490.456.

RETOUCH
"Not Sir, if you revise it, and retouch." ....4.Arbu.64.100.

RETRACING
Gaz'd o'er his Sire, retracing ev'ry line, ...Od.24.270.362.

RETREAT
A soft Retreat from sudden vernal Show'rs; ....1.PSp.98.70.
The lowing Herds to murm'ring Brooks retreat, ...1.PSu.86.79.
In their loose Traces from the Field retreat; ....1.PAu.62.84.
He us'd from Noise and Business to retreat; ....2.ChJM.470.38.
Why rove my thoughts beyond this last retreat? ....2.ElAb.5.319.
Not always humble he who seeks retreat, ...3.Ep1.65A.20.
Ask how from Britain Cæsar made retreat? ....3.Ep1.81A.21.
Ask why from Britain Cæsar made retreat? ....3.Ep1.81B.21.
Not therefore humble he who seeks retreat, ...3.Ep1.65.20.
Ask why from Britain Cæsar would retreat? ....3.Ep1.81.21.
But Wisdom's Triumph is well-tim'd Retreat, ...3.Ep2.225.68.
There, my Retreat the best Companions grace, ...4.HS1.125.17.
But wish you lik'd Retreat a little less; ....4.JD4.87A.33.
Shades, that to Bacon could retreat afford, ...4.HS2.175.69.
The Man, who stretch'd in Isis' calm Retreat ....4.2HE2.116.173.
Yet always wishing to retreat, ...4.HS6.127.257.
Oft in the clear, still Mirrour of Retreat, ...4.EpS2.78.317.
Raptur'd, he gazes round the dear retreat, ...5.DunA1.225.90.
(Haunt of the Muses) made their safe retreat. ....5.DunA2.396.149.
(Haunt of the Muses) made their safe retreat. ....5.DunB2.428.318.
And routed *Reason* finds a safe Retreat in thee. ....6.8.18.18.
In vain to Desarts thy Retreat is made; ....6.84.27.239.
As Godlike *Hector* sees the Prince retreat, ...Il.3.53.191.
The God of Arms and Martial Maid retreat; ....Il.5.46.268.
Slow they retreat, and ev'n retreating fight. ....Il.5.863.307.
'Twas vain to seek Retreat, and vain to fear; ....Il.7.263.377.
The *Greeks,* repuls'd, retreat behind their Wall, ...Il.8.403.416.
Thus the grim Lion his Retreat maintains. ....Il.11.674.65.
What Hopes, what Methods of Retreat remain? ....Il.12.82.84.
Soon as the *Greeks* the Chief's Retreat beheld, ...Il.14.515.188.
They gain th' impervious Rock and safe retreat ....Il.15.310A.209.
No Aids, no Bulwarks your Retreat attend, ...Il.15.896.232.
Breaks thro' the Ranks, and his Retreat pursues: ....Il.16.988.281.
While *Greece* a heavy, thick Retreat maintains, ...Il.17.845.321.
Strook Slaughter back, and cover'd the Retreat. ....Il.21.630.448.
Disdainful of Retreat: High-held before, ...Il.21.687.450.
(Of *Alpheus'* race) the weary youths retreat. ....Od.3.620.117.
Ev'n then, not mindless of his last retreat, ...Od.5.413.192.
A month's reception, and a safe retreat. ....Od.10.14.340.
Our eager sailors seize the fair retreat, ...Od.10.105.345.
Touch'd at his sour retreat, thro' deepest night, ...Od.11.693.419.
The mountains lessen, and retreat the shores; ....Od.11.792.426.
Argos the rich for his retreat he chose, ...Od.15.264.81.
The rest retreat: the victors now advance, ...Od.22.298.300.

RETREATING
Slow they retreat, and ev'n retreating fight. ....Il.5.863.307.
Yet thus, retreating, his Associates fir'd. ....Il.11.713.67.
The *Greek* retreating mourn'd his frustrate Blow, ...Il.13.221.116.
Thus on retreating *Greece* the *Trojans* pour, ...Il.17.817.320.
Him, thus retreating, *Artemis* upbraids, ...Il.21.545.444.
But hence retreating to your domes repair; ....Od.2.285.75.
And to the stern retreating roll the tides. ....Od.2.469.83.
Thro' seas retreating from the sound of war, ...Od.6.10.203.
When seas retreating roar within her caves, ...Od.12.134.438.

RETREATS
The mossie Fountains, and the Green Retreats! ....1.PSu.72.77.
Thy Forests, *Windsor!* and thy green Retreats, ...1.W-F.1.148.
'Tis yours, my Lord, to bless our soft Retreats, ...1.W-F.283.174.
So fierce, these *Greeks* their last Retreats defend. ....Il.12.194.88.
Warn'd, he retreats. Then swift from all sides pour ....Il.16.150.243.
(Not fated yet to die) There safe retreats, ...Il.21.577.446.
And to *Erectheus'* sacred dome retreats. ....Od.7.106.239.
When radiant he advances, or retreats: ....Od.11.18.380.
The homicide retreats to foreign lands; ....Od.23.120.326.

RETRENCH
Can I retrench? Yes, mighty well, ...4.1HE7.75.273.

RETRIEVE

Thy brave Example shall retrieve our Host, ... Il.8.341.413.
And seem already to retrieve the Day. ..... Il.23.529.511.
But grant, oh grant our loss we may retrieve: ..... Od.10.79.343.

RETRIEVES

Small Thought retrieves the Spirits of the Brave. ..... Il.13.156.112.

RETROSPECTIVE

In vain the grave, with retrospective eye, ... 3.Ep1.51A.19.
In vain the Sage, with retrospective eye, ... 3.Ep1.51.19.

RETURN

Might he return, and bless once more our Eyes, ... 1.EOC.462.291.
The Vows you never will return, receive; ..... 1.TrSP.107.398.
And Birds defer their Songs till thy Return: ..... 1.TrSP.174.401.
Return fair Youth, return, and bring along ..... 1.TrSP.238.404.
Return fair Youth, return, and bring along ..... 1.TrSP.238.404.
If you return—ah why these long Delays? ..... 1.TrSP.248.404.
Promise the Skies the bright Return of Day; ..... 1.TrSt.483.430.
When Merchants from th' *Exchange* return in Peace, ... 2.RL*A* 1.87.129.
No less deserv'd a just Return of Praise. ..... 2.TemF.331.280.
They rise, they break, and to that sea return. ..... 3.EOM3.20.94.
Of all thy blameless Life the sole Return ..... 4.Arbu.259.114.
Return well travell'd, and transform'd to Beasts, ... 4.1HE6.123.245.
And courts to courts return it round and round: ..... 5.DunA2.252.130.
And answ'ring Gin-shops sowrer sighs return! ..... 5.DunA3.140.162.
Soon to that mass of Nonsense to return, ... 5.DunB1.241.288.
And courts to courts return it round and round; ..... 5.DunB2.264.308.
And answ'ring gin-shops sowrer sighs return. ..... 5.DunB3.148.327.
Oh take the Husband, or return the Wife! ..... 6.11.82.33.
And to its Ancient *Mirth the* Comic Sock *return.* ..... 6.26ii.8.79.
And never will return, or bring him home. ..... 6.96ii.30Z28.271.
"And never will return, or bring thee home. ..... 6.96ii.38.272.
Return our Thanks. Accept our humble Lays, ... 6.96iii.3.274.
And wak'd and wish'd whole Nights for thy Return? ..... 6.96iv.4.276.
A safe Return was promis'd to our Toils, ... Il.2.143.135.
For our Return we trust the heav'nly Pow'rs; ..... Il.2.314.142.
Ne'er to return was then the common Cry, ... Il.2.352.144.
No more they sigh, inglorious to return, ... Il.2.532.152.
At his Return, a treach'rous Ambush, rose, ... Il.6.232.337.
Return, brave *Ajax,* to thy *Grecian* Friends, ... Il.7.358.381.
A safe Return was promis'd to our toils, ... Il.9.27.433.
Return, *Achilles!* oh return, tho' late, ... Il.9.320.449.
Return, *Achilles!* oh return, tho' late, ... Il.9.320.449.
If I return, I quit immortal Praise ..... Il.9.536.460.
Let these return: Our Voyage, or our Stay, ... Il.9.731.470.
Return then Heroes! and our Answer bear, ... Il.9.763.472.
The Chiefs return; divine *Ulysses* leads. ..... Il.9.774.472.
Hail'd their Return: *Atrides* first begun. ..... Il.9.790.473.
Say shall I stay, or with Dispatch return? ..... Il.10.70.5.
Then (never to return) he sought the Shore, ... Il.10.399.21.
And intercept his hop'd return to *Troy.* ..... Il.10.414.21.
In cruel Chains; till your Return reveal ..... Il.10.514.26.
No more they sigh, inglorious to return, ... Il.11.17.35.
Then swift revert, and Wounds return for Wounds. ..... Il.11.422.53.
When we, victorious, shall to *Greece* return, ... Il.14.593.191.
"What make we here? Return, ye Chiefs, return!" ..... Il.16.247.249.
"What make we here? Return, ye Chiefs, return!" ..... Il.16.247.249.
And safe return him to these Eyes again! ..... Il.16.305.254.
His safe Return, the Winds dispers'd in Air. ..... Il.16.309.254.
The hollow Ships return a deeper Sound. ..... Il.16.333.255.
Incessant swarm, and chas'd, return again. ..... Il.16.782.273.
"Return not, my brave Friend (perhaps he said) ..... Il.16.1013.282.
And for his wish'd Return prepares in vain; ..... Il.17.467.305.
In vain advance! not fated to return. ..... Il.17.565.310.
May glad the Fleets that hope not our return, ... Il.17.718.315.
He never, never must return again. ..... Il.18.78.326.
I cast all hope of my Return away, ... Il.18.130.328.
Return? (said *Hector,* fir'd with stern Disdain) ..... Il.18.333.337.
Now never to return! and doom'd to go ..... Il.21.54.424.
Return the shining Bands of Gods in Arms; ..... Il.21.602.447.
Return in safety to my *Trojan* Friends. ..... Il.21.662.449.
No—If I e'er return, return I must ..... Il.22.150.459.
No—If I e'er return, return I must ..... Il.22.150.459.
The Bath preparing for her Lord's Return: ..... Il.22.571.480.
Forc'd by repeated Insults to return, ... Il.22.644.483.
And the slow Mules the same rough Road return. ..... Il.23.151.495.
To whom we vainly vow'd, at our return, ... Il.23.180.497.
He said: The People to their Ships return: ..... Il.23.199.497.
May the just Gods return another Day. ..... Il.23.750.520.
The King's Return revolving in his Mind, ... Il.24.848.572.
Let all combine t'atchieve his wish'd return: ..... Od.1.99.36.
Shou'd he return, that troop so blithe and bold, ... Od.1.211.43.
To hail *Ulysses'* safe return I came: ..... Od.1.252.45.
But of his wish'd return the care resign; ..... Od.1.350.49.
To bless our safe return we join in pray'r, ... Od.3.193.95.
The father's fortune never to return, ... Od.3.256.98.
And thou return, with disappointed toil, ... Od.3.403.106.
To thy long vows a safe return accord. ..... Od.4.648.150.
You timely will return a welcome guest, ... Od.4.739.153.
My quick return, young *Ithacus* rejoin'd, ... Od.4.811.156.
His wish'd return with happy pow'r befriend, ... Od.4.1011.164.
Will intercept th' unwary Youth's return. ..... Od.4.1078.168.
To bid thee patient his return attend. ..... Od.4.1084.168.
The chief's return shall make the guilty bleed? ..... Od.5.33.172.
'Tis *Jove's* decree *Ulysses* shall return: ..... Od.5.41.172.
Impatient Fate his near return attends, ... Od.5.145.178.
Nor my return the end, nor this the way, ... Od.5.225.182.
I languish to return, and dye at home. ..... Od.5.282.185.
Return the gift, and cast it in the main; ..... Od.5.443.194.
Now on return her care *Nausicaa* bends, ... Od.6.299.225.
Turn and return, and scarce imprint the sand. ..... Od.8.414.286.
And costly presents in return he gave; ..... Od.9.235.316.
For his return with sacrifice and prayer. ..... Od.9.273.318.
And sigh, expecting the return of day. ..... Od.9.363.321.

RETURN (CONTINUED)

And only rich in barren fame return. ..... Od.10.47.341.
But mourn in vain; no prospect of return. ..... Od.10.90.343.
Never, alas! thou never shalt return, ... Od.10.317.359.
And thy lost friends return to humankind. ..... Od.10.356.361.
The lowing herds return; around them throng ..... Od.10.487.367.
And ecchoing hills return the tender cry: ..... Od.10.490.367.
What other joy can equal thy return? ..... Od.10.497.367.
Each breast beats homeward, anxious to return: ..... Od.10.573.370.
So in our palace, at our safe return ..... Od.11.39.381.
They, seal'd with truth return the sure reply, ... Od.11.182.390.
When hand to hand they wound return for wound; ..... Od.11.518.409.
Ev'n to thy Queen disguis'd, unknown, return; ..... Od.11.562.411.
Mean-time the * Goddess our return survey'd ..... Od.12.23.430.
And if the Gods ordain a safe return, ... Od.12.411.451.
'Till his return, no title shall I plead, ... Od.14.178.44.
And the lost glories of his house return. ..... Od.14.189.45.
What means might best his safe return avail, ... Od.14.365.53.
That soon *Ulysses* wou'd return, declar'd, ... Od.14.369.53.
But when arriv'd he thy return shall know, ... Od.15.240.79.
Our debt of safe return, in feast and sacrifice. ..... Od.15.546.96.
Or heav'ns! might He return! (and soon appear ..... Od.16.105.107.
Might he return, I yield my life a prey ..... Od.16.107.108.
Our safe return, and ease a mother's heart. ..... Od.16.141.109.
Our safe return, and back with speed repair: ..... Od.16.163.110.
Her son's return, and ease a parent's heart; ..... Od.16.351.123.
Return, and riot shakes our walls a-new) ..... Od.17.121.137.
How wouldst thou fly, nor ev'n in thought return? ..... Od.18.31.168.
Should he return, what'er my beauties prove, ... Od.18.297.181.
Doom'd to survive, and never to return! ..... Od.19.297.209.
My Lord's return shou'd fate no more retard, ... Od.19.356.211.
Ulysses speaks his own return decreed; ..... Od.19.652.227.
(*Eumæus* in their train) the maids return. ..... Od.20.203.243.
Then, happier thoughts return the nodding scale, ... Od.20.279.246.
Haste and return (*Ulysses* made reply) ..... Od.22.122.292.
And spreads her Lord's return from place to place. ..... Od.22.532.314.
For ev'ry good man yields a just return: ..... Od.24.331.365.
Who knows thy blest, thy wish'd return? oh say, ... Od.24.465.371.
The Chief's return should make the guilty bleed? ..... Od.24.550.374.

RETURN'D

Shook, and return'd the dreadful blast again. ..... 1.TrPA.48.367.
He said; and thus the Queen of Heav'n return'd; ..... 1.TrSt.348.424.
And from his Throne return'd this stern Reply. ..... 1.TrSt.403.426.
And the press'd Watch return'd a silver Sound. ..... 2.RL1.18.146.
And he return'd a friend, who came a foe. ..... 3.EOM3.206.113.
But soon the Cloud return'd—and thus the Sire: ..... 5.DunA3.225.176.
But soon the cloud return'd—and thus the Sire: ..... 5.DunB3.227.331.
The trembling Priest along the Shore return'd, ... Il.1.47.88.
Then in the Sheath return'd the shining Blade. ..... Il.1.292.100.
The raging King return'd his Frowns again. ..... Il.1.328.103.
And thus return'd. Austere *Saturnius,* say, ... Il.1.714.122.
With answering Sighs return'd the plaintive Sound. ..... Il.4.185.230.
No Words the Godlike *Diomed* return'd, ... Il.4.452.241.
The Youths return'd not from the doubtful Plain, ... Il.5.192.276.
There fell they breathless, and return'd no more. ..... Il.6.234.337.
Hector, this heard, return'd without Delay; ..... Il.6.488.350.
But let my Body, to my Friends return'd, ... Il.7.91.367.
With gen'ral Shouts return'd him loud Acclaim. ..... Il.7.481.388.
And sadly slow, to sacred *Troy* return'd. ..... Il.7.511.389.
With Accent weak these tender Words return'd. ..... Il.9.561.461.
He heard, return'd, and took his painted Shield: ..... Il.10.168.9.
He went a Legat, but return'd a Foe: ..... Il.10.342.18.
Return'd triumphant with this Prize of War. ..... Il.10.631.30.
And what surviv'd of *Greece* to *Greece* return'd; ..... Il.12.14.81.
To him then *Hector* with Disdain return'd; ..... Il.12.267.91.
And trembling, these submissive Words return'd. ..... Il.15.40.195.
Return'd to *Ilion,* and excell'd in War: ..... Il.15.649.221.
Thy Friend return'd; and with it, this Reply. ..... Il.16.67.238.
With generous Anguish, and in scorn return'd. ..... Il.17.18.288.
To their black Vessels all the *Greeks* return'd. ..... Il.19.290.384.
The Iv'ry studded Reins, return'd behind, ... Il.19.430.389.
Where the shrill Brass return'd a sharper Sound: ..... Il.20.324.407.
Scamander spoke; the Shores return'd the Sound. ..... Il.21.230.430.
Go then (return'd the Sire) without delay, ... Il.22.239.465.
And to their Caves the whistling *Winds* return'd: ..... Il.23.285.501.
Or safe return'd, the race of glory past, ... Od.1.303.47.
From *Temesé* return'd, your royal court ..... Od.1.410.52.
And in their ships the conqu'ring *Greeks* return'd; ..... Od.3.160.93.
Return'd *Atrides* to the coast of *Greece,* ..... Od.3.395.105.
When *Troy* was ruin'd, had the chief return'd, ... Od.4.230.130.
Mean-time return'd, with dire remorseless sway ..... Od.4.453.141.
(From *Æthiopia's* happy climes return'd) ..... Od.5.364.190.
Or, the charm tasted, had return'd no more. ..... Od.9.114.308.
With joy the sailors view their friends return'd, ... Od.9.549.328.
At length these words with accent low return'd. ..... Od.10.76.343.
Than if return'd to *Ithaca* from *Troy.* ..... Od.10.494.367.
But home return'd, to each ætherial pow'r ..... Od.11.162.389.
Safe he return'd, without one hostile scar; ..... Od.11.656.416.
Yet safe return'd— *Ulysses* led the way. ..... Od.12.251.444.
To *Crete* return'd, an honourable name. ..... Od.14.271.49.
But deem'd enquiry vain, and to their ship return'd. ..... Od.14.390.53.
The full-fed swine return'd with evening home; ..... Od.14.454.57.
But when return'd, the good *Ulysses'* son ..... Od.14.583.65.
And oh! return'd might we *Ulysses* meet! ..... Od.15.174.76.
The Prince return'd. Renown'd in days of yore ..... Od.15.551.96.
With added gifts return'd him glorious home. ..... Od.19.541.223.
At length return'd, some God inspires thy breast ..... Od.19.567.224.
Sudden the tyrant of the skies return'd: ..... Od.19.638.227.
This said, he first return'd: the faithful swains ..... Od.21.258.272.
With high disdain, and sternly thus return'd. ..... Od.22.72.290.
'Till sev'nteen nights and sev'nteen days return'd, ... Od.24.81.352.
Beyond our hopes, and to our wish, return'd! ..... Od.24.461.370.

RETURN'ST

Once more return'st thou from the Realms of Night? ... Il.23.110.492.

RETURNING

Returning Justice lift aloft her Scale; ... 1.Mes.18.114.
Returning Thoughts in endless Circles roll, ... 1.TrSt.75.413.
Foresees with Anguish his returning Heir. ... 1.TrSt.197.418.
As to the Sea returning Rivers roll, ... 2.TemF.430.284.
Own'd his returning Lord, look'd up, and dy'd! ... 6.15.18.52.
The tragic muse, returning, wept her woes. ... 6.107.4.310.
Returning with the twelfth revolving Light. ... Il.1.559.115.
Her, thus returning from the furrow'd Main, ... Il.1.572.115.
And *Greece* returning plow the watry Deep. ... Il.3.357.210.
The *Trojan* Bands returning *Hector* wait, ... Il.7.372.382.
Those Wheels returning ne'er shall mark the Plain; ... Il.12.128.86.
His Sense returning with the coming Breeze; ... Il.15.271.207.
Too late returning, snuffs the Track of Men, ... Il.18.374.339.
Sudden, returning with the Stream of Light, ... Il.20.391.411.
Returning sad, when toilsome day declines. ... Od.1.250.45.
The youthful Hero, with returning light, ... Od.2.3.59.
And safe returning to the *Grecian* host, ... Od.4.353.136.
His ship returning shall my spies explore: ... Od.4.897.160.
Saw them returning with the setting sun. ... Od.7.416.258.
As from some feast a man returning late, ... Od.10.246.354.
'Till we returning shall our guest demand, ... Od.15.583.98.
Came late-returning to his sylvan bow'r. ... Od.16.471.130.
Mean-time returning, with remorseless sway ... Od.17.144.138.
Soon as returning life regains its seat, ... Od.24.407.368.

RETURNS

Just Gods! shall all things yield Returns but Love? ... 1.PAu.76.85.
With sure *Returns* of still *expected Rhymes.* ... 1.EOC.349.279.
The Merchant from th' *Exchange* returns in Peace, ... 2.RL3.23.170.
Mem'ry and fore-cast just returns engage, ... 3.EOM3.143.107.
Amus'd he reads, and then returns the bills ... 5.DunA2.87.108.
He buoys up instant, and returns to light; ... 5.DunA2.284A.136.
Amus'd he reads, and then returns the bills ... 5.DunB2.91.300.
He buoys up instant, and returns to light: ... 5.DunB2.296.310.
Lo! ev'ry finish'd Son returns to thee: ... 5.DunB4.500.391.
Your Slave, and *exit;* but returns with *Rowe,* ... 6.49ii.4.140.
Never for this can just returns be shown; ... 6.105v.3.302.
Eyes the rough Waves, and tir'd returns at last. ... Il.5.739.302.
And *Greece* indignant thro' her Seas returns. ... Il.6.679.361.
War with a fiercer Tide once more returns, ... Il.7.83.367.
Returns no more to wake the silent dead. ... Il.9.531.459.
Returns the Chief, or must our Navy fall? ... Il.9.793.473.
New Force, new Spirit to each Breast returns; ... Il.11.277.47.
With equal Ardour (*Telamon* returns) ... Il.13.107.109.
Swift to his Tent the *Cretan* King returns. ... Il.13.314.120.
Himself returns to his *Patroclus* slain. ... Il.17.792.319.
(Returns *Achilles*) all our Hosts obey! ... Il.19.144.377.
Lo! he returns! Try then, my flying spear! ... Il.21.70.424.
Ring with conflicting Pow'rs, and Heav'n returns the Sound? ... Il.21.509.443.
In vain: Alas! her Lord returns no more! ... Il.22.572.480.
When once we pass, the Soul returns no more. ... Il.23.94.491.
With haughty rage, and sternly thus returns. ... Od.2.94.65.
She spoke: to his high dome the Prince returns, ... Od.2.335.77.
Is this (returns the Prince) for mirth a time? ... Od.2.347.78.
While to the rival train the Prince returns, ... Od.2.428.81.
Full horribly he roars, his voice all heav'n returns. ... Od.8.346.282.
O royal maid, *Ulysses* strait returns, ... Od.8.503.289.
Aghast returns; the messenger of woe, ... Od.10.287.357.
Thus I, and thus the parent shade returns. ... Od.11.218.392.
The Ghost returns: O chief of humankind ... Od.11.499.408.
The swain returns. A tale of sorrows hear; ... Od.16.61.105.
Wretched old man! (with tears the Prince returns) ... Od.16.158.110.
O'er earth (returns the Prince) resounds thy name, ... Od.16.262.117.
And cries aloud, Thy son, oh Queen returns: ... Od.16.355.123.
Returns he? Ambush'd we'll his walk invade, ... Od.16.398.125.
(Returns *Antinous* with retorted eye) ... Od.17.452.155.
And sow'rly smiling, this reply returns. ... Od.17.544.159.
Swift to the Queen returns the gentle swain: ... Od.17.656.164.
Ah me! forbear, returns the Queen, forbear; ... Od.18.209.177.
To whom with filial awe, the Prince returns: ... Od.18.267.179.
Ah me! returns the Queen, when from this shore ... Od.18.293.180.
My King returns; the proud Usurpers dye. ... Od.20.282.247.
Then silent, to the joyous hall returns, ... Od.21.60.262.
And to the seat returns from whence he rose. ... Od.21.174.268.
Now he returns, and first essays his hand ... Od.24.493.371.

REV'RENC'D

Where *Damian* kneeling, rev'renc'd as she past. ... 2.ChJM.600A.44.

REV'RENCE

Their Work, and rev'rence our Superior Will. ... 1.TrSt.410.427.
And hear with Rev'rence an experienc'd Wife! ... 2.ChWB.2.57.
He takes the Gift with rev'rence, and extends ... 2.RL3.131.177.
In rev'rence to the Sins of *Thirty-nine!* ... 4.EpS2.5.313.
Walker with rev'rence took, and lay'd aside. ... 5.DunB4.206.363.
With rev'rence, hope, and love. ... 6.51ii.36.154.
The Priest to rev'rence, and release the Fair. ... Il.1.32.87.
The Priest to rev'rence, and release the Fair; ... Il.1.491.111.
Ulysses seated, greater Rev'rence drew. ... Il.3.274.205.
Hear our Decree, and rev'rence what ye hear; ... Il.8.8.395.
To whom the King: With Rev'rence we allow ... Il.10.136.8.
With rev'rence at the lofty wonder gaz'd: ... Od.6.200.219.
But fear and rev'rence did my steps detain, ... Od.7.392.256.
To bid me rev'rence or regard the Gods. ... Od.9.328.319.
To worth in misery a rev'rence pay, ... Od.11.424.405.
Hear heav'n's commands, and rev'rence what ye hear! ... Od.12.325.447.

REV'REND

Old Father *Thames* advanc'd his rev'rend Head. ... 1.W-F.330.181.
Shakes off the *Dust,* and rears his rev'rend Head! ... 1.EOC.700.319.
With all the Marks of rev'rend Age appears, ... 1.TrVP.46.379.
Then, on their Father's rev'rend Features rest. ... 1.TrSt.632.436.

REV'REND (CONTINUED)

These rev'rend Honours on my Hoary Head; ... 2.ChJM.132.21.
With rev'rend Dulness, and grave Impotence. ... 2.ChJM.175.23.
Our rev'rend Knight was urg'd to Am'rous Play: ... 2.ChJM.522.40.
Behold a rev'rend sire, whom want of grace ... 3.Ep1.228.34.
But rev'rend S[utton], with a meeker air, ... 3.Ep3.107A.100.
A few grey hairs his rev'rend temples crown'd, ... 3.Ep3.327.120.
Tho' coarse was rev'rend, and tho' bare, was black. ... 4.JD4.39.29.
How pale, each Worshipful and rev'rend Guest ... 4.HS2.75.59.
In rev'rend Bishops note some *small Neglects,* ... 4.EpS1.16.298.
In rev'rend S[utto]n note a *small Neglect,* ... 4.EpS1.16A.298.
Ye Rev'rend Atheists!— *F.* Scandal! name them, Who? ... 4.EpS2.18.314.
The rev'rend Flamen in his lengthen'd dress. ... 5.DunA2.330.142.
Thence to the banks where rev'rend Bards repose, ... 5.DunB2.347.314.
They led him soft; each rev'rend Bard arose; ... 5.DunB2.348.314.
The rev'rend Flamen in his lengthen'd dress. ... 5.DunB2.354.314.
Rosy and rev'rend, tho' without a Gown. ... 5.DunB4.496.391.
Furrow'd his rev'rend face, and white his hairs, ... 6.15.6.51.
As her dead Father's rev'rend image past, ... 6.32.31.97.
The King of Men his Rev'rend Priest defy'd, ... Il.1.13.86.
Hail Rev'rend Priest! to Phœbus' awful Dome ... Il.1.576.115.
A rev'rend Horror silenc'd all the Sky. ... Il.1.737.122.
Full of his God, the rev'rend *Calchas* cry'd, ... Il.2.390.145.
Let rev'rend *Priam* in the Truce engage, ... Il.3.145.197.
And next the wisest of the Rev'rend Throng, ... Il.3.196.200.
The Rites now finish'd, rev'rend *Priam* rose, ... Il.3.378.211.
There rev'rend *Nestor* ranks his *Pylian* Bands, ... Il.4.336.236.
And rev'rend Elders, seek the Gods in vain. ... Il.6.142.331.
Slow from his Seat the rev'rend *Priam* rose. ... Il.7.441.386.
A rev'rend Horror silenc'd all the Sky; ... Il.8.36.397.
The rev'rend Charioteer directs the Course, ... Il.8.147.404.
O rev'rend Prince! (*Tydides* thus replies) ... Il.8.177.406.
Wise *Nestor* then his Rev'rend Figure rear'd; ... Il.9.71.435.
The Monarch thus: the Rev'rend *Nestor* then: ... Il.9.215.443.
The rev'rend *Peleus* shall elect my Wife; ... Il.9.517.458.
But here this Night let rev'rend *Phœnix* stay: ... Il.9.551.460.
My second Father, and my rev'rend Guide! ... Il.9.714.469.
In Slumbers sweet the rev'rend *Phœnix* lay. ... Il.9.778.472.
(Five Girls beside the rev'rend Herald told) ... Il.10.373.19.
The cordial Bev'rage rev'rend *Nestor* shares ... Il.11.785.70.
Thy self, *Achilles,* and thy rev'rend Sire ... Il.11.908.76.
The rev'rend *Ocean* and grey *Tethys* reign, ... Il.14.343.179.
Think of each living Father's rev'rend Head; ... Il.15.800.227.
Of rev'rend Dotards, check'd our Glory long: ... Il.15.875.230.
The rev'rend Elders nodded o'er the Case; ... Il.18.586.351.
Thus charg'd the rev'rend Monarch: Wide were flung ... Il.21.627.448.
He strikes his rev'rend Head now white with Age: ... Il.22.44.454.
In Dust the rev'rend Lineaments deform, ... Il.22.104.457.
Achilles this to rev'rend *Nestor* bears, ... Il.23.705.517.
From me, no Harm shall touch thy rev'rend Head; ... Il.24.456.555.
In me, that Father's rev'rend Image trace, ... Il.24.600.562.
The rev'rend Monarch by the Hand he rais'd; ... Il.24.649.563.
Where full before him rev'rend *Priam* sate: ... Il.24.747.568.
Rev'rend old man! lo here confest he stands ... Od.2.47.62.
But chief the rev'rend Sage admir'd; he took ... Od.3.478.110.
The rev'rend *Nestor* with his Queen repos'd. ... Od.3.515.112.
Vouchsafes the rev'rend stranger to display ... Od.8.157.271.
And back to Ocean glance with rev'rend awe. ... Od.10.631.374.
Then sage *Echeneus,* whose grave, rev'rend brow ... Od.11.428.405.
Say if my sire, the rev'rend *Peleus* reigns ... Od.11.605.413.
Thy rev'rend age had met a shameful fate? ... Od.14.44.38.
And rev'rend strangers, modest youth forbears. ... Od.16.46.104.
There, if base scorn insult my rev'rend age, ... Od.16.294.119.
Some rude insult thy rev'rend age may bear; ... Od.17.330.147.
The rev'rend stranger, or the spotless maid; ... Od.18.463.190.
Beside the gate the rev'rend minstrel stands; ... Od.22.369.305.
And sleeps my child? the rev'rend matron cries: ... Od.23.5.318.
His aged limbs, to kiss his rev'rend face, ... Od.24.276.363.
(Rev'rend and wise, whose comprehensive view ... Od.24.518.373.
Son of *Arcesius,* rev'rend warrior, hear! ... Od.24.599.376.

REV'RENT

Rev'rent I touch thee! but with honest zeal; ... 4.EpS2.216.325.
With rev'rent awe, but decent confidence: ... Od.3.24.87.
With rev'rent hand the King presents the gold, ... Od.3.554.114.

REV'RENTLY

They follow rev'rently each wond'rous wight, ... 4.1740.33.333.

REVEAL

But thou be Silent, nor reveal thy State, ... 1.TrUl.184.471.
To these I made no Scruple to reveal. ... 2.ChWB.274.70.
"The Fault he has I fairly shall reveal, ... 4.2HE2.19.165.
To him reveal my joys, and open all my skies. ... 6.21.42.70.
And Truths, invidious to the Great, reveal. ... Il.1.102.92.
Reveal the Cause, and trust a Parent's Care. ... Il.1.475.110.
In cruel Chains; till your Return reveal ... Il.10.514.26.
Whate'er the Cause, reveal thy secret Care, ... Il.16.27.236.
Reveal the Cause, and trust a Parent's Care. ... Il.18.98.327.
The prescient Godhead to reveal the rest. ... Od.4.744.153.
Convene the tribes, the murd'rous plot reveal, ... Od.4.978.163.
The latent cause, oh sacred Seer, reveal! ... Od.11.178.390.
Nor dare the secret of a God reveal: ... Od.11.304.397.
But thou be silent, nor reveal thy state; ... Od.13.351.24.
But the dire secret of my fate reveal. ... Od.15.297.83.
But I the secrets of high Heav'n reveal. ... Od.17.175.140.
Those to whose eyes the Gods their ways reveal, ... Od.17.464.155.
Reveal, obsequious to my first demand, ... Od.19.125.198.

REVEAL'D

Reveal'd; and *God's* eternal Day be thine! ... 1.Mes.104.122.
The Dame by Signs reveal'd her kind Intent, ... 2.ChJM.498.39.
To Maids alone and Children are reveal'd: ... 2.RL1.38.148.
Puts forth one manly Leg, to sight reveal'd; ... 2.RL3.57.172.
In broad Effulgence all below reveal'd, ... 5.DunB4.18.341.
The Monarch's Will not yet reveal'd appears; ... Il.2.229.138.

REVEAL'D (CONTINUED)
And Breast, reveal'd the Queen of soft Desire. ....Il.3.490.215.
Shines forth reveal'd, and animates the Fight. ....Il.4.586.249.
The Seer reveal'd the Counsels of his Mind. ....Il.6.94.328.
The deathful Secret to the King reveal'd. ....Il.6.218.336.
And bending forward, thus reveal'd his Mind. ....Il.8.620.425.
Against the Word, the Will reveal'd of *Jove?* ....Il.12.274.91.
Perhaps to Him: This *Thetis* had reveal'd; ....Il.17.470.305.
And thus, reveal'd—Hear Prince! and understand ....Il.24.563.559.
'Till the twelfth dawn the light of heav'n reveal'd. ....Od.4.987.163.
Reveal'd the landscape and the scene unknown, ...Od.9.175.312.
The hoary Sire in gratitude reveal'd. ....Od.9.241.316.
Are still at hand; and this reveal'd must be ....Od.15.483.93.
Stand forth reveal'd: with him thy cares employ ....Od.16.182.112.
My ineffectual fraud the fourth reveal'd: ....Od.19.175.200.
And wild with transport had reveal'd the wound; ....Od.23.77.322.
Since what no eye has seen thy tongue reveal'd, ...Od.23.245.335.
The fourth, her maid reveal'd th' amazing tale, ...Od.24.169.356.

REVEALING
Soon as the Sun, with all-revealing Ray ....Il.11.870.74.

REVEALS
Dispels the Darkness and reveals the Day. ....1.TrVP.117.381.
But Heav'n reveals not what, or how, or where: ....2.RL1.111.154.
So thy deep Knowledge Dark Designs reveals. ....6.48iv.4.135.
His own bright evidence reveals a God. ....Il.13.104.109.
But when the dawn reveals the rosy East, ...Od.1.474.55.
No fame reveals; but doubtful of his doom, ...Od.4.143.127.
Soon as the morn reveals the roseate east, ...Od.4.784.156.
The red'ning dawn reveals the circling fields ....Od.14.296.50.
The redning dawn reveals the hostile fields ....Od.17.517.157.
Sincere reveals the sanction of the skies: ....Od.19.651.227.

REVEL
And gen'ral Songs the sprightly Revel end. ....Il.18.700.357.
With song and dance the pompous revel end. ....Od.1.204.42.
Yet thro' my court the noise of Revel rings, ...Od.2.61.63.
Who stay'd to revel, and prolong the feast: ....Od.9.48.304.
From noiseful revel far remote she flies, ...Od.15.557.96.
The drunkards revel, and the gluttons feast. ....Od.16.116.108.

REVELATION
Some Revelation hid from you and me. ....3.Ep3.116.101.

REVELLERS
Unwelcome revellers, whose lawless joy ....Od.1.293.47.
Amidst yon' revellers a sudden guest ....Od.17.325.147.
And give yon' impious Revellers to bleed, ...Od.21.220.270.

REVELS
Here keeps her revels with the dancing *Hours;* ....Od.12.4.430.
And hear their midnight revels uncontroul'd? ....Od.16.98.107.
Two sew'rs from day to day the revels wait, ...Od.16.274.118.

REVENG'D
"And France reveng'd of ANNE's and EDWARD's arms!" ....3.Ep3.146.105.
'Till *Helen's* Woes at full reveng'd appear, ...Il.2.422.147.
And where that conduct, which reveng'd the lust ....Od.22.250.298.

REVENGE
The dire, tho' just, Revenge which I prepare ....1.TrSt.405.427.
In *Phlegias'* Doom thy just Revenge appears, ...1.TrSt.851.445.
From fierce *Idomeneus'* Revenge I flew, ...1.TrUl.144.470.
"Here's your Revenge! you love it at your Heart. ....2.ChWB.200.66.
Those restless passions in revenge inspires; ....2.ElAb.82.326.
Whose attributes were Rage, Revenge, or Lust; ....3.EOM3.258.118.
Who breaks with her, provokes Revenge from Hell, ...3.Ep2.129.61.
Between Revenge, and Grief, and Hunger join'd, ...4.2HE2.38.167.
Revenge our Wits and Statesmen on a *Pope.* ....6.48iii.16.135.
Say what revenge on D[enni]s can be had; ....6.116vii.3.328.
Who breaks with her, provokes Revenge from Hell, ...6.154.15.403.
Breathing Revenge, a sudden Night he spread, ...Il.1.65.89.
'Tis sure, the Mighty will revenge at last. ....Il.1.106.92.
Then let Revenge no longer bear the Sway, ...Il.1.285.100.
In his black Thoughts Revenge and Slaughter roll, ...Il.1.638.118.
But breathe Revenge, and for the Combate burn. ....Il.2.533.152.
Breathing Revenge, in Arms they take their Way ....Il.2.643.157.
Revenge and Fury flaming in his Eyes; ....Il.2.712.160.
Arms must revenge, and *Mars* decide the Field. ....Il.3.363.210.
Shall all be vain: When Heav'n's Revenge is slow, ...Il.4.194.230.
The Coursers joins, and breathes Revenge and War. ....Il.5.903.309.
Fierce for Revenge; and *Diomed* attends. ....Il.5.1031.315.
And beg'd Revenge for her insulted Bed: ....Il.6.206.336.
Who conquer'd their Revenge in former Days. ....Il.9.652.467.
But breathe Revenge, and for the Combat burn. ....Il.11.18.35.
Leap'd from the Chariot to revenge his King, ...Il.11.130.41.
My Javelin can revenge so base a Part, ...Il.12.293.92.
And breath'd Revenge, and fir'd the *Grecian* Train. ....Il.13.444.126.
Haste, and revenge it on th' insulting Foe. ....Il.13.589.134.
Fir'd with Revenge, *Polydamas* drew near, ...Il.14.525.188.
Who leaves a Brother to revenge his Fate. ....Il.14.568.190.
Revenge, revenge it on the cruel Foe. ....Il.15.515.217.
Revenge, revenge it on the cruel Foe. ....Il.15.515.217.
Nor on his Corpse revenge her Heroes lost. ....Il.16.670.270.
With great Revenge, and feeds his inward Woes. ....Il.17.152.293.
Then fierce they rally, to Revenge led on ....Il.17.326.300.
Swift to revenge it, sent his angry Lance; ....Il.17.399.302.
And fills with keen Revenge, with fell Despight, ...Il.17.640.312.
A Pleasure now? Revenge itself is lost: ....Il.18.102.328.
Let me revenge it on proud *Hector's* Heart, ...Il.18.119.328.
Wrath and Revenge from Men and Gods remove: ....Il.18.138.329.
Revenge is all my Soul! no meaner Care, ...Il.19.211.381.
What Banquet but Revenge can glad my Mind? ....Il.19.340.386.
Grief and Revenge his furious Heart inspire, ...Il.19.394.388.
Wild with Revenge, insatiable of War. ....Il.21.638.448.

REVENGE (CONTINUED)
Then let revenge your daring mind employ, ...Od.1.384.51.
With great revenge, immortal praise acquir'd? ....Od.1.388.51.
Judge and revenge my right, impartial *Jove!* ....Od.1.483.55.
Big with revenge, the mighty warrior flies: ....Od.2.369.78.
To *Jove* their cause, and their revenge belongs, ...Od.9.323.319.
Revenge, and doubt, and caution, work'd my breast; ....Od.9.378.321.
From fierce *Idomeneus'* revenge I flew, ...Od.13.311.21.
But heav'n will sure revenge, and Gods there are. ....Od.16.139.109.
The cause of suppliants, and revenge of wrong. ....Od.16.441.128.
Schemes of revenge his pond'ring breast elate, ...Od.17.33.134.
And inly form'd revenge: Then back withdrew, ...Od.17.552.159.
If fiends revenge, and Gods assert the poor, ...Od.17.565.160.
Revenge mature for act inflam'd his breast; ....Od.19.3.192.
With dire revenge his thoughtful bosom glows, ...Od.20.7.230.
Nations embattel'd to revenge the slain? ....Od.20.54.234.
Revenge and scorn within his bosom boil: ....Od.20.371.250.
Lest the ripe harvest of revenge begun, ...Od.20.443.254.
Who thus the warrior to revenge inspires. ....Od.22.245.298.

REVENGEFUL
Stern *Thoas,* glaring with revengeful Eyes, ...Il.4.622.250.
Then with revengeful Eyes he scan'd him o'er: ....Il.20.497.415.

REVENGES
The Sire revenges for the Daughter's sake, ...Il.9.634.466.
The God, the God revenges by my hands. ....Od.9.564.329.

REVENGING
But sheath, Obedient, thy revenging Steel. ....Il.1.280.100.
Orestes brandish'd the revenging sword, ...Od.3.391.105.
There the revenging sword shall smite them all; ....Od.22.479.312.

REVER'D
Behold, four *Kings* in Majesty rever'd, ...2.RL3.37.171.
And *Brachmans* deep in desart Woods rever'd. ....2.TemF.100.260.
Whom they rever'd as God to mourn as Man: ....3.EOM3.224.115.
Whose Word is Truth, as sacred and rever'd, ...4.2HE1.27.197.
Deep in his Entrails—I rever'd them there, ...5.DunB4.384.380.
Renown'd for Wisdom, and rever'd for Age; ....Il.2.22.128.
Stern as he was, he yet rever'd the Dead, ...Il.6.527.353.
Let *Phœnix* lead, rever'd for hoary Age, ...Il.9.221.443.
Ev'n *Jove* rever'd the Venerable Dame. ....Il.14.296.176.
Rever'd for Prudence, and with Prudence, bold.) ....Il.17.377.302.
There on the world's extreamest verge rever'd, ...Od.1.33.31.
What time this dome rever'd her prudent Lord; ....Od.1.298.47.
Is like the dictates of a God rever'd. ....Od.4.214.130.
Mirror of constant faith, rever'd, and mourn'd!— ....Od.4.229.130.
Rever'd and awful ev'n in heav'n's abodes, ...Od.13.166.13.
Oh dearest, most rever'd of womankind! ....Od.17.56.135.
(His father's counsellors, rever'd for age.) ....Od.17.81.136.

REVERE
A perjur'd Prince a leaden Saint revere, ...3.Ep1.148.28.
Nor less revere him, Blunderbuss of Law. ....5.DunA3.150.164.
Nor less revere him, blunderbuss of Law. ....5.DunB3.150.327.
Those who revere the Gods, the Gods will bless. ....Il.1.290.100.
Suppress thy Passion, and the King revere: ....Il.4.467.242.
Your brave Associates, and Your-selves revere! ....Il.5.652.299.
Revere thy Roof, and to thy Guests be kind; ....Il.9.754.471.
Have mercy on me, O my Son! Revere ....Il.22.114.457.
The Sons their Father's wretched Age revere, ...Il.24.331.550.
Oh hear the Wretched, and the Gods revere! ....Il.24.625.563.
Your fame revere, but most th' avenging skies. ....Od.2.72.64.
O *Jove,* supreme, whom Gods and men revere! ....Od.4.457.141.
Revere the Gods, and succour the distrest? ....Od.9.206.314.
'Tis what the Gods require: Those Gods revere, ...Od.9.321.319.
Revere the Gods, the Gods avenge the dead! ....Od.11.92.385.
Truth I revere: For Wisdom never lies. ....Od.11.572.411.
Fly the dire regions, and revere the Gods! ....Od.12.329.447.
O *Jove!* supreme! whom men and Gods revere; ....Od.17.148.138.
Shall I my virgin nuptial vow revere; ....Od.19.616.226.
Nor human right, nor wrath divine revere. ....Od.20.274.246.
And by the name on earth I most revere, ...Od.20.405.252.

REVERENCE
Let mutual Reverence mutual Warmth inspire, ...Il.15.668.221.

REVEREND
On *Homer* still he fix'd a reverend Eye, ...2.TemF.202.271.
"Proceed (he cry'd) proceed, my Reverend Brother, ...4.HAdv.41.79.
Then thus, in *Mentor's* reverend form array'd, ...Od.2.448.83.
Or some Celestial in his reverend form, ...Od.4.878.159.
The reverend stranger, and the spotless maid; ....Od.16.114.108.

REVERENTIAL
All, all look up, with reverential Awe, ...4.EpS1.167.309.
With conscious Shame and reverential Fear. ....Il.3.228.203.

REVERES
Reveres *Apollo's* vocal Caves, and owns ....1.TrSt.577.434.
All Heav'n beside reveres thy Sov'reign Sway, ...Il.5.1076.318.
And as he moves the gazing crowd reveres. ....Od.8.194.272.

REVERING
His art revering, gave him back to day; ....Od.11.362.400.

REVERS'D
His Scythe revers'd, and both his Pinions bound. ....2.TemF.148.265.
The Gods (I thought) revers'd their hard Decree, ...Il.9.614.464.
His Shield revers'd o'er the fall'n Warrior lies; ....Il.13.688.137.
The Car revers'd came rat'ling on the Field; ....Il.23.472.509.
By night revers'd the labour of the day. ....Od.2.118.67.
Is then revers'd the sentence of the sky, ...Od.5.368.190.
Each following night revers'd the toils of day. ....Od.24.167.356.

REVERSE

These can divide, and these reverse the State; ....1.TrSt.240.420.
Reverse, O *Jove,* thy too severe Decree, ...1.TrSt.396.426.
Prone for his fav'rites to reverse his laws? ....3.EOM4.122.139.
There Affectations quite reverse the soul. ....3.Ep1.125A.25.
Or Affectations quite reverse the soul. ....3.Ep1.125.25.
And then mistook reverse of wrong for right. ....3.Ep3.200.110.
Reverse your Ornaments, and hang them all ....3.Ep4.31.140.
Some strange Disaster, some reverse of Fate ....Il.22.582.480.
So may the God reverse his purpos'd will, ...Od.13.212.15.
Anon, from heav'n a sad reverse he feels; ....Od.18.161.174.
Scorn not the sad reverse, injurious maid! ....Od.19.98.197.

REVERSION

That scorns the dull Reversion of a Throne; ....1.TrSt.181.418.
Is there no bright reversion in the sky, ...2.Elegy.9.363.
Or quicken'd a Reversion by a *Drug?* ....4.JD4.135.37.

REVERT

Then swift revert, and Wounds return for Wounds. ....Il.11.422.53.

REVERTS

Unwilling parts, and oft' reverts her Eye ....Il.6.641.358.

REVIEW

How oft' review; each finding like a friend ....6.52.21.156.
Review them, and tell Noses; ....6.58.70.174.
Thus may the *Greeks* review their native Shore, ...Il.3.107.194.
So shall the *Greeks* review their native Shore, ...Il.3.328.208.
How shall I e'er review the blest Abodes, ...Il.14.379.180.
Shall I the long, laborious scenes review, ...Od.3.127.92.
Pleas'd with the false review, secure he lies, ...Od.4.609.148.
But would'st thou soon review my native plain? ....Od.6.347.228.
Remembrance sad, whose image to review ....Od.9.13.301.
If to review his country its his fate, ...Od.9.623.332.
Review the series of our lives, and taste ....Od.15.434.90.
They turn, review, and cheapen every toy. ....Od.15.498.94.
(Who never must review his dear domain; ....Od.20.407.252.

REVIEWS

The skilful Nymph reviews her Force with Care; ....2.RL3.45.172.
Reviews his life, and in the strict survey ....6.55.5.166.
With rapture oft the verge of *Greece* reviews, ...Od.4.697.152.

REVIL'D

As for the Volume that revil'd the Dames, ...2.ChWB.434.78.
Conscious of worth revil'd, thy gen'rous mind ....Od.19.438.216.

REVILE

To lash the Great, and Monarchs to revile. ....Il.2.262.140.

REVILERS

And base revilers of our house and name? ....Od.22.498.313.

REVILES

And glorying thus, the prostrate God reviles. ....Il.21.477.441.

REVILING

Whispers are heard, with Taunts reviling loud, ...2.TemF.404.283.
Whispers were heard, with Taunts reviling loud, ...2.TemF.404A.283.

REVISE

"Not Sir, if you revise it, and retouch." ....4.Arbu.64.100.

REVISIT

Let the pale Sire revisit *Thebes,* and bear ....1.TrSt.421.427.
I shall revisit; and that pledge receive, ...Od.1.411.52.
The court revisit and the lawless train: ....Od.16.291.119.

REVIV'D

Are these reviv'd? or is it *Granville* sings? ....1.W-F.282.174.
But at her Smile, the Beau reviv'd again. ....2.RL5.70.206.
The Tale reviv'd, the Lye so soft o'erthrown; ....4.Arbu.350.121.
A past, vamp'd, future, old, reviv'd, new piece, ...5.DunA1.238.91.
A past, vamp'd, future, old, reviv'd, new piece, ...5.DunB1.284.290.

REVIVE

Then *Sculpture* and her *Sister-Arts* revive; ....1.EOC.701.319.
The vivid Em'ralds there revive the Eye; ....2.TemF.250.275.
In downright Charity revive the dead; ....4.2HE2.164.177.
When Dulness, smiling—"Thus revive the Wits! ....5.DunB4.119.353.
Revive the honours of *Rome's* ancient praise; ....6.20.44.67.
Encourag'd by the Sign, the Troops revive, ...Il.8.303.412.

REVIVER

Or prove Reviver of a Schism, ...6.10.81.27.

REVIVES

And love disdain'd revives with fiercer rage. ....1.TrPA.131.371.
A breath revives him, or a breath o'erthrows! ....4.2HE1.301.221.
Whose fragrant Wit revives, as one may say, ...6.48ii.3.134.
Revives their Ardor, turns their Steps from Flight, ...Il.5.607.297.
Revives their Ardour, turns their Steps from flight, ...Il.11.273.47.
Fair hope revives; and eager I addrest ....Od.4.743.153.
When a lov'd Sire revives before their sight, ...Od.5.507.196.

REVIVING

And feed their Fibres with reviving Dew. ....1.TrVP.16.377.
Reviving *Perault,* murd'ring *Boileau,* he ....6.12.4.37.
The kind Deceit, the still-reviving Fire, ...Il.14.250.173.
Reviving sweets repair the mind's decay, ...Od.10.427.365.

REVOLV'D

This, long revolv'd in his Paternal Breast, ...1.TrSt.549.433.
But ev'ry Charm revolv'd within his Mind: ....2.ChJM.245.26.
Still as his Mind revolv'd with vast Delight ....2.ChJM.349.31.

REVOLV'D (CONTINUED)

Here as the Queen revolv'd with careful Eyes ....Il.6.364.344.
These Fates revolv'd in his almighty Mind, ...Il.15.722.223.
But secret I revolv'd the deep design: ....Od.9.500.326.
The beauteous Queen revolv'd with careful eyes ....Od.15.118.74.
Revolv'd his words, and plac'd them in her heart. ....Od.21.384.278.

REVOLVE

Where as the Years revolve, her Altars blaze, ...Il.2.663.158.
But oft revolve the vision in thy heart: ....Od.19.51.195.

REVOLVES

Much she revolves their arts, their ancient praise, ...5.DunA1.95.70.
Much she revolves their arts, their ancient praise, ...5.DunB1.97.276.
A thousand Cares his lab'ring Breast revolves; ....Il.10.23.3.
Secret revolves; and plans the vengeance due. ....Od.17.183.140.

REVOLVING

Who mourn'd her Lord twice ten revolving Years, ...1.TrUl.218.473.
When now the fourth revolving Day was run, ...2.ChJM.400.34.
But ere the tenth revolving Day was run, ...Il.1.73.90.
Returning with the twelfth revolving Light, ...Il.1.559.115.
The tedious Length of nine revolving Years. ....Il.2.361.144.
Condemn'd for ten revolving Years to weep ....Il.8.496.420.
And we beheld, the last revolving Sun? ....Il.10.58.5.
Such Thoughts revolving in his careful Breast, ...Il.11.521.57.
Pay the large Debt of last revolving Sun; ....Il.13.936.149.
The *Bear* revolving, points his golden Eye; ....Il.18.564.349.
And Mother Earth, and Heav'ns revolving Light, ...Il.19.269.383.
Pensive she sate, revolving Fates to come, ...Il.24.113.539.
The King's Return revolving in his Mind, ...Il.24.848.572.
Ægysthus' fate revolving in his breast, ...Od.1.38.31.
Revolving much his father's doubtful fate: ....Od.1.418.52.
That happy clime! where each revolving year ....Od.4.105.124.
'Till heav'n's revolving lamp restores the day. ....Od.4.296.133.
The Bear revolving, points his golden eye; ....Od.5.350.188.
While full of thought, revolving fates to come, ...Od.10.369.362.
Who mourn'd her Lord twice ten revolving years, ...Od.13.385.25.
A few revolving months shou'd waft him o'er, ...Od.14.423.56.
Revolving deep the Suitors' sudden fate. ....Od.17.34.134.
Divided Right; each ninth revolving year ....Od.19.206.202.
Mean-time revolving in his thoughtful mind ....Od.19.454.216.

REWARD

And conscious Virtue, still its own Reward, ...1.TrSt.758.442.
This my Reward, for having cur'd the Blind? ....2.ChJM.761.51.
Which seeks no int'rest, no reward but praise; ....3.EOM2.246.85.
What then? Is the reward of Virtue bread? ....3.EOM4.150.142.
Weak, foolish man! will Heav'n reward us there ....3.EOM4.173.144.
And shall not Britain now reward his toils, ...3.Ep3.125.110.
Or are they both, in this their own reward? ....3.Ep3.336.120.
These write to Lords, some mean reward to get, ...4.JD2.25.133.
Some write to Lords in hope reward to get, ...4.JD2A.29.134.
Gave him much Praise, and some Reward beside. ....4.2HE2.43.167.
And all who knew those dunces to reward. ....5.DunA2.22.98.
And all who knew those Dunces to reward. ....5.DunB2.26.297.
Said, to reward your Pains, ...6.94.70.261.
The due Reward of many a well-fought Field? ....Il.1.158.95.
That caus'd the Contest, shall reward the Toil. ....Il.3.130.196.
False he detain'd, the just Reward of War: ....Il.5.807.304.
First gain the Conquest, then reward the Toil. ....Il.6.88.327.
Forgets my Service and deserv'd Reward. ....Il.8.440.418.
I ask no Presents, no Reward for Love. ....Il.9.192.442.
He asks no Presents, no Reward for Love. ....Il.9.379.451.
Fight or not fight, a like Reward we claim, ...Il.9.418.453.
Dares greatly venture for a rich Reward? ....Il.10.362.19.
And let the *Thracian* Steeds reward our Toil: ....Il.10.533.27.
Or, in reward of thy victorious Hand, ...Il.20.222.403.
No vulgar Victim must reward the Day, ...Il.22.208.464.
First stood the Prizes to reward the Force ....Il.23.327.503.
Robb'd of my Glory and my just Reward, ...Il.23.653.515.
The fifth Reward, the double Bowl, remain'd. ....Il.23.704.517.
To brave *Patroclus* gave the rich Reward. ....Il.23.873.524.
And left the Urn *Ulysses'* rich Reward. ....Il.23.914.525.
Won by destructive Lust (Reward obscene) ....Il.24.40.537.
The day predestin'd to reward his woes. ....Od.1.24.30.
Will guide her passion, and reward the choice ....Od.1.362.50.
Will guide her passion, and reward her choice, ...Od.2.225.72.
With teeming plenty to reward their toil. ....Od.4.240.130.
And ev'ry soldier found a like reward. ....Od.9.46.304.
And with a gen'rous hand reward his stay; ....Od.11.425.405.
Greece to reward her soldier's gallant toils ....Od.11.653.416.
The due reward of fraud and perjury. ....Od.14.442.57.
Reward this stranger's hospitable love, ...Od.15.361.86.
The presence of thy guest shall best reward ....Od.15.587.98.
Envy shall sicken at thy vast reward. ....Od.19.357.211.
Hence, to reward his merit, he shall bear ....Od.21.365.277.
Save then the Poet, and thy self reward; ....Od.22.387.307.
(Their great reward) a Poet in her praise. ....Od.24.225.358.

REWARDED

But thank'd by few, rewarded yet by none, ...2.TemF.302.278.

REWARDS

Of old, those met *Rewards* who cou'd excel, ...1.EOC.510.295.
Of old, those found *Rewards* who cou'd *excel,* ....1.EOC.510A.295.
And what rewards your Virtue, punish mine. ....3.EOM4.144.141.
Rewards, that either would to Virtue bring ....3.EOM4.181.144.
See how the World its Veterans rewards! ....3.Ep2.243.69.
Are no rewards for Want, and Infamy! ....4.HS2.104.61.
"More Honours, more Rewards, attend the Brave"— ....4.2HE2.48.167.
Like are their merits, like rewards they share, ...5.DunA3.179.170.
Like are their merits, like rewards they share, ...5.DunB3.183.329.
Not as the World its pretty Slaves rewards, ...6.86.5A.245.
The hearty Draught rewards, renews their Toil; ....Il.18.633.354.
Thus he rewards you, with this bitter Fate; ....Il.21.147.427.

REWARDS (CONTINUED)
Where high Rewards the vig'rous Youth inflame, ...Il.22.213.464.

REYNARD
Faith I shall give the answer Reynard gave, ...4.1HE1.114.287.

RHADAMANTH
Whence godlike *Rhadamanth* and *Minos* sprung. ....Il.14.368.180.
On wings of winds with *Rhadamanth* they flew: ....Od.7.414.257.

RHADAMANTHUS
Of utmost earth, where *Rhadamanthus* reigns. ....Od.4.766.155.

RHEA
And ancient *Rhea,* Earth's immortal Dame: ....Il.15.211.205.

RHENA
Oïleus' Son whom beauteous *Rhena* bore. ....Il.2.883.165.

RHESUS
Led on by *Rhesus,* great *Eioneus'* Son: ....Il.10.505.26.
Amidst, lay *Rhesus,* stretch'd in Sleep profound, ...Il.10.548.27.
(The Scourge forgot, on *Rhesus* Chariot hung.) ....Il.10.585.28.
Drag off the Car where *Rhesus* Armour lay, ...Il.10.590.28.
For each he wept, but for his *Rhesus* most: ....Il.10.613.29.
Rhesus and *Rhodius* then unite their Rills, ...Il.12.17.82.

RHESUS'
(On *Rhesus'* side accustom'd to attend, ...Il.10.608.29.
Now while on *Rhesus'* Name he calls in vain, ...Il.10.614.29.

RHET'RIC
There, stript, fair *Rhet'ric* languish'd on the ground; ....5.DunB4.24.342.

RHETORICK
And since that thine all Rhetorick exceeds; ....6.2.5.5.

RHEXENOR
From him *Rhexenor* and *Alcinous* came. ....Od.7.81.237.
Daughter of great *Rhexenor!* (thus began ....Od.7.194.245.

RHIGMUS
Rhigmus, whose Race from fruitful *Thracia* came, ...Il.20.561.417.

RHIME
See RYME, RHYME.
D'ye think me good for nothing but to rhime? ....4.2HE2.32.167.
What will it leave me, if it snatch my Rhime? ....4.2HE2.77.171.
Again to rhime, can *London* be the Place? ....4.2HE2.89.171.
How shall I rhime in this eternal Roar? ....4.2HE2.114.173.
Writing a Sonnet, cou'd not rhime; ....6.44.2.123.
(Not plagu'd with headachs, or the want of rhime) ....6.45.42.125.

RHIMERS
In vain, bad Rhimers all mankind reject, ...4.2HE2.153.175.

RHIMES
Leave such to tune their own dull Rhimes, and know ....1.EOC.358.280.
O Goddess, say, shall I deduce my Rhimes ....1.TrSt.5.409.

RHIMING
This jealous, waspish, wrong-head, rhiming Race; ....4.2HE2.148.175.
Call, if you will, bad Rhiming a disease, ...4.2HE2.182.177.

RHINE
And Groves of Lances glitter on the *Rhine,* ....1.W-F.364.186.
Twice taught the *Rhine* beneath his Laws to roll, ...1.TrSt.27.410.
How twice he vanquish'd where the *Rhine* does roll, ...1.TrSt.27A.410.
Or on the Rubicon, or on the Rhine. ....3.EOM4.246.151.
And scarce are seen the prostrate Nile or Rhine, ...6.71.28.203.
And scarce are seen the prostrate Nile and Rhine, ...6.71.28A.203.

RHODES
From *Rhodes* with everlasting Sunshine bright, ...Il.2.795.163.
On happy *Rhodes* the Chief arriv'd at last: ....Il.2.808.163.

RHODIAN
The daring *Rhodian* vents his haughty Boast. ....Il.5.783.303.
The Son of *Hercules,* the *Rhodian* Guide, ...Il.5.802.304.

RHODIUS
Rhesus and *Rhodius* then unite their Rills, ...Il.12.17.82.

RHODOPE'S
Amidst *Rhodope's* Snows: ....6.11.109.34.

RHYM'D
No Rat is rhym'd to death, nor Maid to love: ....4.JD2.22.133.
Who rhym'd for hire, and patroniz'd for pride. ....5.DunB4.102.351.
Shall Royal praise be rhym'd by such a ribald, ...6.116v.1.327.

RHYME
See RYME, RHIME.
And Rhyme with all the *Rage* of *Impotence!* ....1.EOC.609.308.
Slides into Verse, and hitches in a Rhyme, ...4.HS1.78.13.
Like *Lee* or *Budgell,* I will Rhyme and Print. ....4.HS1.100.15.
Or tir'd in search of Truth, or search of Rhyme. ....4.HS2.86.61.
Maggots half-form'd, in rhyme exactly meet, ...5.DunA1.59.67.
Some strain in rhyme; the Muses, on their racks, ...5.DunA3.153.164.
Some free from rhyme or reason, rule or check, ...5.DunA3.155.164.
Maggots half-form'd in rhyme exactly meet, ...5.DunB1.61.274.
Some strain in rhyme; the Muses, on their racks, ...5.DunB3.159.328.
Some free from rhyme or reason, rule or check, ...5.DunB3.161.328.
Plague with Dispute, or persecute with Rhyme. ....5.DunB4.260.369.
In vain you think to 'scape Rhyme-free, ...6.10.38.25.
(Wench, I'd have said did Rhyme not hinder) ....6.10.57.26.

RHYME (CONTINUED)
We form'd this Name, renown'd in Rhyme; ....6.30.56.88.
Grown old in Rhyme 'twere barbarous to discard ....6.34.1.101.
And Parnell, that would, if he had but a Rhyme. ....6.42i.4.116.

RHYME-FREE
In vain you think to 'scape Rhyme-free, ...6.10.38.25.

RHYMES
With sure *Returns* of still *expected Rhymes.* ....1.EOC.349.279.
Short is the Date, alas, of *Modern Rhymes;* ....1.EOC.476.292.
Whose Use old Bards describe in luscious Rhymes, ...2.ChJM.379.33.
A Man was hang'd for very honest Rhymes. ....4.HS1.146.19.
And paid for all my Satires, all my Rhymes: ....4.JD4.6.27.
With rhymes of this *per Cent.* and that *per Year?* ....4.JD2.56.137.
One wou'd move Love; by Rhymes; but Verses charms ....4.JD2A.23.134.
The rhymes and rattles of the Man or Boy: ....4.1HE1.18.279.
Know, there are Rhymes, which (fresh and fresh apply'd) ...4.1HE1.59.283.
How rhymes eternal gingle in their ear! ....5.DunA3.152Z2.164.
This, this is He, foretold by ancient rhymes, ...5.DunA3.317.186.
Where vile Mundungus trucks for viler rhymes; ....5.DunB1.234.287.
This, this is he, foretold by ancient rhymes: ....5.DunB3.319.335.
Forsooth, if Rhymes fall in not right, ...6.58.39.172.
Some frigid Rhymes disburses; ....6.58.54.173.

RHYMING
In twice ten thousand rhyming nights and days, ...5.DunB4.172.358.
To Rhyming and the Devil? ....6.58.24.171.

RHYTION'S
And those who dwell where *Rhytion's* Domes arise, ...Il.2.787.162.

RIBALD
Shall Royal praise be rhym'd by such a ribald, ...6.116v.1.327.

RIBALDRY
Chaucer's worst ribaldry is learn'd by rote, ...4.2HE1.37.197.

RIBALDS
Yet ne'r one sprig of Laurel grac'd these ribalds, ...4.Arbu.163.108.

RIBAND
And Lovers' Hearts with Ends of Riband bound; ....2.RL5.118.209.

RIBB'D
Nor are their Bodies Rocks, nor ribb'd with Steel; ....Il.4.589.249.
So large he built the Raft: then ribb'd it strong ....Od.5.321.187.

RIBBALDS
Yet ne'er one Sprig of Laurel grac'd those Ribbalds, ...6.98.13.283.

RIBBANDS
To sigh for ribbands if thou art so silly, ...3.EOM4.277.154.

RIBBANS
Where Ribbans wave upon the tye, ...6.61.38.182.

RIBBOND
And knots of scarlet Ribbond deck *his* Mane. ....6.9ix.2.22.

RIBBONS
Chequer'd with Ribbons blue and green; ....4.HS6.49.253.

RIBS
The Tokens on my Ribs, in Black and Blue: ....2.ChWB.256.69.
Tho' stiff with Hoops, and arm'd with Ribs of Whale. .....2.RL2.120.167.
Its Womb they deluge, and its Ribs they rend: ....Il.15.443.214.
The ribs and limbs, observant of the rite: ....Od.3.583.116.
Torn was his skin, nor had the ribs been whole, ...Od.5.544.198.
With ribs of steel, and marble heart immur'd. ....Od.19.578.224.

RICH
O'er Golden Sands let rich *Pactolus* flow, ...1.PSp.61.66.
No rich Perfumes refresh the fruitful Field, ...1.PWi.47.92.
Rich Industry sits smiling on the Plains, ...1.W-F.41.152.
No Seas so rich, so gay no Banks appear, ...1.W-F.225.170.
No Seas so rich so full no Streams appear, ...1.W-F.225A.170.
Stretch'd on rich Carpets, on his Iv'ry Throne; ....1.TrSt.614.436.
(While with rich Gums the solemn Altars blaze) ....1.TrSt.614A.437.
Chast tho' not rich; and tho' not nobly born, ...2.ChJM.260.27.
This rich, this am'rous, venerable Knight, ...2.ChJM.481.38.
The three were Old, but rich and fond beside, ...2.ChWB.58.59.
Whence is our Neighbour's Wife so rich and gay? ....2.ChWB.75.60.
If rich, she keeps her Priest, or something worse; ....2.ChWB.87.61.
There's Danger too, you think, in rich Array, ...2.ChWB.140.63.
Rich luscious Wines, that youthful Blood improve, ...2.ChWB.215.67.
And frequent Cups prolong the rich Repast. ....2.RL3.112.176.
Trembling, and conscious of the rich Brocade. ....2.RL3.116.176.
While frequent Cups prolong the rich Repast. ....2.RL3.112A.176.
Or when rich *China* Vessels, fal'n from high, ...2.RL3.159.180.
On the rich Quilt sinks with becoming Woe, ...2.RL4.35.186.
The Poor, the Rich, the Valiant, and the Sage, ...2.TemF.290.277.
The rich is happy in the plenty giv'n, ...3.EOM2.265.87.
The rich are happy in the plenty giv'n ....3.EOM2.265A.87.
More rich, more wise; but who infers from hence ......3.EOM4.51.133.
There, in the rich, the honour'd, fam'd and great, ...3.EOM4.287.155.
To cram the Rich was prodigal expence, ...3.Ep3.187.109.
Of rich and poor makes all the history; ....3.Ep3.288.116.
And tempts by making rich, not making poor. ....3.Ep3.352.122.
And two rich ship-wrecks bless the lucky shore. ....3.Ep3.356.122.
The rich Buffet well-colour'd Serpents grace, ...3.Ep4.153.152.
Tim'rous by Nature, of the Rich in awe, ...4.HS1.7.5.
Yes, while I live, no rich or noble knave ....4.HS1.119.17.
Know, while I live, no rich or noble knave ....4.HS1.119A.17.
So weak a Vessel, and so rich a Prize! ....4.JD4.229.45.
And the rich feast concludes extremely poor: ....4.HS2.34.57.

RICH (CONTINUED)

The things, we know, are neither rich nor rare, 4.Arbu.171.108.
Not that the things are either rich or rare, 4.Arbu.171A.108.
And just as rich as when he serv'd a QUEEN! 4.Arbu.417.127.
Which tho they're rich, are Things that none will wear 4.JD2A.130.144.
Like nets or lime-twigs, for rich Widows hearts? 4.JD2.58.137.
Like rich old Wardrobes, things extremely rare, 4.JD2.123.145.
Rich with the Treasures of each foreign Tongue; 4.2HE2.173.177.
Why, of two Brothers, rich and restless one 4.2HE2.270.183.
Has seiz'd the Court and City, Poor and Rich: 4.2HE1.170.209.
Weds the rich Dulness of some Son of earth? 4.1HE6.43.239.
Upon my word, you must be rich indeed; 4.1HE6.90.243.
"That Jelly's rich, this Malmsey healing, 4.HS6.204.263.
Some win rich Widows by their Chine and Brawn; 4.1HE1.131.289.
Transform themselves so strangely as the Rich? 4.1HE1.153.291.
Rich ev'n when plunder'd, honour'd while oppress'd, 4.1HE1.182.293.
Swear like a Lord? or a *Rich* out-whore a Duke? 4.EpS1.116.306.
Are they not rich? what more can they pretend? 4.EpS2.114.319.
Rich *with* his [Britain], *in* his [Britain] strong, 4.1740.93.337*.
Rich *with* his . . . *in* . . . his strong, 4.1740.93A.337*.
'Twas on the day, when Thorold, rich and grave, 5.DunA1.83.69.
Immortal Rich! how calm he sits at ease 5.DunA3.257.179.
'Twas on the day, when * * rich and grave, 5.DunB1.85.275.
Immortal Rich! how calm he sits at ease 5.DunB3.261.332.
Be rich in ancient brass, tho' not in gold, 5.DunB4.365.378.
In Di'monds, Pearls, and rich Brocades, 6.14v(b).16.50.
In Di'monds, silks, and rich Brocades, 6.14v(b).16A.50.
Nor envies those that on rich Carpets tread. 6.17iii.29.58.
The shining Robes, rich Jewels, Beds of State, 6.19.51.63.
Whose shining scene with rich *Hesperia* vies. 6.20.71.68.
So Pimps grow rich, while Gallants are undone. 6.24ii.2.75.
As Pimps grow rich, while Gallants are undone. 6.34.22.101.
Bring sometimes with you Lady R[ich] 6.61.45.182.
Bring sometimes with you Mistress R[ic]h 6.61.45B.182.
Seem like the lofty Barn of some rich Swain, 6.96ii.13.270.
The *Thing,* we know, is neither rich nor rare, 6.98.21.284.
Not that they're rich, but that they steal. 6.116iii.4.326.
Rich in her Fruits, and in her martial Race. Il.1.206.96.
To rich *Thyestes* next the Prize descends; Il.2.134.134.
And *Arnè* rich, with purple Harvests crown'd; Il.2.606.156.
From those rich Regions where *Cephisus* leads Il.2.622.157.
Which *Bessa, Thronus,* and rich *Cynos* send: Il.2.635.157.
From rich *Aræsus* and *Adrestia's* Tow'rs, Il.2.1004.170.
Where rich *Henetia* breeds her savage Mules, Il.2.1035.171.
Next all unbuckling the rich Mail they wore, Il.3.157.198.
Bring the rich Wine and destin'd Victims down. Il.3.316.208.
Stiff with the rich embroider'd Work around, Il.4.224.232.
A wealthy Priest, but rich without a Fault; Il.5.16.266.
Left the rich Chariot, and his Brother dead; Il.5.28.267.
These, were the rich immortal Prize our own, Il.5.336.283.
Rich with immortal Gold their Trappings shine. Il.5.887.308.
Axylus, hospitable, rich and good: Il.6.16.323.
The mortal Wound of rich *Elatus* gave, Il.6.40.325.
Rich Heaps of Brass shall in thy Tent be told; Il.6.61.326.
The largest Mantle her rich Wardrobes hold, Il.6.113.329.
That rich with *Tyrian* Dye refulgent glow'd. Il.6.274.340.
The rich Pavillions of his fifty Sons, Il.6.307.341.
And burn rich Odors in *Minerva's* Fane. Il.6.339.343.
The *Phrygian* Queen to her rich Wardrobe went, Il.6.358.343.
Guides their rich Labours, and instructs their Hands. Il.6.403.346.
A radiant Belt that rich with Purple glow'd. Il.7.369.382.
Of fragrant Wines the rich *Eunæus* sent Il.7.562.392.
Give me to seize rich *Nestor's* Shield of Gold; Il.8.235.408.
The next rich Honorary Gift be thine: Il.8.350.414.
Floats in rich Waves, and spreads the Court of *Jove.* Il.8.469.419.
(Rich were the Man, whose ample Stores exceed Il.9.163.440.
And rich *Antheia* with her flow'ry Fields: Il.9.200.442.
(Rich were the Man, whose ample Stores exceed Il.9.350.450.
And rich *Antheia* with her flow'ry Fields: Il.9.387.451.
This from *Amyntor,* rich *Ormenus'* Son, Il.10.313.16.
Dares greatly venture for a rich Reward? Il.10.362.19.
Rich was the Son in Brass, and rich in Gold; Il.10.374.19.
Rich was the Son in Brass, and rich in Gold; Il.10.374.19.
Rich silver Plates his shining Car infold; Il.10.508.26.
And rich *Hippodamus* becomes his Prize. Il.11.434.53.
The Son of *Mentor,* rich in gen'rous Steeds. Il.13.228.116.
There rich in Fortune's Gifts, his Acres till'd, Il.14.138.164.
That rich with *Pallas'* labour'd Colours glow'd; Il.14.208.170.
(*Phorbas* the rich, of all the *Trojan* Train Il.14.575.190.
In the rich Belt, as in a starry Zone. Il.16.167.244.
To the rich Coffer, in his shady Tent: Il.16.269.249.
From rich *Pæonia's* Vales the Warrior came, Il.17.402.303.
Charg'd with rich Spoils, to fair *Opuntia's* Shore! Il.18.382.339.
Rich, various Artifice emblaz'd the Field; Il.18.552.348.
Nectareous Drops, and rich Ambrosia showr'd Il.19.40.373.
With their rich Belts their Captive Arms constrains, Il.21.36.423.
From rich *Pæonia's* Vallies I command Il.21.171.428.
To melt the Fat of some rich Sacrifice, Il.21.425.438.
But the rich Mail *Patroclus* lately wore, Il.22.405.472.
Whom rich *Echepolus,* (more rich than brave) Il.23.365.504.
Whom rich *Echepolus,* (more rich than brave) Il.23.365.504.
To brave *Patroclus* gave the rich Reward. Il.23.873.524.
And left the Urn *Ulysses'* rich Reward. Il.23.914.525.
Whoever dares deserve so rich a Prize! Il.23.946.526.
Fledg'd with Ambrosial plumes, and rich with gold, Od.1.125.38.
Of choicest sort and savour, rich repast! Od.1.186.42.
And the rich pledge of plighted faith receive, Od.1.405.52.
Why seek they not the rich *Icarian* dome? Od.2.58.63.
Here jars of oil breath'd forth a rich perfume; Od.2.384.79.
Where winding round the rich *Cydonian* plain, Od.3.372.104.
Sev'n years, the traytor rich *Mycenæ* sway'd, Od.3.388.105.
Deep in a rich Alcove the Prince was laid, Od.3.510.112.
With rich magnificence, the chariot plac'd: Od.4.52.122.
They share the honours of the rich repast. Od.4.80.123.
Before her breath'd a gale of rich perfume. Od.4.158.128.
And that rich vase, with living sculpture wrought, Od.4.179.128.

RICH (CONTINUED)

Rich tapistry, stiff with inwoven gold: Od.4.406.139.
Rich fragrant wines the cheering bowl supply; Od.4.842.158.
For him, the Nymph a rich repast ordains, Od.5.251.183.
A vest and robe, with rich embroid'ry gay: Od.6.254.222.
Here a rich juice the royal vineyard pours; Od.6.355.229.
In virtue rich; in blessing others, blest. Od.7.96.238.
Rich plates of gold the folding doors incase; Od.7.114.240.
Of choicest sort and savour, rich repast! Od.7.237.247.
Her self supply'd the stores and rich array; Od.7.351.253.
And adding a rich dress inwrought with art Od.8.477.288.
And what rich liquors other climates boast. Od.9.411.323.
And only rich in barren fame return. Od.10.47.341.
Of choicest sort and savour, rich repaste! Od.10.440.365.
Rich in refulgent robes, and dropping balmy dews: Od.10.534.369.
Rich with unnumber'd gifts the Pyle shall burn; Od.11.40.381.
No rich embroid'ry shines to grace his bed: Od.11.229.393.
In rich *Orchomenos,* or *Sparta's* court? Od.11.566.411.
Bear the rich viands and the generous wine: Od.12.26.430.
A various casket that, of rich inlay, Od.13.85.5.
Of brass, rich garments, and refulgent ore: Od.13.159.13.
Rich without bounty, guilty without fears! Od.14.100.40.
So rich, so potent, whom you stile your Lord? Od.14.139.42.
Great in the praise, rich in the spoils of war: Od.14.269.49.
Where the rich wardrobe breath'd a costly scent. Od.15.115.74.
Of choicest sort and favour; rich repast! Od.15.155.76.
Argos the rich for his retreat he chose, Od.15.264.81.
Whom Fortune dooms to serve the rich and great. Od.15.343.86.
A blooming train in rich embroid'ry drest, Od.15.351.86.
And her rich vallies wave with golden corn. Od.15.445.92.
Skill'd in rich works, a woman of their land. Od.15.459.93.
And where on heaps the rich manure was spread, Od.17.358.149.
A kid's well fatted entrails, rich with blood: Od.18.144.173.
Rich from the artist's hand! twelve clasps of gold Od.18.339.184.
A bracelet rich with gold, with amber gay, Od.18.343.184.
Constrain'd! a rent-charge on the rich I live; Od.19.92.197.
In the rich woof a hound Mosaic drawn Od.19.265.208.
In rich *Thesprotia,* and the nearer bound Od.19.309.209.
So rich the value of a store so vast Od.19.337.210.
The rich insult him, and the young deride! Od.19.437.216.
And eager all devour the rich repast. Od.20.321.248.
But the rich banquet in the dome prepar'd, Od.20.347.249.
Where treasur'd garments cast a rich perfume; Od.21.54.261.
(With rich inlay the various floor was grac'd) Od.21.172.267.
Feed the rich smokes, high-curling to the skies. Od.21.283.273.
Embroider'd sandals, a rich cloak and vest, Od.21.367.277.
Rich spoils and gifts that blaz'd against the day. Od.24.110.353.
A bowl, that rich with polish'd silver flames, Od.24.322.365.

RICHARD

P. What? like Sir *Richard,* rumbling, rough and fierce, 4.HS1.23.7.
When *Richard Cœur de Lyon* reign'd, 6.79.9.218.

RICHARD'S

It stands on record, that in *Richard's* Times 4.HS1.145.19.

RICHELIEU

What RICHELIEU wanted, LOUIS scarce could gain, 4.EpS2.116.319.

RICHER

Feed fairer Flocks, or richer Fleeces share; 1.PSu.36.75.
Feed fairer Flocks, or richer Fleeces sheer: 1.PSu.36A.75.
(A richer price than if his joyful Isle Od.5.52.174.
Richer than all th' *Achaian* state supplies, Od.21.110.264.

RICHES

Glorious in Arms, in Riches, and in Fame: 1.TrSt.353.424.
Blest with much Sense, more Riches, and some Grace. 2.ChJM.4.15.
But grant him Riches, your demand is o'er? 3.EOM4.157.142.
To whom can Riches give Repute, or Trust, 3.EOM4.185.144.
For *Riches,* can they give but to the Just, 3.EOM4.185A.144.
What Riches give us let us first enquire: 3.Ep3.81A.94.
P. What Riches give us let us then enquire: 3.Ep3.81B.94.
Both fairly owning, Riches in effect, 3.Ep3.17.84.
What Riches give us let us then enquire: 3.Ep3.81.94.
Riches, like insects, when conceal'd they lie, 3.Ep3.171.107.
The Sense to value Riches, with the Art 3.Ep3.219.111.
To gain those Riches he can ne'er enjoy: 3.Ep4.2.134.
Make but his riches equal to his Wit. 4.HOde1.18.151.
For Fame, for Riches, for a noble Wife? 4.1HE6.39.239.
Riches that vex, and Vanities that tire. 6.86.4.245.
Thus at full Ease in Heaps of Riches roll'd, Il.2.281.141.
For Riches much, and more for Virtue fam'd, Il.13.834.145.
With stately Seats, and Riches, blest in vain: Il.16.724.272.
With Riches honour'd, and with Courage blest, Il.17.650.313.
If there be one whose Riches cost him Care, Il.18.349.338.
In Riches once, in Children once excell'd; Il.24.684.565.
These riches are possess'd, but not enjoy'd! Od.4.118.125.
Blest in his riches, in his children more. Od.14.233.47.
Thence charg'd with riches, as increas'd in fame, Od.14.270.49.
For still he lives, and lives with riches blest. Od.15.473.93.
Riches are welcome then, not else, to me. Od.17.95.136.
Know from the bounteous heav'ns all riches flow, Od.18.26.168.

RICHEST

Dipt in the richest Tincture of the Skies, 2.RL2.65.163.
And which not done, the richest must be poor. 4.1HE1.46.281.
And there in autumn's richest purple dy'd. 6.35.25.103.
(Full fifty Acres of the richest Ground, Il.9.693.468.
The richest, once, of *Asia's* wealthy Kings; Il.20.261.404.
With ten pure Talents from the richest Mine; Il.24.286.548.
A veil of richest texture wrought, she wears, Od.1.429.53.
Two lavers from the richest ore refin'd, Od.4.173.128.
And there in autumn's richest purple dy'd. Od.7.166.244.
And labour'd scenes of richest verdure round. Od.24.256.361.

RICHLY

The *Presence* seems, with things so richly odd, ...4.JD4.238.45.

RICHMENS

Well, I cou'd wish that still in Richmens Homes ....4.JD2A.121.142.

RICHMOND

The Richmond Fair ones ne'er will spoil their Looks, ...6.95.3A.264.

RICHMOND'S

Ne *Richmond's* self, from whose tall Front are ey'd ....6.14ii.53.44.
044.Ne *Richmond's* self, from whose tall Front is ey'd ....6.14ii.53A.44.
But *Richmond's* Fair-ones never spoil their Locks, ...6.95.3.264.

RID

No meagre, muse-rid mope, adust and thin, ...5.DunA2.33.100.
How many stages thro' old Monks she rid? ....5.DunA3.44.154.
No meagre, muse-rid mope, adust and thin, ...5.DunB2.37.297.
How many stages thro' old Monks she rid? ....5.DunB3.52.323.
But on the *Maiden's Nipple* when you rid, ...6.96iv.87.278.
Of that luxurious race to rid the land: ....Od.13.430.27.

RIDDLE

The glory, jest, and riddle of the world! ....3.EOM2.18.56.

RIDDLER

Each Songster, Riddler, ev'ry nameless name, ...5.DunB3.157.328.

RIDDLES

If I the *Sphynxe's* Riddles durst explain, ...1.TrSt.93.414.

RIDE

And Ships secure without their Haulsers ride. ....1.TrUl.30.466.
And while on Fame's triumphal Car they ride, ...5.DunB4.133.354.
And while on Fame's triumphant Car they ride, ...5.DunA4.133A.354.
And Cupids ride the Lyon of the Deeps; ....5.DunB4.308.374.
She does in Triumph ride ....6.14v(b).15A.50.
Or manag'd in your Schools, for Fops to ride, ...6.96iii.29.275.
Before the rest let none too rashly ride; ....Il.4.348.237.
Two Sons of *Priam* in one Chariot ride, ...Il.5.204.276.
And thro' the Ranks of Death triumphant ride. ....Il.5.251.279.
In the same Car the Chiefs to Combate ride, ...Il.5.754.303.
Haste, launch thy Chariot, thro' yon Ranks to ride; ....Il.8.455.418.
In the same Car the Brother-Warriors ride, ...Il.11.139.41.
Hold, stay your Steeds—What Madness thus to ride? ....Il.23.507.510.
Ride the wild waves, and quit the safer shore? ....Od.4.941.162.
Some bark's broad bottom to out-ride the storms, ...Od.5.320.187.
In pomp ride forth: for pomp becomes the great, ...Od.6.45.207.
And ride aloft, to Providence resign'd, ...Od.12.501.456.
And ships secure without their haulsers ride. ....Od.13.121.7.
And tilting o'er the bay the vessels ride: ....Od.14.289.49.

RIDER

Fly Pegasæan *Steed*, thy *Rider bear*, ...6.26ii.1.79.

RIDES

Rides in the whirlwind, and directs the storm. ....5.DunA3.260.179.
Rides in the whirlwind, and directs the storm. ....5.DunB3.264.333.
At *Reithrus*, and secure at anchor rides;. ....Od.1.238.44.
Wide o'er the bay, by vessel vessel rides. ....Od.2.333.77.
It rides; and now descends the sailor train. ....Od.2.441.82.
The ready vessel rides, the sailors ready stand. ....Od.2.455.83.
On spiry volumes there a Dragon rides; ....Od.4.619.149.
Where anchor'd in the bay the vessel rides; ....Od.4.1030.166.
Prepar'd to launch the freighted vessel rides; ....Od.15.508.94.

RIDGE

Whose ridge o'erlook'd a shady length of land; ....Od.10.170.349.

RIDGES

Behind, the rising Earth in Ridges roll'd; ....Il.18.635.354.
The new-ear'd Earth in blacker Ridges roll'd; ....Il.18.635A.354.

RIDGY

When lifted on a ridgy wave, he spies ....Od.5.504.196.

RIDICULE

Than ridicule all *Taste*, blaspheme *Quadrille*, ...4.HS1.38.7.
Sacred to Ridicule! his whole Life long, ...4.HS1.79.13.
Judicious Wits spread wide the Ridicule, ...4.EpS1.61.302.
Yet touch'd and sham'd by *Ridicule* alone. ....4.EpS2.211.325.
How quick Ambition hastes to ridicule! ....5.DunB4.547.396.

RIDICULES

Yet is, whate'er she hates or ridicules. ....3.Ep2.120A.60.
Yet is, whate'er she hates and ridicules. ....3.Ep2.120.60.
And ridicules beyond a hundred foes; ....4.Arbu.110.103.
A vile Encomium doubly ridicules; ....4.2HE1.410.229.
Yet is whate'er she hates or ridicules. ....6.154.6.403.

RIDICULOUS

Alive, ridiculous, and dead, forgot! ....3.Ep2.248.70.
Alive, ridiculous; and dead, forgot! ....6.86.10A.245.

RIDICULOUSLY

A Fiend in glee, ridiculously grim. ....5.DunA3.148.163.
A Fiend in glee, ridiculously grim. ....5.DunB3.154.327.

RIDING

The spreading harbours, and the riding fleets; ....Od.7.56.236.

RIDOTTA

Ridotta sips and dances, till she see ....4.HS1.47.9.

RIDPATH

There Ridpath, Roper, cudgell'd might ye view; ....5.DunA2.141.118.
To Dulness, Ridpath is as dear as Mist.) ....5.DunA3.286.184.
To Dulness Ridpath is as dear as Mist.) ....5.DunB1.208.285.
There Ridpath, Roper, cudgell'd might ye view, ...5.DunB2.149.302.

RIFE

Small-Pox is rife, and *Gay* in dreadful fear— ....6.82vi.13.232.

RIFLE

'Till Time shall rifle ev'ry youthful Grace, ...Il.1.41.87.

RIFLED

When the grim Savage to his rifled Den ....Il.18.373.339.
From thy vain journey, to a rifled Isle. ....Od.3.404.106.

RIFTED

On rifted Rocks, the Dragon's late Abodes, ...1.Mes.71.119.
From rifted rocks, and mountains bleak in air. ....Od.9.476.325.
As in the cavern of some rifted den, ...Od.24.9.347.

RIGG'D

A well-rigg'd Ship for *Chrysa's* sacred Shores: ....Il.1.405.107.
With stays and cordage last he rig'd the ship, ...Od.5.331.188.

RIGHT

The *Lines*, tho' touch'd but faintly, are drawn right. ....1.EOC.22.241.
You then whose Judgment the right Course wou'd steer, ...1.EOC.118.252.
If once right Reason drives *that* Cloud away, ...1.EOC.211.264.
And *smooth* or *rough*, with them, is *right* or *wrong*; ....1.EOC.338.277.
And *smooth* or *rough*, with such, is *right,or wrong*; ....1.EOC.338A.277.
By *Chance* go right, they *purposely* go wrong; ....1.EOC.427.288.
But always think the *last* Opinion *right*. ....1.EOC.431.288.
Whose Right it is, *uncensur'd* to be dull; ....1.EOC.589.307.
Not *dully prepossest*, nor *blindly right*; ....1.EOC.634.311.
Not *dully prepossest*, or *blindly right*; ....1.EOC.634A.311.
And *Boileau* still in Right of *Horace* sways. ....1.EOC.714.323.
Patient of Right, familiar in the Throne? ....1.TrSt.261.421.
Defend my Corps, and conquer in my Right; ....1.TrES.311.461.
My Word was this; *Your Honour's in the right*. ....2.ChJM.161.22.
Whom, in our Right, I must, and will oppose. ....2.ChJM.699.48.
Let my good Spouse pay Tribute, do me Right, ...2.ChWB.52.59.
These three right Ancient Venerable Sires. ....2.ChWB.149.63.
I still prevail'd, and wou'd be in the right, ...2.ChWB.164.64.
"And since in Man right Reason bears the Sway, ...2.ChWB.193.65.
He, against this, right sagely wou'd advise, ...2.ChWB.341.73.
May, must be right, as relative to all. ....3.EOM1.52.19.
In both, to reason right is to submit. ....3.EOM1.164.35.
One truth is clear, "Whatever IS, is RIGHT." ....3.EOM1.294.51.
The hard inhabitant contends is right. ....3.EOM2.230.83.
As far as Goose could judge, he reason'd right, ...3.EOM3.46Z3.96.
One must go right, the other may go wrong. ....3.EOM3.94.101.
"And right, too rigid, harden into wrong; ....3.EOM3.193.113.
Man, like his Maker, saw that all was right, ...3.EOM3.232.116.
For Nature knew no right divine in Men, ...3.EOM3.236.116.
His can't be wrong whose life is in the right: ....3.EOM3.306.124.
There needs but thinking right, and meaning well; ....3.EOM4.32.131.
Who risk the most, that take wrong means, or right? ....3.EOM4.86.136.
"Whatever IS, is RIGHT."—THIS world, 'tis true, ...3.EOM4.145.141.
Shew'd erring Pride, WHATEVER IS, IS RIGHT; ....3.EOM4.394.166.
Some gen'ral maxims, or be right by chance. ....3.Ep1.4.15.
Some flying stroke alone can hit 'em right: ....3.Ep2.154.63.
And then mistook reverse of wrong for right. ....3.Ep3.200.110.
He spits fore-right; his haughty Chest before, ...4.JD4.264.47.
"Right, cries his Lordship, for a Rogue in need ....4.HS2.111.63.
Who asks no more (right reasonable Peer) ....4.HAdv.159.89.
Of all mad Creatures, if the Learn'd are right, ...4.Arbu.105.103.
If wrong, I smil'd; if right, I kiss'd the rod. ....4.Arbu.158.107.
Comma's and points they set exactly right, ...4.Arbu.161.108.
Thus far was right, the rest belongs to Heav'n. ....4.Arbu.419.127.
For Right Hereditary tax'd and fin'd, ...4.2HE2.64.169.
And shall we deem him Ancient, right and sound, ...4.2HE1.58.199.
And to be kept in my right wits. ....4.HS6.22.251.
A Country Mouse, right hospitable, ...4.HS6.158.259.
What right, what true, what fit, we justly call, ...4.1HE1.19.279.
Dulness o'er all possess'd her antient right, ...5.DunA1.9.61.
To cavil, censure, dictate, right or wrong, ...5.DunA2.345.142.
Right well mine eyes arede the myster wight, ...5.DunA3.183.170.
Right well mine eyes arede that myster wight, ...5.DunA3.183A.170.
Dulness o'er all possess'd her ancient right, ...5.DunB1.11.269.
This Box my Thunder, this right hand my God? ....5.DunB1.202.284.
"To cavil, censure, dictate, right or wrong, ...5.DunB2.377.315.
"Right well mine eyes arede the myster wight, ...5.DunB3.187.329.
'The RIGHT DIVINE of Kings to govern wrong. ' " ....5.DunB4.188.360.
'*till* drown'd was Sense, and Shame, and Right, and Wrong— ....5.DunB4.625.406.
Take out your Box of right *Brasil*, ...6.10.64.26.
Right then, there passen by the Way, ...6.14i.7.41.
That none had so much Right to be ....6.30.52.88.
If I am right, oh teach my heart ....6.50.29.147.
Still in the right to stay; ....6.50.30.147.
If I am right, thy grace impart ....6.50.29B.147.
Apollo's Imp, right hopeful Youth; ....6.58.17A.171.
Forsooth, if Rhymes fall in not right, ...6.58.39.172.
To be about you, right or wrong; ....6.64.6.189.
Now, that this same it is right sooth, ...6.79.5.218.
Right tall he made himself to show, ...6.79.33.219.
Right did thy Gossip call thee: ....6.79.66.220.
(Right wary He and wise) ....6.94.22.259.
He rais'd and level'd right, ...6.94.54.261.
Left and Right, ...6.96i.29.269.
If wrong, I smile; if right, I kiss the Rod. ....6.98.8.283.
Commas and *Points* they set exactly right; ....6.98.11.283.
Once in his Life M[OOR]E judges right: ....6.116ii.1.326.
Wherefore thy claim resign, allow his right; ....6.116vi.5.327.
Thus far, is right; the rest belongs to Heav'n. ....6.117.14.333.
She would not do the least right thing, ...6.119.2.336.

RIGHT (CONTINUED)
And if he'll visit me, I'll wave my Right. 6.143.4.385.
Dame *Justice,* weighing long the doubtful Right, 6.145.7.388.
Think not to rob me of a Soldier's Right. Il.1.170.95.
And *Jove* himself shall guard a Monarch's Right. Il.1.228.98.
Jove, on the Right, a prosp'rous Signal sent, Il.2.418.147.
Or hast thou injur'd whom thou dar'st not right? Il.3.76.193.
Me too ye Warriors hear, whose fatal Right Il.3.135.196.
Nor thou a Wife and Sister's Right deny; Il.4.87.224.
Thro' his right Hip with forceful Fury cast, Il.5.87.270.
If right I judge, is *Diomed* the bold. Il.5.231.278.
Pernicious, wild, regardless of the Right. Il.5.1075.318.
The brave Defender of thy Country's Right. Il.6.328.342.
This from the Right to Left the Herald bears, Il.7.221.375.
To right, to left, the dext'rous Lance I wield, Il.7.291.378.
Curs'd is the Man, and void of Law and Right, Il.9.87.436.
As from the Right she soar'd, *Ulysses* pray'd, Il.10.325.17.
In his right Shoulder the broad Shaft appear'd, Il.11.630.61.
To speak his Thought, is ev'ry Freeman's Right, Il.12.249.90.
To right, to left, unheeded take your way, Il.12.281.91.
Then first spake *Merion:* Shall we join the Right, Il.13.396.125.
His right, beneath, the cover'd Pole-Axe held; Il.13.766.141.
Go save the Fleets, and conquer in my right. Il.16.90.239.
Defend my Body, conquer in my Right; Il.16.616.268.
Defend my Corpse, and conquer in my Right; Il.16.614A.268.
Who guarded Right, and kept his People free; Il.16.665.270.
A Spear his Left, a Stone employs his Right: Il.16.892.277.
Torn from his Friend, by right of Conquest mine. Il.17.210.295.
His naked Corps: His Arms are *Hector's* Right. Il.18.24.324.
The Prize of him who best adjudg'd the Right. Il.18.590.351.
Beyond the Bounds of Reason and of Right; Il.19.180.379.
To right with Justice, whom with Pow'r they wrong'd. Il.19.182.379.
Arm'd or with Truth or Falshood, Right or Wrong, Il.20.296.406.
These in her Left-Hand lock'd, her Right unty'd Il.21.567.445.
(Their Grandsire's Wealth, by right of Birth their own, Il.22.68.455.
No less fore-right the rapid Chace they held, Il.22.189.463.
In his right Hand he waves the Weapon round, Il.22.403.472.
But urge the Right, and give him all the Reins; Il.23.409.506.
Presents th' occasion, could we use it right. Il.23.494.510.
(For these dim Eyes, perhaps, discern not right) Il.23.553.511.
This Mule my right? th' undoubted Victor I. Il.23.772.520.
And fell a Hero in his Country's Right. Il.24.266.547.
Held in her right, before the Steeds she stands, Il.24.353.551.
Tow'r on the right of yon' æthereal Space. Il.24.364.551.
Tow'r on the right of yon' æthereal Space. Il.24.384.552.
Thus manifest of right, I build my claim Od.1.277.46.
The Lords of *Ithaca* their right pretend. Od.1.320.48.
Judge and revenge my right, impartial *Jove!* Od.1.483.55.
Shou'd factious pow'r dispute my lineal right, Od.1.504.56.
Your private right shou'd impious pow'r invade, Od.1.513.56.
Did he some loan of antient right require, Od.1.519.57.
Judge and assert my right, impartial *Jove!* Od.2.167.70.
If to the right to urge the pilot's toil, Od.3.205.95.
Right well, reply'd the King, your speech displays Od.4.365.137.
If e'er *Ulysses,* to reclaim your right, Od.4.441.140.
Swift on the regal dome descending right, Od.4.1055.167.
Her husband falling in his country's right: Od.8.572.293.
This social right demands: for him the sails Od.8.591.294.
One common right, the great and lowly claims:) Od.8.600.294.
Rude, and unconscious of a stranger's right; Od.9.204.314.
Contemning laws, and trampling on the right. Od.9.251.317.
Still met th' emergence, and determin'd right) Od.14.554.64.
Thus leaving careless thy paternal right Od.15.13.70.
His right-hand held: before the steeds he stands, Od.15.166.76.
Scarce ended thus the Prince, when on the right Od.15.178.77.
Thus speaking, on the right up-soar'd in air Od.15.565.97.
But swear, impartial arbiters of right, Od.18.64.169.
'Tis right; 'tis man's prerogative to give, Od.18.331.183.
This justice, this the social right demands. Od.18.467.191.
Without infringing hospitable right, Od.19.29.193.
Divided Right; each ninth revolving year Od.19.206.202.
The breach of hospitable right may rue. Od.19.371.212.
To the right shoulder-joint the spear apply'd, Od.19.529.221.
When heav'n, auspicious to thy right avow'd, Od.19.579.224.
No conscious blush, no sense of right restrains Od.20.213.243.
Nor human right, nor wrath divine revere. Od.20.274.246.
Of right the Queen refus'd a second Lord: Od.20.394.251.
"From right to left, in order take the bow; Od.21.150.266.
A son's just right. No *Grecian* Prince but I Od.21.371.277.

RIGHT-HAND
His right-hand held: before the steeds he stands, Od.15.166.76.

RIGHTEOUS
Oh righteous Gods! of all the Great, how few 1.TrUl.86.468.
The righteous End were lost for which I wed, 2.ChJM.120.20.
One only just, and righteous, hope to find: 2.ChJM.636.45.
Did but for *David's* Righteous Sake permit; 2.ChJM.691.48.
That righteous Abel was destroy'd by Cain; 3.EOM4.118.139.
But 'twas thy righteous end, asham'd to see 3.Ep3.149A.105.
No, 'twas thy righteous end, asham'd to see 3.Ep3.149.105.
Grave, righteous S[andys] joggs on till, past belief, 4.1740.13.332*.
For thou art Light. In thee the righteous find 6.23.15.73.
Destroy th' Aggressor, aid my righteous Cause, Il.3.435.213.
Oh hadst thou dy'd beneath the righteous Sword Il.3.535.217.
And Judges brib'd, betray the righteous Cause) Il.16.469.261.
And can ye see this righteous Chief attone Il.20.345.408.
With righteous *Æthiops* (uncorrupted Train!) Il.23.256.499.
By righteous *Themis* and by thund'ring *Jove,* Od.2.74.64.
'Till righteous heav'n reclaim her stubborn breast. Od.2.142.68.
Oh righteous Gods! of all the great, how few Od.13.253.18.
And honour justice and the righteous breast. Od.14.102.40.
How wou'd the Gods my righteous toils succeed, Od.14.447.57.
(So dire a fate, ye righteous Gods! avert, Od.15.384.88.
And the sure oracles of righteous *Jove.* Od.16.419.126.
No—by the righteous pow'rs of heav'n I swear, Od.16.456.129.

RIGHTEOUS (CONTINUED)
If thou the stranger's righteous cause decline, Od.18.265.179.
Perhaps by righteous heav'n that I must bleed! Od.18.310.181.
The righteous pow'rs who tread the starry skies, Od.23.13.319.
Blind! to contemn the stranger's righteous cause, Od.23.65.321.
The righteous pow'rs that mortal lots dispose, Od.23.219.333.
Such future scenes th' all-righteous pow'rs display, Od.23.303.337.

RIGHTFUL
The faithful Dog alone his rightful Master knew! 6.15.10.51.
His faithful Dog his rightful Master knew! 6.15.10A.51.
In peace and joy, the people's rightful Lord; Od.1.153.40.
Ulysses will assert his rightful reign. Od.19.353.211.
Tho' myriads leagu'd thy rightful claim contest; Od.20.60.235.
Thy wond'ring eyes shall view: his rightful reign Od.20.291.247.

RIGHTLIER
Or from their deed I rightlier may divine, Od.1.291.47.

RIGHTLY
Pleasure, or wrong or rightly understood, 3.EOM2.91.65.
God sends not ill; if rightly understood, 3.EOM4.113.139.
Tho' many a passenger he rightly call, 3.Ep1.7.16.

RIGHTS
Where Heav'ns Free Subjects might their *Rights* dispute, 1.EOC.548.302.
The Rights a Court attack'd, a Poet sav'd. 4.2HE1.224.215.
From *Rights* of *Subjects,* and the *Poor Man's Cause;* 6.8.32.18.
Severe, if men th' eternal rights evade! Od.4.478.142.
By these no statutes and no rights are known, Od.9.127.310.
The rights and honours of a pow'r divine? Od.13.149.12.
Fall'n ev'n below the rights of woman due! Od.18.319.182.
These are the rights of age, and shou'd be thine. Od.24.301.364.
So civil rights demand; and who begins Od.24.332.365.

RIGID
"And right, too rigid, harden into wrong; 3.EOM3.193.113.
To rigid Justice steel'd his Brother's Breast. Il.6.78.327.
Close to the Works their rigid Siege they laid. Il.12.304.92.
Embracing rigid with implicit Hands: Il.23.823.522.
At ev'ry point their master's rigid will: Od.22.206.297.
The Gods have form'd that rigid heart of stone! Od.23.106.324.

RIGOROUS
Think not by rigorous judgment seiz'd, 6.69ii.1.199.

RILL
The whisp'ring Zephyr, and the purling rill? 3.EOM1.204.40.
And pointed Crystals break the sparkling Rill, 6.142.4.382.
And polished Crystals break the sparkling Rill, 6.142.4A.382.
Unpolish'd Crystals break the sparkling Rill, 6.142.4B.382.
And painted Crystals break the sparkling Rill, 6.142.4C.382.
Whilst pointed Crystals break the sparkling Rill, 6.142.4D.382.
Thro' Desarts wild now pours a weeping Rill; Il.24.774.569.
And ev'ry fountain pours a sev'ral rill, Od.5.91.176.
A rill of Nectar, streaming from the Gods. Od.9.426.323.

RILLS
The grots that eccho to the tinkling rills, 2.ElAb.158.332.
And there the streams in purer rills descend? 3.EOM3.204.113.
With silver-quiv'ring rills mæander'd o'er— 3.Ep4.85.146.
What are the falling Rills, the pendant Shades, 6.81.7A.225.
Axius, that swells with all his neighb'ring Rills, Il.2.1032.171.
As Torrents roll, increas'd by num'rous Rills, Il.4.516.246.
And down their Summits pour'd a hundred Rills: Il.11.238.46.
Rhesus and *Rhodius* then unite their Rills, Il.12.17.82.
Are heard resounding with a hundred Rills) Il.14.322.178.
Axius, who swells with all the neighb'ring Rills, Il.21.175.428.
Soft Rills of Water from the bubbling Springs, Il.21.290.433.
Louder and louder purl the falling Rills, Il.21.296.433.
Whose polish'd Bed receives the falling Rills; Il.22.202.464.
Where gathering into depth from falling rills, Od.6.101.210.
A lucid lake, and thence descends in rills: Od.6.352.229.
In living rills a gushing fountain broke: Od.9.162.312.
The silver *Phæa's* glitt'ring Rills they lost, Od.15.318.85.
A limpid fount; that spread in parting rills Od.17.233.143.
And images the rills, and flowry vales: Od.23.336.340.

RIM
Deep in the Belly's Rim an Entrance found, Il.13.718.138.
Struck thro' the Belly's Rim, the Warrior lies Il.14.521.188.

RIND
Oft on the Rind I carv'd her Am'rous Vows, 1.PAu.67.85.
Now the cleft Rind inserted Graffs receives, 1.TrVP.13.377.
And print warm kisses on the panting rind, 1.TrFD.60.388.
I can no more; the creeping rind invades 1.TrFD.96.390.
He eat himself the Rind and paring. 4.HS6.170.261.

RING
The Woods shall answer, and their Echo ring. 1.PSu.16.73.
No more the Forests ring, or Groves rejoice; 1.W-F.278.174.
Hear, in *all Tongues* consenting Pæans ring! 1.EOC.186.262.
Hear, in *all Tongues* Triumphant *Pæans* ring! 1.EOC.186A.262.
While they ring round the same *unvary'd Chimes,* 1.EOC.348.278.
No more your Groves with my glad Songs shall ring, 1.TrSP.234.404.
The vaulted Roofs with echoing Musick ring, 2.ChJM.320.29.
And ring suspected Vessels ere they buy, 2.ChWB.101.61.
Hang o'er the *Box,* and hover round the *Ring.* 2.RL1.44.149.
For her the Spouse prepares the bridal ring, 2.ElAb.219.338.
That Charm shall grow, while what fatigues the Ring 3.Ep2.251.70.
Or just as gay, at Council, in a ring 3.Ep3.309.119.
Between each Act the trembling salvers ring, 3.Ep4.161.153.
And quits his Mistress, Money, Ring, and Note! 4.HAdv.54.79.
The heroes sit; the vulgar form a ring. 5.DunA2.352.143.
The heroes sit, the vulgar form a ring. 5.DunB2.384.316.

RING (CONTINUED)
She glares in *Balls, Front-boxes,* and the *Ring,* 6.19.53.63.
'Tis with sounds seraphic ring: 6.31ii.15.94.
With *gentle Philips* shall the Vallies ring. 6.40.2.112.
Tho' with the Stoick chief our stage may ring, 6.41.37.114.
The sounding Hinges ring: On either side Il.5.934.311.
The sounding Hinges ring, the Clouds divide; Il.8.484.420.
Now batter'd Breastplates and hack'd Helmets ring, Il.13.630.136.
The Faulchions ring, Shields rattle, Axes sound, Il.15.864.230.
Ranks wedg'd in Ranks; of Arms a steely Ring Il.16.254.249.
Darts show'r'd on Darts, now round the Carcase ring; Il.16.931.279.
And form a Ring, with Scepters in their Hands; Il.18.584.351.
And undistinguish'd blend the flying Ring: Il.18.694.357.
Clang the strong Arms, and ring the Shores around: Il.19.16.372.
Ring with conflicting Pow'rs, and Heav'n returns the Sound? Il.21.509.443.
Meantime the *Grecians* in a Ring beheld Il.23.530.511.
High on a rising Ground, above the Ring, Il.23.533.511.
Amid the Ring each nervous Rival stands, Il.23.822.522.
Then fix'd a Ring the running Reins to guide, Il.24.339.550.
The silver ring she pull'd, the door re-clos'd; Od.1.552.58.
And the gilt roofs with genial triumph ring. Od.4.844.158.
With beating hearts my fellows form a ring. Od.9.452.324.
Swift from their seats, and thick'ning form a ring. Od.18.49.169.
There as he rested, gathering in a ring Od.18.135.172.
The well-aim'd arrow thro' the distant ring, Od.21.4.258.
Forsakes the staple as she pulls the ring; Od.21.48.261.
Loud as a bull makes hill and valley ring, Od.21.51.261.
To speed the flying shaft thro' ev'ry ring, Od.21.102.263.
The feather'd arrow thro' the destin'd ring, Od.21.118.264.
Sung on direct, and thredded ev'ry ring. Od.21.462.282.
Some wound the gate, some ring against the wall; Od.22.303.301.
Thro' ev'ry ring the victor arrow went. Od.24.202.358.

RINGING
With ceaseless Noise the ringing Walls resound: 2.TemF.423.283.
Full on *Atrides'* ringing Shield it flew, Il.3.428.212.
Sprung from his Car; his ringing Arms resound. Il.4.475.242.
Thro' the strong Brass the ringing Javelin thrown, Il.11.547.58.
His Shield emboss'd the ringing Storm sustains, Il.13.700.138.
And on his Buckler caught the ringing Show'r. Il.16.431.259.
Loud o'er the Fields his ringing Arms resound: Il.21.475.441.
From off the ringing Orb, it struck the Ground. Il.22.372.471.

RINGLET
Thro' ev'ry ringlet levelling his view; Od.21.459.282.

RINGLETS
No more my Locks in Ringlets curl'd diffuse 1.TrSP.83.397.
With shining Ringlets the smooth Iv'ry Neck. 2.RL2.22.160.
With shining Ringlets her smooth Iv'ry Neck. 2.RL2.22A.160.
Some thrid the mazy Ringlets of her Hair, 2.RL2.139.168.
These, in two sable Ringlets taught to break, 2.RL4.169.197.
This, in two sable Ringlets taught to break, 2.RL4.169A.197.
The steely Point with golden Ringlets join'd, Il.6.396.346.
Part on her Head in shining Ringlets roll'd, Il.14.205.170.
And hung with Ringlets to receive the Reins: Il.24.336.550.
Such wavy ringlets o'er his shoulders flow! Od.4.202.129.
And gold, the ringlets that command the door. Od.7.117.240.
A length of hair in sable ringlets flows; Od.16.191.112.
An ivory seat with silver ringlets grac'd, Od.19.68.196.
And thro' twelve ringlets the fleet arrow send, Od.21.76.262.
The rival peers the ringlets and the bow. Od.21.82.263.
And here leave fixt the ringlets in a rowe. Od.21.277.273.
Back from his brows in wavy ringlets fly Od.23.155.328.

RINGS
Oft, as in Airy Rings they skim the Heath, 1.W-F.131.162.
But hark! the Groves rejoice, the Forest rings! 1.W-F.281.174.
Rings to the Skies, and ecchoes thro' the Fields, 1.TrES.64.452.
His Brazen Armour rings against the Ground. 1.TrES.128.454.
This Chime still rings in ev'ry Lady's Ear, 2.ChJM.597.43.
And all *Olympus* rings with loud Alarms. 2.RL5.48.203.
In three *Seal-Rings;* which after, melted down, 2.RL5.91.207.
Wide, and more wide, the floating Rings advance, 2.TemF.440.284.
And Bernard! Bernard! rings thro' all the Strand. 5.DunA2.70.106.
And Lintot! Lintot! rings thro' all the Strand. 5.DunA2.70B.106.
Heav'n rings with laughter: Of the laughter vain, 5.DunA2.113.110.
And Bernard! Bernard! rings thro' all the Strand. 5.DunB2.74.299.
Heav'n rings with laughter: Of the laughter vain, 5.DunB2.121.301.
And his broad Buckler rings against the Ground. Il.4.580.249.
His Brazen Armor rings against the Ground. Il.5.74.269.
On Earth he leaps; his Brazen Armor rings. Il.5.604.297.
Two brazen Rings of Work divine were roll'd. Il.5.895.308.
Fix'd to the Wood with circling Rings of Gold: Il.8.618.425.
He falls; his Armour rings against the Ground. Il.11.563.59.
Rings to the Skies, and ecchos thro' the Fields, Il.12.408.96.
His brazen Armour rings against the Ground. Il.12.482.99.
The hollow Helmet rings against the Plain. Il.13.671.137.
The Field rings dreadful with the Clang of Arms; Il.14.32.159.
On the raz'd Shield the falling Ruin rings: Il.14.476.187.
And his broad Buckler rings against the Ground. Il.15.695.222.
The Clash of Armour rings o'er all the Plain. Il.16.694.271.
The well-aim'd Weapon on the Buckler rings, Il.17.46.289.
And golden Rings the double Back-plate join'd: Il.20.480.414.
At every Bound; His clanging Armour rings: Il.21.284.432.
Cast on the Plain the brazen Burthen rings: Il.23.942.526.
Th' imperial Bird descends in airy Rings. Il.24.394.552.
The wat'ry Fairies dance in mazy Rings, Il.24.776.569.
Yet thro' my court the noise of Revel rings, Od.2.61.63.
Eurymachus presents: and ear-rings bright, Od.18.345.184.
Who thro' the rings directs the feather'd reed. Od.19.677.229.
Which held th' alternate brass and silver rings. Od.21.64.262.
One strikes the gate, one rings against the walls; Od.22.285.300.

RIOT
The lamb thy riot dooms to bleed to-day, 3.EOM1.81.23.
'Tis thus we riot, while who sow it, starve. 3.Ep3.24.88.
Enormous riot and mis-rule survey'd. Od.1.139.39.
Waste in wild riot what your land allows, Od.1.479.55.
Safe in my youth, in riot still they grow, Od.2.65.63.
And bid the voice of lawless riot rage. Od.2.82.64.
Waste in wild riot what your land allows, Od.2.163.70.
'Twas riot all among the lawless train; Od.2.337.77.
When lawless gluttons riot, mirth's a crime; Od.2.348.78.
With lawless riot, and mis-rule disgrace; Od.4.430.140.
In riot to consume a wretched heir. Od.4.913.161.
And bowls flow round, and riot wastes the day. Od.9.50.304.
To quaff thy bowls, or riot in thy feasts. Od.10.454.365.
And lordly gluttons riot in thy court. Od.11.149.388.
Scream o'er the fiend, and riot in his blood, Od.11.712.421.
No—sooner far their riot and their lust Od.15.37.71.
Nor harbours Charity where Riot reigns: Od.15.406.89.
But in my absence riot fills the place, Od.15.555.96.
Thy wealth in riot, the delay enjoy. Od.16.339.122.
Return, and riot shakes our walls a-new) Od.17.121.137.
Or dwells humanity where riot reigns? Od.17.391.150.
Yet starving Want amidst the riot weeps. Od.17.542.158.
To curb wild riot and to punish wrong? Od.17.623.162.
When loud uproar and lawless riot cease, Od.17.654.164.
'Twas riot all amid the Suitor-throng, Od.17.685.165.
Eurynome! to go where riot reigns Od.18.195.176.
With rapes and riot to profane my court; Od.20.383.251.
Perithous' roofs with frantick riot rung; Od.21.318.274.
And all was riot, noise, and wild uproar. Od.21.390.279.
Immod'rate riot, and intemp'rate lust! Od.24.526.373.

RIOTERS
Ordain'd for lawless rioters to bleed; Od.14.48.38.

RIOTOUS
My stores in riotous expence devour, Od.1.324.48.

RIOTS
No pulse that riots, and no blood that glows. 2.ElAb.252.340.
Insatiate riots in the sweet repasts, Od.9.108.308.
Their rapine strengthens, and their riots rise: Od.14.114.41.
These lawless riots end in blood and death. Od.18.178.175.
But impotent these riots to repel, Od.18.271.179.
And the wild riots of the Suitor-train. Od.23.328.340.

RIPÈ
From *Ripè, Stratie, Tegea's* bord'ring Towns, Il.2.733.161.

RIP
Next, rip in yellow Gold, a Vineyard shines, Il.18.651.355.

RIPE
Sylvia's like Autumn ripe, yet mild as *May,* 1.PSp.81.69.
When the ripe Colours *soften* and *unite,* 1.EOC.488.294.
He pulls ripe Apples from the bending Boughs. 1.TrVP.40.378.
With that ripe red th'Autumnal Sun bestows, 1.TrVP.101.381.
And their ripe Years in modest Grace maintain'd. 1.TrSt.620.436.
When thus ripe Lyes are to perfection sprung, 2.TemF.479.286.
Tho' stale, not ripe; tho' thin, yet never clear; 5.DunA3.164.167.
Tho' stale, not ripe; tho' thin, yet never clear; 5.DunB3.170.328.
Ripe Politicks the Nation's Barrel fill, 6.48i.3.133*.
At length, ripe Vengeance o'er their Heads impends, Il.4.41.223.
Attend a deed already ripe in fate: Od.20.285.247.
Lest the ripe harvest of revenge begun, Od.20.443.254.
To whom thus firm of soul: If ripe for death, Od.23.305.337.

RIPEN
The rest, succeeding Times shall ripen into Fate. 1.TrSt.428.427.
To ripen counsels, and decide debates, Od.11.622.414.
And yellow apples ripen into gold; Od.11.730.421.
While schemes of vengeance ripen in his breast. Od.14.133.42.

RIPEN'D
And famish'd dies amidst his ripen'd Fields. 1.W-F.56.154.
The last, scarce ripen'd into perfect Man, 3.EOM3.141.107.
Exceed their promise in the ripen'd store, 6.14iv.19.47.
The yellow Harvests of the ripen'd Year, Il.5.120.273.
And like a Flame thro' Fields of ripen'd Corn, Il.18.191.331.
The blooming boy is ripen'd into man; Od.11.556.411.

RIPENESS
Rank as the ripeness of a Rabbit's tail. 4.HS2.28.57.
Thou gav'st that Ripeness, which so soon began, 5.DunB4.287.372.

RIPENING
And *Phœbus* warm the ripening Ore to Gold. 1.W-F.396.190.
'Twas all her Joy the ripening Fruits to tend, 1.TrVP.7.377.
Whom ripening Time, that Turns a Clap to Pox 4.JD2A.53.136.
The ripening Silver in *Alybean* Mines. Il.2.1045.172.
And yet who knows, but ripening lies in fate Od.3.265.98.

RIPENS
But ripens Spirits in cold *Northern Climes;* 1.EOC.401.286.
And ripens Spirits as he ripens Mines, 3.Ep2.290.74.
And ripens Spirits as he ripens Mines, 3.Ep2.290.74.
The red'ning apple ripens here to gold, 6.35.6.103.
The red'ning apple ripens here to gold, Od.7.147.243.

RIPER
Maturely ponder'd in his riper Age; 2.ChJM.78.18.
Procur'd young Husbands in my riper Days. 2.ChWB.208.66.
Scarfs, garters, gold, amuse his riper stage; 3.EOM2.279.88.
Till grown more frugal in his riper days, 4.Arbu.241.113.
To question wisely men of riper years. Od.3.32.87.
With riper beams when *Phœbus* warms the day. Od.17.30.133.

RIPER (CONTINUED)

Thy riper days no growing worth impart, ...Od.18.257.179.

RIPLEY

And needs no Rod but Ripley with a Rule. ....3.Ep4.18.137.
(Should Ripley venture, all the World would smile) ....4.2HE1.186.211.
See under Ripley rise a new White-hall, ...5.DunB3.327.336.

RIPN'D

I burn, I burn, as when thro' ripn'd Corn ....1.TrSP.9.393.

RIPP'D

It ripp'd his Belly with a ghastly Wound, ...Il.13.642.136.

RISE

Now rise, and haste to yonder Woodbine Bow'rs, ...1.PSp.97.70.
Where-e'er you tread, the blushing Flow'rs shall rise, ...1.PSu.75.77.
Here where the *Mountains* less'ning as they rise, ...1.PAu.59.84.
Swift fly the Years, and rise th'expected Morn! ....1.Mes.21.114.
See spicy Clouds from lowly *Saron* rise, ...1.Mes.27.115.
Sink down ye Mountains, and ye Vallies rise: ....1.Mes.34.116.
No more shall Nation against Nation rise, ...1.Mes.57.117.
Then Palaces shall rise; the joyful Son ....1.Mes.63.118.
See Lillies spring, and sudden Verdure rise; ....1.Mes.68.119.
Rise, crown'd with Light, Imperial *Salem* rise! ....1.Mes.85.120.
Rise, crown'd with Light, Imperial *Salem* rise! ....1.Mes.85.120.
Nor saw displeas'd the peaceful Cottage rise. ....1.W-F.86.158.
Make *Windsor* Hills in lofty Numbers rise, ...1.W-F.287.174.
Where *Windsor-Domes* and pompous Turrets rise, ...1.W-F.352.184.
And Temples rise, the beauteous Works of Peace. ....1.W-F.378.187.
And urg'd the rest by equal Steps to rise; ....1.EOC.97.250.
And *rise* to *Faults* true Criticks *dare not mend*; ....1.EOC.153.257.
Which *out of* Nature's *common Order* rise, ...1.EOC.159.258.
New, distant Scenes of *endless* Science rise! ....1.EOC.224.265.
And bid Alternate Passions fall and rise! ....1.EOC.375.283.
Like some fair *Flow'r* that in the *Spring* does rise, ...1.EOC.498A.294.
(Her Guide now lost) no more attempts to *rise*, ...1.EOC.737.325.
Here cornels rise, and in the shady grove ....1.TrPA.74.368.
Nor tastful Herbs that in these Gardens rise ....1.TrVP.102.381.
To rise, and shade her with a sudden green. ....1.TrFD.48.388.
No Sigh to rise, no Tear had pow'r to flow; ....1.TrSP.127.399.
Then frantick rise, and like some Fury rove ....1.TrSP.159.400.
She spoke, and vanish'd with the Voice—I rise, ...1.TrSP.199.402.
Hence Strife shall rise, and mortal War succeed; ....1.TrSt.344.424.
From the damp Earth impervious Vapours rise, ...1.TrSt.486.430.
On that, *Prosymna's* Grove and Temple rise: ....1.TrSt.534.432.
O'er their fair Cheeks the glowing Blushes rise, ...1.TrSt.630.436.
From no blind Zeal or fond Tradition rise; ....1.TrSt.661.438.
Were thine exempt, Debate wou'd rise above, ...1.TrES.244.459.
Arise my Wife, my beauteous Lady rise! ....2.ChJM.527.40.
And dusky Vapors rise, and intercept the Day: ....2.ChJM.801.53.
And *Venus* sets ere *Mercury* can rise: ....2.ChWB.370.75.
And *Venus* sets when *Mercury* does rise: ....2.ChWB.370A.75.
What mighty Contests rise from trivial Things, ...2.RL1.2.144.
What mighty Quarrels rise from trivial Things, ...2.RL1.2A.144.
Heroes' and Heroins' Shouts confus'dly rise, \ ....2.RL5.41.202.
But trust the Muse—she saw it upward rise, ...2.RL5.123.210.
Where Mountains rise, and circling Oceans flow; ....2.TemF.14.254.
There Trees, and intermingl'd Temples rise ....2.TemF.18.254.
Rise white in Air, and glitter o'er the Coast; ....2.TemF.54.256.
The growing Tow'rs like Exhalations rise, ...2.TemF.91.259.
Made visionary Fabricks round them rise, ...2.TemF.103.261.
These massie Columns in a Circle rise, ...2.TemF.244.275.
By just degrees they ev'ry moment rise, ...2.TemF.312.279.
Rise! Muses, rise! add all your tuneful Breath, ...2.TemF.370.281.
Rise! Muses, rise! add all your tuneful Breath, ...2.TemF.370.281.
Alas how chang'd! what sudden horrors rise! ....2.ElAb.99.327.
Rise in the grove, before the altar rise, ...2.ElAb.265.341.
Rise in the grove, before the altar rise, ...2.ElAb.265.341.
Rise *Alps* between us! and whole oceans roll! ....2.ElAb.290.343.
From the full quire when loud *Hosanna's* rise, ...2.ElAb.353.348.
And catch the Manners living as they rise; ....3.EOM1.14.14.
And all that rises, rise in due degree; ....3.EOM1.46.19.
"Seas roll to waft me, suns to light me rise; ....3.EOM1.139.32.
Created half to rise, and half to fall; ....3.EOM2.15.55.
Who saw its fires here rise, and there descend, ...3.EOM2.37.60.
Uncheck'd may rise, and climb from art to art: ....3.EOM2.40.60.
Who mark'd their Points, to rise, and to descend ....3.EOM2.37B.60.
Who saw the Stars here rise, and there descend, ...3.EOM2.37A.60.
And when in act they cease, in prospect rise; ....3.EOM2.124.70.
See! and confess, one comfort still must rise, ...3.EOM2.293.90.
They rise, they break, and to that sea return. ....3.EOM3.20.94.
And still new needs, new helps, new habits rise, ...3.EOM3.137.106.
Saw Gods descend, and fiends infernal rise: ....3.EOM3.254.118.
Oh sons of earth! attempt ye still to rise, ...3.EOM4.73.135.
Honour and shame from no Condition rise; ....3.EOM4.193.145.
Must rise from Individual to the Whole. ....3.EOM4.362.163.
To fall with dignity, with temper rise; ....3.EOM4.378.165.
And Temple rise—then fall again to dust. ....3.Ep2.140.62.
He thinks a Loaf will rise to fifty pound. ....3.Ep3.118.101.
Rise, honest Muse! and sing the MAN of ROSS: ....3.Ep3.250.113.
Who taught that heav'n-directed spire to rise? ....3.Ep3.261.114.
That tells the Waters or to rise, or fall, ...3.Ep4.58.142.
Why *Turnpikes* rise, and now no Cit, nor Clown ....4.JD4.144.37.
Rise from a Clergy, or a City, feast! ....4.HS2.76.59.
Should rise, and say—"Sir *Robert!* or Sir *Paul!* ....4.HAdv.88.83.
And hate for Arts that caus'd himself to rise; ....4.Arbu.200.110.
"And you shall rise up *Otway* for your pains." ....4.2HE2.146.175.
None e'er has risen, and none e'er shall rise. ....4.2HE1.30.197.
How will our Fathers rise up in a rage, ...4.2HE1.125.205.
His servants up, and rise by five a clock, ...4.2HE1.162.209.
Self-centred Sun, and Stars that rise and fall, ...4.1HE6.6.237.
On the broad base of fifty thousand rise, ...4.1HE6.74.241.
Fr. stop! stop! *P.* Must Satire then, nor *rise*, nor *fall* ....4.EpS2.52.315.
Let Flatt'ry sickening see the Incense rise, ...4.EpS2.244.326.
Rise, rise great W[alpole] fated to appear, ...4.1740.43.334.

RISE (CONTINUED)

Rise, rise great W[alpole] fated to appear, ...4.1740.43.334.
Sees momentary monsters rise and fall, ...5.DunA1.81.69.
Where rebel to thy throne if Science rise, ...5.DunA1.157.82.
Where 'gainst thy throne if rebel Science rise, ...5.DunA1.157A.82.
There rival flames with equal glory rise, ...5.DunA3.72.156.
Embody'd dark, what clouds of Vandals rise! ....5.DunA3.78.156.
In dulness strong, th' avenging Vandals rise; ....5.DunA3.78A.156.
Embody'd thick, what clouds of Vandals rise! ....5.DunA3.78B.156.
Behold, and count them, as they rise to light. ....5.DunA3.122.160.
He look'd, and saw a sable Sorc'rer rise, ...5.DunA3.229.176.
The forests dance, the rivers upward rise, ...5.DunA3.241.177.
New wizards rise: here Booth, and Cibber there: ....5.DunA3.262.179.
And from each show rise duller than the last: ....5.DunA3.300.184.
Sees momentary monsters rise and fall, ...5.DunB1.83.275.
"O! when shall rise a Monarch all our own, ...5.DunB1.311.292.
There rival flames with equal glory rise, ...5.DunB3.80.324.
Embody'd dark, what clouds of Vandals rise! ....5.DunB3.86.324.
Behold, and count them, as they rise to light. ....5.DunB3.130.326.
And look'd, and saw a sable Sorc'rer rise, ...5.DunB3.233.331.
The forests dance, the rivers upward rise, ...5.DunB3.245.332.
New wizards rise; I see my Cibber there! ....5.DunB3.266.333.
See under Ripley rise a new White-hall, ...5.DunB3.327.336.
See other Cæsars, other Homers rise; ....5.DunB4.360.378.
True, he had wit, to make their value rise; ....5.DunB4.377.380.
And, as she turns, the colours fall or rise. ....5.DunB4.540.395.
Thus from the ocean first did rise. ....6.5.4.12.
Thus from the waters first did rise. ....6.5.4A.12.
Thus thou may'st Rise, and in thy daring Flight ....6.7.15.16.
Now louder, and yet louder rise, ...6.11.14.30.
The scolding Quean to louder Notes doth rise, ...6.14ii.23.43.
To View a thousand real Blessings rise; ....6.17iii.9.58.
And sees the Rusticks to their Labours rise; ....6.17iii.33.58.
When foes conspiring rise against his rest, ...6.21.37.70.
Oh teach the mind t' ætherial heights to rise, ...6.23.9.73.
Aloft I'm swiftly born, methinks I rise, ...6.26ii.3.79.
Rise higher yet: learn ev'n yourselves to know; ....6.27.14.81.
He bids your breasts with ancient ardour rise, ...6.32.15.96.
See Coronations rise on ev'ry green; ....6.45.34.125.
Or sees the blush of soft *Parthenia* rise, ...6.45.46.126.
Or sees the blush of *Parthenissa* rise, ...6.45.46A.126.
And hate, for Arts that caus'd himself to rise; ....6.49iii.14.143.
Hate him, for Arts that caus'd himself to rise; ....6.49iii.14A.143.
And hate, for Arts which caus'd himself to rise; ....6.49iii.14B.143.
All Nature's Incence rise! ....6.50.52.148.
First from a Worm they take their Rise, ...6.53.19.162.
And greater Gain would rise, ...6.53.30.162.
First from a Worm they took their Rise, ...6.53.19A.162.
Her Gods, and god-like Heroes rise to view, ...6.71.47.204.
In vain my structures rise, my gardens grow, ...6.81.2.225.
I wake, I rise, and shiv'ring with the Frost, ...6.96iv.43.277.
The Windows open; all the Neighbours rise: ....6.96iv.46.277.
And hate for Arts that caus'd himself to rise; ....6.98.50.284.
The heroine rise, to grace the *British* scene. ....6.107.14.310.
As in spite of his Fall, might make Lucifer rise; ....6.122.6.341.
Such, such Emotions should in *Britons* rise, ...6.128.9.355.
And Temple rise,—then fall again to Dust. ....6.154.26.403.
And Scenes of Blood rise dreadful in his Soul. ....Il.1.639.118.
Let *Greece* be humbled, and the *Trojans* rise; ....Il.1.659.118.
Then bids an empty Phantome rise to sight, ...Il.2.7.127.
At whose Command whole Empires rise or fall: ....Il.2.148.135.
On the round Bunch the bloody Tumours rise; ....Il.2.328.143.
Rise, great *Atrides!* and with Courage sway; ....Il.2.410.147.
With Joy they saw the growing Empire rise, ...Il.2.813.163.
But soon to rise in Slaughter, Blood, and War. ....Il.2.846.164.
Obey the Pow'r from whom thy Glories rise: ....Il.3.514.216.
He ceas'd; His Army's loud Applauses rise, ...Il.3.575.219.
He ceas'd; His Army's just Applauses rise, ...Il.3.575A.219.
For know, of all the num'rous Towns that rise ....Il.4.65.224.
Slow from the Main the heavy Vapours rise, ...Il.4.316.235.
Rise in thy Wrath! To Hell's abhorr'd Abodes ....Il.5.555.295.
Beneath the Rage of burning *Sirius* rise, ...Il.5.1060.317.
And bids the Thunder of the Battel rise. ....Il.6.128.330.
They fall successive, and successive rise; ....Il.6.184.335.
Rise, or behold the conqu'ring Flames ascend, ...Il.6.416.347.
And rise the *Hector* of the future Age! ....Il.6.609.357.
What Crowds of Heroes sunk, to rise no more? ....Il.7.395.383.
Shall rise in Vengeance, and lay waste the Plain. ....Il.8.594.424.
Then shine the Vales, the Rocks in Prospect rise, ...Il.8.695.428.
Jove, at whose Nod whole Empires rise or fall, ...Il.9.32.433.
See, full of *Jove,* avenging *Hector* rise! ....Il.9.311.449.
Rise to redeem; ah yet, to conquer, rise! ....Il.9.323.449.
Rise to redeem; ah yet, to conquer, rise! ....Il.9.323.449.
That Heart shall melt, that Courage rise in vain. ....Il.9.325.450.
Her Hearts are strengthen'd, and her Glories rise. ....Il.9.543.460.
The silver *Cynthia* bade *Contention* rise, ...Il.9.657.467.
That great *Achilles* rise and rage again, ...Il.10.119.7.
Rise, son of *Tydeus!* to the brave and strong ....Il.10.180.9.
Three glitt'ring Dragons to the Gorget rise, ...Il.11.33.36.
O'er his dim Sight the misty Vapours rise, ...Il.11.459.54.
As two tall Oaks, before the Wall they rise, ...Il.12.145.86.
Where *Ida's* misty Tops confus'dly rise; ....Il.13.22.105.
On ev'ry side the dusty Whirlwinds rise, ...Il.13.426.126.
When the loud Rusticks rise, and shout from far, ...Il.13.596.134.
O'er his bent Back the bristly Horrors rise, ...Il.13.598.134.
And bids anew the martial Thunder rise. ....Il.13.950.151.
To *Jove's* glad Omen all the *Grecians* rise, ...Il.13.1040.154.
In ev'ry *Greek* a new *Achilles* rise? ....Il.14.58.160.
There on a Fir, whose spiry Branches rise ....Il.14.325.178.
Black from the Blow, and Smoaks of Sulphur rise; ....Il.14.484.187.
To rise afresh, and once more wake the War, ...Il.15.64.197.
Then, nor till then, shall great *Achilles* rise; ....Il.15.74.199.
Again his Pulses beat, his Spirits rise; ....Il.15.272.207.
The *Greeks* expect the Shock; the Clamours rise ....Il.15.354.210.
The roaring Deeps in watry Mountains rise, ...Il.15.441.214.
To rise in Arms, and shine again in War. ....Il.15.465.215.

RISE (CONTINUED)

O'er the high Stern the curling Volumes rise, Il.16.152.243.
All rise in Arms, and with a gen'ral Cry Il.16.318.255.
The Hills shine out, the Rocks in Prospect rise, Il.16.358.257.
He sees for *Greece* the Scale of Conquest rise, Il.16.432.259.
Clouds rise on Clouds, and Heav'n is snatch'd from sight. Il.16.451.260.
From their deep Beds he bids the Rivers rise, Il.16.470.261.
Were thine exempt, Debate would rise above, Il.16.547.265.
And thick'ning round 'em, rise the Hills of Dead. Il.17.417.303.
Then clash their sounding Arms; the Clangors rise, Il.17.482.306.
Rise, Son of *Peleus!* rise divinely brave! Il.18.209.332.
Rise, Son of *Peleus!* rise divinely brave! Il.18.209.332.
Rise, and prevent (if yet thou think of Fame) Il.18.217.332.
So from *Achilles'* Head the Splendours rise, Il.18.253.334.
If great *Achilles* rise in all his Might, Il.18.355.338.
They rise, take Horse, approach, and meet the War; Il.18.616.352.
With silent Glee, the Heaps around him rise. Il.18.646.354.
Now all at once they rise, at once descend, Il.18.690.357.
The King of Men shall rise in publick Sight, Il.19.173.378.
What can they now, if in his Rage he rise? Il.20.40.394.
Tho' all in Arms the peopled City rise, Il.20.201.402.
Rise from the Shades, and brave me on the Field: Il.21.65.424.
Rise to the War! th' insulting Flood requires Il.21.386.436.
As when the Flames beneath a Caldron rise, Il.21.424.437.
Thick beats his Heart, the troubled Motions rise, Il.21.648.449.
As *Hector* sees, unusual Terrors rise, Il.22.179.461.
This hot thro' scorching Clefts is seen to rise, Il.22.197.463.
O'er the proud Citadel at length should rise, Il.22.520.478.
Of sad *Patroclus* rose, or seem'd to rise; Il.23.79.490.
Where to the Day thy silver Fountains rise, Il.23.183.497.
To breathe, and whisper to the Fires to rise. Il.23.243.499.
All from the Banquet rise, and each invites Il.23.250.499.
The *Western Spirit,* and the *North* to rise; Il.23.259.499.
The heaving Deeps in wat'ry Mountains rise: Il.23.267.500.
And a large Vase, where two bright Handles rise, Il.23.331.503.
Fir'd at his Word, the Rival Racers rise; Il.23.355.504.
Next bold *Meriones* was seen to rise, Il.23.425.507.
Rise then some other, and inform my Sight, Il.23.552.511.
What *Greek* shall blame me, if I bid thee rise, Il.23.659.515.
Rise if thou dar'st, before thy Chariot stand, Il.23.661.515.
Swell to each Gripe, and bloody Tumours rise. Il.23.833.522.
Again they rage, again to Combat rise; Il.23.854.523.
And treads each Footstep e'er the Dust can rise: Il.23.894.524.
From the pleas'd Crowd new Peals of Thunder rise, Il.23.1042.530.
Nor here disdain'd the King of Men to rise. Il.23.1051.531.
The Deeps dividing, o'er the Coast they rise, Il.24.127.540.
Yet still one Comfort in his Soul may rise; Il.24.608.562.
Rise then: Let Reason mitigate our Care: Il.24.659.564.
Never to manly Age that Son shall rise, Il.24.914.574.
To see the smoke from his lov'd palace rise, Od.1.75.34.
Rise then ye Peers! with virtuous anger rise! Od.2.71.64.
Rise then ye Peers! with virtuous anger rise! Od.2.71.64.
Rise in my aid! suffice the tears that flow Od.2.77.64.
Where as to life the wond'rous figures rise, Od.2.105.66.
Would'st thou to rise in arms the *Greeks* advise? Od.2.277.74.
Born, the *Ulysses* of thy age to rise! Od.2.308.76.
And did not Heroes from brave Heroes rise, Od.2.314.76.
Shall rise spontaneous in the needful hour. Od.3.36.88.
When imag'd to my soul his sorrows rise. Od.4.136.126.
He ceas'd; a gust of grief began to rise: Od.4.249.131.
Rise on the poop, and fully stretch the sails. Od.4.484.143.
Then rise, and to the feastful hall remove: Od.4.901.160.
Against *Ulysses* shall thy anger rise? Od.5.274.184.
No rains descend, no snowy vapours rise; Od.6.52.207.
Tho' mountains rise between, and oceans roar. Od.6.376.230.
And seize the moment when the breezes rise: Od.7.408.256.
Acroneus, Thoon, and *Eretmeus* rise; Od.8.114.268.
Thine is the guest, invite him thou to rise. Od.8.154.271.
Rise ye *Phæacians,* try your force, he cry'd; Od.8.230.275.
Rise then ye skill'd in measures: let him bear Od.8.287.278.
Light-bounding from the earth, at once they rise, Od.8.303.279.
Where to the pow'r an hundred altars rise, Od.8.397.285.
And bids proud *Ilion* from her ashes rise. Od.8.538.291.
Or where the sun shall set, or where shall rise? Od.10.218.350.
Some smoak I saw amid the forest rise, Od.10.225.351.
The bowl shall sparkle, and the banquet rise; Od.10.346.360.
'Till all the form in full proportion rise, Od.10.467.366.
Then rise and follow where I lead the way. Od.10.504.368.
As from a lethargy at once they rise, Od.10.558.369.
Shall never the dear land in prospect rise, Od.10.562.369.
Rise, rise my mates! 'tis *Circe* gives command; Od.10.655.375.
Rise, rise my mates! 'tis *Circe* gives command; Od.10.655.375.
All rise and follow, yet depart not all, Od.10.657.375.
He first was seen of all the Peers to rise, Od.11.625.414.
New horrors rise! let prudence by thy guide, Od.12.69.433.
Loud storms around and mists eternal rise, Od.12.89.436.
Smooth as the polish of the mirrour rise Od.12.97.436.
Full on its crown a fig's green branches rise, Od.12.127.438.
Or if I rise in arms, can *Scylla* bleed? Od.12.142.439.
Approach! thy soul shall into raptures rise! Od.12.226.443.
And now the glitt'ring mountains rise to view. Od.12.315.447.
When, at the voice of *Jove,* wild whirlwinds rise, Od.12.369.449.
To *Phœbus* shrines shall rise, and altars burn. Od.12.412.451.
Still may thy beams thro' heav'n's bright portals rise, Od.12.454.453.
Like fowl that haunt the floods, they sink, they rise, Od.12.493.456.
Full in their port a shady hill shall rise, Od.13.176.14.
Their rapine strengthens, and their riots rise: Od.14.114.41.
To dear remembrance makes his image rise, Od.14.152.43.
And horse and foot in mingled tumult rise. Od.14.295.50.
Foreseeing from the first the storm wou'd rise; Od.14.515.62.
Let from among us some swift Courier rise, Od.14.562.64.
Rise, son of *Nestor!* for the road prepare, Od.15.55.72.
Where two fair cities rise with equal pride, Od.15.453.92.
And bids the rural throne with osiers rise. Od.16.48.104.
And round the coast circumfluent oceans rise. Od.16.60.105.
Say, do thy subjects in bold faction rise, Od.16.99.107.
Nor leagu'd in factious arms my subjects rise, Od.16.119.108.
We rise terrific to the task of fight. Od.16.289.118.
And noting, ere we rise in vengeance prove Od.16.330.121.
And horse and foot in mingled tumult rise: Od.17.516.157.
Uproots the bearded corn? rise, try the fight, Od.18.36.168.
By just degrees like well-turn'd columns rise: Od.18.77.170.
And sudden flames in ev'ry bosom rise; Od.18.252.179.
The varying hues in gay confusion rise Od.18.338.184.
Gods! should the stern *Ulysses* rise in might, Od.18.426.189.
Distinct in rows the radiant columns rise: Od.19.45.195.
Rise, *Euryclea!* with officious care Od.19.414.214.
Such raptures in my beating bosom rise, Od.20.108.238.
Sated at length they rise, and bid prepare Od.20.465.256.
So timely rise, when morning streaks the east, Od.22.215.297.
Rise then in combat, at my side attend; Od.22.254.299.
Bid the gay youth and sprightly virgins rise, Od.23.130.326.
Let not against thy spouse thine anger rise! Od.23.216.333.
Delightful rise, when angry *Neptune* roars, Od.23.250.335.
Thick clouds of dust o'er all the circle rise, Od.24.89.352.
I, I am he; oh father rise! behold Od.24.375.367.
All *Ithaca* and *Cephalenia* rise? Od.24.414.369.
In throngs they rise, and to the palace crowd; Od.24.476.371.

RISEN

None e'er has risen, and none e'er shall rise. 4.2HE1.30.197.
And thought *Herself* just risen from the Waves. 6.9vi.2.21.

RISES

Still as he rises in th'Æthereal Height, 1.TrSt.642.437.
The Fair each moment rises in her Charms, 2.RL1.140.157.
The Sun first rises o'er the purpled Main, 2.RL2.2.159.
And all that rises, rise in due degree; 3.EOM1.46.19.
Vig'rous he rises; from th' effluvia strong 5.DunA2.97.109.
Instand buoys up, and rises into light; 5.DunA2.284.137.
A branch of Styx here rises from the Shades, 5.DunA2.314.140.
Hell rises, Heav'n descends, and dance on Earth, 5.DunA3.233.177.
Hell rises, Heav'n descends, to dance on Earth, 5.DunA3.233A.177.
Refulgent rises, with a heav'n its own: 5.DunA3.238A.177.
Vig'rous he rises; from th' effluvia strong 5.DunB2.105.300.
A branch of Styx here rises from the Shades, 5.DunB2.338.314.
Hell rises, Heav'n descends, and dance on Earth: 5.DunB3.237.332.
Eager he rises, and in Fancy hears Il.2.51.129.
Gen'rous he rises in the Crown's Defence, Il.2.336.143.
And the white Ruin rises o'er the Plain. Il.12.344.94.
Then stern *Peneleus* rises to the Fight; Il.13.126.110.
Forthwith *Æneas* rises to his Thought; Il.13.576.133.
Lo! *Hector* rises from the *Stygian* Shades! Il.15.325.209.
Of Carnage rises, as the Heroes fall. Il.16.804.274.
And now it rises, now it sinks, by turns. Il.17.421.303.
A gen'ral Clamour rises at the Sight: Il.17.809.320.
And now it rises, now it sinks by turns. Il.18.2.322.
Rises in Arms: Such Grace thy *Greeks* have won. Il.18.420.341.
A Wood of Lances rises round his Head, Il.20.428.412.
Slowly he rises, scarcely breathes with Pain, Il.21.488.441.
Not half so dreadful rises to the Sight Il.22.37.454.
The old Man's Fury rises, and ye die. Il.23.492.510.
Oïlean Ajax rises to the Race; Il.23.882.524.
The ruddy Morning rises o'er the Waves; Il.24.22.535.
When Morning rises? If I take the wood, Od.5.605.201.
Fell *Scylla* rises, in her fury roars, Od.12.123.437.

RISING

Four Figures rising from the Work appear, 1.PSp.37.64.
That threats a Fight, and spurns the rising Sand. 1.PSp.48.65.
Fresh rising Blushes paint the watry Glass, 1.PSu.28.74.
No more the rising *Sun* shall gild the Morn, 1.Mes.99.121.
To the bright Regions of the rising Day; 1.W-F.388.189.
For rising Merit will *buoy up* at last. 1.EOC.461.291.
With *sweeter Notes* each *rising Temple* rung; 1.EOC.703.320.
Embrac'd thy boughs, the rising bark delay'd, 1.TrFD.55.388.
Embrac'd thy boughs, thy rising bark delay'd, 1.TrFD.55A.388.
A rising Empire on a foreign Ground, 1.TrSt.250.421.
The Realms of rising and declining Day, 1.TrSt.278.421.
And rising gild the radiant East again. 1.TrSt.329.424.
And *Pentheus'* Blood enrich'd the rising Ground, 1.TrSt.465.429.
And rising *Cynthia* sheds her silver Light, 1.TrSt.475.430.
Wakes to new Vigor with the rising Day. 1.TrSt.587.434.
With Sculpture grac'd, and rough with rising Gold. 1.TrSt.636.436.
High on her Crown a rising Snake appears, 1.TrSt.708.439.
And breath'd the Freshness of the rising Day, 1.TrSt.694A.439.
High on a Crown a rising Snake appears, 1.TrSt.708A.439.
Shoots up, and All the rising Host appears. 1.TrES.182.456.
But when the rising Star did Heav'n adorn, 1.TrUl.21A.466.
Whose Hills are brighten'd by the rising Sun. 1.TrUl.119.469.
And rising Springs Eternal Verdure yield. 1.TrUl.131.470.
The Vital Sap then rising from below: 2.ChJM.134.21.
Bright as the rising Sun, in Summer's Day, 2.ChJM.345.30.
Clear was the Day, and *Phœbus* rising bright, 2.ChJM.613.44.
While on a Bank reclin'd of rising Green, 2.ChJM.625.45.
She said; a rising Sigh express'd her Woe, 2.ChJM.783.52.
The fierce *Thalestris* fans the rising Fires. 2.RL*A*2.12.132.
Where *Thames* with Pride surveys his rising Tow'rs, 2.RL3.2.169.
He watch'd th' Ideas rising in her Mind, 2.RL3.142.178.
Strange Phantoms rising as the Mists arise; 2.RL4.40.186.
And fierce *Thalestris* fans the rising Fire. 2.RL4.94.191.
Call forth the Greens, and wake the rising Flowers; 2.TemF.2.253.
And Sculpture rising on the roughen'd Gold. 2.TemF.78.258.
Or if no Basis bear my rising Name, 2.TemF.519.289.
And swelling organs lift the rising soul; 2.ElAb.272.342.
Yet shall thy grave with rising flow'rs be drest, 2.Elegy.63.367.
The rising tempest puts in act the soul, 3.EOM2.105.67.
See him from Nature rising slow to Art! 3.EOM3.169.110.
Learns, from this union of the rising Whole, 3.EOM4.337.161.
Or *Flavia's* self in glue (her rising task) 3.Ep2.25A.52.
Or Sappho's self in glue (her rising task) 3.Ep2.25B.52.

RISING (CONTINUED)

Whose rising Forests, not for pride or show, 3.Ep4.187.155.
Shall hail the rising, close the parting day. 4.HOde1.30.153.
Salute the rising, close the parting day. 4.HOde1.30B.153.
Let rising Granaries and Temples here, 4.2HE2.258.183.
Sure fate of all, beneath whose rising ray 4.2HE1.19.195.
Some rising Genius sins up to my Song. 4.EpS2.9.313.
You hurt a man that's rising in the Trade. 4.EpS2.35.314.
And pin'd, unconscious of his rising fate; 5.DunA1.110.76.
Then stretch thy sight o'er all her rising reign, 5.DunA3.57.155.
Then stretch thy sight o'er all her rising reign, 5.DunB3.65.323.
The rising game, and chac'd from flow'r to flow'r. 5.DunB4.426.383.
Yet in the rising blossom promise more. 6.14iv.20.47.
Or, of the Rising or *Meridian* Sun) 6.26i.9.79.
And *Athens* rising near the pole! 6.51i.22.152.
An *Athens* rising near the pole! 6.51i.22A.152.
Rome's pompous glories rising to our thought! 6.52.24.156.
Here, rising bold, the Patriot's honest face; 6.71.57.204.
That darts severe upon a rising Lye, 6.73.6.209.
Th' Assembly seated, rising o'er the rest, Il.1.77.90.
And calm the rising Tempest of his Soul. Il.1.258.99.
Then rising in his Wrath, the Monarch storm'd; Il.1.502.112.
Thus *Vulcan* spoke; and rising with a Bound, Il.1.752.123.
He spoke, and sate; when *Nestor* rising said, Il.2.99.131.
Who rising, high th' Imperial Sceptre rais'd: Il.2.341.143.
And fair *Lilæa* views the rising Flood. Il.2.627.157.
A rising Mount the Work of human Hands, Il.2.983.170.
Where *Erythinus'* rising Clifts are seen, Il.2.1036.172.
The Nations hear, with rising Hopes possest, Il.3.153.198.
His beating Bosom claim'd the rising Fight. Il.4.259.233.
Small at her Birth, but rising ev'ry Hour, Il.4.503.245.
Beneath the rising or the setting Sun. Il.5.331.282.
He spoke, and rising hurl'd his forceful Dart, Il.5.351.283.
The grey Dust, rising with collected Winds, Il.5.615.297.
But *Boreas* rising fresh, with gentle Breath, Il.5.858.307.
He said, and rising, high above the Field Il.7.295.378.
Antenor rising, thus demands their Ear: Il.7.418.385.
At length *Tydides* rose, and rising spoke. Il.7.475.388.
Their rising Bulwarks on the Sea-beat Coast? Il.7.533.391.
And ardent Warriors wait the rising Morn. Il.8.708.429.
And slowly rising, thus the Council mov'd. Il.9.126.438.
The Tent is brightned with the rising Blaze: Il.9.278.447.
Then rising all, with Goblets in their Hands, Il.9.788.472.
The *Trojan* Lines possess'd the rising Ground. Il.11.74.38.
Old *Nestor* rising then, the Hero led Il.11.790.71.
And waits the rising of the fatal Blaze. Il.11.811.72.
Shoots up, and all the rising Host appears. Il.12.536.101.
But *Neptune,* rising from the Seas profound, Il.13.67.108.
New rising Spirits all my Force alarm, Il.13.109.110.
New rising Spirits all the Man alarm, Il.13.109A.110.
Meanwhile with rising Rage the Battel glows, Il.13.225.116.
The rising Combate sounds along the Shore. Il.13.423.126.
While *Neptune* rising from his azure Main, Il.13.442.126.
To Vengeance rising with a sudden Spring, Il.13.487.130.
Then rising in his Rage, he burns to fight: Il.13.592.134.
With rising Wrath, and tumbled Gods on Gods; Il.14.290.176.
And clust'ring *Lotos* swell'd the rising Bed, Il.14.398.182.
Sullen he sate, and curb'd the rising Groan. Il.15.161.202.
What Bulwarks rising between you and Fate? Il.15.895.232.
Now save the Ships, the rising Fires restrain, Il.16.106.240.
Divine *Achilles* view'd the rising Flames, Il.16.154.243.
And round him wide the rising Structure grows. Il.16.259.249.
Their rising Rage *Patroclus'* Breath inspires, Il.16.322.255.
And breath'd a Spirit in his rising Heart. Il.16.650.269.
But where the rising Whirlwind clouds the Plains, Il.16.935.279.
Ourself with rising Spirits swell your Heart. Il.17.517.308.
Less fierce the Winds with rising Flames conspire, Il.17.825.320.
They brought, and plac'd it o'er the rising Flame: Il.18.406.340.
And rising solemn, each his Sentence spoke. Il.18.588.351.
In Arms the glitt'ring Squadron rising round Il.18.611.352.
Behind, the rising Earth in Ridges roll'd; Il.18.635.354.
Achilles (rising in the midst) begun. Il.19.56.374.
When thus, not rising from his lofty Throne, Il.19.79.375.
Let rising Spirits flow from sprightly Juice, Il.19.234.382.
There stuck the Lance. Then rising e'er he threw, Il.20.321.407.
His Heart high-bounding in his rising Breast: Il.20.492.415.
Then rising in his Rage above the Shores, Il.21.257.431.
Broad Elm, and Cypress rising in a Spire; Il.21.410.437.
And the near Hero rising on his Sight! Il.21.616.448.
Like *Jove's* own Lightning, or the rising Sun. Il.22.178.461.
Heap with a rising Pyramid the Plain. Il.23.201.497.
Of rising Earth, Memorial of the Dead. Il.23.320.502.
The Hero, rising, thus addrest the Train. Il.23.340.503.
High on a rising Ground, above the Ring, Il.23.533.511.
He saw; and rising, to the *Greeks* begun. Il.23.540.511.
Achilles rising, thus: Let *Greece* excite Il.23.759.520.
Achilles rising then bespoke the Train: Il.23.878.524.
(*Minerva* rising, gave the Mourner place) Il.24.132.540.
Nor *Jove's* Command, should check the rising Rage. Il.24.735.568.
He said, and rising, chose the Victim Ewe Il.24.786.569.
And hasty, snatches from the rising Blaze. Il.24.791.570.
Watch'd from the rising to the setting Sun) Il.24.1010.577.
The rising and descending Sun surveys) Od.1.32.31.
Indulge my rising grief, whilst these (my friend) Od.1.203.42.
We, with the rising morn our ships unmoor'd, Od.3.185.95.
Then slowly rising, o'er the sandy space Od.3.496.111.
The cave was brighten'd with a rising blaze: Od.5.75.176.
'Till dimm'd with rising grief, they stream'd again. Od.5.108.177.
'Till dimm'd with rising grief, they stream'd again. Od.5.204.181.
And form a Raft, and build the rising ship, Od.5.211.181.
And rising night her friendly shade extends. Od.5.290.185.
The rising forests, and the tufted trees. Od.5.513.197.
Whose shady horrors on a rising brow Od.5.614.201.
The rising fire supplies with busy care, Od.7.8.233.
In sep'rate Islands crown'd with rising spires; Od.7.58.236.
But with the rising day, assembled here, Od.7.250.248.

RISING (CONTINUED)

Perhaps from realms that view the rising day, Od.8.29.263.
And drifts of rising dust involve the sky: Od.8.128.269.
Those to *Aurora* and the rising sun.) Od.9.26.303.
Thick, as the budding leaves or rising flow'rs Od.9.55.304.
And the sea whitens with the rising gale. Od.9.160.312.
And from their mountains rising smokes appear. Od.9.194.313.
We stand discover'd by the rising fires; Od.9.297.318.
My self above them from a rising ground Od.9.455.324.
And rising mountains gain upon our sight. Od.10.33.341.
Cool'd ev'ry breast, and damp'd the rising joy. Od.10.156.347.
O'er the fair web the rising figures shine, Od.10.256.355.
The Goddess rising, asks her guests to stay, Od.10.264.355.
This with one voice declar'd, the rising train Od.10.527.368.
'Till rising up, *Aretè* silence broke, Od.11.416.404.
And the sky reddens with the rising day. Od.11.469.407.
Lest *Gorgon* rising from th' infernal lakes, Od.11.785.425.
Here *Phœbus* rising in th' etherial way, Od.12.5.430.
A rising tomb, the silent dead to grace, Od.12.19.430.
The rising tomb a lofty column bore, Od.12.21.430.
When rising sad and slow, with pensive look, Od.12.188.441.
And toss with rising storms the wat'ry way, Od.12.344.448.
'Till great *Alcinous* rising own'd the sign. Od.13.195.15.
Whose hills are brighten'd by the rising sun, Od.13.286.19.
And rising springs eternal verdure yield. Od.13.298.20.
The trav'ler rising from the banquet gay, Od.15.89.73.
Swift as the word he forms the rising blaze, Od.15.112.74.
Bear it my son! repress thy rising rage: Od.16.295.119.
O friends! he cry'd elate with rising joy, Od.16.370.124.
And rising instant to the Palace mov'd. Od.16.423.127.
Check'd half his might: yet rising to the stroke, Od.18.112.172.
Up-rising early with the purple morn, Od.19.365.212.
Of human race now rising from repose, Od.20.122.239.
But shook his head, and rising wrath restrain'd. Od.20.232.244.
He spoke; then rising, his broad sword unbound, Od.21.123.264.
And unperceiv'd, enjoys the rising fight. Od.22.263.299.
But *Pallas* backward held the rising day, Od.23.260.335.
When slowly-rising, *Halitherses* spoke: Od.24.517.372.

RISK

Who risk the most, that take wrong means, or right? 3.EOM4.86.136.
Why risk the world's great empire for a Punk? 3.Ep1.83.21.
To risk more bravely thy now forfeit Life? Il.10.519.26.

RISQ'D

How sometimes life is risq'd, and always ease: 3.EOM4.274.154.

RISQU'D

Down his own throat he risqu'd the Grecian gold; 5.DunB4.382.380.

RISQUES

Survey the Pangs they bear, the Risques they run, 4.HAdv.51.79.

RITE

Twelve Days the Pow'rs indulge the Genial Rite, Il.1.558.115.
Their Pray'rs perform'd, the Chiefs the Rite pursue, Il.2.502.150.
Or dy'd at least before thy Nuptial Rite! Il.3.58.192.
Two Lambs, devoted by your Country's Rite, Il.3.141.197.
The *Phrygian* Monarch to the Peaceful Rite; Il.3.162.198.
The Rite perform'd, the Chiefs their Thirst allay, Il.9.231.444.
Each Portion parts, and orders ev'ry Rite. Il.9.286.448.
At ev'ry Rite his Share should be increas'd, Il.10.257.13.
And solemn Dance, and *Hymenæal* Rite; Il.18.570.350.
And solemn swear, (observant of the Rite) Il.19.174.378.
Go then ye Chiefs! indulge the genial Rite; Il.19.287.384.
Thus she; and having paid the rite divine, Od.3.76.90.
But call'd untimely (not the sacred rite Od.3.169.94.
Propose departure from the finish'd rite, Od.3.441.108.
Nor was *Minerva* absent from the rite, Od.3.552.114.
The ribs and limbs, observant of the rite: Od.3.583.116.
His house affords the hospitable rite, Od.3.621.118.
"In evil hour the nuptial rite intends, Od.4.1019.165.
Hermes the hospitable rite partook, Od.5.119.178.
Now pleas'd and satiate from the social rite Od.7.248.248.
We sate indulging in the genial rite: Od.9.189.313.
While thoughtless we, indulge the genial rite, Od.9.649.333.
They sate indulging in the genial rite. Od.10.209.350.
But from th' infernal rite thine eye withdraw, Od.10.630.374.
They seize, they kill!—but for the rite divine, Od.12.419.451.
Pious! to guard the hospitable rite, Od.14.313.50.
Observant of the Gods, begins the rite; Od.14.468.58.
They press the *Hymenæan* rite abhorr'd. Od.19.155.200.
To her mean hand assign the friendly rite. Od.19.402.214.
The friendly rite of purity declin'd; Od.19.439.216.
Deaf to Heav'n's voice, the social rite transgrest; Od.21.31.260.
That rite compleat, up-rose the thoughtful man, Od.21.290.274.

RITES

But to your *Isis* all my Rites transfer, 1.TrSt.373.425.
Whose impious Rites disgrace thy mighty Name, 1.TrSt.387.426.
We to thy Name our Annual Rites will pay, 1.TrSt.592.435.
The King once more the solemn Rites requires, 1.TrSt.603.435.
And bad his Daughters at the Rites appear. 1.TrSt.622.436.
Which *Danaus* us'd in sacred Rites of old, 1.TrSt.635.436.
And bad his Daughters to the Rites repair. 1.TrSt.622A.436.
Those Rites discharg'd, his sacred Corps bequeath 1.TrES.330A.461.
These unavailing Rites he may receive, 1.TrES.334.462.
These unvailing Rites he may receive, 1.TrES.334A.462.
To you shall Rites Divine be ever paid, 1.TrUl.246.474.
That ere the Rites are o'er, you may repent! 2.ChJM.281.27.
Trembling, begins the sacred Rites of Pride. 2.RL1.128.155.
Thy fate unpity'd, and thy rites unpaid? 2.Elegy.48.366.
And the wide *East* ador'd with rites divine! 6.20.12.66.
Give all his rites, and all his obsequies! 6.20.38.67.
These little rites, a Stone, a Verse, receive, 6.109.19.314.
These little rites, a Stone and Verse, receive, 6.109.19A.314.

RITES (CONTINUED)
The Army thus in sacred Rites engag'd, ... Il.1.418.107.
The Rites now finish'd, rev'rend *Priam* rose, ... Il.3.378.211.
Where twenty Days in Genial Rites he pass'd. ...... Il.6.270.340.
There first to *Jove* our solemn Rites were paid; ...... Il.11.864.74.
Social we sit, and share the genial Rites. ...... Il.11.911.76.
The violated Rites, the ravish'd Dame, ... Il.13.785.142.
Those Rites discharg'd, his sacred Corpse bequeath ...... Il.16.817.274.
The genial Rites, and hospitable Fare; ...... Il.18.476.344.
That Rites divine should ratify the Band, ... Il.19.317.385.
These his cold Rites, and this his wat'ry Tomb. ...... Il.21.377.436.
Far from our pious Rites, those dear Remains ...... Il.22.124.458.
Peaceful He sleeps, with all our Rites adorn'd, ... Il.22.421.472.
The common Rites of Sepulture bestow, ... Il.22.429.473.
Some Rites remain, to glut our Rage of Grief. ...... Il.23.14.486.
Some Ease at least those pious Rites may give, ... Il.23.57.489.
And bid the Forests fall: (Such Rites are paid ...... Il.23.63.489.
Let my pale Corse the Rites of Burial know, ... Il.23.87.490.
But *Agamemnon,* as the Rites demand, ... Il.23.134.493.
Smear'd with the bloody Rites, he stands on high, ... Il.23.218.498.
The Various Goddess to partake the Rites. ...... Il.23.251.499.
With sable Wine; then, (as the Rites direct). ...... Il.23.296.501.
Now, the same Hero's Funeral Rites to grace, ... Il.23.874.524.
Remains unask'd; what Time the Rites require ...... Il.24.825.571.
Perform, ye *Trojans!* what the Rites require, ... Il.24.985.576.
(Strong Guards and Spies, till all the Rites were done, ... Il.24.1009.577.
With frequent rites, and pure, avow'd thy pow'r, ... Od.1.81.35.
His herds and flocks in feastful rites devour. ...... Od.1.117.37.
And the chaste Queen connubial rites require; ...... Od.1.359.49.
To the pale Shade funereal rites ordain, ... Od.1.379.51.
These rites of *Neptune,* monarch of the deep, ... Od.3.56.89.
The sacred rites and hecatombs to pay, ... Od.3.176.94.
And now, the rites discharg'd, our course we keep ...... Od.3.364.104.
And hospitable rites adorn the dome. ...... Od.3.454.109.
Who grac'd our rites, a more than mortal guest. ...... Od.3.533.113.
While these officious tend the rites divine, ... Od.3.592.116.
To those dear hospitable rites a foe, ... Od.4.41.122.
Let each deplore his dead: the rites of woe ...... Od.4.269.132.
Then from the rites of purity repair, ... Od.4.299.133.
These rites to piety and grief discharg'd, ... Od.4.795.156.
Yet as we fled, our fellows rites we pay'd, ... Od.9.73.305.
And try what social rites a savage lends: ...... Od.9.270.318.
Dire rites alas! and fatal to my friends! ...... Od.9.271.318.
I follow sadly to the magic rites. ...... Od.10.374.362.
To share thy feast-rites, or ascend thy bed; ...... Od.10.404.364.
Four faithful handmaids the soft rites prepare; ...... Od.10.414.364.
Thus solemn rites and holy vows we paid ...... Od.11.43.381.
To whom with tears: These rites, oh mournful shade, ... Od.11.98.385.
In sacred groves celestial rites he pays, ... Od.11.223.392.
The rites, more sacred made by heav'nly song: ...... Od.13.32.2.
To you shall rites divine be ever paid, ... Od.13.413.26.
The Sire with hospitable rites receiv'd, ... Od.14.352.51.
If, after social rites and gifts bestow'd, ... Od.14.445.57.
Nor found the hospitable rites unpay'd. ...... Od.15.213.78.
Well pleas'd the hospitable rites to pay. ...... Od.15.586.98.
Witness the genial rites, and witness all ...... Od.17.178.140.
From nuptial rites they now no more recede, ... Od.19.178.200.
The lunar feast-rites to the God of day. ...... Od.20.195.242.
In due libations, and in rites divine, ... Od.21.279.273.
To the chaste love-rites of the nuptial bed. ...... Od.23.318.339.
"The rites have waited long." The chief commands ...... Od.24.456.370.

RITUAL
Due ritual honours to the Gods I pay: ...... Od.4.588.147.
With ritual hecatombs the Gods adore: ...... Od.4.792.156.
Partook the sacred feast, and ritual honours paid. ...... Od.20.346.249.

RIVAL
But wou'd you sing, and rival *Orpheus'* Strain, ... 1.PSu.81.78.
Nymphs that in Verse no more cou'd rival me, ... 1.TrSP.29.394.
As when two Winds with Rival Force contend, ... 1.TrSt.265.421.
Than issuing forth, the Rival of his Beams ...... 2.RL2.3.159.
Alone can rival, can succeed to thee. ...... 2.ElAb.206.336.
Flam'd forth this rival to, its Sire, the Sun, ... 3.Ep3.12.84.
To him each Rival shall submit, ... 4.HOde1.17.151.
And rival, Curtius! of thy fame and zeal, ... 5.DunA1.195.86.
Stood dauntless Curl, "Behold that rival here! ...... 5.DunA2.54.104.
There rival flames with equal glory rise, ... 5.DunA3.72.156.
Stood dauntless Curl; "Behold that rival here! ...... 5.DunB2.58.298.
There rival flames with equal glory rise, ... 5.DunB3.80.324.
When their bright rival is not there. ...... 6.4iv.15.11.
Ev'n Rival Wits did *Voiture's* Death deplore, ... 6.19.15.62.
Ev'n Rival Wits did *Voiture's* Fate deplore, ... 6.19.15A.62.
Who when two Wits on rival themes contest, ... 6.49iii.23.143.
Who, if two Wits on rival Themes contest, ... 6.98.59.285.
C[IBBE]R and DUCK contend in rival lays: ...... 6.116vi.2.327.
Thou stood'st a Rival of Imperial Pow'r; ...... Il.1.248.98.
What King can bear a Rival in his Sway? ...... Il.1.383.106.
And who his Rival can in Arms subdue, ... Il.3.103.194.
And who his Rival shall in Arms subdue, ... Il.3.324.208.
Each to his Rival yields the Mark unknown, ... Il.7.223.375.
And urge thy Soul to rival Acts with mine: ...... Il.13.308.119.
Fir'd at his Word, the Rival Racers rise. ...... Il.23.355.504.
Tho' thy fierce Rival drove the matchless Steed ...... Il.23.419.506.
But thus upbraids his Rival as he flies; ...... Il.23.519.510.
Amid the Ring each nervous Rival stands, ... Il.23.822.522.
Whose Force with rival Forces to oppose, ... Il.23.993.529.
With rival art, and ardor in their mien, ... Od.1.142.39.
Join to that royal youth's, your rival name, ... Od.1.393.51.
With ardent eyes the rival train they threat, ... Od.2.177.70.
Diverse their steps: The rival rout ascend ...... Od.2.292.75.
Greece, and the rival train thy voice withstand. ...... Od.2.304.76.
While to the rival train the Prince returns, ... Od.2.428.81.
To force the Goddess, and to rival *Jove.* ...... Od.11.718.421.
Hither, intent the rival rout to slay ...... Od.16.256.117.
He said: The rival train his voice approv'd, ... Od.16.422.127.

RIVAL (CONTINUED)
Sudden before the rival pow'rs she stands: ...... Od.16.431.128.
By rival nations courted for their songs; ...... Od.17.467.156.
What bounty gives, without a rival share, ... Od.18.22.168.
In rival crouds contest the glorious prize, ... Od.18.289.180.
In rival tasks beneath the burning rage ...... Od.18.411.188.
"Rebate your loves, each rival suit suspend, ... Od.19.164.200.
For me the rival archers shall contend. ...... Od.19.669.228.
The rival peers the ringlets and the bow. ...... Od.21.82.263.
Shall I, a Queen, by rival chiefs ador'd, ... Od.21.339.276.
With rival loves pursu'd his royal Dame; ...... Od.24.147.355.
Yet a short space, your rival suit suspend, ... Od.24.156.355.

RIVAL'D
Rival'd the hyacinth in vernal bloom. ...... Od.4.182.128.

RIVAL'S
Or with a *Rival's,* or an *Eunuch's* spite. ...... 1.EOC.31.242.
Fall he that must beneath his Rival's Arms, ... Il.3.139.197.
In Thirst of Vengeance, at his Rival's Heart, ... Il.3.466.214.
Go now, once more thy Rival's Rage excite, ... Il.3.539.217.
Or judge me envious of a Rival's Fame. ...... Il.23.656.515.
And stain his Rival's Mail with issuing Gore; ...... Il.23.950.527.

RIVALS
Those hate as *Rivals* all that write; and others ...... 1.EOC.30A.242.
Some hate as *Rivals* all that write; and others ...... 1.EOC.30B.242.
Say, wretched Rivals! what provokes your Rage? ...... 1.TrSt.210.419.
Fear not thy Rivals, tho' for Swiftness known, ... Il.23.381.505.
Compare those Rivals Judgment, and thy own: ...... Il.23.382.505.
She breaks his Rivals Chariot from the Yoke; ...... Il.23.470.509.
When youthful Rivals their full Force extend, ... Il.23.512.510.
Your Rivals, destitute of youthful Force, ... Il.23.525.510.
The Rivals, late so distant on the Green. ...... Il.23.604.513.
The wondring Rivals gaze with cares oppress, ... Od.2.183.71.
Hear all! but chiefly you, oh Rivals! hear. ...... Od.2.190.71.
Yet now the Rivals are my smallest care: ...... Od.2.268.74.
That crowds of rivals for thy mother's charms ...... Od.3.260.98.
Brothers in peace, not rivals in command, ... Od.4.243.130.
Ye Peers and rivals in this noble love! ...... Od.17.556.159.
And *Pallas* now, to raise the rivals fires, ... Od.21.1.257.
Ye peers and rivals in the royal love! ...... Od.21.293.274.

RIVALS'
Go, and succeed! the rivals' aims despise; ...... Od.2.319.76.

RIVELL'D
Shrink his thin Essence like a rivell'd Flower. ...... 2.RL2.132.168.

RIVEN
The riven Armour sends a jarring Sound: ...... Il.13.553.132.
And o'er him high the riven Targe extends, ... Il.20.328.407.

RIVER
O early lost! what Tears the River shed ...... 1.W-F.273.174.
Unmix'd, to his *Sicilian* River glides. ...... 1.TrSt.385.426.
Or fish deny'd, (the River yet un-thaw'd) ...... 4.HS2.14.55.
Or kept from fish, (the River yet un-thaw'd) ...... 4.HS2.14A.55.
A River at my garden's end, ... 4.HS6.4.251.
Like twenty River-Gods with all their Urns. ...... 6.33.6.99.
The River swept him to the briny Main: ...... Il.2.1065.172.
Where some swoln River disembogues his Waves, ... Il.17.311.299.
The River trembles to his utmost Shore, ... Il.17.314.300.
Thus when a River swell'd with sudden Rains ...... Il.17.839.321.
The River here divides the flying Train. ...... Il.21.3.420.
The River here divides the scatt'ring Train. ...... Il.21.3A.420.
Repeated Wounds the red'ning River dy'd, ... Il.21.26.422.
Sprung from a River didst thou boast thy Line, ... Il.21.203.429.
The River thus; and thus the Chief replies. ...... Il.21.240.430.
From all his Deep the bellowing River roars, ... Il.21.258.431.
From all his Deeps the bellowing River roars, ... Il.21.258A.431.
Not a whole River stops the Hero's Course, ... Il.21.354.435.
At length the River rear'd his languid Head, ... Il.21.416.437.
The burning River sends his earnest Pray'r. ...... Il.21.431.438.
And hail'd the river, and its God addrest. ...... Od.5.567.199.
I drew, and casting on the river side ...... Od.10.191.349.

RIVER-GODS
Like twenty River-Gods with all their Urns. ...... 6.33.6.99.

RIVER'S
Along the River's level Meads they stand, ... Il.2.550.153.
A river's mouth, impervious to the wind, ... Od.7.365.254.
First to the field and river's bank to lead, ... Od.9.528.328.

RIVERS
Nor Rivers winding thro' the Vales below, ... 1.PWi.3.88.
As gardens fresh, where running rivers stray, ... 1.TrPA.62.368.
But, ah! like rivers, swift to glide away; ...... 1.TrPA.63.368.
Those from whose Urns the rowling Rivers flow, ... 1.TrSt.288.422.
As to the Sea returning Rivers roll, ... 2.TemF.430.284.
And roll obedient Rivers thro' the Land; ...... 3.Ep4.202.156.
The forests dance, the rivers upward rise, ... 5.DunA3.241.177.
The forests dance, the rivers upward rise, ... 5.DunB3.245.332.
In their old Bounds the Rivers roll again, ... Il.12.35.83.
From their deep Beds he bids the Rivers rise, ... Il.16.470.261.
What Rivers can, *Scamander* might have shown; ...... Il.21.209.430.
The Seas, the Rivers, and the Springs below, ... Il.21.214.430.
And hissing Rivers to their bottoms burn. ...... Il.21.393.436.

RIVETS
The panting *Trojan* rivets to the Ground. ...... Il.20.466.413.

ROAB
See ROBE.
Roab thee in heav'nly vests, and round thee weep. ...... Od.24.76.351.

ROAB'D
And white-roab'd Innocence from Heav'n descend. ... 1.Mes.20.114.

ROAD
Suffice that Reason keep to Nature's road, ... 3.EOM2.115.69.
Yes, Nature's road must ever be prefer'd; ... 3.EOM2.161.74.
Slave to no sect, who takes no private road, ... 3.EOM4.331.160.
We nobly take the high Priori Road, ... 5.DunB4.471.386.
For that Road leads directly to the Heart. ... 6.33.10.99.
For this Road leads directly to the Heart. ... 6.33.10A.99.
Then swiftly sailing, cut the liquid Road. ... Il.1.409.107.
Ulysses follow'd thro' the watry Road, ... Il.2.765.162.
Fast by the Road, his ever-open Door ... Il.6.19.325.
A sudden Road! a long and ample way. ... Il.15.409.213.
As when two Mules, along the rugged Road, ... Il.17.832.321.
Vain hope! to shun him by the self-same Road ... Il.21.653.449.
(A wider Compass) smoak along the Road. ... Il.22.194.463.
With proper Instruments they take the Road, ... Il.23.138.493.
And the slow Mules the same rough Road return. ... Il.23.151.495.
Haste then; yon' narrow Road before our Sight ... Il.23.493.510.
Fast by the Road a Precipice was worn: ... Il.23.500.510.
(The safer road) beside the *Psyrian* isle; ... Od.3.206.95.
Guides of thy road, companions of thy way. ... Od.3.418.107.
They went, and kept the wheel's smooth-beaten road ... Od.10.117.346.
Thy fated road (the magic Pow'r reply'd) ... Od.10.598.372.
Rise, son of *Nestor!* for the road prepare, ... Od.15.55.72.
By road frequented, or by fountain-side. ... Od.15.480.93.
Thus spoke the dame, and homeward took the road. ... Od.15.491.94.
Yon bird that dexter cuts th' aerial road, ... Od.15.573.98.
When first our vessel anchor'd in your road. ... Od.17.185.140.
Along the road conversing side by side, ... Od.17.204.141.
Now pass'd the rugged road, they journey down ... Od.17.230.143.
Nor stirr'd an inch, contemptuous, from the road: ... Od.17.275.145.

ROADS
Where the three Roads the *Phocian* Fields divide: ... 1.TrSt.92.414.

ROAM
Amid her Kindred Stars familiar roam, ... 1.W-F.255.172.
Amidst her Kindred Stars familiar roam, ... 1.W-F.255A.172.
Led by the Sound I roam from Shade to Shade, ... 1.W-F.269.173.
His flocks at random round the forest roam: ... 1.TrPA.20.366.
Range in the woods, and in the vallies roam: ... 1.TrPA.79.368.
Treated, caress'd, where-e'er she's pleas'd to roam— ... 2.ChWB.76.60.
Or lets his Wife abroad with Pilgrims roam, ... 2.ChWB.349.74.
In search of Mischief still on Earth to roam. ... 2.RL1.64.150.
Not Man alone, but all that roam the wood, ... 3.EOM3.119.104.
For foreign glory, foreign joy, they roam; ... 3.Ep2.223.68.
Fool! 'tis in vain from Wit to Wit to roam; ... 6.49ii.15.140.
To court ambitious men may roam, ... 6.61.26.181.
"From Place to Place o'er *Brobdingnag* I'll roam, ... 6.96ii.37.272.
To roam the silent Fields in dead of Night? ... Il.10.456.24.
From Room to Room his pensive Daughters roam; ... Il.24.203.545.
Why roam thy Mules and Steeds the Plains along, ... Il.24.449.555.
Thro' *Troy's* wide Streets abandon'd shall I roam, ... Il.24.979.576.
For this, the god constrains the *Greek* to roam, ... Od.1.96.36.
Whilst heaping unwish'd wealth, I distant roam; ... Od.4.113.125.
Roam the wild Isle in search of rural cates, ... Od.4.498.144.
Shalt yet enjoy, but still art doom'd to roam. ... Od.4.642.149.
To roam the howling desart of the main: ... Od.4.748.153.
Yet ev'ry day, while absent thus I roam, ... Od.5.281.185.
Where mountain wolves and bridled lions roam, ... Od.10.242.352.
No longer now from shore to shore to roam, ... Od.13.7.2.
I seiz'd the proffer (ever fond to roam) ... Od.14.322.50.
Whose hap it was to this our roof to roam, ... Od.14.419.56.
On fond pursuits neglectful while you roam, ... Od.15.15.70.
The blood-stain'd exile, ever doom'd to roam. ... Od.15.301.83.
Patient to roam the street, by hunger led, ... Od.15.330.85.
So pays the wretch, whom fact constrains to roam, ... Od.19.192.201.
Thus lives your Lord; nor longer doom'd to roam: ... Od.19.345.211.
Like thee, in rags obscene decreed to roam! ... Od.20.262.246.

ROAM'ST
Ah whither roam'st thou? much-enduring man! ... Od.10.334.360.

ROAMING
The roaming Lyon meets a bristly Boar, ... Il.16.994.281.

ROAMS
Whene'er *Ulysses* roams the realm of Night, ... Od.1.503.56.
How twice ten years from shore to shore he roams; ... Od.2.205.71.
Far from his country roams my hapless Lord! ... Od.14.50.38.

ROAR
The hollow Winds thro' naked Temples roar; ... 1.W-F.68.156.
Then bow'd and spoke; the Winds forget to roar, ... 1.W-F.353.184.
There *Faction* roar, *Rebellion* bite her Chain, ... 1.W-F.421.193.
The *hoarse, rough Verse* shou'd like the *Torrent* roar. ... 1.EOC.369.282.
He cry'd, and Ætna trembled with the roar! ... 1.TrPA.139.371.
Heav'n trembles, roar the Mountains, thunders all the Ground. .. 1.TrES.66A.452.
Leap the resounding Bars, the flying Hinges roar. ... 1.TrES.198.456.
Like broken Thunders that at distance roar, ... 2.TemF.23.255.
Clouds interpose, waves roar, and winds arise. ... 2.ElAb.246.339.
"A hundred oxen at your levee roar." ... 3.Ep3.46.89.
Then full against his Cornish lands they roar, ... 3.Ep3.355.122.
Or call the winds thro' long Arcades to roar, ... 3.Ep4.35.140.
Shall call the winds thro' long Arcades to roar, ... 3.Ep4.35A.140.
No barking Dog, no Household in a Roar; ... 4.HAdv.168.89.
And others roar aloud, "Subscribe, subscribe." ... 4.Arbu.114.103.
How did they fume, and stamp, and roar, and chafe? ... 4.Arbu.191.109.
Not Winds that round our ruin'd Abbeys roar, ... 4.JD2A.67.138.
How shall I rhime in this eternal Roar? ... 4.2HE2.114.173.
Ah luckless Poet! stretch thy lungs and roar, ... 4.2HE1.324.223.
"God save King Tibbald!" Grubstreet alleys roar. ... 5.DunA1.256.94.
And *Grubstreet* garrets roar, God save the king. ... 5.DunA1.256A.94.
Teach thou the warb'ling Polypheme to roar, ... 5.DunB3.305.334.

ROAR (CONTINUED)
How would they fume, and stamp, and roar, and chafe! ... 6.98.41.284.
Shall hear, and dread my manly Roar. ... 6.135.44.367.
A hundred Bounces manly Roar. ... 6.135.44A.367.
And roar in Numbers worthy *Bounce*. ... 6.135.94.370.
From East and South when Winds begin to roar, ... Il.2.176.137.
That dash'd on broken Rocks tumultuous roar, ... Il.2.472.149.
Roar thro' a thousand Chanels to the Main; ... Il.4.519.246.
Loud, as the Roar encountring Armies yield, ... Il.5.1054.316.
Heaps Waves on Waves, and bids th' *Ægean* roar; ... Il.9.8.431.
Thro' the still Night they march, and hear the roar ... Il.9.237.444.
Or bids the brazen Throat of War to roar; ... Il.10.8.2.
The Care of him who bids the Thunder roar, ... Il.10.652.30.
Heav'n trembles, roar the Mountains, thunders all the Ground. .Il.12.410.96.
Leap the resounding Bars, the flying Hinges roar. ... Il.12.552.101.
Hark! the Gates burst, the brazen Barriers roar! ... Il.13.166.112.
Th' afflicted Deeps, tumultuous, mix and roar; ... Il.13.1003.152.
When lo! the Deeps arise, the Tempests roar, ... Il.14.287.176.
That roar thro' Hell, and bind th' invoking Gods: ... Il.14.306.177.
Roar thro' the Woods, and make whole Forests fall; ... Il.14.460.186.
The Horses thunder, Earth and Ocean roar! ... Il.15.405.212.
So pent by Hills, the wild Winds roar aloud ... Il.16.923.279.
When o'er the slaughter'd Bull they hear him roar, ... Il.17.71.290.
And distant Rocks rebellow to the Roar. ... Il.17.315.300.
Call then thy subject Streams, and bid them roar, ... Il.21.362.435.
Where dash'd on Rocks the broken Billows roar, ... Il.23.71.489.
Forth burst the stormy Band with thundring Roar, ... Il.23.264.500.
The ruffled Seas beneath their Passage roar. ... Il.23.287.501.
As a large Fish, when Winds and Waters roar, ... Il.23.802.521.
The forests murmur, and the surges roar, ... Od.1.64.33.
With ceaseless roar the foaming deep surrounds. ... Od.1.258.45.
The sable billows foam and roar below. ... Od.2.461.83.
Fronts the deep roar of disemboguing *Nile:* ... Od.4.480.143.
Round the descending nymph the waves redounding roar. ... Od.4.578.147.
The rock rush'd sea-ward, with impetuous roar ... Od.4.681.151.
Down rush'd the night. East, west, together roar, ... Od.5.379.190.
Amidst the rocks he hears a hollow roar ... Od.5.516.197.
Roar the wild waves; beneath, is sea profound! ... Od.5.529.198.
Tho' mountains rise between, and oceans roar. ... Od.6.376.230.
The wild winds whistle, and the billows roar; ... Od.7.357.254.
All haste assembled, at his well-known roar, ... Od.9.477.325.
Th' astonisht Savage with a roar replies: ... Od.9.593.330.
It fell, and brush'd the stern: The billows roar, ... Od.9.633.332.
A ghastly band of Giants hear the roar, ... Od.10.137.347.
In swine to grovel, or in lions roar, ... Od.10.512.368.
Who ne'er knew salt, or heard the billows roar, ... Od.11.153.389.
There sullen Lions sternly seem to roar, ... Od.11.753.423.
Hideous her voice, and with less terrors roar ... Od.12.109.436.
When seas retreating roar within her caves, ... Od.12.134.438.
The mounting billows roar: the furious blast ... Od.12.479.455.
The face of things; the winds began to roar; ... Od.14.511.62.
And when the north had ceas'd the stormy roar, ... Od.19.232.204.
Who ne'er knew salt, or heard the billows roar, ... Od.23.286.337.

ROAR'D
Roar'd out for rage, and hurried o'er the plain: ... 1.TrPA.133.371.
He cry'd, he roar'd, he storm'd, he tore his Hair; ... 2.ChJM.756.51.
He cry'd, he roar'd, he rag'd, he tore his Hair: ... 2.ChJM.756A.51.
Roar'd for the Handkerchief that caus'd his Pain. ... 2.RL5.106.208.
Great *D[enni]s* roar'd, like Ox at Slaughter. ... 6.10.62.26.
Like him his Barons rag'd and roar'd, ... 6.79.11.218.
Full thirteen Moons imprison'd roar'd in vain; ... Il.5.477.290.
Involv'd the Mount; the Thunder roar'd aloud; ... Il.17.671.314.
He roar'd: in vain the Dogs, the Men withstood, ... Il.18.673.356.
Impious he roar'd defiance to the Gods: ... Od.4.674.151.
Roar'd the dead limbs; the burning entrails groan'd. ... Od.12.466.453.
So roar'd the lock when it releas'd the spring. ... Od.21.52.261.
He roar'd, and torments gave his soul to hell— ... Od.22.514.314.

ROARING
At once the rushing Winds with roaring Sound ... 1.TrSt.488.430.
The roaring Winds tempestuous Rage restrain; ... 1.TrUl.28.466.
The Mole projected break the roaring Main; ... 3.Ep4.200.156.
Thames wafts it thence to Rufus' roaring hall, ... 5.DunA2.253.130.
Thames wafts it thence to Rufus' roaring hall, ... 5.DunB2.265.308.
Thro' roaring Seas the wond'ring Warriors bear; ... Il.2.744.161.
The Lion's roaring thro' the mid-night Shade; ... Il.11.228.45.
Caresus roaring down the stony Hills, ... Il.12.18.82.
The roaring Main, at her great Master's Call, ... Il.14.453.185.
The roaring Deeps in watry Mountains rise, ... Il.15.441.214.
Thus loudly roaring, and o'erpow'ring all, ... Il.15.444.214.
And puffing loud, the roaring Bellows blew. ... Il.18.438.341.
And bid the roaring Bellows cease to blow. ... Il.18.478.345.
And all the roaring Billows of the Main. ... Il.21.212.430.
The Structure crackles in the roaring Fires, ... Il.23.270.500.
O'er pathless Forests, or the roaring Main. ... Il.24.540.558.
To realms, that rocks and roaring seas divide? ... Od.2.409.80.
High o'er the roaring waves the spreading sails ... Od.2.466.83.
What raging winds? what roaring waters round? ... Od.5.390.191.
To roaring billows, and the warring wind; ... Od.6.206.220.
Has fate oppress'd thee in the roaring waves, ... Od.11.496.408.
Has Fate oppress'd me on the roaring waves! ... Od.11.502.408.
Plows o'er that roaring surge its desp'rate way; ... Od.12.80.435.
'Midst roaring whirlpools, and absorbs the main, ... Od.12.130.438.
And in the roaring whirlpools rush the tides. ... Od.12.510.457.
The roaring wind's tempestuous rage restrain; ... Od.13.119.7.
And whelms th' offenders in the roaring tydes: ... Od.23.358.342.

ROARINGS
Howl to the roarings of the Northern deep. ... 4.2HE1.329.223.
And 'midst the Roarings of the Waters dy'd? ... Il.6.439.348.
And hush the Roarings of the sacred Deep: ... Il.15.217.205.
Fast by the roarings of the main we place; ... Od.12.20.430.
To calm the roarings of the stormy main, ... Od.12.399.450.

ROARS
From Pole to Pole the Thunder roars aloud, 1.TrSt.496.431.
While Thunder roars, and Lightning round him flies. 1.TrSt.525.432.
He foams, he roars, he rends the panting Prey. 1.TrES.20.450.
Deep Groans and hollow Roars rebellow thro' the Wood. 1.TrES.299.460.
And the black Ocean foams and roars below. 1.TrUl.12.465.
Jove's Thunder roars, Heav'n trembles all around; 2.RL5.49.203.
The Trumpet roars, long flaky Flames expire, 2.TemF.414.283.
And here, while Town, and Court, and City roars, 4.2HE2.123.173.
Great Cæsar roars, and hisses in the fires; 5.DunB1.251.289.
And "Coll!" each Butcher roars at Hockley-hole. 5.DunB1.326.294.
When thunder roars, and lightning blasts the plain, 6.21.8.69.
Hark! how the thund'ring Giant roars. 6.78ii.8.216.
In Peals of Thunder now she roars, and now 6.96ii.9.270.
Like Peals of Thunder now she roars, and now 6.96ii.9A.270.
The parted Ocean foams and roars below: Il.1.627.117.
Murmuring they move, as when old *Ocean* roars, Il.2.249.139.
Round the bleak Realms where *Hellespontus* roars, Il.2.1024.171.
Roars thro' the Desart, and demands his Prey. Il.3.562.218.
He foams, he roars; The Shepherd dares not stay, Il.5.178.275.
He foams, he roars, he rends the panting Prey. Il.12.364.94.
Both Armies join: Earth thunders, Ocean roars. Il.14.456.185.
The warring Nations meet, the Battel roars, Il.15.842.229.
Loud roars the Deluge till it meets the Main; Il.16.474.261.
Deep groans, and hollow roars, rebellow thro' the Wood. Il.16.604.267.
And echoing Roars rebellow thro' the Shades. Il.16.918.279.
Roars thro' the Desart, and demands his Young; Il.18.372.339.
A rapid Torrent thro' the Rushes roars: Il.18.668.356.
He groans away his Soul: Not louder roars Il.20.467.413.
This way and that, the spreading Torrent roars; Il.20.573.418.
Part plunge into the Stream: Old *Xanthus* roars, Il.21.9.421.
Roars the resounding Surge with Men and Horse. Il.21.19.422.
From all his Deep the bellowing River roars, Il.21.258.431.
From all his Deeps the bellowing River roars, Il.21.258A.431.
With equal Rage, indignant *Xanthus* roars, Il.21.356.435.
White curl the waves, and the vex'd ocean roars. Od.4.788.156.
Full horribly he roars, his voice all heav'n returns. Od.8.346.282.
Where on *Trinacrian* rocks the Ocean roars, Od.11.134.387.
Fell *Scylla* rises, in her fury roars, Od.12.123.437.
The rough rock roars; tumultuous boil the waves; Od.12.283.446.
The furious tempest roars with dreadful sound: Od.12.373.449.
And the black Ocean foams and roars below. Od.13.103.6.
Delightful rise, when angry *Neptune* roars, Od.23.250.335.
Yet Fate withstands! a sudden tempest roars Od.23.341.341.

ROAST
A Tomb of boil'd, and roast, and flesh, and fish, 4.HS2.70.59.
The Vulgar boil, the Learned roast an Egg; 4.2HE2.85.171.
Roast beef, tho' old, proclaims him stout, 6.150.13.399.
Roast beef tho' cold, proclaims him stout, 6.150.13A.899.
Th' Assistants part, transfix, and roast the rest: Il.1.611.117.
Th' Assistants part, transfix, and roast the rest; Il.2.511.151.
They roast the fragments, and prepare the feast. Od.12.430.451.
His sons divide, and roast with artful care Od.19.492.220.

ROASTED
Had roasted turnips in the Sabin farm. 3.Ep1.219.34.
'Tis known, a Cook-maid roasted *Prior,* 6.10.59.26.

ROASTING
For writing pamphlets, and for roasting Popes; 5.DunA3.282A.183.
For writing Pamphlets, and for roasting Popes; 5.DunB3.284.334.

ROB
Nor Age, nor Blindness, rob me of Delight. 2.ChJM.554.42.
And gets an Act of Parliament to rob? 4.JD4.143.37.
And 'twere a sin to rob them of their Mite. 4.Arbu.162.108.
What rob your Boys? those pretty rogues!— 4.1HE7.27.271.
That those who bind and rob thee, would not kill, 4.1740.17.332.
Or rob the Roman geese of all their glories, 5.DunA1.191.85.
Or rob Rome's ancient geese of all their glories, 5.DunB1.211.285.
And 'twere a Sin to rob them of their *Mite.* 6.98.12.283.
Think not to rob me of a Soldier's Right. Il.1.170.95.
And rob a Subject, than despoil a Foe. Il.1.304.101.
Nor rob the Vultures of one Limb of thee. Il.22.444.474.
Rob not the God, and so propitious gales Od.11.140.387.
Rob not the God! and so propitious gales Od.12.172.440.

ROB'D
First, rob'd in White, the Nymph intent adores 2.RL1.123.155.
The sage *Chaldæans* rob'd in White appear'd, 2.TemF.99.260.
She bathes, and rob'd, the sacred dome ascends; Od.4.1001.164.
Ulysses rob'd him in the cloak and vest. Od.5.294.185.
Rob'd in the garments her own hands had made; Od.7.315.251.
Go bathe, and rob'd in white, ascend the tow'rs; Od.17.60.135.
She bath'd; and rob'd in white, with all her train, Od.17.69.136.
Soon as the morn, new-rob'd in purple light, Od.19.499.220.

ROBB'D
Not ardent Lover robb'd of all his Bliss, 2.RLA2.5.132.
Not ardent Lovers robb'd of all their Bliss, 2.RL4.5.183.
By Spirit robb'd of Pow'r, by Warmth of Friends, 3.Ep2.144.62.
Shou'd D[enni]s print how once you robb'd your Brother, 6.116vii.1.328.
By Spirit, robb'd of Power; by Warmth, of Friends; 6.154.30.403.
Sarpedon's Thigh, had robb'd the Chief of Breath; Il.5.822.305.
Greece, robb'd of him, must bid her Host despair, Il.11.588.60.
So *Pallas* robb'd the Many of their Mind, Il.18.362.339.
Robb'd of the Prize the *Grecian* Suffrage gave, Il.18.517.346.
Robb'd of my Glory and my just Reward, Il.23.653.515.
Whose visual orb *Ulysses* robb'd of light; Od.1.90.36.
By one *Etolian* robb'd of all belief, Od.14.418.56.

ROBB'ST
Thou robb'st me of a Glory justly mine, Il.22.27.453.

ROBBERS
The robbers prize, the prey to lawless might. Od.15.14.70.

ROBE
See ROAB.
A Robe obscene was o'er her Shoulders thrown, 1.TrSt.154.416.
A graceful Robe her slender Body drest, 1.TrUl.104.469.
The rest his many-colour'd Robe conceal'd. 2.RL3.58.172.
That long behind he trails his pompous Robe, 2.RL3.73.173.
Gath'ring his flowing Robe, he seem'd to stand, 2.TemF.240.274.
That Robe of Quality so struts and swells, 3.Ep2.189.65.
He ceas'd, and show'd the robe; the crowd confess 5.DunA2.329.141.
He ceas'd, and spread the robe; the crowd confess 5.DunB2.353.314.
His Purple Robe, bright Ensign of Command. Il.8.269.410.
The radiant Robe her sacred Fingers wove, Il.8.468.419.
Hangs on the Robe, or trembles at the Knee, Il.22.633.482.
The martial Scarf and Robe of Triumph wove. Il.22.657.483.
In the same Robe he living wore, he came, Il.23.80.490.
In the same Robe the Living wore, he came, Il.23.80A.490.
A royal robe he wore with graceful pride, Od.2.5.60.
With flow'rs of gold: an under robe, unbound, Od.5.297.185.
And Kings draw lustre from the robe of state. Od.6.74.208.
A vest and robe, with rich embroid'ry gay: Od.6.254.222.
A vest, a robe, and imitate your King: Od.8.428.287.
Then o'er his limbs a gorgeous robe he spreads, Od.8.493.289.
A graceful robe her slender body drest, Od.13.271.19.
His robe, which spots indelible besmear, Od.13.502.29.
Grac'd with a decent robe he shall retire, Od.17.630.163.
A robe *Antinous* gives of shining dyes, Od.18.337.184.
A robe of military purple flow'd Od.19.262.207.
And regal robe with figur'd gold embost, Od.19.293.209.
These tatter'd weeds (my decent robe resign'd.) Od.19.391.213.

ROBE'S
Foreign her air, her robe's discordant pride 5.DunB4.47.345.

ROBERT
Such as Sir *Robert* would approve— F. Indeed ? 4.HS1.153.21.
Should rise, and say—"Sir *Robert!* or Sir *Paul!* 4.HAdv.88.83.
Go see Sir ROBERT— P. See Sir Robert !— hum 4.EpS1.27.299.
Go see Sir ROBERT— P. See Sir Robert !— hum 4.EpS1.27.299.
And all agree, Sir Robert cannot live. 4.1740.42.334.

ROBERT'S
But let me add, Sir ROBERT's mighty dull, 4.EpS2.133.320.

ROBES
No more my Robes in waving Purple flow, 1.TrSP.81.397.
And with Celestial Robes adorn the mighty Dead. 1.TrES.329.461.
And with Celestial Robes adorn the Dead. 1.TrES.329A.461.
There in long Robes the Royal *Magi* stand, 2.TemF.97.260.
Paint, Marble, Gems, and Robes of *Persian* Dye, 4.2HE2.265.183.
She, tinsel'd o'er in robes of varying hues, 5.DunA1.79.69.
And "Take (he said) these robes which once were mine, 5.DunA2.327.141.
She, tinsel'd o'er in robes of varying hues, 5.DunB1.81.275.
"Receive (he said) those robes which once were mine, 5.DunB2.351.314.
And shameless *Billingsgate* her Robes adorn. 5.DunB4.26.342.
Where *Lillies* smile in virgin robes of white, 6.14iv.5.47.
The shining Robes, rich Jewels, Beds of State, 6.19.51.63.
And with celestial Robes adorn the Dead. Il.16.816.274.
With purple robes inwrought, and still with gold, Od.1.212.43.
In saffron robes the Daughter of the dawn Od.4.586.147.
But bathe, and in imperial robes array'd, Od.4.990.163.
And spotless robes become the young and gay: Od.6.76.208.
Tunics, and stoles, and robes imperial bears. Od.6.88.209.
Then æmulous the royal robes they lave, Od.6.105.211.
And while the robes imbibe the solar ray, Od.6.111.211.
The robes resumes, the glittering car ascends, Od.6.300.225.
And robes like these, so recent and so fair? Od.7.321.251.
My wants, and lent these robes that strike your eyes. Od.7.381.255.
Her wond'rous robes; and full the Goddess blooms. Od.8.402.285.
The vests, the robes, and heaps of shining gold; Od.8.456.288.
A polish'd chest and stately robes to bear, Od.8.461.288.
The robes the vests are rang'd, and heaps of gold: Od.8.476.288.
Rich in refulgent robes, and dropping balmy dews: Od.10.534.369.
Long flowing robes of purest white array Od.10.649.375.
Beneath the seats, soft painted robes they spread, Od.13.88.5.
The gold, the brass, the robes, *Ulysses* brought; Od.13.422.26.
To wash her robes descending to the main, Od.15.461.93.
Sandals, a sword, and robes, respect to prove, Od.16.79.106.
Imperial robes his manly limbs infold: Od.16.187.112.
Then o'er their limbs refulgent robes they threw, Od.17.102.136.
Of decent robes a present has design'd; Od.17.639.163.
Then in such robes as suppliants may require, Od.17.652.164.
Permit me first thy royal robes to bring: Od.22.525.314.

ROBIN
The *Robin-red-breast* till of late had rest, 4.HS2.37.57.

ROBIN-RED-BREAST
The *Robin-red-breast* till of late had rest, 4.HS2.37.57.

ROBOAM
But judg'd *Roboam* his own Son. 6.101.20.290.

ROBS
That *Spain* robs on, and *Dunkirk's* still a Port. 4.JD4.165.39.
Robs the sad Orphan of his Father's Friends: Il.22.629.482.

ROCHESTER
Ev'n mitred *Rochester* would nod the head, 4.Arbu.140.105.

ROCK
Delia, each Cave and ecchoing Rock rebounds. 1.PAu.50.83.
Thyrsis, each Cave and ecchoing Rock rebounds. 1.PAu.50A.83.
The shapeless *Rock,* or hanging *Precipice.* 1.EOC.160.258.

ROCK (CONTINUED)

Hid in a rock, and by my Acis laid, ... 1.TrPA.49.367.
Torn from the rock, which threatned as it flew; .... 1.TrPA.145.372.
No further speech the thundering rock affords, ... 1.TrPA.146.372.
The rock asunder cleav'd, and thro' the chink .... 1.TrPA.155.372.
"There stands a Rock from whose impending Steep .... 1.TrSP.189.402.
The hanging Cliffs of *Scyron's* Rock explores, ... 1.TrSt.470.429.
The mouldring Rock that trembles from on high. .... 1.TrSt.854.445.
But dreads the mouldring Rock that trembles from on high. .... 1.TrSt.854A.445.
Th'unwieldy Rock, the Labour of a God. .... 1.TrES.190.456.
Drives the sharp Rock; the solid Beams give way, ... 1.TrES.196.456.
High on a Rock of Ice the Structure lay, ... 2.TemF.27.255.
The wond'rous Rock like *Parian* Marble shone, ... 2.TemF.29.255.
From the dry rock who bade the waters flow? .... 3.Ep3.254.114.
To rock the Cradle of reposing Age, ... 4.Arbu.409.127.
A Nursing-mother, born to rock the throne! .... 5.DunA1.251Z4.93.
And I, a Nursing-mother, rock the throne, ... 5.DunB1.312.293.
Each staunch Polemic, stubborn as a rock, ... 5.DunB4.195.361.
But in the rock my flowing tears suppress, ... 6.20.31.67.
Still, tho' a rock, can thus relieve her woe, ... 6.20.58.67.
To rock the Cradle of reposing Age, ... 6.117.4.333.
Th' *Olenian* Rock; and where *Alisium* flows; .... Il.2.750.161.
To the close Covert of an arching Rock. .... Il.4.321.236.
A broken Rock the Force of *Pirus* threw, ... Il.4.599.250.
A broken Rock by *Nestor's* Son was thrown, ... Il.5.711.301.
Then *Ajax* seiz'd the Fragment of a Rock, ... Il.7.320.379.
And rush'd on *Teucer* with the lifted Rock. .... Il.8.388.416.
High on a Rock fair *Thryoëssa* stands, ... Il.11.846.74.
Dark'ning the Rock, while with unweary'd Wings .... Il.12.191.88.
Th' unweildy Rock, the Labour of a God. .... Il.12.544.101.
Drives the sharp Rock; the solid Beams give way, ... Il.12.550.101.
The God whose Earthquakes rock the solid Ground, ... Il.13.68.108.
Around the Globe, whose Earthquakes rock the World; .... Il.15.249.206.
Close in the Rock, (not fated yet to die). .... Il.15.311.209.
They gain th' impervious Rock and safe retreat .... Il.15.310A.209.
So some tall Rock o'erhangs the hoary Main, ... Il.15.746.224.
From the tall Rock the sable Waters flow. .... Il.16.6.234.
As on a Rock that overhangs the Main, ... Il.16.494.262.
Large as a Rock, was by his Fury thrown. .... Il.16.501.262.
Deep in a cavern'd Rock my Days were led; .... Il.18.471.344.
But Ocean's God, whose Earthquakes rock the Ground, ... Il.20.339.408.
Her self a Rock, (for such was Heav'ns high Will) .... Il.24.773.569.
The Rock for ever lasts, the Tears for ever flow! .... Il.24.779.569.
There stands a rock, high eminent and steep, ... Od.3.374.104.
The rock rush'd sea-ward, with impetuous roar .... Od.4.681.151.
Safe from the secret rock and adverse storm, ... Od.4.879.159.
With water from the rock, and rosie wine, ... Od.5.214.181.
So the rough rock had shagg'd *Ulysses'* hands. .... Od.5.553.199.
High at its head, from out the cavern'd rock .... Od.9.161.312.
Near this, a fence of marble from the rock, ... Od.9.215.314.
Now driv'n before him, thro' the arching rock, ... Od.9.280.318.
And cautious, thus. Against a dreadful rock, ... Od.9.337.320.
Then stretch'd in length o'er half the cavern'd rock, ... Od.9.354.321.
Could roll the rock. In hopeless grief we lay, ... Od.9.362.321.
Before him march, and pour into the rock: .... Od.9.397.322.
Brain'd on the rock; his second dire repast. .... Od.9.405.322.
Swing round and round, and dash'd from rock to rock, ... Od.9.539.328.
Swing round and round, and dash'd from rock to rock, ... Od.9.539.328.
The Giant spoke, and thro' the hollow rock .... Od.9.543.328.
From the tall hill he rends a pointed rock; .... Od.9.566.329.
Already, when the dreadful rock he threw, ... Od.9.581.330.
The rock o'erwhelms us, and we 'scap'd in vain. .... Od.9.584.330.
A larger rock then heaving from the plain, ... Od.9.631.332.
Where the dark rock o'erhangs th' infernal lake, ... Od.10.612.374.
High in the air the rock its summit shrouds, ... Od.12.87.436.
Full in the center of this rock display'd, ... Od.12.99.436.
Close by, a rock of less enormous height .... Od.12.125.437.
Steer by the higher rock: lest whirl'd around .... Od.12.262.445.
The rough rock roars; tumultuous boil the waves; .... Od.12.283.446.
And high above the rock she spouts the main: .... Od.12.287.446.
The rock rebellows with a thund'ring sound; .... Od.12.290.446.
As from some rock that overhangs the flood, ... Od.12.300.446.
With that, the God whose earthquakes rock the ground .... Od.13.184.15.
And roots her down, as everlasting rock. .... Od.13.189.15.
The entrance with a rock the Goddess clos'd. .... Od.13.424.26.
At the *Coracian* rock he now resides, ... Od.13.469.28.
Where, from the rock, with liquid lapse distills .... Od.17.232.143.
He stood, and mov'd not, like a marble rock; .... Od.17.549.159.
They move, and murmurs run thro' all the rock: .... Od.24.12.347.
And *Leucas'* rock, and *Ocean's* utmost streams, ... Od.24.17.347.

ROCK'D

When rock'd the mountains, and when groan'd the ground, ... 3.EOM3.250.118.

ROCK'S

When *Ajax* strives, some Rock's vast Weight to throw, ... 1.EOC.370.282.
The Rock's high Summit, in the Temple's Shade, ... 2.TemF.47.256.
So Silent Fountains, from a Rock's tall Head, ... Il.9.19.432.
A Rock's round Fragment flies, with Fury born, ... Il.13.192.115.
Some rugged Rock's hard Entrails gave thee Form, ... Il.16.50.237.
A Rock's large Fragment thunder'd on his Head; .... Il.16.706.271.
Then, heav'd on high, a rock's enormous weight .... Od.9.284.318.
As from a hanging rock's tremendous height, ... Od.14.341.51.

ROCKING

Troy's Turrets totter on the rocking Plain; .... Il.20.81.397.

ROCKS

The Hills and Rocks attend my doleful Lay, ... 1.PSu.17.73.
Ev'n Hills and Rocks attend my doleful Lay, ... 1.PSu.17A.73.
Taught Rocks to weep, and made the *Mountains* groan. .... 1.PAu.16.82.
Thro' Rocks and Caves the Name of *Delia* sounds, ... 1.PAu.49.83.
Thro' Rocks and Caves the Name of Thyrsis sounds, ... 1.PAu.49A.83.
The Rocks proclaim th'approaching Deity. .... 1.Mes.32.116.
Be smooth ye Rocks, ye rapid Floods give way! .... 1.Mes.36.116.
On rifted Rocks, the Dragon's late Abodes, ... 1.Mes.71.119.

ROCKS (CONTINUED)

Rocks fall to Dust, and Mountains melt away; .... 1.Mes.106.122.
Stones leap'd to *Form*, and *Rocks* began to *live;* .... 1.EOC.702.319.
The Rocks around, the hanging Roofs above, ... 1.TrSP.164.400.
I go, ye Nymphs! those Rocks and Seas to prove; .... 1.TrSP.201.402.
To Rocks and Seas I fly from *Phaon's* Hate, ... 1.TrSP.205.402.
And hope from Seas and Rocks a milder Fate. .... 1.TrSP.206.402.
Ah! canst thou doom me to the Rocks and Sea, ... 1.TrSP.222.403.
Dash'd on these Rocks, than to thy Bosom prest? .... 1.TrSP.225.403.
Dash'd on sharp Rocks, than to thy Bosom prest? .... 1.TrSP.225A.403.
Dash'd on those Rocks, than to thy Bosom prest? .... 1.TrSP.225B.403.
Sprung from the Rocks, and plung'd into the Main. .... 1.TrSt.18.410.
The dreadful Signal all the Rocks rebound, ... 1.TrSt.163.417.
Sees yawning Rocks in massy Fragments fly, ... 1.TrSt.511.431.
While from torn Rocks the massy Fragments roll'd; .... 1.TrSt.511A.431.
He dreads the Rocks, and Shoals, and Seas, and Skies, ... 1.TrSt.524.432.
And pays in hollow Rocks his awful Vows, ... 1.TrSt.862.446.
The Desart ecchoes, and the Rocks reply: .... 1.TrES.222.458.
Two craggy Rocks, projecting to the Main, ... 1.TrUl.27.466.
Th'emerging Hills and Rocks of *Ithaca*. .... 1.TrUl.24A.466.
To the deaf Rocks, and hoarse-resounding Main. .... 1.TrUl.99.469.
Here naked Rocks, and empty Wastes were seen, ... 2.TemF.15.254.
So *Zembla's* Rocks (the beauteous Work of Frost) .... 2.TemF.53.256.
Ye rugged rocks! which holy knees have worn; .... 2.ElAb.19.320.
The darksom pines that o'er yon' rocks reclin'd .... 2.ElAb.155.332.
And low-brow'd rocks hang nodding o'er the deeps. .... 2.ElAb.244.339.
And Seas, and Rocks, and Skies rebound .... 6.11.47.32.
Eurydice the Rocks, and hollow Mountains rung. .... 6.11.117.34.
"Marbles to them, but rolling Rocks to you. .... 6.96ii.30.271.
Where lingering Drops from Mineral Rocks distill, ... 6.142.3B.382.
And Walls of Rocks, secure my native Reign, ... Il.1.204.96.
The Rocks remurmur, and the Deeps rebound. .... Il.2.252.139.
That dash'd on broken Rocks tumultuous roar, ... Il.2.472.149.
Olyzon's Rocks, or *Mœlibæa's* Fields, ... Il.2.873.165.
Or where *Ithomè*, rough with Rocks, appears; .... Il.2.887.166.
Foam o'er the Rocks, and thunder to the Skies. .... Il.4.483.243.
Nor are their Bodies Rocks, nor ribb'd with Steel; .... Il.4.589.249.
Where chain'd on burning Rocks the *Titans* groan. .... Il.5.1107.320.
Then shine the Vales, the Rocks in Prospect rise, ... Il.8.695.428.
Where o'er the Vales th' *Olenian* Rocks arose; .... Il.11.889.75.
Who rul'd where *Calydon's* white Rocks arise, ... Il.13.287.119.
Him neither Rocks can crush, nor Steel can wound, ... Il.13.412.126.
The Hills shine out, the Rocks in Prospect rise, ... Il.16.358.257.
The Desert echoes, and the Rocks reply: .... Il.16.525.264.
And distant Rocks rebellow to the Roar. .... Il.17.315.300.
The Victim Bull; the Rocks rebellow round, ... Il.20.469.414.
And close in Rocks or winding Caverns lye. .... Il.21.29.422.
With broken Rocks, and with a Load of Dead, ... Il.21.364.435.
Where dash'd on Rocks the broken Billows roar, ... Il.23.71.489.
O'er Hills, o'er Dales, o'er Crags, o'er Rocks, they go: .... Il.23.141.494.
To realms, that rocks and roaring seas divide? .... Od.2.409.80.
Sung dying to the rocks, but sung in vain. .... Od.3.343.103.
That gift our barren rocks will render vain: .... Od.4.822.157.
An ample port the rocks projected form, ... Od.4.1105.169.
She sate and sung; the rocks resound her lays: .... Od.5.74.176.
On rocks and shores consum'd the tedious day; .... Od.5.200.181.
Amidst the rocks he hears a hollow roar .... Od.5.516.197.
All rough with rocks, with foamy billows white. .... Od.5.521.197.
Above, sharp rocks forbid access; around .... Od.5.528.198.
Between the parting rocks at length he spy'd .... Od.5.562.199.
To rocks, to caves, the frighted virgins fly; .... Od.6.166.216.
The spacious basons arching rocks enclose, ... Od.6.315.226.
And clear of rocks. I fainted by the flood; .... Od.7.366.254.
He sends a dreadful groan: the rocks around .... Od.9.469.325.
From rifted rocks, and mountains bleak in air. .... Od.9.476.325.
Our groans the rocks re-murmur'd to the main. .... Od.10.60.342.
Clear of the rocks th' impatient vessel flies; .... Od.10.151.347.
Where rocks controul his waves with ever-during mounds. .... Od.11.14.379.
Where on *Trinacrian* rocks the Ocean roars, ... Od.11.134.387.
High o'er the main two Rocks exalt their brow, ... Od.12.71.433.
Shuns the dire rocks: In vain she cuts the skies, ... Od.12.77.435.
The dire rocks meet, and crush her as she flies; .... Od.12.78.435.
If from yon justling rocks and wavy war .... Od.12.256.444.
Now thro' the rocks, appal'd with deep dismay, ... Od.12.278.445.
Now from the rocks the rapid vessel flies, ... Od.12.312.447.
For on the rocks it bore where *Scylla* raves, ... Od.12.505.457.
Fast by the rocks beheld the desp'rate way: .... Od.12.508.457.
Two craggy rocks projecting to the main, ... Od.13.118.7.
To the deaf rocks, and hoarse-resounding main. .... Od.13.266.18.
And from the lofty brow of rocks by day .... Od.16.382.124.
The justling rocks where fierce *Charybdis* raves, ... Od.23.353.341.

ROCKY

Around whose rocky sides the water flows: .... 1.TrPA.40.367.
Behold the rocky caverns where I dwell, ... 1.TrPA.68.368.
Rent from the Walls, a Rocky Fragment lay; .... 1.TrES.100.453.
And gently plac'd him on the Rocky Shore: .... 1.TrUl.48.467.
With Rocky Mountains, and with Olives crown'd! .... 1.TrUl.227.473.
As from some Rocky Cleft the Shepherd sees .... Il.2.111.132.
These head the Troops that Rocky *Aulis* yields, ... Il.2.590.156.
Crocylia rocky, and *Zacynthus* green. .... Il.2.772.162.
Heav'd with vast Force, a Rocky Fragment wields. .... Il.5.370.284.
Where *Calydon* on rocky Mountains stands, ... Il.9.653.467.
So down the Rampires rolls the rocky Show'r; .... Il.12.180.87.
Rent from the Walls a rocky Fragment lay; .... Il.12.454.98.
Prone down the rocky Steep, he rush'd along; .... Il.13.28.105.
And rocky *Imbrus* breaks the rolling Wave: .... Il.13.52.107.
Then, as a Falcon from the rocky Height, ... Il.13.91.109.
Vent his mad Vengeance on our rocky Walls, ... Il.18.328.337.
The rocky Pavement glitter'd with the Show. .... Il.23.249.499.
And rocky *Imbrus* lifts its pointed Heads, ... Il.24.104.539.
Amid'st an Isle, around whose rocky shore .... Od.1.63.33.
Or the strait course to rocky *Chios* plow, ... Od.3.207.95.
The *Phocæ* swift surround his rocky cave, ... Od.4.544.146.
He wrench'd a rocky fragment from the ground: .... Od.8.210.273.
Strong are her sons, tho' rocky are her shores; .... Od.9.28.303.

ROCKY 222 ROLL'D

ROCKY (CONTINUED)
Removes the rocky mountain from the door, ...Od.9.371.321.
Strong walls of brass the rocky coast confine. ....Od.10.4.339.
And gently plac'd him on the rocky shore. ....Od.13.139.11.
With rocky mountains, and with olives crown'd. ....Od.13.394.26.
He seeks his lodging in the rocky den. ....Od.14.599.66.
Then cautious thro' the rocky reaches wind, ...Od.15.320.85.

ROD
Stretch'd o'er the Poor, and Church, his Iron Rod, ...1.W-F.75.157.
Snatch from his hand the balance and the rod, ...3.EOM1.121.30.
If Calvin feel Heav'n's blessing, or its rod, ...3.EOM4.139.141.
A Wit's a feather, and a Chief a rod; ....3.EOM4.247.151.
And needs no Rod but Ripley with a Rule. ....3.Ep4.18.137.
And needs no Rod but S[taffor]d with a Rule ....3.Ep4.18A.137*.
And needs no Rod but S[heppar]d with a Rule ....3.Ep4.18B.137*.
What Sin of mine cou'd merit such a Rod? ....4.JD4.63.31.
If wrong, I smil'd; if right, I kiss'd the rod. ....4.Arbu.158.107.
And each Blasphemer quite escape the Rod, ...4.EpS2.195.324.
Thine from the birth, and sacred from the rod, ...5.DunB4.283.372.
Can Sins of Moments claim the Rod ....6.50.20Z1.147*.
If wrong, I smile; if right, I kiss the Rod. ....6.98.8.283.
Spreads the red Rod of angry Pestilence, ...6.137.4.373.
Hence, with thy Laurel Crown, and Golden Rod, ...Il.1.37.87.
Let Tyrants govern with an iron rod, ...Od.2.263.74.
But crush the nations with an iron rod, ...Od.5.16.171.
To her, the Pow'r who bears the charming rod. ....Od.5.185.180.
Who bears the virtue of the sleepy rod. ....Od.7.185.244.
(Immortal *Hermes* with the golden rod) ....Od.10.330.360.
Or crush'd by traytors with an iron rod? ....Od.11.213.392.

RODE
Here, like some furious Prophet, *Pindar* rode, ...2.TemF.212.272.
To Needham's quick the voice triumphal rode, ...5.DunB1.323.293.
Rode forth the valiant *Guise;* ....6.79.108.221.
In *Chrysa's* Port now sage *Ulysses* rode; ....Il.1.566.115.
Rode like a Woman to the Field of War. ....Il.2.1063.172.
Tow'ring they rode in one refulgent Car: ....Il.11.426.53.
Old *Nestor* mounts the Seat: Beside him rode ....Il.11.638.62.
Swift fly the mules: nor rode the nymph alone, ...Od.6.97.210.
Once more undaunted on the ruin rode, ...Od.12.525.458.
And rode the storm; 'till by the billows tost, ...Od.19.319.209.

RODRIGO
Now flames old Memnon, now Rodrigo burns, ...5.DunA1.208.87.

ROE
And leap exulting like the bounding Roe. ....1.Mes.44.116.
Thus on a Roe the well-breath'd Beagle flies, ...Il.15.697.222.
They bay the boar, or chase the bounding roe: ....Od.6.122.212.

ROES
But roes and lev'rets, and the fallow deer; ....1.TrPA.87.369.

ROGUE
The rogue and fool by fits is fair and wise, ...3.EOM2.233.83.
A Rogue with Ven'son to a Saint without. ....3.Ep1.139.26.
"Old Cato is as great a Rogue as you." ....3.Ep3.68.93.
The Wretch that trusts them, and the Rogue that cheats. ....3.Ep3.238.112.
So kept the Diamond, and the rogue was bit. ....3.Ep3.364.123.
These I cou'd bear; but not a Rogue so civil, ...4.JD4.56.29.
"Right, cries his Lordship, for a Rogue in need ....4.HS2.111.63.
Lintot, dull rogue! will think your price too much. ....4.Arbu.63.100.
So prompts, and saves a Rogue who cannot read. ....4.JD2.16.133.
But let them write for You, each Rogue impairs ....4.JD2.99.141.
So prompts, and saves some Rogue who cannot read. ....4.JD2.16A.133.
And Bitch and Rogue her Answer was to all; ....6.14ii.40.44.
And Bitch and Rogue her Answer was at all; ....6.14ii.40A.44.
One rogue is usher to another still. ....Od.17.251.143.

ROGUES
What rob your Boys? those pretty rogues!— ....4.1HE7.27.271.
Speak out, and bid me blame no Rogues at all. ....4.EpS2.53.315.
Dash'd by these Rogues, turns *English* common Draught: ....6.60.14.178.
That sturdy Vagrants, Rogues in Rags, ...6.135.21.366.
That Sturdy Beggars, Rogues in Rags, ...6.135.21A.366.
That idle Gypsies, Rogues in Rags, ...6.135.21B.366.

ROLL
Tempt Icy Seas, where scarce the Waters roll, ...1.W-F.389.189.
As Streams roll down, *enlarging* as they flow! ....1.EOC.192.263.
Twice taught the *Rhine* beneath his Laws to roll, ...1.TrSt.27.410.
How twice he vanquish'd where the *Rhine* does roll, ...1.TrSt.27A.410.
Returning Thoughts in endless Circles roll, ...1.TrSt.75.413.
Ev'n those who dwell where Suns at distance roll, ...1.TrSt.812.443.
Instruct the Eyes of young *Coquettes* to roll, ...2.RL1.88.152.
Or roll the Planets thro' the boundless Sky. ....2.RL2.80.165.
Beauties in vain their pretty Eyes may roll; ....2.RL5.33.201.
Pale Suns, unfelt, at distance roll away, ...2.TemF.55.256.
As to the Sea returning Rivers roll, ...2.TemF.430.284.
When from the Censer clouds of fragrance roll, ...2.ElAb.271.342.
While praying, trembling, in the dust I roll, ...2.ElAb.279.342.
Rise *Alps* between us! and whole oceans roll! ....2.ElAb.290.343.
See my lips tremble, and my eye-balls roll, ...2.ElAb.323.345.
And those love-darting eyes must roll no more. ....2.Elegy.34.365.
"Seas roll to waft me, suns to light me rise; ....3.EOM1.139.32.
And if each system in gradation roll, ...3.EOM1.247.45.
Could he, who taught each Planet where to roll, ...3.EOM2.35A.60.
Or wing the sky, or roll along the flood, ...3.EOM3.120.104.
And roll obedient Rivers thro' the Land; ....3.Ep4.202.156.
Not when from Plate to Plate your eyeballs roll, ...4.HS2.7.55.
Teach ev'ry Thought within its bounds to roll, ...4.2HE2.204.179.
(Tho' but, perhaps, a muster-roll of Names) ....4.2HE1.124.205.
Where winds can carry, or where waves can roll, ...4.1HE6.70.241.
So slow th' unprofitable Moments roll, ...4.1HE1.39.281.
Did from Bœotian to Bœotian roll? ....5.DunA3.42.154.

ROLL (CONTINUED)
Roll all their tydes, then back their circles bring; ....5.DunA3.48.154.
Might from Bœotian to Bœotian roll? ....5.DunA3.42A.154.
From shelves to shelves see greedy Vulcan roll, ...5.DunA3.73.156.
See! the dull stars roll round and re-appear. ....5.DunA3.336.192.
When the dull stars roll round and re-appear. ....5.DunA3.336A.192.
Next, o'er his Books his eyes began to roll, ...5.DunB1.127.278.
Back to the Devil the last echoes roll, ...5.DunB1.325.294.
Might from Bœotian to Bœotian roll? ....5.DunB3.50.322.
Roll all their tides, then back their circles bring; ....5.DunB3.56.323.
From shelves to shelves see greedy Vulcan roll, ...5.DunB3.81.324.
See! the dull stars roll round and re-appear. ....5.DunB3.322.335.
Roll in her Vortex, and her pow'r confess. ....5.DunB4.84.349.
Prompt at the call, around the Goddess roll ....5.DunB4.189.360.
See! still thy own, the heavy Canon roll, ...5.DunB4.247.367.
The vulgar herd turn off to roll with Hogs, ...5.DunB4.525.394.
As streams roll down enlarging as they flow. ....6.9ii.2.21.
Roll all their tides, then back their circles bring. ....6.9iii.2.21.
Just when she learns to roll a melting eye, ...6.45.3.124.
While summer suns roll unperceiv'd away? ....6.52.18.156.
Yet should the Muses bid my numbers roll, ...6.52.73.158.
I see thy fountains fall, thy waters roll ....6.106ii.3.307.
"I'll list you in the harmless roll ....6.140.31.379.
In his black Thoughts Revenge and Slaughter roll, ...Il.1.638.118.
But thou, nor they, shall search the Thoughs that roll ....Il.1.710.121.
So roll the Billows to th' *Icarian* Shore, ...Il.2.175.137.
Back to th' Assembly roll the thronging Train, ...Il.2.247.139.
Eternal *Jove!* and you bright Orb that roll ....Il.3.348.209.
Bare his red Arm, and bid the Thunder roll; ....Il.4.201.230.
As Torrents roll, increas'd by num'rous Rills, ...Il.4.516.246.
And roll in smoaking Volumes to the Skies. ....Il.5.620.297.
Or the dark Barrier roll with Ease away. ....Il.5.933.311.
Can *Mars* rebel, and does no Thunder roll? ....Il.5.943.311.
Years might again roll back, my Youth renew, ...Il.7.161.372.
Bar Heav'n with Clouds, or roll those Clouds away. ....Il.8.483.420.
Around her Throne the vivid Planets roll, ...Il.8.691.428.
And the big Tears roll trickling from her Eyes. ....Il.11.160.42.
And o'er the Forests roll the Flood of Fire, ...Il.11.202.44.
Men, Steeds, and Chariots, roll in Heaps along. ....Il.11.619.61.
In their old Bounds the Rivers roll again, ...Il.12.35.83.
They gnash their Tusks, with Fire their Eye-balls roll, ...Il.12.167.87.
Jove sends one Gust, and bids them roll away. ....Il.14.26.158.
The Blood in brisker Tides began to roll, ...Il.17.251.297.
And back the Chariots roll, and Coursers bound, ...Il.18.265.335.
In living Silver seem'd the Waves to roll, ...Il.18.703.357.
His glowing Eye-balls roll with living Fire, ...Il.19.395.388.
But swift *Scamander* roll thee to the Deep, ...Il.21.138.427.
Nor roll their wonted Tribute to the Deep. ....Il.21.236.430.
(So, e're a Storm, the Waters heave and roll) ....Il.21.649.449.
So they, while down their Cheeks the Torrents roll; ....Il.22.126.458.
Delightful roll along my native Coast! ....Il.23.179.497.
And turns him short; till, doubling as they roll, ...Il.23.411.506.
Defil'd with honourable Dust, they roll, ...Il.23.852.523.
Roll back the gather'd Forests to the Town. ....Il.24.992.577.
Gives to the roll of death his glorious name! ....Od.1.218.43.
Oh beat those storms, and roll the seas in vain! ....Od.2.415.81.
And to the stern retreating roll the tides. ....Od.2.469.83.
And the winds whistle, and the surges roll ....Od.3.368.104.
Two, foremost in the roll of *Mars* renown'd, ...Od.4.667.150.
Lost in delight the circling year wou'd roll, ...Od.4.815.157.
And south, and north, roll mountains to the shore. ....Od.5.380.190.
The seas may roll, the tempests rage in vain. ....Od.8.612.295.
The massy load cou'd bear, or roll along) ....Od.9.287.318.
Could roll the rock. In hopeless grief we lay, ...Od.9.362.321.
The boiling billows thund'ring roll below; ....Od.12.72.434.
Then *Jove* in anger bids his thunders roll, ...Od.12.485.456.
Slow seem'd the sun to move, the hours to roll, ...Od.13.37.3.
In home-felt joys delighted roll away; ....Od.13.57.4.
Broad burst the lightnings, deep the thunders roll; ....Od.14.338.51.
Down her fair cheek the tears abundant roll, ...Od.21.386.279.
Before him wide, in mixt effusion roll ....Od.22.99.291.

ROLL'D
The silver Eel, in shining Volumes roll'd, ...1.W-F.143.163.
The figur'd Streams in Waves of Silver roll'd, ...1.W-F.335.182.
Thou, sable *Styx!* whose livid Streams are roll'd ....1.TrSt.83.413.
But at the Summons, roll'd her Eyes around, ...1.TrSt.126.415.
While from torn Rocks the massy Fragments roll'd; ....1.TrSt.511A.431.
Or thro' what Veins our ancient Blood has roll'd? ....1.TrSt.800.443.
Within whose Orb the thick Bull-hides were roll'd, ...1.TrES.9.450.
On which the Labours of the Nymphs were roll'd, ...1.TrUl.37.467.
Forsook th' *Horizon,* and roll'd down the Light; ....2.ChJM.368.32.
And half the Mountain roll'd into a Wall: ....2.TemF.88A.259.
The flying Rumours gather'd as they roll'd, ...2.TemF.468.286.
Thou, who since Yesterday, has roll'd o'er all ....4.JD4.202.43.
He roll'd his eyes that witness'd huge dismay, ...5.DunA1.115.77.
Then down are roll'd the books; stretch'd o'er 'em lies ....5.DunA2.371.145.
Then down are roll'd the books; stretch'd o'er 'em lies ....5.DunB2.403.316.
A small Euphrates thro' the piece is roll'd, ...6.71.29.203.
Oft' roll'd his Eyes around, ...6.79.110.221.
And gloomy Darkness roll'd around his Head. ....Il.1.66.89.
Roll'd the large Orbs of her majestic Eyes, ...Il.1.713.121.
Descending swift, roll'd down the rapid Light. ....Il.1.777.124.
Thus at full Ease in Heaps of Riches roll'd, ...Il.2.281.141.
Strait to the Tree his sanguine Spires he roll'd, ...Il.2.374.145.
Round the vast Orb an hundred Serpents roll'd, ...Il.2.528.151.
And where *Parthenius,* roll'd thro' Banks of Flow'rs, ...Il.2.1040.172.
Roll'd down *Scamander* with the Vulgar Dead. ....Il.2.1049.172.
At this the Goddess roll'd her radiant Eyes, ...Il.4.73.224.
Two brazen Rings of Work divine were roll'd. ....Il.5.895.308.
Dire, black, tremendous! Round the Margin roll'd, ...Il.5.912.309.
And roll'd, with Limbs relax'd, along the Land. ....Il.7.18.363.
What Tears shall down thy silver Beard be roll'd, ...Il.7.149.372.
Rapt by th' Æthereal Steeds the Chariot roll'd; ....Il.8.51.398.
Roll'd the big Thunder o'er the vast Profound: ....Il.8.162.405.
Roll'd on the King his Eyes, and thus begun. ....Il.9.42.433.

ROLL'D (CONTINUED)

A splendid Carpet roll'd beneath his Head. ....Il.10.177.9.
Within whose Orb the thick Bull-Hides were roll'd, ...Il.12.353.94.
Embattel'd roll'd, as *Hector* rush'd along. ....Il.13.62.107.
Enter, and see on heaps the Helmets roll'd, ...Il.13.345.122.
And roll'd the smoaking Entrails to the Ground. ....Il.13.643.136.
The Helm fell off, and roll'd amid the Throng: ....Il.13.730.139.
Part on her Head in shining Ringlets roll'd, ...Il.14.205.170.
Erect, then roll'd along the Sands in Blood. ....Il.14.548.189.
Roll'd in the Ditch the heapy Ruin lay; ....Il.15.408.213.
There lay on Heaps his various Garments roll'd, ...Il.16.270.249.
And roll'd and grovel'd, as to Earth he grew. ....Il.18.32.325.
(Wond'rous to tell) instinct with Spirit roll'd ....Il.18.442.342.
In hissing Flames huge silver Bars are roll'd, ...Il.18.545.348.
Behind, the rising Earth in Ridges roll'd; ....Il.18.635.354.
The new-ear'd Earth in blacker Ridges roll'd; ....Il.18.635A.354.
Those beauteous Fields where *Hyllus'* Waves are roll'd, ...Il.20.451.413.
Till roll'd between the Banks, it lies the Food ....Il.21.221.430.
And turn'd up Bucklers glitter'd as they roll'd. ....Il.21.351.435.
So roll'd up in his Den, the swelling Snake ....Il.22.130.458.
Roll'd at the Feet of unrelenting *Jove!* ....Il.22.286.468.
Achilles, musing as he roll'd his eyes ....Il.22.459.474.
At length he roll'd in Dust, and thus begun: ....Il.22.528.478.
And roll'd his Eyes around the wat'ry Waste. ....Il.23.177.497.
(Roll'd in his Helmet, these *Achilles* throws.) ....Il.23.428.507.
His Car amidst the dusty Whirlwind roll'd, ...Il.23.583.513.
Restless he roll'd around his weary Bed, ...Il.24.9.535.
The golden Vase in purple Palls they roll'd, ...Il.24.1005.577.
Did not the sun, thro' heav'n's wide azure roll'd, ...Od.2.101.66.
"Years roll'd on years my god-like sire decay, ...Od.2.257.74.
And od'rous fumes from loaded altars roll'd. ....Od.3.349.103.
Which round th' intorted horns the gilder roll'd; ....Od.3.555.114.
The fields receding as the chariot roll'd: ....Od.3.628.118.
The splendid car roll'd slow in regal state: ....Od.4.28.121.
And roll'd his eyes around the restless deep; ....Od.5.106.177.
Tow'rd his lov'd coast he roll'd his eyes in vain, ...Od.5.107.177.
And roll'd his eyes o'er all the restless main, ...Od.5.203.181.
And roll'd on leavers, launch'd her in the deep. ....Od.5.332.188.
So roll'd the Float, and so its texture held: ....Od.5.420.192.
The raging God a wat'ry mountain roll'd; ....Od.5.465.195.
'Till the huge surge roll'd off. Then backward sweep ....Od.5.548.198.
There, as the night in silence roll'd away, ...Od.6.21.204.
Twice ten tempestuous nights I roll'd, resign'd ....Od.6.205.220.
Her self the chest prepares: in order roll'd ....Od.8.475.288.
Then bending with full force, around he roll'd ....Od.8.483.288.
To the cave's mouth he roll'd, and clos'd the gate. ....Od.9.285.318.
He roll'd it on the cave, and clos'd the gate. ....Od.9.401.322.
Roll'd back the vessel to the Island's side: ....Od.9.572.330.
'Till evening *Phœbus* roll'd away the light: ....Od.9.651.333.
Spent and o'erwatch'd. Two days and nights roll'd on, ...Od.10.167.348.
The deathful scene, Princes on Princes roll'd! ....Od.11.151.388.
And cleft in fragments, and the fragments roll'd; ....Od.12.209.442.
Now round the mast my mates the fetters roll'd, ...Od.12.214.442.
Thunder'd the deeps, the smoking billows roll'd! ....Od.12.241.443.
The hideous pest, my labouring eyes I roll'd; ....Od.12.275.445.
And setting stars roll'd down the azure plain; ....Od.12.368.449.
On which the labours of the nymphs were roll'd, ...Od.13.128.8.
And all thy fortunes roll'd within his breast. ....Od.15.10.70.
Crunus they pass'd, next *Chalcis* roll'd away, ...Od.15.316.84.
Down to the deep; there roll'd the future food ....Od.15.516.95.
His Lord, when twenty tedious years had roll'd, ...Od.17.397.151.
Down her fair cheek the copious torrent roll'd: ....Od.19.243.206.
Along the pavement roll'd the mutt'ring head. ....Od.22.366.305.
The deathful scene, on Heroes, Heroes roll'd; ....Od.23.390.343.

ROLLI

Rolli the feather to his ear conveys, ...5.DunA2.195.124.
Rolli the feather to his ear conveys, ...5.DunB2.203.305.

ROLLING

Now marks the Course of rolling Orbs on high; ....1.W-F.245.171.
Her sacred Domes involv'd in rolling Fire, ...1.W-F.324.180.
" *Apollo's* Fane surveys the rolling Deep; ....1.TrSP.190.402.
With Dread beheld the rolling Surges sweep ....1.TrSt.59.412.
Now glaring Fiends, and Snakes on rolling Spires, ...2.RL4.43.187.
Sulphureous Flames, and Clouds of rolling Smoke: ....2.TemF.339.280.
And now, on rolling Waters snatch'd away. ....4.HOde1.48.153.
And now, by rolling Waters snatch'd away. ....4.HOde1.48A.153.
And now, by rolling Waters wash'd away. ....4.HOde1.48B.153.
Happier thy fortunes! like a rolling stone, ...5.DunA3.295.184.
Happier thy fortunes! like a rolling stone, ...5.DunB3.293.334.
Rolling in *Mæanders,* ....6.11.100.33.
"Marbles to them, but rolling Rocks to you. ....6.96ii.30.271.
And keep the rolling maggot at a bay. ....6.96ii.30Z52.272.
"And keep the rolling Maggot at a Bay?" ....6.96ii.70.273.
Rolling, and black'ning, Swarms succeeding Swarms, ...Il.2.113.133.
And Thunder rolling shook the Firmament. ....Il.2.419.147.
And *Chalcis,* beaten by the rolling Deep. ....Il.2.778.162.
The rolling Sun descending to the Main ....Il.7.557.392.
Your selves condemn'd ten rolling Years to weep ....Il.8.516.421.
The Walls are scal'd; the rolling Flames arise; ....Il.9.700.468.
And rolling, drew a bloody Trail along. ....Il.11.190.44.
And gulphy *Simois,* rolling to the Main ....Il.12.21.82.
Th' enormous Monsters, rolling o'er the Deep, ...Il.13.43.107.
And rocky *Imbrus* breaks the rolling Wave: ....Il.13.52.107.
From Steep to Steep the rolling Ruin bounds; ....Il.13.195.115.
Wide-rolling, foaming high, and tumbling to the shore. ....Il.13.1005.152.
Of rolling Dust, their winged Wheels employ, ...Il.14.169.165.
And Sheets of rolling Smoke involve the Skies. ....Il.16.153.243.
In fair *Abydos* by the rolling Main.) ....Il.17.657.313.
Beneath its ample Verge. A rolling Cloud ....Il.17.670.314.
The rolling Wheels of *Greece* the Body tore, ...Il.20.455.413.
Swift o'er the rolling Pebbles, down the Hills ....Il.21.295.433.
O'er slaughter'd Heroes, and o'er rolling Steeds. ....Il.21.606.447.
These fix'd up high behind the rolling Wain, ...Il.22.499.477.
Hush'd by the Murmurs of the rolling Deep ....Il.23.76.489.

ROLLING (CONTINUED)

The flound'ring Coursers rolling on the Plain, ...Il.23.517.510.
And o'er the Trenches led the rolling Cars. ....Il.24.550.559.
Beheld the Flames and rolling Smokes arise. ....Il.24.998.577.
A bark to waft me o'er the rolling main; ....Od.2.242.73.
And seek my sire thro' storms and rolling seas! ....Od.2.300.76.
Rolling convulsive on the floor, is seen ....Od.4.952.162.
And stoops incumbent on the rolling deep. ....Od.5.63.174.
Strong with the fear of death. The rolling flood ....Od.5.415.192.
His head, and cast it on the rolling tyde. ....Od.5.591.201.
But smoaky volumes rolling from the ground. ....Od.10.114.346.
And where, slow rolling from the *Stygian* bed, ...Od.10.610.374.
Thus o'er the rolling surge the vessel flies, ...Od.12.1.427.
The solitary shore, and rolling sea. ....Od.13.222.16.
They, high enthron'd above the rolling clouds, ...Od.16.286.118.
On rolling oceans, and in fighting fields, ...Od.17.337.148.
Fast from her eye descends the rolling tear, ...Od.23.37.321.

ROLLS

And Earth rolls back beneath the flying Steed. ....1.W-F.158.164.
And chalky *Wey,* that rolls a milky Wave: ....1.W-F.344.183.
And unregarded Thunder rolls in vain: ....1.TrSt.305.423.
And half the Mountain rolls into a Wall: ....2.TemF.88.259.
Rolls o'er my *Grotto,* and but sooths my Sleep. ....4.HS1.124.17.
One lull'd th' *Exchequer,* and one stunn'd the *Rolls;* ....4.2HE2.130.173.
From morn to night, at Senate, Rolls, and Hall, ...4.1HE6.36.239.
Long Chanc'ry-lane retentive rolls the sound, ...5.DunA2.251.130.
Rolls the large tribute of dead dogs to Thames, ...5.DunA2.260.133.
There, in a dusky vale where Lethe rolls, ...5.DunA3.15.151.
Wings the red lightning, and the thunder rolls. ....5.DunA3.252.178.
Rolls the loud thunder, and the light'ning wings! ....5.DunA3.252A.178.
Long Chanc'ry-lane retentive rolls the sound, ...5.DunB2.263.308.
Rolls the large tribute of dead dogs to Thames, ...5.DunB2.272.309.
Rolls the black troop, and overshades the street, ...5.DunB2.360.315.
Here, in a dusky vale where Lethe rolls, ...5.DunB3.23.321.
Wings the red lightning, and the thunder rolls. ....5.DunB3.256.332.
Or Tyber, now no longer Roman, rolls, ...5.DunB4.299.373.
The Gloom rolls on, the sable Throne behold ....5.DunB4.629A.407.
In ev'ry Town, where *Thamis* rolls his Tyde, ...6.14ii.1.43.
Stretches his little Hands, and rolls his Eyes! ....6.96v.8.280.
Who rolls the Thunder o'er the vaulted Skies. ....Il.1.671.119.
And into *Peneus* rolls his easy Tides; ....Il.2.911.167.
While from the Centre *Hector* rolls his Eyes ....Il.3.121.195.
The Wave behind rolls on the Wave before; ....Il.4.481.243.
Swift down the Steep of Heav'n the Chariot rolls, ...Il.5.958.312.
Where *Celadon* rolls down his rapid Tide. ....Il.7.166.372.
Be witness, *Jove!* whose Thunder rolls on high. ....Il.7.488.388.
Thick Light'nings flash; the mutt'ring Thunder rolls; ....Il.8.95.401.
But let us haste—Night rolls the Hours away, ...Il.10.295.15.
Wide o'er the Field with guideless Fury rolls, ...Il.11.209.44.
Rolls sable Clouds in Heaps on Heaps along; ....Il.11.398.52.
The Storm rolls on, and *Hector* rules the Field: ....Il.11.450.54.
Soft *Minyas* rolls his Waters to the Main. ....Il.11.859.74.
So down the Rampires rolls the rocky Show'r; ....Il.12.180.87.
And speaking rolls her large, majestic Eyes) ....Il.14.298.177.
Where gentle *Xanthus* rolls his easy Tyde, ...Il.14.508.188.
Not with more Rage a Conflagration rolls, ...Il.15.728.224.
There stand the *Trojans,* and here rolls the Deep. ....Il.15.899.232.
And rolls the Cloud to blacken Heav'n with Storms, ...Il.16.435.259.
Then tumbling rolls enormous on the Ground: ....Il.17.591.311.
Troy pours along, and this way rolls our Fate. ....Il.17.800.319.
The rumbling Torrent thro' the Ruin rolls, ...Il.17.829.321.
The sacred Herald rolls the Victim slain ....Il.19.279.384.
Above, the Sire of Gods his Thunder rolls, ...Il.20.75.397.
The sacred Flood that rolls on golden Sands; ....Il.20.100.398.
He grins, he foams, he rolls his Eyes around; ....Il.20.206.402.
So the fierce Coursers, as the Chariot rolls, ...Il.20.581.418.
And rolls behind the Rout a Heap of Clouds) ....Il.21.8.421.
Still swift *Scamander* rolls where'er he flies: ....Il.21.300.433.
And thro surrounding Friends the Chariot rolls. ....Il.24.402.552.
Slow rolls the Chariot thro' the following Tide; ....Il.24.897.573.
And *Wealth* incessant rolls her golden tides. ....Od.1.498.56.
Then stay, my child! Storms beat, and rolls the main; ....Od.2.414.81.
Not unrecorded in the rolls of fame: ....Od.4.276.132.
Rolls clouds on clouds, and stirs the wat'ry world, ...Od.5.376.190.
Together clung, it rolls around the field; ....Od.5.419.192.
Rolls diverse, and in fragments strows the flood. ....Od.5.469.195.
For rough the way, and distant rolls the wave ....Od.6.43.207.
Stranger arise! the sun rolls down the day, ...Od.6.303.225.
The brightest shines in all the rolls of fame: ....Od.8.418.286.
Tho' tempests rage, tho' rolls the swelling main, ...Od.8.611.295.
So blest as thine in all the rolls of Fame; ....Od.11.592.412.
Air thunders, rolls the ocean, groans the ground. ....Od.12.374.449.
And dire *Charybdis* rolls her thund'ring waves. ....Od.12.506.457.
On these, in rolls of fat involv'd with art, ...Od.14.476.58.
Restless his body rolls, to rage resign'd: ....Od.20.31.233.
O'er all the man her eyes she rolls in vain, ...Od.23.97.324.
Who rolls the thunder o'er the vaulted skies) ....Od.24.548.374.

ROMAN

And People Heav'n with *Roman* Deities. ....1.TrSt.46.411.
And witness next what *Roman* Authors tell, ...2.ChJM.675.47.
Tell how the *Roman* Matrons led their Life, ...2.ChWB.343.73.
Bold *Scipio,* Saviour of the *Roman* State, ...2.TemF.163.267.
The *Roman Rostra* deck'd the Consul's Throne: ....2.TemF.239.274.
Above all Greek, above all Roman Fame: ....4.2HE1.26.197.
And Sydney's verse halts ill on Roman feet: ....4.2HE1.98.203.
While *Roman* Spirit charms, and *Attic* Wit: ....4.EpS2.85.317.
C[ompton] that Roman in his nose alone, ...4.1740.65.335.
Or rob the Roman geese of all their glories, ...5.DunA1.191.85.
Roman and Greek Grammarians! know your Better: ....5.DunB4.215.363.
Or Tyber, now no longer Roman, rolls, ...5.DunB4.299.373.
Have stoop'd to serve an haughty *Roman* dame? ....6.20.6.66.
And calls forth *Roman* drops from *British* eyes. ....6.32.16.96.
Stand emulous of Greek and Roman fame? ....6.71.54.204.

ROSE (CONTINUED)
To thy imperial race from woman rose! ....Od.11.542.410.
Rose in his majesty, and noblier trod; ....Od.11.660.416.
Ev'n I who from the Lord of thunders rose, ...Od.11.765.424.
But swarms of spectres rose from deepest hell, ...Od.11.779.425.
And high above it rose the tapering oar. ....Od.12.22.430.
A sudden joy in every bosom rose; ....Od.12.351.448.
All night it rag'd; when morning rose, to land ....Od.12.375.449.
Sulphureous odors rose, and smould'ring smoke. ....Od.12.492.456.
As priest himself, the blameless rustick rose; ....Od.14.481.59.
Nimbly he rose, and cast his garment down; ....Od.14.565.64.
The honest herdsman rose, as this he said, ...Od.14.586.65.
The King from *Helen* rose, and sought his guest. ....Od.15.66.72.
There form'd his empire; there his palace rose. ....Od.15.265.81.
'Till radiant rose the messenger of day. ....Od.15.534.95.
Rose ominous, nor flies without a God: ....Od.15.574.98.
Soon as the Suitors from the banquet rose, ...Od.17.432.153.
Then instant rose, and as he mov'd along ....Od.17.684.165.
Sad *Euryclea* rose: with trembling hand ....Od.19.421.214.
Sated they rose, and all retir'd to rest. ....Od.19.498.220.
There imag'd to her soul *Ulysses* rose; ....Od.19.701.229.
Up-rose, and thus divin'd the vengeance near. ....Od.20.422.253.
And to the seat returns from whence he rose. ....Od.21.174.268.
That rite compleat, up-rose the thoughtful man, ...Od.21.290.274.
The Heroes rose, and dragg'd him from the hall; ....Od.21.320.275.
But ere I spoke, he rose, and check'd the sound. ....Od.23.78.322.
The huge trunc rose, and heav'd into the sky; ....Od.23.194.333.
Ere *Greece* rose dreadful in th' avenging day, ...Od.23.233.334.
Amid the circle first *Eupithes* rose, ...Od.24.483.371.

ROSEATE
I come, I come! prepare your roseate bow'rs, ...2.ElAb.317.345.
I come, ye ghosts! prepare your roseate bow'rs, ...2.ElAb.317A.345.
And roseate Unguents, heav'nly Fragrance! shed: ....Il.23.229.499.
Unbarr'd the portal of the roseate east ....Od.4.412.140.
Soon as the morn reveals the roseate east, ...Od.4.784.156.
Sprinkled with roseate light the dewy lawn; ....Od.17.2.132.

ROSES
Here Western Winds on breathing Roses blow. ....1.PSp.32.63.
Let opening Roses knotted Oaks adorn, ...1.PAu.37.83.
Shows in her Cheek the Roses of Eighteen, ...2.RL4.32.186.
Like Roses that in Desarts bloom and die. ....2.RL4.158.197.
See from my cheek the transient roses fly! ....2.ElAb.331.346.
There the first roses of the year shall blow; ....2.Elegy.66.367.
Pearls on her neck, and roses in her hair, ...5.DunA2.152Z1.120.
The vanquish'd roses lose their pride, ...6.4iv.5.10.
Where opening *Roses* breathing sweets diffuse, ...6.14iv.3.47.

ROSIE
Here Bees from Blossoms sip the rosie Dew, ...1.PSu.69.77.
But ere the Rosie Morn renew'd the Day, ...1.TrUl.154.471.
'Till rosie Morn had purpled o'er the Sky: ....Il.1.623.117.
Now rosie Morn ascends the Court of *Jove,* ....Il.2.59.130.
First rosie *Venus* felt his brutal Rage; ....Il.5.557.295.
Soon as the Morn the rosie *Welkin* Warms ....Il.18.353A.338.
Soon as the Morn the rosie Orient warms ....Il.18.353B.338.
Gave to *Ulysses'* son the rosie wine. ....Od.3.77.90.
With rosie lustre purpled o'er the lawn; ....Od.3.517.112.
(Ambrosial cates, with Nectar rosie red) ....Od.5.118.178.
With water from the rock, and rosie wine, ...Od.5.214.181.
The goblet high with rosie wine they crown'd, ...Od.21.288.273.

ROSS
Rise, honest Muse! and sing the MAN of ROSS: ....3.Ep3.250.113.
The MAN of ROSS, each lisping babe replies. ....3.Ep3.262.115.
The MAN of ROSS divides the weekly bread: ....3.Ep3.264.115.
Is any sick? the MAN of ROSS relieves, ...3.Ep3.269.115.
Din'd with the MAN of ROSS, or my LORD MAY'R. ....4.EpS2.99.318.

ROSTRA
The *Roman Rostra* deck'd the Consul's Throne: ....2.TemF.239.274.

ROSY
Rosy and rev'rend, tho' without a Gown. ....5.DunB4.496.391.
Soon as the rosy Morn had wak'd the Day, ...Il.7.456.387.
Sprinkled with rosy Light the dewy Lawn, ...Il.8.2.394.
But when the rosy Messenger of Day ....Il.9.828.474.
Scarce did the Down his rosy Cheeks invest, ...Il.11.287.48.
That haunts the verdant Gloom, or rosy Bow'r, ...Il.20.12.393.
And now the rosy-finger'd Morn appears, ...Il.23.131.493.
On the mid Pavement pours the rosy Wine, ...Il.24.375.551.
Rosy and fair! as *Phœbus'* silver Bow ....Il.24.956.576.
With rosy Lustre streak'd the dewy Lawn; ....Il.24.1000.577.
But when the dawn reveals the rosy East, ...Od.1.474.55.
In rosy prime with charms attractive grac'd, ...Od.1.543.58.
By ten long years refin'd, and rosy-bright.) ....Od.3.505.112.
With rosy lustre purpled o'er the lawn; ....Od.3.624.118.
Advanc'd her rosy steps; before the bay, ...Od.4.587.147.
When rosy morning call'd them from their rest, ...Od.5.293.185.
Now from her rosy car *Aurora* shed ....Od.6.57.208.
And bad the herald pour the rosy wine. ....Od.7.239.248.
Soon as again the rosy morning shone, ...Od.9.174.312.
Now did the rosy-finger'd morn arise, ...Od.9.364.321.
When rosy morning glimmer'd o'er the dales, ...Od.9.515.327.
But when the rosy morning warm'd the east, ...Od.10.212.350.
And unregarded laughs the rosy wine. ....Od.10.448.365.
Prolong'd the feast, and quaff'd the rosy wine: ....Od.10.565.369.
Now did the rosy-finger'd Morn arise, ...Od.13.21.2.
To fill the goblet high with rosy wine: ....Od.13.65.4.
But ere the rosy morn renew'd the day, ...Od.13.321.23.
In grateful banquet o'er the rosy wine. ....Od.15.540.96.
Then to the Gods the rosy juice he pours, ...Od.18.179.175.
Retire we hence! but crown with rosy wine ....Od.18.464.190.
Nor think thy self exempt: that rosy prime ....Od.19.100.197.
Wine rosy-bright the brimming goblets crown'd, ...Od.20.317.248.

ROSY (CONTINUED)
Now flames the rosy dawn, but *Pallas* shrouds ....Od.23.398.343.

ROSY-BRIGHT
By ten long years refin'd, and rosy-bright.) ....Od.3.505.112.
Wine rosy-bright the brimming goblets crown'd, ...Od.20.317.248.

ROSY-FINGER'D
And now the rosy-finger'd Morn appears, ...Il.23.131.493.
Now did the rosy-finger'd morn arise, ...Od.9.364.321.
Now did the rosy-finger'd Morn arise, ...Od.13.21.2.

ROT
To draw nutrition, propagate, and rot; ....3.EOM2.64.63.
Sufficient Sap, at once to bear and rot. ....6.49i.12.137.
Shall Rot in *Drury-Lane.* ....6.54.20.165.

ROTATION
Oft in the Passions' wild rotation tost, ...3.Ep1.41.18.

ROTE
Chaucer's worst ribaldry is learn'd by rote, ...4.2HE1.37.197.

ROUGH
Rough *Satyrs* dance, and *Pan* applauds the Song: ....1.PSu.50.75.
And *smooth* or *rough,* with them, is *right* or *wrong;* ....1.EOC.338.277.
And *smooth* or *rough,* with such, is *right,or wrong;* ....1.EOC.338A.277.
The *hoarse, rough Verse* shou'd like the *Torrent* roar. ....1.EOC.369.282.
And combs with rakes, his rough, disorder'd hairs: ....1.TrPA.24.366.
By bearded cheeks, and members rough with hair. ....1.TrPA.107.370.
Horrid his Mane, and rough with curling Hairs; ....1.TrSt.568.434.
With Sculpture grac'd, and rough with rising Gold. ....1.TrSt.636.436.
Pointed above, and rough and gross below: ....1.TrES.184.456.
A plain rough Hero turn a crafty Knave? ....3.Ep1.78A.21.
The plain rough Hero turn a crafty Knave? ....3.Ep1.78.21.
Boastful and rough, your first son is a 'Squire; ....3.Ep1.103.22.
And something said of *Chartres* much too rough. ....4.HS1.4.5.
P. What? like Sir *Richard,* rumbling, rough and fierce, ...4.HS1.23.7.
Nay troth, th' *Apostles,* (tho' perhaps too rough) ....4.JD4.76.31.
More rough than forty Germans when they scold. ....4.JD2.62.139.
Has Age but melted the rough parts away, ...4.2HE2.318.187.
Old *England's* Genius, rough with many a Scar, ...4.EpS1.152.309.
Liquids grew rough, and *Mutes* turn'd vocal: ....6.30.8.86.
Soft *B*— and rough *C[ragg]s,* adieu! ....6.47.5.128*.
And rough *Pylenè,* and th' *Olenian* Steep ....Il.2.777.162.
Or where *Ithomè,* rough with Rocks, appears; ....Il.2.887.166.
Eyes the rough Waves, and tir'd returns at last. ....Il.5.739.302.
A Goat's rough Body bore a Lion's Head; ....Il.6.222.337.
Pointed above, and rough and gross below: ....Il.12.538.101.
As the fell Boar on some rough Mountain's Head, ...Il.13.594.134.
Smooths the rough Wood, and levels ev'ry Part; ....Il.15.475.215.
So rough thy Manners, so untam'd thy Mind. ....Il.16.53.237.
Pointed above, and rough and gross below: ....Il.16.894.277.
The rough *Ciconians* learn'd the Trade of War) ....Il.17.78.291.
Bridg'd the rough Flood across: The Hero stay'd ....Il.21.274.432.
Jumping high o'er the Shrubs of the rough Ground, ...Il.23.142.495.
And the slow Mules the same rough Road return. ....Il.23.151.495.
On this, rough *Auster* drove th' impetuous tyde: ....Od.3.377.104.
All rough with rocks, with foamy billows white. ....Od.5.521.197.
So the rough rock had shagg'd *Ulysses'* hands. ....Od.5.553.199.
For rough the way, and distant rolls the wave ....Od.6.43.207.
Rough from the tossing surge *Ulysses* moves; ....Od.6.162.216.
Crown'd with rough thickets, and a nodding wood. ....Od.9.224.316.
The rough rock roars; tumultuous boil the waves; ....Od.12.283.446.
Rein'd the rough storms, and calm'd the tossing floods: ....Od.12.470.454.
The fleecy spoils of sheep, a goat's rough hide ....Od.14.588.65.
To perish in the rough *Trinacrian* sea. ....Od.19.316.209.
Deep in the rough recesses of the wood, ...Od.19.511.221.
Of all that *Ithaca's* rough hills contain, ...Od.21.373.277.

ROUGHEN'D
And Sculpture rising on the roughen'd Gold. ....2.TemF.78.258.

ROUL
Rack'd with convulsive pangs in dust I roul; ....Od.4.726.153.
In her sad breast the Prince's fortunes roul, ...Od.4.1039.166.
High schemes of pow'r in just succession roul.) ....Od.19.326.210.

ROULING
In brooding tempests, and in rouling clouds; ....Od.12.88.436.

ROULS
And in soft mazes rouls a silver Tide: ....Od.11.286.396.
Where rouls yon smoke, yon tumbling ocean raves; ....Od.12.261.445.
Th' insulted Heroe rouls his wrathful eyes, ...Od.19.86.196.

ROUND
Round broken Columns clasping Ivy twin'd; ....1.W-F.69.156.
And Palms Eternal flourish round his Urn. ....1.W-F.312.179.
Where clearer Flames glow round the frozen Pole; ....1.W-F.390.189.
While they ring round the same *unvary'd Chimes,* ....1.EOC.348.278.
His flocks at random round the forest roam: ....1.TrPA.20.366.
Round like a shield, and in the middle plac'd: ....1.TrPA.109.370.
Then round your Neck in wanton Wreaths I twine, ...1.TrSP.149.400.
And *Cadmus* searching round the spacious Sea? ....1.TrSt.8.409.
A Hiss from all the Snaky Tire went round; ....1.TrSt.162.417.
And floated Fields lye undistinguish'd round: ....1.TrSt.499.431.
While Thunder roars, and Lightning round him flies. ....1.TrSt.525.432.
About the Realm she walks her dreadful Round, ...1.TrSt.710.440.
Like some black Tempest gath'ring round the Tow'rs: ....1.TrES.92.453.
He poiz'd, and swung it round; then tost on high, ...1.TrES.103.453.
Releas'd from Sleep; and round him might survey ....1.TrUl.54.467.
And Songs were sung, and flowing Bowls went round; ....2.ChJM.354.31.
And Songs were sung, and Healths went nimbly round; ....2.ChJM.354A.31.
The Servants round stood ready at their Call. ....2.ChJM.405.34.
Was compass'd round with Walls of solid Stone; ....2.ChJM.449.36.

ROUND (CONTINUED)
So featly tripp'd the light-foot Ladies round, 2.ChJM.620.45.
She licks her fair round Face, and frisks abroad 2.ChWB.146.63.
Know then, unnumber'd Spirits round thee fly, 2.RL1.41.148.
Hang o'er the *Box*, and hover round the *Ring*. 2.RL1.44.149.
The lucid Squadrons round the Sails repair: 2.RL2.56.163.
The Berries crackle, and the Mill turns round. 2.RL3.106.175.
Strait hover round the Fair her Airy Band; 2.RL3.113.176.
With earnest Eyes, and round unthinking Face, 2.RL4.125.194.
Why round our Coaches crowd the white-glov'd Beaus, 2.RL5.13.200.
Made visionary Fabricks round them rise, 2.TemF.103.261.
The Wars of *Troy* were round the Pillar seen: 2.TemF.188.271.
Here dragg'd in Triumph round the *Trojan* Wall. 2.TemF.191.271.
The Doves that round the Infant Poet spread 2.TemF.230.274.
Loud Laughs burst out, and bitter Scoffs fly round, 2.TemF.403.282.
With rapid Motion turn'd the Mansion round; 2.TemF.422.283.
Relentless walls! whose darksom round contains 2.ElAb.17.320.
Black Melancholy sits, and round her throws 2.ElAb.165.333.
And round thy phantom glue my clasping arms. 2.ElAb.234.339.
Where round some mould'ring tow'r pale ivy creeps, 2.ElAb.243.339.
While Altars blaze, and Angels tremble round. 2.ElAb.276.342.
Bright clouds descend, and Angels watch thee round, 2.ElAb.340.347.
Or tread the mazy round his follow'rs trod, 3.EOM2.25.58.
Look round our World; behold the chain of Love 3.EOM3.7.92.
Yet make at once their circle round the Sun: 3.EOM3.314.126.
Stuck o'er with titles and hung round with strings, 3.EOM4.205.146.
Plays round the head, but comes not to the heart: 3.EOM4.254.152.
Hemm'd round with Glories, pilfer Cloth or Bread, 3.Ep1.145Z2.27.
Still round and round the Ghosts of Beauty glide, 3.Ep2.241.69.
Still round and round the Ghosts of Beauty glide, 3.Ep2.241.69.
Or water all the Quorum ten miles round? 3.Ep3.42.89.
No noontide-bell invites the country round; 3.Ep3.192.109.
To all their dated Backs he turns you round, 3.Ep4.135.150.
Paint Angels trembling round his *falling Horse?* 4.HS1.28.7.
Shall half the new-built Churches round thee fall? 4.HS2.119.63.
On Broccoli and mutton, round the year; 4.HS2.138.65.
But ey'd him round, and stript off all the Cloaths; 4.HAdv.115.85.
They rave, recite, and madden round the land. 4.Arbu.6.96.
With desp'rate Charcoal round his darken'd walls? 4.Arbu.20.97.
Let Peals of Laughter, *Codrus!* round thee break, 4.Arbu.85.101.
Means not, but blunders round about a meaning: 4.Arbu.186.109.
Not Winds that round our ruin'd Abbeys roar, 4.JD2A.67.138.
There spread round MURRAY all your blooming Loves; 4.HOde1.10.151.
The Boys flock round him, and the People stare: 4.2HE2.120.173.
With Terrors round can Reason hold her throne, 4.2HE2.310.187.
Add one round hundred, and (if that's not fair) 4.1HE6.75.241.
Thro' Taverns, Stews, and Bagnio's take our round, 4.1HE6.119.245.
Hemm'd by a triple Circle round, 4.HS6.48.253.
Turn round to square, and square again to round; 4.1HE1.170.291.
Turn round to square, and square again to round; 4.1HE1.170.291.
Dragg'd in the Dust! his Arms hang idly round, 4.EpS1.153.309.
Or round a Quaker's Beaver cast a Glory. 4.EpS2.97.318.
The way they take is strangely round about. 4.EpS2.125.320.
Four guardian Virtues, round, support her Throne; 5.DunA1.44.65.
Or wafting ginger, round the streets to go, 5.DunA1.201.87.
Or wafting ginger, round the streets to run, 5.DunA1.201A.87.
Raptur'd, he gazes round the dear retreat, 5.DunA1.225.90.
With scarlet hats, wide waving, circles round, 5.DunA2.10.97.
So Jove's bright bow displays its watry round, 5.DunA2.165.121.
And courts to courts return it round and round: 5.DunA2.252.130.
And courts to courts return it round and round: 5.DunA2.252.130.
Round, and more round, o'er all the sea of heads. 5.DunA2.378.146.
Round, and more round, o'er all the sea of heads. 5.DunA2.378.146.
To some fam'd round-house, ever open gate! 5.DunA2.392.148.
Him close she curtain'd round with vapors blue, 5.DunA3.3.150.
Or whirligigs, twirl'd round by skilful swain, 5.DunA3.49.154.
See round the Poles where keener spangles shine, 5.DunA3.61.155.
Shall take thro' Grubstreet her triumphant round, 5.DunA3.128.160.
Round him, each *Science* by its modern type 5.DunA3.191z1.172.
Angel of Dulness, sent to scatter round 5.DunA3.253.178.
See! the dull stars roll round and re-appear. 5.DunA3.336.192.
When the dull stars roll round and re-appear. 5.DunA3.336A.192.
Four guardina Virtues, round, support her throne: 5.DunB1.46.274.
Round him much Embryo, much Abortion lay, 5.DunB1.121.278.
His Peers shine round him with reflected grace, 5.DunB2.9.296.
With scarlet hats wide-waving circled round, 5.DunB2.14.297.
So Jove's bright bow displays its wat'ry round, 5.DunB2.173.304.
And courts to courts return it round and round; 5.DunB2.264.308.
And courts to courts return it round and round; 5.DunB2.264.308.
Round and more round, o'er all the sea of heads. 5.DunB2.410.317.
Round and more round, o'er all the sea of heads. 5.DunB2.410.317.
To some fam'd round-house, ever open gate! 5.DunB2.424.318.
Him close she curtains round with Vapours blue, 5.DunB3.3.320.
Him close she curtain'd round with Vapours blue, 5.DunB3.3A.320.
Or whirligigs, twirl'd round by skilful swain, 5.DunB3.57.323.
See, round the Poles where keener spangles shine, 5.DunB3.69.323.
Shall take thro' Grub-street her triumphant round; 5.DunB3.136.326.
Angel of Dulness, sent to scatter round 5.DunB3.257.332.
See! the dull stars roll round and re-appear. 5.DunB3.322.335.
Now running round the Circle, finds it square. 5.DunB4.34.343.
Led by my hand, he saunter'd Europe round, 5.DunB4.311.374.
Walk round and round, now prying here, now there; 5.DunB4.353.377.
Walk round and round, now prying here, now there; 5.DunB4.353.377.
Others the Syren Sisters warble round, 5.DunB4.541.395.
Others the Syren Sisters compass round, 5.DunB4.541A.395.
While the long solemn Unison went round: 5.DunB4.612.405.
Attentive Blocks stand round you, and admire. 6.7.10.15.
Then oh! she cries, what Slaves I round me see? 6.9vii.4.22.
And oh! she cries, what Slaves I round me see? 6.9x.4A.22.
But oh! she cries, what Slaves I round me see? 6.9x.4B.22.
Transported Demi-Gods stood round, 6.11.42.31.
And Snakes uncurl'd hang list'ning round their Heads. 6.11.70.32.
With *Styx* nine times round her, 6.11.91.33.
The grunting Hogs alarm the Neighbours round, 6.14ii.26.43.
I see protecting Myriads round thee fly, 6.21.23.69.
And verdant olives flourish round the year. 6.35.10.103.

ROUND (CONTINUED)
When thousand Worlds are round. 6.50.24.147.
And deal Damnation round the land, 6.50.27.147.
Whole Systems flaming round 6.50.24A.147.
Or deal Damnation round the land, 6.50.27A.147.
And deal Destruction round the land, 6.50.27B.147.
Call round her tomb each object of desire, 6.52.49.157.
And round the orb in lasting notes be read, 6.71.66.204.
All the plum'd Beau-monde round her gathers; 6.93.9.256.
While the plum'd Beau–monde round her gathers; 6.93.9A.256.
Or tumbl'd from the Toadstool's slippery round 6.96ii.30Z9.271.
"Or tumbled from the Toadstool's slipp'ry Round, 6.96ii.43.272.
When folks might see thee all the Country round 6.96iv.79.278.
Wrapt round and sanctify'd with *Shakespear's* Name; 6.98.18.283.
Means not, but blunders round about a Meaning; 6.98.36.284.
Here lies a round Woman, who thought *mighty odd* 6.124i.1.346.
Sapho enrag'd crys out your Back is round, 6.129.3.357.
And ev'ry opening Virtue blooming round, 6.132.2.362.
And brandish'd round him all his Hundred Hands; Il.1.527.113.
Tost all the Day in rapid Circles round; Il.1.762.123.
Apollo tun'd the Lyre; the *Muses* round Il.1.774.124.
On the round Bunch the bloody Tumours rise; Il.2.328.143.
The Mother last, as round the Nest she flew, Il.2.382.145.
Round the vast Orb an hundred Serpents roll'd, Il.2.528.151.
Like some proud Bull that round the Pastures leads Il.2.566.154.
Say, Virgins, seated round the Throne Divine, Il.2.572.155.
Round the bleak Realms where *Hellespontus* roars, Il.2.1024.171.
Of those who round *Mœonia's* Realms reside, Il.2.1052.172.
A Night of Vapors round the Mountain-Heads, Il.3.16.188.
While round his dauntless Head the *Grecians* pour Il.3.113.195.
And, Master of the Flocks, surveys them round. Il.3.260.204.
And round the Lists the gen'rous Coursers neigh. Il.3.408.212.
Now round the Lists th' admiring Armies stand, Il.3.423.212.
Fair as a God with Odours round him spread Il.3.483.215.
The Maids officious round their Mistress wait, Il.3.526.216.
The stern *Atrides* rages round the Field: Il.3.560.218.
While the full Bowls flow round, the Pow'rs employ Il.4.5.221.
While round the Prince the *Greeks* employ their Care, Il.4.252.232.
Why stand ye gazing round the dreadful Plain, Il.4.278.234.
Alastor, Chromius, Hæmon round him wait, Il.4.340.237.
Such Clamours rose from various Nations round, Il.4.496.244.
Trojans and *Greeks* now gather round the Slain; Il.4.538.247.
Then sudden wav'd his flaming Faulchion round, Il.4.616.250.
He swung it round; and gath'ring Strength to throw, Il.5.373.285.
'Till in the Steely Circle straiten'd round, Il.5.774.303.
Such as the Heav'ns produce: and round the Gold Il.5.894.308.
Dire, black, tremendous! Round the Margin roll'd, Il.5.912.309.
(A warlike Circle) round *Tydides* stand: Il.5.973.313.
With Slaughter red, and raging round the Field. Il.5.1019.315.
Where the broad Cincture girt his Armor round, Il.5.1050.316.
Heap'd round, and heaving under Loads of slain; Il.5.1089.318.
Their consecrated Spears lay scatter'd round, Il.6.165.334.
His Brother-Chief, whose useless Arms lay round, Il.6.399.346.
Apply'd each Nerve, and swinging round on high, Il.7.321.379.
In flaming Circles round their Heads they flew, Il.7.330.380.
Escap'd great *Ajax*, they survey'd him round, Il.7.374.382.
He rais'd his Voice: The Hosts stood list'ning round. Il.7.459.387.
And round the Pile a gen'ral Tomb they rear'd. Il.7.519.389.
In shining Circle round their Father *Jove*, Il.7.527.391.
The Troops exulting sate in order round, Il.8.685.428.
Which round the Board *Menætius'* Son bestor'd; Il.9.284.447.
Has he not fenc'd his guarded Navy round, Il.9.460.455.
And the red Fiends that walk the nightly Round. Il.9.686.468.
He rose, and first he cast his Mantle round, Il.10.27.3.
All sheath'd in Arms, his brave Companions round: Il.10.171.9.
That round the Warrior cast a dreadful Shade; Il.11.44.36.
The vengeful Victor rages round the Fields Il.11.341.49.
And round him deep the steely Circle grows. Il.11.524.57.
With Bands of furious *Trojans* compass'd round. Il.11.593.60.
And glaring round, by tardy Steps withdrew. Il.11.673.65.
Tho' round his Sides a wooden Tempest rain, Il.11.684.65.
While round the Town the fierce *Epeians* stood. Il.11.869.74.
And the deaf Eccho rattles round the Fields. Il.12.182.87.
The dreadful Pass, and round them heap the slain. Il.12.212.88.
And round him rose a Monument of Dead. Il.12.224.89.
His Talons truss'd; alive, and curling round, Il.12.235.89.
Like some black Tempest gath'ring round the Tow'rs; Il.12.446.97.
He poiz'd, and swung it round; then toss'd on high, Il.12.457.98.
He sate; and round him cast his azure Eyes, Il.13.21.105.
There the great Ruler of the azure Round Il.13.53.107.
With well-rang'd Squadrons strongly circled round: Il.13.172.113.
A Rock's round Fragment flies, with Fury born, Il.13.192.115.
Full on the Shield's round Boss the Weapon rung; Il.13.256.117.
That shed a Lustre round th' illumin'd Wall. Il.13.340.122.
Beneath the spacious Targe (a blazing Round, Il.13.513.131.
Round dead *Alcathous* now the Battel rose; Il.13.628.136.
Antilochus, as *Thoon* turn'd him round, Il.13.690.137.
And everlasting Darkness shades him round. Il.13.844.146.
Their Guardians these, the Nations round confess, Il.13.919.148.
But round the Battlements, and round the Plain, Il.13.953.151.
But round the Battlements, and round the Plain, Il.13.953.151.
Shot Terrors round, that wither'd ev'n the Strong. Il.13.1017.153.
And spread a long, unmeasur'd Ruin round. Il.13.1031.153.
Here first she bathes; and round her Body pours Il.14.197.168.
Large Clasps of Gold the Foldings gather'd round, Il.14.209.170.
Call the black Gods that round Saturnus dwell, Il.14.309A.177.
Perfume the Mount, and breathe *Ambrosia* round. Il.14.404.183.
The golden Vision round his sacred Head; Il.14.414.183.
Toss'd round and round, the missive Marble flings; Il.14.475.187.
Toss'd round and round, the missive Marble flings; Il.14.475.187.
But whirling on, with many a fiery round, Il.14.479.187.
In vain an Iron Tempest hisses round; Il.14.497.188.
With watry Drops the Chief they sprinkle round, Il.14.509.188.
Eternal Darkness wrapt the Warrior round, Il.14.613.192.
Round the wide Fields he cast a careful view, Il.15.7.194.
(His sad Associates round with weeping Eyes) Il.15.12.194.

ROUNDELAY
And feebly sung a lusty Roundelay: ....2.ChJM.389.33.

ROUNDLY
What's *roundly smooth,* or *languishingly slow;* ....1.EOC.359.280.

ROUNDS
And gives th' eternal wheels to know their rounds. ....3.Ep3.170.107.
Now tow'r aloft, and course in airy Rounds; ....II.2.544.153.
Where the wan Spectres walk eternal rounds; ....Od.11.584.412.
In giddy rounds the whirling ship is tost, ...Od.14.339.51.

ROUS'D
Rous'd at his name, up rose the bowzy Sire, ...5.DunB4.493.390.

ROUSE
To rouse the *Spartan* I my self decree; ....II.10.128.7.

ROUT
Still press'd the Rout, and still the hindmost slew; ....II.11.232.45.
The *Grecian* Rout, the slaying, and the slain. ....II.11.733.67.
And where he turns, the Rout disperse, or die: ....II.12.52.83.
A Rout undisciplin'd, a straggling Train, ...II.13.141.111.
Stand, and my Spear shall rout their scatt'ring Pow'r, ...II.13.207.115.
To these, glad Conquest, murd'rous Rout to those. ....II.13.393.124.
Loud o'er the Rout was heard the Victor's Cry, ...II.16.454.260.
Of Men, Steeds, Chariots, urg'd the Rout along; ....II.17.824.320.
And rolls behind the Rout a Heap of Clouds) ....II.21.8.421.
Diverse their steps: The rival rout ascend ....Od.2.292.75.
Hither, intent the rival rout to slay ....Od.16.256.117.

ROUTED
Thus when dispers'd a routed Army runs, ...2.RL3.81.173.
And routed *Reason* finds a safe Retreat in thee. ....6.8.18.18.
Their Quibbles routed, and defy'd their Puns; ....6.128.12.356.
Turn back the Routed, and forbid the Flight; ....II.6.100.328.
Amidst the Tumult of the routed Train, ...II.11.161.42.
Thro' the mid Field the routed urge their way. ....II.11.218.45.
Victorious *Ajax* plies the routed Crew; ....II.11.610.61.
So *Jove* once more may drive their routed Train, ...II.12.117.93.
Neptune meanwhile the routed *Greeks* inspir'd; ....II.13.117.110.
And forc'd the routed Ranks to stand the Day. ....II.16.479.261.
Their Fellows routed, toss the distant Spear, ...II.17.437.304.
Her routed Squadrons pant behind their Wall: ....II.21.341.435.

ROUTING
For routing *Triplets,* and restoring *ed.* ....6.98.12Z2.283.

ROUZ'D
Thro' thickest Woods, and rouz'd the Beasts of Prey. ......1.TrSt.529.432.
Rouz'd by the Prince of Air, the whirlwinds sweep ....3.Ep3.353.122.
Lest, rouz'd to Rage, he shake the blest Abodes, ...II.1.748.123.
The Warrior rouz'd, and to th' Entrenchments led. ......II.10.206.10.
Rouz'd with the Cries of Dogs, and Voice of Men; ......II.12.164.87.
He said, and rouz'd the Soul in ev'ry Breast; ....II.13.211.116.
This rouz'd the Soul in ev'ry *Trojan* Breast; ....II.15.590.219.
Rouz'd from his Thicket by a Storm of Darts; ....II.21.678.450.
For angry *Neptune* rouz'd the raging main: ....Od.7.356.253.
Which rouz'd all *Greece* and made the mighty bleed; .....Od.14.273.49.
Rouz'd by the hounds and hunters' mingling cries, ...Od.19.517.221.
The City rouz'd shall to our rescue haste, ...Od.22.91.290.

ROUZE
With equal Warmth, and rouze the Warrior's Fire; ....1.TrES.54.451.
To stir, to rouze, to shake the Soul he comes, ...5.DunB4.67.348.
Rouze the huge Dragon, with a spurn, from rest, ...6.21.31.70.
Unite, and rouze the Sons of *Greece* to Arms. ....II.2.94.131.
And join to rouze the Sons of *Greece* to Arms. ....II.2.106.132.
Succeed to these my Cares, and rouze the rest; ....II.10.200.10.
And rouze, with Flame divine, the *Grecian* Pow'r. ......II.12.314.93.
With equal Warmth, and rouze the Warrior's Fire; ......II.12.398.96.
But most his Hunters rouze his mighty Rage. ....II.13.601.135.
Rouze then thy Forces this important Hour; ....II.22.343.470.
Provok'd to Passion, once more rouz'd to Ire ....II.24.733.568.
Rouze man by man, and animate my crew. ....Od.10.654.375.
To rouze *Ulysses,* points the Suitors' tongues: ....Od.18.396.187.
Ulysses wav'd, to rouze the savage war. ....Od.19.510.221.

ROUZES
Swells all the winds, and rouzes all the storms. ....Od.5.378.190.

ROUZING
Æneas rouzing as the Foe came on, ...II.20.335.407.

ROV'D
Dauntless we rov'd; *Achilles* led the way: ....Od.3.130.92.

ROVE
Here was she seen o'er Airy Wastes to rove, ...1.W-F.167.165.
I seem thro' consecrated Walks to rove, ...1.W-F.267.173.
Then frantick rise, and like some Fury rove ....1.TrSP.159.400.
The bounding Goats and frisking Heyfers rove; ....1.TrUl.129.470.
Why rove my thoughts beyond this last retreat? ....2.ElAb.5.319.
Not always glide thro' gloomy Vales, and rove ....6.17ii.21.56.
Biddel, like thee, might farthest *India* rove; ....6.96iv.19.276.
Thro' thy blest Shades (La Source) I seem to rove ....6.106ii.2.307.
Where the fat Herds in plenteous Pasture rove; ....II.2.735.161.
Constrain'd me from my native realm to rove: ....Od.4.360.137.
Free as the winds I give thee now to rove— ....Od.5.209.181.
Outcast I rove, familiar with the storms! ....Od.6.210.220.
Far from my native coast, I rove alone, ...Od.7.33.235.
Where savage goats thro' pathless thickets rove: ....Od.9.136.311.
O blind to fate! what led thy steps to rove ....Od.11.335.360.
For still distrest I rove from coast to coast, ...Od.11.589.412.
Still must we restless rove, new seas explore, ...Od.12.337.448.
The bounding goats and frisking heifers rove: ....Od.13.296.20.

ROVE (CONTINUED)
Whose fate enquiring, thro' the world we rove; ....Od.15.294.83.

ROVERS
When Sallee Rovers chac'd him on the deep. ....5.DunB4.380.380.
The captive dame *Phæacian* rovers bore, ...Od.7.11.233.

ROVES
With slaught'ring Guns th'unweary'd Fowler roves, ...1.W-F.125.162.
To distant Lands *Vertumnus* never roves; ....1.TrVP.85.380.
Mean time the banish'd *Polynices* roves ....1.TrSt.443.428.
While thro' Poetic scenes the Genius roves, ...5.DunB4.489.390.
"But ah! I fear thy little Fancy roves ....6.96ii.51.273.
As when o'er *Erymanth Diana* roves, ...Od.6.117.211.
As on his banks the maid enamour'd roves, ...Od.11.287.396.

ROVING
For gain, not glory, wing'd his roving flight, ...4.2HE1.71.199.
With roving pyrates o'er th' *Ægyptian* main: ....Od.17.510.157.

ROW
Cloath spice, line trunks, or flutt'ring in a row, ...4.2HE1.418.231.
Chatting and laughing all-a-row, ...4.HS6.136.259.
What passes in the dark third row ....6.61.8.181.
Sev'n were his Ships; each Vessel fifty row, ...II.2.876.165.
Shield touching Shield, a long-refulgent Row; ....II.12.311.93.
Thro' the fair Streets, the Matrons in a Row, ...II.18.575.350.
When justly tim'd with equal sweep they row, ...Od.7.419.258.
Swift row my mates, and shoot along the sea; ....Od.12.235.443.
Their heads above, connected in a row, ...Od.22.503.313.
Full fifty purple figs; and many a row ....Od.24.397.368.

ROW'D
Took down our masts, and row'd our ships to shore. .....Od.9.82.306.
Around his breast a wond'rous Zone is row'd, ...Od.11.751.423.
Swift to the town the well-row'd gally flew: ....Od.15.596.99.

ROWE
"But, for the Passions, Southern sure and Rowe. ....4.2HE1.86.201.
Sooner shall *Rowe* lampoon the UNION ....6.10.45.25.
Had not sage *Rowe* pronounc'd it *Entertaining.* ....6.12.9.37.
To drink and droll be *Rowe* allow'd ....6.47.9.128.
Heaven gives thee for thy Loss of *Rowe,* ....6.47.19.129.
Your Slave, and exit; but returns with *Rowe,* ....6.49ii.4.140.
Dear Rowe, *lets sit and talk of Tragedies:* ....6.49ii.5.140.
Pope to the Closet steps aside with *Rowe.* ....6.49ii.12.140.
Nor *Congreve, Rowe,* nor *Stanyan.* ....6.58.50.173.
Nor *Fenton, Rowe,* not *Stanyan.* ....6.58.50A.173.
Thy reliques, *Rowe,* to this fair urn we trust, ...6.72.1.208.
Thy reliques, *Rowe,* to this fair shrine we trust, ...6.72.1B.208.
Thy reliques, *Rowe,* to this fair tomb we trust, ...6.72.1C.208.
Thy Reliques, *Rowe!* to this sad Shrine we trust, ...6.152.1.400.
A Rowe of six fair Tripods then succeeds; ....II.19.251.383.
And here leave fixt the ringlets in a rowe. ....Od.21.277.273.

ROWERS
To the strong stroke at once the rowers bend. ....Od.2.459.83.

ROWES
To Rowes dear Reliques be this Marble just ....6.72.1A.208.

ROWL
Thro' the fair Scene rowl slow the lingring Streams, ...1.W-F.217.169.
Chariots on Chariots rowl; the clashing Spokes ....II.16.444.260.
The thoughts which rowl within my ravish'd breast, ...Od.1.259.45.
Why rowl those eyes unfriended of repose? ....Od.20.42.234.
Father of Gods and men! whose thunders rowl ....Od.20.141.240.
Nor gives the Sun his golden orb to rowl, ...Od.20.429.254.

ROWL'D
Rowl'd in the bloody Dust, and paw'd the slipp'ry Ground. .....1.TrES.272.459.
Rowl'd in the bloody dust, and paw'd the slip'ry ground. ....II.16.577.267.
With broken force the billows rowl'd away, ...Od.3.378.105.
Here, till the setting sun rowl'd down the light, ...Od.9.188.313.
There, 'till the setting sun rowl'd down the light, ...Od.10.208.350.
Full on his Sire he rowl'd his ardent eyes; ....Od.20.460.255.

ROWLING
The various Seasons of the rowling Year; ....1.PSp.38.64.
But as around his rowling orb he cast, ...1.TrPA.136.371.
High o'er the rowling Heav'ns, a Mansion lyes, ...1.TrSt.276.421.
Those from whose Urns the rowling Rivers flow, ...1.TrSt.288.422.
The Heav'ns, and drives on heaps the rowling Clouds, ...1.TrSt.493.430.
Her twisting Volumes, and her rowling Eyes, ...1.TrSt.728.440.
The rowling Ruins smoak along the Field. ....1.TrES.132.454.
The solitary Shore, and rowling Sea. ....1.TrUl.55.467.
The rowling smokes involve the sacrifice. ....5.DunA1.206.87.
The rowling smokes involve the sacrifice. ....5.DunB1.248.288.
Who fix't thy self amidst the rowling frame, ...6.23.7.73.
His rowling Wheels did run: ....6.79.126.222.
The Goddess spoke: The rowling Waves unclose; ....II.1.562.115.
Beneath the rowling Sun, and starry Skies, ...II.4.66.224.
His Country's Cares lay rowling in his Breast. ....II.10.4.2.
And wrap in rowling Flames the Fleet and Wall. ....II.12.228.89.
The rowling Ruins smoak along the Field. ....II.12.486.99.
She speeds to *Lemnos* o'er the rowling Deep, ...II.14.264.173.
To break the rowling waves, and ruffling storm: ....Od.4.1106.169.
To shield the vessel from the rowling sea; ....Od.5.519.197.
Back to the seas the rowling surge may sweep, ...Od.5.536.198.
And soft receives him from the rowling sea. ....Od.5.579.200.
With living flames his rowling eye-balls glow; ....Od.6.156.216.
Amid the terrors of the rowling main. ....Od.7.331.253.
And all unseen the surge and rowling sea, ...Od.9.170.312.
To the hoarse murmurs of the rowling deep. ....Od.12.10.430.
And thou whose lustre gilds the rowling sphere! ....Od.17.149.139.

ROWLS
And *Erasinus* rowls a Deluge on: ....1.TrSt.501.431.
The Car rowls slowly o'er the dusty Plain. ....1.TrES.280.460.
The Car rowls slowly o'er the dusty Plain. ....Il.16.585.267.
Slow rowls the car before th' attending train. ....Od.6.380.230.
Still as they plead, the fatal lots he rowls, ...Od.11.701.419.
Round his swol'n heart the murm'rous fury rowls; ....Od.20.19.232.

ROWS
Here Files of Pins extend their shining Rows, ...2.RL1.137.156.
Why bows the Side-box from its inmost Rows? ....2.RL5.14.200.
And ever-living Lamps depend in Rows. ....2.TemF.144.265.
Whose Cause-way parts the vale with shady rows? ....3.Ep3.259.114.
With arms expanded Bernard rows his state, ...5.DunB2.67.299.
And mount the Hill in venerable rows: ....6.14iv.14.47.
Ten Rows of azure Steel the Work infold, ...Il.11.31.36.
The Trees in flaming rows to Ashes turn, ...Il.21.408.437.
There casks of wine in rows adorn'd the dome. ....Od.2.385.79.
Two rows of stately dogs, on either hand, ...Od.7.118.240.
Her jaws grin dreadful with three rows of teeth; ....Od.12.113.437.
The King selected from the glitt'ring rows ....Od.15.116.74.
Distinct in rows the radiant columns rise: ....Od.19.45.195.
Thro' rows of shade with various fruitage crown'd, ...Od.24.255.361.

ROWS'D
Rows'd by the woodland nymphs, at early dawn, ...Od.9.178.312.

ROWZ'D
Rowz'd by the light, old Dulness heav'd the head, ...5.DunA1.213.89.
Rowz'd by the light, old Dulness heav'd the head; ....5.DunB1.257.289.
Array'd in Terrors, rowz'd the *Trojan* Pow'rs: ....Il.4.594.249.
Old *Nestor* saw, and rowz'd the Warrior's Rage; ....Il.6.83.327.
Troy rowz'd as soon; for on this dreadful Day ....Il.8.69.398.
Thus while he rowz'd the Fire in ev'ry Breast, ...Il.16.252.249.
And rowzing *Ajax,* rowz'd the list'ning Bands. ....Il.16.680.270.
Rowz'd from my fatal sleep, I long debate ....Od.10.54.342.
Thus *Agelaus* rowz'd the lagging band. ....Od.22.271.299.

ROWZE
Rowze the fleet Hart, and chear the opening Hound. ....1.W-F.150.164.
To rowze the Watchmen of the Publick Weal, ...4.EpS2.217.325.
Or rowze the Furies and awake the War? ....Il.4.22.222.
Shall rowze thy Slaves, and her lost Lord deplore, ...Il.5.503.292.
Rowze all thy *Trojans,* urge thy *Aids* to fight; ....Il.5.597.297.
I go to rowze soft *Paris* to the War; ....Il.6.349.343.
A nobler Charge shall rowze the dawning Day. ....Il.8.652.426.

ROWZES
Morpheus rowzes from his Bed; ....6.11.31.31.
Dull *Morpheus* rowzes from his Bed; ....6.11.31A.31.
The Savage wound, he rowzes at the Smart, ...Il.5.177.275.

ROWZING
Shock just had giv'n himself the rowzing Shake, ...2.RL*A*1.15.127.
Now Lapdogs give themselves the rowzing Shake, ...2.RL1.15.146.
And rowzing *Ajax,* rowz'd the list'ning Bands. ....Il.16.680.270.
Elate her Heart, and rowzing all her Pow'rs, ...Il.17.149.293.

ROYAL
And makes his trembling Slaves the Royal Game. ....1.W-F.64.155.
Of Nature broke; and Royal Perjuries; ....1.TrSt.179.418.
Such was the Discord of the Royal Pair, ...1.TrSt.190.418.
And now the King, his Royal Feast to grace, ...1.TrSt.617.436.
The Royal Nymphs approach divinely bright, ...1.TrSt.624.436.
The Royal Nymphs approach'd divinely bright, ...1.TrSt.624A.436.
His Royal Person from his Friends and Queen, ...1.TrUl.61.468.
Proves the just Victim of his Royal Rage. ....2.RL3.60.172.
There in long Robes the Royal *Magi* stand, ...2.TemF.97.260.
And sweetly flow through all the Royal Line. ....4.HS1.32.7.
With Royal Favourites in Flatt'ry vie, ...4.JD4.60.31.
"He dwells amidst the Royal Family; ....4.JD4.103.33.
You give all royal Witchcraft to the Devil: ....4.2HE2.219.181.
"I cannot like, Dread Sir! your Royal Cave; ....4.1HE1.115.287.
Like Royal Harts, be never more run down? ....4.EpS2.29.314.
She ceas'd. Then swells the Chapel-royal throat: ....5.DunB1.319.293.
His royal Sense, of Op'ra's or the Fair; ....5.DunB4.314.374.
Shall Royal praise be rhym'd by such a ribald, ...6.116v.1.327.
Then might a Royal Youth, and true, ...6.135.77.369.
A Treasure, which, of Royal kind, ...6.135.79.369.
The Brother-Kings, of *Atreus'* Royal Race. ....Il.1.22.86.
Or, if our Royal Pleasure shall ordain, ...Il.1.189.96.
With Fraud, unworthy of a Royal Mind. ....Il.1.196.96.
Thence bear *Briseïs* as our Royal Prize: ....Il.1.423.108.
The Brother Kings of *Atreus'* Royal Race: ....Il.1.489.111.
But Royal Scandal his Delight supreme. ....Il.2.270.140.
And bring the Race of Royal Bastards here, ...Il.2.285.141.
Were led by *Pandarus,* of Royal Blood. ....Il.2.1001.170.
The loveliest Nymph of *Priam's* Royal Race) ....Il.3.168.199.
My House was honour'd with each Royal Guest: ....Il.3.270.205.
The Royal Brother thus his Grief exprest, ...Il.4.183.230.
Honour'd and lov'd like *Priam's* Royal Race: ....Il.5.662.299.
Of Royal *Hecuba,* his Mother Queen. ....Il.6.313.341.
A thousand Measures to the Royal Tent. ....Il.7.563.392.
And drench'd in Royal Blood the thirsty Dart. ....Il.8.368.415.
Superior Sorrows swell'd his Royal Breast; ....Il.9.12.431.
And each well worthy of a Royal Bed; ....Il.9.188.441.
Then from the Royal Tent they take their way; ....Il.9.232.444.
Then from the Royal Tent they took their way; ....Il.9.232A.444.
Patroclus only of the Royal Train, ...Il.9.251.445.
Gifts worthy thee, his Royal Hand prepares; ....Il.9.341.450.
And each well worthy of a Royal Bed; ....Il.9.375.451.
The Royal *Peleus,* when from *Pthia's* Coast ....Il.9.566.461.
Whose luckless Hand his Royal Uncle slew; ....Il.9.682.468.
Pass'd thro the Hosts, and reach'd the Royal Tent. ....Il.9.787.472.
To wake *Atrides* in the Royal Tent. ....Il.10.38.4.
Ev'n to the Royal Tent pursue my way, ...Il.10.385.21.

ROYAL (CONTINUED)
(Whom to his aged Arms, a Royal Slave, ...Il.11.766.69.
Lo! where the Son of Royal *Clytius* lies, ...Il.15.496.216.
Belov'd no less than *Priam's* Royal Race. ....Il.15.651.221.
And is it thus our Royal Kinsman dies? ....Il.15.655.221.
The King of Nations forc'd his royal Slave: ....Il.18.518.346.
To bear the Presents from the royal Tent. ....Il.19.244.383.
Like young *Lycaon,* of the Royal Line, ...Il.20.113.398.
To *Lemnos'* Isle he sold the Royal Slave, ...Il.21.46.424.
(O King of Men!) it claims thy royal Care, ...Il.23.61.489.
When *Hermes* greeting, touch'd his royal Hand, ...Il.24.445.554.
And joyful thus the royal Sire reply'd. ....Il.24.518.557.
These serv'd his Person at the royal Feast, ...Il.24.582.561.
The wond'ring Hero eyes his royal Guest; ....Il.24.797.570.
No less the royal Guest the Hero eyes, ...Il.24.798.570.
Sincere from royal blood, and faith profan'd; ....Od.1.50.33.
Of sandy *Pyle,* the royal Youth shall haste. ....Od.1.119.38.
The stranger Guest the royal Youth beheld. ....Od.1.156.40.
Are you, of manly growth, his royal heir? ....Od.1.268.45.
Unblam'd abundance crown'd the royal board, ...Od.1.297.47.
Of *Ilus* sprung from *Jason's* royal strain, ...Od.1.338.48.
With decent grief the royal dead deplor'd, ...Od.1.382.51.
Join to that royal youth's, your rival name, ...Od.1.393.51.
From *Temesé* return'd, your royal court ....Od.1.410.52.
Mean-time rekindl'd at the royal charms, ...Od.1.465.54.
A royal robe he wore with graceful pride, ...Od.2.5.60.
The royal bed, *Eurynomus* aspires; ....Od.2.28.61.
(His royal hand th' imperial scepter sway'd) ....Od.2.45.62.
If ruin to our royal race ye doom, ...Od.2.83.64.
For three long years the royal fraud behold? ....Od.2.102.66.
"Lest when the Fates his royal ashes claim, ...Od.2.111.67.
And seek my royal sire from shore to shore: ....Od.2.244.73.
The royal dome; while sad the Prince explores ....Od.2.293.75.
The royal suppliant to *Minerva* pray'd. ....Od.2.296.76.
And as he moves with royal anguish mourns. ....Od.2.336.77.
The royal Palace to the Queen convey, ...Od.2.378.79.
To keep my voyage from the royal ear, ...Od.2.419.81.
On *Nestor* first, and *Nestor's* royal line; ....Od.3.71.89.
The royal dame his lawless suit deny'd. ....Od.3.331.102.
When beds of royal state invite your stay? ....Od.3.450.108.
On me, my consort, and my royal line! ....Od.3.489.111.
The Monarch turns him to his royal guest; ....Od.3.603.117.
And speeding, thus address'd the royal ear. ....Od.4.32.121.
The royal portion of the choicest chines ....Od.4.78.123.
Alcandra gave, a pledge of royal grace: ....Od.4.168.128.
And bounteous, from the royal treasure told ....Od.4.175.128.
Say, royal youth, sincere of soul report ....Od.4.421.140.
A suppliant to your royal court I come. ....Od.4.428.140.
With patient ear, oh royal youth, attend ....Od.4.467.142.
Secure of storms, your royal brother past: ....Od.4.684.151.
Magnificent he leads: the royal guest ....Od.4.715.152.
Be *Sparta* honour'd with his royal guest, ...Od.4.802.156.
In dear remembrance of your royal grace, ...Od.4.819.157.
And smiling thus, the royal Youth address'd: ....Od.4.830.158.
Before her dome the royal matron stands, ...Od.4.904.160.
The darling object of your royal care ....Od.4.928.161.
He dar'd not violate your royal ear. ....Od.4.989.163.
To all my hope my royal Lord is lost, ...Od.4.1071.167.
The royal car at early dawn obtain, ...Od.6.41.207.
Then with a filial awe the royal maid ....Od.6.67.208.
And may his child the royal car obtain? ....Od.6.70.208.
Swift at the royal nod th' attending train ....Od.6.85.209.
Then æmulous the royal robes they lave, ...Od.6.105.211.
From great *Alcinous'* royal loins I spring, ...Od.6.237.221.
Close by the stream a royal dress they lay, ...Od.6.253.222.
Attend my royal sire, a radiant band. ....Od.6.306.225.
Here a rich juice the royal vineyard pours; ....Od.6.355.229.
To great *Alcinous* on his royal throne. ....Od.6.360.229.
Her royal hand a wond'rous work designs, ...Od.6.367.229.
My royal father shares the genial hours; ....Od.6.372.229.
And her, *Alcinous* chose his royal mate. ....Od.7.85.238.
Fix'd in amaze before the royal gates. ....Od.7.109.239.
To thee, thy consort, and this royal train, ...Od.7.196.245.
The prudent *Greek)* possess the royal mind. ....Od.7.282.249.
And graceful thus began the royal maid. ....Od.8.498.289.
O royal maid, *Ulysses* strait returns, ...Od.8.503.289.
These ears have heard my royal Sire disclose ....Od.8.617.295.
The royal bark had ten. Our ships compleat ....Od.9.186.313.
And six fair daughters, grac'd the royal bed: ....Od.10.6.339.
Our second progress to my royal friend; ....Od.10.64.342.
And shew'd them where the royal dome appear'd. ....Od.10.126.347.
All pale ascends my royal mother's shade: ....Od.11.105.385.
Say if my spouse maintains her royal trust, ...Od.11.214.392.
The royal partner of fam'd *Cretheus'* bed. ....Od.11.282.395.
Then fruitful, to her *Cretheus'* royal bed ....Od.11.313.397.
The royal *Minos Ariadne* bred, ...Od.11.399.403.
But here this night the royal guest detain, ...Od.11.436.405.
Thro' veins (he cry'd) of royal fathers flow'd; ....Od.11.451.406.
But say, resides my son in royal port, ...Od.11.565.411.
And the bright partner of thy royal throne. ....Od.12.536.459.
These ears have heard my royal sire disclose ....Od.13.198.15.
His royal person from his friends and Queen; ....Od.13.228.17.
For thee he sighs; and to the royal heir ....Od.13.467.28.
Deludes with fallacies the royal ear, ...Od.14.151.43.
Beneath the royal Portico display'd, ...Od.15.5.69.
Himself thy convoy to each royal friend. ....Od.15.94.73.
And now, when thro' the royal dome they pass'd, ...Od.15.146.75.
From *Ithaca,* of royal birth I came, ...Od.15.290.83.
Ulysses' wand'rings to his royal mate; ....Od.15.333.85.
Unwelcome news, or vex the royal ear; ....Od.15.401.88.
Swift from above descends the royal Fair; ....Od.17.45.134.
The stranger's words may ease the royal heart: ....Od.17.603.161.
So finding favour in the royal eye, ...Od.17.640.163.
A Mendicant approach'd the royal gate; ....Od.18.2.166.
(Reply'd the sagest of the royal train) ....Od.18.202.176.
That sadly tore my royal Lord away: ....Od.18.302.181.

ROYAL (CONTINUED)

But when my son grows man, the royal sway	Od.18.313.181.
His royal hands; Each torch refulgent burns	Od.18.392.186.
Of royal grace th' offended Queen may guide;	Od.19.103.197.
The royal bed an elder issue blest,	Od.19.210.203.
My honour'd roof receiv'd the royal guest:	Od.19.227.204.
Then he, with pity touch'd: O Royal Dame!	Od.19.298.209.
The royal object of your dearest care,	Od.19.307.209.
The darling object of your royal love,	Od.19.339.210.
With royal gifts to send you honour'd home!—	Od.19.361.211.
"Receive, she cries, your royal daughter's son;	Od.19.475.219.
Amphithea's arms receiv'd the royal heir;	Od.19.487.220.
But studious to conceal her royal Lord,	Od.19.557.223.
Task'd for the royal board to bolt the bran	Od.20.134.240.
When, early dress'd, advanc'd the royal heir;	Od.20.155.241.
The goodliest goats of all the royal herd	Od.20.219.243.
And with the royal herd protection buy:	Od.20.278.246.
Assent your self, and gain the royal will.	Od.20.392.251.
Whene'er her choice the royal Dame avows,	Od.20.409.252.
Where safe repos'd the royal treasures lay;	Od.21.12.259.
Nor to the royal heart recall in vain	Od.21.89.263.
Ye peers and rivals in the royal love!	Od.21.293.274.
O royal mother! ever-honour'd name!	Od.21.369.277.
Where pil'd on heaps the royal armour lies;	Od.22.127.292.
Stores from the royal magazine I bring,	Od.22.156.294.
Where slumbers soft now close the royal eye;	Od.22.467.311.
Permit me first thy royal robes to bring:	Od.22.525.314.
The royal pair; she guides them, and retires.	Od.23.316.338.
His royal mother, pale *Anticlea's* shade;	Od.23.350.341.
With rival loves pursu'd his royal Dame;	Od.24.147.355.
Lest, when the Fates his royal ashes claim,	Od.24.160.356.
Of *Polypemon's* royal line I spring.	Od.24.356.366.
Dismiss that care, for to the royal bride	Od.24.468.371.

ROYALL

That serves his R[oyal]l H[ighness]	6.94.76.261.

RUB

With thirsty sponge they rub the tables o'er,	Od.22.488.313.

RUBBISH

Bright thro' the rubbish of some hundred years;	4.2HE2.166.177.

RUBICON

Or on the Rubicon, or on the Rhine.	3.EOM4.246.151.

RUBIED

With sanguine drops the walls are rubied round:	Od.20.426.254.

RUBIES

The flaming Rubies shew their sanguine Dye;	2.TemF.251.275.

RUBRIC

What tho' my Name stood rubric on the walls?	4.Arbu.215.111.
Of Curl's chaste press, and Lintot's rubric post,	5.DunA1.38.O64.
Of Curl's chaste press, and Lintot's rubric post:	5.DunB1.40.273.

RUBS

Just as a blockhead rubs his thoughtless skull,	6.41.7.113.

RUBY

The Coral redden, and the Ruby glow,	1.W-F.394.190.
See on these ruby lips the trembling breath,	2.Elegy.31.365.

RUDDER

Ev'n with the rudder in his hand, he fell.	Od.3.360.104.
And to the helm the guiding rudder join'd.	Od.5.326.187.
Swept from the deck, and from the rudder torn,	Od.5.405.192.
Then first my hands did from the rudder part,	Od.10.36.341.

RUDDIER

Did here the trees with ruddier burdens bend,	3.EOM3.203.113.

RUDDY

Fresh are his ruddy Cheeks, his Forehead fair,	2.ChWB.120.62.
The ruddy Gold, the Steel, and shining Brass;	Il.9.478.456.
Which never Man had stain'd with ruddy Wine,	Il.16.274.249.
And Heav'ns high Arch reflects the ruddy Light;	Il.18.252.334.
The ruddy Morning rises o'er the Waves;	Il.24.22.535.
Still as *Aurora's* ruddy Beam is spread,	Il.24.507.557.
Here ruddy brass and gold refulgent blaz'd;	Od.2.382.79.
Thus while he speaks, the ruddy sun descends,	Od.3.421.107.
Then slowly sunk the ruddy globe of light,	Od.3.629.118.
And all the ruddy Orient flames with day:	Od.8.2.260.
A ruddy gleam; whose hilt, a silver blaze;	Od.8.438.287.
'Till ruddy morning purpled o'er the east.	Od.9.653.333.
So speaking, from the ruddy orient shone	Od.10.645.375.

RUDE

While the rude Swain his rural Musick tries,	1.TrSt.689.439.
To save the Powder from too rude a Gale,	2.RL2.93.165.
Or caus'd Suspicion when no Soul was rude,	2.RL4.73.190.
There, on rude Iron Columns smear'd with Blood,	2.TemF.125.264.
Confounds the Civil, keeps the Rude in awe,	4.JD4.270.47.
"I'm quite asham'd—'tis mighty rude	4.HS6.208.263.
Which some rude wind will always discompose;	6.22.4.71.
Or bid the furious *Gaul* be rude no more?	6.51.16.151.
Beneath a rude and nameless stone he lies,	6.72.3.208.
By *Boreas's* rude breath.—	6.100iv.3.289.
Rude from the Furnace, and but shap'd by Fire.	Il.23.976.528.
So the rude *Boreas*, o'er the field new shorn,	Od.5.470.195.
There no rude winds presume to shake the skies,	Od.6.51.207.
Beat by rude blasts, and wet with wintry show'rs,	Od.6.154.216.
Unseen of all the rude *Phæacian* race.	Od.7.52.236.
Tost by rude tempest thro' a war of waves:	Od.8.28.263.
Ill bear the brave a rude ungovern'd tongue,	Od.8.199.273.

RUDE (CONTINUED)

Rude, and unconscious of a stranger's right;	Od.9.204.314.
Rude Pyrates seiz'd, and shipp'd thee o'er the main?	Od.15.419.89.
And the rude insults of ungovern'd tongues.	Od.16.86.106.
To some rude churl, and born by stealth away.	Od.16.241.116.
Some rude insult thy rev'rend age may bear;	Od.17.330.147.
Full on the shoulder the rude weight descends:	Od.18.109.172.
Pierc'd thro' the breast the rude *Ctesippus* bled,	Od.22.316.301.
And the rude licence of ungovern'd tongues,	Od.23.30.320.
But if o'erturn'd by rude, ungovern'd hands,	Od.23.207.333.
(Some surly Islander, of manners rude)	Od.24.307.364.
For godless men, and rude, possess the coast:	Od.24.327.365.

RUDELY

A being darkly wise, and rudely great:	3.EOM2.4.53.
Crawl thro' the Street, shov'd on, or rudely press'd	3.Ep1.230A.35.
Shov'd from the wall perhaps, or rudely press'd	3.Ep1.230.35.
"But rudely press before a Duke.	4.HS6.59.253.
'Those Loving Ladies rudely to traduce.	6.13.21.39.
For whom thus rudely pleads my loud-tongu'd Gate,	6.100i.1.288.
And rudely scatters, far to distance round,	Il.17.332.300.

RUDIMENTS

While yet he learn'd his Rudiments of War.	Il.16.977.281.

RUE

"The Day I meet him, *Nic.* shall rue	6.79.139.222.
"The Day I meet *Nic.* he shall rue	6.79.139A.222.
And all your wrongs the proud oppressors rue!	Od.1.330.48.
The breach of hospitable right may rue.	Od.19.371.212.

RUEFUL

Lo H[orne]ck's fierce, and M[itchell]'s rueful face;	5.DunA3.146A.162.
Yet smiling at his rueful length of face)	5.DunB2.142.302.

RUEFULL

Obscene to sight, the ruefull Racer lay;	Il.23.912.525.

RUFA

Rufa, whose eye quick-glancing o'er the Park,	3.Ep2.21.50.
Agrees as ill with Rufa studying Locke,	3.Ep2.23.51.

RUFA'S

Rufa's at either end a Common-Shoar,	4.HAdv.29.77.

RUFF

Soft on the paper ruff its leaves I spread,	5.DunB4.407.382.
And Ruff compos'd most duly;	6.58.34.172.
And search the shag of Thighatira's Ruff.	6.96ii.30Z2.271.

RUFFIAN

By some stern ruffian, or adultrous wife.	Od.3.292.100.
The ruffian breathing yet on *Argive* ground;	Od.3.319.102.
Or darling son oppress'd by ruffian-force	Od.4.311.134.
May timely intercept their ruffian rage,	Od.4.977.163.

RUFFIAN-FORCE

Or darling son oppress'd by ruffian-force	Od.4.311.134.

RUFFIAN'S

Dread not the railer's laugh, nor ruffian's rage;	Od.20.328.249.

RUFFLED

Where Contemplation prunes her ruffled Wings,	4.JD4.186.41.
Here Contemplation prunes her ruffled Wings,	4.JD4.186A.41.
There Contemplation prunes her ruffled Wings,	4.JD4.186B.41.
The whitening Surface of the ruffled Deep.	Il.2.178.137.
Dispers'd and broken thro' the ruffled Skies.	Il.5.648.299.
The ruffled Seas beneath their Passage roar.	Il.23.287.501.

RUFFLING

To break the rowling waves, and ruffling storm:	Od.4.1106.169.

RUFUL

Yet smiling at his ruful length of face)	5.DunA2.134.115.

RUFUS

Lo *Rufus*, tugging at the deadly Dart,	1.W-F.83.158.

RUFUS'

Thames wafts it thence to Rufus' roaring hall,	5.DunA2.253.130.
Thames wafts it thence to Rufus' roaring hall,	5.DunB2.265.308.

RUG

Who sins with whom? who got his Pension *Rug*,	4.JD4.134.37.

RUGGED

The rugged Soil allows no level Space	1.TrUl.122.470.
Ye rugged rocks! which holy knees have worn;	2.ElAb.19.320.
Where *Ægilipa's* rugged Sides are seen,	Il.2.771.162.
Thro' both the Tendons broke the rugged Stone,	Il.5.377.285.
Some rugged Rock's hard Entrails gave thee Form,	Il.16.50.237.
As when two Mules, along the rugged Road,	Il.17.832.321.
A race of rugged mariners are these;	Od.7.41.235.
The rugged race of savages, unskill'd	Od.9.147.311.
The rugged soil allows no level space	Od.13.289.19.
A rugged staff his trembling hand sustains;	Od.13.505.30.
A rural Portico of rugged stone:	Od.14.10.35.
My feeble step, since rugged is the way.	Od.17.219.142.
Now pass'd the rugged road, they journey down	Od.17.230.143.
And labour made the rugged soil a plain.	Od.24.237.360.

RUIN

O'er Heaps of Ruin stalk'd the stately Hind;	1.W-F.70.156.
The pondrous Ruin crush'd his batter'd Crown.	1.TrES.106.453.
Just in the Jaws of Ruin, and *Codille*.	2.RL3.92.174.

RUIN (CONTINUED)

Atoms or systems into ruin hurl'd, ...3.EOM1.89.25.
How happy! those to ruin, these betray, ...3.EOM4.290.155.
More go to ruin Fortunes, than to raise. ......3.Ep3.202Z2.110.
Could joyn the Arts, to ruin, and to please. ......4.HAdv.6.75.
So odd, my Country's Ruin makes me grave. ......4.EpS2.207.324.
A yawning ruin hangs and nods in air; ......5.DunA1.28.63.
Oh glorious ruin! and *Apelles* burn'd. ......5.DunA3.97Z2.158.
Quite o'er the Banks to their own Ruin force. ......6.17ii.17.56.
Thy Father's Grief, and Ruin of thy Race; ......Il.3.74.193.
Then had his Ruin crown'd *Atrides'* Joy, ...Il.3.459.214.
The Race of *Trojans* in thy Ruin join, ...Il.4.190.230.
And one prodigious Ruin swallow All. ......Il.4.199.230.
Discharg'd the pond'rous Ruin at the Foe. ......Il.5.374.285.
That Pest of *Troy,* that Ruin of our Race! ......Il.6.353.343.
My Mother's Death, the Ruin of my Kind, ...Il.6.575.355.
With Force tempestuous let the Ruin fly: ......Il.7.322.379.
The Ruin vanish'd, and the Name no more ......Il.7.555.392.
Stretch'd in long Ruin, and expos'd to Day) ......Il.11.124.41.
And one refulgent Ruin levells all. ......Il.11.204.44.
Now the last Ruin the whole Host appalls; ......Il.11.403.52.
And whelms the smoaky Ruin in the Waves. ......Il.12.32.82.
And the white Ruin rises o'er the Plain. ......Il.12.344.94.
The pond'rous Ruin crush'd his batter'd Crown. ......Il.12.460.98.
From Steep to Steep the rolling Ruin bounds; ......Il.13.195.115.
And hurl the blazing Ruin at our Head. ......Il.13.409.125.
And hurl the brazen Ruin at our Head. ......Il.13.409A.125*.
Then spreads a length of Ruin o'er the Ground. ......Il.13.496.130.
And spread a long, unmeasur'd Ruin round. ......Il.13.1031.153.
Who, far from *Argos,* wills our Ruin here. ......Il.14.76.161.
On the raz'd Shield the falling Ruin rings: ......Il.14.476.187.
The Mountain-Oak in flaming Ruin lies, ...Il.14.483.187.
And dread the Ruin that impends on all. ......Il.14.598.191.
And one vast Ruin whelm th' *Olympian* State. ......Il.15.155.202.
Roll'd in the Ditch the heapy Ruin lay; ......Il.15.408.213.
The falling Ruin crush'd *Cebrion's* Head, ...Il.16.895.277.
A lovely Ruin, now defac'd and dead. ......Il.17.64.290.
And force th' unwilling God to ruin *Troy.* ......Il.17.387.302.
The rumbling Torrent thro' the Ruin rolls, ...Il.17.829.321.
And these, in Ruin and Confusion hurl'd, ...Il.20.170.400.
Such Ruin theirs, and such Compassion mine. ......Il.21.142.427.
Such pond'rous Ruin shall confound the Place, ...Il.21.374.436.
Corses and Arms to one bright Ruin turn, ...Il.21.392.436.
Swift on the sedgy Reeds the Ruin preys; ......Il.21.406.437.
And in one Ruin sink the *Trojan* Name. ......Il.21.441.438.
The rattling Ruin of the clashing Cars, ...Il.23.516.510.
(Price of his Ruin:) For who dares deny ......Il.23.771.520.
The same stern God to Ruin gives you all. ......Il.24.302.549.
The Scourge and Ruin of my Realm and Race; ......Il.24.631.563.
Shall sink, a smoaking Ruin on the Plain. ......Il.24.917.574.
If ruin to our royal race ye doom, ...Od.2.83.64.
Around their Lord, a mighty ruin! lye: ......Od.4.722.152.
To ruin doom the *Jove*-descended *line:* ......Od.4.996.164.
With what remains, from certain ruin fly, ...Od.10.319.359.
When swift to ruin they invade the prey. ......Od.12.418.451.
The pilot by the tumbling ruin slain, ...Od.12.483.455.
Once more undaunted on the ruin rode, ...Od.12.525.458.
They plan our future ruin, and resort ......Od.24.181.356.
Nor rush to ruin. Justice will prevail. ......Od.24.529.373.

RUIN'D

On Sovereigns ruin'd, or on Friends betray'd, ...2.TemF.409.283.
Not Winds that round our ruin'd Abbeys roar, ...4.JD2A.67.138.
Their ruins ruin'd, and their place no more! ......6.71.22.203.
Thro' ruin'd Moles the rushing Wave resounds, ...Il.5.118.273.
From ancient *Ilus'* ruin'd Monument; ......Il.11.476.55.
The last sad Relick of my ruin'd State, ...Il.22.93.456.
When *Troy* was ruin'd, had the chief return'd, ...Od.4.230.130.

RUIN'S

Or seek some ruin's formidable shade; ......6.52.30.157.

RUINS

Rome's ancient *Genius,* o'er its *Ruins* spread, ...1.EOC.699.319.
The rowling Ruins smoak along the Field. ......1.TrES.132.454.
Where *Troy's* Majestic Ruins strow the Ground. ......1.TrUl.133.470.
But the fall'n Ruins of Another's Fame: ......2.TemF.520.289.
Perhaps, by its own ruins sav'd from flame, ...6.71.15.203.
Their ruins ruin'd, and their place no more! ......6.71.22.203.
Their ruins perish'd, and their place no more! ......6.71.22A.203.
Where mighty Towns in Ruins spread the Plain, ...Il.2.799.163.
While Flames ascend, and mighty Ruins fall. ......Il.5.412.286.
Rais'd on the Ruins of his vengeful Hand: ......Il.5.793.304.
A Country's Ruins! to the Seas are born: ......Il.11.617.61.
And Heaps on Heaps the smoaky Ruins fall. ......Il.12.308.92.
The rowling Ruins smoak along the Field. ......Il.12.486.99.
And whelm in Ruins yon' flagitious Town. ......Il.13.788.142.
Whelm'd in thy Country's Ruins shalt thou fall, ...Il.13.973.152.
The Wall in Ruins, and the *Greeks* in Flight. ......Il.14.20.157.
Lies whelm'd in Ruins of the *Theban* Wall, ...Il.14.128.163.
Those, *Pallas, Jove,* and We, in Ruins laid: ......Il.20.233.403.
And ev'n her crumbling Ruins are no more. ......Il.20.366.410.
Beneath her Ruins! Know, that Hope is vain; ......Il.21.693.450.
I see the Ruins of your smoking Town! ......Il.24.306.549.
And dash the ruins on the ships below: ......Od.10.140.347.
Where *Troy's* majestic ruins strow the ground. ......Od.13.300.20.
And mark the ruins of no vulgar man. ......Od.14.250.48.
The ruins of himself! now worn away ......Od.24.271.362.

RUL'D

Th' Oppressor rul'd Tyrannick where he *durst,* ......1.W-F.74.157.
Jilts rul'd the State, and Statesmen *Farces* writ; ......1.EOC.538.298.
But young and tender Virgins, rul'd with Ease, ...2.ChJM.111.20.
"The Wives of all my Family have rul'd ......2.ChWB.195.66.
"The Wives of all my Race have ever rul'd ......2.ChWB.195A.66.
She rul'd, in native Anarchy, the mind. ......5.DunA1.14.61.

RUL'D (CONTINUED)

In Lud's old walls, tho' long I rul'd renown'd, ...5.DunA3.275.183.
She rul'd, in native Anarchy, the mind. ......5.DunB1.16.270.
In Lud's old walls tho' long I rul'd, renown'd ......5.DunB3.277.333.
Distracting Thoughts by turns his Bosom rul'd, ...Il.1.253.98.
Thus rul'd their Ardour, thus preserv'd their Force, ...Il.4.357.238.
Not thus resistless rul'd the Stream of Fight, ...Il.6.123.330.
Some God, they thought, who rul'd the Fate of Wars, ...Il.6.133.330.
Rag'd on the left, and rul'd the Tyde of War: ......Il.11.621.61.
Who rul'd where *Calydon's* white Rocks arise, ...Il.13.287.119.
He held his Seat, and rul'd the Realms around. ......Il.17.357.301.
From *Hyde's* Walls, he rul'd the Lands below. ......Il.20.444.413.
And rul'd the Fields where silver *Satnio* flow'd) ......Il.21.99.425.
One lash'd the Coursers, while one rul'd the Reins. ......Il.23.738.519.
Who rul'd his subjects with a father's love. ......Od.5.19.172.
(*Eurymedon's* last hope, who rul'd of old ......Od.7.74.237.
And god-like *Neleus* rul'd the *Pylian* plain: ......Od.11.312.397.

RUL'ST

And dead, thou rul'st a King in these abodes. ......Od.11.594.412.

RULE

Th' Intent propos'd, *that Licence* is a *Rule.* ......1.EOC.149.256.
All which, exact to *Rule* were brought about, ...1.EOC.277.271.
In *Words,* as *Fashions,* the same Rule will hold; ......1.EOC.333.276.
To rule in streams to which he was ally'd: ......1.TrPA.150.372.
And you that rule *Sicilia's* happy Plains, ...1.TrSP.69.396.
Each wou'd the sweets of Sovereign Rule devour, ...1.TrSt.182.418.
With Transport views the airy Rule his own, ...1.TrSt.449.428.
He scarce cou'd rule some Idle Appetites; ......2.ChJM.6.15.
He cou'd not rule his Carnal Appetites; ......2.ChJM.6A.15.
Or such a *Wit* as no Man e'er can rule? ......2.ChJM.189.24.
Let Reason's Rule your strong Desires abate, ...2.ChJM.293.28.
"One of us two must rule, and one obey, ...2.ChWB.192.65.
And stood content to rule by wholsome Laws; ......2.ChWB.430.78.
Who rule to Sex to Fifty from Fifteen, ...2.RL4.58.189.
Go, teach Eternal Wisdom how to rule— ......3.EOM2.29.59.
Sure as De-moivre, without rule or line? ......3.EOM3.104.102.
And Man's prerogative to rule, but spare. ......3.EOM3.160.109.
Ask you why *Clodio* broke thro' ev'ry rule? ......3.Ep1.206A.33.
Europe a Woman, Child, or Dotard rule, ...3.Ep1.152.28.
Ask you why Wharton broke thro' ev'ry rule? ......3.Ep1.206.33.
Or, if you rule him, never show you rule ......3.Ep2.262A.71.
Or, if you rule him, never show you rule ......3.Ep2.262A.71.
The grave Sir Gilbert holds it for a rule, ...3.Ep3.103.99.
And needs no Rod but Ripley with a Rule. ......3.Ep4.18.137.
And needs no Rod but S[taffor]d with a Rule ......3.Ep4.18A.137*.
And needs no Rod but S[heppar]d with a Rule ......3.Ep4.18B.137*.
(For I, who hold sage Homer's rule the best, ...4.HS2.159.67.
You think this cruel? take it for a rule, ...4.Arbu.83.101.
Shou'd such a man, too fond to rule alone, ...4.Arbu.197.110.
Yet why? that Father held it for a rule ......4.Arbu.382.125.
If such the Plague and pains to write by rule, ...4.2HE2.180.177.
Then, by the rule that made the Horse-tail bare, ...4.2HE1.63.199.
Or say our fathers never broke a rule; ......4.2HE1.93.203.
Instruct his Family in ev'ry rule, ...4.2HE1.163.209.
Some free from rhyme or reason, rule or check, ...5.DunA3.155.164.
Some free from rhyme or reason, rule or check, ...5.DunB3.161.328.
Senates and Courts with Greek and Latin rule, ...5.DunB4.179.359.
Should such a man, too fond to rule alone, ...6.49iii.11.142.
bidst Fortune rule the World below ......6.50.11A.146*.
Led by some rule, that guides, but not constrains; ......6.52.67.158.
No, trust the Sex's sacred Rule; ......6.64.21.190.
Should such a Man, too fond to rule alone, ...6.98.47.284.
Atheism and Superstition rule by Turns; ......6.99.18.287.
In merry old England it once was a rule, ...6.105vii.1.302.
Sir, I admit your gen'ral Rule ......6.124ii.1.347.
Rule thy own Realms with arbitrary Sway: ......Il.1.236.98.
Rule thou thy self, as more advanc'd in Age. ......Il.1.373.106.
Two valiant Brothers rule th' undaunted Throng, ...Il.2.612.156.
Who rule the Dead, and horrid Woes prepare ......Il.3.352.209.
Till to supply his Place and rule the Car, ...Il.8.157.405.
And ever constant, ever rule Mankind. ......Il.8.533.422.
Unfit for publick Rule, or private Care; ......Il.9.89.437.
And rule the tributary Realms around. ......Il.9.206.442.
And rule the tributary Realms around. ......Il.9.393.452.
Then none (said *Nestor)* shall his Rule withstand, ...Il.10.148.8.
"Let thy just Counsels aid, and rule thy Friend". ......Il.11.919.76.
These rule the *Pthians,* and their Arms employ ......Il.13.875.147.
Inspire the Ranks, and rule the distant War. ......Il.14.152.165.
And those who rule th' inviolable Floods, ...Il.14.315.178.
Lo thus (the Victor cries) we rule the Field, ...Il.14.529.189.
Rule as he will his portion'd Realms on high; ......Il.15.208.204.
Assign'd by Lot, our triple Rule we know; ......Il.15.212.205.
By the just Rule, and the directing Line. ......Il.15.477.215.
The Rule of Men; whose Glory is from Heav'n! ......Il.17.295.299.
Fated to rule, and born a King of Kings. ......Il.19.108.376.
Who rule the Dead, and horrid Woes prepare ......Il.19.271.383.
Mentes my name; I rule the *Taphian* race, ...Od.1.229.43.
There rule, from palace-cares remote and free, ...Od.1.457.54.
And his stern rule the groaning land obey'd; ......Od.3.389.105.
Argos the seat of sovereign rule I chose; ......Od.4.235.130.
Then she. Obedient to my rule, attend: ......Od.4.538.146.
He smooth'd, and squar'd 'em, by the rule and line. ......Od.5.316.186.
Nobles and Chiefs who rule *Phæacia's* states, ...Od.8.11.262.
Say by his rule is my dominion aw'd, ...Od.11.212.392.
Three years thy house their lawless rule has seen, ...Od.13.431.27.
True friendship's laws are by this rule exprest, ...Od.15.83.73.
Whose pious rule a warlike race obey! ......Od.19.130.199.
For Rule mature, *Telemachus* deplores ......Od.19.182.200.
And rule our Palace with an equal sway: ......Od.23.382.343.

RULER

And the mad Ruler to misguide the Day, ...1.TrSt.309.423.
Unmov'd remain'd the Ruler of the Sky, ...1.TrSt.402.426.
Look thro', and trust the Ruler with his Skies, ...4.1HE6.8.237.

RULER (CONTINUED)
To *Neptune,* Ruler of the Seas profound, ... Il.9.239.444.
There the great Ruler of the azure Round ..... Il.13.53.107.
The Sea's great Ruler there, and *Hector* here. ..... Il.14.452.185.
Not by my Arts the Ruler of the Main ..... Il.15.47.196.
The World's great Ruler, felt her venom'd Dart; ..... Il.19.101.376.
This heard the raging Ruler of the main; ..... Od.4.677.151.
These did the Ruler of the deep ordain ..... Od.7.45.235.
Oh Pow'r supreme, oh ruler of the whole! ..... Od.24.543.374.

RULERS
And this the Faith *Phæacia's* Rulers boast? ..... 1.TrUl.85.468.
The sceptred Rulers lead; the following Host ..... Il.2.109.132.
Far other Rulers those proud Steeds demand, ... Il.10.473.24.
Two lordly Rulers of the Wood engage; ..... Il.16.916.279.
To the brave Rulers of the racing Steed; ..... Il.23.342.503.
And scarce their Rulers check their martial Rage. ..... Il.24.494.556.
And scarce their Rulers check the martial Rage. ..... Il.24.494A.556.
The sceptred Rulers. Fear not, but be bold: ..... Od.7.66.237.
With goblets crown'd, the Rulers of the land; ..... Od.7.183.244.
And Chiefs and Rulers, a majestic band. ..... Od.13.217.16.
And this the faith *Phæacia's* rulers boast? ..... Od.13.252.18.

RULES
Those RULES of old *discover'd,* not *devis'd,* ..... 1.EOC.88.249.
Hear how learn'd *Greece* her useful Rules indites, ... 1.EOC.92.250.
From great *Examples useful Rules* were giv'n; ..... 1.EOC.98A.250.
Bold in the Practice of *mistaken Rules,* ..... 1.EOC.110.251.
And Rules as strict his labour'd Work confine, ... 1.EOC.137.255.
Learn hence for Ancient *Rules* a just Esteem; ..... 1.EOC.139.255.
And did his Work to Rules as strict confine, ... 1.EOC.137A.255.
If, where the *Rules* not far enough extend, ... 1.EOC.146.256.
(Since Rules were made but to promote their End) ..... 1.EOC.147.256.
But tho' the *Ancients* thus their *Rules* invade, ... 1.EOC.161.259.
And tho' the *Ancients* thus their *Rules* invade, ... 1.EOC.161A.259.
What the weak Head with strongest Byass rules, ... 1.EOC.203.263.
Neglect the Rules each *Verbal Critick* lays, ... 1.EOC.261.269.
Who durst depart from *Aristotle's* Rules. ..... 1.EOC.272.270.
That durst depart from *Aristotle's* Rules. ..... 1.EOC.272A.270.
And while Self-Love each jealous Writer rules, ... 1.EOC.516.296.
Receiv'd his Rules, and stood convinc'd 'twas fit ..... 1.EOC.651A.313.
The justest *Rules,* and clearest *Method* join'd; ..... 1.EOC.670.315.
The *Rules,* a Nation born to serve, obeys, ... 1.EOC.713.322.
Such was the Muse, whose Rules and Practice tell, ... 1.EOC.723.323.
This nymph compress'd by him who rules the day, ... 1.TrFD.11.386.
Ev'n Fortune rules no more:—Oh servile Land, ... 1.TrSt.241.420.
Thus, if eternal justice rules the ball, ... 2.Elegy.35.365.
Could he, whose rules the rapid Comet bind, ... 3.EOM2.35.60.
Could he, whose rules the whirling Comet bind, ... 3.EOM2.35B.60.
Reason's comparing balance rules the whole. ..... 3.EOM2.60.63.
Ah! if she lend not arms, as well as rules, ... 3.EOM2.151.73.
Or, if she rules him, never shows she rules; ..... 3.Ep2.262.71.
Or, if she rules him, never shows she rules; ..... 3.Ep2.262.71.
Blends, in exception to all gen'ral rules, ... 3.Ep2.275.72.
Yet shall (my Lord) your just, your noble rules ..... 3.Ep4.25.139.
And if they starve, they starve by rules of art. ..... 3.Ep4.38.140.
Just as they are, yet shall noble rules ..... 3.Ep4.25A.139.
Our Court may justly to our Stage give Rules, ... 4.JD4.220.45.
See them survey their Limbs by *Durer's* Rules, ... 4.JD4.240.45.
But strong in sense, and wise without the rules. ..... 4.HS2.10.55.
Suppose that honest Part that rules us all, ... 4.HAdv.87.83.
To Rules of Poetry no more confin'd, ... 4.2HE2.202.179.
Who rules in Cornwall, or who rules in Berks; ..... 4.1HE6.104.243.
Who rules in Cornwall, or who rules in Berks; ..... 4.1HE6.104.243.
And if I pray by Reason's rules, ... 4.HS6.15.251.
Sure, if I spare the Minister, no rules ..... 4.EpS2.146.321.
Actuates, maintains, and rules the moving Frame. ..... 6.17i(b).4.55.
No matter for the Rules of Time and Place: ..... 6.19.28A.63.
Fate rules us: then to Fate give way! ..... 6.24iii(a).3.75.
Ye Gods! what justice rules the ball? ..... 6.51i.25.152.
Authors are judg'd by strange capricious Rules, ... 6.60.1.178.
Theirs are the Rules of *France,* the Plots of *Spain:* ..... 6.60.12.178.
But what avails to lay down rules for sense? ..... 6.106iii.1.307.
Ev'n by that God I swear, who rules the Day; ..... Il.1.109.92.
Wise by his Rules, and happy by his Sway; ..... Il.1.334.104.
Sent by great *Jove* to him who rules the Host, ... Il.2.103.131.
Great *Agamemnon* rules the num'rous Band, ... Il.2.694.159.
And rules them peaceful in a foreign Land: ..... Il.2.810.163.
The *Paphlagonians Pylæmenes* rules. ..... Il.2.1034.171.
Tho' all the rest with stated Rules we bound, ... Il.4.298.235.
The Storm rolls on, and *Hector* rules the Field: ..... Il.11.450.54.
Pensive, the rules the Goddess gave, he weigh'd; ..... Od.1.556.58.
The house of him who rules these happy lands. ..... Od.7.30.235.
Rules this blest realm, repentant I obey! ..... Od.8.436.287.
Each rules his race, his neighbour not his care, ... Od.9.131.311.
Ye perish all! tho' he who rules the main ..... Od.12.135.438.
And witness every pow'r that rules the sky! ..... Od.14.435.56.
The shield of *Jove,* or him who rules the day! ..... Od.18.278.180.
Heav'n rules us yet, and Gods there are above. ..... Od.24.410.368.

RULING
In the clear Mirror of thy ruling *Star* ..... 2.RL1.108.154.
Let ruling Angels from their spheres be hurl'd, ... 3.EOM1.253.46.
To serve mere engines to the ruling Mind? ..... 3.EOM1.262.46.
The Mind's disease, its ruling Passion came; ..... 3.EOM2.138.71.
The ruling Passion, be it what it will, ... 3.EOM2.148Z1.72.
The ruling Passion conquers Reason still. ..... 3.EOM2.148Z2.72.
'Tis in the Ruling Passion: There, alone, ... 3.Ep1.174A.30.
Search then the Ruling Passion: There, alone, ... 3.Ep1.174.30.
Whose ruling Passion was the Lust of Praise; ..... 3.Ep1.181.30.
Shall feel your ruling passion strong in death: ..... 3.Ep1.263.38.
In Men, we various Ruling Passions find, ... 3.Ep2.207.67.
"The ruling Passion, be it what it will, ... 3.Ep3.155.106.
"The ruling Passion conquers Reason still." ..... 3.Ep3.156.106.
The ruling Charge: The Task of Fight be mine. ..... Il.17.547.309.
With hasty hand the ruling reins he drew: ..... Od.3.612.117.

RULING (CONTINUED)
Talk not of ruling in this dol'rous gloom, ... Od.11.595.412.

RUMBLING
P. What? like Sir *Richard,* rumbling, rough and fierce, ... 4.HS1.23.7.
With thunder rumbling from the mustard-bowl, ... 5.DunA2.218.127.
With Thunder rumbling from the mustard bowl, ... 5.DunB2.226.307.
The rumbling Torrent thro' the Ruin rolls, ... Il.17.829.321.
When the tyde rushes from her rumbling caves ..... Od.12.282.446.
Charybdis rumbling from her inmost caves, ... Od.12.521.458.

RUMINATING
And ruminating wrath, he scorns repose. ..... Od.20.8.230.

RUMORS
Some guest arrives, with rumors of her Lord; ..... Od.14.414.56.

RUMOUR
Th'astonish'd Mother when the Rumour came, ... 1.TrSt.697.439.
Not warp'd by Passion, aw'd by Rumour, ... 6.89.5.250.
Not led by custome, mov'd by Rumour, ... 6.89.5A.250.
But guess by Rumour, and but boast we know) ..... Il.2.577.155.
Deaf to the rumour of fallacious fame, ... Od.1.217.43.
The Queen's fond hope inventive rumour cheers, ... Od.1.523.57.

RUMOUR'D
Tis rumour'd, *Budgell* on a time ..... 6.44.1.123.

RUMOURS
In ev'ry Ear incessant Rumours rung, ... 2.TemF.336.280.
The flying Rumours gather'd as they roll'd, ... 2.TemF.468.286.
Is it then true, as distant rumours run, ... Od.3.259.98.

RUMP
(For so she was, as e'er show'd Rump yet, ... 6.10.86.27.
His Rump well pluck'd with Nettles stings, ... 6.93.21.257.

RUMP'D
Goose-rump'd, Hawk-nos'd, Swan-footed, is my Dear? ..... 4.HAdv.122.85.

RUMPLED
Or rumpled Petticoats, or tumbled Beds, ... 2.RL4.72.190.

RUN
She runs, but hopes she does not run unseen, ... 1.PSp.58.66.
And now his Shadow reach'd her as she run, ... 1.W-F.193.168.
Still *run on* Poets in a raging Vein, ... 1.EOC.606.308.
Still *run on* Poets in a frantick Vein, ... 1.EOC.606A.308.
Nay, run to *Altars; there* they'll talk you dead; ..... 1.EOC.624A.310.
A *second* Deluge Learning thus o'er-run, ... 1.EOC.691.317.
Acis too run, and help, oh help! he said, ... 1.TrPA.141.371.
Shall Fortune still in one sad Tenor run, ... 1.TrSP.71.397.
And bids the Year with swifter Motion run. ..... 1.TrSt.454.429.
Th' *Inachian* Streams with headlong Fury run, ... 1.TrSt.500.431.
Run to the Shade, and bark against the Skies. ..... 1.TrSt.647.437.
They hear, they run, and gath'ring at his Call, ... 1.TrES.179.456.
When now the fourth revolving Day was run, ... 2.ChJM.400.34.
His Heav'nly Progress thro' the *Twins* had run; ..... 2.ChJM.610.44.
But once grown sleek, will from her Corner run, ... 2.ChWB.144.63.
The Youths hang o'er their Chariots as they run; ..... 2.TemF.218.272.
And scornful Hisses run thro all the Croud. ..... 2.TemF.405.283.
Planets and Suns run lawless thro' the sky, ... 3.EOM1.252.46.
Instruct the planets in what orbs to run, ... 3.EOM2.21.56.
As Eastern priests in giddy circles run, ... 3.EOM2.27.58.
On their own Axis as the Planets run, ... 3.EOM3.313.126.
To run a Muck, and tilt at all I meet; ..... 4.HS1.70.11.
Run out as fast, as one that pays his Bail, ... 4.JD4.182A.41.
Survey the Pangs they bear, the Risques they run, ... 4.HAdv.51.79.
Nothing so mean for which he can't run mad; ..... 4.HAdv.64.81.
And will you run to Perils, Sword, and Law, ... 4.HAdv.135.87.
From gleaming Swords no shrieking Women run; ..... 4.HAdv.169.89.
It is not Poetry, but Prose run mad: ..... 4.Arbu.188.109.
As shallow streams run dimpling all the way. ..... 4.Arbu.316.118.
Alas! to Grotto's and to Groves we run, ... 4.2HE2.110.173.
The worst of Madmen is a Saint run mad. ..... 4.1HE6.27.239.
Long as the Year's dull circle seems to run, ... 4.1HE1.37.281.
Discharge their Garrets, move their Beds, and run ..... 4.1HE1.157.291.
See thronging Millions to the Pagod run, ... 4.EpS1.157.309.
Like Royal Harts, be never more run down? ..... 4.EpS2.29.314.
As for the rest, each winter up they run, ... 4.1740.29.333.
She saw with joy the line immortal run, ... 5.DunA1.97.71.
Or wafting ginger, round the streets to run, ... 5.DunA1.201A.87.
"So take the hindmost Hell."—He said, and run. ..... 5.DunA2.56.105.
Mears, Warner, Wilkins run: Delusive thought! ..... 5.DunA2.117.111.
And the fresh vomit run for ever green!" ..... 5.DunA2.148.119.
Shall first recall'd run forward to thy mind; ..... 5.DunA3.56A.155.
She saw, with joy, the line immortal run, ... 5.DunB1.99.276.
Now (shame to Fortune!) an ill Run at Play ..... 5.DunB1.113.277.
"So take the hindmost, Hell."—He said, and run. ..... 5.DunB2.60.298.
Mears, Warner, Wilkins run: delusive thought! ..... 5.DunB2.125.301.
And the fresh vomit run for ever green!" ..... 5.DunB2.156.303.
Thrid ev'ry science, run thro' ev'ry school? ..... 5.DunB4.256.369.
To run with Horses, or to hunt with Dogs; ..... 5.DunB4.526.394.
From Stage to Stage the licens'd Earl may run, ... 5.DunB4.587.401.
As Clocks run fastest when most Lead is on. ..... 6.7.4.15.
And run precipitant, with Noise and Strife, ... 6.17ii.5.56.
And bad'st the years in long procession run: ..... 6.23.6.73.
To run so smoothly, one by one ..... 6.30.11A.86.
Some to unload the fertile branches run, ... 6.35.19.103.
Tho the Dean has run from us in manner uncivil; ..... 6.42i.1.116.
Like M[eadow]s run to sermons, ... 6.61.25.181.
Like R— run to sermons, ... 6.61.25A.181.
Like Meadows run to sermons, ... 6.61.25B.181.
The Waves run frighted to the Shores. ..... 6.78ii.7.216.
His rowling Wheels did run: ..... 6.79.126.222.
His trowling Wheels they run: ..... 6.79.126A.222.

RUN (CONTINUED)
Compell'd to run each knavish Jockey's Heat! ... 6.96iii.25.275.
It is not Poetry, but Prose run mad: ... 6.98.38.284.
Her Tongue still run, on credit from her Eyes, ... 6.99.5.286.
Tho' he talk'd much of Virtue, her Head always run ... 6.124i.5.346.
"And run, on ivory, so glib, ... 6.140.22.378.
This day TOM's fair account has run ... 6.150.3.398.
But ere the tenth revolving Day was run, ... Il.1.73.90.
Now nine long Years of mighty *Jove* are run, ... Il.2.161.136.
From Pail to Pail with busie Murmur run ... Il.2.556.154.
The best that e'er on Earth's broad Surface run, ... Il.5.330.282.
On either side run purple to the Main. ... Il.6.6.322.
Too daring Prince! ah whither dost thou run? ... Il.6.510.351.
So shall my Days in one sad Tenor run, ... Il.6.520.352.
Whither, O *Menelaus!* would'st thou run, ... Il.7.127.369.
Whither, oh whither does *Ulysses* run? ... Il.8.117.403.
And yet those Years that since thy Birth have run, ... Il.9.81.436.
Of Sense and Justice, run where Frenzy drives; ... Il.9.493.456.
Large painful Drops from all his Members run, ... Il.11.941.77.
On certain Dangers we too rashly run: ... Il.12.76.84.
They hear, they run, and gath'ring at his Call, ... Il.12.533.101.
Shalt run, forgetful of a Warrior's Fame, ... Il.13.1036.153.
Better from Evils, well foreseen, to run, ... Il.14.86.162.
Whose honour'd Dust (his Race of Glory run) ... Il.14.127.163.
Fall mighty Numbers; mighty Numbers run; ... Il.14.616.192.
Safe in his Art, as side by side they run, ... Il.15.826.228.
For when *Alcmena's* nine long Months were run, ... Il.19.103.376.
Shouts of Applause run rattling thro the Skies. ... Il.23.847.523.
Why teach ye not my rapid Wheels to run, ... Il.24.329.550.
Is it then true, as distant rumours run, ... Od.3.259.98.
Hath journey'd half, and half remains to run; ... Od.4.540.146.
His twelfth diurnal race begins to run. ... Od.4.804.156.
By seas, by wars, so many dangers run, ... Od.5.287.185.
Some to unload the fertile branches run, ... Od.7.160.244.
I wield the gauntlet, and I run the race. ... Od.8.236.275.
These to the north and night's dark regions run, ... Od.9.25.303.
Whither (he cry'd) ah whither will ye run? ... Od.10.509.368.
And now the Moon had run her monthly round, ... Od.12.387.450.
Strait to the lodgments of his herd he run, ... Od.14.85.40.
Not with such transport wou'd my eyes run o'er, ... Od.14.163.43.
That father, for whose sake thy days have run ... Od.16.207.114.
So they aloud: and tears in tides had run, ... Od.16.242.116.
Three days have spent their beams, three nights have run ... Od.17.606.161.
His annual longitude of heav'n shall run; ... Od.19.350.211.
Lo hence I run for other arms to wield, ... Od.22.118.292.
Run good *Eumæus* then, and (what before ... Od.22.172.295.
They move, and murmurs run thro' all the rock: ... Od.24.12.347.
They case their limbs in brass; to arms they run; ... Od.24.534.373.
Heaps rush on heaps; they fight, they drop, they run. ... Od.24.609.377.

RUNDEL
Secker is decent, *Rundel* has a Heart, ... 4.EpS2.71.316.

RUNG
With *sweeter Notes* each *rising Temple* rung; ... 1.EOC.703.320.
He rais'd his Spouse ere Matin Bell was rung, ... 2.ChJM.523.40.
Thrice rung the Bell, the Slipper knock'd the Ground, ... 2.RL1.17.146.
In ev'ry Ear incessant Rumours rung, ... 2.TemF.336.280.
Eurydice the Rocks, and hollow Mountains rung. ... 6.11.117.34.
On his broad Shield the sounding Weapon rung, ... Il.5.343.283.
Shook with his Fall his Brazen Armor rung, ... Il.5.764.303.
And as he march'd, the brazen Buckler rung. ... Il.6.146.331.
The Strokes redoubled on his Buckler rung; ... Il.11.691.66.
Swift from his Seat; his clanging Armour rung. ... Il.12.94.84.
With sounding Strokes their brazen Targets rung: ... Il.12.170.87.
Full on the Shield's round Boss the Weapon rung; ... Il.13.256.117.
And on the tincling Verge more faintly rung. ... Il.13.518.131.
With Shouts incessant Earth and Ocean rung, ... Il.13.1057.155.
Supine he fell; his brazen Helmet rung. ... Il.15.781.226.
His hollow Helm with falling Javelins rung. ... Il.16.133.242.
So fell the Warriors, and so rung their Arms. ... Il.16.772.273.
His bounding Helmet on the Champain rung. ... Il.16.959.280.
Fix'd deep, and loudly in the Buckler rung. ... Il.20.309.407.
The opening Folds; the sounding Hinges rung. ... Il.21.628.448.
Smote on his Knee; the hollow Cuishes rung ... Il.21.700.450.
The brazen Portal in his Passage rung. ... Il.24.398.552.
The vaulted roofs and solid pavement rung. ... Od.10.255.355.
The brazen portals in their passage rung. ... Od.15.217.78.
With *Argus, Argus,* rung the woods around; ... Od.17.353.149.
Perithous' roofs with frantick riot rung; ... Od.21.318.274.

RUNIC
And *Runic* Characters were grav'd around: ... 2.TemF.122.263.

RUNNING
It asks *Discretion* ev'n in *running Mad;* ... 1.EOC.160Z2.258.
As gardens fresh, where running rivers stray, ... 1.TrPA.62.368.
Nonsense precipitate, like running Lead, ... 5.DunB1.123.278.
Now running round the Circle, finds it square. ... 5.DunB4.34.343.
By running Goods, these graceless Owlers gain, ... 6.60.11.178.
Thus fell a reas'ning, not a running. ... 6.67.4.195.
As with swift Step she form'd the running Maze: ... Il.16.219.248.
He purg'd; and wash'd it in the running Stream. ... Il.16.279.249.
Along the Margin winds the running Blaze: ... Il.21.407.437.
As closely following as the running Thread ... Il.23.890.524.
Then fix'd a Ring the running Reins to guide, ... Il.24.339.550.

RUNS
She runs, but hopes she does not run unseen, ... 1.PSp.58.66.
Thus when dispers'd a routed Army runs, ... 2.RL3.81.173.
And a low Murmur runs along the Field. ... 2.TemF.287.277.
Observe how system into system runs, ... 3.EOM1.25.16.
Once on a time (so runs the Fable) ... 4.HS6.157.259.
That tinctur'd as it runs, with Lethe's streams, ... 5.DunA2.315.140.
Another Cynthia her new journey runs, ... 5.DunA3.239.177.
That tinctur'd as it runs with Lethe's streams, ... 5.DunB2.339.314.

RUNS (CONTINUED)
Another Cynthia her new journey runs, ... 5.DunB3.243.332.
O'er ev'ry vein a shudd'ring horror runs; ... 5.DunB4.143.355.
To where the Seine, obsequious as she runs, ... 5.DunB4.297.373.
Some joy still lost, as each vain year runs o'er, ... 6.86.7.245.
Along the Region runs a deaf'ning Sound; ... Il.2.119.133.
He runs, he flies, thro' all the Grecian Train, ... Il.2.224.138.
Or where by *Phœstus* silver *Jardan* runs; ... Il.2.789.162.
And the long Shout runs ecchoing thro' the Skies. ... Il.3.576.219.
O'er these a Range of Marble Structure runs, ... Il.6.306.341.
And all the Coast that runs along the Main. ... Il.9.603.464.
And rapid as it runs, the single Spokes are lost. ... Il.18.696.357.
And runs on crackling Shrubs between the Hills; ... Il.20.570.418.
While fast behind them runs the Blaze of Fire; ... Il.21.15.422.
Fix'd on the Goal his Eye fore-runs the Course, ... Il.23.395.506.
Then to *Noemon* swift she runs, she flies, ... Od.2.434.82.
Frantic thro' clashing swords she runs, she flies, ... Od.8.573.293.
Sudden, the master runs; aloud he calls; ... Od.14.37.37.

RURAL
And *Albion's* Cliffs resound the Rural Lay. ... 1.PSp.6.61.
The Turf with rural Dainties shall be Crown'd, ... 1.PSp.99.70.
Let other Swains attend the Rural Care, ... 1.PSu.35.74.
And yet my Numbers please the rural Throng, ... 1.PSu.49.75.
Hylas and *Ægon* sung their Rural Lays; ... 1.PAu.2.80.
Hylas and *Ægon's* Rural Lays I sing. ... 1.PAu.6.80.
And with fresh Bays her Rural Shrine adorn. ... 1.PWi.20.90.
Eccho no more the rural Song rebounds, ... 1.PWi.41A.92.
Adieu ye Shepherd's rural *Lays* and *Loves,* ... 1.PWi.90.95.
Above the rest a rural Nymph was fam'd, ... 1.W-F.171.165.
Your Rural Cares, and Pleasures, are the same. ... 1.TrVP.95.381.
Lotis the nymph (if rural tales be true) ... 1.TrFD.31.387.
This rural Prince one only Daughter blest, ... 1.TrSt.670.438.
While the rude Swain his rural Musick tries, ... 1.TrSt.689.439.
Our rural Ancestors, with little blest, ... 4.2HE1.241.215.
To him, the Rural Cottage does afford ... 6.17iii.24.58.
A Type of Paradise, the Rural Scene! ... 6.17iii.39.58.
You dream of triumphs in the rural shade; ... 6.45.32.125.
This radiant pile nine rural sisters raise; ... 6.126ii.2.353.
In gather'd Swarms surround the Rural Bow'rs; ... Il.2.555.154.
The Mountain Nymphs the rural Tomb adorn'd, ... Il.6.531.353.
Not one was absent; not a Rural Pow'r ... Il.20.11.393.
For Plowshares, Wheels, and all the rural Trade. ... Il.23.990.529.
To the gay Court a rural shed prefers, ... Od.1.246.44.
On the fat flock and rural dainties feast; ... Od.4.110.125.
Roam the wild Isle in search of rural cates, ... Od.4.498.144.
The Prince in rural bow'r they fondly thought, ... Od.4.864.159.
With him, rest peaceful in the rural cell, ... Od.13.473.29.
A rural Portico of rugged stone: ... Od.14.10.35.
Three now were absent on the rural care; ... Od.14.28.36.
The rural labour or domestick care. ... Od.14.260.49.
And here, unenvy'd, rural dainties taste. ... Od.14.452.57.
The rural tribe in common share the rest, ... Od.14.486.59.
Sate in the Cottage, at their rural feast: ... Od.15.323.85.
Me to the fields, to tend the rural care; ... Od.15.393.88.
And bids the rural throne with osiers rise. ... Od.16.48.104.
'Till then, thy guest amid the rural train ... Od.16.81.106.
To good *Laertes* in his rural court. ... Od.16.165.110.
Or stoop to tasks a rural Lord demands. ... Od.17.25.133.
Our rural victims mount in blazing flames! ... Od.17.285.146.
Of night draws on, go seek the rural bow'r: ... Od.17.677.165.
Those hands in work? to tend the rural trade, ... Od.18.405.188.
At an old swineherd's rural lodge he lay. ... Od.24.178.356.
There stood his mansion of the rural sort, ... Od.24.238.360.
There wait thy faithful band of rural friends, ... Od.24.419.369.
Now sate *Ulysses* at the rural feast, ... Od.24.564.375.

RUSH
The Youth rush eager to the Sylvan War; ... 1.W-F.148.164.
Rush thro' the Thickets, down the Vallies sweep, ... 1.W-F.156.164.
Then foaming pour along, and rush into the *Thames.* ... 1.W-F.218.169.
And half thy Forests rush into my Floods, ... 1.W-F.386.189.
For *Fools* rush in where *Angels* fear to tread. ... 1.EOC.625.310.
Rush thro' the Mounds, and bear the Dams away: ... 1.TrSt.505.431.
Rush to the Foe, and claim the promis'd Fight. ... 1.TrES.56.451.
And rush in Millions on the World below. ... 2.TemF.482.286.
All quit their sphere, and rush into the skies. ... 3.EOM1.124.30.
Planets and Suns rush lawless thro' the sky, ... 3.EOM1.252A.46.
Fools rush into my Head, and so I write. ... 4.HS1.14.5.
Rush Chaplain, Butler, Dogs and all: ... 4.HS6.213.263.
The Monkey-mimicks rush discordant in. ... 5.DunA2.228.128.
Rush to the world, impatient for the day. ... 5.DunA3.22.152.
Shall first recall'd, rush forward to thy mind; ... 5.DunA3.56.155.
And ten-horn'd fiends and Giants rush to war. ... 5.DunA3.232.177.
The Monkey-mimics rush discordant in; ... 5.DunB2.236.307.
Rush to the world, impatient for the day. ... 5.DunB3.30.321.
Shall, first recall'd, rush forward to thy mind: ... 5.DunB3.64.323.
And ten-horn'd fiends and Giants rush to war. ... 5.DunB3.236.332.
Streets, chairs, and coxcombs rush upon my sight; ... 6.45.48.126.
Forth in the Street I rush with frantick Cries: ... 6.96iv.45.277.
The Council breaks, the Warriors rush to Arms. ... Il.2.977.169.
Rush to her Thought, and force a tender Tear. ... Il.3.186.200.
The *Trojans* rush tumultuous to the War; ... Il.4.253.232.
Rush to the Vales, and pour'd along the Plain, ... Il.4.518.246.
Rush to the Fight, and ev'ry Foe controul; ... Il.5.160.274.
The bounding Coursers rush amidst the War. ... Il.5.299.281.
Rush fearless to the Plains, and uncontroul'd ... Il.5.683.300.
At her Command rush forth the Steeds Divine; ... Il.5.886.308.
No longer bent to rush on certain Harms, ... Il.7.141.370.
Forth rush a Tide of *Greeks,* the Passage freed; ... Il.8.315.412.
Then rush behind him, and prevent his Pace. ... Il.10.410.21.
On Heaps the *Trojans* rush, with wild affright, ... Il.10.616.29.
The lighter Arms, rush forward to the Field. ... Il.11.64.37.
Rush to the Foe, and claim the promis'd Fight. ... Il.12.400.96.
Rush like a fiery Torrent o'er the Field, ... Il.13.421.126.
The Hosts rush on; loud Clamours shake the Shore; ... Il.15.404.212.

RUSH (CONTINUED)

In rush the conqu'ring *Greeks* to spoil the slain; ..... Il.15.642.221.
To the black Fount they rush a hideous Throng, ... Il.16.198.247.
Fir'd, they rush on; First *Hector* seeks the Foes, ... Il.16.677.270.
The Lash resounds; the Coursers rush to War. ..... Il.16.888.277.
Not fiercer rush along the gloomy Wood, ... Il.17.811.320.
Let me, this instant, rush into the Fields, ... Il.18.153.330.
Rush sudden; Hills of Slaughter heap the Ground, ... Il.18.612.352.
Earth echoes, and the Nations rush to Arms. ..... Il.20.66.396.
The clust'ring Legions rush into the Flood: ..... Il.21.17.422.
Rush the swift Eastern and the Western Wind: ..... Il.21.389.436.
The herded *Ilians* rush like driven Deer; ..... Il.22.2.452.
And rush beneath the long-descending Stroke? ..... Il.23.762.520.
Unmoor the fleet, and rush into the sea. ..... Od.4.786.156.
They rush into the deep with eager joy, ... Od.6.325.226.
And snatch their oars, and rush into the deep. ..... Od.9.554.328.
Rush to their mothers with unruly joy, ... Od.10.489.367.
They rush to land, and end in feasts the day: ..... Od.12.362.448.
Better to rush at once to shades below, ... Od.12.415.451.
And in the roaring whirlpools rush the tides. ..... Od.12.510.457.
With ready hands they rush to seize their slave; ..... Od.14.378.53.
"Ye rush to arms, and stain the feast with blood: ..... Od.16.315.121.
His teeth all shatter'd rush immix'd with blood. ..... Od.18.117.172.
To rush between, and use the shorten'd sword. ..... Od.22.115.292.
They hear, rush forth, and instant round him stand, ... Od.22.533.314.
Nor rush to ruin. Justice will prevail. ..... Od.24.529.373.
Fierce they rush forth: *Ulysses* leads the way. ..... Od.24.579.376.
Heaps rush on heaps; they fight, they drop, they run. ..... Od.24.609.377.

RUSH'D

'Till bold *Sarpedon* rush'd into the Field; ..... 1.TrES.4.449.
All in a Trice he rush'd on *Guise*, ... 6.79.57.219.
All in a Trice on *Guise* he rush'd, ... 6.79.57A.219.
But now the Servants they rush'd in; ..... 6.79.97.221.
They rush'd to War, and perish'd on the Plain. ..... Il.2.1011.170.
Rush'd to the Bed, impatient for the Joy. ..... Il.3.556.218.
The Foe rush'd furious as he pants for Breath, ... Il.4.606.250.
The Hero rush'd impetuous to the Fight; ..... Il.5.171.275.
In rush'd *Antilochus*, his Aid to bring, ... Il.5.699.301.
Rush'd terrible amidst the Ranks of Fight. ..... Il.5.839.305.
Rush'd on a *Tamarisk's* strong Trunk, and broke ..... Il.6.49.325.
Rush'd forth with *Hector* to the Fields of Fight. ..... Il.6.663.360.
Then rush'd impetuous thro' the *Scæan* Gate. ..... Il.7.2.363.
He rush'd, and on *Ulysses* call'd aloud. ..... Il.8.116.403.
And rush'd on *Teucer* with the lifted Rock. ..... Il.8.388.416.
The lighter Arms, rush'd forward to the Field. ..... Il.11.64A.37.
They rush'd to Fight, and perish'd on the Plain! ..... Il.11.430.53.
Forth from the Portals rush'd th' intrepid Pair, ... Il.12.161.87.
Prone down the rocky Steep, he rush'd along; ..... Il.13.28.105.
Embattel'd roll'd, as *Hector* rush'd along. ..... Il.13.62.107.
He spoke, then rush'd amid the Warrior Crew; ..... Il.14.171.165.
He spoke, then rush'd amid the warring Crew; ..... Il.14.171A.165.
On rush'd bold *Hector*, gloomy as the Night, ... Il.15.394.212.
Then, fir'd to Vengeance, rush'd amidst the Foe; ..... Il.15.534.217.
Hector (this said) rush'd forward on the Foes: ..... Il.15.664.221.
Forth rush'd the Youth, with martial Fury fir'd, ... Il.15.687.222.
And rush'd enrag'd before the *Trojan* Croud: ..... Il.15.833.229.
Like furious, rush'd the *Myrmidonian* Crew, ... Il.16.202.247.
Whole *Troy* embodied, rush'd with Shouts along. ..... Il.17.309.299.
And rush'd to combate, but he rush'd in vain: ..... Il.17.405.303.
And rush'd to combate, but he rush'd in vain: ..... Il.17.405.303.
Rush'd from the Tents with Cries; and gath'ring round ..... Il.18.35.325.
Twelve in the Tumult wedg'd, untimely rush'd ..... Il.18.271.335.
Now perish *Troy!* He said, and rush'd to Fight. ..... Il.19.471.391.
He rush'd impetuous. Such the Lion's Rage, ... Il.20.199.402.
On him *Achilles* rush'd: He fearless stood, ... Il.21.161.428.
Phœbus rush'd forth, the flying Bands to meet, ... Il.21.629.448.
Achilles, like a Lion, rush'd abroad: ..... Il.24.721.567.
If e'er ye rush'd in Crowds, with vast Delight ..... Il.24.878.573.
In rush'd the Suitors with voracious haste: ..... Od.1.190.42.
And o'er the shaded landscape rush'd the night. ..... Od.3.630.118.
The rock rush'd sea-ward, with impetuous roar ..... Od.4.681.151.
Down rush'd the night. East, west, together roar, ... Od.5.379.190.
A mighty wave rush'd o'er him as he spoke, ... Od.5.403.192.
Down rush'd the toils, enwrapping as they lay ..... Od.8.339.282.
How the *Greeks* rush'd tumultuous to the main: ..... Od.8.548.292.
And Night rush'd headlong on the shaded deeps. ..... Od.9.78.306.
But two rush'd out, and to the navy flew. ..... Od.10.134.347.
Unwieldy, out They rush'd, with gen'ral cry, ... Od.10.461.366.
And o'er the shaded billows rush'd the night: ..... Od.11.12.379.
And here thro' sev'n wide portals rush'd the war. ..... Od.11.324.398.
Climb'd the tall bark, and rush'd into the main; ..... Od.12.181.441.
Rush'd with dire noise, and dash'd the sides in twain; ..... Od.12.497.456.
Forth rush'd the swain with hospitable haste. ..... Od.14.84.40.
On earth he rush'd with agonizing pain; ..... Od.19.531.221.
And like a lion rush'd against his Lord: ..... Od.22.94.291.

RUSHED

The Lion rushed thro' the woodland Shade, ... Il.11.601.61.

RUSHES

And like a Deluge rushes in the War. ..... 1.TrES.134.454.
So on *Mæotis'* Marsh, (where Reeds and Rushes ..... 6.26i.1.79.
On *Coon* rushes with his lifted Spear: ..... Il.11.330.49.
And, like a Deluge, rushes in the War. ..... Il.12.488.99.
This said, he rushes where the Combate burns; ..... Il.13.313.120.
Lo, great *Æneas* rushes to the Fight: ..... Il.13.609.135.
Dauntless he rushes where the *Spartan* Lord ..... Il.13.763.141.
With ample Strokes he rushes to the Flood, ... Il.15.300.208.
Dolops, the Son of *Lampus* rushes on, ... Il.15.622.220.
A rapid Torrent thro' the Rushes roars: ..... Il.18.668.356.
A mossy bank with pliant rushes crown'd; ..... Od.5.595.201.
When the tyde rushes from her rumbling caves ..... Od.12.282.446.
And with fresh rushes heap'd an ample bed. ..... Od.14.60.38.
Minerva rushes thro' th' aereal way, ... Od.23.372.343.

RUSHING

At once the rushing Winds with roaring Sound ..... 1.TrSt.488.430.
Now rushing in the furious Chief appears, ... 1.TrES.199.456.
With rushing Troops the Plains are cover'd o'er, ... Il.2.548.153.
With Shouts the *Trojans* rushing from afar ..... Il.3.3.186.
Of arm'd *Tydides* rushing to the War. ..... Il.4.477.242.
Thro' ruin'd Moles the rushing Wave resounds, ... Il.5.118.273.
The rushing Stream his Brazen Armor dy'd, ... Il.5.132.273.
The rushing Chariot, and the bounding Steed. ..... Il.5.275.280.
Safe thro' the rushing Horse and feather'd Flight ..... Il.5.393.285.
Next rushing to the *Dardan* Spoil, detains ..... Il.5.399.286.
Thrice rushing furious, at the Chief he strook; ..... Il.5.529.294.
Now rushing fierce, in equal Arms appear, ... Il.5.1042.316.
There meets the Chariot rushing down the Skies, ... Il.8.505.420.
Then rushing from his Tent, he snatch'd in hast ..... Il.10.154.8.
As scatter'd Lambs the rushing Lion fear. ..... Il.11.490.56.
The Victor rushing to despoil the Dead, ... Il.11.708.66.
Furious he spoke, and rushing to the Wall, ... Il.12.295.92.
Now rushing in the furious Chief appears, ... Il.12.553.101.
Then *Teucer* rushing to despoil the dead, ... Il.13.245.116.
Swift as a Whirlwind rushing to the Fleet, ... Il.13.277.117.
And the fierce Soul came rushing thro' the Wound. ..... Il.14.614.192.
Phœbus himself the rushing Battel led; ..... Il.15.348.210.
As when a Lion, rushing from his Den, ... Il.15.760.225.
Then rushing sudden on his prostrate Prize, ... Il.16.907.279.
And *Mars* himself came rushing on his Soul. ..... Il.17.252.297.
Full in the Mouth is stopp'd the rushing Tide, ... Il.17.312.299.
And thro' the Wound the rushing Entrails broke. ..... Il.17.365.301.
And breaks the Torrent of the rushing Bands. ..... Il.17.838.321.
In its wide Womb they pour the rushing Stream; ..... Il.18.409.340.
The rushing Ocean murmur'd o'er my Head. ..... Il.18.472.344.
Two Lions rushing from the Wood appear'd; ..... Il.18.671.356.
Once stay'd *Achilles*, rushing to the War. ..... Il.19.338.386.
Oft' stay'd *Achilles* rushing to the War. ..... Il.19.338A.386.
Lo great *Æneas* rushing to the War; ..... Il.20.147.400.
Meanwhile the rushing Armies hide the Ground; ..... Il.20.188.402.
Achilles, rushing in with dreadful Cries, ... Il.20.333.407.
The Scene of War came rushing on his Sight. ..... Il.20.392.411.
The rushing Entrails pour'd upon the Ground ..... Il.20.483.414.
His loaded Shield bends to the rushing Tide; ..... Il.21.265.431.
Loud flash the Waters to the rushing Fall ..... Il.21.272.432.
Then fiercely rushing on the daring Foe, ... Il.21.703.450.
With *Troilus*, dreadful on his rushing Car, ... Il.24.322.550.
Then, with a rushing sound, th' Assembly bend ..... Od.2.291.75.
Rushing impetuous forth, we strait prepare ..... Od.4.611.148.
Detains the rushing current of his tydes, ... Od.5.577.200.
Nor wind sharp-piercing, nor the rushing show'r; ..... Od.5.621.201.
Down rushing, it up-turns a hill of ground. ..... Od.8.218.274.
Contract its mouth, and break the rushing tide. ..... Od.10.104.345.
Where *Phlegeton's* loud torrents rushing down, ... Od.10.608.374.
Nor by the axe the rushing forest bends, ... Od.12.13.430.
When in her gulphs the rushing sea subsides, ... Od.12.288.446.
Then rushing to his arms, he kiss'd his boy ..... Od.16.210.114.
To dart the spear, and guide the rushing car ..... Od.18.307.181.
And rushing forth tumultuous reel away. ..... Od.18.473.191.
He thinks the Queen is rushing to his arms. ..... Od.20.115.238.
The wary Chief the rushing foe represt, ... Od.22.95.291.
A Boar fierce-rushing in the sylvan war ..... Od.23.75.322.
Or rushing to his arms, confess her love? ..... Od.23.90.323.

RUSSEL

So Russel did, but could not eat at night, ... 4.1HE6.115.245.

RUSSET

Here in full Light the russet Plains extend; ..... 1.W-F.23.150.

RUSSIAN

"No Lord's anointed, but a Russian Bear." ..... 4.2HE1.389.229.

RUSSLE

Fans clap, Silks russle, and tough Whalebones crack; ..... 2.RL5.40.202.

RUST

Swords, Pikes, and Guns, with everlasting Rust! ..... 4.HS1.74.11.
It is the rust we value, not the gold. ..... 4.2HE1.36.197.
Th' inscription value, but the rust adore; ..... 6.71.36.203.
The sacred rust of twice ten hundred years! ..... 6.71.38.203.

RUST'LING

Thro' breaking Woods her rust'ling Course they hear; ..... Il.10.215.11.

RUSTED

Old *Dolius* too his rusted arms put on; ..... Od.24.574.375.

RUSTIC

That, lac'd with bits of rustic, makes a Front. ..... 3.Ep4.34.140.
And, lac'd with bits of rustic, 'tis a Front. ..... 3.Ep4.34A.140.
Tho' still some traces of our rustic vein ..... 4.2HE1.270.219.
The *Rustic Lout* so like a Brute, ... 6.44.25.123.
The rustic Monarch of the Field descries ..... Il.18.645.354.
And nine sour Dogs compleat the rustic Band. ..... Il.18.670.356.
Where antient *Neleus* sate, a rustic throne; ..... Od.3.521.113.
Some rustic wretch, who liv'd in heav'n's despight, ... Od.9.250.317.
Before the threshold of his rustic gate; ..... Od.14.8.35.
Spurn'd with his rustic heel his King unknown; ..... Od.17.273.145.
Hold, lawless rustic! whither wilt thou go? ..... Od.21.391.279.
Here now arriving, to his rustic band ..... Od.24.244.360.

RUSTICK

As priest himself, the blameless rustick rose; ..... Od.14.481.59.

RUSTICKS

And sees the Rusticks to their Labours rise; ..... 6.17iii.33.58.
When the loud Rusticks rise, and shout from far, ... Il.13.596.134.
Hence to your fields, ye rusticks! hence away, ... Od.21.87.263.

RUSTLING
Stretch their long Necks, and clap their rustling Wings, ...Il.2.543.153.
As when some Shepherd from the rustling Trees ....Il.3.47.190.
But swift thro' rustling Thickets bursts her way; ....Il.11.158.42.
Who hear, from rustling Oaks, thy dark Decrees; ....Il.16.290.253.
Who hear, from rustling Oaks, their dark Decrees; ....Il.16.290A.253.
Then rustling, crackling, crashing, thunder down. ....Il.23.149.495.

RUSTY
From the black Trumpet's rusty Concave broke ....2.TemF.338.280.
Now herald hawker's rusty voice proclaims ....5.DunA2.13A.98.

RUTHLESS
Mars urg'd him on; yet, ruthless in his Hate, ...Il.5.691.300.
The ruthless Victor stripp'd their shining Arms. ....Il.6.34.325.
If Wrath so dreadful fill thy ruthless Mind, ...Il.9.564.461.
And ruthless *Proserpine*, confirm'd his Vow. ....Il.9.585.463.
The ruthless Falchion op'd his tender Side; ....Il.20.544.417.
All but the ruthless Monarch of the Main. ....Od.1.28.30.

RYM'D
Has drunk with *Cibber,* nay has rym'd for *Moor.* ....4.Arbu.373.123.
Has drank with *Cibber,* nay has rym'd for *Moor.* ....4.Arbu.373A.123.

RYME
See RHIME, RHYME.
Then from the *Mint* walks forth the Man of Ryme, ...4.Arbu.13.96.
And promise our best Friends to ryme no more; ....4.2HE1.178.209.
All ryme, and scrawl, and scribble, to a man. ....4.2HE1.188.211.
But most of all, the Zeal of Fools in ryme. ....4.2HE1.407.229.

RYMES
Rymes e'er he wakes, and prints before *Term* ends, ...4.Arbu.43.99.
Or Spite, or Smut, or Rymes, or Blasphemies. ....4.Arbu.322.119.
To know the Poet from the Man of Rymes: ....4.2HE1.341.225.

RYMING
A maudlin Poetess, a ryming Peer, ...4.Arbu.16.97.

S
"To crave your sentiment, if—'s your name. ....4.JD4.67.31.
Not—'s self e'er tells more *Fibs* than I; ....4.2HE1.176.209.
Whom (saving W[alter]) every S. *harper bites,* ....4.1740.26.333*.
Shine in the dignity of F.R.S. ....5.DunB4.570.398.

S*Z
See SHUTZ.
If honest S*z take scandal at a spark, ...4.1HE1.112.287.

S'IL
'Twas *S'il vous plaist, Monsieur.* ....6.14v(b).12.49.
& *S'il vous plaist, Monsieur.* ....6.14v(b).12A.49.

SABAEAN
And heap'd with Products of *Sabæan* Springs! ....1.Mes.94.121.

SABBATH
Ev'n *Sunday* shines no *Sabbath-day* to me: ....4.Arbu.12.96.
Why will you break the Sabbath of my days? ....4.1HE1.3.279.
See Christians, Jews, one heavy sabbath keep; ....5.DunA3.91.157.
See Christians, Jews, one heavy sabbath keep, ...5.DunB3.99.324.
Peaceful sleep out the Sabbath of the Tomb, ...6.86.19.246.

SABBATH-DAY
Ev'n *Sunday* shines no *Sabbath-day* to me: ....4.Arbu.12.96.

SABBATHS
As Hags hold Sabbaths, less for joy than spight, ...3.Ep2.239.69.

SABIN
Had roasted turnips in the Sabin farm. ....3.Ep1.219.34.

SABINUS
Thro' his young Woods how pleas'd Sabinus stray'd, ...3.Ep4.89.146.

SABLE
Like verdant Isles the sable Waste adorn. ....1.W-F.28.150.
Reap their own Fruits, and woo their Sable Loves, ...1.W-F.410.192.
Thou, sable *Styx!* whose livid Streams are roll'd ....1.TrSt.83.413.
The Sable Flock shall fall beneath the Stroke, ...1.TrSt.594.435.
When Night with sable Wings o'erspreads the Ground, ...1.TrSt.711.440.
Now move to War her Sable *Matadores,* ....2.RL3.47.172.
Of *Asia's* Troops, and *Africk's* Sable Sons, ...2.RL3.82.174.
These, in two sable Ringlets taught to break, ...2.RL4.169.197.
This, in two sable Ringlets taught to break, ...2.RL4.169A.197.
What tho' no friends in sable weeds appear, ...2.Elegy.55.367.
With deeper sable blots the silver flood. ....5.DunA2.262.133.
Shaking the horrors of his sable brows, ...5.DunA2.303A.139.
Slow moves the Goddess from the sable flood, ...5.DunA2.331.142.
(Earth's wide extreams) her sable flag display'd; ....5.DunA3.63.155.
He look'd, and saw a sable Sorc'rer rise, ...5.DunA3.229.176.
He look'd, and saw a sable seer arise, ...5.DunA3.229A.176.
With deeper sable blots the silver flood. ....5.DunB2.274.309.
Shaking the horrors of his sable brows, ...5.DunB2.327.313.
Around him wide a sable Army stand, ...5.DunB2.355.314.
(Earth's wide extremes) her sable flag display'd, ...5.DunB3.71.323.
And look'd, and saw a sable Sorc'rer rise, ...5.DunB3.233.331.
Broad hats, and hoods, and caps, a sable shoal: ....5.DunB4.190.360.
She comes! she comes! the sable Throne behold ....5.DunB4.629.407.
The Gloom rolls on, the sable Throne behold ....5.DunB4.629A.407.
Or China's Earth receive the sable Tyde; ....6.82i.4.229.
And dipt them in the sable Well, ...6.140.11.378.
Soon shall the Fair the sable Ship ascend, ...Il.1.185.96.
A sable Cloud conceal'd her from the rest. ....Il.1.266.99.
The sable Fumes in curling Spires arise, ...Il.1.416.107.
He spoke, and awful, bends his sable Brows; ....Il.1.683.119.

SABLE (CONTINUED)
Nor drew his sable Vessels to the Flood. ....Il.2.208.138.
Their Troops in thirty sable Vessels sweep ....Il.2.618.157.
In forty sable Barks they stem'd the Main; ....Il.2.922.167.
Or drink, *Æsepus,* of thy sable Flood; ....Il.2.1000.170.
To *Earth* a sable, to the *Sun* a white, ...Il.3.142.197.
Lay'd their bright Arms along the sable Shore. ....Il.3.158.198.
Death's sable Shade at once o'ercast their Eyes, ...Il.4.626.250.
Like *Pallas* dreadful with her sable Shield, ...Il.5.410.286.
Mars hovers o'er them with his sable Shield, ...Il.5.621.297.
In sable Ships they left their native Soil, ...Il.5.678.300.
Th' avenging Bolt, and shake the sable Shield! ....Il.8.424.417.
Greece on her sable Ships attempt her Flight. ....Il.8.636.426.
In sable Streams soft-trickling Waters shed. ....Il.9.20.432.
The Blood of *Greeks* shall dye the sable Main; ....Il.9.766.472.
The King to *Nestor's* sable Ship repairs; ....Il.10.81.6.
A sable Ewe each Leader should provide, ...Il.10.255.13.
With each a sable Lambkin by her side; ....Il.10.256.13.
The Squadrons spread their sable Wings behind. ....Il.11.66.37.
Rolls sable Clouds in Heaps on Heaps along; ....Il.11.398.52.
The groaning Axle sable Drops distills, ...Il.11.660.63.
The sable Blood in Circles mark'd the Ground. ....Il.11.943.77.
Ev'n when they saw *Troy's* sable Troops impend, ...Il.12.159.87.
The crowded Ships, and sable Seas between. ....Il.13.24.105.
Invokes the sable Subtartarean Pow'rs, ...Il.14.314.178.
Against the sable Ships with flaming Brands, ...Il.15.905.232.
From the tall Rock the sable Waters flow. ....Il.16.6.234.
A sable Scene! The Terrors *Hector* led. ....Il.17.115.292.
(The sable Plumage nodded o'er his Head) ....Il.17.212.295.
Then with his sable Brow he gave the Nod, ...Il.17.245.297.
But now th' Eternal shook his sable Shield, ...Il.17.668.314.
While the long Night extends her sable Reign, ...Il.18.365.339.
And sable look'd, tho form'd of molten Gold. ....Il.18.636.354.
Sable it look'd, tho form'd of molten Gold. ....Il.18.636A.354.
They tore his Flesh, and drank the sable Blood. ....Il.18.674.356.
Purple the Ground, and streak the sable Sand; ....Il.22.507.477.
All to *Achilles'* sable Ship repair, ...Il.23.37.488.
And well-fed Sheep, and sable Oxen slay: ....Il.23.205.498.
With sable Wine; then, (as the Rites direct). ....Il.23.296.501.
Wide o'er the Pyle the sable Wine they throw, ...Il.23.311.502.
Refulgent gliding o'er the sable Deeps. ....Il.24.102.539.
She spake, and veil'd her Head in sable Shade, ...Il.24.122.540.
Adorn'd the matron-brow of sable Night; ....Od.1.534.57.
The sable billows foam and roar below. ....Od.2.461.83.
As *Pallas* will'd, along the sable skies ....Od.4.1053.167.
With water one, and one with sable wine; ....Od.5.338.188.
When *Jove* tremendous in the sable deeps ....Od.7.334.253.
The fatted sheep and sable bulls they slay, ...Od.9.49.304.
A sable ram, the pride of all thy breed. ....Od.10.625.374.
Be next thy care the sable sheep to place ....Od.10.628.374.
The sable ewe, and ram, together bound. ....Od.10.686.376.
Then sable Night ascends, and balmy rest ....Od.12.41.431.
A mark of vengeance on the sable deep: ....Od.13.173.14.
Where *Arethusa's* sable water glides; ....Od.13.470.28.
The sable water and the copious mast ....Od.13.471.29.
The sable crows with intercepted flight ....Od.14.342.51.
Then pour'd of offer'd wine the sable wave: ....Od.14.499.60.
A length of hair in sable ringlets flows; ....Od.16.191.112.
Might see the sable field at once arise! ....Od.18.417.189.
His visage solemn sad, of sable hue: ....Od.19.279.208.
And airy terrors sable ev'ry dream. ....Od.20.103.238.
Your future thought let sable Fate employ; ....Od.20.308.247.
So cow'ring fled the sable heaps of ghosts, ...Od.24.13.347.
And fatted sheep and sable oxen slay; ....Od.24.84.352.
Ulysses parting thro' the sable flood; ....Od.24.362.366.

SABLER
He bears no token of the sabler streams, ...5.DunA2.285.137.
He bears no token of the sabler streams, ...5.DunB2.297.310.

SABRE
With his broad Sabre next, a Chief in Years, ...2.RL3.55.172.
Seam'd o'er with wounds, which his own sabre gave, ...Od.4.335.135.
A sabre, when the warrior press'd to part, ...Od.19.273.208.
A radiant sabre grac'd his purple zone, ...Od.20.157.241.

SACK
Sow'd in a Sack, and plung'd into a Well: ....2.ChJM.588.43.
Know, Eusden thirsts no more for sack or praise; ....5.DunB1.293.291.
Whose game is Whisk, whose treat a toast in sack, ...6.45.24.125.
Oh! save the Salary, and drink the Sack! ....6.116v.6.327.
And Dogs shall tear him, e'er he sack the Town. ....Il.18.332.337.

SACK'D
The noblest Spoil from sack'd *Lyrnessus* born, ...Il.2.842.164.
I sack'd twelve ample Cities on the Main, ...Il.9.432.453.
With a sack'd Palace, and barbaric spoils. ....Od.4.122.126.
With latent heroes sack'd imperial *Troy.* ....Od.8.542.291.
And sack'd the city, and destroy'd the race, ...Od.9.44.304.

SACKCLOTH
They dealt in *Sackcloth,* and turn'd *Cynder-Wenches:* ....6.95.2.264.

SACKS
Elate in Thought, he sacks untaken *Troy:* ....Il.2.46.129.
Ev'n now, the hand of Rapine sacks the dome. ....Od.15.16.70.

SACRED
Fair *Thames* flow gently from thy sacred Spring, ...1.PSp.3.59.
A wondrous *Tree* that Sacred *Monarchs* bears? ....1.PSp.86.69.
In those fair Fields where Sacred *Isis* glides, ...1.PSu.25.73.
Ye *Mantuan* Nymphs, your sacred Succour bring; ....1.PAu.5.80.
Whose sacred Flow'r with Fragrance fills the Skies. ....1.Mes.10.113.
And savage Howlings fill the sacred Quires. ....1.W-F.72.156.
And Wolves with Howling fill the sacred Quires. ....1.W-F.72A.156.
Ye sacred Nine! that all my Soul possess, ...1.W-F.259.173.

SACRED (CONTINUED)

Here noble *Surrey* felt the sacred Rage, ...1.W-F.291.175.
Make sacred *Charles's* Tomb for ever known, ...1.W-F.319.180.
Her sacred Domes involv'd in rolling Fire, ...1.W-F.324.180.
Hail Sacred *Peace!* hail long-expected Days, ...1.W-F.355.185.
Before *his* sacred Name flies ev'ry Fault, ...1.EOC.422.288.
Are Mortals urg'd thro' *Sacred Lust of Praise!* ....1.EOC.521.296.
Are Mortals urg'd by *Sacred Lust of Praise?* ....1.EOC.521A.296.
Pulpits their *Sacred Satire* learn'd to spare, ...1.EOC.550.302.
No Place so Sacred from such Fops is barr'd, ...1.EOC.622.310.
Demand our Song; a sacred Fury fires ....1.TrSt.3.409.
And Sacred Thirst of Sway; and all the Ties ....1.TrSt.178.417.
And sacred Silence reigns, and universal Peace. ....1.TrSt.291.422.
Each sacred Accent bears eternal Weight, ...1.TrSt.298.422.
And stain the sacred Womb where once he lay? ....1.TrSt.333.424.
Nor Victims sink beneath the Sacred Stroke; ....1.TrSt.372.425.
And first to Light expos'd the Sacred Shade. ....1.TrSt.509.431.
O'er all his Bosom sacred Transports reign, ...1.TrSt.579A.434.
Thus, seiz'd with Sacred Fear, the Monarch pray'd; ....1.TrSt.598.435.
Which *Danaus* us'd in sacred Rites of old, ...1.TrSt.635.436.
Those Honours paid, his sacred Corps bequeath ....1.TrES.330.461.
Those Rites discharg'd, his sacred Corps bequeath ....1.TrES.330A.461.
Where endless Honours wait the Sacred Shade. ....1.TrES.349.462.
Divine *Ulysses* was her Sacred Load, ...1.TrUl.15.466.
Sacred to *Phorcys'* Pow'r, whose Name it bears; ....1.TrUl.26.466.
Sacred the South, by which the Gods descend, ...1.TrUl.43.467.
Thy sacred Presence from that Hour I lost; ....1.TrUl.198.472.
Who ventures Sacred Marriage to defame. ....2.ChJM.223A.25.
And join'd my Heart, in Wedlock's sacred Band: ....2.ChJM.582.43.
But since the Sacred Leaves to All are free, ...2.ChJM.677.47.
And one, whose Faith has ever sacred been. ....2.ChJM.704.48.
One fatal stroke the sacred Hair does sever ....2.RL*A*1.117.130.
Trembling, begins the sacred Rites of Pride. ....2.RL1.128.155.
Each Band the number of the Sacred Nine. ....2.RL3.30.171.
The meeting Points the sacred Hair dissever ....2.RL3.153.179.
But by this Lock, this sacred Lock I swear, ...2.RL4.133.194.
His Sacred Head a radiant Zodiack crown'd, ...2.TemF.234.274.
Thus on their Knees address the sacred Fane. ....2.TemF.319.279.
Thus on their Knees address'd the sacred Fane. ....2.TemF.319A.279.
August her deed, and sacred be her fame; ....2.ElAb.78.326.
As with cold lips I kiss'd the sacred veil, ...2.ElAb.111.329.
Ah no—in sacred vestments may'st thou stand, ...2.ElAb.325.346.
What tho' no sacred earth allow thee room, ...2.Elegy.61.367.
The ground, now sacred by thy reliques made. ....2.Elegy.68.368.
Then sacred seem'd th'etherial vault no more; ....3.EOM3.263.119.
Sacred to Ridicule! his whole Life long, ...4.HS1.79.13.
Whose *Satyr's sacred,* and whose Rage *secure.* ....4.JD4.283.49.
And children sacred held a *Martin's* nest, ...4.HS2.38.57.
And hides in sacred Sluttishness the rest. ....4.HAdv.111.85.
No place is sacred, not the Church is free, ...4.Arbu.11.96.
(*Midas,* a sacred Person and a King) ....4.Arbu.70.100.
Sacred to social Life and social Love, ...4.HOde1.22.151.
His House, thy Temple, sacred still to Love ....4.HOde1.22A.151.
And virtuous Alfred, a more sacred Name, ...4.2HE1.8.195.
Whose Word is Truth, as sacred and rever'd, ...4.2HE1.27.197.
"Nothing is Sacred now but Villany." ....4.EpS1.170.309.
O sacred Weapon! left for Truth's defence, ...4.EpS2.212.325.
She bids him wait her to the sacred Dome; ....5.DunA1.221.89.
With mystic words, the sacred Opium shed; ....5.DunA1.242.91.
(As under seas Alphæus' sacred sluice ....5.DunA2.317A.140.
"Dulness is sacred in a sound Divine." ....5.DunA2.328.141.
Thou, yet unborn, hast touch'd this sacred shore; ....5.DunA3.37.154.
She bids him wait her to her sacred Dome: ....5.DunB1.265.289.
With mystic words, the sacred Opium shed. ....5.DunB1.288.290.
"Dulness is sacred in a sound divine." ....5.DunB2.352.314.
Thou, yet unborn, hast touch'd this sacred shore; ....5.DunB3.45.322.
Or vest dull Flatt'ry in the sacred Gown; ....5.DunB4.97.350.
Thine from the birth, and sacred from the rod, ...5.DunB4.283.372.
The Cap and Switch be sacred to his Grace; ....5.DunB4.585.400.
Religion blushing veils her sacred fires, ...5.DunB4.649.409.
Hail sacred spring, whose fruitful stream ....6.6ii.1.14.
From Sacred Union and consent of Things. ....6.11.35Z10.31.
While solemn Airs improve the sacred Fire; ....6.11.129.34.
A thorny crown transpierc'd thy sacred brow, ...6,25.7.77.
To thee, Redeemer! mercy's sacred spring! ....6.25.15.77.
YE shades, where sacred truth is sought; ....6.51i.1.151.
Sacred *Hymen!* these are thine. ....6.51ii.44.154.
Muse! at that name thy sacred sorrows shed, ...6.52.47.157.
No, trust the Sex's sacred Rule; ....6.64.21.190.
The sacred rust of twice ten hundred years! ....6.71.38.203.
And sacred, place by *Dryden's* awful dust: ....6.72.2.208.
Laid Sacred here, by Dryden's awful Dust, ...6.72.2A.208.
Sacred to *Musick* and to *Love.* ....6.82vii.8.233.
This ' *sheffield* rais'd. The sacred Dust below ....6.83.1.237.
Nymph of the Grot, these sacred Springs I keep, ...6.87.1.248.
Thy silent whisper is the sacred test.] ....6.107.32.311.
Whom Heav'n kept sacred from the Proud and Great. ....6.112.4.318.
Yet sacred keep his Friendships, and his Ease. ....6.118.10.335.
Let such, such only, tread this sacred Floor, ...6.142.13.383.
Such only such shall tread the sacred Floor, ...6.142.13A.383.
Such only such may tread this sacred Floor, ...6.142.13B.383.
Let such, such only, tread the sacred Floor, ...6.142.13F.383.
Repuls'd the sacred Sire, and thus reply'd. ....Il.1.34.87.
If e'er with Wreaths I hung thy sacred Fane, ...Il.1.57.88.
But let some Prophet, or some sacred Sage, ...Il.1.83.90.
That sacred Seer whose comprehensive View ....Il.1.93.91.
The King of Kings, shall touch that sacred Head. ....Il.1.116.92.
And joins the sacred Senate of the Skies. ....Il.1.294.101.
Now by this sacred Sceptre, hear me swear, ...Il.1.309.102.
A well-rigg'd Ship for *Chrysa's* sacred Shores: ....Il.1.405.107.
The Army thus in sacred Rites engag'd, ...Il.1.418.107.
To wait his Will two sacred Heralds stood, ...Il.1.420.107.
Ye sacred Ministers of Men and Gods! ....Il.1.435.108.
From *Thebè* sacred to *Apollo's* Name, ...Il.1.478.110.
Ulysses led to *Phœbus* sacred Fane; ....Il.1.573.115.
The sacred Off'ring of the salted Cake; ....Il.1.587.116.

SACRED (CONTINUED)

Whose sacred Eye thy *Tenedos* surveys, ...Il.1.592.116.
The sacred Counsels of his Breast conceal'd. ....Il.1.663.118.
Witness the sacred Honours of our Head, ...Il.1.679.119.
The sacred Counsels of Almighty Mind: ....Il.1.705.121.
Nor break the sacred Union of the Sky: ....Il.1.747.123.
Nine sacred Heralds now proclaiming loud ....Il.2.123.133.
Beside a Fountain's sacred Brink we rais'd ....Il.2.368.145.
The sacred Off'ring of the salted Cake: ....Il.2.487.150.
While the fat Victim feeds the sacred Fire. ....Il.2.509.151.
Or *Thespia* sacred to the God of Day. ....Il.2.599.156.
The sacred Stream unmix'd with Streams below, ...Il.2.913.167.
Sacred and awful! From the dark Abodes ....Il.2.914.167.
Fast by the Foot of *Ida's* sacred Hill: ....Il.2.999.170.
For stern *Achilles* lopt his sacred Head, ...Il.2.1048.172.
On either side a sacred Herald stands, ...Il.3.338.209.
Next to decide by sacred Lots prepare, ...Il.3.392.211.
None stands so dear to *Jove* as sacred *Troy.* ....Il.4.68.224.
So, great *Atrides!* show'd thy sacred Blood, ...Il.4.176.229.
Which stain'd with sacred Blood the blushing Sand. ....Il.5.107.272.
Now, Goddess, now, thy sacred Succour yield. ....Il.5.149.274.
When first for *Troy* I sail'd the sacred Seas, ...Il.5.249.279.
The sacred *Ichor,* and infus'd the Balm. ....Il.5.506.292.
Troy's sacred Walls, nor need a foreign Hand? ....Il.5.578.296.
As when on *Ceres'* sacred Floor the Swain ....Il.5.611.297.
And now the God, from forth his sacred Fane, ...Il.5.627.298.
Yet let me die in *Ilion's* sacred Wall; ....Il.5.846.306.
Taught by the Gods that mov'd his sacred Breast: ....Il.6.92.328.
Unbar the sacred Gates; and seek the Pow'r ....Il.6.111.329.
With brandish'd Steel from *Nyssa's* sacred Grove, ...Il.6.164.334.
Endu'd with Wisdom, sacred Fear, and Truth. ....Il.6.204.336.
Nor stain the sacred Friendship of our Race. ....Il.6.266.339.
Let Chiefs abstain, and spare the sacred Juice ....Il.6.332.342.
Thus told the Dictates of his sacred Breast. ....Il.7.50.365.
The sacred Ministers of Earth and Heav'n: ....Il.7.332.380.
To sacred *Troy,* where all her Princes lay ....Il.7.490.388.
To shed his sacred Light on Earth again, ...Il.7.499.389.
And sadly slow, to sacred *Troy* return'd. ....Il.7.511.389.
There, from his radiant Car, the sacred Sire ....Il.8.61.398.
O'er Heav'ns clear Azure spread the sacred Light; ....Il.8.84.399.
He drop'd the Reins; and shook with sacred Dread, ...Il.8.167.406.
His Eagle, sacred Bird of Heav'n! he sent, ...Il.8.297.411.
The radiant Robe her sacred Fingers wove, ...Il.8.468.419.
Let sacred Heralds sound the solemn Call; ....Il.8.644.426.
O'er Heav'ns clear Azure spreads her sacred Light, ...Il.8.688.428.
O'er Heav'ns clear Azure sheds her sacred Light, ...Il.8.688A.428.
Sev'n sacred Tripods, whose unsully'd Frame ....Il.9.159.440.
And sacred *Pedasus,* for Vines renown'd; ....Il.9.198.442.
The Youth with Wine the sacred Goblets crown'd, ...Il.9.229.444.
And sprinkles sacred Salt from lifted Urns; ....Il.9.282.447.
Sev'n sacred Tripods, whose unsully'd Frame ....Il.9.346.450.
And sacred *Pedasus,* for Vines renown'd; ....Il.9.385.451.
His Age be sacred, and his Will be free. ....Il.9.555.460.
There, till the sacred Morn restor'd the Day, ...Il.9.777.472.
These sacred Heralds and great *Ajax* heard. ....Il.9.807.473.
His Age is sacred, and his Choice is free. ....Il.9.811.473.
And vengeful Anger fill'd his sacred Breast. ....Il.10.605.29.
And gild the Courts of Heav'n with sacred Light. ....Il.11.4.34.
And sacred Night her awful Shade extend. ....Il.11.252.46.
And sacred Night her awful Shade extend. ....Il.11.268.47.
Ye sacred Nine, Celestial Muses! tell, ...Il.11.281.47.
Honey new-press'd, the sacred Flow'r of Wheat, ...Il.11.770.69.
A Goblet sacred to the *Pylian* Kings, ...Il.11.773.69.
To great *Alphæus'* sacred Source we came. ....Il.11.863.74.
While sacred *Troy* the warring Hosts engag'd; ....Il.12.12.81.
Ev'n the sweet Charms of sacred Numbers tire. ....Il.13.798.143.
Sacred to Dress, and Beauty's pleasing Cares: ....Il.14.192.168.
And burns the Sons of Heav'n with sacred Fires! ....Il.14.228.172.
Where the great Parents (sacred Source of Gods!) ....Il.14.230.172.
And stretch the other o'er the sacred Main. ....Il.14.308.177.
Nor seek, unknown to thee, the sacred Cells ....Il.14.353.179.
And be these Moments sacred all to Joy. ....Il.14.358.180.
Sacred to Love and to the genial Hour; ....Il.14.384.181.
The golden Vision round his sacred Head; ....Il.14.414.183.
By the dread Honours of thy sacred Head, ...Il.15.45.196.
To sacred *Ilion* from th' *Idæan* Height. ....Il.15.191.204.
And hush the Roarings of the sacred Deep: ....Il.15.217.205.
This ting'd with Sulphur, sacred first to Flame, ...Il.16.278.249.
Or sacred *Ilion,* thy bright Presence boast, ...Il.16.634.269.
Those Rites discharg'd, his sacred Corpse bequeath ....Il.16.817.274.
Where endless Honours wait the sacred Shade. ....Il.16.836.276.
But flaming *Phœbus* kept the sacred Tow'r. ....Il.16.858.276.
The radiant Spoils to sacred *Ilion* bore. ....Il.17.216.295.
He shook the sacred Honours of his Head; ....Il.17.229.296.
With sacred Darkness shades the Face of all. ....Il.17.523.308.
The sacred Eagle, from his Walks above ....Il.17.763.318.
Their sacred Seats, the glimm'ring *Grotto* fill'd; ....Il.18.66.326.
Haste, and our Fathers sacred Seat attend, ...Il.18.178.331.
Sacred to Vengeance, by this Hand expire; ....Il.18.395.340.
Here sacred Pomp, and genial Feast delight, ...Il.18.569.350.
On Seats of Stone, within the sacred Place, ...Il.18.585.351.
And gild the Courts of Heav'n with sacred Light) ....Il.19.4.371.
Untouch'd it rests, and sacred from Decay. ....Il.19.42.373.
These on the sacred Seats of Council plac'd, ...Il.19.53.374.
Sacred to *Jove,* and yon' bright Orb of Day. ....Il.19.196.379.
And *Greece* around sate thrill'd with sacred Awe. ....Il.19.266.383.
The sacred Herald rolls the Victim slain ....Il.19.279.384.
His ancient Seat beneath the sacred Deeps. ....Il.20.16.393.
Assist them Gods! or *Ilion's* sacred Wall ....Il.20.41.394.
The sacred Flood that rolls on golden Sands; ....Il.20.100.398.
But *Jove* himself, the sacred Source of thine. ....Il.20.139.400.
The sacred *Tros,* of whom the *Trojan* Name. ....Il.20.275.405.
And thick bestrown, lies *Ceres'* sacred Floor, ...Il.20.578.418.
O sacred Stream! thy Word we shall obey; ....Il.21.241.431.
His sacred Arrows in defence of *Troy,* ....Il.21.252.431.
Apollo enters *Ilion's* sacred Town: ....Il.21.598.446.

SACRED (CONTINUED)

By all the sacred Prevalence of Pray'r; ... Il.22.427.473.
Nor all the sacred Prevalence of Pray'r. ... Il.22.436.473.
Yet mine shall sacred last; mine, undecay'd, ... Il.22.489.476.
Sacred to Vengeance, instant shall expire, ... Il.23.31.488.
The grassy Mound, and clip thy sacred Hair. ... Il.23.56.489.
And sacred grew to *Sperchius* honour'd Flood: ... Il.23.175.496.
On his cold Hand the sacred Lock he laid. ... Il.23.191.497.
Nor sacred *Phœbus* less employ'd his Care; ... Il.23.232.499.
To sacred Ocean, and the Floods below: ... Il.23.253.499.
The sacred Relicks to the Tent they bore; ... Il.23.315.502.
Accept thou this, O sacred Sire! (he said) ... Il.23.707.517.
Not one but honours sacred Age and me: ... Il.23.748.520.
But, set apart for sacred Use, commands ... Il.23.1062.533.
Spread o'er the sacred Corse his golden Shield. ... Il.24.33.536.
(The blue-hair'd Sisters of the sacred Main) ... Il.24.112.539.
The sacred Sire of Gods and mortal Man: ... Il.24.136.540.
Vent his mad Vengeance on the sacred Dead: ... Il.24.150.541.
Haste, winged Goddess! to the sacred Town, ... Il.24.179.543.
Thy sacred Bird, cœlestial Augury! ... Il.24.382.552.
(The sacred Messenger of Heav'n reply'd) ... Il.24.466.556.
The stern *Pelides;* and nor sacred Age ... Il.24.734.568.
But now the peaceful Hours of sacred Night ... Il.24.753.568.
Last o'er the Urn the sacred Earth they spread, ... Il.24.1007.577.
Of sacred *Troy,* and raz'd her heav'n-built wall, ... Od.1.4.28.
To sorrow sacred, and secure of fame: ... Od.1.438.53.
(A sacred oath) each proud oppressor slain ... Od.1.485.55.
(A sacred oath) if heav'n the pow'r supply, ... Od.2.169.70.
Untouch'd and sacred may these vessels stand, ... Od.2.396.80.
The sacred Sun, above the waters rais'd, ... Od.3.1.85.
And join'd the band before the sacred fire, ... Od.3.41.88.
Then give thy friend to shed the sacred wine; ... Od.3.59.89.
To see the pref'rence due to sacred age ... Od.3.66.89.
'Tis sacred truth I ask, and ask of thee. ... Od.3.124.91.
But call'd untimely (not the sacred rite ... Od.3.169.94.
The sacred rites and hecatombs to pay, ... Od.3.176.94.
There he, the sweetest of the sacred train, ... Od.3.342.103.
But when to *Sunium's* sacred point we came, ... Od.3.352.103.
Sacred to *Neptune* and the pow'rs divine. ... Od.3,426.107.
The sacred heralds on their hands around ... Od.3.433.108.
Scatters with quiv'ring hand the sacred flour, ... Od.3.565.115.
And sacred wheat upon the victim lay'd, ... Od.3.569.115.
The sacred Sage before his altar stands, ... Od.3.586.116.
Whose sword was sacred to the man he lov'd: ... Od.4.228.130.
A previous pledge of sacred faith obtain'd, ... Od.4.347.136.
A pledge and monument of sacred love. ... Od.4.810.156.
She bathes, and rob'd, the sacred dome ascends; ... Od.4.1001.164.
And gild the courts of heav'n with sacred light. ... Od.5.4.171.
To sacred *Pylos* and to *Sparta* came. ... Od.5.29.172.
Where men frequent, or sacred altars blaze. ... Od.5.128.178.
But hear, oh earth, and hear ye sacred skies! ... Od.5.238.182.
Shone the fifth morn: when from her sacred seat ... Od.5.334.188.
With that, her hand the sacred veil bestows, ... Od.5.446.194.
And binds the sacred cincture round his breast: ... Od.5.475.195.
For sacred ev'n to Gods is Misery: ... Od.5.573.199.
To *Pallas* sacred, shades the holy ground, ... Od.6.350.229.
The grove they reach, where from the sacred shade ... Od.6.383.230.
Now from the sacred thicket where he lay, ... Od.7.17.234.
And to *Erectheus'* sacred dome retreats. ... Od.7.106.239.
Do thou make perfect! sacred be his words! ... Od.7.424.258.
The sacred master of celestial song: ... Od.8.56.264.
A friend is sacred, and I stile him friend. ... Od.8.240.275.
Since Wisdom's sacred guidance he pursues, ... Od.8.423.286.
Who sacred honours to the Bard denies? ... Od.8.524.290.
An off'ring sacred to th' immortal pow'rs: ... Od.8.558.292.
Satiate we slept: But when the sacred dawn ... Od.9.197.314.
In sacred shade his honour'd mansion stood ... Od.9.232.316.
And shed her sacred light along the skies. ... Od.9.365.321.
Milk newly prest, the sacred flow'r of wheat, ... Od.10.270.355.
Or the fair offspring of the sacred floods. ... Od.10.416.364.
To taste the joys of *Circe's* sacred dome. ... Od.10.506.368.
To guard the ship. Seek we the sacred shades ... Od.10.525.368.
And sacred vows, and mystic song, apply'd ... Od.10.636.374.
The sacred draught shall all the dead forbear, ... Od.10.640.374.
By the soft tye and sacred name of friend! ... Od.11.82.385.
The herds are sacred to the God of day, ... Od.11.137.387.
The latent cause, oh sacred Seer, reveal! ... Od.11.178.390.
In sacred groves celestial rites he pays, ... Od.11.223.392.
The sacred *Argo,* fill'd with demigods! ... Od.12.84.435.
Sev'n herds, sev'n flocks enrich the sacred plains, ... Od.12.162.440.
There sacred to the radiant God of day ... Od.12.316.447.
And shed her sacred light along the skies. ... Od.13.22.2.
A victim Oxe beneath the sacred hand ... Od.13.27.2.
The rites, more sacred made by heav'nly song: ... Od.13.32.2.
Divine *Ulysses* was her sacred load, ... Od.13.106.6.
Sacred to *Phorcys'* pow'r, whose name it bears: ... Od.13.117.7.
Sacred the south, by which the Gods descend, ... Od.13.134.8.
Thy sacred presence from that hour I lost: ... Od.13.365.24.
Now seated in the Olive's sacred shade ... Od.13.425.26.
From sacred *Crete,* and from a Sire of Fame: ... Od.14.230.47.
One sacred to the *Nymphs* apart they lay; ... Od.14.484.59.
The sacred act of friendship shall record. ... Od.15.64.72.
Whose boasted Sire was sacred *Alpheus'* heir; ... Od.15.211.78.
(The sacred wine yet foaming on the ground) ... Od.15.279.82.
And skim'd along by *Elis'* sacred coast. ... Od.15.319.85.
This house holds sacred in her ample wall! ... Od.17.179.140.
Here with his goats, (not vow'd to sacred flame, ... Od.17.246.143.
Nymphs of this fountain! to whose sacred names ... Od.17.284.146.
His sacred eloquence in balm distills, ... Od.17.604.161.
The Peers assent: when strait his sacred head ... Od.18.66.170.
And these my *friends shall guard the sacred ties ... Od.18.72.170.
He never dar'd defraud the sacred fane, ... Od.19.428.215.
Of sacred melody confess'd the force; ... Od.19.536.222.
This sacred truth attest each genial pow'r, ... Od.20.287.247.
Partook the sacred feast, and ritual honours paid. ... Od.20.346.249.
Sacred to *Phœbus* is the solemn day, ... Od.21.274.273.

SACRED (CONTINUED)

Oh ev'ry sacred name in one! my friend! ... Od.22.226.297.
For dear to Gods and Men is sacred song. ... Od.22.382.307.
The man divine; forbear that sacred head; ... Od.22.396.307.
But age is sacred, and we spare thy age. ... Od.23.26.320.
Words seal'd with sacred truth, and truth obey: ... Od.23.190.332.
The oxen sacred to the God of day, ... Od.23.356.342.
Or sacred *Elis,* to procure supplies; ... Od.24.496.372.

SACRIFIC'D

The Thighs thus sacrific'd, and Entrails drest, ... Il.1.610.117.
The Thighs thus sacrific'd and Entrails drest, ... Il.2.510.151.
The thighs now sacrific'd, and entrails drest, ... Od.3.590.116.

SACRIFICE

And All to one lov'd Folly Sacrifice. ... 1.EOC.266.270.
The Relicks of a former Sacrifice. ... 1.TrSt.602.435.
And dooms a dreadful Sacrifice to Hell. ... 1.TrSt.750.441.
And swell the pomp of dreadful sacrifice, ... 2.ElAb.354.348.
A solemn Sacrifice, perform'd in state, ... 3.Ep4.157.152.
The rowling smokes involve the sacrifice. ... 5.DunA1.206.87.
The rowling smokes involve the sacrifice. ... 5.DunB1.248.288.
What cannot copious Sacrifice attone? ... 5.DunB4.557.397.
Nor Vows unpaid, nor slighted Sacrifice, ... Il.1.118.92.
Perhaps, with added Sacrifice and Pray'r, ... Il.1.125.93.
And waft the Sacrifice to *Chrysa's* Shores, ... Il.1.183.96.
Aton'd by Sacrifice, desist to wound. ... Il.1.581.115.
And trembling sought the Pow'rs with Sacrifice, ... Il.2.389.145.
With hasty Feasts they sacrifice, and pray ... Il.2.476.149.
Ador'd with Sacrifice and Oxen slain; ... Il.2.662.158.
To punish *Troy* for slighted Sacrifice; ... Il.5.225.278.
And thou must fall, thy Virtue's Sacrifice. ... Il.6.515.351.
A Steer for Sacrifice the King design'd, ... Il.7.380.382.
Are mov'd by Off'rings, Vows, and Sacrifice; ... Il.9.621.465.
In Vengeance of neglected Sacrifice; ... Il.9.658.467.
He rends his Hairs, in sacrifice to *Jove,* ... Il.10.19.2.
And bows his Head to *Hector's* Sacrifice. ... Il.10.54.4.
A Bull to *Jove* he slew in sacrifice, ... Il.11.906.76.
Of Sacrifice, the purple Draught he pour'd ... Il.16.282.250.
Gape wide, and drink our Blood for Sacrifice! ... Il.17.477.306.
Accept, *Patroclus!* this mean sacrifice. ... Il.17.605.311.
Slain by this Hand, sad Sacrifice expire; ... Il.18.395A.340.
To melt the Fat of some rich Sacrifice, ... Il.21.425.438.
Yet let the Sacrifice at least be paid, ... Il.22.660.484.
Full fifty Rams to bleed in Sacrifice, ... Il.23.182.497.
Sad Sacrifice! twelve *Trojan* Captives fell. ... Il.23.215.498.
But *Peleus'* Son intreats, with Sacrifice, ... Il.23.258.499.
Perhaps he sought not Heav'n by Sacrifice, ... Il.23.625.514.
But flies unblest! No grateful Sacrifice, ... Il.23.1021.529.
With Vows of firstling Lambs, and grateful Sacrifice. ... Il.23.1033.530.
While to the final sacrifice they rose. ... Od.3.436.108.
The solemn sacrifice call'd down the guest; ... Od.7.270.249.
For his return with sacrifice and prayer. ... Od.9.273.318.
Averse, beholds the smoaking sacrifice; ... Od.9.646.333.
Then give command the sacrifice to haste, ... Od.10.634.374.
Strait I command the sacrifice to haste, ... Od.11.57.383.
In feast and sacrifice my chosen train ... Od.14.282.49.
Mean-time the Prince with sacrifice adores ... Od.15.248.80.
Our debt of safe return, in feast and sacrifice. ... Od.15.546.96.
Lo! I the ready sacrifice prepare: ... Od.16.201.113.
I see the smokes of sacrifice aspire, ... Od.17.322.147.

SACRIFICES

And on thy Altars Sacrifices lay; ... 1.TrSt.593.435.

SACRIFICING

And ere the sacrificing throng he join'd, ... Od.3.17.87.

SACRILEGIOUS

Above the reach of *Sacrilegious* Hands, ... 1.EOC.182.261.
And tempts once more thy sacrilegious Hands. ... 2.RL4.174.198.
His sacrilegious train, who dar'd to prey ... Od.19.313.209.

SAD

Why sit we sad, when *Phosphor* shines so clear, ... 1.PSp.27.63.
As some sad Turtle his lost Love deplores, ... 1.PAu.19.82.
In Notes more sad than when they sing their own. ... 1.PWi.40.92.
When the sad Pomp along his Banks was led? ... 1.W-F.274.174.
Shall Fortune still in one sad Tenor run, ... 1.TrSP.71.397.
Like some sad Statue, speechless, pale, I stood; ... 1.TrSP.125.399.
While all his sad Companions upward gaze, ... 1.TrSt.644.437.
Let the sad Tale for ever rest untold! ... 1.TrSt.801.443.
And whither, whither its sad Owner flie? ... 1.TrUl.79.468.
Sad in the midst of Triumphs, sigh'd for Pain; ... 2.ChJM.358.31.
And sad Experience leaves no room for Doubt. ... 2.ChJM.630.45.
Sad Chance of War! now, destitute of Aid, ... 2.RL3.63.172.
As Thou, sad Virgin! for thy ravish'd Hair. ... 2.RL4.10.183.
For, that sad moment, when the *Sylphs* withdrew, ... 2.RL4.11.183.
Oh name for ever sad! for ever dear! ... 2.ElAb.31.321.
Led thro' a sad variety of woe: ... 2.ElAb.36.321.
Then share thy pain, allow that sad relief; ... 2.ElAb.49.323.
Canst thou forget that sad, that solemn day, ... 2.ElAb.107.328.
Sad proof how well a lover can obey! ... 2.ElAb.172.334.
When at the close of each sad, sorrowing day, ... 2.ElAb.225.338.
I shriek, start up, the same sad prospect find, ... 2.ElAb.247.339.
See in her Cell sad *Eloisa* spread, ... 2.ElAb.303.344.
Thy place is here, sad sister come away! ... 2.ElAb.310.344.
Thou, *Abelard!* the last sad office pay, ... 2.ElAb.321.345.
In sad similitude of griefs to mine, ... 2.ElAb.360.348.
Let him our sad, our tender story tell; ... 2.ElAb.364.348.
He dies, sad out-cast of each church and state, ... 3.Ep1.204.32.
Yet still a sad, good Christian at her heart. ... 3.Ep2.68.55.
And sad Sir Balaam curses God and dies. ... 3.Ep3.402.125.
And the sad Burthen of some merry Song. ... 4.HS1.80.13.
I sit with sad Civility, I read ... 4.Arbu.37.98.
Hang the sad Verse on CAROLINA'S Urn, ... 4.EpS1.80.304.

SAD (CONTINUED)

But sad examples never fail to move. ....5.DunA1.176.84.
Sooths the sad series of her tedious tale. ....5.DunA3.191z6.172.
The sad Example never fail'd to move. ....5.DunB1.194A.283.
How sweet the periods, neither sad, nor sung! ....5.DunB3.202.330.
There to her heart sad Tragedy addrest ....5.DunB4.37.344.
Oft to her heart sad Tragedy addrest ....5.DunB4.37A.344.
But, sad example! never to escape ....5.DunB4.527.394.
Sad *Orpheus* sought his Consort lost; ....6.11.51Z1.32.
How Rome her own sad Sepulchre appears, ...6.71.2.202.
Beneath her Palm here sad Judæa weeps, ...6.71.26.203.
This sad Decree, no Joy shall last. ....6.78ii.2.216.
To this sad Shrine, who'er thou art, draw near, ...6.85.1.242.
And all we gain, some sad Reflection more; ....6.86.8.245.
Is still a sad good Christian at her Heart. ....6.99.20.287.
Thy Reliques, *Rowe!* to this sad Shrine we trust, ...6.152.1.400.
But sad retiring to the sounding Shore, ...Il.1.455.109.
And his sad Consort beats her breast in vain. ....Il.2.859.165.
The golden Web her own sad Story crown'd, ...Il.3.170.199.
Then, the sad Victim of the Publick Rage. ....Il.3.520.216.
And flatted Vineyards, one sad Waste appear; ....Il.5.121.273.
And the sad Father try'd his Arts in vain; ....Il.5.193.276.
Deck'd in sad Triumph for the mournful Field, ...Il.5.910.309.
Example sad! and Theme of future Song. ....Il.6.449.348.
He said, and past with sad presaging Heart ....Il.6.462.349.
There her sad Eyes in vain her Lord explore, ...Il.6.470.350.
So shall my Days in one sad Tenor run, ...Il.6.520.352.
In one sad Day beheld the Gates of Hell; ....Il.6.535.353.
Heaps fell on Heaps, sad Trophies of his Art, ...Il.8.335.413.
Confus'd, and sad, I wander thus alone, ...Il.10.103.7.
Sad Mothers of unutterable Woes!) ....Il.11.350.50.
There sad he met the brave *Evæmon's* Son, ...Il.11.940.77.
Deplor'd *Amphimachus,* sad Object! lies; ....Il.13.263.117.
And his sad Comrades from the Battel bore; ....Il.13.282.119.
Till sad *Mecistheus* and *Alastor* bore ....Il.13.531.131.
Sunk in his sad Companion's Arms he lay, ...Il.13.817.144.
Such, as to *Promachus'* sad Spouse we bear; ....Il.14.592.191.
(His sad Associates round with weeping Eyes) ....Il.15.12.194.
Great *Hector* view'd him with a sad Survey, ...Il.15.492.216.
Till sad *Polydamas* the Steeds restrain'd, ...Il.15.532.217.
In one sad Sepulchre, one common Fall. ....Il.15.663.221.
Or come sad Tidings from our native Land? ....Il.16.18.235.
We too must yield: The same sad Fate must fall ....Il.17.286.298.
Now lies, a sad Companion of the Dead: ....Il.17.345.301.
The sad *Achilles* how his lov'd one fell: ....Il.17.778.318.
Rose in sad Prospect to his boding Mind. ....Il.18.8.323.
Sad Tydings, Son of *Peleus!* thou must hear; ....Il.18.21.324.
E'er the sad Fruit of thy unhappy Womb ....Il.18.113.328.
Around, his sad Companions melt in Tears: ....Il.18.276.335.
He spoke, and bid the sad Attendants round ....Il.18.403.340.
Slain by this Hand, sad Sacrifice expire; ....Il.18.395A.340.
And sad Posterity repeat the Tale. ....Il.19.66.374.
Slow as she past, beheld with sad survey ....Il.19.297.384.
Beat her sad Breast, and tore her golden Hair; ....Il.19.300.384.
His Son's sad Fate, and drops a tender Tear.) ....Il.19.344.386.
But till the News of my sad Fate invades ....Il.19.358.387.
This Diff'rence only their sad Fates afford, ...Il.20.535.416.
Sad Victims! destin'd to *Patroclus'* Shade. ....Il.21.39.423.
There no sad Mother shall thy Fun'rals weep, ...Il.21.137.427.
While the sad Father on the Rampart stands, ...Il.22.49.454.
What Sorrows then must their sad Mother know, ...Il.22.72.455.
Great *Jove* has plac'd, sad Spectacle of Pain! ....Il.22.84.456.
The last sad Relick of my ruin'd State, ...Il.22.93.456.
The Mother first beheld with sad survey; ....Il.22.511.477.
While the sad Father answers Groans with Groans, ...Il.22.515.477.
Sinks my sad Soul with Sorrow to the Grave. ....Il.22.543.478.
Some Comfort that had been, some sad Relief, ...Il.22.548.479.
O fatal Change! become in one sad Day ....Il.22.560.479.
Sad Product now of hapless Love, remains! ....Il.22.621.482.
Robs the sad Orphan of his Father's Friends: ....Il.22.629.482.
For ever sad, for ever bath'd in Tears; ....Il.22.631.482.
To my sad Soul *Astyanax* appears! ....Il.22.643.483.
Thro' the sad City mourn'd her Hero slain. ....Il.23.2.485.
And twelve sad Victims of the *Trojan* Line ....Il.23.30.488.
Of sad *Patroclus* rose, or seem'd to rise; ....Il.23.79.490.
Sad Sacrifice! twelve *Trojan* Captives fell. ....Il.23.215.498.
Takes a sad Pleasure the last Bones to burn, ...Il.23.276.501.
Next the white Bones his sad Companions place ....Il.23.313.502.
Nor suit, with them, the Games of this sad Day: ....Il.23.348.503.
Sad, as they shar'd in human Grief, they stand, ...Il.23.351.503.
Takes his sad Couch, more unobserv'd to weep, ...Il.24.7.535.
The last sad Honours of a fun'ral Fire? ....Il.24.49.537.
Sad Object as I am for heav'nly Sight! ....Il.24.119.540.
And forth she pac'd, majestically sad. ....Il.24.124.540.
Where the sad Sons beside their Father's Throne ....Il.24.197.545.
(Sad Scene of Woe!) His Face his wrapt Attire ....Il.24.200.545.
Sad *Hecuba* renews, and then replies. ....Il.24.242.546.
No—pent in this sad Palace let us give ....Il.24.255.547.
Lo! the sad Father, frantick with his Pain, ...Il.24.291.548.
Oh send me, Gods! e'er that sad Day shall come, ...Il.24.307.549.
Surviv'd, sad Relicks of his num'rous Line. ....Il.24.316.549.
The sad Attendants load the groaning Wain: ....Il.24.342.550.
Sad *Hecuba* approach'd with anxious Mind; ....Il.24.350.550.
On this sad Subject you enquire too much. ....Il.24.478.556.
In one sad Day beheld the *Stygian* Shades; ....Il.24.760.569.
She stands her own sad Monument of Woe; ....Il.24.778.569.
Sad Dreams of Care yet wand'ring in their Breast: ....Il.24.845.572.
The sad Procession of her hoary Sire, ...Il.24.871.572.
Ev'n to the Palace the sad Pomp they wait: ....Il.24.898.573.
Sad Product now of hapless Love, remains! ....Il.24.913.574.
The sad Companion of thy Mother's Woe; ....Il.24.923.574.
Thence, many Evils his sad Parents bore, ...Il.24.932.575.
Sad *Helen* next in Pomp of Grief appears: ....Il.24.959.576.
Sad *Helen* has no Friend now thou art gone! ....Il.24.978.576.
(Sad spoils of luxury) the Suitors fate. ....Od.1.141.39.
Returning sad, when toilsome day declines. ....Od.1.250.45.

SAD (CONTINUED)

Let not your soul be sunk in sad despair; ....Od.1.255.45.
While sad on foreign shores *Ulysses* treads, ...Od.2.151.69.
The royal dome; while sad the Prince explores ....Od.2.293.75.
Lest the sad tale a mother's life impair, ...Od.2.422.81.
And the sad son's, to suffer and to mourn! ....Od.3.257.98.
Ends the sad evening of a stormy life: ....Od.4.116.125.
That sad Idea wounds my anxious breast! ....Od.4.132.126.
Of sad reflection, and corroding care. ....Od.4.400.139.
With him to share the sad funereal feast. ....Od.4.740.153.
In her sad breast the Prince's fortunes roul, ...Od.4.1039.166.
But sad *Ulysses* by himself apart, ...Od.5.103.177.
Chear the sad heart, not let affliction grieve. ....Od.6.246.222.
Late a sad spectacle of woe, he trod ....Od.6.291.224.
By a sad train of miseries alone ....Od.7.289.250.
Sad from my natal hour my days have ran, ...Od.8.171.271.
Remembrance sad, whose image to review ....Od.9.13.301.
Sad for their loss, but joyful of our life. ....Od.9.72.305.
From *Troy's* fam'd fields, sad wand'rers o'er the main, ...Od.9.307.319.
No ease, no pleasure my sad heart receives, ...Od.9.541.328.
But the sad fate that did our friends destroy ....Od.10.155.347.
Ye sad companions of *Ulysses'* woes! ....Od.10.215.350.
With broken hearts my sad companions stood, ...Od.10.227.351.
Sad, pleasing sight! with tears each eye ran o'er, ...Od.10.471.366.
My sad companions on the beach I found, ...Od.10.483.366.
Leave to repentance and his own sad heart, ...Od.10.524.368.
Must sad *Ulysses* ever be delay'd? ....Od.10.571.370.
Around their lord my sad companions mourn, ...Od.10.572.370.
My sad companions heard in deep despair; ....Od.10.679.376.
Sad at the sight I stand, deep fix'd in woe, ...Od.11.69.383.
There mournful *Phædra* with sad *Procris* moves, ...Od.11.395.403.
Sad *Ariadne,* partner of their woe; ....Od.11.398.403.
For ever sad with proud disdain he pin'd, ...Od.11.667.417.
Pensive and sad I stand, at length accost, ...Od.11.677.418.
They scream, they shriek; sad groans and dismal sounds ....Od.11.781.425.
When rising sad and slow, with pensive look, ...Od.12.188.441.
And whither, whither its sad owner fly? ....Od.13.246.18.
From sad reflection let my soul repose; ....Od.14.194.45.
Chears the sad heart, nor lets affliction grieve. ....Od.15.363.87.
She too, sad Mother! for *Ulysses* lost ....Od.15.382.88.
Thy whole sad story, from its first, declare: ....Od.15.414.89.
Sent the sad sire in solitude to stray; ....Od.16.149.109.
Twice ten sad years o'er earth and ocean tost, ...Od.16.226.114.
Lest a sad prey to ever-musing cares, ...Od.16.352.123.
Then sorrowing, with sad step the Queen retir'd, ...Od.16.465.129.
The sad survivor of his num'rous train, ...Od.17.163.139.
Anon, from heav'n a sad reverse he feels; ....Od.18.161.174.
For *Pallas* seals his doom: All sad he turns ....Od.18.185.175.
Scorn not the sad reverse, injurious maid! ....Od.19.98.197.
His visage solemn sad, of sable hue: ....Od.19.279.208.
And sad similitude of woes ally'd, ...Od.19.400.214.
Sad *Euryclea* rose: with trembling hand ....Od.19.421.214.
Long to protract the sad sepulchral hour; ....Od.19.431.215.
Sad *Philomel,* in bow'ry shades unseen, ...Od.19.605.225.
A sad variety of woes I mourn! ....Od.19.612.226.
Some pitying God (*Ulysses* sad reply'd) ....Od.20.211.243.
The sad remembrance of a perish'd man. ....Od.21.90.263.
Weeps a sad life in solitude away. ....Od.23.388.343.
Led the sad numbers by *Ulysses* slain. ....Od.24.124.354.
Nor his sad consort, on the mournful bier, ...Od.24.346.365.
Then sad in council all the Seniors sate, ...Od.24.481.371.

SADDEN'D

Sate on each Face, and sadden'd ev'ry heart. ....Il.9.4.431.
The bleeding Youth: *Troy* sadden'd at the View. ....Il.14.558.190.
Blank Horror sadden'd each celestial Face. ....Il.15.109.200.

SADDENS

Her gloomy presence saddens all the scene, ...2.ElAb.167.333.
Not the black Fear of Death, that saddens all? ....4.2HE2.309.187.
And a still Horror saddens all the Deeps: ....Il.7.74.366.
And the soul saddens by the use of pain. ....Od.10.551.369.
And solemn horrour saddens every breast. ....Od.11.6.379.

SADDER

In sadder Notes than when they sing their own. ....1.PWi.40A.92.
Love taught my Tears in sadder Notes to flow, ...1.TrSP.7.393.
From furious *Sappho* yet a sadder Fate, ...4.HS1.83A.13.
For sadder Tydings never touch'd thy Ear; ....Il.17.772.318.
A sadder Journey to the Shades below. ....Il.21.55.424.

SADDLE

When, with his Sword at Saddle Bow, ...6.79.107.221.

SADLY

Confus'd, and sadly thus at length replies: ....1.TrSt.797.443.
His Task perform'd, he sadly went his Way, ...2.ChJM.363.31.
Then sadly say, with mutual pity mov'd, ...2.ElAb.351.348.
In a sadly-pleasing Strain ....6.11.5.30.
Is that a Birth-day? ah! tis sadly clear, ...6.86.9B.245.
Or sadly told, how many Hopes lie here! ....6.132.6.362.
So sadly lost, so lately sought in vain. ....Il.1.583.115.
And sadly slow, to sacred *Troy* return'd. ....Il.7.511.389.
And slowly, sadly, to their Fleet repair. ....Il.7.515.389.
Thus sadly slain, th' unhappy *Polydore;* ....Il.20.486.414.
Some Word thou would'st have spoke, which sadly dear, ...Il.24.936.575.
And sadly shar'd the last Sepulcral Feast. ....Il.24.1014.577.
Patient permit the sadly-pleasing strain; ....Od.1.449.54.
We press to hear what sadly he relates. ....Od.10.294.357.
I follow sadly to the magic rites. ....Od.10.374.362.
Sadly they far'd along the sea-beat shore; ....Od.10.683.376.
Thus wailing, slow and sadly she descends, ...Od.18.245.178.
That sadly tore my royal Lord away: ....Od.18.302.181.

SADLY-PLEASING

In a sadly-pleasing Strain .... 6.11.5.30.
Patient permit the sadly-pleasing strain; .... Od.1.449.54.

SADNESS

'Tis all blank sadness, or continual tears. .... 2.ElAb.148.331.
In solemn Sadness, and majestic Grief. .... Il.9.16.431.
And solemn sadness thro' the gloom of hell, ... Od.24.33.348.

SAFE

Safe on my Shore each unmolested Swain .... 1.W-F.369.186.
And Authors think their Reputation safe, ... 1.EOC.450.290.
Nor is *Paul's Church* more safe than *Paul's Church-yard:* .... 1.EOC.623.310.
And send him safe to *Lycia,* distant far .... 1.TrES.233.458.
And safe restor'd me to my Native Land. .... 1.TrUl.83.468.
Safe from the treach'rous Friend, the daring Spark, ... 2.RL1.73.151.
Safe from the treach'rous Friend, and daring Spark, ... 2.RL1.73A.151.
Safe past the *Gnome* thro' this fantastick Band, ... 2.RL4.55.188.
But safe in Desarts from th' Applause of Men, ... 2.TemF.360.281.
Safe in the hand of one disposing Pow'r, ... 3.EOM1.287.50.
Safe is your Secret still in Cloe's ear; .... 3.Ep2.173.64.
How much more safe, dear Countrymen! his State, ... 4.HAdv.61.81.
And swear, not *Addison* himself was safe. .... 4.Arbu.192.109.
How did they swear, not *Addison* was safe. .... 4.Arbu.192A.109.
A safe Companion, and a free; .... 4.1HE7.40.271.
Safe from the Bar, the Pulpit, and the Throne, ... 4.EpS2.210.325.
Safe, where no criticks damn, no duns molest, ... 5.DunA1.249.92.
(Haunt of the Muses) made their safe retreat. .... 5.DunA2.396.149.
Safe in its heaviness, can never stray, ... 5.DunA3.297.184.
Too safe in inborn heaviness to stray, ... 5.DunA3.297A.184.
Safe, where no Critics damn, no duns molest, ... 5.DunB1.295.291.
(Haunt of the Muses) made their safe retreat. .... 5.DunB2.428.318.
Safe in its heaviness, shall never stray, ... 5.DunB3.295.334.
Safe in its heaviness, can never stray, ... 5.DunB3.295A.334.
Safe and unseen the young Æneas past: .... 5.DunB4.290.373.
And routed *Reason* finds a safe Retreat in thee. .... 6.8.18.18.
Thus Dulness, the safe Opiate of the Mind, ... 6.16.1.53.
Safe shall he lye, and hope beneath thy shade. .... 6.21.10.69.
How safe must be the King upon this Throne, ... 6.48ii.5.134.
Sees his past days safe out of fortune's pow'r, ... 6.55.3.166.
He sees past days safe out of fortune's pow'r, ... 6.55.3A.166.
God send the K[ing] safe landing, ... 6.61.51.183.
Cry'd sagely, 'Tis not safe, I hold, ... 6.94.23.259.
Safe from Wound .... 6.96i.35.269.
Safe would I bear him to his Journey's End, ... 6.96iii.35.275.
How would they swear, not *Congreve's* self was safe! .... 6.98.42.284.
A safe Companion, and an easy Friend, ... 6.125.7.350.
Safe is your secret still in Cloë's ear; .... 6.139.17.377.
Safe to the Pleasures of your native Shore. .... Il.1.26.87.
'Till, safe at distance, to his God he prays, ... Il.1.51.88.
Safe in her Vales my warlike Coursers fed: .... Il.1.202.96.
Safe in her Sides the Hecatomb they stow'd, ... Il.1.408.107.
A safe Return was promis'd to our Toils, ... Il.2.143.135.
Safe and inglorious, to our native Shore. .... Il.2.170.136.
Safe from the Fight, in yonder lofty Walls, ... Il.3.482.215.
Or safe to *Troy,* if *Jove* assist the Foe. .... Il.5.283.280.
Safe thro' the rushing Horse and feather'd Flight .... Il.5.393.285.
A safe Return was promis'd to our toils, ... Il.9.27.433.
If safe we land on *Argos* fruitful Shore, ... Il.9.184.441.
If safe we land on *Argos* fruitful Shore, ... Il.9.371.451.
Safe to transport him to his native Plains, ... Il.9.809.473.
Safe may we pass beneath the gloomy Shade, ... Il.10.331.17.
Safe by thy Succour to our Ships convey'd; .... Il.10.332.17.
Safe in their Cares, th' auxiliar Forces sleep, ... Il.10.491.25.
Safe to the Ships, he wisely clear'd the way, ... Il.10.573.28.
Safe from the Darts, the Care of Heav'n he stood, ... Il.11.215.45.
Safe in his Helm (the Gift of *Phœbus'* Hands) .... Il.11.455.54.
Safe in their Arms, the Navy fears no Flame; .... Il.13.407.125.
O'er his safe Head the Javelin idly sung, ... Il.13.517.131.
Safe let us stand; and from the Tumult far, ... Il.14.151.165.
Safe from Access of each intruding Pow'r, ... Il.14.194.168.
They gain th' impervious Rock and safe retreat .... Il.15.310A.209.
Yet leaves his Nation safe, his Children free; .... Il.15.585.219.
Safe in his Art, as side by side they run, ... Il.15.826.228.
And safe return him to these Eyes again! .... Il.16.305.254.
His safe Return, the Winds dispers'd in Air. .... Il.16.309.254.
And send him safe to *Lycia,* distant far .... Il.16.536.265.
Safe to the Navy thro' the Storm of War. .... Il.17.519.308.
Safe thro' the Tempest, to the Tented Shore. .... Il.18.188.331.
More safe to combate in the mingled Band, ... Il.20.433.412.
(Not fated yet to die) There safe retreats, ... Il.21.577.446.
Beneath the pointed Steel; but safe from Harms .... Il.21.701.450.
Safe from Pursuit, and shut from mortal View, ... Il.21.707.451.
There safe, they wipe the briny Drops away, ... Il.22.3.452.
Safe in their Walls are now her Troops bestow'd, ... Il.22.21.453.
Safe in the Crowd he ever scorn'd to wait, ... Il.22.588.480.
Safe thro' the Foe by our Protection led: .... Il.24.188.544.
Safe thro' the Foe by his Protection led: .... Il.24.218.546.
Take this, and pour to *Jove:* that safe from Harms, ... Il.24.355.551.
And safe conduct him to *Achilles'* Tent. .... Il.24.416.553.
Safe to *Pelides'* Tent conduct my way. .... Il.24.528.558.
Safe may'st thou sail, and turn thy Wrath from *Troy;* .... Il.24.702.566.
Safe with his friends to gain his natal shore: .... Od.1.8.28.
To hail *Ulysses'* safe return I came: .... Od.1.252.45.
Or safe return'd, the race of glory past, ... Od.1.303.47.
Their safe experience to the fav'rite child. .... Od.1.402.51.
Safe in my youth, in riot still they grow, ... Od.2.65.63.
Safe in the court, nor tempt the watry way. .... Od.2.290.75.
To bless our safe return we join in pray'r, ... Od.3.193.95.
Safe reach'd the *Mirmydons* their native land, ... Od.3.228.96.
And safe to *Argos'* port his navy brought, ... Od.3.396.105.
Thee to *Atrides* they shall safe convey, ... Od.3.417.106.
And safe returning to the *Grecian* host, ... Od.4.353.136.
There anchor'd vessels safe in harbour lye, ... Od.4.485.143.
To thy long vows a safe return accord. .... Od.4.648.150.
On *Gyræ,* safe *Oilean Ajax* sate, ... Od.4.672.151.

SAFE (CONTINUED)

Safe from the secret rock and adverse storm, ... Od.4.879.159.
That safe recess they gain with happy speed, ... Od.4.1107.169.
Some smooth ascent, or safe-sequester'd bay. .... Od.5.561.199.
Safe in the love of heav'n, an ocean flows .... Od.6.243.221.
But, nymphs, recede! safe chastity denies .... Od.6.263.222.
Safe to transport him to the wish'd-for shore: .... Od.7.255.248.
Restore me safe thro' weary wand'rings tost, ... Od.8.507.289.
Safe as they pass, and safe repass the tides, ... Od.8.614.295.
Safe as they pass, and safe repass the tides, ... Od.8.614.295.
Pursue their flight, but leave them safe to bound .... Od.9.139.311.
'Till safe we anchor'd in the shelter'd bay: .... Od.9.171.312.
A month's reception, and a safe retreat. .... Od.10.14.340.
So in our palace, at our safe return .... Od.11.39.381.
Safe he return'd, without one hostile scar; .... Od.11.656.416.
To live, or perish! to be safe, be wise! .... Od.12.193.441.
Yet safe return'd— *Ulysses* led the way. .... Od.12.251.444.
And if the Gods ordain a safe return, ... Od.12.411.451.
Safe to my home to send your happy guest. .... Od.13.51.3.
Safe in the hollow deck dispose the cates: .... Od.13.87.5.
And safe restor'd me to my native land. .... Od.13.250.18.
Safe through the level seas we sweep our way; .... Od.14.286.49.
What means might best his safe return avail, ... Od.14.365.53.
And safe I slept, till brightly-dawning shone .... Od.14.568.64.
That thou safe sailing from the *Pylian* strand .... Od.15.49.72.
Safe in thy mother's care the vesture lay, ... Od.15.140.75.
And safe conveys thee where thy soul desires. .... Od.15.359.86.
Our debt of safe return, in feast and sacrifice. .... Od.15.546.96.
And safe to sail with ornaments of love. .... Od.16.80.106.
Our safe return, and ease a mother's heart. .... Od.16.141.109.
Our safe return, and back with speed repair: .... Od.16.163.110.
Yet safe he sails! the pow'rs cœlestial give .... Od.16.384.124.
Thence safe I voyag'd to my native shore. .... Od.17.169.139.
Safe in their care, for heav'n protects the just. .... Od.17.681.165.
He, safe at *Ithaca* with joy receiv'd, ... Od.19.542.223.
Ardent to speak the Monarch safe restor'd: .... Od.19.556.223.
Thus anchor'd safe on reason's peaceful coast, ... Od.20.29.233.
Where safe repos'd the royal treasures lay; .... Od.21.12.259.
And safe conveyance to his port of rest. .... Od.21.368.277.
How much more safe the good than evil deed: .... Od.22.414.308.
Restore thee safe, since my *Ulysses* reigns. .... Od.23.276.336.

SAFE-SEQUESTER'D

Some smooth ascent, or safe-sequester'd bay. .... Od.5.561.199.

SAFELY

(This from his Pledge I learn'd, which safely stor'd .... Il.6.275.340.
Their lofty Decks, or safely cleave the Main; .... Il.8.638.426.
Their lofty Decks, and safely cleave the Main; .... Il.8.638A.426.
Sep'rate from all, I safely landed here; .... Od.3.223.96.
(Fool that he was) and let them safely go, ... Od.9.521.328.
Gifts, which to distant ages safely stor'd, ... Od.15.63.72.
Can strangers safely in the court reside, ... Od.16.71.106.

SAFER

Some safer world in depth of woods embrac'd, ... 3.EOM1.105.27.
So much 'tis safer thro' the Camp to go, ... Il.1.303.101.
But safer Plunder thy own Host supplies; .... Il.2.287.141.
(The safer road) beside the *Psyrian* isle; .... Od.3.206.95.
Ride the wild waves, and quit the safer shore? .... Od.4.941.162.
I chose the safer sea, and chanc'd to find .... Od.7.364.254.

SAFEST

And who stands safest, tell me? is it he .... 4.HS2.125.65.
But Sense must sure thy safest Plunder be, ... 6.7.13.16.
Yet, I'll direct the safest means to go: .... Od.5.183.180.

SAFETY

And ships, in safety, wander to and fro. .... 1.TrPA.28.366.
Where shall this Treasure now in Safety lie? .... 1.TrUl.78.468.
But with their Toils their People's Safety bought: .... 2.TemF.160.267.
His safety must his liberty restrain: .... 3.EOM3.277.120.
In Safety, Innocence, and full Repose, ... 6.17iii.18.58.
To whom its Safety a whole People owes, ... Il.2.29.128.
To whom its Safety a whole People owes; .... Il.2.79.130.
Love, Duty, Safety, summon us away, ... Il.2.167.136.
So *Greece* to Combate shall in Safety go, ... Il.7.410.385.
Retires for Safety to the Mother's Arms. .... Il.8.326.413.
Our common Safety must be now the Care; .... Il.8.657.427.
Whatever means of Safety can be sought, ... Il.10.164.9.
A Chief, whose Safety is *Minerva's* Care; .... Il.10.287.14.
Regard thy Safety, and depart in Peace; .... Il.10.595.28.
Atrides mark'd as these their Safety sought, ... Il.11.165.42.
The Cure and Safety of his wounded Friend, ... Il.12.2.80.
Conquest, not Safety, fill the Thoughts of all; .... Il.12.325.93.
And Towns and Empires for their Safety bless. .... Il.13.920.148.
They ask their Safety and their Fame from you: .... Il.15.803.227.
And with his Life his Master's Safety bought. .... Il.17.696.314.
Thy rage in safety thro' the Files of War: .... Il.19.453.391.
Return in safety to my *Trojan* Friends. .... Il.21.662.449.
To whom her Safety and her Fame she ow'd, ... Il.22.558.479.
To lodge in safety with some friendly Hand? .... Il.24.469.556.
On thee attend, thy Safety to maintain, ... Il.24.539.558.
Consult thy Safety, and forgive my Fear, ... Il.24.817.571.
(Whose fame and safety was her constant care .... Od.3.271.99.
The son in safety to his native shore; .... Od.5.35.172.
Huge, horrid, vast! where scarce in safety sails .... Od.5.227.182.
Consult our safety, and put off to sea. .... Od.9.267.317.
Jove safety grants; he grants it to your care. .... Od.12.257.445.
They bore the treasures, and in safety plac'd. .... Od.13.24.2.
Where shall this treasure now in safety lie? .... Od.13.245.17.
In safety to *Dulichium's* friendly court. .... Od.14.439.57.
A wretch in safety to her native shore." .... Od.15.475.93.
Here dwell in safety from the suitors wrongs, ... Od.16.85.106.
In lasting safety from the father's pow'r. .... Od.17.303.146.

SAFFRON

The Saffron Morn, with early Blushes spread, ...Il.11.1.34.
Now shed *Aurora* round her Saffron Ray, ...Il.24.866.572.
In saffron robes the Daughter of the dawn ....Od.4.586.147.
The saffron Morn, with early blushes spread, ...Od.5.1.170.

SAFRON

And when the morn unveils her safron ray, ...Od.12.35.431.

SAGACIOUS

And hound sagacious on the tainted green: ....3.EOM1.214.42.
Sagacious Bub, so late a friend, and there ....4.1740.55.334.
So late a foe, yet more sagacious H[are] ....4.1740.56.335.
A form majestic, and sagacious mind: ....Od.20.85.237.

SAGE

Discours'd in Terms as just, with Looks as Sage, ...1.EOC.269.270.
These weighty Motives *January* the Sage ....2.ChJM.77.18.
Yet you pursue sage *Solomon's* Advice, ...2.ChJM.151.21.
Do what you list, for me; you must be sage, ...2.ChJM.206.24.
How many Pisspots on the Sage she threw; ....2.ChWB.390.76.
The sage *Chaldæans* rob'd in White appear'd, ...2.TemF.99.260.
The sage Historians in white Garments wait; ....2.TemF.146.265.
The Poor, the Rich, the Valiant, and the Sage, ...2.TemF.290.277.
Shall burning Ætna, if a sage requires, ...3.EOM4.123.139.
In vain the Sage, with retrospective eye, ...3.Ep1.51.19.
But, sage historians! 'tis your task to prove ....3.Ep1.85.21.
What made (say Montagne, or more sage Charron!) ....3.Ep1.146.27.
"All this is madness," cries a sober sage: ....3.Ep3.153.106.
His Grace's fate sage Cutler could foresee, ...3.Ep3.315.119.
You'll give me, like a Friend both sage and free, ...4.HS1.9.5.
(A Doctrine sage, but truly none of mine) ....4.HS2.3.55.
(For I, who hold sage Homer's rule the best, ...4.HS2.159.67.
As the sage dame, experienc'd in her trade, ...5.DunA2.125.112.
Wond'ring he gaz'd: When lo! a Sage appears, ...5.DunA3.27.153.
As the sage dame, experienc'd in her trade, ...5.DunB2.133.301.
Wond'ring he gaz'd: When lo! a Sage appears, ...5.DunB3.35.322.
Had not sage *Rowe* pronounc'd it *Entertaining.* ....6.12.9.37.
To make you look as sage as any Sophy. ....6.13.15.39.
The man had courage, was a sage, 'tis true, ...6.41.39.114.
By Saint, by Savage, and by Sage, ...6.50.3.145.
by Christian Saint, by Heathen sage, ...6.50.3A.145.
By Saint, by Savage, or by Sage, ...6.50.3B.145.
But let some Prophet, or some sacred Sage, ...Il.1.83.90.
Uprising slow, the venerable Sage ....Il.1.95.91.
Slow from his Seat arose the *Pylian* Sage; ....Il.1.330.103.
And sage *Ulysses* with the Conduct grac'd: ....Il.1.407.107.
In *Chrysa's* Port now sage *Ulysses* rode; ....Il.1.566.115.
Cloath'd in the Figure of the *Pylian* Sage, ...Il.2.21.128.
Thus spoke the Sage: The Kings without Delay ....Il.2.107.132.
Nestor the Sage conducts his chosen Host: ....Il.2.716.160.
Antenor grave, and sage *Ucalegon,* ....Il.3.197.200.
Slow they proceed: The sage *Ulysses* then ....Il.3.336.209.
Let sage Advice, the Palm of Age, be mine. ....Il.4.379.239.
Sage as thou art, and learn'd in Humankind, ...Il.4.414.240.
Had not sage *Helenus* her State redrest, ...Il.6.91.328.
Sage *Helenus* their secret Counsels knew: ....Il.7.48.365.
Demand the Fight, To whom the *Pylian* Sage: ....Il.7.206.374.
And sage *Idæus* on the Part of *Troy,* ....Il.7.334.380.
O Sage! to *Hector* be these Words address'd. ....Il.7.344.381.
The Sage whose Counsels long had sway'd the rest, ...Il.7.390.383.
'Twas thus the Sage his wholsome Counsel mov'd; ....Il.7.412.385.
Sage *Priam* check'd their Grief: With silent Haste ....Il.7.508.389.
The Glory of the *Greeks,* the *Pylian* Sage. ....Il.8.122.404.
Thus spoke the hoary Sage: the rest obey; ....Il.9.109.437.
Great *Ajax* next, and *Ithacus* the sage. ....Il.9.222.443.
Thy Youth as then in sage Debates unskill'd, ...Il.9.568.462.
To seek sage *Nestor* now the Chief resolves, ...Il.10.24.3.
The sage Protector of the *Greeks* he found ....Il.10.82.6.
O prudent Chief! (the *Pylian* Sage reply'd) ....Il.10.162.9.
(Reply'd the Sage) to praise me, or to blame: ....Il.10.292.15.
Father! not so, (sage *Ithacus* rejoin'd) ....Il.10.654.31.
From sage *Antenor* and *Theano* sprung; ....Il.11.284.48.
Can then the Sons of *Greece* (the Sage rejoind) ....Il.11.800.71.
Such as sage *Chiron,* Sire of *Pharmacy,* ....Il.11.966.78.
But sage *Polydamas,* discreetly brave, ...Il.13.905.148.
Fluctuates, in doubtful Thought, the *Pylian* Sage; ....Il.14.28.158.
Thus he. The sage *Ulysses* thus replies, ...Il.14.88.162.
Thus pray'd the Sage: Th' Eternal gave consent, ...Il.15.436.214.
(The sage Preserver of the *Grecian* Host) ....Il.15.793.226.
Minerva seconds what the Sage inspires. ....Il.15.807.227.
Nestor, Idomeneus, Ulysses sage, ...Il.19.331.386.
So flam'd his fiery Mail. Then wept the Sage; ....Il.22.43.454.
Thus, (nought unsaid) the much-advising Sage ....Il.23.423.506.
The Sage and King, majestically slow. ....Il.24.869.572.
In sage debates, surrounded with his Peers, ...Od.1.113.37.
Where sole of all his train, a Matron sage ....Od.1.247.44.
Pains the sage ear, and hurts the sober eye. ....Od.1.294.47.
Of *Nestor,* hoary Sage, his doom demand; ....Od.1.370.50.
His sage reply, and with her train retires. ....Od.1.460.54.
The lighted torch the sage *Euryclea* bears. ....Od.1.540.57.
Here thou art sage in vain—I better read the skies. ....Od.2.210.72.
Sage *Mentor's* form, and thus like *Mentor* spoke. ....Od.2.306.76.
But now the wise instructions of the sage, ...Od.2.353.78.
How shall I meet, or how accost the Sage, ...Od.3.29.87.
Regarded ever by the just and sage. ....Od.3.67.89.
On themes remote the venerable Sage: ....Od.3.302.101.
But this the hospitable Sage denied. ....Od.3.443.108.
But chief the rev'rend Sage admir'd; he took ....Od.3.478.110.
To these the hospitable Sage, in sign ....Od.3.502.112.
Sage *Nestor* fill'd it, and the sceptre sway'd. ....Od.3.523.113.
The sacred Sage before his altar stands, ...Od.3.586.116.
To crown thy various gifts, the sage assign'd ....Od.4.261.131.
Form'd by the care of that consummate sage, ...Od.4.283.132.
Proclaims you from the sage *Ulysses* sprung. ....Od.4.832.158.
'Tis not, reply'd the Sage, to *Medon* giv'n ....Od.4.944.162.

SAGE (CONTINUED)

The Sage retir'd: Unable to controul ....Od.4.950.162.
Thus to his soul the Sage began to say. ....Od.5.598.201.
Echeneus sage, a venerable man! ....Od.7.209.246.
His sage advice the list'ning King obeys; ....Od.7.224.247.
Sage *Nestor, Periclimenus* the bold, ...Od.11.348.399.
Then sage *Echeneus,* whose grave, rev'rend brow ....Od.11.428.405.
Down sate the Sage; and cautious to withstand, ...Od.14.35.36.
Make the sage frolic, and the serious smile, ...Od.14.521.62.
Eumæus sage approach'd th' imperial throne, ...Od.16.356.123.
With *Antiphus,* and *Halitherses* sage, ...Od.17.80.136.
The sage *Ulysses,* fearful to disclose ....Od.18.110.172.
Such gentle manners, and so sage a mind, ...Od.19.404.214.
To the sage *Greeks* conven'd in *Themis'* court, ...Od.20.180.242.
By sage *Eumæus* born: the purple tide ....Od.20.318.248.
Sage and serene *Telemachus* replies; ....Od.20.403.251.
This said, to sage *Piræus* sped the Seer, ...Od.20.445.254.
(Whose sage decision I with wonder hear) ....Od.21.295.274.
His sage reply, and with her train retir'd: ....Od.21.382.278.
Sage *Polybus,* and stern *Amphimedon,* ....Od.22.267.299.
And sage *Eurynomè,* the couch prepare: ....Od.23.310.338.
And one *Sicilian* matron, old and sage, ...Od.24.242.360.
Sage *Medon* came, and *Phemius* came along; ....Od.24.505.372.

SAGE'S

The merchant's toil, the sage's indolence, ...3.EOM2.172.75.
Vain was the chief's and sage's pride ....4.HOde9.13.159.
He ceas'd; then order'd for the Sage's Bed ....Il.9.733.470.

SAGELY

For sagely hast thou said; Of all Mankind, ...2.ChJM.635.45.
He, against this, right sagely wou'd advise, ...2.ChWB.341.73.
Cry'd sagely, 'Tis not safe, I hold, ...6.94.23.259.

SAGER

N[ewcastle] laugh, or D[orset] sager [sneer] ....4.1740.61.335*.

SAGES

But to my Tale: Some Sages have defin'd ....2.ChJM.440.36.
Than Bramins, Saints, and Sages did before; ....3.Ep3.186.109.
Sages and Chiefs long since had birth ....4.HOde9.9.159.
Groves, where immortal Sages taught; ....6.51i.2.151.
Gods, Emp'rors, Heroes, Sages, Beauties, lie. ....6.71.34.203.
And Chiefs or Sages long to Britain giv'n, ...6.132.13.362.
But ten such Sages as they grant in thee; ....Il.2.443.148.

SAGEST

(Reply'd the sagest of the royal train) ....Od.18.202.176.

SAID

He said; *Alexis,* take this Pipe, the same ....1.PSu.41.75.
What have I said?—where-e'er my *Delia* flies, ...1.PAu.35.82.
What have I said?—where-e'er my Thyrsis flies, ...1.PAu.35A.82.
And said; "Ye Shepherds, sing around my Grave!" ....1.PWi.18.90.
She said, and melting as in Tears she lay, ...1.W-F.203.168.
At length great *ANNA* said—Let Discord cease! ....1.W-F.327.181.
She said, the World obey'd, and all was *Peace!* ....1.W-F.328.181.
And said, a charming female stole that eye. ....1.TrPA.34.366.
This said, he rose, and frantick with his pain, ...1.TrPA.132.371.
Acis too run, and help, oh help! he said, ...1.TrPA.141.371.
Yet this tall Elm, but for his Vine (he said) ....1.TrVP.63.380.
She said, and for her lost *Galanthis* sighs, ...1.TrFD.1.385.
Farewel my Lesbian *Love!* you might have said, ...1.TrSP.113.398.
He said; and thus the Queen of Heav'n return'd; ....1.TrSt.348.424.
He said, his Words the list'ning Chief inspire ....1.TrES.53.451.
Then thus to *Thoos;—Hence* with speed (he said) ....1.TrES.67.452.
Your Aid (said *Thoos) Peteus's* Son demands, ...1.TrES.80Z2.452.
He said, and leap'd from off his lofty Car; ....1.TrES.217.457.
She said; the Cloud-Compeller overcome, ...1.TrES.254.459.
From what far Clime (said she) remote from Fame, ...1.TrUl.116.469.
There goes a Saying, and 'twas shrewdly said, ...2.ChJM.101.19.
There goes a Saying, and 'twas wisely said, ...2.ChJM.101A.19.
He said; the rest in diff'rent Parts divide, ...2.ChJM.139.21.
Heav'n that (said he) inspir'd me first to wed, ...2.ChJM.254.26.
So said they rose, nor more the Work delay'd; ....2.ChJM.299.28.
Here let us walk, he said, observ'd by none, ...2.ChJM.543.41.
For sagely hast thou said; Of all Mankind, ...2.ChJM.635.45.
By ev'ry Word that *Solomon* has said? ....2.ChJM.683.48.
It must be done—I am a King, said he, ...2.ChJM.703.48.
And so has mine, (she said)—I am a Queen! ....2.ChJM.705.48.
And must I languish then (she said) and die, ...2.ChJM.730.50.
This said, his Back against the Trunk he bent; ....2.ChJM.738A.50.
What I have said, quoth he, I must maintain; ....2.ChJM.778.52.
She said; a rising Sigh express'd her Woe, ...2.ChJM.783.52.
Excuse me, Dear, if ought amiss was said, ...2.ChJM.791.53.
For so said *Paul,* and *Paul's* a sound Divine. ....2.ChWB.55.59.
All this I said; but Dreams, Sirs, I had none. ....2.ChWB.304.71.
Rain follows Thunder, that was all he said. ....2.ChWB.392.76.
Soon as he said, My Mistress and my Wife, ...2.ChWB.427.77.
Boast not my Fall (he said) insulting Foe! ....2.RL*A* 2.142.136.
And thus in Whispers said, or seem'd to say. ....2.RL1.26.147.
He said; when *Shock,* who thought she slept too long, ...2.RL1.115.154.
Let Spades be Trumps! she said, and Trumps they were. ....2.RL3.46.172.
She said; then raging to *Sir Plume* repairs, ...2.RL4.121.194.
Which, with a Sigh, she rais'd; and thus she said. ....2.RL4.146.196.
O had I stay'd, and said my Pray'rs at home! ....2.RL4.160.197.
She said: the pitying Audience melt in Tears, ...2.RL5.1.199.
(Said Fame) but high above Desert renown'd: ....2.TemF.325.279.
She said: in Air the trembling Musick floats, ...2.TemF.372.281.
'Tis true, said I, not void of Hopes I came, ...2.TemF.501.287.
How oft', when press'd to marriage, have I said, ...2.ElAb.73.325.
Come, sister come! (it said, or seem'd to say) ....2.ElAb.309.344.
"I give and I devise, (old Euclio said, ...3.Ep1.256.37.
And something said of *Chartres* much too rough. ....4.HS1.4.5.
"What *Speech* esteem you most?"—"The *King's,"* said I, ...4.JD4.68.31.
"Then happy Man who shows the Tombs!" said I, ...4.JD4.102.33.

SAID (CONTINUED)

(Thus said our Friend, and what he said I sing.)	4.HS2.68.59.
(Thus said our Friend, and what he said I sing.)	4.HS2.68.59.
Shut, shut the door, good *John!* fatigu'd I said,	4.Arbu.1.96.
Thus much I've said, I trust without Offence;	4.JD2A.131.144.
Thus much I've said, I trust without offence;	4.JD2.125.145.
You said the same; and are you discontent	4.2HE2.29.167.
But let it (in a word) be said,	4.HS6.195.263.
No sooner said, but from the Hall	4.HS6.212.263.
'Twas what I said to Craggs and Child,	4.1HE7.67.273.
Said, "Tories call'd him Whig, and Whigs a Tory;"	4.EpS1.8.297.
Sure, if they cannot cut, it may be said	4.EpS2.148.321.
So like, that criticks said and courtiers swore,	5.DunA2.45.101.
"So take the hindmost Hell."—He said, and run.	5.DunA2.56.105.
He said, and climb'd a stranded Lighter's height,	5.DunA2.275.135.
And "Take (he said) these robes which once were mine,	5.DunA2.327.141.
How sweet the periods, neither said nor sung!	5.DunA3.198.174.
So like, that critics said, and courtiers swore,	5.DunB2.49.298.
"So take the hindmost, Hell."—He said, and run.	5.DunB2.60.298.
He said, and clim'd a stranded lighter's height,	5.DunB2.287.309.
"Receive (he said) those robes which once were mine,	5.DunB2.351.314.
Fierce as a startled Adder, swell'd, and said,	5.DunB4.373.379.
More she had said, but yawn'd—All Nature nods:	5.DunB4.605A.403.
(Wench, I'd have said did Rhyme not hinder)	6.10.57.26.
(As once you said of you know who)	6.10.94.27.
But those, in which a Learned Author said,	6.13.5.39.
Come, gentle Air! th' Æolian Shepherd said,	6.14iii.1.45.
Stephens prints *Heathen Greek,* 'tis said,	6.29.13.83.
Of *Lintot's* Books this can't be said,	6.29.19.83.
Those printed unknown Tongues, 'tis said,	6.29.7Z1.83.
And gently pressd my hand, and said, Be Ours!—	6.66.4.194.
Said *this* was Flatt'ry, *that* a Fault.	6.77.3.214.
And thus, at Court, he said.	6.94.8.259.
Some said that *D[ou]gl[a]s* sent should be,	6.94.17.259.
And said to him, Good Neighbour,	6.94.38.260.
Said, to reward your Pains,	6.94.70.261.
Why has the Proverb falsly said	6.94.85.262.
When they said	6.96i.13.268.
She said, but broken Accents stopt her Voice,	6.96ii.71.273.
'Tis said, that thou shouldst cleave unto thy Wife;	6.96iv.9.276.
God said, *Let Newton be!* and All was *Light.*	6.111.2.317.
—He said, and dy'd.	6.123.9.344.
"Madness and lust" (said God) "be you his heirs"	6.130.32.359.
Where still so much is said,	6.133.2.363.
So very much is said,	6.133.2A.363.
E'er said of me, is, I can bite:	6.135.20.366.
"And take (she said, and smil'd serene)	6.140.3.378.
What they said, or may say of the Mortal within.	6.144.6.386.
He said and sate: when *Calchas* thus reply'd,	Il.1.91.91.
He said, observant of the blue-ey'd Maid;	Il.1.291.100.
This said, he ceas'd: The King of Men replies;	Il.1.376.106.
He deeply sighing said: To tell my Woe,	Il.1.476.110.
He gave to *Chryses,* thus the Heroe said.	Il.1.575.115.
If e'er, O Father of the Gods! she said,	Il.1.652.118.
She said, and sighing thus the God replies	Il.1.670.119.
He said, and to her Hands the Goblet heav'd,	Il.1.766.124.
The *Phantome* said; then, vanish'd from his sight,	Il.2.43.129.
And, Dost thou sleep, Oh *Atreus'* Son? (he said)	Il.2.76.130.
He spoke, and sate; when *Nestor* rising said,	Il.2.99.131.
He said, and cow'ring as the Dastard bends,	Il.2.326.142.
He said: the Shores with loud Applauses sound,	Il.2.400.145.
He said; the Monarch issu'd his Commands;	Il.2.520.151.
He said. The Challenge *Hector* heard with Joy,	Il.3.109.195.
This said, the many-colour'd Maid inspires	Il.3.183.200.
This said, once more he view'd the Warrior-Train:	Il.3.253.204.
This said, once more he view'd the martial Train:	Il.3.253A.204.
This said, the hoary King no longer stay'd,	Il.3.386.211.
He said, and poiz'd in Air the Jav'lin sent,	Il.3.439.213.
Furious he said, and tow'rd the *Grecian* Crew	Il.3.455.213.
Forsook her Cheek; and, trembling, thus she said.	Il.3.492.215.
They said, while *Pallas* thro' the *Trojan* Throng	Il.4.115.226.
He said: A Leader's and a Brother's Fears	Il.4.220.231.
This said, he stalk'd with ample Strides along,	Il.4.286.234.
He said. With Joy the Monarch march'd before,	Il.4.380.239.
His Cheek with Blushes; and severe, he said.	Il.4.403.240.
He said, and pass'd where great *Tydides* lay,	Il.4.418.240.
He said, then shook the pondrous Lance and flung,	Il.5.342.283.
This said, she wip'd from *Venus'* wounded Palm	Il.5.505.292.
He said: new Courage swell'd each Hero's Heart.	Il.5.572.296.
He said: Both Javelins at an Instant flew:	Il.5.814.305.
He said, nor *Hector* to the Chief replies,	Il.5.848.306.
To whom assenting, thus the Thund'rer said:	Il.5.952.312.
He said; *Saturnia,* ardent to obey,	Il.5.956.312.
She said, and to the Steeds approaching near,	Il.5.1028.315.
He said: Compassion touch'd the Hero's Heart,	Il.6.63.326.
This said, with ample Strides the Hero past;	Il.6.143.331.
Thus having said, the gallant Chiefs alight,	Il.6.288.340.
He said, nor answer'd *Priam's* warlike Son;	Il.6.430.347.
He said, and past with sad presaging Heart	Il.6.462.349.
Thus having said, the glorious Chief resumes	Il.6.638.358.
He said: The Warrior heard the Word with Joy.	Il.7.59.365.
He said, and turn'd his Brother's vengeful Mind,	Il.7.139.370.
Said I in secret? No, your Vows declare,	Il.7.233.376.
He said. The Troops with elevated Eyes,	Il.7.239.376.
He said, and rising, high above the Field	Il.7.295.378.
He said, and rear'd his Sceptre to the Sky.	Il.7.489.388.
Thus said the Chief; and *Nestor,* skill'd in War,	Il.8.143.404.
He said; and hasty, o'er the gasping Throng	Il.8.190.406.
Furious he said; then, bending o'er the Yoke,	Il.8.224.408.
He said, and twang'd the String. The Weapon flies	Il.8.365.414.
What hast thou said, Oh Tyrant of the Skies!	Il.8.575.424.
He said; deep Silence held the *Grecian* Band,	Il.9.39.433.
He said, all approv'd. The Heralds bring	Il.9.227.444.
He said; *Patroclus* o'er the blazing Fire	Il.9.271.446.
This said, each Prince a double Goblet crown'd,	Il.9.771.472.
This said, each parted to his sev'ral Cares;	Il.10.80.6.

SAID (CONTINUED)

The hoary Monarch rais'd his Eyes, and said.	Il.10.89.6.
Then none (said *Nestor)* shall his Rule withstand,	Il.10.148.8.
The Warrior saw the hoary Chief, and said.	Il.10.185.10.
This said, the Hero o'er his Shoulders flung	Il.10.202.10.
Watch thus, and *Greece* shall live—The Hero said;	Il.10.227.12.
Is there (said he) a Chief so greatly brave,	Il.10.241.12.
Is there (he said) a Chief so greatly brave,	Il.10.241A.12.
Hector! (he said) my Courage bids me meet	Il.10.377.20.
He said, and high in Air the Weapon cast,	Il.10.441.23.
This said, the Spoils with dropping Gore defac'd,	Il.10.536.27.
Pallas (this said) her Hero's Bosom warms,	Il.10.558.27.
This said, *Pisander* from the Car he cast,	Il.11.185.43.
She said, and vanish'd: *Hector,* with a Bound,	Il.11.269.47.
He said; the Driver whirls his lengthful Thong;	Il.11.359.50.
Here stand his utmost Force—The Warrior said;	Il.11.451.54.
He said, and forceful pierc'd his spacious Shield;	Il.11.546.58.
The Hero said, His Friend obey'd with haste,	Il.11.754.68.
To his high Seat; the Chief refus'd, and said.	Il.11.791.71.
Peleus said only this,—"My Son! be brave".	Il.11.915.76.
He said, and in his Arms upheld the Chief.	Il.11.977.78.
He said; his Words the list'ning Chief inspire	Il.12.397.96.
Then thus to *Thoos;—hence* with speed, (he said)	Il.12.411.96.
Your Aid (said *Thoos) Peteus'* Son demands,	Il.12.426.97.
He said, and rouz'd the Soul in ev'ry Breast;	Il.13.211.116.
This said, he rushes where the Combate burns;	Il.13.313.120.
Nor vain (said *Merion)* are our martial Toils;	Il.13.347.122.
He said; and *Merion* to th' appointed Place,	Il.13.418.126.
The bold *Deïphobus* approach'd, and said.	Il.13.581.134.
Tore off his Arms, and loud-exulting said.	Il.13.778.141.
This said, he seiz'd (while yet the Carcass heav'd)	Il.13.801.143.
This said; the tow'ring Chief, prepares to go,	Il.13.946.150.
This said; the tow'ring Chief, prepar'd to go,	Il.13.946A.150.
He said, and like a Lion stalk'd along:	Il.13.1056.155.
He said: and seizing *Thrasimedes'* Shield,	Il.14.13.157.
Let Heav'n's dread Empress (*Cytheræa* said)	Il.14.223.172.
Then grant me (said the Queen) those conqu'ring Charms,	Il.14.225.172.
She said. With Awe divine the Queen of Love	Il.14.243.172.
Take this, and with it all thy Wish, she said:	Il.14.254.173.
Swear then (he said) by those tremendous Floods	Il.14.305.177.
For that (said *Jove)* suffice another Day;	Il.14.355.180.
Thus having said, the Pow'r of Slumber flew,	Il.14.417.183.
He said, and Sorrow touch'd each *Argive* Breast:	Il.14.535.189.
The Goddess said, and sullen took her Place;	Il.15.108.200.
Thus, to th' impetuous Homicide she said.	Il.15.145.202.
She said, and sate: the God that gilds the Day,	Il.15.168.203.
And must I then (said she) O Sire of Floods!	Il.15.224.205.
Then *Greece* shall breathe from Toils—The Godhead said;	Il.15.264.207.
Furious he said; the smarting Scourge resounds;	Il.15.402.212.
This said, his eager Javelin sought the Foe:	Il.15.498.216.
Hector (this said) rush'd forward on the Foes:	Il.15.664.221.
Is there (he said) in Arms a Youth like you,	Il.15.682.222.
He said, and backward to the Lines retir'd;	Il.15.686.222.
I haste to bring the Troops—The Hero said;	Il.16.160.244.
She said; the Cloud-compeller overcome,	Il.16.559.266.
This said, *Patroclus* to the Battel flies;	Il.16.763.273.
"Return not, my brave Friend (perhaps he said)	Il.16.1013.282.
Pensive he said; then pressing as he lay	Il.16.1042.283.
He said, and touch'd his Heart. The raging Pair	Il.17.135.293.
He strode along the Field, as thus he said.	Il.17.211.295.
Olympus trembled, and the Godhead said.	Il.17.230.296.
Thus they. While with one Voice the *Trojans* said,	Il.17.480.306.
He said; and breathing in th' immortal Horse	Il.17.524.308.
He said. *Alcimedon,* with active Heat,	Il.17.548.309.
With great *Atrides.* Hither turn (he said)	Il.17.576.311.
Gone is *Antilochus* (the Hero said)	Il.17.793.319.
'Tis well (said *Ajax)* be it then thy Care	Il.17.801.319.
Have try'd it, and have stood. The Hero said.	Il.17.807.320.
Thus to his Soul he said. Ah! what constrains	Il.18.9.323.
She said, and left the Caverns of the Main.	Il.18.85.327.
Thy want of Arms (said *Iris)* well we know,	Il.18.235.333.
Return? (said *Hector,* fir'd with stern Disdain)	Il.18.333.337.
A Footstool at her Feet: then calling, said,	Il.18.459.343.
Thus having said, the Father of the Fires	Il.18.537.347.
And thus, his Hand soft-touching, *Thetis* said.	Il.19.10.371.
He said: His finish'd Wrath with loud Acclaim	Il.19.77.375.
From us (he said) this Day an Infant springs,	Il.19.107.376.
A Youth (said she) of *Jove's* immortal Kind	Il.19.120.377.
Sighing he said: His Grief the Heroes join'd,	Il.19.360.387.
The gen'rous *Xanthus,* as the Words he said,	Il.19.446.390.
Now perish *Troy!* He said, and rush'd to Fight.	Il.19.471.391.
He said, and fir'd their heav'nly Breasts with Rage:	Il.20.43.395.
This said, and Spirit breath'd into his Breast,	Il.20.142.400.
And thus, assembling all the Pow'rs, she said.	Il.20.145.400.
Thus having said, the Tyrant of the Sea	Il.20.172.400.
Now then let others bleed—This said, aloud	Il.20.401.412.
He said: Nor less elate with martial Joy,	Il.20.415.412.
Thus, breathing Rage thro' all the Hero said;	Il.20.427.412.
Are thine no more—Th' insulting Hero said,	Il.20.453.413.
And knock'd his fault'ring Knees, the Hero said.	Il.21.61.424.
Die then—He said; and as the Word he spoke	Il.21.125.426.
Threat'ning he said: The hostile Chiefs advance;	Il.21.179.429.
While the proud Victor thus triumphing said,	Il.21.199.429.
He said; then from the Bank his Jav'lin tore,	Il.21.217.430.
He said; and drove with Fury on the Foe.	Il.21.247.431.
He said; and on the Chief descends amain,	Il.21.378.436.
And thus short-panting, to the God he said.	Il.21.417.437.
She said, and seiz'd her Wrists with eager Rage;	Il.21.566.445.
He said, and stood; collected in his Might;	Il.21.675.450.
He said: With matchless Force the Jav'lin flung	Il.21.699.450.
He said, and acting what no Words could say,	Il.22.108.457.
And thus, fast-falling the salt Tears, she said.	Il.22.113.457.
Fraudful she said; then swiftly march'd before;	Il.22.313.469.
I follow thee—He said, and stripp'd the Slain.	Il.22.462.474.
On his dead Friend's cold Breast, and thus he said.	Il.23.24.488.
Gloomy he said, and (horrible to view)	Il.23.33.488.

SAILORS (CONTINUED)

At once the sailors to their charge arise: ....Od.8.46.264.
With joy the sailors view their friends return'd, ...Od.9.549.328.
The sailors spent with toils their folly mourn, ...Od.10.89.343.
Our eager sailors seize the fair retreat, ...Od.10.105.345.
The sailors catch the word, their oars they seize, ...Od.10.149.347.
With earnest haste my frighted sailors press, ...Od.10.153.347.
The weeping sailors; nor less fierce their joy ....Od.10.493.367.
The sailors waiting, and the ships prepar'd. ....Od.14.370.53.
But other counsels pleas'd the sailors mind: ....Od.14.374.53.
"Swear first (she cry'd) ye sailors! to restore ....Od.15.474.93.
Swift as she ask'd, the ready sailors swore. ....Od.15.476.93.
No sailors there, no vessels to convey, ...Od.17.166.139.
And gulph'd in crouds at once the sailors dye, ...Od.23.252.335.

SAILS

Or under Southern Skies exalt their Sails, ...1.W-F.391.189.
Spread all his Sails, and durst the Deeps explore; ....1.EOC.646.312.
To these fond Eyes restore thy welcome Sails? ....1.TrSP.247.404.
Cupid for thee shall spread the swelling Sails. ....1.TrSP.253.404.
For thee shall *Cupid* spread the swelling Sails. ....1.TrSP.253A.404.
This way and that, the wav'ring Sails they bend, ...1.TrSt.266.421.
Spread their broad Sails, and launch into the Main: .....1.TrUl.2.465.
Thus with spread Sails the winged Gally flies; ....1.TrUl.13.465.
They land my Goods, and hoist their flying Sails. ....1.TrUl.157.471.
The lucid Squadrons round the Sails repair: ....1.RL2.56.163.
He spoke; the Spirits from the Sails descent; ....1.RL2.137.168.
Here Amphitrite sails thro' myrtle bow'rs; ....3.Ep4.123.149.
Or spread their feather'd Sails against the Beams, ...6.26i.8.79.
The Sails they furl'd, they lash'd the Mast aside, ...Il.1.568.115.
Supply'd by *Phœbus,* fill the swelling Sails; ....Il.1.625.117.
Fly, *Grecians* fly, your Sails and Oars employ, ...Il.2.171.136.
The third Day hence, shall *Pthia* greet our Sails, ...Il.9.473.455.
Us too he bids our Oars and Sails employ, ...Il.9.802.473.
No more the Troops, our hoisted Sails in view, ...Il.14.110.163.
There sate *Achilles,* shaded by his Sails, ...Il.18.5.323.
Lo, where yon' Sails their canvas Wings extend, ...Il.19.366.387.
Surround her feet; with these sublime she sails ....Od.1.126.38.
Me from our coast shall spreading sails convey, ...Od.2.404.80.
High o'er the roaring waves the spreading sails ....Od.2.466.83.
And furl their sails, and issue on the land. ....Od.3.14.87.
The God still breathing on my swelling sails; ....Od.3.222.96.
O'er the warm *Libyan* wave to spread my sails: ....Od.4.104.124.
Rise on the poop, and fully stretch the sails. ....Od.4.484.143.
Still with expanded sails we court in vain ....Od.4.489.143.
With sails we wing the masts, our anchors weigh, ...Od.4.785.156.
The desp'rate crew ascend, unfurl the sails; ....Od.4.1033.166.
Huge, horrid, vast! where scarce in safety sails ....Od.5.227.182.
Thy loom, *Calypso!* for the future sails ....Od.5.329.187.
With beating heart *Ulysses* spreads his sails; ....Od.5.344.188.
Then to the Palaces of heav'n she sails, ...Od.6.47.207.
They launch the vessel, and unfurl the sails, ...Od.8.47.264.
Call thee aboard, and stretch the swelling sails. ....Od.8.166.271.
This social right demands: for him the sails ....Od.8.591.294.
With sails outspread we fly th' unequal strife, ...Od.9.71.305.
Our sails we gather'd, cast our cables o'er, ...Od.9.172.312.
He charg'd to fill, and guide the swelling sails: ....Od.10.28.340.
Our oars we shipp'd: all day the swelling sails ....Od.11.9.379.
Attend thy voyage, and impel thy sails: ....Od.11.141.387.
Sing thro' the shrouds, and stretch the swelling sails. ...Od.11.794.426.
Spread your broad sails, and plow the liquid way: ....Od.12.36.431.
O fly the dreadful sight! expand thy sails, ...Od.12.105.436.
Here fills her sails and spreads her oars in vain; ....Od.12.122.437.
Attend thy voyage, and impell thy sails; ....Od.12.173.440.
The friendly Goddess stretch'd the swelling sails; ....Od.12.185.441.
With speed the bark we climb: the spacious sails ....Od.12.471.454.
Thus with spread sails the winged gally flies; ....Od.13.104.6.
They land my goods, and hoist their flying sails. ....Od.13.324.23.
Thro' the mid seas the nimble pinnace sails, ...Od.14.329.51.
To smooth thy passage, and supply thy sails: ....Od.15.42.71.
Their sails they loos'd, they lash'd the mast aside, ...Od.15.537.96.
Telemachus in triumph sails the main. ....Od.16.363.124.
With gather'd sails they stood, and lifted oars. ....Od.16.369.124.
Yet safe he sails! the pow'rs cœlestial give ....Od.16.384.124.
How to the land of *Lote* unblest he sails; ....Od.23.335.340.
How, the loud storms in prison bound, he sails ....Od.23.339.341.

SAINT

See ST.
Meek as a Saint, or haughty as the Devil; ....2.ChJM.187.23.
Full many a Saint, since first the World began, ...2.ChWB.46.58.
To patch, nay ogle, might become a Saint, ...2.RL5.23.201.
Soft as the slumbers of a saint forgiv'n, ...2.ElAb.255.340.
The virtues of a saint at twenty-one! ....3.EOM4.184.144.
A Saint in Crape is twice a Saint in Lawn; ....3.Ep1.88.21.
A Saint in Crape is twice a Saint in Lawn; ....3.Ep1.88.21.
A Rogue with Ven'son to a Saint without. ....3.Ep1.139.26.
A perjur'd Prince a leaden Saint revere, ...3.Ep1.148.28.
"Odious! in woollen! 'twould a Saint provoke, ...3.Ep1.242.36.
Whether the Charmer sinner it, or saint it, ...3.Ep2.15.49.
The worst of Madmen is a Saint run mad. ....4.1HE6.27.239.
Prompt or to guard or stab, to saint or damn, ...5.DunB2.357.315.
Beholds himself a Patriot, Chief, of Saint. ....5.DunB4.536.395.
By Saint, by Savage, and by Sage, ...6.50.3.145.
by Christian Saint, by Heathen sage, ...6.50.3A.145.
By Saint, by Savage, or by Sage, ...6.50.3B.145.
One that should be a Saint, ...6.68.1.196.
The Saint sustain'd it, but the Woman dy'd. ....6.115.10.323.
Pays the last Tribute of a Saint to Heav'n. ....6.132.14.362.

SAINTED

Love's victim then, tho' now a sainted maid: ....2.ElAb.312.344.

SAINTS

May live like Saints, by Heav'ns Consent, and mine. ....2.ChJM.126.20.
And pitying saints, whose statues learn to weep! ....2.ElAb.22.320.

SAINTS (CONTINUED)

Dim and remote the joys of saints I see, ...2.ElAb.71.325.
And Saints with wonder heard the vows I made. ....2.ElAb.114.329.
No silver saints, by dying misers giv'n, ...2.ElAb.137.331.
And Saints embrace thee with a love like mine. ....2.ElAb.342.347.
Than Bramins, Saints, and Sages did before; ....3.Ep3.186.109.
Where sprawl the Saints of Verrio or Laguerre, ...3.Ep4.146.151.
Silent and soft, as Saints remove to Heav'n, ...4.EpS1.93.305.
All that makes Saints of Queens, and Gods of Kings, ...4.EpS2.225.325.
A Church collects the saints of Drury-lane. ....5.DunA2.26.99.
A Church collects the saints of Drury-lane. ....5.DunB2.30.297.
Faith, gallants, board with saints, and bed with sinners. ...6.41.24.114.
(Aye watching o'er his Saints with Eye unseen,) ....6.137.3.373.
This single Crayon, Madam, saints the Queen. ....6.147iii.4.390.

SAINTS'

Than good, in all the *Bible* and *Saints'-Lives.* ....2.ChWB.364.74.

SAINTS'-LIVES

Than good, in all the *Bible* and *Saints'-Lives.* ....2.ChWB.364.74.

SAINTSHIP

The Dev'l was piqu'd such saintship to behold, ...3.Ep3.349.122.

SAITH

What saith my Council learned in the Laws? ....4.HS1.142.19.

SAKE

Did but for *David's* Righteous Sake permit; ....2.ChJM.691.48.
At least, kind Sir, for Charity's sweet sake, ...2.ChJM.732.50.
To follow Virtue ev'n for Virtue's sake. ....2.TemF.365.281.
We grow more partial for th' observer's sake; ....3.Ep1.12.16.
Still *Sapho*—"*Hold!* for God-sake—you'll offend: ......4.Arbu.101.103.
Ev'n those I pardon, for whose sinful sake ....4.JD2.41.135.
Ev'n those I pardon, For whose sinful Sake ....4.JD2A.45.136.
But wish'd it Stilton for his sake; ....4.HS6.168.261.
"But come, for God's sake, live with Men: ....4.HS6.178.261.
"For God's sake, come, and live with Men: ....4.HS6.178A.261.
Fr. Hold Sir! for God's-sake, where's th' Affront to you? ...4.EpS2.157.322.
Who hunger, and who thirst, for scribling sake: ....5.DunA1.48.65.
Who hunger, and who thirst for scribling sake: ....5.DunB1.50.274.
At last in pity, for our sake, ...6.4iii.11.10.
Refine ourselves to Spirit, for your Sake. ....6.82vi.2.232.
With Toils, sustain'd for *Paris'* sake and mine: ....Il.6.445.348.
For much they suffer, for thy sake, in War. ....Il.6.675.360.
The Sire revenges for the Daughter's sake, ...Il.9.634.466.
And inly trembled for his Brother's sake. ....Il.10.282.14.
For *Hector's* sake these Walls he bids thee leave, ...Il.24.211.545.
A Pledge of Gratitude for *Hector's* sake; ....Il.24.526.558.
That father, for whose sake thy days have run ....Od.16.207.114.
O guard it, guard it, for thy servant's sake! ....Od.17.675.165.

SALAMANDER

Beware; your Heart's no *Salamander!* ....6.10.54.26.

SALAMANDER'S

Mount up, and take a *Salamander's* Name. ....2.RL1.60.150.

SALAMINIAN

With these appear the *Salaminian* Bands, ...Il.2.671.158.

SALAMIS

From warlike *Salamis* I drew my Birth, ...Il.7.237.376.

SALARY

Oh! save the Salary, and drink the Sack! ....6.116v.6.327.

SALE

By sale, at least by death, to change their Lord. ....4.2HE2.251.183.

SALEM

Rise, crown'd with Light, Imperial *Salem* rise! ....1.Mes.85.120.

SALESMEN

Poets make Characters, as *Salesmen* Cloaths, ...6.60.25.178.

SALIENT

"The salient spout, far-streaming to the sky; ....5.DunA2.154.120.
"The salient spout, far-streaming to the sky; ....5.DunA2.154A.120.
"The salient spout, far-streaming to the sky; ....5.DunB2.162.303.

SALLADS

With soups unbought and sallads blest his board. ....3.Ep3.184.109.
For Sallads, Tarts, and Pease! ....6.47.48.130.

SALLEE

When Sallee Rovers chac'd him on the deep. ....5.DunB4.380.380.

SALLUST

And yet some Care of *S[allu]st* should be had, ...4.HAdv.63.81.

SALLY

Seek not your Fleet, but sally from the Wall; ....Il.12.326.93.

SALLY'D

Flush'd in his cheek, or sally'd in his blood; ....Od.11.646.416.

SALMON'S

A salmon's belly, Helluo, was thy fate: ....3.Ep1.234.35.

SALMONEUS

Tyro began: whom great *Salmoneus* bred; ....Od.11.281.395.

SALOMON

No Mortal read his *Salomon,* ....6.101.19.290.

SALT

Salt, pepper and mace 6.91.5.253.
And sprinkles sacred Salt from lifted Urns; Il.9.282.447.
And thus, fast-falling the salt Tears, she said. Il.22.113.457.
Who ne'er knew salt, or heard the billows roar, Od.11.153.389.
Who ne'er knew salt, or heard the billows roar, Od.23.286.337.

SALTED

The sacred Off'ring of the salted Cake; Il.1.587.116.
Between their Horns the salted Barley threw, Il.1.600.116.
The sacred Off'ring of the salted Cake: Il.2.487.150.
The salted cakes in canisters are laid, Od.4.1003.164.

SALUBRIOUS

Salubrious Draughts the Warrior's Thirst allay, Il.11.786.70.

SALUTARY

Or bless with salutary arts to heal; Od.17.465.155.

SALUTE

Salute the God in num'rous Hymns of Praise. 1.TrSt.655.437.
When opening Buds salute the welcome Day, 2.TemF.3.253.
Salute the diff'rent Quarters of the Sky. 2.TemF.68.257.
Salute the coming, close the parting day. 4.HOde1.30A.153.
Salute the rising, close the parting day. 4.HOde1.30B.153.
And Gonoëssa's Spires salute the Sky. Il.2.693.159.
Salute his master, and confess his joys. Od.17.363.149.

SALUTES

When warbling Philomel salutes the Spring? 1.PSp.26.63.
Where vast Cythæron's Top salutes the Sky, 1.TrSt.161.416.
And, on his Knees, salutes his Mother Earth; 1.TrUl.237.473.
And in soft Sounds, Your Grace salutes their Ear. 2.RL1.86.152.
Far from his own domain salutes the soil; Od.4.696.152.
And on his knees salutes his mother earth: Od.13.404.26.
But thou, when morn salutes th' aerial plain, Od.16.290.119.

SALVATION

And taught more Pleasant Methods of Salvation; 1.EOC.547.302.
They to Salvation shew the arduous way, 6.2.28.6.

SALVERS

Between each Act the trembling salvers ring, 3.Ep4.161.153.

SAMÈ

Dulichium, Samè, and Zacynthus crown'd Od.9.23.302.

SAM

Ho! Master Sam, quoth Sandys' Sprite, 6.58.37.172.
"To what,(quoth Sam) shall Ovid change?" 6.58.75A.174.

SAMARITAN

The Words addrest to the Samaritan: 2.ChWB.14.57.

SAME

He said; Alexis, take this Pipe, the same 1.PSu.41.75.
And the same Hand that sow'd, shall reap the Field. 1.Mes.66.118.
In the same Shades the Cupids tun'd his Lyre, 1.W-F.295.176.
To the same Notes, of Love, and soft Desire. 1.W-F.296.176.
By her just Standard, which is still the same: 1.EOC.69.246.
By the same Laws which first herself ordain'd. 1.EOC.91.249.
Nature and Homer were, he found, the same: 1.EOC.135.255.
With the same Spirit that its Author writ, 1.EOC.234.266.
In Words, as Fashions, the same Rule will hold; 1.EOC.333.276.
While they ring round the same unvary'd Chimes, 1.EOC.348.278.
From the same Foes, at last, both felt their Doom, 1.EOC.685.317.
And the same Age saw Learning fall, and Rome. 1.EOC.686.317.
Your Rural Cares, and Pleasures, are the same. 1.TrVP.95.381.
And I my self the same rash act had done, 1.TrFD.26.387.
O still the same Ulysses! she rejoin'd, 1.TrUl.166.471.
The same Apostle too has elsewhere own'd 2.ChWB.32.58.
(The same, his ancient Personage to deck, 2.RL5.89.207.
Their Pleas were diff'rent, their Request the same; 2.TemF.292.278.
Prefer'd the same Request, and lowly bow'd, 2.TemF.329.280.
Around the Shrine, and made the same Request: 2.TemF.395.282.
I shriek, start up, the same sad prospect find, 2.ElAb.247.339.
That, chang'd thro' all, and yet in all the same, 3.EOM1.269.47.
Have full as oft no meaning, or the same. 3.EOM2.86.65.
The same ambition can destroy or save, 3.EOM2.201.79.
Yet from the same we learn, in its decline, 3.EOM2.257.86.
And bid Self-Love and Social be the same. 3.EOM3.138Z2.106.
The same his table, and the same his bed; 3.EOM3.153.108.
The same his table, and the same his bed; 3.EOM3.153.108.
In the same temple, the resounding wood, 3.EOM3.155.108.
The same which in a Sire the Sons obey'd; 3.EOM3.213.114.
The same Self-love, in all, becomes the cause 3.EOM3.271.120.
And bade Self-love and Social be the same. 3.EOM3.318.126.
Bliss is the same in subject or in king, 3.EOM4.58.134.
With the same trash mad mortals wish for here? 3.EOM4.174.144.
Heroes are much the same, the points agreed, 3.EOM4.219.147.
The same (my Lord) if Tully's or your own. 3.EOM4.240.150.
That true SELF-LOVE and SOCIAL are the same; 3.EOM4.396.166.
The same adust complexion has impell'd 3.Ep1.59.19.
Tho' the same Sun with all-diffusive rays 3.Ep1.97.22.
See the same man, in vigour, in the gout; 3.Ep1.130.25.
Know, God and Nature only are the same: 3.Ep1.154.28.
With the same spirit that he drinks and whores; 3.Ep1.189.31.
The same for ever! and describ'd by all 3.Ep2.183.65.
We find our tenets just the same at last. 3.Ep3.16.84.
My Life's amusements have been just the same, 4.HS2.153.67.
But not Sir H[erber]t, for he does the same. 4.HAdv.16.75.
And thought a Lye in Verse or Prose the same: 4.Arbu.339.120.
Sense, past thro' him, no longer is the same, 4.JD2.33.135.
You said the same; and you are you discontent 4.2HE2.29.167.
All vast Possessions (just the same the case 4.2HE2.254.183.
Each Individual: His great End the same. 4.2HE2.283.185.

SAME (CONTINUED)

Whether we joy or grieve, the same the curse, 4.1HE6.22.237.
"This same Dessert is not so pleasant: 4.HS6.221.263.
"Well, but the Poor"—the Poor have the same itch: 4.1HE1.154.291.
She's still the same, belov'd, contented thing. 4.EpS1.140.308.
Compar'd, and knew their gen'rous End the same: 4.EpS2.81.317.
Since the whole House did afterwards the same: 4.EpS2.170.323.
The same their talents, and their tasts the same, 5.DunA2.348.143.
The same their talents, and their tasts the same, 5.DunA2.348.143.
Old in new state, another yet the same. 5.DunA3.32.154.
'Tis the same rope at sev'ral ends they twist, 5.DunA3.285.184.
Else all my Prose and Verse were much the same; 5.DunB1.189.283.
'Tis the same rope at different ends they twist; 5.DunB1.207.285.
The same their talents, and their tastes the same; 5.DunB2.380.315.
The same their talents, and their tastes the same; 5.DunB2.380.315.
Old in new state, another yet the same. 5.DunB3.40.322.
To the same notes thy sons shall hum, or snore, 5.DunB4.59.347.
With the same Cement, ever sure to bind, 5.DunB4.267.370.
Then dupe to Party; child and man the same; 5.DunB4.502.391.
From the same cloud we thus descry 6.5.11A.12.
Wit, past thro' thee, no longer is the same, 6.7.11.16.
And the same Stream at once both cools and burns. 6.9v.4.21.
"Be thilke same Thing Maids longen a'ter? 6.14i.24.42.
The pond'rous Ballance keeps its Poize the same, 6.17i(b).3.55.
Thus Voiture's early Care still shone the same, 6.19.69.64.
Gav'st all things to be chang'd, yet ever art the same! 6.23.8.73.
The same mild season gives the blooms to blow, 6.35.15.103.
Within the same did Sandys lurk, 6.58.27.171.
On the same pile the faithful fair expire; 6.69i.2.197.
On the same pile their faithful fair expire; 6.69i.2A.197.
Now, that this same it is right sooth, 6.79.5.218.
"And piss against the same. 6.79.144.223.
Then slyly thrust it up that same, 6.94.43.260.
Reason, you found, and Virtue were the same. 6.96iii.8.267.
Thy Children's Noses all should twang the same. 6.96iv.108.279.
She asks what bosom has not felt the same? 6.107.16.311.
Steer'd the same course to the same quiet shore, 6.109.13.314.
Steer'd the same course to the same quiet shore, 6.109.13.314.
Took the same course to the same quiet shore, 6.109.13A.314.
Took the same course to the same quiet shore, 6.109.13A.314.
Her B[ur]l[ingto]n do just the same. 6.119.12.337.
The same in Habit, and in Mien the same. Il.2.74.130.
The same in Habit, and in Mien the same. Il.2.74.130.
The same their Nation, and their Chief the same. Il.2.836.164.
The same their Nation, and their Chief the same. Il.2.836.164.
Their Height, their Colour, and their Age the same; Il.2.931.167.
(Great Menelaus urg'd the same Request) Il.3.269.205.
My Brothers these; the same our native Shore, Il.3.305.208.
From the same Urn they drink the mingled Wine, Il.3.368.210.
With ours, thy Care and Ardour are the same. Il.4.412.240.
A Phantom rais'd, the same in Shape and Show Il.5.546.294.
In the same Car the Chiefs to Combate ride, Il.5.754.303.
By the same Arm my sev'n brave Brothers fell, Il.6.534.353.
The same I chose for more than vulgar Charms, Il.9.167.441.
The same he chose for more than vulgar Charms, Il.9.354.451.
The Wretch and Hero find their Prize the same; Il.9.419.453.
The same which once King Cinyras possest: Il.11.26.36.
In the same Car the Brother-Warriors ride, Il.11.139.41.
The social Shades the same dark Journey go, Il.11.339.49.
Would the same God had fixt it in his Heart! Il.11.486.56.
And the same Arm that led, concludes the Day; Il.11.892.75.
Last Nestor's Son the same bold Ardour takes, Il.13.129.110.
Not so the Brave—still dauntless, still the same, Il.13.366.123.
The same our Honours, and our Birth the same. Il.15.235.206.
The same our Honours, and our Birth the same. Il.15.235.206.
The same which dead Protesilaus bore, Il.15.856.229.
We too must yield: The same sad Fate must fall Il.17.886.298.
By the same Arm illustrious Podes bled, Il.17.664.313.
The self same Night to both a Being gave, Il.18.297.336.
Gives the same Youth to the same conqu'ring Hand; Il.21.53.424.
Gives the same Youth to the same conqu'ring Hand; Il.21.53.424.
Not the same Mother gave thy Suppliant Breath, Il.21.107.426.
Vain hope! to shun him by the self-same Road Il.21.653.449.
(Her Face, her Gesture, and her Arms the same) Il.22.292.468.
At diff'rent Periods, yet our Fate the same! Il.22.613.481.
In the same Robe he living wore, he came, Il.23.80.490.
In Stature, Voice, and pleasing Look, the same. Il.23.81.490.
In the same Robe the Living wore, he came, Il.23.80A.490.
Alas how diff'rent! yet how like the same! Il.23.129.493.
And the slow Mules the same rough Road return. Il.23.151.495.
(The same renown'd Asteropæus wore) Il.23.640.515.
Now, the same Hero's Funeral Rites to grace, Il.23.874.524.
(The self-same Place beside Patroclus' Pyre, Il.23.909.525.
Their Merits, nor their Honours, are the same. Il.24.86.539.
Content—By the same Hand let me expire! Il.24.277.548.
The same stern God to Ruin gives you all. Il.24.302.549.
In ev'ry Face the self-same Grief is shown, Il.24.884.573.
The same his features, if the same his years. Od.1.270.45.
The same his features, if the same his years. Od.1.270.45.
With equal souls, and sentiments the same. Od.3.158.93.
His port, his features, and his shape the same: Od.4.200.129.
The same my practice, were my fate the same. Od.5.244.183.
The same my practice, were my fate the same. Od.5.244.183.
The same her parents, and her pow'r the same. Od.7.71.237.
The same her parents, and her pow'r the same. Od.7.71.237.
The same mild season gives the blooms to blow, Od.7.156.243.
(From the same lineage stern Æætes came, Od.10.161.348.
From the same fountain Amythaon rose, Od.11.315.397.
Lo! still the same Ulysses is your guide! Od.12.253.444.
O still the same Ulysses! she rejoin'd, Od.13.333.23.
In toils his equal, and in years the same. Od.15.223.79.
The Prince obedient to the same command, Od.19.17.193.
Too like Ulysses, and perhaps the same! Od.19.417.214.
The same you think, have all beholders thought. Od.19.449.216.
In the same moment forth Philætius flies, Od.21.421.280.
In the same urn a sep'rate space contains Od.24.99.353.

SAME (CONTINUED)
The same thy aspect, if the same thy care; ....Od.24.299.364.
The same thy aspect, if the same thy care; ....Od.24.299.364.

SAMIAN
When Reason doubtful, like the Samian letter, ...5.DunB4.151.356.
You, like the *Samian,* visit Lands unknown, ...6.96iii.17.275.
For ambush'd close beneath the *Samian* shore ....Od.4.896.160.
Their sail directed for the *Samian* coast, ...Od.4.1102.169.
Peers from the distant *Samian* shore retort; ....Od.19.150.199.
A *Samian* Peer, more studious than the rest ....Od.20.353.249.

SAMOS
Go, rase my *Samos,* let *Mycenè* fall, ...1.TrSt.368.425.
Between where *Samos* wide his Forests spreads, ...Il.24.103.539.
From *Samos,* circled with th' *Ionian* main, ...Od.1.317.48.
In *Samos* sands, or streights of *Ithaca,* .... Od.15.34.71.
The court proud *Samos* and *Dulichium* fills, ...Od.16.131.109.
Of *Samos;* twenty from *Zacynthus* coast: ....Od.16.271.118.

SAMOS'
To *Samos'* Isle she sent the wedded fair; ....Od.15.392.88.

SAMOTHRACIA
In *Samothracia,* on a Mountain's Brow, ...Il.13.19.105.

SAMPLE
And sends thee One, a Sample of her Host. ....Il.7.280.378.

SAMPLER
She furl'd her Sampler, and hawl'd in her Thread, ...6.96ii.5.270.

SAMSON
How *Samson* fell; and he whom *Dejanire* .... 2.ChWB.381.75.

SAMSON'S
How *Samson's* Heart false *Dalilah* did move, ...2.ChWB.381Z1.75.

SAMUEL
Rather with Samuel I beseech with tears ....6.2.17.6.
S[a]m[uel] M[olyneu]x, Esquire! ....6.58.16A.171.

SANCHO'S
Sancho's dread Doctor and his Wand-were there. ....3.Ep4.160.153.

SANCTIFIED
E'er taught to shine, or sanctified from shame ....6.130.14.358.

SANCTIFIES
'Tis Use alone that sanctifies Expence, ...3.Ep4.179.154.
In you, my *Lord,* Taste sanctifies Expence, ...3.Ep4.179A.154.
Truth guards the Poet, sanctifies the line, ...4.EpS2.246.327.

SANCTIFY
Yet more to sanctify the Word you send, ...Il.9.223.444.

SANCTIFY'D
E'er taught to shine, or sanctify'd from shame! ....3.EOM4.300.156.
Has sanctify'd whole Poems for an age. ....4.2HE1.114.205.
Wrapt round and sanctify'd with *Shakespear's* Name; ....6.98.18.283.
The Scourge of Pride, tho' sanctify'd or great, ...6.118.3.334.

SANCTION
The Stamp of Fate, and Sanction of the God: ....Il.1.685.120.
And add the Sanction of consid'rate Age; ....Il.3.146.197.
Let him demand the Sanction of the Night: ....Il.7.346.381.
That seals his Word; the Sanction of the God. ....Il.17.246.297.
The Sanction of th' assembled pow'rs report: ....Od.1.107.36.
By the firm sanction of his sov'reign will, ...Od.4.327.135.
To the firm sanction of thy fate attend! ....Od.4.639.149.
To the stern sanction of th' offended sky ....Od.4.652.150.
Sincere reveals the sanction of the skies: ....Od.19.651.227.
Vouchsafe the sanction of a sign above. ....Od.20.125.239.
That binds the Fates; the sanction of the God: ....Od.24.561.375.

SANCTITY
To pass my Age in Sanctity and Ease: ....2.ChJM.263.27.

SAND
That threats a Fight, and spurns the rising Sand. ....1.PSp.48.65.
Whose Ghost yet shiv'ring on *Cocytus'* Sand ....1.TrSt.419.427.
(The crooked Keel divides the yellow Sand) ....1.TrUl.46.467.
Build on the wave, or arch beneath the sand? ....3.EOM3.102.102.
Yet tames not this; it sticks to our last sand. ....3.Ep1.225.34.
(The crooked Keel divides the yellow Sand) ....Il.1.631.117.
Thick as Autumnal Leaves, or driving Sand, ...Il.2.970.169.
Broke short: the Fragments glitter'd on the Sand. ....Il.3.448.213.
First *Odius* falls, and bites the bloody Sand, ...Il.5.51.269.
Which stain'd with sacred Blood the blushing Sand. ....Il.5.107.272.
Stretch'd in their Blood lay gasping on the Sand? ....Il.5.865.307.
Vast Drifts of Sand shall change the former Shore; ....Il.7.554.392.
Now smooth'd with Sand, and levell'd by the Flood, ...Il.12.33.82.
The Point broke short, and sparkled in the Sand. ....Il.13.218.116.
Trail'd the long Lance that mark'd with Blood the Sand. ....Il.13.748.140.
A pond'rous Stone up-heaving from the Sand, ...Il.14.472.186.
From the high Poop he tumbles on the Sand, ...Il.15.506.216.
Polydamas laid *Otus* on the Sand, ...Il.15.614.220.
Mark with what Ease they sink into the Sand! ....Il.16.905.279.
The gushing Purple dy'd the thirsty Sand: ....Il.21.132.427.
Purple the Ground, and streak the sable Sand; ....Il.22.507.477.
And trail those graceful Honours on the Sand! ....Il.23.352.504.
And backward hurl'd *Ancæus* on the Sand, ...Il.23.730.519.
At each, nine oxen on the sand lay slain. ....Od.3.10.87.
For each a bed, she scoops the hilly sand: ....Od.4.592.148.
Couch'd on the sunny sand, the monsters sleep: ....Od.4.605.148.
To seek *Ulysses,* pac'd along the sand. ....Od.5.192.180.

SAND (CONTINUED)
No footing sure affords the faithless sand, ...Od.5.530.198.
(The vestures cleans'd o'erspread the shelly sand, ...Od.6.107.211.
Turn and return, and scarce imprint the sand. ....Od.8.414.286.
At once descend, and press the desart sand; ....Od.12.8.430.
Of great *Alcinous* falls, and stains the sand. ....Od.13.28.2.
(The crooked keel divides the yellow sand) ....Od.13.137.9.
The ship arriv'd: Forth-issuing on the sand, ...Od.14.382.53.

SAND'S
Quoth Sand's *To Waste–Paper.* .... 6.58.76A.174.

SANDAL
And on his foot the golden sandal shone. ....Od.20.158.241.

SANDALS
And painted Sandals on her Feet she wore: ....1.TrUl.107.469.
Th' embroider'd Sandals on his Feet were ty'd, ...Il.2.55.129.
Next on his Feet the shining Sandals bound; ....Il.10.28.3.
Last her fair Feet celestial Sandals grace. ....Il.14.215.170.
She said: the sandals of cælestial mold ....Od.1.124.38.
Embroider'd sandals glitter'd as he trod, ...Od.2.7.60.
Clasp'd on his feet th' embroider'd sandals shine, ...Od.4.417.140.
The glancing splendors as their sandals play. ....Od.8.306.279.
And painted Sandals on her Feet she wore. ....Od.13.274.19.
Then from the deck the Prince his sandals takes; ....Od.15.593.99.
Sandals, a sword, and robes, respect to prove, ...Od.16.79.106.
He brac'd his sandals on, and strode away: ....Od.16.167.110.
Fair on his feet the polish'd sandals shine, ...Od.17.5.132.
Embroider'd sandals, a rich cloak and vest, ...Od.21.367.277.

SANDS
O'er Golden Sands let rich *Pactolus* flow, ...1.PSp.61.66.
Red *Iber's* Sands, or *Ister's* foaming Flood; ....1.W-F.368.186.
Clear as a Glass, the shining Sands below; ....1.TrSP.180.401.
The faithless *Syrtes* and the moving Sands; ....1.TrSt.815.443.
Then on the Sands he rang'd his wealthy Store, ...1.TrUl.94.469.
Oft wou'd he say, Who builds his House on Sands, ...2.ChWB.347.74.
Than Leaves on Trees, or Sands upon the Shores; ....2.TemF.425.284.
Pensive they walk along the barren Sands: ....Il.1.427.108.
Beat the loose Sands, and thicken to the Fleet. ....Il.2.184.137.
A lasting Prodigy on *Aulis'* Sands. ....Il.2.385.145.
Supine he tumbles on the crimson'd Sands, ...Il.4.603.250.
Deep drove his Helmet in the Sands, and there ....Il.5.717.301.
Next *Teuthras'* Son distain'd the Sands with Blood, ...Il.6.15.323.
And large Libations drench'd the Sands around. ....Il.9.230.444.
Than Dust in Fields, or Sands along the Shore; ....Il.9.507.458.
And sprinkling, as he past, the Sands with Gore. ....Il.13.681.137.
But Heav'n forsakes not thee: O'er yonder Sands ....Il.14.165.165.
Erect, then roll'd along the Sands in Blood. ....Il.14.548.189.
And draws imagin'd Houses in the Sands; ....Il.15.417.213.
Than keep this hard-got Inch of barren Sands, ...Il.15.606.220.
In strong Convulsions panting on the Sands ....Il.17.366.301.
And *Troy's* black Sands must drink our Blood alike: ....Il.18.386.339.
The sacred Flood that rolls on golden Sands; ....Il.20.100.398.
Tears drop the Sands, and Tears their Arms bedew. ....Il.23.18A.487.
Tears bathe their Arms, and Tears the Sands bedew. ....Il.23.18.487.
Of golden Sleep, and starting from the Sands, ...Il.23.120.492.
A common Structure on the humble Sands; ....Il.23.307.501.
Quits his bright Car, and springs upon the Sands; ....Il.23.590.513.
And calls the Wrestlers to the level Sands: ....Il.23.815.521.
And spread soft hydes upon the yellow sands; ....Od.3.48.88.
His ragged claws are stuck with stones and sands; ....Od.5.552.199.
The desart sands, and now he looks a God. ....Od.6.292.224.
Up-bore my load, and prest the sinking sands ....Od.10.197.350.
Forth on the sands the victim oxen led: ....Od.13.215.16.
Then on the sands he rang'd his wealthy store, ...Od.13.261.18.
In *Samos* sands, or streights of *Ithaca,* .... Od.15.34.71.
Wide o'er the sands are spread the stiff'ning prey ....Od.22.430.309.
Drench with your blood your pillag'd country's sands? ....Od.24.137.354.

SANDY
Waste sandy Vallies, once perplex'd with Thorn, ...1.Mes.73.119.
O'er sandy Wilds were yellow Harvests spread, ...1.W-F.88.158.
In *other Parts* it leaves wide sandy Plains; ....1.EOC.55.245.
With heavy steps he sinks the sandy plain; ....1.TrPA.36.366.
(*Nestor,* whom *Pylos'* sandy Realms obey'd) ....Il.2.100.131.
And those who dwell along the sandy Shore, ...Il.2.690.159.
In ninety Sail, from *Pylos'* sandy Coast, ...Il.2.715.160.
His Troops, neglected on the sandy Shore, ...Il.2.939.168.
The whole Extent to *Pylos'* sandy Plain ....Il.9.201.442.
And now arriv'd, where, on the sandy Bay ....Il.9.243.444.
The whole Extent to *Pylos'* sandy Plain ....Il.9.388.452.
He now lies headless on the sandy Shore. ....Il.10.663.31.
Then the green Fields, and then the sandy Shore; ....Il.12.338.93.
From diff'rent Quarters sweep the sandy Plain; ....Il.13.425.126.
Now great *Sarpedon,* on the sandy Shore, ...Il.16.773.273.
The distant Band, that on the sandy Shore ....Il.17.215.295.
And deep beneath a sandy Mountain hurl'd ....Il.21.372.436.
(Such charge was giv'n 'em) to the sandy Shore; ....Il.23.153.495.
The Hero fixes in the sandy Shore: ....Il.23.1011.529.
Of sandy *Pyle,* the royal Youth shall haste. ....Od.1.119.38.
Thro' the wide Ocean first to sandy *Pyle,* .... Od.1.369.50.
Then slowly rising, o'er the sandy space ....Od.3.496.111.
He trod her footsteps in the sandy shore. ....Od.5.248.183.
And slept secure along the sandy shore. ....Od.9.173.312.
Thus he; then parting prints the sandy shore ....Od.13.80.5.
Thither his son from sandy *Pyle* repairs, ...Od.24.179.356.

SANDYS
Grave, righteous S[andys] joggs on till, past belief, ...4.1740.13.332*.
Within the same did *Sandys* lurk, ...6.58.27.171.
Quoth *Sandys: To Waste-Paper.* .... 6.58.76.174.
Quoth *Sandys: Into Waste*-Paper. ....6.58.76B.174.

SANDYS'
Ho! Master *Sam*, quoth *Sandys'* Sprite, ...6.58.37.172.

SANGAR'S
And *Sangar's* Stream ran purple with their Blood. ....Il.3.250.204.
In *Asius'* Shape, who reign'd by *Sangar's* Flood; ....Il.16.874.277.

SANGER
For who to sing for *Sanger* could refuse? ....6.12.2.37.

SANGER'S
Ozell, at *Sanger's* Call, invok'd his Muse, ...6.12.1.37.
His Numbers such, as Sanger's self might use. ....6.12.3.37.

SANGUIN
All pale and breathless on the sanguin Field. ....Il.8.384.416.
And ey'd him breathless on the sanguin Field. ....Il.8.384A.416.
His Eyes like *Gorgon* shot a sanguin Flame ....Il.8.418.417.
And drinks large Slaughter at her sanguin Eyes: ....Il.11.100.39.
Fires stream in Light'ning from his sanguin Eyes, ...Il.13.599.135.
Meanwhile fresh slaughter bathes the sanguin ground, ...Il.13.682.137.

SANGUINARY
O Peers! the sanguinary scheme suspend: ....Od.20.307.247.

SANGUINE
The flaming Rubies shew their sanguine Dye; ....2.TemF.251.275.
From sanguine *Sew[ell]* down to pidling *T[ibbald]s*: ....6.98.14A.283.
Strait to the Tree his sanguine Spires he roll'd, ...Il.2.374.145.
Now from nocturnal Sweat, and sanguine Stain, ...Il.10.673.31.
As the red Star now shows his sanguine Fires ....Il.11.83.38.
Defends him breathless on the sanguine Field, ...Il.11.333.49.
His sanguine Eyeballs glare with living Fire; ....Il.11.528.57.
A sanguine Torrent steeps the reeking Ground; ....Il.17.415.303.
Soon shall the sanguine Torrent spread so wide, ...Il.18.161.330.
And Earth is delug'd with the sanguine Show'rs. ....Il.20.576.418.
And altars blaze along his sanguine shore. ....Od.4.646.150.
Thick plumage, mingled with a sanguine show'r. ....Od.15.570.98.
With fiery glare his sanguine eye-balls shine, ...Od.19.519.221.
With sanguine drops the walls are rubied round: ....Od.20.426.254.

SANS
Yet swinken nat sans Secresie. ....6.14i.2.41.
Women, tho' nat sans Leacherie, ...6.14i.1A.41.

SAP
Which the kind Soil with milky Sap supplies; ....1.TrVP.103.381.
The Vital Sap then rising from below: ....2.ChJM.134.21.
Sufficient Sap, at once to bear and rot. ....6.49i.12.137.

SAPERTON'S
Join *Cotswold* Hills to *Saperton's* fair Dale, ...4.2HE2.257.183.

SAPHIRE
Loud from a saphire sky his thunder sounds: ....Od.20.128.239.

SAPHIRS
Bright azure Rays from lively Saphirs stream, ...2.TemF.252.275.

SAPHO
Yet once thy *Sapho* cou'd thy Cares employ, ...1.TrSP.49.395.
Those tempting Words were all to *Sapho* us'd. ....1.TrSP.68.396.
For whom should *Sapho* use such Arts as these? ....1.TrSP.87.397.
Still is there cause for *Sapho* still to love: ....1.TrSP.90.397.
No Lover's Gift your *Sapho* cou'd confer, ...1.TrSP.117.398.
No Gift on thee thy *Sapho* cou'd confer, ...1.TrSP.117A.398.
"Haste *Sapho*, haste, from high *Leucadia* throw ....1.TrSP.197.402.
"*Sapho* to *Phœbus* consecrates her Lyre, ...1.TrSP.215.403.
"What suits with *Sapho*, *Phœbus*, suits with thee; ....1.TrSP.216.403.
To distant Seas must tender *Sapho* fly? ....1.TrSP.219.403.
Poor *Sapho* dies while careless *Phaon* stays. ....1.TrSP.249.404.
Still *Sapho*—"*Hold!* for God-sake—you'll offend: ....4.Arbu.101.103.
Still *Sapho*—"*Hold!* nay see you—you'll offend: ....4.Arbu.101A.103.
Sapho can tell you how this Man was bit: ....4.Arbu.369.123.
As who knows Sapho, smiles at other whores. ....4.JD2.6.133.
Sapho enrag'd crys out your Back is round, ...6.129.3.357.
I answer thus—poor Sapho you grow grey, ...6.129.7.357.

SAPHO'S
Can *Phaon's* Eyes forget his *Sapho's* Hand? ....1.TrSP.2.393.
And the wide World resounds with *Sapho's* Praise. ....1.TrSP.32.394.

SAPP'D
The sapp'd Foundations by thy Force shall fall, ...Il.7.552.392.

SAPPHICK
The softer Spirit of the *Sapphick* Muse. ....2.TemF.225.273.

SAPPHO
Or Sappho at her toilet's greasy task, ...3.Ep2.25.52.
With Sappho fragrant at an ev'ning Mask; ....3.Ep2.26.52.
Why she and Sappho raise that monstrous sum? ....3.Ep3.123.102.
From furious *Sappho* scarce a milder Fate, ...4.HS1.83.13.
From furious *Sappho* yet a sadder Fate, ...4.HS1.83A.13.
In *Sappho* touch the *Failing of the Sex*, ...4.EpS1.15.298.
Tho' sprightly Sappho force our love and praise, ...6.106i.1.306.

SAPPHO'S
Or *Sappho's* self in glue (her rising task) ....3.Ep2.25B.52.
As *Sappho's* diamonds with her dirty smock, ...3.Ep2.24.51.

SAPPHOES
And cite those Sapphoes wee admire no more; ....6.43.2.120.

SAPS
If secret Gold saps on from knave to knave. ....3.Ep3.38.88.
The Weight of Waters saps the yielding Wall, ...Il.12.25.82.

SARAH
Like *Sarah* or *Rebecca* lead her Life: ....2.ChJM.312.29.
Like *Sarah* and *Rebecca* lead her Life: ....2.ChJM.312A.29.

SARCENET
Whose sarcenet skirts are edg'd with flamy gold, ...5.DunA3.250.178.

SARON
See spicy Clouds from lowly *Saron* rise, ...1.Mes.27.115.

SARPEDON
'Till bold *Sarpedon* rush'd into the Field; ....1.TrES.4.449.
'Til great *Sarpedon* tow'r'd amid the Field; ....1.TrES.4A.449.
Resolv'd alike, Divine *Sarpedon* glows ....1.TrES.21.450.
Divine *Sarpedon* with Regret beheld ....1.TrES.119.454.
When now *Sarpedon* his brave Friends beheld ....1.TrES.209A.457.
And first *Sarpedon* tost his weighty Lance, ...1.TrES.282.460.
And first *Sarpedon* whirl'd his weighty Lance, ...1.TrES.282A.460.
And from the Fight convey *Sarpedon* slain; ....1.TrES.325.461.
Receiv'd *Sarpedon*, at the God's Command, ...1.TrES.346.462.
Which blameless *Glaucus* and *Sarpedon* lead; ....Il.2.1069.172.
Sarpedon first his ardent Soul express'd, ...Il.5.573.296.
Now meet thy Fate, and by *Sarpedon* slain ....Il.5.812.305.
With Joy *Sarpedon* view'd the wish'd Relief, ...Il.5.840.305.
His mournful Friends divine *Sarpedon* laid: ....Il.5.853.306.
Divine *Sarpedon* the last Band obey'd, ...Il.12.115.85.
Till great *Sarpedon* tow'r'd amid the Field; ....Il.12.348.94.
Resolv'd alike, divine *Sarpedon* glows ....Il.12.365.94.
Divine *Sarpedon* with Regret beheld ....Il.12.473.99.
Ev'n in my lov'd Son, divine *Sarpedon* falls! ....Il.15.72.199.
When now *Sarpedon* his brave Friends beheld ....Il.16.512.263.
And first *Sarpedon* whirl'd his weighty Lance, ...Il.16.587.267.
Low in the Dust is great *Sarpedon* laid, ...Il.16.641.269.
See! where in Dust the great *Sarpedon* lies, ...Il.16.663.270.
Now great *Sarpedon*, on the sandy Shore, ...Il.16.773.273.
And from the Fight convey *Sarpedon* slain; ....Il.16.812.274.
Receiv'd *Sarpedon*, at the God's Command, ...Il.16.833.275.
Thy Friend *Sarpedon* proves his base Neglect: ....Il.17.166.294.
While unreveng'd the great *Sarpedon* falls? ....Il.17.168.294.
Arms, which of late divine *Sarpedon* wore, ...Il.23.943.526.

SARPEDON'S
Sarpedon's Friend; Across the Warrior's Way, ...1.TrES.99.453.
Not unreveng'd to bear *Sarpedon's* Death. ....1.TrES.307.461.
Burns with Desire *Sarpedon's* Strength to prove; ....Il.5.778.303.
Both strook, both wounded, but *Sarpedon's* slew: ....Il.5.815.305.
Sarpedon's Thigh, had robb'd the Chief of Breath; ....Il.5.822.305.
Crown'd with *Sarpedon's* Birth th' Embrace of *Jove*) ....Il.6.244.338.
Sarpedon's Friend; A-cross the Warrior's way, ...Il.12.453.98.
Sarpedon's Friends, *Amisodarus'* Seed; ....Il.16.389.258.
Not unreveng'd to bear *Sarpedon's* Death. ....Il.16.612.268.
Sarpedon's Arms and honour'd Corse again! ....Il.17.180.294.

SARSENET
Whose sarsenet skirts are edg'd with flamy gold, ...5.DunB3.254.332.

SAT
He put on careless Airs, and sat and sung. ....2.ChWB.240.68.
Or sat delighted in the thick'ning shade, ...3.Ep4.90.146.
To see the circle sat, of all unseen. ....Od.20.464.256.

SAT'RIST
This dreaded Sat'rist *Dennis* will confess ....4.Arbu.370.123.

SATAN
And sink downright to *Satan* when I die. ....2.ChJM.118.20.
Wife, son, and daughter, Satan, are thy prize, ...3.Ep3.399A.124.
But Satan now is wiser than of yore, ...3.Ep3.351.122.
Wife, son, and daughter, Satan, are thy own, ...3.Ep3.399.124.
Satan himself feels far less joy than they. ....4.JD2.90.141.

SATANS
Nor *Satans* self shall joy so much as hee ....4.JD2A.92.140.

SATE
The Fair sate panting at a *Courtier's Play*, ...1.EOC.540.299.
He sate, pursu'd by all his flocks of sheep. ....1.TrPA.42.367.
Sate heavy on his Heart, and broke his Rest; ....1.TrSt.550.433.
Justin, who silent sate, and heard the Man, ...2.ChJM.176.23.
The beauteous Dame sate smiling at the Board, ...2.ChJM.341.30.
Restless he sate, invoking ev'ry Pow'r ....2.ChJM.351.31.
And sipt his Cordial as he sate upright: ....2.ChJM.387.33.
And supp'd his Cordial as he sate upright: ....2.ChJM.387B.33.
And close beside him sate the gentle *May*: ....2.ChJM.413.34.
Ev'n tho' the Pope himself had sate at Table. ....2.ChWB.181.65.
Th'impending Woe sate heavy on his Breast. ....2.RL2.54.163.
Nay, *Poll* sate mute, and *Shock* was most Unkind! ....2.RL4.164.197.
Clapt his glad Wings, and sate to view the Fight: ....2.RL5.54.203.
There sate *Zamolxis* with erected Eyes, ...2.TemF.123.264.
The *Mantuan* there in sober Triumph sate, ...2.TemF.200.271.
Sate fix'd in Thought the mighty *Stagyrite*; ....2.TemF.233.274.
'Till then by Nature crown'd, each Patriarch sate, ...3.EOM3.215.114.
I wish'd the man a dinner, and sate still: ....4.Arbu.152.107.
Sate full-blown *Bufo*, puff'd by ev'ry quill; ....4.Arbu.232.112.
Who, tho' the House was up, delighted sate, ...4.2HE2.186.177.
When all their Lordships had sate late.) ....4.HS6.188.261.
And down the Mice sate, *tête à tête* , ...4.HS6.199.263.
She ey'd the Bard, where supperless he sate, ...5.DunA1.109.76.
Studious he sate, with all his books around, ...5.DunA1.111.77.
Great Tibbald sate: The proud Parnassian sneer, ...5.DunA2.5.97.
Who sate the nearest, by the words o'ercome ....5.DunA2.369.145.
Swearing and supperless the Hero sate, ...5.DunB1.115.278.

SATE 248 SATURN'S

SATE (CONTINUED)

Great Cibber sate: the proud Parnassian sneer, ...5.DunB2.5.296.
Who sate the nearest, by the words o'ercome, ...5.DunB2.401.316.
Still with dry Eyes the Tory *Celia* sate, ...6.33.2.99.
Firm on his Front his Beaver sate, ...6.79.25.218.
When on the Monarch's ample Hand you sate, ...6.96iv.99.279.
Where, nobly-pensive, ST. JOHN sate and thought; ....6.142.10.383.
There, nobly-pensive, ST. JOHN sate and thought; ....6.142.10A.383.
Here, nobly-pensive, ST. JOHN sate and thought; ....6.142.10B.383.
He said and sate: when *Calchas* thus reply'd, ...Il.1.91.91.
Then sternly silent sate: With like Disdain, ...Il.1.327.103.
But raging still amidst his Navy sate ....Il.1.634.118.
The Thund'rer sate, where old *Olympus* shrouds ....Il.1.648.118.
He spoke, and sate; when *Nestor* rising said, ...Il.2.99.131.
Trembling he sate, and shrunk in abject Fears, ...Il.2.330.143.
There sate the Seniors of the *Trojan* Race, ...Il.3.191.200.
Both Armies sate, the Combate to survey, ...Il.3.406.212.
They sate, and listen'd to the dying Sounds. ....Il.5.48.268.
To *Mars*, who sate remote, they bent their way; ....Il.5.445.289.
To cool his glowing Wound he sate apart, ...Il.5.990.314.
There sullen sate beneath the Sire of Gods, ...Il.5.1065.317.
Glorious he sate, in Majesty restor'd, ...Il.5.1118.321.
Oppos'd to those, where *Priam's* Daughters sate: ....Il.6.309.341.
Here, hid from human Eyes, thy Brother sate, ...Il.6.422.347.
The *Trojan* Peers in nightly Council sate: ....Il.7.415.385.
The Senior spoke, and sate. To whom reply'd ....Il.7.428.385.
The Troops exulting sate in order round, ...Il.8.685.428.
Sate on each Face, and sadden'd ev'ry heart. ....Il.9.4.431.
Full opposite he sate, and listen'd long ....Il.9.253.445.
There sate the mournful Kings: when *Neleus'* Son, ...Il.10.239.12.
Wrapt in the Blaze of boundless Glory sate; ....Il.11.109.39.
He sate; and round him cast his azure Eyes, ...Il.13.21.105.
Emerg'd, he sate; and mourn'd his *Argives* slain. ....Il.13.26.105.
On golden Clouds th' immortal Synod sate; ....Il.13.662.137.
Sate *Sleep*, in Likeness of the Bird of Night, ...Il.14.328.178.
On *Ida's* Summit sate imperial *Jove:* .... Il.15.6.194.
There sate the Pow'rs in awful Synod plac'd; ....Il.15.92.200.
Sate stedfast Care, and low'ring Discontent. ....Il.15.113.200.
Sullen he sate, and curb'd the rising Groan. ....Il.15.161.202.
She said, and sate: the God that gilds the Day, ...Il.15.168.203.
There sate th' Eternal; He, whose Nod controuls ....Il.15.172.203.
Sate doubtful Conquest hov'ring o'er the Field; ....Il.15.361.210.
Still in the Tent *Patroclus* sate, to tend ....Il.15.452.215.
Shrunk up he sate, with wild and haggard Eye, ...Il.16.488.262.
Beheld with Pity; as apart he sate, ...Il.17.227.296.
There sate *Achilles*, shaded by his Sails, ...Il.18.5.323.
Pensive he sate; for all that Fate design'd, ...Il.18.7.323.
He reach'd the Throne where pensive *Thetis* sate; ....Il.18.492.345.
From his Ambrosial Head, where perch'd she sate, ...Il.19.125.377.
And *Greece* around sate thrill'd with sacred Awe. ....Il.19.266.383.
(The Work of *Vulcan)* sate the Pow'rs around. ....Il.20.18.393.
(The Work of *Vulcan)* sate the Gods around. ....Il.20.18A.393.
In Circle close each heav'nly Party sate, ...Il.20.184.401.
In aid of him, beside the Beech he sate, ...Il.21.645.449.
Sate all the blustring Brethren of the Sky. ....Il.23.247.499.
Concludes; then sate, stiff with unwieldy Age. ....Il.23.424.506.
The Monarch sate; from whence with sure survey ....Il.23.534.511.
Pensive she sate, revolving Fates to come, ...Il.24.113.539.
Sate bath'd in Tears, and answer'd Groan with Groan. ....Il.24.198.545.
(The Work of Soldiers) where the Hero Sate. ....Il.24.556.559.
There sate the Hero; *Alcimus* the brave, ...Il.24.580.560.
Where full before him rev'rend *Priam* sate: ....Il.24.747.568.
Soon as in solemn form th' assembly sate, ...Od.2.11.60.
Then silent sate—at length *Antinous* burns ....Od.2.93.65.
Where sate, encompast with his sons, the Sire. ....Od.3.42.88.
Where *Nestor* sate with youthful *Thrasymed.* .... Od.3.50.89.
Yet what I learn'd, attend; as here I sate, ...Od.3.225.96.
The old man early rose, walk'd forth, and sate ....Od.3.518.112.
Where antient *Neleus* sate, a rustic throne; ....Od.3.521.113.
Where sate *Atrides'* midst his bridal friends, ...Od.4.4.119.
Where circled with his Peers *Atrides* sate: ....Od.4.62.122.
On *Gyræ*, safe *Oilean Ajax* sate, ...Od.4.672.151.
Antinous sate spectator of the sport; ....Od.4.850.158.
She sate and sung; the rocks resound her lays: ....Od.5.74.176.
All on the lonely shore he sate to weep, ...Od.5.105.177.
There sate all desolate, and sigh'd alone, ...Od.5.201.181.
He fill'd the throne where *Mercury* had sate. ....Od.5.250.183.
Plac'd at the helm he sate, and mark'd the skies, ...Od.5.345.188.
Mean-time *Phæacia's* peers in council sate; ....Od.6.65.208.
There next his side the god-like hero sate; ....Od.7.228.247.
Encircled by huge multitudes, he sate: ....Od.8.62.265.
Aloft, the King in pomp Imperial sate. ....Od.8.458.288.
My life, thy gift I boast! He said, and sate ....Od.8.511.290.
We sate indulging in the genial rite: ....Od.9.189.313.
With hands extended in the midst he sate; ....Od.9.496.326.
They sate indulging in the genial rite. ....Od.10.209.350.
Pensive I sate; my tears bedew'd the bed; ....Od.10.589.372.
She sate in silence while the tale I tell, ...Od.12.45.431.
He sate, and ey'd the sun, and wish'd the night; ....Od.13.36.3.
Ulysses found him, busied as he sate ....Od.14.7.35.
Here sate *Eumæus*, and his cares apply'd ....Od.14.25.35.
Down sate the Sage; and cautious to withstand, ...Od.14.35.36.
Then sate companion of the friendly feast, ...Od.14.95.40.
Who sate delighted at his servant's board; ....Od.14.488.59.
He sate, and sweet refection cheer'd his soul. ....Od.14.501.60.
Sate in the Cottage, at their rural feast: ....Od.15.323.85.
There sate the Prince: the feast *Eumæus* spread; ....Od.16.49.104.
He spoke and sate. The Prince with transport flew, ...Od.16.234.114.
With clouded looks, a pale assembly sate. ....Od.16.361.123.
Then moving from the strand, apart they sate, ...Od.16.376.124.
Arriv'd, with wild tumultuous noise they sate ....Od.16.424.127.
Past on, and sate by faithful *Mentor's* side; ....Od.17.79.136.
Lowly she sate, and with dejected view ....Od.17.112.137.
Observant of his voice, *Eumæus* sate ....Od.17.682.165.
While fix'd in thought the pensive Heroe sate, ...Od.18.1.166.
Due-distant for discourse the Heroe sate; ....Od.19.123.198.

SATE (CONTINUED)

And pensive sate, and tears began to flow. ....Od.21.58.262.
There in her chamber as she sate apart, ...Od.21.383.278.
Immur'd we sate, and catch'd each passing sound; ....Od.23.44.321.
Oppos'd, before the shining Fire she sate. ....Od.23.92.323.
Amaz'd she sate, and impotent to speak; ....Od.23.96.324.
Radiant before his gazing Consort sate. ....Od.23.164.328.
Then sad in council all the Seniors sate, ...Od.24.481.371.
Now sate *Ulysses* at the rural feast, ...Od.24.564.375.

SATED

And now (each sated with the genial feast, ...Od.15.158.76.
Sated they rose, and all retir'd to rest. ....Od.19.498.220.
All cheaply sated at another's cost! ....Od.20.216.243.
Sated at length they rise, and bid prepare ....Od.20.465.256.

SATELLITES

Why JOVE's Satellites are less than JOVE? ....3.EOM1.42.18.

SATIATE

In Life's cool evening satiate of applause, ...4.1HE1.9.279.
Now May'rs and Shrieves all hush'd and satiate lay, ...5.DunA1.89.70.
Now May'rs and Shrieves all hush'd and satiate lay, ...5.DunB1.91.276.
The bravest soon are satiate of the Field; ....Il.19.220.382.
Satiate at length with unavailing Woes, ...Il.24.647.563.
Their hunger satiate, and their thirst represt, ...Od.5.255.184.
Now pleas'd and satiate from the social rite ....Od.7.248.248.
Satiate we slept: But when the sacred dawn ....Od.9.197.314.
The banquet past, and satiate ev'ry man, ...Od.15.324.85.

SATIETY

Without satiety, tho' e'er so blest, ...3.EOM4.317.158.
And glutt with full satiety of days; ....6.21.40.70.
To melt in full Satiety of Grief! ....Il.22.549.479.
To full satiety of grief she mourns, ...Od.21.59.262.

SATIRE

Pulpits their *Sacred Satire* learn'd to spare, ...1.EOC.550.302.
There are to whom my Satire seems too bold, ...4.HS1.2.5.
All these, my modest Satire bad *translate*, ...4.Arbu.189.109.
All these, my modest Satire bid *translate*, ... 4.Arbu.189A.109.
Make Satire a Lampoon, and Fiction, Lye. ....4.Arbu.302.117.
Let never honest Man my satire dread, ...4.Arbu.303A.117.
"Satire or Sense alas! can *Sporus* feel? ....4.Arbu.307.118.
" Satire or Shame alas! can *Sporus* feel? ....4.Arbu.307A.118.
"Satire or Sense alas! he cannot feel? ....4.Arbu.307B.118.
Sharp Satire that, and that Pindaric lays? ....4.2HE2.83.171.
Hence Satire rose, that just the medium hit, ...4.2HE1.261.217.
Satire be kind, and let the wretch alone. ....4.1HE1.135.289.
Adieu Distinction, Satire, Warmth, and Truth! ....4.EpS1.64.302.
So—Satire is no more—I feel it die— ....4.EpS1.83.304.
F. Why so? if Satire know its Time and Place, ...4.EpS1.87.305.
But let all Satire in all Changes spare ....4.EpS1.91.305.
Come on then Satire! gen'ral, unconfin'd, ...4.EpS2.14.314.
Down, down, proud Satire! tho' a Realm be spoil'd, ...4.EpS2.38.315.
Fr. stop! stop! *P.* Must Satire then, nor *rise*, nor *fall* ....4.EpS2.52.315.
Down, down, proud Satire! tho' a Land be spoil'd, ...4.EpS2.38A.315.
Praise cannot stoop, like Satire, to the Ground; ....4.EpS2.110.319.
But History and Satire held their head: ....5.DunB4.39Z2.344.
Nor had the gentle Satire caus'd complaining, ...6.12.8A.37.
May *Satire* ne'er befool ye, or beknave ye, ...6.40.9.112.
Should modest Satire bid all these *translate*, ... 6.98.39.284.

SATIRE'S

Satire's my Weapon, but I'm too discreet ....4.HS1.69.11.

SATIRES

See *Libels, Satires—here* you have it—read. ....4.HS1.149.19.
See *Libels, Satires—there* you have it—read. ....4.Hs1.149A.19.
P. Libels and *Satires!* lawless Things indeed! ....4.HS1.150.21.
And paid for all my Satires, all my Rhymes: ....4.JD4.6.27.

SATISFACTION

The windy satisfaction of the tongue. ....Od.4.1092.169.

SATISFIE

And more confound our Choice than satisfie: .... 6.17iii.3.57.

SATISFY'D

No cavern'd Hermit, rests self-satisfy'd. ....3.EOM4.42.132.
Be satisfy'd, I'll do my best:— ....4.HS6.78.255.
Is satisfy'd, secure, and innocent: ....6.16.4.53.
From Nature's temp'rate feast rose satisfy'd, ...6.112.9.318.

SATNIO

And till'd the Banks where silver *Satnio* flow'd. ....Il.6.42.325.
And rul'd the Fields where silver *Satnio* flow'd) ....Il.21.99.425.

SATNIO'S

Amidst her Flocks on *Satnio's* silver Shore) ....Il.14.520.188.

SATNIUS

(*Satnius* the brave, whom beauteous *Neis* bore ....Il.14.519.188.

SATURN

Where curs'd *Iäpetus* and *Saturn* dwell, ...Il.8.599.425.
What-time old *Saturn*, from *Olympus* cast, ...Il.14.234.172.
Three Brother Deities from *Saturn* came, ...Il.15.210.204.
And all the Gods that round old *Saturn* dwell, ...Il.15.254.207.

SATURN'S

To *Saturn's* Son be all your Vows addrest: ....Il.7.230.376.
(Heav'ns awful Empress, *Saturn's* other Heir) ....Il.8.465.419.
Saturn's great Sons in fierce Contention vy'd, ...Il.13.436.126.
Great *Saturn's* Heir, and Empress of the Skies! ....Il.14.277.175.

SATURNIA 249 SAVE

SATURNIA
He said; *Saturnia,* ardent to obey, ...Il.5.956.312.
Saturnia lends the Lash; the Coursers fly; ....Il.8.476.419.
Meantime *Saturnia* from *Olympus'* Brow, ...Il.14.179.165.
Whilst from *Olympus* pleas'd *Saturnia* flew. ....Il.14.258.173.
Sweet pleasing Sleep! (*Saturnia* thus began) ....Il.14.266.174.
Go wait the Thund'rer's Will (*Saturnia* cry'd) ....Il.15.164.202.
Saturnia ask'd an Oath, to vouch the Truth, ...Il.19.109.376.
Saturnia, Majesty of Heav'n, defy'd. ....Il.20.98.398.
(These with a gather'd Mist *Saturnia* shrouds, ...Il.21.7.421.
Ah why, *Saturnia!* must thy Son engage ....Il.21.432.438.
Not so *Saturnia* bore the vaunting Maid; ....Il.21.554.444.

SATURNIA'S
When *Jove,* dispos'd to tempt *Saturnia's* Spleen, ...Il.4.7.221.
That heard, deep Anguish stung *Saturnia's* Soul; ....Il.8.240.409.
Ah yet, will *Venus* aid *Saturnia's* Joy, ...Il.14.221.172.
His warm Intreaty touch'd *Saturnia's* Ear; ....Il.21.442.438.

SATURNIAN
To hatch a new Saturnian age of Lead. ....5.DunA1.26.63.
Th' Augustus born to bring Saturnian times: ....5.DunA3.318.186.
To hatch a new Saturnian age of Lead. ....5.DunB1.28.271.
Th' Augustus born to bring Saturnian times. ....5.DunB3.320.335.
And bring Saturnian days of Lead and Gold. ....5.DunB4.16.341.
And brings the true Saturnian age of lead. ....6.106iv.12.307.

SATURNIUS
And thus return'd. Austere *Saturnius,* say, ...Il.1.714.122.
As the red Comet from *Saturnius* sent ....Il.4.101.225.
Then bids *Saturnius* bear his Oath in mind; ....Il.19.119.376.
But great *Saturnius* is the Source of mine. ....Il.21.204.429.

SATURNUS
Call the black Gods that round Saturnus dwell, ...Il.14.309A.177.

SATYR
Had not her Sister Satyr held her head: ....5.DunB4.42.345.
Nor had the toothless Satyr caus'd complaining, ...6.12.8.37.
Compare De Foe's *Burlesque with* Dryden's *Satyr,* ....6.17iv.11.59.
Censor of Tories, President of Satyr, ...6.48ii.2.134.
But thou too gently hast laid on thy Satyr; ....6.48iii.7.134.
If any Fool is by our Satyr bit, ...6.60.23.178.
Maul'd human *Wit* in one thick Satyr, ...6.101.9.290.
Satyr still just with humour ever new; ....6.125.1Z4.349.

SATYR'S
Whose *Satyr's sacred,* and whose Rage *secure.* ....4.JD4.283.49.

SATYRION
Satyrion near, with hot *Eringo's* stood, ...2.ChJM.377.32.

SATYRIST
Blest Satyrist! who touch'd the Mean so true, ...6.118.7.334.
—Tis not the *sober Satyrist* you should dread, ...6.120.11.339.

SATYRS
Rough *Satyrs* dance, and *Pan* applauds the Song: ....1.PSu.50.75.
Leave dang'rous *Truths* to unsuccessful *Satyrs,* ....1.EOC.592.307.
How oft the *Satyrs* and the wanton *Fawns,* ....1.TrVP.21.378.

SAUCER
With saucer Eyes of Fire, ...6.58.14.171.

SAUL
While tow'ring o'er your Alphabet, like Saul, ...5.DunB4.217.363.

SAUNTER'D
Led by my hand, he saunter'd Europe round, ...5.DunB4.311.374.

SAV'D
But sav'd from Death, our *Argives* yearly pay ....1.TrSt.662.438.
All Europe sav'd, yet Britain not betray'd. ....3.Ep1.143.26.
Curse the sav'd candle, and unop'ning door; ....3.Ep3.196.109.
The wretch, who living sav'd a candle's end: ....3.Ep3.292.117.
The Rights a Court attack'd, a Poet sav'd. ....4.2HE1.224.215.
There sav'd by spice, like mummies, many a year, ...5.DunA1.131.80.
Cou'd Troy be sav'd by any single hand, ...5.DunA1.187.85.
And Quarles is sav'd by Beauties not his own. ....5.DunB1.140.280.
There, sav'd by spice, like Mummies, many a year, ...5.DunB1.151.281.
Could Troy be sav'd by any single hand, ...5.DunB1.197.283.
Embrac'd me on the cross, and sav'd me by thy death. ....6.25.10.77.
Perhaps, by its own ruins sav'd from flame, ...6.71.15.203.
I half could wish this people might be sav'd. ....6.146.4.389.
I half could wish this people should be sav'd. ....6.146.4A.389.
From mortal Madness scarce was sav'd by Flight. ....Il.5.1087.318.
Sav'd I, for this, his Fav'rite *Son distress'd, ...Il.8.441.418.
Her Wives, her Infants by my Labours sav'd; ....Il.9.429.453.
He try'd it once, and scarce was sav'd by Fate. ....Il.9.468.455.
The Warrior heard, he vanquish'd, and he sav'd. ....Il.9.706.469.
And sav'd from Numbers, to his Car conveys. ....Il.11.609.61.
Had sav'd the Father, and now saves the Son. ....Il.15.631.220.
The Fleet once sav'd, desist from farther chace, ...Il.16.116.241.
But when the Fleets are sav'd from Foes and Fire, ...Il.16.302.254.
Has sav'd thee, and the partial God of Light. ....Il.20.520.416.
What Numbers had been sav'd by *Hector's* Flight? ....Il.22.143.459.
Sav'd from the Flames, for hungry Dogs to rend. ....Il.23.225.498.
Thus sav'd from death they gain'd the *Phæstan* shores, ...Od.3.380.105.
Sav'd from the jaws of death by heav'n's decree, ...Od.5.141.178.
And Prudence sav'd him in the needful hour. ....Od.5.557.199.
And sav'd a life of miseries to come!) ....Od.14.304.50.
He heard, he sav'd, he plac'd me at his side; ....Od.14.309.50.
Who sav'd thy father with a friendly part? ....Od.16.443.128.
Ulysses sav'd him from th' avenger's hand. ....Od.16.447.128.
How sav'd from storms *Phæacia's* coast he trod, ...Od.23.365.342.

SAV'RY
Black from the Tents the sav'ry Vapors flew. ....Il.7.559.392.
And wholsome Garlick crown'd the sav'ry Treat. ....Il.11.771.69.
And with keen gust the sav'ry viands share. ....Od.4.300.133.
With hunger keen devours the sav'ry feast; ....Od.14.132.42.
The sav'ry cates on glowing embers cast ....Od.20.33.234.

SAVAGE
Wolves gave thee suck, and savage Tygers fed. ....1.PAu.90.86.
To Savage Beasts and Savage Laws a Prey, ...1.W-F.45.153.
To Savage Beasts and Savage Laws a Prey, ...1.W-F.45.153.
And savage Howlings fill the sacred Quires. ....1.W-F.72.156.
Still fond and proud of *Savage Liberty,* ....1.EOC.650.313.
One savage Heart, or teach it how to love? ....1.TrSP.243.404.
The Savage Hunter, and the haunted Wood; ....1.TrSt.324.423.
Where once his Steeds their savage Banquet found, ...1.TrSt.390.426.
So stalks the Lordly Savage o'er the Plain, ...1.TrES.15.450.
While the grim Savage grinds with foamy Jaws ....1.TrES.297.460.
On savage stocks inserted learn to bear; ....3.EOM2.182.77.
He saves from famine, from the savage saves; ....3.EOM3.64.98.
And turn'd on Man a fiercer savage, Man. ....3.EOM3.168.110.
"A pretty kind of savage Scene! ....4.HS6.177.261.
"But Lord, my Friend, this savage Scene! ....4.HS6.177A.261.
Tyrants no more their savage nature kept, ...6.32.7.96.
By Saint, by Savage, and by Sage, ...6.50.3.145.
By Saint, by Savage, or by Sage, ...6.50.3B.145.
See arts her savage sons controul, ...6.51i.21.152.
To Mountain-wolves and all the Savage race, ...6.65.2.192.
To Mountain Bores and all the Savage race, ...6.65.2A.192.
The savage Race withdrew, nor dar'd ....6.82vii.3.233.
And Wars and Horrors are thy savage Joy. ....Il.1.232.98.
Where rich *Henetia* breeds her savage Mules, ...Il.2.1035.171.
The Lordly Savage rends the panting Prey ....Il.3.40A.190.
In Woods and Wilds to wound the Savage Race; ....Il.5.66.269.
The Savage wound, he rowzes at the Smart, ...Il.5.177.275.
(Fair Nurse of Fountains, and of Savage Game) ....Il.8.58.398.
The Savage seizes, draws, and rends the last: ....Il.11.230.45.
The Lordly Savage vindicates his Prey. ....Il.11.603.61.
So stalks the lordly Savage o'er the Plain, ...Il.12.359.94.
And hardy *Thracians* tame the savage Horse; ....Il.13.8.104.
A Prey to every Savage of the Wood; ....Il.13.144.111.
(Fair Nurse of Fountains and of savage Game) ....Il.15.171.203.
So when a Savage, ranging o'er the Plain, ...Il.15.702.223.
While the grim Savage grinds with foamy Jaws ....Il.16.602.267.
At length the sov'reign Savage wins the Strife, ...Il.16.997.281.
But if the Savage turns his glaring Eye, ...Il.17.815.320.
When the grim Savage to his rifled Den ....Il.18.373.339.
The bleeding Savage tumbles to the Ground: ....Il.19.278.383.
To his bold Spear the Savage turns alone, ...Il.20.204.402.
Thy certain Arrows pierce the savage Race? ....Il.21.562.445.
On their whole War, untam'd the Savage flies; ....Il.21.683.450.
Who hastes to murder with a savage Joy, ...Il.24.54.538.
Among a savage race, whose shelfy bounds ....Od.1.257.45.
Where savage Pyrates seek thro' seas unknown ....Od.3.88.90.
The monarch-savage rends the trembling prey. ....Od.4.454.141.
The mimic force of every savage shape: ....Od.4.564.147.
What savage beasts may wander in the waste? ....Od.5.609.201.
The land of *Cyclops* first; a savage kind, ...Od.9.119.308.
Where savage goats thro' pathless thickets rove: ....Od.9.136.311.
And try what social rites a savage lends: ....Od.9.270.318.
Fools that ye are! (the Savage thus replies, ...Od.9.325.319.
Th' astonisht Savage with a roar replies: ....Od.9.593.330.
Aloft he whirls, to crush the savage prey; ....Od.11.706.420.
Four savage dogs, a watchful guard, attend. ....Od.14.24.35.
The Monarch savage rends the panting prey: ....Od.17.145.138.
Him no fell Savage on the plain withstood, ...Od.17.382.150.
By death dis-rob'd of all their savage pow'rs, ...Od.19.381.212.
With glancing rage the tusky savage tore. ....Od.19.463.218.
Ulysses wav'd, to rouze the savage war. ....Od.19.510.221.
The savage from his leafy sounder flies: ....Od.19.518.221.
The savage renders vain the wound decreed, ...Od.19.523.221.
By savage hands his fleet and friends he lost; ....Od.23.344.341.
Or savage beasts his mangled reliques tear, ...Od.24.342.365.

SAVAGES
No wonder Savages or Subjects slain ....1.W-F.57A.154.
But Subjects starv'd while Savages were fed. ....1.W-F.60A.154.
Which monsters wild, and savages obey! ....1.TrPA.14.366.
(Mother of Savages, whose echoing Hills ....Il.14.321.178.
The rugged race of savages, unskill'd ....Od.9.147.311.

SAVD
Who to be savd by one, must damn the rest. ....6.82ix(b).2.234.

SAVE
In such a Cause disdain'd thy Life to save; ....1.TrSt.754.441.
I have a Soul to save as well as You; ....2.ChJM.578.43.
Help dearest Lord, and save at once the Life ....2.ChJM.724.49.
And bless those Souls my Conduct help'd to save! ....2.ChWB.439.78.
To save the Powder from too rude a Gale, ...2.RL2.93.165.
The same ambition can destroy or save, ...3.EOM2.201.79.
Fame but from death a villain's name can save, ...3.EOM4.249.151.
Truths would you teach, or save a sinking land? ....3.EOM4.265.153.
Now save a People, and now save a Groat. ....3.Ep1.145Z4.27.
Now save a People, and now save a Groat. ....3.Ep1.145Z4.27.
Must then at once (the character to save) ....3.Ep1.77.21.
Save just at dinner—then prefers, no doubt, ...3.Ep1.138.26.
Still tries to save the hallow'd taper's end, ...3.Ep1.239.36.
"Oh, save my Country, Heav'n!" shall be your last. ....3.Ep1.265.38.
Or find some Doctor that would save the life ....3.Ep3.95.97.
His givings rare, save farthings to the poor. ....3.Ep3.348.122.
Save but our *Army!* and let *Jove* incrust ....4.HS1.73.11.
See wretched *Monsieur* flies to save his Throat, ...4.HAdv.53.79.
The Youth might save much Trouble and Expence, ...4.HAdv.67.81.
Have I no Friend to serve, no Soul to save? ....4.Arbu.274.115.
May prompt and save His Life who cannot read: ....4.JD2A.16.132.

SAVE (CONTINUED)

He starves with cold to save them from the Fire; .... 4.JD2.72.139.
Or Gods to save them in a trice! .... 4.HS6.217.263.
Save when they lose a Question, or a Job. .... 4.EpS1.104.305.
To save a Bishop, may I name a Dean? .... 4.EpS2.33.314.
To save thee in th' infectious office *dies.* .... 4.1740.76.336.
Here studious I unlucky moderns save, ... 5.DunA1.161.82.
And save the state by cackling to the Tories? .... 5.DunA1.192.86.
"God save King Tibbald!" Grubstreet alleys roar. .... 5.DunA1.256.94.
And *Grubstreet* garrets roar, God save the king. .... 5.DunA1.256A.94.
And the hoarse nation croak'd, God save King Log! .... 5.DunA1.260.95.
And the loud nation croak'd, God save King Log! .... 5.DunA1.260A.95.
Yet sure had Heav'n decreed to save the State, ... 5.DunB1.195.283.
And cackling save the Monarchy of Tories? .... 5.DunB1.212.285.
"God save king Cibber!" mounts in ev'ry note. .... 5.DunB1.320.293.
Familiar White's , "God save king Colley!" cries; .... 5.DunB1.321.293.
"God save king Colley!" Drury-lane replies: .... 5.DunB1.322.293.
And the hoarse nation croak'd, "God save King Log!" .... 5.DunB1.330.294.
As erst Medea (cruel, so to save!) .... 5.DunB4.121.353.
G—d save the pretty Lady's there! .... 6.10.110.27.
'Tis Thou shalt save him from insidious wrongs, ... 6.21.5.69.
All these were join'd in one, yet fail'd to save .... 6.27.7.81.
And from all Wits that have a Knack Gad save ye. .... 6.40.10.112.
Save Three-pence, and his Soul. .... 6.47.12.128.
To save this Land from dangerous Mystery. .... 6.48iii.6.134.
Who save our Eyesight, or wou'd save our State, ... 6.48iv.12.136.
Who save our Eyesight, or wou'd save our State, ... 6.48iv.12.136.
Save me alike from foolish Pride, ... 6.50.33.148.
The gaudy Dress will save the Fool. .... 6.64.22.190.
Mercy alike to kill or save. .... 6.69ii.8.199.
"No *Sheet* is here to save thee: .... 6.79.78.220.
Of some Dry-Nurse to save her Hen; .... 6.93.18.257.
Those *Spectacles*, ordain'd thine Eyes to save, ... 6.96iv.75.278.
Thus shall you save its half-extinguish'd Life. .... 6.100v.2.289.
Oh! save the Salary, and drink the Sack! .... 6.116v.6.327.
Yes— *Save my Country, Heav'n,* .... 6.123.8.344.
The only way to save 'em from our A[sse]s. .... 6.131ii.2.360.
Could save a Mother's justest Pride from fate, ... 6.132.3.362.
Could save a Parent's justest Pride from fate, ... 6.132.3A.362.
'Tis time to save the few Remains of War. .... Il.1.82.90.
Forc'd to deplore, when impotent to save: .... Il.1.322.103.
Now shameful Flight alone can save the Host, ... Il.2.145.135.
And from Destruction save the *Trojan* Race. .... Il.3.210.201.
To save a trembling, heartless, dastard Race? .... Il.4.285.234.
And save a Life, the Bulwark of our War. .... Il.5.307.281.
Their Wives, their Infants, and their Altars save. .... Il.5.592.296.
Shall save a *Trojan* from our boundless Rage: .... Il.6.72.327.
No Force can then resist, no Flight can save, ... Il.6.630.358.
Oh turn and save from *Hector's* direful Rage .... Il.8.121.403.
And save the Reliques of the *Grecian* Land! .... Il.8.292.411.
But Darkness now, to save the Cowards, falls, ... Il.8.625.425.
Now shameful flight alone can save the Host; .... Il.9.29.433.
To deprecate the Chief, and save the Host. .... Il.9.236.444.
To save thy *Greeks,* and stop the Course of Fate; .... Il.9.321.449.
To save the Ships, the Troops, the Chiefs from Fire. .... Il.9.547.460.
Besought the Chief to save the sinking State; .... Il.9.691.468.
To save our Army, and our Fleets to free, ... Il.9.798.473.
What yet remains to save th' afflicted State. .... Il.10.26.3.
His Life to hazard, and his Country save? .... Il.10.242.13.
The Warrior rescue, and your Country save. .... Il.11.719.67.
To save their Fleet, the last Efforts they try, ... Il.12.173.87.
'Tis yours to save us, if you cease to fear; .... Il.13.75.108.
Prevent this Evil, and your Country save: .... Il.13.155.111.
And save the Reliques of the *Grecian* Name. .... Il.15.435.214.
Ah save his Arms, secure his Obsequies! .... Il.15.497.216.
Go save the Fleets, and conquer in my right. .... Il.16.90.239.
Now save the Ships, the rising Fires restrain, ... Il.16.106.240.
And humble the proud Monarch whom you save. .... Il.16.329.255.
Oh save from hostile Rage his lov'd Remains: .... Il.16.668.270.
To save our present, and our future Race. .... Il.17.265.298.
And save *Patroclus* from the Dogs of *Troy.* .... Il.17.301.299.
To save your *Troy,* tho' Heav'n its Fall ordain? .... Il.17.379.302.
And save the Living from a fiercer Foe. .... Il.17.579.311.
And save our selves, while with impetuous Hate .... Il.17.799.319.
The Host to succour, and thy Friends to save, ... Il.18.165.330.
Assist the Combate, and *Patroclus* save: .... Il.18.210.332.
Or save one Member of the sinking State; .... Il.20.364.410.
Shot down to save her, and redeem her Fame. .... Il.21.642.448.
Save thy dear Life; or if a Soul so brave .... Il.22.78.456.
Neglect that Thought, thy dearer Glory save. .... Il.22.79.456.
And treat on Terms of Peace to save the Town: .... Il.22.157.459.
Some Sense of Duty, some Desire to save. .... Il.24.194.544.
Some Sense of Duty, some Desire to save. .... Il.24.224.546.
And will Omnipotence neglect to save .... Od.1.78.35.
To save the state; and timely to restrain .... Od.1.114.37.
And form sure plans to save the sinking state. .... Od.1.357.49.
With ease can save each object of his love; .... Od.3.286.100.
The pow'r defrauding who vouchsaf'd to save. .... Od.4.676.151.
And to their pow'r to save his race appeal. .... Od.4.979.163.
It was my crime to pity, and to save; .... Od.5.166.180.
And save a suppliant, and a man distrest. .... Od.5.575.200.
Studious to save what human wants require, ... Od.5.632.202.
Him, and his house, heav'n mov'd my mind to save, ... Od.9.234.316.
This way and that, I cast to save my friends, ... Od.9.503.326.
And save the few not fated yet to die. .... Od.10.320.359.
Our task be now thy treasur'd stores to save, ... Od.13.417.26.
Was yet to save th' oppress'd and innocent. .... Od.14.346.51.
To win thy grace: O save us, pow'r divine! .... Od.16.203.113.
Or save his life; and soon his life to save .... Od.18.106.172.
Or save his life; and soon his life to save .... Od.18.106.172.
Save then the Poet, and thy self reward; .... Od.22.387.307.

SAVES

He saves from famine, from the savage saves; .... 3.EOM3.64.98.
He saves from famine, from the savage saves; .... 3.EOM3.64.98.
So prompts, and saves a Rogue who cannot read. .... 4.JD2.16.133.

SAVES (CONTINUED)

So prompts, and saves some Rogue who cannot read. .... 4.JD2.16A.133.
Ev'n *Guthry* saves half *Newgate* by a Dash. .... 4.EpS2.11.313.
Saves in the Moment of the last Despair. .... Il.4.16.221.
Had sav'd the Father, and now saves the Son. .... Il.15.631.220.
Yet stops, and turns, and saves his lov'd Allies. .... Il.16.433.259.
Who saves her Infants from the Rage of War? .... Il.24.919.574.

SAVIL

The Name of *Savil* and of *Boyle.* .... 6.119.16.337.

SAVING

But fix'd *His* Word, *His* saving Pow'r remains: .... 1.Mes.107.122.
This saving counsel, "Keep your Piece nine years." .... 4.Arbu.40.98.
This, this the saving doctrine, preach'd to all, ... 4.1HE1.81.285.
Whom (saving W[alter]) every S. *harper bites,* .... 4.1740.26.333*.
And saving Ignorance enthrones by Laws. .... 5.DunA3.90.157.
And saving Ignorance enthrones by Laws. .... 5.DunB3.98.324.
And o'er his breast extend his saving shield: .... 6.21.14.69.
And owns no Help but from thy saving Hands: .... Il.9.304.449.
If ought from Heav'n with-hold his saving Arm; .... Il.11.927.77.

SAVIOR

The SAVIOR comes! by ancient Bards foretold: .... 1.Mes.37.116.

SAVIOUR

Bold *Scipio,* Saviour of the *Roman* State, ... 2.TemF.163.267.
Thy Country's Saviour, and thy Father's Boast! .... Il.8.342.413.
The people's Saviour, and divinely wise, ... Od.15.269.81.

SAVO'RY

Or mow from racy plumbs the savo'ry blew, ... 6.96ii.30Z47.272.

SAVOUR

Of choicest sort and savour, rich repast! .... Od.1.186.42.
Of choicest sort and savour, rich repast! .... Od.7.237.247.
Of choicest sort and savour, rich repaste! .... Od.10.440.365.

SAVOY

I see the *Savoy* totter to her fall! .... 5.DunA3.324A.189.

SAW

Nor saw displeas'd the peaceful Cottage rise. .... 1.W-F.86.158.
Pan saw and lov'd, and burning with Desire .... 1.W-F.183.166.
Pan saw and lov'd, and furious with Desire .... 1.W-F.183A.166.
She saw her Sons with purple Deaths expire, ... 1.W-F.323.180.
And the same Age saw *Learning* fall, and *Rome.* .... 1.EOC.686.317.
But lo! I saw, (as near her side I stood) .... 1.TrFD.27.387.
I saw, unhappy! what I now relate, ... 1.TrFD.53.388.
And saw where *Teucer* with th' *Ajaces* stood, ... 1.TrES.61.451.
The Maker saw, took pity, and bestow'd .... 2.ChJM.63.17.
She saw him watch the Motions of her Eye, ... 2.ChJM.601.44.
A wiser Monarch never saw the Sun: .... 2.ChJM.632.45.
But when he saw his Bosome-Wife so drest, ... 2.ChJM.752.51.
As with these Eyes I plainy saw thee whor'd; .... 2.ChJM.769.52.
As surely seize thee, as I saw too well. .... 2.ChJM.771.52.
By Heav'n, I swore but what I *thought* I saw. .... 2.ChJM.794.53.
Christ saw a Wedding once, the Scripture says, ... 2.ChWB.9.57.
And saw but one, 'tis thought, in all his Days; .... 2.ChWB.10.57.
I saw, alas! some dread Event impend, ... 2.RL1.109.154.
He saw, he wish'd, and to the Prize aspir'd: .... 2.RL2.30.161.
But trust the Muse—she saw it upward rise, ... 2.RL5.123.210.
Criticks I saw, that other Names deface, ... 2.TemF.37.256.
No weeping orphan saw his father's stores .... 2.ElAb.135.330.
Superior beings, when of late they saw .... 3.EOM2.31.59.
Who saw its fires here rise, and there descend, ... 3.EOM2.37.60.
Who saw the Stars here rise, and there descend, ... 3.EOM2.37A.60.
Saw helpless him from whom their life began: .... 3.EOM3.142.107.
Man, like his Maker, saw that all was right, ... 3.EOM3.232.116.
Saw Gods descend, and fiends infernal rise: .... 3.EOM3.254.118.
Cutler saw tenants break, and houses fall, ... 3.Ep3.323.120.
The Tempter saw his time; the work he ply'd; .... 3.Ep3.369.123.
And quick to swallow me, methought I saw .... 4.JD4.172.39.
Saw such a Scene of *Envy, Sin,* and *Hate.* .... 4.JD4.193A.43.
Who judg'd themselves, and saw with their own Eyes) .... 4.HAdv.113.85.
All for a Thing you ne're so much as *saw?* .... 4.HAdv.136.87.
His Wit all see-saw between *that* and *this,* .... 4.Arbu.323.119.
No Courts he saw, no Suits would ever try, ... 4.Arbu.396.126.
The *Temple* late two Brother Sergeants saw, ... 4.2HE2.127.173.
When twenty Fools I never saw .... 4.HS6.64.255.
She saw with joy the line immortal run, ... 5.DunA1.97.71.
She saw old Pryn in restless Daniel shine, ... 5.DunA1.101.71.
She saw in *N[orto]n* all his father shine, ... 5.DunA1.101A.71.
She saw slow Philips creep like Tate's poor page, ... 5.DunA1.103.72.
Rome in her Capitol saw Querno sit, ... 5.DunA2.11.97.
He look'd, and saw a sable Sorc'rer rise, ... 5.DunA3.229.176.
He look'd, and saw a sable seer arise, ... 5.DunA3.229A.176.
She saw, with joy, the line immortal run, ... 5.DunB1.99.276.
She saw old Pryn in restless Daniel shine, ... 5.DunB1.103.276.
She saw slow Philips creep like Tate's poor page, ... 5.DunB1.105.277.
Rome in her Capitol saw Querno sit, ... 5.DunB2.15.297.
And look'd, and saw a sable Sorc'rer rise, ... 5.DunB3.233.331.
As if he saw St. James's and the Queen. .... 5.DunB4.280.371.
The Sire saw, one by one, his Virtues wake: .... 5.DunB4.285.372.
The Sire saw, smiling, his own Virtues wake: .... 5.DunB4.285A.372.
Europe he saw, and Europe saw him too. .... 5.DunB4.294.373.
Europe he saw, and Europe saw him too. .... 5.DunB4.294.373.
Saw ev'ry Court, heard ev'ry King declare .... 5.DunB4.313.374.
Then look'd, and saw a lazy, lolling sort, ... 5.DunB4.337.376.
I saw, and started from its vernal bow'r .... 5.DunB4.425.383.
Which Theocles in raptur'd vision saw, ... 5.DunB4.488.389.
While *Argo* saw her kindred Trees .... 6.11.40.31.
And *Argo* saw her kindred Trees .... 6.11.40A.31.
Him when he saw—he rose, and crawl'd to meet, ... 6.15.15.51.
Who ne'er saw naked Sword, or look'd in, *Plato.* .... 6.41.44.114.
Saw others happy, and with sighs withdrew; .... 6.45.8.124.

SAW (CONTINUED)
Who saw you in Tower, and since 6.68.7.196.
And Parnell who saw you not since 6.68.9.196.
Hearts so sincere th' Almighty saw well pleas'd, 6.69i.5.198.
Victims so pure Heav'n saw well pleas'd 6.69ii.3.199.
And saw her Cocks well serve her Hens. 6.93.4.256.
You went, you saw, you heard: With Virtue fraught, 6.96iii.21.275.
I saw thee stretch'd on *Lilliputian* Ground; 6.96iv.68.278.
Corneille himself saw, wonder'd, and was fir'd. 6.107.8.310.
Saw nothing to regret, or there to fear; 6.112.8.318.
Saw nothing to regret, Nor there to fear; 6.112.8A.318.
But when I saw such Charity remain, 6.146.3.389.
Judged for themselves, and saw with their own eyes. 6.147i.2.390.
He saw, and sudden to the Goddess cries, Il.1.267A.99.
The Feast disturb'd with Sorrow *Vulcan* saw, Il.1.738.122.
Nor saw what *Jove* and secret Fate design'd, Il.2.48.129.
And saw their blooming Warriors early slain. Il.2.800.163.
With Joy they saw the growing Empire rise, Il.2.813.163.
Great as a God! I saw him once before, Il.3.297.207.
The Shaft infix'd, and saw the gushing Tide: Il.4.179.230.
High at their Head he saw the Chief appear, Il.4.288.234.
The King, who saw their Squadrons yet unmov'd, Il.4.388.239.
I saw him once, when gath'ring martial Pow'rs Il.4.430.240.
And happier, saw the Sev'nfold City fall. Il.4.461.242.
This saw *Ulysses,* and with Grief enrag'd Il.4.567.248.
Nor saw his Country's Peril, nor his own. Il.5.84.270.
Saw the wide Waste of his destructive Hand: Il.5.127.273.
Already in his Hopes he saw him kill'd, Il.5.527.294.
Great *Hector* saw, and raging at the View Il.5.722.302.
But *Hector* saw; and furious at the Sight, Il.5.838.305.
Old *Nestor* saw, and rowz'd the Warrior's Rage; Il.6.83.327.
When now *Minerva* saw her *Argives* slain, Il.7.23.363.
All saw, and fear'd, his huge, tempestuous Sway. Il.7.184.373.
Great *Hector* heard; he saw the flashing Light, Il.8.208.407.
He saw their Soul, and thus his Word imparts. Il.8.556.423.
The Warrior saw the hoary Chief, and said. Il.10.185.10.
I saw his Coursers in proud Triumph go, Il.10.506.26.
Saw *Tydeus'* Son with heav'nly Succour blest, Il.10.604.29.
He rose, and saw the Field deform'd with Blood, Il.10.610.29.
No sooner *Hector* saw the King retir'd, Il.11.365.51.
Th' *Epeians* saw, they trembled, and they fled. Il.11.879.75.
This saw *Polydamas;* who, wisely brave, Il.12.67.83.
Ev'n when they saw *Troy's* sable Troops impend, Il.12.159.87.
And saw where *Teucer* with th' *Ajaces* stood, Il.12.405.96.
Short as he turn'd, I saw the Pow'r appear: Il.13.102.109.
He saw, and shun'd the Death; the forceful Dart Il.13.247.117.
The *Cretan* saw; and stooping, caus'd to glance Il.13.511.131.
The *Cretan* saw, and shun'd the brazen Spear: Il.13.637.136.
There saw the *Trojans* fly, the *Greeks* pursue, Il.15.8.194.
Well-pleas'd the Thund'rer saw their earnest care, Il.15.176.203.
We saw him, late, by thund'ring *Ajax* kill'd; Il.15.326.209.
But when he saw, ascending up the Fleet, Il.15.456.215.
This *Hector* saw, and thus express'd his Joy. Il.15.570.218.
Jove is with us; I saw his Hand, but now, Il.15.574.218.
Hector they saw, and all who fly, or fight, Il.15.812.228.
Troy saw and trembled, as this Helmet blaz'd: Il.16.96.239.
Great *Ajax* saw, and own'd the Hand divine, Il.16.148.243.
Troy saw, and thought the dread *Achilles* nigh, Il.16.336.255.
Thestor was next; who saw the Chief appear, Il.16.486.262.
One instant saw, one Instant overtook Il.17.214.295.
They saw *Achilles,* and in him their Fate. Il.18.292.336.
(Confest we saw him) tore his Arms away. Il.19.459.391.
Once (as I think) you saw this brandish'd Spear Il.20.228.403.
Saw, e'er it fell, th' immeasurable Spear. Il.20.313.407.
Saw the Distress, and mov'd the Pow'rs around. Il.20.340.408.
The Squire who saw expiring on the Ground Il.20.565.418.
Fear touch'd the Queen of Heav'n: She saw dismay'd, Il.21.384.436.
And saw the foremost Steed with sharpen'd Eyes; Il.23.537.511.
He saw; and rising, to the *Greeks* begun. Il.23.540.511.
Achilles saw, and pitying thus begun. Il.23.611.514.
With Joy *Pelides* saw the Honour paid, Il.23.1052.533.
I saw descend the Messenger of *Jove,* Il.24.235.546.
I saw, I heard her, and the Word shall stand. Il.24.274.547.
I saw him, when like *Jove,* his Flames he tost Il.24.481.556.
I saw, but help'd not: Stern *Achilles'* Ire Il.24.483.556.
We saw, as unperceiv'd we took our stand, Od.2.123.67.
Grave *Eteoneus* saw the pomp appear, Od.4.31.121.
Speak you, (who saw) his wonders in the war. Od.4.334.135.
Mentor himself I saw, and much admir'd.— Od.4.882.159.
Saw stately *Ceres* to her passion yield, Od.5.160.179.
The King of Ocean saw, and seeing burn'd, Od.5.363.190.
Leucothea saw, and pity touch'd her breast: Od.5.425.193.
Saw them returning with the setting sun. Od.7.416.258.
They went; but as they ent'ring saw the Queen Od.10.127.347.
Some smoak I saw amid the forest rise, Od.10.225.351.
They saw, they knew me, and with eager pace Od.10.469.366.
And saw that all was grief beneath the sun. Od.10.591.372.
A Queen, to *Troy* she saw our legions pass; Od.11.106.386.
Or saw gay vessel stem the wat'ry plain, Od.11.154.389.
I saw him not; it was not mine to fear. Od.14.256.48.
Nine years we warr'd; the tenth saw *Ilion* fall; Od.14.276.49.
I saw my self the vast unnumber'd store Od.14.359.51.
She saw, she wept, she ran with eager pace, Od.17.41.134.
Distant he saw, across the shady Dome; Od.17.402.152.
Ulysses late he saw, on *Cretan* ground, Od.17.614.162.
The tender drops. *Antinous* saw, and said. Od.21.86.263.
He saw their secret souls, and thus began. Od.21.211.270.
Amaz'd, confounded, as they saw him fall, Od.22.27.287.
Ulysses saw, and thus with transport cry'd. Od.22.224.297.
They saw, they knew him, and with fond embrace Od.22.535.314.
I saw it not, she cries, but heard alone, Od.23.41.321.
Plough'd half his thigh; I saw, I saw the scar, Od.23.76.322.
Plough'd half his thigh; I saw, I saw the scar, Od.23.76.322.
Nor saw gay vessel stem the surgy plain, Od.23.287.337.

SAW'ST
Oh had'st thou dy'd when first thou saw'st the Light, Il.3.57.192.
Saw'st thou the Worthies of the *Grecian* Host? Od.11.461.407.
What years have circled since thou saw'st that guest? Od.24.335.365.

SAWS
To heathnish Authors, Proverbs, and old Saws. 2.ChJM.219.25.
His Saws are toothless, and his Hatchets Lead. 4.EpS2.149.321.

SAXON
Whom ev'n the *Saxon* spar'd, and bloody *Dane,* 1.W-F.77.157.

SAY
Say, *Daphnis,* say, in what glad Soil appears 1.PSp.85.69.
Say, *Daphnis,* say, in what glad Soil appears 1.PSp.85.69.
Say, Shepherd, say, in what glad Soil appears 1.PSp.85A.69.
Say, Shepherd, say, in what glad Soil appears 1.PSp.85A.69.
Say, is not Absence Death to those who love? 1.PAu.30.82.
'Tis hard to say, if greater Want of Skill 1.EOC.1.239.
Once on a time, *La Mancha's* Knight, they say, 1.EOC.267.270.
Ask them the Cause; *They're wiser still,* they say; 1.EOC.436.288.
To hail this tree; and say, with weeping eyes, 1.TrFD.82.389.
Say, lovely Youth, that dost my Heart command, 1.TrSP.1.393.
O Goddess, say, shall I deduce my Rhimes 1.TrSt.5.409.
Say, wretched Rivals! what provokes your Rage? 1.TrSt.210.419.
Say to what End your impious Arms engage? 1.TrSt.211.419.
Say, from what Period then has *Jove* design'd 1.TrSt.381.425.
Say, can those Honours please? and canst thou love 1.TrSt.392.426.
But say, Illustrious Guest (adjoin'd the King) 1.TrSt.790.443.
Say, shall I snatch him from Impending Fate; 1.TrES.232.458.
For long ago, let Priests say what they cou'd, 2.ChJM.7.15.
Grave Authors say, and witty Poets sing, 2.ChJM.21.16.
This Blessing lasts, (if those who try, say true) 2.ChJM.57.17.
And since I speak of Wedlock, let me say, 2.ChJM.127.20.
The Venture's greater, I'll presume to say, 2.ChJM.182.23.
What does my Friend, my dear *Placebo* say? 2.ChJM.221.25.
I say, quoth he, by Heav'n the Man's to blame, 2.ChJM.222.25.
What next ensu'd beseems not me to say; 2.ChJM.383.33.
About this Spring (if ancient Fame say true) 2.ChJM.459.37.
Hark old Sir *Paul* ('twas thus I us'd to say) 2.ChWB.74.60.
If poor (you say) she drains her Husband's Purse; 2.ChWB.86.60.
If you had Wit, you'd say, "Go where you will, 2.ChWB.130.62.
I told'em, *Thus you say,* and *thus you do*— 2.ChWB.150.63.
But all that Score I paid—As how? you'll say, 2.ChWB.231.68.
So bless the good Man's Soul, I say no more. 2.ChWB.252.69.
I (to say truth) was twenty more than he: 2.ChWB.318.72.
Oft wou'd he say, Who builds his House on Sands, 2.ChWB.347.74.
And so do Numbers more, I'll boldly say, 2.ChWB.353.74.
Say what strange Motive, Goddess! cou'd compel 2.RL1.7.145.
Oh say what stranger Cause, yet unexplor'd, 2.RL1.9.145.
And thus in Whispers said, or seem'd to say. 2.RL1.26.147.
'Twas then *Belinda!* if Report say true, 2.RL1.117.154.
Already hear the horrid things they say, 2.RL4.108.192.
Say, why are Beauties prais'd and honour'd most, 2.RL5.9.199.
That Men may say, when we the Front-box grace, 2.RL5.17.200.
I call aloud; it hears not what I say; 2.ElAb.237.339.
Come, sister come! (it said, or seem'd to say) 2.ElAb.309.344.
Then sadly say, with mutual pity mov'd, 2.ElAb.351.348.
There passengers shall stand, and pointing say, 2.Elegy.39.365.
Say first, of God above, or Man below, 3.EOM1.17.14.
Then say not Man's imperfect, Heav'n in fault; 3.EOM1.69.22.
Say rather, Man's as perfect as he ought; 3.EOM1.70.22.
But does he say, the Maker is not *good,* 3.EOM1.108Z1.28.
Say, here he gives too little, there too much; 3.EOM1.116.29.
Say what their use, had he the pow'rs of all? 3.EOM1.178.36.
Say what the use, were finer optics giv'n, 3.EOM1.195.39.
Say what th' advantage of so fine an Eye 3.EOM1.195B.39.
Say, will the falcon, stooping from above, 3.EOM3.53.97.
Say, where full Instinct is th'unerring guide, 3.EOM3.83.100.
Say, in what mortal soil thou deign'st to grow? 3.EOM4.8.128.
Who thus define it, say they more or less 3.EOM4.27.130.
Say, in pursuit of profit or delight, 3.EOM4.85.136.
Say, was it Virtue, more tho' Heav'n ne'er gave, 3.EOM4.103.138.
And which more blest? who chain'd his country, say, 3.EOM4.147.142.
Say, at what part of nature will they stand? 3.EOM4.166.143.
Look next on Greatness; say where Greatness lies? 3.EOM4.217.147.
Say, would'st thou be the Man to whom they fall? 3.EOM4.276.154.
Say, shall my little bark attendant sail, 3.EOM4.385.165.
What made (say Montagne, or more sage Charron!) 3.Ep1.146.27.
Say, what can cause such impotence of mind? 3.Ep2.93.57.
"Say, what can Cloe want?"—she wants a Heart. 3.Ep2.160.64.
What say you? B. Say? Why take it, Gold and all. 3.Ep3.80B.94.
What say you? B. Say? Why take it, Gold and all. 3.Ep3.80B.94.
What say you? "Say? Why take it, Gold and all." 3.Ep3.80.94.
What say you? "Say? Why take it, Gold and all." 3.Ep3.80.94.
"Oh say, what sums that gen'rous hand supply? 3.Ep3.277.116.
Say, for such worth are other worlds prepar'd? 3.Ep3.335.120.
The Lines are weak, another's pleas'd to say, 4.HS1.5.5.
F. Your Plea is good. But still I say, beware! 4.HS1.143.19.
"But as for *Courts,* forgive me if I say, 4.JD4.92.33.
What life in all that ample Body, say, 4.HS2.77.59.
And, what's more rare, a Poet shall say *Grace.* 4.HS2.150.67.
And, what's more rare, the Poet shall say *Grace.* 4.HS2.150A.67.
He too can say, "With Wives I never sin." 4.HAdv.73.81.
Should rise, and say—"Sir *Robert!* or Sir *Paul!* 4.HAdv.88.83.
Tye up the knocker, say I'm sick, I'm dead, 4.Arbu.2.96.
Say, is their Anger, or their Friendship worse? 4.Arbu.30A.98.
(Some say his Queen) was forc'd to speak, or burst. 4.Arbu.72.100.
Say for my comfort, languishing in bed, 4.Arbu.121.104.
I pay my Debts, believe, and say my Pray'rs, 4.Arbu.268.114.
Who tells whate'er you think, whate'er you say, 4.Arbu.297.117.
When doom'd to say his Beads and Ev'ning Song: 4.JD2A.112.142.
When doom'd to say his Beads and Evensong: 4.JD2.106.143.
Not to say worse in pamper'd Churchmens Lives 4.JD2A.88.140.
"To say too much, might do my Honour wrong: 4.2HE2.12.165.
Better (say I) be pleas'd, and play the fool; 4.2HE2.181.177.

SAY (CONTINUED)

Say, can you find out one such Lodger there? ....4.2HE2.223.181.
Say at what age a Poet grows divine? ....4.2HE1.50.199.
Or say our fathers never broke a rule; ....4.2HE1.93.203.
Why then I say, the Publick is a fool. ....4.2HE1.94.203.
Who says in verse what others say in prose; ....4.2HE1.202.211.
That when I aim at praise, they say I bite. ....4.2HE1.409.229.
Say with what eyes we ought at Courts to gaze, ...4.1HE6.16.237.
Now this I'll say, you'll find in me ....4.1HE7.39.271.
Say, does thy blood rebel, thy bosom move ....4.1HE1.55.283.
And say, to which shall our applause belong, ...4.1HE1.97.287.
'Tis all from *Horace:* did not *Horace* say ....4.EpS1.7A.297.
Horace would say, *Sir* Billy *serv'd the Crown,* ....4.EpS1.13.298.
Fr. Tis all a Libel— *Paxton* (Sir) will say. ....4.EpS2.1.313.
Still let me say! No Follower, but a Friend. ....4.EpS2.93.318.
Say great Patricians! (since your selves inspire ....5.DunA1.3.61.
Say from what cause, in vain decry'd and curst, ...5.DunA1.5.61.
Let there be darkness! (the dread pow'r shall say) ....5.DunA3.337Z1.192.
I sing. Say you, her instruments the Great! ....5.DunB1.3.269.
Say how the Goddess bade Britannia sleep, ...5.DunB1.7.269.
Walker! our hat"—nor more he deign'd to say, ...5.DunB4.273.371.
Moses indeed may say the words but Thou ....6.2.19.6.
See! She retires: Nor can we say ....6.4iv.10.10.
That is to say, the Want of Coin. ....6.10.70.26.
(You say) he'd more good Breeding; *Ergo*— ....6.10.90.27.
And one may say of *Dryden* too, ...6.10.93.27.
And fearless say to God— *Thou* art my friend! ....6.21.4.69.
What have you against this to say? ....6.24iii(a).5.75.
To foreign Letters cou'd I say? ....6.30.65.88.
To other Letters cou'd I say? ....6.30.65A.88.
Hark! they whisper; Angels say, ...6.31ii.7.94.
Pallas they say Sprung from the Head of *Jove,* ....6.37.3.106.
Some flatly say, the Book's as ill done, ...6.44.15.123.
Whose fragrant Wit revives, as one may say, ...6.48ii.3.134.
Say, will ye bless the bleak *Atlantic* shore? ....6.51ii.15.151.
Some say from *Pastry Cook* it came, ...6.59.3.177.
To say that at Court there's a Death of all Wit, ...6.62iii.3A.185.
To say that at Court there's a Dearth of all Wit, ...6.62iii.3.185.
They say *A—'s* a Wit, for what? ....6.62vi.1.186.
You say A[rgyle]'s a wit, for what? ....6.62vi.1B.186*.
A[rgyle] they say has wit, for what? ....6.62vi.1C.186*.
Arthur, they say, has wit; for what? ....6.62vi.1F.186 *.
In peevish Fits to have you say, ...6.64.9.189.
And say what Region is our destin'd Seat? ....6.65.6A.192.
Though Dukes they be, to Dukes I say, ...6.79.3.217.
As who should say, alas the Day, ...6.79.67.220.
"If thou hast ought to say, now speak." ....6.79.81A.220.
Say Grace, with your hat off ....6.91.28.254.
Most true it is, I dare to say, ...6.94.1.259.
Say, by what Witchcraft, or what Dæmon led, ...6.96iv.31.277.
Some say the Dev'l himself is in that *Mare:* ....6.96iv.33.277.
They say, on Pope would fall ....6.102.2.294.
All he can say for 't is, he neither made ....6.105vi.3.302.
May truly say, here lies an honest Man. ....6.112.2.318.
Nor let us say, (those English glories gone) ....6.113.11.320.
Say what revenge on D[enni]s can be had; ....6.116vii.3.328.
5. Who tells you all I *mean,* and all I *say;* ....6.120.9.339.
'Tis the first time I dare to say, ...6.121.3.340.
'Tis the first coin I'm bold to say, ...6.121.3A.340.
But that the Worthy and the Good shall say, ...6.125.11.350.
Thanks, dirty Pair! you teach me what to say, ...6.129.5.357.
Can say of me, is, I can bite: ....6.135.20A.366.
"Say what can Cloë want?"—She wants a *Heart:* ....6.139.4.377.
What they said, or may say of the Mortal within. ....6.144.6.386.
Once (says an Author, where, I need not say) ....6.145.1.388.
Say first what Cause? That Pow'r here ....6.155.8Z1.404 *
Say, artful Manager of Heav'n (she cries) ....Il.1.698.120.
And thus return'd. Austere *Saturnius,* say, ...Il.1.714.122.
Say shall we march with our unconquer'd Pow'rs, ...Il.2.283.141.
Say would'st thou seize some valiant Leader's Prize? ....Il.2.288.141.
Say, Virgins, seated round the Throne Divine, ...Il.2.572.155.
Oh say what Heroes, fir'd by Thirst of Fame, ...Il.2.578.155.
Say next O Muse! of all *Achaïa* breeds, ...Il.2.924.167.
Say, was it thus, with such a baffled Mien, ...Il.3.69.192.
But lift thy Eyes, and say, What *Greek* is He ....Il.3.219.202.
Say, tô new Nations must I cross the Main, ...Il.3.495.215.
Her glowing Eyes, and thus began to say. ....Il.3.532.217.
Then say ye Pow'rs! what signal Issue waits ....Il.4.19.222.
Say, is it thus those Honours you requite? ....Il.4.400.239.
Say, Chief, is all thy ancient Valor lost, ...Il.5.575.296.
Say, mighty Father! Shall we scourge his Pride, ...Il.5.950.312.
O *Hector!* say, what great Occasion calls ....Il.6.318.341.
And say, This Chief transcends his Father's Fame: ....Il.6.613.357.
My Heart weeps Blood at what the *Trojans* say, ...Il.6.672.360.
Thus shall he say: "A valiant *Greek* lies there, ...Il.7.101.368.
Exchange some Gift; that *Greece* and *Troy* may say, ...Il.7.363.382.
Then Goddess! say, shall *Hector* glory then, ...Il.8.457.418.
Pallas and *Juno!* say, why heave your Hearts? ....Il.8.557.423.
Say what Success? divine *Laertes* Son! ....Il.9.791.473.
But say, what Hero shall sustain that Task? ....Il.10.45.4.
Say shall I stay, or with Dispatch return? ....Il.10.70.5.
What moves thee, say, when Sleep has clos'd the Sight, ...Il.10.455.24.
But say, be faithful, and the Truth recite! ....Il.10.477.24.
Say, since this Conquest, what their Counsels are? ....Il.10.481.25.
Say thou, whose Praises all our Host proclaim, ...Il.10.640.30.
Say whence these Coursers? by what Chance bestow'd, ...Il.10.642.30.
Say Muse! when *Jove* the *Trojan's* Glory crown'd, ...Il.11.387.51.
Ah! try the utmost that a Friend can say, ...Il.11.922.76.
Say, great *Eurypylus!* shall *Greece* yet stand? ....Il.11.952.77.
A Change so shameful, say what Cause has wrought? ....Il.13.147.111.
O say, in ev'ry Art of Battel skill'd, ...Il.13.327.121.
There hear what *Greece* has on her Part to say. ....Il.13.481.130.
What new Alarm, divine *Machaon* say, ...Il.14.5.157.
Who boldly gives it, and what he shall say, ...Il.14.122.163.
Say, is this Chief, extended on the Plain, ...Il.14.551.189.
O say, when *Neptune* made proud *Ilion* yield, ...Il.14.601.191.

SAY (CONTINUED)

Patroclus, say, what Grief thy Bosom bears, ...Il.16.9.235.
Say, Muses, thron'd above the starry Frame, ...Il.16.140.243.
"Stern Son of *Peleus* (thus ye us'd to say, ...Il.16.242.248.
Say, shall I snatch him from impending Fate, ...Il.16.535.264.
Tho much at parting that great Chief might say, ...Il.16.1011.282.
Say, shall our slaughter'd Bodies guard your Walls ....Il.17.167.294.
Say, is it just (my Friend) that *Hector's* Ear ....Il.17.189.294.
Curs'd be the Man (ev'n private *Greeks* would say) ....Il.17.474.306.
Big with the mighty Grief, he strove to say ....Il.17.783.319.
Patroclus—Ah!—Say Goddess can I boast ....Il.18.101.328.
Was't not enough, ye valiant Warriors say, ...Il.18.335.337.
Say (for I know not) is their Race divine, ...Il.18.421.341.
Say, shall not I one Nation's Fate command, ...Il.18.429.341.
Now since her Presence glads our Mansion, say, ...Il.18.473.344.
Oh *Vulcan!* say, was ever Breast divine ....Il.18.501.345.
He said, and acting what no Words could say, ...Il.22.108.457.
And seiz'd the Beast, and thus began to say: ....Il.23.769.520.
Then call'd his Queen, and thus began to say. ....Il.24.232.546.
Say whither, Father! when each mortal Sight ....Il.24.447.554.
But say, convey'st thou thro' the lonely Plains ....Il.24.467.556.
The King alarm'd. Say what, and whence thou art, ...Il.24.473.556.
But say with speed, if ought of thy Desire ....Il.24.824.571.
But say, yon' jovial Troop so gaily drest, ...Od.1.289.47.
But say, that Stranger-guest who late withdrew, ...Od.1.515.57.
Say then, ye Peers! by whose commands we meet? ....Od.2.35.62.
Or say, does high necessity of state ....Od.2.39.62.
Or who can say (his gamesome mate replies) ....Od.2.372.78.
And whence your race? on what adventure, say, ...Od.3.84.90.
Say, is the fault, thro' tame submission, thine? ....Od.3.262.98.
Say from what scepter'd ancestry ye claim, ...Od.4.73.122.
Say, royal youth, sincere of soul report ....Od.4.421.140.
The bands relax'd, implore the Seer to say ....Od.4.573.147.
Say, son of *Atreus,* say what God inspir'd ....Od.4.625.149.
Say, son of *Atreus,* say what God inspir'd ....Od.4.625.149.
Unfriended of the gales. All-knowing! say ....Od.4.631.149.
My prompt obedience bows. But deign to say, ...Od.4.653.150.
Requested for his speed; but, courteous, say ....Od.4.856.159.
Say, breathes my Lord the blissful realm of light, ...Od.4.1087.168.
Thus to his soul the Sage began to say. ....Od.5.598.201.
Say, with thy garments shall I bend my way ....Od.6.71.208.
Cam'st thou not hither, wond'rous stranger! say, ...Od.7.318.251.
And faithful say, to you the pow'rs belong ....Od.8.289.278.
But say, if that lewd scandal of the sky ....Od.8.387.285.
Say wilt thou bear the Mulct? He instant cries, ...Od.8.389.285.
Say what thy birth, and what the name you bore, ...Od.8.597.294.
Say from what city, from what regions tost, ...Od.8.601.294.
But say thro' what waste regions hast thou stray'd, ...Od.8.625.296.
Say why the fate the *Troy* awak'd thy cares, ...Od.8.629.297.
A theme of future song! Say then if slain ....Od.8.633.297.
What are ye, guests? on what adventure, say, ...Od.9.299.318.
Say 'twas *Ulysses;* 'twas his deed, declare, ...Od.9.589.330.
Say whence, ye Gods, contending nations strive ....Od.10.42.341.
Say shall we seek access? With that they call; ....Od.10.262.355.
What art thou? say! from whence, from whom you came? ....Od.10.387.363.
How shall I tread (I cry'd) ah *Circe!* say, ...Od.10.594.372.
O say what angry pow'r *Elpenor* led ....Od.11.71.383.
But say, why yonder on the lonely strands ....Od.11.174.390.
Or say, since honour call'd thee to the field, ...Od.11.198.391.
Say what distemper gave thee to the dead? ....Od.11.207.391.
Say if my sire, good old *Laertes,* lives? ....Od.11.210.392.
Say by his rule is my dominion aw'd, ...Od.11.212.392.
Say if my spouse maintains her royal trust, ...Od.11.214.392.
But say, upon the dark and dismal coast, ...Od.11.460.407.
Say while the sea, and while the tempest raves, ...Od.11.495.408.
But say, resides my son in royal port, ...Od.11.565.411.
Or say in *Pyle?* for yet he views the light, ...Od.11.567.411.
Then I. Thy suit is vain, nor can I say ....Od.11.569.411.
But say, if in my steps my son proceeds, ...Od.11.601.413.
Say if my sire, the rev'rend *Peleus* reigns ....Od.11.605.413.
Say now, what man is he, the man deplor'd, ...Od.14.138.42.
Say if to us the Gods these Omens send, ...Od.15.188.77.
But say, if in the court the Queen reside ....Od.16.33.103.
Whence father, from what shore this stranger, say? ....Od.16.57.105.
Say, do thy subjects in bold faction rise, ...Od.16.99.107.
What ship transported thee, O father say, ...Od.16.246.116.
Say, if the Suitors measure back the main, ...Od.16.484.130.
Few words she spoke, tho' much she had to say, ...Od.17.50.135.
Say, to my mournful couch shall I ascend? ....Od.17.117.137.
Say wilt thou not (ere yet the Suitor-crew ....Od.17.120.137.
Say wilt thou not the least account afford? ....Od.17.122.137.
And, say (she cries) does fear, or shame, detain ....Od.17.657.164.
Say is it baseness, to decline the foe? ....Od.18.59.169.
Say, if large hire can tempt thee to employ ....Od.18.404.188.
Fierce in the van: Then wou'dst thou, wou'dst thou, say, ...Od.18.420.189.
Say, since *Ulysses* left his natal coast, ...Od.19.9.193.
They're doom'd to bleed; O say, cœlestial maid! ....Od.20.52.234.
Say thou, to whom my youth its nurture owes, ...Od.20.161.241.
Now say sincere, my guest! the Suitor train ....Od.20.208.243.
Say you, whom these forbidden walls inclose, ...Od.21.69.262.
Say, shou'd some fav'ring God restore again ....Od.21.201.269.
But thou sincere! Oh *Euryclea,* say, ...Od.22.456.310.
Say, once more say, is my *Ulysses* here? ....Od.23.38.321.
Say, once more say, is my *Ulysses* here? ....Od.23.38.321.
That hence th' eluded passengers may say, ...Od.23.135.327.
Not unobserv'd: the *Greeks* eluded say ....Od.23.145.328.
'Tis thine, oh Queen, to say: And now impart, ...Od.23.209.333.
Son of *Melanthus!* (he began) Oh say! ....Od.24.129.354.
Say, could one city yield a troop so fair? ....Od.24.132.354.
Say, for the public did ye greatly fall? ....Od.24.139.354.
Who then thy master, say? and whose the land ....Od.24.302.364.
Say, lives he yet, or molders in the grave? ....Od.24.313.364.
Who knows thy blest, thy wish'd return? oh say, ...Od.24.465.371.
Say, hast thou doom'd to this divided state ....Od.24.544.374.

SAY'ST
Horses (thou say'st) and Asses, Men may try, ... 2.ChWB.100.61.
All this thou say'st, and all thou say'st are Lies. .... 2.ChWB.117.62.
All this thou say'st, and all thou say'st are Lies. .... 2.ChWB.117.62.

SAYING
There goes a Saying, and 'twas shrewdly said, ... 2.ChJM.101.19.
There goes a Saying, and 'twas wisely said, ... 2.ChJM.101A.19.

SAYINGS
"What Boy but hears the sayings of old Ben? .... 4.2HE1.80.201.

SAYS
Thus says the King who knew your Wickedness; .... 2.ChJM.639.46.
Whose Reign Indulgent God, says Holy Writ, ... 2.ChJM.690.48.
Christ saw a Wedding once, the Scripture says, ... 2.ChWB.9.57.
"God cannot love (says Blunt, with lifted eyes) .... 3.Ep3.105B.99.
"God cannot love (says Blunt, with tearless eyes) .... 3.Ep3.105.99.
Wou'd go to Mass in jest, (as Story says) .... 4.JD4.16.27.
And says our *Wars thrive ill,* because *delay'd;* .... 4.JD4.163.39.
And if the Dame says yes, the Dress says no. .... 4.HAdv.132.87.
And if the Dame says yes, the Dress says no. .... 4.HAdv.132.87.
But sure no Statute in his favour says, ... 4.2HE2.288.185.
Who says in verse what others say in prose; .... 4.2HE1.202.211.
My *Pylades!* what *Juv'nal* says, no Jest is; .... 6.24iii(b).1.76.
He says, poor Poets lost, while Players won, ... 6.34.21.101.
Says *Addison* to *Steele,* 'Tis Time to go. .... 6.49ii.11.140.
"Has she no Faults then (Envy says) Sir?" .... 6.89.9.250.
"Has she no Faults then (Envy says)?" .... 6.89.9A.250.
But hold! says *Molly,* first let's try, ... 6.94.49.260.
Once (says an Author, where, I need not say) .... 6.145.1.388.
There, take (says *Justice)* take ye each a *Shell.* .... 6.145.10.388.
A man, he says, a man resides with thee, ... Od.5.131.178.

SCABBARD
And from the scabbard drew the shining sword; .... Od.11.28.380.
And in the scabbard plung'd the glitt'ring blade: .... Od.11.123.387.

SCAEA'S
The gentle Steeds thro' *Scæa's* Gates they guide: .... Il.3.333.209.
At *Scæa's* Gates they meet the mourning Wain, ... Il.24.886.573.

SCAEAN
Her silent Footsteps to the *Scæan* Gate. .... Il.3.190.200.
Great *Hector* enter'd at the *Scæan* Gate. .... Il.6.297.341.
And met the Mourner at the *Scæan* Gate. .... Il.6.491.350.
Then rush'd impetuous thro' the *Scæan* Gate. .... Il.7.2.363.
Achilles' Fury at the *Scæan* Gate; .... Il.9.467.455.
Now near the Beech-tree, and the *Scæan* Gates, ... Il.11.223.45.
While *Hector* checking at the *Scæan* Gates .... Il.16.869.277.
There fixt he stood before the *Scæan* Gate; .... Il.22.10.453.
Full at the *Scæan* Gates expects the War; .... Il.22.48.454.
And stretch thee here, before this *Scæan* Gate. .... Il.22.452.474.
Nor ev'n his Stay without the *Scæan* Gate. .... Il.22.565.479.

SCAFFOLD
But quite mistakes the scaffold for the pile. .... 3.Ep1.221.34.
Wait, to the Scaffold, or the silent Cell, ... 6.84.31Z1.239.
She waits, or to the Scaffold, or the Cell, ... 6.84.33.240.

SCAFFOLDS
"Away, away! take all your scaffolds down, ... 4.1HE1.146.289.

SCAL'D
He leapt the Trenches, scal'd a Castle-Wall, ... 4.2HE2.40.167.
The Walls are scal'd; the rolling Flames arise; .... Il.9.700.468.

SCALDING
From his vile Visage wip'd the scalding Tears. .... Il.2.331.143.
When scalding Thirst their burning Bowels wrings. .... Il.16.195.247.

SCALE
Returning Justice lift aloft her Scale; .... 1.Mes.18.114.
With Fates prevailing, turn'd the Scale of Fight. .... 1.TrES.171Z2.455.
Then, in the scale of reas'ning life, 'tis plain .... 3.EOM1.47.19.
Then, in the scale of Life and Sence, 'tis plain .... 3.EOM1.47A.19.
Go, wiser thou! and in thy scale of sense .... 3.EOM1.113.29.
The scale of sensual, mental pow'rs ascends: .... 3.EOM1.208.41.
Thro' gen'ral Life, behold the Scale arise .... 3.EOM1.207A.41.
The scale to measure others wants by thine. .... 3.EOM2.292.90.
See the false scale of Happiness complete! .... 3.EOM4.288.155.
Or helps th' ambitious Hill the heav'n to scale, ... 3.Ep4.59.142.
Poetic Justice, with her lifted scale; .... 5.DunA1.50.66.
Poetic Justice, with her lifted scale, ... 5.DunB1.52.274.
St. A-d-re [*André]* too, the Scale to take .... 6.94.27.260.
While, Scale in Hand, Dame *Justice* past along. .... 6.145.4.388.
To scale our Walls, to wrap our Tow'rs in Flames, ... Il.8.200.407.
Whose Fates are heaviest in the Scale of *Jove.* .... Il.8.662.427.
And level hangs the doubtful Scale of Fight. .... Il.11.436.53.
With Fates prevailing, turn'd the Scale of Fight. .... Il.12.528.101.
Compact, and firm with many a jointed Scale) .... Il.15.629.220.
Then, nor till then, the Scale of War shall turn, ... Il.15.720.223.
He sees for *Greece* the Scale of Conquest rise, ... Il.16.432.259.
With *Jove* averse, had turn'd the Scale of Fate: .... Il.17.373.302.
The Scale of Conquest ever wav'ring lies , ... Il.19.223.382.
Low sinks the Scale surcharg'd with *Hector's* Fate; .... Il.22.275.467.
Then, happier thoughts return the nodding scale, ... Od.20.279.246.
Weigh then my counsels in an equal scale, ... Od.24.528.373.

SCALE'S
Where, one step broken, the great scale's destroy'd: .... 3.EOM1.244.45.

SCALES
Pleas'd, the green Lustre of the Scales survey, ... 1.Mes.83.120.
The yellow Carp, in Scales bedrop'd with Gold, ... 1.W-F.144.163.
As when two Scales are charg'd with doubtful Loads, ... 1.TrES.167.455.

SCALES (CONTINUED)
Now *Jove* suspends his golden Scales in Air, ... 2.RL5.71.206.
His Giant Limbs are arm'd in Scales of Gold. .... 2.TemF.116.262.
"Hear you! in whose grave heads, as equal scales, ... 5.DunA2.335.142.
"Ye Critics! in whose heads, as equal scales, ... 5.DunB2.367.315.
For nothing's left in either of the Scales. .... 6.28.2.82.
And in a Moment scales the lofty Skies. .... Il.5.458.290.
High o'er the dusty Whirlwind scales the Heav'n. .... Il.5.1063.317.
The Sire of Gods his golden Scales suspends, ... Il.8.88.399.
Whose imitated Scales against the Skies .... Il.11.34.36.
As when two Scales are charg'd with doubtful Loads, ... Il.12.521.100.
The Scales of *Jove,* and pants with Awe divine. .... Il.16.800.274.
Jove weighs affairs of earth in dubious scales, ... Od.6.229.220.

SCALING
Raise scaling Engines, and ascend the Wall: .... 1.TrES.180.456.
When scaling Armies climb'd up ev'ry Part, ... 6.96iv.69.278.
Raise scaling Engines, and ascend the Wall: .... Il.12.534.101.

SCALY
With Looks unmov'd, he hopes the Scaly Breed, ... 1.W-F.139.163.
Mending old Nets to catch the scaly Fry; .... 6.14ii.16.43.
Shot forth to View, a scaly Serpent sees; .... Il.3.48.191.
In Shoals before him fly the scaly Train, ... Il.21.31.422.
Now flounce aloft, now dive the scaly Fry, ... Il.21.414.437.
The scaly charge their guardian God surround: .... Od.4.558.146.
Invade him, couch'd amid the scaly fold: .... Od.4.562.147.
New from the corse, the scaly frauds diffuse .... Od.4.597.148.

SCAMANDER
Roll'd down *Scamander* with the Vulgar Dead. .... Il.2.1049.172.
Who near ador'd *Scamander* made Abode, ... Il.5.101.271.
Where Silver *Simois* and *Scamander* join. .... Il.5.965.312.
And deep *Scamander* swells with Heaps of Slain. .... Il.11.623.61.
But call'd *Scamander* by the Sons of Earth. .... Il.20.102.398.
But swift *Scamander* roll thee to the Deep, ... Il.21.138.427.
What Rivers can, *Scamander* might have shown; .... Il.21.209.430.
Scamander spoke; the Shores return'd the Sound. .... Il.21.230.430.
Still swift *Scamander* rolls where'er he flies: .... Il.21.300.433.
Now urge the Course where swift *Scamander* glides: .... Il.21.714.451.

SCAMANDER'S
The Legions crowd *Scamander's* flow'ry Side, ... Il.2.547.153.
Scamandrius, from *Scamander's* honour'd Stream; .... Il.6.501.351.
What Tides of Blood have drench'd *Scamander's* Shore? .... Il.7.394.383.
These to *Scamander's* Bank apart he led, ... Il.8.611.425.
What boots ye now *Scamander's* worship'd Stream, ... Il.21.143.427.
Next by *Scamander's* double Source they bound, ... Il.22.195.463.

SCAMANDRIUS
Then dy'd *Scamandrius,* expert in the Chace, ... Il.5.65.269.
Scamandrius, from *Scamander's* honour'd Stream; .... Il.6.501.351.

SCAN
Know then thyself, presume not God to scan; .... 3.EOM2.1.53.

SCAN'D
Then with revengeful Eyes he scan'd him o'er: .... Il.20.497.415.

SCANDAL
With Scandal arm'd, th'Ignoble Mind's Delight,) .... 1.TrSt.233.420.
Wh[arton], the Shame and Scandal of mankind: .... 3.EOM4.282A.154.
Or her, whose life the Church and Scandal share, ... 3.Ep2.105.58.
The Pleasure miss'd her, and the Scandal hit. .... 3.Ep2.128.61.
Give Virtue scandal, Innocence a fear, ... 4.Arbu.285.116.
"Praise undeserv'd is scandal in disguise:" .... 4.2HE1.413.229.
And quite a scandal not to learn: .... 4.HS6.146.259.
If honest S*z take scandal at a spark, ... 4.1HE1.112.287.
Ye Rev'rend Atheists!— *F.* Scandal! name them, Who? .... 4.EpS2.18.314.
Deem it but Scandal which the jealous raise, ... 6.38.11Z3.108.
Enjoys the *Jest,* and copies *Scandal* out: .... 6.120.6.339.
The Pleasure miss'd her, and the Scandal hit; .... 6.154.14.403.
In Scandal busie, in Reproaches bold: .... Il.2.258.140.
But Royal Scandal his Delight supreme. .... Il.2.270.140.
And fly, the Scandal of thy *Trojan* Host. .... Il.3.60.192.
Shame to your Country, Scandal of your Kind! .... Il.4.276.234.
Women of Greece! Oh Scandal of your Race, ... Il.7.109.369.
But say, if that lewd scandal of the sky .... Od.8.387.285.
(A load and scandal to this happy shore.) .... Od.17.299.146.
Oh sharp in scandal, voluble and vain! .... Od.22.319.301.

SCANDALOUSLY
Yet shun their Fault, who, *Scandalously nice,* .... 1.EOC.556.304.
Still hoarding up, most scandalously nice, ... 6.41.19.114.

SCANDALS
And gath'ring Scandals grew on ev'ry Tongue. .... 2.TemF.337.280.

SCANS
Each Wight who reads not, and but scans and spells, ... 4.Arbu.165.108.
The Wight who reads not, and but scans and spells, ... 4.Arbu.165A.108.
Each Wight who reads not, but who scans and spells, ... 4.Arbu.165B.108.
Who thinks he *reads* when he but *scans* and *spells,* .... 6.98.15.283.

SCANTIER
Here scantier limits the proud Arch confine, ... 6.71.27.203.
Now scantier limits the proud Arch confine, ... 6.71.27A.203.

SCANTY
We leap'd on shore, and with a scanty feast .... Od.10.61.342.
'Tis ours, with good the scanty round to grace. .... Od.19.378.212.

SCAP'D
Unseen I scap'd; and favour'd by the Night, ... 1.TrUl.148.470.
But 'scap'd not *Ajax;* his tempestuous Hand .... Il.14.471.186.
Wretch! Thou hast scap'd again. Once more thy Flight .... Il.20.519.416.

SCAP'D (CONTINUED)
Who scap'd by Flight, or who by Battel fell. ....Il.21.720.451.
And 'scap'd the perils of the gulfy Main. ....Od.1.17.30.
Scarce with these few I scap'd; of all my train, ...Od.9.339.320.
Just 'scap'd impending death, when now again ....Od.9.575.330.
The rock o'erwhelms us, and we 'scap'd in vain. ....Od.9.584.330.
Unseen I 'scap'd; and favour'd by the night ....Od.13.315.21.
Yet 'scap'd he death; and vengeful of his wrong ....Od.15.260.80.

SCAPE
No impious Wretch shall 'scape unpunish'd long, ...2.ChJM.649.46.
Hear this, and tremble! you, who 'scape the Laws. ....4.HS1.118.17.
The Morals blacken'd when the Writings scape; ....4.Arbu.352.121.
Observing, cry'd, "You scape not so, ...4.1HE7.57.271.
On Crimes that scape, or triumph o'er the Law: ....4.EpS1.168.309.
To 'scape my Censure, not expect my Praise: ....4.EpS2.113.319.
And 'scape the martyrdom of jakes and fire; ....5.DunA1.124.78.
How, with less reading than makes felons 'scape, ...5.DunA1.235.90.
And 'scape the martyrdom of jakes and fire: ....5.DunB1.144.280.
How, with less reading than makes felons scape, ...5.DunB1.281.290.
In vain you think to 'scape Rhyme-free, ...6.10.38.25.
And pleas'd to 'scape from Flattery to Wit. ....6.84.12.239.
Ye scape not both; One, headlong from his Car, ...Il.5.349.283.
Give these at least to 'scape from *Hector's* Hand, ...Il.8.291.411.
Trust thy own Cowardice to 'scape their Fire. ....Il.12.288.92.
Shall 'scape with Transport, and with Joy repose. ....Il.19.76.375.
For should he 'scape the Sword, the common Doom, ...Il.22.624.482.
To 'scape the Wars, to *Agamemnon* gave, ...Il.23.366.504.
Hither, to 'scape his chains, my course I steer, ...Od.17.526.158.

SCAPED
None 'scaped him, bosom'd in the gloomy wood; ....Od.17.383.150.

SCAPES
Is but a licens'd Theft that 'scapes the Law. ....Il.24.534.558.

SCAPING
See ESCAPE.
Half-breathless 'scaping to the land, he flew ....Od.16.65.105.

SCAR
Old *England's* Genius, rough with many a Scar, ...4.EpS1.152.309.
Not *Waller's* Wreath can hide the Nation's Scar, ...4.EpS2.230.325.
Safe he return'd, without one hostile scar; ....Od.11.656.416.
The gen'rous motive dignifies the scar. ....Od.17.561.159.
The scar, with which his manly knee was sign'd; ....Od.19.455.216.
The scar, with which his manly knee was sign'd. ....Od.19.461.218.
Deep o'er his knee inseam'd, remain'd the scar: ....Od.19.544.223.
Lo! the broad scar indented on my thigh, ...Od.21.227.270.
The sign conspicuous, and the scar expos'd: ....Od.21.231.270.
Plough'd half his thigh; I saw, I saw the scar, ...Od.23.76.322.
The scar indented by the tusky boar. ....Od.24.385.367.

SCAR'D
Scar'd at the grizly Forms, I sweat, I fly, ...4.JD4.278.49.
Scar'd at the spectre of pale Poverty! ....4.1HE1.70.283.
A dauntless infant! never scar'd with God. ....5.DunB4.284.372.
Scar'd with the Din and Tumult of the Fight, ...Il.6.47.325.
Scar'd at the dazling Helm, and nodding Crest. ....Il.6.597.356.
Scar'd we receded. Forth, with frantic hand ....Od.9.471.325.
Stun my scar'd ears, and pierce hell's utmost bounds. ....Od.11.782.425.

SCARBOROUGHW
Brave S[carborough]w lov'd thee, and was ly'd to death. ....4.1740.78.336.

SCARBROW
And melts to Goodness, need I SCARBROW name? ....4.EpS2.65.316.

SCARCE
Scarce could the Goddess from her Nymph be known, ...1.W-F.175.166.
Tempt Icy Seas, where scarce the Waters roll, ...1.W-F.389.189.
So great the tale, I scarce can count them o'er; ....1.TrPA.80.368.
How, scarce, my ewes their strutting udders bear; ....1.TrPA.83.368.
His pleasures too (tho' that I scarce can bear) ....1.TrPA.123.370.
Scarce to himself, himself is better known. ....1.TrVP.84.380.
O scarce a Youth, yet scarce a tender Boy! ....1.TrSP.103.398.
O scarce a Youth, yet scarce a tender Boy! ....1.TrSP.103.398.
But scarce subsisted to the Second Reign. ....1.TrSt.199.418.
This weary'd Arm can scarce the Bolt sustain, ...1.TrSt.304.423.
He scarce cou'd rule some Idle Appetites; ....2.ChJM.6.15.
That scarce they bent the Flow'rs, or touch'd the Ground. ....2.ChJM.622.45.
When their weak Legs scarce dragg'd 'em out of Doors; ....2.ChWB.155.64.
Not much we fasted, but scarce ever slept. ....2.ChWB.286.70.
I vow'd, I scarce cou'd sleep since first I knew him, ...2.ChWB.300.71.
But to my Tale: A Month scarce past away, ...2.ChWB.329.72.
And scarce detested in his Country's Fate. ....2.TemF.158.266.
Scarce to the Top I stretch'd my aking Sight, ...2.TemF.246.275.
Scarce seem'd her Stature of a Cubit's height, ...2.TemF.259.275.
Scarce any Tale was sooner heard than told; ....2.TemF.469.286.
Heav'n scarce believ'd the conquest it survey'd, ...2.ElAb.113.329.
A thousand movements scarce one purpose gain; ....3.EOM1.54.20.
The last, scarce ripen'd into perfect Man, ...3.EOM3.141.107.
Who ask and reason thus, will scarce conceive ....3.EOM4.163.143.
Born where Heav'n's influence scarce can penetrate: ....3.Ep1.94.22.
Just brought out this, when scarce his tongue could stir, ...3.Ep1.254.37.
Scarce once herself, by turns all Womankind! ....3.Ep2.116.60.
As leaves them scarce a Subject in their Age: ....3.Ep2.222.68.
At last, to follies Youth could scarce defend, ...3.Ep2.235.69.
Scarce H[awle]y's self had sent it to the dogs? ....3.Ep3.54A.90.
There are (I scarce can think it, but am told) ....4.HS1.1.5.
Scarce to wise *Peter* complaisant enough, ...4.HS1.3.5.
They scarce can bear their *Laureate* twice a Year: ....4.HS1.34.7.
From furious *Sappho* scarce a milder Fate, ...4.HS1.83.13.
Scarce was I enter'd, when behold! there came ....4.JD4.24.27.
Act Sins which Prisca's Confessor scarce hears: ....4.JD2.40.135.
I scarce can think him such a worthless thing, ...4.2HE1.209.213.

SCARCE (CONTINUED)
And fluent Shakespear scarce effac'd a line. ....4.2HE1.279.219.
Our Courtier scarce could touch a bit, ...4.HS6.171.261.
And when three Sov'reigns dy'd, could scarce be vext, ...4.EpS1.107.306.
Scarce hurts the Lawyer, but undoes the Scribe. ....4.EpS2.47.315.
What RICHELIEU wanted, LOUIS scarce could gain, ...4.EpS2.116.319.
Writ not, and *Chartres* scarce could write or read, ...4.EpS2.186.324.
How Hints, like spawn, scarce quick in embryo lie, ...5.DunA1.57.67.
Then [Aaron] essay'd: scarce vanish'd out of sight ....5.DunA2.283B.136.
How hints, like spawn, scarce quick in embryo lie, ...5.DunB1.59.274.
Then * essay'd; scarce vanish'd out of sight, ...5.DunB2.295.310.
Then catch'd the Schools; the Hall scarce kept awake; ....5.DunB4.609.404.
'Till Fate scarce felt his gentle Breath suppress, ...6.19.13.62.
'Till Death scarce felt did o'er his Pleasures creep, ...6.19.13A.62.
'Till death scarce felt his gentle Breath suppress, ...6.19.13B.62.
Statues of Men, scarce less alive than they; ....6.71.10.203.
And scarce are seen the prostrate Nile or Rhine, ...6.71.28.203.
And scarce are seen the prostrate Nile and Rhine, ...6.71.28A.203.
Or Virtue's Virtue scarce would last a Day. ....6.82vi.8.232.
My spacious palm in Stature scarce a Span ....6.96ii.30Z41.272.
"My spacious Palm? Of Stature scarce a Span, ...6.96ii.63.273.
Scarce once herself, by Turns all Womankind? ....6.154.2.402.
And scarce ensure the wretched Pow'r to fly. ....Il.2.164.136.
While scarce the Swains their feeding Flocks survey, ...Il.3.19.188.
Th' Immortal Coursers scarce the Labour bore. ....Il.4.40.223.
While scarce the Skies her horrid Head can bound, ...Il.4.504.245.
Now win the Shores, and scarce the Seas remain. ....Il.5.985.314.
And scarce refrain'd when I forbad the War. ....Il.5.1001.314.
From mortal Madness scarce was sav'd by Flight. ....Il.5.1087.318.
Redeem'd too late, she scarce beheld again ....Il.6.540.353.
The Waves scarce heave, the Face of Ocean sleeps, ...Il.7.73.366.
These Words scarce spoke, with gen'rous Ardour prest, ...Il.7.119.369.
Scarce could the Friend his slaughter'd Friend explore, ...Il.7.504.389.
Scarce had his Falchion cut the Reins, and freed ....Il.8.109.403.
Sole should he sit, with scarce a God to Friend, ...Il.8.250.409.
He try'd it once, and scarce was sav'd by Fate. ....Il.9.468.455.
Scarce can my Knees these trembling Limbs sustain, ...Il.10.100.7.
And scarce my Heart support its Load of Pain. ....Il.10.101.7.
Scarce had he pass'd the Steeds and *Trojan* Throng, ...Il.10.401.21.
Till scarce at distance of a Javelin's throw, ...Il.10.425.22.
Ev'n great *Achilles* scarce their Rage can tame, ...Il.10.475.24.
Scarce had he spoke, when lo! the Chiefs appear, ...Il.10.636.30.
Scarce did the Down his rosy Cheeks invest, ...Il.11.287.48.
Scarce from the Field with all their Efforts chas'd, ...Il.11.688.66.
Whose humble Barrier scarce the Foes divides, ...Il.13.856.146.
What Troops, out-number'd scarce the War maintain? ....Il.13.927.149.
Yet scarce an Army stirs him from his Post: ....Il.16.137.243.
There yet scarce spent, it quivers on the Plain, ...Il.16.743.272.
The first Attack the *Grecians* scarce sustain, ...Il.17.324.300.
Scarce their weak Drivers guide them thro' the Fight: ....Il.17.555.309.
Who tremble yet, scarce rescu'd from their Fates, ...Il.17.719.315.
Scarce sev'n Moons gone, lay *Sthenelus* his Wife; ....Il.19.115.376.
Scarce on the Surface curl'd the briny Dew. ....Il.20.273.405.
Great as he is, our Arm he scarce will try, ...Il.20.399.411.
His Back scarce turn'd, the *Pelian* Jav'lin gor'd; ....Il.20.567.418.
Scarce respited from Woes I yet appear, ...Il.21.92.425.
And scarce twelve morning Suns have seen me here; ....Il.21.93.425.
His Feet, upborn, scarce the strong Flood divide, ...Il.21.266.431.
And scarce restrains the Torrent in her Eyes: ....Il.21.574.446.
Tho' strook, tho' wounded, scarce perceives the Pain, ...Il.21.681.450.
The God now distant scarce a Stride before, ...Il.21.715.451.
Scarce the whole People stop his desp'rate Course, ...Il.22.524.478.
Scarce from the Verge of Death recall'd, again ....Il.22.606.481.
When scarce a God redeem'd him from his Hand) ....Il.23.362.504.
Scarce did the Chief the vig'rous Strife propose, ...Il.23.820.522.
Hail, and be blest! For scarce of mortal Kind ....Il.24.463.556.
And scarce their Rulers check their martial Rage. ....Il.24.494.556.
And scarce their Rulers check the martial Rage. ....Il.24.494A.556.
Scarce three strong *Greeks* could lift its mighty Weight, ...Il.24.559.559.
Scarce all my herds their luxury suffice; ....Od.2.63.63.
Scarce all my wine their midnight hours supplies. ....Od.2.64.63.
Still lab'ring on, 'till scarce at last we found ....Od.3.147.92.
Which scarce the sea-fowl in a year o'erfly) ....Od.3.412.106.
Observant of his word. The word scarce spoke, ...Od.3.606.117.
Scarce could *Iäsion* taste her heav'nly charms, ...Od.5.161.179.
Huge, horrid, vast! where scarce in safety sails ....Od.5.227.182.
For scarce in ken appears that distant Isle ....Od.5.456.194.
Now, scarce withdrawn the fierce Earth-shaking pow'r, ...Od.5.488.195.
The soul scarce waking, in the arms of death. ....Od.5.587.200.
Turn and return, and scarce imprint the sand. ....Od.8.414.286.
Scarce twenty measures from the living stream ....Od.9.243.316.
(Scarce twenty four-wheel'd cars, compact and strong, ...Od.9.286.318.
Scarce with these few I scap'd; of all my train, ...Od.9.339.320.
The direful wreck *Ulysses* scarce survives! ....Od.11.144.387.
Ulysses at his country scarce arrives! ....Od.11.145.387.
The wond'rous youths had scarce nine winters told, ...Od.11.381.401.
Touch'd at the sight from tears I scarce refrain, ...Od.11.675.417.
Scarce the fam'd *Argo* pass'd these raging floods, ...Od.12.83.435.
Now scarce four hundred left. These to defend, ...Od.14.23.35.
Scarce ended thus the Prince, when on the right ....Od.15.178.77.
Scarce lifts his eyes, and bows as to a God. ....Od.16.195.113.
Scarce had he spoke, when turning to the strand ....Od.16.366.124.
And scarce those few, for tears, could force their way. ....Od.17.51.135.
Scarce sure of life, look round, and trembling move ....Od.22.419.308.
And scarce the meshy toils the copious draught contain, ...Od.22.427.308.
Pow'rless to speak, I scarce uplift my eyes, ...Od.23.109.325.
How scarce himself surviv'd: He paints the bow'r, ...Od.23.345.341.

SCARCELY
Slowly he rises, scarcely breathes with Pain, ...Il.21.488.441.
And pour to Dogs the Life-blood scarcely warm; ....Il.22.105.457.
His bounding Horses scarcely touch the Fields: ....Il.23.582.513.
The winds were hush'd, the billows scarcely curl'd, ...Od.5.502.196.
The solid gate its fury scarcely bounds; ....Od.21.463.282.

SCARE
Write on, nor let me scare ye; .... 6.58.38.172.
Write on, nor let me scare you; .... 6.58.38A.172.
And scare Lord *Fannys* from his Ear: .... 6.135.76.369.

SCARECROW
Scarecrow to Boys, the breeding Woman's curse; .... 4.JD4.268.47.

SCARES
The *God* whose Ensign scares the Birds of Prey, ... 1.TrVP.23.378.

SCARF
The various-colour'd Scarf, the Shield he rears, ... Il.10.84.6.
The martial Scarf and Robe of Triumph wove. .... Il.22.657.483.
This heav'nly Scarf beneath thy bosom bind, ... Od.5.440.193.
The mindful chief *Leucothea's* scarf unbound; .... Od.5.589.200.

SCARFS
Scarfs, garters, gold, amuse his riper stage; .... 3.EOM2.279.88.

SCARLET
His Purple Crest, and Scarlet-circled Eyes, ... 1.W-F.116.161.
Grow scarlet strawberries to feast my love: .... 1.TrPA.75.368.
At Sermons too I shone in Scarlet gay; .... 2.ChWB.287.71.
Mounts the Tribunal, lifts her scarlet head, ... 4.EpS1.149.309.
With scarlet hats, wide waving, circles round, ... 5.DunA2.10.97.
With scarlet hats wide-waving circled round, ... 5.DunB2.14.297.
And knots of scarlet Ribbond deck *his* Mane. .... 6.9ix.2.22.

SCARLET-CIRCLED
His Purple Crest, and Scarlet-circled Eyes, ... 1.W-F.116.161.

SCARPHE'S
Opus, Calliarus, and *Scarphe's* Bands; .... Il.2.636.157.

SCARR'D
Drop endlong; scarr'd, and black with sulph'rous hue, ... Od.14.343.51.

SCARS
Inglorious Triumphs, and dishonest Scars. .... 1.W-F.326.180.

SCARSDALE
Scarsdale his Bottle, *Darty* his Ham-Pye; .... 4.HS1.46.9.

SCATT'ER
Sent Lightning on our Fleets, and scatt'er Fate?" .... Il.22.470.475.

SCATT'RING
Streak with long Gleams the scatt'ring Shades of Night; .... 1.TrSt.485.430.
But trembling leaves the scatt'ring Flocks a Prey. .... Il.5.179.275.
Swift as a Whirlwind drives the scatt'ring Foes, ... Il.5.850.306.
He, like a Whirlwind, toss'd the scatt'ring Throng, ... Il.12.45.83.
Stand, and my Spear shall rout their scatt'ring Pow'r, ... Il.13.207.115.
Troy's scatt'ring Orders open to the Show'r. .... Il.13.902.148.
The River here divides the scatt'ring Train. .... Il.21.3A.420.
Before him scatt'ring, they prevent his pains, ... Il.21.297.433.
The scatt'ring Arrows rattling from the Case, ... Il.21.571.446.
The leafy honours scatt'ring on the ground; .... Od.11.235.393.
The scatt'ring dogs around at distance bay. .... Od.14.40.37.

SCATTER
A leaf, like Sibyl's, scatter to and fro .... 3.Ep3.75.93.
Scatter your Favours on a Fop, ... 4.1HE7.31.271.
Angel of Dulness, sent to scatter round .... 5.DunA3.253.178.
Angel of Dulness, sent to scatter round .... 5.DunB3.257.332.
And scatter ore the Fields the driving Snow, ... 6.82v.2.231.
To scatter Hosts, and terrify Mankind. .... Il.15.353.210.
Of Geese, that scream, and scatter round the Plain. .... Il.17.529.309.
And scatter o'er the Fields of driving Snow; .... Il.19.381.388.
Thro' yon wide Host this Arm shall scatter Fear, ... Il.20.413.412.
Thee, Vultures wild should scatter round the Shore, ... Il.22.57.455.
And scatter them, ye storms, in empty air! .... Od.8.444.287.
Or screaming vulturs scatter thro' the air: .... Od.24.343.365.

SCATTER'D
Their faded Honours scatter'd on her Bier. .... 1.PWi.32.91.
Born by the Trumpet's Blast, and scatter'd thro the Sky. .... 2.TemF.488.287.
Each Leader now his scatter'd Force conjoins .... Il.2.560.154.
What's He, whose Arms lie scatter'd on the Plain? .... Il.3.254.204.
And all their Race be scatter'd as the Dust! .... Il.3.375.211.
Lo his proud Vessels scatter'd o'er the Main, ... Il.4.216.231.
Their consecrated Spears lay scatter'd round, ... Il.6.165.334.
From the red Field their scatter'd Bodies bear, ... Il.7.400.384.
Their Car in Fragments scatter'd o'er the Sky; .... Il.8.493.420.
Your Car in Fragments scatter'd o'er the Sky; .... Il.8.515.421.
Where thinly scatter'd lay the Heaps of Dead. .... Il.8.612.425.
(Enquir'd the Chief) or scatter'd o'er the Plain? .... Il.10.495.25.
As scatter'd Lambs the rushing Lion fear. .... Il.11.490.56.
My Friends all scatter'd, all the Foes around? .... Il.11.516.57.
The scatter'd Crowds fly frighted o'er the Field; .... Il.11.607.61.
The Ranks lie scatter'd, and the Troops o'erthrown) .... Il.11.665.63.
And here detain the scatter'd Youth of *Troy:* .... Il.13.943.150.
I scatter'd Slaughter from my fatal Bow. .... Il.13.980.152.
Soon shalt thou view the scatter'd *Trojan* Bands .... Il.14.166.165.
These proud in Arms, those scatter'd o'er the Plain; .... Il.15.9.194.
So flies a Herd of Oxen, scatter'd wide, ... Il.15.366.211.
Fly diverse, scatter'd o'er the distant Plain. .... Il.16.347.256.
But *Troy* repuls'd, and scatter'd o'er the Plains, ... Il.16.362.257.
(Or Kids, or Lambs) lie scatter'd o'er the Plain, ... Il.16.421.259.
All pale with Fear, at distance scatter'd round, ... Il.17.73.290.
And here, and there, their scatter'd Arrows light: .... Il.17.433.304.
The *Phrygians* now her scatter'd spoils enjoy, ... Il.18.341.338.
And Stalls, and Folds, and scatter'd Cotts between; .... Il.18.679.356.
Our Force he scatter'd, and our Herds he kill'd; .... Il.20.122.399.
All scatter'd round the Stream (their Mightiest slain) .... Il.21.223.430.
Floating midst scatter'd Arms; while Casques of Gold .... Il.21.350.435.

SCATTER'D (CONTINUED)
Collects the scatter'd Shafts, and fallen Bow, ... Il.21.586.446.
Views, from his Arm, the *Trojans* scatter'd Flight, ... Il.21.615.448.
O'er all the Corse their scatter'd Locks they throw. .... Il.23.166.495.
Kiss his pale Cheek, and rend their scatter'd Hair: .... Il.24.889.573.
Some he destroy'd, some scatter'd as the dust, ... Od.3.163.93.
Planks, Beams, dis-parted fly: the scatter'd wood .... Od.5.468.195.
Tosses and drives the scatter'd heaps of corn. .... Od.5.471.195.
Launch'd his red lightning at our scatter'd ships: .... Od.7.335.253.
The scatter'd wreck the winds blew back again. .... Od.9.341.320.
Or torn by birds are scatter'd thro' the sky. .... Od.14.157.43.
Then distant from the scatter'd Islands steer, ... Od.15.39.71.
The clotted feathers scatter'd from above .... Od.15.568.98.
And scatter'd short, or wide, the points of death; .... Od.22.283.300.
The scatter'd arms that hung around the dome .... Od.24.193.356.
All scatter'd round their glitt'ring weapons lie; .... Od.24.618.377.

SCATTERS
And scatters Blessings from her Dove-like Wing. .... 1.W-F.430.194.
And scatters Deaths around from both her Eyes, ... 2.RL5.58.203.
And undiscerning, scatters Crowns and Chains. .... 2.TemF.297.278.
And may thy God who scatters Darts around, ... Il.1.580.115.
'Till the Mass scatters as the Winds arise, ... Il.5.647.299.
O'erturns, confounds, and scatters all their Bands. .... Il.11.402.52.
And rudely scatters, far to distance round, ... Il.17.332.300.
The tempest scatters, and divides our fleet; .... Od.3.370.104.
Scatters with quiv'ring hand the sacred flour, ... Od.3.565.115.

SCENE
Eternal Beauties grace the shining Scene, ... 1.PWi.71.94.
Here waving Groves a chequer'd Scene display, ... 1.W-F.17.150.
Thro' the fair Scene rowl slow the lingring Streams, ... 1.W-F.217.169.
I view the *Grotto,* once the Scene of Love, ... 1.TrSP.163.400.
Fix'd on the Glorious Scene in wild Amaze, ... 1.TrSt.645.437.
(His Scene of Pleasure, and peculiar Care) .... 2.ChJM.466.37.
Down to the Central Earth, his proper Scene, ... 2.RL4.15.184.
And, join'd, this Intellectual Scene compose. .... 2.TemF.10.253.
Now a clear Sun the shining Scene displays, ... 2.TemF.19.254.
Strait chang'd the Scene, and snatch'd me from the Throne. ... 2.TemF.419.283.
Her gloomy presence saddens all the scene, ... 2.ElAb.167.333.
Amid that scene, if some relenting eye .... 2.ElAb.355.348.
Expatiate free o'er all this scene of Man; .... 3.EOM1.5.11.
Where-e'er he shines, oh Fortune, gild the scene, ... 3.Ep3.245.113.
Tir'd of the scene Parterres and Fountains yield, ... 3.Ep4.87.146.
No artful wildness to perplex the scene; .... 3.Ep4.116.148.
No artful Wilderness to perplex the scene; .... 3.Ep4.116A.148.
Saw such a Scene of *Envy, Sin,* and *Hate.* .... 4.JD4.193A.43.
Where Thames reflects the visionary Scene. .... 4.HOde1.24.153.
Whilst Thames reflects the visionary Scene. .... 4.HOde1.24A.153.
Conspicuous Scene! another yet is nigh, ... 4.1HE6.50.239.
Remov'd from all th' ambitious Scene, ... 4.HS6.27.251.
"A pretty kind of savage Scene! .... 4.HS6.177.261.
"But Lord, my Friend, this savage Scene! .... 4.HS6.177A.261.
The Scene, the Master, opening to my view, ... 4.EpS2.68.316.
Beholds thro' fogs that magnify the scene: .... 5.DunA1.78.68.
Now Night descending, the proud scene was o'er, ... 5.DunA1.87.69.
Now look thro' Fate! behold the scene she draws! .... 5.DunA3.119.160.
Beholds thro' fogs, that magnify the scene. .... 5.DunB1.80.275.
Now Night descending, the proud scene was o'er, ... 5.DunB1.89.276.
Now look thro' Fate! behold the scene she draws! .... 5.DunB3.127.325.
Behold a Scene of Misery and Woe! .... 6.9x.1.22.
Make Life a Scene of Pain, and constant Toil, ... 6.17iii.6.57.
A Type of Paradise, the Rural Scene! .... 6.17iii.39.58.
In ev'ry Scene some Moral let it teach, ... 6.19.23.62.
Whose shining scene with rich *Hesperia* vies. .... 6.20.71.68.
Live o'er each scene, and be what they behold: .... 6.32.4.96.
Our scene precariously subsists too long .... 6.32.41.97.
Your scene precariously subsists too long .... 6.32.41A.97.
In beauteous order terminate the scene. .... 6.35.27.103.
In pensive thought recall the fancy'd scene, ... 6.45.33.125.
And what behind the Scene, ... 6.61.9.181.
Scene of my youthful Loves, and happier hours! .... 6.66.2.194.
My Bed, (the scene of all our former Joys, ... 6.96iv.39.277.
With her th' *Italian* scene first learnt to glow; .... 6.107.5.310.
The heroine rise, to grace the *British* scene. .... 6.107.14.310.
And blest, that timely from our Scene remov'd .... 6.152.9.400.
Approach, and view the wond'rous Scene below! .... Il.3.174.199.
Had some brave Chief this martial Scene beheld, ... Il.4.630.251.
The Field of Combate is no Scene for thee: .... Il.5.434.289.
Me Glory summons to the martial Scene, ... Il.6.634.358.
Such be the Scene from his *Idæan* Bow'r; .... Il.8.252.409.
And not a Cloud o'ercasts the solemn Scene; .... Il.8.690.428.
A pensive Scene! 'till *Tydeus'* warlike Son .... Il.9.41.433.
Discord with Joy the Scene of Death descries, ... Il.11.99.39.
But *Hector,* from this Scene of Slaughter far, ... Il.11.620.61.
Jove sees delighted, and avoids the Scene .... Il.13.13.104.
An Iron Scene gleams dreadful o'er the Fields, ... Il.13.179.114.
Tremendous Scene, that gen'ral Horror gave, ... Il.13.434.126.
His wounded Eyes the Scene of Sorrow knew; .... Il.14.18.157.
Is this a Scene for Love? On *Ida's* Height, ... Il.14.375.180.
The Skies would yield an ampler Scene of Rage, ... Il.15.153.202.
A mournful Witness of this Scene of Woe: .... Il.15.463.215.
The Scene wide-opening to the Blaze of Light. .... Il.15.813.228.
The smiling Scene wide opens to the Sight, ... Il.16.360.257.
As the young Olive, in some Sylvan Scene, ... Il.17.57.290.
A sable Scene! The Terrors *Hector* led. .... Il.17.115.292.
And conscious, look'd thro' all the Scene of Fate. .... Il.17.228.296.
Could blame this Scene; such Rage, such Horror reign'd; .... Il.17.460.305.
Meantime, at distance from the Scene of Blood, ... Il.17.484.306.
And fleecy Flocks, that whiten all the Scene. .... Il.18.680.356.
A splendid Scene! Then *Agamemnon* rose: .... Il.19.258.383.
Suffice, from yonder Mount to view the Scene; .... Il.20.164.400.
The Scene of War came rushing on his Sight. .... Il.20.392.411.
High o'er the Scene of Death *Achilles* stood, ... Il.20.587.418.
Jove, as his Sport, the dreadful Scene descries, ... Il.21.454.439.
To their own Hands commit the frantick Scene, ... Il.21.541.444.

SCENE 256 SCHERIANS

SCENE (CONTINUED)
(Sad Scene of Woe!) His Face his wrapt Attire ....Il.24.200.545.
(A solemn Scene!) at length the Father spoke. ....Il.24.803.570.
Thence all these Tears, and all this Scene of Woe! ....Il.24.931.575.
What lands so distant from that scene of death ....Od.3.237.97.
Some envious pow'r the blissful scene destroys; ....Od.4.245.131.
The man entranc'd wou'd view the deathful scene. ....Od.4.314.134.
Without the grot, a various sylvan scene ....Od.5.80.176.
A scene, where if a God shou'd cast his sight, ...Od.5.95.177.
Thy heart might settle in this scene of ease, ...Od.5.265.184.
Falls by degrees, and forms a beauteous scene; ....Od.6.354.229.
In beauteous order terminate the scene. ....Od.7.168.244.
Th' unwonted scene surprize and rapture drew; ....Od.7.179.244.
The bushing alders form'd a shady scene. ....Od.9.164.312.
Reveal'd the landscape and the scene unknown, ...Od.9.175.312.
The deathful scene, Princes on Princes roll'd! ....Od.11.151.388.
So vile a deed, so dire a scene of blood. ....Od.11.520.409.
Dire *Scylla* there a scene of horror forms, ...Od.12.280.445.
Never, I never, scene so dire survey'd! ....Od.12.309.447.
And plan with all thy arts the scene of fate. ....Od.13.442.27.
One scene of woe; to endless cares consign'd, ...Od.16.208.114.
And plan the scene of death, I bend my way: ....Od.16.257.117.
Be now the scene of instant death decreed: ....Od.16.387.124.
(Scene of their insolence) the Lords resort; ....Od.17.191.140.
And now in humbler scene submit to Fate. ....Od.17.339.148.
Long, long the scene of all my past delight, ...Od.21.79.262.
Far be he banish'd from this stately scene ....Od.21.343.276.
From the dire scene th' exempted two withdraw, ...Od.22.418.308.
(Their life's last scene) they trembling wait their fall. ....Od.22.494.313.
The deathful scene, on Heroes, Heroes roll'd; ....Od.23.390.343.
From all the scene of tumult far away! ....Od.23.392.343.

SCENES
See what Delights in Sylvan Scenes appear! ....1.PSu.59.76.
Bear me, oh bear me to sequester'd Scenes, ...1.W-F.261.173.
To paint anew the flow'ry Sylvan Scenes, ...1.W-F.285.174.
And bring the Scenes of opening Fate to Light. ....1.W-F.426.194.
New, distant Scenes of *endless* Science rise! ....1.EOC.224.265.
Soft Scenes of Solitude no more can please, ...1.TrSP.15.393.
With mournful Looks the blissful Scenes survey'd, ...2.ChJM.61.17.
Now Lakes of liquid Gold, *Elysian* Scenes, ...2.RL4.45.187.
No more these scenes my meditation aid, ...2.ElAb.161.332.
What scenes appear where-e'er I turn my view! ....2.ElAb.263.341.
But nobler scenes Maria's dreams unfold, ...3.Ep3.131.104.
Beheld such Scenes of *Envy, Sin,* and *Hate.* ....4.JD4.193.43.
Back fly the scenes, and enter foot and horse; ....4.2HE1.315.223.
Old scenes of glory, times long cast behind, ...5.DunA3.55.155.
But oh! what scenes, what miracles behind? ....5.DunA3.201Z1.175.
Here lay poor Fletcher's half-eat scenes, and here ....5.DunB1.131.279.
Old scenes of glory, times long cast behind ....5.DunB3.63.323.
While thro' Poetic scenes the Genius roves, ...5.DunB4.489.390.
What Scenes appear'd, ...6.11.54.32.
And *Twick'nam* such, which fairer Scenes enrich, ...6.14ii.49.44.
What flatt'ring scenes our wand'ring fancy wrought, ...6.52.23.156.
In vain fair Thames reflects the double scenes ....6.81.3.225.
And Scenes of Blood rise dreadful in his Soul. ....Il.1.639.118.
What Scenes of Grief and Numbers of the Slain! ....Il.2.50.129.
What Scenes of Grief and Mountains of the Slain! ....Il.2.50A.129.
The Bow'rs of *Ceres,* and the Sylvan Scenes, ...Il.2.850.164.
Jove seals the League, or bloodier Scenes prepares; ....Il.4.113.225.
What Scenes of Slaughter in yon Fields appear! ....Il.9.301.449.
Bright Scenes of Arms, and Works of War appear; ....Il.11.872.74.
The fancy'd Scenes, of *Ilion* wrapt in Flames, ...Il.16.1005.282.
And Scenes of Blood, and agonizing Sounds. ....Il.19.214.381.
Let their warm Heads with Scenes of Battle glow, ...Il.19.235.382.
To fill with Scenes of Death his closing Eyes, ...Il.22.86.456.
[When fierce in arms he sought the scenes of war, ...Od.2.255.74.
Shall I the long, laborious scenes review, ...Od.3.127.92.
What scenes have I survey'd of dreadful view? ....Od.6.262.222.
In scenes of death, by tempest and by war. ....Od.8.206.273.
While scenes of woe rose anxious in my breast, ...Od.10.443.365.
New trains of dangers, and new scenes of woes: ....Od.11.129.387.
The scenes of life recur, and actions past; ....Od.11.181.390.
Thy woes on earth, the wond'rous scenes in hell, ...Od.11.467.407.
If scenes of misery can entertain, ...Od.11.474.407.
The dreadful scenes of *Pluto's* dreary state. ....Od.12.44.431.
Now all at once tremendous scenes unfold; ....Od.12.240.443.
Scenes of lewd loves his wakeful eyes survey, ...Od.20.10.230.
Such future scenes th' all-righteous pow'rs display, ...Od.23.303.337.
And labour'd scenes of richest verdure round. ....Od.24.256.361.

SCENT
At once they gratify their Scent and Taste, ...2.RL3.111.176.
And like sure Spaniels, at first Scent lie down. ....6.82vi.6.232.
Where treasur'd Odors breath'd a costly Scent. ....Il.6.359.343.
Sleek the smooth skin, and scent the snowy limbs. ....Od.6.94.209.
And breathing odours scent the balmy skies. ....Od.8.398.285.
Where the rich wardrobe breath'd a costly scent. ....Od.15.115.74.
His eye how piercing, and his scent how true, ...Od.17.384.150.
To wash, to scent, and purify the room. ....Od.22.475.312.

SCENTED
And ravenous Dogs, allur'd by scented Blood, ...1.TrSt.737.441.

SCENTS
Less fragrant Scents th' unfolding Rose exhales, ...2.TemF.316.279.
There dangling pears exalted scents unfold, ...Od.11.729.421.
Spreads o'er the coast, and scents the tainted gales; ....Od.12.434.452.

SCEPTER
And by this awful Scepter which I bear, ...2.ChJM.648.46.
With his huge Scepter grac'd, and red Attire, ...Il.18.485.345.
Alternate, each th' attesting Scepter took, ...Il.18.587.351.
(His royal hand th' imperial scepter sway'd) ....Od.2.45.62.
Where great *Hippotades* the scepter bore, ...Od.10.2.335.
He sway'd the scepter with imperial state. ....Od.11.346.399.

SCEPTER (CONTINUED)
To fix the scepter stedfast in his hands? ....Od.11.608.413.
Th' imperial scepter, and the regal bed: ....Od.16.134.109.

SCEPTER'D
Whom scepter'd Slaves in golden Harness drew: ....2.TemF.114.262.
Oh true descendent of a scepter'd line! ....Od.1.286.46.
Or came fore-runner of your scepter'd Sire? ....Od.1.520.57.
Say from what scepter'd ancestry ye claim, ...Od.4.73.122.
Than reign the scepter'd monarch of the dead. ....Od.11.600.413.

SCEPTERS
While These exalt their Scepters o'er my Urn; ....1.TrSt.106.414.
The Change of Scepters, and impending Woe; ....1.TrSt.842.444.
They gave thee Scepters, and a wide Command, ...Il.9.53.434.
The Laws and Scepters to thy Hand are giv'n, ...Il.9.129.438.
And form a Ring, with Scepters in their Hands; ....Il.18.584.351.

SCEPTIC
With too much knowledge for the Sceptic side, ...3.EOM2.5.53.

SCEPTRE
Extends the Sceptre and the Laurel Crown. ....Il.1.20.86.
Now by this sacred Sceptre, hear me swear, ...Il.1.309.102.
This Sceptre, form'd by temper'd Steel to prove ....Il.1.313.103.
His Sceptre starr'd with golden Studs around. ....Il.1.326.103.
Held forth the Sceptre and the Laurel Crown, ...Il.1.487.111.
And last his Arm the massy Sceptre loads, ...Il.2.57.129.
High in his Hand the Golden Sceptre blaz'd: ....Il.2.128.133.
The Golden Sceptre, of Celestial Frame, ...Il.2.129.133.
On this bright Sceptre now the King reclin'd, ...Il.2.137.134.
Receiv'd th' Imperial Sceptre of Command, ...Il.2.222.138.
The weighty Sceptre on his Back descends: ....Il.2.327.143.
Who rising, high th' Imperial Sceptre rais'd: ....Il.2.341.143.
He said, and rear'd his Sceptre to the Sky. ....Il.7.489.388.
But first exalt thy Sceptre to the Skies, ...Il.10.379.20.
The Chief then heav'd the golden Sceptre high, ...Il.10.387.21.
Then with his Sceptre that the Deep controuls, ...Il.13.87.109.
The Herald plac'd the Sceptre in his Hands, ...Il.23.647.515.
At least, the sceptre lost, I still shou'd reign ....Od.1.507.56.
And dash'd th' imperial sceptre to the ground. ....Od.2.90.65.
Sage *Nestor* fill'd it, and the sceptre sway'd. ....Od.3.523.113.
Who sway'd the sceptre, where prolific *Nile* ....Od.4.317.134.
No, if this sceptre yet commands the main. ....Od.5.374.190.

SCEPTRED
The Pow'rs of Earth, and sceptred Sons of *Jove.* ....Il.1.369.105.
The sceptred Rulers lead; the following Host ....Il.2.109.132.
Nor rais'd his Head, nor stretch'd his sceptred Hand; ....Il.3.282.207.
The sceptred Kings of *Greece* his Words approv'd. ....Il.7.413.385.
And pleasing thus her sceptred Lord address'd. ....Od.4.184.128.
A pledge the sceptred pow'r of *Sidon* gave, ...Od.4.837.158.
A sceptred Lord, who o'er the fruitful plain ....Od.4.1051.167.
The sceptred Rulers. Fear not, but be bold: ....Od.7.66.237.
Where sceptred *Minos* with impartial hand ....Od.19.205.202.

SCEPTRES
His Feet on Sceptres and *Tiara's* trod, ...2.TemF.153.266.
Thus vanish sceptres, coronets, and balls, ...6.45.39.125.
Then mighty *Prætus Argos'* Sceptres sway'd, ...Il.6.197.336.
Between the Swords their peaceful Sceptres rear'd; ....Il.7.335.380.

SCHEDIUS
Epistrophus and *Schedius* head the War. ....Il.2.621.157.
By *Hector* here the *Phocian Schedius* dy'd; ....Il.15.611.220.
Schedius the brave, of all the *Phocian* Kind ....Il.17.354.301.

SCHEM'D
In vain they schem'd, in vain they bled ....4.HOde9.15.159.

SCHEME
Oh blind to truth, and God's whole scheme below, ...3.EOM4.93.137.
Who sees and follows that great scheme the best, ...3.EOM4.95.137.
Hence the Fool's paradise, the Statesman's scheme, ...5.DunA3.9.150.
Hence the Fool's Paradise, the Statesman's Scheme, ...5.DunB3.9.320.
Intent to form the future Scheme of Fate; ....Il.20.185.401.
The scheme of all our happiness destroy? ....Od.4.889.159.
Each scheme I turn'd, and sharpen'd ev'ry thought; ....Od.9.502.326.
O Peers! the sanguinary scheme suspend: ....Od.20.307.247.
And thus his meditated scheme began. ....Od.21.291.274.

SCHEMES
At the next Bottle, all their Schemes they cease, ...6.17iv.7.59.
To gain Pescennius one employs his schemes, ...6.71.39.203.
A thousand Schemes the Monarch's Mind employ; ....Il.2.45.129.
My Schemes, my Labours, and my Hopes be vain? ....Il.4.36.222.
While schemes of vengeance ripen in his breast. ....Od.14.133.42.
Schemes of revenge his pond'ring breast elate, ...Od.17.33.134.
High schemes of pow'r in just succession roul.) ....Od.19.326.210.
That other feeds on planetary schemes, ...Od.20.453.255.

SCHERIA
In twice ten days shall fertile *Scheria* find, ...Od.5.44.173.
The recreant nation to fair *Scheria* led, ...Od.6.11.203.

SCHERIA'S
Forsaking *Scheria's* ever-pleasing shore, ...Od.7.101.239.
Not more renown'd the men of *Scheria's* Isle, ...Od.7.136.241.

SCHERIAN
High on a throne, amid the *Scherian* pow'rs, ...Od.6.371.229.
(The *Scherian* states) he turn'd, and thus addrest. ....Od.13.46.3.

SCHERIANS
Aghast the *Scherians* stand in deep surprize; ....Od.13.190.15.

SCHISM
Or prove Reviver of a Schism, ...6.10.81.27.

SCHISMATICS
So Schismatics the *plain Believers* quit, ...1.EOC.428.288.
So Schismatics the *dull Believers* quit, ...1.EOC.428A.288.

SCHOENOS
And *Schœnos, Scolos, Græa* near the Main, ...II.2.592.156.

SCHOLAR
A Scholar, or a Wit or two: ....6.29.28.83.

SCHOLAR'S
The *Scholar's Learning,* with the *Courtier's Ease.* .. 1.EOC.668.315.
The *Scholar's Learning,* and the *Courtier's Ease.* .. 1.EOC.668A.315.
The *Scholar's Learning,* with the *Courtier's* wit. .. 1.EOC.668B.315.

SCHOLARS
But cou'd we Women write as Scholars can, ...2.ChWB.366.75.
Those play the Scholars who can't play the Men; ....2.ChWB.371.75.

SCHOLE
See SCHOOL.
From Schole-boy's Tale of fayre *Ireland:* .... 6.14i.4.41.

SCHOLE-BOY'S
From Schole-boy's Tale of fayre *Ireland:* .... 6.14i.4.41.

SCHOLIAST
Thy mighty Scholiast, whose unweary'd pains ....5.DunB4.211.363.

SCHOLIASTS
There, thy good Scholists with unweary'd pains ....5.DunA1.159.82.
"There, dim in clouds, the poreing Scholiasts mark, ...5.DunA3.187.172.
"There, dim in clouds, the poring Scholiasts mark, ...5.DunB3.191.329.
Or chew'd by blind old Scholiasts o'er and o'er. ....5.DunB4.232.365.

SCHOOL
See SCHOLE.
Once *School-Divines* this zealous Isle o'erspread; ....1.EOC.440.288.
Once *School-Divines* our zealous Isle o'erspread; ....1.EOC.440A.288.
Remembers oft the School-boy's simple fare, ...4.HS2.73.59.
I'll e'en leave Verses to the Boys at school: ....4.2HE2.201.179.
And God the Father turns a School-Divine. ....4.2HE1.102.203.
At Court, who hates whate'er he read at School. ....4.2HE1.106.203.
And send his Wife to Church, his Son to school. ....4.2HE1.164.209.
Late as it is, I put my self to school, ...4.1HE1.47.281.
Hervey and Hervey's school, F[ox], H[arr]y, H[into]n, ...4.1740.57.335.
Let him no trifler from his school, ...4.1740.87.337.
And turn the Council to a Grammar School! ....5.DunB4.180.359.
Thrid ev'ry science, run thro' ev'ry school? ....5.DunB4.256.369.
Thro' School and College, thy kind cloud o'ercast, ...5.DunB4.289.372.

SCHOOL-BOY'S
Remembers oft the School-boy's simple fare, ...4.HS2.73.59.

SCHOOL-DIVINE
And God the Father turns a School-Divine. ....4.2HE1.102.203.

SCHOOL-DIVINES
Once *School-Divines* this zealous Isle o'erspread; ....1.EOC.440.288.
Once *School-Divines* our zealous Isle o'erspread; ....1.EOC.440A.288.

SCHOOLMAN'S
Un-learn'd, he knew no Schoolman's subtle Art, ...4.Arbu.398.126.

SCHOOLMEN
Let subtle schoolmen teach these friends to fight, ...3.EOM2.81.64.
Schoolmen new tenements in Hell must make; ....4.JD2.42.135.
Schoolmen new Tenements in Hell must make; ....4.JD2A.46.136.

SCHOOLS
Some are bewilder'd in the Maze of Schools, ...1.EOC.26.242.
As subtle Clerks by many Schools are made, ...2.ChJM.109.20.
Hear Bethel's Sermon, one not vers'd in schools, ...4.HS2.9.55.
Schools, courts, and senates shall my laws obey, ...5.DunA1.251Z5.93.
Each shudd'ring owns the Genius of the Schools; ....5.DunB4.146A.355.
Then catch'd the Schools; the Hall scarce kept awake; ....5.DunB4.609.404.
Or manag'd in your Schools, for Fops to ride, ...6.96iii.29.275.

SCIATICS
Rack'd with Sciatics, martyr'd with the Stone, ...4.1HE6.54.241.

SCIENCE
One *Science* only will one *Genius* fit; ....1.EOC.60.245.
To teach vain Wits a Science *little known,* ....1.EOC.199.263.
To teach vain Wits that Science *little known,* ....1.EOC.199A.263.
New, distant Scenes of *endless* Science rise! ....1.EOC.224.265.
Fir'd with the Charms fair *Science* does impart, ...1.EOC.219A.265.
Who taught that useful Science, to be *good.* ....2.TemF.108.261.
'Tis sure the hardest science to forget! ....2.ElAb.190.335.
His soul proud Science never taught to stray ....3.EOM1.101.27.
The only Science of Mankind is Man. ....3.EOM2.2A.53.
Go, wond'rous creature! mount where Science guides, ...3.EOM2.19.56.
Trace Science then, with Modesty thy guide; ....3.EOM2.43.61.
As hard a science to the Fair as Great! ....3.Ep2.226.68.
And tho' no science, fairly worth the sev'n: ....3.Ep4.44.140.
Where rebel to thy throne if Science rise, ...5.DunA1.157.82.
Where 'gainst thy throne if rebel Science rise, ...5.DunA1.157A.82.
Yet holds the Eel of Science by the Tail. ....5.DunA1.234.90.
And orient Science at a birth begun. ....5.DunA3.66.156.
Where, faint at best, the beams of Science fall. ....5.DunA3.76.156.
"But, where each Science lifts its modern Type, ...5.DunA3.191z1.172.
Round him, each *Science* by its modern type ....5.DunA3.191z1.172.
Yet holds the eel of science by the tail: ....5.DunB1.280.290.

SCIENCE (CONTINUED)
and orient Science their bright course begun: ....5.DunB3.74.323.
And orient Science first their course begun: ....5.DunB3.74A.323.
Where, faint at best, the beams of Science fall: ....5.DunB3.84.324.
"But, where each Science lifts its modern type, ...5.DunB3.195.329.
Beneath her foot-stool, *Science* groans in Chains, ...5.DunB4.21.342.
Thrid ev'ry science, run thro' ev'ry school? ....5.DunB4.256.369.
'Till wrangling *Science* taught it Noise and Show, ...6.8.11.18.
Go now, learn all vast Science can impart: ....6.27.12.81.
Blest in each Science, blest in ev'ry Strain! ....6.84.5.238.
Content with Science in the Vale of Peace. ....6.112.6.318.
Content with Science in the arms of Peace. ....6.112.6A.318.
Skill'd in his Science of the Dart and Bow. ....II.2.877.165.
To whom was Voice, and Sense, and Science given ....II.18.489.345.
I speak from science, and the voice is Fate. ....Od.2.198.71.
Where never science rear'd her lawrel'd head: ....Od.6.12.203.

SCIPIO
Such was the Life great *Scipio* once admir'd, ...1.W-F.257.172.
Bold *Scipio,* Saviour of the *Roman* State, ...2.TemF.163.267.

SCIPIO'S
That very Cæsar, born in Scipio's days, ...3.Ep1.216.33.

SCLAVONIANS
Nor ten *Sclavonians,* scolding, deaf me more ....4.JD2A.68.138.

SCOFFER
Scoffer, behold what gratitude we bear: ....Od.22.322.301.

SCOFFING
And scoffing, thus, to War's victorious Maid. ....II.21.491.441.
Eumæus scoffing, then with keen disdain. ....Od.22.211.297.

SCOFFS
Loud Laughs burst out, and bitter Scoffs fly round, ...2.TemF.403.282.

SCOLD
More rough than forty Germans when they scold. ....4.JD2.62.139.

SCOLDED
How oft she scolded in a Day, he knew, ...2.ChWB.389.76.

SCOLDING
When Airs, and Flights, and Screams, and Scolding fail. ....2.RL5.32.201.
Nor ten *Sclavonians,* scolding, deaf me more ....4.JD2A.68.138.
Now singing shrill, and scolding eft between, ...6.14ii.17.43.
The scolding Quean to louder Notes doth rise, ...6.14ii.23.43.

SCOLDS
Scolds answer foul-mouth'd Scolds; bad Neighbourhood I
    ween. ....6.14ii.18.43.
Scolds answer foul-mouth'd Scolds; bad Neighbourhood I
    ween. ....6.14ii.18.43.
And Curs, Girls, Boys, and Scolds, in the deep Base are
    drown'd ....6.14ii.27.44.
Scolds with her maid, or with her chaplain crams. ....6.41.22.114.

SCOLOS
And *Schœnos, Scolos, Græa* near the Main, ...II.2.592.156.

SCONCE'S
Triumphant *Umbriel* on a Sconce's Height ....2.RL5.53.203.

SCOOP'D
And from the Fibres scoop'd the rooted Ball, ...II.14.578.190.

SCOOPS
Or scoops in circling theatres the Vale, ...3.Ep4.60.142.
For each a bed, she scoops the hilly sand: ....Od.4.592.148.
The grain deep-piercing till it scoops it out: ....Od.9.460.325.

SCOPE
His *Fable, Subject, Scope* in ev'ry Page, ...1.EOC.120.252.

SCORCH
Fires that scorch, yet dare not shine: ....6.51ii.40.154.
Scorch all the Banks! and (till our Voice reclaim) ....II.21.396.436.

SCORCH'D
And scorch'd by Suns, it withers on the Plain. ....II.4.559.248.
So scorch'd with Heat along the desert Shore, ...II.16.993.281.
As the scorch'd Locusts from their Fields retire, ...II.21.14.421.
But *Jove's* swift lightning scorch'd him in her arms. ....Od.5.162.179.
Scorch'd by the sun, or sear'd by heav'nly fire: ....Od.5.308.186.

SCORCHES
By Night he scorches, as he burns by Day. ....1.PSu.92.79.

SCORCHING
Phaon to *Ætna's* scorching Fields retires, ...1.TrSP.11.393.
The scorching Ashes o'er his graceful Head; ....II.18.28.325.
This hot thro' scorching Clefts is seen to rise, ...II.22.197.463.
Sing'd are his brows; the scorching lids grow black; ....Od.9.463.325.
The scorching flames climb round on ev'ry side: ....Od.14.474.58.

SCORE
But all that Score I paid—As how? you'll say, ...2.ChWB.231.68.
Bond is but one, but *Harpax* is a Score. ....4.HS1.44.9.
For, mark th' advantage; just so many score ....4.1HE6.77.241.
And *English Musick* with a dismal score: ....5.DunA3.191z4.172.
Then sighing, thus, "And am I now three-score? ....5.DunB2.285.309.

SCORES
A Tongue that can cheat Widows, cancel Scores, ...4.JD4.58.31.

SCORN

At ev'ry Trifle scorn to take Offence, ... 1.EOC.386.284.
So much they scorn the Crowd, that if the Throng ... 1.EOC.426.288.
If thou all others didst despise and scorn: ... 1.TrPA.119.370.
Ev'n now, when silent Scorn is all they gain, ... 1.TrVP.73.380.
For those, *Aurora Cephalus* might scorn, ... 1.TrSP.97.398.
His Sons with Scorn their Eyeless Father view, ... 1.TrSt.336.424.
The Pride of Fools, and Slaves insulting Scorn. ... 1.TrUl.183.471.
He spoke with Scorn, and turn'd another way— ... 2.ChJM.220.25.
He spoke; and turn'd, with Scorn, another way— ... 2.ChJM.220A.25.
Know then, I scorn your dull Authorities, ... 2.ChJM.696.48.
I'd scorn your Prentice, shou'd you die to-morrow. ... 2.ChWB.123.62.
Free Gifts we scorn, and love what costs us Pains: ... 2.ChWB.260.69.
And view with scorn *Two Pages* and a *Chair.* ... 2.RL1.46.149.
Who would not scorn what Huswife's Cares produce, ... 2.RL5.21.200.
The People's Fable, and the Scorn of all. ... 2.TemF.401.282.
Then teach me, Heaven! to scorn the guilty Bays; ... 2.TemF.521.289.
Himself, his throne, his world, I'd scorn 'em all: ... 2.ElAb.86.326.
From ancient story learn to scorn them all. ... 3.EOM4.286.155.
Clodio, the scorn and wonder of our days, ... 3.Ep1.180A.30.
Wharton, the scorn and wonder of our days, ... 3.Ep1.180.30.
Why then declare Good-nature is her scorn, ... 3.Ep2.59.55.
Your Taste of Follies, with our Scorn of Fools, ... 3.Ep2.276.72.
Toasts live a scorn, and Queens may die a jest. ... 3.Ep2.282.73.
Then scorn a homely dinner, if you can. ... 4.HS2.12.55.
When sharp with Hunger, scorn you to be fed, ... 4.HAdv.149.87.
Alike my scorn, if he succeed or fail, ... 4.Arbu.362.122.
And scorn the Flesh, the Dev'l, and all but Gold. ... 4.JD2.24.133.
Why one like *Bu*— with Pay and Scorn content, ... 4.2HE2.274.185.
Who scorn a Lad should teach his Father skill, ... 4.2HE1.129.205.
But learn, ye Dunces! not to scorn your GOD." ... 5.DunA3.222.176.
But, "Learn, ye DUNCES! not to scorn your GOD" ... 5.DunB3.224.331.
Find Virtue local, all Relation scorn, ... 5.DunB4.479.389.
So Wit, which most to scorn it does pretend, ... 6.16.11.53.
There Censure, Envy, Malice, Scorn, or Hate, ... 6.17iii.12.58.
And suffer scorn, and bend the supple knee; ... 6.22.9.71.
With honest scorn the first fam'd *Cato* view'd ... 6.32.39.97.
Or other's wants with Scorn deride ... 6.50.35B.148.
A scorn of wrangling, yet a zeal for truth; ... 6.57.8.169.
and scorn the Government of Blunderland. ... 6.61.20A.181.
and rashly scorn the realm of Blunderland. ... 6.61.20B.181.
Then scorn to gain a Friend by servile ways, ... 6.73.10.210.
Good Nature, she declar'd it, was her Scorn, ... 6.99.7.286.
On one so old your sword you scorn to draw. ... 6.116vii.6.328.
Who holds Dragoons and Wooden-Shoes in scorn; ... 6.128.20.356.
And scorn the Pranks of Dogs at Court. ... 6.135.14.366.
And scorn a rascal and a coach! ... 6.150.20.399.
And scorn a rascal in a coach! ... 6.150.20A.399.
Once great in Arms, the common Scorn we grow, ... Il.2.153.135.
Scorn all his Joy, and Laughter all his Aim. ... Il.2.260.140.
Long had he liv'd the Scorn of ev'ry *Greek,* ... Il.2.271.140.
I scorn the Coward, and detest his Bed; ... Il.3.508.216.
Fix'd on the Chief with Scorn, and thus he spoke. ... Il.5.309.281.
Fir'd at his Scorn the Queen to *Prætus* fled, ... Il.6.205.336.
Their Sons degen'rate, and their Race a Scorn? ... Il.7.148.371.
Gash'd with dishonest Wounds, the Scorn of Heav'n: ... Il.8.14.395.
And learn to scorn the Wretch they basely fear. ... Il.9.484.456.
'Tis he that offers, and I scorn them all. ... Il.9.509.458.
Else must our Host become the Scorn of *Troy.* ... Il.10.226.12.
And scorn the Guidance of a vulgar Hand; ... Il.10.474.24.
Old as I am, to Age I scorn to yield, ... Il.10.646.30.
With generous Anguish, and in scorn return'd. ... Il.17.18.288.
And bade the Chief reflect, how late with Scorn ... Il.20.115.398.
No: with the common Heap I scorn to fall— ... Il.21.655.449.
Stern had reply'd; fierce Scorn inhancing Scorn ... Il.23.573.512.
Stern had reply'd; fierce Scorn inhancing Scorn ... Il.23.573.512.
And starting into manhood, scorn the boy. ... Od.1.386.51.
"This realm, she flies: *Phæacia* is her scorn. ... Od.6.340.227.
The pride of fools, and slaves insulting scorn. ... Od.13.350.24.
And the blind suitors their destruction scorn. ... Od.13.464.28.
There, if base scorn insult my rev'rend age, ... Od.16.294.119.
From ev'ry great man's gate repuls'd with scorn? ... Od.17.257.144.
While with indignant scorn he sternly spoke, ... Od.18.100.172.
Scorn not the sad reverse, injurious maid! ... Od.19.98.197.
Low-couch'd on earth, the gift of sleep I scorn, ... Od.19.395.213.
And modest worth with noble scorn retires. ... Od.20.168.241.
Your violence and scorn, ye Suitors cease, ... Od.20.332.249.
Revenge and scorn within his bosom boil: ... Od.20.371.250.
Our weakness scorn? *Antinous* thus reply'd. ... Od.21.271.272.
'Tis you that offer, and I scorn them all: ... Od.22.76.290.

SCORN'D

She scorn'd the Praise of Beauty, and the Care; ... 1.W-F.177.166.
And but from *Nature's Fountains* scorn'd to draw: ... 1.EOC.133.254.
Where *wanted,* scorn'd, and envy'd where acquir'd; ... 1.EOC.503A.295.
"In vain he lov'd, relentless *Pyrrha* scorn'd; ... 1.TrSP.194.402.
"Deucalion scorn'd, and *Pyrrha* lov'd in vain. ... 1.TrSP.196.402.
Scorn'd by those slaves his former bounty fed ... 6.15.8.51.
Scorn'd Heaven it self, and durst the Gods deride, ... 6.20.57.67.
He scorn'd to borrow from the Wits of yore; ... 6.34.9.101.
She scorn'd the Champion, but the Man she lov'd. ... Il.3.488.215.
And Faith is scorn'd by all the perjur'd Line. ... Il.4.191.230.
Safe in the Crowd he ever scorn'd to wait, ... Il.22.588.480.
Nor scorn'd the Queen the holy Choir to join, ... Od.3.574.116.
And *Jove's* scorn'd thunder serves to drench our fields) ... Od.9.424.323.
Scorn'd ev'n by man, and (oh severe disgrace) ... Od.13.150.12.
Scorn'd by the young, forgotten by the old, ... Od.24.188.356.

SCORND

From *French?* He scornd it; no, from *Greek.* ... 6.44.8.123.

SCORNFUL

Like these, rejected by the scornful Dame. ... 1.TrVP.28.378.
My scornful Brother with a Smile appears, ... 1.TrSP.135.399.
What sullen Fury clowds his scornful Brow! ... 1.TrSt.255.421.
Not scornful Virgins who their Charms survive, ... 2.RL4.4.183.

SCORNFUL (CONTINUED)

And scornful Hisses run thro all the Croud. ... 2.TemF.405.283.
And scornful Hisses ran thro all the Croud. ... 2.TemF.405A.283.
View him with scornful, yet with jealous eyes, ... 4.Arbu.199.110.
Cast on the prostrate Nine a scornful look, ... 5.DunB4.51.346.
View him with scornful, yet with jealous eyes, ... 6.49iii.13.143.
View him with Jealous, yet with Scornful eyes, ... 6.49iii.13A.143.
View him with scornful, yet with fearful eyes, ... 6.98.49.284.
Gods! how the scornful *Greeks* exult to see ... Il.3.61.192.
(*Ulysses,* with a scornful Smile, replies) ... Il.10.472.24.
Who viewing first his Foes with scornful Eyes, ... Il.20.200.402.
The scornful Dame her Conquest views with Smiles, ... Il.21.476.441.
Scornful, his Hand; and gives him to his Friends; ... Il.23.807.521.
Or scornful Sister with her sweeping Train, ... Il.24.973.576.
This said, and scornful turning from the shore ... Od.10.325.360.
Scornful he spoke, and o'er his shoulder flung ... Od.18.130.172.
There was a day, when with the scornful Great ... Od.18.165.174.
Scornful they heard: *Melantho,* fair and young, ... Od.18.367.185.
Scornful of age, to taunt the virtuous man, ... Od.18.397.187.
Cries one, with scornful leer and mimic voice, ... Od.20.449.255.
The Suitors with a scornful smile survey ... Od.21.407.279.

SCORNING

Thus scorning prophecy, and warn'd in vain, ... 1.TrPA.35.366.
Dunce scorning Dunce beholds the next advance, ... 5.DunB4.137.354.
But I, of mind elate, and scorning fear, ... Od.9.585.330.

SCORNS

That scorns the dull Reversion of a Throne; ... 1.TrSt.181.418.
Scorns not to take our *Argos* in her Way. ... 1.TrSt.811.443.
And she who scorns a Man, must die a Maid; ... 2.RL5.28.201.
And justly CÆSAR scorns the Poet's Lays, ... 4.HS1.35.7.
And scorns all Arms, all Battery—but Gold ... 4.JD2A.28.134.
Eridanus his humble fountain scorns, ... 5.DunA2.174.122.
Eridanus his humble fountain scorns; ... 5.DunB2.182.304.
He slights thy Friendship, thy Proposals scorns, ... Il.9.796.473.
Me, aukward me she scorns, and yields her charms ... Od.8.349.282.
But he that scorns the chains of sleep to wear ... Od.10.96.345.
He shall, I trust; a Heroe scorns despair) ... Od.16.106.108.
And ruminating wrath, he scorns repose. ... Od.20.8.230.

SCOT

A Scot will fight for Christ's Kirk o' the Green; ... 4.2HE1.40.197.
To treat him like her Sister *Scot,* ... 6.101.30.291.

SCOTISTS

Scotists and *Thomists,* now, in Peace remain, ... 1.EOC.444.289.

SCOTLAND

In Scotland, at the Orcades; and there, ... 3.EOM2.223.82.

SCOTO

Ask men's Opinions: Scoto now shall tell ... 3.Ep1.158.28.

SCOTS

Make *Scots* speak Treason, cozen subtlest Whores, ... 4.JD4.59.31.
From Scots to Wight, from Mount to Dover strand. ... 4.JD2.86.141.
From Scots to Wight, From Mount to Dover Strand; ... 4.JD2A.91.140.

SCOTSMAN

Just as a Scotsman does his Plumbs. ... 4.1HE7.24.269.

SCOUNDRELS

Has crept thro' scoundrels ever since the flood, ... 3.EOM4.212.147.

SCOUR

Toss their high Heads, and scour along the Plain; ... 1.TrUl.9.465.
But the rash Youth prepares to scour the Plain: ... Il.10.394.21.
The Wolves, tho' hungry, scour dispers'd away; ... Il.11.602.61.
Stung by the Stroke, the Coursers scour the Fields ... Il.11.656.63.
Scour o'er the Fields, and stretch to reach the Town. ... Il.16.453.260.
Th' amaz'd *Pæonians* scour along the Plain: ... Il.21.224.430.
Toss their high heads, and scour along the plain; ... Od.13.100.6.

SCOUR'D

Can taste no pleasure since his Shield was scour'd; ... 6.71.42.204.

SCOURG'D

As erst he scourg'd *Jessides'* Sin of yore ... 6.137.8.373.
And send thee scourg'd, and howling thro' the Fleet. ... Il.2.325.142.

SCOURGE

But prove the Scourge to lash you on your Way: ... 2.ChJM.288.28.
I was my self the Scourge that caus'd the Smart; ... 2.ChWB.6.57.
Or turns young Ammon loose to scourge mankind? ... 3.EOM1.160.35.
And Tutchin flagrant from the scourge, below: ... 5.DunA2.140.118.
Jacob, the Scourge of Grammar, mark with awe, ... 5.DunA3.149.164.
W[oolsto]n, the scourge of Scripture, mark with awe, ... 5.DunA3.149A.164.
Woolston, the Scourge of Gospel, mark with awe, ... 5.DunA3.149B.164.
And Tutchin flagrant from the scourge below. ... 5.DunB2.148.302.
"Jacob, the scourge of Grammar, mark with awe, ... 5.DunB3.149.327.
The Scourge of Pride, tho' sanctify'd or great, ... 6.118.3.334.
Scourge of thy People, violent and base! ... Il.1.305.101.
Swift at the Scourge th' Ethereal Coursers fly, ... Il.5.926.310.
Say, mighty Father! Shall we scourge his Pride, ... Il.5.950.312.
(The Scourge forgot, on *Rhesus* Chariot hung.) ... Il.10.585.28.
He mounts the Car, the golden Scourge applies; ... Il.13.40.106.
A Scourge to thee, thy Father, and thy Line. ... Il.13.571.133.
To scourge the Wretch insulting them and Heav'n. ... Il.15.229.205.
Furious he said; the smarting Scourge resounds; ... Il.15.402.212.
Strikes from his Hand the Scourge, and renders vain ... Il.23.463.508.
Springs to her Knight, and gives the Scourge again, ... Il.23.468.509.
The driving Scourge high-lifted in thy Hand, ... Il.23.662.516.
The Scourge and Ruin of my Realm and Race; ... Il.24.631.563.
Oppress, destroy, and be the scourge of God; ... Od.2.264.74.
And ev'ry Monarch be the scourge of God: ... Od.5.17.171.

SCOURGE (CONTINUED)
The silver scourge, it glitter'd o'er the field: ....Od.6.378.230.
Scourge thro' the publick street, and cast thee there, ...Od.17.570.160.
The scourge, the scourge shall lash thee into sense. ....Od.18.388.186.
The scourge, the scourge shall lash thee into sense. ....Od.18.388.186.

SCOURGES
The lifted Scourges all at once resound; ....Il.23.438.507.
The foes of peace, and scourges of mankind, ...Od.14.104.41.

SCOURS
Not so, when swift *Camilla* scours the Plain, ...1.EOC.372.282.
Imbibes new life, and scours and stinks along, ...5.DunA2.98.109.
Imbibes new life, and scours and stinks along; ....5.DunB2.106.300.

SCOUT
Encourag'd thus, no idle Scout I go, ...Il.10.383.21.

SCOWR'D
Swift at her call her husband scowr'd away ....Od.10.131.347.

SCRAP
Pregnant with thousands flits the Scrap unseen, ...3.Ep3.77.93.
No rag, no scrap, of all the beau, or wit, ...5.DunA2.111.110.
No rag, no scrap, of all the beau, or wit, ...5.DunB2.119.301.

SCRAPE
A hundred footsteps scrape the marble Hall: ....3.Ep4.152.152.

SCRAPS
On parchment scraps y-fed, and Wormius hight. ....5.DunA3.184.171.
On parchment scraps y-fed, and Wormius hight. ....5.DunB3.188.329.
'Twas but for scraps he ask'd, and ask'd in vain. ....Od.17.259.144.

SCRATCH
Nor could so scratch and tear. ....6.79.32.218.
Nor more could scratch and tear. ....6.79.32A.218.
Nor boast the Scratch thy feeble Arrow gave, ...Il.11.497.56.

SCRATCH'D
Now as he scratch'd to fetch up Thought, ...6.58.29.172.
When now two Ages, he had scratch'd from Fate ....6.108.3B.312.

SCRATCHED
She scratched, bit, and spar'd ne Lace ne Band, ...6.14ii.39.44.
She scratched, bit, and spar'd nor Lace and Band, ...6.14ii.39A.44.

SCRAWL
All ryme, and scrawl, and scribble, to a man. ....4.2HE1.188.211.
Tho' with a Golden Pen you scrawl, ...6.58.7.171.
Tho' with a Golden Pen ye scrawl, ...6.58.7A.171.

SCRAWLS
Is there, who lock'd from Ink and Paper, scrawls ....4.Arbu.19.97.
Is there, who lock'd from pen and Paper, scrawls ....4.Arbu.19A.97.

SCREAM
Scream, like the winding of ten thousand Jacks: ....5.DunA3.154.164.
Scream like the winding of ten thousand jacks: ....5.DunB3.160.328.
And scream thyself as none e'er scream'd before! ....5.DunB3.306.335.
The short thick Sob, loud Scream, and shriller Squawl: ......6.14ii.6.43.
And hov'ring Vulturs scream around their Prey. ....Il.11.571.59.
Of Geese, that scream, and scatter round the Plain. ....Il.17.529.309.
And scream aloft, and skim the deeps below. ....Od.5.87.176.
Scream o'er the fiend, and riot in his blood, ...Od.11.712.421.
They scream, they shriek; sad groans and dismal sounds ....Od.11.781.425.
They cry, they scream, their unfledg'd brood a prey ....Od.16.240.116.
A scream of joy her feeble voice essay'd: ....Od.22.446.309.
And such a scream fill'd all the dismal coasts. ....Od.24.14.347.

SCREAM'D
And scream thyself as none e'er scream'd before! ....5.DunB3.306.335.

SCREAMING
They cuff, they tear, they raise a screaming Cry; ....1.TrES.221.458.
The whimp'ring Girl, and hoarser-screaming Boy, ...6.14ii.21.43.
They cuff, they tear, they raise a screaming Cry; ....Il.16.524.264.
Or fowl that screaming haunt the wat'ry way. ....Od.12.392.450.
Or screaming vulturs scatter thro' the air: ....Od.24.343.365.

SCREAMS
And Screams of Horror rend th' affrighted Skies. ....2.RL3.156.180.
When Airs, and Flights, and Screams, and Scolding fail. ....2.RL5.32.201.
Dismal screams, ...6.11.57.32.
Adonis screams—Ah! Foe to all Mankind! ....6.129.4.357.
Thin, hollow screams, along the deep descent. ....Od.24.8.347.

SCREECHES
With hollow Screeches fled the dire Repast; ....1.TrSt.736.441.

SCREEN
And that describes a charming *Indian Screen;* ....2.RL*A*1.78.129.
And one describes a charming *Indian Screen;* ....2.RL3.14.170.
Be this thy Screen, and this thy Wall of Brass; ....4.1HE1.95.285.
His Friend and Shame, and was a kind of *Screen.* ....4.EpS1.22.299.
(A wat'ry Bulwark) screen the Band who fly. ....Il.21.262.431.
Depending vines the shelving cavern screen, ...Od.5.88.176.

SCREEN'D
And screen'd in Shades from Day's detested Glare, ...2.RL4.22.185.
Screen'd by the Shields of his surrounding Friends. ....Il.4.145.227.
Screen'd from the Foe behind his shining Veil, ...Il.5.391.285.
Tho' screen'd behind *Apollo's* mighty Shield. ....Il.5.528.294.
And screen'd his Brother with a mighty Shade; ....Il.8.398.416.
And screen'd his Brother with the mighty Shade; ....Il.8.398A.416.
Till with a snowy Veil he screen'd the Blaze. ....Il.8.549.422.

SCREEN'D (CONTINUED)
Screen'd by protecting Gods from hostile eyes, ...Od.14.391.54.
Where screen'd from *Boreas,* high-o'erarch'd, they lay. ....Od.14.601.66.

SCREW
Let others screw their Hypocritick Face, ...6.33.7.99.
Let others screw a Hypocritick Face, ...6.33.7A.99.

SCRIBBLE
If *Mævius* Scribble in *Apollo's* spight, ...1.EOC.34.243.
Make some take Physick, others scribble Plays; ....2.RL4.62.189.
But turn a Wit, and scribble verses too? ....4.JD2.54.137.
If I would scribble, rather than repose. ....4.2HE2.71.169.
All ryme, and scrawl, and scribble, to a man. ....4.2HE1.188.211.
And scribble in a *Berlin:* ....6.58.8.171.
Or scribble in a *Berlin:* ·..6.58.8A.171.

SCRIBBLER
In scribbler to have had a place. ....6.42v.6.119.

SCRIBE
Scarce hurts the Lawyer, but undoes the Scribe. ....4.EpS2.47.315.

SCRIBLER
Who shames a Scribler? break one cobweb thro', ...4.Arbu.89.102.
A hireling Scribler, or a hireling Peer, ...4.Arbu.364.122.

SCRIBLERS
Scriblers or Peers, alike are *Mob* to me. ....4.HS1.140.19.
Scriblers like Spiders, break one cobweb thro', ...4.Arbu.89A.102.

SCRIBLERUM
Quaedam quae attinent ad Scriblerum, ...6.42v.3.119.

SCRIBLING
Than when they promise to give *Scribling* o'er. ....1.EOC.595.307.
Who hunger, and who thirst, for scribling sake: ....5.DunA1.48.65.
Who hunger, and who thirst for scribling sake: ....5.DunB1.50.274.

SCRIP
And at his side a wretched scrip was hung, ...Od.13.506.30.
Across his shoulders, then, the scrip he flung, ...Od.17.220.142.
With smiles receiving, on his scrip he lay'd. ....Od.17.429.153.
He fill'd his scrip, and to the threshold sped; ....Od.17.495.156.
Before his feet the well-fill'd scrip he threw, ...Od.17.553.159.
The broad-patch'd scrip; the scrip in tatters hung ....Od.18.131.172.
The broad-patch'd scrip; the scrip in tatters hung ....Od.18.131.172.

SCRIPTURE
Christ saw a Wedding once, the Scripture says, ...2.ChWB.9.57.
F. Why yes: with *Scripture* still you may be free; ....4.EpS1.37.300.
W[oolsto]n, the scourge of Scripture, mark with awe, ...5.DunA3.149A.164.
Full in the middle of the Scripture. ....6.101.14.290.

SCRIPTURES
Heroick *Judeth,* as the Scriptures show, ...2.ChJM.73A.18.
How the first Female (as the Scriptures show) ....2.ChWB.379.75.

SCRIPTUS
Scriptus & in tergo, nec dum finitus Orestes. ....6.24iii(b).2.76.

SCRIV'NER
Will sneaks a Scriv'ner, and exceeding knave: ....3.Ep1.106.22.
No poor Court-badge, great Scriv'ner! fir'd thy brain, ...3.Ep3.147A.105.
'Twas no Court-badge, great Scriv'ner! fir'd thy brain, ...3.Ep3.147B.105.
No gay Court-badge, great Scriv'ner! Fir'd thy brain, ...3.Ep3.147C.105.
No mean Court-badge, great Scriv'ner! fir'd thy brain, ...3.Ep3.147.105.
Slides to a Scriv'ner or a City Knight. ....4.HS2.178.69.

SCRUPLE
Which grave Physicians scruple not to give; ....2.ChJM.376.32.
To these I made no Scruple to reveal. ....2.ChWB.274.70.
Some scruple rose, but thus he eas'd his thought, ...3.Ep3.365.123.
To lend a wife, few here would scruple make, ...6.41.35.114.

SCUD
But I to *Pylos* scud before the gales, ...Od.3.221.96.

SCUDDING
Then scudding swiftly from the dang'rous ground, ...Od.12.238.443.

SCUDS
He bounds aloft, and scuds from Hills to Hills: ....Il.11.597.60.

SCULKING
See sculking Truth in her old cavern lye, ...5.DunA3.347.193.

SCULL
Not Welsted so: drawn endlong by his scull, ...5.DunA2.293.138.
Not so bold Arnall, with a weight of scull, ...5.DunA2.293A.138.
And blunt the sense, and fit it for a scull ....5.DunA3.17.151.

SCULLER
They hire their Sculler, and when once aboard, ...4.1HE1.159.291.

SCULLS
And Sculls are but the Barrels of the Brain. ....6.48i.2.133*.

SCULPTOR'S
A marble Courser by the Sculptor's Hands, ...Il.17.495.307.

SCULPTUR'D
Gold, Silver, Iv'ry, Vases sculptur'd high, ...4.2HE2.264.183.
In sculptur'd Gold two Turtles seem to drink: ....Il.11.777.69.
In sculptur'd gold and labour'd silver stand. ....Od.7.119.240.
Beneath a sculptur'd arch he sits enthron'd, ...Od.8.517.290.

SCULPTUR'D (CONTINUED)
In sculptur'd stone immortaliz'd their care, ... Od.17.237.143.
And *Vulcan's* art enrich'd the sculptur'd gold). .... Od.24.96.352.

SCULPTURE
Then *Sculpture* and her *Sister-Arts* revive; .... 1.EOC.701.319.
With Sculpture grac'd, and rough with rising Gold. .... 1.TrSt.636.436.
And Sculpture rising on the roughen'd Gold. .... 2.TemF.78.258.
In living Sculpture on the Sides were spread .... 2.TemF.204.271.
Or where, by sculpture made for ever known, ... 5.DunA1.119.77.
This with the noblest force of sculpture grac'd, ... 6.20.27.66.
The verse and sculpture bore an equal part, ... 6.71.51.204.
With various Sculpture, and the golden Crest. .... Il.18.708.357.
Against a column, fair with sculpture grac'd; .... Od.1.168.40.
And that rich vase, with living sculpture wrought, ... Od.4.179.128.
The silver vase with living sculpture wrought. .... Od.15.135.75.

SCULPTURES
A Tomb, indeed, with fewer Sculptures grac'd, ... 2.ChWB.247.69.
The polish'd Pillar diff'rent Sculptures grace; .... 2.TemF.226.273.

SCUT
"The little Scut he so pursu'd before, ... 4.HAdv.138.87.

SCYLLA
Where treach'rous *Scylla* cut the Purple Hairs: .... 1.TrSt.469.429.
Here *Scylla* bellows from her dire abodes, ... Od.12.107.436.
Fell *Scylla* rises, in her fury roars, ... Od.12.123.437.
Ah shun the horrid gulph! by *Scylla* fly, ... Od.12.137.438.
Or if I rise in arms, can *Scylla* bleed? .... Od.12.142.439.
Cautious the name of *Scylla* I suppress; .... Od.12.266.445.
Dire *Scylla* there a scene of horror forms, ... Od.12.280.445.
When lo! fierce *Scylla* stoop'd to seize her prey, ... Od.12.294.446.
For on the rocks it bore where *Scylla* raves, ... Od.12.505.457.
And howling *Scylla* whirls her thund'rous waves, ... Od.23.354.341.

SCYLLA'S
Fear the just Gods, and think of *Scylla's* Fate! .... 2.RL3.122.177.
Unseen I pass'd by *Scylla's* dire abodes: .... Od.12.527.458.

SCYRON'S
The hanging Cliffs of *Scyron's* Rock explores, ... 1.TrSt.470.429.

SCYROS
When *Scyros* fell before his conqu'ring Arms. .... Il.9.785.472.
From *Scyros* Isle conduct him o'er the Main, ... Il.19.353.387.
With me from *Scyros* to the field of fame .... Od.11.619.414.

SCYTHE
To trim his beard, th'unweildy scythe prepares; .... 1.TrPA.23.366.
Oft o'er his Back a crooked Scythe is laid, ... 1.TrVP.33.378.
Death with his Scythe cut off the fatal Thread, ... 1.TrSt.745.441.
His Scythe revers'd, and both his Pinions bound. .... 2.TemF.148.265.
Foodless, the scythe along the burthen'd field; .... Od.18.413.189.

SCYTHES
But useless Lances into Scythes shall bend, ... 1.Mes.61.118.

SCYTHIAN
The horrid Forms of *Scythian* Heroes stood, ... 2.TemF.126.264.

SDEATH
Fir'd that the House reject him, "'Sdeath I'll print it .... 4.Arbu.61.100.

SEA
Around his Throne the Sea-born Brothers stood, ... 1.W-F.337.182.
(His Sea-green Mantle waving with the Wind) .... 1.W-F.350.184.
Lost in my Fame, as in the Sea their Streams. .... 1.W-F.362.185.
Come Galatea, from the sea arise, ... 1.TrPA.94.369.
Ah! canst thou doom me to the Rocks and Sea, ... 1.TrSP.222.403.
And *Cadmus* searching round the spacious Sea? .... 1.TrSt.8.409.
And all th'extended Space of Earth, and Air, and Sea. .... 1.TrSt.279.421.
In Storms by Sea, and Combats on the Shore: .... 1.TrUl.18.466.
The solitary Shore, and rowling Sea. .... 1.TrUl.55.467.
For much I fear, long Tracts of Land and Sea .... 1.TrUl.203.472.
Thus to the Sea-green Sisters sends his Pray'r. .... 1.TrUl.239.473.
And tremble at the Sea that froaths below! .... 2.RL2.136.168.
Sooner let Earth, Air, Sea, to *Chaos* fall, ... 2.RL4.119.193.
Why deck;d with all that Land and Sea afford, ... 2.RL5.11.200.
Why deck'd with all that Land and Sea afford, ... 2.RL5.11.200.
As to the Sea returning Rivers roll, ... 2.TemF.430.284.
Of Storms at Sea, and Travels on the Shore, ... 2.TemF.451.285.
Still as the sea, ere winds were taught to blow, ... 2.ElAb.253.340.
Like bubbles on the sea of Matter born, ... 3.EOM3.19.94.
They rise, they break, and to that sea return. .... 3.EOM3.20.94.
On air or sea new motions be imprest, ... 3.EOM4.125.139.
From dirt and sea-weed as proud Venice rose; .... 3.EOM4.292.155.
What made Directors cheat in South-sea year? .... 3.Ep3.119.101.
Un-water'd see the drooping sea-horse mourn, ... 3.Ep4.125.149.
Back to his bounds their subject Sea command, ... 3.Ep4.201.156.
In *South-sea* days not happier, when surmis'd .... 4.HS2.133.65.
Till like the Sea, they compass all the land, ... 4.JD2.85.141.
Out drink the Sea and that bold Wretch outswear, ... 4.JD2A.43.136.
Soon, like the Sea, he'l compass all the Land, ... 4.JD2A.90.140.
Thus in a sea of folly toss'd, ... 4.HS6.125.257.
South-sea Subscriptions take who please, ... 4.1HE7.65.273.
Round, and more round, o'er all the sea of heads. .... 5.DunA2.378.146.
Round and more round, o'er all the sea of heads. .... 5.DunB2.410.317.
Full grown, and from the Sea the Queen of Love; .... 6.37.4.106.
Whose Altar, Earth, Sea, Skies; .... 6.50.50.148.
Might e'en as well be termd the Sea; .... 6.67.18.195.
Come, fill the South-Sea Goblet full; .... 6.80.1.224.
Or Father Francis cross the sea, ... 6.102.7.294.
From dirt and sea-weed as proud Venice rose; .... 6.130.2.358.
Rose from the Flood the Daughter of the Sea; .... Il.1.645.118.
Of those *Calydnæ's* Sea-girt Isles contain; .... Il.2.822.164.

SEA (CONTINUED)
Let him, unactive on the Sea-beat Shore, ... Il.7.277.378.
Their rising Bulwarks on the Sea-beat Coast? .... Il.7.533.391.
Swells o'er the Sea, from *Thracia's* frozen Shore, ... Il.9.7.431.
The Sea with Ships, the Fields with Armies spread, ... Il.11.113.39.
When gath'ring Aids along the *Grecian* Sea, ... Il.11.903.75.
And to the Sea the floating Bulwarks fall. .... Il.12.26.82.
When now the Thund'rer, on the Sea-beat Coast, ... Il.13.1.103.
The Sea subsiding spreads a level Plain, ... Il.13.46.107.
Bring all to Sea, and hoist each Sail for flight. .... Il.14.85.161.
They wing their way, and *Imbrus'* Sea-beat Soil, ... Il.14.318.178.
Then soon the haughty Sea-God shall obey, ... Il.15.55.196.
Command the Sea-God to his watry Reign: .... Il.15.62.197.
And drive the *Grecians* headlong to the Sea. .... Il.15.295.208.
Float in one Sea, and wave before the Wind. .... Il.16.263.249.
And all the Sea-green Sisters of the Deep. .... Il.18.46.325.
The Sea-green Sisters plunge beneath the Wave: .... Il.18.182.331.
An aged Sea-God, Father of his Line, ... Il.20.138.399.
Thus having said, the Tyrant of the Sea .... Il.20.172.400.
An unregarded Carcase to the Sea. .... Il.21.329.434.
And stoops on *Hellespont's* resounding Sea. .... Il.24.424.553.
Of sea-girt *Ithaca*, demands my care: .... Od.1.111.37.
What toils by sea! where dark in quest of prey .... Od.3.129.92.
With *Menelaus*, thro' the curling sea. .... Od.3.351.103.
Which scarce the sea-fowl in a year o'erfly) .... Od.3.412.106.
Learn what I heard the sea-born Seer relate, ... Od.4.471.142.
High o'er a gulphy sea, the *Pharian* Isle .... Od.4.479.142.
Then seek the place the sea-born nymph assign'd, ... Od.4.589.147.
But the bright sea-maid's gentle pow'r implor'd, ... Od.4.599.148.
The rock rush'd sea-ward, with impetuous roar .... Od.4.681.151.
Unmoor the fleet, and rush into the sea. .... Od.4.786.156.
To sea-surrounded realms the Gods assign .... Od.4.827.158.
(The sea-ward prow invites the tardy gales) .... Od.4.1034.166.
The chough, the sea-mew, the loquacious crow, ... Od.5.86.176.
Or habitant of earth, or sea, or sky. .... Od.5.102.177.
On a slight Raft to pass the swelling sea .... Od.5.226.182.
At once the face of earth and sea deforms, ... Od.5.377.190.
On the black sea what perils shou'd ensue. .... Od.5.386.190.
And now the west-wind whirls it o'er the sea. .... Od.5.423.192.
Swift as a Sea-mew springing from the flood, ... Od.5.428.193.
And all was cover'd with the curling sea. .... Od.5.449.194.
This said, his sea-green steeds divide the foam, ... Od.5.486.195.
To shield the vessel from the rowling sea; .... Od.5.519.197.
Roar the wild waves; beneath, is sea profound! .... Od.5.529.198.
And soft receives him from the rowling sea. .... Od.5.579.200.
From lands remote, and o'er a length of sea? .... Od.7.319.251.
A Raft was form'd to cross the surging sea; .... Od.7.350.253.
I chose the safer sea, and chanc'd to find .... Od.7.364.254.
Some mean sea-farer in pursuit of gain; .... Od.8.180.272.
And the sea whitens with the rising gale. .... Od.9.160.312.
And all unseen the surge and rowling sea, ... Od.9.170.312.
The face of things: along the sea-beat shore .... Od.9.196.314.
Fast by the sea a lonely cave we view, ... Od.9.212.314.
Consult our safety, and put off to sea. .... Od.9.267.317.
Now off at sea, and from the shallows clear, ... Od.9.555.328.
The whole sea shook, and refluent beat the shore. .... Od.9.570.330.
With all our force we kept aloof to sea, ... Od.9.635.332.
There disembarking on the green sea-side, ... Od.9.639.333.
At length we reach'd *Æolia's* sea-girt shore, ... Od.10.1.335.
To smooth the deep, or swell the foamy sea. .... Od.10.24.340.
And with desponding hearts put off to sea. .... Od.10.88.343.
Haste to thy vessel on the sea-beat shore, ... Od.10.477.366.
In storms by sea, in perils on the shore; .... Od.10.543.369.
Sadly they far'd along the sea-beat shore; .... Od.10.683.376.
That done, a people far from Sea, explore, ... Od.11.152.388.
There the wide sea with all his billows raves! .... Od.11.195.391.
Say while the sea, and while the tempest raves, ... Od.11.495.408.
Nor while the sea, nor while the tempest raves, ... Od.11.501.408.
And pines with thirst amidst a sea of waves: .... Od.11.722.421.
The Sea-dog and the Dolphin are her food; .... Od.12.118.437.
Swift row my mates, and shoot along the sea; .... Od.12.235.443.
When in her gulphs the rushing sea subsides, ... Od.12.288.446.
'Till now from sea or flood no succour found, ... Od.12.393.450.
Snapt the strong helm, and bore to sea the mast. .... Od.12.499.456.
Just when the sea within her gulphs subsides, ... Od.12.509.457.
In storms by sea, and combats on the shore; .... Od.13.109.6.
The winged Pinnace shot along the sea. .... Od.13.187.15.
The solitary shore, and rolling sea. .... Od.13.222.16.
For much I fear, long tracts of land and sea .... Od.13.370.25.
Thus to the sea-green sisters sends his pray'r. .... Od.13.406.26.
Have wander'd many a sea, and many a land. .... Od.14.145.42.
When all was wild expanse of sea and air; .... Od.14.333.51.
Soft I descended, to the sea apply'd .... Od.14.385.53.
And seize their seats, impatient for the sea. .... Od.15.247.80.
With rapid speed to whirl them o'er the sea. .... Od.15.315.84.
Of fierce sea-wolves, and monsters of the flood. .... Od.15.517.95.
Mount the tall bark, and launch into the sea. .... Od.15.590.98.
Learn what I heard the *sea-born Seer relate, ... Od.17.160.139.
The sea, the land, and shakes the world with arms! .... Od.17.343.148.
And ninety cities crown the sea-born Isle: .... Od.19.197.201.
To perish in the rough *Trinacrian* sea. .... Od.19.316.209.
The sea-green sisters waited on the dame. .... Od.24.66.350.
Far in a lonely nook, beside the sea, ... Od.24.177.356.
Reliev'd our weary'd vessel from the sea. .... Od.24.360.366.

SEA-BEAT
Let him, unactive on the Sea-beat Shore, ... Il.7.277.378.
Their rising Bulwarks on the Sea-beat Coast? .... Il.7.533.391.
When now the Thund'rer, on the Sea-beat Coast, ... Il.13.1.103.
They wing their way, and *Imbrus'* Sea-beat Soil, ... Il.14.318.178.
The face of things: along the sea-beat shore .... Od.9.196.314.
Haste to thy vessel on the sea-beat shore, ... Od.10.477.366.
Sadly they far'd along the sea-beat shore; .... Od.10.683.376.

SEA-BORN
Around his Throne the Sea-born Brothers stood, 1.W-F.337.182.
Learn what I heard the sea-born Seer relate, Od.4.471.142.
Then seek the place the sea-born nymph assign'd, Od.4.589.147.
Learn what I heard the *sea-born Seer relate, Od.17.160.139.
And ninety cities crown the sea-born Isle: Od.19.197.201.

SEA-DOG
The Sea-dog and the Dolphin are her food; Od.12.118.437.

SEA-FARER
Some mean sea-farer in pursuit of gain; Od.8.180.272.

SEA-FOWL
Which scarce the sea-fowl in a year o'erfly) Od.3.412.106.

SEA-GIRT
Of those *Calydnæ's* Sea-girt Isles contain; Il.2.822.164.
Of sea-girt *Ithaca*, demands my care: Od.1.111.37.
At length we reach'd *Æolia's* sea-girt shore, Od.10.1.335.

SEA-GOD
Then soon the haughty Sea-God shall obey, Il.15.55.196.
Command the Sea-God to his watry Reign: Il.15.62.197.
An aged Sea-God, Father of his Line, Il.20.138.399.

SEA-GREEN
(His Sea-green Mantle waving with the Wind) 1.W-F.350.184.
Thus to the Sea-green Sisters sends his Pray'r. 1.TrUl.239.473.
And all the Sea-green Sisters of the Deep. Il.18.46.325.
The Sea-green Sisters plunge beneath the Wave: Il.18.182.331.
This said, his sea-green steeds divide the foam, Od.5.486.195.
Thus to the sea-green sisters sends his pray'r. Od.13.406.26.
The sea-green sisters waited on the dame. Od.24.66.350.

SEA-HORSE
Un-water'd see the drooping sea-horse mourn, 3.Ep4.125.149.

SEA-MAID'S
But the bright sea-maid's gentle pow'r implor'd, Od.4.599.148.

SEA-MEW
The chough, the sea-mew, the loquacious crow, Od.5.86.176.
Swift as a Sea-mew springing from the flood, Od.5.428.193.

SEA-SIDE
There disembarking on the green sea-side, Od.9.639.333.

SEA-SURROUNDED
To sea-surrounded realms the Gods assign Od.4.827.158.

SEA-WARD
The rock rush'd sea-ward, with impetuous roar Od.4.681.151.
(The sea-ward prow invites the tardy gales) Od.4.1034.166.

SEA-WEED
From dirt and sea-weed as proud Venice rose; 3.EOM4.292.155.
From dirt and sea-weed as proud Venice rose; 6.130.2.358.

SEA-WOLVES
Of fierce sea-wolves, and monsters of the flood. Od.15.517.95.

SEA'S
Who view the *Western* Sea's extreamest Bounds, 1.TrSt.816.443.
The Sea's great Ruler there, and *Hector* here. Il.14.452.185.
The sea's smooth face, and cleave the hoary deep; Od.9.116.308.

SEAL
Without their aid, to seal these dying eyes. 1.TrFD.99.390.
And waits 'till pleasing Slumbers seal his Eyes. 1.TrSt.538.433.
I seal the Contract with a holy Kiss, 2.ChJM.565.42.
In three *Seal-Rings;* which after, melted down, 2.RL5.91.207.
To seal the Truce and end the dire Debate. Il.3.321.208.
Black Death, and Fate unpitying, seal his Eyes. Il.16.399.258.
She ceas'd: Ambrosial slumbers seal his eyes; Od.20.65.235.

SEAL-RINGS
In three *Seal-Rings;* which after, melted down, 2.RL5.91.207.

SEAL'D
Nor pass these lips in holy silence seal'd. 2.ElAb.10.319.
Now pleasing *Sleep* had seal'd each mortal Eye, Il.2.1.126.
And his seal'd Eyes for ever lose the Light! Il.5.819.305.
With Tablets seal'd, that told his dire Intent. Il.6.210.336.
The fatal Tablets, till that Instant seal'd, Il.6.217.336.
I gave, and seal'd it with th' Almighty Nod, Il.15.81.199.
Divine *Patroclus!* Death has seal'd his Eyes; Il.22.483.476.
Is seal'd in Sleep, thou wander'st thro' the Night? Il.24.448.555.
Heav'n seal'd my words, and you those deeds behold. Od.2.202.71.
Next these in worth, and firm those urns be seal'd; Od.2.399.80.
A solemn oath impos'd the secret seal'd, Od.4.986.163.
They, seal'd with truth return the sure reply, Od.11.182.390.
And in soft slumber seal'd her flowing eye. Od.16.469.130.
Words seal'd with sacred truth, and truth obey: Od.23.190.332.
Seal'd his cold eyes, or drop'd a tender tear! Od.24.347.365.

SEALS
Or in soft Slumbers seals the wakeful Eye; 1.TrSt.434.428.
Each gentle clerk, and mutt'ring seals his eyes. 5.DunA2.372.145.
Each gentle clerk, and mutt'ring seals his eyes. 5.DunB2.404.316.
This seals thy Suit, and this fulfills thy Vows— Il.1.682.119.
Jove seals the League, or bloodier Scenes prepares; Il.4.113.225.
So from her Babe, when Slumber seals his Eye, Il.4.162.228.
And Death in lasting Slumber seals his Eyes. Il.5.90.270.
And seals in endless Shades his swimming Eyes. Il.6.14.323.
And Sleep eternal seals his swimming Eyes. Il.11.310.48.

SEALS (CONTINUED)
And everlasting Slumber seals his Eyes. Il.13.689.137.
And seals again, by fits, his swimming Eyes. Il.14.514.188.
That seals his Word; the Sanction of the God. Il.17.246.297.
Or in soft Slumbers seals the wakeful Eye; Il.24.422.553.
Or in soft slumber seals the wakeful eye: Od.5.61.174.
Seals ev'ry eye, and calms the troubled breast. Od.12.42.431.
For *Pallas* seals his doom: All sad he turns Od.18.185.175.
Or in soft slumber seals the wakeful eye, Od.24.4.347.

SEAM
Yet hang your lip, to see a Seam awry! 4.1HE1.174.293.

SEAM'D
Seam'd o'er with wounds, which his own sabre gave, Od.4.335.135.

SEAMEN
As Seamen at a Capstain Anchors weigh? 6.96ii.30Z44.272.
"As Seamen at a Capstern Anchors weigh? 6.96ii.66.273.

SEAR'D
Scorch'd by the sun, or sear'd by heav'nly fire: Od.5.308.186.

SEARCH
But feigns a Laugh, to see me search around, 1.PSp.55.66.
In search of *Wit* these lose their *common Sense,* 1.EOC.28.242.
But shoud'st thou search the spacious World around, 2.ChJM.637.45.
In search of Mischief still on Earth to roam. 2.RL1.64.150.
Repair'd to search the gloomy Cave of *Spleen.* 2.RL4.16.184.
Repairs to search the gloomy Cave of *Spleen.* 2.RL4.16A.184.
Yet, in the search, the wisest may mistake, 3.Ep1.210A.33.
Search then the Ruling Passion: There, alone, 3.Ep1.174.30.
Yet, in this search, the wisest may mistake, 3.Ep1.210.33.
Go, search it there, where to be born and die, 3.Ep3.287.116.
Or tir'd in search of Truth, or search of Rhyme. 4.HS2.86.61.
Or tir'd in search of Truth, or search of Rhyme. 4.HS2.86.61.
In search of Vanities from Nature strays: 4.HAdv.99.83.
And search it to the *Bottom.* 6.94.32.260.
And search the shag of Thighatira's Ruff. 6.96ii.30Z2.271.
Search all the House; my *Gulliver* is lost! 6.96iv.44.277.
But thou, nor they, shall search the Thoughs that roll Il.1.710.121.
Vain is the Search, presumptuous and abhorr'd, Il.1.728.122.
But if thou still persist to search my Birth, Il.6.187.335.
Go search your slaughter'd Chiefs on yonder Plain, Il.7.486.388.
Some search the Plain, some fell the sounding Grove: Il.7.495.389.
In Search of Prey she wings the spacious Air, Il.9.426.453.
Hector he sought; in search of *Hector* turn'd Il.20.105.398.
I search to find them, but I search in vain. Il.23.547.511.
I search to find them, but I search in vain. Il.23.547.511.
Who search the Sorrows of a Parent's Heart, Il.24.474.556.
Propitious to the search. Direct your toil Od.1.368.50.
Search, for some thoughts, thy own suggesting mind; Od.3.34.87.
Search all thy stores of faithful memory: Od.3.123.91.
Eludes my search: but when his form I view'd Od.4.343.136.
Roam the wild Isle in search of rural cates, Od.4.498.144.
Whose texture ev'n the search of Gods deceives, Od.8.323.281.
Lest in a search too anxious and too vain Od.15.106.73.
For farther search, his rapid steeds transport Od.17.132.138.
The curious search of *Euryclea's* eye. Od.19.459.217.
Hapless to search! more hapless still to find! Od.21.28.260.
To search the woods for sets of flowry thorn, Od.24.259.361.
May I presume to search thy secret soul? Od.24.542.374.

SEARCH'D
For lost *Europa* search'd the World in vain, 1.TrSt.248.420.
For Pinks and Daisies search'd the flow'ry Plain; 2.ChJM.624.45.
He search'd for coral but he gather'd weeds. 5.DunA2.286Z2.137.
In vain she search'd each Cranny of the House, 6.96ii.15.270.
Thro' Heaps of Carnage search'd the mournful Plain. Il.7.503.389.
And search'd each passing sheep, and felt it o'er, Od.9.497.326.
Search'd the wide country for his wand'ring mares, Od.21.26.260.
Mean-while *Ulysses* search'd the dome, to find Od.22.421.308.

SEARCHES
Spreads his wide arms, and searches round and round: Od.9.494.326.

SEARCHING
And *Cadmus* searching round the spacious Sea? 1.TrSt.8.409.
Thro the thick Files he darts his searching Eyes, Il.4.235.232.
In this attire secure from searching eyes, Od.4.339.136.
And if aright these searching eyes survey, Od.16.494.131.

SEAS
The Seas shall waste; the Skies in Smoke decay; 1.Mes.105.122.
No Seas so rich, so gay no Banks appear, 1.W-F.225.170.
No Seas so rich so full no Streams appear, 1.W-F.225A.170.
Tempt Icy Seas, where scarce the Waters roll, 1.W-F.389.189.
The Time shall come, when free as Seas or Wind 1.W-F.397.190.
And Seas but join the Regions they divide; 1.W-F.400.191.
My father o'er your seas presides; and he 1.TrPA.112.370.
I go, ye Nymphs! those Rocks and Seas to prove; 1.TrSP.201.402.
To Rocks and Seas I fly from *Phaon's* Hate, 1.TrSP.205.402.
And hope from Seas and Rocks a milder Fate. 1.TrSP.206.402.
To distant Seas must tender *Sapho* fly? 1.TrSP.219.403.
Ah let me seek it from the raging Seas: 1.TrSP.257.404.
To raging Seas unpity'd I'll remove, 1.TrSP.258.404.
Ah! let me seek it from the raging Seas: 1.TrSP.257B.404.
Passes the Strait that parts the foaming Seas, 1.TrSt.472.430.
He dreads the Rocks, and Shoals, and Seas, and Skies, 1.TrSt.524.432.
Delights the *Nereids* of the neighb'ring Seas; 1.TrUl.34.466.
Delights the *Nereids* of the neighb'ring Seas; 1.TrUl.229.473.
I stood, methought, betwixt Earth, Seas, and Skies; 2.TemF.11.254.
All various Sounds from Earth, and Seas, and Skies, 2.TemF.433.284.
In seas of flame my plunging soul is drown'd, 2.ElAb.275.342.
"Seas roll to waft me, suns to light me rise; 3.EOM1.139.32.
T' enroll your triumphs o'er the seas and land; 4.2HE1.373.227.

SEAS (CONTINUED)

What seas you travers'd! and what fields you fought! ....4.2HE1.396.229.
Arabian shores, or Indian seas infold? ....4.1HE6.12.237.
The toil, the danger of the Seas; ....4.HS6.37.253.
A place there is, betwixt earth, air and seas, ...5.DunA2.79.107.
(As under seas Alphæus' secret sluice ....5.DunA2.317.140.
(As under seas Alphæus' sacred sluice ....5.DunA2.317A.140.
Her boundless Empire over seas and lands. ....5.DunA3.60.155.
A place there is, betwixt earth, air, and seas, ...5.DunB2.83.299.
(As under seas Alphæus' secret sluice ....5.DunB2.341.314.
Her boundless empire over seas and lands. ....5.DunB3.68.323.
Intrepid then, o'er seas and lands he flew: ....5.DunB4.293.373.
So when the first bold Vessel dar'd the Seas, ...6.11.38.31.
When the first Vessel dar'd the Seas, ...6.11.38A.31.
And Seas, and Rocks, and Skies rebound ....6.11.47.32.
And measure back the Seas we crost before? ....Il.1.80.90.
Swift to the Seas profound the Goddess flies, ...Il.1.688.120.
Twice sixty Warriors thro' the foaming Seas. ....Il.2.609.156.
Thro' roaring Seas the wond'ring Warriors bear; ....Il.2.744.161.
But those who view fair *Elis* o'er the Seas ....Il.2.759.162.
Led nine swift Vessels thro' the foamy Seas; ....Il.2.794.163.
Where many Seas, and many Suff'rings past, ...Il.2.807.163.
To warmer Seas the Cranes embody'd fly, ...Il.3.7.188.
For distant *Troy* refus'd to sail the Seas: ....Il.3.308.208.
First move the whitening Surface of the Seas, ...Il.4.479.243.
When first for *Troy* I sail'd the sacred Seas, ...Il.5.249.279.
Now win the Shores, and scarce the Seas remain. ....Il.5.985.314.
And *Greece* indignant thro' her Seas returns. ....Il.6.679.361.
Wash'd by broad *Hellespont's* resounding Seas, ...Il.7.100.368.
The Town, the Tents, and navigable Seas. ....Il.8.66.398.
Where on her utmost Verge the Seas resound; ....Il.8.598.424.
They gave Dominion o'er the Seas and Land, ...Il.9.54.434.
To *Neptune,* Ruler of the Seas profound, ...Il.9.239.444.
She took, and thunder'd thro' the Seas and Land. ....Il.11.10.35.
A Country's Ruins! to the Seas are born: ....Il.11.617.61.
Convey'd that Freshness the cool Seas exhale; ....Il.11.761.69.
The circling Seas alone absorbing all, ...Il.12.341.93.
The crowded Ships, and sable Seas between. ....Il.13.24.105.
But *Neptune,* rising from the Seas profound, ...Il.13.67.108.
O'er Earth and Seas, and thro' th' aerial way, ...Il.14.350.179.
Deep under Seas, where hoary *Ocean* dwells. ....Il.14.354.180.
Around the Ships: Seas hanging o'er the Shores, ...Il.14.455.185.
Seeks his own Seas, and trembles at our Rage! ....Il.15.251.206.
Burn'd to the bottom of the Seas profound; ....Il.15.253.206.
Burn'd to the bottom of his Seas profound; ....Il.15.253A.206.
As, when black Tempests mix the Seas and Skies, ...Il.15.440.214.
And raging Seas produc'd thee in a Storm, ...Il.16.51.237.
With long-projected Beams the Seas are bright, ...Il.18.251.334.
And when along the level Seas they flew, ...Il.20.272.405.
Not him the Seas unmeasur'd Deeps detain, ...Il.21.68.424.
The Seas, the Rivers, and the Springs below, ...Il.21.214.430.
Across the *Thracian* Seas their Course they bore; ....Il.23.286.501.
The ruffled Seas beneath their Passage roar. ....Il.23.287.501.
Seas, Shores, and Skies with loud Applause resound, ...Il.23.1028.530.
What Seas they measur'd, and what Fields they fought; ....Il.24.14.535.
On stormy seas unnumber'd toils he bore, ...Od.1.7.28.
Of *Phorcys,* dreaded in the sounds and seas:) ....Od.1.93.36.
Measur'd a length of seas, a toilsome length, in vain. ....Od.1.339.48.
A realm defended with incircling seas: ....Od.1.526.57.
And seek my sire thro' storms and rolling seas! ....Od.2.300.76.
Thro' seas and realms companion of thy care. ....Od.2.326.77.
To realms, that rocks and roaring seas divide? ....Od.2.409.80.
Oh beat those storms, and roll the seas in vain! ....Od.2.415.81.
Lo! on the seas prepar'd the vessel stands; ....Od.2.450.83.
Where savage Pyrates seek thro' seas unknown ....Od.3.88.90.
Thro' the mid seas he bids our navy steer, ...Od.3.211.96.
What pow'r becalms th' innavigable seas? ....Od.4.515.145.
The flouncing herd ascending from the seas; ....Od.4.556.146.
To speed a prosp'rous voyage o'er the seas? ....Od.4.634.149.
By seas, by wars, so many dangers run, ...Od.5.287.185.
To *Neptune's* wrath, stern Tyrant of the Seas, ...Od.5.431.193.
Stretch'd wide his eager arms, and shot the seas along. ....Od.5.477.195.
Back to the seas the rowling surge may sweep, ...Od.5.536.198.
Where to the seas the shelving shore declin'd, ...Od.5.564.199.
Thro' seas retreating from the sound of war, ...Od.6.10.203.
Soft he reclines along the murm'ring seas, ...Od.6.283.224.
Unpolish'd men, and boistrous as their seas: ....Od.7.42.235.
Soon as their rage subsides, the seas I brave ....Od.7.360.254.
O'er unknown seas arriv'd from unknown shores. ....Od.8.14.262.
The seas may roll, the tempests rage in vain. ....Od.8.612.295.
The seas to traverse, or the ships to build, ...Od.9.148.311.
Pyrates perhaps, who seek thro' seas unknown ....Od.9.301.318.
Thro' various seas by various perils tost, ...Od.9.309.319.
And sweep with equal strokes the smoaky seas; ....Od.10.150.347.
And all around it only seas and skies! ....Od.10.226.351.
How could thy soul, by realms and seas disjoyn'd, ...Od.11.73.383.
Next, where the Sirens dwell, you plow the seas; ....Od.12.51.431.
These seas o'erpass'd, be wise! but I refrain ....Od.12.67.433.
Thrice in her gulphs the boiling seas subside, ...Od.12.131.438.
When seas retreating roar within her caves, ...Od.12.134.438.
Stretch to the stroke, and brush the working seas. ....Od.12.265.445.
Still must we restless rove, new seas explore, ...Od.12.337.448.
Dance the green *Nereids* of the neighb'ring seas. ....Od.12.378.449.
More dreadful than the tempest, lash'd the seas; ....Od.12.504.457.
Then nine long days I plow'd the calmer seas, ...Od.12.529.458.
Smooth seas, and gentle winds, invite him home. ....Od.13.8.2.
Delights the *Nereids* of the neighb'ring seas; ....Od.13.125.8.
Delights the *Nereids* of the neighb'ring seas: ....Od.13.396.26.
Far on the swelling seas to wander hence? ....Od.14.207.45.
Safe through the level seas we sweep our way; ....Od.14.286.49.
Thro' the mid seas the nimble pinnace sails, ...Od.14.329.51.
O'er seas convey'd me to my native reign: ....Od.16.253.117.
And fish of ev'ry fin thy seas afford: ....Od.19.134.199.
Torn from thy arms, to sail a length of seas; ....Od.23.284.337.
Forc'd a long month the wintry seas to bear, ...Od.24.142.354.

SEASON

Fresh as the Morn, and as the Season fair: ....1.PSp.20.62.
Fresh as the Morn, and as the Season fair, ...1.PSp.17z3.62.
In that cold Season Love but treats his Guest ....2.ChJM.105.19.
Which in due Place and Season, you may hear. ....2.ChJM.513.40.
'Twas now the Season when the glorious Sun ....2.ChJM.609.44.
In that soft Season when descending Showers ....2.TemF.1.253.
Wait but for wings, and in their season, fly. ....3.Ep3.172.107.
The season, when to come, and when to go, ...4.2HE1.360.225.
The Season of green Pease is fled, ...6.10.107.27.
The same mild season gives the blooms to blow, ...6.35.15.103.
Beauty, frail flow'r that ev'ry season fears, ...6.52.57.157.
Must season this knuckle, ...6.91.6.253.
'Tis now no Season for these kind Delays; ....Il.11.792.71.
'Twas now no Season for prolong'd Debate; ....Il.18.291.336.
Some less important Season may suffice, ...Il.19.198.381.
No Season now for calm familiar Talk, ...Il.22.169.460.
But ev'ry season fills the foaming pail. ....Od.4.112.125.
The same mild season gives the blooms to blow, ...Od.7.156.243.
Staid but a season to re-fit his fleet; ....Od.14.422.56.
A gift in season which his wants require. ....Od.17.631.163.
At ev'ning mild (meet season to confer) ....Od.17.662.164.

SEASON'D

To form strong buskins of well-season'd hyde. ....Od.14.26.36.

SEASONS

The various Seasons of the rowling Year; ....1.PSp.38.64.
In vain kind Seasons swell'd the teeming Grain, ...1.W-F.53.154.
But when the circling Seasons in their Train ....Il.21.523.443.
But when the Seasons, following in their train, ...Od.10.556.369.

SEAT

Or chuse thy Seat in *Ilion's* proud Abodes, ...1.TrSt.835.444.
Full in the midst, proud *Fame's* Imperial Seat ....2.TemF.248.275.
Her Head's untouch'd, that noble Seat of Thought: ....3.Ep2.74.56.
The woods recede around the naked seat, ...3.Ep3.209.110.
In Britain's Senate he a seat obtains, ...3.Ep3.393.124.
You'll wish your hill or shelter'd seat again. ....3.Ep4.76.144.
You'll wish your Hill, and shelter'd seat again. ....3.Ep4.76A.144.
Much they extoll'd his Pictures, much his Seat, ...4.Arbu.239.113.
Much they extoll'd the Pictures, much the Seat, ...4.Arbu.239A.113.
Oh, could I see my Country Seat! ....4.HS6.128.259.
And destin'd here th' imperial seat of Fools. ....5.DunA1.36.O64.
And in sweet numbers celebrates the seat. ....5.DunA1.226.90.
High on a gorgeous seat, that far outshone ....5.DunA2.1.96.
There in his seat two spacious Vents appear, ...5.DunA2.81.108.
He chinks his purse, and takes his seat of state: ....5.DunA2.189.124.
Then raptures high the seat of sense o'erflow, ...5.DunA3.5.150.
Her seat imperial, Dulness shall transport. ....5.DunA3.302.185.
And here she plann'd th' Imperial seat of Fools. ....5.DunB1.272.290.
High on a gorgeous seat, that far out-shone ....5.DunB2.1.296.
There in his seat two spacious vents appear, ...5.DunB2.85.299.
He chinks his purse, and takes his seat of state: ....5.DunB2.197.305.
Then raptures high the seat of Sense o'erflow, ...5.DunB3.5.320.
Her seat imperial Dulness shall transport. ....5.DunB3.300.334.
In what new Nation shall we fix our Seat? ....6.65.6.192.
And say what Region is our destin'd Seat? ....6.65.6A.192.
Calls it the Seat of Empire, Arts and Arms! ....6.96v.24.280.
Slow from his Seat arose the *Pylian* Sage; ....Il.1.330.103.
Each takes his Seat, and each receives his Share. ....Il.1.613.117.
Fierce from his Seat, at this *Ulysses* springs, ...Il.2.302.142.
Few Leagues remov'd, we wish our peaceful Seat, ...Il.2.358.144.
Each takes his Seat, and each receives his Share. ....Il.2.513.151.
The *Greeks* and *Trojans* seat on either Hand; ....Il.3.98.194.
He mounts the Seat, *Antenor* at his side; ....Il.3.332.209.
Swift from his Seat he leap'd upon the Ground, ...Il.5.142.274.
Now mount my Seat, and from the Chariot's height ....Il.5.278.280.
Now haste, ascend my Seat, and from the Car ....Il.5.278A.280.
Swift to *Æneas'* empty Seat proceed, ...Il.5.326.282.
She mounts the Seat oppress'd with silent Woe, ...Il.5.455.290.
In well-built *Pheræ* held his lofty Seat: ....Il.5.672.300.
The youthful Victor mounts his empty Seat, ...Il.5.720.301.
Drew from his Seat the martial Charioteer. ....Il.5.1029.315.
He held his Seat; a Friend to Human Race. ....Il.6.18.325.
Our ancient Seat his honour'd Presence grac'd, ...Il.6.269.340.
Each takes his Seat, and each receives his Share. ....Il.7.385.383.
Slow from his Seat the rev'rend *Priam* rose. ....Il.7.441.386.
High on the cloudy Point his Seat he plac'd. ....Il.8.64.398.
Then haste, ascend my Seat, and from the Car ....Il.8.133.404.
Leap'd from his Seat, and laid the Harp aside. ....Il.9.258.445.
Or *Troy* once more must be the Seat of War? ....Il.10.248.13.
Old *Nestor* mounts the Seat: Beside him rode ....Il.11.638.62.
To his high Seat; the Chief refus'd, and said. ....Il.11.791.71.
Swift from his Seat; his clanging Armour rung. ....Il.12.94.84.
Who held his Seat in *Corinth's* stately Town; ....Il.13.835.145.
Victorious *Troy:* Then, starting from his Seat, ...Il.15.457.215.
Hurl'd from the lofty Seat, at distance far, ...Il.15.530.217.
He shifts his Seat, and vaults from one to one; ....Il.15.827.228.
He held his Seat, and rul'd the Realms around. ....Il.17.357.301.
Sole in the Seat the Charioteer remains, ...Il.17.532.309.
To thee I yield the Seat, to thee resign ....Il.17.546.309.
Snatches the Reins, and vaults into the Seat. ....Il.17.549.309.
And o'er his Seat the bloody Trophies hung. ....Il.17.611.312.
Prone from the Seat he tumbles to the Plain; ....Il.17.699.314.
Haste, and our Fathers sacred Seat attend, ...Il.18.178.331.
His ancient Seat beneath the sacred Deeps. ....Il.20.16.393.
Shot headlong from his Seat, beside the Wheel, ...Il.23.473.509.
High on the Seat the Cabinet they bind: ....Il.24.333.550.
He said, and entring, took his Seat of State, ...Il.24.746.568.
He led the Goddess to the sovereign seat, ...Od.1.171.40.
Then drew his seat, familiar, to her side: ....Od.1.174.40.
And soon restore him to his regal seat. ....Od.1.266.45.
His former seat beside the King he found, ...Od.3.598.117.
The glitt'ring seat *Telemachus* ascends; ....Od.3.610.117.
To *Pheræ* now, *Diocleus'* stately seat, ...Od.3.619.117.

SEAT (CONTINUED)
The seat of majesty *Adraste* brings, ... Od.4.161.128.
The sovereign seat then *Jove*-born Helen *press'd,* ... Od.4.183.128.
Argos the seat of sovereign rule I chose; ... Od.4.235.130.
Our sovereign seat a lewd usurping race ... Od.4.429.140.
Of *Jove's* high seat descends with sweepy force, ... Od.4.644.150.
Shone the fifth morn: when from her sacred seat ... Od.5.334.188.
He seis'd the Raft, and leapt into his seat, ... Od.5.414.192.
The seat of Gods, the regions mild of peace, ... Od.6.49.207.
Now mounting the gay seat, the silken reins ... Od.6.95.209.
The splendid seat, the list'ning chief address'd. ... Od.6.302.225.
And seat him fair in some distinguish'd place. ... Od.7.219.247.
And from his seat *Laodamas* remov'd, ... Od.7.226.247.
Then to the Council seat they bend their way, ... Od.8.5.261.
Before his seat a polish'd table shines, ... Od.8.65.265.
Radiant with starry studs, a silver seat ... Od.10.375.362.
Then led and plac'd me on the sov'reign seat, ... Od.10.431.365.
Each from his seat to each Immortal pours, ... Od.13.70.4.
Transported from his seat *Eumæus* sprung, ... Od.16.13.102.
His seat *Ulysses* to the Prince resign'd. ... Od.16.42.104.
There stood an empty seat, where late was plac'd ... Od.17.404.152.
An ivory seat with silver ringlets grac'd, ... Od.19.68.196.
The sovereign seat with graceful air she press'd; ... Od.19.72.196.
A seat soft spread with furry spoils prepare, ... Od.19.119.198.
A seat adorn'd with furry spoils she plac'd: ... Od.19.122.198.
His former seat receiv'd the stranger-guest; ... Od.19.592.225.
A trivet-table, and ignobler seat, ... Od.20.323.248.
With which he nobly may discharge his seat, ... Od.20.363.250.
Resuming then his seat, *Eupitheus'* son ... Od.21.147.265.
And to the seat returns from whence he rose. ... Od.21.174.268.
His seat he takes, his eyes upon his Lord. ... Od.21.426.280.
He spurn'd the seat with fury as he fell, ... Od.22.103.291.
Soon as returning life regains its seat, ... Od.24.407.368.
And strait resum'd his seat) while round him bows ... Od.24.470.371.

SEATED
Th' Assembly seated, rising o'er the rest, ... Il.1.77.90.
Say, Virgins, seated round the Throne Divine, ... Il.2.572.155.
Ulysses seated, greater Rev'rence drew. ... Il.3.274.205.
There *Hector* seated by the Stream he sees, ... Il.15.270.207.
Now graceful seated on her shining throne, ... Od.5.109.177.
A guest, a stranger, seated in the dust! ... Od.7.215.247.
In order seated on their banks, they sweep ... Od.9.209.314.
Now seated in the Olive's sacred shade ... Od.13.425.26.
On chairs and beds in order seated round, ... Od.24.452.370.

SEATS
Oh deign to visit our forsaken Seats, ... 1.PSu.71.77.
Some God conduct you to these blissful Seats, ... 1.PSu.71A.77.
At once the Monarch's and the Muse's Seats, ... 1.W-F.2.148.
And call the Muses to their ancient Seats, ... 1.W-F.284.174.
Grav'd o'er their Seats the Form of *Time* was found, ... 2.TemF.147.265.
Whose Seats the weary Traveller repose? ... 3.Ep3.260.114.
Joy lives not here; to happier seats it flies, ... 6.81.5.225.
And sure if ought below the Seats Divine ... 6.84.21.239.
Yet sure if ought below the Seats Divine ... 6.84.21A.239.
Who climbs these High Seats oh his joy shall be great! ... 6.122.21.342.
And to the Seats Divine her Flight addrest. ... Il.1.646.118.
Or in fair *Tarphe's* Sylvan Seats reside; ... Il.2.639.157.
So from their Seats the Brother-Chiefs are torn, ... Il.5.210.277.
In Seats of Council and the sumptuous Feast: ... Il.8.197.407.
Mix with the Gods, and fill their Seats of Gold. ... Il.8.541.422.
And plac'd in Seats with purple Carpets spread. ... Il.9.266.445.
To quit these Shores, their native Seats enjoy, ... Il.9.540.460.
And took their Seats beneath the shady Tent. ... Il.11.763.69.
With stately Seats, and Riches, blest in vain: ... Il.16.724.272.
Their sacred Seats, the glimm'ring *Grotto* fill'd; ... Il.18.66.326.
On Seats of Stone, within the sacred Place, ... Il.18.585.351.
These on the sacred Seats of Council plac'd, ... Il.19.53.374.
Th' immortal Seats should ne'er behold her more; ... Il.19.128.377.
To their new Seats the Female Captives move; ... Il.19.295.384.
They mount their Seats; the Lots their Place dispose; ... Il.23.427.507.
Arise! O *Thetis,* from thy Seats below. ... Il.24.116.540.
The Goddess seats her by her pensive Son, ... Il.24.161.542.
And all fair *Lesbos'* blissful Seats contain, ... Il.24.686.565.
The seats to range, the fragrant wood to bring, ... Od.3.544.114.
And you who fill the blissful seats above! ... Od.5.13.171.
She past, delighted with the well-known seats; ... Od.7.105.239.
At once the seats they fill: and every eye ... Od.8.17.262.
The Sun ne'er views th' uncomfortable seats, ... Od.11.17.380.
Beneath the seats, soft painted robes they spread, ... Od.13.88.5.
And seize their seats, impatient for the sea. ... Od.15.247.80.
And fresh from bathing, to their seats withdrew. ... Od.17.103.136.
Swift from their seats, and thick'ning form a ring. ... Od.18.49.169.
The seats with purple cloathe in order due; ... Od.20.188.242.

SEC
(That Gay the poor Sec: and that arch Chaplain Parnell, ... 6.42i.5.116.

SECKER
Secker is decent, *Rundel* has a Heart, ... 4.EpS2.71.316.

SECOND
Stretch'd on the Lawn his second Hope survey, ... 1.W-F.81.158.
Now Length of *Fame* (our *second* Life) is lost, ... 1.EOC.480.293.
A *second* Deluge Learning thus o'er-run, ... 1.EOC.691.317.
(My self the offspring of a second bride.) ... 1.TrFD.10.386.
And while her Arms her Second Hope contain, ... 1.TrSt.17.410.
And while her Arms a second Hope contain, ... 1.TrSt.17A.410.
But scarce subsisted to the Second Reign. ... 1.TrSt.199.418.
Spreads in a second Circle, then a third; ... 2.TemF.439.284.
How vain that second Life in others' Breath, ... 2.TemF.505.288.
Yet serves to second too some other use. ... 3.EOM1.56.20.
Perhaps acts second to some sphere unknown, ... 3.EOM1.58.20.
Perhaps acts second to a sphere unknown ... 3.EOM1.58A.20.
On him, their second Providence, they hung, ... 3.EOM3.217.114.

SECOND (CONTINUED)
Without a second, or without a judge: ... 3.EOM4.264.153.
If second qualities for first they take. ... 3.Ep1.211.33.
They seek the second not to lose the first. ... 3.Ep2.214.67.
Then ask'd Ten Thousand for a second Night: ... 4.HAdv.8.75.
Who trades in Frigates of the second Rate? ... 4.HAdv.62.81.
To second, Arbuthnot! thy Art and Care, ... 4.Arbu.133.105.
Still Dunce the second reigns like Dunce the first? ... 5.DunA1.6.61.
A second effort brought but new disgrace, ... 5.DunA2.167.121.
One circle first, and then a second makes, ... 5.DunA2.374.146.
"A second see, by meeker manners known, ... 5.DunA3.135.161.
Still Dunce the second reigns like Dunce the first; ... 5.DunB1.6.269.
A second effort brought but new disgrace, ... 5.DunB2.175.304.
One circle first, and then a second makes; ... 5.DunB2.406.317.
"A second see, by meeker manners known, ... 5.DunB3.143.326.
And, at their second birth, they issue mine." ... 5.DunB4.386.380.
Shrinks to her second cause, and is no more. ... 5.DunB4.644.408.
A second sun thou dost present, ... 6.6ii.13.15.
In five long Years I took no second Spouse; ... 6.96iv.5.276.
My second (Child of Fortune!) waits ... 6.135.59.368.
For whom must *Helen* break her second Vow? ... Il.3.497.215.
And Nerves to second what thy Soul inspires! ... Il.4.363.238.
His Strokes they second, and avert our Spears: ... Il.5.744.302.
Had thence retir'd; and with her second Joy, ... Il.6.466.349.
My second Father, and my rev'rend Guide! ... Il.9.714.469.
To raise my Hopes, and second my Design. ... Il.10.264.13.
The *Spartan* wish'd the second Place to gain, ... Il.10.273.14.
To second these, in close Array combin'd, ... Il.11.65.37.
This Heart and Hand shall second all thy Fires: ... Il.13.986.152.
The trembling, servile, second Race of Heav'n. ... Il.15.223.205.
The second to his Lord in Love and Fame, ... Il.16.179.245.
(*Ajax,* to *Peleus'* Son the second Name, ... Il.17.328.300.
And shall not I, the second Pow'r above, ... Il.18.427.341.
Troy yet shall dare to camp a second Night? ... Il.19.74.375.
Expect a second Summons to the War; ... Il.19.238.382.
The second Victor claims a Mare unbroke, ... Il.23.333.503.
O'er-past *Atrides)* second in the Course. ... Il.23.598.513.
To him the second Honours of the Day. ... Il.23.616.514.
A well-fed Ox was for the second plac'd; ... Il.23.876.524.
The well-fed Bull (the second Prize) he shar'd, ... Il.23.913.525.
Shou'd second love a pleasing flame inspire, ... Od.1.358.49.
And on the board a second banquet rose. ... Od.4.68.122.
"Too late the Queen selects a second lord: ... Od.4.1018.165.
And tender second to a mother's cares. ... Od.7.16.234.
Distinguish'd long, and second now to none! ... Od.7.290.250.
Brain'd on the rock; his second dire repast. ... Od.9.405.322.
Our second progress to my royal friend; ... Od.10.64.342.
Our second hope to great *Achilles* dy'd! ... Od.11.674.417.
Afresh for thee, my second cause of woe! ... Od.14.201.45.
Obtruding on my choice a second Lord, ... Od.19.154.200.
E're second vows my bridal faith profane. ... Od.20.97.237.
Of right the Queen refus'd a second Lord: ... Od.20.394.251.
And second all *Eupithes'* rage inspir'd. ... Od.24.533.373.

SECONDING
He said, and seconding the kind request, ... Od.14.57.38.

SECONDLY
And *secondly,* how innocent a *Belle* ... 4.HAdv.108.85.

SECONDS
These Words he seconds with his flying Lance, ... Il.5.659.299.
Minerva seconds what the Sage inspires. ... Il.15.807.227.
Wakes all our Force, and seconds all our Fires. ... Il.15.879.230.
Of swift removal, seconds my desires. ... Od.17.21.133.

SECRECIE
Ne swinken but with Secrecie: ... 6.14i.2A.41.

SECRESIE
Yet swinken nat sans Secresie. ... 6.14i.2.41.

SECRET
And secret Transport touch'd the conscious Swain. ... 1.W-F.90.159.
In some fair Body thus the secret Soul ... 1.EOC.76B.247.
Their growing Fears in secret Murmurs vent, ... 1.TrSt.225.420.
O'er all his Bosom secret Transports reign, ... 1.TrSt.579.434.
Skill'd in the Laws of Secret Fate above, ... 1.TrSt.839.444.
Consum'd at Heart, and fed a secret Fire. ... 2.ChJM.360.31.
With secret Vows, to favour his Design. ... 2.ChJM.417.35.
By secret Writing to disclose his Pain, ... 2.ChJM.497.39.
Secret, and undescry'd, he took his Way, ... 2.ChJM.537.41.
Such secret Transports warm my melting Heart. ... 2.ChJM.572.43.
That e'er he told a Secret to his Dame. ... 2.ChWB.276.70.
Some secret Truths from Learned Pride conceal'd, ... 2.RL1.37.148.
And secret Passions labour'd in her Breast. ... 2.RL4.2.183.
O let us still the secret Joy partake, ... 2.TemF.364.281.
Each talk'd aloud, or in some secret Place, ... 2.TemF.466.286.
Safe is your Secret still in Cloe's ear; ... 3.Ep2.173.64.
If secret Gold saps on from knave to knave. ... 3.Ep3.38.88.
That secret rare, between th' extremes to move ... 3.Ep3.227.111.
Who in the *Secret,* deals in Stocks secure, ... 4.JD4.140.37.
Out with it, *Dunciad!* let the secret pass, ... 4.Arbu.79.101.
That Secret to each Fool, that he's an Ass: ... 4.Arbu.80.101.
But each man's secret standard in his mind, ... 4.Arbu.176.109.
"'Tis now no secret—I protest ... 4.HS6.118.257.
P. See! now I keep the Secret, and not you. ... 4.EpS2.23.314.
Have still a secret Byass to a Knave: ... 4.EpS2.101.319.
(As under seas Alphæus' secret sluice ... 5.DunA2.317.140.
Thus at her felt approach, and secret might, ... 5.DunA3.345.193.
(As under seas Alphæus' secret sluice ... 5.DunB2.341.314.
Thus at her felt approach, and secret might, ... 5.DunB4.639.407.
While *Procris* panted in the secret shade; ... 6.14iii.2.45.
Tho' secret, yet with copious Grief she mourns, ... 6.33.5.99.
Tho' secret, yet with copious Streams she mourns, ... 6.33.5A.99.
Of secret Jesuits swift shall be the Doom, ... 6.48ii.7.134.

SECRET (CONTINUED)
Resolv'd this *Secret* to explore, ... 6.94.31.260.
But each Man's secret Standard in his Mind, ... 6.98.26.284.
Safe is your secret still in Cloë's ear; .... 6.139.17.377.
Nor saw what *Jove* and secret Fate design'd, ... Il.2.48.129.
Not thus the King in secret Council spoke. .... Il.2.232.138.
Born in the Shades of *Ida's* secret Grove, ... Il.2.994.170.
In secret own'd resistless Beauty's Pow'r: .... Il.3.204.201.
She spoke, and *Helen's* secret Soul was mov'd; .... Il.3.487.215.
Tho' secret Anger swell'd *Minerva's* Breast, ... Il.4.31.222.
Two Heroes led the secret Squadron on, ... Il.4.446.241.
But heard respectful, and in secret burn'd: .... Il.4.453.241.
In secret Woods he won the *Naiad's* Grace, ... Il.6.31.325.
The deathful Secret to the King reveal'd. .... Il.6.218.336.
And mourn'd in secret, his, and *Ilion's* Fate. .... Il.6.423.347.
With secret Pleasure each fond Parent smil'd, ... Il.6.598.356.
Sage *Helenus* their secret Counsels knew: .... Il.7.48.365.
But pray in secret, lest the Foes should hear, ... Il.7.231.376.
Said I in secret? No, your Vows declare, ... Il.7.233.376.
Tho' secret Anger swell'd *Minerva's* Breast, ... Il.8.572.424.
What in my secret Soul is understood, ... Il.9.408.452.
Touch'd with her secret Key, the Doors unfold; .... Il.14.195.168.
And secret there indulge thy soft Desire. .... Il.14.386.181.
Whate'er the Cause, reveal thy secret Care, ... Il.16.27.236.
Her secret Offspring to her Sire she bare; .... Il.16.228.248.
To Fate submitting with a secret Sigh) .... Il.18.164.330.
Secret, dispatch'd her trusty Messenger. .... Il.18.204.331.
Nine Years kept secret in the dark Abode, ... Il.18.469.344.
(Ev'n while he lives, he wastes with secret Woe) .... Il.18.515.346.
A secret Ambush on the Foe prepare: .... Il.18.596.351.
Curs'd the dire Fury, and in secret groan'd. .... Il.19.134.377.
Far on *Olyumpus'* Top in secret State .... Il.20.33.394.
A growing Work employ'd her secret Hours, ... Il.22.568.479.
Where *Thetis* sorrow'd in her secret Cave: .... Il.24.110.539.
Take Gifts in secret, that must shun the Light? .... Il.24.532.558.
Twelve Days, nor Foes, nor secret Ambush dread; .... Il.24.987.577.
A secret pleasure touch'd *Athena's* soul, ... Od.3.65.89.
But my pleas'd bosom glow'd with secret joy: .... Od.4.356.136.
Once more the *Nile,* who from the secret source .... Od.4.643.149.
Spontaneous did you speed his secret course, ... Od.4.870.159.
Safe from the secret rock and adverse storm, ... Od.4.879.159.
A solemn oath impos'd the secret seal'd, ... Od.4.986.163.
And thus in secret to his soul he said. .... Od.5.366.190.
To the calm current of the secret tyde; .... Od.6.252.222.
And secret moves along the crowded space, ... Od.7.51.236.
The silent tear, and heard the secret groan: .... Od.8.92.267.
The silent tear, and heard the secret groan; .... Od.8.584.294.
Joy touch'd my secret soul, and conscious heart, ... Od.9.491.326.
But secret I revolv'd the deep design: .... Od.9.500.326.
Soon might'st thou tell me, where in secret here .... Od.9.537.328.
Lest to the<e> naked secret fraud be meant, ... Od.10.359.361.
Nor dare the secret of a God reveal: .... Od.11.304.397.
When earnest to explore thy secret breast, ... Od.11.547.410.
And sought the secret counsels of the God. .... Od.13.147.12.
These in the secret gloom the chief dispos'd; .... Od.13.423.26.
And secret walk, unknown to mortal eyes. .... Od.13.454.28.
And tempt the secret ambush of the night. .... Od.14.254.48.
To come in pomp, or bear a secret sail? .... Od.14.366.53.
But the dire secret of my fate reveal. .... Od.15.297.83.
My secret soul in all thy sorrow shares: .... Od.15.523.95.
Yet secret go; for numerous are my foes, ... Od.16.142.109.
The secret that thy father lives, retain .... Od.16.324.121.
Steals on his Sire a glance, and secret smiles. .... Od.16.497.131.
But droop'd her head, and drew a secret sigh. .... Od.17.171.139.
Secret revolves; and plans the vengeance due. .... Od.17.183.140.
Heav'n with a secret principle indu'd .... Od.17.252.143.
And the sooth'd heart with secret pleasure fills. .... Od.17.605.161.
A secret instinct moves her troubled breast .... Od.17.635.163.
Consulting secret with the blue-ey'd Maid, ... Od.19.1.192.
To distant rooms, dispos'd with secret care: .... Od.19.6.193.
In council secret with the Martial Maid; .... Od.19.63.195.
But ever for my Lord in secret grieve!— .... Od.19.159.200.
Of secret grief unseals the fruitful source; .... Od.19.190.201.
Ulysses' heart dilates with secret joy. .... Od.20.152.241.
Philætius too relents, but secret shed .... Od.21.85.263.
Shall I the secret of my breast conceal, ... Od.21.199.269.
He saw their secret souls, and thus began. .... Od.21.211.270.
Indecent joy, and feast thy secret soul. .... Od.22.449.309.
Long knew, but lock'd the secret in his breast; .... Od.23.32.320.
May I presume to search thy secret soul? .... Od.24.542.374.

SECRETARY
He marches off, his Grace's Secretary. .... 5.DunA2.212.127.
He marches off, his Grace's Secretary. .... 5.DunB2.220.306.

SECRETLY
And speedy lands, and secretly confers. .... Od.24.180.356.

SECRETS
And find divulg'd the Secrets they wou'd hide. .... 2.ChJM.36.16.
Full well the Secrets of my Soul she knew, ... 2.ChWB.267.69.
Who now partakes the Secrets of the Skies? .... Il.1.699.121.
Cam'st thou the Secrets of our Camp to find, ... Il.10.457.24.
Exploring then the secrets of the state, ... Od.4.351.136.
But I the secrets of high Heav'n reveal. .... Od.17.175.140.
The secrets of the bridal bed are known .... Od.23.241.335.

SECT
To *one small Sect,* and All are *damn'd beside.)* .... 1.EOC.397.285.
Slave to no sect, who takes no private road, ... 3.EOM4.331.160.
Sworn to no Master, of no Sect am I: .... 4.1HE1.24.281.
If I condemn one Sect or part .... 6.50.29A.147.
Except the Sect of *Pythagoreans,* .... 6.135.84.369.

SECUR'D
The Gaul subdu'd, or Property secur'd, ... 4.2HE1.10.195.
Secur'd by mountains of heap'd casuistry: .... 5.DunA3.348.193.
Secur'd the Temper of th' Ætherial Arms. .... Il.20.315.407.
But by our Walls secur'd, repel the Foe. .... Il.22.119.458.
Secur'd the valves. There, wrap'd in silent shade, ... Od.1.555.58.
A double strength of bars secur'd the gates: .... Od.2.390.80.
Secur'd each side: So bound we all the crew. .... Od.9.510.327.
Deep in my soul the truth shall lodge secur'd, ... Od.19.577.224.
Secur'd him from the keen nocturnal air. .... Od.20.178.241.
A double strength of valves secur'd the place, ... Od.22.144.294.
Secur'd the door, and hasty strode away: .... Od.22.218.297.

SECURE
Secure they trust th'unfaithful Field, beset, ... 1.W-F.103.160.
Secure from *Flames,* from *Envy's* fiercer Rage, ... 1.EOC.183.261.
O launch thy Bark, secure of prosp'rous Gales, ... 1.TrSP.252.404.
And Ships secure without their Haulsers ride. .... 1.TrUl.30.466.
Secure from Theft: Then launch'd the Bark again, ... 1.TrUl.51.467.
Besides *Minerva* to secure her Care, ... 1.TrUl.58.468.
Spent with Fatigue, and slept secure on Land; .... 1.TrUl.153.471.
Secure thou seest thy Native Shore at last? .... 1.TrUl.170.471.
Secure at once himself and Heav'n to please; .... 2.ChJM.38.16.
But ah! what Mortal lives of Bliss secure, ... 2.ChJM.475.38.
He turn'd the Key, and made the Gate secure. .... 2.ChJM.542.41.
But now secure the painted Vessel glides, ... 2.RL2.47.162.
Secure to be as blest as thou canst bear: .... 3.EOM1.286.50.
Secure of Peace at least beyond the Grave. .... 4.JD4.4.27.
Secure of Happiness beyond the Grave. .... 4.JD4.4A.27.
Who in the *Secret,* deals in Stocks secure, ... 4.JD4.140.37.
Whose *Satyr's sacred,* and whose Rage *secure.* .... 4.JD4.283.49.
Secure us kindly in our native night. .... 5.DunA1.154.82.
Secure, thro' her, the noble prize to carry, ... 5.DunA2.211.127.
Secure us kindly in our native night. .... 5.DunB1.176.283.
Secure, thro' her, the noble prize to carry, ... 5.DunB2.219.306.
Is satisfy'd, secure, and innocent: .... 6.16.4.53.
Behold, and count them all; secure to find .... 6.96iv.13.276.
Be bold, and count them all; secure to find .... 6.96iv.13A.276.
Secure in dullness, madness, want, and age. .... 6.116vii.8.328.
"Secure the radiant weapons wield; .... 6.140.5.378.
And Walls of Rocks, secure my native Reign, ... Il.1.204.96.
And seize secure; No more *Achilles* draws .... Il.1.394.106.
Mean time, secure within thy Ships from far .... Il.1.552.114.
But part in Peace, secure thy Pray'r is sped: .... Il.1.678.119.
And live the rest secure of future Harms. .... Il.3.140.197.
Secure of me, O King! exhort the rest: .... Il.4.303.235.
Haste to the Fight, secure of just Amends; .... Il.4.416.240.
Secure with these, thro' fighting Fields we go, ... Il.5.282.280.
Secure of fav'ring Gods, he takes the Field; .... Il.5.743.302.
Sit thou secure amidst thy social Band; .... Il.7.133.370.
Next, to secure our Camp, and Naval Pow'rs, ... Il.7.406.384.
Then, to secure the Camp and Naval Pow'rs, ... Il.7.520.389.
Secure behind the *Telamonian* Shield .... Il.8.321.412.
From Age inglorious and black Death secure; .... Il.8.668.427.
Secure of Death, confiding in Despair; .... Il.12.208.88.
Secure in Mail, and sheath'd in shining Steel. .... Il.13.258.117.
Far from the Hunter's Rage secure they lie, ... Il.15.310.209.
Ah save his Arms, secure his Obsequies! .... Il.15.497.216.
Secure of Death, confiding in Despair; .... Il.15.849.229.
Secure I lay, conceal'd from Man and God: .... Il.18.470.344.
Secure, what *Vulcan* can, is ever thine. .... Il.18.532.347.
Secure, no *Grecian* Force transcends thy own. .... Il.20.388.411.
But he secure lyes guarded in the Wall. .... Il.22.380.471.
So shalt thou pass the Goal, secure of Mind, ... Il.23.417.506.
Secure, this Hand shall his whole Frame confound, ... Il.23.777.520.
At *Reithrus,* and secure at anchor rides;. .... Od.1.238.44.
Thou, heedful of advice, secure proceed; .... Od.1.397.51.
To sorrow sacred, and secure of fame: .... Od.1.438.53.
In this attire secure from searching eyes, ... Od.4.339.136.
Pleas'd with the false review, secure he lies, ... Od.4.609.148.
Secure of storms, your royal brother past: .... Od.4.684.151.
I shar'd secure the *Æthiopian* feast. .... Od.5.370.190.
Propitious *Pallas,* to secure her care, ... Od.7.19.234.
Go then secure, thy humble suit prefer, ... Od.7.97.238.
Fear only fools, secure in men of sense: .... Od.8.272.278.
And added magick, to secure my love. .... Od.9.34.303.
And slept secure along the sandy shore. .... Od.9.173.312.
Secure to seize us ere we reach'd the door. .... Od.9.498.326.
Then bring thy friends, secure from future harms, ... Od.10.479.366.
And ships secure without their haulsers ride. .... Od.13.121.7.
Secure from theft: then launch'd the bark again, ... Od.13.142.11.
Besides *Minerva,* to secure her care, ... Od.13.225.16.
Spent with fatigue, and slept secure on land. .... Od.13.320.23.
Secure thou seest thy native shore at last? .... Od.13.337.23.
Secure he sits, near great *Atrides* plac'd; .... Od.13.490.29.
See to the port secure the vessel fly! .... Od.16.371.124.
Yet if injustice never be secure, ... Od.17.564.160.
In their apartments keep; secure the doors: .... Od.19.19.193.
In lodgments first secure his care he view'd, ... Od.20.206.243.
I thoughtless err'd in) well secure that door: .... Od.22.173.295.

SECURELY
He steer'd securely, and discover'd far, ... 1.EOC.647.312.
The Stream of Life shou'd more securely flow .... 6.17ii.18.56.
Securely cas'd the Warrior's Body o'er. .... Il.22.406.472.
First march the heavy Mules, securely slow, ... Il.23.140.494.
Stranger! whoe'er thou art, securely rest .... Od.1.161.40.
Had led, securely crost the dreadful main. .... Od.3.233.97.
But in an inner court, securely clos'd, ... Od.3.514.112.
Securely bid the strongest of the train .... Od.8.225.274.
Securely fetter'd by a silver thong. .... Od.10.26.340.
Thus he: the beeves around securely stray, ... Od.12.417.451.
Stranger (reply'd the Prince) securely rest .... Od.15.304.83.

SECURES
Then dubs Director, and secures his soul. ....3.Ep3.374.123.
No helm secures their course, no pilot guides, ...Od.8.605.295.
He said; from female ken she strait secures ....Od.19.33.194.
Secures the court, and with a cable tyes ....Od.21.422.280.

SECUREST
With Piety, the Soul's securest Guard, ...1.TrSt.757.442.

SECURITY
And place, on good Security, his Gold. ....4.2HE1.168.209.

SEDATE
Compos'd his Posture, and his Look sedate; ....2.TemF.201.271.
Sedate and quiet the comparing lies, ...3.EOM2.69.63.
In vain sedate reflections we would make, ...3.Ep1.33.18.
For *D[avena]nt* circumspect, sedate, ...6.94.5.259.
Compos'd in suff'rings, and in joy sedate, ...6.109.3.314.
But who like thee can boast a Soul sedate, ...Il.3.87.194.
Sedate and silent move the num'rous Bands; ....Il.4.486.243.
Retire then Warriors, but sedate and slow; ....Il.5.746.302.
The *Lycian* Leader, and sedate reply'd. ....Il.17.188.294.
Sedate of soul, his character sustain'd, ...Od.17.551.159.
Not so (*Ulysses* more sedate reply'd) ....Od.22.469.311.

SEDGY
The gulphy *Lee* his sedgy Tresses rears: ....1.W-F.346.184.
Swift on the sedgy Reeds the Ruin preys; ....Il.21.406.437.

SEDITION
Sedition silence, and assert the Throne. ....Il.2.339.143.

SEDLEY
Sprat, Carew, Sedley, and a hundred more, ...4.2HE1.109.205.

SEDUC'D
Seduc'd this soft, this easy Heart of mine!) ....Il.24.967.576.
By bribes seduc'd: and how the Sun, whose eye ....Od.8.311.281.

SEDUCEMENTS
The Nymph's seducements, and the magic bow'r. ....Od.5.11.171.

SEDUCING
Fly unperceiv'd, seducing half the flow'r ....Od.4.890.160.

SEE
But feigns a Laugh, to see me search around, ...1.PSp.55.66.
For see! the gath'ring Flocks to Shelter tend, ...1.PSp.101.70.
See what Delights in Sylvan Scenes appear! ....1.PSu.59.76.
But see, the Shepherds shun the Noon-day Heat, ...1.PSu.85.79.
Oh, skill'd in Nature! see the Hearts of Swains, ...1.PAu.11.81.
See gloomy Clouds obscure the chearful Day! ....1.PWi.30.91.
See, where on Earth the flow'ry Glories lye, ...1.PWi.33.91.
But see! where *Daphne* wondring mounts on high, ...1.PWi.69.93.
But see, *Orion* sheds unwholsome Dews, ...1.PWi.85.95.
See pale *Orion* sheds unwholsome Dews, ...1.PWi.85A.95.
See Nature hasts her earliest Wreaths to bring, ...1.Mes.23.114.
See lofty *Lebanon* his Head advance, ...1.Mes.25.115.
See nodding Forests on the Mountains dance, ...1.Mes.26.115.
See spicy Clouds from lowly *Saron* rise, ...1.Mes.27.115.
See Lillies spring, and sudden Verdure rise; ....1.Mes.68.119.
See, a long Race thy spatious Courts adorn; ....1.Mes.87.121.
See future Sons, and Daughters yet unborn ....1.Mes.88.121.
See barb'rous Nations at thy Gates attend, ...1.Mes.91.121.
See thy bright Altars throng'd with prostrate Kings, ...1.Mes.93.121.
See Heav'n its sparkling Portals wide display, ...1.Mes.97.121.
Where Order in Variety we see, ...1.W-F.15.149.
See *Pan* with Flocks, with Fruits *Pomona* crown'd, ...1.W-F.37.151.
But see the Man who spacious Regions gave ....1.W-F.79.157.
But see the Man whose spacious Regions gave ....1.W-F.79A.157.
See! from the Brake the whirring Pheasant springs, ...1.W-F.111.161.
See! the bold Youth strain up the threatning Steep, ...1.W-F.155.164.
I see, I see where two fair Cities bend ....1.W-F.379.187.
I see, I see where two fair Cities bend ....1.W-F.379.187.
See, from *each Clime* the Learn'd their Incense bring; ....1.EOC.185.262.
Short Views we take, nor see the *Lengths behind,* ....1.EOC.222.265.
Whoever thinks a faultless Piece to see, ...1.EOC.253.268.
And see now *clearer* and now *darker Days)* ....1.EOC.405.287.
Our Sons their Fathers' *failing Language* see, ...1.EOC.482.293.
See *Dionysius Homer's* Thoughts refine, ...1.EOC.665.314.
But see! each *Muse*, in *Leo's* Golden Days, ...1.EOC.697.319.
See how my fruits the loaded branches bend, ...1.TrPA.70.368.
And see my presents, nor the gifts despise. ....1.TrPA.95.369.
And see the Boughs with happy Burthens bend. ....1.TrVP.8.377.
See, while I write, my Words are lost in Tears; ....1.TrSP.109.398.
Ah! canst thou rather see this tender Breast ....1.TrSP.224.403.
Give them to dare, what I might wish to see, ...1.TrSt.118.415.
To punish these, see *Jove* himself descend! ....1.TrSt.316.423.
Yet these in Silence see the Fates fulfil ....1.TrSt.409.427.
But see! the Stars begin to steal away, ...1.TrSt.825.444.
Tho' they cou'd see as far as Ships can sail? ....2.ChJM.501.39.
Than be deluded when a Man can see! ....2.ChJM.503.39.
And well this Honourable Knight you see: ....2.ChJM.644.46.
That this much-injur'd Knight again shou'd see; ....2.ChJM.702.48.
Why was I taught to make my Husband see, ...2.ChJM.762.52.
Alas, my Love, 'tis certain, cou'd you see, ...2.ChJM.774.52.
Alas, my Lord, 'tis certain, cou'd you see, ...2.ChJM.774A.52.
If I but see a Cousin or a Friend, ...2.ChWB.80.60.
"But see! I'm all your own—nay hold—for Shame! ....2.ChWB.203.66.
To see, be seen, to tell, and gather Tales; ....2.ChWB.282.70.
But see! the *Nymph* in Sorrow's Pomp appears, ...2.RL*A*2.59.133.
And see thro' all things with his half-shut Eyes) ....2.RL3.118.176.
Already see you a degraded Toast, ...2.RL4.109.192.
Then see! the *Nymph* in beauteous Grief appears, ...2.RL4.143.196.
See the poor Remnants of these slighted Hairs! ....2.RL4.167.197.
See the poor Remnants of this slighted Hair! ....2.RL4.167A.197.

SEE (CONTINUED)
She smil'd to see the doughty Hero slain, ...2.RL5.69.206.
See fierce *Belinda* on the *Baron* flies, ...2.RL5.75.206.
But see how oft Ambitious Aims are cross'd, ...2.RL5.107.208.
There might you see the length'ning Spires ascend, ...2.TemF.89.259.
Hither, they cry'd, direct your Eyes, and see ....2.TemF.380.282.
While thus I stood, intent to see and hear, ...2.TemF.497.287.
Dim and remote the joys of saints I see, ...2.ElAb.71.325.
See how the force of others' pray'rs I try, ...2.ElAb.149.331.
Cut from the root my perish'd joys I see, ...2.ElAb.258Z1.340.
See in her Cell sad *Eloisa* spread, ...2.ElAb.303.344.
See my lips tremble, and my eye-balls roll, ...2.ElAb.323.345.
Ah then, thy once-lov'd *Eloisa* see! ....2.ElAb.329.346.
See from my cheek the transient roses fly! ....2.ElAb.331.346.
See the last sparkle languish in my eye! ....2.ElAb.332.346.
See on these ruby lips the trembling breath, ...2.Elegy.31.365.
Of Man what see we, but his station here, ...3.EOM1.19.14.
See worlds on worlds compose one universe, ...3.EOM1.24.16.
'Tis but a part we see, and not a whole. ....3.EOM1.60.20.
See, thro' this air, this ocean, and this earth, ...3.EOM1.233.44.
Beast, bird, fish, insect! what no eye can see, ...3.EOM1.239.44.
All Chance, Direction, which thou canst not see; ....3.EOM1.290.50.
Then see how little the remaining sum, ...3.EOM2.51.62.
See anger, zeal and fortitude supply; ....3.EOM2.187.77.
See the blind beggar dance, the cripple sing, ...3.EOM2.267.87.
See some strange comfort ev'ry state attend, ...3.EOM2.271.87.
See some fit Passion ev'ry age supply, ...3.EOM2.273.87.
See! and confess, one comfort still must rise, ...3.EOM2.293.90.
See plastic Nature working to this end, ...3.EOM3.9.93.
See Matter next, with various life endu'd, ...3.EOM3.13.93.
See dying vegetables life sustain, ...3.EOM3.15.93.
See life dissolving vegetate again: ....3.EOM3.16.93.
See, lifeless Matter moving to one End ....3.EOM3.9A.93.
While Man exclaims, "See all things for my use!" ....3.EOM3.45.96.
"See man for mine!" replies a pamper'd goose; ....3.EOM3.46.96.
See then the acting and comparing pow'rs ....3.EOM3.95.101.
See him from Nature rising slow to Art! ....3.EOM3.169.110.
"Here subterranean works and cities see; ....3.EOM3.181.111.
See FALKLAND dies, the virtuous and the just! ....3.EOM4.99.137.
See god-like TURENNE prostrate on the dust! ....3.EOM4.100.137.
See FALKLAND falls, the virtuous and the just! ....3.EOM4.99A.137.
See SIDNEY bleeds amid the martial strife! ....3.EOM4.101.138.
To see all others faults, and feel our own: ....3.EOM4.262.153.
Make fair deductions, see to what they mount. ....3.EOM4.270.153.
See Cromwell, damn'd to everlasting fame! ....3.EOM4.284.155.
See the false scale of Happiness complete! ....3.EOM4.288.155.
Then see them broke with toils, or sunk in ease, ...3.EOM4.297.156.
Then see them broke with toils, or lost in ease, ...3.EOM4.297A.156.
See! the sole bliss Heav'n could on all bestow; ....3.EOM4.327.160.
See, that no being any bliss can know, ...3.EOM4.335.161.
All see 'tis Vice, and itch of vulgar praise. ....3.Ep1.119.24.
See the same man, in vigour, in the gout; ....3.Ep1.130.25.
That pleas'd can see a younger charm, or hear ....3.Ep2.259A.71.
All eyes may see from what the change arose, ...3.Ep2.35.53.
All eyes may see—a Pimple on her nose. ....3.Ep2.36.53.
See Sin in State, majestically drunk, ...3.Ep2.69.55.
None see what Parts of Nature it conceals. ....3.Ep2.190.65.
See how the World its Veterans rewards! ....3.Ep2.243.69.
But 'twas thy righteous end, asham'd to see ....3.Ep3.149A.105.
Oh! that such bulky Bribes as all might see, ...3.Ep3.35.88.
"See Britain sunk in lucre's sordid charms, ...3.Ep3.145.105.
No, 'twas thy righteous end, asham'd to see ....3.Ep3.149.105.
And see, what comfort it affords our end. ....3.Ep3.298.117.
See! sportive fate, to punish aukward pride, ...3.Ep4.19.138.
Or see the stretching branches long to meet! ....3.Ep4.92.146.
Un-water'd see the drooping sea-horse mourn, ...3.Ep4.125.149.
Another age shall see the golden Ear ....3.Ep4.173.154.
And see the stretching branches long to meet! ....3.Ep4.92A.146.
Ridotta sips and dances, till she see ....4.HS1.47.9.
See *Libels, Satires—here* you have it—read. ....4.HS1.149.19.
See *Libels, Satires—there* you have it—read. ....4.Hs1.149A.19.
Our sons shall see it leisurely decay, ...4.JD4.44.29.
"And this, you see, is but my Dishabille—" ....4.JD4.115.35.
Can *gratis* see the *Country*, or the *Town?* ....4.JD4.145.37.
To see themselves fall endlong into Beasts, ...4.JD4.167.39.
I blest my Stars! but still afraid to see ....4.JD4.180A.41.
And bring ev'n me to see the Damn'd at Court. ....4.JD4.191A.43.
I quak'd at heart; and still afraid to see ....4.JD4.180.41.
And force ev'n me to see the Damn'd at Court. ....4.JD4.191.43.
See! where the *British* Youth, engag'd no more ....4.JD4.212.43.
To see those Anticks, *Fopling* and *Courtin:* ....4.JD4.237.45.
See them survey their Limbs by *Durer's* Rules, ...4.JD4.240.45.
For hung with *Deadly Sins* I see the Wall, ...4.JD4.274.49.
Cheap eggs, and herbs, and olives still we see, ...4.HS2.35.57.
What's *Property?* dear Swift! you see it alter ....4.HS2.167.69.
See wretched *Monsieur* flies to save his Throat, ...4.HAdv.53.79.
See good Sir *George* of ragged Livery stript, ...4.HAdv.55.81.
A Lady's Face is all you see undress'd; ....4.HAdv.124.85.
Sir, let me see your works and you no more. ....4.Arbu.68.100.
Still *Sapho—"Hold!* nay see you—you'll offend: ....4.Arbu.101A.103.
Go on, obliging Creatures, make me see ....4.Arbu.119.104.
Left me to see neglected Genius bloom, ...4.Arbu.257.114.
And see what friends, and read what books I please. ....4.Arbu.264.114.
To see what Friends, or read what Books I please; ....4.Arbu.262A.114.
Why am I ask'd, what next shall see the light? ....4.Arbu.271.115.
Why ask, when this or that shall see the light? ....4.Arbu.272A.115.
His Wit all see-saw between *that* and *this,* ....4.Arbu.323.119.
We see no new-built Palaces aspire, ...4.JD2.111.143.
How'ere some pleasure 'tis, this Fool to see ....4.JD2A.69.138.
"My only Son, I'd have him see the World: ....4.2HE2.6.165.
"Go on, my Friend (he cry'd) see yonder Walls! ....4.2HE2.46.167.
See! strow'd with learned dust, his Night-cap on, ...4.2HE2.118.173.
Lord! how we strut thro' *Merlin's* Cave, to see ....4.2HE2.139.175.
To see their Judgments hang upon thy Voice; ....4.1HE6.35.239.
See Ward by batter'd Beaus invited over, ...4.1HE6.56.241.
Rather than so, see Ward invited over, ...4.1HE6.56A.241.

SEE (CONTINUED)

'Tis (let me see) three years and more,	4.HS6.83.255.
Because they see me us'd so well:	4.HS6.102.257.
"See but the fortune of some Folks!	4.HS6.108.257.
Oh, could I see my Country Seat!	4.HS6.128.259.
"As sweet a Cave as one shall see!	4.HS6.175.261.
And you shall see, the first warm Weather,	4.1HE7.19.269.
And liv'd—just as you see I do;	4.1HE7.72.273.
See modest Cibber now has left the Stage:	4.1HE1.6.279.
To either India see the Merchant fly,	4.1HE1.69.283.
See him, with pains of body, pangs of soul,	4.1HE1.71.283.
"Because I see by all the Tracks about,	4.1HE1.116.287.
Yet hang your lip, to see a Seam awry!	4.1HE1.174.293.
And when it comes, the Court see nothing in't.	4.EpS1.2.297.
Why now, this moment, don't I see you steal?	4.EpS1.6.297.
Go see Sir ROBERT— P. See Sir Robert !— hum	4.EpS1.27.299.
Go see Sir ROBERT— P. See Sir Robert !— hum	4.EpS1.27.299.
See thronging Millions to the Pagod run,	4.EpS1.157.309.
See, all our Nobles begging to be Slaves!	4.EpS1.163.309.
See, all our Fools aspiring to be Knaves!	4.EpS1.164.309.
P. See! now I keep the Secret, and not yòu.	4.EpS2.23.314.
I sit and dream I see my CRAGS anew!	4.EpS2.69.316.
To see a Footman kick'd that took his pay:	4.EpS2.151.322.
Yes, I am proud; I must be proud to see	4.EpS2.208.324.
Let Flatt'ry sickening see the Incense rise,	4.EpS2.244.326.
And see what succour from the Patriot Race.	4.1740.4.332.
See Gods with Dæmons in strange league ingage,	5.DunA1.107.76.
But see great Settle to the dust descend,	5.DunA1.185.85.
In one quick flash see Proserpine expire,	5.DunA1.209.87.
I see a King! who leads my chosen sons	5.DunA1.251.93.
I see a chief, who leads my chosen sons,	5.DunA1.251Z1.93.
I see a Monarch proud my race to own!	5.DunA1.251Z3.93.
I see! I see!—" Then rapt, she spoke no more.	5.DunA1.255.94.
I see! I see!—" Then rapt, she spoke no more.	5.DunA1.255.94.
See in the circle next, Eliza plac'd;	5.DunA2.149.119.
True to the bottom, see Concanen creep,	5.DunA2.287.137.
True to the bottom, see *R[oome]* and *Wh[atle]y* creep,	5.DunA2.287B.137.
"Oh born to see what none can see awake!	5.DunA3.35.154.
"Oh born to see what none can see awake!	5.DunA3.35.154.
See round the Poles where keener spangles shine,	5.DunA3.61.155.
From shelves to shelves see greedy Vulcan roll,	5.DunA3.73.156.
"How little, see! that portion of the ball,	5.DunA3.75A.156.
See Alaric's stern port, the martial frame	5.DunA3.83.157.
See, the gold Ostrogoths on Latium fall;	5.DunA3.85.157.
See, the fierce Visigoths on Spain and Gaul.	5.DunA3.86.157.
See, where the Morning gilds the palmy shore,	5.DunA3.87.157.
See Christians, Jews, one heavy sabbath keep;	5.DunA3.91.157.
See, the Cirque falls! th' unpillar'd Temple nods!	5.DunA3.99.158.
See graceless Venus to a Virgin turn'd,	5.DunA3.103.159.
"And see! my son, the hour is on its way,	5.DunA3.115.160.
See all her progeny, illustrious sight!	5.DunA3.121.160.
"A second see, by meeker manners known,	5.DunA3.135.161.
See yet a younger, by his blushes known,	5.DunA3.135A.161.
"See next two slip-shod Muses traipse along,	5.DunA3.141A.162.
Wits, who like Owls see only in the dark,	5.DunA3.188.172.
"See now, what Dulness and her sons admire;	5.DunA3.226.176.
See! what the charms, that smite the simple heart	5.DunA3.227.176.
A godlike youth: See *Jove's* own bolt he flings	5.DunA3.251A.178.
I see th' unfinish'd Dormitory wall,	5.DunA3.323A.189.
I see the *Savoy* totter to her fall!	5.DunA3.324A.189.
Till Thames see Eton's sons for ever play,	5.DunA3.331.191.
See! the dull stars roll round and re-appear.	5.DunA3.336.192.
See sculking Truth in her old cavern lye,	5.DunA3.347.193.
See Physic beg the Stagyrite's defence!	5.DunA3.351.193.
See Metaphysic call for aid on Sence!	5.DunA3.352.193.
See Mystery to Mathematicks fly!	5.DunA3.353.193.
And see! thy very Gazetteers give o'er,	5.DunB1.215.285.
Now, see thy very Gazetteers give o'er,	5.DunB1.215A.285.
Lift up your gates, ye Princes, see him come!	5.DunB1.301.291.
See Cibber enters! haste, and turn the Key.	5.DunB1.300A.291.
See in the circle next, Eliza plac'd,	5.DunB2.157.303.
True to the bottom, see Concanen creep,	5.DunB2.299.310.
"Oh born to see what none can see awake!	5.DunB3.43.322.
"Oh born to see what none can see awake!	5.DunB3.43.322.
See, round the Poles where keener spangles shine,	5.DunB3.69.323.
From shelves to shelves see greedy Vulcan roll,	5.DunB3.81.324.
See Alaric's stern port! the martial frame	5.DunB3.91.324.
See the bold Ostrogoths on Latium fall,	5.DunB3.93.324.
See the fierce Visigoths on Spain and Gaul!	5.DunB3.94.324.
See, where the morning gilds the palmy shore	5.DunB3.95.324.
See Christians, Jews, one heavy sabbath keep,	5.DunB3.99.324.
See, the Cirque falls, th' unpillar'd Temple nods,	5.DunB3.107.325.
See graceless Venus to a Virgin turn'd,	5.DunB3.111.325.
"And see, my son! the hour is on its way,	5.DunB3.123.325.
See all her progeny, illustrious sight!	5.DunB3.129.325.
"A second see, by meeker manners known,	5.DunB3.143.326.
Wits, who like owls, see only in the dark,	5.DunB3.192.329.
"See now, what Dulness and her sons admire!	5.DunB3.228.331.
See what the charms, that smite the simple heart	5.DunB3.229.331.
New wizards rise; I see my Cibber there!	5.DunB3.266.333.
See! the dull stars roll round and re-appear.	5.DunB3.322.335.
See, see, our own true Phœbus wears the bays!	5.DunB3.323.335.
See, see, our own true Phœbus wears the bays!	5.DunB3.323.335.
On Poets' Tombs see Benson's titles writ!	5.DunB3.325.336.
See under Ripley rise a new White-hall,	5.DunB3.327.336.
'Till Thames see Eaton's sons for ever play,	5.DunB3.335.336.
See hairs and pores, examines bit by bit:	5.DunB4.234.366.
Are things which Kuster, Burman, Wasse shall see,	5.DunB4.237.366.
See! still thy own, the heavy Canon roll,	5.DunB4.247.367.
But wherefore waste I words? I see advance	5.DunB4.271.370.
See now, half-cur'd, and perfectly well-bred,	5.DunB4.323.375.
See, to my country happy I restore	5.DunB4.329.375.
See other Cæsars, other Homers rise;	5.DunB4.360.378.
Now see an Attys, now a Cecrops clear,	5.DunB4.363.378.
See Nature in some partial narrow shape,	5.DunB4.455.385.
Whose pious hope aspires to see the day	5.DunB4.461.385.

SEE (CONTINUED)

See all in *Self,* and but for self be born:	5.DunB4.480.389.
Oh hide the God still more! and make us see	5.DunB4.483.389.
Oh hide the God still more! or make us see	5.DunB4.483A.389.
See skulking *Truth* to her old Cavern fled,	5.DunB4.641.407.
See *Mystery* to *Mathematics* fly!	5.DunB4.647.408.
See how the sun in dusky skies	6.4iv.1.10.
See! She retires: Nor can we say	6.4iv.10.10.
And thus thro' mists we see the sun,	6.5.5.12.
With eyes erect the heav'ns to see;	6.6ii.10.14.
Then oh! she cries, what Slaves I round me see?	6.9vii.4.22.
And oh! she cries, what Slaves I round me see?	6.9x.4A.22.
But oh! she cries, what Slaves I round me see?	6.9x.4B.22.
(You see how well I can contrive a	6.10.19.25.
Nay, Mr. *Wycherly* see *Binfield.*	6.10.48.26.
I had to see you some Intent	6.10.67.26.
And see! the tortur'd Ghosts respire,	6.11.64.32.
See shady Forms advance!	6.11.65.32.
See, wild as the Winds, o'er the Desart he flies;	6.11.110.34.
—Ah see, he dies!	6.11.112.34.
I see protecting Myriads round thee fly,	6.21.23.69.
I see him ever, and will ever hear:	6.21.34.70.
To see a piece of failing flesh and blood,	6.41.47.114.
See Coronations rise on ev'ry green;	6.45.34.125.
To see the Good from Ill;	6.50.10.146.
Who all dost see & all dost know	6.50.9A.146.
Who all dost see who all dost know	6.50.9B.146.
To hide the Fault I see;	6.50.38.148.
When I the needy see	6.50.37Z2.148*.
Or hide the Fault I see;	6.50.38B.148.
See arts her savage sons controul,	6.51i.21.152.
Whate'er we think, whate'er we see,	6.53.3.161.
See first the merry P[elham] comes	6.58.43.172.
See, see, ye great New—le comes,	6.58.43A.172.
See, see, ye great New—le comes,	6.58.43A.172.
See there! you're always in my Way!	6.64.10.189.
See Anno quart. of Edward, third.	6.67.12.195.
Holland (for all that I can see)	6.67.17.195.
you'l see in the margin)	6.68.6.196.
See the wild Waste of all-devouring years!	6.71.1.202.
In living medals see her wars enroll'd,	6.71.55.204.
Then future ages with delight shall see	6.71.59.204.
See what ample Strides he takes,	6.78ii.5.216.
Though Dukes they be, yet Dukes shall see,	6.79.3A.217.
Was *Lancastere* to see,	6.79.122.222.
A Sight it was to see;	6.79.134.222.
Thro' Fortune's Cloud One truly Great can see,	6.84.39.240.
One truly Great thro' Fortune's Cloud can see,	6.84.31Z11.240.
About—let me see,—	6.91.25.254.
O'erjoy'd to see what God had sent.	6.93.24.257.
It is; see here's the FUR.	6.94.64.261.
See! and believe your Eyes!	6.96i.16.268.
See him stride	6.96i.17.268.
Shall I ne'er see thee turn my watches key	6.96ii.30Z43.272.
Or laugh to see thee walk with cautious tread,	6.96ii.30Z45.272.
"To see thee leap the Lines, and traverse o'er	6.96ii.62.273.
To see us strain before the Coach and Cart;	6.96iii.24.275.
See how they pat thée with their pretty Paws:	6.96iv.15.276.
'Tis not for that I grieve; no, 'tis to see	6.96iv.59.278.
When folks might see thee all the Country round	6.96iv.79.278.
When in the *Marrow-Bone* I see thee ramm'd;	6.96iv.83.278.
'Tis not for that I grieve; O, 'tis to see	6.96iv.59A.278.
In Miniature see *Nature's* Power appear;	6.96v.1.280.
See, in the Tube he pants, and sprawling lies,	6.96v.7.280.
See who ne'er was or will be half read!	6.101.1.290.
I see thy fountains fall, thy waters roll	6.106ii.3.307.
You please to see, on Twit'nam green,	6.114.7.321.
See Madam! see, the Arts o'erthrown,	6.119.19.337.
See Madam! see, the Arts o'erthrown,	6.119.19.337.
See Madam! all the Arts O'erthrown,	6.119.19B.337.
To see his own Maids serve a new Lord and Master.	6.122.18.342.
Hence see him modest free from pride or shew	6.130.9.358.
See *Bounce,* like *Berecynthia,* crown'd	6.135.45.368.
"In Dryden's Virgil see the print.	6.140.28.379.
You see that Island's Wealth, where only free,	6.142.6Z1A.382.
Or wise *Ulysses* see perform'd our Will,	Il.1.188.96.
My Prize of War, yet tamely see resumed;	Il.1.393.106.
Gods! how the scornful *Greeks* exult to see	Il.3.61.192.
See on the Plain thy *Grecian* Spouse appears,	Il.3.213.202.
(Far as from hence these aged Orbs can see)	Il.3.220.203.
See! bold *Idomeneus* superior tow'rs	Il.3.295.207.
See ready *Pallas* waits thy high Commands,	Il.4.91.224.
I see the God, already, from the Pole	Il.4.200.230.
I see th' Eternal all his Fury shed,	Il.4.202.231.
These see thou shun, thro' all th' embattled Plain,	Il.5.166.275.
If e'er I see my Spouse and Sire again,	Il.5.269.280.
O Friend! two Chiefs of Force immense I see,	Il.5.302.281.
O Son of *Tydeus,* cease! be wise and see	Il.5.533.294.
And unreveng'd see *Priam's* People die?	Il.5.566.295.
If I, unblest, must see my Son no more,	Il.5.844.305.
Yet while my *Hector* still survives, I see	Il.6.544.353.
And see thy Warriors fall, thy Glories end.	Il.6.573.355.
I see thee trembling, weeping, Captive led!	Il.6.579.355.
Some haughty *Greek* who lives thy Tears to see,	Il.6.586.355.
Shall neither hear thee sigh, nor see thee weep.	Il.6.593.355.
Gods! should he see our Warriors trembling stand,	Il.7.155.372.
See the long Walls extending to the Main,	Il.7.534.391.
Some other Sun may see the happier Hour,	Il.8.173.406.
And see his *Trojans* to the Shades descend.	Il.8.251.409.
With Arms unaiding see our *Argives* slain;	Il.8.581.424.
Shall see th' Almighty Thunderer in Arms.	Il.8.587.424.
Shall see his bloody Spoils in Triumph born,	Il.8.664.427.
See! what a Blaze from hostile Tents aspires,	Il.9.103.437.
To see no wholsom Motion be withstood,	Il.9.135.438.
See, full of *Jove,* avenging *Hector* rise!	Il.9.311.449.
See! Heav'n and Earth the raging Chief defies;	Il.9.312.449.

SEE (CONTINUED)

See what Preheminence our Merits gain! ... Il.9.441.454.
Then shall you see our parting Vessels crown'd, ... Il.9.471.455.
See what Effect our low Submissions gain! ... Il.9.738.471.
The *Trojans* see the Youths untimely die, ... Il.11.151.42.
Before great *Ajax,* see the mingled Throng ... Il.11.646.62.
With Grief I see the great *Machaon* bleeds. ... Il.11.797.71.
And see the *Grecians* gasping at their Feet. ... Il.12.122.85.
I trusted in the Gods and you, to see ... Il.13.133.111.
My Heart weeps blood to see your Glory lost! ... Il.13.160.112.
Ah! never may he see his native Land, ... Il.13.303.119.
Enter, and see on heaps the Helmets roll'd, ... Il.13.345.122.
See! on one *Greek* three *Trojan* Ghosts attend, ... Il.13.560.133.
See, as thou mov'st, on Dangers Dangers spread, ... Il.13.923.148.
Shall then proud *Hector* see his Boast fulfill'd, ... Il.14.51.160.
And have I liv'd to see with mournful Eyes ... Il.14.57.160.
Thy Ships first flying with Despair shall see, ... Il.14.112.163.
To see the gath'ring Grudge in ev'ry Breast, ... Il.15.110.200.
See, and be strong! the Thund'rer sends thee Aid. ... Il.15.289.208.
Soon as they see the furious Chief appear, ... Il.15.316.209.
How easy then, to see the sinking State ... Il.15.578.218.
See the thin Reliques of their baffled Band, ... Il.16.91.239.
Press'd by his single Force, let *Hector* see, ... Il.16.300.254.
At once they see, they tremble, and they fly. ... Il.16.337.255.
His Troops, that see their Country's Glory slain, ... Il.16.346.256.
See! where in Dust the great *Sarpedon* lies, ... Il.16.663.270.
This Instant see his short-liv'd Trophies won, ... Il.16.789.274.
Nor unattended, see the Shades below. ... Il.16.796.274.
Ev'n now on Life's last Verge I see thee stand, ... Il.16.1030.283.
I see thee fall, and by *Achilles'* Hand. ... Il.16.1031.283.
And see his Jaws distil with smoaking Gore; ... Il.17.72.290.
See what a Tempest direful *Hector* spreads, ... Il.17.288.299.
All, whom I see not thro' this Cloud of War, ... Il.17.299.299.
The Sun shall see her conquer, till his Fall ... Il.17.522.308.
Give me to see, and *Ajax* asks no more: ... Il.17.730.315.
Ah then, I see thee dying, see thee dead! ... Il.18.124.328.
Ah then, I see thee dying, see thee dead! ... Il.18.124.328.
Aghast they see the living Light'nings play, ... Il.18.267.335.
An aged Father never see me more! ... Il.18.388.340.
Studious to see that Terror of the Plain, ... Il.19.49.373.
I know my Fates: To die, to see no more ... Il.19.468.391.
Ourself will sit, and see the Hand of Fate ... Il.20.34.394.
And trembling see another God of War. ... Il.20.62.396.
And can ye see this righteous Chief attone ... Il.20.345.408.
Sure I shall see yon' Heaps of *Trojans* kill'd ... Il.21.64.424.
Thy well-known Captive, great *Achilles!* see, ... Il.21.84.425.
See! my choak'd Streams no more their Course can keep, ... Il.21.235.430.
Or stain this Lance, or see *Achilles* fall. ... Il.21.246.431.
And gladsome see their last Escape from Fate: ... Il.21.632.448.
These I have yet to see, perhaps yet more! ... Il.22.91.456.
Or if I perish, let her see me fall ... Il.22.152.459.
Now see him flying! to his Fears resign'd, ... Il.22.227.465.
See, where in vain he supplicates above, ... Il.22.285.468.
Their *Hector* on the Pile they should not see, ... Il.22.443.474.
See, if already their deserted Tow'rs ... Il.22.478.475.
Rejoic'd, of all the num'rous *Greeks,* to see ... Il.23.747.520.
Ye see, to *Ajax* I must yield the Prize; ... Il.23.927.526.
I see your Blood the Fields of *Phrygia* drown, ... Il.24.305.549.
I see the Ruins of your smoking Town! ... Il.24.306.549.
His trembling Limbs, his helpless Person, see! ... Il.24.602.562.
See him in me, as helpless and as old! ... Il.24.627.563.
See him, in *Troy,* the pious Care decline ... Il.24.681.565.
A weak old Man to see the Light and live! ... Il.24.704.566.
The tenth shall see the Fun'ral and the Feast; ... Il.24.835.571.
Thy Presence here shou'd stern *Atrides* see, ... Il.24.854.572.
To see the smoke from his lov'd palace rise, ... Od.1.75.34.
I see (I cry'd) his woes, a countless train; ... Od.2.203.71.
I see his friends o'erwhelm'd beneath the main; ... Od.2.204.71.
To see the pref'rence due to sacred age ... Od.3.66.89.
Far as thy mind thro' backward time can see, ... Od.3.122.91.
See there confess'd, *Pisistratus* replies, ... Od.4.209.129.
Jealous, to see their high behests obey'd, ... Od.4.477.142.
His friends, his country he shall see, tho' late; ... Od.5.54.174.
Tho' well I see thy graces far above ... Od.5.277.184.
See! from their thrones thy kindred monarchs sigh! ... Od.6.40.206.
Joyful they see applauding Princes gaze, ... Od.6.187.218.
To see my soil, my son, my friends, again. ... Od.7.304.250.
See the lewd dalliance of the Queen of Love! ... Od.8.348.282.
Why was I born? see how the wanton lies! ... Od.8.353.282.
We see the death from which we cannot move, ... Od.9.350.321.
Now *Æolus,* ye see, augments his store: ... Od.10.48.341.
Or see the wretched for whose loss we mourn. ... Od.10.318.359.
I see! I see, thy bark by *Neptune* tost, ... Od.11.130.387.
I see! I see, thy bark by *Neptune* tost, ... Od.11.130.387.
I see thy friends o'erwhelm'd in liquid graves! ... Od.11.143.387.
Thy eyes shall see him burn with noble fire, ... Od.11.557.411.
The trembling crowds shall see the sudden shade ... Od.13.182.14.
But enter this my homely roof, and see ... Od.14.53.38.
My heart weeps blood, to see a soul so brave ... Od.16.95.107.
Than see the hand of violence invade ... Od.16.113.108.
Than see the wealth of Kings consum'd in waste, ... Od.16.115.108.
Other *Ulysses* shalt thou never see, ... Od.16.224.114.
See to the port secure the vessel fly! ... Od.16.371.124.
I see the smokes of sacrifice aspire, ... Od.17.322.147.
Our walls this twelvemonth should not see the slave. ... Od.17.491.156.
See how with nods assent yon princely train! ... Od.18.16.167.
See ready for the fight, and hand to hand, ... Od.18.46.169.
Might see the sable field at once arise! ... Od.18.417.189.
With'ring at heart to see the weeping Fair, ... Od.19.246.206.
Whilst hope prevail'd to see your Sire restor'd, ... Od.20.393.251.
To see the circle sat, of all unseen. ... Od.20.464.256.
First may'st thou see the springing dawn of light; ... Od.22.214.297.
Amaz'd they see, they tremble, and they fly: ... Od.22.333.302.
Ulysses lives his vanquish'd foes to see; ... Od.23.57.321.
And now, ev'n now it melts! for sure I see ... Od.23.177.329.
They see their Lord, they gaze, and they admire. ... Od.24.451.370.

SEE-SAW

His Wit all see-saw between *that* and *this,* ... 4.Arbu.323.119.

SEE'ST

"See'st thou an Isle, by Palmers, Pilgrims trod, ... 5.DunA3.105A.159.
Thou see'st that Island's Wealth, where only free, ... 6.142.6Z1.382.
See'st thou the *Greeks* by Fates unjust opprest, ... Il.8.244.409.
See'st thou not me, whom Nature's Gifts adorn, ... Il.21.119.426.
Think from some pow'rful Foe thou see'st him fly, ... Il.24.606.562.

SEED

To raise up Seed to bless the Pow'rs above, ... 2.ChJM.121.20.
To raise up Seed t'adore the Pow'rs above, ... 2.ChJM.121A.20.
Is thine alone the seed that strews the plain? ... 3.EOM3.37.96.
Plant of celestial seed! if dropt below, ... 3.EOM4.7.128.
Bids seed-time, harvest, equal course maintain, ... 3.Ep3.167.107.
Then rose the Seed of Chaos, and of Night, ... 5.DunB4.13.340.
Thy Christian Seed, our mutual Flesh and Bone: ... 6.96iv.17.276.
To match the Seed of Cloud-compelling *Jove.* ... Il.2.724.160.
Due Honours to the Seed of *Jove* belong; ... Il.9.639.466.
For proffer'd Peace! And sues his Seed for Grace? ... Il.11.183.43.
And try the Prowess of the Seed of *Jove.* ... Il.13.563.133.
Sarpedon's Friends, *Amisodarus'* Seed; ... Il.16.389.258.
To *Atreus'* Seed, the god-like *Telamon.* ... Il.17.708.315.
The Seed of *Thetis* thus to *Venus'* Son. ... Il.20.213.402.
The King obey'd. The Virgin-seed of *Jove* ... Od.24.629.377.

SEED-TIME

Bids seed-time, harvest, equal course maintain, ... 3.Ep3.167.107.

SEEDS

And Seeds of Gold in *Ophyr's* Mountains glow. ... 1.Mes.96.121.
Most have the *Seeds* of Judgment in their Mind; ... 1.EOC.20.241.
'Tis thine the Seeds of future War to know, ... 1.TrSt.841.444.
Thou dost the Seeds of future War foreknow, ... 1.TrSt.841A.444.
The vital flame, and swells the genial seeds. ... 3.EOM3.118.104.
And shook from out his Pipe the seeds of fire; ... 5.DunB4.494.391.
Pregnant with Plagues, and shedding Seeds of Death, ... Il.5.1059.317.
In embers heap'd, preserves the seeds of fire: ... Od.5.633.202.
With animating breath the seeds of fire; ... Od.9.446.324.
The genuine seeds of Poesy are sown; ... Od.22.384.307.

SEEING

But He the Pow'r, to whose All-seeing Eyes ... 1.TrUl.88.469.
The optics seeing, as the objects seen. ... 3.Ep1.24.17.
All-seeing in thy mists, we want no guide, ... 5.DunB4.469.386.
All-seeing Monarch! whether *Lycia's* Coast ... Il.16.633.269.
At one Regard of his all-seeing Eye, ... Il.17.674.314.
At length are odious to th' all-seeing Mind; ... Il.20.354.408.
Attests th' all-seeing Sovereign of the skies. ... Od.2.425.81.
The King of Ocean saw, and seeing burn'd, ... Od.5.363.190.
That lies beneath the sun's all-seeing ray; ... Od.8.608.295.
But he, the Pow'r to whose all-seeing eyes ... Od.13.255.18.
Consult we first th' all-seeing pow'rs above, ... Od.16.418.126.

SEEK

Feed here my Lambs, I'll seek no distant Field. ... 1.PSp.64.67.
When Swains from Sheering seek their nightly Bow'rs; ... 1.PSu.64.76.
Nor thirsty Heifers seek the gliding Flood. ... 1.PWi.38A.91.
Seek the clear Spring, or haunt the pathless Grove; ... 1.W-F.168.165.
And the new World launch forth to seek the Old. ... 1.W-F.402.191.
But *you* who seek to *give* and *merit* Fame, ... 1.EOC.46.244.
Survey the *Whole,* nor seek slight Faults to find, ... 1.EOC.235.266.
Meanly they seek the Blessing to confine, ... 1.EOC.398.286.
All may allow; but seek your *Friendship* too. ... 1.EOC.565.305.
"Fly hence; and seek the fair *Leucadian* Main; ... 1.TrSP.188.402.
"Fly hence; and seek the far *Leucadian* Main; ... 1.TrSP.188A.402.
Ah let me seek it from the raging Seas: ... 1.TrSP.257.404.
Ah! let me seek it from the raging Seas: ... 1.TrSP.257B.404.
You seek to share in Sorrows not your own; ... 1.TrSt.803.443.
Strait seek their Home, and fly with eager Pace, ... 1.TrUl.214.472.
Seek, and perhaps you'll find, among the Fair, ... 2.ChJM.285.28.
Who seek in love for ought but love alone. ... 2.ElAb.84.326.
Seek an admirer, or would fix a friend. ... 3.EOM4.44.132.
Are giv'n in vain, but what they seek they find) ... 3.EOM4.348.162.
They seek the second not to lose the first. ... 3.Ep2.214.67.
To seek applause by printing what I write: ... 4.2HE2.150A.175.
Here, Wisdom calls: "Seek Virtue first! be bold! ... 4.1HE1.77.285.
Old puns restore, lost blunders nicely seek, ... 5.DunA1.163.82.
For Attic Phrase in Plato let them seek, ... 5.DunB4.227.365.
Encourag'd lovers seek her breast: ... 6.4v.6.11.
Honour *and Wealth, the Joys we seek,*deny ... 6.17iii.1.57.
When I no Favour seek? ... 6.47.34.129.
Of those that seek thy Face; ... 6.50.30A.147.
Or seek some ruin's formidable shade; ... 6.52.30.157.
To *Budgel* seek, or *Carey.* ... 6.58.40.172.
To this the Thund'rer: Seek not thou to find ... Il.1.704.121.
Now seek some skilful Hand whose pow'rful Art ... Il.4.228.232.
Nor seek unpractis'd to direct the Car, ... Il.4.354.238.
To seek her Parents on his flow'ry Side, ... Il.4.547.247.
Unbar the sacred Gates; and seek the Pow'r ... Il.6.111.329.
And rev'rend Elders, seek the Gods in vain. ... Il.6.142.331.
And seek the Gods, t'avert th' impending Woe. ... Il.6.303.341.
To seek his Spouse, his Soul's far dearer Part; ... Il.6.463.349.
'Twas vain to seek Retreat, and vain to fear; ... Il.7.263.377.
Now seek some means his fatal wrath to end, ... Il.9.145.439.
To seek sage *Nestor* now the Chief resolves, ... Il.10.24.3.
Tho' Years and Honours bid thee seek Repose. ... Il.10.187.10.
Tydides spoke—The Man you seek, is here. ... Il.10.260.13.
Perhaps, ev'n now pursu'd, they seek the Shore; ... Il.10.634.30.
Shall seek their Walls, and *Greece* respire again. ... Il.11.933.77.
Seek not, this Day, the *Grecian* Ships to gain; ... Il.12.254.90.
Seek not your Fleet, but sally from the Wall; ... Il.12.326.93.
From Milk, innoxious, seek their simple Food: ... Il.13.12.104.
To seek a surer Javelin in his Tent. ... Il.13.224.116.
Or seek auxiliar Force; at length decreed ... Il.13.574.133.

SEEK (CONTINUED)

Seek not alone t'engross the Gifts of Heav'n. ..... Il.13.914.148.
The Chiefs you seek on yonder Shore lie slain; ..... Il.13.981.152.
Such Counsel if you seek, behold the Man ..... Il.14.121.163.
Nor seek, unknown to thee, the sacred Cells ..... Il.14.353.179.
Some seek the Trench, some skulk behind the Wall, ... Il.15.391.212.
Wounded, they wound; and seek each others Hearts ..... Il.15.862.230.
Grim as voracious Wolves that seek the Springs ..... Il.16.194.246.
We seek our Ramparts, and desert the Day. ..... Il.17.391.302.
Till his spent Coursers seek the Fleet again: ..... Il.18.330.337.
If Sheep or Oxen seek the winding Stream. ..... Il.18.606.352.
If yet thou farther seek to learn my Birth ..... Il.20.252.404.
Confus'dly heap'd, they seek their inmost Caves, ... Il.21.32.422.
The *Grecians* seek their Ships, and clear the Strand, ... Il.23.5.486.
E'er yet from Rest or Food we seek Relief, ... Il.23.13.486.
Seek their black Ships, and clear the crowded Strand; ..... Il.24.2.534.
Seek not to stay me, nor my Soul affright ..... Il.24.267.547.
Nor seek by Tears my steady Soul to bend; ..... Il.24.707.567.
Why seek they not the rich *Icarian* dome? ..... Od.2.58.63.
And seek my royal sire from shore to shore: ..... Od.2.244.73.
And seek my sire thro' storms and rolling seas! ..... Od.2.300.76.
Teach me to seek redress for all my woe, ... Od.2.355.78.
To seek *Ulysses* thro' the wat'ry way. ..... Od.2.405.80.
Where savage Pyrates seek thro' seas unknown ..... Od.3.88.90.
My sire I seek, where-e'er the voice of fame ..... Od.3.100.91.
And seek *Atrides* on the *Spartan* shore. ..... Od.3.406.106.
One seek the harbour where the vessels moor, ... Od.3.536.113.
Their doubtful course to seek a distant friend? ..... Od.4.36.121.
Then seek the place the sea-born nymph assign'd, ... Od.4.589.147.
Seek for his father's fate, but find his own. ..... Od.4.899.160.
So wat'ry fowl, that seek their fishy food, ... Od.5.64.174.
To seek *Ulysses,* pac'd along the sand. ..... Od.5.192.180.
They seek the cisterns where *Phæacian* dames ..... Od.6.99.210.
Seek thou the Queen along the rooms of state; ..... Od.6.366.229.
I seek th' adventure, and forsake the rest. ..... Od.9.228.316.
Pyrates perhaps, who seek thro' seas unknown ..... Od.9.301.318.
Say shall we seek access? With that they call; ..... Od.10.262.355.
Each friend you seek in yon enclosure lies, ... Od.10.337.360.
Seek ye to meet those evils ye shou'd shun? ..... Od.10.510.368.
To guard the ship. Seek we the sacred shades ..... Od.10.525.368.
There seek the *Theban* Bard, depriv'd of sight, ... Od.10.582.371.
To seek *Tiresias'* awful shade below, ... Od.10.677.376.
To seek *Tiresias* in the nether sky, ... Od.11.201.391.
To seek the *Theban,* and consult the Fates: ..... Od.11.588.412.
Strait seek their home, and fly with eager pace ..... Od.13.381.25.
To seek his father's fate, and find his own! ..... Od.14.209.45.
But seek thou first the Master of the swine, ... Od.15.45.72.
Himself will seek thee here, nor wilt thou find ..... Od.15.238.79.
To seek thee, friend, I hither took my way. ..... Od.16.32.103.
Mankind, to seek their own similitude. ..... Od.17.253.143.
And injur'd suppliants seek in vain for aid. ..... Od.17.649.164.
Of night draws on, go seek the rural bow'r: ..... Od.17.677.165.
Seek thou repose; whilst here I sole remain, ... Od.19.54.195.
To seek my Lord among the warrior-train, ... Od.20.96.237.
A plenteous board: Hence! seek another host! ..... Od.20.230.244.
Who in partition seek his realm to share; ..... Od.20.273.246.
If I the prize, if me you seek to wife, ... Od.21.73.262.
To seek *Tiresias* in the vales of death; ..... Od.23.348.341.
A friend I seek, a wise one and a brave, ... Od.24.312.364.

SEEK'ST

"Son! what thou seek'st is in thee. Look, and find ..... 5.DunA3.247.178.
"Son; what thou seek'st is in thee! Look, and find ..... 5.DunB3.251.332.
Seek'st thou some Friend, or nightly Centinel? ..... Il.10.92.6.

SEEKS

A Shepherd's Boy (he seeks no better Name) ..... 1.PSu.1.71.
Seeks freshest Pasture and the purest Air, ... 1.Mes.50.117.
And when in youth he seeks the shady woods, ... 1.TrFD.84.389.
He seeks a Shelter from th'inclement Heav'n, ... 1.TrSt.560.433.
Each individual seeks a sev'ral goal; ..... 3.EOM2.237.84.
Which seeks no int'rest, no reward but praise; ..... 3.EOM2.246.85.
The link dissolves, each seeks a fresh embrace, ... 3.EOM3.129.105.
Not always humble he who seeks retreat, ... 3.Ep1.65A.20.
Not therefore humble he who seeks retreat, ... 3.Ep1.65.20.
Seeks from the Stage his vile Support to gain: ..... 4.JD2A.14.132.
And seeks a surer State, and courts thy gentle Reign. ..... 6.8.15.18.
And 'tis in thee at last that *Wisdom* seeks for Rest. ..... 6.8.24.18.
Nor seeks in vain for succour to the Stream. ..... 6.14iv.26.47.
Which nothing seeks to show, or needs to hide, ... 6.73.2.209.
Paris he seeks, impatient to destroy, ... Il.3.563.219.
But seeks in vain along the Troops of *Troy;* ..... Il.3.564.219.
As when the lordly Lyon seeks his Food ..... Il.5.206.276.
The soul indignant seeks the Realms of Night. ..... Il.5.360.283.
The Soul disdainful seeks the Caves of Night, ... Il.5.818.305.
Pamper'd and proud, he seeks the wonted Tides, ... Il.6.654.359.
This seeks the *Grecian,* that the *Phrygian* Train. ..... Il.7.371.382.
Ulysses seeks the Ships, and shelters there. ..... Il.8.124.404.
Seeks he the Sorrows of our Host to know? ..... Il.11.802.72.
Who seeks ignobly in his Ships to stay, ... Il.13.305.119.
And seeks the Cave of Death's half-Brother, *Sleep.* ..... Il.14.265.173.
Seeks his own Seas, and trembles at our Rage! ..... Il.15.251.206.
Fir'd, they rush on; First *Hector* seeks the Foes, ... Il.16.677.270.
'Tis *Hector* comes; and when he seeks the Prize, ... Il.17.572.311.
Seeks he to meet *Achilles'* Arm in War, ... Il.20.215.403.
She seeks the bridal bow'r: A matron there ..... Od.7.7.233.
Amid these joys, why seeks thy mind to know ..... Od.9.11.301.
He seeks his lodging in the rocky den. ..... Od.14.599.66.
There seeks *Telemachus,* and thus apart ..... Od.17.670.164.
The house they enter, and he seeks the field; ..... Od.24.254.361.

SEEM

Here Earth and Water seem to strive again, ... 1.W-F.12.149.
I seem thro' consecrated Walks to rove, ... 1.W-F.267.173.
Those *Freer Beauties,* ev'n in *Them,* seem Faults: ..... 1.EOC.170.260.
Conceal his Force, nay seem sometimes to *Fly.* ..... 1.EOC.178.261.

SEEM (CONTINUED)

Those oft are *Stratagems* which *Errors* seem, ... 1.EOC.179.261.
Oft *hide* his Force, nay seem sometimes to *Fly.* ..... 1.EOC.178A.261.
Those are but *Stratagems* which *Errors* seem, ... 1.EOC.179A.261.
Mount o'er the Vales, and seem to tread the Sky; ..... 1.EOC.226.265.
And the first *Clouds* and *Mountains* seem the last: ..... 1.EOC.228.265.
The *Sound* must seem an *Eccho* to the *Sense.* ..... 1.EOC.365.281.
As things seem *large* which we thro' *Mists* descry, ... 1.EOC.392.285.
Lest God himself shou'd seem too *Absolute.* ..... 1.EOC.549.302.
The Balls seem wounded with the piercing Ray, ... 2.ChJM.800A.53.
Heav'n knows, how seldom things are what they seem! ..... 2.ChJM.806.54.
'Twill then be Infamy to seem your Friend! ..... 2.RL4.112.192.
And Legislators seem to think in Stone. ..... 2.TemF.74.258.
The fiery Steeds seem starting from the Stone; ..... 2.TemF.219.272.
Thy voice I seem in ev'ry hymn to hear, ... 2.ElAb.269.341.
Is but to please can Pleasure seem a fault? ..... 3.Ep2.212A.67.
That each may seem a Virtue, or a Vice. ..... 3.Ep2.206.67.
Is still to please, can Pleasure seem a fault? ..... 3.Ep2.212.67.
Why, if the Nights seem tedious—take a Wife; ..... 4.HS1.16.5.
To seem but mortal, ev'n in sound Divines. ..... 4.HS2.80.59.
Still to one Bishop *Philips* seem a Wit? ..... 4.Arbu.100.102.
He, who to seem more deep than you or I, ... 4.2HE1.131.207.
He did his best to seem to eat, ... 4.HS6.173.261.
And drooping lillies seem to tell ..... 6.4iv.8.10.
His easie Art may happy Nature seem, ... 6.19.3.62.
Where still in breathing brass they seem to live, ... 6.22.17.72.
Then, when you seem above mankind to soar, ... 6.27.16.81.
And seem a thicker Dew, or thinner Rain; ..... 6.42vi.4.120.
Lean and fretful; would seem wise; ..... 6.70.8.201.
Seem like the lofty Barn of some rich Swain, ... 6.96ii.13.270.
Thus Honey-combs seem Palaces to Bees; ..... 6.96v.29.281.
Made *David* seem so mad and freakish, ... 6.101.17.290.
Thro' thy blest Shades (La Source) I seem to rove ..... 6.106ii.2.307.
Be what ye seem, unanimated Clay! ..... Il.7.115.369.
In sculptur'd Gold two Turtles seem to drink: ..... Il.11.777.69.
And seem to walk on Wings, and tread in Air. ..... Il.13.106.109.
Strong as they seem, embattel'd like a Tow'r. ..... Il.13.208.115.
Two Spies at distance lurk, and watchful seem ..... Il.18.605.352.
Rear high their Horns, and seem to lowe in Gold, ... Il.18.666.356.
As Men in Slumbers seem with speedy pace, ... Il.22.257.466.
Now seem to touch the Sky, and now the Ground. ..... Il.23.446.508.
And seem just mounting on his Car behind; ..... Il.23.458.508.
And seem already to retrieve the Day. ..... Il.23.529.511.
There sullen Lions sternly seem to roar, ... Od.11.753.423.
And the waves flashing seem to burn with fires. ..... Od.12.82.435.
Seem as extinct, and all their splendors lost; ..... Od.12.372.449.
Still let her seem to sail, and seem alone; ..... Od.13.181.14.
Still let her seem to sail, and seem alone; ..... Od.13.181.14.
Bestow, my friend! thou dost not seem the worst ..... Od.17.497.156.
And seem to meet, yet fly, the bridal day, ... Od.18.190.175.
Proud, to seem brave among a coward train! ..... Od.18.424.189.
These gates would seem too narrow for they flight. ..... Od.18.427.189.
But, stranger! as thy days seem full of fate, ... Od.19.184.200.

SEEM'D

Perhaps he seem'd *above* the Critick's Law, ... 1.EOC.132.254.
Faith, Gospel, All, seem'd made to be *disputed,* ..... 1.EOC.442.289.
And, but he seem'd a larger bulk to bear, ... 1.TrPA.161.373.
Who seem'd descended from some Princely Line: ..... 1.TrUl.103.469.
For, by th'Immortal Pow'rs, it *seem'd* too plain— ..... 2.ChJM.779.52.
Of twenty Winters' Age he seem'd to be; ..... 2.ChWB.317.72.
Seem'd to her Ear his winning Lips to lay, ... 2.RL1.25.147.
And thus in Whispers said, or seem'd to say. ..... 2.RL1.26.147.
That seem'd but *Zephyrs* to the Train beneath. ..... 2.RL2.58.163.
'Twas this, the Morning *Omens* seem'd to tell; ..... 2.RL4.161.197.
And seem'd to distant Sight of solid Stone. ..... 2.TemF.30.255.
In Years he seem'd, but not impair'd by Years. ..... 2.TemF.187.270.
A strong Expression most he seem'd t'affect, ... 2.TemF.194.271.
And seem'd to labour with th' inspiring God. ..... 2.TemF.213.272.
Gath'ring his flowing Robe, he seem'd to stand, ... 2.TemF.240.274.
Scarce seem'd her Stature of a Cubit's height, ... 2.TemF.259.275.
What Virtue seem'd, was done for thee alone. ..... 2.TemF.349.280.
And all that Virtue seem'd, was done for thee alone. ..... 2.TemF.349A.280.
With Sparks, that seem'd to set the World on fire. ..... 2.TemF.415.283.
Come, sister come! (it said, or seem'd to say) ..... 2.ElAb.309.344.
Then sacred seem'd th'etherial vault no more; ..... 3.EOM3.263.119.
Ben, old and poor, as little seem'd to heed ..... 4.2HE1.73.199.
And seem'd to emulate great Jacob's pace. ..... 5.DunA2.64.105.
Where the tall Nothing stood, or seem'd to stand; ..... 5.DunA2.102.109.
And to mere mortals seem'd a Priest in drink? ..... 5.DunA2.394.149.
Where the tall Nothing stood, or seem'd to stand; ..... 5.DunB2.110.300.
And to mere mortals seem'd a Priest in drink: ..... 5.DunB2.426.318.
The Goddess smiling seem'd to give consent; ..... 5.DunB4.395.381.
Who all cœlestial seem'd before, ... 6.4iii.8.10.
That seem'd to fill the Name unworthy ..... 6.30.5B.85.
Which seem'd like two broad Suns in misty Skies: ..... 6.96ii.74.273.
Form'd the bright Fringe, and seem'd to burn in Gold. ..... Il.2.529.151.
As one unskill'd or dumb, he seem'd to stand, ... Il.3.281.207.
She seem'd an ancient Maid, well-skill'd to cull ..... Il.3.477.214.
Have ye forgot what seem'd your Dread before? ..... Il.4.591.249.
Distracted with Surprize, she seem'd to fly. ..... Il.6.484.350.
Nor seem'd the Vengeance worthy such a Son; ..... Il.15.30.195.
Her yet-surviving Heroes seem'd to fall. ..... Il.16.992.281.
He seem'd like aged *Periphas* to Sight. ..... Il.17.375.302.
Seem'd as extinct: Day ravish'd from their Eyes, ... Il.17.424.303.
The waving Silver seem'd to blush with Blood. ..... Il.18.618.352.
And each bold Figure seem'd to live, or die. ..... Il.18.626.352.
In living Silver seem'd the Waves to roll, ... Il.18.703.357.
Seem'd sensible of Woe, and droop'd his Head: ..... Il.19.447.390.
Pale *Troy* beheld, and seem'd already lost; ..... Il.20.60.396.
In Voice and Aspect, seem'd the Pow'r divine; ..... Il.20.114.398.
And then the great *Æneas* seem'd to fear. ..... Il.20.229.403.
And as he mov'd, his Figure seem'd on flame. ..... Il.22.398.472.
Of sad *Patroclus* rose, or seem'd to rise; ..... Il.23.79.490.
Living, I seem'd his dearest, tend'rest Care, ... Il.23.85.490.
So swift, it seem'd a Flight, and not a Race. ..... Il.23.588.513.

SEEM'D (CONTINUED)

Seem'd all too mean the Stores he could employ, ... Il.24.289.548.
For sure he seem'd not of terrestrial Line! ..... Il.24.324.550.
He seem'd, fair Offspring of some princely Line! ..... Il.24.426.553.
All mute, yet seem'd to question with their Eyes: ..... Il.24.595.561.
But this of many counsels seem'd the best: ..... Od.9.379.321.
Still as I spoke, the Phantom seem'd to moan, ... Od.11.100.385.
His voice, that list'ning still they seem'd to hear. ..... Od.11.415.404.
His voice, that list'ning still they seem'd to hear. ..... Od.13.2.1.
Slow seem'd the sun to move, the hours to roll, ... Od.13.37.3.
Who seem'd descended from some princely line. ..... Od.13.270.19.

SEEM'ST

Thou seem'st all trembling, shivr'ing, dying, ... 6.31i.7.93.
Thou seem'st all trembling, fainting, dying, ... 6.31i.7A.93.
Tho' great in all, thou seem'st averse to lend ..... Il.13.907.148.

SEEMING

And *speak,* tho' *sure,* with *seeming Diffidence:* ..... 1.EOC.567.305.
O'ercharge the Shoulders of the seeming Swain. ..... 1.TrVP.32.378.
Each seeming want compensated of course, ... 3.EOM1.181.37.
'Tis real good, or seeming, moves them all; ..... 3.EOM2.94.66.
Death still draws nearer, never seeming near. ..... 3.EOM3.76.99.
A polish'd Urn the seeming Virgin bore, ... Od.7.26.235.
The seeming beggar answers with his pray'rs. ..... Od.17.425.153.

SEEMLIER

Are seemlier hid; my thoughtless youth they blame, ... Od.19.21.193.

SEEMLY

Where seemly rang'd in peaceful order stood ..... Od.1.169.40.

SEEMS

And vanquish'd Nature seems to charm no more. ..... 1.PSp.76.68.
And pawing, seems to beat the distant Plain, ... 1.W-F.152.164.
All seems Infected that th' Infected spy, ... 1.EOC.558.304.
Shades all the Banks, and seems it self a Grove; ..... 1.TrSP.182.401.
Heav'n seems improv'd with a superior Ray, ... 1.TrSt.294.422.
Medusa seems to move her languid Eyes, ... 1.TrSt.638.437.
And seems a Match for more than Mortal Force. ..... 1.TrES.204.457.
Seems to reject him, tho' she grants his Pray'r. ..... 2.RL4.80.190.
So Man, who here seems principal alone, ... 3.EOM1.57.20.
There are to whom my Satire seems too bold, ... 4.HS1.2.5.
The *Presence* seems, with things so richly odd, ... 4.JD4.238.45.
But here a Grievance seems to lie, ... 4.HS6.9.251.
Long as the Year's dull circle seems to run, ... 4.1HE1.37.281.
And left-legg'd Jacob seems to emulate. ..... 5.DunB2.68.299.
How lovely sorrow seems, how bright! ..... 6.5.1A.12.
That even humble seems a Term too high. ..... 6.9xi.4.24.
The more it seems to go about, to come ..... 6.17i(a).5.55.
And while he seems to study, thinks of you: ..... 6.45.44.125.
He seems a Monarch, and his Country's Pride. ..... Il.3.225.203.
Ev'n Godlike *Hector* seems himself to fear; ..... Il.4.582.249.
He seems remiss, but bears a valiant Mind; ..... Il.10.139.8.
Rest seems inglorious, and the Night too long. ..... Il.10.181.9.
Distress'd he seems, and no Assistance near: ..... Il.11.585.60.
Now stiff recedes, yet hardly seems to fly, ... Il.11.694.66.
And seems a Match for more than mortal Force. ..... Il.12.558.102.
And seems a moving Mountain topt with Snow. ..... Il.13.948.150.
Girt in surrounding Flames, he seems to fall ..... Il.15.750.224.
(My aukward Form, it seems, displeas'd her Eye) ..... Il.18.464.344.
Buoy'd by some inward Force, he seems to swim, ... Il.19.418.389.
Yet sure he seems, (to judge by Shape and Air,) ..... Il.23.554.511.
Buoy'd by her heav'nly Force, he seems to swim, ... Il.23.903.525.
She seems attentive to their pleaded vows, ... Od.1.321.48.
Thus seems the Palm with stately honours crown'd ..... Od.6.193.218.
O friends, he cries, the stranger seems well-skill'd ..... Od.8.143.270.
How goodly seems it, ever to employ ..... Od.9.7.301.
And yet it swims, or seems to swim, the main! ..... Od.13.193.15.
Freighted, it seems, with toys of ev'ry sort ..... Od.15.456.92.
Seems half to yield, yet flies the bridal hour: ..... Od.16.136.109.
If, as he seems, he was, in better days, ... Od.17.371.150.
Her beauty seems, and only seems, to shade: ..... Od.18.250.179.
Her beauty seems, and only seems, to shade: ..... Od.18.250.179.
In thy whole form *Ulysses* seems exprest: ..... Od.19.443.216.

SEEN

While curling Smokes from Village-Tops are seen, ... 1.PAu.63.84.
Nor envy *Windsor!* since thy Shades have seen ..... 1.W-F.161.164.
Here was she seen o'er Airy Wastes to rove, ... 1.W-F.167.165.
In the clear azure Gleam the Flocks are seen, ... 1.W-F.215.169.
There Kings shall sue, and suppliant States be seen ..... 1.W-F.383.188.
Where late was hair, the shooting leaves are seen ..... 1.TrFD.47.388.
A Serpent from her left was seen to rear ..... 1.TrSt.158.416.
Nor Gems on Bowls emboss'd were seen to shine, ... 1.TrSt.208.419.
Have we not seen (the Blood of *Laius* shed) ..... 1.TrSt.330.424.
Seen with both Eyes, and pinion'd on the Place, ... 2.ChJM.664.47.
Seen with both Eyes, and seiz'd upon the Place, ... 2.ChJM.664A.47.
Forswear the Fact, tho' seen with both his Eyes, ... 2.ChWB.72.59.
Fair to be seen, and rear'd of honest Wood. ..... 2.ChWB.246.68.
To see, be seen, to tell, and gather Tales; ..... 2.ChWB.282.70.
Of airy Elves by Moonlight Shadows seen, ... 2.RL1.31.148.
Clubs, Diamonds, Hearts, in wild Disorder seen, ... 2.RL3.79.173.
Unnumber'd Throngs on ev'ry side are seen ..... 2.RL4.47.187.
If *Hampton-Court* these Eyes had never seen! ..... 2.RL4.150.196.
Here naked Rocks, and empty Wastes were seen, ... 2.TemF.15.254.
The Wars of *Troy* were round the Pillar seen: ..... 2.TemF.188.271.
Then came the smallest Tribe I yet had seen, ... 2.TemF.356.281.
This having heard and seen, some Pow'r unknown ..... 2.TemF.418.283.
Of Prodigies, and Portents seen in Air, ... 2.TemF.452.285.
As, to be hated, needs but to be seen; ..... 3.EOM2.218.82.
Yet seen too oft, familiar with her face, ... 3.EOM2.219.82.
But seen too oft, familiar with her face, ... 3.EOM2.219A.82.
O'er-look'd, seen double, by the fool, and wise. ..... 3.EOM4.6.128.
The optics seeing, as the objects seen. ..... 3.Ep1.24.17.
One certain Portrait may (I grant) be seen, ... 3.Ep2.181.64.

SEEN (CONTINUED)

A Woman's seen in Private life alone: ..... 3.Ep2.200.67.
Smit with the mighty pleasure, to be seen: ..... 3.Ep4.128.149.
In them, as certain to be lov'd as seen, ... 4.HS1.53.9.
"Spirits like you, believe me, shou'd be seen, ... 4.JD4.88.33.
Have you not seen at Guild-hall's narrow Pass, ... 4.2HE2.104.173.
Seen him I have, but in his happier hour ..... 4.EpS1.29.300.
Seen him, uncumber'd with the Venal tribe, ... 4.EpS1.31.300.
Have I in silent wonder seen such things ..... 4.EpS1.109.306.
Glitt'ring with ice here hoary hills are seen, ... 5.DunA1.73.68.
In ev'ry loom our labours shall be seen, ... 5.DunA2.147.119.
That once was Britain—Happy! had she seen ..... 5.DunA3.109.159.
Glitt'ring with ice here hoary hills are seen, ... 5.DunB1.75.275.
In ev'ry loom our labours shall be seen, ... 5.DunB2.155.303.
That once was Britain—Happy! had she seen ..... 5.DunB3.117.325.
Not closer, orb in orb, conglob'd are seen ..... 5.DunB4.79.349.
Soft, as the wily Fox is seen to creep, ... 5.DunB4.351.377.
Thus bred, thus taught, how many have I seen, ... 5.DunB4.505.392.
Thus have I *seen,* in *Araby* the blest, ... 6.9viii.1.22.
And nought was seen, and nought was heard ..... 6.11.51Z3.32.
At ev'ry Door are Sun-brunt Matrons seen, ... 6.14ii.15.43.
So have I seen, in black and white ..... 6.14v(a).19.49.
So have I seen an Insect fair, ... 6.14v(b).19A.50.
And seen the Death of much Immortal Song. ..... 6.34.20.101.
But had they, Miss, your Wit and Beauty seen, ... 6.37.5.106.
But shines himselfe till they are seen no more. ..... 6.43.12.120.
And shines himselfe till they are seen no more. ..... 6.43.12A.121.
That Statesmen have the Worm, is seen ..... 6.53.25.162.
That Statesmen have a Worm, is seen ..... 6.53.25A.162.
Seen with Wit and Beauty seldom. ..... 6.70.3.201.
And scarce are seen the prostrate Nile or Rhine, ... 6.71.28.203.
And scarce are seen the prostrate Nile and Rhine, ... 6.71.28A.203.
"Trembling, I've seen thee dare the Kitten's Paw; ..... 6.96ii.27.271.
But 'tis for *Greece* I fear: For late was seen ..... Il.1.718.122.
Great as the Gods th' exalted Chief was seen, ... Il.2.568.154.
Where *Ægilipa's* rugged Sides are seen, ... Il.2.771.162.
Where *Erythinus'* rising Clifts are seen, ... Il.2.1036.172.
On either side the meeting Hosts are seen, ... Il.3.159.198.
My self, O King! have seen that wondrous Man; ..... Il.3.266.205.
Nor had you seen the King of Men appear ..... Il.4.256.233.
The War's whole Art with Wonder had he seen, ... Il.4.634.251.
These seen, the *Dardan* backward turn'd his Course, ... Il.5.701.301.
Else had'st thou seen me sink on yonder Plain, ... Il.5.1088.318.
Had seen my Death! Why did not Whirlwinds bear ..... Il.6.436.348.
Now lost, now seen, they intercept his way, ... Il.10.429.23.
For seen at distance, and but seen behind, ... Il.11.750.68.
For seen at distance, and but seen behind, ... Il.11.750.68.
Bent with the Weight the nodding Woods are seen, ... Il.12.339.93.
Below, fair *Ilion's* glitt'ring Spires were seen, ... Il.13.23.105.
Now wears a mortal Form; like *Calchas* seen, ... Il.13.69.108.
Her Quarry seen, impetuous at the Sight, ... Il.13.92.109.
As from some far-seen Mountain's airy Crown, ... Il.13.241.116.
Beneath the Chin the Point was seen to glide, ... Il.13.491.130.
(Seen from some Island, o'er the Main afar, ... Il.18.247.334.
A figur'd Dance succeeds: Such once was seen ..... Il.18.681.356.
Which on the far-seen Mountain blazing high, ... Il.19.406.389.
And scarce twelve morning Suns have seen me here; ..... Il.21.93.425.
Lo, what an Aid on *Mars's* Side is seen! ..... Il.21.492.441.
This hot thro' scorching Clefts is seen to rise, ... Il.22.197.463.
The rest around the Margins will be seen, ... Il.23.300.501.
Next bold *Meriones* was seen to rise, ... Il.23.425.507.
(Who thrice has seen the perishable kind ..... Od.3.303.101.
Rolling convulsive on the floor, is seen ..... Od.4.952.162.
Or seen his mother pierc'd with grief expire. ..... Od.4.971.163.
Not without wonder seen. Then thus began, ... Od.7.316.251.
Fields waving high with heavy crops are seen, ... Od.9.153.312.
No more was seen the human form divine, ... Od.10.278.356.
Death thou hast seen in all her ghastly forms; ..... Od.11.516.409.
He first was seen of all the Peers to rise, ... Od.11.625.414.
Now lost, now seen, with shrieks and dreadful cries; ..... Od.12.494.456.
Three years thy house their lawless rule has seen, ... Od.13.431.27.
Else had I seen my native walls in vain, ... Od.13.439.27.
Those foreign keepers guard: and here are seen ..... Od.14.125.42.
But rarely seen, or seen with weeping eyes. ..... Od.15.558.96.
But rarely seen, or seen with weeping eyes. ..... Od.15.558.96.
Enter, oh seldom seen! for lawless pow'rs ..... Od.16.29.103.
Seen or unseen, o'er earth at pleasure move) ..... Od.16.175.111.
Beneath, sequester'd to the nymphs, is seen ..... Od.17.242.143.
Oh had you seen him, vig'rous, bold and young, ... Od.17.380.150.
Takes a last look, and having seen him, dies; ..... Od.17.398.151.
Ill suits it, female virtue to be seen ..... Od.18.217.177.
Since what no eye has seen thy tongue reveal'd, ... Od.23.245.335.
Oft have I seen with solemn fun'ral games ..... Od.24.111.353.

SEER

He look'd, and saw a sable seer arise, ... 5.DunA3.229A.176.
But Annius, crafty Seer, with ebon wand, ... 5.DunB4.347.377.
That sacred Seer whose comprehensive View ..... Il.1.93.91.
The Seer reveal'd the Counsels of his Mind. ..... Il.6.94.328.
Deiphobus, and *Helenus* the Seer: ..... Il.12.108.85.
For thus a skilful Seer would read the Skies. ..... Il.12.266.91.
Not *Calchas* this, the venerable Seer; ..... Il.13.101.109.
Polydus' Son, a Seer of old Renown. ..... Il.13.836.145.
Deiphobus, nor *Helenus* the Seer, ... Il.13.955.151.
Deiphobus, and *Helenus* the Seer: ..... Il.13.983.152.
Nor Augur, Priest, or Seer had been obey'd. ..... Il.24.272.547.
Hippothous, Pammon, Helenus the Seer, ... Il.24.314.549.
To me, no Seer, th' inspiring Gods suggest; ..... Od.1.260.45.
Learn what I heard the sea-born Seer relate, ... Od.4.471.142.
Th' oraculous Seer frequents the *Pharian* coast, ... Od.4.519.145.
What arts can captivate the changeful Seer? ..... Od.4.534.146.
The Seer, while Zephyrs curl the swelling deep, ... Od.4.541.146.
The bands relax'd, implore the Seer to say ..... Od.4.573.147.
Me with reluctance thus the Seer address'd. ..... Od.4.624.149.
A shelfy tract, and long!) O Seer, I cry, ... Od.4.651.150.
(The mighty Seer who on these hills grew old; ..... Od.9.596.331.

SEER (CONTINUED)
These to the rest; but to the *Seer* must bleed Od.10.624.374.
'Till awful from the shades arise the *Seer.* Od.10.641.374.
The latent cause, oh sacred Seer, reveal! Od.11.178.390.
Nor this, replies the Seer, will I conceal. Od.11.179.390.
This dares a Seer, but nought the Seer prevails, Od.11.357.399.
This dares a Seer, but nought the Seer prevails, Od.11.357.399.
The Fates have follow'd as declar'd the Seer. Od.13.206.15.
A Seer he was, from great *Melampus* sprung, Od.15.252.80.
Learn what I heard the *sea-born Seer relate, Od.17.160.139.
When *Theoclymenus* the seer began: Od.17.172.139.
In vision rap'd <rapt>; the * *Hyperesian* Seer Od.20.421.253.
Tax not, (the heav'n-illumin'd Seer rejoin'd) Od.20.437.254.
This said, to sage *Piræus* sped the Seer, Od.20.445.254.
By their dread *Seer, and such my future day. Od.23.304.337.

SEES
From whence he sees his absent Brother fly, 1.TrSt.448.428.
Then sees *Cythæron* towring o'er the Plain, 1.TrSt.466.429.
Sees yawning Rocks in massy Fragments fly, 1.TrSt.511.431.
Sees by Degrees a purer Blush arise, 2.RL1.143.157.
She sees, and trembles at th' approaching Ill, 2.RL3.91.174.
Who sees with equal eye, as God of all, 3.EOM1.87.24.
Sees God in clouds, or hears him in the wind; 3.EOM1.100.27.
That sees immediate good by present sense; 3.EOM2.73.64.
Which sees no more the stroke, or feels the pain, 3.EOM3.67.98.
Who sees and follows that great scheme the best, 3.EOM4.95.137.
He sees, why Nature plants in Man alone 3.EOM4.345.162.
And envies ev'ry sparrow that he sees. 3.Ep1.233.35.
A Park is purchas'd, but the Fair he sees 3.Ep2.39.53.
And when she sees her Friend in deep despair, 3.Ep2.169.64.
Wise Peter sees the World's respect for Gold, 3.Ep3.125.102.
Who sees pale Mammon pine amidst his store, 3.Ep3.173.107.
Sees but a backward steward for the Poor; 3.Ep3.174.107.
Not for himself he sees, or hears, or eats; 3.Ep4.5.134.
Who but must laugh, the Master when he sees, 3.Ep4.107.147.
The suff'ring eye inverted Nature sees, 3.Ep4.119.149.
Poor *Cornus* sees his frantic Wife elope, 4.Arbu.25.97.
And sees at *Cannons* what was never there: 4.Arbu.300.117.
And sees pale Virtue carted in her stead! 4.EpS1.150.309.
Impatient sees his country bought and sold, 4.1740.11.332.
She sees a Mob of Metaphors advance, 5.DunA1.65.67.
Sees momentary monsters rise and fall, 5.DunA1.81.69.
She sees a Mob of Metaphors advance, 5.DunB1.67.275.
Sees momentary monsters rise and fall, 5.DunB1.83.275.
For sure, if Dulness sees a grateful Day, 5.DunB4.181.359.
And sees the Rusticks to their Labours rise; 6.17iii.33.58.
Sees no foul Discords at their Banquets bred, 6.17iii.36.58.
Who sees him act, but envies ev'ry deed? 6.32.25.96.
Or sees the blush of soft *Parthenia* rise, 6.45.46.126.
Or sees the blush of *Parthenissa* rise, 6.45.46A.126.
Sees his past days safe out of fortune's pow'r, 6.55.3.166.
He sees past days safe out of fortune's pow'r, 6.55.3A.166.
Th' Avenger sees, with a delighted Eye, 6.82x.3.236.
He sees his *Britain* with a Mother's Eyes; 6.96v.22.280.
And sees at *C[a]nons* what was never there; 6.120.8.339.
And when she sees her Friend in deep despair, 6.139.13.377.
He sees, and sudden to the Goddess cries, Il.1.267.99.
Pours the black Wine, and sees the Flames aspire; Il.1.608.117.
As from some Rocky Cleft the Shepherd sees Il.2.111.132.
The Fair one's Grief, and sees her falling Tears. Il.2.714.160.
Shot forth to View, a scaly Serpent sees; Il.3.48.191.
As Godlike *Hector* sees the Prince retreat, Il.3.53.191.
Sees what befell, and what may yet befall; Il.3.151.198.
This Day (perhaps the last that sees me here) Il.6.458.348.
This *Hector* sees, as his experienc'd Eyes Il.11.443.54.
Achilles sees us, to the Feast invites; Il.11.910.76.
Jove sees delighted, and avoids the Scene Il.13.13.104.
He sees *Alcathous* in the Front aspire: Il.13.537.132.
And sees superior Posts in meaner Hands. Il.13.579.134.
Achilles sees his Country's Forces fly: Il.14.160.165.
She sees her *Jove,* and trembles at the Sight. Il.14.184.168.
Greece sees, in hope, *Troy's* great Defender slain: Il.14.494.188.
Supreme he sits; and sees, in Pride of Sway, Il.15.116.201.
There *Hector* seated by the Stream he sees, Il.15.270.207.
And sees the watry Mountains break below. Il.15.749.224.
Think, your *Achilles* sees you fight: Be brave, Il.16.328.255.
He sees for *Greece* the Scale of Conquest rise, Il.16.432.259.
And trembling Man sees all his Labours vain! Il.16.475.261.
Sunk with *Troy's* heavy Fates, he sees decline Il.16.799.274.
Alas! who sees not *Jove's* almighty Hand Il.17.709.315.
Looks down, and sees the distant Thicket move; Il.17.764.318.
Let ev'ry *Greek* who sees my Spear confound Il.19.149.377.
Sees with Regret unhappy Mortals die. Il.20.32.394.
Sees, thro' its parting Plates, the upper Air, Il.20.329.407.
This sees *Hippodamas,* and seiz'd with Fright, Il.20.463.413.
The Son of *Peleus* sees, with Joy possest, Il.20.491.415.
The fierce *Achilles* sees me, and I fall: Il.21.666.449.
As *Hector* sees, unusual Terrors rise, Il.22.179.461.
Like a thin Smoke he sees the Spirit fly, Il.23.117.492.
No more *Achilles* sees his native Plain; Il.23.187.497.
And hov'ring o'er, their stretching Shadows sees. Il.23.460.508.
The Fraud celestial *Pallas* sees with Pain, Il.23.467.509.
What sees the Sun, but hapless Heroes Falls? Il.24.690.566.
Now, imag'd in his mind, he sees restor'd Od.1.152.40.
And sees (and labours onward as he sees) Od.5.512.197.
And sees (and labours onward as he sees) Od.5.512.197.
The chief with wonder sees th' extended streets, Od.7.55.236.
Arrive'd, he sees, he grieves, with rage he burns; Od.8.345.282.
And sees me wand'ring still from coast to coast; Od.9.647.333.
Sees with delight the sun's declining ray, Od.13.41.3.
No more I bathe, since he no longer sees Od.18.211.177.
On ev'ry side he sees the labour grow: Od.22.163.295.

SEEST
Thou seest an Island, not to those unknown, 1.TrUl.118.469.
Secure thou seest thy Native Shore at last? 1.TrUl.170.471.
Seest thou these lids that now unfold in vain? Od.9.533.328.
Thou seest an Island, not to those unknown Od.13.285.19.
Secure thou seest thy native shore at last? Od.13.337.23.
The shades thou seest, from yon' fair realms above. Od.24.213.358.

SEINE
To where the Seine, obsequious as she runs, 5.DunB4.297.373.

SEIS'D
He seis'd the Raft, and leapt into his seat, Od.5.414.192.

SEIZ'D
He seiz'd the Wand that causes Sleep to fly, 1.TrSt.433.428.
He seiz'd his Wand that causes Sleep to fly, 1.TrSt.433A.428.
And seiz'd with Horror, in the Shades of Night, 1.TrSt.557.433.
And seiz'd with Horror, 'midst the Shades of Night, 1.TrSt.557A.433.
Thus, seiz'd with Sacred Fear, the Monarch pray'd; 1.TrSt.598.435.
(With Brutal Force he seiz'd my *Trojan* Prey, 1.TrUl.146.470.
The Rage of Jealousie then seiz'd his Mind, 2.ChJM.485.39.
Seen with both Eyes, and seiz'd upon the Place, 2.ChJM.664A.47.
She seiz'd a Twig, and up the Tree she went. 2.ChJM.739.50.
By all those Pow'rs, some Frenzy seiz'd your Mind, 2.ChJM.780.52.
And a new Palsie seiz'd them when I frown'd. 2.ChWB.67.59.
The nimble Juice soon seiz'd his giddy Head, 2.ChWB.405.76.
Not youthful Kings in Battel seiz'd alive, 2.RL4.3.183.
Not more Amazement seiz'd on *Circe's* Guests, 4.JD4.166.39.
"The Hare once seiz'd the Hunter heeds no more 4.HAdv.137.87.
Seiz'd in the Fact, and in her Cuckold's Pow'r, 4.HAdv.171.89.
Seiz'd and ty'd down to judge, how wretched I! 4.Arbu.33.98.
Has seiz'd the Court and City, Poor and Rich: 4.2HE1.170.209.
Became when seiz'd, a Puppy, or an Ape. 5.DunA2.122.111.
Became, when seiz'd, a puppy, or an ape. 5.DunB2.130.301.
And where it fix'd, the beauteous bird I seiz'd: 5.DunB4.430.383.
Seiz'd with dumb joy—then falling by his side, 6.15.17.52.
Sent his own lightning, and the Victims seiz'd. 6.69i.6.198.
Think not by rigorous judgment seiz'd, 6.69ii.1.199.
Achilles seiz'd; to him alone confest; Il.1.265.99.
But now He seiz'd *Briseïs'* heav'nly Charms, Il.1.506.112.
Seiz'd by the beating Wing, the Monster slew: Il.2.383.145.
The valiant Victor seiz'd the golden Prize. Il.2.1067.172.
Then seiz'd the Reins his gentle Steeds to guide, Il.3.388.211.
(Seiz'd by the Crest) th' unhappy Warrior drew; Il.3.456.213.
His polish'd Bow with hasty Rashness seiz'd. Il.4.136.226.
With Horror seiz'd, the King of Men descry'd Il.4.178.230.
Troy seiz'd of *Helen,* and our Glory lost, Il.4.210.231.
Seiz'd to despoil, and dragg'd the Corps along: Il.4.531.246.
Seiz'd with Affright the boldest Foes appear; Il.4.581.249.
Seiz'd with unusual Fear *Idæus* fled, Il.5.27.266.
And seiz'd the Quiver where it idly hung. Il.5.265.280.
Tydides thus. The Goddess, seiz'd with Dread, Il.5.439.289.
Nor Sloth hath seiz'd me, but thy Word restrains: Il.5.1013.315.
Then *Ajax* seiz'd the Fragment of a Rock, Il.7.320.379.
Humbled they stood; pale Horror seiz'd on all, Il.7.574.393.
The *Greeks* beheld, and Transport seiz'd on all: Il.8.302.412.
Each seiz'd a Portion of the Kingly Feast, Il.9.123.438.
With Sorrow seiz'd, in Consternation lost, Il.9.813.473.
Then seiz'd his pond'rous Lance, and strode along. Il.10.204.10.
A sudden Palsy seiz'd his turning Head; Il.10.445.23.
Great *Diomed* himself was seiz'd with Fear, Il.11.447.54.
He spoke, while *Socus* seiz'd with sudden Fright, Il.11.558.58.
I seiz'd his Car, the Van of Battel led; Il.11.878.75.
This said, he seiz'd (while yet the Carcass heav'd) Il.13.801.143.
Fierce as when first by stealth he seiz'd her Charms, Il.14.335.179.
The Victor seiz'd; and as aloft he shook Il.14.585.190.
All *Greece* in Heaps; but one he seiz'd, and slew. Il.15.769.226.
First seiz'd a Ship on that contested Strand; Il.15.855.229.
Already had stern *Hector* seiz'd his Head, Il.17.137.293.
And seiz'd a Bull, the Master of the Herd: Il.18.672.356.
Grief seiz'd the Thund'rer, by his Oath engag'd; Il.19.123.377.
This sees *Hippodamas,* and seiz'd with Fright, Il.20.463.413.
He seiz'd a bending Bough, his Steps to stay; Il.21.269.432.
What Sloath has seiz'd us, when the Fields around Il.21.508.443.
She said, and seiz'd her Wrists with eager Rage; Il.21.566.445.
And seiz'd the Beast, and thus began to say: Il.23.769.520.
A sudden horror seiz'd on either mind: Od.4.863.159.
Or was the vessel seiz'd by fraud or force? Od.4.871.159.
Fear seiz'd his slacken'd limbs and beating heart; Od.5.522.197.
With wonder seiz'd, we view the pleasing ground, Od.9.176.312.
Next seiz'd two wretches more, and headlong cast, Od.9.404.322.
(A beamy blade) then seiz'd the bended bow, Od.10.311.359.
He seiz'd my hand, and gracious thus began. Od.10.333.360.
The Goddess swore: then seiz'd my hand, and led Od.10.411.364.
The tender moment seiz'd, and thus I said. Od.10.569.370.
Or nobly seiz'd thee in the dire alarms Od.11.497.408.
Nor nobly seiz'd me in the dire alarms, Od.11.503.408.
Fear seiz'd the mighty, and unnerv'd the brave; Od.12.245.443.
The lofty figtree seiz'd, and clung around. Od.12.512.457.
(With brutal force he seiz'd my *Trojan* prey, Od.13.313.21.
I seiz'd the proffer (ever fond to roam) Od.14.322.50.
Rude Pyrates seiz'd, and shipp'd thee o'er the main? Od.15.419.89.
She strait pursu'd, and seiz'd my willing arm; Od.15.501.94.
Seiz'd by the hand, and thus prophetic cry'd. Od.15.572.98.
Bore on full stretch, and seiz'd a dappl'd fawn: Od.19.266.208.
A mirthful phrenzy seiz'd the fated crowd; Od.20.415.252.
When Death had seiz'd her prey, thy son attends, Od.23.45.321.
Was heard, and terror seiz'd the *Grecian* train: Od.24.68.350.
Grief seiz'd at once, and wrapt up all the man; Od.24.368.366.
He ran, he seiz'd him with a strict embrace, Od.24.373.367.

SEIZE
Sudden they seize th'amaz'd, defenceless Prize, 1.W-F.109.161.
As surely seize thee, as I saw too well. 2.ChJM.771.52.
Oh had the Youth but been content to seize 2.RL*A*2.19.132.

SEIZE 271 SELF

SEIZE (CONTINUED)

Oh hadst thou, Cruel! been content to seize ....2.RL4.175.198.
Or settling, seize the Sweets the Blossoms yield, ...2.TemF.286.277.
But let heav'n seize it, all at once 'tis fir'd, ...2.ElAb.201.336.
Peace, Fools! or *Gonson* will for Papists seize you, ...4.JD4.256.47.
Now, now I seize, I clasp thy charms, ...4.HOde1.43.153.
I grasp I seize, I clasp thy charms, ...4.HOde1.43A.153.
And now I seize, I clasp thy charms, ...4.HOde1.43B.153.
And bad the nimblest racer seize the prize; ....5.DunA2.32.99.
And bids the nimblest racer seize the prize; ....5.DunA2.32A.99.
To seize his papers, Curl, was next thy care; ....5.DunA2.105.109.
To seize his papers, *C[url]l*, was next thy care; ....5.DunA2.106A.109.
And bade the nimblest racer seize the prize; ....5.DunB2.36.297.
To seize his papers, Curl, was next thy care; ....5.DunB2.113.301.
But could'st thou seize some Tongues that now are free, ...6.8.28.18.
So seize them Flames, or take them *Tonson*. ....6.10.36.25.
This Hand shall seize some other Captive Dame. ....Il.1.176.96.
Ev'n in thy Tent I'll seize the blooming Prize, ...Il.1.245.98.
Atrides, seize not on the beauteous Slave; ....Il.1.362.105.
Seize on *Briseïs*, whom the *Grecians* doom'd ....Il.1.392.106.
And seize secure; No more *Achilles* draws ....Il.1.394.106.
Say would'st thou seize some valiant Leader's Prize? ....Il.2.288.141.
Now seize th' Occasion, now the Troops survey, ...Il.2.518.151.
Then seize th' Occasion, dare the mighty Deed, ...Il.4.129.226.
Haste, seize the Whip, and snatch the guiding Rein; ....Il.5.284.280.
And seize the Coursers of Ætherial Breed. ....Il.5.327.282.
And fierce, to seize it, conqu'ring *Ajax* sprung: ....Il.5.765.303.
What Pity, Sloath should seize a Soul so brave, ...Il.6.670.360.
Give me to seize rich *Nestor's* Shield of Gold; ....Il.8.235.408.
To yonder Camp, or seize some stragling Foe? ....Il.10.244.13.
The panting Warriors seize him as He stands, ...Il.10.447.23.
Urge thou the Slaughter, while I seize the Steeds. ....Il.10.557.27.
To seize, and drew the Corselet from his Breast. ....Il.11.480.55.
Allow'd to seize, but not possess the Prize; ....Il.12.260.90.
To seize his beamy Helm the Victor flies, ...Il.13.253.117.
Deiphobus to seize his Helmet flies, ...Il.13.666.137.
Each valiant *Grecian* seize his broadest Shield; ....Il.14.432.184.
All spring to seize him; Storms of Arrows fly; ....Il.14.495.188.
Repuls'd, they yield; the *Trojans* seize the slain: ....Il.17.325.300.
If Earth at length this active Prince can seize, ...Il.21.72.424.
To seize his treasures, and divide his state, ...Od.2.377.79.
Perhaps may seize thy realm, and share the spoil; ....Od.3.402.106.
And shouting seize the God: our force t'evade ....Od.4.613.148.
And hope and doubt alternate seize her soul. ....Od.4.1040.166.
Majestically fierce, to seize his prey; ....Od.6.158.216.
And seize the moment when the breezes rise: ....Od.7.408.256.
To seize the time, and with a sudden wound ....Od.9.356.321.
Secure to seize us ere we reach'd the door. ....Od.9.498.326.
Our eager sailors seize the fair retreat, ...Od.10.105.345.
The sailors catch the word, their oars they seize, ...Od.10.149.347.
But if his herds ye seize, beneath the waves ....Od.11.142.387.
Dauntless my sword I seize: the airy crew, ...Od.11.277.395.
The fruit he strives to seize: but blasts arise, ...Od.11.731.421.
If but to seize thy arms thou make delay, ...Od.12.153.439.
While yet I speak, at once their oars they seize, ...Od.12.264.445.
'Till the fell fiend arise to seize her prey. ....Od.12.273.445.
When lo! fierce *Scylla* stoop'd to seize her prey, ...Od.12.294.446.
Why seize ye not yon beeves, and fleecy prey? ....Od.12.409.450.
They seize, they kill!—but for the rite divine, ...Od.12.419.451.
With ready hands they rush to seize their slave; ....Od.14.378.53.
To seize thy life shall lurk the murd'rous band, ...Od.15.35.71.
And seize their seats, impatient for the sea. ....Od.15.247.80.
Your drooping eyes with soft oppression seize; ....Od.19.595.225.
Go you, and seize the felon; backward bind ....Od.22.188.296.
Headlong they drop: the fowlers seize the prey. ....Od.22.342.304.
Wise is thy soul, but errors seize the wise; ....Od.23.82.322.

SEIZES

Seizes your Fame, and puts his Laws in force. ....1.EOC.168.259.
Inspir'd he seizes: These an altar raise: ....5.DunA1.137.80.
Inspir'd he seizes: These an altar raise: ....5.DunB1.157.282.
One instinct seizes, and transports away. ....5.DunB4.74.348.
Eager he seizes, and devours the slain, ...Il.3.39.190.
The Savage seizes, draws, and rends the last: ....Il.11.230.45.
Deep Horror seizes ev'ry *Grecian* Breast, ...Il.15.364.211.

SEIZING

He said: and seizing *Thrasimedes'* Shield, ...Il.14.13.157.

SEJANUS

Sejanus, Wolsey, hurt not honest FLEURY, ...4.EpS1.51.301.

SELDOM

True *Taste* as seldom is the *Critick's* Share; ....1.EOC.12.240.
Let it be *seldom*, and *compell'd* by *Need*, ...1.EOC.165.259.
Seldom at *Council*, never in a *War*: ....1.EOC.577.298.
So seldom view'd, and ever in Disguise. ....1.TrUl.190.472.
Heav'n knows, how seldom things are what they seem! ....2.ChJM.806.54.
Love seldom haunts the Breast where Learning lies, ...2.ChWB.369.75.
Seldom at Church ('twas such a busy life) ....3.Ep3.381.124.
Observe how seldom ev'n the best succeed: ....4.2HE1.286.219.
Yet custom (seldom to your favour gain'd) ....6.38.19.108.
Seen with Wit and Beauty seldom. ....6.70.3.201.
So seldom view'd, and ever in disguise! ....Od.13.357.24.
Enter, oh seldom seen! for lawless pow'rs ....Od.16.29.103.

SELDOME

For tho ye seldome write a book ....6.58.68Z3.173.

SELECT

Or from those Meads select unfading Flow'rs, ...1.PWi.74.94.
Select to *Jove*, th' Inviolable King. ....Il.3.144.197.
From all your Troops select the boldest Knight, ...Il.7.87.367.
These to select, *Ulysses*, be thy Care: ....Il.19.192.379.
The Hero's Bones with careful view select: ....Il.23.297.501.
For the chaste Queen select an equal Lord. ....Od.1.383.51.

SELECT (CONTINUED)

Select, in honour of our foreign guest: ....Od.14.458.57.
And from the Peers select the noblest Lord; ....Od.19.622.226.
Select the largest to the pow'rs divine. ....Od.24.247.360.

SELECTED

By Vote selected, to the Gen'ral's Bed. ....Il.1.483.111.
The Thighs, selected to the Gods, divide: ....Il.1.603.117.
The Thighs, selected to the Gods, divide. ....Il.2.505.150.
Fall two, selected to attend their Lord. ....Il.23.213.498.
Selected from my stores, of matchless price ....Od.4.833.158.
Slay the selected beeves, and flea the slain; ....Od.12.424.451.
The King selected from the glitt'ring rows ....Od.15.116.74.
The Lord selected to the nuptial joys, ...Od.20.399.251.

SELECTEST

Shed its selectest Influence from above; ....2.ChJM.429.35.

SELECTS

"Too late the Queen selects a second lord: ....Od.4.1018.165.

SELF

Not *Neptune's* self from all his Streams receives ....1.W-F.223.170.
Not *Neptune's* self from all his Floods receives ....1.W-F.223A.170.
Not *Neptune's* self from all her streams receives ....1.W-F.223B.170.
From Heav'n it self tho' sev'nfold *Nilus* flows, ...1.W-F.359.185.
Be sure *your self* and your own *Reach* to know, ...1.EOC.48.244.
It self unseen, but in th' *Effects*, remains. ....1.EOC.79.248.
Still with *It self compar'd*, his *Text* peruse; ....1.EOC.128.253.
Trust not your self; but your Defects to know, ...1.EOC.213.264.
If *Faith* it self has *diff'rent Dresses* worn, ...1.EOC.446.289.
And while Self-Love each jealous Writer rules, ...1.EOC.516.296.
(Far more than e'er can by your self be guest) ....1.TrVP.81.380.
(My self the offspring of a second bride.) ....1.TrFD.10.386.
And I my self the same rash act had done, ...1.TrFD.26.387.
Not *Bacchus'* self with *Phaon* cou'd compare: ....1.TrSP.26.394.
To Heav'n it self, and Earth's remotest Ends. ....1.TrSP.40.395.
Alas, what more could Fate it self impose, ...1.TrSP.79.397.
Shades all the Banks, and seems it self a Grove; ....1.TrSP.182.401.
And *Phœbus* self is less a God to me. ....1.TrSP.221.403.
Taught by thy self to win the promis'd Reign: ....1.TrSt.94.414.
Then self-condemn'd to Shades of endless Night, ...1.TrSt.99.414.
And Heav'n it self the wandring Chariot burn'd. ....1.TrSt.311.423.
And by thy self the Honour of thy Race. ....1.TrSt.824.444.
To thee my Treasures and my self commend. ....1.TrUl.111.469.
Self-banish'd thence, I sail'd before the Wind, ...1.TrUl.142.470.
But this to me? who, like thy self, excel ....1.TrUl.171.471.
And guard the Wisdom which her self inspires. ....1.TrUl.212.472.
Not *Hester's* self, whose Charms the *Hebrews* sing, ...2.ChJM.343.30.
Nor if she thought her self in Heav'n or Hell. ....2.ChJM.423.35.
I was my self the Scourge that caus'd the Smart; ....2.ChWB.6.57.
I've had, my self, full many a merry Fit, ...2.ChWB.23.57.
Have Goods and Body to your self alone. ....2.ChWB.127.62.
"What? wou'd you have me to your self alone? ....2.ChWB.198.66.
This Clerk, my self, and my good Neighbour *Alce*, ...2.ChWB.281.70.
When, after Millions slain, your self shall die; ....2.RL5.146.211.
And Love it self was banish'd from my Breast, ...2.TemF.6.253.
In Air self-ballanc'd hung the Globe below, ...2.TemF.13.254.
From Time's first Birth, with Time it self shall last; ....2.TemF.50.256.
Around the Shrine it self of *Fame* they stand, ...2.TemF.180.270.
I have not yet forgot my self to stone. ....2.ElAb.24.320.
Renounce my love, my life, my self—and you. ....2.ElAb.204.336.
Oppose thy self to heav'n; dispute my heart; ....2.ElAb.282.343.
Once like thy self, I trembled, wept, and pray'd, ...2.ElAb.311.344.
Devotion's self shall steal a thought from heav'n, ...2.ElAb.357.348.
No self-confounding Faculties to share; ....3.EOM1.191A.38.
Self-love, to urge, and Reason, to restrain; ....3.EOM2.54.62.
Self-love, the spring of motion, acts the soul; ....3.EOM2.59.62.
Self-love still stronger, as its objects nigh; ....3.EOM2.71.63.
Self-love yet stronger, as its objects nigh; ....3.EOM2.71A.63.
Each strengthens Reason, and Self-love restrains. ....3.EOM2.80.64.
Self-love and Reason to one end aspire, ...3.EOM2.87.65.
Modes of Self-love the Passions we may call; ....3.EOM2.93.66.
For, Vice or Virtue, Self directs it still; ....3.EOM2.236.84.
Ev'n mean Self-love becomes, by force divine, ...3.EOM2.291.90.
And bid Self-Love and Social be the same. ....3.EOM3.138Z2.106.
Self-love and Social at her birth began, ...3.EOM3.149.107.
So drives Self-love, thro' just and thro' unjust, ...3.EOM3.269.120.
The same Self-love, in all, becomes the cause ....3.EOM3.271.120.
Forc'd into virtue thus by Self-defence, ...3.EOM3.279.121.
Self-love forsook the path it first pursu'd, ...3.EOM3.281.121.
And bade Self-love and Social be the same. ....3.EOM3.318.126.
No cavern'd Hermit, rests self-satisfy'd. ....3.EOM4.42.132.
One self-approving hour whole years out-weighs ....3.EOM4.255.152.
Self-love thus push'd to social, to divine, ...3.EOM4.353.162.
Self-love but serves the virtuous mind to wake, ...3.EOM4.363.163.
That true SELF-LOVE and SOCIAL are the same; ....3.EOM4.396.166.
Or *Flavia's* self in glue (her rising task) ....3.Ep2.25A.52.
Or Sappho's self in glue (her rising task) ....3.Ep2.25B.52.
Scarce H[awle]y's self had sent it to the dogs? ....3.Ep3.54A.90.
Give Harpax self the blessing of a Friend; ....3.Ep3.94.97.
Of mad Good-nature, and of mean Self-love. ....3.Ep3.228.111.
That live-long wig which Gorgon's self might own, ...3.Ep3.295.117.
Not *Naso's* self more impudently near, ...4.JD4.178A.41.
Not *Fannius* self more impudently near, ...4.JD4.178.41.
Curs'd by thy neighbours, thy Trustees, thy self, ...4.HS2.106.61.
A Self-Tormentor, worse than (in the Play) ....4.HAdv.25.77.
He spins the slight, self-pleasing thread anew; ....4.Arbu.90.102.
Still spin the slight, self-pleasing thread anew; ....4.Arbu.90A.102.
And *St. John's* self (great *Dryden's* friends before) ....4.Arbu.141.105.
Nor *Satans* self shall joy so much as hee ....4.JD2A.92.140.
Who there his Muse, or Self, or Soul attends? ....4.2HE2.90.171.
The Ship it self may make a better figure, ...4.2HE2.298.185.
Not—'s self e'er tells more *Fibs* than I; ....4.2HE1.176.209.
Self-centred Sun, and Stars that rise and fall, ...4.1HE6.6.237.
For Vertue's self may too much Zeal be had; ....4.1HE6.26.239.

SELF (CONTINUED)

Not for your self, but for your Fools and Knaves;	4.1HE6.92.243.
How should I thrust my self between?	4.HS6.50.253.
Late as it is, I put my self to school,	4.1HE1.47.281.
With self-applause her wild creation views,	5.DunA1.80.69.
She looks, and breathes her self into their airs.	5.DunA1.220.89.
And all was hush'd, as Folly's self lay dead.	5.DunA2.386.148.
'None but Thy self can be thy parallel.'	5.DunA3.272.180.
With self-applause her wild creation views;	5.DunB1.82.275.
And all was hush'd, as Folly's self lay dead.	5.DunB2.418.318.
See all in *Self,* and but for self be born:	5.DunB4.480.389.
See all in *Self,* and but for self be born:	5.DunB4.480.389.
Wrapt up in Self, a God without a Thought,	5.DunB4.485.389.
Kind Self-conceit to some her glass applies,	5.DunB4.533.394.
But 'tis thy self alone can give the fire:	6.2.22.6.
Behind thy self thou still dost stay;	6.6ii.6.14.
So, forc'd from Engines, Lead it self can fly,	6.7.17.16.
Thou wert e'er Nature's self began to be,	6.8.2.17.
His Numbers such, as Sanger's self might use.	6.12.3.37.
Ne *Richmond's* self, from whose tall Front are ey'd	6.14ii.53.44.
044.Ne *Richmond's* self, from whose tall Front is ey'd	6.14ii.53A.44.
(Not death it self from me cou'd force a tear,	6.20.35.67.
Scorn'd Heaven it self, and durst the Gods deride,	6.20.57.67.
I share his griefs, and feel my self his pain:	6.21.36.70.
Who fix't thy self amidst the rowling frame,	6.23.7.73.
And on thy self, undazled, fix thy eye.	6.23.12.73.
And on thy self, fix her undazzl'd Eye!	6.23.12A.73.
As *Cato's* self had not disdain'd to hear.	6.32.46.97.
"How strangely you expose your self, my dear!"	6.41.10.113.
Stern *Cato's* self was no relentless spouse.	6.41.30.114.
And that my self am blind:	6.50.8.144.
And I my self am blind:	6.50.8A.146.
A wandring, self-consuming fire.	6.51ii.20.153.
"Know'st thou not me, nor yet thy self?"	6.79.83.220.
Were Virtue's self in Silks,—faith keep away!	6.82vi.7.232.
"Shall I ne'er bear thy self and House again?	6.96ii.60.273.
How would they swear, not *Congreve's* self was safe!	6.98.42.284.
Destin'd and due to wretches self-enslav'd!	6.146.2.389.
Dies between Exigents, and self defence.	6.147iv.4.391.
Dies under Exigents, or self defence.	6.147iv.4A.391.
Achilles self conduct her o'er the Main;	II.1.190.96.
Rule thou thy self, as more advanc'd in Age.	II.1.373.106.
Him must our Hosts, our Chiefs, our Self obey?	II.1.382.106.
My self the first th' assembl'd Chiefs incline	II.1.500.112.
Nor what they offer, thou thy self despise.	II.2.429.148.
My self, O King! have seen that wondrous Man;	II.3.266.205.
Sprung, with thy self, from one Celestial Sire,	II.4.84.224.
When *Priam's* Pow'rs and *Priam's* self shall fall,	II.4.198.230.
Be still thy self; in Arms a mighty Name;	II.4.300.235.
My self will charge this Terror of the Field.	II.5.297.281.
Great *Juno's* self has born her Weight of Pain,	II.5.481.291.
Know thy vain self, nor let their Flatt'ry move	II.5.786.304.
My self will dare the Danger of the Day.	II.7.116.369.
Not *Hector's* self should want an equal Foe.	II.7.190.373.
The King of Men, by *Juno's* self inspir'd,	II.8.266.410.
My self will arm, and thunder at thy side.	II.8.456.418.
When *Juno's* self, and *Pallas* shall appear,	II.8.459.419.
My self will stay, till *Troy* or I expire;	II.9.66.434.
My self, and *Sthenelus,* will fight for Fame;	II.9.67.435.
And with *Orestes'* self divide my Care.	II.9.186.441.
My self will give the Dow'r; so vast a Store,	II.9.193.442.
(My self will name them) to *Pelides'* Tent.	II.9.220.443.
Such as thy self shall chuse; who yield to none,	II.9.368.451.
And with *Orestes'* self divide his Care.	II.9.373.451.
Our self to hoary *Nestor* will repair;	II.10.65.5.
To rouse the *Spartan* I my self decree;	II.10.128.7.
The rest the People shar'd; my self survey'd	II.11.840.73.
My self the foremost; but my Sire deny'd;	II.11.853.74.
Thy self, *Achilles,* and thy rev'rend Sire	II.11.908.76.
Forth-springing instant, darts her self from high,	II.13.93.109.
As *Pallas'* self might view with fixt Delight;	II.13.174.113.
Nor *Asius'* Son, nor *Asius'* self appear.	II.13.956.151.
Self-clos'd behind her shut the Valves of Gold.	II.14.196.168.
Not thus ev'n for thy self I felt Desire,	II.14.371.180.
My self, ye *Greeks!* my self will lead the way.	II.14.436.184.
My self, ye *Greeks!* my self will lead the way.	II.14.436.184.
Thy self a *Greek;* and, once, of *Greeks* best!	II.16.32.236.
As at *Achilles* self! Beneath thy Dart	II.17.235.297.
With *Hector's* self shall equal Honours claim;	II.17.272.298.
Not *Pallas'* self, her Breast when Fury warms,	II.17.458.305.
My self, and my bold Brother will sustain	II.17.803.320.
Beyond Mankind, beyond my self, is slain!	II.18.104.328.
The self same Night to both a Being gave,	II.18.297.336.
Self-mov'd, obedient to the Beck of Gods:	II.18.444.342.
Not by my self, but vengeful *Ate* driv'n;	II.19.92.375.
Vain hope! to shun him by the self-same Road	II.21.653.449.
And spare thy self, thy Father, spare us all!	II.22.77.456.
Rest here: My self will lead the *Trojan* on,	II.22.287.468.
Could I my self the bloody Banquet join!	II.22.437.473.
Prizes which none beside our self could gain,	II.23.343.503.
Antilochus! we shall our self provide.	II.23.638.515.
(The self-same Place beside *Patroclus'* Pyre,	II.23.909.525.
(A Goddess by our self to *Peleus* giv'n,	II.24.78.538.
Fierce as he is, *Achilles* self shall spare	II.24.191.544.
Fierce as he is, *Achilles'* self shall spare	II.24.221.546.
Thy self not young, a weak old Man thy Guide.	II.24.454.555.
Old like thy self, and not unknown to Fame;	II.24.488.556.
To yield thy *Hector* I my self intend:	II.24.708.567.
Her self a Rock, (for such was Heav'ns high Will)	II.24.773.569.
In ev'ry Face the self-same Grief is shown,	II.24.884.573.
For thee I mourn; and mourn my self in thee,	II.24.975.576.
My self assisting in the social joy,	Od.4.331.135.
Heroes in various climes my self have found,	Od.4.367.137.
For who, self-mov'd, with weary wing wou'd sweep	Od.5.125.178.
And self-considering, as he stands, debates;	Od.6.170.216.
Alas! a mortal, like thy self, am I;	Od.7.283.249.

SELF (CONTINUED)

Her self supply'd the stores and rich array;	Od.7.351.253.
Why not her self did she conduct the way,	Od.7.387.255.
Our self we give, memorial of our name:	Od.8.466.288.
Her self the chest prepares: in order roll'd	Od.8.475.288.
In wond'rous ships self-mov'd, instinct with mind;	Od.8.604.294.
My self the fifth. We stand, and wait the hour.	Od.9.395.322.
My self above them from a rising ground	Od.9.455.324.
First I release my self, my fellows last:	Od.9.546.328.
And ah, thy self the rash attempt forbear!	Od.10.316.359.
And steal thy self from life, by slow decays:	Od.11.165.389.
The wife self-murder'd from a beam depends,	Od.11.337.398.
Firm to the mast with chains thy self be bound,	Od.12.63.433.
To warn the thoughtless self-confiding train,	Od.13.174.14.
To thee my treasures and my self commend.	Od.13.278.19.
Self-banish'd thence. I sail'd before the wind,	Od.13.309.21.
But this to me? who, like thy self, excell	Od.13.338.23.
And guard the wisdom which her self inspires.	Od.13.379.25.
If thou but equal to thy self be found,	Od.13.449.27.
Our states my self and *Idomen* employ	Od.14.274.49.
I saw my self the vast unnumber'd store	Od.14.359.51.
The Will it self, Omnipotent, fulfills.	Od.14.497.60.
Or fates peculiar to thy self portend?	Od.15.189.77.
To-morrow for my self I must provide,	Od.15.328.85.
Yet like my self I wish'd thee here preferr'd,	Od.17.209.141.
The Heroe stood self-conquer'd, and endur'd.	Od.17.279.145.
Nor think thy self exempt: that rosy prime	Od.19.100.197.
The vision self-explain'd (the Chief replies).	Od.19.650.227.
Nor dread to name your self the bowyer's prize:	Od.19.684.229.
Your couch to fashion as your self prescribe.	Od.19.698.229.
In self-debate the Suitors doom resolv'd.	Od.20.36.234.
Doubt you the Gods? Lo *Pallas'* self descends,	Od.20.57.235.
Thy self untimely and thy consort dy'd,	Od.20.80.236.
Assent your self, and gain the royal will.	Od.20.392.251.
My self with arms can furnish all the train;	Od.22.155.294.
Self-taught I sing; by heav'n, and heav'n alone	Od.22.383.307.
Save then the Poet, and thy self reward;	Od.22.387.307.
And steal my self from life by slow decays;	Od.23.298.337.
Nothing neglected, but thy self alone.	Od.24.293.364.
When by thy self and by *Anticlia* sent,	Od.24.386.367.
(Oft warn'd by *Mentor* and my self in vain)	Od.24.523.373.
Regard thy self, the living, and the dead.	Od.24.589.376.

SELF-APPLAUSE

With self-applause her wild creation views,	5.DunA1.80.69.
With self-applause her wild creation views;	5.DunB1.82.275.

SELF-APPROVING

One self-approving hour whole years out-weighs	3.EOM4.255.152.

SELF-BALLANC'D

In Air self-ballanc'd hung the Globe below,	2.TemF.13.254.

SELF-BANISH'D

Self-banish'd thence, I sail'd before the Wind,	1.TrUl.142.470.
Self-banish'd thence. I sail'd before the wind,	Od.13.309.21.

SELF-CENTRED

Self-centred Sun, and Stars that rise and fall,	4.1HE6.6.237.

SELF-CLOS'D

Self-clos'd behind her shut the Valves of Gold.	II.14.196.168.

SELF-CONCEIT

Kind Self-conceit to some her glass applies,	5.DunB4.533.394.

SELF-CONDEMN'D

Then self-condemn'd to Shades of endless Night,	1.TrSt.99.414.

SELF-CONFIDING

To warn the thoughtless self-confiding train,	Od.13.174.14.

SELF-CONFOUNDING

No self-confounding Faculties to share;	3.EOM1.191A.38.

SELF-CONQUER'D

The Heroe stood self-conquer'd, and endur'd.	Od.17.279.145.

SELF-CONSIDERING

And self-considering, as he stands, debates;	Od.6.170.216.

SELF-CONSUMING

A wandring, self-consuming fire.	6.51ii.20.153.

SELF-DEBATE

In self-debate the Suitors doom resolv'd.	Od.20.36.234.

SELF-DEFENCE

Forc'd into virtue thus by Self-defence,	3.EOM3.279.121.

SELF-ENSLAV'D

Destin'd and due to wretches self-enslav'd!	6.146.2.389.

SELF-EXPLAIN'D

The vision self-explain'd (the Chief replies.)	Od.19.650.227.

SELF-LOVE

And while Self-Love each jealous Writer rules,	1.EOC.516.296.
Self-love, to urge, and Reason, to restrain;	3.EOM2.54.62.
Self-love, the spring of motion, acts the soul;	3.EOM2.59.62.
Self-love still stronger, as its objects nigh;	3.EOM2.71.63.
Self-love yet stronger, as its objects nigh;	3.EOM2.71A.63.
Each strengthens Reason, and Self-love restrains.	3.EOM2.80.64.
Self-love and Reason to one end aspire,	3.EOM2.87.65.
Modes of Self-love the Passions we may call;	3.EOM2.93.66.
Ev'n mean Self-love becomes, by force divine,	3.EOM2.291.90.

SELF-LOVE (CONTINUED)
And bid Self-Love and Social be the same. ....3.EOM3.138Z2.106.
Self-love and Social at her birth began, ...3.EOM3.149.107.
So drives Self-love, thro' just and thro' unjust, ...3.EOM3.269.120.
The same Self-love, in all, becomes the cause ....3.EOM3.271.120.
Self-love forsook the path it first pursu'd, ...3.EOM3.281.121.
And bade Self-love and Social be the same. ....3.EOM3.318.126.
Self-love thus push'd to social, to divine, ...3.EOM4.353.162.
Self-love but serves the virtuous mind to wake, ...3.EOM4.363.163.
That true SELF-LOVE and SOCIAL are the same; ....3.EOM4.396.166.
Of mad Good-nature, and of mean Self-love. ....3.Ep3.228.111.

SELF-MOV'D
Self-mov'd, obedient to the Beck of Gods: ....Il.18.444.342.
For who, self-mov'd, with weary wing wou'd sweep ....Od.5.125.178.
In wond'rous ships self-mov'd, instinct with mind; ....Od.8.604.294.

SELF-MURDER'D
The wife self-murder'd from a beam depends, ...Od.11.337.398.

SELF-PLEASING
He spins the slight, self-pleasing thread anew; ....4.Arbu.90.102.
Still spin the slight, self-pleasing thread anew; ....4.Arbu.90A.102.

SELF-SAME
Vain hope! to shun him by the self-same Road ....Il.21.653.449.
(The self-same Place beside *Patroclus'* Pyre, ...Il.23.909.525.
In ev'ry Face the self-same Grief is shown, ...Il.24.884.573.

SELF-SATISFY'D
No cavern'd Hermit, rests self-satisfy'd. ....3.EOM4.42.132.

SELF-TAUGHT
Self-taught I sing; by heav'n, and heav'n alone ....Od.22.383.307.

SELF-TORMENTOR
A Self-Tormentor, worse than (in the Play) ....4.HAdv.25.77.

SELFE
Which Natures selfe inspires? ....6.50.20Z4.147*.

SELFISH
Passions, tho' selfish, if their means be fair, ...3.EOM2.97.66.
No selfish motive this profusion draws, ...3.Ep3.205A.110.
A low-born, cell-bred, selfish, servile band, ...5.DunB2.356.315.
My Sons! be proud, be selfish, and be dull. ....5.DunB4.582.400.

SELFISHLY
Who can your Merit selfishly approve, ...4.Arbu.293.117.

SELFISHNESS
Sick of herself thro' very selfishness! ....3.Ep2.146.62.
Sick of herself thro' very Selfishness. ....6.154.32.403.

SELKIRK
Immortal *S[elkir]k,* and grave *De[La* Warr]e! ....4.EpS1.92.305.
P. As *S[elkir]k,* if he lives, will love the 'prince. ....4.EpS2.61.316.
Fr. Strange spleen to *S[elkir]k! P.* Do I wrong the Man? ....4.EpS2.62.316.
Against your worship when had *S[elkir]k* writ? ....4.EpS2.158.322.
Against your worship what has *S[elkir]k* writ? ....4.EpS2.158A.322.
Nor *** talk'd, nor *S[elkirk]* whisper'd more; ....5.DunA2.382A.147*.

SELLÈ'S
From *Ephyr's* Walls, and *Sellè's* winding Shore, ...Il.2.798.163.

SELL
Not ev'ry Man's oblig'd to sell his Store, ...2.ChWB.42.58.
"Wou'd I vouchsafe to sell what Nature gave, ...2.ChWB.201.66.
Sell their presented Partridges, and Fruits, ...4.HS2.51.59.
Is she who shows what Ware she has to sell; ....4.HAdv.109.85.
And sell his Soul for Vanity, ...6.58.23.171.
Stocks thou may'st buy and sell, but always lose; ....6.66.7.194.
And sell to bondage in a foreign land: ....Od.14.327.51.
When slave! to sell thee at a price too dear ....Od.17.297.146.
Dear sell the slaves! demand no greater gain. ....Od.20.458.255.

SELLE'S
From great *Arisba's* Walls and *Selle's* Coast, ...Il.2.1014.171.
The Coursers fed on *Selle's* winding Shore. ....Il.12.112.85.

SELLES'
(Well known in Fight on *Selles'* winding Shore, ...Il.15.627.220.

SELLI
(Whose Groves, the *Selli,* Race austere! surround, ...Il.16.288.252.

SELLS
And silent sells a King, or buys a Queen. ....3.Ep3.78.93.
Last, for his Country's love, he sells his Lands. ....3.Ep3.212.110.
He tells what Strumpet Places sells for Life, ...4.JD4.148.37.
Yet when he sells, the writings he impairs ....4.JD2A.102.140.
But Curst be he, who basely sells a Cause, ...4.JD2A.72.138.

SELVES
Rehearse, ye Muses, what your selves inspir'd. ....1.PAu.56.84.
When we but praise *Our selves* in *Other Men.* ....1.EOC.455.290.
Hear but the Fact, and judge your selves the Case. ....2.ChWB.336.73.
Slaves to your selves, and ev'n fatigu'd with Ease, ...2.TemF.397.282.
At last they steal us from our selves away; ....4.2HE2.73.171.
Then too we hurt our selves, when to defend ....4.2HE1.364.227.
Say great Patricians! (since your selves inspire ....5.DunA1.3.61.
Dare to have sense your selves; assert the stage, ...6.32.43.97.
And fit your selves—like Chaps in *Monmouth-Street.* ....6.60.28.178.
To mix in combate which your selves neglect? ....Il.4.393.239.
Our selves to lessen, while our Sires you raise? ....Il.4.457.242.
Our selves, here fix'd, will make the dang'rous Stand: ....Il.6.104.328.

SELVES (CONTINUED)
Be still your selves, and *Hector* asks no more. ....Il.6.138.330.
Our selves, our Infants, and our City spare! ....Il.6.385.345.
Your selves condemn'd ten rolling Years to weep ....Il.8.516.421.
What for our selves we can, is always ours; ....Il.9.824.474.
Be still your selves, and we shall need no more. ....Il.14.428.184.
Be mindful of your selves, your ancient Fame, ...Il.15.572.218.
Respect your selves, and learn an honest Shame: ....Il.15.667.221.
Your shameful Efforts 'gainst your selves employ, ...Il.17.386.302.
And save our selves, while with impetuous Hate ....Il.17.799.319.
Your selves were present; where this Minstrel-God ....Il.24.81.538.
No, you must feel him too; your selves must fall; ....Il.24.301.549.
Not as He wills, but as our selves incline. ....Od.9.332.320.
Your selves, your wives, your long-descending race, ...Od.13.58.4.
Death to your selves, eternal chains to me. ....Od.15.484.93.
Be mindful of your selves, draw forth your swords, ...Od.22.87.290.

SELY
This sely Clerk full low doth lout: ....6.14i.14.42.

SEMBLANCE
Aerial Semblance, and an empty Shade! ....Il.23.125.493.
With semblance fair th' unhappy men she plac'd. ....Od.10.269.355.
In human semblance. On his bloomy face ....Od.10.331.360.
Impassive semblance, and a flitting shade. ....Od.10.587.372.
With semblance fair invites me to his home: ....Od.14.321.50.
With semblance fair, but inward deep deceit. ....Od.17.77.136.
And thus with semblance mild addrest the crew. ....Od.17.554.159.
Delusive semblance!—But my remnant life ....Od.19.666.228.
Impassive semblance, Images of air! ....Od.24.22.348.

SEMBLANT
Two youths approach, whose semblant features prove ....Od.4.33.121.

SEMELE'S
In flames, like Semele's, be brought to bed, ...5.DunB3.315.335.

SEMELES
In flames, like Semeles, he brought to bed, ...5.DunA3.313.186.

SENATE
Than Cæsar with a senate at his heels. ....3.EOM4.258.152.
P. But bribes a Senate, and the Land's betray'd. ....3.Ep3.34A.88.
But bribes a Senate, and the Land's betray'd. ....3.Ep3.34.88.
In Britain's Senate he a seat obtains, ...3.Ep3.393.124.
F— loves the *Senate, Hockley-Hole* his Brother ....4.HS1.49.9.
Like *Cato,* give his little Senate laws, ...4.Arbu.209.111.
From morn to night, at Senate, Rolls, and Hall, ...4.1HE6.36.239.
And shake alike the Senate and the Field: ....4.EpS2.87.318.
And free at once the Senate and the Throne; ....4.1740.90.337.
Unseen at Church, at Senate, or at Court, ...5.DunB4.338.376.
At Senate, and at Bar, how welcome would'st thou be! ....6.8.30.18.
While *Cato* gives his little senate laws, ...6.32.23.96.
Like Cato, gives his little Senate Laws, ...6.49iii.25.143.
What more could *G[eor]ge* or *S[ena]te* gain? ....6.64.16.190*.
Like *Cato* gives his *little Senate* Laws, ...6.98.61.285.
The Senate heard him, and his Country lov'd. ....6.132.8.362.
And joins the sacred Senate of the Skies. ....Il.1.294.101.
There calls a Senate of the Peers around. ....Il.2.66.130.
A Senate void of Order as of Choice, ...Il.7.416.385.
A Senate void of Union as of Choice, ...Il.7.416A.385.
When *Jove* conven'd the Senate of the Skies, ...Il.8.3.394.
Or mix among the Senate of the Gods? ....Il.14.380.180.
And summons all the Senate of the Skies. ....Il.20.8.393.

SENATE'S
The *S[ena]te's,* and then *H[er]v[e]y's* once agen. ....4.EpS1.72.303.
In vain a nations zeal a senate's cares ....6.130.31.359.

SENATES
Judges and Senates have been bought for gold, ...3.EOM4.187.145.
Tho' wond'ring Senates hung on all he spoke, ...3.Ep1.184.31.
Or ship off Senates to some distant Shore; ....3.Ep3.74A.93.
Or ship off Senates to a distant Shore; ....3.Ep3.74.93.
Senates degen'rate, Patriots disagree, ...3.Ep3.150.105.
Thy Nobles Sl[ave]s, thy Se[nate]s bought with gold. ....4.1740.81.336*.
Schools, courts, and senates shall my laws obey, ...5.DunA1.251Z5.93.
'Till Senates nod to Lullabies divine, ...5.DunB1.317.293.
Senates and Courts with Greek and Latin rule, ...5.DunB4.179.359.
Teach Kings to fiddle, and make Senates dance. ....5.DunB4.598.402.
"In Senates fam'd for many a Speech, ...6.79.89.221.
He talks of Senates, and of Courtly Tribes, ...6.96v.15.280.

SENATOR
The pale Boy-Senator yet tingling stands, ...5.DunB4.147.355.
The Senator at Cricket urge the Ball; ....5.DunB4.592.402.

SENCE
See SENSE.
Then, in the scale of Life and Sence, 'tis plain ....3.EOM1.47A.19.
So the learnd Bard that starves with all his Sence ....4.JD2A.17.134.
See Metaphysic call for aid on Sence! ....5.DunA3.352.193.
And gain in morals what they lose in sence. ....6.82ix(c).2.234.

SEND
And thro' th' *Achaian* Cities send the Sound. ....1.TrSt.164.417.
And to the Shades a Ghost Triumphant send; ....1.TrSt.777.442.
And send him safe to *Lycia,* distant far ....1.TrES.233.458.
And send the Godly in a Pett, to pray. ....2.RL4.64.189.
And send up Vows from *Rosamonda's* Lake. ....2.RL5.136.211.
Cries, "Send me, Gods! a whole Hog *barbecu'd!"* ....4.HS2.26.55.
You love a Verse, take such as I can send. ....4.2HE2.2.165.
And send his Wife to Church, his Son to school. ....4.2HE1.164.209.
"Send for him up, take no excuse. ....4.HS6.36.253.
Send her to Court, you send her to her Grave. ....4.1HE1.119.287.
Send her to Court, you send her to her Grave. ....4.1HE1.119.287.

SEND (CONTINUED)

The Goddess then: "Who best can send on high .... 5.DunA2.153.120.
'Till all tun'd equal, send a gen'ral hum. .... 5.DunA2.354.143.
The Goddess then: "Who best can send on high .... 5.DunB2.161.303.
'Till all tun'd equal, send a gen'ral hum. .... 5.DunB2.386.316.
Send it, I pray, by the next Post, ... 6.10.115.28.
To Heav'n familiar his bold vows shall send, ... 6.21.3.69.
God send the K[ing] safe landing, ... 6.61.51.183.
And send what *A[rgy]le,* would he *write,* might have writ. .... 6.62iii.4.185.
Oh be thou blest with all that Heav'n can send, ... 6.86.1.244.
But send him, honest *Job,* thy *Wife.* .... 6.101.34.291.
To send at a dash all these Nymphs to the Devil? .... 6.122.10.341.
To thee, sweet *Fop,* these Lines I send, ... 6.135.1.366.
To her own *Chrysa* send the black-ey'd Maid. .... Il.1.124.93.
And send thee scourg'd, and howling thro' the Fleet. .... Il.2.325.142.
Full fifty Ships they send, and each conveys .... Il.2.608.156.
Which *Bessa, Thronus,* and rich *Cynos* send: .... Il.2.635.157.
A bloodless Race, that send a feeble Voice. .... Il.3.202.201.
And you whom distant Nations send to War! .... Il.6.136.330.
Whose unber'd Arms, by fits, thick Flashes send. .... Il.8.706.429.
Yet more to sanctify the Word you send, ... Il.9.223.444.
Of all the Warriors yonder Host can send, ... Il.9.269.446.
If mighty *Neptune* send propitious Gales; .... Il.9.474.456.
Why shou'd we Gifts to proud *Achilles* send, ... Il.9.816.474.
To send more Heroes to th' infernal Shade, ... Il.10.589.28.
By *Hector* send our Forces to explore, ... Il.10.662.31.
Less keen those Darts the fierce *Ilythiæ* send, ... Il.11.348.50.
And to their Owners send them nobly back. .... Il.13.381.123.
This, my third Victim, to the Shades I send. .... Il.13.561.133.
Shall send *Patroclus,* but shall send in vain. .... Il.15.70.199.
Shall send *Patroclus,* but shall send in vain. .... Il.15.70.199.
And send him safe to *Lycia,* distant far .... Il.16.536.265.
And send the living *Lycians* to the Dead. .... Il.16.688.271.
The Son of *Panthus,* skill'd the Dart to send, ... Il.17.11.288.
Ah would *Minerva* send me Strength to rear .... Il.17.634.312.
Large Gifts they promise, and their Elders send; .... Il.18.521.346.
To keep, or send the Presents, be thy Care; .... Il.19.145.377.
And the last Blaze send *Ilion* to the Skies. .... Il.22.521.478.
Their Heart, their Eyes, their Voice, they send before; .... Il.23.439.507.
Far as an able Arm the Disk can send, ... Il.23.511.510.
And send their Souls before him as he flies. .... Il.23.898.524.
Oh send me, Gods! e'er that sad Day shall come, ... Il.24.307.549.
His winged Messenger to send from high, ... Il.24.361.551.
My Steps, and send thee, Guardian of my way. .... Il.24.462.556.
May send him thee to chase that Foe away. .... Il.24.611.562.
Thus from my walls the much-lov'd son to send .... Od.3.445.108.
Another to *Laerceus* must we send, ... Od.3.539.113.
Send not to good *Laertes,* nor engage .... Od.4.993.164.
Me now the guardian Goddess deigns to send, ... Od.4.1083.168.
But never, never shall *Calypso* send .... Od.5.179.180.
Or some enormous whale the God may send, ... Od.5.538.198.
A wretched exile to his country send, ... Od.7.200.245.
In haste their heralds send the gifts to bring. .... Od.8.434.287.
If home thou send us, and vouchsafe to spare. .... Od.9.413.323.
And send thee howling to the realms of night! .... Od.9.613.332.
And send out spies the dubious coast to view. .... Od.10.180.349.
Be it my task to send with ample stores .... Od.11.438.406.
Safe to my home to send your happy guest. .... Od.13.51.3.
Then send the stranger to his native shore. .... Od.13.67.4.
And send swift arrows from the bounding string, ... Od.14.262.49.
His guest, and send thee where thy soul desires. .... Od.14.585.65.
Send to the town thy vessel with thy friends, ... Od.15.44.71.
Say if to us the Gods these Omens send, ... Od.15.188.77.
And forth to pasture send the bristly care. .... Od.16.4.102.
Lest heav'n in vengeance send some mightier woe. .... Od.18.129.172.
Send, oh *Diana,* send the sleep of death! .... Od.18.240.178.
Send, oh *Diana,* send the sleep of death! .... Od.18.240.178.
They send their eager souls with ev'ry look, ... Od.18.253.179.
Shall send thee howling all in blood away! .... Od.18.384.186.
With royal gifts to send you honour'd home!— .... Od.19.361.211.
"With gifts of price shall send him joyous home." .... Od.19.483.220.
Thy shaft, and send me joyful to the dead: .... Od.20.95.237.
To some *Sicilian* mart these courtiers send, ... Od.20.456.255.
And thro' twelve ringlets the fleet arrow send, ... Od.21.76.262.
What Souls and Spirits shall it send below? .... Od.21.162.267.
And send us with some humbler wife to live, ... Od.21.169.267.
Far hence thy banish'd consort shall we send; .... Od.22.241.298.

SENDERS

A Pox of all Senders .... 6.42iv.1.118.
A pox on all Senders .... 6.42iv.1A.118.

SENDS

When *Albion* sends her eager Sons to War, ... 1.W-F.106.161.
He sends a Monster, horrible and fell, ... 1.TrSt.705.439.
And sends the brave *Epicles* to the Shades, ... 1.TrES.98.453.
And *Ajax* sends his Jav'lin at the Foe; .... 1.TrES.136.454.
Thus to the Sea-green Sisters sends his Pray'r. .... 1.TrUl.239.473.
Strait the black Clarion sends a horrid Sound, ... 2.TemF.402.282.
A mightier Pow'r the strong direction sends, ... 3.EOM2.165.74.
God sends not ill; if rightly understood, ... 3.EOM4.113.139.
God sends not Ill, 'tis Nature lets it fall .... 3.EOM4.113Z1.139.
Hear then the truth: "'Tis Heav'n each Passion sends, ... 3.Ep3.161.106.
Bids Bubo build, and sends him such a Guide: .... 3.Ep4.20.138.
Bids *Babo* build, and sends him such a Guide: .... 3.Ep4.20A.138.
Pitholeon sends to me: "You know his Grace, ... 4.Arbu.49.99.
My Counsel sends to execute a Deed: .... 4.2HE2.92.171.
His Sister sends, her vot'ress, from above. .... 5.DunA2.208.127.
His sister sends, her vot'ress, from above. .... 5.DunB2.216.306.
And sends the brave *Abantes* to the Wars: .... Il.2.642.157.
And sends thee One, a Sample of her Host. .... Il.7.280.378.
But since what Honour asks, the Gen'ral sends, ... Il.9.645.466.
And sends by those whom most thy Heart commends, ... Il.9.646.466.
Or sends soft Snows to whiten all the Shore, ... Il.10.7.2.
Sends he some Spy, amidst these silent Hours, ... Il.10.43.4.
And sends the brave *Epicles* to the Shades; .... Il.12.452.98.

SENDS (CONTINUED)

And *Ajax* sends his Javelin at the Foe; .... Il.12.490.99.
The riven Armour sends a jarring Sound: .... Il.13.553.132.
Jove sends one Gust, and bids them roll away. .... Il.14.26.158.
Sends forth his active Mind from Place to Place, ... Il.15.88.200.
See, and be strong! the Thund'rer sends thee Aid. .... Il.15.289.208.
This Instant sends thee down to *Pluto's* Coast, ... Il.16.755.273.
And sends his Voice in Thunder to the Skies: .... Il.17.96.291.
Then thro' the Field he sends his Voice aloud, ... Il.17.574.311.
Who sends thee, Goddess! from th' Etherial Skies? .... Il.18.219.332.
The burning River sends his earnest Pray'r. .... Il.21.431.438.
And mounts the Walls, and sends around her View: .... Il.22.595.480.
The Day, that to the Shades the Father sends, ... Il.22.628.482.
With Mules and Waggons sends a chosen Band; .... Il.23.135.493.
And sends before old *Phœnix* to the Place, ... Il.23.435.507.
And *Troy* sends forth one universal Groan. .... Il.24.885.573.
And sends in shouts applauses to the skies. .... Od.8.416.286.
He sends a dreadful groan: the rocks around .... Od.9.469.325.
What wond'rous man heav'n sends us in our guest! .... Od.11.418.405.
Thus to the sea-green sisters sends his pray'r. .... Od.13.406.26.
'Tis *Jove* that sends the stranger and the poor. .... Od.14.68.39.
Sends forth her peers, and every peer a foe: .... Od.16.130.109.
Some God no doubt this strange kindly sends; .... Od.18.400.187.
Or heav'n delusion sends. But hence, away! .... Od.18.456.190.

SENESHAL

The Seneshal rebuk'd in haste withdrew; .... Od.4.47.122.

SENIOR

If there's a Senior, who contemns this Age; .... 6.128.22.356.
The Senior spoke, and sate. To whom reply'd .... Il.7.428.385.
And from the Senior Pow'r, submiss retires; .... Il.21.544.444.
A Senior honour'd, and a Friend belov'd! .... Il.23.720.519.
Meet then the Senior, far renown'd for sense, ... Od.3.23.87.
To these the Senior thus declar'd his will: .... Od.3.530.113.

SENIOR'S

The Senior's judgment all the crowd admire, ... 5.DunA2.277.135.
The Senior's judgment all the crowd admire, ... 5.DunB2.289.309.

SENIORS

There sate the Seniors of the *Trojan* Race, ... Il.3.191.200.
Up rose nine Seniors, chosen to survey .... Od.8.295.279.
Much ask'd the Seniors; till *Piræus* came. .... Od.17.83.136.
Then sad in council all the Seniors sate, ... Od.24.481.371.

SENSATIONS

And quick sensations skip from vein to vein, ... 5.DunA2.204.126.
And quick sensations skip from vein to vein; .... 5.DunB2.212.306.

SENSE

See SENCE.
Whose Sense instructs us, and whose Humour charms, ... 1.PAu.9.81.
To tire our *Patience,* than mis-lead our *Sense:* .... 1.EOC.4.239.
So by *false Learning* is *good Sense* defac'd; .... 1.EOC.25.241.
In search of *Wit* these lose their *common Sense,* .... 1.EOC.28.242.
And mark *that Point* where Sense and Dullness *meet.* .... 1.EOC.51.244.
These leave the Sense, their Learning to display, ... 1.EOC.116.252.
These lost the Sense, their Learning to display, ... 1.EOC.116A.252.
These lost their Sense, their Learning to display, ... 1.EOC.116B.252.
These lose the Sense, their Learning to display, ... 1.EOC.116C.252.
T' *admire* Superior Sense, and *doubt* their own! .... 1.EOC.200.263.
And fills up all the *mighty Void* of *Sense!* .... 1.EOC.210.264.
The *Sense,* they humbly take upon Content. .... 1.EOC.308.274.
Much *Fruit* of *Sense* beneath is rarely found. .... 1.EOC.310.274.
Ancients in *Phrase,* meer Moderns in their *Sense!* .... 1.EOC.325.275.
The *Sound* must seem an *Eccho* to the *Sense.* .... 1.EOC.365.281.
That always shows *Great Pride,* or *Little Sense;* .... 1.EOC.387.284.
For Fools *Admire,* but Men of Sense *Approve;* .... 1.EOC.391.284.
'Twixt Sense and Nonsense daily change their Side. .... 1.EOC.435.288.
And none had *Sense enough to be Confuted.* .... 1.EOC.443.289.
But *Sense* surviv'd, when *merry Jests* were past; .... 1.EOC.460.291.
Good-Nature and *Good-Sense* must ever join; .... 1.EOC.524.297.
That not alone what to your *Sense* is due, ... 1.EOC.564.305.
Be *silent* always when you *doubt* your Sense; .... 1.EOC.566.305.
That only makes *Superior* Sense *belov'd.* .... 1.EOC.577.306.
For the *worst Avarice* is that of *Sense:* .... 1.EOC.579.306.
Strain out the last, dull droppings of their Sense, ... 1.EOC.608.308.
Distrustful *Sense* with modest Caution speaks; .... 1.EOC.626.310.
And without Method *talks* us into Sense, ... 1.EOC.654.313.
The less my Sense, the more my Love appears. .... 1.TrSP.110.398.
Blest with much Sense, more Riches, and some Grace. .... 2.ChJM.4.15.
Conceive me Sirs, nor take my Sense amiss, ... 2.ChJM.113.20.
Who past all Pleasure, damn the Joys of Sense, ... 2.ChJM.174.23.
(Who, tho' not *Faith,* had *Sense* as well as We) .... 2.ChJM.179.23.
That was with Sense, but not with Virtue blest; .... 2.ChJM.240.26.
Imperfect Objects may your Sense beguile: .... 2.ChJM.798.53.
Unless good Sense preserve what Beauty gains: .... 2.RL5.16.200.
Back thro' the paths of pleasing sense I ran, ... 2.ElAb.69.324.
How shall I lose the sin, yet keep the sense, ... 2.ElAb.191.335.
Go, wiser thou! and in thy scale of sense .... 3.EOM1.113.29.
Vast Range of Sense! from Man's imperial race .... 3.EOM1.209A.41.
In the nice bee, what sense so subtly true .... 3.EOM1.219.42.
What thin partitions Sense from Thought divide: .... 3.EOM1.226.43.
And quitting sense call imitating God; .... 3.EOM2.26.58.
That sees immediate good by present sense; .... 3.EOM2.73.64.
And Grace and Virtue, Sense and Reason split, ... 3.EOM2.83.64.
And each vacuity of sense by Pride: .... 3.EOM2.286.89.
Equal is Common Sense, and Common Ease. .... 3.EOM4.34.131.
That such are happier, shocks all common sense. .... 3.EOM4.52.133.
Reason's whole pleasure, all the joys of Sense, ... 3.EOM4.79.136.
All Reason's pleasures, all the joys of Sense, ... 3.EOM4.79A.136.
Grasp the whole worlds of Reason, Life, and Sense, ... 3.EOM4.357.163.
When Sense subsides, and Fancy sports in sleep, ... 3.Ep1.46.18.
(So Darkness strikes the sense no less than Light) .... 3.Ep1.112.23.
Flavia's a Wit, has too much sense to Pray, ... 3.Ep2.87.57.

SENSE (CONTINUED)

To you gave Sense, Good-humour, and a Poet. ....3.Ep2.292.74.
The Sense to value Riches, with the Art ....3.Ep3.219.111.
And something previous ev'n to Taste—'tis Sense: ....3.Ep4.42.140.
Good Sense, which only is the gift of Heav'n, ...3.Ep4.43.140.
Still follow Sense, of ev'ry Art the Soul, ...3.Ep4.65.143.
And Splendor borrows all her rays from Sense. ....3.Ep4.180.154.
Begin with Sense, of ev'ry Art the Soul, ...3.Ep4.65A.143.
For Splendor borrows all her rays from Sense. ....3.Ep4.180A.154.
To wholesome Solitude, the Nurse of Sense: ....4.JD4.185.41.
But strong in sense, and wise without the rules. ....4.HS2.10.55.
Were he a Dupe of only common Sense. ....4.HAdv.68.81.
No Sense to guide, no Reason to enquire, ...4.HAdv.144.87.
While pure Description held the place of Sense? ....4.Arbu.148.106.
And all they want is spirit, taste, and sense. ....4.Arbu.160.108.
And he, who now to sense, now nonsense leaning, ...4.Arbu.185.109.
Or Envy holds a whole Week's war with Sense, ...4.Arbu.252.114.
And show the Sense of it, without the Love; ....4.Arbu.294.117.
"Satire or Sense alas! can *Sporus* feel? ....4.Arbu.307.118.
"Satire or Sense alas! he cannot feel? ....4.Arbu.307B.118.
This Town, I had the Sense to hate it too; ....4.JD2A.2.132.
And hopes no captious Fools will wrest my sense ....4.JD2A.132.144.
This Town, I had the sense to hate it too: ....4.JD2.2.133.
Sense, past thro' him, no longer is the same, ...4.JD2.33.135.
Let no Court-Sycophant pervert my sense, ...4.JD2.126.145.
"Yours *Cowper's* Manner—and yours *Talbot's* Sense." ....4.2HE2.134.175.
(For Use will father what's begot by Sense) ....4.2HE2.170.177.
More on a Reader's sense, than Gazer's eye. ....4.2HE1.351.225.
BARNARD in spirit, sense, and truth abounds. ....4.1HE1.85.285.
At Sense and Virtue, balance all agen. ....4.EpS1.60.302.
And all the well-whipt Cream of Courtly Sense, ...4.EpS1.70.303.
And all I sung should be the *Nation's Sense:* ....4.EpS1.78.304.
But past the Sense of human Miseries, ...4.EpS1.101.305.
CARLETON'S calm Sense, and STANHOPE'S noble Flame, ...4.EpS2.80.317.
Who think a Coxcomb's Honour like his Sense; ....4.EpS2.202.324.
Plung'd for his sense, but found no bottom there; ....5.DunA1.113.77.
Now leave all memory of sense behind: ....5.DunA1.230.90.
And instant, fancy feels th' imputed sense; ....5.DunA2.192.124.
When fancy flags, and sense is at a stand. ....5.DunA2.222.128.
Soft, creeping, words on words, the sense compose, ...5.DunA2.357.143.
Then raptures high the seat of sense o'erflow, ...5.DunA3.5.150.
And blunt the sense, and fit it for a scull ....5.DunA3.17.151.
"Sense, speech, and measure, living tongues and dead, ...5.DunA3.161.165.
The source of Newton's Light, of Bacon's Sense! ....5.DunA3.216.176.
Plung'd for his sense, but found no bottom there, ...5.DunB1.119.278.
Guard the sure barrier between that and Sense; ....5.DunB1.178.283.
And once betray'd me into common sense: ....5.DunB1.188.283.
Now leave all memory of sense behind: ....5.DunB1.276.290.
And, instant, fancy feels th' imputed sense; ....5.DunB2.200.305.
When fancy flags, and sense is at a stand. ....5.DunB2.230.307.
Soft creeping, words on words, the sense compose, ...5.DunB2.389.316.
Then raptures high the seat of Sense o'erflow, ...5.DunB3.5.320.
And blunt the sense, and fit it for a skull ....5.DunB3.25.321.
"Sense, speech, and measure, living tongues and dead, ...5.DunB3.167.328.
The source of Newton's Light, of Bacon's Sense! ....5.DunB3.218.331.
Break all their nerves, and fritter all their sense: ....5.DunB4.56.347.
If Music meanly borrows aid from Sense: ....5.DunB4.64.348.
As Fancy opens the quick springs of Sense, ...5.DunB4.156.357.
In ancient Sense if any needs will deal, ...5.DunB4.229.365.
His royal Sense, of Op'ra's or the Fair; ....5.DunB4.314.374.
Wraps in her Veil, and frees from sense of Shame. ....5.DunB4.336.376.
By common sense to common knowledge bred, ...5.DunB4.467.386.
Lost was the Nation's Sense, nor could be found, ...5.DunB4.611.404.
'*till* drown'd was Sense, and Shame, and Right, and Wrong— ....5.DunB4.625.406.
And *Metaphysic* calls for aid on *Sense!* ....5.DunB4.646.408.
But Sense must sure thy safest Plunder be, ...6.7.13.16.
Afflicted *Sense* thou kindly dost set free, ...6.8.16.18.
Be but to teach the Ignorant more Sense; ....6.16.8.53.
Railing at Men of Sense, to show their Wit; ....6.17iv.10.59.
And pays prodigious dear for—Sense. ....6.29.26.83.
Dare to have sense your selves; assert the stage, ...6.32.43.97.
Unbarrel thy just Sense, and broach thy Wit. ....6.48i.6.133*.
Well spread with Sense, shall be the Nation's Plaister. ....6.48ii.12.134.
Know, Sense, like Charity, *begins at Home.* ....6.49ii.16.140.
Who all my Sense confin'd ....6.50.6.146.
Who hast my Sense confin'd ....6.50.6A.146.
Who last my Sense confin'd ....6.50.6B.146.
Who charm the sense, or mend the heart; ....6.51i.10.151.
Fill'd with the sense of age, the fire of youth; ....6.57.7.169.
To writing of good Sense. ....6.58.12.171.
Blockheads with Reason Men of Sense abhor; ....6.60.5.178.
And all they want is Spirit, Taste, and Sense. ....6.98.10.283.
In Sense still wanting, tho' he lives on Theft, ...6.98.33.284.
Johnson, who now to Sense, now Nonsense leaning, ...6.98.35.284.
Aw'd without Sense, and without Beauty charm'd, ...6.99.2.286.
But what avails to lay down rules for sense? ....6.106iii.1.307.
And thou! whose sense, whose humour, and whose rage, ...6.106iv.1.307.
Blest with plain Reason and with sober Sense; ....6.115.2.322.
The Sense and Taste of one that bears ....6.119.15.337.
The wit & sense of one who bears ....6.119.15A.337.
When you attack my Morals, Sense, or Truth, ...6.129.6.357.
In Manners plain, in Sense alone refind, ...6.134.5.364.
Yet Master *Pope,* whom Truth and Sense ....6.135.87.369.
Yet Master P[ope] Whom Witt and Sense ....6.135.87A.369.
Who Heaven's Lore reject for brutish Sense; ....6.137.7.373.
The good their Virtue might effect, or sense, ...6.147iv.3.391.
The good their Virtue would effect, or sense, ...6.147iv.3A.391.
Who lost to Sense of gen'rous Freedom past ....Il.1.307.102.
Smit with a conscious Sense, retires behind, ...Il.3.45.190.
Just was his Sense, and his Expression plain, ...Il.3.276.205.
With pleasing Sweets his fainting Sense renews, ...Il.3.471.214.
Is this the Chief, who lost to Sense of Shame ....Il.3.533.217.
If yet not lost to all the Sense of Shame, ...Il.6.350.343.
Of Sense and Justice, run where Frenzy drives; ....Il.9.493.456.
Sure Heav'n resumes the little Sense it lent. ....Il.12.272.91.
With Beauty, Sense, and ev'ry Work of Art: ....Il.13.542.132.

SENSE (CONTINUED)

The Sense of Gods with more than mortal Sweets. ....Il.14.202.169.
His Sense returning with the coming Breeze; ....Il.15.271.207.
Nor more in Councils fam'd for solid Sense, ...Il.15.322.209.
His gen'rous Sense he not in vain imparts; ....Il.15.674.222.
To their own Sense condemn'd! and left to chuse ....Il.18.363.339.
To whom was Voice, and Sense, and Science given ....Il.18.489.345.
Yet curst with Sense! a Wretch, whom in his Rage ....Il.22.82.456.
Nor I thy Equal, or in Years, or Sense. ....Il.23.670.516.
Some Sense of Duty, some Desire to save. ....Il.24.194.544.
Some Sense of Duty, some Desire to save. ....Il.24.224.546.
Meet then the Senior, far renown'd for sense, ...Od.3.23.87.
All sense of woe delivers to the wind. ....Od.4.308.134.
With nectar'd drops the sick'ning sense restor'd. ....Od.4.600.148.
But giv'n the sense, to pity, and to feel. ....Od.5.246.183.
Fit words attended on his weighty sense, ...Od.7.212.247.
Some greatly think, some speak with manly sense; ....Od.8.186.272.
Fear only fools, secure in men of sense: ....Od.8.272.278.
He feasted ev'ry sense with ev'ry joy. ....Od.8.490.289.
His sense lay cover'd with the dozy fume; ....Od.9.429.323.
Still curst with sense, their mind remains alone, ...Od.10.280.356.
And take the painful sense of toil away. ....Od.10.428.365.
Nor much for sense, nor much for courage fam'd; ....Od.10.660.375.
Heav'ns! how he charmed us with a flow of sense, ...Od.11.623.414.
What man, or God, deceiv'd his better sense, ...Od.14.206.45.
Let wit cast off the sullen yoke of sense. ....Od.14.525.62.
To read this sign, and mystick sense of heav'n. ....Od.15.193.77.
Fresh to my sense, and always in my mind. ....Od.17.335.147.
O'er all her sense, as the couch she prest, ...Od.18.221.177.
The scourge, the scourge shall lash thee into sense. ....Od.18.388.186.
When woes the waking sense alone assail, ...Od.20.98.237.
No conscious blush, no sense of right restrains ....Od.20.213.243.
To ev'ry sense is lost, to reason blind: ....Od.20.434.254.
Her equal pow'r each faithful sense obeys. ....Od.20.440.254.
Is common sense quite banish'd from thy breast? ....Od.21.310.274.
Mov'd by no weak surmize, but sense of shame, ...Od.21.347.276.
When *Agelaus* thus: Has none the sense ....Od.22.148.294.

SENSE-LESS

A sense-less, worth-less, and unhonour'd crowd; ....4.2HE1.306.221.

SENSELESS

But senseless, lifeless! Idol void and vain! ....5.DunA2.42.100.
But senseless, lifeless! idol void and vain! ....5.DunB2.46.298.
They left their senseless, treating, drunken Host. ....6.17iv.21.59.
Let Men their Days in senseless Strife employ, ...Il.1.744.123.
(Unhappy Change!) now senseless, pale, he found, ...Il.18.281.335.
A senseless Corps! inanimated Clay! ....Il.22.561.479.
Nor vent on senseless Earth thy Vengeance vain, ...Il.24.173.543.
Lay senseless, and supine, amidst the flock. ....Od.9.355.321.

SENSES

No Senses stronger than his brain can bear. ....3.EOM1.192A.38.
On diff'rent senses diff'rent objects strike; ....3.EOM2.128.70.
Steals my senses, shuts my sight, ...6.31ii.10.94.
His Senses wandring to the Verge of Death. ....Il.15.14.194.
And calls his Senses from the Verge of Death. ....Il.15.66.197.
His Eyes flash Sparkles, his stunn'd Senses reel ....Il.16.957.280.
And wrapt his Senses in the Cloud of Grief; ....Il.18.26.325.
Jove plung'd my senses in the death of sleep. ....Od.7.369.254.

SENSIBLE

And sensible soft Melancholy. ....6.89.8.250.
Seem'd sensible of Woe, and droop'd his Head: ....Il.19.447.390.

SENSUAL

The scale of sensual, mental pow'rs ascends: ....3.EOM1.208.41.
Of *sensual,* and of *mental* Faculties. ....3.EOM1.208A.41.

SENT

Sent up in Vapours to the *Baron's* Brain ....2.RL3.119.176.
Chang'd to a Bird, and sent to flit in Air, ...2.RL3.123.177.
Thro undulating Air the Sounds are sent, ...2.TemF.446.285.
Scarce H[awle]y's self had sent it to the dogs? ....3.Ep3.54A.90.
And Gold but sent to keep the fools in play, ...3.Ep3.5.83.
"Sir, Spain has sent a thousand jars of oil; ....3.Ep3.44.89.
Could he himself have sent it to the dogs? ....3.Ep3.54.90.
But duly sent his family and wife. ....3.Ep3.382.124.
Who sent the Thief that stole the Cash, away, ...4.2HE2.25.167.
Who sent the Thief who stole the Cash, away, ...4.2HE2.25A.167.
Who cropt our Ears, and sent them to the King. ....4.EpS1.18.298.
When the last blaze sent Ilion to the skies. ....5.DunA1.212.88.
All vain petitions, sent by winds on high, ...5.DunA2.85B.108.
Angel of Dulness, sent to scatter round ....5.DunA3.253.178.
Sent with a Pass, and vagrant thro' the land; ....5.DunB1.232.287.
When the last blaze sent Ilion to the skies. ....5.DunB1.256.289.
Angel of Dulness, sent to scatter round ....5.DunB3.257.332.
But she, good Goddess, sent to ev'ry child ....5.DunB4.529.394.
Has sent thee down in mercy to mankind, ...6.20.46.67.
Gazettes sent Gratis down, and frank'd, ...6.39.7.110.
In the *Lines* that you sent, are the *Muses* and *Graces;* ....6.62i.1.185.
In the Song that you sent, are the *Muses* and *Graces;* ....6.62i.1A.185.
Sent his own lightning, and the Victims seiz'd. ....6.69i.6.198.
O'erjoy'd to see what God had sent. ....6.93.24.257.
Some said that *D[ou]gl[a]s* sent should be, ...6.94.17.259.
The good Wife to the Surgeon sent, ...6.94.37.260.
He sent him War, or Plague, or Famine sore. ....6.137.10.373.
May TOM, whom heav'n sent down to raise ....6.150.15.399.
'Tis where God sent some that adore him ....6.151.7.399.
Sent by the * Sister and the Wife of *Jove;* ....Il.1.262.99.
Sent in *Jove's* Anger on a slavish Race, ...Il.1.306.101.
The fair *Chruseis* to her Sire was sent, ...Il.1.504.112.
Sent by great *Jove* to him who rules the Host, ...Il.2.103.131.
From *Jove* himself the dreadful Sign was sent. ....Il.2.373.145.
Jove, on the Right, a prosp'rous Signal sent, ...Il.2.418.147.
Whom *Troy* sent forth, the beauteous *Paris* came: ....Il.3.26.189.

SENT (CONTINUED)

He said, and poiz'd in Air the Jav'lin sent, ... Il.3.439.213.
As the red Comet from *Saturnius* sent .... Il.4.101.225.
The Gods (they cry'd) the Gods this Signal sent, ... Il.4.111.225.
Next, sent by *Greece* from where *Asopus* flows, ... Il.4.436.241.
Sent by great *Ajax* to the Shades of Hell; .... Il.4.543.247.
His Lance bold *Thoas,* at the Conqu'ror sent, ... Il.4.610.250.
Whom *Borus* sent (his Son and only Joy) .... Il.5.59.269.
From *Menelaus'* Arm the Weapon sent, ... Il.5.71.269.
Bold *Merion* sent him to the Realms of Hell. .... Il.5.76.270.
Curs'd be the Fate that sent me to the Field, ... Il.5.266.280.
His massy Spear with matchless Fury sent .... Il.5.758.303.
And Numbers more his Sword had sent to Hell: .... Il.5.837.305.
Thy Hands I arm'd, and sent thee forth to War: .... Il.5.1007.315.
Ulysses' Spear *Pidytes* sent to Hell; .... Il.6.36.325.
To *Lycia* the devoted Youth he sent, ... Il.6.209.336.
The breathless Carcase to your Navy sent, ... Il.7.97.368.
Then shall our Herald to th' *Atrides* sent, ... Il.7.448.386.
Of fragrant Wines the rich *Eunæus* sent .... Il.7.562.392.
His Eagle, sacred Bird of Heav'n! he sent, ... Il.8.297.411.
Let chosen Delegates this Hour be sent, ... Il.9.219.443.
He sent thee early to th' *Achaian* Host; .... Il.9.567.461.
On *Oeneus'* Fields she sent a monstrous Boar, ... Il.9.659.467.
She sent Embassadors, a chosen Band, ... Il.9.689.468.
And now th' elected Chiefs whom *Greece* had sent, ... Il.9.786.472.
Ulysses, sudden as the Voice was sent, ... Il.10.158.9.
A long-wing'd Heron great *Minerva* sent; .... Il.10.322.17.
Hector (he thought) had sent, and check'd his hast, ... Il.10.424.22.
Just then a deathful Dream *Minerva* sent; .... Il.10.578.28.
When baleful *Eris,* sent by *Jove's* Command, ... Il.11.5.35.
This glorious Gift he sent, nor sent in vain.) .... Il.11.30.36.
This glorious Gift he sent, nor sent in vain.) .... Il.11.30.36.
Around the Field his feather'd Shafts he sent, ... Il.11.475.55.
Strait to *Mænetius'* much-lov'd Son he sent; .... Il.11.736.68.
Mean time *Patroclus,* by *Achilles* sent, ... Il.11.788.71.
For sure to warn us *Jove* his Omen sent, ... Il.12.255.90.
Him to the Surgeons of the Camp he sent; .... Il.13.283.119.
To these the Warrior sent his Voice around. .... Il.13.607.135.
Sent from an Arm so strong, the missive Wood .... Il.13.638.136.
Sent from his follo'wing Host: The *Grecian* Train .... Il.13.1058.155.
And sent his Voice before his as he flew, ... Il.14.172.165.
And sent to *Argos,* and his native Shore. .... Il.15.34.195.
The distant Hunter sent into his Heart. .... Il.15.699.222.
Sent by great *Ajax* to the Shades of Hell. .... Il.15.909.232.
Now sent to *Troy, Achilles'* Arms to aid, ... Il.16.703.271.
Sent by the great *Æneas'* Arm in vain. .... Il.16.744.272.
Fierce as a Flood of Flame by *Vulcan* sent, ... Il.17.97.291.
O'er all the black Battalions sent his View, ... Il.17.123.292.
Swift thro' the spacious Plain he sent a Look; .... Il.17.213.295.
Sent by great *Ajax* to the Shades of Hell. .... Il.17.349.301.
Swift to revenge it, sent his angry Lance; .... Il.17.399.302.
When from the Ships he sent the *Pylian* Band. .... Il.17.439.304.
The Lord of Thunders sent the blue-ey'd Maid. .... Il.17.615.312.
And sent his Soul with ev'ry Lance he threw. .... Il.17.647.313.
And round on all sides sent his piercing View. .... Il.17.760.318.
To *Troy* I sent him; but the Fates ordain .... Il.18.77.326.
He sent refulgent to the Field of War, ... Il.18.280.335.
To *Troy* I sent him! but his native Shore .... Il.18.513.346.
The Shores resounded with the Voice he sent. .... Il.19.44.373.
This Instant from the Navy shall be sent .... Il.19.139.377.
And now the Delegates *Ulysses* sent, ... Il.19.243.383.
Sent Lightning on our Fleets, and scatt'er Fate?" .... Il.22.470.475.
Has that curst Hand sent headlong to the Tomb? .... Il.22.541.478.
The shining Charger to his Vessel sent. .... Il.23.702.517.
Of *Pluto* sent, a blood-polluted Ghost. .... Od.1.40.31.
Hermes I sent, while yet his soul remain'd .... Od.1.49.32.
Then *Discord,* sent by *Pallas* from above, ... Od.3.165.93.
Was sent to crown the long-protracted joy, ... Od.4.9.120.
Sent many a shade to *Pluto's* dreary coast. .... Od.4.354.136.
By *Jove* the stranger and the poor are sent, ... Od.6.247.222.
Of all my sorrows, sent by heav'n and fate! .... Od.7.325.251.
Of woes unnumber'd, sent by Heav'n and Fate? .... Od.9.16.301.
Three men were sent, deputed from the crew, ... Od.9.99.307.
The three we sent, from off th' inchanting ground .... Od.9.111.308.
Sent a tall stag, descending from the wood, ... Od.10.183.349.
Or has hell's Queen an empty Image sent, ... Od.11.257.394.
Sent with full force, cou'd reach the depth below. .... Od.12.102.436.
Sent by *Alcinous:* Of *Arete's* train .... Od.13.82.5.
To Fame I sent him, to acquire renown: .... Od.13.488.29.
To *Samos'* Isle she sent the wedded fair; .... Od.15.392.88.
A spy was sent their summons to convey: .... Od.15.494.94.
Sent the sad sire in solitude to stray; .... Od.16.149.109.
A stranger sent by Heav'n attends me there; .... Od.17.65.135.
Sent me (to punish my pursuit of gain) .... Od.17.509.157.
His grandsire sent him to the sylvan chace, ... Od.19.465.218.
(Of granted vows a certain signal sent) .... Od.20.144.240.
And sent him sober'd home, with better wit. .... Od.21.322.275.
When by thy self and by *Anticlia* sent, ... Od.24.386.367.
To watch the foe a trusty spy he sent: .... Od.24.566.375.

SENTENC'D

For when he sign'd thy Death, he sentenc'd me. .... 6.96iv.78.278.
Sentenc'd, 'tis true, by his inhuman Doom, ... Il.24.950.575.

SENTENCE

With *Warmth* gives Sentence, yet is always *Just;* .... 1.EOC.678.316.
Demands the Sentence, and contented dies. .... 1.TrSt.702.439.
And tag each Sentence with, *My Life! my Dear!* .... 2.ChWB.109.62.
With some grave Sentence out of Holy Writ. .... 2.ChWB.346.74.
When hungry Judges soon the Sentence sign, ... 2.RL*A*1.85.129.
The hungry Judges soon the Sentence sign, ... 2.RL3.21.170.
While Wits and Templers ev'ry sentence raise, ... 4.Arbu.211.111.
One Tragic sentence if I dare deride .... 4.2HE1.121.205.
While Fops and Templars ev'ry Sentence raise, ... 6.49iii.27.143.
Whilst Wits and Templars ev'ry Sentence raise, ... 6.49iii.27A.143.
While Wits and Templars ev'ry Sentence raise, ... 6.49iii.27B.143.

SENTENCE (CONTINUED)

While Wits and Templars ev'ry Sentence raise, ... 6.98.63.285.
In such base Sentence if thou couch thy Fear, ... Il.14.100.162.
In free Debate, my Friends, your Sentence speak: .... Il.18.299.336.
And rising solemn, each his Sentence spoke. .... Il.18.588.351.
My sentence hear: With stern distaste avow'd, ... Od.1.352.49.
In publick sentence, or in private thought; .... Od.3.156.93.
With vast applause the sentence all approve; .... Od.4.900.160.
Is then revers'd the sentence of the sky, ... Od.5.368.190.
The monster to the sword, part sentence gave .... Od.8.555.292.
This sentence pleas'd: Then all their steps addrest .... Od.13.19.2.
My sentence is gone forth, and 'tis decreed .... Od.18.309.181.
The sentence I propose, ye Peers, attend: .... Od.20.359.249.

SENTENCES

Who knew most *Sentences* was *deepest read;* .... 1.EOC.441.288.

SENTIMENT

"To crave your sentiment, if—'s your name. .... 4.JD4.67.31.
To nobler Sentiment to fire the Brave, ... 6.152.5.400.

SENTIMENTS

For Words well meant, and Sentiments sincere? .... Il.12.246.90.
With equal souls, and sentiments the same. .... Od.3.158.93.

SEP'RATE

Set up themselves, and drove a *sep'rate* Trade: .... 1.EOC.105Z1.251.
And sep'rate from their kindred dregs below; .... 2.Elegy.26.364.
For ever sep'rate, yet for ever near! .... 3.EOM1.224.43.
"Their sep'rate cells and properties maintain. .... 3.EOM3.188.112.
His sep'rate Troops let ev'ry Leader call, ... Il.2.432.148.
In sep'rate Squadrons these their Train divide, ... Il.2.753.161.
Each on the Coals the sep'rate Morsels lays, ... Il.24.790.570.
Sep'rate from all, I safely landed here; .... Od.3.223.96.
In sep'rate Islands crown'd with rising spires; .... Od.7.58.236.
The folded flocks each sep'rate from the rest, ... Od.9.257.317.
To sep'rate mansions, and retir'd to rest. .... Od.13.20.2.
In the same urn a sep'rate space contains .... Od.24.99.353.
Nor had the Sire been sep'rate from the Son. .... Od.24.443.370.

SEPTIMULEIUS

As much as did *Septimuleius;* .... 6.10.74.26.

SEPTUAGINT

Lo here the *Septuagint,—and Paul,* .... 6.39.15.110.

SEPULCHRAL

Sepulchral lyes our holy walls to grace, ... 5.DunA1.41.65.
Sepulchral Lyes, our holy walls to grace, ... 5.DunB1.43.273.
Sepulchral honours to *Elpenor's* shade. .... Od.12.12.430.
Long to protract the sad sepulchral hour; .... Od.19.431.215.

SEPULCHRE

How Rome her own sad Sepulchre appears, ... 6.71.2.202.
In one sad Sepulchre, one common Fall. .... Il.15.663.221.
That done, they bid the Sepulchre aspire, ... Il.23.317.502.

SEPULCHRES

Useless, unseen, as lamps in sepulchres; .... 2.Elegy.20.364.

SEPULCRAL

And sadly shar'd the last Sepulcral Feast. .... Il.24.1014.577.

SEPULTURE

The common Rites of Sepulture bestow, ... Il.22.429.473.

SEQUESTER'D

Bear me, oh bear me to sequester'd Scenes, ... 1.W-F.261.173.
So the struck deer in some sequester'd part .... 6.81.11.226.
So the struck doe in some sequester'd part .... 6.81.11A.226.
Lo! the struck deer in some sequester'd part .... 6.81.11B.226.
But now (what time in some sequester'd Vale .... Il.11.119.39.
(For what's sequester'd from celestial view?) .... Od.4.514.144.
Aside, sequester'd from the vast resort, ... Od.4.849.158.
Some smooth ascent, or safe-sequester'd bay. .... Od.5.561.199.
Beneath, sequester'd to the nymphs, is seen .... Od.17.242.143.
Exil'd for this to some sequester'd den, ... Od.21.393.279.

SERAPH

As the rapt Seraph that adores and burns; .... 3.EOM1.278.49.

SERAPH'S

He asks no Angel's wing, no Seraph's fire; .... 3.EOM1.110.28.
He asks no Angel's wing, or Seraph's fire; .... 3.EOM1.110A.28.
He asks no Angel's wing, nor Seraph's fire; .... 3.EOM1.110B.28.
A Newton's Genius, or a Seraph's flame: .... 5.DunA3.214.175.
For the fair *Hittite,* when on Seraph's Wings .... 6.137.9.373.

SERAPHIC

Where flames refin'd in breasts seraphic glow. .... 2.ElAb.320.345.
With sounds seraphic ring: .... 6.31ii.15.94.

SERAPHIM

As the rapt Seraphim that sings and burns; .... 3.EOM1.278A.49.

SERAPHS

And wings of Seraphs shed divine perfumes; .... 2.ElAb.218.338.

SERENE

The Moon, serene in Glory, mounts the Sky, ... 1.PWi.6.89.
Serene he look'd, and gave an awful Nod, ... 1.TrSt.282.422.
Serene in Torments, unconcern'd in Death; .... 2.ChJM.674.47.
O grace serene! oh virtue heav'nly fair! .... 2.ElAb.297.343.
Serene in Virgin Modesty she shines, ... 3.Ep2.255.70.
Preserve him social, chearful, and serene, ... 4.Arbu.416.127.
But all is quiet, jocund, and serene, ... 6.17iii.38.58.

SERENE (CONTINUED)

While he, serene in thought, shall calm survey ......6.21.19.69.
Serene, in virgin majesty, she shines; ......6.106i.6.306.
Serene, in virgin Modesty, she shines; ......6.106i.6A.306.
"And take (she said, and smil'd serene) ......6.140.3.378.
But who living and dying, serene still and free, ...6.144.7.386.
When not a Breath disturbs the deep Serene; ......II.8.689.428.
Not unrelenting: Then serene began ......II.24.651.564.
Those toils (*Telemachus* serene replies) ......Od.1.495.56.
Wash, and partake serene the friendly feast. ......Od.4.294.133.
From morn to eve, impassive and serene, ...Od.4.313.134.
With look serene I turn'd, and thus began. ......Od.12.247.444.
To whom with grace serene the Queen rejoin'd: ......Od.19.687.229.
Sage and serene *Telemachus* replies; ......Od.20.403.251.

SERENELY

Now setting *Phœbus* shone serenely bright, ...1.PAu.13.81.
The setting Sun now shone serenely bright, ...1.PAu.13A.81.
And in thy Glories more serenely shine; ......1.TrSt.40.411.
Serenely pure, and yet divinely strong, ...4.2HE2.172.177.
Serenely dreadful, and as fix'd as Fate. ......II.5.640.298.

SERENES

Then (while a Smile serenes his awful Brow) ......II.15.178.203.

SERENEST

Grace shines around her with serenest beams, ...2.ElAb.215.337.

SERENISSA

So gentle sleep from *Serenissa* flies, ...6.4i.3.9.
But *Serenissa* must becalm the breast. ......6.4i.14.9.
Ah *Serenissa,* from our arms ......6.4iii.1.10.
When *Serenissa* is away. ......6.4iv.21.11.

SERENISSA'S

No sweets but *Serenissa's* sighs. ......6.4v.4.11.
Go bask in *Serenissa's* eyes, ...6.6i.3.13.

SERENITY

Calm rest, and soft serenity of mind; ......6.23.16.73.

SERGEANT

The Judge to dance his brother Sergeant call; ......5.DunB4.591.401.

SERGEANTS

The *Temple* late two Brother Sergeants saw, ...4.2HE2.127.173.

SERIES

A dreadful Series of Intestine Wars, ...1.W-F.325.180.
And the long Series of succeeding Woe: ......1.TrSt.320.423.
Sooths the sad series of her tedious tale. ......5.DunA3.191z6.172.
Pleas'd with the series of each happy day. ......6.55.7.166.
Or in fair series laurell'd Bards be shown, ...6.71.61.204.
How trace the tedious series of our fate? ......Od.3.140.92.
The mournful series of my father's fate: ......Od.4.436.140.
The long, the mournful series to relate ......Od.7.324.251.
Th' unhappy series of a wand'rer's woe? ......Od.9.12.301.
Review the series of our lives, and taste ......Od.15.434.90.
The series of my toils, to sooth her woe; ......Od.19.57.195.
If the long series of my woes shall end; ......Od.20.121.239.
What-e'er thro' life's whole series I have done ......Od.22.228.297.

SERIOUS

Whether thou chuse Cervantes' serious air, ...5.DunA1.19.62.
Whether thou chuse Cervantes' serious air, ...5.DunB1.21.270.
A long, exact, and serious Comedy, ...6.19.22.62.
Peep'd in your fans, been serious, thus, and cry'd, ...6.41.4.113.
Whether thou choose Cervantes' serious air, ...6.106iv.3.307.
When social mirth unbent his serious soul, ...Od.1.335.48.
Thus serious they: but he who gilds the skies, ...Od.8.373.284.
Make the sage frolic, and the serious smile, ...Od.14.521.62.

SERMON

My tedious Sermon here is at an End. ......2.ChJM.215.25.
And close the Sermon, as beseem'd his Wit, ...2.ChWB.345.73.
And chose the Sermon, as beseem'd his Wit, ...2.ChWB.345A.73.
A standing sermon, at each year's expense, ...3.Ep4.21.139.
Hear Bethel's Sermon, one not vers'd in schools, ...4.HS2.9.55.

SERMONS

At Sermons too I shone in Scarlet gay; ......2.ChJM.287.71.
'Till show'rs of Sermons, Characters, Essays, ...5.DunB2.361.315.
Sermons to *Charles* the First, when Prince; ......6.39.10.110.
Like M[eadow]s run to sermons, ...6.61.25.181.
Like R— run to sermons, ...6.61.25A.181.
Like Meadows run to sermons, ...6.61.25B.181.

SERPENT

But in my Breast the Serpent Love abides. ......1.PSu.68.77.
A Serpent from her left was seen to rear ......1.TrSt.158.416.
A curling Serpent from her left did rear ......1.TrSt.158A.416.
A Bosome Serpent, a Domestick Evil, ...2.ChJM.47.17.
Like Aaron's serpent, swallows up the rest. ......3.EOM2.132.71.
Now serpent-like, in prose he sweeps the ground, ...4.2HE1.100.203.
Should wag two serpent tails in Smithfield fair! ......5.DunA3.290.184.
Should'st wag a serpent-tail in Smithfield fair! ......5.DunB3.288.334.
Herself the ninth: The Serpent as he hung, ...II.2.378.145.
Shot forth to View, a scaly Serpent sees; ......II.3.48.191.
On which a mimic Serpent creeps along, ...II.11.50.36.
A bleeding Serpent, of enormous Size, ...II.12.234.89.
Amidst the Host the fallen Serpent lies: ......II.12.240.90.
Knew all the serpent-mazes of deceit, ...Od.4.342.136.

SERPENT-LIKE

Now serpent-like, in prose he sweeps the ground, ...4.2HE1.100.203.

SERPENT-MAZES

Knew all the serpent-mazes of deceit, ...Od.4.342.136.

SERPENT-TAIL

Should'st wag a serpent-tail in Smithfield fair! ......5.DunB3.288.334.

SERPENT'S

How with the Serpent's Teeth he sow'd the Soil, ...1.TrSt.9.409.

SERPENTS

And harmless Serpents lick the Pilgrim's Feet. ......1.Mes.80.120.
And snatch'd the starting Serpents from the Ground. ......1.TrSt.127.415.
A hundred Serpents guard her horrid Head, ...1.TrSt.145.416.
The rich Buffet well-colour'd Serpents grace, ...3.Ep4.153.152.
Round the vast Orb an hundred Serpents roll'd, ...II.2.528.151.
A Fringe of Serpents hissing guards the Gold: ......II.5.913.309.

SERV'D

And serv'd alike his Vassals and his God. ......1.W-F.76.157.
Which serv'd the past, and must the times to come! ......3.EOM2.52.62.
All serv'd, all serving! nothing stands alone; ......3.EOM3.25.94.
Each serv'd, and serving! nothing stands alone; ......3.EOM3.25A.94.
All serv'd, and serving! nothing stands alone; ......3.EOM3.25B.94.
The Muse but serv'd to ease some Friend, not Wife, ...4.Arbu.131.105.
And just as rich as when he serv'd a QUEEN! ......4.Arbu.417.127.
He serv'd a 'Prenticeship, who sets up shop; ......4.2HE1.181.211.
The Grace-cup serv'd with all decorum: ......4.HS6.138.259.
Horace would say, *Sir* Billy *serv'd the Crown,* ......4.EpS1.13.298.
From us that serv'd so long in vain, ...6.4iii.3.10.
He'd not be serv'd so like a Beast, ...6.30.28.86.
He'd ne'er be serv'd so like a Beast; ......6.30.28B.86.
"Who broke no promise, serv'd no private end, ...6.71.69.204.
Who broke no promise, serv'd no private end, ...6.97.3.282.
Moses he serv'd as *Moses Pharaoh,* ......6.101.21.290.
Serv'd with pure Wheat, and by a Princess' Hand; ......II.8.231.408.
And his the Glory to have serv'd so well. ......II.10.370.19.
Or serv'd to ballast, or to prop the Fleet) ......II.14.474.186.
And thy soft Pleasures serv'd with captive Dames! ......II.16.1006.282.
These serv'd his Person at the royal Feast, ...II.24.582.561.
But serv'd a master of a nobler kind, ...Od.17.377.150.

SERVANT

Pleas'd her best Servant wou'd his Courage try, ...2.ChJM.331.30.
But cou'd not climb, and had no Servant nigh, ...2.ChJM.727.49.
A master, or a servant, or a friend, ...3.EOM2.250.85.
Beast, Man, or Angel, Servant, Lord, or King. ......3.EOM3.302.123.
"In pow'r your Servant, out of pow'r your Friend." ......3.Ep1.161Z2.29.
An humble servant to all human kind, ...3.Ep1.253.37.
[In Pow'r a Servant, out of Pow'r a Friend.] ......4.EpS2.161.322.
Speak, Gracious Lord, oh speak; thy Servant hears: ......6.2.1.5.
For I'm thy Servant, and I'l still be so: ......6.2.2.5.
Speak, gracious Lord, oh speak; thy Servant hears. ......6.2.18.6.
Speak when thou wilt, for still thy Servant hears. ......6.2.34.6.
Like an old servant now cashier'd, he lay; ......6.15.12.51.
The fawning Servant turns a haughty Lord; ......6.19.44.63.
Avenge thy servant, and the *Greeks* destroy. ......II.1.60.88.
His faithful Servant, old *Calesius* dy'd. ......II.6.24.325.
Weak is thy Servant, and thy Coursers slow. ......II.8.132.404.
Great *Hector* sorrows for his Servant kill'd, ...II.8.155.405.
A faithful Servant to a foreign Lord; ......II.15.503.216.
And stretch'd the Servant o'er his dying Lord. ......II.20.568.418.
What his the Suitors? must my servant train ......Od.4.906.160.
O King belov'd of *Jove!* thy servant spare, ...Od.10.315.359.
A faithful servant, and without a fault. ......Od.14.6.35.
The faithful servant joy'd his unknown Lord. ......Od.14.489.59.
A servant added to his absent Lord) ......Od.14.505.61.
Some master, or some servant would allow ......Od.14.574.64.
A faithful servant, by the Prince belov'd! ......Od.15.582.98.
His lord's commands the faithful servant bears; ......Od.17.424.153.
Such servant as your humble choice requires, ...Od.19.407.214.
At once each servant brac'd his armour on; ......Od.22.131.293.
Flow from this tongue, then let thy servant die! ......Od.23.80.322.

SERVANT'S

Since you a servant's ravish'd form bemoan, ...1.TrFD.3.385.
Oft had the Goddess heard her servant's call, ...5.DunB2.97.300.
Such food as falls to simple servant's share; ......Od.14.98.40.
Who sate delighted at his servant's board; ......Od.14.488.59.
O guard it, guard it, for thy servant's sake! ......Od.17.675.165.

SERVANTS

The Servants round stood ready at their Call. ......2.ChJM.405.34.
His servants up, and rise by five a clock, ...4.2HE1.162.209.
The joy their wives, their sons, and servants share, ...4.2HE1.245.215.
But now the Servants they rush'd in; ......6.79.97.221.
Great G[eorge ii]! such servants since thou well can'st lack, ...6.116v.5.327.
The Steeds he left, their trusty Servants hold; ......II.8.145.404.
Not such, my friend, the servants of their feast: ......Od.15.350.86.
Blank and discountenanc'd the servants stand, ...Od.15.402.88.
For like their lawless lords, the servants are. ......Od.17.331.147.
The master gone, the servants what restrains? ......Od.17.390.150.
Wealth, servants, friends, were mine in better days; ......Od.17.503.157.
His servants insults, his invaded bed, ...Od.23.325.340.
Where the few servants that divide his care, ...Od.24.240.360.
Nor servants, absent on another care; ......Od.24.258.361.

SERVE

The *Rules,* a Nation born to serve, obeys, ...1.EOC.713.322.
Quit all his State, descend, and serve again? ......1.TrSt.258.421.
Of honest Parents, and may serve my Turn. ......2.ChJM.261.27.
Paul, knowing One cou'd never serve our Turn, ...2.ChWB.58.58.
That he, and only he, sho'd serve my Turn. ......2.ChWB.295.71.
To serve mere engines to the ruling Mind? ......3.EOM1.262.46.
To serve, not suffer, strengthen, not invade, ...3.EOM3.298.123.
This bids to serve, and that to shun mankind; ......3.EOM4.20.129.
"If—where I'm going—I could serve you, Sir?" ......3.Ep1.255.37.

SERVE 278 SETT'ST

SERVE (CONTINUED)

For well they knew, proud Trappings serve to hide ....4.HAdv.116.85.
Or, when a tight, neat Girl, will serve the Turn, ...4.HAdv.151.87.
Have I no Friend to serve, no Soul to save? ....4.Arbu.274.115.
"His whole Ambition was to serve a Lord, ...4.2HE2.14.165.
Or serve (like other Fools) to fill a room; ....5.DunB1.136.280.
To serve his cause, O Queen! is serving thine. ....5.DunB1.214.285.
To wonder at their Maker, not to serve." ....5.DunB4.458.385.
Serve peopled Towns, and stately Cities grace; ....6.17ii.24.56.
Have stoop'd to serve an haughty *Roman* dame? ....6.20.6.66.
They'll serve no Man alive. ....6.77.8A.214.
And saw her Cocks well serve her Hens. ....6.93.4.256.
Nor like your Capons, serve your Cocks. ....6.93.30.257.
Of some Dry–Nurse to serve for Hen; ....6.93.18A.257.
But if my Life be doom'd to serve the Bad, ...6.96iii.37.275.
Or *Marlb'rough* serve him like a Friend? ....6.101.32.291.
That *Cibber* can serve both for Fool and for Poet. ....6.105vii.4.302.
To see his own Maids serve a new Lord and Master. ....6.122.18.342.
But you yourself may serve to show it, ...6.124ii.3.347.
Lord! never ask who thus could serve ye? ....6.127.3.355.
Who dare to serve their Country, and be poor. ....6.142.14A.383.
Disgrac'd and injur'd by the Man we serve? ....Il.1.212.97.
To live thy Slave, and still to serve in vain, ' ....Il.1.389.106.
May all their Consorts serve promiscuous Lust, ...Il.3.374.211.
For him I serve, of *Myrmidonian* Race; ....Il.24.485.556.
To serve our Prince, it fell on me, the last. ....Il.24.490.556.
Whom Fortune dooms to serve the rich and great. ....Od.15.343.86.
Exact of taste, and serve the feast in state. ....Od.16.275.118.
Its current thence to serve the city brings: ....Od.17.234.143.
Unjust to me and all that serve the state, ...Od.17.472.156.
Their wonted grace, but only serve to weep. ....Od.18.296.180.

SERVES

Yet serves to second too some other use. ....3.EOM1.56.20.
Cares not for service, or but serves when prest, ...3.EOM3.86.100.
This too serves always, Reason never long; ....3.EOM3.93.101.
What serves one will, when many wills rebel? ....3.EOM3.274.120.
Self-love but serves the virtuous mind to wake, ...3.EOM4.363.163.
The Dull, flat Falshood serves for policy, ...3.Ep1.126A.25.
Or Falshood serves the dull for policy, ...3.Ep1.126.25.
Useful, we grant, it serves what life requires, ...3.Ep3.29A.88.
Useful, I grant, it serves what life requires, ...3.Ep3.29.88.
One half-pint bottle serves them both to dine, ...4.HS2.53.59.
Serves but to keep fools pert, and knaves awake: ....5.DunB4.442.383.
That serves his R[oyal]l H[ighness] ....6.94.76.261.
Serves not to slaughter, but provoke the Foe. ....Il.5.263.279.
He serves me most, who serves his Country best. ....Il.10.201.10.
He serves me most, who serves his Country best. ....Il.10.201.10.
And *Jove's* scorn'd thunder serves to drench our fields) ....Od.9.424.323.

SERVICE

Cares not for service, or but serves when prest, ...3.EOM3.86.100.
A War-horse never for the Service chose, ...4.HAdv.114.85.
'Tis for the Service of the Crown, ...4.HS6.34.253.
While vows and service nothing gain'd, ...6.4iii.9.10.
To *Baker* first my Service, pray; ....6.13.26.40.
Abroad in foreign Service to be lost; ....6.17ii.15.56.
And Service, Faith, and Justice plead in vain. ....Il.1.509.112.
Urge all the Ties to former Service ow'd, ...Il.1.512.112.
Forgets my Service and deserv'd Reward. ....Il.8.440.418.
In that sharp Service, singled from the rest, ...Il.13.357.122.
For such Desert what Service can I pay? ....Il.18.474.344.
Sole with *Telemachus* her service ends, ...Od.1.547.58.
His buskins old, in former service torn, ...Od.24.265.361.

SERVICES

Past Services of Friends, good Deeds of Foes, ...6.8.34.19.

SERVILE

Let barb'rous *Ganges* arm a servile Train; ....1.W-F.365.186.
Of all this *Servile Herd* the worst is He ....1.EOC.414.287.
Alike disdain with servile Necks to bear ....1.TrSt.186.418.
Ev'n Fortune rules no more:—Oh servile Land, ...1.TrSt.241.420.
Not proud, nor servile, be one Poet's praise ....4.Arbu.336.120.
Nor proud, nor servile, be one Poet's praise ....4.Arbu.336A.120.
When servile Chaplains cry, that Birth and Place ....4.2HE2.220.181.
A low-born, cell-bred, selfish, servile band, ...5.DunB2.356.315.
Then scorn to gain a Friend by servile ways, ...6.73.10.210.
Tho' next the Servile drop thee next the Vain, ...6.84.31Z4.239.
No Son of *Mars* descend, for servile Gains, ...Il.6.85.327.
The trembling, servile, second Race of Heav'n. ....Il.15.223.205.
Mad as he was, he threaten'd servile Bands, ...Il.21.527.443.
And left me these, a soft and servile Crew, ...Il.24.326.550.
Then to the servile task the Monarch turns ....Od.18.391.186.
Nor servile flatt'ry stain'd the moral lay. ....Od.22.392.307.
Nor speaks thy form a mean or servile mind: ....Od.24.297.364.

SERVING

All serv'd, all serving! nothing stands alone; ....3.EOM3.25.94.
Each serv'd, and serving! nothing stands alone; ....3.EOM3.25A.94.
All serv'd, and serving! nothing stands alone; ....3.EOM3.25B.94.
Since 'twas no form'd Design of serving God: ....4.JD4.18.27.
Tremble before a *noble Serving-Man?* ....4.JD4.199.43.
To serve his cause, O Queen! is serving thine. ....5.DunB1.214.285.

SERVING-MAN

Tremble before a *noble Serving-Man?* ....4.JD4.199.43.

SERVITUDE

Not sunk by sloth, nor rais'd by servitude; ....3.Ep3.222.111.
Some few the foes in servitude detain; ....Od.17.522.158.
And servitude with pleasing tasks deceive; ....Od.22.461.310.

SES

And if unwatch'd is sure t' omit Ses Heires: ....4.JD2A.103.140.
The Deeds, and dextrously omits, *ses Heires:* ....4.JD2.100.141.

SESAMUS

And lofty *Sesamus* invades the Sky; ....Il.2.1039.172.

SESOSTRIS

High on his Car *Sesostris* struck my View, ...2.TemF.113.262.

SESSION

Nor herald sworn, the session to proclaim) ....Od.3.171.94.

SESTOS

And *Sestos* and *Abydos'* neighb'ring Strands, ...Il.2.1013.171.

SET

Set up themselves, and drove a *sep'rate* Trade: ....1.EOC.105Z1.251.
Then clear this Doubt, and set my Mind at ease. ....2.ChJM.275.27.
And set the Strumpet here in open View, ...2.ChJM.653.46.
And old Examples set before my Eyes; ....2.ChWB.342.73.
Wrapt in th' envenom'd Shirt, and set on Fire. ....2.ChWB.382.76.
These set the Head, and those divide the Hair, ...2.RL1.146.158.
With Sparks, that seem'd to set the World on fire. ....2.TemF.415.283.
Full in my view set all the bright abode, ...2.ElAb.127.330.
The less, or greater, set so justly true, ...3.EOM3.291.122.
The less, and greater, set so justly true, ...3.EOM3.291A.122.
And always set the Gem above the Flow'r. ....3.Ep1.100A.22.
And justly set the Gem above the Flow'r. ....3.Ep1.100.22.
Nor in an Hermitage set Dr. Clarke. ....3.Ep4.78.144.
Has Nature set no bounds to wild Desire? ....4.HAdv.143.87.
Comma's and points they set exactly right, ...4.Arbu.161.108.
Now with set-looks to his bilk'd client talk: ....4.JD2A.77.138.
Those Suns of Glory please not till they set. ....4.2HE1.22.195.
Of Land, set out to plant a Wood. ....4.HS6.6.251.
The Beans and Bacon set before 'em, ...4.HS6.137.259.
To set this matter full before you, ...4.1HE7.81.273.
To set this matter full before ye, ...4.1HE7.81A.273.
P. If not the Tradesman who set up to day, ...4.EpS2.36.314.
With-hold the pension, and set up the head; ....5.DunB4.96.350.
Or set on Metaphysic ground to prance, ...5.DunB4.265.370.
Then thus. "From Priest-craft happily set free, ...5.DunB4.499.391.
To set, like him, heav'n too on fire. ....6.5.18.12.
Those eyes shou'd set the world on flame. ....6.5.18A.12.
Afflicted *Sense* thou kindly dost set free, ...6.8.16.18.
Set up with these, he ventur'd on the Town. ....6.49i.7.137.
"Within thy Reach I set the Vinegar? ....6.96ii.18.270.
"Within the reach I set the Vinegar? ....6.96ii.18A.270.
"And shall I set thee on my Hand no more, ...6.96ii.61.273.
Was there no other Way to set him free? ....6.96iv.93.279.
Commas and *Points* they set exactly right; ....6.98.11.283.
Set *Bacchus* from his glassy Prison free, ...6.100vi.2.289.
Before my Children set your Beef, ...6.135.49.368.
Before my Puppyes set your Beef, ...6.135.49A.368.
For nine long Years have set the World in Arms; ....Il.3.206.201.
Assembled Nations, set two Worlds in Arms? ....Il.4.38.223.
And set to View the warring Deities. ....Il.5.165.275.
And set aside the Cause of *Greece* and *Troy?* ....Il.14.222.172.
Shall set in Glory; bids him drive the Foe; ....Il.16.795.274.
Set wide your Portals to the flying Throng. ....Il.21.622.448.
And now the Sun had set upon their Woe; ....Il.23.193.497.
But, set apart for sacred Use, commands ....Il.23.1062.533.
Set up by Jove your Spectacle of Woe? ....Il.24.300.549.
This *Hermes* (such the Pow'r of Gods) set wide; ....Il.24.561.559.
Then set the genial banquet in his view, ...Od.7.222.247.
Jove bids to set the stranger on his way, ...Od.7.404.256.
Or where the sun shall set, or where shall rise? ....Od.10.218.350.
Then hast'ning to the styes set wide the door, ...Od.10.459.366.
Like some fair plant set by a heav'nly hand, ...Od.14.202.45.
Now set the sun, and darken'd all the shore. ....Od.15.506.94.
(An humble side-board set) *Ulysses* shar'd. ....Od.20.348.249.
Against the wall he set the bow unbent: ....Od.22.137.293.
His honour'd harp with care he first set down, ...Od.22.375.306.
Whose guilty glories now are set in blood. ....Od.22.410.307.
Once more the palace set in fair array, ...Od.22.491.313.
Ere the fair Mischief set two worlds in arms, ...Od.23.232.334.
Be all the rest; and set thy soul at ease. ....Od.24.416.369.

SET-LOOKS

Now with set-looks to his bilk'd client talk: ....4.JD2A.77.138.

SETS

So modest Plainness sets off sprightly Wit: ....1.EOC.302.273.
And sets th'avenging Thunderer in Arms. ....1.TrSt.339.424.
And *Venus* sets ere *Mercury* can rise: ....2.ChWB.370.75.
And *Venus* sets when *Mercury* does rise: ....2.ChWB.370A.75.
Its proper bliss, and sets its proper bounds. ....3.EOM3.110.103.
He serv'd a 'Prenticeship, who sets up shop; ....4.2HE1.181.211.
And sets the Passions on the side of Truth; ....4.2HE1.218.213.
And, while he bids thee, sets th' Example too? ....4.1HE1.109.287.
Sets half the World, God knows, against the rest; ....4.EpS1.58.302.
A Poet's form she sets before their eyes, ...5.DunA2.31A.99.
Illumes their light, and sets their flames on fire. ....5.DunA3.256.179.
Illumes their light, and sets their flames on fire. ....5.DunB3.260.332.
But sets up One, a greater, in their Place; ....6.19.38.63.
With strictest Order sets his Train in Arms, ...Il.4.338.236.
The God, whose Light'ning sets the Heav'ns on fire, ...Il.14.333.179.
Nor He, whose Anger sets the World in Arms, ...Il.17.459.305.
Achilles mounts, and sets the Field on Fire; ....Il.19.435.389.
To search the woods for sets of flowry thorn, ...Od.24.259.361.

SETT

When those fair Suns shall sett, as sett they must, ...2.RL5.147.211.
When those fair Suns shall sett, as sett they must, ...2.RL5.147.211.
So to *Ulysses* welcome sett the Sun. ....Od.13.44.3.

SETT'ST

Who sett'st our Entrails free! ....6.53.34.162.

SETTING

Now setting *Phœbus* shone serenely bright,	1.PAu.13.81.
The setting Sun now shone serenely bright,	1.PAu.13A.81.
(His Shadow lengthen'd by the setting Sun)	1.W-F.194.168.
Strike off his Pension, by the setting sun,	3.Ep1.160.29.
Shine, buzz, and fly-blow in the setting-sun.	3.Ep2.28.52.
Beneath the rising or the setting Sun.	II.5.331.282.
Watch'd from the rising to the setting Sun)	II.24.1010.577.
Observ'd, nor heedful of the setting light,	Od.3.170.94.
At dawn, and ending with the setting sun,	Od.4.482.143.
Saw them returning with the setting sun,	Od.7.416.258.
Here, till the setting sun rowl'd down the light,	Od.9.188.313.
There, 'till the setting sun rowl'd down the light,	Od.10.208.350.
And setting stars roll'd down the azure plain;	Od.12.368.449.
Their grief unfinish'd with the setting sun:	Od.16.243.116.
Thus had their joy wept down the setting sun,	Od.21.240.271.

SETTING-SUN

Shine, buzz, and fly-blow in the setting-sun.	3.Ep2.28.52.

SETTLE

As Eusden, Philips, Settle, writ of Kings)	4.2HE1.417.231.
But see great Settle to the dust descend,	5.DunA1.185.85.
Know, Settle, cloy'd with custard and with praise,	5.DunA1.247.92.
Known by the band and suit which Settle wore,	5.DunA3.29.153.
Well purg'd, and worthy Settle, Banks, and Broome.	5.DunB1.146.280.
Known by the band and suit which Settle wore	5.DunB3.37.322.
And Shades Eternal settle o'er his Eyes.	II.4.527.246.
Thy heart might settle in this scene of ease,	Od.5.265.184.

SETTLE'S

But liv'd, in Settle's numbers, one day more.	5.DunA1.88.69.
Yet liv'd, in Settle's numbers, one day more.	5.DunA1.88A.69.
But liv'd, in Settle's numbers, one day more.	5.DunB1.90.276.

SETTLED

And down he settled me with hearty Blows:	2.ChWB.418.77.
And settled Sorrow on his aged Face,	II.21.618.448.
Not break, the settled Temper of thy Soul.	II.23.688.517.

SETTLEMENT

I pass each previous Settlement and Deed,	2.ChJM.305.28.

SETTLES

Then, gather'd, settles on the hoary Deeps;	II.13.1002.152.

SETTLING

Or settling, seize the Sweets the Blossoms yield,	2.TemF.286.277.
With silent Joy the settling Hosts survey:	II.7.66.366.
Thus in thick Orders settling wide around,	II.7.75.366.

SEV'N

And tho' no science, fairly worth the sev'n:	3.Ep4.44.140.
To Books and Study gives sev'n years compleat,	4.2HE2.117.173.
Thron'd on sev'n hills, the Antichrist of Wit.	5.DunA2.12.97.
Thron'd on sev'n hills, the Antichrist of wit.	5.DunB2.16.297.
Up to her godly garret after sev'n,	6.45.21.125.
Three Shillings cost the first, the last sev'n Groats;	6.96iv.53.277.
Sev'n were his Ships; each Vessel fifty row,	II.2.876.165.
By the same Arm my sev'n brave Brothers fell,	II.6.534.353.
Huge was its Orb, with sev'n thick Folds o'ercast,	II.7.267.377.
Sev'n were the Leaders of the nightly Bands,	II.9.117.437.
Sev'n sacred Tripods, whose unsully'd Frame	II.9.159.440.
Sev'n lovely Captives of the *Lesbian* Line,	II.9.165.440.
Sev'n ample Cities shall confess his Sway,	II.9.195.442.
Sev'n sacred Tripods, whose unsully'd Frame	II.9.346.450.
Sev'n lovely Captives of the *Lesbian* Line,	II.9.352.451.
Sev'n ample Cities shall confess thy Sway,	II.9.382.451.
Lo, sev'n are offer'd, and of equal Charms.	II.9.752.471.
Scarce sev'n Moons gone, lay *Sthenelus* his Wife;	II.19.115.376.
Sev'n Captives next a lovely Line compose;	II.19.253.383.
And sev'n broad Acres covers as he lies.	II.21.473.441.
Of sev'n his Sons, by whom the Lot was cast	II.24.489.556.
Sev'n years, the traytor rich *Mycenæ* sway'd,	Od.3.388.105.
I stay reluctant sev'n continu'd years,	Od.7.346.253.
Sev'n golden talents to perfection wrought,	Od.9.236.316.
And here thro' sev'n wide portals rush'd the war.	Od.11.324.398.
Sev'n herds, sev'n flocks enrich the sacred plains,	Od.12.162.440.
Sev'n herds, sev'n flocks enrich the sacred plains,	Od.12.162.440.
On sev'n bright years successive blessings wait;	Od.14.317.50.
In sev'n just portions, pure of hand and heart.	Od.14.483.59.
To him sev'n talents of pure ore I told,	Od.24.320.365.

SEV'NFOLD

From Heav'n it self tho' sev'nfold *Nilus* flows,	1.W-F.359.185.
Then, with his Sev'nfold Shield, he strode away.	1.TrES.88.453.
Oft have we known that sev'nfold Fence to fail,	2.RL2.119.167.
Stole from the Master of the sev'nfold Face:	5.DunB1.244.288.
And happier, saw the Sev'nfold City fall.	II.4.461.242.
Whirl'd the long Lance against the sev'nfold Shield.	II.7.296.378.
Then close beneath the sev'nfold Orb withdrew.	II.8.324.413.
By the broad glitt'ring of the sev'nfold Shield.	II.11.649.62.
Then, with his sev'nfold Shield, he strode away.	II.12.442.97.
Who bore by turns great *Ajax'* sev'nfold Shield;	II.13.886.147.

SEV'NTEEN

Full sev'nteen nights he cut the foamy way;	Od.5.355.189.
In sev'nteen days appear'd your pleasing coast,	Od.7.353.253.
'Till sev'nteen nights and sev'nteen days return'd,	Od.24.81.352.
'Till sev'nteen nights and sev'nteen days return'd,	Od.24.81.352.

SEV'NTH

Till in the sev'nth it fix'd. Then *Ajax* threw,	II.7.299.379.
The sev'nth arose, and now the Sire of Gods	Od.12.469.454.
Six days consum'd; the sev'nth we plow'd the main.	Od.14.283.49.
The sev'nth, the fraudful wretch (no cause descry'd)	Od.15.513.95.

SEV'RAL

Each might his *sev'ral Province* well command,	1.EOC.66.246.
And sev'ral Men impels to sev'ral ends.	3.EOM2.166.75.
And sev'ral Men impels to sev'ral ends.	3.EOM2.166.75.
Each individual seeks a sev'ral goal;	3.EOM2.237.84.
In sev'ral Men we sev'ral Passions find,	3.Ep2.207.A.67.
In sev'ral Men we sev'ral Passions find,	3.Ep2.207.A.67.
'Tis the same rope at sev'ral ends they twist,	5.DunA3.285.184.
(His Friends, each busy'd in his sev'ral Part,	II.5.826.305.
Strait to their sev'ral Cares the *Trojans* move,	II.7.494.388.
This said, each parted to his sev'ral Cares;	II.10.80.6.
And all obey their sev'ral Chief's Commands.	II.12.100.85.
And ev'ry fountain pours a sev'ral rill,	Od.5.91.176.
Compell'd, reluctant, to their sev'ral styes,	Od.14.455.57.
These while on sev'ral tables they dispose,	Od.14.480.59.
"And prove your sev'ral strengths"—The Princes heard,	Od.21.151.266.
The sev'ral trees you gave me long ago.	Od.24.389.368.

SEVE

Explains the *Seve* and *Verdeur* of the Vine.	5.DunB4.556.397.
Explains the *Seve* and Verdure of each Vine.	5.DunB4.556A.397.

SEVEN

How *Pallas* talk'd when she was Seven Years old.	6.37.10.106.
Or follow Girls Seven Hours in Eight?—	6.47.35.129.

SEVENFOLD

Each Chief his sevenfold Shield display'd,	6.11.45.31.

SEVENTY

Has truly liv'd the space of seventy years,	6.55.1Z2.167.

SEVER

One fatal stroke the sacred Hair does sever	2.RL*A*1.117.130.
From the dear man unwilling she must sever,	6.45.5.124.
The Limbs they sever from th' inclosing Hide;	II.1.602.117.
The Limbs they sever from th' inclosing Hyde,	II.2.504.150.
The Limbs they sever from the reeking Hyde,	II.24.788.570.

SEVER'D

This fav'rite Isle, long sever'd from her reign,	5.DunA3.117.160.
This fav'rite Isle, long sever'd from her reign,	5.DunB3.125.325.
Which sever'd from the Trunk (as I from thee)	II.1.311.103.
His sever'd Head was toss'd among the Throng,	II.11.189.43.
Me Fate has sever'd from the Sons of Earth,	II.23.99.491.
Sever'd the bole, and smooth'd the shining grain;	Od.23.200.333.

SEVERAL

As several Garbs with Country, Town, and Court.	1.EOC.323.275.
All to your several states with speed resort;	Od.1.478.55.
And to their several domes to Rest resort.	Od.1.536.57.

SEVERE

And Kings more furious and severe than they:	1.W-F.46.153.
Modestly bold, and Humanly severe?	1.EOC.636.311.
Oh! yeild at last, nor still remain severe;	1.TrPA.114.370.
Reverse, O *Jove*, thy too severe Decree,	1.TrSt.396.426.
From grave to gay, from lively to severe;	3.EOM4.380.165.
Severe to all, but most to Womankind;	6.19.32.63.
That darts severe upon a rising Lye,	6.73.6.209.
Learning not vain, and wisdom not severe	6.75.7.212.
Yet soft his Nature, tho' severe his Lay,	6.118.5.334.
Severe of Morals, of Affections mild,	6.125.1A.349.
Severe of Morals, but of Nature mild;	6.125.1B.349.
Thy Son must fall, by too severe a Doom,	II.1.461.110.
But fond of Glory, with severe Delight,	II.4.258.233.
His Cheek with Blushes; and severe, he said.	II.4.403.240.
He spake, and smil'd severe, for well he knew	II.14.557.190.
That Iron Heart inflexibly severe;	II.24.51.537.
Such is, alas! the Gods severe Decree;	II.24.661.564.
Instinct divine! nor blame severe his choice,	Od.1.445.54.
But truth severe shall dictate to my tongue:	Od.4.470.142.
Severe, if men th' eternal rights evade!	Od.4.478.142.
But with severe rebuke *Antinous* cry'd.	Od.4.1022.165.
Heedless of others, to his own severe.	Od.9.132.311.
Scorn'd ev'n by man, and (oh severe disgrace)	Od.13.150.12.
The wrath of Princes ever is severe.	Od.17.212.142.
Telemachus absorpt in thought severe,	Od.17.582.160.
What words, my son, have pass'd thy lips severe?	Od.19.576.224.
The Chief severe, compelling each to move,	Od.22.486.312.

SEVERELY

Oft, when his Shoe the most severely wrung,	2.ChWB.239.68.
For thee the fates, severely kind, ordain	2.ElAb.249.339.
But how severely with themselves proceed	4.2HE2.157.175.
Yet sure the Best are most severely fated,	6.60.3.178.
Severely bent his Purpose to fulfill,	II.15.100.200.
Severely chaste, or if commenc'd a bride?	Od.16.34.104.
Severely chaste *Penelope* remains,	Od.16.36.104.

SEVERER

But urging Vengeance and severer Fight;	1.TrES.142.454.
But urging Vengeance, and severer Fight;	II.12.496.99.

SEVEREST

And Fate's severest Rage disarm:	6.11.119.34.

SEVERN

And rapid Severn hoarse applause resounds.	3.Ep3.252.114.

SEVIL

And, like true *Sevil* Snuff, awake the Brain.	6.48iv.8.136.

SEW'R

Marshal'd in order due, to each a Sew'r	Od.1.191.42.
Now bid the Sew'r approach, and let us join	Od.21.278.273.

SEW'RS
Two sew'rs from day to day the revels wait, ...Od.16.274.118.

SEWELL
From sanguine *Sew[ell]* down to pidling *T[ibbald]s:* .... 6.98.14A.283.

SEX
Than such as Women on their Sex bestow.) ....1.TrVP.56.379.
Wou'd Men but follow what the Sex advise, ...2.ChJM.67.18.
And all the faithless Sex, for ever to be true. ....2.ChJM.655.46.
And all the Sex in each succeeding Age, ...2.ChJM.660.46.
Who lov'd our Sex, and honour'd all our Kind. ....2.ChJM.693.48.
It is not in our Sex to break our Word. ....2.ChJM.709.49.
Marry who will, our *Sex* is to be Sold! ....2.ChWB.171.65.
Who rule to Sex to Fifty from Fifteen, ...2.RL4.58.189.
Ease, Pleasure, Virtue, All, our Sex resign. ....2.RL4.106.192.
Each sex desires alike, 'till two are one. ....3.EOM3.122.104.
Picks from each sex, to make the Fav'rite blest, ...3.Ep2.273A.72.
That buys your sex a Tyrant o'er itself. ....3.Ep2.288A.73.
Yet mark the fate of a whole Sex of Queens! ....3.Ep2.219.68.
Pleasures the sex, as children Birds, pursue, ...3.Ep2.231.68.
Picks from each sex, to make its Fav'rite blest, ...3.Ep2.273.72.
Which buys your sex a Tyrant o'er itself. ....3.Ep2.288.73.
In *Sappho* touch the *Failing of the Sex,* .... 4.EpS1.15.298.
Too much *your Sex* is by their Forms confin'd, ...6.19.31.63.
Still in Constraint your suff'ring Sex remains, ...6.19.41.63.
But gives your feeble sex, made up of fears, ...6.38.17.108.
From her own sex should mercy find to day! ....6.41.2.113.
Our sex are still forgiving at their heart; ....6.41.12.113.
Frail, fev'rish Sex! their Fit now chills, now burns; ....6.99.17.287.
How quickly all the Sex pursue! ....6.119.18.337.
At this, the Fairest of her Sex obey'd, ...Il.3.521.216.
Go, let thy own soft Sex employ thy Care, ...Il.5.435.289.
Not one of all the Race, not Sex, nor Age, ...Il.6.71.327.
Not one of all the Race, nor Sex, nor Age, ...Il.6.71A.327.
And the least freedom with the sex is shame, ...Od.6.344.228.
The perjur'd sex, and blacken all the race; ....Od.11.538.409.
Nor trust the sex that is so rarely wise; ....Od.11.546.410.
(The sex is ever to a soldier kind.) ....Od.14.246.48.
To whom the King: Ill suits your sex to stay ....Od.18.359.185.
The vulgar of my sex I most exceed ....Od.19.372.212.
Our easy faith, and make the sex their prey: ....Od.23.228.334.
The gen'ral sex shall suffer in her shame, ...Od.24.230.358.

SEX'S
No, trust the Sex's sacred Rule; ....6.64.21.190.

SEXE'S
But she, your Sexe's Mirrour, free from Pride, ...2.ChJM.438.36.
By Heav'n, those Authors are our Sexe's Foes, ...2.ChJM.698.48.
Thy Sexe's Tyrant, with a Tyger's Heart? ....Il.21.560.445.

SEXES
Assume what Sexes and what Shapes they please. ....2.RL1.70.151.

SEXT
Edwardi Sext. or *prim. & quint. Eliz:* .... 4.HS1.148.19.

SH
For some Folks read, but all Folks sh—. ....6.29.30.83.
As one Hog lives on what another sh—. ....6.82ix(e).2.235.

SHADE
And from the Brink his dancing Shade surveys. ....1.PSp.34.63.
Cynthus and *Hybla* yield to *Windsor*-Shade. ....1.PSp.68.67.
And verdant Alders form'd a quiv'ring Shade. ....1.PSu.4.71.
And chast *Diana* haunts the Forest Shade. ....1.PSu.62.76.
Trees, where you sit, shall crowd into a Shade, ...1.PSu.74.77.
Beneath the Shade a spreading Beech displays, ...1.PAu.1.80.
And the low Sun had lengthen'd ev'ry Shade. ....1.PAu.100.87.
While Plants their Shade, or Flow'rs their Odours give, ...1.PWi.83.94.
Arise, the Pines a noxious Shade diffuse; ....1.PWi.86.95.
From Storms a Shelter, and from Heat a Shade. ....1.Mes.16.114.
In genial Spring, beneath the quiv'ring Shade ....1.W-F.135.162.
And *Cynthus'* Top forsook for *Windsor* Shade; ....1.W-F.166.165.
Bath'd in the Springs, or sought the cooling Shade; ....1.W-F.166A.165.
Led by the Sound I roam from Shade to Shade, ...1.W-F.269.173.
Led by the Sound I roam from Shade to Shade, ...1.W-F.269.173.
Pleas'd in the silent Shade with empty Praise; ....1.W-F.432.194.
Envy will *Merit* as its *Shade* pursue, ...1.EOC.466.292.
And sweetly *melt* into just Shade and Light, ...1.EOC.489.294.
This humble Praise, lamented *Shade!* receive, ...1.EOC.733.325.
His downy cheeks with a beginning shade, ...1.TrPA.8.365.
And Wreaths of Hay his Sun-burnt Temples shade; ....1.TrVP.34.378.
Had stood neglected and a barren shade; ....1.TrVP.64.380.
To rise, and shade her with a sudden green. ....1.TrFD.48.388.
There wish'd to grow, and mingle shade with shade. ....1.TrFD.56.388.
There wish'd to grow, and mingle shade with shade. ....1.TrFD.56.388.
A hundred Snakes her gloomy Visage shade, ...1.TrSt.144.416.
And first to Light expos'd the Sacred Shade. ....1.TrSt.509.431.
And first to Light expos'd the Venerable Shade. ....1.TrSt.509A.431.
Run to the Shade, and bark against the Skies. ....1.TrSt.647.437.
Retires from *Argos* to the Sylvan Shade, ...1.TrSt.681.439.
His Bed the Ground, his Canopy the Shade, ...1.TrSt.687.439.
Now flies from *Argos* to the Sylvan Shade, ...1.TrSt.681A.439.
Where endless Honours wait the Sacred Shade. ....1.TrES.349.462.
In the wild Olive's unfrequented Shade; ....1.TrUl.50.467.
And wander'd in the solitary Shade; ....2.ChJM.62.17.
And Airy Musick warbled thro' the Shade. ....2.ChJM.464.37.
As thro' the Moon-light shade they nightly stray, ...2.RL*A*2.177.137.
The Rock's high Summit, in the Temple's Shade, ...2.TemF.47.256.
Start from their Roots, and form a Shade around: ....2.TemF.84.259.
What beck'ning ghost, along the moonlight shade ....2.Elegy.1.362.
What can atone (oh ever-injur'd shade!) ....2.Elegy.47.366.
Taller or stronger than the weeds they shade? ....3.EOM1.40.18.
As, in some well-wrought picture, light and shade, ...3.EOM2.208.81.

SHADE (CONTINUED)
Man walk'd with beast, joint tenant of the shade; ....3.EOM3.152.108.
To all beside as much an empty shade, ...3.EOM4.243.150.
And haunt their slumbers in the pompous shade. ....3.EOM4.304.156.
"Wrap my cold limbs, and shade my lifeless face: ....3.Ep1.245.36.
Your Virtues open fairest in the shade. ....3.Ep2.202.67.
And strength of Shade contends with strength of Light; ....3.Ep4.82.145.
Or sat delighted in the thick'ning shade, ...3.Ep4.90.146.
Now sweep those Alleys they were born to shade. ....3.Ep4.98.146.
And there a Summer-house, that knows no shade; ....3.Ep4.122.149.
First shade a Country, and then raise a Town. ....3.Ep4.190.155.
To wrap me in the Universal Shade; ....4.HS1.96.13.
"Why then for ever buried in the shade? ....4.JD4.87.33.
A shapeless shade! it melted from his sight, ...5.DunA2.103.109.
The King descended to th' Elyzian shade. ....5.DunA3.14.150.
And all the nations cover'd in her shade! ....5.DunA3.64.155.
Shade him from Light, and cover him from Law; ....5.DunB1.314.293.
A shapeless shade, it melted from his sight, ...5.DunB2.111.300.
The King descending, views th' Elysian Shade. ....5.DunB3.14.320.
And all the nations cover'd in her shade! ....5.DunB3.72.323.
And you, my Critics! in the chequer'd shade, ...5.DunB4.125.354.
'Tis in the shade of Arbitrary Sway. ....5.DunB4.182.360.
Now, to thy shade from all their glory shrunk; 5.DunB4.509A.39
Whose trees in summer yield him shade, ...6.1.7.3.
Soft looks of mercy grace the flatt'ring shade, ...6.4ii.4.9.
Had he but once this fairer shade descry'd, ...6.4ii.9.9.
His Numbers rais'd a Shade from Hell, ...6.11.133.34.
While *Procris* panted in the secret shade; ....6.14iii.2.45.
The Garden's Hope, and its expected shade. ....6.14iv.16.47.
Still from *Apollo* vindicates her shade, ...6.14iv.24.47.
To his dear ashes and his honour'd shade, ...6.20.39.67.
And fill the shade with never ceasing lays; ....6.20.67.68.
Safe shall he lye, and hope beneath thy shade. ....6.21.10.69.
You dream of triumphs in the rural shade; ....6.45.32.125.
Or seek some ruin's formidable shade; ....6.52.30.157.
All hail! once pleasing, once inspiring Shade, ...6.66.1.194.
Peace to thy gentle shade, and endless Rest! ....6.72.5.208.
What are the gay parterre, the chequer'd shade, ...6.81.7.225.
The Muse attends thee to the silent Shade: ....6.84.28.239.
The Muse attends thee to thy silent Shade: ....6.84.28A.239.
Fame, and the Muse, pursue thee to the Shade. ....6.84.28B.239.
Till you are Dust like me. ' *he.* Dear Shade! I will: ....6.123.4.343.
And haunt his slumbers in the pompous Shade. .... 6.130.18.358.
Attend the shade of gentle *Buckingham:* .... 6.132.10.362.
Peace to thy gentle Shade, and endless Rest, ...6.152.7.400.
(The Region stretch'd beneath his mighty Shade) ....Il.2.921.167.
Or whom the Vales in Shade of *Tmolus* hide, ...Il.2.1053.172.
To Thieves more grateful than the Midnight Shade; ....Il.3.18.188.
And veil'd her Blushes in a silken Shade; ....Il.3.522.216.
Death's sable Shade at once o'ercast their Eyes, ...Il.4.626.250.
He too had sunk to Death's Eternal Shade; ....Il.5.30.267.
He hides the Hero with his mighty Shade. ....Il.5.366.284.
Oppress'd had sunk to Death's Eternal Shade, ...Il.5.384.285.
Beneath a Beech, *Jove's* consecrated Shade, ...Il.5.852.306.
And *Hippoplacus'* wide-extended Shade) ....Il.6.495.351.
A barren Shade, and in his Honour grow. ....Il.6.533.353.
Radiant they met, beneath the Beechen Shade; ....Il.7.27.364.
At length compos'd they sit, and shade the Ground. ....Il.7.76.366.
But now the Night extends her awful Shade; ....Il.7.341.381.
Since then the Night extends her gloomy Shade, ...Il.7.356.381.
And shot red Light'nings thro' the gloomy Shade: ....Il.7.573.393.
And screen'd his Brother with a mighty Shade; ....Il.8.398.416.
And screen'd his Brother with the mighty Shade; ....Il.8.398A.416.
The *Greeks* rejoicing bless the friendly Shade. ....Il.8.608.425.
Lest under Covert of the Midnight Shade, ...Il.8.649.426.
Their threat'ning Tents already shade our Wall, ...Il.9.306.449.
Guideless, alone, through Night's dark Shade to go, ...Il.10.47.4.
So near, and favour'd by the gloomy Shade. ....Il.10.113.7.
And thus accosted thro' the gloomy Shade. ....Il.10.224.11.
Safe may we pass beneath the gloomy Shade, ...Il.10.331.17.
Thro' the brown Shade the fulgid Weapons shin'd. ....Il.10.547.27.
To send more Heroes to th' infernal Shade, ...Il.10.589.28.
Mean while the Chiefs, arriving at the Shade ....Il.10.618.29.
That round the Warrior cast a dreadful Shade; ....Il.11.44.36.
Shade the black Host, and intercept the Skies. ....Il.11.196.44.
The Lion's roaring thro' the mid-night Shade; ....Il.11.228.45.
And sacred Night her awful Shade extend. ....Il.11.252.46.
And sacred Night her awful Shade extend. ....Il.11.268.47.
The Lion rushed thro' the woodland Shade, ...Il.11.601.61.
How shall he grieve, when to th' eternal Shade ....Il.11.900.75.
He lay collected, in defensive Shade. ....Il.13.516.131.
This Mate shall joy thy melancholy Shade. ....Il.13.526.131.
Their lifted Bucklers cast a dreadful Shade ....Il.13.615.135.
Dark in embow'ring Shade, conceal'd from Sight, ...Il.14.327.178.
He pays due Vengeance to his Kinsman's Shade. ....Il.16.704.271.
Where endless Honours wait the sacred Shade. ....Il.16.836.276.
And shade the Temples of the Man divine. ....Il.16.963.280.
Guards the dead Hero with the dreadful Shade; ....Il.17.144.293.
And thus due Honours purchas'd to his Shade. ....Il.17.182.294.
Poor as it is, some Off'ring to thy Shade. ....Il.17.607.312.
Shall *Hector's* Head be offer'd to thy Shade; ....Il.18.392.340.
And decent cover'd with a linen Shade; ....Il.18.414.340.
Beneath an ample Oak's expanded Shade. ....Il.18.648.355.
Crown the fair Hills that silver *Simois* shade. ....Il.20.183.401.
And left him sleeping in Eternal Shade. ....Il.20.454.413.
Sad Victims! destin'd to *Patroclus'* Shade. ....Il.21.39.423.
Thus is aton'd *Patroclus* honour'd Shade, ...Il.21.149.427.
Far-stretching in the Shade of *Trojan* Tow'rs. ....Il.22.8.453.
Burn on thro' Death, and animate my Shade. ....Il.22.490.476.
On *Priam's* Roof, and *Hippoplacia's* Shade. ....Il.22.611.481.
To Heroes slumb'ring in Eternal Shade) ....Il.23.64.489.
When lo! the Shade before his closing Eyes ....Il.23.78.490.
Whate'er can rest a discontented Shade; ....Il.23.112.492.
In vain to grasp the visionary Shade; ....Il.23.116.492.
Aerial Semblance, and an empty Shade! ....Il.23.125.493.
And where in Shade of consecrated Bow'rs ....Il.23.184.497.

SHADE (CONTINUED)

Twelve *Trojan* Heroes offer'd to thy Shade; ..... Il.23.223.498.
Till I shall follow to th' Infernal Shade. ..... Il.23.305.501.
She spake, and veil'd her Head in sable Shade, ... Il.24.122.540.
So broad, his Pinions stretch'd their ample Shade, ... Il.24.392.552.
So broad, his Pinions stretch their ample Shade, ... Il.24.392A.552.
Thro' the dim Shade the Herald first espies ..... Il.24.433.554.
He groans, and calls on lov'd *Patroclus'* Shade. ..... Il.24.739.568.
And peaceful slept the mighty *Hector's* Shade. ..... Il.24.1016.577.
Supremely tall, and shade the deeps below. ..... Od.1.240.44.
To the pale Shade funereal rites ordain, ... Od.1.379.51.
Secur'd the valves. There, wrap'd in silent shade, ... Od.1.555.58.
"Shall want in death a shroud to grace his shade." ..... Od.2.114.67.
And twylight gray her evening shade extends. ..... Od.3.422.107.
But he descending to th' infernal shade, ... Od.3.522.113.
But when from dewy shade emerging bright, ... Od.4.267.132.
Sent many a shade to *Pluto's* dreary coast. ..... Od.4.354.136.
'Till night with grateful shade involv'd the skies, ... Od.4.582.147.
Or in eternal shade if cold he lies, ... Od.4.749.153.
'Till night with silent shade invests the pole; ..... Od.4.782.156.
His golden circlet in the western shade. ..... Od.4.1036.166.
While pensive in the silent slumb'rous shade, ... Od.4.1045.166.
And nodding cypress form'd a fragrant shade; ..... Od.5.83.176.
And rising night her friendly shade extends. ..... Od.5.290.185.
(Thick strown by tempest thro' the bow'ry shade) ..... Od.5.625.201.
Wrapt in embow'ring shade, *Ulysses* lies, ... Od.6.130.213.
The grove they reach, where from the sacred shade ..... Od.6.383.230.
With ever-during shade these happy eyes! ..... Od.7.306.250.
Now o'er the earth ascends the evening shade: ..... Od.8.452.287.
And thrice we call'd on each unhappy Shade. ..... Od.9.74.305.
Thro' all-surrounding shade our navy brought; ..... Od.9.166.312.
In shelter thick of horrid shade reclin'd; ..... Od.9.219.314.
In sacred shade his honour'd mansion stood ..... Od.9.232.316.
Shot to *Olympus* from the woodland shade. ..... Od.10.368.362.
Impassive semblance, and a flitting shade. ..... Od.10.587.372.
To seek *Tiresias'* awful shade below, ... Od.10.677.376.
New to the realms of death, *Elpenor's* shade: ..... Od.11.66.383.
To whom with tears: These rites, oh mournful shade, ... Od.11.98.385.
The shade withdrew, and mutter'd empty sounds. ..... Od.11.103.385.
All pale ascends my royal mother's shade: ..... Od.11.105.385.
Thus I, and thus the parent shade returns. ..... Od.11.218.392.
Thrice in my arms I strove her shade to bind, ... Od.11.248.393.
Fly'st thou, lov'd shade, while I thus fondly mourn? ..... Od.11.253.394.
O son of woe, the pensive shade rejoyn'd, ... Od.11.259.394.
Then shade to shade in mutual forms succeeds, ... Od.11.279.395.
Then shade to shade in mutual forms succeeds, ... Od.11.279.395.
A lovely shade, *Amphion's* youngest joy! ..... Od.11.342.398.
Now all *Atrides* is an empty shade. ..... Od.11.490.408.
O injur'd shade, I cry'd, what mighty woes ..... Od.11.541.410.
Warn'd by my ills beware, the Shade replies, ... Od.11.545.410.
And tow'ring *Ajax,* an illustrious shade! ..... Od.11.578.412.
Illustrious shade, (I cry'd) of *Peleus'* fates ..... Od.11.615.414.
While yet I spoke, the Shade with transport glow'd, ... Od.11.659.416.
A gloomy shade, the sullen *Ajax* stood; ..... Od.11.666.417.
Ev'n after death? relent, great Shade, relent! ..... Od.11.680.418.
While yet I speak, the shade disdains to stay, ... Od.11.691.418.
A mournful vision! the *Sisyphyan* shade; ..... Od.11.734.422.
Here hovering ghosts, like fowl, his shade surround, ... Od.11.747.423.
The god-like *Theseus,* and *Perithous'* shade; ..... Od.11.778.425.
Sepulchral honours to *Elpenor's* shade. ..... Od.12.12.430.
From the pale ghosts, and hell's tremendous shade. ..... Od.12.24.430.
A yawning cavern casts a dreadful shade: ..... Od.12.100.436.
The words of *Circe* and the *Theban* Shade; ..... Od.12.321.447.
To fly these shores the prescient *Theban* Shade ..... Od.12.326.447.
Then while the night displays her awful shade, ... Od.12.347.448.
From the loud storms to find a *Sylvan* shade; ..... Od.12.396.450.
And o'er the dungeon cast a dreadful shade. ..... Od.12.516.457.
In the wild olive's unfrequented shade, ... Od.13.141.11.
The trembling crowds shall see the sudden shade ..... Od.13.182.14.
Now seated in the Olive's sacred shade ..... Od.13.425.26.
Thro' mazy thickets of the woodland shade, ... Od.14.2.32.
Now cover'd with th' eternal shade of death! ..... Od.14.52.38.
But unapparent as a viewless shade ..... Od.16.173.111.
His black'ning chin receives a deeper shade: ..... Od.16.192.112.
Conceal'd in caverns in the sylvan shade. ..... Od.16.255.117.
Or where he hides in solitude and shade; ..... Od.16.399.125.
And veiling decent with a modest shade ..... Od.16.432.128.
At rest, or wand'ring in his country's shade, ... Od.17.181.140.
Or ere brown ev'ning spreads her chilly shade. ..... Od.17.215.142.
And holy horrors solemnize the shade. ..... Od.17.245.143.
Her beauty seems, and only seems, to shade: ..... Od.18.250.179.
To dress the walk, and form th' embow'ring shade. ..... Od.18.406.188.
Their drooping eyes the slumb'rous shade oppress, ... Od.19.497.220.
When nature's hush'd beneath her brooding shade, ... Od.19.602.225.
'Till soft oblivious shade *Minerva* spread, ... Od.19.703.229.
Beneath the verdure of which awful shade, ... Od.20.344.249.
O race to death devote! with *Stygian* shade ..... Od.20.423.253.
O'er the high crest, and cast a dreadful shade. ..... Od.22.141.293.
And each now wails an unlamented shade. ..... Od.22.455.310.
His royal mother, pale *Anticlea's* shade; ..... Od.23.350.341.
And lov'd *Patroclus* still attends his shade. ..... Od.24.28.348.
(Thus *Agamemnon's* kingly shade rejoin'd) ..... Od.24.52.350.
But *Agamemnon,* thro' the gloomy shade, ... Od.24.127.354.
Thus in the regions of eternal shade ..... Od.24.232.359.
Thro' rows of shade with various fruitage crown'd, ... Od.24.255.361.

SHADED

Sing, while beside the shaded Tomb I mourn, ... 1.PWi.19.90.
O'er dusky Fields and shaded Waters fly, ... 2.TemF.285.277.
Those ancient Woods that shaded all the Ground? ..... 4.JD2A.116.142.
Those ancient Woods, that shaded all the ground? ..... 4.JD2.110.143.
The shaded Tomb of old *Æpytus* stood; ..... Il.2.732.161.
Rest on the Summits of the shaded Hill; ..... Il.5.646.299.
Shaded with Clouds, and circumfus'd in Gold, ... Il.14.390.181.
Portentous shone, and shaded all the Field, ... Il.15.351.210.
That shaded *Ide,* and all the subject Field ..... Il.17.669.314.

SHADED (CONTINUED)

There sate *Achilles,* shaded by his Sails, ... Il.18.5.323.
The Smokes high-curling to the shaded Skies; ..... Il.18.246.334.
And o'er the shaded landscape rush'd the night. ..... Od.3.630.118.
Sonorous thro' the shaded air it sings; ..... Od.8.214.274.
And Night rush'd headlong on the shaded deeps. ..... Od.9.78.306.
High rais'd of stone; a shaded space around: ..... Od.10.241.352.
And o'er the shaded billows rush'd the night: ..... Od.11.12.379.
(The shaded Ocean blacken'd as it spread) ..... Od.14.336.51.
And shaded with a green surrounding grove; ..... Od.17.239.143.

SHADES

'Till in your Native Shades You tune the Lyre: ..... 1.PSp.12.61.
Daphnis and *Strephon* to the Shades retir'd, ... 1.PSp.17z1.62.
Then hid in Shades, eludes her eager Swain; ..... 1.PSp.54.66.
If *Windsor*-Shades *delight the matchless Maid,* ..... 1.PSp.67.67.
To closer Shades the painting Flocks remove, ... 1.PSu.87.79.
For her, the Lymes their pleasing Shades deny; ..... 1.PAu.25.82.
For him, the Lymes their pleasing Shades deny; ..... 1.PAu.25A.82.
And the fleet Shades glide o'er the dusky Green. ..... 1.PAu.64.85.
The Mossie Fountains and the Sylvan Shades, ... 1.Mes.3.112.
Unlock your Springs, and open all your Shades. ..... 1.W-F.4.148.
Thin Trees arise that shun each others Shades. ..... 1.W-F.22.150.
Nor envy *Windsor!* since thy Shades have seen ..... 1.W-F.161.164.
"Let me, O let me, to the Shades repair, ... 1.W-F.201.168.
"My native Shades—there weep, and murmur there." ..... 1.W-F.202.168.
Happy next him who to these Shades retires, ... 1.W-F.237.171.
Who now shall charm the Shades where *Cowley* strung ..... 1.W-F.279.174.
In the same Shades the *Cupids* tun'd his Lyre, ... 1.W-F.295.176.
As Shades more sweetly recommend the Light, ... 1.EOC.301.273.
A painted Mitre shades his furrow'd Brows. ..... 1.TrVP.49.379.
These shades, unknowing of the fates, she sought, ... 1.TrFD.17.386.
Those shades, unknowing of the fates, she sought, ... 1.TrFD.17A.386.
Sport in her shades, and in her shades be fed; ..... 1.TrFD.79.389.
Sport in her shades, and in her shades be fed; ..... 1.TrFD.79.389.
My closing lips, and hides my head in shades: ..... 1.TrFD.97.390.
I find the Shades that veil'd our Joys before, ... 1.TrSP.167.400.
But, *Phaon* gone, those Shades delight no more. ..... 1.TrSP.168.400.
I find the Shades that did our Joys conceal, ... 1.TrSP.167A.400.
Not Him, who made me love those Shades so well, ... 1.TrSP.168A.400.
Night shades the Groves, and all in Silence lye, ... 1.TrSP.175.401.
Shades all the Banks, and seems it self a Grove; ..... 1.TrSP.182.401.
Then self-condemn'd to Shades of endless Night, ... 1.TrSt.99.414.
Thro' Crouds of Airy Shades she wing'd her Flight, ... 1.TrSt.130.415.
Veil'd her fair Glories in the Shades of Night. ..... 1.TrSt.137.415.
Go mount the Winds, and to the Shades repair; ..... 1.TrSt.416.427.
Streak with long Gleams the scatt'ring Shades of Night; ..... 1.TrSt.485.430.
And seiz'd with Horror, in the Shades of Night, ... 1.TrSt.557.433.
And seiz'd with Horror, 'midst the Shades of Night, ... 1.TrSt.557A.433.
Goddess of Shades, beneath whose gloomy Reign ..... 1.TrSt.583.434.
And to the Shades a Ghost Triumphant send; ..... 1.TrSt.777.442.
And sends the brave *Epicles* to the Shades, ... 1.TrES.98.453.
And murm'ring to the Shades the Soul retires. ..... 1.TrES.110A.453.
And his Eyes darken'd with the Shades of Death: ..... 1.TrES.315.461.
So just recov'ring from the Shades of Night, ... 2.ChJM.802.54.
And screen'd in Shades from Day's detested Glare, ... 2.RL4.22.185.
Dreadful, as Hermit's Dreams in haunted Shades, ... 2.RL4.41.186.
These stop'd the Moon, and call'd th' unbody'd Shades ..... 2.TemF.101.260.
Shades ev'ry flow'r, and darkens ev'ry green, ... 2.ElAb.168.333.
The lights and shades, whose well accorded strife ..... 3.EOM2.121.70.
Sighs for the shades—"How charming is a Park!" ..... 3.Ep2.38.53.
Joins willing woods, and varies shades from shades, ... 3.Ep4.62.142.
Joins willing woods, and varies shades from shades, ... 3.Ep4.62.142.
Shades, that to Bacon could retreat afford, ... 4.HS2.175.69.
What Walls can guard me, or what Shades can hide? ..... 4.Arbu.7.96.
And let me in these Shades compose ..... 4.HS6.25.251.
A branch of Styx here rises from the Shades, ... 5.DunA2.314.140.
A branch of Styx here rises from the Shades, ... 5.DunB2.338.314.
Oh punish him, or to th' Elysian shades ..... 5.DunB4.417.382.
Great shades of **, **, **, *, ... 5.DunB4.545A.395.
By the Heroe's armed Shades, ... 6.11.77.33.
This Letter greets you from the Shades; ..... 6.13.1.39.
Basks in the Sun, then to the Shades retires, ... 6.17iii.30.58.
YE shades, where sacred truth is sought; ..... 6.51i.1.151.
And steel now glitters in the Muses shades. ..... 6.51i.8.151.
What are the falling Rills, the pendant Shades, ... 6.81.7A.225.
What are these noontide bowers and solemn shades, ... 6.81.7B.225.
There hid in Shades, and wasting Day by Day, ... 6.81.13A.226.
There hid in Shades, and pining Day by Day, ... 6.81.13B.226.
Ev'n now she shades thy Evening Walk with Bays, ... 6.84.35.240.
Thro' thy blest Shades (La Source) I seem to rove ..... 6.106ii.2.307.
When other Fair ones to the Shades go down, ... 6.110.1A.316.
When other Ladies to the Shades go down, ... 6.110.1B.316.
Late as I slumber'd in the Shades of Night, ... Il.2.71.130.
('Twas where the Plane-tree spread its Shades around) ..... Il.2.370.145.
No Rest, no Respite, 'till the Shades descend; ..... Il.2.459.149.
And *Eleon,* shelter'd by *Olympus'* Shades, ... Il.2.897.166.
Born in the Shades of *Ida's* secret Grove, ... Il.2.994.170.
And Shades Eternal! Let Division cease, ... Il.3.400.211.
And Shades Eternal settle o'er his Eyes. ..... Il.4.527.246.
Sent by great *Ajax* to the Shades of Hell; ..... Il.4.543.247.
His Eye-balls darken with the Shades of Death; ..... Il.4.578.249.
And everlasting Shades his Eyes surround. ..... Il.5.64.269.
I make this Present to the Shades below. ..... Il.5.801.304.
And o'er his Eye-balls swum the Shades of Night. ..... Il.5.857.307.
And seals in endless Shades his swimming Eyes. ..... Il.6.14.323.
Beneath the Beech-Tree's consecrated Shades, ... Il.6.298.341.
Then sunk *Eioneus* to the Shades below, ... Il.7.15.363.
And see his *Trojans* to the Shades descend. ..... Il.8.251.409.
Lest in the Silence and the Shades of Night, ... Il.8.635.426.
Then to their Vessels, thro' the gloomy Shades, ... Il.9.773.472.
Hangs o'er the Fleet, and shades our Walls below? ..... Il.10.183.10.
This, tho' surrounding Shades obscur'd their View, ... Il.10.323.17.
The social Shades the same dark Journey go, ... Il.11.339.49.
And a short Darkness shades his swimming Eyes. ..... Il.11.460.54.
Pallas, descending in the Shades of Night, ... Il.11.850.74.

SHADES (CONTINUED)

And sends the brave *Epicles* to the Shades; ....Il.12.452.98.
And murm'ring to the Shades the Soul retires. ....Il.12.464.98.
This, my third Victim, to the Shades I send. ....Il.13.561.133.
And everlasting Darkness shades him round. ....Il.13.844.146.
Catch the dry Mountain, and its Shades devour. ....Il.14.462.186.
Supine, and Shades eternal veil his Eyes. ....Il.14.522.188.
Infernal *Pluto* sways the Shades below; ....Il.15.213.205.
Had almost sunk me to the Shades below? ....Il.15.285.208.
Lo! *Hector* rises from the *Stygian* Shades! ....Il.15.325.209.
Sent by great *Ajax* to the Shades of Hell. ....Il.15.909.232.
His swimming Eyes eternal Shades surround. ....Il.16.413.259.
And shades the Sun, and blots the golden Skies: ....Il.16.437.259.
And Death involv'd him with the Shades of Hell. ....Il.16.505.262.
And his Eyes darken'd with the Shades of Death: ....Il.16.620.268.
Dispatch'd by *Merion* to the Shades of Death: ....Il.16.734.272.
Your Swords must plunge them to the Shades of Hell. ....Il.16.760.273.
Nor unattended, see the Shades below. ....Il.16.796.274.
To the dark Shades the Soul unwilling glides, ...Il.16.901.278.
And echoing Roars rebellow thro' the Shades. ....Il.16.918.279.
The tender Plant, and withers all its Shades; ....Il.17.62.290.
Sent by great *Ajax* to the Shades of Hell.' ....Il.17.349.301.
With sacred Darkness shades the Face of all. ....Il.17.523.308.
His hastening Soul, and sinks him to the Shades. ....Il.19.359.387.
Beneath the Shades of *Tmolus*, crown'd with Snow, ...Il.20.443.413.
A sadder Journey to the Shades below. ....Il.21.55.424.
Rise from the Shades, and brave me on the Field: ....Il.21.65.424.
The quiver'd Huntress of the *Sylvan* Shades. ....Il.21.546.444.
To *Ida's* Forests and surrounding Shades? ....Il.21.658.449.
If, in the melancholy Shades below, ...Il.22.487.476.
If, in the silent Shades of Hell below, ...Il.22.487A.476.
A sudden Darkness shades her swimming Eyes: ....Il.22.598.480.
The Day, that to the Shades the Father sends, ...Il.22.628.482.
Patroclus bears them to the Shades below. ....Il.23.189.497.
'Twas when, emerging thro' the Shades of Night, ...Il.23.280.501.
In one sad Day beheld the *Stygian* Shades; ....Il.24.760.569.
Dismiss'd thee gently to the Shades below. ....Il.24.957.576.
Or glides a ghost with unapparent shades. ....Od.2.152.69.
Of empty shades, I measure back the main; ....Od.2.250.73.
For when the fav'ring shades of night arise, ...Od.2.402.80.
Brown with o'er-arching shades and pendent woods, ...Od.3.97.90.
To pay whose honours to the Shades of hell ....Od.3.361.104.
So with her young, amid the woodland shades ....Od.4.449.141.
Glide thro' the shades, and bind th' attesting Gods! ....Od.5.240.183.
Or human voice? but issuing from the shades ....Od.6.147.214.
A wreathy foliage, and concealing shades. ....Od.6.152.215.
Where waving shades obscure the mazy streams. ....Od.6.250.222.
To *Pallas* sacred, shades the holy ground, ...Od.6.350.229.
Brown with dark forests, and with shades around. ....Od.10.298.358.
To guard the ship. Seek we the sacred shades ....Od.10.525.368.
But when the shades came on at evening hour, ...Od.10.566.370.
To all the shades around libations pour, ...Od.10.616.374.
Then the wan shades and feeble ghosts implore, ...Od.10.620.374.
Thin airy shoals, and visionary shades. ....Od.10.633.374.
'Till awful from the shades arise the *Seer*. ....Od.10.641.374.
Clouds the dull air, and wraps them round in shades. ....Od.11.20.380.
Now the wan shades we hail, th' infernal Gods, ...Od.11.35.381.
And wither'd Elders, pale and wrinkled shades: ....Od.11.50.383.
'Till awful, from the shades *Tiresias* rose. ....Od.11.64.383.
To glide in shades, and wander with the dead? ....Od.11.72.383.
Both beauteous shades, both hapless in their loves; ....Od.11.396.403.
The heroine shades; they vanish'd at her call. ....Od.11.481.408.
Of warrior Kings, and joyn'd th' illustrious shades. ....Od.11.662.416.
Better to rush at once to shades below, ...Od.12.415.451.
And bear the lamp of heav'n to shades below. ....Od.12.451.452.
From earth remov'd him to the shades below, ...Od.14.237.48.
Nor sink by sickness to the shades below; ....Od.15.447.92.
So with her young, amid the woodland shades, ...Od.17.140.138.
The Chief yet doubts, or to the shades below ....Od.18.104.172.
His golden circlet in the deep'ning shades; ....Od.18.354.184.
Soft slumb'rous shades his drooping eye-lids close, ...Od.19.60.195.
Parnassus, thick perplex'd with horrid shades, ...Od.19.503.220.
Sad *Philomel*, in bow'ry shades unseen, ...Od.19.605.225.
And to the shades devote the Suitor-train. ....Od.20.293.247.
His destin'd prey, and wraps them all in shades. ....Od.22.38.288.
Its bloom eternal in the *Stygian* shades. ....Od.24.118.353.
The shades thou seest, from yon' fair realms above. ....Od.24.213.358.

SHADING

His Tow'ry Helmet, black with shading Plumes. ....Il.6.639.358.

SHADOW

Their Vines a Shadow to their Race shall yield; ....1.Mes.65.118.
And now his Shadow reach'd her as she run, ...1.W-F.193.168.
(His Shadow lengthen'd by the setting Sun) ....1.W-F.194.168.
But like a Shadow, proves the *Substance* true; ....1.EOC.467.292.
But like a Shadow, proves the *Substance* too; ....1.EOC.467A.292.
If not God's image, yet his shadow drew: ....3.EOM3.288.121.
Now to thy gentle shadow all are shrunk, ...5.DunB4.509.392.
Huge moles, whose shadow stretch'd from shore to shore, ...6.71.21.203.

SHADOW'D

Illustrate, if you know, the shadow'd fate. ....Od.19.626.226.

SHADOWS

Project long Shadows o'er the Chrystal Tyde. ....1.W-F.376.187.
Like empty Shadows, pass, and glide away; ....2.ChJM.54.17.
Like flitting Shadows, pass, and glide away; ....2.ChJM.54A.17.
The gliding Shadows o'er the polish'd Glass. ....2.ChJM.237.26.
Of airy Elves by Moonlight Shadows seen, ...2.RL1.31.148.
(Not those which thin, unbody'd Shadows fill, ...6.13.2.39.
'Tis a fear that starts at shadows. ....6.70.4.201.
And Death's dim Shadows swam before his View. ....Il.13.726.139.
And hov'ring o'er, their stretching Shadows sees. ....Il.23.460.508.

SHADOWY

Shines a broad Mirrour thro' the shadowy Cave; ....6.142.2.382.
Host against Host with shadowy Squadrons drew, ...Il.4.510.245.
Host against Host with shadowy Legions drew, ...Il.8.77.399.
Courage resume, the shadowy form reply'd, ...Od.4.1079.168.
A shadowy form! for high in heav'n's abodes ....Od.11.743.423.
Nor solar ray, cou'd pierce the shadowy bow'r, ...Od.19.514.221.

SHADWELL

"How Shadwell hasty, Wycherly was slow; ....4.2HE1.85.201.
And Shadwell nods the poppy on his brows; ....5.DunA2.324.141.
And Shadwell nods the Poppy on his brows. ....5.DunB3.22.321.

SHADWELL'S

In Shadwell's bosom with eternal Rest! ....5.DunB1.240.287.

SHADWELLS

New *S[hadwell]s* and new *M[ilbour]ns* must arise; ....1.EOC.463B.291.

SHADY

At Morn the Plains, at Noon the shady Grove; ....1.PSp.78.68.
Ye shady Beeches, and ye cooling Streams, ...1.PSu.13.72.
The shady Empire shall retain no Trace ....1.W-F.371.186.
Then weary grown, to shady grotts retires, ...1.TrPA.37.366.
Here cornels rise, and in the shady grove ....1.TrPA.74.368.
To her the Shady Grove, the flow'ry Field, ...1.TrVP.5.377.
And when in youth he seeks the shady woods, ...1.TrFD.84.389.
Ascend from Hills, and Plains, and shady Bow'rs; ....1.TrSt.287.422.
Delight in *Cynthus* and the Shady Shore; ....1.TrSt.834.444.
And crowns the pointed Cliffs with shady Boughs. ....1.TrUl.32.466.
Whose Cause-way parts the vale with shady rows? ....3.Ep3.259.114.
See shady Forms advance! ....6.11.65.32.
High *Mycalè*, and *Latmos'* shady Brows, ...Il.2.1057.172.
A shady Light was shot from glimm'ring Shields, ...Il.4.324.236.
And shoot a shady Lustre o'er the Field. ....Il.8.704.428.
Near, and more near, the shady Cohorts prest; ....Il.11.522.57.
And took their Seats beneath the shady Tent. ....Il.11.763.69.
But plac'd aloft, on *Ida's* shady Height ....Il.14.183.168.
And spread the Carnage thro' the shady Gloom. ....Il.15.369.211.
From *Pelion's* shady Brow the Plant entire ....Il.16.174.245.
To the rich Coffer, in his shady Tent: ....Il.16.269.249.
Each fair-hair'd Dryad of the shady Wood, ...Il.20.13.393.
The shady Foot of *Ida's* Fount-ful Hill. ....Il.20.259.404.
Whose shaggy brow o'erhangs the shady deep, ...Od.3.375.104.
Whose shady horrors on a rising brow ....Od.5.614.201.
The fair-hair'd *Dryads* of the shady wood, ...Od.6.145.214.
With shady mountains, spread their isles around. ....Od.9.24.303.
The bushing alders form'd a shady scene. ....Od.9.164.312.
Whose ridge o'erlook'd a shady length of land; ....Od.10.170.349.
Nymphs sprung from fountains, or from shady woods, ...Od.10.415.364.
Here watchful o'er the flocks, in shady bow'rs ....Od.12.170.440.
Swift from the oak they strip the shady pride; ....Od.12.421.451.
A pause of silence hush'd the shady rooms: ....Od.13.3.1.
And crowns the pointed cliffs with shady boughs. ....Od.13.123.7.
Full in their port a shady hill shall rise, ...Od.13.176.14.
The shady grot, that brightned with the God. ....Od.13.420.26.
And lofty *Zacinth* crown'd with shady hills. ....Od.16.132.109.
Distant he saw, across the shady Dome; ....Od.17.402.152.
Zacynthus, green with ever-shady groves, ...Od.19.152.199.

SHAFT

The bearded Shaft the destin'd Passage found, ...1.TrES.113.454.
But first, to speed the Shaft, address thy Vow ....Il.4.131.226.
She turn'd the Shaft, which hissing from above, ...Il.4.166.228.
The Shaft infix'd, and saw the gushing Tide: ....Il.4.179.230.
Pierc'd with a winged Shaft (the Deed of *Troy*) ....Il.4.232.232.
The Shaft he drew, but left the Head behind. ....Il.4.247.232.
The Shaft found Entrance in his Iron Breast, ...Il.5.486.291.
By *Teucer's* Shaft brave *Aretäon* bled, ...Il.6.37.325.
With ev'ry Shaft some hostile Victim slew, ...Il.8.323.413.
Till ev'ry Shaft in *Phrygian* Blood be dy'd. ....Il.8.358.414.
Another Shaft the raging Archer drew; ....Il.8.375.415.
That other Shaft with erring Fury flew, ...Il.8.376.415.
The Shaft already to his Shoulder drew; ....Il.8.390.416.
The Bow-string twang'd; nor flew the Shaft in vain, ...Il.11.481.55.
In his right Shoulder the broad Shaft appear'd, ...Il.11.630.61.
The bearded Shaft the destin'd Passage found, ...Il.12.467.98.
The Shaft of *Merion* mingled with the dead. ....Il.13.814.144.
But skill'd from far the flying Shaft to wing, ...Il.13.893.148.
Down drop'd the Bow: the Shaft with brazen Head ....Il.15.546.217.
The single, he, whose Shaft divides the Cord. ....Il.23.1016.529.
To *Phœbus*, Patron of the Shaft and Bow. ....Il.23.1023.529.
He takes the Bow, directs the Shaft above, ...Il.23.1030.530.
My well-aim'd shaft with death prevents the foe: ....Od.8.250.276.
Great *Philoctetes* taught the shaft to fly. ....Od.8.252.276.
When late stern *Neptune* points the shaft with death; ....Od.11.167.389.
The Goddess aims her shaft, the Nymph expires. ....Od.11.404.404.
Thy shaft, and send me joyful to the dead: ....Od.20.95.237.
To speed the flying shaft thro' ev'ry ring, ...Od.21.102.263.
At distance far the feather'd shaft he throws, ...Od.21.173.268.
He snatch'd the shaft that glitter'd on the board: ....Od.21.455.282.
Then notch'd the shaft, releast, and gave it wing; ....Od.21.460.282.
Thy erring shaft has made our bravest bleed, ...Od.22.33.288.
While yet each shaft flew deathful from his hand: ....Od.22.133.293.
When late stern *Neptune* points the shaft of death; ....Od.23.300.337.

SHAFTED

First silver-shafted *Phœbus* took the Plain ....Il.20.91.398.
The silver-shafted Goddess of the Chace! ....Od.4.160.128.
Nor bent the silver-shafted Queen her bow; ....Od.11.243.393.

SHAFTS

Discharge thy Shafts, this ready Bosom rend, ...1.TrSt.776.442.
By thee the Bow and mortal Shafts are born, ...1.TrSt.837.444.
Thy Shafts aveng'd lewd *Tityus'* guilty Flame, ...1.TrSt.847.445.
God of the Silver Bow! thy Shafts employ, ...Il.1.59.88.

SHAFTS (CONTINUED)
Fierce as he mov'd, his Silver Shafts resound. ....Il.1.64.89.
And *Phœbus* dart his burning Shafts no more. ....Il.1.90.91.
Grac'd with the Present of his Shafts and Bow. ....Il.2.1003.170.
These Shafts, once fatal, carry Death no more. ....Il.5.259.279.
Of sounding Shafts, she bears him from the Fight. ....Il.5.394.285.
Around the Field his feather'd Shafts he sent, ...Il.11.475.55.
Skill'd, or with Shafts to gall the distant Field, ...Il.13.404.125.
Collects the scatter'd Shafts, and fallen Bow, ...Il.21.586.446.
His shafts *Apollo* aim'd; at once they sound, ...Od.11.393.403.
The bounding shafts upon the harness play, ...Od.15.208.78.
Pierc'd with her golden shafts the rere of night; ....Od.19.500.220.
And to his shafts obtend these ample boards, ...Od.22.88.290.
While yet th' auxiliar shafts this hand supply; ....Od.22.123.292.
The best of all the shafts had left alive. ....Od.22.269.299.
First bleeds *Antinous:* thick the shafts resound; ....Od.24.206.358.

SHAG
And search the shag of Thighatira's Ruff. ....6.96ii.30Z2.271.

SHAGG'D
Ye grots and caverns shagg'd with horrid thorn! ....2.ElAb.20.320.
So the rough rock had shagg'd *Ulysses'* hands. ....Od.5.553.199.

SHAGGY
In shaggy Spoils here *Theseus* was beheld, ...2.TemF.79.258.
A shaggy Tap'stry, worthy to be spread ....5.DunA2.135.117.
A shaggy Tap'stry, worthy to be spread ....5.DunB2.143.302.
And from their Hills the shaggy *Centaurs* tore. ....Il.1.357.105.
To distant Dens the shaggy *Centaurs* fled) ....Il.2.903.166.
Obscures the Glade, and nods his shaggy Brows, ...Il.2.919.167.
There high on *Sipylus* his shaggy Brow, ...Il.24.777.569.
With Purple soft, and shaggy Carpets spread; ....Il.24.813.571.
And anchor under *Mimas'* shaggy brow? ....Od.3.208.96.
Whose shaggy brow o'erhangs the shady deep, ...Od.3.375.104.
But cliffs, and shaggy shores, a dreadful sight! ....Od.5.520.197.
And cavern'd ways, the shaggy coast along, ...Od.14.3.32.
A shaggy goat's soft hyde beneath him spread, ...Od.14.59.38.
As many stalls for shaggy goats are rear'd; ....Od.14.123.42.
His shaggy cloak a mountain goat supply'd: ....Od.14.597.66.
With sheep and shaggy goats the porkers bled, ...Od.20.314.248.

SHAK'ST
Who bath'st in Blood, and shak'st the lofty Wall! ....Il.5.40A.267.

SHAKE
Shake the light Blossoms from their blasted Boughs! ....1.TrVP.111.381.
Long Trails of Light, and shake their blazing Hair. ....1.TrSt.844.445.
Shock just had giv'n himself the rowzing Shake, ...2.RL*A*1.15.127.
Now *Shock* had giv'n himself the towzing Shake, ...2.RL1.15A.145.
Now Lapdogs give themselves the rowzing Shake, ...2.RL1.15.146.
And shake all o'er, like a discover'd Spy. ....4.JD4.279.49.
Grave, as when Pris'ners shake the head, and swear ....4.JD2.69.139.
And shake alike the Senate and the Field: ....4.EpS2.87.318.
Or laugh and shake in Rab'lais' easy Chair, ...5.DunA1.20.62.
Let others aim: 'Tis yours to shake the soul ....5.DunA2.217.127.
Or laugh and shake in Rab'lais' easy chair, ...5.DunB1.22.270.
Let others aim: 'Tis yours to shake the soul ....5.DunB2.225.307.
To stir, to rouze, to shake the Soul he comes, ...5.DunB4.67.348.
Eton and Winton shake thro' all their Sons. ....5.DunB4.144.355.
Or Ravenous *Corm'rants* shake their flabby Wings, ...6.26i.6.79.
And shake his Head at Doctor *S[wif]t.* ....6.39.24.111.
Groan and shake; ....6.96i.23.268.
Or laugh and shake in Rab'lais' easy chair, ...6.106iv.4.307.
No Force can shake: What *is,* that *ought* to be. ....Il.1.731.122.
Lest, rouz'd to Rage, he shake the blest Abodes, ...Il.1.748.123.
Must shake, and heavy will the Vengeance fall! ....Il.2.451.149.
And thund'ring Footsteps shake the sounding Shore: ....Il.2.549.153.
Men, Steeds, and Chariots shake the trembling Ground; ....Il.2.980.170.
All pale with Rage, and shake the threat'ning Lance. ....Il.3.426.212.
And shake his *Ægis* o'er their guilty Head. ....Il.4.203.231.
Who bathe in Blood, and shake the lofty Wall! ....Il.5.40.267.
Who bathe in Blood, and shake th' embattel'd Wall! ....Il.5.554.295.
When shouting Millions shake the thund'ring Field. ....Il.5.1055.317.
The solid Earth's eternal Basis shake! ....Il.7.545.391.
Men, Steeds, and Chariots shake the trembling Ground; ....Il.8.73.399.
The stedfast Earth from her Foundations shake, ...Il.8.243.409.
A dreadful Front! they shake the Brands, and threat ....Il.8.264.410.
Th' avenging Bolt, and shake the sable Shield! ....Il.8.424.417.
Th' avenging Bolt, and shake the dreadful Shield! ....Il.8.527.421.
And each immortal Nerve with Horror shake. ....Il.8.565.423.
Has he not Walls no human Force can shake? ....Il.9.459.455.
Th' avenging Bolt, and shake the dreadful Shield. ....Il.10.328.17.
Shake the dry Field, and thunder tow'rd the Fleet. ....Il.11.641.62.
In vain their Clamours shake the ambient Fields, ...Il.12.155.87.
The Forests shake! Earth trembled as he trod, ...Il.13.30.105.
The solid Globe's eternal Basis shake. ....Il.13.302.119.
When twice ten thousand shake the lab'ring Field; ....Il.14.174.165.
Shake my broad *Ægis* on thy active Arm, ...Il.15.259.207.
The Hosts rush on; loud Clamours shake the Shore; ....Il.15.404.212.
With conqu'ring Shouts the *Trojans* shake the Plain, ...Il.16.730.272.
Some, hard and heavy, shake the sounding Shields. ....Il.16.934.279.
And shake the brazen Concave of the Skies. ....Il.17.483.306.
From their high Manes they shake the Dust, and bear ....Il.17.526.308.
The solid Globe's eternal Basis shake. ....Il.20.161.400.
And all her Members shake with sudden Fear; ....Il.22.575.480.
His Friends (while loud Applauses shake the Skies) ....Il.23.1004.529.
And shake the Purpose of my Soul no more. ....Il.24.719.567.
To shake with war proud *Ilion's* lofty tow'rs, ...Od.2.200.71.
Th' avenging bolt, and shake the dreadful shield! ....Od.4.1006.164.
There no rude winds presume to shake the skies, ...Od.6.51.207.
Th' avenging bolt, and shake the dreadful shield; ....Od.6.386.230.
Shake at the weight, and refluent beat the shore. ....Od.9.634.332.
O'er the *Cerulean* Vault, and shake the Pole; ....Od.20.142.240.

SHAKER
The great Earth-shaker thus: To whom replies ....Il.20.357.410.
He said: the Shaker of the earth replies. ....Od.13.171.13.

SHAKES
Shakes off the *Dust,* and rears his rev'rend Head! ....1.EOC.700.319.
It shakes; the pondrous Stones disjoynted yield; ....1.TrES.131.454.
Gloomy as Night, and shakes two shining Spears; ....1.TrES.200.456.
And shakes the waving Forests on his Sides! ....1.TrUl.233.473.
Earth shakes her nodding Tow'rs, the Ground gives way; ....2.RL5.51.203.
The Temple shakes, the sounding Gates unfold, ...2.TemF.137.264.
Shakes all together, and produces—You. ....3.Ep2.280.73.
The Mountain nods, the Forest shakes, ...6.78ii.6.216.
Not * He that shakes the solid Earth so strong: ....Il.1.525.113.
Shakes his Ambrosial Curls, and gives the Nod; ....Il.1.684.120.
And unextinguish'd Laughter shakes the Skies. ....Il.1.771.124.
He shakes the feeble Props of human Trust, ...Il.2.149.135.
Where high *Neritos* shakes his waving Woods, ...Il.2.770.162.
Shakes his huge Spear, and nods his Plumy Crest: ....Il.2.989.170.
High on his Car he shakes the flowing Reins, ...Il.2.1016.171.
The Lots of Fight, and shakes the brazen Urn. ....Il.3.403.211.
And in his Hand a pointed Jav'lin shakes. ....Il.3.420.212.
The Sire whose Thunder shakes the cloudy Skies, ...Il.4.45.223.
And shakes the Sparkles from its blazing Hair: ....Il.4.106.225.
She stalks on Earth, and shakes the World around; ....Il.4.505.245.
Shakes for his Danger, and neglects his own; ....Il.5.694.301.
That shakes a Spear that casts a dreadful Light; ....Il.5.729.302.
But shakes his Plume, and fierce to Combate flies, ...Il.5.849.306.
Thus He who Shakes *Olympus* with his Nod; ....Il.5.1108.320.
Atrides o'er him shakes the vengeful Steel; ....Il.6.54.326.
Fierce in the Front he shakes two dazling Spears; ....Il.6.131.330.
Let Conquest make them ours: Fate shakes their Wall, ...Il.7.478.388.
Then * He, whose Trident shakes the Earth, began. ....Il.7.529.391.
Then with a Voice that shakes the solid Skies, ...Il.8.194.406.
And wide beneath him, all *Olympus* shakes. ....Il.8.553.422.
Who shakes the feeble Props of human Trust, ...Il.9.33.433.
War shakes her Walls, and thunders at her Gates. ....Il.9.688.468.
Then, with his Foot, old *Nestor* gently shakes ....Il.10.178.9.
Whose Thunder shakes the dark aerial Hall. ....Il.10.390.21.
The Navy shakes, and at the dire Alarms ....Il.11.15.35.
It shakes; the pond'rous Stones disjointed yield; ....Il.12.485.99.
Gloomy as Night! and shakes two shiny Spears: ....Il.12.554.102.
This ready Arm, unthinking, shakes the Dart; ....Il.13.111.110.
The long Lance shakes, and vibrates in the Wound: ....Il.13.555.132.
And * he that shakes the solid Earth, gave Aid. ....Il.13.850.146.
Shakes his white Plumes that to the Breezes flow, ...Il.13.947.150.
And such a Clamour shakes the sounding Heav'n. ....Il.14.464.186.
Shakes all the Thrones of Heav'n, and bends the Poles. ....Il.15.119.201.
The trembling World, and shakes the steady Poles. ....Il.15.173.203.
But when aloft he shakes it in the Skies, ...Il.15.362.210.
The Deck approaching, shakes a flaming Brand; ....Il.15.489.216.
Shakes his huge Javelin, and whole Armies fall. ....Il.15.727.224.
The Chief so thunders, and so shakes the Fleet. ....Il.15.759.225.
Now shakes his Spear, now lifts, and now protends, ...Il.15.887.231.
His pointless Spear the Warrior shakes in vain; ....Il.16.146.243.
Patroclus shakes his Lance; but Fate denies. ....Il.16.463.260.
Loose in each Joint; each Nerve with Horror shakes. ....Il.16.969.281.
He shakes, and charges the bold Charioteer. ....Il.16.1045.283.
In vain *Automedon* now shakes the Rein, ...Il.17.488.307.
Shakes down Diseases, Pestilence and War; ....Il.19.413.389.
And now he shakes his great paternal Spear, ...Il.19.420.389.
Beneath, stern *Neptune* shakes the solid Ground, ...Il.20.77.397.
And in his deep Abysses shakes with Fear. ....Il.21.216.430.
Or deep beneath the trembling Thicket shakes; ....Il.22.246.465.
Now shakes his Lance, and braves the Dread of *Troy.* ....Il.22.356.470.
I well discern him, as he shakes the Rein, ...Il.23.562.511.
And unextinguish'd laughter shakes the sky. ....Od.8.366.283.
And shakes the waving forests on his sides. ....Od.13.400.26.
Mean-while *Pisistratus* he gently shakes, ...Od.15.53.72.
Pois'd in his hand the pointed jav'lin shakes. ....Od.15.594.99.
Return, and riot shakes our walls a-new) ....Od.17.121.137.
The sea, the land, and shakes the world with arms! ....Od.17.343.148.
A strong emotion shakes my anguish'd breast; ....Od.19.442.216.

SHAKESPEAR
Call *Tibbald Shakespear,* and he'll swear the Nine ....4.2HE2.137.175.
Shakespear, (whom you and ev'ry Play-house bill ....4.2HE1.69.199.
Or damn all Shakespear, like th' affected fool ....4.2HE1.105.203.
And full in Shakespear, fair in Otway shone: ....4.2HE1.277.219.
And fluent Shakespear scarce effac'd a line. ....4.2HE1.279.219.
And crucify poor Shakespear once a week. ....5.DunA1.164.83.
There hapless Shakespear, yet of Tibbald sore, ...5.DunB1.133.279.
'Twixt Plautus, Fletcher, Shakespear, and Corneille, ...5.DunB1.285.290.
Enter Shakespear, with a loud clap. ....6.148i.2.395.
And near thy *Shakespear* place thy honour'd Bust, ...6.152.2.400.

SHAKESPEAR'S
Preserv'd in *Milton's* or in *Shakespear's* name. ....4.Arbu.168.108.
"Of Shakespear's Nature, and of Cowley's Wit; ....4.2HE1.83.201.
With Shakespear's nature, or with Johnson's art, ...5.DunA2.216.127.
With Shakespear's nature, or with Johnson's art, ...5.DunB2.224.307.
"What! no respect, he cry'd, for Shakespear's page?" ....5.DunB4.114A.352.
Wrapt round and sanctify'd with *Shakespear's* Name; ....6.98.18.283.

SHAKESPEARE
Who study Shakespeare at the Inns of Court, ...5.DunB4.568.398.

SHAKING
Shaking the horrors of his ample brows, ...5.DunA2.303.139.
Shaking the horrors of his sable brows, ...5.DunA2.303A.139.
Shaking the horrors of his sable brows, ...5.DunB2.327.313.
Clad in his Might th' Earth-shaking Pow'r appears; ....Il.14.447.185.
Else had my Wrath, Heav'ns Thrones all shaking round, ...Il.15.252.206.
Thy Force can match the great Earth-shaking Pow'r. ....Il.21.552.444.
Troy feels the Blast along her shaking Walls, ...Il.23.268.500.
Now, scarce withdrawn the fierce Earth-shaking pow'r, ...Od.5.488.195.

SHALL (OMITTED)
1259 ...

SHALLOP
Imported in a shallop not his own: ... Od.20.237.244.

SHALLOW
There *shallow Draughts* intoxicate the Brain, ... 1.EOC.217.264.
As shallow streams run dimpling all the way. ... 4.Arbu.316.118.
Proud Fortune, and look shallow Greatness thro': ... 4.1HE1.108.287.
So from the Sun's broad beam, in shallow urns ... 5.DunB2.11.296.
Shallow, yet swift, the stream of fortune flows, ... 6.22.3.71.
(Such as his shallow wit, he deem'd was mine) ... Od.9.499.326.

SHALLOWS
Our depths who fathoms, or our shallows finds, ... 3.Ep1.29.17.
Now off at sea, and from the shallows clear, ... Od.9.555.328.

SHALT
These thefts, false nymph, thou shalt enjoy no more, ... 1.TrPA.138.371.
Soon shalt thou find, if thou but arm their Hands, ... 1.TrSt.120.415.
Nor shalt thou, *Phœbus,* find a Suppliant here: ... 1.TrSt.760.442.
Thou by some other shalt be laid as low. ... 2.RL5.98.207.
Hell thou shalt move; for Faustus is thy friend: ... 5.DunA3.306.185.
Pluto with Cato thou for her shalt join, ... 5.DunA3.307.185.
Thou Cibber! thou, his Laurel shalt support, ... 5.DunB1.299.291.
On grinning dragons thou shalt mount the wind. ... 5.DunB3.268.333.
Hell thou shalt move; for Faustus is our friend: ... 5.DunB3.308.335.
Pluto with Cato thou for this shalt join, ... 5.DunB3.309.335.
'Tis Thou shalt save him from insidious wrongs, ... 6.21.5.69.
Thou on the fiery Basilisk shalt tread, ... 6.21.29.70.
And thou shalt live; for *Buckingham* commends. ... 6.63.2.188.
Take all thou e're shalt have, a constant Muse: ... 6.66.5.194.
And thou shalt have the Brains. ... 6.94.72.261.
Thou who shalt stop, where *Thames'* translucent Wave ... 6.142.1.382.
Hence shalt thou prove my Might, and curse the Hour, ... Il.1.247.98.
Then shalt thou mourn th' Affront thy Madness gave, ... Il.1.321.103.
What fits thy Knowledge, thou the first shalt know; ... Il.1.708.121.
Her shalt thou wound: So *Pallas* gives Command. ... Il.5.169.275.
Yet long th' inflicted Pangs thou shalt not mourn, ... Il.5.1104.320.
Then shalt thou store (when *Greece* the Spoil divides) ... Il.9.364.451.
There shalt thou live his Son, his Honours share, ... Il.9.372.451.
Her shalt thou wed whom most thy Eyes approve, ... Il.9.378.451.
There shalt thou reign with Pow'r and Justice crown'd, ... Il.9.392.452.
There shalt thou stay (the King of Men reply'd ... Il.10.71.5.
Thou shalt not long the Death deserv'd withstand, ... Il.11.469.55.
Whelm'd in thy Country's Ruins shalt thou fall, ... Il.13.973.152.
Ev'n thou shalt call on *Jove,* and call in vain; ... Il.13.1033.153.
Ev'n thou shalt wish, to aid thy desp'rate Course, ... Il.13.1034.153.
Shalt run, forgetful of a Warrior's Fame, ... Il.13.1036.153.
The Lance of *Hector,* thou shalt meet thy Fate: ... Il.13.1053.155.
Soon shalt thou view the scatter'd *Trojan* Bands ... Il.14.166.165.
But thou a Prey to Vulturs shalt be made! ... Il.16.1009.282.
Insulting Man! thou shalt be soon, as I; ... Il.16.1028.283.
But long thou shalt not thy just Fate withstand, ... Il.20.521.416.
So shalt thou pass the Goal, secure of Mind, ... Il.23.417.506.
Nor shalt thou Death, nor shalt thou Danger dread; ... Il.24.217.546.
Nor shalt thou Death, nor shalt thou Danger dread; ... Il.24.217.546.
Thou too my Son! to barb'rous Climes shalt goe, ... Il.24.922.574.
Shalt yet enjoy, but still art doom'd to roam. ... Od.4.642.149.
Attend, and speedy thou shalt pass the main: ... Od.6.348.229.
So shalt thou view with joy thy natal shore, ... Od.6.375.230.
High-thron'd, and feasting, there thou shalt behold ... Od.7.65.237.
So shalt thou instant reach the realm assign'd, ... Od.8.603.294.
And never shalt thou taste this Nectar more. ... Od.9.416.323.
Never, alas! thou never shalt return, ... Od.10.317.359.
Sooner shalt thou, a stranger to thy shape, ... Od.10.340.360.
Soon shalt thou reach old Ocean's utmost ends, ... Od.10.602.372.
So peaceful shalt thou end thy blissful days, ... Od.11.164.389.
Nor garment shalt thou want, nor ought beside, ... Od.14.578.64.
Other *Ulysses* shalt thou never see, ... Od.16.224.114.
Dearly, full dearly shalt thou buy thy bread, ... Od.17.270.145.
Another *Ægypt,* shalt thou quickly find. ... Od.17.532.158.
To thy own dogs a prey thou shalt be made; ... Od.21.395.279.
Thus, and thus only, shalt thou join thy friend. ... Od.22.243.298.
Nor shalt thou in the day of danger find ... Od.23.127.326.

SHAM'D
Old Cotta sham'd his fortune and his birth, ... 3.Ep3.179.108.
Yet touch'd and sham'd by *Ridicule* alone. ... 4.EpS2.211.325.

SHAME
(The *Glory* of the Priesthood, and the *Shame!*) ... 1.EOC.694.318.
Such inconsistent things are Love and Shame! ... 1.TrSP.142.395.
Their down cast looks a decent Shame confest, ... 1.TrSt.631.436.
What Grief, what Shame must *Glaucus* undergo, ... 1.TrES.308.461.
Enough to shame the gentlest Bard that sings ... 2.ChJM.454.37.
Enough to shame the boldest Bard that sings ... 2.ChJM.454A.37.
"But see! I'm all your own—nay hold—for Shame! ... 2.ChWB.203.66.
Oft has he blush'd from Ear to Ear for Shame, ... 2.ChWB.275.70.
And Husband-Bull—Oh monstrous! fie, for Shame! ... 2.ChWB.386.76.
I can no more; by shame, by rage suppress, ... 2.ElAb.105.328.
But what will grow on Pride, or grow on Shame. ... 3.EOM2.194.78.
But what or grows on Pride, or grows on Shame. ... 3.EOM2.194A.78.
Shame to the virgin, to the matron pride, ... 3.EOM2.242.84.
Honour and shame from no Condition rise; ... 3.EOM4.193.145.
Wh[arton], the Shame and Scandal of mankind: ... 3.EOM4.282A.154.
E'er taught to shine, or sanctify'd from shame! ... 3.EOM4.300.156.
A Tale, that blends their glory with their shame! ... 3.EOM4.308.157.
Where none distinguish twixt your Shame and Pride, ... 3.Ep2.204A.67.
Where none distinguish twixt your Shame or Pride, ... 3.Ep2.204B.67.
There, none distinguish 'twixt your Shame or Pride, ... 3.Ep2.204.67.
To friends, to fortune, to mankind a shame, ... 4.HS2.107.61.
To Shame eternal, or eternal Law. ... 4.HAdv.174.89.
"And shame the Fools—your Int'rest, Sir, with *Lintot."* ... 4.Arbu.62.100.
" Satire or Shame alas! can *Sporus* feel? ... 4.Arbu.307A.118.

SHAME (CONTINUED)
That Flatt'ry, ev'n to Kings, he held a shame, ... 4.Arbu.338.120.
And swear, all shame is lost in George's Age! ... 4.2HE1.126.205.
His Friend and Shame, and was a kind of *Screen.* ... 4.EpS1.22.299.
There, where no Passion, Pride, or Shame transport, ... 4.EpS1.97.305.
Let humble ALLEN, with an aukward Shame, ... 4.EpS1.135.308.
Let low-born ALLEN, with an aukward Shame, ... 4.EpS1.135A.308.
That "Not to be corrupted is the Shame." ... 4.EpS1.160.309.
Now (shame to Fortune!) an ill Run at Play ... 5.DunB1.113.277.
Wraps in her Veil, and frees from sense of Shame. ... 5.DunB4.336.376.
And strait succeeded, leaving shame no room, ... 5.DunB4.531.394.
'*till* drown'd was Sense, and Shame, and Right, and Wrong— .5.DunB4.625.406.
Nay, e'en the Parts of Shame by Name would call: ... 6.14ii.41.44.
Made Slaves by Honour, and made Fools by Shame. ... 6.19.36.63.
A bright example of young *Tarquin's* shame. ... 6.38.22.108.
Where reign our Sires! There, to thy Countrey's Shame, ... 6.96iii.7.274.
'Tis sure some Virtue to conceal its Shame. ... 6.96v.20.280.
Thought by all Heav'n a burning Shame; ... 6.119.10.337.
E'er taught to shine, or sanctified from shame ... 6.130.14.358.
A Tale! that blends the Glory with the Shame ... 6.130.38.359.
What Shame, what Woe is this to *Greece!* what Joy ... Il.1.339.104.
What Shame to *Greece* a fruitless War to wage, ... Il.2.151.135.
Oh lasting Shame in ev'ry future Age! ... Il.2.152.135.
Haste gen'rous *Ithacus!* prevent the Shame, ... Il.2.215.138.
Aw'd by no Shame, by no Respect controul'd, ... Il.2.257.140.
With Shame deserting, heap with vile Disgrace. ... Il.2.349.143.
But vanquish'd! baffled! oh eternal Shame! ... Il.2.363.144.
With conscious Shame and reverential Fear. ... Il.3.228.203.
My Brother once, before my Days of Shame; ... Il.3.237.203.
Else should I merit everlasting Shame, ... Il.3.509.216.
Is this the Chief, who lost to Sense of Shame ... Il.3.533.217.
O'erwhelm me, Earth! and hide a Monarch's Shame. ... Il.4.219.231.
Shame to your Country, Scandal of your Kind! ... Il.4.276.234.
Stung with the Shame, within the winding Way, ... Il.4.444.241.
Struck with Amaze, and Shame, the *Trojan* Crew ... Il.5.35.267.
Meets Death, and worse than Death, Eternal Shame. ... Il.5.658.299.
Inglorious *Argives!* to your Race a Shame, ... Il.5.980.313.
If yet not lost to all the Sense of Shame, ... Il.6.350.343.
On Hate of *Troy,* than conscious Shame and Grief: ... Il.6.421.347.
The Thoughts of Glory past, and present Shame, ... Il.6.588.355.
How great the Shame, when ev'ry Age shall know ... Il.7.111.369.
Thus to the Kings he spoke. What grief, what Shame ... Il.7.145.371.
Back to the Skies with Shame he shall be driv'n, ... Il.8.13.395.
O'erwhelm me Earth! and hide a Warrior's Shame. ... Il.8.182.406.
Await on *Troy,* on *Greece* eternal Shame. ... Il.8.215.407.
Oh *Argives!* Shame of human Race; he cry'd, ... Il.8.274.410.
First let him speak, who first has suffer'd Shame. ... Il.9.44.434.
And stand we deedless, O eternal Shame! ... Il.11.407.53.
What shame, inglorious if I quit the Plain; ... Il.11.514.57.
Or are her Heroes doom'd to die with Shame, ... Il.11.954.77.
With Shame repuls'd, with Grief and Fury driv'n, ... Il.12.183.87.
Another's is the Crime, but yours the Shame. ... Il.13.152.111.
I waste no Anger, for they feel no Shame: ... Il.13.158.112.
While Clouds of friendly Dust conceal thy Shame. ... Il.13.1037.154.
And thou the Shame of any Host but ours! ... Il.14.93.162.
The Wretch relentless, and o'erwhelm with Shame! ... Il.14.164.165.
Back to the Skies would'st thou with Shame be driv'n, ... Il.15.150.202.
Respect your selves, and learn an honest Shame: ... Il.15.667.221.
Meets Death, and worse than Death, eternal Shame. ... Il.15.673.222.
Now manly Shame forbids th' inglorious Flight; ... Il.15.790.226.
With mutual Honour, and with mutual Shame! ... Il.15.797.227.
What Grief, what Shame must *Glaucus* undergo, ... Il.16.613.268.
And in *Patroclus'* Blood efface thy Shame. ... Il.16.882.277.
Oh lasting Shame! to our own Fears a Prey, ... Il.17.390.302.
What Shame to *Greece* for future times to tell, ... Il.17.628.312.
Thy Friend's Disgrace, thy own eternal Shame! ... Il.18.218.332.
Shall ignominious We with shame retire, ... Il.21.510.443.
Honour and Shame th' ungen'rous Thought recall: ... Il.22.139.459.
Shame is not of his Soul; nor understood, ... Il.24.56.538.
Thy erring voice displays thy Mother's shame. ... Od.2.98.65.
Proceed my son! this youthful shame expel; ... Od.3.19.87.
At first with worthy shame and decent pride, ... Od.3.330.102.
For then with dire remorse, and conscious shame, ... Od.4.357.136.
O shame to manhood! shall one daring boy ... Od.4.888.159.
And the least freedom with the sex is shame, ... Od.6.344.228.
And bear the shame, like *Mars,* to share the joy? ... Od.8.376.284.
O envy'd shame! (the smiling Youth rejoin'd,) ... Od.8.377.284.
And free, he cries, oh *Vulcan!* free from shame ... Od.8.383.284.
There humbly stopp'd with conscious shame and awe, ... Od.10.67.342.
Shame touch'd *Eurylochus* his alter'd breast, ... Od.10.529.368.
How ill, alas! do want and shame agree? ... Od.17.423.152.
And, say (she cries) does fear, or shame, detain ... Od.17.657.164.
Shame suits but ill. *Eumæus* thus rejoin'd: ... Od.17.659.164.
His is the suff'rance, but the shame is thine. ... Od.18.266.179.
And custom bids thee without shame receive; ... Od.18.332.183.
With conscious shame they hear the stern rebuke, ... Od.18.389.186.
With their own blood, and intercept the shame; ... Od.20.16.232.
Those arguments I'll use: nor conscious shame, ... Od.20.227.244.
On me, on all, what grief, what shame attends? ... Od.21.265.272.
Mov'd by no weak surmize, but sense of shame, ... Od.21.347.276.
Then to the Prince. Nor have I wrought thee shame; ... Od.21.465.282.
Or shame of men, or dread of Gods above; ... Od.22.48.288.
To these, the nightly prostitutes to shame, ... Od.22.497.313.
The gen'ral sex shall suffer in her shame, ... Od.24.230.358.
Shame to this age, and all that shall succeed! ... Od.24.498.372.
Shame not the line whence glorious you descend, ... Od.24.587.376.

SHAMEFUL
As Shameful sure as *Impotence* in *Love.* ... 1.EOC.533.297.
And wins (oh shameful Chance!) the *Queen* of *Hearts.* ... 2.RL3.88.174.
Nor she a shameful Mother. ... 6.94.84.262.
Now shameful Flight alone can save the Host, ... Il.2.145.135.
Think not the *Greeks* to shameful Flight to bring, ... Il.2.312.142.
Now shameful flight alone can save the Host; ... Il.9.29.433.
Flight, more than shameful, is destructive here. ... Il.13.76.108.
A Change so shameful, say what Cause has wrought? ... Il.13.147.111.

SHAMEFUL (CONTINUED)
Nor Fear with-holds, nor shameful Sloth detains. ....Il.13.294.119.
What shameful Words, (unkingly as thou art) ....Il.14.90.162.
Thus he accosts him. What a shameful Sight! ....Il.16.877.277.
Your shameful Efforts 'gainst your selves employ, ...Il.17.386.302.
Ah no! *Achilles* meets a shameful Fate, ...Il.21.325.434.
To shameful Bondage and unworthy Toils. ....Il.22.62.455.
A shameful fate now hides my hapless head, ...Od.5.401.192.
Thy rev'rend age had met a shameful fate? ....Od.14.44.38.

SHAMELESS
Such shameless *Bards* we have; and yet 'tis true, ...1.EOC.610.309.
Brand the bold Front of shameless, guilty Men, ...4.HS1.106.15.
Shameless as carted Whores, that with a Grace, ...4.JD2A.84.140.
Not so from shameless Curl: Impetuous spread ....5.DunA2.171.122.
Not so from shameless Curl; impetuous spread ....5.DunB2.179.304.
And shameless *Billingsgate* her Robes adorn. ....5.DunB4.26.342.
Tho' shameless as he is, to face these Eyes ....Il.9.487.456.
'Till *Jove* refunds his shameless daughter's dow'r. ....Od.8.358.282.
Shameless they give, who give what's not their own. ....Od.17.536.158.

SHAMES
Who shames a Scribler? break one cobweb thro', ...4.Arbu.89.102.
Of him, whose chatt'ring shames the Monkey tribe; ....5.DunA2.224.128.
Of him, whose chatt'ring shames the Monkey tribe: ....5.DunB2.232.307.

SHAP'D
The Workman join'd, and shap'd the bended Horns, ...Il.4.142.227.
Old *Chiron* rent, and shap'd it for his Sire; ....Il.16.175.245.
Old *Chiron* fell'd, and shap'd it for his Sire; ....Il.19.423.389.
Rude from the Furnace, and but shap'd by Fire. ....Il.23.976.528.

SHAPE
Each Shape he varies, and each Art he tries, ...1.TrVP.43.379.
Add, that he varies ev'ry Shape with ease, ...1.TrVP.92.381.
Or Shape excuses the Defects of Face. ....2.ChWB.97.61.
Admir'd such wisdom in an earthly shape, ...3.EOM2.33.60.
First, Silks and Diamonds veil no finer Shape, ...4.HAdv.106.85.
Her Shape her own, whatever Shape she have, ...4.HAdv.163.89.
Her Shape her own, whatever Shape she have, ...4.HAdv.163.89.
The libel'd Person, and the pictur'd Shape; ....4.Arbu.353.121.
"Observe his Shape how clean! his Locks how curl'd! ....4.2HE2.5.165.
Quarto's, Octavo's, shape the less'ning pyre, ...5.DunA1.141.81.
So Proteus, hunted in a nobler shape, ...5.DunA2.121.111.
Quartos, octavos, shape the less'ning pyre; ....5.DunB1.161.282.
So Proteus, hunted in a nobler shape, ...5.DunB2.129.301.
See Nature in some partial narrow shape, ...5.DunB4.455.385.
Their Infamy, still keep the human shape. ....5.DunB4.528.394.
Virtue confess'd in human shape he draws, ...6.32.17.96.
Here lyes what had nor *Birth,* nor *Shape,* nor *Fame;* ....6.116iv.1.326.
Nireus, in faultless Shape, and blooming Grace, ...Il.2.817.163.
Polites' Shape, the Monarch's Son, she chose, ...Il.2.960.169.
(In Shape a Mortal) pass'd disguis'd along. ....Il.4.116.226.
To shape the Circle of the bending Wheel) ....Il.4.555.248.
A Phantom rais'd, the same in Shape and Show ....Il.5.546.294.
In *Asius'* Shape, who reign'd by *Sangar's* Flood; ....Il.16.874.277.
(In *Mentes* Shape, beneath whose martial Care ....Il.17.77.291.
Assuming *Phœnix'* Shape, on Earth she falls ....Il.17.624.312.
With well-taught Feet: Now shape, in oblique ways, ...Il.18.691.357.
Assumes *Agenor's* Habit, Voice, and Shape, ...Il.21.710.451.
Yet sure he seems, (to judge by Shape and Air,) ....Il.23.554.511.
His port, his features, and his shape the same: ....Od.4.200.129.
The mimic force of every savage shape: ....Od.4.564.147.
But when, his native shape resum'd, he stands ....Od.4.569.147.
A Boar's obscener shape the God belies: ....Od.4.618.149.
Shape the broad sail, or smooth the taper oar; ....Od.6.320.226.
A fathom's length, to shape it and to plain; ....Od.9.385.321.
Sooner shalt thou, a stranger to thy shape, ...Od.10.340.360.

SHAPELESS
The shapeless *Rock,* or hanging *Precipice.* ....1.EOC.160.258.
A shapeless shade! it melted from his sight, ...5.DunA2.103.109.
A shapeless shade, it melted from his sight, ...5.DunB2.111.300.

SHAPELY
The spiry Firr and shapely Box adorn; ....1.Mes.74.119.
With shapely growth *Diana* grac'd their bloom; ....Od.20.86.237.

SHAPES
In various Shapes of *Parsons, Criticks, Beaus;* ....1.EOC.459.291.
Adjusts his shapes; while in the crystal brook ....1.TrPA.25.366.
Those bashful Crimes disguis'd in borrow'd Shapes; ....1.TrSt.359.425.
Assume what Sexes and what Shapes they please. ....2.RL1.70.151.
Still vary Shapes and Dyes; ....6.14v(b).21.50.
But here all Sizes and all Shapes you meet, ...6.60.27.178.
But here all Sizes and all Shapes ye meet, ...6.60.27A.178.
The dext'rous Woodman shapes the stubborn Oaks; ....Il.23.386.505.

SHAR'D
Then shar'd the Tyranny, then lent it aid, ...3.EOM3.247.117.
Then shar'd the Tyranny, and lent it aid, ...3.EOM3.247A.117.
Whose nightly Joys the beauteous *Iphis* shar'd: ....Il.9.783.472.
The rest the People shar'd; my self survey'd ....Il.11.840.73.
Th' unhappy Hero; fled, or shar'd his Fate. ....Il.15.785.226.
They wept, and shar'd in human Miseries. ....Il.17.487.307.
Who shar'd the Gifts of *Ceres* at thy Board, ...Il.21.87.425.
We shar'd the lengthen'd Labours of a Year? ....Il.21.518.443.
Sad, as they shar'd in human Grief, they stand, ...Il.23.351.503.
The well-fed Bull (the second Prize) he shar'd, ...Il.23.913.525.
What Toils they shar'd, what martial Works they wrought, ...Il.24.13.535.
And each indulging shar'd in sweet Repast. ....Il.24.795.570.
And sadly shar'd the last Sepulcral Feast. ....Il.24.1014.577.
With your *Ulysses* shar'd an equal doom! ....Od.1.454.54.
Euryclea, who, great *Ops!* thy lineage shar'd, ...Od.2.392.80.
I, to confirm the mutual joys we shar'd, ...Od.4.233.130.
I shar'd secure the *Æthiopian* feast. ....Od.5.370.190.

SHAR'D (CONTINUED)
And shar'd the lands, and gave the lands their bounds. ....Od.6.16.204.
Their wives made captive, their possessions shar'd, ...Od.9.45.304.
I shar'd his kindness with his lawful race; ....Od.14.235.48.
The Prince and stranger shar'd the genial feast, ...Od.17.114.137.
Before the board whose blessings we have shar'd; ....Od.17.177.140.
Familiar enter'd, and the banquet shar'd; ....Od.17.307.146.
(An humble side-board set) *Ulysses* shar'd. ....Od.20.348.249.

SHARE
Feed fairer Flocks, or richer Fleeces share; ....1.PSu.36.75.
And the broad Faulchion in a Plow-share end. ....1.Mes.62.118.
True *Taste* as seldom is the *Critick's* Share; ....1.EOC.12.240.
Well, he may please himself, and you may share ....1.TrPA.122.370.
For you he lives; and you alone shall share ....1.TrVP.88.380.
To part his Throne and share his Heav'n with thee; ....1.TrSt.42.411.
Th'unwonted Weight, or drag the crooked Share, ...1.TrSt.187.418.
And shall not *Tantalus* his Kingdoms share ....1.TrSt.394.426.
And shall not Tantalus's Kingdoms share ....1.TrSt.394A.426.
You seek to share in Sorrows not your own; ....1.TrSt.803.443.
To share the Danger, and repel the Foe. ....1.TrES.76.452.
To share the Danger, and repell the Foe. ....1.TrES.80Z10.452.
But if her Virtues prove the larger Share, ...2.ChJM.192.24.
The lovely Prize, and share my Bliss with none! ....2.ChJM.265.27.
If to her share some Female Errors fall, ...2.RL2.17.160.
Then share thy pain, allow that sad relief; ....2.ElAb.49.323.
Ah more than share it! give me all thy grief. ....2.ElAb.50.323.
Nor share one pang of all I felt for thee. ....2.ElAb.292.343.
No pow'rs of body or of soul to share, ...3.EOM1.191.38.
No self-confounding Faculties to share; ....3.EOM1.191A.38.
Each has his share; and who would more obtain, ...3.EOM4.47.132.
Or her, whose life the Church and Scandal share, ...3.Ep2.105.58.
"Peeress and Butler share alike the Box, ...3.Ep3.142.105.
Whose table, Wit, or modest Merit share, ...3.Ep3.241.112.
Or, in a mortgage, prove a Lawyer's share, ...4.HS2.169.69.
Or, in a mortgage, prove the Lawyer's share, ...4.HS2.169A.69.
The joy their wives, their sons, and servants share, ...4.2HE1.245.215.
Like are their merits, like rewards they share, ...5.DunA3.179.170.
Like are their merits, like rewards they share, ...5.DunB3.183.329.
His Heart, his Mistress and his Friend did share; ....6.19.9.62.
I share his griefs, and feel my self his pain: ....6.21.36.70.
His double Share in *Cæsar Caius,* ....6.30.32.87.
And till we share your joys, forgive our grief; ....6.109.18.314.
We share with Justice, as with Toil we gain: ....Il.1.160.95.
Why grieves my Son? Thy Anguish let me share, ...Il.1.474.110.
Each takes his Seat, and each receives his Share. ....Il.1.613.117.
Each takes his Seat, and each receives his Share. ....Il.2.513.151.
The Heralds part it, and the Princes share; ....Il.3.343.209.
The Crime's sufficient that they share my Love. ....Il.4.80.224.
A Goddess born to share the Realms above, ...Il.4.85.224.
And only mourn, without my Share of Praise? ....Il.4.207.231.
Fix'd to thy Side, in ev'ry Toil I share, ...Il.4.304.235.
To share the Pleasures of the Genial Feast: ....Il.4.397.239.
And share those Griefs inferior Pow'rs must share; ....Il.5.472.290.
And share those Griefs inferior Pow'rs must share; ....Il.5.472.290.
Foremost he press'd, in glorious Toils to share, ...Il.5.1000.314.
'Tis hers t'offend; and ev'n offending share ....Il.5.1078.318.
Our Troops to hearten, and our Toils to share? ....Il.6.415.347.
No Parent now remains, my Griefs to share, ...Il.6.522.352.
Thy Wife, thy Infant, in thy Danger share: ....Il.6.548.354.
Haste then, in all their glorious Labours share; ....Il.6.674.360.
That both may claim it, and that both may share. ....Il.7.248.376.
That both may claim 'em, and that both may share. ....Il.7.248A.376.
Each takes his Seat, and each receives his Share. ....Il.7.385.383.
There shall he live my Son, our Honours share, ...Il.9.185.441.
There shalt thou live his Son, his Honours share, ...Il.9.372.451.
Nor share his Council, nor his Battel join; ....Il.9.490.456.
And share my Realms, my Honours, and my Heart. ....Il.9.730.470.
Yet must I tax his Sloath, that claims no share ....Il.10.130.7.
At ev'ry Rite his Share should be increas'd, ...Il.10.257.13.
So brave a Task each *Ajax* strove to share, ...Il.10.271.14.
Social we sit, and share the genial Rites. ....Il.11.911.76.
To share the Danger, and repell the Foe. ....Il.12.420.97.
To share the Danger, and repell the Foe. ....Il.12.434.97.
Ev'n now some Energy divine I share, ...Il.13.105.109.
And trace large Furrows with the Shining Share; ....Il.13.882.147.
Advance the Glory which he cannot share, ...Il.14.147.164.
Not *Troy* alone, but haughty *Greece* shall share ....Il.14.563.190.
Your Wives, your Infants, and your Parents share: ....Il.15.799.227.
And speak those Sorrows which a Friend would share. ....Il.16.28.236.
With *Hector* part the Spoil, and share the Fame. ....Il.17.273.298.
Only alas! to share in mortal Woe? ....Il.17.507.308.
Why mourns my Son? thy Anguish let me share, ...Il.18.97.327.
Forth let him bring them, for the Troops to share; ....Il.18.350.338.
Vouchsafe, O *Thetis!* at our Board to share ....Il.18.475.344.
And blame those Virtues which they cannot share. ....Il.22.149.459.
May share our Wealth, and leave our Walls in Peace. ....Il.22.163.459.
Frequent and full, the genial Feast to share. ....Il.23.38.488.
And share your Feast; but, with the Dawn of Day, ...Il.23.60.489.
Bade share the Honours, and surcease the Strife. ....Il.23.970.527.
All stretch'd at ease the genial Banquet share, ...Il.24.3.534.
(Well-pleas'd to share the Feast,) amid the Quire ....Il.24.82.538.
I share thy Banquet, and consent to live. ....Il.24.811.571.
Approach the dome, the social banquet share, ...Od.1.163.40.
True, while my friend is griev'd, his griefs I share; ....Od.2.267.74.
Perhaps may seize thy realm, and share the spoil; ....Od.3.402.106.
The rest may here the pious duty share, ...Od.3.542.114.
They share the honours of the rich repast. ....Od.4.80.123.
And with keen gust the sav'ry viands share. ....Od.4.300.133.
With him to share the sad funereal feast. ....Od.4.740.155.
Lo I thy steps attend, thy labours share. ....Od.6.38.206.
To all that share the blessings of your reign, ...Od.7.197.245.
Invite the Hero to his share of fame. ....Od.8.146.270.
His manly worth, and share the glorious day? ....Od.8.158.271.
And bear the shame, like *Mars,* to share the joy? ....Od.8.376.284.
Twelve Princes in our realm dominion share, ...Od.8.425.286.

SHARE (CONTINUED)
Be swift to give; that he this night may share ....Od.8.429.287.
Our hour was come, to taste our share of pain. ....Od.9.60.304.
Or feels the labours of the crooked share, ...Od.9.142.311.
To share thy feast-rites, or ascend thy bed; ....Od.10.404.364.
Circe in vain invites the feast to share; ....Od.10.441.365.
And share the pleasures of this genial hour. ....Od.10.545.369.
You share the pleasure,—then in bounty share; ....Od.11.423.405.
You share the pleasure,—then in bounty share; ....Od.11.423.405.
Of wand'rings and of woes a wretched share? ....Od.13.481.29.
Of four assistants who his labours share, ...Od.14.27.36.
Then tell me whence thou art? and what the share ....Od.14.55.38.
Such food as falls to simple servant's share; ....Od.14.98.40.
Little alas! was left my wretched share, ...Od.14.240.48.
With him, let us the genial banquet share, ...Od.14.459.57.
The rural tribe in common share the rest, ...Od.14.486.59.
And with my betters claim'd a share of praise. ....Od.14.527.62.
And let yon' mendicant our plenty share: ....Od.17.419.152.
To share our feast, and lead the life of Kings. ....Od.17.457.155.
What bounty gives, without a rival share, ...Od.18.22.168.
They share the meal that earn it ere they taste. ....Od.19.32.194.
Must share the general doom of with'ring time: ....Od.19.101.197.
Her foodful glebe with fierce *Achaians* share; ....Od.19.203.202.
The limbs; then all the tasteful viands share. ....Od.19.493.220.
Who in partition seek his realm to share; ....Od.20.273.246.
I share the doom ye Suitors cannot shun. ....Od.20.444.254.
Or share the feast with due respect, or go ....Od.21.92.263.
Cease the mad strife, and share our bounty here. ....Od.21.332.276.
If yet I share the old man's memory? ....Od.24.249.361.
They share the gladsome board; the roofs resound. ....Od.24.453.370.

SHARES
Shares with his lord the pleasure and the pride: ....3.EOM3.36.95.
To bawd for others, and go Shares with Punk. ....6.49i.26.138.
The Queen of Pleasures shares the Toils of Fight, ...Il.4.14.221.
(To whom the Hind like Shares of Land allows) ....Il.10.421.22.
Who shares his Labours, and defends his side. ....Il.11.583.60.
The cordial Bev'rage rev'rend *Nestor* shares ....Il.11.785.70.
And Shares were parted to each *Pylian* Lord. ....Il.11.829.73.
The shining Shares full many Plowmen guide, ...Il.18.629.354.
Then back the turning Plow-shares cleave the Soil: ....Il.18.634.354.
My royal father shares the genial hours; ....Od.6.372.229.
Portions the food, and each his portion shares. ....Od.8.514.290.
Of these due shares to ev'ry sailor fall; ....Od.9.641.333.
And shares the banquet in superior state, ...Od.11.224.392.
Nor cease the tears, 'till each in slumber shares ....Od.12.365.449.
Whilst *Eteoneus* portions out the shares, ...Od.15.156.76.
My secret soul in all thy sorrow shares: ....Od.15.523.95.
Her Queen endures, polluted joys she shares ....Od.18.372.185.
Dispos'd apart, *Ulysses* shares the treat; ....Od.20.322.248.
He ended, sinking into sleep, and shares ....Od.23.369.343.

SHARON
Sweeter than *Sharon,* in immaculate trim, ...4.JD4.252.47.

SHARP
Sharp *Boreas* blows, and Nature feels Decay, ...1.PWi.87.95.
Dash'd on sharp Rocks, than to thy Bosom prest? ....1.TrSP.225A.403.
Drives the sharp Rock; the solid Beams give way, ...1.TrES.196.456.
Shall feel sharp Vengeance soon o'ertake his Sins, ...2.RL2.125.167.
A sharp accuser, but a helpless friend! ....3.EOM2.154.73.
When sharp with Hunger, scorn you to be fed, ...4.HAdv.149.87.
Sharp Satire that, and that Pindaric lays? ....4.2HE2.83.171.
And the sharp arrows of censorious tongues. ....6.21.6.69.
Sharp was his Voice; which in the shrillest Tone, ...Il.2.273.140.
Fits the sharp Arrow to the well-strung Bow. ....Il.4.147.227.
As when sharp *Boreas* blows abroad, and brings ....Il.12.175.87.
As when high *Jove* his sharp Artill'ry forms, ...Il.12.331.93.
Drives the sharp Rock; the solid Beams give way, ...Il.12.550.101.
In that sharp Service, singled from the rest, ...Il.13.357.122.
Where sharp the Pang, and mortal is the Wound. ....Il.13.719.138.
First the sharp Lance was by *Atrides* thrown; ....Il.13.757.141.
Sharp in his Thigh he felt the piercing Wound; ....Il.16.367.257.
Above, sharp rocks forbid access; around ....Od.5.528.198.
Nor wind sharp-piercing, nor the rushing show'r; ....Od.5.621.201.
Guide the sharp stake, and twirl it round and round. ....Od.9.456.324.
Sharp blew the North; snow whitening all the fields ....Od.14.536.63.
What mutters he? (*Melanthius* sharp rejoins) ....Od.17.294.146.
Twang'd short and sharp, like the shrill swallow's cry. ....Od.21.449.282.
Oh sharp in scandal, voluble and vain! ....Od.22.319.301.

SHARP-PIERCING
Nor wind sharp-piercing, nor the rushing show'r; ....Od.5.621.201.

SHARPEN'D
But as coarse Iron, sharpen'd, mangles more, ...4.JD4.118.35.
With sharpen'd sight pale Antiquaries pore, ...6.71.35.203.
His sharpen'd Spear let ev'ry *Grecian* wield, ...Il.2.454.149.
And bristled thick with sharpen'd Stakes below. ....Il.12.64.83.
And saw the foremost Steed with sharpen'd Eyes; ....Il.23.537.511.
The land at distance, and with sharpen'd eyes. ....Od.5.505.196.
The narrow'r end I sharpen'd to a spire; ....Od.9.386.322.
Each scheme I turn'd, and sharpen'd ev'ry thought; ....Od.9.502.326.
Inspect with sharpen'd sight, ahd frugal care, ...Od.19.25.193.

SHARPER
No Eagle sharper, every Charm to find, ...4.HAdv.120.85.
P. How Sir! not damn the Sharper, but the Dice? ....4.EpS2.13.314.
Where the shrill Brass return'd a sharper Sound: ....Il.20.324.407.

SHARPERS
Thieves, Supercargoes, Sharpers, and Directors. ....4.HS1.72.11.

SHARPEST
Stands on the sharpest Edge of Death or Life: ....Il.10.197.10.
As the bold Bird, endu'd with sharpest Eye ....Il.17.761.318.

SHARPEST (CONTINUED)
Of those who view the Course, not sharpest ey'd, ...Il.23.558.511.

SHATTER'D
The Folds are shatter'd, from the crackling Door ....1.TrES.197.456.
Our shatter'd Barks may yet transport us o'er, ...Il.2.169.136.
The shatter'd Chariot from the crooked Yoke: ....Il.6.50.326.
His Bulk supporting on the shatter'd Shield. ....Il.7.326.380.
The Folds are shatter'd; from the crackling Door ....Il.12.551.101.
His shatter'd Helm, and stretch'd him o'er the Slain. ....Il.16.708.271.
The shatter'd Crest, and Horse-hair, strow the Plain: ....Il.17.341.300.
The Teeth it shatter'd, and the Tongue it rent. ....Il.17.698.314.
With shatter'd vessels, and disabled oars: ....Od.3.381.105.
His teeth all shatter'd rush immix'd with blood. ....Od.18.117.172.

SHAVE
Some plunge in bus'ness, others shave their crowns: ....3.Ep1.56.19.

SHE (OMITTED)
929

SHE'D
To all obliging she'd appear: ....6.14v(b).10.49.

SHE'L
She'l keep thee Book! I lay my Head, ...6.64.19A.190.

SHE'LL
Oblige her, and she'll hate you while you live: ....3.Ep2.138.62.
But die, and she'll adore you—Then the Bust ....3.Ep2.139.62.
Oblige her, and she'll hate you while you live. ....6.154.24.403.
But die, and she'll adore you—then the Bust ....6.154.25.403.

SHE'S
This hour she's *idoliz'd,* the next *abus'd,* ....1.EOC.433.288.
Whether she's chast or rampant, proud or civil; ....2.ChJM.186.23.
Treated, caress'd, where-e'er she's pleas'd to roam— ....2.ChWB.76.60.
Freakish when well, and fretful when she's Sick. ....2.ChWB.91.61.
Because she's honest, and the best of Friends: ....3.Ep2.104.58.
She's still the same, belov'd, contented thing. ....4.EpS1.140.308.
Let *Greatness* own her, and she's mean no more: ....4.EpS1.144.309.
Tell P[ickenbur]g how slim she's grown ....6.61.24.181.
Tell P[ickenbur]g how thin she's grown ....6.61.24A.181.
Tell Buckenburg how thin she's grown ....6.61.24B.181.
Alas she's deaf, and does not hear. ....6.89.12A.250.
And now she's in t'other, she thinks it but *Queer.* ....6.124i.10.347.
She's dead!—but thus she lookd the hour she dy'd, ...6.147iii.2.390.

SHEAR
O'er the congenial dust injoin'd to shear ....Od.4.271.132.

SHEARS
First shears the forehead of the bristly boar, ...Od.14.469.58.

SHEATH
But sheath, Obedient, thy revenging Steel. ....Il.1.280.100.
Then in the Sheath return'd the shining Blade. ....Il.1.292.100.
Your shining Swords within the Sheath restrain, ...Il.3.125.196.
The Baldric studded, and the Sheath enchas'd, ...Il.7.367.382.
Gold was the Hilt, a silver sheath encas'd ....Il.11.41.36.
Whose ivory sheath inwrought with curious pride, ...Od.8.439.287.
Sheath thy bright sword, and join our hands in peace; ....Od.10.396.363.
But sheath thy ponyard, while my tongue relates ....Od.11.120.386.
(Fast by, the rest lay sleeping in the sheath, ...Od.21.456.282.

SHEATH'D
Was sheath'd, and *Israel* liv'd to bless the Lord. ....2.ChJM.76.18.
Was sheath'd, and *Luxury* with *Charles* restor'd; ....4.2HE1.140.207.
And call the Squadrons sheath'd in Brazen Arms: ....Il.2.517.151.
His Cutlace sheath'd beside his pondrous Sword. ....Il.3.341.209.
Sheath'd in bright Arms, but expect Command. ....Il.4.405.240.
Who sheath'd in Brass the *Paphlagonians* led. ....Il.5.706.301.
Sheath'd in bright Arms each adverse Chief came on, ...Il.5.780.303.
Sheath'd in bright Steel the Giant-Warrior shone: ....Il.7.250.376.
Sheath'd in bright Arms let ev'ry Troop engage, ...Il.8.659.427.
All sheath'd in Arms, his brave Companions round: ....Il.10.171.9.
Thus sheath'd in Arms, the Council they forsake, ...Il.10.319.17.
And sheath'd in Arms, expect the dawning Light. ....Il.11.861.74.
Secure in Mail, and sheath'd in shining Steel. ....Il.13.258.117.
Thus sheath'd in shining Brass, in bright Array, ...Il.14.443.184.
Sheath'd in bright Arms, thro' cleaving Ranks he flies, ...Il.17.95.291.
Drew the broad Cutlace sheath'd beside his Sword; ....Il.19.260.383.
Greece sheath'd in Arms, beside her Vessels stood; ....Il.20.2.392.
And sheath'd in Steel, provoke his Foe to fight. ....Il.23.948.526.
He spoke, and sheath'd in arms, incessant flies ....Od.23.393.343.

SHEATHS
The *Spartan* Hero sheaths his Limbs in Arms. ....Il.3.422.212.

SHEAVES
Sheaves heap'd on Sheaves, here thicken up the Ground. ....Il.18.640.354.
Sheaves heap'd on Sheaves, here thicken up the Ground. ....Il.18.640.354.
(Too short to gripe them) the brown Sheaves of Corn. ....Il.18.644.354.

SHED
And in soft Silence shed the kindly Show'r! ....1.Mes.14.114.
O early lost! what Tears the River shed ....1.W-F.273.174.
Oh Fact accurst! What Tears has *Albion* shed, ...1.W-F.321.180.
Have we not seen (the Blood of *Laius* shed) ....1.TrSt.330.424.
O'er all his Limbs *Ambrosial* Odours shed, ...1.TrES.328.461.
Think not my Virtue lost, tho' Time has shed ....2.ChJM.131.21.
Heav'n knows, I shed full many a private Tear, ...2.ChJM.198.24.
Shed its selectest Influence from above; ....2.ChJM.429.35.
To hide the Flood of Tears I did *not* shed. ....2.ChWB.312.72.
At ev'ry Breath were balmy Odours shed, ...2.TemF.314.279.
Love but demands what else were shed in pray 'r; ....2.ElAb.46.322.

SHED (CONTINUED)

And the dim windows shed a solemn light;	2.ElAb.144.331.
And wings of Seraphs shed divine perfumes;	2.ElAb.218.338.
And licks the hand just rais'd to shed his blood.	3.EOM1.84.24.
The Blow unfelt, the Tear he never shed;	4.Arbu.349.120.
Of gentle Blood (part shed in Honour's Cause,	4.Arbu.388.126.
With mystic words, the sacred Opium shed;	5.DunA1.242.91.
With mystic words, the sacred Opium shed.	5.DunB1.288.290.
She pity'd! but her Pity only shed	5.DunB4.345.377.
Thy choicer mists on this assembly shed,	5.DunB4.357.378.
Such tears, as Patriots shed for dying Laws:	6.32.14.96.
Muse! at that name thy sacred sorrows shed,	6.52.47.157.
Shed like this Wine, distain the thirsty Ground;	Il.3.373.211.
That shed Perfumes, and whisp'ring thus addrest.	Il.3.480.215.
I see th' Eternal all his Fury shed,	Il.4.202.231.
The pious Maids their mingled Sorrows shed,	Il.6.646.358.
To shed his sacred Light on Earth again,	Il.7.499.389.
The Wounds they wash'd, their pious Tears they shed,	Il.7.506.389.
Nor less the *Greeks* their pious Sorrows shed,	Il.7.512.389.
O'er the dark Trees a yellower Verdure shed,	Il.8.693.428.
In sable Streams soft-trickling Waters shed.	Il.9.20.432.
To shed *Ulysses'* and my Brother's Blood,	Il.11.182.43.
Those Eyes, that shed insufferable Light,	Il.13.6.104.
On him the War is bent, the Darts are shed,	Il.13.201.115.
That shed a Lustre round th' illumin'd Wall.	Il.13.340.122.
Till *Jove* himself descends, his Bolts to shed,	Il.13.408.125.
And unavailing Tears profusely shed,	Il.13.825.145.
Shed thy soft Dews on *Jove's* immortal Eyes,	Il.14.270.175.
While *Jove* yet rests, while yet my Vapours shed	Il.14.413.183.
And stuck with Darts by warring Heroes shed;	Il.16.775.273.
O'er all his Limbs Ambrosial Odours shed,	Il.16.815.274.
A Flood of Tears, at this, the Goddess shed;	Il.18.123.328.
A Ray divine her heav'nly Presence shed,	Il.9.9.371.
Eternal Sorrows what avails to shed?	Il.19.227.382.
If this be false, Heav'n all its Vengeance shed,	Il.19.275.383.
Trembled the sparkling Plumes, and the loose Glories shed	Il.19.415.389.
Jove by these Hands shall shed thy noble Life;	Il.22.328.469.
And roseate Unguents, heav'nly Fragrance! shed:	Il.23.229.499.
What must be, must be. Bear thy Lot, nor shed	Il.24.692.566.
Now shed *Aurora* round her Saffron Ray,	Il.24.866.572.
To the gay Court a rural shed prefers,	Od.1.246.44.
There, as the waters o'er his hands he shed,	Od.2.295.76.
Then give thy friend to shed the sacred wine;	Od.3.59.89.
And shed ambrosial dews. Fast by the deep,	Od.4.583.147.
Now from her rosy car *Aurora* shed	Od.6.57.208.
On thy soft hours their choicest blessings shed,	Od.6.219.220.
"Heav'n on that hour its choicest influence shed,	Od.6.337.227.
But when the music paus'd, he ceas'd to shed	Od.8.83.267.
Again unmann'd a show'r of sorrow shed:	Od.8.90.267.
The Graces unguents shed, ambrosial show'rs,	Od.8.400.285.
Shed sweets shed unguents, in a show'r of oil:	Od.8.492.289.
Shed sweets shed unguents, in a show'r of oil:	Od.8.492.289.
And shed her sacred light along the skies.	Od.9.365.321.
Wild with despair, I shed a copious tyde	Od.11.251.394.
Then o'er my eyes the Gods soft slumber shed,	Od.12.401.450.
And shed her sacred light along the skies.	Od.13.22.2.
She o'er my limbs old age and wrinkles shed;	Od.16.230.114.
'Tis horrible to shed imperial blood.	Od.16.417.126.
Nourish'd deep anguish, tho' he shed no tear;	Od.17.583.161.
And o'er her eyes ambrosial slumber shed.	Od.19.704.229.
Philætius too relents, but secret shed	Od.21.85.263.
His generous wines dishonour'd shed in vain,	Od.23.327.340.
Then unguents sweet and tepid streams we shed;	Od.24.62.350.
No friend to bathe our wounds! or tears to shed	Od.24.216.358.
Nor could his mother fun'ral unguents shed,	Od.24.344.365.

SHEDDING

Pregnant with Plagues, and shedding Seeds of Death,	Il.5.1059.317.

SHEDS

But see, *Orion* sheds unwholsome Dews,	1.PWi.85.95.
See pale *Orion* sheds unwholsome Dews,	1.PWi.85A.95.
And rising *Cynthia* sheds her silver Light,	1.TrSt.475.430.
And drink the falling tears once other sheds,	2.RalAb.350.348.
Thus from his flaggy Wings when *Notus* sheds	Il.3.15.188.
O'er Heav'ns clear Azure sheds her sacred Light,	Il.8.688A.428.
The balmy oil, a fragrant show'r, he sheds,	Od.6.269.223.
She sheds celestial bloom, regard to draw,	Od.8.21.263.
Warn'd by the God who sheds the golden day,	Od.8.343.282.
Sheds her bright beam, pursue the destin'd way.	Od.12.350.448.
At once his vestures change; at once she sheds	Od.16.478.130.
From limb to limb an air majestic sheds,	Od.18.227.178.
O'er every limb a show'r of fragrance sheds:	Od.23.151.328.

SHEENE

Fair Mirrour of foul Times! whose fragile Sheene	6.137.1.373.

SHEEP

No Lambs or Sheep for Victims I'll impart,	1.PSp.51.66.
The bleating Sheep with my Complaints agree,	1.PSu.19.73.
Who lost my Heart while I preserv'd my Sheep.	1.PAu.80.86.
Explores the lost, the wand'ring Sheep directs,	1.Mes.51.117.
He sate, pursu'd by all his flocks of sheep.	1.TrPA.42.367.
With fleeces sheep, and birds with plumy trains;	1.TrPA.105.370.
And bid *Endymion* nightly tend his Sheep.	1.TrSP.100.398.
Blush'd with the Blood of Sheep and Oxen slain.	1.TrUl.231.473.
Where bask on sunny banks the simple sheep,	5.DunB4.352.377.
Strait from the Town are Sheep and Oxen sought,	Il.8.629.426.
Fat Sheep and Oxen from the Town are led,	Il.8.677.427.
Which Flesh of Porket, Sheep, and Goat contains:	Il.9.274.447.
On Sheep or Goats, resistless in his way,	Il.10.566.27.
On *Ida's* Tops, their Father's fleecy Sheep,	Il.11.142.42.
My Sire three hundred chosen Sheep obtain'd.	Il.11.835.73.
If Sheep or Oxen seek the winding Stream.	Il.18.606.352.
Expires the Goat; the Sheep in Silence dies:	Il.23.42.488.
And well-fed Sheep, and sable Oxen slay:	Il.23.205.498.

SHEEP (CONTINUED)

The fatted sheep and sable bulls they slay,	Od.9.49.304.
Where sheep and goats lay slumb'ring round the shore.	Od.9.214.314.
Or drive a flock of sheep and goats away,	Od.9.266.317.
And search'd each passing sheep, and felt it o'er,	Od.9.497.326.
Fat sheep and goats in throngs we drive before,	Od.9.547.328.
Aboard in haste they heave the wealthy sheep,	Od.9.553.328.
Be next thy care the sable sheep to place	Od.10.628.374.
Dis-bark the sheep, an offering to the Gods;	Od.11.22.380.
Then dy'd the sheep; a purple torrent flow'd,	Od.11.45.381.
Blush'd with the blood of sheep and oxen slain.	Od.13.398.26.
The fleecy spoils of sheep, a goat's rough hide	Od.14.588.65.
In humbler life, the lowing herds and sheep?	Od.15.417.89.
The bellowing oxen, and the bleating sheep;	Od.15.443.92.
Then sheep and goats and bristly porkers bled,	Od.17.201.141.
With sheep and shaggy goats the porkers bled,	Od.20.314.248.
Three hundred sheep, and all the shepherd swains;	Od.21.22.260.
And fatted sheep and sable oxen slay;	Od.24.84.352.

SHEEPHOOK

Far, as a Swain his whirling Sheephook throws,	Il.23.1001.529.

SHEEPISHLY

" *Billy,* my dear! how sheepishly you look!	2.ChWB.183.65.

SHEER

Feed fairer Flocks, or richer Fleeces sheer:	1.PSu.36A.75.

SHEERING

When Swains from Sheering seek their nightly Bow'rs;	1.PSu.64.76.

SHEERS

Fate urg'd the Sheers, and cut the *Sylph* in twain,	2.RL3.151.179.
Uncurl'd it hangs, the fatal Sheers demands;	2.RL4.173.198.
Morsel for dogs! then trimm'd with brazen sheers	Od.22.511.313.

SHEET

Then snatch'd a sheet of Thulè from her bed;	5.DunA1.214.89.
Then snatch'd a sheet of Thulè from her bed,	5.DunB1.258.289.
"No *Sheet* is here to save thee:	6.79.78.220.
The spacious sheet, and stretch it to the wind.	Od.2.465.83.
Like a black sheet the whelming billow spread,	Od.5.466.195.
The spacious sheet, and stretch it to the wind:	Od.11.4.379.
The spacious sheet, and stretch it to the wind.	Od.15.313.84.

SHEETS

By this the Sheets were spread, the Bride undrest,	2.ChJM.381.33.
Who random drawings from your sheets shall take,	3.Ep4.27.140.
Unstain'd, untouch'd, and yet in maiden sheets;	5.DunB1.229.287.
Unstain'd, unstitch'd, and yet in maiden sheets;	5.DunB1.229A.287.
Such Sheets as these, whate'er be the Disaster,	6.48ii.11.134.
By the soft Fannings of the wafting Sheets,	6.82ii.3.230.
While *Jove* descends in sluicy Sheets of Rain,	Il.5.122.273.
Beneath the low-hung Clouds the Sheets of Snow	Il.12.177.87.
And Sheets of rolling Smoke involve the Skies.	Il.16.153.243.
And Sheets of Smoak mount heavy to the Poles.	Il.17.830.321.

SHEFFIELD

The Courtly *Talbot, Somers, Sheffield* read,	4.Arbu.139.105.
Sheffield approves, consenting *Phœbus* bends,	6.63.7.188.
This ' *sheffield* rais'd. The sacred Dust below	6.83.1.237.

SHELF

Here swells the shelf with Ogilby the great:	5.DunA1.121.78.
Here swells the shelf with Ogilby the great;	5.DunB1.141.280.
O all-accomplish'd Cæsar! on thy Shelf	6.147ix.1.392.
'Tis true, Great Bard, thou on my shelf shall lye	6.147ix.3.392.

SHELFY

Among a savage race, whose shelfy bounds	Od.1.257.45.
She ceas'd, and bounding from the shelfy shore,	Od.4.577.147.
A shelfy tract, and long!) O Seer, I cry,	Od.4.651.150.
To bright *Lucina's* fane; the shelfy coast	Od.19.218.204.

SHELL

The Pearly Shell its lucid Glove infold,	1.W-F.395.190.
At all times Just, but when he sign'd the Shell.	2.TemF.173.269.
In all things Just, but when he sign'd the Shell.	2.TemF.173A.269.
Or in a Bean–shell venture from the shore	6.96ii.30Z13.271.
"Thy Bark a Bean-shell, and a Straw thy Oar?	6.96ii.58.273.
There, take (says *Justice)* take ye each a *Shell*.	6.145.10.388.

SHELLS

And smooth as shells that gliding waters wear;	1.TrPA.55.367.
A tribe, with weeds and shells fantastic crown'd,	5.DunB4.398.381.

SHELLY

Stretch'd on the shelly shore, he first surveys	Od.4.555.146.
(The vestures cleans'd o'erspread the shelly sand,	Od.6.107.211.

SHELT'RING

He who beneath thy shelt'ring wing resides,	6.21.1.69.

SHELTER

For see! the gath'ring Flocks to Shelter tend,	1.PSp.101.70.
From Storms a Shelter, and from Heat a Shade.	1.Mes.16.114.
But finds no shelter from his raging fires.	1.TrPA.38.366.
He seeks a Shelter from th'inclement Heav'n,	1.TrSt.560.433.
At once a shelter from her boughs receives,	6.14iv.28.48.
And takes a Shelter from his pointed Fires.	6.17iii.31.58.
And gains the friendly Shelter of the Wood.	Il.15.707.223.
And in thick shelter of innum'rous boughs	Od.5.606.201.
Then took the shelter of the neighb'ring wood.	Od.7.367.254.
In shelter thick of horrid shade reclin'd;	Od.9.219.314.
And took the spreading shelter of the wood.	Od.14.388.53.

SHELTER'D

You'll wish your hill or shelter'd seat again. ... 3.Ep4.76.144.
You'll wish your Hill, and shelter'd seat again. ... 3.Ep4.76A.144.
And *Eleon,* shelter'd by *Olympus'* Shades, ... Il.2.897.166.
'Till safe we anchor'd in the shelter'd bay: ... Od.9.171.312.

SHELTERS

Ulysses seeks the Ships, and shelters there. ... Il.8.124.404.

SHELTRED

Here, in a Grotto, sheltred close from Air, ... 2.RL4.21.185.

SHELVES

These shelves admit not any modern book. ... 3.Ep4.140.151.
Or *Sloane,* or *Woodward's* wondrous Shelves contain; ... 4.JD4.30.29.
And there, the groaning shelves Philemon bends. ... 5.DunA1.134.80.
And here, the groaning shelves Philemon bends. ... 5.DunA1.134A.80.
From shelves to shelves see greedy Vulcan roll, ... 5.DunA3.73.156.
From shelves to shelves see greedy Vulcan roll, ... 5.DunA3.73.156.
With visage from his shelves with dust besprent? ... 5.DunA3.182A.170.
Such with their shelves as due proportion hold, ... 5.DunB1.137.280.
And here the groaning shelves Philemon bends. ... 5.DunB1.154.281.
From shelves to shelves see greedy Vulcan roll, ... 5.DunB3.81.324.
From shelves to shelves see greedy Vulcan roll, ... 5.DunB3.81.324.
The bending shelves with loads of cheeses prest, ... Od.9.256.317.
The loaden shelves afford us full repast; ... Od.9.274.318.

SHELVING

A Lake there was, with shelving banks around, ... 1.TrFD.15.386.
The shelving Walls reflect a glancing Light; ... 1.TrSt.531.432.
In Lines advanc'd along the shelving Strand; ... Il.14.40.159.
Depending vines the shelving cavern screen, ... Od.5.88.176.
Where to the seas the shelving shore declin'd, ... Od.5.564.199.
Where to the main the shelving shore descends; ... Od.10.603.373.

SHEPHERD

Say, Shepherd, say, in what glad Soil appears ... 1.PSp.85A.69.
Ah wretched Shepherd, what avails thy Art, ... 1.PSu.33.74.
Do Lovers dream, or is my Shepherd kind? ... 1.PAu.52A.84.
He comes, my Shepherd comes!—Now cease my Lay, ... 1.PAu.53A.84.
As the good Shepherd tends his fleecy Care, ... 1.Mes.49.117.
Oft in her Glass the musing Shepherd spies ... 1.W-F.211.169.
The poorest shepherd best may tell his store. ... 1.TrPA.81.368.
Come, gentle Air! th' Æolian Shepherd said, ... 6.14iii.1.45.
As from some Rocky Cleft the Shepherd sees ... Il.2.111.132.
Not with more Ease, the spilful Shepherd Swain ... Il.2.562.154.
As when some Shepherd from the rustling Trees ... Il.3.47.190.
The distant Shepherd trembling hears the Sound: ... Il.4.520.246.
If chance some Shepherd with a distant Dart ... Il.5.176.275.
He foams, he roars; The Shepherd dares not stay, ... Il.5.178.275.
Far as a shepherd, from some Point on high, ... Il.5.960.312.
To *Jason,* Shepherd of his People, bore) ... Il.7.565.392.
Has torn the Shepherd's Dog, or Shepherd Swain; ... Il.15.703.223.
And Steers slow-moving, and two Shepherd Swains; ... Il.18.608.352.
And, all amidst them, dead, the Shepherd Swains! ... Il.18.614.352.
What time young *Paris,* simple Shepherd Boy, ... Il.24.39.537.
The shepherd swains with sure abundance blest, ... Od.4.109.125.
A Giant-shepherd here his flock maintains ... Od.9.217.314.
The shepherd quitting here at night the plain, ... Od.10.94.343.
A shepherd meeting thee, the *Oar* surveys, ... Od.11.157.389.
Where *Nestor,* shepherd of his people, reigns. ... Od.17.125.137.
Three hundred sheep, and all the shepherd swains; ... Od.21.22.260.
An Oar my hand must bear; a shepherd eyes ... Od.23.289.337.

SHEPHERD'S

Thy Victim, Love, shall be the Shepherd's Heart, ... 1.PSp.52.66.
A Shepherd's Boy (he seeks no better Name) ... 1.PSu.1.71.
Adieu ye Shepherd's rural *Lays* and *Loves,* ... 1.PWi.90.95.
And trusts her Infant to a Shepherd's Cares. ... 1.TrSt.683.439.
Has torn the Shepherd's Dog, or Shepherd Swain; ... Il.15.703.223.
Thick, as beneath some Shepherd's thatch'd Abode, ... Il.16.779.273.
And adds the herdsman's to the shepherd's care, ... Od.10.97.345.

SHEPHERDS

But see, the Shepherds shun the Noon-day Heat, ... 1.PSu.85.79.
The Shepherds cry, "Thy Flocks are left a Prey—" ... 1.PAu.78.85.
I'll fly from Shepherds, Flocks, and flow'ry Plains.— ... 1.PAu.86.86.
From Shepherds, Flocks, and Plains, I may remove, ... 1.PAu.87.86.
Thus sung the Shepherds till th'Approach of Night, ... 1.PAu.97.87.
And said; "Ye Shepherds, sing around my Grave!" ... 1.PWi.18.90.
And Shepherds gaul him with an Iron War; ... 1.TrES.18.450.
('Midst Flocks and Shepherds) in the silent Grove; ... 6.17ii.22.56.
And Shepherds gaul him with an Iron War; ... Il.12.362.94.
So watchful Shepherds strive to force, in vain, ... Il.18.199.331.

SHEPPARD

And needs no Rod but S[heppar]d with a Rule ... 3.Ep4.18B.137*.

SHERLOCK

While Sherlock, Hare, and Gibson preach in vain. ... 5.DunB3.204.330.

SHERRARDS

You may meet the *Two Champions* who are no Lord
S[herrar]d ... 6.62v.2.186.
You may meet your *Two Champions* who are no Lord
Sherrards. ... 6.62v.2A.186.

SHEW

See SHOW.
Yet he shall find, wou'd time th'occasion shew, ... 1.TrPA.124.370.
Full hearty was his Love, and I can shew ... 2.ChWB.255.69.
The flaming Rubies shew their sanguine Dye; ... 2.TemF.251.275.
Shew by what Laws the wand'ring Planets stray ... 3.EOM2.21A.56.
And shew'd a NEWTON as we shew an Ape. ... 3.EOM2.34.60.
Or tricks to shew the stretch of human brain, ... 3.EOM2.47.61.
Now pox on those who shew a *Court in Wax!* ... 4.JD4.206.43.

SHEW (CONTINUED)

Yet, for the World, she would not shew her Leg! ... 4.HAdv.32.77.
To shew.. ... 4.1740.52.334.
She does but shew her coward face and dies: ... 5.DunA1.158.82.
As half to shew, half veil the deep Intent. ... 5.DunB4.4.339.
And, to excuse it, need but shew the prize; ... 5.DunB4.434.383.
They to Salvation shew the arduous way, ... 6.2.28.6.
Who shew their Parts as *Pentlow* does, ... 6.10.30.25.
With Just Description shew the Soul Divine ... 6.75.9.212.
He still might shew his own. ... 6.94.88.262.
Hence see him modest free from pride or shew ... 6.130.9.358.
The mushrooms shew his wit was sudden! ... 6.150.11.398.
And thou great *Mars,* begin and shew the way. ... Il.15.121.201.
What, and from whence? his name and lineage shew. ... Od.1.516.57.
O, piteous of my fate, vouchsafe to shew, ... Od.4.513.144.
To shew posterity *Elpenor* was. ... Od.11.95.385.
Stranger! may fate a milder aspect shew, ... Od.20.249.245.

SHEW'D

And shew'd a NEWTON as we shew an Ape. ... 3.EOM2.34.60.
Shew'd erring Pride, WHATEVER IS, IS RIGHT; ... 3.EOM4.394.166.
E shew'd, a *Comma* ne'er could claim ... 6.30.19.86.
Who shew'd his breech, to prove 'twas not besh— ... 6.116i.4.325.
And shew'd the Wound by fierce *Tydides* giv'n, ... Il.5.451.289.
And shew'd the Shores, the Navy, and the Main: ... Il.15.811.228.
And shew'd them where the royal dome appear'd. ... Od.10.126.347.
And shew'd its nature and its wond'rous pow'r: ... Od.10.363.362.

SHEWN

Since some have writ, and shewn no Wit at all. ... 6.60.8.178.
What foreign theatres with pride have shewn, ... 6.107.9.310.

SHEWS

Unconquer'd *Cato* shews the Wound he tore, ... 2.TemF.176.269.
Here to her Chosen all her works she shews; ... 5.DunB1.273.290.
But Fop shews Fop superior complaisance. ... 5.DunB4.138.355.
She shews her Grief in a sincerer Place; ... 6.33.8.99.
Deceiv'd by Shews and Forms! ... 6.53.2.161.
Fate shews an old Dog Trick! ... 6.79.62A.220.
Shews every mournful Face with Tears o'erspread, ... Il.23.132.493.
Vain shews of love to veil his felon hate! ... Od.4.712.152.
Ill suits it with your shews of duteous zeal, ... Od.4.966.163.

SHIELD

The Lillies blazing on the Regal Shield. ... 1.W-F.306.178.
Round like a shield, and in the middle plac'd: ... 1.TrPA.109.370.
With his broad Shield oppos'd, he forc'd his way ... 1.TrSt.528.432.
And bears aloft his ample Shield in Air, ... 1.TrES.8.449.
Then, with his Sev'nfold Shield, he strode away. ... 1.TrES.88.453.
To shield his Off-spring, and avert his Fate. ... 1.TrES.140.454.
Each heav'd the Shield, and pois'd the lifted Spear: ... 1.TrES.262.459.
And *Perseus* dreadful with *Minerva's* Shield: ... 2.TemF.80.258.
Each Chief his sevenfold Shield display'd, ... 6.11.45.31.
And o'er his breast extend his saving shield: ... 6.21.14.69.
Can taste no pleasure since his Shield was scour'd; ... 6.71.42.204.
And ev'ry *Grecian* fix his Brazen Shield, ... Il.2.455.149.
With the huge Shield each brawny Arm deprest, ... Il.2.463.149.
The dreadful *Ægis, Jove's* immortal Shield, ... Il.2.526.151.
His figur'd Shield, a shining Orb, he takes, ... Il.3.419.212.
Full on *Atrides'* ringing Shield it flew, ... Il.3.428.212.
Thro' *Paris'* Shield the forceful Weapon went, ... Il.3.440.213.
Now Shield with Shield, with Helmet Helmet clos'd, ... Il.4.508.245.
Now Shield with Shield, with Helmet Helmet clos'd, ... Il.4.508.245.
His Flank, unguarded by his ample Shield, ... Il.4.534.247.
His beamy Shield emits a living Ray; ... Il.5.6.266.
So tow'rs his Helmet, and so flames his Shield. ... Il.5.233.278.
Without a Warrior's Arms, the Spear and Shield! ... Il.5.267.280.
Thine be the Guidance then: With Spear and Shield ... Il.5.296.281.
On his broad Shield the sounding Weapon rung, ... Il.5.343.283.
O'er the fall'n Trunk his ample Shield display'd, ... Il.5.365.284.
Like *Pallas* dreadful with her sable Shield, ... Il.5.410.286.
Tho' screen'd behind *Apollo's* mighty Shield. ... Il.5.528.294.
Mars hovers o'er them with his sable Shield, ... Il.5.621.297.
But now the Monarch's Lance transpierc'd his Shield, ... Il.5.664.300.
His Shield too weak the furious Dart to sustain, ... Il.5.665.300.
A Wood of Spears his ample Shield sustain'd; ... Il.5.767.303.
O'er her broad Shoulders hangs his horrid Shield, ... Il.5.911.309.
Beneath his pond'rous Shield his Sinews bend, ... Il.5.993.314.
And thy fell Daughter with the Shield and Spear: ... Il.5.1073.317.
Bright'ning the Shield, and polishing the Bow. ... Il.6.401.346.
Stern *Telamon* behind his ample Shield ... Il.7.265.377.
And bear thick Battel on my sounding Shield. ... Il.7.292.378.
Whirl'd the long Lance against the sev'nfold Shield. ... Il.7.296.378.
Thro' *Hector's* Shield the forceful Javelin flew, ... Il.7.300.379.
Spouts the black Gore, and dimms his shining Shield. ... Il.7.314.379.
His Bulk supporting on the shatter'd Shield. ... Il.7.326.380.
Give me to seize rich *Nestor's* Shield of Gold; ... Il.8.235.408.
Secure behind the *Telamonian* Shield ... Il.8.321.412.
Moves as he moves, and turns the shining Shield. ... Il.8.328.413.
He fell: But *Ajax* his broad Shield display'd, ... Il.8.397.416.
Th' avenging Bolt, and shake the sable Shield! ... Il.8.424.417.
Th' avenging Bolt, and shake the dreadful Shield! ... Il.8.527.421.
The various-colour'd Scarf, the Shield he rears, ... Il.10.84.6.
He heard, return'd, and took his painted Shield: ... Il.10.168.9.
His Head reclining on his bossy Shield. ... Il.10.173.9.
Th' avenging Bolt, and shake the dreadful Shield. ... Il.10.328.17.
Then help'd by thee, and cover'd by thy Shield, ... Il.10.343.18.
And circling Terrors fill'd the expressive Shield: ... Il.11.48.36.
Great *Hector,* cover'd with his spacious Shield, ... Il.11.81.38.
And o'er the Body spreads his ample Shield. ... Il.11.334.49.
He said, and forceful pierc'd his spacious Shield; ... Il.11.546.58.
But soon as *Ajax* heaves his Tow'r-like Shield, ... Il.11.606.61.
By the broad glitt'ring of the sev'nfold Shield. ... Il.11.649.62.
O'er his broad Back his moony Shield he threw, ... Il.11.672.65.
Shield touching Shield, a long-refulgent Row; ... Il.12.311.93.
Shield touching Shield, a long-refulgent Row; ... Il.12.311.93.

SHIELD (CONTINUED)

And bears aloft his ample Shield in Air; ... Il.12.352.94.
Then, with his sev'nfold Shield, he strode away. ... Il.12.442.97.
To shield his Off-spring, and avert his Fate. ... Il.12.494.99.
Before his wary Steps, his ample Shield. ... Il.13.214.116.
The rest lies rooted in a *Trojan* Shield. ... Il.13.336.121.
Or bear close Battel on the sounding Shield. ... Il.13.405.125.
From his slope Shield, the disappointed Lance. ... Il.13.512.131.
His Shield revers'd o'er the fall'n Warrior lies; ... Il.13.688.137.
His Shield emboss'd the ringing Storm sustains, ... Il.13.700.138.
Nor pierc'd *Pisander* thro' *Atrides'* Shield; ... Il.13.759.141.
His left Arm high oppos'd the shining Shield; ... Il.13.765.141.
Who bore by turns great *Ajax'* sev'nfold Shield; ... Il.13.886.147.
Nor bear the Helm, nor lift the moony Shield; ... Il.13.892.148.
Before him flaming, his enormous Shield ... Il.13.1012.153.
He said: and seizing *Thrasimedes'* Shield, ... Il.14.13.157.
Each valiant *Grecian* seize his broadest Shield; ... Il.14.432.184.
The weaker Warrior takes a lighter Shield. ... Il.14.442.184.
(One brac'd his Shield, and one sustain'd his Sword.) ... Il.14.468.186.
On the raz'd Shield the falling Ruin rings: ... Il.14.476.187.
His following Shield the fallen Chief o'erspread; ... Il.14.489.187.
From frantic *Mars* she snatch'd the Shield and Spear; ... Il.15.143.202.
High-held before him, *Jove's* enormous Shield ... Il.15.350.210.
As long as *Phœbus* bore unmov'd the Shield, ... Il.15.360.210.
Before them flam'd the Shield, and march'd the God. ... Il.15.413.213.
And quit the Quiver for the pond'rous Shield. ... Il.15.557.218.
He pierc'd the Centre of his sounding Shield: ... Il.15.625.220.
Against the Margin of his ample Shield ... Il.15.779.226.
Achilles' Shield his ample Shoulders spread, ... Il.16.168.244.
Shield urg'd on Shield, and Man drove Man along: ... Il.16.261.249.
Shield urg'd on Shield, and Man drove Man along: ... Il.16.261.249.
O'er his broad Shoulders spread the massy Shield; ... Il.16.429.259.
Which pierc'd below the Shield his valiant Heart. ... Il.16.485.262.
Each heav'd the Shield, and pois'd the lifted Spear: ... Il.16.567.266.
The Lance hiss'd harmless o'er his cov'ring Shield, ... Il.16.741.272.
His Spear in Shivers falls: His ample Shield ... Il.16.966.280.
His broad Shield glimmers, and his Lances flame. ... Il.17.10.288.
But soon as *Ajax* rear'd his tow'rlike Shield, ... Il.17.139.293.
Meanwhile great *Ajax* (his broad Shield display'd) ... Il.17.143.293.
Which pass'd the Shield of *Aretus* the young; ... Il.17.585.311.
But now th' Eternal shook his sable Shield, ... Il.17.668.314.
Except the mighty *Telamonian* Shield? ... Il.18.230.332.
Then first he form'd th' immense and solid *Shield;* ... Il.18.551.348.
Two Cities radiant on the Shield appear, ... Il.18.567.350.
Thus the broad Shield complete the Artist crown'd ... Il.18.701.357.
And like the Moon, the broad refulgent Shield ... Il.19.402.388.
Spread o'er his Breast the fencing Shield he bore, ... Il.20.196.402.
(To meet the thund'ring Lance) his dreadful Shield, ... Il.20.311.407.
Compos'd the Shield; of Brass each outward Fold, ... Il.20.319.407.
From great *Æneas'* Shield the Spear he drew, ... Il.20.371.410.
His useless Lance and unavailing Shield) ... Il.21.59.424.
One struck, but pierc'd not the *Vulcanian* Shield; ... Il.21.182.429.
His loaded Shield bends to the rushing Tide; ... Il.21.265.431.
He spoke, and smote the loud-resounding Shield, ... Il.21.464.440.
His Shield (a broad Circumference) he bore; ... Il.21.688.450.
Beneath a Turret, on his Shield reclin'd, ... Il.22.136.458.
The Warrior-Shield, the Helm, and Lance lay down, ... Il.22.156.459.
Unerring, but the heav'nly Shield repell'd ... Il.22.370.471.
Before his Breast the flaming Shield he bears, ... Il.22.394.472.
Before his Breast his flaming Shield he bears, ... Il.22.394A.472.
Thro' the broad Shield, but at the Corselet stay'd: ... Il.23.966.527.
Spread o'er the sacred Corse his golden Shield. ... Il.24.33.536.
Th' avenging bolt, and shake the dreadful shield! ... Od.4.1006.164.
Like a broad shield amid the watry waste. ... Od.5.360.189.
To shield the vessel from the rowling sea; ... Od.5.519.197.
Th' avenging bolt, and shake the dreadful shield; ... Od.6.386.230.
And low on earth my shield and javelin cast, ... Od.14.306.50.
And trusted to my coat and shield alone! ... Od.14.542.63.
A pointed javelin, and a fenceful shield. ... Od.16.321.121.
Each pois'd his shield, and each advanc'd his spear; ... Od.16.493.131.
The shield of *Jove*, or him who rules the day! ... Od.18.278.180.
Should *Jove* dire war unloose, with spear and shield ... Od.18.418.189.
My sure divinity shall bear the shield, ... Od.20.61.235.
For missile jav'lins, and for helm and shield; ... Od.22.119.292.
And now his shoulders bear the massy shield, ... Od.22.138.293.
One hand sustain'd a helm, and one the shield ... Od.22.197.296.
On good *Eumæus'* shield and shoulder glanc'd; ... Od.22.309.301.
Then to his train he gives his spear and shield; ... Od.24.253.361.

SHIELD'S

The Shield's large Orb behind his Shoulder cast, ... Il.6.144.331.
Full on the Shield's round Boss the Weapon rung; ... Il.13.256.117.
And pierc'd the *Dardan* Shield's extremest Bound, ... Il.20.323.407.

SHIELDED

By *Laurels* shielded from the piercing Day: ... 6.14iv.22.47.
While shielded from the Darts, the *Greeks* obtain ... Il.18.273.335.
If shielded to the dreadful fight we move, ... Od.16.282.118.

SHIELDS

In vain he calls, the Din of Helms and Shields ... 1.TrES.63.452.
Shields, helms, and swords all jangle as they hang, ... 6.9i.1.21.
So from the polish'd Arms, and brazen Shields, ... Il.2.538.152.
Pierce the tough Cors'lets and the brazen Shields. ... Il.2.652.158.
Now rest their Spears, or lean upon their Shields; ... Il.3.177.199.
With flaming Shields in martial Circle stood. ... Il.4.122.226.
Screen'd by the Shields of his surrounding Friends. ... Il.4.145.227.
A shady Light was shot from glimm'ring Shields, ... Il.4.324.236.
Shields urg'd on Shields, and Men drove Men along. ... Il.4.485.243.
Shields urg'd on Shields, and Men drove Men along. ... Il.4.485.243.
And *Greece* and *Troy* with clashing Shields engag'd. ... Il.5.550.295.
With bristling Lances, and compacted Shields; ... Il.5.773.303.
Horrid with bristling Spears, and gleaming Shields. ... Il.7.70.366.
From their bor'd Shields the Chiefs their Javelins drew, ... Il.7.305.379.
From their bor'd Shields the Chiefs the Javelins drew, ... Il.7.305A.379.
To Lances, Lances, Shields to Shields oppos'd, ... Il.8.76.399.

SHIELDS (CONTINUED)

To Lances, Lances, Shields to Shields oppos'd, ... Il.8.76.399.
With close-rang'd Chariots, and with thicken'd Shields. ... Il.8.261.409.
Slipp'ry with Blood, o'er Arms and Heaps of Shields, ... Il.10.541.27.
O'er Heaps of Carcasses, and Hills of Shields. ... Il.11.657.63.
O'er heapy Shields, and o'er the prostrate Throng, ... Il.11.886.75.
Trojans and *Greeks* with clashing Shields engage, ... Il.12.3.80.
Helmets, and Shields, and God-like Heroes slain: ... Il.12.22.82.
Now with compacted Shields, in close Array, ... Il.12.119.85.
In vain around them beat their hollow Shields; ... Il.12.156.87.
Heavy, and thick, resound the batter'd Shields, ... Il.12.181.87.
In vain he calls; the Din of Helms and Shields ... Il.12.407.96.
Armour in Armour lock'd, and Shields in Shields, ... Il.13.180.114.
Armour in Armour lock'd, and Shields in Shields, ... Il.13.180.114.
And high-hung spears, and shields that flame with Gold. ... Il.13.346.122.
Dire was the Gleam, of Breastplates, Helms and Shields, ... Il.13.432.126.
And his broad Buckler shields his slaughter'd Friend; ... Il.13.530.131.
With cov'ring Shields (a friendly Circle) stand. ... Il.14.502.188.
Shields touching Shields in order blaze above, ... Il.15.678.222.
Shields touching Shields in order blaze above, ... Il.15.678.222.
The Faulchions ring, Shields rattle, Axes sound, ... Il.15.864.230.
Shields, Helmets rattle, as the Warriors close; ... Il.16.765.273.
Some, hard and heavy, shake the sounding Shields. ... Il.16.934.279.
With brazen Shields in horrid Circle stand: ... Il.17.317.300.
Then o'er their Backs they spread their solid Shields; ... Il.17.559.310.
Cover'd with Shields, beside a silver Flood. ... Il.18.604.352.
So Helms succeeding Helms, so Shields from Shields ... Il.19.384.388.
So Helms succeeding Helms, so Shields from Shields ... Il.19.384.388.
Beneath one Roof of well-compacted Shields ... Il.22.6.453.
Horrid with bristly spears, and glancing shields. ... Od.14.297.50.
Froze with the blast, and gath'ring glaz'd our shields. ... Od.14.537.63.
Lay cover'd by their ample shields at rest. ... Od.14.539.63.
Horrid with bristly spears, and gleaming shields: ... Od.17.518.157.
With shields indented deep in glorious wars. ... Od.19.37.194.
Twelve shields, twelve lances, and twelve helmets bears: ... Od.22.159.294.

SHIFT

They shift the moving Toyshop of their Heart; ... 2.RL1.100.153.
A Weasel once made shift to slink ... 4.1HE7.51.271.
Realms shift their place, and Ocean turns to land. ... 5.DunA1.70.68.
Realms shift their place, and Ocean turns to land. ... 5.DunB1.72.275.
Yet Dew or Rain may wett us to the Shift, ... 6.42vi.5.120.
I know to shift my Ground, remount the Car, ... Il.7.289.378.

SHIFTED

Perhaps the Wind just shifted from the east: ... 3.Ep1.64.20.

SHIFTING

Quick whirls, and shifting eddies, of our minds? ... 3.Ep1.30.17.
With what a shifting gale your course you ply; ... 4.2HE1.298.221.
And Conquest shifting to the *Trojan* Side, ... Il.17.706.315.

SHIFTS

I still have shifts against a Time of Need: ... 2.ChWB.297.71.
He shifts his Place, his Colour comes and goes; ... Il.13.360.123.
He shifts his Seat, and vaults from one to one; ... Il.15.827.228.
Now shifts his Side, impatient for the Day: ... Il.24.18.535.

SHILL

He'd do't; and ne'r stand Shill—I Shall—I, ... 6.44.9.123.

SHILLINGS

In shillings and in pence at first they deal, ... 4.JD2.83.141.
Content but for five shillings in the pound, ... 4.1740.40.334.
Three Shillings cost the first, the last sev'n Groats; ... 6.96iv.53.277.

SHIN'D

If Parts allure thee, think how Bacon shin'd, ... 3.EOM4.281.154.
If Parts allure thee, think how Wh[arton] shin'd, ... 3.EOM4.281A.154.
The Courtier smooth, who forty years had shin'd ... 3.Ep1.252.37.
E'er swell'd on Marble; as in Verse have shin'd ... 4.2HE1.392.229.
Shin'd in Description, he might show it, ... 4.HS6.190.261.
How shin'd the Soul, unconquer'd in the Tow'r! ... 4.EpS2.83.317.
Once brightest shin'd this child of Heat and Air. ... 5.DunB4.424.383.
Where *Hector* march'd, the God of Battels shin'd, ... Il.5.730.302.
Who o'er the Sons of Men in Beauty shin'd, ... Il.6.195.335.
Before him brandish'd, at each Motion shin'd. ... Il.6.397.346.
And in his Hand a pointed Javelin shin'd. ... Il.10.398.21.
Thro' the brown Shade the fulgid Weapons shin'd. ... Il.10.547.27.
Full in the blazing Van great *Hector* shin'd, ... Il.13.1010.153.
With Brass refulgent the broad Surface shin'd, ... Il.17.560.310.
The new-made Car with solid Beauty shin'd; ... Il.24.334.550.
Bright in his hand a pond'rous javelin shin'd; ... Od.2.13.60.
Far o'er the rest thy mighty father shin'd, ... Od.3.149.93.
Of men decay, and thro' three Ages shin'd, ... Od.3.304.101.
Aurora dawn'd, and *Phœbus* shin'd in vain, ... Od.7.371.254.
Nor longer in the heavy eye-ball shin'd ... Od.13.500.29.
In all the youth his father's image shin'd, ... Od.14.204.45.
They reach'd the dome; the dome with marble shin'd. ... Od.16.41.104.
Nought else are all that shin'd on earth before; ... Od.24.23.348.
Not more thy wisdom, than her virtue, shin'd; ... Od.24.220.358.

SHINE

Now Golden Fruits on loaded Branches shine, ... 1.PAu.73.85.
Behold the *Groves* that shine with silver Frost, ... 1.PWi.9.89.
O'erflow thy Courts: The LIGHT HIMSELF shall shine ... 1.Mes.103.122.
Let *Volga's* Banks with Iron Squadrons shine, ... 1.W-F.363.186.
And force *that Sun* but on a *Part* to Shine; ... 1.EOC.399.286.
In all you speak, let Truth and Candor shine: ... 1.EOC.563.305.
These bright, like gold, and those with purple shine; ... 1.TrPA.72.368.
Whose Charms as far all other Nymphs out-shine, ... 1.TrVP.53.379.
And in thy Glories more serenely shine; ... 1.TrSt.40.411.
Nor Gems on Bowls emboss'd were seen to shine, ... 1.TrSt.208.419.
Nor shine their Beauties with superior Grace, ... 1.TrSt.626.436.
And shine more faintly at approaching Day; ... 1.TrSt.826.444.
And on thy Hospitable *Argos* shine. ... 1.TrSt.856.445.

SHINE (CONTINUED)
And op'd those Eyes which brighter shine than they; ....2.RL1.14A.145.
And, like the Sun, they shine on all alike. ....2.RL2.14.160.
The wandring streams that shine between the hills, ...2.ElAb.157.332.
Eternal sun-shine of the spotless mind! ....2.ElAb.209.337.
From opening skies may streaming glories shine, ...2.ElAb.341.347.
Ask for what end the heav'nly bodies shine, ...3.EOM1.131.31.
Of show'rs and sun-shine, as of Man's desires; ....3.EOM1.152.34.
Fair op'ning to some Court's propitious shine, ...3.EOM4.9.128.
The soul's calm sun-shine, and the heart-felt joy, ...3.EOM4.168.143.
Alike or when, or where, they shone, or shine, ...3.EOM4.245.150.
E'er taught to shine, or sanctify'd from shame! ....3.EOM4.300.156.
He'll shine a Tully and a Wilmot too. ....3.Ep1.187.31.
Or drest in smiles of sweet Cecilia shine, ...3.Ep2.13.49.
Shine, buzz, and fly-blow in the setting-sun. ....3.Ep2.28.52.
And shine that Superfluity away. ....4.HS2.116.63.
Nor Kitchen shine with more than usal Fire ....4.JD2A.118.142.
Such as on HOUGH's unsully'd Mitre shine, ...4.EpS2.240.326.
And for that Cause which made your Fathers shine, ...4.EpS2.252.327.
She saw old Pryn in restless Daniel shine, ...5.DunA1.101.71.
She saw in *N[orto]n* all his father shine, ...5.DunA1.101A.71.
See round the Poles where keener spangles shine, ...5.DunA3.61.155.
She saw old Pryn in restless Daniel shine, ...5.DunB1.103.276.
His Peers shine round him with reflected grace, ...5.DunB2.9.296.
See, round the Poles where keener spangles shine, ...5.DunB3.69.323.
Another (for in all what one can shine?) ....5.DunB4.555.397.
Shine in the dignity of F.R.S. ....5.DunB4.570.398.
Nor *public* Flame, nor *private*, dares to shine; ....5.DunB4.651.409.
Are best by thee express'd, and shine in thee alone. ....6.8.39.19.
Here *Orange-* trees with blooms and pendants shine, ...6.14iv.17.47.
In these gay Thoughts the Loves and Graces shine, ...6.19.1.62.
Whom prostrate Kings beheld unrival'd shine, ...6.20.11.66.
Shine through the soul, and drive its clouds away! ....6.23.14.73.
Fires that scorch, yet dare not shine: ....6.51ii.40.154.
Like them to shine thro' long succeeding age, ...6.52.11.156.
Oh lasting as those colours may they shine, ...6.52.63.158.
Touch'd by thy hand, again Rome's glories shine, ...6.71.46.204.
On the cast ore, another Pollio, shine; ....6.71.64.204.
And the whole Princesse in my work should shine. ....6.75.10.212.
Where other Buckhursts, other Dorsets shine, ...6.118.13.335.
E'er taught to shine, or sanctified from shame ....6.130.14.358.
Once more refulgent shine in Brazen Arms. ....Il.2.200.137.
Where *Anemoria's* stately Turrets shine, ...Il.2.625.157.
In equal Arms their Brother-Leaders shine, ...Il.2.1020.171.
Around whose Brow such martial Graces shine, ...Il.3.221.203.
Be bold (she cry'd) in ev'ry Combate shine, ...Il.5.158.274.
Distance immense! between the Pow'rs that shine ....Il.5.535.294.
Rich with immortal Gold their Trappings shine. ....Il.5.887.308.
Then shine the Vales, the Rocks in Prospect rise, ...Il.8.695.428.
To shine in Councils, and in Camps to dare. ....Il.9.571.462.
Inspires her War, and bids her Glory shine. ....Il.9.805.473.
Rang'd at the Ships let all our Squadrons shine, ...Il.9.830.474.
The Stars shine fainter on th' Ætherial Plains, ...Il.10.297.15.
Menœtius thus; "Tho' great *Achilles* shine ....Il.11.916.76.
Some Beam of Comfort yet on *Greece* may shine, ...Il.11.928.77.
Shine 'twixt the Hills, or wander o'er the Plain. ....Il.12.36.83.
For this, behold! in horrid Arms I shine, ...Il.13.307.119.
Lord of a Host, o'er all my Host I shine, ...Il.13.570.133.
A splendid Footstool, and a Throne, that shine ....Il.14.272.175.
Daughters of *Jove!* that on *Olympus* shine, ...Il.14.599.191.
To rise in Arms, and shine again in War. ....Il.15.465.215.
Indulgent *Jove!* how plain thy Favours shine, ...Il.15.576.218.
Some Beam of Comfort yet on *Greece* may shine, ...Il.16.56.237.
The Hills shine out, the Rocks in Prospect rise, ...Il.16.358.257.
Long us'd, untouch'd, in fighting Fields to shine, ...Il.16.962.280.
Hector in proud *Achilles'* Arms shall shine, ...Il.17.209.295.
Where vast *Olympus* starry Summits shine: ....Il.18.180.331.
Where Heav'ns far-beaming, brazen Mansions shine. ....Il.18.434.341.
To shine with Glory, till he shines no more! ....Il.18.530.347.
Goddess (he cry'd) these glorious Arms that shine ....Il.19.25.372.
Long lost to Battel, shine in Arms again. ....Il.19.50.374.
Resume thy Arms, and shine again in War. ....Il.19.142.377.
Thy Praise it is in dreadful Camps to shine, ...Il.19.217.381.
And shine in mazy Wand'rings o'er the Plains. ....Il.21.298.433.
Whose glitt'ring Margins rais'd with Silver shine; ....Il.23.641.515.
Others 'tis own'd, in Fields of Battle shine, ...Il.23.773.520.
Sidonian Artists taught the Frame to shine, ...Il.23.867.524.
Two Tripods next and twice two Chargers shine, ...Il.24.285.548.
But when the tenth fair Morn began to shine, ...Il.24.995.577.
And shine eternal in the sphere of fame— ....Od.1.394.51.
Fullfil our wish, and let thy glory shine ....Od.3.70.89.
Never on man did heav'nly favour shine ....Od.3.273.99.
So guide me, Goddess! so propitious shine ....Od.3.488.111.
Clasp'd on his feet th' embroider'd sandals shine, ...Od.4.417.140.
So when with praise amid the dance they shine, ...Od.6.77.208.
Shine in her hand: Along the sounding plains ....Od.6.96.210.
The warrior Goddess gives his frame to shine ....Od.6.271.223.
And shine before him all the desart way: ....Od.7.274.249.
Wide o'er the world *Alcinous'* glory shine! ....Od.7.425.258.
O'er the fair web the rising figures shine, ...Od.10.256.355.
Thus terribly adorn'd the figures shine, ...Od.11.757.423.
All dreadful bright my limbs in armour shine; ....Od.12.269.445.
This silver bowl, whose costly margins shine ....Od.15.128.75.
Fair on his feet the polish'd sandals shine, ...Od.17.5.132.
With fiery glare his sanguine eye-balls shine, ...Od.19.519.221.
Of sovereign state with faded splendor shine. ....Od.20.244.244.
(With polish'd oak the level pavements shine) ....Od.21.44.261.
The Warrior-Goddess gives his frame to shine ....Od.23.153.328.
Pallas attending gives his frame to shine ....Od.24.427.369.

SHINES
Why sit we sad, when *Phosphor* shines so clear, ...1.PSp.27.63.
Ev'n Spring displeases, when she shines not here, ...1.PSp.83.69.
Clears, and *improves* whate'er it shines upon, ...1.EOC.316.274.
In Arms he shines, conspicuous from afar, ...1.TrES.7.449.
Here ever shines the Godlike *Socrates:* ....2.TemF.171.269.

SHINES (CONTINUED)
Grace shines around her with serenest beams, ...2.ElAb.215.337.
Shines, in exposing Knaves, and painting Fools, ...3.Ep2.119.60.
Serene in Virgin Modesty she shines, ...3.Ep2.255.70.
Where-e'er he shines, oh Fortune, gild the scene, ...3.Ep3.245.113.
Ev'n *Sunday* shines no *Sabbath-day* to me: ....4.Arbu.12.96.
One Simile, that solitary shines ....4.2HE1.111.205.
I follow *Virtue*, where she shines, I praise, ...4.EpS2.95.318.
There, stamp'd with arms, Newcastle shines compleat, ...5.DunA1.122.78.
That shines a Consul, this Commissioner. ....5.DunA3.180.170.
There, stamp'd with arms, Newcastle shines complete: ....5.DunB1.142.280.
That shines a consul, this Commissioner." ....5.DunB3.184.329.
('Tis thus aspiring Dulness ever shines) ....5.DunB4.19.341.
She shines the first of batter'd Jades, ...6.14v(b).17.50.
But shines himselfe till they are seen no more. ....6.43.12.120.
And shines himselfe till they are seen no more. ....6.43.12A.121.
Serene, in virgin majesty, she shines; ....6.106i.6.306.
Serene, in virgin Modesty, she shines; ....6.106i.6A.306.
Where shines great *Strafford's* glittering Star: ....6.135.58.368.
Where shines great *Strafford's* guilded Star: ....6.135.58A.368.
Shines a broad Mirrour thro' the shadowy Cave; ....6.142.2.382.
Shines a broad Mirrour thro' the gloomy Cave; ....6.142.2A.382.
Shines a broad Mirrour thro' the watry Cave; ....6.142.2B.382.
Shines in exposing Knaves and painting Fools, ...6.154.5.403.
But *Thetis'* Son now shines in Arms no more; ....Il.2.938.168.
Shines forth reveal'd, and animates the Fight. ....Il.4.586.249.
High on the Throne he shines: His Coursers fly, ...Il.8.55.398.
While *Phœbus* shines, or Men have tongues to praise? ....Il.10.252.13.
Before the next the graceful *Paris* shines, ...Il.12.105.85.
In Arms he shines, conspicuous from afar, ...Il.12.351.94.
A Dart, whose Point with Brass refulgent shines, ...Il.15.568.218.
To shine with Glory, till he shines no more! ....Il.18.530.347.
Still shines exalted on th' ætherial Plain, ...Il.18.565.349.
Next, rip in yellow Gold, a Vineyard shines, ...Il.18.651.355.
Now shines the tenth bright Morning since I came ....Il.21.173.428.
As radiant *Hesper* shines with keener Light, ...Il.22.399.472.
The living Image of my Father shines. ....Il.24.458.555.
Amid the Circle shines: but hope and fear ....Od.1.150.40.
She shines with fatal excellence, to thee: ....Od.2.140.67.
Above, beneath, around the Palace shines ....Od.4.85.123.
Full shines the father in the filial frame, ...Od.4.199.129.
In thee renew'd the soul of *Nestor* shines: ....Od.4.282.132.
Who shines exalted on th' etherial plain, ...Od.5.351.188.
So shines majestic, and so stately moves, ...Od.6.180.218.
And near, a Forum flank'd with marble shines, ...Od.6.318.226.
Around, a circle of bright damsels shines, ...Od.6.368.229.
Sudden he shines, and manifest to sight. ....Od.7.191.245.
Before his seat a polish'd table shines, ...Od.8.65.265.
The brightest shines in all the rolls of fame: ....Od.8.418.286.
No rich embroid'ry shines to grace his bed: ....Od.11.229.393.
Thro' all his woes the Hero shines confest; ....Od.11.419.405.
Such *Venus* shines, when with a measur'd bound ....Od.18.229.178.
Now *Pallas* shines confess'd; aloft she spreads ....Od.22.330.302.
And the fair dome with polish'd marble shines. ....Od.23.198.333.

SHINING
Eternal Beauties grace the shining Scene, ...1.PWi.71.94.
The vivid Green his shining Plumes unfold; ....1.W-F.117.161.
The silver Eel, in shining Volumes roll'd, ...1.W-F.143.163.
While thro' the Skies his shining Current strays, ...1.W-F.228A.170.
With *Edward's* Acts adorn the shining Page, ...1.W-F.303.177.
His shining Horns diffus'd a golden Gleam: ....1.W-F.332.182.
And glossy Jett is pair'd with shining White. ....1.TrSP.44.395.
Clear as a Glass, the shining Sands below; ....1.TrSP.180.401.
And crowd their shining Ranks to yield thee place; ....1.TrSt.36.411.
A shining Synod of Majestick Gods ....1.TrSt.292.422.
But *Thebes*, where shining in Cœlestial Charms ....1.TrSt.360.425.
Deep in her Breast he plung'd his shining Sword, ...1.TrSt.725.440.
The shining Structures rais'd by lab'ring Gods! ....1.TrSt.836.444.
Gloomy as Night, and shakes two shining Spears; ....1.TrES.200.456.
Her decent Hand a shining Jav'lin bore, ...1.TrUl.106.469.
Here Files of Pins extend their shining Rows, ...2.RL1.137.156.
With shining Ringlets the smooth Iv'ry Neck. ....2.RL2.22.160.
With shining Ringlets her smooth Iv'ry Neck. ....2.RL2.22A.160.
And Particolour'd Troops, a shining Train, ...2.RL3.43.172.
On shining Altars of *Japan* they raise ....2.RL3.107.175.
A two-edg'd Weapon from her shining Case; ....2.RL3.128.177.
Which adds new Glory to the shining Sphere! ....2.RL5.142.211.
Now a clear Sun the shining Scene displays, ...2.TemF.19.254.
Deep hid the shining mischief under ground: ....3.Ep3.10.84.
And half unsheath'd the shining Blade; ....6.11.46.32.
The shining Robes, rich Jewels, Beds of State, ...6.19.51.63.
Whose shining scene with rich *Hesperia* vies. ....6.20.71.68.
Clear as her soul, and shining as her frame; ....6.126ii.4.353.
The Monarch started from his shining Throne; ....Il.1.128.93.
Then in the Sheath return'd the shining Blade. ....Il.1.292.100.
To high *Olympus'* shining Court ascend, ...Il.1.511.112.
The shining Synod of th' Immortals wait ....Il.1.690.120.
The shining Monuments of *Vulcan's* Art: ....Il.1.779.124.
And shining soars and claps her Wings above. ....Il.2.122.133.
In *Hector's* Breast be plung'd this shining Sword, ...Il.2.496.150.
The shining Armies swept along the Ground; ....Il.2.947.168.
The shining Armies sweep along the Ground; ....Il.2.947A.168.
So from the King the shining Warrior flies, ...Il.3.51.191.
Your shining Swords within the Sheath restrain, ...Il.3.125.196.
His figur'd Shield, a shining Orb, he takes, ...Il.3.419.212.
The *Trojan* first his shining Jav'lin threw; ....Il.3.427.212.
And now *Olympus'* shining Gates unfold; ....Il.4.1.220.
A Mountain Goat resign'd the shining Spoil, ...Il.4.138.227.
The shining Whiteness and the *Tyrian* Dye. ....Il.4.175.229.
The shining Barb appear above the Wound. ....Il.4.181.230.
(Fell'd by some Artist with his shining Steel, ...Il.4.554.248.
Screen'd from the Foe behind her shining Veil, ...Il.5.391.285.
Two shining Spears are brandish'd in his Hands; ....Il.5.605.297.
The ruthless Victor stripp'd their shining Arms. ....Il.6.34.325.
A hundred Beeves the shining Purchase bought. ....Il.6.295.341.

SHINING (CONTINUED)

The Priestess then the shining Veil displays, ... Il.6.376.344.
And laves, in Height of Blood, his shining Sides; ... Il.6.655.359.
Spouts the black Gore, and dimms his shining Shield. ... Il.7.314.379.
In shining Circle round their Father *Jove,* ... Il.7.527.391.
And buckled on their shining Arms with Haste. ... Il.8.68.398.
Moves as he moves, and turns the shining Shield. ... Il.8.328.413.
To great *Olympus'* shining Gates she flies, ... Il.8.504.420.
The ruddy Gold, the Steel, and shining Brass; ... Il.9.478.456.
Next on his Feet the shining Sandals bound; ... Il.10.28.3.
The shining Helmet, and the pointed Spears: ... Il.10.85.6.
The shining Greaves his manly Legs inclose; ... Il.10.151.8.
Next him *Ulysses* took a shining Sword, ... Il.10.307.16.
Rich silver Plates his shining Car infold; ... Il.10.508.26.
In shining Greaves, with silver Buckles bound: ... Il.11.24.35.
The shining Blade, and golden Hangers grac'd. ... Il.11.42.36.
The stern *Tydides* strips their shining Arms. ... Il.11.432.53.
Far in the Bay his shining Palace stands, ... Il.13.34.106.
From *Hector's* Hand a shining Javelin fled: ... Il.13.246.116.
Secure in Mail, and sheath'd in shining Steel. ... Il.13.258.117.
Soon as the Foe the shining Chiefs beheld ... Il.13.420.126.
His left Arm high oppos'd the shining Shield; ... Il.13.765.141.
And trace large Furrows with the Shining Share; ... Il.13.882.147.
Part on her Head in shining Ringlets roll'd, ... Il.14.205.170.
Thus sheath'd in shining Brass, in bright Array, ... Il.14.443.184.
Stood shining o'er him, half unseal'd his Sight: ... Il.15.279.207.
When great *Achilles'* shining Armour blaz'd: ... Il.16.335.255.
The shining Circlets of his golden Hair, ... Il.17.53.289.
And in the Victor's Hands the shining Prey. ... Il.17.94.291.
Conceals the Warriors' shining Helms in Night: ... Il.17.319.300.
There plac'd beside her on the shining Frame, ... Il.18.493.345.
The shining Shares full many Plowmen guide, ... Il.18.629.354.
And shot the shining Mischief to the Heart! ... Il.19.62.374.
Shining with Tears, she lifts, and thus she cries. ... Il.19.302.384.
These shining on, in long Procession come ... Il.20.9.393.
Return the shining Bands of Gods in Arms; ... Il.21.602.447.
The Chariots first proceed, a shining Train; ... Il.23.162.495.
Four ample Measures held the shining Frame: ... Il.23.336.503.
On whose broad Front a Blaze of shining white, ... Il.23.538.511.
Of beauteous Handmaids, Steeds, and shining Ore, ... Il.23.630.514.
Such Joy the *Spartan's* shining Face o'erspread, ... Il.23.683.517.
The shining Charger to his Vessel sent. ... Il.23.702.517.
And all the Gods in shining Synod round. ... Il.24.130.540.
Fast from the shining Sluices of her Eyes ... Il.24.960.576.
Now graceful seated on her shining throne, ... Od.5.109.177.
A moment snatch'd the shining form away, ... Od.5.448.194.
Thro' the thick gloom the shining portals blaze; ... Od.6.23.204.
(Their shining veils unbound.) Along the skies ... Od.6.113.211.
With opening streets and shining structures spread, ... Od.7.104.239.
And fill the shining thrones along the bay. ... Od.8.6.261.
The vests, the robes, and heaps of shining gold; ... Od.8.456.288.
Full where the dome its shining valves expands, ... Od.8.495.289.
The keen-edg'd pole-axe, or the shining sword, ... Od.9.466.325.
And from the scabbard drew the shining sword; ... Od.11.28.380.
Lo where he lies, amidst a shining store ... Od.13.158.13.
Her decent hand a shining Javelin bore, ... Od.13.273.19.
The shining veil, and thus endearing said. ... Od.15.137.75.
With copious streams the shining vase supplies ... Od.15.150.76.
And heap'd the shining canisters with bread. ... Od.16.50.104.
Recumbent on the shining thrones of state. ... Od.16.425.127.
Full where the dome its shining valves expands, ... Od.16.430.128.
Her freight a shining band: with martial air ... Od.16.492.130.
Then dis-array'd, the shining bath they sought, ... Od.17.98.136.
The bread from canisters of shining mold ... Od.18.145.173.
Full where the dome its shining valves expands, ... Od.18.247.178.
A robe *Antinous* gives of shining dyes, ... Od.18.337.184.
The shining baldness of his head survey, ... Od.18.401.187.
A two-edg'd faulchion and a shining spear, ... Od.21.366.277.
Telemachus girds on his shining sword. ... Od.21.476.283.
Oppos'd, before the shining Fire she sate. ... Od.23.92.323.
Sever'd the bole, and smooth'd the shining grain; ... Od.23.200.333.

SHINY

Gloomy as Night! and shakes two shiny Spears: ... Il.12.554.102.

SHIP

Thither they bent, and haul'd their Ship to Land, ... 1.TrUl.45.467.
Or ship off Senates to some distant Shore; ... 3.Ep3.74A.93.
Or ship off Senates to a distant Shore; ... 3.Ep3.74.93.
And two rich ship-wrecks bless the lucky shore. ... 3.Ep3.356.122.
The Ship it self may make a better figure, ... 4.2HE2.298.185.
To hurt your Lady-lap-dog-ship; ... 6.135.6.366.
Once chance to hurt your Lap dog ship ... 6.135.6A.366.
Soon shall the Fair the sable Ship ascend, ... Il.1.185.96.
A well-rigg'd Ship for *Chrysa's* sacred Shores: ... Il.1.405.107.
In his black Ship the *Pylian* Prince he found, ... Il.2.65.130.
When the Ship tosses, and the Tempests beat: ... Il.2.359.144.
And point at ev'ry Ship their vengeful Flame! ... Il.9.308.449.
The King to *Nestor's* sable Ship repairs; ... Il.10.81.6.
But those my Ship contains, whence distant far, ... Il.13.349.122.
Above the sides of some tall Ship ascend, ... Il.15.442.214.
And ev'ry Ship sustain'd an equal Tyde. ... Il.15.481.216.
To force our Fleet, or ev'n a Ship to gain, ... Il.15.561.218.
And swell'd with Tempests on the Ship descends; ... Il.15.753.225.
From Ship to Ship thus *Ajax* swiftly flew, ... Il.15.830.229.
From Ship to Ship thus *Ajax* swiftly flew, ... Il.15.830.229.
First seiz'd a Ship on that contested Strand; ... Il.15.855.229.
Close to the Stern of that fam'd Ship, which bore ... Il.16.340.256.
And from the half-burn'd Ship proud *Troy* retires: ... Il.16.349.256.
All to *Achilles'* sable Ship repair, ... Il.23.37.488.
And howling Tempest, stears the fearless Ship; ... Il.23.388.505.
One Ship convey'd us from our native Place; ... Il.24.486.556.
And to what ship I owe the friendly freight? ... Od.1.222.43.
Far from your Capital my ship resides ... Od.1.237.44.
And now they ship their oars, and crown with wine ... Od.2.470.83.
Thy ship and sailors but for orders stay; ... Od.3.414.106.

SHIP (CONTINUED)

I to the ship, to give the orders due, ... Od.3.460.109.
His ship o'erwhelm'd: but frowning on the floods, ... Od.4.673.151.
From his tall ship the King of men descends: ... Od.4.694.151.
My ship equip'd within the neighb'ring port, ... Od.4.854.159.
His ship returning shall my spies explore: ... Od.4.897.160.
And form a Raft, and build the rising ship, ... Od.5.211.181.
The best-built ship, tho' *Jove* inspire the gales. ... Od.5.228.182.
With stays and cordage last he rigg'd the ship, ... Od.5.331.188.
Firm-rooted in the surge a ship should stand ... Od.8.620.296.
Six brave companions from each ship we lost, ... Od.9.69.305.
While, with my single ship, adventurous I ... Od.9.201.314.
My train obey'd me and the ship unty'd. ... Od.9.208.314.
But answer, the good ship that brought ye o'er, ... Od.9.333.320.
The largest ship might claim it for a mast. ... Od.9.383.321.
Know hence what treasures in our ship we lost, ... Od.9.410.323.
And near the ship came thund'ring on the flood. ... Od.9.568.329.
These in my hollow ship the Monarch hung, ... Od.10.25.340.
With weighty steps, 'till at the ship I threw ... Od.10.198.350.
To guard the ship. Seek we the sacred shades ... Od.10.525.368.
The ship we moor on these obscure abodes; ... Od.11.21.380.
My mates ascend the ship; they strike their oars; ... Od.11.791.426.
Thither they bent, and haul'd their ship to land, ... Od.13.136.9.
This then I doom; to fix the gallant ship ... Od.13.172.13.
The swarming people hail their ship to land, ... Od.13.179.14.
Firm-rooted in the surge a ship shou'd stand; ... Od.13.203.15.
And to what ship I owe the friendly freight? ... Od.14.217.45.
In giddy rounds the whirling ship is tost, ... Od.14.339.51.
The ship arriv'd: Forth-issuing on the sand, ... Od.14.382.53.
But deem'd enquiry vain, and to their ship return'd. ... Od.14.390.53.
He climbs the ship, ascends the stern with haste, ... Od.15.308.84.
A ship of *Sidon* anchor'd in our port; ... Od.15.457.92.
(A noble prize!) and to your ship convey. ... Od.15.490.94.
What ship transported thee, O father say, ... Od.16.246.116.
Of *Byblos'* reed, a ship from *Egypt* brought) ... Od.21.424.280.

SHIP-WRECKS

And two rich ship-wrecks bless the lucky shore. ... 3.Ep3.356.122.

SHIP'S

A ship's tough cable, from a column hung; ... Od.22.500.313.

SHIPP'D

Or shipp'd with Ward to ape and monkey lands, ... 5.DunA1.200.86.
Our oars we shipp'd: all day the swelling sails ... Od.11.9.379.
Rude Pyrates seiz'd, and shipp'd thee o'er the main? ... Od.15.419.89.

SHIPPEN

As downright *Shippen,* or as old *Montagne.* ... 4.HS1.52.9.
Is all the help stern S[hippen] wou'd afford. ... 4.1740.16.332*.

SHIPS

Then Ships of uncouth Form shall stem the Tyde, ... 1.W-F.403.191.
And ships, in safety, wander to and fro. ... 1.TrPA.28.366.
A pine which ships might challenge for a mast: ... 1.TrPA.44.367.
And Ships secure without their Haulsers ride. ... 1.TrUl.30.466.
Tho' they cou'd see as far as Ships can sail? ... 2.ChJM.501.39.
Here sailing Ships delight the wand'ring Eyes; ... 2.TemF.17.254.
Some trivial Present to my Ships I bear, ... Il.1.219.97.
Mean time, secure within thy Ships from far ... Il.1.552.114.
The Ships and Tents in mingled Prospect lay. ... Il.1.633.118.
So, from the Tents and Ships, a length'ning Train ... Il.2.117.133.
To fit the Ships, and launch into the Main. ... Il.2.186.137.
Swift to the Ships precipitates her Flight; ... Il.2.204.138.
Desert the Ships, and pour upon the Plain. ... Il.2.248.139.
The hollow Ships each deaf'ning Shout rebound. ... Il.2.401.145.
Who dares, inglorious, in his Ships to stay, ... Il.2.466.149.
Full fifty Ships they send, and each conveys ... Il.2.608.156.
Twice twenty Ships transport the warlike Bands, ... Il.2.653.158.
In twelve black ships to *Troy* they steer their Course, ... Il.2.673.158.
In sixty Ships with *Menelaus* draws: ... Il.2.710.160.
Their Ships, supply'd by *Agamemnon's* Care, ... Il.2.743.161.
Three Ships with *Nireus* sought the *Trojan* Shore, ... Il.2.815.163.
Full fifty Ships beneath *Achilles'* Care ... Il.2.833.164.
His Troops in forty Ships *Podarces* led, ... Il.2.860.165.
In ten black Ships embark'd for *Ilion's* Shore, ... Il.2.868.165.
Sev'n were his Ships; each Vessel fifty row, ... Il.2.876.165.
Leonteus leads, and forty Ships obey. ... Il.2.905.166.
When thy tall Ships triumphant stem'd the Tide, ... Il.3.66.192.
In sable Ships they left their native Soil, ... Il.5.678.300.
With six small Ships, and but a slender Train, ... Il.5.794.304.
Thy hollow Ships his Captive Son detain, ... Il.6.60.326.
Before their Ships, proclaim my Son's Intent: ... Il.7.449.386.
To the black Ships *Idæus* bent his way: ... Il.7.457.387.
Ulysses seeks the Ships, and shelters there. ... Il.8.124.404.
Soon as before yon' hollow Ships we stand, ... Il.8.220.407.
Whose distant Ships the guarded Navy bound. ... Il.8.273.410.
Before the Ships a desp'rate Stand they made, ... Il.8.415.417.
Greece with her Ships, and crown our Toils with Fame: ... Il.8.624.425.
Greece on her sable Ships attempt her Flight. ... Il.8.636.426.
Ships thou hast store, and nearest to the Main, ... Il.9.62.434.
The Ships, the *Greeks,* and all the *Grecian* Name. ... Il.9.315.449.
To save the Ships, the Troops, the Chiefs from Fire. ... Il.9.547.460.
Rang'd at the Ships let all our Squadrons shine, ... Il.9.830.474.
To those tall Ships, remotest of the Fleet, ... Il.10.126.7.
Safe by thy Succour to our Ships convey'd; ... Il.10.332.17.
Vast Heaps of Brass shall in your Ships be told, ... Il.10.451.23.
Safe to the Ships, he wisely clear'd the way, ... Il.10.573.28.
Haste to the Ships, the gotten Spoils enjoy, ... Il.10.596.28.
But *Dolon's* Armour, to his Ships convey'd, ... Il.10.670.31.
Whose Ships remote the guarded Navy bound. ... Il.11.12.35.
The Sea with Ships, the Fields with Armies spread, ... Il.11.113.39.
The *Grecian* Ships his captive Sons detain, ... Il.11.174.43.
Then to her Ships shall flying *Greece* be press'd, ... Il.11.250.46.
Then to her Ships shall flying *Greece* be prest, ... Il.11.266.47.
With twelve black Ships he reach'd *Percope's* Strand, ... Il.11.295.48.

SHIPS (CONTINUED)
Till *Hector's* Arm involve the Ships in Flame? ....Il.11.408.53.
And great *Machaon* to the Ships convey. ....Il.11.635.61.
Thro' intermingled Ships and Tents, he past; ....Il.11.755.68.
Ev'n to the Ships victorious *Troy* pursues, ...Il.11.958.78.
Lead to my Ships, and draw this deadly Dart; ....Il.11.963.78.
Close by their hollow Ships the *Grecians* lay; ....Il.12.42.83.
The flying *Grecians* strove their Ships to gain; ....Il.12.134.86.
Seek not, this Day, the *Grecian* Ships to gain; ....Il.12.254.90.
Tho' all our Chiefs amid yon' Ships expire, ...Il.12.287.92.
The crowded Ships, and sable Seas between. ....Il.13.24.105.
Pant in the Ships; while *Troy* to Conquest calls, ...Il.13.119.110.
Invade your Camps, involve your Ships in Flame? ....Il.13.146.111.
Then to the Ships with surly Speed he went, ...Il.13.223.116.
Who seeks ignobly in his Ships to stay, ...Il.13.305.119.
And thence my Ships transport me thro' the Main; ....Il.13.569.133.
Our Heroes slaughter'd, and our Ships on flame, ...Il.13.786.142.
And what brave Heroes at the Ships lie slain? ....Il.13.928.149.
To yon' tall Ships to bear the *Trojan* Fires; ....Il.13.932.149.
(Their Ships at distance from the Battel stand, ...Il.14.39.159.
Rank above Rank, the crowded Ships they moor; ....Il.14.43.160.
Ev'n to the Ships their conqu'ring Arms extend, ...Il.14.65.160.
And launch what Ships lie nearest to the Main; ....Il.14.82.161.
Thy Ships first flying with Despair shall see, ...Il.14.112.163.
Shall *Hector* thunder at your Ships again? ....Il.14.424.184.
Around the Ships: Seas hanging o'er the Shores, ...Il.14.455.185.
Fly to their Ships and *Hellespont* again: ....Il.15.263.207.
And to the Ships impell thy rapid Horse: ....Il.15.293.208.
Fierce on the Ships above, the Cars below, ...Il.15.448.214.
Nor this the Ships can fire, nor that defend; ....Il.15.485.216.
Then swift invades the Ships, whose beaky Prores ....Il.15.834.229.
Against the sable Ships with flaming Brands, ...Il.15.905.232.
Doom'd in their Ships to sink by Fire and Sword, ...Il.16.25.236.
Shall quit the Ships, and *Greece* respire again. ....Il.16.63.238.
Now *Hector* to my Ships his Battel bears, ...Il.16.85.238.
Behold all *Ilion* on their Ships descends; ....Il.16.93.239.
Now save the Ships, the rising Fires restrain, ...Il.16.106.240.
While restless, raging, in your Ships you lay) ....Il.16.243.248.
Tho' still determin'd, to my Ships confin'd, ...Il.16.296.254.
The hollow Ships return a deeper Sound. ....Il.16.333.255.
So from the Ships, along the dusky Plain, ...Il.16.438.259.
Back to the Ships his destin'd Progress held, ...Il.16.477.261.
Patroclus' Ships the glorious Spoils adorn. ....Il.16.808.274.
When from the Ships he sent the *Pylian* Band. ....Il.17.439.304.
Now to the Ships to force it, now to *Troy.* ....Il.17.457.305.
Achilles in his Ships at distance lay, ...Il.17.462.305.
To great *Achilles* at his Ships she came, ...Il.18.207.331.
That tend the Ships, or guide them o'er the Main, ...Il.19.46.373.
If trembling in the Ships he lags behind. ....Il.19.240.382.
Now issued from the Ships the warrior Train, ...Il.19.378.387.
These his Attendants to the Ships convey'd, ...Il.21.38.423.
The *Grecians* seek their Ships, and clear the Strand, ...Il.23.5.486.
He said: The People to their Ships return: ....Il.23.199.497.
There plac'd 'em round: Then from the Ships proceeds ....Il.23.323.503.
These to the Ships his Train triumphant leads, ...Il.23.595.513.
And to the Ships brave *Merion* bears the Prize. ....Il.23.1043.530.
Seek their black Ships, and clear the crowded Strand; ....Il.24.2.534.
Sought their black Ships, and clear'd the crowded Strand; ....Il.24.2A.534.
On thousand Ships, and wither'd half a Host: ....Il.24.482.556.
On thousand Ships, and wither'd half an Host: ....Il.24.482A.556.
And in their ships the conqu'ring *Greeks* return'd; ....Od.3.160.93.
We, with the rising morn our ships unmoor'd, ...Od.3.185.95.
And measur'd tracts unknown to other ships, ...Od.3.409.106.
There quit the ships, and on the destin'd shore ....Od.4.791.156.
What ships have I, what sailors to convey, ...Od.5.181.180.
Launch'd his red lightning at our scatter'd ships: ....Od.7.335.253.
And ships shall wait thee with the morning ray. ....Od.7.405.256.
Our ships with ease transport thee in a day. ....Od.7.412.257.
In wond'rous ships self-mov'd, instinct with mind; ....Od.8.604.294.
Close at the ships the bloody fight began, ...Od.9.61.304.
Now here, now there, the giddy ships are born, ...Od.9.79.306.
Took down our masts, and row'd our ships to shore. ....Od.9.82.306.
The seas to traverse, or the ships to build, ...Od.9.148.311.
Where ships may rest, unanchor'd and unty'd; ....Od.9.158.312.
In haste our fellows to the ships repair, ...Od.9.180.313.
The royal bark had ten. Our ships compleat ....Od.9.186.313.
Then from their anchors all our ships unbind, ...Od.9.654.333.
And dash the ruins on the ships below: ....Od.10.140.347.
Down to the haven and the ships in haste ....Od.13.23.2.
And ships secure without their haulsers ride. ....Od.13.121.7.
Nine ships I mann'd equip'd with ready stores, ...Od.14.280.49.
The steer-man governs, and the ships obey. ....Od.14.287.49.
The sailors waiting, and the ships prepar'd. ....Od.14.370.53.
By *Ægypt's* silver flood our ships we moor, ...Od.17.511.157.
Back to their ships the frighted host had fled; ....Od.24.69.351.
The rest in ships are wafted o'er the main. ....Od.24.480.371.
With ships he parted and a num'rous train, ...Od.24.491.371.
Those, and their ships he bury'd in the main. ....Od.24.492.371.

SHIPWRACK'D
The shipwrack'd Hero on the *Coan* Coast: ....Il.15.32.195.

SHIPWRACKT
The Monarch's son a shipwrackt wretch reliev'd, ...Od.14.351.51.

SHIPWRECK'D
As to the shipwreck'd mariner, the shores ....Od.23.249.335.

SHIPWRIGHT
As when a Shipwright, with *Palladian* Art, ...Il.15.474.215.
Long and capacious as a shipwright forms ....Od.5.319.187.
As when a shipwright stands his workmen o'er, ...Od.9.457.324.

SHIPWRIGHT'S
To him the Shipwright's and the Builder's Art. ....Il.5.80.270.

SHIRE
Knight of the Post corrupt, or of the Shire, ...4.Arbu.365.122.

SHIRT
Wrapt in th' envenom'd Shirt, and set on Fire. ....2.ChWB.382.76.
But when no Prelate's Lawn with Hair-shirt lin'd, ...4.1HE1.165.291.

SHIRTLESS
Grave mummers! sleeveless some, and shirtless others. ....5.DunA3.108.159.
Grave Mummers! sleeveless some, and shirtless others. ....5.DunB3.116.325.

SHIT
See SH.

SHIV'RING
Whose Ghost yet shiv'ring on *Cocytus'* Sand ....1.TrSt.419.427.
A puny insect, shiv'ring at a breeze! ....3.Ep4.108.148.
Here in one bed two shiv'ring sisters lye, ...5.DunA1.31.63.
I wake, I rise, and shiv'ring with the Frost, ...6.96iv.43.277.
And his Soul shiv'ring at th' Approach of Death. ....Il.21.77.424.
He said; chill horrors shook my shiv'ring soul, ...Od.4.725.152.
And my cold blood hangs shiv'ring in my veins; ....Od.11.784.425.
My shiv'ring blood congeal'd forgot to flow, ...Od.12.310.447.
Fast by my side, and shiv'ring thus I said. ....Od.14.546.63.

SHIVER'D
Pisander's Spear fell shiver'd on the Field. ....Il.13.760.141.
Th' afflicted Monarch shiver'd with Despair; ....Il.24.441.554.

SHIVERING
And a cold fear ran shivering thro' my blood; ....Od.11.56.383.

SHIVERS
His Spear in Shivers falls: His ample Shield ....Il.16.966.280.

SHIVR'ING
Thou seem'st all trembling, shivr'ing, dying, ...6.31i.7.93.

SHOAL
Broad hats, and hoods, and caps, a sable shoal: ....5.DunB4.190.360.
Then what a shoal of lawless men should go ....Od.21.405.279.

SHOALS
He dreads the Rocks, and Shoals, and Seas, and Skies, ...1.TrSt.524.432.
In Shoals before him fly the scaly Train, ...Il.21.31.422.
Thin airy shoals, and visionary shades. ....Od.10.633.374.
Thin, airy shoals of visionary ghosts; ....Od.11.48.383.

SHOAR
See SHORE.
Or Billows murm'ring on the hollow Shoar: ....2.TemF.24.255.
Rufa's at either end a Common-Shoar, ...4.HAdv.29.77.
Fair *Thames* shall hear from shoar to Shoare ....6.135.43A.367.

SHOARE
Fair *Thames* from either ecchoing Shoare ....6.135.43.367.
Fair *Thames* shall hear from shoar to Shoare ....6.135.43A.367.

SHOCK
Shock just had giv'n himself the rowzing Shake, ...2.RLA1.15.127.
Now *Shock* had giv'n himself the towzing Shake, ...2.RL1.15A.145.
He said; when *Shock*, who thought she slept too long, ...2.RL1.115.154.
Or whether Heav'n has doom'd that *Shock* must fall. ....2.RL2.110.166.
Ariel himself shall be the Guard of *Shock.* ....2.RL2.116.166.
Nay, *Poll* sate mute, and *Shock* was most Unkind! ....2.RL4.164.197.
The Shock of Armies, and commence the War. ....Il.4.395.239.
To dare the Shock, or urge the rapid Race: ....Il.5.281.280.
The fiercest Shock of charging Hosts sustain; ....Il.5.638.298.
The hollow Brass resounded with the Shock. ....Il.7.319.379.
So graceful these, and so the Shock they stand ....Il.12.151.87.
At ev'ry Shock the crackling Wood resounds; ....Il.13.196.115.
He felt the Shock, nor more was doom'd to feel, ...Il.13.257.117.
The *Greeks* expect the Shock; the Clamours rise ....Il.15.354.210.
Shock; while the madding Steeds break short their Yokes: ....Il.16.445.260.
In dreadful Shock the mingled Hosts engage. ....Il.16.930.279.
The weighty Shock his Neck and Shoulders feel; ....Il.16.956.280.
The Shock of *Hector* and his charging Train: ....Il.17.804.320.
Troy's black Battalions wait the Shock of Fight. ....Il.20.4.392.
With horrid Clangor shock th' ætherial Arms: ....Il.21.451.439.
His shoulder-blade receiv'd th' ungentle shock; ....Od.17.548.159.
Cluster'd they hang, till at some sudden shock, ...Od.24.11.347.

SHOCK'D
And never shock'd, and never turn'd aside, ...1.EOC.629.310.

SHOCKING
And now with Shouts the shocking Armies clos'd, ...Il.8.75.399.

SHOCKS
That such are happier, shocks all common sense. ....3.EOM4.52.133.
What shocks one part will edify the rest, ...3.EOM4.141.141.
Beauty that shocks you, Parts that none will trust, ...4.Arbu.332.120.
The Simile yet one thing shocks, ...6.93.27Z5.257.
So firmly Proof to all the Shocks of Fate? ....Il.3.88.194.

SHOCKT
Rattle the clatt'ring Cars, and the shockt Axles bound. ....Il.23.143.495.

SHOD
Men bearded, bald, cowl'd, uncowl'd, shod, unshod, ...5.DunA3.106.159.
Men bearded, bald, cowl'd, uncowl'd, shod, unshod, ...5.DunB3.114.325.

SHOE
Oft, when his Shoe the most severely wrung, ...2.ChWB.239.68.

SHOES
Prefer a new Japanner to their shoes, ...4.1HE1.156.291.
Who holds Dragoons and Wooden-Shoes in scorn; ....6.128.20.356.

SHON
Fine as a filmy web beneath it shon ....Od.19.269.208.

SHONE
Now setting *Phœbus* shone serenely bright, ...1.PAu.13.81.
The setting Sun now shone serenely bright, ...1.PAu.13A.81.
Which from the first has shone on *Ages past,* ....1.EOC.402.286.
The Majesty of Heav'n superior shone; ....1.TrSt.281.422.
Sublime in Regal State, *Adrastus* shone, ...1.TrSt.613.436.
And massie Beams in native Marble shone, ...1.TrUl.36.467.
And Mirth and Pleasure shone in ev'ry Face. ....2.ChJM.356.31.
At Sermons too I shone in Scarlet gay; ....2.ChWB.287.71.
A Train of well-drest Youths around her shone, ...2.RLA1.21.127.
Fair Nymphs, and well-drest Youths around her shone, ...2.RL2.5.159.
The wond'rous Rock like *Parian* Marble shone, ...2.TemF.29.255.
There *Ninus* shone, who spread th' *Assyrian* Fame, ...2.TemF.95.260.
There *Cæsar,* grac'd with both *Minerva's,* shone; ....2.TemF.155.266.
High on the first, the mighty *Homer* shone; ....2.TemF.182.270.
Arms and the Man in Golden Cyphers shone. ....2.TemF.209.272.
With equal Rays immortal *Tully* shone, ...2.TemF.238.274.
With various-colour'd Light the Pavement shone, ...2.TemF.254.275.
Shone sweetly lambent with celestial day: ....2.ElAb.64.324.
Alike or when, or where, they shone, or shine, ...3.EOM4.245.150.
And full in Shakespear, fair in Otway shone: ....4.2HE1.277.219.
'Twas here in clouded majesty she shone; ....5.DunA1.43.65.
But high above, more solid Learning shone, ...5.DunA1.127.79.
In clouded Majesty here Dulness shone; ....5.DunB1.45.274.
But, high above, more solid Learning shone, ...5.DunB1.147.281.
High on a gorgeous seat, that far out-shone ....5.DunB2.1.296.
Thus *Voiture's* early Care still shone the same, ...6.19.69.64.
The living Virtue now had shone approv'd, ...6.132.7.362.
The bossie Naves of solid Silver shone; ....Il.5.896.308.
Twelve Domes for them and their lov'd Spouses shone, ...Il.6.310.341.
She chose a Veil that shone superior far, ...Il.6.366.344.
Sheath'd in bright Steel the Giant-Warrior shone: ....Il.7.250.376.
The Sons of *Merops* shone amidst the War; ....Il.11.425.53.
Portentous shone, and shaded all the Field, ...Il.15.351.210.
Emblaz'd with Studs of Gold, his Faulchion shone, ...Il.16.166.244.
There shone the Image of the Master Mind: ....Il.18.557.349.
Long lost to Battel, shone in Arms again. ....Il.20.58.396.
Where'ere he mov'd, the Goddess shone before, ...Il.20.127.399.
And on his Breast the beamy Splendors shone ....Il.22.177.461.
So shone the Point of great *Achilles'* Spear. ....Il.22.402.472.
She shone amidst them, on her painted Bow: ....Il.23.248.499.
Who more than *Peleus* shone in Wealth and Pow'r? ....Il.24.673.565.
The fourth day shone, when all their labours o'er ....Od.3.219.96.
With unguents smooth the lucid marble shone, ...Od.3.520.112.
On the bright eminence young *Nestor* shone, ...Od.4.29.121.
Shone the fifth morn: when from her sacred seat ....Od.5.334.188.
Around, a beavy of bright damsels shone. ....Od.6.98.210.
And shone transcendent o'er the beauteous train. ....Od.6.128.212.
With stars of silver shone the bed of state. ....Od.7.229.247.
Divine *Arete* and *Alcinous* shone. ....Od.7.313.251.
With silver shone the throne; his Lyre well strung ....Od.8.63.265.
Naubolides with grace unequall'd shone, ...Od.8.121.269.
Soon as again the rosy morning shone, ...Od.9.174.312.
And now the third succeeding morning shone. ....Od.10.168.348.
So speaking, from the ruddy orient shone ....Od.10.645.375.
And on the surface shone the holy store. ....Od.11.34.381.
She shone unrival'd with a blaze of charms, ...Od.11.552.411.
None but *Pelides* brighter shone in arms. ....Od.11.580.412.
And massy beams in native marble shone: ....Od.13.127.8.
Around the mansion in a circle shone ....Od.14.9.35.
And safe I slept, till brightly-dawning shone ....Od.14.568.64.
And *Polyphides* on whom *Phœbus* shone ....Od.15.274.82.
"Then, beaming o'er th' illumin'd wall they shone: ....Od.16.310.120.
With ivory silver'd thick the foot-stool shone, ...Od.19.70.196.
In the deep vase, that shone like burnish'd gold, ...Od.19.452.216.
And on his foot the golden sandal shone. ....Od.20.158.241.
There shone high-heap'd the labour'd brass and ore, ...Od.21.13.259.
At once in brazen Panoply they shone, ...Od.22.130.293.
With silver shone, with elephant, and gold. ....Od.23.206.333.
And, still more old, in arms *Laertes* shone. ....Od.24.575.375.

SHOOK
Soon as the Flocks shook off the nightly Dews, ...1.PSp.17.62.
Shook, and return'd the dreadful blast again. ....1.TrPA.48.367.
The trembling tree with sudden horror shook. ....1.TrFD.30.387.
Trembl'd, and shook the Heav'ns and Gods he bore. ....1.TrSt.139.415.
Again *Leucothoë* shook at these Alarms, ...1.TrSt.167.417.
The snowy Fleece; he tost, and shook in Air: ....1.TrES.188.456.
Each Axle groan'd; the bounding Chariot shook; ....1.TrES.274.459.
Each Axle crackled, and the Chariot shook: ....1.TrES.274A.459.
Shook high her flaming Torch, in open Sight, ...2.ChJM.329.30.
The tott'ring *China* shook without a Wind, ...2.RL4.163.197.
The Trumpet sounded, and the Temple shook, ...2.TemF.277.276.
With Heav'n's own thunders shook the world below, ...3.EOM3.267.119.
And shook his head at *Murray,* as a Wit. ....4.2HE2.132.175.
"What shook the stage, and made the people stare?" ....4.2HE1.336.225.
Loud thunder to its bottom shook the bog, ...5.DunA1.259.95.
Hoarse thunder to its bottom shook the bog, ...5.DunA1.259A.95.
Sudden, a burst of thunder shook the flood. ....5.DunA2.301.139.
Loud thunder to its bottom shook the bog, ...5.DunB1.329.294.
When lo! a burst of thunder shook the flood. ....5.DunB2.325.313.
And shook from out his Pipe the seeds of fire; ....5.DunB4.494.391.
He laughd, and shook his Sides so fat: ....6.67.2.195.
And shook the Stage with Thunders all his own! ....6.128.16.356.
When bold Rebellion shook the Realms above, ...Il.1.516.113.
And all *Olympus* to the Centre shook. ....Il.1.687.120.
Nor was the Signal vain that shook the Sky. ....Il.1.721.122.
And Thunder rolling shook the Firmament. ....Il.2.419.147.
And high *Enispè* shook by wintry Wind, ...Il.2.738.161.

SHOOK (CONTINUED)
Two pointed Spears he shook with gallant Grace, ...Il.3.31.189.
Full on his Casque; the crested Helmet shook; ....Il.3.446.213.
The Goddess softly shook her silken Vest ....Il.3.479.214.
Have I, for this, shook *Ilion* with Alarms, ...Il.4.37.222.
He shook his hoary Locks, and thus reply'd. ....Il.4.369.238.
He said, then shook the pondrous Lance and flung, ...Il.5.342.283.
Then with a Voice that shook the vaulted Skies, ...Il.5.431.289.
His blazing Buckler thrice *Apollo* shook: ....Il.5.530.294.
Shook with his Fall his Brazen Armor rung, ...Il.5.764.303.
Shook by her Arm the mighty Javelin bends, ...Il.5.923.310.
No Lance he shook, nor bent the twanging Bow, ...Il.7.171.372.
Old *Nestor* shook the Casque. By Heav'n inspir'd, ...Il.7.219.375.
While the deep Thunder shook th' Aerial Hall. ....Il.7.575.393.
The stedfast Firmament beneath them shook: ....Il.8.50.398.
He drop'd the Reins; and shook with sacred Dread, ...Il.8.167.406.
She shook her Throne that shook the starry Pole: ....Il.8.241.409.
She shook her Throne that shook the starry Pole: ....Il.8.241.409.
Shook by her Arm, the massy Javelin bends; ....Il.8.473.419.
(Still, as he spoke, his Limbs with Horror shook) ....Il.10.462.24.
They shook with Fear, and drop'd the silken Rein; ....Il.11.168.42.
But *Jove* descending shook th' *Idæan* Hills, ...Il.11.237.46.
Then *Neptune* and *Apollo* shook the Shore, ...Il.12.15.81.
The snowy Fleece, he toss'd, and shook in Air: ....Il.12.542.101.
And, at the fourth, the distant *Ægæ* shook. ....Il.13.33.106.
So stood *Idomeneus,* his Javelin shook, ...Il.13.602.135.
That shook the pond'rous Lance, in Act to throw, ...Il.13.735.139.
Whole Nations fear'd: but not an *Argive* shook. ....Il.13.1019.153.
Shook the fix'd Splendours of the Throne of *Jove.* ....Il.13.1061.155.
Great *Jove* awaking, shook the blest Abodes, ...Il.14.289.176.
And at *Prothœnor* shook the trembling Spear; ....Il.14.526.189.
The Victor seiz'd; and as aloft he shook ....Il.14.585.190.
Then with his Hand he shook the mighty Wall; ....Il.15.414.213.
And Peals of Thunder shook the Firmament. ....Il.15.437.214.
The startling Steeds, and shook his eager Reins. ....Il.15.525.217.
And with unmanly Tremblings shook the Car, ...Il.16.491.262.
The gaping Dastard: As the Spear was shook, ...Il.16.498.262.
Each Axle crackled, and the Chariot shook: ....Il.16.579.267.
Troy, at the Loss, thro' all her Legions shook. ....Il.16.672.270.
His blazing *Ægis* thrice *Apollo* shook: ....Il.16.860.276.
He shook the sacred Honours of his Head; ....Il.17.229.296.
But now th' Eternal shook his sable Shield, ...Il.17.668.314.
The Mountain shook, the rapid Stream stood still. ....Il.20.74.397.
And shook his Jav'lin like a waving Flame. ....Il.20.490.415.
And shook two Spears, advancing from the Flood; ....Il.21.162.428.
The Foe thrice tugg'd, and shook the rooted Wood; ....Il.21.191.429.
Shook with her Sighs, and panted on her Breast. ....Il.21.592.446.
The Tumult wak'd him: From his Eyes he shook ....Il.23.292.501.
And echoing Groans that shook the lofty Tent. ....Il.24.158.542.
A sudden Trembling shook his aged Frame: ....Il.24.444.554.
He said; chill horrors shook my shiv'ring soul, ...Od.4.725.152.
Ev'n to her inmost soul the Goddess shook; ....Od.5.147.178.
The raging Monarch shook his azure head, ...Od.5.365.190.
Then shook the Heroe, to despair resign'd, ...Od.5.381.190.
The whole sea shook, and refluent beat the shore. ....Od.9.570.330.
Old Ocean shook, and back his surges flew. ....Od.9.582.330.
Yet as I shook my faulchion o'er the blood, ...Od.11.110.386.
He grasp'd his sword, and shook his glitt'ring spear. ....Od.11.650.416.
And shook astonish'd thro' her hundred states; ....Od.11.684.418.
At once into the main the crew it shook: ....Od.12.491.456.
His pond'rous footstool, shook it at his lord. ....Od.17.493.156.
But shook his thoughtful head, nor more complain'd, ...Od.17.550.159.
But the dark brow of silent sorrow shook: ....Od.17.584.161.
In ev'ry joint the trembling *Irus* shook; ....Od.18.101.172.
He shook the graceful honours of his head; ....Od.18.182.175.
But shook his head, and rising wrath restrain'd. ....Od.20.232.244.
With guilty fears the pale assembly shook. ....Od.22.82.290.
A sudden horror all th' assembly shook, ...Od.24.516.372.
Fear shook the nations. At the voice divine ....Od.24.616.377.

SHOOT
Headlong descend, and shoot into the Deep, ...1.TrES.108.453.
Pursue the Stars that shoot athwart the Night, ...2.RL2.82.165.
Upward the Columns shoot, the Roofs ascend, ...2.TemF.264.276.
A Wild, where weeds and flow'rs promiscuous shoot, ...3.EOM1.7.13.
Or Wild, where weeds and flow'rs promiscuous shoot, ...3.EOM1.7A.13.
Eye Nature's walks, shoot Folly as it flies, ...3.EOM1.13.14.
The surest Virtues thus from Passions shoot, ...3.EOM2.183.77.
Sure never to o'er-shoot, but just to hit, ...3.EOM3.89.101.
And swiftly shoot along the Mall, ...4.HOde1.45.153.
Shoot their long Beams, and kindle half the Skies: ....Il.2.537.152.
And shoot a shady Lustre o'er the Field. ....Il.8.704.428.
Headlong descend, and shoot into the Deep, ...Il.12.462.98.
With naked force, and shoot along the wave, ...Od.7.361.254.
Now griesly forms, shoot o'er the lawns of hell. ....Od.11.708.420.
The slippery sides, and shoot into the skies. ....Od.12.98.436.
And shoot a leafy forest to the skies; ....Od.12.128.438.
Swift row my mates, and shoot along the sea; ....Od.12.235.443.
Yon Archer, comrades, will not shoot in vain; ....Od.22.84.290.
And this bold Archer soon shall shoot no more. ....Od.22.151.294.

SHOOTER'S
Stopt short of Life, and mock'd the Shooter's Art. ....Il.5.139.273.

SHOOTING
Where late was hair, the shooting leaves are seen ....1.TrFD.47.388.
While yet thc Smart was shooting in the Bone. ....2.ChWB.258.69.
Hover, and catch the shooting Stars by Night; ....2.RL2.82A.165.
A *Feather* shooting from another's head, ...5.DunB4.521.394.
As *Phœbus* shooting from th' *Idæan* Brow, ...Il.15.268.207.
The bright far-shooting God who gilds the Day, ...Il.19.458.391.

SHOOTS
To decent Form the lawless Shoots to bring, ...1.TrVP.11.377.
Not half so swiftly shoots along in Air ....1.TrSt.128.415.
When lab'ring with strong Charms, she shoots from high ....1.TrSt.148.416.

SHOOTS (CONTINUED)

And a glad Horror shoots through ev'ry Vein: 1.TrSt.580.434.
Shoots up, and All the rising Host appears. 1.TrES.182.456.
What Pangs, what sudden Shoots distend my Side? 2.ChJM.721.49.
The Sun obliquely shoots his burning Ray; 2.RL3.20.170.
Or breathes thro' air, or shoots beneath the deeps, 3.EOM3.116.104.
In Man, the judgment shoots at flying game, 3.Ep1.155.28.
With annual joy the red'ning shoots to greet, 3.Ep4.91.146.
Wit shoots in vain its momentary fires, 5.DunB4.633.407.
And bath'd in Ocean, shoots a keener Light. Il.5.10.266.
Shoots up, and all the rising Host appears. Il.12.536.101.
Shoots on the Wing, and skims along the Sky: Il.13.94.109.
When lo! a Lyon shoots across the way: Il.15.312.209.
That thrills my Arm and shoots thro ev'ry Vein, Il.16.638.269.
And aims his Claws, and shoots upon his Wings: Il.22.188.463.
Then shoots from heav'n to high *Pieria's* steep, Od.5.62.174.
Shoots from the starry vault thro' fields of air; Od.8.8.261.
From heav'n *Minerva* shoots with guardian cares; Od.18.220.177.

SHOP

He serv'd a 'Prenticeship, who sets up shop; 4.2HE1.181.211.
Her evening cates before his neighbour's shop,) 5.DunA2.68.106.
Her evening cates before his neighbour's shop,) 5.DunB2.72.299.
A Brandy and Tobacco Shop is near, 6.14ii.12.43.

SHOPS

The shops shut up in every street, 4.1HE7.8.269.
And answ'ring Gin-shops sowrer sighs return! 5.DunA3.140.162.
And answ'ring gin-shops sowrer sighs return. 5.DunB3.148.327.

SHORE

See SHOAR.
If *Sylvia* smiles, new Glories gild the Shore, 1.PSp.75.68.
Her Name with Pleasure once she taught the Shore, 1.PWi.43.92.
But tell the Reeds, and tell the vocal Shore, 1.PWi.59.93.
Than the fair Nymphs that gild thy Shore below; 1.W-F.232A.170.
What Kings first breath'd upon her winding Shore, 1.W-F.300.176.
And the hush'd Waves glide softly to the Shore. 1.W-F.354.184.
Safe on my Shore each unmolested Swain 1.W-F.369.186.
Oh stretch thy Reign, fair *Peace!* from Shore to Shore, 1.W-F.407.192.
Oh stretch thy Reign, fair *Peace!* from Shore to Shore, 1.W-F.407.192.
But when loud Surges lash the sounding Shore, 1.EOC.368.282.
But when loud billows lash the sounding Shore, 1.EOC.368A.282.
The mighty *Stagyrite* first left the Shore, 1.EOC.645.311.
Affrighted *Atlas,* on the distant Shore, 1.TrSt.138.415.
Had sung—"Expect thy Sons on *Argos'* Shore, 1.TrSt.547.433.
Delight in *Cynthus* and the Shady Shore; 1.TrSt.834.444.
Oppos'd in Combate on the dusty Shore. 1.TrES.80.452.
With equal Steps bold *Teucer* prest the Shore, 1.TrES.89.453.
The copious Slaughter covers all the Shore, 1.TrES.165.455.
The Shore is heap'd with Death, and Tumult rends the Sky. 1.TrES.208.457.
And, pale in Death, lay groaning on the Shore. 1.TrES.295.460.
Veil'd in a Cloud, to silver *Simois* Shore: 1.TrES.339.462.
In Storms by Sea, and Combats on the Shore: 1.TrUl.18.466.
And gently plac'd him on the Rocky Shore: 1.TrUl.48.467.
The solitary Shore, and rowling Sea. 1.TrUl.55.467.
Another Port appear'd, another Shore, 1.TrUl.65.468.
Ah why forsake *Phæacia's* happy Shore? 1.TrUl.81.468.
A hapless Exile on a Foreign Shore. 1.TrUl.159.471.
Secure thou seest thy Native Shore at last? 1.TrUl.170.471.
An hapless Exile on a Foreign Shore. 1.TrUl.159A.471.
And heard thy Counsels on *Phæacia's* Shore. 1.TrUl.200.472.
The pleasing Prospect of thy Native Shore! 1.TrUl.225.473.
Of Storms at Sea, and Travels on the Shore, 2.TemF.451.285.
Or ship off Senates to some distant Shore; 3.Ep3.74A.93.
Or ship off Senates to a distant Shore; 3.Ep3.74.93.
And two rich ship-wrecks bless the lucky shore. 3.Ep3.356.122.
A verier Monster than on *Africk's* Shore 4.JD4.28.27.
Thou, yet unborn, hast touch'd this sacred shore; 5.DunA3.37.154.
See, where the Morning gilds the palmy shore, 5.DunA3.87.157.
"Proceed great days! till Learning fly the shore, 5.DunA3.329.191.
Thou, yet unborn, hast touch'd this sacred shore; 5.DunB3.45.322.
See, where the morning gilds the palmy shore 5.DunB3.95.324.
"Proceed, great days! 'till Learning fly the shore, 5.DunB3.333.336.
She heard, and drove him to th' Hibernian shore. 5.DunB4.70.348.
To the soft joys of *Nile's* delightful shore. 6.20.10.66.
To what dark, undiscover'd Shore? 6.31i.6.93.
The Play may pass—but that strange creature, *Shore,* 6.41.5.113.
Say, will ye bless the bleak *Atlantic* shore? 6.51i.15.151.
Perhaps ev'n *Britain's* utmost shore 6.51i.19.151.
Huge moles, whose shadow stretch'd from shore to shore, 6.71.21.203.
Huge moles, whose shadow stretch'd from shore to shore, 6.71.21.203.
Or in a Bean-shell venture from the shore 6.96ii.30Z13.271.
"Hast thou for these now ventur'd from the Shore, 6.96ii.57.273.
Steer'd the same course to the same quiet shore, 6.109.13.314.
Took the same course to the same quiet shore, 6.109.13A.314.
On Britains Shore and brought with fav'ring Gods 6.155.2.404.
Whose Limbs unbury'd on the naked Shore Il.1.5.82.
Safe to the Pleasures of your native Shore. Il.1.26.87.
The trembling Priest along the Shore return'd, Il.1.47.88.
Why leave we not the fatal *Trojan* Shore, Il.1.79.90.
My Fleet shall waft me to *Thessalia's* Shore. Il.1.222.97.
The purpled Shore with Mountains of the Dead, Il.1.320.103.
Along the Shore whole Hecatombs were laid, Il.1.414.107.
But sad retiring to the sounding Shore, Il.1.455.109.
Next on the Shore their Hecatomb they land, Il.1.570.115.
Safe and inglorious, to our native Shore. Il.2.170.136.
So roll the Billows to th' *Icarian* Shore, Il.2.175.137.
In Loves and Pleasures on the *Phrygian* Shore. Il.2.295.141.
Gods! let me perish on this hateful Shore, Il.2.320.142.
Behold them weeping for their native Shore! Il.2.354.144.
And foam and thunder on the stony Shore. Il.2.473.149.
And thund'ring Footsteps shake the sounding Shore: Il.2.549.153.
And those who dwell along the sandy Shore, Il.2.690.159.
He led the Warriors from th' *Ætolian* Shore, Il.2.779.162.
From *Ephyr's* Walls, and *Sellè's* winding Shore, Il.2.798.163.

SHORE (CONTINUED)

Three Ships with *Nireus* sought the *Trojan* Shore, Il.2.815.163.
But now inglorious, stretch'd along the Shore, Il.2.837.164.
The first who boldly touch'd the *Trojan* Shore, Il.2.855.165.
In ten black Ships embark'd for *Ilion's* Shore, Il.2.868.165.
His Forces *Medon* led from *Lemnos'* Shore, Il.2.882.165.
His Troops, neglected on the sandy Shore, Il.2.939.168.
Thus may the *Greeks* review their native Shore, Il.3.107.194.
Lay'd their bright Arms along the sable Shore. Il.3.158.198.
With *Menelaus,* on the *Spartan* Shore. Il.3.298.207.
My Brothers these; the same our native Shore, Il.3.305.208.
Adorn'd with Honours in their native Shore, Il.3.313.208.
So shall the *Greeks* review their native Shore, Il.3.328.208.
Be fix'd for ever to the *Trojan* Shore, Il.3.505.215.
Not thus I lov'd thee, when from *Sparta's* Shore Il.3.551.217.
To spread the War, I flew from Shore to Shore; Il.4.39.223.
To spread the War, I flew from Shore to Shore; Il.4.39.223.
Shall dream of Conquests on the hostile Shore; Il.4.209.231.
And found *Menestheus* on the dusty Shore, Il.4.381.239.
The Billows float in order to the Shore, Il.4.480.243.
Amid the Flocks on silver *Simois'* Shore: Il.4.545.247.
Stretch'd on the Shore, and thus neglected dies. Il.4.561.248.
And lay the Boaster grov'ling on the Shore, Il.5.152.274.
My much-lov'd Consort, and my native Shore, Il.5.845.305.
With levell'd Spears along the winding Shore; Il.6.233.337.
With *Helen* touching on the *Tyrian* Shore. Il.6.363.344.
Not all my Brothers gasping on the Shore; Il.6.577.355.
Greece on the Shore shall raise a Monument; Il.7.98.368.
Great *Areïthous,* known from Shore to Shore Il.7.169.372.
Great *Areïthous,* known from Shore to Shore Il.7.169.372.
Let him, unactive on the Sea-beat Shore, Il.7.277.378.
What Tides of Blood have drench'd *Scamander's* Shore? Il.7.394.383.
(Oh had he perish'd e'er they touch'd our Shore) Il.7.465.387.
Nor less the *Greeks,* descending on the Shore, Il.7.496.389.
Vast Drifts of Sand shall change the former Shore; Il.7.554.392.
Your hasty Triumphs on the *Lemnian* Shore? Il.8.277.410.
Our hasty Triumphs on the *Lemnian* Shore? Il.8.277A.410.
To thee my Vows were breath'd from ev'ry Shore; Il.8.286.411.
The batter'd Archer groaning to the Shore. Il.8.400.416.
Stretch'd by some *Argive* on his native Shore: Il.8.436.418.
What mighty *Trojan* then, on yonder Shore, Il.8.461.419.
Full Hecatombs lay burning on the Shore; Il.8.679.427.
Swells o'er the Sea, from *Thracia's* frozen Shore, Il.9.7.431.
If safe we land on *Argos* fruitful Shore, Il.9.184.441.
Of murm'ring Billows on the sounding Shore. Il.9.238.444.
If safe we land on *Argos* fruitful Shore, Il.9.371.451.
The Wealth he left for this detested Shore: Il.9.476.456.
Than Dust in Fields, or Sands along the Shore; Il.9.507.458.
Or sends soft Snows to whiten all the Shore, Il.10.7.2.
Then (never to return) he sought the Shore, Il.10.399.21.
Confine his Course along the Fleet and Shore, Il.10.412.21.
And a low Groan remurmur'd thro' the Shore. Il.10.563.27.
Perhaps, ev'n now pursu'd, they seek the Shore; Il.10.634.30.
He now lies headless on the sandy Shore. Il.10.663.31.
The Warriors standing on the breezy Shore, Il.11.758.69.
Along the Shore with hasty Strides he went; Il.11.935.77.
Far from your Friends, and from your native Shore! Il.11.951.77.
Then *Neptune* and *Apollo* shook the Shore, Il.12.15.81.
With his huge Trident wounds the trembling Shore, Il.12.30.82.
The Coursers fed on *Selle's* winding Shore. Il.12.112.85.
Then the green Fields, and then the sandy Shore; Il.12.338.93.
Oppos'd in Combat on the dusty Shore. Il.12.424.97.
With equal Steps bold *Teucer* press'd the Shore, Il.12.443.97.
The copious Slaughter covers all the Shore, Il.12.519.100.
The Shore is heap'd with Death, and Tumult rends the Sky. Il.12.562.102.
For lo! the fated Time, th' appointed Shore; Il.13.165.112.
The rising Combate sounds along the Shore. Il.13.423.126.
And, fierce in Death, lies foaming on the Shore. Il.13.500.130.
His honour'd Body to the Tented Shore. Il.13.532.131.
To *Troy* they drove him, groaning from the Shore, Il.13.680.137.
The clotted Eye-balls tumble on the Shore. Il.13.776.141.
Thro' filial Love he left his native Shore, Il.13.807.143.
Attends the mournful Pomp along the Shore, Il.13.824.145.
The Chiefs you seek on yonder Shore lie slain; Il.13.981.152.
Wide-rolling, foaming high, and tumbling to the shore. Il.13.1005.152.
That Giant-Corse, extended on the Shore, Il.13.1054.155.
Who landed first lay highest on the Shore.) Il.14.44.160.
O'er fair *Emathia's* ever pleasing Shore, Il.14.260.173.
And drive the Hero to the *Coan* Shore: Il.14.288.176.
So lies great *Hector* prostrate on the Shore; Il.14.487.187.
Now faints anew, low-sinking on the Shore; Il.14.512.188.
Amidst her Flocks on *Satnio's* silver Shore) Il.14.520.188.
And sent to *Argos,* and his native Shore. Il.15.34.195.
The Hosts rush on; loud Clamours shake the Shore; Il.15.404.212.
O *Jove!* if ever, on his native Shore, Il.15.428.213.
One kept the Shore, and one the Vessel trod; Il.15.486.216.
Teucer, behold! extended on the Shore Il.15.510.216.
His Corps fell bleeding on the slipp'ry Shore; Il.15.620.220.
(Well known in Fight on *Selles'* winding Shore, Il.15.627.220.
The first that touch'd th' unhappy *Trojan* Shore: Il.15.857.229.
So warr'd both Armies on th' ensanguin'd Shore, Il.16.1.233.
By *Zephyr* pregnant on the breezy Shore. Il.16.185.245.
From Shore to Shore the doubling Shouts resound, Il.16.332.255.
From Shore to Shore the doubling Shouts resound, Il.16.332.255.
Unblest *Protesilaus* to *Ilion's* Shore, Il.16.341.256.
Some mighty Fish draws panting to the Shore; Il.16.496.262.
And pale in Death, lay groaning on the Shore. Il.16.600.267.
Now great *Sarpedon,* on the sandy Shore, Il.16.773.273.
Veil'd in a Cloud, to silver *Simois'* Shore: Il.16.826.275.
So scorch'd with Heat along the desart Shore, Il.16.993.281.
Instarr'd with Gems and Gold, bestrow the Shore, Il.17.55.289.
The Time allow'd: *Troy* thicken'd on the Shore, Il.17.114.292.
The distant Band, that on the sandy Shore Il.17.215.295.
The River trembles to his utmost Shore, Il.17.314.300.
The Field, and spread her Slaughters to the Shore; Il.17.521.308.
For sure he knows not, distant on the Shore, Il.17.723.315.

SHORE (CONTINUED)

This is not all: *Patroclus* on the Shore, ... Il.17.775.318.
Hear how his Sorrows echo thro' the Shore! ... Il.18.81.327.
Safe thro' the Tempest, to the Tented Shore. ... Il.18.188.331.
Shot in a Whirlwind to the Shore below; ... Il.18.206.331.
Charg'd with rich Spoils, to fair *Opuntia's* Shore! ... Il.18.382.339.
To *Troy* I sent him! but his native Shore ... Il.18.513.346.
Then many a Hero had not press'd the Shore, ... Il.19.63.374.
My much lov'd Parents, and my native Shore— ... Il.19.469.391.
Swept the wide Shore, and drove him to the Plain. ... Il.20.179.401.
But kind *Eëtion* touching on the Shore, ... Il.21.48.424.
Far from his Father, Friends, and native Shore; ... Il.21.89.425.
These *Phrygian* Fields, and press a foreign Shore. ... Il.21.698.450.
Tempts his Pursuit, and wheels about the Shore. ... Il.21.716.451.
Thee, Vultures wild should scatter round the Shore, ... Il.22.57.455.
Be this the Song, slow-moving tow'rd the Shore, ... Il.22.493.476.
Unbath'd he lies, and bleeds along the Shore! ... Il.22.573.480.
Lyes on broad *Hellespont's* resounding Shore: ... Il.23.4.486.
But great *Pelides,* stretch'd along the Shore ... Il.23.70.489.
Now give thy Hand; for to the farther Shore ... Il.23.93.491.
(Such charge was giv'n 'em) to the sandy Shore; ... Il.23.153.495.
So stay'd *Achilles,* circling round the Shore, ... Il.23.278.501.
And up the Champain thunder from the Shore: ... Il.23.440.507.
Tears up the Shore, and thunders tow'rd the Main. ... Il.23.454.508.
Known thro' *Buprasium* and the *Pylian* Shore! ... Il.23.724.519.
By some huge Billow dash'd against the Shore, ... Il.23.803.521.
(O'erturn'd by *Pallas)* where the slipp'ry Shore ... Il.23.907.525.
A burst of Laughter echo'd thro' the Shore. ... Il.23.922.525.
The Hero fixes in the sandy Shore: ... Il.23.1011.529.
With Reeds collected from the marshy Shore; ... Il.24.554.559.
Thou can'st not call him from the *Stygian* Shore, ... Il.24.694.566.
(Those Wives must wait'em) to a foreign Shore! ... Il.24.921.574.
Since *Paris* brought me to the *Trojan* Shore; ... Il.24.965.576.
Safe with his friends to gain his natal shore: ... Od.1.8.28.
(Ah men unbless'd!) to touch that natal shore. ... Od.1.12.29.
Amid'st an Isle, around whose rocky shore ... Od.1.63.33.
Must he, whose altars on the *Phrygian* shore ... Od.1.80.35.
But parting then for that detested shore, ... Od.1.273.46.
Impatient on the hoarse-resounding shore. ... Od.1.396.51.
While storms vindictive intercept the shore. ... Od.1.424.53.
How twice ten years from shore to shore he roams; ... Od.2.205.71.
How twice ten years from shore to shore he roams; ... Od.2.205.71.
And seek my royal sire from shore to shore: ... Od.2.244.73.
And seek my royal sire from shore to shore: ... Od.2.244.73.
The great *Ulysses* reach'd his native shore. ... Od.2.389.80.
Swift to the shore they move: Along the strand ... Od.2.454.83.
Telemachus already prest the shore; ... Od.3.15.87.
Along the shore th' illustrious pair he led, ... Od.3.49.89.
It fits to ask ye, what your native shore, ... Od.3.83.90.
The great *Ulysses;* fam'd from shore to shore ... Od.3.102.91.
The great *Ulysses;* fam'd from shore to shore ... Od.3.102.91.
Nine painful years, on that detested shore ... Od.3.145.92.
Tydides' vessels touch'd the wish'd-for shore: ... Od.3.220.96.
Long-lab'ring gains his natal shore at last; ... Od.3.290.100.
Condemn'd perhaps some foreign shore to tread; ... Od.3.314.101.
And seek *Atrides* on the *Spartan* shore. ... Od.3.406.106.
And the parcht borders of th' *Arabian* shore: ... Od.4.102.124.
As when contending on the *Lesbian* shore ... Od.4.462.142.
Her distance from the shore, the course begun ... Od.4.481.143.
Basks on the breezy shore, in grateful sleep, ... Od.4.542.146.
Stretch'd on the shelly shore, he first surveys ... Od.4.555.146.
She ceas'd, and bounding from the shelfy shore, ... Od.4.577.147.
Along the tended shore, in balmy sleep ... Od.4.584.147.
Nor sight of natal shore, nor regal dome ... Od.4.641.149.
And altars blaze along his sanguine shore. ... Od.4.646.150.
The breathless heroes on their native shore? ... Od.4.660.150.
A whirling gust tumultuous from the shore, ... Od.4.687.151.
My friends attending at the shore I sought. ... Od.4.780.156.
There quit the ships, and on the destin'd shore ... Od.4.791.156.
For ambush'd close beneath the *Samian* shore ... Od.4.896.160.
Ride the wild waves, and quit the safer shore? ... Od.4.941.162.
In all her tackle trim, to quit the shore. ... Od.4.1032.166.
The son in safety to his native shore; ... Od.5.35.172.
All on the lonely shore he sate to weep, ... Od.5.105.177.
And inly pining for his native shore; ... Od.5.195.181.
He trod her footsteps in the sandy shore. ... Od.5.248.183.
And south, and north, roll mountains to the shore. ... Od.5.380.190.
Soon as thy arms the happy shore shall gain, ... Od.5.442.194.
Thus, thus find out the destin'd shore, and then ... Od.5.482.195.
With gentle force impelling to that shore, ... Od.5.494.195.
So joys *Ulysses* at th' appearing shore; ... Od.5.511.197.
Of murm'ring surges breaking on the shore: ... Od.5.517.197.
The Chief, and dash'd him on the craggy shore: ... Od.5.543.198.
(A wider circle, but in sight of shore) ... Od.5.559.199.
Where to the seas the shelving shore declin'd, ... Od.5.564.199.
That moment, fainting as he touch'd the shore, ... Od.5.580.200.
Wide o'er the shore with many a piercing cry ... Od.6.165.216.
But since thou tread'st our hospitable shore, ... Od.6.233.221.
"Perhaps a native of some distant shore, ... Od.6.333.227.
So shalt thou view with joy thy natal shore, ... Od.6.375.230.
Snatch'd from *Epirus,* her sweet native shore, ... Od.7.12.233.
Forsaking *Scheria's* ever-pleasing shore, ... Od.7.101.239.
Safe to transport him to the wish'd-for shore: ... Od.7.255.248.
By heav'n's high will compell'd from shore to shore; ... Od.7.291.250.
By heav'n's high will compell'd from shore to shore; ... Od.7.291.250.
Unblest! to tread that interdicted shore: ... Od.7.333.253.
And storms vindictive intercept the shore. ... Od.7.359.254.
Then female voices from the shore I heard: ... Od.7.374.254.
Then gently waft thee to the pleasing shore, ... Od.7.409.257.
Of thronging multitudes the shore rebounds; ... Od.8.16.262.
The winds from *Ilion* to the *Cicons'* shore, ... Od.9.41.303.
Took down our masts, and row'd our ships to shore. ... Od.9.82.306.
Far in wide ocean, and from sight of shore: ... Od.9.94.306.
The rest in haste forsook the pleasing shore, ... Od.9.113.308.
Or bark of traffic, glides from shore to shore; ... Od.9.146.311.
Or bark of traffic, glides from shore to shore; ... Od.9.146.311.

SHORE (CONTINUED)

And slept secure along the sandy shore. ... Od.9.173.312.
The face of things: along the sea-beat shore ... Od.9.196.314.
Where sheep and goats lay slumb'ring round the shore. ... Od.9.214.314.
My friends advise me, and to quit the shore; ... Od.9.265.317.
Where lies she anchor'd? near, or off the shore? ... Od.9.334.320.
Fast by your shore the gallant vessel broke. ... Od.9.338.320.
We to thy shore the precious freight shall bear, ... Od.9.412.323.
The sons of men shall ne'er approach thy shore, ... Od.9.415.323.
And reach our vessel on the winding shore. ... Od.9.548.328.
The whole sea shook, and refluent beat the shore. ... Od.9.570.330.
From shore to shore, and gird the solid world. ... Od.9.618.332.
From shore to shore, and gird the solid world. ... Od.9.618.332.
Shake at the weight, and refluent beat the shore. ... Od.9.634.332.
Stretch'd on the shore in careless ease we rest, ... Od.9.652.333.
At length we reach'd *Æolia's* sea-girt shore, ... Od.10.1.335.
The tenth presents our welcome native shore: ... Od.10.31.340.
We leap'd on shore, and with a scanty feast ... Od.10.61.342.
And fix'd, without, my haulsers to the shore. ... Od.10.110.346.
And pouring down the mountains, crowd the shore. ... Od.10.138.347.
Was first my thought: but speeding back to shore ... Od.10.178.349.
The face of things, we slept along the shore. ... Od.10.211.350.
This said, and scornful turning from the shore ... Od.10.325.360.
Haste to thy vessel on the sea-beat shore, ... Od.10.477.366.
In storms by sea, in perils on the shore; ... Od.10.543.369.
Where to the main the shelving shore descends; ... Od.10.603.373.
With promis'd off'rings on thy native shore; ... Od.10.621.374.
Your hopes already touch your native shore: ... Od.10.672.375.
Sadly they far'd along the sea-beat shore; ... Od.10.683.376.
And the huge pyle along the shore ascends. ... Od.12.14.430.
Nigh the curst shore, and listen to the lay; ... Od.12.54.432.
And human carnage taints the dreadful shore. ... Od.12.60.432.
Thence to *Trinacria's* shore you bend your way, ... Od.12.160.439.
While to the shore the rapid vessel flies, ... Od.12.218.442.
The sun descending, and so near the shore? ... Od.12.338.448.
Thus I: and while to shore the vessel flies, ... Od.12.359.448.
Past sight of shore, along the surge we bound, ... Od.12.473.454.
No longer now from shore to shore to roam, ... Od.13.7.2.
No longer now from shore to shore to roam, ... Od.13.7.2.
Then send the stranger to his native shore. ... Od.13.67.4.
Thus he; then parting prints the sandy shore ... Od.13.80.5.
In storms by sea, and combats on the shore; ... Od.13.109.6.
And gently plac'd him on the rocky shore. ... Od.13.139.11.
And menac'd vengeance, ere he reach'd his shore; ... Od.13.153.13.
To reach his natal shore was thy decree; ... Od.13.154.13.
With ev'ry stranger pass from shore to shore; ... Od.13.209.15.
With ev'ry stranger pass from shore to shore; ... Od.13.209.15.
The blazing Altars redden all the shore. ... Od.13.219.16.
The solitary shore, and rolling sea. ... Od.13.222.16.
Another port appear'd, another shore, ... Od.13.232.17.
Ah why forsake *Phæacia's* happy shore? ... Od.13.248.18.
A hapless exile on a foreign shore. ... Od.13.326.23.
Secure thou seest thy native shore at last? ... Od.13.337.23.
And heard thy counsels on *Phæacia's* shore. ... Od.13.367.25.
The pleasing prospect of thy native shore. ... Od.13.392.26.
Fierce foes insidious intercept the shore: ... Od.13.493.29.
But Fate condemn'd him to a foreign shore! ... Od.14.77.40.
Again to hail them in their native shore. ... Od.14.164.43.
Shall lov'd *Ulysses* hail this happy shore, ... Od.14.191.45.
Belov'd and honour'd in his native shore; ... Od.14.232.47.
The tenth soft wafts me to *Thesprotia's* shore. ... Od.14.350.51.
Soon as remote from shore they plow the wave, ... Od.14.377.53.
To speed *Ulysses* to his native shore. ... Od.14.471.58.
To launch thy vessel for thy natal shore: ... Od.15.18.70.
The coursers drive; but lash them to the shore. ... Od.15.225.79.
When lo! a wretch ran breathless to the shore, ... Od.15.250.80.
A wretch in safety to her native shore." ... Od.15.475.93.
Now set the sun, and darken'd all the shore. ... Od.15.506.94.
Then on the breezy shore descending, join ... Od.15.539.96.
Whence father, from what shore this stranger, say? ... Od.16.57.105.
As when, contending on the *Lesbian* shore, ... Od.17.153.139.
Thence safe I voyag'd to my native shore. ... Od.17.169.139.
Oh be some God his convoy to our shore! ... Od.17.289.146.
(A load and scandal to this happy shore.) ... Od.17.299.146.
Long, long since perish'd on a distant shore! ... Od.17.379.150.
With boundless treasure, from *Thesprotia's* shore. ... Od.17.617.162.
Ah me! returns the Queen, when from this shore ... Od.18.293.180.
Peers from the distant *Samian* shore retort; ... Od.19.150.199.
He wing'd his voyage to the *Phrygian* shore. ... Od.19.233.204.
Without retinue, to that friendly shore ... Od.19.311.209.
Of luckless friendship on a foreign shore ... Od.21.35.261.
(For *Greece* has beauteous dames on ev'ry shore.) ... Od.21.267.272.
Ulysses vengeful from the *Trojan* shore; ... Od.22.42.288.
Why must I wake to grieve, and curse thy shore? ... Od.23.23.320.
For never must *Ulysses* view this shore; ... Od.23.69.322.
New as they were to that infernal shore, ... Od.24.29.348.
High on the shore the growing hill we raise, ... Od.24.103.353.
When our triumphant navies touch'd your shore; ... Od.24.141.354.
Sunk is the glory of this once-fam'd shore! ... Od.24.328.365.
Our wandring course, and drove us on your shore: ... Od.24.358.366.
Well hop'd we then to meet on this fair shore, ... Od.24.365.366.

SHORES

Blest *Thames's* Shores the brightest Beauties yield, ... 1.PSp.63.67.
And with deep Murmurs fills the sounding Shores; ... 1.PAu.20.82.
And future Navies on thy Shores appear. ... 1.W-F.222.170.
And hears the Murmurs of the diff'rent Shores: ... 1.TrSt.471.430.
Why on those Shores are we with Joy survey'd, ... 1.TrES.33.450.
Why on these Shores are we with Joy survey'd, ... 1.TrES.33A.450.
Far from the *Lycian* Shores, his happy Native Reign. ... 1.TrES.260.459.
And leave the sinking Hills, and less'ning Shores. ... 1.TrUl.4.465.
Ev'n to those Shores is *Ithaca* renown'd, ... 1.TrUl.132.470.
To farthest Shores th' Ambrosial Spirit flies, ... 2.TemF.376.281.
Than Leaves on Trees, or Sands upon the Shores; ... 2.TemF.425.284.
Arabian shores, or Indian seas infold? ... 4.1HE6.12.237.
The Waves run frighted to the Shores. ... 6.78ii.7.216.

SHORES (CONTINUED)

And whose bright Presence gilds thy *Chrysa's* Shores. Il.1.56.88.
And waft the Sacrifice to *Chrysa's* Shores, Il.1.183.96.
A well-rigg'd Ship for *Chrysa's* sacred Shores: Il.1.405.107.
Beheld him mourning on the naked Shores, Il.1.472.110.
To heap the Shores with copious Death, and bring Il.1.534.113.
And heaves huge Surges to the trembling Shores: Il.2.250.139.
He said: the Shores with loud Applauses sound, Il.2.400.145.
Beneath his Conduct sought the *Phrygian* Shores. Il.2.774.162.
And *Boreas* beats the hoarse-resounding Shores. Il.2.1025.171.
Now win the Shores, and scarce the Seas remain. Il.5.985.314.
Shouts of Applause along the Shores resound. Il.8.674.427.
What to these Shores th' assembled Nations draws, Il.9.446.454.
To quit these Shores, their native Seats enjoy, Il.9.540.460.
Why on those Shores are we with Joy survey'd, Il.12.377.95.
The Heav'ns re-echo, and the Shores reply; Il.13.64.107.
Mixt with *Bœotians*, on the Shores of *Troy*. Il.13.876.147.
Around the Ships: Seas hanging o'er the Shores, Il.14.455.185.
To flank the Navy, and the Shores defend. Il.15.345.210.
Exhorts, adjures, to guard these utmost Shores; Il.15.794.226.
And shew'd the Shores, the Navy, and the Main: Il.15.811.228.
Lay rank'd contiguous on the bending Shores. Il.15.835.229.
With streaming Blood the slipp'ry Shores are dy'd, Il.15.866.230.
He, lov'd of *Jove*, had launch'd for *Ilion's* Shores Il.16.206.247.
Far from the *Lycian* Shores, his happy native Reign. Il.16.565.266.
Troy starts astonish'd, and the Shores rebound. Il.18.258.334.
Not long continues to the Shores confin'd, Il.18.308.336.
And speed to Meadows on whose sounding Shores Il.18.667.356.
Clang the strong Arms, and ring the Shores around: Il.19.16.372.
The Shores resounded with the Voice he sent. Il.19.44.373.
Now thro' the trembling Shores *Minerva* calls. Il.20.67.396.
At *Neptunes* Shrine on *Helice's* high Shores Il.20.468.414.
So sweeps the Hero thro' the wasted Shores; Il.20.574.418.
The flashing Billows beat the whiten'd Shores: Il.21.10.421.
Scamander spoke; the Shores return'd the Sound. Il.21.230.430.
Then rising in his Rage above the Shores, Il.21.257.431.
And lifts his Billows, and o'erwhelms his Shores. Il.21.357.435.
Seas, Shores, and Skies with loud Applause resound, Il.23.1028.530.
While sad on foreign shores *Ulysses* treads, Od.2.151.69.
When great *Ulysses* sought the *Phrygian* shores Od.2.199.71.
The neighb'ring main, and sorrowing treads the shores. Od.2.294.76.
Thou to the court ascend; and to the shores Od.2.327.77.
The Goddess shov'd the vessel from the shores, Od.2.438.82.
Us to these shores our filial duty draws, Od.3.98.91.
Thus sav'd from death they gain'd the *Phæstan* shores, Od.3.380.105.
There wander'd *Menelaus* thro' foreign shores, Od.3.384.105.
The tempest drove him to these shores and thee. Od.5.142.178.
On rocks and shores consum'd the tedious day; Od.5.200.181.
But cliffs, and shaggy shores, a dreadful sight! Od.5.520.197.
Where the ports open, or the shores descend, Od.5.535.198.
What sounds are these that gather from the shores? Od.6.143.214.
'Tis death with hostile step these shores to tread; Od.6.242.221.
O'er unknown seas arriv'd from unknown shores. Od.8.14.262.
A speedy voyage to his native shores. Od.8.174.271.
He feigns a journey to the *Lemnian* shores: Od.8.326.281.
To the soft *Cyprian* shores the Goddess moves, Od.8.395.285.
And grant him to his spouse and native shores! Od.8.446.287.
To thy fond wish thy long-expected shores, Od.8.500.289.
While from the shores the winged navy flies: Od.8.550.292.
A widow, and a slave, on foreign shores! Od.8.580.293.
Strong are her sons, tho' rocky are her shores; Od.9.28.303.
The Ocean widen'd, and the shores withdrew. Od.10.53.342.
The jutting shores that swell on either side Od.10.103.345.
Now to the shores we bend, a mournful train, Od.11.1.377.
On distant shores unwept, unburied lye. Od.11.68.383.
Will give thee back to day, and *Circe's* shores: Od.11.86.385.
A prosp'rous voyage to his native shores; Od.11.127.387.
Graze num'rous herds along the verdant shores; Od.11.135.387.
Com'st thou a wand'rer from the *Phrygian* shores? Od.11.197.391.
Nor have these eyes beheld my native shores, Od.11.204.391.
To land *Ulysses* on his native shores. Od.11.413.404.
The stranger from our hospitable shores; Od.11.439.406.
And fitter pomp to hail my native shores: Od.11.447.406.
The mountains lessen, and retreat the shores; Od.11.792.426.
And lo! the *Siren* shores like mists arise. Od.12.201.441.
Warn'd by their awful voice these shores to shun, Od.12.322.447.
To fly these shores the prescient *Theban* Shade Od.12.326.447.
Weary and wet th' *Ogygian* shores I gain, Od.12.531.458.
And leave the sinking hills, and less'ning shores. Od.13.95.5.
Ev'n to those shores is *Ithaca* renown'd, Od.13.299.20.
Intent to voyage to th' *Egyptian* shores; Od.14.281.49.
But first the King dismiss'd me from his shores, Od.14.371.53.
All with obedient haste forsake the shores, Od.15.591.98.
With speed they guide the vessel to the shores; Od.16.346.123.
Full to the bay within the winding shores Od.16.368.124.
Swift at the word descending to the shores, Od.16.374.124.
The *Taphian* pyrates on *Thesprotia's* shores; Od.16.445.128.
Ere yet he trod these shores! to strife he draws Od.18.448.190.
This gift, long since when *Sparta's* shores he trod, Od.21.17.259.
So, when by hollow shores the fisher train Od.22.425.308.
Thy lost *Ulysses* to his native shores, Od.23.168.328.
As to the shipwreck'd mariner, the shores Od.23.249.335.
Thence swift re-sailing to my native shores, Od.23.295.337.
And whirls him groaning from his native shores: Od.23.342.341.
How struggling thro' the surge, he reach'd the shores Od.23.359.342.
Detain'd reluctant from my native shores. Od.23.380.343.

SHORN

And in the new-shorn Field the Partridge feeds, 1.W-F.98.160.
Shorn from the Crest. *Atrides* wav'd his Steel: Il.13.771.141.
Shorn from the Crest, the purple Honours glow. Il.15.635.220.
So the rude *Boreas*, o'er the field new shorn, Od.5.470.195.

SHORT

Shall finish what his short-liv'd Sire begun; 1.Mes.64.118.
Short is his Joy! he feels the fiery Wound, 1.W-F.113.161.

SHORT (CONTINUED)

Strait a short Thunder breaks the frozen Sky. 1.W-F.130.162.
Short Views we take, nor see the *Lengths behind*, 1.EOC.222.265.
Form *short Ideas;* and offend in *Arts* 1.EOC.287.271.
Short is the Date, alas, of *Modern Rhymes;* 1.EOC.476.292.
But soon the Short-liv'd Vanity is lost! 1.EOC.497.294.
It still *looks home*, and *short Excursions* makes; 1.EOC.627.310.
But in low Numbers short Excursions tries: 1.EOC.738.326.
Tho' short my Stature, yet my Name extends 1.TrSP.39.395.
And the short Monarch of a hasty Year 1.TrSt.196.418.
Thought a short Life well lost for endless Fame. 1.TrSt.717.440.
Short is the Date prescrib'd to Mortal Man; 1.TrES.239.458.
And reign'd the short-liv'd Tyrant of his Breast; 2.ChJM.231.25.
How short a Space our Worldly Joys endure? 2.ChJM.476.38.
Madam, 'tis past, and my short Anger o'er; 2.ChJM.789.53.
And just as short of Reason he must fall, 3.EOM3.47.96.
And just as short of Reason Man will fall, 3.EOM3.47A.96.
While still too wide or short is human Wit; 3.EOM3.90.101.
Short and but rare, 'till Man improv'd it all. 3.EOM4.116.139.
Then learned Sir! (to cut the Matter short) 4.HS1.91.13.
I cough like *Horace*, and tho' lean, am short, 4.Arbu.116.104.
They bled, they cupp'd, they purg'd; in short, they cur'd: 4.2HE2.193.179.
What's long or short, each accent where to place, 4.2HE1.207.213.
Who pants for glory finds but short repose, 4.2HE1.300.221.
In short, I'm perfectly content, 4.HS6.29.251.
Chang'd it to August, and (in short) 4.1HE7.3.269.
But you may read it, I stop short. 4.1HE7.84.273.
Weak tho' I am of limb, and short of sight, 4.1HE1.49.283.
In short, that reas'ning, high, immortal Thing, 4.1HE1.185.293.
And Snip-snap short, and Interruption smart. 5.DunA2.232.128.
And Snip-snap short, and Interruption smart, 5.DunB2.240.307.
All my commands are easy, short, and full: 5.DunB4.581.399.
Wits have short Memories, and Dunces none) 5.DunB4.620.406.
Wits have short Memories, and Dulness none) 5.DunB4.620A.406.
The short thick Sob, loud Scream, and shriller Squawl: 6.14ii.6.43.
Long future prospects, and short present joys: 6.22.11.71.
In short, the rest were all in Fray, 6.30.48.87.
There he stopt short, nor since has writ a tittle, 6.49i.9.137.
Some few short Years, no more! 6.53.38.162.
Such, such a man extends his life's short space, 6.55.8.166.
In short Pope and Gay (as 6.68.5.196.
In one short view subjected to your eye 6.71.33.203.
In one short view subjected to our eye 6.71.33A.203.
Though made full short by G—d: 6.79.34.219.
To his poor Babe a Life so short: 6.124iv.2.348.
For tho' we deem the short-liv'd Fury past, Il.1.105.92.
Thy short-liv'd Friendship, and thy groundless Hate. Il.1.238.98.
Sure, to so short a Race of Glory born, Il.1.462.110.
So short a Space the Light of Heav'n to view! Il.1.544.114.
So short a Space, and fill'd with Sorrow too! Il.1.545.114.
To Life so short, and now dishonour'd too. Il.1.657.118.
And, one short Month, endure the Wintry Main? Il.2.357.144.
But now, ye Warriors, take a short Repast; Il.2.452.149.
Broke short: the Fragments glitter'd on the Sand. Il.3.448.213.
Short was his Date! by dreadful *Ajax* slain Il.4.550.247.
Stopt short of Life, and mock'd the Shooter's Art. Il.5.139.273.
Short is his Date, and soon his Glory ends; Il.5.496.291.
A short-liv'd Reptile in the Dust of Earth. Il.5.538.294.
(Each at his Post in Arms) a short Repaste. Il.7.455.387.
Now had the *Grecians* snatch'd a short Repaste, Il.8.67.398.
The Fires they light, to short Repasts they fall, Il.9.119.438.
Then thus in short my fixt Resolves attend, Il.9.414.452.
Short is my Date, but deathless my Renown; Il.9.535.460.
Short of its Crest, and with no Plume o'erspread; Il.10.304.16.
And a short Darkness shades his swimming Eyes. Il.11.460.54.
Stop'd short of Life, nor with his Entrails mix'd. Il.11.550.58.
Without the Gods, how short a Period stands Il.12.9.81.
Short as he turn'd, I saw the Pow'r appear: Il.13.102.109.
The Point broke short, and sparkled in the Sand. Il.13.218.116.
And in short Pantings sobb'd his Soul away; Il.13.818.144.
(Not that short Life which Mortals lead below, Il.13.1047.155.
Tydides cut him short, and thus began. Il.14.120.163.
His Breath, in quick, short Pantings, comes, and goes; Il.16.134.242.
The Sword broke short; but his, *Peneleus* sped Il.16.406.258.
Shock; while the madding Steeds break short their Yokes: Il.16.445.260.
Short is the Date prescrib'd to mortal Man; Il.16.542.265.
This Instant see his short-liv'd Trophies won, Il.16.789.274.
And turn'd him short, and herded in the Croud. Il.16.982.281.
So short a space the Light of Heav'n to view, Il.18.79.327.
So short alas! and fill'd with Anguish too? Il.18.80.327.
And reap what Glory Life's short Harvest yields. Il.18.154.330.
But mighty *Jove* cuts short, with just Disdain, Il.18.383.339.
Grace with immortal Arms this short-liv'd Son, Il.18.528.347.
(Too short to gripe them) the brown Sheaves of Corn. Il.18.644.354.
Nor great *Achilles* grudge this short Delay; Il.19.188.379.
Yet a short Interval, and none shall dare Il.19.237.382.
That spun so short his Life's illustrious Line: Il.20.155.400.
And the short Absence of *Achilles* paid. Il.21.150.427.
And thus short-panting, to the God he said. Il.21.417.437.
Yet a short space the great Avenger stay'd, Il.22.419.472.
And short, or wide, th' ungovern'd Courser drive: Il.23.392.506.
And turns him short; till, doubling as they roll, Il.23.411.506.
And, turn'd too short, he tumbled on the Strand, Il.23.549.511.
And great *Patroclus* in short Triumph bore. Il.23.944.526.
Allow'd their Mules and Steeds a short Repose. Il.24.432.554.
Still in short intervals of pleasing woe, Od.4.127.126.
His speech thus ended short, he frowning rose, Od.4.1027.165.
And the short date of fading charms below; Od.5.280.185.
Then with a short repast relieve their toil, Od.6.109.211.
Short is the time, and lo! ev'n now the gales Od.8.165.271.
So near the pastures, and so short the way, Od.10.98.345.
Let this short memory of grief suffice. Od.10.541.369.
And cruel, enviest thou a short repose? Od.12.336.448.
Why were my cares beguil'd in short repose? Od.12.439.452.
And the short rage of thirst and hunger ceast) Od.15.159.76.
Yet short his date of life! by female pride he dies. Od.15.271.81.

SHORT (CONTINUED)
The night; then down to short repose they lay; ....Od.15.533.95.
And now a short repast prepar'd, they fed, ...Od.16.498.131.
My friend adieu! let this short stay suffice; ....Od.17.7.132.
Short was that doubt; to quell his rage inur'd, ...Od.17.278.145.
Then turning short, disdain'd a further stay, ...Od.18.133.172.
Short woolly curls o'erfleec'd his bending head, ...Od.19.280.208.
Twang'd short and sharp, like the shrill swallow's cry. ....Od.21.449.282.
And scatter'd short, or wide, the points of death; ....Od.22.283.300.
Yet a short space, your rival suit suspend, ...Od.24.156.355.

SHORT-LIV'D
Shall finish what his short-liv'd Sire begun; ....1.Mes.64.118.
But soon the Short-liv'd Vanity is lost! ....1.EOC.497.294.
And reign'd the short-liv'd Tyrant of his Breast; ....2.ChJM.231.25.
For tho' we deem the short-liv'd Fury past, ...Il.1.105.92.
Thy short-liv'd Friendship, and thy groundless Hate. ....Il.1.238.98.
A short-liv'd Reptile in the Dust of Earth. ....Il.5.538.294.
This Instant see his short-liv'd Trophies won, ...Il.16.789.274.
Grace with immortal Arms this short-liv'd Son, ...Il.18.528.347.

SHORT-PANTING
And thus short-panting, to the God he said. ....Il.21.417.437.

SHORTEN
He the least point shoud shorten or omit ....4.JD2A.109.142.

SHORTEN'D
With Faulchions, Axes, Swords, and shorten'd Darts. ....Il.15.863.230.
And raz'd his Shoulder with a shorten'd Spear: ....Il.17.679.314.
This shorten'd of its top, I gave my train ....Od.9.384.321.
His nose they shorten'd, and his ears they slit, ...Od.21.321.275.
To rush between, and use the shorten'd sword. ....Od.22.115.292.
The wretch, and shorten'd of his nose and ears; ....Od.22.512.313.

SHORTER
And now his shorter Breath with sultry Air ....1.W-F.195.168.
Take shorter journies to the day, ...6.6i.6.14.

SHORTLY
Shall shortly want the gen'rous tear he pays; ....2.Elegy.78.368.
Shortly no Lad shall *chuck*, or Lady *vole*, ...4.JD4.146.37.

SHORTNING
Who shortning with a storm of blows thy stay, ...Od.18.383.186.

SHOT
Sol thro' white Curtains shot a tim'rous Ray, ...2.RL1.13.145.
A sudden Star, it shot thro' liquid Air, ...2.RL5.127.210.
That all the Shot of Dulness now must be ....4.JD4.64.31.
Shot to the black abyss, and plung'd down-right. ....5.DunA2.276.135.
Shot to the black abyss, and plung'd down-right. ....5.DunB2.288.309.
And the bright Flame was shot thro' MARCHMONT'S Soul. ....6.142.12.383.
And shot the gen'rous flame thro' Machmont's soul ....6.142.12A.383.
The Pyres thick-flaming shot a dismal Glare. ....Il.1.72.90.
The Fires thick-flaming shot a dismal Glare. ....Il.1.72A.90.
A mighty Dragon shot, of dire Portent; ....Il.2.372.145.
Shot forth to View, a scaly Serpent sees; ....Il.3.48.191.
And shot like Light'ning from *Olympus'* Height. ....Il.4.100.225.
Shot the bright Goddess in a Trail of Light. ....Il.4.108.225.
A shady Light was shot from glimm'ring Shields, ...Il.4.324.236.
Shot down avenging, from the Vault of Stars. ....Il.6.134.330.
Nor shot less swift from *Ilion's* Tow'ry Height: ....Il.7.26.364.
And shot red Light'nings thro' the gloomy Shade: ....Il.7.573.393.
His Eyes like *Gorgon* shot a sanguin Flame ....Il.8.418.417.
I shot from Heav'n, and gave his Arm the Day. ....Il.8.444.418.
Shot from their flashing Points a quiv'ring Light. ....Il.10.175.9.
Shot thro' the Battel in a Moment's Space, ...Il.11.363.50.
Shot heav'n-bred Horror thro' the *Grecian's* Heart; ....Il.11.669.65.
And their bright Arms shot Horror o'er the Plain. ....Il.13.395.124.
Shot Terrors round, that wither'd ev'n the Strong. ....Il.13.1017.153.
Swift from th' *Idæan* Summit shot to Heav'n. ....Il.15.85.199.
A sudden Ray shot beaming o'er the Plain, ...Il.15.810.227.
A sudden Horror shot thro' all the Chief, ...Il.18.25.324.
Shot in a Whirlwind to the Shore below; ....Il.18.206.331.
And shot the shining Mischief to the Heart! ....Il.19.62.374.
Shot the descending Goddess from above. ....Il.19.371.387.
Shot down to save her, and redeem her Fame. ....Il.21.642.448.
Him, as he blazing shot across the Field, ...Il.22.35.454.
Shot trembling Rays that glitter'd o'er the Land; ....Il.22.176.461.
(Flames, as he spoke, shot flashing from his Eyes) ....Il.22.434.473.
Shot headlong from his Seat, beside the Wheel, ...Il.23.473.509.
Shot from the Chariot; while his Coursers stray ....Il.23.550.511.
She plung'd, and instant shot the dark Profound. ....Il.24.106.539.
And in a moment shot into the Skies: ....Il.24.575.560.
Stretch'd wide his eager arms, and shot the seas along. ....Od.5.477.195.
The Goddess shot; *Ulysses* was her care. ....Od.6.20.204.
Shot thro' the western clouds a dewy ray; ....Od.6.382.230.
Shot to *Olympus* from the woodland shade. ....Od.10.368.362.
The winged Pinnace shot along the sea. ....Od.13.187.15.
My naked breast, and shot along the tide. ....Od.14.386.53.
The sun obliquely shot his dewy ray. ....Od.17.688.165.
That shot effulgence like the solar ray, ...Od.18.344.184.
And this mad Archer soon have shot his last. ....Od.22.92.291.
Before *Minerva* shot the livid flames; ....Od.24.623.377.

SHOU'D (OMITTED)
98

SHOUD
He the least point shoud shorten or omit ....4.JD2A.109.142.

SHOUD'ST
But shoud'st thou search the spacious World around, ...2.ChJM.637.45.

SHOULD (OMITTED)
210

SHOULD'RING
Should'ring God's altar a vile image stands, ...3.Ep3.293.117.

SHOULD'ST
"Thou should'st be always thus, resign'd and meek! ....2.ChWB.185.65.
Should'st wag a serpent-tail in Smithfield fair! ....5.DunB3.288.334.
Should'st fall an easy Conquest on the Field. ....Il.3.542.217.
But why should'st thou suspect the War's Success? ....Il.12.285.92.
Should'st thou (but Heav'n avert it!) should'st thou bleed, ...Il.22.121.458.
Should'st thou (but Heav'n avert it!) should'st thou bleed, ...Il.22.121.458.
For should'st thou suffer, pow'rless to relieve ....Od.16.87.106.

SHOULDER
A painted Quiver on her Shoulder sounds, ...1.W-F.179.166.
Which o'er the Warrior's Shoulder took its Course, ...1.TrES.283.460.
Ammon's great Son one shoulder had too high, ...4.Arbu.117.104.
Gay pats my shoulder, and you vanish quite; ....6.45.47.126.
A radiant Baldric, o'er his Shoulder ty'd, ...Il.3.415.212.
Which o'er the Warrior's Shoulder took its Course, ...Il.5.23.266.
And pierc'd his Shoulder as he mounts his Car; ....Il.5.62.269.
On his broad Shoulder fell the forceful Brand, ...Il.5.105.272.
Deep in his Shoulder pierc'd, and drank the Gore: ....Il.5.131.273.
Hypenor's Shoulder his broad Faulchion cleaves. ....Il.5.187.275.
Whose ample Belt that o'er his Shoulder lay, ...Il.5.994.314.
The Shield's large Orb behind his Shoulder cast, ...Il.6.144.331.
Fix'd in the Shoulder as he mounts his Steeds; ....Il.7.20.363.
The Shaft already to his Shoulder drew; ....Il.8.390.416.
Which willful err'd, and o'er his Shoulder past; ....Il.10.442.23.
A radiant Baldrick, o'er his Shoulder ty'd, ...Il.11.39.36.
Pierc'd thro' the Shoulder, first *Deiopis* fell; ....Il.11.531.57.
In his right Shoulder the broad Shaft appear'd, ...Il.11.630.61.
The driving Javelin thro' his Shoulder thrust, ...Il.14.527.189.
Pierc'd thro' the Shoulder as he basely flies. ....Il.15.387.212.
The fourfold Buckler o'er his Shoulder ty'd; ....Il.15.565.218.
Thro' *Dolops'* Shoulder urg'd his forceful Dart, ...Il.15.638.221.
His Shoulder-blade receives the fatal Wound; ....Il.16.344.256.
Between his Arm and Shoulder aims a Blow, ...Il.16.384.258.
Pierc'd thro' the Shoulder as he mounts his Steeds; ....Il.16.411.259.
Which o'er the Warrior's Shoulder took its course, ...Il.16.588.267.
And deep transpiercing, thro' the Shoulder stood; ....Il.17.359.301.
And raz'd his Shoulder with a shorten'd Spear: ....Il.17.679.314.
Nodding, his Head hangs down his Shoulder o'er; ....Il.23.810.521.
The glitt'ring zone athwart his shoulder cast ....Od.4.415.140.
Her ratling quiver from her shoulder sounds: ....Od.6.120.212.
He said, and o'er his shoulder flung the blade. ....Od.8.451.287.
His neck obliquely o'er his shoulder hung, ...Od.9.441.324.
His weighty faulchion o'er his shoulder ty'd: ....Od.14.596.66.
His shoulder-blade receiv'd th' ungentle shock; ....Od.17.548.159.
Full on the shoulder the rude weight descends: ....Od.18.109.172.
Scornful he spoke, and o'er his shoulder flung ....Od.18.130.172.
Full on his shoulder it inflicts a wound, ...Od.18.441.190.
O'er which a promontory-shoulder spread: ....Od.19.281.208.
To the right shoulder-joint the spear apply'd, ...Od.19.529.221.
On good *Eumæus'* shield and shoulder glanc'd; ....Od.22.309.301.

SHOULDER-BLADE
His Shoulder-blade receives the fatal Wound; ....Il.16.344.256.
His shoulder-blade receiv'd th' ungentle shock; ....Od.17.548.159.

SHOULDER-JOINT
To the right shoulder-joint the spear apply'd, ...Od.19.529.221.

SHOULDER'S
Fix'd in the Shoulder's Joint, he reel'd around; ....1.TrES.271.459.

SHOULDERS
Hairs, like a wood, my head and shoulders grace, ...1.TrPA.102.370.
O'ercharge the Shoulders of the seeming Swain. ....1.TrVP.32.378.
A Robe obscene was o'er her Shoulders thrown, ...1.TrSt.154.416.
Oenides' manly Shoulders overspread, ...1.TrSt.572.434.
around her Shoulders flew the waving Vest. ....1.TrUl.105.469.
So lab'ring on, with shoulders, hands, and head, ...5.DunA2.61.105.
By his broad shoulders known, and length of ears, ...5.DunA3.28.153.
So lab'ring on, with shoulders, hands, and head, ...5.DunB2.65.299.
By his broad shoulders known, and length of ears, ...5.DunB3.36.322.
His Mountain-Shoulders half his Breast o'erspread, ...Il.2.265.140.
Down their broad Shoulders falls a Length of Hair; ....Il.2.649.158.
His bended Bow a-cross his Shoulders flung, ...Il.3.29.189.
Broad is his Breast, his Shoulders larger spread, ...Il.3.255.204.
Whose brawny Shoulders, and whose swelling Chest, ...Il.3.291.207.
O'er her broad Shoulders hangs his horrid Shield, ...Il.5.911.309.
His Mane dishevel'd o'er his Shoulders flies; ....Il.6.657.360.
From *Tydeus'* Shoulders strip the costly Load, ...Il.8.236.409.
A Leopard's spotted Hide his Shoulders spread; ....Il.10.35.4.
This said, the Hero o'er his Shoulders flung ....Il.10.202.10.
A Wolf's grey Hide around his Shoulders hung. ....Il.10.396.21.
No mortal Shoulders suit the glorious Load, ...Il.10.510.26.
Between his Shoulders pierc'd the following Dart, ...Il.11.560.59.
From his broad Shoulders tore the Spoils away; ....Il.13.697.138.
Part o'er her Shoulders wav'd like melted Gold. ....Il.14.206.170.
And from the spouting Shoulders struck his Head; ....Il.14.582.190.
His Mane dishevel'd o'er his Shoulders flies; ....Il.15.303.208.
The well-stor'd Quiver on his Shoulders hung: ....Il.15.520.217.
Achilles' Shield his ample Shoulders spread, ...Il.16.168.244.
O'er his broad Shoulders spread the massy Shield; ....Il.16.429.259.
Fix'd in the Shoulders Joint, he reel'd around; ....Il.16.576.267.
The weighty Shock his Neck and Shoulders feel; ....Il.16.956.280.
Full on my Shoulders let their Nostrils blow, ...Il.17.570.310.
Her *Ægis, Pallas* o'er his Shoulders throws; ....Il.18.242.334.
From his broad Shoulders hew'd his crested Head: ....Il.20.558.417.
They eas'd their Shoulders, and dispos'd the Load; ....Il.23.155.495.
Loose on their Shoulders the long Manes reclin'd, ...Il.23.443.508.
Their Bones resound with Blows: Sides, Shoulders, Thighs ....Il.23.832.522.

SHOULDERS (CONTINUED)

His glowing Breath upon his Shoulders plays; ......Il.23.895.524.
Such wavy ringlets o'er his shoulders flow! ......Od.4.202.129.
His limbs how turn'd! how broad his shoulders spread! ......Od.8.148.270.
And the huge body on my shoulders heav'd: ......Od.10.195.350.
I heard, and instant o'er my shoulders flung ......Od.10.309.359.
And full nine cubits broad their shoulders spread. ......Od.11.384.402.
Around her shoulders flew the waving vest, ...Od.13.272.19.
Nor had these shoulders cov'ring, but of steel. ......Od.14.535.63.
Then o'er his ample shoulders whirl'd the cloak, ...Od.15.69.72.
Across his shoulders, then, the scrip he flung, ...Od.17.220.142.
Full many a post have those broad shoulders worn, ...Od.17.256.143.
Broad spread his shoulders, and his nervous thighs ......Od.18.76.170.
His shoulders intercept th' unfriendly rays. ......Od.19.457.217.
His head, his shoulders, and his knees embrac'd: ......Od.21.235.271.
And now his shoulders bear the massy shield, ...Od.22.138.293.
Ill suits this garb the shoulders of a King. ......Od.22.526.314.

SHOULDST

'Tis said, that thou shouldst cleave unto thy Wife; ......6.96iv.9.276.

SHOUT

Such is the shout, the long-applauding note, ...4.2HE1.330.223.
Here fortun'd Curl to slide; loud shout the band, ...5.DunA2.69.106.
Six huntsmen with a shout precede his chair; ......5.DunA2.185.124.
Here fortun'd Curl to slide; loud shout the band, ...5.DunB2.73.299.
Six huntsmen with a shout precede his chair: ......5.DunB2.193.305.
The hollow Ships each deaf'ning Shout rebound. ......Il.2.401.145.
And the long Shout runs echoing thro' the Skies. ......Il.3.576.219.
A gen'ral Shout that all the Region rends. ......Il.4.491.244.
When the loud Rusticks rise, and shout from far, ...Il.13.596.134.
A Shout, that tore Heav'ns Concave, and above ......Il.13.1060.155.
Loud, as the Shout encountring Armies yield, ...Il.14.173.165.
They shout incessant, and the Vales resound. ......Il.17.74.291.
Loud shout the *Trojans*, and renew the Fight. ......Il.17.810.320.
With her own Shout *Minerva* swells the Sound; ......Il.18.257.334.
The *Greeks* accept, and shout *Pelides'* Name. ......Il.19.78.375.
They pant, they stretch, they shout along the Plain. ......Il.23.450.508.
Floats a strong shout along the waves of air. ......Od.6.358.229.
Pleas'd with the din of war, and noble shout of foes. ......Od.11.316.397.
If at the clash of arms, and shout of foes, ...Od.11.603.413.
They storm, they shout, with hasty frenzy fir'd, ...Od.24.532.373.

SHOUTING

Produc'd *Æneas* to the shouting Train; ......Il.5.628.298.
When shouting Millions shake the thund'ring Field. ......Il.5.1055.317.
Of shouting Huntsmen and of clam'rous Hounds; ......Il.11.526.57.
Beset with watchful Dogs, and shouting Swains, ...Il.11.675.65.
The shouting *Argives* strip the Heroes slain. ......Il.17.369.302.
The shouting Host in loud Applauses join'd; ......Il.18.361.339.
Then fierce *Achilles,* shouting to the Skies, ...Il.20.437.413.
Of shouting Hunters, and of clam'rous Hounds, ...Il.21.680.450.
And still'd the Clamour of the shouting Bands. ......Il.23.648.515.
And shouting seize the God: our force t'evade ......Od.4.613.148.

SHOUTS

The War begins; mix'd Shouts and Groans arise; ......1.TrES.95.453.
The War renews, mix'd Shouts and Groans arise; ......1.TrES.95A.453.
The Nymph exulting fills with Shouts the Sky, ...2.RL3.99.174.
Heroes' and Heroins' Shouts confus'dly rise, ...2.RL5.41.202.
Here shouts all Drury, there all Lincoln's-Inn; ......5.DunA3.266.179.
Here shouts all Drury, there all Lincoln's-inn; ......5.DunB3.270.333.
The *Greeks* in Shouts their joint Assent declare ......Il.1.31.87.
With Shouts the *Trojans* rushing from afar ......Il.3.3.186.
And shrilling Shouts and dying Groans arise; ......Il.4.513.246.
The *Greeks* with Shouts press on, and spoil the Dead, ...Il.4.584.249.
And shouts and thunders in the Fields below. ......Il.4.596.250.
And shouts, in *Stentor's* sounding Voice, aloud: ......Il.5.977.313.
While pleas'd amidst the gen'ral Shouts of *Troy,* ......Il.6.614.357.
With gen'ral Shouts return'd him loud Acclaim. ......Il.7.481.388.
And now with Shouts the shocking Armies clos'd, ...Il.8.75.399.
Triumphant Shouts and dying Groans arise; ......Il.8.80.399.
The Shouts of *Trojans* thicken in the Wind; ......Il.8.192.406.
Dreadful he shouts: from Earth a Stone he took, ...Il.8.387.416.
Shouts of Applause along the Shores resound. ......Il.8.674.427.
Hear how with Shouts their Conquest they proclaim, ...Il.9.307.449.
Mean while the Victor's Shouts ascend the Skies; ......Il.9.699.468.
Shouts of Acclaim the list'ning Heroes raise, ...Il.9.834.474.
Now Shouts and Tumults wake the tardy Sun, ...Il.11.67.37.
As swift *Atrides,* with loud Shouts pursu'd, ...Il.11.221.45.
Shouts, as he past, the crystal Regions rend, ...Il.11.445.54.
O Friend! *Ulysses'* Shouts invade my Ear; ......Il.11.584.60.
And Groans of Slaughter mix with Shouts of Fight. ......Il.11.653.63.
The War renews, mix'd Shouts and Groans arise; ......Il.12.449.98.
His Shouts incessant ev'ry *Greek* inspire, ...Il.13.71.108.
But with repeated Shouts his Army fires. ......Il.13.204.115.
And hail, with Shouts, his Progress thro' the Skies: ......Il.13.1041.154.
With Shouts incessant Earth and Ocean rung, ...Il.13.1057.155.
Hark! how the Shouts divide, and how they meet, ...Il.14.7.157.
Loud Shouts of Triumph fill the crowded Plain; ......Il.14.493.188.
Shouts in their Ears, and lightens in their Eyes, ...Il.15.363.211.
So fears the Youth; all *Troy* with Shouts pursue, ...Il.15.708.223.
Ev'n yet, the *Greeks* with piercing Shouts inspires, ...Il.15.888.231.
The Flames my Eyes, the Shouts invade my Ears. ......Il.16.86.238.
From Shore to Shore the doubling Shouts resound, ...Il.16.332.255.
Fierce on the Rear, with Shouts, *Patroclus* flies; ......Il.16.448.260.
With horrid Shouts they circle round the Slain; ......Il.16.693.271.
With conqu'ring Shouts the *Trojans* shake the Plain, ...Il.16.730.272.
Great *Merion* follows, and new Shouts arise: ......Il.16.764.273.
Whole *Troy* embodied, rush'd with Shouts along. ......Il.17.309.299.
With fiercer Shouts his ling'ring Troops he fires, ...Il.18.197.331.
Now shouts to *Simois,* from her beauteous * Hill; ......Il.20.73.397.
And hear his Shouts victorious o'er the Plain. ......Il.23.563.512.
Shouts of Applause run rattling thro the Skies. ......Il.23.847.523.
And sends in shouts applauses to the skies. ......Od.8.416.286.
Tho' arms, or shouts, or dying groans they hear. ......Od.21.255.272.

SHOUTS (CONTINUED)

If arms, or shouts, or dying groans they hear, ...Od.21.416.280.
With dreadful shouts *Ulysses* pour'd along, ...Od.24.620.377.

SHOV'D

Crawl thro' the Street, shov'd on, or rudely press'd ......3.Ep1.230A.35.
Shov'd from the wall perhaps, or rudely press'd ......3.Ep1.230.35.
The Goddess shov'd the vessel from the shores, ...Od.2.438.82.
Again I shov'd her off; our fate to fly, ...Od.9.573.330.

SHOVE

"You ne'er consider whom you shove, ...4.HS6.58.253.
And shove him off as far as e'er we can: ......5.DunB4.474.387.

SHOVES

Comes titt'ring on, and shoves you from the stage: ......4.2HE2.325.187.

SHOW

See SHEW.
The Flocks around a dumb Compassion show, ...1.PSu.6.72.
Nor all his Stars above a Lustre show, ...1.W-F.231.170.
Nor all his Stars a brighter Lustre show, ...1.W-F.231A.170.
Works *without Show,* and *without Pomp* presides: ......1.EOC.75.247.
LEARN then what MORALS Criticks ought to show, ...1.EOC.560.304.
Who to a *Friend* his Faults can freely show, ...1.EOC.637.311.
A Spring there is, whose Silver Waters show, ...1.TrSP.179.401.
In show a youthful Swain, of Form divine, ...1.TrUl.102.469.
Who vers'd in Fortune, fear the flatt'ring Show, ...1.TrUl.209.472.
Heroick *Judeth,* as old *Hebrews* show, ...2.ChJM.73.18.
Heroick *Judeth,* as the Scriptures show, ...2.ChJM.73A.18.
And *Pyramus* and *Thisbe* plainly show ......2.ChJM.516.40.
'Twas charg'd with Fruit that made a goodly Show, ...2.ChJM.603.44.
To show her Furr, and to be *Catterwaw'd.* ......2.ChWB.147.63.
How the first Female (as the Scriptures show) ......2.ChWB.379.75.
In Show like Leaders of the swarthy *Moors.* ......2.RL3.48.172.
Wrapt in a Gown, for Sickness, and for Show. ......2.RL4.36.186.
To midnight dances, and the publick show? ......2.Elegy.58.367.
Infer the Motive from the Deed, and show, ...3.Ep1.53.19.
Not always Actions show the man: we find ......3.Ep1.61.20.
Or, if you rule him, never show you rule ......3.Ep2.262A.71.
Ladies, like variegated Tulips, show, ...3.Ep2.41.53.
And show their zeal, and hide their want of skill. ......3.Ep2.186.65.
Only to show, how many Tastes he wanted. ......3.Ep4.14.137.
You show us, Rome was glorious, not profuse, ...3.Ep4.23.139.
Whose rising Forests, not for pride or show, ...3.Ep4.187.155.
Had no *new Verses,* or *new Suit* to show; ......4.JD4.13.27.
"And tho' the Court show *Vice* exceeding clear, ...4.JD4.96.33.
And show the Sense of it, without the Love; ......4.Arbu.294.117.
But show no mercy to an empty line; ......4.2HE2.175.177.
And call for Pen and Ink to show our Wit. ......4.2HE1.180.211.
Yet let me show, a Poet's of some weight, ...4.2HE1.203.211.
And take it kindly meant to show ......4.HS6.61.253.
Shin'd in Description, he might show it, ...4.HS6.190.261.
But show me one, who has it in his pow'r ......4.1HE1.136.289.
Show there was one who held it in disdain. ......4.EpS1.172.309.
While proud Philosophy repines to show ......5.DunA3.193.173.
And from each show rise duller than the last: ......5.DunA3.300.184.
While proud Philosophy repines to show, ...5.DunB3.197.330.
Show all his paces, not a step advance. ......5.DunB4.266.370.
'Till wrangling *Science* taught it Noise and Show, ...6.8.11.18.
And vary'd *Tulips* show so dazling gay, ...6.14iv.7.47.
Railing at Men of Sense, to show their Wit; ......6.17iv.10.59.
In pitying love we but our weakness show, ...6.32.11.96.
And show, you have the virtue to be mov'd. ......6.32.38.97.
That Mercy I to others show, ...6.50.39.148.
That Mercy show to me. ......6.50.40.148.
As I to others mercy show, ...6.50.39A.148.
Let him hiss loud, to show you all—he's hit. ......6.60.24.178.
But *you* show your *Wit,* whereas *they* show'd their *Tails.* ......6.62ii.2.185.
Which nothing seeks to show, or needs to hide, ...6.73.2.209.
Right tall he made himself to show, ...6.79.33.219.
"O show me, *Flora,* 'midst those Sweets, the Flow'r ......6.96ii.49.273.
But you yourself may serve to show it, ...6.124ii.3.347.
Good without Show, and without weakness kind: ......6.134.6.364.
And where fair *Asinen* and *Hermion* show ......Il.2.680.159.
To whom his Art *Apollo* deign'd to show, ...Il.2.1002.170.
And Crowds stood wond'ring at the passing Show; ......Il.3.68.192.
Soft moving Speech, and pleasing outward Show, ...Il.3.95.194.
But some gay Dancer in the publick Show. ......Il.3.486.215.
A Phantom rais'd, the same in Shape and Show ......Il.5.546.294.
His Eyes delighting with their splendid Show, ...Il.6.400.346.
Thy Hate to *Troy,* is this the Time to show? ......Il.6.406.346.
Till *Greece,* provok'd, from all her Numbers show ......Il.7.45.365.
And call'd *Alcyone;* a Name to show ......Il.9.677.468.
Peace was his Charge; receiv'd with peaceful Show, ...Il.10.341.18.
The bottom bare, (a formidable Show!) ......Il.12.63.83.
Next *Callianira, Callianassa* show ......Il.18.55.326.
Stand in their Porches, and enjoy the Show. ......Il.18.576.350.
A deeper Dye the dangling Clusters show, ...Il.18.653.355.
Unmov'd, the Hero kindles at the Show, ...Il.19.19.372.
How vain that martial Pomp, and dreadful Show, ...Il.21.549.444.
The Sire, superior smil'd; and bade her show, ...Il.21.593.446.
Jove lifts the golden Balances, that show ......Il.22.271.467.
In show an Aid, by hapless *Hector's* Side ......Il.22.293.468.
The rocky Pavement glitter'd with the Show. ......Il.23.249.499.
If yet (Distinction to thy Friend to show, ...Il.23.627.514.
Am I become my People's common Show, ...Il.24.299.549.
I show thee, King! thou tread'st on hostile Land; ......Il.24.717.567.
Show me, fair daughter, (thus the chief demands) ......Od.7.29.235.
In outward show heav'n gives thee to excell, ...Od.8.197.273.
In show a youthful swain, of form divine, ...Od.13.269.18.
Who, vers'd in fortune, fear the flattering show, ...Od.13.376.25.
To him thy presents show, thy words repeat: ......Od.15.175.77.
But mercy to the poor and stranger show, ...Od.18.128.172.
To my lov'd son the snares of death to show, ...Od.18.197.176.
O wise alone in form, and brave in show! ......Od.18.262.179.

SHOW (CONTINUED)
Graceful she said, and bade *Eumæus* show ....Od.21.81.262.
The day that show me, ere I close my eyes, ...Od.24.595.376.

SHOW'D
High on *Parnassus'* Top her Sons she show'd, ...1.EOC.94.250.
Nay show'd his Faults—but when wou'd Poets mend? ....1.EOC.621.309.
But as he march'd, good Gods! he show'd a Pair ....2.ChWB.315.72.
(For none but Lady M—show'd the Rest) ....4.HAdv.125A.85.
Show'd us that France had something to admire. ....4.2HE1.275.219.
But show'd his Breeding, and his Wit, ...4.HS6.172.261.
He ceas'd, and show'd the robe; the crowd confess ....5.DunA2.329.141.
(For so she was, as e'er show'd Rump yet, ...6.10.86.27.
Show'd *Rome* her *Cato's* figure drawn in state; ....6.32.30.97.
But *you* show your *Wit*, whereas *they* show'd their *Tails*. ....6.62ii.2.185.
As show'd, Vice had his Hate and Pity too. ....6.118.8.334.
So, great *Atrides!* show'd thy sacred Blood, ...Il.4.176.229.
Show'd the Celestial Blood, and with a Groan ....Il.5.1066.317.
The faithful Youth his Monarch's Mandate show'd: ....Il.6.216.336.
The Day, that show'd me to the golden Sun, ...Il.6.435.348.
Thy Infant Breast a like Affection show'd; ....Il.9.608.464.
He show'd, and vaunted of his matchless Boy: ....Il.19.106.376.
There on the Spot which great *Achilles* show'd, ...Il.23.154.495.
The Nymph just show'd him, and with tears withdrew. ....Od.5.310.186.
And show'd, as unperceiv'd we took our stand, ...Od.24.170.356.

SHOW'R
And *Jove* consented in a silent Show'r. ....1.PSu.8.72.
And in soft Silence shed the kindly Show'r! ....1.Mes.14.114.
A Show'r of Blood o'er all the fatal Field. ....1.TrES.257.459.
In one abundant show'r of Cent. per Cent., ...3.Ep3.372.123.
From yon old wallnut-tree a show'r shall fall; ....4.HS2.145.67.
Look'd a white lilly sunk beneath a show'r. ....5.DunB4.104.351.
Suckled, and chear'd, with air, and sun, and show'r, ...5.DunB4.406.381.
And soft *Carnations* show'r their balmy dews; ....6.14iv.4.47.
And from soak'd Plumes disperse a briny Show'r, ...6.26i.7.79.
When from the Thatch drips fast a Show'r of Rain. ....6.96ii.14.270.
Their Stones and Arrows in a mingled Show'r. ....Il.3.114.195.
Foretells the ratling Hail, or weighty Show'r, ...Il.10.6.2.
So down the Rampires rolls the rocky Show'r; ....Il.12.180.87.
His Spoils he could not, for the Show'r of Spears. ....Il.13.647.136.
Troy's scatt'ring Orders open to the Show'r. ....Il.13.902.148.
Not when fair *Danae* felt the Show'r of Gold ....Il.14.363.180.
The hissing Brands; thick streams the fiery Show'r; ....Il.16.151.243.
And on his Buckler caught the ringing Show'r. ....Il.16.431.259.
A Show'r of Blood o'er all the fatal Field. ....Il.16.562.266.
Wave their thick Falchions, and their Jav'lins show'r: ....Il.17.818.320.
These Words, attended with a Show'r of Tears, ...Il.21.109.426.
And bending o'er thee, mix'd the tender Show'r! ....Il.22.547.479.
A Show'r of Ashes o'er his Neck and Head. ....Il.24.202.545.
One universal, solemn Show'r began; ....Il.24.645.563.
A Show'r of Tears o'erflows her beauteous Eyes, ...Il.24.874.573.
When-e'er his influence *Jove* vouchsafes to show'r ....Od.4.285.132.
Nor wind sharp-piercing, nor the rushing show'r; ....Od.5.621.201.
The balmy oil, a fragrant show'r, he sheds, ...Od.6.269.223.
Again unmann'd a show'r of sorrow shed: ....Od.8.90.267.
Shed sweets shed unguents, in a show'r of oil: ....Od.8.492.289.
And *Jove* descends in each prolific show'r. ....Od.9.126.310.
Thick plumage, mingled with a sanguine show'r. ....Od.15.570.98.
The tears rain'd copious in a show'r of joy. ....Od.16.16.102.
Nor winter's boreal blast, nor thund'rous show'r, ...Od.19.513.221.
In solemn silence fell the kindly show'r. ....Od.21.237.271.
Before his feet the ratling show'r he threw, ...Od.22.5.286.
Again the foe discharge the steely show'r; ....Od.22.300.300.
O'er every limb a show'r of fragrance sheds: ....Od.23.151.328.
And roof'd defensive of the storm and show'r; ....Od.23.196.333.

SHOW'R'D
Darts show'r'd on Darts, now round the Carcase ring; ....Il.16.931.279.

SHOW'RING
He could no more; The show'ring Darts deny'd ....Il.5.770.303.
Long stands the show'ring Darts, and missile Fires; ....Il.11.678.65.
The show'ring Darts, and Numbers sunk to Hell. ....Il.16.941.280.
(Whose show'ring Arrows, as he cours'd below, ...Il.22.253.466.

SHOW'RS
All Nature mourns, the Skies relent in Show'rs, ...1.PSp.69.68.
A soft Retreat from sudden vernal Show'rs; ....1.PSp.98.70.
And from the *Pleiads* fruitful Show'rs descend. ....1.PSp.102.70.
Not Show'rs to Larks, or Sunshine to the Bee, ...1.PAu.45.83.
Not Show'rs to Larks, nor Sunshine to the Bee, ...1.PAu.45A.83.
Soft Show'rs distill'd, and Suns grew warm in vain; ....1.W-F.54.154.
Which the cold North congeals to haily Show'rs. ....1.TrSt.495.431.
Now Smoaks with Show'rs the misty Mountain-Ground, ...1.TrSt.498.431.
Presents flow'd in apace: With Show'rs of Gold, ...2.ChWB.64.59.
To steal from Rainbows ere they drop in Show'rs ....2.RL2.96.165.
Of show'rs and sun-shine, as of Man's desires; ....3.EOM1.152.34.
All-bounteous, fragrant grains, and golden show'rs, ...5.DunA2.4.97.
Here gay Description Ægypt glads with show'rs, ...5.DunB1.73.275.
All-bounteous, fragrant Grains and Golden show'rs, ...5.DunB2.4.296.
'Till show'rs of Sermons, Characters, Essays, ...5.DunB2.361.315.
So from one cloud soft show'rs we view, ...6.5.9.12.
And Show'rs of Wealth descending from the Skies. ....Il.2.814.163.
As from the Clouds' deep Bosom swell'd with Show'rs, ...Il.11.384.51.
While hissing Darts descend in Iron Show'rs: ....Il.11.697.66.
And half the Skies descend in sluicy Show'rs. ....Il.12.28.82.
Thro' the long Walls the stony Show'rs were heard, ...Il.12.203.88.
And now the Stones descend in heavier Show'rs. ....Il.12.330.93.
Soft Oils of Fragrance, and ambrosial Show'rs: ....Il.14.198.168.
And Earth is loaden with incessant Show'rs, ...Il.16.467.261.
And Earth is delug'd with the sanguine Show'rs. ....Il.20.576.418.
(Such as was that, when show'rs of jav'lins fled ....Od.5.397.191.
Beat by rude blasts, and wet with wintry show'rs, ...Od.6.154.216.
The Graces unguents shed, ambrosial show'rs, ...Od.8.400.285.
O'erspread the land, when spring descends in show'rs: ....Od.9.56.304.

SHOW'RS (CONTINUED)
Who swells the clouds, and gladdens earth with show'rs. ....Od.13.163.13.
With show'rs of stones he drives them far away; ....Od.14.39.37.
And *Jove* descends in deluges of show'rs. ....Od.14.513.62.
But when the storm was spent in plenteous show'rs, ...Od.19.286.209.

SHOW'RY
Like colour'd Rainbows o'er a show'ry Cloud: ....Il.11.36.36.
Commands the Goddess of the show'ry Bow. ....Il.15.179.203.
The various Goddess of the show'ry Bow, ...Il.18.205.331.

SHOWERS
In that soft Season when descending Showers ....2.TemF.1.253.
Here gay Description Ægypt glads with showers; ....5.DunA1.71.68.
Not Showers to Larks so pleasing, ...6.78i.5.215.

SHOWN
Reflect what Truth was in my Passion shown, ...2.ChJM.549.41.
By this no more was meant, than to have shown, ...2.ChJM.679.47.
And Dreams foretel, as Learned Men have shown: ....2.ChWB.303.71.
Or come discolour'd thro' our Passions shown. ....3.Ep1.26.17.
In publick Stations Men sometimes are shown, ...3.Ep2.199A.66.
But grant, in Public Men sometimes are shown, ...3.Ep2.199.66.
Thus others Talents having nicely shown, ...4.JD4.80.31.
Now shown by Cynthia's silver Ray, ...4.HOde1.47.153.
Yet think great Sir! (so many Virtues shown) ....4.2HE1.376.227.
Then sung, how shown him by the nutbrown maids, ...5.DunA2.313.140.
Then sung, how shown him by the Nut-brown maids ....5.DunB2.337.314.
Never by tumbler thro' the hoops was shown ....5.DunB4.257.369.
Or in fair series laurell'd Bards be shown, ...6.71.61.204.
And yet in this no Vanity is shown; ....6.105ii.3.300.
But sure in this no Vanity is shown; ....6.105ii.3A.300.
Never for this can just returns be shown; ....6.105v.3.302.
Me, when the Cares my better Years have shown ....6.117.7.333.
Alas! one bad Example shown, ...6.119.17.337.
And now, this great Example shown, ...6.119.17A.337.
Ah Madam! this Example shown, ...6.119.17B.337.
Alas! one ill Example shown, ...6.119.17C.337.
Such just Examples on Offenders shown, ...Il.2.338.143.
To whom the King. With Justice hast thou shown ....Il.9.147.439.
Think not to live, tho' all the Truth be shown: ....Il.10.517.26.
Proud of the Favours mighty *Jove* has shown, ...Il.12.75.84.
What Rivers can, *Scamander* might have shown; ....Il.21.209.430.
In ev'ry Face the self-same Grief is shown, ...Il.24.884.573.
Nor wonder I, at such profusion shown; ....Od.17.535.158.
Why such profusion of indulgence shown ....Od.20.451.255.
On ev'ry plant and tree thy cares are shown, ...Od.24.292.364.

SHOWR'D
Nectareous Drops, and rich Ambrosia showr'd ....Il.19.40.373.

SHOWR'S
The showr's descend, and lightnings fly. ....6.5.12A.12.
Dark Showr's of Javelins fly from Foes to Foes; ....Il.6.3.322.
Who wings the winds, and darkens heav'n with showr's) ....Od.13.30.2.

SHOWS
Shows most true Mettle when you *check* his Course. ....1.EOC.87.249.
That always shows *Great Pride*, or *Little Sense;* ....1.EOC.387.284.
A Mirrour shows the Figures moving by; ....2.ChJM.235.25.
Th' embroider'd *King* who shows but half his Face, ...2.RL3.76.173.
Shows in her Cheek the Roses of Eighteen, ...2.RL4.32.186.
Or, if she rules him, never shows she rules; ....3.Ep2.262.71.
"Then happy Man who shows the Tombs!" said I, ...4.JD4.102.33.
Meer *Houshold Trash!* of Birth-Nights, Balls and Shows, ...4.JD4.130.35.
Shows *Poland's* Int'rests, takes the *Primate's* ....4.JD4.154A.39.
Is she who shows what Ware she has to sell; ....4.HAdv.109.85.
(For none but Lady M[ohun] shows the Rest) ....4.HAdv.125.85.
Here to her Chosen all her works she shows; ....5.DunA1.227.90.
Nor let false Shows, or empty Titles please: ....6.19.47.63.
Where beauteous *Arenè* her Structures shows, ...Il.2.719.160.
Thy Force like Steel a temper'd Hardness shows, ...Il.3.89.194.
'Till black as Night the swelling Tempest shows, ...Il.4.318.235.
And cease the Strife when *Hector* shows the way. ....Il.7.348.381.
The red'ning Orient shows the coming Day, ...Il.10.296.15.
As the red Star now shows his sanguine Fires ....Il.11.83.38.
Exhorts his Armies, and the Trenches shows. ....Il.12.56.83.
No Force, no Firmness, the pale Coward shows; ....Il.13.359.123.
Good Heav'ns! what active Feats yon' Artist shows, ...Il.16.903.278.
This shows thee, friend, by old experience taught, ...Od.5.235.182.

SHREW
'Tis an ugly envious Shrew, ...6.70.10.201.

SHREWD
Shrewd words, which woud against him clear the doubt ....4.JD2A.107.142.
Or, in Quotation, shrewd Divines leave out ....4.JD2.103.143.

SHREWDLY
There goes a Saying, and 'twas shrewdly said, ...2.ChJM.101.19.

SHREWSBURY
The bow'r of wanton Shrewsbury and love; ....3.Ep3.308.119.
I study'd SHREWSBURY, the wise and great: ....4.EpS2.79.317.

SHRIEK
I shriek, start up, the same sad prospect find, ...2.ElAb.247.339.
That shriek incessant, while the Faulcon hung ....Il.17.847.321.
And the loud shriek redoubles from the main. ....Od.6.136.213.
They scream, they shriek; sad groans and dismal sounds ....Od.11.781.425.

SHRIEK'D
Nor *Grecian* virgins shriek'd his obsequies, ...Od.3.321.102.
And all the dire assembly shriek'd around. ....Od.11.54.383.

SHRIEKING
From gleaming Swords no shrieking Women run; ....4.HAdv.169.89.
The flouncing Steeds and shrieking Warriors drown'd. ....Il.21.13.421.
And shrieking loud denounce approaching fate. ....Od.2.178.70.

SHRIEKS
Not louder Shrieks to pitying Heav'n are cast, ...2.RL3.157.180.
Not louder Shrieks by Dames to Heav'n are cast, ...2.RL3.157A.180.
Shrieks of Woe, ...6.11.59.32.
With piercing Shrieks the Youth resigns his Breath, ...Il.4.577.249.
With tender Shrieks the Goddess fill'd the Place, ...Il.5.427.289.
And on his Knees with piercing Shrieks he fell; ....Il.20.482.414.
With piercing Shrieks his bitter Fate she moans, ...Il.22.514.477.
Whose Shrieks and Clamours fill the vaulted Dome; ....Il.24.204.545.
And swam the stream: Loud shrieks the virgin train, ...Od.6.135.213.
She cries, she shrieks: the fierce insulting foe ....Od.8.577.293.
Chiefs of renown! loud echoing shrieks arise; ....Od.12.296.446.
Now lost, now seen, with shrieks and dreadful cries; ....Od.12.494.456.
He shrieks, he reels, he falls, and breathless lies. ....Od.18.443.190.
Unmanly shrieks precede each dying groan, ...Od.22.345.304.

SHRIEVES
Now May'rs and Shrieves all hush'd and satiate lay, ...5.DunA1.89.70.
Now May'rs and Shrieves in pleasing slumbers lay, ...5.DunA1.89A.70.
Great in her charms! as when on Shrieves and May'rs ....5.DunA1.219.89.
Now May'rs and Shrieves all hush'd and satiate lay, ...5.DunB1.91.276.
Great in her charms! as when on Shrieves and May'rs ....5.DunB1.263.289.

SHRILL
Wind the shrill Horn, or spread the waving Net. ....1.W-F.96.159.
Where the shrill Cries of frantick Matrons sound, ...1.TrSt.464.429.
And the shrill Trumpets mix their Silver Sound; ....2.ChJM.319.29.
The shrill Ecchos rebound: ....6.11.9.30.
Now singing shrill, and scolding eft between, ...6.14ii.17.43.
By the shrill Clang and whistling Wings, they knew. ....Il.10.324.17.
So swift thro' Æther the shrill *Harpye* springs, ...Il.19.372.387.
Where the shrill Brass return'd a sharper Sound: ....Il.20.324.407.
She ceas'd; shrill ecstasies of joy declare ....Od.4.1013.165.
Twang'd short and sharp, like the shrill swallow's cry. ....Od.21.449.282.

SHRILLER
The short thick Sob, loud Scream, and shriller Squawl: ....6.14ii.6.43.

SHRILLEST
Sharp was his Voice; which in the shrillest Tone, ...Il.2.273.140.

SHRILLING
Join to the yelping Treble shrilling Cries; ....6.14ii.22.43.
And her full Pipes those shrilling Cries confound: ....6.14ii.24.43.
And shrilling Shouts and dying Groans arise; ....Il.4.513.246.
As thro' the shrilling Vale, or Mountain Ground, ...Il.16.767.273.
With shrilling Clangor sounds th' Alarm of War; ....Il.18.260.335.
With open Beak and shrilling Cries he springs, ...Il.22.187.463.
The shrilling airs the vaulted roof rebounds, ...Od.1.425.53.
Maids, wives, and matrons, mix a shrilling sound. ....Od.3.573.115.
Wak'd by the shrilling sound, *Ulysses* rose, ...Od.6.137.213.

SHRIN'D
Believe a Goddess shrin'd in ev'ry tree. ....1.TrFD.87.389.
Booth in his cloudy tabernacle shrin'd, ...5.DunA3.263.179.
Booth in his cloudy tabernacle shrin'd, ...5.DunB3.267.333.

SHRINE
And with fresh Bays her Rural Shrine adorn. ....1.PWi.20.90.
On *Phœbus* Shrine my Harp I'll then bestow, ...1.TrSP.212.403.
But view'd the Shrine with a superior Look, ...1.TrSt.755.441.
Honour forbid! at whose unrival'd Shrine ....2.RL4.105.192.
Around the Shrine it self of *Fame* they stand, ...2.TemF.180.270.
On which a Shrine of purest Gold was rear'd; ....2.TemF.197.271.
Here in a Shrine that cast a dazling Light, ...2.TemF.232.274.
(Her Virgin Handmaids) still attend the Shrine: ....2.TemF.271.276.
Millions of suppliant Crowds the Shrine attend, ...2.TemF.288.277.
First at the Shrine the Learned World appear, ...2.TemF.298.278.
Around the Shrine, and made the same Request: ....2.TemF.395.282.
From yonder shrine I heard a hollow sound. ....2.ElAb.308.344.
The shrine with gore unstain'd, with gold undrest, ...3.EOM3.157.109.
J[efferie]s, who bows at Hi[ll]sb[orough]'s hoary Shrine ....4.HAdv.46.79.
Oh All-accomplish'd St. JOHN! deck thy Shrine? ....4.EpS2.139.321.
Touch'd with the Flame that breaks from Virtue's Shrine, ...4.EpS2.233.326.
But chief her shrine where naked Venus keeps, ...5.DunB4.307.374.
I bought them, shrouded in that living shrine, ...5.DunB4.385.380.
Thy reliques, *Rowe*, to this fair shrine we trust, ...6.72.1B.208.
To this sad Shrine, who'er thou art, draw near, ...6.85.1.242.
Thy Reliques, *Rowe!* to this sad Shrine we trust, ...6.152.1.400.
One *Greek* enrich'd thy Shrine with offer'd Gore; ....Il.15.429.214.
That, with his Arms, shall hang before thy Shrine, ...Il.18.393.340.
At *Neptunes* Shrine on *Helice's* high Shores ....Il.20.468.414.
To grace thy *Manes*, and adorn thy Shrine. ....Il.24.745.568.
(The Priest of *Phœbus* at th' *Ismarian* shrine) ....Od.9.231.316.
Lo! gifts of labour'd gold adorn thy shrine, ...Od.16.202.113.
By the sure precept of the sylvan shrine, ...Od.19.341.210.
Whose shrine with weanling lambs he wont to load.) ....Od.19.469.219.

SHRINES
Shrines! where their vigils pale-ey'd virgins keep, ...2.ElAb.21.320.
The shrines all trembled, and the lamps grew pale: ....2.ElAb.112.329.
Our shrines irradiate, or emblaze the floors; ....2.ElAb.136.331.
Still on our Shrines his grateful Off'rings lay, ...Il.24.89.539.
To *Phœbus* shrines shall rise, and altars burn. ....Od.12.412.451.

SHRINK
Shrink his thin Essence like a rivell'd Flower. ....2.RL2.132.168.
What happier natures shrink at with affright, ...3.EOM2.229.83.
Shrink back to my Paternal Cell, ...4.1HE7.76.273.
Shrink, and confess the Genius of the place: ....5.DunB4.146.355.
And all her Triumphs shrink into a Coin: ....6.71.24.203.

SHRINK (CONTINUED)
Back shrink the *Myrmidons* with dread Surprize, ...Il.19.17.372.

SHRINKS
Shrinks to her hidden cause, and is no more: ....5.DunA3.350.193.
Shrinks to her second cause, and is no more. ....5.DunB4.644.408.
Then shrinks to Earth again. ....6.53.8.161.
Neptune shrinks! ....6.96i.44.269.
The wary *Trojan* shrinks, and bending low ....Il.7.303.379.
But shrinks and shudders, when the Thunder flies. ....Il.20.422.412.

SHRIVEL'D
Can these lean shrivel'd limbs unnerv'd with age, ...Od.19.88.196.

SHROUD
Howl o'er the Masts, and sing thro' ev'ry Shroud: ....Il.15.755.225.
"Shall want in death a shroud to grace his shade." ....Od.2.114.67.
Howls o'er the shroud, and rends it from the mast: ....Od.12.480.455.
Haste, rear the mast, the swelling shroud display; ....Od.16.364.124.
Me with his whelming wave let Ocean shroud! ....Od.20.77.236.

SHROUDED
I bought them, shrouded in that living shrine, ...5.DunB4.385.380.

SHROUDS
Once more invades the guilty Dome, and shrouds ....1.TrSt.171.417.
But with a thicker Night black *Auster* shrouds ....1.TrSt.492.430.
Soft o'er the Shrouds Aerial Whispers breathe, ...2.RL2.57.163.
The Thund'rer sate, where old *Olympus* shrouds ....Il.1.648.118.
The Queen of Love her favour'd Champion shrouds ....Il.3.467.214.
Then *Actor's* Sons had dy'd, but *Neptune* shrouds ....Il.11.884.75.
Mars hov'ring o'er his *Troy*, his Terror shrouds ....Il.20.69.396.
But present to his Aid, *Apollo* shrouds ....Il.20.513.416.
(These with a gather'd Mist *Saturnia* shrouds, ...Il.21.7.421.
But jealous of his Fame, *Apollo* shrouds ....Il.21.705.450.
And all the rattling shrouds in fragments torn. ....Od.9.80.306.
Sing thro' the shrouds, and stretch the swelling sails. ....Od.11.794.426.
High in the air the rock its summit shrouds, ...Od.12.87.436.
Now flames the rosy dawn, but *Pallas* shrouds ....Od.23.398.343.

SHROWD
Irresolute of soul, his state to shrowd ....Od.19.343.211.

SHROWDED
His face he shrowded with his purple vest: ....Od.4.152.127.

SHROWDS
'Till coasting nigh the Cape, where *Malea* shrowds ....Od.4.685.151.

SHRUBS
To leaf-less Shrubs the flow'ring Palms succeed, ...1.Mes.75.119.
For Shrubs, when nothing else at top is, ...6.67.9.195.
And root the Shrubs, and lay the Forest bare; ....Il.12.166.87.
And sprinkling all the Shrubs with Drops of Blood; ....Il.13.268.117.
And sprinkling all the Shrubs with dropping Blood; ....Il.13.268A.117.
And runs on crackling Shrubs between the Hills; ....Il.20.570.418.
Jumping high o'er the Shrubs of the rough Ground, ...Il.23.142.495.

SHRUNK
Now to thy gentle shadow all are shrunk, ...5.DunB4.509.392.
Now, to thy shade from all their glory shrunk; 5.DunB4.509A.392
And the huge Boar is shrunk into an Urn: ....5.DunB4.552.396.
Now nothing's left, but wither'd, pale, and shrunk, ...6.49i.25.138.
More, shrunk to *Smith—and* Smith's no name at all. ....6.116iv.4.327.
Trembling he sate, and shrunk in abject Fears, ...Il.2.330.143.
Shrunk up he sate, with wild and haggard Eye, ...Il.16.488.262.
Shrunk with dry Famine, and with Toils declin'd, ...Il.19.165.378.
And the shrunk Waters in their Chanel boil: ....Il.21.401.436.
Spent with fatigue, and shrunk with pining fast, ...Od.7.295.250.
The skin shrunk up, and wither'd at her hand: ....Od.13.497.29.
His sinews shrunk with age, and stiff with toil, ...Od.19.366.212.

SHUDD'RING
O'er ev'ry vein a shudd'ring horror runs; ....5.DunB4.143.355.
Each shudd'ring owns the Genius of the Schools; 5.DunB4.146A.355

SHUDDERS
But shrinks and shudders, when the Thunder flies. ....Il.20.422.412.

SHUN
I shun the Fountains which I sought before. ....1.PSu.30.74.
I'll shun the Fountains which I sought before. ....1.PSu.30A.74.
But see, the Shepherds shun the Noon-day Heat, ...1.PSu.85.79.
The thirsty Heifers shun the gliding Flood. ....1.PWi.38.91.
Thin Trees arise that shun each others Shades. ....1.W-F.22.150.
Avoid *Extreams;* and shun the Fault of such, ...1.EOC.384.284.
'Tis what the *Vicious fear,* the *Virtuous shun;* ....1.EOC.506.295.
Yet shun their Fault, who, *Scandalously nice,* ....1.EOC.556.304.
To shun their poison, and to chuse their food? ....3.EOM3.100.101.
This bids to serve, and that to shun mankind; ....3.EOM4.20.129.
Who most to shun or hate Mankind pretend, ...3.EOM4.43.132.
Pride guides his steps, and bids him shun the great: ....3.Ep1.66.20.
And most contemptible, to shun contempt; ....3.Ep1.195.31.
(For what to shun will no great knowledge need, ...3.Ep3.201.110.
This, or that Person, what avails to shun? ....4.HAdv.77.81.
I shun his Zenith, court his mild Decline; ....4.EpS2.76.317.
This, teach me more than Hell to shun, ...6.50.15.146.
That let me shun ev'n more than Hell ....6.50.15A.146.
—What, touch me not? what, shun a Wife's Embrace? ....6.96iv.2.276.
And thou, from Camps remote, the Danger shun, ...Il.1.548.114.
And shun the Vengeance of th' *Herculean* Race, ...Il.2.804.163.
In yonder Walls that Object let me shun, ...Il.3.382.211.
These see thou shun, thro' all th' embattled Plain, ...Il.5.166.275.
Me dost thou bid to shun the coming Fight, ...Il.5.310.281.
And tempt a Fate which Prudence bids thee shun? ....Il.7.128.369.
And shun Contention, the sure Source of Woe; ....Il.9.335.450.

SHUN (CONTINUED)

No martial Toil I shun, no Danger fear; ....Il.11.411.53.
Than perish in the Danger we may shun. ....Il.14.87.162.
Might only we the vast Destruction shun, ...Il.16.126.242.
I shun great *Ajax?* I desert my Train? ....Il.17.193.294.
And warn'd to shun *Hectorean* Force in vain! ....Il.18.18.324.
The Stroke of Fate the bravest cannot shun: ....Il.18.147.329.
While yet we talk, or but an instant shun. ....Il.19.147.377.
But *Phœbus* warns him from high Heav'n, to shun ......Il.20.431.412.
Vain hope! to shun him by the self-same Road ....Il.21.653.449.
Yet shun *Achilles!* enter yet the Wall, ...Il.22.76.455.
And urge to meet the Fate he cannot shun. ....Il.22.288.468.
Here, where but one could pass, to shun the Throng ....Il.23.501.510.
Ah! may my Sorrows ever shun the Light! ....Il.24.120.540.
Take Gifts in secret, that must shun the Light? ....Il.24.532.558.
Farewell: To shun *Achilles'* Sight I fly; ....Il.24.567.560.
And in *Eubea* shun the woes we fear. ....Od.3.212.96.
Hard toil! the prophet's piercing eye to shun; ....Od.4.596.148.
The care to shun the blast of sland'rous tongues; ....Od.6.328.227.
To shun th' encounter of the vulgar crowd, ...Od.7.21.235.
Nor shun the blessing proffer'd to thy arms, ...Od.10.353.361.
Seek ye to meet those evils ye shou'd shun? ....Od.10.510.368.
Ah shun the horrid gulph! by *Scylla* fly, ...Od.12.137.438.
Warn'd by their awful voice these shores to shun, ...Od.12.322.447.
Constrain'd I act what wisdom bids me shun. ....Od.12.354.448.
And turning sudden, shun the death design'd. ....Od.15.321.85.
To shun the hidden snares of death, and live. ....Od.16.385.124.
Or shun in some black forge the midnight air. ....Od.18.378.186.
Where shall *Ulysses* shun, or how sustain, ...Od.20.53.234.
I share the doom ye Suitors cannot shun. ....Od.20.444.254.
With conscious dread they shun the quiv'ring net: ......Od.22.340.304.
The lot, which all lament, and none can shun! ....Od.24.42.350.

SHUN'D

With flying Coursers shun'd his dreadful Ire: ....Il.8.310.412.
He saw, and shun'd the Death; the forceful Dart ....Il.13.247.117.
The *Cretan* saw, and shun'd the brazen Spear. ....Il.13.637.136.
Shun'd the descending Death; which hissing on, ...Il.17.352.301.
Stooping, he shun'd; the Jav'lin idly fled, ...Il.17.596.311.
But *Hector* shun'd the meditated Blow: ....Il.22.350.470.

SHUNN'D

Not that he shunn'd the doubtful Strife, ...6.79.127.222.
Brave as he was, and shunn'd unequal Force. ....Il.5.702.301.
The Foe reclining, shunn'd the flying Death, ...Il.14.539.189.
But *Ajax* shunn'd the meditated Blow. ....Il.15.499.216.
Patroclus mark'd him as he shunn'd the War, ...Il.16.490.262.

SHUNNING

That shunning Faults, one quiet *Tenour* keep; ....1.EOC.241.267.
Here shunning idleness at once and praise, ...6.126ii.1.353.
So spoke the wretch; but shunning farther fray, ...Od.17.304.146.

SHUNS

Shuns the permitted, the forbid pursues! ....4.HAdv.101.83.
Our author shuns by vulgar springs to move, ...6.32.9.96.
And shuns the Fate he well deserv'd to find. ....Il.3.46.190.
Achilles shuns the Fight; yet some there are ....Il.7.275.378.
Ajax he shuns, thro' all the dire Debate, ...Il.11.666.63.
Nor shuns the Foe, nor turns the Steeds away, ...Il.13.503.130.
His Fate, he stands; nor shuns the Lance of *Crete*. ....Il.13.548.132.
The Boaster flies, and shuns superior Force. ....Il.14.572.190.
The *Dardan* Hero shuns his Foe no more. ....Il.22.314.469.
Not only flies the guilt, but shuns th' offence: ....Od.6.342.228.
Shuns the dire rocks: In vain she cuts the skies, ...Od.12.77.435.
And shuns (who wou'd not?) wicked men in power; ....Od.17.661.164.

SHUT

And see thro' all things with his half-shut Eyes) ....2.RL3.118.176.
Himself shut out, and *Jacob Hall* let in. ....4.HAdv.86.83.
Shut, shut the door, good *John!* fatigu'd I said, ...4.Arbu.1.96.
Shut, shut the door, good *John!* fatigu'd I said, ...4.Arbu.1.96.
The shops shut up in every street, ...4.1HE7.8.269.
and shut out Miles Davies. ....6.68.16.197.
"The Casement it is shut likewise; ....6.79.79.220.
The wide Horizon shut him from their View. ....Il.13.96.109.
Self-clos'd behind her shut the Valves of Gold. ....Il.14.196.168.
Lock fast the brazen Bars, and shut out Death. ....Il.21.626.448.
Safe from Pursuit, and shut from mortal View, ...Il.21.707.451.
Shut from our Walls! I fear, I fear him slain! ....Il.22.587.480.
Shut from the walks of men, to pleasure lost, ...Od.16.156.110.
(The half-shut door conceal'd his lurking foes) ....Od.22.196.296.

SHUTS

Steals my senses, shuts my sight, ...6.31ii.10.94.
And shuts the *Grecians* in their wooden Walls: ....Il.18.344.338.
Pale *Troy* against *Achilles* shuts her Gate; ....Il.21.723.451.
And shuts again; with equal ease dispos'd, ...Od.9.372.321.

SHUTTLE

Forth from her Iv'ry Hand the Shuttle falls, ...Il.22.576.480.
And thro' the loom the golden shuttle guides. ....Od.5.79.176.
The flying shuttle thro' the threads to guide: ....Od.7.139.242.

SHUTZ

See S*Z.
Alas, like Shutz I cannot pun ....6.61.22.181.

SHYLOCK

And ev'ry child hates Shylock, tho' his soul ....3.Ep1.114.23.
Of wretched Shylock, spite of Shylock's Wife: ....3.Ep3.96.97.
Why Shylock wants a meal, the cause is found, ...3.Ep3.117.101.
Plums, and Directors, *Shylock* and his Wife, ...4.HS1.103.15.

SHYLOCK'S

Of wretched Shylock, spite of Shylock's Wife: ....3.Ep3.96.97.
What brought Sir *Shylock's* ill got wealth to waste? ...3.Ep4.15A.137.

SI

'Twas *Si Signior*, 'twas *Yaw Mynheer*, ...6.14v(b).11.49.
'Twas *Si Signior*, & *Yaw Mynheer*, ...6.14v(b).11A.49.

SIBYL

A slip-shod Sibyl led his steps along, ...5.DunB3.15.320.

SIBYL'S

A leaf, like Sibyl's, scatter to and fro ....3.Ep3.75.93.

SICANIA

Some adverse *Dæmon* from *Sicania* bore ....Od.24.357.366.

SICILIA'S

And you that rule *Sicilia's* happy Plains, ...1.TrSP.69.396.

SICILIAN

While on thy Banks *Sicilian* Muses sing; ....1.PSp.4.60.
But ah beware, *Sicilian* Nymphs! nor boast ....1.TrSP.65.396.
Unmix'd, to his *Sicilian* River glides. ....1.TrSt.385.426.
To some *Sicilian* mart these courtiers send, ...Od.20.456.255.
And one *Sicilian* matron, old and sage, ...Od.24.242.360.
The hoary King his old *Sicilian* maid ....Od.24.425.369.
Call'd by the careful old *Sicilian* dame, ...Od.24.449.370.

SICILIANS

The fair *Sicilians* now thy Soul inflame; ....1.TrSP.63.396.

SICK

The Sick and Weak the healing Plant shall aid; ....1.Mes.15.114.
Receiv'd th'Impressions of the Love-sick Squire, ...2.ChJM.432.35.
She took th'Impressions of the Love-sick Squire, ...2.ChJM.432A.35.
Freakish when well, and fretful when she's Sick. ....2.ChWB.91.61.
The Courtier's Promises, and Sick Man's Pray'rs, ...2.RL5.119.209.
Perhaps was sick, in love, or had not din'd. ....3.Ep1.80.21.
Sick of herself thro' very selfishness! ....3.Ep2.146.62.
Health to the sick, and solace to the swain. ....3.Ep3.258.114.
Is any sick? the MAN of Ross relieves, ...3.Ep3.269.115.
Sick of his civil Pride from Morn to Eve; ....3.Ep4.166.153.
As one of *Woodward's* Patients, sick and sore, ...4.JD4.152.37.
Tye up the knocker, say I'm sick, I'm dead, ...4.Arbu.2.96.
But sick of Fops, and Poetry, and Prate, ...4.Arbu.229.112.
Possest with Muse, and sick with Poetry; ....4.JD2A.70.138.
When, sick of Muse, our follies we deplore, ...4.2HE1.177.209.
You humour me when I am sick, ...4.1HE7.5.269.
Now sick alike of Envy and of Praise. ....4.1HE1.4.279.
Grow sick, and damn the Climate—like a Lord. ....4.1HE1.160.291.
At some sick miser's triple-bolted gate, ...5.DunA2.238.129.
At some sick miser's triple-bolted gate, ...5.DunB2.248.307.
Sick was the Sun, the Owl forsook his bow'r, ...5.DunB4.11.340.
My swimming Eyes are sick of Light, ...6.31ii.6Z1.94.
Sick of herself thro' very Selfishness. ....6.154.32.403.

SICK'NING

The Day beheld, and sick'ning at the Sight, ...1.TrSt.136.415.
'Till drooping, sick'ning, dying, they began ....3.EOM3.223.115.
The sick'ning Stars fade off th' æthereal plain; ....5.DunA3.342.192.
The sick'ning stars fade off th'ethereal plain; ....5.DunB4.636.407.
With nectar'd drops the sick'ning sense restor'd. ....Od.4.600.148.
Then pale with fears, and sick'ning at the sight, ...Od.18.86.170.

SICKEN

All pleasures sicken, and all glories sink; ....3.EOM4.46.132.
Envy shall sicken at thy vast reward. ....Od.19.357.211.

SICKEN'D

When Nature sicken'd, and each gale was death? ....3.EOM4.108.138.
Beheld the War, and sicken'd at the Sight; ....Il.6.469.350.

SICKENING

Let Flatt'ry sickening see the Incense rise, ...4.EpS2.244.326.

SICKENS

My bleeding bosom sickens at the sound, ...Od.1.439.53.
She sickens, trembles, falls, and faints away: ....Od.23.212.333.

SICKLES

With bended Sickles stand the Reaper-Train: ....Il.18.638.354.

SICKLY

And raging *Sirius* blasts the sickly Year, ...1.TrSt.748.441.
There *Affectation* with a sickly Mien ....2.RL4.31.186.
With each a sickly brother at his back: ....5.DunB2.306.310.
Not such the sickly beams, which unsincere, ...Od.19.40.194.

SICKNESS

And much his Sickness griev'd his worthy Lord, ...2.ChJM.407.34.
Wrapt in a Gown, for Sickness, and for Show. ....2.RL4.36.186.
Of Peace and War, Health, Sickness, Death, and Life; ....2.TemF.449.285.
And more, the Sickness of long Life, Old-age: ....4.HS2.88.61.
His Life, tho' Long, to sickness past unknown, ...4.Arbu.402.126.
Sickness, its courtship, makes the fair ....6.4iii.5.10.
And by this sickness chuse to tell ....6.4iii.13.10.
Those, Age or Sickness, soon or late, disarms; ....6.19.60.63.
In Wants, in Sickness, shall a *Friend* be nigh, ...6.117.11.333.
Nor sink by sickness to the shades below; ....Od.15.447.92.

SIDE

The Dawn now blushing on the Mountain's Side, ...1.PSp.21.62.
And while *Aurora* gilds the Mountain's Side, ...1.PSp.17z5.62.
In crowding Ranks on ev'ry Side arise, ...1.Mes.89.121.
Than the fair Nymphs that grace thy side below; ....1.W-F.232B.170.

SIDE (CONTINUED)

Behold! th'ascending *Villa's* on my Side ... 1.W-F.375.187.
And Feather'd People crowd my wealthy Side, ... 1.W-F.404.191.
And fain *wou'd* be upon the *Laughing Side:* ... 1.EOC.33.243.
'Twixt Sense and Nonsense daily change their Side. ... 1.EOC.435.288.
Some valuing those of their own *Side,* or *Mind,* ... 1.EOC.452.290.
And *Love to Praise,* with *Reason* on his Side? ... 1.EOC.642.311.
Her private Orchards wall'd on ev'ry side, ... 1.TrVP.19.377.
But lo! I saw, (as near her side I stood) ... 1.TrFD.27.387.
Thus on each side, alas! our tott'ring State ... 1.TrSt.269.421.
Thus strove the Chief on ev'ry side distress'd, ... 1.TrSt.526.432.
On this side *Lerna's* pois'nous Water lies, ... 1.TrSt.533.432.
But *Phœbus* lov'd, and on the Flow'ry Side ... 1.TrSt.676.438.
Two bleeding Babes depending at her Side; ... 1.TrSt.720.440.
From side to side the trembling Balance nods, ... 1.TrES.168.455.
From side to side the trembling Balance nods, ... 1.TrES.168.455.
Two Marble Doors unfold on either side; ... 1.TrUl.42.467.
The knotty Point was urg'd on either Side; ... 2.ChJM.140.21.
The knotty Point was urg'd on ev'ry Side; ... 2.ChJM.140A.21.
The Guests appear in Order, Side by Side, ... 2.ChJM.316.29.
The Guests appear in Order, Side by Side, ... 2.ChJM.316.29.
The joyful Knight survey'd her by his Side, ... 2.ChJM.347.31.
The good old Knight mov'd slowly by her Side. ... 2.ChJM.403.34.
His Wife, not suffer'd from his Side to stray, ... 2.ChJM.487.39.
From thy dear Side I have no Pow'r to part, ... 2.ChJM.571.42.
The Fairies sported on the Garden's Side, ... 2.ChJM.618.45.
What Pangs, what sudden Shoots distend my Side? ... 2.ChJM.721.49.
By pressing Youth attack'd on ev'ry side. ... 2.ChWB.93.61.
If once my Husband's Arm was o'er my Side, ... 2.ChWB.166.64.
I groan'd, and lay extended on my Side; ... 2.ChWB.419.77.
Th'inferior Priestess, at her Altar's side, ... 2.RL1.127.155.
Pain at her Side, and *Megrim* at her Head. ... 2.RL4.24.185.
Pain at her Side, and *Languor* at her Head. ... 2.RL4.24A.185.
Unnumber'd Throngs on ev'ry side are seen ... 2.RL4.47.187.
Why bows the Side-box from its inmost Rows? ... 2.RL5.14.200.
All side in Parties, and begin th' Attack; ... 2.RL5.39.202.
The doubtful Beam long nods from side to side; ... 2.RL5.73.206.
The doubtful Beam long nods from side to side; ... 2.RL5.73.206.
And drew a deadly *Bodkin* from her Side. ... 2.RL5.88.207.
Of *Gothic* Structure was the Northern Side, ... 2.TemF.119.263.
With too much knowledge for the Sceptic side, ... 3.EOM2.5.53.
All, all alike, find Reason on their side. ... 3.EOM2.174.75.
And all alike, find Reason on their side. ... 3.EOM2.174A.75.
There, *Pastorella* by a fountain side: ... 3.Ep2.8A.49.
Is there, Pastora by a fountain side: ... 3.Ep2.8.49.
Stocks and Subscriptions pour on ev'ry side, ... 3.Ep3.370.123.
On ev'ry side you look, behold the Wall! ... 3.Ep4.114.148.
And neither leans on this side, nor on that: ... 4.HS2.62.59.
And neither leans on this side, or on that: ... 4.HS2.62A.59.
A heavy Chest, thick Neck, or heaving Side. ... 4.HAdv.117.85.
With Handkerchief and Orange at my side: ... 4.Arbu.228.112.
And sets the Passions on the side of Truth; ... 4.2HE1.218.213.
Most warp'd to Flatt'ry's side; but some, more nice, ... 4.2HE1.259.217.
Let me but live on this side *Trent:* ... 4.HS6.30.251.
Could I but live on this side *Trent:* ... 4.HS6.30A.251.
Good M[arch]m[on]t's fate tore P[olwar]th from thy side, ... 4.1740.79.336.
There Caxton slept, with Wynkin at his side, ... 5.DunA1.129.79.
And now to this side, now to that, they nod, ... 5.DunA2.363.144.
There Caxton slept, with Wynkyn at his side, ... 5.DunB1.149.281.
And now to this side, now to that they nod, ... 5.DunB2.395.316.
There march'd the bard and blockhead, side by side, ... 5.DunB4.101.351.
There march'd the bard and blockhead, side by side, ... 5.DunB4.101.351.
Thro' both he pass'd, and bow'd from side to side: ... 5.DunB4.108.352.
Thro' both he pass'd, and bow'd from side to side: ... 5.DunB4.108.352.
Some Slave of mine be pinion'd to their side." ... 5.DunB4.134.354.
In flow'rs, the honours of thy side. ... 6.6ii.20.15.
A *Bubble-boy* and *Tompion* at her Side, ... 6.9vii.2.22.
Ne Village is without, on either side, ... 6.14ii.51.44.
Seiz'd with dumb joy—then falling by his side, ... 6.15.17.52.
Thousands on ev'ry side shall yield their breath; ... 6.21.17.69.
Fix'd to one side, but mod'rate to the rest; ... 6.27.4.81.
Now *Europe's* balanc'd, neither Side prevails, ... 6.28.1.82.
Now *Europe's* balanc'd, and no Side prevails, ... 6.28.1A.82.
Here grapes discolour'd on the sunny side, ... 6.35.24.103.
Fix'd to one side, but mod'rate to the rest; ... 6.57.4.169.
And Curio, restless by the Fair-one's side, ... 6.71.43.204.
May wear a Pick-lock at his Side; ... 6.135.34.367.
Iülus' Side, as erst *Evander's,* ... 6.135.73.369.
The starry Faulchion glitter'd at his side; ... Il.2.56.129.
In Tribes and Nations rank'd on either side. ... Il.2.523.151.
The Legions crowd *Scamander's* flow'ry Side, ... Il.2.547.153.
Close, on the left, the bold *Bæotians* side. ... Il.2.629.157.
The Warrior's Toils, and combate by his side. ... Il.2.997.170.
He spoke: in still Suspense on either side ... Il.3.133.196.
On either side the meeting Hosts are seen, ... Il.3.159.198.
The King the first; *Thymætes* at his side; ... Il.3.193.200.
Approach my Child, and grace thy Father's Side. ... Il.3.212.202.
He mounts the Seat, *Antenor* at his side; ... Il.3.332.209.
On either side a sacred Herald stands, ... Il.3.338.209.
And drove to *Troy, Antenor* at his Side. ... Il.3.389.211.
Sustain'd the Sword that glitter'd at his side. ... Il.3.416.212.
Sustains the Sword that glitters at his side ... Il.3.416A.212.
A Hand-maid Goddess at his Side to wait, ... Il.3.503.215.
The fiery Coursers snorted at his side. ... Il.4.263.233.
Fix'd to thy Side, in ev'ry Toil I share, ... Il.4.304.235.
(The warlike *Sthenelus* attends his side) ... Il.4.420.240.
The Sons subdu'd, for Heav'n was on their side. ... Il.4.463.242.
To seek her Parents on his flow'ry Side, ... Il.4.547.247.
Astynous breathless fell, and by his side ... Il.5.184.275.
Glitt'ring in Arms, and combate Side by Side. ... Il.5.205.276.
Glitt'ring in Arms, and combate Side by Side. ... Il.5.205.276.
On Valor's side the Odds of Combate lie, ... Il.5.655.299.
Oresbius last fell groaning at their side: ... Il.5.869.308.
The sounding Hinges ring: On either side ... Il.5.934.311.
And ev'ry side of wav'ring Combate tries; ... Il.5.1025.315.
On either side run purple to the Main. ... Il.6.6.322.

SIDE (CONTINUED)

Breathless the good Man fell, and by his side ... Il.6.23.325.
And conquer'd still, for Heav'n was on his side. ... Il.6.230.337.
My self will arm, and thunder at thy side. ... Il.8.456.418.
And fix'd their Headstalls to his Chariot-side. ... Il.8.676.427.
Never, ah never let me leave thy side! ... Il.9.572.462.
His Armour buckling at his Vessel's side. ... Il.10.40.4.
Watch ev'ry Side, and turn to ev'ry Sound. ... Il.10.218.11.
With each a sable Lambkin by her side; ... Il.10.256.13.
(On *Rhesus'* side accustom'd to attend, ... Il.10.608.29.
Sustain'd the Sword that glitter'd at his side: ... Il.11.40.36.
And falling Ranks are strow'd on ev'ry side. ... Il.11.94.38.
Mean-while on ev'ry side, around the Plain, ... Il.11.225.45.
No more the Youth shall join his Consort's side, ... Il.11.313.49.
Opites next was added to their side, ... Il.11.390.52.
Haste, let us join, and combat side by side. ... Il.11.409.53.
Haste, let us join, and combat side by side. ... Il.11.409.53.
And the red Slaughter spreads on ev'ry side. ... Il.11.530.57.
Plow'd half his side, and bar'd it to the Bone. ... Il.11.548.58.
Who shares his Labours, and defends his side. ... Il.11.583.60.
Down his cleft Side while fresh the Blood distills, ... Il.11.596.60.
Still at my Heart, and ever at my Side! ... Il.11.743.68.
On ev'ry side the crackling Trees they tear, ... Il.12.165.87.
So from each side increas'd the stony Rain, ... Il.12.343.94.
From side to side the trembling Balance nods, ... Il.12.522.101.
From side to side the trembling Balance nods, ... Il.12.522.101.
On ev'ry side the dusty Whirlwinds rise, ... Il.13.426.126.
And glitter'd, extant at the farther side. ... Il.13.492.130.
On ev'ry side the steely Circle grows; ... Il.13.629.136.
While Death's strong Pangs distend his lab'ring Side, ... Il.13.722.139.
A Slings soft Wool, snatch'd from a Soldier's side, ... Il.13.751.140.
Now side by side, with like unweary'd Care, ... Il.13.877.147.
Now side by side, with like unweary'd Care, ... Il.13.877.147.
Far-echoing Clamours bound from side to side; ... Il.13.1042.154.
Far-echoing Clamours bound from side to side; ... Il.13.1042.154.
When now they touch'd the Mead's enamel'd Side, ... Il.14.507.188.
As by his side the groaning Warrior fell, ... Il.14.537.189.
Legions on Legions from each side arise; ... Il.15.446.214.
In Peace, in War, for ever at his side, ... Il.15.504.216.
Then mutual Slaughters spread on either side; ... Il.15.610.220.
And stood by *Meges'* side, a sudden Aid, ... Il.15.637.221.
On Valour's side the odds of Combate lie, ... Il.15.670.221.
And rends his side, fresh-bleeding with the Dart ... Il.15.698.222.
The godlike Hero stalks from side to side. ... Il.15.821.228.
The godlike Hero stalks from side to side. ... Il.15.821.228.
Safe in his Art, as side by side they run, ... Il.15.826.228.
Safe in his Art, as side by side they run, ... Il.15.826.228.
Swift *Pedasus* was added to their side, ... Il.16.186.245.
While crackling Forests fall on ev'ry side. ... Il.16.770.273.
On ev'ry side the busy Combate grows; ... Il.16.776.273.
Fast by his Side, the gen'rous *Spartan* glows ... Il.17.151.293.
The boiling Ocean works from Side to Side, ... Il.17.313.299.
The boiling Ocean works from Side to Side, ... Il.17.313.299.
Strain'd with full Force, and tugg'd from Side to Side, ... Il.17.451.304.
Strain'd with full Force, and tugg'd from Side to Side, ... Il.17.451.304.
And call'd *Æneas* fighting near his Side. ... Il.17.551.309.
Sudden at *Hector's* Side *Apollo* stood, ... Il.17.654.313.
And Conquest shifting to the *Trojan* Side, ... Il.17.706.315.
Nor fear we Armies, fighting Side by Side; ... Il.17.805.320.
Nor fear we Armies, fighting Side by Side; ... Il.17.805.320.
Our Swords kept time, and conquer'd side by side. ... Il.18.402.340.
Our Swords kept time, and conquer'd side by side. ... Il.18.402.340.
And turn their crooked Yokes on ev'ry side. ... Il.18.630.354.
The Leaders press'd the Chief on ev'ry side; ... Il.19.323.386.
That, starr'd with Gems, hung glitt'ring at his side; ... Il.19.401.388.
(The silver Traces sweeping at their side) ... Il.19.428.389.
(Her golden Arrows sounding at her side) ... Il.20.97.398.
First rose *Laomedon* from *Ilus'* Side; ... Il.20.283.406.
Wounded, we wound; and neither side can fail, ... Il.20.298.406.
The ruthless Falchion op'd his tender Side; ... Il.20.544.417.
Then from his side the Sword *Pelides* drew, ... Il.21.189.429.
Now here, now there, he turns on ev'ry side, ... Il.21.285.432.
Lo, what an Aid on *Mars's* Side is seen! ... Il.21.492.441.
In show an Aid, by hapless *Hector's* Side ... Il.22.293.468.
Stood at my side, a pensive, plaintive Ghost; ... Il.23.127.493.
The growing Structure spreads on ev'ry side; ... Il.23.203.498.
He said, and plac'd the Goblet at his side; ... Il.23.717.518.
And grappling close, thy tumble side by side. ... Il.23.851.523.
And grappling close, thy tumble side by side. ... Il.23.851.523.
Shall pay the Stroke, and grace the Striker's Side: ... Il.23.953.527.
Now shifts his Side, impatient for the Day: ... Il.24.18.535.
The hoary Herald help'd him at his Side. ... Il.24.348.550.
Then drew his seat, familiar, to her side: ... Od.1.174.40.
A two-edg'd faulchion threaten'd by his side, ... Od.2.6.60.
Each burns with rancour to the adverse side. ... Od.3.182.94.
And views *Gortyna* on the western side; ... Od.3.376.104.
Fast by his side *Pisistratus* lay spread, ... Od.3.512.112.
Death, present death on ev'ry side appears. ... Od.5.392.191.
Here grapes discolour'd on the sunny side, ... Od.7.165.244.
There next his side the god-like hero sate; ... Od.7.228.247.
Adds graceful terror to the wearer's side. ... Od.8.440.287.
A port there is, inclos'd on either side, ... Od.9.157.312.
This said, I climb'd my vessel's lofty side; ... Od.9.207.314.
Secur'd each side: So bound we all the crew. ... Od.9.510.327.
Roll'd back the vessel to the Island's side: ... Od.9.572.330.
There disembarking on the green sea-side, ... Od.9.639.333.
The jutting shores that swell on either side ... Od.10.103.345.
I drew, and casting on the river side ... Od.10.191.349.
I led the one, and of the other side ... Od.10.234.352.
(These tender words on ev'ry side I hear) ... Od.10.496.367.
First draw thy faulchion, and on ev'ry side ... Od.10.614.374.
And trenching the black earth on ev'ry side, ... Od.11.29.380.
'Till side by side along the dreary coast ... Od.11.575.411.
'Till side by side along the dreary coast ... Od.11.575.411.
Two marble doors unfold on either side; ... Od.13.133.8.
And at his side a wretched scrip was hung, ... Od.13.506.30.

SIDE (CONTINUED)

Jove thunder'd on their side. Our guilty head ...Od.14.298.50.
He heard, he sav'd, he plac'd me at his side; ...Od.14.309.50.
The scorching flames climb round on ev'ry side: ...Od.14.474.58.
Fast by my side, and shiv'ring thus I said. ...Od.14.546.63.
And by his side the guest accepted plac'd. ...Od.15.309.84.
By road frequented, or by fountain-side. ...Od.15.480.93.
To combat by thy side, thy guardian pow'r. ...Od.16.185.112.
Past on, and sate by faithful *Mentor's* side; ...Od.17.79.136.
Along the road conversing side by side, ...Od.17.204.141.
Along the road conversing side by side, ...Od.17.204.141.
Jove thunder'd on their side: our guilty head ...Od.17.519.157.
Ulysses so, from side to side devolv'd, ...Od.20.35.234.
Ulysses so, from side to side devolv'd, ...Od.20.35.234.
(An humble side-board set) *Ulysses* shar'd. ...Od.20.348.249.
On either side awaits a virgin fair; ...Od.21.67.262.
Fast by his father's side he takes his stand; ...Od.21.477.283.
Fast by our side let either faithful swain ...Od.22.120.292.
On ev'ry side he sees the labour grow: ...Od.22.163.295.
And thus address'd *Ulysses* near his side. ...Od.22.179.296.
Fierce on the villain from each side they leapt, ...Od.22.202.297.
The howling felon swung from side to side. ...Od.22.210.297.
The howling felon swung from side to side. ...Od.22.210.297.
In *Mentor's* friendly form she join'd his side; ...Od.22.223.297.
Rise then in combat, at my side attend; ...Od.22.254.299.
Still at his side is *Nestor's* son survey'd, ...Od.24.27.348.
Haste to the cottage by this orchard side. ...Od.24.417.369.
'Twas heav'n that struck, and heav'n was on his side. ...Od.24.515.372.

SIDE-BOARD

(An humble side-board set) *Ulysses* shar'd. ...Od.20.348.249.

SIDE-BOX

Why bows the Side-box from its inmost Rows? ...2.RL5.14.200.

SIDELONG

Thus while she spoke, a sidelong Glance she cast, ...2.ChJM.599.44.

SIDES

Around whose rocky sides the water flows: ...1.TrPA.40.367.
And shakes the waving Forests on his Sides! ...1.TrUl.233.473.
In living Sculpture on the Sides were spread ...2.TemF.204.271.
And various Animals his Sides surround: ...2.TemF.235.274.
To buy both sides, and give thy Country peace. ...3.Ep3.152.106.
Slopes at its foot, the woods its sides embrace, ...4.1HE1.141.289.
He laughd, and shook his Sides so fat: ...6.67.2.195.
Safe in her Sides the Hecatomb they stow'd, ...II.1.408.107.
Where *Ægilipa's* rugged Sides are seen, ...II.2.771.162.
And laves, in Height of Blood, his shining Sides; ...II.6.655.359.
With Gold and Brass his loaded Navy's sides. ...II.9.178.441.
With Gold and Brass thy loaded Navy's sides. ...II.9.365.451.
And from their Sides the Foam descends in Snow; ...II.11.362.50.
Tho' round his Sides a wooden Tempest rain, ...II.11.684.65.
On all sides thick, the Peals of Arms resound. ...II.13.699.138.
To bathe his Sides and cool his fiery Blood: ...II.15.301.208.
Above the sides of some tall Ship ascend, ...II.15.442.214.
On all sides batter'd, yet resists his Pow'r: ...II.15.745.224.
Warn'd, he retreats. Then swift from all sides pour ...II.16.150.243.
And round on all sides sent his piercing View. ...II.17.760.318.
Beneath the Vase, and climbs around the Sides: ...II.18.408.340.
Of these the Sides adorn'd with Swords of Gold, ...II.18.688.356.
Lash'd by his Tail his heaving sides resound; ...II.20.207.402.
The parted Visage falls on equal Sides: ...II.20.446.413.
On all sides round the Forest hurles her Oaks ...II.23.147.495.
Their Bones resound with Blows: Sides, Shoulders, Thighs ...II.23.832.522.
The soul for ever flies: on all sides round ...Od.3.580.116.
These form'd the sides: the deck he fashion'd last; ...Od.5.323.187.
The slippery sides, and shoot into the skies. ...Od.12.98.436.
Rush'd with dire noise, and dash'd the sides in twain; ...Od.12.497.456.
And shakes the waving forests on his sides. ...Od.13.400.26.
Turn'd on all sides, and view'd it o'er and o'er; ...Od.21.428.280.
On all sides thus they double wound on wound, ...Od.22.343.304.

SIDNEY

See SIDNEY bleeds amid the martial strife! ...3.EOM4.101.138.

SIDON

Whom from soft *Sidon* youthful *Paris* bore, ...II.6.362.344.
(*Sidon* the Capital) I stretch'd my toil ...Od.4.99.124.
A pledge the sceptred pow'r of *Sidon* gave, ...Od.4.837.158.
A ship of *Sidon* anchor'd in our port; ...Od.15.457.92.
I too (she cry'd) from glorious *Sidon* came, ...Od.15.466.93.

SIDON'S

From *Sidon's* hospitable Monarch came; ...Od.15.131.75.

SIDONIAN

Sidonian Maids embroider'd ev'ry Part, ...II.6.361.343.
Sidonian Artists taught the Frame to shine, ...II.23.867.524.

SIEGE

In Love's, in Nature's spite, the siege they hold, ...4.JD2.23.133.
In Nature's spight, the Stubborn Siege they hold ...4.JD2A.27.134.
Close to the Works their rigid Siege they laid. ...II.12.304.92.

SIEVE

But like a Sieve let ev'ry blessing thro', ...6.86.6.245.
But like a Sieve let ev'ry Pleasure thro', ...6.86.6B.245.

SIFT

Some turn the mill, or sift the golden grain, ...Od.7.133.241.

SIGH

No Sigh, no Murmur the wide World shall hear, ...1.Mes.45.117.
And kindly sigh for sorrows not your own; ...1.TrFD.4.385.
No Sigh to rise, no Tear had pow'r to flow; ...1.TrSP.127.399.

SIGH (CONTINUED)

And sigh in Silence, lest the World shou'd hear: ...2.ChJM.199.24.
A speaking Sigh, and cast a mournful View; ...2.ChJM.415.35.
A heaving Sigh, and cast a mournful View; ...2.ChJM.415A.35.
Heav'n knows, (with that a tender Sigh she drew) ...2.ChJM.577.43.
Breathe a soft Sigh, and drop a tender Tear; ...2.ChJM.666.47.
She said; a rising Sigh express'd her Woe, ...2.ChJM.783.52.
"Fye, 'tis unmanly thus to sigh and groan; ...2.ChWB.197.66.
Resign'd to Fate, and with a Sigh retir'd, ...2.RL3.146.179.
Which, with a Sigh, she rais'd; and thus she said. ...2.RL4.146.196.
And waft a sigh from *Indus* to the *Pole*. ...2.ElAb.58.323.
That something still which prompts th'eternal sigh, ...3.EOM4.3.128.
To sigh for ribbands if thou art so silly, ...3.EOM4.277.154.
Nor leave one sigh behind them when they die. ...3.Ep2.230.68.
Ready to cast, I yawn, I sigh, and sweat: ...4.JD4.157.39.
Ready to cast, I yawn, I sigh, I sweat: ...4.JD4A.157.39.
To sigh each Bill, about he now must walk; ...4.JD2A.76.138.
My Heir may sigh, and think it want of Grace ...4.2HE2.286.185.
Clos'd their long Glories with a Sigh, to find ...4.2HE1.13.195.
Sigh, while his Chloë, blind to Wit and Worth, ...4.1HE6.42.239.
And thy last sigh was heard when W[yndha]m died. ...4.1740.80.336.
All look, all sigh, and call on Smedley lost; ...5.DunA2.281.136.
All look, all sigh, and call on E[usden] lost; ...5.DunA2.281A.136.
All look, all sigh, and call on Smedley lost; ...5.DunB2.293.310.
A fading Fresco here demands a sigh: ...6.52.34.157.
To sigh unheard in, to the passing winds? ...6.81.10.225.
To sigh unseen into the passing Wind? ...6.81.10A.225.
(A Sigh the Absent claims, the Dead a Tear) ...6.84.14.239.
Without a Sigh, a Trouble, or a Tear; ...6.86.16A.245.
And be thy latest Gasp a Sigh of Love. ...6.86.20A.246.
And the gay Courtier feels the sigh sincere, ...6.113.6.320.
And the gay Courtier feels his sigh sincere, ...6.113.6A.320.
Sigh, with his Captive for his ofspring lost ...6.130.22.358.
Dry pomps and Obsequies without a sigh. ...6.130.26.358.
No more they sigh, inglorious to return, ...II.2.532.152.
Then, with a Sigh that heav'd his manly Breast, ...II.4.182.230.
Her Bosom labour'd with a boding Sigh, ...II.6.508.351.
Shall neither hear thee sigh, nor see thee weep. ...II.6.593.355.
His Princess parts with a prophetick Sigh, ...II.6.640.358.
No more they sigh, inglorious to return, ...II.11.17.35.
But dare not murmur, dare not vent a Sigh; ...II.15.123.201.
A Sigh, that instant, from his Bosom broke, ...II.16.29.236.
Unfortunately Good! a boding Sigh ...II.16.66.238.
And sigh, at distance from the glorious War. ...II.16.640.269.
To Fate submitting with a secret Sigh) ...II.18.164.330.
All comfortless he stands: Then, with a Sigh, ...II.22.377.471.
Sigh back her Sighs, and answer Tear with Tear. ...II.22.663.484.
The Synod griev'd, and gave a pitying sigh, ...Od.2.92.65.
Insensate! with a sigh the King replies, ...Od.4.37.121.
Ulysses! (with a sigh she thus began) ...Od.5.257.184.
See! from their thrones thy kindred monarchs sigh! ...Od.6.40.206.
And sigh, expecting the return of day. ...Od.9.363.321.
I met them with a sigh, and thus bespoke. ...Od.10.670.375.
Sigh for their friends devour'd, and mourn the dead. ...Od.12.364.449.
(Thus good *Eumæus* with a sigh rejoin'd) ...Od.14.396.54.
Alas! (*Eumæus* with a sigh rejoin'd) ...Od.15.344.86.
But droop'd her head, and drew a secret sigh. ...Od.17.171.139.
Oh my dear son!—The father with a sigh: ...Od.22.166.295.
At length *Ulysses* with a sigh replies: ...Od.23.265.336.

SIGH'D

Around the Room, and sigh'd before he spoke:) ...2.ChJM.86.18.
Sad in the midst of Triumphs, sigh'd for Pain; ...2.ChJM.358.31.
And sigh'd full oft, but sigh'd and wept in vain; ...2.ChJM.491.39.
And sigh'd full oft, but sigh'd and wept in vain; ...2.ChJM.491.39.
And sigh'd for Woe, but sigh'd and wept in vain; ...2.ChJM.491A.39.
And sigh'd for Woe, but sigh'd and wept in vain; ...2.ChJM.491A.39.
Sore sigh'd the Knight, to hear his Lady's Cry, ...2.ChJM.726.49.
Then sigh'd and cry'd, *Adieu my Dear, adieu!* ...2.ChWB.424.77.
Or he whose Virtue sigh'd to lose a day? ...3.EOM4.148.142.
And sigh'd) "My lands and tenements to Ned." ...3.Ep1.257:37.
She sigh'd not that They stay'd, but that She went. ...6.45.10.125.
Ambition sigh'd; She found it vain to trust ...6.71.19.203.
He sigh'd; but sighing, rais'd his vengeful Steel, ...II.11.415.53.
And here had sigh'd and sorrow'd out the Day; ...II.24.891.573.
Deep from his inmost soul *Atrides* sigh'd, ...Od.4.445.141.
There sate all desolate, and sigh'd alone, ...Od.5.201.181.
Sigh'd, while he furnish'd the luxurious board, ...Od.14.31.36.
Or sigh'd in exile forth his latest breath, ...Od.14.51.38.
In silent wonder sigh'd unwilling praise. ...Od.19.272.208.
Sigh'd from his mighty soul, and thus began. ...Od.21.263.272.
Deep from his soul he sigh'd, and sorrowing spread ...Od.24.369.366.

SIGH'ST

Yet sigh'st thou now for apples and for cakes? ...3.EOM4.176.144.

SIGHING

She stopp'd, and sighing, Oh good Gods, she cry'd, ...2.ChJM.720.49.
Then sighing, thus. "And I am now threescore? ...5.DunA2.273.135.
Then sighing, thus, "And am I now three-score? ...5.DunB2.285.309.
He deeply sighing said: To tell my Woe, ...II.1.476.110.
She said, and sighing thus the God replies ...II.1.670.119.
And sighing thus bespoke the blue-ey'd Maid. ...II.2.192.137.
And, softly sighing, from the Loom withdrew. ...II.3.188.200.
He sigh'd; but sighing, rais'd his vengeful Steel, ...II.11.415.53.
Who sighing, thus his bleeding Friend address'd. ...II.11.947.77.
Slow he recedes, and sighing, quits the Dead. ...II.17.116.292.
Sighing he said: His Grief the Heroes join'd, ...II.19.360.387.
Fast as he could, he sighing quits the Walls; ...II.21.619.448.
Then sighing, to the Deep his Looks he cast, ...II.23.176.497.
(Thus sighing spoke the Man of many woes) ...Od.7.323.251.
Thus fierce he said: we sighing went our way, ...Od.10.87.343.
Then softly sighing, he the fair address, ...Od.11.295.396.

SIGHS

Go gentle Gales, and bear my Sighs away! 1.PAu.17.82.
Go gentle Gales, and bear my Sighs along! 1.PAu.23.82.
Go gentle Gales, and bear my Sighs away! 1.PAu.31.82.
Go gentle Gales, and bear my Sighs along! 1.PAu.39.83.
Go gentle Gales, and bear my Sighs away! 1.PAu.47.83.
And cease ye Gales to bear my Sighs away! 1.PAu.54.84.
And told in Sighs to all the trembling Trees; 1.PWi.62.93.
Now *Sighs* steal out, and *Tears begin to flow:* 1.EOC.379.283.
She said, and for her lost *Galanthis* sighs, 1.TrFD.1.385.
Thus thro' the trembling boughs in sighs complains. 1.TrFD.68.389.
Gods! can no Pray'rs, no Sighs, no Numbers move 1.TrSP.242.404.
The Winds my Pray'rs, my Sighs, my Numbers bear, 1.TrSP.244.404.
Sighs for his Country; and laments again 1.TrUl.98.469.
And breathes three am'rous Sighs to raise the Fire. 2.RL2.42.162.
She sighs for ever on her pensive Bed, 2.RL4.23.185.
Here sighs a Jar, and there a Goose-pye talks; 2.RL4.52.188.
Sighs, Sobs, and Passions, and the War of Tongues. 2.RL4.84.190.
Repentant sighs, and voluntary pains: 2.ElAb.18.320.
Still breath'd in sighs, still usher'd with a tear. 2.ElAb.32.321.
Griefs to thy griefs, and eccho sighs to thine. 2.ElAb.42.322.
Tears that delight, and sighs that waft to heav'n. 2.ElAb.214.337.
I waste the Matin lamp in sighs for thee, 2.ElAb.267.341.
Sighs for a Sister with unwounded ear; 3.Ep2.260A.71.
Sighs for a Daughter with unwounded ears 3.Ep2.260B.71.
Sighs for the shades—"How charming is a Park!" 3.Ep2.38.53.
Sighs for a Daughter with unwounded ear; 3.Ep2.260.71.
Tenants with sighs the smoakless tow'rs survey, 3.Ep3.193.109.
Sore sighs Sir G[ilbert], starting at the bray 5.DunA2.241.129.
So sighs Sir G[ilber]t, starting at the bray 5.DunA2.241A.129.
Padua with sighs beholds her Livy burn; 5.DunA3.97.158.
And answ'ring Gin-shops sowrer sighs return! 5.DunA3.140.162.
Sore sighs Sir Gilbert, starting at the bray, 5.DunB2.251.307.
Padua, with sighs, beholds her Livy burn, 5.DunB3.105.325.
And answ'ring gin-shops sowrer sighs return. 5.DunB3.148.327.
So us'd to sighs, so long inur'd to tears, 6.4i.11.9.
No sweets but *Serenissa's* sighs. 6.4v.4.11.
The truest Hearts for *Voiture* heav'd with Sighs; 6.19.17.62.
She sighs, and is no *Dutchess* at her Heart. 6.19.56.63.
Two or *Three* Kisses, with *Two* or *Three* Sighs, 6.36.3.104.
Two or *Three* Kisses, and *Two* or *Three* Sighs, 6.36.3A.105.
Two or *Three* Kisses, *Two* or *Three* Sighs, 6.36.3B.105.
Saw others happy, and with sighs withdrew; 6.45.8.124.
Brutus for absent *Portia* sighs, 6.51ii.15.153.
Nor Sighs for Coach and Six. 6.54.4.164.
Sighs for an Otho, and neglects his bride. 6.71.44.204.
Where *British* Sighs from dying WYNDHAM stole, 6.142.11.383.
Here patriot sighs from Wyndham's bosom stole, 6.142.11A.383.
There partiot sighs from Wyndham's bosom stole 6.142.11B.383.
Here Wyndham, thy last Sighs for Liberty 6.142.11C.383.
Here Wyndham, this last Sighs for Liberty 6.142.11D.383.
Here British sighs from dying WYNDHAM stole, 6.142.11F.383.
Here British sighs from Windham's bosom stole 6.142.11G.383.
Sighs from his inmost Soul, and thus replies; Il.4.46.223.
With answering Sighs return'd the plaintive Sound. Il.4.185.230.
Words mixt with Sighs, thus bursting from his Breast. Il.9.22.432.
Sighs following Sighs his inward Fears confest. Il.10.12.2.
Sighs following Sighs his inward Fears confest. Il.10.12.2.
Persuasive Speech, and more persuasive Sighs, Il.14.251.173.
Her mournful Offspring, to his Sighs reply'd; Il.18.92.327.
Shall I not force her Breast to heave with Sighs, Il.18.157.330.
The Tears, and Sighs burst from his swelling Heart. Il.18.370.339.
That done, their Sorrows and their Sighs renew. Il.18.416.341.
Unmov'd, he heard them, and with Sighs deny'd. Il.19.324.386.
Shook with her Sighs, and panted on her Breast. Il.21.592.446.
Sigh back her Sighs, and answer Tear with Tear. Il.22.663.484.
But chief, *Pelides:* thick succeeding Sighs Il.23.21.487.
My only Food my Sorrows and my Sighs! Il.24.809.570.
With plaintive Sighs, and Musick's solemn Sound: Il.24.901.573.
Thus spoke th' inventive Queen, with artful sighs. Od.2.106.66.
Ah! no such hope (the Prince with sighs replies) Od.3.279.99.
Unblest he sighs, detain'd by lawless charms, Od.5.22.172.
With sighs, *Ulysses* heard the words she spoke, Od.5.221.182.
To whom with sighs *Ulysses* gave reply: Od.8.167.271.
Fast fell the tears, and sighs succeeded sighs: Od.8.582.294.
Fast fell the tears, and sighs succeeded sighs: Od.8.582.294.
Deep are his sighs, his visage pale, his dress Od.11.232.393.
Of flowing tears, and thus with sighs reply'd. Od.11.252.394.
To whom with sighs: I pass these dreadful gates Od.11.587.412.
Sighs for his country, and laments again Od.13.265.18.
For thee he sighs; and to the royal heir Od.13.467.28.
Hence springs their confidence, and from our sighs Od.14.113.41.
And end her tears, her sorrows, and her sighs. Od.17.9.132.
And sudden sighs precede approaching woe. Od.20.420.253.
Ah no! with sighs *Penelope* rejoyn'd, Od.23.59.321.
Their sighs were many, and the tumult loud. Od.24.477.371.
As mixing words with sighs, he thus began. Od.24.488.371.

SIGHT

But *Delia* always; absent from her Sight, 1.PSp.79.68.
But *Delia* always; forc'd from *Delia's* Sight, 1.PSp.79A.68.
But since those Graces please thy Sight no more, 1.PSu.29A.74.
Are half so charming as thy Sight to me. 1.PAu.46.83.
Not proud *Olympus* yields a nobler Sight, 1.W-F.33.151.
Pleas'd, in the Gen'ral's Sight, the Host lye down 1.W-F.107A.161.
Fir'd at first Sight with what the *Muse* imparts, 1.EOC.219.265.
Something, whose Truth convinc'd at Sight we find, 1.EOC.299.273.
Foretold the Cyclops he shou'd lose his sight. 1.TrPA.32.366.
To gain her Sight, a thousand Forms he wears, 1.TrVP.29.378.
And prais'd the Beauty of the pleasing Sight. 1.TrVP.62.380.
Nor at first sight, like most, admires the Fair; 1.TrVP.87.380.
This change unknown, astonish'd at the sight 1.TrFD.35.387.
Before my Sight a Watry Virgin stood, 1.TrSP.186.401.
Now wretched *Oedipus,* depriv'd of Sight, 1.TrSt.69.413.
Forc'd from these Orbs the bleeding Balls of Sight. 1.TrSt.100.414.
Tore from these Orbs the bleeding Balls of Sight. 1.TrSt.100A.414.

SIGHT (CONTINUED)

The Day beheld, and sick'ning at the Sight, 1.TrSt.136.415.
Struck with the Sight, and fix'd in deep Amaze, 1.TrSt.575.434.
To Heav'n he lifts his Hands, erects his Sight, 1.TrSt.581.434.
His native Mountains lessen to his Sight; 1.TrSt.643.437.
Unless our Desart Cities please thy Sight, 1.TrSt.774.442.
Jove's heav'nly Daughter stood confess'd to Sight, 1.TrUl.163.471.
Grac'd with thy Sight, and favour'd with thy Aid: 1.TrUl.194.472.
Shook high her flaming Torch, in open Sight, 2.ChJM.329.30.
Old as I am, and now depriv'd of Sight, 2.ChJM.552.42.
And, in the very Act, restore his Sight: 2.ChJM.652.46.
Old as he was, and void of Eye-sight too, 2.ChJM.728.49.
Look'd out, and stood restor'd to sudden Sight. 2.ChJM.749.51.
So Heav'n preserve the Sight it has restor'd, 2.ChJM.768.52.
So help me Fates, as 'tis no perfect Sight, 2.ChJM.776.52.
Strange Phantoms dance around, and skim before your Sight. 2.ChJM.804.54.
His Strength, his Sight, his Life, were lost for Love. 2.ChWB.381Z2.75.
Transparent Forms, too fine for mortal Sight, 2.RL2.61.163.
Puts forth one manly Leg, to sight reveal'd; 2.RL3.57.172.
Hairs less in sight, or any Hairs but these! 2.RL4.176.198.
Charms strike the Sight, but Merit wins the Soul. 2.RL5.34.201.
And seem'd to distant Sight of solid Stone. 2.TemF.30.255.
Scarce to the Top I stretch'd my aking Sight, 2.TemF.246.275.
When on the *Goddess* first I cast my Sight, 2.TemF.258.275.
A sudden Cloud strait snatch'd them from my Sight, 2.TemF.354.280.
'Tis all we beg thee, to conceal from Sight 2.TemF.362.281.
Love, free as air, at sight of human ties, 2.ElAb.75.325.
Priests, Tapers, Temples, swim before my sight: 2.ElAb.274.342.
Why has not Man a microscopic sight? 3.EOM1.193A.38.
What modes of sight betwixt each wide extreme, 3.EOM1.211.41.
Thus gracious CHANDOS is belov'd at sight, 3.Ep1.113.23.
So when the Sun's broad beam has tir'd the sight, 3.Ep2.253.70.
Like a big Wife at sight of loathsome Meat, 4.JD4.156.39.
Painted for sight, and essenc'd for the smell, 4.JD4.226.45.
I kept, like *Asian* Monarchs, from their sight: 4.Arbu.220.111.
At sight of Heirs dissolv'd in Luxury. 4.JD2A.93.140.
The people, sure, the people are the sight! 4.2HE1.323.223.
Weak tho' I am of limb, and short of sight, 4.1HE1.49.283.
A shapeless shade! it melted from his sight, 5.DunA2.103.109.
Then * * try'd, but hardly snatch'd from sight, 5.DunA2.283.136.
H[ill] try'd the next, but hardly snatch'd from sight, 5.DunA2.283A.136
Then [Aaron] essay'd: scarce vanish'd out of sight 5.DunA2.283B.136
Then stretch thy sight o'er all her rising reign, 5.DunA3.57.155.
See all her progeny, illustrious sight! 5.DunA3.121.160.
Dishonest sight! his breeches rent below; 5.DunA3.194.173.
A shapeless shade, it melted from his sight, 5.DunB2.111.300.
Then * essay'd; scarce vanish'd out of sight, 5.DunB2.295.310.
Then stretch thy sight o'er all her rising reign, 5.DunB3.65.323.
See all her progeny, illustrious sight! 5.DunB3.129.325.
Dishonest sight! his breeches rent below; 5.DunB3.198.330.
Attends; all flesh is nothing in his sight! 5.DunB4.550.396.
While mankind boasts superior sight, 6.6ii.9.14.
Steals my senses, shuts my sight, 6.31ii.10.94.
The lessening World forsakes my Sight, 6.31ii.6Z2.94.
No common object to your sight displays, 6.32.19.96.
Streets, chairs, and coxcombs rush upon my sight; 6.45.48.126.
With sharpen'd sight pale Antiquaries pore, 6.71.35.203.
A Sight it was to see; 6.79.134.222.
It could not aid his Sight. 6.94.56.261.
Which frames the Harvest-bug, too small for Sight, 6.96v.3.280.
So while the sun's broad beam yet strikes the sight, 6.106i.4.306.
So when the sun's broad beam has tir'd the sight, 6.106i.4A.306.
Was there a Chief, but melted at the Sight? 6.128.7.355.
Takes, opens, swallows it, before their Sight. 6.145.8.388.
Meantime the radiant Sun, to mortal Sight Il.1.776.124.
Then bids an empty Phantome rise to sight, Il.2.7.127.
The *Phantome* said; then, vanish'd from his sight, Il.2.43.129.
A Dream Divine appear'd before my Sight; Il.2.72.130.
And Hell's Abyss hide nothing from your sight, Il.2.575.155.
Amidst the Plain in sight of *Ilion* stands Il.2.982.170.
Here, in the midst, in either Army's sight, Il.3.127.196.
Full in her *Paris'* Sight the Queen of Love Il.3.529.216.
Between both Armies thus, in open Sight, Il.4.107.225.
Struck at his Sight the *Trojans* backward drew, Il.4.571.249.
When fresh he rears his radiant Orb to Sight, Il.5.9.266.
Struck at the Sight, the mighty *Ajax* glows Il.5.756.303.
But *Hector* saw; and furious at the Sight, Il.5.838.305.
Oh Sight accurst! Shall faithless *Troy* prevail, Il.5.876.308.
Depriv'd of Sight by their avenging Doom, Il.6.171.334.
Beheld the War, and sicken'd at the Sight; Il.6.469.350.
And the vast World hangs trembling in my Sight! Il.8.32.397.
Nor great *Idomeneus* that Sight could bear, Il.8.99.402.
The quiv'ring Steeds fell prostrate at the Sight; Il.8.165.406.
The conscious Swains, rejoicing in the Sight, Il.8.697.428.
Himself, oppos'd t' *Ulysses* full in sight, Il.9.285.448.
And hostile *Troy* was ever full in Sight. Il.10.222.11.
What moves thee, say, when Sleep has clos'd the Sight, Il.10.455.24.
The welcome Sight *Ulysses* first descries, Il.10.550.27.
But sure till now no Coursers struck my Sight Il.10.648.30.
With new-born Day to gladden mortal Sight, Il.11.3.34.
Tears, at the Sight, came starting from his Eye, Il.11.322.49.
Great *Jove* from *Ide* with Slaughter fills his Sight, Il.11.435.53.
O'er his dim Sight the misty Vapours rise, Il.11.459.54.
And gladden'd *Troy* with Sight of hostile Blood. Il.11.577.60.
Each takes new Courage at the Hero's Sight; Il.11.724.67.
Her Quarry seen, impetuous at the Sight, Il.13.92.109.
Stabb'd at the Sight, *Deiphobus* drew nigh, Il.13.509.131.
Paris from far the moving Sight beheld, Il.13.827.145.
And grizly War appears a pleasing Sight. Il.14.178.165.
She sees her *Jove,* and trembles at the Sight. Il.14.184.168.
Dark in embow'ring Shade, conceal'd from Sight, Il.14.327.178.
Expos'd to mortal, and immortal Sight; Il.14.376.180.
Stood shining o'er him, half unseal'd his Sight: Il.15.279.207.
With Anguish *Ajax* views the piercing Sight, Il.15.508.216.
It was not thus, when, at my Sight amaz'd, Il.16.95.239.
The smiling Scene wide opens to the Sight, Il.16.360.257.

SIGHT (CONTINUED)
Clouds rise on Clouds, and Heav'n is snatch'd from sight. ... Il.16.451.260.
Fix'd on the Field his Sight, his Breast debates ... Il.16.785.274.
Thus he accosts him. What a shameful Sight! ... Il.16.877.277.
If yet a *Greek* the Sight of *Hector* dread, ... Il.17.203.295.
Thou stand'st, and Armies tremble at thy Sight ... Il.17.234.297.
Struck at the Sight, recede the *Trojan* Train: ... Il.17.368.301.
He seem'd like aged *Periphas* to Sight. ... Il.17.375.302.
Lo, to my Sight beyond our Hope restor'd, ... Il.17.552.309.
Now, now, *Atrides!* cast around thy Sight, ... Il.17.737.317.
Not with less Quickness, his exerted Sight ... Il.17.767.318.
A gen'ral Clamour rises at the Sight: ... Il.17.809.320.
Two golden Talents lay amidst, in sight, ... Il.18.589.351.
Now forth at once, too swift for sight, they spring, ... Il.18.693.357.
(With new-born Day to gladden mortal Sight, ... Il.19.3.371.
Now call the Hosts, and try, if in our Sight, ... Il.19.73.375.
The King of Men shall rise in publick Sight, ... Il.19.173.378.
The Scene of War came rushing on his Sight. ... Il.20.392.411.
A Cloud of Sorrow overcast his Sight, ... Il.20.487.415.
But nor that Force, nor Form divine to Sight ... Il.21.368.436.
And the near Hero rising on his Sight! ... Il.21.616.448.
Not half so dreadful rises to the Sight ... Il.22.37.454.
Unworthy Sight! The Man, belov'd of Heav'n, ... Il.22.221.464.
Too long, O *Hector!* have I born the Sight ... Il.22.295.468.
And, in his Parents' Sight, now dragg'd along! ... Il.22.510.477.
And is it thou (he answers) to my Sight ... Il.23.109.492.
Haste then; yon' narrow Road before our Sight ... Il.23.493.510.
Like the full Moon, stood obvious to the Sight. ... Il.23.539.511.
Rise then some other, and inform my Sight, ... Il.23.552.511.
Obscene to sight, the ruefull Racer lay; ... Il.23.912.525.
Now grace the Lists before our Army's Sight, ... Il.23.947.526.
Low'ring they meet, tremendous to the Sight; ... Il.23.961.527.
Sad Object as I am for heav'nly Sight! ... Il.24.119.540.
Conceal'd from Sight; With frantick Hands he spread ... Il.24.201.545.
Say whither, Father! when each mortal Sight ... Il.24.447.554.
But can I, absent from my Prince's Sight, ... Il.24.531.558.
Farewell: To shun *Achilles'* Sight I fly; ... Il.24.567.560.
Sudden, (a venerable Sight!) appears; ... Il.24.586.561.
The Sight is granted to thy longing Eyes. ... Il.24.752.568.
She view'd her honours, and enjoy'd the sight. ... Od.3.553.114.
Nor sight of natal shore, nor regal dome ... Od.4.641.149.
When sight of less'ning *Ithaca* was lost, ... Od.4.1101.169.
With new-born day to gladden mortal sight, ... Od.5.3.170.
A scene, where if a God shou'd cast his sight, ... Od.5.95.177.
Then swell'd to sight *Phæacia's* dusky coast, ... Od.5.357.189.
When a lov'd Sire revives before their sight, ... Od.5.507.196.
But cliffs, and shaggy shores, a dreadful sight! ... Od.5.520.197.
(A wider circle, but in sight of shore) ... Od.5.559.199.
Sudden he shines, and manifest to sight. ... Od.7.191.245.
Oh sight (he cry'd) dishonest and unjust! ... Od.7.214.247.
O sight tormenting to an husband's eyes! ... Od.8.354.282.
And none, ah none so lovely to my sight, ... Od.9.29.303.
My absent parents rose before my sight, ... Od.9.37.303.
Far in wide ocean, and from sight of shore: ... Od.9.94.306.
Appall'd at sight of more than mortal man! ... Od.9.305.319.
As sure, as *Neptune* cannot give thee sight. ... Od.9.614.332.
Our sight the whole collected navy chear'd, ... Od.9.637.332.
And rising mountains gain upon our sight. ... Od.10.33.341.
A sudden horror struck their aking sight. ... Od.10.130.347.
Sad, pleasing sight! with tears each eye ran o'er, ... Od.10.471.366.
So round me press'd exulting at my sight, ... Od.10.491.367.
Not that lov'd country for whose sight we mourn, ... Od.10.498.367.
There seek the *Theban* Bard, depriv'd of sight, ... Od.10.582.371.
Astonish'd at the sight, aghast I stood, ... Od.11.55.383.
Sad at the sight I stand, deep fix'd in woe, ... Od.11.69.383.
Struck at the sight I melt with filial woe, ... Od.11.108.386.
The phantom Prophet ceas'd, and sunk from sight ... Od.11.184.390.
Mov'd at the sight, I for a space resign'd ... Od.11.491.408.
Touch'd at the sight from tears I scarce refrain, ... Od.11.675.417.
Should fix me, stiffen'd at the monstrous sight, ... Od.11.787.425.
O fly the dreadful sight! expand thy sails, ... Od.12.105.436.
Veils the dire monster, and confounds the sight. ... Od.12.277.445.
Past sight of shore, along the surge we bound, ... Od.12.473.454.
Jove's heav'nly daughter stood confess'd to sight. ... Od.13.330.23.
Grac'd with thy sight, and favour'd with thy aid. ... Od.13.361.24.
From the loath'd object ev'ry sight shall turn, ... Od.13.463.28.
Soon past beyond their sight, I left the flood, ... Od.14.387.53.
Advanc'd the bird of *Jove:* auspicious sight! ... Od.15.179.77.
Full dexter to the car: the prosp'rous sight ... Od.15.184.77.
O art thou come to bless my longing sight! ... Od.16.24.103.
And Poverty look'd smiling in my sight. ... Od.17.506.157.
Then pale with fears, and sick'ning at the sight, ... Od.18.86.170.
Lest they by sight of swords to fury fir'd, ... Od.19.14.193.
Inspect with sharpen'd sight, and frugal care, ... Od.19.25.193.
The walls where-e'er my wond'ring sight I turn, ... Od.19.46.195.
Can visit unapproach'd by mortal sight. ... Od.19.53.195.
Avaunt, she cry'd, offensive to my sight! ... Od.19.80.196.
'Tis hard, he cries, to bring to sudden sight ... Od.19.257.207.
Then with a change of form eludes their sight, ... Od.22.261.299.
With sight of his *Ulysses* ere he dies; ... Od.23.386.343.
Stood the great son, heart-wounded with the sight: ... Od.24.372.367.
Behold, *Telemachus!* (nor fear the sight) ... Od.24.584.376.

SIGHT'S
But 'till your Sight's establish'd, for a while, ... 2.ChJM.797.53.

SIGHTLESS
And on the sightless Eye-ball pour the Day. ... 1.Mes.40.116.
Of all who blindly creep, or sightless soar; ... 3.EOM1.12.13.
The bursting Balls drop sightless to the Ground. ... Il.16.898.278.
Ev'n he who sightless wants his visual ray, ... Od.8.221.274.

SIGHTS
Pass these to nobler sights lo Henley stands, ... 5.DunA3.195A.173.
Before you pass th' imaginary sights ... 6.45.35.125.

SIGILS
Of *Talismans* and *Sigils* knew the Pow'r, ... 2.TemF.105.261.

SIGN
The Banquet done, the Monarch gives the Sign ... 1.TrSt.633.436.
This heard, to *Damian* strait a Sign she made ... 2.ChJM.535.41.
Assur'd me, *Mars* in *Taurus* was my Sign. ... 2.ChWB.322.72.
When hungry Judges soon the Sentence sign, ... 2.RLA1.85.129.
The hungry Judges soon the Sentence sign, ... 2.RL3.21.170.
(Sure sign, that no spectator shall be drown'd). ... 5.DunA2.166.121.
With that, a Tear (portentous sign of Grace!) ... 5.DunB1.243.288.
(Sure sign, that no spectator shall be drown'd) ... 5.DunB2.174.304.
She wears no Colours (sign of Grace) ... 6.14v(a).13.49.
The faithful, fix'd, irrevocable Sign; ... Il.1.681.119.
From *Jove* himself the dreadful Sign was sent. ... Il.2.373.145.
(A fatal Sign to Armies on the Plain, ... Il.4.103.225.
The King himself (an Honorary Sign) ... Il.7.386.383.
(The Sign of Conquest) and thus urg'd the Fight. ... Il.8.209.407.
Encourag'd by the Sign, the Troops revive, ... Il.8.303.412.
That done, to *Phœnix Ajax* gave the Sign; ... Il.9.291.448.
Just then, in sign she favour'd their Intent, ... Il.10.321.17.
Thro' the red Skies her bloody Sign extends, ... Il.11.7.35.
Plac'd as a Sign to Man amid the Skies.) ... Il.11.38.36.
The leading Sign, th' irrevocable Nod, ... Il.12.275.91.
Without a Sign, his Sword the brave Man draws, ... Il.12.283.92.
Presumptuous *Troy* mistook th' accepting Sign, ... Il.15.438.214.
Confessing *Jove,* and trembling at the Sign; ... Il.16.149.243.
(In sign of Tempests from the troubled Air, ... Il.17.618.312.
When Men distrest hang out the Sign of War) ... Il.18.248.334.
That Sign beheld, and strengthen'd from above, ... Il.24.365.551.
The God propitious gave the guiding sign; ... Od.3.210.96.
To these the hospitable Sage, in sign ... Od.3.502.112.
Thus feasting high, *Alcinous* gave the sign ... Od.7.238.248.
With eager joy, and with a sign addrest. ... Od.8.332.281.
I give the sign, and struggle to be free: ... Od.12.234.443.
The Monarch to *Pontonous* gave the sign, ... Od.13.64.4.
'Till great *Alcinous* rising own'd the sign. ... Od.13.195.15.
To read this sign, and mystick sense of heav'n. ... Od.15.193.77.
Gave her the sign, and to his vessel went. ... Od.15.500.94.
I give the sign: that instant, from beneath, ... Od.16.304.120.
Then gave a sign, and beckon'd him to come. ... Od.17.403.152.
Vouchsafe the sanction of a sign above. ... Od.20.125.239.
Beheld, but with a sign forbade the boy. ... Od.21.136.265.
The sign conspicuous, and the scar expos'd: ... Od.21.231.270.
Amaz'd, *Laertes.* "Give some certain sign, ... Od.24.382.367.
Yet by another sign thy offspring know; ... Od.24.388.368.

SIGN'D
At all times Just, but when he sign'd the Shell. ... 2.TemF.173.269.
In all things Just, but when he sign'd the Shell. ... 2.TemF.173A.269.
"To get my Warrant quickly sign'd: ... 4.HS6.76.255.
Sign'd with that Ichor which from Gods distills. ... 5.DunA2.88.108.
Sign'd with that Ichor which from Gods distils. ... 5.DunB2.92.300.
For when he sign'd thy Death, he sentenc'd me. ... 6.96iv.78.278.
From the sign'd Victims crops the curling Hair, ... Il.3.342.209.
Sign'd to the Troops, to yield his Foe the Way, ... Il.22.269.466.
The scar, with which his manly knee was sign'd; ... Od.19.455.216.
The scar, with which his manly knee was sign'd. ... Od.19.461.218.
Which whizzing high, the wall unseemly sign'd. ... Od.20.369.250.

SIGN'ST
If e'er thou sign'st our Wishes with thy Nod; ... Il.15.432.214.

SIGNAL
The dreadful Signal all the Rocks rebound, ... 1.TrSt.163.417.
High Heav'n with trembling the dread Signal took, ... Il.1.686.120.
Nor was the Signal vain that shook the Sky. ... Il.1.721.122.
This wondrous Signal *Jove* himself displays, ... Il.2.392.145.
Jove, on the Right, a prosp'rous Signal sent, ... Il.2.418.147.
Who dares to tremble on this signal Day, ... Il.2.467.149.
And ev'ry Age record the signal Day. ... Il.3.361.210.
And age to Age record the signal Day. ... Il.3.361A.210.
And Age to Age record this signal Day. ... Il.3.574.219.
Then say ye Pow'rs! what signal Issue waits ... Il.4.19.222.
The Gods (they cry'd) the Gods this Signal sent, ... Il.4.111.225.
But let the Signal be this Moment giv'n; ... Il.4.306.235.
And let some Deed this signal Night adorn, ... Il.10.333.18.
Then gave his Friend the Signal to retire; ... Il.10.586.28.
A signal Omen stopp'd the passing Host, ... Il.12.231.89.
Long weigh'd the Signal, and to *Hector* spoke. ... Il.12.244.90.
Nor dares to combate on this signal Day! ... Il.13.306.119.
Who stops to plunder, in this signal Hour, ... Il.15.400.212.
Gives the loud signal, and the Heav'ns reply. ... Il.20.187.401.
A signal of her Hymenæal choice: ... Od.4.1016.165.
Then gave the signal to the willing guest; ... Od.7.433.258.
Thy signal throw transcends the utmost bound ... Od.8.223.274.
Be, nor by signal nor by word betray'd, ... Od.15.478.93.
(Of granted vows a certain signal sent) ... Od.20.144.240.
Thy lost *Ulysses,* on this signal day? ... Od.23.170.328.

SIGNATURES
With signatures of such majestic grace. ... Od.4.76.123.

SIGNIOR
'Twas *Si Signior,* 'twas *Yaw Mynheer,* ... 6.14v(b).11.49.
'Twas *Si Signior,* & Yaw *Mynheer,* ... 6.14v(b).11A.49.

SIGNS
Where twelve fair Signs in beauteous Order lye? ... 1.PSp.40.64.
Where twelve bright Signs in beauteous Order lye? ... 1.PSp.40A.64.
The Dame by Signs reveal'd her kind Intent, ... 2.ChJM.498.39.
Signs of Remorse, while thus his Spouse he chear'd: ... 2.ChJM.788.53.
Writ underneath the Country Signs; ... 4.HS6.92.255.
"Signs following signs lead on the Mighty Year; ... 5.DunA3.335.191.
"Signs following signs lead on the Mighty Year; ... 5.DunA3.335.191.
Then, when these signs declare the Mighty Year; ... 5.DunA3.335A.191.

SIGNS (CONTINUED)

Signs following signs lead on the mighty year! ....5.DunB3.321.335.
Signs following signs lead on the mighty year! ....5.DunB3.321.335.
The Lots produc'd, each Hero signs his own, ...Il.7.211.374.
But *Jove* averse the Signs of Wrath display'd, ...Il.7.572.392.
The Wrath appeas'd, by happy Signs declares, ...Il.8.295.411.
With signs, she thus express'd her anxious love. ....Od.4.939.162.
No tracks of beasts, or signs of men we found, ...Od.10.113.346.
Now heav'n gave signs of wrath; along the ground ....Od.12.464.453.
Signs from above ensu'd: th' unfolding sky ....Od.21.452.282.
Smit with the signs which all his doubts explain, ...Od.24.401.368.

SILENC'D

The silenc'd Preacher yields to potent strain, ...4.2HE1.237.215.
A rev'rend Horror silenc'd all the Sky. ....Il.1.737.122.
The loudest silenc'd, and the fiercest cool'd. ....Il.2.246.139.
A rev'rend Horror silenc'd all the Sky; ....Il.8.36.397.

SILENCE

But, charm'd to Silence, listens while She sings, ...1.PSp.15.61.
Such Silence waits on *Philomela's* Strains, ...1.PWi.78.94.
And in soft Silence shed the kindly Show'r! ....1.Mes.14.114.
Your Silence there is better than your *Spite,* ....1.EOC.598.308.
Night shades the Groves, and all in Silence lye, ...1.TrSP.175.401.
And sacred Silence reigns, and universal Peace. ....1.TrSt.291.422.
The Monarch then his solemn Silence broke, ...1.TrSt.296.422.
Yet these in Silence see the Fates fulfil ....1.TrSt.409.427.
While on the Deck the Chief in Silence lies, ...1.TrUl.5.465.
And sigh in Silence, lest the World shou'd hear: ....2.ChJM.199.24.
Silence wou'd swell me, and my Heart wou'd break. ....2.ChJM.695.48.
Silence ensu'd, and thus the Nymph began. ....2.RL5.8.199.
Nor ever Silence, Rest or Peace is here. ....2.TemF.435.284.
Nor pass these lips in holy silence seal'd. ....2.ElAb.10.319.
A death-like silence, and a dread repose: ....2.ElAb.166.333.
Silence without, and Fasts within the wall; ....3.Ep3.190.109.
Silence, or hurt, he libels the *Great Man;* ....4.JD4.159.39.
For song, for silence, some expect a bribe ....4.Arbu.113A.103.
To Ease and Silence, ev'ry Muse's Son: ....4.2HE2.111.173.
"Silence, ye Wolves! while Ralph to Cynthia howls, ...5.DunA3.159.165.
King John in silence modestly expires: ....5.DunB1.252.289.
"Silence, ye Wolves! while Ralph to Cynthia howls, ...5.DunB3.165.328.
"O *Cara! Cara!* silence all that train: ....5.DunB4.53.346.
Silence! Coœval with Eternity; ....6.8.1.17.
Silence, the Knave's Repute, the Whore's good Name, ...6.8.25.18.
Then pompous *Silence* reigns, and stills the noisie Laws. ....6.8.33.18.
And drink in silence, or in silence lave! ....6.87.4.248.
And drink in silence, or in silence lave! ....6.87.4.248.
Ah bathe in silence, or in silence lave! ....6.87.4A.248.
Ah bathe in silence, or in silence lave! ....6.87.4A.248.
Asks of the *British Youth—Is* silence there? ....6.107.17.311.
Oh doe but silence Cibber, and the Bells. ....6.131i.6.360.
In unambitious silence be my lot, ...6.147vii.1.391.
In Silence past along the winding Strand ....Il.1.453A.109.
Thus *Thetis* spoke, but *Jove* in Silence held ....Il.1.662.118.
And a still Silence lulls the Camp to Peace. ....Il.2.254.139.
Sedition silence, and assert the Throne. ....Il.2.339.143.
His Silence thus the prudent Hero broke. ....Il.2.347.143.
His Silence here, with Blushes, *Paris* breaks; ....Il.3.85.193.
The Tumult silence, and the Fight suspend. ....Il.3.120.195.
Her sullen Silence, and with Fury spoke. ....Il.4.34.222.
But just Reproof with decent Silence bears. ....Il.5.602.297.
Beside his Coursers, thus her Silence broke. ....Il.5.997.314.
The solemn Silence, and their Pow'rs bespoke. ....Il.7.78.366.
Stern *Menelaus* first the Silence broke, ...Il.7.107.369.
The *Greeks* gave ear, but none the Silence broke, ...Il.7.474.388.
The Sire of Gods his awful Silence broke; ....Il.8.5.395.
Lest in the Silence and the Shades of Night, ...Il.8.635.426.
He said; deep Silence held the *Grecian* Band, ...Il.9.39.433.
Pray, in deep Silence, and with purest Hands. ....Il.9.226.444.
In Silence waiting till he ceas'd the Song. ....Il.9.254.445.
In Silence wrapt, in Consternation drown'd, ...Il.9.557.460.
With that, stern *Ajax* his long Silence broke, ...Il.9.735.470.
The gen'ral Silence, and undaunted spoke. ....Il.9.815.473.
Then first *Polydamas* the Silence broke, ...Il.12.243.90.
Silence that spoke, and Eloquence of Eyes. ....Il.14.252.173.
Hear me ye Sons of *Greece!* with Silence hear! ....Il.19.81.375.
Eternal Silence, and portentous spoke. ....Il.19.451.391.
Sternly they met. The Silence *Hector* broke; ....Il.22.315.469.
Expires the Goat; the Sheep in Silence dies: ....Il.23.42.488.
Each look'd on other, none the Silence broke, ...Il.24.596.561.
Thus gazing long, the Silence neither broke, ...Il.24.802.570.
And moves in Silence thro' the hostile Land. ....Il.24.861.572.
Silence at length the gay *Antinous* broke, ...Od.1.489.55.
'Twas silence all: at last *Ægyptius* spoke; ....Od.2.19.61.
Within these walls inglorious silence reigns. ....Od.2.34.62.
My num'rous woes, in silence let them dwell. ....Od.2.238.73.
But silence soon the son of *Nestor* broke, ...Od.4.257.131.
Then thus his melancholy silence broke. ....Od.5.222.182.
And a dead silence still'd the wat'ry world. ....Od.5.503.196.
There, as the night in silence roll'd away, ...Od.6.21.204.
Silence ensu'd. The eldest first began, ...Od.7.208.246.
Thus they; in silence long my fate I mourn'd, ...Od.10.75.343.
'Till rising up, *Aretè* silence broke, ...Od.11.416.404.
In silence turns, and sullen stalks away. ....Od.11.692.418.
She sate in silence while the tale I tell, ...Od.12.45.431.
A pause of silence hush'd the shady rooms: ....Od.13.3.1.
While on the deck the Chief in silence lies, ...Od.13.96.5.
But *Nestor's* son the chearful silence broke, ...Od.15.186.77.
Be Silence still our guard. The Monarch's spies ....Od.15.481.93.
He fed, and ceas'd when silence held the lyre. ....Od.17.431.153.
'Till silence thus th' imperial matron broke; ....Od.18.254.179.
'Till thus *Amphinomus* the silence broke. ....Od.18.459.190.
In solemn silence fell the kindly show'r. ....Od.21.237.271.
Curious to hear his Queen the silence break: ....Od.23.95.324.
Why thus in silence? why with winning charms ....Od.23.101.324.

SILENT

And *Jove* consented in a silent Show'r. ....1.PSu.8.72.
For ever silent, since despis'd by thee. ....1.PSu.44.75.
Come lovely Nymph, and bless the silent Hours, ...1.PSu.63.76.
While silent Birds forget their tuneful Lays, ...1.PWi.7.89.
In hollow Caves sweet *Echo* silent lies, ...1.PWi.41.92.
Silent, or only to her Name replies, ...1.PWi.42.92.
The balmy *Zephyrs,* silent since her Death, ...1.PWi.49.92.
The patient Fisher takes his silent Stand ....1.W-F.137.163.
Or wandring thoughtful in the silent Wood, ...1.W-F.249.172.
And silent *Darent,* stain'd with *Danish* Blood. ....1.W-F.348.184.
Pleas'd in the silent Shade with empty Praise; ....1.W-F.432.194.
Be *silent* always when you *doubt* your Sense; ....1.EOC.566.305.
Ev'n now, when silent Scorn is all they gain, ...1.TrVP.73.380.
Thro' lonely Plains, and thro' the silent Grove, ...1.TrSP.160.400.
As if the silent Grove, and lonely Plains ....1.TrSP.161.400.
And silent Tears fall trickling from my Eyes. ....1.TrSP.200.402.
Untun'd my Lute, and silent is my Lyre, ...1.TrSP.229.403.
And dark Dominions of the silent Night; ....1.TrSt.131.415.
And brings, descending thro' the silent Air, ...1.TrSt.480.430.
And thus invokes the silent *Queen* of *Night.* ....1.TrSt.582.434.
And silent Hours to various Talk invite. ....1.TrSt.795.443.
To the soft Arms of silent *Sleep* and *Death;* ....1.TrES.331.461.
Of matchless Swiftness, but of silent Pace, ...1.TrES.345.462.
But thou be Silent, nor reveal thy State, ...1.TrUl.184.471.
Justin, who silent sate, and heard the Man, ...2.ChJM.176.23.
'Twas he had summon'd to her silent Bed ....2.RL1.21.147.
Fair Virtue's silent Train: Supreme of these ....2.TemF.170.268.
Tho' cold like you, unmov'd, and silent grown, ...2.ElAb.23.320.
What turns him now a stupid silent dunce? ....3.Ep1.163.29.
And silent sells a King, or buys a Queen. ....3.Ep3.78.93.
Who can't be silent, and who will not lye; ....4.Arbu.34.98.
I can't be silent, and I will not lye; ....4.Arbu.34A.98.
(More silent far) where Kings and Poets lye; ....4.1HE6.51.239.
While with the silent growth of ten per Cent, ...4.1HE1.132.289.
Silent and soft, as Saints remove to Heav'n, ...4.EpS1.93.305.
Have I in silent wonder seen such things ....4.EpS1.109.306.
Yet silent bow'd to Christ's No kingdom here. ....5.DunA2.368.145.
Hung silent down his never-blushing head; ....5.DunA2.385.148.
Silent the monarch gaz'd; yet ask'd in thought 5.DunA3.245A.178
Yet silent bow'd to Christ's No kingdom here. ....5.DunB2.400.316.
Hung silent down his never-blushing head; ....5.DunB2.417.318.
Gone ev'ry blush, and silent all reproach, ...5.DunB4.563.398.
Some, deep Free-Masons, join the silent race ....5.DunB4.571.398.
Let them be silent then; and thou alone ....6.2.31.6.
A poet made the silent wood pursue; ....6.3.11.7.
The silent wood, of old, a poet drew ....6.3.11A.7.
Wake into Voice each silent String, ...6.11.3.29.
And the soft, silent Harmony, that springs ....6.11.35Z9.31.
('Midst Flocks and Shepherds) in the silent Grove; ....6.17ii.22.56.
Were silent, which by Fates Decree ....6.30.10.86.
Were silent, which kind Fate thought worthy ....6.30.10A.86.
Some felt the silent stroke of mould'ring age, ...6.71.11.203.
The Muse attends thee to the silent Shade: ....6.84.28.239.
The Muse attends thee to thy silent Shade: ....6.84.28A.239.
Wait, to the Scaffold, or the silent Cell, ...6.84.31Z1.239.
(Envy be silent and attend!) ....6.89.2.250.
Thy silent whisper is the sacred test.] ....6.107.32.311.
Pensive hast follow'd to the silent tomb, ...6.109.12.314.
Blest Maid; hast follow'd to the silent tomb, ...6.109.12A.314.
Silent he wander'd by the sounding Main: ....Il.1.50.88.
Then sternly silent sate: With like Disdain, ...Il.1.327.103.
At awful Distance long they silent stand, ...Il.1.430.108.
Past silent, as the Heralds held her Hand, ...Il.1.452.109.
Arising silent, wrapt in Holy Fear, ...Il.1.692.120.
Be silent Wretch, and think not here allow'd ....Il.2.241.139.
In silent Pomp he moves along the Main. ....Il.2.700.159.
Who now lay silent in the gloomy Grave: ....Il.2.854.165.
Born on the Banks of *Gyges'* silent Lake. ....Il.2.1055.172.
But silent, breathing Rage, resolv'd, and skill'd ....Il.3.11.188.
Ceas'd is the War, and silent all the Fields. ....Il.3.178.199.
Her silent Footsteps to the *Scæan* Gate. ....Il.3.190.200.
Silent they slept, and heard of Wars no more. ....Il.3.314.208.
Unseen, and silent, from the Train she moves, ...Il.3.523.216.
Sedate and silent move the num'rous Bands; ....Il.4.486.243.
She mounts the Seat oppress'd with silent Woe, ...Il.5.455.290.
Unmov'd and silent, the whole War they wait, ...Il.5.639.298.
Silent the Warrior smil'd, and pleas'd resign'd ....Il.6.504.351.
Till Fate condemns me to the silent Tomb. ....Il.6.627.358.
With silent Joy the settling Hosts survey: ....Il.7.66.366.
Sage *Priam* check'd their Grief: With silent Haste ....Il.7.508.389.
Confus'd and silent, for his Frown they fear'd. ....Il.8.555.423.
So Silent Fountains, from a Rock's tall Head, ...Il.9.19.432.
Silent, unmov'd, in dire Dismay they stand, ...Il.9.40.433.
Returns no more to wake the silent dead. ....Il.9.531.459.
Sends he some Spy, amidst these silent Hours, ...Il.10.43.4.
Thus leads you wandring in the silent Night? ....Il.10.161.9.
In silent State the Consistory crown'd. ....Il.10.232.12.
To roam the silent Fields in dead of Night? ....Il.10.456.24.
Then pours the silent Tempest, thick, and deep: ....Il.12.336.93.
As when old Ocean's silent Surface sleeps, ...Il.14.21.157.
And his hush'd Waves lie silent on the Main. ....Il.14.280.175.
Now to the Navy born on silent Wings, ...Il.14.407.183.
To the soft Arms of silent *Sleep* and *Death;* ....Il.16.818.274.
Of matchless Swiftness, but of silent Pace, ...Il.16.832.275.
The big round Drops cours'd down with silent pace, ...Il.17.497.307.
The youthful Warrior heard with silent Woe, ...Il.17.781.319.
Each beat her Iv'ry Breast with silent Woe, ...Il.18.67.326.
Silent they stood: *Polydamas* at last, ...Il.18.293.336.
Meantime the Townsmen, arm'd with silent Care, ...Il.18.595.351.
With silent Glee, the Heaps around him rise. ....Il.18.646.354.
Silent, he heard the Queen of Woods upbraid: ....Il.21.553.444.
If, in the silent Shades of Hell below, ...Il.22.487A.476.
The Host beheld him, silent with Amaze! ....Il.23.782.520.
A solemn, silent, melancholy Train. ....Il.24.1012.577.
And silent, to the joyous hall repairs. ....Od.1.430.53.

SILENT (CONTINUED)

Such the pleas'd ear will drink with silent joy. Od.1.436.53.
Secur'd the valves. There, wrap'd in silent shade, Od.1.555.58.
Then silent sate—at length *Antinous* burns Od.2.93.65.
'Till night with silent shade invests the pole; Od.4.782.156.
The great event with silent hope attend; Od.4.1025.165.
While pensive in the silent slumb'rous shade, Od.4.1045.166.
Was in the silent gates of sleep confin'd) Od.4.1066.167.
Now in the silent grave the Monarch lay, Od.6.17.204.
But silent march, nor greet the common train Od.7.39.235.
Silent they gaze, and eye the god-like guest. Od.7.193.245.
The silent tear, and heard the secret groan: Od.8.92.267.
The silent tear, and heard the secret groan; Od.8.584.294.
Silent we came, and melancholy lay, Od.10.166.348.
Why sits *Ulysses* silent and apart? Od.10.445.365.
Why is she silent, while her Son is nigh? Od.11.177.390.
And death release me from the silent urn! Od.11.610.413.
The hungry flame devours the silent dead. Od.12.18.430.
A rising tomb, the silent dead to grace, Od.12.19.430.
The silent fisher casts th' insidious food, Od.12.301.446.
But thou be silent, nor reveal thy state; Od.13.351.24.
And inly bleeds, and silent wastes away: Od.13.434.27.
Silent and thoughtful while the board he ey'd, Od.14.134.42.
No more—th' approaching hours of silent night Od.14.449.57.
And void of pain, the silent arrows kill. Od.15.451.92.
But the dark brow of silent sorrow shook: Od.17.584.161.
Their silent journey, since his tale begun, Od.17.607.161.
Nor bury in the silent grave my cares? Od.18.242.178.
Silent, abash'd, they hear the stern rebuke, Od.18.458.190.
In silent wonder sigh'd unwilling praise. Od.19.272.208.
Immur'd within the silent bow'r of *Sleep,* Od.19.656.227.
Then silent, to the joyous hall returns, Od.21.60.262.
Then unperceiv'd and silent, at the board Od.21.425.280.
The lyre, now silent, trembling in his hands; Od.22.370.305.

SILENTLY

His years slide silently away, 6.1.10A.3.

SILENUS

And old *Silenus,* youthful in Decay, 1.TrVP.24.378.
Where Tindal dictates, and Silenus snores." 5.DunB4.492.390.

SILIA

How soft is Silia! fearful to offend, 3.Ep2.29.52.
But spare your censure; Silia does not drink. 3.Ep2.34.52.

SILK

He wrapt in Silk, and laid upon his Heart. 2.ChJM.399.34.
Let *Sporus* tremble—"What? that Thing of silk, 4.Arbu.305.117.
Let *Paris* tremble—"What? that Thing of silk, 4.Arbu.305A.117.
So spins the silk-worm small its slender store, 5.DunB4.253.369.
Or draw to silk Arachne's subtile line; 5.DunB4.590.401.
Misers are Muckworms, Silk-worms Beaus, 6.53.23.162.

SILK-WORM

So spins the silk-worm small its slender store, 5.DunB4.253.369.

SILK-WORMS

Misers are Muckworms, Silk-worms Beaus, 6.53.23.162.

SILKEN

While clog'd he beats his silken Wings in vain; 2.RL2.130.168.
Pours at great Bourbon's feet her silken sons; 5.DunB4.298.373.
The Goddess softly shook her silken Vest Il.3.479.214.
And veil'd her Blushes in a silken Shade; Il.3.522.216.
They shook with Fear, and drop'd the silken Rein; Il.11.168.42.
The bolt, obedient to the silken cord, Od.1.553.58.
The silken fleece impurpl'd for the loom, Od.4.181.128.
Now mounting the gay seat, the silken reins Od.6.95.209.
My limbs, and o'er me cast a silken vest. Od.10.648.375.
The bolt, obedient to the silken string, Od.21.47.261.

SILKS

Fans clap, Silks russle, and tough Whalebones crack; 2.RL5.40.202.
First, Silks and Diamonds veil no finer Shape, 4.HAdv.106.85.
In silks, in crapes, in garters, and in rags; 5.DunA2.18.98.
In silks, in crapes, in Garters, and in rags, 5.DunB2.22.297.
In Di'monds, silks, and rich Brocades, 6.14v(b).16A.50.
Were Virtue's self in Silks,—faith keep away! 6.82vi.7.232.

SILKWORM

So spins the silkworm small its slender store, 5.DunA1.171.84.

SILL

Under this Marble, or under this Sill, 6.144.1.386.

SILLIER

Sillier than *G[i]ld[o]n* cou'dst thou be, 6.64.17.190.

SILLY

To sigh for ribbands if thou art so silly, 3.EOM4.277.154.
The silly bard grows fat, or falls away. 4.2HE1.303.221.

SILV'RY

"Of all th' enamel'd race, whose silv'ry wing 5.DunB4.421.383.

SILVER

Led forth his Flocks along the silver *Thame,* 1.PSu.2.71.
Bewail'd his Fate beside a silver Spring; 1.PSu.2A.71.
Behold the *Groves* that shine with silver Frost, 1.PWi.9.89.
The silver Swans her hapless Fate bemoan, 1.PWi.39.91.
Her Fate remurmur to the silver Flood; 1.PWi.64.93.
The silver Flood, so lately calm, appears 1.PWi.65.93.
Nor Evening *Cynthia* fill her silver Horn, 1.Mes.100.122.
The silver Eel, in shining Volumes roll'd, 1.W-F.143.163.
Here arm'd with Silver Bows, in early Dawn, 1.W-F.169.165.

SILVER (CONTINUED)

In a soft, silver Stream dissolv'd away. 1.W-F.204.168.
The silver Stream her Virgin Coldness keeps, 1.W-F.205.168.
And add new Lustre to her Silver *Star.* 1.W-F.290.175.
The figur'd Streams in Waves of Silver roll'd, 1.W-F.335.182.
The *Kennet* swift, for silver Eels renown'd; 1.W-F.341.183.
His Temples thinly spread with silver Hairs: 1.TrVP.47.379.
A Spring there is, whose Silver Waters show, 1.TrSP.179.401.
Nor Silver Vases took the forming Mold, 1.TrSt.207.419.
And rising *Cynthia* sheds her silver Light, 1.TrSt.475.430.
And bathe in silver Dews thy yellow Hair; 1.TrSt.832.444.
Veil'd in a Cloud, to silver *Simois* Shore: 1.TrES.339.462.
And the shrill Trumpets mix their Silver Sound; 2.ChJM.319.29.
The Silver Key that lock'd the Garden Door. 2.ChJM.468.37.
The Silver Key that op'd the Garden Door. 2.ChJM.468A.37.
And the press'd Watch return'd a silver Sound. 2.RL1.18.146.
The silver Token, and the circled Green, 2.RL1.32.148.
Each Silver Vase in mystic Order laid. 2.RL1.122.155.
Lanch'd on the Bosom of the Silver *Thames.* 2.RL2.4.159.
Form a strong Line about the Silver Bound, 2.RL2.121.167.
The silver Lamp; the fiery Spirits blaze. 2.RL3.108.176.
From silver Spouts the grateful Liquors glide, 2.RL3.109.176.
The silver Lamp, and fiery Spirits blaze. 2.RL3.108A.176.
His Silver Beard wav'd gently o'er his Breast; 2.TemF.185.270.
Four Swans sustain a Carr of Silver bright 2.TemF.210.272.
No silver saints, by dying misers giv'n, 2.ElAb.137.331.
To *Paraclete's* white walls, and silver springs, 2.ElAb.348.348.
While Angels with their silver wings o'ershade 2.Elegy.67.367.
With silver-quiv'ring rills mæander'd o'er— 3.Ep4.85.146.
And now the Chapel's silver bell you hear, 3.Ep4.141.151.
If neither Gems adorn, nor Silver tip 4.HAdv.147.87.
Who to the *Dean* and *silver Bell* can swear, 4.Arbu.299.117.
Thither, the silver-sounding Lyres 4.HOde1.25.153.
Now shown by Cynthia's silver Ray, 4.HOde1.47.153.
Which sounds the Silver Thames along, 4.HOde9.2.159.
Gold, Silver, Iv'ry, Vases sculptur'd high, 4.2HE2.264.183.
And tips with silver all the walls: 4.HS6.192.261.
"As Gold to Silver, Virtue is to Gold." 4.1HE1.78.285.
The silver Thames reflects its marble face. 4.1HE1.142.289.
With deeper sable blots the silver flood. 5.DunA2.262.133.
Slow mov'd the Goddess from the silver flood, 5.DunA2.331A.142.
With deeper sable blots the silver flood. 5.DunB2.274.309.
These silver drops, like morning dew, 6.5.7.12.
All up the silver *Thames,* or all a down; 6.14ii.52.44.
For not the Desk with silver Nails, 6.58.9.171.
While smoking Streams from Silver Spouts shall glide, 6.82i.3.229.
While smoking Streams from Silver Spouts shall flow, 6.82i.3A.229.
With silver sounds, and sweetly tune out time. 6.82xii.2.237.
"Where twin'd the Silver Eel around thy Hook, 6.96ii.21.270.
Villete's soft Voice and St John's silver Lyre. 6.106ii.6.307.
4. Who to the *Dean* and *Silver Bell* can swear, 6.120.7.339.
God of the Silver Bow! thy Shafts employ, Il.1.59.88.
Fierce as he mov'd, his Silver Shafts resound. Il.1.64.89.
God of the Silver Bow, thy Ear incline, Il.1.590.116.
Late had she view'd the Silver-footed Dame, Il.1.696.120.
In close Consult, the Silver-footed Queen. Il.1.719.122.
With Voice alternate aid the silver Sound. Il.1.775.124.
Copæ, and *Thisbè,* fam'd for silver Doves, Il.2.601.156.
His silver Current thro' the flow'ry Meads; Il.2.623.157.
Or *Messè's* Tow'rs for silver Doves renown'd, Il.2.705.159.
His Hand no more awak'd the silver String. Il.2.730.161.
Or where by *Phœstus* silver *Jardan* runs; Il.2.789.162.
And where *Hyperia's* silver Fountains flow. Il.2.895.166.
Yet o'er the silver Surface pure they flow, Il.2.912.167.
And train'd by Him who bears the Silver Bow. Il.2.929.167.
The ripening Silver in *Alybean* Mines. Il.2.1045.172.
Thy curling Tresses, and thy silver Lyre, Il.3.80.193.
With Flow'rs adorn'd, with silver Buckles bound: Il.3.412.212.
With Flow'rs adorn'd, and silver Buckles bound: Il.3.412A.212.
To *Lycian Phœbus* with the Silver Bow, Il.4.132.226.
Amid the Flocks on silver *Simois'* Shore: Il.4.545.247.
This done, the Patron of the Silver Bow Il.5.545.294.
The bossie Naves of solid Silver shone; Il.5.896.308.
Silver the Beam, th' extended Yoke was Gold, Il.5.900.309.
Where Silver *Simois* and *Scamander* join. Il.5.965.312.
And till'd the Banks where silver *Satnio* flow'd. Il.6.42.325.
The Chief arriv'd at *Xanthus'* silver Flood: Il.6.212.336.
What Tears shall down thy silver Beard be roll'd, Il.7.149.372.
With that, a Sword with Stars of Silver grac'd, Il.7.366.382.
And tip with Silver ev'ry Mountain's Head; Il.8.694.428.
Of polish'd Silver with its costly Frame) Il.9.248.445.
And promis'd Comfort to my silver Hairs. Il.9.617.464.
The silver *Cynthia* bade *Contention* rise, Il.9.657.467.
Rich silver Plates his shining Car infold; Il.10.508.26.
And leads them, fasten'd by the silver Reins; Il.10.583.28.
In shining Greaves, with silver Buckles bound: Il.11.24.35.
Gold was the Hilt, a silver sheath encas'd Il.11.41.36.
Within its Concave hung a silver Thong, Il.11.49.36.
But the broad Belt, with Plates of Silver bound, Il.11.303.48.
Amidst her Flocks on *Satnio's* silver Shore) Il.14.520.188.
And call the God that bears the silver Bow. Il.15.60.196.
His manly Legs, with silver Buckles bound Il.16.163.244.
(The Presents of the silver-footed Dame) Il.16.272.249.
Between the Space where silver *Simois* flows, Il.16.480.261.
To *Peleus,* and the silver-footed Dame; Il.16.702.271.
Veil'd in a Cloud, to silver *Simois'* Shore: Il.16.826.275.
Nesæa mild, and Silver *Spio* came. Il.18.48.326.
While the long Pomp the silver Wave divides. Il.18.88.327.
And thus the silver-footed Dame began. Il.18.94.327.
So they. Meanwhile the silver-footed Dame Il.18.431.341.
High on a Throne, with Stars of silver grac'd Il.18.457.343.
And soft receiv'd me on their silver Breast. Il.18.466.344.
He thus address'd the silver-footed Dame. Il.18.494.345.
In hissing Flames huge silver Bars are roll'd, Il.18.545.348.
A silver Chain suspends the massy Round, Il.18.554.348.
To the soft Flute, and Cittern's silver Sound: Il.18.574.350.

SILVER (CONTINUED)
Cover'd with Shields, beside a silver Flood. ... Il.18.604.352.
They fight, they fall, beside the silver Flood; ... Il.18.617.352.
The waving Silver seem'd to blush with Blood. ... Il.18.618.352.
And curl'd on silver Props, in order glow: ... Il.18.654.355.
That glitt'ring gay, from silver Belts depend. ... Il.18.689.357.
In living Silver seem'd the Waves to roll, ... Il.18.703.357.
The silver Cuishes first his Thighs infold; ... Il.19.398.388.
(The silver Traces sweeping at their side) ... Il.19.428.389.
Each azure Sister of the silver Flood; ... Il.20.14.393.
And the chast Huntress of the silver Bow. ... Il.20.54.396.
First silver-shafted *Phœbus* took the Plain ... Il.20.91.398.
Crown the fair Hills that silver *Simois* shade. ... Il.20.183.401.
And rul'd the Fields where silver *Satnio* flow'd) ... Il.21.99.425.
Then to the Godhead of the silver Bow ... Il.21.248.431.
Of pointed Arrows, and the silver Bow! ... Il.21.550.444.
Pity, while yet I live, these silver Hairs; ... Il.22.80.456.
Rent from his Head the silver Locks away. ... Il.22.109.457.
Far-beaming o'er the silver Host of Night, ... Il.22.400.472.
Where to the Day thy silver Fountains rise, ... Il.23.183.497.
Whose glitt'ring Margins rais'd with Silver shine; ... Il.23.641.515.
A silver Urn; that full six Measures held, ... Il.23.865.524.
His Word the silver-footed Queen attends, ... Il.24.155.541.
Their Chariots stopping, at the silver Spring ... Il.24.430.554.
Adjure him by his Father's silver Hairs, ... Il.24.571.560.
Those silver Hairs, that venerable Face; ... Il.24.601.562.
(Old Ocean's Daughter, silver-footed Dame) ... Il.24.710.567.
These by *Apollo's* silver Bow were slain, ... Il.24.761.569.
With silver Fleece, which his Attendants slew. ... Il.24.787.570.
Rosy and fair! as *Phœbus'* silver Bow ... Il.24.956.576.
A silver Laver, of capacious size: ... Od.1.182.41.
Reflecting to the Queen the silver sounds. ... Od.1.426.53.
In slumber clos'd her silver-streaming eyes. ... Od.1.464.54.
The silver ring she pull'd, the door re-clos'd; ... Od.1.552.58.
Who boast experience from these silver hairs; ... Od.3.463.109.
High on a massy vase of silver mold, ... Od.4.65.122.
The silver-shafted Goddess of the Chace! ... Od.4.160.128.
A silver canister divinely wrought, ... Od.4.165.128.
With silver tripods, the kind host assign'd; ... Od.4.174.128.
Not mean the massy mold, of silver grac'd ... Od.4.835.158.
Her eyes restrain the silver-streaming tears: ... Od.4.1000.164.
Or azure daughters of the silver flood? ... Od.6.146.214.
And o'er the silver pours the fusile gold. ... Od.6.278.224.
The silver scourge, it glitter'd o'er the field: ... Od.6.378.230.
The pillars silver, on a brazen base; ... Od.7.115.240.
Silver the lintels deep-projecting o'er, ... Od.7.116.240.
In sculptur'd gold and labour'd silver stand. ... Od.7.119.240.
With stars of silver shone the bed of state. ... Od.7.229.247.
A silver laver, of capacious size. ... Od.7.233.247.
With silver shone the throne; his Lyre well strung ... Od.8.63.265.
A ruddy gleam; whose hilt, a silver blaze; ... Od.8.438.287.
A silver bowl that held a copious draught, ... Od.9.237.316.
Securely fetter'd by a silver thong. ... Od.10.26.340.
She to *Artacia's* silver streams came down, ... Od.10.121.346.
Radiant with starry studs, a silver seat ... Od.10.375.362.
The silver stands with golden flaskets grac'd: ... Od.10.420.364.
A silver laver of capacious size. ... Od.10.436.365.
Nor bent the silver-shafted Queen her bow; ... Od.11.243.393.
And in soft mazes rouls a silver Tide: ... Od.11.286.396.
A bowl; the Prince a silver beaker chose. ... Od.15.117.74.
This silver bowl, whose costly margins shine ... Od.15.128.75.
The silver vase with living sculpture wrought. ... Od.15.135.75.
A silver laver of capacious size. ... Od.15.151.76.
The silver *Phæa's* glitt'ring Rills they lost, ... Od.15.318.85.
They bend the silver bow with tender skill, ... Od.15.450.92.
T'usurp the honours due to silver hairs ... Od.16.45.104.
A silver laver of capacious size. ... Od.17.107.137.
Where silver alders, in high arches twin'd, ... Od.17.240.143.
By *Ægypt's* silver flood our ships we moor, ... Od.17.511.157.
(The partners of her cares) the silver wool; ... Od.18.362.185.
An ivory seat with silver ringlets grac'd, ... Od.19.68.196.
Which held th' alternate brass and silver rings. ... Od.21.64.262.
In slumber clos'd her silver-streaming eyes. ... Od.21.388.279.
Between the laver and the silver throne; ... Od.22.376.306.
And the pale silver glows with fusile gold: ... Od.23.160.328.
With silver shone, with elephant, and gold. ... Od.23.206.333.
The mingled web, whose gold and silver ray ... Od.24.173.356.
A bowl, that rich with polish'd silver flames, ... Od.24.322.365.

SILVER-FOOTED
Late had she view'd the Silver-footed Dame, ... Il.1.696.120.
In close Consult, the Silver-footed Queen. ... Il.1.719.122.
(The Presents of the silver-footed Dame) ... Il.16.272.249.
To *Peleus*, and the silver-footed Dame; ... Il.16.702.271.
And thus the silver-footed Dame began. ... Il.18.94.327.
So they. Meanwhile the silver-footed Dame ... Il.18.431.341.
He thus address'd the silver-footed Dame. ... Il.18.494.345.
His Word the silver-footed Queen attends, ... Il.24.155.541.
(Old Ocean's Daughter, silver-footed Dame) ... Il.24.710.567.

SILVER-QUIV'RING
With silver-quiv'ring rills mæander'd o'er— ... 3.Ep4.85.146.

SILVER-SHAFTED
First silver-shafted *Phœbus* took the Plain ... Il.20.91.398.
The silver-shafted Goddess of the Chace! ... Od.4.160.128.
Nor bent the silver-shafted Queen her bow; ... Od.11.243.393.

SILVER-SOUNDING
Thither, the silver-sounding Lyres ... 4.HOde1.25.153.

SILVER-STREAMING
In slumber clos'd her silver-streaming eyes. ... Od.1.464.54.
Her eyes restrain the silver-streaming tears: ... Od.4.1000.164.
In slumber clos'd her silver-streaming eyes. ... Od.21.388.279.

SILVER'D
To isles of fragrance, lilly-silver'd vales, ... 5.DunB4.303.374.
And smiling calmness silver'd o'er the deep. ... Od.10.108.345.
The hand of Time had silver'd o'er with snow, ... Od.11.429.405.
With ivory silver'd thick the foot-stool shone, ... Od.19.70.196.

SIMILE
One Simile, that solitary shines ... 4.2HE1.111.205.
Fr. This filthy Simile, this beastly Line, ... 4.EpS2.181.323.
(That Simile is not my own, ... 6.10.17.25.
The Simile yet one thing shocks, ... 6.93.27Z5.257.

SIMILES
Figures ill-pair'd, and Similes unlike. ... 5.DunA1.64.67.

SIMILIES
Figures ill pair'd, and Similies unlike. ... 5.DunB1.66.275.

SIMILITUDE
In sad similitude of griefs to mine, ... 2.ElAb.360.348.
In just similitude, the grace and air ... Od.4.192.129.
Mankind, to seek their own similitude. ... Od.17.253.143.
With fair similitude of truth beguiles ... Od.19.235.204.
And sad similitude of woes ally'd, ... Od.19.400.214.

SIMOÏSIUS
In blooming Youth fair *Simoïsius* fell, ... Il.4.542.247.
Fair *Simoïsius*, whom his Mother bore ... Il.4.544.247.
Thus pierc'd by *Ajax*, *Simoïsius* lies ... Il.4.560.248.
He drops the Corps of *Simoïsius* slain, ... Il.4.565.248.

SIMO'S
Turn then from Wits; and look on Simo's Mate, ... 3.Ep2.101.58.

SIMOIS
Veil'd in a Cloud, to silver *Simois* Shore: ... 1.TrES.339.462.
And thence from *Simois* nam'd the lovely Boy. ... Il.4.549.247.
Where Silver *Simois* and *Scamander* join. ... Il.5.965.312.
And gulphy *Simois*, rolling to the Main ... Il.12.21.82.
Between the Space where silver *Simois* flows, ... Il.16.480.261.
Now shouts to *Simois*, from her beauteous * Hill; ... Il.20.73.397.
Crown the fair Hills that silver *Simois* shade. ... Il.20.183.401.
Then thus to *Simois:* Haste, my Brother Flood! ... Il.21.358.435.

SIMOIS'
Amid the Flocks on silver *Simois'* Shore: ... Il.4.545.247.
On *Simois'* Brink Ambrosial Herbage grew. ... Il.5.969.312.
Veil'd in a Cloud, to silver *Simois'* Shore: ... Il.16.826.275.

SIMONY
Not more of Simony beneath black Gowns, ... 4.JD2.81.141.
In Noble's Titles; Pride and Simony, ... 4.JD2A.87.140.

SIMP'RING
With simp'ring Angels, Palms, and Harps divine; ... 3.Ep2.14.49.

SIMPER
The conscious simper, and the jealous leer, ... 5.DunA2.6.97.
The conscious simper, and the jealous leer, ... 5.DunB2.6.296.

SIMPLE
Yet simple Nature to his hope has giv'n, ... 3.EOM1.103.27.
And simple Reason never sought but one: ... 3.EOM3.230.115.
Averted half your Parents simple Pray'r, ... 3.Ep2.286.73.
Remembers oft the School-boy's simple fare, ... 4.HS2.73.59.
Or simple Pride for Flatt'ry makes demands; ... 4.Arbu.253.114.
Have bled and purg'd me to a simple *Vote*. ... 4.2HE2.197.179.
A simple Quaker, or a Quaker's Wife, ... 4.EpS1.133.308.
See! what the charms, that smite the simple heart ... 5.DunA3.227.176.
See what the charms, that smite the simple heart ... 5.DunB3.229.331.
Where bask on sunny banks the simple sheep, ... 5.DunB4.352.377.
When simple *Macer*, now of high Renown, ... 6.49i.1.137.
Your pilf'ring Lord, with simple Pride, ... 6.135.33.367.
As when some simple Swain his Cot forsakes, ... Il.5.734.302.
From Milk, innoxious, seek their simple Food: ... Il.13.12.104.
What time young *Paris*, simple Shepherd Boy, ... Il.24.39.537.
But he, of ancient faith, a simple swain, ... Od.14.30.36.
Such food as falls to simple servant's share; ... Od.14.98.40.

SIMPLES
He hears; and as a Still, with Simples in it, ... 4.JD4.126.35.
Just as a Still, with Simples in it, ... 6.10.15.25.
With various simples cloaths the fat'ned soil. ... Od.4.318.134.

SIMPLES'
(She that all Simples' healing Virtues knew, ... Il.11.876.75.

SIMPLEX
"'Tis *Fornicatio simplex*, and no other: ... 4.HAdv.42.79.

SIMPLICITY
Thus much is left of old Simplicity! ... 4.HS2.36.57.
And strangely lik'd for her *Simplicity:* ... 6.49i.20.138.
In Wit, a Man; Simplicity, a Child; ... 6.125.2.349.
A manly wit, a child's simplicity, ... 6.125.1Z1.349.

SIMPLICIUS
And good Simplicius asks of her advice. ... 3.Ep2.32.52.

SIN
The clear, reflecting Mind, presents his Sin ... 1.TrSt.73.413.
Alas, alas, that ever Love was Sin! ... 2.ChWB.324.72.
Nor could it sure be such a Sin to paint. ... 2.RL5.24.201.
Too soon they taught me 'twas no sin to love. ... 2.ElAb.68.324.
And wait, till 'tis no sin to mix with thine. ... 2.ElAb.176.334.
How shall I lose the sin, yet keep the sense, ... 2.ElAb.191.335.

SIN (CONTINUED)

See Sin in State, majestically drunk, ...3.Ep2.69.55.
What Sin of mine cou'd merit such a Rod? ....4.JD4.63.31.
Convicted of that mortal Sin, a Hole! ....4.JD4.245A.47.
Beheld such Scenes of *Envy, Sin,* and *Hate.* ....4.JD4.193.43.
Saw such a Scene of *Envy, Sin,* and *Hate.* ....4.JD4.193A.43.
To deluge Sin, and drown a Court in Tears. ....4.JD4.285.49.
He too can say, "With Wives I never sin." ....4.HAdv.73.81.
Too hard a Penance for defeated Sin, ...4.HAdv.85.83.
Why did I write? what sin to me unknown ....4.Arbu.125.104.
And 'twere a sin to rob them of their Mite. ....4.Arbu.162.108.
It was a Sin to call our Neighbour Fool, ...4.Arbu.383.126.
Ev'n Poetry, tho tis indeed a Sin ....4.JD2A.7.132.
I grant that Poetry's a crying sin; ....4.JD2.7.133.
True, conscious Honour is to feel no sin, ...4.1HE1.93.285.
All Tyes dissolv'd, and ev'ry Sin forgiv'n, ...4.EpS1.94.305.
This calls the Church to deprecate our Sin, ...4.EpS1.129.307.
—What are you thinking? *Fr.* Faith, the thought's no Sin, ...4.EpS2.122.320.
To *W[alpole]* guilty of some venial Sin, ...4.EpS2.162.322 .
"O born in sin, and forth in folly brought! ....5.DunB1.225.286.
In some close corner of the soul, they sin: ....6.41.18.114.
And Wit and Love no Sin, ...6.61.4.180.
And Love and Wit no Sin, ...6.61.4A.180.
Hackney'd in Sin, we beat about the Town, ...6.82vi.5.232.
Purge all your verses from the sin of wit ....6.82ix(f).2.235.
As decent to *repent* in, as to *sin* in. ....6.95.6.264.
And 'twere a Sin to rob them of their *Mite.* ....6.98.12.283.
As erst he scourg'd *Jessides'* Sin of yore ....6.137.8.373.
With not one sin but poetry, ...6.150.2.398.
"Wretch! this is villany, and this is sin." ....Od.14.110.41.

SINCE

But since those Graces please thy Eyes no more, ...1.PSu.29.74.
But since those Graces please thy Sight no more, ...1.PSu.29A.74.
For ever silent, since despis'd by thee. ....1.PSu.44.75.
The balmy *Zephyrs,* silent since her Death, ...1.PWi.49.92.
Nor envy *Windsor!* since thy Shades have seen ....1.W-F.161.164.
Since Fate relentless stop'd their Heav'nly Voice, ...1.W-F.277.174.
(Since Rules were made but to promote their End) ....1.EOC.147.256.
Since none can compass more than they *Intend;* ....1.EOC.256.268.
Since you a servant's ravish'd form bemoan, ...1.TrFD.3.385.
Farewell! and since I cannot bend to join ....1.TrFD.92.390.
Since *Phaon* fled, I all those Joys resign, ...1.TrSP.236A.404.
Yet since thou wilt thy Sister-Queen controul, ...1.TrSt.366.425.
Since still the Lust of Discord fires thy Soul, ...1.TrSt.367.425.
Nor err from me, since I deserve it all: ....1.TrSt.773.442.
But since, alas, ignoble Age must come, ...1.TrES.47.451.
But since by Counsel all things shou'd be done, ...2.ChJM.95.19.
Since if I found no Pleasure in my Spouse, ...2.ChJM.115.20.
And since I speak of Wedlock, let me say, ...2.ChJM.127.20.
Let none oppose th'Election, since on this ....2.ChJM.256.27.
Since it chastises still what best it loves. ....2.ChJM.283.27.
But since he's blind and old, (a helpless Case) ....2.ChJM.645.46.
But since the Sacred Leaves to All are free, ...2.ChJM.677.47.
I yield it up; but since I gave my Oath, ...2.ChJM.701.48.
For, since Fifteen, in Triumph have I led ....2.ChWB.7.57.
Full many a Saint, since first the World began, ...2.ChWB.46.58.
But since their Wealth (the best they had) was mine, ...2.ChWB.60.59.
"Of *Job's* great Patience since so oft you preach, ...2.ChWB.186.65.
"And since in Man right Reason bears the Sway, ...2.ChWB.193.65.
I vow'd, I scarce cou'd sleep since first I knew him, ...2.ChWB.300.71.
Since all that Man e'er lost, is treasur'd there. ....2.RL*A*2.159.136.
But since, alas! frail Beauty must decay, ...2.RL5.25.201.
Curl'd or uncurl'd, since Locks will turn to grey, ...2.RL5.26.201.
Since painted, or not painted, all shall fade, ...2.RL5.27.201.
Since all things lost on Earth, are treasur'd there. ....2.RL5.114.208.
Since living Virtue is with Envy curst, ...2.TemF.320.279.
Let us (since Life can little more supply ....3.EOM1.3.11.
"Th' exceptions few; some change since all began, ...3.EOM1.147.33.
The gen'ral ORDER, since the whole began, ...3.EOM1.171.36.
But since not every good we can divide, ...3.EOM2.95.66.
Has crept thro' scoundrels ever since the flood, ...3.EOM4.212.147.
Since but to wish more Virtue, is to gain. ....3.EOM4.326.160.
Well then, since with the world we stand or fall ....3.Ep3.79A.94.
Since then, my Lord, on such a World we fall, ...3.Ep3.79.94.
Since 'twas no form'd Design of serving God: ....4.JD4.18.27.
Thou, who since Yesterday, has roll'd o'er all ....4.JD4.202.43.
Tho' Heav'n be praisd, that ever since I knew ....4.JD2A.1.132.
Sages and Chiefs long since had birth ....4.HOde9.9.159.
But (thanks to *Homer)* since I live and thrive, ...4.2HE2.68.169.
Now, or long since, what diff'rence will be found? ....4.2HE2.238.181.
Since HARLEY bid me first attend, ...4.HS6.85.255.
Since the whole House did afterwards the same: ....4.EpS2.170.323.
Say great Patricians! (since your selves inspire ....5.DunA1.3.61.
And all who since, in mild benighted days, ...5.DunA3.45.154.
E'er since Sir Fopling's Periwig was Praise, ...5.DunB1.167.282.
And all who since, in mild benighted days, ...5.DunB3.53.323.
Then thus. "Since Man from beast by Words is known, ...5.DunB4.149.356.
And since my Tongue is in thy praises slow, ...6.2.4.5.
And since that thine all Rhetorick exceeds; ....6.2.5.5.
Since no Reprizals can be made on thee. ....6.7.14.16.
Since 'tis enough we find it so in You. ....6.7.24.16.
Since your Acquaintance with one *Brocas,* ....6.10.9.24.
Since those were slander'd most whom *Ozell* praised: ....6.12.7A.37.
Since not much Wine, much Company, much Food, ...6.17iv.28.60.
A large Concordance, (bound long since,) ....6.39.9.110.
There he stopt short, nor since has writ a tittle, ...6.49i.9.137.
Since quicken'd by thy Breath, ...6.50.42.148.
E'er since our Grandame's Evil; ....6.53.10.161.
Since Worms shall eat ev'n thee. ....6.53.36.162.
Since you have Brains as well as Men, ...6.58.67.173.
Since some have writ, and shewn no Wit at all. ....6.60.8.178.
Who saw you in Tower, and since ....6.68.7.196.
And Parnell who saw you not since ....6.68.9.196.
Since these for your Jury, good ....6.68.13.197.
Can taste no pleasure since his Shield was scour'd; ....6.71.42.204.

SINCE (CONTINUED)

Since my old Friend is grown so great, ...6.74.1.211.
And ah! since Death must that dear Frame destroy, ...6.86.17A.245.
And ah! since Death must that lov'd frame destroy, ...6.86.17C.245.
But since you hatch, pray own your Chicks: ....6.93.28.257.
E'er since the Days of *Eve,* ....6.94.2.259.
Great G[eorge ii]! such servants since thou well can'st lack, ...6.116v.5.327.
Since Great *Achilles* and *Atrides* strove, ...Il.1.7.85.
But since for common Good I yield the Fair, ...Il.1.151.94.
O Parent Goddess! since in early Bloom ....Il.1.460.110.
Now, valiant Chiefs! since Heav'n itself alarms, ...Il.2.93.131.
Since first the Labours of this War begun: ....Il.2.162.136.
Since Earth's wide Regions, Heav'n's unmeasur'd Height, ...Il.2.574.155.
Since fair *Briseis* from his Arms was torn, ...Il.2.841.164.
Who pierc'd long since beneath his Arrows bled; ....Il.4.139.227.
Sprung since thou art from *Jove,* and Heav'nly born. ....Il.5.1105.320.
Since vengeful Goddesses confed'rate join ....Il.7.37.364.
Since then the Night extends her gloomy Shade, ...Il.7.356.381.
Since rallying from our Wall we forc'd the Foe, ...Il.8.359.414.
Long since had *Hector* stain'd these Fields with Gore, ...Il.8.435.418.
And yet those Years that since thy Birth have run, ...Il.9.81.436.
Since more than his my Years, and more my Sway. ....Il.9.214.443.
My Fates long since by *Thetis* were disclos'd, ...Il.9.532.459.
But since what Honour asks, the Gen'ral sends, ...Il.9.645.466.
(Since Cares, like mine, deprive thy Soul of Rest) ....Il.10.107.7.
Say, since this Conquest, what their Counsels are? ....Il.10.481.25.
Since not alike endu'd with Force or Art, ...Il.12.319.93.
But since, alas! ignoble Age must come, ...Il.12.391.96.
But since yon' Ramparts by thy Arms lay low, ...Il.13.979.152.
Long since too vent'rous, at thy bold Command, ...Il.14.283.176.
Since Heav'n commands it (*Ajax* made reply) ....Il.15.554.218.
Since Battel is renounc'd, thy Thoughts employ ....Il.17.159.293.
Ah then, since from this miserable Day ....Il.18.129.328.
Since unreveng'd, a hundred Ghosts demand ....Il.18.131.329.
Since here, for brutal Courage far renown'd, ...Il.18.133.329.
Now since her Presence glads our Mansion, say, ...Il.18.473.344.
(The City since of many-languag'd Men) ....Il.20.257.404.
Ten Days were past, since in his Father's Reign ....Il.21.50.424.
Now shines the tenth bright Morning since I came ....Il.21.173.428.
Since You of all our num'rous Race, alone ....Il.22.303.468.
Since now at length the pow'rful Will of Heav'n ....Il.22.475.475.
Since now no more the Father guards his *Troy.* ....Il.22.653.483.
Since great *Minerva* wings their rapid Way, ...Il.23.485.509.
For since the Goal they doubled, round the Plain ....Il.23.546.511.
(Since great *Tydides* bears the first away) ....Il.23.615.514.
E'er since that Day implacable to *Troy,* ....Il.24.38.537.
Nine Days are past, since all the Court above ....Il.24.141.541.
And we submit, since such the Will of Heav'n. ....Il.24.176.543.
Since Victor of thy Fears, and slighting mine, ...Il.24.357.551.
This the twelfth Evening since he rested there, ...Il.24.505.557.
But since the God his Hand has pleas'd to turn, ...Il.24.688.565.
Here let me grow to Earth! since *Hector* lies ....Il.24.697.566.
Whom most he honour'd, since he lost his Friend; ....Il.24.723.567.
For since the Day that numbred with the Dead ....Il.24.806.570.
Since *Paris* brought me to the *Trojan* Shore; ....Il.24.965.576.
Since all who in th' *Olympian* bow'r reside ....Od.1.103.36.
But since to part, for sweet refection due ....Od.1.403.51.
Since great Ulysses sought the *Phrygian* plains, ...Od.2.33.61.
To whom the Youth. Since then in vain I tell ....Od.2.237.73.
Since he who like a father held his reign, ...Od.2.265.74.
But since thy veins paternal virtue fires, ...Od.2.317.76.
Their state, since last you left your natal land; ....Od.4.528.146.
And take this method, since the best I can. ....Od.5.463.195.
Since wide he wander'd on the wat'ry waste; ....Od.5.497.196.
But since thou tread'st our hospitable shore, ...Od.6.233.221.
Ye Gods! since this worn frame refection knew, ...Od.6.261.222.
Suppliant to her, since first he chose to pray, ...Od.7.386.255.
Since Wisdom's sacred guidance he pursues, ...Od.8.423.286.
(Untasted joy, since that disastrous hour, ...Od.8.487.289.
Cyclop! since human flesh has been thy feast, ...Od.9.408.322.
Long since he menac'd, such was Fate's command; ....Od.9.599.331.
Or (since to dust proud *Troy* submits her tow'rs) ....Od.11.196.391.
Or say, since honour call'd thee to the field, ...Od.11.198.391.
Since in the dust proud *Troy* submits her tow'rs. ....Od.11.205.391.
For since kind heav'n with wealth our realm has blest, ...Od.11.426.405.
Since yet the early hour of night allows ....Od.11.472.407.
For since of womankind so few are just, ...Od.11.563.411.
For real suff'rings since I grieve sincere, ...Od.14.397.55.
Since to be talkative I now commence, ...Od.14.524.62.
Since fix'd are thy resolves, may thund'ring *Jove* ....Od.15.126.75.
Long since, in better days, by *Helen* wove: ....Od.15.139.75.
To such a man since harbour you afford, ...Od.15.368.87.
Since audience mild is deign'd, permit my tongue ....Od.16.93.107.
Nor food nor wine refus'd: but since the day ....Od.16.152.110.
But re-consider, since the wisest err, ...Od.16.334.122.
Adieu! but since this ragged garb can bear ....Od.17.26.133.
My feeble step, since rugged is the way. ....Od.17.219.142.
Long, long since perish'd on a distant shore! ....Od.17.379.150.
Their silent journey, since his tale begun, ...Od.17.607.161.
No more I bathe, since he no longer sees ....Od.18.211.177.
Say, since *Ulysses* left his natal coast, ...Od.19.9.193.
Since my brave brother with his *Cretan* band ....Od.19.225.204.
Or, since mature in manhood, he deplores ....Od.19.619.226.
Estrang'd, since dear *Ulysses* sail'd to *Troy!* ....Od.19.696.229.
Since here resolv'd oppressive these reside, ...Od.20.275.246.
Since daring zeal with cool debate is join'd; ....Od.20.284.247.
Since due regard must wait the Prince's friend, ...Od.20.360.249.
This gift, long since when *Sparta's* shores he trod, ...Od.21.17.259.
But since 'till then, this tryal you delay, ...Od.21.300.274.
Since cold in death th' offender lies; oh spare ....Od.22.66.290.
Since my dear Lord left *Ithaca* for *Troy:* ....Od.23.22.320.
Since what no eye has seen thy tongue reveal'd, ...Od.23.245.335.
Since the just Gods who tread the starry plains ....Od.23.275.336.
Restore thee safe, since my *Ulysses* reigns. ....Od.23.276.336.
What years have circled since thou saw'st that guest? ....Od.24.335.365.
Five years have circled since these eyes pursu'd ....Od.24.361.366.

SINCE (CONTINUED)
Had not long since thy knowing soul decreed, ... Od.24.549.374.
Yet hear the issue: Since *Ulysses'* hand .... Od.24.552.374.

SINCERE
Tho' Learn'd, well-bred; and tho' well-bred, sincere; .... 1.EOC.635.311.
Thus, with an Air sincere, in Fiction bold, ... 1.TrUl.138.470.
To these we owe true friendship, love sincere, ... 3.EOM2.255.86.
Fix'd to no spot is Happiness sincere, ... 3.EOM4.15.129.
The Fool consistent, and the False sincere; .... 3.Ep1.176.30.
Pleasures sincere, and unallay'd with Pain, ... 6.17iii.10.58.
Sincere, tho' prudent; constant, yet resign'd; .... 6.27.2.81.
Whose Soul, sincere and free, ... 6.47.50.130.
But entring learns to be sincere. .... 6.51ii.6.152.
Sincere, tho' prudent, constant, yet resign'd; .... 6.57.2.169.
Hearts so sincere th' Almighty saw well pleas'd, ... 6.69i.5.198.
"Statesman, yet friend to Truth! of soul sincere, ... 6.71.67.204.
"Statesman, yet friend to Truth! in soul sincere, ... 6.71.67A.204.
But candid, free, sincere, as you began, ... 6.73.12.210.
With Greatness easy, and with wit sincere. .... 6.75.8.212.
Statesman, yet Friend to Truth! of Soul sincere, ... 6.97.1.281.
Statesman, yet Friend to Truth! in Sòul sincere, ... 6.97.1A.281.
Just of thy word, in ev'ry thought sincere, ... 6.109.5.314.
Go then, where only bliss sincere is known! .... 6.109.15.314.
Go, just of word, in ev'ry thought sincere, ... 6.109.5A.314.
Just of thy word, and in each thought sincere, ... 6.109.5B.314.
And the gay Courtier feels the sigh sincere. .... 6.113.6.320.
And the gay Courtier feels his sigh sincere, ... 6.113.6A.320.
For never Heart felt Passion more sincere: .... 6.152.4.400.
For Words well meant, and Sentiments sincere? .... Il.12.246.90.
The Happiest taste not Happiness sincere, ... Il.24.671.565.
Sincere from royal blood, and faith profan'd; .... Od.1.50.33.
Sincere, from whence began thy course, recite, ... Od.1.221.43.
But, gen'rous youth! sincere and free declare, ... Od.1.267.45.
Say, royal youth, sincere of soul report .... Od.4.421.140.
Kind the persuasion, and sincere my aim; .... Od.5.243.183.
The social feast of joy, with joy sincere. .... Od.8.430.287.
Thus, with an air sincere, in fiction bold, ... Od.13.305.21.
Sincere from whence begun your course relate, ... Od.14.216.45.
For real suff'rings since I grieve sincere, ... Od.14.397.55.
Sincere the youthful Heroe made reply. .... Od.16.118.108.
For what so easy as to be sincere? .... Od.17.19.133.
By precious gifts the vow sincere display: .... Od.18.323.182.
And, unattended by sincere repose, ... Od.19.600.225.
Sincere reveals the sanction of the skies: .... Od.19.651.227.
Now say sincere, my guest! the Suitor train .... Od.20.208.243.
But thou sincere! Oh *Euryclea,* say, ... Od.22.456.310.

SINCERELY
Words ever pleasing, yet sincerely true, ... 6.125.1Z3.349.
Declare sincerely to no foe's demand .... Od.15.286.82.

SINCERER
She shews her Grief in a sincerer Place; .... 6.33.8.99.
No *British* Miss sincerer Grief has known, ... 6.96ii.3.270.

SINCEREST
The *clearest Head,* and the *sincerest Heart.* .... 1.EOC.732.325.

SINCERITY
For thee she feels sincerity of woe: .... Od.11.550.410.

SINDG'D
See SING'D.
Then the sindg'd members they with skill divide; .... Od.14.475.58.

SINEWS
Beneath his pond'rous Shield his Sinews bend, ... Il.5.993.314.
Confirm'd his Sinews, and restor'd to Fight. .... Il.7.328.380.
His sinews shrunk with age, and stiff with toil, ... Od.19.366.212.
These aged sinews with new vigor strung .... Od.21.207.269.

SINEWY
Who wrench'd the Javelin from his sinewy Thigh. .... Il.5.855.307.
The sinewy Ancles bor'd, the Feet he bound .... Il.17.336.300.
He dropt his sinewy arms: his knees no more .... Od.5.581.200.
Arriv'd, his sinewy arms incessant place .... Od.8.315.281.
Aslope they glanc'd, the sinewy fibres tore, ... Od.19.526.221.
Truss'd with his sinewy pounce a trembling dove; .... Od.20.303.247.
That sinewy fragment at *Ulysses* cast, ... Od.20.366.250.

SINFUL
Weak, sinful Laymen were but Flesh and Blood. .... 2.ChJM.8.15.
Let sinful Batchelors their Woes deplore, ... 2.ChJM.29.16.
Shall I, the Terror of this sinful Town, ... 4.JD4.196.43.
Ev'n those I pardon, for whose sinful sake .... 4.JD2.41.135.
Ev'n those I pardon, For whose sinful Sake .... 4.JD2A.45.136.
I know the Swing of sinful Hack, ... 6.61.12.181.

SING
While on thy Banks *Sicilian* Muses sing; .... 1.PSp.4.60.
Why sit we mute, when early Linnets sing, ... 1.PSp.25.62.
Sing then and *Damon* shall attend the Strain, ... 1.PSp.29.63.
Then sing by turns, by turns the Muses sing, ... 1.PSp.41.64.
Then sing by turns, by turns the Muses sing, ... 1.PSp.41.64.
The Skies to brighten, and the Birds to sing. .... 1.PSp.72.68.
Blest Nymphs, whose Swains those Graces sing so well! .... 1.PSp.96.70.
A Faithful Swain, whom Love had taught to sing, ... 1.PSu.1A.71.
To you I mourn; nor to the Deaf I sing, ... 1.PSu.15.72.
But wou'd you sing, and rival *Orpheus'* Strain, ... 1.PSu.81.78.
Hylas and *Ægon's* Rural Lays I sing. .... 1.PAu.6.80.
Ye Birds, that left by Summer, cease to sing, ... 1.PAu.28.82.
Is not so mournful as the Strains you sing, ... 1.PWi.2.88.
Oh sing of *Daphne's* Fate, and *Daphne's* Praise! .... 1.PWi.8.89.
And said; "Ye Shepherds, sing around my Grave!" .... 1.PWi.18.90.
Sing, while beside the shaded Tomb I mourn, ... 1.PWi.19.90.

SING (CONTINUED)
In Notes more sad than when they sing their own. .... 1.PWi.40.92.
In sadder Notes than when they sing their own. .... 1.PWi.40A.92.
The Dumb shall sing, the Lame his Crutch foregoe, ... 1.Mes.43.116.
What Muse for *Granville* can refuse to sing? .... 1.W-F.6.148.
The Muse shall sing, and what she sings shall last) .... 1.W-F.174.166.
To sing those Honours you deserve to wear, ... 1.W-F.289.175.
Oh wou'dst thou sing what Heroes *Windsor* bore, ... 1.W-F.299.176.
The Muse, whose early Voice you taught to Sing, ... 1.EOC.735.325.
And mighty *Cæsar's* conqu'ring Eagles sing; .... 1.TrSt.24.410.
Shall warm my Breast to sing of *Cæsar's* Fame: .... 1.TrSt.48.411.
And sing, with Horror, his prodigious End. .... 1.TrSt.68.413.
Grave Authors say, and witty Poets sing, ... 2.ChJM.21.16.
(So Poets sing) was present on the Place; .... 2.ChJM.327.30.
Not *Hester's* self, whose Charms the *Hebrews* sing, ... 2.ChJM.343.30.
I sing—This Verse to *Caryll,* Muse! is due; .... 2.RL1.3.144.
With Eyes on Fame for ever fix'd, they sing; .... 2.TemF.272.276.
For her white virgins *Hymenæals* sing; .... 2.ElAb.220.338.
See the blind beggar dance, the cripple sing, ... 3.EOM2.267.87.
Rise, honest Muse! and sing the MAN of ROSS: .... 3.Ep3.250.113.
(Thus said our Friend, and what he said I sing.) .... 4.HS2.68.59.
Why let him Sing—but when you're in the Wrong, ... 4.HAdv.141.87.
To fetch and carry Sing-song up and down; .... 4.Arbu.226.112.
As needy Beggars sing at doors for meat. .... 4.JD2.26.133.
As needy Beggars sing at Doors for Meat .... 4.JD2A.30.134.
Sing thy sonorous Verse—but not aloud. .... 4.2HE2.109.173.
We build, we paint, we sing, we dance as well, ... 4.2HE1.46.197.
Or who shall wander where the Muses sing? .... 4.2HE1.352.225.
To sing, or cease to sing, we never know; .... 4.2HE1.361.227.
To sing, or cease to sing, we never know; .... 4.2HE1.361.227.
Your Arms, your Actions, your Repose to sing! .... 4.2HE1.395.229.
Yet every child another song will sing, ... 4.1HE1.91.285.
For what? to have a Box where Eunuchs sing, ... 4.1HE1.105.287.
Then might I sing without the least Offence, ... 4.EpS1.77.304.
Books and the Man I sing, the first who brings .... 5.DunA1.1.59.
Hence the soft sing-song on Cecilia's day, ... 5.DunA1.40.65.
Why shou'd I sing what bards the nightly Muse 5.DunA2.389.148
Another Durfey, Ward! shall sing in thee. 5.DunA3.138.161
I sing. Say you, her instruments the Great! .... 5.DunB1.3.269.
Why should I sing what bards the nightly Muse 5.DunB2.421.318
Another Durfey, Ward! shall sing in thee. 5.DunB3.146.326
Ye Pow'rs! whose Mysteries restor'd I sing, ... 5.DunB4.5.339.
Why all your Toils? your Sons have learn'd to sing. .... 5.DunB4.546.396.
O sing, and hush the Nations with thy Song! .... 5.DunB4.626.406.
While wretched lovers sing in vain. .... 6.6i.16.14.
Descend ye Nine! descend and sing; .... 6.11.1.29.
For who to sing for *Sanger* could refuse? .... 6.12.2.37.
Fain would my Muse the flow'ry Treasures sing, ... 6.14iv.1.47.
Wit's Queen, (if what the Poets sing be true) .... 6.37.1.106.
Of *gentle Philips* will I ever sing, ... 6.40.1.112.
Nor work, nor play, nor paint, nor sing. .... 6.119.4.336.
Not work, nor play nor paint, nor sing. .... 6.119.4A.336.
And all Mankind, but Cibber, sing thy praise. .... 6.131i.8.360.
To sing Fidelity and Bounce. .... 6.135.94A.370.
"Of those that sing of these poor eyes." .... 6.140.32.379.
And There Triumphant Sing Thy Soverain's Praise. .... 6.147ix.6.392.
Of Woes unnumber'd, heav'nly Goddess, sing! .... Il.1.2.82.
Of all the *Grecian* Woes, O Goddess, sing! .... Il.1.2A.82.
Their Names, their Numbers, and their Chiefs I sing. .... Il.2.585.155.
No more his heav'nly Voice was heard to sing; .... Il.2.729.161.
To raise each Act to Life, and sing with Fire! .... Il.12.206.88.
And o'er their Heads unheeded Javelins sing. .... Il.13.631.136.
Howl o'er the Masts, and sing thro' ev'ry Shroud: .... Il.15.755.225.
The Corps of *Hector,* and your *Pæans* sing. .... Il.22.492.476.
Alternately they sing, alternate flow .... Il.24.902.574.
Phemius, whose voice divine cou'd sweetest sing .... Od.1.199.42.
Then to the Bard aloud: O cease to sing, ... Od.8.93.267.
To dress, to dance, to sing our sole delight, ... Od.8.285.278.
The woe of *Greece,* and sing so well the woe? .... Od.8.534.291.
Th' *Epæan* fabric, fram'd by *Pallas,* sing: .... Od.8.540.291.
Then to the Bard aloud: O cease to sing, ... Od.8.585.294.
Sing thro' the shrouds, and stretch the swelling sails. .... Od.11.794.426.
And the soul hears him, tho' he cease to sing. .... Od.17.613.161.
Then, as some heav'nly minstrel, taught to sing .... Od.21.440.281.
Self-taught I sing; by heav'n, and heav'n alone .... Od.22.383.307.

SING-SONG
To fetch and carry Sing-song up and down; .... 4.Arbu.226.112.
Hence the soft sing-song on Cecilia's day, ... 5.DunA1.40.65.

SING'D
See SINDG'D.
Else, sing'd with Light'ning, had'st thou hence been thrown, ... Il.5.1106.320.
Sing'd are his brows; the scorching lids grow black; .... Od.9.463.325.
These quarter'd, sing'd, and fix'd on forks of wood, ... Od.14.88.40.

SINGE
The Cat, if you but singe her Tabby Skin, ... 2.ChWB.142.63.

SINGERS
And *Ireland,* mother of sweet singers, ... 6.150.7.398.

SINGING
Thus singing as he went, at last he drew .... 2.ChJM.716.49.
With singing, laughing, ogling, and all that. .... 2.RL3.18.170.
But Singing-Girls and Mimicks draw him in. .... 4.HAdv.74.81.
By singing Peers up-held on either hand, ... 5.DunB4.49.346.
To lands of singing, or of dancing slaves, ... 5.DunB4.305.374.
Now singing shrill, and scolding eft between, ... 6.14ii.17.43.
One year may make a singing Swan of *Duck.* .... 6.116v.4.327.
Thro' the thick Storm of singing Spears he flies, ... Il.5.214.277.

SINGING-GIRLS
But Singing-Girls and Mimicks draw him in. .... 4.HAdv.74.81.

SINGLE

But oft in *those*, confin'd to *single Parts*. ... 1.EOC.63.246.
But ev'n in *those*, confin'd to *single Parts*. ... 1.EOC.63A.246.
No single Parts unequally surprize; ... 1.EOC.249.268.
And yet, like me, has but a single eye. ... 1.TrPA.111.370.
And Beauty draws us with a single Hair. ... 2.RL2.28.161.
That single Act gives half the World the Spleen. ... 2.RL4.78.190.
In God's, one single can its end produce; ... 3.EOM1.55.20.
The single atoms each to other tend, ... 3.EOM3.10.93.
A single leaf may waft an Army o'er, ... 3.Ep3.73A.93.
A single leaf can waft an Army o'er, ... 3.Ep3.73B.93.
A single leaf shall waft an Army o'er, ... 3.Ep3.73.93.
A single verse, we quarrel with a friend; ... 4.2HE1.365.227.
Cou'd Troy be sav'd by any single hand, ... 5.DunA1.187.85.
Could Troy be sav'd by any single hand, ... 5.DunB1.197.283.
Not that I'd ask a single drop to mourn ... 6.20.33.67.
This single Crayon, Madam, saints the Queen. ... 6.147iii.4.390.
He dares the *Spartan* King to single Fight; ... Il.3.128.196.
In single Fight to toss the beamy Lance; ... Il.3.180.199.
With *Sparta's* King to meet in single Fray: ... Il.3.538.217.
Greece in her single Heroes strove in vain; ... Il.6.516.351.
To dare the boldest *Greek* to single Fight, ... Il.7.44.365.
A single Warrior 'midst a Host of Foes; ... Il.8.126.404.
Repell the Rage of *Priam's* single Son? ... Il.9.463.455.
Each single *Greek*, in this conclusive Strife, ... Il.10.196.10.
A single Warrior, half an Host sustains: ... Il.11.605.61.
Burn at each Foe, and single ev'ry Prize; ... Il.15.741.224.
Press'd by his single Force, let *Hector* see, ... Il.16.300.254.
And rapid as it runs, the single Spokes are lost. ... Il.18.696.357.
Can last a Hero thro' a single Day? ... Il.19.162.378.
And thin the Squadrons with my single Spear. ... Il.20.414.412.
The single Fight with *Thetis'* god-like Son; ... Il.20.432.412.
In vain a single *Trojan* sues for Grace; ... Il.21.113.426.
The single, he, whose Shaft divides the Cord. ... Il.23.1016.529.
And now a single beam the Chief bestrides; ... Od.5.472.195.
While, with my single ship, adventurous I ... Od.9.201.314.
Whose arm may sink us at a single stroke. ... Od.9.580.330.
What single arm hath prowess to subdue? ... Od.20.50.234.
What single arm with numbers can contend? ... Od.20.384.251.
And Fate to numbers by a single hand. ... Od.22.18.287.
Or com'st thou single, or attend thy train? ... Od.24.352.365.

SINGLED

And singled out a Pear-Tree planted nigh: ... 2.ChJM.602.44.
Have singled out, is *Ithacus* the Wise: ... Il.3.262.204.
These singled from their Troops the Fight maintain, ... Il.5.19.266.
His Friend *Machaon* singled from the rest, ... Il.11.734.67.
In that sharp Service, singled from the rest, ... Il.13.357.122.
Him *Hector* singled, as his Troops he led, ... Il.15.652.221.

SINGLES

He singles out; arrests, and lays him dead. ... Il.15.767.226.

SINGLY

Consider'd *singly*, or behold too *near*, ... 1.EOC.172.260.
And singly fill a fear'd and envy'd Throne! ... 1.TrSt.223.419.
At *Ombre* singly to decide their Doom; ... 2.RL3.27.171.
And singly mad, asperse the Sov'reign Reign. ... Il.2.309.142.
Hector! approach my Arm, and singly know ... Il.7.273.377.
Lives there a Man, who singly dares to go ... Il.10.243.13.
What Danger, singly if I stand the Ground, ... Il.11.515.57.
Singly methinks, yon' tow'ring Chief I meet, ... Il.13.113.110.
And what thou canst not singly, urge the rest. ... Il.13.300.119.
Or singly, *Hector* and his Troops attend? ... Il.17.104.291.
Yet singly, now, the long disputed Prize ... Il.17.662.313.
No God can singly such a Host engage, ... Il.20.407.412.
Great *Hector* singly stay'd; chain'd down by Fate, ... Il.22.9.453.
Against his Rage if singly thou proceed, ... Il.22.120.458.
And singly vanquish'd the *Cadmæan* Race. ... Il.23.788.521.
(Ten double-edg'd, and ten that singly wound.) ... Il.23.1009.529.
Singly to pass thro' Hosts of Foes! to face ... Il.24.247.546.
But great *Achilles* singly clos'd the Gate. ... Il.24.560.559.
Ulysses singly, or all *Greece* in arms. ... Od.3.268.98.
Assistant force, or singly to destroy? ... Od.16.261.117.

SINGS

But, charm'd to Silence, listens while She sings, ... 1.PSp.15.61.
The Captive Bird that sings within thy Bow'r! ... 1.PSu.46.75.
She sings of Friendship, and she sings to thee. ... 1.PAu.12A.81.
She sings of Friendship, and she sings to thee. ... 1.PAu.12A.81.
No more the mounting Larks, while *Daphne* sings, ... 1.PWi.53.92.
The Muse shall sing, and what she sings shall last) ... 1.W-F.174.166.
Are these reviv'd? or is it *Granville* sings? ... 1.W-F.282.174.
Tho' great *Alcæus* more sublimely sings, ... 1.TrSP.33.394.
Of furious Hate surviving Death, she sings, ... 1.TrSt.51.412.
Enough to shame the gentlest Bard that sings ... 2.ChJM.454.37.
Enough to shame the boldest Bard that sings ... 2.ChJM.454A.37.
Th' expiring Swan, and as he sings he dies. ... 2.RL5.66.206.
Here *Orpheus* sings; Trees moving to the Sound ... 2.TemF.83.259.
As the rapt Seraphim that sings and burns; ... 3.EOM1.278A.49.
Is it for thee the lark ascends and sings? ... 3.EOM3.31.95.
Or hears the hawk when Philomela sings? ... 3.EOM3.56.97.
"Love follows flying Game (as *Sucklyn* sings) ... 4.HAdv.139.87.
One sings the Fair; but Songs no longer move, ... 4.JD2.21.133.
Verse prays for Peace, or sings down Pope and Turk. ... 4.2HE1.236.215.
How this or that Italian sings, ... 4.HS6.142.259.
All his Grace preaches, all his Lordship sings, ... 4.EpS2.224.325.
Let Envy howl while Heav'n's whole Chorus sings, ... 4.EpS2.242.326.
(As sings thy great fore-father, Ogilby,) ... 5.DunA1.258.94.
Who sings so loudly, and who sings so long. ... 5.DunA2.256.131.
Who sings so loudly, and who sings so long. ... 5.DunA2.256.131.
(As sings thy great forefather Ogilby) ... 5.DunB1.328.294.
Who sings so loudly, and who sings so long. ... 5.DunB2.268.308.
Who sings so loudly, and who sings so long. ... 5.DunB2.268.308.
(Once swan of Thames, tho' now he sings no more.) ... 5.DunB3.20.321.
And meditates her Charms, and sings her Praise. ... 6.17iii.21.58.

SINGS (CONTINUED)

Tho' now on loftier Themes he sings ... 6.135.89.370.
Tho' now of Mighty Peers he sings ... 6.135.89A.370.
At *Hector's* Breast, and sings along the Skies: ... Il.8.366.414.
With this he sooths his angry Soul, and sings ... Il.9.249.445.
Whose tender Lay the Fate of *Linus* sings; ... Il.18.662.355.
A Bard amid the joyous circle sings ... Od.4.23.121.
Taught by the Gods to please, when high he sings ... Od.8.41.264.
Then fir'd by all the Muse, aloud he sings ... Od.8.69.265.
And sings with unmatch'd force along the skies. ... Od.8.138.270.
Sonorous thro' the shaded air it sings; ... Od.8.214.274.
The loves of *Mars* and *Citherea* sings; ... Od.8.308.280.
For whom my chanter sings, and goblet flows ... Od.13.10.2.
Swift as the word the parting arrow sings, ... Od.22.11.287.
While the sweet Lyrist airs of rapture sings, ... Od.23.133.327.

SINGULAR

As oft the *Learn'd* by being *Singular;* ... 1.EOC.425.288.

SINISTER

The Victor Eagle, whose sinister Flight ... Il.12.257.90.
Sinister to their hope! This omen ey'd ... Od.20.304.247.

SINK

Sink down ye Mountains, and ye Vallies rise: ... 1.Mes.34.116.
The Sun wou'd sink into the Western Main, ... 1.TrSt.328.424.
Nor Victims sink beneath the Sacred Stroke; ... 1.TrSt.372.425.
And sink downright to *Satan* when I die. ... 2.ChJM.118.20.
Waft on the Breeze, or sink in Clouds of Gold. ... 2.RL2.60.163.
And Tow'rs and Temples sink in Floods of Fire. ... 2.TemF.478.286.
To sink oppress with aromatic pain? ... 3.EOM1.200A.40.
All pleasures sicken, and all glories sink; ... 3.EOM4.46.132.
To swell the Terras, or to sink the Grot; ... 3.Ep4.49.142.
Blotch thee all o'er, and sink.. ... 4.1740.84.337.
Down sink the flames, and with a hiss expire. ... 5.DunA1.216.89.
Now sink in sorrows with a tolling Bell. ... 5.DunA2.220.128.
Who but to sink the deeper, rose the higher. ... 5.DunA2.278.135.
How Laurus lay inspir'd beside a sink, ... 5.DunA2.393.149.
How E[usden] lay inspir'd beside a sink, ... 5.DunA2.393A.149.
Down sink the flames, and with a hiss expire. ... 5.DunB1.260.289.
Who but to sink the deeper, rose the higher. ... 5.DunB2.290.309.
How Henley lay inspir'd beside a sink, ... 5.DunB2.425.318.
To sound or sink in *cano*, O or A, ... 5.DunB4.221.364.
Like buoys, that never sink into the flood, ... 5.DunB4.241.366.
But sink, and take deep rooting in my heart. ... 6.2.10.6.
Nor swell too high, nor sink too low. ... 6.11.23.30.
The Furies sink upon their Iron Beds, ... 6.11.69.32.
And neither swell too high, nor sink too low; ... 6.17ii.20.56.
Melting they fall, and sink into the Heart! ... Il.3.286.207.
Else had'st thou seen me sink on yonder Plain, ... Il.5.1088.318.
All sink alike, the Fearful and the Brave. ... Il.6.631.358.
He waits but for the Morn, to sink in Flame ... Il.9.314.449.
Her hosts shall sink, nor his the Pow'r to aid? ... Il.11.901.75.
Shall sink beneath us, smoaking on the Ground; ... Il.13.1030.153.
Doom'd in their Ships to sink by Fire and Sword, ... Il.16.25.236.
Mark with what Ease they sink into the Sand! ... Il.16.905.279.
Now sink in gloomy Clouds the proud Abodes; ... Il.17.827.321.
Ordain'd, to sink me with the Weight of Woe? ... Il.18.12.323.
(My only Offspring) sink into the Grave? ... Il.19.346.386.
Enough—When Heav'n ordains, I sink in Night, ... Il.19.470.391.
I faint, I sink, unequal to the Fight— ... Il.21.419.437.
And in one Ruin sink the *Trojan* Name. ... Il.21.441.438.
And hopes this day to sink the *Trojan* Name ... Il.21.692.450.
And with false Terrors sink another's Mind. ... Il.22.362.470.
Yet suffer not thy Soul to sink with Dread; ... Il.24.455.555.
Shall sink, a smoaking Ruin on the Plain. ... Il.24.917.574.
He, like his sire, may sink depriv'd of breath, ... Od.2.374.78.
The tow'rs of *Pylos* sink, its views decay, ... Od.3.616.117.
Forbid that want shou'd sink me to a lye. ... Od.7.383.255.
Whose arm may sink us at a single stroke. ... Od.9.580.330.
We sink, beneath the circling eddy drown'd. ... Od.12.263.445.
From sleep debarr'd, we sink from woes to woes; ... Od.12.335.448.
Like fowl that haunt the floods, they sink, they rise, ... Od.12.493.456.
Nor sink by sickness to the shades below; ... Od.15.447.92.
I'll grieve, 'till sorrow sink me to the grave! ... Od.20.266.246.
Or sink at once forgotten with the dead. ... Od.24.501.372.

SINKING

Now fainting, sinking, pale, the Nymph appears; ... 1.W-F.191.167.
And thou, kind *Love*, my sinking Limbs sustain, ... 1.TrSP.209.403.
And leave the sinking Hills, and less'ning Shores. ... 1.TrUl.4.465.
Behold him sinking in the Western Main. ... 1.TrUl.121.470.
The sinking Stone at first a Circle makes; ... 2.TemF.437.284.
Truths would you teach, or save a sinking land? ... 3.EOM4.265.153.
To ease th' oppress'd, and raise the sinking heart? ... 3.Ep3.244.113.
I trust that sinking Fund, my Life. ... 4.1HE7.74.273.
Sinking from thought to thought, a vast profound! ... 5.DunA1.112.77.
First he relates, how sinking to the chin, ... 5.DunA2.307.139.
Sinking from thought to thought, a vast profound! ... 5.DunB1.118.278.
First he relates, how sinking to the chin, ... 5.DunB2.331.313.
Or add one Patriot to a sinking state; ... 6.132.4.362.
Besought the Chief to save the sinking State; ... Il.9.691.468.
Not till amidst yon' sinking Navy slain, ... Il.9.765.472.
His Arm and Knee his sinking Bulk sustain; ... Il.11.458.54.
Atrides' Arm the sinking Hero stays, ... Il.11.608.61.
His Load of Armour, sinking to the Ground, ... Il.14.491.188.
Now faints anew, low-sinking on the Shore; ... Il.14.512.188.
How easy then, to see the sinking State ... Il.15.578.218.
The God the *Grecians* sinking Souls deprest, ... Il.16.889.277.
Have forc'd the Pow'rs to spare a sinking State, ... Il.17.382.302.
Who, sinking now with Age, and Sorrow, pays ... Il.18.507.346.
Or save one Member of the sinking State; ... Il.20.364.410.
Their sinking Limbs the fancy'd Course forsake, ... Il.22.259.466.
To raise her sinking with assistant Hands. ... Il.22.605.481.
And form sure plans to save the sinking state. ... Od.1.357.49.
For here retir'd the sinking billows sleep, ... Od.10.107.345.

SINKING (CONTINUED)
Up-bore my load, and prest the sinking sands Od.10.197.350.
And leave the sinking hills, and less'ning shores. Od.13.95.5.
Behold him sinking in the western main. Od.13.288.19.
He ended, sinking into sleep, and shares Od.23.369.343.

SINKS
With heavy steps he sinks the sandy plain; 1.TrPA.36.366.
And Fancy sinks beneath a Weight of Woe. 1.TrSP.231.403.
Down sinks the Warrior, with a thundring Sound, 1.TrES.127.454.
It sinks, and spreads its Honours on the Ground; 1.TrES.291.460.
The graver Prude sinks downward to a *Gnome,* 2.RL1.63.150.
On the rich Quilt sinks with becoming Woe, 2.RL4.35.186.
And boldly sinks into the sounding Strings. 2.TemF.215.272.
Sinks deep within him, and possesses whole, 3.Ep3.373.123.
Sinks the lost Actor in the tawdry load. 4.2HE1.333.223.
Furious he sinks; precipitately dull. 5.DunA2.294.139.
Now sinks in sorrows with a tolling bell; 5.DunB2.228.307.
Nor sinks his Credit lower than it was. 6.34.16.101.
When *Athens* sinks by fates unjust, 6.51i.17.151.
Applauds their Eloquence, but sinks their Fees. 6.96v.18.280.
At length the Tumult sinks, the Noises cease, Il.2.253.139.
So sinks a Tow'r, that long Assaults had stood Il.4.528.246.
And sinks a breathless Carcass on the Plain. Il.4.566.248.
Down sinks the Chief: his clanging Arms resound; Il.4.579A.249.
Down sinks the Warrior with a thundring Sound, Il.5.73.269.
Lo brave *Æneas* sinks beneath his Wound, Il.5.569.295.
He groans in Death, and pondrous sinks to Ground: Il.5.716.301.
Prone on his Face he sinks beside the Wheel; Il.6.53.326.
So sinks the Youth: his beauteous Head, depress'd Il.8.373.415.
Before *Atrides'* Rage so sinks the Foe, Il.11.205.44.
The Warrior sinks, tremendous now no more! Il.12.216.89.
Down sinks the Warrior with a thund'ring Sound, Il.12.481.99.
The panting Thund'rer nods, and sinks to Rest. Il.14.406.183.
He sinks to Earth, and grasps the bloody Dust. Il.14.528.189.
He sinks, with endless Darkness cover'd o'er, Il.16.386.258.
It sinks, and spreads its Honours on the Ground; Il.16.596.267.
Prone sinks the Warrior, and his Arms resound. Il.17.52.289.
And now it rises, now it sinks, by turns. Il.17.421.303.
And now it rises, now it sinks by turns. Il.18.2.322.
His hastening Soul, and sinks him to the Shades. Il.19.359.387.
Low sinks the Scale surcharg'd with *Hector's* Fate; Il.22.275.467.
Heavy with Death it sinks, and Hell receives the Weight. Il.22.276.467.
Sinks my sad Soul with Sorrow to the Grave. Il.22.543.478.
At length he sinks in the soft Arms of Sleep. Il.23.77.490.
From the bent Angle sinks the loaden Weight; Il.24.108.539.
O'erwhelm'd it sinks: while round a smoke expires, Od.12.81.435.
He faints, he sinks, with mighty joys opprest: Od.24.405.368.

SINNER
Whether the Charmer sinner it, or saint it, 3.Ep2.15.49.
So from a sister sinner you shall hear, 6.41.9.113.
and one that's a Sinner, 6.68.2.196.

SINNERS
Thither, where sinners may have rest, I go, 2.ElAb.319.345.
The sinners fall, and bless the vengeful day! 6.21.20.69.
When he the rage of sinners shall sustain, 6.21.35.70.
Faith, gallants, board with saints, and bed with sinners. 6.41.24.114.

SINS
E'er I recount the Sins of these Profane, 1.TrSt.327.424.
Shall feel sharp Vengeance soon o'ertake his Sins, 2.RL2.125.167.
Of ORDER, sins against th' Eternal Cause. 3.EOM1.130.31.
Consistent in our follies and our sins, 3.Ep1.226.34.
She sins with Poets thro' pure Love of Wit. 3.Ep2.76.56.
Who sins with whom? who got his Pension *Rug,* 4.JD4.134.37.
Those venial sins, an Atom, or a Straw: 4.JD4.243.47.
For hung with *Deadly Sins* I see the Wall, 4.JD4.274.49.
Act Sins which Prisca's Confessor scarce hears: 4.JD2.40.135.
And whose strange Sins no Canonist can tell, 4.JD2A.47.136.
In rev'rence to the Sins of *Thirty-nine!* 4.EpS2.5.313.
Some rising Genius sins up to my Song. 4.EpS2.9.313.
Can Sins of Moments claim the Rod 6.50.20Z1.147*.
Can those be Sins with Natures God 6.50.20Z3.147*.
If this can cover multitudes of sins, 6.146.7.389.
And daily Pray'rs attone for daily Sins. Il.9.623.465.
The track of friendship, not pursuing, sins. Od.24.333.365.

SINTHIANS
The *Sinthians* rais'd me on the *Lemnian* Coast. Il.1.765.124.

SINTIANS
Prefers his barb'rous *Sintians* to thy arms! Od.8.336.281.

SIP
Here Bees from Blossoms sip the rosie Dew, 1.PSu.69.77.
And sip with *Nymphs,* their Elemental Tea. 2.RL1.62.150.
Their flow'ry Toils, and sip the fragrant Dew, 2.TemF.283.277.

SIP'D
Some, as she sip'd, the fuming Liquor fann'd, 2.RL3.114.176.

SIPP'D
How here he sipp'd, how there he plunder'd snug 5.DunB1.129.279.
He eat the Sops, she sipp'd the Wine: 6.93.20.257.

SIPS
Ridotta sips and dances, till she see 4.HS1.47.9.
And modest as the maid that sips alone: 5.DunA3.136.161.
And modest as the maid who sips alone: 5.DunA3.136A.161.
And modest as the maid that sips alone; 5.DunB3.144.326.

SIPT
And sipt his Cordial as he sate upright: 2.ChJM.387.33.

SIPYLUS
There high on *Sipylus* his shaggy Brow, Il.24.777.569.

SIR
Such Prudence, Sir, in all your Words appears, 2.ChJM.149.21.
Sir, I have liv'd a Courtier all my Days, 2.ChJM.156.22.
This Sir affects not you, whose ev'ry Word 2.ChJM.166.23.
And therefore, Sir, as you regard your Rest, 2.ChJM.184.23.
Ah gentle Sir, take Warning of a Friend, 2.ChJM.194.24.
And trust me, Sir, the chastest you can chuse 2.ChJM.212.24.
Sir Knight, he cry'd, if this be all you dread, 2.ChJM.278.27.
Then be not, Sir, abandon'd to Despair; 2.ChJM.284.28.
For know, Sir Knight, of gentle Blood I came, 2.ChJM.591.43.
Else why these needless Cautions, Sir, to me? 2.ChJM.595.43.
At least, kind Sir, for Charity's sweet sake, 2.ChJM.732.50.
Then Sir be cautious, nor too rashly deem; 2.ChJM.805.54.
Hark old Sir *Paul* ('twas thus I us'd to say) 2.ChWB.74.60.
Sir, I'm no Fool: Nor shall you, by St. *John,* 2.ChWB.126.62.
She said; then raging to *Sir Plume* repairs, 2.RL4.121.194.
(*Sir Plume,* of *Amber Snuff-box* justly vain, 2.RL4.123.194.
A mournful Glance Sir *Fopling* upwards cast, 2.RL5.63.205.
When bold Sir *Plume* had drawn *Clarissa* down, 2.RL5.67.206.
As bold Sir *Plume* had drawn *Clarissa* down, 2.RL5.67A.206.
Mark how they grace Lord Umbra, or Sir Billy: 3.EOM4.278.154.
"If—where I'm going—I could serve you, Sir?" 3.Ep1.255.37.
Your money, Sir? "My money, Sir, what all? 3.Ep1.258.37.
Your money, Sir? "My money, Sir, what all? 3.Ep1.258.37.
The Manor, Sir?—"The Manor! hold," he cry'd, 3.Ep1.260.37.
'Tis the dear Prince (Sir John) that crowns thy cup, 3.Ep3.207A.110.
"Sir, Spain has sent a thousand jars of oil; 3.Ep3.44.89.
Astride his cheese Sir Morgan might we meet, 3.Ep3.49.90.
The grave Sir Gilbert holds it for a rule, 3.Ep3.103.99.
As well his Grace reply'd, "Like you, Sir John? 3.Ep3.317.119.
Sir Balaam now, he lives like other folks, 3.Ep3.357.122.
Behold Sir Balaam, now a man of spirit, 3.Ep3.375.123.
The Court forsake him, and Sir Balaam hangs: 3.Ep3.398.124.
And sad Sir Balaam curses God and dies. 3.Ep3.402.125.
What brought Sir Visto's ill got wealth to waste? 3.Ep4.15.137.
What brought Sir *Shylock's* ill got wealth to waste? 3.Ep4.15A.137.
P. What? like Sir *Richard,* rumbling, rough and fierce, 4.HS1.23.7.
Then learned Sir! (to cut the Matter short) 4.HS1.91.13.
Such as Sir *Robert* would approve— F. Indeed ? 4.HS1.153.21.
"But the best *Words?"—"O* Sir, the *Dictionary."* 4.JD4.69.31.
"But Sir, of Writers?"—" *Swift,* for closer Style, 4.JD4.72.31.
"Obliging Sir! I love you, I profess, 4.JD4.86A.33.
"Oh! Sir, politely well! nay, let me dye, 4.JD4.112A.35.
"Obliging Sir! for Courts you sure were made: 4.JD4.86.33.
"Ah gentle Sir! you Courtiers so cajol us— 4.JD4.90.33.
"Lord! Sir, a meer *Mechanick!* strangely low, 4.JD4.108.33.
"Oh! Sir, politely so! nay, let me dye, 4.JD4.112.35.
"Not Sir, my only—I have better still, 4.JD4.114.35.
And " *sweet Sir Fopling!* you have so much wit!" 4.JD4.233.45.
Damn him, he's honest, Sir,—and that's enuff. 4.JD4.263.47.
But not Sir *H[erber]t,* for he does the same. 4.HAdv.16.75.
See good Sir *George* of ragged Livery stript, 4.HAdv.55.81.
Sure, worthy Sir, the Diff'rence is not great, 4.HAdv.75.81.
Should rise, and say—"Sir *Robert!* or Sir *Paul!* 4.HAdv.88.83.
Should rise, and say—"Sir *Robert!* or Sir *Paul!* 4.HAdv.88.83.
"Informs you Sir, 'twas when he knew no better. 4.Arbu.52.100.
"And shame the Fools—your Int'rest, Sir, with *Lintot."* 4.Arbu.62.100.
"Not Sir, if you revise it, and retouch." 4.Arbu.64.100.
Sir, let me see your works and you no more. 4.Arbu.68.100.
Such *Ovid's* nose, and "Sir! you have an *Eye—"* 4.Arbu.118.104.
The first Lampoon Sir *Will.* or *Bubo* makes. 4.Arbu.280.115.
Bows and begins.—"This Lad, Sir, is of Blois: 4.2HE2.4.165.
"Sir, he's your Slave, for twenty pound a year. 4.2HE2.8.165.
"But Sir, to you, with what wou'd I not part? 4.2HE2.15.165.
I think Sir Godfry should decide the Suit; 4.2HE2.24.167.
At Ten for certain, Sir, in Bloomsb'ry-Square— 4.2HE2.95.171.
There's a Rehearsal, Sir, exact at One.— 4.2HE2.97.171.
'Twas, "Sir your Law"—and "Sir, your Eloquence"— 4.2HE2.133.175.
'Twas, "Sir your Law"—and "Sir, your Eloquence"— 4.2HE2.133.175.
Yes, Sir, how small soever be my heap, 4.2HE2.284.185.
I wish you joy, Sir, of a Tyrant gone; 4.2HE2.305.187.
Your People, Sir, are partial in the rest. 4.2HE1.32.197.
Yet Sir, reflect, the mischief is not great; 4.2HE1.189.211.
Think of those Authors, Sir, who would rely 4.2HE1.350.225.
Yet think great Sir! (so many Virtues shown) 4.2HE1.376.227.
Faith, Sir, you know as much as I. 4.HS6.116.257.
"Pray take them, Sir,—Enough's a Feast: 4.1HE7.25.269.
"No Sir, you'll leave them to the *Hogs."* 4.1HE7.28.271.
"Lean as you came, Sir, you must go." 4.1HE7.58.273.
Sir, you may spare your Application 4.1HE7.59.273.
"I cannot like, Dread Sir! your Royal Cave; 4.1HE1.115.287.
Sir Job sail'd forth, the evening bright and still, 4.1HE1.138.289.
But *Horace,* Sir, was delicate, was nice; 4.EpS1.11.298.
Horace would say, *Sir* Billy *serv'd the Crown,* 4.EpS1.13.298.
Sir *George* of *some slight Gallantries* suspect. 4.EpS1.15A.298.
Go see Sir ROBERT— P. See Sir Robert !— hum 4.EpS1.27.299.
Go see Sir ROBERT— P. See Sir Robert !— hum 4.EpS1.27.299.
P. Dear Sir, forgive the Prejudice of Youth: 4.EpS1.63.302.
Fr. Tis all a Libel— *Paxton* (Sir) will say. 4.EpS2.1.313.
P. How Sir! not damn the Sharper, but the Dice? 4.EpS2.13.314.
Fr. A Dean, Sir? no: his Fortune is not made, 4.EpS2.34.314.
But Sir, I beg you, for the Love of Vice! 4.EpS2.42.315.
P. If merely to come in, Sir, they go out, 4.EpS2.124.320.
But let me add, Sir ROBERT's mighty dull, 4.EpS2.133.320.
Fr. Hold Sir! for God's-sake, where's th' Affront to you? 4.EpS2.157.322.
No more than of Sir Har[r]y or Sir P[aul]. 4.1740.20.333*.
No more than of Sir Har[r]y or Sir P[aul]. 4.1740.20.333*.
And all agree, Sir Robert cannot live. 4.1740.42.334.
Sore sighs Sir G[ilbert], starting at the bray 5.DunA2.241.129.
So sighs Sir G[ilber]t, starting at the bray 5.DunA2.241A.12
E'er since Sir Fopling's Periwig was Praise, 5.DunB1.167.282.
Sore sighs Sir Gilbert, starting at the bray, 5.DunB2.251.307.
But, Sir, from *Brocas, Fouler,* me, 6.10.37.25.

SIR (CONTINUED)

Sir, you're so stiff in your Opinion, ...6.10.79.27.
You have no Cause to take Offence, Sir, ...6.10.101.27.
The learn'd Sir *William,* or the deep Sir *James.* ....6.48iv.14.136.
The learn'd Sir *William,* or the deep Sir *James.* ....6.48iv.14.136.
And thou be stil'd Sir *Esdras Barnivelt.* ....6.48iv.16.136.
"Sir Duke! be here to Night." ....6.79.48.219.
A double Jest still pleases sweet Sir Harry— ....6.82vi.12.232.
One day I mean to Fill Sir Godfry's tomb, ...6.88.1.249.
"Has she no Faults then (Envy says) Sir?" ....6.89.9.250.
With a cup and a can, Sir, ...6.90.10.251.
You wonder at it—This Sir is the case, ...6.105iii.3.301.
Well, Sir, suppose, the *Busto's* a damn'd head, ...6.105vi.1.302.
Tis granted Sir; the Busto's a damn'd head, ...6.105vi.1A.302.
Sir, I admit your gen'ral Rule ....6.124ii.1.347.
Pray tell me Sir, whose Dog are you? ....6.136.2.372.

SIRACH

The Son of *Sirach* testifies no less. ....2.ChJM.640.46.

SIRE

Shall finish what his short-liv'd Sire begun; ....1.Mes.64.118.
Behold, *Andræmon* and th'unhappy Sire ....1.TrFD.57.388.
My sire, my sister, and my spouse farewell! ....1.TrFD.88.389.
The Sire against the Son his Arrows drew, ...1.TrSt.15.410.
My Sons their old, unhappy Sire despise, ...1.TrSt.103.414.
Thou Sire of Gods and Men, Imperial *Jove!* ....1.TrSt.243.420.
Let the pale Sire revisit *Thebes,* and bear ....1.TrSt.421.427.
Then wild with Anguish, to her Sire she flies; ....1.TrSt.701.439.
Æneas bending with his aged Sire: ....2.TemF.207.272.
The same which in a Sire the Sons obey'd, ...3.EOM3.213.114.
Then, looking up from sire to sire, explor'd ....3.EOM3.225.115.
Then, looking up from sire to sire, explor'd ....3.EOM3.225.115.
Convey'd unbroken faith from sire to son, ...3.EOM3.228.115.
Why, full of days and honour, lives the Sire? ....3.EOM4.106.138.
Behold a rev'rend sire, whom want of grace ....3.Ep1.228.34.
Flam'd forth this rival to, its Sire, the Sun, ...3.Ep3.12.84.
Gross as her sire, and as her mother grave, ...5.DunA1.12.61.
Each sire imprest and glaring in his son; ....5.DunA1.98.71.
And high-born *Howard,* more majestic sire, ...5.DunA1.250Z1.92.
But soon the Cloud return'd—and thus the Sire: ....5.DunA3.225.176.
To whom the Sire: In yonder cloud, behold! ....5.DunA3.249A.178.
Gross as her sire, and as her mother grave, ...5.DunB1.14.270.
Each sire imprest and glaring in his son: ....5.DunB1.100.276.
Not wrap up Oranges, to pelt your sire! ....5.DunB1.236.287.
And high-born Howard, more majestic sire, ...5.DunB1.297.291.
But soon the cloud return'd—and thus the Sire: ....5.DunB3.227.331.
The Sire saw, one by one, his Virtues wake: ....5.DunB4.285.372.
The Sire saw, smiling, his own Virtues wake: ....5.DunB4.285A.372.
Rous'd at his name, up rose the bowzy Sire, ...5.DunB4.493.390.
Sire, Ancestors, Himself. One casts his eyes ....5.DunB4.519.394.
The Sire is made a Peer, the Son a Fool. ....5.DunB4.548.396.
Whether his hoary sire he spies, ...6.51ii.29.153.
Repuls'd the sacred Sire, and thus reply'd. ....Il.1.34.87.
Far from her native Soil, and weeping Sire. ....Il.1.46.88.
The Sire insulted, and his Gifts deny'd: ....Il.1.493.111.
Th' insulted Sire (his God's peculiar Care) ....Il.1.494.111.
The fair *Chruseïs* to her Sire was sent, ...Il.1.504.112.
The Sire of Gods, and all th' Etherial Train, ...Il.1.554.114.
At this, the Sire embrac'd the Maid again, ...Il.1.582.115.
O Sire of Gods and Men! thy Suppliant hear, ...Il.1.666.119.
Full on the Sire the Goddess of the Skies ....Il.1.712.121.
Thou, Goddess-Mother, with our Sire comply, ...Il.1.746.123.
To strong *Dulichium* from his Sire he fled, ...Il.2.763.162.
By mighty *Jove,* the Sire of Men and Gods; ....Il.2.812.163.
The Sire forewarn'd, and prophecy'd their Doom: ....Il.2.1009.170.
Fate urg'd them on! the Sire forwarn'd in vain, ...Il.2.1010.170.
The Sire whose Thunder shakes the cloudy Skies, ...Il.4.45.223.
Sprung, with thy self, from one Celestial Sire, ...Il.4.84.224.
The Sire of Men and Monarch of the Sky ....Il.4.95.225.
Not thus thy Sire the fierce Encounter fear'd; ....Il.4.426.240.
Gods! how the Son degen'rates from the Sire? ....Il.4.451.241.
Stern as his Sire, the Boaster thus begun. ....Il.4.455.242.
Preserv'd the Son, in Pity to the Sire. ....Il.5.32.267.
Nor tempt the Wrath of Heav'ns avenging Sire. ....Il.5.44.268.
If e'er my Godlike Sire deserv'd thy Aid, ...Il.5.147.274.
If e'er I see my Spouse and Sire again, ...Il.5.269.280.
Thus front the Foe, and emulate my Sire. ....Il.5.317.281.
No Infant on his Knees shall call him Sire. ....Il.5.498.291.
The Sire of Gods and Men superior smil'd, ...Il.5.517.293.
The Wretch would brave high Heav'ns immortal Sire, ...Il.5.559.295.
Whose Sire *Diöcleus,* wealthy, brave and great, ...Il.5.671.300.
Jove got such Heroes as my Sire, whose Soul ....Il.5.790.304.
Thy Sire, O Prince! o'erturn'd the *Trojan* State, ...Il.5.804.304.
O Sire! can no Resentment touch thy Soul? ....Il.5.942.311.
There sullen sate beneath the Sire of Gods, ...Il.5.1065.317.
What, or from whence I am, or who my Sire, ...Il.6.179.334.
Or offer Heav'n's great Sire polluted Praise. ....Il.6.337.343.
Lay'd *Thebè* waste, and slew my warlike Sire! ....Il.6.525.352.
Each Name, each Action, and each Hero's Sire? ....Il.7.154.372.
The Sire of Gods his awful Silence broke; ....Il.8.5.395.
There, from his radiant Car, the sacred Sire ....Il.8.61.398.
The Sire of Gods his golden Scales suspends, ...Il.8.88.399.
Oh mighty *Jove!* oh Sire of the distress'd! ....Il.8.282.410.
Young *Ageläus* (*Phradmon* was his Sire) ....Il.8.309.412.
Sprung from an Alien's Bed thy Sire to grace, ...Il.8.343.413.
Troy yet found Grace before th' *Olympian* Sire, ...Il.8.401.416.
But He above, the Sire of Heav'n withstands, ...Il.8.437.418.
Nor dare to combate her's and Natures Sire. ....Il.8.499.420.
And speaks the Mandate of the Sire of Gods. ....Il.8.507.420.
Nor dare to combate her's and Nature's Sire. ....Il.8.519.421.
To lift thy Lance against the Sire of Heav'n? ....Il.8.523A.421.
To win the Damsel, and prevent my Sire. ....Il.9.581.462.
My Sire with Curses loads my hated Head, ...Il.9.582.463.
Your Sire receiv'd me, as his Son caress'd, ...Il.9.600.464.
The Sire revenges for the Daughter's sake, ...Il.9.634.466.

SIRE (CONTINUED)

A Sire the Slaughter of his Son forgives; ....Il.9.745.471.
To ease a Sov'reign, and relieve a Sire. ....Il.10.193.10.
As thou defend'st the Sire, defend the Son. ....Il.10.338.18.
Then to their Sire for ample Sums restor'd; ....Il.11.145.42.
When the kind Sire consign'd his Daughter's Charms ....Il.11.289.48.
My Sire three hundred chosen Sheep obtain'd. ....Il.11.835.73.
My self the foremost; but my Sire deny'd; ....Il.11.853.74.
My Sire deny'd in vain: On foot I fled ....Il.11.856.74.
Thy self, *Achilles,* and thy rev'rend Sire ....Il.11.908.76.
Such as sage *Chiron,* Sire of *Pharmacy,* ....Il.11.966.78.
Vaunts of his Gods, and calls high *Jove* his Sire. ....Il.13.82.108.
The Sire of Earth and Heav'n, by *Thetis* won ....Il.13.438.126.
Great *Æsyetes* was the Hero's Sire; ....Il.13.538.132.
From him, my Sire: from *Calydon* expell'd, ...Il.14.134.164.
Attend, and in the Son, respect the Sire. ....Il.14.144.164.
The Sire of all, old *Ocean,* owns my Reign, ...Il.14.279.175.
And taught Submission to the Sire of Heav'n. ....Il.15.52.196.
Attend the Mandate of the Sire above, ...Il.15.196.204.
And must I then (said she) O Sire of Floods! ....Il.15.224.205.
The Sire of Gods, confirming *Thetis'* Pray'r, ...Il.15.714.223.
Against *Alcides, Copreus* was his Sire: ....Il.15.773.226.
A Son as gen'rous as the Sire was base; ....Il.15.775.226.
A Son as gen'rous as his Sire was base; ....Il.15.775A.226.
Old *Chiron* rent, and shap'd it for his Sire; ....Il.16.175.245.
Her secret Offspring to her Sire she bare; ....Il.16.228.248.
Her Sire caress'd him with a Parent's Care. ....Il.16.229.248.
And pay the Forfeit of their guilty Sire. ....Il.16.393.258.
No more to chear his Spouse, or glad his Sire. ....Il.17.32.289.
So tell our hoary Sire—This Charge she gave: ....Il.18.181.331.
And *Jove* himself, the Sire of Men and Gods, ...Il.19.100.376.
Their mingled Grief the Sire of Heav'n survey'd, ...Il.19.362.387.
Old *Chiron* fell'd, and shap'd it for his Sire; ....Il.19.423.389.
All but old Ocean, hoary Sire! who keeps ....Il.20.15.393.
And question'd thus the Sire of Men and Gods. ....Il.20.22.393.
Hermes, of profitable Arts the Sire, ...Il.20.47.396.
Above, the Sire of Gods his Thunder rolls, ...Il.20.75.397.
The valiant Sons of an unhappy Sire; ....Il.20.532.416.
Who, or from whence? Unhappy is the Sire, ...Il.21.167.428.
Begot my Sire, whose Spear such Glory won: ....Il.21.177.429.
Was not the Mandate of the Sire above ....Il.21.250.431.
The Adamantine *Ægis* of her Sire, ...Il.21.466.440.
No Deed perform'd, to our *Olympian* Sire? ....Il.21.511.443.
And yields to Ocean's hoary Sire, the Prize? ....Il.21.548.444.
The Sire, superior smil'd; and bade her show, ...Il.21.593.446.
And take their Thrones around th' Æthereal Sire. ....Il.21.604.447.
The Sire of Mortals and Immortals spoke. ....Il.22.220.464.
Go then (return'd the Sire) without delay, ...Il.22.239.465.
No more to smile upon his Sire! no Friend ....Il.22.622.482.
Nor idly warns the hoary Sire, nor hears ....Il.23.373.505.
Gen'rous alike, for me, the Sire and Son ....Il.23.695.517.
Accept thou this, O sacred Sire! (he said) ....Il.23.707.517.
To meet his Might, and emulate thy Sire, ...Il.23.784.521.
The Son of *Nestor,* worthy of his Sire. ....Il.23.940.526.
Deny to Consort, Mother, Son, and Sire, ...Il.24.48.537.
Howe'er be Heav'ns almighty Sire obey'd— ....Il.24.121.540.
There in the Light'nings Blaze the Sire they found, ...Il.24.129.540.
The sacred Sire of Gods and mortal Man: ....Il.24.136.540.
And all amidst them lay the hoary Sire, ...Il.24.199.545.
Add to the slaughter'd Son the wretched Sire! ....Il.24.278.548.
Inglorious Sons of an unhappy Sire! ....Il.24.317.549.
'Tis just (said *Priam)* to the Sire above ....Il.24.369.551.
Go, guard the Sire; th' observing Foe prevent, ...Il.24.415.552.
Are true, my Son! (the godlike Sire rejoin'd) ....Il.24.460.555.
Polyctor is my Sire, an honour'd Name, ...Il.24.487.556.
And joyful thus the royal Sire reply'd. ....Il.24.518.557.
Touch'd with the dear Remembrance of his Sire. ....Il.24.635.563.
And now his Sire he mourns, and now his Friend. ....Il.24.643.563.
The Sire obey'd him, trembling and o'er-aw'd. ....Il.24.720.567.
Apart from *Priam,* lest th' unhappy Sire ....Il.24.732.568.
Wak'd with the Word, the trembling Sire arose, ...Il.24.858.572.
The sad Procession of her hoary Sire, ...Il.24.871.572.
Th' assembly thus the Sire supreme addrest; ....Od.1.37.31.
(*Atlas* her sire, to whose far-piercing eye ....Od.1.67.33.
That from his realm retards his god-like Sire: ....Od.1.121.38.
Happier the son, whose hoary sire is blest ....Od.1.281.46.
Soon may your Sire discharge the vengeance due, ...Od.1.329.48.
Or came fore-runner of your scepter'd Sire? ....Od.1.520.57.
No more my Sire will glad these longing eyes: ....Od.1.522.57.
And ease the Sire of half the cares of age. ....Od.2.30.61.
For my lost Sire continual sorrows spring, ...Od.2.53.62.
The dowry; Is *Telemachus* her Sire? ....Od.2.60.63.
For my lost Sire, nor add new woe to woe. ....Od.2.78.64.
Dismiss the Queen; and if her sire approves, ...Od.2.129.67.
And seek my royal sire from shore to shore: ....Od.2.244.73.
"Years roll'd on years my god-like sire decay, ...Od.2.257.74.
And seek my sire thro' storms and rolling seas! ....Od.2.300.76.
He, like his sire, may sink depriv'd of breath, ...Od.2.374.78.
To learn what fates thy wretched sire detain, ...Od.3.21.87.
Where sate, encompast with his sons, the Sire. ....Od.3.42.88.
My sire I seek, where-e'er the voice of fame ....Od.3.100.91.
Art thou the son of that illustrious sire? ....Od.3.151.93.
Thy Sire and I were one; nor vary'd aught ....Od.3.155.93.
How well the son appeas'd his slaughter'd sire! ....Od.3.239.97.
(On whom the virtues of thy sire descend) ....Od.3.243.97.
As those with which *Minerva* mark'd thy sire) ....Od.3.275.99.
Or as my children imitate their sire, ...Od.3.452.109.
Submissive thus the hoary Sire preferr'd ....Od.3.494.111.
My sons! the dictates of your sire fulfil. ....Od.3.531.113.
His good old Sire with sorrow to the tomb ....Od.4.144.127.
Of that heroic sire the youth is sprung, ...Od.4.211.129.
Fast for the Sire the filial sorrows flow; ....Od.4.251.131.
From the great sire transmissive to the race, ...Od.4.287.132.
Proteus her sire divine. With pity press'd, ...Od.4.495.144.
And for the pious sire preserve the son: ....Od.4.1010.164.
When a lov'd Sire revives before their sight, ...Od.5.507.196.

SIRE (CONTINUED)
Will my dread Sire his ear regardful deign, ...Od.6.69.208.
The conscious Sire the dawning blush survey'd, ...Od.6.81.209.
Attend my royal sire, a radiant band. ....Od.6.306.225.
For fast beside it dwells my honour'd sire. ....Od.7.38.235.
And all the children emulate their sire. ....Od.7.89.238.
These ears have heard my royal Sire disclose ....Od.8.617.295.
The hoary Sire in gratitude reveal'd. ....Od.9.241.316.
For him the mighty Sire of Gods assign'd ....Od.10.21.340.
And touch'd the Youths; but their stern Sire reply'd, ...Od.10.82.343.
Say if my sire, good old *Laertes,* lives? ....Od.11.210.392.
Thy sire in solitude foments his care: ....Od.11.226.393.
The Sire denies, and Kings rejected mourn. ....Od.11.352.399.
The sire shall bless his son, the son his sire: ....Od.11.558.411.
The sire shall bless his son, the son his sire: ....Od.11.558.411.
Say if my sire, the rev'rend *Peleus* reigns ....Od.11.605.413.
O Sire of men and Gods, immortal *Jove!* ....Od.12.437.452.
The sev'nth arose, and now the Sire of Gods ....Od.12.469.454.
So *Jove* decreed, (dread Sire of men and Gods.) ....Od.12.528.458.
Shall then no more, O Sire of Gods! be mine ....Od.13.148.12.
These ears have heard my royal sire disclose ....Od.13.198.15.
From sacred *Crete,* and from a Sire of Fame: ....Od.14.230.47.
The Sire with hospitable rites receiv'd, ...Od.14.352.51.
Whose boasted Sire was sacred *Alpheus'* heir; ....Od.15.211.78.
And soon he reach'd the Palace of his Sire. ....Od.15.243.80.
Was once my Sire: tho' now for ever lost ....Od.15.292.83.
And Sire, forsaken on the verge of age; ....Od.15.371.87.
Laertes lives, the miserable sire, ...Od.15.375.87.
As some fond sire who ten long winters grieves, ...Od.16.17.102.
An unblest offspring of a sire unblest! ....Od.16.128.108.
Sent the sad sire in solitude to stray; ....Od.16.149.109.
Thou art not—no, thou can'st not be my sire. ....Od.16.215.114.
Steals on his Sire a glance, and secret smiles. ....Od.16.497.131.
Nor from the sire art thou the son declin'd; ....Od.18.155.173.
And thus the Son the fervent Sire addrest. ....Od.19.4.193.
And rapt with ecstacy the Sire address'd. ....Od.19.43.195.
Be calm, replies the Sire; to none impart, ...Od.19.50.195.
The Prince appoints; but to his Sire assigns ....Od.20.324.248.
From my great Sire too soon devolv'd to me! ....Od.20.331.249.
Nor shou'd thy Sire a Queen his daughter boast, ...Od.20.376.251.
Whilst hope prevail'd to see your Sire restor'd, ...Od.20.393.251.
Full on his Sire he rowl'd his ardent eyes; ....Od.20.460.255.
The fourth had drawn it. The great Sire with joy ....Od.21.135.265.
With speedy ardour to his Sire he flies, ...Od.22.116.292.
And four broad bucklers, to his Sire he bears: ....Od.22.129.292.
The sire and son's great acts, with-held the day; ....Od.22.258.299.
His sire approaches, and the bard defends. ....Od.22.394.307.
Gaz'd o'er his Sire, retracing ev'ry line, ...Od.24.270.362.
Then to his Sire with beating heart he moves, ...Od.24.283.363.
These floods of sorrow, oh my Sire, restrain! ....Od.24.379.367.
Nor had the Sire been sep'rate from the Son. ....Od.24.443.370.
Who nurs'd the children, and now tends the sire: ....Od.24.450.370.

SIRE'S
The Son expiring in the Sire's Embrace; ....Il.22.545.479.
To the sire's merit give the son's request. ....Od.4.444.141.
Her kindred's wishes, and her Sire's commands; ....Od.15.20.70.
And with the sire's and son's commix thy blood. ....Od.22.238.298.

SIREN
See SYREN.
And lo! the *Siren* shores like mists arise. ....Od.12.201.441.
Our swift approach the *Siren* quire descries; ....Od.12.219.442.
Then how unharm'd he past the *Siren*-coasts, ...Od.23.352.341.

SIREN-COASTS
Then how unharm'd he past the *Siren*-coasts, ...Od.23.352.341.

SIRENS
Next, where the Sirens dwell, you plow the seas; ....Od.12.51.431.
In flow'ry meads the sportive *Sirens* play, ...Od.12.194.441.

SIRES
This too, *Let Men their Sires and Mothers leave,* .... 2.ChWB.19.57.
These three right Ancient Venerable Sires. ....2.ChWB.149.63.
The mothers nurse it, and the sires defend; ....3.EOM3.126.105.
Why should not we be wiser than our Sires? ....4.2HE1.44.197.
And to debase the Sons, exalts the Sires. ....4.2HE1.134.207.
Sons, Sires, and Grandsires, all will wear the Bays, ...4.2HE1.171.209.
Where reign our Sires! There, to thy Countrey's Shame, ...6.96iii.7.274.
Which own'd, would all their Sires and Sons disgrace. ....6.96iii.16.275.
Our selves to lessen, while our Sires you raise? ....Il.4.457.242.
Sons, Sires, and Wives, an undistinguish'd Prey. ....Il.5.596.297.
Unhappy they, and born of luckless Sires, ...Il.6.157.333.
Before my Eyes my mighty Sires to place, ...Il.6.259.339.
To bid the Sires with hoary Honours crown'd, ...Il.8.645.426.
Its Touch makes Orphans, bathes the cheeks of Sires, ...Il.11.502.56.
Of their great sires, and most their sires disgrace. ....Od.2.316.76.
Of their great sires, and most their sires disgrace. ....Od.2.316.76.
'Till our consenting sires a spouse provide ....Od.6.345.228.
How lov'd of *Jove* he crown'd our sires with praise, ...Od.8.279.278.

SIRIAN
Against the Solar Beam and *Sirian* Fire. ....Il.23.235.499.

SIRIUS
The sultry *Sirius* burns the thirsty Plains, ...1.PSu.21.73.
And raging *Sirius* blasts the sickly Year, ...1.TrSt.748.441.
Beneath the Rage of burning *Sirius* rise, ...Il.5.1060.317.

SIRIUS'
As warring Winds, in *Sirius'* sultry Reign, ...Il.13.424.126.

SIRREVERENCE
Ev'n to their own S[ir]r[e]v[ere]nce in a Carr? ....4.2HE2.107.173.

SIRS
Conceive me Sirs, nor take my Sense amiss, ...2.ChJM.113.20.
Now Sirs you know to what I stand inclin'd, ...2.ChJM.137.21.
We, Sirs, are Fools; and must resign the Cause ....2.ChJM.218.25.
All this I said; but Dreams, Sirs, I had none. ....2.ChWB.304.71.
'Far be it, Sirs, from my more civill Muse, ...6.13.20.39.
Believe him, Sirs h'has known the World too long, ...6.34.19A.101.

SISE-RAH
And *Deborah,* as she *Sise-rah:* .... 6.101.22.290.

SISERA
Or dext'rous *Deb'rah Sisera*-him ....6.101.28.291.

SISERA-HIM
Or dext'rous *Deb'rah Sisera*-him ....6.101.28.291.

SISTER
Then *Sculpture* and her *Sister-Arts* revive; ....1.EOC.701.319.
My trembling sister strove to urge her flight, ...1.TrFD.36.387.
My sire, my sister, and my spouse farewell! ....1.TrFD.88.389.
Yet since thou wilt thy Sister-Queen controul, ...1.TrSt.366.425.
He thus bespoke his Sister and his Queen. ....1.TrES.226.458.
The Sister-Lock now sits uncouth, alone, ...2.RL4.171.198.
Thus her blind Sister, fickle *Fortune* reigns, ...2.TemF.296.278.
Ah let thy handmaid, sister, daughter move, ...2.ElAb.153.332.
Come, sister come! (it said, or seem'd to say) ....2.ElAb.309.344.
Thy place is here, sad sister come away! ....2.ElAb.310.344.
Sighs for a Sister with unwounded ear; ....3.Ep2.260A.71.
She turns her very Sister to a Job, ...4.HAdv.21.77.
Who starves a Sister, or forswears a Debt? ....4.EpS1.112.306.
Who starv'd a Sister, who forswore a Debt, ...4.EpS2.20.314.
Grieve not at ought our sister realm acquires: ....5.DunA1.24.62.
His Sister sends, her vot'ress, from above. ....5.DunA2.208.127.
His sister sends, her vot'ress, from above. ....5.DunB2.216.306.
Had not her Sister Satyr held her head: ....5.DunB4.42.345.
Sister Spirit, come away. ....6.31ii.8.94.
So from a sister sinner you shall hear, ...6.41.9.113.
Smit with the love of Sister-arts we came, ...6.52.13.156.
The tender sister, daughter friend and wife; ....6.52.52.157.
To treat him like her Sister *Scot,* .... 6.101.30.291.
Sent by the * Sister and the Wife of *Jove;* .... Il.1.262.99.
Discord! dire Sister of the slaught'ring Pow'r, ...Il.4.502.244.
(*Theano's* Sister) to his youthful Arms. ....Il.11.290.48.
Obey'd the Sister and the Wife of *Jove:* .... Il.14.244.172.
No weeping Sister his cold Eye shall close, ...Il.15.398.212.
He thus bespoke his Sister and his Queen. ....Il.16.529.264.
Their Sister Looks; *Dexamene* the slow, ...Il.18.56.326.
Oh had'st thou still, a Sister of the Main, ...Il.18.109.328.
Ye Sister *Nereids!* to your Deeps descend, ...Il.18.177.331.
(His Wife and Sister) spoke almighty *Jove.* .... Il.18.418.341.
Her Sister Captives echo'd Groan for Groan, ...Il.19.321.385.
Each azure Sister of the silver Flood; ....Il.20.14.393.
The quiver'd *Dian,* Sister of the Day, ...Il.20.96.398.
And he, but from a Sister of the Main; ....Il.20.137.399.
Or scornful Sister with her sweeping Train, ...Il.24.973.576.
To calm the Queen the Phantom-sister flies. ....Od.4.1054.167.
O sister, to my soul for ever dear, ...Od.4.1067.167.
But now an azure sister of the main) ....Od.5.427.193.
With sister-fruits; one fertile, one was wild. ....Od.5.619.201.
Two sister Goddesses possess the plain, ...Od.12.166.440.

SISTER-ARTS
Then *Sculpture* and her *Sister-Arts* revive; ....1.EOC.701.319.
Smit with the love of Sister-arts we came, ...6.52.13.156.

SISTER-FRUITS
With sister-fruits; one fertile, one was wild. ....Od.5.619.201.

SISTER-LOCK
The Sister-Lock now sits uncouth, alone, ...2.RL4.171.198.

SISTER-QUEEN
Yet since thou wilt thy Sister-Queen controul, ...1.TrSt.366.425.

SISTER'S
A nearer woe, a sister's stranger fate. ....1.TrFD.6.385.
Thy Wife and Sister's Tutelary Care? ....1.TrSt.395.426.
She, who can own a Sister's charms, or hears ....3.Ep2.259B.71.
She, who can love a Sister's charms, or hear ....3.Ep2.259.71.
Oft her gay Sister's life and spirit fled; ....5.DunB4.39Z1.344.
Asham'd to combate in their Sister's Cause. ....Il.3.310.208.
Nor thou a Wife and Sister's Right deny; ....Il.4.87.224.
That caus'd these Woes, deserves a Sister's Name! ....Il.6.433.348.

SISTERS
So from my Birth the *Sisters* fix'd my Doom, ...1.TrSP.91.397.
Thus to the Sea-green Sisters sends his Pray'r. ....1.TrUl.239.473.
Here in one bed two shiv'ring sisters lye, ...5.DunA1.31.63.
While all your smutty sisters walk the streets. ....5.DunB1.230.287.
Let Bawdry, Bilingsgate, two sisters dear, ...5.DunB1.307A.292
Others the Syren Sisters warble round, ...5.DunB4.541.395.
Others the Syren Sisters compass round, ...5.DunB4.541A.395
How wilt thou now the fatal Sisters move? ....6.11.95.33.
Oh heav'n-born sisters! source of art! ....6.51i.9.151.
This radiant pile nine rural sisters raise; ....6.126ii.2.353.
Or sought her Sisters in the *Trojan* Court? ....Il.6.477.350.
His Sisters follow'd; ev'n the vengeful Dame, ...Il.9.696.468.
And all the Sea-green Sisters of the Deep. ....Il.18.46.325.
Hear me, and judge, ye Sisters of the Main! ....Il.18.69.326.
The Sea-green Sisters plunge beneath the Wave: ....Il.18.182.331.
Around, a Train of weeping Sisters stands, ...Il.22.604.481.
(The blue-hair'd Sisters of the sacred Main) ....Il.24.112.539.
These sons their sisters wed, and all remain ....Od.10.7.339.
Thus to the sea-green sisters sends his pray'r. ....Od.13.406.26.
The sea-green sisters waited on the dame. ....Od.24.66.350.

SISTRUM
Rattling an ancient Sistrum at his head. ....5.DunB4.374.379.

SISYPHUS
Æolian Sisyphus, with Wisdom blest, ...Il.6.191.335.

SISYPHYAN
A mournful vision! the *Sisyphyan* shade; ....Od.11.734.422.

SIT
Why sit we mute, when early Linnets sing, ...1.PSp.25.62.
Why sit we sad, when *Phosphor* shines so clear, ...1.PSp.27.63.
Trees, where you sit, shall crowd into a Shade, ...1.PSu.74.77.
I sit in Tatters, and immur'd at home! ....2.ChWB.77.60.
Then down they sit, and in their Dotage write, ...2.ChWB.374.75.
Descend, and sit on each important Card: ....2.RL3.32.171.
Where Age and Want sit smiling at the gate: ....3.Ep3.266.115.
I sit with sad Civility, I read ....4.Arbu.37.98.
And sit attentive to his own applause; ....4.Arbu.210.111.
I sit and dream I see my CRAGS anew! ....4.EpS2.69.316.
Rome in her Capitol saw Querno sit, ...5.DunA2.11.97.
To him we grant our amplest pow'rs to sit ....5.DunA2.343.142.
To him we grant our ample pow'rs to sit ....5.DunA2.343A.142.
The heroes sit; the vulgar form a ring. ....5.DunA2.352.143.
B[enson] sole Judge of Architecture sit, ...5.DunA3.321.188.
Or chair'd at White's amidst the Doctors sit, ...5.DunB1.203.284.
Rome in her Capitol saw Querno sit, ...5.DunB2.15.297.
"To him we grant our amplest pow'rs to sit ....5.DunB2.375.315.
The heroes sit, the vulgar form a ring. ....5.DunB2.384.316.
So by each Bard an Alderman shall sit, ...5.DunB4.131.354.
Sit still a Moment; pray be easy— ....6.10.2.24.
Dear Rowe, *lets sit and talk of Tragedies:* 6.49ii.5.140.
I wish the Man a Dinner, and sit still; ....6.49iii.2.142.
I wish the Wretch a Dinner, and sit still; ....6.49iii.2A.142.
And on that Chair did sit; ....6.79.70.220.
I wish the Man a Dinner, and sit still. ....6.98.2.283.
But high in Heav'n they sit, and gaze from far, ...Il.4.11.221.
Apart they sit, their deep Designs employ, ...Il.4.29.222.
Whose Crimes sit heavy on her perjur'd Head; ....Il.4.271.234.
They sit conceal'd, and wait the future Fight. ....Il.7.68.366.
At length compos'd they sit, and shade the Ground. ....Il.7.76.366.
Sit thou secure amidst thy social Band; ....Il.7.133.370.
Sole should he sit, with scarce a God to Friend, ...Il.8.250.409.
But greater Cares sit heavy on our Souls, ...Il.9.299.449.
They sit, rejoicing in her Aid divine, ...Il.10.679.32.
Social we sit, and share the genial Rites. ....Il.11.911.76.
In haste, and standing; for to sit they fear'd. ....Il.18.290.336.
Ourself will sit, and see the Hand of Fate ....Il.20.34.394.
Sleepless they sit, impatient to engage, ...Il.24.493.556.
Why here once more in solemn council sit? ....Od.2.36.62.
We sit, and trust the pilot and the wind. ....Od.9.88.306.
We sit expecting. Lo! he comes at last. ....Od.9.275.318.
Thus might we sit, with social goblets crown'd, ...Od.14.225.46.
O'er the protracted feast the Suitors sit, ...Od.20.447.254.
To sit distinguish'd, with our presence grac'd, ...Od.21.312.274.

SITE
And stately *Corinth's* pleasing Site surveys. ....1.TrSt.473.430.
Its Site uncertain, if in Earth or Air; ....2.TemF.421.283.
And fair *Mantinea's* ever-pleasing Site; ....Il.2.739.161.

SITS
Rich Industry sits smiling on the Plains, ...1.W-F.41.152.
The Chimney keeps, and sits content within; ....2.ChWB.143.63.
The Sister-Lock now sits uncouth, alone, ...2.RL4.171.198.
Fame sits aloft, and points them out their Course, ...2.TemF.483.286.
Black Melancholy sits, and round her throws ....2.ElAb.165.333.
Still sits at squat, and peeps not from its hole. ....3.Ep1.115.24.
Tho' daring Milton sits Sublime, ...4.HOde9.5.159.
Good C[ornbury] hopes, and candidly sits still. ....4.1740.18.332*.
On this he sits, to that he leans his ear, ...5.DunA2.82.108.
Old Bavius sits, to dip poetic souls, ...5.DunA3.16.151.
Immortal Rich! how calm he sits at ease ....5.DunA3.257.179.
On this he sits, to that he leans his ear, ...5.DunB2.86.300.
Sits Mother Osborne, stupify'd to stone! ....5.DunB2.312.311.
Old Bavius sits, to dip poetic souls, ...5.DunB3.24.321.
Immortal Rich! how calm he sits at ease ....5.DunB3.261.332.
Our Midas sits Lord Chancellor of Plays! ....5.DunB3.324.335.
Proud grief sits swelling in her eyes: ....6.5.2.12.
Close to the best known Author, *Umbra* sits, ...6.49ii.1.140.
E'en sits him down, and writes to honest *T[ickell]* ....6.49ii.14.140.
And sits attentive to his own Applause; ....6.49iii.26.143.
And sits attentive to his own Applause; ....6.98.62.285.
He sits superior, and the Chariot flies. ....Il.13.41.107.
Supreme he sits; and sees, in Pride of Sway, ...Il.15.116.201.
Why sits great *Hector* from the Field so far, ...Il.15.276.207.
Unknown to him who sits remote on high, ...Il.18.223.332.
All comfortless he sits, and wails his Friend: ....Il.19.367.387.
Beneath a sculptur'd arch he sits enthron'd, ...Od.8.517.290.
First down he sits, to milk the woolly dams, ...Od.9.402.322.
Why sits *Ulysses* silent and apart? ....Od.10.445.365.
Secure he sits, near great *Atrides* plac'd; ....Od.13.490.29.
The pensive mother sits in humble state; ....Od.17.111.137.

SITTING
And sitting down, to milk his flocks prepares; ....Od.9.289.318.
Now sitting as he was, the chord he drew, ...Od.21.458.282.

SIX
Or in a Coach and Six the *British* Fair, ...2.RL3.164.181.
Six pompous Columns o'er the rest aspire; ....2.TemF.179.270.
Then give Humility a coach and six, ...3.EOM4.170.143.
And give Humility a coach and six? ....3.EOM4.170A.143.
Bear home six Whores, and make his Lady weep? ....3.Ep3.60.91.
"I'll now give six-pence where I gave a groat, ...3.Ep3.366.123.
For life, six hundred pounds a year, ...4.HS6.2.251.

SIX (CONTINUED)
To spend six months with Statesmen here. ....4.HS6.32.253.
Six huntsmen with a shout precede his chair; ....5.DunA2.185.124.
Six huntsmen with a shout precede his chair: ....5.DunB2.193.305.
Nor Sighs for Coach and Six. ....6.54.4.164.
On Sunday at Six, in the Street that's call'd *Gerrard,* ....6.62v.1.186.
For Six-pence, I'd have giv'n a thousand Pound. ....6.96iv.80.278.
And strains, from hard bound Brains, six Lines a Year; ....6.98.32.284.
A Tower there is, where six Maidens do dwell; ....6.122.1.341.
Who by six such fair Maidens at once is possest. ....6.122.4.341.
With six small Ships, and but a slender Train, ...Il.5.794.304.
Thro' six Bull-hides the furious Weapon drove, ...Il.7.298.379.
A Rowe of six fair Tripods then succeeds; ....Il.19.251.383.
Of six years Age, unconscious of the Yoke, ...Il.23.756.520.
Of twice six Oxen its reputed Price; ....Il.23.817.521.
A silver Urn; that full six Measures held, ...Il.23.865.524.
Six youthful Sons, as many blooming Maids ....Il.24.759.569.
'Till twice six times descends the lamp of day: ....Od.2.421.81.
Six brave companions from each ship we lost, ...Od.9.69.305.
Six blooming youths, in private grandeur bred, ...Od.10.5.339.
And six fair daughters, grac'd the royal bed: ....Od.10.6.339.
Six days and nights a doubtful course we steer, ...Od.10.91.343.
Six horrid necks she rears, and six terrific heads; ....Od.12.112.437.
Six horrid necks she rears, and six terrific heads; ....Od.12.112.437.
At once six mouths expands, at once six men devours. ....Od.12.124.437.
At once six mouths expands, at once six men devours. ....Od.12.124.437.
'Tis better six to lose, than all to die. ....Od.12.138.438.
Her six mouths yawn, and six are snatch'd away. ....Od.12.155.439.
Her six mouths yawn, and six are snatch'd away. ....Od.12.155.439.
Stretch'd her dire jaws and swept six men away; ....Od.12.295.446.
Six guilty days my wretched mates employ ....Od.12.467.454.
Six days consum'd; the sev'nth we plow'd the main. ....Od.14.283.49.
Six calmy days and six smooth nights we sail, ...Od.15.511.94.
Six calmy days and six smooth nights we sail, ...Od.15.511.94.
Twice twenty six, all peers of mighty name, ...Od.16.269.118.
Six are their menial train: twice twelve the boast ....Od.16.270.118.
Six beams, oppos'd to six in equal space: ....Od.19.671.228.
Six beams, oppos'd to six in equal space: ....Od.19.671.228.
Sure thro' six circlets flew the whizzing dart. ....Od.19.673.229.
With *Demoptolemus:* These six survive, ...Od.22.268.299.
One sure of six shall reach *Ulysses'* heart: ....Od.22.277.300.
Of these, twice six pursue their wicked way, ...Od.22.462.310.
And six were all the sons of *Dolius'* race: ....Od.24.573.375.

SIX-PENCE
"I'll now give six-pence where I gave a groat, ...3.Ep3.366.123.
For Six-pence, I'd have giv'n a thousand Pound. ....6.96iv.80.278.

SIXPENCE
If vile D[evonshire] lov'd Sixpence, more than he. ....4.2HE2.229A.181.
If vile Van-muck lov'd Sixpence, more than he. ....4.2HE2.229.181.
They ne'er gave *Sixpence* for *two Lines,* .... 6.29.23.83.

SIXTEEN
E'er sixteen passing years had overlaid ....1.TrPA.7.365.
And sixteen Palms his Brows large Honours spread: ....Il.4.141.227.

SIXTY
But in due Time, when Sixty Years were o'er, ...2.ChJM.9.15.
How oft by these at sixty are undone ....3.EOM4.183.144.
Full sixty years the World has been her Trade, ...3.Ep2.123.60.
Full sixty Years the World has been her Trade, ...6.154.9.403.
Twice sixty Warriors thro' the foaming Seas. ....Il.2.609.156.
In sixty Ships with *Menelaus* draws: ....Il.2.710.160.
In sixty Sail th' *Arcadian* Bands unite. ....Il.2.740.161.

SIZE
How great I look'd! of what a godlike size! ....1.TrPA.98.369.
But swell'd to larger Size, the more I gaz'd, ...2.TemF.260.275.
Volumes, whose size the space exactly fill'd; ....5.DunA1.117.77.
Of these twelve volumes, twelve of amplest size, ...5.DunA1.135.80.
"His be yon Juno of majestic size, ...5.DunA2.155.120.
That on his vigor and superior size. ....5.DunA2.162.121.
Of these twelve volumes, twelve of amplest size, ...5.DunB1.155.281.
"His be yon Juno of majestic size, ...5.DunB2.163.303.
One on his vigour and superior size. ....5.DunB2.170.304.
And some things of little size, ...6.18.4.61.
Is a thing of little size, ...6.18.9.61.
And some things else of little size, ...6.18.4A.61.
And swells his bloated Corps to largest size. ....6.26i.15.79.
Reach thy Size? ....6.96i.4.268.
"Equal in Size to Cells of Honeycombs. ....6.96ii.56.273.
A bleeding Serpent, of enormous Size, ...Il.12.234.89.
His Port majestick, and his ample Size: ....Il.15.815.228.
Thund'ring he falls; a Mass of monstrous Size, ...Il.21.472.441.
His manly Beauty, and superiour Size: ....Il.22.466.474.
Of twenty Measures its capacious Size. ....Il.23.332.503.
Whose Weight and Size the circling *Greeks* admire, ...Il.23.975.528.
His god-like Aspect and majestick Size; ....Il.24.799.570.
A silver Laver, of capacious size: ....Od.1.182.41.
Like the *Telemachus,* in voice and size, ...Od.2.430.81.
A silver laver, of capacious size. ....Od.7.233.247.
Of size enormous, and terrific mien, ...Od.10.128.347.
The joyful crew survey his mighty size, ...Od.10.204.350.
A silver laver of capacious size. ....Od.10.436.365.
Proud of their strength and more than mortal size, ...Od.11.385.402.
There huge *Orion* of portentous size, ...Od.11.703.419.
A silver laver of capacious size. ....Od.15.151.76.
A silver laver of capacious size. ....Od.17.107.137.
Dimension'd equal to his size, exprest ....Od.19.276.208.

SIZES
But here all Sizes and all Shapes you meet, ...6.60.27.178.
But here all Sizes and all Shapes ye meet, ...6.60.27A.178.

SKELTON
And beastly Skelton Heads of Houses quote: 4.2HE1.38.197.

SKETCH
But as the slightest Sketch, if justly trac'd, 1.EOC.23.241.
Strike in the sketch, or in the picture glow; 6.52.44.157.

SKEW'R
Or whiten'd Wall provoke the Skew'r to write, 4.HS1.98.13.

SKIE
See SKY.
With louder Clamours rend the vaulted Skie: 2.ChJM.755.51.
With such loud Clamours rend the vaulted Skie: 2.ChJM.755A.51.

SKIES
All Nature mourns, the Skies relent in Show'rs, 1.PSp.69.68.
The Skies to brighten, and the Birds to sing. 1.PSp.72.68.
Lose the low Vales, and steal into the Skies. 1.PAu.60.84.
The Skies yet blushing with departing Light, 1.PAu.98.87.
No grateful Dews descend from Ev'ning Skies, 1.PWi.45.92.
Whose sacred Flow'r with Fragrance fills the Skies. 1.Mes.10.113.
And *Carmel's* flow'ry Top perfumes the Skies! 1.Mes.28.115.
Lo Earth receives him from the bending Skies! 1.Mes.33.116.
Demanding Life, impatient for the Skies! 1.Mes.90.121.
The Seas shall waste; the Skies in Smoke decay; 1.Mes.105.122.
Who claim'd the Skies, dispeopled Air and Floods, 1.W-F.47.153.
The headlong Mountains and the downward Skies, 1.W-F.212.169.
While led along the Skies his Current strays, 1.W-F.228.170.
While thro' the Skies his shining Current strays, 1.W-F.228A.170.
Bids his free Soul expatiate in the Skies, 1.W-F.254.172.
And lift her Turrets nearer to the Skies; 1.W-F.288.175.
Or under Southern Skies exalt their Sails, 1.W-F.391.189.
Encourag'd thus, Witt's *Titans* brav'd the Skies, 1.EOC.552.304.
Not Jove himself (your Jove that sways the skies) 1.TrPA.99.369.
Venus for those had rapt thee to the Skies, 1.TrSP.101.398.
Tho' all the Skies, ambitious of thy Sway, 1.TrSt.37.411.
Resign to *Jove* his Empire of the Skies, 1.TrSt.45.411.
The Wretch then lifted to th'unpitying Skies 1.TrSt.77.413.
There spreads her dusky Pinions to the Skies. 1.TrSt.135.415.
Far in the bright Recesses of the Skies, 1.TrSt.275.421.
Those golden Wings that cut the yielding Skies; 1.TrSt.430.428.
And draws a radiant Circle o'er the Skies. 1.TrSt.442.428.
Promise the Skies the bright Return of Day; 1.TrSt.483.430.
Encrease the Darkness and involve the Skies. 1.TrSt.487.430.
He dreads the Rocks, and Shoals, and Seas, and Skies, 1.TrSt.524.432.
Run to the Shade, and bark against the Skies. 1.TrSt.647.437.
Rings to the Skies, and ecchoes thro' the Fields, 1.TrES.64.452.
Tumultuous Clamour mounts, and thickens in the Skies. 1.TrES.96.453.
What Words are these, O Sov'reign of the Skies? 1.TrES.238.458.
Less swift, an Eagle cuts the liquid Skies: 1.TrUl.14.466.
Then to the Skies your mounting Soul shall go, 2.ChJM.289.28.
Dipt in the richest Tincture of the Skies, 2.RL2.65.163.
And Screams of Horror rend th' affrighted Skies. 2.RL3.156.180.
And base, and treble Voices strike the Skies. 2.RL5.42.202.
The Skies bespangling with dishevel'd Light. 2.RL5.130A.210.
And pleas'd pursue its Progress thro' the Skies. 2.RL5.132.211.
This *Partridge* soon shall view in cloudless Skies, 2.RL5.137.211.
I stood, methought, betwixt Earth, Seas, and Skies; 2.TemF.11.254.
And the huge Columns heave into the Skies. 2.TemF.92.259.
O'er which a pompous Dome invades the Skies: 2.TemF.245.275.
Fill the wide Earth, and gain upon the Skies. 2.TemF.313.279.
Loud as the Burst of Cannon rends the Skies, 2.TemF.334.280.
The pois'nous Vapor blots the purple Skies, 2.TemF.340.280.
Sweet to the World, and grateful to the Skies. 2.TemF.377.281.
The Queen assents, the Trumpet rends the Skies, 2.TemF.392.282.
As Flames by Nature to the Skies ascend, 2.TemF.428.284.
All various Sounds from Earth, and Seas, and Skies, 2.TemF.433.284.
Sudden you mount! you becken from the skies; 2.ElAb.245.339.
Blot out each bright Idea of the skies. 2.ElAb.284.343.
From opening skies may streaming glories shine, 2.ElAb.341.347.
All quit their sphere, and rush into the skies. 3.EOM1.124.30.
"My foot-stool earth, my canopy the skies." 3.EOM1.140.32.
As much eternal springs and cloudless skies, 3.EOM1.153.34.
Study a Mite, not comprehend the Skies? 3.EOM1.196A.39.
She, from the rending earth and bursting skies, 3.EOM3.253.118.
By mountains pil'd on mountains, to the skies? 3.EOM4.74.135.
P. Where London's column, pointing at the skies 3.Ep3.339A.121.
But well-dispers'd, is Incense to the Skies. 3.Ep3.236.111.
Not to the skies in useless columns tost, 3.Ep3.255.114.
Where London's column, pointing at the skies 3.Ep3.339.121.
Look thro', and trust the Ruler with his Skies, 4.1HE6.8.237.
Advance thy golden Mountain to the skies; 4.1HE6.73.241.
Sweet to the World, and grateful to the Skies: 4.EpS2.245.326.
When the last blaze sent Ilion to the skies. 5.DunA1.212.88.
Walls, steeples, skies, bray back to him again: 5.DunA2.248.130.
Soon as they dawn, from Hyperborean skies, 5.DunA3.77.156.
Against her throne, from Hyperborean skies, 5.DunA3.77A.156.
Whales sport in woods, and dolphins in the skies, 5.DunA3.242.177.
When the last blaze sent Ilion to the skies. 5.DunB1.256.289.
Walls, steeples, skies, bray back to him again. 5.DunB2.260.308.
Soon as they dawn, from Hyperborean skies 5.DunB3.85.324.
Whales sport in woods, and dolphins in the skies; 5.DunB3.246.332.
See how the sun in dusky skies 6.4iv.1.10.
And to the skies its incense throws. 6.4iv.18.11.
As the soft dews of morning skies 6.5.7A.12.
And pleas'd, look downward to the Skies. 6.6ii.16.15.
And fill with spreading Sounds the Skies; 6.11.15.30.
And Seas, and Rocks, and Skies rebound 6.11.47.32.
To him reveal my joys, and open all my skies. 6.21.42.70.
And view familiar, in its native skies, 6.23.10.73.
And view familiar, in her native skies, 6.23.10A.73.
From storms defended, and inclement skies: 6.35.2.103.
Whose Altar, Earth, Sea, Skies; 6.50.50.148.
Bestreak'd with Blood the Skies; 6.79.106.221.
Whose dazling Lustre whitens all the Skies. 6.82v.4.231.

SKIES (CONTINUED)
Propt the Skies: 6.96i.15.268.
Which seem'd like two broad Suns in misty Skies: 6.96ii.74.273.
"It came from Bertrand's not the skies; 6.140.15.378.
To calm thy Fury I forsake the Skies: Il.1.274.100.
To calm thy Fury I forsook the Skies: Il.1.274A.100.
And joins the sacred Senate of the Skies. Il.1.294.101.
And waft their grateful Odours to the Skies. Il.1.417.107.
Thro' wondring Skies enormous stalk'd along; Il.1.524.113.
Who rolls the Thunder o'er the vaulted Skies. Il.1.671.119.
Jove to his starry Mansion in the Skies. Il.1.689.120.
Who now partakes the Secrets of the Skies? Il.1.699.121.
Full on the Sire the Goddess of the Skies Il.1.712.121.
And unextinguish'd Laughter shakes the Skies. Il.1.771.124.
The doubling Clamours eccho to the Skies. Il.2.188.137.
Shoot their long Beams, and kindle half the Skies: Il.2.537.152.
Or white *Lycastus* glitters to the Skies, Il.2.788.162.
And Show'rs of Wealth descending from the Skies. Il.2.814.163.
Floats the wide Field, and blazes to the Skies. Il.2.949.168.
The Tumult thickens, and the Skies resound. Il.2.981.170.
Meantime, to beauteous *Helen* from the Skies Il.3.165.199.
The raging Warrior to the spacious Skies Il.3.449.213.
His Spouse, or Slave; and mount the Skies no more. Il.3.506.215.
And the long Shout runs ecchoing thro' the Skies. Il.3.576.219.
The Sire whose Thunder shakes the cloudy Skies, Il.4.45.223.
Haste, leave the Skies, fulfil thy stern Desire, Il.4.53.223.
Beneath the rowling Sun, and starry Skies, Il.4.66.224.
Spread in dim Streams, and sail along the Skies, Il.4.317.235.
Foam o'er the Rocks, and thunder to the Skies. Il.4.483.243.
While scarce the Skies her horrid Head can bound, Il.4.504.245.
Like the red Star that fires th' Autumnal Skies, Il.5.8.266.
Or God incens'd, who quits the distant Skies Il.5.224.278.
Or if that Chief, some Guardian of the Skies Il.5.235.278.
Then with a Voice that shook the vaulted Skies, Il.5.431.289.
Her Brother's Car, to mount the distant Skies, Il.5.450.289.
And in a Moment scales the lofty Skies. Il.5.458.290.
And roll in smoaking Volumes to the Skies. Il.5.620.297.
Along the Skies their gloomy Lines display, Il.5.642.299.
Dispers'd and broken thro' the ruffled Skies. Il.5.648.299.
And brings along the Furies of the Skies. Il.5.725.302.
The Carnage *Juno* from the Skies survey'd, Il.5.874.308.
The Sun's bright Portals and the Skies command, Il.5.931.311.
The Chariot mounts, where deep in ambient Skies, Il.5.936.311.
Choak the parch'd Earth, and blacken all the Skies; Il.5.1061.317.
Of all the Gods who tread the spangled Skies, Il.5.1096.319.
This Pest he slaughter'd (for he read the Skies, Il.6.225.337.
To the pure Skies these horrid Hands to raise, Il.6.336.343.
His Head now freed, he tosses to the Skies; Il.6.656.359.
I left, for this, the Council of the Skies: Il.7.40.364.
Implore the God whose Thunder rends the Skies. Il.7.240.376.
That clouds the World, and blackens half the Skies. Il.7.543.391.
When *Jove* conven'd the Senate of the Skies, Il.8.3.394.
Back to the Skies with Shame he shall be driv'n, Il.8.13.395.
The Tumult thickens, and the Skies resound. Il.8.74.399.
Low sunk on Earth, the *Trojan* strikes the Skies. Il.8.92.401.
The God in Terrors, and the Skies on fire. Il.8.98.402.
This Day, averse, the Sov'reign of the Skies Il.8.171.406.
Then with a Voice that shakes the solid Skies, Il.8.194.406.
At *Hector's* Breast, and sings along the Skies: Il.8.366.414.
So spoke th' imperial Regent of the Skies; Il.8.433.418.
The Sun's bright Portals and the Skies command; Il.8.481.420.
There meets the Chariot rushing down the Skies, Il.8.505.420.
Who shall the Sov'reign of the Skies controul? Il.8.562.423.
What hast thou said, Oh Tyrant of the Skies! Il.8.575.424.
Who swells the Clouds, and blackens all the Skies. Il.8.585.424.
A Flood of Glory bursts from all the Skies: Il.8.696.428.
Jove's Arm, display'd, asserts her from the Skies; Il.9.542.460.
Mean while the Victor's Shouts ascend the Skies; Il.9.699.468.
The Heroes pray'd, and *Pallas* from the Skies, Il.10.351.18.
But first exalt thy Sceptre to the Skies, Il.10.379.20.
These great *Ulysses* lifting to the Skies, Il.10.530.26.
Blest as ye are, the fav'rites of the Skies; Il.10.651.30.
Thro' the red Skies her bloody Sign extends, Il.11.7.35.
Whose imitated Scales against the Skies Il.11.34.36.
Plac'd as a Sign to Man amid the Skies.) Il.11.38.36.
Flash from his Arms as Light'ning from the Skies. Il.11.88.38.
Shade the black Host, and intercept the Skies. Il.11.196.44.
Now to the Skies the foaming Billows rears, Il.11.399.52.
And half the Skies descend in sluicy Show'rs. Il.12.28.82.
And the Turf trembles, and the Skies resound. Il.12.60.83.
His following Host with Clamours rend the Skies: Il.12.138.86.
Their Roots in Earth, their Heads amidst the Skies, Il.12.146.86.
Jove's Bird on sounding Pinions beat the Skies; Il.12.233.89.
Dismiss'd his Conquest in the middle Skies, Il.12.259.90.
For thus a skilful Seer would read the Skies. Il.12.266.91.
Redoubling Clamours thunder in the Skies. Il.12.298.92.
He stills the Winds, and bids the Skies to sleep; Il.12.335.93.
Rings to the Skies, and ecchos thro' the Fields, Il.12.408.96.
Tumultuous Clamour mounts, and thickens in the Skies. Il.12.450.98.
And level'd at the Skies with pointing Rays, Il.13.185.114.
And *Pleuron's* chalky Cliffs emblaze the Skies. Il.13.288.119.
In streamy Sparkles, kindling all the Skies, Il.13.321.120.
And the dry Fields are lifted to the Skies: Il.13.427.126.
But *Jove* the greater, First-born of the Skies, Il.13.447.126.
O thou, great Father! Lord of Earth and Skies, Il.13.789.142.
And hail, with Shouts, his Progress thro' the Skies: Il.13.1041.154.
And lifts the *Trojan* Glory to the Skies. Il.14.80.161.
Great *Saturn's* Heir, and Empress of the Skies! Il.14.277.175.
Hear, and obey the Mistress of the Skies, Il.14.301.177.
To join its Summit to the neighb'ring Skies, Il.14.326.178.
Like Light'ning flashing thro' the frighted Skies. Il.14.446.185.
By fits he breathes, half views the fleeting Skies, Il.14.513.188.
The foodful Earth, and all-infolding Skies, Il.15.42.195.
Think'st thou with me? fair Empress of the Skies! Il.15.53.196.
Enough thou know'st the Tyrant of the Skies, Il.15.99.200.
And damp th' eternal Banquets of the Skies. Il.15.107.200.

SKIES 317 SKILL

SKIES (CONTINUED)

Arms, that reflect a Radiance thro' the Skies. ....Il.15.137.202.
Back to the Skies would'st thou with Shame be driv'n, ...Il.15.150.202.
The Skies would yield an ampler Scene of Rage, ...Il.15.153.202.
Drive thro' the Skies, when *Boreas* fiercely blows; ....Il.15.193.204.
What means the haughty Sov'reign of the Skies, ...Il.15.206.204.
That drives a Turtle thro' the liquid Skies; ....Il.15.267.207.
His Head now freed, he tosses to the Skies; ....Il.15.302.208.
From diff'rent parts, and mingle in the Skies. ....Il.15.355.210.
But when aloft he shakes it in the Skies, ...Il.15.362.210.
Experienc'd *Nestor* chief obtests the Skies, ...Il.15.426.213.
As, when black Tempests mix the Seas and Skies, ...Il.15.440.214.
To view the Navy blazing to the Skies; ....Il.15.719.223.
And Sheets of rolling Smoke involve the Skies. ....Il.16.153.243.
And shades the Sun, and blots the golden Skies: ....Il.16.437.259.
Tumultuous Clamour fills the Fields and Skies; ....Il.16.449.260.
And opens all the Floodgates of the Skies: ....Il.16.471.261.
What Words are these, O Sov'reign of the Skies? ....Il.16.541.265.
Supine, and wildly gazing on the Skies, ...Il.16.1016.282.
And sends his Voice in Thunder to the Skies: ....Il.17.96.291.
The *Grecian* marking, as it cut the Skies, ...Il.17.351.301.
And all Heav'n's Splendors blotted from the Skies. ....Il.17.425.303.
And shake the brazen Concave of the Skies. ....Il.17.483.306.
The drooping Cattel dread th' impending Skies, ...Il.17.620.312.
Thrice to the Skies the *Trojan* Clamours flew. ....Il.18.194.331.
Who sends thee, Goddess! from th' Etherial Skies? ....Il.18.219.332.
The Smokes high-curling to the shaded Skies; ....Il.18.246.334.
Reflecting Blaze on Blaze, against the Skies. ....Il.18.254.334.
And bears the blazing Present through the Skies. ....Il.18.712.357.
His Hands uplifted to th' attesting Skies, ...Il.19.263.383.
Whose dazling Lustre whitens all the Skies: ....Il.19.383.388.
With Splendor flame the Skies, and laugh the Fields around. ..Il.19.389.388.
And summons all the Senate of the Skies. ....Il.20.8.393.
This Day, we call the Council of the Skies ....Il.20.30.394.
Then fierce *Achilles,* shouting to the Skies, ...Il.20.437.413.
Fires the high Woods, and blazes to the Skies, ...Il.20.572.418.
Its erring Fury hiss'd along the Skies; ....Il.21.186.429.
Go matchless Goddess! triumph in the Skies, ...Il.21.583.446.
He lifts his wither'd Arms; obtests the Skies; ....Il.22.45.454.
(The swiftest Racer of the liquid Skies) ....Il.22.184.463.
With Exhalations steaming to the Skies; ....Il.22.198.463.
And stoops impetuous from the cleaving Skies. ....Il.22.242.465.
And the last Blaze send *Ilion* to the Skies. ....Il.22.521.478.
He call'd th' Aerial Pow'rs, along the Skies ....Il.23.242.499.
To the wide Main then stooping from the Skies, ...Il.23.266.500.
Shouts of Applause run rattling thro the Skies. ....Il.23.847.523.
His Friends (while loud Applauses shake the Skies) ....Il.23.1004.529.
Seas, Shores, and Skies with loud Applause resound, ...Il.23.1028.530.
Implores the God to speed it thro' the Skies, ...Il.23.1032.530.
But not deserted by the pitying Skies. ....Il.24.29.536.
And th' unrelenting Empress of the Skies: ....Il.24.37.537.
If equal Honours by the partial Skies ....Il.24.70.538.
He added not: And *Iris* from the Skies ....Il.24.99.539.
Calls *Jove* his *Thetis* to the hated Skies? ....Il.24.118.540.
And touch with momentary Flight the Skies. ....Il.24.128.540.
O favor'd of the Skies! (Thus answer'd then ....Il.24.501.557.
And in a moment shot into the Skies: ....Il.24.575.560.
To whom the King. Oh favour'd of the Skies! ....Il.24.696.566.
And soon as Morning paints the Eastern Skies, ...Il.24.751.568.
Assist him, *Jove!* thou regent of the skies! ....Od.2.42.62.
Your fame revere, but most th' avenging skies. ....Od.2.72.64.
Here thou art sage in vain—I better read the skies. ....Od.2.210.72.
O Goddess! who descending from the skies ....Od.2.297.76.
Attests th' all-seeing Sovereign of the skies. ....Od.2.425.81.
Nor earth had hid his carcase from the skies, ...Od.3.320.102.
Sudden the Thund'rer blackens all the skies, ...Od.3.367.104.
And soars an Eagle thro' the liquid skies. ....Od.3.475.110.
O happy Youth! and favour'd of the skies, ...Od.3.480.110.
When purple light shall next suffuse the skies, ...Od.4.550.146.
'Till night with grateful shade involv'd the skies, ...Od.4.582.147.
Thus 'till the sun had travel'd half the skies, ...Od.4.601.148.
And all th' offended synod of the skies; ....Od.4.636.149.
As *Pallas* will'd, along the sable skies ....Od.4.1053.167.
I speak not all the counsel of the skies: ....Od.4.1090.168.
But hear, oh earth, and hear ye sacred skies! ....Od.5.238.182.
Whose leafless summits to the skies aspire, ...Od.5.307.185.
To curl old Ocean, and to warm the skies. ....Od.5.342.188.
Plac'd at the helm he sate, and mark'd the skies, ...Od.5.345.188.
There no rude winds presume to shake the skies, ...Od.6.51.207.
(Their shining veils unbound.) Along the skies ....Od.6.113.211.
Mean time (the care and fav'rite of the skies) ....Od.6.129.213.
If from the skies a Goddess, or if earth ....Od.6.175.216.
Thou visit earth, a daughter of the skies, ...Od.6.178.218.
"Or rather, some descendant of the skies; ....Od.6.335.227.
The mist objected, and condens'd the skies) ....Od.7.54.236.
From storms defended, and inclement skies: ....Od.7.143.243.
Beyond these tracts, and under other skies, ...Od.7.327.252.
The wakeful mariners shall watch the skies, ...Od.7.407.256.
And sings with unmatch'd force along the skies. ....Od.8.138.270.
The crowd gaze upward while it cleaves the skies. ....Od.8.216.274.
Their feet half-viewless quiver in the skies: ....Od.8.304.279.
Stung to the soul, indignant thro' the skies ....Od.8.313.281.
Thus serious they: but he who gilds the skies, ...Od.8.373.284.
And breathing odours scent the balmy skies. ....Od.8.398.285.
And sends in shouts applauses to the skies. ....Od.8.416.286.
Crown him with ev'ry joy, ye fav'ring skies; ....Od.8.448.287.
Lives there a man beneath the spacious skies, ...Od.8.523.290.
How blazing tents illumin'd half the skies, ...Od.8.549.292.
And shed her sacred light along the skies. ....Od.9.365.321.
With hands uplifted to the starry skies. ....Od.9.616.332.
But the great God, whose thunder rends the skies, ...Od.9.645.333.
Edg'd round with cliffs, high-pointing to the skies; ....Od.10.102.345.
And mingled horrors eccho to the skies. ....Od.10.142.347.
And all around it only seas and skies! ....Od.10.226.351.
Ev'n when keen winter freezes in the skies, ...Od.11.230.393.
His bed the leaves, his canopy the skies. ....Od.11.237.393.

SKIES (CONTINUED)

Like a vain dream to these infernal skies. ....Od.11.268.394.
The Gods they challenge, and affect the skies; ....Od.11.386.402.
Or pale and wan beholds these nether skies? ....Od.11.571.411.
Toss it on high, and whirl it to the skies. ....Od.11.732.421.
There in the bright assemblies of the skies, ...Od.11.745.423.
Shuns the dire rocks: In vain she cuts the skies, ...Od.12.77.435.
Beat its bleak brow, and intercept the skies. ....Od.12.90.436.
The slippery sides, and shoot into the skies. ....Od.12.98.436.
And shoot a leafy forest to the skies; ....Od.12.128.438.
I turn, and view them quivering in the skies; ....Od.12.297.446.
And sudden lifts it quivering to the skies: ....Od.12.303.447.
Lash the wild surge, and bluster in the skies; ....Od.12.342.448.
With hands uplifted they attest the skies; ....Od.12.360.448.
And clouds and double darkness veil the skies; ....Od.12.370.449.
Vengeance, ye Gods! or I the skies forego, ...Od.12.450.452.
The joy of earth, and glory of the skies; ....Od.12.455.453.
The gloomy West, and whistles in the skies. ....Od.12.478.455.
And shed her sacred light along the skies. ....Od.13.22.2.
Less swift an eagle cuts the liquid skies: ....Od.13.105.6.
Belov'd by *Jove,* and him who gilds the skies, ...Od.15.270.81.
Expect me with the morn, to pay the skies ....Od.15.545.96.
Were every wish indulg'd by fav'ring skies, ...Od.16.160.110.
Thro' the wide fields of air, and cleaves the skies; ....Od.16.169.111.
Then why (she said) O favour'd of the skies! ....Od.16.180.112.
What need of aids, if favour'd by the skies? ....Od.16.281.118.
The care of Gods and fav'rite of the skies. ....Od.16.379.124.
If they forbid, I war not with the skies. ....Od.16.421.127.
Holy repast! That instant from the skies ....Od.16.474.130.
Wander, perhaps, some inmate of the skies; ....Od.17.577.160.
Here boundless wrongs the starry skies invade, ...Od.17.648.164.
With bursts of laughter rend the vaulted skies: ....Od.18.119.172.
Then to the skies her flight *Minerva* bends, ...Od.18.233.178.
Resign'd the skies, and night involv'd the pole. ....Od.19.496.220.
Full twenty annual suns in distant skies: ....Od.19.566.224.
Sudden the tyrant of the skies return'd: ....Od.19.638.227.
Sincere reveals the sanction of the skies: ....Od.19.651.227.
The Goddess pleas'd, regains her natal skies. ....Od.20.67.235.
I deem it sure a vision of the skies. ....Od.20.109.238.
The tyrant, not the father of the skies! ....Od.20.252.245.
Feed the rich smokes, high-curling to the skies. ....Od.21.283.273.
And take it He, the favour'd of the skies! ....Od.21.299.274.
The righteous pow'rs who tread the starry skies, ...Od.23.13.319.
And the mixt clamour thunders in the skies. ....Od.24.90.352.
And all the wing'd good omens of the skies. ....Od.24.364.366.
Who rolls the thunder o'er the vaulted skies) ....Od.24.548.374.

SKILFUL

As skilful Divers from some Airy Steep ....1.TrES.107.453.
The skilful Nymph reviews her Force with Care; ....2.RL3.45.172.
Or whirligigs, twirl'd round by skilful swain, ...5.DunA3.49.154.
Or whirligigs, twirl'd round by skilful swain, ...5.DunB3.57.323.
"So skilful and those Hands so taper; ....6.119.6.336.
Now seek some skilful Hand whose pow'rful Art ....Il.4.228.232.
The skilful Archer wide survey'd the Field, ...Il.8.322.413.
As when two skilful Hounds the Lev'ret winde, ...Il.10.427.22.
For thus a skilful Seer would read the Skies. ....Il.12.266.91.
As skilful Divers, from some airy Steep, ...Il.12.461.98.
What skilful Divers are our *Phrygian* Foes! ....Il.16.904.278.
What if the Gods, the Skilful to confound, ...Il.23.623.514.
Those, who in skilful Archery contend ....Il.23.1006.529.
And skilful *Teucer:* In the Helm they threw ....Il.23.1018.529.
Artist divine, whose skilful hands infold ....Od.3.540.114.
So dress'd and manag'd by thy skilful hand? ....Od.24.303.364.

SKILFULL

Use, use (cry'd Jove) those skilfull Eyes, ...6.119.5B.336.

SKILL

'Tis hard to say, if greater Want of Skill ....1.EOC.1.239.
And show their zeal, and hide their want of skill. ....3.Ep2.186.65.
Oh filthy check on all industrious skill, ...3.Ep3.63.92.
Where half the skill is decently to hide. ....3.Ep4.54.142.
I curse such lavish cost, and little skill, ...3.Ep4.167.153.
Who scorn a Lad should teach his Father skill, ...4.2HE1.129.205.
Shall *Ward* draw Contracts with a Statesman's skill? ....4.EpS1.119.306.
Such skill in passing all, and touching none. ....5.DunB4.258.369.
So just thy skill, so regular my rage. ....6.52.12.156.
Ah *Moore!* thy Skill were well employ'd, ...6.53.29.162.
For the Dame, by her Skill in Affairs Astronomical, ...6.124i.7.346.
To these his Skill their * Parent-God imparts, ...Il.2.890.166.
No Strength or Skill, but just in Time, be try'd: ....Il.4.349.237.
Thy Father's Skill, O *Phereclus,* was thine, ...Il.5.77.270.
Thy matchless Skill, thy yet-unrival'd Fame, ...Il.5.220.278.
To human Force and human Skill, the Field: ....Il.6.2.322.
The Parts transfixes, and with Skill divides. ....Il.9.276.447.
The Skill of War to us not idly giv'n, ...Il.13.1024.153.
With Skill divine had *Vulcan* form'd the Bow'r, ...Il.14.193.168.
With various Skill and high Embroid'ry grac'd. ....Il.14.246.173.
With Skill divine has *Vulcan* form'd thy Bow'r, ...Il.14.383.181.
The martial Leaders, with like Skill and Care, ...Il.15.478.216.
(Others in Council fam'd for nobler Skill, ...Il.18.135.329.
Neptune and *Jove* on thee conferr'd the Skill, ...Il.23.377.505.
While with sure Skill, tho' with inferior Steeds, ...Il.23.393.506.
With tardier Coursers, and inferior Skill. ....Il.23.608.514.
Whose dext'rous Skill directs the flying Dart. ....Il.23.1049.531.
With Skill prepare them, and in Parts divide: ....Il.24.789.570.
His skill divine, a breathing statue lives; ....Od.6.276.224.
For not the bow they bend, nor boast the skill ....Od.6.321.226.
With skill the virgin guides th' embroider'd rein, ...Od.6.379.230.
Than works of female skill their women's pride, ...Od.7.138.242.
But gave him skill to raise the lofty lay. ....Od.8.60.265.
Expert in ev'ry art, I boast the skill ....Od.8.247.275.
Thy praise was just; their skill transcends thy praise. ....Od.8.420.286.
Inimitably wrought with skill divine. ....Od.11.758.423.
Then the sindg'd members they with skill divide; ....Od.14.475.58.

SKILL (CONTINUED)

The skill of weather and of winds unknown,	Od.14.541.63.
They bend the silver bow with tender skill,	Od.15.450.92.
Fame speaks the *Trojans* bold; they boast the skill	Od.18.305.181.
Their strength and skill the Suitors shall assay:	Od.19.675.229.
(His perfect skill the wond'ring gazers ey'd)	Od.21.127.264.
(For his gift) the skill to bend the bow.	Od.21.285.273.
His heav'nly skill, a breathing image lives;	Od.23.158.328.
Great is thy skill, oh father! great thy toil,	Od.24.287.363.

SKILL'D

Once I was skill'd in ev'ry Herb that grew,	1.PSu.31.74.
Oh, skill'd in Nature! see the Hearts of Swains,	1.PAu.11.81.
Tho' skill'd in Fate and dark Futurity,	1.TrSt.552.433.
Skill'd in the Laws of Secret Fate above,	1.TrSt.839.444.
Skill'd in th'illustrious Labours of the Loom.	1.TrUl.165.471.
You should be better skill'd in Nocks,	6.93.29.257.
Oh next him skill'd to draw the tender Tear,	6.152.3.400.
Skill'd in each Art, and crown'd with ev'ry Grace.	II.1.142.93.
Experience'd *Nestor*, in Persuasion skill'd,	II.1.331.103.
Th' experienc'd *Nestor*, in Persuasion skill'd,	II.1.331A.103.
Skill'd to direct the flying Dart aright;	II.2.632.157.
Skill'd in his Science of the Dart and Bow.	II.2.877.165.
Old *Merops* Sons; whom skill'd in Fates to come	II.2.1008.170.
Skill'd in the Fight their crooked Bows to bend;	II.2.1029.171.
But silent, breathing Rage, resolv'd, and skill'd	II.3.11.188.
She seem'd an ancient Maid, well-skill'd to cull	II.3.477.214.
Græa, her Fav'rite Maid, well-skill'd to cull	II.3.477A.214.
And fears *Ulysses*, skill'd in ev'ry Art?	II.4.391.239.
Skill'd in the Bow, on Foot I sought the War,	II.5.242.278.
Thus said the Chief; and *Nestor*, skill'd in War,	II.8.143.404.
Skill'd in each Art, unmatch'd in Form divine,	II.9.166.441.
Skill'd in each Art, unmatch'd in Form divine,	II.9.353.451.
In deep Prophetic Arts their Father skill'd,	II.11.427.53.
Not deeper skill'd in ev'ry martial Slight,	II.11.541.58.
A wise Physician, skill'd our Wounds to heal,	II.11.636.62.
O say, in ev'ry Art of Battel skill'd,	II.13.327.121.
Skill'd, or with Shafts to gall the distant Field,	II.13.404.125.
But skill'd from far the flying Shaft to wing,	II.13.893.148.
Skill'd in Pursuit, and swiftest in the Chace.	II.14.618.192.
Skill'd to direct the Javelin's distant Flight,	II.15.320.209.
(Skill'd in the Manage of the bounding Steed)	II.15.823.228.
Skill'd in the Dart in vain, his Sons expire,	II.16.392.258.
And skill'd in Dancing to dispute the Prize,	II.16.746.272.
Skill'd in the Dart, and matchless in the Course:	II.16.975.281.
The Son of *Panthus*, skill'd the Dart to send,	II.17.11.288.
How skill'd he was in each obliging Art;	II.17.755.318.
Skill'd to discern the Future by the past,	II.18.294.336.
Skill'd in the Needle, and the lab'ring Loom;	II.23.330.503.
And skill'd to manage the high-bounding Steed.	II.23.358.504.
Nor skill'd, nor studious, with prophetic eye	Od.1.261.45.
And better skill'd in dark events to come)	Od.5.219.182.
O friends, he cries, the stranger seems well-skill'd	Od.8.143.270.
Studious of freight, in naval trade well skill'd,	Od.8.181.272.
Skill'd in heroic exercise, I claim	Od.8.201.273.
Rise then ye skill'd in measures: let him bear	Od.8.287.278.
Skill'd in the dance, tall youths, a blooming band,	Od.8.301.279.
All expert soldiers, skill'd on foot to dare,	Od.9.57.304.
Skill'd the dark fates of mortals to declare,	Od.9.597.331.
Where dwelt th' enchantress skill'd in herbs of pow'r;	Od.10.328.360.
Skill'd in smooth tales, and artful to deceive,	Od.11.453.406.
Skill'd in th' illustrious labours of the loom.	Od.13.332.23.
Skill'd in rich works, a woman of their land.	Od.15.459.93.
Skill'd in th' illustrious labours of the loom.	Od.16.171.111.
Medon, and *Phemius* skill'd in heav'nly song.	Od.16.273.118.
And, skill'd in female works, four lovely dames.	Od.24.323.365.

SKILLFUL

That Quarter most the skillful *Greeks* annoy,	II.6.550.354.

SKIM

Oft, as in Airy Rings they skim the Heath,	1.W-F.131.162.
Strange Phantoms dance around, and skim before your Sight.	2.ChJM.804.54.
And airy Spectres skim before their Eyes;	2.TemF.104.261.
Or skim the flow'ry Meads of *Asphodill:*)	6.13.4.39.
And scream aloft, and skim the deeps below.	Od.5.87.176.
The ball dismiss'd, in dance they skim the strand,	Od.8.413.286.
Sudden shall skim along the dusky glades	Od.10.632.374.

SKIM'D

And skim'd along by *Elis'* sacred coast.	Od.15.319.85.

SKIMMING

So skimming the fat off,	6.91.27.254.
Then skimming the fat off,	6.91.27A.254.
These lightly skimming, when they swept the Plain,	II.20.270.405.

SKIMS

Flies o'er th'unbending Corn, and skims along the Main.	1.EOC.373.283.
Shoots on the Wing, and skims along the Sky:	II.13.94.109.

SKIN

A *Lyon's* yellow Skin the *Theban* wears,	1.TrSt.567.434.
The Cat, if you but singe her Tabby Skin,	2.ChWB.142.63.
But having amply stuff'd his skin,	4.1HE7.53.271.
In a dun night-gown of his own loose skin,	5.DunA2.34.100.
In a dun night-gown of his own loose skin;	5.DunB2.38.297.
But Purg'd shall be to Skin and Bone,	6.54.15.165.
And fear'd to tan his Skin.	6.79.28.218.
And raz'd the Skin and drew the Purple Gore.	II.4.169.229.
And stripp'd the Skin, and crack'd the solid Bone.	II.5.378.285.
And the transparent Skin with Crimson stain'd.	II.5.420.287.
From the rent Skin the Warrior tuggs again	II.5.1052.316.
Hung by the Skin: the Body sunk to Dust.	II.16.409.258.
Torn was his skin, nor had the ribs been whole,	Od.5.544.198.
Sleek the smooth skin, and scent the snowy limbs.	Od.6.94.209.

SKIN (CONTINUED)

O'er thy smooth skin a bark of wrinkles spread,	Od.13.457.28.
The skin shrunk up, and wither'd at her hand:	Od.13.497.29.

SKINS

Then fill'd two goat-skins with her hands divine,	Od.5.337.188.
And form'd of fleecy skins his humble bed:	Od.20.2.230.
And fleecy skins compos'd an humble bed:	Od.20.176.241.

SKIP

Had he thy Reason, would he skip and play?	3.EOM1.82.24.
And quick sensations skip from vein to vein,	5.DunA2.204.126.
And quick sensations skip from vein to vein;	5.DunB2.212.306.

SKIPS

Our Courtier skips from dish to dish,	4.HS6.200A.263.

SKIRMISH

And skirmish wide: So *Nestor* gave Command,	II.17.438.304.

SKIRTS

Whose sarcenet skirts are edg'd with flamy gold,	5.DunA3.250.178.
Whose sarcenet skirts are edg'd with flamy gold,	5.DunB3.254.332.

SKREEN

Swift at the word he cast his skreen aside,	Od.22.404.307.

SKULK

Gaming and Grub-street skulk behind the King.	5.DunB1.310.292.
In vain they skulk behind their boasted Wall,	II.8.216.407.
Some seek the Trench, some skulk behind the Wall,	II.15.391.212.

SKULKING

See skulking *Truth* to her old Cavern fled,	5.DunB4.641.407.

SKULL

Not so bold Arnall; with a weight of skull,	5.DunB2.315.312.
And blunt the sense, and fit it for a skull	5.DunB3.25.321.
The Poize of Dulness to the heavy Skull,	6.17i(a).1.55.
Just as a blockhead rubs his thoughtless skull,	6.41.7.113.
Resistless drove the batter'd Skull before,	II.20.461.413.

SKY

See SKIE.

And what is That, which binds the Radiant Sky,	1.PSp.39.64.
The Moon, serene in Glory, mounts the Sky,	1.PWi.6.89.
Above the Clouds, above the Starry Sky.	1.PWi.70.94.
Nor yet, when moist *Arcturus* clouds the Sky,	1.W-F.119.161.
Strait a short Thunder breaks the frozen Sky.	1.W-F.130.162.
When the fierce Eagle cleaves the liquid Sky;	1.W-F.186.167.
Mount o'er the Vales, and seem to tread the Sky;	1.EOC.226.265.
The sun all objects views beneath the sky,	1.TrPA.110.370.
A fiery Gleam, and reddens all the Sky.	1.TrSt.149.416.
Where vast *Cythæron's* Top salutes the Sky,	1.TrSt.161.416.
And force unwilling Vengeance from the Sky?	1.TrSt.301.422.
Unmov'd remain'd the Ruler of the Sky,	1.TrSt.402.426.
And win by turns the Kingdom of the Sky:	1.TrSt.491.430.
Th'intrepid *Theban* hears the bursting Sky,	1.TrSt.510.431.
It flew with Force, and labour'd up the Sky;	1.TrES.104.453.
The Shore is heap'd with Death, and Tumult rends the Sky.	1.TrES.208.457.
And Night's dark Mantle overspread the Sky.	2.ChJM.370.32.
The Sun adorns the Fields, and brightens all the Sky.	2.ChJM.530.41.
The light *Militia* of the lower Sky;	2.RL1.42.149.
While melting Musick steals upon the Sky,	2.RL2.49.162.
Or roll the Planets thro' the boundless Sky.	2.RL2.80.165.
The Nymph exulting fills with Shouts the Sky,	2.RL3.99.174.
Till the bright Mountains prop th' incumbent Sky:	2.TemF.58.256.
Salute the diff'rent Quarters of the Sky.	2.TemF.68.257.
When the wing'd Colonies first tempt the Sky,	2.TemF.284.277.
Born by the Trumpet's Blast, and scatter'd thro the Sky.	2.TemF.488.287.
Fresh blooming hope, gay daughter of the sky!	2.ElAb.299.343.
Is there no bright reversion in the sky,	2.Elegy.9.363.
Fate snatch'd her early to the pitying sky.	2.Elegy.24.364.
But thinks, admitted to that equal sky,	3.EOM1.111.28.
T' inspect a Mote, not comprehend the Sky?	3.EOM1.196B.39.
Planets and Suns run lawless thro' the sky,	3.EOM1.252.46.
Planets and Suns rush lawless thro' the sky,	3.EOM1.252A.46.
Or wing the sky, or roll along the flood,	3.EOM3.120.104.
And keep a while one Parent from the Sky!	4.Arbu.413.127.
And pond'rous slugs cut swiftly thro' the sky;	5.DunA1.178.84.
All vain petitions, mounting to the sky,	5.DunA2.85.108.
Whose vain petitions, mounting to the sky,	5.DunA2.85A.108.
"The salient spout, far-streaming to the sky;	5.DunA2.154.120.
"The salient spout, fair-streaming to the sky;	5.DunA2.154A.120.
In homage, to the mother of the sky,	5.DunA3.124.160.
And pond'rous slugs cut swiftly thro the sky;	5.DunB1.182.283.
Go, purify'd by flames ascend the sky,	5.DunB1.227.286.
All vain petitions, mounting to the sky,	5.DunB2.89.300.
"The salient spout, far-streaming to the sky;	5.DunB2.162.303.
In homage to the Mother of the sky,	5.DunB3.132.326.
And pondrous Slugs move nimbly thro' the Sky.	6.7.18.16.
And all the bright *Militia* of the sky,	6.21.24.69.
And with my Head Sublime *can reach the Sky.*	6.26ii.4.79.
To what new clime, what distant sky	6.51i.13.151.
So soard Eliah to the Sky.	6.69ii.4Z2.199.
Lofty Poet! touch the Sky.	6.96i.50.269.
Receiv'd the weapons of the sky;	6.140.10.378.
Beneath a nobler roof, the sky.	6.141.8.380.
'Till rosie Morn had purpled o'er the Sky:	II.1.623.117.
Nor was the Signal vain that shook the Sky.	II.1.721.122.
A rev'rend Horror silenc'd all the Sky.	II.1.737.122.
Nor break the sacred Union of the Sky:	II.1.747.123.
And *Gonoëssa's* Spires salute the Sky.	II.2.693.159.
And lofty *Sesamus* invades the Sky;	II.2.1039.172.
With Noise, and Order, thro' the mid-way Sky;	II.3.8.188.
While thus their Pray'rs united mount the Sky;	II.3.370.211.

SKY (CONTINUED)

The Sire of Men and Monarch of the Sky .... Il.4.95.225.
While the smooth Chariot cuts the liquid Sky. .... Il.5.927.310.
He said, and rear'd his Sceptre to the Sky. .... Il.7.489.388.
A rev'rend Horror silenc'd all the Sky; .... Il.8.36.397.
Between th' extended Earth and starry Sky. .... Il.8.56.398.
Smooth glides the Chariot thro' the liquid Sky. .... Il.8.477.419.
Their Car in Fragments scatter'd o'er the Sky; .... Il.8.493.420.
Your Car in Fragments scatter'd o'er the Sky; .... Il.8.515.421.
Flame thro' the Vast of Air, and reach the Sky. .... Il.8.545.422.
Wide o'er the Field, high-blazing to the Sky, ... Il.8.631.426.
Your Eyes shall view, when Morning paints the Sky .... Il.9.800.473.
Attesting thus the Monarch of the Sky. .... Il.10.388.21.
Now soil'd with Dust, and naked to the Sky, ... Il.11.135.41.
Ye Vagrants of the Sky! your Wings extend, ... Il.12.279.91.
It flew with Force, and labour'd up the Sky; .... Il.12.458.98.
The Shore is heap'd with Death, and Tumult rends the Sky. .... Il.12.562.102.
Shoots on the Wing, and skims along the Sky: .... Il.13.94.109.
Thick Stones and Arrows intercept the Sky, ... Il.13.900.148.
Weighs down the Cloud, and blackens in the Sky, ... Il.14.24.158.
Had hurl'd indignant to the nether Sky, ... Il.14.292.176.
Why comes my Goddess from th' æthereal Sky, ... Il.14.339.179.
The Sport of Heav'n, and Fable of the Sky! .... Il.14.378.180.
And thicker Javelins intercept the Sky. .... Il.14.496.188.
From the vast Concave of the spangled Sky, ... Il.15.24.195.
What Claim was here the Tyrant of the Sky? .... Il.15.219.205.
Of all that wing the mid Aerial Sky, ... Il.17.762.318.
Unknown to all the Synod of the Sky. .... Il.18.224.332.
When my proud Mother hurl'd me from the Sky, ... Il.18.463.344.
To which, around the Axle of the Sky, ... Il.18.563.349.
By *Hector* slain, their Faces to the Sky, ... Il.19.201.381.
Streams from some lonely Watch-tow'r to the Sky: .... Il.19.407.389.
The *Dardan* Prince, and bore him thro' the Sky, ... Il.20.374.410.
'Tis not in me, tho' favour'd by the Sky, ... Il.20.405.412.
As when Autumnal *Boreas* sweeps the Sky, ... Il.21.402.437.
Or gasping, turn their Bellies to the Sky. .... Il.21.415.437.
And the red Vapours purple all the Sky. .... Il.21.610.447.
The gazing Gods lean forward from the Sky: .... Il.22.218.464.
Sate all the blustring Brethren of the Sky. .... Il.23.247.499.
Now seem to touch the Sky, and now the Ground. .... Il.23.446.508.
That teach the Disk to sound along the Sky. .... Il.23.982.528.
If such thy Will, dispatch from yonder Sky .... Il.24.381.551.
Uncommon are such Favours of the Sky, ... Il.24.568.560.
To judge the winged Omens of the sky. .... Od.1.262.45.
Abrupt, with eagle-speed she cut the sky; .... Od.1.413.52.
And clang their wings, and hovering beat the sky; .... Od.2.176.70.
Full tow'rd the east, and mount into the sky. .... Od.2.182.71.
With thy wise dreams, and fables of the sky. .... Od.2.208.72.
The whistling winds already wak'd the sky; .... Od.3.213.96.
The best, the dearest fav'rite of the sky .... Od.3.295.100.
(A length of Ocean and unbounded sky, ... Od.3.411.106.
Aurora streaks the sky with orient light, ... Od.4.268.132.
Whate'er thy title in thy native sky, ... Od.4.508.144.
To the stern sanction of th' offended sky .... Od.4.652.150.
Then met th' eternal Synod of the sky, ... Od.5.5.171.
Or habitant of earth, or sea, or sky. .... Od.5.102.177.
What mov'd this journey from my native sky, ... Od.5.121.178.
Thus having said, he cut the cleaving sky, ... Od.5.189.180.
To which, around the axle of the sky .... Od.5.349.188.
Is then revers'd the sentence of the sky, ... Od.5.368.190.
And hush'd the blust'ring brethren of the sky. .... Od.5.491.195.
Tho' *Boreas* rag'd along th' inclement sky. .... Od.5.627.202.
To guard the wretched from th' inclement sky: .... Od.6.216.220.
That breath'd a fragrance thro' the balmy sky. .... Od.6.256.222.
(By *Neptune* aw'd) apparent from the sky: .... Od.6.392.230.
Blue metals crown'd, in colours of the sky: .... Od.7.113.240.
No glorious native of yon azure sky: .... Od.7.284.250.
Gaz'd, as before some brother of the sky. .... Od.8.18.262.
Curious to learn the counsels of the sky, ... Od.8.77.266.
And drifts of rising dust involve the sky: .... Od.8.128.269.
She spoke: and momentary mounts the sky: .... Od.8.227.274.
And unextinguish'd laughter shakes the sky. .... Od.8.366.283.
But say, if that lewd scandal of the sky .... Od.8.387.285.
And loud applauses rend the vaulted sky. .... Od.8.404.285.
And bending backward whirls it to the sky; .... Od.8.410.286.
Where happy as the Gods that range the sky, ... Od.8.489.289.
Tho' clouds and darkness veil th' encumber'd sky, ... Od.8.609.295.
The pow'rs below, the blessed in the sky; .... Od.10.358.361.
The dolesome passage to th' infernal sky. .... Od.11.24.380.
His cold remains all naked to the sky .... Od.11.67.383.
Above, below, on earth and in the sky! .... Od.11.139.387.
To seek *Tiresias* in the nether sky, ... Od.11.201.391.
By turns they visit this etherial sky, ... Od.11.371.401.
And the sky reddens with the rising day. .... Od.11.469.407.
There figs sky-dy'd, a purple hue disclose, ... Od.11.727.421.
The sky for ever low'rs, for ever clouds remain. .... Od.12.94.436.
So pant the wretches, struggling in the sky, ... Od.12.305.447.
And all above is sky, and ocean all around! .... Od.12.474.454.
All unsustain'd between the wave and sky, ... Od.12.517.457.
Or torn by birds are scatter'd thro' the sky. .... Od.14.157.43.
And witness every pow'r that rules the sky! .... Od.14.435.56.
Their wrongs and blasphemies ascend the sky, ... Od.15.348.86.
And cloath the naked from th' inclement sky. .... Od.16.84.106.
Nor I, alas! descendent of the sky. .... Od.16.205.113.
Outcasts of earth, to breathe an unknown sky? .... Od.16.395.125.
Mean-time they heard, soft-circling in the sky, ... Od.17.310.146.
Ev'n till the morning lamp adorns the sky; .... Od.18.364.185.
Then wild uproar and clamour mounts the sky, ... Od.18.444.190.
O Queen! no vulgar vision of the sky .... Od.19.641.227.
Loud from a saphire sky his thunder sounds: .... Od.20.128.239.
Big with their doom denounc'd in earth and sky .... Od.20.151.241.
Signs from above ensu'd: th' unfolding sky .... Od.21.452.282.
The huge trunc rose, and heav'd into the sky; .... Od.23.194.333.
Then, when the surge in thunder mounts the sky, ... Od.23.251.335.
Pallas, and *Jove,* and him who gilds the sky! .... Od.24.434.369.

SKY-DY'D

There figs sky-dy'd, a purple hue disclose, ... Od.11.727.421.

SLACK

Taught nor to slack, nor strain its tender strings, ... 3.EOM3.290.121.
Taught not to slack, nor strain its tender strings, ... 3.EOM3.290A.121.
Nor slack nor strain the tender Strings; .... 6.11.35Z6.31.
Headlong he tumbles: His slack Nerves unbound .... Il.7.21.363.
And his slack Knees desert their dying Load. .... Il.11.707.66.
Down dropp'd the leg, from her slack hand releas'd! .... Od.19.547.223.

SLACKEN'D

His slacken'd Knees receiv'd the numbing Stroke; .... Il.7.324.379.
His slacken'd Hand deserts the Lance it bore; .... Il.14.488.187.
Fear seiz'd his slacken'd limbs and beating heart; .... Od.5.522.197.

SLAIN

What wonder then, a Beast or Subject slain .... 1.W-F.57.154.
No wonder Savages or Subjects slain .... 1.W-F.57A.154.
Which these dire Hands from my slain Father tore; .... 1.TrSt.114.415.
Where Earth-born Brothers were by Brothers slain? .... 1.TrSt.252.421.
Had slain his Brother, leaves his Native Land, ... 1.TrSt.556.433.
When by a thousand Darts the *Python* slain .... 1.TrSt.664.438.
Th' *Inachians* view the Slain with vast Surprize, ... 1.TrSt.727.440.
Th' *Inachians* view'd the Slain with vast Surprize, ... 1.TrSt.727A.440.
Laments his Son, predestin'd to be slain, ... 1.TrES.259.459.
And from the Fight convey *Sarpedon* slain; .... 1.TrES.325.461.
Blush'd with the Blood of Sheep and Oxen slain. .... 1.TrUl.231.473.
How some with Swords their sleeping Lords have slain, ... 2.ChWB.407.76.
Oh thou hast slain me for my Wealth (I cry'd) .... 2.ChWB.420.77.
She smil'd to see the doughty Hero slain, ... 2.RL5.69.206.
When, after Millions slain, your self shall die; .... 2.RL5.146.211.
Than favour'd Man by touch etherial slain. .... 3.EOM3.68.98.
The favour'd Man by touch etherial slain, ... 3.EOM3.68A.98*.
Had brav'd the *Goth,* and many a *Vandal* slain, ... 6.128.2.355.
The Souls of mighty Chiefs untimely slain; .... Il.1.4.82.
Or fed the Flames with Fat of Oxen slain; .... Il.1.58.88.
For much the Goddess mourn'd her Heroes slain. .... Il.1.76.90.
The Spoils of Cities raz'd, and Warriors slain, ... Il.1.159.95.
And glut his Vengeance with my People slain. .... Il.1.725.122.
What Scenes of Grief and Numbers of the Slain! .... Il.2.50.129.
What Scenes of Grief and Mountains of the Slain! .... Il.2.50A.129.
And bravest Chiefs, in *Helen's* Quarrel slain, ... Il.2.197.137.
As many Birds as by the Snake were slain, ... Il.2.394.145.
Ador'd with Sacrifice and Oxen slain; .... Il.2.662.158.
And saw their blooming Warriors early slain. .... Il.2.800.163.
Fool that he was! by fierce *Achilles* slain, ... Il.2.1064.172.
Eager he seizes, and devours the slain, ... Il.3.39.190.
Hear, and be Witness. If, by *Paris* slain, ... Il.3.354.210.
Thy Country's Foe, the *Grecian* Glory slain? .... Il.4.128.226.
To fight for *Greece,* and conquer to be slain? .... Il.4.189.230.
And unreveng'd, his mighty Brother slain." .... Il.4.217.231.
Such as I was, when *Ereuthalion* slain .... Il.4.372.238.
Trojans and *Greeks* now gather round the Slain; .... Il.4.538.247.
Short was his Date! by dreadful *Ajax* slain .... Il.4.550.247.
He drops the Corps of *Simoïsius* slain, ... Il.4.565.248.
Or slain, or fled, the Sons of *Dares* view: .... Il.5.36.267.
Those slain he left; and sprung with noble Rage .... Il.5.188.275.
T' avenge *Atrides:* Now, untimely slain, ... Il.5.679.300.
Struck with the Thought, should *Helen's* Lord be slain, ... Il.5.695.301.
Now meet thy Fate, and by *Sarpedon* slain .... Il.5.812.305.
The *Greeks* with slain *Tlepolemus* retir'd; .... Il.5.828.305.
What rash Destruction! and what Heroes slain? .... Il.5.945.311.
Just then Gigantic *Periphas* lay slain, ... Il.5.1038.316.
Heap'd round, and heaving under Loads of slain; .... Il.5.1089.318.
By great *Euryalus* was *Dresus* slain, ... Il.6.25.325.
Melanthius by *Eurypylus* was slain; .... Il.6.43.325.
When Fame shall tell, that not in Battel slain .... Il.6.59.326.
Forth from the slain he tugg'd the reeking Dart. .... Il.6.82.327.
His Eldest-born by raging *Mars* was slain, ... Il.6.251.339.
Now Hosts oppose thee, and thou must be slain! .... Il.6.517.351.
Of Heroes slain he bears the reeking Spoils, ... Il.6.611.357.
When now *Minerva* saw her *Argives* slain, ... Il.7.23.363.
Here if I fall, by chance of Battel slain, ... Il.7.89.367.
By *Hector* slain, the mighty Man of War[."] .... Il.7.102.368.
And gratify the *Manes* of the slain. .... Il.7.487.388.
No God consulted, and no Victim slain! .... Il.7.535.391.
With Arms unaiding mourn our *Argives* slain; .... Il.8.44.397.
My Glory ravish'd, and my People slain! .... Il.8.285.410.
With *Chromius, Dætor, Ophelestes* slain: .... Il.8.332.413.
Triumphant now, now miserably slain, ... Il.8.530.421.
With Arms unaiding see our *Argives* slain; .... Il.8.581.424.
That stern *Achilles* (his *Patroclus* slain) .... Il.8.593.424.
The Day may come, when all our Warriors slain, ... Il.9.324.450.
This Beast (when many a Chief his Tusks had slain) .... Il.9.661.467.
The Heroes slain, the Palaces o'erthrown, ... Il.9.704.469.
Not till amidst yon' sinking Navy slain, ... Il.9.765.472.
Thro' Dust, thro' Blood, o'er Arms, and Hills of Slain. .... Il.10.356.18.
Or nightly Pillager that strips the slain. .... Il.10.408.21.
The Sons of false *Antimachus* were slain; .... Il.11.162.42.
Soon as he hears, that not in Battel slain, ... Il.11.173.43.
Now by the Foot the flying Foot were slain, ... Il.11.193.44.
Oh worthy better Fate! oh early slain! .... Il.11.311.49.
There slain, they left them in eternal Night; .... Il.11.419.53.
By *Tydeus'* Lance *Agastrophus* was slain, ... Il.11.437.53.
Then thus *Ulysses,* gazing on the Slain. .... Il.11.564.59.
And deep *Scamander* swells with Heaps of Slain. .... Il.11.623.61.
While here (he cry'd) the flying *Greeks* are slain; .... Il.11.644.62.
The *Grecian* Rout, the slaying, and the slain. .... Il.11.733.67.
For *Neleus'* Sons *Alcides'* Rage had slain; .... Il.11.832.73.
A Bull *Alphæus;* and a Bull was slain .... Il.11.866.74.
Their Pow'rs neglected and no Victim slain, ... Il.12.7.81.
But when her Sons were slain, her City burn'd, ... Il.12.13.81.
Helmets, and Shields, and God-like Heroes slain: .... Il.12.22.82.
The dreadful Pass, and round them heap the slain. .... Il.12.212.88.
Emerg'd, he sate; and mourn'd his *Argives* slain. .... Il.13.26.105.

SLAIN 320 SLAUGHTER

SLAIN (CONTINUED)
The Spoils contested, and bear off the slain. ....Il.13.260.117.
And pierc'd with Sorrow for his * Grandson slain, ...Il.13.274.117.
Yet hand to hand I fight, and spoil the slain; ....Il.13.343.122.
First by his Hand *Othryoneus* was slain, ...Il.13.457.128.
Then *Idomen,* insulting o'er the slain; ....Il.13.558.133.
For slain *Ascalaphus* commenc'd the Fray. ....Il.13.665.137.
Expell'd and exil'd, for her Brother slain.) ....Il.13.874.147.
And what brave Heroes at the Ships lie slain? ....Il.13.928.149.
The Chiefs you seek on yonder Shore lie slain; ....Il.13.981.152.
Greece sees, in hope, *Troy's* great Defender slain: ....Il.14.494.188.
A worthy Vengeance for *Prothœnor* slain? ....Il.14.552.189.
The God of Battels dares avenge the slain; ....Il.15.131.201.
And not content that half of *Greece* lie slain, ...Il.15.328.209.
These drink the Life of gen'rous Warriors slain; ....Il.15.358.210.
Stretch'd on one Heap, the Victors spoil the slain. ....Il.15.389.212.
The gallant Man, tho' slain in Fight he be, ...Il.15.584.219.
In rush the conqu'ring *Greeks* to spoil the slain; ....Il.15.642.221.
Bright with the Blaze, and red with Heroes slain: ....Il.15.851.229.
His Troops, that see their Country's Glory slain, ...Il.16.346.256.
Slain by two Brothers, thus two Brothers bleed, ...Il.16.388.258.
Laments his Son, predestin'd to be slain, ...Il.16.564.266.
Unguided now, their mighty Master slain. ....Il.16.628.268.
With horrid Shouts they circle round the Slain; ....Il.16.693.271.
His shatter'd Helm, and stretch'd him o'er the Slain. ....Il.16.708.271.
Th' *Achaians* sorrow for their Hero slain; ....Il.16.729.272.
The Prize contested, and despoil the Slain. ....Il.16.806.274.
And from the Fight convey *Sarpedon* slain; ....Il.16.812.274.
Who first, brave Hero! by that Arm was slain, ...Il.16.847.276.
Pierc'd thro' the dauntless Heart, then tumbles slain; ....Il.16.911.279.
Turn, and behold the brave *Euphorbus* slain! ....Il.17.84.291.
By *Sparta* slain! for ever now suppress ....Il.17.85.291.
Slain in my Cause, and for my Honour slain, ...Il.17.102.291.
Slain in my Cause, and for my Honour slain, ...Il.17.102.291.
Lies slain the great *Achilles'* dearer Part: ....Il.17.236.297.
Whatever Hand shall win *Patroclus* slain, ...Il.17.270.298.
Repuls'd, they yield; the *Trojans* seize the slain: ....Il.17.325.300.
Phorcys, as slain *Hippothous* he defends, ...Il.17.362.301.
The shouting *Argives* strip the Heroes slain. ....Il.17.369.302.
Asteropeus with Grief beheld the Slain, ...Il.17.404.303.
Their god-like Master slain before their Eyes, ...Il.17.486.307.
Alas! thy Friend is slain, and *Hector* wields ....Il.17.538.309.
But left their slain Companion in his Blood: ....Il.17.603.311.
The Arms are *Hector's,* who despoil'd the Slain. ....Il.17.780.319.
Himself returns to his *Patroclus* slain. ....Il.17.792.319.
Beyond Mankind, beyond my self, is slain! ....Il.18.104.328.
For soon alas! that wretched Offspring slain, ...Il.18.115.328.
Thrice the slain Hero by the Foot he drew; ....Il.18.193.331.
The hungry Lion from a Carcase slain. ....Il.18.200.331.
The long-contended Carcase of the Slain. ....Il.18.274.335.
Slain by this Hand, sad Sacrifice expire; ....Il.18.395A.340.
Then slain by *Phœbus* (*Hector* had the Name) ....Il.18.525.346.
The Subject of Debate, a Townsman slain: ....Il.18.578.350.
Fresh as in Life, the Carcase of the Slain. ....Il.19.34.373.
Then in the Nostrils of the Slain she pour'd ....Il.19.39.373.
By *Hector* slain, their Faces to the Sky, ...Il.19.201.381.
The sacred Herald rolls the Victim slain ....Il.19.279.384.
And dry'd my Sorrows for a Husband slain; ....Il.19.314.385.
While thus *Achilles* glories o'er the Slain. ....Il.20.448.413.
But vaunts not long, with all his Swiftness slain. ....Il.20.478.414.
Thus sadly slain, th' unhappy *Polydore;* ....Il.20.486.414.
With that, he gluts his Rage on Numbers slain: ....Il.20.525.416.
In vain your immolated Bulls are slain, ...Il.21.145.427.
All scatter'd round the Stream (their Mightiest slain) ....Il.21.223.430.
Huge Heaps of Slain disgorges on the Coast, ...Il.21.259.431.
Increas'd with Gore, and swelling with the Slain. ....Il.21.379.436.
Like others fly, and be like others slain? ....Il.21.652.449.
Methinks already I behold thee slain, ...Il.22.53.454.
My Heroes slain, my Bridal Bed o'erturn'd, ...Il.22.88.456.
I feel my Folly in my People slain. ....Il.22.145.459.
Hector, whose Zeal whole Hecatombs has slain, ...Il.22.224.464.
Or let him bear, by stern *Pelides* slain, ...Il.22.231.465.
Who fear'd no Vengeance for *Patroclus* slain: ....Il.22.416.472.
I follow thee—He said, and stripp'd the Slain. ....Il.22.462.474.
High o'er the Slain the great *Achilles* stands, ...Il.22.471.475.
The Souls of Heroes, their great *Hector* slain? ....Il.22.480.475.
Shut from our Walls! I fear, I fear him slain! ....Il.22.587.480.
Thro' the sad City mourn'd her Hero slain. ....Il.23.2.485.
While those deputed to inter the Slain ....Il.23.200.497.
His Threat, and guard inviolate the Slain: ....Il.23.227.498.
The Giant by *Achilles* slain, he stow'd ....Il.23.979.528.
Has *Hector* ting'd with Blood of Victims slain? ....Il.24.45.537.
But yield to Ransom, and restore the Slain. ....Il.24.174.543.
The Corps of *Hector,* at yon' Navy slain. ....Il.24.238.546.
And what his Mercy, thy slain Sons declare; ....Il.24.252.547.
Wretch that I am! my bravest Offspring slain, ...Il.24.319.549.
Next with the Gifts (the Price of *Hector* slain) ....Il.24.341.550.
Thy matchless Son, her Guard and Glory, slain! ....Il.24.472.556.
The best, the bravest of my Sons are slain! ....Il.24.613.562.
Him too thy Rage has slain! beneath thy Steel ....Il.24.620.562.
These by *Apollo's* silver Bow were slain, ...Il.24.761.569.
Hang on the Wheels, and grovel round the Slain. ....Il.24.887.573.
For *Ilion* now (her great Defender slain) ....Il.24.916.574.
Or Son, or Brother, by great *Hector* slain; ....Il.24.927.575.
(The Tomb of him thy warlike Arm had slain) ....Il.24.952.576.
(A sacred oath) each proud oppressor slain ....Od.1.485.55.
Boar bled by boar, and goat by goat lay slain. ....Od.2.338.77.
At each, nine oxen on the sand lay slain. ....Od.3.10.87.
Whether in fields by hostile fury slain, ...Od.3.108.91.
There hecatombs of bulls to *Neptune* slain ....Od.3.217.96.
Extended pale, by swarthy *Memnon* slain! ....Od.4.256.131.
No vows had we prefer'd, nor victim slain! ....Od.4.475.142.
Just hecatombs with due devotion slain, ...Od.4.637.149.
Telemachus in thought already slain! ....Od.4.1100.169.
Happy! thrice happy! who in battle slain ....Od.5.393.191.
A theme of future song! Say then if slain ....Od.8.633.297.

SLAIN (CONTINUED)
Ghastly with wounds the forms of warriors slain ....Od.11.51.383.
The god-like leaders, who in battle slain, ...Od.11.462.407.
When lo! advanc'd the forms of Heroes slain ....Od.11.482.408.
And swell'd the ground with mountains of the slain, ...Od.11.612.414.
How, lost thro' love, *Eurypylus* was slain, ...Od.11.635.415.
Slay the selected beeves, and flea the slain; ....Od.12.424.451.
Slain are those herds which I with pride survey, ...Od.12.447.452.
Beeves, slain by heaps, along the ocean bleed. ....Od.12.463.453.
The pilot by the tumbling ruin slain, ...Od.12.483.455.
Blush'd with the blood of sheep and oxen slain. ....Od.13.398.26.
Like great *Atrides,* just restor'd and slain. ....Od.13.440.27.
Of perfect Hecatombs in order slain: ....Od.19.429.215.
Nations embattel'd to revenge the slain? ....Od.20.54.234.
The rest must perish, their great leader slain. ....Od.22.279.300.
By the bold son *Amphimedon* was slain: ....Od.22.314.301.
Wrapt in a new-slain Oxe's ample hide: ....Od.22.403.307.
By one be slain, tho' by an Heroe's hand? ....Od.23.40.321.
Sleepless devours each word; and hears, how slain ....Od.23.333.340.
And friends in battle slain, heroic ghosts! ....Od.23.351.341.
Midst heaps of heroes in thy quarrel slain: ....Od.24.54.350.
Led the sad numbers by *Ulysses* slain. ....Od.24.124.354.
Stretch'd in our palace, by these hands lie slain. ....Od.24.381.367.
Weeping they bear the mangled heaps of slain, ...Od.24.478.371.
Has slain the Suitors, heav'n shall bless the land. ....Od.24.553.374.

SLAND'ROUS
What tho' this sland'rous *Jew,* this *Solomon,* ....2.ChJM.669.47.
The care to shun the blast of sland'rous tongues; ....Od.6.328.227.
A gen'rous heart repairs a sland'rous tongue. ....Od.8.432.287.
And dumb for ever be thy sland'rous tongue! ....Od.17.546.159.

SLANDER
To slander Wives, and Wedlock's holy Name. ....2.ChJM.223.25.
But strait the direful Trump of Slander sounds, ...2.TemF.332.280.
Slander or Poyson, dread from *Delia's* Rage, ...4.HS1.81.13.
Who loves a Lye, lame slander helps about, ...4.Arbu.289.116.
Slander beside her, like a Magpye, chatters, ...6.14ii.33.44.
To prove the heroe.—Slander stings the brave. ....Od.8.208.273.

SLANDER'D
Of all her Dears she never slander'd one, ...3.Ep2.175.64.
Full ten years slander'd, did he once reply? ....4.Arbu.374.123.
Slander'd the Ancients first, then *Wycherley;* ....6.12.5.37.
For those were slander'd most whom *Ozell* prais'd: ....6.12.7.37.
Since those were slander'd most whom *Ozell* praised: ....6.12.7A.37.
Of all her Dears she never slander'd one, ...6.139.19.377.

SLANDROUS
Let not the Wise these slandrous Words regard, ...2.ChJM.49.17.

SLASHING
From slashing *Bentley* down to pidling *Tibalds.* ....4.Arbu.164.108.
Like slashing Bentley with his desp'rate Hook; ....4.2HE1.104.203.
From slashing *B[entle]y* down to pidling *T[ibbald]s:* ....6.98.14.283.

SLAUGHT'RING
With slaught'ring Guns th'unweary'd Fowler roves, ...1.W-F.125.162.
Discord! dire Sister of the slaught'ring Pow'r, ...Il.4.502.244.
Still slaught'ring on, the King of Men proceeds; ....Il.11.199.44.
Collecting Spoils, and slaught'ring all along, ...Il.11.887.75.
Those slaught'ring Arms, so us'd to bathe in Blood, ...Il.18.368.339.
Thro' falling Squadrons bear my slaught'ring Sword, ...Il.19.444.390.
His slaught'ring Hands, yet red with Blood, he laid ....Il.23.23.488.
Our slaught'ring Arm, and bid the Hosts obey. ....Il.24.827.571.

SLAUGHTER
The copious Slaughter covers all the Shore, ...1.TrES.165.455.
Great *D[enni]s* roar'd, like Ox at Slaughter. ....6.10.62.26.
When flush'd with Slaughter, *Hector* comes, to spread ....Il.1.319.103.
In Blood and Slaughter shall repent at last. ....Il.1.449.109.
In his black Thoughts Revenge and Slaughter roll, ...Il.1.638.118.
But soon to rise in Slaughter, Blood, and War. ....Il.2.846.164.
The bold *Antilochus* the Slaughter led, ...Il.4.522.246.
With copious Slaughter all the Fields are red, ...Il.4.628.250.
Serves not to slaughter, but provoke the Foe. ....Il.5.263.279.
And stretch the Slaughter to the Gates of *Troy?* ....Il.5.568.295.
Mars, red with Slaughter, aids our hated Foes: ....Il.5.882.308.
Smile on the Slaughter, and enjoy my Woe. ....Il.5.947.311.
With Slaughter red, and raging round the Field. ....Il.5.1019.315.
The Waste of Slaughter, and the Rage of Fight, ...Il.5.1099.319.
Both breathing Slaughter, both resolv'd in Arms. ....Il.7.4.363.
Still swells the Slaughter, and still grows the Rage! ....Il.8.432.418.
What Scenes of Slaughter in yon Fields appear! ....Il.9.301.449.
A Sire the Slaughter of his Son forgives; ....Il.9.745.471.
Urge thou the Slaughter, while I seize the Steeds. ....Il.10.557.27.
Enough, my Son, from farther Slaughter cease, ...Il.10.594.28.
And drinks large Slaughter at her sanguin Eyes: ....Il.11.100.39.
Great *Agamemnon* then the Slaughter led, ...Il.11.127.41.
Great *Jove* from *Ide* with Slaughter fills his Sight, ...Il.11.435.53.
Shall breathe from Slaughter, and in combat stand, ...Il.11.488.56.
And the red Slaughter spreads on ev'ry side. ....Il.11.530.57.
But *Hector,* from this Scene of Slaughter far, ...Il.11.620.61.
And Groans of Slaughter mix with Shouts of Fight. ....Il.11.653.63.
The copious Slaughter covers all the Shore, ...Il.12.519.100.
And breathing Slaughter, follow'd to the War. ....Il.13.383.123.
Arm'd with wild Terrors, and to Slaughter bred, ...Il.13.595.134.
Meanwhile fresh slaughter bathes the sanguin ground, ...Il.13.682.137.
In Thirst of Slaughter, and in Lust of Fight. ....Il.13.800.143.
I scatter'd Slaughter from my fatal Bow. ....Il.13.980.152.
Or breathe from Slaughter in the Fields of Air. ....Il.15.183.203.
Bath'd *Greece* in Slaughter, and her Battel gor'd, ...Il.15.283.207.
Heaps fall on Heaps: the Slaughter *Hector* leads; ....Il.15.372.211.
And o'er the Slaughter stalks gigantic Death. ....Il.15.393.212.
Commands your Slaughter, or proclaims your Death. ....Il.16.104.239.
And gorg'd with Slaughter, still they thirst for more. ....Il.16.201.247.

SLAUGHTER 321 SLAVES

SLAUGHTER (CONTINUED)
And turns the Slaughter on the conqu'ring Bands. ....Il.16.483.262.
Haste, strip his Arms, the Slaughter round him spread, ...Il.16.687.271.
The Slaughter, *Elasus* and *Mulius* crown'd: ....Il.16.854.276.
And breathing Slaughter, pours amid the Foes. ....Il.16.947.280.
For him the Slaughter to the Fleet they spread, ...Il.18.211.332.
Rush sudden; Hills of Slaughter heap the Ground, ...Il.18.612.352.
Now tir'd with Slaughter, from the *Trojan* Band ....Il.21.34.422.
Strook Slaughter back, and cover'd the Retreat. ....Il.21.630.448.
And vengeful slaughter, fierce for human blood. ....Od.8.562.293.
Of war and slaughter, and the clash of arms? ....Od.11.498.408.
Of war and slaughter, and the clash of arms. ....Od.11.504.408.
Thus by the goary arm of slaughter falls ....Od.11.509.408.
So the grim Lion from the slaughter comes, ...Od.22.440.309.
Our floors with death, and push'd the slaughter on; ....Od.24.442.370.
"From mutual slaughter: *Peace* descends to spare." ....Od.24.615.377.

SLAUGHTER'D
In Heaps his slaughter'd Sons into the Deep. ....1.TrSt.60.412.
And there, in Flames the slaughter'd Victims fry. ....1.TrSt.612.436.
And there, in Flames the slaughter'd Victims fly. ....1.TrSt.612A.436.
Whole slaughter'd hecatombs, and floods of wine, ...3.Ep3.203A.110.
What slaughter'd hecatombs, what floods of wine, ...3.Ep3.203.110.
And slaughter'd Heroes groan around their Lord! ....Il.2.497.150.
But on his Car the slaughter'd Victims laid, ...Il.3.387.211.
Those fifty slaughter'd in the gloomy Vale, ...Il.4.448.241.
And slaughter'd Heroes swell the dreadful Tide. ....Il.4.515.246.
To guard his slaughter'd Friend, *Æneas* flies, ...Il.5.361.283.
This Pest he slaughter'd (for he read the Skies, ...Il.6.225.337.
While we to Flames our slaughter'd Friends bequeathe, ...Il.7.399.383.
Her slaughter'd Heroes, and their Bones in-urn. ....Il.7.451.386.
Our slaughter'd Heroes, and their Bones in-urn. ....Il.7.471.387.
Go search your slaughter'd Chiefs on yonder Plain, ...Il.7.486.388.
Scarce could the Friend his slaughter'd Friend explore, ...Il.7.504.389.
And slaughter'd Heroes swell the dreadful Tide. ....Il.8.82.399.
Back by the Foot each slaughter'd Warrior drew; ....Il.10.571.28.
Snatch'd from devouring Hounds, a slaughter'd Fawn, ...Il.13.266.117.
And his broad Buckler shields his slaughter'd Friend; ....Il.13.530.131.
Our Heroes slaughter'd, and our Ships on flame, ...Il.13.786.142.
And Groans of slaughter'd *Greeks* to Heav'n ascend. ....Il.14.66.160.
As *Promachus* his slaughter'd Brother draws, ...Il.14.560.190.
Stern *Mars*, with Anguish for this slaughter'd Son, ...Il.15.126.201.
And slaughter'd Heroes swell the dreadful Tyde. ....Il.15.867.230.
(When some tall Stag fresh-slaughter'd in the Wood ....Il.16.196.247.
To guard the Reliques of my slaughter'd Friend. ....Il.16.644.269.
And stretch him breathless on his slaughter'd Son; ....Il.16.790.274.
Thus for some slaughter'd Hind, with equal Rage, ...Il.16.915.279.
When o'er the slaughter'd Bull they hear him roar, ...Il.17.71.290.
Say, shall our slaughter'd Bodies guard your Walls ....Il.17.167.294.
As when a slaughter'd Bull's yet reeking Hyde, ...Il.17.450.304.
But ah! the Relicks of my slaughter'd Friend! ....Il.19.28.372.
And I succeed to slaughter'd *Polydore*. ....Il.21.102.426.
And my swift Soul o'ertake my slaughter'd Friend! ....Il.21.324.434.
O'er slaughter'd Heroes, and o'er rolling Steeds. ....Il.21.606.447.
Yon' Line of slaughter'd *Trojans* lately trod. ....Il.21.654.449.
Or, worse than slaughter'd, sold in distant Isles ....Il.22.61.455.
Where late the slaughter'd Victims fed the Fire) ....Il.23.910.525.
Add to the slaughter'd Son the wretched Sire! ....Il.24.278.548.
How well the son appeas'd his slaughter'd sire! ....Od.3.239.97.
From slaughter'd gluttons to release the dome. ....Od.15.201.78.
Forgot the slaughter'd brother, and the son: ....Od.24.555.374.

SLAUGHTERS
And wond'ring view the Slaughters of the Night. ....Il.10.617.29.
And all the Slaughters that must stain the Day. ....Il.11.72.37.
Tir'd with th' incessant Slaughters of the Fight. ....Il.13.888.147.
What Youth he slaughters under *Ilion's* Walls? ....Il.15.71.199.
Then mutual Slaughters spread on either side; ....Il.15.610.220.
Where'er he moves, the growing Slaughters spread ....Il.16.510.262.
The Field, and spread her Slaughters to the Shore; ....Il.17.521.308.
Content, thy Slaughters could amaze a God. ....Il.21.238.430.
A Lion, not a Man, who slaughters wide ....Il.24.52.537.

SLAV'RY
Till Conquest cease, and Slav'ry be no more: ....1.W-F.408.192.

SLAVE
This Slave the Floor, and That the Table spreads; ....1.TrSt.608.435.
Whor'd by my Slave—Perfidious Wretch! may Hell ....2.ChJM.770.52.
Confess'd within the slave of love and man. ....2.ElAb.178.334.
This hour a slave, the next a deity. ....3.EOM1.68.21.
Envy, to which th'ignoble mind's a slave, ...3.EOM2.191.78.
Slave to no sect, who takes no private road, ...3.EOM4.331.160.
He dreads a death-bed like the meanest slave: ....3.Ep1.68.20.
A fool to Pleasure, yet a slave to Fame: ....3.Ep2.62A.55.
A fool to Pleasure, and a slave to Fame: ....3.Ep2.62.55.
The Slave that digs it, and the Slave that hides. ....3.Ep3.112.101.
The Slave that digs it, and the Slave that hides. ....3.Ep3.112.101.
Un-plac'd, un-pension'd, no Man's Heir, or Slave? ....4.HS1.116.17.
His Wit confirms him but a Slave the more, ...4.HAdv.65.81.
"Sir, he's your Slave, for twenty pound a year. ....4.2HE2.8.165.
Then hire a Slave, (or if you will, a Lord) ....4.1HE6.99.243.
Slave to a Wife or Vassal to a Punk, ...4.1HE1.62.283.
A Pension, or such Harness for a slave ....4.1HE1.87.285.
Adieu to Virtue if you're once a Slave: ....4.1HE1.118.287.
COBHAM'S a Coward, POLWARTH is a Slave, ...4.EpS2.130.320.
Fr. You're strangely proud. *P.* So proud I am no Slave: ....4.EpS2.205.324.
Some Slave of mine be pinion'd to their side." ....5.DunB4.134.354.
First slave to Words, then vassal to a Name, ...5.DunB4.501.391.
A Monarch's half, and half a Harlot's slave. ....5.DunB4.512.392.
T'o'ercome the slave your eyes have doom'd to Death ....6.3.2A.7.
Who flies the tyrant to relieve the slave? ....6.4i.6.9.
Nor, tho' her slave, thy lot deplore; ....6.6i.9.14.
Forgot of ev'ry friend, and ev'ry slave! ....6.22.24.72.
So when your slave, at some dear, idle time, ...6.45.41.125.
Your Slave, and *exit;* but returns with *Rowe*, ... 6.49ii.4.140.

SLAVE (CONTINUED)
Or, if your Slave you think to bless, ...6.64.11.189.
A Fool to Pleasure, yet a Slave to Fame; ....6.99.10.287.
A Fool to Pleasure, and a Slave to Fame; ....6.99.10A.287.
To let no noble Slave come near, ...6.135.75.369.
For never *Briton* more disdain'd a Slave! ....6.152.6.400.
Inglorious Slave to Int'rest, ever join'd ....Il.1.195.96.
But know, proud Monarch, I'm thy Slave no more; ....Il.1.221.97.
Atrides, seize not on the beauteous Slave; ....Il.1.362.105.
To live thy Slave, and still to serve in vain, ...Il.1.389.106.
Must want a *Trojan* Slave to pour the Wine. ....Il.2.158.136.
Be still thou Slave! and to thy Betters yield; ....Il.2.237.138.
Have we not known thee, Slave! of all our Host, ...Il.2.310.142.
His Spouse, or Slave; and mount the Skies no more. ....Il.3.506.215.
Or Godlike *Paris* live a Woman's Slave! ....Il.6.671.360.
Some Brass or Iron, some an Oxe, or Slave. ....Il.7.569.392.
Slave as she was, my Soul ador'd the Dame. ....Il.9.453.454.
And that resum'd; the fair *Lyrnessian* Slave. ....Il.9.482.456.
One Woman-Slave was ravish'd from thy Arms: ....Il.9.751.471.
Disgrac'd, dishonour'd, like the vilest Slave! ....Il.9.762.472.
(Whom to his aged Arms, a Royal Slave, ...Il.11.766.69.
But thou can'st live, for thou can'st be a Slave. ....Il.12.290.92.
Ill-fated *Paris!* Slave to Womankind, ...Il.13.965.151.
Disgrac'd, dishonour'd, like the meanest Slave. ....Il.16.81.238.
The King of Nations forc'd his royal Slave: ....Il.18.518.346.
To *Lemnos'* Isle he sold the Royal Slave, ...Il.21.46.424.
In vain each Slave with duteous Care attends, ...Il.24.293.549.
Driv'n hence a Slave before the Victor's Sword; ....Il.24.924.575.
In the vile habit of a village slave, ...Od.4.336.136.
Bid *Dolius* quick attend, the faithful slave ....Od.4.972.163.
A widow, and a slave, on foreign shores! ....Od.8.580.293.
'Twas on no coward, no ignoble slave, ...Od.9.559.329.
A slave to some poor hind that toils for bread; ....Od.11.599.412.
To a base Monarch still a slave confin'd, ...Od.11.767.424.
Slave to the insolence of youthful Lords! ....Od.14.72.39.
To whom whate'er his slave enjoys is ow'd, ...Od.14.75.39.
With ready hands they rush to seize their slave; ....Od.14.378.53.
(*Eumæus'* proper treasure bought this slave, ...Od.14.503.60.
Live to base insolence of pow'r a slave. ....Od.16.96.107.
For any office could the slave be good, ...Od.17.262.145.
When slave! to sell thee at a price too dear ....Od.17.297.146.
Makes man a slave, takes half his worth away. ....Od.17.393.151.
Our walls this twelvemonth should not see the slave. ....Od.17.491.156.
From all thou beg'st, a bold audacious slave; ....Od.17.533.158.
And thus with just reproach address'd the slave. ....Od.18.125.172.
Instant the flying sail the slave shall wing ....Od.18.141.173.
Slave, I with justice might deserve the wrong, ...Od.18.430.189.
Swift from the dome conduct the slave away; ....Od.20.435.254.
Because the Priest is born a peaceful slave. ....Od.21.180.268.
We dread the censure of the meanest slave, ...Od.21.349.276.
Proceed false slave, and slight their empty words; ....Od.21.399.279.

SLAVE'S
Due pains shall punish then this slave's offence, ...Od.17.290.146.

SLAVER
It is the Slaver kills, and not the Bite. ....4.Arbu.106.103.

SLAVES
(For wiser Brutes were backward to be Slaves.) ....1.W-F.50.153.
And makes his trembling Slaves the Royal Game. ....1.W-F.64.155.
When all were Slaves thou cou'dst around survey, ...1.TrSt.221.419.
Still prone to change, tho' still the Slaves of State, ...1.TrSt.226.420.
Fortune's tame Fools, and Slaves in ev'ry Reign! ....1.TrSt.264.421.
The Pride of Fools, and Slaves insulting Scorn. ....1.TrUl.183.471.
Love in these Labyrinths his Slaves detains, ...2.RL2.23.160.
Whom scepter'd Slaves in golden Harness drew: ....2.TemF.114.262.
Slaves to your selves, and ev'n fatigu'd with Ease, ...2.TemF.397.282.
Where slaves once more their native land behold, ...3.EOM1.107.28.
And Gods of Conqu'rors, Slaves of Subjects made: ....3.EOM3.248.117.
What can ennoble sots, or slaves, or cowards? ....3.EOM4.215.147.
All the made trade of Fools and Slaves for Gold? ....4.1HE6.13.237.
As Pride in Slaves, and Avarice in Kings, ...4.EpS1.110.306.
See, all our Nobles begging to be Slaves! ....4.EpS1.163.309.
Thy Nobles Sl[ave]s, thy Se[nate]s bought with gold. ....4.1740.81.336*.
To lands of singing, or of dancing slaves, ...5.DunB4.305.374.
Born for First Ministers, as Slaves for Kings, ...5.DunB4.602.403.
Venus beheld her, 'midst her Crowd of Slaves, ...6.9vi.1.21.
Then oh! she cries, what Slaves I round me see? ....6.9vii.4.22.
And oh! she cries, what Slaves I round me see? ....6.9x.4A.22.
But oh! she cries, what Slaves I round me see? ....6.9x.4B.22.
Scorn'd by those slaves his former bounty fed ....6.15.8.51.
Made Slaves by Honour, and made Fools by Shame. ....6.19.36.63.
And men, once ignorant, are slaves. ....6.51i.28.152.
Where mix'd with Slaves the groaning Martyr toil'd; ....6.71.6.202.
Not as the World its pretty Slaves rewards, ...6.86.5A.245.
Yes, we are slaves—but yet, by Reason's Force, ...6.96iii.31.275.
(That Trick of Tyrants) may be born by Slaves. ....Il.1.162.95.
Shall rowze thy Slaves, and her lost Lord deplore, ...Il.5.503.292.
And meditates new Cheats on all his Slaves: ....Il.9.486.456.
Stand but as Slaves before a noble Mind. ....Il.9.495.457.
Meantime *Achilles'* Slaves prepar'd a Bed, ...Il.9.775.472.
The Slaves their Master's slow approach survey'd, ...Il.11.978.78.
Gods as we are, we are but slaves to *Jove* .... Od.5.176.180.
Rank'd with his slaves, on earth the Monarch lies: ....Od.11.231.393.
The pride of fools, and slaves insulting scorn. ....Od.13.350.24.
Then to the slaves—Now from the herd the best ....Od.14.457.57.
Yet busied with his slaves, to ease his woe, ...Od.16.150.109.
Slaves to a boy, go, flatter and obey. ....Od.16.403.125.
He, (when *Piræus* ask'd for slaves to bring ....Od.17.86.136.
A Palace, wealth, and slaves, I late possess'd, ...Od.19.94.197.
Twelve female slaves the gift of *Ceres* grind; ....Od.20.133.240.
Dear sell the slaves! demand no greater gain. ....Od.20.458.255.

SLAVISH
Sent in *Jove's* Anger on a slavish Race, ... Il.1.306.101.

SLAY
Shall *David* as *Uriah* slay him, ... 6.101.27.291.
Ev'n there, the hindmost of their Rear I slay, ... Il.11.891.75.
And well-fed Sheep, and sable Oxen slay: .... Il.23.205.498.
The fatted sheep and sable bulls they slay, ... Od.9.49.304.
Slay the due Victim in the genial hour: .... Od.11.163.389.
Arise unanimous; arise and slay! .... Od.12.410.450.
Slay the selected beeves, and flea the slain; .... Od.12.424.451.
Hither, intent the rival rout to slay .... Od.16.256.117.
Breathes there a man who dares that Heroe slay, ... Od.16.454.129.
Their garments, and succinct the victims slay. .... Od.17.200.141.
Then all with speed succinct the victims slay: .... Od.20.313.248.
To slay thy son, thy kingdoms to divide, ... Od.22.64.289.
Him, if this arm be pow'rful, shall I slay? .... Od.22.181.296.
What hop'st thou here? Thee first the sword shall slay, ... Od.22.239.298.
Due victims slay to all th' æthereal pow'rs. .... Od.23.296.337.
The cave of death! How his companions slay .... Od.23.355.341.
And fatted sheep and sable oxen slay; .... Od.24.84.352.

SLAYING
The *Grecian* Rout, the slaying, and the slain. .... Il.11.733.67.

SLEEK
But once grown sleek, will from her Corner run, ... 2.ChWB.144.63.
Their flowing Manes, and sleek their glossy Neck. .... Il.23.350.503.
Sleek the smooth skin, and scent the snowy limbs. .... Od.6.94.209.
A sleek and idle race is all their care. .... Od.17.389.150.

SLEEP
Not balmy Sleep to Lab'rers faint with Pain, ... 1.PAu.44.83.
The Trumpets sleep, while chearful Horns are blown, ... 1.W-F.373.187.
We cannot *blame* indeed—but we may *sleep.* .... 1.EOC.242.267.
The Reader's threaten'd (not in vain) with *Sleep.* .... 1.EOC.353.279.
For those might *Cynthia* lengthen *Phaon's* Sleep. .... 1.TrSP.99.398.
He seiz'd the Wand that causes Sleep to fly, ... 1.TrSt.433.428.
He seiz'd his Wand that causes Sleep to fly, ... 1.TrSt.433A.428.
All Birds and Beasts lye hush'd; Sleep steals away .... 1.TrSt.478.430.
Let *Sleep* and *Death* convey, by thy Command, ... 1.TrES.248.459.
To the soft Arms of silent *Sleep* and *Death;* .... 1.TrES.331.461.
Then *Sleep* and *Death,* two Twins of winged Race, ... 1.TrES.344.462.
All which soft Sleep now banish'd from his Breast; .... 1.TrUl.19.466.
Releas'd from Sleep; and round him might survey .... 1.TrUl.54.467.
While in th'Embrace of pleasing Sleep I lay, ... 1.TrUl.155.471.
Sleep fled his Eyes, and Peace forsook his Breast; .... 2.ChJM.393.34.
Thus when from Sleep we first our Eyes display, ... 2.ChJM.799.53.
I vow'd, I scarce cou'd sleep since first I knew him, ... 2.ChWB.300.71.
As balmy Sleep had charm'd my Cares to Rest, ... 2.TemF.5.253.
There sleep forgot, with mighty Tyrants gone, ... 2.TemF.352.280.
These must not sleep in Darkness and in Death. .... 2.TemF.371.281.
But all is calm in this eternal sleep; .... 2.ElAb.313.344.
And close confin'd to their own palace sleep. .... 2.Elegy.22.364.
And close confin'd in their own palace sleep. .... 2.Elegy.22A.364.
When Sense subsides, and Fancy sports in sleep, ... 3.Ep1.46.18.
And for my Soul I cannot sleep a wink. .... 4.HS1.12.5.
Rolls o'er my *Grotto,* and but sooths my Sleep. .... 4.HS1.124.17.
Can sleep without a Poem in my head, ... 4.Arbu.269.115.
Peace stole her wing, and wrapt the world in sleep; .... 4.2HE1.401.229.
Sleep, or peruse some ancient Book, ... 4.HS6.130.259.
Hiss if he hiss, and if he slumber, sleep. .... 4.1740.36.334.
Where nameless somethings in their causes sleep, ... 5.DunA1.54.66.
Sleepless themselves to give their readers sleep. .... 5.DunA1.92.70.
Thus the soft gifts of Sleep conclude the day, ... 5.DunA2.387.148.
And all the Western World believe and sleep. .... 5.DunA3.92.157.
Say how the Goddess bade Britannia sleep, ... 5.DunB1.7.269.
Where nameless Somethings in their causes sleep, ... 5.DunB1.56.274.
Sleepless themselves, to give their readers sleep. .... 5.DunB1.94.276.
And all be sleep, as at an Ode of thine." .... 5.DunB1.318.293.
There, all from Paul's to Aldgate drink and sleep. .... 5.DunB2.346.314.
Thus the soft gifts of Sleep conclude the day, ... 5.DunB2.419.318.
And all the western world believe and sleep. .... 5.DunB3.100.324.
Arrest him, Empress; or you sleep no more"— .... 5.DunB4.69.348.
While the Great Mother bids Britannia sleep, ... 5.DunB4.627Z1.407.
Sound sleep by night; study and ease .... 6.1.13.3.
So gentle sleep from *Serenissa* flies, ... 6.4i.3.9.
All rest in Peace at last, and sleep eternally. .... 6.8.42.19.
As smiling Infants sport themselves to Sleep. .... 6.19.14A.62.
Lull'd by these fountains the distrest may sleep; .... 6.20.63.67.
I'll sleep, or Infants at the Breast, ... 6.31ii.6Z10.95.
Ye Harlots, sleep at Ease! .... 6.47.4.128.
Nor Sleep to Toil so easing .... 6.78i.7.215.
Not Sleep to Toil so easing .... 6.78i.7A.215.
No Sleep to Toil so easing .... 6.78i.7B.215.
Peaceful sleep out the Sabbath of the Tomb, ... 6.86.19.246.
And to the Murmur of these Waters sleep; .... 6.87.2.248.
In peace let one poor Poet sleep, ... 6.138.2.376.
Now pleasing *Sleep* had seal'd each mortal Eye, ... Il.2.1.126.
And, Dost thou sleep, Oh *Atreus'* Son? (he said) .... Il.2.76.130.
Starting from Sleep with a distracted Air, ... Il.5.502.292.
Thy *Hector* wrapt in everlasting Sleep, ... Il.6.592.355.
Shall, raz'd and lost, in long Oblivion sleep. .... Il.7.540.391.
Then late refresh'd with Sleep from Toils of Fight, ... Il.7.578.393.
Till Sleep descending o'er the Tents, bestows .... Il.9.836.474.
And lost in Sleep the Labours of the Day: .... Il.10.2.1.
While others sleep, thus range the Camp alone? .... Il.10.91.6.
No Taste of Sleep these heavy Eyes have known; .... Il.10.102.7.
Each sunk in Sleep, extended on the Field, ... Il.10.172.9.
And couching close, repell invading Sleep. .... Il.10.210.11.
What moves thee, say, when Sleep has clos'd the Sight, ... Il.10.455.24.
Where stand his Coursers? In what Quarter sleep .... Il.10.479.25.
Safe in their Cares, th' auxiliar Forces sleep, ... Il.10.491.25.
Then sleep those Aids among the *Trojan* Train, ... Il.10.494.25.
And eas'd in Sleep the Labours of the Day, ... Il.10.543.27.
Amidst, lay *Rhesus,* stretch'd in Sleep profound, ... Il.10.548.27.

SLEEP (CONTINUED)
And Sleep eternal seals his swimming Eyes. .... Il.11.310.48.
He stills the Winds, and bids the Skies to sleep; .... Il.12.335.93.
(While the Winds sleep) his Breast receiv'd the Stroke. .... Il.13.550.132.
And seeks the Cave of Death's half-Brother, *Sleep.* .... Il.14.265.173.
Sweet pleasing Sleep! (*Saturnia* thus began) .... Il.14.266.174.
Jove's awful Temples in the Dew of Sleep? .... Il.14.282.176.
Sate *Sleep,* in Likeness of the Bird of Night, ... Il.14.328.178.
To *Neptune's* Ear soft *Sleep* his Message brings; .... Il.14.408.183.
Thus wakens *Hector* from the Sleep of Death? .... Il.15.281.207.
Let *Sleep* and *Death* convey, by thy Command, ... Il.16.551.265.
To the soft Arms of silent *Sleep* and *Death;* .... Il.16.818.274.
Then *Sleep* and *Death,* two *Twins* of winged Race, ... Il.16.831.275.
Then ease in Sleep the Labours of the Day. .... Il.23.69.489.
At length he sinks in the soft Arms of Sleep. .... Il.23.77.490.
Of golden Sleep, and starting from the Sands, ... Il.23.120.492.
And sunk to Quiet in th' Embrace of Sleep, ... Il.23.289.501.
Nor tastes the Gifts of all-composing Sleep. .... Il.24.8.535.
There Sleep at last o'ercomes the Hero's Eyes; .... Il.24.27.536.
Then grasps the Wand that causes Sleep to fly, ... Il.24.421.553.
Is seal'd in Sleep, thou wander'st thro' the Night? .... Il.24.448.555.
My careful Temples in the Dew of Sleep: .... Il.24.805.570.
Soft Sleep a Stranger to my weeping Eyes, ... Il.24.808.570.
Then he: Now Father sleep, but sleep not here, ... Il.24.816.571.
Then he: Now Father sleep, but sleep not here, ... Il.24.816.571.
Now Gods and Men the Gifts of Sleep partake; .... Il.24.846.572.
Now dost thou sleep, when *Hector* is restor'd? .... Il.24.852.572.
In his pavilion there to sleep repairs; .... Od.1.539.57.
And soft approach the balmy hours of sleep: .... Od.3.428.107.
And to the gifts of balmy sleep repairs. .... Od.3.509.112.
And pleas'd they sleep (the blessing of the night.) .... Od.3.622.118.
But now let sleep the painful waste repair .... Od.4.399.139.
Basks on the breezy shore, in grateful sleep, ... Od.4.542.146.
Their number summ'd, repos'd in sleep profound .... Od.4.557.146.
Along the tended shore, in balmy sleep .... Od.4.584.147.
Couch'd on the sunny sand, the monsters sleep: .... Od.4.605.148.
Was in the silent gates of sleep confin'd) .... Od.4.1066.167.
He grasps the wand that causes sleep to fly, ... Od.5.60.174.
Nor clos'd in sleep his ever-watchful eyes. .... Od.5.346.188.
Enjoy the comfort gentle sleep allows; .... Od.5.607.201.
And to the gifts of balmy sleep repairs. .... Od.7.310.251.
Jove plung'd my senses in the death of sleep. .... Od.7.369.254.
Prest with the weight of sleep that tames the strong: .... Od.9.442.324.
Of sleep, oppress thee, or by fraud or pow'r? .... Od.9.482.325.
Of sleep, oppresses me with fraudful pow'r. .... Od.9.486.326.
Rowz'd from my fatal sleep, I long debate .... Od.10.54.342.
Me, lock'd in sleep, my faithless crew bereft .... Od.10.77.343.
But he that scorns the chains of sleep to wear .... Od.10.96.345.
For here retir'd the sinking billows sleep, ... Od.10.107.345.
With sleep repair'd the long debauch of night: .... Od.10.664.375.
There worn and wasted, lose our cares in sleep .... Od.12.9.430.
Hush'd the loud winds, and charm'd the waves to sleep. .... Od.12.205.441.
From sleep debarr'd, we sink from woes to woes; .... Od.12.335.448.
All which soft sleep now banish'd from his breast, ... Od.13.110.6.
Releas'd from sleep, and round him might survey .... Od.13.221.16.
While in th' embrace of pleasing sleep I lay, ... Od.13.322.23.
In sleep profound the Son of *Nestor* lies; .... Od.15.7.70.
Let those whom sleep invites, the call obey, ... Od.15.430.89.
Wrapt in th' embrace of sleep, the faithful train .... Od.16.252.117.
And in soft sleep forgot the cares of day. .... Od.16.501.131.
Howe'er 'tis well! that Sleep a-while can free .... Od.18.237.178.
Send, oh *Diana,* send the sleep of death! .... Od.18.240.178.
In sweet oblivion let my sorrow sleep! .... Od.19.140.199.
Low-couch'd on earth, the gift of sleep I scorn, ... Od.19.395.213.
When from the downy bands of sleep releas'd, ... Od.19.647.227.
Immur'd within the silent bow'r of *Sleep,* .... Od.19.656.227.
Not so the Queen; The downy bands of sleep .... Od.20.68.235.
Never did I a sleep so sweet enjoy, ... Od.23.21.319.
He ended, sinking into sleep, and shares .... Od.23.369.343.
The golden wand, that causes sleep to fly, ... Od.24.3.345.
Soft sleep, fair garments, and the joys of wine, ... Od.24.300.364.

SLEEP'S
Sleep's all-subduing charm who dares defy, ... 5.DunA2.341.142.
Sleep's all-subduing pow'r who dares defy, ... 5.DunA2.341A.142.
"Sleep's all-subduing charms who dares defy, ... 5.DunB2.373.315.
At length with Love and Sleep's soft Pow'r oppress, ... Il.14.405.183.
Nor sleep's soft pow'r can close my streaming eyes, ... Od.4.135.126.
Sleep's gentle pow'rs her drooping eyes invade; .... Od.4.1046.166.
To render sleep's soft blessing unsincere? .... Od.4.1060.167.
(Restless and early sleep's soft bands they broke) .... Od.24.506.372.

SLEEP'ST
But sleep'st thou now? when from yon' Hill the Foe .... Il.10.182.9.
And sleep'st thou Father! (thus the Vision said) .... Il.24.851.572.
And sleep'st thou, careless of the bridal day? .... Od.6.30.205.

SLEEPER
Full endlong from the roof the sleeper fell, ... Od.10.667.375.

SLEEPING
Now sleeping Flocks on their soft Fleeces lye, ... 1.PWi.5.89.
And bids renew the Feasts, and wake the sleeping Fires. .... 1.TrSt.604A.435.
Ulysses sleeping, on his Couch they bore, ... 1.TrUl.47.467.
How some with Swords their sleeping Lords have slain, ... 2.ChWB.407.76.
How shall he keep, what, sleeping or awake, ... 3.EOM3.275.120.
To your fraternal care, our sleeping friends. .... 5.DunB4.440.383.
Folly by thee lies sleeping in the Breast, ... 6.8.23.18.
And in a Desart sleeping lay; .... 6.82vii.2.233.
The Camp he travers'd thro' the sleeping Crowd, ... Il.10.156.8.
Let younger *Greeks* our sleeping Warriors wake; .... Il.10.188.10.
Sleeping he dy'd, with all his Guards around, ... Il.10.658.31.
And left him sleeping in Eternal Shade. .... Il.20.454.413.
Ulysses sleeping on his couch they bore, ... Od.13.138.9.
Awake the sleeping fires, their meal prepare, ... Od.16.3.100.
(Fast by, the rest lay sleeping in the sheath, ... Od.21.456.282.

SLEEPLESS
Before the sleepless Tyrant's guarded Gate; ....1.TrSt.205.419.
And sleepless Lovers, just at Twelve, awake: ....2.RL1.16.146.
Sleepless themselves to give their readers sleep. ....5.DunA1.92.70.
Sleepless themselves, to give their readers sleep. ....5.DunB1.94.276.
Long sleepless Nights in heavy Arms I stood, ...Il.9.430.453.
Sleepless they sit, impatient to engage, ...Il.24.493.556.
Sleepless I watch; for I have learn'd to bear. ....Od.18.366.185.
Sleepless devours each word; and hears, how slain ....Od.23.333.340.

SLEEPS
And fast beside him, once-fear'd *Edward* sleeps: ....1.W-F.314.179.
And sleeps thy Thunder in the Realms above? ....1.TrSt.110.414.
Then conscience sleeps, and leaving nature free, ...2.ElAb.227.338.
'Till tir'd he sleeps, and Life's poor play is o'er! ....3.EOM2.282.88.
The temp'rate sleeps, and spirits light as air! ....4.HS2.74.59.
Nor sleeps one error in its father's grave, ...5.DunA1.162.82.
Th' unconscious flood sleeps o'er thee like a lake. ....5.DunA2.292.138.
Lo where Mœotis sleeps, and hardly flows ....5.DunA3.79.156.
He sleeps among the dull of ancient days; ....5.DunB1.294.291.
Th' unconscious stream sleeps o'er thee like a lake. ....5.DunB2.304.310.
Lo! where Mæotis sleeps, and hardly flows ....5.DunB3.87.324.
In troubled waters, but now sleeps in Port. ....5.DunB4.202.362.
Where sleeps my Grildrig, in the fragrant Bower. ....6.96ii.30Z18.271.
"Where sleeps my *Grildrig* in the fragrant Bow'r! ....6.96ii.50A.273.
"Where sleeps my *Grildrig* in his fragrant Bow'r! ....6.96ii.50.273.
Where sleeps my Gulliver? *O tell me where?* ....6.96iv.47.277.
And peaceful sleeps the liquid Element, ...Il.5.644.299.
The Waves scarce heave, the Face of Ocean sleeps, ...Il.7.73.366.
Sleeps balmy Blessing, Love's endearing Joy; ....Il.13.796.143.
As when old Ocean's silent Surface sleeps, ...Il.14.21.157.
Peaceful He sleeps, with all our Rites adorn'd, ...Il.22.421.472.
And sleeps *Achilles,* (thus the Phantom said) ....Il.23.83.490.
Sleeps my *Achilles,* his *Patroclus* dead? ....Il.23.84.490.
Cries to the Gods, and vengeance sleeps too long. ....Od.2.70.64.
Of the high porch, *Ulysses* sleeps profound: ....Od.7.436.258.
And sleeps my child? the rev'rend matron cries: ....Od.23.5.318.

SLEEPY
The sleepy Eye, that spoke the melting soul. ....4.2HE1.150.209.
Who bears the virtue of the sleepy rod. ....Od.7.185.244.

SLEEVE
Some fold the Sleeve, whilst others plait the Gown; ....2.RL1.147.158.
Some fold the Sleeve, while others plait the Gown; ....2.RL1.147A.158.

SLEEVELESS
Grave mummers! sleeveless some, and shirtless others. ....5.DunA3.108.159.
Grave Mummers! sleeveless some, and shirtless others. ....5.DunB3.116.325.

SLEEVES
Nor Nightgown without Sleeves, avails ....6.58.11A.171.

SLEIGHT
What Sleight is that, which Love will not explore? ....2.ChJM.515.40.

SLENDER
O let my Muse her slender Reed inspire, ...1.PSp.11.61.
A graceful Robe her slender Body drest, ...1.TrUl.104.469.
And mighty Hearts are held in slender Chains. ....2.RL2.24.161.
So spins the silkworm small its slender store, ...5.DunA1.171.84.
So spins the silk-worm small its slender store, ...5.DunB4.253.369.
Our Hearts may bear its slender Chain a Day, ...6.19.64.64.
First on his Limbs a slender Vest he drew, ...Il.2.53.129.
With six small Ships, and but a slender Train, ...Il.5.794.304.
A graceful robe her slender body drest, ...Od.13.271.19.

SLEPT
And there deluded *Argus* slept and bled; ....1.TrSt.355.425.
Spent with Fatigue, and slept secure on Land; ....1.TrUl.153.471.
Not much we fasted, but scarce ever slept. ....2.ChWB.286.70.
If e'er I slept, I dream'd of him alone, ...2.ChWB.302.71.
He said; when *Shock,* who thought she slept too long, ...2.RL1.115.154.
The Queen of *Midas* slept, and so may I. ....4.Arbu.82.101.
He slept, poor Dog! and lost it, to a doit. ....4.2HE2.36.167.
Command old words that long have slept, to wake, ...4.2HE2.167.177.
There Caxton slept, with Wynkin at his side, ...5.DunA1.129.79.
Slept first, the distant nodded to the hum. ....5.DunA2.370.145.
There Caxton slept, with Wynkyn at his side, ...5.DunB1.149.281.
Slept first; the distant nodded to the hum. ....5.DunB2.402.316.
Unfinish'd Treaties in each Office slept; ....5.DunB4.616.405.
'Twas one vast Nothing, All, and All slept fast in thee. ....6.8.3.17.
Silent they slept, and heard of Wars no more. ....Il.3.314.208.
Achilles slept; and in his warm Embrace ....Il.9.780.472.
In Arms we slept, beside the winding Flood, ...Il.11.868.74.
And peaceful slept the mighty *Hector's* Shade. ....Il.24.1016.577.
And slept beneath the pompous Colonnade; ....Od.3.511.112.
And slept delighted with the gifts of love. ....Od.5.292.185.
All night I slept, oblivious of my pain; ....Od.7.370.254.
And slept secure along the sandy shore. ....Od.9.173.312.
Satiate we slept: But when the sacred dawn ....Od.9.197.314.
The face of things, we slept along the shore. ....Od.10.211.350.
Spent with fatigue, and slept secure on land. ....Od.13.320.23.
Where the fat porkers slept beneath the sun; ....Od.14.86.40.
And safe I slept, till brightly-dawning shone ....Od.14.568.64.
And there the quiver, where now guiltless slept ....Od.21.15.259.

SLEW
Thy Hand slew *Python;* and the Dame who lost ....1.TrSt.849.445.
Whose Son, the swift *Orsilochus,* I slew, ...1.TrUl.145.470.
Preserv'd the *Jews,* and slew th' *Assyrian* Foe: ....2.ChJM.74.18.
And with their Heads to Heav'n the Victims slew: ....Il.1.601.117.
Seiz'd by the beating Wing, the Monster slew: ....Il.2.383.145.
The Barley sprinkled, and the Victim slew. ....Il.2.503.150.
Alcides' Uncle, old *Lycimnius,* slew; ....Il.2.802.163.
And the bold Sons of great *Evenus* slew. ....Il.2.844.164.

SLEW (CONTINUED)
With that, the Chief the tender Victims slew, ...Il.3.364.210.
The sounding Darts in Iron Tempests slew, ...Il.4.511.245.
And *Leucus,* lov'd by wise *Ulysses,* slew. ....Il.4.564.248.
And some bold Chieftain ev'ry Leader slew: ....Il.5.50.268.
And two brave Leaders at an Instant slew; ....Il.5.183.275.
And first two Leaders valiant *Hector* slew, ...Il.5.751.302.
Both strook, both wounded, but *Sarpedon's* slew: ....Il.5.815.305.
The God who slew him, leaves his prostrate Prize ....Il.5.1040.316.
Nine Days he feasted, and nine Bulls he slew. ....Il.6.214.336.
(Fiercest of Men) and those the Warrior slew. ....Il.6.228.337.
Lay'd *Thebè* waste, and slew my warlike Sire! ....Il.6.525.352.
Him not by manly Force *Lycurgus* slew, ...Il.7.173.372.
Beheld the finish'd Work. Their Bulls they slew; ....Il.7.558.392.
With ev'ry Shaft some hostile Victim slew, ...Il.8.323.413.
Thus following *Hector* still the hindmost slew. ....Il.8.412.417.
Whose luckless Hand his Royal Uncle slew; ....Il.9.682.468.
Ulysses following, as his Part'ner slew, ...Il.10.570.28.
Whose hostile King the brave *Tydides* slew; ....Il.10.657.31.
And slew *Bienor* at his People's Head: ....Il.11.128.41.
And slew the Children for the Father's Fault; ....Il.11.166.42.
Still press'd the Rout, and still the hindmost slew; ....Il.11.232.45.
And first *Doryclus, Priam's* Son, he slew, ...Il.11.611.61.
A Bull to *Jove* he slew in sacrifice, ...Il.11.906.76.
And the bold Son of *Pylæmenes* slew. ....Il.13.804.143.
Bold *Merion, Morys* and *Hippotion* slew. ....Il.14.608.191.
And thee, brave *Clonius!* great *Agenor* slew. ....Il.15.385.211.
All *Greece* in Heaps; but one he seiz'd, and slew. ....Il.15.769.226.
Now ev'ry *Greek* some hostile Hero slew, ...Il.16.364.257.
The flying *Lycians, Glaucus* met, and slew; ....Il.16.726.272.
And thrice three Heroes at each Onset slew. ....Il.16.949.280.
The Man, that slew *Achilles,* in his Friend! ....Il.20.494.415.
Thrasius, Astypylus, and *Mnesus* slew; ....Il.21.226.430.
All those relentless *Mars* untimely slew, ...Il.24.325.550.
With silver Fleece, which his Attendants slew. ....Il.24.787.570.
Slew the dire pair, and gave to fun'ral flame ....Od.3.392.105.
One for his food the raging glutton slew, ...Od.10.133.347.
Whose son, the swift *Orsilochus,* I slew: ....Od.13.312.21.
Of my own tribe an *Argive* wretch I slew; ....Od.15.298.83.
Great *Demoptolemus, Ulysses* slew; ....Od.22.293.300.

SLICES
Then clap four slices of Pilaster on't, ...3.Ep4.33.140.

SLIDD'RING
Slidd'ring, and stagg'ring. On the Border stood ....Il.21.267.431.

SLIDE
Parts answ'ring parts shall slide into a whole, ...3.Ep4.66.143.
I fear'd th'Infection slide from him to me, ...4.JD4.170.39.
I felt th'Infection slide from him to me, ...4.JD4.170A.39.
Back to my native Moderation slide, ...4.1HE1.33.281.
Here fortun'd Curl to slide; loud shout the band, ...5.DunA2.69.106.
Here fortun'd Curl to slide; loud shout the band, ...5.DunB2.73.299.
Hours, days, and years slide soft away, ...6.1.10.3.
His years slide silently away, ...6.1.10A.3.
Hours, days, and years slide swift away, ...6.1.10B.3.

SLIDES
Slides into Verse, and hitches in a Rhyme, ...4.HS1.78.13.
Slides to a Scriv'ner or a City Knight. ....4.HS2.178.69.
Wash'd from beneath him, slides the slimy Soil; ....Il.21.310.433.

SLIDING
Now sliding Streams the thirsty Plants renew, ...1.TrVP.15.377.
A sliding Noose, and waver'd in the Wind. ....2.ChWB.396.76.
When lo! a Harlot form soft sliding by, ...5.DunB4.45.345.
And many a Boat soft sliding to and fro. ....6.14ii.4.43.

SLIGHT
Survey the *Whole,* nor seek slight Faults to find, ...1.EOC.235.266.
For his embraces you the Cyclops slight. ....1.TrPA.121.370.
I, for a few slight Spots, am not so nice. ....2.ChWB.39.58.
Slight is the Subject, but not so the Praise, ...2.RL1.5.144.
Slight Lines of Hair surprize the Finny Prey, ...2.RL2.26.161.
Some dire Disaster, or by Force, or Slight, ...2.RL2.103.166.
And live there Men who slight immortal Fame? ....2.TemF.366.281.
Nor Fame I slight, nor for her Favours call; ....2.TemF.513.288.
'Tis mine to wash a few slight Stains; but theirs ....4.JD4.284.49.
He spins the slight, self-pleasing thread anew; ....4.Arbu.90.102.
Still spin the slight, self-pleasing thread anew; ....4.Arbu.90A.102.
Sir *George* of *some slight Gallantries* suspect. ....4.EpS1.15A.298.
Not deeper skill'd in ev'ry martial Slight, ...Il.11.541.58.
These shall I slight? and guide my wav'ring Mind ....Il.12.277.91.
Sweeps the slight Works and fashion'd Domes away. ....Il.15.419.213.
And the slight Cov'ring of expanded Hydes. ....Il.20.326.407.
On a slight Raft to pass the swelling sea ....Od.5.226.182.
To slight the poor, or ought humane despise. ....Od.14.66.39.
They slight the pledges of their former vows; ....Od.15.26.71.
Proceed false slave, and slight their empty words; ....Od.21.399.279.

SLIGHTED
See the poor Remnants of these slighted Hairs! ....2.RL4.167.197.
See the poor Remnants of this slighted Hair! ....2.RL4.167A.197.
Nor Vows unpaid, nor slighted Sacrifice, ...Il.1.118.92.
To punish *Troy* for slighted Sacrifice; ....Il.5.225.278.
High o'er their slighted Trench our Steeds shall bound, ...Il.8.218.407.
Thy Country slighted in her last Distress, ...Il.16.42.237.
And ev'n these slighted charms might learn to please. ....Od.5.266.184.

SLIGHTEST
But as the slightest Sketch, if justly trac'd, ...1.EOC.23.241.

SLIGHTING
Since Victor of thy Fears, and slighting mine, ...Il.24.357.551.

SLIGHTLY
And slightly on her Breast the Wanton strook: ....II.21.497.442.

SLIGHTS
The other slights, for Women, Sports, and Wines, ...4.2HE2.272.185.
Mocks our Attempts, and slights our just Demands. ....II.8.438.418.
He slights thy Friendship, thy Proposals scorns, ...II.9.796.473.

SLILY
No Commentator can more slily pass ....4.JD2.101.141.

SLIM
Tell P[ickenbur]g how slim she's grown ....6.61.24.181.

SLIMY
The Sun e're got, or slimy *Nilus* bore, ...4.JD4.29.29.
Wash'd from beneath him, slides the slimy Soil; ....II.21.310.433.
Was clogg'd with slimy Dung, and mingled Gore. ....II.23.908.525.

SLING
Or whirl the sounding Pebble from the Sling, ...II.13.894.148.
Axes to cut, and Ropes to sling the Load. ....II.23.139.493.

SLINGS
A Slings soft Wool, snatch'd from a Soldier's side, ...II.13.751.140.

SLINK
A Weasel once made shift to slink ....4.1HE7.51.271.

SLIP
Give me some Slip of this most blissful Tree, ...2.ChWB.399.76.

SLIP-SHOD
"Lo next two slip-shod Muses traipse along, ...5.DunA3.141.162.
"See next two slip-shod Muses traipse along, ...5.DunA3.141A.162.
A slip-shod Sibyl led his steps along, ...5.DunB3.15.320.

SLIP'D
That slip'd thro' Cracks and Zig-zags of the Head; ....5.DunB1.124.278.

SLIP'RY
Rowl'd in the bloody dust, and paw'd the slip'ry ground. ....II.16.577.267.

SLIPP'RY
Rowl'd in the bloody Dust, and paw'd the slipp'ry Ground. .....1.TrES.272.459.
Steep its Ascent, and slipp'ry was the Way; ....2.TemF.28.255.
"Or tumbled from the Toadstool's slipp'ry Round, ...6.96ii.43.272.
With streaming Blood the slipp'ry Fields are dy'd, ...II.4.514.246.
With streaming Blood the slipp'ry Fields are dy'd, ...II.8.81.399.
Slipp'ry with Blood, o'er Arms and Heaps of Shields, ...II.10.541.27.
His Corps fell bleeding on the slipp'ry Shore, ...II.15.620.220.
With streaming Blood the slipp'ry Shores are dy'd, ...II.15.866.230.
(O'erturn'd by *Pallas*) where the slipp'ry Shore ....II.23.907.525.

SLIPPER
Thrice the wrought Slipper knock'd against the Ground, ...2.RL1.17A.145.
Thrice rung the Bell, the Slipper knock'd the Ground, ...2.RL1.17.146.

SLIPPERY
Or tumbl'd from the Toadstool's slippery round ....6.96ii.30Z9.271.
The slippery sides, and shoot into the skies. ....Od.12.98.436.

SLIPT
Thrice thro' my arms she slipt like empty wind, ...Od.11.249.393.

SLIT
His nose they shorten'd, and his ears they slit, ...Od.21.321.275.

SLOANE
And Books for Mead, and Butterflies for Sloane. ....3.Ep4.10.136.
And Books for Mead, and Rarities for Sloane. ....3.Ep4.10A.136.
Or *Sloane*, or *Woodward's* wondrous Shelves contain; ....4.JD4.30.29.

SLOATH
Sloath unfolds her Arms and wakes; ....6.11.32.31.
Sloath from its Lethargy awakes, ...6.11.32A.31.
What Pity, Sloath should seize a Soul so brave, ...II.6.670.360.
Yet must I tax his Sloath, that claims no share ....II.10.130.7.
What Sloath has seiz'd us, when the Fields around ....II.21.508.443.

SLOATHFUL
Still, with your Voice, the sloathful Soldiers raise, ...II.10.74.5.

SLOP'D
Nor 'till oblique he slop'd his evening ray, ...Od.7.372.254.

SLOPE
Imbrown the Slope, and nod on the Parterre, ...3.Ep4.174.154.
Imbrown thy Slope, and nod on thy Parterre, ...3.Ep4.174A.154.
From his slope Shield, the disappointed Lance. ....II.13.512.131.

SLOPES
And when up ten steep slopes you've dragg'd your thighs, ...3.Ep4.131.150.
Slopes at its foot, the woods its sides embrace, ...4.1HE1.141.289.

SLOPING
Of hanging mountains, and of sloping greens: ....6.81.4.225.
(A race divided, whom with sloping rays ....Od.1.31.31.
And now, declining with his sloping wheels, ...Od.2.436.82.
Her sloping hills the mantling vines adorn, ...Od.15.444.92.

SLOTH
Ev'n av'rice, prudence; sloth, philosophy; ....3.EOM2.188.77.
Not sunk by sloth, nor rais'd by servitude; ....3.Ep3.222.111.
But Thee or Fear deterrs, or Sloth detains; ....II.5.1008.315.
Nor Sloth hath seiz'd me, but thy Word restrains: ....II.5.1013.315.

SLOTH (CONTINUED)
Nor Fear with-holds, nor shameful Sloth detains. ....II.13.294.119.
Not for thy sloth, I deem thy Lord unkind; ....Od.24.296.364.

SLOTHFUL
Be furious, envious, slothful, mad or drunk, ...4.1HE1.61.283.

SLOVEN
You laugh, half Beau half Sloven if I stand, ...4.1HE1.161.291.

SLOW
While yon slow Oxen turn the furrow'd Plain. ....1.PSp.30.63.
Thro' the fair Scene rowl slow the lingring Streams, ...1.W-F.217.169.
The *Loddon* slow, with verdant Alders crown'd: ....1.W-F.342.183.
That like a wounded Snake, drags its slow length along. ....1.EOC.357.280.
What's *roundly smooth*, or *languishingly slow;* ....1.EOC.359.280.
The Line too *labours*, and the Words move *slow;* ....1.EOC.371.282.
By slow degrees, and cover all below: ....1.TrFD.44A.387.
Pensive and slow, with sudden Grief opprest ....1.TrUl.68.468.
See him from Nature rising slow to Art! ....3.EOM3.169.110.
All sly slow things, with circumspective eyes: ....3.EOM4.226.148.
"How Shadwell hasty, Wycherly was slow; ....4.2HE1.85.201.
So slow th' unprofitable Moments roll, ...4.1HE1.39.281.
She saw slow Philips creep like Tate's poor page, ...5.DunA1.103.72.
Next Smedley div'd; slow circles dimpled o'er ....5.DunA2.279.135.
Next *E[usden]* div'd; slow circles dimpled o'er ....5.DunA2.279A.135.
Slow moves the Goddess from the sable flood, ...5.DunA2.331.142.
Slow mov'd the Goddess from the silver flood, ...5.DunA2.331A.142.
She saw slow Philips creep like Tate's poor page, ...5.DunB1.105.277.
Next Smedley div'd; slow circles dimpled o'er ....5.DunB2.291.309.
Slow rose a form, in majesty of Mud; ....5.DunB2.326.313.
Let others creep by timid steps, and slow, ...5.DunB4.465.386.
And since my Tongue is in thy praises slow, ...6.2.4.5.
Who slow, and leisurely rehearse, ...6.10.13.24.
While in more lengthen'd Notes and slow, ...6.11.10.30.
In more lengthen'd Notes and slow, ...6.11.10A.30.
In constant Motion, nor too swift nor slow, ...6.17ii.19.56.
We'll not be slow to visit Dr. Swift. ....6.42vi.6.120.
Count the slow clock, and dine exact at noon; ....6.45.18.125.
The Blockhead is a Slow-worm; ....6.53.14.161.
Uprising slow, the venerable Sage ....II.1.95.91.
Slow from his Seat arose the *Pylian* Sage; ....II.1.330.103.
And oft look'd back, slow-moving o'er the Strand. .....II.1.453.109.
If Fate resists, or if our Arms are slow, ...II.2.438.148.
Advanc'd with Steps majestically slow. ....II.3.112.195.
Slow they proceed: The sage *Ulysses* then ....II.3.336.209.
Him *Helen* follow'd slow with bashful Charms, ...II.3.557.218.
Shall all be vain: When Heav'n's Revenge is slow, ...II.4.194.230.
Slow from the Main the heavy Vapours rise, ...II.4.316.235.
Slow he gave way, the rest tumultuous fled; ....II.4.583.249.
I hate the cumbrous Chariot's slow Advance, ...II.5.314.281.
Retire then Warriors, but sedate and slow; ....II.5.746.302.
Slow they retreat, and ev'n retreating fight. ....II.5.863.307.
The Train majestically slow proceeds. ....II.6.369.344.
That stream'd at ev'ry Look: then, moving slow, ...II.6.642.358.
Slow from his Seat the rev'rend *Priam* rose. ....II.7.441.386.
And sadly slow, to sacred *Troy* return'd. ....II.7.511.389.
Weak is thy Servant, and thy Coursers slow. ....II.8.132.404.
While *Pray'rs*, to heal her Wrongs, move slow behind. ....II.9.630.465.
Then sow'rly slow th' indignant Beast retires. ....II.11.679.65.
As the slow Beast with heavy Strength indu'd, ...II.11.682.65.
Now the slow Course of all-impairing Time ....II.11.814.72.
The Slaves their Master's show approach survey'd, ...II.11.978.78.
His tir'd, slow Steps, he drags from off the Field. ....II.13.653.136.
In slow Procession bore from off the Plain. ....II.13.822.144.
By Arms abroad, or slow Disease at home: ....II.13.838.145.
Slow moving on; *Atrides* leads the way. ....II.14.154.165.
Slow he recedes, and sighing, quits the Dead. ....II.17.116.292.
Next him *Idomeneus*, now more with Age, ...II.17.304.299.
Their Sister Looks; *Dexamene* the slow, ...II.18.56.326.
And Steers slow-moving, and two Shepherd Swains; .....II.18.608.352.
Slow as she past, beheld with sad survey ....II.19.297.384.
Where the slow *Caucons* close the Rear of Fight. .....II.20.378.410.
Be this the Song, slow-moving tow'rd the Shore, ...II.22.493.476.
First march the heavy Mules, securely slow, ...II.23.140.494.
And the slow Mules the same rough Road return. ......II.23.151.495.
But slow, and past their Vigour, are my Steeds. ....II.23.380.505.
Slow dragg'd the Steeds his batter'd Chariot on: ......II.23.610.514.
May the slow Mules and fun'ral Car command. ....II.24.186.544.
May the slow Mules and fun'ral Car command. ....II.24.216.546.
On his slow Wheels the following People wait, ...II.24.403.552.
The Sage and King, majestically slow. ....II.24.869.572.
Slow rolls the Chariot thro' the following Tide; ....II.24.897.573.
The splendid car roll'd slow in regal state: ....Od.4.28.121.
For eight slow-circling years by tempests tost, ...Od.4.97.124.
Slow-pacing thrice around th' insidious pile; ....Od.4.378.139.
Slow rowls the car before th' attending train. ....Od.6.380.230.
While the slow mules draw on th' imperial maid: ......Od.7.2.232.
More swift than *Mars,* and more than *Vulcan* slow? ....Od.8.370.283.
Now far the last, with pensive pace and slow ....Od.9.531.328.
Eurylochus with pensive steps and slow, ...Od.10.286.357.
And where, slow rolling from the *Stygian* bed, ...Od.10.610.374.
And steal thy self from life, by slow decays, ...Od.11.165.389.
Has life's fair lamp declin'd by slow decays, ...Od.11.208.392.
Nor came my fate by ling'ring pains and slow, ...Od.11.242.393.
And near them walk'd, with solemn pace and slow, ...Od.11.397.403.
When rising sad and slow, with pensive look, ...Od.12.188.441.
But dreadful most, when by a slow decay ....Od.12.405.450.
Slow seem'd the sun to move, the hours to roll, ...Od.13.37.3.
Pensive and slow, with sudden grief opprest ....Od.13.235.17.
To give another's is thy hand so slow? ....Od.17.486.156.
Thus wailing, slow and sadly she descends, ...Od.18.245.178.
And slow behind her damsel train attends. ....Od.18.350.184.
Thus slow, to fly with rapture to his arms? ....Od.23.102.324.
And steal my self from life by slow decays; ....Od.23.298.337.
When, moving slow, the regal form they view'd ....Od.24.31.348.

SLOW-CIRCLING
For eight slow-circling years by tempests tost, ... Od.4.97.124.

SLOW-MOVING
And oft look'd back, slow-moving o'er the Strand. ..... Il.1.453.109.
And Steers slow-moving, and two Shepherd Swains; ..... Il.18.608.352.
Be this the Song, slow-moving tow'rd the Shore, ... Il.22.493.476.

SLOW-PACING
Slow-pacing thrice around th' insidious pile; ..... Od.4.378.139.

SLOW-WORM
The Blockhead is a Slow-worm; ..... 6.53.14.161.

SLOWLY
Disabl'd *Glaucus* slowly quit the Field; ..... 1.TrES.120.454.
The Car rowls slowly o'er the dusty Plain. ..... 1.TrES.280.460.
The good old Knight mov'd slowly by her Side. ..... 2.ChJM.403.34.
Spreads his black Wings, and slowly mounts to Day. ..... 2.RL4.88.191.
How oft' our slowly-growing works impart, ... 6.52.19.156.
In sullen Fury slowly quits the Prize. ..... Il.4.623.250.
And slowly, sadly, to their Fleet repair. ..... Il.7.515.389.
And slowly rising, thus the Council mov'd. ..... Il.9.126.438.
And stirs but slowly when he stirs at last. ..... Il.11.689.66.
Disabl'd *Glaucus* slowly quit the Field; ..... Il.12.474.99.
The Car rowls slowly o'er the dusty Plain. ..... Il.16.585.267.
Slowly he rises, scarcely breathes with Pain, ... Il.21.488.441.
Then slowly rising, o'er the sandy space ..... Od.3.496.111.
Then slowly sunk the ruddy globe of light, ... Od.3.629.118.
When slowly-rising, *Halitherses* spoke: ..... Od.24.517.372.

SLOWLY-GROWING
How oft' our slowly-growing works impart, ... 6.52.19.156.

SLOWLY-RISING
When slowly-rising, *Halitherses* spoke: ..... Od.24.517.372.

SLOWNESS
Not thro' our Crime, or Slowness in the Course; ..... Il.19.456.391.

SLUGS
And pond'rous slugs cut swiftly thro' the sky; ..... 5.DunA1.178.84.
And pond'rous slugs cut swiftly thro the sky; ..... 5.DunB1.182.283.
And pondrous Slugs move nimbly thro' the Sky. ..... 6.7.18.16.

SLUICE
The King of Dykes! than whom, no sluice of mud ..... 5.DunA2.261.133.
(As under seas Alphæus' secret sluice ..... 5.DunA2.317.140.
(As under seas Alphæus' sacred sluice ..... 5.DunA2.317A.140.
The King of dykes! than whom no sluice of mud ..... 5.DunB2.273.309.
(As under seas Alphæus' secret sluice ..... 5.DunB2.341.314.

SLUICES
Releas'd th'impetuous Sluices of the Main,— ..... 1.TrSt.313.423.
Fast from the shining Sluices of her Eyes ..... Il.24.960.576.
And dry the tearful sluices of Despair: ..... Od.4.306.134.
So from the sluices of *Ulysses'* eyes ..... Od.8.581.294.

SLUICY
While *Jove* descends in sluicy Sheets of Rain, ... Il.5.122.273.
And half the Skies descend in sluicy Show'rs. ..... Il.12.28.82.

SLUMB'RING
And goad the Prelate slumb'ring in his Stall. ..... 4.EpS2.219.325.
Did slumb'ring visit, and convey to stews; ..... 5.DunB2.422.318.
The slumb'ring Chief, and in these Words awakes. ..... Il.10.179.9.
To Heroes slumb'ring in Eternal Shade) ..... Il.23.64.489.
Where sheep and goats lay slumb'ring round the shore. ..... Od.9.214.314.
To fix the slumb'ring monster to the ground, ... Od.9.357.321.
And with these words the slumb'ring youth awakes. ..... Od.15.54.72.

SLUMB'ROUS
While pensive in the silent slumb'rous shade, ... Od.4.1045.166.
Soft slumb'rous shades his drooping eye-lids close, ... Od.19.60.195.
Their drooping eyes the slumb'rous shade oppress, ... Od.19.497.220.

SLUMBER
(That ev'n in Slumber caus'd her Cheek to glow) ..... 2.RL1.24.147.
Hiss if he hiss, and if he slumber, sleep. ..... 4.1740.36.334.
Where slumber Abbots, purple as their wines: ..... 5.DunB4.302.373.
So from her Babe, when Slumber seals his Eye, ... Il.4.162.228.
And Death in lasting Slumber seals his Eyes. ..... Il.5.90.270.
At this, soft Slumber from his Eyelids fled; ..... Il.10.184.10.
And everlasting Slumber seals his Eyes. ..... Il.13.689.137.
Thus having said, the Pow'r of Slumber flew, ... Il.14.417.183.
Unwilling Slumber, and the Chiefs bespoke. ..... Il.23.293.501.
And pours deep Slumber on their watchful Eyes: ..... Il.24.548.559.
In slumber clos'd her silver-streaming eyes. ..... Od.1.464.54.
Or in soft slumber seals the wakeful eye: ..... Od.5.61.174.
In slumber wore the heavy night away, ... Od.5.199.181.
'Till then, let slumber close thy careful eyes; ..... Od.7.406.256.
When slumber next should tame the man of blood. ..... Od.9.393.322.
Sweet time of slumber! be the night obey'd! ..... Od.12.348.448.
Nor cease the tears, 'till each in slumber shares ..... Od.12.365.449.
Then o'er my eyes the Gods soft slumber shed, ... Od.12.401.450.
'Twas then soft slumber fled my troubled brain: ..... Od.12.431.451.
O fatal slumber, paid with lasting woes! ..... Od.12.440.452.
And in soft slumber seal'd her flowing eye. ..... Od.16.469.130.
And o'er her eyes ambrosial slumber shed. ..... Od.19.704.229.
In slumber clos'd her silver-streaming eyes. ..... Od.21.388.279.
Soon as soft slumber eas'd the toils of day, ... Od.23.371.343.
Or in soft slumber seals the wakeful eye, ... Od.24.4.347.

SLUMBER'D
And *Juno* slumber'd on the golden Bed. ..... Il.1.781.125.
Th' Immortals slumber'd on their Thrones above; ..... Il.2.3.126.

SLUMBER'D (CONTINUED)
Late as I slumber'd in the Shades of Night, ... Il.2.71.130.

SLUMBERS
Or in soft Slumbers seals the wakeful Eye; ..... 1.TrSt.434.428.
And waits 'till pleasing Slumbers seal his Eyes. ..... 1.TrSt.538.433.
To call soft Slumbers on his infant Eyes. ..... 1.TrSt.690.439.
And pleasing Slumbers steal upon his Eyes. ..... 1.TrUl.6.465.
While purer Slumbers spread their golden Wings) ..... 2.TemF.8.253.
'Obedient slumbers that can wake and weep'; ..... 2.ElAb.212.337.
Soft as the slumbers of a saint forgiv'n, ... 2.ElAb.255.340.
And haunt their slumbers in the pompous shade. ..... 3.EOM4.304.156.
A Statesman's slumbers how this speech would spoil! ..... 3.Ep3.43.89.
Now May'rs and Shrieves in pleasing slumbers lay, ... 5.DunA1.89A.70.
Which most conduce to sooth the soul in slumbers, ... 5.DunA2.337.142.
"Which most conduce to sooth the soul in slumbers, ... 5.DunB2.369.315.
Soft be his Slumbers! But may this suffice ..... 6.17iv.22.60.
Ah spare my Slumbers, gently tread the Cave! ..... 6.87.3.248.
And haunt his slumbers in the pompous Shade. ..... 6.130.18.358.
In Slumbers sweet the rev'rend *Phœnix* lay. ..... Il.9.778.472.
O Pow'r of Slumbers! hear, and favour still. ..... Il.14.269.175.
Their Feet unwash'd, their Slumbers on the Ground; ..... Il.16.289.253.
As Men in Slumbers seem with speedy pace, ... Il.22.257.466.
And pleasing Slumbers quiet all their Care. ..... Il.24.4.534.
Or in soft Slumbers seals the wakeful Eye; ..... Il.24.422.553.
And peaceful slumbers close my mother's eyes, ... Od.2.403.80.
And leaden slumbers press his drooping eyes. ..... Od.4.610.148.
'Till *Pallas* pour'd soft slumbers on his eyes; ..... Od.5.635.202.
And peaceful slumbers calm'd his anxious breast; ..... Od.6.2.203.
Rose instant from the slumbers of the night; ..... Od.8.4.261.
Lest, in thy slumbers on the watry main, ... Od.8.481.288.
Thus breaks our slumbers, and disturbs the night? ..... Od.9.480.325.
And pleasing slumbers steal upon his eyes. ..... Od.13.97.5.
She ceas'd: Ambrosial slumbers seal his eyes; ..... Od.20.65.235.
Where slumbers soft now close the royal eye; ..... Od.22.467.311.

SLUMBRING
Did slumbring visit, and convey to stews? ..... 5.DunA2.390.148.
And all lay slumbring in the dusky bow'r; ..... Od.10.567.370.

SLUMBROUS
There every eye with slumbrous chains she bound, ... Od.2.444.82.
The downy fleece to form the slumbrous bed; ..... Od.4.404.139.

SLUNK
So slunk to *Cambden* House so high, ... 6.79.131.222.

SLUT
That Bag—which *Jenny,* wanton Slut , ... 6.94.77.261.
Not touch me! never Neighbour call'd me Slut! ..... 6.96iv.25.277.

SLUTS
These filthy Sluts, their Jordans ne'er abscond ..... 6.96ii.30Z3.271.

SLUTTISHNESS
And hides in sacred Sluttishness the rest. ..... 4.HAdv.111.85.

SLY
All sly slow things, with circumspective eyes: ..... 3.EOM4.226.148.
A Quaker? sly: A Presbyterian? sow'r: ..... 3.Ep1.108.23.
Nor sly Informer watch my Words to draw ..... 4.JD2A.133.144.
No sly Informer watch these words to draw ..... 4.JD2.127.145.
His sly, polite, insinuating stile ..... 4.EpS1.19.298.
Her, sly *Cyllenius* lov'd; on her would gaze, ... Il.16.218.248.
Answer'd evasive of the sly request. ..... Od.1.530.57.

SLYLY
Then slyly thrust it up *that same,* ..... 6.94.43.260.

SMACKING
Then gives a smacking buss, and cries—No words! ..... 6.45.26.125.

SMALL
Thus (if small Things we may with great compare) ..... 1.W-F.105.160.
To *one small Sect,* and All are *damn'd beside.)* ..... 1.EOC.397.285.
Or the small Pillow grace a Lady's Bed, ... 2.RL3.166.181.
Charm'd the Small-pox, or chas'd old Age away; ..... 2.RL5.20.200.
To him no high, no low, no great, no small; ..... 3.EOM1.279.49.
So, when small humors gather to a gout, ... 3.EOM2.159.74.
"Learn each small People's genius, policies, ... 3.EOM3.183.111.
Where small and great, where weak and mighty, made ..... 3.EOM3.297.123.
Fortune in Men has some small diff'rence made, ... 3.EOM4.195.145.
In the small circle of our foes or friends; ..... 3.EOM4.242.150.
As the small pebble stirs the peaceful lake; ..... 3.EOM4.364.164.
Spleen, Vapours, or Small-pox, above them all, ... 3.Ep2.267.72.
Yet for *small Turbots* such esteem profess? ..... 4.HS2.23.55.
Ev'n such small Critics some regard may claim, ... 4.Arbu.167.108.
'Tis to small purpose that you hold your tongue, ... 4.2HE2.155.175.
A worthy Member, no small Fool, a Lord; ..... 4.2HE2.185.177.
Yes, Sir, how small soever be my heap, ... 4.2HE2.284.185.
"Both small and great, both you and I: ..... 4.HS6.180.261.
As want of figure, and a small Estate. ..... 4.1HE1.68.283.
In rev'rend Bishops note some *small Neglects,* ..... 4.EpS1.16.298.
In rev'rend S[utto]n note a *small Neglect,* ..... 4.EpS1.16A.298.
Alas! the small Discredit of a Bribe ..... 4.EpS2.46.315.
So spins the silkworm small its slender store, ... 5.DunA1.171.84.
Small thanks to France and none to Rome or Greece, ... 5.DunA1.237.91.
Thus the small jett which hasty hands unlock, ... 5.DunA2.169.122.
Small thanks to France, and none to Rome or Greece, ... 5.DunB1.283.290.
Thus the small jett, which hasty hands unlock, ... 5.DunB2.177.304.
With mincing step, small voice, and languid eye; ..... 5.DunB4.46.345.
So spins the silk-worm small its slender store, ... 5.DunB4.253.369.
Till, by degrees, remote and small, ... 6.11.18.30.
They print their Names in Letters small, ... 6.29.9.83.
This small, well-polish'd gem, the work of years! ..... 6.52.40.157.
The Great Ones are thought mad, the Small Ones Fools: ..... 6.60.2.178.

SMALL (CONTINUED)
A small Euphrates thro' the piece is roll'd, ... 6.71.29.203.
Small-Pox is rife, and *Gay* in dreadful fear— .... 6.82vi.13.232.
For it maketh things small: .... 6.91.18.253.
In small pieces cut it, ... 6.91.3A.253.
That maketh things small: .... 6.91.18A.253.
Which frames the Harvest-bug, too small for Sight, ... 6.96v.3.280.
A Prize as small, O Tyrant! match'd with thine, ... Il.1.215.97.
So small their Number, that if Wars were ceas'd, ... Il.2.155.135.
But few his Troops, and small his Strength in Arms. .... Il.2.820.164.
Nor yet appear his Care and Conduct small; .... Il.3.257.204.
Small at her Birth, but rising ev'ry Hour, ... Il.4.503.245.
With six small Ships, and but a slender Train, ... Il.5.794.304.
Small Aid to *Troy* thy feeble Force can be, ... Il.5.798.304.
Small Thought retrieves the Spirits of the Brave. .... Il.13.156.112.
Small Stock of Iron needs that Man provide; .... Il.23.987.528.
Small tract of fertile lawn, the least to mine. .... Od.4.828.158.
A small but verdant Isle appear'd in view, ... Od.4.1103.169.
Small is the faith, the Prince and Queen ascribe .... Od.14.146.42.
Small is the comfort from the Queen to hear .... Od.15.400.88.

SMALL-POX
Charm'd the Small-pox, or chas'd old Age away; .... 2.RL5.20.200.
Spleen, Vapours, or Small-pox, above them all, ... 3.Ep2.267.72.
Small-Pox is rife, and *Gay* in dreadful fear— .... 6.82vi.13.232.

SMALLER
The males without (a smaller race) remain'd; .... Od.14.20.35.

SMALLEST
Then came the smallest Tribe I yet had seen, ... 2.TemF.356.281.
Yet now the Rivals are my smallest care: .... Od.2.268.74.
The smallest portion of a wasteful board, ... Od.17.540.158.

SMAR
A smar Free-thinker? all things in an hour. .... 3.Ep1.109.23.

SMART
Pan came, and ask'd, what Magick caus'd my Smart, ... 1.PAu.81.86.
I was my self the Scourge that caus'd the Smart; .... 2.ChWB.6.57.
While yet the Smart was shooting in the Bone. .... 2.ChWB.258.69.
To smart and agonize at ev'ry pore? .... 3.EOM1.198.40.
F. A hundred smart in *Timon* and in *Balaam:* .... 4.HS1.42.9.
"Men only feel the Smart, but not the Vice." .... 4.2HE2.217.179.
And Snip-snap short, and Interruption smart. .... 5.DunA2.232.128.
And Snip-snap short, and Interruption smart, ... 5.DunB2.240.307.
Here a bright *Redcoat,* there a smart *Toupee.* .... 6.9vii.5.22.
These *smart, new Characters* supplyd. .... 6.44.22.123.
Goodly and smart,—with Ears of *Issachar.* .... 6.60.30.179.
Each pretty Carecter with pleasing Smart .... 6.82iv.1.231.
Our Tails may smart for what you hatch. .... 6.93.27Z4.257.
The Savage wound, he rowzes at the Smart, ... Il.5.177.275.
Stung with the Smart, all panting with the Pain, ... Il.11.351.50.
Then raging with intolerable Smart, ... Il.11.574.59.
As faintly reeling he confess'd the Smart; .... Il.11.944.77.
With healing Balms the raging Smart allay, ... Il.11.965.78.
Mad with the Smart, he drops the fatal Prey, ... Il.12.237.90.
His painful Arm, yet useless with the Smart .... Il.16.629.269.
Pow'rful alike to ease the Wretche's Smart; .... Il.16.635.269.

SMARTING
Furious he said; the smarting Scourge resounds; .... Il.15.402.212.
Athwart the fiery steeds the smarting thong; .... Od.15.207.78.

SMARTS
And he that smarts has Reason to complain. .... 2.ChJM.205.24.
No creature smarts so little as a Fool. .... 4.Arbu.84.101.

SMEAR'D
There, on rude Iron Columns smear'd with Blood, ... 2.TemF.125.264.
Next his grim idol smear'd with human blood; .... 3.EOM3.266.119.
Smear'd with the bloody Rites, he stands on high, ... Il.23.218.498.

SMEDLEY
Next Smedley div'd; slow circles dimpled o'er .... 5.DunA2.279.135.
All look, all sigh, and call on Smedley lost; .... 5.DunA2.281.136.
Smedley in vain resounds thro' all the coast. .... 5.DunA2.282.136.
Lo Smedley rose, in majesty of mud! .... 5.DunA2.302.139.
Next Smedley div'd; slow circles dimpled o'er .... 5.DunB2.291.309.
All look, all sigh, and call on Smedley lost; .... 5.DunB2.293.310.
Smedley in vain resounds thro' all the coast. .... 5.DunB2.294.310.

SMELL
At once they gratifie their Smell and Taste, ... 2.RL*A*1.95.130.
Of smell, the headlong lioness between, ... 3.EOM1.213.41.
Painted for sight, and essenc'd for the smell, ... 4.JD4.226.45.
Myrtles have lost their balmy smell, ... 6.4iv.7.10.
Can smell a Plaister, or an Issue. .... 6.135.32.367.

SMELLING
Woolwich and *Wapping,* smelling strong of Pitch; .... 6.14ii.47.44.

SMIL'D
And Virgins *smil'd* at what they *blush'd* before— .... 1.EOC.543.299.
And danc'd around, and smil'd on ev'ry Knight: .... 2.ChJM.330.30.
If I but smil'd, a sudden Youth they found, ... 2.ChWB.66.59.
Belinda smil'd, and all the World was gay. .... 2.RL2.52.162.
She smil'd to see the doughty Hero slain, ... 2.RL5.69.206.
You rais'd these hallow'd walls; the desert smil'd, ... 2.ElAb.133.330.
When the *Queen* frown'd, or smil'd, he knows; and what .... 4.JD4.132.37.
If wrong, I smil'd; if right, I kiss'd the rod. .... 4.Arbu.158.107.
Who prais'd my Modesty, and smil'd. .... 4.1HE7.68.273.
Smiling on all, and smil'd on by a Queen. .... 5.DunB4.506.392.
"And take (she said, and smil'd serene) .... 6.140.3.378.
The Sire of Gods and Men superior smil'd, ... Il.5.517.293.
Silent the Warrior smil'd, and pleas'd resign'd .... Il.6.504.351.

SMIL'D (CONTINUED)
With secret Pleasure each fond Parent smil'd, ... Il.6.598.356.
Grimly he smil'd; Earth trembled as he strode: .... Il.7.256.377.
And smil'd superior on his Best-belov'd. .... Il.8.48.398.
He spake, and smil'd severe, for well he knew .... Il.14.557.190.
The Sire, superior smil'd; and bade her show, ... Il.21.593.446.
Achilles smil'd: The Gift propos'd (he cry'd) .... Il.23.637.515.
Alike their leaves, but not alike they smil'd .... Od.5.618.201.
And youthful smil'd; but in the low disguise .... Od.7.27.235.
Youth smil'd celestial, with each opening grace. .... Od.10.332.360.

SMILE
If *Delia* smile, the Flow'rs begin to spring, ... 1.PSp.71.68.
Amaze th'unlearn'd, and make the Learned *Smile.* .... 1.EOC.327.275.
My scornful Brother with a Smile appears, ... 1.TrSP.135.399.
But at her Smile, the Beau reviv'd again. .... 2.RL5.70.206.
"The King would smile on you—at least the Queen?" .... 4.JD4.89.33.
He past it o'er; affects an easy Smile .... 4.JD4.122.35.
He past it o'er; put on an easy Smile .... 4.JD4.122A.35.
Care, if a livery'd Lord or smile or frown? .... 4.JD4.197.43.
Let but the Ladies smile, and they are blest; .... 4.JD4.254.47.
Poor guiltless I! and can I chuse but smile, ... 4.Arbu.281.116.
Make Languor smile, and smooth the Bed of Death, ... 4.Arbu.411.127.
(Should Ripley venture, all the World would smile) .... 4.2HE1.186.211.
Th' engaging Smile, the Gaiety, ... 4.1HE7.46.271.
Could please at Court, and make AUGUSTUS smile: .... 4.EpS1.20.299.
Could please at Court, and made AUGUSTUS smile: .... 4.EpS1.20A.299.
Smile without Art, and win without a Bribe. .... 4.EpS1.32.300.
Where *Lillies* smile in virgin robes of white, ... 6.14iv.5.47.
Then smile Belinda at reproachful tongues, ... 6.38.25.108.
Glow in thy heart, and smile upon thy face. .... 6.86.14.245.
If wrong, I smile; if right, I kiss the Rod. .... 6.98.8.283.
Make Languor smile, and smooth the Bed of Death. .... 6.117.6.333.
And smile propitious, and unbend thy Bow. .... Il.1.597.116.
Which, with a Smile, the white-arm'd Queen receiv'd. .... Il.1.767.124.
Juno and *Pallas* with a Smile survey'd, ... Il.5.507.292.
Smile on the Slaughter, and enjoy my Woe. .... Il.5.947.311.
Hush'd to Repose, and with a Smile survey'd. .... Il.6.619.357.
She mingled with the Smile a tender Tear. .... Il.6.621.357.
(*Ulysses,* with a scornful Smile, replies) .... Il.10.472.24.
(Th' immortal Father with a Smile replies!) .... Il.15.54.196.
Then (while a Smile serenes his awful Brow) .... Il.15.178.203.
Thus she, and *Juno* with a Smile approv'd. .... Il.21.505.442.
Smile on the Sun; now, wither on the Ground: .... Il.21.540.444.
No more to smile upon his Sire! no Friend .... Il.22.622.482.
Constrain'd a smile, and thus ambiguous spoke. .... Od.1.490.55.
And thus deriding, with a smile addrest. .... Od.2.340.77.
Is it, ye pow'rs that smile at human harms! .... Od.11.255.394.
Make the sage frolic, and the serious smile, ... Od.14.521.62.
Thus with a transient smile the matron cries. .... Od.18.194.176.
The Chief indignant grins a ghastly smile; .... Od.20.370.250.
The Suitors with a scornful smile survey .... Od.21.407.279.

SMILES
If *Sylvia* smiles, new Glories gild the Shore, ... 1.PSp.75.68.
With pleasing Smiles to view the God-like Man; .... 1.TrUl.161.471.
Repairs her Smiles, awakens ev'ry Grace, ... 2.RL1.141.157.
Favours to none, to all she Smiles extends, ... 2.RL2.11.160.
The Smiles of Harlots, and the Tears of Heirs, ... 2.RL5.120.209.
Or failing, smiles in exile or in chains, ... 3.EOM4.234.148.
Earth smiles around, with boundless bounty blest, ... 3.EOM4.371.164.
Or drest in smiles of sweet Cecilia shine, ... 3.Ep2.13.49.
Eternal Smiles his Emptiness betray, ... 4.Arbu.315.118.
As who knows Sapho, smiles at other whores. .... 4.JD2.6.133.
The Goddess smiles on Whig and Tory race, ... 5.DunA3.284.183.
Our Goddess smiles on Whig and Tory race, ... 5.DunA3.284A.183.
The *Smiles* and *Loves* had dy'd in *Voiture's* Death, ... 6.19.19.62.
Pleas'd while with Smiles his happy Lines you view, ... 6.19.75.64.
Each pleasing *Blount* shall endless smiles bestow, ... 6.52.61.158.
The play full smiles around the dimpled mouth .... 6.75.1.211.
As these Dear Smiles to me. .... 6.78i.8.215.
Smiles on the Vomit, and enjoys the Purge. .... 6.82x.6.236.
M[oo]re always smiles whenever he recites; .... 6.105ii.1.300.
He smiles (you think) approving what he writes; .... 6.105ii.2.300.
The *Greeks* with Smiles the polish'd Trophy view. .... Il.3.464.214.
Led by the Goddess of the Smiles and Loves. .... Il.3.524.216.
Sweet Smiles are thine and kind endearing Charms, ... Il.5.521.293.
And calls the Mother of the *Smiles* and *Loves.* .... Il.14.218.171.
With Smiles she took the Charm; and smiling prest .... Il.14.255.173.
Smiles on her Lips a spleenful Joy exprest, ... Il.15.111.200.
But you, when Fortune smiles, when *Jove* declares .... Il.17.384.302.
The scornful Dame her Conquest views with Smiles, ... Il.21.476.441.
The *Smiles* and *Love's* unconquerable Queen! .... Il.21.493.441.
Stern winter smiles on that auspicious clime: .... Od.4.769.155.
Him, while he spoke, with smiles *Calypso* ey'd, ... Od.5.233.182.
With pleasing smiles to view the god-like man. .... Od.13.328.23.
Steals on his Sire a glance, and secret smiles. .... Od.16.497.131.
With smiles receiving, on his scrip he lay'd. .... Od.17.429.153.
The Peers with smiles addrest their unknown King: .... Od.18.136.173.
Hides fraud in smiles, while death is ambush'd there. .... Od.18.200.176.
Smiles dew'd with tears the pleasing strife exprest .... Od.19.550.223.

SMILING
The smiling Infant in his Hand shall take .... 1.Mes.81.120.
Rich Industry sits smiling on the Plains, ... 1.W-F.41.152.
Her smiling babe (a pleasing charge) she prest .... 1.TrFD.19.386.
The beauteous Dame sate smiling at the Board, ... 2.ChJM.341.30.
Here smiling *Loves* and *Bacchanals* appear, ... 2.TemF.228.273.
Those smiling eyes, attemp'ring ev'ry ray, ... 2.ElAb.63.324.
Love, Hope, and Joy, fair pleasure's smiling train, ... 3.EOM2.117.69.
Where Age and Want sit smiling at the gate: .... 3.Ep3.266.115.
Shall call the smiling Loves, and young Desires; .... 4.HOde1.26.153.
Shall call the smiling Loves, and soft Desires; .... 4.HOde1.26A.153.
And smiling, whispers to the next, ... 4.HS6.52.253.
Yet smiling at his rueful length of face) .... 5.DunA2.134.115.
And the pleas'd dame soft-smiling leads away. .... 5.DunA2.180.123.

SMILING (CONTINUED)
And the pleas'd dame soft-smiling lead'st away. ....5.DunA2.180A.123.
Yet smiling at his rueful length of face) ....5.DunB2.142.302.
And the pleas'd dame, soft-smiling, lead'st away. ....5.DunB2.188.304.
When Dulness, smiling—"Thus revive the Wits! ....5.DunB4.119.353.
The Sire saw, smiling, his own Virtues wake: ....5.DunB4.285A.372.
The Goddess smiling seem'd to give consent; ....5.DunB4.395.381.
Smiling on all, and smil'd on by a Queen. ....5.DunB4.506.392.
As smiling Infants sport themselves to Rest: ....6.19.14.62.
As smiling Infants sport themselves to Sleep. ....6.19.14A.62.
Or views his smiling progeny; ....6.51ii.32.153.
His only Hope hung smiling at her Breast, ...Il.6.497.351.
And last with Flour the smiling Surface strows. ....Il.11.783.70.
With Smiles she took the Charm; and smiling prest ....Il.14.255.173.
She ceas'd, and smiling with superior Love, ...Il.14.387.181.
The smiling Scene wide opens to the Sight, ...Il.16.360.257.
And smiling, thus the wat'ry Queen address'd. ....Il.18.452.343.
(Fair Maids, and blooming Youths) that smiling bear ....Il.18.659.355.
Minerva smiling heard, the Pair o'ertook, ...Il.21.496.442.
A happier lot the smiling fates decree: ....Od.4.762.155.
And smiling thus, the royal Youth address'd: ....Od.4.830.158.
When the gay morn unveils her smiling ray: ....Od.6.36.206.
And smiling thus bespoke the blooming maid. ....Od.6.82.209.
O envy'd shame! (the smiling Youth rejoin'd,) ....Od.8.377.284.
And smiling calmness silver'd o'er the deep. ....Od.10.108.345.
The King with smiling looks his joy exprest, ...Od.14.136.42.
And smiling round celestial Youth attends. ....Od.15.353.86.
I follow'd smiling, innocent of harm. ....Od.15.502.94.
And Poverty look'd smiling in my sight. ....Od.17.506.157.
And sow'rly smiling, this reply returns. ....Od.17.544.159.
The smiling Queen the happy omen blest: ....Od.17.626.163.

SMINTHEUS
O *Smintheus!* sprung from fair *Latona's* Line, ...Il.1.53.88.

SMIT
Smit with her varying plumage, spare the dove? ....3.EOM3.54.97.
Smit with the mighty pleasure, to be seen: ....3.Ep4.128.149.
Smit with his mien, the Mud-nymphs suck'd him in: ....5.DunA2.308.139.
And smit with love of Poesy and Prate. ....5.DunA2.350.143.
Smit with his mien, the Mud-nymphs suck'd him in: ....5.DunB2.332.313.
And smit with love of Poesy and Prate. ....5.DunB2.382.316.
Smit with the love of Sister-arts we came, ...6.52.13.156.
Smit with his Countrey's Love, I've heard him prate ....6.96v.9.280.
And smit with Love of Honourable Deeds. ....Il.1.354.105.
Smit with a conscious Sense, retires behind, ...Il.3.45.190.
Thus to their Bulwarks, smit with Panick, Fear, ...Il.22.1.452.
Smit with the signs which all his doubts explain, ...Od.24.401.368.

SMITE
See! what the charms, that smite the simple heart ....5.DunA3.227.176.
See what the charms, that smite the simple heart ....5.DunB3.229.331.
There the revenging sword shall smite them all; ....Od.22.479.312.

SMITES
He smites the Steeds; the rapid Chariot flies; ....Il.22.503.477.

SMITH
(Who are to me both *Smith* and *Johnson)* .... 6.10.35.25.
More, shrunk to *Smith—and* Smith's no name at all. ....6.116iv.4.327.
The dextrous smith the tools already drew: ....Od.3.549.114.

SMITH'S
More, shrunk to *Smith—and* Smith's no name at all. ....6.116iv.4.327.

SMITHFIELD
The Smithfield Muses to the Ear of Kings. ....5.DunA1.2.59.
Should wag two serpent tails in Smithfield fair. ....5.DunA3.290.184.
The Smithfield Muses to the ear of Kings, ...5.DunB1.2.267.
Should'st wag a serpent-tail in Smithfield fair! ....5.DunB3.288.334.

SMOAK
See SMOKE.
The rowling Ruins smoak along the Field. ....1.TrES.132.454.
Till their proud Navy wrapt in Smoak and Fires, ...Il.8.222.407.
The rowling Ruins smoak along the Field. ....Il.12.486.99.
And Sheets of Smoak mount heavy to the Poles. ....Il.17.830.321.
Let his last Spirit smoak upon my Dart; ....Il.18.120.328.
Obscure in Smoak, his Forges flaming round, ...Il.18.436.341.
The Waters foam, the heavy Smoak aspires: ....Il.21.427.438.
(A wider Compass) smoak along the Road. ....Il.22.194.463.
Then Clouds of Foot that smoak along the Plain; ....Il.23.163.495.
Some smoak I saw amid the forest rise, ...Od.10.225.351.

SMOAK'D
And lo! two puddings smoak'd upon the board. ....3.Ep3.360.123.
His gushing Entrails smoak'd upon the Ground, ...Il.4.608.250.
What Altar smoak'd not with our Victims Gore? ....Il.8.287.411.
While the black Vessels smoak'd with human Gore. ....Il.16.2.233.
Their equal pace, and smoak'd along the field. ....Od.3.615.117.

SMOAK'ED
The *Spartan* Hero's Chariot smoak'ed along. ....Il.23.502.510.

SMOAKING
Or smoaking forth, a hundred Hawkers load, ...4.Arbu.217.111.
The stream, and smoaking, flourish'd o'er his head. ....5.DunA2.172.122.
His Eye-Balls burn, he wounds the smoaking Plain, ...6.9ix.1.22.
And *Troy's* proud Walls lie smoaking on the Ground. ....Il.4.333.236.
And roll in smoaking Volumes to the Skies. ....Il.5.620.297.
The smoaking Steel, *Mars* bellows with the Pain: ....Il.5.1053.316.
The Victim falls, they strip the smoaking Hide, ...Il.7.382.382.
Each from the Yoke the smoaking Steeds unty'd, ...Il.8.675.427.
Above the Coals the smoaking Fragments turns, ...Il.9.281.447.
And twelve lay smoaking on the *Trojan* Plain: ....Il.9.433.453.
Defends him breathless on the smoaking Field, ...Il.11.333A.49.

SMOAKING (CONTINUED)
And roll'd the smoaking Entrails to the Ground. ....Il.13.643.136.
Shall sink beneath us, smoaking on the Ground; ....Il.13.1030.153.
And best Defence, lies smoaking on the Ground: ....Il.14.64.160.
And best Defence, lies smoaking in the Dust; ....Il.14.74.161.
The Coursers fly; the smoaking Chariot bounds: ....Il.15.403.212.
Plung'd in his Throat the smoaking Weapon lies; ....Il.16.398.258.
The trembling Limbs, and sucks the smoaking Blood; ....Il.16.603.267.
And see his Jaws distil with smoaking Gore; ....Il.17.72.290.
Warm'd in the Brain the smoaking Weapon lies, ...Il.20.551.417.
Black bloody Drops the smoaking Chariot die: ....Il.20.584.418.
Release your smoaking Coursers from the Car; ....Il.23.10.486.
The smoaking Chariots, rapid as they bound, ...Il.23.445.508.
Shall sink, a smoaking Ruin on the Plain. ....Il.24.917.574.
With smoaking thighs, and offering to the God. ....Od.3.12.87.
Averse, beholds the smoaking sacrifice; ....Od.9.646.333.
And smoaking back the tasteful viands drew, ...Od.14.90.40.
And o'er the coals the smoaking fragments lays. ....Od.15.113.74.

SMOAKLESS
Tenants with sighs the smoakless tow'rs survey, ...3.Ep3.193.109.

SMOAKS
Now Smoaks with Show'rs the misty Mountain-Ground, ...1.TrSt.498.431.
Drives the swift Steeds; the Chariot smoaks along. ....Il.8.191.406.
The Horses fly; the Chariot smoaks along. ....Il.11.360.50.
Still gath'ring Force, it smoaks; and, urg'd amain, ...Il.13.197.115.
Smoaks in the Dust, and ploughs into the Ground. ....Il.14.480.187.
Black from the Blow, and Smoaks of Sulphur rise; ....Il.14.484.187.
Smoaks thro' the Ranks, o'ertakes the flying War, ...Il.16.461.260.
Thunders impetuous down, and smoaks along the ground. ....Od.11.738.422.

SMOAKY
But in a smoaky Cloud the God of Fire ....Il.5.31.267.
And whelms the smoaky Ruin in the Waves. ....Il.12.32.82.
And Heaps on Heaps the smoaky Ruins fall. ....Il.12.308.92.
Then swift as Wind, o'er *Lemnos* smoaky Isle, ...Il.14.317.178.
But smoaky volumes rolling from the ground. ....Od.10.114.346.
And sweep with equal strokes the smoaky seas; ....Od.10.150.347.

SMOCK
As *Flavia's* diamonds with her dirty smock, ...3.Ep2.24A.51.
As Sappho's diamonds with her dirty smock, ...3.Ep2.24.51.
Did ever Smock-face act so vile a Part? ....4.Arbu.326A.119.
And wear a cleaner Smock. ....6.14v(a).6.48.

SMOCK-FACE
Did ever Smock-face act so vile a Part? ....4.Arbu.326A.119.

SMOCKS
They use white Powder, and wear Holland-Smocks. ....6.95.4.264.

SMOK'D
And all the cavern smok'd with streaming blood. ....Od.11.46.381.
When *Troy's* proud bulwarks smok'd upon the ground, ...Od.11.652.416.

SMOKE
See SMOAK.
The Seas shall waste; the Skies in Smoke decay; ....1.Mes.105.122.
Her Fanes no more with Eastern Incense smoke, ...1.TrSt.371.425.
Let Altars blaze and Temples smoke for her; ....1.TrSt.374.425.
And fill thy Temples with a grateful Smoke: ....1.TrSt.595.435.
Sulphureous Flames, and Clouds of rolling Smoke: ....2.TemF.339.280.
Where spices smoke beneath the burning Line, ...5.DunA3.62.155.
Where spices smoke beneath the burning Line, ...5.DunB3.70.323.
Let Altars smoke, and Hecatombs be paid. ....Il.1.88.91.
Now vanish'd like their Smoke: The Faith of Men! ....Il.2.407.147.
Shall fill thy Temple with a grateful Smoke. ....Il.6.383.345.
And Sheets of rolling Smoke involve the Skies. ....Il.16.153.243.
Flew to the Fleet, involv'd in Fire and Smoke. ....Il.16.331.255.
Clear'd from the Smoke the joyful Navy lies; ....Il.16.350.256.
And *Hector's* Blood shall smoke upon thy Lance. ....Il.21.343.435.
Like a thin Smoke he sees the Spirit fly, ...Il.23.117.492.
To see the smoke from his lov'd palace rise, ...Od.1.75.34.
A yearling bullock to thy name shall smoke, ...Od.3.490.111.
His batter'd brains shou'd on the pavement smoke. ....Od.9.540.328.
A stream of curling smoke ascending blue, ...Od.10.174.349.
O'erwhelm'd it sinks: while round a smoke expires, ...Od.12.81.435.
Where rouls yon smoke, yon tumbling ocean raves; ....Od.12.261.445.
Sulphureous odors rose, and smould'ring smoke. ....Od.12.492.456.
Obscene with smoke, their beamy lustre lost, ...Od.19.10.193.
In clouds of smoke, rais'd by the noble fray, ...Od.24.55.350.

SMOKES
While curling Smokes from Village-Tops are seen, ...1.PAu.63.84.
The rowling smokes involve the sacrifice. ....5.DunA1.206.87.
The rowling smokes involve the sacrifice. ....5.DunB1.248.288.
And Metaphysic smokes involve the Pole. ....5.DunB4.248.368.
The Fires are kindled, and the Smokes ascend; ....Il.2.475.149.
The Smokes high-curling to the shaded Skies; ....Il.18.246.334.
Now from the well-fed Swine black Smokes aspire, ...Il.23.39.488.
Smokes, nor as yet the sullen Flames arise; ....Il.23.237.499.
Beheld the Flames and rolling Smokes arise. ....Il.24.998.577.
Streams the black blood, and smokes upon the ground. ....Od.3.581.116.
And from their mountains rising smokes appear. ....Od.9.194.313.
His blood in vengeance smokes upon my spear. ....Od.16.457.129.
I see the smokes of sacrifice aspire, ...Od.17.322.147.
Feed the rich smokes, high-curling to the skies. ....Od.21.283.273.

SMOKING
The trembling Limbs, and sucks the smoking Blood; ....1.TrES.298.460.
While *China's* Earth receives the smoking Tyde. ....2.RL3.110.176.
And *China's* Earth receives the smoking Tyde. ....2.RL3.110A.176.
The stream, and smoking flourish'd o'er his head. ....5.DunB2.180.304.
While smoking Streams from Silver Spouts shall glide, ...6.82i.3.229.
While smoking Streams from Silver Spouts shall flow, ...6.82i.3A.229.

SMOKING 328 SNATCH

SMOKING (CONTINUED)
Nor ever from our smoking Altar ceast ....Il.24.91.539.
I see the Ruins of your smoking Town! ....Il.24.306.425.549.
An ample vase receives the smoking wave, ...Od.10.425.365.
Thunder'd the deeps, the smoking billows roll'd! ....Od.12.241.443.
And oft *Ulysses* smoking victims laid. ....Od.22.374.306.

SMOKY
Driv'n from the Land before the smoky Cloud, ...Il.21.16.422.

SMOOTH
Be smooth ye Rocks, ye rapid Floods give way! ....1.Mes.36.116.
And *smooth* or *rough,* with them, is *right* or *wrong;* .... 1.EOC.338.277.
And *smooth* or *rough,* with such, is *right,or wrong;* .... 1.EOC.338A.277.
What's *roundly smooth,* or *languishingly slow;* .... 1.EOC.359.280.
And the *smooth Stream* in *smoother Numbers* flows; ....1.EOC.367.282.
And smooth as shells that gliding waters wear; ....1.TrPA.55.367.
Venus for thee shall smooth her native Main. ....1.TrSP.251.404.
With shining Ringlets the smooth Iv'ry Neck. ....2.RL2.22.160.
With shining Ringlets her smooth Iv'ry Neck. ....2.RL2.22A.160.
Smooth flow the Waves, the Zephyrs gently play, ...2.RL2.51.162.
As on the smooth Expanse of Chrystal Lakes, ...2.TemF.436.284.
And smooth my passage to the realms of day: ....2.ElAb.322.345.
The Courtier smooth, who forty years had shin'd ....3.Ep1.252.37.
Let *Carolina* smooth the tuneful Lay, ...4.HS1.30.7.
Make Languor smile, and smooth the Bed of Death, ...4.Arbu.411.127.
I learn to smooth and harmonize my Mind, ...4.2HE2.203.179.
Waller was smooth; but Dryden taught to join ....4.2HE1.267.217.
Wafts the smooth Eunuch and enamour'd swain. ....5.DunB4.310.374.
Direct each step, and smooth the path to Heaven. ....6.21.28.70.
A *Chrysostom* to smooth thy Band in: ....6.39.12.110.
Make Languor smile, and smooth the Bed of Death. ....6.117.6.333.
"You'd write as smooth again on glass, ...6.140.21.378.
Cut down it lies, tall, smooth, and largely spread, ...Il.4.556.248.
While the smooth Chariot cuts the liquid Sky. ....Il.5.927.310.
Smooth as the sailing Doves they glide along. ....Il.5.971.313.
Smooth glides the Chariot thro' the liquid Sky. ....Il.8.477.419.
Raz'd the smooth Cone, and thence obliquely glanc'd. ....Il.11.454.54.
As smooth of Face as fraudulent of Mind! ....Il.13.966.151.
Smooth-gliding without Step, above the Heads, ...Il.20.375.410.
With dissonance, the smooth melodious strain. ....Od.1.472.55.
Let neither flatt'ry smooth, nor pity hide. ....Od.3.115.91.
With unguents smooth the lucid marble shone, ...Od.3.520.112.
The smooth-hair'd horses, and the rapid car, ...Od.3.605.117.
Now sailing smooth the level surface sweep, ...Od.5.66.175.
And double-edg'd; the handle smooth and plain, ...Od.5.301.185.
Then glassy smooth lay all the liquid plain, ...Od.5.501.196.
Some smooth ascent, or safe-sequester'd bay. ....Od.5.561.199.
Sleek the smooth skin, and scent the snowy limbs. ....Od.6.94.209.
Shape the broad sail, or smooth the taper oar; ....Od.6.320.226.
Descends smooth-gliding from the Courts of *Jove,* .... Od.8.330.281.
The sea's smooth face, and cleave the hoary deep; ....Od.9.116.308.
Neptune's smooth face, and cleave the yielding deep. ....Od.9.210.314.
To smooth the deep, or swell the foamy sea. ....Od.10.24.340.
They went, and kept the wheel's smooth-beaten road ....Od.10.117.346.
Fix the smooth oar, and bid me live to fame. ....Od.11.97.385.
Smooth flows the gentle stream with wanton pride, ...Od.11.285.396.
Skill'd in smooth tales, and artful to deceive, ...Od.11.453.406.
Smooth as the polish of the mirrour rise ....Od.12.97.436.
Smooth seas, and gentle winds, invite him home. ....Od.13.8.2.
O'er thy smooth skin a bark of wrinkles spread, ...Od.13.457.28.
To smooth thy passage, and supply thy sails: ....Od.15.42.71.
A smooth-tongu'd sailor won her to his mind; ....Od.15.462.93.
Six calmy days and six smooth nights we sail, ...Od.15.511.94.
Thus smooth he ended, yet his death conspir'd: ....Od.16.464.129.
With unguents smooth, of polisht marble wrought; ....Od.17.99.136.
Who smooth of tongue, in purpose insincere, ...Od.18.199.176.

SMOOTH-BEATEN
They went, and kept the wheel's smooth-beaten road ....Od.10.117.346.

SMOOTH-GLIDING
Smooth-gliding without Step, above the Heads, ...Il.20.375.410.
Descends smooth-gliding from the Courts of *Jove,* .... Od.8.330.281.

SMOOTH-HAIR'D
The smooth-hair'd horses, and the rapid car, ...Od.3.605.117.

SMOOTH-TONGU'D
A smooth-tongu'd sailor won her to his mind; ....Od.15.462.93.

SMOOTH'D
Smooth'd ev'ry brow, and open'd ev'ry soul: ....4.2HE1.248.217.
'Twas form'd of Horn, and smooth'd with artful Toil; ....Il.4.137.227.
Now smooth'd with Sand, and levell'd by the Flood, ...Il.12.33.82.
(For God had smooth'd the waters of the deep) ....Od.3.190.95.
He smooth'd, and squar'd 'em, by the rule and line. ....Od.5.316.186.
Some Demon calm'd the Air, and smooth'd the deep, ...Od.12.204.441.
(Smooth'd by the workman to a polish'd plain) ....Od.17.416.152.
Sever'd the bole, and smooth'd the shining grain; ....Od.23.200.333.

SMOOTHER
And the *smooth Stream* in *smoother Numbers* flows; ....1.EOC.367.282.

SMOOTHLY
So sweetly warble, or so smoothly flow. ....1.PWi.4.89.
Now smoothly steers through Air his equal Flight, ...1.TrSt.439.428.
So sweetly mawkish, and so smoothly dull; ....5.DunA3.165.167.
So sweetly mawkish, and so smoothly dull; ....5.DunB3.171.328.
Chim'd in so smoothly, one by one, ...6.30.11.86.
To run so smoothly, one by one ....6.30.11A.86.
She smoothly gliding swims th' harmonious round, ...Od.18.230.178.

SMOOTHS
Smooths the rough Wood, and levels ev'ry Part; ....Il.15.475.215.
Before the wand'rer smooths the wat'ry way, ...Od.5.578.200.

SMOTE
Smote ev'ry Brain, and wither'd ev'ry Bay; ....5.DunB4.10.340.
And smote him on the Ear. ....6.79.60.219.
Smote by the Arm of *Jove,* and dire Dismay, ...Il.12.41.83.
Smote by the Arm of *Jove,* with dire Dismay, ...Il.12.41A.83.
And smote his Temples, with an Arm so strong ....Il.13.729.139.
Smote his rebelling Breast, and fierce begun. ....Il.15.127.201.
And smote his Thigh, and thus aloud exclaims. ....Il.16.155.244.
He spoke, and smote the loud-resounding Shield, ...Il.21.464.440.
Smote on his Knee; the hollow Cuishes rung ....Il.21.700.450.

SMOTH'RING
And all in clouds of smoth'ring sulphur lost. ....Od.14.340.51.

SMOTHER
Could they these *Rabbits* smother; ....6.94.82.262.

SMOTHERS
O'ertakes the flying boy, and smothers half his words. ....1.TrPA.147.372.

SMOULD'RING
Sulphureous odors rose, and smould'ring smoke. ....Od.12.492.456.
Imbrown'd with vapor of the smould'ring flame. ....Od.19.22.193.

SMUT
Or Spite, or Smut, or Rymes, or Blasphemies. ....4.Arbu.322.119.

SMUTTY
While all your smutty sisters walk the streets. ....5.DunB1.230.287.

SNACKS
At last he whispers "Do, and we go snacks." ....4.Arbu.66.100.

SNAKE
The crested Basilisk and speckled Snake; ....1.Mes.82.120.
That like a wounded Snake, drags its slow length along. ....1.EOC.357.280.
High on her Crown a rising Snake appears, ...1.TrSt.708.439.
High on a Crown a rising Snake appears, ...1.TrSt.708A.439.
As many Birds as by the Snake were slain, ...Il.2.394.145.
So roll'd up in his Den, the swelling Snake ....Il.22.130.458.

SNAKES
There hateful *Envy* her own Snakes shall feel, ...1.W-F.419.193.
Her Snakes, unty'd, Sulphureous Waters drink; ....1.TrSt.125.415.
A hundred Snakes her gloomy Visage shade, ...1.TrSt.144.416.
Now glaring Fiends, and Snakes on rolling Spires, ...2.RL4.43.187.
List'ning *Envy* drops her Snakes; ....6.11.33.31.
And list'ning *Envy* drops her Snakes; ....6.11.33A.31.
And Snakes uncurl'd hang list'ning round their Heads. ....6.11.70.32.
Why start you? are they Snakes? or have they Claws? ....6.96iv.16.276.
With horrors arm'd, and curls of hissing snakes, ...Od.11.786.425.

SNAKY
A Hiss from all the Snaky Tire went round; ....1.TrSt.162.417.

SNAP
And Snip-snap short, and Interruption smart. ....5.DunA2.232.128.
And Snip-snap short, and Interruption smart, ...5.DunB2.240.307.
And, when they think not of you—snap! ....6.135.18.366.

SNAPPISH
The snappish Cur, (the Passengers annoy) ....6.14ii.19.43.

SNAPT
Then snapt his box, and strok'd his belly down: ....5.DunB4.495.391.
And snapt the spinal joint, and wak'd in hell. ....Od.10.668.375.
Snapt the strong helm, and bore to sea the mast. ....Od.12.499.456.

SNARE
Is mark'd to perish in a deathful snare: ....Od.4.929.161.
Thus on some tree hung struggling in the snare, ...Od.22.505.313.

SNARES
To his immortal dome the finish'd snares. ....Od.8.320.281.
In vain they strive, th' entangling snares deny ....Od.8.341.282.
Then to the snares his force the God applies; ....Od.8.393.285.
For thee their snares the Suitor Lords shall lay ....Od.15.33.71.
To shun the hidden snares of death, and live. ....Od.16.385.124.
To my lov'd son the snares of death to show, ...Od.18.197.176.
Helpless amid the snares of death I tread, ...Od.18.273.179.
When the wide field extended snares beset, ...Od.22.339.303.

SNATCH
And *snatch* a *Grace* beyond the Reach of Art, ...1.EOC.155.258.
Say, shall I snatch him from Impending Fate; ....1.TrES.232.458.
Snatch me, just mounting, from the blest abode, ...2.ElAb.287.343.
Snatch from his hand the balance and the rod, ...3.EOM1.121.30.
When half our knowledge we must snatch, not take. ....3.Ep1.34.18.
What will it leave me, if it snatch my Rhime? ....4.2HE2.77.171.
Glad, like a Boy, to snatch the first good day, ...4.2HE2.294.185.
And snatch me, o'er the earth, or thro' the air, ...4.2HE1.346.225.
Th' unbalanc'd Mind, and snatch the Man away; ....4.1HE6.25.239.
I'll stretch my arm, and snatch him to my breast. ....6.21.38.70.
Snatch to thy Holy Hill of Spotless Bay, ...6.155.7.404.
And dar'st thou threat to snatch my Prize away, ...Il.1.213.97.
and kind Embraces snatch the hasty Joy. ....Il.3.550.217.
Haste, seize the Whip, and snatch the guiding Rein; ....Il.5.284.280.
And snatch the Glory from his lifted Lance. ....Il.10.438.23.
Say, shall I snatch him from impending Fate, ...Il.16.535.264.
Whether to snatch him from impending Fate, ...Il.22.230.465.
Should snatch the Glory from his lifted Lance, ...Il.22.268.466.
By Stealth to snatch him from th' insulting Foe: ....Il.24.35.536.
Howe'er by Stealth to snatch the Corse away, ...Il.24.93.539.
O snatch the Moments yet within thy Pow'r, ...Il.24.167.542.
Oh snatch some portion of these acts from fate, ...Od.1.13.29.
And snatch their oars, and rush into the deep. ....Od.9.554.328.

SNATCH (CONTINUED)
Snatch me, ye whirlwinds! far from humane race, ...Od.20.74.236.

SNATCH'D
And snatch'd the starting Serpents from the Ground. ....1.TrSt.127.415.
Sudden these Honours shall be snatch'd away, ...2.RL3.103.175.
Which snatch'd my best, my fav'rite Curl away! ....2.RL4.148.196.
A sudden Cloud strait snatch'd them from my Sight, ...2.TemF.354.280.
Strait chang'd the Scene, and snatch'd me from the Throne. ...2.TemF.419.283.
Fancy restores what vengeance snatch'd away, ...2.ElAb.226.338.
Fate snatch'd her early to the pitying sky. ....2.Elegy.24.364.
And now, on rolling Waters snatch'd away. ....4.HOde1.48.153.
And now, by rolling Waters snatch'd away. ....4.HOde1.48A.153.
Then snatch'd a sheet of Thulè from her bed; ....5.DunA1.214.89.
That suit, an unpaid Taylor snatch'd away! ....5.DunA2.110.110.
Then * * try'd, but hardly snatch'd from sight, ...5.DunA2.283.136.
H[ill] try'd the next, but hardly snatch'd from sight, ...5.DunA2.283A.136.
Then snatch'd a sheet of Thulè from her bed, ...5.DunB1.258.289.
That suit an unpay'd taylor snatch'd away. ....5.DunB2.118.301.
And snatch'd them in Cœlestial fire. ....6.69ii.4.199.
Now for two ages having snatch'd from fate ....6.108.3.312.
When now two Ages, he had snatch'd from Fate ....6.108.3A.312.
Depriv'd his Eyes, and snatch'd his Voice away; ....Il.2.728.160.
As if some God had snatch'd their Voice away. ....Il.4.489.243.
She snatch'd the Reins, she lash'd with all her Force, ...Il.5.1034.316.
The Monarch spoke: the Warriors snatch'd with haste ....Il.7.454.387.
Now had the *Grecians* snatch'd a short Repaste, ...Il.8.67.398.
Then rushing from his Tent, he snatch'd in hast ....Il.10.154.8.
One Instant snatch'd his trembling Soul to Hell, ...Il.10.526.26.
Snatch'd from devouring Hounds, a slaughter'd Fawn, ...Il.13.266.117.
Swift as the Word bold *Merion* snatch'd a Spear, ...Il.13.382.123.
A Slings soft Wool, snatch'd from a Soldier's side, ...Il.13.751.140.
Then snatch'd a Lance, and issu'd from the Door. ....Il.14.16.157.
From frantic *Mars* she snatch'd the Shield and Spear; ....Il.15.143.202.
Clouds rise on Clouds, and Heav'n is snatch'd from sight. ....Il.16.451.260.
He snatch'd the Fury-Goddess of Debate, ...Il.19.126.377.
Whom Heaven enamour'd snatch'd to upper Air, ...Il.20.279.406.
That done, with Force divine, he snatch'd on high ....Il.20.373.410.
Snatch'd from his Hope, the Glories of the Day. ....Il.23.466.509.
For ever snatch'd from our desiring Eyes! ....Il.23.710.518.
And snatch'd the Reins, and whirl'd the Lash around: ....Il.24.542.558.
Snatch'd in thy Bloom from these desiring Eyes! ....Il.24.909.574.
Now snatch'd by Harpies to the dreary coast, ...Od.1.309.47.
Already snatch'd by Fate, and the black doom of death! ....Od.3.300.100.
Too early snatch'd by fate ere known to me! ....Od.4.279.132.
A moment snatch'd the shining form away, ...Od.5.448.194.
Snatch'd from *Epirus,* her sweet native shore, ...Od.7.12.233.
Snatch'd two, unhappy! of my martial band; ....Od.9.343.320.
Snatch'd in the whirl, the hurried navy flew, ...Od.10.52.342.
Her six mouths yawn, and six are snatch'd away. ....Od.12.155.439.
Now snatch'd by Harpies to the dreary coast, ...Od.14.407.55.
Snatch'd for his beauty to the thrones above: ....Od.15.273.82.
Snatch'd thee an infant from thy native land! ....Od.15.411.89.
Snatch'd from thy parents arms, thy parents eyes, ...Od.15.412.89.
But snatch'd by pyrates from my native place, ...Od.15.468.93.
So snatch'd from all our cares!—Tell, hast thou known ....Od.17.54.135.
Wing'd *Harpies* snatch'd th' unguarded charge away, ...Od.20.92.237.
He snatch'd the shaft that glitter'd on the board: ....Od.21.455.282.
The Bow he snatch'd, and in an instant bent; ....Od.24.201.358.

SNATCHES
Snatches the Reins, and vaults into the Seat. ....Il.17.549.309.
Snatches his Life amid the Clouds of Air. ....Il.17.766.318.
And hasty, snatches from the rising Blaze. ....Il.24.791.570.
Two more he snatches, murders, and devours. ....Od.9.369.321.

SNEAK
Patrons, who sneak from living worth to dead, ...5.DunB4.95.350.

SNEAK'D
So K[ent] so B[erkeley] sneak'd into the grave, ...5.DunB4.511.392.

SNEAKING
Con. Philips cries, "A sneaking Dog I hate." ....4.HAdv.11.75.
When Int'rest calls off all her sneaking Train, ...6.84.31.239.
Tho' Int'rest calls off all her sneaking Train, ...6.84.31Z3.239.
Thus thou may'st help the sneaking Elf: ....6.116ii.7.326.

SNEAKS
Will sneaks a Scriv'ner, and exceeding knave: ....3.Ep1.106.22.

SNEER
Lost the arch'd eye-brown, or *Parnassian* sneer? ....4.Arbu.96.102.
And without sneering, teach the rest to sneer; ....4.Arbu.202.110.
Did not the Sneer of more impartial men ....4.EpS1.59.302.
N[ewcastle] laugh, or D[orset] sager [sneer] ....4.1740.61.335*.
Great Tibbald sate: The proud Parnassian sneer, ...5.DunA2.5.97.
Great Tibbald nods: The proud Parnassian sneer, ...5.DunA2.5A.97.
Great Cibber sate: the proud Parnassian sneer, ...5.DunB2.5.296.
And without sneering, teach the rest to sneer; ....6.49iii.16.143.
And without sneering, teach the rest to sneer; ....6.98.52.284.

SNEERING
And without sneering, teach the rest to sneer; ....4.Arbu.202.110.
Lo sneering G[oo]de, half malice and half whim, ...5.DunA3.147.163.
Lo sneering Goode, half malice and half whim, ...5.DunB3.153.327.
And without sneering, teach the rest to sneer; ....6.49iii.16.143.
And without sneering, teach the rest to sneer; ....6.98.52.284.

SNEERS
Sneers at another, in toupee or gown; ....5.DunB4.88.349.

SNEEZ'D
She spoke, *Telemachus* then sneez'd aloud; ....Od.17.624.162.

SNIP
And Snip-snap short, and Interruption smart. ....5.DunA2.232.128.
And Snip-snap short, and Interruption smart, ...5.DunB2.240.307.

SNIP-SNAP
And Snip-snap short, and Interruption smart. ....5.DunA2.232.128.
And Snip-snap short, and Interruption smart, ...5.DunB2.240.307.

SNOR'D
The lumpish Husband snor'd away the Night, ...2.ChJM.420.35.

SNORE
To the same notes thy sons shall hum, or snore, ...5.DunB4.59.347.

SNORES
Where Tindal dictates, and Silenus snores." ....5.DunB4.492.390.

SNORING
Dropt his huge head, and snoring lay supine. ....Od.9.440.324.

SNORT
But snort and tremble at the Gulph beneath; ....Il.12.58.83.

SNORTED
The fiery Coursers snorted at his side. ....Il.4.263.233.

SNOW
Thus Trees are crown'd with Blossoms white as Snow, ...2.ChJM.133.21.
And melt down Ancients like a heap of snow: ....4.2HE1.65.199.
And heavy harvests nod beneath the snow. ....5.DunA1.76.68.
And heavy harvests nod beneath the snow. ....5.DunB1.78.275.
Mount in dark volumes, and descend in snow. ....5.DunB2.364.315.
And scatter ore the Fields the driving Snow, ...6.82v.2.231.
To great *Olympus* crown'd with fleecy Snow. ....Il.1.551.114.
Where *Titan* hides his hoary Head in Snow, ...Il.2.894.166.
Swift as the Wind, and white as Winter-Snow: ....Il.10.507.26.
Swift as the Wind, and white as Winter-Snow. ....Il.10.601.29.
And from their Sides the Foam descends in Snow; ....Il.11.362.50.
Beneath the low-hung Clouds the Sheets of Snow ....Il.12.177.87.
O'er their huge Limbs the Foam descends in Snow, ...Il.13.883.147.
And seems a moving Mountain topt with Snow. ....Il.13.948.150.
Than new fal'n Snow, and dazling as the Light. ....Il.14.214.170.
And scatter o'er the Fields of driving Snow; ....Il.19.381.388.
Beneath the Shades of *Tmolus,* crown'd with Snow, ...Il.20.443.413.
Mold the round hail, or flake the fleecy snow; ....Od.4.772.155.
The hand of Time had silver'd o'er with snow, ...Od.11.429.405.
Sharp blew the North; snow whitening all the fields ....Od.14.536.63.
A team of twenty geese, (a snow-white train!) ....Od.19.627.226.

SNOW-WHITE
A team of twenty geese, (a snow-white train!) ....Od.19.627.226.

SNOWIE
Once gave new Beauties to the snowie Neck. ....2.RL4.170.198.
The snowie Fleece, and wind the twisted Wool.) ....Il.3.478.214.
As down thy snowie Thigh distill'd the streaming Flood. ....Il.4.177.229.
Her snowie Hand the razing Steel profan'd, ...Il.5.419.287.
While the fat Herds and snowie Flocks they fed, ...Il.6.536.353.

SNOWS
Th' Eternal Snows appear already past, ...1.EOC.227.265.
Eternal Snows the growing Mass supply, ...2.TemF.57.256.
The freezing Tanais thro' a waste of Snows, ...5.DunA3.80.156.
Mid snows of paper, and fierce hail of pease; ....5.DunA3.258.179.
The freezing Tanais thro' a waste of snows, ...5.DunB3.88.324.
'Mid snows of paper, and fierce hail of pease; ....5.DunB3.262.332.
Amidst *Rhodope's* Snows: ....6.11.109.34.
Soft as the Fleeces of descending Snows ....Il.3.284.207.
Her Arms whose Whiteness match the falling Snows. ....Il.5.390.285.
Her Arms whose Whiteness match'd the falling Snows. ....Il.5.390A.285.
Or sends soft Snows to whiten all the Shore, ...Il.10.7.2.
O'er *Hæmus'* Hills with Snows eternal crown'd; ....Il.14.261.173.
Swift as the rat'ling Hail, or fleecy Snows ....Il.15.192.204.
Like Crystal clear, and cold as Winter-Snows. ....Il.22.200.463.
As snows collected on the mountain freeze; ....Od.19.238.205.

SNOWY
And snowy Mountains thy bright Presence boast; ....1.TrSt.830.444.
The snowy Fleece; he tost, and shook in Air: ....1.TrES.188.456.
Parrhasia, on her snowy Cliffs reclin'd, ...Il.2.737.161.
O'er her fair Face a snowy Veil she threw, ...Il.3.187.200.
There with her snowy Hand the Queen restrains ....Il.5.940.311.
So decent Urns their snowy Bones may keep, ...Il.7.402.384.
Till with a snowy Veil he screen'd the Blaze. ....Il.8.549.422.
Ulysses now the snowy Steeds detains, ...Il.10.582.28.
Their snowy Limbs and beauteous Bodies lie. ....Il.11.136.41.
And nurs'd in *Thrace* where snowy Flocks are fed. ....Il.11.286.48.
A Snowy Inundation hides the Plain; ....Il.12.334.93.
The snowy Fleece, he toss'd, and shook in Air: ....Il.12.542.101.
The pow'rful *Cestus* to her snowy Breast. ....Il.14.256.173.
Lifts the gay Head, in snowy Flourets fair, ...Il.17.59.290.
Swift from *Olympus'* snowy Summit flies, ...Il.18.711.357.
And from *Olympus'* snowy Tops descends. ....Il.24.156.542.
The snowy Bones his Friends and Brothers place ....Il.24.1003.577.
In snowy waves flow'd glitt'ring on the ground. ....Od.5.298.185.
No rains descend, no snowy vapours rise; ....Od.6.52.207.
The snowy fleece, or twist the purpled wool. ....Od.6.64.208.
Sleek the smooth skin, and scent the snowy limbs. ....Od.6.94.209.
Their snowy lustre whitens all the strand.) ....Od.6.108.211.
Forth from her snowy hand *Nausicaa* threw ....Od.6.133.213.
Stretch'd out her snowy hand, and thus she spoke: ....Od.11.417.405.
We then collect thy snowy bones, and place ....Od.24.93.352.

SNUFF
Snuff, or the *Fan,* supply each Pause of Chat, ...2.RL3.17.170.
(*Sir Plume,* of *Amber Snuff-box* justly vain, ...2.RL4.123.194.

SNUFF (CONTINUED)

He first the Snuff-box open'd, then the Case, ... 2.RL4.126.194.
A Charge of *Snuff* the wily Virgin threw; .... 2.RL5.82.206.
And Beaus' in *Snuff-boxes* and *Tweezer-Cases.* .... 2.RL5.116.209.
My Wig all powder, and all snuff my Band; .... 4.1HE1.162.291.
Snuff just three Times, and read again.) .... 6.10.66.26.
And, like true *Sevil* Snuff, awake the Brain. .... 6.48iv.8.136.
The pack impatient snuff the tainted gale; .... Od.19.507.221.

SNUFF-BOX

(*Sir Plume,* of *Amber Snuff-box* justly vain, ... 2.RL4.123.194.
He first the Snuff-box open'd, then the Case, ... 2.RL4.126.194.

SNUFF-BOXES

And Beaus' in *Snuff-boxes* and *Tweezer-Cases.* .... 2.RL5.116.209.

SNUFFS

He snuffs the Females in the distant Plain, ... Il.6.658.360.
He snuffs the Females in the well known Plain, ... Il.15.304.208.
Too late returning, snuffs the Track of Men, ... Il.18.374.339.

SNUG

How here he sipp'd, how there he plunder'd snug .... 5.DunB1.129.279.

SNUG'S

"For Snug's the word: My dear! we'll live in Town." .... 4.1HE1.147.289.

SO

So when the Nightingale to Rest removes, ... 1.PSp.13.61.
Why sit we sad, when *Phosphor* shines so clear, ... 1.PSp.27.63.
Blest Nymphs, whose Swains those Graces sing so well! .... 1.PSp.96.70.
Are half so charming as thy Sight to me. .... 1.PAu.46.83.
So dies her Love, and so my Hopes decay. .... 1.PAu.70.85.
So dies her Love, and so my Hopes decay. .... 1.PAu.70.85.
Is not so mournful as the Strains you sing, ... 1.PWi.2.88.
So sweetly warble, or so smoothly flow. .... 1.PWi.4.89.
So sweetly warble, or so smoothly flow. .... 1.PWi.4.89.
So may kind Rains their vital Moisture yield, ... 1.PWi.15.89.
The silver Flood, so lately calm, appears .... 1.PWi.65.93.
The Groves of *Eden,* vanish'd now so long, ... 1.W-F.7.148.
Not half so swift the trembling Doves can fly, ... 1.W-F.185.167.
Not half so swiftly the fierce Eagle moves, ... 1.W-F.187.167.
No Seas so rich, so gay no Banks appear, ... 1.W-F.225.170.
No Seas so rich, so gay no Banks appear, ... 1.W-F.225.170.
No Lake so gentle, and no Spring so clear. .... 1.W-F.226.170.
No Lake so gentle, and no Spring so clear. .... 1.W-F.226.170.
Nor *Po* so swells the fabling Poet's Lays, ... 1.W-F.227.170.
No Seas so rich so full no Streams appear, ... 1.W-F.225A.170.
No Seas so rich so full no Streams appear, ... 1.W-F.225A.170.
So by *false Learning* is *good Sense* defac'd; .... 1.EOC.25.241.
Their Generation's so *equivocal:* .... 1.EOC.43.243.
So *vast* is Art, so *narrow* Human Wit: .... 1.EOC.61.246.
So *vast* is Art, so *narrow* Human Wit: .... 1.EOC.61.246.
So modern *Pothecaries,* taught the Art .... 1.EOC.108.251.
Nor Time nor Moths e'er spoil'd so much as they: .... 1.EOC.113.252.
In Praise so just, let ev'ry Voice be join'd, ... 1.EOC.187.262.
So pleas'd at first, the towring *Alps* we try, ... 1.EOC.225.265.
Our Author, happy in a Judge so nice, ... 1.EOC.273.270.
Not so by Heav'n (he answers in a Rage) .... 1.EOC.281.271.
So vast a Throng the Stage can ne'er contain. .... 1.EOC.283.271.
The Stage can ne'er so vast a Throng contain. .... 1.EOC.283A.271.
What oft was *Thought,* but ne'er so well *Exprest,* .... 1.EOC.298.273.
So modest Plainness sets off sprightly Wit: .... 1.EOC.302.273.
Such *labour'd Nothings,* in so *strange* a Style, ... 1.EOC.326.275.
And but so mimick ancient Wits at best, ... 1.EOC.331.276.
Not so, when swift *Camilla* scours the Plain, ... 1.EOC.372.282.
So much they scorn the Crowd, that if the Throng .... 1.EOC.426.288.
So Schismatics the *plain Believers* quit, ... 1.EOC.428.288.
We think our *Fathers* Fools, so *wise* we grow; .... 1.EOC.438.288.
Our *wiser Sons,* no doubt, will think *us* so. .... 1.EOC.439.288.
So Schismatics the *dull Believers* quit, ... 1.EOC.428A.288.
So when the faithful *Pencil* has design'd .... 1.EOC.484.293.
If *Wit* so much from *Ign'rance* undergo, ... 1.EOC.508.295.
Ah ne'er so *dire* a *Thirst of Glory* boast, ... 1.EOC.522.297.
Who, if *once wrong,* will needs be *always so;* .... 1.EOC.569.305.
That, if *once wrong,* will needs be *always so;* .... 1.EOC.569A.305.
Nor be so *Civil* as to prove *Unjust;* .... 1.EOC.581.306.
For who can *rail* so long as they can *write?* .... 1.EOC.599.308.
And *lash'd* so long, like *Tops,* are lash'd *asleep.* .... 1.EOC.601.308.
No Place so Sacred from such Fops is barr'd, ... 1.EOC.622.310.
Know from whose arms you fly so fast away. .... 1.TrPA.67.368.
So great the tale, I scarce can count them o'er; .... 1.TrPA.80.368.
I'm not so monst'rous; I my face did view .... 1.TrPA.96.369.
Is half so mighty, half so large, my love; .... 1.TrPA.100.369.
Is half so mighty, half so large, my love; .... 1.TrPA.100.369.
So bulls in forests hunt their absent loves, ... 1.TrPA.134.371.
Oh crown so constant and so pure a Fire! .... 1.TrVP.105.381.
Oh crown so constant and so pure a Fire! .... 1.TrVP.105.381.
So may no Frost, when early Buds appear, ... 1.TrVP.108.381.
Such, and so bright an Aspect now he bears, ... 1.TrVP.114.381.
That wandring Heart which I so lately lost; .... 1.TrSP.66.396.
And still increase the Woes so soon begun? .... 1.TrSP.72.397.
So from my Birth the *Sisters* fix'd my Doom, ... 1.TrSP.91.397.
Not Him, who made me love those Shades so well, ... 1.TrSP.168A.400.
This Breast which once, in vain! you lik'd so well; .... 1.TrSP.226.403.
Not half so swiftly shoots along in Air .... 1.TrSt.128.415.
So fares a Sailor on the stormy Main, ... 1.TrSt.520.432.
Behold him here, for whom, so many Days, ... 1.TrSt.763.442.
So prest with Hunger, from the Mountain's Brow, ... 1.TrES.13.450.
So stalks the Lordly Savage o'er the Plain, ... 1.TrES.15.450.
So falls *Epicles;* then in Groans expires, ... 1.TrES.109.453.
So Conquest loth for either to declare, ... 1.TrES.171.455.
So stood the War, till *Hector's* matchless Might .... 1.TrES.171Z1.455.
Not so *Patroclus* never-erring Dart; .... 1.TrES.285.460.
So lyes a Bull beneath the Lion's Paws, ... 1.TrES.296.460.
So mounts the bounding Vessel o'er the Main: .... 1.TrUl.10.465.

SO (CONTINUED)

For so the Gods ordain'd, to keep unseen .... 1.TrUl.60.468.
So seldom view'd, and ever in Disguise. .... 1.TrUl.190.472.
So spake the Goddess, and the Prospect clear'd, ... 1.TrUl.234.473.
But what so pure, which envious Tongues will spare? .... 2.ChJM.43.17.
His Friends were summon'd, on a Point so nice, ... 2.ChJM.81.18.
So may my Soul arrive at Ease and Rest, ... 2.ChJM.154.22.
Th'assuming Wit, who deems himself so wise .... 2.ChJM.162.22.
Pleasing to God, and shou'd be so to Man; .... 2.ChJM.169.23.
Her will I wed, if gracious Heav'n so please; .... 2.ChJM.262.27.
Now shou'd the Nuptial Pleasures prove so great, ... 2.ChJM.272.27.
And to my fervent Pray'rs so far consent, ... 2.ChJM.280.27.
So said they rose, nor more the Work delay'd; .... 2.ChJM.299.28.
(So Poets sing) was present on the Place; .... 2.ChJM.327.30.
So kind a Bridegroom, or so bright a Bride. .... 2.ChJM.334.30.
So kind a Bridegroom, or so bright a Bride. .... 2.ChJM.334.30.
E're look'd so lovely on her *Persian* King: .... 2.ChJM.344.30.
So keen he was, and eager to possess: .... 2.ChJM.374.32.
Then briskly sprung from Bed, with Heart so light, ... 2.ChJM.385.33.
Argus himself, so cautious and so wise, ... 2.ChJM.505.39.
Argus himself, so cautious and so wise, ... 2.ChJM.505.39.
So many an honest Husband may, 'tis known, ... 2.ChJM.506.40.
So may my Soul have Joy, as thou, my Wife, ... 2.ChJM.545.41.
It so befel, in that fair Morning-tide, ... 2.ChJM.617.45.
So featly tripp'd the light-foot Ladies round, ... 2.ChJM.620.45.
The Knights so nimbly o'er the Greensword bound, ... 2.ChJM.621.45.
So may some Wildfire on your Bodies fall, ... 2.ChJM.641.46.
And will you so, reply'd the Queen, indeed? .... 2.ChJM.656.46.
And so has mine, (she said)—I am a Queen! .... 2.ChJM.705.48.
O for that tempting Fruit, so fresh, so green; .... 2.ChJM.722.49.
O for that tempting Fruit, so fresh, so green; .... 2.ChJM.722.49.
But when he saw his Bosome-Wife so drest, ... 2.ChJM.752.51.
So Heav'n preserve the Sight it has restor'd, ... 2.ChJM.768.52.
So help me Fates, as 'tis no perfect Sight, ... 2.ChJM.776.52.
Wretch that I am, that e'er I was so Kind! .... 2.ChJM.782.52.
So just recov'ring from the Shades of Night, ... 2.ChJM.802.54.
None judge so wrong as those who think amiss. .... 2.ChJM.810.54.
To be so well deluded by their Wives. .... 2.ChJM.820.54.
I, for a few slight Spots, am not so nice. .... 2.ChWB.39.58.
But by your Leave, Divines, so am not I. .... 2.ChWB.45.58.
For so said *Paul,* and *Paul's* a sound Divine. .... 2.ChWB.55.59.
To lye so boldly as we Women can. .... 2.ChWB.71.59.
Whence is our Neighbour's Wife so rich and gay? .... 2.ChWB.75.60.
Why to her House do'st thou so oft repair? .... 2.ChWB.78.60.
Art thou so Am'rous? and is she so fair? .... 2.ChWB.79.60.
Art thou so Am'rous? and is she so fair? .... 2.ChWB.79.60.
Art thou so Amorous? Is she so fair? .... 2.ChWB.79A.60.
Art thou so Amorous? Is she so fair? .... 2.ChWB.79A.60.
There swims no Goose so gray, but, soon or late, ... 2.ChWB.98.61.
What? so familiar with your Spouse? I cry'd: .... 2.ChWB.167.64.
"Of *Job's* great Patience since so oft you preach, ... 2.ChWB.186.65.
"Well shou'd you practise, who so well can teach. .... 2.ChWB.187.65.
But I so drest, and danc'd, and drank, and din'd; .... 2.ChWB.233.68.
And view'd a Friend, with Eyes so very kind, ... 2.ChWB.234.68.
So bless the good Man's Soul, I say no more. .... 2.ChWB.252.69.
It so befell, in Holy Time of *Lent,* .... 2.ChWB.277.70.
We grew so intimate, I can't tell how, ... 2.ChWB.292.71.
Of Legs and Feet, so clean, so strong, so fair! .... 2.ChWB.316.72.
Of Legs and Feet, so clean, so strong, so fair! .... 2.ChWB.316.72.
Of Legs and Feet, so clean, so strong, so fair! .... 2.ChWB.316.72.
And wou'd be so, in spight of all he swore. .... 2.ChWB.340.73.
And so do Numbers more, I'll boldly say, ... 2.ChWB.353.74.
Slight is the Subject, but not so the Praise, ... 2.RL1.5.144.
In Tasks so bold, can Little Men engage, ... 2.RL1.11.145.
So Ladies in Romance assist their Knight, ... 2.RL3.129.177.
So long my Honour, Name, and Praise shall live! .... 2.RL3.170.182.
Who speaks so well shou'd ever speak in vain. .... 2.RL4.132.194.
But *Umbriel,* hateful *Gnome!* forbears not so; .... 2.RL4.141.196.
Not half so fixt the *Trojan* cou'd remain, ... 2.RL5.5.199.
So spoke the Dame, but no Applause ensu'd; .... 2.RL5.35.201.
So when bold *Homer* makes the Gods engage, ... 2.RL5.45.202.
Those Eyes are made so killing—*was* his last: .... 2.RL5.64.205.
Rather than so, ah let me still survive, ... 2.RL5.101.207.
Not fierce *Othello* in so loud a Strain .... 2.RL5.105.208.
So Heav'n decrees! with Heav'n who can contest? .... 2.RL5.112.208.
(So *Rome's* great Founder to the Heav'ns withdrew, ... 2.RL5.125.210.
Not *Berenice's* Locks first rose so bright, ... 2.RL5.129.210.
So *Zembla's* Rocks (the beauteous Work of Frost) .... 2.TemF.53.256.
So large it spread, and swell'd to such a Height. .... 2.TemF.247.275.
So soft, tho high, so loud, and yet so clear, ... 2.TemF.374.281.
So soft, tho high, so loud, and yet so clear, ... 2.TemF.374.281.
So soft, tho high, so loud, and yet so clear, ... 2.TemF.374.281.
So from a Spark, that kindled first by Chance, ... 2.TemF.475.286.
And long 'twas doubtful, both so closely pent, ... 2.TemF.491.287.
For who so fond as youthful Bards of Fame? .... 2.TemF.502.288.
So hard to gain, so easy to be lost: .... 2.TemF.504.288.
So hard to gain, so easy to be lost: .... 2.TemF.504.288.
But if the Purchase costs so dear a Price, ... 2.TemF.515.289.
For hearts so touch'd, so pierc'd, so lost as mine. .... 2.ElAb.196.336.
For hearts so touch'd, so pierc'd, so lost as mine. .... 2.ElAb.196.336.
For hearts so touch'd, so pierc'd, so lost as mine. .... 2.ElAb.196.336.
Such if there be, who loves so long, so well; .... 2.ElAb.363.348.
Such if there be, who loves so long, so well; .... 2.ElAb.363.348.
So flew the soul to its congenial place, ... 2.Elegy.27.365.
So perish all, whose breast ne'er learn'd to glow .... 2.Elegy.45.366.
So peaceful rests, without a stone, a name, ... 2.Elegy.69.368.
Why form'd so weak, so little, and so blind! .... 3.EOM1.36.18.
Why form'd so weak, so little, and so blind! .... 3.EOM1.36.18.
Why form'd so weak, so little, and so blind! .... 3.EOM1.36.18.
Why made so weak, so little, and so blind! .... 3.EOM1.36A.18.
Why made so weak, so little, and so blind! .... 3.EOM1.36A.18.
Why made so weak, so little, and so blind! .... 3.EOM1.36A.18.
And all the question (wrangle e'er so long) .... 3.EOM1.49.19.
So Man, who here seems principal alone, ... 3.EOM1.57.20.
The blest today is as completely so, ... 3.EOM1.75.23.
26.And he that's bless'd to day, as fully so, ... 3.EOM1.75A.23.

SO (CONTINUED)

So justly all proportion'd to each state; .... 3.EOM1.183B.37.
Say what th' advantage of so fine an Eye .... 3.EOM1.195B.39.
Or touch, so tremblingly alive all o'er, ... 3.EOM1.197C.39.
In the nice bee, what sense so subtly true .... 3.EOM1.219.42.
So, cast and mingled with his very frame, ... 3.EOM2.137.71.
So, when small humors gather to a gout, ... 3.EOM2.159.74.
80.Tho' oft so mix'd, the difference is too nice .... 3.EOM2.209A.81.
And oft so mix, the diff'rence is too nice .... 3.EOM2.209.81.
Ask your own heart, and nothing is so plain; .... 3.EOM2.215.81.
Vice is a monster of so frightful mien, ... 3.EOM2.217.81.
The hour conceal'd, and so remote the fear, ... 3.EOM3.75.99.
So from the first eternal ORDER ran, ... 3.EOM3.113.103.
So drives Self-love, thro' just and thro' unjust, ... 3.EOM3.269.120.
The less, or greater, set so justly true, ... 3.EOM3.291.122.
The less, and greater, set so justly true, ... 3.EOM3.291A.122.
So two consistent motions act the Soul; .... 3.EOM3.315.126.
Which still so near us, yet beyond us lies, ... 3.EOM4.5.128.
Or why so long (in life if long can be) .... 3.EOM4.109.138.
But still this world (so fitted for the knave) .... 3.EOM4.131.140.
Thy boasted Blood, a thousand years or so, ... 3.EOM4.207A.146.
Nor own, your fathers have been fools so long. .... 3.EOM4.214.147.
Not own, your fathers have been fools so long. .... 3.EOM4.214A.147.
To sigh for ribbands if thou art so silly, ... 3.EOM4.277.154.
Without satiety, tho' e'er so blest, ... 3.EOM4.317.158.
(So Darkness fills the eye no less than Light) .... 3.Ep1.112A.23.
The coxcomb bird, so talkative and grave, ... 3.Ep1.5.15.
Others so very close, they're hid from none; .... 3.Ep1.111.23.
(So Darkness strikes the sense no less than Light) .... 3.Ep1.112.23.
Shall parts so various aim at nothing new? .... 3.Ep1.186.31.
Nothing so true as what you once let fall, ... 3.Ep2.1.46.
So morning Insects that in muck begun, ... 3.Ep2.27.52.
Yet ne'er so sure our passion to create, ... 3.Ep2.51.54.
So Philomed“e, lect'ring all mankind .... 3.Ep2.83.57.
No Ass so meek; no Ass so obstinate: .... 3.Ep2.102.58.
No Ass so meek, no Ass so obstinate: .... 3.Ep2.102.58.
So much the Fury still out-ran the Wit, ... 3.Ep2.127.61.
So very reasonable, so unmov'd, ... 3.Ep2.165.64.
So very reasonable, so unmov'd, ... 3.Ep2.165.64.
That Robe of Quality so struts and swells, ... 3.Ep2.189.65.
Weakness or Delicacy; all so nice, ... 3.Ep2.205.67.
In Youth they conquer, with so wild a rage, ... 3.Ep2.221.68.
So these their merry, miserable Night; .... 3.Ep2.240.69.
So when the Sun's broad beam has tir'd the sight, ... 3.Ep2.253.70.
Blest paper-credit! that advanc'd so high! .... 3.Ep3.69A.93.
(Whom with a wig so wild, and mien so maz'd, ... 3.Ep3.51.90.
(Whom with a wig so wild, and mien so maz'd, ... 3.Ep3.51.90.
Or soft Adonis, so perfum'd and fine, ... 3.Ep3.61.91.
To live on Ven'son when it sold so dear. .... 3.Ep3.120.101.
"(So long by watchful Ministers withstood) .... 3.Ep3.138.104.
Not so his Son, he mark'd this oversight, ... 3.Ep3.199.109.
"What all so wish, but want the pow'r to do! .... 3.Ep3.276.116.
Religious, punctual, frugal, and so forth; .... 3.Ep3.343.122.
So kept the Diamond, and the rogue was bit. .... 3.Ep3.364.123.
"And am so clear too of all other vice." .... 3.Ep3.368.123.
There (so the Dev'l ordain'd) one Christmas-tide .... 3.Ep3.383.124.
My Lady falls to play; so bad her chance, ... 3.Ep3.395.124.
So proud, so grand, of that stupendous air, ... 3.Ep4.101.147.
So proud, so grand, of that stupendous air, ... 3.Ep4.101.147.
So quick retires each flying course, you'd swear .... 3.Ep4.159.153.
And swear no Day was ever past so ill. .... 3.Ep4.168.153.
Fools rush into my Head, and so I write. .... 4.HS1.14.5.
But touch me, and no Minister so sore. .... 4.HS1.76.13.
So drink with *Waters*, or with *Chartres* eat, ... 4.HS1.89.13.
So drink with Walters, or with *Chartres* eat, ... 4.HS1.89B.13.
Laws are explain'd by Men—so have a care. .... 4.HS1.144.19.
Yet went to COURT!—the Dev'l wou'd have it so. .... 4.JD4.14.27.
So was I punish'd, as if full as *proud*, ... 4.JD4.19.27.
So Time, that changes all things, had ordain'd! .... 4.JD4.43.29.
These I cou'd bear; but not a Rogue so civil, ... 4.JD4.56.29.
Good common Linguists, and so *Panurge* was: .... 4.JD4.75.31.
Till I cry'd out, "You prove yourself so able, ... 4.JD4.82.33.
"For had they found a Linguist half so good, ... 4.JD4.84.33.
"Ah gentle Sir! you Courtiers so cajol us— .... 4.JD4.90.33.
"So much *alone*, (to speak plain Truth between us) .... 4.JD4.90A.33.
"And coarse of Phrase—your *English* all are so. .... 4.JD4.109.35.
"Oh! Sir, politely so! nay, let me dye, ... 4.JD4.112.35.
So when you plague a Fool, 'tis still the Curse, ... 4.JD4.120.35.
As the fair Fields they sold to look so fine. .... 4.JD4.217.45.
So weak a Vessel, and so rich a Prize! .... 4.JD4.229.45.
So weak a Vessel, and so rich a Prize! .... 4.JD4.229.45.
And " *sweet Sir Fopling!* you have so much wit!" .... 4.JD4.233.45.
The *Presence* seems, with things so richly odd, ... 4.JD4.238.45.
So first to preach a white-glov'd Chaplain goes, ... 4.JD4.250.47.
Frighted, I quit the Room, but leave it so, ... 4.JD4.272.49.
Courts are too much for Wits so weak as mine; .... 4.JD4.280.49.
Courts are no match for Wits so weak as mine; .... 4.JD4.280A.49.
Till *Becca-ficos* sold so dev'lish dear .... 4.HS2.39.57.
Is what two souls so gen'rous cannot bear; .... 4.HS2.58.59.
Not so: a Buck was then a week's repast, ... 4.HS2.93.61.
Not so, who of Ten Thousand gull'd her Knight, ... 4.HAdv.7.75.
Yet starves herself, so little her own Friend, ... 4.HAdv.23.77.
Nothing in Nature is so lewd as *Peg*, ... 4.HAdv.31.77.
Nothing so mean for which he can't run mad; .... 4.HAdv.64.81.
To all defects, *Ty[rawle]y* not so blind: .... 4.HAdv.121.85*.
All for a Thing you ne're so much as *saw?* .... 4.HAdv.136.87.
"The little Scut he so pursu'd before, ... 4.HAdv.138.87.
So *B[athurs]t* cries, Philosopher and Rake! .... 4.HAdv.158.89.
The Queen of *Midas* slept, and so may I. .... 4.Arbu.82.101.
No creature smarts so little as a Fool. .... 4.Arbu.84.101.
"Just so immortal *Maro* held his head:" .... 4.Arbu.122.104.
And he, whose Fustian's so sublimely bad, ... 4.Arbu.187.109.
And so obliging that he ne'er oblig'd; .... 4.Arbu.208.110.
Poems I heeded (now be-rym'd so long) .... 4.Arbu.221.111.
So, when a Statesman wants a Day's defence, ... 4.Arbu.251.114.
Oh let me live my own! and die so too! .... 4.Arbu.261.114.

SO (CONTINUED)

There let me live my own, and die so too, ... 4.Arbu.263A.114.
So well-bred Spaniels civilly delight .... 4.Arbu.313.118.
Did ever Smock-face act so vile a Part? .... 4.Arbu.326A.119.
The Tale reviv'd, the Lye so oft o'erthrown; .... 4.Arbu.350.121.
The Tales of Vengeance; Lyes so oft o'erthrown; .... 4.Arbu.350A.121.
So humble, he has knock'd at *Tibbald's* door, ... 4.Arbu.372.123.
One supreme State, so excellently ill; .... 4.JD2A.4.132.
So vast our best Divines, we must confess, ... 4.JD2A.100.140.
So *Luther* thought the *Pater noster* long, ... 4.JD2A.111.142.
One Giant-Vice, so excellently ill, ... 4.JD2.4.133.
So prompts, and saves a Rogue who cannot read. .... 4.JD2.16.133.
Those write because all write, and so have still .... 4.JD2.27.133.
Curs'd be the Wretch! so venal and so vain; .... 4.JD2.63.139.
Curs'd be the Wretch! so venal and so vain; .... 4.JD2.63.139.
And steal so little, few perceive they steal; .... 4.JD2.84.141.
So vast, our new Divines, we must confess, ... 4.JD2.97.141.
So Luther thought the Paternoster long, ... 4.JD2.105.143.
So prompts, and saves some Rogue who cannot read. .... 4.JD2.16A.133.
So the learnd Bard that starves with all his Sence .... 4.JD2A.17.134.
Well let Them pass and so may those that use .... 4.JD2A.41.136.
Language so harsh, 'tis sure enough to tear .... 4.JD2A.65.138.
Nor *Satans* self shall joy so much as hee .... 4.JD2A.92.140.
Why words so flowing, thoughts so free, ... 4.HOde1.39.153.
Why words so flowing, thoughts so free, ... 4.HOde1.39.153.
Cou'd you complain, my Friend, he prov'd so bad? .... 4.2HE2.22.165.
But knottier Points we knew not half so well, ... 4.2HE2.58.169.
Not quite so well however as one ought; .... 4.2HE2.100.171.
So stiff, so mute! some Statue, you would swear, ... 4.2HE2.121.173.
So stiff, so mute! some Statue, you would swear, ... 4.2HE2.121.173.
Then polish all, with so much life and ease, ... 4.2HE2.176.177.
A man so poor wou'd live without a *Place:* .... 4.2HE2.287.185.
Has Life no sourness, drawn so near its end? .... 4.2HE2.316.187.
And each true Briton is to Ben so civil, ... 4.2HE1.41.197.
Shall we, or shall we not, account him so, ... 4.2HE1.51.199.
And, having once been wrong, will be so still. .... 4.2HE1.130.207.
Or what remain'd, so worthy to be read .... 4.2HE1.137.207.
I, who so oft renounce the Muses, lye, ... 4.2HE1.175.209.
Had he beheld an Audience gape so wide. .... 4.2HE1.321.223.
Let Bear or Elephant be e'er so white, ... 4.2HE1.322.223.
Yet think great Sir! (so many Virtues shown) .... 4.2HE1.376.227.
So well in paint and stone they judg'd of merit: .... 4.2HE1.384.227.
"To make men happy, and to keep them so." .... 4.1HE6.2.237.
So take it in the very words of *Creech.]* .... 4.1HE6.4.237.
If not so pleas'd, at Council-board rejoyce, ... 4.1HE6.34.239.
So known, so honour'd, at the House of Lords; .... 4.1HE6.49.239.
So known, so honour'd, at the House of Lords; .... 4.1HE6.49.239.
For, mark th' advantage; just so many score .... 4.1HE6.77.241.
Rather than so, see Ward invited over, ... 4.1HE6.56A.241.
So Russel did, but could not eat at night, ... 4.1HE6.115.245.
It is but so much more in debt, ... 4.HS6.41.253.
"So eager to express your love, ... 4.HS6.57.253.
Because they see me us'd so well: .... 4.HS6.102.257.
"My Lord and he are grown so great, ... 4.HS6.105.257.
Once on a time (so runs the Fable) .... 4.HS6.157.259.
"To eat so much—but all's so good. .... 4.HS6.209.263.
"To eat so much—but all's so good. .... 4.HS6.209.263.
"This same Dessert is not so pleasant: .... 4.HS6.221.263.
And kept you up so oft till one; .... 4.1HE7.48.271.
Observing, cry'd, "You scape not so, ... 4.1HE7.57.271.
So bought an Annual Rent or two. .... 4.1HE7.71.273.
So slow th' unprofitable Moments roll, ... 4.1HE1.39.281.
But to the world, no bugbear is so great, ... 4.1HE1.67.283.
But wretched Bug, his *Honour*, and so forth. .... 4.1HE1.90.285.
Bestia and Bug, Their *Honours*, and so forth. .... 4.1HE1.90A.285.
But Bug and D[e]l[orain], Their *Honours*, and so forth. .... 4.1HE1.90B.285*.
Who know themselves so little what to do? .... 4.1HE1.123.289.
Transform themselves so strangely as the Rich? .... 4.1HE1.153.291.
Is half so incoherent as my Mind, ... 4.1HE1.166.291.
If any ask you, "Who's the Man, so near .... 4.EpS1.45.301.
So much the better, you may laugh the more. .... 4.EpS1.56.302.
So *Latin*, yet so *English* all the while, ... 4.EpS1.74.304.
So *Latin*, yet so *English* all the while, ... 4.EpS1.74.304.
So—Satire is no more—I feel it die— .... 4.EpS1.83.304.
F. Why so? if Satire know its Time and Place, ... 4.EpS1.87.305.
And so may'st Thou, Illustrious *Passeran!* .... 4.EpS1.124.307.
Feign what I will, and paint it e'er so strong, ... 4.EpS2.8.313.
Fr. Then why so few commended? P. Not so fierce& .... 4.EpS2.104.319.
Fr. Then why so few commended? P. Not so fierce& .... 4.EpS2.104.319.
P. I only call those Knaves who are so now. .... 4.EpS2.127.320.
Quite turns my Stomach— *P.* So does Flatt'ry mine; .... 4.EpS2.182.323.
Fr. You're strangely proud. *P.* So proud I am no Slave: .... 4.EpS2.205.324.
So impudent, I own myself no Knave: .... 4.EpS2.206.324.
So odd, my Country's Ruin makes me grave. .... 4.EpS2.207.324.
Not so, when diadem'd with Rays divine, ... 4.EpS2.232.326.
And C[hesterfiel]d who speaks so well and writes, ... 4.1740.25.333.
So geese to gander prone obedience keep, ... 4.1740.35.334.
Sagacious Bub, so late a friend, and there .... 4.1740.55.334.
So late a foe, yet more sagacious H[are] .... 4.1740.56.335.
These wond'rous works; so Jove and Fate require) .... 5.DunA1.4.61.
So watchful Bruin forms with plastic care .... 5.DunA1.99.71.
Or which fond authors were so good to gild; .... 5.DunA1.118.77.
So spins the silkworm small its slender store, ... 5.DunA1.171.84.
So gravest precepts may successless prove, ... 5.DunA1.175.84.
So written precepts may successless prove, ... 5.DunA1.175A.84.
So graver precepts may successless prove, ... 5.DunA1.175B.84.
So spirits ending their terrestrial race, ... 5.DunA1.223.90.
So when Jove's block descended from on high, ... 5.DunA1.257.94.
But now, so ANNE and Piety ordain, ... 5.DunA2.25.99.
A Fool, so just a copy of a Wit; .... 5.DunA2.44.101.
So like, that critics said and courtiers swore, ... 5.DunA2.45.101.
"So take the hindmost Hell."—He said, and run. .... 5.DunA2.56.105.
So lab'ring on, with shoulders, hands, and head, ... 5.DunA2.61.105.
That once so flutter'd, and that once so writ. .... 5.DunA2.112.110.
That once so flutter'd, and that once so writ. .... 5.DunA2.112.110.
So Proteus, hunted in a nobler shape, ... 5.DunA2.121.111.

SO (CONTINUED)

So shall each hostile name become our own, 5.DunA2.131.113.
So Jove's bright bow displays its watry round, 5.DunA2.165.121.
Not so from shameless Curl: Impetuous spread 5.DunA2.171.122.
So, (fam'd like thee for turbulence and horns,) 5.DunA2.173.122.
A moan so loud, that all the Guild awake, 5.DunA2.240.129.
So swells each Windpipe; Ass intones to Ass, 5.DunA2.243.129.
So sighs Sir G[ilber]t, starting at the bray 5.DunA2.241A.129.
Who sings so loudly, and who sings so long. 5.DunA2.256.131.
Who sings so loudly, and who sings so long. 5.DunA2.256.131.
Not Welsted so: drawn endlong by his scull, 5.DunA2.293.138.
Not so bold Arnall, with a weight of scull, 5.DunA2.293A.138.
So from the mid-most the nutation spreads 5.DunA2.377.146.
So sweetly mawkish, and so smoothly dull; 5.DunA3.165.167.
So sweetly mawkish, and so smoothly dull; 5.DunA3.165.167.
(So may the fates preserve the ears you lend) 5.DunA3.212.175.
(So may the fates preserve the ears ye lend). 5.DunA3.212A.175.
So watchful Bruin forms, with plastic care, 5.DunB1.101.276.
This brazen Brightness, to the 'Squire so dear; 5.DunB1.219.286.
So Spirits ending their terrestrial race, 5.DunB1.267.290.
So when Jove's block descended from on high 5.DunB1.327.294.
So from the Sun's broad beam, in shallow urns 5.DunB2.11.296.
But now (so ANNE and Piety ordain) 5.DunB2.29.297.
A fool, so just a copy of a wit; 5.DunB2.48.298.
So like, that critics said, and courtiers swore, 5.DunB2.49.298.
"So take the hindmost, Hell."—He said, and run. 5.DunB2.60.298.
So lab'ring on, with shoulders, hands, and head, 5.DunB2.65.299.
That once so flutter'd, and that once so writ. 5.DunB2.120.301.
That once so flutter'd, and that once so writ. 5.DunB2.120.301.
So Proteus, hunted in a nobler shape, 5.DunB2.129.301.
So shall each hostile name become our own, 5.DunB2.139.302.
So Jove's bright bow displays its wat'ry round, 5.DunB2.173.304.
Not so from shameless Curl; impetuous spread 5.DunB2.179.304.
So (fam'd like thee for turbulence and horns) 5.DunB2.181.304.
A moan so loud, that all the guild awake; 5.DunB2.250.307.
So swells each wind-pipe, Ass intones to Ass, 5.DunB2.253.307.
Who sings so loudly, and who sings so long. 5.DunB2.268.308.
Who sings so loudly, and who sings so long. 5.DunB2.268.308.
Not so bold Arnall; with a weight of skull, 5.DunB2.315.312.
So clouds replenish'd from some bog below, 5.DunB2.363.315.
So from the mid-most the nutation spreads 5.DunB2.409.317.
So sweetly mawkish, and so smoothly dull; 5.DunB3.171.328.
So sweetly mawkish, and so smoothly dull; 5.DunB3.171.328.
(So may the fates preserve the ears you lend) 5.DunB3.214.331.
(Not half so pleas'd when Goodman prophesy'd) 5.DunB3.232.331.
Of darkness visible so much be lent, 5.DunB4.3.339.
As erst Medea (cruel, so to save!) 5.DunB4.121.353.
So by each Bard an Alderman shall sit, 5.DunB4.131.354.
So upright Quakers please both Man and God. 5.DunB4.208.363.
So spins the silk-worm small its slender store, 5.DunB4.253.369.
Thou gav'st that Ripeness, which so soon began, 5.DunB4.287.372.
And ceas'd so soon, he ne'er was Boy, nor Man. 5.DunB4.288.372.
So may the sons of sons of sons of whores, 5.DunB4.332.376.
So he; but pious, whisper'd first his pray'r. 5.DunB4.354.377.
So shall each youth, assisted by our eyes, 5.DunB4.359.378.
So back to Pollio, hand in hand, they went. 5.DunB4.396.381.
Of nought so certain as our *Reason* still, 5.DunB4.481.389.
Of nought so doubtful as of *Soul* and *Will.* 5.DunB4.482.389.
So K[ent] so B[erkeley] sneak'd into the grave, 5.DunB4.511.392.
So K[ent] so B[erkeley] sneak'd into the grave, 5.DunB4.511.392.
For I'm thy Servant, and I'l still be so: 6.2.2.5.
So gentle sleep from *Serenissa* flies, 6.4i.3.9.
So us'd to sighs, so long inur'd to tears, 6.4i.11.9.
So us'd to sighs, so long inur'd to tears, 6.4i.11.9.
From us that serv'd so long in vain, 6.4iii.3.10.
Shall heav'n so soon the prize obtain? 6.4iii.4.10.
So spicy gales at once betray 6.4v.7.11.
So from one cloud soft show'rs we view, 6.5.9.12.
So like a *Phaëton* appears, 6.5.14.12.
So these mild drops from *Celia's* eyes 6.5.9A.12.
(Tho' ne'er so weighty) reach a wondrous height; 6.7.16.16.
So, forc'd from Engines, Lead it self can fly, 6.7.17.16.
Since 'tis enough we find it so in You. 6.7.24.16.
So swift,—this moment here, the next 'tis gone, 6.9iv.1.21.
So imperceptible the motion. 6.9iv.2.21.
I'd call them Mountains, but can't call them so, 6.9xi.1.23.
While the fair Vales beneath so humbly lie, 6.9xi.3.23.
(For so one sure may call that Head, 6.10.27.25.
So seize them Flames, or take them *Tonson.* 6.10.36.25.
But burnt so long, may soon turn Tinder, 6.10.55.26.
And so be fir'd by any Cinder– 6.10.56.26.
Shou'd it so prove, yet who'd admire? 6.10.58.26.
But who so dear will buy the Lead, 6.10.75.26.
Sir, you're so stiff in your Opinion, 6.10.79.27.
(For so she was, as e'er show'd Rump yet, 6.10.86.27.
Is, I've been well a Week, or so. 6.10.106.27.
So when the first bold Vessel dar'd the Seas, 6.11.38.31.
And so remain, for ever and for ay, 6.13.30.40.
How can ye, Mothers, vex your Children so? 6.14ii.7.43.
And vary'd *Tulips* show so dazling gay, 6.14iv.7.47.
Such Nastiness and so much Pride 6.14v(a).8.48.
So have I seen, in black and white 6.14v(a).19.49.
So have I known those Insects fair, 6.14v(b).19.50.
(Which curious *Germans* hold so rare,) 6.14v(b).20.50.
So have I seen an Insect fair, 6.14v(b).19A.50.
So Wit, which most to scorn it does pretend, 6.16.11.53.
So Clocks to Lead their nimble Motions owe, 6.17i(b).1.55.
So Waters putrifie with Rest, and lose 6.17ii.9.56.
So to mine Host, the greatest Jest, they past, 6.17iv.17.59.
What, shou'd a *Queen,* so long the boast of fame, 6.20.5.66.
Howe're she liv'd none ever dy'd so well. 6.20.16.66.
A fate so glorious, and so nobly born, 6.20.34.67.
A fate so glorious, and so nobly born, 6.20.34.67.
As children birds, so men their bliss pursue, 6.22.5.71.
So Pimps grow rich, while Gallants are undone. 6.24ii.2.75.
So on *Mæotis'* Marsh, (where Reeds and Rushes 6.26i.1.79.

SO (CONTINUED)

All fair, and not so much as read. 6.29.20.83.
Others account 'em but so so; 6.29.2.82.
Others account 'em but so so; 6.29.2.82.
Chim'd in so smoothly, one by one, 6.30.11.86.
So hop'd to stand no less than he 6.30.17.86.
He'd not be serv'd so like a Beast; 6.30.28.86.
To run so smoothly, one by one 6.30.11A.86.
So hop'd to stand as well as he 6.30.17A.86.
He'd ne'er be us'd so like a Beast; 6.30.28A.86.
He'd ne'er be serv'd so like a Beast; 6.30.28B.86.
Yet they'd resign that Post so high, 6.30.40.87.
That none had so much Right to be 6.30.52.88.
I can't—indeed now—I so hate a whore— 6.41.6.113.
So from a sister sinner you shall hear, 6.41.9.113.
And did not wicked custom so contrive, 6.41.13.113.
Yet if a friend a night, or so, should need her, 6.41.33.114.
In all the rest so impudently good: 6.41.48.114.
The *Rustic Lout* so like a Brute, 6.44.25.123.
And the *fond Fop* so clean contrary, 6.44.27.123.
So when your slave, at some dear, idle time, 6.45.41.125.
And so may starve with me. 6.47.52.130.
So thy deep Knowledge Dark Designs reveals. 6.48iv.4.135.
So some coarse Country Wench, almost decay'd, 6.49i.15.138.
And so obliging, that he ne'r oblig'd: 6.49iii.22.143.
Mean tho' I am, not wholly so 6.50.41.148.
Mean as I am, not wholly so 6.50.41A.148.
So mix'd our studies, and so join'd our name, 6.52.10.156.
So mix'd our studies, and so join'd our name, 6.52.10.156.
So just thy skill, so regular my rage. 6.52.12.156.
So just thy skill, so regular my rage. 6.52.12.156.
Ev'n so all Things shall prosper well, 6.54.11.164.
That hereto was so civil; 6.58.22.171.
Forth popp'd the *Sprite* so thin; 6.58.30.172.
Abroad with such as are not so. 6.61.48.182.
Abroad with those that are not so 6.61.48A.182.
And so fair Maids, our ballad ends, 6.61.50A.183.
He laughd, and shook his Sides so fat: 6.67.2.195.
Hearts so sincere th' Almighty saw well pleas'd, 6.69i.5.198.
A pair so faithful could expire; 6.69ii.2.199.
Victims so pure Heav'n saw well pleas'd 6.69ii.3.199.
So soard Eliah to the Sky. 6.69ii.4Z2.199.
Since my old Friend is grown so great, 6.74.1.211.
So would I draw (but oh, 'tis vain to try 6.75.3.211.
Not Showers to Larks so pleasing, 6.78i.5.215.
Nor Sleep to Toil so easing 6.78i.7.215.
Not Sleep to Toil so easing 6.78i.7A.215.
No Sleep to Toil so easing 6.78i.7B.215.
So broad, it hid his Chin; 6.79.26.218.
No Vixen Civet-Cat so sweet, 6.79.31.218.
Nor could so scratch and tear. 6.79.32.218.
So sore the Gout have I. 6.79.52.219.
And so down fell Duke *Nic.* 6.79.64.220.
Did wave his Wand so white, 6.79.118.222.
All in that dreadful Hour, so calm 6.79.121.222.
And so he did—for to *New Court* 6.79.125.222.
So slunk to *Cambden* House so high, 6.79.131.222.
So slunk to *Cambden* House so high, 6.79.131.222.
Did wave his Hand so white, 6.79.118A.222.
"So that each Pisser-by shall read, 6.79.143.223.
So the struck deer in some sequester'd part 6.81.11.226.
So the struck doe in some sequester'd part 6.81.11A.226.
So long her Honour, Name, and Praise shall last! 6.82i.8.229.
For authors now are so conceited grown 6.82ix(f).3.235.
So when Curll's Stomach the strong Drench o'ercame, 6.82x.1.236.
So Ireland change thy tone, 6.90.12.251.
So skimming the fat off, 6.91.27.254.
With Eyes so piercing, yet so pleasant, 6.93.7.256.
With Eyes so piercing, yet so pleasant, 6.93.7.256.
Yet tender was this Hen so fair, 6.93.15.257.
Bears *Rabbits,—Gad!* so plentiful, 6.94.11.259.
'Tis pity that two Squires so Gent— 6.94.39.260.
'Tis so unsav'ry a-Bit.) 6.94.48.260.
But all about was so opake, 6.94.55.261.
And so the Work was o'er. 6.94.68.261.
So shall I, 6.96i.49.269.
What *Redriff* Wife so long hath kept her Vows? 6.96iv.6.276.
If so, our *Dean* shall drive him forth by Pray'r. 6.96iv.34.277.
So call'd on *Brobdingnag's* stupendous Coast, 6.96iv.98.279.
Nay, wou'd kind *Jove* my Organs so dispose, 6.96iv.105.279.
So might I find my loving Spouse of course 6.96iv.109.279.
And he, whose Fustian's so sublimely bad, 6.98.37.284.
And so obliging that he ne'er oblig'd: 6.98.58.285.
Made *David* seem so mad and freakish, 6.101.17.290.
So there's an end of honest *Jack.* 6.103.2.295.
So little Justice here he found, 6.103.3.295.
The rest God knows—so does the Devil. 6.104i.2.297.
Both were so forward, each would write, 6.105iv.3.301.
So dull, each hung an A[rse] 6.105iv.4.301.
So *Amphisb na,* we have read 6.105iv.5A.301.
But now we're so frugal, I'd have you to know it, 6.105vii.3.302.
So while the sun's broad beam yet strikes the sight, 6.106i.4.306.
So when the sun's broad beam has tir'd the sight, 6.106i.4A.306.
So unaffected, so compos'd a mind, 6.115.7.323.
So unaffected, so compos'd a mind, 6.115.7.323.
So firm yet soft, so strong yet so refin'd, 6.115.8.323.
So firm yet soft, so strong yet so refin'd, 6.115.8.323.
So firm yet soft, so strong yet so refin'd, 6.115.8.323.
Of one so poor you cannot take the law; 6.116vii.5.328.
On one so old your sword you scorn to draw. 6.116vii.6.328.
Blest Satyrist! who touch'd the Mean so true, 6.118.7.334.
"So skilful and those Hands so taper; 6.119.6.336.
"So skilful and those Hands so taper; 6.119.6.336.
"That head acute, and Hands so taper; 6.119.6A.336.
"That Head so quick, those Hands so taper; 6.119.6B.336.
"That Head so quick, those Hands so taper; 6.119.6B.336.

SO (CONTINUED)

So sunk proud *Asius* in that deathful Day, Il.13.497A.130.
His lab'ring Heart, heaves, with so strong a bound, Il.13.554.132.
To him, ambitious of so great an Aid, Il.13.580.134.
So stood *Idomeneus*, his Javelin shook, Il.13.602.135.
So joys *Æneas*, and his native Band Il.13.626.136.
Sent from an Arm so strong, the missive Wood Il.13.638.136.
And smote his Temples, with an Arm so strong Il.13.729.139.
So from the Steel that guards *Atrides'* Heart, Il.13.743.140.
Not so discourag'd, to the Future blind, Il.13.761.141.
So when two lordly Bulls, with equal Toil, Il.13.879.147.
And great *Othryoneus*, so fear'd of late? Il.13.970.151.
So may the Gods on *Hector* Life bestow, Il.13.1046.155.
Gerenian Nestor then. So Fate has will'd; Il.14.59.160.
Lives there a Man so dead to Fame, who dares Il.14.102.162.
The Monarch's Daughter there (so *Jove* ordain'd) Il.14.136.164.
So may he perish, so may *Jove* disclaim Il.14.163.165.
So may he perish, so may *Jove* disclaim Il.14.163.165.
Which held so long that ancient Pair in Peace. Il.14.238.172.
Which held so long this ancient Pair in Peace. Il.14.348.179.
Ne'er did my Soul so strong a Passion prove, Il.14.359.180.
Not half so loud the bellowing Deeps resound, Il.14.457.185.
So lies great *Hector* prostrate on the Shore; Il.14.487.187.
So just the Stroke, that yet the Body stood Il.14.547.189.
So swift flew *Juno* to the blest Abodes, Il.15.90.200.
So from the Clouds descending *Iris* falls; Il.15.194.204.
Not half so swift the sailing Falcon flies, Il.15.266.207.
Why sits great *Hector* from the Field so far, Il.15.276.207.
So *Greece*, that late in conq'ring Troops pursu'd. Il.15.314.209.
So flies a Herd of Oxen, scatter'd wide, Il.15.366.211.
So strong to fight, so active to pursue? Il.15.683.222.
So strong to fight, so active to pursue? Il.15.683.222.
So when a Savage, ranging o'er the Plain, Il.15.702.223.
So fears the Youth; all *Troy* with Shouts pursue, Il.15.708.223.
So *Mars*, when human Crimes for Vengeance call, Il.15.726.223.
So some tall Rock o'erhangs the hoary Main, Il.15.746.224.
So pale the *Greeks* the Eyes of *Hector* meet, Il.15.758.225.
The Chief so thunders, and so shakes the Fleet. Il.15.759.225.
The Chief so thunders, and so shakes the Fleet. Il.15.759.225.
So when a Horseman from the watry Mead Il.15.822.228.
So the strong Eagle from his airy Height Il.15.836.229.
Thou wouldst have thought, so furious was their Fire, Il.15.844.229.
Ev'n *Ajax* paus'd (so thick the Javelins fly) Il.15.882.231.
So well the Chief his Naval Weapon sped, Il.15.906.232.
So warr'd both Armies on th' ensanguin'd Shore, Il.16.1.233.
That flows so fast in these unmanly Tears? Il.16.10.235.
So rough thy Manners, so untam'd thy Mind. Il.16.53.237.
So rough thy Manners, so untam'd thy Mind. Il.16.53.237.
So thick, the Darts an Iron Tempest rain'd: Il.16.131.242.
Full on the Lance a Stroke so justly sped, Il.16.144.243.
No Hand so sure of all th' *Emathian* Line, Il.16.232.248.
Think what Reproach these Ears endur'd so long, Il.16.241.248.
"Whose Rage defrauds us of so fam'd a Field. Il.16.245.249.
So Helm to Helm, and Crest to Crest they throng, Il.16.260.249.
So loud their Clamours, and so keen their Arms. Il.16.321.255.
So loud their Clamours, and so keen their Arms. Il.16.321.255.
So when thick Clouds inwrap the Mountain's Head, Il.16.354.256.
The Head, divided by a Stroke so just, Il.16.408.258.
So from the Ships, along the dusky Plain, Il.16.438.259.
Not so *Patroclus'* never erring Dart; Il.16.590.267.
So lies a Bull beneath the Lion's Paws, Il.16.601.267.
So far the *Trojans* from their Lines retir'd; Il.16.719.272.
So fell the Warriors, and so rung their Arms. Il.16.772.273.
So fell the Warriors, and so rung their Arms. Il.16.772.273.
(So *Jove* decreed!) At length the *Greeks* obtain Il.16.805.274.
So spoke the God who darts celestial Fires: Il.16.867.277.
Should soon convince thee of so false a Fear. Il.16.880.277.
So spoke th' inspiring God; then took his flight, Il.16.885.277.
So pent by Hills, the wild Winds roar aloud Il.16.923.279.
The last, black Remnant of so bright a Line. Il.16.951.280.
So scorch'd with Heat along the desart Shore, Il.16.993.281.
Patroclus thus, so many Chiefs o'erthrown, Il.16.999.281.
So many Lives effus'd, expires his own. Il.16.1000.281.
Too long amus'd with a Pursuit so vain, Il.17.83.291.
So from the Fold th' unwilling Lion parts, Il.17.117.292.
'Twas not for State we summon'd you so far, Il.17.262.298.
So thro' the Thicket bursts the Mountain Boar, Il.17.331.300.
And skirmish wide: So *Nestor* gave Command, Il.17.438.304.
So tugging round the Corps both Armies stood; Il.17.454.304.
So flies a Vulture thro' the clam'rous Train Il.17.528.309.
So looks the Lion o'er a mangled Boar, Il.17.608.312.
So burns the vengeful Hornet (Soul all o'er) Il.17.642.313.
Not so our Spears: incessant tho' they rain, Il.17.713.315.
So turns the Lion from the nightly Fold, Il.17.741.317.
So mov'd *Atrides* from his dang'rous Place Il.17.749.317.
So parts the Chief; from Rank to Rank he flew, Il.17.759.318.
So these—Behind, the Bulk of *Ajax* stands, Il.17.837.321.
So from the *Trojan* Chiefs the *Grecians* fly, Il.17.849.321.
Is this the Day, which Heav'n so long ago Il.18.11.323.
(So *Thetis* warn'd) when by a *Trojan* Hand, Il.18.13.323.
So short a space the Light of Heav'n to view, Il.18.79.327.
So short alas! and fill'd with Anguish too? Il.18.80.327.
So shall *Achilles* fall! stretch'd pale and dead, Il.18.151.329.
Soon shall the sanguine Torrent spread so wide, Il.18.161.330.
So tell our hoary Sire—This Charge she gave: Il.18.181.331.
So watchful Shepherds strive to force, in vain, Il.18.199.331.
So from *Achilles'* Head the Splendours rise, Il.18.253.334.
So high his brazen Voice the Hero rear'd: Il.18.263.335.
I deem'd not *Greece* so dreadful, while engag'd Il.18.303.336.
So may his Rage be tir'd, and labour'd down; Il.18.331.337.
So *Pallas* robb'd the Many of their Mind, Il.18.362.339.
Those slaught'ring Arms, so us'd to bathe in Blood, Il.18.368.339.
So grieves *Achilles;* and impetuous vents Il.18.377.339.
So they. Meanwhile the silver-footed Dame Il.18.431.341.
(So long a Stranger) to these honour'd Walls? Il.18.496.345.
So pierc'd with Sorrows, so o'erwhelm'd as mine? Il.18.502.345.

SO (CONTINUED)

So pierc'd with Sorrows, so o'erwhelm'd as mine? Il.18.502.345.
So whirls a Wheel, in giddy Circle tost, Il.18.695.357.
So swift thro' Æther the shrill *Harpye* springs, Il.19.372.387.
So Helms succeeding Helms, so Shields from Shields Il.19.384.388.
So Helms succeeding Helms, so Shields from Shields Il.19.384.388.
So to Night-wand'ring Sailors, pale with Fears, Il.19.404.389.
So stream'd the golden Honours from his Head, Il.19.414.389.
When strange to tell! (So *Juno* will'd) he broke Il.19.450.390.
With unabated Rage—So let it be! Il.19.466.391.
That spun so short his Life's illustrious Line: Il.20.155.400.
Against the Might of Man, so feeble known, Il.20.162.400.
Not so *Pelides;* furious to engage, Il.20.198.402.
So fierce *Achilles* on *Æneas* flies; Il.20.210.402.
So stands *Æneas*, and his Force defies. Il.20.211.402.
Why comes *Æneas* thro' the Ranks so far? Il.20.214.402.
But can *Achilles* be so soon forgot? Il.20.227.403.
Proclaim'd so loudly by the Voice of Fame, Il.20.245.404.
So voluble a Weapon is the Tongue; Il.20.297.406.
A Fate so near him, chills his Soul with Fright, Il.20.331.407.
To spare a Form, an Age so like thy own! Il.20.540.417.
So sweeps the Hero thro' the wasted Shores; Il.20.574.418.
So the fierce Coursers, as the Chariot rolls, Il.20.581.418.
So plung'd in *Xanthus* by *Achilles'* Force, Il.21.18.422.
So the huge *Dolphin* tempesting the Main, Il.21.30.422.
As now the Captive, whom so late I bound Il.21.66.424.
So perish *Troy*, and all the *Trojan* Line! Il.21.141.427.
So ends thy Glory! Such the Fate they prove Il.21.201.429.
So when a Peasant to his Garden brings Il.21.289.432.
So oft' the Surge, in wat'ry Mountains spread, Il.21.305.433.
That blaze so dreadful in each *Trojan* Eye; Il.21.371.436.
So look'd the Field, so whiten'd was the Ground, Il.21.404.437.
So look'd the Field, so whiten'd was the Ground, Il.21.404.437.
So boils th' imprison'd Flood, forbid to flow, Il.21.428.438.
So dread, so fierce, as *Venus* is to me; Il.21.503.442.
So dread, so fierce, as *Venus* is to me; Il.21.503.442.
Nor mix Immortals in a Cause so mean. Il.21.542.444.
Not so *Saturnia* bore the vaunting Maid; Il.21.554.444.
So, when the Falcon wings her way above, Il.21.575.446.
So rag'd *Achilles:* Death and dire Dismay, Il.21.611.447.
(So, e're a Storm, the Waters heave and roll) Il.21.649.449.
So may I reach, conceal'd, the cooling Flood, Il.21.659.449.
So from some deep grown Wood a Panther starts, Il.21.677.450.
So the proud Courser, victor of the prize, Il.22.33.453.
Not half so dreadful rises to the Sight Il.22.37.454.
So flam'd his fiery Mail. Then wept the Sage; Il.22.43.454.
Save thy dear Life; or if a Soul so brave Il.22.78.456.
So they, while down their Cheeks the Torrents roll; Il.22.126.458.
So roll'd up in his Den, the swelling Snake Il.22.130.458.
So oft' *Achilles* turns him to the Plain: Il.22.255.466.
With Fate itself so long to hold the Course? Il.22.264.466.
Great *Hector* falls; that *Hector* fam'd so far, Il.22.281.467.
'Tis so—Heav'n wills it, and my Hour is nigh! Il.22.378.471.
So *Jove's* bold Bird, high-balanc'd in the Air, Il.22.391.471.
So shone the Point of great *Achilles'* Spear. Il.22.402.472.
So spake the mournful Dame: Her Matrons hear, Il.22.662.484.
This Night my Friend, so late in Battel lost, Il.23.126.493.
So vow'd my Father, but he vow'd in vain; Il.23.186.497.
So spake he, threat'ning: But the Gods made vain Il.23.226.498.
Not so, (the Dame reply'd) I haste to go Il.23.252.499.
So stay'd *Achilles*, circling round the Shore, Il.23.278.501.
So watch'd the Flames, till now they flam'd no more. Il.23.279.501.
So watch'd the Flames, till now they flame no more. Il.23.279A.501*.
So shalt thou pass the Goal, secure of Mind, Il.23.417.506.
So far *Antilochus!* thy Chariot flew Il.23.513.510.
So swift, it seem'd a Flight, and not a Race. Il.23.588.513.
Such, and so narrow now the Space between Il.23.603.513.
The Rivals, late so distant on the Green. Il.23.604.513.
So soon swift *Æthe* her lost Ground regain'd, Il.23.605.513.
O *Peleus* Son! the Mare so justly mine. Il.23.622.514.
An Act so rash (*Antilochus*) has stain'd. Il.23.652.515.
So not a Leader shall our Conduct blame, Il.23.655.515.
What needs appealing in a Fact so plain? Il.23.658.515.
So spoke *Antilochus;* and at the Word Il.23.677.516.
Those due distinctions thou so well can'st pay, Il.23.749.520.
So let his Friends be nigh, a needful Train Il.23.779.520.
Now prove that Prowess you have prov'd so well. Il.23.859.523.
Whoever dares deserve so rich a Prize! Il.23.946.526.
So past them all the rapid Circle flies: Il.23.1003.529.
Not so *Achilles:* He, to Grief resign'd, Il.24.5.534.
The Form so pleasing, and the Heart so kind, Il.24.11.535.
The Form so pleasing, and the Heart so kind, Il.24.11.535.
So past the Goddess thro' the closing Wave, Il.24.109.539.
By Stealth should bear him, but we will'd not so: Il.24.144.541.
Alone, for so we will: No *Trojan* near; Il.24.183.544.
Some Thought there must be, in a Soul so brave, Il.24.193.544.
Alone, for so he wills: No *Trojan* near, Il.24.213.546.
Some Thought there must be, in a Soul so brave, Il.24.223.546.
So brave! so many fall'n! To calm his Rage Il.24.253.547.
So brave! so many fall'n! To calm his Rage Il.24.253.547.
To raise our Hands, for who so good as *Jove?* Il.24.370.551.
So shall thy Suppliant, strengthen'd from above, Il.24.385.552.
So broad, his Pinions stretch'd their ample Shade, Il.24.392.552.
So broad, his Pinions stretch their ample Shade, Il.24.392A.552.
Thro' *Grecian* Foes, so num'rous and so strong? Il.24.450.555.
Thro' *Grecian* Foes, so num'rous and so strong? Il.24.450.555.
And know so well how god-like *Hector* dy'd? Il.24.475.556.
A Life so grateful, still regard him dead. Il.24.516.557.
Tho' not so wretched: There he yields to me, Il.24.628.563.
So shall thy Pity and Forbearance give Il.24.703.566.
So was her Pride chastiz'd by Wrath divine, Il.24.763.569.
T'inter thy *Hector?* For, so long we stay Il.24.826.571.
So spoke the Fair, with Sorrow-streaming Eye: Il.24.981.576.
So may the Man of blood be doom'd to bleed! Od.1.60.33.
Griev'd that a Visitant so long shou'd wait Od.1.157.40.
Shou'd he return, that troop so blithe and bold, Od.1.211.43.

SO (CONTINUED)

But say, yon' jovial Troop so gaily drest, ... Od.1.289.47.
Who now (so heav'n decrees) is doom'd to mourn, ... Od.1.299.47.
(For so of old my father's court he grac'd, ... Od.1.334.48.
So Fathers speak (persuasive speech and mild!) .... Od.1.401.51.
So bright a genius with the toils of state! .... Od.1.494.56.
So soon forgot, was just and mild in vain! .... Od.2.266.74.
So like your voices, and your words so wise, ... Od.3.153.93.
So like your voices, and your words so wise, ... Od.3.153.93.
Not so the King of Men: he will'd to stay; .... Od.3.175.94.
(So *Jove,* that urg'd us to our fate, ordain'd.) .... Od.3.184.95.
And rais'd new discord. Then (so Heav'n decreed) .... Od.3.195.95.
What lands so distant from that scene of death .... Od.3.237.97.
So fell *Ægysthus;* and may'st thou, my friend, ... Od.3.242.97.
With rays so strong, distinguish'd, and divine, ... Od.3.274.99.
So might she love thee, so thy soul inspire! .... Od.3.276.99.
So might she love thee, so thy soul inspire! .... Od.3.276.99.
So spake *Jove's* daughter, the celestial maid. .... Od.3.431.108.
So guide me, Goddess! so propitious shine .... Od.3.488.111.
So guide me, Goddess! so propitious shine .... Od.3.488.111.
So wrought, as *Pallas* might with pride behold. .... Od.3.556.114.
Oh! had the Gods so large a boon deny'd, ... Od.4.123.126.
So moves, adorn'd with each attractive grace, ... Od.4.159.128.
These drugs, so friendly to the joys of life, ... Od.4.315.134.
(For so the common care of *Greece* requir'd) .... Od.4.390.139.
So with her young, amid the woodland shades .... Od.4.449.141.
So with his batt'ning flocks the careful swain .... Od.4.559.146.
So, whilst he feeds luxurious in the stall, ... Od.4.719.152.
Charm'd by your speech, so graceful and humane, ... Od.4.814.157.
O early worth! a soul so wise, and young, ... Od.4.831.158.
So when the wood-man's toyl her cave surrounds .... Od.4.1041.166.
How in a realm so distant shou'd you know .... Od.4.1069.167.
So wat'ry fowl, that seek their fishy food, ... Od.5.64.174.
What pow'r so great, to dare to disobey? .... Od.5.130.178.
Strait to dismiss: so Destiny commands: .... Od.5.144.178.
So when *Aurora* sought *Orion's* love, ... Od.5.155.179.
So when the covert of the thrice-ear'd field .... Od.5.159.179.
For what so dreadful as the wrath of *Jove?* .... Od.5.188.180.
By seas, by wars, so many dangers run, ... Od.5.287.185.
So large he built the Raft: then ribb'd it strong .... Od.5.321.187.
So roll'd the Float, and so its texture held: .... Od.5.420.192.
So roll'd the Float, and so its texture held: .... Od.5.420.192.
So the rude *Boreas,* o'er the field new shorn, ... Od.5.470.195.
So joys *Ulysses* at th' appearing shore; .... Od.5.511.197.
So the rough rock had shagg'd *Ulysses'* hands. .... Od.5.553.199.
The verdant Arch so close its texture kept: .... Od.5.622.201.
So when with praise amid the dance they shine, ... Od.6.77.208.
So shines majestic, and so stately moves, ... Od.6.180.218.
So shines majestic, and so stately moves, ... Od.6.180.218.
So breathes an air divine! But if thy race .... Od.6.181.218.
A plant so stately, or a nymph so fair. .... Od.6.202.219.
A plant so stately, or a nymph so fair. .... Od.6.202.219.
So may the Gods who heav'n and earth controul, ... Od.6.217.220.
So *Pallas* his heroic frame improves .... Od.6.279.224.
So shalt thou view with joy thy natal shore, ... Od.6.375.230.
No bird so light, no thought so swift as they. .... Od.7.48.235.
No bird so light, no thought so swift as they. .... Od.7.48.235.
(So *Pallas* order'd, *Pallas* to their eyes .... Od.7.53.236.
So may the Gods your better days increase, ... Od.7.202.246.
So reign for ever on your country's breast, ... Od.7.204.246.
So near approach we their celestial kind, ... Od.7.277.249.
And robes like these, so recent and so fair? .... Od.7.321.251.
And robes like these, so recent and so fair? .... Od.7.321.251.
To crown the feast, so wills the bounteous King. .... Od.8.54.264.
None wield the gauntlet with so dire a sway, ... Od.8.101.267.
None in the leap spring with so strong a bound, ... Od.8.103.268.
So may dread *Jove* (whose arm in vengeance forms .... Od.8.505.289.
The woe of *Greece,* and sing so well the woe? .... Od.8.534.291.
So from the sluices of *Ulysses'* eyes .... Od.8.581.294.
So shalt thou instant reach the realm assign'd, ... Od.8.603.294.
And none, ah none so lovely to my sight, ... Od.9.29.303.
I then advis'd to fly: not so the rest, ... Od.9.47.304.
Now Fortune changes (so the fates ordain) .... Od.9.59.304.
A deed so rash had finish'd all our fate, ... Od.9.360.321.
Green from the wood; of height and bulk so vast, ... Od.9.382.321.
(So fortune chanc'd, or so some God design'd) .... Od.9.399.322.
(So fortune chanc'd, or so some God design'd) .... Od.9.399.322.
In his broad eye so whirls the fiery wood; .... Od.9.461.325.
Secur'd each side: So bound we all the crew. .... Od.9.510.327.
(So much the love of home possess'd my heart) .... Od.10.37.341.
So near the pastures, and so short the way, ... Od.10.98.345.
So near the pastures, and so short the way, ... Od.10.98.345.
So shall thy tedious toils a respite find, ... Od.10.355.361.
So round me press'd exulting at my sight, ... Od.10.491.367.
So speaking, from the ruddy orient shone .... Od.10.645.375.
So shall a barren heifer from the stall .... Od.11.37.381.
So in our palace, at our safe return .... Od.11.39.381.
So shall a Ram, the largest of the breed, ... Od.11.41.381.
Rob not the God, and so propitious gales .... Od.11.140.387.
So peaceful shalt thou end thy blissful days, ... Od.11.164.389.
He ceas'd: but left so charming on their ear .... Od.11.414.404.
So vile a deed, so dire a scene of blood. .... Od.11.520.409.
So vile a deed, so dire a scene of blood. .... Od.11.520.409.
Nor trust the sex that is so rarely wise; .... Od.11.546.410.
For since of womankind so few are just, ... Od.11.563.411.
So blest as thine in all the rolls of Fame; .... Od.11.592.412.
O dear-bought honour with so brave a life! .... Od.11.672.417.
Rob not the God! and so propitious gales .... Od.12.172.440.
So the foul monster lifts her prey on high, ... Od.12.304.447.
So pant the wretches, struggling in the sky, ... Od.12.305.447.
Never, I never, scene so dire survey'd! .... Od.12.309.447.
The sun descending, and so near the shore? .... Od.12.338.448.
So will'd some Demon, minister of woes! .... Od.12.352.448.
A deed so dreadful all the Gods alarms, ... Od.12.441.452.
So to the beam the Bat tenacious clings, ... Od.12.513.457.
So *Jove* decreed, (dread Sire of men and Gods.) .... Od.12.528.458.

SO (CONTINUED)

And what so tedious as a twice-told tale? .... Od.12.538.459.
He ceas'd; but left so pleasing on their ear .... Od.13.1.1.
So to *Ulysses* welcome sett the Sun. .... Od.13.44.3.
So may I find, when all my wand'rings cease, ... Od.13.54.4.
So mounts the bounding vessel o'er the main. .... Od.13.101.6.
So may the God reverse his purpos'd will, ... Od.13.212.15.
For so the Gods ordain'd, to keep unseen .... Od.13.227.17.
So seldom view'd, and ever in disguise! .... Od.13.357.24.
So spake the Goddess, and the prospect clear'd, ... Od.13.401.26.
So look'd the Chief, so mov'd! To mortal eyes .... Od.13.508.30.
So look'd the Chief, so mov'd! To mortal eyes .... Od.13.508.30.
So just reception from a heart so kind: .... Od.14.62.38.
So just reception from a heart so kind: .... Od.14.62.38.
He trod so fatally the paths of Fame. .... Od.14.82.40.
So rich, so potent, whom you stile your Lord? .... Od.14.139.42.
So rich, so potent, whom you stile your Lord? .... Od.14.139.42.
Who (so the Gods, and so the Fates ordain'd) .... Od.14.144.42.
Who (so the Gods, and so the Fates ordain'd) .... Od.14.144.42.
So perish'd he: and left (for ever lost) .... Od.14.158.43.
So mild a master never shall I find: .... Od.14.160.43.
If so, a cloak and vesture be my meed; .... Od.14.177.44.
So will'd the God who gives and takes away. .... Od.14.279.49.
So from the deck are hurl'd the ghastly crew. .... Od.14.344.51.
If with desire so strong thy bosom glows, ... Od.15.75.72.
So shall thy god-like father, toss'd in vain .... Od.15.198.78.
How sprung a thought so monstrous in thy mind? .... Od.15.345.86.
(So dire a fate, ye righteous Gods! avert, ... Od.15.384.88.
So left perhaps to tend the fleecy train, ... Od.15.418.89.
While I, so many wand'rings past and woes, ... Od.15.530.95.
So past in pleasing dialogue away .... Od.15.532.95.
So round the youth his arms *Eumæus* spread, ... Od.16.21.103.
Not so—(exclaims the Prince with decent grace) .... Od.16.43.104.
My heart weeps blood, to see a soul so brave .... Od.16.95.107.
Yet cease to go—what man so blest but mourns? .... Od.16.159.110.
So they aloud: and tears in tides had run, ... Od.16.242.116.
So *Pallas* wills—but thou my son, explain .... Od.16.258.117.
"I bear them hence (so *Jove* my soul inspires) .... Od.16.312.120.
For what so easy as to be sincere? .... Od.17.19.133.
So ill th' inclemencies of morning air, ... Od.17.27.133.
So snatch'd from all our cares!—Tell, hast thou known .... Od.17.54.135.
(So Heav'n decreed) ingag'd the Great in arms. .... Od.17.135.138.
So with her young, amid the woodland shades, ... Od.17.140.138.
So shall our bounties speak a grateful mind; .... Od.17.187.140.
So spoke the wretch; but shunning farther fray, ... Od.17.304.146.
Not *Argus* so (*Eumæus* thus rejoin'd) .... Od.17.376.150.
So clos'd for ever faithful *Argus'* eyes! .... Od.17.399.151.
It is not so with Want! how few that feed .... Od.17.470.156.
To give another's is thy hand so slow? .... Od.17.486.156.
So much more sweet, to spoil, than to bestow? .... Od.17.487.156.
Nor all can give so much as thou canst crave. .... Od.17.534.158.
"So may these impious fall, by fate oppress!" .... Od.17.627.163.
So finding favour in the royal eye, ... Od.17.640.163.
A tongue so flippant, with a throat so wide! .... Od.18.33.168.
A tongue so flippant, with a throat so wide! .... Od.18.33.168.
So food and rayment constant will I give: .... Od.18.407.188.
Not so a youth who deals the goblet round, ... Od.18.440.190.
And, Why so turbulent of soul? he cries; .... Od.19.87.196.
So pays the wretch, whom fact constrains to roam, ... Od.19.192.201.
So, melted with the pleasing tale he told, ... Od.19.242.206.
So rich the value of a store so vast .... Od.19.337.210.
So rich the value of a store so vast .... Od.19.337.210.
Such gentle manners, and so sage a mind, ... Od.19.404.214.
So in nocturnal solitude forlorn, ... Od.19.611.226.
So by my choice avow'd, at length decide .... Od.19.623.226.
So, when the sun restores the purple day, ... Od.19.674.229.
And bays the stranger groom: so wrath comprest .... Od.20.21.232.
Ulysses so, from side to side devolv'd, ... Od.20.35.234.
Not so the Queen; The downy bands of sleep .... Od.20.68.235.
So *Pandarus,* thy hopes, three orphan fair .... Od.20.78.236.
Aw'd by the Prince, so haughty, brave, and young, ... Od.20.334.249.
But who so vain of faith, so blind to fate, ... Od.20.395.251.
But who so vain of faith, so blind to fate, ... Od.20.395.251.
So roar'd the lock when it releas'd the spring. .... Od.21.52.261.
But baffled thus! confess'd so far below .... Od.21.268.272.
Not so, *Eurymachus:* That no man draws .... Od.21.272.273.
So end our night: Before the day shall spring, ... Od.21.280.273.
So shall the patron of these arts bestow .... Od.21.284.273.
A hope so idle never touch'd his brain: .... Od.21.341.276.
Then ease your bosoms of a fear so vain. .... Od.21.342.276.
Who wrongs his Princess with a thought so mean. .... Od.21.344.276.
O fair! and wisest of so fair a kind! .... Od.21.345.276.
What? hopes the fool to please so many lords? .... Od.21.400.279.
Its owner absent, and untry'd so long. .... Od.21.430.281.
So the great Master drew the mighty bow: .... Od.21.445.281.
Not so content, with bolder frenzy fir'd, ... Od.22.45.288.
(So need compells.) Then all united strive .... Od.22.89.290.
So near adjoins, that one may guard the strait. .... Od.22.153.294.
No so (reply'd *Ulysses)* leave him there, ... Od.22.184.296.
So study'd tortures his vile days shall end. .... Od.22.192.296.
So drawn aloft, athwart the column ty'd, ... Od.22.209.297.
So timely rise, when morning streaks the east, ... Od.22.215.297.
(So speed 'em heav'n) our jav'lins at the foe. .... Od.22.289.300.
Not lessen'd of their force (so light the wound) .... Od.22.310.301.
Not half so keen, fierce vulturs of the chace .... Od.22.337.303.
So, when by hollow shores the fisher train .... Od.22.425.308.
So the grim Lion from the slaughter comes, ... Od.22.440.309.
Not so (*Ulysses* more sedate reply'd) .... Od.22.469.311.
So with the Suitors let 'em mix in dust, ... Od.22.480.312.
A fate so pure, as by the martial sword? .... Od.22.496.313.
So ends the bloody business of the day. .... Od.22.516.314.
Never did I a sleep so sweet enjoy, ... Od.23.21.319.
So *Pallas* his heroic form improves .... Od.23.161.328.
So cow'ring fled the sable heaps of ghosts, ... Od.24.13.347.
Condemn'd to pay the great arrear so soon, ... Od.24.41.349.
What cause compell'd so many, and so gay, ... Od.24.130.354.

SO (CONTINUED)
What cause compell'd so many, and so gay, ... Od.24.130.354.
Say, could one city yield a troop so fair? ... Od.24.132.354.
Not so: his judgment takes the winding way ... Od.24.279.363.
Age so advanc'd may some indulgence claim. ... Od.24.295.364.
So dress'd and manag'd by thy skilful hand? ... Od.24.303.364.
For so reported the first man I view'd, ... Od.24.306.364.
So civil rights demand; and who begins ... Od.24.332.365.
Thy son, so long desir'd, so long detain'd, ... Od.24.377.367.
Thy son, so long desir'd, so long detain'd, ... Od.24.377.367.
'Tis so—the Suitors for their wrongs have paid— ... Od.24.411.369.
So spoke *Telemachus:* the gallant boy ... Od.24.592.376.
So *Pallas* spoke: The mandate from above ... Od.24.628.377.

SOAK
With melted lard they soak the weapon o'er, ... Od.21.185.268.

SOAK'D
And from soak'd Plumes disperse a briny Show'r, ... 6.26i.7.79.

SOAR
Of all who blindly creep, or sightless soar; ... 3.EOM1.12.13.
Hope humbly then; with trembling pinions soar; ... 3.EOM1.91.25.
What would this Man? Now upward will he soar, ... 3.EOM1.173.36.
Go, soar with Plato to th' empyreal sphere, ... 3.EOM2.23.57.
Perhaps more high some daring son may soar, ... 5.DunB4.599.402.
Go tuneful bird, forbear to soar, ... 6.6i.1.13.
Then, when you seem above mankind to soar, ... 6.27.16.81.
O'er earth and ocean wide prepar'd to soar, ... Od.1.128.38.

SOAR'D
High o'er the wond'ring Hosts he soar'd above, ... Il.8.299.412.
As from the Right she soar'd, *Ulysses* pray'd, ... Il.10.325.17.
Thus speaking, on the right up-soar'd in air ... Od.15.565.97.
Not to this troop, I fear, that phantom soar'd, ... Od.19.664.228.

SOARD
So soard Eliah to the Sky. ... 6.69ii.4Z2.199.

SOARING
Swift as an Arrow soaring from the Bow! ... 2.ChJM.290.28.
And following with his Eye the soaring Dove, ... Il.23.1031.530.

SOARS
And shining soars and claps her Wings above. ... Il.2.122.133.
And soars an Eagle thro' the liquid skies. ... Od.3.475.110.

SOB
The short thick Sob, loud Scream, and shriller Squawl: ... 6.14ii.6.43.
Bathe thy cold Face, and sob upon thy Breast! ... Il.18.398.340.

SOBB'D
She sobb'd a Storm, and wip'd her flowing Eyes, ... 6.96ii.73.273.
And in short Pantings sobb'd his Soul away; ... Il.13.818.144.

SOBER
And charm'd with virtuous Joys, and sober Life, ... 2.ChJM.79.18.
For when thy Charms my sober Thoughts engage, ... 2.ChJM.569.42.
He ceas'd, and *May* with sober Grace reply'd; ... 2.ChJM.575A.43.
The *Mantuan* there in sober Triumph sate, ... 2.TemF.200.271.
As sober Lanesb'row dancing in the gout. ... 3.Ep1.251.37.
All mild ascends the Moon's more sober light, ... 3.Ep2.254.70.
"All this is madness," cries a sober sage: ... 3.Ep3.153.106.
There dwelt a Citizen of sober fame, ... 3.Ep3.341.121.
There sober Thought pursu'd th'amusing theme ... 4.JD4.188.41.
Here still Reflection led on sober Thought, ... 4.JD4.188A.41.
Did some more sober Critic come abroad? ... 4.Arbu.157.107.
Nor circle sober fifty with thy Charms. ... 4.HOde1.6.151.
Nor circle sober fifty with your Charms. ... 4.HOde1.6A.151.
In all but this, a man of sober Life, ... 4.2HE2.188.177.
I ask these sober questions of my Heart. ... 4.2HE2.211.179.
Walk sober off; before a sprightlier Age ... 4.2HE2.324.187.
Time was, a sober Englishman wou'd knock ... 4.2HE1.161.209.
Of sober face, with learned dust besprent? ... 5.DunA3.182.170.
Of sober face, with learned dust besprent?" ... 5.DunB3.186.329.
But sober History restrain'd her rage, ... 5.DunB4.39.344.
The decent Knight retir'd with sober rage, ... 5.DunB4.113.352.
He may indeed (if sober all this time) ... 5.DunB4.259.369.
For sober, studious Days; ... 6.47.46.130.
The sober Follies of the Wise and Great; ... 6.84.10.238.
In *Yorkshire* dwelt a sober Yeoman, ... 6.93.1.256.
Should some more sober Criticks come abroad, ... 6.98.7.283.
All mild appears the moon's more sober light, ... 6.106i.5.306.
All mild ascends the moon's more sober light, ... 6.106i.5A.306.
Blest with plain Reason and with sober Sense; ... 6.115.2.322.
—Tis not the *sober Satyrist* you should dread, ... 6.120.11.339.
Descend in all her sober charms; ... 6.140.2.378.
" *Athenian Queen!* and *sober charms!* ... 6.140.25.379.
For happy Counsels flow from sober Feasts. ... Il.9.100.437.
And clad the dusky Fields in sober Gray; ... Il.24.428.554.
Pains the sage ear, and hurts the sober eye. ... Od.1.294.47.
The sober train attended and obey'd. ... Od.3.432.108.

SOBER'D
And sent him sober'd home, with better wit. ... Od.21.322.275.

SOBERLY
His Thirst and Hunger soberly represt. ... Il.9.290.448.

SOBERS
And drinking *largely* sobers us again. ... 1.EOC.218.265.

SOBS
Sighs, Sobs, and Passions, and the War of Tongues. ... 2.RL4.84.190.
Stretch'd on the Plain, he sobs away his Breath, ... Il.13.644.136.
He sobs his Soul out in the Gush of Blood. ... Il.16.419.259.

SOBS (CONTINUED)
And sobs of joy re-eccho'd thro' the bow'r: ... Od.10.472.366.
And with their sobs the vaulted roofs resound. ... Od.10.538.369.

SOCIAL
And bid Self-Love and Social be the same. ... 3.EOM3.138Z2.1
Self-love and Social at her birth began, ... 3.EOM3.149.107.
"Here too all forms of social union find, ... 3.EOM3.179.111.
And bade Self-love and Social be the same. ... 3.EOM3.318.126.
Self-love thus push'd to social, to divine, ... 3.EOM4.353.162.
That true SELF-LOVE and SOCIAL are the same; ... 3.EOM4.396.166.
Preserve him social, chearful, and serene, ... 4.Arbu.416.127.
Sacred to social Life and social Love, ... 4.HOde1.22.151.
Sacred to social Life and social Love, ... 4.HOde1.22.151.
Of Social Pleasure, ill-exchang'd for Pow'r; ... 4.EpS1.30.300.
Oh source of ev'ry social tye, ... 6.51ii.25.153.
Thy martial spirit, or thy Social love! ... 6.113.8.320.
In Life, with ev'ry social Grace adorn'd, ... 6.134.9.364.
Sit thou secure amidst thy social Band; ... Il.7.133.370.
Then each, indulging in the social Feast, ... Il.9.289.448.
Molus receiv'd, the Pledge of social Ties; ... Il.10.316.17.
The social Shades the same dark Journey go, ... Il.11.339.49.
Social we sit, and share the genial Rites. ... Il.11.911.76.
Supine he falls, and to his social Train ... Il.13.694.138.
Preserve his Arms, preserve his social Train, ... Il.16.304.254.
Retires for Succour to his social Train, ... Il.16.985.281.
Approach the dome, the social banquet share, ... Od.1.163.40.
Or number'd in my Father's social train? ... Od.1.224.43.
When social mirth unbent his serious soul, ... Od.1.335.48.
High in *Ulysses'* social list inroll'd. ... Od.1.528.57.
Of social welcome, mix'd the racy wine, ... Od.3.503.112.
What time the *Greeks* combin'd their social arms, ... Od.4.195.129.
My self assisting in the social joy, ... Od.4.331.135.
Now pleas'd and satiate from the social rite ... Od.7.248.248.
With social intercourse, and face to face, ... Od.7.275.249.
The social feast of joy, with joy sincere. ... Od.8.430.287.
This social right demands: for him the sails ... Od.8.591.294.
Man's social days in union, and in joy? ... Od.9.8.301.
And try what social rites a savage lends: ... Od.9.270.318.
And social joys, the late-transform'd repairs: ... Od.10.532.369.
And ev'ry God inspiring social love! ... Od.14.183.44.
Thus might we sit, with social goblets crown'd, ... Od.14.225.46.
If, after social rites and gifts bestow'd, ... Od.14.445.57.
Sweet is thy converse to each social ear; ... Od.15.355.86.
Nor less the father pour'd a social flood; ... Od.16.236.114.
This justice, this the social right demands. ... Od.18.467.191.
Then with *Telemachus* the social feast ... Od.19.368.212.
I ne'er discern'd, before this social hour. ... Od.19.406.214.
The social feast, and drain the cheering bowl: ... Od.20.327.249.
Deaf to Heav'n's voice, the social rite transgrest; ... Od.21.31.260.

SOCIETIES
Cities were built, Societies were made: ... 3.EOM3.200.113.

SOCIETY
B. Trade it may help, Society extend; ... 3.Ep3.31A.88.
Trade it may help, Society extend; ... 3.Ep3.31.88.
That NATURE our Society adores, ... 5.DunB4.491.390.
Thy sweet Society, thy winning Care, ... Il.19.337.386.
Far from the sweet society of men, ... Od.21.394.279.

SOCINIAN
I wish you do not turn *Socinian;* ... 6.10.80.27.

SOCINUS
Did all the Dregs of bold *Socinus* drain; ... 1.EOC.545.300.

SOCK
And to its Ancient *Mirth the* Comic Sock *return.* ... 6.26ii.8.79.

SOCRATES
Here ever shines the Godlike *Socrates:* ... 2.TemF.171.269.
Like Socrates, that Man is great indeed. ... 3.EOM4.236.148.

SOCUS
But to his Aid his Brother *Socus* flies, ... Il.11.537.57.
Socus, the brave, the gen'rous, and the wise: ... Il.11.538.57.
He spoke, while *Socus* seiz'd with sudden Fright, ... Il.11.558.58.

SOE'ER
Curst be the Verse, how well soe'er it flow, ... 4.Arbu.283.116.
What Pow'r soe'er provokes our lifted Hand, ... Il.8.567.423.

SOEVER
How merrily soever others fare? ... 2.ChWB.135.63.
Yes, Sir, how small soever be my heap, ... 4.2HE2.284.185.

SOFT
A soft Retreat from sudden vernal Show'rs; ... 1.PSp.98.70.
Soft as he mourn'd, the Streams forgot to flow, ... 1.PSu.5.71.
Now sleeping Flocks on their soft Fleeces lye, ... 1.PWi.5.89.
And in soft Silence shed the kindly Show'r! ... 1.Mes.14.114.
Soft Show'rs distill'd, and Suns grew warm in vain; ... 1.W-F.54.154.
In a soft, silver Stream dissolv'd away. ... 1.W-F.204.168.
I hear soft Musick dye along the Grove; ... 1.W-F.268.173.
And hear soft Musick dye along the Grove; ... 1.W-F.268A.173.
'Tis yours, my Lord, to bless our soft Retreats, ... 1.W-F.283.174.
To the same Notes, of Love, and soft Desire: ... 1.W-F.296.176.
The *Memory's* soft Figures melt away. ... 1.EOC.59.245.
Soft is the Strain when *Zephyr* gently blows, ... 1.EOC.366.282.
And soft as down upon the breast of swans: ... 1.TrPA.61.367.
Let soft Compassion touch your gentle Mind; ... 1.TrVP.106.381.
In her soft Breast consenting Passions move, ... 1.TrVP.122.382.
Soft Scenes of Solitude no more can please, ... 1.TrSP.15.393.
Spread thy soft Wings, and waft me o'er the Main, ... 1.TrSP.210.403.
Or in soft Slumbers seals the wakeful Eye; ... 1.TrSt.434.428.

SOFT (CONTINUED)
To call soft Slumbers on his infant Eyes. 1.TrSt.690.439.
To the soft Arms of silent *Sleep* and *Death;* 1.TrES.331.461.
All which soft Sleep now banish'd from his Breast; 1.TrUl.19.466.
Soft Rains and kindly Dews refresh the Field, 1.TrUl.130.470.
Yet led astray by *Venus'* soft Delights, 2.ChJM.5.15.
The breathing Flute's soft Notes are heard around, 2.ChJM.318.29.
On her soft Couch uneasily she lay: 2.ChJM.419.35.
And wasted in the soft, infectious Fire. 2.ChJM.433.35.
With pleasing Poison, and with soft Deceit! 2.ChJM.480.38.
And in soft Murmurs tell the Trees their Pain; 2.ChJM.528.41.
Breathe a soft Sigh, and drop a tender Tear; 2.ChJM.666.47.
And in soft Bosoms dwells such mighty Rage? 2.RL1.12.145.
Thence, by a soft Transition, we repair 2.RL1.49.149.
Soft yielding Minds to Water glide away, 2.RL1.61.150.
And in soft Sounds, *Your Grace* salutes their Ear. 2.RL1.86.152.
Soft o'er the Shrouds Aerial Whispers breathe, 2.RL2.57.163.
Soft Sorrows, melting Griefs, and flowing Tears. 2.RL4.86.190.
In that soft Season when descending Showers 2.TemF.1.253.
So soft, tho high, so loud, and yet so clear, 2.TemF.374.281.
On neighb'ring Air a soft Impression make; 2.TemF.443.284.
Speed the soft intercourse from soul to soul, 2.ElAb.57.323.
Ye soft illusions, dear deceits, arise! 2.ElAb.240.339.
Soft as the slumbers of a saint forgiv'n, 2.ElAb.255.340.
With ev'ry bead I drop too soft a tear. 2.ElAb.270.342.
Matter too soft a lasting mark to bear, 3.Ep2.3.46.
How soft is Silia! fearful to offend, 3.Ep2.29.52.
On the soft Passion, and the Taste refin'd, 3.Ep2.84.57.
Or soft Adonis, so perfum'd and fine, 3.Ep3.61.91.
Soft and Agreeable come never there. 3.Ep4.102.147.
But soft—by regular approach—not yet— 3.Ep4.129.149.
To rest, the Cushion and soft Dean invite, 3.Ep4.149.151.
He came by soft Transition to his own: 4.JD4.81A.31.
Lull'd by soft Zephyrs thro' the broken Pane, 4.Arbu.42.99.
Soft were my Numbers, who could take offence 4.Arbu.147.106.
Fed with soft Dedication all day long, 4.Arbu.233.112.
Or from the soft-ey'd Virgin steal a tear! 4.Arbu.286.116.
Yet soft by Nature, more a Dupe than Wit, 4.Arbu.368.123.
Pierce the soft lab'rinth of a Lady's ear 4.JD2.55.137.
Ah sound no more thy soft alarms, 4.HOde1.5.151.
Ah sound no more your soft alarms, 4.HOde1.5A.151.
Ah sound no more the soft alarms, 4.HOde1.5B.151.
Shall call the smiling Loves, and soft Desires; 4.HOde1.26A.153.
Forms the soft bosom with the gentlest art, 4.2HE1.219.213.
Britain to soft refinements less a foe, 4.2HE1.265.217.
Silent and soft, as Saints remove to Heav'n, 4.EpS1.93.305.
Hence the soft sing-song on Cecilia's day, 5.DunA1.40.65.
And the pleas'd dame soft-smiling leads away. 5.DunA2.180.123.
And the pleas'd dame soft-smiling lead'st away. 5.DunA2.180A.123.
Strives to extract from his soft, giving palm; 5.DunA2.200.126.
They led him soft; how all the bards arose; 5.DunA2.322.141.
Soft, creeping, words on words, the sense compose, 5.DunA2.357.143.
As to soft gales top-heavy pines bow low 5.DunA2.359.143.
Thus the soft gifts of Sleep conclude the day, 5.DunA2.387.148.
And soft besprinkled with Cimmerian dew. 5.DunA3.4.150.
And the pleas'd dame, soft-smiling, lead'st away. 5.DunB2.188.304.
Strives to extract from his soft, giving palm; 5.DunB2.208.306.
They led him soft; each rev'rend Bard arose; 5.DunB2.348.314.
Soft creeping, words on words, the sense compose, 5.DunB2.389.316.
As to soft gales top-heavy pines bow low 5.DunB2.391.316.
Thus the soft gifts of Sleep conclude the day, 5.DunB2.419.318.
And soft besprinkles with Cimmerian dew. 5.DunB3.4.320.
And soft besprinkled with Cimmerian dew. 5.DunB3.4A.320.
Soft on her lap her Laureat son reclines. 5.DunB4.20.341.
When lo! a Harlot form soft sliding by, 5.DunB4.45.345.
Soft, as the wily Fox is seen to creep, 5.DunB4.351.377.
(Reply'd soft Annius) this our paunch before 5.DunB4.388.380.
And Douglas lend his soft, obstetric hand." 5.DunB4.394.380.
Soft on the paper ruff its leaves I spread, 5.DunB4.407.382.
Hours, days, and years slide soft away, 6.1.10.3.
Soft looks of mercy grace the flatt'ring shade, 6.4ii.4.9.
So from one cloud soft show'rs we view, 6.5.9.12.
As the soft dews of morning skies 6.5.7A.12.
Hark! the Numbers, soft and clear, 6.11.12.30.
Music her soft, assuasive Voice applies; 6.11.25.30.
And the soft, silent Harmony, that springs 6.11.35Z9.31.
And many a Boat soft sliding to and fro. 6.14ii.4.43.
And soft *Carnations* show'r their balmy dews; 6.14iv.4.47.
Soft be his Slumbers! But may this be all. 6.17iv.22.60.
To the soft joys of *Nile's* delightful shore. 6.20.10.66.
Calm rest, and soft serenity of mind; 6.23.16.73.
I hear around soft Musick play, 6.31ii.6Z7.95.
Wou'd you enjoy soft nights and solid dinners? 6.41.23.114.
Or sees the blush of soft *Parthenia* rise, 6.45.46.126.
Soft *B*— and rough *C[ragg]s,* adieu! 6.47.5.128*.
Love, soft intruder, enters here, 6.51ii.5.152.
And soft *Belinda's* blush for ever glow. 6.52.62.158.
Soft without weakness, without glaring gay; 6.52.66.158.
Come these soft lines, with nothing Stiff in 6.61.5.180.
But soft recesses of uneasy minds, 6.81.9.225.
But soft recesses for th' uneasy Mind, 6.81.9A.225.
By the soft Fannings of the wafting Sheets, 6.82ii.3.230.
In some soft Dream, or Extasy of joy: 6.86.18.245.
In some soft Dream may thy mild Soul remove, 6.86.19A.246.
Or let thy soul in some soft dream remove, 6.86.19B.246.
Let the mild soul in some soft dream remove, 6.86.19C.246.
And sensible soft Melancholy. 6.89.8.250.
Soft as the Speaking Trumpet's mellow Noise: 6.96ii.72.273.
Villete's soft Voice and St John's silver Lyre. 6.106ii.6.307.
O soft Humanity, in Age belov'd! 6.113.4.320.
So firm yet soft, so strong yet so refin'd, 6.115.8.323.
Me long,ah long! may these soft Cares engage; 6.117.3.333.
Yet soft his Nature, tho' severe his Lay, 6.118.5.334.
This whispers soft his Vengeance to controul, Il.1.257.99.
Yet these with soft, persuasive Arts I sway'd, Il.1.358.105.
She, in soft Sorrows, and in pensive Thought, Il.1.451.109.

SOFT (CONTINUED)
Thy graceful Form instilling soft Desire, Il.3.79.193.
Soft moving Speech, and pleasing outward Show, Il.3.95.194.
Soft as the Fleeces of descending Snows Il.3.284.207.
And Breast, reveal'd the Queen of soft Desire. Il.3.490.215.
Or carry Wars to some soft *Asian* Plain? Il.3.496.215.
He knew soft Combates suit the tender Dame, Il.5.413.286.
Go, let thy own soft Sex employ thy Care, Il.5.435.289.
Raz'd her soft Hand with this lamented Wound. Il.5.516.293.
E're yet their Wives soft Arms the Cowards gain, Il.6.101.328.
I go to rowze soft *Paris* to the War; Il.6.349.343.
Whom from soft *Sidon* youthful *Paris* bore, Il.6.362.344.
Whom each soft Charm and early Grace adorn, Il.6.498.351.
Soft on her fragrant Breast the Babe she laid, Il.6.618.357.
Thro' all her Train the soft Infection ran, Il.6.645.358.
(Soft *Zephyr* curling the wide wat'ry Plain) Il.7.72.366.
In sable Streams soft-trickling Waters shed. Il.9.20.432.
With Fleeces, Carpets, and soft Linen spread: Il.9.776.472.
Or sends soft Snows to whiten all the Shore, Il.10.7.2.
Alike deny'd the Gifts of soft Repose, Il.10.32.4.
At this, soft Slumber from his Eyelids fled; Il.10.184.10.
Soft Wool within; without, in order spread, Il.10.311.16.
Soft, at just distance, both the Chiefs pursue. Il.10.418.21.
Soft *Minyas* rolls his Waters to the Main. Il.11.859.74.
A Slings soft Wool, snatch'd from a Soldier's side, Il.13.751.140.
Soft Oils of Fragrance, and ambrosial Show'rs: Il.14.198.168.
Shed thy soft Dews on *Jove's* immortal Eyes, Il.14.270.175.
And secret there indulge thy soft Desire. Il.14.386.181.
Thick new-born Vi'lets a soft Carpet spread, Il.14.397.182.
Steep'd in soft Joys, and circumfus'd with Air; Il.14.402.183.
At length with Love and Sleep's soft Pow'r opprest, Il.14.405.183.
To *Neptune's* Ear soft *Sleep* his Message brings; Il.14.408.183.
Thy soft Deceits, and well-dissembled Love. Il.15.38.195.
Their Pain, soft Arts of Pharmacy can ease, Il.16.38.237.
But sure thou spring'st not from a soft Embrace, Il.16.47.237.
To the soft Arms of silent *Sleep* and *Death;* Il.16.818.274.
Sunk in soft Dust the mighty Chief remains, Il.16.936.279.
And thy soft Pleasures serv'd with captive Dames! Il.16.1006.282.
And the blue Languish of soft *Alia's* Eye. Il.18.50.326.
And the soft Tears to trickle from her Eyes? Il.18.158.330.
Observ'd her ent'ring; her soft Hand she press'd, Il.18.451.343.
And soft receiv'd me on their silver Breast. Il.18.466.344.
To the soft Flute, and Cittern's silver Sound: Il.18.574.350.
Tune soft the Voice, and answer to the Strain. Il.18.664.355.
The Maids in soft Cymarrs of Linen drest; Il.18.685.356.
And thus, his Hand soft-touching, *Thetis* said. Il.19.10.371.
If ever yet soft Pity touch'd thy mind, Il.21.105.426.
Soft Rills of Water from the bubbling Springs, Il.21.290.433.
And soft re-murmur in their wonted Bed. Il.21.447.438.
Sunk soft in Down upon the Nurse's Breast, Il.22.649.483.
At length he sinks in the soft Arms of Sleep. Il.23.77.490.
And left me these, a soft and servile Crew, Il.24.326.550.
Or in soft Slumbers seals the wakeful Eye; Il.24.422.553.
These Words soft Pity in the Chief inspire, Il.24.634.563.
Soft Sleep a Stranger to my weeping Eyes, Il.24.808.570.
With Purple soft, and shaggy Carpets spread; Il.24.813.571.
Seduc'd this soft, this easy Heart of mine!) Il.24.967.576.
Successless all her soft caresses prove, Od.1.73.34.
And spread soft hydes upon the yellow sands; Od.3.48.88.
In whom stern courage with soft virtue join'd, Od.3.137.92.
And soft approach the balmy hours of sleep: Od.3.428.107.
Suffic'd, soft-whispering thus to *Nestor's* son, Od.4.81.123.
Nor sleep's soft pow'r can close my streaming eyes, Od.4.135.126.
In her soft hands the beauteous *Phylo* brought: Od.4.166.128.
And o'er soft palls of purple grain unfold Od.4.405.139.
Heav'ns! wou'd a soft, inglorious, dastard train Od.4.447.141.
To render sleep's soft blessing unsincere? Od.4.1060.167.
Or in soft slumber seals the wakeful eye: Od.5.61.174.
For now the soft Enchantress pleas'd no more: Od.5.196.181.
Approaching soft; and thus the chief addrest. Od.5.206.181.
Less soft my feature, less august my frame? Od.5.270.184.
And bear him soft on broken waves away; Od.5.493.195.
And soft receives him from the rowling sea. Od.5.579.200.
Where on the flow'ry herb as soft he lay, Od.5.597.201.
'Till *Pallas* pour'd soft slumbers on his eyes; Od.5.635.202.
In elder times the soft *Phæacian* train Od.6.5.203.
And give soft transport to a parent's heart. Od.6.34.206.
Odour divine! whose soft refreshing streams Od.6.93.209.
Oh let soft pity touch thy gen'rous mind! Od.6.212.220.
On thy soft hours their choicest blessings shed, Od.6.219.220.
Soft he reclines along the murm'ring seas, Od.6.283.224.
There, soft-extended, to the murm'ring sound Od.7.435.258.
To soft affliction all his manly mind: Od.8.80.267.
And the soft Lyre to grace our pastimes bear. Od.8.292.278.
Come, my belov'd! and taste the soft delights; Od.8.333.281.
To the soft *Cyprian* shores the Goddess moves, Od.8.395.285.
Four faithful handmaids the soft rites prepare; Od.10.414.364.
Fair, pensive youths, and soft-enamour'd maids, Od.11.49.383.
By the soft tye and sacred name of friend! Od.11.82.385.
And in soft mazes rouls a silver Tide: Od.11.286.396.
There with soft step the fair *Alcmena* trod, Od.11.325.398.
Soft, as some song divine, thy story flows, Od.11.458.407.
Time for discourse, and time for soft repose, Od.11.473.407.
To soft affliction all my manly mind, Od.11.492.408.
To meet soft quiet and repose at home; Od.11.536.409.
Touch the soft lyre, and tune the vocal lay; Od.12.195.441.
Then o'er my eyes the Gods soft slumber shed, Od.12.401.450.
'Twas then soft slumber fled my troubled brain: Od.12.431.451.
Beneath the seats, soft painted robes they spread, Od.13.88.5.
All which soft sleep now banish'd from his breast, Od.13.110.6.
By soft *Phæacians,* my degen'rate race! Od.13.151.13.
Soft rains and kindly dews refresh the field, Od.13.297.20.
A shaggy goat's soft hyde beneath him spread, Od.14.59.38.
Less soft my mother, less my father kind. Od.14.162.43.
The tenth soft wafts me to *Thesprotia's* shore. Od.14.350.51.
Soft I descended, to the sea apply'd Od.14.385.53.

SOFT (CONTINUED)
Hush thee, he cry'd, (soft-whisp'ring in my ear) .... Od.14.555.64.
A part we consecrate to soft repose, ... Od.15.427.89.
In form, a virgin in soft beauty's bloom, ... Od.16.170.111.
Soft were his words; his actions wisdom sway'd; .... Od.16.414.126.
And in soft slumber seal'd her flowing eye. .... Od.16.469.130.
And in soft sleep forgot the cares of day. .... Od.16.501.131.
Heav'ns! would a soft, inglorious, dastard train .... Od.17.138.138.
Mean-time they heard, soft-circling in the sky, ... Od.17.310.146.
Soft pity touch'd the mighty master's soul; .... Od.17.364.149.
(Immortal gifts! to kindle soft desires) .... Od.18.226.178.
With soft forgetfulness, a wretch like me; .... Od.18.238.178.
With the soft fondness of a daughter bred) .... Od.18.370.185.
Soft slumb'rous shades his drooping eye-lids close, ... Od.19.60.195.
A seat soft spread with furry spoils prepare, ... Od.19.119.198.
Your drooping eyes with soft oppression seize; .... Od.19.595.225.
'Till soft oblivious shade *Minerva* spread, ... Od.19.703.229.
Whilst night extends her soft oblivious veil, ... Od.20.99.237.
Then to the lute's soft voice prolong the night, ... Od.21.473.283.
On that soft pillow, from that envy'd height .... Od.22.213.297.
Persuasive, thus, with accent soft began. .... Od.22.378.306.
Where slumbers soft now close the royal eye; .... Od.22.467.311.
While the soft hours stole unperceiv'd away; .... Od.23.322.339.
Soon as soft slumber eas'd the toils of day, ... Od.23.371.343.
Or in soft slumber seals the wakeful eye, ... Od.24.4.347.
Of question distant, and of soft essay, ... Od.24.280.363.
Soft sleep, fair garments, and the joys of wine, ... Od.24.300.364.
(Restless and early sleep's soft bands they broke) .... Od.24.506.372.

SOFT-CIRCLING
Mean-time they heard, soft-circling in the sky, ... Od.17.310.146.

SOFT-ENAMOUR'D
Fair, pensive youths, and soft-enamour'd maids, ... Od.11.49.383.

SOFT-EXTENDED
There, soft-extended, to the murm'ring sound .... Od.7.435.258.

SOFT-EY'D
Or from the soft-ey'd Virgin steal a tear! .... 4.Arbu.286.116.

SOFT-SMILING
And the pleas'd dame soft-smiling leads away. .... 5.DunA2.180.123.
And the pleas'd dame soft-smiling lead'st away. .... 5.DunA2.180A.123.
And the pleas'd dame, soft-smiling, lead'st away. .... 5.DunB2.188.304.

SOFT-TOUCHING
And thus, his Hand soft-touching, *Thetis* said. .... Il.19.10.371.

SOFT-TRICKLING
In sable Streams soft-trickling Waters shed. .... Il.9.20.432.

SOFT-WHISP'RING
Hush thee, he cry'd, (soft-whisp'ring in my ear) .... Od.14.555.64.

SOFT-WHISPERING
Suffic'd, soft-whispering thus to *Nestor's* son, ... Od.4.81.123.

SOFT'NING
Firm wisdom interdicts the soft'ning tear. .... Od.19.250.206.

SOFTEN
When the ripe Colours *soften* and *unite,* .... 1.EOC.488.294.
If white and black blend, soften, and unite .... 3.EOM2.213.81.
Musick can soften Pain to Ease, ... 6.11.120.34.
And arts but soften us to feel thy flame. .... 6.51ii.4.152.
Breath'd from the Gods to soften human pain) .... Od.17.611.161.

SOFTEN'D
And soften'd Sounds along the Waters die. .... 2.RL2.50.162.
Yet, mix'd and soften'd, in his work unite: .... 3.EOM2.112.68.
Then Marble soften'd into life grew warm, ... 4.2HE1.147.207.
And soften'd Mortals learn'd the Arts of Peace. .... 6.11.35Z2.31.
The soften'd Chief with kind Compassion view'd, ... Il.6.622.357.
With Pity soften'd, and with Fury swell'd: .... Il.13.828.145.
Thy gentle Accents soften'd all my Pain. .... Il.24.974.576.
And soften'd his stern soul to tender love. .... Od.11.328.398.
And melting pity soften'd ev'ry face; .... Od.17.593.161.

SOFTENS
When Musick softens, and when Dancing fires? .... 2.RL1.76.151.
Bid her be all that chears or softens life, ... 6.52.51.157.
Softens Defects, and heightens all its Charms, ... 6.96v.23.280.
Sooths weary Life, and softens human Pain. .... Il.24.166.542.

SOFTER
Let softer Strains Ill-fated *Henry* mourn, ... 1.W-F.311.179.
Within, the Waves in softer Murmurs glide, ... 1.TrUl.29.466.
Th' expressive Emblem of their softer Pow'r; .... 2.RL3.40.171.
The softer Spirit of the *Sapphick* Muse. .... 2.TemF.225.273.
Its last best work, creates this softer Man; .... 3.Ep2.272A.72.
Its last best work, It forms a softer Man; .... 3.Ep2.272B.72.
Its last best work, but forms a softer Man; .... 3.Ep2.272.72.
But the good Bishop, with a softer air, ... 3.Ep3.107C.100.
F. Then all your Muse's softer Art display, ... 4.HS1.29.7.
How pleasing ATTERBURY's softer hour! .... 4.EpS2.82.317.
How young Lutetia, softer than the down, ... 5.DunA2.309.139.
How young Lutetia, softer than the down, ... 5.DunB2.333.313.
Caracci's strength, *Coreggio's* softer line, ... 6.52.37.157.
A softer wonder my pleas'd soul surveys, ... 6.106i.2.306.
Yet softer Honours, and less noisy Fame .... 6.132.9.362.
Brac'd in, and fitted to his softer Breast; .... Il.3.414.212.
These softer Moments let Delights employ, ... Il.3.549.217.
Thee milder Arts befit, and softer Wars, ... Il.5.520.293.
Let softer Cares the present Hour employ, ... Il.14.357.180.
And *Chromius* last; but of the softer race, ... Od.11.349.399.

SOFTER (CONTINUED)
Within, the waves in softer murmurs glide, ... Od.13.120.7.

SOFTEST
The Muses teach me all their softest Lays, ... 1.TrSP.31.394.
Think not your softest Numbers can display .... 2.ChJM.337.30.
And dwells such Rage in softest Bosoms then? .... 2.RL1.11A.145.
With softest Manners, gentlest Arts, adorn'd! .... 6.84.4.238.
Of softest manners, unaffected mind, ... 6.109.7.314.
Warm with the softest Wool, and doubly lin'd. .... Il.10.153.8.
Of softest Texture, and inwrought with Gold; .... Il.24.1006.577.
Of softest woof, is bright *Alcippe's* care. .... Od.4.164.128.

SOFTLY
And the hush'd Waves glide softly to the Shore. .... 1.W-F.354.184.
And softly lay me on the Waves below! .... 1.TrSP.208.403.
And softly curse the Tyrants whom they fear. .... 1.TrSt.229.420.
Then softly whisper'd in her faithful Ear, ... 1.TrSt.621.436.
Where, as she try'd his Pulse, he softly drew .... 2.ChJM.414.35.
Or softly glide by the Canal, ... 4.HOde1.46.153.
And, softly sighing, from the Loom withdrew. .... Il.3.188.200.
The Goddess softly shook her silken Vest .... Il.3.479.214.
Then softly sighing, he the fair addrest, ... Od.11.295.396.
But when the softly-stealing pace of time .... Od.15.390.88.

SOFTLY-STEALING
But when the softly-stealing pace of time .... Od.15.390.88.

SOFTNESS
Her moving Softness, and majestick Grace. .... 2.ChJM.249.26.
Courage with Softness, Modesty with Pride, ... 3.Ep2.278.72.
Th' infectious Softness thro' the Heroes ran; .... Il.24.644.563.
To softness lost, to spousal love unknown, ... Od.23.105.324.

SOHOE
Befringe the rails of Bedlam and Sohoe. .... 4.2HE1.419.231.

SOIL
Say, *Daphnis,* say, in what glad Soil appears .... 1.PSp.85.69.
Say, Shepherd, say, in what glad Soil appears .... 1.PSp.85A.69.
Which the kind Soil with milky Sap supplies; .... 1.TrVP.103.381.
How with the Serpent's Teeth he sow'd the Soil, ... 1.TrSt.9.409.
The rugged Soil allows no level Space .... 1.TrUl.122.470.
For 'twas from *Crete,* my Native Soil, I came; .... 1.TrUl.141.470.
Say, in what mortal soil thou deign'st to grow? .... 3.EOM4.8.128.
We ought to blame the culture, not the soil: .... 3.EOM4.14.129.
The knave deserves it, when he tills the soil, ... 3.EOM4.152.142.
In life's low vale, the soil the virtues like, ... 3.Ep1.95.22.
Who then shall grace, or who improve the Soil? .... 3.Ep4.177.154.
Yet to their Lord owe more than to the soil; .... 3.Ep4.184.154.
Has what the frugal, dirty soil affords, ... 4.EpS2.174.323.
(The soil that arts and infant letters bore) .... 5.DunA3.88.157.
(The soil that arts and infant letters bore) .... 5.DunB3.96.324.
Far from her native Soil, and weeping Sire. .... Il.1.46.88.
Whose fruitful Soil luxuriant Harvests grace, ... Il.1.205.96.
The Men who *Glaphyra's* fair Soil partake, ... Il.2.864.165.
In sable Ships they left their native Soil, ... Il.5.678.300.
Amphius Apæsus' happy Soil possess'd, ... Il.5.760.303.
Bold are the men, and gen'rous is the Soil; .... Il.9.204.442.
Bold are the Men, and gen'rous is the Soil; .... Il.9.391.452.
Force the bright Plowshare thro' the fallow Soil, ... Il.13.880.147.
They wing their way, and *Imbrus'* Sea-beat Soil, ... Il.14.318.178.
On the hard Soil his groaning Breast he threw, ... Il.18.31.325.
Then back the turning Plow-shares cleave the Soil: .... Il.18.634.354.
Wash'd from beneath him, slides the slimy Soil; .... Il.21.310.433.
At once consumes the dead, and dries the Soil; .... Il.21.400.436.
The bard they banish'd from his native soil, ... Od.3.340.103.
To them my vassals had resign'd a soil, ... Od.4.239.130.
With various simples cloaths the fat'ned soil. .... Od.4.318.134.
Far from his own domain salutes the soil; .... Od.4.696.152.
To see my soil, my son, my friends, again. .... Od.7.304.250.
My native soil is *Ithaca* the fair, ... Od.9.21.302.
The soil untill'd a ready harvest yields, ... Od.9.123.310.
Nor knows the soil to feed the fleecy care, ... Od.9.141.311.
Gaze on the coast, nor cultivate the soil, ... Od.9.149.311.
Whose oxen long have torn the furrow'd soil, ... Od.13.40.3.
The rugged soil allows no level space .... Od.13.289.19.
For 'twas from *Crete* my native soil I came, ... Od.13.308.21.
Crete awes the circling waves, a fruitful soil! .... Od.19.196.201.
"To view his mother's soil, my *Delphic* dome .... Od.19.482.220.
And labour made the rugged soil a plain. .... Od.24.237.360.
Thy careful hand is stamp'd on all the soil, ... Od.24.288.363.
An absent Heroe's bed they sought to soil, ... Od.24.524.373.

SOIL'D
I tore my Gown, I soil'd my Locks with Dust, ... 2.ChWB.309.71.
Now soil'd with Dust, and naked to the Sky, ... Il.11.135.41.
The Body soil'd with Dust, and black with Gore, ... Il.23.3.485.

SOILS
And soils its verdant Tresses on the Ground: .... Il.13.243.116.

SOJOURN
By thy sweet Sojourn in those virtuous Climes, ... 6.96iii.6.274.

SOJOURN'D
While here I sojourn'd, oft I heard the fame .... Od.14.355.51.

SOL
For envy'd Wit, like *Sol* Eclips'd, makes known .... 1.EOC.468.292.
Sol thro' white Curtains shot a tim'rous Ray, ... 2.RL1.13.145.
Sol thro' white Curtains did his Beams display, ... 2.RL1.13A.145.
Now flaming from the *Zenith, Sol* had driv'n .... Il.16.938.280.
And now the gates where ev'ning *Sol* descends, ... Od.24.16.347.
Their latent buds, and *Sol* exalts the juice. .... Od.24.400.368.

SOL'S
For *Sol's* is now the only ray. ....6.4iv.12.10.
To *Sol's* bright Isle our voyage we pursue, ...Od.12.314.447.

SOLA
Solus cum Sola, with his sprightly *May.* .... 2.ChJM.472.38.

SOLACE
Amidst his Ease, his Solace and Delight, ...2.ChJM.482.38.
Art far the dearest Solace of my Life; ....2.ChJM.546.41.
Health to the sick, and solace to the swain. ....3.Ep3.258.114.
For matrimonial Solace dies a martyr. ....4.1HE1.151.291.
And solace of the thirsty swain. ....6.6ii.4.14.

SOLAR
Far as the solar walk, or milky way; ....3.EOM1.102.27.
Against the Solar Beam and *Sirian* Fire. ....Il.23.235.499.
And while the robes imbibe the solar ray, ...Od.6.111.211.
That shot effulgence like the solar ray, ...Od.18.344.184.
Nor solar ray, cou'd pierce the shadowy bow'r, ...Od.19.514.221.

SOLD
Marry who will, our *Sex* is to be Sold! ....2.ChWB.171.65.
Esteem and Love were never to be sold. ....3.EOM4.188.145.
To live on Ven'son when it sold so dear. ....3.Ep3.120.101.
And therefore hopes this Nation may be sold: ....3.Ep3.126.102.
'Twas very want that sold them for two pound. ....3.Ep3.328.120.
As the fair Fields they sold to look so fine. ....4.JD4.217.45.
Till *Becca-ficos* sold so dev'lish dear ....4.HS2.39.57.
My lands are sold, my Father's house is gone; ....4.HS2.155.67.
All Worldly's Hens, nay Partridge, sold to town, ...4.2HE2.234.181.
All He[athco]te's Hens, nay Partridge, sold to town, ...4.2HE2.234A.181.
Just half the land would buy, and half be sold: ....4.1HE1.125.289.
Impatient sees his country bought and sold, ...4.1740.11.332.
The Clergy perjur'd, thy whole People sold. ....4.1740.82.336.
And keep his Lares, tho' his house be sold; ....5.DunB4.366.378.
Poor *Y[ounge]r's* sold for Fifty Pound, ...6.47.31.129.
"To some Lord's Daughter sold the living Toy; ....6.96ii.34.272.
He, who for Bribes his faithless Counsels sold, ...Il.11.163.42.
To *Lemnos'* Isle he sold the Royal Slave, ...Il.21.46.424.
And sold to *Lemnos,* stalks on *Trojan* Ground! ....Il.21.67.424.
Or, worse than slaughter'd, sold in distant Isles ....Il.22.61.455.
Achilles bound, and sold to foreign Lands, ...Il.24.947.575.
There *Eriphylè* weeps, who loosely sold ....Od.11.406.404.
The *Taphians* sold me to this man's embrace. ....Od.15.469.93.
Sold to *Laertes,* by divine command, ...Od.15.520.95.

SOLDIER
A Soldier now, he with his Sword appears; ....1.TrVP.41.378.
Tom struts a Soldier, open, bold, and brave; ....3.Ep1.105.22.
In ANNA's Wars, a Soldier poor and old, ...4.2HE2.33.167.
The Soldier breath'd the Gallantries of France, ...4.2HE1.145.207.
And (tho' no Soldier) useful to the State. ....4.2HE1.204.211.
In Soldier, Churchman, Patriot, Man in Pow'r, ...4.EpS1.161.309.
A common Soldier, but who clubb'd his *Mite?* .... 6.128.8.355.
'Till ev'ry Soldier grasp a *Phrygian* Wife, ...Il.2.421.147.
What Chief, or Soldier, of the num'rous Band, ...Il.2.434.148.
For thee the Soldier bleeds, the Matron mourns, ...Il.6.412.347.
With which a wounded Soldier touch'd his Breast, ...Il.13.280.119.
And ev'ry soldier found a like reward. ....Od.9.46.304.
He quaff'd the gore: and strait his soldier knew, ...Od.11.485.408.
(The sex is ever to a soldier kind.) ....Od.14.246.48.

SOLDIER'S
Think not to rob me of a Soldier's Right. ....Il.1.170.95.
Whose just Division crown'd the Soldier's Toils; ....Il.1.481.111.
And knowing this, I know a Soldier's Part. ....Il.11.520.57.
A Slings soft Wool, snatch'd from a Soldier's side, ...Il.13.751.140.
Greece to reward her soldier's gallant toils ....Od.11.653.416.

SOLDIERS
Crowns were reserv'd to grace the *Soldiers* too. ....1.EOC.513.296.
With Mobs, and Duns, and Soldiers, at their doors; ....4.2HE2.124.173.
The Chiefs advises, and the Soldiers warms. ....Il.4.339.236.
Some few my Soldiers had, himself the rest. ....Il.9.437.454.
Still, with your Voice, the sloathful Soldiers raise, ...Il.10.74.5.
The Soldiers Baseness, or the Gen'ral's Fault? ....Il.13.148.111.
While War hangs doubtful, while his Soldiers fight? ....Il.14.107.162.
(The Work of Soldiers) where the Hero Sate. ....Il.24.556.559.
All expert soldiers, skill'd on foot to dare, ...Od.9.57.304.
The leader's rashness made the soldiers bleed. ....Od.10.516.368.
With him the strength of war, the soldiers pride, ...Od.11.673.417.

SOLDIERS'
Spread their cold Poison thro' our Soldiers' Breasts, ...Il.12.292.92.

SOLE
From Love, the sole Disease thou canst not cure! ....1.PSu.12.72.
Sole judge of Truth, in endless Error hurl'd: ....3.EOM2.17.56.
See! the sole bliss Heav'n could on all bestow; ....3.EOM4.327.160.
Of all thy blameless Life the sole Return ....4.Arbu.259.114.
Sole Dread of Folly, Vice, and Insolence! ....4.EpS2.213.325.
B[enson] sole Judge of Architecture sit, ...5.DunA3.321.188.
THOU art my God, sole object of my love; ....6.25.1.77.
To One sole Monarch *Jove* commits the Sway; ....Il.2.243.139.
Sole should he sit, with scarce a God to Friend, ...Il.8.250.409.
Those, my sole Oracles, inspire my Rage: ....Il.16.73.238.
Sole in the Seat the Charioteer remains, ...Il.17.532.309.
And *Jove's* sole Favour gives him all his Fame. ....Il.21.674.450.
Your sole Defence, your guardian Pow'r is gone! ....Il.24.304.549.
Ulysses, sole of all the victor train, ...Od.1.18.30.
Where sole of all his train, a Matron sage ....Od.1.247.44.
Sole o'er my vassals, and domestic train. ....Od.1.508.56.
Sole with *Telemachus* her service ends, ...Od.1.547.58.
Sole witness of the deed I now declare; ....Od.4.333.135.
Me sole the daughter of the deep address'd; ....Od.4.496.144.

SOLE (CONTINUED)
Ægisthus sole survives to boast the deed. ....Od.4.724.152.
Sole in an isle, encircled by the main, ...Od.5.20.172.
Sole on a plank, on boiling surges tost, ...Od.7.337.253.
Sole in the race the contest I decline, ...Od.8.263.276.
To dress, to dance, to sing our sole delight, ...Od.8.285.278.
O sole belov'd! command thy menial train ....Od.8.460.288.
Ulysses sole with air majestic stands, ...Od.13.72.4.
Sole, and all comfortless he wastes away, ...Od.15.380.87.
Sole in an Isle, imprison'd by the main, ...Od.17.162.139.
The sole attendant on the genial day. ....Od.18.55.169.
Seek thou repose; whilst here I sole remain, ...Od.19.54.195.
Partaking free, my sole-invited guest; ....Od.19.369.212.
The sole attendant on our genial bow'r.) ....Od.23.244.335.

SOLE-INVITED
Partaking free, my sole-invited guest; ....Od.19.369.212.

SOLELY
Has God, thou fool! work'd solely for thy good, ...3.EOM3.27.95.

SOLEMN
In solemn State the Consistory crown'd: ....1.TrSt.285.422.
The Monarch then his solemn Silence broke, ...1.TrSt.296.422.
Wide o'er the World in solemn Pomp she drew ....1.TrSt.476.430.
The King once more the solemn Rites requires, ...1.TrSt.603.435.
These solemn Feasts propitious *Phœbus* please, ...1.TrSt.788.443.
While *Visits* shall be paid on solemn Days, ...2.RL3.167.181.
Canst thou forget that sad, that solemn day, ...2.ElAb.107.328.
And the dim windows shed a solemn light; ....2.ElAb.144.331.
A solemn Sacrifice, perform'd in state, ...3.Ep4.157.152.
And what a solemn face if he denies! ....4.JD2.68.139.
While the long solemn Unison went round: ....5.DunB4.612.405.
The deep, majestick, solemn Organs blow. ....6.11.11.30.
While solemn Airs improve the sacred Fire; ....6.11.129.34.
What are these noontide bowers and solemn shades, ...6.81.7B.225.
With pure Lustrations, and with solemn Pray'rs. ....Il.1.411.107.
Where at his solemn Altar, as the Maid ....Il.1.574.115.
And solemn Voice, the Priest directs his Pray'r. ....Il.1.589.116.
When thus the King prefers his solemn Pray'r. ....Il.2.488.150.
The solemn Truce, a fatal Truce to thee! ....Il.4.187.230.
The solemn Council best becomes the Old: ....Il.4.377.239.
The solemn Silence, and their Pow'rs bespoke. ....Il.7.78.366.
Let sacred Heralds sound the solemn Call; ....Il.8.644.426.
And not a Cloud o'ercasts the solemn Scene; ....Il.8.690.428.
In solemn Sadness, and majestic Grief. ....Il.9.16.431.
And solemn swear those Charms were never mine; ....Il.9.172.441.
Pleas'd with the solemn Harp's harmonious Sound. ....Il.9.246.444.
And solemn swear those Charms were only thine; ....Il.9.359.451.
With solemn Fun'rals and a lasting Tomb. ....Il.11.573.59.
There first to *Jove* our solemn Rites were paid; ....Il.11.864.74.
And solemn Dance, and *Hymenæal* Rite; ....Il.18.570.350.
And rising solemn, each his Sentence spoke. ....Il.18.588.351.
Pronounc'd those solemn Words that bind a God. ....Il.19.112.376.
And solemn swear, (observant of the Rite) ....Il.19.174.378.
Greece honours not with solemn Fasts the Dead: ....Il.19.228.382.
The solemn Words a deep Attention draw, ...Il.19.265.383.
Hear then my solemn Oath, to yield to Fate ....Il.21.438.438.
Ev'n now our solemn Hecatombs attend, ...Il.23.254.499.
Victorious then in ev'ry solemn Game ....Il.23.725.519.
With solemn Pace thro' various Rooms he went, ...Il.24.578.560.
One universal, solemn Show'r began; ....Il.24.645.563.
(A solemn Scene!) at length the Father spoke. ....Il.24.803.570.
With plaintive Sighs, and Musick's solemn Sound: ....Il.24.901.573.
A solemn, silent, melancholy Train. ....Il.24.1012.577.
Soon as in solemn form th' assembly sate, ...Od.2.11.60.
Why here once more in solemn council sit? ....Od.2.36.62.
The due libation and the solemn prayer: ....Od.3.58.89.
Tho' at the solemn midnight hour he rose, ...Od.4.968.163.
A solemn oath impos'd the secret seal'd, ...Od.4.986.163.
Swear, by the solemn oath that binds the Gods. ....Od.5.232.182.
All *Greece* had paid my solemn fun'rals then, ...Od.5.399.192.
The solemn sacrifice call'd down the guest; ....Od.7.270.249.
Expert to conquer in the solemn games. ....Od.8.160.271.
These solemn vows and holy off'rings paid ....Od.10.626.374.
And solemn horrour saddens every breast. ....Od.11.6.379.
Thus solemn rites and holy vows we paid ....Od.11.43.381.
And near them walk'd, with solemn pace and slow, ...Od.11.397.403.
Attesting solemn all the pow'rs divine, ...Od.14.368.53.
A solemn compact let us ratify, ...Od.14.434.56.
In solemn speed the bird majestick flew ....Od.15.183.77.
With pure libations, and with solemn pray'r; ....Od.15.283.82.
The Prince thus interrupts the solemn woe. ....Od.16.245.116.
His visage solemn sad, of sable hue: ....Od.19.279.208.
In solemn silence fell the kindly show'r. ....Od.21.237.271.
Sacred to *Phœbus* is the solemn day, ...Od.21.274.273.
And solemn sadness thro' the gloom of hell, ...Od.24.33.348.
Oft have I seen with solemn fun'ral games ....Od.24.111.353.

SOLEMNITIES
Great was the Cause; our old Solemnities ....1.TrSt.660.438.

SOLEMNIZ'D
An added pudding solemniz'd the Lord's: ....3.Ep3.346.122.

SOLEMNIZE
And holy horrors solemnize the shade. ....Od.17.245.143.

SOLEMNLY
And, tho' I solemnly declare ....4.HS6.121.257.

SOLEUM
Much to her mind the soleum feast recalls, ...5.DunA1.93A.70.

SOLICITOUS
Solicitous for others Ends, 6.47.41.130.

SOLID
The solid Pow'r of *Understanding* fails; 1.EOC.57.245.
On lofty Beams of solid Timber hung. 1.TrES.194.456.
Drives the sharp Rock; the solid Beams give way, 1.TrES.196.456.
Where the strong Fibres bind the solid Heart. 1.TrES.287.460.
One solid Comfort, our Eternal Wife, 2.ChJM.55.17.
Was compass'd round with Walls of solid Stone; 2.ChJM.449.36.
The solid Comforts of a virtuous Life. 2.ChJM.558.42.
And seem'd to distant Sight of solid Stone. 2.TemF.30.255.
One solid dish his week-day meal affords, 3.Ep3.345.122.
What solid Happiness, what empty Pride? 4.HAdv.145.87.
And solid pudding against empty praise. 5.DunA1.52.66.
But high above, more solid Learning shone, 5.DunA1.127.79.
Of solid proof, impenetrably dull. 5.DunA3.18.151.
Half thro' the solid darkness of his soul; 5.DunA3.224.176.
And solid pudding against empty praise. 5.DunB1.54.274.
But, high above, more solid Learning shone, 5.DunB1.147.281.
Of solid proof, impenetrably dull: 5.DunB3.26.321.
Half thro' the solid darkness of his soul; 5.DunB3.226.331.
On passive paper, or on solid brick. 5.DunB4.130.354.
Wou'd you enjoy soft nights and solid dinners? 6.41.23.114.
Not * He that shakes the solid Earth so strong: Il.1.525.113.
Burst the strong Nerves, and crash'd the solid Bone: Il.4.602.250.
And stripp'd the Skin, and crack'd the solid Bone. Il.5.378.285.
The bossie Naves of solid Silver shone; Il.5.896.308.
Of tough Bull-hides; of solid Brass the last. Il.7.268.377.
The solid Earth's eternal Basis shake! Il.7.545.391.
Then with a Voice that shakes the solid Skies, Il.8.194.406.
His solid Arms, refulgent, flame with Gold; Il.10.509.26.
Upheave the Piles that prop the solid Wall; Il.12.307.92.
On lofty Beams of solid Timber hung. Il.12.548.101.
Drives the sharp Rock; the solid Beams give way, Il.12.550.101.
The God whose Earthquakes rock the solid Ground, Il.13.68.108.
The solid Globe's eternal Basis shake. Il.13.302.119.
And * he that shakes the solid Earth, gave Aid. Il.13.850.146.
Of him, whose Trident rends the solid Ground. Il.14.176.165.
Nor more in Councils fam'd for solid Sense, Il.15.322.209.
Where the strong Fibres bind the solid Heart. Il.16.592.267.
Then o'er their Backs they spread their solid Shields; Il.17.559.310.
And stubborn Brass, and Tin, and solid Gold: Il.18.546.348.
Then first he form'd th' immense and solid *Shield;* Il.18.551.348.
Beneath, stern *Neptune* shakes the solid Ground, Il.20.77.397.
The solid Globe's eternal Basis shake. Il.20.161.400.
Fixt on the Center stands their solid Base. Il.23.829.522.
The new-made Car with solid Beauty shin'd; Il.24.334.550.
A solid Pine-tree barr'd of wond'rous Length; Il.24.558.559.
The burnish'd laver flames with solid gold; Od.4.66.122.
In solid gold the purple vintage flows, Od.4.67.122.
Nor entrails, flesh, nor solid bone remains. Od.9.349.320.
From shore to shore, and gird the solid world. Od.9.618.332.
The vaulted roofs and solid pavement rung. Od.10.255.355.
A weighty ax, and cleft the solid oak; Od.14.464.58.
The solid gate its fury scarcely bounds; Od.21.463.282.
Pierc'd thro' and thro', the solid gate resounds. Od.21.464.282.

SOLINUS
Manilius or Solinus shall supply: 5.DunB4.226.365.

SOLITARY
The solitary Shore, and rowling Sea. 1.TrUl.55.467.
And wander'd in the solitary Shade: 2.ChJM.62.17.
Lost in a convent's solitary gloom! 2.ElAb.38.322.
One Simile, that solitary shines 4.2HE1.111.205.
To muse, and spill her solitary Tea, 6.45.16.125.
There as the solitary Mourner raves, Il.24.21.535.
Far from the rest, and solitary reigns, Od.9.218.314.
As down the hill I solitary go, Od.10.181.349.
The solitary shore, and rolling sea. Od.13.222.16.
While pensive in this solitary den, Od.14.409.55.

SOLITUDE
Soft Scenes of Solitude no more can please, 1.TrSP.15.393.
To wholesome Solitude, the Nurse of Sense. 4.JD4.185.41.
But if to Solitude we turn our Eyes, 6.17iii.8.58.
Thy sire in solitude foments his care: Od.11.226.393.
Sent the sad sire in solitude to stray; Od.16.149.109.
Or where he hides in solitude and shade; Od.16.399.125.
So in nocturnal solitude forlorn, Od.19.611.226.
Weeps a sad life in solitude away. Od.23.388.343.

SOLITUDES
In these deep solitudes and awful cells, 2.ElAb.1.319.

SOLLICIT
Repent old pleasures, and sollicit new: 2.ElAb.186.335.
Forgetting their Interest, now humbly sollicit 6.42i.7.116.

SOLLICITES
The Spear sollicites, and the Bandage bound; Il.13.750.140.

SOLO
With nothing but a Solo in his head; 5.DunB4.324.375.

SOLOMON
Heav'n rest thy Spirit, noble *Solomon,* 2.ChJM.631.45.
What tho' this sland'rous *Jew,* this *Solomon,* 2.ChJM.669.47.
By ev'ry Word that *Solomon* has said? 2.ChJM.683.48.
More Wives than One by *Solomon* were try'd, 2.ChWB.21.57.

SOLOMON'S
Yet you pursue sage *Solomon's* Advice, 2.ChJM.151.21.
Solomon's Proverbs, *Eloïsa's* Loves; 2.ChWB.361.74.

SOLUS
Solus cum Sola, with his sprightly *May.* 2.ChJM.472.38.
"But *Tully* has it, *Nunquam minus solus:*" 4.JD4.91.33.

SOLVE
Who solve these Questions beyond all Dispute; 2.ChJM.296.28.
But let them read, and solve me, if they can, 2.ChWB.13.57.

SOLYMÉ'S
From far, on *Solymé's* aerial brow, Od.5.362.189.

SOLYMA
Ye Nymphs of *Solyma!* begin the Song: 1.Mes.1.112.

SOLYMAEAN
Then met in Arms the *Solymæan* Crew, Il.6.227.337.
In Combate on the *Solymæan* Plain. Il.6.252.339.

SOME
O were I made by some transforming Pow'r, 1.PSu.45.75.
Some God conduct you to these blissful Seats, 1.PSu.71A.77.
As some sad Turtle his lost Love deplores, 1.PAu.19.82.
In some still Ev'ning, when the whisp'ring Breeze 1.PWi.79.94.
As some coy Nymph her Lover's warm Address 1.W-F.19.150.
Some thoughtless Town, with Ease and Plenty blest, 1.W-F.107.161.
Sudden, before some unsuspecting Town, 1.W-F.108A.161.
Some few in *that,* but Numbers err in *this,* 1.EOC.5.239.
Some are bewilder'd in the Maze of Schools, 1.EOC.26.242.
And some made *Coxcombs* Nature meant but *Fools.* 1.EOC.27.242.
Some hate as *Rivals* all that write; and others 1.EOC.30B.242.
Some have at first for *Wits,* then *Poets* past, 1.EOC.36.243.
Some neither can for *Wits* nor *Criticks* pass, 1.EOC.38.243.
In some fair Body thus th' informing Soul 1.EOC.76.247.
In some fair Body thus the sprightly Soul 1.EOC.76A.247.
In some fair Body thus the secret Soul 1.EOC.76B.247.
Some, to whom Heav'n in Wit has been profuse, 1.EOC.80.248.
Some on the Leaves of ancient Authors prey, 1.EOC.112.251.
Some dryly plain, without Invention's Aid, 1.EOC.114.252.
Some Beauties yet, no Precepts can declare, 1.EOC.141.255.
Some LUCKY LICENCE answers to the full 1.EOC.148.256.
In *Prospects,* thus, some *Objects* please our Eyes, 1.EOC.158.258.
Some Figures *monstrous* and *mis-shap'd* appear, 1.EOC.171.260.
Oh may some Spark of *your* Cœlestial Fire 1.EOC.195.263.
Thus when we view some well-proportion'd Dome, 1.EOC.247.268.
For *not* to know some Trifles, is a Praise. 1.EOC.262.269.
Most Criticks, fond of some subservient Art, 1.EOC.263.269.
Some to *Conceit* alone their Taste confine, 1.EOC.289.271.
Some by *Old Words* to Fame have made Pretence; 1.EOC.324.275.
Not mend their Minds; as some to *Church* repair, 1.EOC.342.277.
With some *unmeaning* Thing they call a *Thought,* 1.EOC.355.279.
When *Ajax* strives, some Rock's vast Weight to throw, 1.EOC.370.282.
Some *foreign* Writers, some our *own* despise; 1.EOC.394.285.
Some *foreign* Writers, some our *own* despise; 1.EOC.394.285.
Some the *French* Writers, some our *own* despise; 1.EOC.394A.285.
Some the *French* Writers, some our *own* despise; 1.EOC.394A.285.
Some ne'er advance a Judgment of their own, 1.EOC.408.287.
Some judge of Authors' *Names,* not *Works,* and then 1.EOC.412.287.
In some starv'd Hackny Sonneteer, or me? 1.EOC.419.287.
Some praise at Morning what they blame at Night; 1.EOC.430.288.
Some valuing those of their own *Side,* or *Mind,* 1.EOC.452.290.
Some *bright Idea* of the Master's Mind, 1.EOC.485.294.
Like some fair *Flow'r* the early *Spring* supplies, 1.EOC.498.294.
Some *fair Idea* of the Master's Mind, 1.EOC.485A.294.
Like some fair *Flow'r* that in the *Spring* does rise, 1.EOC.498A.294.
Sure *some* to *vex,* but never *all* to *please;* 1.EOC.505.295.
Employ their Pains to spurn some others down; 1.EOC.515.296.
But if in Noble Minds some Dregs remain, 1.EOC.526.297.
Some positive persisting Fops we know, 1.EOC.568.305.
Like some *fierce Tyrant* in *Old Tapestry!* 1.EOC.587.307.
Yet *some* there were, among the *sounder Few* 1.EOC.719.323.
Let some kind nurse supply a mother's care: 1.TrFD.77.389.
Like some sad Statue, speechless, pale, I stood; 1.TrSP.125.399.
Then frantick rise, and like some Fury rove 1.TrSP.159.400.
Thou *Fury,* then, some lasting Curse entail, 1.TrSt.111.414.
Blind as I am, some glorious Villany! 1.TrSt.119.415.
Cou'dst thou some great, proportion'd Mischief frame, 1.TrSt.122.415.
On flow'ry Herbs in some green Covert laid, 1.TrSt.686.439.
Some few like him, inspir'd with Martial flame, 1.TrSt.716.440.
Some with vast Beams the squallid Corps engage, 1.TrSt.733.440.
Like some black Tempest gath'ring round the Tow'rs: 1.TrES.92.453.
As skilful Divers from some Airy Steep 1.TrES.107.453.
The Chief who fear'd some Foe's insulting Boast 1.TrES.115.454.
(While some laborious Matron, just and poor, 1.TrES.168Z1.455.
Hewn for the Mast of some great Admiral, 1.TrES.289.460.
Or Pine (fit Mast for some great Admiral) 1.TrES.289A.460.
Some juster Prince perhaps had entertain'd, 1.TrUl.82.468.
Who seem'd descended from some Princely Line: 1.TrUl.103.469.
With Joy to thee, as to some God, I bend, 1.TrUl.110.469.
Or some fair Isle which *Neptune's* Arms surround? 1.TrUl.115.469.
Blest with much Sense, more Riches, and some Grace. 2.ChJM.4.15.
He scarce cou'd rule some Idle Appetites; 2.ChJM.6.15.
Some wicked Wits have libell'd all the Fair: 2.ChJM.44.17.
Some prais'd with Wit, and some with Reason blam'd. 2.ChJM.142.21.
Some prais'd with Wit, and some with Reason blam'd. 2.ChJM.142.21.
Thus, in some publick *Forum* fix'd on high, 2.ChJM.234.25.
Or that some Star, with Aspect kind to Love, 2.ChJM.428.35.
Had some fierce Tyrant in her stead been found, 2.ChJM.436.36.
But to my Tale: Some Sages have defin'd 2.ChJM.440.36.
By means of this, some Wonder shall appear, 2.ChJM.512.40.
So may some Wildfire on your Bodies fall, 2.ChJM.641.46.
Or some devouring Plague consume you all, 2.ChJM.642.46.
But some faint Glimm'ring of a doubtful Light. 2.ChJM.777.52.
By all those Pow'rs, some Frenzy seiz'd your Mind, 2.ChJM.780.52.
Whence some infer, whose Conscience is too nice, 2.ChWB.11.57.
Or else her Wit some Fool-Gallant procures, 2.ChWB.95.61.
She finds some honest Gander for her Mate. 2.ChWB.99.61.

SOME (CONTINUED)

With some grave Sentence out of Holy Writ. ....2.ChWB.346.74.
Give me some Slip of this most blissful Tree, ...2.ChWB.399.76.
How some with Swords their sleeping Lords have slain, ...2.ChWB.407.76.
And some have hammer'd Nails into their Brain, ...2.ChWB.408.77.
And some have drench'd them with a deadly Potion; ....2.ChWB.409.77.
Some secret Truths from Learned Pride conceal'd, ...2.RL1.37.148.
Rejects Mankind, is by some *Sylph* embrac'd: ....2.RL1.68.151.
Some Nymphs there are, too conscious of their Face, ...2.RL1.79.151.
I saw, alas! some dread Event impend, ...2.RL1.109.154.
Some fold the Sleeve, whilst others plait the Gown; ....2.RL1.147.158.
Some fold the Sleeve, while others plait the Gown; ....2.RL1.147A.158.
If to her share some Female Errors fall, ...2.RL2.17.160.
Some to the Sun their Insect-Wings unfold, ...2.RL2.59.163.
Some in the Fields of purest *Æther* play, ...2.RL2.77.164.
Some guide the Course of wandring Orbs on high, ...2.RL2.79.164.
Some less refin'd, beneath the Moon's pale Light ....2.RL2.81.165.
Some dire Disaster, or by Force, or Slight, ...2.RL2.103.166.
Or some frail *China* Jar receive a Flaw, ...2.RL2.106.166.
Some, Orb in Orb, around the Nymph extend, ...2.RL2.138.168.
Some thrid the mazy Ringlets of her Hair, ...2.RL2.139.168.
Some hang upon the Pendants of her Ear; ....2.RL2.140.168.
And now, (as oft in some distemper'd State) ....2.RL3.93.174.
Some, as she sip'd, the fuming Liquor fann'd, ...2.RL3.114.176.
Some o'er her Lap their careful Plumes display'd, ...2.RL3.115.176.
Make some take Physick, others scribble Plays; ....2.RL4.62.189.
In some lone Isle, or distant *Northern* Land; ....2.RL4.154.196.
Thou by some other shalt be laid as low. ....2.RL5.98.207.
Some thought it mounted to the Lunar Sphere, ...2.RL5.113.208.
Some fresh ingrav'd appear'd of Wits renown'd; ....2.TemF.35.255.
Enlarges some, and others multiplies. ....2.TemF.134.264.
Here, like some furious Prophet, *Pindar* rode, ...2.TemF.212.272.
Some she disgrac'd, and some with Honours crown'd; ....2.TemF.294.278.
Some she disgrac'd, and some with Honours crown'd; ....2.TemF.294.278.
This having heard and seen, some Pow'r unknown ....2.TemF.418.283.
Each talk'd aloud, or in some secret Place, ...2.TemF.466.286.
Some to remain, and some to perish soon, ...2.TemF.485.287.
Some to remain, and some to perish soon, ...2.TemF.485.287.
Some dire misfortune follows close behind. ....2.ElAb.34.321.
Heav'n first taught letters for some wretch's aid, ...2.ElAb.51.323.
Some banish'd lover, or some captive maid; ....2.ElAb.52.323.
Some banish'd lover, or some captive maid; ....2.ElAb.52.323.
Some emanation of th' all-beauteous Mind. ....2.ElAb.62.324.
Where round some mould'ring tow'r pale ivy creeps, ...2.ElAb.243.339.
Propt on some tomb, a neighbour of the dead! ....2.ElAb.304.344.
Propt in some tomb, a neighbour of the dead! ....2.ElAb.304A.344.
Amid that scene, if some relenting eye ....2.ElAb.355.348.
And sure if fate some future Bard shall join ....2.ElAb.359.348.
Yet serves to second too some other use. ....3.EOM1.56.20.
Perhaps acts second to some sphere unknown, ...3.EOM1.58.20.
Touches some wheel, or verges to some goal; ....3.EOM1.59.20.
Touches some wheel, or verges to some goal; ....3.EOM1.59.20.
Some safer world in depth of woods embrac'd, ...3.EOM1.105.27.
Some happier island in the watry waste, ...3.EOM1.106.28.
"Th' exceptions few; some change since all began, ...3.EOM1.147.33.
Exalt their kind, and take some Virtue's name. ....3.EOM2.100.67.
In this weak queen, some fav'rite still obey. ....3.EOM2.150.73.
Lust, thro' some certain strainers well refin'd, ...3.EOM2.189.77.
In Man they join to some mysterious use; ....3.EOM2.206.80.
As, in some well-wrought picture, light and shade, ...3.EOM2.208.81.
See some strange comfort ev'ry state attend, ...3.EOM2.271.87.
See some fit Passion ev'ry age supply, ...3.EOM2.273.87.
Some livelier play-thing gives his youth delight, ...3.EOM2.277.88.
For some his Int'rest prompts him to provide, ...3.EOM3.59.98.
Fair op'ning to some Court's propitious shine, ...3.EOM4.9.128.
Some place the bliss in action, some in ease, ...3.EOM4.21.129.
Some place the bliss in action, some in ease, ...3.EOM4.21.129.
Some sunk to Beasts, find pleasure end in pain; ....3.EOM4.23.130.
Some swell'd to Gods, confess ev'n Virtue vain; ....3.EOM4.24.130.
But some way leans and hearkens to the kind. ....3.EOM4.40.131.
Some are, and must be, greater than the rest, ...3.EOM4.50.133.
Some are, and must be, mightier than the rest, ...3.EOM4.50A.133.
Think we, like some weak Prince, th'Eternal Cause, ...3.EOM4.121.139.
Or some old temple, nodding to its fall, ...3.EOM4.129.140.
Fortune in Men has some small diff'rence made, ...3.EOM4.195.145.
Some greedy minion, or imperious wife, ...3.EOM4.302.156.
But touches some above, and some below; ....3.EOM4.336.161.
But touches some above, and some below; ....3.EOM4.336.161.
Some gen'ral maxims, or be right by chance. ....3.Ep1.4.15.
There's some Peculiar in each leaf and grain, ...3.Ep1.15.17.
Some unmark'd fibre, or some varying vein: ....3.Ep1.16.17.
Some unmark'd fibre, or some varying vein: ....3.Ep1.16.17.
Some plunge in bus'ness, others shave their crowns: ....3.Ep1.56.19.
True, some are open, and to all men known; ....3.Ep1.110.23.
Some God, or Spirit he has lately found, ...3.Ep1.164.29.
Some wand'ring touches some reflected light, ...3.Ep2.153A.63.
Some wand'ring touches some reflected light, ...3.Ep2.153A.63.
Some wand'ring touch, or some reflected light, ...3.Ep2.153.63.
Some wand'ring touch, or some reflected light, ...3.Ep2.153.63.
Some flying stroke alone can hit 'em right: ....3.Ep2.154.63.
Men, some to Bus'ness, some to Pleasure take; ....3.Ep2.215.67.
Men, some to Bus'ness, some to Pleasure take; ....3.Ep2.215.67.
Men, some to Quiet, some to public Strife; ....3.Ep2.217.68.
Men, some to Quiet, some to public Strife; ....3.Ep2.217.68.
To squander some, and some to hide agen. ....3.Ep3.14A.84.
To squander some, and some to hide agen. ....3.Ep3.14A.84.
Or ship off Senates to some distant Shore; ....3.Ep3.74A.93.
Some War, some Plague, some Famine they foresee, ...3.Ep3.115A.101.
Some War, some Plague, some Famine they foresee, ...3.Ep3.115A.101.
Some War, some Plague, some Famine they foresee, ...3.Ep3.115A.101.
For some to heap, and some to throw away. ....3.Ep3.6.83.
For some to heap, and some to throw away. ....3.Ep3.6.83.
Pity mistakes for some poor tradesman craz'd). ....3.Ep3.52.90.
Or find some Doctor that would save the life ....3.Ep3.95.97.
To some, indeed, Heav'n grants the happier fate, ...3.Ep3.99.98.
Some War, some Plague, or Famine they foresee, ...3.Ep3.115.101.

SOME (CONTINUED)

Some War, some Plague, or Famine they foresee, ...3.Ep3.115.101.
Some Revelation hid from you and me. ....3.Ep3.116.101.
Like some lone Chartreux stands the good old Hall, ...3.Ep3.189.109.
Some scruple rose, but thus he eas'd his thought, ...3.Ep3.365.123.
Some Dæmon whisper'd, "Visto! have a Taste." ....3.Ep4.16.137.
Load some vain Church with old Theatric state, ...3.Ep4.29.140.
On some patch'd dog-hole ek'd with ends of wall, ...3.Ep4.32.140.
Lo some are Vellom, and the rest as good ....3.Ep4.137.150.
Some Dæmon whisper'd, "Knights should have a Taste." ....3.Ep4.16A.137.
Who-e'er offends, at some unlucky Time ....4.HS1.77.13.
And the sad Burthen of some merry Song. ....4.HS1.80.13.
But some excising Courtier will have Toll. ....4.JD4.147.37.
As in the Pox, some give it, to get free; ....4.JD4.171.39.
Bear me, some God! oh quickly bear me hence ....4.JD4.184.41.
No wonder some Folks bow, and think them *Kings.* .... 4.JD4.211.43.
The Mosque of *Mahound,* or some queer *Pa-god.* .... 4.JD4.239.45.
But on some lucky day (as when they found ....4.HS2.55.59.
Not but we may exceed, some Holy time, ...4.HS2.85.61.
Ill Health some just indulgence may engage, ...4.HS2.87.61.
At best, it falls to some ungracious Son ....4.HS2.173.69.
Some damn the Jade, and some the Cullies blame, ...4.HAdv.15.75.
Some damn the Jade, and some the Cullies blame, ...4.HAdv.15.75.
Some feel no Flames but at the *Court* or *Ball,* .... 4.HAdv.37.79.
And yet some Care of *S[allu]st* should be had, ...4.HAdv.63.81.
Z—ds! let some Eunuch or Platonic take— ....4.HAdv.157.87.
(Some say his Queen) was forc'd to speak, or burst. ....4.Arbu.72.100.
For song, for silence, some expect a bribe ....4.Arbu.113A.103.
The Muse but serv'd to ease some Friend, not Wife, ...4.Arbu.131.105.
Did some more sober Critic come abroad? ....4.Arbu.157.107.
Ev'n such small Critics some regard may claim, ...4.Arbu.167.108.
Such piece-meal Critics some regard may claim, ...4.Arbu.167A.108.
And flatter'd ev'ry day, and some days eat: ....4.Arbu.240.113.
He pay'd some Bards with Port, and some with Praise, ...4.Arbu.242.113.
He pay'd some Bards with Port, and some with Praise, ...4.Arbu.242.113.
To some a dry Rehearsal was assign'd, ...4.Arbu.243.113.
May some choice Patron bless each gray goose quill! ....4.Arbu.249.114.
Some Beasts were kill'd, tho' not whole Hecatombs: ....4.JD2A.122.142.
Thus as the pipes of some carv'd Organ move, ...4.JD2.17.133.
These write to Lords, some mean reward to get, ...4.JD2.25.133.
Some beasts were kill'd, tho' not whole hecatombs, ...4.JD2.116.143.
So prompts, and saves some Rogue who cannot read. ....4.JD2.16A.133.
Some write to Lords in hope reward to get, ...4.JD2A.29.134.
Some write, because all write; and thus have stil ....4.JD2A.31.134.
How'ere some pleasure 'tis, this Fool to see ....4.JD2A.69.138.
Shall bless thy name at least some twice a day, ...4.HOde1.30C.153.
Gave him much Praise, and some Reward beside. ....4.2HE2.43.167.
So stiff, so mute! some Statue, you would swear, ...4.2HE2.121.173.
Bright thro' the rubbish of some hundred years; ....4.2HE2.166.177.
I, who at some times spend, at others spare, ...4.2HE2.290.185.
Did not some grave Examples yet remain, ...4.2HE1.128.205.
Yet let me show, a Poet's of some weight, ...4.2HE1.203.211.
And speak in publick with some sort of grace. ....4.2HE1.208.213.
Unless he praise some monster of a King, ...4.2HE1.210.213.
And in our own (excuse some Courtly stains) ....4.2HE1.215.213.
And in our own (excuse some Courtly strains) ....4.2HE1.215A.213.
Most warp'd to Flatt'ry's side; but some, more nice, ...4.2HE1.259.217.
Tho' still some traces of our rustic vein ....4.2HE1.270.219.
Some doubt, if equal pains or equal fire ....4.2HE1.282.219.
Be call'd to Court, to plan some work divine, ...4.2HE1.374.227.
Or chuse at least some Minister of Grace, ...4.2HE1.378.227.
Weds the rich Dulness of some Son of earth? ....4.1HE6.43.239.
Some Wag observes me thus perplext, ...4.HS6.51.253.
About some great Affair, at Two— ....4.HS6.74.255.
Yet some I know with envy swell, ...4.HS6.101.257.
"I wonder what some people mean; ....4.HS6.104.257.
"See but the fortune of some Folks! ....4.HS6.108.257.
Of some Express arriv'd at Court, ...4.HS6.110.257.
Sleep, or peruse some ancient Book, ...4.HS6.130.259.
Hold out some months 'twixt Sun and Fire, ...4.1HE7.18.269.
"Eat some, and pocket up the rest—" ....4.1HE7.26.269.
And feel some comfort, not to be a fool. ....4.1HE1.48.283.
The rest, some farm the Poor-box, some the Pews; ....4.1HE1.128.289.
The rest, some farm the Poor-box, some the Pews; ....4.1HE1.128.289.
Some keep Assemblies, and wou'd keep the Stews; ....4.1HE1.129.289.
Some with fat Bucks on childless Dotards fawn; ....4.1HE1.130.289.
Some win rich Widows by their Chine and Brawn; ....4.1HE1.131.289.
Now let some whimzy, or that Dev'l within ....4.1HE1.143.289.
The Fool whose Wife elopes some thrice a quarter, ...4.1HE1.150.291.
In rev'rend Bishops note some *small Neglects,* .... 4.EpS1.16.298.
Sir *George* of *some slight Gallantries* suspect. .... 4.EpS1.15A.298.
A Joke on JEKYL, or some odd *Old Whig,* .... 4.EpS1.39.300.
But well may put some Statesmen in a fury. ....4.EpS1.52.302.
These, may some gentle, ministerial Wing ....4.EpS1.95.305.
Some rising Genius sins up to my Song. ....4.EpS2.9.313.
Else might he take to Virtue some years hence— ....4.EpS2.60.315.
Some, in their choice of Friends (nay, look not grave) ....4.EpS2.100.318.
To *W[alpole]* guilty of some venial Sin, ...4.EpS2.162.322 .
All gaze with ardour: some, a Poet's name, ...5.DunA2.47.102.
Some beg an eastern, some a western wind: ....5.DunA2.84.108.
Some beg an eastern, some a western wind: ....5.DunA2.84.108.
Some for an eastern, some a western wind: ....5.DunA2.84A.108.
Some for an eastern, some a western wind: ....5.DunA2.84A.108.
At some sick miser's triple-bolted gate, ...5.DunA2.238.129.
To some fam'd round-house, ever open gate! ....5.DunA2.392.148.
Till Peter's Keys some christen'd Jove adorn, ...5.DunA3.101.159.
Grave mummers! sleeveless some, and shirtless others. ....5.DunA3.108.159.
Some strain in rhyme; the Muses, on their racks, ...5.DunA3.153.164.
Some free from rhyme or reason, rule or check, ...5.DunA3.155.164.
And carry'd off in some Dog's tail at last. ....5.DunA3.294A.184.
And hang some curious cobweb in its stead! ....5.DunB1.180.283.
Some Dæmon stole my pen (forgive th' offence) ....5.DunB1.187.283.
Hold—to some Minister I more incline; ....5.DunB1.213A.285.
All gaze with ardour: Some a poet's name, ...5.DunB2.51.298.
Some beg an eastern, some a western wind: ....5.DunB2.88.300.
Some beg an eastern, some a western wind: ....5.DunB2.88.300.

SOME 342 SOME

SOME (CONTINUED)

At some sick miser's triple-bolted gate, ...5.DunB2.248.307.
So clouds replenish'd from some bog below, ...5.DunB2.363.315.
To some fam'd round-house, ever open gate! ....5.DunB2.424.318.
'Till Peter's keys some christ'ned Jove adorn, ...5.DunB3.109.325.
Grave Mummers! sleeveless some, and shirtless others. ....5.DunB3.116.325.
Some strain in rhyme; the Muses, on their racks, ...5.DunB3.159.328.
Some free from rhyme or reason, rule or check, ...5.DunB3.161.328.
And carry'd off in some Dog's tail at last. ....5.DunB3.292.334.
Some Slave of mine be pinion'd to their side." ....5.DunB4.134.354.
Else sure some Bard, to our eternal praise, ...5.DunB4.171.357.
"Oh (cry'd the Goddess) for some pedant Reign! ....5.DunB4.175.358.
Some gentle JAMES, to bless the land again; ....5.DunB4.176.358.
"What tho' we let some better sort sort of fool ....5.DunB4.255.369.
Some would have spoken, but the voice was drown'd ....5.DunB4.277.371.
Each with some wond'rous gift approach'd the Pow'r, ...5.DunB4.399.381.
Yet by some object ev'ry brain is stirr'd; ....5.DunB4.445.384.
See Nature in some partial narrow shape, ...5.DunB4.455.385.
Thrust some Mechanic Cause into his place; ....5.DunB4.475.387.
Kind Self-conceit to some her glass applies, ...5.DunB4.533.394.
On some, a Priest succinct in amice white ....5.DunB4.549.396.
Some, deep Free-Masons, join the silent race ....5.DunB4.571.398.
Some Botanists, or Florists at the least, ...5.DunB4.573.399.
Perhaps more high some daring son may soar, ...5.DunB4.599.402.
But could'st thou seize some Tongues that now are free, ...6.8.28.18.
I'm told, you think to take a Step some ....6.10.49.26.
I had to see you some Intent ....6.10.67.26.
He had some Fancy, and cou'd write; ....6.10.95.27.
Some play, some eat, some cack against the Wall, ...6.14ii.8.43.
Some play, some eat, some cack against the Wall, ...6.14ii.8.43.
Some play, some eat, some cack against the Wall, ...6.14ii.8.43.
Yet in some Things methinks she fails, ...6.14v(a).4.48.
Like some free Port of Trade: ....6.14v(b).3.49.
As some free Port of Trade: ....6.14v(b).3A.49.
Descanted, some on this Thing, some on that; ....6.17iv.2.59.
Descanted, some on this Thing, some on that; ....6.17iv.2.59.
Some, over each Orac'lous Glass, fore-doom ....6.17iv.3.59.
And some things of little size, ...6.18.4.61.
And some things else of little size, ...6.18.4A.61.
In ev'ry Scene some Moral let it teach, ...6.19.23.62.
Whole Years neglected for some Months ador'd, ...6.19.43.63.
Which some rude wind will always discompose; ....6.22.4.71.
Glares on some Traveller's unwary steps, ...6.26i.11.79.
Some *Stephens* to the rest prefer, ...6.29.3A.82.
And some esteem *Old*-Elzevir; ....6.29.4.83.
Which some can't construe, some can't read: ....6.29.14.83.
Which some can't construe, some can't read: ....6.29.14.83.
For some Folks read, but all Folks sh—. ....6.29.30.83.
Which some can't construe, most can't read; ....6.29.7Z2.83.
Some *Colinæus* praise, some *Bleau,* ....6.29.1.82.
Some *Colinæus* praise, some *Bleau,* ....6.29.1.82.
Some *Plantin* to the rest prefer, ...6.29.3.82.
Some to unload the fertile branches run, ...6.35.19.103.
Some dry the black'ning clusters in the sun, ...6.35.20.103.
If on some meaner head this Lock had grown, ...6.38.3.107.
But yet if some, with Malice more than Wit, ...6.38.11Z1.107.
Pray heartily for some new Gift, ...6.39.23.111.
In some close corner of the soul, they sin: ....6.41.18.114.
Some flatly say, the Book's as ill done, ...6.44.15.123.
But faith I fear, some Folks beside ....6.44.21.123.
As some fond virgin, whom her mother's care ....6.45.1.124.
Some Squire, perhaps, you take delight to rack; ....6.45.23.125.
In some fair evening, on your elbow laid, ...6.45.31.125.
So when your slave, at some dear, idle time, ...6.45.41.125.
Rack your Inventions some, and some *in time* translate. ....6.48iii.14.135.
Rack your Inventions some, and some *in time* translate. ....6.48iii.14.135.
Some Ends of Verse his Betters might afford, ...6.49i.5.137.
Some end of Verse his Betters did afford, ...6.49i.5A.137.
So some coarse Country Wench, almost decay'd, ...6.49i.15.138.
'Till some new Tyrant lifts his purple hand, ...6.51i.23.152.
Some *Athens* perishes, some *Tully* bleeds. ....6.51i.32.152.
Some *Athens* perishes, some *Tully* bleeds. ....6.51i.32.152.
Some *Athens* perishes, or some *Tully* bleeds. ....6.51i.32A.152.
Some *Athens* perishes, or some *Tully* bleeds. ....6.51i.32A.152.
Whether thy hand strike out some free design, ...6.52.3.156.
Or seek some ruin's formidable shade; ....6.52.30.157.
Led by some rule, that guides, but not constrains; ....6.52.67.158.
Some few short Years, no more! ....6.53.38.162.
Some Worms suit all Conditions; ....6.53.22A.162.
Some frigid Rhymes disburses; ....6.58.54.173.
Some frigid lines disturbs; ....6.58.54A.173.
Some say from *Pastry Cook* it came, ...6.59.3.177.
And some from *Cat* and *Fiddle.* ....6.59.4.177.
Since some have writ, and shewn no Wit at all. ....6.60.8.178.
Some Wit you have and more may learn, ...6.61.31.182.
Some felt the silent stroke of mould'ring age, ...6.71.11.203.
Some hostile fury, some religious rage; ....6.71.12.203.
Some hostile fury, some religious rage; ....6.71.12.203.
Some bury'd marble half preserves a name; ....6.71.16.203.
"And (what some awe must give ye, ...6.79.90.221.
So the struck deer in some sequester'd part ....6.81.11.226.
So the struck doe in some sequester'd part ....6.81.11A.226.
Lo! the struck deer in some sequester'd part ....6.81.11B.226.
Thus, Madam, most Men talk, and some Men do: ....6.82vi.9.232.
Some strangely wonder you're not fond to marry— ....6.82vi.11.232.
Some who grow dull religious strait commence ....6.82ix(c).1.234.
Woud you your writings to some Palates fit ....6.82ix(f).1.235.
Some joy still lost, as each vain year runs o'er, ...6.86.7.245.
And all we gain, some sad Reflection more; ....6.86.8.245.
In some soft Dream, or Extasy of joy: ....6.86.18.245.
And all we gain, some pensive Notion more; ....6.86.8B.245.
Die by some sudden Extasy of Joy. ....6.86.18B.245.
In some soft Dream may thy mild Soul remove, ...6.86.19A.246.
Or let thy soul in some soft dream remove, ...6.86.19B.246.
Let the mild soul in some soft dream remove, ...6.86.19C.246.
Some sprigs of that bed ....6.91.11.253.

SOME (CONTINUED)

Of some Dry-Nurse to save her Hen; ....6.93.18.257.
Of some Dry-Nurse to serve for Hen; ....6.93.18A.257.
Some said that *D[ou]gl[a]s* sent should be, ...6.94.17.259.
Some talk'd of *W[a]lk[e]r's* Merit, ...6.94.18.259*.
Seem like the lofty Barn of some rich Swain, ...6.96ii.13.270.
Or by some Flea with mortal venom stung? ....6.96ii.30Z6.271.
"To some Lord's Daughter sold the living Toy; ....6.96ii.34.272.
Some say the Dev'l himself is in that *Mare:* ....6.96iv.33.277.
Some think you mad, some think you are possest ....6.96iv.35.277.
Some think you mad, some think you are possest ....6.96iv.35.277.
These, for some Moments when you deign to quit, ...6.96iv.61.278.
'Tis sure some Virtue to conceal its Shame. ....6.96v.20.280.
Should some more sober Criticks come abroad, ...6.98.7.283.
Yet ev'n this Creature may some Notice claim, ...6.98.17.283.
But some odd Graces and fine Flights she had, ...6.99.3.286.
Men, some to Business, some to Pleasure take. ....6.99.15.287.
Men, some to Business, some to Pleasure take. ....6.99.15.287.
Bring forth some Remnant of *Promethean* theft, ...6.100iv.1.289.
Still leave some ancient virtues to our age: ....6.113.10.320.
Some morning-walks along the Mall, ...6.114.3.321.
Shall some kind Hand, like B***'s or thine, ...6.117.9.333.
Some Vices were too high but none too low ....6.130.10.358.
(Tho' some of *J—'s* hungry Breed) ....6.135.52.368.
Shall call their Friend some Ages hence, ...6.135.88.369.
'Tis where God sent some that adore him, ...6.151.7.399.
But let some Prophet, or some sacred Sage, ...Il.1.83.90.
But let some Prophet, or some sacred Sage, ...Il.1.83.90.
Still must that Tongue some wounding Message bring, ...Il.1.133.93.
This Hand shall seize some other Captive Dame. ....Il.1.176.96.
And some deputed Prince the Charge attend; ....Il.1.186.96.
Some trivial Present to my Ships I bear, ...Il.1.219.97.
Some Marks of Honour on my Son bestow, ...Il.1.654.118.
As from some Rocky Cleft the Shepherd sees ....Il.2.111.132.
Say would'st thou seize some valiant Leader's Prize? ....Il.2.288.141.
Some Captive Fair, to bless thy Kingly Bed? ....Il.2.290.141.
We may be wanted on some busie Day, ...Il.2.296.142.
Suppose some Hero should his Spoils resign, ...Il.2.318.142.
As on some Mountain, thro' the lofty Grove ....Il.2.534.152.
Like some proud Bull that round the Pastures leads ....Il.2.566.154.
As when some Shepherd from the rustling Trees ....Il.3.47.190.
Like Steel, uplifted by some strenuous Swain, ...Il.3.91.194.
Tho' some of larger Stature tread the Green, ...Il.3.223.203.
Perhaps their Sword some nobler Quarrel draws, ...Il.3.309.208.
But some gay Dancer in the publick Show. ....Il.3.486.215.
Or carry Wars to some soft *Asian* Plain? ....Il.3.496.215.
So some fell Lion whom the Woods obey, ...Il.3.561.218.
Yet some Distinction *Juno* might require, ...Il.4.83.224.
And Fate now labours with some vast Event: ....Il.4.112.225.
As when some stately Trappings are decreed, ...Il.4.170.229.
While some proud *Trojan* thus insulting cries, ...Il.4.212.231.
Now seek some skilful Hand whose pow'rful Art ....Il.4.228.232.
Pierc'd by some *Lycian* or *Dardanian* Bow, ...Il.4.240.232.
As if some God had snatch'd their Voice away. ....Il.4.489.243.
(Fell'd by some Artist with his shining Steel, ...Il.4.554.248.
Had some brave Chief this martial Scene beheld, ...Il.4.630.251.
And some bold Chieftain ev'ry Leader slew: ....Il.5.50.268.
If chance some Shepherd with a distant Dart ....Il.5.176.275.
Or if that Chief, some Guardian of the Skies ....Il.5.235.278.
And, but some God, some angry God withstands, ...Il.5.240.278.
And, but some God, some angry God withstands, ...Il.5.240.278.
Strong as thou art, some God may yet be found, ...Il.5.499.292.
To quit her Country for some Youth of *Troy;* ....Il.5.514.293.
He dreads his Fury, and some Steps retires. ....Il.5.540.294.
As when some simple Swain his Cot forsakes, ...Il.5.734.302.
Far as a shepherd, from some Point on high, ...Il.5.960.312.
Some God, they thought, who rul'd the Fate of Wars, ...Il.6.133.330.
Warm'd with some Virtue, some Regard of Fame! ....Il.6.443.348.
Warm'd with some Virtue, some Regard of Fame! ....Il.6.443.348.
This Day, some God who hates our *Trojan* Land ....Il.6.460.349.
Some haughty *Greek* who lives thy Tears to see, ...Il.6.586.355.
What my Soul prompts, and what some God commands. ....Il.7.80.367.
Which when some future Mariner surveys, ...Il.7.99.368.
Greece in our Cause shall arm some pow'rful Hand. ....Il.7.134.370.
Achilles shuns the Fight; yet some there are ....Il.7.275.378.
Some future Day shall lengthen out the Strife, ...Il.7.354.381.
Exchange some Gift; that *Greece* and *Troy* may say, ...Il.7.363.382.
Some Space at least permit the War to breathe, ...Il.7.398.383.
Some search the Plain, some fell the sounding Grove: ....Il.7.495.389.
Some search the Plain, some fell the sounding Grove: ....Il.7.495.389.
Some Brass or Iron, some an Oxe, or Slave. ....Il.7.569.392.
Some Brass or Iron, some an Oxe, or Slave. ....Il.7.569.392.
Some other Sun may see the happier Hour, ...Il.8.173.406.
With ev'ry Shaft some hostile Victim slew, ...Il.8.323.413.
Some golden Tripod, or distinguish'd Car, ...Il.8.351.414.
Or some fair Captive whom thy Eyes approve ....Il.8.353.414.
But sure some God denies me to destroy ....Il.8.363.414.
Stretch'd by some *Argive* on his native Shore: ....Il.8.436.418.
Some future Day, perhaps he may be mov'd ....Il.8.453.418.
She claims some Title to transgress our Will. ....Il.8.501.420.
She claims some Title to transgress his Will: ....Il.8.521.421.
Some hostile Wound let ev'ry Dart bestow, ...Il.8.639.426.
Some lasting Token of the *Phrygian* Foe, ...Il.8.640.426.
Some line the Trench, and others man the Wall. ....Il.9.120.438.
Now seek some means his fatal wrath to end, ...Il.9.145.439.
Yet some Redress to suppliant *Greece* afford, ...Il.9.398.452.
Some few my Soldiers had, himself the rest. ....Il.9.437.454.
Some Present too to ev'ry Prince was paid; ....Il.9.438.454.
Some greater *Greek* let those high Nuptials grace, ...Il.9.514.458.
I thought (but some kind God that Thought suppress) ....Il.9.588.463.
Sends he some Spy, amidst these silent Hours, ...Il.10.43.4.
Seek'st thou some Friend, or nightly Centinel? ....Il.10.92.6.
Some other be dispatch'd, of nimbler Feet, ...Il.10.125.7.
To yonder Camp, or seize some stragling Foe? ....Il.10.244.13.
Some God within commands, and I obey. ....Il.10.262.13.
But let some other chosen Warrior join, ...Il.10.263.13.

SOME (CONTINUED)

And let some Deed this signal Night adorn, ...Il.10.333.18.
O Friend! I hear some Step of hostile Feet, ...Il.10.405.21.
Some Spy perhaps, to lurk beside the Main; ....Il.10.407.21.
Lest on the Foe some forward *Greek* advance, ...Il.10.437.23.
Or art some Wretch by hopes of Plunder led, ...Il.10.459.24.
Shall we dismiss thee, in some future Strife ....Il.10.518.26.
Perhaps some Horses of the *Trojan* Breed ....Il.10.628.30.
Some God, I deem, conferr'd the glorious Prize, ...Il.10.650.30.
As sweating Reapers in some wealthy Field, ...Il.11.89.38.
But now (what time in some sequester'd Vale ....Il.11.119.39.
Finds, on some grassy Lare, the couching Fawns, ...Il.11.154.42.
He bleeds! (he cries) some God has sped my Dart; ....Il.11.485.56.
Where this but lights, some noble Life expires, ...Il.11.501.56.
Then furious thus, (but first some Steps withdrew.) ....Il.11.552.58.
As when some Huntsman with a flying Spear, ...Il.11.594.60.
In some wide Field by Troops of Boys pursu'd, ...Il.11.683.65.
Some fav'ring God *Achilles'* Heart may move; ....Il.11.924.76.
If some dire Oracle his Breast alarm, ...Il.11.926.77.
Some Beam of Comfort yet on *Greece* may shine, ...Il.11.928.77.
Till some wide Wound lets out their mighty Soul. ....Il.12.168.87.
Like some black Tempest gath'ring round the Tow'rs; ....Il.12.446.97.
As skilful Divers, from some airy Steep, ...Il.12.461.98.
The Chief, who fear'd some Foe's insulting Boast ....Il.12.469.98.
(While some laborious Matron, just and poor, ...Il.12.523.101.
If yet some heav'nly Pow'r your Breast excite, ...Il.13.83.108.
Some God, my Friend, some God in human form ....Il.13.99.109.
Some God, my Friend, some God in human form ....Il.13.99.109.
Ev'n now some Energy divine I share, ...Il.13.105.109.
As from some Mountain's craggy Forehead torn, ...Il.13.191.114.
As from some far-seen Mountain's airy Crown, ...Il.13.241.116.
On some important Message art thou bound, ...Il.13.329.121.
Or bleeds my Friend by some unhappy Wound? ....Il.13.330.121.
And were some Ambush for the Foes design'd, ...Il.13.355.122.
Or Pine, fit Mast for some great Admiral, ...Il.13.494.130.
Or find some Foe whom Heav'n and he shall doom ....Il.13.535.132.
Fixt as some Column, or deep-rooted Oak, ...Il.13.549.132.
To call some Hero to partake the Deed. ....Il.13.575.133.
As the fell Boar on some rough Mountain's Head, ...Il.13.594.134.
There, for some luckier *Greek* it rests a Prize, ...Il.13.731.139.
As on some ample Barn's well-harden'd Floor, ...Il.13.739.139.
(Like some vile Worm extended on the Ground) ....Il.13.819.144.
To some the Pow'rs of bloody War belong, ...Il.13.915.148.
To some, sweet Music, and the Charm of Song; ....Il.13.916.148.
Some cold in Death, some groaning on the Ground, ...Il.13.958.151.
Some cold in Death, some groaning on the Ground, ...Il.13.958.151.
Some low in Dust (a mournful Object) lay, ...Il.13.959.151.
High on the Wall some breath'd their Souls away. ....Il.13.960.151.
Some Lines, methinks, may make his Lineage known, ...Il.14.555.190.
As some way-faring Man, who wanders o'er ....Il.15.86.199.
Some seek the Trench, some skulk behind the Wall, ...Il.15.391.212.
Some seek the Trench, some skulk behind the Wall, ...Il.15.391.212.
The sportive Wanton, pleas'd with some new Play, ...Il.15.418.213.
Above the sides of some tall Ship ascend, ...Il.15.442.214.
Perhaps some fav'ring God his Soul may bend; ....Il.15.466.215.
Some God prevents our destin'd Enterprize: ....Il.15.549.217.
Some God, propitious to the *Trojan* Foe, ...Il.15.550.218.
Lift the bold Lance, and make some *Trojan* bleed. ....Il.15.685.222.
So some tall Rock o'erhangs the hoary Main, ...Il.15.746.224.
Amidst the Plain of some wide-water'd Fen, ...Il.15.761.225.
Some lordly Bull (the rest despers'd and fled) ....Il.15.766.226.
To some great City thro' the publick way; ....Il.15.825.228.
Or may some meaner Cause thy Pity claim? ....Il.16.23.236.
Some rugged Rock's hard Entrails gave thee Form, ...Il.16.50.237.
If some dire Oracle thy Breast alarm, ...Il.16.54.237.
Some Beam of Comfort yet on *Greece* may shine, ...Il.16.56.237.
Some adverse God thy Rashness may destroy; ....Il.16.118.241.
Some God, like *Phœbus*, ever kind to *Troy*. ....Il.16.119.241.
(When some tall Stag fresh-slaughter'd in the Wood ....Il.16.196.247.
Now ev'ry *Greek* some hostile Hero slew, ...Il.16.364.257.
Some mighty Fish draws panting to the Shore; ....Il.16.496.262.
Or Pine (fit Mast for some great Admiral) ....Il.16.594.267.
Thick, as beneath some Shepherd's thatch'd Abode, ...Il.16.779.273.
Thus for some slaughter'd Hind, with equal Rage, ...Il.16.915.279.
In the deep Bosom of some gloomy Wood; ....Il.16.924.279.
Stones follow Stones; some clatter on the Fields, ...Il.16.933.279.
Some, hard and heavy, shake the sounding Shields. ....Il.16.934.279.
As the young Olive, in some Sylvan Scene, ...Il.17.57.290.
Flies, as before some Mountain Lion's Ire ....Il.17.69.290.
Thus in the Center of some gloomy Wood, ...Il.17.146.293.
Where some swoln River disembogues his Waves, ...Il.17.311.299.
On some good Man, or Woman unreprov'd ....Il.17.493.307.
Cleaves the broad Forehead of some brawny Bull; ....Il.17.589.311.
Poor as it is, some Off'ring to thy Shade. ....Il.17.607.312.
Some Hero too must be dispatch'd, to bear ....Il.17.721.315.
To whelm some City under Waves of Fire, ...Il.17.826.321.
Drag some vast Beam, or Mast's unwieldy Length; ....Il.17.834.321.
Some interposing Hill the Stream divides, ...Il.17.841.321.
Like some fair Olive, by my careful Hand ....Il.18.75.326.
Shall I not force some widow'd Dame to tear ....Il.18.155.330.
As when from some beleaguer'd Town arise ....Il.18.245.334.
(Seen from some Island, o'er the Main afar, ...Il.18.247.334.
Like some fair Plant beneath my careful Hand ....Il.18.511.346.
Some less important Season may suffice, ...Il.19.198.381.
Streams from some lonely Watch-tow'r to the Sky: ....Il.19.407.389.
Buoy'd by some inward Force, he seems to swim, ...Il.19.418.389.
Our favour'd Hero, let some Pow'r descend. ....Il.20.151.400.
But lest some adverse God now cross his Way, ...Il.20.156.400.
Till at the length, by some brave Youth defy'd, ...Il.20.203.402.
Has *Troy* propos'd some spacious Tract of Land? ....Il.20.223.403.
To one that fears thee, some unwarlike Boy: ....Il.20.241.404.
To one that dreads thee, some unwarlike Boy: ....Il.20.500.415.
Some Pity to a Suppliant's Name afford, ...Il.21.86.425.
Some Dæmon urges! 'tis my Doom to die! ....Il.21.104.426.
Whose ev'ry Wave some wat'ry Monster brings, ...Il.21.139.427.
Like some vile Swain, whom, on a rainy Day, ...Il.21.327.434.

SOME (CONTINUED)

To melt the Fat of some rich Sacrifice, ...Il.21.425.438.
Some proud in Triumph, some with Rage on fire; ....Il.21.603.447.
Some proud in Triumph, some with Rage on fire; ....Il.21.603.447.
The Pale Inhabitants, some fall, some fly; ....Il.21.609.447.
The Pale Inhabitants, some fall, some fly; ....Il.21.609.447.
So from some deep grown Wood a Panther starts, ...Il.21.677.450.
Thro' the thick Gloom of some tempestuous Night ....Il.22.38.454.
Struck by some God, he fears, recedes, and flies. ....Il.22.180.461.
As when some Hero's Fun'rals are decreed ....Il.22.211.464.
(Some golden Tripod, or some lovely Dame) ....Il.22.214.464.
(Some golden Tripod, or some lovely Dame) ....Il.22.214.464.
And great *Achilles*, lest some *Greek's* Advance ....Il.22.267.466.
But now some God within me bids me try ....Il.22.319.469.
While some ignobler, the great Dead deface ....Il.22.467.474.
Some Comfort that had been, some sad Relief, ...Il.22.548.479.
Some Comfort that had been, some sad Relief, ...Il.22.548.479.
Some strange Disaster, some reverse of Fate ....Il.22.582.480.
Some strange Disaster, some reverse of Fate ....Il.22.582.480.
Some Stranger plows his patrimonial Field. ....Il.22.627.482.
Some Rites remain, to glut our Rage of Grief. ....Il.23.14.486.
Some Ease at least those pious Rites may give, ...Il.23.57.489.
Hereafter *Greece* some nobler Work may raise, ...Il.23.308.502.
Of some once-stately Oak the last Remains, ...Il.23.401.506.
(Some Tomb perhaps of old, the Dead to grace; ....Il.23.405.506.
Those, tho' the swiftest, by some God with-held, ...Il.23.544.511.
Rise then some other, and inform my Sight, ...Il.23.552.511.
Some Gift must grace *Eumelus;* view thy Store ....Il.23.629.514.
Stand forth some Man, to bear the Bowl away! ....Il.23.770.520.
By some huge Billow dash'd against the Shore, ...Il.23.803.521.
Some aged Herald, who with gentle Hand, ...Il.24.185.544.
Some Thought there must be, in a Soul so brave, ...Il.24.193.544.
Some Sense of Duty, some Desire to save. ....Il.24.194.544.
Some Sense of Duty, some Desire to save. ....Il.24.194.544.
Some aged Herald, who with gentle Hand ....Il.24.215.546.
Some Thought there must be, in a Soul so brave, ...Il.24.223.546.
Some Sense of Duty, some Desire to save. ....Il.24.224.546.
Some Sense of Duty, some Desire to save. ....Il.24.224.546.
Wide as appears some Palace Gate display'd, ...Il.24.391.552.
He seem'd, fair Offspring of some princely Line! ....Il.24.426.553.
I mark some Foes Advance: O King! beware; ....Il.24.435.554.
To lodge in safety with some friendly Hand? ....Il.24.469.556.
(Tho' many a Wound they gave) Some heav'nly Care, ...Il.24.513.557.
Some Hand divine, preserves him ever fair: ....Il.24.514.557.
Just gains some Frontier, breathless, pale! amaz'd! ....Il.24.592.561.
Yet now perhaps, some Turn of human Fate ....Il.24.604.562.
Think from some pow'rful Foe thou see'st him fly, ...Il.24.606.562.
Some God impells with Courage not thy own: ....Il.24.712.567.
Condemn'd to toil for some inhuman Lord. ....Il.24.925.575.
Or else some *Greek* whose Father prest the Plain, ...Il.24.926.575.
Some Word thou would'st have spoke, which sadly dear, ...Il.24.936.575.
If some proud Brother ey'd me with Disdain, ...Il.24.972.576.
Oh snatch some portion of these acts from fate, ...Od.1.13.29.
But still the frown of some cælestial pow'r ....Od.1.253.45.
Some other *Greeks* a fairer claim may plead; ....Od.1.505.56.
Did he some loan of antient right require, ...Od.1.519.57.
Arrives some message of invading foes? ....Od.2.38.62.
Inspire some Patriot, and demand debate! ....Od.2.40.62.
From him some bribe thy venal tongue requires, ...Od.2.217.72.
Search, for some thoughts, thy own suggesting mind; ....Od.3.34.87.
The youth of *Pylos,* some on pointed wood ....Od.3.43.88.
Transfix'd the fragments, some prepar'd the food. ....Od.3.44.88.
Some he destroy'd, some scatter'd as the dust, ...Od.3.163.93.
Some he destroy'd, some scatter'd as the dust, ...Od.3.163.93.
Some God this arm with equal prowess bless! ....Od.3.250.97.
Mov'd by some Oracle, or voice divine? ....Od.3.264.98.
By some stern ruffian, or adultrous wife. ....Od.3.292.100.
Condemn'd perhaps some foreign shore to tread; ....Od.3.314.101.
Me, as some needy peasant, would ye leave, ...Od.3.447.108.
Let one, dispatchful, bid some swain to lead ....Od.3.534.113.
Whether he wanders on some firendless coast, ...Od.4.141.127.
Some envious pow'r the blissful scene destroys; ....Od.4.245.131.
Some Dæmon anxious for the *Trojan* doom, ...Od.4.375.137.
Some heav'nly pow'r averse my stay constrains: ....Od.4.512.144.
Some whirl the disk, and some the jav'lin dart. ....Od.4.848.158.
Some whirl the disk, and some the jav'lin dart. ....Od.4.848.158.
Or some Celestial in his reverend form, ...Od.4.878.159.
For them to form some exquisite repast? ....Od.4.908.161.
Some Kings with arbitrary rage devour, ...Od.4.918.161.
To know, if some inhabitant of heav'n, ...Od.4.945.162.
The chief shall honour as some heav'nly guest, ...Od.5.48.174.
Some other motive, Goddess! sways thy mind, ...Od.5.223.182.
(Some close design, or turn of womankind) ....Od.5.224.182.
Some bark's broad bottom to out-ride the storms, ...Od.5.320.187.
Had some distinguish'd day renown'd my fall; ....Od.5.396.191.
Fixt by some Dæmon to his bed of pain, ...Od.5.509.196.
Or some enormous whale the God may send, ...Od.5.538.198.
Some smooth ascent, or safe-sequester'd bay. ....Od.5.561.199.
As some poor peasant, fated to reside ....Od.5.630.202.
Spares only to inflict some mightier woe! ....Od.6.208.220.
As by some artist to whom *Vulcan* gives ....Od.6.275.224.
This land of joy: his steps some Godhead leads: ....Od.6.288.224.
"Perhaps a native of some distant shore, ...Od.6.333.227.
"Or rather, some descendant of the skies; ....Od.6.335.227.
Some turn the mill, or sift the golden grain, ...Od.7.133.241.
Some ply the loom; their busy fingers move ....Od.7.134.241.
Some to unload the fertile branches run, ...Od.7.160.244.
Some dry the black'ning clusters in the sun, ...Od.7.161.244.
And seat him fair in some distinguish'd place. ....Od.7.219.247.
Gracious approach us some immortal pow'r; ....Od.7.266.248.
Some high event the conscious Gods design. ....Od.7.268.248.
Oft with some favour'd traveller they stray, ...Od.7.273.249.
Gaz'd, as before some brother of the sky. ....Od.8.18.262.
Some mean sea-farer in pursuit of gain; ....Od.8.180.272.
Some greatly think, some speak with manly sense; ....Od.8.186.272.
Some greatly think, some speak with manly sense; ....Od.8.186.272.

SOME (CONTINUED)

As some fond matron views in mortal fight .... Od.8.571.293.
Some dear-lov'd brother press'd the *Phrygian* plain? .... Od.8.634.297.
Or bled some friend? who bore a brother's part, ... Od.8.635.297.
Hither some fav'ring God, beyond our thought, ... Od.9.165.312.
As some lone mountain's monstrous growth he stood, ... Od.9.223.316.
Which now some ages from his race conceal'd, ... Od.9.240.316.
Of some fell monster, fierce with barb'rous pow'r, ... Od.9.249.317.
Some rustic wretch, who liv'd in heav'n's despight, ... Od.9.250.317.
At least some hospitable gift bestow; .... Od.9.319.319.
(So fortune chanc'd, or so some God design'd) .... Od.9.399.322.
Urg'd by some present God, they swift let fall .... Od.9.453.324.
Who plye the wimble, some huge beam to bore; .... Od.9.458.324.
I deem'd some godlike Giant to behold, ... Od.9.601.331.
Some vessel, not his own, transport him o'er; .... Od.9.626.332.
(Not yielding to some bulky mountain's height) .... Od.10.129.347.
Some God directing, to this peaceful bay .... Od.10.165.348.
Some pow'r divine who pities human woe .... Od.10.182.349.
Some smoak I saw amid the forest rise, ... Od.10.225.351.
As from some feast a man returning late, ... Od.10.246.354.
Rejoycing round, some morsel to receive, ... Od.10.248.354.
Some hoard of grief close harbour'd at his heart. .... Od.10.446.365.
Soft, as some song divine, thy story flows, ... Od.11.458.407.
Thick as the boars, which some luxurious lord .... Od.11.513.409.
Unfold some trifle, but conceal the rest. .... Od.11.548.410.
A slave to some poor hind that toils for bread; .... Od.11.599.412.
O Prince attend! some fav'ring pow'r be kind, ... Od.12.49.431.
Some Demon calm'd the Air, and smooth'd the deep, ... Od.12.204.441.
As from some rock that overhangs the flood, ... Od.12.300.446.
Some mighty woe relentless heav'n forbodes: .... Od.12.328.447.
O cruel thou! some fury sure has steel'd .... Od.12.333.448.
So will'd some Demon, minister of woes! .... Od.12.352.448.
Some juster Prince perhaps had entertain'd, ... Od.13.249.18.
Who seem'd descended from some princely line. .... Od.13.270.19.
With joy to thee, as to some God, I bend, ... Od.13.277.19.
Or some fair isle which *Neptune's* arms surround? .... Od.13.282.19.
Some voice of God close whisp'ring from within, ... Od.14.109.41.
But these, no doubt, some oracle explore, ... Od.14.111.41.
Like some fair plant set by a heav'nly hand, ... Od.14.202.45.
Oh! had he perisht on some well-fought day, ... Od.14.401.55.
Some guest arrives, with rumors of her Lord; .... Od.14.414.56.
Some in the flames, bestrow'd with flour, they threw; .... Od.14.478.59.
Some cut in fragments, from the forks they drew: .... Od.14.479.59.
Let from among us some swift Courier rise, ... Od.14.562.64.
Some friend would fence me from the winter's rage. .... Od.14.571.64.
Some master, or some servant would allow .... Od.14.574.64.
Some master, or some servant would allow .... Od.14.574.64.
Let o'er thy house some chosen maid preside, ... Od.15.29.71.
Some choice domestic viands to prepare; .... Od.15.88.73.
Without some pledge, some monument of love; .... Od.15.96.73.
Without some pledge, some monument of love; .... Od.15.96.73.
To thee, as to some God, I'll temples raise, ... Od.15.204.78.
Not undeserving, some support obtain. .... Od.15.335.85.
Doom'd a fair prize to grace some Prince's board, ... Od.15.420.89.
Or yet more distant, to some Lord apply? .... Od.15.550.96.
Some well-known friend (*Eumæus)* bends this way; .... Od.16.9.102.
As some fond sire who ten long winters grieves, ... Od.16.17.102.
And let some handmaid of her train resort .... Od.16.164.110.
To some rude churl, and born by stealth away. .... Od.16.241.116.
Some God has told them, or themselves survey .... Od.16.372.124.
To some blest Prince, the Prince decreed by Heav'n. .... Od.16.407.126.
Lead on: but help me to some staff to stay .... Od.17.218.142.
Some whey, to wash his bowels, he might earn. .... Od.17.265.145.
Oh be some God his convoy to our shore! .... Od.17.289.146.
Or some brave Suitor's sword, might pierce the heart .... Od.17.301.146.
Some rude insult thy rev'rend age may bear; .... Od.17.330.147.
Some care his Age deserves: Or was he priz'd .... Od.17.372.150.
Some few the foes in servitude detain; .... Od.17.522.158.
From *Mars* impartial some broad wound we bear; .... Od.17.560.159.
All, ev'n the worst, condemn'd; and some reprov'd. .... Od.17.573.160.
Wander, perhaps, some inmate of the skies; .... Od.17.577.160.
As when some heav'n-taught Poet charms the ear, ... Od.17.609.161.
Some light, and sooth her soul's eternal pain. .... Od.17.637.163.
Like some vile swine's, that greedy of his prey .... Od.18.35.168.
Lest heav'n in vengeance send some mightier woe. .... Od.18.129.172.
O may'st thou, favour'd by some guardian pow'r, ... Od.18.175.175.
Some joy remains: To thee a son is giv'n, ... Od.18.207.177.
Or shun in some black forge the midnight air. .... Od.18.378.186.
Some God no doubt this strange kindly sends; .... Od.18.400.187.
Some visitant of pure etherial race, ... Od.19.48.195.
The golden goblets some, and some restor'd .... Od.19.74.196.
The golden goblets some, and some restor'd .... Od.19.74.196.
To some new channel soon, the changeful tide .... Od.19.102.197.
This art, instinct by some cœlestial pow'r, ... Od.19.160.200.
Some wretch reluctant views aerial light, ... Od.19.401.214.
At length return'd, some God inspires thy breast .... Od.19.567.224.
Let some refresh the vase's sullied mold; .... Od.20.190.242.
Some bid the goblets boast their native gold: .... Od.20.191.242.
Some to the spring, with each a jar, repair, ... Od.20.192.242.
Some wield the sounding ax; the dodder'd oaks .... Od.20.200.243.
Some pitying God (*Ulysses* sad reply'd) .... Od.20.211.243.
Or haply perish'd on some distant coast, ... Od.20.263.246.
Now, to some foreign clime inclin'd to fly, ... Od.20.277.246.
To some *Sicilian* mart these courtiers send, ... Od.20.456.255.
Then thus *Telemachus.* Some God I find .... Od.21.105.263.
With each new sun to some new hope a prey, ... Od.21.165.267.
And send us with some humbler wife to live, ... Od.21.169.267.
Say, shou'd some fav'ring God restore again .... Od.21.201.269.
Some may betray, and yonder walls may hear. .... Od.21.245.271.
Some moments you, and let me lead the way. .... Od.21.247.271.
At ev'ry portal let some matron wait, ... Od.21.252.272.
And some respect *Telemachus* may claim. .... Od.21.336.276.
Exil'd for this to some sequester'd den, ... Od.21.393.279.
At ev'ry portal let some matron wait, ... Od.21.413.280.
While some deriding—How he turns the bow! .... Od.21.431.281.
Some other like it sure the man must know, ... Od.21.432.281.

SOME (CONTINUED)

Then, as some heav'nly minstrel, taught to sing .... Od.21.440.281.
To some new strain when he adapts the lyre, ... Od.21.442.281.
Some, turn'd by *Pallas,* on the threshold fall, ... Od.22.302.301.
Some wound the gate, some ring against the wall; .... Od.22.303.301.
Some wound the gate, some ring against the wall; .... Od.22.303.301.
Some weak, or pond'rous with the brazen head, ... Od.22.304.301.
Thus on some tree hung struggling in the snare, ... Od.22.505.313.
Ah no! some God the Suitors deaths decreed, ... Od.23.63.321.
Some God descends, and by his hand they bleed; .... Od.23.64.321.
As by some artist to whom *Vulcan* gives .... Od.23.157.328.
Vast as some mighty column's bulk on high .... Od.23.193.332.
As in the cavern of some rifted den, ... Od.24.9.347.
Cluster'd they hang, till at some sudden shock, ... Od.24.11.347.
Or well-defending some beleaguer'd wall, ... Od.24.138.354.
Some God assisted, and unmann'd us all: .... Od.24.209.358.
Age so advanc'd may some indulgence claim. .... Od.24.295.364.
(Some surly Islander, of manners rude) .... Od.24.307.364.
Some adverse *Dæmon* from *Sicania* bore .... Od.24.357.366.
Amaz'd, *Laertes.* "Give some certain sign, ... Od.24.382.367.
His mod'rate words some better minds persuade: .... Od.24.530.373.
Some fall to earth, and some confus'dly fly. .... Od.24.619.377.
Some fall to earth, and some confus'dly fly. .... Od.24.619.377.

SOMERS

The Courtly *Talbot, Somers, Sheffield* read, ... 4.Arbu.139.105.

SOMETHING

Something, whose Truth convinc'd at Sight we find, ... 1.EOC.299.273.
If rich, she keeps her Priest, or something worse; .... 2.ChWB.87.61.
"'Tis something difficult, I must allow, ... 2.ChWB.188A.65.
And all who told it, added something new, ... 2.TemF.470.286.
That something still which prompts th'eternal sigh, ... 3.EOM4.3.128.
Something as dim to our internal view, ... 3.Ep1.49.18.
'Tis true, but something in her was forgot .... 3.Ep2.158A.64.
Something there is more needful than Expence, ... 3.Ep4.41.140.
And something previous ev'n to Taste—'tis Sense: .... 3.Ep4.42.140.
And something said of *Chartres* much too rough. .... 4.HS1.4.5.
Hartshorn, or something that shall close your Eyes. .... 4.HS1.20.7.
He calls for something bitter, something sour, ... 4.HS2.33.57.
He calls for something bitter, something sour, ... 4.HS2.33.57.
(Cries prating *Balbus)* "something will come out." .... 4.Arbu.276.115.
Years foll'wing Years, steal something ev'ry day, ... 4.2HE2.72.171.
Show'd us that France had something to admire. .... 4.2HE1.275.219.
Something, which for your Honour they may cheat, ... 4.1HE6.93.243.
Something in Verse as true as Prose; .... 4.HS6.26.251.
But something much more our concern, ... 4.HS6.145.259.
And all are clear, that something must be done. .... 4.1740.30.333.
Something betwixt a H[eidegger] and Owl) .... 5.DunA1.244.92.
Something betwixt a Heideggre and owl,) .... 5.DunB1.290.290.
Author of something yet more great than Letter; .... 5.DunB4.216.363.
Read something of a diff'rent Nature, ... 6.10.5.24.
Something to blame, and something to commend? .... 6.52.22.156.
Something to blame, and something to commend? .... 6.52.22.156.
Something to deck their pretty Babes and Spouses; .... 6.96iv.56.278.
"Do something exquisite, and wise—" .... 6.119.7.336.
"Do something very fine, and wise—" .... 6.119.7A.336.
Upon something or other, she found better *Fun.* .... 6.124i.6.346.
'Tis true, but something in her was *forgot.* .... 6.139.2.377.

SOMETHINGS

Where nameless somethings in their causes sleep, ... 5.DunA1.54.66.
Where nameless Somethings in their causes sleep, ... 5.DunB1.56.274.

SOMETIMES

Great Wits sometimes may *gloriously offend,* .... 1.EOC.152.257.
Conceal his Force, nay seem sometimes to *Fly.* .... 1.EOC.178.261.
Oft *hide* his Force, nay seem sometimes to *Fly.* .... 1.EOC.178A.261.
As Men of Breeding, sometimes Men of Wit, ... 1.EOC.259.269.
'Tis best sometimes your Censure to restrain, ... 1.EOC.596.308.
Sometimes his Pruning-hook corrects the Vines, ... 1.TrVP.37.378.
Dost sometimes Counsel take—and sometimes *Tea.* .... 2.RL3.8.169.
Dost sometimes Counsel take—and sometimes *Tea.* .... 2.RL3.8.169.
"But sometimes Virtue starves, while Vice is fed." .... 3.EOM4.149.142.
How sometimes life is risq'd, and always ease: .... 3.EOM4.274.154.
In publick Stations Men sometimes are shown, ... 3.Ep2.199A.66.
But grant, in Public Men sometimes are shown, ... 3.Ep2.199.66.
Sometimes to call a Minister my Friend: .... 4.Arbu.266.114.
Such they'll degrade; and sometimes, in its stead, ... 4.2HE2.163.177.
Sometimes the Folly benefits mankind; .... 4.2HE1.191.211.
('Tis Reason's voice, which sometimes one can hear) .... 4.1HE1.12.279.
Sometimes a Patriot, active in debate, ... 4.1HE1.27.281.
Sometimes, with Aristippus, or St. Paul, ... 4.1HE1.31.281.
As gods sometimes descend from heav'n and deign .... 6.4i.1.9.
Bring sometimes with you Lady R[ich] .... 6.61.45.182.
And sometimes Mistress H[owar]d, ... 6.61.46.182.
Bring sometimes with you Mistress R[ic]h .... 6.61.45B.182.
The weakest Woman sometimes may .... 6.94.3.259.

SOMEWHAT

Not to go back, is somewhat to advance, ... 4.1HE1.53.283.

SOMEWHERE

There must be, somewhere, such a rank as Man; .... 3.EOM1.48.19.

SOMMERS

Thus SOMMERS once, and HALIFAX were mine. .... 4.EpS2.77.317.

SOMNUS

With Gold unfading, *Somnus,* shall be thine; .... Il.14.273.175.
Had *Somnus* dry'd the balmy dews away. .... Od.7.373.254.

SOMNUS'

For *Juno's* Love, and *Somnus'* pleasing Ties, ... Il.14.415.183.

SON

A *Virgin* shall conceive, a *Virgin* bear a Son! .... 1.Mes.8.113.
Then Palaces shall rise; the joyful Son .... 1.Mes.63.118.
While, at each Change, the Son of *Lybian Jove* .... 1.EOC.376.283.
When the fair Consort of her son replies. .... 1.TrFD.2.385.
Of these she crop'd, to please her infant son; .... 1.TrFD.25.387.
My son, thy mother's parting kiss receive, ... 1.TrFD.94.390.
The Sire against the Son his Arrows drew, ... 1.TrSt.15.410.
When by the Son the trembling Father dy'd, ... 1.TrSt.91.414.
The murd'ring Son ascend his Parent's Bed, ... 1.TrSt.331.424.
Thus, thro' the parting Clouds the Son of *May* .... 1.TrSt.437.428.
Heav'n had not crown his Wishes with a Son, ... 1.TrSt.543.433.
Jocasta's Son, and *Thebes* my Native Place. .... 1.TrSt.805.443.
Replies—Ah why forbears the Son to Name .... 1.TrSt.808.443.
His God-like Son, and urg'd him on to Fame. .... 1.TrES.6.449.
His matchless Son, and urg'd him on to Fame. .... 1.TrES.6A.449.
Your Aid (said *Thoos) Peteus's* Son demands, ... 1.TrES.80Z2.452.
My God-like Son shall press the *Phrygian* Plain: .... 1.TrES.228.458.
Laments his Son, predestin'd to be slain, ... 1.TrES.259.459.
Whose Son, the swift *Orsilochus,* I slew, ... 1.TrUl.145.470.
The growing Virtues of my youthful Son, ... 1.TrUl.245.474.
His Father's Blessing from an Elder Son: .... 2.ChJM.70.18.
The Son of *Sirach* testifies no less. .... 2.ChJM.640.46.
Convey'd unbroken faith from sire to son, ... 3.EOM3.228.115.
Tell me, if Virtue made the Son expire, ... 3.EOM4.105.138.
As that the virtuous son is ill at ease, ... 3.EOM4.119.139.
Boastful and rough, your first son is a 'Squire; .... 3.Ep1.103.22.
By his own son, that passes by unbless'd: .... 3.Ep1.231.35.
Wife, son, and daughter, Satan, are thy prize, ... 3.Ep3.399A.124.
T' enrich a Bastard, or a Son they hate. .... 3.Ep3.100.98.
Not so his Son, he mark'd this oversight, ... 3.Ep3.199.109.
First, for his Son a gay Commission buys, ... 3.Ep3.389.124.
Wife, son, and daughter, Satan, are thy own, ... 3.Ep3.399.124.
A lost Bank-bill, or heard their Son was drown'd) .... 4.HS2.56.59.
"Pity! to build, without a son or wife: .... 4.HS2.163.67.
At best, it falls to some ungracious Son .... 4.HS2.173.69.
The Wretch, whose Av'rice drove his *Son* away. .... 4.HAdv.26.77.
Arthur, whose giddy Son neglects the Laws, ... 4.Arbu.23.97.
Ammon's great Son one shoulder had too high, ... 4.Arbu.117.104.
"My only Son, I'd have him see the World: .... 4.2HE2.6.165.
To read in Greek, the Wrath of Peleus' Son. .... 4.2HE2.53.169.
To Ease and Silence, ev'ry Muse's Son: .... 4.2HE2.111.173.
And send his Wife to Church, his Son to school. .... 4.2HE1.164.209.
Weds the rich Dulness of some Son of earth? .... 4.1HE6.43.239.
Adopt him Son, or Cozen at the least, ... 4.1HE6.108.245.
Ye Gods! shall *Cibber's* Son, without rebuke .... 4.EpS1.115.306.
And offer Country, Parent, Wife, or Son! .... 4.EpS1.158.309.
Each Mother asks it for her Booby Son, ... 4.EpS2.107.319.
Each sire imprest and glaring in his son; .... 5.DunA1.98.71.
My son! the promis'd land expects thy reign. .... 5.DunA1.246.92.
To him the Goddess. "Son! thy grief lay down, ... 5.DunA2.123.112.
(Tho' one his son dissuades, and one his wife) .... 5.DunA2.160.121.
Thus the great Father to the greater Son. .... 5.DunA3.34.154.
"And see! my son, the hour is on its way, ... 5.DunA3.115.160.
A hundred sons, and ev'ry son a God: .... 5.DunA3.126.160.
"Son! what thou seek'st is in thee. Look, and find .... 5.DunA3.247.178.
"And are these wonders, Son, to thee unknown? .... 5.DunA3.269.180.
The Mighty Mother, and her Son who brings .... 5.DunB1.1.267.
Each sire imprest and glaring in his son: .... 5.DunB1.100.276.
My son! the promis'd land expects thy reign. .... 5.DunB1.292.291.
Folly, my son, has still a Friend at Court. .... 5.DunB1.300.291.
To grace her dauntless Son, she now proclaims .... 5.DunB2.17A.297.
To him the Goddess: "Son! thy grief lay down, ... 5.DunB2.131.301.
(Tho' this his Son dissuades, and that his Wife.) .... 5.DunB2.168.304.
Thus the great Father to the greater Son. .... 5.DunB3.42.322.
"And see, my son! the hour is on its way, ... 5.DunB3.123.325.
An hundred sons, and ev'ry son a God: .... 5.DunB3.134.326.
"Son; what thou seek'st is in thee! Look, and find .... 5.DunB3.251.332.
"And are these wonders, Son, to thee unknown? .... 5.DunB3.273.333.
Soft on her lap her Laureat son reclines. .... 5.DunB4.20.341.
"Receive, great Empress! thy accomplish'd Son: .... 5.DunB4.282.372.
Lo! ev'ry finish'd Son returns to thee: .... 5.DunB4.500.391.
The Sire is made a Peer, the Son a Fool. .... 5.DunB4.548.396.
Perhaps more high some daring son may soar, ... 5.DunB4.599.402.
As son, as father, brother, husband, friend! .... 6.51ii.28.153.
As son, as father, husband, friend! .... 6.5iii.28A.152.
Here lies the Friend most lov'd, the Son most dear: .... 6.85.2.242.
If ever Friend, if ever Son were dear! .... 6.85.2A.242.
If ever Friend, if ever Son was dear! .... 6.85.2B.242.
If ever Son, if ever Friend was dear; .... 6.85.2C.242.
Here lies the Friend most wept, the Son most dear: .... 6.85.2D.242.
But judg'd *Roboam* his own Son. .... 6.101.20.290.
No son nor Grandson shall the line sustain .... 6.130.29.358.
The pious Son, fond Husband, faithful Friend: .... 6.134.4.364.
The Wrath of *Peleus'* Son the direful Spring .... Il.1.1A.82.
Latona's Son a dire Contagion spread, ... Il.1.11.86.
And dread avenging *Phœbus,* Son of *Jove.* .... Il.1.30.87.
Inspir'd by *Juno, Thetis'* God-like Son .... Il.1.74.90.
From *Atreus'* Son? Then let those Eyes that view .... Il.1.271.100.
Thy Son must fall, by too severe a Doom, ... Il.1.461.110.
If yon proud Monarch thus thy Son defies, ... Il.1.466.110.
Why grieves my Son? Thy Anguish let me share, ... Il.1.474.110.
But Goddess! thou, thy suppliant Son attend, ... Il.1.510.112.
Unhappy Son! (fair *Thetis* thus replies, ... Il.1.540.113.
Which now, alas! too nearly threats my Son. .... Il.1.549.114.
Some Marks of Honour on my Son bestow, ... Il.1.654.118.
To grace her fierce, inexorable Son? .... Il.1.723.122.
To honour *Thetis'* Son he bends his Care, ... Il.2.5.127.
Oh *Atreus'* Son! canst thou indulge thy Rest? .... Il.2.26.128.
And, Dost thou sleep, Oh *Atreus'* Son? (he said) .... Il.2.76.130.
And is it thus, divine *Laertes'* Son! .... Il.2.209.138.
And let these Eyes behold my Son no more; .... Il.2.321.142.
Next came *Idomeneus* and *Tydeus'* Son, ... Il.2.482.149.
Ajax the less, *Oïleus'* valiant Son; .... Il.2.631.157.
(*Ancæus'* Son) the mighty Squadron led. .... Il.2.742.161.
(*Eurytus'* this, and that *Teätus'* Son) .... Il.2.756.161.

SON (CONTINUED)

Thoas came next, *Andræmon's* valiant Son, ... Il.2.775.162.
Tlepolemus, the Son of *Hercules,* .... Il.2.793.162.
Iphiclus' Son, and Brother to the Dead; .... Il.2.861.165.
Oïleus' Son whom beauteous *Rhena* bore. .... Il.2.883.165.
But *Thetis'* Son now shines in Arms no more; .... Il.2.938.168.
Polites' Shape, the Monarch's Son, she chose, ... Il.2.960.169.
Anchises' Son, by *Venus'* stol'n Embrace, ... Il.2.993.170.
When *Atreus'* Son harangu'd the list'ning Train, ... Il.3.275.205.
Paris thy Son, and *Sparta's* King advance, ... Il.3.322.208.
Nor view the Danger of so dear a Son. .... Il.3.383.211.
Two Pow'rs Divine the Son of *Atreus* aid, ... Il.4.9.221.
Amidst the Ranks *Lycaön's* Son she found, ... Il.4.119.226.
Can *Peteus'* Son forget a Warrior's Part, ... Il.4.390.239.
Oh Son of *Tydeus!* (He, whose Strength could tame .... Il.4.422.240.
Gods! how the Son degen'rates from the Sire? .... Il.4.451.241.
Not so fierce *Capaneus'* undaunted Son, ... Il.4.454.241.
Old *Priam's* Son, *Democoon* was his Name; .... Il.4.574.249.
Preserv'd the Son, in Pity to the Sire. .... Il.5.32.267.
Whom *Borus* sent (his Son and only Joy) .... Il.5.59.269.
At length he found *Lycaon's* mighty Son; .... Il.5.216.278.
O Prince (*Lycaon's* valiant Son reply'd) .... Il.5.288.281.
About her much-lov'd Son her Arms she throws, ... Il.5.389.285.
Amphitryon's Son infix'd the deadly Dart, ... Il.5.483.291.
O Son of *Tydeus,* cease! be wise and see .... Il.5.533.294.
He thus advancing, *Nestor's* valiant Son .... Il.5.693.301.
A broken Rock by *Nestor's* Son was thrown, ... Il.5.711.301.
Alcides' Offspring meets the Son of *Jove.* .... Il.5.779.303.
Jove's great Descendent, and his greater Son. .... Il.5.781.303.
Who style thee Son of Cloud-compelling *Jove.* .... Il.5.787.304.
The Son of *Hercules,* the *Rhodian* Guide, ... Il.5.802.304.
Doubtful if *Jove's* great Son he should pursue, ... Il.5.830.305.
If I, unblest, must see my Son no more, ... Il.5.844.305.
Then threw the Force of *Tydeus'* warlike Son; .... Il.5.1048.316.
She gives th' Example, and her Son pursues. .... Il.5.1103.320.
Next *Teuthras'* Son distain'd the Sands with Blood, ... Il.6.15.323.
And *Nestor's* Son laid stern *Ablerus* dead. .... Il.6.38.325.
Thy hollow Ships his Captive Son detain, ... Il.6.60.326.
No Son of *Mars* descend, for servile Gains, ... Il.6.85.327.
When daring *Glaucus* and great *Tydeus'* Son .... Il.6.148.333.
(Reply'd the Chief) can *Tydeus'* Son enquire? .... Il.6.180.334.
Then call'd *Ephyre: Glaucus* was his Son; .... Il.6.193.335.
Long in a strict Embrace she held her Son, ... Il.6.316.341.
My Son from Fight, when *Greece* surrounds our Walls? .... Il.6.319.341.
He said, nor answer'd *Priam's* warlike Son; .... Il.6.430.347.
Ah too forgetful of thy Wife and Son! .... Il.6.511.351.
And all ye deathless Pow'rs! protect my Son! .... Il.6.605.356.
The Son of *Priam,* glorying in his Might, ... Il.6.662.360.
On great *Menesthius, Areïthous'* Son; .... Il.7.12.363.
O Son of *Priam!* let thy faithful Ear .... Il.7.51.365.
And trembling met this dreadful Son of War. .... Il.7.132.370.
To *Saturn's* Son be all your Vows addrest: .... Il.7.230.376.
O Son of *Telamon,* thy Country's Pride! .... Il.7.283.378.
Oh Flight unworthy great *Laertes'* Son! .... Il.8.118.403.
Euæmon's Son next issues to the Foe, ... Il.8.319.412.
And the brave Son repays his Cares with Fame. .... Il.8.346.414.
Sav'd I, for this, his Fav'rite *Son distress'd, ... Il.8.441.418.
To grace her gloomy, fierce, resenting Son, ... Il.8.451.418.
A pensive Scene! 'till *Tydeus'* warlike Son .... Il.9.41.433.
Would hardly stile thee *Nestor's* youngest Son. .... Il.9.82.436.
His Son was first to pass the lofty Mound, ... Il.9.111.437.
There shall he live my Son, our Honours share, ... Il.9.185.441.
With like Surprize arose *Menætius'* Son: .... Il.9.259.445.
Which round the Board *Menætius'* Son bestor'd; .... Il.9.284.447.
His parting Son, these Accents were his last. .... Il.9.329.450.
There shalt thou live his Son, his Honours share, ... Il.9.372.451.
Repell the Rage of *Priam's* single Son? .... Il.9.463.455.
The Son of *Peleus* ceas'd: The Chiefs around .... Il.9.556.460.
Your Sire receiv'd me, as his Son caress'd, ... Il.9.600.464.
Let me (my Son) an ancient Fact unfold, ... Il.9.649.466.
On her own Son to wreak her Brother's Death: .... Il.9.684.468.
A Sire the Slaughter of his Son forgives; .... Il.9.745.471.
Say what Success? divine *Laertes* Son! .... Il.9.791.473.
Whose Son, with *Merion,* o'er the Watch presides.) .... Il.10.68.5.
O Son of *Neleus* (thus the King rejoin'd) .... Il.10.94.6.
Rise, Son of *Tydeus!* to the brave and strong .... Il.10.180.9.
His Son, and godlike *Merion* march'd behind, ... Il.10.229.12.
There sate the mournful Kings: when *Neleus'* Son, ... Il.10.239.12.
This from *Amyntor,* rich *Ormenus'* Son, ... Il.10.313.16.
As thou defend'st the Sire, defend the Son. .... Il.10.338.18.
Rich was the Son in Brass, and rich in Gold; .... Il.10.374.19.
Ulysses thus, and thus *Eumedes'* Son: .... Il.10.484.25.
Led on by *Rhesus,* great *Eioneus'* Son: .... Il.10.505.26.
While unresolv'd the Son of *Tydeus* stands, ... Il.10.592.28.
Enough, my Son, from farther Slaughter cease, ... Il.10.594.28.
Saw *Tydeus'* Son with heav'nly Succour blest, ... Il.10.604.29.
The Goddess then: O Son of *Priam* hear! .... Il.11.257.46.
Charops, the Son of *Hippasus,* was near; .... Il.11.535.57.
Fam'd Son of *Hippasus!* there press the Plain; .... Il.11.565.59.
And first *Doryclus, Priam's* Son, he slew, ... Il.11.611.61.
Glory of *Greece,* old *Neleus'* valiant Son! .... Il.11.633.61.
Strait to *Mænetius'* much-lov'd Son he sent; .... Il.11.736.68.
Old *Neleus* glory'd in his conqu'ring Son. .... Il.11.827.73.
King *Augias'* Son, and Spouse of *Agamede:* .... Il.11.875.75.
Peleus said only this,—"My Son! be brave". .... Il.11.915.76.
There sad he met the brave *Evæmon's* Son, ... Il.11.940.77.
His matchless Son, and urg'd him on to Fame. .... Il.12.350.94.
Your Aid (said *Thoos) Peteus'* Son demands, ... Il.12.426.97.
Th' inspiring God, *Oïleus'* active Son .... Il.13.97.109.
Last *Nestor's* Son the same bold Ardour takes, ... Il.13.129.110.
The Son of *Mentor,* rich in gen'rous Steeds. .... Il.13.228.116.
Cteatus' Son, of *Neptune's* boasted Line; .... Il.13.249.117.
Cteatus' Son, of *Neptune's* forceful Line; .... Il.13.249A.117*.
In *Thoas'* Voice, *Andræmon's* valiant Son, ... Il.13.286.119.
Terror, his best lov'd Son, attends his Course, ... Il.13.386.124.
To crown with Glory *Peleus'* godlike Son, ... Il.13.439.126.

SON (CONTINUED)

Remain the Prize of *Nestor's* youthful Son. Il.13.508.130.
Touch'd ev'ry *Greek,* but *Nestor's* Son the most. Il.13.528.131.
The Son of *Mars* fell gasping on the Ground, Il.13.658.137.
The Son of *Asius, Adamas,* drew near, Il.13.710.138.
And the bold Son of *Pylæmenes* slew. Il.13.804.143.
Polydus' Son, a Seer of old Renown. Il.13.836.145.
Iphyclus' Son: and that (*Oïleus)* thine: Il.13.870.147.
To *Panthus'* Son, at *Hector's* high Command, Il.13.951.151.
Nor *Asius'* Son, nor *Asius'* self appear. Il.13.956.151.
The godlike Father, and th' intrepid Son? Il.13.968.151.
(That Day, the Son his Father's Buckler bore) Il.14.15.157.
Hear then in me the great *Oenides'* Son, Il.14.126.163.
Attend, and in the Son, respect the Sire. Il.14.144.164.
His conqu'ring Son, *Alcides,* plow'd the Main: Il.14.286.176.
Like great *Alcides,* his all-conqu'ring Son? Il.14.300.177.
Pierc'd by whose Point, the Son of *Enops* bled; Il.14.518.188.
Anetor's Brother, or perhaps his Son. Il.14.556.190.
Phalces and *Mermer, Nestor's* Son o'erthrew. Il.14.607.191.
But stretch'd in heaps before *Oïleus'* Son, Il.14.615.192.
Nor seem'd the Vengeance worthy such a Son; Il.15.30.195.
Ev'n my lov'd Son, divine *Sarpedon* falls! Il.15.72.199.
Stern *Mars,* with Anguish for this slaughter'd Son, Il.15.126.201.
Go thou my Son! the trembling *Greeks* alarm, Il.15.258.207.
His Will divine the Son of *Jove* obey'd. Il.15.265.207.
Thus to bold *Hector* spoke the Son of *Jove,* Il.15.296.208.
The Son of *Clytius,* in his daring Hand, Il.15.488.216.
Lo! where the Son of Royal *Clytius* lies, Il.15.496.216.
Clytus, Pisenor's Son, renown'd in Fame, Il.15.522.217.
Dolops, the Son of *Lampus* rushes on, Il.15.622.220.
Had sav'd the Father, and now saves the Son. Il.15.631.220.
Warms the bold Son of *Nestor* in his Cause. Il.15.681.222.
The Son redeem'd the Honours of the Race, Il.15.774.226.
A Son as gen'rous as the Sire was base; Il.15.775.226.
A Son as gen'rous as his Sire was base; Il.15.775A.226.
Eurypylus, Tydides, Artreus' Son, Il.16.35.236.
No longer flames the Lance of *Tydeus'* Son; Il.16.101.239.
The Son of *Borus,* that espous'd the Dame. Il.16.215.247.
The Son confess'd his Father's heav'nly Race, Il.16.222.248.
"Stern Son of *Peleus* (thus ye us'd to say, Il.16.242.248.
But *Peleus'* Son; and *Peleus'* Son to none Il.16.276.249.
But *Peleus'* Son; and *Peleus'* Son to none Il.16.276.249.
My godlike Son shall press the *Phrygian* Plain: Il.16.531.264.
Laments his Son, predestin'd to be slain, Il.16.564.266.
And round his Son confounds the warring Hosts, Il.16.697.271.
Agacleus' Son, from *Budium's* lofty Walls: Il.16.700.271.
O Friend (*Menœtius'* Son this Answer gave) Il.16.757.273.
And stretch him breathless on his slaughter'd Son; Il.16.790.274.
The Son of *Panthus,* skill'd the Dart to send, Il.17.11.288.
(*Ajax,* to *Peleus'* Son the second Name, Il.17.328.300.
The Son of *Lethus,* brave *Pelasgus'* Heir, Il.17.334.300.
Stretch'd in the Dust the great *Iphytus'* Son, Il.17.353.301.
The rest, in pity to her Son, conceal'd. Il.17.471.305.
For not by you shall *Priam's* Son be born Il.17.513.308.
The Son of *Venus* to the Counsel yields; Il.17.558.310.
O Chief, Oh Father! (*Atreus'* Son replies) Il.17.630.312.
(Bold Son of Air and Heat) on angry Wings Il.17.644.313.
Eëtion's Son, and *Podes* was his Name; Il.17.649.313.
Like *Phœnops, Asius'* Son, appear'd the God; Il.17.655.313.
The Son of *Priam* whirl'd the missive Wood; Il.17.688.314.
Stood *Nestor's* Son, the Messenger of Woe: Il.18.4.322.
Sad Tydings, Son of *Peleus!* thou must hear; Il.18.21.324.
While *Nestor's* Son sustains a manlier Part, Il.18.37.325.
Why mourns my Son? thy late-preferr'd Request Il.18.95.327.
Why mourns my Son? thy Anguish let me share, Il.18.97.327.
The great *Alcides, Jove's* unequal'd Son, Il.18.148.329.
My Son (Cœrulean *Thetis* made reply, Il.18.163.330.
Rise, Son of *Peleus!* rise divinely brave! Il.18.209.332.
The gallant Chief defends *Menœtius'* Son, Il.18.233.333.
The Son of *Panthus,* thus exprest his Fears; Il.18.295.336.
At last thy Will prevails: Great *Peleus'* Son Il.18.419.341.
Grace with immortal Arms this short-liv'd Son, Il.18.528.347.
Swift to her Son: Her Son she finds in Tears, Il.19.6.371.
Swift to her Son: Her Son she finds in Tears, Il.19.6.371.
Suppress (my Son) this Rage of Grief, and know Il.19.11.371.
(The Azure Goddess to her Son reply'd) Il.19.32.373.
He too sore wounded by *Agenor's* Son. Il.19.55.374.
And *Jove* expected his immortal Son; Il.19.104.376.
The Son of *Peleus* thus: And thus replies Il.19.153.378.
What boastful Son of War, without that Stay, Il.19.161.378.
Against *Latona* march'd the Son of *May;* Il.20.95.398.
To whom the Son of *Jove,* That God implore, Il.20.134.399.
The Seed of *Thetis* thus to *Venus'* Son. Il.20.213.402.
To this *Anchises'* Son. Such Words employ Il.20.240.404.
Nor dread the Vaunts of *Peleus'* haughty Son; Il.20.418.412.
The single Fight with *Thetis'* god-like Son; Il.20.432.412.
The Son of *Peleus* sees, with Joy possest, Il.20.491.415.
(The Son of *Pireus,* an illustrious Name,) Il.20.562.417.
The Son of *Priam,* whom the Hero's Hand Il.21.42.423.
Where *Jason's* Son the Price demanded gave; Il.21.47.424.
The Son of *Pelagon,* whose lofty Line Il.21.157.428.
Whose Son encounters our resistless Ire. Il.21.168.428.
O Son of *Peleus!* what avails to trace Il.21.169.428.
Now lift thy Arm, and try that Hero's Son! Il.21.178.429.
But *Jove* he dreads, nor wars against his Son. Il.21.210.430.
The yellow Flood began: O Son of *Jove!* Il.21.249.431.
But most of *Thetis,* must her Son complain; Il.21.318.434.
O Son of *Peleus!* Lo thy Gods appear! Il.21.333.435.
Ah why, *Saturnia!* must thy Son engage Il.21.432.438.
And what (he cries) has *Peleus'* Son in view, Il.22.15.453.
He calls his much lov'd Son with feeble Cries; Il.22.46.454.
The Son, resolv'd *Achilles'* Force to dare, Il.22.47.454.
Hector! my lov'd, my dearest, bravest Son! Il.22.52.454.
Have mercy on me, O my Son! Revere Il.22.114.457.
Enough, O Son of *Peleus! Troy* has view'd Il.22.317.469.
Great *Jove* deserts me, and the Son of *Jove,* Il.22.384.471.
And bow before the Murd'rer of my Son. Il.22.533.478.

SON (CONTINUED)

The Son expiring in the Sire's Embrace; Il.22.545.479.
But *Peleus'* Son intreats, with Sacrifice, Il.23.258.499.
Mourns o'er the Ashes of an only Son, Il.23.275.501.
Peleus receiv'd, and on his Son bestow'd.) Il.23.346.503.
Experienc'd *Nestor* gives his Son the Reins, Il.23.371.505.
The prudent Son with unattending Ears. Il.23.374.505.
My Son! tho' youthful Ardor fire thy Breast, Il.23.375.505.
Experienc'd *Nestor* gives the Son the Reins, Il.23.371A.505.
To fell extreams. But *Thetis'* god-like Son, Il.23.574.512.
Last came, *Admetus!* thy unhappy Son; Il.23.609.514.
O *Peleus* Son! the Mare so justly mine. Il.23.622.514.
Not without Cause incens'd at *Nestor's* Son, Il.23.649.515.
Gen'rous alike, for me, the Sire and Son Il.23.695.517.
Wisely and well, my Son, thy Words have prov'd Il.23.719.518.
Go thou, my Son! by gen'rous Friendship led, Il.23.743.519.
His youthful Equals, *Nestor's* Son the last. Il.23.884.524.
The Son of *Nestor,* worthy of his Sire. Il.23.940.526.
Fierce, at the Word, uprose great *Tydeus'* Son, Il.23.957.527.
Deny to Consort, Mother, Son, and Sire, Il.24.48.537.
To lose a Friend, a Brother, or a Son, Il.24.60.538.
If *Thetis'* Son must no Distinction know, Il.24.72.538.
Her furious Son from *Priam* to receive Il.24.97.539.
We will, thy Son himself the Corse restore, Il.24.145.541.
The Goddess seats her by her pensive Son, Il.24.161.542.
And urge her Monarch to redeem his Son; Il.24.180.543.
To Dogs, to Vultures, and to *Peleus'* Son! Il.24.260.547.
Add to the slaughter'd Son the wretched Sire! Il.24.278.548.
And speed my Journey to redeem my Son? Il.24.330.550.
Are true, my Son! (the godlike Sire rejoin'd) Il.24.460.555.
Thy matchless Son, her Guard and Glory, slain! Il.24.472.556.
My Son forgot not, in exalted Pow'r; Il.24.522.558.
His Son, his Mother! urge him to bestow Il.24.572.560.
He hears his Son still lives to glad his Eyes; Il.24.609.562.
A Father one, and one a Son, deplore: Il.24.641.563.
An only Son! and he (alas!) ordain'd Il.24.679.565.
One only Son! and he (alas!) ordain'd Il.24.679A.565.
Lo! to thy Pray'r restor'd, thy breathless Son: Il.24.749.568.
My hapless Son, the Dust has been my Bed, Il.24.807.570.
An only Son, once Comfort of our Pains, Il.24.912.574.
Never to manly Age that Son shall rise, Il.24.914.574.
Thou too my Son! to barb'rous Climes shalt goe, Il.24.922.574.
Or Son, or Brother, by great *Hector* slain; Il.24.927.575.
Afflicts the chief, t'avenge his Giant son Od.1.89.35.
Ulysses' Son: but happier he, whom fate Od.1.279.46.
Happier the son, whose hoary sire is blest Od.1.281.46.
Had with transmissive honour grac'd his Son. Od.1.308.47.
Oh son of *Polybus!* the Prince replies, Od.1.521.57.
(Daughter of Ops, the just *Pisenor's* son, Od.1.541.57.
Ye lov'd the father; go, the son attend. Od.2.288.75.
If to the son the father's worth descends, Od.2.309.76.
Oh whither, whither flies my son? she cry'd, Od.2.408.80.
Proceed my son! this youthful shame expel; Od.3.19.87.
Gave to *Ulysses'* son the rosie wine. Od.3.77.90.
Lo at thy knee his suppliant son appears. Od.3.111.91.
There too my son—ah once my best delight, Od.3.135.92.
Art thou the son of that illustrious sire? Od.3.151.93.
How well the son appeas'd his slaughter'd sire! Od.3.239.97.
Thus he, and *Nestor* took the word: My son, Od.3.258.98.
The happy son, will, as the father, aid, Od.3.270.99.
O son of *Neleus!* awful *Nestor,* tell Od.3.308.101.
Hence warn'd, my son beware! nor idly stand Od.3.398.106.
Thus from my walls the much-lov'd son to send Od.3.445.108.
And be thy son companion of his way. Od.3.473.110.
That day, to great *Achilles'* son resign'd Od.4.7.120.
And fast beside him great *Ulysses'* son: Od.4.30.121.
Suffic'd, soft-whispering thus to *Nestor's* son, Od.4.81.123.
View my friend's son? (the King exulting cries) Od.4.226.130.
Son of my friend, by glorious toils approv'd, Od.4.227.130.
But silence soon the son of *Nestor* broke, Od.4.257.131.
Or darling son oppress'd by ruffian-force Od.4.311.134.
Say, son of *Atreus,* say what God inspir'd Od.4.625.149.
What third brave son of *Mars* the fates constrain Od.4.747.153.
Laertes' son: girt with circumfluous tides, Od.4.753.154.
To thee the Son of *Jove,* and beauteous *Helen's* Lord. Od.4.776.155.
Why rashly wou'd my son his fate explore, Od.4.940.162.
And for the pious sire preserve the son: Od.4.1010.164.
"When o'er her son disastrous death impends." Od.4.1020.165.
Thy son, the Gods propitious will restore, Od.4.1063.167.
My darling son is fled! an easy prey Od.4.1075.168.
His only son, their ambush'd fraud employ, Od.5.27.172.
The son in safety to his native shore; Od.5.35.172.
'Tis ours this son of sorrow to relieve, Od.6.245.222.
No son surviv'd; *Arete* heir'd his state, Od.7.84.237.
To see my soil, my son, my friends, again. Od.7.304.250.
Nor thou unwilling to be call'd my son. Od.7.400.256.
Thither of old, Earth's * Giant-son to view, Od.7.413.257.
Laertes' son, of *Ithaca* the fair; Od.9.590.330.
Th' immortal father no less boasts the son. Od.9.608.331.
And if th' unhappy *Cyclop* be thy Son; Od.9.620.332.
Laertes' son, of Ithaca the fair. Od.9.622.332.
Son of *Laertes!* (then the Queen began) Od.10.475.366.
Regardless of her son the Parent stood. Od.11.111.386.
Unmindful of her son, *Anticlea* stands? Od.11.175.390.
Why is she silent, while her Son is nigh? Od.11.177.390.
Com'st thou, my son, alive, to realms beneath, Od.11.190.391.
If yet *Telemachus,* my son, survives? Od.11.211.392.
For thee, my son, I wept my life away; Od.11.240.393.
Thou, thou my son wert my disease and death; Od.11.245.393.
Unkindly with my love my son conspir'd, Od.11.246.393.
O son of woe, the pensive shade rejoyn'd, Od.11.259.394.
And *Megara,* who charm'd the son of *Jove,* Od.11.327.398.
With her own son she joyn'd in nuptial bands, Od.11.331.398.
Thence to her son the choicest plagues she brings, Od.11.339.398.
Thy infant son her fragrant bosom prest, Od.11.553.411.
The sire shall bless his son, the son his sire: Od.11.558.411.

SON (CONTINUED)

The sire shall bless his son, the son his sire: .... Od.11.558.411.
But say, resides my son in royal port, ... Od.11.565.411.
But say, if in my steps my son proceeds, ... Od.11.601.413.
The wars and wisdom of thy gallant son: .... Od.11.618.414.
Whose son, the swift *Orsilochus,* I slew: .... Od.13.312.21.
The growing virtues of my youthful son, ... Od.13.412.26.
Son of *Laertes!* much-experienc'd man! .... Od.13.428.27.
Estrange thee from thy own, thy son, thy wife; .... Od.13.462.28.
The Monarch's son a shipwrackt wretch reliev'd, ... Od.14.351.51.
Had with transmissive honours grac'd his son. .... Od.14.406.55.
Another to the winged son of *May:* .... Od.14.485.59.
Upstarted *Thoas* strait, *Andræmon's* son, ... Od.14.564.64.
But when return'd, the good *Ulysses'* son .... Od.14.583.65.
With *Nestor's* Son, *Telemachus* was lay'd; .... Od.15.6.70.
In sleep profound the Son of *Nestor* lies; .... Od.15.7.70.
Rise, son of *Nestor!* for the road prepare, ... Od.15.55.72.
Mean-time the King, his Son, and *Helen,* went .... Od.15.114.74.
Atrides' son the purple draught prepares. .... Od.15.157.76.
Ulysses' son, with his illustrious friend, ... Od.15.160.76.
But *Nestor's* son the chearful silence broke, ... Od.15.186.77.
To *Nestor's* heir *Ulysses'* god-like son: .... Od.15.219.78.
Who knows the son of sorrow to relieve, ... Od.15.362.86.
From foreign climes an only son receives, ... Od.16.18.102.
To thee my son the suppliant I resign, ... Od.16.67.105.
The mournful hour that tore his son away .... Od.16.148.109.
Why to thy god-like son this long disguise? .... Od.16.181.112.
I am thy father. O my son! my son! .... Od.16.206.114.
I am thy father. O my son! my son! .... Od.16.206.114.
I am *Ulysses,* I (my son) am He. .... Od.16.225.114.
So *Pallas* wills—but thou my son, explain .... Od.16.258.117.
Bear it my son! repress thy rising rage: .... Od.16.295.119.
Bear it my son! howe'er thy heart rebel. .... Od.16.297.120.
By that regard a son his father owes; .... Od.16.323.121.
And cries aloud, Thy son, oh Queen returns: .... Od.16.355.123.
And my friend's son lives dearest to my heart. .... Od.16.461.129.
Ulysses and his son had drest with art .... Od.16.472.130.
Hangs o'er her son; in his embraces dies; .... Od.17.48.135.
When thus the Queen. My son! my only friend! .... Od.17.116.137.
Of the proud son; as that we stand this hour .... Od.17.302.146.
The thoughtful Son beheld, and call'd his swain: .... Od.17.417.152.
This said, the portion from his son convey'd .... Od.17.428.153.
Of my great mistress, and her god-like son. .... Od.17.475.156.
Nor from the sire art thou the son declin'd; .... Od.18.155.173.
To my lov'd son the snares of death to show, ... Od.18.197.176.
Go warn thy son, nor be the warning vain, ... Od.18.201.176.
Some joy remains: To thee a son is giv'n, ... Od.18.207.177.
O why, my son, why now no more appears .... Od.18.255.179.
But when my son grows man, the royal sway .... Od.18.313.181.
And thus the Son the fervent Sire addrest. .... Od.19.4.193.
Auxiliar to his son, *Ulysses* bears .... Od.19.35.194.
His son *Deucalion* bore successive sway; .... Od.19.208.203.
His son, who gave me first to view the day! .... Od.19.209.203.
Son of my love, and Monarch of my cares! .... Od.19.424.215.
"Receive, she cries, your royal daughter's son; .... Od.19.475.219.
At length abrupt—my son!—my King!—she cry'd. .... Od.19.553.223.
What words, my son, have pass'd thy lips severe? .... Od.19.576.224.
Resuming then his seat, *Eupitheus'* son .... Od.21.147.265.
To slay thy son, thy kingdoms to divide, ... Od.22.64.289.
Oh my dear son!—The father with a sigh: .... Od.22.166.295.
Or (as my thought misgives) by *Dolius'* son. .... Od.22.175.295.
What for thy country now, thy Queen, thy son? .... Od.22.253.299.
Damastor's son, bold *Agelaus,* leads .... Od.22.264.299.
With these, *Pisander* great *Polyctor's* son, ... Od.22.266.299.
By the bold son *Amphimedon* was slain: .... Od.22.314.301.
And let thy son attest, nor sordid pay .... Od.22.391.307.
If yet he breathes, permit thy son to give .... Od.22.399.307.
Be bold, on friendship and my son rely; .... Od.22.412.307.
And now the King commands his son to call .... Od.22.432.309.
The son observant not a moment stays: .... Od.22.434.309.
(My son) full fifty of the handmaid train, ... Od.22.459.310.
To you my son, and you, my faithful swains; .... Od.22.473.312.
He, he is thine! thy son, his latent guest .... Od.23.31.320.
When Death had seiz'd her prey, thy son attends, ... Od.23.45.321.
Indulge, my son, the cautions of the wise; .... Od.23.114.325.
Thy coward son degen'rate lag behind. .... Od.23.128.326.
To wake his son; and bid his friends arise. .... Od.23.394.343.
Still at his side is *Nestor's* son survey'd, ... Od.24.27.348.
Had with transmissive glories grac'd thy son. .... Od.24.48.350.
O son of *Peleus!* greater than mankind! .... Od.24.51.350.
Son of *Melanthus!* (he began) Oh say! .... Od.24.129.354.
Thither his son from sandy *Pyle* repairs, ... Od.24.179.356.
First came the son; the father next succeeds, ... Od.24.183.356.
And martial son, *Ulysses* gave command. .... Od.24.245.360.
Wretch that he was! and that I am! my son! .... Od.24.337.365.
Then thus the Son. From *Alybas* I came, ... Od.24.353.366.
Stood the great son, heart-wounded with the sight: .... Od.24.372.367.
Thy son, with twenty winters now grown old; .... Od.24.376.367.
Thy son, so long desir'd, so long detain'd, ... Od.24.377.367.
His gazing son admires the god-like grace, ... Od.24.429.369.
Nor had the Sire been sep'rate from the Son. .... Od.24.443.370.
Fierce for his son, he breathes his threats in air; .... Od.24.538.373.
Forgot the slaughter'd brother, and the son: .... Od.24.555.374.
A son of *Dolius* on the message went, ... Od.24.567.375.
Swell with new joy, and thus his son addrest. .... Od.24.583.376.
A son and grandson of th' *Arcesian* name .... Od.24.596.376.
Son of *Arcesius,* rev'rend warrior, hear! .... Od.24.599.376.
Before the father and the conqu'ring son .... Od.24.608.376.

SON'S

His Son's fine Taste an op'ner Vista loves, ... 3.Ep4.93.146.
'Twas in the Son's Defence the Mother bled. .... Il.5.468.290.
Before their Ships, proclaim my Son's Intent: .... Il.7.449.386.
Whose Son's great Arm alone the Weapon wields, ... Il.16.176.245.
Full oft' the God his Son's hard Toils bemoan'd, ... Il.19.133.377.
His Son's sad Fate, and drops a tender Tear.) .... Il.19.344.386.

SON'S (CONTINUED)

And wept her god-like Son's approaching Doom: .... Il.24.114.539.
My Son's dear Relicks? what befalls him dead? .... Il.24.498.557.
The son's destruction waits the mother's fame: .... Od.2.144.68.
Beneath *Achilles'* warlike son's command. .... Od.3.229.96.
And the sad son's, to suffer and to mourn! .... Od.3.257.98.
To the sire's merit give the son's request. .... Od.4.444.141.
Makes her with hope her son's arrival wait. .... Od.4.1098.169.
Her son's return, and ease a parent's heart; .... Od.16.351.123.
Thy husband's wonder, and thy son's to raise, ... Od.18.191.175.
And joining to my son's my menial train, ... Od.19.617.226.
A son's just right. No *Grecian* Prince but I .... Od.21.371.277.
And with the sire's and son's commix thy blood. .... Od.22.238.298.
The sire and son's great acts, with-held the day; .... Od.22.258.299.

SONG

Rough *Satyrs* dance, and *Pan* applauds the Song: .... 1.PSu.50.75.
For her, the feather'd Quires neglect their Song; .... 1.PAu.24.82.
For him, the feather'd Quires neglect their Song; .... 1.PAu.24A.82.
The Birds shall cease to tune their Ev'ning Song, ... 1.PAu.40.83.
And bade his Willows learn the moving Song. .... 1.PWi.14.89.
Eccho no more the rural Song rebounds, ... 1.PWi.41A.92.
Ye Nymphs of *Solyma!* begin the Song: .... 1.Mes.1.112.
Live in Description, and look green in Song: .... 1.W-F.8.149.
Still in thy Song shou'd vanquish'd *France* appear, ... 1.W-F.309.178.
But most by *Numbers* judge a Poet's Song, ... 1.EOC.337.276.
A *needless Alexandrine* ends the Song, ... 1.EOC.356.280.
And found my Kisses sweeter than my Song. .... 1.TrSP.56.396.
Joy to my Soul, and Vigour to my Song: .... 1.TrSP.239.404.
Demand our Song; a sacred Fury fires .... 1.TrSt.3.409.
And fix, O Muse! the Barrier of thy Song, ... 1.TrSt.20.410.
For gentle Lays, and joyous Nuptial Song; .... 2.ChJM.336.30.
This was his Song; Oh kind and constant be, ... 2.ChJM.714.49.
With Dance and Song we kept the Nuptial Day. .... 2.ChWB.330.73.
One dy'd in *Metaphor,* and one in *Song.* .... 2.RL5.60.204.
Oh master of the poet, and the song! .... 3.EOM4.374.164.
And the sad Burthen of some merry Song. .... 4.HS1.80.13.
In Flow'r of Age you perish for a Song! .... 4.HS1.102.15.
The World's good word is better than a Song) .... 4.HS2.102.61.
Think ye to cure the Mischief with a Song? .... 4.HAdv.142.87.
Think you to cure the Mischief with a Song? .... 4.HAdv.142A.87.
The World had wanted many an idle Song) .... 4.Arbu.28.98.
For song, for silence, some expect a bribe .... 4.Arbu.113A.103.
No more than Thou, great GEORGE! a Birth-day Song. .... 4.Arbu.222.112.
To fetch and carry Sing-song up and down; .... 4.Arbu.226.112.
Horace and he went hand in hand in song. .... 4.Arbu.234.112.
But stoop'd to Truth, and moraliz'd his song: .... 4.Arbu.341.120.
He stoop'd to Truth, and moraliz'd his song: .... 4.Arbu.341A.120.
If there be Force in Virtue, or in Song. .... 4.Arbu.387.126.
When doom'd to say his Beads and Ev'ning Song: .... 4.JD2A.112.142.
Exalt the Dance, or animate the Song; .... 4.HOde1.28.153.
Exalt the Dance, and animate the Song; .... 4.HOde1.28A.153.
Above the reach of vulgar Song; .... 4.HOde9.4.159.
"A perfect Genius at an Opera-Song— .... 4.2HE2.11.165.
And all our Grace at Table is a Song. .... 4.2HE1.174.209.
What will a Child learn sooner than a song? .... 4.2HE1.205.213.
And Heav'n is won by violence of Song. .... 4.2HE1.240.215.
Yet every child another song will sing, ... 4.1HE1.91.285.
This new Court jargon, or the good old song? .... 4.1HE1.98.287.
Some rising Genius sins up to my Song. .... 4.EpS2.9.313.
Hence the soft sing-song on Cecilia's day, ... 5.DunA1.40.65.
And hail him victor in both gifts of Song, ... 5.DunA2.255.131.
In lofty madness, meditating song, ... 5.DunA3.142.162.
All hail him victor in both gifts of song, ... 5.DunB2.267.308.
In lofty madness meditating song; .... 5.DunB3.16.321.
Then take at once the Poet and the Song. .... 5.DunB4.8.340.
O sing, and hush the Nations with thy Song! .... 5.DunB4.626.406.
Thus Song could prevail .... 6.11.87.33.
On *French* translation, and *Italian* song. .... 6.32.42.97.
And seen the Death of much Immortal Song. .... 6.34.20.101.
Became the Subject of great *Homer's* song; .... 6.38.8.107.
Too bright your Form, and too renown'd his Song, ... 6.38.11Z5.108.
Look sow'r, and hum a song—as you may now. .... 6.45.50A.126.
Moral *Truth,* and mystic *Song!* .... 6.51i.12.151.
In the Song that you sent, are the *Muses* and *Graces;* .... 6.62i.1A.185.
To Lordings proud I tune my Song, ... 6.79.1A.217.
In vain his consort bribes for venal song .... 6.130.28.358.
Me, far from meaner Care or meaner Song, ... 6.155.6.404.
Apollo listens, and approves the Song. .... Il.1.621.117.
In Feasts Ambrosial, and Celestial Song. .... Il.1.773.124.
Example sad! and Theme of future Song. .... Il.6.449.348.
In Silence waiting till he ceas'd the Song. .... Il.9.254.445.
With Horror sounds the loud *Orthian* Song: .... Il.11.14.35.
To some, sweet Music, and the Charm of Song; .... Il.13.916.148.
Be this the Song, slow-moving tow'rd the Shore, ... Il.22.493.476.
With song and dance the pompous revel end. .... Od.1.204.42.
Hush'd in attention to the warbled song. .... Od.1.420.52.
The chanter's soul and raptur'd song inspire; .... Od.1.444.54.
Ye deedless boasters! and the song attend: .... Od.1.470.55.
The song is noise, and impious is the feast. .... Od.2.350.78.
In honour's limits (such the pow'r of Song) .... Od.3.337.103.
While she with work and song the time divides, ... Od.5.78.176.
The sacred master of celestial song: .... Od.8.56.264.
From that fierce wrath the noble song arose, ... Od.8.71.266.
Touch'd at the song, *Ulysses* strait resign'd .... Od.8.79.266.
Transported with the song, the list'ning train .... Od.8.87.267.
Of heav'nly song has crown'd the genial hour! .... Od.8.96.267.
To race, to sail, to dance, to chaunt the song. .... Od.8.290.278.
Hear the sweet song, and taste the feast in peace. .... Od.8.464.288.
The song recals past horrours to my eyes, ... Od.8.537.291.
A theme of future song! Say then if slain .... Od.8.633.297.
Of dreadful Magic, and commanding Song. .... Od.10.164.348.
And sacred vows, and mystic song, apply'd .... Od.10.636.374.
And mutter'd vows, and mystic song apply'd .... Od.11.59.383.
Soft, as some song divine, thy story flows, ... Od.11.458.407.
Their song is death, and makes destruction please. .... Od.12.52.432.

SONG (CONTINUED)
Be stop'd against the song! 'tis death to hear! .... Od.12.62.433.
And thus the sweet deluders tune the song. .... Od.12.221.442.
The song instructs the soul, and charms the ear. .... Od.12.225.443.
The rites, more sacred made by heav'nly song: .... Od.13.32.2.
Medon, and *Phemius* skill'd in heav'nly song. .... Od.16.273.118.
They feast, they dance, and raise the mirthful song. .... Od.17.686.165.
For dear to Gods and Men is sacred song. .... Od.22.382.307.
Example dread! and theme of tragic song! .... Od.24.229.358.

SONGS
And Birds defer their Songs till thy Return: .... 1.TrSP.174.401.
No more your Groves with my glad Songs shall ring, ... 1.TrSP.234.404.
And Songs were sung, and flowing Bowls went round; .... 2.ChJM.354.31.
And Songs were sung, and Healths went nimbly round; .... 2.ChJM.354A.31.
One sings the Fair; but Songs no longer move, ... 4.JD2.21.133.
Composing Songs, for Fools to get by heart? .... 4.2HE2.126.173.
Songs, sonnets, epigrams the winds uplift, ... 5.DunA2.107.109.
Songs, sonnets, epigrams the winds uplift, ... 5.DunB2.115.301.
Our songs by our captivity; .... 6.6i.14.14.
Still warm our hearts, and still inspire our songs. .... 6.38.26.108.
Nor lends to Wanton Songs an Ear, ... 6.54.3.164.
And gen'ral Songs the sprightly Revel end. .... Il.18.700.357.
By rival nations courted for their songs; .... Od.17.467.156.

SONGSTER
Each Songster, Riddler, ev'ry nameless name, ... 5.DunB3.157.328.

SONNET
Compos'd a Sonnet to the lovely *May;* .... 2.ChJM.397.34.
Writing a Sonnet, cou'd not rhime; .... 6.44.2.123.

SONNETEER
In some starv'd Hackny Sonneteer, or me? .... 1.EOC.419.287.

SONNETS
Songs, sonnets, epigrams the winds uplift, ... 5.DunA2.107.109.
Songs, sonnets, epigrams the winds uplift, ... 5.DunB2.115.301.

SONOROUS
Sing thy sonorous Verse—but not aloud. .... 4.2HE2.109.173.
But far o'er all, sonorous Blackmore's strain, ... 5.DunA2.247.129.
But far o'er all, sonorous Blackmore's strain; .... 5.DunB2.259.308.
Sonorous thro' the shaded air it sings; .... Od.8.214.274.

SONS
See future Sons, and Daughters yet unborn .... 1.Mes.88.121.
When *Albion* sends her eager Sons to War, ... 1.W-F.106.161.
She saw her Sons with purple Deaths expire, ... 1.W-F.323.180.
No more my Sons shall dye with *British* Blood .... 1.W-F.367.186.
High on *Parnassus'* Top her Sons she show'd, ... 1.EOC.94.250.
The last, the meanest of your Sons inspire, ... 1.EOC.196.263.
Our *wiser Sons,* no doubt, will think *us* so. .... 1.EOC.439.288.
Our Sons their Fathers' *failing Language* see, ... 1.EOC.482.293.
In Heaps his slaughter'd Sons into the Deep. .... 1.TrSt.60.412.
My Sons their old, unhappy Sire despise, ... 1.TrSt.103.414.
These Sons, ye Gods! who with flagitious Pride .... 1.TrSt.107.414.
His Sons with Scorn their Eyeless Father view, ... 1.TrSt.336.424.
Avenging on the Sons the Father's Crimes, ... 1.TrSt.378.425.
Thy Plagues, and curse 'em with such Sons as those. .... 1.TrSt.399.426.
Had sung—"Expect thy Sons on *Argos'* Shore, ... 1.TrSt.547.433.
The guiding Godhead, and his future Sons. .... 1.TrSt.578.434.
If on the Sons the Parents' Crimes descend, ... 1.TrSt.820.444.
How many Sons of Gods, foredoom'd to Death, ... 1.TrES.242.458.
Than all the Sons of *Adam* cou'd redress. .... 2.ChWB.368.75.
Then all the Sons of *Adam* can redress. .... 2.ChWB.368A.75.
Of *Asia's* Troops, and *Africk's* Sable Sons, ... 2.RL3.82.174.
The same which in a Sire the Sons obey'd, ... 3.EOM3.213.114.
Oh sons of earth! attempt ye still to rise, ... 3.EOM4.73.135.
Whose sons shall blush their fathers were thy foes, ... 3.EOM4.388.165.
By his own Sons that pass him by unbless'd: .... 3.Ep1.231A.35.
Our sons shall see it leisurely decay, ... 4.JD4.44.29.
Tho' justly Greece her eldest sons admires, ... 4.2HE1.43.197.
And to debase the Sons, exalts the Sires. .... 4.2HE1.134.207.
Sons, Sires, and Grandsires, all will wear the Bays, ... 4.2HE1.171.209.
The joy their wives, their sons, and servants share, ... 4.2HE1.245.215.
I see a King! who leads my chosen sons .... 5.DunA1.251.93.
I see a chief, who leads my chosen sons, ... 5.DunA1.251Z1.93.
She summons all her sons: an endless band .... 5.DunA2.15.98.
The sons of *Dulness* meet: An endless band .... 5.DunA2.15A.98.
And learn, my sons, the wond'rous pow'r of Noise. .... 5.DunA2.214.127.
What Dulness dropt among her sons impress .... 5.DunA2.375.146.
The North by myriads pours her mighty sons, ... 5.DunA3.81.157.
No fiercer sons, had Easter never been. .... 5.DunA3.110.159.
A hundred sons, and ev'ry son a God: .... 5.DunA3.126.160.
Behold a hundred sons, and each a dunce. .... 5.DunA3.130.161.
Embrace, embrace my Sons! be foes no more! .... 5.DunA3.171.167.
"Yet oh my sons! a father's words attend: .... 5.DunA3.211.175.
"See now, what Dulness and her sons admire; .... 5.DunA3.226.176.
Till Thames see Eton's sons for ever play, ... 5.DunA3.331.191.
The sons of *Isis* reel! the towns-mens sport; .... 5.DunA3.333A.191.
And thou! his Aid de camp, lead on my sons, ... 5.DunB1.305.291.
And now the Queen, to glad her sons, proclaims .... 5.DunB2.17.297.
And learn, my sons, the wond'rous pow'r of Noise. .... 5.DunB2.222.306.
Sons of a Day! just buoyant on the flood, ... 5.DunB2.307.310.
What Dulness dropt among her sons impress .... 5.DunB2.407.317.
The North by myriads pours her mighty sons, ... 5.DunB3.89.324.
No fiercer sons, had Easter never been. .... 5.DunB3.118.325.
An hundred sons, and ev'ry son a God: .... 5.DunB3.134.326.
Behold an hundred sons, and each a Dunce. .... 5.DunB3.138.326.
Embrace, embrace my sons! be foes no more! .... 5.DunB3.177.329.
"Yet oh, my sons! a father's words attend: .... 5.DunB3.213.330.
"See now, what Dulness and her sons admire! .... 5.DunB3.228.331.
'Till Thames see Eaton's sons for ever play, ... 5.DunB3.335.336.
To the same notes thy sons shall hum, or snore, ... 5.DunB4.59.347.
Who pay her homage in her sons, the Great; .... 5.DunB4.92.349.

SONS (CONTINUED)
But spread, my sons, your glory thin or thick, ... 5.DunB4.129.354.
Eton and Winton shake thro' all their Sons. .... 5.DunB4.144.355.
O! if my sons may learn one earthly thing, ... 5.DunB4.183.360.
To lull the sons of Marg'ret and Clare-hall, ... 5.DunB4.200.362.
Pours at great Bourbon's feet her silken sons; .... 5.DunB4.298.373.
So may the sons of sons of sons of whores, ... 5.DunB4.332.376.
So may the sons of sons of sons of whores, ... 5.DunB4.332.376.
So may the sons of sons of sons of whores, ... 5.DunB4.332.376.
"My sons! (she answer'd) both have done your parts: .... 5.DunB4.437.383.
"O! would the Sons of Men once think their Eyes .... 5.DunB4.453.385.
Why all your Toils? your Sons have learn'd to sing. .... 5.DunB4.546.396.
My Sons! be proud, be selfish, and be dull. .... 5.DunB4.582.400.
Thy Pestle braining all the Sons of *Rome.* .... 6.48ii.8.134.
O *Button!* summon all thy Sons of Wit! .... 6.48iii.12.135.
See arts her savage sons controul, ... 6.51i.21.152.
Which own'd, would all their Sires and Sons disgrace. .... 6.96iii.16.275.
Against the *Gothick* Sons of frozen Verse; .... 6.128.14.356.
Apollo's genuine Sons thy fame shall raise .... 6.131i.7.360.
A hundred Sons! and not one *Fop.* .... 6.135.48.368.
That two, my tallest Sons, might grace .... 6.135.71.369.
Arts Arms and Honour to her Ancient Sons: .... 6.155.3.404.
The Pow'rs of Earth, and sceptred Sons of *Jove.* .... Il.1.369.105.
Unite, and rouze the Sons of *Greece* to Arms. .... Il.2.94.131.
And join to rouze the Sons of *Greece* to Arms. .... Il.2.106.132.
Ye Sons of *Mars,* partake your Leader's Care, ... Il.2.139.135.
Sons of *Astyochè* the Heav'nly Fair, ... Il.2.614.157.
Eubœa next her martial Sons prepares, ... Il.2.641.157.
For now the Sons of *Oeneus* were no more! .... Il.2.780.162.
Crete's hundred Cities pour forth all her Sons. .... Il.2.790.162.
And the bold Sons of great *Evenus* slew. .... Il.2.844.164.
Old *Merops* Sons; whom skill'd in Fates to come .... Il.2.1008.170.
When, to the Van, before the Sons of Fame .... Il.3.25.189.
His Sons are faithless, headlong in Debate, ... Il.3.147.198.
Bleed all his Sons, and *Ilion* float with Gore, ... Il.4.56.223.
Her Sons and Matrons *Greece* shall lead in Chains, ... Il.4.272.234.
The Sons subdu'd, for Heav'n was on their side. .... Il.4.463.242.
The Sons of *Dares* first the Combate sought, ... Il.5.15.266.
The Sons to Toils of glorious Battel bred; .... Il.5.18.266.
Or slain, or fled, the Sons of *Dares* view: .... Il.5.36.267.
Sons of *Eurydamas,* who wise and old, ... Il.5.190.275.
Two Sons of *Priam* in one Chariot ride, ... Il.5.204.276.
Tydeus' and *Atreus'* Sons their Points have found, ... Il.5.260.279.
How long, ye Sons of *Priam!* will ye fly, ... Il.5.565.295.
Sons, Sires, and Wives, an undistinguish'd Prey. .... Il.5.596.297.
Who o'er the Sons of Men in Beauty shin'd, ... Il.6.195.335.
With two brave Sons and one fair Daughter bless'd; .... Il.6.242.338.
Beheld the Sons of *Greece* untimely fall.) .... Il.6.278.340.
For Husbands, Brothers, Sons, engag'd in War. .... Il.6.301.341.
The rich Pavillions of his fifty Sons, ... Il.6.307.341.
How would the Sons of *Troy,* in Arms renown'd, ... Il.6.562.354.
What Art shall calm the furious Sons of War? .... Il.7.42.364.
Their Sons degen'rate, and their Race a Scorn? .... Il.7.148.371.
Forbear, my Sons! your farther Force to prove, ... Il.7.337.380.
There, to the Sons of *Mars,* in Council found, ... Il.7.458.387.
Ye Sons of *Atreus,* and ye *Greeks,* give ear! .... Il.7.460.387.
Nor *Priam,* nor his Sons obtain'd their Grace; .... Il.8.683.427.
Ye Sons of *Greece!* partake your Leader's Care, ... Il.9.23.432.
These Toils, my Subjects and my Sons might bear, ... Il.10.191.10.
'Tis well, my Sons, your nightly Cares employ, ... Il.10.225.12.
Nor less bold *Hector,* and the Sons of *Troy,* .... Il.10.357.18.
Two Sons of *Priam* next to Battel move, ... Il.11.137.41.
The Sons of false *Antimachus* were slain; .... Il.11.162.42.
The *Grecian* Ships his captive Sons detain, ... Il.11.174.43.
The Sons of *Merops* shone amidst the War; .... Il.11.425.53.
Whose Sons now tremble at his darted Spear, ... Il.11.489.56.
Can then the Sons of *Greece* (the Sage rejoind) .... Il.11.800.71.
For *Neleus'* Sons *Alcides'* Rage had slain; .... Il.11.832.73.
The Sons of *Actor* at their Army's Head .... Il.11.844.74.
Then *Actor's* Sons had dy'd, but *Neptune* shrouds .... Il.11.884.75.
But when her Sons were slain, her City burn'd, ... Il.12.13.81.
The Sons of *Priam* with the third appear, ... Il.12.107.85.
Antenor's Sons the forth Battalion guide, ... Il.12.113.85.
Troy and her Sons may find a gen'ral Grave, ... Il.12.289.92.
E're yet to *Troy* the Sons of *Greece* were led, ... Il.13.229.116.
With *Priam's* Sons, a Guardian of the Throne, ... Il.13.237.116.
Leads forth th' embattel'd Sons of *Crete* to War; .... Il.13.334.121.
Saturn's great Sons in fierce Contention vy'd, ... Il.13.436.126.
O'er spacious *Crete,* and her bold Sons I reign, ... Il.13.568.133.
With three bold Sons was gen'rous *Prothous* blest, ... Il.14.130.164.
And burns the Sons of Heav'n with sacred Fires! .... Il.14.228.172.
Pours new Destruction on her Sons again? .... Il.15.329.210.
Once Sons of *Mars,* and Thunderbolts of War! .... Il.15.891.231.
In equal Arms two Sons of *Nestor* stand, ... Il.16.376.257.
Skill'd in the Dart in vain, his Sons expire, ... Il.16.392.258.
How many Sons of Gods, foredoom'd to Death, ... Il.16.545.265.
Not empty Boasts the Sons of *Troy* repell, ... Il.16.759.273.
These Sons of *Panthus* vent their haughty Mind. .... Il.17.26.288.
Meanwhile the Sons of *Nestor,* in the Rear, ... Il.17.436.304.
Hear me ye Sons of *Greece!* with Silence hear! .... Il.19.81.375.
The Sons of *Nestor, Phyleus'* valiant Heir, ... Il.19.245.383.
But call'd *Scamander* by the Sons of Earth. .... Il.20.102.398.
Sons he has many, those thy Pride may quell; .... Il.20.220.403.
And 'tis his Fault to love those Sons too well. .... Il.20.221.403.
Three Sons renown'd adorn'd his nuptial Bed, ... Il.20.276.406.
The two remaining Sons the Line divide: .... Il.20.282.406.
No two of Earth's degen'rate Sons could raise. .... Il.20.338.407.
And Sons succeeding Sons, the lasting Line sustain. .... Il.20.356.408.
And Sons succeeding Sons, the lasting Line sustain. .... Il.20.356.408.
Of all his Sons, the dearest, and the last. .... Il.20.474.414.
The valiant Sons of an unhappy Sire; .... Il.20.532.416.
Two Sons (alas, unhappy Sons) she bore, ... Il.21.100.426.
Two Sons (alas, unhappy Sons) she bore, ... Il.21.100.426.
But least, the Sons of *Priam's* hateful Race. .... Il.21.114.426.
Who strive presumptuous with the Sons of *Jove.* .... Il.21.202.429.
Till *Troy* receive her flying Sons , till all .... Il.21.340.435.

SONS (CONTINUED)

SOON

SOON (CONTINUED)

SOON (CONTINUED)
Soon as it rose, his furious Steeds he join'd; ... Il.24.23.535.
And soon as Morning paints the Eastern Skies, ... Il.24.751.568.
Soon may the aged Cheeks in Tears be drown'd, ... Il.24.784.569.
Soon as *Aurora,* Daughter of the Dawn, ... Il.24.999.577.
And soon restore him to his regal seat. ... Od.1.266.45.
Soon may kind heav'n a sure relief provide, ... Od.1.328.48.
Soon may your Sire discharge the vengeance due, ... Od.1.329.48.
Soon shou'd yon' boasters cease their haughty strife, ... Od.1.348.49.
Soon as in solemn form th' assembly sate, ... Od.2.11.60.
So soon forgot, was just and mild in vain! ... Od.2.266.74.
Soon shou'd their hopes in humble dust be laid, ... Od.3.277.99.
Soon as *Malæa's* misty tops arise, ... Od.3.366.104.
And soon as morning paints the fields of light, ... Od.3.467.109.
Soon as due vows on ev'ry part were pay'd, ... Od.3.568.115.
But silence soon the son of *Nestor* broke, ... Od.4.257.131.
Soon as the morn, in orient purple drest, ... Od.4.411.140.
Ulysses soon shall re-assert his claim. ... Od.4.456.141.
Such to our wish the warrior soon restore, ... Od.4.461.142.
Then soon th' invaders of his bed and throne, ... Od.4.465.142.
His various arts he soon resumes in aid: ... Od.4.614.148.
Soon as the morn reveals the roseate east, ... Od.4.784.156.
He soon his rashness shall with life atone, ... Od.4.898.160.
Soon as thy arms the happy shore shall gain, ... Od.5.442.194.
Soon as warm life its wonted office found, ... Od.5.588.200.
But would'st thou soon review thy native plain? ... Od.6.347.228.
Soon as their rage subsides, the seas I brave ... Od.7.360.254.
Soon as again the rosy morning shone, ... Od.9.174.312.
Soon might'st thou tell me, where in secret here ... Od.9.537.328.
And soon the known *Æolian* coast regain: ... Od.10.59.342.
But soon his sons their well-known guest descry'd, ... Od.10.69.342.
Soon in the luscious feast themselves they lost, ... Od.10.274.356.
Soon as she strikes her wand, and gives the word, ... Od.10.349.361.
Soon shalt thou reach old Ocean's utmost ends, ... Od.10.602.372.
For well I know that soon the heav'nly pow'rs ... Od.11.85.385.
Soon as the morn restor'd the day, we pay'd ... Od.12.11.430.
All, soon or late, are doom'd that path to tread; ... Od.12.31.431.
Soon as *Ulysses* near th' enclosure drew, ... Od.14.33.36.
That soon *Ulysses* wou'd return, declar'd, ... Od.14.369.53.
Soon as remote from shore they plow the wave, ... Od.14.377.53.
Soon past beyond their sight, I left the flood, ... Od.14.387.53.
Full soon th' inclemency of Heav'n I feel, ... Od.14.534.63.
As soon as his approach the Heroe knew, ... Od.15.67.72.
But soon as morning from her orient bed ... Od.15.214.78.
To *Pylos* soon they came; when thus begun ... Od.15.218.78.
Brooks no repulse, nor cou'dst thou soon depart: ... Od.15.237.79.
And soon he reach'd the Palace of his Sire. ... Od.15.243.80.
Soon shall my bounties speak a grateful mind, ... Od.15.578.98.
And soon each envy'd happiness attend ... Od.15.579.98.
Soon as the Morning blush'd along the plains, ... Od.16.1.100.
Or heav'ns! might He return! (and soon appear ... Od.16.105.107.
Soon as *Aurora,* daughter of the dawn, ... Od.17.1.132.
Such to our wish the warrior soon restore, ... Od.17.152.139.
Then soon th' invaders of his bed, and throne, ... Od.17.156.139.
Soon as the Suitors from the banquet rose, ... Od.17.432.153.
Or save his life; and soon his life to save ... Od.18.106.172.
To some new channel soon, the changeful tide ... Od.19.102.197.
Soon will he grace this dear paternal dome. ... Od.19.346.211.
Soon as the morn, new-rob'd in purple light, ... Od.19.499.220.
Soon with redoubl'd force the wound repay'd; ... Od.19.528.221.
Soon, with consummate joy to crown his pray'r, ... Od.20.130.240.
Dispatch! for soon the Suitors will assay ... Od.20.194.242.
Soon from the fount, with each a brimming urn, ... Od.20.202.243.
With deeds consummate soon the promis'd joys! ... Od.20.295.247.
From my great Sire too soon devolv'd to me! ... Od.20.331.249.
But soon to fly the messengers of death) ... Od.21.457.282.
And this mad Archer soon have shot his last. ... Od.22.92.291.
Soon as his store of flying fates was spent, ... Od.22.136.293.
And this bold Archer soon shall shoot no more. ... Od.22.151.294.
Soon as her eyes the welcome object met, ... Od.22.444.309.
Soon fled the soul impure, and left behind ... Od.22.507.313.
Soon as soft slumber eas'd the toils of day, ... Od.23.371.343.
Condemn'd to pay the great arrear so soon, ... Od.24.41.349.
Soon as absorpt in all-embracing flame ... Od.24.91.352.
Soon as returning life regains its seat, ... Od.24.407.368.

SOONER
Wounds, Charms, and *Ardors,* were no sooner read, ... 2.RL1.119.154.
Sooner shall Grass in *Hide*-Park Circus *grow,* ... 2.RL4.117.193.
Sooner let Earth, Air, Sea, to *Chaos* fall, ... 2.RL4.119.193.
Scarce any Tale was sooner heard than told; ... 2.TemF.469.286.
What will a Child learn sooner than a song? ... 4.2HE1.205.213.
No sooner said, but from the Hall ... 4.HS6.212.263.
Ask ye their names? I sooner could disclose ... 5.DunB2.309A.310.
Sooner shall Major-General cease ... 6.10.41.25.
Sooner shall *Rowe* lampoon the UNION ... 6.10.45.25.
And in th' impetuous Course themselves the sooner drain: ... 6.17ii.13.56.
Sooner I'd quit my Part in thee, ... 6.30.25.86.
Sooner we'd quit our Part in thee, ... 6.30.25A.86.
Who'd sooner quit our Part in thee, ... 6.30.25B.86.
No sooner *Hector* saw the King retir'd, ... Il.11.365.51.
No sooner had he spoke, but thund'ring near ... Il.23.579.513.
No sooner freed, and thro' th' enclosure past, ... Od.9.545.328.
Sooner shalt thou, a stranger to thy shape, ... Od.10.340.360.
In vain! far sooner all the murth'rous brood ... Od.13.494.29.
No—sooner far their riot and their lust ... Od.15.37.71.

SOONEST
Why, nature, dost thou soonest fire ... 6.51ii.11.153.

SOOTE
But, as he glozeth with Speeches soote, ... 6.14i.17.42.

SOOTERKINS
Fruits of dull Heat, and Sooterkins of Wit. ... 5.DunB1.126.278.

SOOTH
To sooth my Hopes and mitigate my Woes. ... 1.TrUl.206.472.
To sooth his Cares, and free from Noise and Strife ... 2.ChJM.27.16.
The well-sung woes will sooth my pensive ghost; ... 2.ElAb.365.348.
The well-sung woes shall sooth my pensive ghost; ... 2.ElAb.365A.348.
Which most conduce to sooth the soul in slumbers, ... 5.DunA2.337.142.
"Which most conduce to sooth the soul in slumbers, ... 5.DunB2.369.315.
Now, that this same it is right sooth, ... 6.79.5.218.
Or *Glumglum's* humbler Title sooth thy Ear: ... 6.96iv.104.279.
To sooth a Consort's and a Parent's Woe. ... Il.17.42.289.
To sooth a Father's and a Mother's Woe; ... Il.22.430.473.
And sooth my Sorrows, while I bear to live. ... Il.23.58.489.
With Words to sooth the miserable Man. ... Il.24.652.564.
And sooth the vanquish'd with a victor's pray'r. ... Od.4.572.147.
To sooth my hopes, and mitigate my woes. ... Od.13.373.25.
Some light, and sooth her soul's eternal pain. ... Od.17.637.163.
To sooth their fears a specious reason feign: ... Od.19.8.193.
The series of my toils, to sooth her woe. ... Od.19.57.195.
To sooth my grief, he haply may record: ... Od.19.114.198.
With tender sympathy to sooth my soul, ... Od.19.635.227.

SOOTH'D
Thus have I sooth'd my Griefs, and thus have paid ... Il.17.606.311.
Sooth'd the frail Queen, and poyson'd all her heart. ... Od.3.329.102.
And the sooth'd heart with secret pleasure fills. ... Od.17.605.161.

SOOTHING
As soothing Folly, or exalting Vice: ... 2.TemF.516.289.

SOOTHS
Ye Pow'rs, what pleasing Frensie sooths my Mind! ... 1.PAu.51.83.
Rolls o'er my *Grotto,* and but sooths my Sleep. ... 4.HS1.124.17.
Sooths the sad series of her tedious tale. ... 5.DunA3.191z6.172.
With this he sooths his angry Soul, and sings ... Il.9.249.445.
Now plies the Lash, and sooths and threats in vain; ... Il.17.489.307.
Sooths weary Life, and softens human Pain. ... Il.24.166.542.
Who sooths to dear delight his anxious mind: ... Od.1.72.34.

SOOTY
Swift on his sooty Pinions flitts the *Gnome,* ... 2.RL4.17.184.
Then with a Sponge the sooty Workman drest ... Il.18.483.345.

SOPHISTRY
Destroy his Fib, or Sophistry; in vain, ... 4.Arbu.91.102.
His blunted Arms by *Sophistry* are born, ... 5.DunB4.25.342.
The Parson's Cant, the Lawyer's Sophistry, ... 6.8.40.19.

SOPHONISBA
With arts arising *Sophonisba* rose: ... 6.107.3.310.

SOPHS
Three Cambridge Sophs and three pert Templars came, ... 5.DunA2.347.143.
Three College Sophs, and three pert Templars came, ... 5.DunB2.379.315.

SOPHY
To make you look as sage as any Sophy. ... 6.13.15.39.

SOPS
He eat the Sops, she sipp'd the Wine: ... 6.93.20.257.
He eat the Sops, she drank the Wine: ... 6.93.20A.257.

SORC'RER
He look'd, and saw a sable Sorc'rer rise, ... 5.DunA3.229.176.
And look'd, and saw a sable Sorc'rer rise, ... 5.DunB3.233.331.

SORDID
"See Britain sunk in lucre's sordid charms, ... 3.Ep3.145.105.
Plain, but not sordid, tho' not splendid, clean. ... 4.HS2.48.57.
And pleas'd, if sordid Want be far away. ... 4.2HE2.295.185.
Obscene with reptiles, took his sordid bed. ... Od.17.359.149.
And let thy son attest, nor sordid pay ... Od.22.391.307.

SORE
Sore sigh'd the Knight, to hear his Lady's Cry, ... 2.ChJM.726.49.
How sore I gall'd him, only Heav'n cou'd know, ... 2.ChWB.241.68.
But touch me, and no Minister so sore. ... 4.HS1.76.13.
And Itch most hurts, when anger'd to a Sore; ... 4.JD4.119.35.
As one of *Woodward's* Patients, sick and sore, ... 4.JD4.152.37.
But 'faith your very Friends will soon be sore; ... 4.EpS1.23.299.
Laugh at your Friends, and if your Friends are sore, ... 4.EpS1.55.302.
Sore sighs Sir G[ilbert], starting at the bray ... 5.DunA2.241.129.
There hapless Shakespear, yet of Tibbald sore, ... 5.DunB1.133.279.
Sore sighs Sir Gilbert, starting at the bray, ... 5.DunB2.251.307.
The Ducke sore tickleth his Erse Roote: ... 6.14i.18.42.
In woful wise did sore affright ... 6.58.15.171.
So sore the Gout have I. ... 6.79.52.219.
Sore mutt'ring all the way, ... 6.79.138.222.
Made *Jeremy* full sore to cry, ... 6.101.23.290.
He sent him War, or Plague, or Famine sore. ... 6.137.10.373.
Press'd as we are, and sore of former Fight, ... Il.6.105.328.
The prudent Chief in sore Distress they found, ... Il.11.592.60.
Tho' sore of Battel, tho' with Wounds oppress'd, ... Il.14.145.164.
Stiff with Fatigue, and fretted sore with Wounds; ... Il.17.744.317.
(Tho' sore distrest) to aid the *Pylian* Bands; ... Il.17.790.319.
He too sore wounded by *Agenor's* Son. ... Il.19.55.374.
Injurious men! who while my soul is sore ... Od.3.252.97.

SORER
And is not mine, my Friend, a sorer case, ... 4.Arbu.73.100.

SORREL
What mean those Visits to the *Sorrel Mare?* ... 6.96iv.30.277.
The Neighbours answer, *With the Sorrel Mare.* ... 6.96iv.48.277.
The *Groom* and *Sorrel Mare* preferr'd to me! ... 6.96iv.60.278.

SORROW
Enur'd to Sorrow from my tender Years, 1.TrSP.73.397.
But touch'd with Sorrow for the Dead, too late, 1.TrSt.703.439.
But clear they wrinkled Brown, and quit thy Sorrow, 2.ChWB.122.62.
I never (to my sorrow I declare) 4.EpS2.98.318.
While Wren with sorrow to the grave descends, 5.DunA3.325.189.
While Wren with sorrow to the grave descends, 5.DunB3.329.336.
While *Celia's* tears make sorrow bright, 6.5.1.12.
How lovely sorrow seems, how bright! 6.5.1A.12.
Before my Sorrow be quite lost. 6.10.116.28.
Yet lovely in her Sorrow still appears: 6.96ii.11.270.
So short a Space, and fill'd with Sorrow too! Il.1.545.114.
The Feast disturb'd with Sorrow *Vulcan* saw, Il.1.738.122.
The *Grecian's* Sorrow, and the *Dardan's* Joy. Il.4.233.232.
Fear on her Cheek, and Sorrow in her Eye. Il.6.485.350.
(Down his white Beard a Stream of Sorrow flows) Il.9.559.460.
With Sorrow seiz'd, in Consternation lost, Il.9.813.473.
And pierc'd with Sorrow for his * Grandson slain, Il.13.274.117.
His wounded Eyes the Scene of Sorrow knew; Il.14.18.157.
He said, and Sorrow touch'd each *Argive* Breast: Il.14.535.189.
Th' *Achaians* sorrow for their Hero slain; Il.16.729.272.
What Sorrow dictates, but no Word found way. Il.17.784.319.
Who, sinking now with Age, and Sorrow, pays Il.18.507.346.
What greater Sorrow could afflict my Breast, Il.19.341.386.
A Cloud of Sorrow overcast his Sight, Il.20.487.415.
And settled Sorrow on his aged Face, Il.21.618.448.
Ah! let me, let me go where Sorrow calls; Il.22.530.478.
Sinks my sad Soul with Sorrow to the Grave. Il.22.543.478.
A while they sorrow, then dismiss their Care; Il.24.62.538.
So spoke the Fair, with Sorrow-streaming Eye: Il.24.981.576.
On all around th' infectious Sorrow grows; Il.24.983.576.
To sorrow sacred, and secure of fame: Od.1.438.53.
And gen'rous wine, which thoughtful sorrow flies. Od.2.330.77.
A private sorrow, not a publick cause. Od.3.99.91.
His good old Sire with sorrow to the tomb Od.4.144.127.
Above restraint the tide of sorrow rose: Od.4.206.129.
Provoke new sorrow from these grateful eyes. Od.4.750.154.
But ah how chang'd! from thence my sorrow flows; Od.6.197.219.
'Tis ours this son of sorrow to relieve, Od.6.245.222.
Again unmann'd a show'r of sorrow shed: Od.8.90.267.
Their wistful eyes in floods of sorrow drown'd. Od.10.484.366.
Or learn'd to sorrow for a country lost. Od.10.547.369.
And bow his age with sorrow to the tomb! Od.11.239.393.
And tender sorrow thrills in ev'ry vein; Od.11.676.417.
While yet I spoke, a sudden sorrow ran Od.12.330.447.
What sorrow had been mine, if at my gate Od.14.43.38.
Who knows the son of sorrow to relieve, Od.15.362.86.
Another's sorrow may thy ear enjoy, Od.15.424.89.
My secret soul in all thy sorrow shares: Od.15.523.95.
As the bold eagle with fierce sorrow stung, Od.16.238.114.
But the dark brow of silent sorrow shook: Od.17.584.161.
(Suspending sorrow with celestial strain Od.17.610.161.
Then, while the streaming sorrow dims her eyes, Od.18.193.176.
Tears but indulge the sorrow, not redress. Od.18.206.177.
In sweet oblivion let my sorrow sleep! Od.19.140.199.
But inward on my soul let sorrow prey; Od.19.194.201.
Down her pale cheek new-streaming sorrow flows: Od.19.702.229.
I'll grieve, 'till sorrow sink me to the grave! Od.20.266.246.
I shall not sorrow for a mother lost; Od.21.120.264.
We drank the cup of sorrow mix'd with tears, Od.23.378.343.
These floods of sorrow, oh my Sire, restrain! Od.24.379.367.
Spoke when he ceas'd: dumb sorrow touch'd them all. Od.24.503.372.

SORROW-STREAMING
So spoke the Fair, with Sorrow-streaming Eye: Il.24.981.576.

SORROW'D
Requir'd his Arm, he sorrow'd unredrest. Il.18.520.346.
Stung to the Soul, he sorrow'd, and he rag'd. Il.19.124.377.
Of this Distress, and sorrow'd in thy Flight: Il.22.296.468.
Where *Thetis* sorrow'd in her secret Cave: Il.24.110.539.
And here had sigh'd and sorrow'd out the Day; Il.24.891.573.
Much have I sorrow'd, but my master more. Od.14.78.40.

SORROW'S
But see! the *Nymph* in Sorrow's Pomp appears, 2.RL*A*2.59.133.
Alike devote to sorrow's dire extreme Od.4.1061.167.

SORROWING
When at the close of each sad, sorrowing day, 2.ElAb.225.338.
And left him sorrowing on the lonely Coast, Il.1.564.115.
The sorrowing Friends his frantick Rage obey. Il.24.310.549.
The neighb'ring main, and sorrowing treads the shores. Od.2.294.76.
Then sorrowing, with sad step the Queen retir'd, Od.16.465.129.
In every sorrowing soul I pour'd delight, Od.17.505.157.
Deep from his soul he sigh'd, and sorrowing spread Od.24.369.366.

SORROWS
And kindly sigh for sorrows not your own; 1.TrFD.4.385.
You seek to share in Sorrows not your own; 1.TrSt.803.443.
Soft Sorrows, melting Griefs, and flowing Tears. 2.RL4.86.190.
He breaks the Vial whence the Sorrows flow. 2.RL4.142.196.
Take back that grace, those sorrows, and those tears, 2.ElAb.285.343.
Now sink in sorrows with a tolling Bell. 5.DunA2.220.128.
Now sinks in sorrows with a tolling bell; 5.DunB2.228.307.
Muse! at that name thy sacred sorrows shed, 6.52.47.157.
And with a Father's Sorrows mix his own! 6.85.8.242.
And *Europe* taste thy Sorrows in a Dish. 6.96ii.78.274.
And *Europe* taste thy Sorrows in her Dish. 6.96ii.78A.274.
She, in soft Sorrows, and in pensive Thought, Il.1.451.109.
And thus the Sorrows of his Soul explores. Il.1.473.110.
Troy yet should flourish, and my Sorrows end. Il.6.355.343.
And end with Sorrows as they first begun. Il.6.521.352.
Why with untimely Sorrows heaves thy Heart? Il.6.625.357.
The pious Maids their mingled Sorrows shed, Il.6.646.358.
Nor less the *Greeks* their pious Sorrows shed, Il.7.512.389.

SORROWS (CONTINUED)
Great *Hector* sorrows for his Servant kill'd, Il.8.155.405.
Superior Sorrows swell'd his Royal Breast; Il.9.12.431.
Th' afflicted Pair, their Sorrows to proclaim, Il.9.675.468.
For him these Sorrows? for my mortal Foe? Il.9.724.470.
Anxious he sorrows for th' endanger'd Host. Il.10.18.2.
Seeks he the Sorrows of our Host to know? Il.11.802.72.
The Toils, the Sorrows, and the Wounds of War. Il.14.564.190.
With bitter Groans his Sorrows he exprest, Il.15.458.215.
Thy melting Sorrows thus pursue thy Friend? Il.16.16.235.
And speak those Sorrows which a Friend would share. Il.16.28.236.
Till *Thetis'* Sorrows thus began to flow. Il.18.68.326.
Hear how his Sorrows echo thro' the Shore! Il.18.81.327.
Had caus'd such Sorrows past, and Woes to come. Il.18.114.328.
New Woes, new Sorrows shall create again: Il.18.116.328.
Pours unavailing Sorrows o'er the Dead. Il.18.278.335.
That done, their Sorrows and their Sighs renew. Il.18.416.341.
So pierc'd with Sorrows, so o'erwhelm'd as mine? Il.18.502.345.
Their Sov'reign's Sorrows in their own exprest. Il.19.8.371.
Eternal Sorrows what avails to shed? Il.19.227.382.
Sorrows on Sorrows, never doom'd to end! Il.19.308.385.
Sorrows on Sorrows, never doom'd to end! Il.19.308.385.
And dry'd my Sorrows for a Husband slain; Il.19.314.385.
He groans, he raves, he sorrows from his Soul. Il.19.334.386.
What Sorrows then must their sad Mother know, Il.22.72.455.
Yet all their Sorrows turn not *Hector's* Heart: Il.22.111.457.
And thrice their Sorrows and Laments renew; Il.23.17.487.
And sooth my Sorrows, while I bear to live. Il.23.58.489.
Once more afresh the *Grecian* Sorrows flow: Il.23.192.497.
Ah! may my Sorrows ever shun the Light! Il.24.120.540.
Ev'n *Juno* sought her Sorrows to console, Il.24.133.540.
Maternal Sorrows, long, ah long, to last! Il.24.138.540.
How long, unhappy! shall thy Sorrows flow, Il.24.163.542.
Still, still for *Hector* let our Sorrows flow, Il.24.257.547.
Who search the Sorrows of a Parent's Heart, Il.24.474.556.
These unavailing Sorrows o'er the Dead; Il.24.693.566.
A Parent once, whose Sorrows equal'd thine: Il.24.758.569.
My only Food my Sorrows and my Sighs! Il.24.809.570.
Nine Days to vent our Sorrows I request, Il.24.834.571.
Now meet him dead, and let your Sorrows flow! Il.24.880.573.
Then pour your boundless Sorrows o'er the Dead. Il.24.895.573.
While deeper Sorrows groan from each full Heart, Il.24.904.574.
Thy Pity check'd my Sorrows in their Flow: Il.24.971.576.
The sorrows of your inmost soul relate; Od.1.356.49.
Then swelling sorrows burst their former bounds, Od.1.461.54.
Ægyptius, by his age and sorrows broke: Od.2.20.61.
For my lost Sire continual sorrows spring, Od.2.53.62.
O friend! what sorrows dost thou bring to mind? Od.3.126.92.
Happier his lot, who, many sorrows past, Od.3.289.100.
When imag'd to my soul his sorrows rise. Od.4.136.126.
Fast for the Sire the filial sorrows flow; Od.4.251.131.
To woe! Did ever sorrows equal mine? Od.4.959.163.
From what deep source my ceaseless sorrows flow? Od.4.1070.167.
Pour'd the big sorrows of his swelling heart; Od.5.104.177.
With echoing sorrows made the mountains groan, Od.5.202.181.
No more in sorrows languish life away: Od.5.208.181.
Of all my sorrows, sent by heav'n and fate! Od.7.325.251.
That bath'd, our guest may bid his sorrows cease, Od.8.463.288.
And down my cheek the pious sorrows flow. Od.11.109.386.
Thus in a tyde of tears our sorrows flow, Od.11.573.411.
Enough my master's sorrows, and my own. Od.14.46.38.
And calls the springing sorrows from her eyes. Od.14.153.43.
Alas, *Telemachus!* my sorrows flow Od.14.200.45.
Unhappy guest! whose sorrows touch my mind! Od.14.395.54.
The swain returns. A tale of sorrows hear; Od.16.61.105.
Nor ceas'd, 'till *Pallas* bid her sorrows fly, Od.16.468.130.
And end her tears, her sorrows, and her sighs. Od.17.9.132.
But why these sorrows, when my Lord arrives? Od.23.239.335.
And moves the sorrows to enhance the joys. Od.24.282.363.

SORT
For diff'rent *Styles* with diff'rent *Subjects* sort, 1.EOC.322.275.
Take the most strong, and sort them as you can. 3.Ep1.72.20.
Each is a sort of *Virtue,* and of *Vice.* 3.Ep2.206A.67.
Hast thou, O *Sun!* beheld an emptier sort, 4.JD4.204.43.
And speak in publick with some sort of grace. 4.2HE1.208.213.
Bubo observes, he lash'd no sort of *Vice:* 4.EpS1.12.298.
"What tho' we let some better sort sort of fool 5.DunB4.255.369.
"What tho' we let some better sort sort of fool 5.DunB4.255.369.
Then look'd, and saw a lazy, lolling sort, 5.DunB4.337.376.
Her children first of more distinguish'd sort, 5.DunB4.567.398.
But Fate dispos'd them in this humble sort, 6.126ii.7.353.
When Laureates make Odes, do you ask of what sort? 6.153.1.402.
Of choicest sort and savour, rich repast! Od.1.186.42.
Of choicest sort and savour, rich repast! Od.7.237.247.
Of choicest sort and savour, rich repaste! Od.10.440.365.
Of choicest sort and favour; rich repast! Od.15.155.76.
Freighted, it seems, with toys of ev'ry sort Od.15.456.92.
There stood his mansion of the rural sort, Od.24.238.360.

SORTS
Grant but as many sorts of Mind as Moss. 3.Ep1.18.17.
Then in plain prose, were made two sorts of Men, 3.Ep3.13A.84.
Then careful Heav'n supply'd two sorts of Men, 3.Ep3.13.84.

SOT
The sot a hero, lunatic a king; 3.EOM2.268.87.
A Fop their Passion, but their Prize a Sot, 3.Ep2.247.70.
"D'ye think me, noble Gen'ral, such a Sot? 4.2HE2.50.167.
On every learned Sot; 6.47.14.129.
A Fop their Passion, but their Prize a Sot; 6.86.9A.245.

SOTS
Concluding all were desp'rate Sots and Fools, 1.EOC.271.270.
What can ennoble sots, or slaves, or cowards? 3.EOM4.215.147.

SOUGHT

I shun the Fountains which I sought before. 1.PSu.30.74.
I'll shun the Fountains which I sought before. 1.PSu.30A.74.
Bath'd in the Springs, or sought the cooling Shade; 1.W-F.166A.165.
These shades, unknowing of the fates, she sought, 1.TrFD.17.386.
Those shades, unknowing of the fates, she sought, 1.TrFD.17A.386.
And sought around his Native Realm in vain; 1.TrUl.71.468.
And sought no Treasure but thy Heart alone. 2.ChJM.551.41.
Just in that instant, anxious *Ariel* sought 2.RL3.139.178.
Who sought no more than on his Foe to die. 2.RL5.78.206.
In ev'ry place is sought, but sought in vain: 2.RL5.110.208.
In ev'ry place is sought, but sought in vain: 2.RL5.110.208.
Long have we sought t'instruct and please Mankind, 2.TemF.300.278.
And simple Reason never sought but one: 3.EOM3.230.115.
I sought no homage from the Race that write; 4.Arbu.219.111.
Sad *Orpheus* sought his Consort lost; 6.11.51Z1.32.
First sought a Poet's Fortune in the Town: 6.49i.2.137.
YE shades, where sacred truth is sought; 6.51i.1.151.
Who broke no promise, sought no private end, 6.97.3A.282.
While he but sought his Author's Fame to further, 6.116viii.5.328.
For *Chryses* sought with costly Gifts to gain Il.1.15.86.
The Priest of *Phœbus* sought by Gifts to gain Il.1.484.111.
So sadly lost, so lately sought in vain. Il.1.583.115.
And trembling sought the Pow'rs with Sacrifice, Il.2.389.145.
Beneath his Conduct sought the *Phrygian* Shores. Il.2.774.162.
Three Ships with *Nireus* sought the *Trojan* Shore, Il.2.815.163.
Whom long my Eyes have sought, but sought in vain; Il.3.302.207.
Whom long my Eyes have sought, but sought in vain; Il.3.302.207.
A peaceful Guest, he sought *Mycenæ's* Tow'rs; Il.4.431.241.
The Sons of *Dares* first the Combate sought, Il.5.15.266.
Skill'd in the Bow, on Foot I sought the War, Il.5.242.278.
Those heav'nly Steeds the Hero sought so far, Il.5.806.304.
Wild with his Pain, he sought the bright Abodes, Il.5.1064.317.
While *Bacchus* headlong sought the briny Flood, Il.6.167.334.
By his Decree I sought the *Trojan* Town, Il.6.255.339.
At home he sought her, but he sought in vain; Il.6.464.349.
At home he sought her, but he sought in vain; Il.6.464.349.
Or sought her Sisters in the *Trojan* Court? Il.6.477.350.
Sought her own Palace, and indulg'd her Woe. Il.6.643.358.
Hector inspir'd he sought: To him addrest, Il.7.49.365.
Of ev'ry Chief who sought this glorious War, Il.7.152.372.
Strait from the Town be Sheep and Oxen sought, Il.8.629.426.
Long e'er the rest, he rose, and sought my Tent. Il.10.143.8.
Whatever means of Safety can be sought, Il.10.164.9.
Of *Greece* he left, and sought the *Theban* Tow'rs, Il.10.340.18.
Then (never to return) he sought the Shore, Il.10.399.21.
Atrides mark'd as these their Safety sought, Il.11.165.42.
Cassandra's Love he sought with Boasts of Pow'r, Il.13.461.128.
For him, in *Troy's* remotest Lines, he sought, Il.13.577.133.
Fac'd ev'ry Foe, and ev'ry Danger sought; Il.13.705.138.
Me chief he sought, and from the Realms on high Il.14.291.176.
This said, his eager Javelin sought the Foe: Il.15.498.216.
With Gifts of Price he sought and won the Dame; Il.16.227.248.
Till on the Left the Chief he sought, he found; Il.17.769.318.
Achilles sought his Tent. His Train before Il.19.291.384.
Then, swift ascending, sought the bright Abodes. Il.19.377.387.
Hector he sought; in search of *Hector* turn'd Il.20.105.398.
Approach'd, and sought his Knees with suppliant Tears; Il.21.75.424.
Where, all confus'd, she sought the Sov'reign God; Il.21.590.446.
And sought for Glory in the Jaws of Fate: Il.22.589.480.
Perhaps he sought not Heav'n by Sacrifice, Il.23.625.514.
Sought their black Ships, and clear'd the crowded Strand; Il.24.2A.534.
Ev'n *Juno* sought her Sorrows to console, Il.24.133.540.
Since great Ulysses sought the *Phrygian* plains, Od.2.33.61.
When great *Ulysses* sought the *Phrygian* shores Od.2.199.71.
[When fierce in arms he sought the scenes of war, Od.2.255.74.
We sought direction of the pow'r divine: Od.3.209.96.
My friends attending at the shore I sought. Od.4.780.156.
Nor took a kind adieu, nor sought consent!— Od.4.964.163.
So when *Aurora* sought *Orion's* love, Od.5.155.179.
The Queen she sought: the Queen her hours bestow'd Od.6.61.208.
Forsook by thee, in vain I sought thy aid Od.6.387.230.
And sought the deep recesses of the den. Od.9.279.318.
Access we sought, nor was access deny'd: Od.10.301.358.
With gifts unnumber'd *Neleus* sought her arms, Od.11.343.399.
With haughty stalk he sought the distant glades Od.11.661.416.
And sought the secret counsels of the God. Od.13.147.12.
And sought, around, his native realm in vain: Od.13.238.17.
The closest caverns of the grot she sought; Od.13.421.26.
Eumæus at his Sylvan lodge he sought, Od.14.5.35.
They sought repaste; while to th' unhappy kind, Od.14.383.53.
The King from *Helen* rose, and sought his guest. Od.15.66.72.
To *Bias'* arms) he sought a foreign air; Od.15.263.80.
Then dis-array'd, the shining bath they sought, Od.17.98.136.
Round the wide world are sought those men divine Od.17.462.155.
Ulysses sought: with fond affection dear Od.19.486.220.
Bright *Cytherea* sought the bow'r of *Jove;* Od.20.89.237.
How long in vain *Penelope* we sought? Od.21.167.267.
Trembling they sought their guilty heads to hide, Od.22.55.289.
An absent Heroe's bed they sought to soil, Od.24.524.373.

SOUL

Bids his free Soul expatiate in the Skies, 1.W-F.254.172.
Ye sacred Nine! that all my Soul possess, 1.W-F.259.173.
Thus in the *Soul* while *Memory* prevails, 1.EOC.56.245.
In some fair Body thus th' informing Soul 1.EOC.76.247.
In some fair Body thus the sprightly Soul 1.EOC.76A.247.
In some fair Body thus the secret Soul 1.EOC.76B.247.
Gen'rous Converse; a *Soul* exempt from *Pride;* 1.EOC.641.311.
No more my Soul a Charm in Musick finds, 1.TrSP.13.393.
The fair *Sicilians* now thy Soul inflame; 1.TrSP.63.396.
By Charms like thine which all my Soul have won, 1.TrSP.95.398.
Joy to my Soul, and Vigour to my Song: 1.TrSP.239.404.
And thousand Furies haunt his guilty Soul. 1.TrSt.76.413.
Stung to the Soul, the Brothers start from Rest, 1.TrSt.174.417.
What Joys, oh Tyrant! swell'd thy Soul that Day, 1.TrSt.220.419.

SOUL (CONTINUED)

Since still the Lust of Discord fires thy Soul, 1.TrSt.367.425.
'Twas thus I deem'd thy haughty Soul wou'd bear 1.TrSt.404.427.
In fighting Fields, nor urge thy Soul to War. 1.TrES.46.451.
And murm'ring from the Corps th'unwilling Soul retires. 1.TrES.110.453.
And murm'ring to the Shades the Soul retires. 1.TrES.110A.453.
And when th'ascending Soul has wing'd her Flight, 1.TrES.247.459.
And the Soul issu'd in the Purple Flood. 1.TrES.321.461.
My Soul abhors the tastless, dry Embrace, 2.ChJM.103.19.
So may my Soul arrive at Ease and Rest, 2.ChJM.154.22.
The Charms of Wedlock all his Soul imploy: 2.ChJM.229.25.
Touch'd to the Quick, and tickl'd at the Soul. 2.ChJM.277.27.
Then to the Skies your mounting Soul shall go, 2.ChJM.289.28.
Cou'd swell the Soul to Rage, and fire the Martial Train. 2.ChJM.325.30.
His lovely Mistress all his Soul possest, 2.ChJM.361.31.
So may my Soul have Joy, as thou, my Wife, 2.ChJM.545.41.
I have a Soul to save as well as You; 2.ChJM.578.43.
Now, by my Mother's Soul, it is decreed, 2.ChJM.657.46.
With all my Soul, he thus reply'd again; 2.ChJM.736.50.
For, on my Soul, amends shall soon be made: 2.ChJM.792.53.
To clear my Quail-pipe, and refresh my Soul, 2.ChWB.213.67.
His Soul, I hope, enjoys eternal Glory, 2.ChWB.237.68.
His Soul, I hope, enjoys perpetual Glory, 2.ChWB.237A.68.
So bless the good Man's Soul, I say no more. 2.ChWB.252.69.
Full well the Secrets of my Soul she knew, 2.ChWB.267.69.
Can never be a Mouse of any Soul. 2.ChWB.299.71.
He wept, kind Soul! and stoop'd to kiss my Face; 2.ChWB.422.77.
While her rackt Soul Repose and Peace requires, 2.RL*A*2.11.132.
'Tis these that early taint the Female Soul, 2.RL1.87.152.
Or caus'd Suspicion when no Soul was rude, 2.RL4.73.190.
Charms strike the Sight, but Merit wins the Soul. 2.RL5.34.201.
Warm from the soul, and faithful to its fires, 2.ElAb.54.323.
Speed the soft intercourse from soul to soul, 2.ElAb.57.323.
Speed the soft intercourse from soul to soul, 2.ElAb.57.323.
And make my soul quit *Abelard* for God. 2.ElAb.128.330.
Ere such a soul regains its peaceful state, 2.ElAb.197.336.
Far other dreams my erring soul employ, 2.ElAb.223.338.
All my loose soul unbounded springs to thee. 2.ElAb.228.338.
Stain all my soul, and wanton in my eyes! 2.ElAb.266.341.
And swelling organs lift the rising soul; 2.ElAb.272.342.
In seas of flame my plunging soul is drown'd, 2.ElAb.275.342.
And dawning grace is opening on my soul: 2.ElAb.280.342.
Suck my last breath, and catch my flying soul! 2.ElAb.324.346.
Suck my last breath, and catch the flying soul! 2.ElAb.324A.346.
Why bade ye else, ye Pow'rs! her soul aspire 2.Elegy.11.363.
So flew the soul to its congenial place, 2.Elegy.27.365.
Ev'n he, whose soul now melts in mournful lays, 2.Elegy.77.368.
Gradations just, has thy pervading soul 3.EOM1.31.17.
And Centres just, has thy pervading soul 3.EOM1.31A.17.
The soul, uneasy and confin'd from home, 3.EOM1.97.26.
The soul, uneasy and confin'd at home, 3.EOM1.97A.26.
His soul proud Science never taught to stray 3.EOM1.101.27.
No pow'rs of body or of soul to share, 3.EOM1.191.38.
Whose body Nature is, and God the soul; 3.EOM1.268.47.
Breathes in our soul, informs our mortal part, 3.EOM1.275.48.
Describe or fix one movement of the Soul? 3.EOM2.36A.60.
Self-love, the spring of motion, acts the soul; 3.EOM2.59.62.
The rising tempest puts in act the soul, 3.EOM2.105.67.
Soon flows to this, in body and in soul. 3.EOM2.140.71.
The fiery soul abhor'd in Catiline, 3.EOM2.199.79.
One all-extending, all-preserving Soul 3.EOM3.22.94.
So two consistent motions act the Soul; 3.EOM3.315.126.
One common blessing, as one common soul. 3.EOM4.62.134.
The first, last purpose of the human soul; 3.EOM4.338.161.
And opens still, and opens on his soul, 3.EOM4.342.161.
God loves from Whole to Parts: but human soul 3.EOM4.361.163.
There Affectations quite reverse the soul. 3.Ep1.125A.25.
To ease the Soul of one oppressive weight, 3.Ep1.57.19.
And ev'ry child hates Shylock, tho' his soul 3.Ep1.114.23.
Or Affectations quite reverse the soul. 3.Ep1.125.25.
Mercy! cries Helluo, mercy on my soul! 3.Ep1.236.35.
Then all for Death, that Opiate of the soul! 3.Ep2.91.57.
That life of pleasure, and that soul of whim! 3.Ep3.306.118.
Then dubs Director, and secures his soul. 3.Ep3.374.123.
Still follow Sense, of ev'ry Art the Soul, 3.Ep4.65.143.
Make the soul dance upon a Jig to Heaven. 3.Ep4.144.151.
Begin with Sense, of ev'ry Art the Soul, 3.Ep4.65A.143.
And for my Soul I cannot sleep a wink. 4.HS1.12.5.
The Soul stood forth, nor kept a Thought within; 4.HS1.54.9.
The Feast of Reason and the Flow of Soul: 4.HS1.128.17.
What Terrors wou'd distract each conscious Soul 4.JD4.244A.47.
But oh! what Terrors must distract a Soul 4.JD4.244B.47.
And the free Soul looks down to pity Kings. 4.JD4.187.41.
But oh! what Terrors must distract the Soul, 4.JD4.244.47.
What tho' his Soul be Bullet, Body Buff? 4.JD4.262A.47.
The Soul subsides; and wickedly inclines 4.HS2.79.59.
A Clerk, foredoom'd his Father's soul to cross, 4.Arbu.17.97.
Have I no Friend to serve, no Soul to save? 4.Arbu.274.115.
His Father, Mother, Body, Soul, and Muse. 4.Arbu.381.125.
And all the kind Deceivers of the soul! 4.HOde1.36.153.
And all the dear Deceivers of the Soul! 4.HOde1.36A.153.
Who there his Muse, or Self, or Soul attends? 4.2HE2.90.171.
And keep the equal Measure of the Soul. 4.2HE2.205.179.
One, driv'n by strong Benevolence of Soul, 4.2HE2.276.185.
The sleepy Eye, that spoke the melting soul. 4.2HE1.150.209.
Smooth'd ev'ry brow, and open'd ev'ry soul: 4.2HE1.248.217.
Yet lov'd his Friend, and had a Soul; 4.HS6.162.261.
That lock up all the Functions of my soul; 4.1HE1.40.281.
(Between the Fits) this Fever of the soul: 4.1HE1.58.283.
See him, with pains of body, pangs of soul, 4.1HE1.71.283.
How shin'd the Soul, unconquer'd in the Tow'r! 4.EpS2.83.317.
O thou, of business the directing soul, 5.DunA1.147.81.
Let others aim: 'Tis yours to shake the soul 5.DunA2.217.127.
Which most conduce to sooth the soul in slumbers, 5.DunA2.337.142.
Who knows how long, thy transmigrating soul 5.DunA3.41.154.
And lick up all their Physick of the Soul. 5.DunA3.74.156.

SOUL (CONTINUED)

Half thro' the solid darkness of his soul; 5.DunA3.224.176.
Joy fills his soul, joy innocent of thought: 5.DunA3.245.178.
O thou! of Bus'ness the directing soul! 5.DunB1.169.282.
Let others aim: 'Tis yours to shake the soul 5.DunB2.225.307.
"Which most conduce to sooth the soul in slumbers, 5.DunB2.369.315.
Who knows how long thy transmigrating soul 5.DunB3.49.322.
And lick up all their Physic of the Soul. 5.DunB3.82.324.
Half thro' the solid darkness of his soul; 5.DunB3.226.331.
Joy fills his soul, joy innocent of thought; 5.DunB3.249.332.
To stir, to rouze, to shake the Soul he comes, 5.DunB4.67.348.
Without the soul, the Muse's Hypocrit. 5.DunB4.100.351.
The boyd's harmony, the beaming soul, 5.DunB4.236.366.
Her too receive (for her my soul adores) 5.DunB4.331.375.
Dismiss my soul, where no Carnation fades." 5.DunB4.418.382.
The common Soul, of Heav'n's more frugal make, 5.DunB4.441.383.
Of nought so doubtful as of *Soul* and *Will.* 5.DunB4.482.389.
However from my Soul I judge 6.10.97.27.
Or when the Soul is press'd with Cares 6.11.26.30.
Or when the Soul is sunk with Cares 6.11.26A.30.
Passions no more the Soul engage, 6.11.34A.31.
Hers lift the Soul to Heav'n. 6.11.134.34.
Or teach the soul of *Cleopatra* fear) 6.20.36.67.
At length, my soul! thy fruitless hopes give o'er, 6.22.1.71.
Eternal Reason! whose presiding soul 6.23.3.73.
Shine through the soul, and drive its clouds away! 6.23.14.73.
Tell me, my Soul, can this be Death? 6.31ii.12.94.
The hov'ring Soul is on the Wing; 6.31ii.6Z5.94.
To wake the soul by tender strokes of art, 6.32.1.96.
In some close corner of the soul, they sin: 6.41.18.114.
Save Three-pence, and his Soul. 6.47.12.128.
Whose Soul, sincere and free, 6.47.50.130.
'Twas all th' Ambition his great Soul could feel, 6.49i.3.137.
'Twas all th' Ambition his high Soul could feel, 6.49i.3A.137.
Strong as their charms, and gentle as their soul; 6.52.74.158.
And sell his Soul for Vanity, 6.58.23.171.
"Statesman, yet friend to Truth! of soul sincere, 6.71.67.204.
"Statesman, yet friend to Truth! in soul sincere, 6.71.67A.204.
A soul as full of Worth, as void of Pride, 6.73.1.209.
With Just Description shew the Soul Divine 6.75.9.212.
Inly she bleeds, and pants her Soul away. 6.81.14A.226.
Inly he bleeds, and pants his Soul away. 6.81.14B.226.
Inly he bleeds, and melts his soul away. 6.81.14C.226.
Can touch Immortals, 'tis a Soul like thine: 6.84.22.239.
A Soul supreme, in each hard Instance try'd, 6.84.23.239.
In some soft Dream may thy mild Soul remove, 6.86.19A.246.
Or let thy soul in some soft dream remove, 6.86.19B.246.
Let the mild soul in some soft dream remove, 6.86.19C.246.
Statesman, yet Friend to Truth! of Soul sincere, 6.97.1.281.
Statesman, yet Friend to Truth! in Soul sincere, 6.97.1A.281.
But ev'ry Woman's in her Soul a Rake. 6.99.16.287.
A softer wonder my pleas'd soul surveys, 6.106i.2.306.
What pleasing Phrensy steals away my Soul? 6.106ii.1.307.
Passion and Pride were to her soul unknown, 6.115.5.322.
In this World, she despis'd every Soul she met here, 6.124i.9.347.
Clear as her soul, and shining as her frame; 6.126ii.4.353.
Clean as her soul, and spotless as her frame; 6.126ii.4A.353.
Clear as her soul, and spotless as her frame; 6.126ii.4B.353.
"Come, if you'll be a quiet soul, 6.140.29.379.
And the bright Flame was shot thro' MARCHMONT'S Soul. 6.142.12.383.
And shot the gen'rous flame thro' Machmont's soul 6.142.12A.383.
Thy Soul enjoys that Liberty it lov'd. 6.152.10.400.
Thy Soul enjoys the Liberty it lov'd. 6.152.10A.400.
To whom *Pelides.* From thy inmost Soul Il.1.107.92.
Strife and Debate thy restless Soul employ, Il.1.231.98.
And calm the rising Tempest of his Soul. Il.1.258.99.
Then rage in Bitterness of Soul, to know Il.1.323.103.
But that imperious, that unconquer'd Soul, Il.1.378.106.
And thus the Sorrows of his Soul explores. Il.1.473.110.
And Scenes of Blood rise dreadful in his Soul. Il.1.639.118.
Deep in the close Recesses of my Soul. Il.1.711.121.
His Figure such as might his Soul proclaim; Il.2.263.140.
But ill thy Soul supplies a Form so fair. Il.3.64.192.
But who like thee can boast a Soul sedate, Il.3.87.194.
She spoke, and *Helen's* secret Soul was mov'd; Il.3.487.215.
Mix'd with thy Soul, and all dissolv'd away. Il.3.554.218.
Sighs from his inmost Soul, and thus replies; Il.4.46.223.
Possess his Soul, which thus the *Spartan* chears: Il.4.221.231.
And Nerves to second what thy Soul inspires! Il.4.363.238.
If glorious Deeds afford thy Soul delight, Il.4.406.240.
The Soul comes floating in a Tide of Gore. Il.4.537.247.
But *Pallas* now *Tydides* Soul inspires, Il.5.1.263.
Wake each Paternal Virtue in thy Soul: Il.5.161.274.
Know, 'tis not honest in my Soul to fear, Il.5.312.281.
The soul indignant seeks the Realms of Night. Il.5.360.283.
Sarpedon first his ardent Soul express'd, Il.5.573.296.
The grizly Wound dismiss'd his Soul to Hell, Il.5.667.300.
Jove got such Heroes as my Sire, whose Soul Il.5.790.304.
The Soul disdainful seeks the Caves of Night, Il.5.818.305.
The fainting Soul stood ready wing'd for Flight, Il.5.856.307.
O Sire! can no Resentment touch thy Soul? Il.5.942.311.
And all thy Mother in thy Soul rebells. Il.5.1101.319.
Then with a plenteous Draught refresh thy Soul, Il.6.325.342.
But he who found not whom his Soul desir'd, Il.6.472.350.
My Soul impells me to th' embattel'd Plains; Il.6.567.354.
What Pity, Sloath should seize a Soul so brave, Il.6.670.360.
To her the God: Great *Hector's* Soul incite Il.7.43.364.
What my Soul prompts, and what some God commands. Il.7.80.367.
Not void of Soul, and not unskill'd in War: Il.7.276.378.
To whom great *Ajax* his high Soul express'd. Il.7.343.381.
And each brave Foe was in his Soul a Friend". Il.7.365.382.
That heard, deep Anguish stung *Saturnia's* Soul; Il.8.240.409.
His Vows, in Bitterness of Soul preferr'd; Il.8.294.411.
Nor urge a Soul already fill'd with fire. Il.8.356.414.
He saw their Soul, and thus his Word imparts. Il.8.556.423.
They gave thee not—a brave and virtuous Soul. Il.9.56.434.

SOUL (CONTINUED)

But bold of Soul, when headlong Fury fir'd, Il.9.143.439.
If Gifts immense his mighty Soul can bow, Il.9.155.439.
And sure all this may move his mighty Soul. Il.9.208.442.
With this he sooths his angry Soul, and sings Il.9.249.445.
Mix purer Wine, and open ev'ry Soul. Il.9.268.445.
What in my secret Soul is understood, Il.9.408.452.
My Spoil alone his greedy Soul delights; Il.9.442.454.
Slave as she was, my Soul ador'd the Dame. Il.9.453.454.
And early Wisdom to thy Soul convey'd: Il.9.605.464.
And Gifts can conquer ev'ry Soul but thine. Il.9.748.471.
Oh Soul of Battels, and thy People's Guide! Il.9.757.471.
Or strive with Pray'rs his haughty Soul to bend? Il.9.817.474.
(Since Cares, like mine, deprive thy Soul of Rest) Il.10.107.7.
Wond'rous old Man! whose Soul no Respite knows, Il.10.186.10.
One Instant snatch'd his trembling Soul to Hell, Il.10.526.26.
Or if thy Soul aspire to fiercer Deeds, Il.10.556.27.
His Soul rekindled, and awak'd his Worth. Il.11.406.53.
And questions thus his own unconquer'd Soul. Il.11.512.56.
Till some wide Wound lets out their mighty Soul. Il.12.168.87.
So bodes my Soul, and bids me thus advise; Il.12.265.91.
And free the Soul that quivers in thy Heart. Il.12.294.92.
In fighting Fields, nor urge thy Soul to War. Il.12.390.96.
And murm'ring to the Shades the Soul retires. Il.12.464.98.
My Soul is kindled, and my Bosom burns; Il.13.108.109.
He said, and rouz'd the Soul in ev'ry Breast; Il.13.211.116.
And urge thy Soul to rival Acts with mine: Il.13.308.119.
Inglorious here, my Soul abhors to stay, Il.13.331.121.
And fix'd his Soul, to conquer or to die: Il.13.369.123.
He spoke, and all as with one Soul obey'd; Il.13.614.135.
And in short Pantings sobb'd his Soul away; Il.13.818.144.
The Soul came issuing at the narrow Vent: Il.13.842.145.
Go then, successful, where thy Soul inspires; Il.13.985.152.
Could charm the Cares of *Nestor's* watchful Soul: Il.14.2.156.
Mix'd with her Soul, and melted in her Arms. Il.14.336.179.
Ne'er did my Soul so strong a Passion prove, Il.14.359.180.
The Soul of *Ajax* burn'd above the rest. Il.14.536.189.
And the fierce Soul came rushing thro' the Wound. Il.14.614.192.
And anxious asks, what Cares disturb her Soul? Il.15.97.200.
Perhaps some fav'ring God his Soul may bend; Il.15.466.215.
This rouz'd the Soul in ev'ry *Trojan* Breast: Il.15.590.219.
Not more the Mother's Soul that Infant warms, Il.16.13.235.
May never Rage like thine my Soul enslave, Il.16.40.237.
A Soul well-suiting that tempestuous Kind, Il.16.52.237.
This Day shall give you all your Soul demands; Il.16.250.249.
Two Friends, two Bodies with one Soul inspir'd. Il.16.267.249.
And vents his Soul effus'd with gushing Gore. Il.16.387.258.
He sobs his Soul out in the Gush of Blood. Il.16.419.259.
And when th' ascending Soul has wing'd her flight, Il.16.550.265.
And the Soul issu'd in the purple Flood. Il.16.626.268.
The Soul, exhaling, issu'd at the vent. Il.16.738.272.
To the dark Shades the Soul unwilling glides, Il.16.901.278.
He faints; the Soul unwilling wings her way, Il.16.1032.283.
Deep in great *Hector's* Soul: Thro' all the War Il.17.90.291.
(Such, as shou'd burn in ev'ry Soul, that draws Il.17.175.294.
And *Mars* himself came rushing on his Soul. Il.17.252.297.
And stands the Center and the Soul of all: Il.17.413.303.
Thus fell the Youth; the Air his Soul receiv'd, Il.17.592.311.
What more desires my Soul, than here, unmov'd, Il.17.632.312.
So burns the vengeful Hornet (Soul all o'er) Il.17.642.313.
And sent his Soul with ev'ry Lance he threw. Il.17.647.313.
Thus to his Soul he said. Ah! what constrains Il.18.9.323.
Sweet to the Soul, as Hony to the Taste; Il.18.140.329.
Stung to the Soul, he sorrow'd, and he rag'd. Il.19.124.377.
With Limbs and Soul untam'd, he tires a War. Il.19.168.378.
Revenge is all my Soul! no meaner Care, Il.19.211.381.
He groans, he raves, he sorrows from his Soul. Il.19.334.386.
His hastening Soul, and sinks him to the Shades. Il.19.359.387.
But *Jove* alone endues the Soul with Worth: Il.20.291.406.
A Fate so near him, chills his Soul with Fright, Il.20.331.407.
He groans away his Soul: Not louder roars Il.20.467.413.
His Soul no longer brook'd the distant Fight, Il.20.488.415.
And for the Soul an ample Passage made. Il.20.530.416.
And his Soul shiv'ring at th' Approach of Death. Il.21.77.424.
And my swift Soul o'ertake my slaughter'd Friend! Il.21.324.434.
He stops, and questions thus his mighty Soul. Il.21.650.449.
One only Soul informs that dreadful Frame: Il.21.673.450.
Save thy dear Life; or if a Soul so brave Il.22.78.456.
But fix'd remains the Purpose of his Soul: Il.22.127.458.
And with them turns the rais'd Spectator's Soul. Il.22.216.464.
Collect thy Soul, and call forth all thy Pow'r. Il.22.344.470.
My Soul shall bravely issue from my Breast. Il.22.366.471.
Nor less *Achilles* his fierce Soul prepares; Il.22.393.471.
By thy own Soul! by those who gave thee Breath! Il.22.426.473.
Can his dear Image from my Soul depart, Il.22.485.476.
Then his fell Soul a Thought of Vengeance bred, Il.22.495.476.
Sinks my sad Soul with Sorrow to the Grave. Il.22.543.478.
To my sad Soul *Astyanax* appears! Il.22.643.483.
When once we pass, the Soul returns no more. Il.23.94.491.
All Night, *Achilles* hails *Patroclus* Soul, Il.23.272.500.
At the near Prize each gathers all his Soul, Il.23.452.508.
And please a Soul, desirous to bestow,) Il.23.628.514.
Joy swells his Soul, as when the vernal Grain Il.23.679.516.
Not break, the settled Temper of thy Soul. Il.23.688.517.
I yield; that all may know, my Soul can bend, Il.23.697.517.
Still breathing Strife, and unsubdu'd of Soul: Il.23.853.523.
The panting Chief to *Pallas* lifts his Soul: Il.23.900.525.
And all his Soul on his *Patroclus* fed: Il.24.10.535.
Shame is not of his Soul; nor understood, Il.24.56.538.
Some Thought there must be, in a Soul so brave, Il.24.193.544.
Some Thought there must be, in a Soul so brave, Il.24.223.546.
Seek not to stay me, nor my Soul affright Il.24.267.547.
Heav'n, or thy Soul, inspire this bold Design: Il.24.358.551.
Yet suffer not thy Soul to sink with Dread; Il.24.455.555.
Respecting him, my Soul abjures th' Offence; Il.24.535.558.
Yet still one Comfort in his Soul may rise; Il.24.608.562.

SOUL (CONTINUED)

Nor seek by Tears my steady Soul to bend; .... Il.24.707.567.
And shake the Purpose of my Soul no more. .... Il.24.719.567.
My Soul might keep, or utter with a Tear; .... Il.24.937.575.
Hermes I sent, while yet his soul remain'd .... Od.1.49.32.
While his fond soul these fancied triumphs swell'd, ... Od.1.155.40.
And then the purpose of thy soul declare. .... Od.1.164.40.
Let not your soul be sunk in sad despair; .... Od.1.255.45.
When social mirth unbent his serious soul, ... Od.1.335.48.
With friendlier zeal my father's soul was fir'd, ... Od.1.344.49.
The sorrows of your inmost soul relate; .... Od.1.356.49.
But if his soul hath wing'd the destin'd flight, ... Od.1.376.50.
The chanter's soul and raptur'd song inspire; .... Od.1.444.54.
And in his raptured soul the Vision glows. .... Od.1.558.58.
A length of days his soul with prudence crown'd, ... Od.2.21.61.
Tho' with a grace divine her soul is blest, ... Od.2.133.67.
Gods! how my soul is mov'd with just disdain? .... Od.2.272.74.
And all *Penelope* thy soul inspires, ... Od.2.318.76.
Indulge the genial hour, unbend thy soul, ... Od.2.343.77.
A secret pleasure touch'd *Athena's* soul, ... Od.3.65.89.
Injurious men! who while my soul is sore .... Od.3.252.97.
So might she love thee, so thy soul inspire! .... Od.3.276.99.
The soul for ever flies: on all sides round .... Od.3.580.116.
Whence with incessant grief my soul annoy'd, ... Od.4.117.125.
When imag'd to my soul his sorrows rise. .... Od.4.136.126.
The soul of friendship to my hope is lost, ... Od.4.247.131.
This unavailing impotence of soul. .... Od.4.264.131.
In thee renew'd the soul of *Nestor* shines: .... Od.4.282.132.
Mean-time with genial joy to warm the soul, ... Od.4.301.133.
And oft in bitterness of soul deplor'd .... Od.4.361.137.
Spoke loud the languish of his yerning soul: .... Od.4.388.139.
Say, royal youth, sincere of soul report .... Od.4.421.140.
Deep from his inmost soul *Atrides* sigh'd, ... Od.4.445.141.
Three chosen chiefs of dauntless soul command: .... Od.4.552.146.
He said; chill horrors shook my shiv'ring soul, ... Od.4.725.152.
My gloomy soul receives a gleam of joy. .... Od.4.742.153.
While deep attention fix'd my list'ning soul. .... Od.4.816.157.
O early worth! a soul so wise, and young, ... Od.4.831.158.
In the young soul illustrious thought to raise, ... Od.4.914.161.
More dreadful than your boding soul divines: .... Od.4.926.161.
The mighty griefs that swell her lab'ring soul, ... Od.4.951.162.
And hope and doubt alternate seize her soul. .... Od.4.1040.166.
O sister, to my soul for ever dear, ... Od.4.1067.167.
Is not already in thy soul decreed, ... Od.5.32.172.
Ev'n to her inmost soul the Goddess shook; .... Od.5.147.178.
Swear then, thou mean'st not what my soul forebodes; .... Od.5.231.182.
And thus in secret to his soul he said. .... Od.5.366.190.
As thus he commun'd with his soul apart. .... Od.5.523.197.
But instant *Pallas* enter'd in his soul. .... Od.5.545.198.
The soul scarce waking, in the arms of death. .... Od.5.587.200.
Thus to his soul the Sage began to say. .... Od.5.598.201.
Crown the chaste wishes of thy virtuous soul, ... Od.6.218.220.
Wise is thy soul, but man is born to bear: .... Od.6.228.220.
Bear, with a soul resign'd, the will of *Jove;* .... Od.6.231.221.
But hear, tho' wisdom in thy soul presides, ... Od.6.307.225.
There stops, and anxious with his soul debates, ... Od.7.108.239.
Joy touch'd my soul: My soul was joy'd in vain, ... Od.7.355.253.
Joy touch'd my soul: My soul was joy'd in vain, ... Od.7.355.253.
Far from my soul (he cry'd) the Gods efface .... Od.7.395.256.
Where thy soul rests, and labour is no more. .... Od.7.410.257.
O forward to proclaim thy soul unwise! .... Od.8.184.272.
And, youth, my gen'rous soul resents the wrong: .... Od.8.200.273.
Stung to the soul, indignant thro' the skies .... Od.8.313.281.
O more than man! thy soul the Muse inspires, ... Od.8.531.291.
My soul foreboded I should find the bow'r .... Od.9.248.317.
My soul impells me; and in act I stand .... Od.9.358.321.
Thrice drain'd, and pour'd the deluge on his soul. .... Od.9.428.323.
Joy touch'd my secret soul, and conscious heart, ... Od.9.491.326.
For *Greece,* for home, and all thy soul held dear? .... Od.10.74.343.
With drugs of force to darken all the soul: .... Od.10.273.356.
And the full soul bursts copious from his eye. .... Od.10.292.357.
She mixt the potion, fraudulent of soul; .... Od.10.377.362.
Swear, in thy soul no latent frauds remain, ... Od.10.409.364.
The bath, the feast, their fainting soul renews; .... Od.10.533.369.
And the soul saddens by the use of pain. .... Od.10.551.369.
Gave to retain th' unseparated soul: .... Od.10.585.372.
To hate the light and life my soul begun, ... Od.10.590.372.
The youngest of our band, a vulgar soul .... Od.10.661.375.
How could thy soul, by realms and seas disjoyn'd, ... Od.11.73.383.
Lux'd the neck joynt—my soul descends to hell. .... Od.11.80.385.
Strait all the mother in her soul awakes, ... Od.11.188.390.
But, when thy soul from her sweet mansion fled, ... Od.11.206.391.
While the impassive soul reluctant flies .... Od.11.267.394.
And soften'd his stern soul to tender love. .... Od.11.328.398.
And her foul soul to blackest Hell descends; .... Od.11.338.398.
To raise a bounty noble as thy soul; .... Od.11.445.406.
Thy better soul abhors the liar's part, ... Od.11.454.406.
Steal thro' the ear, and win upon the soul; .... Od.11.457.407.
Glows in our veins, and opens ev'ry soul, ... Od.11.522.409.
And calm the raging tempest of thy soul. .... Od.11.690.418.
The song instructs the soul, and charms the ear. .... Od.12.225.443.
Approach! thy soul shall into raptures rise! .... Od.12.226.443.
My soul takes wing to meet the heav'nly strain; .... Od.12.233.443.
That stubborn soul, by toil untaught to yield! .... Od.12.334.448.
My wrath is kindled, and my soul in flames. .... Od.12.461.453.
His native home deep-imag'd in his soul. .... Od.13.38.3.
Then, then be present, and my soul inspire .... Od.13.443.27.
To this *Minerva.* Be thy soul at rest; .... Od.13.486.29.
Joy touch'd the Hero's tender soul, to find .... Od.14.61.38.
My soul detests him as the gates of hell. .... Od.14.181.44.
From sad reflection let my soul repose; .... Od.14.194.45.
But works of peace my soul disdain'd to bear, ... Od.14.259.48.
He sate, and sweet refection cheer'd his soul. .... Od.14.501.60.
His guest, and send thee where thy soul desires. .... Od.14.585.65.
And safe conveys thee where thy soul desires. .... Od.15.359.86.
My secret soul in all thy sorrow shares: .... Od.15.523.95.

SOUL (CONTINUED)

My heart weeps blood, to see a soul so brave .... Od.16.95.107.
The thinking mind, my soul to vengeance fires; .... Od.16.303.120.
"I bear them hence (so *Jove* my soul inspires) .... Od.16.312.120.
Stung to the soul, abash'd, confounded stand; .... Od.16.359.123.
O prudent Princess! bid thy soul confide. .... Od.16.453.129.
My gen'rous soul abhors th' ungrateful part, ... Od.16.460.129.
Thy mandate born, my soul disdain'd to stay. .... Od.16.489.130.
Soft pity touch'd the mighty master's soul; .... Od.17.364.149.
(Not but his soul, resentful as humane, ... Od.17.436.154.
In every sorrowing soul I pour'd delight, ... Od.17.505.157.
Sedate of soul, his character sustain'd, ... Od.17.551.159.
And the soul hears him, tho' he cease to sing. .... Od.17.613.161.
The tongue speaks wisely, when the soul is wise; .... Od.18.152.173.
Stung to the soul, o'ercast with holy dread, ... Od.18.181.175.
Thy soul, *Penelope,* from heav'n inspires; .... Od.18.188.175.
I feel an impulse, tho' my soul disdains; .... Od.18.196.176.
That warmth of soul that urg'd thy younger years? .... Od.18.256.179.
That gen'rous soul with just resentment burns, ... Od.18.268.179.
I bear their outrage, tho' my soul rebell: .... Od.18.272.179.
My soul with woes, that long, ah long must last! .... Od.18.300.181.
Proceeds this boldness from a turn of soul, ... Od.18.379.186.
But idly thus thy soul prefers to live, ... Od.18.408.188.
Whence this unguarded openness of soul, ... Od.18.454.190.
Dishonest wounds, or violence of soul, ... Od.19.15.193.
And, Why so turbulent of soul? he cries; .... Od.19.87.196.
My gate, an emblem of my open soul, ... Od.19.96.197.
To thee the purpose of my soul I told, ... Od.19.111.198.
But inward on my soul let sorrow prey; .... Od.19.194.201.
Eurybates! in whose large soul alone .... Od.19.282.208.
I not the fondness of your soul reprove .... Od.19.301.209.
But your wise Lord, (in whose capacious soul .... Od.19.325.210.
Irresolute of soul, his state to shrowd .... Od.19.343.211.
Of gentle soul, to human race a friend; .... Od.19.384.212.
No ceas'd discourse (the banquet of the soul) .... Od.19.494.220.
Deep in my soul the truth shall lodge secur'd, ... Od.19.577.224.
With tender sympathy to sooth my soul, ... Od.19.635.227.
There imag'd to her soul *Ulysses* rose; .... Od.19.701.229.
Tempest of wrath his soul no longer tost; .... Od.20.30.233.
And thus in bitterness of soul divin'd. .... Od.20.140.240.
He said, but in his soul fond joys arise, ... Od.21.100.263.
Or (as my soul now dictates) shall I tell? .... Od.21.200.269.
Sigh'd from his mighty soul, and thus began. .... Od.21.263.272.
On her *Ulysses* then she fix'd her soul, ... Od.21.385.279.
Wretch that he was, of unprophetic soul! .... Od.22.13.287.
And the fierce soul to darkness div'd, and hell. .... Od.22.104.291.
O King! to mercy be thy soul inclin'd, ... Od.22.379.306.
'Till the warm sun exhales their soul away. .... Od.22.431.309.
Indecent joy, and feast thy secret soul. .... Od.22.449.309.
Soon fled the soul impure, and left behind .... Od.22.507.313.
He roar'd, and torments gave his soul to hell— .... Od.22.514.314.
To whom with warmth: My soul a lie disdains; .... Od.23.27.320.
Wise is thy soul, but errors seize the wise; .... Od.23.82.322.
Fix'd in my soul as when he sail'd to *Troy,* .... Od.23.179.329.
Pour out my soul, and dye within thy arms! .... Od.23.226.333.
Touch'd to the soul the King with rapture hears, ... Od.23.247.335.
To whom thus firm of soul: If ripe for death, ... Od.23.305.337.
And pour at once the torrent of his soul? .... Od.24.278.363.
Deep from his soul he sigh'd, and sorrowing spread .... Od.24.369.366.
Be all the rest; and set thy soul at ease. .... Od.24.416.369.
May I presume to search thy secret soul? .... Od.24.542.374.
Had not long since thy knowing soul decreed, ... Od.24.549.374.

SOUL'S

With Piety, the Soul's securest Guard, ... 1.TrSt.757.442.
'Tis what concerns my Soul's Eternal Bliss; .... 2.ChJM.114.20.
The soul's calm sun-shine, and the heart-felt joy, ... 3.EOM4.168.143.
Tho' his Soul's Bullet, and his Body Buff! .... 4.JD4.262.47.
The Combate urges, and my Soul's on fire. .... Il.6.453.348.
To seek his Spouse, his Soul's far dearer Part; .... Il.6.463.349.
Andromache! my Soul's far better Part, ... Il.6.624.357.
My Rage rekindles, and my Soul's on flame, ... Il.9.760.472.
Or yet, with many a Soul's untimely flight, ... Il.16.791.274.
Some light, and sooth her soul's eternal pain. .... Od.17.637.163.

SOULS

And draws the Aromatick Souls of Flow'rs. .... 1.W-F.244.171.
For as in *Bodies,* thus in *Souls,* we find .... 1.EOC.207.264.
Express the Discord of the Souls they bear: .... 1.TrSt.54.412.
Their kindred Souls to mutual Hate and War. .... 1.TrSt.117.415.
And bless those Souls my Conduct help'd to save! .... 2.ChWB.439.78.
And lodge such daring Souls in Little Men? .... 2.RL1.12A.145.
To their first Elements their Souls retire: .... 2.RL1.58.150.
To their first Elements the Souls retire: .... 2.RL1.58A.150.
Oh happy state! when souls each other draw, ... 2.ElAb.91.327.
Most souls, 'tis true, but peep out once an age, ... 2.Elegy.17.363.
Lo these were they, whose souls the Furies steel'd, ... 2.Elegy.41.366.
Who first taught souls enslav'd, and realms undone, ... 3.EOM3.241.116.
Such as the souls of cowards might conceive, ... 3.EOM3.259.118.
Congenial souls! whose life one Av'rice joins, ... 3.Ep3.133.104.
Is what two souls so gen'rous cannot bear; .... 4.HS2.58.59.
With equal Talents, these congenial Souls .... 4.2HE2.129.173.
Old Bavius sits, to dip poetic souls, ... 5.DunA3.16.151.
Old Bavius sits, to dip poetic souls, ... 5.DunB3.24.321.
Vain of Italian Arts, Italian Souls: .... 5.DunB4.300.373.
Of Souls the greater Part, Heav'ns common make, ... 5.DunB4.441A.383.
An hundred Souls of Turkeys in a pye; .... 5.DunB4.594.402.
By those happy Souls who dwell .... 6.11.74.33.
Born on the swelling Notes our Souls aspire, ... 6.11.128.34.
Exalted Souls, inform'd with purer Fire! .... 6.27.11.81.
Their Souls on Wings of Lightning fly .... 6.69ii.4Z1.199.
By Travel, generous Souls enlarge the Mind, ... 6.96v.11.280.
rejoyn Ye Kindred Souls, and flame on high, ... 6.109.16Z1.314.
The Souls of mighty Chiefs untimely slain; .... Il.1.4.82.
Restore our Blood, and raise the Warrior's Souls, ... Il.4.297.235.
Such Souls as burn in your exalted Breast! .... Il.4.331.236.

SOULS (CONTINUED)

Whose Coward Souls your manly Form disgrace. Il.7.110.369.
Lest Thirst of Glory your brave Souls divide, Il.7.207.374.
Their Strength he withers, and unmans their Souls. Il.8.96.402.
But feast their Souls on *Ilion's* Woes to come. Il.8.571.424.
But greater Cares sit heavy on our Souls, Il.9.299.449.
Discharge their Souls of half the Fears of War. Il.10.493.25.
Breaking their Ranks, and crushing out their Souls; Il.11.210.44.
He touch'd the Chiefs, and steel'd their manly Souls; Il.13.88.109.
High on the Wall some breath'd their Souls away. Il.13.960.151.
Arms cannot much: Tho' *Mars* our Souls incite, Il.14.69.160.
Breathe their brave Souls out, in another's War. Il.16.662.270.
The God the *Grecians* sinking Souls deprest, Il.16.889.277.
And copious Banquets, glad your weary Souls. Il.19.206.381.
Tread down whole Ranks, and crush out Hero's Souls. Il.20.582.418.
The Souls of Heroes, their great *Hector* slain? Il.22.480.475.
Still may our Souls, O gen'rous Youth! agree, Il.23.685.517.
And send their Souls before him as he flies. Il.23.898.524.
With equal souls, and sentiments the same. Od.3.158.93.
And steals with modest violence our souls, Od.8.190.272.
Still burns thy rage? and can brave souls resent Od.11.679.418.
Absolves the just, and dooms the guilty souls. Od.11.702.419.
This day adjourn your cares; exalt your souls, Od.12.33.431.
The Chief retiring. Souls, like that in thee, Od.17.537.158.
They send their eager souls with ev'ry look, Od.18.253.179.
The Suitors souls, insensate of their doom! Od.20.414.252.
What Souls and Spirits shall it send below? Od.21.162.267.
He saw their secret souls, and thus began. Od.21.211.270.
And rest at last, where souls unbodied dwell Od.24.19.348.

SOUND

Begin, the Vales shall Echo to the Sound. 1.PSp.44A.65.
'Tis he th'obstructed Paths of Sound shall clear, 1.Mes.41.116.
Led by the Sound I roam from Shade to Shade, 1.W-F.269.173.
Nations *unborn* your mighty Names shall sound, 1.EOC.193.263.
The *Sound* must seem an *Eccho* to the *Sense*. 1.EOC.365.281.
And the *World's Victor* stood subdu'd by *Sound!* 1.EOC.381.284.
Insulting waters yield a murmuring sound: 1.TrPA.158.372.
And thro' th' *Achaian* Cities send the Sound. 1.TrSt.164.417.
Let weeping *Nilus* hear the Timbrel sound. 1.TrSt.376.425.
Where the shrill Cries of frantick Matrons sound, 1.TrSt.464.429.
At once the rushing Winds with roaring Sound 1.TrSt.488.430.
With noisie Care and various Tumult sound. 1.TrSt.606.435.
Our Feasts enhanc'd with Musick's sprightly Sound? 1.TrES.32.450.
Down sinks the Warrior, with a thundring Sound, 1.TrES.127.454.
Nods, groans, and reels, 'till with a crackling Sound 1.TrES.290.460.
Nods to the Axe, till with a groaning Sound 1.TrES.290A.460.
My Limbs are active, still I'm sound at Heart, 2.ChJM.129.20.
And the shrill Trumpets mix their Silver Sound; 2.ChJM.319.29.
For so said *Paul*, and *Paul's* a sound Divine. 2.ChWB.55.59.
And sound suspected Vessels ere they buy, 2.ChWB.101A.61.
And the press'd Watch return'd a silver Sound. 2.RL1.18.146.
And Wits take Lodgings in the Sound of *Bow;* 2.RL4.118.193.
Sudden I heard a wild promiscuous Sound, 2.TemF.22.255.
Here *Orpheus* sings; Trees moving to the Sound 2.TemF.83.259.
From Pole to Pole the Winds diffuse the Sound, 2.TemF.308.279.
Strait the black Clarion sends a horrid Sound, 2.TemF.402.282.
At the dread Sound, pale Mortals stood aghast, 2.TemF.416.283.
Thus ev'ry Voice and Sound, when first they break, 2.TemF.442.284.
From yonder shrine I heard a hollow sound. 2.ElAb.308.344.
She, 'midst the light'ning's blaze, and thunder's sound, 3.EOM3.249.117.
No rafter'd roofs with dance and tabor sound, 3.Ep3.191.109.
Rend with tremendous Sound your ears asunder, 4.HS1.25.7.
Rend with tremendous Sound our ears asunder, 4.HS1.25A.7.
Turns you from sound Philosophy aside; 4.HS2.6.55.
To seem but mortal, ev'n in sound Divines. 4.HS2.80.59.
Ah sound no more thy soft alarms, 4.HOde1.5.151.
Ah sound no more your soft alarms, 4.HOde1.5A.151.
Ah sound no more the soft alarms, 4.HOde1.5B.151.
And shall we deem him Ancient, right and sound, 4.2HE1.58.199.
I can't but think 'twould sound more clever, 4.HS6.11.251.
Sound forth, my Brayers, and the welkin rend." 5.DunA2.236.129.
Long Chanc'ry-lane retentive rolls the sound, 5.DunA2.251.130.
"Dulness is sacred in a sound Divine." 5.DunA2.328.141.
Sound, sound ye Viols, be the Cat-call dumb! 5.DunB1.302.291.
Sound, sound ye Viols, be the Cat-call dumb! 5.DunB1.302.291.
Sound forth my Brayers, and the welkin rend." 5.DunB2.246.307.
High Sound, attemp'red to the vocal nose; 5.DunB2.256.308.
Long Chanc'ry-lane retentive rolls the sound, 5.DunB2.263.308.
"Dulness is sacred in a sound divine." 5.DunB2.352.314.
To sound or sink in *cano*, O or A, 5.DunB4.221.364.
And last turn'd *Air*, the Echo of a Sound! 5.DunB4.322.374.
And empty heads console with empty sound. 5.DunB4.542.395.
Sound sleep by night; study and ease 6.1.13.3.
And sound formidinous with angry clang. 6.9i.2.21.
Let the loud Trumpet sound, 6.11.7.30.
Now louder, they sound, 6.11.14A.30.
And Men grew Heroes at the Sound, 6.11.43.31.
And to her Maker's Praise confin'd the Sound. 6.11.125.34.
A hearty Stomach, and sound Lady; 6.13.13.39.
Then wake with Transport at the Sound! 6.31ii.6Z12.95.
Then wake with pleasure at the Sound! 6.31ii.6Z12A.95.
With Voice alternate aid the silver Sound. Il.1.775.124.
Along the Region runs a deaf'ning Sound; Il.2.119.133.
The groaning Banks are burst with bellowing Sound, Il.2.251.139.
He said: the Shores with loud Applauses sound, Il.2.400.145.
Now bid thy Heralds sound the loud Alarms, Il.2.516.151.
With answering Sighs return'd the plaintive Sound. Il.4.185.230.
No Sound, no Whisper, but the Chief's Commands, Il.4.487.243.
No Sound, no Whisper, but their Chief's Commands, Il.4.487A.243.
Mix'd was the Murmur, and confus'd the Sound. Il.4.497.244.
The distant Shepherd trembling hears the Sound: Il.4.520.246.
Down sinks the Warrior with a thundring Sound, Il.5.73.269.
Thro' such a Space of Air, with thund'ring Sound, Il.5.962.312.
And Earth and Heav'n rebellow to the Sound. Il.5.1057.317.
But sound ungrateful in a Warrior's Ears: Il.7.431.386.

SOUND (CONTINUED)

Thou, in thy Time, more sound Advice hast giv'n; Il.7.434.386.
Inclos'd had bled: but *Jove* with awful Sound Il.8.161.405.
To *Ajax* and *Achilles* reach'd the Sound, Il.8.272.410.
Let sacred Heralds sound the solemn Call; Il.8.644.426.
Pleas'd with the solemn Harp's harmonious Sound. Il.9.246.444.
Watch ev'ry Side, and turn to ev'ry Sound. Il.10.218.11.
Old *Nestor* first perceiv'd th' approaching Sound, Il.10.624.29.
Ev'n *Ajax* and *Achilles* heard the Sound, Il.11.11.35.
Our Feasts enhanc'd with Music's sprightly Sound? Il.12.376.95.
Down sinks the Warrior with a thund'ring Sound, Il.12.481.99.
The riven Armour sends a jarring Sound: Il.13.553.132.
Such was the Voice, and such the thund'ring Sound Il.14.175.165.
Clanks on the Field; a dead, and hollow Sound. Il.14.492.188.
Thick sound the Keels; the Storm of Arrows flies. Il.15.447.214.
And issu'd at his Breast. With thund'ring Sound Il.15.640.221.
The Faulchions ring, Shields rattle, Axes sound, Il.15.864.230.
The hollow Ships return a deeper Sound. Il.16.333.255.
Nods to the Axe, till with a groaning Sound Il.16.595.267.
Asteropæus kindled at the Sound, Il.17.258.297.
The Field re-echo'd the distressful Sound. Il.17.293.299.
With her own Shout *Minerva* swells the Sound; Il.18.257.334.
To the soft Flute, and Cittern's silver Sound: Il.18.574.350.
Alarm'd, transported, at the well-known Sound, Il.19.47.373.
The trampled Center yields a hollow Sound: Il.20.189.402.
Where the shrill Brass return'd a sharper Sound: Il.20.324.407.
And Ocean listens to the grateful Sound. Il.20.470.414.
Deep groan'd the Waters with the dying Sound; Il.21.25.422.
Deep groan the Waters with the dying Sound; Il.21.25A.422.
Scamander spoke; the Shores return'd the Sound. Il.21.230.430.
Now bursting on his Head with thund'ring Sound, Il.21.263.431.
The bubbling Waters yield a hissing Sound. Il.21.423.437.
Heav'n in loud Thunder bids the Trumpet sound; Il.21.452.439.
Ring with conflicting Pow'rs, and Heav'n returns the Sound? Il.21.509.443.
That teach the Disk to sound along the Sky. Il.23.982.528.
With plaintive Sighs, and Musick's solemn Sound: Il.24.901.573.
My bleeding bosom sickens at the sound, Od.1.439.53.
Then, with a rushing sound, th' Assembly bend Od.2.291.75.
His pond'rous hammer, and his anvil sound, Od.3.550.114.
Maids, wives, and matrons, mix a shrilling sound. Od.3.573.115.
A furious onset with the sound of war. Od.4.612.148.
And now, as near approaching as the sound Od.5.514.197.
Thro' seas retreating from the sound of war, Od.6.10.203.
Wak'd by the shrilling sound, *Ulysses* rose, Od.6.137.213.
Why cease I strait to learn what sound invades? Od.6.148.214.
The tongues of all with transport sound her praise, Od.7.92.238.
There, soft-extended, to the murm'ring sound Od.7.435.258.
His shafts *Apollo* aim'd; at once they sound, Od.11.393.403.
And clang their pinions with terrific sound; Od.11.748.423.
Nor trust thy virtue to th' enchanting sound. Od.12.64.433.
The Gods allow to hear the dangerous sound. Od.12.197.441.
That dreadful sound had chill'd the boldest breast. Od.12.267.445.
The rock rebellows with a thund'ring sound; Od.12.290.446.
Strait to my anxious thoughts the sound convey'd Od.12.320.447.
The furious tempest roars with dreadful sound: Od.12.373.449.
The south-east blust'ring with a dreadful sound; Od.12.388.450.
Crept the raw hides, and with a bellowing sound Od.12.465.453.
And the wide portal echoes to the sound. Od.15.163.76.
Lifts to the sound his ear, and rears his head. Od.17.347.148.
With speaking eyes, and voice of plaintive sound, Od.17.438.154.
With deaden'd sound, one on the threshold falls, Od.22.284.300.
Immur'd we sate, and catch'd each passing sound; Od.23.44.321.
But ere I spoke, he rose, and check'd the sound. Od.23.78.322.

SOUNDED

The Trumpet sounded, and the Temple shook, 2.TemF.277.276.

SOUNDER

Yet *some* there were, among the *sounder Few* 1.EOC.719.323.
The savage from his leafy sounder flies: Od.19.518.221.

SOUNDEST

And soundest Casuists doubt, like you and me? 3.Ep3.2.83.

SOUNDING

And with deep Murmurs fills the sounding Shores; 1.PAu.20.82.
Now close behind his sounding Steps she hears; 1.W-F.192.168.
But when loud Surges lash the sounding Shore, 1.EOC.368.282.
But when loud billows lash the sounding Shore, 1.EOC.368A.282.
Let sounding axes lop my limbs away, 1.TrFD.74.389.
And strikes with bolder Rage the sounding Strings, 1.TrSP.34.394.
Stoop with their sounding Pinions to the Fight; 1.TrES.220.458.
Two sounding Darts the *Lycian* Leader threw, 1.TrES.267.459.
Nor *Joab* the sounding Clarion cou'd inspire, 2.ChJM.323.29.
The Temple shakes, the sounding Gates unfold, 2.TemF.137.264.
And boldly sinks into the sounding Strings. 2.TemF.215.272.
Long-sounding isles, and intermingled graves, 2.ElAb.164.333.
Thither, the silver-sounding Lyres 4.HOde1.25.153.
And empty words she gave, and sounding strain, 5.DunA2.41.100.
And empty words she gave, and sounding strain, 5.DunB2.45.298.
And sweep the sounding Lyre! 6.11.4.29.
I'd call thee *Houyhnhnm*, that high sounding Name, 6.96iv.107.279.
Silent he wander'd by the sounding Main: Il.1.50.88.
But sad retiring to the sounding Shore, Il.1.455.109.
And thund'ring Footsteps shake the sounding Shore: Il.2.549.153.
The sounding Darts in Iron Tempests slew, Il.4.511.245.
And first bold *Phegeus* cast his sounding Spear, Il.5.22.266.
On his broad Shield the sounding Weapon rung, Il.5.343.283.
Of sounding Shafts, she bears him from the Fight. Il.5.394.285.
Of sounding Brass; the polish'd Axle Steel. Il.5.891.308.
The sounding Hinges ring: On either side Il.5.934.311.
And shouts, in *Stentor's* sounding Voice, aloud: Il.5.977.313.
And bear thick Battel on my sounding Shield. Il.7.292.378.
Some search the Plain, some fell the sounding Grove: Il.7.495.389.
The sounding Darts in Iron Tempests flew, Il.8.78.399.
The Steeds that startle at his sounding Arms. Il.8.382.416.

SOUNDING (CONTINUED)
The sounding Hinges ring, the Clouds divide; ....Il.8.484.420.
Of murm'ring Billows on the sounding Shore. ....Il.9.238.444.
He lends the Lash; the Steeds with sounding Feet ....Il.11.640.62.
With sounding Strokes their brazen Targets rung: ....Il.12.170.87.
Jove's Bird on sounding Pinions beat the Skies; ....Il.12.233.89.
Or bear close Battel on the sounding Shield. ....Il.13.405.125.
Or whirl the sounding Pebble from the Sling, ...Il.13.894.148.
On sounding Wings a dexter Eagle flew. ....Il.13.1039.154.
Beyond the missile Javelin's sounding Flight, ...Il.14.150.165.
And such a Clamour shakes the sounding Heav'n. ....Il.14.464.186.
He pierc'd the Centre of his sounding Shield: ....Il.15.625.220.
Thick beats the Combate on the sounding Prores. ....Il.15.843.229.
Ajax no more the sounding Storm sustain'd, ...Il.16.130.242.
The brazen Head falls sounding on the Plain. ....Il.16.147.243.
Two sounding Darts the *Lycian* Leader threw; ....Il.16.572.266.
Some, hard and heavy, shake the sounding Shields. ....Il.16.934.279.
And hear the Thunder of the sounding Steeds. ....Il.17.196.295.
Then clash their sounding Arms; the Clangors rise, ...Il.17.482.306.
He spoke, and high the sounding Jav'lin flung, ...Il.17.584.311.
And speed to Meadows on whose sounding Shores ....Il.18.667.356.
(Her golden Arrows sounding at her side) ....Il.20.97.398.
(As from a Sycamore, his sounding Steel ....Il.21.44.423.
(As on a Fig-tree Top, his sounding Steel ....Il.21.44A.423.
The opening Folds; the sounding Hinges rung. ....Il.21.628.448.
With quicker Steps the sounding Champain beat. ....Il.23.496.510.
Swift from the String the sounding Arrow flies; ....Il.23.1020.529.
And from the sounding portico they flew. ....Od.3.626.118.
Shine in her hand: Along the sounding plains ....Od.6.96.210.
Once more harmonious strike the sounding string, ...Od.8.539.291.
Thy sounding voice directs his aim again; ....Od.9.583.330.
This said, the sounding strokes his horses fire, ...Od.15.242.80.
Long as the minstrel swept the sounding wire, ...Od.17.430.153.
Dash'd from his hand the sounding goblet flies, ...Od.18.442.190.
Some wield the sounding ax; the dodder'd oaks ....Od.20.200.243.
Drop harmless, on the pavement sounding dead. ....Od.22.305.301.
The sounding portals instant they display; ....Od.22.436.309.

SOUNDS
Thro' Rocks and Caves the Name of *Delia* sounds, ...1.PAu.49.83.
Thro' Rocks and Caves the Name of Thyrsis sounds, ...1.PAu.49A.83.
Her Name alone the mournful *Eccho* sounds, ...1.PWi.42A.92.
A painted Quiver on her Shoulder sounds, ...1.W-F.179.166.
In *Sounds* and jingling *Syllables* grown old, ...1.EOC.605.308.
And in soft Sounds, *Your Grace* salutes their Ear. ....2.RL1.86.152.
And soften'd Sounds along the Waters die. ....2.RL2.50.162.
To sweeter Sounds, and temper'd *Pindar's* Fire: ....2.TemF.223.273.
Of various Tongues the mingled Sounds were heard; ....2.TemF.280.277.
But strait the direful Trump of Slander sounds, ...2.TemF.332.280.
All various Sounds from Earth, and Seas, and Skies, ...2.TemF.433.284.
Thro undulating Air the Sounds are sent, ...2.TemF.446.285.
To sounds of heav'nly harps, she dies away, ...2.ElAb.221.338.
From sounds to things, from fancy to the heart; ....3.EOM4.392.166.
Which sounds the Silver Thames along, ...4.HOde9.2.159.
High sounds, attempred to the vocal nose. ....5.DunA2.246.129.
And fill with spreading Sounds the Skies; ....6.11.15.30.
Warriors she fires with animated Sounds; ....6.11.28.30.
Warriors she fires by sprightly Sounds; ....6.11.28A.30.
What Sounds were heard, ...6.11.53.32.
With sounds seraphic ring: ....6.31ii.15.94.
With silver sounds, and sweetly tune out time. ....6.82xii.2.237.
Sounds the tough Horn, and twangs the quiv'ring String. ....Il.4.157.228.
The Peace infring'd, nor heard the Sounds of War; ....Il.4.385.239.
They sate, and listen'd to the dying Sounds. ....Il.5.48.268.
Each sounds your Praise, and War is all your own. ....Il.7.340.381.
With Horror sounds the loud *Orthian* Song: ....Il.11.14.35.
The rising Combate sounds along the Shore. ....Il.13.423.126.
And thick and heavy sounds the Storm of Blows. ....Il.16.766.273.
The Gods inspire it, and it sounds thy Death. ....Il.16.1027.283.
With shrilling Clangor sounds th' Alarm of War; ....Il.18.260.335.
And Scenes of Blood, and agonizing Sounds. ....Il.19.214.381.
Vary'd each Face; then Discord sounds Alarms, ...Il.20.65.396.
Untaught to fear or fly, he hears the Sounds ....Il.21.679.450.
Loud sounds the Axe, redoubling Strokes on Strokes; ....Il.23.146.495.
Loud sounds the Axe, rebounding Strokes on Strokes; ....Il.23.146A.495.
Of *Phorcys*, dreaded in the sounds and seas) ....Od.1.93.36.
Reflecting to the Queen the silver sounds. ....Od.1.426.53.
The pleasing sounds each latent warrior warm'd, ...Od.4.381.139.
Her ratling quiver from her shoulder sounds: ....Od.6.120.212.
What sounds are these that gather from the shores? ....Od.6.143.214.
She spoke, and sudden with tumultuous sounds ....Od.8.15.262.
To rapturous sounds, at hand *Pontonous* hung: ....Od.8.64.265.
Earth sounds my wisdom, and high heav'n my fame. ....Od.9.20.302.
His voice like thunder thro' the cavern sounds: ....Od.9.303.318.
The shade withdrew, and mutter'd empty sounds. ....Od.11.103.385.
They scream, they shriek; sad groans and dismal sounds ....Od.11.781.425.
'Till dying off, the distant sounds decay: ....Od.12.237.443.
And *Itylus* sounds warbling o'er the plains; ....Od.19.607.226.
The sounds assault *Ulysses'* wakeful ear; ....Od.20.112.238.
Loud from a saphire sky his thunder sounds: ....Od.20.128.239.
And if unusual sounds invade their ear, ...Od.21.415.280.
The voice, attun'd to instrumental sounds, ...Od.23.143.328.

SOUP
From soup to sweet-wine, and God bless the King. ....3.Ep4.162.153.

SOUPE
And drown his Lands and Manors in a Soupe. ....5.DunB4.596.402.

SOUPS
With soups unbought and sallads blest his board. ....3.Ep3.184.109.

SOUR
See SOWR.
He calls for something bitter, something sour, ...4.HS2.33.57.
Z—ds, you're as sour as *Cato Censor!* ....6.10.102.27.

SOUR (CONTINUED)
And nine sour Dogs compleat the rustic Band. ....Il.18.670.356.
Sour with debauch, a reeling tribe, they came. ....Od.3.172.94.
Touch'd at his sour retreat, thro' deepest night, ...Od.11.693.419.

SOURCE
At once the *Source,* and *End,* and *Test* of *Art.* ....1.EOC.73.247.
And stir within me ev'ry source of love. ....2.ElAb.232.339.
The source of Newton's Light, of Bacon's Sense! ....5.DunA3.216.176.
The source of Newton's Light, of Bacon's Sense! ....5.DunB3.218.331.
Mother of Arrogance, and Source of Pride! ....5.DunB4.470.386.
The source of good; thy splendor to descry, ...6.23.11.73.
Oh heav'n-born sisters! source of art! ....6.51i.9.151.
Oh source of ev'ry social tye, ...6.51ii.25.153.
Thro' thy blest Shades (La Source) I seem to rove ....6.106ii.2.307.
Thou Source of Light! whom *Tenedos* adores, ...Il.1.55.88.
And shun Contention, the sure Source of Woe; ....Il.9.335.450.
To great *Alphæus'* sacred Source we came. ....Il.11.863.74.
And *Xanthus* foaming from his fruitful Source; ....Il.12.20.82.
Gods of one Source, of one ethereal Race, ...Il.13.445.126.
Fast-flowing from its Source, as prone he lay, ...Il.13.556.133.
Where the great Parents (sacred Source of Gods!) ....Il.14.230.172.
Beheld, and thus bespoke the Source of Light. ....Il.15.247.206.
But *Jove* himself, the sacred Source of thine. ....Il.20.139.400.
He, Source of Pow'r and Might! with boundless Sway, ...Il.20.292.406.
Flows from the Source of *Axius,* Stream divine! ....Il.21.158.428.
But great *Saturnius* is the Source of mine. ....Il.21.204.429.
Next by *Scamander's* double Source they bound, ...Il.22.195.463.
The Source of Evil one, and one of Good; ....Il.24.664.565.
The wretched Source of all this Misery! ....Il.24.976.576.
The source of pow'r on earth deriv'd to Kings! ....Od.1.58.33.
Their blood devolving from the source of *Jove.* ....Od.4.34.121.
Once more the *Nile,* who from the secret source ....Od.4.643.149.
From what deep source my ceaseless sorrows flow? ....Od.4.1070.167.
O fatal voyage, source of all my woes!) ....Od.6.198.219.
Source of my life, I cry'd, from earth I fly ....Od.11.200.391.
Where graze thy herds, illustrious Source of day! ....Od.12.161.439.
To whom the thund'ring Pow'r: O source of day! ....Od.12.452.453.
Of secret grief unseals the fruitful source; ....Od.19.190.201.
By *Jove,* the source of good, supreme in pow'r! ....Od.19.347.211.
And Prince! to stop the source of future ill, ...Od.20.391.251.
The Archer's strife; the source of future woes, ...Od.24.196.358.

SOURCES
And from their Sources boil her hundred Floods. ....Il.20.80.397.

SOURNESS
Has Life no sourness, drawn so near its end? ....4.2HE2.316.187.

SOUTH
When the South glows with his Meridian Ray, ...1.TrSt.214.419.
Sacred the South, by which the Gods descend, ...1.TrUl.43.467.
But on the South a long Majestic Race ....2.TemF.109.261.
Thus flying East and West, and North and South, ...2.TemF.473.286.
What made Directors cheat in South-sea year? ....3.Ep3.119.101.
Oh blast it, South-winds! till a stench exhale, ...4.HS2.27.55.
In *South-sea* days not happier, when surmis'd ....4.HS2.133.65.
South-sea Subscriptions take who please, ...4.1HE7.65.273.
"Thence to the South extend thy gladden'd eyes; ....5.DunA3.71.156.
"Thence to the South as far extend thy eyes; ....5.DunA3.71A.156.
"Thence to the south extend thy gladden'd eyes; ....5.DunB3.79.324.
And South beheld that Master-piece of Man." ....5.DunB4.174.358.
Come, fill the South-Sea Goblet full; ....6.80.1.224.
From East and South when Winds begin to roar, ...Il.2.176.137.
And south, and north, roll mountains to the shore. ....Od.5.380.190.
And now the south, and now the north, bear sway, ...Od.5.421.192.
Oh should the fierce south-west his rage display, ...Od.12.343.448.
The south-east blust'ring with a dreadful sound; ....Od.12.388.450.
Sacred the south, by which the Gods descend, ...Od.13.134.8.

SOUTH-EAST
The south-east blust'ring with a dreadful sound; ....Od.12.388.450.

SOUTH-SEA
What made Directors cheat in South-sea year? ....3.Ep3.119.101.
In *South-sea* days not happier, when surmis'd ....4.HS2.133.65.
South-sea Subscriptions take who please, ...4.1HE7.65.273.
Come, fill the South-Sea Goblet full; ....6.80.1.224.

SOUTH-WEST
Oh should the fierce south-west his rage display, ...Od.12.343.448.

SOUTH-WINDS
Oh blast it, South-winds! till a stench exhale, ...4.HS2.27.55.

SOUTHERN
Or under Southern Skies exalt their Sails, ...1.W-F.391.189.
Which not alone the *Southern Wit* sublimes, ...1.EOC.400.286.
"But, for the Passions, Southern sure and Rowe. ....4.2HE1.86.201.
Then warp my voyage on the southern gales, ...Od.4.103.124.
Now sunk the West, and now a southern breeze ....Od.12.503.457.

SOUTHERNE
Argyle his Praise, when *Southerne* wrote, ...6.77.1.214.

SOUTHWARD
Then southward let your Bard retire, ...4.1HE7.17.269.

SOV'REIGN
His Sov'reign favours, and his Country loves; ....1.W-F.236.171.
Such, they may cry, deserve the Sov'reign State, ...1.TrES.41.451.
What Words are these, O Sov'reign of the Skies? ....1.TrES.238.458.
Pleasure the Sov'reign Bliss of Humankind: ....2.ChJM.441.36.
Ye Sov'reign Wives! give Ear, and understand; ....2.ChWB.68.59.
He prov'd a Rebel to my Sov'reign Will: ....2.ChWB.334.73.
A sov'reign being but a sov'reign good. ....3.EOM3.238.116.

SOV'REIGN (CONTINUED)
A sov'reign being but a sov'reign good. ....3.EOM3.238.116.
Such was the Sov'reign Doom, and such the Will of *Jove.* ....Il.1.8.85.
Let Kings be just, and Sov'reign Pow'r preside. ....Il.1.365.105.
And singly mad, asperse the Sov'reign Reign. ....Il.2.309.142.
But chief *Tydides* bore the Sov'reign Sway; ....Il.2.684.159.
Then suck'd the Blood, and Sov'reign Balm infus'd, ...Il.4.250.232.
All Heav'n beside reveres thy Sov'reign Sway, ...Il.5.1076.318.
This Day, averse, the Sov'reign of the Skies ....Il.8.171.406.
Who shall the Sov'reign of the Skies controul? ....Il.8.562.423.
Thro' too much Def'rence to our Sov'reign Sway, ...Il.10.140.8.
To ease a Sov'reign, and relieve a Sire. ....Il.10.193.10.
Such, they may cry, deserve the sov'reign State, ...Il.12.385.95.
And comes it ev'n from him, whose sov'reign Sway ....Il.14.104.162.
What means the haughty Sov'reign of the Skies, ...Il.15.206.204.
What Words are these, O Sov'reign of the Skies? ....Il.16.541.265.
At length the sov'reign Savage wins the Strife, ...Il.16.997.281.
Came halting forth the Sov'reign of the Fire: ....Il.18.486.345.
Stretch not henceforth, O Prince! thy sov'reign Might, ...Il.19.179.379.
And *Vulcan,* the black Sov'reign of the Fire: ....Il.20.48.396.
Where, all confus'd, she sought the Sov'reign God; ....Il.21.590.446.
(Dire Pomp of sov'reign Wretchedness!) must fall, ...Il.22.94.456.
Let the strong Sov'reign of the plumy Race ....Il.24.363.551.
Let the strong Sov'reign of the plumy Race ....Il.24.383.552.
The First of Men in sov'reign Misery. ....Il.24.629.563.
For *Polybus* her Lord, (whose sov'reign sway ....Od.4.169.128.
Temper'd with drugs of sov'reign use, t'assuage ....Od.4.303.134.
By the firm sanction of his sov'reign will, ...Od.4.327.135.
The sov'reign of the herd is doom'd to fall. ....Od.4.720.152.
Around their sov'reign wept the menial fair, ...Od.4.956.162.
Such is our sov'reign Will, and such is Fate. ....Od.5.55.174.
Then led and plac'd me on the sov'reign seat, ...Od.10.431.365.
As thus the plumy sov'reign of the air ....Od.15.194.78.
When thus the Sov'reign from her chair of state: ....Od.19.124.198.
Phedon the fact affirm'd, whose sov'reign sway ....Od.19.329.210.
The sov'reign step a beauteous train attends: ....Od.19.700.229.

SOV'REIGN'S
Trembling they stood before their Sov'reign's Look; ....Il.8.37.397.
Their Sov'reign's Sorrows in their own exprest. ....Il.19.8.371.
Her keen reproach had reach'd the Sov'reign's ear; ....Od.19.109.197.

SOV'REIGNS
And when three Sov'reigns dy'd, could scarce be vext, ...4.EpS1.107.306.

SOVERAIN'S
And There Triumphant Sing Thy Soverain's Praise. ....6.147ix.6.392.

SOVEREIGN
Each wou'd the sweets of Sovereign Rule devour, ...1.TrSt.182.418.
That Sovereign Goodness dwells in *Him* alone ....2.ChJM.680.47.
He led the Goddess to the sovereign seat, ...Od.1.171.40.
Attests th' all-seeing Sovereign of the skies. ....Od.2.425.81.
The sovereign seat then *Jove*-born Helen *press'd,* ....Od.4.183.128.
Argos the seat of sovereign rule I chose; ....Od.4.235.130.
Our sovereign seat a lewd usurping race ....Od.4.429.140.
Thus while he spoke, the sovereign plant he drew, ...Od.10.361.361.
No longer durst sustain the sovereign look. ....Od.18.390.186.
The sovereign seat with graceful air she press'd; ....Od.19.72.196.
Your sovereign Will my duty bids obey. ....Od.19.195.201.
Of sovereign state with faded splendor shine. ....Od.20.244.244.
Now press the sovereign dame with warm desire ....Od.20.397.251.

SOVEREIGN'S
Perhaps, yet vibrates on his SOVEREIGN's Ear— ....4.Arbu.357.122.
Their sovereign's step a virgin train attends: ....Od.1.428.53.

SOVEREIGNS
On Sovereigns ruin'd, or on Friends betray'd, ...2.TemF.409.283.

SOW
In *Pharian* Fields to sow the Golden Grain; ....1.TrSt.860.446.
'Tis thus we riot, while who sow it, starve. ....3.Ep3.24.88.
Untaught to plant, to turn the glebe and sow, ...Od.9.121.310.

SOW'D
And the same Hand that sow'd, shall reap the Field. ....1.Mes.66.118.
How with the Serpent's Teeth he sow'd the Soil, ...1.TrSt.9.409.
Sow'd in a Sack, and plung'd into a Well: ....2.ChJM.588.43.

SOW'R
Not yet purg'd off, of Spleen and sow'r Disdain, ...1.EOC.527.297.
A Quaker? sly: A Presbyterian? sow'r: ....3.Ep1.108.23.
Look sow'r, and hum a tune—as you may now. ....6.45.50.126.
Look sow'r, and hum a song—as you may now. ....6.45.50A.126.
And Streams of Sweat down their sow'r Foreheads flow. ....Il.13.884.147.
Sow'r he departs, and quits th' untasted Prey. ....Il.17.748.317.
Sullen and sow'r with discontented mien ....Od.11.329.398.

SOW'RLY
Now gayly Mad, now sow'rly Splenatick, ...2.ChWB.90.61.
Then sow'rly slow th' indignant Beast retires. ....Il.11.679.65.
Thus sow'rly waild' he, sputt'ring Dirt and Gore; ....Il.23.921.525.
And sow'rly smiling, this reply returns. ....Od.17.544.159.
Behind him sow'rly stalk'd. Without delay ....Od.20.183.242.

SOWN
There lay the sword-knot *Sylvia's* Hands had sown, ...2.RL2.39Z1.161.
The genuine seeds of Poesy are sown; ....Od.22.384.307.

SOWR
See SOUR.
As Heav'n's blest beam turns vinegar more sowr; ....3.EOM2.148.72.

SOWRER
And answ'ring Gin-shops sowrer sighs return! ....5.DunA3.140.162.
And answ'ring gin-shops sowrer sighs return. ....5.DunB3.148.327.

SOWS
'Tis thus we eat the bread another sows: ....3.Ep3.22.85.

SOWSE
But sowse the Cabbidge with a bounteous heart. ....4.HS2.60.59.

SOWSING
Then stoops, and sowsing on the quiv'ring Hare, ...Il.17.765.318.

SOWZE
Spread thy broad wing, and sowze on all the Kind. ....4.EpS2.15.314.

SOWZING
The sowzing Prelate, or the sweating Peer, ...4.1740.70.336.

SOY
"Your only wearing is your *Padua-soy."* .... 4.JD4.113.35.

SOYL
The soyl that nurs'd us, and that gave us breath: ....Od.10.499.367.

SPACE
What tho' the Stars contract their Heav'nly Space, ...1.TrSt.35.411.
And all th'extended Space of Earth, and Air, and Sea. ....1.TrSt.279.421.
Then pouring after, thro' the gaping Space ....1.TrES.205.457.
Urg'd by fierce Drivers thro' the dusty Space, ...1.TrUl.8.465.
The rugged Soil allows no level Space ....1.TrUl.122.470.
How short a Space our Worldly Joys endure? ....2.ChJM.476.38.
His time a moment, and a point his space. ....3.EOM1.72.22.
Enough, that Virtue fill'd the space between; ....3.Ep3.289.116.
Volumes, whose size the space exactly fill'd; ....5.DunA1.117.77.
In that wide space the Goddess took her stand, ...5.DunA2.23A.99.
Now to pure Space lifts her extatic state, ...5.DunB4.33.343.
Or bind in Matter, or diffuse in Space. ....5.DunB4.476.388.
Four acres was th' allotted space of ground, ...6.35.3.103.
To Thee, whose Temple is all Space, ...6.50.49.148.
Such, such a man extends his life's short space, ...6.55.8.166.
Has truly liv'd the space of seventy years, ...6.55.1Z2.167.
So short a Space the Light of Heav'n to view! ....Il.1.544.114.
So short a Space, and fill'd with Sorrow too! ....Il.1.545.114.
Then let a mid-way Space our Hosts divide, ...Il.3.99.194.
With Lances fix'd, and close the Space between. ....Il.3.160.198.
The middle Space suspected Troops supply, ...Il.4.344.237.
Thro' such a Space of Air, with thund'ring Sound, ...Il.5.962.312.
The *Lycians* grant a chosen Space of Ground, ...Il.6.239.337.
Some Space at least permit the War to breathe, ...Il.7.398.383.
From Space to Space be ample Gates around, ...Il.7.408.385.
From Space to Space be ample Gates around, ...Il.7.408.385.
From Space to Space were ample Gates around, ...Il.7.522.390.
From Space to Space were ample Gates around, ...Il.7.522.390.
But in his inner Tent, an ampler Space, ...Il.9.779.472.
Yet let him pass, and win a little Space; ....Il.10.409.21.
So distant they, and such the Space between, ...Il.10.419.22.
An empty Space where late the Coursers stood, ...Il.10.611.29.
Shot thro' the Battel in a Moment's Space, ...Il.11.363.50.
No Space for Combat in yon' narrow Bounds. ....Il.12.74.84.
Then pouring after thro' the gaping Space, ...Il.12.559.102.
Æneas heard, and for a Space resign'd ....Il.13.590.134.
Joins Hill to Dale, and measures Space with Space: ....Il.15.89.200.
Joins Hill to Dale, and measures Space with Space: ....Il.15.89.200.
O'er the dread Fosse (a late-impervious Space) ....Il.15.410.213.
Stand to your Arms, maintain this arduous Space! ....Il.15.495.216.
Then cleans'd his Hands; and fixing for a Space ....Il.16.280.250.
Between the Space where silver *Simois* flows, ...Il.16.480.261.
So short a space the Light of Heav'n to view, ...Il.18.79.327.
Yet, my *Patroclus!* yet a space I stay, ...Il.18.389.340.
Amid both Hosts (a dreadful Space) appear ....Il.20.192.402.
And for a Moment's space, suspend the Day: ....Il.22.322.469.
Yet a short space the great Avenger stay'd, ...Il.22.419.472.
Such, and so narrow now the Space between ....Il.23.603.513.
Their Tops connected, but at wider space ....Il.23.828.522.
Leonteus next a little space surpast, ...Il.23.997.529.
Tow'r on the right of yon' æthereal Space. ....Il.24.364.551.
Tow'r on the right of yon' æthereal Space. ....Il.24.384.552.
Th' aerial space, and mounts the winged gales: ....Od.1.127.38.
Then slowly rising, o'er the sandy space ....Od.3.496.111.
No *Greek* an equal space had e'er possest ....Od.4.231.130.
From space to space, and nail'd the planks along; ....Od.5.322.187.
From space to space, and nail'd the planks along; ....Od.5.322.187.
And secret moves along the crowded space, ...Od.7.51.236.
Fair thrones within from space to space were rais'd, ...Od.7.124.240.
Fair thrones within from space to space were rais'd, ...Od.7.124.240.
Four acres was th' allotted space of ground, ...Od.7.144.243.
Before the rest, what space the hinds allow ....Od.8.129.269.
To glory give the space thou hast to stay; ....Od.8.164.271.
High rais'd of stone; a shaded space around: ....Od.10.241.352.
Mov'd at the sight, I for a space resign'd ....Od.11.491.408.
Urg'd by fierce drivers thro' the dusty space, ...Od.13.99.6.
The rugged soil allows no level space ....Od.13.289.19.
Frequent and thick. Within the space, were rear'd ....Od.14.17.35.
A few hours space permit me here to stay; ....Od.17.28.133.
Wait for a space without, but wait not long; ....Od.17.328.147.
Let for a space the pensive Queen attend, ...Od.17.650.164.
From space to space the torch wide-beaming burns, ...Od.18.357.184.
From space to space the torch wide-beaming burns, ...Od.18.357.184.
Twelve days, while *Boreas* vex'd th' aerial space, ...Od.19.230.204.
Beneath the feastful bow'r. A narrow space ....Od.19.376.212.
Six beams, oppos'd to six in equal space: ....Od.19.671.228.
Tost thro' the void, illimitable space: ....Od.20.75.236.
And bore it, regular from space to space: ....Od.23.202.333.
And bore it, regular from space to space: ....Od.23.202.333.
In the same urn a sep'rate space contains ....Od.24.99.353.

SPACE (CONTINUED)
Yet a short space, your rival suit suspend, Od.24.156.355.

SPACIOUS
See SPATIOUS.
But see the Man who spacious Regions gave 1.W-F.79.157.
But see the Man whose spacious Regions gave 1.W-F.79A.157.
Let old *Arcadia* boast her spacious Plain, 1.W-F.159A.164.
And *Cadmus* searching round the spacious Sea? 1.TrSt.8.409.
Far from the Town, a spacious Port appears, 1.TrUl.25.466.
His spacious Garden, made to yield to none, 2.ChJM.448.36.
But shoud'st thou search the spacious World around, 2.ChJM.637.45.
Full in the Passage of each spacious Gate 2.TemF.145.265.
Not less in Number were the spacious Doors, 2.TemF.424.283.
There in his seat two spacious Vents appear, 5.DunA2.81.108.
There in his seat two spacious vents appear, 5.DunB2.85.299.
Close to the gates a spacious garden lies, 6.35.1.103.
My spacious palm in Stature scarce a Span 6.96ii.30Z41.272.
"Doors, Windows, Chimnies, and the spacious Rooms, 6.96ii.55.273.
"My spacious Palm? Of Stature scarce a Span, 6.96ii.63.273.
Who plow the spacious *Orchomenian* Plain. Il.2.611.156.
From *Pthia's* spacious Vales, and *Hella*, blest Il.2.831.164.
His Fame for Wisdom fills the spacious Earth. Il.3.264.204.
The raging Warrior to the spacious Skies Il.3.449.213.
There veil'd in spacious Coverlets they stand; Il.5.246.279.
Then hear a Tale that fills the spacious Earth. Il.6.188.335.
In Search of Prey she wings the spacious Air, Il.9.426.453.
My Travels thence thro' spacious *Greece* extend; Il.9.598.464.
Great *Hector*, cover'd with his spacious Shield, Il.11.81.38.
He said, and forceful pierc'd his spacious Shield; Il.11.546.58.
Beneath the spacious Targe (a blazing Round, Il.13.513.131.
O'er spacious *Crete*, and her bold Sons I reign, Il.13.568.133.
Swift thro' the spacious Plain he sent a Look; Il.17.213.295.
And thick Bull-hides the Spacious Concave lin'd. Il.17.561.310.
Has *Troy* propos'd some spacious Tract of Land? Il.20.223.403.
(A Tale resounded thro' the spacious Earth) Il.20.253.404.
Three thousand Mares his spacious Pastures bred, Il.20.262.405.
To distant *Sparta* and the spacious waste Od.1.118.37.
Others apart, the spacious hall prepare, Od.1.146.40.
The spacious loom, and mix'd the various thread: Od.2.104.66.
Full in the openings of the spacious main Od.2.440.82.
The spacious sheet, and stretch it to the wind. Od.2.465.83.
Close ambush'd nigh the spacious hall he plac'd. Od.4.710.152.
The lucid wave a spacious bason fills. Od.6.102.210.
The spacious basons arching rocks enclose, Od.6.315.226.
Close to the gates a spacious Garden lies, Od.7.142.242.
With instant care they mark a spacious round, Od.8.297.279.
Commands her train a spacious vase to bring, Od.8.470.288.
The spacious vase with ample streams suffice, Od.8.471.288.
Lives there a man beneath the spacious skies, Od.8.523.290.
Rear but the mast, the spacious sail display, Od.10.600.372.
The spacious sheet, and stretch it to the wind: Od.11.4.379.
Around, a spacious arch of waves he throws, Od.11.291.396.
With speed the bark we climb: the spacious sails Od.12.471.454.
Far from the town a spacious port appears, Od.13.116.7.
Thro' spacious *Argos*, and the Realms of *Greece*, Od.15.92.73.
The spacious sheet, and stretch it to the wind. Od.15.313.84.
In spacious *Crete* he drew his natal air: Od.16.62.105.
Who o'er *Dulichium* stretch'd his spacious reign, Od.16.410.126.
Athwart the spacious square each tries his art Od.17.192.140.
Thick swarms the spacious hall with howling ghosts, Od.20.427.254.
The spacious valve, with art inwrought, conjoins; Od.23.197.333.
A spacious loom, and mix'd the various thread; Od.24.153.355.

SPADE
Falls undistinguish'd by the Victor *Spade!* 2.RL3.64.172.
And marks the future Current with his Spade, Il.21.294.433.
And marks their future Current with his Spade, Il.21.294A.433.

SPADES
Let Spades be Trumps! she said, and Trumps they were. 2.RL3.46.172.
The hoary Majesty of *Spades* appears; 2.RL3.56.172.
Th' Imperial Consort of the Crown of *Spades*. 2.RL3.68.173.

SPADILLIO
Spadillio first, unconquerable Lord! 2.RL3.49.172.

SPADO
In thy defence I'll draw *Toledo's* Spado. 6.48iv.10.136.

SPAIN
"Sir, Spain has sent a thousand jars of oil; 3.Ep3.44.89.
Almost as quickly, as he conquer'd *Spain*. 4.HS1.132.19.
That *Spain* robs on, and *Dunkirk's* still a Port. 4.JD4.165.39.
See, the fierce Visigoths on Spain and Gaul. 5.DunA3.86.157.
See the fierce Visigoths on Spain and Gaul! 5.DunB3.94.324.
Thy Politicks should ope the Eyes of *Spain*, 6.48iv.7.136.
Theirs are the Rules of *France*, the Plots of *Spain:* 6.60.12.178.

SPAKE
He spake; and speaking, leaps from off the Car; 1.TrES.217A.457.
So spake the Goddess, and the Prospect clear'd, 1.TrUl.234.473.
Thus then to Man the voice of Nature spake— 3.EOM3.171.110.
Words, that wise *Bacon*, or brave *Raleigh* spake; 4.2HE2.168.177.
Such as wise *Bacon*, or brave *Raleigh* spake; 4.2HE2.168A.177.
Te-he cry'd Ladies; Clerke nought spake: 6.14i.21.42.
Then *Jove* thus spake: With Care and Pain 6.30.55.88.
Then *Jove* spake thus with Care and Pain 6.30.55A.88.
Thus have I spoke, and what I spake is Fate. Il.8.491.420.
Let Worth determine here. The Monarch spake, Il.10.281.14.
Then first spake *Merion:* Shall we join the Right, Il.13.396.125.
He spake, and smil'd severe, for well he knew Il.14.557.190.
He spake; and speaking, leaps from off the Car; Il.16.520.263.
Come, and receive thy Fate! He spake no more. Il.20.498.415.
Thus while he spake, the *Trojan* pale with Fears Il.21.74.424.
Thine is the Glory doom'd. Thus spake the Gods; Il.21.344.435.

SPAKE (CONTINUED)
So spake the mournful Dame: Her Matrons hear, Il.22.662.484.
So spake he, threat'ning: But the Gods made vain Il.23.226.498.
Thus spake the Youth, nor did his Words offend; Il.23.635.515.
Proud of the Gift, thus spake the Full of Days: Il.23.751.520.
She spake, and veil'd her Head in sable Shade, Il.24.122.540.
He spake, and to her hand preferr'd the bowl: Od.3.64.89.
So spake *Jove's* daughter, the celestial maid. Od.3.431.108.
So spake the Goddess, and the prospect clear'd, Od.13.401.26.
She spake, then touch'd him with her pow'rful wand: Od.13.496.29.

SPAN
Shall *Jove*, for one, extend the narrow Span, 1.TrES.240.458.
Yet not to Earth's contracted Span, 6.50.21.147.
But if to Earth's contracted Span, 6.50.21A.147.
But not to Earth's contracted Span, 6.50.21B.147.
My spacious palm in Stature scarce a Span 6.96ii.30Z41.272.
"My spacious Palm? Of Stature scarce a Span, 6.96ii.63.273.
Great *Jove* in Justice should this Span adorn: Il.1.463.110.
There ends thy narrow Span assign'd by Fate, Il.11.566.59.
Shall *Jove*, for one, extend the narrow Span, Il.16.543.265.

SPANGLED
Yon spangled Arch glows with the starry Train, 1.TrSt.584.434.
Of all the Gods who tread the spangled Skies, Il.5.1096.319.
From the vast Concave of the spangled Sky, Il.15.24.195.

SPANGLES
When falling Dews with Spangles deck'd the Glade, 1.PAu.99.87.
See round the Poles where keener spangles shine, 5.DunA3.61.155.
See, round the Poles where keener spangles shine, 5.DunB3.69.323.

SPANIARD
And own, the *Spaniard* did a *waggish thing*, 4.EpS1.17.298.
Spaniard or *French* came to her; 6.14v(b).9.49.
The *Spaniard* hides his Ponyard in his Cloke, 6.48iv.1.135.
Spaniard and *French* abuse to the World's End, 6.60.21.178.

SPANIEL
Before his Lord the ready Spaniel bounds, 1.W-F.99.160.
Who, tho' no Spaniel, am a Friend. 6.135.2.366.

SPANIELS
So well-bred Spaniels civilly delight 4.Arbu.313.118.
And like sure Spaniels, at first Scent lie down. 6.82vi.6.232.

SPANISH
And for plain *Spanish* quit *Brasil;* 6.10.44.25.
But ev'n as Coughs thy *Spanish* Liquorish heals, 6.48iv.3.135.
Thy Works in *Spanish* shou'd have been translated, 6.48iv.6.136.
With *Spanish* Wool he dy'd his Cheek, 6.79.29.218.

SPAR'D
Whom ev'n the *Saxon* spar'd, and bloody *Dane*, 1.W-F.77.157.
She scratched, bit, and spar'd ne Lace ne Band, 6.14ii.39.44.
She scratched, bit, and spar'd nor Lace and Band, 6.14ii.39A.44.
He spar'd but one to bear the dreadful Tale. Il.4.449.241.
And curs'd the treach'rous Lance that spar'd a Foe; Il.13.222.116.
But spar'd a while the destin'd *Trojan* Tow'rs: Il.13.441.126.
Well was the Crime, and well the Vengeance spar'd; Il.15.256.207.
The glorious Gift; and, for *Lycaon* spar'd, Il.23.872.524.
For thy stern Father never spar'd a Foe: Il.24.930.575.
Phemius alone the hand of vengeance spar'd, Od.22.367.305.

SPARAGRASS
A curious *Fowl* and *Sparagrass* I chose, 6.96iv.51.277.

SPARE
Pulpits their *Sacred Satire* learn'd to spare, 1.EOC.550.302.
But what so pure, which envious Tongues will spare? 2.ChJM.43.17.
What Time wou'd spare, from Steel receives its date, 2.RL3.171.182.
My hands shall rend what ev'n thy own did spare. 2.RL4.168A.197.
Tears still are mine, and those I need not spare, 2.ElAb.45.322.
Smit with her varying plumage, spare the dove? 3.EOM3.54.97.
And Man's prerogative to rule, but spare. 3.EOM3.160.109.
But spare your censure; Silia does not drink. 3.Ep2.34.52.
This year a Reservoir, to keep and spare, 3.Ep3.175.107.
At such a feast old vinegar to spare, 4.HS2.57.59.
Hear this! and spare his Family, *James More!* 4.Arbu.385.126.
Ah spare me, Venus! let me, let me rest! 4.HOde1.2.151.
O spare me, Venus! let me, let me rest 4.HOde1.2A.151.
Spare me, ah Spare! no more the man 4.HOde1.3A.151.
Spare me, ah Spare! no more the man 4.HOde1.3A.151.
Their own strict Judges, not a word they spare 4.2HE2.159.175.
I, who at some times spend, at others spare, 4.2HE2.290.185.
Sir, you may spare your Application 4.1HE7.59.273.
But let all Satire in all Changes spare 4.EpS1.91.305.
Spare then the Person, and expose the Vice. 4.EpS2.12.314.
Admit your Law to spare the Knight requires; 4.EpS2.30.314.
Sure, if I spare the Minister, no rules 4.EpS2.146.321.
Heav'n had decreed to spare the Grubstreet-state. 5.DunA1.184.85.
This incense bribes the god to spare; 6.4v.2.11.
That heav'n, the threaten'd world to spare, 6.5.15.12.
But spare old *England*, lest you hurt a Friend. 6.60.22.178.
Ah spare my Slumbers, gently tread the Cave! 6.87.3.248.
No, none of these—Heav'n spare his Life! 6.101.33.291.
Yet this, like their old one, for nothing will spare, 6.122.19.342.
The Plague destroying whom the Sword would spare, Il.1.81.90.
The Priest may pardon, and the God may spare. Il.1.126.93.
But spare the Weakness of my feeble Age: Il.3.381.211.
Shall Heav'n by Peace the bleeding Kingdoms spare, Il.4.21.222.
If Man, destroy; if God, entreat to spare. Il.5.229.278.
Oh spare my Youth, and for the Life I owe Il.6.57.326.
Our Wives, our Infants, and our City spare, Il.6.118.330.
Let Chiefs abstain, and spare the sacred Juice Il.6.332.342.
Our Wives, our Infants, and our City spare, Il.6.345.343.

SPARE (CONTINUED)
Our selves, our Infants, and our City spare! .....Il.6.385.345.
Thy just Rebukes, yet learn to spare them now. .....Il.10.137.8.
O spare my Youth, and for the Breath I owe, ...Il.10.449.23.
Oh spare our Youth, and for the Life we owe, ...Il.11.171.43.
Have forc'd the Pow'rs to spare a sinking State, ...Il.17.382.302.
Fate claim'd *Achilles,* but might spare his Friend. .....Il.19.350.386.
Good as he is, to immolate or spare .....Il.20.359.410.
To spare a Form, an Age so like thy own! .....Il.20.540.417.
And spare thy self, thy Father, spare us all! .....Il.22.77.456.
And spare thy self, thy Father, spare us all! .....Il.22.77.456.
Not those who gave me Breath shou'd bid me spare, ...Il.22.435.473.
Fierce as he is, *Achilles* self shall spare .....Il.24.191.544.
Fierce as he is, *Achilles'* self shall spare .....Il.24.221.546.
Alas! my Lord! he knows not how to spare, ...Il.24.251.547.
To spare thy Age; and offer all in vain! .....Il.24.857.572.
And grief destroy what time a while would spare. .....Od.2.423.81.
Heav'n bad the deep to spare! but heav'n my foe .....Od.6.207.220.
Destroys perhaps the strength that time wou'd spare: .....Od.8.150.271.
If home thou send us, and vouchsafe to spare. .....Od.9.413.323.
O King belov'd of *Jove!* thy servant spare, ...Od.10.315.359.
Receive the suppliant! spare my destin'd blood! .....Od.15.303.83.
The lewd to death devote, the virtuous spare. .....Od.19.582.224.
Since cold in death th' offender lies; oh spare .....Od.22.66.290.
Oh spare an Augur's consecrated head, ...Od.22.355.304.
And spare the Poet's ever-gentle kind. .....Od.22.380.306.
Medon the herald too our arms may spare, ...Od.22.397.307.
But age is sacred, and we spare thy age. .....Od.23.26.320.
"From mutual slaughter: *Peace* descends to spare." .....Od.24.615.377.

SPARES
My hands shall rend what ev'n thy Rapine spares: .....2.RL4.168.197.
Pluto, the grizly God who never spares, ...Il.9.209.442.
Spares only to inflict some mightier woe! .....Od.6.208.220.

SPARETH
That never spareth none. .....6.82viii.4.233.

SPARING
Yet to his Guest tho' no way sparing, ...4.HS6.169.261.
The weary Wood-man spreads his sparing Meal, ...Il.11.120.41.

SPARK
Oh may some Spark of *your* Cœlestial Fire .....1.EOC.195.263.
In pure good Will I took this jovial Spark, ...2.ChWB.263.69.
Safe from the treach'rous Friend, the daring Spark, ...2.RL1.73.151.
Safe from the treach'rous Friend, and daring Spark, ...2.RL1.73A.151.
So from a Spark, that kindled first by Chance, ...2.TemF.475.286.
Papillia, wedded to her am'rous spark .....3.Ep2.37A.53.
Attracts each light gay meteor of a Spark, ...3.Ep2.22.50.
Papillia, wedded to her doating spark, ...3.Ep2.37.53.
A Spark too fickle, or a Spouse too kind. .....3.Ep2.94.57.
A grain of Courage, or a spark of Spirit, ...4.2HE2.227.181.
If honest S*z take scandal at a spark, ...4.1HE1.112.287.
Nor *human* Spark is left, nor Glimpse *divine!* .....5.DunB4.652.409.
Vital spark of heav'nly flame! .....6.31ii.1.94.
And hear a spark, yet think no danger nigh; .....6.45.4.124.

SPARKLE
Blaze on the Brims, and sparkle in the Wine— .....1.TrSt.209.419.
See the last sparkle languish in my eye! .....2.ElAb.332.346.
Glow in thy heart, and sparkle in thy face. .....6.86.14A.245.
Known by the Flames that sparkle from her Eyes. .....Il.1.268.99.
Let the Steel sparkle, and the Jav'lin fly: .....Il.22.310.469.
The bowl shall sparkle, and the banquet rise; .....Od.10.346.360.

SPARKLED
Known by the Flames that sparkled from her Eyes. .....Il.1.268A.99.
Fair *Venus'* Neck, her Eyes that sparkled Fire, ...Il.3.489.215.
The Point broke short, and sparkled in the Sand. .....Il.13.218.116.
The gilded Horsehair sparkled in the Sun, ...Il.22.396.472.
While kindling Anger sparkled in his Eyes) .....Il.24.706.566.
(Green as it was) and sparkled fiery red. .....Od.9.450.324.

SPARKLES
From private Sparkles raise the gen'ral Flame, ...3.EOM3.138Z1.106.
And shakes the Sparkles from its blazing Hair: .....Il.4.106.225.
While streamy Sparkles, restless as he flies, ...Il.11.87.38.
In streamy Sparkles, kindling all the Skies, ...Il.13.321.120.
His Eyes flash Sparkles, his stunn'd Senses reel .....Il.16.957.280.

SPARKLING
See Heav'n its sparkling Portals wide display, ...1.Mes.97.121.
Now his *fierce Eyes* with *sparkling Fury* glow; .....1.EOC.378.283.
Nor on my Hand the sparkling Diamonds glow, ...1.TrSP.82.397.
To fill the Goblet high with sparkling Wine, ...1.TrSt.634.436.
On her white Breast a sparkling *Cross* she wore, ...2.RL2.7.159.
With that, he lifted thrice the sparkling brand, ...5.DunA1.203.87.
Their Wit still sparkling and their Flames still warm. .....6.19.72.64.
And pointed Crystals break the sparkling Rill, ...6.142.4.382.
And polished Crystals break the sparkling Rill, ...6.142.4A.382.
Unpolish'd Crystals break the sparkling Rill, ...6.142.4B.382.
And painted Crystals break the sparkling Rill, ...6.142.4C.382.
Whilst pointed Crystals break the sparkling Rill, ...6.142.4D.382.
The double Bowl with sparkling *Nectar* crown'd, ...Il.1.753.123.
With Indignation sparkling in his Eyes, ...Il.2.304.142.
In thirty Sail the sparkling Waves divide, ...Il.2.888.166.
Trembled the sparkling Plumes, and the loose Glories shed .....Il.19.415.389.
Such quick regards his sparkling eyes bestow; .....Od.4.201.129.
Rage sparkling in his eyes, and burning in his breast. .....Od.4.887.159.
Indulge the taste, and drein the sparkling bowls: .....Od.12.34.431.

SPARKS
These Sparks with aukward Vanity display .....1.EOC.329.275.
Where yet thin Fumes from dying Sparks arise, ...1.TrSt.600.435.
With Sparks, that seem'd to set the World on fire. .....2.TemF.415.283.

SPARKS (CONTINUED)
Heav'ns twinkling Sparks draw light, and point their horns. .....5.DunB2.12.296.
Heav'ns Starry Sparks draw light, and point their horns. .....5.DunB2.12A.296.

SPARROW
A hero perish, or a sparrow fall, ...3.EOM1.88.25.
And envies ev'ry sparrow that he sees. .....3.Ep1.233.35.
Her Squirrel missing, or her Sparrow flown. .....6.96ii.4.270.
Her Squirrel missing, or the sparrow flown. .....6.96ii.4A.270.

SPARTA
By *Sparta* slain! for ever now suppress .....Il.17.85.291.
And in his well-known Voice to *Sparta* calls. .....Il.17.625.312.
To distant *Sparta* and the spacious waste .....Od.1.118.37.
The realms of *Pyle* and *Sparta* to explore, ...Od.2.243.73.
To *Pyle* or *Sparta* to demand supplies, ...Od.2.368.78.
Go then; to *Sparta* take the watry way, ...Od.3.413.106.
Let thy strong coursers swift to *Sparta* bear; .....Od.3.471.110.
And now proud *Sparta* with their wheels resounds, ...Od.4.1.119.
Sparta, whose walls a range of hills surrounds: .....Od.4.2.119.
Is *Sparta* blest, and these desiring eyes .....Od.4.225.130.
Be *Sparta* honour'd with his royal guest, ...Od.4.802.156.
To sacred *Pylos* and to *Sparta* came. .....Od.5.29.172.
To *Sparta,* still with female beauty gay: .....Od.13.476.29.
For know, to *Sparta* thy lov'd offspring came, ...Od.13.477.29.
To *Sparta* flies, *Telemachus* her care. .....Od.13.511.30.

SPARTA'S
Paris alone and *Sparta's* King advance, ...Il.3.179.199.
Paris thy Son, and *Sparta's* King advance, ...Il.3.322.208.
With *Sparta's* King to meet in single Fray: .....Il.3.538.217.
Not thus I lov'd thee, when from *Sparta's* Shore .....Il.3.551.217.
Let *Sparta's* Treasures be this Hour restor'd, ...Il.7.422.385.
To *Sparta's* Queen of old the radiant vase .....Od.4.167.128.
In rich *Orchomenos,* or *Sparta's* court? .....Od.11.566.411.
This gift, long since when *Sparta's* shores he trod, ...Od.21.17.259.

SPARTAN
And level with the Dust the *Spartan* Wall: .....1.TrSt.369.425.
Nor envy'd *Paris* with the *Spartan* Bride: .....2.ChJM.348.31.
With *Agis,* not the last of *Spartan* Names: .....2.TemF.175.269.
"No Lessons now are taught the *Spartan* way: .....4.JD4.93.33.
You met th' Approaches of the *Spartan* Queen, ...Il.3.70.192.
By *Paris* there the *Spartan* King be fought, ...Il.3.101.194.
He dares the *Spartan* King to single Fight; .....Il.3.128.196.
Each Army stood: The *Spartan* Chief reply'd. .....Il.3.134.196.
These, when the *Spartan* Queen approach'd the Tow'r, ...Il.3.203.201.
Erect, the *Spartan* most engag'd our View, ...Il.3.273.205.
With *Menelaus,* on the *Spartan* Shore. .....Il.3.298.207.
The *Spartan* Hero sheaths his Limbs in Arms. .....Il.3.422.212.
Be therefore now the *Spartan* Wealth restor'd, ...Il.3.571.219.
Mycenæ, Argos, and the *Spartan* Wall; .....Il.4.77.224.
Nor less the *Spartan* fear'd, before he found .....Il.4.180.230.
Possess his Soul, which thus the *Spartan* chears: .....Il.4.221.231.
His speedy Succour to the *Spartan* King; .....Il.4.231.232.
And fall or conquer by the *Spartan* King. .....Il.5.700.301.
Beneath the *Spartan* Spear, a living Prize. .....Il.6.46.325.
And there the vengeful *Spartan* fires his Train. .....Il.6.555.354.
The graceful Husband of the *Spartan* Bride. .....Il.7.429.385.
Their proffer'd Wealth, nor ev'n the *Spartan* Dame. .....Il.7.477.388.
Joyful they met; the *Spartan* thus begun: .....Il.10.41.4.
To whom the *Spartan:* These thy Orders born, ...Il.10.69.5.
To rouse the *Spartan* I my self decree; .....Il.10.128.7.
The *Spartan* wish'd the second Place to gain, ...Il.10.273.14.
Dauntless he rushes where the *Spartan* Lord .....Il.13.763.141.
Against the Target of the *Spartan* King; .....Il.13.810.144.
Meantime their Fight the *Spartan* King survey'd, ...Il.15.636.221.
The fiery *Spartan* first, with loud Applause, ...Il.15.680.222.
Thy Breast, unarm'd, receiv'd the *Spartan* Lance. .....Il.16.371.257.
The *Trojan* thus: The *Spartan* Monarch burn'd .....Il.17.17.288.
While the fierce *Spartan* tore his Arms away. .....Il.17.66.290.
Now enter'd in the *Spartan* Ranks, he turn'd .....Il.17.121.292.
Fast by his Side, the gen'rous *Spartan* glows .....Il.17.151.293.
The *Spartan* Hero's Chariot smoak'ed along. .....Il.23.502.510.
Thence speed your voyage to the *Spartan* strand, ...Od.1.371.50.
And seek *Atrides* on the *Spartan* shore. .....Od.3.406.106.
Accept this welcome to the *Spartan* court; .....Od.4.70.122.
What cause hath led you to the *Spartan* court? .....Od.4.422.140.
From *Pyle* re-sailing and the *Spartan* court, ...Od.4.931.162.
The *Spartan* King; how *Ithacus* attends, ...Od.8.566.293.
Nor think of flight before the *Spartan* King .....Od.15.61.72.
And in these words the *Spartan* chief bespoke. .....Od.15.187.77.
The regal presents of the *Spartan* Lord; .....Od.15.233.79.
The gifts and treasures of the *Spartan* King) .....Od.17.87.136.
My lengthen'd journey to the *Spartan* court. .....Od.17.133.138.

SPARTAN'S
Amidst his Triumph to the *Spartan's* Heart? .....Il.4.126.226.
Such Joy the *Spartan's* shining Face o'erspread, ...Il.23.683.517.

SPARTANS
The hardy *Spartans,* exercis'd in Arms: .....Il.2.702.159.

SPATIOUS
See SPACIOUS.
See, a long Race thy spatious Courts adorn; .....1.Mes.87.121.

SPATTER'D
Shall lick their mangled Master's spatter'd Gore. .....Il.22.97.456.

SPAWN
How Hints, like spawn, scarce quick in embryo lie, ...5.DunA1.57.67.
How hints, like spawn, scarce quick in embryo lie, ...5.DunB1.59.274.

SPEAK

In all you speak, let Truth and Candor shine: 1.EOC.563.305.
And *speak,* tho' *sure,* with *seeming Diffidence:* 1.EOC.567.305.
Speak when you're *sure,* yet speak with *Diffidence;* 1.EOC.567A.305.
Speak when you're *sure,* yet speak with *Diffidence;* 1.EOC.567A.305.
But *Appius* reddens at each Word you speak, 1.EOC.585.306.
She ceas'd at once to speak, and ceas'd to be; 1.TrFD.100.390.
A thousand tender Words, I hear and speak; 1.TrSP.151.400.
And since I speak of Wedlock, let me say, 2.ChJM.127.20.
Let ev'ry Friend with Freedom speak his Mind. 2.ChJM.138.21.
If what I speak my noble Lord offend, 2.ChJM.214.24.
Well, I'm a Woman, and as such must speak; 2.ChJM.694.48.
Thus shall ye speak, and exercise Command. 2.ChWB.69.59.
Who speaks so well shou'd ever speak in vain. 2.RL4.132.194.
In Act to speak, and graceful, stretch'd his Hand: 2.TemF.241.274.
They live, they speak, they breathe what love inspires, 2.ElAb.53.323.
Let tears, and burning blushes speak the rest. 2.ElAb.106.328.
Make *Scots* speak Treason, cozen subtlest Whores, 4.JD4.59.31.
"So much *alone,* (to speak plain Truth between us) 4.JD4.90A.33.
(Some say his Queen) was forc'd to speak, or burst. 4.Arbu.72.100.
And speak in publick with some sort of grace. 4.2HE1.208.213.
Speak out, and bid me blame no Rogues at all. 4.EpS2.53.315.
Speak the loud language Princes.. 4.1740.45.334.
Thrice Budgel aim'd to speak, but thrice suppress 5.DunA2.365.144.
Thrice Budgel aim'd to speak, but thrice suppress 5.DunB2.397.316.
Let Friend affect to speak as Terence spoke, 5.DunB4.223.364.
The Convocation gap'd, but could not speak: 5.DunB4.610.404.
Speak, Gracious Lord, oh speak; thy Servant hears: 6.2.1.5.
Speak, Gracious Lord, oh speak; thy Servant hears: 6.2.1.5.
Speak words of Comfort in my willing Ears; 6.2.3.5.
Speak thou in words, but let me speak in deeds! 6.2.6.5.
Speak thou in words, but let me speak in deeds! 6.2.6.5.
Nor speak alone, but give me grace to hear 6.2.7.6.
Moses himself, speak thou, that I may live. 6.2.16.6.
Speak, gracious Lord, oh speak; thy Servant hears. 6.2.18.6.
Speak, gracious Lord, oh speak; thy Servant hears. 6.2.18.6.
Thou without them may'st speak and profit too; 6.2.23.6.
(My God) speak comfort to my ravish'd Ears; 6.2.32.6.
Speak when thou wilt, for still thy Servant hears. 6.2.34.6.
And from those pretty Things you speak have told, 6.37.9.106.
"If thou hast ought to speak, speak out." 6.79.81.220.
"If thou hast ought to speak, speak out." 6.79.81.220.
"If thou hast ought to say, now speak." 6.79.81A.220.
If *Pope* must tell what *HARCOURT* cannot speak? 6.85.6.242.
When *Pope* must tell what *HARCOURT* cannot speak? 6.85.6A.242.
O teach me, Dear, new Words to speak my Flame; 6.96iv.95.279.
And 'tis certain, dear Cibber, that you may *speak last;* 6.149.2A.397.
For I must speak what Wisdom would conceal, Il.1.101.92.
Speak what thou know'st, and speak without controul. Il.1.108.92.
Speak what thou know'st, and speak without controul. Il.1.108.92.
Loth to advance, or speak their hard Command; Il.1.431.108.
Vext when he spoke, yet still they heard him speak. Il.2.272.140.
For thus I speak, and what I speak shall stand; Il.8.566.423.
For thus I speak, and what I speak shall stand; Il.8.566.423.
First let him speak, who first has suffer'd Shame. Il.9.44.434.
Age bids me speak; nor shall th' Advice I bring Il.9.85.436.
Thee, Prince! it fits alike to speak and hear, Il.9.133.438.
What art thou, speak, that on Designs unknown Il.10.90.6.
To speak his Thought, is ev'ry Freeman's Right, Il.12.249.90.
Speak it in Whispers, lest a *Greek* should hear. Il.14.101.162.
May speak to Councils and assembled Kings. Il.14.125.163.
Speak her Request, and deem her Will obey'd. Il.14.224.172.
Nor speak him vulgar, nor of vulgar Race; Il.14.554.190.
Absent, by me they speak, by me they sue; Il.15.802.227.
And speak those Sorrows which a Friend would share. Il.16.28.236.
To speak, beseems the Council; but to dare Il.16.761.273.
In free Debate, my Friends, your Sentence speak: Il.18.299.336.
Two, while I speak, my Eyes in vain explore, Il.22.63.455.
Thy Words, that speak Benevolence of Mind Il.24.459.555.
So Fathers speak (persuasive speech and mild!) Od.1.401.51.
Speak him descended of no vulgar race: Od.1.518.57.
(I speak aloud, that ev'ry *Greek* may hear) Od.2.128.67.
I speak from science, and the voice is Fate. Od.2.198.71.
Speak they their lineage, or their names declare? Od.4.186.128.
Speak you, (who saw) his wonders in the war. Od.4.334.135.
Observe, and in the truths I speak confide: Od.4.518.145.
He thus; O were the woes you speak the worst! Od.4.924.161.
Horrid to speak! in ambush is decreed Od.4.932.162.
I speak not all the counsel of the skies: Od.4.1090.168.
In act to speak, *Laodamas* ascends: Od.8.142.270.
Some greatly think, some speak with manly sense; Od.8.186.272.
And bitter fate. To speak he made essay, Od.10.288.357.
While yet I speak, the shade disdains to stay, Od.11.691.418.
In act to speak the * Pow'r of magic stands, Od.12.27.430.
While yet I speak the winged gally flies, Od.12.200.441.
While yet I speak, at once their oars they seize, Od.12.264.445.
All press to speak, all question with their eyes. Od.13.191.15.
Nor speak I rashly but with faith averr'd, Od.14.175.44.
And what I speak attesting heav'n has heard. Od.14.176.44.
Speak not a word, least any *Greek* may hear— Od.14.556.64.
Soon shall my bounties speak a grateful mind, Od.15.578.98.
So shall our bounties speak a grateful mind; Od.17.187.140.
His bulk and beauty speak no vulgar praise; Od.17.370.150.
May what I speak your princely minds approve, Od.17.555.159.
With wonder gaze, and gazing speak aloud; Od.18.81.170.
That speak disdain, the wanton thus replies. Od.18.374.185.
Due-distant for us both to speak, and hear. Od.19.120.198.
Yet, while I speak, the mighty woe suspend; Od.19.305.209.
Ardent to speak the Monarch safe restor'd: Od.19.556.223.
Speak him descended from no vulgar race. Od.21.362.277.
Amaz'd she sate, and impotent to speak; Od.23.96.324.
Pow'rless to speak, I scarce uplift my eyes, Od.23.109.325.
The world conspires to speak *Ulysses* wise; Od.23.124.326.
That I forbore, thus, thus, to speak my love; Od.23.224.333.
When thou must learn what I must speak with tears? Od.23.282.337.

SPEAK'ST

"Speak'st thou of Syrian Princes? Traitor base! 5.DunB4.375.379.
What-ere thou speak'st, let this be understood; 6.2.35.6.

SPEAKER

"And perfect *Speaker?*"—"Onslow, past dispute." 4.JD4.71.31.
Wrong the best Speaker, and the justest Cause. Il.19.86.375.

SPEAKING

He spake; and speaking, leaps from off the Car; 1.TrES.217A.457.
A speaking Sigh, and cast a mournful View; 2.ChJM.415.35.
He spoke, and speaking, in proud Triumph spread 2.RL4.139.195.
"And get by speaking Truth of Monarchs dead, 4.JD4.106.33.
Soft as the Speaking Trumpet's mellow Noise: 6.96ii.72.273.
In Arts of Council, and in speaking well! Il.2.441.148.
Then speaking thus the King of Kings arose; Il.3.567.219.
The Head, yet speaking, mutter'd as it fell. Il.10.527.26.
And speaking rolls her large, majestic Eyes) Il.14.298.177.
Thus speaking, furious from the Field he strode, Il.15.244.206.
He spoke; and speaking, swifter than the Wind Il.15.468.215.
He spake; and speaking, leaps from off the Car; Il.16.520.263.
But speaking tears the want of words supply, Od.10.291.357.
So speaking, from the ruddy orient shone Od.10.645.375.
Thus speaking, with dispatchful hand he took Od.14.463.58.
Thus speaking, on the right up-soar'd in air Od.15.565.97.
With speaking eyes, and voice of plaintive sound, Od.17.438.154.
Thus speaking, on the floor the bow he plac'd, Od.21.171.267.
Thus speaking, from the ground the sword he took Od.22.363.304.
Thus speaking, on the circling wall he strung Od.22.499.313.

SPEAKS

Distrustful *Sense* with modest Caution speaks; 1.EOC.626.310.
This speaks the Glory of the *British Queen,* 2.RL*A*1.77.129.
When *Florio* speaks, what Virgin could withstand, 2.RL1.97.152.
One speaks the Glory of the *British Queen,* 2.RL3.13.170.
Who speaks so well shou'd ever speak in vain. 2.RL4.132.194.
Tho' what he learns, he speaks and may advance 3.Ep1.3.15.
She speaks, behaves, and acts just as she ought; 3.Ep2.161.64.
This Thing has *travell'd,* speaks each Language too, 4.JD4.46.29.
Thus Bethel spoke, who always speaks his thought, 4.HS2.129.65.
Whether in florid Impotence he speaks, 4.Arbu.317.118.
Of Ch[andos] W[inchilsea] who speaks at all, 4.1740.19.332*.
And C[hesterfiel]d who speaks so well and writes, 4.1740.25.333.
When he speaks, 6.96i.39.269.
Our laughter, *R[oom]e,* whene'er he speaks, provokes; 6.105iii.1A.301.
She speaks, behaves, and acts just as she ought; 6.139.5.377.
'Tis just, my Brother, what your Anger speaks: Il.3.86.193.
But, when he speaks, what Elocution flows! Il.3.283.207.
'Tis *Hector* speaks, and calls the Gods to hear: Il.7.86.367.
And speaks the Mandate of the Sire of Gods. Il.8.507.420.
This speaks my Grief; this headless Lance I wield; Il.13.335.121.
And Nature speaks at ev'ry Pause of Art. Il.24.905.574.
The present Synod speaks its author wise; Od.2.41.62.
While yet he speaks, *Telemachus* replies. Od.2.147.68.
Thus while he speaks, the ruddy sun descends, Od.3.421.107.
Speaks thee descendent of etherial race: Od.4.510.144.
Speaks from thy tongue and ev'ry action guides; Od.6.308.225.
He speaks reserv'dly, but he speaks with force, Od.8.191.272.
He speaks reserv'dly, but he speaks with force, Od.8.191.272.
And owning her *Ulysses,* thus she speaks. Od.11.189.390.
And as he speaks the tears descend in dew. Od.11.582.412.
What tydings, friend? what speaks the voice of fame? Od.16.483.130.
The tongue speaks wisely, when the soul is wise; Od.18.152.173.
Speaks thee an Heroe from an Heroe sprung: Od.18.260.179.
Fame speaks the *Trojans* bold; they boast the skill Od.18.305.181.
While yet she speaks, the gay *Antinous* cries, Od.18.329.183.
While yet he speaks, *Eurymachus* replies, Od.18.428.189.
Ulysses speaks his own return decreed; Od.19.652.227.
Or speaks their deed a bounteous mind humane? Od.20.210.243.
And Folly, with the tongue of Wisdom speaks. Od.23.18.319.
Thus speaks the Queen, and no reply attends, Od.23.87.323.
Thus speaks the Queen, still dubious, with disguise; Od.23.183.330.
While yet he speaks, her pow'rs of life decay, Od.23.211.333.
Hangs round her neck and speaks his joy in tears. Od.23.248.335.
Nor speaks thy form a mean or servile mind: Od.24.297.364.

SPEAR

And bleed for ever under *Britain's* Spear. 1.W-F.310.179.
The Hook she bore, instead of *Cynthia's* Spear, 1.TrVP.9.377.
The Spear, pursu'd by gushing Streams of Gore; 1.TrES.126.454.
Each heav'd the Shield, and pois'd the lifted Spear: 1.TrES.262.459.
Present the Spear, and arm him for the Fight. 2.RL3.130.177.
Present their Spear, and arm him for the Fight. 2.RL3.130A.177.
An ignominious cross, the nails, the spear: 6.25.6.77.
His sharpen'd Spear let ev'ry *Grecian* wield, Il.2.454.149.
Shakes his huge Spear, and nods his Plumy Crest: Il.2.989.170.
Then with his Spear restrain'd the Youth of *Troy,* Il.3.110.195.
Who first shall launce his pointed Spear in Air. Il.3.393.211.
Arm'd with his Spear, he meditates the Wound, Il.4.569.248.
Cold thro' his Temples glides the whizzing Spear; Il.4.576.249.
Th' *Ætolian* Warrior tugg'd his weighty Spear: Il.4.615.250.
And first bold *Phegeus* cast his sounding Spear, Il.5.22.266.
The Spear of *Merion* mingled with the Dead. Il.5.86.270.
Full in his Nape infix'd the fatal Spear; Il.5.96.271.
Tho' now determin'd by *Tydides'* Spear. Il.5.195.276.
Without a Warrior's Arms, the Spear and Shield! Il.5.267.280.
Take thou the Spear, the Chariot's Care be mine. Il.5.287.280.
Thine be the Guidance then: With Spear and Shield Il.5.296.281.
The Spear may enter where the Arrow fail'd. Il.5.341.283.
Thy Dart has err'd, and now my Spear be try'd: Il.5.348.283.
His Spear extending where the Carcass lies; Il.5.362.284.
Whose Spear ill-fated makes a Goddess bleed, Il.5.494.291.
That shakes a Spear that casts a dreadful Light; Il.5.729.302.
His massy Spear with matchless Fury sent Il.5.758.303.
Pierc'd by my Spear to endless Darkness go! Il.5.800.304.
From warring Gods thou bad'st me turn my Spear, Il.5.1014.315.

SPEAR (CONTINUED)
And thy fell Daughter with the Shield and Spear: .....Il.5.1073.317.
Ulysses' Spear *Pidytes* sent to Hell; .....Il.6.36.325.
Beneath the *Spartan* Spear, a living Prize. .....Il.6.46.325.
Enough of *Greeks* shall die thy Spear with Gore; .....Il.6.284.340.
Break thou *Tydides'* Spear, and let him fall .....Il.6.380.345.
A Spear the Hero bore of wondrous Strength, ...Il.6.394.346.
By *Glaucus'* Spear the bold *Iphinous* bleeds, ...Il.7.19.363.
Then with his Spear restrain'd the Youth of *Troy,* .....Il.7.60.365.
Drove thro' the *Trojan* Targe the knotty Spear; .....Il.7.312.379.
The thirsty Fury of my flying Spear. .....Il.8.142.404.
Fierce he drove on; *Tydides* whirl'd his Spear. .....Il.8.150.405.
The Spear with erring Haste mistook its way, ...Il.8.151.405.
A massy Spear he bore of mighty Strength, ...Il.8.615.425.
The Wolf's grey Hide, th' unbended Bow and Spear; .....Il.10.529.26.
But when, or wounded by the Spear, or Dart, ...Il.11.247.46.
But when, or wounded by the Spear, or Dart, ...Il.11.263.47.
Atrides first discharg'd the missive Spear; .....Il.11.299.48.
Then with his Spear, unseen, his Time he took, ...Il.11.325.49.
On *Coon* rushes with his lifted Spear: .....Il.11.330.49.
Whose Sons now tremble at his darted Spear, ...Il.11.489.56.
Ulysses reach'd him with the fatal Spear; .....Il.11.536.57.
By *Pallas'* Care, the Spear, tho' deep infix'd, ...Il.11.549.58.
As when some Huntsman with a flying Spear, ...Il.11.594.60.
The Spear, pursu'd by gushing Streams of Gore; .....Il.12.480.99.
Stand, and my Spear shall rout their scatt'ring Pow'r, ...Il.13.207.115.
On the rais'd Orb to distance bore the Spear: .....Il.13.220.116.
He groans beneath the *Telamonian* Spear. .....Il.13.240.116.
Nor trust the Dart, or aim th' uncertain Spear, ...Il.13.342.122.
Swift as the Word bold *Merion* snatch'd a Spear, ...Il.13.382.123.
Full on his Throat discharg'd the forceful Spear: .....Il.13.490.130.
Ev'n then, the Spear the vig'rous Arm confest. .....Il.13.519.131.
The *Cretan* saw, and shun'd the brazen Spear: .....Il.13.637.136.
The forceful Spear his hollow Corselet broke, ...Il.13.641.136.
And on his loaded Arm discharg'd his Spear: .....Il.13.669.137.
And struck his Target with the brazen Spear, ...Il.13.711.138.
But *Merion's* Spear o'ertook him as he flew, ...Il.13.717.138.
The Spear, the Conqu'ror from his Body drew, ...Il.13.725.139.
The Spear sollicites, and the Bandage bound; .....Il.13.750.140.
Pisander's Spear fell shiver'd on the Field. .....Il.13.760.141.
His unsuccessful Spear he chanc'd to fling .....Il.13.809.143.
For not the Spear the Locrian Squadrons wield .....Il.13.891A.148.
Each now disabled by a hostile Spear. .....Il.13.984.152.
His strongest Spear each valiant *Grecian* wield, ...Il.14.431.184.
And at *Prothœnor* shook the trembling Spear; .....Il.14.526.189.
Propt on that Spear to which thou ow'st thy Fall, ...Il.14.533.189.
But young *Ilioneus* receiv'd the Spear, ...Il.14.573.190.
From frantic *Mars* she snatch'd the Shield and Spear; .....Il.15.143.202.
But *Crœsmus'* Bosom took the flying Spear; .....Il.15.619.220.
Due to stern *Pallas,* and *Pelides'* Spear. .....Il.15.737.224.
Now shakes his Spear, now lifts, and now protends, ...Il.15.887.231.
Where furious *Ajax* ply'd his Ashen Spear, ...Il.16.143.243.
His pointless Spear the Warrior shakes in vain; .....Il.16.146.243.
To wing the Spear, or aim the distant Dart; .....Il.16.231.248.
Then first thy Spear, divine *Patroclus!* flew, ...Il.16.338.255.
The brazen-pointed Spear, with Vigour thrown, ...Il.16.368.257.
The gaping Dastard: As the Spear was shook, ...Il.16.498.262.
Each heav'd the Shield, and pois'd the lifted Spear: .....Il.16.567.266.
I stand unable to sustain the Spear, ...Il.16.639.269.
His Spear *Æneas* at the Victor threw, ...Il.16.739.272.
My Spear, the destin'd Passage had it found, ...Il.16.747.273.
Were thine my Vigour, this successful Spear .....Il.16.879.277.
A Spear his Left, a Stone employs his Right: .....Il.16.892.277.
His Spear in Shivers falls: His ample Shield .....Il.16.966.280.
His vent'rous Spear first drew the Hero's Gore; .....Il.16.978.281.
Thus, by an Arm divine, and mortal Spear, ...Il.16.983.281.
And upwards cast the Corps: The reeking Spear .....Il.16.1044.283.
Their Fellows routed, toss the distant Spear, ...Il.17.437.304.
And the Spear trembled as his Entrails heav'd. .....Il.17.593.311.
Deep rooted in the Ground, the forceful Spear .....Il.17.598.311.
Thro' his broad Belt the Spear a Passage found, ...Il.17.652.313.
And raz'd his Shoulder with a shorten'd Spear: .....Il.17.679.314.
But erring from its Aim, th' impetuous Spear .....Il.17.689.314.
Lame with their Wounds, and leaning on the Spear; .....Il.19.52.374.
Let ev'ry *Greek* who sees my Spear confound .....Il.19.149.377.
And now he shakes his great paternal Spear, ...Il.19.420.389.
A Spear which stern *Achilles* only wields, ...Il.19.424.389.
Observ'd the Fury of his flying Spear; .....Il.20.120.399.
To his bold Spear the Savage turns alone, ...Il.20.204.402.
Once (as I think) you saw this brandish'd Spear .....Il.20.228.403.
Receive this Answer: 'Tis my flying Spear. .....Il.20.307.407.
Saw, e'er it fell, th' immeasurable Spear. .....Il.20.313.407.
The forceful Spear of great *Achilles* flew, ...Il.20.322.407.
And at his Back perceives the quiv'ring Spear: .....Il.20.330.407.
From great *Æneas'* Shield the Spear he drew, ...Il.20.371.410.
My Spear, that parted on the Wings of Wind, ...Il.20.394.411.
And thin the Squadrons with my single Spear. .....Il.20.414.412.
No more shall *Hector's* and *Pelides'* Spear .....Il.20.495.415.
The Spear a fourth time bury'd in the Cloud, ...Il.20.517.416.
That one the Spear destroy'd, and one the Sword. .....Il.20.536.416.
Thro' *Mulius'* Head then drove th' impetuous Spear, ...Il.20.547.417.
Succeeds to Fate: The Spear his Belly rends; .....Il.20.563.417.
Lo! he returns! Try then, my flying spear! .....Il.21.70.424.
Achilles rais'd the Spear, prepar'd to wound; .....Il.21.78.424.
And while above the Spear suspended stood, ...Il.21.80.424.
For ah! one Spear shall drink each Brother's Gore, ...Il.21.101.426.
When by the Spear, the Arrow, or the Dart, ...Il.21.122.426.
His Hand forgot its Grasp, and left the Spear; .....Il.21.127.426.
Begot my Sire, whose Spear such Glory won: .....Il.21.177.429.
Deep in the swelling Bank was driv'n the Spear, ...Il.21.187.429.
The fourth, he tries to break the Spear in vain; .....Il.21.193.429.
Far as a Spear can fly, *Achilles* springs .....Il.21.283.432.
Might *Hector's* Spear this dauntless Bosom rend, ...Il.21.323.434.
The Pow'r of Battels lifts his brazen Spear, ...Il.21.456.440.
Enrag'd *Achilles* follows with his Spear; .....Il.21.637.448.
He stoop'd, while o'er his Head the flying Spear .....Il.22.351.470.

SPEAR (CONTINUED)
He calls *Deïphobus,* demands a Spear, ...Il.22.375.471.
So shone the Point of great *Achilles'* Spear. .....Il.22.402.472.
Phyleus and *Polydorus,* with the Spear. .....Il.23.732.519.
Next these a Buckler, Spear and Helm, he brings, ...Il.23.941.526.
A furious Pass the Spear of *Ajax* made .....Il.23.965.527.
A Massy Spear amid the Circle plac'd, ...Il.23.1045.531.
The King to *Merion* gives the brazen Spear: .....Il.23.1061.533.
A glitt'ring spear wav'd awful in her hand. .....Od.1.137.39.
The spear receiving from her hand, he plac'd .....Od.1.167.40.
Each hand tremendous with a brazen spear, ...Od.1.332.48.
His spear, indignant for such high disdain, ...Od.4.678.151.
In fighting fields as far the spear I throw, ...Od.8.261.276.
I climb'd a cliff, with spear and sword in hand, ...Od.10.169.348.
I lanc'd my spear, and with a sudden wound .....Od.10.187.349.
The bloody spear, his gather'd feet I ty'd .....Od.10.192.349.
Then leaning on the spear with both my hands, ...Od.10.196.350.
He grasp'd his sword, and shook his glitt'ring spear. .....Od.11.650.416.
Prepar'd to whirl the whizzing spear I stay, ...Od.12.272.445.
With his broad spear, the dread of dogs and men, ...Od.14.598.66.
Takes from the stranger's hand the glitt'ring spear: .....Od.15.307.83.
His blood in vengeance smokes upon my spear. .....Od.16.457.129.
Each pois'd his shield, and each advanc'd his spear; .....Od.16.493.131.
He props his spear against the pillar'd wall; .....Od.17.36.134.
To dart the spear, and guide the rushing car .....Od.18.307.181.
Should *Jove* dire war unloose, with spear and shield .....Od.18.418.189.
And foremost of the train, his cornel spear .....Od.19.509.221.
To the right shoulder-joint the spear apply'd, ...Od.19.529.221.
With manly grasp he wav'd a martial spear, ...Od.20.156.241.
Fall'n guiltless of the mark, my certain spear .....Od.20.374.251.
A two-edg'd faulchion and a shining spear, ...Od.21.366.277.
Thy spear, *Telemachus!* prevents th' attack, ...Od.22.107.291.
The long incumbrance of the weighty spear .....Od.22.113.292.
And from *Ctesippus'* arm the spear elanc'd .....Od.22.308.301.
Thy death, ennobled by *Ulysses'* spear. .....Od.22.313.301.
The victim's heel is answer'd with this spear. .....Od.22.323.301.
Then to his train he gives his spear and shield; .....Od.24.253.361.
Full at *Eupithes* drove the deathful spear: .....Od.24.605.376.

SPEARS
The Youth surround her with extended Spears; .....1.TrSt.723.440.
Around the Works a Wood of glitt'ring Spears .....1.TrES.181.456.
Gloomy as Night, and shakes two shining Spears; .....1.TrES.200.456.
Propt on their Bodkin Spears, the Sprights survey .....2.RL5.55.203.
With nodding Plumes and Groves of waving Spears. .....Il.2.182.137.
But with protended Spears in fighting Fields, ...Il.2.651.158.
Two pointed Spears he shook with gallant Grace, ...Il.3.31.189.
Now rest their Spears, or lean upon their Shields; .....Il.3.177.199.
With Spears erect, a moving Iron Wood; Il.4.323.236
Thro' the thick Storm of singing Spears he flies, ...Il.5.214.277.
Two shining Spears are brandish'd in his Hands; .....Il.5.605.297.
The Spears already tremble in their Hand; .....Il.5.698.301.
His Strokes they second, and avert our Spears: .....Il.5.744.302.
A Wood of Spears his ample Shield sustain'd; .....Il.5.767.303.
Fierce in the Front he shakes two dazling Spears; .....Il.6.131.330.
Their consecrated Spears lay scatter'd round, ...Il.6.165.334.
With levell'd Spears along the winding Shore; .....Il.6.233.337.
Horrid with bristling Spears, and gleaming Shields. .....Il.7.70.366.
And with th' *Arcadian* Spears my Prowess try'd, ...Il.7.165.372.
And each bold Chief a hundred Spears commands. .....Il.9.118.437.
The shining Helmet, and the pointed Spears: .....Il.10.85.6.
A Wood of Spears stood by, that fixt upright, ...Il.10.174.9.
Betwixt the Camp and him our Spears employ, ...Il.10.413.21.
Who spread their Bucklers, and advance their Spears, ...Il.11.721.67.
Around the Works a Wood of glitt'ring Spears .....Il.12.535.101.
Gloomy as Night! and shakes two shiny Spears: .....Il.12.554.102.
Spears lean on Spears, on Targets Targets throng, ...Il.13.181.114.
Spears lean on Spears, on Targets Targets throng, ...Il.13.181.114.
Spears I have store, (and *Trojan* Lances all) .....Il.13.339.121.
And high-hung spears, and shields that flame with Gold. .....Il.13.346.122.
Go—from my conquer'd Spears, the choicest take, ...Il.13.380.123.
Bristled with upright Spears, that flash'd afar; .....Il.13.431.126.
His Spoils he could not, for the Show'r of Spears. .....Il.13.647.136.
Supported on their Spears, they took their way, ...Il.14.45.160.
They join, they thicken, they protend their Spears; .....Il.17.275.298.
And hemm'd with bristled Spears, the *Grecians* stood; .....Il.17.408.303.
Not so our Spears: incessant tho' they rain, ...Il.17.713.315.
On their own Spears, by their own Chariots crush'd: .....Il.18.272.335.
Broad-glitt'ring Breastplates, Spears with pointed Rays .....Il.19.386.388.
And shook two Spears, advancing from the Flood; .....Il.21.162.428.
Arm'd with protended Spears, my native Band; .....Il.21.172.428.
Amidst a war of spears in foreign lands, ...Od.11.478.408.
Tho' spears in iron tempests rain'd around, ...Od.11.657.416.
Horrid with bristly spears, and glancing shields. .....Od.14.297.50.
Horrid with bristly spears, and gleaming shields: .....Od.17.518.157.
The plumy-crested helms, and pointed spears, ...Od.19.36.194.
Four brazen helmets, eight refulgent spears, ...Od.22.128.292.
A blaze of bucklers, and a wood of spears. .....Od.22.161.295.

SPECIAL
To Fifty chosen *Sylphs,* of special Note, ...2.RL2.117.166.
He'd recommend her, as a special breeder. .....6.41.34.114.

SPECIES
Murders their species, and betrays his own. .....3.EOM3.164.109.

SPECIOUS
In vain the Chiefs contriv'd a specious way, ...1.TrSt.192.418.
The board with specious miracles he loads, ...5.DunB4.553.396.
To sooth their fears a specious reason feign: .....Od.19.8.193.

SPECKLED
The crested Basilisk and speckled Snake; .....1.Mes.82.120.
Transform'd to *Combs,* the speckled and the white. .....2.RL1.136.156.
In Form a God! the Panther's speckled Hyde .....Il.3.27.189.

SPECTACLE
Lay Fortune-struck, a Spectacle of Woe! .... 6.128.3.355.
Great *Jove* has plac'd, sad Spectacle of Pain! .... Il.22.84.456.
Set up by Jove your Spectacle of Woe? .... Il.24.300.549.
Late a sad spectacle of woe, he trod .... Od.6.291.224.

SPECTACLES
Those *Spectacles,* ordain'd thine Eyes to save, ... 6.96iv.75.278.

SPECTATOR
(Sure sign, that no spectator shall be drown'd). .... 5.DunA2.166.121.
(Sure sign, that no spectator shall be drown'd) .... 5.DunB2.174.304.
He'd write in Prose—To the *Spectator.* .... 6.44.4.123.
Antinous sate spectator of the sport; .... Od.4.850.158.

SPECTATOR'S
And with them turns the rais'd Spectator's Soul. .... Il.22.216.464.

SPECTATORS
The tame Spectators of his Deeds of War. .... Il.4.12.221.
Vision divine! The throng'd spectators gaze .... Od.3.476.110.

SPECTRE
Scar'd at the spectre of pale Poverty! .... 4.1HE1.70.283.
When lo! a Spectre rose, whose index-hand .... 5.DunB4.139.355.
But, stern as Ajax' spectre, strode away. .... 5.DunB4.274.371.
Around the Spectre bloody Wars are wag'd, ... Il.5.549.295.
And add one Spectre to the Realms below! .... Il.11.557.58.
And forc'd the stubborn spectre to reply; .... Od.11.695.419.
A tow'ring spectre of gigantic mold, ... Od.11.742.423.
Or glide a spectre in the realms beneath? .... Od.17.131.138.

SPECTRES
And the pale Spectres trembled at her View: .... 1.TrSt.133.415.
Pale Spectres, gaping Tombs, and Purple Fires: .... 2.RL4.44.187.
And airy Spectres skim before their Eyes; .... 2.TemF.104.261.
And the pale Spectres dance! .... 6.11.68.32.
But here and there th' unbody'd Spectres chace .... Il.23.90.490.
Shall drive the spectres from forbidden ground: .... Od.10.639.374.
Know; to the spectres, that thy bev'rage taste, ... Od.11.180.390.
Where the wan Spectres walk eternal rounds; .... Od.11.584.412.
Around ten thousand thousand spectres stand .... Od.11.699.419.
But swarms of spectres rose from deepest hell, ... Od.11.779.425.
Trembling the Spectres glide, and plaintive vent .... Od.24.7.347.

SPED
The duteous Knight in this fair Garden sped. .... 2.ChJM.474.38.
In this fair Garden he perform'd and sped. .... 2.ChJM.474A.38.
A dire Dilemma! either way I'm sped, ... 4.Arbu.31.98.
But part in Peace, secure thy Pray'r is sped: .... Il.1.678.119.
He bleeds! (he cries) some God has sped my Dart; .... Il.11.485.56.
And thus (he cries) behold thy Promise sped! .... Il.13.472.129.
Oïlean Ajax first his Javelin sped, ... Il.14.517.188.
Medon and *Iäsus, Æneas* sped; .... Il.15.376.211.
So well the Chief his Naval Weapon sped, ... Il.15.906.232.
Full on the Lance a Stroke so justly sped, ... Il.16.144.243.
The Sword broke short; but his, *Peneleus* sped .... Il.16.406.258.
He spoke, *Patroclus* march'd, and thus he sped. .... Il.16.1015.282.
Full on his Neck the falling Falchion sped, ... Il.20.557.417.
Behind him, diligently close, he sped, ... Il.23.889.524.
He fill'd his scrip, and to the threshold sped; .... Od.17.495.156.
His course to *Ithaca* this Heroe sped, ... Od.19.470.219.
This said, to sage *Piræus* sped the Seer, ... Od.20.445.254.
But from the threshold shall his darts be sped, ... Od.22.85.290.
Full thro' his neck the weighty faulchion sped: .... Od.22.365.305.

SPEECH
Our Speech, our Colour, and our strange Attire! .... 1.W-F.406.192.
No further speech the thundering rock affords, ... 1.TrPA.146.372.
Artful in Speech, in Action, and in Mind! .... 1.TrUl.168.471.
A Statesman's slumbers how this speech would spoil! .... 3.Ep3.43.89.
"What *Speech* esteem you most?"—"The *King's,"* said I, ... 4.JD4.68.31.
[Plain Truth, dear MURRAY, needs no flow'rs of speech, ... 4.1HE6.3.237.
Whose Speech you took, and gave it to a Friend? .... 4.EpS2.167.323.
Utter'd a speech, and ask'd their friends to dine; .... 4.1740.38.334.
"Sense, speech, and measure, living tongues and dead, ... 5.DunA3.161.165.
"Sense, speech, and measure, living tongues and dead, ... 5.DunB3.167.328.
The tongue mov'd gently first, and Speech was low, ... 6.8.10.18.
Yet *Speech,* ev'n there, submissively withdraws .... 6.8.31.18.
There learn'd she Speech from Tongues that never cease. .... 6.14ii.32.44.
And ev'ry speech in Z—nds end, ... 6.61.18.181.
And ev'ry speech with Z—nds end, ... 6.61.18A.181.
"In Senates fam'd for many a Speech, ... 6.79.89.221.
Here on the Monarch's Speech *Achilles* broke, ... Il.1.386.106.
And artful thus pronounc'd the Speech design'd. .... Il.2.138.134.
Atrides' Speech. The mighty Numbers move. .... Il.2.174.136.
Soft moving Speech, and pleasing outward Show, ... Il.3.95.194.
To whom the *Cretan* thus his Speech addrest; .... Il.4.302.235.
The God of Battels, and this Speech addrest. .... Il.5.38.267.
Her Speech new Fury to their Hearts convey'd; .... Il.5.986.314.
His Speech addressing to the Godlike Man. .... Il.9.294.448.
A faithful Speech, that knows nor Art, nor Fear; .... Il.9.407.452.
Their Speech, their Counsels, and Designs to hear? .... Il.10.246.13.
Persuasive Speech, and more persuasive Sighs, ... Il.14.251.173.
From whence this boding Speech, the stern Decree .... Il.16.1038.283.
From such a Warrior such a Speech shou'd hear? .... Il.17.190.294.
Of Speech, Unhappy! from the dying Hour. .... Il.22.412.472.
Th' Effect succeeds the Speech. *Pelides* cries, ... Il.23.935.526.
Yet hear this certain speech, nor deem it vain; .... Od.1.263.45.
So Fathers speak (persuasive speech and mild!) .... Od.1.401.51.
Unskill'd in speech, nor yet mature of age? .... Od.3.30.87.
Right well, reply'd the King, your speech displays .... Od.4.365.137.
And thus benevolent his speech address'd. .... Od.4.420.140.
Charm'd by your speech, so graceful and humane, ... Od.4.814.157.
Gentle of speech, beneficent of mind? .... Od.4.917.161.
The Queen her speech with calm attention hears, ... Od.4.999.164.

SPEECH (CONTINUED)
His speech thus ended short, he frowning rose, ... Od.4.1027.165.
There stopp'd the Goddess, and her speech renew'd. .... Od.7.62.236.
While thus my fraudful speech I reassume. .... Od.9.430.323.
And wou'd but Fate the pow'r of speech afford! .... Od.9.536.328.
Artful in speech, in action, and in mind! .... Od.13.335.23.
How will each speech his grateful wonder raise? .... Od.15.176.77.
His speech the tempest of her grief restor'd; .... Od.19.284.208.
I ratifie my speech; before the sun .... Od.19.349.211.
In all thy speech what pleasing force I find! .... Od.19.688.229.
Then to the King this friendly speech renew'd: .... Od.20.207.243.

SPEECHES
But, as he glozeth with Speeches soote, ... 6.14i.17.42.

SPEECHLESS
Like some sad Statue, speechless, pale, I stood; .... 1.TrSP.125.399.
To find that Speechless Stone where Dryden lies. .... 6.72.4A.208.
A speechless interval of grief ensues, ... Od.19.251.207.

SPEED
Hang o'er their Coursers Heads with eager Speed, ... 1.W-F.157.164.
As from the God with fearful Speed she flew, ... 1.W-F.189A.167.
As did the God with equal Speed pursue. .... 1.W-F.190A.167.
Restrain his Fury, than provoke his Speed; .... 1.EOC.85.249.
Does with glad Speed the well-known Journey go, ... 1.TrSt.142A.415.
With eager Speed the well-known Journey took, ... 1.TrSt.142.416.
Then thus to *Thoos;—Hence* with speed (he said) .... 1.TrES.67.452.
To speed his Bliss, and haste the happy Hour. .... 2.ChJM.352.31.
Speed the soft intercourse from soul to soul, ... 2.ElAb.57.323.
Welcome the coming, speed the going guest.) .... 4.HS2.160.67.
Speed your Flight! .... 6.96i.30.269.
Haste, launch thy Vessels, fly with Speed away, ... Il.1.235.98.
With equal Speed, and fir'd by equal Charms, ... Il.3.421.212.
But first, to speed the Shaft, address thy Vow .... Il.4.131.226.
The Prizes purchas'd by their winged Speed) .... Il.9.164.440.
The Prizes purchas'd by their winged Speed) .... Il.9.351.450.
Now speed thy hasty Course along the Fleet, ... Il.10.63.5.
Mages for Strength, *Oïleus* fam'd for Speed. .... Il.10.124.7.
Meges the bold, with *Ajax* fam'd for speed, ... Il.10.205.10.
Oh speed our Labours, and direct our ways! .... Il.10.535.27.
That Path they take, and speed to reach the Town. .... Il.11.220.45.
Ascend thy Chariot, haste with speed away, ... Il.11.634.61.
Hear then ye Warriors! and obey with speed; .... Il.12.87.84.
The moving Legions speed their headlong way: .... Il.12.120.85.
Then thus to *Thoos;—hence* with speed, (he said) .... Il.12.411.96.
Then to the Ships with surly Speed he went, ... Il.13.223.116.
Speed to the Town, and leave the War behind. .... Il.14.506.188.
If Thought of Man can match the Speed of Gods. .... Il.15.91.200.
Sprung from the Wind, and like the Wind in speed; .... Il.16.183.245.
Forbear, he cry'd, with fruitless Speed to chace .... Il.17.79.291.
From Danger now with swiftest Speed they flew, ... Il.17.530.309.
And now to Conquest with like Speed pursue; .... Il.17.531.309.
And speed to Meadows on whose sounding Shores .... Il.18.667.356.
Not all his Speed escapes the rapid Floods; .... Il.21.301.433.
While all the flying Troops their Speed employ, ... Il.21.717.451.
With mortal Speed a Godhead to pursue? .... Il.22.16.453.
Float in their Speed, and dance upon the Wind: .... Il.23.444.508.
Ulysses next; and he whose Speed surpast .... Il.23.883.524.
Implores the God to speed it thro' the Skies, ... Il.23.1032.530.
And speed my Journey to redeem my Son? .... Il.24.330.550.
But say with speed, if ought of thy Desire .... Il.24.824.571.
Must speed, obedient to their high command. .... Od.1.109.36.
With friendly speed, induc'd by erring fame, ... Od.1.251.45.
Thence speed your voyage to the *Spartan* strand, ... Od.1.371.50.
Homeward with pious speed repass the main, ... Od.1.378.50.
Abrupt, with eagle-speed she cut the sky; .... Od.1.413.52.
All to your several states with speed resort; .... Od.1.478.55.
And lo, with speed we plow the watry way; .... Od.2.323.76.
Shall speed aboard, a valiant chosen band. .... Od.2.332.77.
With speed divine from street to street she flies. .... Od.2.431.81.
Th' impatient mariner thy speed demands. .... Od.2.451.83.
With speed the mast they rear, with speed unbind .... Od.2.464.83.
With speed the mast they rear, with speed unbind .... Od.2.464.83.
She spoke, and led the way with swiftest speed: .... Od.3.39.88.
With strength and speed superior form'd, in fight .... Od.4.277.132.
With joy impetuous, to the port I speed: .... Od.4.580.147.
To speed a prosp'rous voyage o'er the seas? .... Od.4.634.149.
The sprightly courser, or indulge his speed: .... Od.4.826.158.
Requested for his speed; but, courteous, say .... Od.4.856.159.
For *Elis* I shou'd sail with utmost speed, ... Od.4.858.159.
Spontaneous did you speed his secret course, ... Od.4.870.159.
To tend the fruit-groves: With incessant speed .... Od.4.974.163.
Her pious speed a female train attends: .... Od.4.1002.164.
That safe recess they gain with happy speed, ... Od.4.1107.169.
We in the course unrival'd speed display, ... Od.8.283.278.
With speed to learn what men possess'd the land. .... Od.10.116.346.
I speed my passage to th' enchanted dome: .... Od.10.370.362.
With ready speed the joyful crew obey: .... Od.10.507.368.
I heard inces'd, and first resolv'd to speed .... Od.10.517.368.
To speed our course, and waft us o'er the floods, ... Od.11.36.381.
But from the dark dominions speed thy way, ... Od.11.269.394.
I speed my flight, and to my mates repair. .... Od.11.790.426.
Back to the bark I speed along the main. .... Od.12.432.451.
With speed the bark we climb: the spacious sails .... Od.12.472.454.
To speed *Ulysses* to his native shore. .... Od.14.471.58.
Shall prompt our speed, and point the ready way. .... Od.15.60.72.
Nor check our speed, impatient of delay. .... Od.15.74.72.
Welcome the coming, speed the parting guest. .... Od.15.84.73.
Mean-time may'st thou with happiest speed regain .... Od.15.142.75.
In solemn speed the bird majestick flew .... Od.15.183.77.
With speed be gone, (said he) call ev'ry mate, ... Od.15.234.79.
With speed the mast they rear, with speed unbind .... Od.15.312.84.
With speed the mast they rear, with speed unbind .... Od.15.312.84.
With rapid speed to whirl them o'er the sea. .... Od.15.315.84.
And deems thee lost: shall I my speed employ .... Od.16.146.109.

SPEED (CONTINUED)

But to the Queen with speed dispatchful bear ....Od.16.162.110.
Our safe return, and back with speed repair: ....Od.16.163.110.
With speed they guide the vessel to the shores; ....Od.16.346.123.
With speed debarking land the naval stores; ....Od.16.347.123.
Now let us speed; my friend, no more my guest! ....Od.17.208.141.
Hence dotard, hence! and timely speed thy way, ...Od.18.14.167.
The gifts of love; with speed they take the way. ....Od.18.336.184.
To speed his voyage to the *Grecian* strand. ....Od.19.324.210.
And springs impetuous with opponent speed: ....Od.19.524.221.
Diana! speed thy deathful ebon dart, ...Od.20.72.235.
Be such my lot! Or thou *Diana* speed ....Od.20.94.237.
Then all with speed succinct the victims slay: ....Od.20.313.248.
But vengeful *Pallas* with preventing speed ....Od.20.467.256.
To speed the flying shaft thro' ev'ry ring, ...Od.21.102.263.
With speed *Telemachus* obeys, and flies ....Od.22.126.292.
(So speed 'em heav'n) our jav'lins at the foe. ....Od.22.289.300.
The aged Governess with speed obeys: ....Od.22.435.309.

SPEEDED

The Heroe speeded to the *Cnossian* court: ....Od.19.221.204.

SPEEDIEST

The speediest succour from my guardian hand; ....Od.15.105.73.

SPEEDING

Strong *Thrasymed* discharg'd the speeding blow ....Od.3.570.115.
And speeding, thus address'd the royal ear. ....Od.4.32.121.
Then speeding back, involv'd in various thought, ...Od.4.779.155.
Was first my thought: but speeding back to shore ....Od.10.178.349.

SPEEDS

Swift as the Word, the Herald speeds along ....1.TrES.77.452.
Speeds on the Wings of Winds thro' liquid Air; ....Il.2.957.169.
A pointed Lance, and speeds from Band to Band; ....Il.11.272.47.
Tydides mounts, and to the Navy speeds. ....Il.11.508.56.
Swift as the Word, the Herald speeds along ....Il.12.421.97.
She speeds to *Lemnos* o'er the rowling Deep, ...Il.14.264.173.
Achilles speeds from Tent to Tent, and warms ....Il.16.190.246.
He, like the warlike Eagle speeds his Pace, ...Il.21.281.432.
To the cleft Cavern speeds the gentle Dove, ...Il.21.576.446.
Down to the strand he speeds with haughty strides, ...Od.4.1029.166.
The Nurse with eager rapture speeds her way; ....Od.23.2.316.

SPEEDY

His speedy Succour to the *Spartan* King; ....Il.4.231.232.
The speedy Javelin drove from Back to Breast. ....Il.5.54.269.
On speedy Measures then employ your Thought; ....Il.14.67.160.
The speedy Council at his Word adjourn'd; ....Il.19.289.384.
(Such as in Races crown the speedy Strife) ....Il.22.209.464.
As Men in Slumbers seem with speedy pace, ...Il.22.257.466.
Than who too speedy, hastes to end his life ....Od.3.291.100.
That care be fate's, a speedy passage thine. ....Od.4.734.153.
Attend, and speedy thou shalt pass the main: ....Od.6.348.229.
A speedy voyage to his native shores. ....Od.8.174.271.
Now (cry'd *Telemachus*) with speedy care ....Od.15.244.80.
My anxious parents urge a speedy choice, ...Od.19.180.200.
With speedy ardour to his Sire he flies, ...Od.22.116.292.
And speedy lands, and secretly confers. ....Od.24.180.356.

SPELLS

Each Wight who reads not, and but scans and spells, ...4.Arbu.165.108.
The Wight who reads not, and but scans and spells, ...4.Arbu.165A.108.
Each Wight who reads not, but who scans and spells, ...4.Arbu.165B.108.
Know, there are Words, and Spells, which can controll ....4.1HE1.57.283.
Who thinks he *reads* when he but *scans* and *spells,* ....6.98.15.283.
The spells of *Circe,* and her magic pow'r; ....Od.23.346.341.

SPENCER

See SPENSER.
In Spencer native Muses play; ....4.HOde9.6.159.

SPEND

And here in Dalliance spend the livelong Day, ...2.ChJM.471.38.
I'd spend my dearest Blood to ease thy Pain. ....2.ChJM.737.50.
They might (were Harpax not too wise to spend) ....3.Ep3.93.97.
I, who at some times spend, at others spare, ...4.2HE2.290.185.
To spend six months with Statesmen here. ....4.HS6.32.253.
"Then spend your life in Joy and Sport, ...4.HS6.181.261.
For Want of you, we spend our random Wit on ....6.82vi.3.232.

SPENDS

Steals much, spends little, yet has nothing left: ....4.Arbu.184.109.
Steals much, spends little, yet has nothing left: ....6.98.34.284.
Nor deaden'd there its giddy Fury spends, ...Il.14.478.187.

SPENSER

See SPENCER.
Spenser himself affects the obsolete, ...4.2HE1.97.203.

SPENT

While lab'ring Oxen, spent with Toil and Heat, ...1.PAu.61.84.
On the cold Marble spent with Toil he lies, ...1.TrSt.537.432.
And spent, in empty Air, its dying Force. ....1.TrES.284.460.
Spent with Fatigue, and slept secure on Land; ....1.TrUl.153.471.
The constant Tenour of whose well-spent Days ....2.TemF.330.280.
Spent in a sudden storm of lust, ...6.51ii.18.153.
And the gay Conscience of a life well spent, ...6.86.12.245.
And the glad Conscience of a life well spent, ...6.86.12A.245.
And each spent Courser at the Chariot blow. ....Il.2.465.149.
And spent in empty Air its erring Force. ....Il.5.24.266.
When now the *North* his boist'rous Rage has spent, ...Il.5.643.299.
Spent as thou art with long laborious Fight, ...Il.6.327.342.
And all your Masters well-spent Care repay. ....Il.8.229.408.
And spent with Toil neglect the Watch of Night? ....Il.10.366.19.
Spent and o'erpow'r'd, he barely breathes at most; ....Il.16.136.242.

SPENT (CONTINUED)

And spent in empty Air its dying Force. ....Il.16.589.267.
There yet scarce spent, it quivers on the Plain, ...Il.16.743.272.
In long Vibrations spent its Fury there. ....Il.17.599.311.
Till his spent Coursers seek the Fleet again: ....Il.18.330.337.
Sung innocent, and spent its Force in Air. ....Il.22.352.470.
Suffice it to have spend with swift decay ....Od.2.351.78.
Thus spent already, how shall nature bear ....Od.5.602.201.
Spent with fatigue, and shrunk with pining fast, ...Od.7.295.250.
The sailors spent with toils their folly mourn, ...Od.10.89.343.
Spent and o'erwatch'd. Two days and nights roll'd on, ...Od.10.167.348.
As weary plowman spent with stubborn toil, ...Od.13.39.3.
Spent with fatigue, and slept secure on land. ....Od.13.320.23.
Three days have spent their beams, three nights have run ....Od.17.606.161.
But when the storm was spent in plenteous show'rs, ...Od.19.286.209.
Soon as his store of flying fates was spent, ...Od.22.136.293.

SPERCHIUS

Divine *Sperchius! Jove*-descended *Flood!* ....Il.16.212.247.
And sacred grew to *Sperchius* honour'd Flood: ....Il.23.175.496.
Sperchius! whose Waves in mazy Errors lost ....Il.23.178.497.

SPEW

And gaping Tritons spew to wash your face. ....3.Ep4.154.152.

SPHEARS

End in the starry vault, and prop the sphears.) ....Od.1.70.34.

SPHERE

Some thought it mounted to the Lunar Sphere, ...2.RL5.113.208.
Which adds new Glory to the shining Sphere! ....2.RL5.142.211.
Perhaps acts second to some sphere unknown, ...3.EOM1.58.20.
Perhaps acts second to a sphere unknown ....3.EOM1.58A.20.
If to be perfect in a certain sphere, ...3.EOM1.73.22.
All quit their sphere, and rush into the skies. ....3.EOM1.124.30.
Submit—In this, or any other sphere, ...3.EOM1.285.50.
Go, soar with Plato to th' empyreal sphere, ...3.EOM2.23.57.
When those blue eyes first open'd on the sphere; ....3.Ep2.284.73.
I meddle, Goddess! only in my sphere. ....5.DunB4.432.383.
The baby, in that sunny sphere ....6.5.13.12.
The Field of Combate is the Sphere for Men. ....Il.6.635.358.
When all the starry Train emblaze the Sphere: ....Il.22.401.472.
And shine eternal in the sphere of fame— ....Od.1.394.51.
And *thou, to whom 'tis giv'n to gild the sphere! ....Od.4.458.142.
And thou whose lustre gilds the rowling sphere! ....Od.17.149.139.
Gild the gross vapor of this nether sphere! ....Od.19.41.194.
Or globes of iron fix'd in either sphere; ....Od.19.249.206.

SPHERES

And all the trembling Spheres confess'd the God. ....1.TrSt.283.422.
Ye know the Spheres and various Tasks assign'd, ...2.RL2.75.164.
Who measur'd Earth, describ'd the Starry Spheres, ...2.TemF.111.262.
And stunn'd him with the music of the spheres, ...3.EOM1.202.40.
Let ruling Angels from their spheres be hurl'd, ...3.EOM1.253.46.

SPHYNXE'S

If I the *Sphynxe's* Riddles durst explain, ...1.TrSt.93.414.

SPICE

Like Frigates fraught with Spice and Cochine'l, ...4.JD4.227.45.
Cloath space, line trunks, or flutt'ring in a row, ...4.2HE1.418.231.
There sav'd by spice, like mummies, many a year, ...5.DunA1.131.80.
There, sav'd by spice, like Mummies, many a year, ...5.DunB1.151.281.

SPICES

With od'rous Spices they perfum'd the Place, ...2.ChJM.355.31.
Or Spices breathing in *Arabian* Gales. ....2.TemF.317.279.
For Indian spices, for Peruvian gold, ...4.1HE6.71.241.
Where spices smoke beneath the burning Line, ...5.DunA3.62.155.
Where spices smoke beneath the burning Line, ...5.DunB3.70.323.

SPICY

See spicy Clouds from lowly *Saron* rise, ...1.Mes.27.115.
For thee, *Idume's* spicy Forests blow; ....1.Mes.95.121.
Led by new Stars, and born by spicy Gales! ....1.W-F.392.190.
Full oft I drain'd the Spicy Nut-brown Bowl; ....2.ChWB.214.67.
Full oft I drain'd the Spicy Nut-brown Bowl ....2.ChWB.214A.67.
So spicy gales at once betray ....6.4v.7.11.

SPIDER

Who made the spider parallels design, ...3.EOM3.103.102.
Thin, as the filmy threads the spider weaves. ....Od.8.324.281.

SPIDER'S

The spider's touch, how exquisitely fine! ....3.EOM1.217.42.
Art thou in Spider's web, entangled hung? ....6.96ii.30Z5.271.

SPIDERS

Scriblers like Spiders, break one cobweb thro', ...4.Arbu.89A.102.

SPIED

Not to be spied of Ladies gent. ....6.14i.10.41.

SPIES

See SPYES.
Oft in her Glass the musing Shepherd spies ....1.W-F.211.169.
I heed not, I, the Bolts, the Locks, the Spies. ....2.ChWB.129.62.
He spies me out. I whisper, gracious God! ....4.JD4.62.31.
Spies, Guardians, Guests, old Women, Aunts, and Cozens& ....4.HAdv.129.85.
Himself among the storied Chiefs he spies, ...5.DunA2.143.118.
Himself amongst the storied Chiefs he spies, ...5.DunA2.143A.118.
Himself among the story'd chiefs he spies, ...5.DunB2.151.302.
Veils his fair glories, while he spies ....6.4iv.2.10.
Whether his hoary sire he spies, ...6.51ii.29.153.
To keep off Flatt'rers, Spies, and Panders, ...6.135.74.369.
Not far, great *Hector* on the Dust he spies, ...Il.15.11.194.

SPIES (CONTINUED)

Two Spies at distance lurk, and watchful seem ... Il.18.605.352.
When now the gen'rous Youth *Achilles* spies, ... Il.21.647.449.
One place at length he spies, to let in Fate, ... Il.22.407.472.
(Strong Guards and Spies, till all the Rites were done, ... Il.24.1009.577.
His ship returning shall my spies explore: ... Od.4.897.160.
When lifted on a ridgy wave, he spies ... Od.5.504.196.
And send out spies the dubious coast to view. ... Od.10.180.349.
And spies commission to explore the land. ... Od.14.291.50.
Be Silence still our guard. The Monarch's spies ... Od.15.481.93.
Our spies commission'd strait the coast explore, ... Od.17.512.157.
Befriended by my own domestic spies, ... Od.19.176.200.

SPIGHT

See SPITE.
If *Mævius* Scribble in *Apollo's* spight, ... 1.EOC.34.243.
(Whom Envy to the Great, and vulgar Spight ... 1.TrSt.232.420.
And, spight of all its Praises, must declare, ... 2.ChJM.196.24.
Tho' watch'd, and captive, yet in spight of all, ... 2.ChJM.518.40.
One you shall quit—in spight of both your Eyes— ... 2.ChWB.128.62.
And wou'd be so, in spight of all he swore. ... 2.ChWB.340.73.
As Hags hold Sabbaths, less for joy than spight, ... 3.Ep2.239.69.
In Nature's spight, the Stubborn Siege they hold ... 4.JD2A.27.134.
In spight of Witches, Devils, Dreams, and Fire? ... 4.2HE2.313.187.
And all their Spight on active Pomp display. ... 6.17iii.15.58.

SPIKY

The spiky Wheels thro' Heaps of Carnage tore; ... Il.20.585.418.

SPILFUL

Not with more Ease, the spilful Shepherd Swain ... Il.2.562.154.

SPILL

To muse, and spill her solitary Tea, ... 6.45.16.125.

SPILT

And have whole Streams of Blood been spilt in vain? ... Il.14.99.162.

SPIN

To spin, to weep, and cully Human Race. ... 2.ChWB.161.64.
Still spin the slight, self-pleasing thread anew; ... 4.Arbu.90A.102.
Spin all your Cobwebs o'er the Eye of Day! ... 4.EpS2.222.325.
And spin thy future with a whiter clue! ... Od.20.250.245.

SPINAGE

Both Spinage and Endive, ... 6.91.14.253.

SPINAL

Forth from the Bone the spinal Marrow flies, ... Il.20.559.417.
And snapt the spinal joint, and wak'd in hell. ... Od.10.668.375.

SPINDLE

There guide the Spindle, and direct the Loom: ... Il.6.633.358.
The Spindle follows, and displays the Charms ... Il.23.891.524.
In curious works; the whirling spindle glow'd ... Od.6.62.208.
While with the purple orb the spindle glows. ... Od.6.370.229.
Go, with the Queen the spindle guide, or cull ... Od.18.361.185.

SPINS

Lord *Fanny* spins a thousand such a Day. ... 4.HS1.6.5.
He spins the slight, self-pleasing thread anew; ... 4.Arbu.90.102.
So spins the silkworm small its slender store, ... 5.DunA1.171.84.
So spins the silk-worm small its slender store, ... 5.DunB4.253.369.
Urg'd on all hands it nimbly spins about, ... Od.9.459.325.

SPINSTER'S

Of the fair Spinster's Breast, and moving Arms: ... Il.23.892.524.

SPIO

Nesæa mild, and Silver *Spio* came. ... Il.18.48.326.

SPIRE

Who taught that heav'n-directed spire to rise? ... 3.Ep3.261.114.
And last, a little Ajax tips the spire. ... 5.DunA1.142.81.
A twisted Birth-day Ode completes the spire. ... 5.DunB1.162.282.
Broad Elm, and Cypress rising in a Spire; ... Il.21.410.437.
Cassandra first beholds, from *Ilion's* Spire, ... Il.24.870.572.
The narrow'r end I sharpen'd to a spire; ... Od.9.386.322.

SPIRES

Behold! *Augusta's* glitt'ring Spires increase, ... 1.W-F.377.187.
Now glaring Fiends, and Snakes on rolling Spires, ... 2.RL4.43.187.
There might you see the length'ning Spires ascend, ... 2.TemF.89.259.
Vales, Spires, meandring Streams, and *Windsor's* tow'ry Pride. .6.14ii.54.44.
The sable Fumes in curling Spires arise, ... Il.1.416.107.
Strait to the Tree his sanguine Spires he roll'd, ... Il.2.374.145.
Low in the Dust be laid yon' hostile Spires, ... Il.2.494.150.
And *Gonoëssa's* Spires salute the Sky. ... Il.2.693.159.
Gleam on the Walls, and tremble on the Spires. ... Il.8.702.428.
They, pale with Terror, mark its Spires unroll'd, ... Il.12.241.90.
Below, fair *Ilion's* glitt'ring Spires were seen, ... Il.13.23.105.
From her Foundations curling to her Spires, ... Il.22.519.478.
In sep'rate Islands crown'd with rising spires; ... Od.7.58.236.

SPIRIT

Whose Judgment sways us, and whose Spirit warms! ... 1.PAu.10.81.
Th' Æthereal Spirit o'er its Leaves shall move, ... 1.Mes.11.113.
With the same Spirit that its Author *writ,* ... 1.EOC.234.266.
Heav'n rest thy Spirit, noble *Solomon,* ... 2.ChJM.631.45.
Whatever Spirit, careless of his Charge, ... 2.RL2.123.167.
The softer Spirit of the *Sapphick* Muse. ... 2.TemF.225.273.
To farthest Shores th' Ambrosial Spirit flies, ... 2.TemF.376.281.
Or moving spirit bade the waters flow; ... 2.ElAb.254.340.
In each low wind methinks a Spirit calls, ... 2.ElAb.305.344.
Ethereal Essence, Spirit, Substance, Man, ... 3.EOM1.238A.44.
Wit, Spirit, Faculties, but make it worse; ... 3.EOM2.146.72.

SPIRIT (CONTINUED)

One thinks on Calvin Heav'n's own spirit fell, ... 3.EOM4.137.141.
Or Public Spirit its great cure, a Crown. ... 3.EOM4.172.144.
Correct with spirit, eloquent with ease, ... 3.EOM4.381.165.
Some God, or Spirit he has lately found, ... 3.Ep1.164.29.
With the same spirit that he drinks and whores; ... 3.Ep1.189.31.
With too much Spirit to be e'er at ease, ... 3.Ep2.96.58.
By Spirit robb'd of Pow'r, by Warmth of Friends, ... 3.Ep2.144.62.
Behold Sir Balaam, now a man of spirit, ... 3.Ep3.375.123.
And all they want is spirit, taste, and sense. ... 4.Arbu.160.108.
Yours *Milton's* Genius, and mine *Homer's* Spirit. ... 4.2HE2.136.175.
A grain of Courage, or a spark of Spirit, ... 4.2HE2.227.181.
Not but the Tragic spirit was our own, ... 4.2HE1.276.219.
But Kings in Wit may want discerning spirit. ... 4.2HE1.385.227.
BARNARD in spirit, sense, and truth abounds. ... 4.1HE1.85.285.
While *Roman* Spirit charms, and *Attic* Wit: ... 4.EpS2.85.317.
Spirit of *Arnall!* aid me while I lye. ... 4.EpS2.129.320.
And pour'd her Spirit o'er the land and deep. ... 5.DunB1.8.269.
Oft her gay Sister's life and spirit fled; ... 5.DunB4.39Z1.344
Intrigu'd with glory, and with spirit whor'd; ... 5.DunB4.316.374.
And pours her Spirit o'er the Land and Deep. ... 5.DunB4.627Z2.40
Must give the Spirit, and the Life inspire; ... 6.2.20.6.
Ah fleeting Spirit! wand'ring Fire, ... 6.31i.1.93.
Sister Spirit, come away. ... 6.31ii.8.94.
The balmy spirit of the western gale ... 6.35.11.103.
That thou hast done, with *Life* and *Spirit.* ... 6.44.30.123.
Refine ourselves to Spirit, for your Sake. ... 6.82vi.2.232.
Calm ev'ry thought, and spirit ev'ry Grace, ... 6.86.13A.245.
And all they want is Spirit, Taste, and Sense. ... 6.98.10.283.
Thy martial spirit, or thy Social love! ... 6.113.8.320.
By Spirit, robb'd of Power; by Warmth, of Friends; ... 6.154.30.403.
The vital Spirit issu'd at the Wound, ... Il.3.366.210.
His Arms resound, the Spirit wings its way. ... Il.5.56.269.
Recall'd his Spirit from the Gates of Death. ... Il.5.859.307.
Thy high Commands must spirit all our Wars. ... Il.9.98.437.
But from our Lips the vital Spirit fled, ... Il.9.530.459.
While Life's warm Spirit beats within my Breast. ... Il.9.720.470.
New Force, new Spirit to each Breast returns; ... Il.11.277.47.
Their Breasts no more the vital Spirit warms; ... Il.11.431.53.
The Spirit of a God my Breast inspire, ... Il.12.205.88.
Spirit divine! whose Exhalation greets ... Il.14.201.169.
And breath'd a Spirit in his rising Heart. ... Il.16.650.269.
Did such a Spirit as the Gods impart ... Il.17.173.294.
Excessive Spirit, urg'd 'em to the Course; ... Il.17.525.308.
Let his last Spirit smoak upon my Dart; ... Il.18.120.328.
(Wond'rous to tell) instinct with Spirit roll'd ... Il.18.442.342.
In those wide Wounds thro' which his Spirit fled, ... Il.19.29.372.
This said, and Spirit breath'd into his Breast, ... Il.20.142.400.
And his Eye darkens, and his Spirit flies: ... Il.21.198.429.
To the dark Realm the Spirit wings its Way, ... Il.22.455.474.
Long as the vital Spirit moves my Heart? ... Il.22.486.476.
Oh had thy gentle Spirit past in Peace, ... Il.22.544.479.
Till then, the Spirit finds no resting place, ... Il.23.89.490.
Like a thin Smoke he sees the Spirit fly, ... Il.23.117.492.
And calls the Spirit with a dreadful Cry. ... Il.23.219.498.
Invok'd the Gods whose Spirit moves the Air, ... Il.23.239.499.
The *Western Spirit,* and the *North* to rise; ... Il.23.259.499.
Minerva's Spirit drives his matchless Pace, ... Il.23.479.509.
The Coursers fly with Spirit not their own. ... Il.24.544.558.
The balmy spirit of the western gale ... Od.7.152.243.
As while the spirit in this bosom glows, ... Od.8.509.290.
Each drooping spirit with bold words repair, ... Od.9.447.324.
Thro' the wide wound the vital spirit flies. ... Od.10.190.349.
And breath'd his manly spirit thro' the wound. ... Od.11.686.418.
Down drop'd he groaning, and the spirit fled. ... Od.14.473.58.

SPIRIT'S

That e'er deserv'd a watchful Spirit's Care; ... 2.RL2.102.166.

SPIRITLESS

A heartless, spiritless, inglorious Crew: ... Il.7.114.369.

SPIRITS

And purer Spirits swell the sprightly Flood, ... 1.W-F.94.159.
With Spirits feeds, with Vigour fills the whole, ... 1.EOC.77.248.
What wants in *Blood* and *Spirits,* swell'd with *Wind;* ... 1.EOC.208.264.
But ripens Spirits in cold *Northern Climes,* ... 1.EOC.401.286.
Where guilty Spirits feel Eternal Pain; ... 1.TrSt.82.413.
Know then, unnumber'd Spirits round thee fly, ... 2.RL1.41.148.
For Spirits, freed from mortal Laws, with ease ... 2.RL1.69.151.
Haste then ye Spirits! to your Charge repair; ... 2.RL2.111.166.
He spoke; the Spirits from the Sails descent; ... 2.RL2.137.168.
The silver Lamp; the fiery Spirits blaze. ... 2.RL3.108.176.
The silver Lamp, and fiery Spirits blaze. ... 2.RL3.108A.176.
As into air the purer spirits flow, ... 2.Elegy.25.364.
From brutes what men, from men what spirits know: ... 3.EOM1.79.23.
And ripens Spirits as he ripens Mines, ... 3.Ep2.290.74.
"Spirits like you, believe me, shou'd be seen, ... 4.JD4.88.33.
The temp'rate sleeps, and spirits light as air! ... 4.HS2.74.59.
So spirits ending their terrestrial race, ... 5.DunA1.223.90.
So Spirits ending their terrestrial race, ... 5.DunB1.267.290.
Drowns my spirits, draws my breath? ... 6.31ii.11.94.
Exhaust thy Spirits, and thy Arms unbrace. ... Il.4.365.238.
His Nerves confirm'd, his languid Spirits chear'd; ... Il.5.155.274.
And draw new Spirits from the gen'rous Bowl; ... Il.6.326.342.
(For Strength consists in Spirits and in Blood, ... Il.9.826.474.
New rising Spirits all my Force alarm, ... Il.13.109.110.
New rising Spirits all the Man alarm, ... Il.13.109A.110.
Small Thought retrieves the Spirits of the Brave. ... Il.13.156.112.
Again his Pulses beat, his Spirits rise; ... Il.15.272.207.
But let the few whom brisker Spirits warm, ... Il.15.334.210.
And breathes fierce Spirits in his following Band. ... Il.15.841.229.
And pour'd swift Spirits thro' each *Trojan* Breast. ... Il.16.890.277.
Ourself with rising Spirits swell your Heart. ... Il.17.517.308.
Strength is deriv'd from Spirits and from Blood, ... Il.19.159.378.
Let rising Spirits flow from sprightly Juice, ... Il.19.234.382.

SPIRITS 365 SPOIL'D

SPIRITS (CONTINUED)
She, unresisting, fell; (her Spirits fled) ....Il.21.498.442.
And next, the Losers Spirits to restore, ...Il.23.818.521.
What Souls and Spirits shall it send below? ....Od.21.162.267.

SPIRITUAL
As Spiritual one, as the other is Carnal), ...6.42i.6.116.

SPIRTS
Spirts in the gard'ner's eyes who turns the cock. ....5.DunA2.170.122.
Spirts in the gard'ner's eyes who turns the cock. ....5.DunB2.178.304.

SPIRY
The spiry Firr and shapely Box adorn; ....1.Mes.74.119.
These moss-grown domes with spiry turrets crown'd, ...2.ElAb.142.331.
There on a Fir, whose spiry Branches rise ....Il.14.325.178.
On spiry volumes there a Dragon rides; ....Od.4.619.149.
Her spiry cliffs amid surrounding clouds; ....Od.4.686.151.
And spiry tops, the tufted trees above, ...Od.10.175.349.

SPIT
The spit of fortune too! her cruel hand ....Od.15.410.89.

SPITE
See SPIGHT.
Or with a *Rival's,* or an *Eunuch's* spite. ....1.EOC.31.242.
Applause, in spite of trivial Faults, is due. ....1.EOC.258.269.
Your Silence there is better than your *Spite,* ....1.EOC.598.308.
Unbiass'd, or by *Favour* or by *Spite;* ....1.EOC.633.311.
Liv'd an unspotted Maid in spite of Man: ....2.ChWB.47.58.
Spite of his haughty Mien, and barb'rous Pride: ....2.RL3.70.173.
Sudden he view'd, in spite of all her Art, ...2.RL3.143.178.
And, spite of Pride, in erring Reason's spite, ...3.EOM1.293.51.
And, spite of Pride, in erring Reason's spite, ...3.EOM1.293.51.
And, spite of Pride, and in thy Reason's spite, ...3.EOM1.293A.51.
And, spite of Pride, and in thy Reason's spite, ...3.EOM1.293A.51.
And hell was built on spite, and heav'n on pride. ....3.EOM3.262.119.
Of wretched Shylock, spite of Shylock's Wife: ....3.Ep3.96.97.
Or Spite, or Smut, or Rymes, or Blasphemies. ....4.Arbu.322.119.
In Love's, in Nature's spite, the siege they hold, ...4.JD2.23.133.
Spite of thyself a glorious minister! ....4.1740.44.334.
Begone ye Criticks, and restrain your Spite, ...6.7.1.15.
And *Winter's* Coolness spite of *Summer's* rays. ....6.14iv.30.48.
In spite of the Carle ....6.42iv.10.118.
For me, I think (in spite of Blunders) ....6.44.19.123.
Why Faith, in Spite of all my Brags, ...6.74.7.211.
Burnet and *Ducket,* friends in spite, ...6.105iv.1.301.
When, *D[u]ck[e]t B[u]rn[e]t,* friends in spite, ...6.105iv.1A.301.
As in spite of his Fall, might make Lucifer rise; ....6.122.6.341.
The worst that Envy, or that Spite ....6.135.19.366.
Ungracious Gods! with spite and envy curst! ....Od.5.149.178.

SPITS
What tho' (the use of barb'rous spits forgot) ....3.Ep3.181.109.
He spits fore-right; his haughty Chest before, ...4.JD4.264.47.
Half Froth, half Venom, spits himself abroad, ...4.Arbu.320.119.

SPITTING
With *Envy,* (spitting Cat,) dread Foe to Peace: ....6.14ii.34.44.

SPLAY
And splay-foot verse, remain'd, and will remain. ....4.2HE1.271.219.

SPLAY-FOOT
And splay-foot verse, remain'd, and will remain. ....4.2HE1.271.219.

SPLEEN
Not yet purg'd off, of Spleen and sow'r Disdain, ...1.EOC.527.297.
This *Justin* heard, nor cou'd his Spleen controul, ...2.ChJM.276.27.
Repair'd to search the gloomy Cave of *Spleen.* ....2.RL4.16.184.
Repairs to search the gloomy Cave of *Spleen.* ....2.RL4.16A.184.
Of Bodies chang'd to various Forms by *Spleen.* ....2.RL4.48.187.
That single Act gives half the World the Spleen. ....2.RL4.78.190.
From spleen, from obstinacy, hate, or fear! ....3.EOM2.186.77.
While one there is that charms us with his Spleen. ....3.Ep1.121A.24.
While one there is who charms us with his Spleen. ....3.Ep1.121.24.
Spleen, Vapours, or Small-pox, above them all, ...3.Ep2.267.72.
"You'll die of Spleen"..Excuse me, *Nunquam minus..* ....4.JD4.91A.33.
'Twou'd burst ev'n *Heraclitus* with the Spleen, ...4.JD4.236.45.
Nor puff'd by Pride, nor sunk by Spleen. ....4.HS6.28.251.
But give the Knight (or give his Lady) spleen; ....4.1HE1.145.289.
Fr. Strange spleen to *S[elkir]k! P.* Do I wrong the Man? ....4.EpS2.62.316.
And much good News, and little Spleen as may be; ....6.13.12.39.
Poor Vadius, long with learned spleen devour'd, ...6.71.41.204.
Wit like religion is with spleen profest; ....6.82ix(b).1A.234.
Spleen to Mankind his envious Heart possest, ...Il.2.267.140.
When *Jove,* dispos'd to tempt *Saturnia's* Spleen, ...Il.4.7.221.
Renew'd th' attack, incontinent of spleen: ....Od.19.79.196.

SPLEENFUL
Smiles on her Lips a spleenful Joy exprest, ...Il.15.111.200.

SPLEENWORT
A Branch of healing *Spleenwort* in his hand. ....2.RL4.56.188.

SPLENATICK
Now gayly Mad, now sow'rly Splenatick, ...2.ChWB.90.61.
Why not when I am splenatick? ....4.1HE7.6.269.

SPLENDID
And all is *splendid Poverty* at best. ....4.JD4.225.45.
Plain, but not sordid, tho' not splendid, clean. ....4.HS2.48.57.
Our Birth-day Nobles splendid Livery: ....4.1HE6.33.239.
His Eyes delighting with their splendid Show, ...Il.6.400.346.
A splendid Carpet roll'd beneath his Head. ....Il.10.177.9.
Him his swift Coursers, on his splendid Car ....Il.13.678.137.

SPLENDID (CONTINUED)
A splendid Footstool, and a Throne, that shine ....Il.14.272.175.
High on the splendid Car: One glorious Prize ....Il.17.514.308.
A splendid Scene! Then *Agamemnon* rose: ....Il.19.258.383.
Two splendid Mantles, and a Carpet spread, ...Il.24.728.568.
(In age his equal) on a splendid bed: ....Od.3.513.112.
The splendid car roll'd slow in regal state: ....Od.4.28.121.
The splendid seat, the list'ning chief address'd. ....Od.6.302.225.
Remain'd: Beside him, on a splendid throne, ...Od.7.312.251.
At night each pair on splendid carpets lay, ...Od.10.11.340.
The splendid mantle round him first he threw, ...Od.15.68.72.
With furry spoils of beasts the splendid beds: ....Od.17.40.134.
With splendid palls the downy fleece adorn: ....Od.19.364.212.
With splendid palls, and canopies of state: ....Od.19.394.213.
Reach'd, in its splendid case, the bow unstrung: ....Od.21.56.262.

SPLENDOR
Not ice or crystal equal splendor yield, ...1.TrPA.56.367.
With Splendor, Charity; with Plenty, Health; ....3.Ep3.225.111.
And Splendor borrows all her rays from Sense. ....3.Ep4.180.154.
For Splendor borrows all her rays from Sense. ....3.Ep4.180A.154.
The source of good; thy splendor to descry, ...6.23.11.73.
A gleamy Splendor flash'd along the Fields. ....Il.2.539.152.
With Splendor flame the Skies, and laugh the Fields around. ..Il.19.389.388.
Of sovereign state with faded splendor shine. ....Od.20.244.244.

SPLENDORS
And all Heav'n's Splendors blotted from the Skies. ....Il.17.425.303.
And on his Breast the beamy Splendors shone ....Il.22.177.461.
The firmament with living splendors glows. ....Od.6.54.208.
The front appear'd with radiant splendors gay, ...Od.7.110.240.
The glancing splendors as their sandals play. ....Od.8.306.279.
Whose worth the splendors of thy race adorns, ...Od.8.504.289.
Seem as extinct, and all their splendors lost; ....Od.12.372.449.

SPLENDOUR
For *Jove* his Splendour round the Chief had thrown, ...Il.15.734.224.

SPLENDOURS
Shook the fix'd Splendours of the Throne of *Jove.* ....Il.13.1061.155.
So from *Achilles'* Head the Splendours rise, ...Il.18.253.334.

SPLINTER'D
Splinter'd on Earth flew half the broken Wood. ....Il.13.715.138.

SPLIT
And Grace and Virtue, Sense and Reason split, ...3.EOM2.83.64.
Each had a Gravity wou'd make you split, ...4.2HE2.131.175.
Ingenious Writer, lest thy Barrel split, ...6.48i.5.133*.

SPLITTING
The splitting Raft the furious tempest tore; ....Od.7.358.254.

SPOIL
And decks the Goddess with the glitt'ring Spoil. ....2.RL1.132.156.
But oh! if e'er thy *Gnome* could spoil a Grace, ...2.RL4.67.189.
Rests on his Club, and holds th' *Hesperian* Spoil. ....2.TemF.82.259.
Sure, if they catch, to spoil the Toy at most, ...3.Ep2.233.69.
A Statesman's slumbers how this speech would spoil! ....3.Ep3.43.89.
To spoil the nation's last great trade, Quadrille! ....3.Ep3.64.92.
A Hackney-Coach my chance to spoil a Thought, ...4.2HE2.101.171.
But *Richmond's* Fair-ones never spoil their Locks, ...6.95.3.264.
The Richmond Fair ones ne'er will spoil their Looks, ...6.95.3A.264.
But sure you'll find it hard to spoil ....6.119.14.337.
The golden Spoil, and thine the lovely Dames. ....Il.2.278.141.
The noblest Spoil from sack'd *Lyrnessus* born, ...Il.2.842.164.
And wills, that *Helen* and the ravish'd Spoil ....Il.3.129.196.
A Mountain Goat resign'd the shining Spoil, ...Il.4.138.227.
The *Greeks* with Shouts press on, and spoil the Dead, ...Il.4.584.249.
To spoil his Arms the Victor strove in vain; ....Il.4.619.250.
Next rushing to the *Dardan* Spoil, detains ....Il.5.399.286.
To spoil his glitt'ring Arms, and Plumy Pride. ....Il.5.771.303.
Behold yon' glitt'ring Host, your future Spoil! ....Il.6.87.327.
His radiant Arms preserv'd from hostile Spoil, ...Il.6.528.353.
Be his my Spoil, and his these Arms remain; ....Il.7.90.367.
Then shall he store (when *Greece* the spoil divides) ....Il.9.177.441.
Then shalt thou store (when *Greece* the Spoil divides) ....Il.9.364.451.
My Spoil alone his greedy Soul delights; ....Il.9.442.454.
Great Queen of Arms! receive this hostile Spoil, ...Il.10.532.27.
The Spoil of Foes, or Present of a God? ....Il.10.643.30.
Swift to the Spoil the hasty Victor falls, ...Il.11.149.42.
Yet hand to hand I fight, and spoil the slain; ....Il.13.343.122.
Stretch'd on one Heap, the Victors spoil the slain. ....Il.15.389.212.
In rush the conqu'ring *Greeks* to spoil the slain; ....Il.15.642.221.
And crowd to spoil the Dead: The *Greeks* oppose: ....Il.16.731.272.
To spoil the Carcase fierce *Patroclus* flies: ....Il.16.908.279.
With *Hector* part the Spoil, and share the Fame. ....Il.17.273.298.
Perhaps may seize thy realm, and share the spoil; ....Od.3.402.106.
Receiv'd him charg'd with *Ilion's* noble spoil) ....Od.5.53.174.
We land our cattle, and the spoil divide: ....Od.9.640.333.
A prize more worth than *Ilion's* noble spoil. ....Od.13.161.13.
So much more sweet, to spoil, than to bestow? ....Od.17.487.156.
(The remnants of the spoil the suitor-crowd ....Od.20.3.230.
While to your lust and spoil a guardless prey, ...Od.22.43.288.
Brass, gold, and treasures shall the spoil defray, ...Od.22.68.290.
An absent Heroe's wealth they made their spoil: ....Od.24.525.373.

SPOIL'D
Nor Time nor Moths e'er spoil'd so much as they: ....1.EOC.113.252.
Spoil'd of his Kingdom, and depriv'd of Eyes; ....1.TrSt.104.414.
If these spoil'd Arms adorn a *Grecian* Foe? ....1.TrES.309.461.
The wasting Moth ne'er spoil'd my best Array; ....2.ChWB.288.71.
Down, down, proud Satire! tho' a Realm be spoil'd, ...4.EpS2.38.315.
Down, down, proud Satire! tho' a Land be spoil'd, ...4.EpS2.38A.315.
Nor has one ATTERBURY spoil'd the flock. ....5.DunB4.246.367.
Spoil'd his own language, and acquir'd no more; ....5.DunB4.320.374.

SPOIL'D (CONTINUED)
Imperial wonders rais'd on Nations spoil'd, 6.71.5.202.
But now is spoil'd clean, 6.90.6.251.
Atrides spoil'd, and left them on the Plain; Il.11.133.41.
If these spoil'd Arms adorn a *Grecian* Foe? Il.16.614.268.
In thy spoil'd Palace, and exhausted land; Od.22.60.289.

SPOILERS
Be You the spoilers, and our wealth consume. Od.2.84.64.
Haste from the court, ye spoilers, haste away: Od.2.162.70.
Of haughty spoilers, insolently vain; Od.18.172.175.

SPOILS
And of their fragrant Physick spoils the Fields: 1.W-F.242.171.
E're yet adorn'd with *Nemea's* dreadful Spoils. 1.TrSt.570.434.
In shaggy Spoils here *Theseus* was beheld, 2.TemF.79.258.
Britain, that pays her Patriots with her Spoils? 3.Ep3.216.111.
Whose spoils this paper offers to your eye, 5.DunB4.435.383.
Which spoils full many a good Design, 6.10.69.26.
The spoils of nations, and the pomp of wars, 6.32.28.96.
Stretch'd on the spoils of plunder'd palaces 6.130.12.358.
The Spoils of Cities raz'd, and Warriors slain, Il.1.159.95.
The Spoils of *Ilion* shall thy Loss requite, Il.1.164.95.
Ulysses' Spoils, or ev'n thy own be mine. Il.1.178.96.
What Spoils, what Conquests shall *Atrides* gain? Il.1.224.97.
With Treasure loaded and triumphant Spoils, Il.1.480.111.
Renown'd, triumphant, and enrich'd with Spoils. Il.2.144.135.
Suppose some Hero should his Spoils resign, Il.2.318.142.
Art thou that Hero, could those Spoils be thine? Il.2.319.142.
Encreas'd the Spoils of gallant *Diomed.* Il.5.34.267.
Of Heroes slain he bears the reeking Spoils, Il.6.611.357.
The Spoils and Treasures he to *Ilion* bore, Il.7.464.387.
Shall see his bloody Spoils in Triumph born, Il.8.664.427.
With Conquest honour'd, and enrich'd with Spoils: Il.9.28.433.
The Wealth I gather'd, and the Spoils I made. Il.9.435.454.
Thither the Spoils of this long War shall pass, Il.9.477.456.
Then, for his Spoils, a new Debate arose, Il.9.663.467.
A Lion's yellow Spoils his Back conceal'd; Il.10.29.3.
A Lion's Spoils, that to his Ankles hung; Il.10.203.10.
No Spoils enrich it, and no Studs adorn.) Il.10.306.16.
This said, the Spoils with dropping Gore defac'd, Il.10.536.27.
Haste to the Ships, the gotten Spoils enjoy, Il.10.596.28.
Where late the Spoils of *Hector's* Spy were laid, Il.10.619.29.
These other Spoils from conquer'd *Dolon* came, Il.10.660.31.
Or lay the Spoils of Conquest at her Feet, Il.11.316.49.
Collecting Spoils, and slaught'ring all along, Il.11.887.75.
The Spoils contested, and bear off the slain. Il.13.260.117.
We too can boast of no ignoble Spoils. Il.13.348.122.
His Spoils he could not, for the Show'r of Spears. Il.13.647.136.
From his broad Shoulders tore the Spoils away; Il.13.697.138.
Patroclus' Ships the glorious Spoils adorn. Il.16.808.274.
To me the Spoils my Prowess won, resign; Il.17.15.288.
On these thy conquer'd Spoils I shall bestow, Il.17.41.289.
The radiant Spoils to sacred *Ilion* bore. Il.17.216.295.
Insulting *Hector* bears the Spoils on high, Il.18.169.330.
The *Phrygians* now her scatter'd spoils enjoy, Il.18.341.338.
Charg'd with rich Spoils, to fair *Opuntia's* Shore! Il.18.382.339.
Spoils of my Arms, and thine; when, wasting wide, Il.18.401.340.
Among his Spoils this memorable Load. Il.23.980.528.
(Sad spoils of luxury) the Suitors fate. Od.1.141.39.
The spoils of elephants the roofs inlay, Od.4.87.123.
With a sack'd Palace, and barbaric spoils. Od.4.122.126.
Then from her azure car, the finny spoils Od.4.593.148.
Beneath the finny spoils extended prone, Od.4.595.148.
Long have his coffers groan'd with *Trojan* spoils; Od.10.44.341.
And in our grotto's stow thy spoils and arms. Od.10.480.366.
Heap'd high his navy with unnumber'd spoils. Od.11.654.416.
Ev'n these, when of their ill-got spoils possess'd, Od.14.107.41.
Great in the praise, rich in the spoils of war: Od.14.269.49.
The fleecy spoils of sheep, a goat's rough hide Od.14.588.65.
Instant the swain the spoils of beasts supplies, Od.16.47.104.
With furry spoils of beasts the splendid beds: Od.17.40.134.
A seat soft spread with furry spoils prepare, Od.19.119.198.
A seat adorn'd with furry spoils she plac'd: Od.19.122.198.
To throng my empty'd folds, with gifts or spoils. Od.23.384.343.
Rich spoils and gifts that blaz'd against the day. Od.24.110.353.

SPOKE
Thus *Daphnis* spoke, and *Strephon* thus reply'd. 1.PSp.22.62.
Then bow'd and spoke; the Winds forget to roar, 1.W-F.353.184.
She spoke, and vanish'd with the Voice—I rise, 1.TrSP.199.402.
The still Creation listen'd while he spoke, 1.TrSt.297.422.
Fir'd with the Thirst of Glory, thus he spoke. 1.TrES.26.450.
Spoke from his Throne the Cloud-compelling *Jove:* 1.TrES.323.461.
And, as he spoke, the Tears began to flow. 1.TrUl.73.468.
Thus while he spoke, the blue-ey'd Maid began 1.TrUl.160.471.
Around the Room, and sigh'd before he spoke:) 2.ChJM.86.18.
He spoke with Scorn, and turn'd another way— 2.ChJM.220.25.
He spoke; and turn'd, with Scorn, another way— 2.ChJM.220A.25.
Weak was her Voice, as while she spoke she cry'd. 2.ChJM.576.43.
Thus while she spoke, a sidelong Glance she cast, 2.ChJM.599.44.
Jove ne'er spoke Oracle more true than this, 2.ChJM.809.54.
But when my Point was gain'd, then thus I spoke, 2.ChWB.182.65.
He spoke; the Spirits from the Sails descent; 2.RL2.137.168.
"Give her the Hair"—he spoke, and rapp'd his Box. 2.RL4.130.194.
He spoke, and speaking, in proud Triumph spread 2.RL4.139.195.
So spoke the Dame, but no Applause ensu'd; 2.RL5.35.201.
Or spoke aloud, or whisper'd in the Ear; 2.TemF.434.284.
Great Nature spoke; observant Men obey'd; 3.EOM3.199.113.
Tho' wond'ring Senates hung on all he spoke, 3.Ep1.184.31.
(Were the last words that poor Narcissa spoke) 3.Ep1.243.36.
From the crack'd bag the dropping Guinea spoke, 3.Ep3.66.92.
Mistake, confound, object, at all he spoke. 4.JD4.117.35.
Thus Bethel spoke, who always speaks his thought, 4.HS2.129.65.
The sleepy Eye, that spoke the melting soul. 4.2HE1.150.209.
Clatt'ring their sticks, before ten lines are spoke, 4.2HE1.308.221.

SPOKE (CONTINUED)
Or what was spoke at CRESSY and POITIERS? 4.1HE1.100.287.
I see! I see!—" Then rapt, she spoke no more. 5.DunA1.255.94.
He spoke, and who with Lintot shall contend? 5.DunA2.52.103.
He spoke: and who with Lintot shall contend? 5.DunB2.56.298.
Then thus in quaint Recitativo spoke. 5.DunB4.52.346.
Let Friend affect to speak as Terence spoke, 5.DunB4.223.364.
More she had spoke, but yawn'd—All Nature nods: 5.DunB4.605.403.
Or Midwife *Word* gave Aid, and spoke the Infant forth. 6.8.6.17.
Fierce in this Cause, the *Letters* spoke all, 6.30.7.86.
Fierce in the Cause, the *Letters* spoke all, 6.30.7A.86.
She spoke, but broken Accents stopt her Voice, 6.96ii.71A.273.
Thus spoke the Prudence and the Fears of Age. Il.1.96.91.
The Prophet spoke; when with a gloomy Frown, Il.1.127.93.
He spoke; and furious, hurl'd against the Ground Il.1.325.103.
When *Nestor* spoke, they listen'd and obey'd. Il.1.359.105.
And furious, thus, and interrupting spoke. Il.1.387.106.
The Goddess spoke: The rowling Waves unclose; Il.1.562.115.
Thus *Thetis* spoke, but *Jove* in Silence held Il.1.662.118.
He spoke, and awful, bends his sable Brows; Il.1.683.119.
The Thund'rer spoke, nor durst the Queen reply; Il.1.736.122.
Thus *Vulcan* spoke; and rising with a Bound, Il.1.752.123.
The Vision spoke, and past in Air away. Il.2.92.131.
He spoke, and sate; when *Nestor* rising said, Il.2.99.131.
Thus spoke the Sage: The Kings without Delay Il.2.107.132.
Not thus the King in secret Council spoke. Il.2.232.138.
Vext when he spoke, yet still they heard him speak. Il.2.272.140.
Then deeply thoughtful, pausing e'er he spoke, Il.2.346.143.
Thus spoke the Prophet, thus the Fates succeed. Il.2.397.145.
The Monarch spoke: and strait a Murmur rose, Il.2.470.149.
He spoke: in still Suspense on either side Il.3.133.196.
He spoke no more than just the Thing he ought. Il.3.278.206.
So spoke the Fair, nor knew her Brothers Doom, Il.3.311.208.
She spoke, and *Helen's* secret Soul was mov'd; Il.3.487.215.
Thus having spoke, th' enamour'd *Phrygian* Boy Il.3.555.218.
Thus while he spoke, the Queen of Heav'n enrag'd Il.4.27.222.
Her sullen Silence, and with Fury spoke. Il.4.34.222.
So spoke the Master of the martial Art, Il.4.360.238.
He spoke, and ardent, on the trembling Ground Il.4.474.242.
So spoke he, boastful; but the winged Dart Il.5.138.273.
Fix'd on the Chief with Scorn, and thus he spoke. Il.5.309.281.
Thus while they spoke, the Foe came furious on, Il.5.338.283.
He spoke, and rising hurl'd his forceful Dart, Il.5.351.283.
So spoke the God who darts Celestial Fires; Il.5.539.294.
Thus haughty spoke. The *Lycian* King reply'd. Il.5.803.304.
She spoke: *Minerva* burns to meet the War: Il.5.884.308.
The Monarch spoke: the Words with Warmth addrest Il.6.77.327.
He spoke, and Transport fill'd *Tydides'* Heart; Il.6.261.339.
The Prince beheld, and high-resenting spoke. Il.6.405.346.
Hung on his Hand, and then dejected spoke; Il.6.507.351.
Thus having spoke, th' illustrious Chief of *Troy* Il.6.594.355.
He spoke, and fondly gazing on her Charms Il.6.616.357.
So spoke the Guardian of the *Trojan* State, Il.7.1.363.
The Gods have spoke it, and their Voice is Fate. Il.7.58.365.
And inly groaning, thus opprobrious spoke. Il.7.108.369.
These Words scarce spoke, with gen'rous Ardour prest, Il.7.119.369.
Thus to the Kings he spoke. What grief, what Shame Il.7.145.371.
The Senior spoke, and sate. To whom reply'd Il.7.428.385.
The Monarch spoke: the Warriors snatch'd with haste Il.7.454.387.
At length *Tydides* rose, and rising spoke. Il.7.475.388.
Thus spoke the hoary Monarch of the Deep. Il.7.541.391.
The Heav'ns attentive trembled as he spoke. Il.8.6.395.
Th' Almighty spoke, nor durst the Pow'rs reply, Il.8.35.397.
At length his Best-belov'd, the Pow'r of *Wisdom,* spoke. Il.8.38.397.
Encourag'd his proud Steeds, while thus he spoke. Il.8.225.408.
So spoke th' imperial Regent of the Skies; Il.8.433.418.
Thus have I spoke, and what I spake is Fate. Il.8.491.420.
She spoke, and backward turn'd her Steeds of Light, Il.8.534.422.
The Leader spoke. From all his Hosts around Il.8.673.427.
He spoke: the Host in still Attention heard. Il.9.72.435.
Thus spoke the hoary Sage: the rest obey; Il.9.109.437.
Then *Nestor* spoke, for Wisdom long approv'd, Il.9.125.438.
And thus, impatient, to *Ulysses* spoke. Il.9.736.470.
Well hast thou spoke; but at the Tyrant's Name, Il.9.759.471.
The gen'ral Silence, and undaunted spoke. Il.9.815.473.
Tydides spoke—The Man you seek, is here. Il.10.260.13.
Thus having spoke, with gen'rous Ardour prest, Il.10.299.15.
(Still, as he spoke, his Limbs with Horror shook) Il.10.462.24.
Sternly he spoke, and as the Wretch prepar'd Il.10.522.26.
Scarce had he spoke, when lo! the Chiefs appear, Il.10.636.30.
Ev'n *Jove,* whose Thunder spoke his Wrath, distill'd Il.11.69.37.
He spoke, and *Iris* at his Word obey'd; Il.11.253.46.
He spoke, while *Socus* seiz'd with sudden Fright, Il.11.558.58.
Thus having spoke, the Driver's Lash resounds; Il.11.654.63.
Thus spoke your Father at *Thessalia's* Court; Il.11.920.76.
Long weigh'd the Signal, and to *Hector* spoke. Il.12.244.90.
(Fierce as he spoke, his Eyes with Fury burn'd) Il.12.268.91.
Furious he spoke, and rushing to the Wall, Il.12.295.92.
Fir'd with the Thirst of Glory, thus he spoke. Il.12.370.95.
He spoke, and dragg'd the goary Corse away. Il.13.482.130.
He spoke, and all as with one Soul obey'd; Il.13.614.135.
As thus he spoke, behold in open View, Il.13.1038.154.
And thus the venerable Hero spoke. Il.14.158.165.
He spoke, then rush'd amid the Warrior Crew; Il.14.171.165.
And thus the venerable Warrior spoke. Il.14.158A.165.
He spoke, then rush'd amid the warring Crew; Il.14.171A.165.
Silence that spoke, and Eloquence of Eyes. Il.14.252.173.
Then press'd her Hand, and thus with Transport spoke. Il.14.338.179.
He spoke; the Goddess with the charming Eyes Il.14.373.180.
Gazing he spoke, and kindling at the view, Il.14.393.181.
The goary Visage, thus insulting spoke, Il.14.586.190.
Dreadful he spoke, then toss'd the Head on high; Il.14.595.191.
And thus, incens'd, to fraudful *Juno* spoke, Il.15.16.194.
The Thund'rer spoke: Imperial *Juno* mourn'd, Il.15.39.195.
Th' Almighty spoke; the Goddess wing'd her Flight Il.15.190.203.
Thus to bold *Hector* spoke the Son of *Jove,* Il.15.296.208.

SPOKE (CONTINUED)

The Warrior spoke, the list'ning *Greeks* obey, ... Il.15.338.210.
He spoke; and speaking, swifter than the Wind .... Il.15.468.215.
He spoke, and round him breath'd heroic Fires; .... Il.15.806.227.
He spoke—The Warriors, at his fierce Command, ... Il.15.880.230.
Raging he spoke; nor farther wastes his Breath, ... Il.15.902.232.
Thus spoke, indulgent to his best belov'd. .... Il.16.8.234.
Another follow'd, and *Patroclus* spoke. .... Il.16.30.236.
Joyful they heard, and kindling as he spoke .... Il.16.330.255.
He spoke; each Leader in his Grief partook, ... Il.16.671.270.
Spoke from this Throne the Cloud-compelling *Jove.* .... Il.16.810.274.
So spoke the God who darts celestial Fires: .... Il.16.867.277.
So spoke th' inspiring God; then took his flight, ... Il.16.885.277.
He spoke, *Patroclus* march'd, and thus he sped. .... Il.16.1015.282.
Thus having spoke, *Apollo* wing'd his Flight .... Il.17.87.291.
He spoke, and foremost to the Combat flew: .... Il.17.394.302.
While thus relenting to the Steeds he spoke. .... Il.17.503.308.
He spoke, and high the sounding Jav'lin flung, ... Il.17.584.311.
With Tears the Hero spoke, and at his Pray'r .... Il.17.733.317.
She spoke, and past in Air. The Hero rose; .... Il.18.241.333.
He spoke, and bid the sad Attendants round .... Il.18.403.340.
(His Wife and Sister) spoke almighty *Jove.* .... Il.18.418.341.
And rising solemn, each his Sentence spoke. .... Il.18.588.351.
He spoke, and from the Warriors turn'd his Face: .... Il.19.329.386.
He spoke, and sudden as the Word of *Jove* .... Il.19.370.387.
Eternal Silence, and portentous spoke. .... Il.19.451.391.
He spoke. With all his Force the Jav'lin flung, ... Il.20.308.407.
Lopp'd the green Arms to spoke a Chariot Wheel) .... Il.21.45.424.
Die then—He said; and as the Word he spoke .... Il.21.125.426.
Scamander spoke; the Shores return'd the Sound. .... Il.21.230.430.
He spoke in vain—The Chief without Dismay .... Il.21.255.431.
He spoke, and smote the loud-resounding Shield, ... Il.21.464.440.
The Goddess spoke, and turn'd her Eyes away .... Il.21.484.441.
He spoke; and past: *Latona,* stooping low, ... Il.21.585.446.
The Sire of Mortals and Immortals spoke. .... Il.22.220.464.
His dreadful Plumage nodded as he spoke. .... Il.22.316.469.
He spoke, and lanch'd his Jav'lin at the Foe; .... Il.22.349.470.
(Flames, as he spoke, shot flashing from his Eyes) .... Il.22.434.473.
She spoke; and furious, with distracted Pace, ... Il.22.592.480.
He spoke; they hear him, and the Word obey; .... Il.23.67.489.
Thus while he spoke, each Eye grew big with Tears: .... Il.23.130.493.
But to the King of Men thus spoke the Chief. .... Il.23.194.497.
No sooner had he spoke, but thund'ring near .... Il.23.579.513.
So spoke *Antilochus;* and at the Word .... Il.23.677.516.
The Giant spoke; and in a stupid Gaze .... Il.23.781.520.
Thus to *Ulysses* spoke great *Telamon.* .... Il.23.839.523.
To Heav'n assembled, thus *Apollo* spoke. .... Il.24.43.537.
She spoke, and vanish'd. *Priam* bids prepare .... Il.24.225.546.
He spoke, and bad th' attendant Handmaid bring .... Il.24.371.551.
Thus *Priam* spoke, and *Hermes* thus reply'd. .... Il.24.476.556.
Thus spoke to *Priam* the cœlestial Guide, ... Il.24.517.557.
Till thus at last the Kingly Suppliant spoke, ... Il.24.597.561.
(A solemn Scene!) at length the Father spoke. .... Il.24.803.570.
Some Word thou would'st have spoke, which sadly dear, ... Il.24.936.575.
Thus spoke the Dame, and melted into Tears. .... Il.24.958.576.
So spoke the Fair, with Sorrow-streaming Eye: .... Il.24.981.576.
He spoke; and at his Word, the *Trojan* Train .... Il.24.989.577.
Constrain'd a smile, and thus ambiguous spoke. .... Od.1.490.55.
'Twas silence all: at last *Ægyptius* spoke; .... Od.2.19.61.
And as he stood, he spoke and wept by turns. .... Od.2.32.61.
He spoke. *Telemachus* with transport glows, ... Od.2.43.62.
While thus he spoke, with rage and grief he frown'd, ... Od.2.89.65.
Thus spoke th' inventive Queen, with artful sighs. .... Od.2.106.66.
That flash'd with rage; and as he spoke, he frown'd. .... Od.2.260.74.
While yet he spoke, *Leocritus* rejoyn'd: .... Od.2.275.74.
Sage *Mentor's* form, and thus like *Mentor* spoke. .... Od.2.306.76.
She spoke: to his high dome the Prince returns, ... Od.2.335.77.
He spoke and frown'd, nor longer deign'd to stay, ... Od.2.361.78.
While yet he spoke, she fill'd the walls with cries, ... Od.2.406.80.
Spoke to *Telemachus* the martial Maid. .... Od.2.449.83.
Swift as she spoke, with rapid pace she leads. .... Od.2.452.83.
She spoke, and led the way with swiftest speed: .... Od.3.39.88.
Well hast thou spoke (the blue-ey'd maid replies) .... Od.3.455.109.
The hand of young *Telemachus,* and spoke. .... Od.3.479.110.
Observant of his word. The word scarce spoke, ... Od.3.606.117.
While thus pathetic to the Prince he spoke, ... Od.4.149.127.
And melting with fraternal pity spoke. .... Od.4.258.131.
Your accent varying as their spouses spoke: .... Od.4.380.139.
Spoke loud the languish of his yerning soul: .... Od.4.388.139.
He spoke. The God who mounts the winged winds .... Od.5.56.174.
Thus having spoke, the nymph the table spread, ... Od.5.117.177.
Divine refection! then recruited, spoke. .... Od.5.120.178.
With sighs, *Ulysses* heard the words she spoke, ... Od.5.221.182.
Him, while he spoke, with smiles *Calypso* ey'd, ... Od.5.233.182.
Thus spoke *Calypso* to her god-like guest. .... Od.5.256.184.
Thus while he spoke, the beamy Sun descends, ... Od.5.289.185.
He spoke, and high the forky Trident hurl'd, ... Od.5.375.190.
A mighty wave rush'd o'er him as he spoke, ... Od.5.403.192.
From *Dymas* sprung, and thus the vision spoke: .... Od.6.28.205.
Thus having spoke, th' unknown celestial leads: .... Od.7.49.236.
(Thus sighing spoke the Man of many woes) .... Od.7.323.251.
She spoke, and sudden with tumultuous sounds .... Od.8.15.262.
Thus spoke the Prince: th' attending Peers obey, ... Od.8.43.264.
Thus spoke the King; th' attending Peers obey: .... Od.8.105.268.
Well hast thou spoke, (*Euryalus* replies) .... Od.8.153.271.
He made obeysance, and thus spoke aloud. .... Od.8.156.271.
She spoke: and momentary mounts the sky: .... Od.8.227.274.
Well hast thou spoke, and well thy gen'rous tongue .... Od.8.269.277.
Then mutual, thus they spoke: Behold on wrong .... Od.8.367.283.
Thus spoke to *Ithacus:* To guard with bands .... Od.8.479.288.
The Giant spoke, and thro' the hollow rock .... Od.9.543.328.
Thus while he spoke, the sovereign plant he drew, ... Od.10.361.361.
And ere I spoke the tears began to flow. .... Od.11.70.383.
Still as I spoke, the Phantom seem'd to moan, ... Od.11.100.385.
While yet he spoke, the Prophet I obey'd, ... Od.11.122.387.
Thus while she spoke, in swarms hell's Empress brings .... Od.11.273.395.

SPOKE (CONTINUED)

And as he spoke her tender hand he prest. .... Od.11.296.396.
Stretch'd out her snowy hand, and thus she spoke: .... Od.11.417.405.
While yet I spoke, the Shade with transport glow'd, ... Od.11.659.416.
And turning his grim visage, sternly spoke. .... Od.11.760.424.
The Goddess spoke; in feasts we waste the day, ... Od.12.39.431.
Thus to the melancholy train I spoke: .... Od.12.189.441.
While yet I spoke, a sudden sorrow ran .... Od.12.330.447.
The Monarch spoke: they trembled and obey'd, ... Od.13.214.16.
And as he spoke, the tears began to flow. .... Od.13.240.17.
Thus while he spoke, the blue-ey'd maid began .... Od.13.327.23.
Then future means consult—she spoke, and trod .... Od.13.419.26.
Thus spoke the faithful swain, and thus rejoin'd .... Od.14.171.43.
With artful preface to his host he spoke. .... Od.14.517.62.
Well hast thou spoke (rejoin'd th' attentive swain) .... Od.14.576.64.
Thus spoke the Goddess, and resum'd her flight .... Od.15.51.72.
Thus spoke the dame, and homeward took the road. .... Od.15.491.94.
While yet he spoke, the Prince advancing drew .... Od.16.11.102.
While yet he spoke, impatient of delay .... Od.16.166.110.
He spoke and sate. The Prince with transport flew, ... Od.16.234.114.
Jove grants henceforth, if thou hast spoke from *Jove?* .... Od.16.343.122.
Scarce had he spoke, when turning to the strand .... Od.16.366.124.
Few words she spoke, tho' much she had to say, ... Od.17.50.135.
He ey'd the stranger, and imperious spoke. .... Od.17.249.143.
So spoke the wretch; but shunning farther fray, ... Od.17.304.146.
Then turning to *Antinous,* thus he spoke. .... Od.17.479.156.
He spoke, and lifting high above the board .... Od.17.492.156.
While thus his mother to her virgins spoke. .... Od.17.585.161.
Amidst her maids thus spoke the prudent Queen, ... Od.17.596.161.
She spoke, *Telemachus* then sneez'd aloud; .... Od.17.624.162.
Thus spoke *Penelope. Eumæus* flies .... Od.17.632.163.
While with indignant scorn he sternly spoke, ... Od.18.100.172.
Scornful he spoke, and o'er his shoulder flung .... Od.18.130.172.
Which spoke *Ulysses* to his realm restor'd: .... Od.19.665.228.
He spoke; then rising, his broad sword unbound, ... Od.21.123.264.
Then thus with accent mild *Ulysses* spoke: .... Od.21.197.269.
Vulturs shall tear thee—Thus incens'd they spoke, ... Od.22.35.288.
That wither'd all their hearts, *Ulysses* spoke. .... Od.22.40.288.
And die I trust ye shall—He sternly spoke: .... Od.22.81.290.
Swift as he spoke, he drew his traytor sword, ... Od.22.93.291.
While yet they spoke, in quest of arms again .... Od.22.176.296.
She spoke; but willing longer to survey .... Od.22.257.299.
He spoke: at once their fiery lances flew: .... Od.22.292.300.
While yet she spoke, the Queen in transport sprung .... Od.23.35.320.
But ere I spoke, he rose, and check'd the sound. .... Od.23.78.322.
This spoke the King: Th' observant train obey, ... Od.23.139.327.
He spoke, and sheath'd in arms, incessant flies .... Od.23.393.343.
But *Nestor* spoke, they listen'd, and obey'd. .... Od.24.70.351.
Spoke when he ceas'd: dumb sorrow touch'd them all. .... Od.24.503.372.
When slowly-rising, *Halitherses* spoke: .... Od.24.517.372.
So spoke *Telemachus:* the gallant boy .... Od.24.592.376.
So *Pallas* spoke: The mandate from above .... Od.24.628.377.

SPOKEN

"But has he spoken?" Not a syllable. .... 4.2HE1.335.223.
Some would have spoken, but the voice was drown'd .... 5.DunB4.277.371.

SPOKES

Eight brazen Spokes in radiant Order flame; .... Il.5.892.308.
Chariots on Chariots rowl; the clashing Spokes .... Il.16.444.260.
And rapid as it runs, the single Spokes are lost. .... Il.18.696.357.

SPONGE

Then with a Sponge the sooty Workman drest .... Il.18.483.345.
And let th' abstersive sponge the board renew: .... Od.20.189.242.
With thirsty sponge they rub the tables o'er, ... Od.22.488.313.

SPONTANEOUS

Spontaneous beauties all around advance, ... 3.Ep4.67.143.
Heav'n Gates spontaneous open to the Pow'rs, ... Il.5.928.310.
Heav'n-Gates spontaneous open to the Pow'rs, ... Il.8.478.419.
Conform'd spontaneous, and around him clos'd; .... Il.17.248.297.
Shall rise spontaneous in the needful hour. .... Od.3.36.88.
Spontaneous did you speed his secret course, ... Od.4.870.159.
Spontaneous wines from weighty clusters pour, ... Od.9.125.310.
Spontaneous to the Suitors' feast preferr'd: .... Od.20.220.244.
Then down each cheek the tears spontaneous flow, ... Od.20.419.253.

SPOON

Or o'er cold coffee trifle with the spoon, ... 6.45.17.125.

SPOONS

The Board's with Cups and Spoons, alternate, crown'd; .... 2.RL*A*1.89.130.
For lo! the Board with Cups and Spoons is crown'd, ... 2.RL3.105.175.

SPORT

Nor blush to sport on *Windsor's* blissful Plains: .... 1.PSp.2.59.
The wanton Victims of his *Sport* remain. .... 1.W-F.78.157.
Or where ye Muses sport on *Cooper's* Hill. .... 1.W-F.264.173.
Contending Wits become the *Sport of Fools:* .... 1.EOC.517.296.
Sport in her shades, and in her shades be fed; .... 1.TrFD.79.389.
Sport with her Tail, and wanton in the Sun; .... 2.ChWB.145.63.
And sport and flutter in the Fields of Air. .... 2.RL1.66.151.
Destroy all creatures for thy sport or gust, ... 3.EOM1.117.29.
No wonder then, when all was Love and Sport, ... 4.2HE1.151.209.
Or Virtue, or Religion turn to sport, ... 4.2HE1.211.213.
"Then spend your life in Joy and Sport, ... 4.HS6.181.261.
Whales sport in woods, and dolphins in the skies, ... 5.DunA3.242.177.
Till Isis' Elders reel, their Pupils' sport; .... 5.DunA3.333.191.
The sons of *Isis* reel! the towns-mens sport; .... 5.DunA3.333A.191.
Whales sport in woods, and dolphins in the skies; .... 5.DunB3.246.332.
'Till Isis' Elders reel, their pupils' sport, ... 5.DunB3.337.336.
Where Bentley late tempestuous wont to sport .... 5.DunB4.201.362.
As smiling Infants sport themselves to Rest: .... 6.19.14.62.
As smiling Infants sport themselves to Sleep. .... 6.19.14A.62.
The birds shall sport amidst the bending sprays, ... 6.20.66.68.

SPORT (CONTINUED)

Who think the Turk and Pope a sport .... 6.61.3.180.
Who think both Turk and Pope a sport .... 6.61.3A.180.
We Country Dogs love nobler Sport, ... 6.135.13.366.
The Sport and Insult of the Hostile Train. .... Il.6.102.328.
The Sport of Heav'n, and Fable of the Sky! .... Il.14.378.180.
And make my future Life the Sport of Fate. .... Il.21.316.434.
Jove, as his Sport, the dreadful Scene descries, ... Il.21.454.439.
Antinous sate spectator of the sport; .... Od.4.850.158.
The sport of winds, and driv'n from ev'ry coast, ... Od.5.170.180.
They sport, they feast; *Nausicaa* lifts her voice, ... Od.6.115.211.
Fierce in the sport, along the mountain brow .... Od.6.121.212.
In verdant meads they sport, and wide around .... Od.12.57.432.

SPORTED

The Fairies sported on the Garden's Side, ... 2.ChJM.618.45.
With Princes sported, and on Dainties fed, ... Il.22.647.483.

SPORTING

O'er the green mead the sporting virgins play: .... Od.6.112.211.

SPORTIVE

Both doom'd alike for sportive Tyrants bled, ... 1.W-F.59.154.
See! sportive fate, to punish aukward pride, ... 3.Ep4.19.138.
His papers all, the sportive winds up-lift .... 5.DunA2.107A.109.
In empty Air their sportive Jav'lins throw, ... Il.2.940.168.
The sportive Wanton, pleas'd with some new Play, ... Il.15.418.213.
In flow'ry meads the sportive *Sirens* play, ... Od.12.194.441.
Propose the sportive lot, the Chief replies, ... Od.19.683.229.

SPORTS

The dapper Elves their Moonlight Sports pursue; .... 2.ChJM.460.37.
When Sense subsides, and Fancy sports in sleep, ... 3.Ep1.46.18.
The other slights, for Women, Sports, and Wines, ... 4.2HE2.272.185.
"Now turn to diff'rent sports (the Goddess cries) .... 5.DunA2.213.127.
"Now turn to diff'rent sports (the Goddess cries) .... 5.DunB2.221.306.
The coursers for the champian sports, retain; .... Od.4.821.157.
Ill the gay sports with troubled hearts agree: .... Od.8.170.271.
The sports of glory to the brave belong, ... Od.8.176.271.
Then to the sports his sons the King commands, ... Od.8.405.285.

SPORUS

Let *Sporus* tremble—"What? that Thing of silk, ... 4.Arbu.305.117.
" *Sporus*, that mere white Curd of Ass's milk? .... 4.Arbu.306.117.
"Satire or Sense alas! can *Sporus* feel? .... 4.Arbu.307.118.
" Satire or Shame alas! can *Sporus* feel? .... 4.Arbu.307A.118.
Sporus at Court, or *Japhet* in a Jayl, ... 4.Arbu.363.122.

SPOT

Full in the Center of this Spot of Ground, ... 2.ChJM.456A.37.
Fair without Spot, whose ev'ry charming Part .... 2.ChJM.531.41.
Fix'd like a plant on his peculiar spot, ... 3.EOM2.63.63.
Fix'd to no spot is Happiness sincere, ... 3.EOM4.15.129.
"Yet Cloe sure was form'd without a spot—" .... 3.Ep2.157.63.
Fair without spot; than greas'd by grocer's hands, ... 5.DunA1.199.86.
Thinks Worth, Wit, Learning, to that Spot confin'd; .... 6.96v.26.280.
"Yet Cloë sure was form'd without a Spot—" .... 6.139.1.377.
The Spot, where *Hector* stop'd his Rage before, ... Il.10.234.12.
And mark'd the Spot where *Ilion's* Tow'rs arise; .... Il.11.112.39.
The Hour, the Spot, to conquer, or to fall. .... Il.13.168.112.
This Spot is all you have, to lose or keep; .... Il.15.898.232.
Fixt on the Spot they war; and wounded, wound; .... Il.17.414.303.
There on the Spot which great *Achilles* show'd, ... Il.23.154.495.
And not one empty spot escapes thy care. .... Od.24.291.363.

SPOTLESS

Fair was her Face, and spotless was her Mind, ... 1.TrSt.672.438.
Eternal sun-shine of the spotless mind! .... 2.ElAb.209.337.
Then mix this Dust with thine—O spotless Ghost! .... 6.123.5.343.
The glitt'ring emblem of each spotless dame, ... 6.126ii.3.353.
Clean as her soul, and spotless as her frame; .... 6.126ii.4A.353.
Clear as her soul, and spotless as her frame; .... 6.126ii.4B.353.
Snatch to thy Holy Hill of Spotless Bay, ... 6.155.7.404.
Unransom'd here receive the spotless Fair; .... Il.1.578.115.
You, with your Matrons, go! a spotless Train, ... Il.6.338.343
That spotless as she came, the Maid removes, ... Il.19.175.379.
"The *Grecian* matrons taint my spotless fame; .... Od.2.112.67.
In youth by *Nestor* lov'd, of spotless fame, ... Od.3.576.116.
And spotless robes become the young and gay: .... Od.6.76.208.
Thus with vile censure taint my spotless name. .... Od.6.330.227.
(Reply'd the swain for spotless faith divine) .... Od.14.444.57.
The reverend stranger, and the spotless maid; .... Od.16.114.108.
The rev'rend stranger, or the spotless maid; .... Od.18.463.190.
For spotless faith, and deeds of martial fame: .... Od.19.467.219.
The *Grecian* matrons taint my spotless fame; .... Od.24.161.356.

SPOTS

I, for a few slight Spots, am not so nice. .... 2.ChWB.39.58.
Such happy Spots the nice admirer take, ... 3.Ep2.43A.53.
Their happy Spots the nice admirer take, ... 3.Ep2.43.53.
In me what Spots (for Spots I have) appear, ... 4.HS1.55.9.
In me what Spots (for Spots I have) appear, ... 4.HS1.55.9.
His robe, which spots indelible besmear, ... Od.13.502.29.

SPOTTED

Her spotted Breast, and gaping Womb imbru'd .... 1.TrSt.729.440.
A Leopard's spotted Hide his Shoulders spread; .... Il.10.35.4.
Nor Panther braves his spotted Foe in Fight, ... Il.17.22.288.
Sudden, our bands a spotted Pard restrain: .... Od.4.616.148.

SPOUSAL

Thy spousal ornament neglected lies; .... Od.6.31.205.
'Till *Hymen* lights the torch of spousal love. .... Od.18.334.184.
To him the spousal honour is decreed, ... Od.19.676.229.
To softness lost, to spousal love unknown, ... Od.23.105.324.
Lo! the Queen weds! we hear the spousal lay! .... Od.23.136.327.

SPOUSAL (CONTINUED)

Lo! the Queen weds! we hear the spousal lay! .... Od.23.146.328.
Has steel'd that heart, averse to spousal love! .... Od.23.166.328.
(My father's present in the spousal hour, ... Od.23.243.335.

SPOUSE

My sire, my sister, and my spouse farewell! .... 1.TrFD.88.389.
Tho' Fortune change, his constant Spouse remains, ... 2.ChJM.41.17.
Since if I found no Pleasure in my Spouse, ... 2.ChJM.115.20.
He kiss'd his balmy Spouse, with wanton Play, ... 2.ChJM.388.33.
Who pray'd his Spouse, attended by her Train, ... 2.ChJM.408.34.
He rais'd his Spouse ere Matin Bell was rung, ... 2.ChJM.523.40.
Have Comfort, Spouse, nor think thy Lord unkind; .... 2.ChJM.567.42.
As one whose Thoughts were on his Spouse intent; .... 2.ChJM.751.51.
Signs of Remorse, while thus his Spouse he chear'd: .... 2.ChJM.788.53.
A fruitful Wife, and a believing Spouse. .... 2.ChJM.816.54.
For when my transitory Spouse, unkind, ... 2.ChWB.25.58.
Let my good Spouse pay Tribute, do me Right, ... 2.ChWB.52.59.
"Dear Spouse, I credit not the Tales they tell. .... 2.ChWB.131.62.
What? so familiar with your Spouse? I cry'd: .... 2.ChWB.167.64.
"Approach my Spouse, and let me kiss thy Cheek; .... 2.ChWB.184.65.
My fourth dear Spouse was not exceeding true; .... 2.ChWB.229.68.
It pleas'd the Lord to take my Spouse at last! .... 2.ChWB.308.71.
My Spouse (who was, you know, to Learning bred) .... 2.ChWB.355.74.
Brought her own Spouse and all his Race to Woe; .... 2.ChWB.380.75.
Ah wretch! believ'd the spouse of God in vain, ... 2.ElAb.177.334.
For her the Spouse prepares the bridal ring, ... 2.ElAb.219.338.
A Spark too fickle, or a Spouse too kind. .... 3.Ep2.94.57.
No zealous Pastor blame a failing Spouse, ... 4.EpS2.193.324.
Stern *Cato's* self was no relentless spouse: .... 6.41.30.114.
Thy Pigmy Island and thy tiny Spouse .... 6.96ii.30Z33.272.
"Thy Pigmy Children, and thy tiny Spouse, ... 6.96ii.53.273.
In five long Years I took no second Spouse; .... 6.96iv.5.276.
So might I find my loving Spouse of course .... 6.96iv.109.279.
Shall *Troy*, shall *Priam*, and th' Adult'rous Spouse, ... Il.2.195.137.
See on the Plain thy *Grecian* Spouse appears, ... Il.3.213.202.
His Spouse, or Slave; and mount the Skies no more. .... Il.3.506.215.
Whose gen'rous Spouse, *Theano*, heav'nly Fair, ... Il.5.93.271.
If e'er I see my Spouse and Sire again, ... Il.5.269.280.
Helen at least a braver Spouse might claim, ... Il.6.442.348.
To seek his Spouse, his Soul's far dearer Part; .... Il.6.463.349.
For this my Spouse of great *Aëtion's* Line .... Il.8.232.408.
My Spouse alone must bless his lustful Nights: .... Il.9.443.454.
(The Spouse of *Helen*, the fair Cause of War) .... Il.11.474.55.
The Spouse of *Helen* dealing Darts around, ... Il.11.628.61.
King *Augias'* Son, and Spouse of *Agamede:* .... Il.11.875.75.
His Spouse *Hippodamè*, divinely fair, ... Il.13.539.132.
Such, as to *Promachus'* sad Spouse we bear; .... Il.14.592.191.
No more to chear his Spouse, or glad his Sire. .... Il.17.32.289.
And Spouse, a Widow in her bridal Bed. .... Il.17.40.289.
Charis, his Spouse, a Grace divinely fair, ... Il.18.449.342.
Abash'd, she names his own Imperial Spouse; .... Il.21.595.446.
Nor Spouse nor Mother grace thee with a Tear; .... Il.22.123.458.
Tho' to his breast his spouse with transport flies, ... Od.2.283.75.
Ev'n to the temple stalk'd th' adult'rous spouse, ... Od.3.346.103.
This man my spouse, or such a spouse as he! .... Od.6.294.225.
This man my spouse, or such a spouse as he! .... Od.6.294.225.
"That gave a foreign spouse to crown her bed! .... Od.6.338.227.
'Till our consenting sires a spouse provide .... Od.6.345.228.
Thy absent spouse neglectful of thy charms .... Od.8.335.281.
And grant him to his spouse and native shores! .... Od.8.446.287.
Say if my spouse maintains her royal trust, ... Od.11.214.392.
Lost in the children of the present spouse .... Od.15.25.71.
He grasp'd my hand, and oh my spouse! I leave .... Od.18.303.181.
My bridal gifts shall load the future spouse: .... Od.20.410.252.
Let not against thy spouse thine anger rise! .... Od.23.216.333.
Heav'n, by the *Theban* ghost, thy spouse decrees .... Od.23.283.337.
Then instant his fair spouse *Ulysses* led .... Od.23.317.338.
All he unfolds: His list'ning spouse turns pale .... Od.23.331.340.

SPOUSE'S

A Neighbour's Madness, or his Spouse's, ... 4.HS6.143.259.
Or meets his spouse's fonder eye; .... 6.51ii.31.153.

SPOUSELESS

To tempt the spouseless Queen with am'rous wiles, ... Od.1.315.47.

SPOUSES

What Sums from these old Spouses I cou'd raise, ... 2.ChWB.207.66.
What Sums from these first Spouses I cou'd raise, ... 2.ChWB.207A.66.
"Or others Spouses, like my Lord of— .... 4.HAdv.44.79.
Can never fail Cuckolding *Two* or *Three* Spouses. .... 6.36.7.104.
Something to deck their pretty Babes and Spouses; .... 6.96iv.56.278.
Twelve Domes for them and their lov'd Spouses shone, ... Il.6.310.341.
Wounds, that long hence may ask their Spouses Care, ... Il.8.641.426.
Your accent varying as their spouses spoke: .... Od.4.380.139.

SPOUT

One bent; the Handle this, and that the Spout: .... 2.RL4.50.188.
"The salient spout, far-streaming to the sky; .... 5.DunA2.154.120.
"The salient spout, fair-streaming to the sky; .... 5.DunA2.154A.120.
"The salient spout, far-streaming to the sky; .... 5.DunB2.162.303.
His mouth and nostrils spout a purple flood, ... Od.18.116.172.

SPOUTING

The next a Fountain, spouting thro' his Heir, ... 3.Ep3.176.107.
The Dart a Tyde of spouting Gore pursu'd, ... Il.11.576.60.
Forc'd from their ghastly Orbs, and spouting Gore, ... Il.13.775.141.
And from the spouting Shoulders struck his Head; .... Il.14.582.190.
His Arm falls spouting on the Dust below: .... Il.16.385.258.
One raz'd *Achilles* Hand; the spouting Blood .... Il.21.183.429.
His quiv'ring limbs, and quaff'd his spouting gore. .... Od.2.26.61.
Of two, his cutlace launch'd the spouting blood; .... Od.14.87.40.
A stream of gore burst spouting from his nose; .... Od.22.22.287.
(Not unreveng'd) and quaff'd the spouting gore; .... Od.23.338.341.

SPOUTS

From silver Spouts the grateful Liquors glide, ...2.RL3.109.176.
While opening Hell spouts wild-fire at your head. ....5.DunA3.314.186.
While op'ning Hell spouts wild-fire at your head. ....5.DunB3.316.335.
While smoking Streams from Silver Spouts shall glide, ...6.82i.3.229.
While smoking Streams from Silver Spouts shall flow, ...6.82i.3A.229.
Spouts the black Gore, and dimms his shining Shield. ....Il.7.314.379.
From the pierc'd pupil spouts the boiling blood; ....Od.9.462.325.
And high above the rock she spouts the main: ....Od.12.287.446.

SPRAT

Sprat, Carew, Sedley, and a hundred more, ...4.2HE1.109.205.
Doth many a stinking Sprat and Herring lie; ....6.14ii.11.43.
Cod, Whiting, Oyster, Mackrel, Sprat, or Plaice: ....6.14ii.31.44.

SPRAWL

Where sprawl the Saints of Verrio or Laguerre, ...3.Ep4.146.151.

SPRAWLING

See, in the Tube he pants, and sprawling lies, ...6.96v.7.280.

SPRAWLS

Grim in convulsive agonies he sprawls: ....Od.22.23.287.

SPRAY

Hear how the Birds, on ev'ry bloomy Spray, ...1.PSp.23.62.

SPRAYS

Or hush'd with Wonder, hearken from the Sprays: ....1.PWi.56.93.
The birds shall sport amidst the bending sprays, ...6.20.66.68.

SPREAD

O'er sandy Wilds were yellow Harvests spread, ...1.W-F.88.158.
Wind the shrill Horn, or spread the waving Net. ....1.W-F.96.159.
Spread all his Sails, and durst the Deeps explore; ....1.EOC.646.312.
Rome's ancient *Genius*, o'er its *Ruins* spread, ...1.EOC.699.319.
His Temples thinly spread with silver Hairs: ....1.TrVP.47.379.
The curling Vine her swelling Clusters spread; ....1.TrVP.60.379.
Spread thy soft Wings, and waft me o'er the Main, ...1.TrSP.210.403.
Cupid for thee shall spread the swelling Sails. ....1.TrSP.253.404.
For thee shall *Cupid* spread the swelling Sails. ....1.TrSP.253A.404.
When all my Glories o'er her Limbs were spread, ...1.TrSt.362.425.
When direful Meteors spread thro' glowing Air ....1.TrSt.843.445.
Spread their broad Sails, and launch into the Main: ....1.TrUl.2.465.
Thus with spread Sails the winged Gally flies; ....1.TrUl.13.465.
By this the Sheets were spread, the Bride undrest, ...2.ChJM.381.33.
A Crystal Fountain spread its Streams around, ...2.ChJM.457.37.
Before my Face my Handkerchief I spread, ...2.ChWB.311.72.
His Giant Limbs in State unwieldy spread? ....2.RL3.72.173.
This just behind *Belinda's* Neck he spread, ...2.RL3.133.178.
O wretched Maid! she spread her Hands, and cry'd, ...2.RL4.95.191.
He spoke, and speaking, in proud Triumph spread ....2.RL4.139.195.
While purer Slumbers spread their golden Wings) ....2.TemF.8.253.
Yet wide was spread their Fame in Ages past, ...2.TemF.33.255.
Spread, and grow brighter with the Length of Days. ....2.TemF.52.256.
There *Ninus* shone, who spread th' *Assyrian* Fame, ...2.TemF.204.271.
In living Sculpture on the Sides were spread ....2.TemF.230.274.
The Doves that round the Infant Poet spread ....2.TemF.247.275.
So large it spread, and swell'd to such a Height. ....2.TemF.315.279.
Which still grew sweeter as they wider spread: ....2.TemF.447.285.
And spread o'er all the fluid Element. ....2.TemF.472.286.
In ev'ry Ear it spread, on ev'ry Tongue it grew. ....2.ElAb.303.344.
See in her Cell sad *Eloisa* spread, ...2.ElAb.303.344.
All spread their charms, but charm not all alike; ....3.EOM2.127.70.
As the mind opens, and its functions spread, ...3.EOM2.142.72.
For him as kindly spread the flow'ry lawn. ....3.EOM3.30.95.
Still spread the int'rest, and preserv'd the kind. ....3.EOM3.146.107.
"Spread the thin oar, and catch the driving gale. ....3.EOM3.178.111.
"Spread like a low-born mist, and blot the Sun; ....3.Ep3.140.105.
Fond to spread Friendships, but to cover Heats, ...4.HS1.136.19.
Then, like the Sun, let Bounty spread her ray, ...4.HS2.115.63.
Hath not indulgent Nature spread a Feast, ...4.HAdv.96.83.
To spread about the Itch of Verse and Praise; ....4.Arbu.224.112.
Abuse on all he lov'd, or lov'd him, spread, ...4.Arbu.354.121.
Th' Abuse on all he lov'd, or lov'd him, spread, ...4.Arbu.354A.121.
Or court a Wife, spread out his wily parts, ...4.JD2.57.137.
To court a Wife, and spread his wily parts, ...4.JD2.57A.137.
To court a Wife, or spread his wily parts, ...4.JD2.57B.137.
There spread round MURRAY all your blooming Loves; ....4.HOde1.10.151.
Shall spread thy Conquests over half the kind: ....4.HOde1.16B.151.
Judicious Wits spread wide the Ridicule, ...4.EpS1.61.302.
Spread thy broad wing, and sowze on all the Kind. ....4.EpS2.15.314.
Here pleas'd behold her mighty wings out-spread, ...5.DunA1.25.63.
Who spread a healing mist before the mind, ...5.DunA1.152.82.
Wide as a windmill all his figure spread, ...5.DunA2.62.105.
A shaggy Tap'stry, worthy to be spread ....5.DunA2.135.117.
Gives him a cov'ring worthy to be spread ....5.DunA2.135A.117.
Not so from shameless Curl: Impetuous spread ....5.DunA2.171.122.
Oh spread thy Influence, but restrain thy Rage! ....5.DunA3.114.160.
Here pleas'd behold her mighty wings out-spread ....5.DunB1.27.271.
Still spread a healing mist before the mind; ....5.DunB1.174.283.
Wide as a wind-mill all his figures spread, ...5.DunB2.66.299.
A shaggy Tap'stry, worthy to be spread ....5.DunB2.143.302.
Not so from shameless Curl; impetuous spread ....5.DunB2.179.304.
He ceas'd, and spread the robe; the crowd confess ....5.DunB2.353.314.
Oh spread thy influence, but restrain thy Rage. ....5.DunB3.122.325.
But spread, my sons, your glory thin or thick, ...5.DunB4.129.354.
Soft on the paper ruff its leaves I spread, ...5.DunB4.407.382.
Wide, and more wide, it spread o'er all the realm; ....5.DunB4.613.405.
On her large Squab you find her spread, ...6.14v(a).10.48.
Or spread their feather'd Sails against the Beams, ...6.26i.8.79.
While the spread Fan o'ershades your closing eyes; ....6.45.37.125.
Well spread with Sense, shall be the Nation's Plaister. ....6.48ii.12.134.
With nodding arches, broken temples spread! ....6.71.3.202.
Myrtles and *Bays* around me spread, ...6.82vii.6.233.
Then spread her Hands, and with a Bounce let fall ....6.96ii.7.270.

SPREAD (CONTINUED)

Within the Kingcup now his limbs are spread ....6.96ii.30Z15.271.
"Within the King-Cup if thy Limbs are spread, ...6.96ii.47.273.
Then spread those Morals which the *Houyhnhnms* taught. ....6.96iii.22.275.
In future Ages how their Fame will spread, ...6.98.12Z1.283.
Latona's Son a dire Contagion spread, ...Il.1.11.86.
Breathing Revenge, a sudden Night he spread, ...Il.1.65.89.
But Plagues shall spread, and Fun'ral Fires increase, ...Il.1.122.93.
When flush'd with Slaughter, *Hector* comes, to spread ....Il.1.319.103.
Then spread the Tables, the Repast prepare, ...Il.1.612.117.
Dusky they spread, a close-embody'd Crowd, ...Il.2.115.133.
('Twas where the Plane-tree spread its Shades around) ....Il.2.370.145.
Then spread the Tables, the Repast prepare, ...Il.2.512.151.
Jove o'er his Eyes celestial Glories spread, ...Il.2.570.155.
Where mighty Towns in Ruins spread the Plain, ...Il.2.799.163.
Broad is his Breast, his Shoulders larger spread, ...Il.3.255.204.
Fair as a God with Odours round him spread ....Il.3.483.215.
To spread the War, I flew from Shore to Shore; ....Il.4.39.223.
And sixteen Palms his Brows large Honours spread: ....Il.4.141.227.
Spread in dim Streams, and sail along the Skies, ...Il.4.317.235.
Cut down it lies, tall, smooth, and largely spread, ...Il.4.556.248.
But first, to hide her Heav'nly Visage, spread ....Il.5.1036.316.
Before the Goddess' honour'd Knees be spread; ....Il.6.115.329.
Behind, a Dragon's fiery Tail was spread; ....Il.6.221.337.
Before the Goddess' honour'd Knees be spread, ...Il.6.342.343.
Wide shall it spread, and last thro' Ages long, ...Il.6.448.348.
Then spread the Tables, the Repast prepare, ...Il.7.384.382.
O'er Heav'ns clear Azure spread the sacred Light; ....Il.8.84.399.
Spread all your Canvas, all your Oars employ, ...Il.9.37.433.
And plac'd in Seats with purple Carpets spread. ....Il.9.266.445.
A warmer Couch with num'rous Carpets spread. ....Il.9.734.470.
With Fleeces, Carpets, and soft Linen spread: ....Il.9.776.472.
A Leopard's spotted Hide his Shoulders spread; ....Il.10.35.4.
(The Plain beside with mangled Corps was spread, ...Il.10.237.12.
Soft Wool within; without, in order spread, ...Il.10.311.16.
The Saffron Morn, with early Blushes spread, ...Il.11.1.34.
The Squadrons spread their sable Wings behind. ....Il.11.66.37.
The Sea with Ships, the Fields with Armies spread, ...Il.11.113.39.
O'er Heav'ns pure Azure spread the growing Light, ...Il.11.116.39.
Who spread their Bucklers, and advance their Spears, ...Il.11.721.67.
Spread their cold Poison thro' our Soldiers' Breasts, ...Il.12.292.92.
See, as thou mov'st, on Dangers Dangers spread, ...Il.13.923.148.
And spread a long, unmeasur'd Ruin round. ....Il.13.1031.153.
O'er other Gods I spread my easy Chain; ....Il.14.278.175.
Thick new-born Vi'lets a soft Carpet spread, ...Il.14.397.182.
Swift his broad Faulchion fierce *Peneleus* spread, ...Il.14.581.190.
And spread the Carnage thro' the shady Gloom. ....Il.15.369.211.
And spread your Glory with the Navy's Flame. ....Il.15.573.218.
Then mutual Slaughters spread on either side; ....Il.15.610.220.
Achilles' Shield his ample Shoulders spread, ...Il.16.168.244.
O'er Heav'ns Expanse like one black Cieling spread; ....Il.16.355.257.
O'er his broad Shoulders spread the massy Shield; ....Il.16.429.259.
Where'er he moves, the growing Slaughters spread ....Il.16.510.262.
Haste, strip his Arms, the Slaughter round him spread, ...Il.16.687.271.
On the cold Earth divine *Patroclus* spread, ...Il.17.1.286.
He drops *Patroclus'* Foot, and o'er him spread ....Il.17.344.301.
Rank within Rank, on Buckler Buckler spread, ...Il.17.407.303.
Unclouded there, th' Aerial Azure spread, ...Il.17.428.304.
But Death and Darkness o'er the Carcase spread, ...Il.17.434.304.
Trail'd on the Dust beneath the Yoke were spread, ...Il.17.500.308.
The Field, and spread her Slaughters to the Shore; ....Il.17.521.308.
Then o'er their Backs they spread their solid Shields; ....Il.17.559.310.
Cast on the Ground, with furious Hands he spread ....Il.18.27.325.
Soon shall the sanguine Torrent spread so wide, ...Il.18.161.330.
For him the Slaughter to the Fleet they spread, ...Il.18.211.332.
That, in my Friends Defence, has *Ajax* spread, ...Il.18.231.333.
Around his Brows a golden Cloud she spread; ....Il.18.243.334.
Those in the Tents the Squires industrious spread; ....Il.19.293.384.
Once spread th' inviting Banquet in our Tents; ....Il.19.336.386.
Hast spread th' inviting Banquet in our Tents; ....Il.19.336A.386.
Spread o'er his Breast the fencing Shield he bore, ...Il.20.196.402.
So oft' the Surge, in wat'ry Mountains spread, ...Il.21.305.433.
O'er all th' expanded Plain the Waters spread; ....Il.21.348.435.
Again, the branching Streams begin to spread, ...Il.21.446.438.
On Earth together lay the Lovers spread. ....Il.21.499.442.
Now where the Fig-trees spread their Umbrage broad, ...Il.22.193.463.
But not as yet the fatal News had spread ....Il.22.562.479.
And the pil'd Victims round the Body spread. ....Il.23.207.498.
A Moment hung, and spread her Pinions there, ...Il.23.1040.530.
Spread o'er the sacred Corse his golden Shield. ....Il.24.33.536.
Conceal'd from Sight; With frantick Hands he spread ....Il.24.201.545.
Still as *Aurora's* ruddy Beam is spread, ...Il.24.507.557.
Two splendid Mantles, and a Carpet spread, ...Il.24.728.568.
This done, the Garments o'er the Corse they spread; ....Il.24.736.568.
With Purple soft, and shaggy Carpets spread; ....Il.24.813.571.
Last o'er the Urn the sacred Earth they spread, ...Il.24.1007.577.
(A purple carpet spread the pavement wide) ....Od.1.173.40.
They wash. The tables in fair order spread, ...Od.1.183.41.
While she, laborious in delusion, spread ....Od.2.103.66.
Derisive taunts were spread from guest to guest, ...Od.2.364.78.
And spread soft hydes upon the yellow sands; ....Od.3.48.88.
For *Tenedos* we spread our eager oars, ...Od.3.191.95.
Fast by his side *Pisistratus* lay spread, ...Od.3.512.112.
O'er the warm *Libyan* wave to spread my sails: ....Od.4.104.124.
To spread the pall beneath the regal chair ....Od.4.163.128.
Beneath an ample Portico, they spread ....Od.4.403.139.
When spread the Prince his sail for distant *Pyle?* ....Od.4.867.159.
The saffron Morn, with early blushes spread, ...Od.5.1.170.
Thus having spoke, the nymph the table spread, ...Od.5.117.177.
And spread my glory with the sons of men. ....Od.5.400.192.
Like a black sheet the whelming billow spread, ...Od.5.466.195.
Around him spread a veil of thicken'd air; ....Od.7.20.234.
With opening streets and shining structures spread, ...Od.7.104.239.
The table next in regal order spread, ...Od.7.234.247.
And the thick carpets spread with busy care. ....Od.7.430.258.
His limbs how turn'd! how broad his shoulders spread! ....Od.8.148.270.

SPREAD (CONTINUED)

With shady mountains, spread their isles around. ....Od.9.24.303.
O'er heav'n's pure azure spread the growing light, ...Od.9.64.305.
We rear the masts, we spread the canvas wings; ....Od.9.86.306.
Then spread our hasty banquet on the ground. ....Od.9.98.307.
His flocks, obedient, spread o'er all the hills. ....Od.9.375.321.
With carpets spread; a footstool at my feet. ....Od.10.432.365.
I wash'd. The table in fair order spread, ...Od.10.437.365.
Cocytus' lamentable waters spread; ....Od.10.611.374.
And full nine cubits broad their shoulders spread. ....Od.11.384.402.
Trees of all kinds delicious fruitage spread; ....Od.11.726.421.
Fierce o'er the Pyre, by fanning breezes spread, ...Od.12.17.430.
Spread your broad sails, and plow the liquid way: ....Od.12.36.431.
Thro' every breast, and spread from man to man, ...Od.12.331.447.
Beneath the seats, soft painted robes they spread, ...Od.13.88.5.
Thus with spread sails the winged gally flies, ...Od.13.104.6.
O'er thy smooth skin a bark of wrinkles spread, ...Od.13.457.28.
A swift old-age o'er all his members spread; ....Od.13.498.29.
A shaggy goat's soft hyde beneath him spread, ...Od.14.59.38.
In foreign fields I spread my glory far, ...Od.14.268.49.
We turn'd to flight; the gath'ring vengeance spread ....Od.14.299.50.
(The shaded Ocean blacken'd as it spread) ....Od.14.336.51.
There, clad in arms, along the marshes spread, ...Od.14.532.63.
They wash. The tables in fair order spread, ...Od.15.152.76.
And plac'd in order, spread their equal oars. ....Od.15.592.98.
So round the youth his arms *Eumæus* spread, ...Od.16.21.103.
There sate the Prince: the feast *Eumæus* spread; ....Od.16.49.104.
They wash: the table, in fair order spread, ...Od.17.108.137.
And the proud steer was o'er the marble spread. ....Od.17.202.141.
A limpid fount; that spread in parting rills ....Od.17.233.143.
To cringe, to whine, his idle hands to spread, ...Od.17.266.145.
And where on heaps the rich manure was spread, ...Od.17.358.149.
Before him instant was the banquet spread, ...Od.17.408.152.
We turn'd to flight; the gath'ring vengeance spread ....Od.17.520.157.
Broad spread his shoulders, and his nervous thighs ....Od.18.76.170.
A seat soft spread with furry spoils prepare, ...Od.19.119.198.
O'er which a promontory-shoulder spread: ....Od.19.281.208.
'Till soft oblivious shade *Minerva* spread, ...Od.19.703.229.
An ample hide divine *Ulysses* spread, ...Od.20.1.230.
A hide beneath the portico was spread, ...Od.20.175.241.
And the proud steer was on the marble spread. ....Od.20.315.248.
Wide o'er the sands are spread the stiff'ning prey ....Od.22.430.309.
Haste, *Euryclea*, and dispatchful spread ....Od.23.171.328.
This hand the wonder fram'd; An olive spread ....Od.23.191.332.
Her hand, laborious in delusion, spread ....Od.24.152.355.
Cold and neglected, spread the marble floor. ....Od.24.215.358.
Deep from his soul he sigh'd, and sorrowing spread ....Od.24.369.366.
Now flying Fame the swift report had spread ....Od.24.474.371.
Wide o'er the world their martial fame was spread; ....Od.24.588.376.

SPREAD'ST

Who spread'st thy Empire o'er each God and Man; ....Il.14.267.175.

SPREADING

Beneath the Shade a spreading Beech displays, ...1.PAu.1.80.
Where tow'ring Oaks their spreading Honours rear, ...1.W-F.221A.170.
But *catch* the *spreading Notion* of the Town; ....1.EOC.409.287.
By driving Winds the spreading Flames are born! ....1.TrSP.10.393.
Again grown proud, the spreading rose ....6.4iv.16.11.
And fill with spreading Sounds the Skies; ....6.11.15.30.
With ample Forehead, and with spreading Horns, ...Il.10.349.18.
High on a spreading Tamarisk he plac'd; ....Il.10.537.27.
Whose spreading Arms with leafy Honours crown'd, ...Il.12.147.86.
Arm, e'er our Vessels catch the spreading Flame; ....Il.16.158.244.
Patroclus' Arm forbids the spreading Fires, ...Il.16.348.256.
Chearing his Men, and spreading Deaths around. ....Il.17.770.318.
This way and that, the spreading Torrent roars; ....Il.20.573.418.
(Which spreading Tam'risks on the Margin hide) ....Il.21.21.422.
A spreading Elm, that overhung the Flood; ....Il.21.268.431.
But when arriv'd at *Ida's* spreading Woods, ...Il.23.144.495.
Me from our coast shall spreading sails convey, ...Od.2.404.80.
High o'er the roaring waves the spreading sails ....Od.2.466.83.
The spreading harbours, and the riding fleets; ....Od.7.56.236.
Brown with o'er-arching pine, and spreading oak. ....Od.9.216.314.
The spreading clamor to their city flies, ...Od.14.294.50.
And took the spreading shelter of the wood ....Od.14.388.53.
The spreading clamor to their city flies, ...Od.17.515.157.

SPREADS

Its gawdy Colours spreads on *ev'ry place*; ....1.EOC.312.274.
A flow'ry *Lotos* spreads its Arms above, ...1.TrSP.181.401.
There spreads her dusky Pinions to the Skies. ....1.TrSt.135.415.
And o'er the *Theban* Palace spreads her Wings, ...1.TrSt.170.417.
And spreads its ancient Poysons o'er the Grounds; ....1.TrSt.503.431.
This Slave the Floor, and That the Table spreads; ....1.TrSt.608.435.
It sinks, and spreads its Honours on the Ground; ....1.TrES.291.460.
Soon as she spreads her Hand, th' Aerial Guard ....2.RL3.31.171.
A livid Paleness spreads o'er all her Look; ....2.RL3.90.174.
The Peer now spreads the glitt'ring *Forfex* wide, ...2.RL3.147.179.
Spreads his black Wings, and slowly mounts to Day. ....2.RL4.88.191.
Spreads in a second Circle, then a third; ....2.TemF.439.284.
Spreads his light wings, and in a moment flies. ....2.ElAb.76.326.
"Suckles each herb, and spreads out ev'ry flow'r; ....3.EOM1.134.32.
Spreads undivided, operates unspent, ...3.EOM1.274.48.
Another still, and still another spreads, ...3.EOM4.366.164.
That spreads and swells in puff'd Prosperity, ...4.HS2.126.65.
Spreads her Fore-Buttocks to the Navel bare. ....4.HAdv.34.79.
So from the mid-most the nutation spreads ....5.DunA2.377.146.
So from the mid-most the nutation spreads ....5.DunB2.409.317.
3. Who spreads a *Tale*, a *Libel* hands about, ...6.120.5.339.
Spreads the red Rod of angry Pestilence, ...6.137.4.373.
Around his Temples spreads his golden Wing, ...Il.2.23.128.
Spreads all the Beach, and wide o'ershades the Plain: ....Il.2.118.133.
The gath'ring Murmur spreads; their trampling Feet ....Il.2.183.137.
He calls the Gods, and spreads his lifted Hands. ....Il.3.345.209.
And spreads for Aid his unavailing Hands. ....Il.4.605.250.

SPREADS (CONTINUED)

Spreads the wide Fan to clear the golden Grain, ...Il.5.612.297.
'Tis now enough: now Glory spreads her Charms, ...Il.6.424.347.
Then *Jove* from *Ida's* Top his Horrors spreads; ....Il.8.93.401.
Floats in rich Waves, and spreads the Court of *Jove*. ....Il.8.469.419.
O'er Heav'ns clear Azure spreads her sacred Light, ...Il.8.688.428.
(That spreads her Conquest o'er a thousand States, ...Il.9.502.458.
The gath'ring Tumult spreads o'er all the Plain; ....Il.10.615.29.
The weary Wood-man spreads his sparing Meal, ...Il.11.120.41.
And o'er the Body spreads his ample Shield. ....Il.11.334.49.
And the red Slaughter spreads on ev'ry side. ....Il.11.530.57.
The Sea subsiding spreads a level Plain, ...Il.13.46.107.
Then spreads a length of Ruin o'er the Ground. ....Il.13.496.130.
Spreads his imploring Arms, but spreads in vain. ....Il.13.695.138.
Spreads his imploring Arms, but spreads in vain. ....Il.13.695.138.
Still grows, and spreads, and thickens round the King. ......Il.16.255.249.
It sinks, and spreads its Honours on the Ground; ....Il.16.596.267.
See what a Tempest direful *Hector* spreads, ...Il.17.288.299.
This heard, o'er *Hector* spreads a Cloud of Woe, ...Il.17.666.314.
Spreads his broad Waters o'er the level Plains, ...Il.17.840.321.
The growing Structure spreads on ev'ry side; ....Il.23.203.498.
Between where *Samos* wide his Forests spreads, ...Il.24.103.539.
With beating heart *Ulysses* spreads his sails; ....Od.5.344.188.
Around his loins the verdant cincture spreads ....Od.6.151.214.
Then o'er his limbs a gorgeous robe he spreads, ...Od.8.493.289.
Torn limb from limb, he spreads his horrid feast, ...Od.9.346.320.
Spreads his wide arms, and searches round and round: ....Od.9.494.326.
Here fills her sails and spreads her oars in vain; ....Od.12.122.437.
That God who spreads the radiant beams of light, ...Od.12.385.449.
Spreads o'er the coast, and scents the tainted gales; ....Od.12.434.452.
He spreads; and adds a mantle thick and wide; ....Od.14.589.65.
His eye first glanc'd where *Euryclea* spreads ....Od.17.39.134.
Or ere brown ev'ning spreads her chilly shade. ....Od.17.215.142.
And the pure ivory o'er her bosom spreads. ....Od.18.228.178.
With vast increase beneath my care it spreads, ...Od.20.269.246.
Spreads o'er an ample board a bullock's hide. ....Od.21.184.268.
And spreads the pavement with a mingled flood ....Od.22.25.287.
Now *Pallas* shines confess'd; aloft she spreads ....Od.22.330.302.
And spreads her Lord's return from place to place. ....Od.22.532.314.
Their loves in vain; old *Dolius* spreads his hands, ...Od.24.457.370.

SPRIG

Yet ne'r one sprig of Laurel grac'd these ribalds, ...4.Arbu.163.108.
Yet ne'er one Sprig of Laurel grac'd those Ribbalds, ...6.98.13.283.

SPRIGHT

See SPRITE.
Umbriel, a dusky melancholy Spright, ...2.RL4.13.183.

SPRIGHTLIER

Walk sober off; before a sprightlier Age ....4.2HE2.324.187.

SPRIGHTLY

The sprightly *Sylvia* trips along the Green, ...1.PSp.57.66.
And purer Spirits swell the sprightly Flood, ...1.W-F.94.159.
In some fair Body thus the sprightly Soul ....1.EOC.76A.247.
So modest Plainness sets off sprightly Wit: ....1.EOC.302.273.
Our Feasts enhanc'd with Musick's sprightly Sound? ....1.TrES.32.450.
Nor fierce *Theodamas*, whose sprightly Strain ....2.ChJM.324.29.
Solus cum Sola, with his sprightly *May*. ....2.ChJM.472.38.
Fair *Venus* gave me Fire and sprightly Grace, ...2.ChWB.325.72.
Her lively Looks a sprightly Mind disclose, ...2.RL2.9.159.
Sprightly our Nights, polite are all our Days; ....2.TemF.383.282.
With every sprightly, every decent part; ....4.HOde1.12.151.
The sprightly Wit, the lively Eye, ...4.1HE7.45.271.
Warriors she fires by sprightly Sounds; ....6.11.28A.30.
Just when his fancy points your sprightly eyes, ...6.45.45.125.
They pall *Moliere's* and *Lopez* sprightly strain, ...6.60.15.178.
Tho' sprightly Sappho force our love and praise, ...6.106i.1.306.
With equal Triumph, sprightly, bold and gay, ...Il.6.660.360.
Our Feasts enhanc'd with Music's sprightly Sound? ....Il.12.376.95.
And gen'ral Songs the sprightly Revel end. ....Il.18.700.357.
Let rising Spirits flow from sprightly Juice, ...Il.19.234.382.
Boreas, enamour'd of the sprightly Train, ...Il.20.264.405.
Four sprightly Coursers, with a deadly Groan ....Il.23.210.498.
O'er the full banquet, and the sprightly bowl) ....Od.1.336.48.
Mean time the Lyre rejoins the sprightly lay; ....Od.1.531.57.
Two sprightly youths to form the bounding dance. ....Od.4.26.121.
Three sprightly coursers, and a polish'd car: ....Od.4.806.156.
The sprightly courser, or indulge his speed: ....Od.4.826.158.
And sprightly damsels trim the rays by turns. ....Od.18.358.184.
Bid the gay youth and sprightly virgins rise, ...Od.23.130.326.
And fair-zon'd damsels form the sprightly dance. ....Od.23.142.328.
And now the blooming youths and sprightly fair ....Od.23.319.339.

SPRIGHTS

While tuneful Sprights a merry Consort made, ...2.ChJM.463.37.
The Sprights of fiery Termagants in Flame ....2.RL1.59.150.
Swift to the Lock a thousand Sprights repair, ...2.RL3.135.178.
Propt on their Bodkin Spears, the Sprights survey ....2.RL5.55.203.

SPRIGS

Some sprigs of that bed ....6.91.11.253.

SPRINDGES

With hairy Sprindges we the Birds betray, ...2.RL2.25.161.

SPRING

Fair *Thames* flow gently from thy sacred Spring, ...1.PSp.3.59.
When warbling *Philomel* salutes the Spring? ....1.PSp.26.63.
Now Hawthorns blossom, now the Daisies spring, ...1.PSp.42.65.
If *Delia* smile, the Flow'rs begin to spring, ...1.PSp.71.68.
In Spring the Fields, in Autumn Hills I love, ...1.PSp.77.68.
Ev'n Spring displeases, when she shines not here, ...1.PSp.83.69.
But blest with her, 'tis Spring throughout the Year. ....1.PSp.84.69.
Bewail'd his Fate beside a silver Spring; ....1.PSu.2A.71.

SPRING (CONTINUED)

As in the Crystal Spring I view my Face, ...1.PSu.27.74.
The Nymphs forsaking ev'ry Cave and Spring, ...1.PSu.51.76.
Ye Flow'rs that droop, forsaken by the Spring, ...1.PAu.27.82.
Let Spring attend, and sudden Flow'rs arise; ....1.PAu.36.82.
Thyrsis, the Musick of that murm'ring Spring ....1.PWi.1.88.
Ye gentle *Muses* leave your Crystal Spring, ...1.PWi.21.90.
Oh spring to Light, Auspicious Babe, be born! ....1.Mes.22.114.
With all the Incence of the breathing Spring: ....1.Mes.24.115.
See Lillies spring, and sudden Verdure rise; ....1.Mes.68.119.
In genial Spring, beneath the quiv'ring Shade ....1.W-F.135.162.
Seek the clear Spring, or haunt the pathless Grove; ....1.W-F.168.165.
No Lake so gentle, and no Spring so clear. ....1.W-F.226.170.
Where Peace descending bids her Olives spring, ...1.W-F.429.194.
And trace the Muses *upward* to their *Spring;* ....1.EOC.127.253.
Drink deep, or taste not the *Pierian* Spring: ....1.EOC.216.264.
Like some fair *Flow'r* the early *Spring* supplies, ...1.EOC.498.294.
Like some fair *Flow'r* that in the *Spring* does rise, ...1.EOC.498A.294.
And teach th'obedient Branches where to spring. ....1.TrVP.12.377.
The spring was new, and all the verdant boughs ....1.TrFD.22.386.
A Spring there is, whose Silver Waters show, ...1.TrSP.179.401.
What Name you bear, from what high Race you spring? ....1.TrSt.791.443.
About this Spring (if ancient Fame say true) ....2.ChJM.459.37.
Thick as the Bees, that with the Spring renew ....2.TemF.282.277.
Self-love, the spring of motion, acts the soul; ....3.EOM2.59.62.
Our spring of action to ourselves is lost: ....3.Ep1.42.18.
Weigh well the Cause from whence these Evils spring, ...4.HAdv.102.83.
'Tis sung, when *Midas'* Ears began to spring, ...4.Arbu.69.100.
Who climb their Mountain, or who taste their spring? ....4.2HE1.353.225.
If weak the pleasure that from these can spring, ...4.1HE6.18.237.
As man's mæanders to the vital spring ....5.DunA3.47.154.
Hence Miscellanies spring, the weekly boast ....5.DunB1.39.273.
As man's Mæanders to the vital spring ....5.DunB3.55.323.
Lay'd this gay daughter of the Spring in dust. ....5.DunB4.416.382.
Waves to the tepid Zephyrs of the spring, ...5.DunB4.422.383.
Hail sacred spring, whose fruitful stream ....6.6ii.1.14.
As man's meanders to the vital spring ....6.9iii.1.21.
And humble glories of the youthful Spring; ....6.14iv.2.47.
New greens shall spring, new flow'rs around me grow, ...6.20.68.68.
To thee, Redeemer! mercy's sacred spring! ....6.25.15.77.
Achilles' Wrath, to Greece the direful Spring ....Il.1.1.82.
The Wrath of *Peleus'* Son the direful Spring ....Il.1.1A.82.
The Tears spring starting from his haggard Eyes: ....Il.2.329.143.
Thick as in Spring the Flow'rs adorn the Land, ...Il.2.551.153.
Another Race the following Spring supplies, ...Il.6.183.335.
The Weight of Waters from *Hyperia's* Spring. ....Il.6.583.355.
And give this Arm the Spring which once it knew: ....Il.7.162.372.
Before the Coursers with a sudden Spring ....Il.8.127.404.
The Gods, O Chief! from whom our honours spring, ...Il.9.51.434.
The cleansing Water from the living Spring. ....Il.9.228.444.
And spring to Earth: the *Greeks* dismiss their Fear: ....Il.10.637.30.
Whose Squire *Oïleus,* with a sudden spring, ...Il.11.129.41.
If from *Antimachus* ye spring, ye die: ....Il.11.180.43.
The laughing *Trojan,* with a joyful Spring ....Il.11.483.55.
So two wild Boars spring furious from their Den, ...Il.12.163.87.
To Vengeance rising with a sudden Spring, ...Il.13.487.130.
All spring to seize him; Storms of Arrows fly; ....Il.14.495.188.
(Thy Brother, *Hecuba!* from *Dymas* spring; ....Il.16.875.277.
Fast by the Spring; they both dispute the Flood, ...Il.16.995.281.
Now forth at once, too swift for sight, they spring, ...Il.18.693.357.
The purest Water of the living Spring; ....Il.24.372.551.
Their Chariots stopping, at the silver Spring ....Il.24.430.554.
For my lost Sire continual sorrows spring, ...Od.2.53.62.
And limpid waters from the living spring. ....Od.3.545.114.
From great *Alcinous'* royal loins I spring, ...Od.6.237.221.
None in the leap spring with so strong a bound, ...Od.8.103.268.
O'erspread the land, when spring descends in show'rs: ....Od.9.56.304.
When lo! they met, beside a crystal spring, ...Od.10.119.346.
And living water from the chrystal spring. ....Od.10.619.374.
Then living waters from the chrystal spring; ....Od.11.32.381.
Farewell! and joys successive ever spring ....Od.13.78.5.
Gives from our stock an only branch to spring: ....Od.16.124.108.
Why urge we not to blows? Well-pleas'd they spring ....Od.18.48.169.
Some to the spring, with each a jar, repair, ...Od.20.192.242.
Of twenty virgins to the spring repair: ....Od.20.197.243.
So roar'd the lock when it releas'd the spring. ....Od.21.52.261.
From his full eyes the tears unbidden spring, ...Od.21.83.263.
So end our night: Before the day shall spring, ...Od.21.280.273.
The cleansing waters from the limpid spring: ....Od.21.287.273.
When sultry days, and long, succeed the gentle spring. ....Od.22.336.302.
Of *Polypemon's* royal line I spring. ....Od.24.356.366.

SPRING'ST

But sure thou spring'st not from a soft Embrace, ...Il.16.47.237.

SPRINGING

That crown'd with tufted Trees and springing Corn, ...1.W-F.27.150.
A springing tree for *Dryope* they find, ...1.TrFD.59.388.
Fix'd in the Forehead where the springing Mane ....Il.8.105.402.
Forth-springing instant, darts her self from high, ...Il.13.93.109.
But *Pallas* springing thro' the bright Abode, ...Il.15.140.202.
Lifts the green Ear above the springing Plain, ...Il.23.680.516.
The friendly Gods a springing gale inlarg'd: ....Od.4.796.156.
Swift as a Sea-mew springing from the flood, ...Od.5.428.193.
His brother springing with an active bound ....Od.8.411.286.
And calls the springing sorrows from her eyes. ....Od.14.153.43.
Check not with fallacies the springing tear; ....Od.14.398.55.
Up-springing from his couch, with active haste ....Od.20.116.238.
With springing hope the Heroe's heart rebounds. ....Od.20.129.240.
First may'st thou see the springing dawn of light; ....Od.22.214.297.

SPRINGS

The *Thistle* springs, to which the *Lilly* yields? ....1.PSp.90.69.
And heap'd with Products of *Sabæan* Springs! ....1.Mes.94.121.
Unlock your Springs, and open all your Shades. ....1.W-F.4.148.
See! from the Brake the whirring Pheasant springs, ...1.W-F.111.161.

SPRINGS (CONTINUED)

Bath'd in the Springs, or sought the cooling Shade; ....1.W-F.166A.165.
And found the springs that ne'er till then deny'd ....1.TrFD.51.388.
Headlong from thence the glowing Fury springs, ...1.TrSt.169.417.
Now springs aloft, and tow'rs th'Ethereal Height, ...1.TrSt.440.428.
He springs to Fight, and flies upon the Foes. ....1.TrES.122.454.
And rising Springs Eternal Verdure yield. ....1.TrUl.131.470.
And a new Vigour springs in ev'ry Part. ....2.ChJM.130.21.
Of painted Meadows, and of purling Springs. ....2.ChJM.455.37.
What dire Offence from am'rous Causes springs, ...2.RL1.1.144.
He springs to Vengeance with an eager pace, ...2.RL3.97.174.
And each warm wish springs mutual from the heart. ....2.ElAb.96.327.
All my loose soul unbounded springs to thee. ....2.ElAb.228.338.
To *Paraclete's* white walls, and silver springs, ...2.ElAb.348.348.
Hope springs eternal in the human breast: ....3.EOM1.95.26.
"For me, health gushes from a thousand springs; ....3.EOM1.138.32.
As much eternal springs and cloudless skies, ...3.EOM1.153.34.
From pride, from pride, our very reas'ning springs; ....3.EOM1.161.35.
Such is the World's great harmony, that springs ....3.EOM3.295.122.
On morning wings how active springs the Mind, ...4.HS2.81.59.
Hence springs each weekly Muse, the living boast ....5.DunA1.37.O64.
As Fancy opens the quick springs of Sense, ...5.DunB4.156.357.
And the soft, silent Harmony, that springs ....6.11.35Z9.31.
The Springs above urg'd by the Weight below; ....6.17i(b).2.55.
Our author shuns by vulgar springs to move, ...6.32.9.96.
Nymph of the Grot, these sacred Springs I keep, ...6.87.1.248.
From whom the Pow'r of Laws and Justice springs: ....Il.1.315.103.
Jove loves our Chief, from *Jove* his Honour springs; ....Il.2.233.138.
Fierce from his Seat, at this *Ulysses* springs, ...Il.2.302.142.
That o'er the Windings of *Cayster's* Springs, ...Il.2.542.153.
Heleon and *Hylè,* which the Springs o'erflow; ....Il.2.596.156.
From his proud Car the Prince impetuous springs; ....Il.5.603.297.
And springs, exulting, to his Fields again. ....Il.6.659.360.
Springs from the Mountains tow'rd the guarded Fold: ....Il.10.214.11.
Springs from his Chariot on the trembling Ground, ...Il.11.270.47.
Now fierce for Fame, before the Ranks he springs. ....Il.11.297.48.
And springs the foremost with his lifted Dart: ....Il.11.380.51.
And dauntless springs beneath a Cloud of Darts; ....Il.11.703.66.
He springs to Fight, and flies upon the Foes. ....Il.12.476.99.
Springs thro' the Ranks to fall, and fall by thee, ...Il.13.754.141.
As when from gloomy Clouds a Whirlwind springs, ...Il.13.999.152.
A Youth, who from the mighty *Tydeus* springs, ...Il.14.124.163.
And springs, exulting, to his Fields again: ....Il.15.305.209.
Grim as voracious Wolves that seek the Springs ....Il.16.194.246.
Springs to the Front, and guards him from the Foe: ....Il.17.4.287.
Struck 'twixt the Horns, he springs with many a Bound, ...Il.17.590.311.
From us (he said) this Day an Infant springs, ...Il.19.107.376.
Is this Day born: From *Sthenelus* he springs, ...Il.19.121.377.
So swift thro' Æther the shrill *Harpye* springs, ...Il.19.372.387.
From *Dardanus,* great *Erichthonius* springs, ...Il.20.260.404.
Fierce as he springs, the Sword his Head divides; ....Il.20.445.413.
Meanwhile the Hero springs in Arms, to dare ....Il.21.155.428.
The Seas, the Rivers, and the Springs below, ...Il.21.214.430.
Far as a Spear can fly, *Achilles* springs ....Il.21.283.432.
Soft Rills of Water from the bubbling Springs, ...Il.21.290.433.
He springs impetuous, and invades the Field: ....Il.21.347.435.
With open Beak and shrilling Cries he springs, ...Il.22.187.463.
Springs to her Knight, and gives the Scourge again, ...Il.23.468.509.
Quits his bright Car, and springs upon the Sands; ....Il.23.590.513.
Springs from a Goddess, by a Man's Embrace; ....Il.24.77.538.
Where round the Bed whence *Acheloüs* springs ....Il.24.775.569.
O thou! from whom the whole creation springs, ...Od.1.57.33.
Replenish'd from the cool, translucent springs; ....Od.1.180.41.
The purest product of the chrystal springs; ....Od.4.64.122.
Alternate all partake the grateful springs: ....Od.4.298.133.
Whilst limpid springs the failing cask supply. ....Od.4.486.143.
Springs o'er the fence, and dissipates the fold. ....Od.6.160.216.
Replenish'd from the cool translucent springs, ...Od.7.231.247.
We climb'd the beach, and springs of water found, ...Od.9.97.307.
Replenish'd from the cool, translucent springs; ....Od.10.434.365.
And rising springs eternal verdure yield. ....Od.13.298.20.
Hence springs their confidence, and from our sighs ....Od.14.113.41.
Replete with water from the chrystal springs; ....Od.15.149.75.
No profit springs beneath usurping pow'rs; ....Od.15.404.89.
Forward he springs, and clasps the favourite boy: ....Od.16.20.103.
Wild springs the vine, no more the garden blows. ....Od.16.155.110.
Replenish'd from the pure, translucent springs; ....Od.17.105.137.
Descend to swell the springs, and feed the flow'rs! ....Od.17.283.146.
He said: replenish'd from the purest springs, ...Od.19.450.216.
And springs impetuous with opponent speed: ....Od.19.524.221.
Again the matron springs with eager pace, ...Od.22.531.314.
(From old experience *Nestor's* counsel springs, ...Od.24.71.351.
Springs to his master with a warm embrace, ...Od.24.458.370.

SPRINKLE

In *Jove's* high Name to sprinkle on the Ground, ...Il.6.323.342.
To sprinkle to the Gods, its better Use. ....Il.6.333.342.
With watry Drops the Chief they sprinkle round, ...Il.14.509.188.

SPRINKLED

The first Libations sprinkled on the Ground; ....1.TrSt.649.437.
The Room was sprinkled, and the Bed was blest. ....2.ChJM.382.33.
The Barley sprinkled, and the Victim slew. ....Il.2.503.150.
Sprinkled with rosy Light the dewy Lawn, ...Il.8.2.394.
And sprinkled large Libation on the ground. ....Od.3.507.112.
A sudden frost was sprinkled on his head; ....Od.13.499.29.
Sprinkled with roseate light the dewy lawn; ....Od.17.2.132.

SPRINKLES

And sprinkles sacred Salt from lifted Urns; ....Il.9.282.447.
He sprinkles healing Balmes, to Anguish kind, ...Il.15.454.215.
And the stream sprinkles: From the curling brows ....Od.3.566.115.

SPRINKLING

Where *Pæon* sprinkling heav'nly Balm around, ...Il.5.489.291.
And sprinkling all the Shrubs with Drops of Blood; ....Il.13.268.117.

SPRINKLING (CONTINUED)
And sprinkling all the Shrubs with dropping Blood; .....Il.13.268A.117.
And sprinkling, as he past, the Sands with Gore. .....Il.13.681.137.

SPRITE
See SPRIGHT.
A watchful Sprite, and *Ariel* is my Name. .....2.RL1.106.153.
Forth popp'd the *Sprite* so thin; .....6.58.30.172.
Ho! Master *Sam,* quoth *Sandys'* Sprite, ...6.58.37.172.

SPRUNG
Sprung the rank Weed, and thriv'd with large Increase; .....1.EOC.535.297.
Long reeds sprung up as on a fountain's brink: .....1.TrPA.156.372.
Or how from joyning Stones the City sprung, ...1.TrSt.11.409.
Sprung from the Rocks, and plung'd into the Main. .....1.TrSt.18.410.
Aloft she sprung, and steer'd to *Thebes* her Flight; .....1.TrSt.141.415.
Then briskly sprung from Bed, with Heart so light, ...2.ChJM.385.33.
When thus ripe Lyes are to perfection sprung, ...2.TemF.479.286.
Sprung it from piety, or from despair? .....2.ElAb.180.334.
Ambition first sprung from your blest abodes; .....2.Elegy.13.363.
Each Parent sprung—"What Fortune, pray?"— Their own, ...4.Arbu.390.126.
Each Parent sprung—"What Fortune, pray?"— their own, ...4.Arbu.390A.126.
Who sprung from Kings shall know less joy than I. .....4.Arbu.405.127.
Norton, from Daniel and Ostrœa sprung, ...5.DunA2.383.148.
Tho' born at *Wapping,* and from *Daniel* sprung, ...5.DunA2.384A.148.
Norton, from Daniel and Ostrœa sprung, ...5.DunB2.415.317.
Pallas they say Sprung from the Head of *Jove,* .....6.37.3.106.
Sprung the fierce Strife, from what offended Pow'r? .....Il.1.10.85.
O *Smintheus!* sprung from fair *Latona's* Line, ...Il.1.53.88.
That kindred Deep, from whence his Mother sprung. .....Il.1.457.109.
Diores sprung from *Amarynceus'* Line; .....Il.2.757.161.
Sprung from the God, by *Thessalus* the King. .....Il.2.828.164.
Sprung from *Pirithous* of immortal Race, ...Il.2.900.166.
Sprung from *Trezenian Ceus,* lov'd by *Jove.* .....Il.2.1027.171.
Sprung, with thy self, from one Celestial Sire, ...Il.4.84.224.
Sprung from his Car; his ringing Arms resound. .....Il.4.475.242.
Sprung from the brave *Dolopion's* mighty Line, ...Il.5.100.271.
Those slain he left; and sprung with noble Rage .....Il.5.188.275.
And great *Æneas,* sprung from Race Divine! .....Il.5.305.281.
Sprung from *Alpheus,* plenteous Stream! that yields .....Il.5.673.300.
And fierce, to seize it, conqu'ring *Ajax* sprung: .....Il.5.765.303.
Sprung since thou art from *Jove,* and Heav'nly born. .....Il.5.1105.320.
From a fair *Naiad* and *Bucolion* sprung: .....Il.6.28.325.
Sprung tho' he was from more than mortal Bed; .....Il.6.122.330.
With haste to meet him sprung the joyful Fair, ...Il.6.492.351.
Sprung from the fair *Philomeda's* Embrace, ...Il.7.13.363.
Sprung from such Fathers, who such Numbers sway; .....Il.7.193.373.
Sprung from an Alien's Bed thy Sire to grace, ...Il.8.343.413.
(She from *Marpessa* sprung, divinely fair, ...Il.9.671.467.
Sprung from no God, and of no Goddess born, ...Il.10.60.5.
Achilles sprung from an immortal Dame. .....Il.10.476.24.
From sage *Antenor* and *Theano* sprung; .....Il.11.284.48.
This Counsel pleas'd: the God-like *Hector* sprung .....Il.12.93.84.
Sprung from a God, and more than Mortal bold; .....Il.13.610.135.
Whence godlike *Rhadamanth* and *Minos* sprung. .....Il.14.368.180.
This sprung from *Phelus,* and th' *Athenians* led; .....Il.15.377.211.
Sprung from the Tent, and left the War behind. .....Il.15.469.215.
Sprung from the Race of old *Laomedon,* .....Il.15.623.220.
The Hero most, from *Hicetaon* sprung, ...Il.15.644.221.
He struck his hasty Foot: his Heels up-sprung; .....Il.15.780.226.
Sprung from the Wind, and like the Wind in speed; .....Il.16.183.245.
Sprung on the *Trojan* and the *Lycian* Band; .....Il.16.711.271.
From *Panthus* sprung, *Euphorbus* was his Name; .....Il.16.973.281.
Sprung to his Car, and measur'd back the Field. .....Il.17.140.293.
High on the Chariot at one Bound he sprung, ...Il.17.610.312.
Sprung from my Bed a god-like Hero came, ...Il.18.73.326.
Sprung from my Bed a god-like Hero came, ...Il.18.509.346.
Hence sprung twelve others of unrival'd Kind, ...Il.20.268.405.
From great *Assaracus* sprung *Capys,* He .....Il.20.288.406.
I sprung from *Priam,* and *Laothöe* fair, ...Il.21.96.425.
Sprung from a Hero, from a Goddess born; .....Il.21.120.426.
Sprung from a River didst thou boast thy Line, ...Il.21.203.429.
Two from one Mother sprung, my *Polydore,* .....Il.22.64.455.
Sprung to their Car; and with united Pains .....Il.23.737.519.
Swift on his Car th' impatient Monarch sprung; .....Il.24.397.552.
Swift on the Car th' impatient Monarch sprung; Il.24.397A.552*
Sprung thro' the Gates of Light, and gave the Day: .....Il.24.867.572.
Of *Ilus* sprung from *Jason's* royal strain, ...Od.1.338.48.
Of that heroic sire the youth is sprung, ...Od.4.211.129.
From *Pæon* sprung, their patron-god imparts .....Od.4.321.134.
Proclaims you from the sage *Ulysses* sprung. .....Od.4.832.158.
Oh sprung from Gods! in wisdom more than man. .....Od.5.258.184.
From *Dymas* sprung, and thus the vision spoke: .....Od.6.28.205.
Blest is the father from whose loins you sprung, ...Od.6.183.218.
For know, from Ocean's God *Nausithous* sprung, ...Od.7.72.237.
And three brave sons, from great *Alcinous* sprung. .....Od.8.124.269.
Clytonius sprung: he wing'd the rapid way, ...Od.8.131.270.
Amphialus sprung forward with a bound, ...Od.8.135.270.
Sprung from the fruitful genius of the ground; .....Od.9.152.311.
Nymphs sprung from fountains, or from shady woods, ...Od.10.415.364.
Hence sprung *Amphion,* hence brave *Zethus* came, ...Od.11.319.397.
Hence *Pollux* sprung who wields with furious sway .....Od.11.367.400.
Hence *Ephialtes,* hence stern *Otus* sprung, ...Od.11.377.401.
From *Phœbus* and the bright *Neæra* sprung; .....Od.12.169.440.
Up sprung a brisker breeze; with freshning gales .....Od.12.184.441.
Sprung of a handmaid, from a bought embrace, ...Od.14.234.47.
Sprung in his mind the momentary wit; .....Od.14.552.63.
They join'd the steeds and on the chariot sprung; .....Od.15.216.78.
A Seer he was, from great *Melampus* sprung, ...Od.15.252.80.
From him sprung *Theoclymenus,* who found .....Od.15.278.82.
How sprung a thought so monstrous in thy mind? .....Od.15.345.86.
Transported from his seat *Eumæus* sprung, ...Od.16.13.102.
O that I were from great *Ulysses* sprung, ...Od.16.103.107.
Speaks thee an Heroe from an Heroe sprung: .....Od.18.260.179.
(*Melantho,* from the loins of *Dolius* sprung, ...Od.18.368.185.
Sprung to the Prince, embrac'd his knee with tears, ...Od.22.405.307.

SPRUNG (CONTINUED)
While yet she spoke, the Queen in transport sprung .....Od.23.35.320.

SPUN
"Lord *Fanny* spun a thousand lines a day? .....4.EpS1.8A.297.
To night, our home-spun author would be true, ...6.107.19.311.
That spun so short his Life's illustrious Line: .....Il.20.155.400.
Spun forth, in Earth the fasten'd Weapon stood. .....Il.21.184.429.

SPUNGY
Apply thine Engine to the spungy Door, ...6.100vi.1.289.

SPUR
'Tis more to *guide* than *spur* the Muse's Steed; .....1.EOC.84.248.
What? shall each spur-gall'd Hackney of the Day, ...4.EpS2.140.321.
Came whip and spur, and dash'd thro' thin and thick .....5.DunB4.197.361.

SPUR-GALL'D
What? shall each spur-gall'd Hackney of the Day, ...4.EpS2.140.321.

SPURN
Employ their Pains to spurn some others down; .....1.EOC.515.296.
Rouze the huge Dragon, with a spurn, from rest, ...6.21.31.70.
When wild *Barbarians* spurn her dust; .....6.51i.18.151.
Lest his Spurn .....6.96i.25.268.
The headlong Coursers spurn his empty Car; .....Il.15.531.217.
Spurn the hoar Head of unresisting Age, ...Il.22.103.457.

SPURN'D
The fierce *Atrides* spurn'd him as he bled, ...Il.13.777.141.
He added not, but mounting spurn'd the plain, ...Od.11.307.397.
Spurn'd with his rustic heel his King unknown; .....Od.17.273.145.
Spurn'd, but not mov'd: He, like a pillar stood, ...Od.17.274.145.
Before him spurn'd, the loaded table falls, ...Od.22.24.287.
He spurn'd the seat with fury as he fell, ...Od.22.103.291.

SPURNING
With spurning heels and with a butting head. .....3.Ep3.56.91.

SPURNS
That threats a Fight, and spurns the rising Sand. .....1.PSp.48.65.
(And spurns the Dust where *Menelaus* lies) .....Il.4.213.231.
Admits the Lance: He falls, and spurns the Field; .....Il.4.535.247.
The Steeds fly back: He falls, and spurns the Plain. .....Il.8.154.405.

SPUTT'RING
Thus sow'rly waild' he, sputt'ring Dirt and Gore; .....Il.23.921.525.

SPY
All seems Infected that th' Infected spy, ...1.EOC.558.304.
Were all to spy what Damsels they bedight. .....2.ChWB.157.64.
No Pimp of Pleasure, and no Spy of State, ...4.HS1.134.19.
Then as a licens'd Spy, whom nothing can .....4.JD4.158.39.
And shake all o'er, like a discover'd Spy. .....4.JD4.279.49.
Ev'n in a Bishop I can spy Desert; .....4.EpS2.70.316.
Sends he some Spy, amidst these silent Hours, ...Il.10.43.4.
Some Spy perhaps, to lurk beside the Main; .....Il.10.407.21.
Along the Path the Spy unwary flew; .....Il.10.417.21.
To whom the Spy: Their Pow'rs they thus dispose: .....Il.10.496.25.
Where late the Spoils of *Hector's* Spy were laid, ...Il.10.619.29.
Ev'n yet, methinks, the gliding Ghosts I spy, ...Il.15.286.208.
But such a Chief I spy not thro' the Host: .....Il.17.725.315.
A Spy distinguish'd from his airy stand; .....Od.4.700.152.
A spy was sent their summons to convey: .....Od.15.494.94.
A day-devourer, and an ev'ning-spy! .....Od.19.83.196.
To watch the foe a trusty spy he sent: .....Od.24.566.375.

SPY'D
Full many an Age old *Hymen* had not spy'd .....2.ChJM.333.30.
The longing Dame look'd up, and spy'd her Love .....2.ChJM.718.49.
Let not each beauty ev'ry where be spy'd, ...3.Ep4.53.142.
His very Minister who spy'd them first, ...4.Arbu.71.100.
At length he spy'd the Merry-men brown, ...6.79.115.221.
Achilles, starting as the Chiefs he spy'd, ...Il.9.257.445.
Between the parting rocks at length he spy'd .....Od.5.562.199.
The monster's club within the cave I spy'd, ...Od.9.380.321.
With graceful port advancing now I spy'd .....Od.11.365.400.

SPYES
See SPIES.
Instead of Spyes, & Pimps, & Panders, ...6.135.74A.369.

SQUAB
On her large Squab you find her spread, ...6.14v(a).10.48.

SQUADRON
(*Ancœus'* Son) the mighty Squadron led. .....Il.2.742.161.
Two Heroes led the secret Squadron on, ...Il.4.446.241.
A wakeful Squadron, each in Arms prepar'd: .....Il.10.208.11.
And Gold their Armour: These the Squadron led, ...Il.18.601.351.
In Arms the glitt'ring Squadron rising round .....Il.18.611.352.

SQUADRON'D
Thy squadron'd vineyards well thy art declare, ...Od.24.289.363.

SQUADRONS
Let *Volga's* Banks with Iron Squadrons shine, ...1.W-F.363.186.
His fainting Squadrons to new Fury warms. .....1.TrES.144.454.
The lucid Squadrons round the Sails repair: .....2.RL2.56.163.
And call the Squadrons sheath'd in Brazen Arms: .....Il.2.517.151.
So throng'd, so close, the *Grecian* Squadrons stood .....Il.2.558.154.
Fierce *Ajax* led the *Locrian* Squadrons on, ...Il.2.630.157.
In sep'rate Squadrons these their Train divide, ...Il.2.753.161.
The moving Squadrons blacken all the Strand. .....Il.2.971.169.
Whose Squadrons, led from black *Æsepus'* Flood, ...Il.4.121.226.
Such, and so thick, th' embattel'd Squadrons stood, ...Il.4.322.236.

SQUADRONS (CONTINUED)
The King, who saw their Squadrons yet unmov'd, ...Il.4.388.239.
Host against Host with shadowy Squadrons drew, ...Il.4.510.245.
The Squadrons part; th' expecting *Trojans* stand. ....Il.7.62.366.
Awake thy Squadrons to new Toils of Fight. ....Il.7.397.383.
Squadrons on Squadrons cloud the dusky Plain: ....Il.8.72.399.
Squadrons on Squadrons cloud the dusky Plain: ....Il.8.72.399.
Squadrons on Squadrons drives, and fills the Fields ....Il.8.260.409.
Squadrons on Squadrons drives, and fills the Fields ....Il.8.260.409.
Rang'd at the Ships let all our Squadrons shine, ...Il.9.830.474.
Arriving where the *Thracian* Squadrons lay, ...Il.10.542.27.
The Squadrons spread their sable Wings behind. ....Il.11.66.37.
Whole Squadrons vanish, and proud Heads lie low. ....Il.11.206.44.
Mark how this way yon' bending Squadrons yield! ....Il.11.449.54.
(Young as they were) the vengeful Squadrons led. ....Il.11.845.74.
His fainting Squadrons to new Fury warms. ....Il.12.498.99.
With well-rang'd Squadrons strongly circled round: ....Il.13.172.113.
The *Locrian* Squadrons nor the Jav'lin wield, ...Il.13.891.148.
For not the Spear the Locrian Squadrons wield ....Il.13.891A.148.
And driv'n his conqu'ring Squadrons from the Field. ....Il.15.20.194.
The martial Squadrons close on either Hand: ....Il.16.690.271.
Come, thro' yon' Squadrons let us hew the Way, ...Il.17.201.295.
Thro' falling Squadrons bear my slaught'ring Sword, ...Il.19.444.390.
And thin the Squadrons with my single Spear. ....Il.20.414.412.
Her routed Squadrons pant behind their Wall: ....Il.21.341.435.
Let the leagu'd Squadrons to their Posts retire. ....Il.23.66.489.
Strait in three squadrons all our crew we part, ...Od.9.182.313.

SQUALID
In squalid vests with many a gaping rent, ...Od.17.412.152.

SQUALLID
Some with vast Beams the squallid Corps engage, ...1.TrSt.733.440.

SQUALLS
My vixen Mistress squalls; ....6.47.22.129.

SQUANDER
To squander some, and some to hide agen. ....3.Ep3.14A.84.
To squander these, and those to hide agen. ....3.Ep3.14.84.
Nor could Profusion squander all in kind. ....3.Ep3.48.90.
O squander not thy Grief, those Tears command ....6.96ii.75.273.

SQUAR'D
He smooth'd, and squar'd 'em, by the rule and line. ....Od.5.316.186.

SQUARE
At Ten for certain, Sir, in Bloomsb'ry-Square— ....4.2HE2.95.171.
Add fifty more, and bring it to a square. ....4.1HE6.76.241.
Turn round to square, and square again to round; ....4.1HE1.170.291.
Turn round to square, and square again to round; ....4.1HE1.170.291.
Now running round the Circle, finds it square. ....5.DunB4.34.343.
Thro' yon' square Body, and that black Array: ....Il.13.206.115.
Athwart the spacious square each tries his art ....Od.17.192.140.

SQUAT
Still sits at squat, and peeps not from its hole. ....3.Ep1.115.24.

SQUAWL
The short thick Sob, loud Scream, and shriller Squawl: ....6.14ii.6.43.

SQUAWLE
And gaping Infants squawle to hear the rest. ....6.96iv.66.278.

SQUEAKS
Squeaks like a high-stretch'd Lutestring, and replies: ....4.JD4.99.33.
And, as the Prompter breathes, the Puppet squeaks; ....4.Arbu.318.118.

SQUEEZE
If gentle *Damon* did not squeeze her Hand? ....2.RL1.98.152.

SQUEEZES
Two or *Three* Squeezes, and *Two* or *Three* Towses, ...6.36.5.104.
Two or *Three* Squeezes, *Two* or *Three* Towses, ...6.36.5A.105.

SQUEEZINGS
Ev'n to the Dregs and *Squeezings* of the *Brain;* ....1.EOC.607.308.

SQUINTING
On *Jenkin* too you cast a squinting Eye; ....2.ChWB.118.62.
And motly, squinting *Harvequini's,* ....6.135.40.367.
And motly, squinting Harlequini's, ...6.135.40A.367.

SQUIRE
Damian alone, the Knight's obsequious Squire, ...2.ChJM.359.31.
But anxious Cares the pensive Squire opprest, ...2.ChJM.392.33.
The Squire alone was absent from the Board, ...2.ChJM.406.34.
Receiv'd th'Impressions of the Love-sick Squire, ...2.ChJM.432.35.
She took th'Impressions of the Love-sick Squire, ...2.ChJM.432A.35.
Nor less Impatience vex'd her Am'rous Squire, ...2.ChJM.494.39.
And gave th'Impression to the trusty Squire. ....2.ChJM.511.40.
To haste before; the gentle Squire obey'd: ....2.ChJM.536.41.
Thither th'obsequious Squire address'd his Pace, ...2.ChJM.605.44.
His Squire shall cuckold him before your Face. ....2.ChJM.646.46.
Boastful and rough, your first son is a 'Squire; ....3.Ep1.103.22.
Fill the capacious Squire, and deep Divine! ....3.Ep3.204.110.
This brazen Brightness, to the 'Squire so dear; ....5.DunB1.219.286.
The sturdy Squire to Gallic masters stoop, ...5.DunB4.595.402.
Drink with the 'Squire, and kiss his Wife; ....6.39.18.111.
Hum half a tune, tell stories to the squire; ....6.45.20.125.
Some Squire, perhaps, you take delight to rack; ....6.45.23.125.
A Wit and courtly 'Squire. ....6.58.16.171.
This 'Squire he dropp'd his Pen full soon, ...6.58.35.172.
"To what, (quoth 'Squire) shall *Ovid* change?" ....6.58.75.174.
On Tiptoe then the Squire he stood, ...6.94.57.261.
Is it full grown? The Squire reply'd, ...6.94.63.261.

SQUIRE (CONTINUED)
Whose Squire *Oïleus,* with a sudden spring, ...Il.11.129.41.
He mounts the Car, and gives his Squire the Rein: ....Il.11.352.50.
(His valu'd Coursers, to his Squire consign'd, ...Il.13.485.130.
Strook to the Dust the Squire, and Charioteer ....Il.17.690.314.
But the brave Squire the ready Coursers brought, ...Il.17.695.314.
All bright in heav'nly Arms, above his Squire ....Il.19.434.389.
The Squire who saw expiring on the Ground ....Il.20.565.418.

SQUIRES
Knights, Squires, and Steeds, must enter on the ....1.EOC.282.271.
What could they more than Knights and Squires confound, ...3.Ep3.41.89.
As Beasts of Nature may we hunt the Squires? ....4.EpS2.31.314.
Then Lords and Lordings, 'Squires and Knights, ...6.58.45.172.
Next Lords and Lordings, 'Squires and Knights, ...6.58.45A.172.
'Tis pity that two Squires so Gent— ....6.94.39.260.
The Squires restrain'd: The Foot, with those who wield ....Il.11.63.37.
Those in the Tents the Squires industrious spread; ....Il.19.293.384.
All mount their Chariots, Combatants and Squires. ....Il.23.161.495.

SQUIRREL
Her Squirrel missing, or her Sparrow flown. ....6.96ii.4.270.
Her Squirrel missing, or the sparrow flown. ....6.96ii.4A.270.

SQUIRT
Two Cupids squirt before: a Lake behind ....3.Ep4.111.148.

ST
See SAINT.
Sir, I'm no Fool: Nor shall you, by St. *John,* ....2.ChWB.126.62.
Valerius, whole; and of St. *Jerome,* Part; ....2.ChWB.359.74.
Awake, my Sᴛ. Jᴏʜɴ! leave all meaner things ....3.EOM1.1.11.
And fled from Monarchs, Sᴛ. Jᴏʜɴ! dwells with thee. ....3.EOM4.18.129.
Drive to St. James's a whole herd of swine? ....3.Ep3.62.92.
The well-bred cuckolds in St. James's air: ....3.Ep3.388.124.
And one more Pensioner St. Stephen gains. ....3.Ep3.394.124.
There *St. John* mingles with my friendly Bowl, ...4.HS1.127.17.
And *St. John's* self (great *Dryden's* friends before) ....4.Arbu.141.105.
St John, whose love indulg'd my labours past ....4.1HE1.1.279.
Sometimes, with Aristippus, or St. Paul, ...4.1HE1.31.281.
From low St. James's up to high St. Paul; ....4.1HE1.82.285.
From low St. James's up to high St. Paul; ....4.1HE1.82.285.
If such a Doctrine, in St. James's air, ...4.1HE1.110.287.
St. Jᴏʜɴ has ever been a wealthy Fool— ....4.EpS2.132.320.
Oh All-accomplish'd St. Jᴏʜɴ! deck thy Shrine? ....4.EpS2.139.321.
As if he saw St. James's and the Queen. ....5.DunB4.280.371.
(St. James's first, for leaden Gilbert preach'd) ....5.DunB4.608.404.
Garth at *St James's,* and at *White's,* ....6.58.47.172.
St. A-d-re [*André]* too, the Scale to take ....6.94.27.260.
Is it alive? *St. A-d-re* [*André]* cry'd; ....6.94.61.261.
And now two Legs *St. A-d-re* [*André]* got, ...6.94.65.261.
St. A-nd-re [*André]* shall dissect the Head, ...6.94.71.261.
Villete's soft Voice and Sᵗ John's silver Lyre. ....6.106iii.6.307.
Where, nobly-pensive, Sᴛ. Jᴏʜɴ sate and thought; ....6.142.10.383.
There, nobly-pensive, Sᴛ. Jᴏʜɴ sate and thought; ....6.142.10A.383.
Here, nobly-pensive, Sᴛ. Jᴏʜɴ sate and thought; ....6.142.10B.383.

ST JOHN
See ST.

STAB
Prompt or to guard or stab, to saint or damn, ...5.DunB2.357.315.
"This steel shall stab it to the heart." ....6.140.8.378.

STAB'D
Stab'd by a murd'rous hand *Atrides* dy'd, ...Od.11.505.408.
O'er the full bowl, the traitor stab'd his guest; ....Od.11.508.408.

STABB'D
Should Dennis publish, you had stabb'd your Brother, ...6.116vii.1A.328.
Stabb'd at the Sight, *Deiphobus* drew nigh, ...Il.13.509.131.
Stabb'd in his Palace if your Prince must fall, ...Od.17.91.136.

STABLE
Or with his hound comes hollowing from the stable, ...6.45.27.125.
Why then that dirty Stable-boy thy Care? ....6.96iv.29.277.

STABLE-BOY
Why then that dirty Stable-boy thy Care? ....6.96iv.29.277.

STAFF
Before his feet his pondrous staff he cast; ....1.TrPA.43.367.
Prop'd on his Staff, and stooping as he goes, ...1.TrVP.48.379.
With Staff and Pumps the Marquis lead the Race; ....5.DunB4.586.400.
Lay by your White Staff and gray Habit, ...6.42iv.15.118.
Lay down your White Staff and gray Habit, ...6.42iv.15A.118.
To guide his steps he bore a staff of gold; ....Od.11.113.386.
A rugged staff his trembling hand sustains; ....Od.13.505.30.
Lead on: but help me to some staff to stay ....Od.17.218.142.
A staff *Eumæus* gave. Along the way ....Od.17.222.142.
Propt on a staff, a beggar old and bare, ...Od.17.228.143.
Doubtful, or with his staff to strike him dead, ...Od.17.276.145.
Propt on a staff, and trembling as he went. ....Od.17.413.152.
Then to his hand a staff the victor gave, ...Od.18.124.172.
Propt on a staff, deform'd with age and care, ...Od.24.185.356.

STAFFORD
And needs no Rod but S[taffor]d with a Rule ....3.Ep4.18A.137*.

STAG
(When some tall Stag fresh-slaughter'd in the Wood ....Il.16.196.247.
(The steer or stag:) or with keen hunger bold ....Od.6.159.216.
Sent a tall stag, descending from the wood, ...Od.10.183.349.
Swift as a stag, and as a lion strong, ...Od.17.381.150.

STAG'S
A stag's torn hide is lapt around his reins: ....Od.13.504.30.

STAGE
As e'er cou'd *Dennis*, of the *Grecian* Stage; ....1.EOC.270.270.
As e'er cou'd *Dennis*, of the Laws o' th' Stage; ....1.EOC.270B.270.
As e'er cou'd *Dennis*, of th' *Athenian* stage; ....1.EOC.270C.270.
Knights, Squires, and Steeds, must enter on the ....1.EOC.282.271.
So vast a Throng the Stage can ne'er contain. ....1.EOC.283.271.
The Stage can ne'er so vast a Throng contain. ....1.EOC.283A.271.
And drove those *Holy Vandals* off the Stage. ....1.EOC.696.319.
Scarfs, garters, gold, amuse his riper stage; ....3.EOM2.279.88.
Well, if it be my time to quit the Stage, ...4.JD4.1.27.
Our Court may justly to our Stage give Rules, ...4.JD4.220.45.
If I approve, "Commend it to the Stage." ....4.Arbu.58.100.
Seeks from the Stage his vile Support to gain: ....4.JD2A.14.132.
Comes titt'ring on, and shoves you from the stage: ....4.2HE2.325.187.
"These, only these, support to the crouded stage, ...4.2HE1.87.201.
The stage how loosely does Astræa tread, ...4.2HE1.290.219.
Farewel the stage! if just as thrives the Play, ...4.2HE1.302.221.
"What shook the stage, and made the people stare?" ....4.2HE1.336.225.
See modest Cibber now has left the Stage: ....4.1HE1.6.279.
Whom all Lord Chamberlains allow the Stage: ....4.EpS1.42.301.
Boyer the State, and Law the Stage gave o'er, ...5.DunA2.381.146.
And a new Cibber shall the Stage adorn. ....5.DunA3.134.161.
Oh great Restorer of the good old Stage, ...5.DunA3.201.175.
Thy stage shall stand, ensure it but from Fire. ....5.DunA3.310.185.
Bays, form'd by nature Stage and Town to bless, ...5.DunB1.109.277.
Did on the stage my Fops appear confin'd? ....5.DunB1.191.283.
Boyer the State, and Law the Stage gave o'er, ...5.DunB2.413.317.
And a new Cibber shall the stage adorn. ....5.DunB3.142.326.
Oh great Restorer of the good old Stage, ...5.DunB3.205.330.
Thy stage shall stand, ensure it but from Fire. ....5.DunB3.312.335.
Wake the dull Church, and lull the ranting Stage; ....5.DunB4.58.347.
From Stage to Stage the licens'd Earl may run, ...5.DunB4.587.401.
From Stage to Stage the licens'd Earl may run, ...5.DunB4.587.401.
For this the Tragic Muse first trod the stage, ...6.32.5.96.
Dare to have sense your selves; assert the stage, ...6.32.43.97.
Tho' with the Stoick chief our stage may ring, ...6.41.37.114.
And thus upon the Stage 'tis fairly *thrown,* ....6.60.37.179.
And shook the Stage with Thunders all his own! ....6.128.16.356.
And, on that Stage of War, the Cause be try'd: ....Il.3.100.194.
Stage above stage th' imperial structure stands, ...Od.17.316.147.
Stage above stage th' imperial structure stands, ...Od.17.316.147.

STAGES
How many stages thro' old Monks she rid? ....5.DunA3.44.154.
How many stages thro' old Monks she rid? ....5.DunB3.52.323.

STAGG'RING
Sunk on his Knees and stagg'ring with his Pains, ...Il.5.379.285.
But yet so stunn'd, that stagg'ring on the Plain, ...Il.11.457.54.
Approaching dealt a stagg'ring Blow behind. ....Il.16.955.280.
Slidd'ring, and stagg'ring. On the Border stood ....Il.21.267.431.
Stagg'ring I reel'd, and as I reel'd I fell, ...Od.11.79.385.
Pow'rless to move, his stagg'ring feet deny ....Od.18.283.180.

STAGYRITE
As if the *Stagyrite* o'erlook'd each Line. ....1.EOC.138.255.
Yes, or we must renounce the *Stagyrite*. ....1.EOC.280.271.
The mighty *Stagyrite* first left the Shore, ...1.EOC.645.311.
Sate fix'd in Thought the mighty *Stagyrite;* ....2.TemF.233.274.

STAGYRITE'S
See Physic beg the Stagyrite's defence! ....5.DunA3.351.193.

STAID
Than mine, to find a Subject staid and wise, ...4.JD4.168.39.
Soon as he clears whate'er their passage staid, ...Il.21.293.433.
Staid but a season to re-fit his fleet; ....Od.14.422.56.

STAIN
And stain the sacred Womb where once he lay? ....1.TrSt.333.424.
Oh Stain to Honour! oh Disgrace of Arms! ....1.TrES.212.457.
Oh Stain to Honour! oh Disgrace to Arms! ....1.TrES.212A.457.
Or stain her Honour, or her new Brocade, ...2.RL2.107.166.
Stain all my soul, and wanton in my eyes! ....2.ElAb.266.341.
Wash Bladen white, and expiate Hay's stain. ....5.DunB4.560.397.
Rash, impious Man! to stain the blest Abodes, ...Il.5.491.291.
Nor stain the sacred Friendship of our Race. ....Il.6.266.339.
And hopes, thy Deeds shall wipe the Stain away. ....Il.6.673.360.
Now from nocturnal Sweat, and sanguine Stain, ...Il.10.673.31.
And all the Slaughters that must stain the Day. ....Il.11.72.37.
Oh Stain to Honour! of Disgrace to Arms! ....Il.16.515.263.
Or stain this Lance, or see *Achilles* fall. ....Il.21.246.431.
Great as thou art, ev'n thou may'st stain with Gore ....Il.21.697.450.
And stain the Pavement of my regal Hall; ....Il.22.95.456.
And stain his Rival's Mail with issuing Gore; ....Il.23.950.527.
Shall with inglorious gore this marble stain. ....Od.1.486.55.
T'avenge the stain of my ill-fated charms! ....Od.4.196.129.
If I am lame, that stain my natal hour ....Od.8.351.282.
What human victims stain the feast-ful floor! ....Od.13.451.27.
"Ye rush to arms, and stain the feast with blood: ....Od.16.315.121.
The stain of manhood, of a coward mind: ....Od.18.4.166.
What marks of luxury the marble stain! ....Od.20.186.242.
Nor stain with grief the pleasures of the day; ....Od.21.88.263.

STAIN'D
And silent *Darent*, stain'd with *Danish* Blood. ....1.W-F.348.184.
With monstrous Mixture stain'd my Mother's Bed, ...1.TrSt.96.414.
Blood stain'd her Cheeks, and from her Mouth there came ....1.TrSt.150.416.
Th'exulting Mother stain'd with Filial Blood; ....1.TrSt.323.423.
But stain'd with blood, or ill exchanged for gold, ...3.EOM4.296.156.
How hurt he you? he only stain'd the Gown. ....4.EpS2.165.323.
But stain'd with Blood, or ill exchang'd for ....6.130.6.358.
For this with Falshoods is my Honour stain'd; ....Il.1.137.93.

STAIN'D (CONTINUED)
When by the blood-stain'd Hand *Minerva* prest ....Il.5.37.267.
Which stain'd with sacred Blood the blushing Sand. ....Il.5.107.272.
And the transparent Skin with Crimson stain'd. ....Il.5.420.287.
Long since had *Hector* stain'd these Fields with Gore, ...Il.8.435.418.
His Coursers steep'd in Sweat, and stain'd with Gore, ...Il.11.728.67.
Which never Man had stain'd with ruddy Wine, ...Il.16.274.249.
Achilles' Plume is stain'd with Dust and Gore; ....Il.16.960.280.
An Act so rash (*Antilochus*) has stain'd. ....Il.23.652.515.
I stain'd my hospitable hearth with blood. ....Od.14.446.57.
The blood-stain'd exile, ever doom'd to roam. ....Od.15.301.83.
Nor servile flatt'ry stain'd the moral lay. ....Od.22.392.307.

STAINS
Swift Trouts, diversify'd with Crimson Stains, ...1.W-F.145.163.
'Tis mine to wash a few slight Stains; but theirs ....4.JD4.284.49.
And in our own (excuse some Courtly stains) ....4.2HE1.215.213.
My Lord and me as far as Stains, ...4.HS6.96.257.
That counts your Beauties only by your Stains, ...4.EpS2.221.325.
When black Ambition stains a Publick Cause, ...4.EpS2.228.325.
Stains the pure Iv'ry with a lively Red; ....Il.4.173.229.
Majestical in Death! No Stains are found ....Il.24.511.557.
Of great *Alcinous* falls, and stains the sand. ....Od.13.28.2.
From stains of luxury the polish'd board: ....Od.19.75.196.

STAIR
And may descend to *Mordington* from *Stair:* ....4.EpS2.239.326.
The prudent Queen the lofty stair ascends, ...Od.21.7.258.

STAIRS
And gingling down the back-stairs, told the crew, ...3.Ep3.67.93.
And Climb the dark Stairs to your Friends who have none: ....6.42iii.4.117.
He said; and mounting up the lofty stairs, ...Od.22.158.294.

STAKE
I'll stake yon' Lamb that near the Fountain plays, ...1.PSp.33.63.
I'll stake my Lamb that near the Fountain plays, ...1.PSp.33A.63.
Mean, empty Boast! but shall the *Lycians* stake ....Il.17.163.293.
A Goblet or a Tripod let us stake, ...Il.23.569.512.
The stake now glow'd beneath the burning bed ....Od.9.449.324.
Guide the sharp stake, and twirl it round and round. ....Od.9.456.324.
Thus in his eyeball hiss'd the plunging stake. ....Od.9.468.325.
A knotty stake then aiming at his head, ...Od.14.472.58.

STAKES
Shall then Uxorio, if the stakes he sweep, ...3.Ep3.59.91.
And bristled thick with sharpen'd Stakes below. ....Il.12.64.83.
The Stakes beneath, the *Grecian* Walls behind? ....Il.12.72.84.

STALE
And own *stale Nonsense* which they ne'er invent. ....1.EOC.411.287.
Of a stale Virgin with a Winter Face; ....2.ChJM.104.19.
Tho' stale, not ripe; tho' thin, yet never clear; ....5.DunA3.164.167.
Tho' stale, not ripe; tho' thin, yet never clear; ....5.DunB3.170.328.

STALK
Majestically stalk; ....6.14v(a).21.49.
With haughty stalk he sought the distant glades ....Od.11.661.416.

STALK'D
O'er Heaps of Ruin stalk'd the stately Hind; ....1.W-F.70.156.
Thro' wondring Skies enormous stalk'd along; ....Il.1.524.113.
He boldly stalk'd, the foremost on the Plain, ...Il.3.34.189.
This said, he stalk'd with ample Strides along, ...Il.4.286.234.
Him, as he stalk'd, the *Cretan* Javelin found; ....Il.13.467.128.
Thus stalk'd he, dreadful; Death was in his Look; ....Il.13.1018.153.
He said, and like a Lion stalk'd along: ....Il.13.1056.155.
Fate stalk'd amidst them, grim with human Gore. ....Il.18.624.352.
Of old, she stalk'd amid the bright Abodes; ....Il.19.99.376.
Ev'n to the temple stalk'd th' adult'rous spouse, ...Od.3.346.103.
My haughty step, I stalk'd the vally o'er. ....Od.10.326.360.
Stalk'd with majestic port, a martial train: ....Od.11.52.383.
But turning stalk'd with giant strides away. ....Od.11.774.424.
Behind him sow'rly stalk'd. Without delay ....Od.20.183.242.

STALKED
Stalked through a mead of daffodillies ....6.157.2.406.

STALKING
Who proudly stalking, leaves the herds at large, ...Od.17.292.146.

STALKS
So stalks the Lordly Savage o'er the Plain, ...1.TrES.15.450.
A third majestically stalks ....6.135.61.368.
She stalks on Earth, and shakes the World around; ....Il.4.505.245.
As the grim Lyon stalks around his Prey. ....Il.5.364.284.
So stalks in Arms the grizly God of *Thrace,* ....Il.7.252.376.
So stalks the lordly Savage o'er the Plain, ...Il.12.359.94.
Stalks the proud Ram, the Father of the Fold: ....Il.13.623.135.
And o'er the Slaughter stalks gigantic Death. ....Il.15.393.212.
The godlike Hero stalks from side to side. ....Il.15.821.228.
With ample Strides he stalks from Place to Place. ....Il.16.655.270.
Stalks careless on, with unregarding Pride; ....Il.20.202.402.
And sold to *Lemnos,* stalks on *Trojan* Ground! ....Il.21.67.424.
In silence turns, and sullen stalks away. ....Od.11.692.418.

STALL
And goad the Prelate slumb'ring in his Stall. ....4.EpS2.219.325.
But Fate with Butchers plac'd thy priestly Stall, ...5.DunA3.205.175.
But fate with butchers plac'd thy priestly stall, ...5.DunB3.209.330.
Her Mouth was black as Bull-Dogs at the Stall: ....6.14ii.38.44.
Breaks from his Stall, and beats the trembling Ground; ....Il.6.653.359.
Breaks from his Stall, and pours along the Ground; ....Il.15.299.208.
Prime of the flock, and choicest of the stall: ....Od.4.432.140.
So, whilst he feeds luxurious in the stall, ...Od.4.719.152.
So shall a barren heifer from the stall ....Od.11.37.381.

STALLS
Four of this Race his ample Stalls contain, Il.5.334.282.
Depopulate the Stalls and waste the Fold; Il.5.684.300.
For this, high fed in plenteous Stalls ye stand, Il.8.230.408.
There ty'd, they rest in high Celestial Stalls; Il.8.538.422.
The matchless Steeds his ample Stalls adorn: Il.10.667.31.
Repuls'd by Numbers from the nightly Stalls, Il.11.676.65.
And Stalls, and Folds, and scatter'd Cotts between; Il.18.679.356.
The foaming Coursers to the Stalls they led. Il.19.294.384.
The stately Oxe, and bleeds within the stalls. Od.11.510.408.
As many stalls for shaggy goats are rear'd; Od.14.123.42.

STAMP
How did they fume, and stamp, and roar, and chafe? 4.Arbu.191.109.
To hear each mortal stamp and swear 6.61.17.181.
To hear each mortal stamp and stare 6.61.17A.181.
How would they fume, and stamp, and roar, and chafe! 6.98.41.284.
The Stamp of Fate, and Sanction of the God: Il.1.685.120.

STAMP'D
There, stamp'd with arms, Newcastle shines compleat, 5.DunA1.122.78.
There, stamp'd with arms, Newcastle shines complete: 5.DunB1.142.280.
Thy careful hand is stamp'd on all the soil, Od.24.288.363.

STANCH
May stanch th' Effusion and extract the Dart. Il.4.229.232.

STAND
A Milk-white Bull shall at your Altars stand, 1.PSp.47.65.
Here *Ceres'* Gifts in waving Prospect stand, 1.W-F.39.152.
The patient Fisher takes his silent Stand 1.W-F.137.163.
But when the Fury took her Stand on high, 1.TrSt.160.416.
Now Sirs you know to what I stand inclin'd, 2.ChJM.137.21.
Men shou'd stand mark'd with far more Wickedness, 2.ChWB.367.75.
Here living *Teapots* stand, one Arm held out, 2.RL4.49.188.
There in long Robes the Royal *Magi* stand, 2.TemF.97.260.
Around the Shrine it self of *Fame* they stand, 2.TemF.180.270.
Gath'ring his flowing Robe, he seem'd to stand, 2.TemF.240.274.
Which still unfolded stand, by Night, by Day, 2.TemF.426.284.
Ah no—in sacred vestments may'st thou stand, 2.ElAb.325.346.
There passengers shall stand, and pointing say, 2.Elegy.39.365.
Say, at what part of nature will they stand? 3.EOM4.166.143.
Well then, since with the world we stand or fall 3.Ep3.79A.94.
There, English Bounty yet a-while may stand, 3.Ep3.247.113.
Abhor, a *Perpetuity* should stand: 4.2HE2.247.183.
Desiring I would stand their friend. 4.HS6.66.255.
They stand amaz'd, and think me grown 4.HS6.123.257.
From him whose quills stand quiver'd at his ear, 4.1HE1.83.285.
You laugh, half Beau half Sloven if I stand, 4.1HE1.161.291.
Europe's just balance and our own may stand, 4.1740.97.337.
His gray-goose-weapon must have made her stand. 5.DunA1.188.85.
That gray-goose-weapon must have made her stand. 5.DunA1.188A.85.
Amid that Area wide she took her stand, 5.DunA2.23.99.
In that wide space the Goddess took her stand, 5.DunA2.23A.99.
Where the tall Nothing stood, or seem'd to stand; 5.DunA2.102.109.
When fancy flags, and sense is at a stand. 5.DunA2.222.128.
Thy stage shall stand, ensure it but from Fire. 5.DunA3.310.185.
Great Cibber's brazen, brainless brothers stand; 5.DunB1.32.271.
This grey-goose weapon must have made her stand. 5.DunB1.198.283.
Amid that area wide they took their stand, 5.DunB2.27.297.
Where the tall Nothing stood, or seem'd to stand; 5.DunB2.110.300.
When fancy flags, and sense is at a stand. 5.DunB2.230.307.
Around him wide a sable Army stand, 5.DunB2.355.314.
Thy stage shall stand, ensure it but from Fire. 5.DunB3.312.335.
She tripp'd and laugh'd, too pretty much to stand; 5.DunB4.50.346.
We never suffer it to stand too wide. 5.DunB4.154.356.
There all the Learn'd shall at the labour stand, 5.DunB4.393.380.
Attentive Blocks stand round you, and admire. 6.7.10.15.
Of Gods and heroes, made a Woman stand; 6.20.30.67.
So hop'd to stand no less than he 6.30.17.86.
So hop'd to stand as well as he 6.30.17A.86.
He'd do't; and ne'r stand Shill—I Shall—I, 6.44.9.123.
I wish the Man a Dinner, and stand still; 6.49iii.2B.142.
He Flourish still and Stand, 6.54.10.164.
Stand emulous of Greek and Roman fame? 6.71.54.204.
I cannot go, nor yet can stand, 6.79.51.219.
Let me stand, 6.96i.48.269.
At awful Distance long they silent stand, Il.1.430.108.
Trembling they stand, while *Jove* assumes the Throne, Il.1.694.120.
Stand forth that *Greek!* and hoist his Sail to fly; Il.2.426.147.
Along the River's level Meads they stand, Il.2.550.153.
With these *Arcesilaus* and *Clonius* stand, Il.2.588.155.
A hundred Vessels in long Order stand, Il.2.695.159.
Where *Æpy* high, and little *Pteleon* stand; Il.2.718.160.
Unstain'd with Blood his cover'd Chariots stand; Il.2.942.168.
Now Front to Front the hostile Armies stand, Il.3.23.189.
Yet, wou'd'st thou have the proffer'd Combate stand, Il.3.97.194.
As one unskill'd or dumb, he seem'd to stand, Il.3.281.207.
Now round the Lists th' admiring Armies stand, Il.3.423.212.
Why stand ye gazing round the dreadful Plain, Il.4.278.234.
Why stand you distant, and the rest expect Il.4.392.239.
Take back th' unjust Reproach! Behold we stand Il.4.404.240.
As when the fleecy Flocks unnumber'd stand Il.4.492.244.
There veil'd in spacious Coverlets they stand; Il.5.246.279.
That propt alone by *Priam's* Race should stand Il.5.577.296.
Remote they stand, while Alien Troops engage, Il.5.581.296.
They turn, they stand: The *Greeks* their Fury dare, Il.5.609.297.
Already met the threat'ning Heroes stand; Il.5.697.301.
Troy felt his Arm, and yon' proud Ramparts stand Il.5.792.304.
Commission'd in alternate Watch they stand, Il.5.930.311.
Commission'd in alternate Watch to stand, Il.5.930A.311.
(A warlike Circle) round *Tydides* stand: Il.5.973.313.
Our selves, here fix'd, will make the dang'rous Stand: Il.6.104.328.
To stand the first in Worth as in Command, Il.6.257.339.
The Squadrons part; th' expecting *Trojans* stand. Il.7.62.366.
Gods! should he see our Warriors trembling stand, Il.7.155.372.

STAND (CONTINUED)
Can you stand trembling, and desert the Day? Il.7.194.373.
With these *Eurypylus* and *Thoas* stand, Il.7.203.374.
To stop his Coursers, and to stand the Fight; Il.8.205.407.
Soon as before yon' hollow Ships we stand, Il.8.220.407.
For this, high fed in plenteous Stalls ye stand, Il.8.230.408.
Compacted Troops stand wedg'd in firm Array, Il.8.263.410.
Before the Ships a desp'rate Stand they made, Il.8.415.417.
Commission'd in alternate Watch they stand, Il.8.480.419.
Commission'd in alternate Watch to stand, Il.8.480A.419.
This is his Word; and know his Word shall stand. Il.8.511.421.
For thus I speak, and what I speak shall stand; Il.8.566.423.
And arm in vain: For what I will, shall stand. Il.8.604.425.
Silent, unmov'd, in dire Dismay they stand, Il.9.40.433.
Stand but as Slaves before a noble Mind. Il.9.495.457.
Or at my Knee, by *Phœnix* wouldst thou stand; Il.9.610.464.
Just there, th' impetuous Homicide shall stand, Il.9.769.472.
In the dread Front let great *Atrides* stand, Il.9.832.474.
To whom the King. In such Distress we stand, Il.10.49.4.
Stand off, approach not, but thy Purpose tell. Il.10.93.6.
Where stand his Coursers? In what Quarter sleep Il.10.479.25.
The Horses yok'd beside each Warrior stand. Il.10.545.27.
High on *Ulysses'* Bark her horrid Stand Il.11.9.35.
They stand to Arms: the *Greeks* their Onset dare, Il.11.275.47.
And stand we deedless, O eternal Shame! Il.11.407.53.
Here stand his utmost Force—The Warrior said; Il.11.451.54.
Shall breathe from Slaughter, and in combat stand, Il.11.488.56.
What Danger, singly if I stand the Ground, Il.11.515.57.
To guard their wounded Friend: While thus they stand Il.11.722.67.
The publick Mart and Courts of Justice stand, Il.11.937.77.
Say, great *Eurypylus!* shall *Greece* yet stand? Il.11.952.77.
So graceful these, and so the Shock they stand Il.12.151.87.
Urge those who stand, and those who faint excite; Il.12.323.93.
Fav'ring descends, the wills to stand the Storm. Il.13.100.109.
While Tears of Rage stand burning in their Eye. Il.13.122.110.
Repuls'd he stands; nor from his Stand retires; Il.13.203.115.
Stand, and my Spear shall rout their scatt'ring Pow'r, Il.13.207.115.
Stand we to talk, when Glory calls to Arms? Il.13.379.123.
For thee, tho' Hell's black Portals stand display'd, Il.13.525.131.
His Troops unpractis'd in the Fights of Stand Il.13.890A.147.
(Their Ships at distance from the Battel stand, Il.14.39.159.
Safe let us stand; and from the Tumult far, Il.14.151.165.
Brace on your firmest Helms, and stand to Arms: Il.14.430.184.
Stiff with Amaze the pale Beholders stand, Il.14.485.187.
With cov'ring Shields (a friendly Circle) stand. Il.14.502.188.
There in the Father's awful Presence stand, Il.15.166.203.
How shall his Rashness stand the dire Alarms, Il.15.186.203.
How shall thy Rashness stand the dire Alarms, Il.15.202.204.
Stand the First Onset, and provoke the Storm: Il.15.335.210.
Stand to your Arms, maintain this arduous Space! Il.15.495.216.
Why stand you distant, nor attempt a Deed? Il.15.684.222.
Wedg'd in one Body at the Tents they stand, Il.15.788.226.
There stand the *Trojans*, and here rolls the Deep. Il.15.899.232.
All breathing Death, around their Chief they stand, Il.16.192.246.
In equal Arms two Sons of *Nestor* stand, Il.16.376.257.
And forc'd the routed Ranks to stand the Day. Il.16.479.261.
I stand unable to sustain the Spear, Il.16.639.269.
Ev'n now on Life's last Verge I see thee stand, Il.16.1030.283.
To stand a Trophy of his Fame in War. Il.17.142.293.
'Tis time to try if *Ilion's* State can stand Il.17.161.293.
With brazen Shields in horrid Circle stand: Il.17.317.300.
Can such Opponents stand, when we assail? Il.17.556.310.
Unhelp'd we stand, unequal to engage Il.17.580.311.
His be the Danger: I shall stand the Fight. Il.18.356.338.
Before, deep fix'd, th' eternal Anvils stand; Il.18.547.348.
Stand in their Porches, and enjoy the Show. Il.18.576.350.
For this, or that, the partial People stand: Il.18.582.351.
Of trembling Parents on the Turrets stand. Il.18.598.351.
With bended Sickles stand the Reaper-Train: Il.18.638.354.
Four golden Herdsmen as their Guardians stand, Il.18.669.356.
For how shall Mortal stand the dire Alarms, Il.20.158.400.
Like us they stand, encompass'd with the Crowd, Il.20.302.406.
Hector alone shall stand his fatal Chance, Il.21.342.435.
Stand I to doubt, within the reach of Fate? Il.21.664.449.
It fits us now a noble Stand to make, Il.22.297.468.
The martial *Myrmidons* confus'dly stand: Il.23.73.489.
Thy Altars stand, perfum'd with native Flow'rs! Il.23.185.497.
Sad, as they shar'd in human Grief, they stand, Il.23.351.503.
They stand in order, an impatient Train; Il.23.433.507.
Rise if thou dar'st, before thy Chariot stand, Il.23.661.515.
Stand forth some Man, to bear the Bowl away! Il.23.770.520.
Stand forth, and bear these Prizes from the Plain. Il.23.880.524.
Rang'd in a Line the ready Racers stand; Il.23.885.524.
Stand forth the bravest of our Host! (he cries) Il.23.945.526.
The dreadful Chiefs amid the Circle stand: Il.23.960.527.
I saw, I heard her, and the Word shall stand. Il.24.274.547.
Nor stand confest to frail Mortality. Il.24.569.560.
We saw, as unperceiv'd we took our stand, Od.2.123.67.
Dumb ye all stand, and not one tongue affords Od.2.273.74.
Untouch'd and sacred may these vessels stand, Od.2.396.80.
She bids the Mariners prepar'd to stand, Od.2.432.81.
The ready vessel rides, the sailors ready stand. Od.2.455.83.
Full for the port the *Ithacensians* stand, Od.3.13.87.
Prepar'd I stand: he was but born to try Od.3.116.91.
Hence warn'd, my son beware! nor idly stand Od.3.398.106.
A Spy distinguish'd from his airy stand; Od.4.700.152.
Stand still confest, tho' distant far they lie Od.5.101.177.
To stem too rapid, and too deep to stand. Od.5.531.198.
Raptur'd I stand! for earth ne'er knew to bear Od.6.201.219.
Unconscious of what air I breathe, I stand Od.6.213.220.
In sculptur'd gold and labour'd silver stand. Od.7.119.240.
Night now approaching, in the palace stand Od.7.182.244.
Rang'd in a line the ready racers stand, Od.8.125.269.
Stand forth, ye champions, who the gauntlet wield, Od.8.233.275.
Stand forth ye wrestlers who these pastimes grace! Od.8.235.275.
Graceful before the heav'nly minstrel stand; Od.8.302.279.

STAND (CONTINUED)

Firm-rooted in the surge a ship should stand .... Od.8.620.296.
We stand discover'd by the rising fires; .... Od.9.297.318.
My soul impells me; and in act I stand .... Od.9.358.321.
My self the fifth. We stand, and wait the hour. .... Od.9.395.322.
Big tears of transport stand in ev'ry eye: .... Od.9.551.328.
Celestial as thou art, yet stand deny'd: .... Od.10.407.364.
Untouch'd before thee stand the cates divine, ... Od.10.447.365.
And stand majestic, and recall'd to men. .... Od.10.464.366.
Then pale and pensive stand, with cares opprest, ... Od.11.5.379.
Sad at the sight I stand, deep fix'd in woe, ... Od.11.69.383.
Pensive and sad I stand, at length accost, ... Od.11.677.418.
Around ten thousand thousand spectres stand .... Od.11.699.419.
Resolv'd I stand! and haply had survey'd .... Od.11.777.425.
Around we stand, a melancholy train, ... Od.12.15.430.
Jaggy they stand, the gaping den of death: .... Od.12.114.437.
High on the deck I take my dang'rous stand, ... Od.12.270.445.
Firm at the helm I stand, when fierce the main .... Od.12.496.456.
Sure fixt on Virtue may your nation stand, ... Od.13.60.4.
Aghast the *Scherians* stand in deep surprize; .... Od.13.190.15.
Firm-rooted in the surge a ship shou'd stand; .... Od.13.203.15.
The gather'd tribes before the Altars stand, ... Od.13.216.16.
Tho' leagu'd against me hundred Heroes stand, ... Od.13.445.27.
(The Prince reply'd) stand fixt in fate above; .... Od.15.203.78.
Blank and discountenanc'd the servants stand, ... Od.15.402.88.
Stand forth reveal'd: with him thy cares employ .... Od.16.182.112.
Can we alone in furious battle stand, ... Od.16.266.117.
Stung to the soul, abash'd, confounded stand; .... Od.16.359.123.
Of the proud son; as that we stand this hour .... Od.17.302.146.
I stand: the hand of violence is here: .... Od.17.647.164.
Yon surly mendicants contentious stand; .... Od.18.47.169.
Swear, to stand neutral while we cope in fight. .... Od.18.65.169.
Beneath thy roof, and cou'dst thou tamely stand? .... Od.18.264.179.
That anchor'd in his port the vessels stand, ... Od.19.333.210.
To know thy King, and here I stand confest. .... Od.19.568.224.
Then, with a manly pace, he took his stand; .... Od.21.129.264.
Fast by his father's side he takes his stand; .... Od.21.477.283.
Around their King a faithful guard they stand, ... Od.22.132.293.
Amidst the carnage desp'rate as they stand, ... Od.22.270.299.
They hear, rush forth, and instant round him stand, ... Od.22.533.314.
Around thee stand the daughters of the deep, ... Od.24.75.351.
And show'd, as unperceiv'd we took our stand, ... Od.24.170.356.
Trembling with warmth, the hoary heroes stand, ... Od.24.576.375.

STAND'ST

Thou stand'st unshook amidst a bursting World. .... 4.Arbu.88.101.
Thou stand'st, and Armies tremble at thy Sight .... Il.17.234.297.

STANDARD

And high in Air *Britannia's* Standard flies. .... 1.W-F.110.161.
By her just Standard, which is still the same: .... 1.EOC.69.246.
And figs, from standard and Espalier join: .... 4.HS2.147.67.
But each man's secret standard in his mind, ... 4.Arbu.176.109.
Tore down a Standard, took the Fort and all. .... 4.2HE2.41.167.
Let standard-Authors, thus, like trophies born, ... 5.DunB4.123.353.
But each Man's secret Standard in his Mind, ... 6.98.26.284.
They name the standard of their dearest vow. .... Od.20.46.234.

STANDARD-AUTHORS

Let standard-Authors, thus, like trophies born, ... 5.DunB4.123.353.

STANDER

Distressful Beauty melts each Stander-by; .... Il.24.982.576.

STANDER-BY

Distressful Beauty melts each Stander-by; .... Il.24.982.576.

STANDERS

They, tho' but Standers-by too, mutter'd; .... 6.30.50.87.
They (tho' meer Standers by) too mutter'd .... 6.30.50A.87.
Ev'n they (meer Standers by) too mutter'd; .... 6.30.50B.87.

STANDERS-BY

They, tho' but Standers-by too, mutter'd; .... 6.30.50.87.

STANDING

Great standing miracle! that Heav'n assign'd .... 3.EOM3.77.99.
That Man was made the standing jest of Heav'n; .... 3.Ep3.4.83.
A standing sermon, at each year's expense, ... 3.Ep4.21.139.
Before, and after Standing Armies came. .... 4.HS2.154.67.
A Chronicle of antient standing; .... 6.39.11.110.
To Armies that are Standing. .... 6.61.53.183.
The dauntless King yet standing firm he found, ... Il.4.244.232.
He came, and standing in the midst, explain'd .... Il.7.492.388.
The Warriors standing on the breezy Shore, ... Il.11.758.69.
In standing Fight he mates *Achilles'* Force, ... Il.13.414.126.
In standing Fight he yet maintains his Force: .... Il.13.651.136.
And bold to combate in the standing Fight; .... Il.15.321.209.
Stern *Hector* wav'd his Sword; and standing near .... Il.16.142.243.
Th' immortal Mother, standing close beside .... Il.18.91.327.
In haste, and standing; for to sit they fear'd. .... Il.18.290.336.

STANDISH

Nor Standish well japan'd, avails .... 6.58.11.171.
"A standish, steel and golden pen; .... 6.140.14.378.

STANDS

Still green with Bays each *ancient* Altar stands, ... 1.EOC.181.261.
"There stands a Rock from whose impending Steep .... 1.TrSP.189.402.
And doubtful still, and still distracted stands, ... 1.TrSt.271.421.
The noble *Tydeus* stands confess'd, and known .... 1.TrSt.792.443.
Already on the Verge of Death he stands, ... 1.TrES.229.458.
And now, unveil'd, the *Toilet* stands display'd, ... 2.RL1.121.155.
There stands a Structure of Majestick Frame, ... 2.RL3.3.169.
On this Foundation *Fame's* high Temple stands; .... 2.TemF.61.256.
Nature stands check'd; Religion disapproves; .... 2.ElAb.259.341.

STANDS (CONTINUED)

All serv'd, all serving! nothing stands alone; .... 3.EOM3.25.94.
Each serv'd, and serving! nothing stands alone; 3.EOM3.25A.94
All serv'd, and serving! nothing stands alone; .... 3.EOM3.25B.94.
The only point where human bliss stands still, ... 3.EOM4.311.157
The prospect clears and *Clodio* stands confest. .... 3.Ep1.179A.30.
The prospect clears, and Wharton stands confest. .... 3.Ep1.179.30.
Like some lone Chartreux stands the good old Hall, ... 3.Ep3.189.109.
Should'ring God's altar a vile image stands, ... 3.Ep3.293.117.
It stands on record, that in *Richard's* Times .... 4.HS1.145.19.
It stands on record, that in ancient Times .... 4.HS1.145A.19.
And who stands safest, tell me? is it he .... 4.HS2.125.65.
That turn'd ten thousand Verses, now stands still. .... 4.2HE2.79.171.
The Play stands still; damn action and discourse, ... 4.2HE1.314.223.
When Truth stands trembling on the edge of Law: .... 4.EpS2.249.327.
How Time himself stands still at her command, ... 5.DunA1.69.68.
In office here fair Cloacina stands, ... 5.DunA2.89.108.
Fair as before her works she stands confess'd, ... 5.DunA2.151.12
In naked majesty great Dennis stands, ... 5.DunA2.271.13
In naked majesty Oldmixon stands, ... 5.DunA2.271B.1
Stands known; *Divinity* with box and pipe, ... 5.DunA3.191z2.1
Imbrown'd with native Bronze, lo Henley stands, ... 5.DunA3.195.17
Pass these to nobler sights lo Henley stands, ... 5.DunA3.195A.1
How Time himself stands still at her command, ... 5.DunB1.71.275.
In office here fair Cloacina stands, ... 5.DunB2.93.300.
Fair as before her works she stands confess'd, ... 5.DunB2.159.303
In naked majesty Oldmixon stands, ... 5.DunB2.283.309
Imbrown'd with native bronze, lo! Henly stands, ... 5.DunB3.199.330
Strong in new Arms, lo! Giant Handel stands, ... 5.DunB4.65.348.
The pale Boy-Senator yet tingling stands, ... 5.DunB4.147.355
Stands our Digamma, and o'er-tops them all. 5.DunB4.218.364
—Just while your Coffee stands a Cooling. .... 6.10.8.24.
Thy stone, O *Sysiphus,* stands still; .... 6.11.66.32.
But LINTOT stands in Capital: .... 6.29.10.83.
Stands in the streets, abstracted from the crew, ... 6.45.43.125.
And what never stands still, ... 6.91.10.253.
He stands the Guardian of the Place .... 6.135.58Z2.368.
Suppliant the Venerable Father stands, ... Il.1.17.86.
With Giant-Pride at *Jove's* high Throne he stands, ... Il.1.526.113.
The Priest himself before his Altar stands, ... Il.1.606.117.
If you submit, the Thund'rer stands appeas'd; .... Il.1.750.123.
Nor long surviv'd; to Marble turn'd he stands .... Il.2.384.145.
And those who dwell where pleasing *Augia* stands, ... Il.2.637.157.
Amidst the Plain in sight of *Ilion* stands .... Il.2.982.170.
On either side a sacred Herald stands, ... Il.3.338.209.
None stands so dear to *Jove* as sacred *Troy.* .... Il.4.68.224.
And finds *Machaön,* where sublime he stands .... Il.4.236.232.
With whom the firm *Athenian* Phalanx stands; .... Il.4.382.239.
While *Hector* idle stands, nor bids the Brave .... Il.5.591.296.
Amaz'd no less the great *Tydides* stands; .... Il.5.740.302.
A City stands on *Argos'* utmost Bound, ... Il.6.189.335.
Near *Priam's* Court and *Hector's* Palace stands .... Il.6.392.346.
Beside him, *Helen* with her Virgins stands, ... Il.6.402.346.
Confiding in our want of Worth, he stands, ... Il.9.59.434.
Blest in his Love, this wond'rous Hero stands; .... Il.9.151.439.
Greece on the Brink of Fate all doubtful stands, ... Il.9.303.449.
Where *Calydon* on rocky Mountains stands, ... Il.9.653.467.
He stands relentless, and rejects 'em all. .... Il.9.698.468.
Lo here the wretched *Agamemnon* stands, ... Il.10.96.6.
Stands on the sharpest Edge of Death or Life: .... Il.10.197.10.
How can I doubt, while great *Ulysses* stands .... Il.10.285.14.
The panting Warriors seize him as He stands, ... Il.10.447.23.
While unresolv'd the Son of *Tydeus* stands, ... Il.10.592.28.
Encumber'd with the Dart, *Atrides* stands, ... Il.11.305.48.
Without a Wound the *Trojan* Hero stands; .... Il.11.456.54.
Now on the Field *Ulysses* stands alone, ... Il.11.509.56.
But stands collected in himself and whole, ... Il.11.511.56.
Long stands the show'ring Darts, and missile Fires; .... Il.11.678.65.
Confiding now in bulky Strength he stands, ... Il.11.692.66.
This Hour he stands the Mark of hostile Rage, ... Il.11.716.67.
High on a Rock fair *Thryoëssa* stands, ... Il.11.846.74.
Of two fam'd Surgeons, *Podalirius* stands .... Il.11.968.78.
Without the Gods, how short a Period stands .... Il.12.9.81.
Fierce of his Might, a Boar or Lion stands; .... Il.12.48.83.
Greece on her Rampart stands the fierce Alarms; .... Il.12.309.93.
Far in the Bay his shining Palace stands, ... Il.13.34.106.
Repuls'd he stands, nor from his Stand retires; .... Il.13.203.115.
The Fear of each, or Valour, stands confest. .... Il.13.358.123.
With chatt'ring Teeth he stands, and stiff'ning Hair, ... Il.13.364.123.
Stands all aghast his trembling Char<i>oteer, ... Il.13.502.130.
His Fate, he stands; nor shuns the Lance of *Crete.* .... Il.13.548.132.
Where he, inces'd at partial *Priam,* stands, ... Il.13.578.133.
Troy's great Defender stands alone unaw'd, ... Il.14.449.185.
Easy, as when ashore an Infant stands, ... Il.15.416.213.
Nor fights like others, fix'd to certain Stands, ... Il.15.818.228.
Yet where the Oars are plac'd, he stands to wait .... Il.15.884.231.
Alone, untouch'd, *Pelides'* Javelin stands, ... Il.16.172.244.
High in the midst the great *Achilles* stands, ... Il.16.204.247.
All grim in Dust and Blood, *Patroclus* stands, ... Il.16.482.262.
Already on the Verge of Death he stands, ... Il.16.532.264.
Renew'd by Art divine, the Hero stands, ... Il.16.651.269.
But o'er the Dead the fierce *Patroclus* stands, ... Il.16.679.270.
Stupid he stares, and all-assistless stands: .... Il.16.970.281.
Now blazing in th' immortal Arms he stands, ... Il.17.219.296.
And stands the Center and the Soul of all: .... Il.17.413.303.
Lays its eternal Weight; or fix'd as stands .... Il.17.494.307.
Swift fled the Youth: nor *Menelaus* stands, ... Il.17.789.319.
So these—Behind, the Bulk of *Ajax* stands, ... Il.17.837.321.
High o'er the Host, all terrible he stands, ... Il.19.438.389.
And Death stands ardent on the Edge of War. .... Il.20.28.393.
With fiery *Vulcan* last in Battle stands .... Il.20.99.398.
So stands *Æneas,* and his Force defies. .... Il.20.211.402.
Lo! on the Brink of Fate *Æneas* stands, ... Il.20.341.408.
Bent as he stands, he tumbles to the Plain; .... Il.21.194.429.
High on a Turret hoary *Priam* stands, ... Il.21.613.447.
And such his Valour, that who stands must die. .... Il.21.668.449.

STANDS (CONTINUED)

He stands impassive in th' Æthereal Arms. ... Il.21.702.450.
While the sad Father on the Rampart stands, ... Il.22.49.454.
Resolv'd he stands, and with a fiery Glance ... Il.22.128.458.
All comfortless he stands: Then, with a Sigh, ... Il.22.377.471.
High o'er the Slain the great *Achilles* stands, ... Il.22.471.475.
Around, a Train of weeping Sisters stands, ... Il.22.604.481.
But great *Achilles* stands apart in Pray'r, ... Il.23.172.496.
Smear'd with the bloody Rites, he stands on high, ... Il.23.218.498.
Now Victor at the Goal *Tydides* stands, ... Il.23.589.513.
Next stands a Goblet, massy, large and round. ... Il.23.758.520.
Amid the Circle now each Champion stands, ... Il.23.793.521.
Amid the Ring each nervous Rival stands, ... Il.23.822.522.
Fixt on the Center stands their solid Base. ... Il.23.829.522.
It stands the Prize of Swiftness in the Race. ... Il.23.875.524.
Held in her right, before the Steeds she stands, ... Il.24.353.551.
She stands her own sad Monument of Woe; ... Il.24.778.569.
Rev'rend old man! lo here confest he stands ... Od.2.47.62.
Lo! on the seas prepar'd the vessel stands; ... Od.2.450.83.
There stands a rock, high eminent and steep, ... Od.3.374.104.
The sacred Sage before his altar stands, ... Od.3.586.116.
But when, his native shape resum'd, he stands ... Od.4.569.147.
Before her dome the royal matron stands, ... Od.4.904.160.
The big round tear stands trembling in her eye, ... Od.4.936.162.
Close to her head the pleasing vision stands, ... Od.4.1057.167.
He stands suspended, and explores his mind. ... Od.5.451.194.
And self-considering, as he stands, debates; ... Od.6.170.216.
For Misery, oh Queen, before thee stands! ... Od.6.204.220.
Each blooming youth before the monarch stands: ... Od.8.406.285.
Nausicaa blooming as a Goddess stands, ... Od.8.496.289.
As when a shipwright stands his workmen o'er, ... Od.9.457.324.
The silver stands with golden flaskets grac'd: ... Od.10.420.364.
Unmindful of her son, *Anticlea* stands? ... Od.11.175.390.
Indignant in the dark recess he stands, ... Od.11.647.416.
Gloomy as night he stands, in act to throw ... Od.11.749.423.
In act to speak the * Pow'r of magic stands, ... Od.12.27.430.
Impervious to the step of man it stands, ... Od.12.95.436.
Ulysses sole with air majestic stands, ... Od.13.72.4.
And suppliant stands, invoking every pow'r ... Od.14.470.58.
His right-hand held: before the steeds he stands, ... Od.15.166.76.
Dauntless the King before the Goddess stands. ... Od.16.179.112.
Sudden before the rival pow'rs she stands: ... Od.16.431.128.
Stage above stage th' imperial structure stands, ... Od.17.316.147.
Now front to front each frowning champion stands, ... Od.18.102.172.
Radiant before the gazing Peers she stands; ... Od.18.248.178.
Guard he his guest beneath whose roof he stands: ... Od.18.466.190.
And moveless, as a marble fountain, stands. ... Od.21.239.271.
Before the flame *Eurymachus* now stands, ... Od.21.260.272.
And bless, in all to which he stands inclin'd, ... Od.21.436.281.
The Heroe stands opprest with mighty woe, ... Od.22.162.295.
Beside the gate the rev'rend minstrel stands; ... Od.22.369.305.
O Prince! O Friend! lo here thy *Medon* stands; ... Od.22.407.307.
Or still inviolate the olive stands, ... Od.23.208.333.

STANHOPE'S

CARLETON'S calm Sense, and STANHOPE'S noble Flame, ... 4.EpS2.80.317.

STANYAN

Nor *Congreve, Rowe,* nor *Stanyan,* ... 6.58.50.173.
Nor *Fenton, Rowe,* not *Stanyan,* ... 6.58.50A.173.

STANZA

And each *exalted* Stanza *teems* with *Thought!* ... 1.EOC.423.288.
Who pens a Stanza when he should *engross?* ... 4.Arbu.18.97.

STAPLE

Forsakes the staple as she pulls the ring; ... Od.21.48.261.

STAPLE'S

To the strong staple's inmost depth restor'd, ... Od.1.554.58.

STAR

And add new Lustre to her Silver *Star.* ... 1.W-F.290.175.
Led by the Light of the *Mæonian Star.* ... 1.EOC.648.312.
The gliding Lightning, or descending Star. ... 1.TrSt.129.415.
When not a Star its friendly Lustre keeps, ... 1.TrSt.522.432.
But when the morning Star with early Ray ... 1.TrUl.21.466.
But when the rising Star did Heav'n adorn, ... 1.TrUl.21A.466.
Or that some Star, with Aspect kind to Love, ... 2.ChJM.428.35.
In the clear Mirror of thy ruling *Star* ... 2.RL1.108.154.
A sudden Star, it shot thro' liquid Air, ... 2.RL5.127.210.
The *Julian* Star, and Great *Augustus* here. ... 2.TemF.229.273.
What vary'd being peoples ev'ry star, ... 3.EOM1.27.16.
A godless Regent tremble at a Star? ... 3.Ep1.149.28.
Bare the mean Heart that lurks beneath a Star; ... 4.HS1.108.15.
The Dog-star rages! nay 'tis past a doubt, ... 4.Arbu.3.96.
Each Star of meaner merit fades away; ... 4.2HE1.20.195.
Nor *Boileau* turn the Feather to a Star. ... 4.EpS2.231.326.
Up to a *Star,* and like Endymion dies: ... 5.DunB4.520.394.
Where shines great *Strafford's* glittering Star: ... 6.135.58.368.
Where shines great *Strafford's* guilded Star: ... 6.135.58A.368.
Like the red Star that fires th' Autumnal Skies, ... Il.5.8.266.
And glow'd refulgent as the Morning Star. ... Il.6.367.344.
Fair as the new-born Star that gilds the Morn. ... Il.6.499.351.
As the red Star now shows his sanguine Fires ... Il.11.83.38.
Each Gemm illumin'd with a triple Star. ... Il.14.212.170.
Like the red Star, that from his flaming Hair ... Il.19.412.389.
For sure one Star its baneful Beam display'd ... Il.22.610.481.
But when the Star of Eve, with golden light ... Od.1.533.57.
But when the morning star with early ray ... Od.13.112.6.
The javelin, pointed with a star of brass) ... Od.16.40.104.

STAR'D

And wild Impatience star'd in ev'ry Face: ... 2.TemF.467.286.
Miss star'd; and gray Ducke crieth *Quaake.* ... 6.14i.22.42.

STAR'S

Now flam'd the Dog-star's unpropitious ray, ... 5.DunB4.9.340.
'Twas when the Dog-star's unpropitious ray, ... 5.DunB4.9A.340.

STARE

While the Fops envy, and the Ladies stare! ... 2.RL4.104.192.
And paid a Tradesman once to make him stare, ... 3.Ep2.56.55.
On painted Cielings you devoutly stare, ... 3.Ep4.145.151.
The Boys flock round him, and the People stare: ... 4.2HE2.120.173.
Whereat the Gentleman began to stare— ... 4.2HE2.194.179.
"What shook the stage, and made the people stare?" ... 4.2HE1.336.225.
Shou'd chance to make the well-drest Rabble stare; ... 4.1HE1.111.287.
He grins, and looks broad nonsense with a stare. ... 5.DunA2.186.124.
He grins, and looks broad nonsense with a stare. ... 5.DunB2.194.305.
Appear, and stare you in the Face: ... 6.29.12.83.
Come here in crowds, and stare the strumpet down. ... 6.41.50.114.
To hear each mortal stamp and stare ... 6.61.17A.181.
And yet why, Madam Dives, at your lot should you stare? ... 6.122.11.341.
But why, Madame Dives, at your lot should you stare? ... 6.122.11A.341.
Terror and Death in his wild Eye-balls stare; ... Il.13.363.123.
His eyes look stern, and cast a gloomy stare; ... Od.19.247.206.

STARERS

Of stupid starers, and of loud huzzas; ... 3.EOM4.256.152.

STARES

And *stares, Tremendous!* with a *threatning Eye,* ... 1.EOC.586.306.
The drivers quarrel, and the master stares. ... 4.1740.74.336.
Greater he looks, and more than mortal stares; ... 5.DunA2.305.139.
Greater he looks, and more than mortal stares: ... 5.DunB2.329.313.
Stupid he stares, and all-assistless stands: ... Il.16.970.281.

STARING

Such waxen Noses, stately, staring things, ... 4.JD4.210.43.
Without a staring Reason on his Brows? ... 4.EpS2.194.324.
With tresses staring from poetic dreams, ... 5.DunA3.143.162.
Her tresses staring from Poetic dreams, ... 5.DunB3.17.321.
King, Queen and Nation, staring with Amaze, ... 6.96iv.72.278.

STARK

My L[or]d complains, that *P[ope]* (stark mad with Gardens) ... 6.143.1.385.

STARR'D

"Ah Dennis! Gildon ah! what ill-starr'd rage ... 5.DunA3.167.167.
"Ah Dennis! Gildon ah! what ill-starr'd rage ... 5.DunB3.173.328.
His Sceptre starr'd with golden Studs around. ... Il.1.326.103.
That, starr'd with Gems, hung glitt'ring at his side; ... Il.19.401.388.

STARRY

Above the Clouds, above the Starry Sky. ... 1.PWi.70.94.
Full in the midst, and on a Starry Throne, ... 1.TrSt.280.422.
And veil'd the Starry Glories of his Head: ... 1.TrSt.432.428.
Yon spangled Arch glows with the starry Train, ... 1.TrSt.584.434.
Who measur'd Earth, describ'd the Starry Spheres, ... 2.TemF.111.262.
Heav'ns Starry Sparks draw light, and point their horns. ... 5.DunB2.12A.296.
The starry eyes of heav'n delight ... 6.6ii.11.14.
Jove to his starry Mansion in the Skies. ... Il.1.689.120.
Then to their starry Domes the Gods depart, ... Il.1.778.124.
The starry Faulchion glitter'd at his side; ... Il.2.56.129.
Beneath the rowling Sun, and starry Skies, ... Il.4.66.224.
Between th' extended Earth and starry Poles. ... Il.5.959.312.
Between th' extended Earth and starry Sky. ... Il.8.56.398.
She shook her Throne that shook the starry Pole: ... Il.8.241.409.
Not all the Gods that crown the starry Pole. ... Il.8.563.423.
O'er the wide Clouds, and o'er the starry Plain, ... Il.15.214.205.
Say, Muses, thron'd above the starry Frame, ... Il.16.140.243.
In the rich Belt, as in a starry Zone. ... Il.16.167.244.
And loud Acclaim the starry Region rends. ... Il.16.353.256.
Where vast *Olympus* starry Summits shine: ... Il.18.180.331.
The starry Lights that Heav'ns high Convex crown'd; ... Il.18.560.349.
From bright *Olympus* and the starry Heav'n: ... Il.19.130.377.
The Gods to Council in the starry Hall: ... Il.20.6.393.
When all the starry Train emblaze the Sphere: ... Il.22.401.472.
End in the starry vault, and prop the sphears.) ... Od.1.70.34.
A starry fauchion low-depending grac'd, ... Od.4.416.140.
Shoots from the starry vault thro' fields of air; ... Od.8.8.261.
Then as withdrawing from the starry bow'rs, ... Od.8.325.281.
Stern *Vulcan* homeward treads the starry way: ... Od.8.344.282.
With these gay *Hermes* trod the starry plain; ... Od.8.363.283.
With hands uplifted to the starry skies. ... Od.9.616.332.
Radiant with starry studs, a silver seat ... Od.10.375.362.
Here boundless wrongs the starry skies invade, ... Od.17.648.164.
'Till *Hesperus* leads forth the starry train; ... Od.18.352.184.
Is bounded only by the starry frame: ... Od.19.128.199.
When the pale Empress of yon' starry train ... Od.19.351.211.
My echoing griefs the starry vault invade. ... Od.19.603.225.
The righteous pow'rs who tread the starry skies, ... Od.23.13.319.
Since the just Gods who tread the starry plains ... Od.23.275.336.

STARS

Nor all his Stars above a Lustre show, ... 1.W-F.231.170.
Nor all his Stars a brighter Lustre show, ... 1.W-F.231A.170.
Amid her Kindred Stars familiar roam, ... 1.W-F.255.172.
Amidst her Kindred Stars familiar roam, ... 1.W-F.255A.172.
That *Thames's* Glory to the Stars shall raise! ... 1.W-F.356.185.
Which *Thames's* Glory to the Stars shall raise! ... 1.W-F.356A.185.
Led by new Stars, and born by spicy Gales! ... 1.W-F.392.190.
What tho' the Stars contract their Heav'nly Space, ... 1.TrSt.35.411.
On golden Wings, the *Phrygian* to the Stars; ... 1.TrSt.641.437.
But see! the Stars begin to steal away, ... 1.TrSt.825.444.
As, thank my Stars, in modest Truth I may, ... 2.ChJM.128.20.
While glitt'ring Stars his absent Beams supply, ... 2.ChJM.369.32.
(My Husband, thank my Stars, was out of Town) ... 2.ChWB.279.70.
As the Stars order'd, such my Life has been: ... 2.ChWB.323.72.
And Garters, Stars, and Coronets appear, ... 2.RL1.85.152.
Pursue the Stars that shoot athwart the Night, ... 2.RL2.82.165.

STARS (CONTINUED)
Hover, and catch the shooting Stars by Night; ....2.RL2.82A.165.
And mid'st the Stars inscribe *Belinda's* Name! ....2.RL5.150.212.
As Heaven with Stars, the Roof with Jewels glows, ...2.TemF.143.265.
Of Fires and Plagues, and Stars with blazing Hair, ...2.TemF.453.285.
Glows in the stars, and blossoms in the trees, ...3.EOM1.272.48.
Who saw the Stars here rise, and there descend, ...3.EOM2.37A.60.
Nor asks of God, but of her Stars to give ....3.Ep2.89.57.
Ye little Stars! hide your diminish'd rays. ....3.Ep3.282.116.
I blest my Stars! but still afraid to see ....4.JD4.180A.41.
There (thank my Stars) my whole Commission ends, ...4.Arbu.59.100.
Yes; thank my stars! as early as I knew ....4.JD2.1.133.
(Like twinkling Stars the Miscellanies o'er) ....4.2HE1.110.205.
Self-centred Sun, and Stars that rise and fall, ...4.1HE6.6.237.
Or Popularity, or Stars and Strings? ....4.1HE6.14.237.
Far other *Stars* than *and** wear, ...4.EpS2.238.326.
Thick as the stars of night, or morning dews, ...5.DunA3.24.152.
Thick as the stars of night, and morning dews, ...5.DunA3.24A.152.
Yon stars, yon suns, he rears at pleasure higher, ...5.DunA3.255.179.
See! the dull stars roll round and re-appear. ....5.DunA3.336.192.
The sick'ning Stars fade off th' æthereal plain; ....5.DunA3.342.192.
When the dull stars roll round and re-appear. ....5.DunA3.336A.192.
Thick as the stars of night, or morning dews, ...5.DunB3.32.322.
Yon stars, yon suns, he rears at pleasure higher, ...5.DunB3.259.332.
See! the dull stars roll round and re-appear. ....5.DunB3.322.335.
The sick'ning stars fade off th'ethereal plain; ....5.DunB4.636.407.
The stars that fall from *Celia's* eye, ...6.5.11.12.
And thanks his stars he was not born a fool; ....6.41.8.113.
Light to the Stars the Sun does thus restore, ...6.43.11.120.
But were there One whom better Stars conspire ....6.49iii.7.142.
But should there One whose better Stars conspire ....6.49iii.7A.142.
But *Hymen's* flames like stars unite; ....6.51ii.21A.153.
O would the Stars, to ease my Bonds, ordain, ...6.96iii.33.275.
Shot down avenging, from the Vault of Stars. ....Il.6.134.330.
With that, a Sword with Stars of Silver grac'd, ...Il.7.366.382.
And Stars unnumber'd gild the glowing Pole, ...Il.8.692.428.
The Stars shine fainter on th' Ætherial Plains, ...Il.10.297.15.
Achilles' Glory to the Stars to raise; ....Il.15.82.199.
High on a Throne, with Stars of silver grac'd ....Il.18.457.343.
And o'er the feebler Stars exerts his Rays; ....Il.22.40.454.
What Stars concurring blest his natal Hour? ....Il.24.674.565.
With stars of silver shone the bed of state. ....Od.7.229.247.
The evening stars still mount th' ethereal plains. ....Od.11.465.407.
'Till in the vault of heav'n the stars decay, ...Od.11.468.407.
And setting stars roll'd down the azure plain; ....Od.12.368.449.
The moon, the stars, the bright ætherial host ....Od.12.371.449.
And the stars faded at approaching light; ....Od.14.544.63.
With triple stars, that cast a trembling light. ....Od.18.346.184.

START
Zoilus again would start up from the Dead. ....1.EOC.465.292.
Stung to the Soul, the Brothers start from Rest, ...1.TrSt.174.417.
And the pale Ghosts start at the Flash of Day! ....2.RL5.52.203.
Start from their Roots, and form a Shade around: ....2.TemF.84.259.
I shriek, start up, the same sad prospect find, ...2.ElAb.247.339.
Start ev'n from Difficulty, strike from Chance; ....3.Ep4.68.143.
Why start you? are they Snakes? or have they Claws? ....6.96iv.16.276.
Both Armies start, and trembling gaze around; ....Il.5.1056.317.
Of Hounds and Men; they start, they gaze around; ....Il.10.217.11.
Should start, and tremble at the Heaps of dead. ....Il.10.575.28.
Now clasp his clay-cold Limbs: Then gushing start ....Il.18.369.339.
All start at once; *Oïleus* led the Race; ....Il.23.887.524.
Start from the goal, and vanish o'er the strand: ....Od.8.126.269.
Yet at thy words I start, in wonder lost; ....Od.16.264.117.

STARTED
I saw, and started from its vernal bow'r ....5.DunB4.425.383.
The Monarch started from his shining Throne; ....Il.1.128.93.
Up-started fierce: But far before the rest ....Il.7.197.373.
Back started the pale throngs, and trembling stood. ....Od.11.62.383.

STARTING
And snatch'd the starting Serpents from the Ground. ....1.TrSt.127.415.
The starting Coursers, and restrain their Rage, ...1.TrES.276.460.
Sudden, with starting Tears each Eye o'erflows, ...2.RL5.85.207.
The fiery Steeds seem starting from the Stone; ....2.TemF.219.272.
And the wise Justice starting from his chair ....4.JD4.36.29.
Sore sighs Sir G[ilbert], starting at the bray ....5.DunA2.241.129.
So sighs Sir G[ilber]t, starting at the bray ....5.DunA2.241A.129.
Sore sighs Sir Gilbert, starting at the bray, ...5.DunB2.251.307.
The Tears spring starting from his haggard Eyes: ....Il.2.329.143.
The starting Coursers tremble with Affright; ....Il.5.359.283.
Starting from Sleep with a distracted Air, ...Il.5.502.292.
Achilles, starting as the Chiefs he spy'd, ...Il.9.257.445.
Tears, at the Sight, came starting from his Eye, ...Il.11.322.49.
Victorious *Troy:* Then, starting from his Seat, ...Il.15.457.215.
The starting Coursers, and restrain their Rage, ...Il.16.581.267.
Of golden Sleep, and starting from the Sands, ...Il.23.120.492.
The Hero said, and starting from his Place ....Il.23.881.524.
Then starting up, disconsolate he goes ....Il.24.19.535.
And starting into manhood, scorn the boy. ....Od.1.386.51.
And starting from their couchés loudly cry'd, ...Od.10.70.342.

STARTLE
I loath a Whore, and startle at the Name. ....2.ChJM.592.43.
The Steeds that startle at his sounding Arms. ....Il.8.382.416.

STARTLED
And startled Nature trembled with the Blast. ....2.TemF.417.283.
Fierce as a startled Adder, swell'd, and said, ...5.DunB4.373.379.
His startled Ears th' encreasing Cries attend; ....Il.14.3.156.
No more their Way the startled Horses held; ....Il.23.471.509.

STARTLING
The startling Steeds, and shook his eager Reins. ....Il.15.525.217.

STARTS
And Starts, amidst the thirsty Wilds, to hear ....1.Mes.69.119.
And ere he starts, a thousand Steps are lost. ....1.W-F.154.164.
Starts from her Trance, and trims her wither'd Bays! ....1.EOC.698.319.
A *Cheat!* a *Whore!* who starts not at the Name, ...3.EOM2.220Z1.82.
Up starts a Palace, lo! th' obedient base ....4.1HE1.140.289.
'Tis a fear that starts at shadows. ....6.70.4.201.
Trembling and pale, he starts with wild Affright, ...Il.3.49.191.
Awakes, starts up, and issues from his Tent. ....Il.10.159.9.
Each Bosom boils, each Warrior starts to Arms. ....Il.11.16.35.
Starts from her azure Throne to calm the God. ....Il.15.141.202.
Troy starts astonish'd, and the Shores rebound. ....Il.18.258.334.
So from some deep grown Wood a Panther starts, ...Il.21.677.450.
Ev'n Nature starts, and what ye ask denies. ....Od.2.148.69.

STARV'D
But while the Subject starv'd, the Beast was fed. ....1.W-F.60.154.
But Subjects starv'd while Savages were fed. ....1.W-F.60A.154.
But that the subject starv'd, the beast was fed. ....1.W-F.60B.154.
In some starv'd Hackny Sonneteer, or me? ....1.EOC.419.287.
Who starv'd a Sister, who forswore a Debt, ...4.EpS2.20.314.
Who starv'd a Mother, who forswore a Debt, ...4.EpS2.20A.314.

STARV'LING
Twelve starv'ling bards of these degen'rate days. ....5.DunB2.40.298.

STARVE
'Tis thus we riot, while who sow it, starve. ....3.Ep3.24.88.
And if they starve, they starve by rules of art. ....3.Ep4.38.140.
And if they starve, they starve by rules of art. ....3.Ep4.38.140.
He help'd to bury whom he help'd to starve. ....4.Arbu.248.113.
He help'd to bury him he help'd to starve. ....4.Arbu.248A.113.
To catch and then to starve by way of Cure: ....4.JD2A.10.132.
In which none 'ere cou'd surfiet, none could starve ....4.JD2A.126.142.
In which none e'er could surfeit, none could starve. ....4.JD2.120.143.
Fatten the Courtier, starve the learned band, ...5.DunB1.315.293.
Rather to starve, as they are us'd to do, ...6.17iv.25.60.
There starve and pray, for that's the way to heav'n. ....6.45.22.125.
And so may starve with me. ....6.47.52.130.
Wits starve as useless to a Common weal ....6.82ix(d).1.235.
And starve by strolling, not by work to thrive. ....Od.18.409.188.

STARVELING
Twelve starveling bards of these degen'rate days. ....5.DunA2.36.100.

STARVES
"But sometimes Virtue starves, while Vice is fed." ....3.EOM4.149.142.
P. Who starves by Nobles, or with Nobles eats? ....3.Ep3.237A.112.
"The wretch he starves"—and piously denies: ....3.Ep3.106.100.
Who starves by Nobles, or with Nobles eats? ....3.Ep3.237.112.
Yet starves herself, so little her own Friend, ...4.HAdv.23.77.
He starves with cold to save them from the Fire; ....4.JD2.72.139.
So the learnd Bard that starves with all his Sence ....4.JD2A.17.134.
Who starves a Sister, or forswears a Debt? ....4.EpS1.112.306.
Who starves a Mother, or forswears a Debt? ....4.EpS1.112A.306.

STARVING
And starving Wolves, ran howling to the Wood. ....1.TrSt.738.441.
With starving Wolves, ran howling to the Wood. ....1.TrSt.738A.441.
The starving chemist in his golden views ....3.EOM2.269.87.
In plenty starving, tantaliz'd in state, ...3.Ep4.163.153.
But that the cure is starving, all allow. ....4.JD2.10.133.
Twelve starving bards of these degen'rate days. ....5.DunA2.36A.100.
Yet starving Want amidst the riot weeps. ....Od.17.542.158.

STATE
Parties in *Wit* attend on those of *State*, ...1.EOC.456.290.
Jilts rul'd the State, and Statesmen *Farces* writ; ....1.EOC.538.298.
Unjust Decree! while This enjoys the State, ...1.TrSt.194.418.
Still prone to change, tho' still the Slaves of State, ...1.TrSt.226.420.
These can divide, and these reverse the State; ....1.TrSt.240.420.
From the first Birth of our unhappy State; ....1.TrSt.246.420.
Quit all his State, descend, and serve again? ....1.TrSt.258.421.
Thus on each side, alas! our tott'ring State ....1.TrSt.269.421.
In solemn State the Consistory crown'd: ....1.TrSt.285.422.
But two fair Daughters heir'd his State and Throne. ....1.TrSt.544.433.
Oh thou who freest me from my doubtful State, ...1.TrSt.588.434.
Sublime in Regal State, *Adrastus* shone, ...1.TrSt.613.436.
Such, they may cry, deserve the Sov'reign State, ...1.TrES.41.451.
But thou be Silent, nor reveal thy State, ...1.TrUl.184.471.
Who knows too well the State you thus commend ....2.ChJM.195.24.
To match the Blessings of the future State, ...2.ChJM.273.27.
Good Heav'n no doubt the nuptial State approves, ...2.ChJM.282.27.
And, plac'd in State, the Bridegroom and the Bride. ....2.ChJM.317.29.
His Giant Limbs in State unwieldy spread? ....2.RL3.72.173.
And now, (as oft in some distemper'd State) ....2.RL3.93.174.
Unmov'd, superior still in every State; ....2.TemF.157.266.
Bold *Scipio*, Saviour of the *Roman* State, ...2.TemF.163.267.
Of Turns of Fortune, Changes in the State, ...2.TemF.454.285.
Oh happy state! when souls each other draw, ...2.ElAb.91.327.
Ere such a soul regains its peaceful state, ...2.ElAb.197.336.
Like Eastern Kings a lazy state they keep, ...2.Elegy.21.364.
His knowledge measur'd to his state and place, ...3.EOM1.71.22.
His Being measur'd to his state and place, ...3.EOM1.71A.22.
All but the page prescrib'd, their present state; ....3.EOM1.78.23.
26.If to be perfect in a certain State, ...3.EOM1.73A.22.
Till he's exalted to what state he wou'd? ....3.EOM1.108Z2.28.
All in exact proportion to the state; ....3.EOM1.183.37.
So justly all proportion'd to each state; ....3.EOM1.183B.37.
All in exact proportion to their state; ....3.EOM1.183A.37.
But what his nature and his state can bear. ....3.EOM1.192.38.
Plac'd on this isthmus of a middle state, ...3.EOM2.3.53.
Go, measure earth, weigh air, and state the tides; ....3.EOM2.20.56.
See some strange comfort ev'ry state attend, ...3.EOM2.271.87.
Nor think, in NATURE'S STATE they blindly trod; ....3.EOM3.147.107.
The state of Nature was the reign of God: ....3.EOM3.148.107.

STATE (CONTINUED)

"Mark what unvary'd laws preserve each state, 3.EOM3.189.112.
"Mark what unvary'd laws preserve their state, 3.EOM3.189A.112.
Here rose one little state; another near 3.EOM3.201.113.
King, priest, and parent of his growing state; 3.EOM3.216.114.
Th'according music of a well-mix'd State. 3.EOM3.294.122.
This quits an Empire, that embroils a State: 3.Ep1.58.19.
He dies, sad out-cast of each church and state, 3.Ep1.204.32.
See Sin in State, majestically drunk, 3.Ep2.69.55.
Who feeds yon Alms-house, neat, but void of state, 3.Ep3.265A.115.
He feeds yon Alms-house, neat, but void of state, 3.Ep3.265B.115.
Behold yon Alms-house, neat, but void of state, 3.Ep3.265.115.
Load some vain Church with old Theatric state, 3.Ep4.29.140.
A solemn Sacrifice, perform'd in state, 3.Ep4.157.152.
In plenty starving, tantaliz'd in state, 3.Ep4.163.153.
No Pimp of Pleasure, and no Spy of State, 4.HS1.134.19.
And knows what's fit for ev'ry State to do; 4.JD4.47.29.
Not *Dante* dreaming all th'Infernal State, 4.JD4.192.43.
He knows to live, who keeps the middle state, 4.HS2.61.59.
"In me 'tis noble, suits my birth and state, 4.HS2.113.63.
How much more safe, dear Countrymen! his State, 4.HAdv.61.81.
To *Bufo* left the whole *Castalian* State. 4.Arbu.230.112.
A Knave's a Knave, to me, in ev'ry State, 4.Arbu.361.122.
One supreme State, so excellently ill; 4.JD2A.4.132.
Yet poor, disarm'd and helpless is their State 4.JD2A.11.132.
Yet like the Papists is the Poets state, 4.JD2.11.133.
Vain of this State, what does my Coxcomb do 4.JD2A.59.136.
Now all for Pleasure, now for Church and State; 4.2HE1.158.209.
These Madmen never hurt the Church or State: 4.2HE1.190.211.
And (tho' no Soldier) useful to the State. 4.2HE1.204.211.
But not this part of the poetic state 4.2HE1.348.225.
Go then, and if you can, admire the state 4.1HE6.28.239.
Mix with the World, and battle for the State, 4.1HE1.28.281.
Made fit companions for the Sword of State. 4.1740.68.335.
The lumb'ring carriage of thy broken State? 4.1740.72.336.
Heav'n had decreed to spare the Grubstreet-state. 5.DunA1.184.85.
And save the state by cackling to the Tories? 5.DunA1.192.86.
He chinks his purse, and takes his seat of state: 5.DunA2.189.124.
Boyer the State, and Law the Stage gave o'er, 5.DunA2.381.146.
T[raver]s and *T[rapp]* the church and state gave o'er, 5.DunA2.381A.146.
Who prouder march'd, with magistrates in state, 5.DunA2.391.148.
Or prouder march'd with magistrates in state, 5.DunA2.391A.148.
Old in new state, another yet the same. 5.DunA3.32.154.
What mortal knows his pre-existent state? 5.DunA3.40.154.
Yet sure had Heav'n decreed to save the State, 5.DunB1.195.283.
O! pass more innocent, in infant state, 5.DunB1.237.287.
With arms expanded Bernard rows his state, 5.DunB2.67.299.
He chinks his purse, and takes his seat of state: 5.DunB2.197.305.
Boyer the State, and Law the Stage gave o'er, 5.DunB2.413.317.
Who prouder march'd, with magistrates in state, 5.DunB2.423.318.
Old in new state, another yet the same. 5.DunB3.40.322.
What mortal knows his pre-existent state? 5.DunB3.48.322.
Now to pure Space lifts her extatic state, 5.DunB4.33.343.
Nor absent they, no members of her state, 5.DunB4.91.349.
To lug the pond'rous volume off in state.] 5.DunB4.118.353.
And seeks a surer State, and courts thy gentle Reign. 6.8.15.18.
How Church and State should be oblig'd to thee! 6.8.29.18.
The Musick of a well-tun'd State, 6.11.35Z5.31.
That lies and stinks in State. 6.14v(a).12.48.
And Agents from each foreign State, 6.14v(b).5.49.
And Envoys from each foreign State, 6.14v(b).5A.49.
And varying still in State Æ form 6.14v(b).22A.50.
Cannot affect Us in our tranquil State: 6.17iii.13.58.
The shining Robes, rich Jewels, Beds of State, 6.19.51.63.
Pride, Pomp, and State but reach her outward Part, 6.19.55.63.
And greatly falling with a falling state! 6.32.22.96.
Show'd *Rome* her *Cato's* figure drawn in state; 6.32.30.97.
Who save our Eyesight, or wou'd save our State, 6.48iv.12.136.
In every age, in every state! 6.51i.30.152.
As to be Minister of State, 6.74.2.211.
For *Swift* and him, despis'd the Farce of State, 6.84.9.238.
And hollow'd in his Ear Intrigues of State: 6.96iv.100.279.
Of Laws and Manners in his Pigmy State. 6.96v.10.280.
Of Fops in Learning, and of Knaves in State: 6.118.4.334.
Or add one Patriot to a sinking state; 6.132.4.362.
My master wants no Key of State, 6.135.35.367.
The best, the bravest of the *Grecian* State. Il.1.342.105.
The coming God, and from their Thrones of State Il.1.691.120.
In vain the Partner of Imperial State. Il.1.701.121.
The wretched Quarrels of the mortal State Il.1.742.123.
Peace, factious Monster, born to vex the State, Il.2.306.142.
And Youth itself an empty wav'ring State: Il.3.148.198.
Successful Monarch of a mighty State! Il.3.242.204.
Arise, O Father of the *Trojan* State! Il.3.319.208.
Renounce the Glories of thy Heav'nly State, Il.3.504.215.
To *Phrygia's* Monarch, and the *Phrygian* State! Il.4.48.223.
(Which oh avert from our unhappy State! Il.5.226.278.
Haste, Warrior, haste! preserve thy threaten'd State; Il.5.593.296.
Thy Sire, O Prince! o'erturn'd the *Trojan* State, Il.5.804.304.
Had not sage *Helenus* her State redrest, Il.6.91.328.
Meantime the Guardian of the *Trojan* State, Il.6.296.341.
In fifty Chambers lodg'd; and Rooms of State Il.6.308.341.
Thro' Streets of Palaces and Walks of State; Il.6.490.350.
So spoke the Guardian of the *Trojan* State, Il.7.1.363.
A worthy Champion for the *Grecian* State. Il.7.216.375.
And hail with Joy the Champion of their State: Il.7.373.382.
But ah! permit to pity human State; Il.8.41.397.
Th' Eternal Thunderer, state thron'd in Gold. Il.8.551.422.
Wise, weighty Counsels aid a State distrest, Il.9.101.437.
Besought the Chief to save the sinking State; Il.9.691.468.
What yet remains to save th' afflicted State. Il.10.26.3.
Forget we now our State and lofty Birth; Il.10.76.6.
In silent State the Consistory crown'd. Il.10.232.12.
The State of *Pyle* was sunk to last Despair, Il.11.830.73.
Such, they may cry, deserve the sov'reign State, Il.12.385.95.
And one vast Ruin whelm th' *Olympian* State. Il.15.155.202.

STATE (CONTINUED)

Tho' yet thy State require Redress (he cries) Il.15.460.215.
How easy then, to see the sinking State Il.15.578.218.
Entails a Debt on all the grateful State; Il.15.586.219.
'Tis time to try if *Ilion's* State can stand Il.17.161.293.
'Twas not for State we summon'd you so far, Il.17.262.298.
Have forc'd the Pow'rs to spare a sinking State, Il.17.382.302.
Circled their arching Necks, and wav'd in State, Il.17.499.307.
Circled their arched Necks, and wav'd in State, Il.17.499A.307*.
How more than wretched in th' immortal State! Il.18.72.326.
High on a Bed of State extended laid, Il.18.413.340.
Of thee, of me, of all the *Grecian* State, Il.19.58.374.
In State unmov'd, the King of Men begun. Il.19.80.375.
Thus to convene the whole ætherial State? Il.20.25.393.
Far on *Olyumpus'* Top in secret State Il.20.33.394.
Or save one Member of the sinking State; Il.20.364.410.
Unaided *Ilion,* and her destin'd State, Il.21.439.438.
Howe'er, 'tis better, fighting for the State, Il.21.669.449.
The last sad Relick of my ruin'd State, Il.22.93.456.
To such I call the Gods! One constant state Il.22.339.470.
The wretched Monarch of the falling State Il.22.522.478.
(Ye Gods avert it) threats the *Trojan* State. Il.22.583.480.
Our State asks Counsel; is it best to fly? Il.24.438.554.
And, fenc'd with Palisades, a Hall of State, Il.24.555.559.
Expells him helpless from his peaceful State; Il.24.605.562.
He said, and entring, took his Seat of State, Il.24.746.568.
They weep, and place him on the Bed of State. Il.24.899.573.
To save the state; and timely to restrain Od.1.114.37.
Her feet supported with a stool of state; Od.1.172.40.
And form sure plans to save the sinking state. Od.1.357.49.
So bright a genius with the toils of state! Od.1.494.56.
From his high dome himself descends in state. Od.2.12.60.
Or say, does high necessity of state Od.2.39.62.
To seize his treasures, and divide his state, Od.2.377.79.
Who call'd to council all th' *Achaian* state, Od.3.168.94.
An hour of vengeance for th' afflicted state; Od.3.266.98.
When beds of royal state invite your stay? Od.3.450.108.
And presents, such as suit the state of Kings. Od.3.609.117.
Resembling *Venus* in attractive state. Od.4.20.121.
The splendid car roll'd slow in regal state: Od.4.28.121.
Refresh'd, they wait them to the bow'r of state, Od.4.61.122.
The gifts of heav'n to guard thy hoary state. Od.4.292.132.
Exploring then the secrets of the state, Od.4.351.136.
At *Helen's* beck prepare the room of state: Od.4.402.139.
Their state, since last you left your natal land; Od.4.528.146.
Ægisthus govern'd in paternal state. Od.4.692.151.
His stores ye ravage and usurp his state. Od.4.923.161.
Our other column of the state is born: Od.4.963.163.
In toils of state the miseries of age: Od.4.994.164.
Heart-wounded, to the bed of state withdrew: Od.4.1038.166.
At the cool cave arriv'd, they took their state; Od.5.249.183.
And Majesty derives a grace from State. Od.6.46.207.
From his high dome the King descends in state, Od.6.66.208.
And Kings draw lustre from the robe of state. Od.6.74.208.
The good exult, and heav'n is in our state. Od.6.226.220.
Where in high state the nobles of the land Od.6.305.225.
Seek thou the Queen along the rooms of state; Od.6.366.229.
No son surviv'd; *Arete* heir'd his state, Od.7.84.237.
With stars of silver shone the bed of state. Od.7.229.247.
In state they move; *Alcinous* leads the way: Od.8.44.264.
High on a radiant throne sublime in state, Od.8.61.265.
In state they move, *Alcinous* leads the way: Od.8.106.268.
Then to the radiant thrones they move in state: Od.8.457.288.
Fast by *Alcinous* on a throne of state. Od.8.512.290.
And shares the banquet in superior state, Od.11.224.392.
He sway'd the scepter with imperial state. Od.11.346.399.
The dreadful scenes of *Pluto's* dreary state. Od.12.44.431.
A gen'ral tribute, which the State shall owe. Od.13.18.2.
But thou be silent, nor reveal thy state; Od.13.351.24.
My state he pity'd, and my tears he dry'd, Od.14.310.50.
Exact of taste, and serve the feast in state. Od.16.275.118.
Recumbent on the shining thrones of state. Od.16.425.127.
The pensive mother sits in humble state; Od.17.111.137.
What noble beast in this abandon'd state Od.17.368.150.
Such dogs, and men there are, meer things of state, Od.17.374.150.
Unjust to me and all that serve the state, Od.17.472.156.
Once I enjoy'd in luxury of state Od.17.501.157.
And fed recumbent on a chair of state. Od.17.683.165.
Such was thy father! an imperial state, Od.18.153.173.
I swell'd in pomp, and arrogance of state; Od.18.166.174.
The Queen, descending from her bow'r of state. Od.19.65.195.
Into the woman-state asquint to pry; Od.19.82.196.
And beg, degraded from superior state! Od.19.91.197.
When thus the Sov'reign from her chair of state: Od.19.124.198.
I live regardless of my state-affairs: Od.19.157.200.
"A pall of state, the ornament of death. Od.19.167.200.
'Till copious wealth might guard his regal state. Od.19.328.210.
Irresolute of soul, his state to shrowd Od.19.343.211.
Those who to cruel wrong their state abuse, Od.19.379.212.
With splendid palls, and canopies of state: Od.19.394.213.
Nor wou'd he court repose in downy state, Od.20.173.241.
Of sovereign state with faded splendor shine. Od.20.244.244.
Ulysses from his state a wand'rer still, Od.20.257.245.
To think he still survives to claim the state? Od.20.396.251.
Messena's state from *Ithaca* detains Od.21.21.259.
To the proud Suitors bears in pensive state Od.21.61.262.
Richer than all th' *Achaian* state supplies, Od.21.110.264.
Then gliding thro' the marble valves in state, Od.23.91.323.
More high he treads, and issuing forth in state, Od.23.163.328.
Fram'd by his hand, and be it drest in state! Od.23.182.329.
Com'st thou the first, to view this dreary state? Od.24.39.349.
Say, hast thou doom'd to this divided state Od.24.544.374.

STATE-AFFAIRS

I live regardless of my state-affairs: Od.19.157.200.

STATE'S
Argyle, the State's whole Thunder born to wield, ...4.EpS2.86.318.

STATED
Tho' all the rest with stated Rules we bound, ...II.4.298.235.

STATELIEST
A tree of stateliest growth, and yet undry'd, ...Od.9.381.321.
A barren cow, the stateliest of the Isle, ...Od.10.622.374.

STATELY
O'er Heaps of Ruin stalk'd the stately Hind; ....1.W-F.70.156.
Leaves deck the stately trees; and man is fair, ...1.TrPA.106.370.
And stately *Corinth's* pleasing Site surveys. ....1.TrSt.473.430.
Then as the stately Pine, or Poplar tall, ...1.TrES.288.460.
His House was stately, his Retinue gay, ...2.ChJM.446.36.
Such waxen Noses, stately, staring things, ...4.JD4.210.43.
"Lest stiff, and stately, void of fire, or force, ...4.1HE1.15.279.
"Lest stiff, and stately, void of fire, and force, ...4.1HE1.15A.279.
A stately, worthless Animal, ...6.14v(a).22.49.
Serve peopled Towns, and stately Cities grace; ....6.17ii.24.56.
Attending each with stately Pace, ...6.135.72.369.
Where *Anemoria's* stately Turrets shine, ...II.2.625.157.
The stately Ram thus measures o'er the Ground, ...II.3.259.204.
The stately Quarry on the Cliffs lay dead, ...II.4.140.227.
As when some stately Trappings are decreed, ...II.4.170.229.
Rais'd high the Head, with stately Branches crown'd, ...II.4.553.248.
And now to *Priam's* stately Courts he came, ...II.6.304.341.
From the blind Thicket wounds a stately Deer; ....II.11.595.60.
High on the Hills appears their stately Form, ...II.12.149.87.
The stately Car, and labours out his Breath. ....II.13.506.130.
Who held his Seat in *Corinth's* stately Town; ....II.13.835.145.
With stately Seats, and Riches, blest in vain: ....II.16.724.272.
A Train of Oxen, Mules, and stately Steeds, ...II.23.324.503.
Of some once-stately Oak the last Remains, ...II.23.401.506.
A stately Mule, as yet by Toils unbroke, ...II.23.755.520.
(Whose stately steeds luxuriant pastures bless) ....Od.3.327.102.
To *Pheræ* now, *Diocleus'* stately seat, ...Od.3.619.117.
And last, sublime his stately growth he rears, ...Od.4.621.149.
Saw stately *Ceres* to her passion yield, ...Od.5.160.179.
Above the nymphs she treads with stately grace; ....Od.6.124.212.
So shines majestic, and so stately moves, ...Od.6.180.218.
When stately in the dance you swim th' harmonious maze. ....Od.6.188.218.
Thus seems the Palm with stately honours crown'd ....Od.6.193.218.
A plant so stately, or a nymph so fair. ....Od.6.202.219.
Two rows of stately dogs, on either hand, ...Od.7.118.240.
A polish'd chest and stately robes to bear, ...Od.8.461.288.
And first with stately step at evening hour ....Od.9.529.328.
The next proud *Lamos'* stately tow'rs appear, ...Od.10.92.343.
The stately Oxe, and bleeds within the stalls. ....Od.11.510.408.
Thy stately palace, and thy wide domain. ....Od.15.143.75.
Whose stately growth five flow'ry summers fed: ....Od.19.491.220.
A stately breed! and blackens far the meads. ....Od.20.270.246.
Far be he banish'd from this stately scene ....Od.21.343.276.

STATES
There Kings shall sue, and suppliant States be seen ....1.W-F.383.188.
Who calls the council, states the certain day, ...3.EOM3.107.103.
Thus States were form'd; the name of King unknown, ...3.EOM3.209.114.
All states can reach it, and all heads conceive; ....3.EOM4.30.130.
May pocket States, or fetch or carry Kings; ....3.Ep3.72A.93.
Can pocket States, or fetch or carry Kings; ....3.Ep3.72B.93.
Can pocket States, can fetch or carry Kings; ....3.Ep3.72.93.
Wants reach all States; they beg but better drest, ...4.JD4.224.45.
Now all her various States worn out ....6.14v(b).13A.50.
Celestial States, Immortal Gods! give ear, ...II.8.7.395.
Assembled States, and Lords of Earth obey, ...II.9.128.438.
(That spreads her Conquest o'er a thousand States, ...II.9.502.458.
Their Manners noted, and their States survey'd. ....Od.1.6.28.
All to your several states with speed resort; ....Od.1.478.55.
Next gather the *Pylian* states their just desires, ...Od.3.72.89.
Nobles and Chiefs who rule *Phæacia's* states, ...Od.8.11.262.
When *Greece* assembled all her hundred states ....Od.11.621.414.
And shook astonish'd thro' her hundred states, ...Od.11.684.418.
(The *Scherian* states) he turn'd, and thus addrest. ....Od.13.46.3.
Our states my self and *Idomen* employ ....Od.14.274.49.
Strike, ere the States conven'd the foe betray, ...Od.16.392.125.
These States invite, and mighty Kings admire, ...Od.17.468.156.
Should *Greece* thro' all her hundred states survey ....Od.18.287.180.

STATESMAN
Fear to the statesman, rashness to the chief, ...3.EOM2.243.84.
"Statesman and Patriot ply alike the stocks, ...3.Ep3.141.105.
So, when a Statesman wants a Day's defence, ...4.Arbu.251.114.
The bribing Statesman— *Fr.* Hold! too high you go. ....4.EpS2.24.314.
Gray Statesman, or green Wits; ....6.59.6.177.
"Statesman, yet friend to Truth! of soul sincere, ...6.71.67.204.
"Statesman, yet friend to Truth! in soul sincere, ...6.71.67A.204.
Fond to forget the Statesman in the Friend; ....6.84.8.238.
Statesman, yet Friend to Truth! of soul sincere, ...6.97.1.281.
Statesman, yet Friend to Truth! in Soul sincere, ...6.97.1A.281.

STATESMAN'S
A Statesman's slumbers how this speech would spoil! ....3.Ep3.43.89.
Trims *Europe's* Balance, tops the Statesman's part, ...4.JD4.154.39.
Shall *Ward* draw Contracts with a Statesman's skill? ....4.EpS1.119.306.
Hence the Fool's paradise, the Statesman's scheme, ...5.DunA3.9.150.
Hence the Fool's Paradise, the Statesman's Scheme, ...5.DunB3.9.320.

STATESMEN
Jilts rul'd the State, and Statesmen *Farces* writ; ....1.EOC.538.298.
Here *Britain's* Statesmen oft the Fall foredoom ....2.RL3.5.169.
When statesmen, heroes, kings, in dust repose, ...3.EOM4.387.165.
Of mimick'd Statesmen, and the Merry King. ....3.Ep3.310A.119.
Of mimick'd Statesmen, and their merry King. ....3.Ep3.310.119.
Chiefs, out of War, and Statesmen, out of Place. ....4.HS1.126.17.

STATESMEN (CONTINUED)
To spend six months with Statesmen here. ....4.HS6.32.253.
But well may put some Statesmen in a fury. ....4.EpS1.52.302.
Ye Statesmen, Priests, of one Religion all! ....4.EpS2.16.314.
Revenge our Wits and Statesmen on a *Pope.* ....6.48iii.16.135.
That Statesmen have the Worm, is seen ....6.53.25.162.
That Statesmen have a Worm, is seen ....6.53.25A.162.

STATION
Of Man what see we, but his station here, ...3.EOM1.19.14.
But only what my Station fits, ...4.HS6.21.251.
(Their Naval Station where th' *Ajaces* keep, ...II.13.854.146.

STATIONER
Be thine, my stationer! this magic gift; ....5.DunA2.129.112.
Be thine, my stationer! this magic gift; ....5.DunB2.137.301.

STATIONERS
With Authors, Stationers obey'd the call, ...5.DunA2.27.99.
With Authors, Stationers obey'd the call, ...5.DunB2.31.297.

STATIONS
The Stations duly, and the Vigils kept; ....2.ChWB.285.70.
In publick Stations Men sometimes are shown, ...3.Ep2.199A.66.
Fit for all Stations and in each content ....6.16.3.53.
Fit for all Stations and in all content ....6.16.3A.53.

STATUE
Like some sad Statue, speechless, pale, I stood; ....1.TrSP.125.399.
So stiff, so mute! some Statue, you would swear, ...4.2HE2.121.173.
Whoe're thou art whom this fair statue charms, ...6.20.1.66.
His skill divine, a breathing statue lives; ....Od.6.276.224.

STATUES
The fourfold Walls in breathing Statues grace: ....2.TemF.72A.258.
Between the Statues Obelisks were plac'd, ...2.TemF.117.262.
Your Statues moulder'd, and your Names unknown. ....2.TemF.353.280.
And pitying saints, whose statues learn to weep! ....2.ElAb.22.320.
For Pembroke Statues, dirty Gods, and Coins; ....3.Ep4.8.134.
Trees cut to Statues, Statues thick as trees, ...3.Ep4.120.149.
Trees cut to Statues, Statues thick as trees, ...3.Ep4.120.149.
For *Fountain* Statues, and for *Curio* Coins ....3.Ep4.8A.134.
For Fountain Statues, and for Pembroke Coins ....3.Ep4.8B.134.
Lo statues, temples, theatres o'erturned, ...5.DunA3.97Z1.158.
Grots, Statues, Urns, and *Jo—n's Dog* and *Bitch:* ....6.14ii.50.44.
Statues of Men, scarce less alive than they; ....6.71.10.203.

STATURE
Tho' short my Stature, yet my Name extends ....1.TrSP.39.395.
Scarce seem'd her Stature of a Cubit's height, ...2.TemF.259.275.
My spacious palm in Stature scarce a Span ....6.96ii.30Z41.272.
"My spacious Palm? Of Stature scarce a Span, ...6.96ii.63.273.
Tho' some of larger Stature tread the Green, ...II.3.223.203.
And lofty Stature far exceed the rest? ....II.3.292.207.
In graceful Stature next, and next in Fame.) ....II.17.329.300.
In Stature, Voice, and pleasing Look, the same. ....II.23.81.490.
Of human birth, in stature, or in face; ....Od.9.222.315.
A man in stature, still a boy in heart! ....Od.18.258.179.
The stature of our guest, his port, his face, ...Od.21.361.277.

STATUTE
Consult the Statute: *quart.* I think it is, ...4.HS1.147.19.
In the vast reach of our huge Statute Law ....4.JD2A.134.144.
But sure no Statute in his favour says, ...4.2HE2.288.185.

STATUTES
One of our Giant *Statutes* ope its Jaw! ....4.JD4.173.41.
At length, by wholesom dread of statutes bound, ...4.2HE1.257.217.
By these no statutes and no rights are known, ...Od.9.127.310.

STAUNCH
Each staunch Polemic, stubborn as a rock, ...5.DunB4.195.361.

STAY
Curs'd be the Fields that cause my *Delia's* Stay: ....1.PAu.32.82.
Curs'd be the Fields that cause my Thyrsis' Stay: ....1.PAu.32A.82.
Yet stay, great *Cæsar!* and vouchsate to reign ....1.TrSt.43.411.
Vain Fortune's Favours, never at a Stay, ...2.ChJM.53.17.
Barbarian stay! that bloody stroke restrain; ....2.ElAb.103.328.
Barbarian stay! that bloody hand restrain; ....2.ElAb.103A.328.
Yet here for ever, ever must I stay; ....2.ElAb.171.333.
Nor will Life's stream for Observation stay, ...3.Ep1.31A.18.
Life's stream for Observation will not stay, ...3.Ep1.31.18.
Yet, yet a while, at Court my H[erv]y stay! ....5.DunB1.299A.291.
Behind thy self thou still dost stay; ....6.6ii.6.14.
Our utmost bound, and our eternal stay! ....6.23.20.73.
Why should I stay? Both Parties rage; ....6.47.21.129.
Still in the right to stay; ....6.50.30.147.
But I and M[arlbor]o' stay at home. ....6.61.27.181.
Corinna still, and *Fulvia* stay in Town. ....6.110.2.316.
Still Cloë, Flavia, Delia, stay in Town: ....6.110.2A.316.
Still *Flavia, Chloris, Celia* stay in Town; ....6.110.2B.316.
Then well may this long Stay provoke their Tears, ...II.2.360.144.
Who dares, inglorious, in his Ships to stay, ...II.2.466.149.
Yet *Helen* bids thee stay, lest thou unskill'd ....II.3.541.217.
Presume not thou the lifted Bolt to stay, ...II.4.63.224.
He foams, he roars; The Shepherd dares not stay, ...II.5.178.275.
His Shield too weak the furious Dart to stay, ...II.5.665.300.
If chance a swelling Brook his Passage stay, ...II.5.736.302.
Stay, till I bring the Cup with *Bacchus* crown'd, ...II.6.322.342.
My Wife, my Infant, claim a Moment's Stay; ....II.6.457.348.
But stay my *Hector* here, and guard his *Troy.* ....II.6.559.354.
The graceful *Paris* first excus'd his Stay. ....II.6.665.360.
Nor cou'd the strongest Hands his Fury stay; ....II.7.183.373.
Here *Greece* shall stay; or if all *Greece* retire, ...II.9.65.434.
My self will stay, till *Troy* or I expire; ....II.9.66.434.

STAY (CONTINUED)

Here, if I stay, before the *Trojan* Town, ...Il.9.534.460.
But here this Night let rev'rend *Phœnix* stay: ....Il.9.551.460.
How shall thy Friend, thy *Phœnix,* stay behind? ....Il.9.565.461.
Nor stay, till yonder Fleets ascend in Fire: ....Il.9.710.469.
And here I stay, (if such his high Behest) ....Il.9.719.470.
Let these return: Our Voyage, or our Stay, ...Il.9.731.470.
Say shall I stay, or with Dispatch return? ....Il.10.70.5.
There shalt thou stay (the King of Men reply'd ....Il.10.71.5.
The frighted Hind beholds, and dares not stay, ...Il.11.157.42.
And voted *Helen's* Stay, for *Paris'* Gold. ....Il.11.164.42.
Lo! angry *Jove* forbids your Chief to stay, ...Il.11.357.50.
Infrangible, immortal: There they stay: ....Il.13.57.107.
Who seeks ignobly in his Ships to stay, ...Il.13.305.119.
Inglorious here, my Soul abhors to stay, ...Il.13.331.121.
(Thus arm'd) not *Hector* shall our Presence stay; ....Il.14.435.184.
Patroclus gone, I stay but half behind. ....Il.16.297.254.
Fools stay to feel it, and are wise too late. ....Il.17.36.289.
Yet, yet awhile, thy gen'rous Ardor stay; ....Il.18.171.330.
Unwilling as I am, of force I stay, ...Il.18.227.332.
Yet, my *Patroclus!* yet a space I stay, ...Il.18.389.340.
While *Trojan* Captives here thy Mourners stay, ...Il.18.399.340.
Her Charms *Alcmena's* coming Labours stay , ...Il.19.117.376.
What boastful Son of War, without that Stay, ...Il.19.161.378.
Here then awhile let *Greece* assembled stay, ...Il.19.187.379.
Æneas was the first who dar'd to stay; ....Il.20.109.398.
Fools stay to feel it, and are wise too late. ....Il.20.239.404.
He seiz'd a bending Bough, his Steps to stay; ....Il.21.269.432.
Stay, and the furious Flood shall cease to rave; ....Il.21.336.435.
No stop, no stay; no thought to ask, or tell, ...Il.21.719.451.
Ah stay not, stay not! guardless and alone; ....Il.22.51.454.
Ah stay not, stay not! guardless and alone; ....Il.22.51.454.
My Friends embrac'd my Knees, adjur'd my stay, ...Il.22.307.468.
Yet on the Verge of Battel let us stay, ...Il.22.321.469.
Nor ev'n his Stay without the *Scæan* Gate. ....Il.22.565.479.
Howe'er, reluctant as I am, I stay, ...Il.23.59.489.
Hold, stay your Steeds—What Madness thus to ride? ....Il.23.507.510.
Seek not to stay me, nor my Soul affright ....Il.24.267.547.
T'inter thy *Hector?* For, so long we stay ....Il.24.826.571.
Calypso in her caves constrain'd his stay, ...Od.1.21.30.
But my Associates now my stay deplore, ...Od.1.395.51.
If this displease, why urge ye here your stay? ....Od.2.161.70.
Why cease we then the wrath of heav'n to stay? ....Od.2.195.71.
But yet, I trust, the boaster means to stay ....Od.2.289.75.
He spoke and frown'd, nor longer deign'd to stay, ...Od.2.361.78.
Then stay, my child! Storms beat, and rolls the main; ....Od.2.414.81.
Not so the King of Men: he will'd to stay; ....Od.3.175.94.
Thy ship and sailors but for orders stay; ....Od.3.414.106.
When beds of royal state invite your stay? ....Od.3.450.108.
To keep his stay conceal'd; the chief declar'd ....Od.4.349.136.
Some heav'nly pow'r averse my stay constrains: ....Od.4.512.144.
With that the Goddess deign'd no longer stay, ...Od.7.99.238.
She brib'd my stay with more than human charms; ....Od.7.341.253.
I stay reluctant sev'n continu'd years, ...Od.7.346.253.
But if reluctant, who shall force thy stay? ....Od.7.403.256.
To glory give the space thou hast to stay; ....Od.8.164.271.
In vain *Calypso* long constrain'd my stay, ...Od.9.31.303.
The Goddess rising, asks her guests to stay, ...Od.10.264.355.
The Goddess mild invites the guests to stay: ....Od.10.303.359.
Alone *Eurylochus* persuades their stay. ....Od.10.508.368.
And with a gen'rous hand reward his stay; ....Od.11.425.405.
To whom the Prince: This night with joy I stay, ...Od.11.442.406.
If thou the circling year my stay controul, ...Od.11.444.406.
While yet I speak, the shade disdains to stay, ...Od.11.691.418.
Thus he, nor deign'd for our reply to stay, ...Od.11.773.424.
Unblest the man, whom music wins to stay ....Od.12.53.432.
O stay, oh pride of *Greece! Ulysses* stay! ....Od.12.222.442.
O stay, oh pride of *Greece! Ulysses* stay! ....Od.12.222.442.
O stay, and learn new wisdom from the wise! ....Od.12.231.443.
Prepar'd to whirl the whizzing spear I stay, ...Od.12.272.445.
One only month my wife enjoy'd my stay; ....Od.14.278.49.
Yet stay, my friends, and in your chariot take ....Od.15.85.73.
Stay then: no eye askance beholds thee here; ....Od.15.354.86.
(If long thy stay) the absence of my Lord. ....Od.15.588.98.
Thy mandate born, my soul disdain'd to stay. ....Od.16.489.130.
My friend adieu! let this short stay suffice; ....Od.17.7.132.
A few hours space permit me here to stay; ....Od.17.28.133.
Lead on: but help me to some staff to stay ....Od.17.218.142.
Chearly they fare: Behind, the keepers stay; ....Od.17.223.142.
Chuse you to mingle, while behind I stay? ....Od.17.326.147.
Lest dragg'd in vengeance, thou repent thy stay; ....Od.18.15.167.
Grant him unrival'd in these walls to stay, ...Od.18.54.169.
Then turning short, disdain'd a further stay, ...Od.18.133.172.
To whom the King: Ill suits your sex to stay ....Od.18.359.185.
Who shortning with a storm of blows thy stay, ...Od.18.383.186.
Re-enter then, not all at once, but stay ....Od.21.246.271.
Where the gay blooming Nymph constrain'd his stay, ...Od.23.361.342.
Thou with thy Maids within the Palace stay, ...Od.23.391.343.
Nor farther conference vouchsaf'd to stay; ....Od.24.308.364.

STAY'D

O had I stay'd, and said my Pray'rs at home! ....2.RL4.160.197.
She sigh'd not that They stay'd, but that She went. ....6.45.10.125.
Just as in Anguish of Suspence he stay'd, ...Il.1.259.99.
This said, the hoary King no longer stay'd, ...Il.3.386.211.
No longer with his warlike Steeds he stay'd, ...Il.4.260.233.
He stay'd, and turning, thus address'd his Bands. ....Il.5.741.302.
But stay'd his Hand when Thirst and Hunger ceast. ....Il.9.124.438.
Untouch'd she stay'd, uninjur'd she removes, ...Il.9.173.441.
Untouch'd she stay'd, uninjur'd she removes, ...Il.9.360.451.
On his rais'd Arm by two strong Braces stay'd) ....Il.13.515.131.
Supported on his better Hand he stay'd; ....Il.16.631.269.
But while inglorious in her Walls we stay'd, ...Il.18.339.338.
Once stay'd *Achilles,* rushing to the War. ....Il.19.338.386.
Oft' stay'd *Achilles* rushing to the War. ....Il.19.338A.386.
Her lofty Walls not long our Progress stay'd; ....Il.20.232.403.

STAY'D (CONTINUED)

Bridg'd the rough Flood across: The Hero stay'd ....Il.21.274.432.
Great *Hector* singly stay'd; chain'd down by Fate, ...Il.22.9.453.
Yet a short space the great Avenger stay'd, ...Il.22.419.472.
So stay'd *Achilles,* circling round the Shore, ...Il.23.278.501.
Thro' the broad Shield, but at the Corselet stay'd: ....Il.23.966.527.
The King of Men, and at his bidding stay'd. ....Od.3.188.95.
He there, tho' late, to please the Monarch, stay'd. ....Od.3.198.95.
Joy touch'd the Messenger of heav'n: he stay'd ....Od.5.97.177.
Who stay'd to revel, and prolong the feast: ....Od.9.48.304.
Not one, or male or female, stay'd behind; ....Od.9.398.322.
Arriv'd, before the lofty gates I stay'd; ....Od.10.371.362.
Domestic in his faithless roof I stay'd, ...Od.14.323.50.
How lov'd, how honour'd in this court he stay'd, ...Od.14.357.51.
With him all night the youthful strangers stay'd, ...Od.15.212.78.
Still in the dome divine *Ulysses* stay'd: ....Od.19.2.192.
Whilst, forming plans of death, *Ulysses* stay'd, ...Od.19.62.195.
They part, and join him; but the number stay'd. ....Od.24.531.373.

STAYS

His Praise is lost, who stays till *All* commend; ....1.EOC.475.292.
Poor *Sapho* dies while careless *Phaon* stays. ....1.TrSP.249.404.
Stays 'till we call, and then not often near; ....3.EOM3.87.100.
Between each Drop it gives, stays half a Minute; ....4.JD4.127.35.
Stays will obstruct above, and Hoops below, ...4.HAdv.131.87.
Betwixt each Drop stays half a Minute. ....6.10.16.25.
Where *Summer's* beauty midst of *Winter* stays, ...6.14iv.29.48.
Atrides' Arm the sinking Hero stays, ...Il.11.608.61.
The great *Achilles* with Impatience stays. ....Il.11.793.71.
Ev'n till the Flames consume our Fleet, he stays, ...Il.11.810.72.
With stays and cordage last he rigg'd the ship, ...Od.5.331.188.
The turning wheel before the Palace stays. ....Od.7.4.233.
Who drives the free, or stays the hasty friend; ....Od.15.82.73.
The son observant not a moment stays: ....Od.22.434.309.

STEAD

Had some fierce Tyrant in her stead been found, ...2.ChJM.436.36.
But all such babling blockheads in his stead. ....4.Arbu.304.117.
Such they'll degrade; and sometimes, in its stead, ...4.2HE2.163.177.
And sees pale Virtue carted in her stead! ....4.EpS1.150.309.
And hang some curious cobweb in its stead! ....5.DunB1.180.283.
Yet have we oft discover'd in their stead, ...6.7.7.15.
And Artichoaks reign in their Stead. ....6.10.108.27.
But such a *babling Coxcomb* in his stead. ....6.120.12.339.
Whatever an Heir, or a Friend in his stead, ...6.144.3.386.

STEADY

See STEDDY.
The trembling World, and shakes the steady Poles. ....Il.15.173.203.
His Hand unerring steers the steady Horse, ...Il.23.396.506.
Nor seek by Tears my steady Soul to bend; ....Il.24.707.567.
Of surging waves, and steer the steady course) ....Od.5.328.187.

STEAL

Lose the low Vales, and steal into the Skies. ....1.PAu.60.84.
Now *Sighs* steal out, and *Tears begin to flow:* ....1.EOC.379.283.
With *him,* most Authors steal their Works, or buy; ....1.EOC.618.309.
But see! the Stars begin to steal away, ...1.TrSt.825.444.
And pleasing Slumbers steal upon his Eyes. ....1.TrUl.6.465.
To steal from Rainbows ere they drop in Show'rs ....2.RL2.96.165.
Devotion's self shall steal a thought from heav'n, ...2.ElAb.357.348.
Or from the soft-ey'd Virgin steal a tear! ....4.Arbu.286.116.
And steal so little, few perceive they steal; ....4.JD2.84.141.
And steal so little, few perceive they steal; ....4.JD2.84.141.
"(Cou'd you o'erlook but that)—it is, to steal. ....4.2HE2.20.165.
Years foll'wing Years, steal something ev'ry day, ...4.2HE2.72.171.
At last they steal us from our selves away; ....4.2HE2.73.171.
How shall the Muse, from such a Monarch, steal ....4.2HE1.5.195.
Why now, this moment, don't I see you steal? ....4.EpS1.6.297.
From foolish Greeks to steal them, was as wise; ....5.DunB4.378.380.
Steal from the world, and not a stone ....6.1.19.4.
Gently steal upon the Ear; ....6.11.13.30.
(You may buy it, or steal, ...6.91.2.253.
Not that they're rich, but that they steal. ....6.116iii.4.326.
While your fine Whelps learn all to steal, ...6.135.55.368.
I steal no Conquest from a noble Foe. ....Il.7.294.378.
Steal from corroding care one transient day, ...Od.8.163.271.
And steal thy self from life, by slow decays: ....Od.11.165.389.
Steal thro' the ear, and win upon the soul; ....Od.11.457.407.
And pleasing slumbers steal upon his eyes. ....Od.13.97.5.
And steal my self from life by slow decays; ....Od.23.298.337.

STEALING

Stealing the Papers thence she put ....6.94.79.261.
But when the softly-stealing pace of time ....Od.15.390.88.

STEALS

All Birds and Beasts lye hush'd; Sleep steals away ....1.TrSt.478.430.
While melting Musick steals upon the Sky, ...2.RL2.49.162.
Thy image steals between my God and me, ...2.ElAb.268.341.
Steals much, spends little, yet has nothing left: ....4.Arbu.184.109.
Steals down my cheek th'involuntary Tear? ....4.HOde1.38.153.
Steals my senses, shuts my sight, ...6.31ii.10.94.
Steals much, spends little, yet has nothing left: ....6.98.34.284.
What pleasing Phrensy steals away my Soul? ....6.106ii.1.307.
And steals with modest violence our souls, ...Od.8.190.272.
Steals on his Sire a glance, and secret smiles. ....Od.16.497.131.
Time steals away with unregarded wing, ...Od.17.612.161.
Perhaps he makes them, or perhaps he steals.— ....Od.21.434.281.

STEALTH

Do good by stealth, and blush to find it Fame. ....4.EpS1.136.308.
Fierce as when first by stealth he seiz'd her Charms, ...Il.14.335.179.
By Stealth to snatch him from th' insulting Foe: ....Il.24.35.536.
Howe'er by Stealth to snatch the Corse away, ...Il.24.93.539.
By Stealth should bear him, but we will'd not so: ....Il.24.144.541.

STEALTH (CONTINUED)
To some rude churl, and born by stealth away. .... Od.16.241.116.

STEAM
An oily steam, and taints the noon-tide gales. .... Od.4.548.146.

STEAMING
Blue steaming Poisons, and a Length of Flame; .... 1.TrSt.151.416.
With Exhalations steaming to the Skies; .... Il.22.198.463.
The banquet steaming, and the goblets crown'd: .... Od.10.66.342.

STEAMS
As o'er the fragrant Steams she bends her Head: .... 2.RL3.134.178.
While fragrant Steams the bended Head shall chear; .... 6.82i.6.229.
That drawn by milky Steams, at Ev'ning Hours, ... Il.2.554.154.
Fast by the Brink, within the Steams of Hell; .... Il.8.600.425.

STEARS
And howling Tempest, stears the fearless Ship; .... Il.23.388.505.

STEDDY
See STEADY.
Ere Wit oblique had broke that steddy light, ... 3.EOM3.231.115.
Or he, who bids thee face with steddy view .... 4.1HE1.107.287.
To steer the bounding bark with steddy toil, ... Od.3.356.103.

STEDFAST
The stern *Achilles,* stedfast in his Hate; .... Il.1.635.118.
The stedfast Firmament beneath them shook: .... Il.8.50.398.
The stedfast Earth from her Foundations shake, ... Il.8.243.409.
Sate stedfast Care, and low'ring Discontent. .... Il.15.113.200.
Heav'n's stedfast purpose, and thy future fates. .... Od.11.121.387.
The stedfast purpose of th' Almighty will. .... Od.11.364.400.
To fix the scepter stedfast in his hands? .... Od.11.608.413.

STEED
And Earth rolls back beneath the flying Steed. .... 1.W-F.158.164.
'Tis more to *guide* than *spur* the Muse's Steed; .... 1.EOC.84.248.
The next more fatal pierc'd *Achilles'* Steed, ... 1.TrES.269.459.
The next transpierc'd *Achilles'* mortal Steed, ... 1.TrES.269A.459.
Th'incumber'd Chariot from the dying Steed: .... 1.TrES.278.460.
When the proud steed shall know why Man restrains .... 3.EOM1.61.21.
The bounding steed you pompously bestride, ... 3.EOM3.35.95.
The milky heifer and deserving steed; .... 3.Ep4.186.155.
To fix him graceful on the bounding Steed: .... 4.2HE1.383.227.
Fly Pegasæan *Steed, thy Rider bear,* .... 6.26ii.1.79.
A *Wife* that makes Conserves; a *Steed* .... 6.39.3.110.
Man and Steed: .... 6.96i.27.268.
To grace a Monarch on his bounding Steed, ... Il.4.171.229.
He gives Command to curb the fiery Steed, ... Il.4.346.237.
The bounding Steed, in Arms a mighty Name) .... Il.4.423.240.
. The rushing Chariot, and the bounding Steed. .... Il.5.275.280.
Th' incumber'd Chariot from the dying Steed, ... Il.8.110.403.
As when the pamper'd Steed, with Reins unbound, ... Il.15.298.208.
(Skill'd in the Manage of the bounding Steed) .... Il.15.823.228.
The next transpierc'd *Achilles'* mortal Steed, ... Il.16.574.266.
Th' incumber'd Chariot from the dying Steed: .... Il.16.583.267.
To the brave Rulers of the racing Steed; .... Il.23.342.503.
And skill'd to manage the high-bounding Steed. .... Il.23.358.504.
A little bending to the left-hand Steed; .... Il.23.408.506.
Tho' thy fierce Rival drove the matchless Steed .... Il.23.419.506.
And saw the foremost Steed with sharpen'd Eyes; .... Il.23.537.511.
When the vast fabric of the Steed we rear'd! .... Od.4.374.137.
To quit the steed we both impatient press, ... Od.4.383.139.
All *Troy* up-heav'd the steed: of diff'ring mind, ... Od.8.553.292.
He sung the *Greeks* stern-issuing from the steed, ... Od.8.563.293.
Curbs the proud steed, reluctant to the rein: .... Od.11.370.401.

STEEDS
Knights, Squires, and Steeds, must enter on the .... 1.EOC.282.271.
The comely steeds are grac'd with flowing manes; .... 1.TrPA.104.370.
For this, I suffer'd *Phœbus'* Steeds to stray, ... 1.TrSt.308.423.
Where once his Steeds their savage Banquet found, ... 1.TrSt.390.426.
The fiery Steeds seem starting from the Stone; .... 2.TemF.219.272.
And turn th' unwilling steeds another way: .... 3.Ep3.194.109.
The Duke in Wrath call'd for his Steeds, ... 6.79.53.219.
Let all excite the fiery Steeds of War, ... Il.2.456.149.
Who bravest fought, or rein'd the noblest Steeds? .... Il.2.925.167.
And his, th' unrival'd Race of Heav'nly Steeds) .... Il.2.937.168.
Men, Steeds, and Chariots shake the trembling Ground; .... Il.2.980.170.
Much fam'd for gen'rous Steeds, for Beauty more. .... Il.3.108.195.
Within the Lines they drew their Steeds around, ... Il.3.155.198.
Much fam'd for gen'rous Steeds, for Beauty more. .... Il.3.329.208.
The gentle Steeds thro' *Scæa's* Gates they guide: .... Il.3.333.209.
Then seiz'd the Reins his gentle Steeds to guide, ... Il.3.388.211.
No longer with his warlike Steeds he stay'd, ... Il.4.260.233.
Urge their swift Steeds to face the coming War) .... Il.4.267.234.
His Steeds and Chariots wedg'd in firm Array: .... Il.4.419.240.
Your foaming Steeds urge headlong on the Foes! .... Il.4.588.249.
These from their Steeds, *Tydides* on the Plain. .... Il.5.20.266.
The Steeds and Chariot, to the Navy led, ... Il.5.33.267.
Hither ye *Trojans,* hither drive your Steeds! .... Il.5.134.273.
Their Steeds and Chariot to the Navy born. .... Il.5.211.277.
And thought the Steeds (your large Supplies unknown) .... Il.5.254.279.
Observe my Father's Steeds, renown'd in Fight, ... Il.5.279.280.
Observe my Father's Steeds, renown'd in War. .... Il.5.279A.280.
As thine the Steeds, be thine the Task to guide. .... Il.5.289.281.
Nor shall yon' Steeds that fierce to Fight convey .... Il.5.318.281.
His panting Steeds, remov'd from out the War, ... Il.5.397.286.
And, rein'd with Gold, his foaming Steeds before. .... Il.5.448.289.
From trampling Steeds, and thundring Charioteers, ... Il.5.618.297.
Those heav'nly Steeds the Hero sought so far, ... Il.5.806.304.
For manag'd Steeds, and *Trechus* press'd the Ground; .... Il.5.867.307.
At her Command rush forth the Steeds Divine; .... Il.5.938.308.
The fiery Steeds, and thus to *Jove* complains. .... Il.5.941.311.
Lash'd her white Steeds along th' Aerial Way. .... Il.5.957.312.

STEEDS (CONTINUED)
There *Juno* stop'd, and (her fair Steeds unloos'd) .... Il.5.966.312.
The King beside his panting Steeds she found, ... Il.5.988.314.
She said, and to the Steeds approaching near, ... Il.5.1028.315.
His headlong Steeds, precipitate in Flight, ... Il.6.48.325.
(*Argos* the fair for warlike Steeds renown'd) .... Il.6.190.335.
Fix'd in the Shoulder as he mounts his Steeds; .... Il.7.20.363.
Rapt by th' Æthereal Steeds the Chariot roll'd; .... Il.8.51.398.
Of Gods and Men releas'd the Steeds of Fire: .... Il.8.62.398.
Blue ambient Mists th' immortal Steeds embrac'd; .... Il.8.63.398.
Men, Steeds, and Chariots shake the trembling Ground; .... Il.8.73.399.
Observe the Steeds of *Tros,* renown'd in War, ... Il.8.134.404.
The Steeds he left, their trusty Servants hold; .... Il.8.145.404.
The Steeds fly back: He falls, and spurns the Plain. .... Il.8.154.405.
The quiv'ring Steeds fell prostrate at the Sight; .... Il.8.165.406.
Drives the swift Steeds; the Chariot smoaks along. .... Il.8.191.406.
High o'er their slighted Trench our Steeds shall bound, ... Il.8.218.407.
Encourag'd his proud Steeds, while thus he spoke. .... Il.8.225.408.
The Steeds that startle at his sounding Arms. .... Il.8.382.416.
She ceas'd, and *Juno* rein'd the Steeds with Care; .... Il.8.464.419.
She ceas'd, and *Juno* rein'd her Steeds with Care; .... Il.8.464A.419.
She spoke, and backward turn'd her Steeds of Light, ... Il.8.534.422.
Our Steeds to forage, and refresh our Pow'rs. .... Il.8.628.425.
Each from the Yoke the smoaking Steeds unty'd, ... Il.8.675.427.
Twelve Steeds unmatch'd in Fleetness and in Force, ... Il.9.161.440.
Twelve Steeds unmatch'd in Fleetness and in Force, ... Il.9.348.450.
And Steeds unrival'd on the dusty Plain; .... Il.9.529.459.
His the fair Steeds that all the rest excell, ... Il.10.369.19.
And him alone th' immortal Steeds adorn. .... Il.10.392.21.
Scarce had he pass'd the Steeds and *Trojan* Throng, ... Il.10.401.21.
And those swift Steeds that sweep the Ranks of War, ... Il.10.466.24.
Far other Rulers those proud Steeds demand, ... Il.10.473.24.
And let the *Thracian* Steeds reward our Toil: .... Il.10.533.27.
And the white Steeds behind his Chariot bound. .... Il.10.549.27.
Approach the Chariot, and the Steeds untye; .... Il.10.555.27.
Urge thou the Slaughter, while I seize the Steeds. .... Il.10.557.27.
Lest the fierce Steeds, not yet to Battels bred, ... Il.10.574.28.
Ulysses now the snowy Steeds detains, ... Il.10.582.28.
Methinks the Noise of tramp'ling Steeds I hear .... Il.10.626.30.
Not those fair Steeds so radiant and so gay, ... Il.10.644.30.
Of *Thracian* Lineage are the Steeds ye view, ... Il.10.656.31.
The matchless Steeds his ample Stalls adorn: .... Il.10.667.31.
The brass-hoof'd Steeds tumultuous plunge and bound, ... Il.11.197.44.
The Steeds fly trembling from his waving Sword; .... Il.11.207.44.
Now on yon' Ranks impell your foaming Steeds; .... Il.11.373.51.
His Steeds too distant, and the Foe too nigh; .... Il.11.440.53.
Men, Steeds, and Chariots, roll in Heaps along. .... Il.11.619.61.
He lends the Lash; the Steeds with sounding Feet .... Il.11.640.62.
Thither, O *Hector,* thither urge thy Steeds; .... Il.11.650.62.
The panting Steeds *Eurymedon* unbound. .... Il.11.757.69.
Was born from combat by thy foaming Steeds? .... Il.11.796.71.
And thrice the Number of unrival'd Steeds, ... Il.11.824.73.
The panting Steeds impatient Fury breathe, ... Il.12.57.83.
Back from the Trenches let your Steeds be led; .... Il.12.88.84.
This having reach'd, his brass-hoof'd Steeds he reins, ... Il.13.36.106.
Stop'd his swift Chariot, and his Steeds unbound, ... Il.13.54.107.
The Son of *Mentor,* rich in gen'rous Steeds. .... Il.13.228.116.
Nor shuns the Foe, nor turns the Steeds away, ... Il.13.503.130.
Thus *Asius'* Steeds (their mighty Master gone) .... Il.13.507.130.
And not her Steeds and flaming Chariot nigh? .... Il.14.340.179.
The Steeds, prepar'd my Chariot to convey .... Il.14.349.179.
Now Steeds, and Men, and Cars, tumultuous pass. .... Il.15.411.213.
The startling Steeds, and shook his eager Reins. .... Il.15.525.217.
Till sad *Polydamas* the Steeds restrain'd, ... Il.15.532.217.
Pierc'd thro' the Shoulder as he mounts his Steeds; .... Il.16.411.259.
Shock; while the madding Steeds break short their Yokes: .... Il.16.445.260.
Th' affrighted Steeds, their dying Lords cast down, ... Il.16.452.260.
No Stop, no Check, the Steeds of *Peleus* knew; .... Il.16.458.260.
His flying Steeds the *Myrmidons* detain, ... Il.16.627.268.
And hear the Thunder of the sounding Steeds. .... Il.17.196.295.
The pensive Steeds of great *Achilles* stood; .... Il.17.485.306.
While thus relenting to the Steeds he spoke. .... Il.17.503.308.
No *Greek* like him, the heav'nly Steeds restrains, ... Il.17.542.309.
The glorious Steeds our ready Arms invite, ... Il.17.554.309.
Each hopes the Conquest of the lofty Steeds: .... Il.17.563.310.
The Men, the Steeds, the Armies all are lost .... Il.17.726.315.
Who near him wheeling, drove his Steeds along; .... Il.17.786.319.
Of Men, Steeds, Chariots, urg'd the Rout along: .... Il.17.824.320.
And Steeds and Men lye mingled on the Ground. .... Il.18.266.335.
Whom late, triumphant with his Steeds and Car, ... Il.18.279.335.
Their Steeds unharness'd from the weary Car) .... Il.18.288.335.
His Arms, his Steeds, his Forces to employ; .... Il.18.523.346.
And twice the Number of high-bounding Steeds: .... Il.19.252.383.
And thunders to his Steeds these dread Commands. .... Il.19.439.389.
Steeds cas'd in Mail, and Chiefs in Armour bright, ... Il.20.190.402.
Of warring Heroes, and of bounding Steeds. .... Il.20.376.410.
His prostrate Master, rein'd the Steeds around; .... Il.20.566.418.
The flouncing Steeds and shrieking Warriors drown'd. .... Il.21.13.421.
O'er slaughter'd Heroes, and o'er rolling Steeds. .... Il.21.606.447.
He smites the Steeds; the rapid Chariot flies; .... Il.22.503.477.
Unbrac'd their Armour, and the Steeds unbound. .... Il.23.36.488.
Promiscuous, steeds, and immolated Men) .... Il.23.301.501.
A Train of Oxen, Mules, and stately Steeds, ... Il.23.324.503.
The Steeds of *Tros* beneath his Yoke compell'd, ... Il.23.360.504.
But slow, and past their Vigour, are my Steeds. .... Il.23.380.505.
While with sure Skill, tho' with inferior Steeds, ... Il.23.393.506.
First flew *Eumelus* on *Pheretian* Steeds; .... Il.23.455.508.
And fills his Steeds with Vigour. At a Stroke, ... Il.23.469.509.
While thus young *Nestor* animates his Steeds. .... Il.23.482.509.
Hold, stay your Steeds—What Madness thus to ride? .... Il.23.507.510.
Then to his Steeds with all his Force he cries; .... Il.23.523.510.
And yield the Glory yours—The Steeds obey; .... Il.23.527.511.
And other Steeds, than lately led the Way? .... Il.23.543.511.
Eumelus' Steeds high-bounding in the Chace, ... Il.23.560.511.
And lo! th' approaching Steeds your Contest end. .... Il.23.578.512.
From the hot Steeds the sweaty Torrents stream; .... Il.23.591.513.

STEEDS (CONTINUED)
The Chief himself unyokes the panting Steeds. ....Il.23.596.513.
Slow dragg'd the Steeds his batter'd Chariot on: ....Il.23.610.514.
Of beauteous Handmaids, Steeds, and shining Ore, ...Il.23.630.514.
And touch thy Steeds, and swear, thy whole Intent ....Il.23.663.516.
Soon as it rose, his furious Steeds he join'd; ....Il.24.23.535.
Held in her right, before the Steeds she stands, ...Il.24.353.551.
The King himself his gentle Steeds controuls, ...Il.24.401.552.
Allow'd their Mules and Steeds a short Repose. ....Il.24.432.554.
Why roam thy Mules and Steeds the Plains along, ...Il.24.449.555.
(Whose stately steeds luxuriant pastures bless) ....Od.3.327.102.
My steeds, my chariots, and my sons attend: ....Od.3.416.106.
With steeds, and gilded cars, a gorgeous train ....Od.4.11.121.
This said, his sea-green steeds divide the foam, ...Od.5.486.195.
Along the court the fiery steeds rebound, ...Od.15.162.76.
His right-hand held: before the steeds he stands, ...Od.15.166.76.
Athwart the fiery steeds the smarting thong; ....Od.15.207.78.
They join'd the steeds and on the chariot sprung; ....Od.15.216.78.
For farther search, his rapid steeds transport ....Od.17.132.138.
Whose flaming steeds, emerging thro' the night, ...Od.23.263.336.

STEEL
Nor Fields with gleaming Steel be cover'd o'er; ....1.Mes.59.118.
Or Fields with gleaming Steel be cover'd o'er; ....1.Mes.59A.118.
The browzing cattel, or the piercing steel. ....1.TrFD.91.390.
The Vengeance due to this unlucky Steel? ....1.TrSt.771.442.
Deep in his Breast he plung'd the pointed Steel, ...1.TrES.124.454.
What Time wou'd spare, from Steel receives its date, ...2.RL3.171.182.
Steel cou'd the Labour of the Gods destroy, ...2.RL3.173.182.
Steel cou'd the Works of mortal Pride confound, ...2.RL3.175.182.
The conqu'ring Force of unresisted Steel? ....2.RL3.178.182.
Steel did the Labour of the Gods destroy, ...2.RL3.173A.182.
Like Crystal faithful to the graving Steel: ....2.TemF.46.256.
The fatal Steel unjustly was apply'd, ...4.HAdv.83.83.
To wear red Stockings, and to dine with *St[eel]* ....6.49i.4.137.
And steel now glitters in the Muses shades. ....6.51i.8.151.
John Dunton, Steel, or any one. ....6.58.52.173.
"This steel shall stab it to the heart." ....6.140.8.378.
"A standish, steel and golden pen; ....6.140.14.378.
But sheath, Obedient, thy revenging Steel. ....Il.1.280.100.
This Sceptre, form'd by temper'd Steel to prove ....Il.1.313.103.
Thy Force like Steel a temper'd Hardness shows, ...Il.3.89.194.
Like Steel, uplifted by some strenuous Swain, ...Il.3.91.194.
The brittle Steel, unfaithful to his Hand, ...Il.3.447.213.
(Fell'd by some Artist with his shining Steel, ...Il.4.554.248.
Nor are their Bodies Rocks, nor ribb'd with Steel; ....Il.4.589.249.
The great *Idomeneus'* protended Steel; ....Il.5.58.269.
Her snowie Hand the razing Steel profan'd, ...Il.5.419.287.
Of sounding Brass; the polish'd Axle Steel. ....Il.5.891.308.
The smoaking Steel, *Mars* bellows with the Pain: ....Il.5.1053.316.
Atrides o'er him shakes the vengeful Steel; ....Il.6.54.326.
And Steel well-temper'd, and persuasive Gold. ....Il.6.62.326.
With brandish'd Steel from *Nyssa's* sacred Grove, ...Il.6.164.334.
Sheath'd in bright Steel the Giant-Warrior shone: ....Il.7.250.376.
The Point was Steel, refulgent to behold, ...Il.8.617A.425.
The ruddy Gold, the Steel, and shining Brass; ....Il.9.478.456.
And Steel well temper'd, and refulgent Gold. ....Il.10.452.23.
Whose visionary Steel his Bosom tore: ....Il.10.580.28.
Ten Rows of azure Steel the Work infold, ...Il.11.31.36.
And steel well-temper'd, and persuasive Gold. ....Il.11.176.43.
The thrilling Steel transpierc'd the brawny Part, ...Il.11.327.49.
He sigh'd; but sighing, rais'd his vengeful Steel, ...Il.11.415.53.
Fate wings its Flight, and Death is on the Steel, ...Il.11.500.56.
Patroclus cut the forky Steel away. ....Il.11.981.79.
First *Damasus,* by *Polypœtes'* Steel, ...Il.12.213.88.
Deep in his Breast he plung'd the pointed Steel; ....Il.12.478.99.
Subdu'd by Steel, a tall Ash tumbles down, ...Il.13.242.116.
Secure in Mail, and sheath'd in shining Steel. ....Il.13.258.117.
Him neither Rocks can crush, nor Steel can wound, ...Il.13.412.126.
But harmless bounded from the plated Steel. ....Il.13.738.139.
So from the Steel that guards *Atrides'* Heart, ...Il.13.743.140.
Shorn from the Crest. *Atrides* wav'd his Steel: ....Il.13.771.141.
At the fierce Foe he launch'd his piercing Steel; ....Il.14.538.189.
Pierc'd in the Flank by *Menelaus'* Steel, ...Il.14.611.192.
His open'd Mouth receiv'd the *Cretan* Steel: ....Il.16.415.259.
Yet 'twas but late, beneath my conqu'ring Steel ....Il.17.27.289.
Not tho' his Heart were Steel, his Hands were Fire; ....Il.20.424.412.
That Fire, that Steel, your *Hector* shou'd withstand, ...Il.20.425.412.
Th' impatient Steel with full-descending Sway ....Il.20.459.413.
Forth thro' the Navel burst the thrilling Steel; ....Il.20.481.414.
(As from a Sycamore, his sounding Steel ....Il.21.44.423.
(As on a Fig-tree Top, his sounding Steel ....Il.21.44A.423.
(Like all the Sons of Earth) the Force of Steel; ....Il.21.672.450.
Beneath the pointed Steel; but safe from Harms ....Il.21.701.450.
Let the Steel sparkle, and the Jav'lin fly: ....Il.22.310.469.
And sheath'd in Steel, provoke his Foe to fight. ....Il.23.948.526.
Clad in refulgent Steel on either hand, ...Il.23.959.527.
(Oh Heart of Steel!) the Murd'rer of thy Race! ....Il.24.248.546.
Him too thy Rage has slain! beneath thy Steel ....Il.24.620.562.
Heav'n sure has arm'd thee with a Heart of Steel, ...Il.24.657.564.
Bait the barb'd steel, and from the fishy flood ....Od.4.499.144.
Heav'n has not curst me with a heart of steel, ...Od.5.245.183.
Before the rest I rais'd my ready steel; ....Od.14.257.48.
Of steel elab'rate, and refulgent ore, ...Od.14.360.51.
Nor had these shoulders cov'ring, but of steel. ....Od.14.535.63.
With ribs of steel, and marble heart immur'd. ....Od.19.578.224.
With steel and polish'd elephant adorn'd: ....Od.21.10.259.
Ulysses brandish'd high his vengeful steel, ...Od.22.324.301.
His hands and feet last felt the cruel steel: ....Od.22.513.314.

STEEL'D
Lo these were they, whose souls the Furies steel'd, ...2.Elegy.41.366.
To rigid Justice steel'd his Brother's Breast. ....Il.6.78.327.
The Gods that unrelenting Breast have steel'd, ...Il.9.749.471.
He touch'd the Chiefs, and steel'd their manly Souls; ....Il.13.88.109.
The Furies that relentless Breast have steel'd, ...Il.22.447.474.

STEEL'D (CONTINUED)
A weighty axe, with truest temper steel'd, ...Od.5.300.185.
O cruel thou! some fury sure has steel'd ....Od.12.333.448.
Has steel'd that heart, averse to spousal love! ....Od.23.166.328.

STEEL'S
Pray between Friends, was not that *Steel's?* .... 6.44.24.123.

STEELE
Then up comes *Steele;* he turns upon his *Heel,* .... 6.49ii.7.140.
And in a Moment fastens upon *Steele.* .... 6.49ii.8.140.
Says *Addison* to *Steele,* 'Tis Time to go. ....6.49ii.11.140.

STEELS
But sure relentless folly steels thy breast, ...Od.4.39.122.

STEELY
Where to the steely Point the Reed was join'd, ...Il.4.246.232.
'Till in the Steely Circle straiten'd round, ...Il.5.774.303.
The steely Point with golden Ringlets join'd, ...Il.6.396.346.
Beneath his steely Casque he felt the Blow ....Il.7.16.363.
His steely Lance, that lighten'd as he past. ....Il.10.155.8.
And in his Hands two steely Javelins wields, ...Il.11.55.37.
And round him deep the steely Circle grows. ....Il.11.524.57.
On ev'ry side the steely Circle grows; ....Il.13.629.136.
Ranks wedg'd in Ranks; of Arms a steely Ring ....Il.16.254.249.
Instant convey those steely stores of war ....Od.19.5.193.
Again the foe discharge the steely show'r; ....Od.22.300.300.

STEEP
See! the bold Youth strain up the threatning Steep, ...1.W-F.155.164.
High in the midst, upon this airy steep ....1.TrPA.41.367.
"There stands a Rock from whose impending Steep ....1.TrSP.189.402.
Then wheeling down the Steep of Heav'n he flies, ...1.TrSt.441.428.
As skilful Divers from some Airy Steep ....1.TrES.107.453.
Steep its Ascent, and slipp'ry was the Way; ....2.TemF.28.255.
And when up ten steep slopes you've dragg'd your thighs, ...3.Ep4.131.150.
Loud as the Wolves on Orcas' stormy steep, ...4.2HE1.328.223.
And rough *Pylenè,* and th' *Olenian* Steep ....Il.2.777.162.
Swift down the Steep of Heav'n the Chariot rolls, ...Il.5.958.312.
Or far, oh far from steep *Olympus* thrown, ...Il.8.15.395.
Prone down the Steep of Heav'n their Course they guide. ....Il.8.485.420.
Vast was the Leap, and headlong hung the Steep; ....Il.12.62.83.
As skilful Divers, from some airy Steep, ...Il.12.461.98.
Prone down the rocky Steep, he rush'd along; ....Il.13.28.105.
From Steep to Steep the rolling Ruin bounds; ....Il.13.195.115.
From Steep to Steep the rolling Ruin bounds; ....Il.13.195.115.
Then taking wing from *Athos'* lofty Steep, ...Il.14.263.173.
But how, unbidden, shall I dare to steep ....Il.14.281.175.
From the steep Mountain with exerted Strength ....Il.17.833.321.
Still edging near, and bears him tow'rd the Steep. ....Il.23.504.510.
Permit me now, belov'd of *Jove!* to steep ....Il.24.804.570.
There stands a rock, high eminent and steep, ...Od.3.374.104.
Then shoots from heav'n to high *Pieria's* steep, ...Od.5.62.174.
Climb the steep surge, and thro' the tempest fly; ....Od.6.326.227.
And climb the steep ascent to upper day; ....Od.11.270.395.

STEEP'D
So oft' has steep'd the strength'ning Grain in Wine. ....Il.8.233.408.
His Coursers steep'd in Sweat, and stain'd with Gore, ...Il.11.728.67.
Steep'd in soft Joys, and circumfus'd with Air; ....Il.14.402.183.
Steep'd in their Blood, and in the Dust outspread, ...Il.24.767.569.
All steep'd in blood, all gasping on the ground. ....Od.22.424.308.

STEEPLES
Walls, steeples, skies, bray back to him again: ....5.DunA2.248.130.
Walls, steeples, skies, bray back to him again. ....5.DunB2.260.308.

STEEPS
Steeps Earth in purple, gluts the Birds of Air, ...Il.11.503.56.
Steeps *Troy* in Blood, and ranges round the Plain; ....Il.15.48.196.
Steeps *Troy* in Blood, and rages round the Plain; ....Il.15.48A.196.
A sanguine Torrent steeps the reeking Ground; ....Il.17.415.303.

STEEPY
Arriving then by Ætna's steepy height, ...1.TrPA.31.366.
To *Ilion's* steepy Tow'r she bent her way, ...Il.6.480.350.
In vain they labour up the steepy Mound; ....Il.16.446.260.

STEER
The Steer and Lion at one Crib shall meet; ....1.Mes.79.119.
You then whose Judgment the right Course wou'd steer, ...1.EOC.118.252.
Part pays, and justly, the deserving steer: ....3.EOM3.40.96.
Form'd by thy converse, happily to steer ....3.EOM4.379.165.
Can the light packhorse, or the heavy steer, ...4.1740.69.336.
Poiz'd with a tail, may steer on Wilkins' wings. ....5.DunB4.452.384.
A Steer of five Years' Age, large limb'd, and fed, ...Il.2.478.149.
In twelve black ships to *Troy* they steer their Course, ...Il.2.673.158.
A Steer for Sacrifice the King design'd, ...Il.7.380.382.
A youthful Steer shall fall beneath the Stroke, ...Il.10.347.18.
I steer my voyage to the *Brutian* strand; ....Od.1.234.43.
Thro' the mid seas he bids our navy steer, ...Od.3.211.96.
To steer the bounding bark with steddy toil, ...Od.3.356.103.
Of surging waves, and steer the steady course) ....Od.5.328.187.
(The steer or stag:) or with keen hunger bold ....Od.6.159.216.
Six days and nights a doubtful course we steer, ...Od.10.91.343.
Steer by the higher rock: lest whirl'd around ....Od.12.262.445.
The steer-man governs, and the ships obey. ....Od.14.287.49.
Then distant from the scatter'd Islands steer, ...Od.15.39.71.
And the proud steer was o'er the marble spread. ....Od.17.202.141.
Hither, to 'scape his chains, my course I steer, ...Od.17.526.158.
A steer to form the sumptuous banquet bled, ...Od.19.490.220.
A steer ungrateful to the bull's embrace, ...Od.20.235.244.
And the proud steer was on the marble spread. ....Od.20.315.248.
He said; and of the steer before him plac'd, ...Od.20.365.250.

STEER-MAN
The steer-man governs, and the ships obey. ....Od.14.287.49.

STEER'D
He steer'd securely, and discover'd far, ...1.EOC.647.312.
Aloft she sprung, and steer'd to *Thebes* her Flight; ....1.TrSt.141.415.
Steer'd the same course to the same quiet shore, ...6.109.13.314.

STEERING
Then steering backward from the *Pharian* Isle, ...Od.4.789.156.

STEERMAN'S
While yet he exercis'd the steerman's art, ...Od.3.358.103.

STEERS
Like one who late unyok'd the sweating Steers. ....1.TrVP.36.378.
She mounts aloft, and steers to *Thebes* her Flight, ...1.TrSt.141A.415.
As stubborn Steers by brawny Plowmen broke, ...1.TrSt.184.418.
Now smoothly steers through Air his equal Flight, ...1.TrSt.439.428.
And Steers slow-moving, and two Shepherd Swains; ....Il.18.608.352.
The trampling Steers beat out th' unnumber'd Grain. ....Il.20.580.418.
His Hand unerring steers the steady Horse, ...Il.23.396.506.
Thus arm'd, swift *Hermes* steers his airy way, ...Il.24.423.553.
When steers he home, or why this long delay? ....Od.4.857.159.
With steers of equal strength, th' allotted grounds; ....Od.18.415.189.

STEM
Then Ships of uncouth Form shall stem the Tyde, ...1.W-F.403.191.
Full fifty more from *Athens* stem the Main, ...Il.2.655.158.
Thus all the night they stem the liquid way, ...Od.2.474.84.
But I, determin'd, stem the foamy floods, ...Od.3.199.95.
To stem too rapid, and too deep to stand. ....Od.5.531.198.
Or saw gay vessel stem the wat'ry plain, ...Od.11.154.389.
We bend our course, and stem the desp'rate way; ....Od.12.279.445.
The fifth fair morn we stem th' *Egyptian* tide, ...Od.14.288.49.
Th' eluded Suitors stem the wat'ry way. ....Od.16.495.131.
Nor saw gay vessel stem the surgy plain, ...Od.23.287.337.

STEM'D
In forty sable Barks they stem'd the Main; ....Il.2.922.167.
When thy tall Ships triumphant stem'd the Tide, ...Il.3.66.192.
Ere *Greece* assembled stem'd the tydes to *Troy;* ....Od.1.272.46.

STEMM'D
Stemm'd the *wild Torrent* of a *barb'rous Age,* ....1.EOC.695.319.

STENCH
Oh blast it, South-winds! till a stench exhale, ...4.HS2.27.55.
Unsavoury stench of oil, and brackish ooze: ....Od.4.598.148.

STENELAUS
At *Stenelaus* flew the weighty Stone, ...Il.16.714.271.

STENTOR
Stentor the strong, endu'd with Brazen Lungs, ...Il.5.978.313.

STENTOR'S
And shouts, in *Stentor's* sounding Voice, aloud: ....Il.5.977.313.

STEP
Invites my step, and points to yonder glade? ....2.Elegy.2.362.
Where, one step broken, the great scale's destroy'd: ....3.EOM1.244.45.
With mincing step, small voice, and languid eye; ....5.DunB4.46.345.
Show all his paces, not a step advance. ....5.DunB4.266.370.
I'm told, you think to take a Step some ....6.10.49.26.
Direct each step, and smooth the path to Heaven. ....6.21.28.70.
Each Step they trod, I felt upon my Heart. ....6.96iv.70.278.
Her parting Step? If to the Fane she went, ...Il.6.475.350.
Each Step of passing Feet increas'd th' Affright; ....Il.10.221.11.
O Friend! I hear some Step of hostile Feet, ...Il.10.405.21.
While his swoln Heart at ev'ry Step rebell'd, ...Il.11.681.65.
As with swift Step she form'd the running Maze: ....Il.16.219.248.
With many a Step the Lioness surrounds ....Il.17.147.293.
Nor yields a Step, nor from his Post retires: ....Il.18.198.331.
Smooth-gliding without Step, above the Heads, ...Il.20.375.410.
At ev'ry Step, before *Achilles* stood ....Il.21.382.436.
Thus step by step, where'er the *Trojan* wheel'd, ...Il.22.249.465.
Thus step by step, where'er the *Trojan* wheel'd, ...Il.22.249.465.
Nodding at ev'ry Step: (*Vulcanian* Frame!) ....Il.22.397.472.
Mourn at each Step, and give him up to Fate, ...Il.24.404.552.
Their sovereign's step a virgin train attends: ....Od.1.428.53.
With rapid step the Goddess urg'd her way; ....Od.2.443.82.
'Tis death with hostile step these shores to tread; ....Od.6.242.221.
His step a Virgin met, and stood before: ....Od.7.25.235.
And first with stately step at evening hour ....Od.9.529.328.
My haughty step, I stalk'd the vally o'er. ....Od.10.326.360.
There with soft step the fair *Alcmena* trod, ...Od.11.325.398.
With many a weary step, and many a groan, ...Od.11.735.422.
Impervious to the step of man it stands, ...Od.12.95.436.
With friendly step precedes his unknown guest, ...Od.14.58.38.
Heard his resounding step, and instant said: ....Od.16.8.102.
To human step our land impervious lies, ...Od.16.59.105.
Then sorrowing, with sad step the Queen retir'd, ...Od.16.465.129.
The marble pavement with his step resounds: ....Od.17.38.134.
My feeble step, since rugged is the way. ....Od.17.219.142.
Turn'd his proud step, and left them on their way. ....Od.17.305.146.
His ev'ry step and ev'ry thought is wise. ....Od.17.665.164.
The sov'reign step a beauteous train attends: ....Od.19.700.229.
By many an easy step, the matron went; ....Od.21.42.261.
At ev'ry step debates, her Lord to prove? ....Od.23.89.323.
With backward step he hastens to the bow'r, ...Od.24.570.375.

STEP'D
With that, they step'd aside, and stoop'd their head, ...Il.10.415.21.
Step'd back, and doubted or to live, or die. ....Il.15.883.231.

STEPDAME
By his fierce Stepdame from his Father's Reign ....Il.13.873.147.

STEPHEN
And one more Pensioner St. Stephen gains. ....3.Ep3.394.124.
No Poets there, but *Stephen,* you, and me. ....4.2HE2.140.175.

STEPHENS
Some *Stephens* to the rest prefer, ...6.29.3A.82.
Stephens prints *Heathen Greek,* 'tis said, ...6.29.13.83.

STEPS
And ere he starts, a thousand Steps are lost. ....1.W-F.154.164.
Now close behind his sounding Steps she hears; ....1.W-F.192.168.
And urg'd the rest by equal Steps to rise; ....1.EOC.97.250.
Pride, where Wit fails, steps in to our Defence, ...1.EOC.209.264.
False Steps but help them to renew the Race, ...1.EOC.602.308.
With heavy steps he sinks the sandy plain; ....1.TrPA.36.366.
Till led by Fate, the *Theban's* Steps he treads, ...1.TrSt.561.433.
With equal Steps bold *Teucer* prest the Shore, ...1.TrES.89.453.
By easier Steps, to where the Pear-Tree grew: ....2.ChJM.717.49.
An *Ace* of Hearts steps forth: The *King* unseen ....2.RL3.95.174.
Mark by what wretched steps their glory grows, ...3.EOM4.291.155.
Pride guides his steps, and bids him shun the great: ....3.Ep1.66.20.
With steps unequal L[into]t urg'd the race, ...5.DunA2.63A.105.
A slip-shod Sibyl led his steps along, ...5.DunB3.15.320.
Let others creep by timid steps, and slow, ...5.DunB4.465.386.
Glares on some Traveller's unwary steps, ...6.26i.11.79.
Pope to the Closet steps aside with *Rowe.* ....6.49ii.12.140.
'Tis hers, the brave Man's latest Steps to trace, ...6.84.29.239.
'Tis theirs, the brave Man's latest Steps to trace, ...6.84.29A.239.
*Mark by what wretched steps Great * * grows,* ....6.130.1.358.
Advanc'd with Steps majestically slow. ....Il.3.112.195.
The Nations bleed, where-e'er her Steps she turns, ...Il.4.506.245.
He dreads his Fury, and some Steps retires. ....Il.5.540.294.
Revives their Ardor, turns their Steps from Flight, ...Il.5.607.297.
If Heav'n our Steps to foreign Lands incline, ...Il.6.280.340.
Revives their Ardour, turns their Steps from flight, ...Il.11.273.47.
Before him steps, and bending draws the Dart: ....Il.11.506.56.
Then furious thus, (but first some Steps withdrew.) ....Il.11.552.58.
And glaring round, by tardy Steps withdrew. ....Il.11.673.65.
With equal Steps bold *Teucer* press'd the Shore, ...Il.12.443.97.
I mark'd his parting, and the Steps he trod, ...Il.13.103.109.
Before his wary Steps, his ample Shield. ....Il.13.214.116.
His tir'd, slow Steps, he drags from off the Field. ....Il.13.653.136.
By tardy Steps ascending from the Fleet. ....Il.14.36.159.
Go, guide thy darksome Steps, to *Pluto's* dreary Hall! ....Il.14.534.189.
The Monarch's Steps two Female Forms uphold, ...Il.18.487.345.
He seiz'd a bending Bough, his Steps to stay; ....Il.21.269.432.
With high and haughty steps he towr'd along. ....Il.22.32.453.
Flies thro' the Dome, (the Maids her Steps pursue) ....Il.22.594.480.
With Steps unwilling, to the regal Tent. ....Il.23.48.489.
With quicker Steps the sounding Champain beat. ....Il.23.496.510.
My Steps, and send thee, Guardian of my way. ....Il.24.462.556.
And while the fav'ring Gods our Steps survey, ...Il.24.527.558.
Turn here your steps, and here your eyes employ, ...Il.24.876.573.
With feeble steps from marshalling his Vines ....Od.1.249.45.
With equal steps the paths of glory trace; ....Od.1.392.51.
To this his steps the thoughtful Prince inclin'd; ....Od.1.538.57.
Ulysses comes, and death his steps attends. ....Od.2.192.71.
Diverse their steps: The rival rout ascend ....Od.2.292.75.
He to thy palace shall thy steps pursue; ....Od.3.459.109.
Declines his trembling steps; untimely care ....Od.4.145:127.
Advanc'd her rosy steps; before the bay, ...Od.4.587.147.
Lo I thy steps attend, thy labours share. ....Od.6.38.206.
Attends his steps: th' astonish'd virgins gaze. ....Od.6.282.224.
This land of joy: his steps some Godhead leads: ....Od.6.288.224.
But fear and rev'rence did my steps detain, ...Od.7.392.256.
With weighty steps, 'till at the ship I threw ....Od.10.198.350.
Eurylochus with pensive steps and slow, ...Od.10.286.357.
O blind to fate! what led thy steps to rove ....Od.10.335.360.
To guide his steps he bore a staff of gold; ....Od.11.113.386.
Tread you my steps: 'Tis mine to lead the race, ...Od.11.440.406.
But say, if in my steps my son proceeds, ...Od.11.601.413.
This sentence pleas'd: Then all their steps addrest ....Od.13.19.2.
His steps I hear; the dogs familiar play. ....Od.16.10.102.
Her hasty steps a damsel train attends. ....Od.16.429.128.
My steps *Eumæus* shall to town convey, ...Od.17.29.133.
Instant, *Hippodamè* our steps attend; ....Od.18.216.177.
Wak'd at their steps, her flowing eyes unclose; ....Od.18.235.178.
His steps impetuous to the portal press'd; ....Od.20.159.241.
Unguided hence my trembling steps I bend, ...Od.20.441.254.
Then to repose her steps the Matron bends, ...Od.23.313.338.

STEPT
Chloe stept in, and kill'd him with a Frown; ....2.RL5.68.206.
Stept from its Pedestal to take the Air. ....4.2HE2.122.173.
Stern *Polypœtes* stept before the Throng, ...Il.23.991.529.
Thus laden, o'er the threshold as he stept, ...Od.22.201.297.

STERLING
Nor think your Verses Sterling, ...6.58.6.171.

STERN
Europa's Rape, *Agenor's* stern Decree, ...1.TrSt.7.409.
And from his Throne return'd this stern Reply. ....1.TrSt.403.426.
In sullen Majesty, and stern Disdain: ....1.TrES.16.450.
Back to the Stern the parted Billows flow, ...1.TrUl.11.465.
There stern religion quench'd th' unwilling flame, ...2.ElAb.39.322.
Is all the help stern S[hippen] wou'd afford. ....4.1740.16.332*.
See Alaric's stern port, the martial frame ....5.DunA3.83.157.
See Alaric's stern port! the martial frame ....5.DunB3.91.324.
But, stern as Ajax' spectre, strode away. ....5.DunB4.274.371.
High on the Stern the *Thracian* rais'd his Strain, ...6.11.39.31.
Stern *Proserpine* relented, ...6.11.85.33.
Stern *Cato's* self was no relentless spouse: ....6.41.30.114.

STERN (CONTINUED)

the stern Achilles .... 6.157.1.406*.
At this, *Pelides* frowning stern, reply'd: .... Il.1.193.96.
That adverse Gods commit to stern Debate .... Il.1.341.105.
At this, they ceas'd; the stern Debate expir'd: .... Il.1.400.107.
The stern *Achilles*, stedfast in his Hate; .... Il.1.635.118.
While stern *Achilles* in his Wrath retir'd: .... Il.2.935.167.
For stern *Achilles* lopt his sacred Head, ... Il.2.1048.172.
The stern *Atrides* rages round the Field: .... Il.3.560.218.
Haste, leave the Skies, fulfil thy stern Desire, ... Il.4.53.223.
To whom with stern Reproach the Monarch cry'd. .... Il.4.421.240.
Stern as his Sire, the Boaster thus begun. .... Il.4.455.242.
Stern *Thoas*, glaring with revengeful Eyes, ... Il.4.622.250.
Stern Pow'r of War! by whom the Mighty fall, ... Il.5.39.267.
Not with less Fury stern *Tydides* flew, ... Il.5.182.275.
And stern *Lycaon's* warlike Race begun. .... Il.5.339.283.
Stern *Mars* attentive hears the Queen complain, ... Il.5.453.289.
Stern Pow'r of Arms! by whom the Mighty fall, ... Il.5.553.295.
Stern *Diomed* with either *Ajax* stood, ... Il.5.635.298.
Mars, stern Destroyer! and *Bellona* dread, ... Il.5.726.302.
The Lord of Thunders view'd, and stern bespoke. .... Il.5.1093.318.
To stern *Tydides* now he falls a Prey, ... Il.6.21.325.
And *Nestor's* Son laid stern *Ablerus* dead. .... Il.6.38.325.
Stern *Agamemnon* swift to Vengeance flies, ... Il.6.66.327.
Stern as he was, he yet rever'd the Dead, ... Il.6.527.353.
Now breathe thy Rage, and hush the stern Debate: .... Il.7.34.364.
Stern *Menelaus* first the Silence broke, ... Il.7.107.369.
Stern *Telamon* behind his ample Shield .... Il.7.265.377.
Nor each stern *Ajax*, Thunderbolts of War: .... Il.8.100.402.
By stern *Eurystheus* with long Labours press'd? .... Il.8.442.418.
That stern *Achilles* (his *Patroclus* slain) .... Il.8.593.424.
And calm the Rage of stern *Æacides*. .... Il.9.242.444.
Attend the stern Reply. Then *Phœnix* rose; .... Il.9.558.460.
To her the Chief retir'd from stern Debate, ... Il.9.679.468.
Thus he: The stern *Achilles* thus reply'd. .... Il.9.713.469.
With that, stern *Ajax* his long Silence broke, ... Il.9.735.470.
Stern, and unpitying! if a Brother bleed, ... Il.9.743.471.
Attend the stern Reply. *Tydides* broke .... Il.9.814.473.
High on the painted Stern *Ulysses* laid, ... Il.10.671.31.
The vengeful Monarch gave this stern Reply; .... Il.11.179.43.
Not with less Fury stern *Atrides* flew, ... Il.11.231.45.
Stern *Hector's* Conquests in the middle Plain .... Il.11.423.53.
The stern *Tydides* strips their shining Arms. .... Il.11.432.53.
So turn'd stern *Ajax*, by whole Hosts repell'd, ... Il.11.680.65.
And stern *Eurypylus*, already bleed. .... Il.11.807.72.
Fear'd for my Youth expos'd to stern Alarms; .... Il.11.854.74.
The God of Ocean, marching stern before, ... Il.12.29.82.
In sullen Majesty, and stern Disdain: .... Il.12.360.94.
Then stern *Peneleus* rises to the Fight; .... Il.13.126.110.
The God of Ocean, fir'd with stern Disdain, ... Il.13.273.117.
Arm'd with stern Boldness, and enormous Force; .... Il.13.387.124.
Warr'd on the King of Heav'n with stern Disdain, ... Il.13.443.126.
Cebrion, Phalces, stern *Orthæus* stood, ... Il.13.994.152.
While stern *Achilles* in his Wrath retires. .... Il.14.426.184.
Such stern Decrees, such threatned Woes to come, ... Il.15.105.200.
Stern *Mars*, with Anguish for this slaughter'd Son, ... Il.15.126.201.
As stretch'd in Dust before the Stern he lay. .... Il.15.493.216.
Fierce to fulfill the stern Decrees of *Jove*: .... Il.15.713.223.
Due to stern *Pallas*, and *Pelides'* Spear: .... Il.15.737.224.
The Minister of stern *Euristheus'* Ire .... Il.15.772.226.
Grasps the high Stern, and gives this loud Command. .... Il.15.869.230.
The luckless Warrior at his Stern lay dead: .... Il.15.907.232.
Stern *Hector* wav'd his Sword; and standing near .... Il.16.142.243.
O'er the high Stern the curling Volumes rise, ... Il.16.152.243.
This stern Remembrance to his Troops he gave: .... Il.16.238.248.
"Stern Son of *Peleus* (thus ye us'd to say, ... Il.16.242.248.
Back to his Tent the stern *Achilles* flies, ... Il.16.310.254.
Close to the Stern of that fam'd Ship, which bore .... Il.16.340.256.
Jove view'd the Combate with a stern Survey, ... Il.16.783.274.
Stern *Hector* fastens on the Warrior's Head, ... Il.16.919.279.
Stern *Hector*, as the bleeding Chief he views, ... Il.16.987.281.
From whence this boding Speech, the stern Decree .... Il.16.1038.283.
Already had stern *Hector* seiz'd his Head, ... Il.17.137.293.
Return? (said *Hector*, fir'd with stern Disdain) .... Il.18.333.337.
Stern in superior Grief *Pelides* stood; .... Il.18.367.339.
For this (the stern *Æacides* replies) .... Il.19.197.379.
When the stern Fury of the War is o'er, ... Il.19.199.381.
A Spear which stern *Achilles* only wields, ... Il.19.424.389.
Beneath, stern *Neptune* shakes the solid Ground, ... Il.20.77.397.
E'er yet the stern Encounter join'd, begun .... Il.20.212.402.
With Menace stern the fraudful King defy'd .... Il.21.525.443.
Or let him bear, by stern *Pelides* slain, ... Il.22.231.465.
To stern *Pelides*, and triumphing, cries. .... Il.22.278.467.
The just Conditions of this stern Debate. .... Il.22.324.469.
While thus triumphing, stern *Achilles* cries. .... Il.22.414.472.
And the stern purpose of his Mind unfolds. .... Il.23.8.486.
Stern had reply'd; fierce Scorn inhancing Scorn .... Il.23.573.512.
Stern *Polypœtes* stept before the Throng, ... Il.23.991.529.
And bear what stern *Achilles* may receive: .... Il.24.182.544.
And bear what stern *Achilles* may receive: .... Il.24.212.545.
The same stern God to Ruin gives you all. .... Il.24.302.549.
To stern *Achilles* now direct my ways, ... Il.24.379.551.
I saw, but help'd not: Stern *Achilles'* Ire .... Il.24.483.556.
If then thou art of stern *Pelides'* Train, ... Il.24.495.557.
Whatever Pity that stern Heart can know. .... Il.24.573.560.
The stern *Pelides*; and nor sacred Age .... Il.24.734.568.
Thy Presence here shou'd stern *Atrides* see, ... Il.24.854.572.
For thy stern Father never spar'd a Foe: .... Il.24.930.575.
My sentence hear: With stern distaste avow'd, ... Od.1.352.49.
Stern as he rose, he cast his eyes around .... Od.2.259.74.
Should great *Ulysses* stern appear in arms, ... Od.2.281.74.
Ill suits gay youth the stern, heroic part. .... Od.2.342.77.
Doom'd by the stern *Telemachus* to dye? .... Od.2.367.78.
The Prince and Goddess to the stern ascend; .... Od.2.458.83.
And to the stern retreating roll the tides. .... Od.2.469.83.
In whom stern courage with soft virtue join'd, ... Od.3.137.92.

STERN (CONTINUED)

(Stern daughter of the great Avenger *Jove*) .... Od.3.166.94.
By some stern ruffian, or adultrous wife. .... Od.3.292.100.
And his stern rule the groaning land obey'd; .... Od.3.389.105.
To *Jove*, (with stern regard the God replies,) .... Od.4.635.149.
To the stern sanction of th' offended sky .... Od.4.652.150.
Stern winter smiles on that auspicious clime: .... Od.4.769.155.
To *Neptune's* wrath, stern Tyrant of the Seas, ... Od.5.431.193.
Stern *Neptune* ey'd him, and contemptuous said: .... Od.5.479.195.
Stern God! who rag'd with vengeance unrestrain'd, ... Od.6.393.230.
The stern debate *Atrides* hears with joy: .... Od.8.74.266.
How the stern God enamour'd with her charms .... Od.8.309.280.
Stern *Vulcan* homeward treads the starry way: .... Od.8.344.282.
How stern *Ulysses*, furious to destroy, ... Od.8.541.291.
Came the stern *Greeks* by *Troy's* assisting hands: .... Od.8.552.292.
He sung the *Greeks* stern-issuing from the steed, ... Od.8.563.293.
Ev'n the stern God that o'er the waves presides, ... Od.8.613.295.
It fell, and brush'd the stern: The billows roar, ... Od.9.633.332.
And touch'd the Youths; but their stern Sire reply'd, ... Od.10.82.343.
(From the same lineage stern *Ææetes* came, ... Od.10.161.348.
I answer'd stern. Inglorious then remain, ... Od.10.321.359.
When late stern *Neptune* points the shaft with death; .... Od.11.167.389.
And soften'd his stern soul to tender love. .... Od.11.328.398.
Hence *Ephialtes*, hence stern *Otus* sprung, ... Od.11.377.401.
By stern *Ægysthus*, a majestic train, ... Od.11.483.408.
With martial port he strode, and stern delight; .... Od.11.630.414.
When the stern eyes of Heroes dropp'd a tear; .... Od.11.644.416.
Stern *Minos* waves a mace of burnish'd gold; .... Od.11.698.419.
Stern beasts in trains that by his truncheon fell, ... Od.11.707.420.
He climb'd the lofty stern; then gently prest .... Od.13.90.5.
Back to the stern the parted billows flow, ... Od.13.102.6.
Stern *Neptune* rag'd; and how by his command .... Od.13.202.15.
He climbs the ship, ascends the stern with haste, ... Od.15.308.84.
Ere yet we mingle in the stern debate. .... Od.16.279.118.
" *Ulysses* view'd with stern heroic joy; .... Od.16.309.120.
Storms have I past, and many a stern debate; .... Od.17.338.148.
To whom with stern regards: O insolence, ... Od.18.20.167.
For sure I am, if stern *Ulysses* breathe, ... Od.18.177.175.
With conscious shame they hear the stern rebuke, ... Od.18.389.186.
Gods! should the stern *Ulysses* rise in might, ... Od.18.426.189.
To whom the stern *Telemachus* uprose: .... Od.18.452.190.
Silent, abash'd, they hear the stern rebuke, ... Od.18.458.190.
His eyes look stern, and cast a gloomy stare; .... Od.19.247.206.
Sage *Polybus*, and stern *Amphimedon*, ... Od.22.267.299.
On heaps of death the stern *Ulysses* stood, ... Od.22.438.309.
Stern as the surly lion o'er his prey, ... Od.23.50.321.
When late stern *Neptune* points the shaft of death; .... Od.23.300.337.
Doom'd by stern *Jove*, at home to end my life, ... Od.24.121.353.
Or peaceful amity, or stern debate? .... Od.24.545.374.

STERN-ISSUING

He sung the *Greeks* stern-issuing from the steed, ... Od.8.563.293.

STERNER

And sterner *Cassius* melts at *Junia's* eyes. .... 6.51ii.16.153.

STERNHOLD

Hopkins and Sternhold glad the heart with Psalms; .... 4.2HE1.230.215.
Sternhold himself he *out-Sternholded*, ... 6.101.16.290.

STERNHOLDED

Sternhold himself he *out-Sternholded*, ... 6.101.16.290.

STERNLY

Patroclus lights, and sternly waits the War. .... 1.TrES.218.457.
Then sternly silent sate: With like Disdain, ... Il.1.327.103.
He views the Wretch, and sternly thus replies. .... Il.2.305.142.
Forc'd he gives way, and sternly quits the Ground. .... Il.5.775.303.
Sternly he spoke, and as the Wretch prepar'd .... Il.10.522.26.
Patroclus lights, and sternly waits the War. .... Il.16.521.263.
He sternly views him, and triumphing cries. .... Il.16.1002.281.
Sternly they met. The Silence *Hector* broke; .... Il.22.315.469.
Observant of the Gods, and sternly just, ... Od.1.342.49.
With haughty rage, and sternly thus returns. .... Od.2.94.65.
Sternly his head withdrew, and strode away. .... Od.2.362.78.
There sullen Lions sternly seem to roar, ... Od.11.753.423.
And turning his grim visage, sternly spoke. .... Od.11.760.424.
Telemachus uprais'd, and sternly said. .... Od.18.67.170.
While with indignant scorn he sternly spoke, ... Od.18.100.172.
With high disdain, and sternly thus return'd. .... Od.22.72.290.
And die I trust ye shall—He sternly spoke: .... Od.22.81.290.

STERNS

Wall'd round with Sterns, a gloomy, desp'rate Band. .... Il.15.789.226.

STEW

To make a wash, would hardly stew a child, ... 3.Ep2.54.55.

STEWARD

Sees but a backward steward for the Poor; .... 3.Ep3.174.107.
In order due, the steward of the feast, ... Od.17.405.152.

STEWING

In a Stewing pan put it. .... 6.91.4.253.

STEWS

Thro' Taverns, Stews, and Bagnio's take our round, ... 4.1HE6.119.245.
Some keep Assemblies, and wou'd keep the Stews; .... 4.1HE1.129.289.
Did slumbring visit, and convey to stews? .... 5.DunA2.390.148.
Did slumb'ring visit, and convey to stews; .... 5.DunB2.422.318.
The Stews and Palace equally explor'd, ... 5.DunB4.315.374.

STHENELUS

Great *Sthenelus*, and greater *Diomed*, ... Il.2.683.159.
(The warlike *Sthenelus* attends his side) .... Il.4.420.240.
The helping Hand of *Sthenelus* requir'd; .... Il.5.141.273.

STHENELUS (CONTINUED)

Their fierce Approach bold *Sthenelus* espy'd, ... Il.5.300.281.
Nor *Sthenelus,* with unassisting Hands, ... Il.5.395.285.
Eurymedon and *Sthenelus* the bold. .... Il.8.146.404.
My self, and *Sthenelus,* will fight for Fame; .... Il.9.67.435.
Scarce sev'n Moons gone, lay *Sthenelus* his Wife; .... Il.19.115.376.
Is this Day born: From *Sthenelus* he springs, ... Il.19.121.377.
With Joy brave *Sthenelus* receives the Prize, ... Il.23.593.513.

STICHIUS

(*Stichius* the brave, *Menestheus* the divine,) .... Il.13.262.117.
The Flow'r of *Athens, Stichius, Phidas* led, ... Il.13.863.147.
First great *Arcesilas,* then *Stichius* bleeds; .... Il.15.373.211.

STICK

Stick to the Bar and barefac'd plead the Cause .... 4.JD2A.83.140.
Buy every stick of Wood that lends them heat, ... 4.2HE2.242.183.
To stick the Doctor's Chair into the Throne, ... 5.DunB4.177.359.
no Stick to beat him— .... 6.68.12.196.
"As not to stick at fool or ass, ... 6.140.23.378.

STICKING

The Lance, yet sticking thro' the bleeding Eye, ... Il.14.584.190.

STICKS

Yet tames not this; it sticks to our last sand. .... 3.Ep1.225.34.
Clatt'ring their sticks, before ten lines are spoke, ... 4.2HE1.308.221.
To him who notches Sticks at Westminster. .... 4.1HE1.84.285.
The needy Poet sticks to all he meets, ... 5.DunA3.292.184.
The needy Poet sticks to all he meets, ... 5.DunB3.290.334.
Collective Bodies of strait Sticks. .... 6.67.6.195.
Can stoop to pick up *Strings* and *Sticks.* .... 6.135.12.366.
Has sworn by *Sticks* (the Poet's Oath, ... 6.135.91.370.
The Javelin sticks, and from the Chariot draws: .... Il.16.493.262.

STIFF

A Boar's stiff Hyde, of *Calydonian* Breed, ... 1.TrSt.571.434.
Tho' stiff with Hoops, and arm'd with Ribs of Whale. .... 2.RL2.120.167.
In errant Pride continue stiff, and burn? .... 4.HAdv.152.87.
So stiff, so mute! some Statue, you would swear, ... 4.2HE2.121.173.
"Lest stiff, and stately, void of fire, or force, ... 4.1HE1.15.279.
"Lest stiff, and stately, void of fire, and force, ... 4.1HE1.15A.279.
Sir, you're so stiff in your Opinion, ... 6.10.79.27.
Come these soft lines, with nothing Stiff in .... 6.61.5.180.
Come these lines, with nothing Stiff in .... 6.61.5A.180.
Stiff with the rich embroider'd Work around, ... Il.4.224.232.
But when the Wound grew stiff with clotted Blood, ... Il.11.346.50.
Now stiff recedes, yet hardly seems to fly, ... Il.11.694.66.
Depriv'd of Motion, stiff with stupid Fear, ... Il.13.501.130.
Heavy with cumb'rous Arms, stiff with cold Age, ... Il.13.649.136.
Stiff with Amaze the pale Beholders stand, ... Il.14.485.187.
And costly Furs, and Carpets stiff with Gold. .... Il.16.271.249.
Lo! stiff with clotted Blood, and Pierc'd with Pain, ... Il.16.637.269.
Stiff with Fatigue, and fretted sore with Wounds; .... Il.17.744.317.
Concludes; then sate, stiff with unwieldy Age. .... Il.23.424.506.
And twelve fair Veils, and Garments stiff with Gold. .... Il.24.284.548.
Rich tapistry, stiff with inwoven gold: .... Od.4.406.139.
Stiff are my weary joints; and I resign .... Od.8.264.277.
Of horn the stiff relentless balls appear, ... Od.19.248.206.
His sinews shrunk with age, and stiff with toil, ... Od.19.366.212.
Twelve cloaks, twelve vests, twelve tunicks stiff with gold, ... Od.24.321.365.

STIFF'NING

Her stiff'ning feet were rooted in the ground: .... 1.TrFD.40.387.
Her stiff'ning feet were rooted to the ground: .... 1.TrFD.40A.387.
With chatt'ring Teeth he stands, and stiff'ning Hair, ... Il.13.364.123.
Wide o'er the sands are spread the stiff'ning prey .... Od.22.430.309.

STIFFEN'D

And his Eyes stiffen'd at the Hand of Death; .... Il.22.454.474.
Should fix me, stiffen'd at the monstrous sight, ... Od.11.787.425.

STIFFENS

He burns, he stiffens with collected Ire, ... Il.22.134.458.

STIFFER

A gally measures; when the stiffer gales .... Od.4.483.143.

STIL

There's yet in this, as in all Evills stil, ... 4.JD2A.3.132.
Some write, because all write; and thus have stil .... 4.JD2A.31.134.

STIL'D

Who stil'd the gentle Damsels in his Strain .... 6.13.17.39.
And thou be stil'd Sir *Esdras Barnivelt.* .... 6.48iv.16.136.

STILE

Their Praise is still— *The Stile is excellent:* .... 1.EOC.307.274.
With matchless Impudence they stile a Wife .... 2.ChJM.45.17.
His sly, polite, insinuating stile .... 4.EpS1.19.298.
O come, that easy *Ciceronian* stile, ... 4.EpS1.73.303.
Would hardly stile thee *Nestor's* youngest Son. .... Il.9.82.436.
A friend is sacred, and I stile him friend. .... Od.8.240.275.
So rich, so potent, whom you stile your Lord? .... Od.14.139.42.

STILL

In some still Ev'ning, when the whisp'ring Breeze .... 1.PWi.79.94.
Still bears the Name the hapless Virgin bore, ... 1.W-F.207.168.
Where *Jove,* subdu'd by mortal Passion still, ... 1.W-F.233.170.
Hear *Jove* himself, subdu'd by Beauty still, ... 1.W-F.233A.170.
Still in thy Song shou'd vanquish'd *France* appear, ... 1.W-F.309.178.
All *Fools* have still an Itching to deride, ... 1.EOC.32.243.
There are, who *judge* still *worse* than he can *write.* .... 1.EOC.35.243.
All such have still an Itching to deride, ... 1.EOC.32A.243.
By vain Ambition still to make them more: .... 1.EOC.65.246.
By her just Standard, which is still the same: .... 1.EOC.69.246.

STILL (CONTINUED)

Unerring Nature, still divinely bright, ... 1.EOC.70.246.
By vain Ambition still t'extend them more: .... 1.EOC.65A.246.
Which still *presides,* yet never does *Appear;* .... 1.EOC.75A.247.
Are *Nature* still, but *Nature Methodiz'd;* .... 1.EOC.89.249.
Still with *It self compar'd,* his *Text* peruse; .... 1.EOC.128.253.
But Care in Poetry must still be had, ... 1.EOC.160Z1.258.
Still green with Bays each *ancient* Altar stands, ... 1.EOC.181.261.
Still make the *Whole* depend upon a *Part,* .... 1.EOC.264.269.
Their Praise is still— *The Stile is excellent:* .... 1.EOC.307.274.
Expression is the *Dress* of *Thought,* and still .... 1.EOC.318.274.
With sure *Returns* of still *expected Rhymes.* .... 1.EOC.349.279.
Who still are pleas'd *too little,* or *too much.* .... 1.EOC.385.284.
But blame the *False,* and value still the *True.* .... 1.EOC.407.287.
Ask them the Cause; *They're wiser still,* they say; .... 1.EOC.436.288.
And still to Morrow's wiser than to Day. .... 1.EOC.437.288.
Still make themselves the measure of Mankind; .... 1.EOC.453.290.
Then most our *Trouble* still when most *admir'd,* .... 1.EOC.502.295.
And still the more we *give,* the more *requir'd;* .... 1.EOC.503.295.
Still most our trouble when the most admir'd; .... 1.EOC.502C.295.
The most our trouble still when most admir'd; .... 1.EOC.502D.295.
The more we *give,* the more is still *requir'd:* .... 1.EOC.503B.295.
But still the *Worst* with most Regret commend, ... 1.EOC.518.296.
'Tis not enough your Counsel still be *true,* .... 1.EOC.572.305.
'Twere well, might Criticks still this Freedom take; .... 1.EOC.584.306.
Still humming on, their drowzy Course they keep, ... 1.EOC.600.308.
Still *run on* Poets in a raging Vein, ... 1.EOC.606.308.
Still humming on, their old dull Course they keep, ... 1.EOC.600A.308.
Still *run on* Poets in a frantick Vein, ... 1.EOC.606A.308.
With his own Tongue still edifies his Ears, ... 1.EOC.614.309.
It still *looks home,* and *short Excursions* makes; .... 1.EOC.627.310.
Still *pleas'd* to *teach,* and yet not *proud* to *know?* .... 1.EOC.632.311.
Still fond and proud of *Savage Liberty,* .... 1.EOC.650.313.
Horace still charms with graceful Negligence, ... 1.EOC.653.313.
Still fit for Use, and ready at Command. .... 1.EOC.674.316.
And *Arts* still *follow'd* where her *Eagles flew;* .... 1.EOC.684.317.
And *Boileau* still in Right of *Horace* sways. .... 1.EOC.714.323.
We still defy'd the *Romans,* as *of old.* .... 1.EOC.718.323.
Still pleas'd to *praise,* yet not afraid to *blame,* .... 1.EOC.742.326.
In words like these, which still my mind retains. .... 1.TrPA.52.367.
Oh! yeild at last, nor still remain severe; .... 1.TrPA.114.370.
That still the best and dearest Gift remains. .... 1.TrVP.99.381.
A flow'ry plant, which still preserves her name. .... 1.TrFD.34.387.
You still enjoy'd, and yet you still desir'd, ... 1.TrSP.60.396.
You still enjoy'd, and yet you still desir'd, ... 1.TrSP.60.396.
Still all those Joys to my Remembrance move, ... 1.TrSP.51A.396.
Shall Fortune still in one sad Tenor run, ... 1.TrSP.71.397.
And still increase the Woes so soon begun? .... 1.TrSP.72.397.
Still is there cause for *Sapho* still to love: .... 1.TrSP.90.397.
Still is there cause for *Sapho* still to love: .... 1.TrSP.90.397.
Still prone to change, tho' still the Slaves of State, ... 1.TrSt.226.420.
Still prone to change, tho' still the Slaves of State, ... 1.TrSt.226.420.
And still to change whom chang'd we still must fear? .... 1.TrSt.238.420.
And still to change whom chang'd we still must fear? .... 1.TrSt.238.420.
Where exil'd Tyrants still by turns command! .... 1.TrSt.242.420.
And doubtful still, and still distracted stands, ... 1.TrSt.271.421.
And doubtful still, and still distracted stands, ... 1.TrSt.271.421.
The still Creation listen'd while he spoke, ... 1.TrSt.297.422.
Since still the Lust of Discord fires thy Soul, ... 1.TrSt.367.425.
Thus still his Courage, with his Toils, encreas'd; .... 1.TrSt.527.432.
Be present still, oh Goddess! in our Aid; .... 1.TrSt.590.435.
Still as he rises in th'Æthereal Height, ... 1.TrSt.642.437.
Happy! and happy still She might have prov'd, ... 1.TrSt.674.438.
And conscious Virtue, still its own Reward, ... 1.TrSt.758.442.
These Honours, still renew'd, his antient Wrath appease. .... 1.TrSt.789.443.
For still th'Opprest are his peculiar Care: .... 1.TrUl.91.469.
All these he found, but still, in Error lost, ... 1.TrUl.96.469.
O still the same *Ulysses!* she rejoin'd, ... 1.TrUl.166.471.
These Thoughts he fortify'd with Reasons still, ... 2.ChJM.19.16.
And many Heads are wiser still than one; .... 2.ChJM.96.19.
My Limbs are active, still I'm sound at Heart, ... 2.ChJM.129.20.
As still I hold your own Advice the best. .... 2.ChJM.155.22.
And have observ'd this useful Maxim still, ... 2.ChJM.158.22.
Still one by one, in swift Succession, pass .... 2.ChJM.236.25.
Since it chastises still what best it loves. .... 2.ChJM.283.27.
Provided still, you moderate your Joy, ... 2.ChJM.291.28.
When Fortune favours still the Fair are kind. .... 2.ChJM.304.28.
Still as his Mind revolv'd with vast Delight .... 2.ChJM.349.31.
But faithless still, and wav'ring as the Wind! .... 2.ChJM.478.38.
This Chime still rings in ev'ry Lady's Ear, ... 2.ChJM.597.43.
'Tis but a Counsel—and we Women still .... 2.ChWB.34.58.
And Feasts still kept upon my Wedding-Day: .... 2.ChWB.113.62.
I still prevail'd, and wou'd be in the right, ... 2.ChWB.164.64.
In Country Dances still I bore the Bell, ... 2.ChWB.211.66.
Still warms me to the Bottom of my Heart. .... 2.ChWB.224.67.
I still have shifts against a Time of Need: .... 2.ChWB.297.71.
But vig'rous still, a lively buxom Dame, ... 2.ChWB.319.72.
But oft repented, and repent it still; .... 2.ChWB.333.73.
When still he read, and laugh'd, and read again, ... 2.ChWB.413.77.
And still burn on, in *Cupid's* Flames, *Alive.* .... 2.RL*A*2.147.136.
Belinda still her downy Pillow prest, ... 2.RL1.19.147.
The Fair and Innocent shall still believe. .... 2.RL1.40.148.
Succeeding Vanities she still regards, ... 2.RL1.53.149.
In search of Mischief still on Earth to roam. .... 2.RL1.64.150.
And keep good Humour still whate'er we lose? .... 2.RL5.30.201.
Rather than so, ah let me still survive, ... 2.RL5.101.207.
Unmov'd, superior still in every State; .... 2.TemF.157.266.
On *Homer* still he fix'd a reverend Eye, ... 2.TemF.202.271.
(Her Virgin Handmaids) still attend the Shrine: .... 2.TemF.271.276.
Which still grew sweeter as they wider spread: .... 2.TemF.315.279.
O let us still the secret Joy partake, ... 2.TemF.364.281.
But Mortals! know, 'tis still our greatest Pride, ... 2.TemF.368.281.
But still in Fancy vanquish'd ev'ry Maid; .... 2.TemF.387.282.
Which still unfolded stand, by Night, by Day, ... 2.TemF.426.284.
And follow still where Fortune leads the way; .... 2.TemF.518.289.
Her heart still dictates, and her hand obeys. .... 2.ElAb.16.320.

STILL (CONTINUED)

Still rebel nature holds out half my heart; ... 2.ElAb.26.321.
Still breath'd in sighs, still usher'd with a tear. ... 2.ElAb.32.321.
Still breath'd in sighs, still usher'd with a tear. ... 2.ElAb.32.321.
Tears still are mine, and those I need not spare, ... 2.ElAb.45.322.
Those still at least are left thee to bestow. ... 2.ElAb.120.329.
Still on that breast enamour'd let me lie, ... 2.ElAb.121.329.
Still drink delicious poison from thy eye, ... 2.ElAb.122.329.
Still as the sea, ere winds were taught to blow, ... 2.ElAb.253.340.
Pride still is aiming at the blest abodes, ... 3.EOM1.125.30.
How would he wish that Heav'n had left him still ... 3.EOM1.203.40.
Still by himself abus'd, or disabus'd; ... 3.EOM2.14.55.
And to their proper operation still, ... 3.EOM2.57.62.
Self-love still stronger, as its objects nigh; ... 3.EOM2.71.63.
Reason still use, to Reason still attend: ... 3.EOM2.78.64.
Reason still use, to Reason still attend: ... 3.EOM2.78.64.
Nor God alone in the still calm we find, ... 3.EOM2.109.68.
Present to grasp, and future still to find, ... 3.EOM2.125.70.
The ruling Passion conquers Reason still. ... 3.EOM2.148Z2.72.
In this weak queen, some fav'rite still obey. ... 3.EOM2.150.73.
Reason is here no guide, but still a guard: ... 3.EOM2.162.74.
For, Vice or Virtue, Self directs it still; ... 3.EOM2.236.84.
Wants, frailties, passions, closer still ally ... 3.EOM2.253.85.
Pleas'd with this bauble still, as that before; ... 3.EOM2.281.88.
In Folly's cup still laughs the bubble, joy; ... 3.EOM2.288.89.
One prospect lost, another still we gain; ... 3.EOM2.289.89.
See! and confess, one comfort still must rise, ... 3.EOM2.293.90.
Press to one centre still, the gen'ral Good. ... 3.EOM3.14.93.
Grant that the pow'rful still the weak controul, ... 3.EOM3.49.97.
Death still draws nearer, never seeming near. ... 3.EOM3.76.99.
While still too wide or short is human Wit; ... 3.EOM3.90.101.
Reflection, Reason, still the ties improve, ... 3.EOM3.133.106.
And still new needs, new helps, new habits rise, ... 3.EOM3.137.106.
Still as one brood, and as another rose, ... 3.EOM3.139.107.
Still spread the int'rest, and preserv'd the kind. ... 3.EOM3.146.107.
"Still for the strong too weak, the weak too strong. ... 3.EOM3.194.113.
That something still which prompts th'eternal sigh, ... 3.EOM4.3.128.
Which still so near us, yet beyond us lies, ... 3.EOM4.5.128.
Oh sons of earth! attempt ye still to rise, ... 3.EOM4.73.135.
Heav'n still with laughter the vain toil surveys, ... 3.EOM4.75.135.
But still this world (so fitted for the knave) ... 3.EOM4.131.140.
Not one looks backward, onward still he goes, ... 3.EOM4.223.148.
Think, and if still the things thy envy call, ... 3.EOM4.275.154.
The only point where human bliss stands still, ... 3.EOM4.311.157.
And opens still, and opens on his soul, ... 3.EOM4.342.161.
Another still, and still another spreads, ... 3.EOM4.366.164.
Another still, and still another spreads, ... 3.EOM4.366.164.
Affections? they still take a wider range: ... 3.Ep1.172A.29.
Still to his wench he creeps on knocking knees, ... 3.Ep1.232A.35.
A Judge is just, a Chanc'lor juster still; ... 3.Ep1.89.22.
Still sits at squat, and peeps not from its hole. ... 3.Ep1.115.24.
Opinions? they still take a wider range: ... 3.Ep1.172.29.
His Passion still, to covet gen'ral praise, ... 3.Ep1.196.32.
And (harder still) flagitious, yet not great! ... 3.Ep1.205.33.
Still to his wench he crawls on knocking knees, ... 3.Ep1.232.35.
Still tries to save the hallow'd taper's end, ... 3.Ep1.239.36.
Strange graces still, and stranger flights she had, ... 3.Ep2.49.54.
Yet still a sad, good Christian at her heart. ... 3.Ep2.68.55.
So much the Fury still out-ran the Wit, ... 3.Ep2.127.61.
Safe is your Secret still in Cloe's ear; ... 3.Ep2.173.64.
Is still to please, can Pleasure seem a fault? ... 3.Ep2.212.67.
Still out of reach, yet never out of view, ... 3.Ep2.232.68.
Still round and round the Ghosts of Beauty glide, ... 3.Ep2.241.69.
Woman's at best a Contradiction still. ... 3.Ep2.270.72.
Still, as of old, incumber'd Villainy! ... 3.Ep3.36.88.
"The ruling Passion conquers Reason still." ... 3.Ep3.156.106.
Still follow Sense, of ev'ry Art the Soul, ... 3.Ep4.65.143.
F. Better be *Cibber,* I'll maintain it still, ... 4.HS1.37.7.
The fewer still you name, you wound the more; ... 4.HS1.43.9.
F. Your Plea is good. But still I say, beware! ... 4.HS1.143.19.
"Not Sir, my only—I have better still, ... 4.JD4.114.35.
So when you plague a Fool, 'tis still the Curse, ... 4.JD4.120.35.
He hears; and as a Still, with Simples in it, ... 4.JD4.126.35.
And last (which proves him wiser still than all) ... 4.JD4.150.37.
That *Spain* robs on, and *Dunkirk's* still a Port. ... 4.JD4.165.39.
I blest my Stars! but still afraid to see ... 4.JD4.180A.41.
I quak'd at heart; and still afraid to see ... 4.JD4.180.41.
Here still Reflection led on sober Thought, ... 4.JD4.188A.41.
Will chuse a *Pheasant* still before a *Hen;* ... 4.HS2.18.55.
Cheap eggs, and herbs, and olives still we see, ... 4.HS2.35.57.
Let Us be fix'd, and our own Masters still. ... 4.HS2.180.69.
And pity Men of Pleasure still in Pain! ... 4.HAdv.50.79.
And has not *Colly* still his Lord, and Whore? ... 4.Arbu.97.102.
Does not one Table *Bavius* still admit? ... 4.Arbu.99.102.
Still to one Bishop *Philips* seem a Wit? ... 4.Arbu.100.102.
Still spin the slight, self-pleasing thread anew; ... 4.Arbu.90A.102.
Does not one Table Arnall still admit? ... 4.Arbu.99A.102.
Still *Sapho—"Hold!* for God-sake—you'll offend: ... 4.Arbu.101.103.
Still *Sapho—"Hold!* nay see you—you'll offend: ... 4.Arbu.101A.103.
I wish'd the man a dinner, and sate still: ... 4.Arbu.152.107.
He, who still wanting tho' he lives on theft, ... 4.Arbu.183.109.
And others (harder still) he pay'd in kind. ... 4.Arbu.244.113.
But still the Great have kindness in reserve, ... 4.Arbu.247.113.
May ev'ry *Bavius* have his *Bufo* still! ... 4.Arbu.250.114.
"No, such a Genius never can lye still," ... 4.Arbu.278.115.
Why will the Town imagine still I write? ... 4.Arbu.271A.115.
The Whisper that to Greatness still too near, ... 4.Arbu.356.122.
Well, I cou'd wish that still in Richmens Homes ... 4.JD2A.121.142.
Yet here, as ev'n in Hell, there must be still ... 4.JD2.3.133.
Those write because all write, and so have still ... 4.JD2.27.133.
Well, I could wish, that still in lordly domes ... 4.JD2.115.143.
His House, thy Temple, sacred still to Love ... 4.HOde1.22A.151.
The still-believing, still-renew'd desire; ... 4.HOde1.34.153.
The still-believing, still-renew'd desire; ... 4.HOde1.34.153.
—But why? ah tell me, still too dear! ... 4.HOde1.37A.153.
—But why? ah Celia still too dear! ... 4.HOde1.37B.153.
—But why? ah PATTY, still too dear! ... 4.HOde1.37C.153.
That turn'd ten thousand Verses, now stands still. ... 4.2HE2.79.171.
Yet still, not heeding what your Heart can teach, ... 4.2HE2.224.181.
That God of Nature, who, within us still, ... 4.2HE2.280.185.
Had still this Monster to subdue at last. ... 4.2HE1.18.195.
But still I love the language of his Heart. ... 4.2HE1.78.201.
And, having once been wrong, will be so still. ... 4.2HE1.130.207.
Tho' still some traces of our rustic vein ... 4.2HE1.270.219.
There still remains to mortify a Wit, ... 4.2HE1.304.221.
The Play stands still; damn action and discourse, ... 4.2HE1.314.223.
Still, still be getting, never, never rest. ... 4.1HE6.96.243.
Still, still be getting, never, never rest. ... 4.1HE6.96.243.
Still true to Virtue, and as warm as true: ... 4.1HE1.30.281.
That keep me from Myself; and still delay ... 4.1HE1.41.281.
There, London's voice: "Get Mony, Mony still! ... 4.1HE1.79.285.
Sir Job sail'd forth, the evening bright and still, ... 4.1HE1.138.289.
F. Why yes: with *Scripture* still you may be free; ... 4.EpS1.37.300.
These nothing hurts; they keep their Fashion still, ... 4.EpS1.43.301.
You still may lash the Greatest—in Disgrace: ... 4.EpS1.88.305.
She's still the same, belov'd, contented thing. ... 4.EpS1.140.308.
Still better, Ministers; or if the thing ... 4.EpS2.50.315.
Oft in the clear, still Mirrour of Retreat, ... 4.EpS2.78.317.
Still let me say! No Follower, but a Friend. ... 4.EpS2.93.318.
Have still a secret Byass to a Knave: ... 4.EpS2.101.319.
Good C[ornbury] hopes, and candidly sits still. ... 4.1740.18.332*.
Tho' still he travels on no bad pretence, ... 4.1740.51.334.
Nor like his..still a.. ... 4.1740.88.337.
Still Dunce the second reigns like Dunce the first? ... 5.DunA1.6.61.
Still her old empire to confirm, she tries, ... 5.DunA1.15.61.
How Time himself stands still at her command, ... 5.DunA1.69.68.
Ah! still o'er Britain stretch that peaceful wand, ... 5.DunA1.155.82.
The very worsted still look'd black and blue: ... 5.DunA2.142.118.
Still happy Impudence obtains the prize. ... 5.DunA2.178.123.
Still break the benches, Henley! with thy strain, ... 5.DunA3.199.174.
Thy giddy dulness still shall lumber on, ... 5.DunA3.296.184.
Thy giddy dulness still may lumber on, ... 5.DunA3.296A.184.
Still Dunce the second reigns like Dunce the first; ... 5.DunB1.6.269.
Still her old Empire to restore she tries, ... 5.DunB1.17.270.
How Time himself stands still at her command, ... 5.DunB1.71.275.
Still spread a healing mist before the mind; ... 5.DunB1.174.283.
What then remains? Ourself. Still, still remain ... 5.DunB1.217.286.
What then remains? Ourself. Still, still remain ... 5.DunB1.217.286.
Folly, my son, has still a Friend at Court. ... 5.DunB1.300.291.
The very worsted still look'd black and blue. ... 5.DunB2.150.302.
Still happy Impudence obtains the prize. ... 5.DunB2.186.304.
Benlowes, propitious still to blockheads, bows; ... 5.DunB3.21.321.
Still break the benches, Henley! with thy strain, ... 5.DunB3.203.330.
Thy giddy dulness still shall lumber on, ... 5.DunB3.294.334.
And what the last? a very Poet still. ... 5.DunB4.164.357.
Each fierce Logician, still expelling Locke, ... 5.DunB4.196.361.
'Tis true, on Words is still our whole debate, ... 5.DunB4.219.364.
See! still thy own, the heavy Canon roll, ... 5.DunB4.247.367.
"Grant, gracious Goddess! grant me still to cheat, ... 5.DunB4.355.377.
O may thy cloud still cover the deceit! ... 5.DunB4.356.378.
Still bears them, faithful; and that thus I eat, ... 5.DunB4.389.380.
Make Nature still incroach upon his plan; ... 5.DunB4.473.387.
Of nought so certain as our *Reason* still, ... 5.DunB4.481.389.
Oh hide the God still more! and make us see ... 5.DunB4.483.389.
Oh hide the God still more! or make us see ... 5.DunB4.483A.389.
Bounded by Nature, narrow'd still by Art, ... 5.DunB4.503.392.
Their Infamy, still keep the human shape. ... 5.DunB4.528.394.
For I'm thy Servant, and I'l still be so: ... 6.2.2.5.
Speak when thou wilt, for still thy Servant hears. ... 6.2.34.6.
Behind thy self thou still dost stay; ... 6.6ii.6.14.
Sit still a Moment; pray be easy— ... 6.10.2.24.
Just as a Still, with Simples in it, ... 6.10.15.25.
Thy stone, O *Sysiphus,* stands still; ... 6.11.66.32.
Eurydice still trembled on his Tongue, ... 6.11.114.34.
Still from *Apollo* vindicates her shade, ... 6.14iv.24.47.
Still turns her beauties from th' invading beam, ... 6.14iv.25.47.
Still changing Names, Religions, Climes, ... 6.14v(b).14.50.
Still vary Shapes and Dyes; ... 6.14v(b).21.50.
Still gain new Titles with new Forms; ... 6.14v(b).22.50.
And varying still in State Æ form ... 6.14v(b).22A.50.
Still with Esteem no less convers'd than read; ... 6.19.7.62.
And more Diverting still than Regular, ... 6.19.26.63.
Still in Constraint your suff'ring Sex remains, ... 6.19.41.63.
Still makes new Conquests, and maintains the past: ... 6.19.62.64.
Thus *Voiture's* early Care still shone the same, ... 6.19.69.64.
Their Wit still sparkling and their Flames still warm. ... 6.19.72.64.
Their Wit still sparkling and their Flames still warm. ... 6.19.72.64.
Still to charm those who charm the World beside. ... 6.19.80.64.
Still, tho' a rock, can thus relieve her woe, ... 6.20.58.67.
Still out of reach, tho' ever in their view. ... 6.22.6.71.
Where still in breathing brass they seem to live, ... 6.22.17.72.
Thou who did'st form, and form'd dost still sustain ... 6.23.1A.73.
Such is, and shall be still, my love to thee— ... 6.25.14.77.
Still to keep Company with *U;* ... 6.30.16.86.
Still with dry Eyes the Tory *Celia* sate, ... 6.33.2.99.
Th' advent'rous Lover is successful still, ... 6.34.5.101.
Still warm our hearts, and still inspire our songs. ... 6.38.26.108.
Still warm our hearts, and still inspire our songs. ... 6.38.26.108.
Our sex are still forgiving at their heart; ... 6.41.12.113.
Still hoarding up, most scandalously nice, ... 6.41.19.114.
Vext to be still in town, I knit my brow, ... 6.45.49.126.
Still idle, with a busy Air, ... 6.47.37.129.
None can like thee its Fermentation still. ... 6.48i.4.133*.
Still may those Honours be as justly dealt, ... 6.48iv.15.136.
I wish the Man a Dinner, and sit still; ... 6.49iii.2.142.
I wish the Wretch a Dinner, and sit still; ... 6.49iii.2A.142.
I wish the Man a Dinner, and stand still; ... 6.49iii.2B.142.
Still in the right to stay; ... 6.50.30.147.
Still, when the lust of tyrant pow'r succeeds, ... 6.51i.31.152.
Yet still how faint by precept is exprest ... 6.52.41.157.
Yet still her charms in breathing paint engage; ... 6.52.55.157.

STILL 389 STOCKS

STILL (CONTINUED)

Or if they still must live, from me remove ....Od.4.910.161.
Stand still confest, tho' distant far they lie ....Od.5.101.177.
Still to your own ætherial race the worst! ....Od.5.150.178.
Still I can suffer; Their high will be done! ....Od.5.288.185.
Struck with amaze, yet still to doubt inclin'd, ...Od.5.450.194.
Insulting still, inquisitive, and loud. ....Od.7.22.235.
And still to live, beyond the pow'r of years. ....Od.7.123.240.
But still long-weary'd nature wants repair; ....Od.7.294.250.
My craving bowels still require repaste. ....Od.7.296.250.
Still, further still, I bid the Discus fly. ....Od.8.232.275.
Still, further still, I bid the Discus fly. ....Od.8.232.275.
The ewes still folded, with distended thighs ....Od.9.517.327.
And sees me wand'ring still from coast to coast; ....Od.9.647.333.
If still to live, or desp'rate plunge to Fate: ....Od.10.55.342.
Still curst with sense, their mind remains alone, ...Od.10.280.356.
Still heav'd their hearts, and still their eyes ran o'er. ....Od.10.684.376.
Still heav'd their hearts, and still their eyes ran o'er. ....Od.10.684.376.
Still as I spoke, the Phantom seem'd to moan, ...Od.11.100.385.
Still in the dark abodes of death I stood, ...Od.11.186.390.
His voice, that list'ning still they seem'd to hear. ....Od.11.415.404.
The evening stars still mount th' ethereal plains. ....Od.11.465.407.
For still distrest I rove from coast to coast, ...Od.11.589.412.
Still burns thy rage? and can brave souls resent ....Od.11.679.418.
Still as they plead, the fatal lots he rowls, ...Od.11.701.419.
Such, such was I! still tost from care to care, ...Od.11.763.424.
To a base Monarch still a slave confin'd, ...Od.11.767.424.
Still are new toils and war thy dire delight? ....Od.12.144.439.
Lo! still the same *Ulysses* is your guide! ....Od.12.253.444.
Still must we restless rove, new seas explore, ...Od.12.337.448.
Still may thy beams thro' heav'n's bright portals rise, ...Od.12.454.453.
His voice, that list'ning still they seem'd to hear. ....Od.13.2.1.
Then thus: O Queen farewell! be still possest ....Od.13.74.4.
Of dear remembrance, blessing still and blest! ....Od.13.75.4.
Still let her seem to sail, and seem alone; ....Od.13.181.14.
For still th' oppress'd are his peculiar care. ....Od.13.258.18.
All these he found, but still in error lost ....Od.13.263.18.
O still the same *Ulysses!* she rejoin'd, ...Od.13.333.23.
To *Sparta,* still with female beauty gay: ....Od.13.476.29.
For needy strangers still to flatt'ry fly, ...Od.14.148.42.
I liv'd (and happy still had liv'd) a guest. ....Od.14.316.50.
Still met th' emergence, and determin'd right) ....Od.14.554.64.
Still the succeeding flame expells the last. ....Od.15.28.71.
(For still to thee his loyal thoughts incline) ....Od.15.46.72.
What grateful thoughts still in this bosom glow, ...Od.15.169.76.
For still he lives, and lives with riches blest. ....Od.15.473.93.
Be Silence still our guard. The Monarch's spies ....Od.15.481.93.
Are still at hand; and this reveal'd must be ....Od.15.483.93.
Or still in ambush thirst for blood in vain? ....Od.16.485.130.
Or still in ambush thirst in vain for blood, ...Od.16.487.130.
And still his words live perfect in my mind. ....Od.17.137.138.
One rogue is usher to another still. ....Od.17.251.143.
Still curst by fortune, and insulted here! ....Od.17.527.158.
A man in stature, still a boy in heart! ....Od.18.258.179.
Still in the dome divine *Ulysses* stay'd: ....Od.19.2.192.
And bless the Pow'r that still delights to bless. ....Od.19.136.199.
The night still ravell'd, what the day renew'd. ....Od.19.173.200.
Still turn'd the toilsome mill with anxious mind; ....Od.20.139.240.
Still treat they worth with lordly dull disdain; ....Od.20.209.243.
Here, vagrant still! offensive to my Lords! ....Od.20.225.244.
Ulysses from his state a wand'rer still, ...Od.20.257.245.
Or if each other's wrongs ye still support, ...Od.20.382.251.
To think he still survives to claim the state? ....Od.20.396.251.
Hapless to search! more hapless still to find! ....Od.21.28.260.
And still to last, the vision of my night! ....Od.21.80.262.
And still (all infant as I was) retain ....Od.21.98.263.
Yet still to-morrow falser than to-day. ....Od.21.166.267.
Still the tough bow unmov'd. The lofty man ....Od.21.262.272.
Would add our blood. Injustice still proceeds. ....Od.22.291.300.
Still undishonour'd or by word or deed ....Od.22.350.304.
Thus speaks the Queen, still dubious, with disguise; ....Od.23.183.330.
Or still inviolate the olive stands, ...Od.23.208.333.
Yet still a master ghost, the rest he aw'd, ...Od.24.25.348.
Still at his side is *Nestor's* son survey'd, ...Od.24.27.348.
And lov'd *Patroclus* still attends his shade. ....Od.24.28.348.
With age, yet still majestic in decay! ....Od.24.272.362.
Who digging round the plant still hangs his head, ...Od.24.285.363.
My strength were still, as once in better days; ....Od.24.436.369.
And, still more old, in arms *Laertes* shone. ....Od.24.575.375.

STILL-BELIEVING

The still-believing, still-renew'd desire; ....4.HOde1.34.153.

STILL-RENEW'D

The still-believing, still-renew'd desire; ....4.HOde1.34.153.

STILL-REVIVING

The kind Deceit, the still-reviving Fire, ...Il.14.250.173.

STILL-SURVIVING

Thy still-surviving Sons may sue for thee, ...Il.24.855.572.

STILL'D

Or still'd thy infant Clamours at this Breast; ....Il.22.117.457.
And still'd the Clamour of the shouting Bands. ....Il.23.648.515.
And a dead silence still'd the wat'ry world. ....Od.5.503.196.

STILLS

Then pompous *Silence* reigns, and stills the noisie Laws. ....6.8.33.18.
He stills the Winds, and bids the Skies to sleep; ....Il.12.335.93.
And stills the Bellows, and (in order laid) ....Il.18.481.345.
To take repast, and stills the wordy war; ....Od.12.520.457.

STILTON

But wish'd it Stilton for his sake; ....4.HS6.168.261.

STILTS

This, prose on stilts; that, poetry fall'n lame. ....5.DunB1.190.283.

STING

And with their forky Tongue, and pointless Sting shall play. ....1.Mes.84A.120.
Produc'd the point that left a sting behind; ....4.2HE1.252.217.
O Death! where is thy Sting? ....6.31ii.18.94.
Where mighty Death! Oh where's thy Sting? ....6.31ii.6Z6.94.
Like oxen madden'd by the breeze's sting, ...Od.22.335.302.

STINGS

This painted Child of Dirt that stinks and stings; ....4.Arbu.310.118.
His Rump well pluck'd with Nettles stings, ...6.93.21.257.
They strike th' Assailants, and infix their Stings; ....Il.12.192.88.
Whet all their Stings, and call forth all their Rage; ....Il.16.317.255.
Untam'd, untir'd, he turns, attacks, and stings: ....Il.17.645.313.
And the barb'd Jav'lin stings his Breast in vain: ....Il.21.682.450.
To prove the heroe.—Slander stings the brave. ....Od.8.208.273.
And the fiends haunt him with a thousands stings. ....Od.11.340.398.
The gripes of poverty, and stings of care. ....Od.18.150.173.

STINK

In heaps, like Ambergrise, a stink it lies, ...3.Ep3.235.111.
If this is priz'd for *sweetness,* that for *stink?* ....4.HS2.30.57.
The sweetest thing will stink that he can eat ....4.HS2.32A.57.
Oyl, tho' it stink, they drop by drop impart, ...4.HS2.59.59.
In Dirt and darkness hundreds stink content. ....4.1HE1.133.289.

STINKING

Doth many a stinking Sprat and Herring lie; ....6.14ii.11.43.
(Whatever stinking Fops suppose) ....6.135.30.367.

STINKS

This painted Child of Dirt that stinks and stings; ....4.Arbu.310.118.
Imbibes new life, and scours and stinks along, ...5.DunA2.98.109.
Imbibes new life, and scours and stinks along; ....5.DunB2.106.300.
Who like his Cheops stinks above the ground, ...5.DunB4.372.379.
That lies and stinks in State. ....6.14v(a).12.48.

STINT

And sure the certain Stint was ne'er defin'd. ....2.ChWB.16.57.

STINTED

To just three millions stinted modest Gage. ....3.Ep3.130.103.

STIR

And stir within me ev'ry source of love. ....2.ElAb.232.339.
Just brought out this, when scarce his tongue could stir, ...3.Ep1.254.37.
Once break their Rest, or stir them from their Place; ....4.EpS1.100.305.
No noise, no stir, no motion can'st thou make, ...5.DunA2.291.138.
No noise, no stir, no motion can'st thou make, ...5.DunB2.303.310.
To stir, to rouze, to shake the Soul he comes, ...5.DunB4.67.348.
It is; I feel it stir. ....6.94.62.261.
Sudden I stir the embers, and inspire ....Od.9.445.324.

STIR'D

The trembling Surface, by the Motion stir'd, ...2.TemF.438.284.
And yet the dullest brain, if gently stir'd, ...5.DunB4.445A.384.

STIRR'D

Yet by some object ev'ry brain is stirr'd; ....5.DunB4.445.384.
He barely stirr'd him, but he could not raise: ....Il.23.849.523.
The sudden tumult stirr'd him where he lay, ...Od.10.665.375.
Nor stirr'd an inch, contemptuous, from the road: ....Od.17.275.145.

STIRRUP

And from the Stirrup stretch'd, to find ....6.79.111.221.
And from his Stirrup stretch'd, to find ....6.79.111A.221.

STIRS

As the small pebble stirs the peaceful lake; ....3.EOM4.364.164.
Stirs all the Ranks, and fires the *Trojan* Train; ....Il.5.562.295.
And stirs but slowly when he stirs at last. ....Il.11.689.66.
And stirs but slowly when he stirs at last. ....Il.11.689.66.
As when an Earthquake stirs the nodding Grove; ....Il.13.184.114.
Yet scarce an Army stirs him from his Post: ....Il.16.137.243.
Rolls clouds on clouds, and stirs the wat'ry world, ...Od.5.376.190.

STOB US

What Gellius or Stob us cook'd before, ...5.DunB4.231A.365.

STOBAEUS

What Gellius or Stobæus hash'd before, ...5.DunB4.231.365.

STOCK

The Gods shall of our Stock take care: ....6.80.2.224.
Small Stock of Iron needs that Man provide; ....Il.23.987.528.
A stock by daily luxury decreast; ....Od.14.22.35.
Gives from our stock an only branch to spring: ....Od.16.124.108.

STOCKING

At am'rous Flavio is the Stocking thrown? ....4.1HE1.148.291.

STOCKINGS

To wear red Stockings, and to dine with *St[eel]* ....6.49i.4.137.

STOCKS

On savage stocks inserted learn to bear; ....3.EOM2.182.77.
"Statesman and Patriot ply alike the stocks, ...3.Ep3.141.105.
Stocks and Subscriptions pour on ev'ry side, ...3.Ep3.370.123.
Who in the *Secret,* deals in Stocks secure, ...4.JD4.140.37.
Fufidia thrives in Money, Land, and Stocks: ....4.HAdv.18.77.
Stocks thou may'st buy and sell, but always lose; ....6.66.7.194.

STOIC'S
With too much weakness for the Stoic's pride, ... 3.EOM2.6.53.
With too much weakness for a Stoic's pride, ... 3.EOM2.6A.53.

STOICK
Tho' with the Stoick chief our stage may ring, ... 6.41.37.114.
The Stoick husband was the glorious thing. .... 6.41.38.114.

STOICS
In lazy Apathy let Stoics boast .... 3.EOM2.101.67.

STOL'N
Stol'n from a Duel, follow'd by a Nun, ... 5.DunB4.327.375.
Anchises' Son, by *Venus'* stol'n Embrace, ... Il.2.993.170.
The vig'rous Offspring of a stol'n Embrace, ... Il.8.344.414.
(Young *Ajax* Brother, by a stol'n Embrace; .... Il.13.871.147.
Brave *Megapenthes,* from a stol'n amour .... Od.4.15.121.

STOLE
And said, a charming female stole that eye. .... 1.TrPA.34.366.
An honest factor stole a Gem away: .... 3.Ep3.362.123.
Who sent the Thief that stole the Cash, away, ... 4.2HE2.25.167.
Who sent the Thief who stole the Cash, away, ... 4.2HE2.25A.167.
Lely on animated Canvas stole .... 4.2HE1.149.207.
Peace stole her wing, and wrapt the world in sleep; .... 4.2HE1.401.229.
Thus he, for then a ray of Reason stole .... 5.DunA3.223.176.
In pleasing memory of all he stole, ... 5.DunB1.128.279.
Some Dæmon stole my pen (forgive th' offence) .... 5.DunB1.187.283.
Stole from the Master of the sev'nfold Face: .... 5.DunB1.244.288.
Thus he, for then a ray of Reason stole .... 5.DunB3.225.331.
Where *British* Sighs from dying WYNDHAM stole, ... 6.142.11.383.
Here patriot sighs from Wyndham's bosom stole, ... 6.142.11A.383.
There partiot sighs from Wyndham's bosom stole .... 6.142.11B.383.
Here British groans from dying WYNDHAM stole, ... 6.142.11E.383.
Here British sighs from dying WYNDHAM stole, ... 6.142.11F.383.
Here British sighs from Windham's bosom stole .... 6.142.11G.383.
To Wyndham's breast the patriot passion stole .... 6.142.11H.383.
Here, stole the Honest Tear from Marchmont's Eye .... 6.142.12B.383.
Hence great *Anchises* stole a Breed unknown .... Il.5.332.282.
Each stole a Tear for what he left behind. .... Il.19.361.387.
Adown his cheek a tear unbidden stole, ... Od.17.365.149.
Stole unperceiv'd; he turn'd his head, and dry'd .... Od.17.366.149.
To the high chamber stole the faithless swain, ... Od.22.177.296.
While the soft hours stole unperceiv'd away; .... Od.23.322.339.

STOLES
Tunics, and stoles, and robes imperial bears. .... Od.6.88.209.

STOMACH
First Health: The stomach (cram'd from ev'ry dish, ... 4.HS2.69.59.
Quite turns my Stomach— *P.* So does Flatt'ry mine; .... 4.EpS2.182.323.
A hearty Stomach, and sound Lady; .... 6.13.13.39.
So when Curll's Stomach the strong Drench o'ercame, ... 6.82x.1.236.
Of giant stomach, and of famish'd face. .... Od.17.455.155.

STOMACHS
Those *Heads* as *Stomachs* are not sure the best .... 1.EOC.388.284.

STONE
Inscribe a Verse on this relenting Stone: .... 1.PWi.26.90.
(Obscure the Place, and uninscrib'd the Stone) .... 1.W-F.320.180.
The Cyclops follow'd, and a stone he threw, ... 1.TrPA.144.372.
His body press'd beneath the stone, the blood .... 1.TrPA.151.372.
Than *Phrygian* Marble or the *Parian* Stone. .... 1.TrSP.166.400.
No *Grecian* Stone the pompous Arches grac'd; .... 1.TrSt.203.418.
Nor *Grecian* Stone the pompous Arches grac'd; .... 1.TrSt.203A.418.
A pondrous Stone bold *Hector* heav'd to throw, ... 1.TrES.183.456.
Where Bowls and Urns were form'd of living Stone, ... 1.TrUl.35.467.
Was compass'd round with Walls of solid Stone; .... 2.ChJM.449.36.
And seem'd to distant Sight of solid Stone. .... 2.TemF.30.255.
And Legislators seem to think in Stone. .... 2.TemF.74.258.
The fiery Steeds seem starting from the Stone; .... 2.TemF.219.272.
The sinking Stone at first a Circle makes; .... 2.TemF.437.284.
I have not yet forgot my self to stone. .... 2.ElAb.24.320.
Glance on the stone where our cold reliques lie, ... 2.ElAb.356.348.
So peaceful rests, without a stone, a name, ... 2.Elegy.69.368.
B. And what? no monument, inscription, stone? .... 3.Ep3.283A.116.
"And what? no monument, inscription, stone? .... 3.Ep3.283.116.
Eternal buckle takes in Parian stone. .... 3.Ep3.296.117.
So well in paint and stone they judg'd of merit: .... 4.2HE1.384.227.
Rack'd with Sciatics, martyr'd with the Stone, ... 4.1HE6.54.241.
Happier thy fortunes! like a rolling stone, ... 5.DunA3.295.184.
Sits Mother Osborne, stupify'd to stone! .... 5.DunB2.312.311.
Happier thy fortunes! like a rolling stone, ... 5.DunB3.293.334.
"Leave not a foot of verse, a foot of stone, ... 5.DunB4.127.354.
Steal from the world, and not a stone .... 6.1.19.4.
Thy stone, O *Sysiphus,* stands still; .... 6.11.66.32.
This breathing stone immortaliz'd my woe: .... 6.20.26.66.
Beneath a rude and nameless stone he lies, ... 6.72.3.208.
To find that Speechless Stone where Dryden lies. .... 6.72.4A.208.
Look down upon this Stone; .... 6.82viii.2.233.
Oh let thy once-lov'd Friend inscribe thy Stone, ... 6.85.7.242.
Let then thy once-lov'd Friend inscribe thy Stone, ... 6.85.7A.242.
Yet let thy once-lov'd Friend inscribe thy Stone, ... 6.85.7B.242.
A stone of two foot; .... 6.90.9.251.
In the green Thicket of a Mossy stone? .... 6.96ii.30Z8.271.
"In the green Thicket of a Mossy Stone, ... 6.96ii.42.272.
These little rites, a Stone, a Verse, receive, ... 6.109.19.314.
These little rites, a Stone and Verse, receive, ... 6.109.19A.314.
This modest Stone what few vain Marbles can .... 6.112.1.318.
The modest Stone what few vain Marbles can .... 6.112.1A.318.
The last true Briton lies beneath this stone. .... 6.113.12.320.
With tears inscribes this monumental Stone, ... 6.152.13.400.
Full on his Ankle dropt the pond'rous Stone, ... Il.4.601.250.
Thro' both the Tendons broke the rugged Stone, ... Il.5.377.285.
His bended Arm receiv'd the falling Stone, ... Il.5.712.301.

STONE (CONTINUED)
Of equal Beauty, and of polish'd Stone. .... Il.6.311.341.
The Stone shall tell your vanquish'd Hero's Name, ... Il.7.103.368.
In his strong Hand up-heav'd a flinty Stone, ... Il.7.316.379.
Full on the Brazen Boss the Stone descends; .... Il.7.318.379.
The huge Stone thund'ring thro' his Buckler broke; .... Il.7.323.379.
Dreadful he shouts: from Earth a Stone he took, ... Il.8.387.416.
The furious Chief discharg'd the craggy Stone. .... Il.8.394.416.
By the long Lance, the Sword, or pond'rous Stone, ... Il.11.343.49.
(By the long Lance, the Sword, or pondrous Stone, ... Il.11.664.63.
A pond'rous Stone bold *Hector* heav'd to throw, ... Il.12.537.101.
(Which from the stubborn Stone a Torrent rends) .... Il.13.193.115.
A pond'rous Stone up-heaving from the Sand, ... Il.14.472.186.
Heav'd from the lowest Stone; and bury All, ... Il.15.662.221.
Next on *Eryalus* he flies; a Stone .... Il.16.500.262.
At *Stenelaus* flew the weighty Stone, ... Il.16.714.271.
A Spear his Left, a Stone employs his Right: .... Il.16.892.277.
Still as a Tomb-stone, never to be mov'd, ... Il.17.492.307.
On Seats of Stone, within the sacred Place, ... Il.18.585.351.
(With Force collected) heaves a mighty Stone: .... Il.20.336.407.
A Stone, the Limit of the neigh'bring Land, ... Il.21.469.440.
Then from the lowest Stone shall *Troy* be mov'd— .... Il.21.504.442.
(For *Jove* had turn'd the Nation all to Stone:) .... Il.24.770.569.
His praise, eternal on the faithful stone, ... Od.1.307.47.
On polish'd stone before his Palace gate: .... Od.3.519.112.
And deep intrenchments, and high walls of stone, ... Od.7.59.236.
At last, the stone removing from the gate, ... Od.9.495.326.
High rais'd of stone; a shaded space around: .... Od.10.241.352.
Up the high hill he heaves a huge round stone; .... Od.11.736.422.
The huge round stone, resulting with a bound, ... Od.11.737.422.
Where bowls and urns were form'd of living stone, ... Od.13.126.8.
Fix her for ever, a memorial stone: .... Od.13.180.14.
A rural Portico of rugged stone: .... Od.14.10.35.
The wall was stone from neighbouring quarries born, ... Od.14.13.35.
His praise, eternal on the faithful stone, ... Od.14.405.55.
In sculptur'd stone immortaliz'd their care, ... Od.17.237.143.
And his crush'd forehead marks the stone with gore. .... Od.22.111.292.
His batter'd front and brains besmear the stone. .... Od.22.329.302.
And a red deluge floats the reeking stone. .... Od.22.346.304.
The Gods have form'd that rigid heart of stone! .... Od.23.106.324.
Thy praise eternal on the faithful stone .... Od.24.47.350.

STONE'S
Then heaving high the stone's unwieldy weight, ... Od.9.400.322.

STONES
Stones leap'd to *Form,* and *Rocks* began to *live;* .... 1.EOC.702.319.
Or how from joyning Stones the City sprung, ... 1.TrSt.11.409.
It shakes; the pondrous Stones disjoynted yield; .... 1.TrES.131.454.
And Trees, and Stones, and Farms, and Farmer fall. .... 4.2HE2.263.183.
Thinks that but words, and this but brick and stones? .... 4.1HE6.66.241.
Lord! Lord! how rattl'd then thy Stones, ... 6.79.55.219.
Their Stones and Arrows in a mingled Show'r. .... Il.3.114.195.
Vast Stones and Piles from their Foundation heaves, ... Il.12.31.82.
And Stones and Darts in mingled Tempests fly. .... Il.12.174.87.
And now the Stones descend in heavier Show'rs. .... Il.12.330.93.
It shakes; the pond'rous Stones disjointed yield; .... Il.12.485.99.
Thick Stones and Arrows intercept the Sky, ... Il.13.900.148.
While Stones and Darts in mingled Tempest flew; .... Il.15.709.223.
Compacted Stones the thick'ning Work compose, ... Il.16.258.249.
Stones follow Stones; some clatter on the Fields, ... Il.16.933.279.
Stones follow Stones; some clatter on the Fields, ... Il.16.933.279.
Inclos'd with Stones conspicuous from afar, ... Il.23.403.506.
His ragged claws are stuck with stones and sands; .... Od.5.552.199.
With show'rs of stones he drives them far away; .... Od.14.39.37.
And batter'd brains and blood besmear the stones. .... Od.24.211.358.

STONY
And foam and thunder on the stony Shore. .... Il.2.473.149.
Caresus roaring down the stony Hills, ... Il.12.18.82.
Thro' the long Walls the stony Show'rs were heard, ... Il.12.203.88.
So from each side increas'd the stony Rain, ... Il.12.343.94.
Clear of the stony Heap direct the Course; .... Il.23.414.506.
And dash'd like dogs against the stony floor: .... Od.9.344.320.
A stony image, in eternal night! .... Od.11.788.425.

STOOD
Around his Throne the Sea-born Brothers stood, ... 1.W-F.337.182.
And the *World's Victor* stood subdu'd by *Sound!* .... 1.EOC.381.284.
Receiv'd his Laws, and stood convinc'd 'twas fit .... 1.EOC.651.313.
Receiv'd his Rules, and stood convinc'd 'twas fit .... 1.EOC.651A.313.
Had stood neglected and a barren shade; .... 1.TrVP.64.380.
But lo! I saw, (as near her side I stood) .... 1.TrFD.27.387.
And stood the helpless witness of thy fate; .... 1.TrFD.54.388.
Like some sad Statue, speechless, pale, I stood; .... 1.TrSP.125.399.
Before my Sight a Watry Virgin stood, ... 1.TrSP.186.401.
She stood and cry'd, "O you that love in vain! .... 1.TrSP.187.401.
Who raise thy Temples where the Chariot stood .... 1.TrSt.388.426.
Oblique his Tusks, erect his Bristles stood, ... 1.TrSt.573.434.
And saw where *Teucer* with th' *Ajaces* stood, ... 1.TrES.61.451.
Fix'd in his Belt the feather'd Weapon stood, ... 1.TrES.137.454.
So stood the War, till *Hector's* matchless Might .... 1.TrES.171Z1.455.
Then with erected Eyes stood fix'd in Woe, ... 1.TrUl.72.468.
Celestial *Pallas,* stood before his Eyes; .... 1.TrUl.101.469.
Jove's heav'nly Daughter stood confess'd to Sight, ... 1.TrUl.163.471.
Satyrion near, with hot *Eringo's* stood, ... 2.ChJM.377.32.
The Servants round stood ready at their Call. .... 2.ChJM.405.34.
Look'd out, and stood restor'd to sudden Sight. .... 2.ChJM.749.51.
And stood content to rule by wholsome Laws; .... 2.ChWB.430.78.
Here stood *Ill-nature* like an *ancient Maid,* .... 2.RL4.27.185.
I stood, methought, betwixt Earth, Seas, and Skies; .... 2.TemF.11.254.
Superior, and alone, *Confucius* stood, ... 2.TemF.107.261.
The horrid Forms of *Scythian* Heroes stood, ... 2.TemF.126.264.
Within, stood Heroes who thro' loud Alarms .... 2.TemF.149.265.
High o'er the rest *Epaminondas* stood; .... 2.TemF.161.267.
At the dread Sound, pale Mortals stood aghast, ... 2.TemF.416.283.

STOOD (CONTINUED)

While thus I stood, intent to see and hear, ... 2.TemF.497.287.
Unbrib'd, unbloody, stood the blameless priest: ... 3.EOM3.158.109.
The Soul stood forth, nor kept a Thought within; ... 4.HS1.54.9.
"I make no question but the *Tow'r* had stood." ... 4.JD4.85.33.
Stood just a-tilt, the *Minister* came by. ... 4.JD4.175.41.
What tho' my Name stood rubric on the walls? ... 4.Arbu.215.111.
And a true *Pindar* stood without a head) ... 4.Arbu.236.112.
He stood the furious Foe, the timid Friend, ... 4.Arbu.343.120.
Here stood her Opium, here she nurs'd her Owls, ... 5.DunA1.35.O64.
Stood dauntless Curl, "Behold that rival here! ... 5.DunA2.54.104.
Full in the middle way there stood a lake, ... 5.DunA2.65.105.
Where the tall Nothing stood, or seem'd to stand; ... 5.DunA2.102.109.
Earless on high, stood un-abash'd Defoe, ... 5.DunA2.139.117.
Earless on high, stood pillory'd *D[efoe],* ... 5.DunA2.139A.117.
Here stood her Opium, here she nurs'd her Owls, ... 5.DunB1.271.290.
Stood dauntless Curl; "Behold that rival here! ... 5.DunB2.58.298.
Full in the middle way there stood a lake, ... 5.DunB2.69.299.
Where the tall Nothing stood, or seem'd to stand; ... 5.DunB2.110.300.
Earless on high, stood unabash'd De Foe, ... 5.DunB2.147.302.
Compos'd he stood, bold Benson thrust him by: ... 5.DunB4.110.352.
Th' Accus'd stood forth, and thus address'd the Queen. ... 5.DunB4.420.382.
Transported Demi-Gods stood round, ... 6.11.42.31.
Deny'd to reign, I stood resolv'd to die, ... 6.20.13.66.
In vain your guiltless laurels stood, ... 6.51i.5.151.
Stood Paramount in Pride; ... 6.79.22.218.
On Tiptoe then the Squire he stood, ... 6.94.57.261.
Stood up to dash each vain Pretender's Hope, ... 6.128.17.356.
Behind she stood, and by the Golden Hair ... Il.1.264.99.
To wait his Will two sacred Heralds stood, ... Il.1.420.107.
Suppliant the Goddess stood: One Hand she plac'd ... Il.1.650.118.
Oppress'd with gen'rous Grief the Heroe stood, ... Il.2.207.138.
So throng'd, so close, the *Grecian* Squadrons stood ... Il.2.558.154.
Where *Pytho, Daulis, Cyparissus* stood, ... Il.2.626.157.
The shaded Tomb of old *Æpytus* stood; ... Il.2.732.161.
Last under *Prothous* the *Magnesians* stood, ... Il.2.916.167.
And Crowds stood wond'ring at the passing Show; ... Il.3.68.192.
Each Army stood: The *Spartan* Chief reply'd. ... Il.3.134.196.
Against the Manlike *Amazons* we stood, ... Il.3.249.204.
With flaming Shields in martial Circle stood. ... Il.4.122.226.
Such, and so thick, th' embattel'd Squadrons stood, ... Il.4.322.236.
The Tumult late begun, they stood intent ... Il.4.386.239.
So sinks a Tow'r, that long Assaults had stood ... Il.4.528.246.
A Chief stood nigh who from *Abydos* came, ... Il.4.573.249.
And quiv'ring in his heaving Bosom stood: ... Il.4.613.250.
Beside him stood his Lance, distain'd with Gore, ... Il.5.447.289.
There stopp'd the Car, and there the Coursers stood, ... Il.5.459.290.
Meantime on *Ilion's* Tow'r *Apollo* stood, ... Il.5.551.295.
Erect he stood, and vig'rous from his Wound: ... Il.5.630.298.
Stern *Diomed* with either *Ajax* stood, ... Il.5.635.298.
Atrides mark'd him where sublime he stood; ... Il.5.707.301.
The Head stood fix'd, the quiv'ring Legs in Air: ... Il.5.718.301.
Full in the Boaster's Neck the Weapon stood, ... Il.5.816.305.
The fainting Soul stood ready wing'd for Flight, ... Il.5.856.307.
While near *Tydides* stood th' *Athenian* Maid: ... Il.5.987.314.
He stood suspended with the lifted Dart: ... Il.6.64.326.
Where *Hector* stood, with great *Æneas* join'd, ... Il.6.93.328.
Pensive she stood on *Ilion's* Tow'ry Height, ... Il.6.468.349.
Stood in the Gates, and ask'd what way she bent ... Il.6.474.350.
The Nurse stood near, in whose Embraces prest ... Il.6.496.351.
And the big Tear stood trembling in her Eye. ... Il.6.509.351.
He stood, the Bulwark of the *Grecian* Band. ... Il.7.258.377.
All *Troy* stood trembling at the mighty Man. ... Il.7.260.377.
He rais'd his Voice: The Hosts stood list'ning round. ... Il.7.459.387.
Strong Piles infix'd stood adverse to the Foe. ... Il.7.525.390.
Humbled they stood; pale Horror seiz'd on all, ... Il.7.574.393.
Trembling they stood before their Sov'reign's Look; ... Il.8.37.397.
That wither'd all their Host: Like *Mars* he stood, ... Il.8.419.417.
The *Hours* unloos'd them, panting as they stood, ... Il.8.536.422.
There stood the Chariot beaming forth its Rays, ... Il.8.548.422.
With more than vulgar Grief he stood oppress'd; ... Il.9.21.432.
The *Greeks* stood witness, all our Army heard. ... Il.9.50.434.
Next him *Ascalaphus, Iälmen,* stood, ... Il.9.113.437.
Long sleepless Nights in heavy Arms I stood, ... Il.9.430.453.
A Wood of Spears stood by, that fixt upright, ... Il.10.174.9.
The Wretch stood prop'd, and quiver'd as he stood; ... Il.10.444.23.
The Wretch stood prop'd, and quiver'd as he stood; ... Il.10.444.23.
Doubtful he stood, or with his reeking Blade ... Il.10.588.28.
An empty Space where late the Coursers stood, ... Il.10.611.29.
There wise *Polydamas* and *Hector* stood; ... Il.11.75.38.
The daring Wretch who once in Council stood ... Il.11.181.43.
Safe from the Darts, the Care of Heav'n he stood, ... Il.11.215.45.
And thro' his Arm stood forth the barbed Dart. ... Il.11.328.49.
Stood check'd a while, and *Greece* respir'd again. ... Il.11.424.53.
Amaz'd he stood, with Terrors not his own. ... Il.11.671.65.
In his broad Buckler many a Weapon stood, ... Il.11.698.66.
Fix'd in his nervous Thigh the Weapon stood, ... Il.11.710.66.
Unheard approach'd, and stood before the Tent. ... Il.11.789.71.
While round the Town the fierce *Epeians* stood. ... Il.11.869.74.
This stood, while *Hector* and *Achilles* rag'd, ... Il.12.11.81.
No Fragment tells where once the Wonder stood; ... Il.12.34.83.
As yet the Bulwark stood, and brav'd the Storm; ... Il.12.38.83.
In Arms with these the mighty *Asius* stood, ... Il.12.109.85.
Oppos'd their Breasts, and stood themselves the War. ... Il.12.162.87.
These on the farther Bank now stood and gaz'd, ... Il.12.229.89.
And saw where *Teucer* with th' *Ajaces* stood, ... Il.12.405.96.
Fix'd in his Belt the feather'd Weapon stood, ... Il.12.491.99.
So stood the War, till *Hector's* matchless Might ... Il.12.527.101.
So stood *Idomeneus,* his Javelin shook, ... Il.13.602.135.
Like Gods of War, dispensing Fate, they stood, ... Il.13.634.136.
Stuck deep in Earth, and quiver'd where it stood. ... Il.13.639.136.
In the broad Buckler half the Weapon stood; ... Il.13.714.138.
And this stood adverse with the bended Bow: ... Il.13.736.139.
Cebrion, Phalces, stern *Orthæus* stood, ... Il.13.994.152.
Beside him sudden, unperceiv'd he stood, ... Il.14.409.183.
So just the Stroke, that yet the Body stood ... Il.14.547.189.

STOOD (CONTINUED)

Stood shining o'er him, half unseal'd his Sight: ... Il.15.279.207.
And stood by *Meges'* side, a sudden Aid, ... Il.15.637.221.
For this in Arms the warring Nations stood, ... Il.15.858.229.
The War stood still, and all around them gaz'd, ... Il.16.334.255.
The great *Pæonian,* bold *Pyrechmes,* stood; ... Il.16.342.256.
A living Prize not long the *Trojan* stood; ... Il.16.396.258.
Nor stood to combate, nor had Force to fly: ... Il.16.489.262.
Apollo heard; and suppliant as he stood, ... Il.16.647.269.
Thus while he thought, beside him *Phœbus* stood, ... Il.16.873.277.
Nor tho' disarm'd, *Patroclus'* Fury stood: ... Il.16.980.281.
Where lab'ring on the left the Warrior stood, ... Il.17.125.292.
And now before, and now behind he stood: ... Il.17.145.293.
And deep transpiercing, thro' the Shoulder stood; ... Il.17.359.301.
And hemm'd with bristled Spears, the *Grecians* stood; ... Il.17.408.303.
So tugging round the Corps both Armies stood; ... Il.17.454.304.
The pensive Steeds of great *Achilles* stood; ... Il.17.485.306.
Restive they stood, and obstinate in Woe: ... Il.17.491.307.
No longer *Hector* with his *Trojans* stood, ... Il.17.602.311.
There stood a *Trojan* not unknown to Fame, ... Il.17.648.313.
Sudden at *Hector's* Side *Apollo* stood, ... Il.17.654.313.
High on his Chariot as the *Cretan* stood, ... Il.17.687.314.
Have try'd it, and have stood. The Hero said. ... Il.17.807.320.
Stood *Nestor's* Son, the Messenger of Woe: ... Il.18.4.322.
Silent they stood: *Polydamas* at last, ... Il.18.293.336.
Stern in superior Grief *Pelides* stood; ... Il.18.367.339.
Stood prompt to move, the Azure Goddess came: ... Il.18.448.342.
(The crystal Drops stood trembling in her Eyes) ... Il.18.500.345.
A Place for Ambush fit, they found, and stood ... Il.18.603.352.
There Tumult, there Contention stood confest; ... Il.18.619.352.
Trembling he stood before the golden Wain, ... Il.19.448.390.
Greece sheath'd in Arms, beside her Vessels stood; ... Il.20.2.392.
Dreadful he stood in Front of all his Host; ... Il.20.59.396.
The Mountain shook, the rapid Stream stood still. ... Il.20.74.397.
Advanc'd upon the Field there stood a Mound ... Il.20.174.401.
And stood all impotent, expecting Fate: ... Il.20.556.417.
High o'er the Scene of Death *Achilles* stood, ... Il.20.587.418.
The young *Lycaon* in his Passage stood; ... Il.21.41.423.
And while above the Spear suspended stood, ... Il.21.80.424.
On him *Achilles* rush'd: He fearless stood, ... Il.21.161.428.
Spun forth, in Earth the fasten'd Weapon stood. ... Il.21.184.429.
Repulsive of his Might the Weapon stood: ... Il.21.192.429.
Slidd'ring, and stagg'ring. On the Border stood ... Il.21.267.431.
At ev'ry Step, before *Achilles* stood ... Il.21.382.436.
He said, and stood; collected in his Might; ... Il.21.675.450.
Then graceful as he stood, in act to throw ... Il.21.689.450.
There fixt he stood before the *Scæan* Gate; ... Il.22.10.453.
He stood, and question'd thus his mighty Mind. ... Il.22.137.458.
Proud on his Car th' insulting Victor stood, ... Il.22.501.477.
Stood at my side, a pensive, plaintive Ghost; ... Il.23.127.493.
But fast beside *Achilles* stood in Pray'r, ... Il.23.238.499.
Of thronging *Grecians* round *Achilles* stood; ... Il.23.291.501.
First stood the Prizes to reward the Force ... Il.23.327.503.
Like the full Moon, stood obvious to the Sight. ... Il.23.539.511.
Oppos'd in Arms not long they idly stood, ... Il.23.963.527.
Each stood in order: First *Epæus* threw; ... Il.23.995.529.
Stood proud to Hymn, and tune his youthful Lyre. ... Il.24.83.538.
Pale grew his Face, and upright stood his Hair; ... Il.24.442.554.
Around, at awful distance, stood the rest. ... Il.24.583.561.
Thus stood th' Attendants stupid with Surprize; ... Il.24.594.561.
Two Urns by *Jove's* high Throne have ever stood, ... Il.24.663.564.
Where seemly rang'd in peaceful order stood ... Od.1.169.40.
His Father's throne he fill'd: while distant stood ... Od.2.17.61.
And as he stood, he spoke and wept by turns. ... Od.2.32.61.
To tread the walks of death he stood prepar'd, ... Od.2.311.76.
Untouch'd they stood, 'till his long labours o'er ... Od.2.388.80.
At nine green Theatres the *Pylians* stood, ... Od.3.8.86.
In act to strike: Before him *Perseus* stood, ... Od.3.562.115.
I stood restor'd, and tears had ceas'd to flow; ... Od.4.730.153.
On the lone Island's utmost verge there stood ... Od.5.305.185.
All radiant on the Raft the Goddess stood: ... Od.5.429.193.
Thus long debating in himself he stood: ... Od.5.612.201.
All but the Nymph: the nymph stood fix'd alone, ... Od.6.167.216.
Raptur'd I stood, and as this hour amaz'd, ... Od.6.199.219.
His step a Virgin met, and stood before: ... Od.7.25.235.
Then manifest of heav'n the vision stood, ... Od.7.271.249.
As some lone mountain's monstrous growth he stood, ... Od.9.223.316.
In sacred shade his honour'd mansion stood ... Od.9.232.316.
With broken hearts my sad companions stood, ... Od.10.227.351.
Now on the threshold of the dome they stood, ... Od.10.252.354.
Astonish'd at the sight, aghast I stood, ... Od.11.55.383.
Back started the pale throngs, and trembling stood. ... Od.11.62.383.
Regardless of her son the Parent stood. ... Od.11.111.386.
Still in the dark abodes of death I stood, ... Od.11.186.390.
Ghost throng'd on ghost (a dire assembly) stood! ... Od.11.276.395.
Here ramparts stood, there tow'rs rose high in air, ... Od.11.323.398.
Heav'd on *Olympus* tott'ring *Ossa* stood; ... Od.11.387.402.
Of god-like Heroes who uninjur'd stood ... Od.11.477.408.
A gloomy shade, the sullen *Ajax* stood; ... Od.11.666.417.
There war and havoc the destruction stood, ... Od.11.755.423.
All trembling, deafen'd, and aghast we stood! ... Od.12.243.443.
Aghast I stood, a monument of woe! ... Od.12.311.447.
Before the throne of mighty *Jove* he stood; ... Od.13.146.12.
Then with erected eyes stood fix'd in woe, ... Od.13.239.17.
Celestial *Pallas,* stood before his eyes; ... Od.13.268.18.
Jove's heav'nly daughter stood confess'd to sight. ... Od.13.330.23.
Ev'n now a Vision stood before my eye, ... Od.14.560.64.
He took th' occasion as they stood intent, ... Od.15.499.94.
Has stood our Father's hospitable door; ... Od.15.552.96.
Alone to *Ithacus* she stood display'd, ... Od.16.172.111.
With gather'd sails they stood, and lifted oars. ... Od.16.369.124.
Spurn'd, but not mov'd: He, like a pillar stood, ... Od.17.274.145.
The Heroe stood self-conquer'd, and endur'd. ... Od.17.279.145.
There stood an empty seat, where late was plac'd ... Od.17.404.152.
He stood, and mov'd not, like a marble rock; ... Od.17.549.159.
And his flesh trembled as aghast he stood: ... Od.18.89.171.

STOOD (CONTINUED)
Absorpt in thought, on vengeance fix'd he stood. ....Od.18.394.186.
A lofty copse, the growth of ages, stood: ....Od.19.512.221.
Eager they view'd; with joy they stood amaz'd; ....Od.21.232.271.
Thus dreadful he. Confus'd the Suitors stood, ...Od.22.53.289.
There stood a window near, whence looking down ....Od.22.142.293.
On heaps of death the stern *Ulysses* stood, ...Od.22.438.309.
There terrible in arms *Ulysses* stood, ...Od.23.47.321.
Fierce on the threshold then in arms he stood; ....Od.24.203.358.
There stood his mansion of the rural sort, ...Od.24.238.360.
In this array the kingly Gard'ner stood, ...Od.24.267.361.
Doubtful he stood, if instant to embrace ....Od.24.275.363.
Stood the great son, heart-wounded with the sight: ....Od.24.372.367.
Who now before him, now beside him stood, ...Od.24.512.372.
Stood in the way, and at a glance beheld ....Od.24.568.375.

STOOD'ST
Thou stood'st a Rival of Imperial Pow'r; ....Il.1.248.98.
That thou stood'st forth, of all th' Æthereal Host, ...Il.1.515.113.

STOOL
"My foot-stool earth, my canopy the skies." ....3.EOM1.140.32.
Beneath her foot-stool, *Science* groans in Chains, ...5.DunB4.21.342.
Her feet supported with a stool of state; ....Od.1.172.40.
With ivory silver'd thick the foot-stool shone, ...Od.19.70.196.

STOOP
Wou'd all but *stoop* to what they *understand*. .... 1.EOC.67.246.
Stoop with their sounding Pinions to the Fight; ....1.TrES.220.458.
Stoop with re-sounding Pinions to the Fight; ....1.TrES.220A.458.
Do you but stoop, and leave the rest to me. ....2.ChJM.735.50.
And learned Athens to our Art must stoop, ...4.2HE1.47.197.
P. The brib'd Elector— *Fr.* There you stoop too low. ....4.EpS2.25.314.
Praise cannot stoop, like Satire, to the Ground; ....4.EpS2.110.319.
The sturdy Squire to Gallic masters stoop, ...5.DunB4.595.402.
Can stoop to pick up *Strings* and *Sticks*. .... 6.135.12.366.
Yet stoop to bless a child or wife: ....6.141.10.381.
So *Greece* shall stoop before our conqu'ring Pow'r, ...Il.12.91.84.
Stoop with re-sounding Pinions to the Fight; ....Il.16.523.264.
Troy shall not stoop ev'n to *Achilles'* Hand. ....Il.16.866.277.
They stoop not, these, to mortal man's Command, ...Il.17.81.291.
Or stoop to none but great *Achilles'* Hand. ....Il.17.82.291.
Or stoop to tasks a rural Lord demands. ....Od.17.25.133.
Stoop from the mountains on the feather'd race, ...Od.22.338.303.

STOOP'D
He wept, kind Soul! and stoop'd to kiss my Face; ....2.ChWB.422.77.
But stoop'd to Truth, and moraliz'd his song: ....4.Arbu.341.120.
He stoop'd to Truth, and moraliz'd his song: ....4.Arbu.341A.120.
Have stoop'd to serve an haughty *Roman* dame? ....6.20.6.66.
He stoop'd to Reason, and his Rage resign'd. ....Il.7.140.370.
With that, they step'd aside, and stoop'd their head, ...Il.10.415.21.
None stoop'd a Thought to base inglorious Flight; ....Il.11.95.39.
The *Trojan* stoop'd, the Javelin pass'd in Air. ....Il.11.300.48.
Just as he stoop'd, *Agastrophus's* Crest ....Il.11.479.55.
Now *Troy* had stoop'd beneath his matchless Pow'r, ...Il.16.857.276.
That Plume, which never stoop'd to Earth before, ...Il.16.961.280.
He stoop'd, while o'er his Head the flying Spear ....Il.22.351.470.
When lo! fierce *Scylla* stoop'd to seize her prey, ...Od.12.294.446.

STOOPING
Prop'd on his Staff, and stooping as he goes, ...1.TrVP.48.379.
When tender Youth has wedded stooping Age. ....2.ChJM.340.30.
There great *Alcides* stooping with his Toil, ...2.TemF.81.258.
Say, will the falcon, stooping from above, ...3.EOM3.53.97.
Yet ceas'd not *Hector* thus; but, stooping down, ...Il.7.315.379.
The *Cretan* saw; and stooping, caus'd to glance ....Il.13.511.131.
The Victor stooping, from the Death withdrew: ....Il.15.617.220.
And stooping, darkens with his Wings the Flood. ....Il.15.839.229.
Who stooping forward from the Death withdrew; ....Il.16.740.272.
Stooping, he shun'd; the Jav'lin idly fled, ...Il.17.596.311.
The youngest Hope of *Priam's* stooping Age: ....Il.20.472.414.
Jove's Cyprian Daughter stooping on the Land, ...Il.21.486.441.
He spoke; and past: *Latona*, stooping low, ...Il.21.585.446.
To the wide Main then stooping from the Skies, ...Il.23.266.500.
As stooping dexter with resounding Wings ....Il.24.393.552.
And stooping enter'd at the lowly door. ....Od.24.422.369.

STOOPS
And while the Muse now stoops, or now ascends, ...3.EOM4.375.164.
Th' Address, the Delicacy—stoops at once, ...3.Ep2.85.57.
And stoops from Angels to the Dregs of Earth: ....4.EpS1.142.309.
Then fierce *Tydides* stoops; and from the Fields ....Il.5.369.284.
Stoops down impetuous, while they light for Food, ...Il.15.838.229.
Then stoops, and sowsing on the quiv'ring Hare, ...Il.17.765.318.
And stoops impetuous from the cleaving Skies. ....Il.22.242.465.
Stoops from the Clouds to truss the quiv'ring Hare. ....Il.22.392.471.
And stoops on *Hellespont's* resounding Sea. ....Il.24.424.553.
And stoops incumbent on the rolling deep. ....Od.5.63.174.
Stoops to the ground, and disappoints the blow. ....Od.18.439.189.

STOP
Might stop the Progress of his warlike Host, ...1.TrES.116.454.
They stop the Chariot, and they board the Barge. ....4.Arbu.10.96.
Stop, or turn nonsense at one glance of Thee? ....4.HOde1.40.153.
Stop, or turn nonsense at one glance from Thee? ....4.HOde1.40A.153.
To stop my ears to their confounded stuff. ....4.2HE2.152.175.
But you may read it, I stop short. ....4.1HE7.84.273.
To stop thy foolish views, thy long desires, ...4.1HE1.75.283.
Fr. stop! stop! *P.* Must Satire then, nor *rise*, nor *fall* ....4.EpS2.52.315.
Fr. stop! stop! *P.* Must Satire then, nor *rise*, nor *fall* ....4.EpS2.52.315.
Let it not stop when entred at the Ear ....6.2.9.6.
Your Nose you stop, your Eyes you turn away. ....6.96iv.8.276.
"Nor stop at Flattery or Fib. ....6.140.24.378.
Thou who shalt stop, where *Thames'* translucent Wave ....6.142.1.382.
You who shall stop, where *Thames'* translucent Wave ....6.142.1A.382.

STOP (CONTINUED)
Practis'd alike to turn, to stop, to chace, ...Il.5.280.280.
Practis'd alike to turn, to stop, to chace, ...Il.8.135.404.
To stop his Coursers, and to stand the Fight; ....Il.8.205.407.
Thaumantia! mount the Winds, and stop their Car; ....Il.8.488.420.
To save thy *Greeks*, and stop the Course of Fate; ....Il.9.321.449.
Might stop the Progress of his warlike Host, ...Il.12.470.98.
And stop the *Trojans*, tho' impell'd by *Jove*. ....Il.15.679.222.
If ought from *Jove*, or *Thetis*, stop thy Arm, ...Il.16.55.237.
No Stop, no Check, the Steeds of *Peleus* knew; ....Il.16.458.260.
Flies any *Trojan?* I shall stop his Flight. ....Il.18.346.338.
And stop the Babe, just issuing to the Day. ....Il.19.118.376.
No Stop, no Check, no Aid! With feeble pace, ...Il.21.617.448.
No stop, no stay; no thought to ask, or tell, ...Il.21.719.451.
Scarce the whole People stop his desp'rate Course, ...Il.22.524.478.
And Prince! to stop the source of future ill, ...Od.20.391.251.
Ah stop the Heroe's unresisted hands, ...Od.22.408.307.

STOP'D
Since Fate relentless stop'd their Heav'nly Voice, ...1.W-F.277.174.
You stop'd with Kisses my inchanting Tongue, ...1.TrSP.55.396.
Grief chill'd my Breast, and stop'd my freezing Blood; ....1.TrSP.126.399.
These stop'd the Moon, and call'd th' unbody'd Shades ....2.TemF.101.260.
'Till Death untimely stop'd his tuneful Tongue. ....6.84.2.238.
When Death untimely stop'd his tuneful Tongue. ....6.84.2A.238.
There *Juno* stop'd, and (her fair Steeds unloos'd) ....Il.5.966.312.
The Spot, where *Hector* stop'd his Rage before, ...Il.10.234.12.
Stop'd short of Life, nor with his Entrails mix'd. ....Il.11.550.58.
Stop'd his swift Chariot, and his Steeds unbound, ...Il.13.54.107.
Resistless when he rag'd, and when he stop'd, unmov'd. ....Il.13.200.115.
Be stop'd against the song! 'tis death to hear! ....Od.12.62.433.

STOP'ST
O Thou who stop'st, where *Thames'* translucent Wave ....6.142.1B.382.

STOPP'D
She stopp'd, and sighing, Oh good Gods, she cry'd, ...2.ChJM.720.49.
But *Fate* and *Jove* had stopp'd the *Baron's* Ears. ....2.RL5.2.199.
I'm stopp'd by all the fools I meet, ...4.HS6.111.257.
There stopp'd the Car, and there the Coursers stood, ...Il.5.459.290.
Stopp'd at *Ulysses'* Tent, and call'd aloud. ....Il.10.157.8.
When brave *Tydides* stopp'd; a gen'rous Thought ....Il.10.435.23.
Nor stopp'd the Fury of his vengeful Hand, ...Il.10.568.28.
Ulysses stopp'd; to him *Tydides* bore ....Il.10.620.29.
And stopp'd my Chariot, and detain'd my Arms. ....Il.11.855.74.
Till *Pallas* stopp'd us where *Alisium* flows. ....Il.11.890.75.
A signal Omen stopp'd the passing Host, ...Il.12.231.89.
Then stopp'd, and panted, where the Chariots lie; ....Il.15.3.193.
Stopp'd in the Tumult *Cleobulus* lies, ...Il.16.394.258.
Full in the Mouth is stopp'd the rushing Tide, ...Il.17.312.299.
But stopp'd, and rested, by the third repell'd; ....Il.20.317.407.
And stopp'd *Demuchus*, great *Philetor's* Heir, ...Il.20.528.416.
There stopp'd the Goddess, and her speech renew'd. ....Od.7.62.236.
There humbly stopp'd with conscious shame and awe, ...Od.10.67.342.
The Suitors stopp'd, and gaz'd the Heroe o'er. ....Od.24.30.348.

STOPPEN
And stoppen, and lough, and callen out,— ....6.14i.13.42.

STOPPING
Their Chariots stopping, at the silver Spring ....Il.24.430.554.

STOPS
These touch the vocal Stops, and those the trembling String. ..2.ChJM.321.29.
There stops the Instinct, and there ends the care; ....3.EOM3.128.105.
Nor stops, for one bad Cork, his Butler's pay, ...4.HS2.63.59.
—but here she stops, she yawns, she nods;— ....5.DunB4.605B.403.
Confus'd he stops, a Length of Country past, ...Il.5.738.302.
There stops—So *Hector:* Their whole Force he prov'd, ...Il.13.199.115.
Who stops to plunder, in this signal Hour, ...Il.15.400.212.
Yet stops, and turns, and saves his lov'd Allies. ....Il.16.433.259.
Apollo dreadful stops thy middle way; ....Il.16.952.280.
Not a whole River stops the Hero's Course, ...Il.21.354.435.
He stops, and questions thus his mighty Soul. ....Il.21.650.449.
Grief stops his Voice, a Torrent drowns his Eyes; ....Il.23.477.509.
And *Nestor's* Youngest stops the vents of breath, ...Od.3.579.116.
There stops, and anxious with his soul debates, ...Od.7.108.239.

STOPT
Be stopt in *Vials*, or transfixt with *Pins;* .... 2.RL2.126.167.
And love's warm tyde for ever stopt in thee. ....2.ElAb.258Z2.340.
Then urg'd by C[artere]t, or by C[artere]t stopt, ...4.1740.31.333.
Here stopt the Goddess; and in pomp proclaims ....5.DunB2.365.315.
It stopt, I stopt; it mov'd, I mov'd again. ....5.DunB4.428.383.
It stopt, I stopt; it mov'd, I mov'd again. ....5.DunB4.428.383.
There he stopt short, nor since has writ a tittle, ...6.49i.9.137.
Here stopt by hasty Death, Alexis lies, ...6.82xi.1.236.
She said, but broken Accents stopt her Voice, ...6.96ii.71.273.
She spoke, but broken Accents stopt her Voice, ...6.96ii.71A.273.
Stopt short of Life, and mock'd the Shooter's Art. ....Il.5.139.273.
One Hand embrac'd them close, one stopt the Dart; ....Il.21.82.425.
But first before *Antinous* stopt, and said. ....Od.17.496.156.
Then stopt the Goddess, trembled, and retir'd. ....Od.24.625.377.

STOR'D
His court with nettles, moats with cresses stor'd, ...3.Ep3.183.109.
His Study! with what Authors is it stor'd? ....3.Ep4.133.150.
(This from his Pledge I learn'd, which safely stor'd ....Il.6.275.340.
A Bow and Quiver, with bright Arrows stor'd: ....Il.10.308.16.
The well-stor'd Quiver on his Shoulders hung: ....Il.15.520.217.
With wine and viands I the vessel stor'd: ....Od.4.985.163.
And the full decks with copious viands stor'd. ....Od.5.340.188.
A Palace stor'd with treasures shou'd be thine. ....Od.7.402.256.
And brought another with provisions stor'd. ....Od.9.247.317.
Gifts, which to distant ages safely stor'd, ...Od.15.63.72.
There, while within the poop with care he stor'd ....Od.15.232.79.

STOR'D (CONTINUED)

Not large, but fruitful; stor'd with grass to keep .... Od.15.442.91.
With flocks and herds each grassy plain is stor'd; .... Od.19.133.199.

STORE

Th'industrious Bees neglect their Golden Store; .... 1.PWi.51.92.
Of ancient Writ unlocks the learned Store, ... 1.W-F.247.172.
There are whom Heav'n has blest with store of Wit, ... 1.EOC.80A.248.
The poorest shepherd best may tell his store. .... 1.TrPA.81.368.
With nice Exactness weighs her woolly Store) .... 1.TrES.168Z2.455.
Then on the Sands he rang'd his wealthy Store, ... 1.TrUl.94.469.
Those that are blest with Store of Grace Divine .... 2.ChJM.125.20.
Not ev'ry Man's oblig'd to sell his Store, ... 2.ChWB.42.58.
With store of Pray'rs, for Mornings, Nights, and Noons, ... 2.RL4.29.185.
Of Loss and Gain, of Famine and of Store, ... 2.TemF.450.285.
When Catiline by rapine swell'd his store, ... 3.Ep1.212.33.
To Heirs unknown descends th' unnumber'd store .... 3.Ep2.149A.62.
To Heirs unknown descends th' unguarded store .... 3.Ep2.149.62.
Glorious Ambition! Peter, swell thy store, ... 3.Ep3.127.102.
Who sees pale Mammon pine amidst his store, ... 3.Ep3.173.107.
No Wit to flatter, left of all his store! .... 3.Ep3.311.119.
Oh Impudence of wealth! with all thy store, ... 4.HS2.117.63.
'Tis one thing madly to disperse my store, ... 4.2HE2.292.185.
I ask not to increase my store; .... 4.HS6.8.251.
So spins the silkworm small its slender store, ... 5.DunA1.171.84.
So spins the silk-worm small its slender store, ... 5.DunB4.253.369.
Dropt the dull lumber of the Latin store, ... 5.DunB4.319.374.
Exceed their promise in the ripen'd store, ... 6.14iv.19.47.
October, store, and best *Virginia,* .... 6.39.5.110.
October, store, the best *Virginia,* .... 6.39.5A.110.
To Heirs unknown, descends th' unnumber'd Store, ... 6.154.35.403.
And bribe thy Friendship with a boundless Store. .... Il.1.284.100.
Hence let us fly, and let him waste his Store .... Il.2.294.141.
And where *Pellenè* yields her fleecy Store, ... Il.2.691.159.
To Strangers now descends his heapy Store, ... Il.5.202.276.
Ships thou hast store, and nearest to the Main, ... Il.9.62.434.
Then shall he store (when *Greece* the spoil divides) .... Il.9.177.441.
My self will give the Dow'r; so vast a Store, ... Il.9.193.442.
The proffer'd Presents, an exhaustless Store. .... Il.9.343.450.
Then shalt thou store (when *Greece* the Spoil divides) .... Il.9.364.451.
Himself will give the Dow'r; so vast a Store, ... Il.9.380.451.
On whom his Passion, lavish of his Store, ... Il.11.317.49.
Then *Ida's* Summits pour'd their wat'ry Store; .... Il.12.16.82.
With nice Exactness weighs her woolly Store) .... Il.12.524.101.
Spears I have store, (and *Trojan* Lances all) .... Il.13.339.121.
From all thy Fountains swell thy wat'ry Store, ... Il.21.363.435.
And add half *Ilion's* yet remaining Store, ... Il.22.161.459.
Shou'd *Troy,* to bribe me, bring forth all her Store, ... Il.22.439.473.
Some Gift must grace *Eumelus;* view thy Store .... Il.23.629.514.
What yet most precious of thy Store remains, ... Il.24.468.556.
The strength of wheat, and wines, and ample store. .... Od.2.427.81.
And when he heard the long disastrous store .... Od.4.203.129.
Replete with mail, and military store, ... Od.4.1031.166.
His vessels loaded with a plenteous store .... Od.5.50.174.
To store the vessel let the care be mine, ... Od.5.213.181.
This store, with joy the patient Heroe found, ... Od.5.628.202.
Where the bold youth, the num'rous fleets to store, ... Od.6.319.226.
With fresh provision hence our fleet to store .... Od.9.264.317.
Now *Æolus,* ye see, augments his store: .... Od.10.48.341.
And on the surface shone the holy store. .... Od.11.34.381.
He pours his wat'ry store, the Virgin burns; .... Od.11.284.396.
Lo where he lies, amidst a shining store .... Od.13.158.13.
Then on the sands he rang'd his wealthy store, ... Od.13.261.18.
I saw my self the vast unnumber'd store .... Od.14.359.51.
Fraught with bold warriors and a boundless store. .... Od.14.424.56.
With store to heap above him, and below, ... Od.14.590.65.
Welcom'd with gifts of price, a sumless store! .... Od.19.312.209.
So rich the value of a store so vast .... Od.19.337.210.
With wither'd foliage strew'd, a heapy store! .... Od.19.515.221.
And quiver'd deaths, a formidable store; .... Od.22.4.286.
Soon as his store of flying fates was spent, ... Od.22.136.293.
Sudden his eyes releas'd their wat'ry store; .... Od.24.273.363.

STORES

No weeping orphan saw his father's stores .... 2.ElAb.135.330.
"How those in common all their Stores bestow, ... 3.EOM3.185A.112.
(Rich were the Man, whose ample Stores exceed .... Il.9.163.440.
(Rich were the Man, whose ample Stores exceed .... Il.9.350.450.
Sunk were her Treasures, and her Stores decay'd; .... Il.18.340.338.
From forth his open'd Stores, this said, he drew .... Il.24.281.548.
Seem'd all too mean the Stores he could employ, ... Il.24.289.548.
Thou, as thou may'st, these boundless Stores enjoy; .... Il.24.701.566.
His treasur'd stores these Cormorants consume, ... Od.1.207.42.
My stores in riotous expence devour, ... Od.1.324.48.
Your patrimonial stores in peace possess; .... Od.1.511.56.
Threat on, till all thy stores in waste decay. .... Od.2.232.72.
(When night advances) bear the naval stores; .... Od.2.328.77.
And stow'd within its womb the naval stores. .... Od.2.439.82.
He bids them bring their stores: th' attending train .... Od.2.456.83.
Search all thy stores of faithful memory: .... Od.3.123.91.
And brought our captives and our stores aboard; .... Od.3.186.95.
Amassing gold, and gath'ring naval stores; .... Od.3.385.105.
His drooping vigour, and exhausted stores. .... Od.4.492.143.
Selected from my stores, of matchless price .... Od.4.833.158.
His stores ye ravage and usurp his state. .... Od.4.923.161.
Her self supply'd the stores and rich array; .... Od.7.351.253.
Low lies our Isle, yet blest in fruitful stores; .... Od.9.27.303.
Be it my task to send with ample stores .... Od.11.438.406.
The circling year I wait, with ampler stores .... Od.11.446.406.
Our task be now thy treasur'd stores to save, ... Od.13.417.26.
Nine ships I mann'd equip'd with ready stores, ... Od.14.280.49.
For fair *Dulichium* crown'd with fruitful stores; .... Od.14.372.53.
Hence therefore, while thy stores thy own remain; .... Od.15.23.71.
My stores expos'd and fenceless house demand .... Od.15.104.73.
Their stores compleat, and ready now to weigh, ... Od.15.493.94.
With speed debarking land the naval stores; .... Od.16.347.123.

STORES (CONTINUED)

They moor the vessel and unlade the stores: .... Od.16.375.124.
Instant convey those steely stores of war .... Od.19.5.193.
These swarthy arms among the covert stores .... Od.19.20.193.
His dome dishonour'd, and exhausted stores.— .... Od.19.183.200.
His dome dishonour'd, and exhausted stores; .... Od.19.620.226.
Stores from the royal magazine I bring, ... Od.22.156.294.

STORIED

Himself among the storied Chiefs he spies, ... 5.DunA2.143.118.
Himself amongst the storied Chiefs he spies, ... 5.DunA2.143A.118.
To wound with storied grief the filial ear: .... Od.4.440.140.
The storied labours of thy father's friend: .... Od.4.468.142.
The storied labours of my wand'ring Lord, ... Od.19.113.198.
When time shall prove the storied blessing true: .... Od.19.355.211.

STORIES

Who tell us these troublesome stories, ... 6.42iv.3.118.
Hum half a tune, tell stories to the squire; .... 6.45.20.125.

STORK

Who bid the stork, Columbus-like, explore .... 3.EOM3.105.102.
The Haunt of the voracious *Stork* or *Bittern,* .... 6.26i.4.79.

STORM

The Storm the dark *Lycean* Groves display'd, ... 1.TrSt.508.431.
Menestheus from on high the Storm beheld, ... 1.TrES.57.451.
Nor Heat could melt, nor beating Storm invade. .... 2.TemF.48.256.
He mounts the storm, and walks upon the wind. .... 3.EOM2.110.68.
Nor more a storm her Hate than Gratitude. .... 3.Ep2.132.61.
A Pedant makes; the Storm of *Gonson's* Lungs, ... 4.JD4.53.29.
As drives the storm, at any door I knock, ... 4.1HE1.25.281.
Rides in the whirlwind, and directs the storm. .... 5.DunA3.260.179.
Rides in the whirlwind, and directs the storm. .... 5.DunB3.264.333.
Spent in a sudden storm of lust, ... 6.51ii.18.153.
She sobb'd a Storm, and wip'd her flowing Eyes, ... 6.96ii.73.273.
No more a Storm her Hate, than Gratitude: .... 6.154.18.403.
A Swain surveys the gath'ring Storm below; .... Il.4.315.235.
He dreads th' impending Storm, and drives his Flock .... Il.4.320.236.
Till, with the growing Storm, the Deeps arise, ... Il.4.482.243.
Thro' the thick Storm of singing Spears he flies, ... Il.5.214.277.
Nestor alone amidst the Storm remain'd. .... Il.8.102.402.
The Storm of hissing Javelins pours behind. .... Il.8.193.406.
A sudden Storm the purple Ocean sweeps, ... Il.11.385.51.
The Storm rolls on, and *Hector* rules the Field: .... Il.11.450.54.
As yet the Bulwark stood, and brav'd the Storm; .... Il.12.38.83.
And hissing Javelins rain an Iron Storm: .... Il.12.50.83.
And their deep Roots for ever brave the Storm. .... Il.12.150.87.
Menestheus from on high the Storm beheld, ... Il.12.401.96.
Fav'ring descends, the wills to stand the Storm. .... Il.13.100.109.
Trembling before th' impending Storm they lie, ... Il.13.121.110.
His Shield emboss'd the ringing Storm sustains, ... Il.13.700.138.
Stand the First Onset, and provoke the Storm: .... Il.15.335.210.
Thick sound the Keels; the Storm of Arrows flies. .... Il.15.447.214.
And raging Seas produc'd thee in a Storm, ... Il.16.51.237.
How the Cloud blackens, how the Storm impends! .... Il.16.94.239.
Ajax no more the sounding Storm sustain'd, ... Il.16.130.242.
Observ'd the Storm of Darts the *Grecians* pour, ... Il.16.430.259.
And thick and heavy sounds the Storm of Blows. .... Il.16.766.273.
Atrides from the Voice the Storm divin'd, ... Il.17.99.291.
Forc'd by loud Clamours, and a Storm of Darts; .... Il.17.118.292.
Great *Ajax* mark'd the growing Storm from far, ... Il.17.280.298.
Safe to the Navy thro' the Storm of War. .... Il.17.519.308.
This weary'd Arm, and ward the Storm of War! .... Il.17.635.312.
Behind them rages all the Storm of War; .... Il.17.822.320.
Loud howls the Storm, and drives them o'er the Main. .... Il.19.409.389.
(So, e're a Storm, the Waters heave and roll) .... Il.21.649.449.
Rouz'd from his Thicket by a Storm of Darts; .... Il.21.678.450.
When the storm thickens, and the billows boil) .... Od.3.357.103.
Part, the storm urges on the coast of *Creet,* .... Od.3.371.104.
In battel calm he guides the rapid storm, ... Od.4.371.137.
Safe from the secret rock and adverse storm, ... Od.4.879.159.
To break the rowling waves, and ruffling storm: .... Od.4.1106.169.
On whose high branches, waving with the storm, ... Od.5.84.176.
A man, an outcast to the storm and wave, ... Od.5.165.179.
Forsake thy float, and leave it to the storm: .... Od.5.435.193.
A sure defence from every storm that blows. .... Od.6.316.226.
Me *Pallas* gave to lead the martial storm, ... Od.14.251.48.
The driving storm the wat'ry west-wind pours, ... Od.14.512.62.
Foreseeing from the first the storm wou'd rise; .... Od.14.515.62.
Who shortning with a storm of blows thy stay, ... Od.18.383.186.
But when the storm was spent in plenteous show'rs, ... Od.19.286.209.
And rode the storm; 'till by the billows tost, ... Od.19.319.209.
The storm past innocent. The god-like man .... Od.22.286.300.
And roof'd defensive of the storm and show'r; .... Od.23.196.333.
They storm, they shout, with hasty frenzy fir'd, ... Od.24.532.373.

STORM'D

Cities laid waste, they storm'd the Dens and Caves, ... 1.W-F.49.153.
Tho' there the Brazen Tow'r was storm'd of old, ... 1.TrSt.356.425.
He cry'd, he roar'd, he storm'd, he tore his Hair; .... 2.ChJM.756.51.
Ambition humbled, mighty Cities storm'd, ... 4.2HE1.11.195.
Then rising in his Wrath, the Monarch storm'd; .... Il.1.502.112.
With fewer Troops we storm'd the *Theban* Wall, ... Il.4.460.242.
Now storm'd before him, and now rag'd behind. .... Il.5.731.302.
Here storm'd Contention, and here Fury frown'd; .... Il.5.916.310.
A Princess rap'd transcends a Navy storm'd: .... Il.13.782.142.
Which oft, in Cities storm'd, and Battels won, ... Il.15.630.220.
And proud *Nericus* trembled as I storm'd. .... Od.24.438.369.

STORMS

From Storms a Shelter, and from Heat a Shade. .... 1.Mes.16.114.
That driv'n by Storms, and pouring o'er the Plain, ... 1.TrSt.514.432.
In Storms by Sea, and Combats on the Shore: .... 1.TrUl.18.466.
Blue *Neptune* storms, the bellowing Deeps resound; .... 2.RL5.50.203.
Nor was the Work impair'd by Storms alone, ... 2.TemF.41.256.

STORMS (CONTINUED)

Of Storms at Sea, and Travels on the Shore, ...2.TemF.451.285.
Who heaves old Ocean, and who wings the storms, ...3.EOM1.158.35.
Sudden, she storms! she raves! You tip the wink, ...3.Ep2.33.52.
Whirlpools and storms his circling arm invest, ...5.DunA2.295.139.
Whirlpools and storms his circling arm invest, ...5.DunB2.317.312.
A brave man struggling in the storms of fate, ...6.32.21.96.
From storms defended, and inclement skies: ....6.35.2.103.
Swift as a Flood of Fire, when Storms arise, ...Il.2.948.168.
Fierce *Discord* storms, *Apollo* loud exclaims, ...Il.5.633.298.
Now storms the Victor at the *Trojan* Wall; ....Il.11.235.46.
As when a western Whirlwind, charg'd with Storms, ...Il.11.395.52.
And opes his cloudy Magazine of Storms; ....Il.12.332.93.
All spring to seize him; Storms of Arrows fly; ....Il.14.495.188.
Of Strength defensive against Winds and Storms, ...Il.16.257.249.
And rolls the Cloud to blacken Heav'n with Storms, ...Il.16.435.259.
Æneas storms, and *Hector* foams with Rage: ....Il.17.844.321.
The forky Bolt, and blackens Heav'n with Storms, ...Il.22.234.465.
Proof to the wintry Winds and howling Storms, ...Il.23.827.522.
Hath plac'd beneath the storms which toss the great! ....Od.1.280.46.
While storms vindictive intercept the shore. ....Od.1.424.53.
And seek my sire thro' storms and rolling seas! ....Od.2.300.76.
Then stay, my child! Storms beat, and rolls the main; ....Od.2.414.81.
Oh beat those storms, and roll the seas in vain! ....Od.2.415.81.
Secure of storms, your royal brother past: ....Od.4.684.151.
To the fierce storms, or men more fierce than they: ....Od.4.1076.168.
The clouds of night, and darkens heav'n with storms) ....Od.5.31.172.
With storms pursu'd them thro' the liquid world. ....Od.5.138.178.
Some bark's broad bottom to out-ride the storms, ...Od.5.320.187.
Swells all the winds, and rouzes all the storms. ....Od.5.378.190.
Urg'd on by want, and recent from the storms; ....Od.6.163.216.
Outcast I rove, familiar with the storms! ....Od.6.210.220.
From storms defended, and inclement skies: ....Od.7.143.243.
And storms vindictive intercept the shore. ....Od.7.359.254.
Man must decay, when man contends with storms. ....Od.8.152.271.
By storms and hunger worn: Age well may fail, ...Od.8.265.277.
When storms and hunger both at once assail. ....Od.8.266.277.
And scatter them, ye storms, in empty air! ....Od.8.444.287.
The written bolt, and blackens heav'n with storms,) ....Od.8.506.289.
Drives clouds on clouds, and blackens heav'n with storms: ......Od.9.76.306.
And forc'd by storms, unwilling, on your coast; ....Od.9.310.319.
His word alone the list'ning storms obey, ...Od.10.23.340.
In storms by sea, in perils on the shore; ....Od.10.543.369.
When war has thunder'd with its loudest storms, ...Od.11.515.409.
Loud storms around and mists eternal rise, ...Od.12.89.436.
O friends! Oh often try'd in adverse storms! ....Od.12.248.444.
And here *Charybdis* fills the deep with storms. ....Od.12.281.446.
And toss with rising storms the wat'ry way, ...Od.12.344.448.
From the loud storms to find a *Sylvan* shade; ....Od.12.396.450.
Rein'd the rough storms, and calm'd the tossing floods: ....Od.12.470.454.
Full o'er our heads, and blackens heav'n with storms. ....Od.12.476.455.
In storms by sea, and combats on the shore; ....Od.13.109.6.
Storms have I past, and many a stern debate; ....Od.17.338.148.
How, the loud storms in prison bound, he sails ....Od.23.339.341.
How sav'd from storms *Phæacia's* coast he trod, ...Od.23.365.342.

STORMY

So fares a Sailor on the stormy Main, ...1.TrSt.520.432.
Loud as the Wolves on Orcas' stormy steep, ...4.2HE1.328.223.
Thus loud lamented to the stormy Main. ....Il.1.459.110.
When stormy Winds disclose the dark Profound; ....Il.14.458.186.
Forth burst the stormy Band with thundring Roar, ...Il.23.264.500.
On stormy seas unnumber'd toils he bore, ...Od.1.7.28.
To naval arts inur'd, and stormy toil. ....Od.1.232.43.
Ends the sad evening of a stormy life: ....Od.4.116.125.
To calm the roarings of the stormy main, ...Od.12.399.450.
And when the north had ceas'd the stormy roar, ...Od.19.232.204.
Or did the rage of stormy *Neptune* sweep ....Od.24.134.354.

STORY

What tho' this King (as ancient Story boasts) ....2.ChJM.684.48.
What tho' this King (as *Hebrew* Story boasts). ....2.ChJM.684A.48.
And to the Knight our Story turns again, ...2.ChJM.711.49.
Let him our sad, our tender story tell, ...2.ElAb.364.348.
From ancient story learn to scorn them all. ....3.EOM4.286.155.
Wou'd go to Mass in jest, (as Story says) ....4.JD4.16.27.
He had a Story of *two Mice.* ....4.HS6.156.259.
Our old Friend Swift will tell his Story. ....4.1HE7.82.273.
She views the story with attentive eyes, ...6.14iii.13.46.
The golden Web her own sad Story crown'd, ...Il.3.170.199.
This is not half the Story of our Woe. ....Il.11.803.72.
No story I unfold of public woes, ...Od.2.49.62.
Have learnt his fate, the whole dark story clear: ....Od.3.113.91.
A story, fruitful of disastrous fate: ....Od.4.800.156.
Distant his mournful story to declare, ...Od.6.171.216.
A dreadful story big with future woes, ...Od.8.618.295.
Each others face, and each his story told: ....Od.10.536.369.
To thy chaste bride the wond'rous story tell, ...Od.11.271.395.
Soft, as some song divine, thy story flows, ...Od.11.458.407.
And print th' important story on thy mind! ....Od.12.50.431.
A dreadful story, big with future woes; ....Od.13.199.15.
The cautious Chief his ready story told. ....Od.14.219.46.
Thy whole sad story, from its first, declare: ....Od.15.414.89.
A story fruitful of events, attend: ....Od.15.423.89.
Touch'd at the dreadful story she descends; ....Od.16.428.128.
Nor claim my story 'till the sun descend; ....Od.17.651.164.
A dreadful story of approaching woes? ....Od.23.280.337.
A mournful story of domestic woes, ...Od.23.324.339.

STORY'D

The trophy'd arches, story'd halls invade, ...3.EOM4.303.156.
Himself among the story'd chiefs he spies, ...5.DunB2.151.302.
The trophy'd Arches, story'd Halls invade, ...6.130.17.358.

STOUT

Roast beef, tho' old, proclaims him stout, ...6.150.13.399.
Roast beef tho' cold, proclaims him stout, ...6.150.13A.399.

STOW

A Work to wonder at—perhaps a Stow. ....3.Ep4.70.143.
The Bishop stow (Pontific Luxury!) ....5.DunB4.593.402.
And in our grotto's stow thy spoils and arms. ....Od.10.480.366.

STOW'D

Safe in her Sides the Hecatomb they stow'd, ...Il.1.408.107.
Beneath the Deck the destin'd Victims stow'd: ....Il.1.567.115.
The Giant by *Achilles* slain, he stow'd ....Il.23.979.528.
And stow'd within its womb the naval stores. ....Od.2.439.82.

STOWE

While you, to measure merits, look in Stowe, ...4.2HE1.66.199.

STOWS

More than ten *Holingsheds,* or *Halls,* or *Stows.* ....4.JD4.131.35.

STRAFFORD

With Oxford, Cowper, Noble Strafford by: ....6.147ix.4.392.

STRAFFORD'S

Where shines great *Strafford's* glittering Star: ....6.135.58.368.
Where shines great *Strafford's* guilded Star: ....6.135.58A.368.

STRAGGLING

A Rout undisciplin'd, a straggling Train, ...Il.13.141.111.

STRAGLERS

And the loose Straglers to their Ranks confines. ....1.TrVP.38.378.

STRAGLING

To yonder Camp, or seize some stragling Foe? ....Il.10.244.13.

STRAIGHT

See STRAIGHT.
Like eyes a-squint, look every way but straight. ....6.38.11Z8.108.

STRAIN

Sing then and *Damon* shall attend the Strain, ...1.PSp.29.63.
But wou'd you sing, and rival *Orpheus'* Strain, ...1.PSu.81.78.
Resound ye Hills, resound my mournful Strain! ....1.PAu.57.84.
Resound ye Hills, resound my mournful Strain! ....1.PAu.71.85.
Here shall I try the sweet *Alexis'* Strain, ...1.PWi.11.89.
See! the bold Youth strain up the threatning Steep, ...1.W-F.155.164.
Soft is the Strain when *Zephyr* gently blows, ...1.EOC.366.282.
Strain out the last, dull droppings of their Sense, ...1.EOC.608.308.
With mournful *Philomel* I join my Strain, ...1.TrSP.177.401.
Nor fierce *Theodamas,* whose sprightly Strain ....2.ChJM.324.29.
The only Strain a Wife must hope to hear. ....2.ChJM.598.44.
We leave them here in this Heroick Strain, ...2.ChJM.710.49.
Not fierce *Othello* in so loud a Strain ....2.RL5.105.208.
Taught nor to slack, nor strain its tender strings, ...3.EOM3.290.121.
Taught not to slack, nor strain its tender strings, ...3.EOM3.290A.121.
Could pension'd *Boileau* lash in honest Strain ....4.HS1.111.15.
All fly to *Twit'nam,* and in humble strain ....4.Arbu.21.97.
The silenc'd Preacher yields to potent strain, ...4.2HE1.237.215.
With feasts, and off'rings, and a thankful strain: ....4.2HE1.244.215.
As when Belinda rais'd my Strain. ....4.1HE7.50.271.
And empty words she gave, and sounding strain, ...5.DunA2.41.100.
But far o'er all, sonorous Blackmore's strain, ...5.DunA2.247.129.
Some strain in rhyme; the Muses, on their racks, ...5.DunA3.153.164.
Still break the benches, Henley! with thy strain, ...5.DunA3.199.174.
As one by one, at dread Medæa's strain, ...5.DunA3.341.192.
And empty words she gave, and sounding strain, ...5.DunB2.45.298.
But far o'er all, sonorous Blackmore's strain, ...5.DunB2.259.308.
Some strain in rhyme; the Muses, on their racks, ...5.DunB3.159.328.
Still break the benches, Henley! with thy strain, ...5.DunB3.203.330.
With French Libation, and Italian Strain, ...5.DunB4.559.397.
As one by one, at dread Medea's strain, ...5.DunB4.635.407.
In a sadly-pleasing Strain ....6.11.5.30.
High on the Stern the *Thracian* rais'd his Strain, ...6.11.39.31.
Nor slack nor strain the tender Strings; ....6.11.35Z6.31.
The *Thracian* rais'd his Strain, ...6.11.39A.31.
Who stil'd the gentle Damsels in his Strain ....6.13.17.39.
They pall *Moliere's* and *Lopez* sprightly strain, ...6.60.15.178.
Blest in each Science, blest in ev'ry Strain! ....6.84.5.238.
To see us strain before the Coach and Cart; ....6.96iii.24.275.
To me, Perfidious! this lamenting Strain? ....Il.5.1094.318.
Plac'd in his Tent, attends the lofty Strain: ....Il.9.252.445.
The far-fam'd Hero of Pæonian Strain; ....Il.11.438.53.
From whence this Menace, this insulting Strain, ...Il.13.1044.155.
Unhappy Coursers of immortal Strain! ....Il.17.504.308.
Tune soft the Voice, and answer to the Strain. ....Il.18.664.355.
With *Lycomedes* of *Creiontian* Strain, ...Il.19.247.383.
Xanthus and *Balius!* of *Podarges'* Strain, ...Il.19.440.390.
Then thus the Hero of *Anchises'* Strain. ....Il.20.117.398.
From heav'nly *Venus* thou deriv'st thy Strain, ...Il.20.136.399.
Mean Fame, alas! for one of heav'nly Strain, ...Il.22.29.453.
No less the lab'ring Heroes pant and strain; ....Il.22.261.466.
Of *Ilus* sprung from *Jason's* royal strain, ...Od.1.338.48.
Patient permit the sadly-pleasing strain; ....Od.1.449.54.
With dissonance, the smooth melodious strain. ....Od.1.472.55.
Whilst warbling to the varied strain, advance ....Od.4.25.121.
Who strait propitious, in prophetic strain ....Od.4.575.147.
(Herself a mortal once, of *Cadmus'* strain, ...Od.5.426.193.
Again with loud applause demand the strain: ....Od.8.88.267.
Full of the God he rais'd his lofty strain, ...Od.8.547.292.
The heav'n-taught Poet, and enchanting strain: ....Od.9.4.301.
Each nerve to strain, each bending oar to ply. ....Od.10.148.347.
Her mother *Persè,* of old Ocean's strain, ...Od.10.159.348.
Then every ear I barr'd against the strain, ...Od.12.212.442.
My soul takes wing to meet the heav'nly strain; ....Od.12.233.443.

STRAIN (CONTINUED)

Strain ev'ry nerve, and bid the vessel fly. ... Od.12.255.444.
(For *Phemius* to the Lyre attun'd the strain.) ... Od.17.312.147.
Whence, great *Telemachus!* this lofty strain? ... Od.17.488.156.
(Suspending sorrow with celestial strain ... Od.17.610.161.
Then to the dance they form the vocal strain, ... Od.18.351.184.
To some new strain when he adapts the lyre, ... Od.21.442.281.
Round thee, the *Muses,* with alternate strain, ... Od.24.77.351.

STRAIN'D

For this with Fillets strain'd your tender Head, ... 2.RL4.101.192.
The Youth already strain'd the forceful Yew; ... Il.8.389.416.
Strain'd with full Force, and tugg'd from Side to Side, ... Il.17.451.304.
Be every fetter strain'd, and added band to band. ... Od.12.66.433.
Be ev'ry fetter strain'd, be added band to band. ... Od.12.199.441.
He strain'd him close, as to his breast he grew. ... Od.16.213.114.
Near the high top he strain'd it strongly round, ... Od.22.501.313.
And strain'd him close, as to his breast she grew; ... Od.23.214.333.

STRAINERS

Lust, thro' some certain strainers well refin'd, ... 3.EOM2.189.77.

STRAINING

But most, when straining with too weak a wing, ... 4.2HE1.368.227.
For straining more, it flies in his own face; ... 5.DunA2.168.122.
He said; and straining, heav'd him off the Ground ... Il.23.842.523.

STRAINS

First in these Fields I try the Sylvan Strains, ... 1.PSp.1.59.
With *Waller's* Strains, or *Granville's* moving Lays! ... 1.PSp.46.65.
Resound ye Hills, resound my mournful Strains! ... 1.PAu.85.86.
No more ye Hills, no more resound my Strains! ... 1.PAu.96.87.
Is not so mournful as the Strains you sing, ... 1.PWi.2.88.
Such Silence waits on *Philomela's* Strains, ... 1.PWi.78.94.
To heav'nly Themes sublimer Strains belong. ... 1.Mes.2.112.
Let softer Strains Ill-fated *Henry* mourn, ... 1.W-F.311.179.
My humble Muse, in unambitious Strains, ... 1.W-F.427.194.
First in these Fields I sung the Sylvan Strains. ... 1.W-F.434.194.
My yielding Heart keeps Measure to my Strains. ... 1.TrSP.94.398.
My Heart relents, and answers to my Strains. ... 1.TrSP.94A.398.
My beating heart keeps measure to my strains. ... 1.TrSP.94B.398.
And strains from hard-bound brains eight lines a-year: ... 4.Arbu.182.109.
"Or, I'm content, allow me *Dryden's* strains, ... 4.2HE2.145.175.
And in our own (excuse some Courtly strains) ... 4.2HE1.215A.213.
Implore your help in these pathetic strains: ... 4.2HE1.232.215.
And I'm not us'd to Panegyric strains: ... 4.2HE1.405.229.
Make Horace flat, and humble Maro's strains; ... 5.DunA1.160.82.
Made Horace dull, and humbled Milton's strains. ... 5.DunB4.212.363.
In vain he strains to reach your Ear, ... 6.10.23.25.
The Strains decay, ... 6.11.19.30.
And strains, from hard bound Brains, six Lines a Year; ... 6.98.32.284.
Close to his Breast he strains the Nerve below, ... Il.4.154.228.
And strains his aged Arm to lash the Horse. ... Il.8.148.404.
High strains, responsive to the vocal string. ... Od.1.200.42.
Strains to his bosom his long-absent boy. ... Od.17.129.138.
To vernal airs attunes her varied strains; ... Od.19.606.226.
With tender hands the stubborn horn he strains, ... Od.21.157.267.
Relaxes, strains, and draws them to and fro; ... Od.21.444.281.

STRAIT

Strait a short Thunder breaks the frozen Sky. ... 1.W-F.130.162.
More strait than alders, taller than the planes; ... 1.TrPA.60.367.
Strait from the hollow cliff, and yawning ground, ... 1.TrPA.157.372.
He strait assum'd his Native Form again; ... 1.TrVP.113.381.
And strait a voice, while yet a voice remains, ... 1.TrFD.67.388.
Strait with the Rage of all their Race possest, ... 1.TrSt.173.417.
Passes the Strait that parts the foaming Seas, ... 1.TrSt.472.430.
Strait to the Fort great *Ajax* turn'd his Care, ... 1.TrES.81.453.
Strait seek their Home, and fly with eager Pace, ... 1.TrUl.214.472.
The Foe once gone, our Knight wou'd strait undress, ... 2.ChJM.373A.32.
This heard, to *Damian* strait a Sign she made ... 2.ChJM.535.41.
Strait on the Tree his eager Eyes he bent, ... 2.ChJM.750.51.
We strait struck Hands; the Bargain was agreed; ... 2.ChWB.296.71.
He summons strait his Denizens of Air; ... 2.RL2.55.163.
Strait the three Bands prepare in Arms to join, ... 2.RL3.29.171.
Strait hover round the Fair her Airy Band; ... 2.RL3.113.176.
But strait the direful Trump of Slander sounds, ... 2.TemF.332.280.
A sudden Cloud strait snatch'd them from my Sight, ... 2.TemF.354.280.
Strait the black Clarion sends a horrid Sound, ... 2.TemF.402.282.
Strait chang'd the Scene, and snatch'd me from the Throne. ... 2.TemF.419.283.
The centre mov'd, a circle strait succeeds, ... 3.EOM4.365.164.
Glad of a quarrel, strait I clap the door, ... 4.Arbu.67.100.
Glad of a quarrel, strait I clapt the door, ... 4.Arbu.67A.100.
And strait succeeded, leaving shame no room, ... 5.DunB4.531.394.
Rage strait Collects his Venom all at once, ... 6.26i.14.79.
Collective Bodies of strait Sticks. ... 6.67.6.195.
Some who grow dull religious strait commence ... 6.82ix(c).1.234.
Tho strait be the passage, and narrow the Gate; ... 6.122.22.345.
Strait to the Tree his sanguine Spires he roll'd, ... Il.2.374.145.
The Monarch spoke: and strait a Murmur rose, ... Il.2.470.149.
Strait to the Tents the Troops dispersing bend, ... Il.2.474.149.
Strait the loud Heralds call the gath'ring Bands. ... Il.2.521.151.
Struck with her Presence, strait the livly Red ... Il.3.491.215.
Strait the broad Belt with gay Embroid'ry grac'd ... Il.4.248.232.
Like Mountain Firs, as tall and strait as they. ... Il.5.688.300.
Strait to their sev'ral Cares the *Trojans* move, ... Il.7.494.388.
Strait from the Town be Sheep and Oxen sought, ... Il.8.629.426.
Strait to *Tydides'* high Pavilion born, ... Il.10.666.31.
Strait to *Mænetius'* much-lov'd Son he sent; ... Il.11.736.68.
Strait to the Fort great *Ajax* turn'd his Care, ... Il.12.435.97.
What Aids expect you in this utmost Strait? ... Il.15.894.232.
Let *Greece,* redeem'd from this destructive Strait, ... Il.16.120.241.
Or the strait course to rocky *Chios* plow, ... Od.3.207.95.
Strait be the coursers from the car releast, ... Od.4.45.122.
Ceasing, benevolent he strait assigns ... Od.4.77.123.
Ulysses strait with indignation fir'd, ... Od.4.389.139.

STRAIT (CONTINUED)

Struck with the kind reproach, I strait reply; ... Od.4.507.144.
Who strait propitious, in prophetic strain ... Od.4.575.147.
Rushing impetuous forth, we strait prepare ... Od.4.611.148.
Strait to dismiss: so Destiny commands: ... Od.5.144.178.
He pray'd, and strait the gentle stream subsides, ... Od.5.576.200.
Why cease I strait to learn what sound invades? ... Od.6.148.214.
Touch'd at the song, *Ulysses* strait resign'd ... Od.8.79.266.
O royal maid, *Ulysses* strait returns, ... Od.8.503.289.
Strait in three squadrons all our crew we part, ... Od.9.182.313.
That done, two chosen heralds strait attend ... Od.10.63.342.
In equal parts I strait divide my band, ... Od.10.232.351.
Strait I command the sacrifice to haste, ... Od.11.57.383.
Strait the flea'd victims to the flames are cast, ... Od.11.58.383.
Strait all the mother in her soul awakes, ... Od.11.188.390.
He quaff'd the gore: and strait his soldier knew, ... Od.11.485.408.
Strait from the direful coast to purer air ... Od.11.789.425.
Strait to my anxious thoughts the sound convey'd ... Od.12.320.447.
Strait seek their home, and fly with eager pace ... Od.13.381.25.
Strait to the lodgments of his herd he run, ... Od.14.85.40.
And, where my hopes invite me, strait transport ... Od.14.438.57.
Upstarted *Thoas* strait, *Andræmon's* son, ... Od.14.564.64.
She strait pursu'd, and seiz'd my willing arm; ... Od.15.501.94.
Strait to the Queen and Palace shall I fly, ... Od.15.549.96.
Mark well my voice, *Ulysses* strait replies: ... Od.16.280.118.
Strait to the feast-full palace he repair'd, ... Od.17.306.146.
Our spies commission'd strait the coast explore, ... Od.17.512.157.
The Peers assent: when strait his sacred head ... Od.18.66.170.
He said; from female ken she strait secures ... Od.19.33.194.
The laver strait with busy care she brings: ... Od.19.451.216.
Strait to the guardian of the bristly kind ... Od.20.239.244.
From council strait th' assenting peerage ceas'd, ... Od.20.310.247.
Impatient strait to flesh his virgin-sword, ... Od.20.461.255.
His ardour strait th' obedient Prince suppress, ... Od.21.137.265.
So near adjoins, that one may guard the strait. ... Od.22.153.294.
"Bring sulphur strait and fire" (the Monarch cries) ... Od.22.527.314.
And strait resum'd his seat) while round him bows ... Od.24.470.371.

STRAITEN

Gasps, as they straiten at each end the cord, ... 5.DunB4.29.343.

STRAITEN'D

Might fail of Forage in the straiten'd Town: ... Il.5.255.279.
Fix'd to the Chariot by the straiten'd Rein; ... Il.5.325.282.
He fix'd with straiten'd Traces to the Car. ... Il.5.398.286.
'Till in the Steely Circle straiten'd round, ... Il.5.774.303.

STRAITS

These Straits demand our last Remains of Might. ... Il.6.106.328.

STRAND

Expects its Passage to the farther Strand: ... 1.TrSt.420.427.
From Scots to Wight, from Mount to Dover strand. ... 4.JD2.86.141.
From Scots to Wight, From Mount to Dover Strand; ... 4.JD2A.91.140.
Where the tall May-pole once o'erlook'd the Strand; ... 5.DunA2.24.99.
And Bernard! Bernard! rings thro' all the Strand. ... 5.DunA2.70.106.
And Lintot! Lintot! rings thro' all the Strand. ... 5.DunA2.70B.106.
Where the tall may-pole once o'er-look'd the Strand; ... 5.DunB2.28.297.
And Bernard! Bernard! rings thro' all the Strand. ... 5.DunB2.74.299.
Perhaps neglected, on the dang'rous strand ... 6.96ii.30Z21.271.
And oft look'd back, slow-moving o'er the Strand. ... Il.1.453.109.
In Silence past along the winding Strand ... Il.1.453A.109.
Chruseïs last descending on the Strand. ... Il.1.571.115.
Th' Immortal Coursers graze along the Strand; ... Il.2.943.168.
The moving Squadrons blacken all the Strand. ... Il.2.971.169.
Had stretch'd thee breathless on the hostile Strand; ... Il.7.122.369.
With twelve black Ships he reach'd *Percope's* Strand, ... Il.11.295.48.
Soon as he came, where, on the crouded Strand, ... Il.11.936.77.
But feed the Vulturs on this hateful Strand, ... Il.13.304.119.
And clad in Arms that lighten'd all the Strand, ... Il.13.316.120.
In Lines advanc'd along the shelving Strand; ... Il.14.40.159.
First seiz'd a Ship on that contested Strand; ... Il.15.855.229.
Such Conf'rence held the Chiefs; while on the Strand, ... Il.16.128.242.
Then, two by two, ascended up the Strand. ... Il.18.90.327.
Achilles to the Strand obedient went; ... Il.19.43.373.
The *Grecians* seek their Ships, and clear the Strand, ... Il.23.5.486.
And, turn'd too short, he tumbled on the Strand, ... Il.23.549.511.
Seek their black Ships, and clear the crowded Strand; ... Il.24.2.534.
Sought their black Ships, and clear'd the crowded Strand; ... Il.24.2A.534.
I steer my voyage to the *Brutian* strand; ... Od.1.234.43.
Thence speed your voyage to the *Spartan* strand, ... Od.1.371.50.
When Night descends, embodyed on the strand. ... Od.2.433.82.
Swift to the shore they move: Along the strand ... Od.2.454.83.
Arriv'd, to form along th' appointed strand ... Od.4.591.147.
The flocks of Ocean to the strand repair: ... Od.4.604.148.
Him thus exulting on the distant strand, ... Od.4.699.152.
Instant prepare me, on the neighb'ring strand, ... Od.4.894.160.
Down to the strand he speeds with haughty strides, ... Od.4.1029.166.
Their snowy lustre whitens all the strand.) ... Od.6.108.211.
Start from the goal, and vanish o'er the strand: ... Od.8.126.269.
The ball dismiss'd, in dance they skim the strand, ... Od.8.413.286.
I quit the place, and hasten to the strand. ... Od.10.482.366.
By woman here thou tread'st this mournful strand, ... Od.11.543.410.
We haul'd our bark, and moor'd it on the strand, ... Od.12.376.449.
Ev'n when with transport black'ning all the strand, ... Od.13.178.14.
Much doubting, yet compell'd, I quit the strand. ... Od.14.328.51.
That thou safe sailing from the *Pylian* strand ... Od.15.49.72.
And lash'd his panting coursers to the strand. ... Od.15.231.79.
Scarce had he spoke, when turning to the strand ... Od.16.366.124.
Then moving from the strand, apart they sate, ... Od.16.376.124.
Vain hope! ten suns had warm'd the western strand, ... Od.19.224.204.
To speed his voyage to the *Grecian* strand. ... Od.19.324.210.
All pale, with ooze deform'd, he views the strand, ... Od.23.255.335.

STRANDED
He said, and climb'd a stranded Lighter's height, ...5.DunA2.275.135.
He said, and clim'd a stranded lighter's height, ...5.DunB2.287.309.

STRANDS
And *Sestos* and *Abydos'* neighb'ring Strands, ...Il.2.1013.171.
And now the Fleet, arriv'd from *Lemnos'* Strands, ...Il.7.560.392.
But say, why yonder on the lonely strands ....Od.11.174.390.

STRANGE
Our Speech, our Colour, and our strange Attire! ....1.W-F.406.192.
But *more advanc'd,* behold with strange Surprize ....1.EOC.223.265.
But *more advanc'd,* survey with strange Surprize ....1.EOC.223A.265.
Such *labour'd Nothings,* in so *strange* a Style, ...1.EOC.326.275.
Strange Phantoms dance around, and skim before your Sight. .2.ChJM.804.54.
If, by strange Chance, a modest Blush be rais'd, ...2.ChWB.110.62.
Read in this Book, aloud, with strange Delight, ...2.ChWB.378.75.
Say what strange Motive, Goddess! cou'd compel ....2.RL1.7.145.
Strange Phantoms rising as the Mists arise; ....2.RL4.40.186.
Pleas'd with the strange Success, vast Numbers prest ....2.TemF.394.282.
See some strange comfort ev'ry state attend, ...3.EOM2.271.87.
The whole strange purpose of their lives, to find ....3.EOM4.221.148.
Strange graces still, and stranger flights she had, ...3.Ep2.49.54.
Strange! by the Means defeated of the Ends, ...3.Ep2.143.62.
'Tis strange, the Miser should his Cares employ, ...3.Ep4.1.134.
Is it less strange, the Prodigal should waste ....3.Ep4.3.134.
Has yet a strange Ambition to *look worse:* .... 4.JD4.269.47.
A Plague, whose strange Infection men are sure, ...4.JD2A.9.132.
Of whose strange crimes no Canonist can tell ....4.JD2.43.135.
And whose strange Sins no Canonist can tell, ...4.JD2A.47.136.
There flies about a strange report ....4.HS6.109.257.
And wear their strange old Virtue as they will. ....4.EpS1.44.301.
Fr. Strange spleen to *S[elkir]k! P.* Do I wrong the Man? ....4.EpS2.62.316.
See Gods with Dæmons in strange league ingage, ...5.DunA1.107.76.
And turn strange Hieroglyphicks there; ....6.30.61.88.
The Play may pass—but that strange creature, *Shore,* .... 6.41.5.113.
Those strange examples ne'er were made to fit ye, ...6.41.41.114.
A strange *Metamorphosis.* ....6.58.72.174.
A *Metamorphosis* more strange ....6.58.73.174.
Authors are judg'd by strange capricious Rules, ...6.60.1.178.
In this strange Town a different Course we take, ...6.82vi.1.232.
Pallas, you give yourself strange Airs; ....6.119.13.337.
Strange! by the Means defeated of the Ends. ....6.154.29.403.
When strange to tell! (So *Juno* will'd) he broke ....Il.19.450.390.
Some strange Disaster, some reverse of Fate ....Il.22.582.480.
Th' unquiet night strange projects entertain'd; ....Od.3.183.94.
By what strange fraud *Ægysthus* wrought, relate, ...Od.3.310.101.
Not prone to ill, nor strange to foreign guest, ...Od.9.103.307.
What hurts thee, *Polypheme?* what strange affright ....Od.9.479.325.
Bear on thy back an *Oar:* with strange amaze ....Od.11.156.389.
Some God no doubt this strange kindly sends; ....Od.18.400.187.
The unknown instrument with strange surprize, ...Od.23.290.337.

STRANGELY
"Lord! Sir, a meer *Mechanick!* strangely low, ...4.JD4.108.33.
Transform themselves so strangely as the Rich? ....4.1HE1.153.291.
You laugh, if Coat and Breeches strangely vary, ...4.1HE1.163.291.
The way they take is strangely round about. ....4.EpS2.125.320.
Fr. You're strangely proud. *P.* So proud I am no Slave: ....4.EpS2.205.324.
"How strangely you expose your self, my dear!" ....6.41.10.113.
And strangely lik'd for her *Simplicity:* .... 6.49i.20.138.
Some strangely wonder you're not fond to marry— ....6.82vi.11.232.

STRANGER
A nearer woe, a sister's stranger fate. ....1.TrFD.6.385.
Arriv'st thou here, a Stranger to our Name? ....1.TrUl.117.469.
Oh say what stranger Cause, yet unexplor'd, ...2.RL1.9.145.
Strange graces still, and stranger flights she had, ...3.Ep2.49.54.
"Permit (he cries) no stranger to your fame ....4.JD4.66.31.
All the Court fill'd with stranger things than he, ...4.JD4.181.41.
Bless me! a Packet.—"'Tis a stranger sues, ...4.Arbu.55.100.
Stranger to Civil and Religious Rage, ...4.Arbu.394.126.
O long a stranger, Venus! let me rest ....4.HOde1.2B.151.
Nurs'd the young Stranger with a Mother's Care. ....Il.5.94.271.
His Daughter gave, the Stranger to detain, ...Il.6.237.337.
Nor lives in *Greece* a Stranger to his Name. ....Il.14.142.161.
Till now a Stranger, in a happy Hour ....Il.18.455.343.
(So long a Stranger) to these honour'd Walls? ....Il.18.496.345.
Some Stranger plows his patrimonial Field. ....Il.22.627.482.
Soft Sleep a Stranger to my weeping Eyes, ...Il.24.808.570.
The stranger Guest the royal Youth beheld. ....Od.1.156.40.
Stranger! whoe'er thou art, securely rest ....Od.1.161.40.
But say, that Stranger-guest who late withdrew, ...Od.1.515.57.
That stranger-guest the *Taphian* realm obeys, ...Od.1.525.57.
Thee first it fits, oh stranger! to prepare ....Od.3.57.89.
Too long a stranger to thy native land; ....Od.3.399.106.
Here shall the wand'ring stranger find his home, ...Od.3.453.109.
They came, and near him plac'd the stranger-guest. ....Od.3.529.113.
Obdurate to reject the stranger-guest; ....Od.4.40.122.
'Till now a stranger, in a happy hour ....Od.5.115.177.
To whom the Nymph: O stranger cease thy care, ...Od.6.227.220.
By *Jove* the stranger and the poor are sent, ...Od.6.247.222.
Not without Care divine the stranger treads ....Od.6.287.224.
Stranger arise! the sun rolls down the day, ...Od.6.303.225.
"What stranger this, whom thus *Nausicaa* leads? ....Od.6.331.227.
A wretched stranger, and of all unknown! ....Od.7.34.235.
Succeeds, and ev'n a stranger recommends. ....Od.7.68.237.
A guest, a stranger, seated in the dust! ....Od.7.215.247.
And give the stranger-guest a stranger's due. ....Od.7.223.247.
Cam'st thou not hither, wond'rous stranger! say, ...Od.7.318.251.
Whate'er is honest, Stranger, I approve. ....Od.7.397.256.
Jove bids to set the stranger on his way, ...Od.7.404.256.
Your present aid this godlike stranger craves, ...Od.8.27.263.
That pleas'd th' admiring stranger may proclaim ....Od.8.99.267.
O friends, he cries, the stranger seems well-skill'd ....Od.8.143.270.
Vouchsafes the rev'rend stranger to display ....Od.8.157.271.

STRANGER (CONTINUED)
Give to the stranger-guest a stranger's dues: ....Od.8.424.286.
Hail god-like stranger! and when heav'n restores ....Od.8.499.289.
Receive the stranger as a brother's blood. ....Od.8.594.294.
The poor and stranger are their constant care; ....Od.9.322.319.
Sooner shalt thou, a stranger to thy shape, ...Od.10.340.360.
The stranger from our hospitable shores; ....Od.11.439.406.
Then send the stranger to his native shore. ....Od.13.67.4.
With ev'ry stranger pass from shore to shore; ....Od.13.209.15.
Arriv'st thou here a stranger to our name? ....Od.13.284.19.
Unhappy stranger! (thus the faithful swain ....Od.14.41.37.
'Tis *Jove* that sends the stranger and the poor. ....Od.14.68.39.
To Fame no stranger, nor perhaps to me; ....Od.14.143.42.
With guileful art a stranger to betray, ...Od.14.326.50.
And bless the hand that made a stranger bleed? ....Od.14.448.57.
High on a throne the King each stranger plac'd. ....Od.15.147.75.
His ardent vows, the stranger thus addrest. ....Od.15.281.82.
The Stranger then. Nor shall I ought conceal, ...Od.15.296.83.
Stranger (reply'd the Prince) securely rest ....Od.15.304.83.
Mean-time, protection to thy stranger-friend? ....Od.15.548.96.
No other roof a stranger shou'd receive, ...Od.15.553.96.
Whence father, from what shore this stranger, say? ....Od.16.57.105.
However, stranger! from our grace receive ....Od.16.77.106.
The reverend stranger, and the spotless maid; ....Od.16.114.108.
A nation ever to the stranger kind; ....Od.16.251.117.
This hapless stranger to the city lead; ....Od.17.11.133.
A stranger sent by Heav'n attends me there; ....Od.17.65.135.
The stranger-guest pursu'd him close behind; ....Od.17.84.136.
And in his hand the willing stranger led. ....Od.17.97.136.
The Prince and stranger shar'd the genial feast, ...Od.17.114.137.
He ey'd the stranger, and imperious spoke. ....Od.17.249.143.
My Lords! this stranger of gigantic port ....Od.17.446.155.
Thus drives the stranger from our court and land. ....Od.17.481.156.
Ill fits the stranger and the poor to wound. ....Od.17.575.160.
(Replies the Queen) the stranger beg'd their grace, ...Od.17.592.161.
Then to *Eumæus:* Bring the stranger, fly! ....Od.17.628.163.
The cautious stranger? With the begging kind ....Od.17.658.164.
Stranger, if prompted to chastize the wrong ....Od.18.68.170.
But mercy to the poor and stranger show, ...Od.18.128.172.
Stranger, may *Jove* aid all th' aereal pow'rs, ...Od.18.137.173.
Heav'ns! could a stranger feel oppression's hand ....Od.18.263.179.
O had this stranger sunk to realms beneath, ...Od.18.446.190.
The rev'rend stranger, or the spotless maid; ....Od.18.463.190.
Eurynomè, regard the stranger friend: ....Od.19.118.198.
Receive no stranger-guest, no poor relieve; ....Od.19.158.200.
But, stranger! as thy days seem full of fate, ...Od.19.184.200.
Stranger! that e'er thy hospitable roof ....Od.19.253.207.
Now wash the stranger, and the bed prepare; ....Od.19.363.211.
If, stranger! I permit that mean attire, ...Od.19.375.212.
His former seat receiv'd the stranger-guest; ....Od.19.592.225.
And bays the stranger groom: so wrath comprest ....Od.20.21.232.
Bestow'd the stranger guest? Or waits he griev'd, ...Od.20.163.241.
Stranger! may fate a milder aspect shew, ...Od.20.249.245.
Like thee, poor stranger guest, deny'd his home! ....Od.20.261.246.
His menial train attend the stranger guest; ....Od.20.350.249.
'Tis impious, Prince! to harm the stranger-guest, ...Od.21.334.276.
Accept a wand'ring stranger for my Lord? ....Od.21.340.276.
That stranger, patient of the Suitors wrongs, ...Od.23.29.320.
Thy ancient friend, oh stranger, is no more! ....Od.24.329.365.
But tell me, stranger, be the truth confest, ...Od.24.334.365.

STRANGER-FRIEND
Mean-time, protection to thy stranger-friend? ....Od.15.548.96.

STRANGER-GUEST
But say, that Stranger-guest who late withdrew, ...Od.1.515.57.
That stranger-guest the *Taphian* realm obeys, ...Od.1.525.57.
They came, and near him plac'd the stranger-guest. ....Od.3.529.113.
Obdurate to reject the stranger-guest; ....Od.4.40.122.
And give the stranger-guest a stranger's due. ....Od.7.223.247.
Give to the stranger-guest a stranger's dues: ....Od.8.424.286.
The stranger-guest pursu'd him close behind; ....Od.17.84.136.
Receive no stranger-guest, no poor relieve; ....Od.19.158.200.
His former seat receiv'd the stranger-guest; ....Od.19.592.225.
'Tis impious, Prince! to harm the stranger-guest, ...Od.21.334.276.

STRANGER'S
His only daughter in a stranger's pow'r, ...3.Ep3.325.120.
Shall cease to blush withstranger's gore, ...6.51i.20.152.
Old as he was, ador'd a Stranger's Charms. ....Il.9.579.462.
And give the stranger-guest a stranger's due. ....Od.7.223.247.
And heav'n propitiate in the stranger's cause: ....Od.7.253.248.
Give to the stranger-guest a stranger's dues: ....Od.8.424.286.
Rude, and unconscious of a stranger's right; ....Od.9.204.314.
As well thou claim'st a grateful stranger's love! ....Od.14.491.59.
And drew before the hearth the stranger's bed: ....Od.14.587.65.
Takes from the stranger's hand the glitt'ring spear: ....Od.15.307.83.
Reward this stranger's hospitable love, ...Od.15.361.86.
Nor bears the modest Queen a stranger's face, ...Od.15.556.96.
If this raise anger in the stranger's thought, ...Od.17.16.133.
The stranger's words may ease the royal heart: ....Od.17.603.161.
If thou the stranger's righteous cause decline, ...Od.18.265.179.
Blind! to contemn the stranger's righteous cause, ...Od.23.65.321.

STRANGERS
The Courtly Train, the Strangers, and the rest, ...1.TrSt.652.437.
By strangers honour'd, and by strangers mourn'd! ....2.Elegy.54.367.
By strangers honour'd, and by strangers mourn'd! ....2.Elegy.54.367.
To Strangers now descends his heapy Store, ...Il.5.202.276.
Let none to strangers honours due disclaim; ....Od.8.39.264.
Or strangers, distant far from our abodes, ...Od.9.327.319.
With joy the Maid th' unwary strangers heard, ...Od.10.125.346.
Strangers thy guides! nor there thy labours end, ...Od.11.146.388.
For needy strangers still to flatt'ry fly, ...Od.14.148.42.
With him all night the youthful strangers stay'd, ...Od.15.212.78.
And rev'rend strangers, modest youth forbears. ....Od.16.46.104.

STRANGERS (CONTINUED)
Can strangers safely in the court reside, ...Od.16.71.106.

STRATAGEM
By Murmuring, Wheedling, Stratagem and Force, ...2.ChWB.163.64.
One Stratagem has fail'd, and others will: ....Il.9.548.460.

STRATAGEMS
Those oft are *Stratagems* which *Errors* seem, ...1.EOC.179.261.
Those are but *Stratagems* which *Errors* seem, ...1.EOC.179A.261.
New Stratagems, the radiant Lock to gain. ....2.RL3.120.176.
What stratagems we form'd, what toils we bore? ....Od.3.146.92.

STRATIE
From *Ripè, Stratie, Tegea's* bord'ring Towns, ...Il.2.733.161.

STRATIUS
First *Echephron* and *Stratius* quit their bed; ....Od.3.526.113.
Stratius and *Echephron* the victim led; ....Od.3.560.115.

STRAW
Pleas'd with a rattle, tickled with a straw: ....3.EOM2.276.88.
On once a flock-bed, but repair'd with straw, ...3.Ep3.301.118.
Each idle Atom, or erroneous Straw; ....4.JD4.243A.47.
Those venial sins, an Atom, or a Straw; ....4.JD4.243.47.
Hence, from the straw where Bedlam's Prophet nods, ...5.DunA3.7.150.
Like the vile straw that's blown about the streets ....5.DunA3.291.184.
Hence, from the straw where Bedlam's Prophet nods, ...5.DunB3.7.320.
Like the vile straw that's blown about the streets, ...5.DunB3.289.334.
"Thy Bark a Bean-shell, and a Straw thy Oar? ....6.96ii.58.273.
That *Bedlam* and clean *Stratius* will suit you best: ....6.96iv.36.277.
That *Straw*, that *Straw* would heighten the Disease. ....6.96iv.38.277.
That *Straw*, that *Straw* would heighten the Disease. ....6.96iv.38.277.
That *Bedlam* and clean Straw would suit you best: ....6.96iv.36A.277.
His Sword and Pen not worth a Straw, ...6.116ii.2.326.

STRAWBERRIES
Grow scarlet strawberries to feast my love: ....1.TrPA.75.368.

STRAWS
Of hairs, or straws, or dirt, or grubs, or worms; ....4.Arbu.170.108.
Of Hairs, or Straws, or Dirt, or Grubs, or Worms: ....6.98.20.284.

STRAWY
And brush the dangerous deep with strawy Oar? ....6.96ii.30Z14.271.

STRAY
Where stray ye Muses, in what Lawn or Grove, ...1.PSu.23.73.
As gardens fresh, where running rivers stray, ...1.TrPA.62.368.
For this, I suffer'd *Phœbus'* Steeds to stray, ...1.TrSt.308.423.
Fame, that delights around the World to stray, ...1.TrSt.810.443.
O tell a Wretch, in Exile doom'd to stray, ...1.TrUl.112.469.
His Wife, not suffer'd from his Side to stray, ...2.ChJM.487.39.
But now no longer from our Tale to stray; ....2.ChJM.520.40.
As thro' the Moon-light shade they nightly stray, ...2.RL*A*2.177.137.
Oft when the World imagine Women stray, ...2.RL1.91.152.
His soul proud Science never taught to stray ....3.EOM1.101.27.
Shew by what Laws the wand'ring Planets stray ....3.EOM2.21A.56.
Safe in its heaviness, can never stray, ...5.DunA3.297.184.
Too safe in inborn heaviness to stray, ...5.DunA3.297A.184.
Safe in its heaviness, shall never stray, ...5.DunB3.295.334.
Safe in its heaviness, can never stray, ...5.DunB3.295A.334.
Lo the glad gales o'er all her beauties stray, ...6.14iii.5.45.
While yet a Child, I chanc'd to stray, ...6.82vii.1.233.
Or in the Meads of *Haliartus* stray, ...Il.2.598.156.
Wide o'er th' *Aleian* Field he chose to stray, ...Il.6.247.338.
His piercing Eyes thro' all the Battel stray, ...Il.13.1015.153.
Shot from the Chariot; while his Coursers stray ....Il.23.550.511.
Vagrants of air, and unforeboding stray. ....Od.2.212.72.
Where thro' the vales the mazy waters stray? ....Od.6.72.208.
Oft with some favour'd traveller they stray, ...Od.7.273.249.
For thee thro' hell's eternal dungeons stray: ....Od.11.241.393.
Graze the fair herds, the flocks promiscuous stray; ....Od.12.317.447.
Thus he: the beeves around securely stray, ...Od.12.417.451.
O tell a wretch in exile doom'd to stray, ...Od.13.279.19.
Sent the sad sire in solitude to stray; ....Od.16.149.109.

STRAY'D
In Woods bright *Venus* with *Adonis* stray'd. ....1.PSu.61.76.
Here too, 'tis sung, of old *Diana* stray'd, ...1.W-F.165.165.
Here, as old Bards have sung, *Diana* stray'd, ...1.W-F.165A.165.
Beyond the Forest's verdant Limits stray'd, ...1.W-F.182.166.
But following Wits from that Intention stray'd; ....1.EOC.104.251.
Thro' his young Woods how pleas'd Sabinus stray'd, ...3.Ep4.89.146.
Where the kind Muses met me as I stray'd, ...6.66.3.194.
Or where thro' flow'ry *Tempè Peneus* stray'd, ...Il.2.920.167.
Wand'ring from clime to clime, observant stray'd, ...Od.1.5.28.
But say thro' what waste regions hast thou stray'd, ...Od.8.625.296.
A friendly pair! near these the * *Pylian* stray'd, ...Od.11.577.412.
Pensive and pale from grove to grove I stray'd, ...Od.12.395.450.
But He, deep-musing, o'er the mountains stray'd, ...Od.14.1.32.
Too long in vain, too widely hast thou stray'd. ....Od.15.12.70.

STRAYS
While led along the Skies his Current strays, ...1.W-F.228.170.
While thro' the Skies his shining Current strays, ...1.W-F.228A.170.
In search of Vanities from Nature strays: ....4.HAdv.99.83.
And where the far-fam'd *Hippemolgian* strays, ...Il.13.9.104.
Devious, from care to care incessant strays. ....Od.19.614.226.

STREAK
Streak with long Gleams the scatt'ring Shades of Night; ....1.TrSt.485.430.
Purple the Ground, and streak the sable Sand; ....Il.22.507.477.

STREAK'D
And fleecy Clouds were streak'd with Purple Light; ....1.PAu.14.81.
Had streak'd the Azure Firmament with Light; ....2.ChJM.614.44.
Now, e're the Morn had streak'd with red'ning Light ....Il.7.516.389.
With rosy Lustre streak'd the dewy Lawn; ....Il.24.1000.577.

STREAKS
Aurora streaks the sky with orient light, ...Od.4.268.132.
So timely rise, when morning streaks the east, ...Od.22.215.297.

STREAM
Ye weeping *Loves*, the Stream with Myrtles hide, ...1.PWi.23.90.
In a soft, silver Stream dissolv'd away. ....1.W-F.204.168.
The silver Stream her Virgin Coldness keeps, ...1.W-F.205.168.
His Tresses dropt with Dews, and o'er the Stream ....1.W-F.331.182.
And the *smooth Stream* in *smoother Numbers* flows; ....1.EOC.367.282.
A troubled stream; the troubled stream was clear'd; ....1.TrPA.154.372.
A troubled stream; the troubled stream was clear'd; ....1.TrPA.154.372.
His wandring Stream, and thro' the briny Tydes, ...1.TrSt.384.426.
Of *Nemea's* Stream the yielding Fair enjoy'd: ....1.TrSt.677.438.
From the wide Wound gush'd out a Stream of Blood, ...1.TrES.320.461.
Bright azure Rays from lively Saphirs stream, ...2.TemF.252.275.
We sail'd in Tempests down the Stream of Life; ....2.TemF.345.280.
Oh! while along the stream of Time thy name ....3.EOM4.383.165.
Nor will Life's stream for Observation stay, ...3.Ep1.31A.18.
Life's stream for Observation will not stay, ...3.Ep1.31.18.
A painted Mistress, or a purling Stream. ....4.Arbu.150.107.
The stream, and smoaking, flourish'd o'er his head. ....5.DunA2.172.122.
"The stream, be his the Weekly Journals, bound. ....5.DunA2.268.134.
The stream, and smoking flourish'd o'er his head. ....5.DunB2.180.304.
"The stream, be his the Weekly Journals bound, ...5.DunB2.280.309.
Th' unconscious stream sleeps o'er thee like a lake. ....5.DunB2.304.310.
Hail sacred spring, whose fruitful stream ....6.6ii.1.14.
Thy stream, like his, is never past, ...6.6ii.7.14.
And the same Stream at once both cools and burns. ....6.9v.4.21.
Where ever and anon, the Stream is ey'd, ...6.14ii.3.43.
Nor seeks in vain for succour to the Stream. ....6.14iv.26.47.
The stream at once preserves her virgin leaves, ...6.14iv.27.48.
The Stream of Life shou'd more securely flow ....6.17ii.18.56.
Shallow, yet swift, the stream of fortune flows, ...6.22.3.71.
Commanding tears to stream thro' ev'ry age; ....6.32.6.96.
Shall stream in Vengeance on my reeking Blade. ....Il.1.399.107.
The sacred Stream unmix'd with Streams below, ...Il.2.913.167.
From *Practius'* Stream, *Percotè's* Pasture Lands, ...Il.2.1012.171.
And *Sangar's* Stream ran purple with their Blood. ....Il.3.250.204.
Priest of the Stream, and honour'd as a God. ....Il.5.102.271.
The rushing Stream his Brazen Armor dy'd, ...Il.5.132.273.
From the clear Vein a Stream immortal flow'd, ...Il.5.421.287.
Such Stream as issues from a wounded God; ....Il.5.422.287.
Sprung from *Alpheus*, plenteous Stream! that yields ....Il.5.673.300.
To Curds coagulates the liquid Stream, ...Il.5.1113.321.
Not thus resistless rul'd the Stream of Fight, ...Il.6.123.330.
Scamandrius, from *Scamander's* honour'd Stream; ....Il.6.501.351.
(Down his white Beard a Stream of Sorrow flows) ....Il.9.559.460.
Where e'er he pass'd, a purple Stream pursu'd; ....Il.10.560.27.
The Stream they pass'd, and pitch'd their Tents below. ....Il.11.849.74.
Fires stream in Light'ning from his sanguin Eyes, ...Il.13.599.135.
Stream into Life, whence *Perseus* brave and bold. ....Il.14.364.180.
There *Hector* seated by the Stream he sees, ...Il.15.270.207.
He purg'd; and wash'd it in the running Stream. ....Il.16.279.249.
From the wide Wound gush'd out a Stream of Blood, ...Il.16.625.268.
Some interposing Hill the Stream divides, ...Il.17.841.321.
A Stream of Glory flam'd above his Head. ....Il.18.244.334.
In its wide Womb they pour the rushing Stream; ....Il.18.409.340.
If Sheep or Oxen seek the winding Stream. ....Il.18.606.352.
And flash incessant like a Stream of Fire: ....Il.19.22.372.
Mix in one Stream, reflecting Blaze on Blaze: ....Il.19.387.388.
The Mountain shook, the rapid Stream stood still. ....Il.20.74.397.
Sudden, returning with the Stream of Light, ...Il.20.391.411.
And now to *Xanthus'* gliding Stream they drove, ...Il.21.1.420.
Part plunge into the Stream: Old *Xanthus* roars, ...Il.21.9.421.
As trembling, panting, from the Stream he fled, ...Il.21.60.424.
The Victor to the Stream the Carcass gave, ...Il.21.133.427.
What boots ye now *Scamander's* worship'd Stream, ...Il.21.143.427.
Flows from the Source of *Axius*, Stream divine! ....Il.21.158.428.
As he that thunders to the Stream that flows. ....Il.21.208.430.
All scatter'd round the Stream (their Mightiest slain) ....Il.21.223.430.
O sacred Stream! thy Word we shall obey; ....Il.21.241.431.
In one promiscuous Stream, the reeking Blood. ....Il.23.44.488.
Drives, thro' a Stream of Dust, the Charioteer; ....Il.23.580.513.
From the hot Steeds the sweaty Torrents stream; ....Il.23.591.513.
And all the Eyes of *Ilion* stream around. ....Il.24.785.569.
When now to *Xanthus'* yellow Stream they drove, ...Il.24.862.572.
And pour, above, the consecrated stream. ....Od.3.438.108.
And the stream sprinkles: From the curling brows ....Od.3.566.115.
Or glides with liquid lapse a murm'ring stream, ...Od.4.565.147.
Here, from our strict embrace a Stream he glides: ....Od.4.620.149.
We gain the stream of *Jove*-descended Nile: ....Od.4.790.156.
A falling stream with gentler waters glide; ....Od.5.563.199.
Whoe'er thou art, before whose stream unknown ....Od.5.568.199.
He pray'd, and strait the gentle stream subsides, ...Od.5.576.200.
Now parting from the stream, *Ulysses* found ....Od.5.594.201.
Here by the stream if I the night out-wear, ...Od.5.601.201.
Wav'd high, and frown'd upon the stream below. ....Od.5.615.201.
Haste, to the limpid stream direct thy way, ...Od.6.35.206.
Haste to the stream! companion of thy care ....Od.6.37.206.
And swam the stream: Loud shrieks the virgin train, ...Od.6.135.213.
Close by the stream a royal dress they lay, ...Od.6.253.222.
Such was the wine: to quench whose fervent stream, ...Od.9.242.316.
Scarce twenty measures from the living stream ....Od.9.243.316.
Half the white stream to hard'ning cheese he prest, ...Od.9.292.318.
A stream of curling smoke ascending blue, ...Od.10.174.349.
Smooth flows the gentle stream with wanton pride, ...Od.11.285.396.
Or foam the goblet with a purple stream. ....Od.15.341.86.
Drink the cool stream, and tremble to the wind. ....Od.17.241.143.
Ends in a stream, and murmurs thro' the vales: ....Od.19.241.206.

STREAM (CONTINUED)
What time the sun, from ocean's peaceful stream, ...Od.19.505.221.
My pitying eyes effus'd a plenteous stream, ...Od.19.633.227.
That stream of eloquence shou'd cease to flow. ......Od.20.339.249.
A stream of gore burst spouting from his nose; ......Od.22.22.287.

STREAM'D
While *Dacian* Mountains stream'd with barb'rous Blood; ......1.TrSt.26.410.
That stream'd at ev'ry Look: then, moving slow, ...Il.6.642.358.
So stream'd the golden Honours from his Head, ...Il.19.414.389.
And all the Eyes of *Ilion* stream'd around. ......Il.22.551.479.
'Till dimm'd with rising grief, they stream'd again. ......Od.5.108.177.
'Till dimm'd with rising grief, they stream'd again. ......Od.5.204.181.

STREAMING
He grasp'd the Dust, distain'd with streaming Gore, ...1.TrES.294.460.
From opening skies may streaming glories shine, ...2.ElAb.341.347.
"The salient spout, far-streaming to the sky; ......5.DunA2.154.120.
"The salient spout, fair-streaming to the sky; ......5.DunA2.154A.120.
"The salient spout, far-streaming to the sky; ......5.DunB2.162.303.
As down thy snowie Thigh distill'd the streaming Flood. ......Il.4.177.229.
With streaming Blood the slipp'ry Fields are dy'd, ...Il.4.514.246.
Low at his Knee, she begg'd, with streaming Eyes, ...Il.5.449.289.
With streaming Blood the slipp'ry Fields are dy'd, ...Il.8.81.399.
He grinds the Dust distain'd with streaming Gore, ...Il.13.499.130.
With streaming Blood the slipp'ry Shores are dy'd, ...Il.15.866.230.
The streaming Tears fall copious from his Eyes; ......Il.16.4.234.
He grasp'd the Dust distain'd with streaming Gore, ...Il.16.599.267.
So spoke the Fair, with Sorrow-streaming Eye: ......Il.24.981.576.
And plac'd aloft: while all, with streaming Eyes, ...Il.24.997.577.
Then grateful *Greece* with streaming eyes wou'd raise ......Od.1.305.47.
In slumber clos'd her silver-streaming eyes. ......Od.1.464.54.
Nor sleep's soft pow'r can close my streaming eyes, ...Od.4.135.126.
From the brave youth the streaming passion broke: ......Od.4.150.127.
When streaming grief his faded cheek bedew'd. ......Od.4.756.154.
Her eyes restrain the silver-streaming tears: ......Od.4.1000.164.
With streaming eyes in briny torrents drown'd, ...Od.5.194.180.
And fountains streaming down the fruitful plain. ......Od.9.156.312.
A rill of Nectar, streaming from the Gods. ......Od.9.426.323.
And all the cavern smok'd with streaming blood. ......Od.11.46.381.
That grateful *Greece* with streaming eyes might raise ......Od.14.403.55.
With streaming eyes all comfortless deplor'd, ...Od.16.466.129.
Then, while the streaming sorrow dims her eyes, ...Od.18.193.176.
His further flank with streaming purple dy'd: ......Od.19.530.221.
Down her pale cheek new-streaming sorrow flows: ......Od.19.702.229.
In slumber clos'd her silver-streaming eyes. ......Od.21.388.279.
Beam o'er the eastern hills with streaming light. ......Od.23.264.336.
Then grateful *Greece* with streaming eyes might raise ......Od.24.45.350.

STREAMS
Soft as he mourn'd, the Streams forgot to flow, ...1.PSu.5.71.
There while he mourn'd, the Streams forgot to flow, ...1.PSu.5A.71.
Ye shady Beeches, and ye cooling Streams, ...1.PSu.13.72.
And headlong Streams hang list'ning in their Fall! ......1.PSu.84.79.
And Streams to murmur, e'er I cease to love. ......1.PAu.42.83.
No more the Streams their Murmurs shall forbear, ...1.PWi.57.93.
Adieu ye *Vales*, ye *Mountains, Streams* and *Groves,* ......1.PWi.89.95.
Our plenteous Streams a various Race supply; ......1.W-F.141.163.
Thro' the fair Scene rowl slow the lingring Streams, ...1.W-F.217.169.
Not *Neptune's* self from all his Streams receives ......1.W-F.223.170.
Not *Neptune's* self from all her streams receives ......1.W-F.223B.170.
No Seas so rich so full no Streams appear, ...1.W-F.225A.170.
The figur'd Streams in Waves of Silver roll'd, ...1.W-F.335.182.
Cole, whose dark Streams his flow'ry Islands lave; ......1.W-F.343.183.
Cole, whose clear Streams his flow'ry Islands lave; ......1.W-F.343A.183.
Tho' *Tyber's* Streams immortal *Rome* behold, ...1.W-F.357.185.
Lost in my Fame, as in the Sea their Streams. ......1.W-F.362.185.
As Streams roll down, *enlarging* as they flow! ......1.EOC.192.263.
If *Chrystal Streams with pleasing Murmurs creep,* ......1.EOC.352.279.
To rule in streams to which he was ally'd: ......1.TrPA.150.372.
The Streams and Fountains, no Delights cou'd yield; ......1.TrVP.6.377.
Now sliding Streams the thirsty Plants renew, ...1.TrVP.15.377.
Thou, sable *Styx!* whose livid Streams are roll'd ......1.TrSt.83.413.
Th' *Inachian* Streams with headlong Fury run, ...1.TrSt.500.431.
(Transfix'd as o'er *Castalia's* Streams he hung, ...1.TrSt.666.438.
Where *Xanthus'* Streams enrich the *Lycian* Plain? ......1.TrES.28.450.
The Spear, pursu'd by gushing Streams of Gore; ......1.TrES.126.454.
Ye Streams, beyond my Hopes beheld again! ......1.TrUl.241.473.
A Crystal Fountain spread its Streams around, ...2.ChJM.457.37.
He pierc'd the glitt'ring Clouds with golden Streams, ...2.ChJM.615.44.
While Fish in Streams, or Birds delight in Air, ...2.RL3.163.180.
The wandring streams that shine between the hills, ...2.ElAb.157.332.
And there the streams in purer rills descend? ......3.EOM3.204.113.
In lavish streams to quench a Country's thirst, ...3.Ep3.177.108.
As shallow streams run dimpling all the way. ......4.Arbu.316.118.
To where Fleet-ditch with disemboguing streams ......5.DunA2.259.133.
He bears no token of the sabler streams, ...5.DunA2.285.137.
That tinctur'd as it runs, with Lethe's streams, ...5.DunA2.315.140.
And never wash'd, but in Castalia's streams: ......5.DunA3.144.162.
To where Fleet-ditch with disemboguing streams ......5.DunB2.271.308.
He bears no token of the sabler streams, ...5.DunB2.297.310.
That tinctur'd as it runs with Lethe's streams, ...5.DunB2.339.314.
And never wash'd, but in Castalia's streams. ......5.DunB3.18.321.
As many quit the streams that murm'ring fall ......5.DunB4.199.362.
Thy streams were once th' impartial test ......6.6ii.17.15.
As streams roll down enlarging as they flow. ......6.9ii.2.21.
By the Streams that ever flow, ...6.11.71.33.
Vales, Spires, meandring Streams, and *Windsor's* tow'ry Pride. ......6.14ii.54.44.
Or else their Streams, when hinder'd in their Course, ...6.17ii.16.56.
These to the birds refreshing streams may yield; ......6.20.65.67.
Large Gulps of Aganippe's *streams I'll draw,* ......6.26ii.5.79.
Tho' secret, yet with copious Streams she mourns, ...6.33.5A.99.
This thro' the gardens leads its streams around, ...6.35.29.103.
To various use their various streams they bring, ...6.35.33.104.
Thence endless streams of fair ideas flow, ...6.52.43.157.
Those gliding streams, and evening colonades, ...6.81.8B.225.

STREAMS (CONTINUED)
While smoking Streams from Silver Spouts shall glide, ...6.82i.3.229.
While smoking Streams from Silver Spouts shall flow, ...6.82i.3A.229.
And *Thryon's* Walls *Alphëus'* Streams inclose: ......Il.2.720.160.
The sacred Stream unmix'd with Streams below, ...Il.2.913.167.
Spread in dim Streams, and sail along the Skies, ...Il.4.317.235.
Th' unweary'd Blaze incessant Streams supplies, ...Il.5.7.266.
While *Troy's* fam'd <*> Streams that bound the deathful Plain ......Il.6.5.322.
In sable Streams soft-trickling Waters shed. ......Il.9.20.432.
Not far the Streams of fam'd *Alphæus* flow; ......Il.11.848.74.
Where *Xanthus'* Streams enrich the *Lycian* Plain, ...Il.12.372.95.
The Spear, pursu'd by gushing Streams of Gore; ......Il.12.480.99.
And Streams of Sweat down their sow'r Foreheads flow. ......Il.13.884.147.
And have whole Streams of Blood been spilt in vain? ......Il.14.99.162.
They hail her Queen; the *Nectar* streams around. ......Il.15.95.200.
The hissing Brands; thick streams the fiery Show'r; ......Il.16.151.243.
And Streams, and Vales, and Forests strike the Eyes, ...Il.16.359.257.
Streams from some lonely Watch-tow'r to the Sky: ......Il.19.407.389.
Xanthus whose Streams in golden Currents flow, ...Il.20.53.396.
See! my choak'd Streams no more their Course can keep, ...Il.21.235.430.
And feed with pregnant Streams the Plants and Flow'rs; ......Il.21.292.433.
Call then thy subject Streams, and bid them roar, ...Il.21.362.435.
Again, the branching Streams begin to spread, ...Il.21.446.438.
The streams of *Jardan* issue to the main. ......Od.3.373.104.
Streams the black blood, and smokes upon the ground. ......Od.3.581.116.
Fast streams a tide from beauteous *Helen's* eyes; ......Od.4.250.131.
The vital streams a chilling horror froze: ......Od.4.935.162.
Odour divine! whose soft refreshing streams ......Od.6.93.209.
Wash their fair garments in the limpid streams; ......Od.6.100.210.
Where waving shades obscure the mazy streams. ......Od.6.250.222.
This thro' the gardens leads its streams around, ...Od.7.170.244.
To various use their various streams they bring, ...Od.7.174.244.
Whose polish'd vase with copious streams supplies ......Od.7.232.247.
The spacious vase with ample streams suffice, ...Od.8.471.288.
There belcht the mingled streams of wine and blood, ...Od.9.443.324.
She to *Artacia's* silver streams came down, ...Od.10.121.346.
(*Artacia's* streams alone supply the town:) ......Od.10.122.346.
And mingling streams eternal murmurs make. ......Od.10.613.374.
Ye streams, beyond my hopes beheld again! ......Od.13.408.26.
With copious streams the shining vase supplies ......Od.15.150.76.
With copious streams that golden ew'r supplies ......Od.17.106.137.
And *Leucas'* rock, and *Ocean's* utmost streams, ...Od.24.17.347.
Then unguents sweet and tepid streams we shed; ......Od.24.62.350.

STREAMY
While streamy Sparkles, restless as he flies, ...Il.11.87.38.
In streamy Sparkles, kindling all the Skies, ...Il.13.321.120.
His nodding Helm emits a streamy Ray; ......Il.13.1014.153.

STREET
Crawl thro' the Street, shov'd on, or rudely press'd ......3.Ep1.230A.35.
And Worldly crying coals from street to street, ...3.Ep3.50.90.
And Worldly crying coals from street to street, ...3.Ep3.50.90.
And catechis'd in ev'ry street. ......4.HS6.112.257.
The shops shut up in every street, ...4.1HE7.8.269.
"And oh! (he cry'd) what street, what lane, but knows ......5.DunA2.145.119.
And New-year Odes, and all the Grub-street race. ......5.DunB1.44.274.
Gaming and Grub-street skulk behind the King. ......5.DunB1.310.292.
"And oh! (he cry'd) what street, what lane but knows, ...5.DunB2.153.303.
Rolls the black troop, and overshades the street, ...5.DunB2.360.315.
Shall take thro' Grub-street her triumphant round; ......5.DunB3.136.326.
And fit your selves—like Chaps in *Monmouth-Street.* ......6.60.28.178.
On Sunday at Six, in the Street that's call'd *Gerrard,* ......6.62v.1.186.
Forth in the Street I rush with frantick Cries: ......6.96iv.45.277.
Along the Street the new-made Brides are led, ...Il.18.571.350.
With speed divine from street to street she flies. ......Od.2.431.81.
With speed divine from street to street she flies. ......Od.2.431.81.
Thro' the proud street she moves, the publick gaze; ......Od.7.3.232.
When thro' the street she gracious deigns to move, ...Od.7.90.238.
Patient to roam the street, by hunger led, ...Od.15.330.85.
Scourge thro' the publick street, and cast thee there, ...Od.17.570.160.

STREETS
For you, he walks the streets thro' rain or dust, ...4.JD2.73.139.
"Oh but a Wit can study in the Streets, ...4.2HE2.98.171.
Or wafting ginger, round the streets to go, ...5.DunA1.201.87.
Or wafting ginger, round the streets to run, ...5.DunA1.201A.87.
Streets pav'd with Heroes, Tyber choak'd with Gods! ......5.DunA3.100.158.
Like the vile straw that's blown about the streets ......5.DunA3.291.184.
While all your smutty sisters walk the streets. ......5.DunB1.230.287.
Streets pav'd with Heroes, Tyber choak'd with Gods: ......5.DunB3.108.325.
Like the vile straw that's blown about the streets, ...5.DunB3.289.334.
Stands in the streets, abstracted from the crew, ...6.45.43.125.
Streets, chairs, and coxcombs rush upon my sight; ......6.45.48.126.
Thro' Streets of Palaces and Walks of State; ......Il.6.490.350.
Thro' the fair Streets, the Matrons in a Row, ...Il.18.575.350.
Women alone, when in the Streets they jar, ...Il.20.300.406.
Thro' *Troy's* wide Streets abandon'd shall I roam, ...Il.24.979.576.
The chief with wonder sees th' extended streets, ...Od.7.55.236.
With opening streets and shining structures spread, ...Od.7.104.239.

STREIGHT
See STRAIGHT.
Breaks the wild waves, and forms a dang'rous streight; ......Od.12.126.437.

STREIGHTEN'D
Then streighten'd cords involv'd his body round; ......Od.22.208.297.

STREIGHTS
In *Samos* sands, or streights of *Ithaca,* ......Od.15.34.71.

STRENGTH
Where *Denham's* Strength, and *Waller's* Sweetness join. ......1.EOC.361.280.
With all his strength the giant-lover blows; ......1.TrPA.46.367.
The strength and fury of a giant foe. ......1.TrPA.125.370.

STRENGTH (CONTINUED)

Their Strength united best may help to bear 1.TrES.69.452.
Your Strength, united, best may help to bear 1.TrES.80Z3.452.
O where, ye *Lycians*, is the Strength you boast, 1.TrES.145.455.
The Task be mine the Hero's Strength to try, 1.TrES.215.457.
The Task be mine this Hero's Strength to try, 1.TrES.215A.457.
His Strength, his Sight, his Life, were lost for Love. 2.ChWB.381Z2.75.
But this bold Lord, with manly Strength indu'd, 2.RL5.79.206.
To want the strength of bulls, the fur of bears. 3.EOM1.176.36.
Most strength the moving principle requires; 3.EOM2.67.63.
But strength of mind is Exercise, not Rest: 3.EOM2.104.67.
Gives all the strength and colour of our life. 3.EOM2.122.70.
Grows with his growth, and strengthens with his strength: 3.EOM2.136.71.
'Till one Man's weakness grows the strength of all. 3.EOM2.252.85.
The strength he gains is from th'embrace he gives. 3.EOM3.312.126.
In this one Passion man can strength enjoy, 3.Ep1.222.34.
And strength of Shade contends with strength of Light; 3.Ep4.82.145.
And strength of Shade contends with strength of Light; 3.Ep4.82.145.
Each Man an *Ascapart*, of Strength to toss 4.JD4.276.49.
But none but you can give us Strength to walk; 6.2.29.6.
At once our Strength, our Aid, our guide, our way, 6.23.19A.73.
With strength of body, artifice of mind; 6.38.16.108.
And each from each contract new strength and light. 6.52.16.156.
Caracci's strength, *Coreggio's* softer line, 6.52.37.157.
If thou hast Strength, 'twas Heav'n that Strength bestow'd, Il.1.233.98.
If thou hast Strength, 'twas Heav'n that Strength bestow'd, Il.1.233.98.
Like Gods in Strength, and of a Goddess born; Il.1.367.105.
So shall Authority with Strength be join'd. Il.1.371.106.
Th' united Strength of all the Gods above Il.1.734.122.
Warriors like you, with Strength and Wisdom blest, Il.2.227.138.
His Strength like *Neptune*, and like *Mars* his Mien, Il.2.569.155.
The Strength of *Mars* the blushing Maid compress) Il.2.617.157.
The Strength and Glory of th' *Epean* Name. Il.2.752.161.
But few his Troops, and small his Strength in Arms. Il.2.820.164.
(His was the Strength that mortal Might exceeds, Il.2.936.167.
And Strength of Numbers, to this *Grecian* Race. Il.3.252.204.
What Chief is that with Giant Strength endu'd, Il.3.290.207.
Himself a Host: the *Grecian* Strength and Pride. Il.3.294.207.
Himself an Host: the *Grecian* Strength and Pride. Il.3.294A.207.
The warlike *Pandarus*, for strength renown'd; Il.4.120.226.
The Foot (the Strength of War) he rang'd behind; Il.4.343.237.
No Strength or Skill, but just in Time, be try'd: Il.4.349.237.
Oh! had'st thou Strength to match thy brave Desires, Il.4.362.238.
That Strength which once in boiling Youth I knew; Il.4.371.238.
Oh Son of *Tydeus!* (He, whose Strength could tame Il.4.422.240.
Strength swells thy boiling Breast, infus'd by me, Il.5.162.274.
He swung it round; and gath'ring Strength to throw, Il.5.373.285.
Burns with Desire *Sarpedon's* Strength to prove; Il.5.778.303.
Be mindful of the Strength your Fathers bore; Il.6.137.330.
A Spear the Hero bore of wondrous Strength, Il.6.394.346.
Known is thy Courage, and thy Strength confest. Il.6.669.360.
What Strength thou hast, and what the *Grecian* Foe. Il.7.274.378.
It reach'd his Neck, with matchless Strength impell'd; Il.7.313.379.
With Strength of Body, and with Worth of Mind! Il.7.351.381.
Their Strength he withers, and unmans their Souls. Il.8.96.402.
What Strength I have, be now in Battel try'd, Il.8.357.414.
Strength and Omnipotence invest thy Throne; Il.8.576.424.
A massy Spear he bore of mighty Strength, Il.8.615.425.
Such Strength of Body, with such Force of Mind; Il.9.74.436.
My Child! with Strength, with Glory and Success, Il.9.330.450.
(For Strength consists in Spirits and in Blood, Il.9.826.474.
Mages for Strength, *Oïleus* fam'd for Speed. Il.10.124.7.
With all his Strength the Youth directs his Dart; Il.11.302.48.
As the slow Beast with heavy Strength indu'd, Il.11.682.65.
Confiding now in bulky Strength he stands, Il.11.692.66.
Oh! had I still that Strength my Youth possess'd, Il.11.816.72.
"In Strength superior, and of Race divine, Il.11.917.76.
Their Strength, united, best may help to bear Il.12.413.96.
Your Strength, united, best may help to bear Il.12.427.97.
O where, ye *Lycians!* is the Strength you boast? Il.12.499.99.
There, *Greece* has strength: but this, this Part o'erthrown, Il.13.79.108.
Her Strength were vain; I dread for you alone. Il.13.80.108.
Strength, not their own, the Touch divine imparts, Il.13.89.109.
And lay the Strength of Tyrants on the Ground: Il.13.389.124.
With his full Strength he bent his angry Bow, Il.13.831.145.
There join'd, the whole *Bœotian* Strength remains, Il.13.859.146.
To combate; Strength is of the Gods alone. Il.13.990.152.
Swell his bold Heart, and urge his Strength to War: Il.15.261.207.
Like Strength is felt, from Hope, and from Despair, Il.15.852.229.
Who, like in Strength, in Swiftness, and in Grace, Il.16.188.246.
Such their dread Strength, and such their deathful View. Il.16.203.247.
Of Strength defensive against Winds and Storms, Il.16.257.249.
The Task be mine this Hero's Strength to try, Il.16.518.263.
In little *Panope* for Strength renown'd, Il.17.356.301.
While *Greeks* and *Ilians* equal Strength employ, Il.17.456.305.
Ah would *Minerva* send me Strength to rear Il.17.634.312.
What human Strength and Prudence can supply; Il.17.716.315.
From the steep Mountain with exerted Strength Il.17.833.321.
And Heav'n with Strength supply the mighty Rage! Il.19.38.373.
Strength is deriv'd from Spirits and from Blood, Il.19.159.378.
Courage may prompt; but, ebbing out his Strength, Il.19.163.378.
But built anew with Strength-conferring Fare, Il.19.167.378.
Let gen'rous Food Supplies of Strength produce, Il.19.233.382.
For ev'ry Man has equal Strength to rail: Il.20.299.406.
Endu'd his Knees with strength, his Nerves with Pow'r: Il.22.266.466.
Then low in Dust thy Strength and Glory lay'd. Il.22.420.472.
It is not Strength, but Art, obtains the Prize, Il.23.383.505.
Too true it is, deserted of my Strength, Il.23.721.519.
O'erturn the Strength of *Ajax* on the Ground; Il.23.835.522.
Nor could the Strength of *Ajax* overthrow Il.23.836.522.
With matchless Strength; that time *Ulysses* found Il.23.843.523.
The Strength t'evade, and where the Nerves combine, Il.23.844.523.
Nor weary out your gen'rous Strength in vain. Il.23.857.523.
And third, the Strength of god-like *Ajax* cast. Il.23.998.529.
In Strength of Rage and Impotence of Pride, Il.24.53.538.
Large was the Door, whose well-compacted Strength Il.24.557.559.

STRENGTH (CONTINUED)

A Strength proportion'd to the Woes you feel. Il.24.658.564.
Yet would your pow'rs in vain our strength oppose; Od.2.279.74.
Bread, that decaying man with strength supplies, Od.2.329.77.
A double strength of bars secur'd the gates: Od.2.390.80.
The strength of wheat, and wines, and ample store. Od.2.427.81.
With strength and speed superior form'd, in fight Od.4.277.132.
With naked strength, and plunge into the wave. Od.5.437.193.
Join to the help of Gods the strength of man, Od.5.462.195.
There round his tribes a strength of wall he rais'd, Od.6.13.204.
With forceful strength a branch the Heroe rends; Od.6.150.214.
With conscious strength elate, he bends his way Od.6.157.216.
A strength of wall the guarded city bounds: Od.6.312.226.
With strength the future prize of fame to play, Od.8.23.263.
Incessant in the games your strength display, Od.8.97.267.
Destroys perhaps the strength that time wou'd spare: Od.8.150.271.
This youth with strength enormous bids it fly, Od.8.409.285.
Who not by strength subdu'd me, but by wine. Od.9.604.331.
Amazing strength, these poysons to sustain! Od.10.389.363.
Proud of their strength and more than mortal size, Od.11.385.402.
His substance vanish'd, and his strength decay'd, Od.11.489.408.
With him the strength of war, the soldiers pride, Od.11.673.417.
Now I the strength of *Hercules* behold, Od.11.741.423.
Pale hunger wastes the manly strength away. Od.12.406.450.
Now wasting years my former strength confound, Od.14.247.48.
Oh were my strength as then, as then my age! Od.14.570.64.
Wither the strength of man, and awe the Gods. Od.16.287.118.
Is pil'd with viands and the strength of bread. Od.17.109.137.
To him, his swiftness and his strength were vain; Od.17.350.148.
Gods! how his nerves a matchless strength proclaim: Od.18.84.170.
To-day with pow'r elate, in strength he blooms; Od.18.159.174.
With steers of equal strength, th' allotted grounds; Od.18.415.189.
Of strength superior to the toil assign'd.— Od.19.413.214.
Their strength and skill the Suitors shall assay: Od.19.675.229.
From the pure flour (the growth and strength of man) Od.20.135.240.
The lawless wretch, the man of brutal strength, Od.21.30.260.
The port, the strength, the grandeur of the man! Od.21.99.263.
Heir of my Father's strength, as well as throne. Od.21.122.264.
Vain all their art, and all their strength as vain; Od.21.187.268.
Ulysses' strength, as not to bend his bow! Od.21.269.272.
Sufficient strength to draw the mighty bow? Od.21.338.276.
A double strength of valves secur'd the place, Od.22.144.294.
Alas for this! what mortal strength can move Od.23.185.332.
But strength of youth, or valour of the brave Od.24.113.353.
My strength were still, as once in better days; Od.24.436.369.

STRENGTH-CONFERRING

But built anew with Strength-conferring Fare, Il.19.167.378.

STRENGTH'NING

So oft' has steep'd the strength'ning Grain in Wine. Il.8.233.408.
And strength'ning Bread, and gen'rous Wine be brought. Il.8.630.426.
Let *Hecamede* the strength'ning Bath prepare, Il.14.10.157.

STRENGTHEN

To serve, not suffer, strengthen, not invade, 3.EOM3.298.123.
Each strengthen each, and all encourage all. Il.2.433.148.
If e'er he bore the sword to strengthen ill, Od.2.79.64.
Their orchard-bounds to strengthen and adorn. Od.24.260.361.

STRENGTHEN'D

Her Hearts are strengthen'd, and her Glories rise. Il.9.543.460.
Rage edg'd his Sword, and strengthen'd ev'ry Blow. Il.15.535.217.
That Sign beheld, and strengthen'd from above, Il.24.365.551.
So shall thy Suppliant, strengthen'd from above, Il.24.385.552.
With friendships strengthen'd, and with honors grac'd. Od.13.491.29.

STRENGTHENS

Whose *own Example* strengthens all his Laws, 1.EOC.679.316.
Each strengthens Reason, and Self-love restrains. 3.EOM2.80.64.
Grows with his growth, and strengthens with his strength: 3.EOM2.136.71.
Swells all their Hearts, and strengthens all their Hands. Il.15.717.223.
Their rapine strengthens, and their riots rise: Od.14.114.41.

STRENGTHS

"And prove your sev'ral strengths"—The Princes heard, Od.21.151.266.

STRENUOUS

Like Steel, uplifted by some strenuous Swain, Il.3.91.194.

STREPHON

Thus *Daphnis* spoke, and *Strephon* thus reply'd. 1.PSp.22.62.
Daphnis and *Strephon* to the Shades retir'd, 1.PSp.17z1.62.
The Bowl to *Strephon*, and the Lamb to thee: 1.PSp.94.70.

STRETCH

Stretch his long Triumphs down thro' ev'ry Age, 1.W-F.304.177.
Oh stretch thy Reign, fair *Peace!* from Shore to Shore, 1.W-F.407.192.
Nor yet attempt to stretch thy bolder Wing, 1.TrSt.23.410.
I stretch my empty arms; it glides away: 2.ElAb.238.339.
Or tricks to shew the stretch of human brain, 3.EOM2.47.61.
Let his plantations stretch from down to down, 3.Ep4.189.155.
Shall stretch thy Conquests over half the kind: 4.HOde1.16.151.
Shall stretch his Conquest over half the kind: 4.HOde1.16A.151.
And stretch the Ray to Ages yet unborn. 4.2HE1.228.215.
Ah luckless Poet! stretch thy lungs and roar, 4.2HE1.324.223.
Ah! still o'er Britain stretch that peaceful wand, 5.DunA1.155.82.
At ev'ry line, they stretch, they yawn, they doze. 5.DunA2.358.143.
Then stretch thy sight o'er all her rising reign, 5.DunA3.57.155.
Now stretch thy view, and open all thy mind. 5.DunA3.201Z2.175.
At ev'ry line they stretch, they yawn, they doze. 5.DunB2.390.316.
Then stretch thy sight o'er all her rising reign, 5.DunB3.65.323.
I'll stretch my arm, and snatch him to my breast. 6.21.38.70.
I stretch my Hand, no *Gulliver* is there! 6.96iv.42.277.
Stretch their long Necks, and clap their rustling Wings, Il.2.543.153.
To stretch thee pale and gasping on the Ground; Il.5.500.292.

STRETCH (CONTINUED)

And stretch the Slaughter to the Gates of *Troy?* Il.5.568.295.
Shall stretch your daring Champion in the Dust; Il.7.94.367.
Ye strive in vain! If I but stretch this Hand, Il.8.29.397.
This Arm shall reach thy Heart, and stretch thee dead. Il.8.203.407.
And stretch the dreadful *Hector* at my Feet. Il.13.114.110.
And stretch the other o'er the sacred Main. Il.14.308.177.
At his full Stretch, as the tough String he drew, Il.15.544.217.
Scour o'er the Fields, and stretch to reach the Town. Il.16.453.260.
An Arm as strong may stretch thee in the Dust. Il.16.752.273.
And stretch him breathless on his slaughter'd Son; Il.16.790.274.
The brawny Curriers stretch; and labour o'er Il.17.452.304.
Stretch not henceforth, O Prince! thy sov'reign Might, Il.19.179.379.
Now o'er the Fields they stretch with lengthen'd Strides, Il.21.713.451.
Or let us stretch *Achilles* on the Field, Il.22.311.469.
And stretch thee here, before this *Scæan* Gate. Il.22.452.474.
They pant, they stretch, they shout along the Plain. Il.23.450.508.
So broad, his Pinions stretch their ample Shade, Il.24.392A.552.
Stretch their broad plumes, and float upon the wind. Od.2.174.70.
The spacious sheet, and stretch it to the wind. Od.2.465.83.
Rise on the poop, and fully stretch the sails. Od.4.484.143.
And stretch the swelling canvas to the gales; Od.8.48.264.
Call thee aboard, and stretch the swelling sails. Od.8.166.271.
Each nerve we stretch, and ev'ry oar we ply. Od.9.574.330.
The spacious sheet, and stretch it to the wind: Od.11.4.379.
And stretch the Giant-monsters o'er the ground. Od.11.394.403.
Sing thro' the shrouds, and stretch the swelling sails. Od.11.794.426.
Stretch to the stroke, and brush the working seas. Od.12.265.445.
The spacious sheet, and stretch it to the wind. Od.15.313.84.
Bore on full stretch, and seiz'd a dappl'd fawn: Od.19.266.208.
And o'er the past, *Oblivion* stretch her wing. Od.24.557.375.

STRETCH'D

Stretch'd o'er the Poor, and Church, his Iron Rod, 1.W-F.75.157.
Stretch'd on the Lawn his second Hope survey, 1.W-F.81.158.
And stretch'd his Empire to the frozen Pole; 1.TrSt.28.411.
Stretch'd on rich Carpets, on his Iv'ry Throne; 1.TrSt.614.436.
With Orbs unroll'd lay stretch'd o'er all the Plain, 1.TrSt.665A.438.
Before his Chariot stretch'd his Form divine: 1.TrES.293.460.
Eliza stretch'd upon the fun'ral Pyre, 2.TemF.206.272.
With Heads advanc'd, and Pinions stretch'd for Flight: 2.TemF.211.272.
In Act to speak, and graceful, stretch'd his Hand: 2.TemF.241.274.
Scarce to the Top I stretch'd my aking Sight, 2.TemF.246.275.
Squeaks like a high-stretch'd Lutestring, and replies: 4.JD4.99.33.
The Man, who stretch'd in Isis' calm Retreat 4.2HE2.116.173.
Stretch'd to relieve the Idiot and the Poor, 4.2HE1.226.215.
And now the Victor stretch'd his eager hand 5.DunA2.101.109.
Then down are roll'd the books; stretch'd o'er 'em lies 5.DunA2.371.145.
And stretch'd on bulks, as usual, Poets lay. 5.DunA2.388.148.
And now the victor stretch'd his eager hand 5.DunB2.109.300.
Then down are roll'd the books; stretch'd o'er 'em lies 5.DunB2.403.316.
And stretch'd on bulks, as usual, Poets lay. 5.DunB2.420.318.
His stretch'd-out arm display'd a Volume fair; 5.DunB4.106.351.
Stretch'd on the rack of a too easy chair, 5.DunB4.342.377.
Huge moles, whose shadow stretch'd from shore to shore, 6.71.21.203.
And from the Stirrup stretch'd, to find 6.79.111.221.
And from his Stirrup stretch'd, to find 6.79.111A.221.
There, stretch'd unseen in coverts hid from day, 6.81.13.226.
I saw thee stretch'd on *Lilliputian* Ground; 6.96iv.68.278.
Here view him stretch'd. The Microscope explains, 6.96v.5.280.
Stretch'd on the spoils of plunder'd palaces 6.130.12.358.
Stretch'd forth in honour's nobler bed, 6.141.7.380.
Stretch'd out in honour's nobler bed, 6.141.7A.380.
Then part, where stretch'd along the winding Bay Il.1.632.118.
Stretch'd in the Tents the *Grecian* Leaders lie, Il.2.2.126.
Stretch'd his black Jaws, and crash'd the crying Young; Il.2.379.145.
But now inglorious, stretch'd along the Shore, Il.2.837.164.
(The Region stretch'd beneath his mighty Shade) Il.2.921.167.
Nor rais'd his Head, nor stretch'd his sceptred Hand; Il.3.282.207.
Stretch'd on the Shore, and thus neglected dies. Il.4.561.248.
But pierc'd his Breast, and stretch'd him on the Plain. Il.5.26.266.
Stretch'd in their Blood lay gasping on the Sand? Il.5.865.307.
Stretch'd where he fell, and at *Tydides* flies. Il.5.1041.316.
The Monarch's Javelin stretch'd him in the Dust. Il.6.80.327.
Stretch'd his fond Arms to clasp the lovely Boy. Il.6.595.355.
Had stretch'd thee breathless on the hostile Strand; Il.7.122.369
That Day had stretch'd beneath his matchless Hand Il.8.113.403.
Stretch'd by some *Argive* on his native Shore: Il.8.436.418.
Great *Meleager* stretch'd along the Plain. Il.9.662.467.
Stretch'd in his Bed, with all his Arms around; Il.10.83.6.
Amidst, lay *Rhesus*, stretch'd in Sleep profound, Il.10.548.27.
Stretch'd in long Ruin, and expos'd to Day) Il.11.124.41.
Which pierc'd his Brain, & stretch'd him on the Ground: Il.11.132.41.
Stretch'd in the Dust th' unhappy Warrior lies, Il.11.309.48.
And stretch'd the great *Itymonæus* dead! Il.11.819.72.
There stretch'd at length the wounded Hero lay, Il.11.980.79.
Is stretch'd on both, and close-compell'd they dye. Il.13.454.128.
Is stretch'd on both, and Heaps on Heaps they dye. Il.13.454A.128.
And stretch'd before his much-lov'd Coursers lay. Il.13.498.130.
Stretch'd on the Plain, he sobs away his Breath, Il.13.644.136.
But stretch'd in heaps before *Oïleus'* Son, Il.14.615.192.
Stretch'd on one Heap, the Victors spoil the slain. Il.15.389.212.
As stretch'd in Dust before the Stern he lay. Il.15.493.216.
It stretch'd in Dust unhappy *Lycophron:* Il.15.501.216.
Before his Chariot stretch'd his Form divine: Il.16.598.267.
Stretch'd by *Patroclus'* Arm on yonder Plains, Il.16.667.270.
His shatter'd Helm, and stretch'd him o'er the Slain. Il.16.708.271.
Wide o'er the Land was stretch'd his large Domain, Il.16.723.272.
And stretch'd in Death, forgets the guiding Reins! Il.16.937.279.
Stretch'd in the Dust the great *Iphytus'* Son, Il.17.353.301.
So shall *Achilles* fall! stretch'd pale and dead, Il.18.151.329.
Stretch'd forth, and gash'd with many a gaping Wound. Il.18.282.335.
Here stretch'd in Ranks the level'd Swarths are found, Il.18.639.354.
Stretch'd o'er *Patroclus'* Corse; while all the rest Il.19.7.371.
Far on his out-stretch'd Arm, *Pelides* held Il.20.310.407.
And stretch'd the Servant o'er his dying Lord. Il.20.568.418.

STRETCH'D (CONTINUED)

Stretch'd like a Hero, by a Hero's Arm! Il.21.322.434.
And stretch'd beneath that Fury of the Plain. Il.22.54.455.
At last is *Hector* stretch'd upon the Plain, Il.22.415.472.
The bloody *Hector* stretch'd before thy Feet. Il.23.28.488.
But great *Pelides*, stretch'd along the Shore Il.23.70.489.
All stretch'd at ease the genial Banquet share, Il.24.3.534.
So broad, his Pinions stretch'd their ample Shade, Il.24.392.552.
Those, *Cynthia's* Arrows stretch'd upon the Plain. Il.24.762.569.
Her breathless Brother stretch'd upon the Bier: Il.24.873.573.
Stretch'd on the downy fleece, no rest he knows, Od.1.557.58.
He, stretch'd at ease in *Argos'* calm recess, Od.3.326.102.
(*Sidon* the Capital) I stretch'd my toil Od.4.99.124.
Stretch'd on the shelly shore, he first surveys Od.4.555.146.
Of *Thessaly* wide stretch'd his ample reign:) Od.4.1052.167.
Stretch'd wide his eager arms, and shot the seas along. Od.5.477.195.
He stretch'd his hand the prudent chief to raise, Od.7.225.247.
Then stretch'd in length o'er half the cavern'd rock, Od.9.354.321.
Stretch'd on the shore in careless ease we rest, Od.9.652.333.
Stretch'd forth, and panting in the sunny ray. Od.10.186.349.
This hand had stretch'd him breathless on the ground; Od.10.520.368.
O'er proud *Iölcos Pelias* stretch'd his reign, Od.11.311.397.
Stretch'd out her snowy hand, and thus she spoke: Od.11.417.405.
His arms he stretch'd; his arms the touch deceive, Od.11.487.408.
The friendly Goddess stretch'd the swelling sails; Od.12.185.441.
Stretch'd her dire jaws and swept six men away; Od.12.295.446.
They call, and aid with out-stretch'd arms implore: Od.12.298.446.
In vain they call! those arms are stretch'd no more. Od.12.299.446.
Who o'er *Dulichium* stretch'd his spacious reign, Od.16.410.126.
Stretch'd forth in wrath, shall drive thee from the land. Od.21.402.279.
Then prostrate stretch'd before the dreadful man, Od.22.377.306.
Stretch'd in a long oblivion of their lust. Od.22.481.312.
Stretch'd in our palace, by these hands lie slain. Od.24.381.367.

STRETCH'D-OUT

His stretch'd-out arm display'd a Volume fair; 5.DunB4.106.351.

STRETCHES

Curl stretches after Gay, but Gay is gone, 5.DunA2.119.111
Curl stretches after Gay, but Gay is gone, 5.DunB2.127.301
Stretches his little Hands, and rolls his Eyes! 6.96v.8.280.
Moves into Ranks, and stretches o'er the Land. Il.3.2.186.
Moves on in Rank, and stretches o'er the Land. Il.13.627.136.
And bless the hand that stretches forth the bread. Od.17.13.133.

STRETCHING

Or see the stretching branches long to meet! 3.Ep4.92.146.
And see the stretching branches long to meet! 3.Ep4.92A.146.
Far-stretching in the Shade of *Trojan* Tow'rs. Il.22.8.453.
And hov'ring o'er, their stretching Shadows sees. Il.23.460.508.

STREW'D

With wither'd foliage strew'd, a heapy store! Od.19.515.221.

STREWS

Is thine alone the seed that strews the plain? 3.EOM3.37.96.
My Muse attending strews thy path with Bays, 6.84.31Z7.239.

STRICT

And Rules as strict his labour'd Work confine, 1.EOC.137.255.
And did his Work to Rules as strict confine, 1.EOC.137A.255.
Nay, were they taken in a strict Embrace, 2.ChJM.663.47.
His own strict Judge, and Patron of Mankind. 2.TemF.167.268.
The strict Companions are for ever join'd, 2.TemF.495.287.
Bring then these blessings to a strict account, 3.EOM4.269.153.
Their own strict Judges, not a word they spare 4.2HE2.159.175.
"Behold yon Pair, in strict embraces join'd; 5.DunA3.173.168.
"Behold yon Pair, in strict embraces join'd; 5.DunB3.179.329.
Let the strict Life of graver Mortals be 6.19.21.62.
Reviews his life, and in the strict survey 6.55.5.166.
Long in a strict Embrace she held her Son, Il.6.316.341.
By Orders strict the Charioteers enjoin'd, Il.12.97.84.
While thy strict Hand his Fellows Head restrains, Il.23.410.506.
Here, from our strict embrace a Stream he glides: Od.4.620.149.
To thy strict charge, *Philætius!* we consign Od.21.256.272.
He ran, he seiz'd him with a strict embrace, Od.24.373.367.

STRICTEST

With strictest Order sets his Train in Arms, Il.4.338.236.

STRICTLY

Tho' not too strictly bound to Time and Place: 6.19.28.63.

STRICTURE

Within the stricture of this palace wall Od.22.186.296.

STRIDE

And masculine her Stride. 6.14v(a).18.49.
See him stride 6.96i.17.268.
The Field he measur'd with a larger Stride. Il.13.466.128.
The tow'ring *Ajax*, with an ample Stride, Il.13.1020.153.
High on the Decks, with vast gigantic Stride, Il.15.820.228.
The God now distant scarce a Stride before, Il.21.715.451.
But left the mansion with a lofty stride: Od.17.32.134.

STRIDES

Vice with such Giant-strides comes on amain, 4.EpS2.6.313.
See what ample Strides he takes, 6.78ii.5.216.
This said, he stalk'd with ample Strides along, Il.4.286.234.
This said, with ample Strides the Hero past; Il.6.143.331.
Along the Shore with hasty Strides he went; Il.11.935.77.
From Realm to Realm three ample Strides he took, Il.13.32.106.
With ample Strides he stalks from Place to Place. Il.16.655.270.
With tow'ring Strides *Æneas* first advanc'd; Il.20.194.402.
With heavier Strides, that lengthen tow'rd the Town. Il.21.636.448.
Now o'er the Fields they stretch with lengthen'd Strides, Il.21.713.451.

STRIDES (CONTINUED)

Down to the strand he speeds with haughty strides, ... Od.4.1029.166.
But turning stalk'd with giant strides away. .... Od.11.774.424.

STRIDING

Then striding forward with a furious bound, ... Od.8.209.273.

STRIFE

For *Wit* and *Judgment* often are at strife, ... 1.EOC.82.248.
For *Wit* and *Judgment* ever are at strife, ... 1.EOC.82A.248.
Hence Strife shall rise, and mortal War succeed; .... 1.TrSt.344.424.
To sooth his Cares, and free from Noise and Strife .... 2.ChJM.27.16.
"Who puts a Period to Domestick Strife! .... 2.ChWB.191.65.
For thee (they cry'd) amidst Alarms and Strife, ... 2.TemF.344.280.
There various News I heard, of Love and Strife, ... 2.TemF.448.285.
But ALL subsists by elemental strife; .... 3.EOM1.169.36.
The lights and shades, whose well accorded strife .... 3.EOM2.121.70.
See SIDNEY bleeds amid the martial strife! .... 3.EOM4.101.138.
Give each a System, all must be at strife; .... 3.EOM4.142Z1.141.
Add Nature's, Custom's, Reason's, Passion's strife, ... 3.Ep1.21.17.
Men, some to Quiet, some to public Strife; .... 3.Ep2.217.68.
Born to no Pride, inheriting no Strife, ... 4.Arbu.392.126.
Till friend with friend, and families at strife, ... 4.2HE1.253.217.
But wherefore all this labour, all this strife? .... 4.1HE6.38.239.
When (each Opinion with the next at strife, ... 4.1HE1.167.291.
Chetwood and Curl accept the glorious strife, ... 5.DunA2.159.121.
Chapman and Curl accept the glorious strife, ... 5.DunA2.1059B.121.
Osborn and Curl accept the glorious strife, ... 5.DunA2.159C.121.
Osborne and Curl accept the glorious strife, ... 5.DunB2.167.303.
And run precipitant, with Noise and Strife, ... 6.17ii.5.56.
Alone, remov'd from Grandeur and from Strife, ... 6.17iii.16.58.
Cease, fond Nature, cease thy strife, ... 6.31ii.5.94.
Not that he shunn'd the doubtful Strife, ... 6.79.127.222.
From office, business, news, and strife: .... 6.114.10.321.
The Cause of Strife remov'd so rarely well, ... 6.145.9.388.
Sprung the fierce Strife, from what offended Pow'r? .... Il.1.10.85.
Strife and Debate thy restless Soul employ, ... Il.1.231.98.
Let Men their Days in senseless Strife employ, ... Il.1.744.123.
Encourag'd hence, maintain the glorious Strife, ... Il.2.420.147.
Left to *Atrides,* (Victor in the Strife) .... Il.3.499.215.
Tho' great *Atrides* gain'd the glorious Strife. .... Il.4.18.221.
'Tis Man's bold Task the gen'rous Strife to try, ... Il.7.117.369.
And cease the Strife when *Hector* shows the way. .... Il.7.348.381.
Some future Day shall lengthen out the Strife, ... Il.7.354.381.
There deaf for ever to the martial Strife, ... Il.9.522.458.
Each single *Greek,* in this conclusive Strife, ... Il.10.196.10.
Shall we dismiss thee, in some future Strife .... Il.10.518.26.
Else should this Hand, this Hour, decide the Strife, ... Il.13.612.135.
For Strife, I hear, has made the Union cease, ... Il.14.237.172.
For Strife, I hear, has made that Union cease .... Il.14.347.179.
And better far, in one decisive Strife, ... Il.15.604.220.
At length the sov'reign Savage wins the Strife, ... Il.16.997.281.
No longer then defer the glorious Strife, ... Il.17.43.289.
For *Troy,* for *Troy,* shall henceforth be the Strife, ... Il.18.311.336.
That doom'd our Strife, and doom'd the *Greeks* to fall. .... Il.19.286.384.
'Tis not in Words the glorious strife can end. .... Il.20.251.404.
While these by *Juno's* Will the Strife resign, ... Il.21.448.439.
(Such as in Races crown the speedy Strife) .... Il.22.209.464.
To them I swear; if Victor in the Strife .... Il.22.327.469.
No Thought but Rage, and never-ceasing Strife, ... Il.22.341.470.
Scarce did the Chief the vig'rous Strife propose, ... Il.23.820.522.
While the long Strife ev'n tir'd the Lookers-on, ... Il.23.838.522.
Still breathing Strife, and unsubdu'd of Soul: .... Il.23.853.523.
Bade share the Honours, and surcease the Strife. .... Il.23.970.527.
Soon shou'd yon' boasters cease their haughty strife, ... Od.1.348.49.
With dear esteem: to wise, with jealous strife .... Od.1.545.58.
With sails outspread we fly th' unequal strife, ... Od.9.71.305.
O why was I victorious in the strife! .... Od.11.671.417.
With winds and waves I held unequal strife; .... Od.14.348.51.
Oppress'd by numbers in the glorious strife, ... Od.16.110.108.
Ere yet he trod these shores! to strife he draws .... Od.18.448.190.
Smiles dew'd with tears the pleasing strife exprest .... Od.19.550.223.
Heav'n shall determine in a gameful strife: .... Od.19.667.228.
Shall end the strife, and win th' imperial dame; .... Od.21.5.258.
Hear the conditions, and commence the strife. .... Od.21.74.262.
'Till the next dawn this ill-tim'd strife forgoe, ... Od.21.276.273.
Cease the mad strife, and share our bounty here. .... Od.21.332.276.
The strife-full bow, and gives it to the King. .... Od.21.410.279.
Nor ceas'd the strife, 'till *Jove* himself oppos'd, ... Od.24.58.350.
The Archer's strife; the source of future woes, ... Od.24.196.358.

STRIFE-FULL

The strife-full bow, and gives it to the King. .... Od.21.410.279.

STRIFES

Shall human Strifes celestial Minds divide? .... Il.14.220.172.

STRIKE

At once they bend, and strike their equal Oars, ... 1.TrUl.3.465.
And strike to Dust th'aspiring Tow'rs of *Troy;* .... 2.RL*A*1.138.131.
Bright as the Sun, her Eyes the Gazers strike, ... 2.RL2.13.160.
And strike to Dust th' Imperial Tow'rs of *Troy;* .... 2.RL3.174.182.
Charms strike the Sight, but Merit wins the Soul. .... 2.RL5.34.201.
And base, and treble Voices strike the Skies. .... 2.RL5.42.202.
From Nature's chain whatever link you strike, ... 3.EOM1.245.45.
On diff'rent senses diff'rent objects strike; .... 3.EOM2.128.70.
That touching one must strike the other too; .... 3.EOM3.292.122.
They please as Beauties, here as Wonders strike. .... 3.Ep1.96.22.
Strike off his Pension, by the setting sun, ... 3.Ep1.160.29.
Start ev'n from Difficulty, strike from Chance; .... 3.Ep4.68.143.
Let but a comely Fore-hand strike the Eye: .... 4.HAdv.119.85.
Willing to wound, and yet afraid to strike, ... 4.Arbu.203.110.
Fr. Yes, strike that *Wild,* I'll justify the blow. .... 4.EpS2.54.315.
P. Strike? why the man was hang'd ten years ago: .... 4.EpS2.55.315.
There motley Images her fancy strike, ... 5.DunA1.63.67.
There motley Images her fancy strike, ... 5.DunB1.65.275.

STRIKE (CONTINUED)

When love would strike th' offending fair, ... 6.4v.1.11.
When you, like *Orpheus,* strike the warbling Lyre, ... 6.7.9.15.
That strike the Subjects answ'ring Heart; .... 6.11.35Z8.31.
Or pleas'd to wound, and yet afraid to strike, ... 6.49iii.17.143.
Willing to wound, and yet afraid to strike, ... 6.49iii.17A.143.
Wishing to wound, and yet afraid to strike, ... 6.49iii.17B.143.
Or pleas'd to wound, but yet afraid to strike, ... 6.49iii.17C.143.
Whether thy hand strike out some free design, ... 6.52.3.156.
Strike in the sketch, or in the picture glow; .... 6.52.44.157.
Wishing to wound, and yet afraid to strike, ... 6.98.53.285.
Jove but prepares to strike the fiercer Blow. .... Il.4.195.230.
Loud, and more loud, the Clamours strike their Ear .... Il.10.216.11.
They strike th' Assailants, and infix their Stings; .... Il.12.192.88.
'Tis but the Wish to strike before the rest. .... Il.13.371.123.
Depart I must: What Horrors strike my Eyes? .... Il.15.461.215.
From the proud Archer strike his vaunted Bow. .... Il.15.575.218.
And Streams, and Vales, and Forests strike the Eyes, ... Il.16.359.257.
One Fate the Warrior and the Friend shall strike, ... Il.18.385.339.
And level'd Thunder strike my guilty Head! .... Il.19.276.383.
Then thus, amaz'd: What Wonders strike my Mind! .... Il.20.393.411.
Ye mighty Gods! what Wonders strike my View: .... Il.21.62.424.
His batter'd Face and Elbows strike the Ground; .... Il.23.475.509.
In act to strike: Before him *Perseus* stood, ... Od.3.562.115.
My wants, and lent these robes that strike your eyes. .... Od.7.381.255.
Once more harmonious strike the sounding string, ... Od.8.539.291.
Or chearful voice of mortal strike the ear? .... Od.10.172.349.
My mates ascend the ship; they strike their oars; .... Od.11.791.426.
At once they bend, and strike their equal oars, ... Od.13.94.5.
Is he not wise? know this, and strike the blow. .... Od.16.389.124.
Strike, ere the States conven'd the foe betray, ... Od.16.392.125.
Doubtful, or with his staff to strike him dead, ... Od.17.276.145.

STRIKER'S

Shall pay the Stroke, and grace the Striker's Side: .... Il.23.953.527.

STRIKES

And strikes with bolder Rage the sounding Strings, ... 1.TrSP.34.394.
Strikes, and behold a sudden *Thebes* aspire! .... 2.TemF.86.259.
Strikes, and beholds a sudden *Thebes* aspire; .... 2.TemF.86A.259.
(So Darkness strikes the sense no less than Light) .... 3.Ep1.112.23.
Noble and young, who strikes the heart .... 4.HOde1.11.151.
But hark! he strikes the golden Lyre; .... 6.11.63.32.
And strikes a blush thro' frontless Flattery. .... 6.73.7.209.
So while the sun's broad beam yet strikes the sight, ... 6.106i.4.306.
Low sunk on Earth, the *Trojan* strikes the Skies. .... Il.8.92.401.
Strikes the blue Mountains with her golden Ray, ... Il.9.829.474.
First of the Field, great *Ajax* strikes their Eyes, ... Il.15.814.228.
Strikes the fresh Garland from the Victor's Brow! .... Il.17.200.295.
With loud-resounding Arms he strikes the Plain; .... Il.20.447.413.
He strikes his rev'rend Head now white with Age: .... Il.22.44.454.
Strikes from his Hand the Scourge, and renders vain .... Il.23.463.508.
Whose Weapon strikes yon' flutt'ring Bird, shall bear .... Il.23.1014.529.
Methinks *Ulysses* strikes my wond'ring eyes: .... Od.4.198.129.
Soon as she strikes her wand, and gives the word, ... Od.10.349.361.
And vengeance strikes whom heav'n has doom'd to fall. .... Od.16.301.120.
And now his city strikes the Monarch's eyes, ... Od.17.226.142.
One strikes the gate, one rings against the walls; .... Od.22.285.300.
The Lyrist strikes the string; gay youths advance, ... Od.23.141.327.

STRIKING

And striking Watches the tenth Hour resound. .... 2.RL1.18A.145.
He boarding her, she striking sail to him. .... 4.JD4.231.45.
Striking their pensive bosoms— *Here* lies GAY. .... 6.125.12.350.
Striking their aching hearts— *Here* lies GAY. .... 6.125.12A.350.
Striking their aching bosoms— *Here* lies GAY. .... 6.125.12B.350.

STRING

No more these Hands shall touch the trembling String: .... 1.TrSP.235.404.
These touch the vocal Stops, and those the trembling String. .... 2.ChJM.321.29.
For Fame they raise the Voice, and tune the String. .... 2.TemF.273.276.
On each enervate string they taught the Note .... 4.2HE1.153.209.
Wake into Voice each silent String, ... 6.11.3.29.
One dip the pencil, and one string the lyre. .... 6.52.70.158.
His Hand no more awak'd the silver String. .... Il.2.730.161.
Sounds the tough Horn, and twangs the quiv'ring String. .... Il.4.157.228.
He said, and twang'd the String. The Weapon flies .... Il.8.365.414.
Then *Jove* shall string his Arm, and fire his Breast, ... Il.11.249.46.
Then *Jove* shall string thy Arm, and fire thy Breast, ... Il.11.265.47.
The Bow-string twang'd; nor flew the Shaft in vain, ... Il.11.481.55.
Breathe in your Hearts, and string your Arms to Fight, ... Il.13.84.108.
At his full Stretch, as the tough String he drew, ... Il.15.544.217.
Confirm his Heart, and string his Arm to War: .... Il.16.299.254.
Now Flights of Arrows bounding from the String: .... Il.16.932.279.
Swift from the String the sounding Arrow flies; .... Il.23.1020.529.
A-down the Main-mast fell the parted String, ... Il.23.1026.530.
High strains, responsive to the vocal string. .... Od.1.200.42.
Dumb be thy voice, and mute th' harmonious string; .... Od.8.94.267.
Once more harmonious strike the sounding string, ... Od.8.539.291.
Dumb be thy voice, and mute the tuneful string: .... Od.8.586.294.
And send swift arrows from the bounding string, ... Od.14.262.49.
The bolt, obedient to the silken string, ... Od.21.47.261.
High notes responsive to the trembling string, ... Od.21.441.281.
The bending horns, and one the string essay'd. .... Od.21.447.281.
From his essaying hand the string let fly .... Od.21.448.281.
The whizzing arrow vanish'd from the string, ... Od.21.461.282.
The Lyrist strikes the string; gay youths advance, ... Od.23.141.327.
The twanging string, and try'd the stubborn yew: .... Od.24.198.358.

STRINGS

And strikes with bolder Rage the sounding Strings, ... 1.TrSP.34.394.
And boldly sinks into the sounding Strings. .... 2.TemF.215.272.
Taught nor to slack, nor strain its tender strings, ... 3.EOM3.290.121.
Taught not to slack, nor strain its tender strings, ... 3.EOM3.290A.121.
Stuck o'er with titles and hung round with strings, ... 3.EOM4.205.146.
Or Popularity, or Stars and Strings? .... 4.1HE6.14.237.

STRINGS (CONTINUED)
Nor slack nor strain the tender Strings; 6.11.35Z6.31.
Can stoop to pick up *Strings* and *Sticks.* 6.135.12.366.
Swells their bold Hearts, and strings their nervous Arms; Il.2.531.152.
To these a Youth awakes the warbling Strings, Il.18.661.355.
High airs, attemper'd to the vocal strings; Od.4.24.121.
The vocal lay responsive to the strings. Od.8.42.264.
Mean-time the Bard alternate to the strings Od.8.307.279.
He fights, subdues: for *Pallas* strings his arms. Od.8.568.293.
And forms the dance responsive to the strings. Od.23.134.327.

STRIP
First strip off all her equipage of Pride, 3.EOM2.44.61.
If QUEENSBERRY to strip there's no compelling, 3.Ep2.193.66.
And I not strip the Gilding off a Knave, 4.HS1.115.17.
"Here strip my children! here at once leap in! 5.DunA2.263.133.
"Here strip, my children! here at once leap in, 5.DunB2.275.309.
And strip white *Ceres* of her nut-brown Coat. 6.100vi.3.289.
To strip those Arms thou ill deserv'st to wear, Il.2.323.142.
The Victim falls, they strip the smoaking Hide, Il.7.382.382.
From *Tydeus'* Shoulders strip the costly Load, Il.8.236.409.
Haste, strip his Arms, the Slaughter round him spread, Il.16.687.271.
The shouting *Argives* strip the Heroes slain. Il.17.369.302.
For vulgar parents cannot strip their race Od.4.75.123.
Strip off thy garments; *Neptune's* fury brave Od.5.436.193.
Swift from the oak they strip the shady pride; Od.12.421.451.

STRIP'D
He left huge Lintot, and out-strip'd the wind. 5.DunB2.62.298.

STRIPLING
The fainting Stripling sunk, before the Stroke; Il.21.126.426.
Gay, stripling youths the brimming goblets crown'd. Od.1.194.42.

STRIPP'D
And stripp'd the Skin, and crack'd the solid Bone. Il.5.378.285.
The ruthless Victor stripp'd their shining Arms. Il.6.34.325.
I follow thee—He said, and stripp'd the Slain. Il.22.462.474.
(Stripp'd of my own) and to the vessel bound. Od.14.380.53.

STRIPS
Or nightly Pillager that strips the slain. Il.10.408.21.
The stern *Tydides* strips their shining Arms. Il.11.432.53.
Strips his bright Arms, *Oïleus* lops his Head: Il.13.270.117.

STRIPT
See good Sir *George* of ragged Livery stript, 4.HAdv.55.81.
K— of his Footman's borrow'd Livery stript, 4.HAdv.55A.81.
But ey'd him round, and stript off all the Cloaths; 4.HAdv.115.85.
He left huge Lintot, and out-stript the wind. 5.DunA2.58.105.
There, stript, fair *Rhet'ric* languish'd on the ground; 5.DunB4.24.342.
And stript, their Features to his Mind recalls. Il.11.150.42.
Stript of its Arms alone (the Conqu'rors Due) Il.22.330.470.
Stript of his rags, he blaz'd out like a God. Od.22.2.284.

STRIV'ST
Striv'st thou with *Jove?* Thou are already lost. Il.15.147.202.
Striv'st thou with him, by whom all Pow'r is giv'n? Il.15.204.204.

STRIVE
Here Earth and Water seem to strive again, 1.W-F.12.149.
Where Wigs with Wigs, with Sword-knots Sword-knots strive, 2.RL1.101.153.
Nor strive with all the Tempest in my teeth. 4.2HE2.301.187.
Strive to my list to add one Monarch more; 5.DunB4.600A.403.
To Please her shall her Husband strive 6.54.5.164.
Ah, no! 'tis vain to strive—It will not be. 6.85.9Z1.242.
As Courtiers should, whene'er they strive 6.94.35.260.
Nor rashly strive where human Force is vain. Il.5.167.275.
While thus they strive, *Tlepolemus* the great Il.5.776.303.
That Pass *Tydides, Ajax* strive to gain, Il.6.554.354.
Strive all, of mortal and immortal Birth, Il.8.27.397.
Ye strive in vain! If I but stretch this Hand, Il.8.29.397.
Or strive with Pray'rs his haughty Soul to bend? Il.9.817.474.
But strive, tho' num'rous, to repulse in vain. Il.15.471.215.
So watchful Shepherds strive to force, in vain, Il.18.199.331.
And *Phœnix;* strive to calm his Grief and Rage Il.19.332.386.
Who strive presumptuous with the Sons of *Jove.* Il.21.202.429.
In vain unskilfull to the Goal they strive, Il.23.391.506.
Why with our wiser Elders should we strive? Il.23.925.526.
In vain they strive, th' entangling snares deny Od.8.341.282.
Say whence, ye Gods, contending nations strive Od.10.42.341.
My sword I strive to wield, but strive in vain; Od.11.528.409.
My sword I strive to wield, but strive in vain; Od.11.528.409.
And strive to gain the bark; but *Jove* denies. Od.12.495.456.
Yet strive by pray'r and counsel to restrain Od.16.298.120.
Their lawless insults, tho' thou strive in vain: Od.16.299.120.
Take it who will, he cries, I strive no more. Od.21.160.267.
(So need compells.) Then all united strive Od.22.89.290.
Strive for fair Virtue, and contest for Fame! Od.24.597.376.

STRIVES
When *Ajax* strives, some Rock's vast Weight to throw, 1.EOC.370.282.
Heav'n, when it strives to polish all it can 3.Ep2.271.72.
Invention strives to be before in vain; 4.EpS2.7.313.
Strives to extract from his soft, giving palm; 5.DunA2.200.126.
Strives to extract from his soft, giving palm; 5.DunB2.208.306.
Who strives to please the Fair *against her Will:* 6.34.6.101.
That strives to learn what Heav'n resolves to hide; Il.1.727.122.
Strives he with me, by whom his Pow'r was giv'n, Il.15.188.203.
The fruit he strives to seize: but blasts arise, Od.11.731.421.

STRODE
Then, with his Sev'nfold Shield, he strode away. 1.TrES.88.453.
But, stern as Ajax' spectre, strode away. 5.DunB4.274.371.
Strode where the foremost of the Foes engag'd; Il.4.568.248.
Grimly he smil'd; Earth trembled as he strode: Il.7.256.377.

STRODE (CONTINUED)
Then seiz'd his pond'rous Lance, and strode along. Il.10.204.10.
Then, with his sev'nfold Shield, he strode away. Il.12.442.97.
Thus speaking, furious from the Field he strode, Il.15.244.206.
He strode along the Field, as thus he said. Il.17.211.295.
Exhorting loud thro' all the Field he strode, Il.17.253.297.
Sternly his head withdrew, and strode away. Od.2.362.78.
The brethren cry'd, and instant strode away. Od.9.490.326.
With martial port he strode, and stern delight; Od.11.630.414.
He brac'd his sandals on, and strode away: Od.16.167.110.
This said, the honest herdsman strode before: Od.17.394.151.
When fierce the Heroe o'er the threshold strode; Od.22.1.284.
Secur'd the door, and hasty strode away: Od.22.218.297.
As o'er the heaps of death *Ulysses* strode, Od.24.510.372.

STROK'D
Then snapt his box, and strok'd his belly down: 5.DunB4.495.391.

STROKE
Nor Victims sink beneath the Sacred Stroke; 1.TrSt.372.425.
The Sable Flock shall fall beneath the Stroke, 1.TrSt.594.435.
One fatal stroke the sacred Hair does sever 2.RL*A*1.117.130.
Barbarian stay! that bloody stroke restrain; 2.ElAb.103.328.
Which sees no more the stroke, or feels the pain, 3.EOM3.67.98.
Not less foresees the stroke, or feels the pain. 3.EOM3.67A.98*.
Some flying stroke alone can hit 'em right: 3.Ep2.154.63.
Paulo's free stroke, and *Titian's* warmth divine. 6.52.38.157.
Free as thy stroke, yet faultless as thy line! 6.52.64.158.
Some felt the silent stroke of mould'ring age, 6.71.11.203.
The Stroke had fix'd him to the Gates of Hell, Il.5.239.278.
Taught by this Stroke, renounce the War's Alarms, Il.5.437.289.
His thundring Arm a deadly Stroke imprest Il.6.11.323.
His slacken'd Knees receiv'd the numbing Stroke; Il.7.324.379.
A youthful Steer shall fall beneath the Stroke, Il.10.347.18.
With humble Blandishment to stroke his Beard, Il.10.523.26.
Stung by the Stroke, the Coursers scour the Fields Il.11.656.63.
The Faulchion strook, and Fate pursu'd the Stroke; Il.12.222.89.
Bold *Merion* aim'd a Stroke (nor aim'd it wide) Il.13.215.116.
(While the Winds sleep) his Breast receiv'd the Stroke. Il.13.550.132.
Before the pond'rous Stroke his Corselet yields, Il.13.551.132.
But *Oenomas* receiv'd the *Cretan's* stroke, Il.13.640.136.
So just the Stroke, that yet the Body stood Il.14.547.189.
Full on the Lance a Stroke so justly sped, Il.16.144.243.
The Head, divided by a Stroke so just, Il.16.408.258.
The hollow Armour burst before the Stroke, Il.17.364.301.
The Stroke of Fate the bravest cannot shun: Il.18.147.329.
Or with these Hands the cruel Stroke repell, Il.18.534.347.
With sweeping Stroke the Mowers strow the Lands; Il.18.641.354.
I cou'd not this, this cruel Stroke attend; Il.19.349.386.
The fainting Stripling sunk, before the Stroke; Il.21.126.426.
The stunning Stroke his stubborn Nerves unbound; Il.21.474.441.
And fills his Steeds with Vigour. At a Stroke, Il.23.469.509.
And rush beneath the long-descending Stroke? Il.23.762.520.
Shall pay the Stroke, and grace the Striker's Side: Il.23.953.527.
To the strong stroke at once the rowers bend. Od.2.459.83.
Whose arm may sink us at a single stroke. Od.9.580.330.
Then bending to the stroke, their oars they drew Od.12.182.441.
Lash'd by the stroke the frothy waters fly. Od.12.207.441.
Then bending to the stroke, the active train Od.12.216.442.
Stretch to the stroke, and brush the working seas. Od.12.265.445.
The God arrests her with a sudden stroke, Od.13.188.15.
And strong with pales, by many a weary stroke Od.14.15.35.
Check'd half his might: yet rising to the stroke, Od.18.112.172.
While each to Chance ascrib'd the wond'rous stroke, Od.22.36.288.
Thus shall one stroke the glory lost regain: Od.22.278.300.

STROKES
Loud Strokes are heard, and ratling Arms resound, 1.TrES.164.455.
To wake the soul by tender strokes of art, 6.32.1.96.
Your Weapons enter, and your Strokes they feel. Il.4.590.249.
His Strokes they second, and avert our Spears: Il.5.744.302.
The Strokes redoubled on his Buckler rung; Il.11.691.66.
The Strokes yet echo'd of contending Pow'rs; Il.12.39.83.
With sounding Strokes their brazen Targets rung: Il.12.170.87.
Loud Strokes are heard, and ratling Arms resound, Il.12.518.100.
With ample Strokes he rushes to the Flood, Il.15.300.208.
And thick, strong Strokes, the doubling Vaults rebound. Il.18.550.348.
Loud sounds the Axe, redoubling Strokes on Strokes; Il.23.146.495.
Loud sounds the Axe, redoubling Strokes on Strokes; Il.23.146.495.
Loud sounds the Axe, rebounding Strokes on Strokes; Il.23.146A.495.
Loud sounds the Axe, rebounding Strokes on Strokes; Il.23.146A.495.
'Tis more by Art, than Force of num'rous Strokes, Il.23.385.505.
With hasty strokes the hoarse-resounding deep; Od.9.657.333.
And sweep with equal strokes the smoaky seas; Od.10.150.347.
This said, the sounding strokes his horses fire, Od.15.242.80.
Divide, obedient to the forceful strokes. Od.20.201.243.

STROLL'D
Your wine lock'd up, your Butler stroll'd abroad, 4.HS2.13.55.

STROLLING
And starve by strolling, not by work to thrive. Od.18.409.188.
"In came a Beggar of the strolling crew, Od.21.353.276.

STRONG
When lab'ring with strong Charms, she shoots from high 1.TrSt.148.416.
Whose fatal Bow the strong *Pandion* bore. 1.TrES.90.453.
Not two strong Men th'enormous Weight cou'd raise, 1.TrES.185.456.
With Iron Bars and brazen Hinges strong, 1.TrES.193.456.
From strong *Patroclus'* Hand the Jav'lin fled, 1.TrES.263.459.
Where the strong Fibres bind the solid Heart. 1.TrES.287.460.
Let Reason's Rule your strong Desires abate, 2.ChJM.293.28.
Of Legs and Feet, so clean, so strong, so fair! 2.ChWB.316.72.
Form a strong Line about the Silver Bound, 2.RL2.121.167.
A strong Expression most he seem'd t'affect, 2.TemF.194.271.
The strong connections, nice dependencies, 3.EOM1.30.17.

STRONG (CONTINUED)

At best more watchful this, but that more strong. ...3.EOM2.76.64.
As strong or weak, the organs of the frame; ...3.EOM2.130.70.
She but removes weak passions for the strong: ...3.EOM2.158.74.
A mightier Pow'r the strong direction sends, ...3.EOM2.165.74.
Or (oft more strong than all) the love of ease; ...3.EOM2.170.75.
Strong grows the Virtue with his nature mix'd; ...3.EOM2.178.76.
"Still for the strong too weak, the weak too strong. ...3.EOM3.194.113.
"Still for the strong too weak, the weak too strong. ...3.EOM3.194.113.
Take the most strong, and sort them as you can. ...3.Ep1.72.20.
Tho' strong the bend, yet quick the turns of mind: ...3.Ep1.123.25.
Shall feel your ruling passion strong in death: ...3.Ep1.263.38.
But strong in sense, and wise without the rules. ...4.HS2.10.55.
Serenely pure, and yet divinely strong, ...4.2HE2.172.177.
One, driv'n by strong Benevolence of Soul, ...4.2HE2.276.185.
Milton's strong pinion now not Heav'n can bound, ...4.2HE1.99.203.
May yield, God knows, to strong Temptation. ...4.HS6.184.261.
Feign what I will, and paint it e'er so strong, ...4.EpS2.8.313.
The strong Antipathy of Good to Bad. ...4.EpS2.198.324.
Rich *with* his [Britain], *in* his [Britain] strong, ...4.1740.93.337*.
Rich *with* his . . . *in* . . . his strong, ...4.1740.93A.337*.
One clasp'd in wood, and one in strong cow-hide. ...5.DunA1.130.80.
Vig'rous he rises; from th' effluvia strong ...5.DunA2.97.109.
In dulness strong, th' avenging Vandals rise; ...5.DunA3.78A.156.
From the strong fate of drams if thou get free, ...5.DunA3.137.161.
Heady, not strong, and foaming tho' not full. ...5.DunA3.166.167.
One clasp'd in wood, and one in strong cow-hide; ...5.DunB1.150.281.
Vig'rous he rises; from th' effluvia strong ...5.DunB2.105.300.
From the strong fate of drams if thou get free, ...5.DunB3.145.326.
Heady, not strong; o'erflowing, tho' not full. ...5.DunB3.172.328.
Suspend a while your Force inertly strong, ...5.DunB4.7.340.
Strong in new Arms, lo! Giant Handel stands, ...5.DunB4.65.348.
And strong impulsive gravity of Head: ...5.DunB4.76.348.
Love, strong as Death, the Poet led ...6.11.51.32.
Strong Drink was drunk, and Gambolls play'd, ...6.13.6.39.
Woolwich and *Wapping*, smelling strong of Pitch; ...6.14ii.47.44.
This binds in Ties more easie, yet more strong, ...6.19.67.64.
Strong as their charms, and gentle as their soul; ...6.52.74.158.
And strong as *Hercules*. ...6.76.4.212.
So when Curll's Stomach the strong Drench o'ercame, ...6.82x.1.236.
So firm yet soft, so strong yet so refin'd, ...6.115.8.323.
Both fierce, both hungry, the Dispute grew strong, ...6.145.3.388.
Not * He that shakes the solid Earth so strong: ...Il.1.525.113.
Iälmen and *Ascalaphus* the strong: ...Il.2.613.157.
From *Chalcis'* Walls, and strong *Eretria;* ...Il.2.644.157.
Whom strong *Tyrinthè's* lofty Walls surround, ...Il.2.678.159.
To strong *Dulichium* from his Sire he fled, ...Il.2.763.162.
Casus the strong, and *Crapathus* the fair; ...Il.2.824.164.
Panthus, and *Hicetäon,* once the strong, ...Il.3.195.200.
Burst the strong Nerves, and crash'd the solid Bone: ...Il.4.602.250.
Thus from high Hills the Torrents swift and strong ...Il.5.116.272.
Bends their strong Necks, and tears them to the Ground. ...Il.5.209.276.
But while my Nerves are strong, my Force entire, ...Il.5.316.281.
Not two strong Men th' enormous Weight could raise, ...Il.5.371.284.
Strong as thou art, some God may yet be found, ...Il.5.499.292.
To meet whose Point was strong *Deicoon's* Chance; ...Il.5.660.299.
Stentor the strong, endu'd with Brazen Lungs, ...Il.5.978.313.
Far from the Car, the strong immortal Lance. ...Il.5.1047.316.
And two fair Infants crown'd his strong Embrace.) ...Il.6.32.325.
Rush'd on a *Tamarisk's* strong Trunk, and broke ...Il.6.49.325.
Oeneus the strong, *Bellerophon* the bold: ...Il.6.268.340.
Troy's strong Defence, unconquer'd *Pallas,* aid! ...Il.6.379.345.
In his strong Hand up-heav'd a flinty Stone, ...Il.7.316.379.
Strong Piles infix'd stood adverse to the Foe. ...Il.7.525.390.
Strong God of Ocean! Thou, whose Rage can make ...Il.7.544.391.
Whose strong Embrace holds Heav'n, and Earth, and Main: ...Il.8.26.397.
With Terror cloath'd, and more than mortal strong. ...Il.8.406.416.
Their strong Distress the Wife of *Jove* survey'd; ...Il.8.421.417.
Huge, pond'rous, strong! that when her Fury burns, ...Il.8.474.419.
Or strong Necessity, or urgent Fear: ...Il.9.262.445.
Strong Guards they plac'd, and watch'd nine Nights entire; ...Il.9.594.464.
The strong *Dolopians* thenceforth own'd my Reign, ...Il.9.602.464.
Due Honours calm the fierce, and bend the strong. ...Il.9.640.466.
Strong as they were, the bold *Curetes* fail'd, ...Il.9.665.467.
For strong *Necessity* our Toils demands, ...Il.10.134.8.
Rise, Son of *Tydeus!* to the brave and strong ...Il.10.180.9.
Then grinding Tortures his strong Bosom rend, ...Il.11.347.50.
Then with a Voice which Fury made more strong, ...Il.11.353.50.
The Gust continu'd, violent, and strong, ...Il.11.397.52.
Thro' the strong Brass the ringing Javelin thrown, ...Il.11.547.58.
Strong as he is; yet, one oppos'd to all, ...Il.11.586.60.
On strong *Pandocus* next inflicts a Wound, ...Il.11.612.61.
The Foot alone this strong Defence could force, ...Il.12.65.83.
Strong in themselves, but stronger in his Aid, ...Il.12.303.92.
Strong in themselves, but stronger in their Aid, ...Il.12.303A.92.
Whose fatal Bow the strong *Pandion* bore. ...Il.12.444.97.
Not two strong Men th' enormous Weight could raise, ...Il.12.539.101.
With Iron Bars and Brazen Hinges strong, ...Il.12.547.101.
Strong as they seem, embattel'd like a Tow'r. ...Il.13.208.115.
Indissolubly strong, the fatal Tye ...Il.13.453.128.
On his rais'd Arm by two strong Braces stay'd) ...Il.13.515.131.
His lab'ring Heart, heaves, with so strong a bound, ...Il.13.554.132.
Sent from an Arm so strong, the missive Wood ...Il.13.638.136.
While Death's strong Pangs distend his lab'ring Side, ...Il.13.722.139.
And smote his Temples, with an Arm so strong ...Il.13.729.139.
Meges the strong th' *Epeian* Bands controul'd, ...Il.13.865.147.
Shot Terrors round, that wither'd ev'n the Strong. ...Il.13.1017.153.
Ne'er did my Soul so strong a Passion prove, ...Il.14.359.180.
The pond'rous Targe be wielded by the strong. ...Il.14.434.184.
The strong and cumb'rous Arms the valiant wield, ...Il.14.441.184.
Strong *Periphætes* and *Prothoön* bled, ...Il.14.609.192.
See, and be strong! the Thund'rer sends thee Aid. ...Il.15.289.208.
Strong to impell the Flight of many a Dart. ...Il.15.553.218.
So strong to fight, so active to pursue? ...Il.15.683.222.
So the strong Eagle from his airy Height ...Il.15.836.229.
Strong *Echeclœus,* blest in all those Charms ...Il.16.224.248.

STRONG (CONTINUED)

From strong *Patroclus'* Hand the Javelin fled, ...Il.16.568.266.
Where the strong Fibres bind the solid Heart. ...Il.16.592.267.
Strong as you are, 'tis mortal Force you trust, ...Il.16.751.273.
An Arm as strong may stretch thee in the Dust. ...Il.16.752.273.
The Strong he withers, and confounds the Bold, ...Il.17.198.295.
In strong Convulsions panting on the Sands ...Il.17.366.301.
Whether the Weak or Strong discharge the Dart, ...Il.17.711.315.
While his strong Lance around him heaps the Dead: ...Il.18.232.333.
And thick, strong Strokes, the doubling Vaults rebound. ...Il.18.550.348.
Clang the strong Arms, and ring the Shores around: ...Il.19.16.372.
With strong Repast to hearten' ev'ry Band; ...Il.19.170.378.
Tho' strong in Battel as a brazen Tow'r. ...Il.20.133.399.
Thro' two strong Plates the Point is Passage held, ...Il.20.316.407.
Earth, whose strong Grasp has held down *Hercules*. ...Il.21.73.424.
His Feet, upborn, scarce the strong Flood divide, ...Il.21.266.431.
And strong, and many, are the Sons of *Troy*. ...Il.21.696.450.
Then to the City, terrible and strong, ...Il.22.31.453.
While strong Affliction gives the Feeble Force: ...Il.22.525.478.
Melts their strong Hearts, and bids their Eyes to flow. ...Il.23.20.487.
Like two strong Rafters which the Builder forms ...Il.23.826.522.
And great *Leonteus,* more than mortal strong; ...Il.23.992.529.
Let the strong Sov'reign of the plumy Race ...Il.24.363.551.
Let the strong Sov'reign of the plumy Race ...Il.24.383.552.
Thro' *Grecian* Foes, so num'rous and so strong? ...Il.24.450.555.
Scarce three strong *Greeks* could lift its mighty Weight, ...Il.24.559.559.
(Strong Guards and Spies, till all the Rites were done, ...Il.24.1009.577.
Nor let *Antinous* rage, if strong desire ...Od.1.499.56.
To the strong staple's inmost depth restor'd, ...Od.1.554.58.
You make the Arm of Violence too strong. ...Od.2.88.65.
To the strong stroke at once the rowers bend. ...Od.2.459.83.
With rays so strong, distinguish'd, and divine, ...Od.3.274.99.
Let thy strong coursers swift to *Sparta* bear; ...Od.3.471.110.
And the strong tongs to turn the metal round. ...Od.3.551.114.
Strong *Thrasymed* discharg'd the speeding blow ...Od.3.570.115.
For strong the God, and perfected in guile. ...Od.4.554.146.
And twelve young mules, a strong laborious race, ...Od.4.860.159.
So large he built the Raft: then ribb'd it strong ...Od.5.321.187.
Strong with the fear of death. The rolling flood ...Od.5.415.192.
Floats a strong shout along the waves of air. ...Od.6.358.229.
None in the leap spring with so strong a bound, ...Od.8.103.268.
With these came forth *Ambasineus* the strong; ...Od.8.123.269.
From *Elatreus'* strong arm the Discus flies, ...Od.8.137.270.
Indissolubly strong! then instant bears ...Od.8.319.281.
To that fair Lecher, the strong God of arms. ...Od.8.350.282.
Swift vengeance waits: and Art subdues the strong! ...Od.8.368.283.
Strong are her sons, tho' rocky are her shores; ...Od.9.28.303.
Strong was the tyde, which by the northern blast ...Od.9.91.306.
(Scarce twenty four-wheel'd cars, compact and strong, ...Od.9.286.318.
Prest with the weight of sleep that tames the strong: ...Od.9.442.324.
Strong were the Rams, with native purple fair, ...Od.9.505.326.
The strong concussion on the heaving tyde ...Od.9.571.330.
Strong walls of brass the rocky coast confine. ...Od.10.4.339.
Wild, furious herds, unconquerably strong! ...Od.11.356.399.
More fierce than Giants, more than Giants strong; ...Od.11.378.401.
Ply the strong oar, and catch the nimble gales; ...Od.12.106.436.
Lend his strong aid, his aid he lends in vain. ...Od.12.136.438.
Deathless the pest! impenetrably strong! ...Od.12.148.439.
Snapt the strong helm, and bore to sea the mast. ...Od.12.499.456.
Know, I am with thee, strong in all my might. ...Od.13.448.27.
And strong with pales, by many a weary stroke ...Od.14.15.35.
To form strong buskins of well-season'd hyde. ...Od.14.26.36.
Once I was strong (wou'd heav'n restore those days) ...Od.14.526.62.
If with desire so strong thy bosom glows, ...Od.15.75.72.
But when a length of years unnerves the strong, ...Od.15.448.92.
(Child of his age) with strong paternal joy ...Od.16.19.103.
With the strong raptures of a parent's joy. ...Od.16.211.114.
Now strong as youth, magnificent I tread. ...Od.16.231.114.
Such aids expect, he cries, when strong in might ...Od.16.288.118.
And the strong gates defy a host of foes. ...Od.17.319.147.
Swift as a stag, and as a lion strong, ...Od.17.381.150.
For where's an arm, like thine *Ulysses!* strong, ...Od.17.622.162.
Of this bold insolent, confide, be strong! ...Od.18.69.170.
Then girding his strong loins, the King prepares ...Od.18.74.170.
And each strong joint *Minerva* knits more strong, ...Od.18.79.170.
And each strong joint *Minerva* knits more strong, ...Od.18.79.170.
Thy well-knit frame unprofitably strong, ...Od.18.259.179.
A strong emotion shakes my anguish'd breast; ...Od.19.442.216.
On this, his body by strong cords extend, ...Od.22.190.296.
Trembling with agonies of strong delight ...Od.24.371.367.
Swift as an eagle, as an eagle strong. ...Od.24.621.377.

STRONGER

Taller or stronger than the weeds they shade? ...3.EOM1.40.18.
No Senses stronger than his brain can bear. ...3.EOM1.192A.38.
Self-love still stronger, as its objects nigh; ...3.EOM2.71.63.
Self-love yet stronger, as its objects nigh; ...3.EOM2.71A.63.
The action of the stronger to suspend ...3.EOM2.77.64.
A weaker may surprise, a stronger take? ...3.EOM3.276.120.
We prize the stronger effort of his pow'r, ...3.Ep1.99.22.
Strong in themselves, but stronger in his Aid, ...Il.12.303.92.
Strong in themselves, but stronger in their Aid, ...Il.12.303A.92.
But doom'd to *Hector's* stronger Force to yield! ...Il.15.778.226.
The golden Sun pour'd forth a stronger Ray, ...Il.17.430.304.
(The Mighty fled, pursu'd by stronger Might) ...Il.22.206.464.
But stronger Love impell'd, and I obey. ...Il.22.308.468.

STRONGEST

What the weak Head with strongest Byass rules, ...1.EOC.203.263.
In modern Ages not the strongest Swain ...1.TrES.101.453.
And strongest motive to assist the rest. ...3.EOM4.352.162.
Poor *Colley,* thy Reas'ning is none of the strongest, ...6.149.3.397.
But your reas'ning, God help you! is none of the strongest, ...6.149.3A.397.
Strongest of Men, they pierc'd the Mountain Boar, ...Il.1.355.105.
The strongest Warrior of th' *Ætolian* Train; ...Il.5.1039.316.
And dar'd the Trial of the strongest Hands; ...Il.7.182.373.

STRONGEST (CONTINUED)

Nor cou'd the strongest Hands his Fury stay; .... Il.7.183.373.
Pierc'd the deep Ranks; their strongest Battel tore; .... Il.8.307.412.
In modern Ages not the strongest Swain .... Il.12.455.98.
His strongest Spear each valiant *Grecian* wield, ... Il.14.431.184.
(Swiftest and strongest of th' aerial Race) .... Il.21.282.432.
Securely bid the strongest of the train .... Od.8.225.274.
Arise to throw: the strongest throws in vain. .... Od.8.226.274.
If with this throw the strongest Caster vye, ... Od.8.231.275.
And mules, the strongest of the lab'ring kind; .... Od.21.27.260.
The strongest, bravest, greatest of mankind. .... Od.24.38.349.

STRONGLY

Converse and Love mankind might strongly draw, ... 3.EOM3.207.114.
Then strongly fencing ill-got wealth by law, ... 4.JD2.93.141.
With well-rang'd Squadrons strongly circled round: .... Il.13.172.113.
The utmost gate. (The cable strongly wrought .... Od.21.423.280.
Near the high top he strain'd it strongly round, ... Od.22.501.313.

STROOK

See STRUCK.
Whose Wounds yet fresh, with bloody Hands he strook, ... 1.TrSt.79.413.
But fierce *Atrides* wav'd his Sword and strook .... Il.3.445.213.
The first who strook a valiant *Trojan* dead: .... Il.4.523.246.
Thrice rushing furious, at the Chief he strook; .... Il.5.529.294.
Both strook, both wounded, but *Sarpedon's* slew: .... Il.5.815.305.
Strook thro' the Back the *Phrygian* fell oppress'd; .... Il.8.311.412.
Aim'd at the King, and near his Elbow strook. .... Il.11.326.49.
The Faulchion strook, and Fate pursu'd the Stroke; .... Il.12.222.89.
And trembling strook, and rooted in the Field, ... Il.16.742.272.
Thrice at the Battlements *Patroclus* strook, ... Il.16.859.276.
He strook, he wounded, but he durst no more; .... Il.16.979.281.
Strook to the Dust the Squire, and Charioteer .... Il.17.690.314.
And slightly on her Breast the Wanton strook: .... Il.21.497.442.
Strook Slaughter back, and cover'd the Retreat. .... Il.21.630.448.
Tho' strook, tho' wounded, scarce perceives the Pain, ... Il.21.681.450.
His Ankle strook: The Giant fell supine: .... Il.23.845.523.

STROVE

My trembling sister strove to urge her flight, ... 1.TrFD.36.387.
In vain to free her fasten'd feet she strove, ... 1.TrFD.41.387.
Or long before, with early Valour strove .... 1.TrSt.29.411.
Thus strove the Chief on ev'ry side distress'd, ... 1.TrSt.526.432.
Where tawdry yellow strove with dirty red, ... 3.Ep3.304.118.
Who in your own *Despite* has strove to please ye. .... 6.34.8.101.
Since Great *Achilles* and *Atrides* strove, ... Il.1.7.85.
'Till vain of Mortal's empty Praise, he strove .... Il.2.723.160.
But while he strove to tug th' inserted Dart, ... Il.4.532.246.
To spoil his Arms the Victor strove in vain; .... Il.4.619.250.
And strove to tempt him from the Paths of Fame: .... Il.6.202.336.
Greece in her single Heroes strove in vain; .... Il.6.516.351.
So brave a Task each *Ajax* strove to share, ... Il.10.271.14.
Bold *Merion* strove, and *Nestor's* valiant Heir; .... Il.10.272.14.
Wing'd with his Fears, on Foot he strove to fly, ... Il.11.439.53.
The flying *Grecians* strove their Ships to gain; .... Il.12.134.86.
His circling Friends, who strove to guard too late .... Il.15.784.226.
Big with the mighty Grief, he strove to say .... Il.17.783.319.
There with commutual zeal we both had strove, ... Od.4.241.130.
With all her charms as vainly *Circe* strove, ... Od.9.33.303.
Thrice in my arms I strove her shade to bind, ... Od.11.248.393.
With haughty love th' audacious monster strove .... Od.11.717.421.
He knew his Lord; he knew, and strove to meet, ... Od.17.360.149.
In vain he strove, to crawl; and kiss his feet; .... Od.17.361.149.
He strove to drive the man of mighty woes. .... Od.18.13.167.
Against the fondness of my heart I strove, ... Od.23.229.334.

STROW

Where *Troy's* Majestic Ruins strow the Ground. .... 1.TrUl.133.470.
With Throngs promiscuous strow the level Green. .... 2.RL3.80.173.
With falling Woods to strow the wasted Plain. .... Il.3.92.194.
And her dead Warriors strow the mournful Plains. .... Il.4.273.234.
The shatter'd Crest, and Horse-hair, strow the Plain: .... Il.17.341.300.
With sweeping Stroke the Mowers strow the Lands; .... Il.18.641.354.
Tho' vast the Heaps that strow the crimson Plain, ... Il.19.221.382.
And o'er th' ingredients strow the hallow'd flour: .... Od.10.617.374.
Where *Troy's* majestic ruins strow the ground. .... Od.13.300.20.
And heaps on heaps the wretches strow the ground; .... Od.24.207.358.

STROW'D

See! strow'd with learned dust, his Night-cap on, ... 4.2HE2.118.173.
Alastor, Chromius, Halius strow'd the Plain, ... Il.5.835.305.
And falling Ranks are strow'd on ev'ry side. .... Il.11.94.38.
Strow'd in bright Heaps, their Arms and Armour lay; .... Il.17.852.321.
Sudden, full twenty on the plain are strow'd, ... Od.5.313.186.
And hid it in the dust that strow'd the cave. .... Od.9.388.322.
O'er these was strow'd the consecrated flour, ... Od.11.33.381.
Heaps strow'd on heaps beneath his fauchion groan'd, ... Od.11.631.414.
Strow'd o'er with morsels cut from ev'ry part. .... Od.12.426.451.

STROWN

(Thick strown by tempest thro' the bow'ry shade) .... Od.5.625.201.

STROWS

He strows a Bed of glowing Embers wide, ... Il.9.280.447.
And last with Flour the smiling Surface strows. .... Il.11.783.70.
Nor less *Leonteus* strows the Field with Death; .... Il.12.218.89.
Drops from his Arm: his Baldrick strows the Field: .... Il.16.967.281.
Rolls diverse, and in fragments strows the flood. .... Od.5.469.195.
The mast and acorn, brutal food! and strows .... Od.10.283.356.

STRUCK

See STROOK.
And glitt'ring Thoughts struck out at ev'ry Line; .... 1.EOC.290.271.
Struck with the Sight, and fix'd in deep Amaze, ... 1.TrSt.575.434.
Struck blind by thee, resigns his Days to Grief, ... 2.ChJM.483.38.
We strait struck Hands; the Bargain was agreed; .... 2.ChWB.296.71.

STRUCK (CONTINUED)

Nay once by Heav'n he struck me on the Face: .... 2.ChWB.335.73.
High on his Car *Sesostris* struck my View, ... 2.TemF.113.262.
Be struck with bright Brocade, or Tyrian Dye, ... 4.1HE6.32.239.
The moon-struck Prophet felt the madding hour: .... 5.DunB4.12.340.
First struck out this, and then that Thought; .... 6.77.2.214.
So the struck deer in some sequester'd part .... 6.81.11.226.
So the struck doe in some sequester'd part .... 6.81.11A.226.
Lo! the struck deer in some sequester'd part .... 6.81.11B.226.
Lay Fortune-struck, a Spectacle of Woe! .... 6.128.3.355.
Struck with her Presence, strait the livly Red .... Il.3.491.215.
Struck with his gen'rous Wrath, the King replies; .... Il.4.410.240.
Struck at his Sight the *Trojans* backward drew, ... Il.4.571.249.
Struck with Amaze, and Shame, the *Trojan* Crew .... Il.5.35.267.
Struck with the Thought, should *Helen's* Lord be slain, ... Il.5.695.301.
Struck at the Sight, the mighty *Ajax* glows .... Il.5.756.303.
But sure till now no Coursers struck my Sight .... Il.10.648.30.
And struck his Target with the brazen Spear, ... Il.13.711.138.
Struck thro' the Belly's Rim, the Warrior lies .... Il.14.521.188.
Heart-piercing Anguish struck the *Grecian* Host, ... Il.14.569.190.
And from the spouting Shoulders struck his Head; .... Il.14.582.190.
Struck for th' immortal Race with timely Fear, ... Il.15.142.202.
Struck by an Arm unseen, it burst in two; .... Il.15.545.217.
Has, from my Arm unfailing, struck the Bow, ... Il.15.551.218.
He struck his hasty Foot: his Heels up-sprung; .... Il.15.780.226.
Struck from the Car, falls headlong on the Plain. .... Il.16.900.278.
Struck at the Sight, recede the *Trojan* Train: .... Il.17.368.301.
Struck 'twixt the Horns, he springs with many a Bound, ... Il.17.590.311.
Struck from the Walls, the Echoes float on high, ... Il.18.261.335.
Struck where the crossing Belts unite behind, ... Il.20.479.414.
Thrice struck *Pelides* with indignant Heart, ... Il.20.515.416.
One struck, but pierc'd not the *Vulcanian* Shield; .... Il.21.182.429.
Struck thro' with Wounds, all honest on the Breast. .... Il.22.101.456.
Struck by some God, he fears, recedes, and flies. .... Il.22.180.461.
From off the ringing Orb, it struck the Ground. .... Il.22.372.471.
Struck with the kind reproach, I strait reply; .... Od.4.507.144.
Struck with amaze, yet still to doubt inclin'd, ... Od.5.450.194.
A sudden horror struck their aking sight. .... Od.10.130.347.
Struck with unusual fear, she trembling cries, ... Od.10.385.363.
Struck at the word, my very heart was dead: .... Od.10.588.372.
Struck at the sight I melt with filial woe, ... Od.11.108.386.
Struck with despair, with trembling hearts we view'd .... Od.12.292.446.
Struck at the news, thy azure mother came; .... Od.24.65.350.
'Twas heav'n that struck, and heav'n was on his side. .... Od.24.515.372.

STRUCTURE

There stands a Structure of Majestick Frame, ... 2.RL3.3.169.
High on a Rock of Ice the Structure lay, ... 2.TemF.27.255.
Of various Structure, but of equal Grace: .... 2.TemF.66.257.
Of *Gothic* Structure was the Northern Side, ... 2.TemF.119.263.
Before my View appear'd a Structure fair, ... 2.TemF.420.283.
Then lights the structure, with averted eyes; .... 5.DunA1.205.87.
Then lights the structure, with averted eyes: .... 5.DunB1.247.288.
O'er these a Range of Marble Structure runs, ... Il.6.306.341.
The pompous Structure, and the Town commands, ... Il.6.393.346.
And nigh the Fleet a Fun'ral Structure rear: .... Il.7.401.384.
And round him wide the rising Structure grows. .... Il.16.259.249.
The growing Structure spreads on ev'ry side; .... Il.23.203.498.
The Structure crackles in the roaring Fires, ... Il.23.270.500.
A common Structure on the humble Sands; .... Il.23.307.501.
And high in Air a Sylvan Structure raise. .... Il.24.994.577.
A tow'ring structure to the palace join'd; .... Od.1.537.57.
Stage above stage th' imperial structure stands, ... Od.17.316.147.

STRUCTURES

The shining Structures rais'd by lab'ring Gods! .... 1.TrSt.836.444.
In vain my structures rise, my gardens grow, ... 6.81.2.225.
'Till *Troy's* proud Structures shou'd in Ashes lie. .... Il.2.353.144.
Where beauteous *Arenè* her Structures shows, ... Il.2.719.160.
And yon' fair Structures level with the Ground? .... Il.4.52.223.
Those radiant Structures rais'd by lab'ring Gods, ... Il.7.539.391.
Lay yon' proud Structures level with the Plain, ... Il.15.241.206.
With opening streets and shining structures spread, ... Od.7.104.239.
Who publick structures raise, or who design; .... Od.17.463.155.

STRUGGLE

But after many a hearty Struggle past, ... 2.ChWB.425.77.
To toil and struggle thro' the well-fought Day. .... Il.13.4.103.
I give the sign, and struggle to be free: .... Od.12.234.443.
They pant, and struggle in the moving gold. .... Od.19.268.208.

STRUGGLES

And as she struggles, only moves above; .... 1.TrFD.42.387.

STRUGGLING

Who gently drawn, and struggling less and less, ... 5.DunB4.83.349.
A brave man struggling in the storms of fate, ... 6.32.21.96.
Struggling he follow'd, while th' embroider'd Thong .... Il.3.457.213.
From earth they rear him, struggling now with death; .... Od.3.578.116.
Compress'd their force, and lock'd each struggling blast: .... Od.10.20.340.
So pant the wretches, struggling in the sky, ... Od.12.305.447.
Thus on some tree hung struggling in the snare, ... Od.22.505.313.
How struggling thro' the surge, he reach'd the shores .... Od.23.359.342.

STRUGLING

Who grasps the strugling Heifer's Lunar Horns. .... 1.TrSt.864.446.
By Strugling with a Man upon a Tree? .... 2.ChJM.763.52.
If this be Strugling, by this holy Light, ... 2.ChJM.766.52.
'Tis Strugling with a Vengeance, (quoth the Knight:) .... 2.ChJM.767.52.

STRUMPET

And set the Strumpet here in open View, ... 2.ChJM.653.46.
He tells what Strumpet Places sells for Life, ... 4.JD4.148.37.
Destroy'd alike with Strumpet, Maid, or Wife. .... 4.HAdv.80.83.
Quarrel with *Dryden* for a Strumpet, ... 6.10.85.27.
Come here in crowds, and stare the strumpet down. .... 6.41.50.114.

STRUMPETS 405 STUMBLES

STRUMPETS
Than ev'n in Brothels venal Strumpets are. ....4.JD2A.75.138.

STRUNG
Who now shall charm the Shades where *Cowley* strung ....1.W-F.279.174.
Fits the sharp Arrow to the well-strung Bow. ....Il.4.147.227.
For *Pallas* strung his Arm, and edg'd his Sword. ....Il.4.443.241.
In evil Hour these bended Horns I strung, ...Il.5.264.280.
But while my Nerves are strung, my Force entire, ...Il.5.316A.281.
Breath'd in his Heart, and strung his nervous Arms; ....Il.10.559.27.
Where the knit Nerves the pliant Elbow strung; ....Il.20.554.417.
With silver shone the throne; his Lyre well strung ....Od.8.63.265.
Or that these wither'd nerves like thine were strung; ....Od.16.104.107.
Swell o'er his well-strung limbs, and brace his frame! ....Od.18.85.170.
These aged nerves with new-born vigor strung, ...Od.20.296.247.
These aged sinews with new vigor strung ....Od.21.207.269.
Thus speaking, on the circling wall he strung ....Od.22.499.313.

STRUT
And why not Players strut in Courtiers Cloaths? ....4.JD4.222.45.
Lord! how we strut thro' *Merlin's* Cave, to see ....4.2HE2.139.175.
I neither strut with ev'ry fav'ring breath, ...4.2HE2.300.185.

STRUTS
Tom struts a Soldier, open, bold, and brave; ....3.Ep1.105.22.
That Robe of Quality so struts and swells, ...3.Ep2.189.65.
Now trips a Lady, and now struts a Lord. ....4.Arbu.329.119.
He struts Adonis, and affects grimace: ....5.DunA2.194.124.
He struts Adonis, and affects grimace: ....5.DunB2.202.305.

STRUTTING
How, scarce, my ewes their strutting udders bear; ....1.TrPA.83.368.

STUART
And Peace and Plenty tell, a STUART reigns. ....1.W-F.42.152.

STUBBLE
Moliere's old stubble in a moment flames. ....5.DunB1.254.289.
Then o'er the Stubble up the Mountain flies, ...Il.20.571.418.
Yet by the stubble you may guess the grain, ...Od.14.249.48.

STUBBORN
As stubborn Steers by brawny Plowmen broke, ...1.TrSt.184.418.
But if thou must reform the stubborn Times, ...1.TrSt.377.425.
Two stubborn Swains with Blows dispute their Bounds; ....1.TrES.158.455.
Stubborn as any Lionness was I: ....2.ChWB.337.73.
Nor pray'rs nor fasts its stubborn pulse restrain, ...2.ElAb.27.321.
Or tames the Genius of the stubborn Plain, ...4.HS1.131.19.
In Nature's spight, the Stubborn Siege they hold ....4.JD2A.27.134.
Each staunch Polemic, stubborn as a rock, ...5.DunB4.195.361.
By nature yielding, stubborn but for Fame; ....6.19.35.63.
The stubborn God, inflexible and hard, ...Il.8.439.418.
Its stubborn Purpose, and his Friends disdains. ....Il.9.742.471.
Two stubborn Swains with Blows dispute their Bounds; ....Il.12.512.100.
(Which from the stubborn Stone a Torrent rends) ....Il.13.193.115.
Join'd to one Yoke, the stubborn Earth they tear, ...Il.13.881.147.
The stubborn Arms (by *Jove's* Command dispos'd) ....Il.17.247.297.
And stubborn Brass, and Tin, and solid Gold: ....Il.18.546.348.
The stubborn Bristles from the Victim's Brow ....Il.19.261.383.
The stunning Stroke his stubborn Nerves unbound; ....Il.21.474.441.
The dext'rous Woodman shapes the stubborn Oaks; ....Il.23.386.505.
'Till righteous heav'n reclaim her stubborn breast. ....Od.2.142.68.
And forc'd the stubborn spectre to reply; ....Od.11.695.419.
That stubborn soul, by toil untaught to yield! ....Od.12.334.448.
As weary plowman spent with stubborn toil, ...Od.13.39.3.
Of stubborn labour hewn from heart of oak; ....Od.14.16.35.
The pyre to build, the stubborn oak to rend; ....Od.15.339.86.
That stubborn horn which brave *Ulysses* drew. ....Od.21.95.263.
With tender hands the stubborn horn he strains, ...Od.21.157.267.
The stubborn horn resisted all his pains: ....Od.21.158.267.
Stubborn the breast that with no transport glows, ...Od.23.103.324.
The twanging string, and try'd the stubborn yew: ....Od.24.198.358.

STUCCO
Grotesco roofs, and Stucco floors: ....4.HS6.194.263.
For your damn'd Stucco has no chink) ....4.HS6.219.263.

STUCK
Stuck o'er with titles and hung round with strings, ...3.EOM4.205.146.
He stuck to Poverty with Peace of Mind; ....4.2HE2.65.169.
And stuck her Needle into *Grildrig's* Bed; ....6.96ii.6.270.
Helms stuck to Helms, and Man drove Man along. ....Il.13.182.114.
Stuck deep in Earth, and quiver'd where it stood. ....Il.13.639.136.
And stuck with Darts by warring Heroes shed; ....Il.16.775.273.
Then in the lower Belly stuck the Dart. ....Il.17.587.311.
That trembled as it stuck; nor void of Fear ....Il.20.312.407.
There stuck the Lance. Then rising e'er he threw, ...Il.20.321.407.
And stuck adherent, and suspended hung: ....Od.5.547.198.
His ragged claws are stuck with stones and sands; ....Od.5.552.199.
The men, like fish, they stuck upon the flood, ...Od.10.143.347.

STUDDED
From his numb'd Hand the Iv'ry-studded Reins ....Il.5.713.301.
The Baldric studded, and the Sheath enchas'd, ...Il.7.367.382.
The Iv'ry studded Reins, return'd behind, ...Il.19.430.389.
With him the Sword and studded Belt remains. ....Il.23.972.528.
And studded amber darts a golden ray: ....Od.4.88.123.

STUDENT
How Index-learning turns no student pale, ...5.DunA1.233.90.
How Index-learning turns no student pale, ...5.DunB1.279.290.

STUDIES
He vainly studies every art to please: ....1.TrPA.22.366.
Who studies now but discontented *May?* ....2.ChJM.418.35.
With Studies pale, with Midnight Vigils blind; ....2.TemF.301.278.

STUDIES (CONTINUED)
Happy my Studies, when by these approv'd! ....4.Arbu.143.106.
So mix'd our studies, and so join'd our name, ...6.52.10.156.
Nor blush, these studies thy regard engage; ....6.71.49.204.

STUDIOUS
More studious to divide than to unite, ...3.EOM2.82.64.
'Twas then, the studious head or gen'rous mind, ...3.EOM3.283.121.
Studious he sate, with all his books around, ...5.DunA1.111.77.
Here studious I unlucky moderns save, ...5.DunA1.161.82.
Cost studious *Cabalists* more Time. ....6.30.58.88.
Cost studious Providence more Time. ....6.30.58B.88.
For sober, studious Days; ....6.47.46.130.
(Studious in ev'ry Thing to please thy Taste) ....6.96iv.50.277.
Now coy and studious in no Point to fall, ...6.99.11.287.
With witty Malice, studious to defame, ...Il.2.259.140.
A Prince and People studious of their Gain. ....Il.5.873.308.
The milk-white Coursers studious to convey ....Il.10.572.28.
For ever studious in promoting Ill! ....Il.15.18.194.
An Angler, studious of the Line and Cane, ...Il.16.495.262.
Studious to see that Terror of the Plain, ...Il.19.49.373.
Nor skill'd, nor studious, with prophetic eye ....Od.1.261.45.
Studious thy country's worthies to defame, ...Od.2.97.65.
The work she ply'd; but studious of delay, ...Od.2.117.67.
The winged vessel studious I prepare, ...Od.2.325.77.
Studious to ease thy grief, our care provides ....Od.2.345.77.
Then studious she prepares the choicest flour, ...Od.2.426.81.
Studious to veil the grief, in vain represt, ...Od.4.151.127.
If studious of your realms, you then demand ....Od.4.527.146.
Studious to learn his absent father's doom. ....Od.4.949.162.
And now fierce traytors, studious to destroy ....Od.5.26.172.
Studious to save what human wants require, ...Od.5.632.202.
Studious of freight, in naval trade well skill'd, ...Od.8.181.272.
Around the dungeon, studious to behold ....Od.12.274.445.
Studious of rest and warmth, *Ulysses* lies, ...Od.14.514.62.
The gen'rous lovers, studious to succeed, ...Od.18.321.182.
Studious of peace; and *Æthon* is my name. ....Od.19.214.203.
But studious to conceal her royal Lord, ...Od.19.557.223.
A *Samian* Peer, more studious than the rest ....Od.20.353.249.
The work she ply'd; but studious of delay, ...Od.24.166.356.

STUDIOUSLY
Approach. Great NATURE studiously behold! ....6.142.7.382.

STUDS
With glitt'ring Studs about; ....6.58.26.171.
His Sceptre starr'd with golden Studs around. ....Il.1.326.103.
No Spoils enrich it, and no Studs adorn.) ....Il.10.306.16.
From eldest Times: emboss'd with Studs of Gold, ...Il.11.774.69.
Distinct with Studs; and brazen was the Blade) ....Il.13.768.141.
A pond'rous Mace, with Studs of Iron crown'd, ...Il.15.816.228.
Emblaz'd with Studs of Gold, his Faulchion shone, ...Il.16.166.244.
(A *Thracian* Blade, distinct with Studs of Gold) ....Il.23.952.527.
Radiant with starry studs, a silver seat ....Od.10.375.362.

STUDY
Successive Study, Exercise and Ease. ....1.W-F.240.171.
Be *Homer's* Works your *Study,* and *Delight,* ....1.EOC.124.253.
Study a Mite, not comprehend the Skies? ....3.EOM1.196A.39.
The proper study of Mankind is Man. ....3.EOM2.2.53.
Who from his study rails at human kind; ....3.Ep1.2.15.
Just at his Study-door he'll bless your eyes. ....3.Ep4.132.150.
His Study! with what Authors is it stor'd? ....3.Ep4.133.150.
Pains, reading, study, are their just pretence, ...4.Arbu.159.108.
"Oh but a Wit can study in the Streets, ...4.2HE2.98.171.
To Books and Study gives sev'n years compleat, ...4.2HE2.117.173.
And Reason giv'n them but to study *Flies!* ....5.DunB4.454.385.
Who study Shakespeare at the Inns of Court, ...5.DunB4.568.398.
Sound sleep by night; study and ease ....6.1.13.3.
Repose at night; study and ease ....6.1.13A.3.
And while he seems to study, thinks of you: ....6.45.44.125.
Pains, Reading, Study, are their just Pretence, ...6.98.9.283.

STUDY-DOOR
Just at his Study-door he'll bless your eyes. ....3.Ep4.132.150.

STUDY'D
And study'd Men, their Manners, and their Ways; ....2.ChJM.157.22.
Our Knight (who study'd much, we may suppose) ....2.ChJM.442.36.
I study'd SHREWSBURY, the wise and great: ....4.EpS2.79.317.
Here thy well-study'd Marbles fix our eye; ....6.52.33.157.
So study'd tortures his vile days shall end. ....Od.22.192.296.

STUDYING
Agrees as ill with Rufa studying Locke, ...3.Ep2.23.51.

STUFF
What *woful stuff* this Madrigal wou'd be, ...1.EOC.418.287.
Becomes the stuff of which our dream is wrought: ....3.Ep1.48.18.
To stop my ears to their confounded stuff. ....4.2HE2.152.175.
For thee I dim these eyes, and stuff this head, ...5.DunA1.165.83.
For thee we dim the eyes, and stuff the head ....5.DunB4.249.368.
For thee they dim their eyes and stuff their head. ....5.DunB4.249A.368.
With that pure Stuff from whence we rose, ...6.53.12Z3.161.
Has writ such stuff, as none e'er writ before. ....6.116i.2.325.

STUFF'D
But having amply stuff'd his skin, ...4.1HE7.53.271.

STUFFS
He stuffs and swills, and stuffs again. ....4.HS6.207.263.
He stuffs and swills, and stuffs again. ....4.HS6.207.263.

STUMBLES
Unhappy *Ajax* stumbles on the Plain; ....Il.23.906.525.

STUMBLING
As after *Stumbling,* Jades will *mend* their Pace. 1.EOC.603.308.

STUMM
Let not the *Whigs Geneva's* Stumm infuse, 6.48i.8.133*.

STUN
Stun my scar'd ears, and pierce hell's utmost bounds. Od.11.782.425.

STUNG
And stung with anguish bellow through the groves. 1.TrPA.135.371.
Stung with my Love, and furious with Despair, 1.TrSP.139.399.
Stung to the Soul, the Brothers start from Rest, 1.TrSt.174.417.
As stung his Heart, and made his Marrow fry 2.ChWB.235.68.
And no man wonders he's not stung by Pug: 4.HS1.88.13.
Or by some Flea with mortal venom stung? 6.96ii.30Z6.271.
Stung with the Shame, within the winding Way, Il.4.444.241.
Stung to the Heart the gen'rous *Hector* hears, Il.5.601.297.
Curl'd o'er the Brow, it stung him to the Brain; Il.8.106.402.
That heard, deep Anguish stung *Saturnia's* Soul; Il.8.240.409.
Stung with the Smart, all panting with the Pain, Il.11.351.50.
Stung by the Stroke, the Coursers scour the Fields Il.11.656.63.
He stung the Bird, whose Throat receiv'd the Wound: Il.12.236.90.
At *Jove* incens'd, with Grief and Fury stung, Il.13.27.105.
Stung with fierce Hunger, each the Prey invades, Il.16.917.279.
The Lion thus, with dreadful Anguish stung, Il.18.371.339.
Stung to the Soul, he sorrow'd, and he rag'd. Il.19.124.377.
Stung with new Ardor, thus by Heav'n impell'd, Il.21.346.435.
With grief and rage the mother-lion stung, Od.4.1043.166.
Stung to the soul, indignant thro' the skies Od.8.313.281.
But heedless of those cares, with anguish stung, Od.9.519.327.
And the lost arms for ever stung his mind; Od.11.668.417.
When stung with hunger she embroils the flood, Od.12.117.437.
As the bold eagle with fierce sorrow stung, Od.16.238.114.
Stung to the soul, abash'd, confounded stand; Od.16.359.123.
Stung to the soul, o'ercast with holy dread, Od.18.181.175.
Yet him, my guest, thy venom'd rage hath stung; Od.19.115.198.
His heart with rage this new dishonour stung, Od.20.13.231.
The great *Eurytion* when this frenzy stung, Od.21.317.274.

STUNN'D
And stunn'd him with the music of the spheres, 3.EOM1.202.40.
One lull'd th' *Exchequer,* and one stunn'd the *Rolls;* 4.2HE2.130.173.
Stunn'd with his giddy Larum half the town. 5.DunB4.292.373.
But yet so stunn'd, that stagg'ring on the Plain, Il.11.457.54.
Stunn'd in the Whirl, and breathless with the Fall. Il.15.28.195.
His Eyes flash Sparkles, his stunn'd Senses reel Il.16.957.280.

STUNNING
The stunning Stroke his stubborn Nerves unbound; Il.21.474.441.
Down drop'd he stupid from the stunning wound, Od.18.114.172.

STUNTED
Like stunted hide-bound Trees, that just have got 6.49i.11.137.

STUPEFACTION
Firm Impudence, or Stupefaction mild; 5.DunB4.530.394.

STUPENDOUS
Of massy Substance and stupendous Frame, 1.TrES.192.456.
Stupendous Pile! not rear'd by mortal Hands. 2.TemF.62.256.
All are but parts of one stupendous whole, 3.EOM1.267.47.
So proud, so grand, of that stupendous air, 3.Ep4.101.147.
Far, as loud Bow's stupendous bells resound, 5.DunA3.276.183.
Far as loud Bow's stupendous bells resound; 5.DunB3.278.333.
So call'd on *Brobdingnag's* stupendous Coast, 6.96iv.98.279.
Rais'd on arch'd Columns of stupendous Frame; Il.6.305.341.
Of massy Substance and stupendous Frame; Il.12.546.101.
A massy Caldron of stupendous Frame Il.18.405.340.

STUPID
Fix'd in a stupid Lethargy of Woe. 1.TrSP.128.399.
The Crowd in stupid Wonder fix'd appear, 1.TrSt.731.440.
Of stupid starers, and of loud huzzas; 3.EOM4.256.152.
What turns him now a stupid silent dunce? 3.Ep1.163.29.
The stupid World, like *Assa fetida.* 6.48ii.4.134.
No—let the stupid Prince, whom *Jove* deprives Il.9.492.456.
Depriv'd of Motion, stiff with stupid Fear, Il.13.501.130.
Stupid he stares, and all-assistless stands: Il.16.970.281.
The Giant spoke; and in a stupid Gaze Il.23.781.520.
Thus stood th' Attendants stupid with Surprize; Il.24.594.561.
Down drop'd he stupid from the stunning wound, Od.18.114.172.

STUPIFY'D
Sits Mother Osborne, stupify'd to stone! 5.DunB2.312.311.

STURDY
The sturdy Squire to Gallic masters stoop, 5.DunB4.595.402.
A desp'rate Bulwark, sturdy, firm, and fierce, 6.128.13.356.
That sturdy Vagrants, Rogues in Rags, 6.135.21.366.
That Sturdy Beggars, Rogues in Rags, 6.135.21A.366.
The Victim-Ox the sturdy Youth prepare; Il.18.649.355.
The sturdy Woodmen equal Burthens bore Il.23.152.495.

STURGEON
Who has not learn'd, fresh Sturgeon and Ham-pye 4.HS2.103.61.
Who has not learn'd, fresh Sturgeon or Ham-pye 4.HS2.103A.61.

STUTTER'D
Dipthongs, and Tripthongs, swore and stutter'd, 6.30.51.88.

STUTTERING
Part of the Name of stuttering *T*— 6.30.53.88.

STY
Hard by a Sty, beneath a Roof of Thatch, 6.14ii.28.44.
To hogs transforms 'em, and the Sty receives. Od.10.277.356.

STYES
All lost their form, and habitants of styes. Od.10.338.360.
Then hast'ning to the styes set wide the door, Od.10.459.366.
Compell'd, reluctant, to their sev'ral styes, Od.14.455.57.

STYGIAN
Free, and a Princess, to the *Stygian* coast. 6.20.18.66.
Lo! *Hector* rises from the *Stygian* Shades! Il.15.325.209.
Go, wait thy Brother to the *Stygian* Gloom; Il.17.34.289.
To wait thy Brother to the *Stygian* Gloom; Il.17.34A.289.
All pale they wander on the *Stygian* Coast; Il.22.71.455.
Thou can'st not call him from the *Stygian* Shore, Il.24.694.566.
In one sad Day beheld the *Stygian* Shades; Il.24.760.569.
Free, and a Hero, to the *Stygian* Coast. Il.24.949.575.
What *Greeks,* now wand'ring in the *Stygian* gloom, Od.1.453.54.
Or glides in *Stygian* gloom a pensive ghost, Od.4.142.127.
And where, slow rolling from the *Stygian* bed, Od.10.610.374.
Com'st thou alive to view the *Stygian* bounds, Od.11.583.412.
There *Tantalus* along the *Stygian* bounds Od.11.719.421.
In *Stygian* gloom he glides a pensive ghost! Od.15.293.83.
In *Stygian* gloom he glides a pensive ghost! Od.20.264.246.
O race to death devote! with *Stygian* shade Od.20.423.253.
Its bloom eternal in the *Stygian* shades. Od.24.118.353.

STYL'D
And styl'd the Consort of the thund'ring *Jove.* Il.4.86.224.

STYLE
Such *labour'd Nothings,* in so *strange* a Style, 1.EOC.326.275.
A vile Conceit in pompous Style exprest, 1.EOC.320A.27
How the *Wit brightens!* How the *Style refines!* 1.EOC.421.288.
Whether the Style of *Titan* please thee more, 1.TrSt.857.445.
The Doctor's Wormwood Style, the Hash of Tongues, 4.JD4.52.29.
"But Sir, of Writers?"—" *Swift,* for closer Style, 4.JD4.72.31.
At all my Peevishness, and turns his Style. 4.JD4.123.35.
At all my Peevishness, and chang'd his Style. 4.JD4.123A.35.
When ev'ry Coxcomb knows me by my *Style?* 4.Arbu.282.116.
Style the divine, the matchless, what you will) 4.2HE1.70.199.
(Now, if you're weary of my Style, 6.10.63.26.
Whether the Style of *Grildrig* please thee most, 6.96iv.97.279.
But chief he glory'd with licentious Style Il.2.261.140.
Who style thee Son of Cloud-compelling *Jove.* Il.5.787.304.

STYLES
For diff'rent *Styles* with diff'rent *Subjects* sort, 1.EOC.322.275.
The lofty styles of happy, glorious great, 6.22.19.72.

STYMPHELUS
And *Stymphelus* with her surrounding Grove; Il.2.736.161.

STYPTICK
The Wound he wash'd, the Styptick Juice infus'd. Il.11.983.79.

STYPTICKS
Or Alom- *Stypticks* with contracting Power 2.RL2.131.168.

STYRIAN
The fair *Carystos,* and the *Styrian* Ground; Il.2.646.157.

STYX
Thou, sable *Styx!* whose livid Streams are roll'd 1.TrSt.83.413.
For by the black infernal *Styx* I swear, 1.TrSt.411.427.
A branch of Styx here rises from the Shades, 5.DunA2.314.14
A branch of Styx here rises from the Shades, 5.DunB2.338.31
With *Styx* nine times round her, 6.11.91.33.
Should the *Greek* quarrel too, by *Styx,* I 6.30.68.88.
Has sworn by Styx (the Poet's Oath, 6.135.91A.370.
Styx pours them forth, the dreadful Oath of Gods! Il.2.915.167.
Nor *Styx* been cross'd, nor Hell explor'd in vain. Il.8.448.418.
By thy black Waves, tremendous *Styx!* that flow Il.15.43.195.
And thou oh *Styx!* whose formidable floods Od.5.239.183.

SUËIL
These Aldus printed, those Du Suëil has bound. 3.Ep4.136.150.

SU'D
He su'd to All, but chief implor'd for Grace Il.1.21.86.
To her I su'd; she pity'd my distress; Od.7.376.254.

SUBDU'D
Where *Jove,* subdu'd by mortal Passion still, 1.W-F.233.170.
Hear *Jove* himself, subdu'd by Beauty still, 1.W-F.233A.170
And the *World's Victor* stood subdu'd by *Sound!* 1.EOC.381.284.
She with one Finger and a Thumb subdu'd: 2.RL5.80.206.
The greater Part by hostile Time subdu'd; 2.TemF.32.255.
The *Youth* that all things but himself subdu'd; 2.TemF.152.266.
The pow'rs of all subdu'd by thee alone, 3.EOM1.231.44.
The Gaul subdu'd, or Property secur'd, 4.2HE1.10.195.
Rome learning arts from *Greece,* whom she subdu'd; 6.32.40.97.
Whose Virgin-Charms subdu'd the God of War: Il.2.615.157.
Dar'd and subdu'd, before their haughty Lord; Il.4.442.241.
The Sons subdu'd, for Heav'n was on their side. Il.4.463.242.
If now subdu'd they meditate their Flight, Il.10.365.19.
If now subdu'd, you fix your Hopes on Flight, Il.10.469.24.
Subdu'd by Steel, a tall Ash tumbles down, Il.13.242.116.
Who not by strength subdu'd me, but by wine. Od.9.604.331.

SUBDUE
Deign to be lov'd, and ev'ry Heart subdue! 1.TrVP.69.380.
Oh come! oh teach me nature to subdue, 2.ElAb.203.336.
The young disease, that must subdue at length, 3.EOM2.135.71.
Had still this Monster to subdue at last. 4.2HE1.18.195.

SUBDUE (CONTINUED)

And who his Rival can in Arms subdue, ...Il.3.103.194.
And who his Rival shall in Arms subdue, ...Il.3.324.208.
To calm thy Passions, and subdue thy Rage: ....Il.9.333.450.
Think, and subdue! on Dastards dead to Fame ....Il.13.157.112.
Is it in vain our conqu'ring Arms subdue? ....Il.21.63.424.
What single arm hath prowess to subdue? ....Od.20.50.234.

SUBDUES

Fights and subdues in quarrels not her own. ....6.43.8.120.
Swift vengeance waits: and Art subdues the strong! ....Od.8.368.283.
He fights, subdues: for *Pallas* strings his arms. ....Od.8.568.293.
The choicest portion who subdues his foe; ....Od.18.53.169.

SUBDUING

Sleep's all-subduing charm who dares defy, ...5.DunA2.341.142.
Sleep's all-subduing pow'r who dares defy, ...5.DunA2.341A.142.
"Sleep's all-subduing charms who dares defy, ...5.DunB2.373.315.
But all-subduing *Pallas* lent her pow'r, ...Od.5.556.199.

SUBJECT

What wonder then, a Beast or Subject slain ....1.W-F.57.154.
But while the Subject starv'd, the Beast was fed. ....1.W-F.60.154.
But that the subject starv'd, the beast was fed. ....1.W-F.60B.154.
His *Fable, Subject, Scope* in ev'ry Page, ...1.EOC.120.252.
Made him observe the *Subject* and the *Plot,* ....1.EOC.275.270.
Slight is the Subject, but not so the Praise, ...2.RL1.5.144.
These ever new, nor subject to Decays, ...2.TemF.51.256.
Subject, compound them, follow her and God. ....3.EOM4.2.116.69.
Bliss is the same in subject or in king, ...3.EOM4.58.134.
As leaves them scarce a Subject in their Age: ....3.Ep2.222.68.
Back to his bounds their subject Sea command, ...3.Ep4.201.156.
Than mine, to find a Subject staid and wise, ...4.JD4.168.39.
Became the Subject of great *Homer's* song; ....6.38.8.107.
That Kings are subject to the Gods alone. ....Il.1.250.98.
And rob a Subject, than despoil a Foe. ....Il.1.304.101.
His Subject-Herds, the Monarch of the Meads. ....Il.2.567.154.
And next *Ulysses,* with his Subject Bands. ....Il.4.383.239.
There left a Subject to the Wind and Rain ....Il.4.558.248.
The meanest Subject of our Realms above? ....Il.7.547.391.
Thence his broad Eye the subject World surveys, ...Il.8.65.398.
That shaded *Ide,* and all the subject Field ....Il.17.669.314.
The Subject of Debate, a Townsman slain: ....Il.18.578.350.
But this, no more the Subject of Debate, ...Il.19.67.374.
Is *Greece* and *Troy* the Subject in debate? ....Il.20.26.393.
Call then thy subject Streams, and bid them roar, ...Il.21.362.435.
On this sad Subject you enquire too much. ....Il.24.478.556.
Or nations subject to the western ray. ....Od.8.30.263.
An Isle, whose hills their subject fields survey; ....Od.9.134.311.
From o'er the porch, appear'd the subject town. ....Od.22.143.294.

SUBJECT-HERDS

His Subject-Herds, the Monarch of the Meads. ....Il.2.567.154.

SUBJECTED

Subjected these to those, or all to thee? ....3.EOM1.230.44.
In one short view subjected to your eye ....6.71.33.203.
In one short view subjected to our eye ....6.71.33A.203.
By Force subjected to a Man's Embrace, ...Il.18.506.346.

SUBJECTS

No wonder Savages or Subjects slain ....1.W-F.57A.154.
But Subjects starv'd while Savages were fed. ....1.W-F.60A.154.
Succeeding Monarchs heard the Subjects Cries, ...1.W-F.85.158.
For diff'rent *Styles* with diff'rent *Subjects* sort, ..1.EOC.322.275.
Where Heav'ns Free Subjects might their *Rights* dispute, ..1.EOC.548.302.
His Subjects Faith, and Queen's suspected Love, ...1.TrUl.217.473.
We, wretched subjects tho' to lawful sway, ...3.EOM2.149.73.
And Gods of Conqu'rors, Slaves of Subjects made: ....3.EOM3.248.117.
From *Rights* of *Subjects,* and the *Poor Man's Cause;* ..6.8.32.18.
That strike the Subjects answ'ring Heart; ....6.11.35Z8.31.
These Censures o'er, to different Subjects next, ...6.17iv.15.59.
Bold is the Task, when Subjects grown too wise ....Il.1.103.92.
Subjects all *Argos,* and controuls the Main. ....Il.2.136.134.
These Toils, my Subjects and my Sons might bear, ...Il.10.191.10.
Pass we to other subjects; and engage ....Od.3.301.100.
Who rul'd his subjects with a father's love. ....Od.5.19.172.
In subjects happy! with surprize I gaze; ....Od.8.419.286.
His subjects faith, and Queen's suspected love; ....Od.13.384.25.
Say, do thy subjects in bold faction rise, ...Od.16.99.107.
Nor leagu'd in factious arms my subjects rise, ...Od.16.119.108.
Thy other wants her subjects shall supply. ....Od.17.641.163.

SUBLIME

And *Is himself* that great *Sublime* he draws. ....1.EOC.680.316.
Sublime in Regal State, *Adrastus* shone, ...1.TrSt.613.436.
Tho' daring Milton sits Sublime, ...4.HOde9.5.159.
And with my Head Sublime *can reach the Sky.* ....6.26ii.4.79.
And finds *Machaön,* where sublime he stands ....Il.4.236.232.
Atrides mark'd him where sublime he stood; ....Il.5.707.301.
Surround her feet; with these sublime she sails ....Od.1.126.38.
And last, sublime his stately growth he rears, ...Od.4.621.149.
Supreme in might, sublime in majesty. ....Od.5.7.171.
Sublime to bear thee o'er the gloomy deep. ....Od.5.212.181.
High on a radiant throne sublime in state, ...Od.8.61.265.

SUBLIMELY

Tho' great *Alcæus* more sublimely sings, ...1.TrSP.33.394.
And he, whose Fustian's so sublimely bad, ...4.Arbu.187.109.
And he, whose Fustian's so sublimely bad, ...6.98.37.284.

SUBLIMER

To heav'nly Themes sublimer Strains belong. ....1.Mes.2.112.

SUBLIMES

Which not alone the *Southern Wit* sublimes, ...1.EOC.400.286.

SUBMISS

From Fields forbidden we submiss refrain, ...Il.8.43.397.
From Fields forbidden we submiss refrain, ...Il.8.580.424.
Submiss, Immortals! all he wills, obey; ....Il.15.120.201.
And from the Senior Pow'r, submiss retires; Il.21.544.444

SUBMISSION

"I'm all submission, what you'd have it, make it." ....4.Arbu.46.99.
Obey, ye *Grecians!* with Submission wait, ...Il.2.398.145.
And taught Submission to the Sire of Heav'n. ....Il.15.52.196.
Say, is the fault, thro' tame submission, thine? ....Od.3.262.98.
But to *Jove's* will submission we must pay; ....Od.5.129.178.

SUBMISSIONS

See what Effect our low Submissions gain! ....Il.9.738.471.

SUBMISSIVE

Oh wretched we, a vile submissive Train, ...1.TrSt.263.421.
In manner submissive most humbly do pray, ...6.42iii.2.117.
And trembling, these submissive Words return'd. ....Il.15.40.195.
Submissive I desist, if thou command, ...Il.21.436.438.
Submissive thus the hoary Sire preferr'd ....Od.3.494.111.
Approach'd him passing, and submissive said; ....Od.6.68.208.
But if submissive you resign the sway, ...Od.16.402.125.

SUBMISSIVELY

Yet *Speech,* ev'n there, submissively withdraws ....6.8.31.18.

SUBMIT

Let Female Fears submit to Female Fires! ....1.TrSP.204.402.
And Monuments, like Men, submit to Fate! ....2.RL3.172.182.
In both, to reason right is to submit. ....3.EOM1.164.35.
Submit—In this, or any other sphere, ...3.EOM1.285.50.
To him each Rival shall submit, ...4.HOde1.17.151.
Should I submit to each unjust Decree: ....Il.1.390.106.
Submit he must; or if they will not part, ...Il.1.424.108.
Goddess submit, nor dare our Will withstand, ...Il.1.732.122.
If you submit, the Thund'rer stands appeas'd; ....Il.1.750.123.
Whate'er our Master craves, submit we must, ...Il.2.291.141.
The Great will glory to submit to *Jove.* ....Il.8.176.406.
Submit and tremble at the hand of *Jove.* ....Il.8.257.409.
Glad I submit, whoe'er, or young or old, ...Il.14.118.163.
And we submit, since such the Will of Heav'n. ....Il.24.176.543.
And now in humbler scene submit to Fate. ....Od.17.339.148.

SUBMITS

Lo! *Jove* again submits me to thy Hands, ...Il.21.94.425.
Then to the mother's teats submits the lambs. ....Od.9.291.318.
And to the mother's teat submits the lambs. ....Od.9.367.321.
Or (since to dust proud *Troy* submits her tow'rs) .....Od.11.196.391.
Since in the dust proud *Troy* submits her tow'rs. .....Od.11.205.391.

SUBMITTED

Thy Charms submitted to a mortal Love: ....Il.18.108.328.

SUBMITTING

Please by receiving, by submitting sway ....3.Ep2.263A.71.
Charms by accepting, by submitting sways, ...3.Ep2.263.71.
To Fate submitting with a secret Sigh) ....Il.18.164.330.

SUBSCRIBE

And others roar aloud, "Subscribe, subscribe." ....4.Arbu.114.103.
And others roar aloud, "Subscribe, subscribe." ....4.Arbu.114.103.

SUBSCRIPTIONS

Stocks and Subscriptions pour on ev'ry side, ...3.Ep3.370.123.
South-sea Subscriptions take who please, ...4.1HE7.65.273.

SUBSERVIENT

Most Criticks, fond of some subservient Art, ...1.EOC.263.269.
Subservient to *New-market's* annual cheat! ....6.96iii.26.275.

SUBSIDE

At length the Wits mount up, the Hairs subside. ....2.RL5.74.206.
He foams a Patriot to subside a Peer; ....4.1740.10.332.
Then, when that languid Flames at length subside, ...Il.9.279.447.
The surges now subside, the tempest ends; ....Od.4.693.151.
Thrice in her gulphs the boiling seas subside, ...Od.12.131.438.

SUBSIDED

How barb'rous rage subsided at your word, ...4.2HE1.398.229.

SUBSIDES

When Sense subsides, and Fancy sports in sleep, ...3.Ep1.46.18.
The Soul subsides; and wickedly inclines ....4.HS2.79.59.
And deep subsides the ashy Heap below. ....Il.23.312.502.
He pray'd, and strait the gentle stream subsides, ...Od.5.576.200.
Soon as their rage subsides, the seas I brave ....Od.7.360.254.
When in her gulphs the rushing sea subsides, ...Od.12.288.446.
Just when the sea within her gulphs subsides, ...Od.12.509.457.

SUBSIDING

The Sea subsiding spreads a level Plain, ...Il.13.46.107.

SUBSIST

Subsist not in the good of one, but all. ....3.EOM4.38.131.
N, by whom Names subsist, declar'd, ...6.30.13.86.

SUBSISTED

But scarce subsisted to the Second Reign. ....1.TrSt.199.418.

SUBSISTS
But ALL subsists by elemental strife; ... 3.EOM1.169.36.
Our scene precariously subsists too long ... 6.32.41.97.
Your scene precariously subsists too long ... 6.32.41A.97.
The Form subsists, without the Body's Aid, ... Il.23.124.492.

SUBSTANCE
But like a Shadow, proves the *Substance* true; ... 1.EOC.467.292.
But like a Shadow, proves the *Substance* too; ... 1.EOC.467A.292.
Of massy Substance and stupendous Frame, ... 1.TrES.192.456.
And give up all his Substance to the Poor; ... 2.ChWB.43.58.
(But Airy Substance soon unites again) ... 2.RL3.152.179.
Ethereal Essence, Spirit, Substance, Man, ... 3.EOM1.238A.44.
Of massy Substance and stupendous Frame; ... Il.12.546.101.
No more the substance of the man remains, ... Od.11.263.394.
His substance vanish'd, and his strength decay'd, ... Od.11.489.408.

SUBSTANTIAL
And two substantial Meals a day were made. ... 6.13.7.39.
But 'tis substantial Happiness to *eat*— ... 6.34.26.101.

SUBTARTAREAN
Invokes the sable Subtartarean Pow'rs, ... Il.14.314.178.

SUBTERFUGE
What farther Subterfuge, what Hopes remain? ... Il.11.513.57.
No farther Subterfuge, no farther Chance; ... Il.22.345.470.

SUBTERRANEAN
"Here subterranean works and cities see; ... 3.EOM3.181.111.

SUBTILE
Or draw to silk Arachne's subtile line; ... 5.DunB4.590.401.

SUBTLE
As subtle Clerks by many Schools are made, ... 2.ChJM.109.20.
Let subtle schoolmen teach these friends to fight, ... 3.EOM2.81.64.
A subtle Minister may make of that? ... 4.JD4.133.37.
Un-learn'd, he knew no Schoolman's subtle Art, ... 4.Arbu.398.126.
This subtle Thief of Life, this paltry Time, ... 4.2HE2.76.171.

SUBTLEST
Make *Scots* speak Treason, cozen subtlest Whores, ... 4.JD4.59.31.

SUBTLY
In the nice bee, what sense so subtly true ... 3.EOM1.219.42.

SUBVERTING
Thy Pride once promis'd, of subverting *Troy;* ... Il.16.1004.282.

SUCCEED
To leaf-less Shrubs the flow'ring Palms succeed, ... 1.Mes.75.119.
Hence Strife shall rise, and mortal War succeed; ... 1.TrSt.344.424.
Alone can rival, can succeed to thee. ... 2.ElAb.206.336.
Alike my scorn, if he succeed or fail, ... 4.Arbu.362.122.
Observe how seldom ev'n the best succeed: ... 4.2HE1.286.219.
Nor Emulations, nor Disgusts succeed: ... 6.17iii.37.58.
Thus spoke the Prophet, thus the Fates succeed. ... Il.2.397.145.
To these succeed *Aspledon's* martial Train, ... Il.2.610.156.
To these the Youth of *Phylacè* succeed, ... Il.2.847.164.
The Forces last in fair Array succeed, ... Il.2.1068.172.
Aim at his Breast, and may that Aim succeed! ... Il.4.130.226.
The Field shall prove how Perjuries succeed, ... Il.4.308.235.
Pleas'd may ye hear (so Heav'n succeed my Pray'rs) ... Il.7.462.387.
Th' *Atridæ* first, th' *Ajaces* next succeed: ... Il.8.316.412.
Succeed to these my Cares, and rouze the rest; ... Il.10.200.10.
(So may, ye Gods! my pious Hopes succeed) ... Il.10.629.30.
His Wife live honour'd, all his Race succeed; ... Il.15.588.219.
Amphoterus, and *Erymas* succeed, ... Il.16.508.262.
Perhaps *Apollo* shall thy Arms succeed, ... Il.16.883.277.
Here then my Anger ends: Let War succeed, ... Il.19.71.374.
And I succeed to slaughter'd *Polydore.* ... Il.21.102.426.
And now succeed the Gifts, ordain'd to grace ... Il.23.863.524.
Go, and succeed! the rivals' aims despise; ... Od.2.319.76.
More near and deep, domestic woes succeed! ... Od.9.628.332.
Calls, to succeed his cares, the watchful swain; ... Od.10.95.345.
How wou'd the Gods my righteous toils succeed, ... Od.14.447.57.
Succeed the Omen, Gods! (the youth rejoin'd) ... Od.15.577.98.
Succeed those omens Heav'n! (the Queen rejoin'd) ... Od.17.186.140.
Succeed my wish; your votary restore: ... Od.17.288.146.
Inspire him *Jove!* in ev'ry wish succeed! ... Od.17.427.153.
The gen'rous lovers, studious to succeed, ... Od.18.321.182.
Hear then my friends! If *Jove* this arm succeed, ... Od.21.219.270.
When sultry days, and long, succeed the gentle spring. ... Od.22.336.302.
Shame to this age, and all that shall succeed! ... Od.24.498.372.
'Tis done, and at thy will the Fates succeed. ... Od.24.551.374.

SUCCEEDED
That pleas'd a God, succeeded to her arms. ... 1.TrFD.14.386.
And strait succeeded, leaving shame no room, ... 5.DunB4.531.394.
That pleas'd a God, succeeded to her Arms; ... Il.16.225.248.
Fast fell the tears, and sighs succeeded sighs: ... Od.8.582.294.
Tear follow'd tear, and groan succeeded groan. ... Od.11.101.385.

SUCCEEDING
Succeeding Monarchs heard the Subjects Cries, ... 1.W-F.85.158.
Thus long succeeding Criticks justly reign'd, ... 1.EOC.681.316.
And the long Series of succeeding Woe: ... 1.TrSt.320.423.
The rest, succeeding Times shall ripen into Fate. ... 1.TrSt.428.427.
And all the Sex in each succeeding Age, ... 2.ChJM.660.46.
Succeeding Vanities she still regards, ... 2.RL1.53.149.
Like them to shine thro' long succeeding age, ... 6.52.11.156.
Rolling, and black'ning, Swarms succeeding Swarms, ... Il.2.113.133.
What Fame were his thro' all succeeding Days, ... Il.10.251.13.
No Voice succeeding, he perceiv'd the Foe. ... Il.10.426.22.
Whether (the Gods succeeding our Desires) ... Il.13.931.149.

SUCCEEDING (CONTINUED)
The long-succeeding Numbers who can name? ... Il.17.306.299.
So Helms succeeding Helms, so Shields from Shields ... Il.19.384.388.
And Sons succeeding Sons, the lasting Line sustain. ... Il.20.356.408.
And beat against it, Wave succeeding Wave; ... Il.21.220.430.
To leave him wretched the succeeding Day. ... Il.22.637.482.
But chief, *Pelides:* thick succeeding Sighs ... Il.23.21.487.
No Race succeeding to imperial Sway: ... Il.24.678.565.
These Toils continue nine succeeding Days, ... Il.24.993.577.
And now the third succeeding morning shone. ... Od.10.168.348.
Still the succeeding flame expells the last. ... Od.15.28.71.
To flames we gave thee, the succeeding day, ... Od.24.83.352.
And next his sons, a long-succeeding train. ... Od.24.447.370.

SUCCEEDS
When milder Autumn Summer's Heat succeeds, ... 1.W-F.97.159.
And to fair *Argos'* open Court succeeds. ... 1.TrSt.562.434.
Another love succeeds, another race. ... 3.EOM3.130.105
But just disease to luxury succeeds, ... 3.EOM3.165.109
The centre mov'd, a circle strait succeeds, ... 3.EOM4.365.164
Far worse unhappy *D[iape]r* succeeds, ... 5.DunA2.286Z1.
Still, when the lust of tyrant pow'r succeeds, ... 6.51i.31.152.
By fits one Flash succeeds, as one expires, ... Il.10.9.2.
Accords their Vow, succeeds their Enterprize. ... Il.10.352.18.
Cleft thro' the Head, his Brother's Fate succeeds. ... Il.11.148.42.
Forth flows the Blood; an eager Pang succeeds; ... Il.11.507.56.
And Toil to Toil, and Woe succeeds to Woe. ... Il.16.139.243.
Adrestus first; *Autonous* then succeeds, ... Il.16.851.276.
Them *Chromius* follows, *Aretus* succeeds, ... Il.17.562.310.
A figur'd Dance succeeds: Such once was seen ... Il.18.681.356.
A Rowe of six fair Tripods then succeeds; ... Il.19.251.383.
Succeeds to Fate: The Spear his Belly rends; ... Il.20.563.417.
With those of *Tros,* bold *Diomed* succeeds: ... Il.23.456.508.
The next, tho' distant, *Menelas* succeeds; ... Il.23.481.509.
Such once I was! Now to these Tasks succeeds ... Il.23.739.519.
Th' Effect succeeds the Speech. *Pelides* cries, ... Il.23.935.526.
Thought follows Thought, and Tear succeeds to Tear. ... Il.24.16.535.
The filial tears, but woe succeeds to woe: ... Od.1.314.47.
Succeeds, and ev'n a stranger recommends. ... Od.7.68.237.
Then shade to shade in mutual forms succeeds, ... Od.11.279.395.
Now, wav'ring doubt succeeds to long despair; ... Od.19.615.226.
The guilty war; *Eurynomus* succeeds; ... Od.22.265.299.
First came the son; the father next succeeds, ... Od.24.183.356.

SUCCESS
With greater Passion, but with like Success; ... 1.TrVP.28A.378.
For when Success a Lover's Toil attends, ... 2.RL2.33.161.
Pleas'd with the strange Success, vast Numbers prest ... 2.TemF.394.282.
And act, and be, a Coxcomb with success. ... 5.DunB1.110.277.
When Crimes provoke us, Heav'n Success denies; ... Il.3.453.213.
Our Brother's Arms the just Success have found: ... Il.3.570.219.
Soon should our Arms with just Success be crown'd, ... Il.4.332.236.
'Tis Man's to fight, but Heav'ns to give Success. ... Il.6.427.347.
So hope Success, or dread the dire Effect. ... Il.7.427.385.
Heard ye the Voice of *Jove?* Success and Fame ... Il.8.214.407.
My Child! with Strength, with Glory and Success, ... Il.9.330.450.
Say what Success? divine *Laertes* Son! ... Il.9.791.473.
But why should'st thou suspect the War's Success? ... Il.12.285.92.
Vain are thy Vaunts, Success is still from Heav'n; ... Il.16.754.273.
And such Success mere human Wit attend: ... Il.18.426.341.
But Heav'n alone confers Success in War: ... Il.20.504.415.
Success; and humbles, or confirms the wise) ... Od.2.76.64.
O'er the wide waves success thy ways attends: ... Od.2.310.76.
And crown our voyage with desir'd success. ... Od.3.75.90.
While kindling transports glow'd at our success; ... Od.10.154.347.
With what success, 'tis *Jove's* alone to know, ... Od.15.563.97.
Hope ye success? undaunted crush the foe. ... Od.16.388.124.

SUCCESSES
Unlike Successes equal Merits found. ... 2.TemF.295.278.
No joy no pleasure from successes past ... 6.130.19.358.
Fierce as they are, by long Successes vain; ... Il.15.560.218.

SUCCESSFUL
And all successful, jealous Friends at best. ... 2.TemF.512.288.
Th' advent'rous Lover is successful still, ... 6.34.5.101.
While ev'ry Joy, successful Youth! is thine, ... 6.117.1.333.
And view, with Envy, our successful Wars. ... Il.2.415.147.
Successful Monarch of a mighty State! ... Il.3.242.204.
So when triumphant from successful Toils, ... Il.6.610.357.
If the proud *Grecians* thus successful boast ... Il.7.532.391.
Go then, successful, where thy Soul inspires; ... Il.13.985.152.
"The old, yet still successful, Cheat of Love"; ... Il.14.188.168.
To *Ida's* Top successful *Juno* flies: ... Il.14.331.179.
Were thine my Vigour, this successful Spear ... Il.16.879.277.
Three years successful in my art conceal'd, ... Od.19.174.200.
Our force successful shall our threat make good, ... Od.22.237.298.
Successful toils, and battles bravely won? ... Od.24.120.353.

SUCCESSFULLY
In useful Craft successfully refin'd; ... 1.TrUl.167.471.
In useful craft successfully refin'd! ... Od.13.334.23.

SUCCESSION
Still one by one, in swift Succession, pass ... 2.ChJM.236.25.
In *sure Succession* to the Day of Doom: ... 4.JD4.161.39.
And sure succession down from Heywood's days. ... 5.DunA1.96.70.
And sure succession down from Heywood's days. ... 5.DunB1.98.276.
To prove a dull *Succession* to be true, ... 6.7.23.16.
High schemes of pow'r in just succession roul.) ... Od.19.326.210.

SUCCESSIVE
Successive Study, Exercise and Ease. ... 1.W-F.240.171.
They fall successive, and successive rise; ... Il.6.184.335.
They fall successive, and successive rise; ... Il.6.184.335.
Farewell! and joys successive ever spring ... Od.13.78.5.

SUCCESSIVE (CONTINUED)

On sev'n bright years successive blessings wait; ....Od.14.317.50.
Each Peer successive his libation pours ....Od.18.470.191.
His son *Deucalion* bore successive sway; ....Od.19.208.203.

SUCCESSIVELY

On which three Wives successively had twin'd ....2.ChWB.395.76.

SUCCESSLESS

So gravest precepts may successless prove, ...5.DunA1.175.84.
So written precepts may successless prove, ...5.DunA1.175A.84.
So graver precepts may successless prove, ...5.DunA1.175B.84.
On Heaps they tumble with successless haste; ....Il.11.229.45.
Lest Arts and Blandishments successless prove, ...Il.15.37.195.
Successless all her soft caresses prove, ...Od.1.73.34.
But all her blandishments successless prove, ...Od.7.344.253.

SUCCINCT

Four *Knaves* in Garbs succinct, a trusty Band, ...2.RL3.41.171.
On some, a Priest succinct in amice white ....5.DunB4.549.396.
His Words succinct, yet full, without a Fault; ....Il.3.277.205.
His vest succinct then girding round his waste, ...Od.14.83.40.
Their garments, and succinct the victims slay. ....Od.17.200.141.
Then all with speed succinct the victims slay: ....Od.20.313.248.

SUCCOUR

Ye *Mantuan* Nymphs, your sacred Succour bring; ....1.PAu.5.80.
And see what succour from the Patriot Race. ....4.1740.4.332.
Nor seeks in vain for succour to the Stream. ....6.14iv.26.47.
His speedy Succour to the *Spartan* King; ....Il.4.231.232.
Swift to his Succour thro' the Ranks he ran: ....Il.4.243.232.
Now, Goddess, now, thy sacred Succour yield. ....Il.5.149.274.
Safe by thy Succour to our Ships convey'd; ....Il.10.332.17.
These *Troy* but lately to her Succour won, ...Il.10.504.26.
Saw *Tydeus'* Son with heav'nly Succour blest, ...Il.10.604.29.
Now wants that Succour which so oft' he lent. ....Il.11.971.78.
Two, not the worst; nor ev'n this Succour vain. ....Il.13.310.119.
Or to the Left our wanted Succour lend? ....Il.13.398.125.
Thy lofty Birth no Succour could impart, ...Il.14.541.189.
But thou, 0 God of Health! thy Succour lend, ...Il.16.643.269.
Retires for Succour to his social Train, ...Il.16.985.281.
Now pale and dead, shall succour *Greece* no more. ....Il.17.776.318.
The Host to succour, and thy Friends to save, ...Il.18.165.330.
Succour like this a mortal Arm might lend, ...Il.18.425.341.
And as your Minds direct, your Succour lend ....Il.20.36.394.
No Refuge now, no Succour from above; ....Il.22.383.471.
Still succour Mortals, and attend their Pray'rs; ....Il.24.412.552.
Revere the Gods, and succour the distrest? ....Od.9.206.314.
Low at thy knee thy succour we implore; ....Od.9.317.319.
'Till now from sea or flood no succour found, ...Od.12.393.450.
The speediest succour from my guardian hand; ....Od.15.105.73.
Come, ever welcome, and thy succour lend; ....Od.22.225.297.

SUCH

Such Silence waits on *Philomela's* Strains, ...1.PWi.78.94.
Such was the Life great *Scipio* once admir'd, ...1.W-F.257.172.
Let such teach others who themselves excell, ...1.EOC.15.240.
All such have still an Itching to deride, ...1.EOC.32A.243.
But in such Lays as neither *ebb*, nor *flow*, ...1.EOC.239.267.
Such *labour'd Nothings*, in so *strange* a Style, ...1.EOC.326.275.
And *smooth* or *rough*, with such, is *right,or wrong;* ....1.EOC.338A.277.
Leave such to tune their own dull Rhimes, and know ....1.EOC.358.280.
Avoid *Extreams;* and shun the Fault of such, ...1.EOC.384.284.
And such as *Chaucer* is, shall *Dryden* be. ....1.EOC.483.293.
And such were *Prais'd* who but *endeavour'd well:* ....1.EOC.511.295.
And such were *Prais'd* as but *endeavour'd well:* ....1.EOC.511A.295.
Such without *Wit* are Poets when they please, ...1.EOC.590.307.
Such shameless *Bards* we have; and yet 'tis true, ...1.EOC.610.309.
No Place so Sacred from such Fops is barr'd, ...1.EOC.622.310.
Such once were *Criticks*, such the Happy *Few*, ...1.EOC.643.311.
Such once were *Criticks*, such the Happy *Few*, ...1.EOC.643.311.
Such was the Muse, whose Rules and Practice tell, ...1.EOC.723.323.
Such was *Roscomon—not* more *learn'd* than *good,* ....1.EOC.725.324.
Such late was *Walsh,—the* Muse's Judge and Friend, ...1.EOC.729.325.
Than such as Women on their Sex bestow.) ....1.TrVP.56.379.
What Nymph cou'd e'er attract such Crowds as you? ....1.TrVP.70.380.
Such, and so bright an Aspect now he bears, ...1.TrVP.114.381.
But such as merit, such as equal thine, ...1.TrSP.46.395.
But such as merit, such as equal thine, ...1.TrSP.46.395.
For whom should *Sapho* use such Arts as these? ....1.TrSP.87.397.
Such inconsistent things are Love and Shame! ....1.TrSP.142.399.
Such Rays from *Phœbe's* bloody Circle flow, ...1.TrSt.147.416.
Such Light does *Phœbe's* bloody Orb bestow, ...1.TrSt.147A.416.
Such was the Discord of the Royal Pair, ...1.TrSt.190.418.
Not all those Realms cou'd for such Crimes suffice, ...1.TrSt.216A.419.
Thy Plagues, and curse 'em with such Sons as those. ....1.TrSt.399.426.
Such once employ'd *Alcides'* youthful Toils, ...1.TrSt.569.434.
Such was *Diana's*, such *Minerva's* Face; ....1.TrSt.625.436.
Such was *Diana's*, such *Minerva's* Face; ....1.TrSt.625.436.
In such a Cause disdain'd thy Life to save; ....1.TrSt.754.441.
Such Numbers fell by Pestilential Air! ....1.TrSt.766.442.
If such Inclemency in Heav'n can dwell; ....1.TrSt.769.442.
With such amazing Virtue durst engage. ....1.TrSt.783.442.
Such, they may cry, deserve the Sov'reign State, ...1.TrES.41.451.
Such Men as live in these degen'rate Days. ....1.TrES.186.456.
Such Prudence, Sir, in all your Words appears, ...2.ChJM.149.21.
Or such a *Wit* as no Man e'er can rule? ....2.ChJM.189.24.
The Joys are such as far transcend your Rage, ...2.ChJM.339.30.
Such secret Transports warm my melting Heart. ....2.ChJM.572.43.
That in my Presence offers such a Wrong. ....2.ChJM.650.46.
Well, I'm a Woman, and as such must speak; ....2.ChJM.694.48.
His Rage was such, as cannot be exprest: ....2.ChJM.753.51.
With such loud Clamours rend the vaulted Skie: ....2.ChJM.755A.51.
Such as are perfect, may, I can't deny; ....2.ChWB.44.58.
Let such (a God's Name) with fine Wheat be fed, ...2.ChWB.48.58.
As the Stars order'd, such my Life has been: ....2.ChWB.323.72.

SUCH (CONTINUED)

I took him such a Box as turn'd him blue, ...2.ChWB.423.77.
And in soft Bosoms dwells such mighty Rage? ....2.RL1.12.145.
And dwells such Rage in softest Bosoms then? ....2.RL1.11A.145.
And lodge such daring Souls in Little Men? ....2.RL1.12A.145.
E'er felt such Rage, Resentment and Despair, ...2.RL4.9.183.
The Fair-ones feel such Maladies as these, ...2.RL4.37.186.
Was it for this you took such constant Care ....2.RL4.97.191.
Nor could it sure be such a Sin to paint. ....2.RL5.24.201.
With such a Prize no Mortal must be blest, ...2.RL5.111.208.
Shall draw such Envy as the Lock you lost. ....2.RL5.144.211.
So large it spread, and swell'd to such a Height. ....2.TemF.247.275.
Such was her Form, as antient Bards have told, ...2.TemF.266.276.
But such plain roofs as piety could raise, ...2.ElAb.139.331.
Ere such a soul regains its peaceful state, ...2.ElAb.197.336.
Such if there be, who loves so long, so well; ....2.ElAb.363.348.
There must be, somewhere, such a rank as Man; ....3.EOM1.48.19.
Call Imperfection what thou fancy'st such, ...3.EOM1.115.29.
Alike in ignorance, his reason such, ...3.EOM2.11.55.
Admir'd such wisdom in an earthly shape, ...3.EOM2.33.60.
To Man imparts it; but with such a view ....3.EOM3.73.99.
Such as the souls of cowards might conceive, ...3.EOM3.259.118.
Such is the World's great harmony, that springs ....3.EOM3.295.122.
That such are happier, shocks all common sense. ....3.EOM4.52.133.
As well as dream such trifles are assign'd, ...3.EOM4.179.144.
And yet the fate of all extremes are such, ...3.Ep1.9A.16.
And yet the fate of all extremes is such, ...3.Ep1.9.16.
What will you do with such as disagree? ....3.Ep1.75.21.
Such in those moments as in all the past, ...3.Ep1.264.38.
Such happy Spots the nice admirer take, ...3.Ep2.43A.53.
Cries, "oh! how charming if there's no such place!" ....3.Ep2.108A.58.
Ev'n such is Woman's Fame: with this unblest, ...3.Ep2.281A.73.
Such this day's doctrine—in another fit ....3.Ep2.75.56.
Say, what can cause such impotence of mind? ....3.Ep2.93.57.
Cries, "Ah! how charming if there's no such place!" ....3.Ep2.108.58.
Oh! that such bulky Bribes as all might see, ...3.Ep3.35.88.
Since then, my Lord, on such a World we fall, ...3.Ep3.79.94.
For tho' such motives Folly you may call, ...3.Ep3.159.106.
Say, for such worth are other worlds prepar'd? ....3.Ep3.335.120.
The Dev'l was piqu'd such saintship to behold, ...3.Ep3.349.122.
Seldom at Church ('twas such a busy life) ....3.Ep3.381.124.
Bids Bubo build, and sends him such a Guide: ....3.Ep4.20.138.
Greatness, with Timon, dwells in such a draught ....3.Ep4.103.147.
I curse such lavish cost, and little skill, ...3.Ep4.167.153.
Proud to accomplish what such hands design'd, ...3.Ep4.196.156.
Bids *Babo* build, and sends him such a Guide: ....3.Ep4.20A.138.
Greatness, with Timon, dwells with such a draught ....3.Ep4.103A.147.
Lord *Fanny* spins a thousand such a Day. ....4.HS1.6.5.
Such as a *King* might read, a *Bishop* write, ...4.HS1.152.21.
Such as Sir *Robert* would approve— F. Indeed? ....4.HS1.153.21.
In such a Cause the Plaintiff will be hiss'd, ...4.HS1.155.21.
Such was my Fate; whom Heav'n adjudg'd as *proud,* ....4.JD4.19A.27.
Such was the Wight: Th' apparel on his back ....4.JD4.38.29.
What Sin of mine cou'd merit such a Rod? ....4.JD4.63.31.
Beheld such Scenes of *Envy, Sin,* and *Hate.* ....4.JD4.193.43.
Than such as swell this Bladder of a Court? ....4.JD4.205.43.
Such painted Puppets, such a varnish'd Race ....4.JD4.208.43.
Such painted Puppets, such a varnish'd Race ....4.JD4.208.43.
Such waxen Noses, stately, staring things, ...4.JD4.210.43.
Saw such a Scene of *Envy, Sin,* and *Hate.* ....4.JD4.193A.43.
Such Wits and Beauties are not prais'd for nought, ...4.JD4.234.45.
From such alone the Great Rebukes endure, ...4.JD4.282.49.
Yet for *small Turbots* such esteem profess? ....4.HS2.23.55.
At such a feast old vinegar to spare, ...4.HS2.57.59.
May no such Praise (cries *J[efferie]s)* e'er be mine! ....4.HAdv.45.79.
"Such Nicety, as Lady or Lord *Fanny?—* ....4.HAdv.92.83.
Then, lest Repentence punish such a Life, ...4.HAdv.104.83.
Such *Ovid's* nose, and "Sir! you have an *Eye—"* ....4.Arbu.118.104.
Ev'n such small Critics some regard may claim, ...4.Arbu.167.108.
Such piece-meal Critics some regard may claim, ...4.Arbu.167A.108.
And own'd, that nine such Poets made a *Tate.* ....4.Arbu.190.109.
Peace to all such! but were there One whose fires ....4.Arbu.193.109.
Shou'd such a man, too fond to rule alone, ...4.Arbu.197.110.
Who but must laugh, if such a man there be? ....4.Arbu.213.111.
"No, such a Genius never can lye still," ....4.Arbu.278.115.
But all such babling blockheads in his stead. ....4.Arbu.304.117.
'Tis such a bounty as was never known, ...4.JD2.65.139.
You love a Verse, take such as I can send. ....4.2HE2.2.165.
Faith, in such case, if you should prosecute, ...4.2HE2.23.165.
Nay worse, to ask for Verse at such a time! ....4.2HE2.31.167.
This put the Man in such a desp'rate Mind, ...4.2HE2.37.167.
"D'ye think me, noble Gen'ral, such a Sot? ....4.2HE2.50.167.
Hard Task! to hit the Palate of such Guests, ...4.2HE2.86.171.
Go, lofty Poet! and in such a Croud, ...4.2HE2.108.173.
The Men, who write such Verse as we can read? ....4.2HE2.158.175.
Such they'll degrade; and sometimes, in its stead, ...4.2HE2.163.177.
If such the Plague and pains to write by rule, ...4.2HE2.180.177.
Such as wise *Bacon*, or brave *Raleigh* spake; ....4.2HE2.168A.177.
Say, can you find out one such Lodger there? ....4.2HE2.223.181.
Heathcote himself, and such large-acred Men, ...4.2HE2.240.181.
Leave such to trifle with more grace and ease, ...4.2HE2.326.187.
How shall the Muse, from such a Monarch, steal ....4.2HE1.5.195.
I scarce can think him such a worthless thing, ...4.2HE1.209.213.
Such is the shout, the long-applauding note, ...4.2HE1.330.223.
Not with such Majesty, such bold relief, ...4.2HE1.390.229.
Not with such Majesty, such bold relief, ...4.2HE1.390.229.
(Like Journals, Odes, and such forgotten things ....4.2HE1.416.231.
And then such Friends—as cannot fail to last. ....4.1HE6.80.243.
Now, in such exigencies not to need, ...4.1HE6.89.243.
Such tattle often entertains ....4.HS6.95.257.
Cheese, such as men in Suffolk make, ...4.HS6.167.261.
Was ever such a happy Swain? ....4.HS6.206.263.
I'm no such Beast, nor his Relation; ....4.1HE7.60.273.
A Pension, or such Harness for a slave ....4.1HE1.87.285.
If such a Doctrine, in St. James's air, ...4.1HE1.110.287.
Have I in silent wonder seen such things ....4.EpS1.109.306.

SUCH (CONTINUED)

Yet may this Verse (if such a Verse remain) ....4.EpS1.171.309.
Vice with such Giant-strides comes on amain, ...4.EpS2.6.313.
Than such as *Anstis* casts into the Grave; ....4.EpS2.237.326.
Such as on HOUGH's unsully'd Mitre shine, ...4.EpS2.240.326.
With all such reading as was never read; ....5.DunA1.166.83.
Had heav'n decreed such works a longer date, ...5.DunA1.183.85.
But such a bulk as no twelve bards could raise, ...5.DunA2.35.100.
(Such was her wont, at early dawn to drop ....5.DunA2.67.106.
Such happy arts attention can command, ...5.DunA2.221.128.
Such, as from lab'ring lungs th' Enthusiast blows, ...5.DunA2.245.129.
If there be man who o'er such works can wake, ...5.DunA2.340.142.
No more the Monarch could such raptures bear; ....5.DunA3.357A.193.
Such with their shelves as due proportion hold, ...5.DunB1.137.280.
But such a bulk as no twelve bards could raise, ...5.DunB2.39.298.
(Such was her wont, at early dawn to drop ....5.DunB2.71.299.
Such happy arts attention can command, ...5.DunB2.229.307.
Such as from lab'ring lungs th' Enthusiast blows, ...5.DunB2.255.308.
Or such as bellow from the deep Divine; ....5.DunB2.257.308.
"If there be man, who o'er such works can wake, ...5.DunB2.372.315.
With all such reading as was never read:, ...5.DunB4.250.368.
Such skill in passing all, and touching none. ....5.DunB4.258.369.
Did Nature's pencil ever blend such rays, ...5.DunB4.411.382.
Such vary'd light in one promiscuous blaze? ....5.DunB4.412.382.
Such as Lucretius drew, a God like Thee: ....5.DunB4.484.389.
With such a Gust will I receive thy word. ....6.2.12.6.
Deaf to the Voice of such a *Gorgon,* ....6.10.26.25.
Such Friends, if such there are, as you, ...6.10.32.25.
Such Friends, if such there are, as you, ...6.10.32.25.
Such, who read *Heinsius* and *Masson,* ....6.10.33.25.
His Numbers such, as Sanger's self might use. ....6.12.3.37.
Such place hath *Deptford,* Navy-building Town, ...6.14ii.46.44.
Such *Lambeth,* Envy of each Band and Gown, ...6.14ii.48.44.
And *Twick'nam* such, which fairer Scenes enrich, ...6.14ii.49.44.
Such Nastiness and so much Pride ....6.14v(a).8.48.
Her Learning and good Breeding such, ...6.14v(b).7.49.
Such wholsome Foods as Nature's Wants supply, ...6.17iii.26.58.
Such charms has death when join'd with liberty. ....6.20.14.66.
For me, and such as me, thou deign'st to bear ....6.25.5.77.
Such as then was, and is, thy love to me, ...6.25.13.77.
Such is, and shall be still, my love to thee— ....6.25.14.77.
Such tears, as Patriots shed for dying Laws: ....6.32.14.96.
Such Plays alone should please a *British* ear, ...6.32.45.97.
Such plays alone should win a *British* ear, ...6.32.45A.97.
Such praise is yours—and such shall you possess, ...6.38.23.108.
Such praise is yours—and such shall you possess, ...6.38.23.108.
Such rage without betrays the fire within; ....6.41.17.114.
And sure such kind good creatures may be living. ....6.41.28.114.
Was he discouragd? no such matter; ....6.44.3.123.
About them both why keep we such a pother? ....6.46.3.127.
About them both why make we such a pother? ....6.46.3A.127.
Such Sheets as these, whate'er be the Disaster, ...6.48ii.11.134.
Hunger, not Malice, makes such Authors print, ...6.49iii.5.142.
Should such a man, too fond to rule alone, ...6.49iii.11.142.
Should such a One, too fond to Reign alone, ...6.49iii.11A.142.
Should such a man, too fond to Reign alone, ...6.49iii.11B.142.
Should such a One, resolv'd to Reign alone, ...6.49iii.11C.142.
Should such a man, be fond to Reign alone, ...6.49iii.11D.142.
What pity, Heav'n! if such a Man there be? ....6.49iii.29.143.
Who but must Grieve, if such a man there be? ....6.49iii.29A.143.
Who but must Grieve if such a One there be? ....6.49iii.29B.143.
Who would not laugh if such a Man there be? ....6.49iii.29C.143.
No wicked Whores shall have such Luck ....6.54.13.165.
Such, such a man extends his life's short space, ...6.55.8.166.
Such, such a man extends his life's short space, ...6.55.8.166.
Such this man was; who now, from earth remov'd, ...6.57.11.169.
To keep this Cap, for such as will, to wear; ....6.60.34.179.
Where's such ado with Townsend. ....6.61.16.181.
There's such ado with Townsend. ....6.61.16A.181.
Abroad with such as are not so. ....6.61.48.182.
Alas! if I am such a Creature, ...6.74.5.211.
(Such Honour did them prick) ....6.79.14.218.
Was never such a loving Pair, ...6.79.39.219.
Never was such a loving Pair, ...6.79.39A.219.
I will not cope against such odds, ...6.79.99.221.
Wit is like faith by such warm Fools profest ....6.82ix(b).1.234.
Wit like religion by such Fools profest. ....6.82ix(b).1C.234.
Such were the Notes, thy once-lov'd Poet sung, ...6.84.1.238.
There was such Flutt'ring, Chuckling, Crowing: ....6.93.12.257.
Such, Lady *Mary,* are your Tricks; ....6.93.27.257.
Such, Lady Mary, are your Tricks, ...6.93.27Z1.257.
You dress not such a *Rabbit,* ....6.94.46.260.
When Pride in such contemptuous Beings lies, ...6.96v.31.281.
And own that nine such Poets make a *Tate;* ....6.98.40.284.
Peace to all such! but were there one, whose Fires ....6.98.43.284.
Should such a Man, too fond to rule alone, ...6.98.47.284.
What Pity, Heav'n! if such a Man there be. ....6.98.65.285.
Has writ such stuff, as none e'er writ before. ....6.116i.2.325.
Shall Royal praise be rhym'd by such a ribald, ...6.116v.1.327.
Great G[eorge ii]! such servants since thou well can'st lack, ...6.116v.5.327.
But such a *babling Coxcomb* in his stead. ....6.120.12.339.
Who by six such fair Maidens at once is possest. ....6.122.4.341.
And such a polish as disgraces Art; ....6.126ii.6.353.
And such a polish as disgraceth Art; ....6.126ii.6A.353.
Such, such Emotions should in *Britons* rise, ...6.128.9.355.
Such, such Emotions should in *Britons* rise, ...6.128.9.355.
And that to towze such Things as *flutter,* ....6.135.23.367.
When all such Dogs have had their Days, ...6.135.37.367.
Such thoughts, as prompt the brave to lie, ...6.141.6.380.
Such flames, as high in patriots burn, ...6.141.9.381.
And such as wicked kings may mourn, ...6.141.11.381.
Let such, such only, tread this sacred Floor, ...6.142.13.383.
Let such, such only, tread this sacred Floor, ...6.142.13.383.
Such only such shall tread the sacred Floor, ...6.142.13A.383.
Such only such shall tread the sacred Floor, ...6.142.13A.383.
Such only such may tread this sacred Floor, ...6.142.13B.383.

SUCH (CONTINUED)

Such only such may tread this sacred Floor, ...6.142.13B.383.
Let such, such only, tread this Poet's Floor, ...6.142.13C.383.
Let such, such only, tread this Poet's Floor, ...6.142.13C.383.
Let such, such only, tread the Poet's Floor, ...6.142.13D.383.
Let such, such only, tread the Poet's Floor, ...6.142.13D.383.
Let such, such only, tread their Poet's Floor, ...6.142.13E.383.
Let such, such only, tread their Poet's Floor, ...6.142.13E.383.
Let such, such only, tread the sacred Floor, ...6.142.13F.383.
Let such, such only, tread the sacred Floor, ...6.142.13F.383.
But when I saw such Charity remain, ...6.146.3.389.
Such was the Sov'reign Doom, and such the Will of *Jove.* ..... Il.1.8.85.
Such was the Sov'reign Doom, and such the Will of *Jove.* ..... Il.1.8.85.
Such as a King might ask; and let it be ....Il.1.173.96.
There want not Chiefs in such a Cause to fight, ...Il.1.227.98.
To Pow'r superior none such Hatred bear: ....Il.1.230.98.
Such, as no more these aged Eyes shall view! ....Il.1.346.105.
The *Greeks* to know the Curse of such a King: ....Il.1.535.113.
His Figure such as might his Soul proclaim; ....Il.2.263.140.
Such just Examples on Offenders shown, ...Il.2.338.143.
Not such at *Argos* was their gen'rous Vow, ...Il.2.350.144.
Such was the Will of *Jove;* and hence we dare ....Il.2.386.145.
But ten such Sages as they grant in thee; ....Il.2.443.148.
Such Wisdom soon should *Priam's* Force destroy, ...Il.2.444.148.
Such were the Chiefs, and such the *Grecian* Train. ....Il.2.923.167.
Such were the Chiefs, and such the *Grecian* Train. ....Il.2.923.167.
But ne'er 'till now such Numbers charg'd a Field. ....Il.2.969.169.
Say, was it thus, with such a baffled Mien, ...Il.3.69.192.
They cry'd, No wonder such Celestial Charms ....Il.3.205.201.
Around whose Brow such martial Graces shine, ...Il.3.221.203.
Such mighty Woes on perjur'd Princes wait; ....Il.4.204.231.
"Such are the Trophies *Greece* from *Ilion* brings, ...Il.4.214.231.
And such the Conquests of her King of Kings! ....Il.4.215.231.
Brave Men! he cries (to such who boldly dare ....Il.4.266.234.
Such, and so thick, th' embattel'd Squadrons stood, ...Il.4.322.236.
O Heroes! worthy such a dauntless Train, ...Il.4.326.236.
Such Souls as burn in your exalted Breast! ....Il.4.331.236.
Such as I was, when *Ereuthalion* slain ....Il.4.372.238.
Such *Tydeus* was, and such his martial Fire; ....Il.4.450.241.
Such *Tydeus* was, and such his martial Fire; ....Il.4.450.241.
Such Clamours rose from various Nations round, ...Il.4.496.244.
Such Glories *Pallas* on the Chief bestow'd, ...Il.5.11.266.
Such, from his Arms, the fierce Effulgence flow'd: ....Il.5.12.266.
Such Coursers whirl him o'er the dusty Field, ...Il.5.232.278.
Such Men as live in these degen'rate Days. ....Il.5.372.285.
Such Stream as issues from a wounded God; ....Il.5.422.287.
With great *Æneas;* such the Form he bore, ...Il.5.547.295.
And such in Fight the radiant Arms he wore. ....Il.5.548.295.
Such Cares thy Friends deserve, and such thy Foes. ....Il.5.600.297.
Such Cares thy Friends deserve, and such thy Foes. ....Il.5.600.297.
Jove got such Heroes as my Sire, whose Soul ....Il.5.790.304.
Such as the Heav'ns produce: and round the Gold ....Il.5.894.308.
Thro' such a Space of Air, with thund'ring Sound, ...Il.5.962.312.
Such was their Look as Lions bath'd in Blood, ...Il.5.974.313.
Such Nerves I gave him, and such Force in Fight. ....Il.5.1005.314.
Such Nerves I gave him, and such Force in Fight. ....Il.5.1005.314.
In such a Cloud the God from Combate driv'n, ...Il.5.1062.317.
Such, and so soon, th' Ætherial Texture join'd. ....Il.5.1115.321.
For sure such Courage Length of Life denies, ...Il.6.514.351.
And such the hard Condition of our Birth. ....Il.6.629.358.
Sprung from such Fathers, who such Numbers sway; ....Il.7.193.373.
Sprung from such Fathers, who such Numbers sway; ....Il.7.193.373.
In such a Voice as fills the Earth and Air. ....Il.7.234.376.
Such as I am, I come to prove thy Might; ....Il.7.281.378.
For such I reign, unbounded and above; ....Il.8.33.397.
And such are Men, and Gods, compar'd to *Jove.* ....Il.8.34.397.
Such be the Scene from his *Idæan* Bow'r; ....Il.8.252.409.
For such is Fate, nor can'st thou turn its Course ....Il.8.595.424.
Such various Passions urg'd the troubled Host. ....Il.9.10.431.
Such Strength of Body, with such Force of Mind; ....Il.9.74.436.
Such Strength of Body, with such Force of Mind; ....Il.9.74.436.
And such a Monarch as can chuse the best. ....Il.9.102.437.
Such as himself will chuse, who yield to none, ...Il.9.181.441.
Such are thy Offers as a Prince may take, ...Il.9.217.443.
And such as fits a gen'rous King to make. ....Il.9.218.443.
Such as thy self shall chuse; who yield to none, ...Il.9.368.451.
Such are the Proffers which this Day we bring, ...Il.9.394.452.
Such the Repentance of a suppliant King. ....Il.9.395.452.
For thankless *Greece* such Hardships have I brav'd, ...Il.9.428.453.
When *Hector's* Prowess no such Wonders wrought; ....Il.9.465.455.
His Gifts are hateful: Kings of such a Kind ....Il.9.494.456.
Thy Friend, believe me, no such Gifts demands, ...Il.9.715.469.
And here I stay, (if such his high Behest) ....Il.9.719.470.
Such was his Word; What farther he declar'd, ...Il.9.806.473.
Such bold Exploits uncommon Courage ask, ...Il.10.46.4.
To whom the King. In such Distress we stand, ...Il.10.49.4.
Such wond'rous Deeds as *Hector's* Hand has done, ...Il.10.57.4.
Yet such his Acts, as *Greeks* unborn shall tell, ...Il.10.61.5.
(Such as by Youths unus'd to Arms, are worn; ....Il.10.305.16.
So distant they, and such the Space between, ...Il.10.419.22.
So fast, and with such Fears, the *Trojan* flew; ....Il.10.431.23.
Such Hands may wound, but not incense a Man. ....Il.11.496.56.
And leaves such Objects as distract the Fair. ....Il.11.504.56.
Such Thoughts revolving in his careful Breast, ...Il.11.521.57.
Such then I was, impell'd by youthful Blood; ....Il.11.896.75.
Such gentle Force the fiercest Minds obey; ....Il.11.923.76.
Such as sage *Chiron,* Sire of *Pharmacy,* ....Il.11.966.78.
Such their proud Hopes, but all their Hopes were vain! ....Il.12.140.86.
Such, they may cry, deserve the sov'reign State, ...Il.12.385.95.
Such Men as live in these degen'rate Days. ....Il.12.540.101.
Such his loud Voice, and such his manly Mien; ....Il.13.70.108.
Such his loud Voice, and such his manly Mien; ....Il.13.70.108.
Such, and so swift, the Pow'r of Ocean flew; ....Il.13.95.109.
And falls our Fleet by such inglorious Hands? ....Il.13.140.111.
In such Assays, thy blameless Worth is known, ...Il.13.372.123.
Such as may teach, 'twas still thy brave Delight ....Il.13.376.123.

SUCH (CONTINUED)

Such is the Help thy Arms to *Ilion* bring, ... Il.13.473.129.
And such the Contract of the *Phrygian* King! ... Il.13.474.129.
For such an Aid what will not *Argos* give? ... Il.13.476.130.
In such bold Feats your impious Might approve, ... Il.13.783.142.
With such a Tyde superior Virtue sway'd, ... Il.13.849.146.
But such as those of *Jove's* high Lineage born, ... Il.13.1048.155.
Such was his Threat, ah now too soon made good, ... Il.14.53.160.
In such Distress if Counsel profit ought; ... Il.14.68.160.
In such base Sentence if thou couch thy Fear, ... Il.14.100.162.
To think such Meanness, or the Thought declares? ... Il.14.103.162.
Such Counsel if you seek, behold the Man ... Il.14.121.163.
Such *Tydeus* was, the foremost once in Fame! ... Il.14.141.164.
Such was the Voice, and such the thund'ring Sound ... Il.14.175.165.
Such was the Voice, and such the thund'ring Sound ... Il.14.175.165.
If such thy Will, to that Recess retire, ... Il.14.385.181.
With such a Rage the meeting Hosts are driv'n, ... Il.14.463.186.
And such a Clamour shakes the sounding Heav'n. ... Il.14.464.186.
He pierc'd his Heart—Such Fate attends you all, ... Il.14.561.190.
Such, as the House of *Promachus* must know; ... Il.14.590.191.
Such, as to *Promachus'* sad Spouse we bear; ... Il.14.592.191.
Nor seem'd the Vengeance worthy such a Son; ... Il.15.30.195.
Such was our Word, and Fate the Word obeys. ... Il.15.83.199.
Such stern Decrees, such threatned Woes to come, ... Il.15.105.200.
Such stern Decrees, such threatned Woes to come, ... Il.15.105.200.
Ev'n Pow'r immense had found such Battel hard. ... Il.15.257.207.
Thus point your Arms; and when such Foes appear, ... Il.15.336.210.
Nor was such Glory due to *Teucer's* Hands. ... Il.15.543.217.
Such is the Fate of *Greece,* and such is ours: ... Il.15.580.218.
Such is the Fate of *Greece,* and such is ours: ... Il.15.580.218.
Still press'd, and press'd by such inglorious Hands. ... Il.15.607.220.
Such Conf'rence held the Chiefs; while on the Strand, ... Il.16.128.242.
Such their dread Strength, and such their deathful View. ... Il.16.203.247.
Such their dread Strength, and such their deathful View. ... Il.16.203.247.
Such was *Menestheus,* but mis-call'd by Fame ... Il.16.214.247.
Such were your words—Now Warriors grieve no more, ... Il.16.248.249.
Such is the Force of more than mortal Hands! ... Il.16.971.281.
Sure where such partial Favour Heav'n bestow'd, ... Il.17.105.291.
Did such a Spirit as the Gods impart ... Il.17.173.294.
(Such, as shou'd burn in ev'ry Soul, that draws ... Il.17.175.294.
From such a Warrior such a Speech shou'd hear? ... Il.17.190.294.
From such a Warrior such a Speech shou'd hear? ... Il.17.190.294.
Such o'er *Patroclus* Body hung the Night, ... Il.17.426.303.
Could blame this Scene; such Rage, such Horror reign'd; ... Il.17.460.305.
Could blame this Scene; such Rage, such Horror reign'd; ... Il.17.460.305.
Such, *Jove* to honour the great Dead ordain'd. ... Il.17.461.305.
Can such Opponents stand, when we assail? ... Il.17.556.310.
In such a Form the Goddess round her drew ... Il.17.622.312.
But such a Chief I spy not thro' the Host: ... Il.17.725.315.
Such the wild Terror, and the mingled Cry. ... Il.17.850.321.
Such Horror *Jove* imprest! Yet still proceeds ... Il.17.853.321.
Had caus'd such Sorrows past, and Woes to come. ... Il.18.114.328.
Rises in Arms: Such Grace thy *Greeks* have won. ... Il.18.420.341.
And such Success mere human Wit attend: ... Il.18.426.341.
For such Desert what Service can I pay? ... Il.18.474.344.
Of Works divine (such Wonders are in Heav'n!) ... Il.18.490.345.
For *Thetis* only such a Weight of Care? ... Il.18.504.346.
A figur'd Dance succeeds: Such once was seen ... Il.18.681.356.
Such War th' Immortals wage: Such Horrors rend ... Il.20.89.397.
Such War th' Immortals wage: Such Horrors rend ... Il.20.89.397.
He rush'd impetuous. Such the Lion's Rage, ... Il.20.199.402.
To this *Anchises'* Son. Such Words employ ... Il.20.240.404.
Such we disdain; the best may be defy'd ... Il.20.242.404.
Such *Erichthonius* was: From him there came ... Il.20.274.405.
Such is our Race: 'Tis Fortune gives us Birth, ... Il.20.290.406.
No God can singly such a Host engage, ... Il.20.407.412.
Hector, undaunted, thus. Such Words employ ... Il.20.499.415.
Such we could give, defying and defy'd, ... Il.20.501.415.
Such is the Lust of never-dying Fame! ... Il.20.590.418.
That barr such numbers from their native Plain: ... Il.21.69.424.
Such Ruin theirs, and such Compassion mine. ... Il.21.142.427.
Such Ruin theirs, and such Compassion mine. ... Il.21.142.427.
Begot my Sire, whose Spear such Glory won: ... Il.21.177.429.
So ends thy Glory! Such the Fate they prove ... Il.21.201.429.
Such pond'rous Ruin shall confound the Place, ... Il.21.374.436.
To *Grecian* Gods such let the *Phrygian* be, ... Il.21.502.442.
Troy Walls I rais'd (for such were *Jove's* Commands) ... Il.21.519.443.
Such is his Swiftness, 'tis in vain to fly, ... Il.21.667.449.
And such his Valour, that who stands must die. ... Il.21.668.449.
(Such as in Races crown the speedy Strife) ... Il.22.209.464.
Such Pacts, as Lambs and rabid Wolves combine, ... Il.22.337.470.
Such Leagues, as Men and furious Lions join, ... Il.22.338.470.
To such I call the Gods! One constant state ... Il.22.339.470.
For such a Warrior *Thetis* aids their Woe, ... Il.23.19.487.
And bid the Forests fall: (Such Rites are paid ... Il.23.63.489.
(Such charge was giv'n 'em) to the sandy Shore; ... Il.23.153.495.
Such, and so narrow now the Space between ... Il.23.603.513.
Such Joy the *Spartan's* shining Face o'erspread, ... Il.23.683.517.
Such once I was! Now to these Tasks succeeds ... Il.23.739.519.
And we submit, since such the Will of Heav'n. ... Il.24.176.543.
If such thy Will, dispatch from yonder Sky ... Il.24.381.551.
This *Hermes* (such the Pow'r of Gods) set wide; ... Il.24.561.559.
Uncommon are such Favours of the Sky, ... Il.24.568.560.
Such is, alas! the Gods severe Decree; ... Il.24.661.564.
Her self a Rock, (for such was Heav'ns high Will) ... Il.24.773.569.
Such Griefs, O King! have other Parents known; ... Il.24.780.569.
Should such report thy honour'd Person here, ... Il.24.822.571.
Such Honours *Ilion* to her Hero paid, ... Il.24.1015.577.
Such was that face, on which I dwelt with joy ... Od.1.271.45.
Appear'd he now with such heroic port, ... Od.1.346.49.
Such the pleas'd ear will drink with silent joy. ... Od.1.436.53.
Such railing eloquence, and war of words. ... Od.2.96.65.
Such numbers fell, such Heroes sunk to night: ... Od.3.132.92.
Such numbers fell, such Heroes sunk to night: ... Od.3.132.92.
Ah! no such hope (the Prince with sighs replies) ... Od.3.279.99.
(By force he could not) such a Heroe's fate? ... Od.3.311.101.

SUCH (CONTINUED)

In honour's limits (such the pow'r of Song) ... Od.3.337.103.
Of such a heroe, and of such a friend? ... Od.3.446.108.
Of such a heroe, and of such a friend? ... Od.3.446.108.
And presents, such as suit the state of Kings. ... Od.3.609.117.
With signatures of such majestic grace. ... Od.4.76.123.
Such, and not nobler, in the realms above ... Od.4.89.123.
Such quick regards his sparkling eyes bestow; ... Od.4.201.129.
Such wavy ringlets o'er his shoulders flow! ... Od.4.202.129.
Such, happy *Nestor!* was thy glorious doom; ... Od.4.289.132.
Such to our wish the warrior soon restore, ... Od.4.461.142.
His spear, indignant for such high disdain, ... Od.4.678.151.
Such is our sov'reign Will, and such is Fate. ... Od.5.55.174.
Such is our sov'reign Will, and such is Fate. ... Od.5.55.174.
Such length of ocean and unmeasur'd deep? ... Od.5.126.178.
Such as the mortal life of man sustains: ... Od.5.252.183.
(Such as was that, when show'rs of jav'lins fled ... Od.5.397.191.
Great as he is, such virtue shall devour. ... Od.5.433.193.
(For many such on *Amphitrite* attend) ... Od.5.539.198.
To such a miracle of charms ally'd: ... Od.6.186.218.
Such finish'd grace! I gaze and I adore! ... Od.6.192.218.
This man my spouse, or such a spouse as he! ... Od.6.294.225.
Such were the glories which the Gods ordain'd ... Od.7.176.244.
Let no such thought (with modest grace rejoin'd ... Od.7.281.249.
Who from such youth cou'd hope consid'rate care? ... Od.7.378.254.
Such as thou art, thy thought and mine were one, ... Od.7.399.256.
In such alliance could'st thou wish to join, ... Od.7.401.256.
Such was my boast, while vigour crown'd my days, ... Od.8.203.273.
In such heroic games I yield to none, ... Od.8.237.275.
By fate impos'd; such me my parent bore: ... Od.8.352.282.
Or such who harbour pity in their breast, ... Od.9.205.314.
Such was the wine: to quench whose fervent stream, ... Od.9.242.316.
Such was our fate, and such high *Jove's* command! ... Od.9.312.319.
Such was our fate, and such high *Jove's* command! ... Od.9.312.319.
Such as th' unblest *Cyclopean* climes produce, ... Od.9.422.323.
(Such as his shallow wit, he deem'd was mine) ... Od.9.499.326.
While such a monster as vile *Noman* lives. ... Od.9.542.328.
Long since he menac'd, such was Fate's command; ... Od.9.599.331.
(Such as the good man ever us'd to give.) ... Od.10.249.354.
We went, *Ulysses!* (such was thy command) ... Od.10.295.357.
Such be your minds as ere ye left your coast, ... Od.10.546.369.
Grac'd with such honours as become the Great. ... Od.11.225.393.
All, all are such, when life the body leaves; ... Od.11.262.394.
Such were they Youths! had they to manhood grown, ... Od.11.389.403.
O King! for such thou art, and sure thy blood ... Od.11.450.406.
And such was mine! who basely plung'd her sword ... Od.11.533.409.
Such, such was I! still tost from care to care, ... Od.11.763.424.
Such, such was I! still tost from care to care, ... Od.11.763.424.
If such thy will—We will it, *Jove* replies. ... Od.13.177.14.
Accept such treatment as a swain affords, ... Od.14.71.39.
Such food as falls to simple servant's share; ... Od.14.98.40.
Late with such affluence and possessions blest, ... Od.14.140.42.
Such thou may'st be. But he whose name you crave ... Od.14.154.43.
Not with such transport wou'd my eyes run o'er, ... Od.14.163.43.
But such was Heav'n's high will! Know then I came ... Od.14.229.46.
Such end the wicked found! But *Jove's* intent ... Od.14.345.51.
By many such have I been warn'd; but chief ... Od.14.417.56.
Not for such ends my house and heart are free, ... Od.14.429.56.
Such are the tasks of men of mean estate, ... Od.15.342.86.
Not such, my friend, the servants of their feast: ... Od.15.350.86.
To such a man since harbour you afford, ... Od.15.368.87.
But one choice blessing (such is *Jove's* high will) ... Od.15.524.95.
Such honours as befit a Prince to give; ... Od.16.78.106.
Heav'n such illusion only can impose, ... Od.16.216.114.
With such a foe th' unequal fight to try, ... Od.16.276.118.
Such aids expect, he cries, when strong in might ... Od.16.288.118.
Such be the plea, and by the plea deceive: ... Od.16.318.121.
Such to our wish the warrior soon restore, ... Od.17.152.139.
And such as suits the dictate of my mind. ... Od.17.217.142.
Such dogs, and men there are, meer things of state, ... Od.17.374.150.
Such, when *Ulysses* left his natal coast; ... Od.17.386.150.
With such an image touch'd of human woe; ... Od.17.441.155.
Such guests *Eumæus* to his country brings, ... Od.17.456.155.
But chief to Poets such respect belongs, ... Od.17.466.155.
Nor wonder I, at such profusion shown; ... Od.17.535.158.
Ill suit such forms of grace and dignity. ... Od.17.538.158.
Then in such robes as suppliants may require, ... Od.17.652.164.
O that such baseness should disgrace the light! ... Od.18.90.171.
Such was thy father! an imperial state, ... Od.18.153.173.
Such as in fondness parents ask of heav'n. ... Od.18.208.177.
Such *Venus* shines, when with a measur'd bound ... Od.18.229.178.
Such were his words; and *Hymen* now prepares ... Od.18.315.182.
Not such the sickly beams, which unsincere, ... Od.19.40.194.
For such a Lord! who crown'd your virgin-love ... Od.19.302.209.
Such gentle manners, and so sage a mind, ... Od.19.404.214.
Such servant as your humble choice requires, ... Od.19.407.214.
Be such my lot! Or thou *Diana* speed ... Od.20.94.237.
Such raptures in my beating bosom rise, ... Od.20.108.238.
What guest is he, of such majestic air? ... Od.20.241.244.
And with my life such vile dishonours end. ... Od.20.386.251.
From me, ye Gods! avert such dire disgrace. ... Od.20.412.252.
Why such profusion of indulgence shown ... Od.20.451.255.
(For heav'n forbid, such weakness should endure) ... Od.21.140.265.
Such fate I prophesy our guest attends, ... Od.21.325.275.
Nor shall these walls such insolence contain; ... Od.21.327.275.
With such good fortune as he now shall find. ... Od.21.437.281.
He knows them all; in all such truth appears, ... Od.22.537.315.
Such future scenes th' all-righteous pow'rs display, ... Od.23.303.337.
By their dread *Seer, and such my future day. ... Od.23.304.337.
And such a scream fill'd all the dismal coasts. ... Od.24.14.347.
Such were the games by azure *Thetis* given, ... Od.24.115.353.
And such thy honours, oh belov'd of heaven! ... Od.24.116.353.
Inform thy guest; for such I was of yore ... Od.24.140.354.
Not such, oh *Tyndarus!* thy daughter's deed, ... Od.24.226.358.
"(If such thou art) to manifest thee mine." ... Od.24.383.367.
Such were I now, not absent from your deed ... Od.24.439.370.

SUCK

Wolves gave thee suck, and savage Tygers fed.	1.PAu.90.86.
Or suck the Mists in grosser Air below,	2.RL2.83.165.
Suck my last breath, and catch my flying soul!	2.ElAb.324.346.
Suck my last breath, and catch the flying soul!	2.ElAb.324A.346.
Suck the thread in, then yield it out again:	5.DunA3.50.155.
Suck the thread in, then yield it out again:	5.DunB3.58.323.
From me they suck a little Grace.	6.135.54.368.
Thy bloated Corse, and suck thy goary Wound:	II.21.136.427.

SUCK'D

And suck'd new Poisons with his triple Tongue)	1.TrSt.667.438.
Smit with his mien, the Mud-nymphs suck'd him in:	5.DunA2.308.139.
And suck'd all o'er, like an industrious Bug.	5.DunB1.130.279.
Smit with his mien, the Mud-nymphs suck'd him in:	5.DunB2.332.313.
Then suck'd the Blood, and Sov'reign Balm infus'd,	II.4.250.232.

SUCKLE

And suckle Armies, and dry-nurse the land:	5.DunB1.316.293.

SUCKLED

Suckled, and chear'd, with air, and sun, and show'r,	5.DunB4.406.381.

SUCKLES

"Suckles each herb, and spreads out ev'ry flow'r;	3.EOM1.134.32.
"Suckles each herb, and swells out ev'ry flow'r;	3.EOM1.134A.32.

SUCKLYN

"Love follows flying Game (as Sucklyn sings)	4.HAdv.139.87.

SUCKS

The trembling Limbs, and sucks the smoking Blood;	1.TrES.298.460.
The trembling Limbs, and sucks the smoking Blood;	II.16.603.267.
He sucks the marrow, and the blood he drains,	Od.9.348.320.

SUDDEN

A soft Retreat from sudden vernal Show'rs;	1.PSp.98.70.
Let Spring attend, and sudden Flow'rs arise;	1.PAu.36.82.
See Lillies spring, and sudden Verdure rise;	1.Mes.68.119.
Sudden they seize th'amaz'd, defenceless Prize,	1.W-F.109.161.
Sudden, before some unsuspecting Town,	1.W-F.108A.161.
A sudden Passion in her Breast did move,	1.TrVP.122A.382.
The trembling tree with sudden horror shook.	1.TrFD.30.387.
To rise, and shade her with a sudden green.	1.TrFD.48.388.
Their milky moisture, on a sudden dry'd.	1.TrFD.52.388.
(With sudden Grief her lab'ring Bosom burn'd)	1.TrSt.349.424.
His sudden Fall the entangled Harness broke;	1.TrES.273.459.
Pensive and slow, with sudden Grief opprest,	1.TrUl.68.468.
Sudden, invited by auspicious Gales,	1.TrUl.156.471.
What Pangs, what sudden Shoots distend my Side?	2.ChJM.721.49.
Look'd out, and stood restor'd to sudden Sight.	2.ChJM.749.51.
Your swimming Eyes are drunk with sudden Light,	2.ChJM.803.54.
If I but smil'd, a sudden Youth they found,	2.ChWB.66.59.
Sudden these Honours shall be snatch'd away,	2.RL3.103.175.
Sudden he view'd, in spite of all her Art,	2.RL3.143.178.
Sudden, with starting Tears each Eye o'erflows,	2.RL5.85.207.
A sudden Star, it shot thro' liquid Air,	2.RL5.127.210.
Sudden I heard a wild promiscuous Sound,	2.TemF.22.255.
Strikes, and behold a sudden Thebes aspire!	2.TemF.86.259.
Strikes, and beholds a sudden Thebes aspire;	2.TemF.86A.259.
A sudden Cloud strait snatch'd them from my Sight,	2.TemF.354.280.
Alas how chang'd! what sudden horrors rise!	2.ElAb.99.327.
Sudden you mount! you becken from the skies;	2.ElAb.245.339.
On all the line a sudden vengeance waits,	2.Elegy.37.365.
Sudden, she storms! she raves! You tip the wink,	3.Ep2.33.52.
Sudden she flies, and whelms it o'er the pyre;	5.DunA1.215.89.
Sudden, a burst of thunder shook the flood.	5.DunA2.301.139.
All sudden, Gorgons hiss, and Dragons glare,	5.DunA3.231.177.
Sudden she flies, and whelms it o'er the pyre;	5.DunB1.259.289.
All sudden, Gorgons hiss, and Dragons glare,	5.DunB3.235.331.
Spent in a sudden storm of lust,	6.51ii.18.153.
Live well and fear no sudden fate;	6.69ii.5.199.
Die by a sudden Extacy of Joy!	6.86.18A.245.
Die by some sudden Extasy of Joy.	6.86.18B.245.
The mushrooms shew his wit was sudden!	6.150.11.398.
Breathing Revenge, a sudden Night he spread,	1.65.89.
He sees, and sudden to the Goddess cries,	II.1.267.99.
He saw, and sudden to the Goddess cries,	II.1.267A.99.
Their sudden Friendship by her Arts may cease,	II.4.93.225.
Then sudden wav'd his flaming Faulchion round,	II.4.616.250.
A sudden Cloud comes swimming o'er his Eyes.	II.5.382.285.
Sudden the Fluids fix, the Parts combin'd;	II.5.1114.321.
No more—be sudden, and begin the Fight.	II.7.282.378.
Before the Coursers with a sudden Spring	II.8.127.404.
Headlong he falls; his sudden Fall alarms	II.8.381.416.
Else may the sudden Foe our Works invade,	II.10.112.7.
Ulysses, sudden as the Voice was sent,	II.10.158.9.
What new Distress, what sudden Cause of Fright	II.10.160.9.
A sudden Palsy seiz'd his turning Head;	II.10.445.23.
Whose Squire Oïleus, with a sudden spring,	II.11.129.41.
A sudden Storm the purple Ocean sweeps,	II.11.385.51.
He spoke, while Socus seiz'd with sudden Fright,	II.11.558.58.
Then sudden wav'd his unresisted Sword;	II.12.220.89.
To Vengeance rising with a sudden Spring,	II.13.487.130.
Then sudden mix'd among the warring Crew,	II.13.803.143.
And sudden Hyacinths the Turf bestrow,	II.14.399.183.
Beside him sudden, unperceiv'd he stood,	II.14.409.183.
A sudden Road! a long and ample way.	II.15.409.213.
And stood by Meges' side, a sudden Aid,	II.15.637.221.
The Troops of Troy recede with sudden Fear,	II.15.690.222.
A sudden Ray shot beaming o'er the Plain,	II.15.810.227.
Sudden, the Thund'rer, with a flashing Ray,	II.16.356.257.
His sudden Fall th' entangled Harness broke;	II.16.578.267.
Pierc'd thro' the Bosom with a sudden Wound,	II.16.727.272.
Then rushing sudden on his prostrate Prize,	II.16.907.279.
Thro' all his Veins a sudden Vigour flew,	II.17.250.297.

SUDDEN (CONTINUED)

Sudden at Hector's Side Apollo stood,	II.17.654.313.
Thus when a River swell'd with sudden Rains	II.17.839.321.
A sudden Horror shot thro' all the Chief,	II.18.25.324.
A sudden Council call'd: Each Chief appear'd	II.18.289.335.
Rush sudden; Hills of Slaughter heap the Ground,	II.18.612.352.
He spoke, and sudden as the Word of Jove	II.19.370.387.
Sudden, returning with the Stream of Light,	II.20.391.411.
Sudden, Achilles his broad Sword display'd,	II.21.129.426.
And sudden Joy confus'd, and mix'd Affright:	II.21.722.451.
The sudden Clouds of circling Dust arise.	II.22.504.477.
And all her Members shake with sudden Fear;	II.22.575.480.
A sudden Darkness shades her swimming Eyes:	II.22.598.480.
Then sudden dropt, and left her Life in Air.	II.23.1041.530.
A sudden Trembling shook his aged Frame;	II.24.444.554.
Sudden, (a venerable Sight!) appears,	II.24.586.561.
Approaching sudden to our open'd Tent,	II.24.820.571.
Sudden the Thund'rer blackens all the skies,	Od.3.367.104.
Sudden, our bands a spotted Pard restrain:	Od.4.616.148.
A sudden horror seiz'd on either mind:	Od.4.863.159.
Sudden she sunk beneath the weighty woes;	Od.4.934.162.
Sudden, full twenty on the plain are strow'd,	Od.5.313.186.
Sudden he shines, and manifest to sight.	Od.7.191.245.
She spoke, and sudden with tumultuous sounds	Od.8.15.262.
Sudden th' irremeable way he trod,	Od.8.259.276.
A sudden blaze, and lighted all the cave:	Od.9.296.318.
To seize the time, and with a sudden wound	Od.9.356.321.
Sudden I stir the embers, and inspire	Od.9.445.324.
A sudden horror struck their aking sight.	Od.10.130.347.
I lanc'd my spear, and with a sudden wound	Od.10.187.349.
Then sudden whirling like a waving flame	Od.10.383.363.
Sudden shall skim along the dusky glades	Od.10.632.374.
The sudden tumult stirr'd him where he lay,	Od.10.665.375.
Or swift expir'd it, in a sudden blaze?	Od.11.209.392.
And sudden lifts it quivering to the skies:	Od.12.303.447.
While yet I spoke, a sudden sorrow ran	Od.12.330.447.
A sudden joy in every bosom rose;	Od.12.351.448.
Sudden I drop'd amidst the flashing main;	Od.12.524.458.
The trembling crowds shall see the sudden shade	Od.13.182.14.
The God arrests her with a sudden stroke,	Od.13.188.15.
Pensive and slow, with sudden grief opprest	Od.13.235.17.
Sudden, invited by auspicious gales,	Od.13.323.23.
A sudden frost was sprinkled on his head;	Od.13.499.29.
Sudden, the master runs; aloud he calls;	Od.14.37.37.
Sudden I jogg'd Ulysses, who was laid	Od.14.545.63.
And turning sudden, shun the death design'd.	Od.15.321.85.
A sudden trust from sudden liking grew;	Od.15.464.93.
A sudden trust from sudden liking grew;	Od.15.464.93.
Sudden before the rival pow'rs she stands:	Od.16.431.128.
Revolving deep the Suitors' sudden fate.	Od.17.34.134.
Amidst yon' revellers a sudden guest	Od.17.325.147.
Sudden she lightens in their dazled eyes,	Od.18.251.179.
And sudden flames in ev'ry bosom rise;	Od.18.252.179.
'Tis hard, he cries, to bring to sudden sight	Od.19.257.207.
Sudden the tyrant of the skies return'd:	Od.19.638.227.
Mis-judging of the cause, a sudden fear	Od.20.113.238.
And sudden sighs precede approaching woe.	Od.20.420.253.
All arm, and sudden round the hall appears	Od.22.160.295.
A sudden youth, and give her wings to fly.	Od.23.4.318.
Yet Fate withstands! a sudden tempest roars	Od.23.341.341.
Cluster'd they hang, till at some sudden shock,	Od.24.11.347.
His sudden rapture) in thy Consort blest!	Od.24.219.358.
Sudden his eyes releas'd their wat'ry store;	Od.24.273.363.
A sudden horror all th' assembly shook,	Od.24.516.372.

SUDDENLY

Then suddenly was heard along the main	Od.12.318.447.

SUE

There Kings shall sue, and suppliant States be seen	1.W-F.383.188.
To Jupiter did humbly sue,	6.30.35.87.
And sue for Vengeance to the Thund'ring God.	II.1.513.112.
And Kings that sue to mix their Blood with mine.	II.9.519.458.
Permit not these to sue, and sue in vain;	II.9.648.466.
Permit not these to sue, and sue in vain!	II.9.648.466.
Him it behov'd to ev'ry Chief to sue,	II.10.132.8.
Absent, by me they speak, by me they sue;	II.15.802.227.
With Gifts to sue; and offer to his Hands	II.24.153.541.
Thy still-surviving Sons may sue for thee,	II.24.855.572.
By adverse destiny constrain'd to sue	Od.4.217.130.

SUERTYSHIP

That only suertyship has brought them there:	4.JD2A.79.138.

SUES

Bless me! a Packet.—"'Tis a stranger sues,	4.Arbu.55.100.
Althæa sues; His Friends before him fall;	II.9.697.468.
And sues to Him that ever lives above:	II.10.20.3.
For proffer'd Peace! And sues his Seed for Grace?	II.11.183.43.
In vain a single Trojan sues for Grace;	II.21.113.426.
For counsel and redress, he sues to you.	Od.4.218.130.
Yet sues importunate to loose the God:	Od.8.382.284.
When Neptune sues, my part is to obey.	Od.8.392.285.

SUFF'RANCE

His is the suff'rance, but the shame is thine.	Od.18.266.179.

SUFF'RER

When the poor Suff'rer humbly mourn'd his Case,	4.HAdv.94.83.

SUFF'RERS

And certain Laws, by Suff'rers thought unjust,	4.2HE2.60.169.

SUFF'RING

Much-suff'ring Heroes next their Honours claim,	2.TemF.168.268.
Much-suff'ring Heroes, of less noisy Fame,	2.TemF.169A.268.

SUFF'RING (CONTINUED)
Why doing, suff'ring, check'd, impell'd; and why .... 3.EOM1.67.21.
The suff'ring eye inverted Nature sees, ... 3.Ep4.119.149.
Here all his suff'ring brotherhood retire, ... 5.DunA1.123.78.
Here all his suff'ring brotherhood retire, ... 5.DunB1.143.280.
Still in Constraint your suff'ring Sex remains, ... 6.19.41.63.
If no Regard thy suff'ring Country claim, ... Il.9.400.452.
And while the Fate of suff'ring *Greece* he mourn'd, ... Il.9.560.461.
Methinks my suff'ring Country's Voice I hear, ... Il.22.146.459.
For valour much, for hardy suff'ring more. .... Od.3.103.91.
Howe'er the noble, suff'ring mind, may grieve .... Od.7.297.250.
The suff'ring chief at this began to melt; .... Od.15.408.89.
Oh suff'ring consort of the suff'ring man! .... Od.17.173.140.
Oh suff'ring consort of the suff'ring man! .... Od.17.173.140.
Poor suff'ring heart! he cry'd, support the pain .... Od.20.23.232.
The suff'ring Heroe felt his patient breast .... Od.24.582.376.

SUFF'RINGS
And can these suff'rings fail my heart to move? .... 6.25.11.77.
Compos'd in suff'rings, and in joy sedate, ... 6.109.3.314.
Where many Seas, and many Suff'rings past, ... Il.2.807.163.
No Crime of thine our present Suff'rings draws, ... Il.3.215.202.
Be it thro' toils and suff'rings, long and late; .... Od.9.624.332.
And when at home from foreign suff'rings freed, ... Od.9.627.332.
For real suff'rings since I grieve sincere, ... Od.14.397.55.

SUFFER
Or who could suffer Being here below? .... 3.EOM1.80.23.
To serve, not suffer, strengthen, not invade, ... 3.EOM3.298.123.
B. Who suffer thus, mere Charity should own, ... 3.Ep3.113A.101.
Who suffer thus, mere Charity should own, ... 3.Ep3.113.101.
Much do I suffer, much, to keep in peace .... 4.2HE2.147.175.
We never suffer it to stand too wide. .... 5.DunB4.154.356.
And suffer scorn, and bend the supple knee; .... 6.22.9.71.
And suffer, rather than my People fall. .... Il.1.148.94.
Oh suffer not the Foe to bear away .... Il.5.842.305.
For much they suffer, for thy sake, in War. .... Il.6.675.360.
Condemn'd to suffer the full Force of Fate, ... Il.8.427.417.
So much had suffer'd, and must suffer more. .... Il.10.34.4.
And suffer not his Dart to fall in vain. .... Il.20.131.399.
Ah suffer that my Bones may rest with thine! .... Il.23.104.491.
Yet suffer not thy Soul to sink with Dread; .... Il.24.455.555.
But thou alas! may'st live, to suffer more! .... Il.24.695.566.
The lot of man; to suffer, and to die. .... Od.3.117.91.
And the sad son's, to suffer and to mourn! .... Od.3.257.98.
For him, to suffer, and for me, to mourn! .... Od.4.140.127.
Still I can suffer; Their high will be done! .... Od.5.288.185.
Then must he suffer what the Fates ordain; .... Od.7.262.248.
With heav'n's high will prepar'd to suffer more. .... Od.7.292.250.
Pleas'd will I suffer all the Gods ordain, ... Od.7.303.250.
Must he too suffer? he, oh Goddess! bear .... Od.13.480.29.
For should'st thou suffer, pow'rless to relieve .... Od.16.87.106.
But for meer want, how hard to suffer wrong? .... Od.17.562.159.
The gen'ral sex shall suffer in her shame, ... Od.24.230.358.
'Twas his to suffer, and 'tis mine to mourn! .... Od.24.339.365.

SUFFER'D
For this, I suffer'd *Phœbus'* Steeds to stray, ... 1.TrSt.308.423.
His Wife, not suffer'd from his Side to stray, ... 2.ChJM.487.39.
First let him speak, who first has suffer'd Shame. .... Il.9.44.434.
So much had suffer'd, and must suffer more. .... Il.10.34.4.
Have greatly suffer'd, and have greatly done. .... Il.23.696.517.
For he who much has suffer'd, much will know; .... Od.15.436.90.
Patient he suffer'd with a constant mind. .... Od.24.190.356.

SUFFERING
The suffering virtue of the wise and brave? .... Od.1.79.35.

SUFFERS
Nor suffers *Horace* more in wrong *Translations* .... 1.EOC.663.314.
The Man who suffers, loudly may complain; .... Il.1.179.96.
Yet suffers least, and sways the wav'ring Fight; .... Il.17.419.303.
He suffers ev'ry Lance to fall in vain. .... Il.17.714.315.
And the good suffers, while the bad prevails: .... Od.6.230.221.
He suffers who gives surety for th' unjust: .... Od.8.386.284.
These he decrees, and he but suffers those: .... Od.14.495.60.

SUFFIC'D
Suffic'd it not, that thy long Labours past .... 1.TrUl.169.471.
Suffic'd, soft-whispering thus to *Nestor's* son, ... Od.4.81.123.
To cool one cup suffic'd: the goblet crown'd .... Od.9.244.317.
Suffic'd it not, that thy long labours past .... Od.13.336.23.
With wine suffic'd me, and with dainties fed: .... Od.16.459.129.
A bowl of gen'rous wine suffic'd the guest; .... Od.20.171.241.
Suffic'd it not within the palace plac'd .... Od.21.311.274.

SUFFICE
Remove your hands, the bark shall soon suffice .... 1.TrFD.98.390.
For Crimes like these, not all those Realms suffice, ... 1.TrSt.216.419.
Not all those Realms cou'd for such Crimes suffice, ... 1.TrSt.216A.419.
Suffice that Reason keep to Nature's road, ... 3.EOM2.115.69.
Soft be his Slumbers! But may this suffice .... 6.17iv.22.60.
Let this suffice; th' immutable Decree .... Il.1.730.122.
Suffice, to Night, these Orders to obey; .... Il.8.651.426.
Yet wherefore doubtful? Let this Truth suffice; .... Il.11.517.57.
For that (said *Jove)* suffice another Day; .... Il.14.355.180.
Thy Arms no less suffice the Lance to wield, ... Il.15.556.218.
Some less important Season may suffice, ... Il.19.198.381.
Suffice, from yonder Mount to view the Scene; .... Il.20.164.400.
Suffice thy Father's Merits, and thy own: .... Il.23.694.517.
Suffice, we know and we partake thy Cares: .... Il.24.139.540.
Scarce all my herds their luxury suffice; .... Od.2.63.63.
Rise in my aid! suffice the tears that flow .... Od.2.77.64.
Suffice it to have spend with swift decay .... Od.2.351.78.
The wants of nature with repast suffice, ... Od.4.581.147.
The spacious vase with ample streams suffice, ... Od.8.471.288.

SUFFICE (CONTINUED)
Let this short memory of grief suffice. .... Od.10.541.369.
Suffice it in this exigence alone .... Od.16.340.122.
My friend adieu! let this short stay suffice; .... Od.17.7.132.
For me, suffice the approbation won .... Od.17.474.156.
Suffice it thee thy Monarch to conceal. .... Od.19.586.224.

SUFFICES
Suffices Fulness to the swelling Grain; .... 1.TrUl.125.470.
Suffices fulness to the swelling grain: .... Od.13.292.19.
For here one vest suffices ev'ry swain; .... Od.14.581.65.

SUFFICIENT
Doubt not, sufficient will be left at Night. .... 2.ChWB.137.63.
Teach but that one, sufficient for a King; .... 5.DunB4.184.360.
Sufficient Sap, at once to bear and rot. .... 6.49i.12.137.
The Crime's sufficient that they share my Love. .... Il.4.80.224.
Sufficient they (*Telemachus* rejoin'd) .... Od.16.284.118.
Sufficient strength to draw the mighty bow? .... Od.21.338.276.
For us sufficient is another care: .... Od.22.185.296.

SUFFOLK
Cheese, such as men in Suffolk make, ... 4.HS6.167.261.

SUFFRAGE
That Prize the *Greeks* by common Suffrage gave: .... Il.1.363.105.
Robb'd of the Prize the *Grecian* Suffrage gave, ... Il.18.517.346.
And to their suffrage gain the filial voice: .... Od.19.181.200.
You join your suffrage to the public vote; .... Od.19.448.216.

SUFFUSE
When purple light shall next suffuse the skies, ... Od.4.550.146.

SUGGEST
Is this a Gen'ral's Voice, that would suggest .... Il.9.57.434.
If ought of use thy waking Thoughts suggest, ... Il.10.106.7.
Nor ought a Mother's Caution can suggest; .... Il.16.70.238.
Far be the Omen which my Thoughts suggest! .... Il.22.584.480.
To me, no Seer, th' inspiring Gods suggest; .... Od.1.260.45.
Then would that busy head no broils suggest, ... Od.2.215.72.
What I suggest thy wisdom will perform; .... Od.5.434.193.
Suggest, that *Jove* the peaceful thought inspir'd, ... Od.19.13.193.

SUGGESTING
Search, for some thoughts, thy own suggesting mind; .... Od.3.34.87.

SUGGESTS
Yet should the Fears that wary Mind suggests .... Il.12.291.92.
But thou, the Counsel Heav'n suggests, attend! .... Il.21.338.435.

SUIDAS
I poach in Suidas for unlicens'd Greek. .... 5.DunB4.228.365.

SUIT
At *Hester's* Suit, the Persecuting Sword .... 2.ChJM.75.18.
Had no *new Verses,* or *new Suit* to show; .... 4.JD4.13.27.
The suit, if by the fashion one might guess, ... 4.JD4.40.29.
I think Sir Godfry should decide the Suit; .... 4.2HE2.24.167.
Or when from Court a birth-day suit bestow'd .... 4.2HE1.332.223.
Others, a sword-knot and lac'd suit inflame. .... 5.DunA2.48.103.
Th' embroider'd Suit, at least, he deem'd his prey; .... 5.DunA2.109.110.
That suit, an unpaid Taylor snatch'd away! .... 5.DunA2.110.110.
Known by the band and suit which Settle wore, ... 5.DunA3.29.153.
(His only suit) for twice three years before: .... 5.DunA3.30.154.
Others a sword-knot and lac'd suit inflame. .... 5.DunB2.52.298.
Th'embroider'd suit at least he deem'd his prey; .... 5.DunB2.117.301.
That suit an unpay'd taylor snatch'd away. .... 5.DunB2.118.301.
Known by the band and suit which Settle wore .... 5.DunB3.37.322.
(His only suit) for twice three years before: .... 5.DunB3.38.322.
In a translated Suit, then tries the Town, ... 6.49i.21.138.
Thus Worms suit all Conditions; .... 6.53.22.162.
Some Worms suit all Conditions; .... 6.53.22A.162.
That *Bedlam* and clean Straw will suit you best: .... 6.96iv.36.277.
That *Bedlam* and clean Straw would suit you best: .... 6.96iv.36A.277.
This suit dear TIBBALD kindly hatch; .... 6.116ii.6.326.
Yet (what I can) to move thy Suit I'll go, ... Il.1.550.114.
This seals thy Suit, and this fulfills thy Vows— .... Il.1.682.119.
At *Juno's* Suit the Heav'nly Factions end. .... Il.2.16.128.
At *Juno's* Suit the Heav'nly Factions end. .... Il.2.38.129.
At *Juno's* Suit the Heav'nly Factions end. .... Il.2.88.130.
He knew soft Combates suit the tender Dame, ... Il.5.413.286.
The Cloud-compelling God her Suit approv'd, ... Il.8.47.398.
At *Thetis'* Suit the partial Thund'rer nods. .... Il.8.450.418.
When Man rejects the humble Suit they make, ... Il.9.633.465.
No mortal Shoulders suit the glorious Load, ... Il.10.510.26.
Nor suit, with them, the Games of this sad Day: .... Il.23.348.503.
But never from this nobler suit we cease; .... Od.2.235.73.
The royal dame his lawless suit deny'd. .... Od.3.331.102.
And presents, such as suit the state of Kings. .... Od.3.609.117.
To move thy suit, *Telemachus,* delay, ... Od.4.295.133.
Thus to the Goddess mild my suit I end. .... Od.4.537.146.
Go then secure, thy humble suit prefer, ... Od.7.97.238.
His pleaded reason, and the suit he mov'd. .... Od.7.308.251.
The King with mighty gifts my suit approv'd. .... Od.10.18.340.
His baneful suit pollutes these bless'd abodes, ... Od.10.85.343.
My knees, and weeping thus his suit address'd. .... Od.10.314.359.
Then I. Thy suit is vain, nor can I say .... Od.11.569.411.
Ill suit such forms of grace and dignity. .... Od.17.538.158.
"Rebate your loves, each rival suit suspend, ... Od.19.164.200.
Our common suit nor granted, nor deny'd; .... Od.24.149.355.
Yet a short space, your rival suit suspend, ... Od.24.156.355.

SUITABLE
Appears more *decent* as more *suitable;* .... 1.EOC.319.274.

SUITING
A Soul well-suiting that tempestuous Kind, ...Il.16.52.237.
Ah why th' ill-suiting pastime must I try? ....Od.8.168.271.

SUITOR
To ev'ry Suitor lie in ev'ry thing, ...4.JD2A.80.138.
The bold intrusion of the Suitor-train; ....Od.1.115.37.
Far from the Suitor-train, a brutal crowd, ...Od.1.175.41.
To their own districts drive the Suitor-crowd: ....Od.1.353.49.
By fraud or force the Suitor-train destroy, ...Od.1.385.51.
At length compos'd, he join'd the suitor-throng, ...Od.1.419.52.
Mean-while, in *Ithaca,* the Suitor-powrs ....Od.4.845.158.
The suitor-train thy early'st care demand, ...Od.13.429.27.
The fourth drove victims to the suitor-train: ....Od.14.29.36.
For thee their snares the Suitor Lords shall lay ....Od.15.33.71.
Then measur'd back the way—The suitor band ....Od.16.358.123.
Abash'd, the suitor train his voice attends; ....Od.16.408.126.
Say wilt thou not (ere yet the Suitor-crew ....Od.17.120.137.
Portions like mine if ev'ry Suitor gave, ...Od.17.490.156.
The haughty Suitor with resentment burns, ...Od.17.543.159.
(The Suitor cry'd) or force shall drag thee hence, ...Od.17.569.160.
And parting, to the Suitor pow'rs descends: ....Od.17.669.164.
'Twas riot all amid the Suitor-throng, ...Od.17.685.165.
Thus with loud laughter to the Suitor-train. ....Od.18.43.169.
(Attendant on her chief): the Suitor-crowd ....Od.18.80.170.
The Suitor-train, and raise a thirst to give; ....Od.18.326.183.
The cause demanded by the Suitor-train, ...Od.19.7.193.
The woof unwrought the Suitor-train surprize. ....Od.19.177.200.
And prostrate to my sword the Suitor-train; ....Od.19.572.224.
Shall prostrate to thy sword the Suitor-crowd; ....Od.19.580.224.
(The remnants of the spoil the suitor-crowd ....Od.20.3.230.
Instant, O *Jove!* confound the Suitor train, ...Od.20.147.240.
Now say sincere, my guest! the Suitor train ....Od.20.208.243.
And to the shades devote the Suitor-train. ....Od.20.293.247.
The Suitor now had vanish'd in a ghost: ....Od.20.377.251.
And artful, thus the Suitor-train addrest. ....Od.21.138.265.
He, only he of all the Suitor-throng, ...Od.21.155.266.
And thus terrific, to the Suitor crew. ....Od.22.6.286.
'Till pale as yonder wretch each Suitor lies. ....Od.22.78.290.
And the wild riots of the Suitor-train. ....Od.23.328.340.
The vengeance is compleat; the Suitor-train, ...Od.24.380.367.

SUITOR-CREW
Say wilt thou not (ere yet the Suitor-crew ....Od.17.120.137.

SUITOR-CROWD
To their own districts drive the Suitor-crowd: ....Od.1.353.49.
(Attendant on her chief): the Suitor-crowd ....Od.18.80.170.
Shall prostrate to thy sword the Suitor-crowd; ....Od.19.580.224.
(The remnants of the spoil the suitor-crowd ....Od.20.3.230.

SUITOR-POWRS
Mean-while, in *Ithaca,* the Suitor-powrs ....Od.4.845.158.

SUITOR-THRONG
At length compos'd, he join'd the suitor-throng, ...Od.1.419.52.
'Twas riot all amid the Suitor-throng, ...Od.17.685.165.
He, only he of all the Suitor-throng, ...Od.21.155.266.

SUITOR-TRAIN
The bold intrusion of the Suitor-train; ....Od.1.115.37.
Far from the Suitor-train, a brutal crowd, ...Od.1.175.41.
By fraud or force the Suitor-train destroy, ...Od.1.385.51.
The suitor-train thy early'st care demand, ...Od.13.429.27.
The fourth drove victims to the suitor-train: ....Od.14.29.36.
Thus with loud laughter to the Suitor-train. ....Od.18.43.169.
The Suitor-train, and raise a thirst to give; ....Od.18.326.183.
The cause demanded by the Suitor-train, ...Od.19.7.193.
The woof unwrought the Suitor-train surprize. ....Od.19.177.200.
And prostrate to my sword the Suitor-train; ....Od.19.572.224.
And to the shades devote the Suitor-train. ....Od.20.293.247.
And artful, thus the Suitor-train addrest. ....Od.21.138.265.
And the wild riots of the Suitor-train. ....Od.23.328.340.
The vengeance is compleat; the Suitor-train, ...Od.24.380.367.

SUITOR'S
Or some brave Suitor's sword, might pierce the heart ....Od.17.301.146.

SUITORS
Till the proud Suitors, for their Crimes, afford ....1.TrUl.62.468.
(Sad spoils of luxury) the Suitors fate. ....Od.1.141.39.
In rush'd the Suitors with voracious haste: ....Od.1.190.42.
And the proud Suitors shall its force confess: ....Od.3.251.97.
The Suitors quit, and all to council came: ....Od.4.885.159.
What will the Suitors? must my servant train ....Od.4.906.160.
And on the suitors let thy wrath descend. ....Od.4.1012.164.
The Suitors heard, and deem'd the mirthful voice ....Od.4.1015.165.
Mean-time the Suitors plow the wat'ry plain, ...Od.4.1099.169.
Till the proud suitors for their crimes afford ....Od.13.229.17.
And the blind suitors their destruction scorn. ....Od.13.464.28.
Doom'd to supply the Suitors wastful feast, ...Od.14.21.35.
All to the suitors wastful board preferr'd. ....Od.14.130.42.
Or mingling with the suitors haughty train, ...Od.15.334.85.
Here dwell in safety from the suitors wrongs, ...Od.16.85.106.
Say, if the Suitors measure back the main, ...Od.16.484.130.
Escap'd my care: where lawless Suitors sway, ...Od.16.488.130.
Th' eluded Suitors stem the wat'ry way. ....Od.16.495.131.
Him, gath'ring round, the haughty Suitors greet ....Od.17.76.136.
Soon as the Suitors from the banquet rose, ...Od.17.432.153.
With flatt'ring hopes the Suitors to betray, ...Od.18.189.175.
That yon' proud Suitors, who licentious tread ....Od.18.279.180.
Portend the Suitors fated to my sword. ....Od.19.645.227.
And by his sword the Suitors sure to bleed. ....Od.19.653.227.
Their strength and skill the Suitors shall assay: ....Od.19.675.229.
In self-debate the Suitors doom resolv'd. ....Od.20.36.234.
Dispatch! for soon the Suitors will assay ....Od.20.194.242.

SUITORS (CONTINUED)
Magnificent, and blithe, the Suitors come. ....Od.20.199.243.
Mean-time the Suitors urge the Prince's fate, ...Od.20.300.247.
Your violence and scorn, ye Suitors cease, ...Od.20.332.249.
The Suitors souls, insensate of their doom! ....Od.20.414.252.
I share the doom ye Suitors cannot shun. ....Od.20.444.254.
O'er the protracted feast the Suitors sit, ...Od.20.447.254.
To the proud Suitors bears in pensive state ....Od.21.61.262.
Come then ye Suitors! and dispute a prize ....Od.21.109.264.
To the proud Suitors, or your ancient Lord? ....Od.21.204.269.
The haughty Suitors will deny the bow; ....Od.21.249.272.
Rage flash'd in lightning from the Suitors eyes, ...Od.21.307.274.
If heav'n and *Phœbus* lend the Suitors aid. ....Od.21.396.279.
Th' oppressive Suitors from my walls expell! ....Od.21.404.279.
The Suitors with a scornful smile survey ....Od.21.407.279.
Thus dreadful he. Confus'd the Suitors stood, ...Od.22.53.289.
To drive thy victims to the Suitors feast. ....Od.22.216.297.
So with the Suitors let 'em mix in dust, ...Od.22.480.312.
Ulysses comes! The Suitors are no more! ....Od.23.8.319.
That stranger, patient of the Suitors wrongs, ...Od.23.29.320.
And the dead Suitors almost swam in blood; ....Od.23.48.321.
Ah no! some God the Suitors deaths decreed, ...Od.23.63.321.
But learn we instant how the Suitors trod ....Od.23.85.322.
The Suitors death unknown, 'till we remove ....Od.23.137.327.
The Suitors stopp'd, and gaz'd the Heroe o'er. ....Od.24.30.348.
Then, to her Suitors bade his Queen propose ....Od.24.195.357.
'Tis so—the Suitors for their wrongs have paid— ....Od.24.411.369.
When the last sun beheld the Suitors bleed, ...Od.24.440.370.
Thro' all the city, of the Suitors dead. ....Od.24.475.371.
Has slain the Suitors, heav'n shall bless the land. ....Od.24.553.374.

SUITORS'
Revolving deep the Suitors' sudden fate. ....Od.17.34.134.
Then let him circle round the Suitors' board, ...Od.17.420.152.
To rouze *Ulysses,* points the Suitors' tongues: ....Od.18.396.187.
Avow'd, and falsify the Suitors' claim. ....Od.19.686.229.
Spontaneous to the Suitors' feast preferr'd: ....Od.20.220.244.

SUITS
"What suits with *Sapho, Phœbus,* suits with thee; ....1.TrSP.216.403.
"What suits with *Sapho, Phœbus,* suits with thee; ....1.TrSP.216.403.
Know, all enjoy that pow'r which suits them best; ....3.EOM3.80.100.
Suits Tyrants, Plunderers, but suits not me. ....4.JD4.195.43.
Suits Tyrants, Plunderers, but suits not me. ....4.JD4.195.43.
"In me 'tis noble, suits my birth and state, ...4.HS2.113.63.
No Courts he saw, no Suits would ever try, ...4.Arbu.396.126.
Ill suits a Chief who mighty Nations guides, ...Il.2.77A.130.
Ill suits it now the Joys of Love to know, ...Il.3.511.216.
A cruel Heart ill suits a manly Mind: ....Il.9.619.464.
But ill this Insult suits a prudent Mind. ....Il.17.192.294.
Suits not my Greatness, or superior Age. ....Il.21.513.443.
Ill suits the Wisdom of celestial Mind: ....Il.21.536.444.
Ill suits gay youth the stern, heroic part. ....Od.2.342.77.
Ill suits it with your shews of duteous zeal, ...Od.4.966.163.
As suits the purpose of th' eternal will. ....Od.8.624.296.
And such as suits the dictate of my mind. ....Od.17.217.142.
Shame suits but ill. *Eumæus* thus rejoin'd: ....Od.17.659.164.
Ill suits it, female virtue to be seen ....Od.18.217.177.
To whom the King: Ill suits your sex to stay ....Od.18.359.185.
No vulgar task! Ill suits this courtly crew ....Od.21.94.263.
Ill suits this garb the shoulders of a King. ....Od.22.526.314.

SULLEN
And sullen *Mole,* that hides his diving Flood; ....1.W-F.347.184.
What sullen Fury clowds his scornful Brow! ....1.TrSt.255.421.
Impervious Clouds conceal'd thy sullen Rays; ....1.TrSt.764.442.
In sullen Majesty, and stern Disdain: ....1.TrES.16.450.
No cheerful Breeze this sullen Region knows, ...2.RL4.19.184.
Dull sullen pris'ners in the body's cage: ....2.Elegy.18.364.
Sullen Moans, ...6.11.60.32.
Sullen you turn from both, and call for *Oats.* ....6.96iv.54.277.
Sullen you turn'd from both, and call'd for *Oats.* ....6.96iv.54A.277.
The Chiefs in sullen Majesty retir'd. ....Il.1.401.107.
Her sullen Silence, and with Fury spoke. ....Il.4.34.222.
In sullen Fury slowly quits the Prize. ....Il.4.623.250.
There sullen sate beneath the Sire of Gods, ...Il.5.1065.317.
Ungrateful Prospect to the sullen Pow'r! ....Il.8.253.409.
In sullen Majesty, and stern Disdain: ....Il.12.360.94.
The Goddess said, and sullen took her Place; ....Il.15.108.200.
Sullen he sate, and curb'd the rising Groan. ....Il.15.161.202.
Smokes, nor as yet the sullen Flames arise; ....Il.23.237.499.
Sullen and sow'r with discontented mien ....Od.11.329.398.
A gloomy shade, the sullen *Ajax* stood; ....Od.11.666.417.
In silence turns, and sullen stalks away. ....Od.11.692.418.
There sullen Lions sternly seem to roar, ...Od.11.753.423.
Let wit cast off the sullen yoke of sense. ....Od.14.525.62.

SULLIED
Let some refresh the vase's sullied mold; ....Od.20.190.242.

SULLY'D
As ever sully'd the fair face of Light, ...2.RL4.14.183.

SULPH'ROUS
Drop endlong; scarr'd, and black with sulph'rous hue, ...Od.14.343.51.

SULPHUR
Not sulphur-tipt, emblaze an Ale-house fire; ....5.DunB1.235.287.
The Ground before him flam'd with Sulphur blew; ....Il.8.164.405.
Black from the Blow, and Smoaks of Sulphur rise; ....Il.14.484.187.
This ting'd with Sulphur, sacred first to Flame, ...Il.16.278.249.
And all in clouds of smoth'ring sulphur lost. ....Od.14.340.51.
Bring hither fire, and hither sulphur bring, ...Od.22.518.314.
"Bring sulphur strait and fire" (the Monarch cries) ....Od.22.527.314.
With fire and sulphur, cure of noxious fumes, ...Od.22.529.314.

SULPHUR-TIPT
Not sulphur-tipt, emblaze an Ale-house fire; ....5.DunB1.235.287.

SULPHUREOUS
Her Snakes, unty'd, Sulphureous Waters drink; ....1.TrSt.125.415.
Sulphureous Flames, and Clouds of rolling Smoke: ....2.TemF.339.280.
Sulphureous odors rose, and smould'ring smoke. ....Od.12.492.456.
Glorious in gore!—now with sulphureous fires, ...Od.23.51.321.

SULTRY
The sultry *Sirius* burns the thirsty Plains, ...1.PSu.21.73.
When weary Reapers quit the sultry Field, ...1.PSu.65.77.
And now his shorter Breath with sultry Air ....1.W-F.195.168.
A Night of sultry Clouds involv'd around ....1.TrSt.742.441.
To this sweet Place, in Summer's sultry Heat, ...2.ChJM.469.37.
Who hung with woods yon mountain's sultry brow? ....3.Ep3.253.114.
As Vapors blown by *Auster's* sultry Breath, ...Il.5.1058.317.
As warring Winds, in *Sirius'* sultry Reign, ...Il.13.424.126.
Full on his Neck he feels the sultry Breeze, ...Il.23.459.508.
When sultry days, and long, succeed the gentle spring. ....Od.22.336.302.

SUM
Then see how little the remaining sum, ...3.EOM2.51.62.
Why she and Lesbia raise that monstrous sum? ....3.Ep3.123A.102.
Why she and Sappho raise that monstrous sum? ....3.Ep3.123.102.
To *sum the whole,—the Close of all.* ....6.39.16.110.
Convok'd to Council, weigh the Sum of things. ....Il.13.930.149.
(In order told, we make the sum compleat.) ....Od.4.608.148.
A mighty sum of ill-persuading gold: ....Od.4.702.152.
What sum, what prize from *Æolus* I brought? ....Od.10.40.341.

SUMLESS
The sumless treasure of exhausted mines: ....Od.4.86.123.
Welcom'd with gifts of price, a sumless store! ....Od.19.312.209.

SUMM'D
Their number summ'd, repos'd in sleep profound ....Od.4.557.146.

SUMMER
Ye Birds, that left by Summer, cease to sing, ...1.PAu.28.82.
Which summer suns, and winter frosts expel. ....1.TrPA.69.368.
And there a Summer-house, that knows no shade; ....3.Ep4.122.149.
Whose trees in summer yield him shade, ...6.1.7.3.
While summer suns roll unperceiv'd away? ....6.52.18.156.
In Summer-Days like Grashoppers rejoice, ...Il.3.201.200.
Resplendent as the blaze of summer-noon, ...Od.4.55.122.
Glows with th' autumnal or the summer ray, ...Od.12.92.436.
The summer and the autumn glows in vain, ...Od.12.93.436.
Of summer suns, were both constrain'd to wield ....Od.18.412.188.
In wavy gold thy summer vales are dress'd; ....Od.19.131.199.

SUMMER-DAYS
In Summer-Days like Grashoppers rejoice, ...Il.3.201.200.

SUMMER-HOUSE
And there a Summer-house, that knows no shade; ....3.Ep4.122.149.

SUMMER-NOON
Resplendent as the blaze of summer-noon, ...Od.4.55.122.

SUMMER'S
When milder Autumn Summer's Heat succeeds, ...1.W-F.97.159.
More sweet than winter's sun, or summer's air, ...1.TrPA.54.367.
Bright as the rising Sun, in Summer's Day, ...2.ChJM.345.30.
To this sweet Place, in Summer's sultry Heat, ...2.ChJM.469.37.
It happ'd, that once upon a Summer's Day, ...2.ChJM.521.40.
That laugh'd down many a Summer's Sun, ...4.1HE7.47.271.
Where *Summer's* beauty midst of *Winter* stays, ...6.14iv.29.48.
And *Winter's* Coolness spite of *Summer's* rays. ....6.14iv.30.48.
The wandring Nation of a Summer's Day, ...Il.2.553.154.
That the green Banks in Summer's Heat o'erflows, ...Il.22.199.463.

SUMMERS
Whose stately growth five flow'ry summers fed: ....Od.19.491.220.

SUMMIT
Whose verdant summit fragrant myrtles crown'd. ....1.TrFD.16.386.
And climbing, in the Summit took his Place: ....2.ChJM.606.44.
Whose tow'ring Summit ambient Clouds conceal'd. ....2.TemF.26.255.
The Rock's high Summit, in the Temple's Shade, ...2.TemF.47.256.
Where the wild Figs th' adjoining Summit crown, ...Il.11.219.45.
To join its Summit to the neighb'ring Skies, ...Il.14.326.178.
On *Ida's* Summit sate imperial *Jove:* ....Il.15.6.194.
Swift from th' *Idæan* Summit shot to Heav'n. ....Il.15.85.199.
On yon' tall Summit of the fount-ful *Ide:* ....Il.15.165.203.
Swift from *Olympus'* snowy Summit flies, ...Il.18.711.357.
Th' aerial summit from the marble base: ....Od.4.680.151.
High in the air the rock its summit shrouds, ...Od.12.87.436.

SUMMITS
High *Teree's* Summits, and *Pityea's* Bow'rs; ....Il.2.1005.170.
Rest on the Summits of the shaded Hill; ....Il.5.646.299.
Where o'er her pointed Summits proudly rais'd, ...Il.8.59.398.
On *Ida's* Summits thunder'd from above. ....Il.8.207.407.
From *Ida's* Summits to th' *Olympian* Height. ....Il.8.543.422.
And down their Summits pour'd a hundred Rills: ....Il.11.238.46.
Then *Ida's* Summits pour'd their wat'ry Store; ....Il.12.16.82.
Where vast *Olympus* starry Summits shine: ....Il.18.180.331.
Thro' all their Summits tremble *Ida's* Woods, ...Il.20.79.397.
From *Ida's* Summits, and the Tow'rs of *Troy:* ....Il.22.226.464.
Whose leafless summits to the skies aspire, ...Od.5.307.185.

SUMMON
They summon all her Race: An endless band ....5.DunB2.19.297.
O *Button!* summon all thy Sons of Wit! ....6.48iii.12.135.
To range the Camp, and summon all the Bands: ....Il.2.62.130.

SUMMON (CONTINUED)
Love, Duty, Safety, summon us away, ...Il.2.167.136.
But haste, and summon to our Courts above ....Il.24.95.539.

SUMMON'D
His Friends were summon'd, on a Point so nice, ...2.ChJM.81.18.
Once more in haste he summon'd ev'ry Friend, ...2.ChJM.252.26.
'Twas he had summon'd to her silent Bed ....2.RL1.21.147.
And all the Nations, summon'd at the Call, ...2.TemF.278.276.
And all the Nations summon'd to the Throne. ....5.DunB4.72.348.
The Gods had summon'd to th' *Olympian* Height. ....Il.1.641.118.
This heard, she gave Command; and summon'd came ....Il.6.356.343.
'Twas not for State we summon'd you so far, ...Il.17.262.298.
She call'd aloud, and summon'd *Vulcan's* Aid. ....Il.21.385.436.
My men I summon'd, and these words addrest. ....Od.10.213.350.
Now summon'd *Proserpine* to hell's black hall ....Od.11.480.408.

SUMMONS
But at the Summons, roll'd her Eyes around, ...1.TrSt.126.415.
He summons strait his Denizens of Air; ....2.RL2.55.163.
That summons you to all the Pride of Pray'r: ....3.Ep4.142.151.
She summons all her sons: an endless band ....5.DunA2.15.98.
Her Criticks there she summons, and proclaims ....5.DunA2.333.142.
Me Glory summons to the martial Scene, ...Il.6.634.358.
Expect a second Summons to the War; ....Il.19.238.382.
And summons all the Senate of the Skies. ....Il.20.8.393.
Heard the loud Summons, and forsook the Main, ...Il.20.20.393.
With joyous pride the summons I'd obey. ....Od.1.502.56.
A spy was sent their summons to convey: ....Od.15.494.94.

SUMPTUOUS
Westward, a sumptuous Frontispiece appear'd, ...2.TemF.75.258.
In Seats of Council and the sumptuous Feast: ....Il.8.197.407.
That done, a sumptuous Banquet shall be made, ...Il.19.177.379.
A sumptuous Banquet at our Tent attends. ....Il.23.956.527.
The sumptuous viands, and the flav'rous wines. ....Od.6.90.209.
A steer to form the sumptuous banquet bled, ...Od.19.490.220.

SUMS
What Sums from these old Spouses I cou'd raise, ...2.ChWB.207.66.
What Sums from these first Spouses I cou'd raise, ...2.ChWB.207A.66.
"Oh say, what sums that gen'rous hand supply? ....3.Ep3.277.116.
Where all cry out, "What sums are thrown away!" ....3.Ep4.100.147.
Then to their Sire for ample Sums restor'd; ....Il.11.145.42.
Now Sums immense thy Mercy shall repay. ....Il.21.91.425.

SUN
Where dancing Sun-beams on the Waters play'd, ...1.PSu.3.71.
But soon the Sun with milder Rays descends ....1.PSu.89.79.
The setting Sun now shone serenely bright, ...1.PAu.13A.81.
And the low Sun had lengthen'd ev'ry Shade. ....1.PAu.100.87.
No more the rising *Sun* shall gild the Morn, ...1.Mes.99.121.
(His Shadow lengthen'd by the setting Sun) ....1.W-F.194.168.
But true *Expression,* like th' unchanging *Sun,* ....1.EOC.315.274.
And force *that Sun* but on a *Part* to Shine; ....1.EOC.399.286.
When first that Sun too powerful Beams displays, ...1.EOC.470.292.
More sweet than winter's sun, or summer's air, ...1.TrPA.54.367.
The sun all objects views beneath the sky, ...1.TrPA.110.370.
And Wreaths of Hay his Sun-burnt Temples shade; ....1.TrVP.34.378.
With that ripe red th'Autumnal Sun bestows, ...1.TrVP.101.381.
As when thro' Clouds th'emerging Sun appears, ...1.TrVP.115.381.
The Sun wou'd sink into the Western Main, ...1.TrSt.328.424.
He chides the lazy Progress of the Sun, ...1.TrSt.453.429.
(Where late the Sun did *Atreus'* Crimes detest ....1.TrSt.460.429.
The Sun descending, the *Phæacian* Train ....1.TrUl.1.465.
Whose Hills are brighten'd by the rising Sun. ....1.TrUl.119.469.
The meekest Creature that beholds the Sun! ....2.ChJM.203.24.
Bright as the rising Sun, in Summer's Day, ...2.ChJM.345.30.
The weary Sun, as Learned Poets write, ...2.ChJM.367.32.
('Twas *June,* and *Cancer* had receiv'd the Sun) ....2.ChJM.401.34.
The Sun adorns the Fields, and brightens all the Sky. ....2.ChJM.530.41.
Make your own Terms; and ere to-morrow's Sun ....2.ChJM.563.42.
'Twas now the Season when the glorious Sun ....2.ChJM.609.44.
A wiser Monarch never saw the Sun: ....2.ChJM.632.45.
Sport with her Tail, and wanton in the Sun; ....2.ChWB.145.63.
Ere to the Main this Morning Sun descend. ....2.RL1.110.154.
The Sun first rises o'er the purpled Main, ...2.RL2.2.159.
Bright as the Sun, her Eyes the Gazers strike, ...2.RL2.13.160.
And, like the Sun, they shine on all alike. ....2.RL2.14.160.
The Sun-beams trembling on the floating Tydes, ...2.RL2.48.162.
Some to the Sun their Insect-Wings unfold, ...2.RL2.59.163.
His Purple Pinions opening to the Sun, ...2.RL2.71.164.
The Sun obliquely shoots his burning Ray; ....2.RL3.20.170.
Now a clear Sun the shining Scene displays, ...2.TemF.19.254.
But felt th'Approaches of too warm a Sun; ....2.TemF.42.256.
Eternal sun-shine of the spotless mind! ....2.ElAb.209.337.
Of show'rs and sun-shine, as of Man's desires; ....3.EOM1.152.34.
Warms in the sun, refreshes in the breeze, ...3.EOM1.271.48.
Correct old Time, and regulate the Sun; ....3.EOM2.22.57.
Correct old Time, and teach the Sun his way; ....3.EOM2.22A.57.
And turn their heads to imitate the Sun. ....3.EOM2.28.58.
Yet make at once their circle round the Sun: ....3.EOM3.314.126.
The soul's calm sun-shine, and the heart-felt joy, ...3.EOM4.168.143.
Tho' the same Sun with all-diffusive rays ....3.Ep1.97.22.
Strike off his Pension, by the setting sun, ...3.Ep1.160.29.
Shine, buzz, and fly-blow in the setting-sun. ....3.Ep2.28.52.
Flam'd forth this rival to, its Sire, the Sun, ...3.Ep3.12.84.
"Spread like a low-born mist, and blot the Sun; ....3.Ep3.140.105.
The Sun e're got, or slimy *Nilus* bore, ...4.JD4.29.29.
Hast thou, O *Sun!* beheld an emptier sort, ...4.JD4.204.43.
Then, like the Sun, let Bounty spread her ray, ...4.HS2.115.63.
He walks, an Object new beneath the Sun! ....4.2HE2.119.173.
Ploughs, burns, manures, and toils from Sun to Sun; ....4.2HE2.271.185.
Ploughs, burns, manures, and toils from Sun to Sun; ....4.2HE2.271.185.
Self-centred Sun, and Stars that rise and fall, ...4.1HE6.6.237.
Hold out some months 'twixt Sun and Fire, ...4.1HE7.18.269.

SUN (CONTINUED)

That laugh'd down many a Summer's Sun, ...4.1HE7.47.271.
"Far Eastward cast thine eye, from whence the Sun ....5.DunA3.65.156.
"Far Eastward cast thy eye, from whence the Sun ....5.DunA3.65A.156.
"Far eastward cast thine eye, from whence the Sun ......5.DunB3.73.323.
Sick was the Sun, the Owl forsook his bow'r, ...5.DunB4.11.340.
Suckled, and chear'd, with air, and sun, and show'r, ...5.DunB4.406.381.
Turn'd to the Sun, she casts a thousand dyes, ...5.DunB4.539.395.
Pair'd with his Fellow-Charioteer the Sun; ....5.DunB4.588.401.
See how the sun in dusky skies ....6.4iv.1.10.
The sun (next those the fairest light) ....6.5.3.12.
And thus thro' mists we see the sun, ...6.5.5.12.
And thus thro' mists we view the sun, ...6.5.5A.12.
And the bright sun admire no more; ....6.6i.2.13.
A second sun thou dost present, ...6.6ii.13.15.
At ev'ry Door are Sun-brunt Matrons seen, ...6.14ii.15.43.
Basks in the Sun, then to the Shades retires, ...6.17iii.30.58.
Or, of the Rising or *Meridian* Sun) ....6.26i.9.79.
Some dry the black'ning clusters in the sun, ...6.35.20.103.
Light to the Stars the Sun does thus restore, ...6.43.11.120.
All else beneath the Sun, ...6.50.46.148.
Productive as the Sun. ....6.51ii.24.153.
And now the Sun declining low ....6.79.105.221.
Which wings the Sun-born Insects of the Air, ...6.96v.2.280.
And, un-observed, the glaring sun declines. ....6.106i.7.306.
The *Pæans* lengthen'd 'till the Sun descends: ....Il.1.619.117.
Nor 'till the Sun descended, touch'd the Ground: ....Il.1.763.123.
Meantime the radiant Sun, to mortal Sight ....Il.1.776.124.
Hear! and before the burning Sun descends, ...Il.2.492.150.
The gilded Legions glitt'ring in the Sun. ....Il.2.557.154.
From those far Regions where the Sun refines ....Il.2.1044.172.
To *Earth* a sable, to the *Sun* a white, ...Il.3.142.197.
Lean'd on the Walls, and bask'd before the Sun. ....Il.3.198.200.
Beneath the rowling Sun, and starry Skies, ...Il.4.66.224.
Beneath the rising or the setting Sun. ....Il.5.331.282.
The Day, that show'd me to the golden Sun, ...Il.6.435.348.
Till the new Sun restores the chearful Light: ....Il.7.447.386.
The rolling Sun descending to the Main ....Il.7.557.392.
But when the Sun the Height of Heav'n ascends; ....Il.8.87.399.
Some other Sun may see the happier Hour, ...Il.8.173.406.
The Morning Sun, awak'd by loud Alarms, ...Il.8.586.424.
No Sun e'er gilds the gloomy Horrors there, ...Il.8.601.425.
Let num'rous Fires the absent Sun supply; ....Il.8.632.426.
Like *Pallas* worship'd, like the Sun renown'd; ....Il.8.670.427.
And we beheld, the last revolving Sun? ....Il.10.58.5.
Now Shouts and Tumults wake the tardy Sun, ...Il.11.67.37.
Till to the Main the burning Sun descend, ...Il.11.251.46.
Till to the Main the burning Sun descend, ...Il.11.267.47.
Thence, e'er the Sun advanc'd his noonday Flame, ...Il.11.862.74.
Soon as the Sun, with all-revealing Ray ....Il.11.870.74.
Pay the large Debt of last revolving Sun; ....Il.13.936.149.
Like the broad Sun, illumin'd all the Field: ....Il.13.1013.153.
Not ev'n the Sun, who darts thro' Heav'n his Rays, ...Il.14.391.181.
And shades the Sun, and blots the golden Skies: ....Il.16.437.259.
The Sun, the Moon, and all th' Etherial Host ....Il.17.423.303.
The golden Sun pour'd forth a stronger Ray, ...Il.17.430.304.
The Sun shall see her conquer, till his Fall ....Il.17.522.308.
Forth burst the Sun with all-enlight'ning Ray; ....Il.17.735.317.
Soon as the Sun in Ocean hides his Rays, ...Il.18.249.334.
If but the Morrow's Sun behold us here, ...Il.18.315.336.
Th' unweary'd Sun, the Moon compleatly round; ....Il.18.559.349.
Till yonder Sun descend, ah let me pay ....Il.19.327.386.
Smile on the Sun; now, wither on the Ground: ....Il.21.540.444.
Like *Jove's* own Lightning, or the rising Sun. ....Il.22.178.461.
The gilded Horsehair sparkled in the Sun, ...Il.22.396.472.
And now the Sun had set upon their Woe; ....Il.23.193.497.
What sees the Sun, but hapless Heroes Falls? ....Il.24.690.566.
Watch'd from the rising to the setting Sun) ....Il.24.1010.577.
The rising and descending Sun surveys) ....Od.1.32.31.
Did not the sun, thro' heav'n's wide azure roll'd, ...Od.2.101.66.
While thrice the sun his annual journey made, ...Od.2.119.67.
Down sunk the Sun behind the western hills. ....Od.2.437.82.
The sacred Sun, above the waters rais'd, ...Od.3.1.85.
Thus while he speaks, the ruddy sun descends, ...Od.3.421.107.
Then sunk the Sun, and darken'd all the way. ....Od.3.618.117.
At dawn, and ending with the setting sun, ...Od.4.482.143.
And now the twentieth sun descending, laves ....Od.4.487.143.
When thro' the Zone of heav'n the mounted sun ......Od.4.539.146.
Thus 'till the sun had travel'd half the skies, ...Od.4.601.148.
To view the sun, or breathe the vital air. ....Od.4.728.153.
'Till from his eastern goal, the joyous sun ....Od.4.803.156.
Thus while he spoke, the beamy Sun descends, ...Od.5.289.185.
Scorch'd by the sun, or sear'd by heav'nly fire: .....Od.5.308.186.
Stranger arise! the sun rolls down the day, ...Od.6.303.225.
Some dry the black'ning clusters in the sun, ...Od.7.161.244.
Saw them returning with the setting sun. ....Od.7.416.258.
By bribes seduc'd: and how the Sun, whose eye ......Od.8.311.281.
Those to *Aurora* and the rising sun.) ....Od.9.26.303.
Long as the morning sun increasing bright ....Od.9.63.305.
Here, till the setting sun rowl'd down the light, ...Od.9.188.313.
Now sunk the sun, and darkness cover'd o'er ....Od.9.195.314.
Thus from the Sun descended, and the Main. ....Od.10.160.348.
There, 'till the setting sun rowl'd down the light, ...Od.10.208.350.
Or where the sun shall set, or where shall rise? ......Od.10.218.350.
And saw that all was grief beneath the sun. ....Od.10.591.372.
Now sunk the Sun from his aerial height, ...Od.11.11.379.
The Sun ne'er views th' uncomfortable seats, ...Od.11.17.380.
'Till the sun flames along th' etherial plain; ....Od.11.437.405.
The sun descending, and so near the shore? ....Od.12.338.448.
When the tenth sun descended to the main. ....Od.12.532.458.
He sate, and ey'd the sun, and wish'd the night; ....Od.13.36.3.
Slow seem'd the sun to move, the hours to roll, ...Od.13.37.3.
So to *Ulysses* welcome sett the Sun. ....Od.13.44.3.
Whose hills are brighten'd by the rising sun, ...Od.13.286.19.
Where the fat porkers slept beneath the sun; ....Od.14.86.40.
'Till the swift sun his annual circle made. ....Od.14.324.50.

SUN (CONTINUED)

Beneath the sun prolong they yet their breath, ...Od.15.372.87.
Now set the sun, and darken'd all the shore. ....Od.15.506.94.
Their grief unfinish'd with the setting sun: ....Od.16.243.116.
Wide as the sun displays his vital fire. ....Od.17.469.156.
Nor claim my story 'till the sun descend; ....Od.17.651.164.
The sun obliquely shot his dewy ray. ....Od.17.688.165.
A vest, that dazzl'd like a cloudless sun: ....Od.19.270.208.
I ratifie my speech; before the sun ....Od.19.349.211.
What time the sun, from ocean's peaceful stream, ...Od.19.505.221.
So, when the sun restores the purple day, ...Od.19.674.229.
Nor gives the Sun his golden orb to rowl, ...Od.20.429.254.
With each new sun to some new hope a prey, ...Od.21.165.267.
Thus had their joy wept down the setting sun, ...Od.21.240.271.
'Till the warm sun exhales their soul away. ....Od.22.431.309.
When the last sun beheld the Suitors bleed, ...Od.24.440.370.
The broad effulgence blazes in the sun. ....Od.24.535.373.

SUN-BEAMS

Where dancing Sun-beams on the Waters play'd, ...1.PSu.3.71.
The Sun-beams trembling on the floating Tydes, ...2.RL2.48.162.

SUN-BORN

Which wings the Sun-born Insects of the Air, ...6.96v.2.280.

SUN-BRUNT

At ev'ry Door are Sun-brunt Matrons seen, ...6.14ii.15.43.

SUN-BURNT

And Wreaths of Hay his Sun-burnt Temples shade; ....1.TrVP.34.378.

SUN-SET

Eyes the calm Sun-set of thy Various Day, ...6.84.38.240.

SUN-SHINE

Eternal sun-shine of the spotless mind! ....2.ElAb.209.337.
Of show'rs and sun-shine, as of Man's desires; ....3.EOM1.152.34.
The soul's calm sun-shine, and the heart-felt joy, ...3.EOM4.168.143.

SUN'S

The Sun's mild Lustre warms the vital Air; ....1.PSp.74.68.
So when the Sun's broad beam has tir'd the sight, ...3.Ep2.253.70.
So from the Sun's broad beam, in shallow urns ......5.DunB2.11.296.
So while the sun's broad beam yet strikes the sight, ..6.106i.4.306.
So when the sun's broad beam has tir'd the sight, ...6.106i.4A.306.
The Sun's bright Portals and the Skies command, ...Il.5.931.311.
Where-e'er the Sun's refulgent Rays are cast, ...Il.7.548.392.
The Sun's bright Portals and the Skies command; .....Il.8.481.420.
Nor here the sun's meridian rays had pow'r, ...Od.5.620.201.
That lies beneath the sun's all-seeing ray; ....Od.8.608.295.
Melting I heard; yet 'till the sun's decline ....Od.10.564.369.
Whate'er beneath the sun's bright journey lies. ......Od.12.230.443.
Sees with delight the sun's declining ray, ...Od.13.41.3.
The Sun's diurnal, and his annual race.) ....Od.15.441.91.

SUNDAY

His Compting-house employ'd the Sunday-morn; ......3.Ep3.380.124.
Ev'n *Sunday* shines no *Sabbath-day* to me: ....4.Arbu.12.96.
On Sunday at Six, in the Street that's call'd *Gerrard*, ..6.62v.1.186.

SUNDAY-MORN

His Compting-house employ'd the Sunday-morn; ......3.Ep3.380.124.

SUNDAYS

On Sundays preach, and eat, his Fill; ....6.39.19.111.

SUNDERLAND

To hear 'em rail at honest Sunderland ....6.61.19.181.
To hear you rail at honest S[underlan]d ....6.61.19A.181.
To hear them rail at honest Sunderland ....6.61.19B.181.

SUNG

Hylas and *Ægon* sung their Rural Lays; ....1.PAu.2.80.
Next *Ægon* sung, while *Windsor* Groves admir'd; ...1.PAu.55.84.
Thus sung the Shepherds till th'Approach of Night, ...1.PAu.97.87.
Here too, 'tis sung, of old *Diana* stray'd, ...1.W-F.165.165.
Here, as old Bards have sung, *Diana* stray'd, ...1.W-F.165A.165.
Here his first Lays Majestick *Denham* sung; ....1.W-F.271.173.
His living Harp, and lofty *Denham* sung? ....1.W-F.280.174.
First in these Fields I sung the Sylvan Strains. ......1.W-F.434.194.
When first young *Maro* sung of *Kings* and *Wars*, ..1.EOC.130A.254.
Yet *judg'd* with *Coolness* tho' he sung with *Fire;* .1.EOC.659.314.
A *Raphael* painted, and a *Vida* sung! ....1.EOC.704.320.
While to his reeds he sung his amorous pains, ...1.TrPA.51.367.
"Here She who sung, to Him that did inspire, ...1.TrSP.214.403.
While to his Harp Divine *Amphion* sung? ....1.TrSt.12.409.
Had sung—"Expect thy Sons on *Argos'* Shore, ...1.TrSt.547.433.
And Songs were sung, and flowing Bowls went round; ..2.ChJM.354.31.
And Songs were sung, and Healths went nimbly round; ..2.ChJM.354A.31.
'Tis sung, he labour'd 'till the dawning Day, ...2.ChJM.384.33.
And feebly sung a lusty Roundelay: ....2.ChJM.389.33.
High Mass was sung; they feasted in the Hall; ....2.ChJM.404.34.
Well sung sweet *Ovid*, in the Days of yore, ...2.ChJM.514.40.
And thus his Morning Canticle he sung. ....2.ChJM.524.40.
Sung merrier than the Cuckow or the Jay: ....2.ChJM.713.49.
And sung as sweet as Evening *Philomel*. ....2.ChWB.212.67.
He put on careless Airs, and sat and sung. ....2.ChWB.240.68.
And Youths that dy'd to be by Poets sung. ....2.TemF.128.264.
Guiltless I gaz'd; heav'n listen'd while you sung; .....2.ElAb.65.324.
The well-sung woes will sooth my pensive ghost; .....2.ElAb.365.348.
The well-sung woes shall sooth my pensive ghost; ....2.ElAb.365A.348.
Poets themselves must fall, like those they sung; .....2.Elegy.75.368.
'Tis sung, when *Midas'* Ears began to spring, ...4.Arbu.69.100.
And all I sung should be the *Nation's Sense:* ....4.EpS1.78.304.
What City-Swans once sung within the walls; ....5.DunA1.94.70.
Then sung, how shown him by the nutbrown maids, ...5.DunA2.313.140.

SUNG 417 SUPERIOR

SUNG (CONTINUED)
How sweet the periods, neither said nor sung! .... 5.DunA3.198.174.
What City Swans once sung within the walls; .... 5.DunB1.96.276.
Then sung, how shown him by the Nut-brown maids .... 5.DunB2.337.314.
How sweet the periods, neither sad, nor sung! .... 5.DunB3.202.330.
He sung, and Hell consented .... 6.11.83.33.
Yet ev'n in Death *Eurydice* he sung, ... 6.11.113.34.
And these be sung 'till *Granville's Myra* die; .... 6.52.76.158.
Such were the Notes, thy once-lov'd Poet sung, ... 6.84.1.238.
Who first sung *Arthur,* then sung *Alfred,* .... 6.101.2.290.
Who first sung *Arthur,* then sung *Alfred,* .... 6.101.2.290.
Around their Heads the whistling Javelins sung; .... Il.12.169.87.
Sung on, and pierc'd *Amphimachus* his Heart, ... Il.13.248.117.
O'er his safe Head the Javelin idly sung, ... Il.13.517.131.
And Arrows leaping from the Bowstring sung; .... Il.15.357.210.
Then hiss'd his Arrow, and the Bowstring sung. .... Il.15.521.217.
Sung innocent, and spent its Force in Air. .... Il.22.352.470.
From *Polypætes* Arm, the *Discus* sung: .... Il.23.1000.529.
Sung dying to the rocks, but sung in vain. .... Od.3.343.103.
Sung dying to the rocks, but sung in vain. .... Od.3.343.103.
She sate and sung; the rocks resound her lays: .... Od.5.74.176.
Thus sung the Bard: *Ulysses* hears with joy, ... Od.8.403.285.
He sung the *Greeks* stern-issuing from the steed, ... Od.8.563.293.
Thus while he sung, *Ulysses'* griefs renew, ... Od.8.569.293.
He whirl'd it round; it sung across the main: .... Od.9.632.332.
Plac'd at her loom within, the Goddess sung; .... Od.10.254.354.
Sung on direct, and thredded ev'ry ring. .... Od.21.462.282.
Each sung along, and drop'd upon the ground. .... Od.22.311.301.
That here I sung, was force and not desire; .... Od.22.389.307.

SUNIUM'S
But when to *Sunium's* sacred point we came, ... Od.3.352.103.

SUNK
In her sunk Eye-balls dreadful Meteors glow, ... 1.TrSt.146.416.
Sunk in *Thalestris'* Arms the Nymph he found, ... 2.RL4.89.191.
Cry'd *Dapperwit,* and sunk beside his Chair. .... 2.RL5.62.205.
And each Majestic Phantom sunk in Night. .... 2.TemF.355.280.
Some sunk to Beasts, find pleasure end in pain; .... 3.EOM4.23.130.
Lamented DIGBY! sunk thee to the grave? .... 3.EOM4.104.138.
And all that rais'd the Hero, sunk the Man. .... 3.EOM4.294.155.
Then see them broke with toils, or sunk in ease, ... 3.EOM4.297.156.
"See Britain sunk in lucre's sordid charms, ... 3.Ep3.145.105.
Not sunk by sloth, nor rais'd by servitude; .... 3.Ep3.222.111.
For ever sunk too low, or born too high! .... 4.2HE1.299.221.
Nor puff'd by Pride, nor sunk by Spleen. .... 4.HS6.28.251.
There sunk Thalia, nerveless, cold, and dead, ... 5.DunB4.41.345.
There sunk Thalia, nerveless, faint, and dead, ... 5.DunB4.41A.345.
Look'd a white lilly sunk beneath a show'r. .... 5.DunB4.104.351.
There TALBOT sunk, and was a Wit no more! .... 5.DunB4.168.357.
Or when the Soul is sunk with Cares .... 6.11.26A.30.
"Or sunk within the Peach's Down, repose? .... 6.96ii.46.273.
Next in three Books, sunk human *Nature,* .... 6.101.10.290.
And all that rais'd the Hero sunk the Man. .... 6.130.4.358.
Be *Priam's* Palace sunk in *Grecian* Fires, ... Il.2.495.150.
He too had sunk to Death's Eternal Shade; .... Il.5.30.267.
Down sunk the Priest: the Purple Hand of Death .... Il.5.108.272.
Sunk on his Knees and stagg'ring with his Pains, ... Il.5.379.285.
Oppress'd had sunk to Death's Eternal Shade, ... Il.5.384.285.
His flying Coursers, sunk to endless Night: .... Il.5.710.301.
Then sunk unpity'd to the dire Abodes, ... Il.6.173.334.
Why sunk I not beneath the whelming Tyde, ... Il.6.438.348.
Then sunk *Eioneus* to the Shades below, ... Il.7.15.363.
What Crowds of Heroes sunk, to rise no more? .... Il.7.395.383.
Low sunk on Earth, the *Trojan* strikes the Skies. .... Il.8.92.401.
Bold *Hamopäon* breathless sunk to Ground; .... Il.8.333.413.
Now deep in Ocean sunk the Lamp of Light, ... Il.8.605.425.
When *Lesbos* sunk beneath the Hero's Arms. .... Il.9.168.441.
When *Lesbos* sunk beneath thy conqu'ring Arms. .... Il.9.355.451.
Each sunk in Sleep, extended on the Field, ... Il.10.172.9.
Opheltius, Orus, sunk to endless Night, ... Il.11.392.52.
Next *Ennomus* and *Thoon* sunk to Hell; .... Il.11.532.57.
The State of *Pyle* was sunk to last Despair, ... Il.11.830.73.
The Walls were rais'd, the Trenches sunk in vain. .... Il.12.8.81.
Greece sunk they thought, and this their fatal Hour; .... Il.13.123.110.
So sunk proud *Asius* in that dreadful Day, ... Il.13.497.130.
So sunk proud *Asius* in that deathful Day, ... Il.13.497A.130.
Sunk in his sad Companion's Arms he lay, ... Il.13.817.144.
While sunk in Love's entrancing Joys he lies. .... Il.14.271.175.
Had almost sunk me to the Shades below? .... Il.15.285.208.
Push'd at the Bank: Down sunk th' enormous Mound: .... Il.15.407.213.
There pierc'd by *Ajax,* sunk *Laodamas,* .... Il.15.612.220.
It sunk, and rooted in the *Grecian* Hearts. .... Il.15.675.222.
Hung by the Skin: the Body sunk to Dust. .... Il.16.409.258.
Which sunk him to the dead: when *Troy,* too near .... Il.16.715.271.
Sunk with *Troy's* heavy Fates, he sees decline .... Il.16.799.274.
Then sunk *Pylartes* to eternal Night; .... Il.16.855.276.
Sunk in soft Dust the mighty Chief remains, ... Il.16.936.279.
The show'ring Darts, and Numbers sunk to Hell. .... Il.16.941.280.
With him all *Greece* was sunk; that Moment all .... Il.16.991.281.
Oppos'd me fairly, they had sunk in Fight: .... Il.16.1023.282.
Had sunk each Heart with Terror and Dismay. .... Il.17.128.292.
And sunk the Victim of all-conqu'ring Death. .... Il.18.150.329.
Sunk were her Treasures, and her Stores decay'd; .... Il.18.340.338.
Else had I sunk oppress'd in fatal Fight, ... Il.20.125.399.
Sunk in one Instant to the nether World; .... Il.20.534.416.
And sunk in Dust, the Corps extended lies. .... Il.20.560.417.
The fainting Stripling sunk, before the Stroke; .... Il.21.126.426.
Sunk soft in Down upon the Nurse's Breast, ... Il.22.649.483.
Then sunk the Blaze, the Pyle no longer burn'd, ... Il.23.284.501.
And sunk to Quiet in th' Embrace of Sleep, ... Il.23.289.501.
Sunk was his Heart; his Colour went and came; .... Il.24.443.554.
Let not your soul be sunk in sad despair; .... Od.1.255.45.
Sunk is the Hero, and his glory lost! .... Od.1.310.47.
Down sunk the Sun behind the western hills. .... Od.2.437.82.
Or sunk by tempests in the gulphy main? .... Od.3.109.91.

SUNK (CONTINUED)
Such numbers fell, such Heroes sunk to night: .... Od.3.132.92.
Down sunk the heavy beast: the females round .... Od.3.572.115.
Then sunk the Sun, and darken'd all the way. .... Od.3.618.117.
Then slowly sunk the ruddy globe of light, ... Od.3.629.118.
His vessel sunk, and dear companions lost, ... Od.4.759.155.
Sudden she sunk beneath the weighty woes; .... Od.4.934.162.
There all his vessels sunk beneath the wave! .... Od.5.139.178.
And sunk his brave companions in the main. .... Od.5.168.180.
And sunk amidst 'em heap'd the leaves around. .... Od.5.629.202.
While thus the weary Wand'rer sunk to rest, ... Od.6.1.203.
And sunk transported on the conscious bed. .... Od.8.338.282.
Now sunk the sun, and darkness cover'd o'er .... Od.9.195.314.
Ill fits it me, whose friends are sunk to beasts, ... Od.10.453.365.
Tir'd with long toil, we willing sunk to rest. .... Od.10.553.369.
Now sunk the Sun from his aerial height, ... Od.11.11.379.
The phantom Prophet ceas'd, and sunk from sight .... Od.11.184.390.
Ev'n she had sunk, but *Jove's* imperial bride .... Od.12.85.435.
Sunk were at once the winds; the air above, ... Od.12.202.441.
Now sunk the West, and now a southern breeze .... Od.12.503.457.
Sunk is the Heroe, and his glory lost! .... Od.14.408.55.
Sunk the fair City by the rage of war, ... Od.15.415.89.
Nor wine nor food he tastes; but sunk in woes, ... Od.16.154.110.
O had this stranger sunk to realms beneath, ... Od.18.446.190.
Sunk was each heart, and pale was ev'ry face. .... Od.21.451.282.
Fate, and their crime, have sunk them to the dust; .... Od.22.451.310.
Oh! better hadst thou sunk in *Trojan* ground, ... Od.24.43.350.
Sunk what was mortal of thy mighty name, ... Od.24.92.352.
Sunk is the glory of this once-fam'd shore! .... Od.24.328.365.

SUNNY
Where bask on sunny banks the simple sheep, ... 5.DunB4.352.377.
The baby, in that sunny sphere .... 6.5.13.12.
Here grapes discolour'd on the sunny side, ... 6.35.24.103.
Couch'd on the sunny sand, the monsters sleep: .... Od.4.605.148.
Here grapes discolour'd on the sunny side, ... Od.7.165.244.
Stretch'd forth, and panting in the sunny ray. .... Od.10.186.349.

SUNS
Soft Show'rs distill'd, and Suns grew warm in vain; .... 1.W-F.54.154.
Which summer suns, and winter frosts expel. .... 1.TrPA.69.368.
Ev'n those who dwell where Suns at distance roll, ... 1.TrSt.812.443.
When those fair Suns shall sett, as sett they must, ... 2.RL5.147.211.
Pale Suns, unfelt, at distance roll away, ... 2.TemF.55.256.
What other planets circle other suns, ... 3.EOM1.26.16.
What other planets and what other suns, ... 3.EOM1.26A.16.
"Seas roll to waft me, suns to light me rise; .... 3.EOM1.139.32.
From burning suns when livid deaths descend, ... 3.EOM1.142.32.
Planets and Suns run lawless thro' the sky, ... 3.EOM1.252.46.
Planets and Suns rush lawless thro' the sky, ... 3.EOM1.252A.46.
Three thousand Suns went down on *Welsted's* Lye: .... 4.Arbu.375.123.
Those Suns of Glory please not till they set. .... 4.2HE1.22.195.
And other planets circle other suns: .... 5.DunA3.240.177.
Yon stars, yon suns, he rears at pleasure higher, ... 5.DunA3.255.179.
And other planets circle other suns. .... 5.DunB3.244.332.
Yon stars, yon suns, he rears at pleasure higher, ... 5.DunB3.259.332.
While summer suns roll unperceiv'd away? .... 6.52.18.156.
Which seem'd like two broad Suns in misty Skies: .... 6.96ii.74.273.
And scorch'd by Suns, it withers on the Plain. .... Il.4.559.248.
Or where the Suns arise, or where descend; .... Il.12.280.91.
And scarce twelve morning Suns have seen me here; .... Il.21.93.425.
Of summer suns, were both constrain'd to wield .... Od.18.412.188.
Vain hope! ten suns had warm'd the western strand, ... Od.19.224.204.
Full twenty annual suns in distant skies: .... Od.19.566.224.

SUNSETT
The calmer Sunsett of thy Various Day; .... 6.84.31Z10.240.

SUNSHINE
Not Show'rs to Larks, or Sunshine to the Bee, ... 1.PAu.45.83.
Not Show'rs to Larks, nor Sunshine to the Bee, ... 1.PAu.45A.83.
Nor Sunshine to the Bee; .... 6.78i.6.215.
From *Rhodes* with everlasting Sunshine bright, ... Il.2.795.163.
The rest in Sunshine fought, and open Light: .... Il.17.427.303.

SUP
Or when I sup, or when I dine, ... 4.HS6.134.259.
Bid me with Pollio sup, as well as dine: .... 5.DunB4.392.380.
To sup, like Jove, with blameless Ethiopians .... 6.42ii.2.117.
And Sup with us on Mirth or Quiet, ... 6.61.34.182.
And Sup with us on Mirth on Quiet, ... 6.61.34A.182.
And Sup with us on Mirth and Quiet, ... 6.61.34B.182.
And Sup with us on Milk and Quiet, ... 6.61.34C.182.

SUPER
The head that turns at super-lunar things, ... 5.DunB4.451.384.

SUPER-LUNAR
The head that turns at super-lunar things, ... 5.DunB4.451.384.

SUPERCARGOES
Thieves, Supercargoes, Sharpers, and Directors. .... 4.HS1.72.11.

SUPERFICIAL
The thin Undress of superficial Light, ... 6.14iv.6.47.

SUPERFLUITY
And shine that Superfluity away. .... 4.HS2.116.63.
A noble superfluity it craves, ... 4.1HE6.91.243.

SUPERFLUOUS
In all the madness of superfluous health, ... 3.EOM3.3.92.

SUPERIOR
But lost, dissolv'd in thy superior Rays; .... 1.Mes.101.122.
T' *admire* Superior Sense, and *doubt* their own! .... 1.EOC.200.263.

SUPERIOR (CONTINUED)

That only makes *Superior* Sense *belov'd.* ..... 1.EOC.577.306.
The Majesty of Heav'n superior shone; ..... 1.TrSt.281.422.
Heav'n seems improv'd with a superior Ray, ... 1.TrSt.294.422.
Their Work, and rev'rence our Superior Will. ..... 1.TrSt.410.427.
Nor shine their Beauties with superior Grace, ... 1.TrSt.626.436.
But view'd the Shrine with a superior Look, ... 1.TrSt.755.441.
Unless great Acts superior Merit prove, ... 1.TrES.35.451.
'Till *Hector* came, to whose Superior Might ..... 1.TrES.173.456.
Superior by the Head, was *Ariel* plac'd; ..... 2.RL2.70.164.
Superior, and alone, *Confucius* stood, ... 2.TemF.107.261.
Unmov'd, superior still in every State; ..... 2.TemF.157.266.
Superior Worlds, and look all Nature thro'. ..... 2.TemF.237.274.
We here appeal to thy superior Throne: ..... 2.TemF.303.278.
From thee to Nothing!—On superior pow'rs ..... 3.EOM1.241.45.
Superior beings, when of late they saw ..... 3.EOM2.31.59.
Alas what wonder! Man's superior part ..... 3.EOM2.39.60.
In Parts superior what advantage lies? ..... 3.EOM4.259.152.
That on his vigor and superior size. ..... 5.DunA2.162.121.
One on his vigour and superior size. ..... 5.DunB2.170.304.
There mov'd Montalto with superior air; ..... 5.DunB4.105.351.
But Fop shews Fop superior complaisance. ..... 5.DunB4.138.355.
While mankind boasts superior sight, ... 6.6ii.9.14.
To Pow'r superior none such Hatred bear: ..... Il.1.230.98.
Superior once of all the tuneful Race, ... Il.2.722.160.
See! bold *Idomeneus* superior tow'rs ..... Il.3.295.207.
Immortal *Jove!* high Heav'n's superior Lord, ... Il.3.396.211.
Of Pow'r superior why should I complain? ..... Il.4.81.224.
The Sire of Gods and Men superior smil'd, ... Il.5.517.293.
O'er all the Gods, superior and alone. ..... Il.5.939.311.
Fast by the Throne of Heav'ns superior Lord. ..... Il.5.1119.321.
She chose a Veil that shone superior far, ... Il.6.366.344.
That Day, *Atrides!* a superior Hand ..... Il.7.121.369.
O Father of Mankind, Superior Lord! ..... Il.7.241.376.
Whom Heav'n adorns, superior to thy Kind, ... Il.7.350.381.
And smil'd superior on his Best-belov'd. ..... Il.8.48.398.
No more let Beings of superior Birth ..... Il.8.528.421.
Superior Sorrows swell'd his Royal Breast; ..... Il.9.12.431.
Monarch of Nations! whose superior Sway ..... Il.9.127.438.
Mean-while apart, superior, and alone, ... Il.11.107.39.
"In Strength superior, and of Race divine, ... Il.11.917.76.
Unless great Acts superior Merit prove, ... Il.12.379.95.
He sits superior, and the Chariot flies. ..... Il.13.41.107.
For this, of *Jove's* superior Might afraid, ... Il.13.449.127.
And sees superior Posts in meaner Hands. ..... Il.13.579.134.
With such a Tyde superior Virtue sway'd, ... Il.13.849.146.
Wait under *Ide:* Of thy superior Pow'r ..... Il.14.351.179.
She ceas'd, and smiling with superior Love, ... Il.14.387.181.
The Boaster flies, and shuns superior Force. ..... Il.14.572.190.
Our elder Birthright, and superior Sway. ..... Il.15.185.203.
His elder Birthright, and superior Sway. ..... Il.15.201.204.
Soon as *Achilles,* with superior Care, ... Il.16.236.248.
And with superior Vengeance, greatly glows. ..... Il.16.678.270.
Laugh'st thou not, *Jove!* from thy superior Throne, ... Il.17.19.288.
Dead, he protects him with superior Care, ... Il.17.322.300.
Stern in superior Grief *Pelides* stood; ..... Il.18.367.339.
August, Divine, Superior by the Head! ..... Il.18.602.352.
I know thy Force to mine superior far; ..... Il.20.503.415.
The Race of these superior far to those, ... Il.21.207.430.
Suits not my Greatness, or superior Age. ..... Il.21.513.443.
The Sire, superior smil'd; and bade her show, ... Il.21.593.446.
Superior as thou art, forgive th' Offence, ... Il.23.669.516.
To wave Contention with superior Sway; ..... Il.23.690.517.
For *Phœbus* watch'd it with superior Care, ... Il.24.30.536.
With that superior attribute controul ..... Od.4.263.131.
With strength and speed superior form'd, in fight ..... Od.4.277.132.
Who bound, obedient to superior force, ... Od.4.525.145.
Vain efforts! with superior pow'r compress'd, ... Od.4.623.149.
But when superior to the rage of woe, ... Od.4.729.153.
And high descent, superior to the rest; ..... Od.4.852.158.
From ev'ry dome by pomp superior known; ..... Od.6.364.229.
Superior in the leap, a length of ground: ..... Od.8.136.270.
Alone superior in the field of *Troy,* ..... Od.8.251.276.
And shares the banquet in superior state, ... Od.11.224.392.
Nor dread superior *Jove,* to whom belong ..... Od.16.440.128.
And beg, degraded from superior state! ..... Od.19.91.197.
Of strength superior to the toil assign'd.— ..... Od.19.413.214.

SUPERIOR'S

Superior's Death! an Equal, what a Curse! ..... 6.154.21.403.

SUPERIORS

Superiors? death! an Equal, what a curse! ..... 3.Ep2.135A.61.
Superiors? death! if Equals? what a curse! ..... 3.Ep2.135B.61.
Superiors? death! and Equals? what a curse! ..... 3.Ep2.135.61.
Before his Pride must his Superiors fall, ... Il.1.380.106.

SUPERIOUR

O King of Nations! whose superiour Sway ..... Il.19.143.377.
His manly Beauty, and superiour Size: ..... Il.22.466.474.

SUPERSTITION

Ev'n superstition loses ev'ry fear: ..... 2.ElAb.315.344.
'Till Superstition taught the tyrant awe, ... 3.EOM3.246.117.
A gen'rous faith, from superstition free, ... 6.57.9.169.
Atheism and Superstition rule by Turns; ..... 6.99.18.287.

SUPERSTITITION

With *Tyranny,* then *Superstitition* join'd, ... 1.EOC.687.317.

SUPINE

Thus fell the King; and laid on Earth Supine, ... 1.TrES.292.460.
Supine he tumbles on the crimson'd Sands, ... Il.4.603.250.
Can *Jove,* supine, flagitious Facts survey, ... Il.5.1068.317.
Supine he fell: Those Arms which *Mars* before ..... Il.7.177.372.
And pierc'd his Breast: supine he breath'd his last. ..... Il.11.186.43.

SUPINE (CONTINUED)

Supine he falls, and to his social Train ..... Il.13.694.138.
Supine, and Shades eternal veil his Eyes. ..... Il.14.522.188.
Supine he fell; his brazen Helmet rung. ..... Il.15.781.226.
Thus fell the King; and laid on Earth supine, ... Il.16.597.267.
Supine, and wildly gazing on the Skies, ... Il.16.1016.282.
His Ankle strook: The Giant fell supine: ..... Il.23.845.523.
And now supine, now prone, the Hero lay, ... Il.24.17.535.
Lay senseless, and supine, amidst the flock. ..... Od.9.355.321.
Dropt his huge head, and snoring lay supine. ..... Od.9.440.324.
There lay the King, and all the rest supine; ..... Od.14.592.66.

SUPINELY

Supinely falls, and grasps the bloody Dust. ..... Il.11.534A.57.

SUPP'D

And supp'd his Cordial as he sate upright: ..... 2.ChJM.387B.33.

SUPPERLESS

She ey'd the Bard, where supperless he sate, ... 5.DunA1.109.76.
Swearing and supperless the Hero sate, ... 5.DunB1.115.278.

SUPPERS

(Tho' Dinners oft they want and Suppers too) ..... 6.17iv.24.60.

SUPPLE

And suffer scorn, and bend the supple knee; ..... 6.22.9.71.
Aukward and supple, each Devoir to pay, ... 6.49i.17.138.
Their Joints they supple with dissolving Oil, ... Il.10.676.32.
Chafe ev'ry knot, and supple ev'ry pore. ..... Od.21.186.268.

SUPPLIANT

There Kings shall sue, and suppliant States be seen ..... 1.W-F.383.188.
Who more propitious to the suppliant Crowd, ... 1.TrSt.260.421.
Nor shalt thou, *Phœbus,* find a Suppliant here: ..... 1.TrSt.760.442.
Then, with his suppliant Hands upheld in Air, ... 1.TrUl.238.473.
Millions of suppliant Crowds the Shrine attend, ... 2.TemF.288.277.
Let not a suppliant Queen entreat in vain, ... 6.20.50.67.
Suppliant the Venerable Father stands, ... Il.1.17.86.
But Goddess! thou, thy suppliant Son attend, ... Il.1.510.112.
A Suppliant I from great *Atrides* come: ..... Il.1.577.115.
Suppliant the Goddess stood: One Hand she plac'd ..... Il.1.650.118.
O Sire of Gods and Men! thy Suppliant hear, ... Il.1.666.119.
The fallen Chief in suppliant Posture press'd ..... Il.6.55.326.
Such the Repentance of a suppliant King. ..... Il.9.395.452.
Yet some Redress to suppliant *Greece* afford, ... Il.9.398.452.
His suppliant Father, aged *Oeneus,* came; ..... Il.9.695.468.
Apollo heard; and suppliant as he stood, ... Il.16.647.269.
Who chas'd for Murder thence, a Suppliant came ..... Il.16.701.271.
Approach'd, and sought his Knees with suppliant Tears; ..... Il.21.75.424.
Not the same Mother gave thy Suppliant Breath, ... Il.21.107.426.
So shall thy Suppliant, strengthen'd from above, ... Il.24.385.552.
Till thus at last the Kingly Suppliant spoke, ... Il.24.597.561.
Suppliant my Childrens Murd'rer to implore, ... Il.24.632.563.
Release my Knees, thy suppliant Arts give o'er, ... Il.24.718.567.
The royal suppliant to *Minerva* pray'd. ..... Od.2.296.76.
There, suppliant to the Monarch of the flood, ... Od.3.7.86.
Suppliant he pray'd. And now the victims drest ..... Od.3.78.90.
Lo at thy knee his suppliant son appears. ..... Od.3.111.91.
A suppliant to your royal court I come. ..... Od.4.428.140.
She ceas'd, and suppliant thus I made reply; ..... Od.4.531.146.
I bend, a suppliant at thy wat'ry throne, ... Od.5.569.199.
And save a suppliant, and a man distrest. ..... Od.5.575.200.
Aw'd from access, I lift my suppliant hands; ..... Od.6.203.219.
The patient, heav'nly man thus suppliant pray'd ..... Od.7.1.232.
A suppliant bends: oh pity human woe! ..... Od.7.198.245.
To raise the lowly suppliant from the ground ..... Od.7.216.247.
Suppliant to her, since first he chose to pray, ... Od.7.386.255.
Who suppliant to the King and Peers, implores ..... Od.8.173.271.
I came a suppliant to fair *Circe's* bed, ... Od.10.568.370.
Then with his suppliant hands upheld in air, ... Od.13.405.26.
And suppliant stands, invoking every pow'r ..... Od.14.470.58.
Meet, for the wand'ring suppliant to provide. ..... Od.14.579.64.
Receive the suppliant! spare my destin'd blood! ..... Od.15.303.83.
To thee my son the suppliant I resign, ... Od.16.67.105.
Whom, to the Gods when suppliant fathers bow, ... Od.20.45.234.
Thy suppliant people, and receive their pray'r! ..... Od.22.67.290.
O gracious hear, nor let thy suppliant bleed; ..... Od.22.349.304.

SUPPLIANT'S

The first thus open'd: "Hear thy suppliant's call, ... 5.DunB4.403.381.
In vain he begs thee with a Suppliant's Moan, ... Il.20.539.416.
Some Pity to a Suppliant's Name afford, ... Il.21.86.425.
First to the Queen prefer a suppliant's claim, ... Od.7.69.237.
I meet the Monarch with a suppliant's face, ... Od.14.307.50.
To tempt their bounties with a suppliant's art, ... Od.17.434.154.
Base to insult who bears a suppliant's name, ... Od.21.335.276.

SUPPLIANTS

(Two wretched Suppliants) and for Mercy call? ..... Il.24.440.554.
Victors of late, but humble suppliants now! ..... Od.9.316.319.
The cause of suppliants, and revenge of wrong. ..... Od.16.441.128.
And injur'd suppliants seek in vain for aid. ..... Od.17.649.164.
Then in such robes as suppliants may require, ... Od.17.652.164.

SUPPLICATE

Com'st thou to supplicate th' Almighty Pow'r, ... Il.6.320.342.
Dubious to supplicate the chief, or fly ..... Od.22.371.305.

SUPPLICATES

See, where in vain he supplicates above, ... Il.22.285.468.

SUPPLICATING

They fill the Dome with supplicating Cries. ..... Il.6.375.344.
With piercing Cries, and supplicating Tears: ..... Il.9.702.469.
Thus, blind to Fate! with supplicating Breath, ... Il.16.64.238.

SUPPLIES

Like some fair *Flow'r* the early *Spring* supplies, ... 1.EOC.498.294.
Which the kind Soil with milky Sap supplies; .... 1.TrVP.103.381.
Abundantly supplies us all our Life: .... 2.ChJM.56.17.
His charitable Vanity supplies. .... 3.Ep4.172.153.
Thy charitable Vanity supplies. .... 3.Ep4.172A.153.
What thanks, what praise, if Peter but supplies! .... 4.JD2.67.139.
What thanks, what praise, If Coscus but supplies! .... 4.JD2.67A.139.
Each dropping pear a following pear supplies, ... 6.35.13.103.
The People one, and one supplies the King. .... 6.35.34.104.
Thence beauty, waking all her forms, supplies .... 6.52.45.157.
One grateful woman to thy fame supplies .... 6.72.7.208.
But safer Plunder thy own Host supplies; .... Il.2.287.141.
But ill thy Soul supplies a Form so fair. .... Il.3.64.192.
Th' unweary'd Blaze incessant Streams supplies, ... Il.5.7.266.
And thought the Steeds (your large Supplies unknown) .... Il.5.254.279.
Nor Wine's inflaming Juice supplies their Veins.) .... Il.5.426.289.
Another Race the following Spring supplies, ... Il.6.183.335.
And with th' untasted Food supplies her Care: .... Il.9.427.453.
Let gen'rous Food Supplies of Strength produce, ... Il.19.233.382.
With copious water the bright vase supplies .... Od.1.181.41.
Scarce all my wine their midnight hours supplies. .... Od.2.64.63.
Bread, that decaying man with strength supplies, ... Od.2.329.77.
To *Pyle* or *Sparta* to demand supplies, ... Od.2.368.78.
And asks a bark: the chief a bark supplies. .... Od.2.435.82.
But neither mead nor plain supplies, to feed .... Od.4.825.158.
Words to her dumb complaint a pause supplies, ... Od.4.954.162.
The Goddess last a gentle breeze supplies, ... Od.5.341.188.
The rising fire supplies with busy care, ... Od.7.8.233.
Each dropping pear a following pear supplies, ... Od.7.154.243.
The People one, and one supplies the King. .... Od.7.175.244.
Whose polish'd vase with copious streams supplies .... Od.7.232.247.
She gave me life, reliev'd with just supplies .... Od.7.380.255.
But wisdom the defect of form supplies: .... Od.8.188.272.
With copious water the bright vase supplies .... Od.10.435.365.
Immense supplies for ages yet to come! .... Od.14.362.51.
Haste to the Gen'ral, and demand supplies. .... Od.14.563.64.
No friend in *Ithaca* my place supplies, ... Od.15.102.73.
With copious streams the shining vase supplies .... Od.15.150.76.
Instant the swain the spoils of beasts supplies, ... Od.16.47.104.
With copious streams that golden ew'r supplies .... Od.17.106.137.
The pleasure past supplies a copious theme .... Od.19.681.229.
Richer than all th' *Achaian* state supplies, ... Od.21.110.264.
Or sacred *Elis,* to procure supplies; .... Od.24.496.372.

SUPPLY

Our plenteous Streams a various Race supply; .... 1.W-F.141.163.
Art from that Fund each *just Supply* provides, ... 1.EOC.74.247.
Let some kind nurse supply a mother's care: .... 1.TrFD.77.389.
Incite the Living, and supply the Dead. .... 1.TrES.305.461.
While glitt'ring Stars his absent Beams supply, ... 2.ChJM.369.32.
Snuff, or the *Fan,* supply each Pause of Chat, ... 2.RL3.17.170.
Eternal Snows the growing Mass supply, ... 2.TemF.57.256.
Let us (since Life can little more supply .... 3.EOM1.3.11.
See anger, zeal and fortitude supply; .... 3.EOM2.187.77.
See some fit Passion ev'ry age supply, ... 3.EOM2.273.87.
All forms that perish other forms supply, ... 3.EOM3.17.93.
Blest paper-credit! last and best supply! .... 3.Ep3.69.93.
"Oh say, what sums that gen'rous hand supply? .... 3.Ep3.277.116.
Let Courtly Wits to Wits afford supply, ... 4.EpS2.171.323.
Esteem the public love his best supply, ... 4.1740.91.337.
With reams abundant this abode supply; .... 5.DunA2.86.108.
With reams abundant this abode supply; .... 5.DunB2.90.300.
Manilius or Solinus shall supply: .... 5.DunB4.226.365.
Whose flocks supply him with attire, ... 6.1.6.3.
Such wholsome Foods as Nature's Wants supply, ... 6.17iii.26.58.
That begged with Letters to supply .... 6.30.5A.85.
And vanquish'd realms supply recording gold? .... 6.71.56.204.
And life itself can nothing more supply .... 6.147viii.1.392.
The middle Space suspected Troops supply, ... Il.4.344.237.
Till to supply his Place and rule the Car, ... Il.8.157.405.
Let num'rous Fires the absent Sun supply; .... Il.8.632.426.
Incite the Living, and supply the Dead. .... Il.16.610.268.
What human Strength and Prudence can supply; .... Il.17.716.315.
What Force of Thought and Reason can supply; .... Il.18.322.337.
And Heav'n with Strength supply the mighty Rage! .... Il.19.38.373.
No more shall *Nestor's* Hand your Food supply, ... Il.23.491.510.
A menial train the flowing bowl supply: .... Od.1.145.39.
(A sacred oath) if heav'n the pow'r supply, ... Od.2.169.70.
Whilst limpid springs the failing cask supply. .... Od.4.486.143.
Rich fragrant wines the cheering bowl supply; .... Od.4.842.158.
Propitious to my wants, a Vest supply .... Od.6.215.220.
Then food supply, and bathe his fainting limbs .... Od.6.249.222.
Then unguents in a vase of gold supply, ... Od.6.255.222.
(*Artacia's* streams alone supply the town:) .... Od.10.122.346.
But speaking tears the want of words supply, ... Od.10.291.357.
Doom'd to supply the Suitors wastful feast, ... Od.14.21.35.
To smooth thy passage, and supply thy sails: .... Od.15.42.71.
'Tis mine with food the hungry to supply, ... Od.16.83.106.
Supply the limpid wave, and fragrant oil: .... Od.17.101.136.
Supply his absence, and attend the herd. .... Od.17.225.142.
Thy other wants her subjects shall supply. .... Od.17.641.163.
Be it my task the torches to supply .... Od.18.363.185.
While yet th' auxiliar shafts this hand supply; .... Od.22.123.292.
The transports of her faithful heart supply .... Od.23.3.316.

SUPPLY'D

Is well by Wit's more lasting Flames supply'd. .... 1.TrSP.38.395.
Is well by Wit's more lasting Charms supply'd. .... 1.TrSP.38A.395.
Each want of happiness by Hope supply'd, ... 3.EOM2.285.89.
Then careful Heav'n supply'd two sorts of Men, ... 3.Ep3.13.84.
Her Trade supported, and supply'd her Laws; .... 4.2HE1.222.213.
My tears the want of off'rings had supply'd; .... 6.20.41.67.
One Grateful woman to thy fame supply'd .... 6.72.7A.208.
"While Pepper-Water-Worms thy Bait supply'd; .... 6.96ii.20.270.
Supply'd by *Phœbus,* fill the swelling Sails; .... Il.1.625.117.

SUPPLY'D (CONTINUED)

Their Ships, supply'd by *Agamemnon's* Care, ... Il.2.743.161.
And well the plenteous Freight supply'd the Host: .... Il.7.567.392.
At once the Tent and Ligature supply'd. .... Il.13.752.141.
His Hinds and Swains whole years shall be supply'd .... Il.23.988.528.
And Life, the just equivalent, supply'd .... Od.4.124.126.
Supply'd the cloth, capacious of the gales. .... Od.5.330.187.
The maids the viand, and the bowl supply'd: .... Od.6.296.225.
Her self supply'd the stores and rich array; .... Od.7.351.253.
We thus supply'd, (for twelve were all the fleet.) .... Od.9.187.313.
Reserv'd in bowls, supply'd his nightly feast. .... Od.9.294.318.
(The twining bands the *Cyclop's* bed supply'd) .... Od.9.508.327.
With twining osiers which the bank supply'd. .... Od.10.193.349.
A freshning breeze the * Magic pow'r supply'd, ... Od.11.7.379.
And verdant leaves the flow'ry cake supply'd. .... Od.12.422.451.
A willing widow's copious wealth supply'd. .... Od.14.243.48.
His shaggy cloak a mountain goat supply'd: .... Od.14.597.66.
And constant, *Jove* supply'd the gentle gale. .... Od.15.512.94.
But four Cœlestials both your cares supply'd. .... Od.20.81.236.
Melanthius from an ample jar supply'd: .... Od.20.319.248.
And hence the villain has supply'd their war. .... Od.22.171.295.

SUPPLYD

These *smart, new Characters* supplyd. .... 6.44.22.123.

SUPPLYING

For thee supplying, in the worst of days, ... 5.DunA1.167.83.

SUPPORT

And fix'd support the Weight of all the War: .... 1.TrES.154.455.
The Ease, Support, and Lustre of your Life, ... 4.HAdv.79.83.
Seeks from the Stage his vile Support to gain: .... 4.JD2A.14.132.
"These, only these, support to the crouded stage, ... 4.2HE1.87.201.
"Harley, the Nation's great Support,"— .... 4.1HE7.83.273.
Four guardian Virtues, round, support her Throne; .... 5.DunA1.44.65.
Four guardina Virtues, round, support her throne: .... 5.DunB1.46.274.
Thou Cibber! thou, his Laurel shalt support, ... 5.DunB1.299.291.
Support his front, and Oaths bring up the rear: .... 5.DunB1.308.292.
For 'tis a Pleasure to support a Friend. .... 6.96iii.36.275.
Let Clarke make half his life the poor's support, ... 6.147vi.1.391.
Trust in his Omen, and support the War. .... Il.2.387.145.
The Nerves unbrac'd support his Limbs no more; .... Il.4.536.247.
And scarce my Heart support its Load of Pain. .... Il.10.101.7.
Two Feet support it, and four Handles hold; .... Il.11.775.69.
And fix'd support the Weight of all the Fight. .... Il.12.508.100.
To head my *Lycians,* and support the Fight. .... Il.16.646.269.
Whose Arms support him, reeling thro' the Throng, ... Il.23.808.521.
Not undeserving, some support obtain. .... Od.15.335.85.
Poor suff'ring heart! he cry'd, support the pain .... Od.20.23.232.
Or if each other's wrongs ye still support, ... Od.20.382.251.
Support him, round the lov'd *Ulysses* thrown; .... Od.24.404.368.

SUPPORTED

Man, like the gen'rous vine, supported lives; .... 3.EOM3.311.125.
Her Trade supported, and supply'd her Laws; .... 4.2HE1.222.213.
Supported by the Chiefs on either Hand, ... Il.1.452A.109.
Supported on their Spears, they took their way, ... Il.14.45.160.
Supported on his better Hand he stay'd; .... Il.16.631.269.
On these supported, with unequal Gait, ... Il.18.491.345.
Her feet supported with a stool of state; .... Od.1.172.40.
Perhaps supported at another's board, ... Od.14.49.38.

SUPPORTING

His Bulk supporting on the shatter'd Shield. .... Il.7.326.380.
Supporting with his Hands the Hero's Head, ... Il.23.168.496.
And then (supporting on his arm his head) .... Od.14.557.64.

SUPPORTS

And drawn supports, upheld by God, or thee? .... 3.EOM1.34.17.
The Wood supports the Plain, the parts unite, ... 3.Ep4.81.145.
Supports with homely food his drooping age, ... Od.1.248.45.

SUPPOSE

Our Knight (who study'd much, we may suppose) .... 2.ChJM.442.36.
Our Fathers prais'd rank Ven'son. You suppose .... 4.HS2.91.61.
Suppose that honest Part that rules us all, ... 4.HAdv.87.83.
Suppose he wants a year, will you compound? .... 4.2HE1.57.199.
Of little use the Man you may suppose, ... 4.2HE1.201.211.
Suppose I censure—you know what I mean— .... 4.EpS2.32.314.
Well, Sir, suppose, the *Busto's* a damn'd head, ... 6.105vi.1.302.
Suppose, that *Pope's* an Elf; .... 6.105vi.2.302.
Suppose the Man an Elf; .... 6.105vi.2B.302.
(Whatever stinking Fops suppose) .... 6.135.30.367.
Suppose some Hero should his Spoils resign, ... Il.2.318.142.
And yet suppose these Measures I forego, ... Il.22.154.459.

SUPPRESS

Suppress them, or miscall them Policy? .... 3.Ep1.76A.21.
Suppress them, half, or call them Policy? .... 3.Ep1.76.21.
Hard as it is, my Vengeance I suppress: .... Il.1.289.100.
Suppress thy Passion, and the King revere: .... Il.4.467.242.
Suppress (my Son) this Rage of Grief, and know .... Il.19.11.371.
Suppress thy Impulse, nor reject Advice. .... Il.24.368.551.
When great *Ulysses* shall suppress these harms, ... Od.3.267.98.
The tyde of flowing tears a-while suppress; .... Od.18.205.177.

SUPPRESS'D

Clos'd his dim Eye, and Fate suppress'd his Breath. .... Il.5.109.272.
He ceas'd; the Fates suppress'd his lab'ring Breath, ... Il.16.619.268.

SUPPREST

He ceas'd; the Fates suppress his lab'ring Breath, ... 1.TrES.314.461.
I can no more; by shame, by rage suppress, ... 2.ElAb.105.328.
Thrice Budgel aim'd to speak, but thrice suppress .... 5.DunA2.365.144.
Thrice Budgel aim'd to speak, but thrice suppress .... 5.DunB2.397.316.
'Till Fate scarce felt his gentle Breath suppress, ... 6.19.13.62.

SUPPREST (CONTINUED)

'Till death scarce felt his gentle Breath supprest, ...6.19.13B.62.
But in the rock my flowing tears supprest, ...6.20.31.67.
Soon as the Rage of Hunger was supprest, ...II.2.514.151.
The prudent Goddess yet her Wrath supprest, ...II.4.32.222.
I thought (but some kind God that Thought supprest) ....II.9.588.463.
By *Sparta* slain! for ever now supprest ....II.17.85.291.
He ceas'd. The Fates supprest his lab'ring Breath, ...II.22.453.474.
The rage of thirst and hunger now supprest, ...Od.3.602.117.
Compos'd at length, the gushing tears supprest, ...Od.10.592.372.
Cautious the name of *Scylla* I supprest; ....Od.12.266.445.
His ardour strait th' obedient Prince supprest, ...Od.21.137.265.

SUPREAM

He, who Supream in Judgment, as in Wit, ...1.EOC.657.314.

SUPREME

All Wealth, all Honours, the supreme Degree ....2.ChJM.633.45.
Fair Virtue's silent Train: Supreme of these ....2.TemF.170.268.
One supreme State, so excellently ill; ....4.JD2A.4.132.
Tyrant supreme! shall three Estates command, ...5.DunB4.603.403.
A Soul supreme, in each hard Instance try'd, ...6.84.23.239.
But Royal Scandal his Delight supreme. ....II.2.270.140.
Supreme of Gods! unbounded, and alone! ....II.2.491.150.
Supreme of Gods! unbounded, and alone: ....II.7.244.376.
Supreme he sits; and sees, in Pride of Sway, ...II.15.116.201.
Himself supreme in Valour, as in Sway. ....II.16.209.247.
Oh thou Supreme! high-thron'd, all Height above! ....II.16.284.250.
And whom the *Greeks* supreme by Conquest know, ...II.23.764.520.
Thee first in Virtue, as in Pow'r supreme, ...II.23.1054.533.
Th' assembly thus the Sire supreme addrest; ....Od.1.37.31.
O *Jove*, supreme, whom Gods and men revere! ....Od.4.457.141.
To fate's supreme dispose the dead resign, ...Od.4.733.153.
Supreme in might, sublime in majesty. ....Od.5.7.171.
O'er whom supreme, imperial pow'r I bear: ....Od.8.426.286.
Nor yet forgot old Ocean's dread Supreme ....Od.13.144.12.
O *Jove!* supreme! whom men and Gods revere; ....Od.17.148.138.
"Shou'd He, long honour'd in supreme command, ...Od.19.170.200.
By *Jove*, the source of good, supreme in pow'r! ....Od.19.347.211.
(The God supreme, to whose eternal eye ....Od.20.90.237.
O *Jove* supreme, the raptur'd swain replies, ...Od.20.294.247.
Should he, long honour'd with supreme command, ...Od.24.162.356.
Oh Pow'r supreme, oh ruler of the whole! ....Od.24.543.374.

SUPREMELY

Supremely blest, the poet in his muse. ....3.EOM2.270.87.
And every Dog's Supremely blest. ....6.135.61Z2.368.
And more than Men, or Gods, supremely wise, ...II.13.448.127.
Above the Thought of Man, supremely wise! ....II.13.790.142.
Supremely tall, and shade the deeps below. ....Od.1.240.44.
Unchang'd, immortal, and supremely blest! ....Od.4.94.124.
The Gods, when they supremely bless, bestow ....Od.6.223.220.
Dear to us all, to me supremely dear! ....Od.23.62.321.

SUPREMEST

Thron'd in omnipotence, supremest *Jove* ....Od.4.325.134.

SURCEASE

Bade share the Honours, and surcease the Strife. ....II.23.970.527.

SURCHARG'D

Low sinks the Scale surcharg'd with *Hector's* Fate; ....II.22.275.467.
Each to a crib with choicest grain surcharg'd; ....Od.4.50.122.

SURCINGLE

Gave him the cassock, surcingle, and vest; ....5.DunA2.326.141.
Gave him the cassock, surcingle, and vest. ....5.DunB2.350.314.

SURE

Be sure *your self* and your own *Reach* to know, ...1.EOC.48.244.
Sure to hate most the Men from whom they *learn'd.* ....1.EOC.107.251.
With sure *Returns* of still *expected Rhymes.* ....1.EOC.349.279.
Those *Heads* as *Stomachs* are not sure the best ....1.EOC.388.284.
Sure *some* to vex, but never *all* to *please;* ....1.EOC.505.295.
As Shameful sure as *Impotence* in *Love.* ....1.EOC.533.297.
And *speak,* tho' *sure,* with *seeming Diffidence:* ....1.EOC.567.305.
Speak when you're *sure,* yet speak with *Diffidence;* ....1.EOC.567A.305.
The *Muses* sure *Longinus* did inspire, ...1.EOC.675A.316.
Sure 'twas not much to bid one kind Adieu, ...1.TrSP.111.398.
And sure the Monarch whom they have, to hate; ....1.TrSt.227.420.
To sure Destruction dooms the *Grecian* Wall; ....1.TrES.24.450.
To sure Destruction dooms th' aspiring Wall; ....1.TrES.24A.450.
And cautious sure; for Wisdom is in Age: ....2.ChJM.207.24.
My Joys are full, my Happiness is sure. ....2.ChJM.267.27.
And made all sure enough with Holiness. ....2.ChJM.314.29.
The poor Adorer sure had hang'd, or drown'd: ....2.ChJM.437.36.
'Tis better sure, when Blind, deceiv'd to be, ...2.ChJM.502.39.
Blind as he was, not doubting All was sure, ...2.ChJM.541.41.
And lastly that which sure your Mind must move, ...2.ChJM.561.42.
But sure it was a merrier Fit, she swore, ...2.ChJM.746.51.
And sure the certain Stint was ne'er defin'd. ....2.ChWB.16.57.
Sure to be lov'd, I took no Pains to please, ...2.ChWB.62.59.
Be sure my fine Complexion must be prais'd: ....2.ChWB.111.62.
For 'tis as sure as Cold ingenders Hail, ...2.ChWB.217.67.
And many more than sure the Church approves. ....2.ChWB.362.74.
Nor could it sure be such a Sin to paint. ....2.RL5.24.201.
This sure is bliss (if bliss on earth there be) ....2.ElAb.97.327.
'Tis sure the hardest science to forget! ....2.ElAb.190.335.
And sure if fate some future Bard shall join ....2.ElAb.359.348.
Sure never to o'er-shoot, but just to hit, ...3.EOM3.89.101.
Sure by quick Nature happiness to gain, ...3.EOM3.91.101.
Sure as De-moivre, without rule or line? ....3.EOM3.104.102.
How much of other each is sure to cost; ....3.EOM4.271.153.
"One would not, sure, be frightful when one's dead— ....3.Ep1.246.36.
Yet ne'er so sure our passion to create, ...3.Ep2.51.54.
"Yet Cloe sure was form'd without a spot—" ....3.Ep2.157.63.

SURE (CONTINUED)

Sure, if they catch, to spoil the Toy at most, ...3.Ep2.233.69.
Yet sure, of qualities deserving praise, ...3.Ep3.202Z1.110.
Constant at Church, and Change; his gains were sure, ...3.Ep3.347.122.
He came by sure Transition to his own: ....4.JD4.81.31.
Well met (he cries) and happy sure for each, ...4.JD4.66A.31.
"Obliging Sir! for Courts you sure were made: ....4.JD4.86.33.
In *sure Succession* to the Day of Doom: ....4.JD4.161.39.
Sure, worthy Sir, the Diff'rence is not great, ...4.HAdv.75.81.
Our ancient Kings (and sure those Kings were wise, ...4.HAdv.112.85.
"I too could write, and sure am twice as tall, ...4.Arbu.103A.103.
And when I die, be sure you let me know ....4.Arbu.123.104.
A Plague, whose strange Infection men are sure, ...4.JD2A.9.132.
And if unwatch'd is sure t' omit Ses Heires: ....4.JD2A.103.140.
Language so harsh, 'tis sure enough to tear ....4.JD2A.65.138.
(And little sure imported to remove, ...4.2HE2.56.169.
Sure I should want the Care of ten *Monroes,* ....4.2HE2.70.169.
But sure no Statute in his favour says, ...4.2HE2.288.185.
Sure fate of all, beneath whose rising ray ....4.2HE1.19.195.
"But, for the Passions, Southern sure and Rowe. ....4.2HE1.86.201.
With laughter sure Democritus had dy'd, ...4.2HE1.320.223.
The people, sure, the people are the sight! ....4.2HE1.323.223.
The Man that loves and laughs, must sure do well. ....4.1HE6.129.246.
Then better sure it Charity becomes ....4.EpS2.48.315.
Sure, if I spare the Minister, no rules ....4.EpS2.146.321.
Sure, if they cannot cut, it may be said ....4.EpS2.148.321.
To lie in bed, but sure they lay too long. ....4.1740.22.333.
And sure succession down from Heywood's days. ....5.DunA1.96.70.
(Sure sign, that no spectator shall be drown'd). ....5.DunA2.166.121.
The sure fore-runner of her gentle sway. ....5.DunA3.304.185.
And sure succession down from Heywood's days. ....5.DunB1.98.276.
Guard the sure barrier between that and Sense; ....5.DunB1.178.283.
Yet sure had Heav'n decreed to save the State, ...5.DunB1.195.283.
(Sure sign, that no spectator shall be drown'd) ....5.DunB2.174.304.
The sure fore-runner of her gentle sway: ....5.DunB2.302.334.
None need a guide, by sure Attraction led, ...5.DunB4.75.348.
Else sure some Bard, to our eternal praise, ...5.DunB4.171.357.
For sure, if Dulness sees a grateful Day, ...5.DunB4.181.359.
Be sure I give them Fragments, not a Meal; ....5.DunB4.230.365.
With the same Cement, ever sure to bind, ...5.DunB4.267.370.
Sure you, the goddess we adore, ...6.4iii.7.10.
But Sense must sure thy safest Plunder be, ...6.7.13.16.
Sure *Bavius* copy'd *Mævius* to the full, ...6.7.19.16.
(For so one sure may call that Head, ...6.10.27.25.
Sure to charm all was his peculiar Fate, ...6.19.5.62.
Sure just and modest this request appears, ...6.20.52.67.
And sure such kind good creatures may be living. ....6.41.28.114.
Yet sure the Best are most severely fated, ...6.60.3.178.
And like sure Spaniels, at first Scent lie down. ....6.82vi.6.232.
And sure if ought below the Seats Divine ....6.84.21.239.
Yet sure if ought below the Seats Divine ....6.84.21A.239.
"Sure in that Lake he dropt—My *Grilly's* drown'd"— ....6.96ii.23.270.
And Mistress *Biddel* sure is Fifty three. ....6.96iv.24.276.
'Tis sure some Virtue to conceal its Shame. ....6.96v.20.280.
But sure in this no Vanity is shown; ....6.105ii.3A.300.
And sure a *Printer* is his Match, ...6.116ii.8.326.
But sure you'll find it hard to spoil ....6.119.14.337.
And sure of all Devils this must be the best, ...6.122.3.341.
O! sure to King George 'tis a dismal disaster, ...6.122.17.342.
Sure *Bounce* is one you never read of. ....6.135.8.366.
"Yet Cloë sure was form'd without a Spot—" ....6.139.1.377.
Our ancient kings (and sure those kings were wise) ....6.147i.1.390.
Of sure Protection by thy Pow'r and Sword. ....II.1.100.92.
'Tis sure, the Mighty will revenge at last. ....II.1.106.92.
Sure, to so short a Race of Glory born, ...II.1.462.110.
For sure such Courage Length of Life denies, ...II.6.514.351.
But sure some God denies me to destroy ....II.8.363.414.
And sure all this may move his mighty Soul. ....II.9.208.442.
And shun Contention, the sure Source of Woe; ....II.9.335.450.
Sure ev'ry wise and worthy Man will love. ....II.9.451.454.
But sure till now no Coursers struck my Sight ....II.10.648.30.
And, sure of Glory, dare immortal Deeds. ....II.11.374.51.
For sure to warn us *Jove* his Omen sent, ...II.12.255.90.
Sure Heav'n resumes the little Sense it lent. ....II.12.272.91.
To sure Destruction dooms th' aspiring Wall; ....II.12.368.94.
But sure thou spring'st not from a soft Embrace, ...II.16.47.237.
No Hand so sure of all th' *Emathian* Line, ...II.16.232.248.
Sure where such partial Favour Heav'n bestow'd, ...II.17.105.291.
For sure he knows not, distant on the Shore, ...II.17.723.315.
The bravest sure that ever bore the Name; ....II.18.510.346.
Sure, tho' he wars for *Troy,* he claims our Aid. ....II.20.348.408.
But Pow'rs cœlestial sure this Foe defend. ....II.20.398.411.
Sure I shall see yon' Heaps of *Trojans* kill'd ....II.21.64.424.
Yet sure He too is mortal; He may feel ....II.21.671.450.
Sure of the Vapour in the tainted Dews, ...II.22.247.465.
Invades my Ear? 'Tis sure my Mother's Voice. ....II.22.579.480.
For sure one Star its baneful Beam display'd ....II.22.610.481.
While with sure Skill, tho' with inferior Steeds, ...II.23.393.506.
The Monarch sate; from whence with sure survey ....II.23.534.511.
Lie sure disabled in the middle Field: ....II.23.545.511.
Yet sure he seems, (to judge by Shape and Air,) ....II.23.554.511.
For sure he seem'd not of terrestrial Line! ....II.24.324.550.
Heav'n sure has arm'd thee with a Heart of Steel, ...II.24.657.564.
For sure *Ulysses* in your look appears, ...Od.1.269.45.
Sure-founded on a fair Maternal fame, ...Od.1.278.46.
Soon may kind heav'n a sure relief provide, ...Od.1.328.48.
And form sure plans to save the sinking state. ....Od.1.357.49.
A sure presage from ev'ry wing that flew. ....Od.2.188.71.
Destruction sure o'er all your heads impends; ....Od.2.191.71.
And sure he will: For Wisdom never lies. ....Od.3.26.87.
Or sure *Ægystus* had not dar'd the deed. ....Od.3.315.101.
And sure he will, for *Menelas* is wise. ....Od.3.420.107.
But sure relentless folly steels thy breast, ...Od.4.39.122.
The shepherd swains with sure abundance blest, ...Od.4.109.125.
A Goddess sure! for more than mortal grace ....Od.4.509.144.
Recoiling, on his head is sure to fall. ....Od.4.893.160.

SURE (CONTINUED)

No footing sure affords the faithless sand, ...Od.5.530.198.
Would *Jove* destroy him, sure he had been driv'n ......Od.6.289.224.
A sure defence from every storm that blows. ....Od.6.316.226.
The sure enclosure folds the genial bed; ....Od.8.322.281.
(Tho' sure our vine the largest cluster yields, ...Od.9.423.323.
As sure, as *Neptune* cannot give thee sight. ....Od.9.614.332.
They, seal'd with truth return the sure reply, ...Od.11.182.390.
O King! for such thou art, and sure thy blood ....Od.11.450.406.
But sure the eye of Time beholds no name ....Od.11.591.412.
O cruel thou! some fury sure has steel'd ....Od.12.333.448.
Sure fixt on Virtue may your nation stand, ...Od.13.60.4.
(Sure fate of ev'ry mortal excellence!) ....Od.13.77.5.
Yet sure the Gods their impious acts detest, ...Od.14.101.40.
Find sure tormentors in the guilty breast; ....Od.14.108.41.
Much woe to all, but sure to me the most. ....Od.14.159.43.
(And sure the thought was dictated by *Jove*, ...Od.14.302.50.
And sure the warning Vision was from high: ....Od.14.561.64.
Fate owes thee sure a miserable end! ....Od.15.347.86.
But heav'n will sure revenge, and Gods there are. ......Od.16.139.109.
Who loves his Prince; for sure you merit love. ....Od.16.331.121.
And the sure oracles of righteous *Jove*. ....Od.16.419.126.
Of this sure Auguries the Gods bestow'd, ...Od.17.184.140.
And with sure eyes inspecting all mankind. ....Od.17.581.160.
Sure of defeat, before the Peers engage; ....Od.18.38.168.
For sure I am, if stern *Ulysses* breathe, ...Od.18.177.175.
By the sure precept of the sylvan shrine. ....Od.19.341.210.
"A sure memorial of my dreaded fame ....Od.19.479.220.
And by his sword the Suitors sure to bleed. ....Od.19.653.227.
Sure thro' six circlets flew the whizzing dart. ....Od.19.673.229.
My sure divinity shall bear the shield, ...Od.20.61.235.
I deem it sure a vision of the skies. ....Od.20.109.238.
The Peers reproach the sure Divine of Fate; ....Od.20.432.254.
Some other like it sure the man must know, ...Od.21.432.281.
One sure of six shall reach *Ulysses'* heart: ....Od.22.277.300.
Scarce sure of life, look round, and trembling move ....Od.22.419.308.
Time shall the truth to sure remembrance bring: ....Od.23.115.325.
And now, ev'n now it melts! for sure I see ....Od.23.177.329.
Then hear sure evidence, while we display ....Od.23.189.332.
Conducted sure by heav'n! for heav'n alone ....Od.24.462.370.

SURE-FOUNDED

Sure-founded on a fair Maternal fame, ...Od.1.278.46.

SURELY

As surely seize thee, as I saw too well. ....2.ChJM.771.52.
(And surely, Heav'n and I are of a mind) ....3.Ep3.8.83.
"Yet surely, surely, these were famous men! ....4.2HE1.79.201.
"Yet surely, surely, these were famous men! ....4.2HE1.79.201.
Nor could that fabled dart more surely wound: ....6.14iii.8.46.
Nor did that fabled dart more surely wound: ....6.14iii.8A.46.
Oh! that as surely great *Apollo's* dart, ...Od.17.300.146.

SURER

And seeks a surer State, and courts thy gentle Reign. ..6.8.15.18.
And guides it surer to the Mark in view; ....6.17i(a).4.55.
To seek a surer Javelin in his Tent. ....Il.13.224.116.
Or if a surer, great *Patroclus!* thine. ....Il.16.233.248.
What earthly can implore a surer aid? ....Od.4.1082.168.

SUREST

The surest Virtues thus from Passions shoot, ...3.EOM2.183.77.
And that the Rampart, late our surest Trust, ...Il.14.73.161.

SURETY

He suffers who gives surety for th' unjust: ....Od.8.386.284.

SURETYSHIP

'Twas only Suretyship that brought 'em there. ....4.JD2.70.139.

SURFACE

The trembling Surface, by the Motion stir'd, ...2.TemF.438.284.
On Learning's surface we but lie and nod. ....5.DunB4.242.366.
The whitening Surface of the ruffled Deep. ....Il.2.178.137.
Yet o'er the silver Surface pure they flow, ...Il.2.912.167.
First move the whitening Surface of the Seas, ...Il.4.479.243.
The best that e'er on Earth's broad Surface run, ...Il.5.330.282.
Its Surface bristled with a quiv'ring Wood; ....Il.11.699.66.
And last with Flour the smiling Surface strows. ....Il.11.783.70.
His whirling Wheels the glassy Surface sweep; ....Il.13.42.107.
As when old Ocean's silent Surface sleeps, ...Il.14.21.157.
The extended Surface, drunk with Fat and Gore; ....Il.17.453.304.
With Brass refulgent the broad Surface shin'd, ...Il.17.560.310.
And god-like Labours on the Surface rose. ....Il.18.556.348.
Scarce on the Surface curl'd the briny Dew. ....Il.20.273.405.
Now sailing smooth the level surface sweep, ...Od.5.66.175.
And on the surface shone the holy store. ....Od.11.34.381.

SURFEIT

In which none e'er could surfeit, none could starve. ..4.JD2.120.143.

SURFIET

In which none 'ere cou'd surfiet, none could starve ...4.JD2A.126.142.

SURGE

The surge, and plunge his Father in the deep; ....3.Ep3.354.122.
Now breaks the Surge, and wide the bottom bares. ....Il.11.400.52.
Roars the resounding Surge with Men and Horse. ....Il.21.19.422.
Ploughs thro' the boiling Surge his desp'rate Way. ....Il.21.256.431.
So oft' the Surge, in wat'ry Mountains spread, ...Il.21.305.433.
Charge the black Surge, and pour it on his Head. ......Il.21.365.435.
The crimson Surge, and delug'd him with Blood. ....Il.21.383.436.
The crooked keel the parting surge divides, ...Od.2.468.83.
Far on the swelling surge the chief was born: ....Od.5.406.192.
Heav'd on the surge with intermitting breath, ...Od.5.498.196.
Back to the seas the rowling surge may sweep, ...Od.5.536.198.

SURGE (CONTINUED)

'Till the huge surge roll'd off. Then backward sweep ..Od.5.548.198.
Beyond the beating surge his course he bore, ...Od.5.558.199.
Rough from the tossing surge *Ulysses* moves; ....Od.6.162.216.
Climb the steep surge, and thro' the tempest fly; .....Od.6.326.227.
The surge impell'd me on a craggy coast. ....Od.7.363.254.
Firm-rooted in the surge a ship should stand ....Od.8.620.296.
And all unseen the surge and rowling sea, ...Od.9.170.312.
Thus o'er the rolling surge the vessel flies, ...Od.12.1.427.
Plows o'er that roaring surge its desp'rate way; ......Od.12.80.435.
Lash the wild surge, and bluster in the skies; ....Od.12.342.448.
Past sight of shore, along the surge we bound, ...Od.12.473.454.
Heav'd by the surge and wafted by the breeze. ....Od.12.530.458.
Firm-rooted in the surge a ship shou'd stand; ....Od.13.203.15.
Then, when the surge in thunder mounts the sky, ...Od.23.251.335.
How struggling thro' the surge, he reach'd the shores ...Od.23.359.342.

SURGEON

The good Wife to the Surgeon sent, ...6.94.37.260.
The Surgeon with a *Rabbit* came, ...6.94.41.260.

SURGEONS

Of two fam'd Surgeons, *Podalirius* stands ....Il.11.968.78.
Him to the Surgeons of the Camp he sent; ....Il.13.283.119.

SURGES

But when loud Surges lash the sounding Shore, ...1.EOC.368.282.
With Dread beheld the rolling Surges sweep ....1.TrSt.59.412.
And heaves huge Surges to the trembling Shores: ....Il.2.250.139.
Loud as the Surges when the Tempest blows, ...Il.2.471.149.
Between where *Tenedos* the Surges lave, ...Il.13.51.107.
The forests murmur, and the surges roar, ...Od.1.64.33.
And the winds whistle, and the surges roll ....Od.3.368.104.
The surges now subside, the tempest ends; ....Od.4.693.151.
The fleet swift tilting o'er the surges flew, ...Od.4.797.156.
Of murm'ring surges breaking on the shore: ....Od.5.517.197.
Sole on a plank, on boiling surges tost, ...Od.7.337.253.
Old Ocean shook, and back his surges flew. ....Od.9.582.330.

SURGING

High o'er the surging Tide, by Leaps and Bounds, ...Il.21.352.435.
Of surging waves, and steer the steady course) ....Od.5.328.187.
A Raft was form'd to cross the surging sea; ....Od.7.350.253.

SURGY

This toilsom voyage o'er the surgy main? ....Od.4.424.140.
A Lion now, he curls a surgy mane; ....Od.4.615.148.
From *Cephalenia* cross the surgy main ....Od.20.233.244.
Nor saw gay vessel stem the surgy plain, ...Od.23.287.337.

SURLY

Which made old Ben, and surly Dennis swear, ...4.2HE1.388.229.
Another in a surly fit, ...4.HS6.55.253.
Then to the Ships with surly Speed he went, ...Il.13.223.116.
A surly vagrant of the giant kind, ...Od.18.3.166.
Yon surly mendicants contentious stand; ....Od.18.47.169.
Stern as the surly lion o'er his prey, ...Od.23.50.321.
(Some surly Islander, of manners rude) ....Od.24.307.364.

SURMIS'D

In *South-sea* days not happier, when surmis'd ....4.HS2.133.65.

SURMIZE

'Tis impious to surmize, the pow'rs divine ....Od.4.995.164.
(For watchful Age is ready to surmize) ....Od.15.482.93.
Mov'd by no weak surmize, but sense of shame, ...Od.21.347.276.

SURMIZES

Hence guilty joys, distastes, surmizes, ...6.51ii.37.154.

SURPASS'D

No less, than Mortals are surpass'd by thine: ....1.TrUl.174.471.
Whose Throat surpass'd the Force of fifty Tongues. ...Il.5.979.313.
Surpass'd the Nymphs of *Troy's* illustrious Race) ..Il.6.315.341.
None but *Orion* e'er surpass'd their height. ....Od.11.380.401.
No less than mortals are surpass'd by thine. ....Od.13.341.24.

SURPAST

Melas and *Agrius*, but (who surpast ....Il.14.132.164.
(Whose Feet for Swiftness in the Race surpast) ....Il.20.473.414.
Behold! the Man whose matchless Art surpast ....Il.23.612.514.
Surpast *Iphyclus* in the swift Career, ...Il.23.731.519.
Ulysses next; and he whose Speed surpast ....Il.23.883.524.
Leonteus next a little space surpast, ...Il.23.997.529.
Whose well-taught mind the present age surpast, ...Od.7.210.247.

SURPRISE

A weaker may surprise, a stronger take? ....3.EOM3.276.120.
That view vouchsaf'd, let instant death surprise .....Od.7.305.250.

SURPRIZ'D

Surpriz'd at this, her trembling hand she heaves ......1.TrFD.45.387.
Surpriz'd at better, or surpriz'd at worse. ....4.1HE6.23.237.
Surpriz'd at better, or surpriz'd at worse. ....4.1HE6.23.237.
Confus'd, unactive, or surpriz'd with Fear; ....Il.4.257.233.
Surpriz'd the Monarch feels, yet void of Fear ....Il.11.329.49.

SURPRIZE

The Swain in barren Deserts with surprize ....1.Mes.67.118.
But *more advanc'd*, behold with strange Surprize ....1.EOC.223.265.
But *more advanc'd*, survey with strange Surprize ....1.EOC.223A.265.
No single Parts unequally surprize; ....1.EOC.249.268.
Hear how *Timotheus'* vary'd Lays surprize, ...1.EOC.374.283.
Hear how *Timotheus'* various Lays surprize, ...1.EOC.374A.283.
To pass the Fences, and surprize the Fair? ....1.TrVP.26.378.
Whom wou'd not all those blooming Charms surprize, ...1.TrSP.21.394.

SURPRIZE (CONTINUED)
And views their Arms and Habit with Surprize. 1.TrSt.566.434.
Th' *Inachians* view the Slain with vast Surprize, 1.TrSt.727.440.
Th' *Inachians* view'd the Slain with vast Surprize, 1.TrSt.727A.440.
Slight Lines of Hair surprize the Finny Prey, 2.RL2.26.161.
Already half turn'd Traytor by surprize. 4.JD4.169.39.
Procure a *Taste* to double the surprize, 4.1HE6.30.239.
Thus *Churchill's* race shall other hearts surprize, 6.52.59.157.
Wond'ring we hear, and fix'd in deep Surprize Il.3.287.207.
Distracted with Surprize, she seem'd to fly, Il.6.484.350.
With like Surprize arose *Menætius'* Son: Il.9.259.445.
Thus watch'd the *Grecians,* cautious of Surprize, Il.10.219.11.
The God of War had own'd a just Surprize. Il.13.176.113.
As soon shall freeze Mankind with dire Surprize, Il.15.106.200.
Back shrink the *Myrmidons* with dread Surprize, Il.19.17.372.
Thus stood th' Attendants stupid with Surprize; Il.24.594.561.
And view'd his filial love with vast surprize; Od.4.154.127.
To that recess, commodious for surprize, Od.4.549.146.
The ministers of blood in dark surprize: Od.4.708.152.
Th' unwonted scene surprize and rapture drew; Od.7.179.244.
In subjects happy! with surprize I gaze; Od.8.419.286.
Or thieves insidious thy fair flock surprize? Od.9.483.325.
Aghast the *Scherians* stand in deep surprize; Od.13.190.15.
Then with surprize (surprize chastis'd by fears) Od.16.196.113.
Then with surprize (surprize chastis'd by fears) Od.16.196.113.
What miracle thus dazzles with surprize! Od.19.44.195.
The woof unwrought the Suitor-train surprize. Od.19.177.200.
With joy, and vast surprize, th' applauding train Od.19.532.221.
Ulysses will surprize th' unfinish'd game Od.19.685.229.
The unknown instrument with strange surprize, Od.23.290.337.

SURPRIZES
Surprizes, varies, and conceals the Bounds. 3.Ep4.56.142.
Dangers, doubts, delays, surprizes; 6.51ii.39.154.

SURREY
Here noble *Surrey* felt the sacred Rage, 1.W-F.291.175.
Surrey, the *Granville* of a former Age: 1.W-F.292.175.

SURROUND
Swarm o'er the Lawns, the Forest Walks surround, 1.W-F.149.164.
And this fair Vine, but that her Arms surround 1.TrVP.65.380.
The Youth surround her with extended Spears; 1.TrSt.723.440.
Or some fair Isle which *Neptune's* Arms surround? 1.TrUl.115.469.
The Female Tribe surround him as he lay, 2.ChJM.412.34.
The busy *Sylphs* surround their darling Care; 2.RL1.145.157.
And various Animals his Sides surround; 2.TemF.235.274.
Of these a gloomy Tribe surround the Throne, 2.TemF.412.283.
The Youth with Instruments surround the Fire: Il.1.609.117.
The Chiefs surround the destin'd Beast, and take Il.2.486.150.
In gather'd Swarms surround the Rural Bow'rs; Il.2.555.154.
Whom strong *Tyrinthè's* lofty Walls surround, Il.2.678.159.
And everlasting Shades his Eyes surround. Il.5.64.269.
Where Lakes surround low *Hylè's* watry Plain; Il.5.872.308.
When the Fight rages, and the Flames surround? Il.8.281.410.
Attend his Order, and their Prince surround. Il.8.614.425.
And beardless Youths, our Battlements surround. Il.8.646.426.
And beardless Youths, the Battlements surround. Il.8.646A.426.
But bid in Whispers: These surround their Chief, Il.9.15.431.
Whose liquid Arms the mighty Glove surround, Il.9.240.444.
Ten Zones of Brass its ample Brims surround, Il.11.45.36.
Wild Mountain-Wolves the fainting Beast surround; Il.11.599.60.
(Whose Groves, the *Selli,* Race austere! surround, Il.16.288.252.
His swimming Eyes eternal Shades surround. Il.16.413.259.
Lie there, *Lycaon!* let the Fish surround Il.21.135.427.
With kindled Flames the Tripod-Vase surround; Il.23.50.489.
Swear by that God whose liquid Arms surround Il.23.665.516.
War, and the Blood of Men, surround thy Walls! Il.24.691.566.
Again the mournful Crowds surround the Pyre, Il.24.1001.577.
Surround her feet; with these sublime she sails Od.1.126.38.
The youth with instruments surround the fire. Od.3.589.116.
While this gay friendly troop the King surround, Od.4.21.121.
The *Phocæ* swift surround his rocky cave, Od.4.544.146.
The scaly charge their guardian God surround: Od.4.558.146.
Refulgent pedestals the walls surround, Od.7.128.241.
Tho' bold in open field, they yet surround Od.11.321.398.
Here hovering ghosts, like fowl, his shade surround, Od.11.747.423.
Or some fair isle which *Neptune's* arms surround? Od.13.282.19.
Now all the sons of warlike *Greece* surround Od.24.101.353.

SURROUNDED
Now with Furies surrounded, 6.11.106.34.
This Hour surrounded by the *Trojan* Bands; Il.11.969.78.
In sage debates, surrounded with his Peers, Od.1.113.37.
Had fall'n surrounded with his warlike train; Od.1.302.47.
To sea-surrounded realms the Gods assign Od.4.827.158.

SURROUNDING
The Bow'ry Mazes and surrounding Greens; 1.W-F.262.173.
Of Bow'ry Mazes and surrounding Greens; 1.W-F.262A.173.
To Bow'ry Mazes and surrounding Greens; 1.W-F.262B.173.
And *Stymphelus* with her surrounding Grove; Il.2.736.161.
Screen'd by the Shields of his surrounding Friends. Il.4.145.227.
This, tho' surrounding Shades obscur'd their View, Il.10.323.17.
Girt in surrounding Flames, he seems to fall Il.15.750.224.
Who 'midst surrounding Frosts, and Vapours chill, Il.16.286.252.
To *Ida's* Forests and surrounding Shades? Il.21.658.449.
Begirt with Heroes, and surrounding Bands; Il.22.472.475.
And thro surrounding Friends the Chariot rolls. Il.24.402.552.
Her spiry cliffs amid surrounding clouds; Od.4.686.151.
Thro' all-surrounding shade our navy brought; Od.9.166.312.
Thus in surrounding floods conceal'd he proves Od.11.293.396.
And shaded with a green surrounding grove; Od.17.239.143.

SURROUNDS
Which flaming *Phlegeton* surrounds, 6.11.50.32.
My Son from Fight, when *Greece* surrounds our Walls? Il.6.319.341.
But now the last Despair surrounds our Host; Il.10.194.10.
So fares a Boar, whom all the Troop surrounds Il.11.525.57.
With many a Step the Lioness surrounds Il.17.147.293.
With ceaseless roar the foaming deep surrounds. Od.1.258.45.
Sparta, whose walls a range of hills surrounds: Od.4.2.119.
So when the wood-man's toyl her cave surrounds Od.4.1041.166.
A sylvan train the huntress Queen surrounds, Od.6.119.212.
Now care surrounds me, and my force decays; Od.8.204.273.
But as my waving sword the blood surrounds, Od.11.102.385.
Pallas, unconquer'd maid, my frame surrounds Od.16.228.114.

SURVEY
Pleas'd, the green Lustre of the Scales survey, 1.Mes.83.120.
Stretch'd on the Lawn his second Hope survey, 1.W-F.81.158.
With joyful Pride survey our lofty Woods, 1.W-F.220A.169.
Survey the Region, and confess her Home! 1.W-F.256.172.
But *those attain'd,* we tremble to survey 1.EOC.229.265.
But *more advanc'd,* survey with strange Surprize 1.EOC.223A.265.
Survey the *Whole,* nor seek slight Faults to find, 1.EOC.235.266.
The Face of Nature we no more Survey, 1.EOC.313.274.
When all were Slaves thou cou'dst around survey, 1.TrSt.221.419.
Whence, far below, the Gods at once survey 1.TrSt.277.421.
Like distant Clouds the Mariners survey 1.TrUl.23A.466.
Releas'd from Sleep; and round him might survey 1.TrUl.54.467.
What Air I breath, what Country I survey? 1.TrUl.113.469.
Methinks already I your Tears survey, 2.RL4.107.192.
Propt on their Bodkin Spears, the Sprights survey 2.RL5.55.203.
This the *Beau-monde* shall from the *Mall* survey, 2.RL5.133.211.
Neptune and *Jove* survey the rapid Race: 2.TemF.217.272.
There, at one Passage, oft you might survey 2.TemF.489.287.
Tenants with sighs the smoakless tow'rs survey, 3.Ep3.193.109.
See them survey their Limbs by *Durer's* Rules, 4.JD4.240.45.
Survey the Pangs they bear, the Risques they run, 4.HAdv.51.79.
Survey both Worlds, intrepid and entire, 4.2HE2.312.187.
While he, serene in thought, shall calm survey 6.21.19.69.
Reviews his life, and in the strict survey 6.55.5.166.
Fanes, which admiring Gods with pride survey, 6.71.9.203.
With jealous Eyes thy close Access survey; Il.1.677.119.
Now seize th' Occasion, now the Troops survey, Il.2.518.151.
While scarce the Swains their feeding Flocks survey, Il.3.19.188.
The King of Kings, *Atrides,* you survey, Il.3.235.203.
Both Armies sate, the Combate to survey, Il.3.406.212.
And can you, Chiefs! without a Blush survey Il.4.398.239.
Can *Jove,* supine, flagitious Facts survey, Il.5.1068.317.
With silent Joy the settling Hosts survey: Il.7.66.366.
Who, all my Motions, all my Toils survey! Il.10.330.17.
The Woes of Men unwilling to survey, Il.11.71.37.
Heav'ns! what a prodigy these Eyes survey, Il.13.137.111.
Great *Hector* view'd him with a sad Survey, Il.15.492.216.
A Troop of Wolves th' unguarded Charge survey, Il.16.422.259.
Jove view'd the Combate with a stern Survey, Il.16.783.274.
With Emulation, what I act, survey, Il.19.151.378.
Slow as she past, beheld with sad survey Il.19.297.384.
The Mother first beheld with sad survey; Il.22.511.477.
Rage fills his Eye with Anguish, to survey Il.23.465.508.
And now *Antilochus,* with nice survey, Il.23.497.510.
The Monarch sate; from whence with sure survey Il.23.534.511.
Or can ye, all, another Chief survey, Il.23.542.511.
For the fam'd Twins, impatient to survey Il.23.735.519.
And, cloth'd anew, the following Games survey. Il.23.862.523.
Great are my Hazards; but the Gods survey Il.24.461.555.
And while the fav'ring Gods our Steps survey, Il.24.527.558.
With longing eyes, observing, to survey Od.5.560.199.
Up rose nine Seniors, chosen to survey Od.8.295.279.
Ulysses gaz'd, astonish'd to survey Od.8.305.279.
An Isle, whose hills their subject fields survey; Od.9.134.311.
The joyful crew survey his mighty size, Od.10.204.350.
The paths of Gods what mortal can survey? Od.10.689.376.
The wond'rous kind a length of age survey, Od.12.164.440.
Slain are those herds which I with pride survey, Od.12.447.452.
Releas'd from sleep, and round him might survey Od.13.221.16.
What air I breathe, what country I survey? Od.13.280.19.
His ancient realms *Ulysses* shall survey, Od.14.187.45.
My swains to visit, and the works survey. Od.15.544.96.
Some God has told them, or themselves survey Od.16.372.124.
Took in the ocean with a broad survey: Od.16.383.124.
And if aright these searching eyes survey, Od.16.494.131.
Should *Greece* thro' all her hundred states survey Od.18.287.180.
The shining baldness of his head survey, Od.18.401.187.
But first the *Ulyssean* wealth survey: Od.19.336.210.
Scenes of lewd loves his wakeful eyes survey, Od.20.10.230.
Thy wish produc'd in act, with pleas'd survey, Od.20.290.247.
Floating in gore, portentous to survey! Od.20.417.253.
The Suitors with a scornful smile survey Od.21.407.279.
She spoke; but willing longer to survey Od.22.257.299.
Arise, and bless thee with the glad survey! Od.23.10.319.
Thy heart had leap'd the Heroe to survey, Od.23.49.321.
The works of Gods what mortal can survey, Od.23.83.322.
Canst thou, oh cruel, unconcern'd survey Od.23.169.328.

SURVEY'D
The Gardens enter'd, and the Fruits survey'd, 1.TrVP.51.379.
The Nymph survey'd him and beheld the Grace 1.TrVP.120A.382.
Why on those Shores are we with Joy survey'd, 1.TrES.33.450.
Why on these Shores are we with Joy survey'd, 1.TrES.33A.450.
With mournful Looks the blissful Scenes survey'd, 2.ChJM.61.17.
The joyful Knight survey'd her by his Side, 2.ChJM.347.31.
Heav'n scarce believ'd the conquest it survey'd, 2.ElAb.113.329.
But *Jove's* Imperial Queen their Flight survey'd, Il.2.191.137.
Juno and *Pallas* with a Smile survey'd, Il.5.507.292.
The Carnage *Juno* from the Skies survey'd, Il.5.874.308.
Hush'd to Repose, and with a Smile survey'd. Il.6.619.357.
Escap'd great *Ajax,* they survey'd him round, Il.7.374.382.

SURVEY'D (CONTINUED)
The skilful Archer wide survey'd the Field, ... Il.8.322.413.
Their strong Distress the Wife of *Jove* survey'd; ... Il.8.421.417.
But *Jove* incens'd from *Ida's* Top survey'd, ... Il.8.486.420.
Nestor with Joy the Wakeful Band survey'd, ... Il.10.223.11.
Survey'd the various Fortune of the War. ... Il.11.643.62.
The rest the People shar'd; my self survey'd ... Il.11.840.73.
The Slaves their Master's slow approach survey'd, ... Il.11.978.78.
Why on those Shores are we with Joy survey'd, ... Il.12.377.95.
With Joy the glorious Conflict she survey'd, ... Il.14.181.168.
Meantime their Fight the *Spartan* King survey'd, ... Il.15.636.221.
Their mingled Grief the Sire of Heav'n survey'd, ... Il.19.362.387.
His vent'rous Act the white-arm'd Queen survey'd, ... Il.20.144.400.
This the bright Empress of the Heav'ns survey'd, ... Il.21.490.441.
Their Manners noted, and their States survey'd. ... Od.1.6.28.
Enormous riot and mis-rule survey'd. ... Od.1.139.39.
The conscious lamp the midnight fraud survey'd; ... Od.2.120.67.
And many-languag'd nations has survey'd; ... Od.3.408.106.
Entranc'd, and all the blissful haunt survey'd. ... Od.5.98.177.
The conscious Sire the dawning blush survey'd, ... Od.6.81.209.
What scenes have I survey'd of dreadful view? ... Od.6.262.222.
The wond'ring Nymph his glorious port survey'd, ... Od.6.285.224.
The Queen, on nearer view, the guest survey'd ... Od.7.314.251.
With wond'ring eyes the heroe she survey'd, ... Od.8.497.289.
What customs noted, and what coasts survey'd? ... Od.8.626.296.
There, wand'ring thro' the gloom I first survey'd, ... Od.11.65.383.
There as the wond'rous visions I survey'd, ... Od.11.104.385.
I turn'd my eye, and as I turn'd survey'd ... Od.11.733.422.
Resolv'd I stand! and haply had survey'd ... Od.11.777.425.
Mean-time the * Goddess our return survey'd ... Od.12.23.430.
Never, I never, scene so dire survey'd! ... Od.12.309.447.
Their gentle blandishment the King survey'd, ... Od.16.7.102.
Amphinomus survey'd th' associate band; ... Od.16.367.124.
How in the doleful mansions he survey'd ... Od.23.349.341.
Still at his side is *Nestor's* son survey'd, ... Od.24.27.348.
His ancient host *Amphimedon* survey'd; ... Od.24.128.354.

SURVEY'ST
With joyful Pride survey'st our lofty Woods, ... 1.W-F.220.169.

SURVEYING
All good, all-wise, and all-surveying *Jove!* ... Il.19.268.383.

SURVEYS
And from the Brink his dancing Shade surveys. ... 1.PSp.34.63.
The Nymph surveys him, and beholds the Grace ... 1.TrVP.120.382.
" *Apollo's* Fane surveys the rolling Deep; ... 1.TrSP.190.402.
And stately *Corinth's* pleasing Site surveys. ... 1.TrSt.473.430.
The King surveys his Guests with curious Eyes, ... 1.TrSt.565.434.
The King th'accomplish'd Oracle surveys, ... 1.TrSt.576.434.
Where *Thames* with Pride surveys his rising Tow'rs, ... 2.RL3.2.169.
Heav'n still with laughter the vain toil surveys, ... 3.EOM4.75.135.
And, Milo-like, surveys his arms and hands, ... 5.DunA2.272.135.
Surveys around her in the blest abode. ... 5.DunA3.125.160.
And Milo-like surveys his arms and hands; ... 5.DunB2.284.309.
Surveys around her, in the blest abode, ... 5.DunB3.133.326.
Surveys its beauties, whence its beauties grow; ... 6.14iv.10.47.
Luxurious Nature's Wealth in Thought surveys, ... 6.17iii.20.58.
But what with pleasure heav'n itself surveys; ... 6.32.20.96.
A softer wonder my pleas'd soul surveys, ... 6.106i.2.306.
Whose sacred Eye thy *Tenedos* surveys, ... Il.1.592.116.
And, Master of the Flocks, surveys them round. ... Il.3.260.204.
A Swain surveys the gath'ring Storm below; ... Il.4.315.235.
Which when some future Mariner surveys, ... Il.7.99.368.
Surveys th' Inscription with rejoicing Eyes, ... Il.7.225.375.
Thence his broad Eye the subject World surveys, ... Il.8.65.398.
Now o'er the Fields, dejected, he surveys ... Il.10.13.2.
Surveys the Tow'rs, and meditates their Fall. ... Il.11.236.46.
With Joy the Swain surveys them, as he leads ... Il.13.624.135.
Great *Jove* surveys her with desiring Eyes: ... Il.14.332.179.
And whose broad Eye th' extended Earth surveys. ... Il.14.392.181.
Surveys thy desolated Realms below, ... Il.24.360.551.
The rising and descending Sun surveys) ... Od.1.32.31.
Meantime the lofty rooms the Prince surveys, ... Od.2.380.79.
Stretch'd on the shelly shore, he first surveys ... Od.4.555.146.
Surveys his charge, unknowing of deceit: ... Od.4.607.148.
Who all surveys with his extensive eye, ... Od.11.138.387.
A shepherd meeting thee, the *Oar* surveys, ... Od.11.157.389.
Your deeds with quick impartial eye surveys; ... Od.19.107.197.
That wide th' extended *Hellespont* surveys; ... Od.24.104.353.

SURVIV'D
But *Sense* surviv'd, when *merry Jests* were past; ... 1.EOC.460.291.
When *Patriarch-Wits* surviv'd a *thousand Years;* ... 1.EOC.479.293.
Nor long surviv'd; to Marble turn'd he stands ... Il.2.384.145.
Hippolochus surviv'd; from him I came, ... Il.6.253.339.
And what surviv'd of *Greece* to *Greece* return'd; ... Il.12.14.81.
But (*Jove* assisting) I surviv'd the Day. ... Il.20.124.399.
Surviv'd, sad Relicks of his num'rous Line. ... Il.24.316.549.
All who the Wars of ten long years surviv'd, ... Od.1.16.30.
No son surviv'd; *Arete* heir'd his state, ... Od.7.84.237.
How scarce himself surviv'd: He paints the bow'r, ... Od.23.345.341.

SURVIVE
And Love of *Ombre,* after Death survive. ... 2.RL1.56.150.
Not scornful Virgins who their Charms survive, ... 2.RL4.4.183.
Rather than so, ah let me still survive, ... 2.RL5.101.207.
Ev'n in those tombs where their proud names survive, ... 6.22.16.72.
And not a *Greek* of all the Race survive; ... Il.16.125.242.
I hop'd *Patroclus* might survive, to rear ... Il.19.351.387.
Doom'd to survive, and never to return! ... Od.19.297.209.
With *Demoptolemus:* These six survive, ... Od.22.268.299.

SURVIVES
Late fled the Field, and yet survives his Fame? ... Il.3.534.217.
Yet while my *Hector* still survives, I see ... Il.6.544.353.

SURVIVES (CONTINUED)
If yet *Antilochus* survives the Fight, ... Il.17.738.317.
Ægisthus sole survives to boast the deed. ... Od.4.724.152.
From *Ithaca,* and wond'rous woes survives; ... Od.4.752.154.
The direful wreck *Ulysses* scarce survives! ... Od.11.144.387.
If yet *Telemachus,* my son, survives? ... Od.11.211.392.
"Not one survives to breath<e> to-morrow's air." ... Od.17.589.161.
To think he still survives to claim the state? ... Od.20.396.251.
Dear to mankind thy fame survives, nor fades ... Od.24.117.353.

SURVIVING
Of furious Hate surviving Death, she sings, ... 1.TrSt.51.412.
Her yet-surviving Heroes seem'd to fall. ... Il.16.992.281.
Thy still-surviving Sons may sue for thee, ... Il.24.855.572.

SURVIVOR
The sad survivor of his num'rous train, ... Od.17.163.139.

SUSPECT
And learn from thence their Ladies to suspect: ... 2.ChJM.594.43.
Sir *George* of *some slight Gallantries* suspect. ... 4.EpS1.15A.298.
Why did I not suspect Hippina's Muff ... 6.96ii.30Z1.271.
But why should'st thou suspect the War's Success? ... Il.12.285.92.
Nor fear an Ambush, nor suspect a Foe. ... Il.18.610.352.
Nor blame her faultless, nor suspect of pride: ... Od.7.390.255.

SUSPECTED
His Subjects Faith, and Queen's suspected Love, ... 1.TrUl.217.473.
And ring suspected Vessels ere they buy, ... 2.ChWB.101.61.
And sound suspected Vessels ere they buy, ... 2.ChWB.101A.61.
The middle Space suspected Troops supply, ... Il.4.344.237.
His subjects faith, and Queen's suspected love; ... Od.13.384.25.
The miscreant we suspected takes that way; ... Od.22.180.296.

SUSPECTING
Suspecting fraud, more prudently remain'd. ... Od.10.267.355.

SUSPENCE
Just as in Anguish of Suspence he stay'd, ... Il.1.259.99.
In this suspence bright *Helen* grac'd the room; ... Od.4.157.127.

SUSPEND
Shall list'ning in mid Air suspend their Wings; ... 1.PWi.54.93.
The action of the stronger to suspend ... 3.EOM2.77.64.
Suspend a while your Force inertly strong, ... 5.DunB4.7.340.
The Monarch's Will, suspend the list'ning Crowd. ... Il.2.124.133.
The Tumult silence, and the Fight suspend. ... Il.3.120.195.
Braces of Gold suspend the moving Throne: ... Il.5.897.308.
This Day, the Business of the Field suspend; ... Il.7.35.364.
The warring Nations to suspend their Rage; ... Il.7.54.365.
Awhile your loud, untimely Joy suspend, ... Il.19.83.375.
Nor breathe from Combate, nor thy Sword suspend, ... Il.21.339.435.
And for a Moment's space, suspend the Day: ... Il.22.322.469.
Till then, our Arms suspend the Fall of *Troy.* ... Il.24.839.572.
"Rebate your loves, each rival suit suspend, ... Od.19.164.200.
Yet, while I speak, the mighty woe suspend; ... Od.19.305.209.
Suspend the restful hour with sweet discourse. ... Od.19.597.225.
O Peers! the sanguinary scheme suspend: ... Od.20.307.247.
And on a column near the roof suspend; ... Od.22.191.296.
Yet a short space, your rival suit suspend, ... Od.24.156.355.

SUSPENDED
He stood suspended with the lifted Dart: ... Il.6.64.326.
Felt his great Heart suspended in his Breast: ... Il.7.262.377.
Or holds their Fury in suspended Reins: ... Il.17.543.309.
And while above the Spear suspended stood, ... Il.21.80.424.
He stands suspended, and explores his mind. ... Od.5.451.194.
And stuck adherent, and suspended hung: ... Od.5.547.198.
O'er my suspended woe thy words prevail, ... Od.19.689.229.

SUSPENDING
(Suspending sorrow with celestial strain ... Od.17.610.161.

SUSPENDS
'Till poiz'd aloft, the resting Beam suspends ... 1.TrES.169.455.
Now *Jove* suspends his golden Scales in Air, ... 2.RL5.71.206.
The Sire of Gods his golden Scales suspends, ... Il.8.88.399.
Till pois'd aloft, the resting Beam suspends ... Il.12.525.101.
While his high Law suspends the Pow'rs of Heav'n. ... Il.13.16.104.
A silver Chain suspends the massy Round, ... Il.18.554.348.
Suspends around, low-bending o'er the Pile. ... Il.23.209.498.
No truce the warfare of my heart suspends! ... Od.20.101.237.

SUSPENSE
A cool suspense from pleasure and from pain; ... 2.ElAb.250.339.
He spoke: in still Suspense on either side ... Il.3.133.196.

SUSPICION
On bare *Suspicion* thus to treat your Bride; ... 2.ChJM.796.53.
Or caus'd Suspicion when no Soul was rude, ... 2.RL4.73.190.
Lest rash suspicion might alarm thy mind: ... Od.7.393.256.
All wrath ill-grounded, and suspicion base! ... Od.7.396.256.

SUSPICIONS
But vile Suspicions had aspers'd her Fame; ... 2.ChJM.239.26.

SUSPICIOUS
And Hate, engender'd by suspicious Fears; ... 1.TrSt.177.417.
A tim'rous foe, and a suspicious friend, ... 4.Arbu.206.110.
A tim'rous Foe, and a suspicious Friend, ... 6.98.56.285.

SUSPITIOUS
A tim'rous Foe and a suspitious Friend: ... 6.49iii.20.143.

SUSTAIN
And thou, kind *Love,* my sinking Limbs sustain, ...1.TrSP.209.403.
This weary'd Arm can scarce the Bolt sustain, ...1.TrSt.304.423.
This Hand unaided shall the War sustain: ......1.TrES.214.457.
The Nerves unbrac'd no more his Bulk sustain, ...1.TrES.265.459.
And four fair *Queens* whose hands sustain a Flow'r, ...2.RL3.39.171.
Four Swans sustain a Carr of Silver bright ......2.TemF.210.272.
See dying vegetables life sustain, ...3.EOM3.15.93.
While You, great Patron of Mankind, sustain ......4.2HE1.1.195.
When he the rage of sinners shall sustain, ...6.21.35.70.
O Thou, whose all-creating hands sustain ......6.23.1.73.
Thou who did'st form, and form'd dost still sustain ......6.23.1A.73.
No son nor Grandson shall the line sustain ......6.130.29.358.
Not long the deathful Dart he can sustain; ......Il.5.136.273.
The Warrior's Fury let this Arm sustain; ......Il.5.285.280.
Unnumber'd Woes Mankind from us sustain, ...Il.5.473.290.
The fiercest Shock of charging Hosts sustain; ......Il.5.638.298.
Sustain thy Life, and Human be thy Birth; ......Il.6.176.334.
But say, what Hero shall sustain that Task? ......Il.10.45.4.
Scarce can my Knees these trembling Limbs sustain, ...Il.10.100.7.
His Arm and Knee his sinking Bulk sustain; ......Il.11.458.54.
Let the great Parent Earth one Hand sustain, ...Il.14.307.177.
Th' embody'd *Greeks* the fierce Attack sustain, ...Il.15.470.215.
This Hand, unaided, shall the War sustain: ......Il.16.517.263.
The Nerves unbrac'd no more his Bulk sustain, ...Il.16.570.266.
I stand unable to sustain the Spear, ...Il.16.639.269.
The first Attack the *Grecians* scarce sustain, ...Il.17.324.300.
But bids bold *Thrasymede* those troops sustain; ......Il.17.791.319.
My self, and my bold Brother will sustain ......Il.17.803.320.
As oft' th' *Ajaces* his Assault sustain; ......Il.18.195.331.
What mortal Man *Achilles* can sustain? ......Il.20.129.399.
And Sons succeeding Sons, the lasting Line sustain. ......Il.20.356.408.
That high thro' Fields of Air his Flight sustain, ...Il.24.419.553.
For I alone sustain their naval cares, ...Od.3.462.109.
Still must the wrong'd *Telemachus* sustain, ...Od.4.221.130.
Sustain those Peers, the reliques of our host, ...Od.4.655.150.
That high thro' fields of air his flight sustain ......Od.5.58.174.
Thus then I judge: while yet the planks sustain ......Od.5.458.194.
Amazing strength, these poysons to sustain! ......Od.10.389.363.
No longer durst sustain the sovereign look. ......Od.18.390.186.
Else if the Gods my vengeful arm sustain, ...Od.19.571.224.
Where shall *Ulysses* shun, or how sustain, ...Od.20.53.234.
In arms attend us, and their part sustain. ......Od.22.121.292.
Decree us to sustain a length of woes, ...Od.23.220.333.
His heart within him melts; his knees sustain ......Od.24.402.368.

SUSTAIN'D
The Saint sustain'd it, but the Woman dy'd. ......6.115.10.323.
Sustain'd the Sword that glitter'd at his side. ......Il.3.416.212.
A Wood of Spears his ample Shield sustain'd; ......Il.5.767.303.
With Toils, sustain'd for *Paris'* sake and mine: ......Il.6.445.348.
Nor He, the King of Men, th' Alarm sustain'd; ......Il.8.101.402.
Sustain'd the Sword that glitter'd at his side: ......Il.11.40.36.
And all the Gates sustain'd an equal Tide; ......Il.12.202.88.
(One brac'd his Shield, and one sustain'd his Sword.) ......Il.14.468.186.
And ev'ry Ship sustain'd an equal Tyde. ......Il.15.481.216.
An Exile long, sustain'd at *Ajax'* Board, ...Il.15.502.216.
Ajax no more the sounding Storm sustain'd, ...Il.16.130.242.
Felt pity enter, and sustain'd her part. ......Od.10.474.366.
Sedate of soul, his character sustain'd, ...Od.17.551.159.
His tender bloom to manly growth sustain'd: ......Od.19.410.214.
To violate the life thy youth sustain'd? ......Od.19.564.224.
Great are thy wrongs, and much hast thou sustain'd ......Od.22.59.289.
One hand sustain'd a helm, and one the shield ......Od.22.197.296.

SUSTAINING
With gen'rous Wine, and all-sustaining Bread. ......Il.8.678.427.
And life-sustaining bread, and fair array, ...Od.5.215.182.

SUSTAINS
Each Motion guides, and ev'ry Nerve sustains; ......1.EOC.78.248.
Sustains the Sword that glitters at his side ......Il.3.416A.212.
His falling Bulk his bended Arm sustains; ......Il.5.380.285.
(For not the Bread of Man their Life sustains, ...Il.5.425.289.
The Brazen Vase *Automedon* sustains, ...Il.9.273.447.
A single Warrior, half an Host sustains: ......Il.11.605.61.
His Shield emboss'd the ringing Storm sustains, ...Il.13.700.138.
While *Nestor's* Son sustains a manlier Part, ...Il.18.37.325.
The mournful Mother next sustains her Part. ......Il.24.942.575.
Such as the mortal life of man sustains: ......Od.5.252.183.
No more my heart the dismal din sustains, ...Od.11.783.425.
A rugged staff his trembling hand sustains; ......Od.13.505.30.

SUTTON
But rev'rend S[utton], with a meeker air, ...3.Ep3.107A.100.
Who live like S[u]tt[o]n, or who die like Chartres, ...4.JD2.36.135.
In rev'rend S [utto]n note a *small Neglect,* ......4.EpS1.16A.298.

SWAIN
Then hid in Shades, eludes her eager Swain; ......1.PSp.54.66.
A Faithful Swain, whom Love had taught to sing, ...1.PSu.1A.71.
Not bubling Fountains to the thirsty Swain, ...1.PAu.43.83.
The Swain in barren Desarts with surprize ......1.Mes.67.118.
The Swain with Tears his frustrate Labour yields, ...1.W-F.55.154.
The Swain with Tears to Beasts his Labour yields, ...1.W-F.55A.154.
And secret Transport touch'd the conscious Swain. ......1.W-F.90.159.
Safe on my Shore each unmolested Swain ......1.W-F.369.186.
O'ercharge the Shoulders of the seeming Swain. ......1.TrVP.32.378.
While the rude Swain his rural Musick tries, ...1.TrSt.689.439.
Or great *Osyris,* who first taught the Swain ......1.TrSt.859.446.
In modern Ages not the strongest Swain ......1.TrES.101.453.
Yet this, as easie as a Swain wou'd bear ......1.TrES.187.456.
Yet this, as easie as a Swain could bear ......1.TrES.187A.456.
In show a youthful Swain, of Form divine, ...1.TrUl.102.469.
Health to the sick, and solace to the swain. ......3.Ep3.258.114.
Was ever such a happy Swain? ......4.HS6.206.263.

SWAIN (CONTINUED)
Or whirligigs, twirl'd round by skilful swain, ...5.DunA3.49.154.
Or whirligigs, twirl'd round by skilful swain, ...5.DunB3.57.323.
Wafts the smooth Eunuch and enamour'd swain. ......5.DunB4.310.374.
And solace of the thirsty swain. ......6.6ii.4.14.
If Wit or Critick blame the tender Swain, ...6.13.16.39.
While at her feet her swain expiring lies. ......6.14iii.4.45.
Seem like the lofty Barn of some rich Swain, ...6.96ii.13.270.
Not with more Ease, the spilful Shepherd Swain ......Il.2.562.154.
Like Steel, uplifted by some strenuous Swain, ...Il.3.91.194.
A Swain surveys the gath'ring Storm below; ......Il.4.315.235.
As when on *Ceres'* sacred Floor the Swain ......Il.5.611.297.
As when some simple Swain his Cot forsakes, ...Il.5.734.302.
In modern Ages not the strongest Swain ......Il.12.455.98.
Yet this, as easy as a Swain could bear ......Il.12.541.101.
With Joy the Swain surveys them, as he leads ......Il.13.624.135.
No Swain to guard 'em, and no Day to guide, ...Il.15.367.211.
Has torn the Shepherd's Dog, or Shepherd Swain; ......Il.15.703.223.
As when the Flocks, neglected by the Swain ......Il.16.420.259.
Like some vile Swain, whom, on a rainy Day, ...Il.21.327.434.
Far, as a Swain his whirling Sheephook throws, ...Il.23.1001.529.
Let one, dispatchful, bid some swain to lead ......Od.3.534.113.
So with his batt'ning flocks the careful swain ......Od.4.559.146.
Calls, to succeed his cares, the watchful swain; ......Od.10.95.345.
In show a youthful swain, of form divine, ...Od.13.269.18.
True to his charge, a loyal swain and kind: ......Od.13.466.28.
But he, of ancient faith, a simple swain, ...Od.14.30.36.
Unhappy stranger! (thus the faithful swain ......Od.14.41.37.
The swain reply'd. It never was our guise ......Od.14.65.38.
Accept such treatment as a swain affords, ...Od.14.71.39.
Forth rush'd the swain with hospitable haste. ......Od.14.84.40.
Thus spoke the faithful swain, and thus rejoin'd ......Od.14.171.43.
And why, oh swain of unbelieving mind! ......Od.14.431.56.
(Reply'd the swain for spotless faith divine) ......Od.14.444.57.
The swain, whom acts of piety delight, ...Od.14.467.58.
Be then thy thanks, (the bounteous swain reply'd) ......Od.14.492.60.
Well hast thou spoke (rejoin'd th' attentive swain) ......Od.14.576.64.
For here one vest suffices ev'ry swain; ......Od.14.581.65.
To whom the Swain. Attend what you enquire. ......Od.15.374.87.
And reach'd the mansion of his faithful swain. ......Od.15.598.99.
Instant the swain the spoils of beasts supplies, ...Od.16.47.104.
The swain returns. A tale of sorrows hear; ......Od.16.61.105.
To whom the swain. I hear, and I obey: ......Od.16.144.109.
Lest to the Queen the swain with transport fly, ...Od.16.480.130.
Proceed *Ulysses* and the faithful swain: ......Od.17.205.141.
To no brave prize aspir'd the worthless swain, ...Od.17.258.144.
Ulysses harkned, then addrest the swain. ......Od.17.313.147.
The thoughtful Son beheld, and call'd his swain: ......Od.17.417.152.
To whom the hospitable swain rejoin'd: ......Od.17.458.155.
Swift to the Queen returns the gentle swain: ......Od.17.656.164.
Philætius late arriv'd, a faithful swain. ......Od.20.234.244.
O *Jove* supreme, the raptur'd swain replies, ...Od.20.294.247.
Fast by our side let either faithful swain ......Od.22.120.292.
To the high chamber stole the faithless swain, ...Od.22.177.296.
There pass thy pleasing night, oh gentle swain! ......Od.22.212.297.
And *Polybus* renown'd the faithful swain. ......Od.22.315.301.

SWAINS
Two Swains, whom Love kept wakeful, and the Muse, ...1.PSp.18.62.
Blest Swains, whose Nymphs in ev'ry Grace excell; ......1.PSp.95.70.
Blest Nymphs, whose Swains those Graces sing so well! ......1.PSp.96.70.
Let other Swains attend the Rural Care, ...1.PSu.35.74.
For you the Swains the fairest Flow'rs design, ...1.PSu.55.76.
When Swains from Sheering seek their nightly Bow'rs; ......1.PSu.64.76.
Oh, skill'd in Nature! see the Hearts of Swains, ...1.PAu.11.81.
The Fields are ravish'd from th'industrious Swains, ...1.W-F.65.155.
Ye vig'rous Swains! while Youth ferments your Blood, ...1.W-F.93.159.
Enough for me, that to the listning Swains ......1.W-F.433.194.
Two stubborn Swains with Blows dispute their Bounds; ......1.TrES.158.455.
While scarce the Swains their feeding Flocks survey, ...Il.3.19.188.
The conscious Swains, rejoicing in the Sight, ...Il.8.697.428.
Beset with watchful Dogs, and shouting Swains, ...Il.11.675.65.
Then, from my Fury fled the trembling Swains, ...Il.11.820.73.
Two stubborn Swains with Blows dispute their Bounds; ......Il.12.512.100.
The village Curs, and trembling Swains retire; ......Il.17.70.290.
And Steers slow-moving, and two Shepherd Swains; ......Il.18.608.352.
And, all amidst them, dead, the Shepherd Swains! ......Il.18.614.352.
His Hinds and Swains whole years shall be supply'd ......Il.23.988.528.
The shepherd swains with sure abundance blest, ...Od.4.109.125.
Proud are the lords, and wretched are the swains. ......Od.15.407.89.
My swains to visit, and the works survey. ......Od.15.544.96.
Ulysses, and the Monarch of the Swains, ...Od.16.2.100.
Thus He: and thus the Monarch of the Swains; ......Od.16.35.104.
Three hundred sheep, and all the shepherd swains; ......Od.21.22.260.
This said, he first return'd: the faithful swains ......Od.21.258.272.
The ready swains obey'd with joyful haste, ...Od.22.193.296.
Active and pleas'd, the zealous swains fulfil ......Od.22.205.297.
To you my son, and you, my faithful swains; ......Od.22.473.312.
(The swains unite their toil) the walls, the floor ......Od.22.489.313.
The swains and young *Telemachus* they found, ...Od.24.423.369.
The swains, fatigu'd with labours of the day; ......Od.24.445.370.

SWALLOW
When earthquakes swallow, or when tempests sweep ......3.EOM1.143.33.
And quick to swallow me, methought I saw ......4.JD4.172.39.
And one prodigious Ruin swallow All. ......Il.4.199.230.
And one devouring Vengeance swallow all. ......Il.13.974.152.
Swift as a swallow sweeps the liquid way, ...Od.13.186.15.
Perch'd like a swallow on a rafter's height, ...Od.22.262.299.

SWALLOW'D
The rebel race, and death had swallow'd all; ......Od.24.611.377.

SWALLOW'S
Twang'd short and sharp, like the shrill swallow's cry. ......Od.21.449.282.

SWALLOWS
Like Aaron's serpent, swallows up the rest. ....3.EOM2.132.71.
And swallows roost in Nilus' dusty Urn. ....3.Ep4.126.149.
Till one wide Conflagration swallows all. ....5.DunA3.236.177.
'Till one wide conflagration swallows all. ....5.DunB3.240.332.
Takes, opens, swallows it, before their Sight. ....6.145.8.388.

SWAM
And swam to Empire thro' the purple Flood. ....2.TemF.347.280.
And Death's dim Shadows swam before his View. ....Il.13.726.139.
And swam the stream: Loud shrieks the virgin train, ...Od.6.135.213.
And the dead Suitors almost swam in blood; ....Od.23.48.321.

SWAN
Th' expiring Swan, and as he sings he dies. ....2.RL5.66.206.
And there a naked Leda with a Swan. ....3.Ep2.10A.49.
Is there, a naked Leda with a Swan. ....3.Ep2.10.49.
Goose-rump'd, Hawk-nos'd, Swan-footed, is my Dear? ....4.HAdv.122.85.
Taylor, sweet Swan of Thames, majestic bows; ....5.DunA2.323A.141.
(Once swan of Thames, tho' now he sings no more.) ....5.DunB3.20.321.
One year may make a singing Swan of *Duck*. ....6.116v.4.327.
Fast by the limpid lake my swan-like train ....Od.19.648.227.

SWAN-FOOTED
Goose-rump'd, Hawk-nos'd, Swan-footed, is my Dear? ....4.HAdv.122.85.

SWAN-LIKE
Fast by the limpid lake my swan-like train ....Od.19.648.227.

SWAN'S
Who marks the Swan's or Crane's embody'd Flight, ...Il.15.837.229.

SWANS
The silver Swans her hapless Fate bemoan, ...1.PWi.39.91.
His drooping Swans on ev'ry Note expire, ...1.W-F.275.174.
And soft as down upon the breast of swans: ....1.TrPA.61.367.
Four Swans sustain a Carr of Silver bright ....2.TemF.210.272.
What City-Swans once sung within the walls; ....5.DunA1.94.70.
And mounts far off, among the swans of Thames. ....5.DunA2.286.137.
What City Swans once sung within the walls; ....5.DunB1.96.276.
And mounts far off among the Swans of Thames. ....5.DunB2.298.310.
Or milk-white Swans in *Asius'* watry Plains, ...Il.2.541.152.

SWARM
Swarm o'er the Lawns, the Forest Walks surround, ...1.W-F.149.164.
A Swarm of Drones, that buzz'd about your Head. ....6.7.8.15.
Incessant swarm, and chas'd, return again. ....Il.16.782.273.
There, in the *Forum* swarm a num'rous Train; ....Il.18.577.350.

SWARM'D
These, and a thousand more swarm'd o'er the ground, ...Od.11.53.383.

SWARMING
The swarming Populace the Chief detains, ...Il.23.321.502.
The swarming people hail their ship to land, ...Od.13.179.14.

SWARMS
Rolling, and black'ning, Swarms succeeding Swarms, ...Il.2.113.133.
Rolling, and black'ning, Swarms succeeding Swarms, ...Il.2.113.133.
In gather'd Swarms surround the Rural Bow'rs; ....Il.2.555.154.
And swarms victorious o'er their yielding Walls: ....Il.13.120.110.
In Swarms the guiltless Traveller engage, ...Il.16.316.255.
Thus from the Tents the fervent Legion swarms, ...Il.16.320.255.
Now swarms the populace; a countless throng, ...Od.8.111.268.
With early morn the gather'd country swarms, ...Od.9.53.304.
Thus while she spoke, in swarms hell's Empress brings ....Od.11.273.395.
But swarms of spectres rose from deepest hell, ...Od.11.779.425.
Thick swarms the spacious hall with howling ghosts, ...Od.20.427.254.

SWARTHS
Here stretch'd in Ranks the level'd Swarths are found, ...Il.18.639.354.

SWARTHY
In Show like Leaders of the swarthy *Moors*. ....2.RL3.48.172.
Extended pale, by swarthy *Memnon* slain! ....Od.4.256.131.
These swarthy arms among the covert stores ....Od.19.20.193.

SWAY
But *Fancy's* boundless Empire own'd his Sway. ....1.EOC.648Z2.312.
Great queen of love! how boundless is thy sway; ....1.TrPA.13.366.
Tho' all the Skies, ambitious of thy Sway, ...1.TrSt.37.411.
And Sacred Thirst of Sway; and all the Ties ....1.TrSt.178.417.
To govern *Thebes* by their Alternate Sway; ....1.TrSt.193.418.
And one of those who groan beneath the Sway ....1.TrSt.230.420.
Then thundring thro' the Planks, with forceful Sway, ...1.TrES.195.456.
Abridg'd her Pleasures, and confin'd her Sway. ....2.ChJM.489.39.
"And since in Man right Reason bears the Sway, ...2.ChWB.193.65.
Oh! if the Muse must flatter lawless Sway, ...2.TemF.517.289.
We, wretched subjects tho' to lawful sway, ...3.EOM2.149.73.
"Yet go! and thus o'er all the creatures sway, ...3.EOM3.195.113.
'Till common int'rest plac'd the sway in one. ....3.EOM3.210.114.
Please by receiving, by submitting sway ....3.Ep2.263A.71.
The Love of Pleasure, and the Love of Sway. ....3.Ep2.210.67.
But art thou one, whom new opinions sway, ...4.1HE6.63.241.
'Till *Albion*, as *Hibernia*, bless my sway. ....5.DunA1.251Z6.93.
That lifts our Goddess to imperial sway: ....5.DunA3.116.160.
The sure fore-runner of her gentle sway. ....5.DunA3.304.185.
That lifts our Goddess to imperial sway; ....5.DunB3.124.325.
The sure fore-runner of her gentle sway: ....5.DunB3.302.334.
The young, the old, who feel her inward sway, ...5.DunB4.73.348.
'Tis in the shade of Arbitrary Sway. ....5.DunB4.182.360.
Thine was the Sway, e'er Heav'n was form'd or Earth, ...6.8.4.17.
Wide o'er th' aerial Vault extends thy sway, ...6.65.3.192.
Wide o'er th' Æthereal Walks extends thy sway, ...6.65.3A.192.
Rule thy own Realms with arbitrary Sway: ....Il.1.236.98.
Then let Revenge no longer bear the Sway, ...Il.1.285.100.

SWAY (CONTINUED)
Wise by his Rules, and happy by his Sway; ....Il.1.334.104.
What King can bear a Rival in his Sway? ....Il.1.383.106.
Go, lest the haughty Partner of my Sway ....Il.1.676.119.
From whence this Wrath, or who controuls thy Sway? ....Il.1.715.122.
To One sole Monarch *Jove* commits the Sway; ....Il.2.243.139.
Rise, great *Atrides!* and with Courage sway; ....Il.2.410.147.
But chief *Tydides* bore the Sov'reign Sway; ....Il.2.684.159.
Cos, where *Eurypylus* possest the Sway, ...Il.2.825.164.
With *Polypætes* join'd in equal Sway ....Il.2.904.166.
Young *Amphius* and *Adrastus'* equal Sway; ....Il.2.1007.170.
Great in the War, and great in Arts of Sway. ....Il.3.236.203.
Who high on *Ida's* holy Mountain sway, ...Il.3.347.209.
In fat *Bœotia* held his wealthy Sway, ...Il.5.871.308.
All Heav'n beside reveres thy Sov'reign Sway, ...Il.5.1076.318.
All saw, and fear'd, his huge, tempestuous Sway. ....Il.7.184.373.
Sprung from such Fathers, who such Numbers sway; ....Il.7.193.373.
Great is thy Sway, and weighty are thy Cares; ....Il.9.97.437.
Monarch of Nations! whose superior Sway ....Il.9.127.438.
Sev'n ample Cities shall confess his Sway, ...Il.9.195.442.
Since more than his my Years, and more my Sway. ....Il.9.214.443.
Sev'n ample Cities shall confess thy Sway, ...Il.9.382.451.
Content with just hereditary Sway; ....Il.9.521.458.
Or *Troy* once held, in Peace and Pride of Sway, ...Il.9.526.459.
Oh let not headlong Passion bear the Sway; ....Il.9.637.466.
Thro' too much Def'rence to our Sov'reign Sway, ...Il.10.140.8.
And all I move, deferring to thy Sway, ...Il.12.251.90.
Then thund'ring thro' the Planks, with forceful Sway, ...Il.12.549.101.
Oh were thy Sway the Curse of meaner Pow'rs, ...Il.14.92.162.
And comes it ev'n from him, whose sov'reign Sway ....Il.14.104.162.
Supreme he sits; and sees, in Pride of Sway, ...Il.15.116.201.
Our elder Birthright, and superior Sway. ....Il.15.185.203.
His elder Birthright, and superior Sway. ....Il.15.201.204.
Himself supreme in Valour, as in Sway. ....Il.16.209.247.
O King of Nations! whose superiour Sway ....Il.19.143.377.
He, Source of Pow'r and Might! with boundless Sway, ...Il.20.292.406.
Th' impatient Steel with full-descending Sway ....Il.20.459.413.
For lo! he comes, with unresisted Sway; ....Il.21.623.448.
To wave Contention with superior Sway; ....Il.23.690.517.
Beneath that pond'rous Arm's resistless Sway ....Il.23.800.521.
No Race succeeding to imperial Sway: ....Il.24.678.565.
Elect by *Jove* his Delegate of sway, ...Od.1.501.56.
While lawless feasters in thy palace sway; ....Od.3.401.106.
Me would ye leave, who boast imperial sway, ...Od.3.449.108.
For *Polybus* her Lord, (whose sov'reign sway ....Od.4.169.128.
Mean-time return'd, with dire remorseless sway ....Od.4.453.141.
Free from that law, beneath whose mortal sway ....Od.4.763.155.
Let Kings no more with gentle mercy sway, ...Od.5.14.171.
And next, a wedge to drive with sweepy sway: ....Od.5.303.185.
And now the south, and now the north, bear sway, ...Od.5.421.192.
The dryer blasts alone of *Boreas* sway, ...Od.5.492.195.
And wise *Alcinous* held the regal sway. ....Od.6.18.204.
None wield the gauntlet with so dire a sway, ...Od.8.101.267.
And *Laodame* whirls high, with dreadful sway, ...Od.8.139.270.
Then thus *Euryalus:* O Prince, whose sway ....Od.8.435.287.
Then thus *Ulysses.* Thou, whom first in sway ....Od.9.1.298.
Hence *Pollux* sprung who wields with furious sway ....Od.11.367.400.
O Monarch great in virtue as in sway! ....Od.11.443.406.
A pond'rous mace of brass with direful sway ....Od.11.705.420.
Nor all the monarchs whose far-dreaded sway ....Od.14.119.41.
And *Ctesius* there, my father, holds the sway. ....Od.15.455.92.
To thine, for ages, heav'n decrees the sway. ....Od.15.576.98.
But if submissive you resign the sway, ...Od.16.402.125.
Escap'd my care: where lawless Suitors sway, ...Od.16.488.130.
Mean-time returning, with remorseless sway ....Od.17.144.138.
Thy finish'd charms, all *Greece* would own thy sway, ...Od.18.288.180.
But when my son grows man, the royal sway ....Od.18.313.181.
Consummate pattern of imperial sway, ...Od.19.129.199.
His son *Deucalion* bore successive sway; ....Od.19.208.203.
Phedon the fact affirm'd, whose sov'reign sway ....Od.19.329.210.
Each fav'rite fowl he pounc'd with deathful sway, ...Od.19.631.227.
And human thought, with unresisted sway, ...Od.23.15.319.
And rule our Palace with an equal sway: ....Od.23.382.343.

SWAY'D
And ev'n the Elements a Tyrant sway'd? ....1.W-F.52.153.
Or sway'd by Envy, or through Pride of Mind, ...6.96iii.14.275.
Yet these with soft, persuasive Arts I sway'd, ...Il.1.358.105.
(*Athens* the fair, where great *Erectheus* sway'd, ...Il.2.657.158.
There the brave Chief who mighty Numbers sway'd ....Il.5.383.285.
Then mighty *Prætus Argos'* Sceptres sway'd, ...Il.6.197.336.
(*Cilician Thebè* great *Aëtion* sway'd, ...Il.6.494.351.
The Sage whose Counsels long had sway'd the rest, ...Il.7.390.383.
With such a Tyde superior Virtue sway'd, ...Il.13.849.146.
By his own Ardour, his own Pity sway'd ....Il.15.49.196.
If, (e'er the Day when by mad Passion sway'd, ...Il.19.59.374.
(His royal hand th' imperial scepter sway'd) ....Od.2.45.62.
Wise as he was, by various Counsels sway'd, ...Od.3.197.95.
Sev'n years, the traytor rich *Mycenæ* sway'd, ...Od.3.388.105.
Sage *Nestor* fill'd it, and the sceptre sway'd. ....Od.3.523.113.
Who sway'd the sceptre, where prolific *Nile* ....Od.4.317.134.
But fearful to offend, by wisdom sway'd, ...Od.6.173.216.
By justice sway'd, by tender pity prest: ....Od.10.452.365.
He sway'd the scepter with imperial state. ....Od.11.346.399.
But sway'd by lust of gain, and headlong will, ...Od.14.292.50.
Soft were his words; his actions wisdom sway'd; ....Od.16.414.126.

SWAYS
Whose Judgment sways us, and whose Spirit warms! ....1.PAu.10.81.
Whose Judgment sways us, and whose Rapture warms! ....1.PAu.10A.81.
And *Boileau* still in Right of *Horace* sways. ....1.EOC.714.323.
Not Jove himself (your Jove that sways the skies) ....1.TrPA.99.369.
Adrastus here his happy People sways, ...1.TrSt.539.433.
Charms by accepting, by submitting sways, ...3.Ep2.263.71.
Infernal *Pluto* sways the Shades below; ....Il.15.213.205.
Yet suffers least, and sways the wav'ring Fight; ....Il.17.419.303.

SWAYS (CONTINUED)
Ev'n * He whose Trident sways the watry Reign, ... Il.20.19.393.
Some other motive, Goddess! sways thy mind, ... Od.5.223.182.
The King resolves, for mercy sways the brave. ..... Od.18.107.172.

SWEAR
I swear by all th'unpitying pow'rs of heav'n, ... 1.TrFD.70.389.
For by the black infernal *Styx* I swear, ... 1.TrSt.411.427.
And swear no Mortal's happier in a Wife; ..... 2.ChJM.201.24.
Then hear, my Lord, and witness what I swear. ..... 2.ChJM.584.43.
Now, by my own dread Majesty I swear, ... 2.ChJM.647.46.
All they shall need is to protest, and swear, ... 2.ChJM.665.47.
They need no more but to protest, and swear, ... 2.ChJM.665A.47.
But by this Lock, this sacred Lock I swear, ... 2.RL4.133.194.
So quick retires each flying course, you'd swear ..... 3.Ep4.159.153.
And swear no Day was ever past so ill. ..... 3.Ep4.168.153.
At night, wou'd swear him dropt out of the moon, ... 4.JD4.33.29.
And swear, not *Addison* himself was safe. ..... 4.Arbu.192.109.
How did they swear, not *Addison* was safe. ..... 4.Arbu.192A.109.
Who to the *Dean* and *silver Bell* can swear, ... 4.Arbu.299.117.
Out-usure Jews, or Irishmen out-swear; ..... 4.JD2.38.135.
Grave, as when Pris'ners shake the head, and swear ..... 4.JD2.69.139.
To no more purpose, than when pris'ners swear ..... 4.JD2A.78.138.
So stiff, so mute! some Statue, you would swear, ... 4.2HE2.121.173.
Call *Tibbald Shakespear,* and he'll swear the Nine ..... 4.2HE2.137.175.
And swear, all shame is lost in George's Age! ..... 4.2HE1.126.205.
Which made old Ben, and surly Dennis swear, ... 4.2HE1.388.229.
Swear like a Lord? or a *Rich* out-whore a Duke? ..... 4.EpS1.116.306.
Letters, you swear, no more you'l be ..... 6.30.62A.88.
To hear each mortal stamp and swear ..... 6.61.17.181.
How would they swear, not *Congreve's* self was safe! ..... 6.98.42.284.
4. Who to the *Dean* and *Silver Bell* can swear, ... 6.120.7.339.
Ev'n by that God I swear, who rules the Day; ..... Il.1.109.92.
Now by this sacred Sceptre, hear me swear, ... Il.1.309.102.
By this I swear, when bleeding *Greece* again ..... Il.1.317.103.
For perjur'd Kings, and all who falsely swear! ..... Il.3.353.209.
And swear the Firstlings of thy Flock to pay ..... Il.4.133.226.
And solemn swear those Charms were never mine; ..... Il.9.172.441.
And solemn swear those Charms were only thine; ..... Il.9.359.451.
And swear to grant me the demanded Prize; ..... Il.10.380.20.
Swear then (he said) by those tremendous Floods ..... Il.14.305.177.
And solemn swear, (observant of the Rite) ..... Il.19.174.378.
And Heav'n regard me as I justly swear! ..... Il.19.186.379.
For perjur'd Kings, and all who falsely swear! ..... Il.19.272.383.
To them I swear; if Victor in the Strife ..... Il.22.327.469.
And touch thy Steeds, and swear, thy whole Intent ..... Il.23.663.516.
Swear by that God whose liquid Arms surround ..... Il.23.665.516.
But by the pow'rs that hate the perjur'd, swear, ... Od.2.418.81.
Swear then, thou mean'st not what my soul forebodes; ..... Od.5.231.182.
Swear, by the solemn oath that binds the Gods. ..... Od.5.232.182.
But swear her first by those dread oaths that tie ..... Od.10.357.361.
Or swear that oath by which the Gods are ty'd, ... Od.10.408.364.
Swear, in thy soul no latent frauds remain, ... Od.10.409.364.
Swear, by the Vow which never can be vain. ..... Od.10.410.364.
"Swear first (she cry'd) ye sailors! to restore ..... Od.15.474.93.
No—by the righteous pow'rs of heav'n I swear, ... Od.16.456.129.
But swear, impartial arbiters of right, ... Od.18.64.169.
Swear, to stand neutral while we cope in fight. ..... Od.18.65.169.
By great *Ulysses,* and his woes I swear! ..... Od.20.406.252.

SWEARING
Swearing and supperless the Hero sate, ... 5.DunB1.115.278.

SWEARS
Swears every *Place entail'd* for Years to come, ... 4.JD4.160.39.
"That's *Velvet* for a *King!"* the Flattr'er swears; ..... 4.JD4.218.45.
Swears, like Albutius, a good Cook away; ..... 4.HS2.64.59.
What tho he swears tis all his own, and new; ..... 4.JD2A.37.134.
He swears but Truth, to give the Divel his due: ..... 4.JD2A.38.134.
He swears the Muses met him at the Devil. ..... 4.2HE1.42.197.
Alas! the people curse, the carman swears, ... 4.1740.73.336.

SWEAT
And finds the Heroes, bath'd in Sweat and Gore, ... 1.TrES.79.452.
They tugg, they sweat, but neither gain, nor yield, ... 1.TrES.159.455.
First thro' the length of yon hot Terrace sweat, ... 3.Ep4.130.150.
Ready to cast, I yawn, I sigh, and sweat: ..... 4.JD4.157.39.
Ready to cast, I yawn, I sigh, I sweat: ..... 4.JD4.157A.39.
Scar'd at the grizly Forms, I sweat, I fly, ... 4.JD4.278.49.
Nor at Rehearsals sweat, and mouth'd, and cry'd, ... 4.Arbu.227.112.
Tho' mine the Sweat and Danger of the Day. ..... Il.1.218.97.
They toil, they sweat, thick Clouds of Dust arise, ... Il.2.187.137.
'Till bath'd in Sweat be ev'ry manly Breast, ... Il.2.462.149.
Large Drops of Sweat from all his Limbs descend, ... Il.5.992.314.
And sweat laborious Days in Dust and Blood. ..... Il.9.431.453.
Now from nocturnal Sweat, and sanguine Stain, ... Il.10.673.31.
All drown'd in Sweat the panting Mother flies, ... Il.11.159.42.
His Coursers steep'd in Sweat, and stain'd with Gore, ... Il.11.728.67.
To dry their Sweat, and wash away the Gore, ... Il.11.759.69.
And finds the Heroes, bath'd in Sweat and Gore, ... Il.12.423.97.
They tugg, they sweat; but neither gain, nor yield, ... Il.12.513.100.
A dropping Sweat creeps cold on ev'ry Part; ..... Il.13.361.123.
And Streams of Sweat down their sow'r Foreheads flow. ..... Il.13.884.147.
Asks Toil, and Sweat, and Blood: Their utmost Might ..... Il.15.562.218.
And painful Sweat from all his Members flows. ..... Il.16.135.242.
O'erlabour'd now, with Dust, and Sweat and Gore, ... Il.17.446.304.
The mangled Body bath'd in Sweat and Blood: ..... Il.17.455.305.
The Heroes sweat beneath their honour'd Load: ..... Il.17.831.321.
Inly they groan, big Drops of Sweat distill, ... Il.17.835.321.
While bath'd in Sweat from Fire to Fire he flew, ... Il.18.437.341.
And painful Sweat from all their Members flows. ..... Il.23.797.521.
The humid Sweat from ev'ry Pore descends; ..... Il.23.831.522.
Dust mounts in clouds, and sweat descends in dews. ..... Od.11.740.422.

SWEATING
Sweating he walks, while Loads of golden Grain ..... 1.TrVP.31.378.
Like one who late unyok'd the sweating Steers. ..... 1.TrVP.36.378.
The sowzing Prelate, or the sweating Peer, ... 4.1740.70.336.
As sweating Reapers in some wealthy Field, ... Il.11.89.38.
The third time labour'd by the sweating Hind; ..... Il.18.628.354.

SWEATS
For you he sweats and labours at the Laws, ... 4.JD2.75.139.
While bloody sweats from ev'ry member flow. ..... 6.25.8.77.
The husband toils the Adulterer sweats in vain: ..... 6.130.30.359.
Mean while *Patroclus* sweats the Fire to raise; ..... Il.9.277.447.

SWEATY
From the hot Steeds the sweaty Torrents stream; ..... Il.23.591.513.

SWEDE
From Macedonia's madman to the Swede; ..... 3.EOM4.220.148.

SWEEP
Rush thro' the Thickets, down the Vallies sweep, ... 1.W-F.156.164.
With Dread beheld the rolling Surges sweep ..... 1.TrSt.59.412.
When earthquakes swallow, or when tempests sweep ..... 3.EOM1.143.33.
Shall then Uxorio, if the stakes he sweep, ... 3.Ep3.59.91.
Rouz'd by the Prince of Air, the whirlwinds sweep ..... 3.Ep3.353.122.
Now sweep those Alleys they were born to shade. ..... 3.Ep4.98.146.
And sweep the sounding Lyre! ..... 6.11.4.29.
To sweep the wicked and their Counsels hence; ..... 6.137.5.373.
Burst their dark Mansions in the Clouds, and sweep ..... Il.2.177.137.
Their Troops in thirty sable Vessels sweep ..... Il.2.618.157.
The shining Armies sweep along the Ground; ..... Il.2.947A.168.
Deluge whole Fields, and sweep the Trees along, ... Il.5.117.273.
Full o'er your Tow'rs shall fall, and sweep away ..... Il.5.595.297.
And *Troy's* proud Dames whose Garments sweep the Ground, ... Il.6.563.354.
And those swift Steeds that sweep the Ranks of War, ... Il.10.466.24.
His whirling Wheels the glassy Surface sweep; ..... Il.13.42.107.
From diff'rent Quarters sweep the sandy Plain; ..... Il.13.425.126.
Now sailing smooth the level surface sweep, ... Od.5.66.175.
For who, self-mov'd, with weary wing wou'd sweep ..... Od.5.125.178.
Back to the seas the rowling surge may sweep, ... Od.5.536.198.
'Till the huge surge roll'd off. Then backward sweep ..... Od.5.548.198.
When justly tim'd with equal sweep they row, ... Od.7.419.258.
Now plac'd in order, on their banks they sweep ..... Od.9.115.308.
In order seated on their banks, they sweep ..... Od.9.209.314.
Now rang'd in order on our banks, we sweep ..... Od.9.656.333.
And sweep with equal strokes the smoaky seas; ..... Od.10.150.347.
Safe through the level seas we sweep our way; ..... Od.14.286.49.
Aboard they heave us, mount their decks, and sweep ..... Od.15.509.94.
Sweep with their arching nets the hoary main, ... Od.22.426.308.
Or did the rage of stormy *Neptune* sweep ..... Od.24.134.354.

SWEEPING
While Peers and Dukes, and all their sweeping Train, ... 2.RL1.84.152.
With sweeping Glories glides along in Air, ... Il.4.105.225.
The proud *Ionians* with their sweeping Trains, ... Il.13.860.146.
With sweeping Stroke the Mowers strow the Lands; ..... Il.18.641.354.
(The silver Traces sweeping at their side) ..... Il.19.428.389.
Or scornful Sister with her sweeping Train, ... Il.24.973.576.

SWEEPS
Till hov'ring o'er 'em sweeps the swelling Net. ..... 1.W-F.104.160.
Now serpent-like, in prose he sweeps the ground, ... 4.2HE1.100.203.
Sweeps the wide Earth, and tramples o'er Mankind, ... Il.9.629.465.
A sudden Storm the purple Ocean sweeps, ... Il.11.385.51.
Wide o'er the blasted Fields the Tempest sweeps, ... Il.13.1001.152.
Sweeps the slight Works and fashion'd Domes away. ..... Il.15.419.213.
That sweeps the Fields, depopulates the Fold; ..... Il.16.910.279.
So sweeps the Hero thro' the wasted Shores; ..... Il.20.574.418.
Crossing a Ford, the Torrent sweeps away, ... Il.21.328.434.
As when Autumnal *Boreas* sweeps the Sky, ... Il.21.402.437.
Meteorous the Face of Ocean sweeps, ... Il.24.101.539.
Wide o'er the waste the rage of *Boreas* sweeps, ... Od.9.77.306.
The gushing tempest sweeps the Ocean round; ..... Od.10.51.342.
Swift as a swallow sweeps the liquid way, ... Od.13.186.15.
Whose luxury whole patrimonies sweeps, ... Od.17.541.158.

SWEEPY
The sweepy Crest hung floating in the Wind: ..... Il.19.411.389.
Of *Jove's* high seat descends with sweepy force, ... Od.4.644.150.
And next, a wedge to drive with sweepy sway: ..... Od.5.303.185.

SWEET
Here shall I try the sweet *Alexis'* Strain, ... 1.PWi.11.89.
In hollow Caves sweet *Echo* silent lies, ... 1.PWi.41.92.
More sweet than winter's sun, or summer's air, ... 1.TrPA.54.367.
But when with Day the sweet Delusions fly, ... 1.TrSP.155.400.
A sweet Forgetfulness of Human Care. ..... 1.TrSt.481.430.
Whether to sweet *Castalia* thou repair, ... 1.TrSt.831.444.
And with the Perfumes of sweet *Ambrosial* Dews, ... 1.TrES.342.462.
The sweet Delusion kindly you impose, ... 1.TrUl.205.472.
Her sweet Behaviour, her enchanting Face, ... 2.ChJM.248.26.
To this sweet Place, in Summer's sultry Heat, ... 2.ChJM.469.37.
Well sung sweet *Ovid,* in the Days of yore, ... 2.ChJM.514.40.
At least, kind Sir, for Charity's sweet sake, ... 2.ChJM.732.50.
And sung as sweet as Evening *Philomel.* ..... 2.ChWB.212.67.
The Notes at first were rather sweet than loud: ..... 2.TemF.311.279.
Sweet to the World, and grateful to the Skies. ..... 2.TemF.377.281.
Or drest in smiles of sweet Cecilia shine, ... 3.Ep2.13.49.
Or who in sweet vicissitude appears ..... 3.Ep2.109.58.
From soup to sweet-wine, and God bless the King. ..... 3.Ep4.162.153.
And " *sweet Sir Fopling! you have so much wit!"* ..... 4.JD4.233.45.
Sweet *Moll* and *Jack* are Civet-Cat and Boar: ..... 4.HAdv.30.77.
And there in sweet oblivion drown ..... 4.HS6.131.259.
"As sweet a Cave as one shall see! ..... 4.HS6.175.261.
Lull'd with the sweet *Nepenthe* of a Court; ..... 4.EpS1.98.305.
Sweet to the World, and grateful to the Skies: ..... 4.EpS2.245.326.

SWEET (CONTINUED)

And in sweet numbers celebrates the seat. ..... 5.DunA1.226.90.
Taylor, sweet bird of Thames, majestic bows, ... 5.DunA2.323.141.
Taylor, sweet Swan of Thames, majestic bows; ..... 5.DunA2.323A.141.
How sweet the periods, neither said nor sung! ..... 5.DunA3.198.174.
Each Cygnet sweet of Bath and Tunbridge race, ... 5.DunB3.155.327.
How sweet the periods, neither sad, nor sung! ..... 5.DunB3.202.330.
How sweet an Ovid, MURRAY was our boast! ..... 5.DunB4.169.357.
Together mix'd; sweet recreation, ... 6.1.14.3.
Around in sweet Meanders wildly range, ... 6.17ii.25.56.
To the sweet Name of *Tom D'Urfy*. ..... 6.30.12.86.
No Vixen Civet-Cat so sweet, ... 6.79.31.218.
No Vixen Civet-Cat more sweet, ... 6.79.31A.218.
A double Jest still pleases sweet Sir Harry— ..... 6.82vi.12.232.
By thy sweet Sojourn in those virtuous Climes, ... 6.96iii.6.274.
Was *Flimnap's* Dame more sweet in *Lilliput?* ..... 6.96iv.26.277.
And (at due distance) sweet Discourse admit, ... 6.96iv.62.278.
And sweet Adonis—you have lost a Tooth. ..... 6.129.8.357.
To thee, sweet *Fop*, these Lines I send, ... 6.135.1.366.
And *Ireland*, mother of sweet singers, ... 6.150.7.398.
Words, sweet as Honey, from his Lips distill'd: ..... Il.1.332.103.
Sweet *Pyrrhasus*, with blooming Flourets crown'd, ... Il.2.851.164.
Sweet Smiles are thine and kind endearing Charms, ... Il.5.521.293.
In Slumbers sweet the rev'rend *Phœnix* lay. ..... Il.9.778.472.
Ev'n the sweet Charms of sacred Numbers tire. ..... Il.13.798.143.
To some, sweet Music, and the Charm of Song; ..... Il.13.916.148.
Sweet pleasing Sleep! (*Saturnia* thus began) ..... Il.14.266.174.
And with Perfumes of sweet Ambrosial Dews, ... Il.16.829.275.
Sweet to the Soul, as Hony to the Taste; ..... Il.18.140.329.
Thy sweet Society, thy winning Care, ... Il.19.337.386.
With Nectar sweet, (Refection of the Gods!) ..... Il.19.376.387.
And each indulging shar'd in sweet Repast. ..... Il.24.795.570.
With sweet, reluctant, amorous delay: ..... Od.1.22.30.
Glowing cælestial-sweet with godlike grace, ... Od.1.149.40.
Light is the dance, and double sweet the lays, ... Od.1.205.42.
But since to part, for sweet refection due ..... Od.1.403.51.
Obey that sweet compulsion, nor profane ..... Od.1.471.55.
To taint the joys of sweet, connubial life. ..... Od.1.546.58.
Sweet *Polycaste*, took the pleasing toil ..... Od.3.594.116.
And sweet discourse, the banquet of the mind. ..... Od.4.330.135.
And love, the only sweet of life, destroy. ..... Od.5.152.178.
And golden dreams (the gift of sweet repose) ..... Od.5.636.202.
And warbling sweet, makes earth and heav'n rejoice. ..... Od.6.116.211.
Snatch'd from *Epirus*, her sweet native shore, ... Od.7.12.233.
Yet eager would I bless the sweet disgrace. ..... Od.8.380.284.
Hear the sweet song, and taste the feast in peace. ..... Od.8.464.288.
How sweet the products of a peaceful reign? ..... Od.9.3.298.
With sweet, reluctant, amorous delay; ..... Od.9.32.303.
Insatiate riots in the sweet repasts, ... Od.9.108.308.
To the sweet transports of the genial bed. ..... Od.10.412.364.
But, when thy soul from her sweet mansion fled, ... Od.11.206.391.
And thus the sweet deluders tune the song. ..... Od.12.221.442.
Thus the sweet charmers warbled o'er the main; ..... Od.12.232.443.
Sweet time of slumber! be the night obey'd! ..... Od.12.348.448.
A sweet forgetfulness of human cares. ..... Od.12.366.449.
The sweet delusion kindly you impose, ... Od.13.372.25.
He sate, and sweet refection cheer'd his soul. ..... Od.14.501.60.
'Tis sweet to play the fool in time and place, ... Od.14.519.62.
Sweet is thy converse to each social ear; ..... Od.15.355.86.
Now did the hour of sweet repaste arrive, ... Od.17.194.141.
Sweet Airs ascend, and heav'nly minstrelsie; ..... Od.17.311.147.
So much more sweet, to spoil, than to bestow? ..... Od.17.487.156.
Sweet blooms the Prince beneath *Apollo's* care; ..... Od.19.106.197.
In sweet oblivion let my sorrow sleep! ..... Od.19.140.199.
Suspend the restful hour with sweet discourse. ..... Od.19.597.225.
Far from the sweet society of men, ... Od.21.394.279.
In sweet repaste the present hour imploy, ... Od.21.471.283.
Phemius the sweet, the heav'n-instructed bard. ..... Od.22.368.305.
Ev'n He indulges the sweet joy of tears. ..... Od.22.538.315.
Never did I a sleep so sweet enjoy, ... Od.23.21.319.
While the sweet Lyrist airs of rapture sings, ... Od.23.133.327.
With sweet reluctant amorous delay; ..... Od.23.362.342.
A sweet forgetfulness of all his cares. ..... Od.23.370.343.
Then unguents sweet and tepid streams we shed; ..... Od.24.62.350.

SWEET-WINE

From soup to sweet-wine, and God bless the King. ..... 3.Ep4.162.153.

SWEETEN'D

Has sweeten'd all thy bitter draught of ill: ..... Od.15.525.95.

SWEETER

Lament the Ceasing of a sweeter Breath. ..... 1.PWi.50.92.
A sweeter Musick than their own to hear, ... 1.PWi.58.93.
With *sweeter Notes* each *rising Temple* rung; ..... 1.EOC.703.320.
And found my Kisses sweeter than my Song. ..... 1.TrSP.56.396.
To sweeter Sounds, and temper'd *Pindar's* Fire: ..... 2.TemF.223.273.
Which still grew sweeter as they wider spread: ..... 2.TemF.315.279.
Sweeter than *Sharon*, in immaculate trim, ... 4.JD4.252.47.
Discourse, the sweeter banquet of the mind; ..... Od.15.433.90.

SWEETEST

"Oh 'tis the sweetest of all earthly things ..... 4.JD4.100.33.
He finds no relish in the sweetest Meat; ..... 4.HS2.32.57.
He'll find no relish in the sweetest Meat; ..... 4.HS2.31A.57.
The sweetest thing will stink that he can eat ..... 4.HS2.32A.57.
He'll find no relish in the sweetest Meat; ..... 4.HS2.32B.57.
Than eat the sweetest by themselves at home. ..... 4.HS2.96.61.
(That sweetest Music to an honest ear; ..... 4.HS2.100.61.
Phemius, whose voice divine cou'd sweetest sing ..... Od.1.199.42.
There he, the sweetest of the sacred train, ... Od.3.342.103.

SWEETLY

So sweetly warble, or so smoothly flow. ..... 1.PWi.4.89.
Ev'n I more sweetly pass my careless Days, ... 1.W-F.431.194.
As Shades more sweetly recommend the Light, ... 1.EOC.301.273.

SWEETLY (CONTINUED)

And sweetly *melt* into just Shade and Light, ... 1.EOC.489.294.
Shone sweetly lambent with celestial day: ..... 2.ElAb.64.324.
And sweetly flow through all the Royal Line. ..... 4.HS1.32.7.
So sweetly mawkish, and so smoothly dull; ..... 5.DunA3.165.167.
So sweetly mawkish, and so smoothly dull; ..... 5.DunB3.171.328.
With silver sounds, and sweetly tune out time. ..... 6.82xii.2.237.

SWEETNESS

Fair *Daphne's* dead, and Sweetness is no more! ..... 1.PWi.52.92.
Where *Denham's* Strength, and *Waller's* Sweetness join. ..... 1.EOC.361.280.
The costly Sweetness of *Arabian* Dews, ... 1.TrSP.84.397.
Where Filial Love with Virgin Sweetness join'd. ..... 1.TrSt.673.438.
Yet graceful Ease, and Sweetness void of Pride, ... 2.RL2.15.160.
If this is priz'd for *sweetness*, that for *stink?* ..... 4.HS2.30.57.
What thy cælestial Sweetness does impart; ..... 6.2.8.6.
At once their Motion, Sweetness, and their Use; ..... 6.17ii.10.56.
They, from the Sweetness of that Radiant Look, ... 6.37.7.106.
An Angel's sweetness, or *Bridgewater's* eyes. ..... 6.52.46.157.

SWEETS

While opening Blooms diffuse their Sweets around. ..... 1.PSp.100.70.
But your *Alexis* knows no Sweets but you. ..... 1.PSu.70.77.
Each wou'd the sweets of Sovereign Rule devour, ... 1.TrSt.182.418.
Or settling, seize the Sweets the Blossoms yield, ... 2.TemF.286.277.
How much her sweets their own excel. ..... 6.4iv.9.10.
And with fresh sweets perfume the air, ... 6.4iv.14.11.
No sweets but *Serenissa's* sighs. ..... 6.4v.4.11.
Where opening *Roses* breathing sweets diffuse, ... 6.14iv.3.47.
To breath the Sweets of pure Parnassian *Air,* ..... 6.26ii.2.79.
"O show me, *Flora*, 'midst those Sweets, the Flow'r ..... 6.96ii.49.273.
With pleasing Sweets his fainting Sense renews, ... Il.3.471.214.
The Sense of Gods with more than mortal Sweets. ..... Il.14.202.169.
He felt the Sweets of Liberty again; ..... Il.21.51.424.
Shed sweets shed unguents, in a show'r of oil: ..... Od.8.492.289.
Reviving sweets repair the mind's decay, ... Od.10.427.365.

SWELL

And grateful Clusters swell with floods of Wine; ..... 1.PAu.74.85.
And swell the future Harvest of the Field! ..... 1.PWi.16.89.
And swell the future Harvest of thy Field! ..... 1.PWi.16A.89.
And purer Spirits swell the sprightly Flood, ... 1.W-F.94.159.
Who swell with Tributary Urns his Flood. ..... 1.W-F.338.183.
That swell with Tributary Urns his Flood. ..... 1.W-F.338A.183.
Now swell to Rage, now melt in Tears again. ..... 1.TrSP.132.399.
Cou'd swell the Soul to Rage, and fire the Martial Train. ..... 2.ChJM.325.30.
Silence wou'd swell me, and my Heart wou'd break. ..... 2.ChJM.695.48.
Lord! how you swell, and rage like any Fiend! ..... 2.ChWB.81.60.
These swell their Prospects and exalt their Pride, ... 2.RL1.81.151.
Who swell their Prospects and exalt their Pride, ... 2.RL1.81A.151.
The Domes swell up, the widening Arches bend, ... 2.TemF.90.259.
And on the Winds triumphant swell the Notes; ..... 2.TemF.373.281.
And up the Winds triumphant swell the Notes; ..... 2.TemF.373A.281.
And swell the pomp of dreadful sacrifice, ... 2.ElAb.354.348.
Loves of his own and raptures swell the note: ..... 3.EOM3.34.95.
Glorious Ambition! Peter, swell thy store, ... 3.Ep3.127.102.
"What mines, to swell that boundless charity?" ..... 3.Ep3.278.116.
To swell the Terras, or to sink the Grot; ..... 3.Ep4.49.142.
Than such as swell this Bladder of a Court? ..... 4.JD4.205.43.
Yet some I know with envy swell, ... 4.HS6.101.257.
With horns and trumpets now to madness swell, ... 5.DunA2.219.128.
With horns and trumpets now to madness swell, ... 5.DunB2.227.307.
Exulting in Triumph now swell the bold Notes, ... 6.11.16.30.
Nor swell too high, nor sink too low. ..... 6.11.23.30.
And neither swell too high, nor sink too low; ..... 6.17ii.20.56.
When gath'ring tempests swell the raging main, ... 6.21.7.69.
Swell with Praise ..... 6.96i.6.268.
And slaughter'd Heroes swell the dreadful Tide. ..... Il.4.515.246.
And slaughter'd Heroes swell the dreadful Tide. ..... Il.8.82.399.
Vain Dreams of Conquest swell his haughty Mind; ..... Il.13.762.141.
Swell his bold Heart, and urge his Strength to War: ..... Il.15.261.207.
And slaughter'd Heroes swell the dreadful Tyde. ..... Il.15.867.230.
Great *Jove*, to swell the Horrors of the Flight, ... Il.16.695.271.
Ourself with rising Spirits swell your Heart. ..... Il.17.517.308.
From all thy Fountains swell thy wat'ry Store, ... Il.21.363.435.
Swell to each Gripe, and bloody Tumours rise. ..... Il.23.833.522.
Bow the tall mast, and swell before the gales; ..... Od.2.467.83.
The mighty griefs that swell her lab'ring soul, ... Od.4.951.162.
To smooth the deep, or swell the foamy sea. ..... Od.10.24.340.
The jutting shores that swell on either side ..... Od.10.103.345.
Swell the fat herd; luxuriant, large repaste! ..... Od.13.472.29.
Descend to swell the springs, and feed the flow'rs! ..... Od.17.283.146.
Swell o'er his well-strung limbs, and brace his frame! ..... Od.18.85.170.
The tides of lust that swell their boiling veins: ..... Od.20.214.243.
Cicons on *Cicons* swell th' ensanguin'd plain; ..... Od.23.334.340.
Swell with new joy, and thus his son addrest. ..... Od.24.583.376.

SWELL'D

Swell'd with new Passion, and o'erflows with Tears; ..... 1.PWi.66.93.
In vain kind Seasons swell'd the teeming Grain, ... 1.W-F.53.154.
What wants in *Blood* and *Spirits*, swell'd with *Wind;* ..... 1.EOC.208.264.
Here as I lay, and swell'd with Tears the Flood, ... 1.TrSP.185.401.
What Joys, oh Tyrant! swell'd thy Soul that Day, ... 1.TrSt.220.419.
That, from his exil'd Brother, swell'd with Pride ..... 1.TrSt.423.427.
Long time I heard, and swell'd, and blush'd, and frown'd, ... 2.ChWB.411.77.
So large it spread, and swell'd to such a Height. ..... 2.TemF.247.275.
But swell'd to larger Size, the more I gaz'd, ... 2.TemF.260.275.
Some swell'd to Gods, confess ev'n Virtue vain; ..... 3.EOM4.24.130.
When Catiline by rapine swell'd his store, ... 3.Ep1.212.33.
E'er swell'd on Marble; as in Verse have shin'd ..... 4.2HE1.392.229.
Prose swell'd to verse, Verse loitring into prose; ..... 5.DunA1.228.90.
Prose swell'd to verse, verse loit'ring into prose: ..... 5.DunB1.274.290.
Fierce as a startled Adder, swell'd, and said, ... 5.DunB4.373.379.
His Heart swell'd high, and labour'd in his Breast. ..... Il.1.252.98.
Tho' secret Anger swell'd *Minerva's* Breast, ... Il.4.31.222.
He said: new Courage swell'd each Hero's Heart. ..... Il.5.572.296.

SWELL'D (CONTINUED)

Tho' secret Anger swell'd *Minerva's* Breast, ... Il.8.572.424.
Superior Sorrows swell'd his Royal Breast; .... Il.9.12.431.
As from the Clouds' deep Bosom swell'd with Show'rs, ... Il.11.384.51.
As when a Torrent, swell'd with wintry Rains, ... Il.11.614.61.
Swell'd with false Hopes, with mad Ambition vain! .... Il.13.458.128.
With Pity soften'd, and with Fury swell'd: .... Il.13.828.145.
And clust'ring *Lotos* swell'd the rising Bed, ... Il.14.398.182.
And swell'd with Tempests on the Ship descends; .... Il.15.753.225.
Thus when a River swell'd with sudden Rains .... Il.17.839.321.
Each *Argive* Bosom swell'd with manly Joy, ... Il.20.56.396.
But when the Pow'rs descending swell'd the Fight, ... Il.20.63.396.
But swell'd his Bosom with undaunted Might, ... Il.20.111.398.
With equal Ardor bold *Tydides* swell'd .... Il.23.359.504.
While his fond soul these fancied triumphs swell'd, ... Od.1.155.40.
Then swell'd to sight *Phæacia's* dusky coast, ... Od.5.357.189.
His swoln heart heav'd; his bloated body swell'd: .... Od.5.583.200.
And swell'd the ground with mountains of the slain, ... Od.11.612.414.
I swell'd in pomp, and arrogance of state; .... Od.18.166.174.
And swell'd the bleeding mountain on the ground. .... Od.22.135.293.

SWELLING

And swelling Clusters bend the curling Vines: .... 1.PSp.36.64.
Till hov'ring o'er 'em sweeps the swelling Net. .... 1.W-F.104.160.
His swelling Waters, and alternate Tydes; .... 1.W-F.334.182.
Whole Nations enter with each swelling Tyde, ... 1.W-F.399.191.
The curling Vine her swelling Clusters spread; .... 1.TrVP.60.379.
Cupid for thee shall spread the swelling Sails. .... 1.TrSP.253.404.
For thee shall *Cupid* spread the swelling Sails. .... 1.TrSP.253A.404.
And *Thetis,* near *Ismenos'* swelling Flood, ... 1.TrSt.58.412.
Suffices Fulness to the swelling Grain; .... 1.TrUl.125.470.
And warm the swelling Veins to Feats of Love: .... 2.ChWB.216.67.
Full o'er their Heads the swelling Bag he rent, ... 2.RL4.91.191.
And swelling organs lift the rising soul; .... 2.ElAb.272.342.
Proud grief sits swelling in her eyes: .... 6.5.2.12.
Born on the swelling Notes our Souls aspire, ... 6.11.128.34.
And fearless crush the swelling Aspick's head, ... 6.21.30.70.
The swelling Billows bore him from the Land, ... 6.96ii.30Z22.271.
Supply'd by *Phœbus,* fill the swelling Sails; .... Il.1.625.117.
Whose brawny Shoulders, and whose swelling Chest, ... Il.3.291.207.
'Till black as Night the swelling Tempest shows, ... Il.4.318.235.
If chance a swelling Brook his Passage stay, ... Il.5.736.302.
And Pray'rs will burst that swelling Heart with Pride. .... Il.9.819.474.
And driving down, the swelling Bladder rends: .... Il.13.816.144.
A golden Zone her swelling Bosom bound. .... Il.14.210.170.
The Tears, and Sighs burst from his swelling Heart. .... Il.18.370.339.
Deep in the swelling Bank was driv'n the Spear, ... Il.21.187.429.
Increas'd with Gore, and swelling with the Slain. .... Il.21.379.436.
So roll'd up in his Den, the swelling Snake .... Il.22.130.458.
High in the midst they heap the swelling Bed .... Il.23.319.502.
Then swelling sorrows burst their former bounds, ... Od.1.461.54.
The bark, to waft thee o'er the swelling tides. .... Od.2.346.77.
The God still breathing on my swelling sails; .... Od.3.222.96.
The Seer, while Zephyrs curl the swelling deep, ... Od.4.541.146.
Pour'd the big sorrows of his swelling heart; .... Od.5.104.177.
On a slight Raft to pass the swelling sea .... Od.5.226.182.
Her swelling loins a radiant Zone embrac'd .... Od.5.296.185.
'Tis *Jove* himself the swelling tempest rears; .... Od.5.391.191.
Far on the swelling surge the chief was born: .... Od.5.406.192.
And stretch the swelling canvas to the gales; .... Od.8.48.264.
Call thee aboard, and stretch the swelling sails. .... Od.8.166.271.
Tho' tempests rage, tho' rolls the swelling main, ... Od.8.611.295.
He charg'd to fill, and guide the swelling sails: .... Od.10.28.340.
His swelling heart deny'd the words their way: .... Od.10.290.357.
Our oars we shipp'd: all day the swelling sails .... Od.11.9.379.
Sing thro' the shrouds, and stretch the swelling sails. .... Od.11.794.426.
The friendly Goddess stretch'd the swelling sails; .... Od.12.185.441.
The swelling couch, and lay compos'd to rest. .... Od.13.91.5.
Suffices fulness to the swelling grain: .... Od.13.292.19.
Far on the swelling seas to wander hence? .... Od.14.207.45.
Haste, rear the mast, the swelling shroud display; .... Od.16.364.124.
Down from the swelling loins, the vest unbound .... Od.18.341.184.

SWELLS

Nor *Po* so swells the fabling Poet's Lays, ... 1.W-F.227.170.
Not fabled *Po* more swells the Poets Lays, ... 1.W-F.227A.170.
Tho' foaming *Hermus* swells with Tydes of Gold, ... 1.W-F.358.185.
And swells on an imaginary Throne. .... 1.TrSt.450.428.
The foaming *Lerna* swells above its Bounds, ... 1.TrSt.502.431.
And swells her Breast with Conquests yet to come. .... 2.RL3.28.171.
"Suckles each herb, and swells out ev'ry flow'r; .... 3.EOM1.134A.32.
The vital flame, and swells the genial seeds. .... 3.EOM3.118.104.
That Robe of Quality so struts and swells, ... 3.Ep2.189.65.
That spreads and swells in puff'd Prosperity, ... 4.HS2.126.65.
Here swells the shelf with Ogilby the great: .... 5.DunA1.121.78.
So swells each Windpipe; Ass intones to Ass, ... 5.DunA2.243.129.
Here swells the shelf with Ogilby the great; .... 5.DunB1.141.280.
She ceas'd. Then swells the Chapel-royal throat: .... 5.DunB1.319.293.
So swells each wind-pipe, Ass intones to Ass, ... 5.DunB2.253.307.
And swells his bloated Corps to largest size. .... 6.26i.15.79.
Swells their bold Hearts, and strings their nervous Arms; .... Il.2.531.152.
Axius, that swells with all his neigh'bring Rills, ... Il.2.1032.171.
Strength swells thy boiling Breast, infus'd by me, ... Il.5.162.274.
This swells the Tumult and the Rage of Fight; .... Il.5.728.302.
Nor swells thy Heart in that immortal Breast? .... Il.8.245.409.
Still swells the Slaughter, and still grows the Rage! .... Il.8.432.418.
Who swells the Clouds, and blackens all the Skies. .... Il.8.585.424.
Swells o'er the Sea, from *Thracia's* frozen Shore, ... Il.9.7.431.
Swells the red Horrors of this direful Plain: .... Il.11.102.39.
And deep *Scamander* swells with Heaps of Slain. .... Il.11.623.61.
Each burns for Fame, and swells with martial Pride; .... Il.11.852.74.
Prompts their light limbs, and swells their daring hearts. .... Il.13.90.109.
Swells all their Hearts, and strengthens all their Hands. .... Il.15.717.223.
That all shall know, *Achilles* swells the Tide. .... Il.18.162.330.
With her own Shout *Minerva* swells the Sound; .... Il.18.257.334.
And plenteous *Hermus* swells with Tides of Gold, ... Il.20.452.413.

SWELLS (CONTINUED)

With Fury swells the violated Flood. .... Il.21.152.427.
Axius, who swells with all the neigh'bring Rills, ... Il.21.175.428.
Joy swells his Soul, as when the vernal Grain .... Il.23.679.516.
The weeping Monarch swells the mighty woe: .... Od.4.252.131.
Swells all the winds, and rouzes all the storms. .... Od.5.378.190.
Swells his bold heart, his bosom nobly glows? .... Od.11.604.413.
Who swells the clouds, and gladdens earth with show'rs. .... Od.13.163.13.
Is it that vanquish'd *Irus* swells thy mind? .... Od.18.381.186.

SWEPT

Swept Herds, and Hinds, and Houses to the Main. .... 1.TrSt.515.432.
Led off two captive Trumps, and swept the Board. .... 2.RL3.50.172.
Where things destroy'd are swept to things unborn." .... 5.DunB1.242.288.
Swept to the War, the Lumber of a Land. .... Il.2.240.139.
The shining Armies swept along the Ground; .... Il.2.947.168.
The River swept him to the briny Main: .... Il.2.1065.172.
A moving Cloud, swept on, and hid the Plain. .... Il.3.22.189.
And follow'd where *Tydides* swept the Plain. .... Il.5.406.286.
Fierce as a Whirlwind now I swept the Field: .... Il.11.881.75.
Whole Fields are drown'd, and Mountains swept away; .... Il.16.473.261.
Swept the wide Shore, and drove him to the Plain. .... Il.20.179.401.
These lightly skimming, when they swept the Plain, ... Il.20.270.405.
And ignominious as it swept the Field, ... Il.24.32.536.
Nine Cubits long the Traces swept the Ground; .... Il.24.337.550.
Swept from the deck, and from the rudder torn, ... Od.5.405.192.
Swept from the earth, he perish'd in his prime; .... Od.8.258.276.
Stretch'd her dire jaws and swept six men away; .... Od.12.295.446.
Long as the minstrel swept the sounding wire, ... Od.17.430.153.

SWIFT

Swift fly the Years, and rise th'expected Morn! .... 1.Mes.21.114.
Swift Trouts, diversify'd with Crimson Stains, ... 1.W-F.145.163.
Not half so swift the trembling Doves can fly, ... 1.W-F.185.167.
The *Kennet* swift, for silver Eels renown'd; .... 1.W-F.341.183.
Not so, when swift *Camilla* scours the Plain, ... 1.EOC.372.282.
But, ah! like rivers, swift to glide away; .... 1.TrPA.63.368.
Swift as the wind before pursuing love; .... 1.TrPA.65.368.
Swift as she past, the flitting Ghosts withdrew, ... 1.TrSt.132.415.
And the swift Hounds, affrighted as he flies, ... 1.TrSt.646.437.
Swift as the Word, the Herald speeds along .... 1.TrES.77.452.
Swift to the Battlement the Victor flies, ... 1.TrES.129.454.
Swift to the Field precipitates his Flight; .... 1.TrES.337.462.
Less swift, an Eagle cuts the liquid Skies: .... 1.TrUl.14.466.
Whose Son, the swift *Orsilochus,* I slew, ... 1.TrUl.145.470.
Still one by one, in swift Succession, pass .... 2.ChJM.236.25.
Swift as an Arrow soaring from the Bow! .... 2.ChJM.290.28.
Swift to the Lock a thousand Sprights repair, ... 2.RL3.135.178.
Swift on his sooty Pinions flitts the *Gnome,* .... 2.RL4.17.184.
And swift as Lightning to the Combate flies. .... 2.RL5.38.202.
"But Sir, of Writers?"—" *Swift,* for closer Style, ... 4.JD4.72.31.
"Pray heav'n it last! (cries Swift) as you go on; .... 4.HS2.161.67.
What's *Property?* dear Swift! you see it alter .... 4.HS2.167.69.
And *Congreve* lov'd, and *Swift* endur'd my Lays; .... 4.Arbu.138.105.
"I found him close with *Swift"—"Indeed?* no doubt" .... 4.Arbu.275.115.
And leave on SWIFT this grateful verse ingrav'd, ... 4.2HE1.223.213.
And Swift cry wisely, "Vive la Bagatelle!" .... 4.1HE6.128.246.
Our old Friend Swift will tell his Story. .... 4.1HE7.82.273.
Swift as a bard the bailiff leaves behind, ... 5.DunA2.57.105.
And whisk 'em back to Evans, Young, and Swift. .... 5.DunA2.108.109.
And whisk 'em back to *G[ay],* to *Y[oung],* to *S[wift].* 5.DunA2.108A.109
Cook shall be Prior, and Concanen, Swift, ... 5.DunA2.130.112.
Swift as it mounts, all follow with their eyes; .... 5.DunA2.177.123.
Swift to whose hand a winged volume flies: .... 5.DunA3.230.176.
Hibernian Politicks, O Swift, thy doom, ... 5.DunA3.327.190.
Hibernian Politicks, O Swift, thy fate, ... 5.DunA3.327A.190.
Mourn not, my SWIFT, at ought our Realm acquires, ... 5.DunB1.26.271.
Swift as a bard the bailiff leaves behind, ... 5.DunB2.61.298.
And whisk 'em back to Evans, Young, and Swift. .... 5.DunB2.116.301.
Cook shall be Prior, and Concanen, Swift: .... 5.DunB2.138.301.
Swift as it mounts, all follow with their eyes: .... 5.DunB2.185.304.
Swift to whose hand a winged volume flies: .... 5.DunB3.234.331.
Hibernian Politics, O Swift! thy fate; .... 5.DunB3.331.336.
Hours, days, and years slide swift away, ... 6.1.10B.3.
So swift,—this moment here, the next 'tis gone, ... 6.9iv.1.21.
In constant Motion, nor too swift nor slow, ... 6.17ii.19.56.
Shallow, yet swift, the stream of fortune flows, ... 6.22.3.71.
And shake his Head at Doctor *S[wif]t.* .... 6.39.24.111.
We'll not be slow to visit Dr. Swift. .... 6.42vi.6.120.
Of secret Jesuits swift shall be the Doom, ... 6.48ii.7.134.
For *Swift* and him, despis'd the Farce of State, ... 6.84.9.238.
Jonathan Swift .... 6.90.1.251.
Minerva swift descended from above, ... Il.1.261.99.
The Goddess swift to high *Olympus* flies, ... Il.1.293.100.
Above the bounding Billows swift they flew, ... Il.1.628.117.
Swift to the Seas profound the Goddess flies, ... Il.1.688.120.
Descending swift, roll'd down the rapid Light. .... Il.1.777.124.
Swift as the Word the vain *Illusion* fled, ... Il.2.19.128.
Swift to the Ships precipitates her Flight; .... Il.2.204.138.
Swift in Pursuit, and active in the Fight. .... Il.2.633.157.
Led nine swift Vessels thro' the foamy Seas; .... Il.2.794.163.
Prothous the swift, of old *Tenthredon's* Blood; .... Il.2.917.167.
Swift as a Flood of Fire, when Storms arise, ... Il.2.948.168.
Swift march the *Greeks:* the rapid Dust around .... Il.3.13.188.
Swift-gliding Mists the dusky Fields invade, ... Il.3.17.188.
Herald be swift, and bid *Machaön* bring .... Il.4.230.232.
With hasty Zeal the swift *Talthybius* flies; .... Il.4.234.232.
Swift to his Succour thro' the Ranks he ran: .... Il.4.243.232.
Urge their swift Steeds to face the coming War) .... Il.4.267.234.
From *Meges'* Force the swift *Pedæus* fled, ... Il.5.91.270.
Swift thro' his crackling Jaws the Weapon glides, ... Il.5.97.271.
Thus from high Hills the Torrents swift and strong .... Il.5.116.272.
Swift to the Mark the thirsty Arrow flew, ... Il.5.129.273.
Swift from his Seat he leap'd upon the Ground, ... Il.5.142.274.
Nor join'd swift Horses to the rapid Car. .... Il.5.243.279.
Swift to *Æneas'* empty Seat proceed, ... Il.5.326.282.

SWIFT (CONTINUED)

SWIFT (CONTINUED)

SWIFT-GLIDING

SWIFT-WING'D

SWIFTER
And bids the Year with swifter Motion run. ......1.TrSt.454.429.
And swifter than *His* Arms, give *Victory:* ......6.17iv.6.59.
Swifter than Thought the Wheels instinctive fly, ...Il.8.544.422.
Thro' broken Orders, swifter than the Wind, ...Il.11.441.53.
His foaming Coursers, swifter than the Wind, ...Il.14.505.188.
He spoke; and speaking, swifter than the Wind ......Il.15.468.215.
Deserts his Chariot for a swifter Flight: ......Il.20.464.413.
Achilles only boasts a swifter Pace: ......Il.23.932.526.
Or swifter in the race devour the way: ......Od.8.102.268.

SWIFTEST
The heaviest Muse the swiftest Course has gone, ...6.7.3.15.
Skill'd in Pursuit, and swiftest in the Chace. ......Il.14.618.192.
From Danger now with swiftest Speed they flew, ...Il.17.530.309.
(Swiftest and strongest of th' aerial Race) ......Il.21.282.432.
Incens'd, we heav'nward fled with swiftest wing, ...Il.21.529.443.
(The swiftest Racer of the liquid Skies) ......Il.22.184.463.
Those, tho' the swiftest, by some God with-held, ...Il.23.544.511.
She spoke, and led the way with swiftest speed: ......Od.3.39.88.
Or you, the swiftest racers of the field! ......Od.8.234.275.
No bird of air, no dove of swiftest wing, ...Od.12.75.435.
The swiftest racer of the azure plain ......Od.12.121.437.

SWIFTLY
Not half so swiftly the fierce Eagle moves, ...1.W-F.187.167.
Not half so swiftly shoots along in Air ......1.TrSt.128.415.
And swiftly shoot along the Mall, ...4.HOde1.45.153.
And pond'rous slugs cut swiftly thro' the sky; ......5.DunA1.178.84.
And pond'rous slugs cut swiftly thro the sky; ......5.DunB1.182.283.
Aloft I'm swiftly born, methinks I rise, ...6.26ii.3.79.
Then swiftly sailing, cut the liquid Road. ......Il.1.409.107.
From Ship to Ship thus *Ajax* swiftly flew, ...Il.15.830.229.
Thus they above: While swiftly gliding down, ...Il.21.597.446.
The panting Coursers swiftly turn the Goal, ...Il.22.215.464.
Fraudful she said; then swiftly march'd before; ......Il.22.313.469.
Then scudding swiftly from the dang'rous ground, ...Od.12.238.443.

SWIFTNESS
Of matchless Swiftness, but of silent Pace, ...1.TrES.345.462.
Here with degrees of swiftness, there of force; ......3.EOM1.182.37.
Here due degrees of swiftness, there of force; ......3.EOM1.182A.37.
A Wretch, whose Swiftness was his only Fame, ...Il.10.661.31.
Or thank that Swiftness which outstrips the Death. ......Il.11.466.54.
Excell'd alone in Swiftness in the Course. ......Il.13.415.126.
Who, like in Strength, in Swiftness, and in Grace, ...Il.16.188.246.
And heir'd his Mother's Swiftness, in the Chace. ......Il.16.223.248.
Of matchless Swiftness, but of silent Pace, ...Il.16.832.275.
Ourself will Swiftness to your Nerves impart, ...Il.17.516.308.
No—could our Swiftness o'er the Winds prevail, ...Il.19.460.391.
(Whose Feet for Swiftness in the Race surpast) ......Il.20.473.414.
To vaunt his Swiftness, wheels around the Plain, ...Il.20.477.414.
But vaunts not long, with all his Swiftness slain. ......Il.20.478.414.
Such is his Swiftness, 'tis in vain to fly, ...Il.21.667.449.
Fear not thy Rivals, tho' for Swiftness known, ...Il.23.381.505.
And leave unskilful Swiftness far behind. ......Il.23.418.506.
Your Swiftness? Vanquish'd by a female Foe? ......Il.23.488.509.
It stands the Prize of Swiftness in the Race. ......Il.23.875.524.
Who hopes the Palm of Swiftness to obtain, ...Il.23.879.524.
With rapid swiftness cut the liquid way, ...Od.3.215.96.
To him, his swiftness and his strength were vain; ......Od.17.350.148.

SWILL
And swill in Acorn cups the morning dew, ...6.96ii.30Z48.272.

SWILL'D
A milky deluge next the giant swill'd; ......Od.9.353.321.
Delighted swill'd the large, luxurious draught. ......Od.9.418.323.
'Midst the swill'd insolence of lust and pride? ......Od.16.72.106.
Then swill'd with wine, with noise the crowds obey, ...Od.18.472.191.

SWILLS
He stuffs and swills, and stuffs again. ......4.HS6.207.263.

SWIM
Priests, Tapers, Temples, swim before my sight: ......2.ElAb.274.342.
And Hell's black Horrors swim before my Eye. ......Il.15.287.208.
Buoy'd by some inward Force, he seems to swim, ...Il.19.418.389.
Buoy'd by her heav'nly Force, he seems to swim, ...Il.23.903.525.
When stately in the dance you swim th' harmonious maze. ......Od.6.188.218.
And yet it swims, or seems to swim, the main! ......Od.13.193.15.

SWIMMING
Your swimming Eyes are drunk with sudden Light, ...2.ChJM.803.54.
My swimming Eyes are sick of Light, ...6.31ii.6Z1.94.
A sudden Cloud comes swimming o'er his Eyes. ......Il.5.382.285.
And seals in endless Shades his swimming Eyes. ......Il.6.14.323.
And Sleep eternal seals his swimming Eyes. ......Il.11.310.48.
And a short Darkness shades his swimming Eyes. ......Il.11.460.54.
And seals again, by fits, his swimming Eyes. ......Il.14.514.188.
His swimming Eyes eternal Shades surround. ......Il.16.413.259.
A sudden Darkness shades her swimming Eyes: ......Il.22.598.480.

SWIMS
There swims no Goose so gray, but, soon or late, ...2.ChWB.98.61.
Or swims along the fluid atmosphere, ...5.DunB4.423.383.
And swims before his Eyes the many-colour'd Light. ......Il.20.332.407.
The pavement swims with brains and mingled gore. ......Od.9.345.320.
And yet it swims, or seems to swim, the main! ......Od.13.193.15.
She smoothly gliding swims th' harmonious round, ...Od.18.230.178.

SWINE
How Instinct varies in the grov'ling swine, ...3.EOM1.221.43.
Drive to St. James's a whole herd of swine? ......3.Ep3.62.92.
On fat of Rams, black Bulls, and brawny Swine, ...Il.9.592.464.
Fifty white Flocks, full fifty Herds of Swine, ...Il.11.822.73.

SWINE (CONTINUED)
Now from the well-fed Swine black Smokes aspire, ...Il.23.39.488.
Head, face and members bristle into swine: ......Od.10.279.356.
In swine to grovel, or in lions roar, ...Od.10.512.368.
The full-fed swine return'd with evening home; ......Od.14.454.57.
All, but the careful master of the swine: ......Od.14.593.66.
But seek thou first the Master of the swine, ...Od.15.45.72.
And thus he greets the master of the swine. ......Od.17.6.132.
Where goes the swine-herd with that ill-look'd guest? ......Od.17.254.143.
Enter the house, and of the bristly swine ......Od.24.246.360.

SWINE-HERD
Where goes the swine-herd with that ill-look'd guest? ......Od.17.254.143.

SWINE'S
Like some vile swine's, that greedy of his prey ......Od.18.35.168.

SWINEHERD
And is this present, swineherd! of thy hand? ......Od.17.450.155.

SWINEHERD'S
At an old swineherd's rural lodge he lay. ......Od.24.178.356.

SWING
I know the Swing of sinful Hack, ...6.61.12.181.
Swing round and round, and dash'd from rock to rock, ...Od.9.539.328.

SWINGING
Apply'd each Nerve, and swinging round on high, ...Il.7.321.379.

SWINGS
Full twenty Cubits long, he swings around. ......Il.15.817.228.

SWINKEN
Yet swinken nat sans Secresie. ......6.14i.2.41.
Ne swinken but with Secrecie: ......6.14i.2A.41.

SWISS
Heav'n's Swiss, who fight for any God, or Man. ......5.DunB2.358.315.

SWITCH
The Cap and Switch be sacred to his Grace; ......5.DunB4.585.400.

SWITZ
A Switz, a High-dutch, or a Low-dutch Bear— ......4.1HE1.63.283.

SWOL'N
Round his swol'n heart the murm'rous fury rowls; ......Od.20.19.232.

SWOLN
While his swoln Heart at ev'ry Step rebell'd, ...Il.11.681.65.
Where some swoln River disembogues his Waves, ...Il.17.311.299.
His swoln heart heav'd; his bloated body swell'd: ......Od.5.583.200.

SWORD
A Soldier now, he with his Sword appears; ......1.TrVP.41.378.
Deep in her Breast he plung'd his shining Sword, ...1.TrSt.725.440.
Divides the Traces with his Sword, and freed ......1.TrES.277.460.
At *Hester's* Suit, the Persecuting Sword ......2.ChJM.75.18.
Where Wigs with Wigs, with Sword-knots Sword-knots strive, .2.RL1.101.153.
Where Wigs with Wigs, with Sword-knots Sword-knots strive, .2.RL1.101.153.
There lay the sword-knot *Sylvia's* Hands had sown, ...2.RL2.39Z1.161.
Why dimly gleams the visionary sword? ......2.Elegy.4.362.
Justice a Conq'ror's sword, or Truth a gown, ...3.EOM4.171.143.
And will you run to Perils, Sword, and Law, ...4.HAdv.135.87.
In Days of Ease, when now the weary Sword ......4.2HE1.139.207.
And Nations wonder'd while they dropp'd the sword! ......4.2HE1.399.229.
A Monarch's sword when mad Vain-glory draws, ...4.EpS2.229.325.
To purge and let thee blood, with fire and sword, ...4.1740.15.332.
Made fit companions for the Sword of State. ......4.1740.68.335.
Others, a sword-knot and lac'd suit inflame. ......5.DunA2.48.103.
How keen the war, if Dulness draw the sword! ......5.DunA3.112.160.
How keen the war, if Dulness whet the sword! ......5.DunA3.112A.160.
Others a sword-knot and lac'd suit inflame. ......5.DunB2.52.298.
How keen the war, if Dulness draw the sword! ......5.DunB3.120.325.
And honour'd *Cæsar's* less than *Cato's* sword. ......6.32.36.97.
Who ne'er saw naked Sword, or look'd in, *Plato.* ......6.41.44.114.
When, with his Sword at Saddle Bow, ...6.79.107.221.
His Sword and Pen not worth a Straw, ...6.116ii.2.326.
On one so old your sword you scorn to draw. ......6.116vii.6.328.
The Plague destroying whom the Sword would spare, ...Il.1.81.90.
Of sure Protection by thy Pow'r and Sword. ......Il.1.100.92.
Shall form an Ambush, or shall lift the Sword? ......Il.1.198.96.
That prompts his Hand to draw the deadly Sword, ...Il.1.255.98.
His conqu'ring Sword in any Woman's Cause. ......Il.1.395.107.
In *Hector's* Breast be plung'd this shining Sword, ...Il.2.496.150.
His Sword beside him negligently hung, ...Il.3.30.189.
Perhaps their Sword some nobler Quarrel draws, ...Il.3.309.208.
His Cutlace sheath'd beside his pondrous Sword. ......Il.3.341.209.
Sustain'd the Sword that glitter'd at his side. ......Il.3.416.212.
Sustains the Sword that glitters at his side ......Il.3.416A.212.
But fierce *Atrides* wav'd his Sword and strook ......Il.3.445.213.
Oh hadst thou dy'd beneath the righteous Sword ......Il.3.535.217.
For *Pallas* strung his Arm, and edg'd his Sword. ......Il.4.443.241.
And Numbers more his Sword had sent to Hell: ......Il.5.837.305.
Conquest to Day my happier Sword may bless, ...Il.6.426.347.
Troy fled, she heard, before the *Grecian* Sword; ......Il.6.482.350.
With that, a Sword with Stars of Silver grac'd, ...Il.7.366.382.
Not ev'n a *Phrygian* Dame, who dreads the Sword ......Il.8.188.406.
Accept the Presents; draw thy conqu'ring Sword; ......Il.9.711.469.
Next him *Ulysses* took a shining Sword, ...Il.10.307.16.
Sustain'd the Sword that glitter'd at his side: ......Il.11.40.36.
But now to perish by *Atrides'* Sword: ......Il.11.146.42.
The Steeds fly trembling from his waving Sword; ......Il.11.207.44.
At once, his weighty Sword discharg'd a Wound ......Il.11.307.48.
By the long Lance, the Sword, or pond'rous Stone, ...Il.11.343.49.

SWORD (CONTINUED)

His Death ennobled by *Ulysses'* Sword. ....Il.11.418.53.
His Sword deforms the beauteous Ranks of Fight. ....Il.11.627.61.
(By the long Lance, the Sword, or pondrous Stone, ...Il.11.664.63.
Then sudden wav'd his unresisted Sword; ....Il.12.220.89.
Without a Sign, his Sword the brave Man draws, ...Il.12.283.92.
Like Light'ning brandish'd his far-beaming Sword. ....Il.13.764.141.
(One brac'd his Shield, and one sustain'd his Sword.) ....Il.14.468.186.
Has Fame not told, how, while my trusty Sword ....Il.15.282.207.
Rage edg'd his Sword, and strengthen'd ev'ry Blow. ....Il.15.535.217.
Doom'd in their Ships to sink by Fire and Sword, ...Il.16.25.236.
Stern *Hector* wav'd his Sword; and standing near ....Il.16.142.243.
The Sword broke short; but his, *Peneleus* sped ....Il.16.406.258.
Divides the Traces with his Sword, and freed ....Il.16.582.267.
The Sword for Glory, and his Country's Cause) ....Il.17.176.294.
Drew the broad Cutlace sheath'd beside his Sword; ....Il.19.260.383.
The brazen Sword a various Baldrick ty'd, ...Il.19.400.388.
Thro' falling Squadrons bear my slaught'ring Sword, ...Il.19.444.390.
That fell this instant, vanish'd from my Sword! ....Il.20.396.411.
Fierce as he springs, the Sword his Head divides; ....Il.20.445.413.
That one the Spear destroy'd, and one the Sword. ....Il.20.536.416.
Thy Life *Echeclus!* next the Sword bereaves, ...Il.20.549.417.
Arm'd with his Sword, high-brandish'd o'er the Waves; ....Il.21.23.422.
Sudden, *Achilles* his broad Sword display'd, ...Il.21.129.426.
Then from his side the Sword *Pelides* drew, ...Il.21.189.429.
Nor breathe from Combate, nor thy Sword suspend, ...Il.21.339.435.
Fierce, at the Word, his weighty Sword he drew, ...Il.22.389.471.
For should he 'scape the Sword, the common Doom, ...Il.22.624.482.
The Sword, *Asteropeus* possest of old, ...Il.23.951.527.
With him the Sword and studded Belt remains. ....Il.23.972.528.
Driv'n hence a Slave before the Victor's Sword; ....Il.24.924.575.
The proud Oppressors fly the vengeful sword. ....Od.1.154.40.
His virgin sword Ægysthus' veins imbru'd; ....Od.1.389.51.
If e'er he bore the sword to strengthen ill, ...Od.2.79.64.
If e'er he join'd thy council, or thy sword, ...Od.3.120.91.
Orestes brandish'd the revenging sword, ...Od.3.391.105.
Whose sword was sacred to the man he lov'd: ....Od.4.228.130.
But lives a victim for thy vengeful sword; ....Od.4.736.153.
Tho' to the sword I bow this hoary head, ...Od.4.981.163.
Be his this sword, whose blade of brass displays ....Od.8.437.287.
He said, and to his hand the sword consign'd; ....Od.8.441.287.
And never, never may'st thou want this sword! ....Od.8.450.287.
The monster to the sword, part sentence gave ....Od.8.555.292.
To draw the sword; but Wisdom held my hand. ....Od.9.359.321.
The keen-edg'd pole-axe, or the shining sword, ...Od.9.466.325.
My sword our cables cut, I call'd to weigh; ....Od.10.146.347.
I climb'd a cliff, with spear and sword in hand, ...Od.10.169.348.
Draw forth and brandish thy refulgent sword, ...Od.10.350.361.
Sheath thy bright sword, and join our hands in peace; ....Od.10.396.363.
And from the scabbard drew the shining sword; ....Od.11.28.380.
But as my waving sword the blood surrounds, ...Od.11.102.385.
Dauntless my sword I seize: the airy crew, ...Od.11.277.395.
My sword I strive to wield, but strive in vain; ....Od.11.528.409.
And such was mine! who basely plung'd her sword ....Od.11.533.409.
He grasp'd his sword, and shook his glitt'ring spear. ....Od.11.650.416.
Sandals, a sword, and robes, respect to prove, ...Od.16.79.106.
Yet leave for each of us a sword to wield, ...Od.16.320.121.
Or some brave Suitor's sword, might pierce the heart ....Od.17.301.146.
If when the sword our country's quarrel draws, ...Od.17.558.159.
And prostrate to my sword the Suitor-train; ....Od.19.572.224.
Shall prostrate to thy sword the Suitor-crowd; ....Od.19.580.224.
Portend the Suitors fated to my sword. ....Od.19.645.227.
And by his sword the Suitors sure to bleed. ....Od.19.653.227.
And edge thy sword to reap the glorious field. ....Od.20.62.235.
Impatient strait to flesh his virgin-sword, ...Od.20.461.255.
Receiv'd a pointed sword and missile dart: ....Od.21.34.261.
He spoke; then rising, his broad sword unbound, ...Od.21.123.264.
Telemachus girds on his shining sword. ....Od.21.476.283.
Swift as he spoke, he drew his traytor sword, ...Od.22.93.291.
His failing hand deserts the lifted sword, ...Od.22.97.291.
To rush between, and use the shorten'd sword. ....Od.22.115.292.
What hop'st thou here? Thee first the sword shall slay, ...Od.22.239.298.
Thus speaking, from the ground the sword he took ....Od.22.363.304.
There the revenging sword shall smite them all; ....Od.22.479.312.
A fate so pure, as by the martial sword? ....Od.22.496.313.
Now by the sword and now the jav'lin fall ....Od.24.610.377.

SWORD-KNOT

There lay the sword-knot *Sylvia's* Hands had sown, ...2.RL2.39Z1.161.
Others, a sword-knot and lac'd suit inflame. ....5.DunA2.48.103.
Others a sword-knot and lac'd suit inflame. ....5.DunB2.52.298.

SWORD-KNOTS

Where Wigs with Wigs, with Sword-knots Sword-knots strive, .2.RL1.101.153.
Where Wigs with Wigs, with Sword-knots Sword-knots strive, .2.RL1.101.153.

SWORDS

How some with Swords their sleeping Lords have slain, ...2.ChWB.407.76.
Swords, Pikes, and Guns, with everlasting Rust! ....4.HS1.74.11.
From gleaming Swords no shrieking Women run; ....4.HAdv.169.89.
(Pomps without guilt, of bloodless swords and maces, ...5.DunA1.85.69.
(Pomps without guilt, of bloodless swords and maces, ...5.DunB1.87.275.
Shields, helms, and swords all jangle as they hang, ...6.9i.1.21.
Your shining Swords within the Sheath restrain, ...Il.3.125.196.
And Swords around him innocently play, ...Il.4.633.251.
The Swords wave harmless, and the Javelins fail: ....Il.5.392.285.
Between the Swords their peaceful Sceptres rear'd, ...Il.7.335.380.
With Faulchions, Axes, Swords, and shorten'd Darts. ....Il.15.863.230.
Swords flash in Air, or glitter on the Ground; ....Il.15.865.230.
Lo there the *Trojans!* bath your Swords in Gore! ....Il.16.249.249.
Now, met in Arms, their eager Swords they drew, ...Il.16.403.258.
Your Swords must plunge them to the Shades of Hell. ....Il.16.760.273.
Our Swords kept time, and conquer'd side by side. ....Il.18.402.340.
Of these the Sides adorn'd with Swords of Gold, ...Il.18.688.356.
Insult the Brave, who tremble at their Swords: ....Il.20.420.412.
Frantic thro' clashing swords she runs, she flies, ...Od.8.573.293.

SWORDS (CONTINUED)

"Oft ready swords in luckless hour incite ....Od.16.316.121.
Lest they by sight of swords to fury fir'd, ...Od.19.14.193.
On me let all your lifted swords descend, ...Od.20.385.251.
Be mindful of your selves, draw forth your swords, ...Od.22.87.290.

SWORE

But sure it was a merrier Fit, she swore, ...2.ChJM.746.51.
By Heav'n, I swore but what I *thought* I saw. ....2.ChJM.794.53.
And told'em false, but *Jenkin* swore 'twas true. ....2.ChWB.151.63.
And swore the Rambles that I took by Night, ...2.ChWB.156.64.
And wou'd be so, in spight of all he swore. ....2.ChWB.340.73.
So like, that criticks said and courtiers swore, ...5.DunA2.45.101.
So like, that critics said, and courtiers swore, ...5.DunB2.49.298.
"Witness great Ammon! by whose horns I swore, ...5.DunB4.387.380.
P protested, puff'd, and swore, ...6.30.27.86.
B and *L* swore Bl—and W—s ....6.30.42.87.
G swore, by G—d, it ne'er should be; ....6.30.44.87.
G swore, by G—d, it shou'd not be; ....6.30.44A.87.
Dipthongs, and Tripthongs, swore and stutter'd, ...6.30.51.88.
Those Hands we plighted, and those Oaths we swore, ...Il.4.193.230.
Thus *Hector* swore: the Gods were call'd in vain; ....Il.10.393.21.
The dread, th' irrevocable Oath he swore, ...Il.19.127.377.
They urg'd in vain; the Chief refus'd, and swore. ....Il.23.52.489.
The Goddess swore: then seiz'd my hand, and led ....Od.10.411.364.
Against yon destin'd head in vain I swore, ...Od.13.152.13.
He swore, *Ulysses* on the coast of *Crete* ....Od.14.421.56.
Swift as she ask'd, the ready sailors swore. ....Od.15.476.93.

SWORN

And durst be sworn he had Bewitch'd me to him: ....2.ChWB.301.71.
Sworn to no Master, of no Sect am I: ....4.1HE1.24.281.
Sworn foe to Myst'ry, yet divinely dark; ....5.DunB4.460.385.
You would have sworn this Hen a Pheasant. ....6.93.8.256.
Has sworn by *Sticks* (the Poet's Oath, ...6.135.91.370.
Has sworn by Styx (the Poet's Oath, ...6.135.91A.370.
The Ties of Faith, the sworn Alliance broke, ...Il.7.424.385.
Have sworn Destruction to the *Trojan* Kind; ....Il.20.362.410.
Which *Troy* shall, sworn, produce; that injur'd *Greece* ....Il.22.162.459.
Nor herald sworn, the session to proclaim) ....Od.3.171.94.
Who in a league of blood associates sworn, ...Od.4.1077.168.
When sworn that oath which never can be vain? ....Od.10.450.365.

SWUM

And o'er his Eye-balls swum the Shades of Night. ....Il.5.857.307.

SWUNG

He poiz'd, and swung it round; then tost on high, ...1.TrES.103.453.
He swung it round; and gath'ring Strength to throw, ...Il.5.373.285.
He poiz'd, and swung it round; then toss'd on high, ...Il.12.457.98.
The howling felon swung from side to side. ....Od.22.210.297.

SYCAMORE

(As from a Sycamore, his sounding Steel ....Il.21.44.423.

SYCOPHANT

Let no Court-Sycophant pervert my sense, ...4.JD2.126.145.
Or each new-pension'd Sycophant, pretend ....4.EpS2.142.321.

SYDNEY'S

And Sydney's verse halts ill on Roman feet: ....4.2HE1.98.203.

SYLLABLE

"But has he spoken?" Not a syllable. ....4.2HE1.335.223.

SYLLABLES

These *Equal Syllables* alone require, ...1.EOC.344.277.
In *Sounds* and jingling *Syllables* grown old, ...1.EOC.605.308.
Each Word-catcher that lives on syllables, ...4.Arbu.166.108.
The Word-catcher that lives on syllables, ...4.Arbu.166A.108.
Those four proud Syllables alone ....6.30.9.86.
Those happy Syllables alone ....6.30.9A.86.
A Word-catcher, that lives on Syllables. ....6.98.16.283.

SYLPH

Her Guardian *Sylph* prolong'd the balmy Rest. ....2.RL1.20.147.
Rejects Mankind, is by some *Sylph* embrac'd: ....2.RL1.68.151.
'Tis but their *Sylph*, the wise Celestials know, ...2.RL1.77.151.
Warn'd by thy *Sylph*, oh Pious Maid beware! ....2.RL1.112.154.
Warn'd by the *Sylph*, oh Pious Maid beware! ....2.RL1.112A.154.
All but the *Sylph—With* careful Thoughts opprest, ...2.RL2.53.163.
A wretched *Sylph* too fondly interpos'd; ....2.RL3.150.179.
Fate urg'd the Sheers, and cut the *Sylph* in twain, ...2.RL3.151.179.
A *Sylph* too warn'd me of the Threats of Fate, ...2.RL4.165.197.

SYLPHIDS

Ye *Sylphs* and *Sylphids*, to your Chief give Ear, ...2.RL2.73.164.

SYLPHS

The light Coquettes in *Sylphs* aloft repair, ...2.RL1.65.150.
The *Sylphs* thro' mystick Mazes guide their Way, ...2.RL1.92.152.
Oh blind to Truth! the *Sylphs* contrive it all. ....2.RL1.104.153.
The busy *Sylphs* surround their darling Care; ....2.RL1.145.157.
Ye *Sylphs* and *Sylphids*, to your Chief give Ear, ...2.RL2.73.164.
To Fifty chosen *Sylphs*, of special Note, ...2.RL2.117.166.
For *Sylphs*, yet mindful of their ancient Race, ...2.RL3.35.171.
For, that sad moment, when the *Sylphs* withdrew, ...2.RL4.11.183.
The *Sylphs* behold it kindling as it flies, ...2.RL5.131.211.

SYLVAN

First in these Fields I try the Sylvan Strains, ...1.PSp.1.59.
See what Delights in Sylvan Scenes appear! ....1.PSu.59.76.
Adieu my Flocks, farewell ye *Sylvan* Crew! ....1.PWi.91.95.
The Mossie Fountains and the Sylvan Shades, ...1.Mes.3.112.
Invite my Lays. Be present, Sylvan Maids! ....1.W-F.3.148.
The Youth rush eager to the Sylvan War; ....1.W-F.148.164.

T' (CONTINUED)
T'import twelve mares which there luxurious feed, ...Od.4.859.159.
Why cease ye then t' implore the pow'rś above, ...Od.12.407.450.
'Tis his alone t'avenge the wrongs I bear; ....Od.13.257.18.
T'usurp the honours due to silver hairs ....Od.16.45.104.
Swift to the Queen a herald flies, t'impart ....Od.16.350.123.
T' explore the conduct of the female train: ....Od.19.55.195.
T'insult the dead is cruel and unjust; ....Od.22.450.309.
But when, arising in his wrath t'obey ....Od.24.191.356.

TABBY
The Cat, if you but singe her Tabby Skin, ...2.ChWB.142.63.

TABERNACLE
Booth in his cloudy tabernacle shrin'd, ...5.DunA3.263.179.
Booth in his cloudy tabernacle shrin'd, ...5.DunB3.267.333.

TABLE
This Slave the Floor, and That the Table spreads; ....1.TrSt.608.435.
Old Fish at Table, but young Flesh in Bed. ....2.ChJM.102.19.
Ev'n tho' the Pope himself had sate at Table. ....2.ChWB.181.65.
Who for thy table feeds the wanton fawn, ...3.EOM3.29.95.
The same his table, and the same his bed; ....3.EOM3.153.108.
Whose table, Wit, or modest Merit share, ...3.Ep3.241.112.
Does not one Table *Bavius* still admit? ....4.Arbu.99.102.
Does not one Table Arnall still admit? ....4.Arbu.99A.102.
And all our Grace at Table is a Song. ....4.2HE1.174.209.
Makes love with nods, and knees beneath a table; ....6.45.28.125.
A table with a cloth of bays; ....6.150.6.398.
A Table first with azure Feet she plac'd; ....Il.11.768.69.
One Table fed you, and one Roof contain'd. ....Il.13.587.134.
One House receiv'd us, and one Table fed; ....Il.23.106.491.
Thus having spoke, the nymph the table spread, ...Od.5.117.177.
The table next in regal order spread, ...Od.7.234.247.
Before his seat a polish'd table shines, ...Od.8.65.265.
I wash'd. The table in fair order spread, ...Od.10.437.365.
Confer, and wines and cates the table grace; ....Od.14.223.46.
With earth's whole tribute the bright table bends, ...Od.15.352.86.
One roof contain'd us, and one table fed. ....Od.15.389.88.
(The guests not enter'd, but the table crown'd) ....Od.15.504.94.
They wash: the table, in fair order spread, ...Od.17.108.137.
A trivet-table, and ignobler seat, ...Od.20.323.248.
Before him spurn'd, the loaded table falls, ...Od.22.24.287.
Beneath a table, trembling with dismay, ...Od.22.401.307.
These (ev'ry table cleans'd, and ev'ry throne, ...Od.22.476.312.

TABLES
Then spread the Tables, the Repast prepare, ...Il.1.612.117.
Then spread the Tables, the Repast prepare, ...Il.2.512.151.
Then spread the Tables, the Repast prepare, ...Il.7.384.382.
They wash. The tables in fair order spread, ...Od.1.183.41.
These while on sev'ral tables they dispose, ...Od.14.480.59.
They wash. The tables in fair order spread, ...Od.15.152.76.
With thirsty sponge they rub the tables o'er, ...Od.22.488.313.

TABLETS
With Tablets seal'd, that told his dire Intent. ....Il.6.210.336.
The fatal Tablets, till that Instant seal'd, ...Il.6.217.336.

TABOR
No rafter'd roofs with dance and tabor sound, ...3.Ep3.191.109.

TACKLE
In all her tackle trim, to quit the shore. ....Od.4.1032.166.

TAENARUS
To th'Iron Gates of *Tænarus* she flies, ...1.TrSt.134.415.

TAFFETY
But mere tuff-taffety what now remained; ....4.JD4.42.29.

TAG
And tag each Sentence with, *My Life! my Dear!* .... 2.ChWB.109.62.

TAIL
Sport with her Tail, and wanton in the Sun; ....2.ChWB.145.63.
A Liqu'rish Mouth must have a Lech'rous Tail; ....2.ChWB.218.67.
With all th' embroid'ry plaister'd at thy tail? ....3.Ep3.92.97.
The Monkey-Tail that wags behind his Head ....4.JD4.247A.47.
Rank as the ripeness of a Rabbit's tail. ....4.HS2.28.57.
Then, by the rule that made the Horse-tail bare, ...4.2HE1.63.199.
"Pray dip your Whiskers and your Tail in". ....4.HS6.205.263.
From tail to mouth, they feed, and they carouse; ....4.EpS2.179.323.
Yet holds the Eel of science by the Tail. ....5.DunA1.234.90.
In the Dog's tail his progress ends at last. ....5.DunA3.294.184.
And carry'd off in some Dog's tail at last. ....5.DunA3.294A.184.
Yet holds the eel of science by the tail: ....5.DunB1.280.290.
Should'st wag a serpent-tail in Smithfield fair! ....5.DunB3.288.334.
And carry'd off in some Dog's tail at last. ....5.DunB3.292.334.
Poiz'd with a tail, may steer on Wilkins' wings. ....5.DunB4.452.384.
That plies the Tongue, and wags the Tail, ...6.14v(a).23.49.
The Nymph whose Tail is all on Flame ....6.53.15.161.
Tho, once my Tail in wanton play, ...6.135.3.366.
My Tail indeed 'twas but in play ....6.135.3A.366.
Shall wag her Tail within the Grave. ....6.135.82.369.
Behind, a Dragon's fiery Tail was spread; ....Il.6.221.337.
Lash'd by his Tail his heaving sides resound; ....Il.20.207.402.
And brushing with his Tail the whirling Wheel. ....Il.23.602.513.
Yet (all he could) his tail, his ears, his eyes ....Od.17.362.149.

TAILS
Those Monkey-Tails that wag behind their Head! ....4.JD4.247.47.
Those Monkey-Tails that wagd behind their Head! ....4.JD4.247B.47.
And one is fired by Heads, and one by Tails; ....4.HAdv.36.79.
Should wag two serpent tails in Smithfield fair. ....5.DunA3.290.184.
But *you* show your *Wit,* whereas *they* show'd their *Tails.* ....6.62ii.2.185.

TAILS (CONTINUED)
Our Tails may smart for what you hatch. ....6.93.27Z4.257.
For both Heads are but Tails. ....6.105iv.8.301.
And wag their tails, and fawning lick their feet. ....Od.10.245.354.

TAINT
Pure let them be, and free from Taint of Vice; ....2.ChWB.38.58.
'Tis these that early taint the Female Soul, ...2.RL1.87.152.
To taint with deadly drugs the barbed dart; ....Od.1.341.48.
To taint the joys of sweet, connubial life. ....Od.1.546.58.
"The *Grecian* matrons taint my spotless fame; ....Od.2.112.67.
Thus with vile censure taint my spotless name. ....Od.6.330.227.
The *Grecian* matrons taint my spotless fame; ....Od.24.161.356.

TAINTED
But when the tainted Gales the Game betray, ...1.W-F.101.160.
And hound sagacious on the tainted green: ....3.EOM1.214.42.
Sure of the Vapour in the tainted Dews, ...Il.22.247.465.
Spreads o'er the coast, and scents the tainted gales; ....Od.12.434.452.
To winde the vapour in the tainted dew? ....Od.17.385.150.
The pack impatient snuff the tainted gale; ....Od.19.507.221.

TAINTING
Preserv'd from gaping Wounds, and tainting Air; ....Il.24.31.536.

TAINTS
And rarely Av'rice taints the tuneful mind. ....4.2HE1.192.211.
Taints the red Air with Fevers, Plagues, and Death. ....Il.22.42.454.
Of vegetable venom, taints the plain; ....Od.4.320.134.
An oily steam, and taints the noon-tide gales. ....Od.4.548.146.
And human carnage taints the dreadful shore. ....Od.12.60.432.

TAKE
He said; *Alexis,* take this Pipe, the same ....1.PSu.41.75.
The smiling Infant in his Hand shall take ....1.Mes.81.120.
Thus *Pegasus,* a nearer way to take, ...1.EOC.150.257.
Short Views we take, nor see the *Lengths behind,* .... 1.EOC.222.265.
The *Sense,* they humbly take upon Content. ....1.EOC.308.274.
At ev'ry Trifle scorn to take Offence, ...1.EOC.386.284.
What wonder *Modes* in *Wit* shou'd take their Turn? ....1.EOC.447.289.
'Twere well, might Criticks still this Freedom take; ....1.EOC.584.306.
As without *Learning* they can take *Degrees.* .... 1.EOC.591.307.
Our Criticks take a contrary Extream, ...1.EOC.661.314.
And take at least the Love you will not give. ....1.TrSP.108.398.
And take at least the Love thou wilt not give. ....1.TrSP.108A.398.
A thousand melting Kisses, give, and take: ....1.TrSP.152.400.
Scorns not to take our *Argos* in her Way. ....1.TrSt.811.443.
Will take a Wife, and live in Holy Ease. ....2.ChJM.94.19.
Conceive me Sirs, nor take my Sense amiss, ...2.ChJM.113.20.
Think not I dote; 'tis Time to take a Wife, ...2.ChJM.123.20.
Ah gentle Sir, take Warning of a Friend, ...2.ChJM.194.24.
He look'd, he languish'd, and cou'd take no Rest: ....2.ChJM.362.31.
Vouchsafe the Trunk between your Arms to take; ....2.ChJM.733.50.
Vouchsafe the Bole between your Arms to take; ....2.ChJM.733A.50.
Let all wise Husbands hence Example take; ....2.ChJM.818.54.
I'll take the next good Christian I can find. ....2.ChWB.27.58.
Take which we like, the Counsel, or our Will. ....2.ChWB.35.58.
But Wives, a random Choice, untry'd they take; ....2.ChWB.102.61.
"Take all the Freedoms of a married Life; ....2.ChWB.132.62.
Tho' all the Day I give and take Delight, ...2.ChWB.136.63.
Tho' all the Day I take and give Delight, ...2.ChWB.136A.63.
"Why take me Love! take all and ev'ry part! ....2.ChWB.199.66.
"Why take me Love! take all and ev'ry part! ....2.ChWB.199.66.
It pleas'd the Lord to take my Spouse at last! ....2.ChWB.308.71.
Yet I forgive thee—Take my last Embrace. ....2.ChWB.421.77.
And Nymphs prepar'd their *Chocolate* to take; ....2.RL1.16A.145.
Mount up, and take a *Salamander's* Name. ....2.RL1.60.150.
Dost sometimes Counsel take—and sometimes *Tea.* .... 2.RL3.8.169.
While Nymphs take Treats, or Assignations give, ...2.RL3.169.182.
Make some take Physick, others scribble Plays; ....2.RL4.62.189.
And Wits take Lodgings in the Sound of *Bow;* .... 2.RL4.118.193.
This, the blest Lover shall for *Venus* take, ...2.RL5.135.211.
Nor foes nor fortune take this pow'r away. ....2.ElAb.43.322.
Take back that grace, those sorrows, and those tears, ...2.ElAb.285.343.
Take back my fruitless penitence and pray'rs, ...2.ElAb.286.343.
Exalt their kind, and take some Virtue's name. ....3.EOM2.100.67.
"Go, from the Creatures thy instructions take: ....3.EOM3.172.110.
A weaker may surprise, a stronger take? ....3.EOM3.276.120.
Take Nature's path, and mad Opinion's leave, ...3.EOM4.29.130.
Who risk the most, that take wrong means, or right? ....3.EOM4.86.136.
Men in their loose unguarded hours they take, ...3.EOM4.227.148.
Take ev'ry creature in, of ev'ry kind; ....3.EOM4.370.164.
Affections? they still take a wider range: ....3.Ep1.172A.29.
All Manners take a tincture from our own, ...3.Ep1.25.17.
When half our knowledge we must snatch, not take. ....3.Ep1.34.18.
Take the most strong, and sort them as you can. ....3.Ep1.72.20.
Int'rest o'ercome, or Policy take place: ....3.Ep1.169.29.
Opinions? they still take a wider range: ....3.Ep1.172.29.
If second qualities for first they take. ....3.Ep1.211.33.
Such happy Spots the nice admirer take, ...3.Ep2.43A.53.
Their happy Spots the nice admirer take, ...3.Ep2.43.53.
And Atheism and Religion take their turns; ....3.Ep2.66.55.
'Tis from a Handmaid we must take a Helen. ....3.Ep2.194.66.
Men, some to Bus'ness, some to Pleasure take; ....3.Ep2.215.67.
Come take it as we find it, Gold and all." ....3.Ep3.80A.94.
What say you? B. Say? Why take it, Gold and all. ....3.Ep3.80B.94.
What say you? "Say? Why take it, Gold and all." ....3.Ep3.80.94.
And who would take the Poor from Providence? ....3.Ep3.188.109.
Who random drawings from your sheets shall take, ...3.Ep4.27.140.
Treated, caress'd, and tir'd, I take my leave, ...3.Ep4.165.153.
Why, if the Nights seem tedious—take a Wife; ....4.HS1.16.5.
Will club their Testers, now, to take your Life! ....4.HS1.104.15.
A Popish plot, shall for a Jesuit take; ....4.JD4.35.29.
Z—ds! let some Eunuch or Platonic take— ....4.HAdv.157.87.
"The Piece you think is incorrect: why take it, ...4.Arbu.45.99.
You think this cruel? take it for a rule, ...4.Arbu.83.101.

TAKE (CONTINUED)

Soft were my Numbers, who could take offence ... 4.Arbu.147.106.
Blest be the *Great!* for those they take away, ... 4.Arbu.255.114.
You love a Verse, take such as I can send. ... 4.2HE2.2.165.
"Take him with all his Virtues, on my word; ... 4.2HE2.13.165.
"Let him take Castles who has ne'er a Groat." ... 4.2HE2.51.167.
Stept from its Pedestal to take the Air. ... 4.2HE2.122.173.
Weave Laurel Crowns, and take what Names we please. ... 4.2HE2.142.175.
My Friends? he cry'd, p—x take you for your care! ... 4.2HE2.195.179.
So take it in the very words of *Creech.]* ... 4.1HE6.4.237.
To whom to nod, whom take into your Coach, ... 4.1HE6.102.243.
Thro' Taverns, Stews, and Bagnio's take our round, ... 4.1HE6.119.245.
E'en take the Counsel which I gave you first: ... 4.1HE6.131.246.
"Send for him up, take no excuse. ... 4.HS6.36.253.
And take it kindly meant to show ... 4.HS6.61.253.
Wou'd take me in his Coach to chat, ... 4.HS6.87.255.
"Pray take them, Sir,—Enough's a Feast: ... 4.1HE7.25.269.
South-sea Subscriptions take who please, ... 4.1HE7.65.273.
"Friend Pope! be prudent, let your Muse take breath, ... 4.1HE1.13.279.
If honest S*z take scandal at a spark, ... 4.1HE1.112.287.
"Away, away! take all your scaffolds down, ... 4.1HE1.146.289.
Else might he take to Virtue some years hence— ... 4.EpS2.60.315.
The way they take is strangely round about. ... 4.EpS2.125.320.
And begg'd, he'd take the pains to kick the rest. ... 4.EpS2.155.322.
Take up th' Attorney's (once my better) Guide? ... 5.DunA1.190.85.
"So take the hindmost Hell."—He said, and run. ... 5.DunA2.56.105.
And "Take (he said) these robes which once were mine, ... 5.DunA2.327.141.
Shall take thro' Grubstreet her triumphant round, ... 5.DunA3.128.160.
"Now Bavius, take the poppy from thy brow, ... 5.DunA3.315.186.
And laughs to think Monroe would take her down, ... 5.DunB1.30.271.
Take up the Bible, once my better guide? ... 5.DunB1.200.284.
"So take the hindmost, Hell."—He said, and run. ... 5.DunB2.60.298.
Shall take thro' Grub-street her triumphant round; ... 5.DunB3.136.326.
"Now Bavius take the poppy from thy brow, ... 5.DunB3.317.335.
Then take at once the Poet and the Song. ... 5.DunB4.8.340.
Then take him to devellop, if you can, ... 5.DunB4.269.370.
We nobly take the high Priori Road, ... 5.DunB4.471.386.
Then take them all, oh take them to thy breast! ... 5.DunB4.515.393.
Then take them all, oh take them to thy breast! ... 5.DunB4.515.393.
Contending Princes take them in their Coach. ... 5.DunB4.564A.398.
But sink, and take deep rooting in my heart. ... 6.2.10.6.
Let her whom fear denies repose to take, ... 6.4i.9.9.
Descend an human form to take, ... 6.4iii.12.10.
Take shorter journies to the day, ... 6.6i.6.14.
So seize them Flames, or take them *Tonson.* ... 6.10.36.25.
Tydcombe take Oaths on the Communion; ... 6.10.46.26.
I'm told, you think to take a Step some ... 6.10.49.26.
Take out your Box of right *Brasil,* ... 6.10.64.26.
You have no Cause to take Offence, Sir, ... 6.10.101.27.
Oh take the Husband, or return the Wife! ... 6.11.82.33.
Go fathom Nature, take the Heights of Art! ... 6.27.13.81.
But pray which of you all would take her back? ... 6.41.36.114.
And the Devil may take their Duke. ... 6.42iv.12.118.
Then come and take part in ... 6.42iv.13.118.
The Devil may take their Duke. ... 6.42iv.12A.118.
Give us our earl, the devil take their duke. ... 6.42v.2.119.
Come then, my lord, and take your part in ... 6.42v.7.119.
Ev'n while you write, you take that praise away, ... 6.43.10.120.
Some Squire, perhaps, you take delight to rack; ... 6.45.23.125.
What tender passions take their turns, ... 6.51ii.33.154.
First from a Worm they take their Rise, ... 6.53.19.162.
We take no Measure of your Fops and Beaus; ... 6.60.26.178.
And take off Ladies Limitations. ... 6.61.55.183.
But take off Ladies Limitations. ... 6.61.55A.183.
Take all thou e're shalt have, a constant Muse: ... 6.66.5.194.
But if you will not take my word, ... 6.67.11.195.
As if he meant to take the Air, ... 6.79.123.222.
Or only take a Fee. ... 6.79.124.222.
The Gods shall of our Stock take care: ... 6.80.2.224.
In this strange Town a different Course we take, ... 6.82vi.1.232.
Take a knuckle of Veal ... 6.91.1.253.
You'd take her for a Warren. ... 6.94.12.259.
St. A-d-re [André] too, the Scale to take ... 6.94.27.260.
(Ye *Guildford* Inn-keepers take heed ... 6.94.45.260.
Troops take Heed! ... 6.96i.28.269.
Men, some to Business, some to Pleasure take. ... 6.99.15.287.
Yet take these tears, Mortality's relief, ... 6.109.17.314.
Of one so poor you cannot take the law; ... 6.116vii.5.328.
"And take (she said, and smil'd serene) ... 6.140.3.378.
"Take at this hand celestial arms: ... 6.140.4.378.
"But, Friend, take heed whom you attack; ... 6.140.17.378.
There, take (says *Justice)* take ye each a *Shell.* ... 6.145.10.388.
There, take (says *Justice)* take ye each a *Shell.* ... 6.145.10.388.
To take the only way to be forgiven. ... 6.146.8.389.
With Water purify their Hands, and take ... Il.1.586.116.
And all thy Counsels take the destin'd Course. ... Il.1.717.122.
But now, ye Warriors, take a short Repast; ... Il.2.452.149.
The Chiefs surround the destin'd Beast, and take ... Il.2.486.150.
Breathing Revenge, in Arms they take their Way ... Il.2.643.157.
Take back th' unjust Reproach! Behold we stand ... Il.4.404.240.
Take thou the Spear, the Chariot's Care be mine. ... Il.5.287.280.
Haste all, and take the gen'rous Warrior's Part. ... Il.5.571.296.
Now take Refreshment as the Hour demands: ... Il.7.445.386.
Oh take not, Friends! defrauded of your Fame, ... Il.7.476.388.
Your Hearts shall tremble, if our Arms we take, ... Il.8.564.423.
Such are thy Offers as a Prince may take, ... Il.9.217.443.
Then from the Royal Tent they take their way; ... Il.9.232.444.
And dark thro' Paths oblique their Progress take. ... Il.10.320.17.
What Watch they keep, and what Resolves they take: ... Il.10.364.19.
To learn what Counsels, what Resolves you take, ... Il.10.466.24.
That Path they take, and speed to reach the Town. ... Il.11.220.45.
Then back to *Pyle* triumphant take my way. ... Il.11.893.75.
To right, to left, unheeded take your way, ... Il.12.281.91.
Go—from my conquer'd Spears, the choicest take, ... Il.13.380.123.
Take this, and with it all thy Wish, she said: ... Il.14.254.173.
Shall take new Courage, and disdain to fly. ... Il.18.240.333.

TAKE (CONTINUED)

Take due Refreshment, and the Watch attend. ... Il.18.348.338.
They rise, take Horse, approach, and meet the War; ... Il.18.616.352.
And take their Thrones around th' Æthereal Sire. ... Il.21.604.447.
But when within the Walls our Troops take Breath, ... Il.21.625.448.
With proper Instruments they take the Road, ... Il.23.138.493.
Should our immortal Coursers take the Plain; ... Il.23.344.503.
This narrow way? Take larger Field (he cry'd) ... Il.23.508.510.
Take thou this Token of a grateful Heart, ... Il.23.711.518.
While pleas'd I take the Gift thy Hands present, ... Il.23.745.519.
Who farthest hurls it, take it as his Prize: ... Il.23.984.528.
Take then the Prize, but let brave *Merion* bear ... Il.23.1058.533.
Take this, and pour to *Jove:* that safe from Harms, ... Il.24.355.551.
But thou, oh gen'rous Youth! this Goblet take, ... Il.24.525.558.
Take Gifts in secret, that must shun the Light? ... Il.24.532.558.
His Corse, and take the Gifts: I ask no more. ... Il.24.700.566.
To ask our Counsel or our Orders take, ... Il.24.819.571.
Go then; to *Sparta* take the watry way, ... Od.3.413.106.
And duteous take the orders of the day. ... Od.3.525.113.
I take the present of the promis'd Vase; ... Od.4.820.157.
Then take repast, 'till *Hesperus* display'd ... Od.4.1035.166.
And take this method, since the best I can. ... Od.5.463.195.
When Morning rises? If I take the wood, ... Od.5.605.201.
Comply'd to take the balmy gifts of rest; ... Od.10.35.341.
Then take the antidote the Gods bestow. ... Od.10.342.360.
Take this, nor from the faithless feast abstain, ... Od.10.347.360.
And take the painful sense of toil away. ... Od.10.428.365.
High on the deck I take my dang'rous stand, ... Od.12.270.445.
To take repast, and stills the wordy war; ... Od.12.520.457.
Take with free welcome what our hands prepare, ... Od.14.97.40.
And from the banquet take the bowls away. ... Od.14.507.61.
But in the morning take thy cloaths again, ... Od.14.580.64.
Yet stay, my friends, and in your chariot take ... Od.15.85.73.
Or we perhaps might take him off thy hands. ... Od.17.261.144.
Take that, ere yet thou quit this princely throng: ... Od.17.545.159.
These sons of murder thirst thy life to take; ... Od.17.674.165.
The gifts of love; with speed they take the way. ... Od.18.336.184.
"From right to left, in order take the bow; ... Od.21.150.266.
Take it who will, he cries, I strive no more. ... Od.21.160.267.
And take it He, the favour'd of the skies! ... Od.21.299.274.
To the base court the females take their way; ... Od.22.492.313.
They wash, and to *Ulysses* take their way, ... Od.22.515.314.
Depress or raise, enlarge or take away: ... Od.23.16.319.
And take the banquet which our cares provide: ... Od.24.418.369.
Then all beneath their father take their place, ... Od.24.472.371.

TAKEN

And turtles taken from their airy nest. ... 1.TrPA.89.369.
Nay, were they taken in a strict Embrace, ... 2.ChJM.663.47.
Shall only Man be taken in the gross? ... 3.Ep1.17.17.
For, to be taken, is the Dev'll in Hell; ... 4.HAdv.177.89.

TAKES

The patient Fisher takes his silent Stand ... 1.W-F.137.163.
When Fancy gives what Absence takes away, ... 1.TrSP.146.400.
Which from the neighb'ring *Hampton* takes its Name. ... 2.RL3.4.169.
He takes the Gift with rev'rence, and extends ... 2.RL3.131.177.
Each Virtue in each Passion takes its turn; ... 3.EOM3.136.106.
Is blest in what it takes, and what it gives; ... 3.EOM4.314.158.
Slave to no sect, who takes no private road, ... 3.EOM4.331.160.
He takes his chirping pint, he cracks his jokes: ... 3.Ep3.358A.123.
Eternal buckle takes in Parian stone. ... 3.Ep3.296.117.
He takes his chirping pint, and cracks his jokes: ... 3.Ep3.358.123.
He must repair it; takes a bribe from France; ... 3.Ep3.396.124.
Shows *Poland's* Int'rests, takes the *Primate's* ... 4.JD4.154A.39.
The Chanc'ry takes your rents for twenty year: ... 4.HS2.172.69.
For food digested takes another name. ... 4.JD2.34.135.
Takes God to witness he affects your Cause, ... 4.JD2.76.141.
Takes the whole House upon the Poet's day. ... 4.1HE6.88.243.
And damns the market where he takes no gold. ... 4.1740.12.332.
And ductile dulness new meanders takes; ... 5.DunA1.62.67.
He chinks his purse, and takes his seat of state: ... 5.DunA2.189.124
"Mark first the youth who takes the foremost place, ... 5.DunA3.131.161.
"Mark first that youth who takes the foremost place, ... 5.DunA3.131A.16
And ductile dulness new meanders takes; ... 5.DunB1.64.274.
He chinks his purse, and takes his seat of state: ... 5.DunB2.197.305.
"Mark first that Youth who takes the foremost place, ... 5.DunB3.139.326.
As Meat digested takes a diff'rent Name; ... 6.7.12.16.
No Pains it takes, and no Offence it gives, ... 6.16.5.53.
And takes a Shelter from his pointed Fires. ... 6.17iii.31.58.
Yet takes one kiss before she parts for ever: ... 6.45.6.124.
That this Maid takes in Hand. ... 6.54.12.164.
Let him that takes it, wear it as his own. ... 6.60.38.179.
See what ample Strides he takes, ... 6.78ii.5.216.
Takes, opens, swallows it, before their Sight. ... 6.145.8.388.
Each takes his Seat, and each receives his Share. ... Il.1.613.117.
Each takes his Seat, and each receives his Share. ... Il.2.513.151.
His figur'd Shield, a shining Orb, he takes, ... Il.3.419.212.
And wide thro' Fens an unknown Journey takes; ... Il.5.735.302.
Secure of fav'ring Gods, he takes the Field; ... Il.5.743.302.
Each takes his Seat, and each receives his Share. ... Il.7.385.383.
Each takes new Courage at the Hero's Sight; ... Il.11.724.67.
Last *Nestor's* Son the same bold Ardour takes, ... Il.13.129.110.
The weaker Warrior takes a lighter Shield. ... Il.14.442.184.
All human Courage, gives, or takes away. ... Il.20.293.406.
To the forbidden Field he takes his Flight ... Il.20.475.414.
Takes a sad Pleasure the last Bones to burn, ... Il.23.276.501.
Takes the last Prize, and takes it with a Jest. ... Il.23.924.525.
Takes the last Prize, and takes it with a Jest. ... Il.23.924.525.
He takes the Bow, directs the Shaft above, ... Il.23.1030.530.
Takes his sad Couch, more unobserv'd to weep, ... Il.24.7.535.
Of four vast *Phocæ* takes, to veil her wiles; ... Od.4.594.148.
Who takes the kind, and pays th' ungrateful part; ... Od.8.242.275.
And when the Autumn takes his annual round, ... Od.11.234.393.
My soul takes wing to meet the heav'nly strain; ... Od.12.233.443.
So will'd the God who gives and takes away. ... Od.14.279.49.

TAKES (CONTINUED)

Takes from the stranger's hand the glitt'ring spear:	Od.15.307.83.
Then from the deck the Prince his sandals takes;	Od.15.593.99.
Makes man a slave, takes half his worth away.	Od.17.393.151.
Takes a last look, and having seen him, dies;	Od.17.398.151.
His seat he takes, his eyes upon his Lord.	Od.21.426.280.
Fast by his father's side he takes his stand;	Od.21.477.283.
The miscreant we suspected takes that way;	Od.22.180.296.
Not so: his judgment takes the winding way	Od.24.279.363.

TAKING

Whose Wife, a clean, pains-taking Woman,	6.93.2.256.
Then taking wing from *Athos'* lofty Steep,	Il.14.263.173.

TALBOT

The Courtly *Talbot, Somers, Sheffield* read,	4.Arbu.139.105.
There TALBOT sunk, and was a Wit no more!	5.DunB4.168.357.

TALBOT'S

"Yours *Cowper's* Manner—and yours *Talbot's* Sense."	4.2HE2.134.175.

TALE

So great the tale, I scarce can count them o'er;	1.TrPA.80.368.
Let the sad Tale for ever rest untold!	1.TrSt.801.443.
His ready Tale th'inventive Hero told.	1.TrUl.139.470.
But to my Tale: Some Sages have defin'd	2.ChJM.440.36.
But now no longer from our Tale to stray;	2.ChJM.520.40.
Where let us leave them, and our Tale pursue.	2.ChJM.608.44.
Tho' blunt my Tale, yet honest is my Mind.	2.ChJM.743.51.
Thus ends our Tale, whose Moral next to make,	2.ChJM.817.54.
But to my Tale: A Month scarce past away,	2.ChWB.329.72.
Scarce any Tale was sooner heard than told;	2.TemF.469.286.
A Tale, that blends their glory with their shame!	3.EOM4.308.157.
Or tell a Tale?—A Tale—it follows thus.	3.Ep3.338A.120.
Or tell a Tale?—A Tale—it follows thus.	3.Ep3.338B.120.
But you are tir'd—I'll tell a tale.—B. A greed.	3.Ep3.338B.120.
But you are tir'd—I'll tell a tale. Agreed.	3.Ep3.338.120.
Who turns a *Persian* Tale for half a crown,	4.Arbu.180.109.
The Tale reviv'd, the Lye so oft o'erthrown;	4.Arbu.350.121.
A Tale extreamly *a propos:*	4.HS6.154.259.
Old James himself unfinish'd left his tale,	5.DunA2.380.146.
And *** himself unfinish'd left his tale.	5.DunA2.380A.146.
Motteux himself unfinish'd left his tale,	5.DunA2.380B.146.
Sooths the sad series of her tedious tale.	5.DunA3.191z6.172.
Motteux himself unfinish'd left his tale,	5.DunB2.412.317.
From Schole-boy's Tale of fayre *Ireland:*	6.14i.4.41.
This in our Tale is plain y-fond,	6.14i.3A.41.
There are, 'tis true, who tell another tale,	6.41.15.113.
Who turns a *Persian* Tale for half a Crown,	6.98.30.284.
3. Who spreads a *Tale, a Libel* hands about,	6.120.5.339.
A Tale! that blends the Glory with the Shame	6.130.38.359.
He spar'd but one to bear the dreadful Tale.	Il.4.449.241.
Then hear a Tale that fills the spacious Earth.	Il.6.188.335.
Nor shall a *Trojan* live to tell the Tale.	Il.12.86.84.
Haste, to his Father let the Tale be told:	Il.14.588.190.
And tells the melancholy Tale with Tears.	Il.18.20.324.
And sad Posterity repeat the Tale.	Il.19.66.374.
(A Tale resounded thro' the spacious Earth)	Il.20.253.404.
The fourth, her maid unfolds th' amazing tale.	Od.2.122.67.
Lest the sad tale a mother's life impair,	Od.2.422.81.
And leave half-heard the melancholy tale.	Od.3.144.92.
Fruitful of deeds, the copious tale is long,	Od.4.469.142.
I've heard with pain, but oh! the tale pursue;	Od.4.746.153.
But to the Queen thy mournful tale disclose,	Od.6.373.229.
Your eyes shall witness and confirm my tale,	Od.7.417.258.
Just to the tale, as present at the fray,	Od.8.535.291.
If faithful thou record the tale of fame,	Od.8.543.291.
Unequal to the melancholy tale:	Od.11.409.404.
Thy tale with raptures I could hear thee tell,	Od.11.466.407.
She sate in silence while the tale I tell,	Od.12.45.431.
And what so tedious as a twice-told tale?	Od.12.538.459.
His ready tale th' inventive hero told.	Od.13.306.21.
Or from the fluent tongue produce the tale,	Od.14.221.46.
Ere yet to *Nestor* I the tale relate:	Od.15.235.79.
A tale from falshood free, not free from woe.	Od.15.289.83.
The swain returns. A tale of sorrows hear;	Od.16.61.105.
Their silent journey, since his tale begun,	Od.17.607.161.
So, melted with the pleasing tale he told,	Od.19.242.206.
Truth forms my tale; to pleasing truth attend.	Od.19.306.209.
I part reluctant from the pleasing tale.	Od.19.690.229.
Not one! compleat the bloody tale he found,	Od.22.423.308.
The King alternate a dire tale relates,	Od.23.329.340.
With pleasing horror at the dreadful tale,	Od.23.332.340.
The fourth, her maid reveal'd th' amazing tale,	Od.24.169.356.

TALENT

And use the copious Talent it has giv'n;	2.ChWB.51.59.
'Tis a Bear's Talent not to kick, but hug,	4.HS1.87.13.
Blest with each Talent and each Art to please,	4.Arbu.195.109.
Blest with each Talent, and each Art to please	6.49iii.9A.142.
Blest with each Talent, and each Art to please,	6.98.45.284.
And half a Talent must content the last.	Il.23.877.524.
Receive a Talent of the purest Gold.	Il.23.938.526.
Bring gold, a pledge of love, a talent bring;	Od.8.427.286.

TALENTS

Our bolder Talents in full view display'd,	3.Ep2.201A.67.
Our bolder Talents in full light display'd,	3.Ep2.201.67.
Thus others Talents having nicely shown,	4.JD4.80.31.
These are the talents that adorn them all,	4.JD2.79.141.
With equal Talents, these congenial Souls	4.2HE2.129.173.
The same their talents, and their tasts the same,	5.DunA2.348.143.
The same their talents, and their tastes the same;	5.DunA2.380.315.
Whate'er the talents, or howe'er design'd,	5.DunB4.161.357.
Phryne had Talents for Mankind,	6.14v(b).1.49.
Phryne had Talents to oblige Mankind,	6.14v(b).1A.49.

TALENTS (CONTINUED)

Who born with Talents, bred in Arts to please,	6.49iii.9.142.
With wrangling Talents form'd for foul Debate:	Il.2.307.142.
Ten weighty Talents of the purest Gold,	Il.9.157.440.
Ten weighty Talents of the purest Gold,	Il.9.344.450.
Two golden Talents lay amidst, in sight,	Il.18.589.351.
First of the Train, the golden Talents bore:	Il.19.256.383.
Two golden Talents for the fourth were plac'd;	Il.23.337.503.
Like these, have Talents to regain the Friend?	Il.23.692.517.
The golden Talents *Merion* next obtain'd;	Il.23.703.517.
With ten pure Talents from the richest Mine;	Il.24.286.548.
Ten equal talents of refulgent gold.	Od.4.176.128.
Sev'n golden talents to perfection wrought,	Od.9.236.316.
The various thoughts and talents of mankind,	Od.14.265.49.
To him sev'n talents of pure ore I told,	Od.24.320.365.

TALES

From *Dryden's Fables* down to *Durfey's Tales.*	1.EOC.617.309.
Lotis the nymph (if rural tales be true)	1.TrFD.31.387.
"Dear Spouse, I credit not the Tales they tell.	2.ChWB.131.62.
To see, be seen, to tell, and gather Tales;	2.ChWB.282.70.
But when no End of these vile Tales I found,	2.ChWB.412.77.
Of unknown Dutchesses leud Tales we tell,	2.TemF.388.282.
With home-born Lyes, or Tales from foreign Lands;	2.TemF.465.286.
In Puns, or Politicks, or Tales, or Lyes,	4.Arbu.321.119.
The Tales of Vengeance; Lyes so oft o'erthrown;	4.Arbu.350A.121.
They shall like *Persian* Tales be read,	6.58.55.173.
Skill'd in smooth tales, and artful to deceive,	Od.11.453.406.

TALISMANS

Of *Talismans* and *Sigils* knew the Pow'r,	2.TemF.105.261.

TALK

They talk of *Principles,* but Notions prize,	1.EOC.265.270.
They talk of *Principles,* but Parts they prize,	1.EOC.265A.270.
Nay, fly to *Altars; there* they'll talk you dead;	1.EOC.624.310.
Nay, run to *Altars; there* they'll talk you dead;	1.EOC.624A.310.
And silent Hours to various Talk invite.	1.TrSt.795.443.
In various Talk the chearful hours they past,	2.RLA.1.75.129.
In various Talk th' instructive hours they past,	2.RL3.11.169.
And more than Echoes talk along the walls.	2.ElAb.306.344.
But talk with *Celsus, Celsus* will advise	4.HS1.19.7.
"To gaze on Princes, and to talk of Kings!"	4.JD4.101.33.
"Of all our *Harries,* all our *Edwards* talk,	4.JD4.105.33.
Lets talk, my friends, but talk before we dine:	4.HS2.4.55.
Lets talk, my friends, but talk before we dine:	4.HS2.4.55.
Now with set-looks to his bilk'd client talk:	4.JD2A.77.138.
Talk what you will of Taste, my Friend, you'll find,	4.2HE2.268.183.
You give the Practise, they but give the Talk.	6.2.30.6.
To talk of War, and live in Peace;	6.10.42.25.
All Flutter, Pride, and Talk.	6.14v(a).24.49.
Talk with Church-Wardens about Pews,	6.39.22.111.
Dear Rowe, lets sit and talk of Tragedies:	6.49ii.5.140.
They may talk of the *Goddesses* in *Ida* Vales,	6.62ii.1.185.
Thus, Madam, most Men talk, and some Men do:	6.82vi.9.232.
Mind not their learned whims and idle talk,	6.126i.3.353.
Ye talk like Children, not like Heroes dare.	Il.2.403.146.
Stand we to talk, when Glory calls to Arms?	Il.13.379.123.
While yet we talk, or but an instant shun	Il.19.147.377.
Talk not of Life, or Ransom, (he replies)	Il.21.111.426.
No Season now for calm familiar Talk,	Il.22.169.460.
Talk not of Oaths (the dreadful Chief replies,	Il.22.333.470.
Talk not of ruling in this dol'rous gloom,	Od.11.595.412.
A part in pleasing talk we entertain;	Od.15.428.89.
Oh talk not, talk not of vain beauty's care!	Od.18.210.177.
Oh talk not, talk not of vain beauty's care!	Od.18.210.177.

TALK'D

Each talk'd aloud, or in some secret Place,	2.TemF.466.286.
Nor Motteux talk'd, nor Naso whisper'd more;	5.DunA2.382.147.
Nor *** talk'd, nor *S[elkirk]* whisper'd more;	5.DunA2.382A.147*.
Nor Kelsey talk'd, nor Naso whisper'd more;	5.DunA2.382B.147.
How *Pallas* talk'd when she was Seven Years old.	6.37.10.106.
Some talk'd of *W[a]lk[e]r's* Merit,	6.94.18.259*.
Tho' he talk'd much of Virtue, her Head always run	6.124i.5.346.

TALKATIVE

The coxcomb bird, so talkative and grave,	3.Ep1.5.15.
Since to be talkative I now commence,	Od.14.524.62.

TALKE

"Then trust on Mon, whose yerde can *talke.*"	6.14i.26.42.

TALKEN

They asken that, and talken this,	6.14i.15.42.

TALKER

That gay Free-thinker, a fine talker once,	3.Ep1.162.29.

TALKERS

Talkers, I've learn'd to bear; *Motteux* I knew,	4.JD4.50.29.

TALKS

And without Method *talks* us into Sense,	1.EOC.654.313.
Here sighs a Jar, and there a Goose-pye talks;	2.RL4.52.188.
And talks *Gazettes* and *Post-Boys* o'er by heart.	4.JD4.155.39.
"Not one but nods, and talks of Johnson's Art,	4.2HE1.82.201.
He hears loud Oracles, and talks with Gods.	5.DunA3.8.150.
He hears loud Oracles, and talks with Gods:	5.DunB3.8.320.
Tho' *Artimesia* talks, by Fits,	6.14v(a).1.48.
He talks of Senates, and of Courtly Tribes,	6.96v.15.280.

TALL

Yet this tall Elm, but for his Vine (he said)	1.TrVP.63.380.
Then as the stately Pine, or Poplar tall,	1.TrES.288.460.
Then, as the Mountain Oak, or Poplar tall,	1.TrES.288A.460.

TALL (CONTINUED)

Cæsar and Tall-boy, Charles and Charlema'ne. ....3.Ep2.78.56.
Like a tall bully, lifts the head, and lyes; ....3.Ep3.340.121.
"I too could write, and I am twice as tall, ...4.Arbu.103.103.
"I too could write, and sure am twice as tall, ...4.Arbu.103A.103.
To a tall house near Lincoln's-Inn: ....4.HS6.186.261.
Where the tall May-pole once o'erlook'd the Strand; ....5.DunA2.24.99.
Where the tall Nothing stood, or seem'd to stand; ....5.DunA2.102.109.
Where the tall may-pole once o'er-look'd the Strand; ....5.DunB2.28.297.
Where the tall Nothing stood, or seem'd to stand; ....5.DunB2.110.300.
Ne *Richmond's* self, from whose tall Front are ey'd ....6.14ii.53.44.
044.Ne *Richmond's* self, from whose tall Front is ey'd ....6.14ii.53A.44.
Tall thriving trees confess'd the fruitful mold; ....6.35.5.103.
Right tall he made himself to show, ...6.79.33.219.
The King of Kings, majestically tall, ...II.2.564.154.
When thy tall Ships triumphant stem'd the Tide, ...II.3.66.192.
So tall, so awful, and almost Divine? ....II.3.222.203.
'Till yon' tall Vessels blaze with *Trojan* Fire? ....II.4.283.234.
Cut down it lies, tall, smooth, and largely spread, ...II.4.556.248.
Like Mountain Firs, as tall and strait as they. ....II.5.688.300.
So Silent Fountains, from a Rock's tall Head, ...II.9.19.432.
To those tall Ships, remotest of the Fleet, ...II.10.126.7.
Crops the tall Harvest, and lays waste the Plain; ....II.11.685.65.
Where the tall Fleet of great *Ulysses* lies, ...II.11.938.77.
As two tall Oaks, before the Wall they rise; ....II.12.145.86.
Subdu'd by Steel, a tall Ash tumbles down, ...II.13.242.116.
As when the Mountain Oak, or Poplar tall, ...II.13.493.130.
To yon' tall Ships to bear the *Trojan* Fires; ....II.13.932.149.
On yon' tall Summit of the fount-ful *Ide:* ....II.15.165.203.
Above the sides of some tall Ship ascend, ...II.15.442.214.
So some tall Rock o'erhangs the hoary Main, ...II.15.746.224.
From the tall Rock the sable Waters flow. ....II.16.6.234.
(When some tall Stag fresh-slaughter'd in the Wood ....II.16.196.247.
Then, as the Mountain Oak, or Poplar tall, ...II.16.593.267.
To the tall Top a milk-white Dove they tye, ...II.23.1012.529.
Supremely tall, and shade the deeps below. ....Od.1.240.44.
Load the tall bark, and launch into the main. ....Od.2.457.83.
Bow the tall mast, and swell before the gales; ....Od.2.467.83.
But five tall barks the winds and waters tost ....Od.3.382.105.
From his tall ship the King of men descends: ....Od.4.694.151.
But the tall mast above the vessel rear, ...Od.6.323.226.
Tall thriving trees confess'd the fruitful mold; ....Od.7.146.243.
Launch the tall bark, and order ev'ry oar, ...Od.8.35.263.
Skill'd in the dance, tall youths, a blooming band, ...Od.8.301.279.
From the tall hill he rends a pointed rock; ....Od.9.566.329.
Sent a tall stag, descending from the wood, ...Od.10.183.349.
Climb the tall bark, and launch into the main: ....Od.11.2.377.
Climb'd the tall bark, and rush'd into the main; ....Od.12.181.441.
Mount the tall bark, and launch into the sea. ....Od.15.590.98.

TALL-BOY

Cæsar and Tall-boy, Charles and Charlema'ne. ....3.Ep2.78.56.

TALLER

More strait than alders, taller than the planes; ....1.TrPA.60.367.
Taller or stronger than the weeds they shade? ....3.EOM1.40.18.

TALLEST

That two, my tallest Sons, might grace ....6.135.71.369.

TALONS

A Fawn his Talons truss'd (divine Portent) ....II.8.298.412.
His Talons truss'd; alive, and curling round, ...II.12.235.89.
A milkwhite fowle his clinching talons bore, ...Od.15.180.77.

TALTHYBIUS

Talthybius and *Eurybates* the good. ....II.1.421.108.
Talthybius hastens to the Fleet, to bring ....II.3.163.198.
With hasty Zeal the swift *Talthybius* flies; ....II.4.234.232.
Divine *Talthybius* whom the *Greeks* employ, ...II.7.333.380.
Talthybius shall the Victim Boar convey , ...II.19.195.379.
The Boar *Talthybius* held: The *Grecian* Lord ....II.19.259.383.

TALTHYBIUS'

The glitt'ring Charger to *Talthybius'* Hands. ....II.23.1063.533.

TAM'D

How twice he tam'd proud *Ister's* rapid Flood, ...1.TrSt.25.410.
Who Cities rais'd, or tam'd a monstrous Race; ....2.TemF.71.257.
Came back, and tam'd the Brutes he left behind. ....6.96iii.20.275.
Are tam'd to Wrongs, or this had been thy last. ....II.1.308.102.
Him with Reproof he check'd, or tam'd with Blows. ....II.2.236.138.
Nor tam'd by manners, nor by laws confin'd: ....Od.9.120.310.
(By magic tam'd) familiar to the dome. ....Od.10.243.354.

TAM'RISK

The flow'ry *Lotos,* and the Tam'risk burn, ...II.21.409.437.

TAM'RISKS

(Which spreading Tam'risks on the Margin hide) ....II.21.21.422.

TAMARISK

High on a spreading Tamarisk he plac'd; ....II.10.537.27.

TAMARISK'S

Rush'd on a *Tamarisk's* strong Trunk, and broke ....II.6.49.325.

TAME

The winding *Isis,* and the fruitful *Tame:* ....1.W-F.340.183.
Fortune's tame Fools, and Slaves in ev'ry Reign! ....1.TrSt.264.421.
Grow gentle, tractable, and tame as Geese. ....2.ChJM.668.47.
Like Puppy tame that uses ....6.58.18.171.
Court Puppy tame that uses ....6.58.18A.171.
With tame Content, and Thou possest of thine? ....II.1.168.95.
The tame Spectators of his Deeds of War. ....II.4.12.221.
Oh Son of *Tydeus!* (He, whose Strength could tame ....II.4.422.240.

TAME (CONTINUED)

To tame the Monster-God *Minerva* knows, ...II.5.954.312.
Ev'n great *Achilles* scarce their Rage can tame, ...II.10.475.24.
If 'tis his Will our haughty Foes to tame, ...II.12.77.84.
And hardy *Thracians* tame the savage Horse; ....II.13.8.104.
These can the Rage of haughty *Hector* tame; ....II.13.406.125.
Impow'r'd the Wrath of Gods and Men to tame, ...II.14.295.176.
No Force could tame them, and no Toil could tire; ....II.15.845.229.
Patroclus, while he liv'd, their Rage cou'd tame, ...II.17.546.98.
Say, is the fault, thro' tame submission, thine? ....Od.3.262.98.
When slumber next should tame the man of blood. ....Od.9.393.322.

TAMELY

New Lords they madly make, then tamely bear, ...1.TrSt.228.420.
Madly they make new Lords, then tamely bear, ...1.TrSt.228A.420.
My Prize of War, yet tamely see resumed; ....II.1.393.106.
One Hero's Loss too tamely you deplore, ...II.14.427.184.
Think not (he cries) I tamely will resign ....II.23.621.514.
Beneath thy roof, and cou'dst thou tamely stand? ....Od.18.264.179.

TAMER

Then he. "Great Tamer of all human art! ....5.DunA1.143.81.
Then he, "Great Tamer of all Wit and Art! 5.DunA1.143A.8
Then he: "Great Tamer of all human art! ....5.DunB1.163.282.

TAMES

Yet tames not this; it sticks to our last sand. ....3.Ep1.225.34.
Or tames the Genius of the stubborn Plain, ...4.HS1.131.19.
Prest with the weight of sleep that tames the strong: ....Od.9.442.324.

TAN

And fear'd to tan his Skin. ....6.79.28.218.

TANAIS

The freezing Tanais thro' a waste of Snows, ...5.DunA3.80.156.
The freezing Tanais thro' a waste of snows, ...5.DunB3.88.324.

TANTALIZ'D

In plenty starving, tantaliz'd in state, ...3.Ep4.163.153.

TANTALUS

The guilty Realms of *Tantalus* shall bleed; ....1.TrSt.345.424.
And shall not *Tantalus* his Kingdoms share ....1.TrSt.394.426.
There *Tantalus* along the *Stygian* bounds ....Od.11.719.421.

TANTALUS'S

And shall not Tantalus's Kingdoms share ....1.TrSt.394A.426.

TAP'STRY

A shaggy Tap'stry, worthy to be spread ....5.DunA2.135.117.
A shaggy Tap'stry, worthy to be spread ....5.DunB2.143.302.

TAPE

With tape-typ'd curtains, never meant to draw, ...3.Ep3.302.118.

TAPE-TYP'D

With tape-typ'd curtains, never meant to draw, ...3.Ep3.302.118.

TAPER

To light a Taper at a Neighbour's Fire. ....2.ChWB.139.63.
The hallow'd taper trembling in thy hand, ...2.ElAb.326.346.
Taper legs, and tempting thighs, ...6.18.7.61.
"So skilful and those Hands so taper; ....6.119.6.336.
"That head acute, and Hands so taper; ....6.119.6A.336.
"That Head so quick, those Hands so taper; ....6.119.6B.336.
And beaten Gold each taper Point adorns. ....II.4.143.227.
Whose taper tops refulgent Gold adorns. ....II.10.350.18.
Then o'er the vessel rais'd the taper mast, ...Od.5.324.187.
Shape the broad sail, or smooth the taper oar; ....Od.6.320.226.
But who the lighted taper will provide, ...Od.19.27.193.

TAPER'S

Still tries to save the hallow'd taper's end, ...3.Ep1.239.36.

TAPERING

And high above it rose the tapering oar. ....Od.12.22.430.

TAPERS

Priests, Tapers, Temples, swim before my sight: ....2.ElAb.274.342.
Redeem'd from tapers and defrauded pyes, ...5.DunA1.136.80.
Redeem'd from tapers and defrauded pies, ...5.DunB1.156.282.
With tapers flaming day his train attends, ...Od.19.58.195.

TAPESTRY

Like some *fierce Tyrant* in *Old Tapestry!* ....1.EOC.587.307.
As *Herod's* Hang-dogs in old Tapestry, ...4.JD4.267.47.

TAPHIAN

(*Mentes,* the Monarch of the *Taphian* land) ....Od.1.136.38.
Mentes my name; I rule the *Taphian* race, ...Od.1.229.43.
As then conspicuous at the *Taphian* court; ....Od.1.347.49.
That stranger-guest the *Taphian* realm obeys, ...Od.1.525.57.
The *Taphian* pyrates on *Thesprotia's* shores; ....Od.16.445.128.

TAPHIANS

The *Taphians* sold me to this man's embrace. ....Od.15.469.93.

TAPHOS

And led from *Taphos,* to attend his board, ...Od.14.504.60.

TAPISTRY

Rich tapistry, stiff with inwoven gold: ....Od.4.406.139.

TARDIER

With tardier Coursers, and inferior Skill. ....II.23.608.514.

TARDY
To Virtue's Work provoke the tardy Hall, ... 4.EpS2.218.325.
The gen'rous *Greeks* recede with tardy Pace, ... Il.5.860.307.
Now Shouts and Tumults wake the tardy Sun, ... Il.11.67.37.
And glaring round, by tardy Steps withdrew. .... Il.11.673.65.
By tardy Steps ascending from the Fleet. .... Il.14.36.159.
(The sea-ward prow invites the tardy gales) .... Od.4.1034.166.
Wakeful to weep and watch the tardy dawn .... Od.19.694.229.

TARGE
Drove thro' the *Trojan* Targe the knotty Spear; .... Il.7.312.379.
Beneath the spacious Targe (a blazing Round, ... Il.13.513.131.
And while beneath his Targe he flash'd along, ... Il.13.1016.153.
The pond'rous Targe be wielded by the strong. .... Il.14.434.184.
And o'er him high the riven Targe extends, ... Il.20.328.407.

TARGET
And struck his Target with the brazen Spear, ... Il.13.711.138.
Against the Target of the *Spartan* King; .... Il.13.810.144.

TARGETS
With sounding Strokes their brazen Targets rung: .... Il.12.170.87.
Spears lean on Spears, on Targets Targets throng, ... Il.13.181.114.
Spears lean on Spears, on Targets Targets throng, ... Il.13.181.114.

TARNE
From fruitful *Tarne* to the Fields of *Troy*. .... Il.5.60.269.

TARPHE'S
Or in fair *Tarphe's* Sylvan Seats reside; .... Il.2.639.157.

TARQUIN'S
A bright example of young *Tarquin's* shame. .... 6.38.22.108.

TARTAR
He, whose long Wall the wand'ring Tartar bounds. .... 5.DunA3.68.156.
He, whose long wall the wand'ring Tartar bounds; .... 5.DunB3.76.324.

TARTAREAN
That drives the Dead to dark *Tartarean* Coasts, ... 1.TrSt.435.428.
Infernal *Furies*, and *Tartarean* Gods, ... Il.3.351.209.
Low in the dark, *Tartarean* Gulf shall groan, ... Il.8.16.395.
The victims, vow'd to each *Tartarean* pow'r, ... Od.11.25.380.

TARTS
For Sallads, Tarts, and Pease! .... 6.47.48.130.

TASK
For 'tis but *half* a *Judge's Task*, to *Know*. .... 1.EOC.561.304.
Th' o'erlabour'd *Cyclop* from his Task retires; .... 1.TrSt.306.423.
The Task be mine the Hero's Strength to try, ... 1.TrES.215.457.
The Task be mine this Hero's Strength to try, ... 1.TrES.215A.457.
Glaucus, be bold, Thy Task be first to dare .... 1.TrES.302.460.
His Task perform'd, he sadly went his Way, ... 2.ChJM.363.31.
No happier task these faded eyes pursue, ... 2.ElAb.47.322.
Unequal task! a passion to resign, ... 2.ElAb.195.336.
Active its task, it prompts, impels, inspires. .... 3.EOM2.68.63.
But, sage historians! 'tis your task to prove .... 3.Ep1.85.21.
Or *Flavia's* self in glue (her rising task) .... 3.Ep2.25A.52.
Or Sappho's self in glue (her rising task) .... 3.Ep2.25B.52.
Or Sappho at her toilet's greazy task, ... 3.Ep2.25.52.
But what to follow, is a task indeed.) .... 3.Ep3.202.110.
Hard Task! to hit the Palate of such Guests, ... 4.2HE2.86.171.
That task, which as we follow, or despise, ... 4.1HE1.43.281.
But random Praise—the Task can ne'er be done, ... 4.EpS2.106.319.
Now at his head the dext'rous task commence, ... 5.DunA2.191.124.
Now at his head the dextrous task commence, ... 5.DunB2.199.305.
"Be that my task (replies a gloomy Clerk, ... 5.DunB4.459.385.
Bold is the Task, when Subjects grown too wise .... Il.1.103.92.
As thine the Steeds, be thine the Task to guide. .... Il.5.289.281.
Their Task perform'd, and mix among the Gods. .... Il.5.1121.321.
'Tis Man's bold Task the gen'rous Strife to try, ... Il.7.117.369.
This Task let *Ajax* or *Tydides* prove, ... Il.7.217.375.
But say, what Hero shall sustain that Task? .... Il.10.45.4.
So brave a Task each *Ajax* strove to share, ... Il.10.271.14.
Far other Task! than when they wont to keep .... Il.11.141.41.
The Task be mine this Hero's Strength to try, ... Il.16.518.263.
Glaucus, be bold; thy Task be first to dare .... Il.16.607.268.
In glorious Action, is the Task of War. .... Il.16.762.273.
The ruling Charge: The Task of Fight be mine. .... Il.17.547.309.
That Day, no common Task his Labour claim'd; .... Il.18.439.341.
Thy Task it was, to feed the bellowing Droves .... Il.21.521.443.
Let others for the noble Task prepare, ... Il.23.353.504.
Griev'd as he was, he not this Task deny'd; .... Il.24.347.550.
"A task of grief, his ornaments of death. .... Od.2.110.66.
Awful th' approach, and hard the task appears, ... Od.3.31.87.
Not added years on years my task could close, ... Od.3.141.92.
My task is done; the mansion you enquire .... Od.7.63.236.
Hard is the task, oh Princess! you impose: .... Od.7.322.251.
Instant you sailors to this task attend, ... Od.8.37.264.
And mine shall be the task, henceforth to raise .... Od.8.545.291.
The task thus finish'd of his morning hours, ... Od.9.368.321.
Be it my task to send with ample stores .... Od.11.438.406.
Our task be now thy treasur'd stores to save, ... Od.13.417.26.
While here, (ungrateful task!) his herds I feed, ... Od.14.47.38.
His task it was the wheaten loaves to lay, ... Od.14.506.61.
Hard task, he cries, thy virtue gives thy friend, ... Od.16.69.105.
We rise terrific to the task of fight. .... Od.16.289.118.
Be it my task the torches to supply .... Od.18.363.185.
Then to the servile task the Monarch turns .... Od.18.391.186.
Your other task, ye menial train, forbear; .... Od.19.362.211.
Hard is the task, and rare, the Queen rejoin'd, ... Od.19.654.227.
One maid, unequal to the task assign'd, ... Od.20.138.240.
No vulgar task! Ill suits this courtly crew .... Od.21.94.263.
Three times, unequal to the task, gave way: .... Od.21.132.264.
Retire oh Queen! thy houshold task resume, ... Od.21.377.277.

TASK (CONTINUED)
Th' offending females to that task we doom, ... Od.22.474.312.
Urg'd the dire task imperious from above. .... Od.22.487.313.
A task of grief, his ornaments of death: .... Od.24.159.356.

TASK'D
Task'd for the royal board to bolt the bran .... Od.20.134.240.

TASKS
In Tasks so bold, can Little Men engage, ... 2.RL1.11.145.
Ye know the Spheres and various Tasks assign'd, ... 2.RL2.75.164.
Just as absurd, to mourn the tasks or pains .... 3.EOM1.265.47.
How oft' in pleasing tasks we wear the day, ... 6.52.17.156.
Then all dispersing, various Tasks attend; .... Il.3.527.216.
No more—but hasten to thy Tasks at home, ... Il.6.632.358.
Such once I was! Now to these Tasks succeeds .... Il.23.739.519.
Such are the tasks of men of mean estate, ... Od.15.342.86.
Or stoop to tasks a rural Lord demands. .... Od.17.25.133.
In rival tasks beneath the burning rage .... Od.18.411.188.
To diff'rent tasks their toil the Nymphs addres'd: .... Od.19.73.196.
And servitude with pleasing tasks deceive; .... Od.22.461.310.

TASSELS
With empty Hands no Tassels you can lure, ... 2.ChWB.172.65.

TAST
The Birds obscene, that nightly flock'd to Tast, ... 1.TrSt.735.441.
Or grateful Bitters shall delight the Tast; .... 6.82i.7.229.

TASTE
True *Taste* as seldom is the *Critick's* Share; .... 1.EOC.12.240.
How far your *Genius, Taste,* and *Learning* go; .... 1.EOC.49.244.
Drink deep, or taste not the *Pierian* Spring: .... 1.EOC.216.264.
Some to *Conceit* alone their Taste confine, ... 1.EOC.289.271.
'Tis not enough, Taste, Judgment, Learning, join; .... 1.EOC.562.305.
Blest with a *Taste* exact, yet unconfin'd; .... 1.EOC.639.311.
He views his Food, wou'd taste, yet dares not try; .... 1.TrSt.853A.445.
And taste not half the Bliss the Gods bestow. .... 1.TrUl.210.472.
Once, ere he dy'd, to taste the blissful Life .... 2.ChJM.17.15.
At once they gratifie their Smell and Taste, ... 2.RL*A* 1.95.130.
To taste awhile the Pleasures of a Court; .... 2.RL3.10.169.
At once they gratify their Scent and Taste, ... 2.RL3.111.176.
Where none learn *Ombre,* none e'er taste *Bohea!* .... 2.RL4.156.197.
This taste the honey, and not wound the flow'r: .... 3.EOM2.90.65.
But these less taste them, as they worse obtain. .... 3.EOM4.84.136.
Which who but feels can taste, but thinks can know: .... 3.EOM4.328.160.
The Nose of Hautgout, and the Tip of Taste, ... 3.Ep2.80.57.
On the soft Passion, and the Taste refin'd, ... 3.Ep2.84.57.
Your Taste of Follies, with our Scorn of Fools, ... 3.Ep2.276.72.
His wealth, to purchase what he ne'er can taste? .... 3.Ep4.4.134.
Some Dæmon whisper'd, "Visto! have a Taste." .... 3.Ep4.16.137.
Heav'n visits with a Taste the wealthy fool, ... 3.Ep4.17.137.
And something previous ev'n to Taste—'tis Sense: .... 3.Ep4.42.140.
His Son's fine Taste an op'ner Vista loves, ... 3.Ep4.93.146.
Some Dæmon whisper'd, "Knights should have a Taste." .... 3.Ep4.16A.137.
In you, my *Lord,* Taste sanctifies Expence, ... 3.Ep4.179A.154.
Than ridicule all *Taste,* blaspheme *Quadrille,* .... 4.HS1.38.7.
"To have a Taste, is Insolence indeed: .... 4.HS2.112.63.
But diff'rent Taste in diff'rent Men prevails, ... 4.HAdv.35.79.
And all they want is spirit, taste, and sense. .... 4.Arbu.160.108.
Talk what you will of Taste, my Friend, you'll find, ... 4.2HE2.268.183.
In every Taste of foreign Courts improv'd, ... 4.2HE1.141.207.
He, from the taste obscene reclaims our Youth, ... 4.2HE1.217.213.
Farce once the taste of Mobs, but now of Lords; .... 4.2HE1.311.221.
(For Taste, eternal wanderer, now flies .... 4.2HE1.312.221.
Farce, long the taste of Mobs, but now of Lords; .... 4.2HE1.311A.221.
Ever the taste of Mobs, but now of Lords; .... 4.2HE1.311B.221.
(Taste, that eternal wanderer, which flies .... 4.2HE1.312A.221.
Who climb their Mountain, or who taste their spring? .... 4.2HE1.353.225.
Procure a *Taste* to double the surprize, ... 4.1HE6.30.239.
Then his nice taste directs our Operas: .... 5.DunA2.196.124.
Thy dragons Magistrates and Peers shall taste, ... 5.DunA3.299.184.
Then his nice taste directs our Operas: .... 5.DunB2.204.305.
Thee shall the Patriot, thee the Courtier taste, ... 5.DunB3.297.334.
Can taste no pleasure since his Shield was scour'd; .... 6.71.42.204.
And *Europe* taste thy Sorrows in a Dish. .... 6.96ii.78.274.
And *Europe* taste thy Sorrows in her Dish. .... 6.96ii.78A.274.
(Studious in ev'ry Thing to please thy Taste) .... 6.96iv.50.277.
And all they want is Spirit, Taste, and Sense. .... 6.98.10.283.
The Sense and Taste of one that bears .... 6.119.15.337.
No Taste of Sleep these heavy Eyes have known; .... Il.10.102.7.
With Goat's-milk Cheese a flav'rous Taste bestows, ... Il.11.782.70.
Sweet to the Soul, as Hony to the Taste; .... Il.18.140.329.
Approach, and taste the Dainties of the Bow'r. .... Il.18.456.343.
Let not my Palate know the Taste of Food, ... Il.19.207.381.
To taste the bad, unmix'd, is curst indeed; .... Il.24.668.565.
The Happiest taste not Happiness sincere, ... Il.24.671.565.
Viands of various kinds allure the taste, ... Od.1.185.41.
The luscious wines dishonour'd lose their taste, ... Od.2.349.78.
They taste the entrails, and the altars load .... Od.3.11.87.
Must taste that cup, for man is born to die. .... Od.3.296.100.
Approach, and taste the dainties of my bow'r. .... Od.5.116.177.
Scarce could *Iäsion* taste her heav'nly charms, ... Od.5.161.179.
Viands of various kinds invite the taste, ... Od.7.236.247.
Come, my belov'd! and taste the soft delights; .... Od.8.333.281.
Hear the sweet song, and taste the feast in peace. .... Od.8.464.288.
Our hour was come, to taste our share of pain. .... Od.9.60.304.
And never shalt thou taste this Nectar more. .... Od.9.416.323.
Ascend her bed, and taste celestial charms: .... Od.10.354.361.
Viands of various kinds allure the taste, ... Od.10.439.365.
To taste the joys of *Circe's* sacred dome. .... Od.10.506.368.
Know; to the spectres, that thy bev'rage taste, ... Od.11.180.390.
Indulge the taste, and drein the sparkling bowls: .... Od.12.34.431.
And taste not half the bliss the Gods bestow. .... Od.13.377.25.
Or when, to taste her hospitable board, ... Od.14.413.56.
And here, unenvy'd, rural dainties taste. .... Od.14.452.57.

TASTE (CONTINUED)
Viands of various kinds allure the taste ....Od.15.154.76.
Review the series of our lives, and taste ....Od.15.434.90.
Exact of taste, and serve the feast in state. ....Od.16.275.118.
They share the meal that earn it ere they taste. ....Od.19.32.194.

TASTED
Then first the Flamen tasted living food; ....3.EOM3.265.119.
She tasted, and resign'd it: Then began ....Il.24.135.540.
Or, the charm tasted, had return'd no more. ....Od.9.114.308.

TASTEFUL
The bowl, and tasteful viands tempt in vain, ...Od.4.134.126.
And smoaking back the tasteful viands drew, ...Od.14.90.40.
To turn the tasteful viand o'er the flame; ....Od.15.340.86.
A kid's well-fatted entrails (tasteful food!) ....Od.18.51.169.
The limbs; then all the tasteful viands share. ....Od.19.493.220.
The tasteful inwards, and nectareous wines. ....Od.20.325.249.

TASTES
And tastes the good without the fall to ill; ; ....3.EOM4.312.157.
Only to show, how many Tastes he wanted. ....3.Ep4.14.137.
Yet Wit ne'er tastes, and Beauty ne'er enjoys, ...4.Arbu.312.118.
Tastes for his Friend of Fowl and Fish; ....4.HS6.201.263.
The same their talents, and their tastes the same; ....5.DunB2.380.315.
Which whoso tastes, forgets his former friends, ...5.DunB4.518.394.
Nor tastes the Gifts of all-composing Sleep. ....Il.24.8.535.
(Thence call'd Lotophagi) which whoso tastes, ...Od.9.107.308.
Nor wine nor food he tastes; but sunk in woes, ...Od.16.154.110.

TASTFUL
Nor tastful Herbs that in these Gardens rise, ...1.TrVP.102.381.

TASTLESS
My Soul abhors the tastless, dry Embrace, ...2.ChJM.103.19.

TASTS
The same their talents, and their tasts the same, ...5.DunA2.348.143.

TATE
And own'd, that nine such Poets made a Tate. ....4.Arbu.190.109.
To the mild Limbo of our Father Tate: ....5.DunB1.238.287.
And be like Tate and Brady. ....6.58.64.173.
And own that nine such Poets make a Tate; ....6.98.40.284.

TATE'S
She saw slow Philips creep like Tate's poor page, ...5.DunA1.103.72.
She saw slow Philips creep like Tate's poor page, ...5.DunB1.105.277.

TATTER'D
Where wave the tatter'd ensigns of Rag-Fair, ...5.DunA1.27.63.
Then with these tatter'd rags they wrapt me round, ...Od.14.379.53.
Yet tatter'd as I look, I challeng'd then ....Od.14.572.64.
An aged mendicant in tatter'd weeds. ....Od.16.293.119.
These tatter'd weeds (my decent robe resign'd.) ....Od.19.391.213.
Adjusting to his limbs the tatter'd vest, ...Od.19.591.225.

TATTERS
I sit in Tatters, and immur'd at home! ....2.ChWB.77.60.
And vexing ev'ry Wight, tears Cloaths and all to Tatters. .6.14ii.36.44.
The broad-patch'd scrip; the scrip in tatters hung .....Od.18.131.172.

TATTLE
Such tattle often entertains ....4.HS6.95.257.

TAUGHT
A Faithful Swain, whom Love had taught to sing, ...1.PSu.1A.71.
That taught the Groves my Rosalinda's Name— ....1.PSu.42.75.
Taught Rocks to weep, and made the Mountains groan. ..1.PAu.16.82.
Her Name with Pleasure once she taught the Shore, ..1.PWi.43.92.
(Beasts, taught by us, their Fellow Beasts pursue, ...1.W-F.123A.162.
And taught the World, with Reason to Admire. ....1.EOC.101.250.
So modern Pothecaries, taught the Art ....1.EOC.108.251.
And taught more Pleasant Methods of Salvation; .....1.EOC.547.302.
Men must be taught as if you taught them not; ....1.EOC.574.306.
Men must be taught as if you taught them not; ....1.EOC.574.306.
The Muse, whose early Voice you taught to Sing, ...1.EOC.735.325.
None taught the Trees a nobler Race to bear, ...1.TrVP.3.377.
Love taught my Tears in sadder Notes to flow, ...1.TrSP.7.393.
Twice taught the Rhine beneath his Laws to roll, ...1.TrSt.27.410.
Taught by thy self to win the promis'd Reign; ....1.TrSt.94.414.
Or great Osyris, who first taught the Swain ....1.TrSt.859.446.
That taught by great Examples, all may try ....1.TrES.312.461.
Who taught thee Arts, Alcinous to persuade, ...1.TrUl.177.471.
Why was I taught to make my Husband see, ...2.ChJM.762.52.
Of all the Nurse and all the Priest have taught, ...2.RL1.30.147.
These, in two sable Ringlets taught to break, ...2.RL4.169.197.
This, in two sable Ringlets taught to break, ...2.RL4.169A.197.
Who taught that useful Science, to be good. ....2.TemF.108.261.
And wise Aurelius, in whose well-taught Mind ....2.TemF.165.268.
Nor tears, for ages, taught to flow in vain, ...2.ElAb.28.321.
Heav'n first taught letters for some wretch's aid, ...2.ElAb.51.323.
Too soon they taught me 'twas no sin to love. ....2.ElAb.68.324.
Of all affliction taught a lover yet, ...2.ElAb.189.335.
Still as the sea, ere winds were taught to blow, ...2.ElAb.253.340.
His soul proud Science never taught to stray ....3.EOM1.101.27.
Could he, who taught each Planet where to roll, ...3.EOM2.35A.60.
Taught half by Reason, half by mere decay, ...3.EOM2.259.86.
Who taught the nations of the field and wood ....3.EOM3.99.101.
Who taught the nations of the field and flood ....3.EOM3.99A.101.
Taught to command the fire, controul the flood, ...3.EOM3.220.115.
Who first taught souls enslav'd, and realms undone, ..3.EOM3.241.116.
'Till Superstition taught the tyrant awe, ...3.EOM3.246.117.
She taught the weak to bend, the proud to pray, ...3.EOM3.251.118.
Taught Pow'r's due use to People and to Kings, ...3.EOM3.289.121.
Taught nor to slack, nor strain its tender strings, ...3.EOM3.290.121.

TAUGHT (CONTINUED)
Taught not to slack, nor strain its tender strings, ...3.EOM3.290A.
E'er taught to shine, or sanctify'd from shame! ....3.EOM4.300.1?
With too much Quickness ever to be taught, ...3.Ep2.97.58.
That, Nature gives; and where the lesson taught .....3.Ep2.211.67.
Who taught that heav'n-directed spire to rise? ....3.Ep3.261.114.
"No Lessons now are taught the Spartan way: ....4.JD4.93.33.
Taught on the Wings of Truth, to fly 4.HOde9.3.159
Besides, my Father taught me from a Lad, ...4.2HE2.54.169.
On each enervate string they taught the Note ....4.2HE1.153.20?
Waller was smooth; but Dryden taught to join ....4.2HE1.267.21?
And taught his Romans, in much better metre, ...4.EpS1.9.297.
How new-born Nonsense first is taught to cry, ...5.DunA1.58.67
As taught by Venus, Paris learnt the art 5.DunA2.209.1
How new-born nonsense first is taught to cry, ...5.DunB1.60.27?
As taught by Venus, Paris learnt the art ....5.DunB2.217.3?
Then taught by Hermes, and divinely bold, ...5.DunB4.381.3?
Thus bred, thus taught, how many have I seen, ...5.DunB4.505.3?
Taught by your hand, can charm no less than he; .....6.3.10.7.
And Chærilus taught Codrus to be dull; ....6.7.20.16.
'Till wrangling Science taught it Noise and Show, ...6.8.11.18.
Amphion taught contending Kings, ...6.11.35Z3.31.
Groves, where immortal Sages taught; ....6.51i.2.151.
Then spread those Morals which the Houyhnhnms taught. .6.96iii.22.275.
And the first tears for her were taught to flow. ....6.107.6.310.
Kneller, by Heav'n and not a Master taught, ...6.108.1.312.
E'er taught to shine, or sanctified from shame ....6.130.14.358.
Diana taught him all her Sylvan Arts, ...Il.5.67.269.
Taught by this Stroke, renounce the War's Alarms, ...Il.5.437.289.
Taught by the Gods that mov'd his sacred Breast: .....Il.6.92.328.
Not thus Achilles taught our Hosts to dread, ...Il.6.121.330.
Is it for him these Tears are taught to flow, ...Il.9.723.470.
Go now to Nestor, and from him be taught ....Il.11.748.68.
Once taught Achilles, and Achilles thee. ....Il.11.967.78.
Thus, Trojans, thus, at length be taught to fear; ......Il.13.779.141.
And taught to conquer, or to fall in Fight; ....Il.14.95.162.
Whom Hermes lov'd, and taught the Arts of Gain) ...Il.14.576.190.
And taught Submission to the Sire of Heav'n. ....Il.15.52.196.
And where the Bow, which Phœbus taught to bend? ...Il.15.517.217.
That taught by great Examples, all may try ....Il.16.617.268.
The Chief who taught our lofty Walls to yield, ...Il.16.683.270.
With well-taught Feet: Now shape, in oblique ways, ...Il.18.691.357.
Sidonian Artists taught the Frame to shine, ...Il.23.867.524.
By great Ulysses taught the path to fame: ....Od.2.24.61.
Brave Philoctetes, taught to wing the dart; ....Od.3.231.97.
Taught by a Master of the tuneful kind: ....Od.3.333.102.
This shows thee, friend, by old experience taught, ...Od.5.235.182.
By Pallas taught, he frames the wond'rous mold, ...Od.6.277.224.
Whose well-taught mind the present age surpast, ...Od.7.210.247.
Taught by the Gods to please, when high he sings .....Od.8.41.264.
Great Philoctetes taught the shaft to fly. ....Od.8.252.276.
Or taught the labours of the dreadful day: ....Od.8.536.291.
The heav'n-taught Poet, and enchanting strain: ....Od.9.4.301.
Who taught proud Troy and all her sons to bow; ....Od.9.315.319.
Ulysses, taught by labours to be wise, ...Od.10.540.369.
O taught to bear the wrongs of base mankind! ....Od.11.762.424.
Who taught thee arts, Alcinous to persuade, ...Od.13.344.24.
O thou! whom Age has taught to understand, ...Od.14.425.56.
And taught mankind the counsels of the God. ....Od.15.277.82.
As when some heav'n-taught Poet charms the ear, ...Od.17.609.161.
Yet taught by time, my heart has learn'd to glow ......Od.18.269.179.
With that fam'd bow Ulysses taught to bend, ...Od.19.668.228.
And Pallas taught the texture of the loom. ....Od.20.87.237.
Nor in the front of battle taught to bend, ...Od.21.39.261.
Then, as some heav'nly minstrel, taught to sing ....Od.21.440.281.
Self-taught I sing; by heav'n, and heav'n alone ....Od.22.383.307.
Thou, with the heav'n-taught bard, in peace resort ...Od.22.415.308.
Taught by my care to cull the fleece, or weave, ...Od.22.460.310.
By Pallas taught, he frames the wond'rous mold, ...Od.23.159.328.
But thou! whom years have taught to understand, ...Od.24.310.364.

TAUNT
Scornful of age, to taunt the virtuous man, ...Od.18.397.187.

TAUNTS
Whispers are heard, with Taunts reviling loud, ...2.TemF.404.28?
Whispers were heard, with Taunts reviling loud, ...2.TemF.404A.2
And Taunts alternate innocently flew. 4.2HE1.250.217
Thus with injurious Taunts attack'd the Throne. ......Il.2.274.140.
With Wounds ungen'rous, or with Taunts disgrace. ....Il.22.468.475.
Derisive taunts were spread from guest to guest, ...Od.2.364.78.
With ire-full taunts each other they oppose, ...Od.3.179.94.
With taunts the distant giant I accost, ...Od.9.557.329.
Thus with new taunts insult the monster's ear. ....Od.9.586.330.

TAURUS
Assur'd me, Mars in Taurus was my Sign. 2.ChWB.322.72

TAVERNS
Thro' Taverns, Stews, and Bagnio's take our round, ...4.1HE6.119.245?

TAW
"Nay, mix with Children, as they play'd at Taw; .....6.96ii.28.271.

TAWDRY
Where tawdry yellow strove with dirty red, ...3.Ep3.304.118.
His daughter flaunts a Viscount's tawdry wife; ....3.Ep3.391.124.
Sinks the lost Actor in the tawdry load. ....4.2HE1.333.223?

TAWNY
Her tawny Young, beset by Men and Hounds; ....Il.17.148.293.

TAX
Fear most to tax an Honourable Fool, ...1.EOC.588.307.
I levied first a Tax upon his Need, ...2.ChWB.168.64?
To tax Directors, who (thank God) have Plums; ....4.EpS2.49.315.

TAX (CONTINUED)
Yet must I tax his Sloath, that claims no share ....Il.10.130.7.
Tax not, (the heav'n-illumin'd Seer rejoin'd) ....Od.20.437.254.

TAX'D
I tax'd them oft with Wenching and Amours, ...2.ChWB.154.64.
Tho' double-tax'd, how little have I lost? ....4.HS2.152.67.
For Right Hereditary tax'd and fin'd, ...4.2HE2.64.169.

TAXATIONS
Of old Mismanagements, Taxations new— ....2.TemF.456.285.

TAXES
P. Of Debts, and Taxes, Wife and Children clear, ...3.Ep3.279A.116.
Of Debts, and Taxes, Wife and Children clear, ...3.Ep3.279.116.

TAYLOR
Now deep in Taylor and the Book of Martyrs, ...3.Ep2.63.55.
That suit, an unpaid Taylor snatch'd away! ....5.DunA2.110.110.
Taylor, sweet bird of Thames, majestic bows, ...5.DunA2.323.141.
Taylor, sweet Swan of Thames, majestic bows; ....5.DunA2.323A.141.
That suit an unpay'd taylor snatch'd away. ....5.DunB2.118.301.
Taylor, their better Charon, lends an oar, ...5.DunB3.19.321.
Now deep in *Taylor* and the *Book of Martyrs,* ....6.99.13.287.
Bring me what Nature, Taylor to the *Bear,* ....6.100iii.1.289.

TEÄTUS'
(*Eurytus'* this, and that *Teätus'* Son) ....Il.2.756.161.

TE
Disputes of *Me* or *Te,* of *aut* or *at,* .... 5.DunB4.220.364.

TE-HE
Te-he cry'd Ladies; Clerke nought spake: ....6.14i.21.42.

TEA
And sip with *Nymphs,* their Elemental Tea. ....2.RL1.62.150.
Dost sometimes Counsel take—and sometimes *Tea.* .... 2.RL3.8.169.
To muse, and spill her solitary Tea, ...6.45.16.125.
"A Dish of Tea like Milk-Pail on thy Head? ....6.96ii.68.273.

TEACH
Let such teach others who themselves excell, ...1.EOC.15.240.
Are *nameless Graces* which no Methods teach, ...1.EOC.144.256.
To teach vain Wits a Science *little known,* .... 1.EOC.199.263.
To teach vain Wits that Science *little known,* .... 1.EOC.199A.263.
Still *pleas'd* to *teach,* and yet not *proud* to *know?* .... 1.EOC.632.311.
His *Precepts* teach but what his *Works* inspire. .... 1.EOC.660.314.
And teach th'obedient Branches where to spring. ....1.TrVP.12.377.
Teach him, when first his infant voice shall frame ....1.TrFD.80.389.
The Muses teach me all their softest Lays, ...1.TrSP.31.394.
One savage Heart, or teach it how to love? ....1.TrSP.243.404.
"Well shou'd you practise, who so well can teach. ....2.ChWB.187.65.
Teach Infant-Cheeks a bidden Blush to know, ...2.RL1.89.152.
Then teach me, Heaven! to scorn the guilty Bays; ....2.TemF.521.289.
Oh come! oh teach me nature to subdue, ...2.ElAb.203.336.
Teach me at once, and learn of me to die. ....2.ElAb.328.346.
Correct old Time, and teach the Sun his way; ....3.EOM2.22A.57.
Go, teach Eternal Wisdom how to rule— ....3.EOM2.29.59.
Let subtle schoolmen teach these friends to fight, ...3.EOM2.81.64.
Teach us to mourn our Nature, not to mend, ...3.EOM2.153.73.
Truths would you teach, or save a sinking land? ....3.EOM4.265.153.
Teach me, like thee, in various nature wise, ...3.EOM4.377.165.
Oh teach us, BATHURST! yet unspoil'd by wealth! ....3.Ep3.226.111.
For I am pleas'd to learn, and you to teach; ....4.JD4.67A.31.
And teach, the Being you preserv'd, to bear. ....4.Arbu.134.105.
And without sneering, teach the rest to sneer; ....4.Arbu.202.110.
Teach ev'ry Thought within its bounds to roll, ...4.2HE2.204.179.
Yet still, not heeding what your Heart can teach, ...4.2HE2.224.181.
Who scorn a Lad should teach his Father skill, ...4.2HE1.129.205.
To teach their frugal Virtues to his Heir; ....4.2HE1.166.209.
What better teach a Foreigner the tongue? ....4.2HE1.206.213.
Yet lest you think I railly more than teach, ...4.2HE1.338.225.
Or teach the melancholy Muse to mourn, ...4.EpS1.79.304.
Teach Oaths to Gamesters, and to Nobles Wit? ....5.DunB1.204.284.
Teach Oaths to Gamesters, and to Nobles—Wit? ....5.DunB1.204A.284.
Teach thou the warb'ling Polypheme to roar, ...5.DunB3.305.334.
Words are Man's province, Words we teach alone. ....5.DunB4.150.356.
Teach but that one, sufficient for a King; ....5.DunB4.184.360.
Teach Kings to fiddle, and make Senates dance. ....5.DunB4.598.402.
They teach the Misteries thou dost open lay; ....6.2.26.6.
Be but to teach the Ignorant more Sense; ....6.16.8.53.
In ev'ry Scene some Moral let it teach, ...6.19.23.62.
Or teach the soul of *Cleopatra* fear) ....6.20.36.67.
Oh teach the mind t' ætherial heights to rise, ...6.23.9.73.
And without sneering, teach the rest to sneer; ....6.49iii.16.143.
This, teach me more than Hell to shun, ...6.50.15.146.
If I am right, oh teach my heart ....6.50.29.147.
Teach me to feel another's Woe; ....6.50.37.148.
And teach dull *Harlequins* to grin in vain. ....6.60.16.178.
(Mark the Doctrine I teach) ....6.91.24.254.
O teach me, Dear, new Words to speak my Flame; ....6.96iv.95.279.
Teach me to wooe thee by thy best-lov'd Name! ....6.96iv.96.279.
And without sneering, teach the rest to sneer; ....6.98.52.284.
At once can teach, delight, and lash the age, ...6.106iv.2.307.
Thanks, dirty Pair! you teach me what to say, ...6.129.5.357.
To teach the *Greeks* to murmur at their Lord? ....Il.1.136.93.
And teach our Mother what the Gods require: ....Il.6.108.329.
He bade me teach thee all the ways of War. ....Il.9.570.462.
Such as may teach, 'twas still thy brave Delight ....Il.13.376.123.
That teach the Disk to sound along the Sky. ....Il.23.982.528.
Why teach ye not my rapid Wheels to run, ...Il.24.329.550.
And teach him Mercy when a Father prays. ....Il.24.380.551.
Teach me to seek redress for all my woe, ...Od.2.355.78.
Will teach you to repass th' unmeasur'd main. ....Od.4.576.147.
Or teach the fluttering sail to float in air; ....Od.6.324.226.

TEACH (CONTINUED)
Teach them thy consort, bid thy sons attend; ....Od.8.278.278.

TEACHER
Wait the great teacher Death, and God adore! ....3.EOM1.92.25.

TEACHES
Good Humour only teaches Charms to last, ...6.19.61.64.

TEAM
The *Pleiads, Hyads,* with the Northern Team; ....Il.18.561.349.
There view'd the *Pleiads,* and the northern Team, ...Od.5.347.188.
A team of twenty geese, (a snow-white train!) ....Od.19.627.226.

TEAMS
As when two Teams of Mules divide the Green, ...Il.10.420.22.

TEAPOTS
Here living *Teapots* stand, one Arm held out, ...2.RL4.49.188.

TEAR
From ev'ry Face he wipes off ev'ry Tear. ....1.Mes.46.117.
I'll from his bleeding breast his entrails tear, ...1.TrPA.126.370.
From ev'ry leaf distills a trickling tear, ...1.TrFD.66.388.
No Tear did you, no parting Kiss receive, ...1.TrSP.115.398.
No Sigh to rise, no Tear had pow'r to flow; ....1.TrSP.127.399.
I from the Root thy guilty Race will tear, ...1.TrSt.340.424.
They cuff, they tear, they raise a screaming Cry; ....1.TrES.221.458.
Heav'n knows, I shed full many a private Tear, ...2.ChJM.198.24.
Breathe a soft Sigh, and drop a tender Tear; ....2.ChJM.666.47.
Still breath'd in sighs, still usher'd with a tear. ....2.ElAb.32.321.
With ev'ry bead I drop too soft a tear. ....2.ElAb.270.342.
Assist the Fiends and tear me from my God! ....2.ElAb.288.343.
One human tear shall drop, and be forgiv'n. ....2.ElAb.358.348.
No friend's complaint, no kind domestic tear ....2.Elegy.49.367.
Shall shortly want the gen'rous tear he pays; ....2.Elegy.78.368.
And the last pang shall tear thee from his heart, ...2.Elegy.80.368.
Or from the soft-ey'd Virgin steal a tear! ....4.Arbu.286.116.
The Blow unfelt, the Tear he never shed; ....4.Arbu.349.120.
Language so harsh, 'tis sure enough to tear ....4.JD2A.65.138.
Steals down my cheek th'involuntary Tear? ....4.HOde1.38.153.
With Pity, and with Terror, tear my heart; ....4.2HE1.345.225.
With that, a Tear (portentous sign of Grace!) ....5.DunB1.243.288.
Nor cou'd'st thou, CHESTERFIELD! a tear refuse, ...5.DunB4.43.345.
(Not death it self from me cou'd force a tear, ...6.20.35.67.
Nor could so scratch and tear. ....6.79.32.218.
Nor more could scratch and tear. ....6.79.32A.218.
(A Sigh the Absent claims, the Dead a Tear) ....6.84.14.239.
Without a Sigh, a Trouble, or a Tear; ....6.86.16A.245.
"As Children tear the Wings of Flies away: ....6.96ii.36.272.
For thee the hardy Vet'ran drops a tear, ...6.113.5.320.
This weeping marble had not ask'd thy Tear, ...6.132.5.362.
Here, stole the Honest Tear from Marchmont's Eye ....6.142.12B.383.
Oh next him skill'd to draw the tender Tear, ...6.152.3.400.
Ourself in Arms shall tear her from his Heart. ....Il.1.425.108.
And *Troy's* proud Matrons render Tear for Tear. ....Il.2.423.147.
And *Troy's* proud Matrons render Tear for Tear. ....Il.2.423.147.
Rush to her Thought, and force a tender Tear. ....Il.3.186.200.
Demands a parting Word, a tender Tear: ....Il.6.459.348.
And the big Tear stood trembling in her Eye. ....Il.6.509.351.
She mingled with the Smile a tender Tear. ....Il.6.621.357.
To tear his Country, and his Kind destroy! ....Il.9.92.437.
The furry Helmet from his Brow they tear, ...Il.10.528.26.
As the bold Hunter chears his Hounds to tear ....Il.11.377.51.
But hungry Birds shall tear those Balls away, ...Il.11.570.59.
On ev'ry side the crackling Trees they tear, ...Il.12.165.87.
Join'd to one Yoke, the stubborn Earth they tear, ...Il.13.881.147.
The Birds shall tear him, and the Dogs devour. ....Il.15.401.212.
They cuff, they tear, they raise a screaming Cry; ....Il.16.524.264.
Shall I not force some widow'd Dame to tear ....Il.18.155.330.
And Dogs shall tear him, e'er he sack the Town. ....Il.18.332.337.
His Son's sad Fate, and drops a tender Tear.) ....Il.19.344.386.
Each stole a Tear for what he left behind. ....Il.19.361.387.
Nor Spouse nor Mother grace thee with a Tear; ....Il.22.123.458.
Ah, leave me not for *Grecian* Dogs to tear! ....Il.22.428.473.
The Wretch obeys, retiring with a Tear. ....Il.22.641.483.
Sigh back her Sighs, and answer Tear with Tear. ....Il.22.663.484.
Sigh back her Sighs, and answer Tear with Tear. ....Il.22.663.484.
Thought follows Thought, and Tear succeeds to Tear. ....Il.24.16.535.
Thought follows Thought, and Tear succeeds to Tear. ....Il.24.16.535.
My Soul might keep, or utter with a Tear; ....Il.24.937.575.
(Painful vicissitude!) his bosom tear. ....Od.1.151.40.
The big round tear hung trembling in his eye: ....Od.2.91.65.
They cuff, they tear, their cheeks and necks they rend, ...Od.2.179.70.
Indulge the tribute of a grateful tear. ....Od.4.130.126.
His purple garment veil'd the falling tear. ....Od.4.208.129.
The graceful curl, and drop the tender tear. ....Od.4.272.132.
The big round tear stands trembling in her eye, ...Od.4.936.162.
The flowing tear, and rais'd his drooping head: ....Od.8.84.267.
The silent tear, and heard the secret groan: ....Od.8.92.267.
The silent tear, and heard the secret groan; ....Od.8.584.294.
The tribute of a tear is all I crave, ...Od.11.89.385.
Tear follow'd tear, and groan succeeded groan. ....Od.11.101.385.
Tear follow'd tear, and groan succeeded groan. ....Od.11.101.385.
When the stern eyes of Heroes dropp'd a tear; ....Od.11.644.416.
Check not with fallacies the springing tear; ....Od.14.398.55.
Adown his cheek a tear unbidden stole, ...Od.17.365.149.
A mangled carcase for the hounds to tear. ....Od.17.571.160.
Nourish'd deep anguish, tho' he shed no tear; ....Od.17.583.161.
The tear she wipes, and thus renews her woes. ....Od.18.236.178.
A winy vapour melting in a tear. ....Od.19.143.199.
Firm wisdom interdicts the soft'ning tear. ....Od.19.250.206.
With tear-full eyes o'er all their master gaz'd: ....Od.21.233.271.
Vulturs shall tear thee—Thus incens'd they spoke, ...Od.22.35.288.
Each vents a groan, and drops a tender tear; ....Od.22.483.312.
Fast from her eye descends the rolling tear, ...Od.23.37.321.

TEAR (CONTINUED)
Or savage beasts his mangled reliques tear, ...Od.24.342.365.
Seal'd his cold eyes, or drop'd a tender tear! ....Od.24.347.365.

TEAR-FUL
With Tear-ful Eyes, and with dejected Heart. ....Il.17.788.319.

TEAR-FULL
With tear-full eyes o'er all their master gaz'd: ....Od.21.233.271.

TEARFUL
And dry the tearful sluices of Despair: ....Od.4.306.134.
She veils the torrent of her tearful eyes; ....Od.19.422.214.

TEARING
His radiant Armour tearing from the Dead: ....Il.21.200.429.

TEARLESS
"God cannot love (says Blunt, with tearless eyes) ....3.Ep3.105.99.

TEARS
Swell'd with new Passion, and o'erflows with Tears; ....1.PWi.66.93.
He wipes the Tears for ever from our Eyes. ....1.Mes.45Z2.117.
The Swain with Tears his frustrate Labour yields, ...1.W-F.55.154.
The Swain with Tears to Beasts his Labour yields, ...1.W-F.55A.154.
She said, and melting as in Tears she lay, ...1.W-F.203.168.
And with Celestial Tears augments the Waves. ....1.W-F.210.169.
O early lost! what Tears the River shed ....1.W-F.273.174.
Oh Fact accurst! What Tears has *Albion* shed, ...1.W-F.321.180.
Now *Sighs* steal out, and *Tears begin to flow:* ....1.EOC.379.283.
Let me (if tears and grief permit) relate ....1.TrFD.5.385.
Prostrate, with tears their kindred plant bedew, ...1.TrFD.61.388.
Love taught my Tears in sadder Notes to flow, ...1.TrSP.7.393.
My Parent's Ashes drank my early Tears. ....1.TrSP.74.397.
See, while I write, my Words are lost in Tears; ....1.TrSP.109.398.
Now swell to Rage, now melt in Tears again. ....1.TrSP.132.399.
Insults my Woes, and triumphs in my Tears, ...1.TrSP.136.399.
And all with Tears the with'ring Herbs bedew. ....1.TrSP.172.401.
Here as I lay, and swell'd with Tears the Flood, ...1.TrSP.185.401.
And silent Tears fall trickling from my Eyes. ....1.TrSP.200.402.
Their tortur'd Minds repining Envy tears, ...1.TrSt.176.417.
And, as he spoke, the Tears began to flow. ....1.TrUl.73.468.
And wastes the Days in Grief, the Nights in Tears. ....1.TrUl.219.473.
Full oft in Tears did hapless *May* complain, ...2.ChJM.490.39.
The ready Tears apace began to flow, ...2.ChJM.784.52.
To hide the Flood of Tears I did *not* shed. ....2.ChWB.312.72.
Which not the Tears of brightest Eyes could ease: ....2.RL4.76.190.
Soft Sorrows, melting Griefs, and flowing Tears. ....2.RL4.86.190.
Methinks already I your Tears survey, ...2.RL4.107.192.
Her Eyes half-languishing, half-drown'd in Tears; ....2.RL4.144.196.
She said: the pitying Audience melt in Tears, ...2.RL5.1.199.
Sudden, with starting Tears each Eye o'erflows, ...2.RL5.85.207.
The Smiles of Harlots, and the Tears of Heirs, ...2.RL5.120.209.
Already written—wash it out, my tears! ....2.ElAb.14.320.
Nor tears, for ages, taught to flow in vain. ....2.ElAb.28.321.
Tears still are mine, and those I need not spare, ...2.ElAb.45.322.
Let tears, and burning blushes speak the rest. ....2.ElAb.106.328.
Canst thou forget what tears that moment fell, ...2.ElAb.109.329.
'Tis all blank sadness, or continual tears. ....2.ElAb.148.331.
Tears that delight, and sighs that waft to heav'n. ....2.ElAb.214.337.
Take back that grace, those sorrows, and those tears, ...2.ElAb.285.343.
And drink the falling tears each other sheds, ...2.ElAb.350.348.
There shall the morn her earliest tears bestow, ...2.Elegy.65.367.
As Justice tears his body from the grave, ...3.EOM4.250.151.
Less pleasing far than Virtue's very tears. ....3.EOM4.320.159.
All bath'd in tears—"Oh odious, odious Trees!" ....3.Ep2.40.53.
Of Mirth and Opium, Ratafie and Tears, ...3.Ep2.110.58.
To deluge Sin, and drown a Court in Tears. ....4.JD4.285.49.
And all the Court in Tears, and half the Town, ...4.HAdv.3.75.
All Tears are wip'd for ever from all Eyes; ....4.EpS1.102.305.
Then gush'd the tears, as from the Trojan's eyes ....5.DunA1.211.88.
Tears gush'd again, as from pale Priam's eyes ....5.DunB1.255.289.
Dropping with Infant's blood, and Mother's tears. ....5.DunB4.142.355.
Rather with Samuel I beseech with tears ....6.2.17.6.
So us'd to sighs, so long inur'd to tears, ...6.4i.11.9.
While *Celia's* tears make sorrow bright, ...6.5.1.12.
Thought fit to drown him in her tears: ....6.5.16.12.
And vexing ev'ry Wight, tears Cloaths and all to Tatters. ....6.14ii.36.44.
But in the rock my flowing tears suppress, ...6.20.31.67.
Those tears, which only cou'd have eas'd my breast. ....6.20.32.67.
My tears eternal tribute shou'd be paid: ....6.20.40.67.
My tears the want of off'rings had supply'd; ....6.20.41.67.
Nor is it much to give me back my tears; ....6.20.53.67.
And tears eternal from the marble flow. ....6.20.59.67.
Commanding tears to stream thro' ev'ry age; ....6.32.6.96.
Here tears shall flow from a more gen'rous cause, ...6.32.13.96.
Such tears, as Patriots shed for dying Laws: ....6.32.14.96.
The triumph ceas'd—Tears gush'd from ev'ry eye; ....6.32.33.97.
But while her Pride forbids her Tears to flow, ...6.33.3.99.
Although her Pride forbade her Tears to flow, ...6.33.3B.99.
No guard but virtue, no redress but tears. ....6.38.18.108.
And civil madness tears them from the land. ....6.51i.24.152.
Hence false tears, deceits, disguises, ...6.51ii.38.154.
False oaths, false tears, deceits, disguises, ...6.51ii.38A.154.
Those tears eternal, that embalm the dead: ....6.52.48.157.
Her Locks dishevell'd, and her Flood of Tears ....6.96ii.12.270.
O squander not thy Grief, those Tears command ....6.96ii.75.273.
And the first tears for her were taught to flow. ....6.107.6.310.
Yet take these tears, Mortality's relief, ...6.109.17.314.
Bath'd in unmeaning unrepentant tears ....6.130.24.358.
With tears inscribes this monumental Stone, ...6.152.13.400.
And Pray'rs, and Tears, and Bribes shall plead in vain; ....Il.1.40.87.
There, bath'd in Tears of Anger and Disdain, ...Il.1.458.109.
While Tears Celestial trickle from her Eyes) ....Il.1.541.114.
While Tears Celestial trickled from her Eyes) ....Il.1.541A.114.
The Tears spring starting from his haggard Eyes: ....Il.2.329.143.

TEARS (CONTINUED)
From his vile Visage wip'd the scalding Tears. ....Il.2.331.143.
Then well may this long Stay provoke their Tears, ...Il.2.360.144.
The Fair one's Grief, and sees her falling Tears. ....Il.2.714.160.
And leaves the Father unavailing Tears: ....Il.5.201.276.
Bends their strong Necks, and tears them to the Ground. ....Il.5.209.276.
O'erwhelm'd with Anguish and dissolv'd in Tears; ....Il.5.462.290.
Some haughty *Greek* who lives thy Tears to see, ...Il.6.586.355.
There, while her Tears deplor'd the Godlike Man, ...Il.6.644.358.
What Tears shall down thy silver Beard be roll'd, ...Il.7.149.372.
The Wounds they wash'd, their pious Tears they shed, ...Il.7.506.389.
He begg'd, with Tears he begg'd, in deep Dismay; ....Il.8.443.418.
With piercing Cries, and supplicating Tears: ....Il.9.702.469.
Is it for him these Tears are taught to flow, ...Il.9.723.470.
To claim the Tears of *Trojans* yet unborn. ....Il.10.334.18.
And with unmanly Tears his Life demands. ....Il.10.448.23.
And the big Tears roll trickling from her Eyes. ....Il.11.160.42.
These Words, attended with a Flood of Tears, ...Il.11.177.43.
Tears, at the Sight, came starting from his Eye, ...Il.11.322.49.
While Tears of Rage stand burning in their Eye. ....Il.13.122.110.
The Victor from his Breast the Weapon tears; ....Il.13.646.136.
And unavailing Tears profusely shed, ...Il.13.825.145.
The streaming Tears fall copious from his Eyes; ....Il.16.4.234.
That flows so fast in these unmanly Tears? ....Il.16.10.235.
With joyful Tears to welcome *Hector* home; ....Il.17.242.297.
With Tears the Hero spoke, and at his Pray'r ....Il.17.733.317.
From his fair Eyes the Tears began to flow; ....Il.17.782.319.
And tells the melancholy Tale with Tears. ....Il.18.20.324.
Those he deforms with Dust, and these he tears: ....Il.18.30.325.
All bath'd in Tears, the melancholy Train ....Il.18.86.327.
A Flood of Tears, at this, the Goddess shed; ....Il.18.123.328.
And the soft Tears to trickle from her Eyes? ....Il.18.158.330.
Around, his sad Companions melt in Tears: ....Il.18.276.335.
The Tears, and Sighs burst from his swelling Heart. ....Il.18.370.339.
Swift to her Son: Her Son she finds in Tears, ...Il.19.6.371.
Shining with Tears, she lifts, and thus she cries. ....Il.19.302.384.
Accept these grateful Tears! For thee they flow, ...Il.19.319.385.
And Tears shall trickle from cœlestial Eyes: ....Il.20.249.404.
Approach'd, and sought his Knees with suppliant Tears; ....Il.21.75.424.
These Words, attended with a Show'r of Tears, ...Il.21.109.426.
And tears his Hunter,or beneath him dies. ....Il.21.684.450.
And thus, fast-falling the salt Tears, she said. ....Il.22.113.457.
Tears after Tears his mournful Cheeks o'erflow, ...Il.22.516.478.
Tears after Tears his mournful Cheeks o'erflow, ...Il.22.516.478.
Grief tears his Heart, and drives him to and fro, ...Il.22.526.478.
(A mourning Princess, and a Train in Tears) ....Il.22.553.479.
For ever sad, for ever bath'd in Tears; ....Il.22.631.482.
Thus wretched, thus retiring all in Tears, ...Il.22.642.483.
Tears drop the Sands, and Tears their Arms bedew. ....Il.23.18A.487.
Tears drop the Sands, and Tears their Arms bedew. ....Il.23.18A.487.
Tears bathe their Arms, and Tears the Sands bedew. ....Il.23.18.487.
Tears bathe their Arms, and Tears the Sands bedew. ....Il.23.18.487.
Thus while he spoke, each Eye grew big with Tears: ....Il.23.130.493.
Shews every mournful Face with Tears o'erspread, ...Il.23.132.493.
And pour in Tears, e'er yet they close the Urn. ....Il.23.277.501.
With Tears collected, in the golden Vase. ....Il.23.314.502.
Tears up the Shore, and thunders tow'rd the Main. ....Il.23.454.508.
Sate bath'd in Tears, and answer'd Groan with Groan. ....Il.24.198.545.
And my last Tears flow mingled with his Blood! ....Il.24.280.548.
The mourning Matron dries her tim'rous Tears. ....Il.24.396.552.
Embrac'd his Knees, and bath'd his Hands in Tears; ....Il.24.587.561.
Nor seek by Tears my steady Soul to bend; ....Il.24.707.567.
The Rock for ever lasts, the Tears for ever flow! ....Il.24.779.569.
Soon may the aged Cheeks in Tears be drown'd, ...Il.24.784.569.
A Show'r of Tears o'erflows her beauteous Eyes, ...Il.24.874.573.
Th' obedient Tears, melodious in their Woe. ....Il.24.903.574.
Thence all these Tears, and all this Scene of Woe! ....Il.24.931.575.
Thus spoke the Dame, and melted into Tears. ....Il.24.958.576.
(With Tears collected) in a golden Vase; ....Il.24.1004.577.
The filial tears, but woe succeeds to woe: ....Od.1.314.47.
Familiar now with grief, your tears refrain, ...Od.1.450.54.
Rise in my aid! suffice the tears that flow ....Od.2.77.64.
And tears ran trickling from her aged eyes. ....Od.2.407.80.
Thy cheeks, *Pisistratus,* the tears bedew, ...Od.4.253.131.
Thy breast will heave, and tears eternal flow. ....Od.4.664.150.
And the dear turf with tears of joy bedews. ....Od.4.698.152.
I stood restor'd, and tears had ceas'd to flow; ....Od.4.730.153.
Her eyes restrain the silver-streaming tears: ....Od.4.1000.164.
The Nymph just show'd him, and with tears withdrew. ....Od.5.310.186.
And water her ambrosial couch with tears. ....Od.7.347.253.
Tears bathe his cheeks, and tears the ground bedew: ....Od.8.570.293.
Tears bathe his cheeks, and tears the ground bedew: ....Od.8.570.293.
And bathes with floods of tears the gaping wound; ....Od.8.576.293.
Fast fell the tears, and sighs succeeded sighs: ....Od.8.582.294.
To ev'ry note his tears responsive flow, ...Od.8.587.294.
Why heav'd thy bosom, and why flow'd thy tears? ....Od.8.630.297.
Big tears of transport stand in ev'ry eye: ....Od.9.551.328.
Glad for the living, for the dead in tears. ....Od.9.659.333.
Presaging tears apace began to rain; ....Od.10.230.351.
But tears in mortal miseries are vain. ....Od.10.231.351.
But speaking tears the want of words supply, ...Od.10.291.357.
Sad, pleasing sight! with tears each eye ran o'er, ...Od.10.471.366.
Then gushing tears the narrative confound, ...Od.10.537.369.
Their tears flow round me, and my heart complies. ....Od.10.575.370.
Pensive I sate; my tears bedew'd the bed; ....Od.10.589.372.
Compos'd at length, the gushing tears suppress, ...Od.10.592.372.
To earth they fell; the tears began to rain; ....Od.10.681.376.
But tears in mortal miseries are vain. ....Od.10.682.376.
And ere I spoke the tears began to flow. ....Od.11.70.383.
To whom with tears: These rites, oh mournful shade, ...Od.11.98.385.
Of flowing tears, and thus with sighs reply'd. ....Od.11.252.394.
At last with tears—O what relentless doom ....Od.11.493.408.
Thus in a tyde of tears our sorrows flow, ...Od.11.573.411.
And as he speaks the tears descend in dew. ....Od.11.582.412.
Touch'd at the sight from tears I scarce refrain, ...Od.11.675.417.
Nor cease the tears, 'till each in slumber shares ....Od.12.365.449.

TEARS (CONTINUED)

Tears up the deck; then all at once descends: Od.12.482.455.
And as he spoke, the tears began to flow. Od.13.240.17.
And wastes the days in grief, the nights in tears. Od.13.386.25.
My state he pity'd, and my tears he dry'd, Od.14.310.50.
And here the tears, and there the goblets flow. Od.14.416.56.
The tears rain'd copious in a show'r of joy. Od.16.16.102.
Wretched old man! (with tears the Prince returns) Od.16.158.110.
Tears bathe his cheek, and tears the ground bedew: Od.16.212.114.
Tears bathe his cheek, and tears the ground bedew: Od.16.212.114.
Hung round his neck, while tears his cheek bedew; Od.16.235.114.
So they aloud: and tears in tides had run, Od.16.242.116.
And end her tears, her sorrows, and her sighs. Od.17.9.132.
To wipe the tears from all afflicted eyes, Od.17.14.133.
With wild entrancement, and ecstatic tears. Od.17.44.134.
And scarce those few, for tears, could force their way. Od.17.51.135.
Cease with those tears to melt a manly mind, Od.17.57.135.
The couch, for ever water'd with my tears) Od.17.119.137.
The tyde of flowing tears a-while suppress; Od.18.205.177.
Tears but indulge the sorrow, not redress. Od.18.206.177.
Why must I waste a tedious life in tears, Od.18.241.178.
And tears repeat their long-forgotten course! Od.19.191.201.
From her bright eyes the tears unbounded flow. Od.19.237.205.
Smiles dew'd with tears the pleasing strife exprest Od.19.550.223.
Fresh flow my tears, and shall for ever flow! Od.20.260.246.
Then down each cheek the tears spontaneous flow, Od.20.419.253.
With tears your wan distorted cheeks are drown'd; Od.20.425.253.
And pensive sate, and tears began to flow. Od.21.58.262.
And with her veil conceals the coming tears: Od.21.66.262.
From his full eyes the tears unbidden spring, Od.21.83.263.
Enough her precious tears already flow— Od.21.91.263.
Tears follow'd tears; no word was in their pow'r, Od.21.236.271.
Tears follow'd tears; no word was in their pow'r, Od.21.236.271.
Down her fair cheek the tears abundant roll, Od.21.386.279.
Sprung to the Prince, embrac'd his knee with tears, Od.22.405.307.
Ev'n He indulges the sweet joy of tears. Od.22.538.315.
The tears pour'd down amain: And oh, she cries, Od.23.215.333.
Hangs round her neck and speaks his joy in tears. Od.23.248.335.
When thou must learn what I must speak with tears? Od.23.282.337.
We drank the cup of sorrow mix'd with tears, Od.23.378.343.
Tears flow'd from ev'ry eye, and o'er the dead Od.24.63.350.
And iron-hearted Heroes melt in tears. Od.24.80.352.
No friend to bathe our wounds! or tears to shed Od.24.216.358.
(His venerable eyes bedimm'd with tears) Od.24.325.365.
Big was his eye with tears, his heart with woes: Od.24.484.371.
Here ceas'd he, but indignant tears let fall Od.24.502.372.

TEAT

And to the mother's teat submits the lambs. Od.9.367.321.

TEATS

Then to the mother's teats submits the lambs. Od.9.291.318.

TEAZE

To a good honest Junta that never will teaze you. 6.42iii.6.117.
Has but one way to teaze—by *Law.* 6.116ii.5.326.

TEDIOUS

Fain wou'd he cast a tedious Age away, 1.TrSt.451.429.
Yet had his Mind, thro' tedious Absence, lost 1.TrUl.56.467.
My tedious Sermon here is at an End. 2.ChJM.215.25.
Why, if the Nights seem tedious—take a Wife; 4.HS1.16.5.
Tir'd with a tedious March, one luckless night, 4.2HE2.35.167.
Sooths the sad series of her tedious tale. 5.DunA3.191z6.172.
Have I for this thy tedious Absence born, 6.96iv.3.276.
The tedious Length of nine revolving Years. Il.2.361.144.
His tedious Toils, and hoary Hairs demand Il.9.552.460.
How trace the tedious series of our fate? Od.3.140.92.
On rocks and shores consum'd the tedious day; Od.5.200.181.
Two tedious days and two long nights we lay, Od.9.83.306.
So shall thy tedious toils a respite find, Od.10.355.361.
Thro' tedious toils to view thy native coast. Od.12.177.440.
And what so tedious as a twice-told tale? Od.12.538.459.
Yet had his mind thro' tedious absence lost Od.13.223.16.
Eludes the labours of the tedious way. Od.15.90.73.
In tedious cares, and weeps the night away. Od.16.38.104.
His Lord, when twenty tedious years had roll'd, Od.17.397.151.
Why must I waste a tedious life in tears, Od.18.241.178.

TEEM'D

Of vice, who teem'd with many a dead-born jest; Od.20.354.249.

TEEMING

Now bright *Arcturus* glads the teeming Grain, 1.PAu.72.85.
If teeming Ewes encrease my fleecy Breed. 1.PWi.82.94.
In vain kind Seasons swell'd the teeming Grain, 1.W-F.53.154.
A teeming Mistress, but a barren Bride. 3.Ep2.72.56.
But from the teeming Furrow took his Birth, Il.2.659.158.
(The Pow'rs that cause the teeming Matron's Throes, Il.11.349.50.
All teeming Females, and of gen'rous Breeds. Il.11.825.73.
The teeming Ewes a triple offspring bear; Od.4.106.125.
With teeming plenty to reward their toil. Od.4.240.130.

TEEMS

And each *exalted* Stanza *teems* with *Thought!* 1.EOC.423.288.

TEETH

How with the Serpent's Teeth he sow'd the Soil, 1.TrSt.9.409.
Nor strive with all the Tempest in my teeth. 4.2HE2.301.187.
And the cold Tongue and grinning Teeth divides. Il.5.98.271.
A Boar's white Teeth grinn'd horrid o'er his Head. Il.10.312.16.
His loose Teeth chatter'd, and his Colour fled: Il.10.446.23.
With chatt'ring Teeth he stands, and stiff'ning Hair, Il.13.364.123.
Crash'd the thin Bones, and drown'd the Teeth in Gore: Il.16.417.259.
The Teeth it shatter'd, and the Tongue it rent. Il.17.698.314.
He grinds his Teeth, and furious with Delay Il.19.396.388.

TEETH (CONTINUED)

He calls up all his Rage; he grinds his Teeth, Il.20.208.402.
Her jaws grin dreadful with three rows of teeth; Od.12.113.437.
Why cease I, Gods! to dash those teeth away, Od.18.34.168.
His teeth all shatter'd rush immix'd with blood. Od.18.117.172.

TEGEA'S

From *Ripè, Stratie, Tegea's* bord'ring Towns, Il.2.733.161.

TEIZE

Then presently he falls to teize, 4.HS6.79.255.
Thy Fools no more I'll teize: 6.47.2.128.

TELAMON

Let *Telamon* at least our Tow'rs defend, 1.TrES.74.452.
At least, let *Telamon* those Tow'rs defend, 1.TrES.80Z8.452.
Ajax the less, and *Ajax Telamon;* Il.2.483.150.
Whom the Gigantic *Telamon* commands; Il.2.672.158.
Grant thou, that *Telamon* may bear away Il.7.245.376.
Stern *Telamon* behind his ample Shield Il.7.265.377.
O Son of *Telamon,* thy Country's Pride! Il.7.283.378.
Alarm'd, to *Ajax Telamon* he cry'd, Il.11.582.60.
Let *Telamon,* at least, our Tow'rs defend, Il.12.418.96.
At least, let *Telamon* those Tow'rs defend, Il.12.432.97.
Perceiv'd the first, and thus to *Telamon.* Il.13.98.109.
With equal Ardour (*Telamon* returns) Il.13.107.109.
By the swift Rage of *Ajax Telamon.* Il.17.327.300.
To *Atreus'* Seed, the god-like *Telamon.* Il.17.708.315.
Thus to *Ulysses* spoke great *Telamon.* Il.23.839.523.
And the huge Bulk of *Ajax Telamon.* Il.23.958.527.

TELAMON'S

But pierc'd by *Telamon's* huge Lance expires; Il.15.490.216.

TELAMONIAN

Secure behind the *Telamonian* Shield Il.8.321.412.
He groans beneath the *Telamonian* Spear. Il.13.240.116.
Thus in the Van, the *Telamonian* Train Il.13.897.148.
The *Telamonian* Lance his Belly rends; Il.17.363.301.
Except the mighty *Telamonian* Shield? Il.18.230.332.

TELEMACHUS

Mean time *Telemachus,* the blooming heir Od.1.110.36.
There young *Telemachus,* his bloomy face Od.1.148.40.
But bold *Telemachus* assum'd the man. Od.1.468.55.
Those toils (*Telemachus* serene replies) Od.1.495.56.
Sole with *Telemachus* her service ends, Od.1.547.58.
He spoke. *Telemachus* with transport glows, Od.2.43.62.
The dowry; Is *Telemachus* her Sire? Od.2.60.63.
While yet he speaks, *Telemachus* replies. Od.2.147.68.
Nor fire to rage *Telemachus* his breast. Od.2.216.72.
Telemachus may bid the Queen repair Od.2.223.72.
Doom'd by the stern *Telemachus* to dye? Od.2.367.78.
Like the *Telemachus,* in voice and size, Od.2.430.81.
Spoke to *Telemachus* the martial Maid. Od.2.449.83.
Telemachus already prest the shore; Od.3.15.87.
Last deign *Telemachus* and me to bless, Od.3.74.89.
And let thy words *Telemachus* persuade: Od.3.458.109.
The hand of young *Telemachus,* and spoke. Od.3.479.110.
And bring thy friends, *Telemachus!* a-shore, Od.3.537.113.
The glitt'ring seat *Telemachus* ascends; Od.3.610.117.
Of young *Telemachus!* the lovely boy, Od.4.193.129.
Still must the wrong'd *Telemachus* sustain, Od.4.221.130.
To move thy suit, *Telemachus,* delay, Od.4.295.133.
Inclement fate! *Telemachus* replies, Od.4.395.139.
Instant to young *Telemachus* he press'd, Od.4.419.140.
Telemachus in thought already slain! Od.4.1100.169.
By lov'd *Telemachus* his blooming years! Od.11.84.385.
If yet *Telemachus,* my son, survives? Od.11.211.392.
Thee in *Telemachus* thy realm obeys; Od.11.222.392.
To *Sparta* flies, *Telemachus* her care. Od.13.511.30.
Not young *Telemachus,* his blooming heir. Od.14.199.45.
Alas, *Telemachus!* my sorrows flow Od.14.200.45.
With *Nestor's* Son, *Telemachus* was lay'd; Od.15.6.70.
When, Oh *Telemachus!* (the Goddess said) Od.15.11.70.
Now (cry'd *Telemachus)* with speedy care Od.15.244.80.
Telemachus: whom as to heav'n he prest Od.15.280.82.
Prepare then, said *Telemachus,* to know Od.15.288.83.
'Till good *Telemachus* accepts his guest Od.15.357.86.
Of young *Telemachus* approach'd the land; Od.15.536.96.
The man, who calls *Telemachus* his friend. Od.15.580.98.
Escap'd *Telemachus:* (the pow'rs above Od.16.174.111.
Sufficient they (*Telemachus* rejoin'd) Od.16.284.118.
Telemachus in triumph sails the main. Od.16.363.124.
Thus he: nor ought *Telemachus* reply'd, Od.17.31.134.
Whom when *Telemachus* beheld, he join'd. Od.17.85.136.
And now *Telemachus,* the first of all Od.17.400.152.
Blest be *Telemachus!* in ev'ry deed! Od.17.426.153.
To him *Telemachus.* No more incense Od.17.476.156.
Whence, great *Telemachus!* this lofty strain? Od.17.488.156.
Telemachus absorpt in thought severe, Od.17.582.160.
She spoke, *Telemachus* then sneez'd aloud; Od.17.624.162.
There seeks *Telemachus,* and thus apart Od.17.670.164.
Telemachus uprais'd, and sternly said. Od.18.67.170.
That instant makes *Telemachus* his foe; Od.18.71.170.
In vain! by great *Telemachus* he falls, Od.18.184.175.
Know, to *Telemachus* I tell th' offence: Od.18.387.186.
To whom the stern *Telemachus* uprose: Od.18.452.190.
Not with *Telemachus,* but truth contends; Od.18.461.190.
For Rule mature, *Telemachus* deplores Od.19.182.200.
Then with *Telemachus* the social feast Od.19.368.212.
Sage and serene *Telemachus* replies; Od.20.403.251.
Then thus *Telemachus.* Some God I find Od.21.105.263.
And each on young *Telemachus* attend, Od.21.224.270.
And some respect *Telemachus* may claim. Od.21.336.276.
Permit me (cries *Telemachus)* to claim Od.21.370.277.

TELEMACHUS (CONTINUED)

But bold *Telemachus* thus urg'd him on. .... Od.21.398.279.
Hear what *Telemachus* enjoyns (he cry'd) .... Od.21.412.280.
Telemachus girds on his shining sword. .... Od.21.476.283.
Thy spear, *Telemachus!* prevents th' attack, ... Od.22.107.291.
With speed *Telemachus* obeys, and flies .... Od.22.126.292.
Thy hand, *Telemachus,* it lightly raz'd; .... Od.22.307.301.
The moving words *Telemachus* attends, ... Od.22.393.307.
Nor fits it that *Telemachus* command .... Od.22.464.311.
He lives to thy *Telemachus* and thee! .... Od.23.58.321.
At length *Telemachus—Oh* who can find .... Od.23.99.324.
O my *Telemachus!* the Queen rejoin'd, ... Od.23.107.325.
Be that thy care, *Telemachus* replies, ... Od.23.123.326.
In vain we threat; *Telemachus* commands: .... Od.24.200.358.
And there the young *Telemachus* attends. .... Od.24.420.369.
The swains and young *Telemachus* they found, ... Od.24.423.369.
Behold, *Telemachus!* (nor fear the sight) .... Od.24.584.376.
So spoke *Telemachus:* the gallant boy .... Od.24.592.376.

TELEMUS

It chanc'd prophetick Telemus, who knew .... 1.TrPA.29.366.
This, *Telemus Eurymedes* foretold, ... Od.9.595.330.

TELESCOPE

By Help of Telescope. .... 6.94.52.260.

TELL

Tell me but this, and I'll disclaim the Prize, ... 1.PSp.87.69.
Nay tell me first, in what more happy Fields .... 1.PSp.89.69.
But tell the Reeds, and tell the vocal Shore, ... 1.PWi.59.93.
But tell the Reeds, and tell the vocal Shore, ... 1.PWi.59.93.
And Peace and Plenty tell, a STUART reigns. .... 1.W-F.42.152.
To tell 'em, wou'd a *hundred Tongues* require, ... 1.EOC.44.244.
Such was the Muse, whose Rules and Practice tell, ... 1.EOC.723.323.
The poorest shepherd best may tell his store. .... 1.TrPA.81.368.
Tell 'em, I charg'd them with my latest Breath, ... 1.TrES.306.461.
O tell a Wretch, in Exile doom'd to stray, ... 1.TrUl.112.469.
And tell what more thou must from Fate expect; .... 1.TrUl.181.471.
Tell me, oh tell, is this my Native Place? .... 1.TrUl.202.472.
Tell me, oh tell, is this my Native Place? .... 1.TrUl.202.472.
In worldly Follies, which I blush to tell; .... 2.ChJM.90.19.
He wanted Art to hide, and Means to tell. .... 2.ChJM.395.34.
What then he did, I'll not presume to tell, ... 2.ChJM.422.35.
What then he did, I not presume to tell, ... 2.ChJM.422A.35.
And in soft Murmurs tell the Trees their Pain; .... 2.ChJM.528.41.
And witness next what *Roman* Authors tell, ... 2.ChJM.675.47.
'Tis Truth I tell, tho' not in Phrase refin'd; .... 2.ChJM.742.51.
You tell me, to preserve your Wife's good Grace, ... 2.ChWB.106.61.
"Dear Spouse, I credit not the Tales they tell. .... 2.ChWB.131.62.
To see, be seen, to tell, and gather Tales; .... 2.ChWB.282.70.
We grew so intimate, I can't tell how, ... 2.ChWB.292.71.
Who bid me tell this Lye—and twenty more. .... 2.ChWB.306.71.
Tell how the *Roman* Matrons led their Life, ... 2.ChWB.343.73.
'Twas this, the Morning *Omens* seem'd to tell; .... 2.RL4.161.197.
Of unknown Dutchesses leud Tales we tell, ... 2.TemF.388.282.
Let him our sad, our tender story tell; .... 2.ElAb.364.348.
Oh ever beauteous, ever friendly! tell, ... 2.Elegy.5.362.
May tell why Heav'n has made us as we are. .... 3.EOM1.28.16.
May tell why Heav'n made all things as they are. .... 3.EOM1.28A.16.
What can she more than tell us we are fools? .... 3.EOM2.152.73.
Tell me, if Virtue made the Son expire, ... 3.EOM4.105.138.
But who, but God, can tell us who they are? .... 3.EOM4.136.140.
I'll tell you, friend! a Wise man and a Fool. .... 3.EOM4.200.145.
Tell (for You can) what is it to be wise? .... 3.EOM4.260.152.
Ask men's Opinions: J[ohnsto]n now shall tell .... 3.Ep1.158A.28.
Ask men's Opinions: Jaunssen now shall tell .... 3.Ep1.158B.28.
Ask men's Opinions: Scoto now shall tell .... 3.Ep1.158.28.
Or tell a Tale?—A Tale—it follows thus. .... 3.Ep3.338A.120.
But you are tir'd—I'll tell a tale.—B. A greed. .... 3.Ep3.338B.120.
Arise, and tell me, was thy death more bless'd? .... 3.Ep3.322.120.
But you are tir'd—I'll tell a tale. Agreed. .... 3.Ep3.338.120.
This, all who know me, know; who love me, tell; .... 4.HS1.138.19.
Cry, by your Priesthood tell me what you are? .... 4.JD4.37.29.
He asks, "What *News?"* I tell him of new Plays, ... 4.JD4.124.35.
And buy a Rope, that future times may tell .... 4.HS2.109.63.
And who stands safest, tell me? is it he .... 4.HS2.125.65.
But why all this? I'll tell ye, 'tis my Theme: .... 4.HAdv.27.77.
This Truth, let *L[iddel], J[effer]ys, O[nslo]w* tell. .... 4.HAdv.178.89.
Dear Doctor! tell me, is not this a curse? .... 4.Arbu.29A.98.
And knowing *Walsh,* would tell me I could write; .... 4.Arbu.136.105.
Neglected die! and tell it on his Tomb; .... 4.Arbu.258.114.
Sapho can tell you how this Man was bit: .... 4.Arbu.369.123.
Of whose strange crimes no Canonist can tell .... 4.JD2.43.135.
And whose strange Sins no Canonist can tell, ... 4.JD2A.47.136.
—But why? ah tell me, ah too dear! .... 4.HOde1.37.153.
—But why? ah tell me, still too dear! .... 4.HOde1.37A.153.
You tell the Doctor; when the more you have, ... 4.2HE2.213.179.
Let Ireland tell, how Wit upheld her cause, ... 4.2HE1.221.213.
Tell me if Congreve's Fools are Fools indeed? .... 4.2HE1.287.219.
I guess; and, with their leave, will tell the fault: .... 4.2HE1.357.225.
Tell at your Levee, as the Crouds approach, ... 4.1HE6.161.243.
'Tis one to me—"Then tell us, pray, ... 4.HS6.119.257.
Tell how the Moon-beam trembling falls .... 4.HS6.191.261.
And 'tis but just, I'll tell you wherefore, ... 4.1HE7.33.271.
And 'tis but just, I'll tell ye wherefore, ... 4.1HE7.33A.271.
Our old Friend Swift will tell his Story. .... 4.1HE7.82.273.
Tell me, which Knave is lawful Game, which not? .... 4.EpS2.27.314.
For works like these let deathless Journals tell, ... 5.DunA3.271.180.
I tell the naked fact without disguise, ... 5.DunB4.433.383.
And breaks our rest, to tell us what's a clock. .... 5.DunB4.444.384.
O Muse! relate (for you can tell alone, ... 5.DunB4.619.405.
Tell where I lye. .... 6.1.20.4.
And by this sickness chuse to tell .... 6.4iii.13.10.
And drooping lillies seem to tell .... 6.4iv.8.10.
But which, I cannot tell you truly. .... 6.10.118.28.
Of *Orpheus* now no more let Poets tell, ... 6.11.131.34.

TELL (CONTINUED)

Let future times of *Cleopatra* tell, ... 6.20.15.66.
—Now, dreadful Critic! tell me pray, ... 6.24iii(a).4.75.
Tell me, my Soul, can this be Death? .... 6.31ii.12.94.
This Lock, of which late ages now shall tell, ... 6.38.13.107.
There are, 'tis true, who tell another tale, ... 6.41.15.113.
Who tell us these troublesome stories, ... 6.42iv.3.118.
Hum half a tune, tell stories to the squire; .... 6.45.20.125.
To tell Men things they never *knew at all.* .... 6.48iii.4.134.
Ye all can tell a Fable. .... 6.58.68Z4.173.
Review them, and tell Noses; .... 6.58.70.174.
Tell P[ickenbur]g how slim she's grown .... 6.61.24.181.
Tell P[ickenbur]g how thin she's grown .... 6.61.24A.181.
Tell Buckenburg how thin she's grown .... 6.61.24B.181.
They may tell of three Goddesses in *Ida* Vales, ... 6.62ii.1A.185.
Tell me, by all the melting joys of Love, ... 6.82ii.1.230.
By all these tender Adjurations tell me, ... 6.82ii.5.230.
Nor fears to tell, that MORTIMER is He. .... 6.84.40.240.
And dares to tell, that Mortimer is He. .... 6.84.31Z12.240.
If *Pope* must tell what *HARCOURT* cannot speak? .... 6.85.6.242.
When *Pope* must tell what *HARCOURT* cannot speak? .... 6.85.6A.242.
Where sleeps my Gulliver? *O tell me where?* .... 6.96iv.47.277.
And let me tell you, have a Nose .... 6.135.29.367.
Pray tell me Sir, whose Dog are you? .... 6.136.2.372.
"I tell ye, fool, there's nothing in't: .... 6.140.26.379.
"That dares tell neither Truth nor Lies, ... 6.140.30.379.
He deeply sighing said: To tell my Woe, ... Il.1.476.110.
Permit thy Daughter, gracious *Jove!* to tell .... Il.5.509.292.
When Fame shall tell, that not in Battel slain .... Il.6.59.326.
The Stone shall tell your vanquish'd Hero's Name, ... Il.7.103.368.
Oh would to tell th' immortal Pow'rs above, ... Il.7.159.372.
Who dares think one thing, and another tell, ... Il.9.412.452.
Then tell him; loud, that all the *Greeks* may hear, ... Il.9.483.456.
Tell him, all Terms, all Commerce I decline, ... Il.9.489.456.
Yet such his Acts, as *Greeks* unborn shall tell, ... Il.10.61.5.
Stand off, approach not, but thy Purpose tell. .... Il.10.93.6.
Their other Princes? tell what Watch they keep? .... Il.10.480.25.
The Truth or Falshood of the News I tell. .... Il.10.515.26.
Ye sacred Nine, Celestial Muses! tell, ... Il.11.281.47.
Tell him, not great *Machaon* bleeds alone, ... Il.11.804.72.
Nor shall a *Trojan* live to tell the Tale. .... Il.12.86.84.
I tell the faithful Dictates of my Breast. .... Il.12.248.90.
Than thou hast mine! Oh tell me, to what end .... Il.16.15.235.
Tell 'em, I charg'd them with my latest Breath .... Il.16.611.268.
What Shame to *Greece* for future times to tell, ... Il.17.628.312.
Fly to the Fleet, this Instant fly, and tell .... Il.17.777.318.
So tell our hoary Sire—This Charge she gave: .... Il.18.181.331.
(Wond'rous to tell) instinct with Spirit roll'd .... Il.18.442.342.
When strange to tell! (So *Juno* will'd) he broke .... Il.19.450.390.
No stop, no stay; no thought to ask, or tell, ... Il.21.719.451.
Then last of all, and horrible to tell, ... Il.23.214.498.
Tell him he tempts the Wrath of Heav'n too far: .... Il.24.148.541.
Tell me thy Thought: My Heart impells to go .... Il.24.239.546.
Ah tell me truly, where, oh where are laid .... Il.24.497.557.
To whom the Youth. Since then in vain I tell .... Od.2.237.73.
An honest business never blush to tell. .... Od.3.20.87.
Oh tell me *Mentor!* tell me faithful guide, ... Od.3.27.87.
Oh tell me *Mentor!* tell me faithful guide, ... Od.3.27.87.
O son of *Neleus!* awful *Nestor,* tell .... Od.3.308.101.
Will tell *Ulysses'* bold exploit in *Troy:* .... Od.4.332.135.
To good *Laertes* tell. Experienc'd age .... Od.4.976.163.
Tell then whence art thou? whence that Princely air? .... Od.7.320.251.
Soon might'st thou tell me, where in secret here .... Od.9.537.328.
And not a man appears to tell their fate. .... Od.10.308.359.
O more than human! tell thy race, thy name. .... Od.10.388.363.
To thy chaste bride the wond'rous story tell, ... Od.11.271.395.
Thy tale with raptures I could hear thee tell, ... Od.11.466.407.
The time would fail should I in order tell .... Od.11.633.415.
She sate in silence while the tale I tell, ... Od.12.45.431.
O tell a wretch in exile doom'd to stray, ... Od.13.279.19.
And tell what more thou must from fate expect. .... Od.13.348.24.
Tell me, oh tell, is this my native place? .... Od.13.369.25.
Tell me, oh tell, is this my native place? .... Od.13.369.25.
And all you ask his faithful tongue shall tell. .... Od.13.474.29.
Then tell me whence thou art? and what the share .... Od.14.55.38.
Whom Want itself can force untruths to tell, ... Od.14.180.44.
But tell me, dost thou Prince, dost thou behold .... Od.16.97.107.
I tell thee all, my child, my only joy! .... Od.16.249.117.
So snatch'd from all our cares!—Tell, hast thou known .... Od.17.54.135.
Thy father's fate, and tell me all thy own. .... Od.17.55.135.
What human knowledge could, those Kings might tell; .... Od.17.174.140.
Know, to *Telemachus* I tell th' offence: .... Od.18.387.186.
Or (as my soul now dictates) shall I tell? .... Od.21.200.269.
But chief oh tell me (what I question most) .... Od.24.304.364.
But tell me, stranger, be the truth confest, ... Od.24.334.365.
But tell me, who thou art? and what thy race? .... Od.24.348.365.

TELLS

And think, for once, a Woman tells you true. .... 2.ChWB.4.57.
That tells my Faults, I hate him mortally: .... 2.ChWB.352.74.
That tells the Waters or to rise, or fall, ... 3.Ep4.58.142.
He tells what Strumpet Places sells for Life, ... 4.JD4.148.37.
Who tells whate'er you think, whate'er you say, ... 4.Arbu.297.117.
Not—'s self e'er tells more *Fibs* than I; .... 4.2HE1.176.209.
Tells me I have more Zeal than Wit, ... 4.HS6.56.253.
Tells all their names, lays down the law, ... 4.HS6.202.263.
Tells us, that *Cato* dearly lov'd his wife: .... 6.41.32.114.
Of hireling Lawyers tells the just Decrees, ... 6.96v.17.280.
5. Who tells you all I *mean,* and all I *say;* .... 6.120.9.339.
So *Pallas* tells me, and forbids to fly. .... Il.5.321.282.
No Fragment tells where once the Wonder stood; .... Il.12.34.83.
And tells me, *Jove* asserts the *Trojan* Arms. .... Il.17.393.302.
And tells the melancholy Tale with Tears. .... Il.18.20.324.
That tells, the great *Ulysses* is no more. .... Od.14.112.41.
And tells the news. They arm with all their pow'r. .... Od.24.571.375.

TEMESÉ
From *Temesé* return'd, your royal court ... Od.1.410.52.

TEMPÈ
Or where thro' flow'ry *Tempè Peneus* stray'd, ... Il.2.920.167.

TEMP'RANCE
Healthy by Temp'rance and by Exercise: ... 4.Arbu.401.126.

TEMP'RATE
As Men for ever temp'rate, calm, and wise. ... 3.EOM1.154.34.
The temp'rate sleeps, and spirits light as air! ... 4.HS2.74.59.
From Nature's temp'rate feast rose satisfy'd, ... 6.112.9.318.

TEMP'RING
With native Humour temp'ring virtuous Rage, ... 6.125.3.350.

TEMPER
These 'tis enough to temper and employ; ... 3.EOM2.113.69.
To fall with dignity, with temper rise; ... 3.EOM4.378.165.
Oh! blest with Temper, whose unclouded ray ... 3.Ep2.257.71.
Various of Temper, as of Face or Frame, ... 4.2HE2.282.185.
By Musick, Minds an equal Temper know, ... 6.11.22.30.
The morals blameless, and the temper free, ... 6.125.1Z2.349.
No Bound, no Law thy fiery Temper quells, ... Il.5.1100.319.
Thou know'st the fiery Temper of my Friend. ... Il.11.799.71.
Secur'd the Temper of th' Ætherial Arms. ... Il.20.315.407.
Not break, the settled Temper of thy Soul. ... Il.23.688.517.
A weighty axe, with truest temper steel'd, ... Od.5.300.185.
And as when Arm'rers temper in the ford ... Od.9.465.325.

TEMPER'D
To sweeter Sounds, and temper'd *Pindar's* Fire: ... 2.TemF.223.273.
This Sceptre, form'd by temper'd Steel to prove ... Il.1.313.103.
Thy Force like Steel a temper'd Hardness shows, ... Il.3.89.194.
And Steel well-temper'd, and persuasive Gold. ... Il.6.62.326.
And Steel well temper'd, and refulgent Gold. ... Il.10.452.23.
And steel well-temper'd, and persuasive Gold. ... Il.11.176.43.
Temper'd in this, the Nymph of Form divine ... Il.11.780.70.
Temper'd with drugs of sov'reign use, t'assuage ... Od.4.303.134.
For temper'd drugs and poysons shall be vain. ... Od.10.348.360.
New wine and milk, with honey temper'd, bring, ... Od.10.618.374.
New wine, with honey-temper'd milk, we bring, ... Od.11.31.380.

TEMPERANCE
But Health consists with Temperance alone, ... 3.EOM4.81.136.
Now hear what blessings Temperance can bring: ... 4.HS2.67.59.
Nor one that Temperance advance, ... 4.1HE7.61.273.
Calm Temperance, whose blessings those partake ... 5.DunA1.47.65.
Calm Temperance, whose blessings those partake ... 5.DunB1.49.274.

TEMPERATES
The boiling fluid temperates the cold. ... Od.19.453.216.

TEMPERS
On various Tempers act by various ways, ... 2.RL4.61.189.
Like years, like tempers, and their Prince's love. ... Od.3.465.109.
Tempers the fates of human race above; ... Od.4.326.135.
Then in a bowl he tempers gen'rous wines, ... Od.16.53.105.

TEMPEST
From whose dark Womb a ratling Tempest pours, ... 1.TrSt.494.431.
Then down on Earth a ratling Tempest pours, ... 1.TrSt.494A.431.
Now by the Fury of the Tempest driv'n, ... 1.TrSt.559.433.
Like some black Tempest gath'ring round the Tow'rs: ... 1.TrES.92.453.
The rising tempest puts in act the soul, ... 3.EOM2.105.67.
Nor strive with all the Tempest in my teeth. ... 4.2HE2.301.187.
And calm the rising Tempest of his Soul. ... Il.1.258.99.
Loud as the Surges when the Tempest blows, ... Il.2.471.149.
'Till black as Night the swelling Tempest shows, ... Il.4.318.235.
Around his Head an Iron Tempest rain'd; ... Il.5.766.303.
A double Tempest of the West and North ... Il.9.6.431.
Tho' round his Sides a wooden Tempest rain, ... Il.11.684.65.
Forbid the Tempest, and protect the Ground; ... Il.12.148.87.
Then pours the silent Tempest, thick, and deep: ... Il.12.336.93.
Like some black Tempest gath'ring round the Tow'rs; ... Il.12.446.97.
Where, like a Tempest, dark'ning Heav'n around, ... Il.13.59.107.
The mingled Tempest on the Foes they pour; ... Il.13.901.148.
Wide o'er the blasted Fields the Tempest sweeps, ... Il.13.1001.152.
While yet th' expected Tempest hangs on high, ... Il.14.23.158.
In vain an Iron Tempest hisses round; ... Il.14.497.188.
While Stones and Darts in mingled Tempest flew; ... Il.15.709.223.
Unmov'd it hears, above, the Tempest blow, ... Il.15.748.224.
So thick, the Darts an Iron Tempest rain'd: ... Il.16.131.242.
As when the Hand of *Jove* a Tempest forms, ... Il.16.434.259.
While on each Host with equal Tempest fell ... Il.16.940.280.
See what a Tempest direful *Hector* spreads, ... Il.17.288.299.
Safe thro' the Tempest, to the Tented Shore. ... Il.18.188.331.
They raise a Tempest, or they gently blow. ... Il.18.544.348.
Clamors on Clamors tempest all the Air, ... Il.20.429.412.
Till on the Pyle the gather'd Tempest falls. ... Il.23.269.500.
And howling Tempest, stears the fearless Ship; ... Il.23.388.505.
The tempest scatters, and divides our fleet; ... Od.3.370.104.
The surges now subside, the tempest ends; ... Od.4.693.151.
The tempest drove him to these shores and thee. ... Od.5.142.178.
'Tis *Jove* himself the swelling tempest rears; ... Od.5.391.191.
While by the howling tempest rent in twain ... Od.5.407.192.
But when their texture to the tempest yields, ... Od.5.460.195.
(Thick strown by tempest thro' the bow'ry shade) ... Od.5.625.201.
Climb the steep surge, and thro' the tempest fly; ... Od.6.326.227.
The splitting Raft the furious tempest tore; ... Od.7.358.254.
Tost by rude tempest thro' a war of waves: ... Od.8.28.263.
In scenes of death, by tempest and by war. ... Od.8.206.273.
Nine days our fleet th' uncertain tempest bore ... Od.9.93.306.
The gushing tempest sweeps the Ocean round; ... Od.10.51.342.
Say while the sea, and while the tempest raves, ... Od.11.495.408.

TEMPEST (CONTINUED)
Nor while the sea, nor while the tempest raves, ... Od.11.501.408.
And calm the raging tempest of thy soul. ... Od.11.690.418.
The furious tempest roars with dreadful sound: ... Od.12.373.449.
More dreadful than the tempest, lash'd the seas; ... Od.12.504.457.
For *Pyle* or *Elis* bound: but tempest tost ... Od.13.317.22.
And guard each quarter as the tempest blow. ... Od.14.591.65.
His speech the tempest of her grief restor'd; ... Od.19.284.208.
Tempest of wrath his soul no longer tost; ... Od.20.30.233.
If one more happy, while the tempest raves ... Od.23.253.335.
Yet Fate withstands! a sudden tempest roars ... Od.23.341.341.
'Till *Jove* in wrath the ratling Tempest guides, ... Od.23.357.342.

TEMPEST'S
The tempest's Lord, and tyrant of the wind; ... Od.10.22.340.

TEMPESTING
So the huge *Dolphin* tempesting the Main, ... Il.21.30.422.

TEMPESTS
For *Pyle* or *Elis* bound; but Tempests tost, ... 1.TrUl.150.470.
The Winter's past, the Clouds and Tempests fly, ... 2.ChJM.529.41.
Or brew fierce Tempests on the wintry Main, ... 2.RL2.85.165.
We sail'd in Tempests down the Stream of Life; ... 2.TemF.345.280.
When earthquakes swallow, or when tempests sweep ... 3.EOM1.143.33.
Prescient, the tides or tempests to withstand, ... 3.EOM3.101.102.
Are winds the tempests dreadful to her ears? ... 6.4i.12.9.
Long kept by wars, and long by tempests tost, ... 6.15.2.51.
When gath'ring tempests swell the raging main, ... 6.21.7.69.
When the Ship tosses, and the Tempests beat: ... Il.2.359.144.
The sounding Darts in Iron Tempests slew, ... Il.4.511.245.
The sounding Darts in Iron Tempests flew, ... Il.8.78.399.
And, wrapt in Tempests, o'er the Fleet descends. ... Il.11.8.35.
And Stones and Darts in mingled Tempests fly. ... Il.12.174.87.
When lo! the Deeps arise, the Tempests roar, ... Il.14.287.176.
As, when black Tempests mix the Seas and Skies, ... Il.15.440.214.
And swell'd with Tempests on the Ship descends; ... Il.15.753.225.
(In sign of Tempests from the troubled Air, ... Il.17.618.312.
In gloomy Tempests, and a Night of Clouds: ... Il.20.70.396.
Or sunk by tempests in the gulphy main? ... Od.3.109.91.
For eight slow-circling years by tempests tost, ... Od.4.97.124.
Fell by disastrous fate; by tempests tost, ... Od.4.669.150.
Now from my fond embrace by tempests torn, ... Od.4.962.163.
Tho' tempests rage, tho' rolls the swelling main, ... Od.8.611.295.
The seas may roll, the tempests rage in vain. ... Od.8.612.295.
Tho' spears in iron tempests rain'd around, ... Od.11.657.416.
In brooding tempests, and in rouling clouds; ... Od.12.88.436.
And all in tempests the dire evening clos'd. ... Od.24.59.350.

TEMPESTUOUS
The roaring Winds tempestuous Rage restrain; ... 1.TrUl.28.466.
Where Bentley late tempestuous wont to sport ... 5.DunB4.201.362.
All saw, and fear'd, his huge, tempestuous Sway. ... Il.7.184.373.
With Force tempestuous let the Ruin fly: ... Il.7.322.379.
But 'scap'd not *Ajax;* his tempestuous Hand ... Il.14.471.186.
A Soul well-suiting that tempestuous Kind, ... Il.16.52.237.
Thro' the thick Gloom of some tempestuous Night ... Il.22.38.454.
Twice ten tempestuous nights I roll'd, resign'd ... Od.6.205.220.
Couch'd to the earth, tempestuous as it flies, ... Od.8.215.274.
The roaring wind's tempestuous rage restrain; ... Od.13.119.7.

TEMPLARS
The Tribe of Templars, Play'rs, Apothecaries, ... 4.HAdv.1.75.
Three Cambridge Sophs and three pert Templars came, ... 5.DunA2.347.143.
Three College Sophs, and three pert Templars came, ... 5.DunB2.379.315.
While Fops and Templars ev'ry Sentence raise, ... 6.49iii.27.143.
Whilst Wits and Templars ev'ry Sentence raise, ... 6.49iii.27A.143.
While Wits and Templars ev'ry Sentence raise, ... 6.49iii.27B.143.
While Wits and Templars ev'ry Sentence raise, ... 6.98.63.285.

TEMPLE
Walk in thy Light, and in thy Temple bend. ... 1.Mes.92.121.
With *sweeter Notes* each *rising Temple* rung; ... 1.EOC.703.320.
To *Cyrrha's* Temple on that fatal Day, ... 1.TrSt.90.414.
On that, *Prosymna's* Grove and Temple rise: ... 1.TrSt.534.432.
Thence we these Altars in his Temple raise, ... 1.TrSt.786.443.
Build a fair Temple to the Lord of Hosts; ... 2.ChJM.685.48.
On this Foundation *Fame's* high Temple stands; ... 2.TemF.61.256.
The Temple shakes, the sounding Gates unfold, ... 2.TemF.137.264.
With her, the Temple ev'ry Moment grew, ... 2.TemF.262.276.
The Trumpet sounded, and the Temple shook, ... 2.TemF.277.276.
In the same temple, the resounding wood, ... 3.EOM3.155.108.
Or some old temple, nodding to its fall, ... 3.EOM4.129.140.
And Temple too—then fall again to dust. ... 3.Ep2.140A.62.
And Temple rise—then fall again to dust. ... 3.Ep2.140.62.
No, 'tis a Temple, and a Hecatomb. ... 3.Ep4.156.152.
For Quoits, both *Temple-Bar* and *Charing-Cross.* ... 4.JD4.277.49.
His House, thy Temple, sacred still to Love ... 4.HOde1.22A.151.
The *Temple* late two Brother Sergeants saw, ... 4.2HE2.127.173.
And ope's the Temple of Eternity; ... 4.EpS2.235.326.
See, the Cirque falls! th' unpillar'd Temple nods! ... 5.DunA3.99.158.
From her black grottos near the Temple-wall, ... 5.DunB2.98.300.
Here brisker vapours o'er the Temple creep, ... 5.DunB2.345.314.
See, the Cirque falls, th' unpillar'd Temple nods, ... 5.DunB3.107.325.
To Thee, whose Temple is all Space, ... 6.50.49.148.
And Temple rise,—then fall again to Dust. ... 6.154.26.403.
Shall fill thy Temple with a grateful Smoke. ... Il.6.383.345.
On *Phœbus'* Temple I'll his Arms bestow: ... Il.7.96.367.
Ev'n to the temple stalk'd th' adult'rous spouse, ... Od.3.346.103.
Crown'd with the temple of th' *Athenian* dame; ... Od.3.353.103.

TEMPLE-BAR
For Quoits, both *Temple-Bar* and *Charing-Cross.* ... 4.JD4.277.49.

TEMPLE-WALL
From her black grottos near the Temple-wall, 5.DunB2.98.300.

TEMPLE'S
The Rock's high Summit, in the Temple's Shade, 2.TemF.47.256.
In Ranks adorn'd the Temple's outward Face; 2.TemF.131.264.
But in her Temple's last recess inclos'd, 5.DunA3.1.150.
But in her Temple's last recess inclos'd 5.DunB3.1.320.

TEMPLERS
While Wits and Templers ev'ry sentence raise, 4.Arbu.211.111.

TEMPLES
The hollow Winds thro' naked Temples roar; 1.W-F.68.156.
And Temples rise, the beauteous Works of Peace. 1.W-F.378.187.
Whose horned temples reedy wreaths inclose; 1.TrPA.160.373.
And Wreaths of Hay his Sun-burnt Temples shade; 1.TrVP.34.378.
His Temples thinly spread with silver Hairs: 1.TrVP.47.379.
Let Altars blaze and Temples smoke for her; 1.TrSt.374.425.
Who raise thy Temples where the Chariot stood 1.TrSt.388.426.
And fill thy Temples with a grateful Smoke: 1.TrSt.595.435.
Let Wreaths of Triumph now my Temples twine, 2.RL3.161.180.
There Trees, and intermingl'd Temples rise: 2.TemF.18.254.
And Tow'rs and Temples sink in Floods of Fire. 2.TemF.478.286.
Priests, Tapers, Temples, swim before my sight: 2.ElAb.274.342.
A few grey hairs his rev'rend temples crown'd, 3.Ep3.327.120.
Bid Temples, worthier of the God, ascend; 3.Ep4.198.156.
And Temples, worthier of the God, ascend; 3.Ep4.198A.156.
Let rising Granaries and Temples here, 4.2HE2.258.183.
Lo statues, temples, theatres o'erturned, 5.DunA3.97Z1.158.
Where shall we next thy lasting Temples raise, 6.65.7A.192.
With nodding arches, broken temples spread! 6.71.3.202.
Around his Temples spreads his golden Wing, Il.2.23.128.
Cold thro' his Temples glides the whizzing Spear; Il.4.576.249.
Meanwhile his Temples feel a deadly Wound; Il.5.715.301.
(Thy Gift, *Meriones*) his Temples crown'd; Il.10.310.16.
And now *Ulysses'* thoughtful Temples press'd. Il.10.318.17.
And from his Temples rends the glitt'ring Prize; Il.13.667.137.
And smote his Temples, with an Arm so strong Il.13.729.139.
Jove's awful Temples in the Dew of Sleep? Il.14.282.176.
The radiant Helmet on his Temples burns, Il.15.732.224.
And shade the Temples of the Man divine. Il.16.963.280.
Now crack the blazing Temples of the Gods; Il.17.828.321.
About her Temples flies the busy Bow; Il.21.569.446.
My careful Temples in the Dew of Sleep: Il.24.805.570.
To heav'n the glitt'ring domes and temples blaz'd; Od.6.14.204.
To thee, as to some God, I'll temples raise, Od.15.204.78.

TEMPT
And nodding tempt the joyful Reaper's Hand, 1.W-F.40.152.
Tempt Icy Seas, where scarce the Waters roll, 1.W-F.389.189.
In *fearless Youth* we tempt the Heights of Arts, 1.EOC.220.265.
When the wing'd Colonies first tempt the Sky, 2.TemF.284.277.
And long'd to tempt him like good Job of old: 3.Ep3.350.122.
"This prize is mine; who tempt it, are my foes; 5.DunA2.50.103.
"This prize is mine; who tempt it are my foes; 5.DunB2.54.298.
When *Jove*, dispos'd to tempt *Saturnia's* Spleen, Il.4.7.221.
Nor tempt the Wrath of Heav'ns avenging Sire. Il.5.44.268.
Who tempt our Fury when *Minerva* fires! Il.6.158.333.
And strove to tempt him from the Paths of Fame: Il.6.202.336.
And tempt a Fate which Prudence bids thee shun? Il.7.128.369.
Celestial Minds to tempt the Wrath of *Jove?* Il.8.509.420.
Nor tempt too far the hostile Gods of *Troy.* Il.10.597.29.
Warrior! desist, nor tempt an equal Blow: Il.17.14.288.
Nor tempt too near the Terrors of his Hand. Il.20.434.412.
Forbids to tempt the Wrath of Heav'n too far, Il.24.170.543.
You tempt me, Father, and with Pity touch: Il.24.477.556.
To tempt my Youth, for apt is Youth to err: Il.24.530.558.
To tempt the spouseless Queen with am'rous wiles, Od.1.315.47.
Safe in the court, nor tempt the watry way. Od.2.290.75.
The bowl, and tasteful viands tempt in vain, Od.4.134.126.
Alone, unfriended, will I tempt my way; Od.10.323.360.
And tempt the secret ambush of the night. Od.14.254.48.
To tempt the dangers of forbidding night? Od.15.58.72.
To tempt their bounties with a suppliant's art, Od.17.434.154.
Say, if large hire can tempt thee to employ Od.18.404.188.

TEMPTATION
May yield, God knows, to strong Temptation. 4.HS6.184.261.
Above Temptation, in a low Estate, 6.125.5.350.

TEMPTATIONS
Thicker than arguments, temptations throng, 3.EOM2.75.64.

TEMPTED
In vain she tempted the relentless Youth, Il.6.203.336.
Tho' tempted chaste, and obstinately just? Od.11.215.392.

TEMPTER
The Tempter saw his time; the work he ply'd; 3.Ep3.369.123.
Eve's Tempter thus the Rabbins have exprest, 4.Arbu.330.119.

TEMPTING
Nor be with all those tempting Words abus'd, 1.TrSP.67.396.
Those tempting Words were all to *Sapho* us'd. 1.TrSP.68.396.
O for that tempting Fruit, so fresh, so green; 2.ChJM.722.49.
Just then, *Clarissa* drew with tempting Grace 2.RL3.127.177.
Fair eyes, and tempting looks (which yet I view!) 2.ElAb.295.343.
Or Garden, tempting with forbidden fruit. 3.EOM1.8.13.
Taper legs, and tempting thighs, 6.18.7.61.
And points to *Diomed* the tempting Prize. Il.10.551.27.

TEMPTS
And tempts once more thy sacrilegious Hands. 2.RL4.174.198.
The knave deserves it when he tempts the main, 3.EOM4.153.142.
And tempts by making rich, not making poor. 3.Ep3.352.122.

TEMPTS (CONTINUED)
Let him who tempts me, dread those dire Abodes; Il.8.21.396.
Tempts his Pursuit, and wheels about the Shore. Il.21.716.451.
By Fate, exceeds; and tempts the Wrath of Heav'n: Il.24.65.538.
Tell him he tempts the Wrath of Heav'n too far: Il.24.148.541.
The winds and waves he tempts in early bloom, Od.4.948.162.

TEN
Ten Censure wrong for one who Writes amiss; 1.EOC.6.239.
And ten low Words oft creep in one dull Line, 1.EOC.347.278.
Now, e'er ten Moons their Orb with Light adorn, 1.TrSt.678.438.
And e'er ten Moons their Orb with Light adorn, 1.TrSt.678A.438.
Thro' ten Years Wand'ring, and thro' ten Years War; 1.TrUl.176.471.
Thro' ten Years Wand'ring, and thro' ten Years War; 1.TrUl.176.471.
Who mourn'd her Lord twice ten revolving Years, 1.TrUl.218.473.
Happy! ah ten times happy, had I been, 2.RL4.149.196.
26.As who began ten thousand years ago. 3.EOM1.76A.23.
Tenth or ten thousandth, breaks the chain alike. 3.EOM1.246.45.
Contracts, inverts, and gives ten thousand dyes. 3.Ep1.28.17.
Or water all the Quorum ten miles round? 3.Ep3.42.89.
Behold Villario's ten-years toil compleat; 3.Ep4.79.145.
And when up ten steep slopes you've dragg'd your thighs, 3.Ep4.131.150.
More than ten *Holingsheds*, or *Halls*, or *Stows*. 4.JD4.131.35.
'Tis true, for ten days hence'twill be *King Lear's*. 4.JD4.219.45.
Not so, who of Ten Thousand gull'd her Knight, 4.HAdv.7.75.
Then ask'd Ten Thousand for a second Night: 4.HAdv.8.75.
For Int'rest, ten *per Cent.* her constant Rate is; 4.HAdv.19.77.
My Friendship, and a Prologue, and ten Pound. 4.Arbu.48.99.
Alas! 'tis ten times worse when they *repent.* 4.Arbu.108.103.
Trust me, 'tis ten times worse when they *repent.* 4.Arbu.108A.103.
Full ten years slander'd, did he once reply? 4.Arbu.374.123.
Nor ten *Sclavonians*, scolding, deaf me more 4.JD2A.68.138.
Sure I should want the Care of ten *Monroes*, 4.2HE2.70.169.
That turn'd ten thousand Verses, now stands still. 4.2HE2.79.171.
At Ten for certain, Sir, in Bloomsb'ry-Square— 4.2HE2.95.171.
Clatt'ring their sticks, before ten lines are spoke, 4.2HE1.308.221.
And if we will recite nine hours in ten, 4.2HE1.362.227.
While with the silent growth of ten per Cent, 4.1HE1.132.289.
Ten Metropolitans in preaching well; 4.EpS1.132.307.
Are what ten thousand envy and adore. 4.EpS1.166.309.
P. Strike? why the man was hang'd ten years ago: 4.EpS2.55.315.
Scream, like the winding of ten thousand Jacks: 5.DunA3.154.164.
And ten-horn'd fiends and Giants rush to war. 5.DunA3.232.177.
And ten-horn'd fiends and Giants threaten war. 5.DunA3.232A.177
Scream like the winding of ten thousand jacks: 5.DunB3.160.328.
And ten-horn'd fiends and Giants rush to war. 5.DunB3.236.332.
And Pope's, ten years to comment and translate. 5.DunB3.332.336.
But held in ten-fold bonds the *Muses* lie, 5.DunB4.35.343.
In twice ten thousand rhyming nights and days, 5.DunB4.172.358.
Ten Miles from Town, t' a Place call'd *Epsom*, 6.10.50.26.
Ten times more like him, I profess, 6.10.103.27.
And twice ten thousand bite the ground in death; 6.21.18.69.
The sacred rust of twice ten hundred years! 6.71.38.203.
'Tis ten to one he'll ne'er come back. 6.103.4.295.
As, tho ten Devils rose, they could make them to fall. 6.122.8.341.
But ten such Sages as they grant in thee; Il.2.443.148.
Each leads ten Vessels thro' the yielding Tide. Il.2.754.161.
In ten black Ships embark'd for *Ilion's* Shore, Il.2.868.165.
Ten polish'd Chariots I possess'd at home, Il.5.244.279.
And twice ten Coursers wait their Lord's Command. Il.5.247.279.
Of full ten Cubits was the Lance's Length, Il.6.395.346.
Condemn'd for ten revolving Years to weep Il.8.496.420.
Your selves condemn'd ten rolling Years to weep Il.8.516.421.
Of full ten Cubits was the Lance's Length; Il.8.616.425.
Ten weighty Talents of the purest Gold, Il.9.157.440.
And twice ten Vases of refulgent Mold; Il.9.158.440.
Ten weighty Talents of the purest Gold, Il.9.344.450.
And twice ten Vases of refulgent Mold; Il.9.345.450.
Ten Rows of azure Steel the Work infold, Il.11.31.36.
Twice ten of Tin, the twelve of ductile Gold; Il.11.32.36.
Ten Zones of Brass its ample Brims surround, Il.11.45.36.
And twice ten Bosses the bright Convex crown'd; Il.11.46.36.
When twice ten thousand shake the lab'ring Field; Il.14.174.165.
Haste, bring the Flames! the Toil of ten long Years Il.15.870.230.
Twice ten bright Vases in the midst they laid; Il.19.250.383.
Ten Days were past, since in his Father's Reign Il.21.50.424.
And twice ten Axes casts amidst the Round, Il.23.1008.529.
(Ten double-edg'd, and ten that singly wound.) Il.23.1009.529.
(Ten double-edg'd, and ten that singly wound.) Il.23.1009.529.
With ten pure Talents from the richest Mine; Il.24.286.548.
Now twice ten Years (unhappy Years) are o'er Il.24.964.576.
All who the Wars of ten long years surviv'd, Od.1.16.30.
How twice ten years from shore to shore he roams; Od.2.205.71.
Now twice ten years are past, and now he comes! Od.2.206.71.
And twice ten measures of the choicest flour Od.2.400.80.
Oh then, if ever thro' the ten years war Od.3.118.91.
By ten long years refin'd, and rosy-bright.) Od.3.505.112.
Ten equal talents of refulgent gold. Od.4.176.128.
In twice ten days shall fertile *Scheria* find, Od.5.44.173.
Twice ten tempestuous nights I roll'd, resign'd Od.6.205.220.
The royal bark had ten. Our ships compleat Od.9.186.313.
Around ten thousand thousand spectres stand Od.11.699.419.
Thro' ten years wand'ring, and thro' ten years war; Od.13.343.24.
Thro' ten years wand'ring, and thro' ten years war; Od.13.343.24.
Who mourn'd her Lord twice ten revolving years, Od.13.385.25.
Thro' the long dangers of the ten-years war. Od.15.171.76.
As some fond sire who ten long winters grieves, Od.16.17.102.
Twice ten sad years o'er earth and ocean tost, Od.16.226.114.
Vain hope! ten suns had warm'd the western strand, Od.19.224.204.
When the brave partners of thy ten years toil Od.20.26.233.
Your own *Ulysses!* twice ten years detain'd Od.21.213.270.
When twice ten years are past of mighty woes: Od.23.104.324.
And ten, that red with blushing apples glow'd; Od.24.396.368.

TEN-FOLD

But held in ten-fold bonds the *Muses* lie, ... 5.DunB4.35.343.

TEN-HORN'D

And ten-horn'd fiends and Giants rush to war. ... 5.DunA3.232.177.
And ten-horn'd fiends and Giants threaten war. ... 5.DunA3.232A.177.
And ten-horn'd fiends and Giants rush to war. ... 5.DunB3.236.332.

TEN-YEARS

Behold Villario's ten-years toil compleat; ... 3.Ep4.79.145.
Thro' the long dangers of the ten-years war. ... Od.15.171.76.

TENACIOUS

So to the beam the Bat tenacious clings, ... Od.12.513.457.

TENANT

Man walk'd with beast, joint tenant of the shade; ... 3.EOM3.152.108.

TENANTS

Tenants with sighs the smoakless tow'rs survey, ... 3.Ep3.193.109.
Cutler saw tenants break, and houses fall, ... 3.Ep3.323.120.
Whose chearful Tenants bless their yearly toil, ... 3.Ep4.183.154.

TEND

For see! the gath'ring Flocks to Shelter tend, ... 1.PSp.101.70.
Shall tend the Flocks, or reap the bearded Grain; ... 1.W-F.370.186.
'Twas all her Joy the ripening Fruits to tend, ... 1.TrVP.7.377.
And bid *Endymion* nightly tend his Sheep. ... 1.TrSP.100.398.
Our humbler Province is to tend the Fair, ... 2.RL2.91.165.
Do thou, *Crispissa,* tend her fav'rite Lock; ... 2.RL2.115.166.
As weighty Bodies to the Center tend, ... 2.TemF.429.284.
The single atoms each to other tend, ... 3.EOM3.10.93.
What care to tend, to lodge, to cram, to treat him, ... 3.EOM3.46Z1.96.
To bliss alike by that direction tend, ... 3.EOM3.81.100.
Thee they regard alone; to thee they tend; ... 6.23.17.73.
Thee we regard alone, to thee we tend; ... 6.23.17A.73.
Still in the Tent *Patroclus* sate, to tend ... Il.15.452.215.
That tend the Ships, or guide them o'er the Main, ... Il.19.46.373.
While these officious tend the rites divine, ... Od.3.592.116.
To tend the fruit-groves: With incessant speed ... Od.4.974.163.
Forth hasted he to tend his bristly care: ... Od.14.594.66.
Me to the fields, to tend the rural care; ... Od.15.393.88.
So left perhaps to tend the fleecy train, ... Od.15.418.89.
Those hands in work? to tend the rural trade, ... Od.18.405.188.
Tend, with thy maids, the labors of the loom; ... Od.21.378.278.

TEND'REST

Living, I seem'd his dearest, tend'rest Care, ... Il.23.85.490.

TENDED

Along the tended shore, in balmy sleep ... Od.4.584.147.
(His flock the Giant tended on the green) ... Od.9.253.317.

TENDER

Their artless Passions, and their tender Pains. ... 1.PAu.12.81.
To *Delia's* Ear the tender Notes convey! ... 1.PAu.18.82.
To *Thyrsis* Ear the tender Notes convey! ... 1.PAu.18A.82.
The tender Lambs he raises in his Arms, ... 1.Mes.53.117.
Prescrib'd her Heights, and prun'd her tender Wing, ... 1.EOC.736.325.
What tender lambkins here my folds contain, ... 1.TrPA.84.368.
And one whose tender Care if far above ... 1.TrVP.79.380.
Her tender mother's only hope and pride, ... 1.TrFD.9.386.
Enur'd to Sorrow from my tender Years, ... 1.TrSP.73.397.
Cupid's light Darts my tender Bosom move, ... 1.TrSP.89.397.
O scarce a Youth, yet scarce a tender Boy! ... 1.TrSP.103.398.
A thousand tender Words, I hear and speak; ... 1.TrSP.151.400.
To distant Seas must tender *Sapho* fly? ... 1.TrSP.219.403.
Ah! canst thou rather see this tender Breast ... 1.TrSP.224.403.
Or Men, whose Bosom tender Pity warms? ... 1.TrUl.77.468.
But young and tender Virgins, rul'd with Ease, ... 2.ChJM.111.20.
Her tender Age, her Form divinely Fair, ... 2.ChJM.246.26.
When tender Youth has wedded stooping Age. ... 2.ChJM.340.30.
Whatever was the Cause, the tender Dame ... 2.ChJM.430.35.
Heav'n knows, (with that a tender Sigh she drew) ... 2.ChJM.577.43.
Breathe a soft Sigh, and drop a tender Tear; ... 2.ChJM.666.47.
Come down, and vex your tender Heart no more: ... 2.ChJM.790.53.
"Their tender Husbands, and their Passions cool'd. ... 2.ChWB.196.66.
What tender Maid but must a Victim fall ... 2.RL1.95.152.
With tender *Billet-doux* he lights the Pyre, ... 2.RL2.41.162.
For this with Fillets strain'd your tender Head, ... 2.RL4.101.192.
And, all those tender names in one, thy love! ... 2.ElAb.154.332.
Let him our sad, our tender story tell; ... 2.ElAb.364.348.
To bear too tender, or too firm a heart, ... 2.Elegy.7.363.
Taught nor to slack, nor strain its tender strings, ... 3.EOM3.290.121.
Taught not to slack, nor strain its tender strings, ... 3.EOM3.290A.121.
Me, let the tender Office long engage ... 4.Arbu.408.127.
The tender Labyrinth of a Virgins Ear: ... 4.JD2A.66.138.
To touch Achilles' only tender part; ... 5.DunA2.210.127.
To touch Achilles' only tender part; ... 5.DunB2.218.306.
For here no frowns make tender love afraid, ... 6.4ii.3.9.
Was ravisht from the tender vine; ... 6.6ii.22.15.
Nor slack nor strain the tender Strings; ... 6.11.35Z6.31.
If Wit or Critick blame the tender Swain, ... 6.13.16.39.
That long hast warm'd my tender Breast, ... 6.31i.2.93.
To wake the soul by tender strokes of art, ... 6.32.1.96.
He draws him gentle, tender, and forgiving, ... 6.41.27.114.
What tender passions take their turns, ... 6.51ii.33.154.
The tender sister, daughter, friend and wife; ... 6.52.52.157.
By all these tender Adjurations tell me, ... 6.82ii.5.230.
Till Death unfelt that tender frame destroy, ... 6.86.17.245.
Yet tender was this Hen so fair, ... 6.93.15.257.
Oh next him skill'd to draw the tender Tear, ... 6.152.3.400.
Our weeping Wives, our tender Children call: ... Il.2.166.136.
what Heart but melts to leave the tender Train, ... Il.2.356.144.
Rush to her Thought, and force a tender Tear. ... Il.3.186.200.
With that, the Chief the tender Victims slew, ... Il.3.364.210.

TENDER (CONTINUED)

He knew soft Combates suit the tender Dame, ... Il.5.413.286.
With tender Shrieks the Goddess fill'd the Place, ... Il.5.427.289.
The tender Bosome of a *Grecian* Dame, ... Il.5.512.292.
And press'd his Hand, and tender thus begun. ... Il.6.317.341.
Demands a parting Word, a tender Tear: ... Il.6.459.348.
To tender Passions all his mighty Mind: ... Il.6.505.351.
No Father's Aid, no Mother's tender Care. ... Il.6.523.352.
She mingled with the Smile a tender Tear. ... Il.6.621.357.
With Accent weak these tender Words return'd. ... Il.9.561.461.
The tender Labours, the compliant Cares; ... Il.9.613.464.
Thy dying Eyes no tender Mother close, ... Il.11.569.59.
To tender Pity all his manly Mind; ... Il.13.591.134.
In their kind Arms my tender years were past; ... Il.14.233.172.
I owe the nursing of my tender Years. ... Il.14.346.179.
Our Fathers live, (our first, most tender Care) ... Il.16.19.236.
Nor ever tender Goddess brought thee forth. ... Il.16.49.237.
The tender Plant, and withers all its Shades; ... Il.17.62.290.
And ill requites his Parent's tender Care. ... Il.17.347.301.
I go at least to bear a tender part, ... Il.18.83.327.
Whose tender Lay the Fate of *Linus* sings; ... Il.18.662.355.
Once tender Friend of my distracted Mind! ... Il.19.304.385.
His Son's sad Fate, and drops a tender Tear.) ... Il.19.344.386.
My tender Orphan with a Parent's Care, ... Il.19.352.387.
Nor ply'd the Grass, nor bent the tender Grain; ... Il.20.271.405.
The ruthless Falchion op'd his tender Side; ... Il.20.544.417.
Lent to the wounded God her tender Hand: ... Il.21.487.441.
To her, *Latona* hasts with tender Care; ... Il.21.579.446.
And bending o'er thee, mix'd the tender Show'r! ... Il.22.547.479.
And why was all that tender Care bestow'd? ... Il.22.615.481.
He, who with tender Delicacy bred, ... Il.22.646.483.
She prest his Hand, and tender thus begun. ... Il.24.162.542.
With tender pity touch'd, the Goddess cry'd: ... Od.1.327.48.
His tender theme the charming Lyrist chose ... Od.1.421.53.
Of this to learn, opprest with tender fears ... Od.3.110.91.
With ample forehead, and yet tender horns ... Od.3.492.111.
Wastes all her widow'd hours in tender moan. ... Od.4.148.127.
Dubious to press the tender theme, or wait ... Od.4.155.127.
The graceful curl, and drop the tender tear. ... Od.4.272.132.
Leaves in that fatal laire the tender fawns, ... Od.4.451.141.
His hand the King with tender passion press'd, ... Od.4.829.158.
Of yester dawn disclos'd the tender day, ... Od.4.881.159.
At length, in tender language interwove ... Od.4.938.162.
Or men, whose bosom tender pity warms? ... Od.6.142.214.
And tender second to a mother's cares. ... Od.7.16.234.
Or men, whose bosom tender pity warms? ... Od.8.628.296.
But that distinguish'd from my tender years, ... Od.9.433.324.
By justice sway'd, by tender pity prest: ... Od.10.452.365.
And ecchoing hills return the tender cry: ... Od.10.490.367.
(These tender words on ev'ry side I hear) ... Od.10.496.367.
The tender moment seiz'd, and thus I said. ... Od.10.569.370.
And as he spoke her tender hand he prest. ... Od.11.296.396.
And soften'd his stern soul to tender love. ... Od.11.328.398.
And from his eyes pour'd down the tender dew; ... Od.11.486.408.
And tender sorrow thrills in ev'ry vein; ... Od.11.676.417.
Or Men, whose bosom tender pity warms? ... Od.13.244.17.
Joy touch'd the Hero's tender soul, to find ... Od.14.61.38.
What cares his Mother's tender breast engage, ... Od.15.370.87.
Torn from th' embraces of his tender wife, ... Od.15.379.87.
They bend the silver bow with tender skill, ... Od.15.450.92.
Leaves in that fatal lair her tender fawns, ... Od.17.142.138.
'Till thus the Queen the tender theme renews. ... Od.19.252.207.
His tender bloom to manly growth sustain'd: ... Od.19.410.214.
With tender sympathy to sooth my soul, ... Od.19.635.227.
Venus in tender delicacy rears ... Od.20.82.236.
The tender drops. *Antinous* saw, and said. ... Od.21.86.263.
With tender hands the stubborn horn he strains, ... Od.21.157.267.
Each vents a groan, and drops a tender tear; ... Od.22.483.312.
Ah no! she cries, a tender heart I bear, ... Od.23.175.329.
And with a tender pleasantry reproves: ... Od.24.284.363.
Seal'd his cold eyes, or drop'd a tender tear! ... Od.24.347.365.

TENDERLY

And *Brutus* tenderly reproves. ... 6.51ii.8.152.

TENDERNESS

In equal tenderness her sons conspire, ... Od.7.88.238.
All arts of tenderness to him are known, ... Od.17.126.137.

TENDON

The Tendon burst beneath the pondrous Blow, ... Il.8.395A.416.

TENDONS

Thro' both the Tendons broke the rugged Stone, ... Il.5.377.285.

TENDS

As the good Shepherd tends his fleecy Care, ... 1.Mes.49.117.
That tends to make one worthy Man my foe, ... 4.Arbu.284.116.
But tends to raise that Pow'r which I obey. ... Il.12.252.90.
His wounded Brother good *Polites* tends; ... Il.13.675.137.
With constant duty tends his drooping age. ... Od.24.243.360.
Who nurs'd the children, and now tends the sire: ... Od.24.450.370.

TENEDOS

Thou Source of Light! whom *Tenedos* adores, ... Il.1.55.88.
Whose sacred Eye thy *Tenedos* surveys, ... Il.1.592.116.
Between where *Tenedos* the Surges lave, ... Il.13.51.107.
For *Tenedos* we spread our eager oars, ... Od.3.191.95.

TENEMENTS

And sigh'd) "My lands and tenements to Ned." ... 3.Ep1.257.37.
And Lands and Tenements go down her Throat. ... 4.HAdv.14.75.
Schoolmen new tenements in Hell must make; ... 4.JD2.42.135.
Schoolmen new Tenements in Hell must make; ... 4.JD2A.46.136.

TENETS

Tenets with Books, and Principles with Times. ....3.Ep1.167.29.
We find our tenets just the same at last. ....3.Ep3.16.84.

TENFOLD

With tenfold Ardor now invades the Plain, ...Il.5.172.275.

TENOR

Shall Fortune still in one sad Tenor run, ...1.TrSP.71.397.
So shall my Days in one sad Tenor run, ...Il.6.520.352.

TENOUR

That shunning Faults, one quiet *Tenour* keep; ....1.EOC.241.267.
The constant Tenour of whose well-spent Days ....2.TemF.330.280.
If ought disturb the Tenour of his Breast, ...Il.13.370.123.

TENS

All rank'd by Tens; whole Decads when they dine ......Il.2.157.136.

TENT

Ev'n in thy Tent I'll seize the blooming Prize, ...Il.1.245.98.
Haste to the fierce *Achilles'* Tent (he cries) ....Il.1.422.108.
Arriv'd, the Heroe in his Tent they find, ...Il.1.428.108.
To *Agamemnon's* ample Tent repair. ....Il.2.10.127.
Rich Heaps of Brass shall in thy Tent be told; ....Il.6.61.326.
A thousand Measures to the Royal Tent. ....Il.7.563.392.
Conven'd the Princes in his ample Tent; ....Il.9.122.438.
When from *Pelides'* Tent you forc'd the Maid, ...Il.9.141.439.
(My self will name them) to *Pelides'* Tent: ....Il.9.220.443.
Then from the Royal Tent they take their way; ....Il.9.232.444.
Then from the Royal Tent they took their way; ......Il.9.232A.444.
Plac'd in his Tent, attends the lofty Strain: ....Il.9.252.445.
To his high Tent; the great *Ulysses* leads. ....Il.9.256.445.
The Tent is brightned with the rising Blaze: ....Il.9.278.447.
That, *Agamemnon's* regal Tent affords; ....Il.9.298.449.
But in his inner Tent, an ampler Space, ...Il.9.779.472.
Pass'd thro the Hosts, and reach'd the Royal Tent. ...Il.9.787.472.
But *Phœnix* in his Tent the Chief retains, ...Il.9.808.473.
To wake *Atrides* in the Royal Tent. ....Il.10.38.4.
Long e'er the rest, he rose, and sought my Tent. ....Il.10.143.8.
Then rushing from his Tent, he snatch'd in hast ....Il.10.154.8.
Stopp'd at *Ulysses'* Tent, and call'd aloud. ....Il.10.157.8.
Awakes, starts up, and issues from his Tent. ....Il.10.159.9.
Without his Tent, bold *Diomed* they found, ...Il.10.170.9.
Ev'n to the Royal Tent pursue my way, ...Il.10.385.21.
Hector, the Peers assembling in his Tent, ...Il.10.486.25.
A warlike Form appear'd before his Tent, ...Il.10.579.28.
The wounded Monarch at his Tent they place. ......Il.11.364.51.
Graceful as *Mars, Patroclus* quits his Tent, ...Il.11.737.68.
And took their Seats beneath the shady Tent. ......Il.11.763.69.
Unheard approach'd, and stood before the Tent. ....Il.11.789.71.
This touch'd his gen'rous Heart, and from the Tent ..Il.11.934.77.
And great *Machaon,* wounded in his Tent, ...Il.11.970.78.
To seek a surer Javelin in his Tent. ....Il.13.224.116.
That Office paid, he issu'd from his Tent, ...Il.13.284.119.
Swift to his Tent the *Cretan* King returns. ....Il.13.314.120.
Him, near his Tent, *Meriones* attends; ....Il.13.325.120.
The wanted Weapons; those my Tent can give. .....Il.13.338.121.
At once the Tent and Ligature supply'd. ....Il.13.752.141.
Still in the Tent *Patroclus* sate, to tend ....Il.15.452.215.
Sprung from the Tent, and left the War behind. ...Il.15.469.215.
Lies pierc'd with Wounds, and bleeding in his Tent. .Il.16.34.236.
Achilles speeds from Tent to Tent, and warms .....Il.16.190.246.
Achilles speeds from Tent to Tent, and warms .....Il.16.190.246.
To the rich Coffer, in his shady Tent: ....Il.16.269.249.
Back to his Tent the stern *Achilles* flies, ...Il.16.310.254.
Whate'er *Ulysses* promis'd at thy Tent: ....Il.19.140.377.
To bear the Presents from the royal Tent. ....Il.19.244.383.
Achilles sought his Tent. His Train before ....Il.19.291.384.
With Steps unwilling, to the regal Tent. ....Il.23.48.489.
The sacred Relicks to the Tent they bore; ....Il.23.315.502.
A sumptuous Banquet at our Tent attends. ....Il.23.956.527.
Was *Hector* dragg'd, then hurry'd to the Tent. .....Il.24.26.536.
And echoing Groans that shook the lofty Tent. ....Il.24.158.542.
And safe conduct him to *Achilles'* Tent. ....Il.24.416.553.
But whole he lies, neglected in the Tent: ....Il.24.504.557.
Safe to *Pelides'* Tent conduct my way. ....Il.24.528.558.
And now approach'd *Pelides'* lofty Tent. ....Il.24.552.559.
And found *Achilles* in his inner Tent: ....Il.24.579.560.
And led the hoary Herald to the Tent; ....Il.24.725.568.
Approaching sudden to our open'd Tent, ...Il.24.820.571.
The Old Man's Fears, and turn'd within the Tent; ..Il.24.841.572.

TENTED

His honour'd Body to the Tented Shore. ....Il.13.532.131.
Safe thro' the Tempest, to the Tented Shore. ......Il.18.188.331.
The foe deceiv'd, he pass'd the tented plain, ...Od.4.337.136.

TENTH

And striking Watches the tenth Hour resound. .....2.RL1.18A.145.
Tenth or ten thousandth, breaks the chain alike. ...3.EOM1.246.45.
But ere the tenth revolving Day was run, ...Il.1.73.90.
But wait the Tenth, for *Ilion's* Fall decreed: ......Il.2.396.145.
But when the tenth bright Morning Orient glow'd, ..Il.6.215.336.
The tenth, I forc'd the Gates, unseen of all; ....Il.9.596.464.
Now shines the tenth bright Morning since I came ..Il.21.173.428.
But when the tenth cœlestial Morning broke; ....Il.24.42.537.
The tenth shall see the Fun'ral and the Feast; ......Il.24.835.571.
But when the tenth fair Morn began to shine, ...Il.24.995.577.
Their force on *Ilion,* in the tenth destroy'd) ......Od.5.134.178.
The tenth we touch'd, by various errors tost, ...Od.9.95.306.
The tenth presents our welcome native shore: .....Od.10.31.340.
When the tenth sun descended to the main. ....Od.12.532.458.
Nine years we warr'd; the tenth saw *Ilion* fall; ...Od.14.276.49.
The tenth soft wafts me to *Thesprotia's* shore. ...Od.14.350.51.

TENTHREDON'S

Prothous the swift, of old *Tenthredon's* Blood; ....Il.2.917.167.

TENTS

Where near his Tents his hollow Vessels lay. ......Il.1.403.107.
The Ships and Tents in mingled Prospect lay. .....Il.1.633.118.
Stretch'd in the Tents the *Grecian* Leaders lie, ...Il.2.2.126.
So, from the Tents and Ships, a length'ning Train ...Il.2.117.133.
Thy Tents are crowded, and thy Chests o'erflow. ...Il.2.280.141.
Strait to the Tents the Troops dispersing bend, ...Il.2.474.149.
The Fields, the Tents, the Navy, and the Bay. .....Il.2.963.169.
Black from the Tents the sav'ry Vapors flew. ......Il.7.559.392.
The Town, the Tents, and navigable Seas. ....Il.8.66.398.
Toil'd thro' the Tents, and all his Army fir'd, ...Il.8.267.410.
See! what a Blaze from hostile Tents aspires, ...Il.9.103.437.
The *Myrmidonian* Tents and Vessels lay; ....Il.9.244.444.
Their threat'ning Tents already shade our Wall, ...Il.9.306.449.
Till Sleep descending o'er the Tents, bestows ......Il.9.836.474.
Thro' intermingled Ships and Tents, he past; .....Il.11.755.68.
The Stream they pass'd, and pitch'd their Tents below. ..Il.11.849.74.
Force, to the Fleet and Tents, th' impervious way. ..Il.15.473.215.
Wedg'd in one Body at the Tents they stand, ...Il.15.788.226.
Thus from the Tents the fervent Legion swarms, ...Il.16.320.255.
Rush'd from the Tents with Cries; and gath'ring round ..Il.18.35.325.
Those in the Tents the Squires industrious spread; ..Il.19.293.384.
Once spread th' inviting Banquet in our Tents; ....Il.19.336.386.
Hast spread th' inviting Banquet in our Tents; ....Il.19.336A.386.
How blazing tents illumin'd half the skies, ...Od.8.549.292.

TENURE

(Unsure the Tenure, but how vast the Fine!) ......2.TemF.508.288.

TEOPHRASTE

Has kept his word, Here's *Teophraste.* ....6.44.12.123.

TEPID

Waves to the tepid Zephyrs of the spring, ...5.DunB4.422.383.
Then unguents sweet and tepid streams we shed; ...Od.24.62.350.

TEREE'S

High *Teree's* Summits, and *Pityea's* Bow'rs; ......Il.2.1005.170.

TERENCE

The Art of *Terence,* and *Menander's* Fire; ....1.PAu.8.81.
Let Friend affect to speak as Terence spoke, ...5.DunB4.223.364.

TEREUS

Of *Tereus* she, of *Phaon* I complain. ....1.TrSP.178.401.

TERGO

Scriptus & in tergo, nec dum finitus Orestes. ......6.24iii(b).2.76.

TERM

Do what you list the Term of all your Life: ....2.ChWB.428.77.
Verse-man or Prose-man, term me which you will, ...4.HS1.64.11.
Rymes e'er he wakes, and prints before *Term* ends, ..4.Arbu.43.99.
That even humble seems a Term too high. ....6.9xi.4.24.
Fix'd is the Term to all the Race of Earth, ...Il.6.628.358.

TERM'D

Is aptly term'd a Glow-worm: ....6.53.16.161.

TERMAGANTS

The Sprights of fiery Termagants in Flame ....2.RL1.59.150.

TERMD

Might e'en as well be termd the Sea; ....6.67.18.195.

TERMINATE

In beauteous order terminate the scene. ....6.35.27.103.
In beauteous order terminate the scene. ....Od.7.168.244.

TERMS

Discours'd in Terms as just, with Looks as Sage, ...1.EOC.269.270.
Make your own Terms; and ere to-morrow's Sun ...2.ChJM.563.42.
The whole Artill'ry of the Terms of War, ...4.JD4.54.29.
'Allyes and Lanes are Terms too vile and base, ...6.13.22.39.
Tell him, all Terms, all Commerce I decline, ...Il.9.489.456.
Were these not paid thee by the Terms we bring, ...Il.9.641.466.
To die, or conquer, are the Terms of War. ....Il.17.269.298.
And treat on Terms of Peace to save the Town: ....Il.22.157.459.
Hence with those coward terms; Or fight or fly, ...Od.22.79.290.

TERRACE

First thro' the length of yon hot Terrace sweat, ...3.Ep4.130.150.

TERRACES

And Nero's Terraces desert their walls: ....3.Ep4.72.144.

TERRAS

To swell the Terras, or to sink the Grot; ....3.Ep4.49.142.
A Terras-walk, and half a Rood ....4.HS6.5.251.

TERRAS-WALK

A Terras-walk, and half a Rood ....4.HS6.5.251.

TERRESTRIAL

So spirits ending their terrestrial race, ...5.DunA1.223.90.
So Spirits ending their terrestrial race, ...5.DunB1.267.290.
Unlike our gross, diseas'd, terrestrial Blood: ......Il.5.424.288.
For sure he seem'd not of terrestrial Line! ....Il.24.324.550.

TERRESTRIALS

But Heav'n that knows what all terrestrials need, ...Od.19.691.229.

TERRIBLE 447 TH'

TERRIBLE
Rush'd terrible amidst the Ranks of Fight. ..... Il.5.839.305.
Expiring, pale, and terrible no more, ... Il.8.462.419.
Thus breathing Death, in terrible Array, ... Il.13.187.114.
Adorn'd in all his terrible Array, ... Il.16.170.244.
Swift as a Lion, terrible and bold, ... Il.16.909.279.
High o'er the Host, all terrible he stands, ... Il.19.438.389.
Then to the City, terrible and strong, ... Il.22.31.453.
Expects the Hero's terrible Advance. ..... Il.22.129.458.
These two-edg'd Axes, terrible in War; ..... Il.23.1015.529.
Once swift of foot, and terrible in fight, ... Od.3.136.92.
Host mov'd tow'rd host in terrible array, ... Od.11.628.414.
There terrible, affright the dogs, and reign ..... Od.18.126.172.
There terrible in arms *Ulysses* stood, ... Od.23.47.321.

TERRIBLY
Thus terribly adorn'd the figures shine, ... Od.11.757.423.
Her bosom terribly o'erlooks the tyde. ..... Od.12.116.437.
Dreadful he glares, and terribly he foams, ... Od.22.441.309.

TERRIFIC
In Arms Terrific their huge Limbs they drest. ..... Il.10.300.15.
A grim, terrific, formidable Band: ..... Il.16.193.246.
Terrific Glory! for his burning Breath ..... Il.22.41.454.
Descends terrific from he mountain's brow, ... Od.6.155.216.
Euryalus, like *Mars* terrific, rose, ... Od.8.119.268.
Of size enormous, and terrific mien, ... Od.10.128.347.
And clang their pinions with terrific sound; ..... Od.11.748.423.
Six horrid necks she rears, and six terrific heads; ..... Od.12.112.437.
We rise terrific to the task of fight. ..... Od.16.289.118.
And thus terrific, to the Suitor crew. ..... Od.22.6.286.
Great, and terrific ev'n in death you lay, ... Od.24.56.350.

TERRIFIES
Or terrifies th' offending World with Wars: ..... Il.13.320.120.

TERRIFY
To scatter Hosts, and terrify Mankind. ..... Il.15.353.210.

TERROR
Gigantick *Pride,* pale *Terror,* gloomy *Care,* ..... 1.W-F.415.193.
Ev'n he, the terror of his native grove, ... 1.TrPA.17.366.
Alive, the Pride and Terror of the Wood. ..... 1.TrSt.574.434.
And less of Terror in their Looks appears. ..... 1.TrSt.628.436.
Shall I, the Terror of this sinful Town, ... 4.JD4.196.43.
With Pity, and with Terror, tear my heart; ..... 4.2HE1.345.225.
Pale *Flight* around, and dreadful *Terror* reign; ..... Il.4.500.244.
My self will charge this Terror of the Field. ..... Il.5.297.281.
Or foaming Boars, the Terror of the Wood. ..... Il.5.975.313.
Or foaming Boars, the Terror of the Wood. ..... Il.7.308.379.
With Terror cloath'd, and more than mortal strong. ..... Il.8.406.416.
(That Terror the the *Greeks,* that Man of Men) ..... Il.8.458.419.
They, pale with Terror, mark its Spires unroll'd, ... Il.12.241.90.
He fills the *Greeks* with Terror and Dismay, ... Il.12.301.92.
Terror and Death in his wild Eye-balls stare; ..... Il.13.363.123.
Terror, his best lov'd Son, attends his Course, ... Il.13.386.124.
Dire *Flight* and *Terror* drove the *Trojan* Train. ..... Il.16.439.259.
Had sunk each Heart with Terror and Dismay. ..... Il.17.128.292.
A Chief, once thought no Terror of the Field; ..... Il.17.661.313.
Such the wild Terror, and the mingled Cry. ..... Il.17.850.321.
Studious to see that Terror of the Plain, ... Il.19.49.373.
While great *Achilles,* (Terror of the Plain) ..... Il.20.57.396.
Mars hov'ring o'er his *Troy,* his Terror shrouds ..... Il.20.69.396.
How from that Arm of Terror shall I fly? ..... Il.21.103.426.
Immers'd remain this Terror of the World. ..... Il.21.373.436.
What, shall I fly this Terror of the Plain? ..... Il.21.651.449.
Glorious, my Country's Terror laid in Dust: ..... Il.22.151.459.
With terror wing'd conveys the dread report. ..... Od.4.706.152.
No less a terror, from the neighb'ring groves ..... Od.6.161.216.
Adds graceful terror to the wearer's side. ..... Od.8.440.287.
Yet mix'd with terror at the bold emprize. ..... Od.21.308.274.
Was heard, and terror seiz'd the *Grecian* train: ..... Od.24.68.350.

TERRORS
What Terrors wou'd distract each conscious Soul ..... 4.JD4.244A.47.
But oh! what Terrors must distract a Soul ..... 4.JD4.244B.47.
But oh! what Terrors must distract the Soul, ... 4.JD4.244.47.
With Terrors round can Reason hold her throne, ... 4.2HE2.310.187.
Array'd in Terrors, rowz'd the *Trojan* Pow'rs: ..... Il.4.594.249.
Here all the Terrors of grim War appear, ... Il.5.914.310.
The glitt'ring Terrors from his Brows unbound, ... Il.6.600.356.
The God in Terrors, and the Skies on fire. ..... Il.8.98.402.
And circling Terrors fill'd the expressive Shield: ..... Il.11.48.36.
Amaz'd he stood, with Terrors not his own. ..... Il.11.671.65.
Arm'd with wild Terrors, and to Slaughter bred, ... Il.13.595.134.
Shot Terrors round, that wither'd ev'n the Strong. ..... Il.13.1017.153.
And own the Terrors of th' Almighty Hand! ..... Il.14.486.187.
Nor thus the Boar (those Terrors of the Plain) ..... Il.17.23.288.
A sable Scene! The Terrors *Hector* led. ..... Il.17.115.292.
Thou dar'st not meet the Terrors of his Eye; ..... Il.17.185.294.
And the red Terrors of the blazing Brands: ..... Il.17.746.317.
But tho unarm'd, yet clad in Terrors, go! ..... Il.18.236.333.
Detains those Terrors, keeps that Arm from Fight; ..... Il.18.314.336.
That Arm, those Terrors, we shall feel, not fear; ..... Il.18.316.336.
Dread the grim Terrors, and at distance bay. ..... Il.18.676.356.
Nor tempt too near the Terrors of his Hand. ..... Il.20.434.412.
And Toils, and Terrors, fill'd the dreadful Day. ..... Il.21.612.447.
As *Hector* sees, unusual Terrors rise, ... Il.22.179.461.
And with false Terrors sink another's Mind. ..... Il.22.362.470.
And live; give all thy terrors to the wind. ..... Od.5.441.194.
Amid the terrors of the rowling main. ..... Od.7.331.253.
Will you the terrors of the dome explore, ... Od.10.511.368.
Hideous her voice, and with less terrors roar ..... Od.12.109.436.
And doubles all the terrors of the main. ..... Od.12.340.448.
And airy terrors sable ev'ry dream. ..... Od.20.103.238.

TERTULLIAN
Chrysippus and *Tertullian; Ovid's* Art; ..... 2.ChWB.360.74.

TEST
At once the *Source,* and *End,* and *Test* of *Art.* ..... 1.EOC.73.247.
Thy streams were once th' impartial test ..... 6.6ii.17.15.
Thy silent whisper is the sacred test.] ..... 6.107.32.311.

TESTERS
Will club their Testers, now, to take your Life! ..... 4.HS1.104.15.

TESTIFIES
The Son of *Sirach* testifies no less. ..... 2.ChJM.640.46.

TETHYS
Ocean and *Tethys* their old Empire keep, ... Il.14.231.172.
The rev'rend *Ocean* and grey *Tethys* reign, ... Il.14.343.179.

TEUCER
And saw where *Teucer* with th' *Ajaces* stood, ... 1.TrES.61.451.
And *Teucer* haste, with his unerring Bow, ... 1.TrES.75.452.
And *Teucer* haste, with his unerring Bow, ... 1.TrES.80Z9.452.
With equal Steps bold *Teucer* prest the Shore, ... 1.TrES.89.453.
At once bold *Teucer* draws the twanging Bow, ... 1.TrES.135.454.
And last young *Teucer* with his bended Bow. ..... Il.8.320.412.
And rush'd on *Teucer* with the lifted Rock. ..... Il.8.388.416.
And saw where *Teucer* with th' *Ajaces* stood, ... Il.12.405.96.
And *Teucer* haste with his unerring Bow, ... Il.12.419.97.
And *Teucer* haste, with his unerring Bow, ... Il.12.433.97.
With equal Steps bold *Teucer* press'd the Shore, ... Il.12.443.97.
At once bold *Teucer* draws the twanging Bow, ... Il.12.489.99.
Teucer and *Leitus* first his Words excite; ..... Il.13.125.110.
Him *Teucer* pierc'd between the Throat and Ear; ..... Il.13.239.116.
Then *Teucer* rushing to despoil the dead, ... Il.13.245.116.
And gallant *Teucer* deals Destruction there: ..... Il.13.403.125.
Each *Ajax, Teucer, Merion,* gave command, ... Il.15.340.210.
Teucer, behold! extended on the Shore ..... Il.15.510.216.
Impatient *Teucer,* hastening to his Aid, ... Il.15.518.217.
Once more bold *Teucer,* in his Country's Cause, ... Il.15.536.217.
Then *Teucer* laid his faithless Bow aside; ..... Il.15.564.218.
And skilful *Teucer:* In the Helm they threw ..... Il.23.1018.529.

TEUCER'S
From *Teucer's* Hand a winged Arrow flew, ... 1.TrES.112.453.
By *Teucer's* Shaft brave *Aretäon* bled, ... Il.6.37.325.
Who first by *Teucer's* mortal Arrows bled? ..... Il.8.329.413.
From *Teucer's* Hand a winged Arrow flew; ..... Il.12.466.98.
By *Teucer's* Arm the warlike *Imbrius* bleeds, ... Il.13.227.116.
By *Teucer's* Arrows mingled with the dead. ..... Il.14.610.192.
Nor was such Glory due to *Teucer's* Hands. ..... Il.15.543.217.
Inflicted late by *Teucer's* deadly Dart, ... Il.16.630.269.

TEUTHRAS
Teuthras the great, *Orestes* the renown'd ..... Il.5.866.307.

TEUTHRAS'
Next *Teuthras'* Son distain'd the Sands with Blood, ... Il.6.15.323.

TEXT
Still with *It self compar'd,* his *Text* peruse; ..... 1.EOC.128.253.
And that's a Text I clearly understand. ..... 2.ChWB.18.57.
Publish the present Age, but where my Text ..... 4.HS1.59.11.
'Till rallying all, the Feast became the Text; ..... 6.17iv.16.59.
The *Polygott—three Parts,—my Text,* ..... 6.39.13.110.
Three Parts—the Polyglott,—my *Text,* ..... 6.39.13A.110.

TEXTS
And Men interpret *Texts,* why shou'd not We? ..... 2.ChJM.678.47.
Nor disputant, in vouching Texts, leave out ..... 4.JD2A.106.142.

TEXTURE
Such, and so soon, th' Ætherial Texture join'd. ..... Il.5.1115.321.
Of softest Texture, and inwrought with Gold; ..... Il.24.1006.577.
A veil of richest texture wrought, she wears, ... Od.1.429.53.
So roll'd the Float, and so its texture held: ..... Od.5.420.192.
But when their texture to the tempest yields, ... Od.5.460.195.
The verdant Arch so close its texture kept: ..... Od.5.622.201.
Whose texture ev'n the search of Gods deceives, ... Od.8.323.281.
And *Pallas* taught the texture of the loom. ..... Od.20.87.237.

TEXTURES
Thin glitt'ring Textures of the filmy Dew; ..... 2.RL2.64.163.
The various Textures and the various Dies, ... Il.6.365.344.
Her various textures of unnumber'd dies, ... Od.15.119.74.

TH'
And all th' Aerial Audience clap their Wings ..... 1.PSp.16.61.
Thus sung the Shepherds till th'Approach of Night, ... 1.PAu.97.87.
Th'industrious Bees neglect their Golden Store; ..... 1.PWi.51.92.
The Dreams of *Pindus* and th' *Aonian* Maids, ... 1.Mes.4.112.
Th' Æthereal Spirit o'er its Leaves shall move, ... 1.Mes.11.113.
Swift fly the Years, and rise th'expected Morn! ..... 1.Mes.21.114.
The Rocks proclaim th'approaching Deity. ..... 1.Mes.32.116.
'Tis he th'obstructed Paths of Sound shall clear, ... 1.Mes.41.116.
And bid new Musick charm th'unfolding Ear. ..... 1.Mes.42.116.
And Hell's grim Tyrant feel th'eternal Wound. ..... 1.Mes.48.117.
Here blushing *Flora* paints th'enamel'd Ground, ... 1.W-F.38.151.
The Fields are ravish'd from th'industrious Swains, ... 1.W-F.65.155.
Th' Oppressor rul'd Tyrannick where he *durst,* ..... 1.W-F.74.157.
The Forests wonder'd at th'unusual Grain, ... 1.W-F.89.158.
Secure they trust th'unfaithful Field, beset, ... 1.W-F.103.160.
Sudden they seize th'amaz'd, defenceless Prize, ... 1.W-F.109.161.
With slaught'ring Guns th'unweary'd Fowler roves, ... 1.W-F.125.162.
Th'impatient Courser pants in ev'ry Vein, ... 1.W-F.151.164.
Th'Immortal Huntress, and her Virgin Train; ..... 1.W-F.160.164.
Whom not th'extended *Albion* could contain, ... 1.W-F.315.179.

TH' (CONTINUED)

And blended lie th' Oppressor and th' Opprest! … 1.W-F.318.179.
And blended lie th' Oppressor and th' Opprest! … 1.W-F.318.179.
Behold! th'ascending *Villa's* on my Side … 1.W-F.375.187.
But, of the two, less dang'rous is th' Offence, … 1.EOC.3.239.
In some fair Body thus th' informing Soul … 1.EOC.76.247.
It self unseen, but in th' *Effects,* remains. … 1.EOC.79.248.
Held from afar, aloft, th' Immortal Prize, … 1.EOC.96.250.
Th' Intent propos'd, *that Licence* is a *Rule.* … 1.EOC.149.256.
But with th' *Occasion* and the *Place* comply, … 1.EOC.177.261.
Th' Eternal Snows appear already past, … 1.EOC.227.265.
Th' *increasing* Prospect *tires* our wandring Eyes, … 1.EOC.231.265.
Is not th' Exactness of peculiar Parts; … 1.EOC.244.267.
All comes *united* to th' admiring Eyes; … 1.EOC.250.268.
As e'er cou'd *Dennis,* of the Laws o' th' Stage; … 1.EOC.270B.270.
As e'er cou'd *Dennis,* of th' *Athenian* stage; … 1.EOC.270C.270.
But true *Expression,* like th' unchanging *Sun,* … 1.EOC.315.274.
Amaze th'unlearn'd, and make the Learned *Smile.* … 1.EOC.327.275.
Flies o'er th'unbending Corn, and skims along the Main. … 1.EOC.373.283.
Th' *opposing Body's* Grossness, not its *own.* … 1.EOC.469.292.
All seems Infected that th' Infected spy, … 1.EOC.558.304.
Content, if hence th' Unlearn'd their Wants may view, … 1.EOC.739.326.
To trim his beard, th'unweildy scythe prepares; … 1.TrPA.23.366.
Yet he shall find, wou'd time th'occasion shew, … 1.TrPA.124.370.
And teach th'obedient Branches where to spring. … 1.TrVP.12.377.
With that ripe red th'Autumnal Sun bestows, … 1.TrVP.101.381.
As when thro' Clouds th'emerging Sun appears, … 1.TrVP.115.381.
She feels th'encroaching bark around her grow … 1.TrFD.43.387.
Behold, *Andræmon* and th'unhappy Sire … 1.TrFD.57.388.
I swear by all th'unpitying pow'rs of heav'n, … 1.TrFD.70.389.
But when its way th'impetuous Passion found, … 1.TrSP.129.399.
Th'Alternate Reign destroy'd by Impious Arms, … 1.TrSt.2.409.
Whose fatal Rage th'unhappy Monarch found; … 1.TrSt.14.410.
The Wretch then lifted to th'unpitying Skies … 1.TrSt.77.413.
To th'Iron Gates of *Tænarus* she flies, … 1.TrSt.134.415.
And thro' th' *Achaian* Cities send the Sound. … 1.TrSt.164.417.
Th'unwonted Weight, or drag the crooked Share, … 1.TrSt.187.418.
With Scandal arm'd, th'Ignoble Mind's Delight,) … 1.TrSt.233.420.
Is this th'Eternal Doom decreed above? … 1.TrSt.244.420.
What lofty Looks th'unrival'd Monarch bears! … 1.TrSt.253.421.
And now th'Almighty Father of the Gods … 1.TrSt.273.421.
And all th'extended Space of Earth, and Air, and Sea. … 1.TrSt.279.421.
Triumphant o'er th'eluded Rage of *Jove!* … 1.TrSt.303.422.
Th' o'erlabour'd *Cyclop* from his Task retires; … 1.TrSt.306.423.
Th' *Æolian* Forge exhausted of its Fires. … 1.TrSt.307.423.
Releas'd th'impetuous Sluices of the Main,— … 1.TrSt.313.423.
Th'exulting Mother stain'd with Filial Blood; … 1.TrSt.323.423.
And sets th'avenging Thunderer in Arms. … 1.TrSt.339.424.
'Tis fix'd; th'irrevocable Doom of *Jove;* … 1.TrSt.413.427.
Now springs aloft, and tow'rs th'Ethereal Height, … 1.TrSt.440.428.
(His *Thebes* abandon'd) thro' th' *Aonian* Groves, … 1.TrSt.444.428.
Burst from th' *Æolian* Caves, and rend the Ground, … 1.TrSt.489.430.
Th' *Inachian* Streams with headlong Fury run, … 1.TrSt.500.431.
Th'intrepid *Theban* hears the bursting Sky, … 1.TrSt.510.431.
He seeks a Shelter from th'inclement Heav'n, … 1.TrSt.560.433.
The King th'accomplish'd Oracle surveys, … 1.TrSt.576.434.
Till Nature quicken'd by th'Inspiring Ray, … 1.TrSt.586.434.
Still as he rises in th'Æthereal Height, … 1.TrSt.642.437.
Th'illustrious Off-spring of the God was born. … 1.TrSt.679.438.
Th'astonish'd Mother when the Rumour came, … 1.TrSt.697.439.
Th' *Inachians* view the Slain with vast Surprize, … 1.TrSt.727.440.
Th' *Inachians* view'd the Slain with vast Surprize, … 1.TrSt.727A.440.
But if th'abandon'd Race of Human-kind … 1.TrSt.767.442.
And from the wondring God th'unwilling Youth retir'd. … 1.TrSt.785.443.
Th'Immortal Victim of thy Mother's Fame; … 1.TrSt.848.445.
Whose Purple Rays th' *Achæmenes* adore; … 1.TrSt.858.446.
To sure Destruction dooms th' aspiring Wall; … 1.TrES.24A.450.
What Aid appear'd t'avert th'approaching War, … 1.TrES.60.451.
And saw where *Teucer* with th' *Ajaces* stood, … 1.TrES.61.451.
Prepar'd to labour in th'unequal Fight; … 1.TrES.94.453.
Fierce *Ajax* first th'advancing Host invades, … 1.TrES.97.453.
Cou'd heave th'unwieldy Burthen from the Plain: … 1.TrES.102.453.
And murm'ring from the Corps th'unwilling Soul retires. … 1.TrES.110.453.
Retir'd reluctant from th'unfinish'd Fight. … 1.TrES.118.454.
They join, they thicken, and th'Assault renew; … 1.TrES.152.455.
Unmov'd, th'embody'd *Greeks* their Fury dare, … 1.TrES.153.455.
Not two strong Men th'enormous Weight cou'd raise, … 1.TrES.185.456.
Th'unwieldy Rock, the Labour of a God. … 1.TrES.190.456.
And when th'ascending Soul has wing'd her Flight, … 1.TrES.247.459.
Th'incumber'd Chariot from the dying Steed: … 1.TrES.278.460.
Th'insulting Victor with Disdain bestrode … 1.TrES.316.461.
His Manly Members in th'Immortal Vest, … 1.TrES.341.462.
Th'emerging Hills and Rocks of *Ithaca.* … 1.TrUl.24A.466.
For still th'Opprest are his peculiar Care: … 1.TrUl.91.469.
His ready Tale th'inventive Hero told. … 1.TrUl.139.470.
While in th'Embrace of pleasing Sleep I lay, … 1.TrUl.155.471.
Skill'd in th'illustrious Labours of the Loom. … 1.TrUl.165.471.
But by th'Almighty Author of thy Race, … 1.TrUl.201.472.
Preserv'd the *Jews,* and slew th' *Assyrian* Foe: … 2.ChJM.74.18.
Twice-marry'd Dames are Mistresses o' th' Trade: … 2.ChJM.110.20.
Th'assuming Wit, who deems himself so wise … 2.ChJM.162.22.
But, by th' Immortal Pow'rs, I feel the Pain, … 2.ChJM.204.24.
Let none oppose th'Election, since on this … 2.ChJM.256.27.
Forth came the Priest, and bade th'obedient Wife … 2.ChJM.311.29.
Th' entrancing Raptures of th' approaching Night; … 2.ChJM.350.31.
Th' entrancing Raptures of th' approaching Night; … 2.ChJM.350.31.
Forsook th' *Horizon,* and roll'd down the Light; … 2.ChJM.368.32.
But first thought fit th' Assistance to receive, … 2.ChJM.375.32.
Yet hoping Time th'Occasion might betray, … 2.ChJM.396.34.
Th'obliging Dames obey'd with one Consent; … 2.ChJM.410.34.
Receiv'd th'Impressions of the Love-sick Squire, … 2.ChJM.432.35.
She took th'Impressions of the Love-sick Squire, … 2.ChJM.432A.35.
And gave th'Impression to the trusty Squire. … 2.ChJM.511.40.
Thither th'obsequious Squire address'd his Pace, … 2.ChJM.605.44.
For, by th'Immortal Pow'rs, it *seem'd* too plain— … 2.ChJM.779.52.
Wrapt in th' envenom'd Shirt, and set on Fire. … 2.ChWB.382.76.

TH' (CONTINUED)

When Merchants from th' *Exchange* return in Peace, … 2.RL*A*1.87.129.
And strike to Dust th'aspiring Tow'rs of *Troy;* … 2.RL*A*1.138.131.
Th'inferior Priestess, at her Altar's side, … 2.RL1.127.155.
Not with more Glories, in th' Etherial Plain, … 2.RL2.1.159.
Th' Adventrous *Baron* the bright Locks admir'd, … 2.RL2.29.161.
Th'impending Woe sate heavy on his Breast. … 2.RL2.54.163.
By Laws Eternal, to th' Aerial Kind. … 2.RL2.76.164.
Nor let th' imprison'd Essences exhale, … 2.RL2.94.165.
We trust th'important Charge, the *Petticoat:* … 2.RL2.118.167.
In various Talk th' instructive hours they past, … 2.RL3.11.169.
The Merchant from th' *Exchange* returns in Peace, … 2.RL3.23.170.
Soon as she spreads her Hand, th' Aerial Guard … 2.RL3.31.171.
Th' expressive Emblem of their softer Pow'r; … 2.RL3.40.171.
Th' Imperial Consort of the Crown of *Spades.* … 2.RL3.68.173.
Th' embroider'd *King* who shows but half his Face, … 2.RL3.76.173.
She sees, and trembles at th' approaching Ill, … 2.RL3.91.174.
He watch'd th' Ideas rising in her Mind, … 2.RL3.142.178.
And Screams of Horror rend th' affrighted Skies. … 2.RL3.156.180.
And strike to Dust th' Imperial Tow'rs of *Troy;* … 2.RL3.174.182.
Who give th' *Hysteric* or *Poetic* Fit, … 2.RL4.60.189.
And shall this Prize, th' inestimable Prize, … 2.RL4.113.193.
All side in Parties, and begin th' Attack; … 2.RL5.39.202.
Th' expiring Swan, and as he sings he dies. … 2.RL5.66.206.
Nor fear'd the Chief th'unequal Fight to try, … 2.RL5.77.206.
Now meet thy Fate, th'incens'd Virago cry'd, … 2.RL5.87A.207.
And hence th' Egregious Wizard shall foredoom … 2.RL5.139.211.
But felt th'Approaches of too warm a Sun; … 2.TemF.42.256.
And on th' impassive Ice the Lightnings play: … 2.TemF.56.256.
Till the bright Mountains prop th' incumbent Sky: … 2.TemF.58.256.
Rests on his Club, and holds th' *Hesperian* Spoil. … 2.TemF.82.259.
There *Ninus* shone, who spread th' *Assyrian* Fame, … 2.TemF.95.260.
These stop'd the Moon, and call'd th' unbody'd Shades … 2.TemF.101.260.
And seem'd to labour with th' inspiring God. … 2.TemF.213.272.
Here happy *Horace* tun'd th' *Ausonian* Lyre … 2.TemF.222.273.
Less fragrant Scents th' unfolding Rose exhales, … 2.TemF.316.279.
And give each Deed th' exact intrinsic Worth. … 2.TemF.323.279.
Let fuller Notes th' applauding World amaze, … 2.TemF.326.279.
But safe in Desarts from th' Applause of Men, … 2.TemF.360.281.
To farthest Shores th' Ambrosial Spirit flies, … 2.TemF.376.281.
And beg to make th' immortal Treasons known. … 2.TemF.413.283.
Th' Estate which Wits inherit after Death! … 2.TemF.506.288.
There stern religion quench'd th' unwilling flame, … 2.ElAb.39.322.
Some emanation of th' all-beauteous Mind. … 2.ElAb.62.324.
And love th' offender, yet detest th' offence? … 2.ElAb.192.335.
And love th' offender, yet detest th' offence? … 2.ElAb.192.335.
For her th' unfading rose of *Eden* blooms, … 2.ElAb.217.337.
To light the dead, and warm th' unfruitful urn. … 2.ElAb.262.341.
Of ORDER, sins against th' Eternal Cause. … 3.EOM1.130.31.
"Th' exceptions few; some change since all began, … 3.EOM1.147.33.
Say what th' advantage of so fine an Eye … 3.EOM1.195B.39.
Yet never pass th' insuperable line! … 3.EOM1.228.44.
Alike essential to th' amazing whole; … 3.EOM1.248.45.
Great in the earth, as in th' æthereal frame, … 3.EOM1.270.48.
Go, soar with Plato to th' empyreal sphere, … 3.EOM2.23.57.
Expunge the whole, or lop th'excrescent parts … 3.EOM2.49.61.
Th' Eternal Art educing good from ill, … 3.EOM2.175.76.
Envy, to which th'ignoble mind's a slave, … 3.EOM2.191.78.
But where th'Extreme of Vice, was ne'er agreed: … 3.EOM2.221.82.
Few in th'extreme, but all in the degree; … 3.EOM2.232.83.
That disappoints th'effect of ev'ry vice: … 3.EOM2.240.84.
Th'extensive blessing of his luxury. … 3.EOM3.62.98.
Say, where full Instinct is th'unerring guide, … 3.EOM3.83.100.
Draw forth the monsters of th'abyss profound, … 3.EOM3.221.115.
Or fetch th'aerial eagle to the ground. … 3.EOM3.222.115.
LOVE all the faith, and all th'allegiance then; … 3.EOM3.235.116.
Th' enormous faith of many made for one; … 3.EOM3.242.117.
Then sacred seem'd th'etherial vault no more; … 3.EOM3.263.119.
Th'according music of a well-mix'd State. … 3.EOM3.294.122.
The strength he gains is from th'embrace he gives. … 3.EOM3.312.126.
That something still which prompts th'eternal sigh, … 3.EOM4.3.128.
If while th'Unhappy hope, the Happy fear … 3.EOM4.70A.135.
Count all th'advantage prosp'rous Vice attains, … 3.EOM4.89.136.
Think we, like some weak Prince, th'Eternal Cause, … 3.EOM4.121.139.
Pursues that Chain which links th'immense design, … 3.EOM4.333.161.
Wide and more wide, th'o'erflowings of the mind … 3.EOM4.369.164.
Who but detests th'Endearments of *Courtine* … 3.Ep1.120A.24.
We grow more partial for th' observer's sake; … 3.Ep1.12.16.
Would from th' apparent What conclude the Why, … 3.Ep1.52.19.
In vain th' observer eyes the builder's toil, … 3.Ep1.220.34.
To Heirs unknown descends th' unnumber'd store … 3.Ep2.149A.62.
Th' Address, the Delicacy—stoops at once, … 3.Ep2.85.57.
To Heirs unknown descends th' unguarded store … 3.Ep2.149.62.
Th' exactest traits of Body or of Mind, … 3.Ep2.191.65.
No grace of Heav'n or token of th' Elect; … 3.Ep3.18.84.
With all th' embroid'ry plaister'd at thy tail? … 3.Ep3.92.97.
And one fate buries in th' Asturian Mines. … 3.Ep3.134.104.
And gives th' eternal wheels to know their rounds. … 3.Ep3.170.107.
And turn th' unwilling steeds another way: … 3.Ep3.194.109.
That secret rare, between th' extremes to move … 3.Ep3.227.111.
To ease th' oppress'd, and raise the sinking heart? … 3.Ep3.244.113.
Or helps th' ambitious Hill the heav'n to scale, … 3.Ep4.59.142.
Now breaks or now directs, th' intending Lines; … 3.Ep4.63.143.
Till Kings call forth th' Idea's of your mind, … 3.Ep4.195.155.
Till Kings call forth th' Idea's of thy mind, … 3.Ep4.195A.155.
And He, whose Lightning pierc'd th' *Iberian* Lines, … 4.HS1.129.17.
Such was the Wight: Th' apparel on his back … 4.JD4.38.29.
Nay troth, th' *Apostles,* (tho' perhaps too rough) … 4.JD4.76.31.
And cheats th'unknowing Widow, and the Poor? … 4.JD4.141.37.
I fear'd th'Infection slide from him to me, … 4.JD4.170.39.
I felt th'Infection slide from him to me, … 4.JD4.170A.39.
There sober Thought pursu'd th'amusing theme … 4.JD4.188.41.
Not *Dante* dreaming all th'Infernal State, … 4.JD4.192.43.
What push'd poor *Ellis* on th' Imperial Whore? … 4.HAdv.81.83.
They'l praise her *Elbow, Heel,* or *Tip o' th' Ear.* … 4.HAdv.123.85.
Th' imputed Trash, and Dulness not his own; … 4.Arbu.351.121.

TH' (CONTINUED)

Th' impatient Weapon whizzes on the Wing, ... Il.4.156.228.
The watchful Mother wafts th' envenom'd Fly. ... Il.4.163.228.
I see th' Eternal all his Fury shed, ... Il.4.202.231.
May stanch th' Effusion and extract the Dart. ... Il.4.229.232.
He dreads th' impending Storm, and drives his Flock ... Il.4.320.236.
Such, and so thick, th' embattel'd Squadrons stood, ... Il.4.322.236.
Thus to th' experienc'd Prince *Atrides* cry'd; ... Il.4.368.238.
To watch the Motion, dubious of th' Event. ... Il.4.387.239.
Take back th' unjust Reproach! Behold we stand ... Il.4.404.240.
Him, the bold * Leader of th' *Abantian* Throng ... Il.4.530.246.
But while he strove to tug th' inserted Dart, ... Il.4.532.246.
Th' *Ætolian* Warrior tugg'd his weighty Spear: ... Il.4.615.250.
And one the Leader of th' *Epeian* Race; ... Il.4.625.250.
Th' unweary'd Blaze incessant Streams supplies, ... Il.5.7.266.
Like the red Star that fires th' Autumnal Skies, ... Il.5.8.266.
Her Words allay th' impetuous Warrior's Heat, ... Il.5.45.268.
These see thou shun, thro' all th' embattled Plain, ... Il.5.166.275.
Not two strong Men th' enormous Weight could raise, ... Il.5.371.284.
Where to the Hip th' inserted Thigh unites, ... Il.5.375.285.
She bore *Anchises* in th' *Idæan* Grove, ... Il.5.386.285.
Th' Ambrosial Veil which all the Graces wove; ... Il.5.418.287.
But with the Gods (th' immortal Gods) engage. ... Il.5.470.290.
Th' imperial Partner of the heav'nly Reign; ... Il.5.482.291.
Who bathe in Blood, and shake th' embattel'd Wall! ... Il.5.554.295.
So when th' embattel'd Clouds in dark Array ... Il.5.641.298.
Silver the Beam, th' extended Yoke was Gold, ... Il.5.900.309.
And golden Reins th' immortal Coursers hold. ... Il.5.901.309.
The Goddess thus th' imperial Car ascends; ... Il.5.922.310.
Swift at the Scourge th' Ethereal Coursers fly, ... Il.5.926.310.
Involve in Clouds th' Eternal Gates of Day, ... Il.5.932.311.
And drive from Fight th' impetuous Homicide? ... Il.5.951.312.
Lash'd her white Steeds along th' Aerial Way. ... Il.5.957.312.
Between th' extended Earth and starry Poles. ... Il.5.959.312.
At ev'ry Leap th' Immortal Coursers bound. ... Il.5.963.312.
While near *Tydides* stood th' *Athenian* Maid: ... Il.5.987.314.
The strongest Warrior of th' *Ætolian* Train; ... Il.5.1039.316.
From *Mars* his Arm th' enormous Weapon fled: ... Il.5.1045.316.
Thus pour'd his Plaints before th' immortal Throne. ... Il.5.1067.317.
Against th' Immortals lifts his raging Hand: ... Il.5.1083.318.
She gives th' Example, and her Son pursues. ... Il.5.1103.320.
Yet long th' inflicted Pangs thou shalt not mourn, ... Il.5.1104.320.
And heal'd th' immortal Flesh, and clos'd the Wound. ... Il.5.1111.320.
Such, and so soon, th' Ætherial Texture join'd. ... Il.5.1115.321.
Now Heav'n forsakes the Fight: Th' Immortals yield ... Il.6.1.322.
And hew'd th' enormous Giant to the Ground; ... Il.6.10.323.
That hew'd th' enormous Giant to the Ground; ... Il.6.10A.323.
Ye gen'rous Chiefs! on whom th' Immortals lay ... Il.6.95.328.
Direct the Queen to lead th' assembled Train ... Il.6.109.329.
Where Fame is reap'd amid th' embattel'd Field; ... Il.6.154.333.
Nor fail'd the Crime th' Immortals Wrath to move, ... Il.6.169.334.
(Th' Immortals blest with endless Ease above) ... Il.6.170.334.
Crown'd with *Sarpedon's* Birth th' Embrace of *Jove)* ... Il.6.244.338.
Wide o'er th' *Aleian* Field he chose to stray, ... Il.6.247.338.
And seek the Gods, t'avert th' impending Woe. ... Il.6.303.341.
Com'st thou to supplicate th' Almighty Pow'r, ... Il.6.320.342.
Not to the Court (reply'd th' Attendant Train) ... Il.6.478.350.
Thou, from this Tow'r defend th' important Post; ... Il.6.552.354.
My Soul impells me to th' embattel'd Plains; ... Il.6.567.354.
Thus having spoke, th' illustrious Chief of *Troy* ... Il.6.594.355.
O Thou! whose Glory fills th' Ætherial Throne, ... Il.6.604.356.
Jove bids at length th' expected Gales arise; ... Il.7.7.363.
The Squadrons part; th' expecting *Trojans* stand. ... Il.7.62.366.
Th' *Athenian* Maid, and glorious God of Day, ... Il.7.65.366.
The mightiest Warrior of th' *Achaian* Name ... Il.7.135.370.
Oh would to tell th' immortal Pow'rs above, ... Il.7.159.372.
And with th' *Arcadian* Spears my Prowess try'd, ... Il.7.165.372.
The Flow'r of *Greece,* th' Examples of our Host, ... Il.7.192.373.
Surveys th' Inscription with rejoicing Eyes, ... Il.7.225.375.
Then shall our Herald to th' *Atrides* sent, ... Il.7.448.386.
Th' admiring Chiefs, and all the *Grecian* Name, ... Il.7.480.388.
To wait th' Event, the Herald bent his way. ... Il.7.491.388.
Th' Almighty Thund'rer with a Frown replies, ... Il.7.542.391.
While the deep Thunder shook th' Aerial Hall. ... Il.7.575.393.
As deep beneath th' Infernal Centre hurl'd, ... Il.8.19.396.
As from that Centre to th' Æthereal World. ... Il.8.20.396.
And know, th' Almighty is the God of Gods. ... Il.8.22.396.
Join all, and try th' Omnipotence of *Jove:* ... Il.8.24.396.
Th' Almighty spoke, nor durst the Pow'rs reply, ... Il.8.35.397.
Rapt by th' Æthereal Steeds the Chariot roll'd; ... Il.8.51.398.
Between th' extended Earth and starry Sky. ... Il.8.56.398.
Blue ambient Mists th' immortal Steeds embrac'd; ... Il.8.63.398.
Nor He, the King of Men, th' Alarm sustain'd; ... Il.8.101.402.
Th' incumber'd Chariot from the dying Steed, ... Il.8.110.403.
Great Perils, Father! wait th' unequal Fight; ... Il.8.129.404.
Thus, turning, warn'd th' intrepid *Diomed.* ... Il.8.168.406.
Th' *Atridæ* first, th' *Ajaces* next succeed: ... Il.8.316.412.
Th' *Atridæ* first, th' *Ajaces* next succeed: ... Il.8.316.412.
Troy yet found Grace before th' *Olympian* Sire, ... Il.8.401.416.
Th' avenging Bolt, and shake the sable Shield! ... Il.8.424.417.
So spoke th' imperial Regent of the Skies; ... Il.8.433.418.
Close, or unfold, th' Eternal Gates of Day; ... Il.8.482.420.
Th' avenging Bolt, and shake the dreadful Shield! ... Il.8.527.421.
From *Ida's* Summits to th' *Olympian* Height. ... Il.8.543.422.
Th' Eternal Thunderer, state thron'd in Gold. ... Il.8.551.422.
Trembling afar th' offending Pow'rs appear'd, ... Il.8.554.423.
Cut off, and exil'd from th' Æthereal Race. ... Il.8.569.423.
Shall see th' Almighty Thunderer in Arms. ... Il.8.587.424.
Th' assembled Chiefs, descending on the Ground, ... Il.8.613.425.
Th' insidious Foe the naked Town invade. ... Il.8.650.426.
Ungrateful Off'ring to th' immortal Pow'rs, ... Il.8.681.427.
Heaps Waves on Waves, and bids th' *Ægean* roar; ... Il.9.8.431.
Nor from a Friend th' unkind Reproach appear'd, ... Il.9.49.434.
Go thou inglorious! from th' embattel'd Plain; ... Il.9.61.434.
Age bids me speak; nor shall th' Advice I bring ... Il.9.85.436.
Th' immortal Deeds of Heroes and of Kings. ... Il.9.250.445.

TH' (CONTINUED)

The first fat Off'rings, to th' Immortals due, ... Il.9.287.448.
Proud *Hector,* now, th' unequal Fight demands, ... Il.9.404.452.
But now th' unfruitful Glories charm no more. ... Il.9.417.453.
And with th' untasted Food supplies her Care: ... Il.9.427.453.
What to these Shores th' assembled Nations draws, ... Il.9.446.454.
The World's great Empress on th' *Ægyptian* Plain, ... Il.9.501.458.
He sent thee early to th' *Achaian* Host; ... Il.9.567.461.
Once fought th' *Ætolian* and *Curetian* Bands; ... Il.9.654.467.
Th' afflicted Pair, their Sorrows to proclaim, ... Il.9.675.468.
Althæa's Hate th' unhappy Warrior drew, ... Il.9.681.468.
Th' *Ætolians,* long disdain'd, now took their turn, ... Il.9.707.469.
Just there, th' impetuous Homicide shall stand, ... Il.9.769.472.
And now th' elected Chiefs whom *Greece* had sent, ... Il.9.786.472.
The Peers and Leaders of th' *Achaian* Bands ... Il.9.789.472.
Anxious he sorrows for th' endanger'd Host. ... Il.10.18.2.
What yet remains to save th' afflicted State. ... Il.10.26.3.
Th' unhappy Gen'ral of the *Grecian* Bands; ... Il.10.97.7.
And the wise Counsels of th' eternal Mind? ... Il.10.117.7.
The Warrior rouz'd, and to th' Entrenchments led. ... Il.10.206.10.
Th' unweary'd Watch their list'ning Leaders keep, ... Il.10.209.11.
Each Step of passing Feet increas'd th' Affright; ... Il.10.221.11.
The Trenches past, th' assembl'd Kings around ... Il.10.231.12.
The Stars shine fainter on th' Ætherial Plains, ... Il.10.297.15.
Th' avenging Bolt, and shake the dreadful Shield. ... Il.10.328.17.
Thro' the black Horrors of th' ensanguin'd Plain ... Il.10.355.18.
Th' assembled Peers their lofty Chief inclos'd; ... Il.10.359.19.
Th' immortal Coursers, and the glitt'ring Car, ... Il.10.381.20.
And him alone th' immortal Steeds adorn. ... Il.10.392.21.
When, on the hollow way, th' approaching Tread ... Il.10.403.21.
When now few Furrows part th' approaching Ploughs. ... Il.10.422.22.
Safe in their Cares, th' auxiliar Forces sleep, ... Il.10.491.25.
The Wolf's grey Hide, th' unbended Bow and Spear; ... Il.10.529.26.
To send more Heroes to th' infernal Shade, ... Il.10.589.28.
Old *Nestor* first perceiv'd th' approaching Sound, ... Il.10.624.29.
Till in three Heads th' embroider'd Monster ends. ... Il.11.52.36.
And fair Proportion match'd th' etherial Race. ... Il.11.80.38.
Discord alone, of all th' immortal Train, ... Il.11.101.39.
Rang'd in bright Order on th' *Olympian* Hill; ... Il.11.104.39.
Th' eternal Monarch, on his awful Throne, ... Il.11.108.39.
Where the wild Figs th' adjoining Summit crown, ... Il.11.219.45.
But *Jove* descending shook th' *Idæan* Hills, ... Il.11.237.46.
Th' unkindled Light'ning in his Hand he took, ... Il.11.239.46.
Stretch'd in the Dust th' unhappy Warrior lies, ... Il.11.309.48.
And wing'd an Arrow at th' unwary Foe; ... Il.11.478.55.
Then sow'rly slow th' indignant Beast retires. ... Il.11.679.65.
When this bold Arm th' *Epeian* Pow'rs oppress'd, ... Il.11.817.72.
Th' *Epeians* saw, they trembled, and they fled. ... Il.11.879.75.
Where o'er the Vales th' *Olenian* Rocks arose; ... Il.11.889.75.
How shall he grieve, when to th' eternal Shade ... Il.11.900.75.
Th' Event of Things the Gods alone can view. ... Il.11.973.78.
With Gods averse th' ill-fated Works arose; ... Il.12.6.81.
Th' Advice of wise *Polydamas* obey'd; ... Il.12.124.85.
Forth from the Portals rush'd th' intrepid Pair, ... Il.12.161.87.
They strike th' Assailants, and infix their Stings; ... Il.12.192.88.
The leading Sign, th' irrevocable Nod, ... Il.12.275.91.
To sure Destruction dooms th' aspiring Wall; ... Il.12.368.94.
What Aid appear'd t' avert th' approaching War, ... Il.12.404.96.
And saw where *Teucer* with th' *Ajaces* stood, ... Il.12.405.96.
Prepar'd to labour in th' unequal Fight; ... Il.12.448.97.
Fierce *Ajax* first th' advancing Host invades, ... Il.12.451.98.
Could heave th' unwieldy Burthen from the Plain. ... Il.12.456.98.
Retir'd reluctant from th' unfinish'd Fight. ... Il.12.472.98.
They join, they thicken, and th' Assault renew; ... Il.12.506.100.
Unmov'd th' embody'd *Greeks* their Fury dare, ... Il.12.507.100.
Not two strong Men th' enormous Weight could raise, ... Il.12.539.101.
Th' unweildy Rock, the Labour of a God. ... Il.12.544.101.
And felt the Footsteps of th' immortal God. ... Il.13.31.105.
Th' enormous Monsters, rolling o'er the Deep, ... Il.13.43.107.
Th' impatient *Trojans,* in a gloomy Throng, ... Il.13.61.107.
But most th' *Ajaces,* adding Fire to Fire. ... Il.13.72.108.
Th' inspiring God, *Oïleus'* active Son ... Il.13.97.109.
Trembling before th' impending Storm they lie, ... Il.13.121.110.
And *Merion* next, th' impulsive Fury found; ... Il.13.128.110.
For lo! the fated Time, th' appointed Shore; ... Il.13.165.112.
Between the Leaders of th' *Athenian* Line, ... Il.13.261.117.
Where's now th' imperious Vaunt, the daring Boast ... Il.13.289.119.
Fierce on the Foe th' impetuous Hero drove; ... Il.13.317.120.
Or terrifies th' offending World with Wars: ... Il.13.320.120.
And glows with Prospects of th' approaching Day. ... Il.13.332.121.
Leads forth th' embattel'd Sons of *Crete* to War; ... Il.13.334.121.
That shed a Lustre round th' illumin'd Wall. ... Il.13.340.122.
Nor trust the Dart, or aim th' uncertain Spear, ... Il.13.342.122.
Whom *Ajax* fells not on th' ensanguin'd Ground. ... Il.13.413.126.
He said; and *Merion* to th' appointed Place, ... Il.13.418.126.
Proud of himself, and of th' imagin'd Bride, ... Il.13.465.128.
Haste, and revenge it on th' insulting Foe. ... Il.13.589.134.
Th' assisting Forces of his native Bands: ... Il.13.617.135.
In order follow all th' embody'd Train; ... Il.13.620.135.
On golden Clouds th' immortal Synod sate; ... Il.13.662.137.
Th' exulting Victor leaping where he lay, ... Il.13.696.138.
And blunts the Javelin of th' eluded Foe. ... Il.13.713.138.
Atrides, watchful of th' unwary Foe, ... Il.13.745.140.
Without th' Assistance, or the Fear of *Jove.* ... Il.13.784.142.
And Conquest hovers o'er th' *Achaian* Bands: ... Il.13.848.146.
(Their Naval Station where th' *Ajaces* keep, ... Il.13.854.146.
Locrians and *Pthians,* and th' *Epæan* Force; ... Il.13.861.146.
Meges the strong th' *Epeian* Bands controul'd, ... Il.13.865.147.
Tir'd with th' incessant Slaughters of the Fight. ... Il.13.888.147.
Opprobrious, thus, th' impatient Chief reprov'd. ... Il.13.964.151.
The godlike Father, and th' intrepid Son? ... Il.13.968.151.
Black Fate hangs o'er thee from th' avenging Gods, ... Il.13.971.151.
Th' afflicted Deeps, tumultuous, mix and roar; ... Il.13.1003.152.
His startled Ears th' encreasing Cries attend; ... Il.14.3.156.
While I th' Adventures of the Day explore. ... Il.14.12.157.
While yet th' expected Tempest hangs on high, ... Il.14.23.158.

TH' (CONTINUED)

O Grace and Glory of th' *Achaian* Name! ...... Il.14.49.160.
Not he that thunders from th' aerial Bow'r, ... Il.14.61.160.
Thro' Heav'n, thro' Earth, and all th' aerial Way; ...... Il.14.200.169.
Forth from the Dome th' Imperial Goddess moves, ... Il.14.217.171.
That roar thro' Hell, and bind th' invoking Gods: ...... Il.14.306.177.
The Queen assents, and from th' infernal Bow'rs ...... Il.14.313.178.
And those who rule th' inviolable Floods, ... Il.14.315.178.
Why comes my Goddess from th' æthereal Sky, ... Il.14.339.179.
O'er Earth and Seas, and thro' th' aerial way, ... Il.14.350.179.
To ask Consent, I leave th' *Olympian* Bow'r; ...... Il.14.352.179.
And whose broad Eye th' extended Earth surveys. ...... Il.14.392.181.
Now, *Neptune!* now, the' important Hour employ, ... Il.14.411.183.
Clad in his Might th' Earth-shaking Pow'r appears; ...... Il.14.447.185.
Less loud the Winds, that from th' *Æolian* Hall ...... Il.14.459.186.
And own the Terrors of th' Almighty Hand! ...... Il.14.486.187.
Thou first, great *Ajax!* on th' ensanguin'd Plain ...... Il.14.605.191.
O thou, still adverse to th' eternal Will, ... Il.15.17.194.
Our Pow'r immense, and brave th' Almighty Hand? ...... Il.15.22.194.
Headlong I hurl'd them from th' *Olympian* Hall, ... Il.15.27.195.
Nor pull th' unwilling Vengeance on thy Head, ... Il.15.36.195.
(Th' immortal Father with a Smile replies!) ...... Il.15.54.196.
To yon' bright Synod on th' *Olympian* Hill; ...... Il.15.58.196.
Let her descend, and from th' embattel'd Plain ...... Il.15.61.196.
I gave, and seal'd it with th' Almighty Nod, ... Il.15.81.199.
The trembling Queen (th' Almighty Order giv'n) ...... Il.15.84.199.
Swift from th' *Idæan* Summit shot to Heav'n. ...... Il.15.85.199.
But *Jove* shall thunder thro' th' Ethereal Dome, ... Il.15.104.200.
And damp th' eternal Banquets of the Skies. ...... Il.15.107.200.
Struck for th' immortal Race with timely Fear, ... Il.15.142.202.
Thus, to th' impetuous Homicide she said. ...... Il.15.145.202.
And one vast Ruin whelm th' *Olympian* State. ...... Il.15.155.202.
There sate th' Eternal; He, whose Nod controuls ...... Il.15.172.203.
Th' Almighty spoke; the Goddess wing'd her Flight ...... Il.15.190.203.
To sacred *Ilion* from th' *Idæan* Height. ...... Il.15.191.204.
He breaks his Faith with half th' ethereal Race; ...... Il.15.239.206.
Howe'er th' Offence by other Gods be past, ... Il.15.242.206.
Let *Ilion* conquer, till th' *Achaian* Train ...... Il.15.262.207.
As *Phœbus* shooting from th' *Idæan* Brow, ... Il.15.268.207.
Thoas, the bravest of th' *Ætolian* Force: ...... Il.15.319.209.
They gain th' impervious Rock and safe retreat ...... Il.15.310A.209.
Vulcan to *Jove* th' immortal Gift consign'd, ... Il.15.352.210.
This sprung from *Phelus,* and th' *Athenians* led; ...... Il.15.377.211.
Push'd at the Bank: Down sunk th' enormous Mound: ...... Il.15.407.213.
Thus pray'd the Sage: Th' Eternal gave consent, ... Il.15.436.214.
Presumptuous *Troy* mistook th' accepting Sign, ... Il.15.438.214.
Th' embody'd *Greeks* the fierce Attack sustain, ... Il.15.470.215.
Force, to the Fleet and Tents, th' impervious way. ...... Il.15.473.215.
Thund'ring he falls, and drops th' extinguish'd Fires. ...... Il.15.491.216.
Drove thro' the thickest of th' embattel'd Plains ...... Il.15.524.217.
Th' all-wise Disposer of the Fates of Men, ... Il.15.541.217.
Th' astonish'd Archer to great *Ajax* cries; ...... Il.15.548.217.
The fierce Commander of th' *Epeian* Band. ...... Il.15.615.220.
On the fall'n Chief th' invading *Trojan* prest, ... Il.15.782.226.
Th' unhappy Hero; fled, or shar'd his Fate. ...... Il.15.785.226.
Now manly Shame forbids th' inglorious Flight; ...... Il.15.790.226.
The first that touch'd th' unhappy *Trojan* Shore: ...... Il.15.857.229.
So warr'd both Armies on th' ensanguin'd Shore, ... Il.16.1.233.
Had not th' injurious King our Friendship lost, ... Il.16.97.239.
And from thy Deeds expects, th' *Achaian* Host ...... Il.16.110.240.
Oh! would to all th' immortal Pow'rs above, ... Il.16.122.241.
And only we destroy th' accursed Town! ...... Il.16.127.242.
A mortal Courser match'd th' immortal Race. ...... Il.16.189.246.
No Hand so sure of all th' *Emathian* Line, ... Il.16.232.248.
And all th' unmeasur'd *Æther* flames with Light. ...... Il.16.361.257.
A Troop of Wolves th' unguarded Charge survey, ... Il.16.422.259.
Dark o'er the Fields th' ascending Vapour flies, ... Il.16.436.259.
Th' affrighted Steeds, their dying Lords cast down, ... Il.16.452.260.
From Bank to Bank th' immortal Coursers flew, ... Il.16.459.260.
(When guilty Mortals break th' eternal Laws, ... Il.16.468.261.
Th' impetuous Torrents from their Hills obey, ... Il.16.472.261.
And when th' ascending Soul has wing'd her flight, ... Il.16.550.265.
His sudden Fall th' entangled Harness broke; ...... Il.16.578.267.
Th' incumber'd Chariot from the dying Steed: ...... Il.16.583.267.
Th' insulting Victor with Disdain bestrode ...... Il.16.621.268.
And owns th' Assistance of immortal Hands. ...... Il.16.652.269.
Th' *Achaians* sorrow for their Hero slain; ...... Il.16.729.272.
His manly Members in th' immortal Vest; ...... Il.16.828.275.
So spoke th' inspiring God; then took his flight, ... Il.16.885.277.
Far from his Rage th' immortal Coursers drove; ...... Il.16.1048.283.
Th' immortal Coursers were the Gift of *Jove.* ...... Il.16.1049.283.
So from the Fold th' unwilling Lion parts, ... Il.17.117.292.
And doom'd to *Trojan* Dogs th' unhappy Dead; ...... Il.17.138.293.
Now blazing in th' immortal Arms he stands, ... Il.17.219.296.
And force th' unwilling God to ruin *Troy.* ...... Il.17.387.302.
The Sun, the Moon, and all th' Etherial Host ...... Il.17.423.303.
Unclouded there, th' Aerial Azure spread, ... Il.17.428.304.
He said; and breathing in th' immortal Horse ...... Il.17.524.308.
Implores th' Eternal, and collects his Might. ...... Il.17.567.310.
And calls th' *Ajaces* from the warring Croud, ... Il.17.575.311.
Is only mine: th' Event belongs to *Jove.* ...... Il.17.583.311.
The drooping Cattel dread th' impending Skies, ... Il.17.620.312.
But now th' Eternal shook his sable Shield, ... Il.17.668.314.
Th' affrighted Hills from their Foundations nod, ... Il.17.672.314.
But erring from its Aim, th' impetuous Spear ...... Il.17.689.314.
Sow'r he departs, and quits th' untasted Prey. ...... Il.17.748.317.
How *Ilion* triumphs, and th' *Achaians* mourn. ...... Il.17.774.318.
Th' enormous Timber lumbring down the Hill. ...... Il.17.836.321.
And wretched I, th' unwilling Messenger! ...... Il.18.22.324.
How more than wretched in th' immortal State! ...... Il.18.72.326.
Th' immortal Mother, standing close beside ...... Il.18.91.327.
'Tis not in Fate th' Alternate now to give; ...... Il.18.117.328.
As oft' th' *Ajaces* his Assault sustain; ...... Il.18.195.331.
And all the Glories of th' extended Day; ...... Il.18.202.331.
Who sends thee, Goddess! from th' Etherial Skies? ...... Il.18.219.332.
Th' immortal Empress of the Realms above; ...... Il.18.222.332.

TH' (CONTINUED)

With shrilling Clangor sounds th' Alarm of War; ...... Il.18.260.335.
In Ocean's Waves th' unwilling Light of Day ...... Il.18.284.335.
And from their Labours eas'd th' *Achaian* Band. ...... Il.18.286.335.
What Words are these (th' Imperial Dame replies, ... Il.18.423.341.
Before, deep fix'd, th' eternal Anvils stand; ...... Il.18.547.348.
Then first he form'd th' immense and solid *Shield;* ...... Il.18.551.348.
Th' unweary'd Sun, the Moon compleatly round; ...... Il.18.559.349.
Still shines exalted on th' ætherial Plain, ... Il.18.565.349.
Th' appointed Heralds still the noisy Bands, ... Il.18.583.351.
Alternate, each th' attesting Scepter took, ... Il.18.587.351.
And Pales of glitt'ring Tin th' Enclosure grace. ...... Il.18.656.355.
The purple Product of th' Autumnal Year. ...... Il.18.660.355.
She, as a Falcon cuts th' Aerial way, ... Il.18.710.357.
Th' immortal Arms the Goddess-Mother bears ...... Il.19.5.371.
On all th' immortal Artist had design'd. ...... Il.19.24.372.
To Gods and Goddesses th' unruly Joy ...... Il.19.105.376.
The dread, th' irrevocable Oath he swore, ... Il.19.127.377.
Th' immortal Seats should ne'er behold her more; ...... Il.19.128.377.
His Hands uplifted to th' attesting Skies, ... Il.19.263.383.
Once spread th' inviting Banquet in our Tents; ...... Il.19.336.386.
Hast spread th' inviting Banquet in our Tents; ...... Il.19.336A.386.
Forg'd on th' Eternal Anvils of the God. ...... Il.19.393.388.
O'erlooks th' embattled Host, and hopes the bloody Day. ...... Il.19.397.388.
Th' immortal Coursers, and the radiant Car, ... Il.19.427.389.
Not brighter, *Phœbus* in th' Æthereal Way, ... Il.19.436.389.
His fate-ful Voice. Th' intrepid Chief reply'd ...... Il.19.465.391.
Th' infernal Monarch rear'd his horrid Head, ... Il.20.84.397.
Such War th' Immortals wage: Such Horrors rend ...... Il.20.89.397.
Th' Immortals guard him thro' the dreadful Plain, ... Il.20.130.399.
Thro' the thick Troops th' embolden'd Hero prest: ...... Il.20.143.400.
But if th' Armipotent, or God of Light, ... Il.20.166.400.
The Grace and Glory of th' Ambrosial Feast. ...... Il.20.281.406.
Saw, e'er it fell, th' immeasurable Spear. ...... Il.20.313.407.
Secur'd the Temper of th' Ætherial Arms. ...... Il.20.315.407.
At length are odious to th' all-seeing Mind; ...... Il.20.354.408.
Th' Imperial Goddess with the radiant Eyes. ...... Il.20.358.410.
Are thine no more—Th' insulting Hero said, ... Il.20.453.413.
Th' impatient Steel with full-descending Sway ...... Il.20.459.413.
Thus sadly slain, th' unhappy *Polydore;* ...... Il.20.486.414.
Then *Dryops* tumbled to th' ensanguin'd Plain, ... Il.20.526.416.
Gigantic Chief! Deep gash'd th' enormous Blade, ... Il.20.529.416.
Thro' *Mulius'* Head then drove th' impetuous Spear, ... Il.20.547.417.
The trampling Steers beat out th' unnumber'd Grain. ...... Il.20.580.418.
And his Soul shiv'ring at th' Approach of Death. ...... Il.21.77.424.
Th' Eternal Ocean, from whose Fountains flow ...... Il.21.213.430.
Th' amaz'd *Pæonians* scour along the Plain: ...... Il.21.224.430.
(Swiftest and strongest of th' aerial Race) ...... Il.21.282.432.
O'er all th' expanded Plain the Waters spread; ...... Il.21.348.435.
Rise to the War! th' insulting Flood requires ...... Il.21.386.436.
Exert th' unweary'd Furies of the Flame! ...... Il.21.397.436.
So boils th' imprison'd Flood, forbid to flow, ... Il.21.428.438.
She bade th' Ignipotent his Rage forbear, ... Il.21.443.438.
Infest a God: Th' obedient Flame withdraws: ...... Il.21.445.438.
With horrid Clangor shock th' ætherial Arms: ...... Il.21.451.439.
Weeping she grasp'd his Knees: Th' Ambrosial Vest ...... Il.21.591.446.
And take their Thrones around th' Æthereal Sire. ...... Il.21.604.447.
He stands impassive in th' Æthereal Arms. ...... Il.21.702.450.
To all th' Immortals hateful as to me! ...... Il.22.56A.455.
Honour and Shame th' ungen'rous Thought recall: ...... Il.22.139.459.
Obliquely wheeling thro' th' aerial Way; ...... Il.22.186.463.
And hopes th' Assistance of his pitying Friends, ... Il.22.252.466.
Then *Hector,* fainting at th' approach of Death. ...... Il.22.425.473.
Proud on his Car th' insulting Victor stood, ... Il.22.501.477.
Th' attending Heralds, as by Office bound, ... Il.23.49.489.
But here and there th' unbody'd Spectres chace ...... Il.23.90.490.
Forbid to cross th' irremeable Flood. ...... Il.23.92.490.
Part of himself; th' immortal Mind remains: ...... Il.23.123.492.
Bends o'er th' extended Body of the Dead. ...... Il.23.169.496.
Patroclus decent, on th' appointed Ground ...... Il.23.170.496.
The Body decent, on th' appointed Ground ...... Il.23.170A.496.
He call'd th' Aerial Pow'rs, along the Skies ...... Il.23.242.499.
Far on th' extreamest Limits of the Main. ...... Il.23.257.499.
The Morning Planet told th' approach of Light; ...... Il.23.281.501.
And sunk to Quiet in th' Embrace of Sleep, ... Il.23.289.501.
Ye Kings and Princes of th' *Achaian* Name! ...... Il.23.294.501.
Till I shall follow to th' Infernal Shade. ...... Il.23.305.501.
And short, or wide, th' ungovern'd Courser drive: ...... Il.23.392.506.
Prone on the Dust th' unhappy Master fell; ...... Il.23.474.509.
Presents th' occasion, could we use it right. ...... Il.23.494.510.
And lo! th' approaching Steeds your Contest end. ...... Il.23.578.512.
Th' Award opposes, and asserts his Claim. ...... Il.23.620.514.
And vindicate by Oath th' ill-gotten Prize. ...... Il.23.660.515.
Superior as thou art, forgive th' Offence, ... Il.23.669.516.
This Mule my right? th' undoubted Victor I. ...... Il.23.772.520.
Th' admiring *Greeks* loud Acclamations raise, ... Il.23.896.524.
Th' Effect succeeds the Speech. *Pelides* cries, ... Il.23.935.526.
While foul in Dust th' unhonour'd Carcase lies, ... Il.24.28.536.
By Stealth to snatch him from th' insulting Foe: ...... Il.24.35.536.
And th' unrelenting Empress of the Skies: ...... Il.24.37.537.
Then thus the Thund'rer checks th' imperial Dame: ...... Il.24.84.539.
While thus they commun'd, from the' *Olympian* Bow'rs ...... Il.24.177.543.
Had any mortal Voice th' Injuction laid, ... Il.24.271.547.
He spoke, and bad th' attendant Handmaid bring ...... Il.24.371.551.
Th' imperial Bird descends in airy Rings. ...... Il.24.394.552.
Swift on his Car th' impatient Monarch sprung; ...... Il.24.397.552.
Go, guard the Sire; th' observing Foe prevent, ... Il.24.415.552.
Swift on the Car th' impatient Monarch sprung: ...... Il.24.397A.552*.
Th' afflicted Monarch shiver'd with Despair; ...... Il.24.441.554.
Respecting him, my Soul abjures th' Offence; ...... Il.24.535.558.
Before th' inspiring God that urg'd them on, ... Il.24.543.558.
Thus stood th' Attendants stupid with Surprize; ...... Il.24.594.561.
Th' infectious Softness thro' the Heroes ran; ...... Il.24.644.563.
Apart from *Priam,* lest th' unhappy Sire ...... Il.24.732.568.
Those boasted twelve th' avenging two destroy'd. ...... Il.24.766.569.
Th' unhappy Race the Honours of a Grave. ...... Il.24.772.569.

TH' (CONTINUED)

Th' obedient Tears, melodious in their Woe. Il.24.903.574.
And by th' Immortals ev'n in Death belov'd! Il.24.945.575.
On all around th' infectious Sorrow grows; Il.24.983.576.
Th' assembly thus the Sire supreme addrest; Od.1.37.31.
Did Fate, or we, th' adult'rous act constrain? Od.1.46.32.
Th' eternal columns which on earth he rears Od.1.69.34.
Since all who in th' *Olympian* bow'r reside Od.1.103.36.
Let *Hermes* to th' *Atlantic* isle <*> repair; Od.1.105.36.
The Sanction of th' assembled pow'rs report: Od.1.107.36.
Th' aerial space, and mounts the winged gales: Od.1.127.38.
And to the dome th' unknown Cælestial leads. Od.1.166.40.
Delicious wines th' attending herald brought; Od.1.187.42.
But ah I dream!—th' appointed hour is fled, Od.1.215.43.
To me, no Seer, th' inspiring Gods suggest; Od.1.260.45.
From *Samos,* circled with th' *Ionian* main, Od.1.317.48.
For young *Atrides* to th' *Achaian* coast Od.1.372.50.
Then first he recognis'd th' Ætherial guest; Od.1.415.52.
By him, and all th' immortal thrones above, Od.1.484.55.
Thus he, tho' conscious of th' ætherial Guest, Od.1.529.57.
Rose anxious from th' inquietudes of Night. Od.2.4.59.
Soon as in solemn form th' assembly sate, Od.2.11.60.
(His royal hand th' imperial scepter sway'd) Od.2.45.62.
Your fame revere, but most th' avenging skies. Od.2.72.64.
But while your Sons commit th' unpunish'd wrong, Od.2.87.65.
And dash'd th' imperial sceptre to the ground. Od.2.90.65.
Thus spoke th' inventive Queen, with artful sighs. Od.2.106.66.
The fourth, her maid unfolds th' amazing tale. Od.2.122.67.
By him, and all th' immortal host above, Od.2.168.70.
Above th' assembled Peers they wheel on high, Od.2.175.70.
Prescient he view'd th' aerial tracts, and drew Od.2.187.71.
Unnumber'd Birds glide thro' th' aerial way, Od.2.211.72.
Then, with a rushing sound, th' Assembly bend Od.2.291.75.
Where lay the treasures of th' *Ithacian* race: Od.2.381.79.
Attests th' all-seeing Sovereign of the skies. Od.2.425.81.
Th' impatient mariner thy speed demands. Od.2.451.83.
He bids them bring their stores: th' attending train Od.2.456.83.
The Chief his orders gives; th' obedient band Od.2.462.83.
Awful th' approach, and hard the task appears, Od.3.31.87.
Along the shore th' illustrious pair he led, Od.3.49.89.
Alike to Council or th' Assembly came, Od.3.157.93.
And turn th' event, confounding human pride: Od.3.162.93.
Who call'd to council all th' *Achaian* state, Od.3.168.94.
Th' unquiet night strange projects entertain'd; Od.3.183.94.
Ev'n to th' unhappy, that unjustly bleed, Od.3.240.97.
An hour of vengeance for th' afflicted state; Od.3.266.98.
Ev'n to the temple stalk'd th' adult'rous spouse, Od.3.346.103.
Crown'd with the temple of th' *Athenian* dame; Od.3.353.103.
On this, rough *Auster* drove th' impetuous tyde: Od.3.377.104.
Far from their fellows, on th' *Ægyptian* coast. Od.3.383.105.
The youthful Hero and th' *Athenian* maid Od.3.440.108.
But he descending to th' infernal shade, Od.3.522.113.
Which round th' intorted horns the gilder roll'd; Od.3.555.114.
Th' assistants part, transfix, and broil the rest. Od.3.591.116.
And the parcht borders of th' *Arabian* shore: Od.4.102.124.
With vast munificence th' imperial guest: Od.4.172.128.
Charm'd with that virtuous draught, th' exalted mind Od.4.307.134.
I view'd th' effects of that disastrous flame, Od.4.358.137.
Which kindled by th' imperious Queen of love, Od.4.359.137.
Slow-pacing thrice around th' insidious pile; Od.4.378.139.
Then thro' th' illumin'd dome, to balmy rest Od.4.407.140.
Th' obsequious Herald guides each princely guest: Od.4.408.140.
Th' imperial mantle o'er his vest he threw; Od.4.414.140.
Clasp'd on his feet th' embroider'd sandals shine, Od.4.417.140.
And all to mount th' imperial bed aspire. Od.4.434.140.
Then soon th' invaders of his bed and throne, Od.4.465.142.
Long on th' *Ægyptian* coast by calms confin'd Od.4.473.142.
Severe, if men th' eternal rights evade! Od.4.478.142.
Appease th' afflictive fierce desire of food. Od.4.500.144.
What pow'r becalms th' innavigable seas? Od.4.515.145.
Th' oraculous Seer frequents the *Pharian* coast, Od.4.519.145.
For perilous th' assay, unheard the toil, Od.4.535.146.
There wallowing warm, th' enormous herd exhales Od.4.547.146.
Will teach you to repass th' unmeasur'd main. Od.4.576.147.
Arriv'd, to form along th' appointed strand Od.4.591.147.
And all th' offended synod of the skies; Od.4.636.149.
To the stern sanction of th' offended sky Od.4.652.150.
Th' aerial summit from the marble base: Od.4.680.151.
Ingulf'd, and to th'abyss the boaster bore. Od.4.682.151.
Th' enamour'd Goddess, or elude her love: Od.4.758.154.
Fill the wide circle of th' eternal year: Od.4.768.155.
Confounded and appall'd, th' unfinish'd game Od.4.884.159.
Antinous first th' assembled Peers addrest, Od.4.886.159.
Th' allotted labours of the day refrain, Od.4.907.161.
I own me conscious of th' unpleasing deed: Od.4.983.163.
Dreading th' effect of a fond mother's fear, Od.4.988.163.
Th' avenging bolt, and shake the dreadful shield! Od.4.1006.164.
Will intercept th' unwary Youth's return. Od.4.1078.168.
And *Asteris* th' advancing Pilot knew: Od.4.1104.169.
Then met th' eternal Synod of the sky, Od.5.5.171.
Pallas, to these, deplores th' unequal fates Od.5.8.171.
Nor oars to cut th' immeasurable way. Od.5.25.172.
Glide thro' the shades, and bind th' attesting Gods! Od.5.240.183.
Who shines exalted on th' etherial plain, Od.5.351.188.
Now to, now fro, before th' autumnal blast; Od.5.418.192.
So joys *Ulysses* at th' appearing shore; Od.5.511.197.
These eyes at last behold th' unhop'd-for coast, Od.5.525.197.
Th' unhappy man; ev'n Fate had been in vain: Od.5.555.199.
Tho' *Boreas* rag'd along th' inclement sky. Od.5.627.202.
Hither the Goddess wing'd th' aereal way, Od.6.55.208.
Swift at the royal nod th' attending train Od.6.85.209.
When stately in the dance you swim th' harmonious maze. Od.6.188.218.
To guard the wretched from th' inclement sky: Od.6.216.220.
Attends his steps: th' astonish'd virgins gaze. Od.6.282.224.
"Won by her pray'r, th' aereal bridegroom flies. Od.6.336.227.
Not only flies the guilt, but shuns th' offence: Od.6.342.228.

TH' (CONTINUED)

Th' unguarded virgin as unchaste I blame, Od.6.343.228.
With skill the virgin guides th' embroider'd rein, Od.6.379.230.
Slow rowls the car before th' attending train. Od.6.380.230.
Th' avenging bolt, and shake the dreadful shield; Od.6.386.230.
While the slow mules draw on th' imperial maid: Od.7.2.232.
To shun th' encounter of the vulgar crowd, Od.7.21.235.
Thus having spoke, th' unknown celestial leads: Od.7.49.236.
The chief with wonder sees th' extended streets, Od.7.55.236.
To heal divisions, to relieve th' oppress; Od.7.95.238.
Four acres was th' allotted space of ground, Od.7.144.243.
With all th' united labours of the year; Od.7.159.244.
Th' unwonted scene surprize and rapture drew; Od.7.179.244.
And prostrate fell before th' Imperial dame. Od.7.189.245.
'Tis what the happy to th' unhappy owe. Od.7.199.245.
And join'd to that th' experience of the last. Od.7.211.247.
But if descended from th' *Olympian* bow'r, Od.7.265.248.
Th' assembled Peers with gen'ral praise approv'd Od.7.307.251.
Heav'n drove my wreck th' *Ogygian* Isle to find, Od.7.338.253.
She bade me follow in th' attendant train; Od.7.391.255.
Thus he. No word th' experienc'd man replies, Od.7.421.258.
Thus spoke the Prince: th' attending Peers obey, Od.8.43.264.
Dumb be thy voice, and mute th' harmonious string; Od.8.94.267.
That pleas'd th' admiring stranger may proclaim Od.8.99.267.
Thus spoke the King; th' attending Peers obey: Od.8.105.268.
And bore th' unrival'd honours of the day. Od.8.132.270.
To try th' illustrious labours of the field: Od.8.144.270.
Ah why th' ill-suiting pastime must I try? Od.8.168.271.
But dreads th' athletic labours of the field. Od.8.182.272.
While others beauteous as th' æthereal kind, Od.8.195.273.
Fierce from his arm th' enormous load he flings; Od.8.213.274.
Who takes the kind, and pays th' ungrateful part; Od.8.242.275.
Sudden th' irremeable way he trod, Od.8.259.276.
Or boast the glories of th' athletic field; Od.8.282.278.
And level for the dance th' allotted ground; Od.8.298.279.
Th' eternal anvil on the massy base. Od.8.316.281.
In vain they strive, th' entangling snares deny Od.8.341.282.
Dwells there a God on all th' *Olympian* brow Od.8.369.283.
He suffers who gives surety for th' unjust: Od.8.386.284.
Th' assembly gazes with astonish'd eyes, Od.8.415.286.
Th' assenting Peers, obedient to the King, Od.8.433.287.
The precious gifts th' illustrious heralds bear, Od.8.453.287.
And to the court th' embody'd Peers repair. Od.8.454.288.
The Muse indulgent loves th' harmonious kind: Od.8.526.290.
Th' *Epæan* fabric, fram'd by *Pallas,* sing: Od.8.540.291.
Th' unwise award to lodge it in the tow'rs, Od.8.557.292.
An off'ring sacred to th' immortal pow'rs: Od.8.558.292.
Th' unwise prevail, they lodge it in the walls, Od.8.559.292.
Floating in air, invite th' impelling gales: Od.8.592.294.
Tho' clouds and darkness veil th' encumber'd sky, Od.8.609.295.
As suits the purpose of th' eternal will. Od.8.624.296.
Th' unhappy series of a wand'rer's woe? Od.9.12.301.
With sails outspread we fly th' unequal strife, Od.9.71.305.
Nine days our fleet th' uncertain tempest bore Od.9.93.306.
The three we sent, from off th' inchanting ground Od.9.111.308.
Unlearn'd in all th' industrious arts of toil. Od.9.150.311.
Nor glimmer'd *Phœbe* in th' ethereal plain: Od.9.168.312.
I seek th' adventure, and forsake the rest. Od.9.228.316.
(The Priest of *Phœbus* at th' *Ismarian* shrine) Od.9.231.316.
Came tumbling, heaps on heaps, th' unnumber'd flock: Od.9.281.318.
'Tis what the happy to th' unhappy owe: Od.9.320.319.
Such as th' unblest *Cyclopean* climes produce, Od.9.422.323.
Does any mortal in th' unguarded hour Od.9.481.325.
Pleas'd with th' effect of conduct and of art. Od.9.492.326.
No sooner freed, and thro' th' enclosure past, Od.9.545.328.
Th' astonisht Savage with a roar replies: Od.9.593.330.
Th' immortal father no less boasts the son. Od.9.608.331.
And if th' unhappy *Cyclop* be thy Son; Od.9.620.332.
And angry *Neptune* heard th' unrighteous pray'r. Od.9.630.332.
With joy the Maid th' unwary strangers heard, Od.10.125.346.
Clear of the rocks th' impatient vessel flies; Od.10.151.347.
Now dropp'd our anchors in th' *Ææan* bay, Od.10.157.347.
The far-fam'd brother of th' enchantress dame) Od.10.162.348.
With semblance fair th' unhappy men she plac'd. Od.10.269.355.
Where dwelt th' enchantress skill'd in herbs of pow'r; Od.10.328.360.
Where on th' all-bearing earth unmark'd it grew, Od.10.362.362.
But all is easy to th' ethereal kind. Od.10.366.362.
I speed my passage to th' enchanted dome: Od.10.370.362.
To tread th' uncomfortable paths beneath, Od.10.580.371.
Gave to retain th' unseparated soul: Od.10.585.372.
Where the dark rock o'erhangs th' infernal lake, Od.10.612.374.
And o'er th' ingredients strow the hallow'd flour: Od.10.617.374.
But from th' infernal rite thine eye withdraw, Od.10.630.374.
To tread th' uncomfortable paths beneath, Od.10.675.376.
The Sun ne'er views th' uncomfortable seats, Od.11.17.380.
The dolesome passage to th' infernal sky. Od.11.24.380.
Now the wan shades we hail, th' infernal Gods, Od.11.35.381.
But in thy breast th' important truth conceal, Od.11.303.397.
Who blest th' Almighty Thund'rer in her arms; Od.11.318.397.
Jocasta frown'd, th' incestuous *Theban* Queen; Od.11.330.398.
In lofty *Thebes* he wore th' imperial crown, Od.11.335.398.
The stedfast purpose of th' Almighty will. Od.11.364.400.
And *Castor* glorious on th' embattled plain Od.11.369.401.
'Till the sun flames along th' etherial plain; Od.11.437.405.
The evening stars still mount th' ethereal plains. Od.11.465.407.
'Twas mine on *Troy* to pour th' imprison'd war: Od.11.642.416.
Of warrior Kings, and joyn'd th' illustrious shades. Od.11.662.416.
With accents mild, th' inexorable ghost. Od.11.678.418.
Th' immortal liver grows, and gives th' immortal feast. Od.11.714.421.
Th' immortal liver grows, and gives th' immortal feast. Od.11.714.421.
With haughty love th' audacious monster strove Od.11.717.421.
Th' aerial arrow from the twanging bow. Od.11.750.423.
Lest *Gorgon* rising from th' infernal lakes, Od.11.785.425.
'Till from the waves th' *Ææan* hills arise. Od.12.2.427.
Here *Phœbus* rising in th' etherial way, Od.12.5.430.
And print th' important story on thy mind! Od.12.50.431.

TH' (CONTINUED)

Nor trust thy virtue to th' enchanting sound. ....Od.12.64.433.
That bears *Ambrosia* to th' Ætherial King, ...Od.12.76.435.
Glows with th' autumnal or the summer ray, ...Od.12.92.436.
Th' aereal region now grew warm with day, ...Od.12.210.442.
Eternal mists obscure th' aereal plain, ...Od.12.286.446.
The silent fisher casts th' insidious food, ...Od.12.301.446.
With pray'r they now address th' æthereal train, ...Od.12.423.451.
Mean-time *Lampetiè* mounts th' aereal way, ...Od.12.443.452.
To dash th' offenders in the whelming tyde. ....Od.12.457.453.
Loos'd from the yards invite th' impelling gales. ....Od.12.472.454.
Weary and wet th' *Ogygian* shores I gain, ...Od.12.531.458.
To *Jove* th' Eternal, (pow'r above all pow'rs! ....Od.13.29.2.
The luscious wine th' obedient herald brought; ....Od.13.68.4.
Whom glory circles in th' *Olympian* bow'rs. ....Od.13.71.4.
From all th' eluded dangers of the deep! ....Od.13.157.13.
To whom the Father of th' immortal pow'rs, ...Od.13.162.13.
For still th' oppress'd are his peculiar care. ....Od.13.258.18.
His ready tale th' inventive hero told. ....Od.13.306.21.
While in th' embrace of pleasing sleep I lay, ...Od.13.322.23.
Skill'd in th' illustrious labours of the loom. ....Od.13.332.23.
But, by th' almighty author of thy race, ...Od.13.368.25.
Soon as *Ulysses* near th' enclosure drew, ...Od.14.33.36.
Let fall th' offensive truncheon from his hand. ....Od.14.36.37.
Now cover'd with th' eternal shade of death! ....Od.14.52.38.
Intent to voyage to th' *Egyptian* shores; ....Od.14.281.49.
The fifth fair morn we stem th' *Egyptian* tide, ...Od.14.288.49.
Was yet to save th' opprest and innocent. ....Od.14.346.51.
They sought repaste; while to th' unhappy kind, ...Od.14.383.53.
No more—th' approaching hours of silent night ....Od.14.449.57.
Full soon th' inclemency of Heav'n I feel, ...Od.14.534.63.
Still met th' emergence, and determin'd right) ....Od.14.554.64.
Well hast thou spoke (rejoin'd th' attentive swain) ....Od.14.576.64.
A golden ew'r th' attendant damsel brings, ...Od.15.148.75.
The chief his orders gives: th' obedient band ....Od.15.310.84.
Torn from th' embraces of his tender wife, ...Od.15.379.87.
He took ıh' occasion as they stood intent, ...Od.15.499.94.
Th' observing Augur took the Prince aside, ...Od.15.571.98.
Yon bird that dexter cuts th' aerial road, ...Od.15.573.98.
And cloath the naked from th' inclement sky. ....Od.16.84.106.
Th' imperial scepter, and the regal bed: ....Od.16.134.109.
Skill'd in th' illustrious labours of the loom. ....Od.16.171.111.
Wrapt in th' embrace of sleep, the faithful train ....Od.16.252.117.
The names, and numbers of th' audacious train; ....Od.16.259.117.
With such a foe th' unequal fight to try, ...Od.16.276.118.
But thou, when morn salutes th' aerial plain, ...Od.16.290.119.
"Then, beaming o'er th' illumin'd wall they shone: ....Od.16.310.120.
Th' associates of the Prince repass'd the bay; ....Od.16.345.122.
Th' uncautious Herald with impatience burns, ...Od.16.354.123.
Eumæus sage approach'd th' imperial throne, ...Od.16.356.123.
Amphinomus survey'd th' associate band; ....Od.16.367.124.
Consult we first th' all-seeing pow'rs above, ...Od.16.418.126.
Renown'd for wisdom, by th' abuse accurst! ....Od.16.435.128.
Ulysses sav'd him from th' avenger's hand. ....Od.16.447.128.
My gen'rous soul abhors th' ungrateful part, ...Od.16.460.129.
Unable to contain th' unruly joy. ....Od.16.481.130.
But from th' *Hermæan* height I cast a view, ...Od.16.490.130.
Th' eluded Suitors stem the wat'ry way. ....Od.16.495.131.
So ill th' inclemencies of morning air, ...Od.17.27.133.
Arriving now before th' Imperial hall, ...Od.17.35.134.
With all thy handmaids thank th' immortal Pow'rs; ....Od.17.61.135.
While to th' assembled council I repair; ....Od.17.64.135.
Then soon th' invaders of his bed, and throne, ...Od.17.156.139.
Nor oars to cut th' immeasurable way— ....Od.17.167.139.
Daughters of *Jove!* who from th' ætherial bow'rs ....Od.17.282.145.
Stage above stage th' imperial structure stands, ...Od.17.316.147.
And learn the gen'rous from th' ignoble heart; ....Od.17.435.154.
Dooms to full vengeance all th' offending train) ....Od.17.437.154.
With roving pyrates o'er th' *Ægyptian* main: ....Od.17.510.157.
His shoulder-blade receiv'd th' ungentle shock; ....Od.17.548.159.
Much of th' experienc'd man I long to hear, ...Od.17.598.161.
Irus, a name expressive of th' employ. ....Od.18.11.167.
Th' injurious *Greek* that dares attempt a blow, ...Od.18.70.170.
Black fate impends, and this th' avenging hour! ....Od.18.83.170.
They dragg'd th' unwilling *Irus* to the fight; ....Od.18.87.170.
Stranger, may *Jove* aid all th' aereal pow'rs, ...Od.18.137.173.
She smoothly gliding swims th' harmonious round, ...Od.18.230.178.
'Till silence thus th' imperial matron broke; ....Od.18.254.179.
Th' afflictive hand of wrathful *Jove* to bear: ....Od.18.317.182.
Know, to *Telemachus* I tell th' offence: ....Od.18.387.186.
To dress the walk, and form th' embow'ring shade. ....Od.18.406.188.
With steers of equal strength, th' allotted grounds; ....Od.18.415.189.
And nodding helm, I tread th' ensanguin'd field, ...Od.18.419.189.
To the blest Gods that fill th' aereal bow'rs, ...Od.18.471.191.
His bright alcove th' obsequious youth ascends: ....Od.19.59.195.
These to remove th'expiring embers came, ...Od.19.76.196.
Renew'd th' attack, incontinent of spleen: ....Od.19.79.196.
Th' insulted Heroe rouls his wrathful eyes, ...Od.19.86.196.
Of royal grace th' offended Queen may guide; ....Od.19.103.197.
Twelve days, while *Boreas* vex'd th' aerial space, ...Od.19.230.204.
His shoulders intercept th' unfriendly rays. ....Od.19.457.217.
Thus cautious, in th' obscure he hop'd to fly ....Od.19.458.217.
With joy, and vast surprize, th' applauding train ....Od.19.532.221.
When *Euryclea* found, th' ablution ceas'd; ....Od.19.546.223.
She to the fount conveys th' exhausted vase: ....Od.19.588.224.
Ulysses will surprize th' unfinish'd game ....Od.19.685.229.
Wing'd *Harpies* snatch'd th' unguarded charge away, ...Od.20.92.237.
And let th' abstersive sponge the board renew: ....Od.20.189.242.
Dim thro' th' eclipse of fate, the rays divine ....Od.20.243.244.
From council strait th' assenting peerage ceas'd, ...Od.20.310.247.
Had not th' inglorious wound thy malice aim'd ....Od.20.373.251.
No clouds of error dim th' etherial rays, ...Od.20.439.254.
Shall end the strife, and win th' imperial dame; ....Od.21.5.258.
Th' unbended bow, and arrows wing'd with Fate. ....Od.21.62.262.
Which held th' alternate brass and silver rings. ....Od.21.64.262.
Richer than all th' *Achaian* state supplies, ...Od.21.110.264.

TH' (CONTINUED)

His ardour strait th' obedient Prince suppress, ...Od.21.137.265.
Fatal to all, but to th' aggressor first. ....Od.21.324.275.
What if th' Immortals on the man bestow ....Od.21.337.276.
Th' oppressive Suitors from my walls expell! ....Od.21.404.279.
Signs from above ensu'd: th' unfolding sky ....Od.21.452.282.
Since cold in death th' offender lies; oh spare ....Od.22.66.290.
Th' untasted viands, and the jovial bowl. ....Od.22.100.291.
Thy spear, *Telemachus!* prevents th' attack, ...Od.22.107.291.
While yet th' auxiliar shafts this hand supply; ....Od.22.123.292.
Driv'n from the gate, th' important pass be lost. ....Od.22.125.292.
Th' event of actions and our fates are known: ....Od.22.321.301.
Full oft was check'd th' injustice of the rest: ....Od.22.352.304.
From the dire scene th' exempted two withdraw, ...Od.22.418.308.
If yet there live of all th' offending kind. ....Od.22.422.308.
Th' offending females to that task we doom, ...Od.22.474.312.
Wash'd with th' effusive wave, are purg'd of gore. ....Od.22.490.313.
By us, in heaps th' illustrious peerage falls, ...Od.23.121.326.
Th' important deed our whole attention calls. ....Od.23.122.326.
That hence th' eluded passengers may say, ...Od.23.135.327.
This spoke the King: Th' observant train obey, ...Od.23.139.327.
For me, and me alone, th' imperial bed: ....Od.23.172.329.
Th' enormous burthen, who but heav'n above? ....Od.23.186.332.
Ere *Greece* rose dreadful in th' avenging day, ...Od.23.233.334.
For, to *Tiresias* thro' th' eternal gates ....Od.23.269.336.
Due victims slay to all th' æthereal pow'rs. ....Od.23.296.337.
Such future scenes th' all-righteous pow'rs display, ...Od.23.303.337.
Cicons on *Cicons* swell th' ensanguin'd plain; ....Od.23.334.340.
And whelms th' offenders in the roaring tydes: ....Od.23.358.342.
Minerva rushes thro' th' aereal way, ...Od.23.372.343.
Thou, for thy Lord; while me th' immortal pow'rs ....Od.23.379.343.
With oils and honey blaze th' augmented fires, ...Od.24.85.352.
That wide th' extended *Hellespont* surveys; ....Od.24.104.353.
The fourth, her maid reveal'd th' amazing tale, ...Od.24.169.356.
Nor wail'd his father o'er th' untimely dead, ...Od.24.345.365.
And *Medon* first th' assembled chiefs bespoke. ....Od.24.507.372.
A sudden horror all th' assembly shook, ...Od.24.516.372.
Th' offence was great, the punishment was just. ....Od.24.527.373.
None now the kindred of th' unjust shall own; ....Od.24.554.374.
And prompt to execute th' eternal will, ...Od.24.562.375.
Descended *Pallas* from th' *Olympian* hill. ....Od.24.563.375.
A son and grandson of th' *Arcesian* name ....Od.24.596.376.

THALESTRIS

The fierce *Thalestris* fans the rising Fires. ....2.RL*A* 2.12.132.
And fierce *Thalestris* fans the rising Fire. ....2.RL4.94.191.
In vain *Thalestris* with Reproach assails, ...2.RL5.3.199.
Belinda frown'd, *Thalestris* call'd her Prude. ....2.RL5.36.201.
To Arms, to Arms! the bold *Thalestris* cries, ...2.RL5.37A.201.
While thro' the Press enrag'd *Thalestris* flies, ...2.RL5.57.203.

THALESTRIS'

Sunk in *Thalestris'* Arms the Nymph he found, ...2.RL4.89.191.

THALIA

There sunk Thalia, nerveless, cold, and dead, ...5.DunB4.41.345.
There sunk Thalia, nerveless, faint, and dead, ...5.DunB4.41A.345.
Thalia, Glauce, (ev'ry wat'ry Name) ....Il.18.47.325.

THALPIUS

One was *Amphimachus,* and *Thalpius* one; ....Il.2.755.161.

THAMAYRIS'

And *Dorion,* fam'd for *Thamayris'* Disgrace, ...Il.2.721.160.

THAME

Led forth his Flocks along the silver *Thame,* .... 1.PSu.2.71.

THAMES

Fair *Thames* flow gently from thy sacred Spring, ...1.PSp.3.59.
Where gentle *Thames* his winding Waters leads ....1.PSu.3A.71.
Thames heard the Numbers as he flow'd along, ...1.PWi.13.89.
Thy Offspring, *Thames!* the fair *Lodona* nam'd, ...1.W-F.172.165.
In vain on Father *Thames* she calls for Aid, ...1.W-F.197.168.
In vain on Father *Thames* she call'd for Aid, ...1.W-F.197A.168.
Then foaming pour along, and rush into the *Thames.* .... 1.W-F.218.169.
While lasts the Mountain, or while *Thames* shall flow) ....1.W-F.266.173.
Old Father *Thames* advanc'd his rev'rend Head. ....1.W-F.330.181.
Unbounded *Thames* shall flow for all Mankind, ...1.W-F.398.191.
Lanch'd on the Bosom of the Silver *Thames.* .... 2.RL2.4.159.
Where *Thames* with Pride surveys his rising Tow'rs, ...2.RL3.2.169.
But gudgeons, flounders, what my Thames affords. ....4.HS2.142.67.
Where Thames reflects the visionary Scene. ....4.HOde1.24.153.
Whilst Thames reflects the visionary Scene. ....4.HOde1.24A.153.
Which sounds the Silver Thames along, ...4.HOde9.2.159.
The silver Thames reflects its marble face. ....4.1HE1.142.289.
Thames wafts it thence to Rufus' roaring hall, ...5.DunA2.253.130.
Rolls the large tribute of dead dogs to Thames, ...5.DunA2.260.133.
And mounts far off, among the swans of Thames. ....5.DunA2.286.137.
Pours into Thames: Each city-bowl is full ....5.DunA2.319.140.
Taylor, sweet bird of Thames, majestic bows, ...5.DunA2.323.141.
Taylor, sweet Swan of Thames, majestic bows; ....5.DunA2.323A.141.
Till Thames see Eton's sons for ever play, ...5.DunA3.331.191.
Thames wafts it thence to Rufus' roaring hall, ...5.DunB2.265.308.
Rolls the large tribute of dead dogs to Thames, ...5.DunB2.272.309.
And mounts far off among the Swans of Thames. ....5.DunB2.298.310.
Pours into Thames: and hence the mingled wave ....5.DunB2.343.314.
(Once swan of Thames, tho' now he sings no more.) ....5.DunB3.20.321.
'Till Thames see Eaton's sons for ever play, ...5.DunB3.335.336.
All up the silver *Thames,* or all a down; ....6.14ii.52.44.
In vain fair Thames reflects the double scenes ....6.81.3.225.
Fair *Thames* from either ecchoing Shoare ....6.135.43.367.
Fair *Thames* shall hear from shoar to Shoare ....6.135.43A.367.

THAMES'

Thou who shalt stop, where *Thames'* translucent Wave ....6.142.1.382.
You who shall stop, where *Thames'* translucent Wave ....6.142.1A.382.
O Thou who stop'st, where *Thames'* translucent Wave ....6.142.1B.382.

THAMES'S

Blest *Thames's* Shores the brightest Beauties yield, ...1.PSp.63.67.
To *Thames's* Banks which fragrant Breezes fill, ...1.W-F.263.173.
That *Thames's* Glory to the Stars shall raise! ....1.W-F.356.185.
Which *Thames's* Glory to the Stars shall raise! ....1.W-F.356A.185.
Give me on *Thames's* Banks, in honest Ease, ...4.Arbu.261A.114.

THAMIS

In ev'ry Town, where *Thamis* rolls his Tyde, ...6.14ii.1.43.

THAN

More bright than Noon, yet fresh as early Day, ...1.PSp.82.69.
Why art thou prouder and more hard than they? ....1.PSu.18.73.
More fell than Tygers on the *Lybian* Plain; ....1.PAu.90A.86.
In Notes more sad than when they sing their own. ....1.PWi.40.92.
In sadder Notes than when they sing their own. ....1.PWi.40A.92.
A sweeter Musick than their own to hear, ...1.PWi.58.93.
Than what more humble Mountains offer here, ...1.W-F.35.151.
And Kings more furious and severe than they: ....1.W-F.46.153.
A wealthier Tribute, than to thine he gives. ....1.W-F.224.170.
Than thine, which visits *Windsor's* fam'd Abodes, ...1.W-F.229A.170.
Than the fair Nymphs that gild thy Shore below; ....1.W-F.232A.170.
Than the fair Nymphs that grace thy side below; ....1.W-F.232B.170.
Or looks on Heav'n with more than mortal Eyes, ...1.W-F.253.172.
To tire our *Patience,* than mis-lead our *Sense:* ....1.EOC.4.239.
There are, who *judge* still *worse* than he can *write.* ....1.EOC.35.243.
'Tis more to *guide* than *spur* the Muse's Steed; ....1.EOC.84.248.
Restrain his Fury, than provoke his Speed; ....1.EOC.85.249.
Since none can compass more than they *Intend;* ....1.EOC.256.268.
Thus Criticks, of less *Judgment* than *Caprice,* ....1.EOC.285.271.
For *Works* may have more *Wit* than does 'em good, ...1.EOC.303.274.
And still to Morrow's wiser than to Day. ....1.EOC.437.288.
Blunt Truths more Mischief than *nice Falshoods* do; ....1.EOC.573.306.
Than when they promise to give *Scribling* o'er. ....1.EOC.595.307.
Your Silence there is better than your *Spite,* ....1.EOC.598.308.
Nor is *Paul's Church* more safe than *Paul's Church-yard:* ....1.EOC.623.310.
But less to please the Eye, than arm the Hand, ...1.EOC.673.316.
Such was *Roscomon—not* more *learn'd* than *good,* ....1.EOC.725.324.
Oh! lovely nymph, and more than lilies fair, ...1.TrPA.53.367.
More sweet than winter's sun, or summer's air, ...1.TrPA.54.367.
O far more pleasing than the flow'ry field! ....1.TrPA.57.367.
Than grapes mature, or blushing apples are; ....1.TrPA.59.367.
More strait than alders, taller than the planes; ....1.TrPA.60.367.
More strait than alders, taller than the planes; ....1.TrPA.60.367.
Your beauty charms a greater man than Jove. ....1.TrPA.101.369.
And yields an Off-spring more than Nature gives; ....1.TrVP.14.377.
Than such as Women on their Sex bestow.) ....1.TrVP.56.379.
(Far more than e'er can by your self be guest) ....1.TrVP.81.380.
While I consume with more than *Ætna's* Fires! ....1.TrSP.12.393.
Than ev'n those Gods contend in Charms with thee. ....1.TrSP.30.394.
And found my Kisses sweeter than my Song. ....1.TrSP.56.396.
And the last Joy was dearer than the rest. ....1.TrSP.58.396.
O Night more pleasing than the brightest Day, ...1.TrSP.145.400.
Than *Phrygian* Marble or the *Parian* Stone. ....1.TrSP.166.400.
Thy Charms than those may far more pow'rful be, ...1.TrSP.220.403.
O far more faithless and more hard than they? ....1.TrSP.223.403.
Dash'd on these Rocks, than to thy Bosom prest? ....1.TrSP.225.403.
Dash'd on sharp Rocks, than to thy Bosom prest? ....1.TrSP.225A.403.
Dash'd on those Rocks, than to thy Bosom prest? ....1.TrSP.225B.403.
Be this the Cause of more than mortal Hate; ....1.TrSt.427.427.
Was more, alas! than cruel Fate wou'd give! ....1.TrSt.692.439.
Which claims no less the Fearful than the Brave, ...1.TrES.44.451.
And seems a Match for more than Mortal Force. ....1.TrES.204.457.
No less, than Mortals are surpass'd by thine: ....1.TrUl.174.471.
And many Heads are wiser still than one; ....2.ChJM.96.19.
To give your Person than your Goods away: ....2.ChJM.183.23.
No less in Wedlock than in Liberty. ....2.ChJM.332.30.
Than be deluded when a Man can see! ....2.ChJM.503.39.
To die this Instant, than to lose thy Love. ....2.ChJM.548.41.
Or die the Death I dread no less than Hell, ...2.ChJM.587.43.
By this no more was meant, than to have shown, ...2.ChJM.679.47.
Sung merrier than the Cuckow or the Jay: ....2.ChJM.713.49.
Than in her Life she ever felt before. ....2.ChJM.747.51.
Jove ne'er spoke Oracle more true than this, ...2.ChJM.809.54.
More Wives than One by *Solomon* were try'd, ...2.ChWB.21.57.
Declar'd 'twas better far to Wed, than Burn. ....2.ChWB.29.58.
Than that *Mausolus'* Pious Widow plac'd, ...2.ChWB.248.69.
Better than e'er our Parish Priest cou'd do. ....2.ChWB.268.69.
I (to say truth) was twenty more than he: ....2.ChWB.318.72.
And many more than sure the Church approves. ....2.ChWB.362.74.
Than good, in all the *Bible* and *Saints'-Lives.* ....2.ChWB.364.74.
Than all the Sons of *Adam* cou'd redress. ....2.ChWB.368.75.
And op'd those Eyes which brighter shine than they; ....2.RL1.14A.145.
A Youth more glitt'ring than a *Birth-night Beau,* ....2.RL1.23.147.
Than issuing forth, the Rival of his Beams ....2.RL2.3.159.
Belinda burns with more than mortal Ire, ...2.RL4.93.191.
With more than usual Lightning in her Eyes; ....2.RL5.76.206.
Who sought no more than on his Foe to die. ....2.RL5.78.206.
Rather than so, ah let me still survive, ...2.RL5.101.207.
Not more by Envy than Excess of Praise. ....2.TemF.44.256.
The Notes at first were rather sweet than loud: ....2.TemF.311.279.
Than Leaves on Trees, or Sands upon the Shores; ....2.TemF.425.284.
Scarce any Tale was sooner heard than told; ....2.TemF.469.286.
And is my *Abelard* less kind than they? ....2.ElAb.44.322.
Ah more than share it! give me all thy grief. ....2.ElAb.50.323.
More fond than mistress, make me that to thee! ....2.ElAb.90.327.
And more than Echoes talk along the walls. ....2.ElAb.306.344.
Than just to look about us and to die) ....3.EOM1.4.11.
Taller or stronger than the weeds they shade? ....3.EOM1.40.18.
Why JOVE's Satellites are less than JOVE? ....3.EOM1.42.18.
And little less than Angel, would be more; ....3.EOM1.174.36.

THAN (CONTINUED)

No Senses stronger than his brain can bear. ....3.EOM1.192A.38.
Thicker than arguments, temptations throng, ...3.EOM2.75.64.
More studious to divide than to unite, ...3.EOM2.82.64.
What can she more than tell us we are fools? ....3.EOM2.152.73.
And treat this passion more as friend than foe: ....3.EOM2.164.74.
Or (oft more strong than all) the love of ease; ....3.EOM2.170.75.
But thinks his neighbour farther gone than he. ....3.EOM2.226.82.
Than favour'd Man by touch etherial slain. ....3.EOM3.68.98.
To Pow'r unseen, and mightier far than they: ....3.EOM3.252.118.
Than this, that Happiness is Happiness? ....3.EOM4.28.130.
Some are, and must be, greater than the rest, ...3.EOM4.50.133.
Some are, and must be, mightier than the rest, ...3.EOM4.50A.133.
"What differ more (you cry) than crown and cowl?" ....3.EOM4.199.145.
Yet ne'er looks forward farther than his nose. ....3.EOM4.224.148.
Yet ne'er looks forward further than his nose. ....3.EOM4.224A.148.
Than Cæsar with a senate at his heels. ....3.EOM4.258.152.
Less pleasing far than Virtue's very tears. ....3.EOM4.320.159.
(So Darkness fills the eye no less than Light) ....3.Ep1.112A.23.
(So Darkness strikes the sense no less than Light) ....3.Ep1.112.23.
A Fool, with more of Wit than half mankind, ...3.Ep1.200.32.
Less Wit than Mimic, more a Wit than wise: ....3.Ep2.48.54.
Less Wit than Mimic, more a Wit than wise: ....3.Ep2.48.54.
For true No-meaning puzzles more than Wit. ....3.Ep2.114.59.
Nor more a storm her Hate than Gratitude. ....3.Ep2.132.61.
As Hags hold Sabbaths, less for joy than spight, ...3.Ep2.239.69.
More go to ruin Fortunes, than to raise. ....3.Ep3.202Z2.110.
What could they more than Knights and Squires confound, ...3.Ep3.41.89.
Is this too little? would you more than live? ....3.Ep3.83.94.
Alas! 'tis more than Turner finds they give. ....3.Ep3.84.94.
Alas! 'tis more than (all his Visions past) ....3.Ep3.85.94.
Than ev'n that Passion, if it has no Aim; ....3.Ep3.158.106.
Than Bramins, Saints, and Sages did before; ....3.Ep3.186.109.
His word would pass for more than he was worth. ....3.Ep3.344.122.
But Satan now is wiser than of yore, ...3.Ep3.351.122.
Than his fine Wife, alas! or finer Whore. ....3.Ep4.12.136.
Something there is more needful than Expence, ...3.Ep4.41.140.
Yet to their Lord owe more than to the soil; ....3.Ep4.184.154.
Than his fine Wife (my Lord) or finer Whore. ....3.Ep4.12A.136.
Than ridicule all *Taste,* blaspheme *Quadrille,* ....4.HS1.38.7.
A verier Monster than on *Africk's* Shore ....4.JD4.28.27.
More than ten *Holingsheds,* or *Halls,* or *Stows.* ....4.JD4.131.35.
And last (which proves him wiser still than all) ....4.JD4.150.37.
Than mine, to find a Subject staid and wise, ...4.JD4.168.39.
All the Court fill'd with stranger things than he, ...4.JD4.181.41.
Than such as swell this Bladder of a Court? ....4.JD4.205.43.
Sweeter than *Sharon,* in immaculate trim, ...4.JD4.252.47.
And lin'd with *Giants,* deadlier than 'em all: ....4.JD4.275.49.
Oldfield, with more than Harpy throat endu'd, ...4.HS2.25.55.
Than eat the sweetest by themselves at home. ....4.HS2.96.61.
The World's good word is better than a Song) ....4.HS2.102.61.
The Lord of thousands, than if now *Excis'd;* ....4.HS2.134.65.
Than in five acres now of rented land. ....4.HS2.136.65.
The Lord of thousands, than ev'n now *Excis'd;* ....4.HS2.134A.65.
A Self-Tormentor, worse than (in the Play) ....4.HAdv.25.77.
"Better than lust for Boys, with *Pope* and *Turk,* ....4.HAdv.43.79.
Yea, tho' the Blessing's more than he can use, ...4.HAdv.100.83.
Or plumper Thigh, than lurk in humble Crape: ....4.HAdv.107.85.
Than not to wait too long, nor pay too dear. ....4.HAdv.160.89.
"But Foes like these!"—One Flatt'rer's worse than all; ....4.Arbu.104.103.
"But all these foes!"—One Flatt'rer's worse than all; ....4.Arbu.104A.103.
No more than Thou, great GEORGE! a Birth-day Song. ....4.Arbu.222.112.
Yet soft by Nature, more a Dupe than Wit, ...4.Arbu.368.123.
And better got than *Bestia's* from the Throne. ....4.Arbu.391.126.
And better got than Clodio's from the Throne. ....4.Arbu.391A.126.
And better got than *Bestia's* from a Throne. ....4.Arbu.391B.126.
Who sprung from Kings shall know less joy than I. ....4.Arbu.405.127.
Pity the rest, than I abhorrd before ....4.JD2A.6.132.
Nor Kitchen shine with more than usal Fire ....4.JD2A.118.142.
More pert, more proud, more positive than he. ....4.JD2.52.137.
More rough than forty Germans when they scold. ....4.JD2.62.139.
Satan himself feels far less joy than they. ....4.JD2.90.141.
Than Civil Codes, with all their glosses, are: ....4.JD2.96.141.
That acts more Crimes than Confessors e'er hear. ....4.JD2A.44.136.
More pert, more proud, more positive than he. ....4.JD2A.58.136.
Than ev'n in Brothels venal Strumpets are. ....4.JD2A.75.138.
To no more purpose, than when pris'ners swear ....4.JD2A.78.138.
Than these in him; by these he lives and thrives ....4.JD2A.89.140.
Than Civil Laws, with all their Glosses, are: ....4.JD2A.99.140.
If I would scribble, rather than repose. ....4.2HE2.71.169.
If vile D[evonshire] lov'd Sixpence, more than he. ....4.2HE2.229A.181.
If vile Van-muck lov'd Sixpence, more than he. ....4.2HE2.229.181.
Why should not we be wiser than our Sires? ....4.2HE1.44.197.
But let them own, that greater faults than we ....4.2HE1.95.203.
He, who to seem more deep than you or I, ...4.2HE1.131.207.
Not—'s self e'er tells more *Fibs* than I; ....4.2HE1.176.209.
What will a Child learn sooner than a song? ....4.2HE1.205.213.
No whiter page than Addison remains. ....4.2HE1.216.213.
Yet lest you think I railly more than teach, ...4.2HE1.338.225.
Inrage, compose, with more than magic Art, ...4.2HE1.344.225.
More on a Reader's sense, than Gazer's eye. ....4.2HE1.351.225.
Shall be no more than TULLY, or than HYDE! ....4.1HE6.53.241.
Shall be no more than TULLY, or than HYDE! ....4.1HE6.53.241.
Rather than so, see Ward invited over, ...4.1HE6.56A.241.
Tells me I have more Zeal than Wit, ...4.HS6.56.253.
I know no more than my Lord Mayor, ...4.HS6.122.257.
That less admires the Palace than the Park; ....4.1HE1.113.287.
Just less than Jove, and much above a King, ...4.1HE1.186.293.
No *Gazeteer* more innocent than I! ....4.EpS1.84.305.
Arraign no mightier Thief than wretched *Wild,* ....4.EpS2.39.315.
The poor and friendless Villain, than the Great? ....4.EpS2.45.315.
Than such as *Anstis* casts into the Grave; ....4.EpS2.237.326.
Far other *Stars* than *and** wear, ...4.EpS2.238.326.
No more than of Sir Har[r]y or Sir P[aul]. ....4.1740.20.333*.
This, the Great Mother dearer held than all ....5.DunA1.33.O64.
Fair without spot; than greas'd by grocer's hands, ...5.DunA1.199.86.

THAN (CONTINUED)

How, with less reading than makes felons 'scape, 5.DunA1.235.90.
Less human genius than God gives an ape, 5.DunA1.236.91.
The King of Dykes! than whom, no sluice of mud 5.DunA2.261.133.
Greater he looks, and more than mortal stares; 5.DunA2.305.139.
How young Lutetia, softer than the down, 5.DunA2.309.139.
And from each show rise duller than the last: 5.DunA3.300.184.
This the Great Mother dearer held than all 5.DunB1.269.290.
How, with less reading than makes felons scape, 5.DunB1.281.290.
Less human genius than God gives an ape, 5.DunB1.282.290.
The King of dykes! than whom no sluice of mud 5.DunB2.273.309.
The name of these blind puppies than of those. 5.DunB2.310A.310.
Greater he looks, and more than mortal stares: 5.DunB2.329.313.
How young Lutetia, softer than the down, 5.DunB2.333.313.
And ev'ry year be duller than the last. 5.DunB3.298.334.
Author of something yet more great than Letter; 5.DunB4.216.363.
In Folly's Cap, than Wisdom's grave disguise. 5.DunB4.240.366.
Taught by your hand, can charm no less than he; 6.3.10.7.
Than *Ev'ning Post,* or *Observator;* 6.10.6.24.
Than to the wicked Works of *Whiston;* 6.10.22.25.
Than I'm like *Aristophanes.* 6.10.104.27.
And more confound our Choice than satisfie: 6.17iii.3.57.
And swifter than *His* Arms, give *Victory:* 6.17iv.6.59.
Than dine with Fools, that on their Guests will force 6.17iv.26.60.
Yet what more than all we prize 6.18.8.61.
But what more than all we prize 6.18.8A.61.
Still with Esteem no less convers'd than read; 6.19.7.62.
And more Diverting still than Regular, 6.19.26.63.
So hop'd to stand no less than he 6.30.17.86.
Than be no Part in *Tom D'Urfy.* 6.30.26.86.
Than be no Part of *Tom* D'Urfey. 6.30.26A.86.
Rather than Letters longer be, 6.30.62.88.
No less than *Pythagorick Y,* 6.30.73.88.
And honour'd *Cæsar's* less than *Cato's* sword. 6.32.36.97.
Nor sinks his Credit lower than it was. 6.34.16.101.
But yet if some, with Malice more than Wit, 6.38.11Z1.107.
Are better than the Bishop's Blessing. 6.39.2.110.
This, teach me more than Hell to shun, 6.50.15.146.
That, more than Heav'n pursue. 6.50.16.146.
That let me shun ev'n more than Hell 6.50.15A.146.
This more than Heaven persu 6.50.16A.146.
And finish'd more thro' happiness than pains! 6.52.68.158.
Than all his Books can vapour; 6.58.74.174.
From Court than Gay or me, 6.61.32.182.
This more than pays whole years of thankless pain; 6.63.5.188.
Sillier than *G[i]ld[o]n* cou'dst thou be, 6.64.17.190.
Statues of Men, scarce less alive than they; 6.71.10.203.
"Than all the Line of *Lancastere* 6.79.87.220.
And hatch'd more Chicks than she could rear. 6.93.16.257.
Better two Heads than one; 6.94.86.262.
At least thy Consort's cleaner than thy *Groom.* 6.96iv.28.277.
More pert than witty, more a Wit than wise. 6.99.6.286.
More pert than witty, more a Wit than wise. 6.99.6.286.
O more than Fortune, Friends, or Country lost! 6.123.6.344.
Than to bestow a Word on *Kings,* 6.135.90.370.
When freedom is more dear than life. 6.141.12.381.
Than just to plan our projects, and to die. 6.147viii.2.392.
No more a Storm her Hate, than Gratitude: 6.154.18.403.
And suffer, rather than my People fall. Il.1.148.94.
And rob a Subject, than despoil a Foe. Il.1.304.101.
Theseus, endu'd with more than mortal Might, Il.1.349.105.
Not less their Number, than th' embody'd Cranes, Il.2.540.152.
To Thieves more grateful than the Midnight Shade; Il.3.18.188.
A better Fate, than vainly thus to boast, Il.3.59.192.
He spoke no more than just the Thing he ought. Il.3.278.206.
The World's Aversion, than their Love before; Il.3.518.216.
Than Godlike *Priam,* or than *Priam's* Race. Il.4.70.224.
Than Godlike *Priam,* or than *Priam's* Race. Il.4.70.224.
More dear than all th' extended Earth contains, Il.4.76.224.
With great Examples more than loud Commands. Il.4.329.236.
Far more than Heirs of all our Parent's Fame, Il.4.464.242.
A more than mortal Voice was heard aloud. Il.5.532.294.
Meets Death, and worse than Death, Eternal Shame. Il.5.658.299.
Sprung tho' he was from more than mortal Bed; Il.6.122.330.
On Hate of *Troy,* than conscious Shame and Grief: Il.6.421.347.
Great *Hector's* Arm is mightier far than thine. Il.7.130.369.
Go, less than Woman in the Form of Man! Il.8.199.407.
With Terror cloath'd, and more than mortal strong. Il.8.406.416.
Swifter than Thought the Wheels instinctive fly, Il.8.544.422.
With more than vulgar Grief he stood opprest; Il.9.21.432.
Is more than Armies, and himself an Host. Il.9.150.439.
The same I chose for more than vulgar Charms, Il.9.167.441.
Since more than his my Years, and more my Sway. Il.9.214.443.
To me more dear than all that bear the Name. Il.9.264.445.
The same he chose for more than vulgar Charms, Il.9.354.451.
Than Dust in Fields, or Sands along the Shore; Il.9.507.458.
And matchless *Idas,* more than Man in War; Il.9.672.467.
No less a Bribe than great *Achilles'* Car, Il.10.465.24.
Far other Task! than when they wont to keep Il.11.141.41.
More grateful, now, to Vulturs than their Wives! Il.11.212.44.
Thro' broken Orders, swifter than the Wind, Il.11.441.53.
Than worn to Toils, and active in the Fight! Il.11.542.58.
Is more than Armies to the publick Weal. Il.11.637.62.
But he more brave than all the Hosts he led. Il.12.118.85.
Which claims no less the fearful than the brave, Il.12.388.96.
And seems a Match for more than mortal Force. Il.12.558.102.
Flight, more than shameful, is destructive here. Il.13.76.108.
Great must he be, of more than human Birth, Il.13.410.125.
And more than Men, or Gods, supremely wise, Il.13.448.127.
Sprung from a God, and more than Mortal bold; Il.13.610.135.
Than perish in the Danger we may shun. Il.14.87.162.
The Sense of Gods with more than mortal Sweets. Il.14.202.169.
Than new fal'n Snow, and dazling as the Light. Il.14.214.170.
His foaming Coursers, swifter than the Wind, Il.14.505.188.
Than winning Words and heav'nly Eloquence. Il.15.323.209.
He spoke; and speaking, swifter than the Wind Il.15.468.215.

THAN (CONTINUED)

Than keep this hard-got Inch of barren Sands, Il.15.606.220.
Belov'd no less than *Priam's* Royal Race. Il.15.651.221.
Meets Death, and worse than Death, eternal Shame. Il.15.673.222.
Bids him with more than mortal Fury glow, Il.15.724.223.
Than thou hast mine! Oh tell me, to what end Il.16.15.235.
More for their Country's Wounds, than for their own. Il.16.37.236.
Than when in Autumn *Jove* his Fury pours, Il.16.466.260.
A more than mortal Voice was heard aloud. Il.16.862.277.
Such is the Force of more than mortal Hands! Il.16.971.281.
Was more than Heav'n had destin'd to his Friend, Il.17.469.305.
Than Man more weak, calamitous, and blind? Il.17.511.308.
What more desires my Soul, than here, unmov'd, Il.17.632.312.
How more than wretched in th' immortal State! Il.18.72.326.
More useful to preserve, than I to kill) Il.18.136.329.
Than left the Plunder of our Country's Foes. Il.18.352.338.
Achilles glow'd with more than mortal Rage: Il.20.104.398.
Meantime, to mix in more than mortal Fight, Il.21.506.442.
To all the Gods no dearer than to me! Il.22.56.455.
Or, worse than slaughter'd, sold in distant Isles Il.22.61.455.
Dearer than all that own a Brother's Name; Il.22.300.468.
No less, than if the Rage of hostile Fires Il.22.518.478.
Oh more than Brother! Think each Office paid, Il.23.111.492.
Whom rich *Echepolus,* (more rich than brave) Il.23.365.504.
And to be swift is less than to be wise: Il.23.384.505.
'Tis more by Art, than Force of num'rous Strokes, Il.23.385.505.
And other Steeds, than lately led the Way? Il.23.543.511.
Than to the Courser in his swift Career Il.23.600.513.
Antilochus, more hum'rous than the rest, Il.23.923.525.
Must yet be more than Hero, more than Man. Il.23.934.526.
Must yet be more than Hero, more than Man. Il.23.934.526.
Must yet be more than Hero, or than Man. Il.23.934A.526.
Must yet be more than Hero, or than Man. Il.23.934A.526.
And great *Leonteus,* more than mortal strong; Il.23.992.529.
And last great *Hector,* more than Man divine, Il.24.323.550.
Who more than *Peleus* shone in Wealth and Pow'r? Il.24.673.565.
Great *Polypheme,* of more than mortal might! Od.1.91.36.
Happier than I, to future empire born, Od.1.283.46.
More pow'rful advocates than vain complaints. Od.2.68.64.
In wond'rous arts than woman more renown'd, Od.2.135.67.
And more than woman with deep wisdom crown'd; Od.2.136.67.
For wealth and beauty less than virtue please. Od.2.236.73.
Than who too speedy, hastes to end his life Od.3.291.100.
Than she, the daughter of almighty *Jove,* Od.3.485.111.
Who grac'd our rites, a more than mortal guest. Od.3.533.113.
But oh! *Ulysses—deeper* than the rest Od.4.131.126.
A Goddess sure! for more than mortal grace Od.4.509.144.
More dreadful than your boding soul divines: Od.4.926.161.
To the fierce storms, or men more fierce than they: Od.4.1076.168.
(A richer price than if his joyful Isle Od.5.52.174.
(The Gods alas more mighty far than I, Od.5.218.182.
Oh sprung from Gods! in wisdom more than man. Od.5.258.184.
Than works of female skill their women's pride, Od.7.138.242.
She brib'd my stay with more than human charms; Od.7.341.253.
Than the swift race, or conflict of the field? Od.8.162.271.
In public more than mortal he appears, Od.8.193.272.
Than what *Phæacia's* sons discharg'd in air. Od.8.212.274.
More swift than *Mars,* and more than *Vulcan* slow? Od.8.370.283.
More swift than *Mars,* and more than *Vulcan* slow? Od.8.370.283.
O more than man! thy soul the Muse inspires, Od.8.531.291.
Appall'd at sight of more than mortal man! Od.9.305.319.
Nor nearer than the gate presum'd to draw. Od.10.68.342.
O more than human! tell thy race, thy name. Od.10.388.363.
Than if return'd to *Ithaca* from *Troy.* Od.10.494.367.
More fierce than Giants, more than Giants strong; Od.11.378.401.
More fierce than Giants, more than Giants strong; Od.11.378.401.
Proud of their strength and more than mortal size, Od.11.385.402.
Than reign the scepter'd monarch of the dead. Od.11.600.413.
'Tis better six to lose, than all to die. Od.12.138.438.
More dreadful than the tempest, lash'd the seas; Od.12.504.457.
A prize more worth than *Ilion's* noble spoil. Od.13.161.13.
No less than mortals are surpass'd by thine. Od.13.341.24.
Than when two friends, alone, in peaceful place Od.14.222.46.
When now was wasted more than half the night, Od.14.543.63.
Nor other hands than ours the welcome give. Od.15.554.96.
Rather than bear dishonour worse than death, Od.16.112.108.
Rather than bear dishonour worse than death, Od.16.112.108.
Than see the hand of violence invade Od.16.113.108.
Than see the wealth of Kings consum'd in waste, Od.16.115.108.
More hopes of comfort than the lonely field. Od.17.23.133.
Better a friend possess them, than a foe: Od.17.93.136.
To beg, than work, he better understands; Od.17.260.144.
So much more sweet, to spoil, than to bestow? Od.17.487.156.
Another Isle than *Cyprus* more unkind, Od.17.531.158.
O justly lov'd, and not more fair than wise! Od.18.286.180.
Offspring of Kings, and more than woman wise! Od.18.330.183.
Himself adorn'd with more than mortal grace: Od.19.304.209.
Blows have more energy than airy words; Od.20.226.244.
A *Samian* Peer, more studious than the rest Od.20.353.249.
Richer than all th' *Achaian* state supplies, Od.21.110.264.
Than all proud *Argos,* or *Mycæna* knows, Od.21.111.264.
Than all our Isles or Continents enclose: Od.21.112.264.
Nature her debt, than disappointed live, Od.21.164.267.
Yet still to-morrow falser than to-day. Od.21.166.267.
And wants and insults, make me less than man? Od.21.306.274.
Better than that, if thou approve our chear, Od.21.331.276.
How much more safe the good than evil deed: Od.22.414.308.
O son of *Peleus!* greater than mankind! Od.24.51.350.
Not more thy wisdom, than her virtue, shin'd; Od.24.220.358.
Not more thy patience, than her constant mind. Od.24.221.358.

THANK

As, thank my Stars, in modest Truth I may, 2.ChJM.128.20.
And thank the Pow'rs, I may possess alone 2.ChJM.264.27.
(My Husband, thank my Stars, was out of Town) 2.ChWB.279.70.
There (thank my Stars) my whole Commission ends, 4.Arbu.59.100.

THANK (CONTINUED)

Yes; thank my stars! as early as I knew ....4.JD2.1.133.
There are who have not—and thank Heav'n there are ....4.2HE2.266.183.
To tax Directors, who (thank God) have Plums; ....4.EpS2.49.315.
Once more thank *Phœbus* for thy forfeit Breath, ...Il.11.465.54.
Or thank that Swiftness which outstrips the Death. ....Il.11.466.54.
Yet for my Sons I thank ye Gods! 'twas well: ....Il.22.98.456.
With all thy handmaids thank th' immortal Pow'rs; ....Od.17.61.135.

THANK'D

But thank'd by few, rewarded yet by none, ...2.TemF.302.278.
For which thy Patron's weekly thank'd: ....6.39.8.110.
Then thank'd Her for Her Kindness; ....6.94.74.261.
Thank'd Heav'n that he had liv'd, and that he dy'd. ....6.112.10.318.

THANKFUL

With feasts, and off'rings, and a thankful strain: ....4.2HE1.244.215.

THANKLESS

His thankless Country leaves him to her Laws. ....3.Ep3.218.111.
This more than pays whole years of thankless pain; ....6.63.5.188.
What a whole thankless land to his denies. ....6.72.8.208.
What a whole thankless land to his deny'd. ....6.72.8A.208.
For thankless *Greece* such Hardships have I brav'd, ...Il.9.428.453.
What from thy thankless Arms can we expect? ....Il.17.165.294.

THANKS

And crown'd with Corn, their Thanks to *Ceres* yield. ....1.PSu.66.77.
Each paid his Thanks, and decently retir'd. ....2.ChJM.372.32.
(Reply'd the Dame:) Are these the Thanks I find? ....2.ChJM.781.52.
He thanks you not, his pride was in Picquette, ...3.Ep1.144A.27.
He thanks you not, his pride is in Picquette, ...3.Ep1.144.27.
What thanks, what praise, if Peter but supplies! ....4.JD2.67.139.
What thanks, what praise, If Coscus but supplies! ....4.JD2.67A.139.
But (thanks to *Homer*) since I live and thrive, ...4.2HE2.68.169.
"I have a thousand thanks to give— ....4.HS6.210.263.
Small thanks to France and none to Rome or Greece, ...5.DunA1.237.91.
Small thanks to France, and none to Rome or Greece, ...5.DunB1.283.290.
And thanks his stars he was not born a fool; ....6.41.8.113.
Return our Thanks. Accept our humble Lays, ...6.96iii.3.274.
Thanks, dirty Pair! you teach me what to say, ...6.129.5.357.
Divine *Idomeneus!* what Thanks we owe ....Il.4.292.235.
There to high *Jove* were publick Thanks assign'd ....Il.11.894.75.
With impious thanks and mockery of vows, ...Od.3.347.103.
Be then thy thanks, (the bounteous swain reply'd) ....Od.14.492.60.
Thanks to thy care! whose absolute command ....Od.17.480.156.
Thanks to my friend, he cries; but now the hour ....Od.17.676.165.
Whát thanks! what boon! reply'd the Queen, are due, ...Od.19.354.211.

THAT (OMITTED)

2177

THAT'S

And that's a Text I clearly understand. ....2.ChWB.18.57.
And give up all that's Female to the Devil. ....2.ChWB.85.60.
26.And he that's bless'd to day, as fully so, ...3.EOM1.75A.23.
Last night, her Lord was all that's good and great, ...3.Ep1.588.412.
"That's *Velvet* for a *King!*" the Flattr'er swears; ....4.JD4.218.45.
Damn him, he's honest, Sir,—and that's enuff. ....4.JD4.263.47.
That's all these Lovers have for their Estate! ....4.HAdv.12.75.
A Property, that's yours on which you live. ....4.2HE2.231.181.
Add one round hundred, and (if that's not fair) ....4.1HE6.75.241.
He's arm'd without that's innocent within; ....4.1HE1.94.285.
P. Why that's the thing you bid me not to do. ....4.EpS2.19.314.
You hurt a man that's rising in the Trade. ....4.EpS2.35.314.
Like the vile straw that's blown about the streets ....5.DunA3.291.184.
Like the vile straw that's blown about the streets, ...5.DunB3.289.334.
The Doctor, and He that's nam'd next to the Devil, ...6.42i.2.116.
There starve and pray, for that's the way to heav'n. ....6.45.22.125.
On Sunday at Six, in the Street that's call'd *Gerrard,* ....6.62v.1.186.
and one that's a Sinner, ...6.68.2.196.
I know the thing that's most uncommon; ....6.89.1.250.
I know a thing that's most uncommon; ....6.89.1A.250.
That's a boiling hot kettle, ...6.91.22A.254.
Behold this Narrative that's here; ....6.94.15.259.
That's made of nothing but a Lady's *Corn.* ....6.96iv.58.278.
Last Night her Lord was all that's good and great; ....6.154.27.403.

THATCH

Hard by a Sty, beneath a Roof of Thatch, ...6.14ii.28.44.
When from the Thatch drips fast a Show'r of Rain. ....6.96ii.14.270.

THATCH'D

Thick, as beneath some Shepherd's thatch'd Abode, ...Il.16.779.273.

THAUMACIA

The Troops *Methonè,* or *Thaumacia* yields, ...Il.2.872.165.

THAUMANTIA

Thaumantia! mount the Winds, and stop their Car; ....Il.8.488.420.

THE<E

Lest to the <e> naked secret fraud be meant, ...Od.10.359.361.

THE (OMITTED)

28754

THEANO

Whose gen'rous Spouse, *Theano,* heav'nly Fair, ...Il.5.93.271.
Antenor's Consort, fair *Theano,* waits ....Il.6.372.344.
From sage *Antenor* and *Theano* sprung; ....Il.11.284.48.

THEANO'S

(*Theano's* Sister) to his youthful Arms. ....Il.11.290.48.

THEATRE

'Till each fam'd Theatre my empire own, ...5.DunA1.253.93.
Till rais'd from Booths to Theatre, to Court, ...5.DunA3.301.185.
'Till rais'd from booths, to Theatre, to Court, ...5.DunB3.299.334.

THEATRES

Or scoops in circling theatres the Vale, ...3.Ep4.60.142.
To Theatres, and to Rehearsals throng, ...4.2HE1.173.209.
To Op'ra's, Theatres, Rehearsals throng, ...4.2HE1.173A.209.
Lo statues, temples, theatres o'erturned, ...5.DunA3.97Z1.158.
Contending Theatres our empire raise, ...5.DunA3.267.179.
Contending Theatres our empire raise, ...5.DunB3.271.333.
Huge Theatres, that now unpeopled Woods, ...6.71.7.202.
What foreign theatres with pride have shewn, ...6.107.9.310.
At nine green Theatres the *Pylians* stood, ...Od.3.8.86.

THEATRIC

Load some vain Church with old Theatric state, ...3.Ep4.29.140.

THEATRICALLY

Her Voice theatrically loud, ...6.14v(a).17.49.

THEBÈ

From *Thebè* sacred to *Apollo's* Name, ...Il.1.478.110.
(*Cilician Thebè* great *Aëtion* sway'd, ...Il.6.494.351.
Lay'd *Thebè* waste, and slew my warlike Sire! ....Il.6.525.352.

THEBÈ'S

And they whom *Thebè's* well-built Walls inclose, ...Il.2.604.156.
For *Tydeus* left me young, when *Thebè's* Wall ....Il.6.277.340.

THEBAE

(The well-wrought Harp from conquer'd *Thebæ* came, ...Il.9.247.445.

THEBAN

In *Theban* Wars an humbler Theme may chuse: ....1.TrSt.50.411.
And o'er the *Theban* Palace spreads her Wings, ...1.TrSt.170.417.
And at the *Theban* Palace did alight, ...1.TrSt.170A.417.
The *Theban* Kings their Line from *Cadmus* trace, ...1.TrSt.317.423.
In dire Alliance with the *Theban* Line; ....1.TrSt.343.424.
Th'intrepid *Theban* hears the bursting Sky, ...1.TrSt.510.431.
Thither with haste the *Theban* Hero flies; ....1.TrSt.532.432.
A Lyon's yellow Skin the *Theban* wears, ...1.TrSt.567.434.
The *Theban* bends on Earth his gloomy Eyes, ...1.TrSt.796.443.
The gen'rous *Pedasus,* of *Theban* Breed; ....1.TrES.720.459.
Then, when the Chief the *Theban* Walls o'erthrew, ...Il.2.843.164.
Forewarn'd the Horrors of the *Theban* War. ....Il.4.435.241.
With fewer Troops we storm'd the *Theban* Wall, ...Il.4.460.242.
And feast encircled by the *Theban* Foe; ....Il.5.1003.314.
Of *Greece* he left, and sought the *Theban* Tow'rs, ...Il.10.340.18.
Lies whelm'd in Ruins of the *Theban* Wall, ...Il.14.128.163.
Not thus I burn'd for either *Theban* Dame, ...Il.14.365.180.
The gen'rous *Pedasus,* of *Theban* Breed; ....Il.16.575.267.
In *Theban* Games the noblest Trophy bore, ...Il.23.786.521.
There seek the *Theban* Bard, depriv'd of sight, ...Od.10.582.371.
When lo! the mighty *Theban* I behold; ....Od.11.112.386.
Jocasta frown'd, th' incestuous *Theban* Queen; ....Od.11.330.398.
To seek the *Theban,* and consult the Fates: ....Od.11.538.412.
The words of *Circe* and the *Theban* Shade; ....Od.12.321.447.
To fly these shores the prescient *Theban* Shade ....Od.12.326.447.
Heav'n, by the *Theban* ghost, thy spouse decrees ....Od.23.283.337.

THEBAN'S

Till led by Fate, the *Theban's* Steps he treads, ...1.TrSt.561.433.

THEBES

Fraternal Rage, the guilty *Thebes* Alarms, ...1.TrSt.1.409.
Or shall I *Juno's* Hate to *Thebes* resound, ...1.TrSt.13.409.
Aloft she sprung, and steer'd to *Thebes* her Flight; ....1.TrSt.141.415.
She mounts aloft, and steers to *Thebes* her Flight, ...1.TrSt.141A.415.
To govern *Thebes* by their Alternate Sway, ...1.TrSt.193.418.
Exclaim'd—O *Thebes!* for thee what Fates remain, ...1.TrSt.234.420.
But *Thebes,* where shining in Cœlestial Charms ....1.TrSt.360.425.
Curs'd *Thebes* the Vengeance it deserves, may prove,— ....1.TrSt.364.425.
No less *Dione* might for *Thebes* contend, ...1.TrSt.407.427.
Let the pale Sire revisit *Thebes,* and bear ....1.TrSt.421.427.
(His *Thebes* abandon'd) thro' th' *Aonian* Groves, ...1.TrSt.444.428.
Forbidden *Thebes* appears before his Eye, ...1.TrSt.447.428.
Jocasta's Son, and *Thebes* my Native Place. ....1.TrSt.805.443.
Strikes, and behold a sudden *Thebes* aspire! ....2.TemF.86.259.
Strikes, and beholds a sudden *Thebes* aspire; ....2.TemF.86A.259.
To Thebes, to Athens, when he will, and where. ....4.2HE1.347.225.
The wealthy tribes of *Pharian Thebes* obey) ....Od.4.170.128.
Founders of *Thebes,* and men of mighty name; ....Od.11.320.398.
In lofty *Thebes* he wore th' imperial crown, ...Od.11.335.398.

THEBES'

Thebes' hostile Walls, unguarded and alone, ...Il.4.438.241.
Not all proud *Thebes'* unrival'd Walls contain, ...Il.9.500.457.

THEE

The Bowl to *Strephon,* and the Lamb to thee: ....1.PSp.94.70.
They parch'd with Heat, and I inflam'd by thee. ....1.PSu.20.73.
For ever silent, since despis'd by thee. ....1.PSu.44.75.
She sings of Friendship, and she sings to thee. ....1.PAu.12A.81.
I know thee Love! on foreign Mountains bred, ...1.PAu.89.86.
Wolves gave thee suck, and savage Tygers fed. ....1.PAu.90.86.
Oh mighty Love, what Magick is like thee! ....1.PAu.84A.86.
I know thee Love! wild as the raging Main, ...1.PAu.89A.86.
To thee, bright Goddess, of a Lamb shall bleed, ...1.PWi.81.94.
For thee, *Idume's* spicy Forests blow; ....1.Mes.95.121.
And break upon thee in a Flood of Day! ....1.Mes.98.121.
Exil'd by Thee from Earth to deepest Hell, ...1.W-F.413.192.
Thee, bold *Longinus!* all the Nine inspire, ...1.EOC.675.316.
For thee shall bear their fruits, and offer all to thee! ....1.TrPA.77.368.
For thee shall bear their fruits, and offer all to thee! ....1.TrPA.77.368.

THEE (CONTINUED)

And these, dear nymph, are kept to play with thee: ....1.TrPA.91.369.
The face was all that now remain'd of thee; ....1.TrFD.63.388.
Than ev'n those Gods contend in Charms with thee. ....1.TrSP.30.394.
But Thee, the last and greatest of my Woes? ....1.TrSP.80.397.
Venus for those had rapt thee to the Skies, ...1.TrSP.101.398.
But *Mars* on thee might look with *Venus'* Eyes. ....1.TrSP.102.398.
No Gift on thee thy *Sapho* cou'd confer, ...1.TrSP.117A.398.
And Love, the God that ever waits on thee, ...1.TrSP.122.399.
For thee the fading Trees appear to mourn, ...1.TrSP.173.401.
"What suits with *Sapho, Phœbus,* suits with thee; ....1.TrSP.216.403.
Absent from thee, the Poet's Flame expires, ...1.TrSP.240.404.
Venus for thee shall smooth her native Main. ....1.TrSP.251.404.
Cupid for thee shall spread the swelling Sails. ....1.TrSP.253.404.
For thee shall *Cupid* spread the swelling Sails. ....1.TrSP.253A.404.
From thee to those, unpity'd, I'll remove, ...1.TrSP.258A.404.
And crowd their shining Ranks to yield thee place; ....1.TrSt.36.411.
Conspire to court thee from our World away; ....1.TrSt.38.411.
To part his Throne and share his Heav'n with thee; ....1.TrSt.42.411.
For Hell and Thee begot an impious Brood, ...1.TrSt.97.414.
If worthy Thee, and what Thou might'st inspire! ....1.TrSt.102.414.
Exclaim'd—O *Thebes!* for thee what Fates remain, ...1.TrSt.234.420.
Nor doom to War a Race deriv'd from thee; ....1.TrSt.397.426.
This, great *Amphiaraus,* lay hid from thee, ...1.TrSt.551.433.
By thee the Bow and mortal Shafts are born, ...1.TrSt.837.444.
Whether the Style of *Titan* please thee more, ...1.TrSt.857.445.
Like thee to vanquish, or like me to die. ....1.TrES.313.461.
With Joy to thee, as to some God, I bend, ...1.TrUl.110.469.
To thee my Treasures and my self commend. ....1.TrUl.111.469.
Who taught thee Arts, *Alcinous* to persuade, ...1.TrUl.177.471.
He who discerns thee must be truly wise, ...1.TrUl.189.472.
Once more 'twas giv'n thee to behold thy Coast: ....1.TrUl.221.473.
Struck blind by thee, resigns his Days to Grief, ...2.ChJM.483.38.
When Un-endow'd, I took thee for my own, ...2.ChJM.550.41.
The Loss of thee is what I only fear. ....2.ChJM.556.42.
Of Earthly Bliss, was well bestow'd on thee! ....2.ChJM.634.45.
Constant and kind I'll ever prove to thee. ....2.ChJM.715.49.
As with these Eyes I plainy saw thee whor'd; ....2.ChJM.769.52.
As surely seize thee, as I saw too well. ....2.ChJM.771.52.
"I know thee for a virtuous, faithful Wife." ....2.ChWB.133.62.
Yet I forgive thee—Take my last Embrace. ....2.ChWB.421.77.
Know then, unnumber'd Spirits round thee fly, ...2.RL1.41.148.
The Drops to thee, *Brillante,* we consign; ....2.RL2.113.166.
For thee (they cry'd) amidst Alarms and Strife, ...2.TemF.344.280.
For thee whole Nations fill'd with Flames and Blood, ...2.TemF.346.280.
What Virtue seem'd, was done for thee alone. ....2.TemF.349.280.
And all that Virtue seem'd, was done for thee alone. ....2.TemF.349A.280.
'Tis all we beg thee, to conceal from Sight ....2.TemF.362.281.
My fancy form'd thee of Angelick kind, ...2.ElAb.61.324.
Nor envy them, that heav'n I lose for thee. ....2.ElAb.72.325.
More fond than mistress, make me that to thee! ....2.ElAb.90.327.
Those still at least are left thee to bestow. ....2.ElAb.120.329.
By thee to mountains, wilds, and deserts led. ....2.ElAb.132.330.
Now think of thee, and curse my innocence. ....2.ElAb.188.335.
Alone can rival, can succeed to thee. ....2.ElAb.206.336.
All my loose soul unbounded springs to thee. ....2.ElAb.228.338.
I hear thee, view thee, gaze o'er all thy charms, ...2.ElAb.233.339.
I hear thee, view thee, gaze o'er all thy charms, ...2.ElAb.233.339.
For thee the fates, severely kind, ordain ....2.ElAb.249.339.
And love's warm tyde for ever stopt in thee. ....2.ElAb.258Z2.340.
I waste the Matin lamp in sighs for thee, ...2.ElAb.267.341.
One thought of thee puts all the pomp to flight, ...2.ElAb.273.342.
Nor share one pang of all I felt for thee. ....2.ElAb.292.343.
Bright clouds descend, and Angels watch thee round, ...2.ElAb.340.347.
And Saints embrace thee with a love like mine. ....2.ElAb.342.347.
What tho' no sacred earth allow thee room, ...2.Elegy.61.367.
How lov'd, how honour'd once, avails thee not, ...2.Elegy.71.368.
A heap of dust alone remains of thee; ....2.Elegy.73.368.
And the last pang shall tear thee from his heart, ...2.Elegy.80.368.
And drawn supports, upheld by God, or thee? ....3.EOM1.34.17.
What future bliss, he gives not thee to know, ...3.EOM1.93.25.
What bliss above, he gives not thee to know, ...3.EOM1.93A.25.
Subjected these to those, or all to thee? ....3.EOM1.230.44.
The pow'rs of all subdu'd by thee alone, ...3.EOM1.231.44.
No glass can reach! from Infinite to thee, ...3.EOM1.240.45.
From thee to Nothing!—On superior pow'rs ....3.EOM1.241.45.
All this dread ORDER break—for whom? for thee? ....3.EOM1.257.46.
All this dread ORDER shall it break? for thee? ....3.EOM1.257A.46.
Of blindness, weakness, Heav'n bestows on thee. ....3.EOM1.284.49.
All Nature is but Art, unknown to thee; ....3.EOM1.289.50.
Is it for thee the lark ascends and sings? ....3.EOM3.31.95.
Is it for thee the linnet pours his throat? ....3.EOM3.33.95.
And fled from Monarchs, ST. JOHN! dwells with thee. ....3.EOM4.18.129.
And fled from Monarchs, *Lelius!* dwells with thee. ....3.EOM4.18A.129.
Lamented DIGBY! sunk thee to the grave? ....3.EOM4.104.138.
If Parts allure thee, think how Bacon shin'd, ...3.EOM4.281.154.
If Parts allure thee, think how Wh[arton] shin'd, ...3.EOM4.281A.154.
Gives thee to make thy neighbour's blessing thine. ....3.EOM4.354.162.
Teach me, like thee, in various nature wise, ...3.EOM4.377.165.
That urg'd by thee, i turn'd the tuneful art ....3.EOM4.391.166.
And Zeal for his great House which eats thee up. ....3.Ep3.208A.110.
Gold imp'd by thee, can compass hardest things, ...3.Ep3.71.93.
O my fair Mistress, *Truth!* Shall I quit thee, ...4.JD4.200.43.
Shall half the new-built Churches round thee fall? ....4.HS2.119.63.
Let Peals of Laughter, *Codrus!* round thee break, ...4.Arbu.85.101.
Welcome for thee, fair Virtue! all the past: ....4.Arbu.358.122.
For thee, fair Virtue! welcome ev'n the *last!* ....4.Arbu.359.122.
Stop, or turn nonsense at one glance of Thee? ....4.HOde1.40.153.
Thee, drest in Fancy's airy beam, ...4.HOde1.41.153.
Stop, or turn nonsense at one glance from Thee? ....4.HOde1.40A.153.
To Thee, the World its present homage pays, ...4.2HE1.23.195.
That Bear or Elephant shall heed thee more; ....4.2HE1.325.223.
Or he, who bids thee face with steddy view ....4.1HE1.107.287.
And, while he bids thee, sets th' Example too? ....4.1HE1.109.287.
The Muse may give thee, but the Gods must guide. ....4.EpS2.215.325.
Rev'rent I touch thee! but with honest zeal; ....4.EpS2.216.325.

THEE (CONTINUED)

Control, decides, insults thee every hour, ...4.1740.7.332.
To purge and let thee blood, with fire and sword, ...4.1740.15.332.
That those who bind and rob thee, would not kill, ...4.1740.17.332.
G[owe]r, C[obha]m, B[athurs]t, pay thee due regards, ...4.1740.23.333.
Finds thee, at best, the butt to crack his joke on. ....4.1740.28.333.
The plague is on thee, Britain, and who tries ....4.1740.75.336.
To save thee in th' infectious office *dies.* ....4.1740.76.336.
Brave S[carborough]w lov'd thee, and was ly'd to death. ....4.1740.78.336.
Blotch thee all o'er, and sink.. ....4.1740.84.337.
For thee I dim these eyes, and stuff this head, ...5.DunA1.165.83.
For thee supplying, in the worst of days, ...5.DunA1.167.83.
For thee explain a thing till all men doubt it, ...5.DunA1.169.84.
So, (fam'd like thee for turbulence and horns,) ....5.DunA2.173.122.
Th' unconscious flood sleeps o'er thee like a lake. ....5.DunA2.292.138.
The hand of Bavius drench'd thee o'er and o'er. ....5.DunA3.38.154.
Shall in thee centre, from thee circulate. ....5.DunA3.52.155.
Shall in thee centre, from thee circulate. ....5.DunA3.52.155.
Another Durfey, Ward! shall sing in thee. ....5.DunA3.138.161.
Thee shall each Ale-house, thee each Gill-house mourn, ...5.DunA3.139.162.
Thee shall each Ale-house, thee each Gill-house mourn, ...5.DunA3.139.162.
For thee each Ale-house and each Gill-house mourn, ...5.DunA3.139A.162.
For thee each Ale-house, thee each Gill-house mourn, ...5.DunA3.139B.162.
For thee each Ale-house, thee each Gill-house mourn, ...5.DunA3.139B.162.
And bade thee live, to crown Britannia's praise, ...5.DunA3.207.175.
"Son! what thou seek'st is in thee. Look, and find ....5.DunA3.247.178.
"And are these wonders, Son, to thee unknown? ....5.DunA3.269.180.
Unknown to thee? These wonders are thy own. ....5.DunA3.270.180.
So (fam'd like thee for turbulence and horns) ....5.DunB2.181.304.
Th' unconscious stream sleeps o'er thee like a lake. ....5.DunB2.304.310.
The hand of Bavius drench'd thee o'er and o'er. ....5.DunB3.46.322.
Shall in thee centre, from thee circulate. ....5.DunB3.60.323.
Shall in thee centre, from thee circulate. ....5.DunB3.60.323.
Another Durfey, Ward! shall sing in thee. ....5.DunB3.146.326.
Thee shall each ale-house, thee each gill-house mourn, ...5.DunB3.147.326.
Thee shall each ale-house, thee each gill-house mourn, ...5.DunB3.147.326.
And bade thee live, to crown Britannia's praise, ...5.DunB3.211.330.
"Son; what thou seek'st is in thee! Look, and find ....5.DunB3.251.332.
"And are these wonders, Son, to thee unknown? ....5.DunB3.273.333.
Unknown to thee? These wonders are thy own. ....5.DunB3.274.333.
Thee shall the Patriot, thee the Courtier taste, ...5.DunB3.297.334.
Thee shall the Patriot, thee the Courtier taste, ...5.DunB3.297.334.
Thou wept'st, and with thee wept each gentle Muse. ....5.DunB4.44.345.
For thee we dim the eyes, and stuff the head ....5.DunB4.249.368.
For thee they dim their eyes and stuff their head. ....5.DunB4.249A.368.
For thee explain a thing till all men doubt it, ...5.DunB4.251.369.
Thee too, my Paridel! she mark'd thee there, ...5.DunB4.341.376.
Thee too, my Paridel! she mark'd thee there, ...5.DunB4.341.376.
Such as Lucretius drew, a God like Thee: ....5.DunB4.484.389.
Lo! ev'ry finish'd Son returns to thee: ....5.DunB4.500.391.
To thee the most rebellious things on earth: ....5.DunB4.508.392.
Made just for thee, as all beside for Kings. – – – ....5.DunB4.604A.403.
Our Love to thee his fervent Breath may blow, ...6.2.21.6.
But without thee, what could the Prophets do? ....6.2.24.6.
She gains from us, as now from thee, ...6.6i.13.14.
To gaze upon themselves in thee. ....6.6ii.12.14.
Of thee they drank, till blushing fruit ....6.6ii.21.15.
And man, like thee, was impollute, ...6.6ii.23.15.
Wit, past thro' thee, no longer is the same, ...6.7.11.16.
Since no Reprizals can be made on thee. ....6.7.14.16.
'Twas one vast Nothing, All, and All slept fast in thee. ....6.8.3.17.
Then various Elements against thee join'd, ...6.8.7.17.
But Rebel Wit deserts thee oft in vain; ....6.8.13.18.
And routed *Reason* finds a safe Retreat in thee. ....6.8.18.18.
With thee in private modest *Dulness* lies, ...6.8.19.18.
Folly by thee lies sleeping in the Breast, ...6.8.23.18.
And 'tis in thee at last that *Wisdom* seeks for Rest. ....6.8.24.18.
Thy very want of Tongue makes thee a kind of Fame. ....6.8.27.18.
How Church and State should be oblig'd to thee! ....6.8.29.18.
Are best by thee express'd, and shine in thee alone. ....6.8.39.19.
Are best by thee express'd, and shine in thee alone. ....6.8.39.19.
Lord's Quibble, Critick's Jest; all end in thee, ...6.8.41.19.
Has sent thee down in mercy to mankind, ...6.20.46.67.
If all the Gods entrust thee to bestow ....6.20.48.67.
No harms can reach thee, and no force shall move. ....6.21.22.69.
I see protecting Myriads round thee fly, ...6.21.23.69.
Raise in their arms, and waft thee on their wing, ...6.21.26.69.
For thou art Light. In thee the righteous find ....6.23.15.73.
Thee they regard alone; to thee they tend; ....6.23.17.73.
Thee they regard alone; to thee they tend; ....6.23.17.73.
Thee we regard alone, to thee we tend; ....6.23.17A.73.
Thee we regard alone, to thee we tend; ....6.23.17A.73.
Which they who love thee not must undergo. ....6.25.4.77.
Such is, and shall be still, my love to thee— ....6.25.14.77.
To thee, Redeemer! mercy's sacred spring! ....6.25.15.77.
Which those who love thee not must undergo. ....6.25.4A.77.
Sooner I'd quit my Part in thee, ...6.30.25.86.
Sooner we'd quit our Part in thee, ...6.30.25A.86.
Who'd sooner quit our Part in thee, ...6.30.25B.86.
Heaven gives thee for thy Loss of *Rowe,* ....6.47.19.129.
None can like thee its Fermentation still. ....6.48i.4.133*.
This was reserv'd, Great *Barnivelt,* for Thee, ...6.48iii.5.134.
Or think Thee Lord alone of Man, ...6.50.23.147.
Nor think Thee Lord alone of Man, ...6.50.23A.147.
To Thee, whose Temple is all Space, ...6.50.49.148.
With thee, on *Raphael's* Monument I mourn, ...6.52.27.157.
With thee repose, where *Tully* once was laid, ...6.52.29.157.
Since Worms shall eat ev'n thee. ....6.53.36.162.
Nay, did all *J[a]c[o]b* breath in thee, ...6.64.18.190.
She keeps thee, Book! I'll lay my Head, ...6.64.19.190.
Nay, did James Baker breath in thee, ...6.64.18A.190.
She'l keep thee Book! I lay my Head, ...6.64.19A.190.
Know, Kings and Fortune cannot make thee more. ....6.73.9.210.
Right did thy Gossip call thee: ....6.79.66.220.
When *John* of *Guise* shall maul thee. ....6.79.68.220.
For on thee did he clap his Chair, ...6.79.69.220.

THEE (CONTINUED)

And angry Gods, shall wreak this Wrong on thee; Il.22.450.474.
And stretch thee here, before this *Scæan* Gate. Il.22.452.474.
I follow thee—He said, and stripp'd the Slain. Il.22.462.474.
Or why reflects my Mind on ought but thee Il.22.482.476.
Thee, *Hector!* last: Thy Loss (divinely brave) Il.22.542.478.
And bending o'er thee, mix'd the tender Show'r! Il.22.547.479.
Useless to thee, from this accursed Day! Il.22.659.484.
Till on the Pyre I place thee; till I rear Il.23.55.489.
Thee too it waits; before the *Trojan* Wall Il.23.101.491.
The Gods have lov'd thee, and with Arts have blest. Il.23.376.505.
Neptune and *Jove* on thee conferr'd the Skill, Il.23.377.505.
What *Greek* shall blame me, if I bid thee rise, Il.23.659.515.
Hateful to thee, and to the Gods forsworn. Il.23.676.516.
'Tis now *Atrides'* turn to yield to thee. Il.23.686.517.
For ah! how few, who should like thee offend, Il.23.691.517.
Like thee, have Talents to regain the Friend? Il.23.692.517.
Or let me lift thee, Chief, or lift thou me: Il.23.840.523.
Thee first in Virtue, as in Pow'r supreme, Il.23.1054.533.
And know thee both their Greatest, and their Best. Il.23.1057.533.
Then hye thee to him, and our Mandate bear; Il.24.147.541.
From *Jove* I come, *Jove* makes thee still his Care: Il.24.210.545.
For *Hector's* sake these Walls he bids thee leave, Il.24.211.545.
Thee *Hermes* to *Pelides* shall convey, Il.24.219.546.
His Grace restore thee to our Roof, and Arms, Il.24.356.551.
If ever Pity touch'd thee for Mankind. Il.24.414.552.
From *Greece* I'll guard thee too; for in those Lines Il.24.457.555.
My Steps, and send thee, Guardian of my way. Il.24.462.556.
Thee, far as *Argos,* pleas'd I could convey; Il.24.537.558.
On thee attend, thy Safety to maintain, Il.24.539.558.
May send him thee to chase that Foe away. Il.24.611.562.
Heav'n sure has arm'd thee with a Heart of Steel, Il.24.657.564.
I show thee, King! thou tread'st on hostile Land; Il.24.717.567.
Perchance behold thee, and our Grace prevent. Il.24.821.571.
This, of thy Grace, accord: To thee are known Il.24.830.571.
Thy still-surviving Sons may sue for thee, Il.24.855.572.
And hurl thee headlong from the Tow'rs of *Troy.* Il.24.929.575.
Dismiss'd thee gently to the Shades below. Il.24.957.576.
Yet was it ne'er my Fate, from thee to find Il.24.968.576.
For thee I mourn; and mourn my self in thee, Il.24.975.576.
For thee I mourn; and mourn my self in thee, Il.24.975.576.
She shines with fatal excellence, to thee: Od.2.140.67.
With thee, the bowl we drain, indulge the feast, Od.2.141.68.
My pow'r shall guard thee, and my hand convey: Od.2.324.77.
The best I chuse, to waft thee o'er the tides. Od.2.334.77.
The bark, to waft thee o'er the swelling tides. Od.2.346.77.
Thee first it fits, oh stranger! to prepare Od.3.57.89.
Long time with thee before proud *Ilion's* wall Od.3.104.91.
In arms he fought; with thee beheld her fall. Od.3.105.91.
'Tis sacred truth I ask, and ask of thee. Od.3.124.91.
With joy I grasp thee, and with love admire: Od.3.152.93.
Who finds thee younger must consult his eyes. Od.3.154.93.
Or leagu'd against thee, do thy people join, Od.3.263.98.
So might she love thee, so thy soul inspire! Od.3.276.99.
Thee to *Atrides* they shall safe convey, Od.3.417.106.
Too long, mis-judging, have I thought thee wise: Od.4.38.122.
I boast a witness of his worth in thee. Od.4.280.132.
In thee renew'd the soul of *Nestor* shines: Od.4.282.132.
Around thee full of years, thy offspring bloom, Od.4.290.132.
Speaks thee descendent of etherial race: Od.4.510.144.
But oh belov'd by heav'n! reserv'd to thee Od.4.761.155.
To thee the Son of *Jove,* and beauteous *Helen's* Lord. Od.4.776.155.
And bid thee cease his absence to deplore. Od.4.1064.167.
To bid thee patient his return attend. Od.4.1084.168.
A man, he says, a man resides with thee, Od.5.131.178.
The tempest drove him to these shores and thee. Od.5.142.178.
Free as the winds I give thee now to rove— Od.5.209.181.
Sublime to bear thee o'er the gloomy deep. Od.5.212.181.
And prosp'rous gales to waft thee on thy way. Od.5.216.182.
In peace shall land thee at thy native home. Od.5.220.182.
This shows thee, friend, by old experience taught, Od.5.235.182.
What fate yet dooms thee, yet, to undergo; Od.5.264.184.
To thee from *Neptune* and the raging main. Od.5.571.199.
To thee I bend! if in that bright disguise Od.6.177.217.
For Misery, oh Queen, before thee stands! Od.6.204.220.
Forsook by thee, in vain I sought thy aid Od.6.387.230.
To thee, thy consort, and this royal train, Od.7.196.245.
Like thee in beauty, nor in virtue less. Od.7.377.254.
And ships shall wait thee with the morning ray. Od.7.405.256.
Then gently waft thee to the pleasing shore, Od.7.409.257.
Our ships with ease transport thee in a day. Od.7.412.257.
Father, arise! for thee thy port proclaims Od.8.159.271.
Call thee aboard, and stretch the swelling sails. Od.8.166.271.
In outward show heav'n gives thee to excell, Od.8.197.273.
To thee, my Goddess, I address my vows, Od.8.510.290.
Who hopes thee, Monarch! for his future guest. Od.9.18.301.
And learn, our pow'r proceeds with thee and thine, Od.9.331.320.
What hurts thee, *Polypheme?* what strange affright Od.9.479.325.
Of sleep, oppress thee, or by fraud or pow'r? Od.9.482.325.
"If no man hurt thee, but the hand divine Od.9.487.326.
"Inflict disease, it fits thee to resign: Od.9.488.326.
And send thee howling to the realms of night! Od.9.613.332.
As sure, as *Neptune* cannot give thee sight. Od.9.614.332.
Shall guard thee, and avert the evil hour. Od.10.344.360.
Or magic bind thee, cold and impotent. Od.10.360.361.
Untouch'd before thee stand the cates divine, Od.10.447.365.
The northern winds shall wing thee on thy way. Od.10.601.372.
But lend me aid, I now conjure thee lend, Od.11.81.385.
Will give thee back to day, and *Circe's* shores: Od.11.86.385.
Thee yet alive, companion of the dead? Od.11.119.386.
A shepherd meeting thee, the *Oar* surveys, Od.11.157.389.
Or say, since honour call'd thee to the field, Od.11.198.391.
Say what distemper gave thee to the dead? Od.11.207.391.
Thee, ever thee, thy faithful consort mourns; Od.11.219.392.
Thee, ever thee, thy faithful consort mourns; Od.11.219.392.
Thee she by night, and thee by day bewails. Od.11.221.392.

THEE (CONTINUED)

Thee she by night, and thee by day bewails. Od.11.221.392.
Thee in *Telemachus* thy realm obeys; Od.11.222.392.
For thee, my son, I wept my life away; Od.11.240.393.
For thee thro' hell's eternal dungeons stray: Od.11.241.393.
For thee I liv'd, for absent thee expir'd. Od.11.247.393.
For thee I liv'd, for absent thee expir'd. Od.11.247.393.
'Tis not the Queen of Hell who thee deceives: Od.11.261.394.
Two brother heroes shall from thee be born; Od.11.300.396.
Thy tale with raptures I could hear thee tell, Od.11.466.407.
Imperial Phantom, bow'd thee to the tomb? Od.11.494.408.
Has fate oppress'd thee in the roaring waves, Od.11.496.408.
Or nobly seiz'd thee in the dire alarms Od.11.497.408.
For thee she feels sincerity of woe: Od.11.550.410.
Alive, we hail'd thee with our guardian Gods, Od.11.593.412.
Accurs'd our army with the loss of thee! Od.11.682.418.
With thee we fell; *Greece* wept thy hapless fates, Od.11.683.418.
Jove hated *Greece,* and punish'd *Greece* in thee! Od.11.688.418.
And guard thee thro' the tumult of the floods. Od.12.159.439.
My following fates to thee oh King, are known, Od.12.535.459.
'Till age and death shall gently call thee hence, Od.13.76.5.
To thee, to thine, the people, and the King! Od.13.79.5.
Mild I obey'd, for who shall war with thee? Od.13.155.13.
With joy to thee, as to some God, I bend, Od.13.277.19.
To thee my treasures and my self commend. Od.13.278.19.
Who taught thee arts, *Alcinous* to persuade, Od.13.344.24.
He who discerns thee must be truely wise, Od.13.356.24.
Once more 'twas giv'n thee to behold thy coast: Od.13.388.25.
Know, I am with thee, strong in all my might. Od.13.448.27.
It fits thee now to wear a dark disguise, Od.13.453.28.
Estrange thee from thy own, thy son, thy wife; Od.13.462.28.
For thee he sighs; and to the royal heir Od.13.467.28.
Afresh for thee, my second cause of woe! Od.14.201.45.
Hush thee, he cry'd, (soft-whisp'ring in my ear) Od.14.555.64.
His guest, and send thee where thy soul desires. Od.14.585.65.
'Till heav'n decrees to bless thee in a bride. Od.15.30.71.
For thee their snares the Suitor Lords shall lay Od.15.33.71.
(For still to thee his loyal thoughts incline) Od.15.46.72.
To thee we now consign the precious load, Od.15.132.75.
To thee, as to some God, I'll temples raise, Od.15.204.78.
Himself will seek thee here, nor wilt thou find Od.15.238.79.
Fate owes thee sure a miserable end! Od.15.347.86.
Stay then: no eye askance beholds thee here; Od.15.354.86.
And safe conveys thee where thy soul desires. Od.15.359.86.
Snatch'd thee an infant from thy native land! Od.15.411.89.
Rude Pyrates seiz'd, and shipp'd thee o'er the main? Od.15.419.89.
Too much detain thee from these sylvan bow'rs. Od.16.30.103.
To seek thee, friend, I hither took my way. Od.16.32.103.
To thee my son the suppliant I resign, Od.16.67.105.
And deems thee lost: shall I my speed employ Od.16.146.109.
What ship transported thee, O father say, Od.16.246.116.
And what blest hands have oar'd thee on the way? Od.16.247.116.
I tell thee all, my child, my only joy! Od.16.249.117.
Thy deeds denote thee of the basest kind. Od.16.437.128.
Yet like my self I wish'd thee here preferr'd, Od.17.209.141.
When slave! to sell thee at a price too dear Od.17.297.146.
Must be my care; and hence transport thee o'er, Od.17.298.146.
And I shall praise thee thro' the boundless earth. Od.17.500.157.
The Chief retiring. Souls, like that in thee, Od.17.537.158.
(The Suitor cry'd) or force shall drag thee hence, Od.17.569.160.
Scourge thro' the publick street, and cast thee there, Od.17.570.160.
The Queen invites thee, venerable guest! Od.17.634.163.
Of her long-absent Lord from thee to gain Od.17.636.163.
I ask, what harms not thee, to breathe this air: Od.18.23.168.
Some joy remains: To thee a son is giv'n, Od.18.207.177.
For thee I mourn till death dissolves my frame. Od.18.244.178.
Speaks thee an Heroe from an Heroe sprung: Od.18.260.179.
My father, mother, all, I trust to thee; Od.18.311.181.
And custom bids thee without shame receive; Od.18.332.183.
A foe may meet thee of a braver kind, Od.18.382.186.
Shall send thee howling all in blood away! Od.18.384.186.
The scourge, the scourge shall lash thee into sense. Od.18.388.186.
Say, if large hire can tempt thee to employ Od.18.404.188.
To thee the purpose of my soul I told, Od.19.111.198.
Thy Port asserts thee of distinguish'd race; Od.19.186.200.
What pangs for thee this wretched bosom bears! Od.19.425.215.
Perhaps, like thee, poor guest! in wanton pride Od.19.436.216.
None imag'd e'er like thee my master lost. Od.19.445.216.
This heav'n-discover'd truth to thee consign'd, Od.19.569.224.
Suffice it thee thy Monarch to conceal. Od.19.586.224.
The geese (a glutton race) by thee deplor'd, Od.19.644.227.
Like thee, poor stranger guest, deny'd his home! Od.20.261.246.
Like thee, in rags obscene decreed to roam! Od.20.262.246.
Had made thee buy the brutal triumph dear: Od.20.375.251.
Stretch'd forth in wrath, shall drive thee from the land. Od.21.402.279.
Then to the Prince. Nor have I wrought thee shame; Od.21.465.282.
Vulturs shall tear thee—Thus incens'd they spoke, Od.22.35.288.
What hop'st thou here? Thee first the sword shall slay, Od.22.239.298.
Fate doom'd thee next, *Eurydamas,* to bear Od.22.312.301.
Arise, and bless thee with the glad survey! Od.23.10.319.
O *Troy—may* never tongue pronounce thee more! Od.23.24.320.
He lives to thy *Telemachus* and thee! Od.23.58.321.
Once more *Ulysses* my belov'd in thee! Od.23.178.329.
To thee, to me, to *Actoris* alone, Od.23.242.335.
Restore thee safe, since my *Ulysses* reigns. Od.23.276.336.
Around thee stand the daughters of the deep, Od.24.75.351.
Roab thee in heav'nly vests, and round thee weep. Od.24.76.351.
Roab thee in heav'nly vests, and round thee weep. Od.24.76.351.
Round thee, the *Muses,* with alternate strain, Od.24.77.351.
To flames we gave thee, the succeeding day, Od.24.83.352.
The Gods assented; and around thee lay Od.24.109.353.
"(If such thou art) to manifest thee mine." Od.24.383.367.

THEFT

Secure from Theft: Then launch'd the Bark again, 1.TrUl.51.467.
He, who still wanting tho' he lives on theft, 4.Arbu.183.109.

THEFT (CONTINUED)
In Sense still wanting, tho' he lives on Theft, 6.98.33.284.
Bring forth some Remnant of *Promethean* theft, 6.100iv.1.289.
Is but a licens'd Theft that 'scapes the Law. Il.24.534.558.
Secure from theft: then launch'd the bark again, Od.13.142.11.

THEFTS
These thefts, false nymph, thou shalt enjoy no more, 1.TrPA.138.371.

THEIR (OMITTED)
2287

THEIRS
Art shall be theirs to varnish an Offence, 2.ChJM.661.46.
'Tis mine to wash a few slight Stains; but theirs 4.JD4.284.49.
Or others Ease and theirs alike destroy, 6.17ii.7.56.
And reading wish, like theirs, our fate and fame, 6.52.9.156.
Condemn a Play of theirs, and they evade it, 6.60.9.178.
Theirs are the Rules of *France,* the Plots of *Spain:* 6.60.12.178.
Theirs is the Vanity, the Learning thine: 6.71.45.204.
'Tis theirs, the brave Man's latest Steps to trace, 6.84.29A.239.
And what extinguish'd theirs, encreas'd my Flame. 6.96iv.74.278.
Think all the Business of the Earth is theirs. 6.96v.28.281.
Theirs are his Omens, and his Thunder theirs. Il.9.310.449.
Theirs are his Omens, and his Thunder theirs. Il.9.310.449.
Such Ruin theirs, and such Compassion mine. Il.21.142.427.
Remember theirs, and mitigate thy own. Il.24.781.569.
But now no crime is theirs: this wrong proceeds Od.18.275.179.

THEM (OMITTED)
340

THEME
In *Theban* Wars an humbler Theme may chuse: 1.TrSt.50.411.
Marriage, the Theme on which they all declaim'd, 2.ChJM.141.21.
There sober Thought pursu'd th'amusing theme 4.JD4.188.41.
But why all this? I'll tell ye, 'tis my Theme: 4.HAdv.27.77.
But why all this? Beloved, 'tis my Theme: 4.HAdv.27A.77.
Like gentle *Fanny's* was my flow'ry Theme, 4.Arbu.149.107.
Like gentle *Damon's* was my flow'ry Theme, 4.Arbu.149A.107.
The melancholy poets theme, 6.6ii.3.14.
And hers, when freedom is the theme, to write. 6.107.12.310.
Ulysses or *Achilles* still his Theme; Il.2.269.140.
Example sad! and Theme of future Song. Il.6.449.348.
His tender theme the charming Lyrist chose Od.1.421.53.
My wars, the copious theme of ev'ry tongue, Od.4.119.125.
Dubious to press the tender theme, or wait Od.4.155.127.
A theme of future song! Say then if slain Od.8.633.297.
'Till thus the Queen the tender theme renews. Od.19.252.207.
The pleasure past supplies a copious theme Od.19.681.229.
The night renews the day-distracting theme, Od.20.102.237.
Example dread! and theme of tragic song! Od.24.229.358.

THEMES
To heav'nly Themes sublimer Strains belong. 1.Mes.2.112.
These now no more shall be the Muse's Themes, 1.W-F.361.185.
Themes of my Verse, and Objects of my Flames, 1.TrSP.233.404.
Who when two Wits on rival themes contest, 6.49iii.23.143.
Who, if two Wits on rival Themes contest, 6.98.59.285.
Tho' now on loftier Themes he sings 6.135.89.370.
On themes remote the venerable Sage: Od.3.302.101.

THEMIS
Fair *Themis* first presents the golden Bowl, Il.15.96.200.
Then *Jove* to *Themis* gives Command, to call Il.20.5.392.
By righteous *Themis* and by thund'ring *Jove,* Od.2.74.64.
(*Themis,* who gives to councils, or denies Od.2.75.64.

THEMIS'
To the sage *Greeks* conven'd in *Themis'* court, Od.20.180.242.

THEMSELVES
Let such teach others who themselves excell, 1.EOC.15.240.
Set up themselves, and drove a *sep'rate* Trade: 1.EOC.105Z1.251.
(As *Kings* dispense with *Laws* Themselves have made) 1.EOC.162.259.
Still make themselves the measure of Mankind; 1.EOC.453.290.
Now Lapdogs give themselves the rowzing Shake, 2.RL1.15.146.
Those Acts of Goodness, which themselves requite. 2.TemF.363.281.
Poets themselves must fall, like those they sung; 2.Elegy.75.368.
They love themselves, a third time, in their race. 3.EOM3.124.105.
All love themselves, a third time, in their race. 3.EOM3.124A.105.
'Till jarring int'rests of themselves create 3.EOM3.293.122.
And jarring int'rests of themselves create 3.EOM3.293A.122.
Not that themselves are wise, but others weak. 3.EOM4.228.148.
Nor that themselves are wise, but others weak. 3.EOM4.228A.148.
Jones and Palladio to themselves restore, 3.Ep4.193.155.
To see themselves fall endlong into Beasts, 4.JD4.167.39.
Than eat the sweetest by themselves at home. 4.HS2.96.61.
Who judg'd themselves, and saw with their own Eyes) 4.HAdv.113.85.
Large as the Fields themselves, and larger far 4.JD2.95.141.
Large as his Fields themselves, and huger far 4.JD2A.98.140.
They treat themselves with most profound respect; 4.2HE2.154.175.
But how severely with themselves proceed 4.2HE2.157.175.
Who know themselves so little what to do? 4.1HE1.123.289.
Transform themselves so strangely as the Rich? 4.1HE1.153.291.
Sleepless themselves to give their readers sleep. 5.DunA1.92.70.
Sleepless themselves, to give their readers sleep. 5.DunB1.94.276.
Which in all others they themselves destroy? 6.4i.8.9.
To gaze upon themselves in thee. 6.6ii.12.14.
To lose themselves by what shou'd them maintain, 6.17ii.12.56.
And in th' impetuous Course themselves the sooner drain: 6.17ii.13.56.
Trifles themselves are Elegant in him. 6.19.4.62.
As smiling Infants sport themselves to Rest: 6.19.14.62.
As smiling Infants sport themselves to Sleep. 6.19.14A.62.
The Learn'd themselves we Book-Worms name; 6.53.13.161.
Judged for themselves, and saw with their own eyes. 6.147i.2.390.

THEMSELVES (CONTINUED)
But helpless tremble for themselves, and fly. Il.11.152.42.
Oppos'd their Breasts, and stood themselves the War. Il.12.162.87.
Strong in themselves, but stronger in his Aid, Il.12.303.92.
Strong in themselves, but stronger in their Aid, Il.12.303A.92.
Themselves abandon'd, shall the Fight pursue, Il.14.111.163.
With helpful Hands themselves assist the Train. Il.14.440.184.
And by their Parents, by themselves, implores. Il.15.795.226.
Lost are those Arms the Gods themselves bestow'd Il.18.105.328.
The Gods themselves at length relenting, gave Il.24.771.569.
Soon in the luscious feast themselves they lost, Od.10.274.356.
The pitying Gods themselves my chains unbind. Od.14.384.53.
Some God has told them, or themselves survey Od.16.372.124.

THEN (OMITTED)
1537

THENCE
Thence form your Judgment, thence your Maxims bring, 1.EOC.126.253.
Thence form your Judgment, thence your Maxims bring, 1.EOC.126.253.
Thence form your Judgment, thence your Notions bring, 1.EOC.126A.253.
Thence form your Judgment, thence your Notions bring, 1.EOC.126A.253.
Thence Arts o'er all the *Northern World* advance; 1.EOC.711.322.
The flight of birds, and thence presages drew, 1.TrPA.30.366.
And thence exerting his refulgent Ray, 1.TrVP.116.381.
Headlong from thence the glowing Fury springs, 1.TrSt.169.417.
Headlong from thence the Fury urg'd her Flight, 1.TrSt.169A.417.
Begin from thence, where first *Alphëus* hides 1.TrSt.383.426.
And thence declining gently to the Main. 1.TrSt.467.429.
Thence we these Altars in his Temple raise, 1.TrSt.786.443.
Thence, from the War, the breathless Hero bore, 1.TrES.338.462.
To count these *Presents,* and from thence to prove 1.TrUl.92.469.
Self-banish'd thence, I sail'd before the Wind, 1.TrUl.142.470.
And learn from thence their Ladies to suspect: 2.ChJM.594.43.
Thence, by a soft Transition, we repair 2.RL1.49.149.
Thence to their Images on earth it flows, 2.Elegy.15.363.
Thence comes your mutton, and these chicks my own: 4.HS2.144.67.
Thames wafts it thence to Rufus' roaring hall, 5.DunA2.253.130.
"Thence to the South extend thy gladden'd eyes; 5.DunA3.71.156.
"Thence to the South as far extend thy eyes; 5.DunA3.71A.156.
Thence a new world, to Nature's laws unknown, 5.DunA3.237.177.
Thames wafts it thence to Rufus' roaring hall, 5.DunB2.265.308.
Thence to the banks where rev'rend Bards repose, 5.DunB2.347.314.
Thence to the banks where Bards departed doze 5.DunB2.314A.314.
"Thence to the south extend thy gladden'd eyes; 5.DunB3.79.324.
Thence a new world to Nature's laws unknown, 5.DunB3.241.332.
Thence bursting glorious, all at once let down, 5.DunB4.291.373.
And thence its current on the town bestows; 6.35.32.104.
Thence endless streams of fair ideas flow, 6.52.43.157.
Thence beauty, waking all her forms, supplies 6.52.45.157.
Stealing the Papers thence she put 6.94.79.261.
Yet thence to think I'd bite your Head off! 6.135.7.366.
But thence to think I'le bite your Head off! 6.135.7A.366.
Thence bear *Briseïs* as our Royal Prize: Il.1.423.108.
And points the Crime, and thence derives the Woes: Il.1.499.112.
And thence to *Troy* his hardy Warriors led. Il.2.764.162.
And thence from *Simois* nam'd the lovely Boy. Il.4.549.247.
Thence glancing downward lopp'd his Holy Hand, Il.5.106.272.
Thence, to relieve the fainting *Argive* Throng, Il.5.970.312.
Had thence retir'd; and with her second Joy, Il.6.466.349.
Thence his broad Eye the subject World surveys, Il.8.65.398.
My Travels thence thro' spacious *Greece* extend; Il.9.598.464.
The Neighbour Nations thence commencing Foes. Il.9.664.467.
Thence the black Fury thro' the *Grecian* Throng Il.11.13.35.
Thence took the long, laborious March by Land. Il.11.296.48.
Raz'd the smooth Cone, and thence obliquely glanc'd. Il.11.454.54.
Thence, e'er the Sun advanc'd his noonday Flame, Il.11.862.74.
From thence, two Javelins glitt'ring in his Hand, Il.13.315.120.
And thence these Trophies and these Arms I gain. Il.13.344.122.
And thence my Ships transport me thro' the Main; Il.13.569.133.
O'er high *Pieria* thence her Course she bore, Il.14.259.173.
From thence he took a Bowl, of antique Frame, Il.16.273.249.
Who chas'd for Murder thence, a Suppliant came Il.16.701.271.
Thence from the War the breathless Hero bore, Il.16.825.275.
Thence on the nether World the Fury fell; Il.19.131.377.
And learn from thence the Business of the Day. Il.19.152.378.
Thence on the Gods of *Troy* we swift descend: Il.20.168.400.
An ample Present let him thence receive, Il.23.631.514.
From thence the Cup of mortal Man he fills, Il.24.665.565.
Thence all these Tears, and all this Scene of Woe! Il.24.931.575.
Thence, many Evils his sad Parents bore, Il.24.932.575.
Thence to re-visit your imperial dome, Od.1.241.44.
Thence speed your voyage to the *Spartan* strand, Od.1.371.50.
Thence to the bath, a beauteous pile, descend; Od.4.58.122.
But ah how chang'd! from thence my sorrow flows; Od.6.197.219.
A lucid lake, and thence descends in rills: Od.6.352.229.
Thence, where proud *Athens* rears her tow'ry head, Od.7.103.239.
And thence its current on the town bestows; Od.7.173.244.
Thence to the Queen. O partner of our reign, Od.8.459.288.
(Thence call'd *Lotophagi)* which whoso tastes, Od.9.107.308.
From thence we climb'd a point, whose airy brow Od.10.111.346.
And thence our fortunes and our fates to know. Od.10.678.376.
And thence had glided, viewless as the air: Od.10.688.376.
Thence to her son the choicest plagues she brings, Od.11.339.398.
Thence to *Trinacria's* shore you bend your way, Od.12.160.439.
To count these presents, and from thence to prove Od.13.259.18.
Self-banish'd thence. I sail'd before the wind, Od.13.309.21.
Thence charg'd with riches, as increas'd in fame, Od.14.270.49.
Thence born to *Ithaca* by wave and wind; Od.15.519.95.
Thence safe I voyag'd to my native shore. Od.17.169.139.
Its current thence to serve the city brings: Od.17.234.143.
Was journey'd thence to *Dodonæan Jove;* Od.19.340.210.
Constrain'd, the choicest beeves I thence import, Od.20.271.246.
Thence thro' his breast its bloody passage tore; Od.22.109.292.
To mount yon window, and alarm from thence Od.22.149.294.
Thence all descend in pomp and proud array, Od.23.131.327.

THENCE (CONTINUED)
Thence swift re-sailing to my native shores, ...Od.23.295.337.

THENCEFORTH
The strong *Dolopians* thenceforth own'd my Reign, ...Il.9.602.464.

THEOCLES
Which Theocles in raptur'd vision saw, ...5.DunB4.488.389.

THEOCLYMENUS
From him sprung *Theoclymenus,* who found ....Od.15.278.82.
Then *Theoclymenus.* But who shall lend ....Od.15.547.96.
When *Theoclymenus* the seer began: ....Od.17.172.139.

THEODAMAS
Nor fierce *Theodamas,* whose sprightly Strain ....2.ChJM.324.29.

THEORY
To Practice now from Theory repair. ....5.DunB4.580.399.

THERE (OMITTED)
724

THERE'S
For there's a *Happiness* as well as *Care.* ....1.EOC.142.255.
There's Danger in assembling Fire and Tow, ...2.ChWB.30.58.
There's Danger too, you think, in rich Array, ...2.ChWB.140.63.
There's not a blessing Individuals find, ...3.EOM4.39.131.
There's some Peculiar in each leaf and grain, ...3.Ep1.15.17.
Cries, "oh! how charming if there's no such place!" ....3.Ep2.108A.58.
Cries, "Ah! how charming if there's no such place!" ....3.Ep2.108.58.
If QUEENSBERRY to strip there's no compelling, ...3.Ep2.193.66.
There's yet in this, as in all Evills stil, ...4.JD2A.3.132.
There's a Rehearsal, Sir, exact at One.— ....4.2HE2.97.171.
There's nothing blackens like the ink of fools; ....4.2HE1.411.229.
That carries double when there's need: ....6.39.4.110.
That carries double if there's need: ....6.39.4A.110.
There's such ado with Townsend. ....6.61.16A.181.
To say that at Court there's a Death of all Wit, ...6.62iii.3A.185.
To say that at Court there's a Dearth of all Wit, ...6.62iii.3.185.
There's Captain *Pennel,* absent half his Life, ...6.96iv.21.276.
So there's an end of honest *Jack.* ....6.103.2.295.
Knock as you please, there's no body at home. ....6.124iii.2.348.
If there's a *Briton,* then, true bred and born, ...6.128.19.356.
If there's a Critick of distinguish'd Rage; ....6.128.21.356.
If there's a Senior, who contemns this Age; ....6.128.22.356.
"I tell ye, fool, there's nothing in't: ....6.140.26.379.

THEREFORE
And therefore, Sir, as you regard your Rest, ...2.ChJM.184.23.
Who does a kindness, is not therefore kind; ....3.Ep1.62.20.
Not therefore humble he who seeks retreat, ...3.Ep1.65.20.
Who combats bravely is not therefore brave, ...3.Ep1.67.20.
Who reasons wisely is not therefore wise, ...3.Ep1.69.20.
And therefore hopes this Nation may be sold: ....3.Ep3.126.102.
Is therefore fit to have a *Government?* ....4.JD4.139.37.
Therefore, dear Friend, at my Advice give o'er ....6.7.21.16.
Et cæt'ra therefore, we decree, ...6.30.81.89.
Timid and therefore treacherous to the last ....6.130.20.358.
Be therefore now the *Spartan* Wealth restor'd, ...Il.3.571.219.
Hence therefore, while thy stores thy own remain; ....Od.15.23.71.
For worthless beauty? therefore now despis'd? ....Od.17.373.150.

THEREIN
And look'd, as if he meant therein ....6.79.71.220.

THERSILOCHUS
The great *Thersilochus* like Fury found, ...Il.17.257.297.
Mydon, Thersilochus, with *Ænius* fell; ....Il.21.227.430.

THERSITES
Thersites only clamour'd in the Throng, ...Il.2.255.139.

THESE (OMITTED)
839

THESES
And Demonstration thin, and Theses thick, ...5.DunB2.241.307.

THESEUS
In shaggy Spoils here *Theseus* was beheld, ...2.TemF.79.258.
Theseus, endu'd with more than mortal Might, ...Il.1.349.105.
She *Theseus* lov'd; from *Crete* with *Theseus* fled; ....Od.11.400.403.
She *Theseus* lov'd; from *Crete* with *Theseus* fled; ....Od.11.400.403.
The god-like *Theseus,* and *Perithous'* shade; ....Od.11.778.425.

THESPIA
Or *Thespia* sacred to the God of Day. ....Il.2.599.156.

THESPROT
From *Thesprot* mariners, a murd'rous crew. ....Od.16.66.105.

THESPROTIA
In rich *Thesprotia,* and the nearer bound ....Od.19.309.209.

THESPROTIA'S
The tenth soft wafts me to *Thesprotia's* shore. ....Od.14.350.51.
The *Taphian* pyrates on *Thesprotia's* shores; ....Od.16.445.128.
With boundless treasure, from *Thesprotia's* shore. ....Od.17.617.162.

THESPROTIAN
Thesprotian tribes, a duteous race, obey: ....Od.19.330.210.

THESSALIA
Thessalia there, and *Greece,* oppose their Arms. ....Il.16.692.271.

THESSALIA'S
My Fleet shall waft me to *Thessalia's* Shore. ....Il.1.222.97.
Thus spoke your Father at *Thessalia's* Court; ....Il.11.920.76.

THESSALIAN
Thessalian Nymphs there are, of Form divine, ...Il.9.518.458.

THESSALIANS
Thessalians all, tho' various in their Name, ...Il.2.835.164.

THESSALUS
Sprung from the God, by *Thessalus* the King. ....Il.2.828.164.

THESSALY
Of *Thessaly* wide stretch'd his ample reign:) ....Od.4.1052.167.
Of *Thessaly,* his name I heard renown'd: ....Od.19.310.209.

THESTOR
Thestor was next; who saw the Chief appear, ...Il.16.486.262.

THETIS
And *Thetis,* near *Ismenos'* swelling Flood, ...1.TrSt.58.412.
Unhappy Son! (fair *Thetis* thus replies, ...Il.1.540.113.
Thus *Thetis* spoke, but *Jove* in Silence held ....Il.1.662.118.
Is wretched *Thetis* least the Care of *Jove?* ....Il.1.669.119.
Jove to his *Thetis* nothing could deny, ...Il.1.720.122.
My Fates long since by *Thetis* were disclos'd, ...Il.9.532.459.
The Sire of Earth and Heav'n, by *Thetis* won ....Il.13.438.126.
If ought from *Jove,* or *Thetis,* stop thy Arm, ...Il.16.55.237.
Hear, as of old! Thou gav'st, at *Thetis* Pray'r, ...Il.16.292.253.
Perhaps to Him: This *Thetis* had reveal'd; ....Il.17.470.305.
(So *Thetis* warn'd) when by a *Trojan* Hand, ...Il.18.13.323.
How just a Cause has *Thetis* to complain! ....Il.18.70.326.
My Son (Cœrulean *Thetis* made reply, ...Il.18.163.330.
Thetis once more ascends the blest Abodes, ...Il.18.183.331.
Till *Thetis* bring me at the dawn of Day. ....Il.18.228.332.
Vulcan draw near, 'tis *Thetis* asks your Aid. ....Il.18.460.343.
Thetis (reply'd the God) our Pow'rs may claim, ...Il.18.461.343.
Vouchsafe, O *Thetis!* at our Board to share ....Il.18.475.344.
He reach'd the Throne where pensive *Thetis* sate; ....Il.18.492.345.
'Tis thine, fair *Thetis,* the Command to lay, ...Il.18.497.345.
For *Thetis* only such a Weight of Care? ....Il.18.504.346.
And thus, his Hand soft-touching, *Thetis* said. ....Il.19.10.371.
The Seed of *Thetis* thus to *Venus'* Son. ....Il.20.213.402.
But most of *Thetis,* must her Son complain; ....Il.21.318.434.
For such a Warrior *Thetis* aids their Woe, ...Il.23.19.487.
We will not: *Thetis* guards it Night and Day. ....Il.24.94.539.
Where *Thetis* sorrow'd in her secret Cave: ....Il.24.110.539.
Arise! O *Thetis,* from thy Seats below. ....Il.24.116.540.
Calls *Jove* his *Thetis* to the hated Skies? ....Il.24.118.540.
Thetis approach'd with Anguish in her Face, ...Il.24.131.540.
Thou com'st fair *Thetis,* but with Grief o'ercast, ...Il.24.137.540.
Tho' to the contest *Thetis* gave the laws, ...Od.11.669.417.
"Forbear your flight: Fair *Thetis* from the main ....Od.24.73.351.
(The vase to *Thetis Bacchus* gave of old, ...Od.24.95.352.
Thetis herself to all our peers proclaims ....Od.24.107.353.
Such were the games by azure *Thetis* given, ...Od.24.115.353.

THETIS'
Inspir'd by *Juno, Thetis'* God-like Son ....Il.1.74.90.
To honour *Thetis'* Son he bends his Care, ...Il.2.5.127.
But *Thetis'* Son now shines in Arms no more; ....Il.2.938.168.
And *Thetis'* Arms receiv'd the trembling God. ....Il.6.168.334.
At *Thetis'* Suit the partial Thund'rer nods. ....Il.8.450.418.
The Sire of Gods, confirming *Thetis'* Pray'r, ...Il.15.714.223.
Till *Thetis'* Sorrows thus began to flow. ....Il.18.68.326.
At *Thetis'* Feet the finish'd Labour lay; ....Il.18.709.357.
Thetis' this Day, or *Venus'* Offspring dies, ...Il.20.248.404.
The single Fight with *Thetis'* god-like Son; ....Il.20.432.412.
To fell extreams. But *Thetis'* god-like Son, ...Il.23.574.512.
If *Thetis'* Son must no Distinction know, ...Il.24.72.538.

THEY (OMITTED)
1449

THEY'D
They'd prove the Father from whose Loins they came. ....1.TrSt.123.415.
Yet they'd resign that Post so high, ...6.30.40.87.

THEY'L
They'l praise her *Elbow, Heel,* or *Tip o' th' Ear.* ....4.HAdv.123.85.

THEY'LL
Nay, fly to *Altars; there* they'll talk you dead; ....1.EOC.624.310.
Nay, run to *Altars; there* they'll talk you dead; ....1.EOC.624A.310.
They'll never poison you, they'll only cheat. ....4.HS1.90.13.
They'll never poison you, they'll only cheat. ....4.HS1.90.13.
Such they'll degrade; and sometimes, in its stead, ...4.2HE2.163.177.
They'll fit no Man alive. ....6.77.8.214.
They'll serve no Man alive. ....6.77.8A.214.

THEY'RE
Ask them the Cause; *They're* wiser still, they say; ....1.EOC.436.288.
Others so very close, they're hid from none; ....3.Ep1.111.23.
Which tho' they're rich, are Things that none will wear ....4.JD2A.130.144.
And that they're Coppice calld, when dock'd, ...6.67.13.195.
Not that they're rich, but that they steal. ....6.116iii.4.326.
But then they're so blithe and so buxome withall, ...6.122.7.341.
Do you ask if they're good, or are evil? ....6.153.2.402.
They're doom'd to bleed; O say, cœlestial maid! ....Od.20.52.234.

THEY'VE
Nor dare to practise till they've learn'd to dance. ....4.2HE1.184.211.

THICK

He from thick Films shall purge the visual Ray, ... 1.Mes.39.116.
Thro' the thick Desarts headlong urg'd his Flight: .... 1.TrSt.558.433.
Within whose Orb the thick Bull-hides were roll'd, ... 1.TrES.9.450.
Thick as the Bees, that with the Spring renew .... 2.TemF.282.277.
Trees cut to Statues, Statues thick as trees, ... 3.Ep4.120.149.
A heavy Chest, thick Neck, or heaving Side. .... 4.HAdv.117.85.
Away they come, thro' thick and thin, ... 4.HS6.185.261.
From him the next receives it, thick or thin, ... 4.EpS2.175.323.
"Here prove who best can dash thro' thick and thin, ... 5.DunA2.264.133.
Thick as the stars of night, or morning dews, ... 5.DunA3.24.152.
As thick as bees o'er vernal blossoms fly, ... 5.DunA3.25.152.
As thick as eggs at Ward in Pillory. .... 5.DunA3.26.152.
Thick as the stars of night, and morning dews, ... 5.DunA3.24A.152.
Embody'd thick, what clouds of Vandals rise! .... 5.DunA3.78B.156.
And Demonstration thin, and Theses thick, ... 5.DunB2.241.307.
"Here prove who best can dash thro' thick and thin, ... 5.DunB2.276.309.
Thick as the stars of night, or morning dews, ... 5.DunB3.32.322.
As thick as bees o'er vernal blossoms fly, ... 5.DunB3.33.322.
As thick as eggs at Ward in Pillory. .... 5.DunB3.34.322.
But spread, my sons, your glory thin or thick, ... 5.DunB4.129.354.
Thick and more thick the black blockade extends, ... 5.DunB4.191.360.
Thick and more thick the black blockade extends, ... 5.DunB4.191.360.
Came whip and spur, and dash'd thro' thin and thick .... 5.DunB4.197.361.
Then thick as Locusts black'ning all the ground, ... 5.DunB4.397.381.
The short thick Sob, loud Scream, and shriller Squawl: .... 6.14ii.6.43.
Maul'd human *Wit* in one thick Satyr, ... 6.101.9.290.
The Pyres thick-flaming shot a dismal Glare. .... Il.1.72.90.
The Fires thick-flaming shot a dismal Glare. .... Il.1.72A.90.
They toil, they sweat, thick Clouds of Dust arise, ... Il.2.187.137.
Thick as in Spring the Flow'rs adorn the Land, ... Il.2.551.153.
Or Leaves the Trees; or thick as Insects play, ... Il.2.552.153.
Thick as Autumnal Leaves, or driving Sand, ... Il.2.970.169.
With piercing Frosts, or thick-descending Rain, ... Il.3.6.188.
Thro the thick Files he darts his searching Eyes, ... Il.4.235.232.
Such, and so thick, th' embattel'd Squadrons stood, ... Il.4.322.236.
So to the Fight the thick *Battalions* throng, ... Il.4.484.243.
Thro' the thick Storm of singing Spears he flies, ... Il.5.214.277.
Broke the thick Ranks, and turn'd the doubtful Day. .... Il.6.8.323.
Thus in thick Orders settling wide around, ... Il.7.75.366.
Huge was its Orb, with sev'n thick Folds o'ercast, ... Il.7.267.377.
And bear thick Battel on my sounding Shield. .... Il.7.292.378.
Thick Light'nings flash; the mutt'ring Thunder rolls; .... Il.8.95.401.
Whose unber'd Arms, by fits, thick Flashes send. .... Il.8.706.429.
And Heav'n flames thick with momentary Fires. .... Il.10.10.2.
Thick fall the heapy Harvests at their Feet. .... Il.11.92.38.
From the dry Fields thick Clouds of Dust arise. .... Il.11.195.44.
And the thick Thunder beats the lab'ring Ground. .... Il.11.198.44.
Thick on his Hide the hollow Blows resound, ... Il.11.686.65.
And bristled thick with sharpen'd Stakes below. .... Il.12.64.83.
Heavy, and thick, resound the batter'd Shields, ... Il.12.181.87.
Then pours the silent Tempest, thick, and deep: .... Il.12.336.93.
Within whose Orb the thick Bull-Hides were roll'd, ... Il.12.353.94.
Thick with Bull-hides, and brazen Orbits bound, ... Il.13.514.131.
Thick with Bull-hides, with brazen Orbits bound, ... Il.13.514A.131.
On all sides thick, the Peals of Arms resound. .... Il.13.699.138.
His heaving Heart beats thick, as ebbing Life decays. .... Il.13.724.139.
Thick Stones and Arrows intercept the Sky, ... Il.13.900.148.
Thus Rank on Rank the thick Battalions throng, ... Il.13.1006.153.
Thick new-born Vi'lets a soft Carpet spread, ... Il.14.397.182.
Mount the thick *Trojans* up the *Grecian* Wall; .... Il.15.445.214.
Thick sound the Keels; the Storm of Arrows flies. .... Il.15.447.214.
Thick beats the Combate on the sounding Prores. .... Il.15.843.229.
Ev'n *Ajax* paus'd (so thick the Javelins fly) .... Il.15.882.231.
So thick, the Darts an Iron Tempest rain'd: .... Il.16.131.242.
The hissing Brands; thick streams the fiery Show'r; .... Il.16.151.243.
Thick, undistinguish'd Plumes, together join'd, ... Il.16.262.249.
So when thick Clouds inwrap the Mountain's Head, ... Il.16.354.256.
Thick Drifts of Dust involve their rapid Flight, ... Il.16.450.260.
And thick and heavy sounds the Storm of Blows. .... Il.16.766.273.
Thick, as beneath some Shepherd's thatch'd Abode, ... Il.16.779.273.
Pierce the thick Battel, and provoke the War. .... Il.17.136.293.
In one thick Darkness all the Fight was lost; .... Il.17.422.303.
And thick and heavy grows the Work of Death: .... Il.17.445.304.
And thick Bull-hides the Spacious Concave lin'd. .... Il.17.561.310.
Wave their thick Falchions, and their Jav'lins show'r: .... Il.17.818.320.
While *Greece* a heavy, thick Retreat maintains, ... Il.17.845.321.
Thick on the Hills the flaming Beacons blaze; .... Il.18.250.334.
And the round Bulwarks, and thick Tow'rs reply: .... Il.18.262.335.
And thick, strong Strokes, the doubling Vaults rebound. .... Il.18.550.348.
Thick beats the Center as the Coursers bound, ... Il.19.388.388.
Thro' the thick Troops th' embolden'd Hero prest: .... Il.20.143.400.
And casts thick Darkness o'er *Achilles'* Eyes. .... Il.20.370.410.
And thick bestrown, lies *Ceres'* sacred Floor, ... Il.20.578.418.
And thick the groaning Axles dropp'd with Gore. .... Il.20.586.418.
Of the thick Foliage. The large Trunk display'd .... Il.21.273.432.
Thick beats his Heart, the troubled Motions rise, ... Il.21.648.449.
Thro' the thick Gloom of some tempestuous Night .... Il.22.38.454.
But chief, *Pelides:* thick succeeding Sighs .... Il.23.21.487.
Thick, where they drive, the dusty Clouds arise, ... Il.23.441.507.
When thronging thick to bask in open air, ... Od.4.603.148.
And in thick shelter of innum'rous boughs .... Od.5.606.201.
(Thick strown by tempest thro' the bow'ry shade) .... Od.5.625.201.
Thro' the thick gloom the shining portals blaze; .... Od.6.23.204.
And the thick carpets spread with busy care. .... Od.7.430.258.
Thick, as the budding leaves or rising flow'rs .... Od.9.55.304.
In shelter thick of horrid shade reclin'd; .... Od.9.219.314.
Thick, and more thick they gather round the blood, ... Od.11.275.395.
Thick, and more thick they gather round the blood, ... Od.11.275.395.
Thick as the boars, which some luxurious lord .... Od.11.513.409.
Thro' the thick gloom his friend *Achilles* knew, ... Od.11.581.412.
Frequent and thick. Within the space, were rear'd .... Od.14.17.35.
He spreads; and adds a mantle thick and wide; .... Od.14.589.65.
Thick plumage, mingled with a sanguine show'r. .... Od.15.570.98.
Thick o'er the board the plenteous viands lay, ... Od.16.51.104.
With ivory silver'd thick the foot-stool shone, ... Od.19.70.196.

THICK (CONTINUED)

Parnassus, thick perplex'd with horrid shades, ... Od.19.503.220.
Thick swarms the spacious hall with howling ghosts, ... Od.20.427.254.
All black with dust and cover'd thick with blood. .... Od.22.439.309.
His thick large locks, of *Hyacinthine* dye. .... Od.23.156.328.
Thick clouds of dust o'er all the circle rise, ... Od.24.89.352.
First bleeds *Antinous:* thick the shafts resound; .... Od.24.206.358.

THICK-DESCENDING

With piercing Frosts, or thick-descending Rain, ... Il.3.6.188.

THICK-FLAMING

The Pyres thick-flaming shot a dismal Glare. .... Il.1.72.90.
The Fires thick-flaming shot a dismal Glare. .... Il.1.72A.90.

THICK'NING

Or sat delighted in the thick'ning shade, ... 3.Ep4.90.146.
Thick'ning this way, and gath'ring on my Ear; .... Il.10.627.30.
Thick'ning their Ranks, and form a deep Array. .... Il.15.339.210.
Compacted Stones the thick'ning Work compose, ... Il.16.258.249.
And thick'ning round 'em, rise the Hills of Dead. .... Il.17.417.303.
When thick'ning darkness clos'd the doubtful day; .... Od.15.317.85.
Swift from their seats, and thick'ning form a ring. .... Od.18.49.169.

THICKEN

They join, they thicken, and th'Assault renew; .... 1.TrES.152.455.
Beat the loose Sands, and thicken to the Fleet. .... Il.2.184.137.
The Shouts of *Trojans* thicken in the Wind; .... Il.8.192.406.
They join, they thicken, and th' Assault renew; .... Il.12.506.100.
And now come full, thicken to the Fleet! .... Il.14.8.157.
They join, they throng, they thicken at his Call, ... Il.15.676.222.
They join, they thicken, they protend their Spears; .... Il.17.275.298.
Sheaves heap'd on Sheaves, here thicken up the Ground. .... Il.18.640.354.
They join, they throng, they thicken to the War. .... Il.20.430.412.

THICKEN'D

Diffus'd around a Veil of thicken'd Air: .... 1.TrUl.59.468.
Lost and confus'd amidst the thicken'd Day: .... Il.3.20.189.
With close-rang'd Chariots, and with thicken'd Shields. .... Il.8.261.409.
The Time allow'd: *Troy* thicken'd on the Shore, ... Il.17.114.292.
Around him spread a veil of thicken'd air; .... Od.7.20.234.
Diffus'd around a veil of thicken'd air: .... Od.13.226.17.

THICKENS

Tumultuous Clamour mounts, and thickens in the Skies. .... 1.TrES.96.453.
The Tumult thickens, and the Skies resound. .... Il.2.981.170.
The Tumult thickens, and the Skies resound. .... Il.8.74.399.
Tumultuous Clamour mounts, and thickens in the Skies. .... Il.12.450.98.
The Tumult thickens, and the Clamour grows. .... Il.13.226.116.
Still grows, and spreads, and thickens round the King. .... Il.16.255.249.
When the storm thickens, and the billows boil) .... Od.3.357.103.

THICKER

But with a thicker Night black *Auster* shrouds .... 1.TrSt.492.430.
Thicker than arguments, temptations throng, ... 3.EOM2.75.64.
And seem a thicker Dew, or thinner Rain; .... 6.42vi.4.120.
And thicker Javelins intercept the Sky. .... Il.14.496.188.

THICKEST

Now range the Hills, the thickest Woods beset, ... 1.W-F.95A.159.
Thro' thickest Woods, and rouz'd the Beasts of Prey. .... 1.TrSt.529.432.
But pour them thickest on the noble head. 5.DunB4.358.37
And plung'd amid the thickest *Trojans* lies. .... Il.3.52.191.
Behold me plunging in the thickest Fight. .... Il.4.407.240.
Where the Fight burns, and where the thickest rage. .... Il.5.14.266.
Then, where the thickest fought, the Victor flew; .... Il.11.191.44.
Then plung'd amidst the thickest Ranks of Fight. .... Il.11.420.53.
Here *Hector* plunging thro' the thickest Fight .... Il.11.662.63.
Then fierce they mingle where the thickest rage. .... Il.13.992.152.
Drove thro' the thickest of th' embattel'd Plains .... Il.15.524.217.
Still at the closest Ranks, the thickest Fight, ... Il.15.742.224.
Where the War bleeds, and where the thickest die. .... Il.16.455.260.
Alone, unaided, in the thickest War? .... Il.17.537.309.

THICKET

In the green Thicket of a Mossy stone? .... 6.96ii.30Z8.271.
"In the green Thicket of a Mossy Stone, ... 6.96ii.42.272.
Whose guileful Javelin from the Thicket flew, ... Il.7.174.372.
From the blind Thicket wounds a stately Deer; .... Il.11.595.60.
This way and that, the ratt'ling Thicket bends, ... Il.16.927.279.
So thro' the Thicket bursts the Mountain Boar, ... Il.17.331.300.
Looks down, and sees the distant Thicket move; .... Il.17.764.318.
Rouz'd from his Thicket by a Storm of Darts; .... Il.21.678.450.
Or deep beneath the trembling Thicket shakes; .... Il.22.246.465.
Now from the sacred thicket where he lay, ... Od.7.17.234.
Thro' the lone thicket, and the desart land. .... Od.10.296.358.

THICKETS

Rush thro' the Thickets, down the Vallies sweep, ... 1.W-F.156.164.
"Learn from the birds what food the thickets yield; 3.EOM3.173.110
They pierce my Thickets, thro' my Grot they glide, ... 4.Arbu.8.96.
But swift thro' rustling Thickets bursts her way; .... Il.11.158.42.
Headlong. Deep-echoing groan the Thickets brown; .... Il.23.148.495.
Where savage goats thro' pathless thickets rove: .... Od.9.136.311.
Crown'd with rough thickets, and a nodding wood. .... Od.9.224.316.
A length of thickets, and entangled wood. .... Od.10.224.351.
Thro' mazy thickets of the woodland shade, ... Od.14.2.32.

THIEF

The Thief condemn'd, in law already dead, ... 4.JD2.15.133.
Who sent the Thief that stole the Cash, away, ... 4.2HE2.25.167.
Who sent the Thief who stole the Cash, away, ... 4.2HE2.25A.167.
This subtle Thief of Life, this paltry Time, ... 4.2HE2.76.171.
Arraign no mightier Thief than wretched *Wild*, ... 4.EpS2.39.315.
He finds himself companion with a thief. .... 4.1740.14.332.
Not one true *Bounce* will be a Thief; .... 6.135.50.368.

THIEVES
Thieves, Supercargoes, Sharpers, and Directors. 4.HS1.72.11.
Plunder'd by Thieves, or Lawyers which is worse, 4.HAdv.57.81.
To Thieves more grateful than the Midnight Shade; Il.3.18.188.
Or thieves insidious thy fair flock surprize? Od.9.483.325.
Did nightly thieves, or Pyrates cruel bands, Od.24.136.354.

THIGH
Or plumper Thigh, than lurk in humble Crape: 4.HAdv.107.85.
May measure there the Breast, the Hip, the Thigh! 4.HAdv.134.87.
As down thy snowie Thigh distill'd the streaming Flood. Il.4.177.229.
Where to the Hip th' inserted Thigh unites, Il.5.375.285.
Sarpedon's Thigh, had robb'd the Chief of Breath; Il.5.822.305.
Who wrench'd the Javelin from his sinewy Thigh. Il.5.855.307.
Fix'd in his nervous Thigh the Weapon stood, Il.11.710.66.
And smote his Thigh, and thus aloud exclaims. Il.16.155.244.
Sharp in his Thigh he felt the piercing Wound; Il.16.367.257.
The Thigh transfix'd, and broke the brittle Bone: Il.16.369.257.
His Blow prevented, and transpierc'd his Thigh, Il.16.373.257.
Lo! the broad scar indented on my thigh, Od.21.227.270.
Plough'd half his thigh; I saw, I saw the scar, Od.23.76.322.

THIGHATIRA'S
And search the shag of Thighatira's Ruff. 6.96ii.30Z2.271.

THIGHS
And when up ten steep slopes you've dragg'd your thighs, 3.Ep4.131.150.
Little legs, and little thighs, 6.18.3.61.
Taper legs, and tempting thighs, 6.18.7.61.
The Thighs, selected to the Gods, divide: Il.1.603.117.
The Thighs thus sacrific'd, and Entrails drest, Il.1.610.117.
The Thighs, selected to the Gods, divide. Il.2.505.150.
The Thighs thus sacrific'd and Entrails drest, Il.2.510.151.
The Purple Cuishes clasp his Thighs around, Il.3.411.212.
And pour'd Libations on the flaming Thighs. Il.11.907.76.
The silver Cuishes first his Thighs infold; Il.19.398.388.
Their Bones resound with Blows: Sides, Shoulders, Thighs Il.23.832.522.
With smoaking thighs, and offering to the God. Od.3.12.87.
The thighs now sacrific'd, and entrails drest, Od.3.590.116.
The ewes still folded, with distended thighs Od.9.517.327.
The thighs, with fat involv'd, divide with art, Od.12.425.451.
The thighs thus offer'd, and the entrails drest, Od.12.429.451.
Broad spread his shoulders, and his nervous thighs Od.18.76.170.
Let then to *Phœbus'* name the fatted thighs Od.21.282.273.

THILKE
Thilke moral shall ye understond, 6.14i.3.41.
"Be thilke same Thing Maids longen a'ter? 6.14i.24.42.

THIN
Thin Trees arise that shun each others Shades. 1.W-F.22.150.
Where yet thin Fumes from dying Sparks arise, 1.TrSt.600.435.
Thin glitt'ring Textures of the filmy Dew; 2.RL2.64.163.
Shrink his thin Essence like a rivell'd Flower. 2.RL2.132.168.
What thin partitions Sense from Thought divide: 3.EOM1.226.43.
"Spread the thin oar, and catch the driving gale. 3.EOM3.178.111.
Thron'd in the Centre of his thin designs; 4.Arbu.93.102.
Thron'd in the Centre of their thin designs; 4.Arbu.93A.102.
Away they come, thro' thick and thin, 4.HS6.185.261.
And a thin Court that wants your Face, 4.1HE7.12.269.
From him the next receives it, thick or thin, 4.EpS2.175.323.
No meagre, muse-rid mope, adust and thin, 5.DunA2.33.100.
"Here prove who best can dash thro' thick and thin, 5.DunA2.264.133.
Tho' stale, not ripe; tho' thin, yet never clear; 5.DunA3.164.167.
Blank'd his bold visage, and a thin Third day: 5.DunB1.114.278.
No meagre, muse-rid mope, adust and thin, 5.DunB2.37.297.
And Demonstration thin, and Theses thick, 5.DunB2.241.307.
"Here prove who best can dash thro' thick and thin, 5.DunB2.276.309.
Tho' stale, not ripe; tho' thin, yet never clear; 5.DunB3.170.328.
But spread, my sons, your glory thin or thick, 5.DunB4.129.354.
Came whip and spur, and dash'd thro' thin and thick 5.DunB4.197.361.
(Not those which thin, unbody'd Shadows fill, 6.13.2.39.
The thin Undress of superficial Light, 6.14iv.6.47.
Forth popp'd the *Sprite* so thin; 6.58.30.172.
Tell P[ickenbur]g how thin she's grown 6.61.24A.181.
Tell Buckenburg how thin she's grown 6.61.24B.181.
Thin Hairs bestrew'd his long mis-shapen Head. Il.2.266.140.
See the thin Reliques of their baffled Band, Il.16.91.239.
Crash'd the thin Bones, and drown'd the Teeth in Gore: Il.16.417.259.
Thro' the thin Verge the *Pelian* Weapon glides, Il.20.325.407.
And thin the Squadrons with my single Spear. Il.20.414.412.
Like a thin Smoke he sees the Spirit fly, Il.23.117.492.
Thin herbage for the mountain-goat to browze, Od.4.824.158.
Thin, as the filmy threads the spider weaves. Od.8.324.281.
Thin airy shoals, and visionary shades. Od.10.633.374.
Thin, airy shoals of visionary ghosts; Od.11.48.383.
Now a thin form is all *Anticlea* was! Od.11.107.386.
Thin, hollow screams, along the deep descent. Od.24.8.347.

THINE
For *Sylvia*, charming *Sylvia* shall be thine. 1.PSp.92.70.
Reveal'd; and *God's* eternal Day be thine! 1.Mes.104.122.
A wealthier Tribute, than to thine he gives. 1.W-F.224.170.
As thine, which visits *Windsor's* fam'd Abodes, 1.W-F.229.170.
Than thine, which visits *Windsor's* fam'd Abodes, 1.W-F.229A.170.
(The *World's* just Wonder, and ev'n *thine O Rome!)* 1.EOC.248.268.
And these and those, my dearest, shall be thine. 1.TrPA.73.368.
As other Gardens are excell'd by thine! 1.TrVP.54.379.
All other Loves are lost in only thine, 1.TrSP.19.394.
But such as merit, such as equal thine, 1.TrSP.46.395.
By Charms like thine which all my Soul have won, 1.TrSP.95.398.
Tho' *Phœbus* longs to mix his Rays with thine, 1.TrSt.39.411.
How mean a Fate, unhappy Child! is thine? 1.TrSt.684.439.
Be this thy Comfort, that 'tis thine t'efface 1.TrSt.822.444.
'Tis thine the Seeds of future War to know, 1.TrSt.841.444.
Were thine exempt, Debate wou'd rise above, 1.TrES.244.459.

THINE (CONTINUED)
No less, than Mortals are surpass'd by thine: 1.TrUl.174.471.
And, *Momentilla*, let the Watch be thine; 2.RL2.114.166.
Griefs to thy griefs, and eccho sighs to thine. 2.ElAb.42.322.
And wait, till 'tis no sin to mix with thine. 2.ElAb.176.334.
Compar'd, half-reas'ning elephant, with thine: 3.EOM1.222.43.
Compar'd with thine, half-reas'ning Elephant! 3.EOM1.222A.43.
The scale to measure others wants by thine. 3.EOM2.292.90.
Is thine alone the seed that strews the plain? 3.EOM3.37.96.
Thine the full harvest of the golden year? 3.EOM3.39.96.
Gives thee to make thy neighbour's blessing thine. 3.EOM4.354.162.
To raise the Thought and touch the Heart, be thine! 3.Ep2.250.70.
O Friend! may each Domestick Bliss be thine! 4.Arbu.406.127.
Dear *Cibber!* never match'd one Ode of thine. 4.2HE2.138.175.
It brighten'd CRAGS's, and may darken thine: 4.1HE6.45.239.
Or beam, good DIGBY! from a Heart like thine. 4.EpS2.241.326.
O thou! whatever Title please thine ear, 5.DunA1.17.62.
Yes, from this moment, mighty Mist! am thine, 5.DunA1.194.86.
Be thine, my stationer! this magic gift; 5.DunA2.129.112.
"Far Eastward cast thine eye, from whence the Sun 5.DunA3.65.156.
"Flow Welsted, flow! like thine inspirer, Beer, 5.DunA3.163.166.
O Thou! whatever title please thine ear, 5.DunB1.19.270.
To serve his cause, O Queen! is serving thine. 5.DunB1.214.285.
And all be sleep, as at an Ode of thine." 5.DunB1.318.293.
Be thine, my stationer! this magic gift; 5.DunB2.137.301.
There Webster! peal'd thy voice, and Whitfield! thine. 5.DunB2.258.308.
"Far eastward cast thine eye, from whence the Sun 5.DunB3.73.323.
"Flow Welsted, flow! like thine inspirer, Beer, 5.DunB3.169.328.
Thine is the genuine head of many a house, 5.DunB4.243.367.
Thine from the birth, and sacred from the rod, 5.DunB4.283.372.
Prop thine, O Empress! like each neighbour Throne, 5.DunB4.333.376.
Nay, Mahomet! the Pigeon at thine ear; 5.DunB4.364.378.
Forbear! nor hope to make that Monarch thine: 5.DunB4.602A.403.
And since that thine all Rhetorick exceeds; 6.2.5.5.
And clips, like thine, his wav'ring wings. 6.6i.12.14.
Thine was the Sway, e'er Heav'n was form'd or Earth, 6.8.4.17.
No Crime was thine, if 'tis no Crime to love. 6.11.96.33.
Not thine, Immortal *Neufgermain!* 6.30.57.88.
Sacred *Hymen!* these are thine. 6.51ii.44.154.
This verse be thine, my friend, nor thou refuse 6.52.1.156.
Theirs is the Vanity, the Learning thine: 6.71.45.204.
Can touch Immortals, 'tis a Soul like thine: 6.84.22.239.
Those *Spectacles*, ordain'd thine Eyes to save, 6.96iv.75.278.
Lord! when the *Giant-Babe* that Head of thine 6.96iv.81.278.
Apply thine Engine to the spungy Door, 6.100vi.1.289.
Attend whatever title please thine ear, 6.106iv.7.307.
Whate'er he draws to please, must all be thine. 6.107.30.311.
Go live! for heav'ns Eternal year is thine, 6.109.9.314.
While ev'ry Joy, successful Youth! is thine, 6.117.1.333.
Shall some kind Hand, like B***'s or thine, 6.117.9.333.
Then mix this Dust with thine—O spotless Ghost! 6.123.5.343.
With tame Content, and Thou possest of thine? Il.1.168.95.
But thine, Ungrateful, and thy Brother's Cause? Il.1.210.97.
A Prize as small, O Tyrant! match'd with thine, Il.1.215.97.
Thine in each Conquest is the wealthy Prey, Il.1.217.97.
'Tis mine to threaten, Prince, and thine to fear. Il.1.240.98.
Thine to look on, and bid the Valiant dye. Il.1.302.101.
'Tis thine whate'er the Warrior's Breast inflames, Il.2.277.141.
The golden Spoil, and thine the lovely Dames. Il.2.278.141.
Art thou that Hero, could those Spoils be thine? Il.2.319.142.
No Crime of thine our present Suff'rings draws, Il.3.215.202.
Then *Paris*, thine leap'd forth, by fatal Chance Il.3.404.211.
What Praise were thine, cou'd'st thou direct thy Dart Il.4.125.226.
To Worth like thine? what Praise shall we bestow? Il.4.293.235.
Thy Father's Skill, O *Phereclus*, was thine, Il.5.77.270.
As thine the Steeds, be thine the Task to guide. Il.5.289.281.
As thine the Steeds, be thine the Task to guide. Il.5.289.281.
Thine be the Guidance then: With Spear and Shield Il.5.296.281.
Sweet Smiles are thine and kind endearing Charms, Il.5.521.293.
How vast the Diff'rence of their Deeds and thine? Il.5.789.304.
My Guest in *Argos* thou, and I in *Lycia* thine. Il.6.281.340.
As thine, *Andromache!* thy Griefs I dread; Il.6.578.355.
And Woes, of which so large a Part was thine! Il.6.581.355.
Great *Hector's* Arm is mightier far than thine. Il.7.130.369.
And Gifts unceasing on thine Altars lay. Il.8.247.409.
What Rage, what Madness, furious Queen! is thine? Il.8.255.409.
The next rich Honorary Gift be thine: Il.8.350.414.
'Tis thine to punish; ours to grieve alone. Il.8.577.424.
But follow it, and make the Wisdom thine. Il.9.138.438.
The Virtues of Humanity be thine— Il.9.337.450.
And solemn swear those Charms were only thine; Il.9.359.451.
These instant shall be thine; and if the Pow'rs Il.9.362.451.
And Gifts can conquer ev'ry Soul but thine. Il.9.748.471.
In this great Enterprize, is only thine. Il.10.278.14.
So still continue to the Race thine Aid! Il.10.346.18.
And count *Atrides'* fairest Daughter thine. Il.13.478.130.
Iphyclus' Son: and that (*Oïleus)* thine: Il.13.870.147.
With Gold unfading, *Somnus*, shall be thine; Il.14.273.175.
For know, thy lov'd one shall be ever thine, Il.14.303.177.
May never Rage like thine my Soul enslave, Il.16.40.237.
Or if a surer, great *Patroclus!* thine. Il.16.233.248.
Were thine exempt, Debate would rise above, Il.16.547.265.
Were thine my Vigour, this successful Spear Il.16.879.277.
Jove's and *Apollo's* is this Deed, not thine; Il.16.1019.282.
Spoils of my Arms, and thine; when, wasting wide, Il.18.401.340.
'Tis thine, fair *Thetis*, the Command to lay, Il.18.497.345.
Secure, what *Vulcan* can, is ever thine. Il.18.532.347.
Before the *Grecian* Peers renounce thine Ire: Il.19.36.373.
But *Jove* himself, the sacred Source of thine. Il.20.139.400.
Are thine no more—Th' insulting Hero said, Il.20.453.413.
O first of Mortals! (for the Gods are thine) Il.21.231.430.
Thine is the Glory doom'd. Thus spake the Gods; Il.21.344.435.
Thine, or my Fate: I kill thee, or I die. Il.22.320.469.
Ah suffer that my Bones may rest with thine! Il.23.104.491.
Add Perjury to Fraud, and make it thine.— Il.23.522.510.
No vulgar Gift) *Eumelus*, shall be thine. Il.23.642.515.

THINE (CONTINUED)
The Mare, or ought thou ask'st, be freely thine, ...Il.23.674.516.
Tho' 'tis not thine to hurl the distant Dart, ...Il.23.712.518.
Of his weak Age, to live the Curse of thine! ....Il.24.682.565.
The Gifts the Father gave, be ever thine, ...Il.24.744.568.
A Parent once, whose Sorrows equal'd thine: ....Il.24.758.569.
My praise the precept is, be thine the deed. ....Od.1.398.51.
And *Halitherses!* thine: be each his friend; ....Od.2.287.75.
Say, is the fault, thro' tame submission, thine? ....Od.3.262.98.
What words are these, and what imprudence thine? ....Od.3.283.100.
Confest, is thine, as once thy father's aid. ....Od.3.487.111.
That care be fate's, a speedy passage thine. ....Od.4.734.153.
Elysium shall be thine; the blissful plains ....Od.4.765.155.
A Palace stor'd with treasures shou'd be thine. ....Od.7.402.256.
The conquest, great *Euryalus,* is thine. ....Od.8.134.270.
Thine is the guest, invite him thou to rise. ....Od.8.154.271.
And learn, our pow'r proceeds with thee and thine, ...Od.9.331.320.
More! give me more, he cry'd: the boon be thine, ...Od.9.419.323.
If thine I am nor thou my birth disown, ...Od.9.619.332.
And Love and love-born confidence be thine. ....Od.10.398.363.
But from th' infernal rite thine eye withdraw, ...Od.10.630.374.
So blest as thine in all the rolls of Fame; ....Od.11.592.412.
Or if of nobler, *Memnon,* it was thine. ....Od.11.638.416.
'Tis thine alone (thy friends and navy lost) ....Od.12.176.440.
To thee, to thine, the people, and the King! ....Od.13.79.5.
(Weak, daring creatures!) is not vengeance thine? ....Od.13.169.13.
No less than mortals are surpass'd by thine. ....Od.13.341.24.
Nor shall that meed be thine, nor ever more ....Od.14.190.45.
Not thine, *Ulysses!* Care unseal'd his eyes; ....Od.15.8.70.
Enchas'd with gold, this valu'd gift be thine; ....Od.15.129.75.
Whatever frugal nature needs, is thine, ...Od.15.528.95.
No race but thine shall *Ithaca* obey, ...Od.15.575.98.
To thine, for ages, heav'n decrees the sway. ....Od.15.576.98.
I gave him my protection, grant him thine. ....Od.16.68.105.
Or that these wither'd nerves like thine were strung; ....Od.16.104.107.
For where's an arm, like thine *Ulysses!* strong, ...Od.17.622.162.
His is the suff'rance, but the shame is thine. ....Od.18.266.179.
Wretch! is not thine: the arrows of the King ....Od.21.103.263.
The court's main gate: To guard that pass be thine. ....Od.21.257.272.
Fierce *Elatus* by thine, *Eumæus,* falls; ....Od.22.296.300.
'Tis thine to merit, mine is to record. ....Od.22.388.307.
He, he is thine! thy son, his latent guest ....Od.23.31.320.
For Wisdom all is thine! lo I obey, ...Od.23.125.326.
'Tis thine, oh Queen, to say: And now impart, ...Od.23.209.333.
Let not against thy spouse thine anger rise! ....Od.23.216.333.
O let me, let me not thine anger move, ...Od.23.223.333.
These are the rights of age, and shou'd be thine. ....Od.24.301.364.

THING
A *little Learning* is a dang'rous Thing; ....1.EOC.215.264.
With some *unmeaning* Thing they call a *Thought,* ....1.EOC.355.279.
That honest Wedlock is a glorious Thing: ....2.ChJM.22.16.
"Let that frail Thing, weak Woman, have her way. ....2.ChWB.194.65.
Or done a thing that might have cost his Life, ...2.ChWB.271.70.
Or who would learn one earthly Thing of Use? ....2.RL5.22.200.
Some livelier play-thing gives his youth delight, ...3.EOM2.277.88.
Its only thinking thing this turn of mind. ....3.EOM3.78.99.
To trust in ev'ry thing, or doubt of all. ....3.EOM4.26.130.
Condition, circumstance is not the thing; ....3.EOM4.57.134.
Add Health and Pow'r, and ev'ry earthly thing; ....3.EOM4.159.143.
No joy, or be destructive of the thing: ....3.EOM4.182.144.
A thing beyond us, ev'n before our death. ....3.EOM4.238.150.
From Peer or Bishop 'tis no easy thing ....3.Ep2.195.66.
Flaunts and goes down, an unregarded thing. ....3.Ep2.252.70.
F. You could not do a worse thing for your Life. ....4.HS1.15.5.
A Thing which *Adam* had been pos'd to name; ....4.JD4.25.27.
This Thing has *travell'd,* speaks each Language too, ...4.JD4.46.29.
The sweetest thing will stink that he can eat ....4.HS2.32A.57.
And always thinks the very thing he ought: ....4.HS2.130.65.
"A Thing descended from the Conqueror? ....4.HAdv.90.83.
'Tis in thyself, and not in God's good Thing: ....4.HAdv.103.83.
All for a Thing you ne're so much as *saw?* ....4.HAdv.136.87.
"The Thing at hand is of all Things the *best.* ....4.HAdv.154.87.
Let *Sporus* tremble—"What? that Thing of silk, ...4.Arbu.305.117.
Let *Paris* tremble—"What? that Thing of silk, ...4.Arbu.305A.117.
Amphibious Thing! that acting either Part, ...4.Arbu.326.119.
And lyes to every Lord in every thing, ...4.JD2.77.141.
To ev'ry Suitor lie in ev'ry thing, ...4.JD2A.80.138.
'Tis one thing madly to disperse my store, ...4.2HE2.292.185.
Allow him but his Play-thing of a Pen, ...4.2HE1.193.211.
I scarce can think him such a worthless thing, ...4.2HE1.209.213.
The fear to want them is as weak a thing: ....4.1HE6.19.237.
In short, that reas'ning, high, immortal Thing, ...4.1HE1.185.293.
And own, the *Spaniard* did a *waggish thing,* ....4.EpS1.17.298.
She's still the same, belov'd, contented thing. ....4.EpS1.140.308.
P. Why that's the thing you bid me not to do. ....4.EpS2.19.314.
Still better, Ministers; or if the thing ....4.EpS2.50.315.
For thee explain a thing till all men doubt it, ...5.DunA1.169.84.
O! if my sons may learn one earthly thing, ...5.DunB4.183.360.
For thee explain a thing till all men doubt it, ...5.DunB4.251.369.
Lost is his God, his Country, ev'ry thing; ....5.DunB4.523.394.
"Be thilke same Thing Maids longen a'ter? ....6.14i.24.42.
A prating Thing, a Magpy height, ...6.14v(a).20.49.
Descanted, some on this Thing, some on that; ....6.17iv.2.59.
Is a thing of little size, ...6.18.9.61.
A vain, unquiet, glitt'ring, wretched Thing! ....6.19.54.63.
The Stoick husband was the glorious thing. ....6.41.38.114.
I know the thing that's most uncommon; ....6.89.1.250.
I know a thing that's most uncommon; ....6.89.1A.250.
The Simile yet one thing shocks, ...6.93.27Z5.257.
(Studious in ev'ry Thing to please thy Taste) ....6.96iv.50.277.
The *Thing,* we know, is neither rich nor rare, ...6.98.21.284.
She would not do the least right thing, ...6.119.2.336.
What earthly thing will woman do? ....6.119.18B.337.
You wonder Who this Thing has writ, ...6.127.1.355.
You ask me Who this Thing has writ, ...6.127.1A.355.

THING (CONTINUED)
O Nash! more blest in ev'ry other thing, ...6.131i.1.360.
Fye, naughty thing! where e'er you come ....6.135.15A.366.
He spoke no more than just the Thing he ought. ....Il.3.278.206.
Who dares think one thing, and another tell, ...Il.9.412.452.

THINGS
And all things flourish where you turn your Eyes. ....1.PSu.76.78.
Just Gods! shall all things yield Returns but Love? ....1.PAu.76.85.
How all things listen, while thy Muse complains! ....1.PWi.77.94.
And where, tho' all things differ, all agree. ....1.W-F.16.150.
Thus (if small Things we may with great compare) ....1.W-F.105.160.
Unfinish'd Things, one knows not what to call, ...1.EOC.42.243.
Nature to all things fix'd the Limits fit, ...1.EOC.52.244.
As things seem *large* which we thro' *Mists* descry, ...1.EOC.392.285.
Unhappy *Wit,* like most mistaken Things, ...1.EOC.494.294.
And Things *unknown* propos'd as Things *forgot:* ....1.EOC.575.306.
And Things *unknown* propos'd as Things *forgot:* ....1.EOC.575.306.
And Things *ne'er known* propos'd as Things *forgot:* 1.EOC.575A.306
And Things *ne'er known* propos'd as Things *forgot:* 1.EOC.575A.306
Such inconsistent things are Love and Shame! ....1.TrSP.142.399.
And all things wake to Life and Joy, but I, ...1.TrSP.156.400.
All things wou'd prosper, all the World grow wise. ....2.ChJM.68.18.
But since by Counsel all things shou'd be done, ...2.ChJM.95.19.
Heav'n knows, how seldom things are what they seem! ....2.ChJM.806.54.
What mighty Contests rise from trivial Things, ...2.RL1.2.144.
What mighty Quarrels rise from trivial Things, ...2.RL1.2A.144.
Nor bound thy narrow Views to Things below. ....2.RL1.36.148.
And see thro' all things with his half-shut Eyes) ....2.RL3.118.176.
Already hear the horrid things they say, ...2.RL4.108.192.
Since all things lost on Earth, are treasur'd there. ....2.RL5.114.208.
The *Youth* that all things but himself subdu'd; ....2.TemF.152.266.
In all things Just, but when he sign'd the Shell. 2.TemF.173A.26
Conceal, disdain—do all things but forget. ....2.ElAb.200.336.
Awake, my St. John! leave all meaner things ....3.EOM1.1.11.
Awake, my Lælius! leave all meaner things ....3.EOM1.1A.11.
May tell why Heav'n made all things as they are. 3.EOM1.28A.16
Account for moral as for nat'ral things: ....3.EOM1.162.35.
Great lord of all things, yet a prey to all; ....3.EOM2.16.55.
While Man exclaims, "See all things for my use!" ....3.EOM3.45.96.
Union the bond of all things, and of Man. 3.EOM3.150.108
From Order, Union, full Consent of things! 3.EOM3.296.123
From Union, Order, full Consent of things! 3.EOM3.296A.1
All sly slow things, with circumspective eyes: 3.EOM4.226.148
Think, and if still the things thy envy call, ...3.EOM4.275.154
From sounds to things, from fancy to the heart; 3.EOM4.392.166
A smar Free-thinker? all things in an hour. ....3.Ep1.109.23.
Time, that on all things lays his lenient hand, ...3.Ep1.224.34.
Woman and Fool are two hard things to hit, ...3.Ep2.113.59.
Gold imp'd with this, may compass hardest things, ...3.Ep3.71A.93.
Gold imp'd with this, can compass hardest things, ...3.Ep3.71B.93.
Gold imp'd by thee, can compass hardest things, ...3.Ep3.71.93.
Things change their titles, as our manners turn: ....3.Ep3.379.123.
And pompous buildings once were things of Use. ....3.Ep4.24.139.
P. Libels and *Satires!* lawless Things indeed! ....4.HS1.150.21.
So Time, that changes all things, had ordain'd! ....4.JD4.43.29.
"Oh 'tis the sweetest of all earthly things ....4.JD4.100.33.
All the Court fill'd with stranger things than he, ...4.JD4.181.41.
Such waxen Noses, stately, staring things, ...4.JD4.210.43.
The *Presence* seems, with things so richly odd, ...4.JD4.238.45.
Prodigious! how the Things *Protest, Protest:* ....4.JD4.255.47.
"The Thing at hand is of all Things the *best.* ....4.HAdv.154.87.
Three things another's modest wishes bound, ...4.Arbu.47.99.
"Good friend forbear! you deal in dang'rous things, ...4.Arbu.75.101.
The things, we know, are neither rich nor rare, ...4.Arbu.171.108.
Not that the things are either rich or rare, ...4.Arbu.171A.108
Which tho they're rich, are Things that none will wear ....4.JD2A.130.144.
Like rich old Wardrobes, things extremely rare, ...4.JD2.123.145.
(Like Journals, Odes, and such forgotten things ....4.2HE1.416.231.
Here no man prates of idle things, ...4.HS6.141.259.
You give the things you never care for. ....4.1HE7.34.271.
You gave the things you never care for. ....4.1HE7.34A.271.
Have I in silent wonder seen such things ....4.EpS1.109.306.
Is it for *Bond* or *Peter* (paltry Things!) ....4.EpS1.121.307.
Is it for *W[a]rd* or *Peter* (paltry Things!) 4.EpS1.121A.307
C[arteret], his own proud dupe, thinks Monarchs things ....4.1740.5.332.
Where things destroy'd are swept to things unborn." 5.DunB1.242.288
Where things destroy'd are swept to things unborn." 5.DunB1.242.288
Are things which Kuster, Burman, Wasse shall see, ...5.DunB4.237.366
The head that turns at super-lunar things, ...5.DunB4.451.384
To thee the most rebellious things on earth: 5.DunB4.508.392
And nobly conscious, Princes are but things 5.DunB4.601.403
Blind with Ambition! to think Princes things 5.DunB4.603A.4
From Sacred Union and consent of Things. ....6.11.35Z10.31.
Yet in some Things methinks she fails, ...6.14v(a).4.48.
And some things of little size, ...6.18.4.61.
And some things else of little size, ...6.18.4A.61.
Gav'st all things to be chang'd, yet ever art the same! ....6.23.8.73.
Two or *Three* civil Things, *Two* or *Three* Vows, ...6.36.2.104.
And from those pretty Things you speak have told, ...6.37.9.106.
How things are priz'd, which once belong'd to you: ....6.38.2.107.
Parson, these Things in thy possessing ....6.39.1.110.
We'd be the best, good-natur'd things alive. ....6.41.14.113.
And loves you best of all things—but his horse. ....6.45.30.125.
To tell Men things they never *knew at all.* ....6.48iii.4.134.
O First of Things! least understood! ....6.50.5A.146.
Ev'n so all Things shall prosper well, ...6.54.11.164.
To call things Woods, for what grows und'r 'em. ....6.67.8.195.
For it maketh things small: ....6.91.18.253.
That maketh things small: ....6.91.18A.253.
And the babes play-things that adorn thy house. ....6.96ii.30Z34.272.
"The Baby Play-things that adorn thy House, ...6.96ii.54.273.
And that to towze such Things as *flutter,* ....6.135.23.367.
(For Gods can all things) in a Veil of Clouds. ....Il.3.468.214.
Th' Event of Things the Gods alone can view. ....Il.11.973.78.
The best of Things beyond their Measure, cloy; ....Il.13.795.143.

THINKS (CONTINUED)
Thinks Worth, Wit, Learning, to that Spot confin'd; ......6.96v.26.280.
Who thinks he *reads* when he but *scans* and *spells,* ......6.98.15.283.
And now she's in t'other, she thinks it but *Queer.* ......6.124i.10.347.
Thus while he thinks, *Antilochus* appears, ...Il.18.19.324.
Just when he holds or thinks he holds his Prey, ...Il.22.185.463.
There fondly thinks the Gods conclude his toil! ......Od.4.695.151.
His fair ones arms—he thinks her, once, too nigh. ......Od.8.356.282.
He thinks the Queen is rushing to his arms. ......Od.20.115.238.

THINLY
His Temples thinly spread with silver Hairs: ......1.TrVP.47.379.
Where thinly scatter'd lay the Heaps of Dead. ......Il.8.612.425.

THINNER
And seem a thicker Dew, or thinner Rain; ......6.42vi.4.120.
The Ranks grow thinner as his Arrows fly, ...Il.8.338.413.
The fishes pant, and gasp in thinner air; ......Od.22.429.309.

THIRD
A Third dispels the Darkness of the Night, ...1.TrSt.609.436.
A third interprets Motions, Looks, and Eyes; ......2.RL3.15.170.
Spreads in a second Circle, then a third; ......2.TemF.439.284.
They love themselves, a third time, in their race. ......3.EOM3.124.105.
All love themselves, a third time, in their race. ......3.EOM3.124A.105.
I would be with you, June the third; ......4.1HE7.2.269.
Drops to the third who nuzzles close behind; ......4.EpS2.178.323.
'Till genial Jacob, or a warm Third-day ......5.DunA1.55.66.
'Till genial Jacob, or a warm Third day, ...5.DunB1.57.274.
Blank'd his bold visage, and a thin Third day: ......5.DunB1.114.278.
The third mad passion of thy doting age. ......5.DunB3.304.334.
Till the third watchman toll; ......6.47.10.128.
What passes in the dark third row ......6.61.8.181.
On thy third Reign look down; disclose our Fate, ...6.65.5.192.
On thy third Realm *look down;* unfold our Fate, ...6.65.5A.192.
See Anno quart. of Edward, third. ......6.67.12.195.
A third majestically stalks ......6.135.61.368.
And now th' Example of the third remain'd. ......Il.1.336.104.
Prepare ye *Trojans!* while a third we bring ......Il.3.143.197.
And these descended in the third Degree. ......Il.5.676.300.
The third Day hence, shall *Pthia* greet our Sails, ...Il.9.473.455.
And of Night's Empire but a third remains. ......Il.10.298.15.
The Sons of *Priam* with the third appear, ...Il.12.107.85.
This, my third Victim, to the Shades I send. ......Il.13.561.133.
His First-born I, the third from *Jupiter:* ......Il.13.567.133.
Euphorbus next; the third mean Part thy own. ......Il.16.1025.282.
The third time labour'd by the sweating Hind; ......Il.18.628.354.
But stopp'd, and rested, by the third repell'd; ......Il.20.317.407.
The third, a Charger yet untouch'd by Flame; ......Il.23.335.503.
The third bold Game *Achilles* next demands, ...Il.23.814.521.
And third, the Strength of god-like *Ajax* cast. ......Il.23.998.529.
A third lives wretched on a distant coast. ......Od.4.670.150.
What third brave son of *Mars* the fates constrain ......Od.4.747.153.
The third fair morn now blaz'd upon the main; ......Od.5.500.196.
But the third morning when *Aurora* brings, ...Od.9.85.306.
And now the third succeeding morning shone. ......Od.10.168.348.
The third in wisdom where they all were wise; ......Od.11.626.414.
And bread and wine the third. The chearful mates ......Od.13.86.5.

THIRD-DAY
'Till genial Jacob, or a warm Third-day ......5.DunA1.55.66.

THIRST
And gasping Furies thirst for Blood in vain. ......1.W-F.422.193.
Ah ne'er so *dire* a *Thirst of Glory* boast, ...1.EOC.522.297.
And Sacred Thirst of Sway; and all the Ties ......1.TrSt.178.417.
Fir'd with the Thirst of Glory, thus he spoke. ......1.TrES.26.450.
Belinda now, whom Thirst of Fame invites, ...2.RL3.25.171.
No fiends torment, no Christians thirst for gold! ......3.EOM1.108.28.
No fiends torment, nor Christians thirst for gold! ......3.EOM1.108A.28.
In lavish streams to quench a Country's thirst, ...3.Ep3.177.108.
And envy'd Thirst and Hunger to the Poor. ......4.1HE6.117.245.
Who hunger, and who thirst, for scribling sake: ......5.DunA1.48.65.
Who hunger, and who thirst for scribling sake: ......5.DunB1.50.274.
Due to his Merit, and brave Thirst of Praise. ......6.108.6.312.
Fir'd with the Thirst which Virtuous Envy breeds, ...Il.1.353.105.
What grieves the Monarch? Is it Thirst of Gold? ......Il.2.282.141.
In radiant Arms, and thirst for *Trojan* Blood. ......Il.2.559.154.
Oh say what Heroes, fir'd by Thirst of Fame, ...Il.2.578.155.
In Thirst of Vengeance, at his Rival's Heart, ...Il.3.466.214.
Let *Priam* bleed! If yet thou thirst for more, ...Il.4.55.223.
So fought each Host, with Thirst of Glory fir'd, ...Il.4.636.251.
With Thirst of Vengeance, and assaults the Foes. ......Il.5.757.303.
Lest Thirst of Glory your brave Souls divide, ...Il.7.207.374.
But stay'd his Hand when Thirst and Hunger ceast. ......Il.9.124.438.
The Rite perform'd, the Chiefs their Thirst allay, ...Il.9.231.444.
His Thirst and Hunger soberly represt. ......Il.9.290.448.
Salubrious Draughts the Warrior's Thirst allay, ...Il.11.786.70.
Fir'd with the Thirst of Glory, thus he spoke. ......Il.12.370.95.
In Thirst of Slaughter, and in Lust of Fight. ......Il.13.800.143.
Those guiltless fall, and thirst for Blood in vain. ......Il.15.359.210.
In the first Ranks indulge thy Thirst of Fame, ...Il.15.558.218.
When scalding Thirst their burning Bowels wrings. ......Il.16.195.247.
And gorg'd with Slaughter, still they thirst for more. ......Il.16.201.247.
Amid the Ranks, with mutual Thirst of Fame, ...Il.16.400.258.
And the torn Boar resigns his Thirst and Life. ......Il.16.998.281.
With Rage insatiate and with Thirst of Blood, ...Il.17.812.320.
E'er Thirst and Want his Forces have oppress, ...Il.19.368.387.
Thither, all parch'd with Thirst, a heartless Train, ...Il.21.633.448.
The Rage of Hunger and of Thirst allay, ...Il.23.68.489.
And *Greece* shall praise thy gen'rous Thirst to give. ......Il.23.632.514.
Relate, if business, or the thirst of gain ......Od.3.86.90.
And now, their thirst by copious draughts allay'd, ...Od.3.439.108.
The rage of thirst and hunger now suppress, ...Od.3.602.117.
Their hunger satiate, and their thirst represt, ...Od.5.255.184.
And with the generous vintage thirst asswag'd. ......Od.6.298.225.

THIRST (CONTINUED)
Our thirst and hunger hastily repress'd; ......Od.10.62.342.
And pines with thirst amidst a sea of waves: ......Od.11.722.421.
And the short rage of thirst and hunger ceast) ......Od.15.159.76.
And now, the rage of thirst and hunger fled, ...Od.16.55.105.
Or still in ambush thirst for blood in vain? ......Od.16.485.130.
Or still in ambush thirst in vain for blood, ...Od.16.487.130.
'Till now the rage of thirst and hunger ceast. ......Od.17.115.137.
Unfinish'd yet, and yet I thirst to hear! ......Od.17.608.161.
These sons of murder thirst thy life to take; ......Od.17.674.165.
The Suitor-train, and raise a thirst to give; ......Od.18.326.183.
The rage of hunger and of thirst represt: ......Od.24.565.375.

THIRSTED
Pour'd forth the darts, that thirsted for our blood, ...Od.24.204.358.

THIRSTING
But oh! thus furious, thirsting thus for gore, ...Od.9.414.323.

THIRSTS
And thirsts and hungers only at one End: ......4.HAdv.24.77.
Know, Eusden thirsts no more for sack or praise; 5.DunB1.293.291
Marks the dry Dust, and thirsts for Blood in vain. ......Il.11.701.66.
Drinks the dry Dust, and thirsts for Blood in vain. ......Il.11.701A.66.
Prints the dry Dust, and thirsts for Blood in vain. ......Il.11.701B.66.

THIRSTY
The sultry *Sirius* burns the thirsty Plains, ...1.PSu.21.73.
Not bubling Fountains to the thirsty Swain, ...1.PAu.43.83.
The thirsty Heifers shun the gliding Flood. ......1.PWi.38.91.
Nor thirsty Heifers seek the gliding Flood. ......1.PWi.38A.91.
And Starts, amidst the thirsty Wilds, to hear ......1.Mes.69.119.
Now sliding Streams the thirsty Plants renew, ...1.TrVP.15.377.
And solace of the thirsty swain. ......6.6ii.4.14.
And while the Dogstar burns the thirsty field, ...6.20.64.67.
Shed like this Wine, distain the thirsty Ground; ......Il.3.373.211.
Swift to the Mark the thirsty Arrow flew, ...Il.5.129.273.
And large Libations drench'd the thirsty Ground; ......Il.7.577.393.
The thirsty Fury of my flying Spear. ......Il.8.142.404.
And drench'd in Royal Blood the thirsty Dart. ......Il.8.368.415.
His thirsty Faulchion, fat with hostile Blood, ...Il.10.561.27.
The thirsty Faulchion drank his reeking Blood: ......Il.16.397.258.
Repuls'd in vain, and thirsty still of Gore; ......Il.17.643.313.
Longing to dip its thirsty Point in Blood; ......Il.21.81.425.
The gushing Purple dy'd the thirsty Sand: ......Il.21.132.427.
And thirsty all of one man's blood they flew; ......Od.22.281.300.
With thirsty sponge they rub the tables o'er, ...Od.22.488.313.

THIRTEEN
Full thirteen Moons imprison'd roar'd in vain; ......Il.5.477.290.

THIRTEENTH
The twelfth or thirteenth Day of *July,* ...... 6.10.117.28.

THIRTY
After an hundred and thirty years' nap, ...6.148i.1.395.
Their Troops in thirty sable Vessels sweep ......Il.2.618.157.
Next thirty Galleys cleave the liquid Plain, ...Il.2.821.164.
In thirty Sail the sparkling Waves divide, ...Il.2.888.166.

THIRTY-NINE
In rev'rence to the Sins of *Thirty-nine!* ...... 4.EpS2.5.313.

THIRTY-THOUSANDTH
Digest his thirty-thousandth dinner; ......6.150.18.399.
Digest this thirty-thousandth dinner; ......6.150.18A.399.

THIS (OMITTED)
1629

THISBÈ
Copæ, and *Thisbè,* fam'd for silver Doves, ...Il.2.601.156.

THISBE
And *Pyramus* and *Thisbe* plainly show ......2.ChJM.516.40.

THISTLE
The *Thistle* springs, to which the *Lilly* yields? ......1.PSp.90.69.

THITHER
Thither with haste the *Theban* Hero flies; ......1.TrSt.532.432.
Thither the *Lycian* Princes bend their Course, ...1.TrES.80Z5.452.
Thither they bent, and haul'd their Ship to Land, ...1.TrUl.45.467.
Thither th'obsequious Squire address'd his Pace, ...2.ChJM.605.44.
Thither, where sinners may have rest, I go, ...2.ElAb.319.345.
Thither, the silver-sounding Lyres ......4.HOde1.25.153.
Thither the Spoils of this long War shall pass, ...Il.9.477.456.
My beauteous Captives thither I'll convey, ...Il.9.479.456.
Thither, O *Hector,* thither urge thy Steeds; ......Il.11.650.62.
Thither, O *Hector,* thither urge thy Steeds; ......Il.11.650.62.
Thither, exulting in his Force, he flies; ......Il.12.137.86.
Thither the *Lycian* Princes bend their Course, ...Il.12.429.97.
Thither, all parch'd with Thirst, a heartless Train, ...Il.21.633.448.
Thither of old, Earth's * Giant-son to view, ...Od.7.413.257.
Two with our herald thither we command, ...Od.10.115.346.
Thither to haste, the region to explore, ...Od.10.177.349.
Thither they bent, and haul'd their ship to land, ...Od.13.136.9.
Me thither in disguise *Eumæus* leads, ...Od.16.292.119.
Thither his son from sandy *Pyle* repairs, ...Od.24.179.356.

THOÖSA
Him young *Thoösa* bore, (the bright increase ......Od.1.92.36.

THO (OMITTED)
16

THO' (OMITTED)
376

THOA
Thoa, Pherusa, Doto, Melita; ... Il.18.53.326.

THOAS
Thoas came next, *Andræmon's* valiant Son, ... Il.2.775.162.
His Lance bold *Thoas* at the Conqu'ror sent, ... Il.4.610.250.
Stern *Thoas,* glaring with revengeful Eyes, ... Il.4.622.250.
With these *Eurypylus* and *Thoas* stand, ... Il.7.203.374.
Thoas, Deïpyrus, in Arms renown'd, ... Il.13.127.110.
Thoas with Grief observ'd his dreadful Course, ... Il.15.318.209.
Thoas, the bravest of th' *Ætolian* Force: ... Il.15.319.209.
Headlong he fell. Next *Thoas* was thy Chance, ... Il.16.370.257.
Thoas and *Merion,* Thunderbolts of War, ... Il.19.246.383.
And gave to *Thoas* at the *Lemnian* Port: ... Il.23.870.524.
Upstarted *Thoas* strait, *Andræmon's* son, ... Od.14.564.64.

THOAS'
To *Thoas'* Care now trust the martial Train, ... Il.2.783.162.
In *Thoas'* Voice, *Andræmon's* valiant Son, ... Il.13.286.119.

THOMAS
H[aywood] and T[homas], Glories of their race! ... 5.DunA3.145A.162*.
In the great Name of *Thomas Durfy.* ... 6.30.12B.86.
Wou'd each hope to be *O* in *Thomas;* ... 6.30.71.88.

THOMISTS
Scotists and *Thomists,* now, in Peace remain, ... 1.EOC.444.289.

THONE'S
Bright *Helen* learn'd from *Thone's* imperial wife; ... Od.4.316.134.

THONG
Struggling he follow'd, while th' embroider'd Thong ... Il.3.457.213.
Within its Concave hung a silver Thong, ... Il.11.49.36.
He said; the Driver whirls his lengthful Thong; ... Il.11.359.50.
Securely fetter'd by a silver thong. ... Od.10.26.340.
Wide-patch'd, and knotted to a twisted thong. ... Od.13.507.30.
Athwart the fiery steeds the smarting thong; ... Od.15.207.78.
Wide patch'd, and fasten'd by a twisted thong. ... Od.17.221.142.
Ill joyn'd, and knotted to a twisted thong. ... Od.18.132.172.

THONGS
With Thongs, inserted thro' the double Wound: ... Il.17.337.300.
With Thongs inserted thro' the double Wound; ... Il.22.498.477.
They said: and (oh curs'd fate!) the thongs unbound; ... Od.10.50.341.
Thongs of tough hides, that boast a purple dye; ... Od.23.204.333.

THOON
Young *Xanthus* next and *Thoon* felt his Rage, ... Il.5.196.276.
Next *Ennomus* and *Thoon* sunk to Hell; ... Il.11.532.57.
And *Oenomaus* and *Thoon* close the Rear; ... Il.12.154.87.
Antilochus, as *Thoon* turn'd him round, ... Il.13.690.137.
Acroneus, Thoon, and *Eretmeus* rise; ... Od.8.114.268.

THOOS
Then thus to *Thoos;—Hence* with speed (he said) ... 1.TrES.67.452.
Your Aid (said *Thoos) Peteus's* Son demands, ... 1.TrES.80Z2.452.
Then thus to *Thoos;—hence* with speed, (he said) ... Il.12.411.96.
Your Aid (said *Thoos) Peteus'* Son demands, ... Il.12.426.97.

THORN
And liquid Amber drop from ev'ry Thorn. ... 1.PAu.38.83.
Waste sandy Vallies, once perplex'd with Thorn, ... 1.Mes.73.119.
Ye grots and caverns shagg'd with horrid thorn! ... 2.ElAb.20.320.
Encircled with a fence of native thorn, ... Od.14.14.35.
To search the woods for sets of flowry thorn, ... Od.24.259.361.
But well repair'd; and gloves against the thorn. ... Od.24.266.361.

THORNS
When, of a hundred thorns, you pull out one? ... 4.2HE2.321.187.
As when a heap of gather'd thorns is cast ... Od.5.417.192.

THORNY
A thorny crown transpierc'd thy sacred brow, ... 6.25.7.77.
The thorny wilds the wood-men fierce assail: ... Od.19.508.221.
My mind reflective, in a thorny maze ... Od.19.613.226.

THOROLD
'Twas on the day, when Thorold, rich and grave, ... 5.DunA1.83.69.

THOSE (OMITTED)
578

THOU
From Love, the sole Disease thou canst not cure! ... 1.PSu.12.72.
Why art thou prouder and more hard than they? ... 1.PSu.18.73.
Thou, whom the Nine with *Plautus'* Wit inspire, ... 1.PAu.7.80.
Thou wert from *Ætna's* burning Entrails torn, ... 1.PAu.91.86.
Delight no more—O Thou my Voice inspire ... 1.Mes.5.112.
Thou too, great Father of the *British* Floods! ... 1.W-F.219.169.
Oh wou'dst thou sing what Heroes *Windsor* bore, ... 1.W-F.299.176.
Be thou the *first* true Merit to befriend; ... 1.EOC.474.292.
If thou all others didst despise and scorn: ... 1.TrPA.119.370.
These thefts, false nymph, thou shalt enjoy no more, ... 1.TrPA.138.371.
If to no Charms thou wilt thy Heart resign, ... 1.TrSP.45.395.
By none alas! by none thou can'st be mov'd, ... 1.TrSP.47.395.
And take at least the Love thou wilt not give. ... 1.TrSP.108A.398.
'Tis thou art all my Care and my Delight, ... 1.TrSP.143.399.
And thou, kind *Love,* my sinking Limbs sustain, ... 1.TrSP.209.403.
Ah! canst thou doom me to the Rocks and Sea, ... 1.TrSP.222.403.
Ah! canst thou rather see this tender Breast ... 1.TrSP.224.403.
And Thou, great Heir of all thy Father's Fame, ... 1.TrSt.31.411.
What Hero, *Clio!* wilt thou first relate? ... 1.TrSt.61.412.

THOU (CONTINUED)
Thou, sable *Styx!* whose livid Streams are roll'd ... 1.TrSt.83.413.
If worthy Thee, and what Thou might'st inspire! ... 1.TrSt.102.414.
Art thou a Father, unregarding *Jove!* ... 1.TrSt.109.414.
Thou *Fury,* then, some lasting Curse entail, ... 1.TrSt.111.414.
Soon shalt thou find, if thou but arm their Hands, ... 1.TrSt.120.415.
Soon shalt thou find, if thou but arm their Hands, ... 1.TrSt.120.415.
Cou'dst thou some great, proportion'd Mischief frame, ... 1.TrSt.122.415.
When all were Slaves thou cou'dst around survey, ... 1.TrSt.221.419.
Thou Sire of Gods and Men, Imperial *Jove!* ... 1.TrSt.243.420.
On thy own Offspring hast thou fix'd this Fate, ... 1.TrSt.245.420.
Thou know'st those Regions my Protection claim, ... 1.TrSt.352.424.
Thou cam'st Triumphant to a Mortal's Arms, ... 1.TrSt.361.425.
Yet since thou wilt thy Sister-Queen controul, ... 1.TrSt.366.425.
But if thou must reform the stubborn Times, ... 1.TrSt.377.425.
Say, can those Honours please? and canst thou love ... 1.TrSt.392.426.
Oh thou who freest me from my doubtful State, ... 1.TrSt.588.434.
Proceed, and firm those Omens thou hast made! ... 1.TrSt.591.435.
Nor shalt thou, *Phœbus,* find a Suppliant here: ... 1.TrSt.760.442.
Whether to sweet *Castalia* thou repair, ... 1.TrSt.831.444.
Thou dost the Seeds of future War foreknow, ... 1.TrSt.841A.444.
Thou art, that wander'st in this desart Place, ... 1.TrUl.109.469.
Arriv'st thou here, a Stranger to our Name? ... 1.TrUl.117.469.
Thou seest an Island, not to those unknown, ... 1.TrUl.118.469.
Secure thou seest thy Native Shore at last? ... 1.TrUl.170.471.
Know'st thou not me, who made thy Life my Care, ... 1.TrUl.175.471.
And tell what more thou must from Fate expect; ... 1.TrUl.181.471.
But thou be Silent, nor reveal thy State, ... 1.TrUl.184.471.
So may my Soul have Joy, as thou, my Wife, ... 2.ChJM.545.41.
While thou art faithful to thy own true Knight, ... 2.ChJM.553.42.
Whilst thou art faithful to thy own true Knight, ... 2.ChJM.553A.42.
For sagely hast thou said; Of all Mankind, ... 2.ChJM.635.45.
But shoud'st thou search the spacious World around, ... 2.ChJM.637.45.
Death! Hell! and Furies! what dost Thou do there? ... 2.ChJM.757.51.
Why to her House do'st thou so oft repair? ... 2.ChWB.78.60.
Art thou so Am'rous? and is she so fair? ... 2.ChWB.79.60.
Art thou so Amorous? Is she so fair? ... 2.ChWB.79A.60.
Horses (thou say'st) and Asses, Men may try, ... 2.ChWB.100.61.
All this thou say'st, and all thou say'st are Lies. ... 2.ChWB.117.62.
All this thou say'st, and all thou say'st are Lies. ... 2.ChWB.117.62.
"Thou should'st be always thus, resign'd and meek! ... 2.ChWB.185.65.
Oh thou hast slain me for my Wealth (I cry'd) ... 2.ChWB.420.77.
Fairest of Mortals, thou distinguish'd Care ... 2.RL1.27.147.
Think what an Equipage thou hast in Air, ... 2.RL1.45.149.
Do thou, *Crispissa,* tend her fav'rite Lock; ... 2.RL2.115.166.
Here Thou, Great *Anna!* whom three Realms obey, ... 2.RL3.7.169.
As Thou, sad Virgin! for thy ravish'd Hair. ... 2.RL4.10.183.
Oh hadst thou, Cruel! been content to seize ... 2.RL4.175.198.
Thou by some other shalt be laid as low. ... 2.RL5.98.207.
Do thou, just Goddess, call our Merits forth, ... 2.TemF.322.279.
Art thou, fond Youth, a Candidate for Praise? ... 2.TemF.500.287.
Thou know'st how guiltless first I met thy flame, ... 2.ElAb.59.323.
Canst thou forget that sad, that solemn day, ... 2.ElAb.107.328.
Canst thou forget what tears that moment fell, ... 2.ElAb.109.329.
Give all thou canst—and let me dream the rest. ... 2.ElAb.124.330.
Come thou, my father, brother, husband, friend! ... 2.ElAb.152.332.
Come *Abelard!* for what hast thou to dread? ... 2.ElAb.257.340.
Ev'n thou art cold—yet *Eloisa* loves. ... 2.ElAb.260.341.
Come, if thou dar'st, all charming as thou art! ... 2.ElAb.281.342.
Come, if thou dar'st, all charming as thou art! ... 2.ElAb.281.342.
Thou, *Abelard!* the last sad office pay, ... 2.ElAb.321.345.
Ah no—in sacred vestments may'st thou stand, ... 2.ElAb.325.346.
But thou, false guardian of a charge too good, ... 2.Elegy.29.365.
Thou, mean deserter of thy brother's blood! ... 2.Elegy.30.365.
'Tis all thou art, and all the proud shall be! ... 2.Elegy.74.368.
The Muse forgot, and thou belov'd no more! ... 2.Elegy.82.368.
Presumptuous Man! the reason wouldst thou find, ... 3.EOM1.35.17.
First, if thou canst, the harder reason guess, ... 3.EOM1.37.18.
Go, wiser thou! and in thy scale of sense ... 3.EOM1.113.29.
Call Imperfection what thou fancy'st such, ... 3.EOM1.115.29.
Yet thou unhappy, think 'tis He's unjust; ... 3.EOM1.118A.29.
Secure to be as blest as thou canst bear: ... 3.EOM1.286.50.
All Chance, Direction, which thou canst not see; ... 3.EOM1.290.50.
But most be present, if thou preach or pray. ... 3.EOM3.6A.92.
Has God, thou fool! work'd solely for thy good, ... 3.EOM3.27.95.
Thou too must perish, when thy feast is o'er! ... 3.EOM3.70.99.
Say, in what mortal soil thou deign'st to grow? ... 3.EOM4.8.128.
Yet sigh'st thou now for apples and for cakes? ... 3.EOM4.176.144.
That thou may'st be by kings, or whores of kings. ... 3.EOM4.206.146.
Say, would'st thou be the Man to whom they fall? ... 3.EOM4.276.154.
To sigh for ribbands if thou art so silly, ... 3.EOM4.277.154.
Thou wert my guide, philosopher, and friend? ... 3.EOM4.390.166.
Yet thou proceed; be fallen Arts thy care, ... 3.Ep4.191A.155.
Thou, who since Yesterday, has roll'd o'er all ... 4.JD4.202.43.
Hast thou, O *Sun!* beheld an emptier sort, ... 4.JD4.204.43.
Thou hast at least bestow'd one penny well. ... 4.HS2.110.63.
How dar'st thou let one worthy man be poor? ... 4.HS2.118.63.
Friend thro' my Life, (which did'st not thou prolong, ... 4.Arbu.27A.98.
Thou unconcern'd canst hear the mighty Crack. ... 4.Arbu.86.101.
Thou stand'st unshook amidst a bursting World. ... 4.Arbu.88.101.
No more than Thou, great George! a Birth-day Song. ... 4.Arbu.222.112.
Man? and *for ever?* Wretch! what wou'dst thou have? ... 4.2HE2.252.183.
Can'st thou endure a Foe, forgive a Friend? ... 4.2HE2.317.187.
Grac'd as thou art, with all the Pow'r of Words, ... 4.1HE6.48.239.
But art thou one, whom new opinions sway, ... 4.1HE6.63.241.
Wilt thou do nothing for a nobler end, ... 4.1HE1.73.283.
Barnard, thou art a *Cit,* with all thy worth; ... 4.1HE1.89.285.
And so may'st Thou, Illustrious *Passeran!* ... 4.EpS1.124.307.
What help from J[ekyll]s opiates canst thou draw ... 4.1740.63.335*.
O thou! whatever Title please thine ear, ... 5.DunA1.17.62.
Whether thou chuse Cervantes' serious air, ... 5.DunA1.19.62.
O thou, of business the directing soul, ... 5.DunA1.147.81.
Thou triumph'st, victor of the high-wrought day, ... 5.DunA2.179.123.
The more thou ticklest, gripes his fist the faster. ... 5.DunA2.202.126.
No noise, no stir, no motion can'st thou make, ... 5.DunA2.291.138.
Thou, yet unborn, hast touch'd this sacred shore; ... 5.DunA3.37.154.

THOU (CONTINUED)

What Gifts from *Troy,* for *Paris* wou'd'st thou gain, ... Il.4.127.226.
Wert thou expos'd to all the hostile Train, ... Il.4.188.230.
But thou, alas! deserv'st a happier Fate. ..... Il.4.205.231.
Oh! had'st thou Strength to match thy brave Desires, ... Il.4.362.238.
What once thou wert, oh ever might'st thou be. ..... Il.4.366.238.
What once thou wert, oh ever might'st thou be. ..... Il.4.366.238.
Who dares to act whate'er thou dar'st to view. ..... Il.4.409.240.
Sage as thou art, and learn'd in Humankind, ... Il.4.414.240.
Can'st thou, remote, the mingling Hosts descry ..... Il.4.424.240.
Whose Arrow wounds the Chief thou guard'st in Fight; ..... Il.5.151.274.
These see thou shun, thro' all th' embattled Plain, ... Il.5.166.275.
Her shalt thou wound: So *Pallas* gives Command. ..... Il.5.169.275.
Take thou the Spear, the Chariot's Care be mine. ..... Il.5.287.280.
Me dost thou bid to shun the coming Fight, ... Il.5.310.281.
Me would'st thou move to base inglorious Flight? ..... Il.5.311.281.
Prince, thou art met. Tho' late in vain assail'd, ... Il.5.340.283.
But thou (tho' *Pallas* urg'd thy frantic Deed) ..... Il.5.493.291.
Know thou, whoe'er with heav'nly Pow'r contends, ... Il.5.495.291.
Strong as thou art, some God may yet be found, ... Il.5.499.292.
But what art thou? who deedless look'st around, ... Il.5.796.304.
But wert thou greater, thou must yield to me. ..... Il.5.799.304.
But wert thou greater, thou must yield to me. ..... Il.5.799.304.
Thou too no less hast been my constant Care; ..... Il.5.1006.314.
Not Fear, thou know'st, withholds me from the Plains, ... Il.5.1012.315.
From warring Gods thou bad'st me turn my Spear, ... Il.5.1014.315.
Thou gav'st that Fury to the Realms of Light, ... Il.5.1074.318.
So boundless she, and thou so partial grown, ... Il.5.1080.318.
Else had'st thou seen me sink on yonder Plain, ... Il.5.1088.318.
Thou most unjust, most odious in our Eyes! ..... Il.5.1097.319.
Yet long th' inflicted Pangs thou shalt not mourn, ... Il.5.1104.320.
Sprung since thou art from *Jove,* and Heav'nly born. ..... Il.5.1105.320.
Else, sing'd with Light'ning, had'st thou hence been thrown, ... Il.5.1106.320.
Well hast thou known proud *Troy's* perfidious Land, ... Il.6.69.327.
Meanwhile, thou *Hector* to the Town retire, ... Il.6.107.328.
What art thou, boldest of the Race of Man? ..... Il.6.152.333.
Yet far before the Troops thou dar'st appear, ... Il.6.155.333.
But if from Heav'n, Celestial thou descend; ..... Il.6.159.333.
Bold as thou art, too prodigal of Breath, ... Il.6.177.334.
But if thou still persist to search my Birth, ... Il.6.187.335.
My Guest in *Argos* thou, and I in *Lycia* thine. ..... Il.6.281.340.
But Thou and *Diomed* be Foes no more. ..... Il.6.285.340.
Com'st thou to supplicate th' Almighty Pow'r, ... Il.6.320.342.
Spent as thou art with long laborious Fight, ... Il.6.327.342.
Break thou *Tydides'* Spear, and let him fall ..... Il.6.380.345.
But thou, atton'd by Penitence and Pray'r, ... Il.6.384.345.
Urge thou thy Knight to march where Glory calls, ... Il.6.454.348.
Too daring Prince! ah whither dost thou run? ..... Il.6.510.351.
And think'st thou not how wretched we shall be, ... Il.6.512.351.
And thou must fall, thy Virtue's Sacrifice. ..... Il.6.515.351.
Now Hosts oppose thee, and thou must be slain! ..... Il.6.517.351.
Thou, from this Tow'r defend th' important Post; ..... Il.6.552.354.
The Day when thou, Imperial *Troy!* must bend, ... Il.6.572.354.
O Thou! whose Glory fills th' Ætherial Throne, ... Il.6.604.356.
Once more impetuous dost thou bend thy way, ... Il.7.31.364.
Whither, O *Menelaus!* would'st thou run, ... Il.7.127.369.
Griev'd tho' thou art, forbear the rash Design; ..... Il.7.129.369.
Sit thou secure amidst thy social Band; ..... Il.7.133.370.
Grant thou Almighty! in whose Hand is Fate, ... Il.7.215.375.
Grant thou, that *Telamon* may bear away ..... Il.7.245.376.
What Strength thou hast, and what the *Grecian* Foe. ..... Il.7.274.378.
Me, as a Boy or Woman would'st thou fright, ... Il.7.285.378.
Thou meet'st a Chief deserving of thy Arms, ... Il.7.287.378.
Thou, in thy Time, more sound Advice hast giv'n; ..... Il.7.434.386.
Herald! in him thou hear'st the Voice of *Greece.* ..... Il.7.483.388.
Strong God of Ocean! Thou, whose Rage can make ..... Il.7.544.391.
Thou Fate! fulfill it; and ye Pow'rs! approve. ..... Il.8.10.395.
Leave thou thy Chariot to our faithful Train: ..... Il.8.138.404.
And thou, *Podargus!* prove thy gen'rous Race: ..... Il.8.227.408.
And thus to *Neptune:* Thou! whose Force can make ..... Il.8.242.409.
See'st thou the *Greeks* by Fates unjust oppress, ... Il.8.244.409.
What hast thou said, Oh Tyrant of the Skies! ..... Il.8.575.424.
For such is Fate, nor can'st thou turn its Course ..... Il.8.595.424.
Fly, if thou wilt, to Earth's remotest Bound, ... Il.8.597.424.
Thou first, and thou alone, in Fields of Fight, ... Il.9.47.434.
Thou first, and thou alone, in Fields of Fight, ... Il.9.47.434.
Go thou inglorious! from th' embattel'd Plain; ..... Il.9.61.434.
Ships thou hast store, and nearest to the Main, ... Il.9.62.434.
Kings thou canst blame; a bold, but prudent Youth; ..... Il.9.79.436.
But thou, O King, to Council call the old: ..... Il.9.96.437.
To whom the King. With Justice hast thou shown ..... Il.9.147.439.
Trust that to Heav'n—but thou, thy Cares engage ..... Il.9.332.450.
If thou wilt yield to great *Atrides'* Pray'rs, ... Il.9.340.450.
Then shalt thou store (when *Greece* the Spoil divides) ..... Il.9.364.451.
There shalt thou live his Son, his Honours share, ... Il.9.372.451.
Her shalt thou wed whom most thy Eyes approve, ... Il.9.378.451.
There shalt thou reign with Pow'r and Justice crown'd, ... Il.9.392.452.
But if all this relentless thou disdain, ... Il.9.396.452.
Divine *Achilles!* wilt thou then retire, ... Il.9.562.461.
Great as thou art, my Lessons made thee brave, ... Il.9.606.464.
Or at my Knee, by *Phœnix* wouldst thou stand; ..... Il.9.610.464.
Well hast thou spoke; but at the Tyrant's Name, ... Il.9.759.471.
There shalt thou stay (the King of Men reply'd ..... Il.10.71.5.
What art thou, speak, that on Designs unknown ..... Il.10.90.6.
Seek'st thou some Friend, or nightly Centinel? ..... Il.10.92.6.
Wise as thou art, be now thy Wisdom try'd: ..... Il.10.163.9.
But sleep'st thou now? when from yon' Hill the Foe ..... Il.10.182.9.
Thou first of Warriors, and thou best of Friends, ... Il.10.276.14.
Thou first of Warriors, and thou best of Friends, ... Il.10.276.14.
0 thou! for ever present in my way, ... Il.10.329.17.
As thou defend'st the Sire, defend the Son. ..... Il.10.338.18.
Be witness thou! immortal Lord of all! ..... Il.10.389.21.
Then thus aloud: Whoe'er thou art, remain; ..... Il.10.439.23.
Whoe'er thou art, be bold, nor fear to die. ..... Il.10.454.23.
Cam'st thou the Secrets of our Camp to find, ... Il.10.457.24.
Or that again our Camps thou may'st explore? ..... Il.10.520.26.

THOU (CONTINUED)

No—once a Traytor, thou betray'st no more. ..... Il.10.521.26.
Urge thou the Slaughter, while I seize the Steeds. ..... Il.10.557.27.
Say thou, whose Praises all our Host proclaim, ... Il.10.640.30.
Thou living Glory of the *Grecian* Name! ..... Il.10.641.30.
Thou shalt not long the Death deserv'd withstand, ... Il.11.469.55.
He, dauntless, thus: Thou Conqu'ror of the Fair, ... Il.11.491.56.
Thou Woman-Warrior with the curling Hair; ..... Il.11.492.56.
Thou hast but done what Boys or Women can; ..... Il.11.495.56.
Not so this Dart, which thou may'st one day feel; ..... Il.11.499.56.
Or thou beneath this Lance must press the Field— ..... Il.11.545.58.
Thou know'st the fiery Temper of my Friend. ..... Il.11.799.71.
If thou but lead the *Myrmidonian* Line; ..... Il.11.929.77.
Clad in *Achilles'* Arms, if thou appear, ... Il.11.930.77.
But thou, *Patroclus!* act a friendly Part, ... Il.11.962.78.
Oh thou! bold Leader of our *Trojan* Bands, ... Il.12.69.84.
Oh thou! brave Leader of our *Trojan* Bands, ... Il.12.69A.84.
Or if the Purpose of thy Heart thou vent, ... Il.12.271.91.
But why should'st thou suspect the War's Success? ..... Il.12.285.92.
But thou can'st live, for thou can'st be a Slave. ..... Il.12.290.92.
But thou can'st live, for thou can'st be a Slave. ..... Il.12.290.92.
And what thou canst not singly, urge the rest. ..... Il.13.300.119.
On some important Message art thou bound, ... Il.13.329.121.
O thou, great Father! Lord of Earth and Skies, ... Il.13.789.142.
Tho' great in all, thou seem'st averse to lend ..... Il.13.907.148.
See, as thou mov'st, on Dangers Dangers spread, ... Il.13.923.148.
Whelm'd in thy Country's Ruins shalt thou fall, ... Il.13.973.152.
Ev'n thou shalt call on *Jove,* and call in vain; ..... Il.13.1033.153.
Ev'n thou shalt wish, to aid thy desp'rate Course, ... Il.13.1034.153.
And thou, Imperious! if thy Madness wait ..... Il.13.1052.155.
The Lance of *Hector,* thou shalt meet thy Fate: ..... Il.13.1053.155.
What shameful Words, (unkingly as thou art) ..... Il.14.90.162.
And thou the Shame of any Host but ours! ..... Il.14.93.162.
And wilt thou thus desert the *Trojan* Plain? ..... Il.14.98.162.
In such base Sentence if thou couch thy Fear, ... Il.14.100.162.
Thou giv'st the Foe: all *Greece* becomes their Prize. ..... Il.14.109.163.
Soon shalt thou view the scatter'd *Trojan* Bands ..... Il.14.166.165.
Think'st thou that *Troy* has *Jove's* high Favour won, ... Il.14.299.177.
Propt on that Spear to which thou ow'st thy Fall, ... Il.14.533.189.
Thou first, great *Ajax!* on th' ensanguin'd Plain ..... Il.14.605.191.
O thou, still adverse to th' eternal Will, ... Il.15.17.194.
Can'st thou, unhappy in thy Wiles! withstand ..... Il.15.21.194.
Hast thou forgot, when bound and fix'd on high, ... Il.15.23.194.
Think'st thou with me? fair Empress of the Skies! ..... Il.15.53.196.
Enough thou know'st the Tyrant of the Skies, ... Il.15.99.200.
Go thou, the Feasts of Heav'n attend thy Call; ..... Il.15.102.200.
And thou great *Mars,* begin and shew the way. ..... Il.15.121.201.
By what wild Passion, Furious! art thou tost? ..... Il.15.146.202.
Striv'st thou with *Jove?* Thou are already lost. ..... Il.15.147.202.
Striv'st thou with *Jove?* Thou are already lost. ..... Il.15.147.202.
Back to the Skies would'st thou with Shame be driv'n, ... Il.15.150.202.
Striv'st thou with him, by whom all Pow'r is giv'n? ..... Il.15.204.204.
And art thou Equal to the Lord of Heav'n? ..... Il.15.205.204.
Go thou my Son! the trembling *Greeks* alarm, ... Il.15.258.207.
If e'er thou sign'st our Wishes with thy Nod; ..... Il.15.432.214.
Thou wouldst have thought, so furious was their Fire, ... Il.15.844.229.
'Twas thou, bold *Hector!* whose resistless Hand ..... Il.15.854.229.
Than thou hast mine! Oh tell me, to what end ..... Il.16.15.235.
Griev'st thou for me, or for my martial Band? ..... Il.16.17.235.
But sure thou spring'st not from a soft Embrace, ... Il.16.47.237.
Thou beg'st his Arms, and in his Arms, thy Death. ..... Il.16.65.238.
Oh thou Supreme! high-thron'd, all Height above! ..... Il.16.284.250.
Hear, as of old! Thou gav'st, at *Thetis* Pray'r, ... Il.16.292.253.
But thou, 0 God of Health! thy Succour lend, ... Il.16.643.269.
For thou, tho' distant, can'st restore my Might, ... Il.16.645.269.
Swift as thou art (the raging Hero cries) ..... Il.16.745.272.
But thou a Prey to Vulturs shalt be made! ..... Il.16.1009.282.
But thou Imperious! hear my latest Breath; ..... Il.16.1026.282.
Insulting Man! thou shalt be soon, as I; ..... Il.16.1028.283.
Laugh'st thou not, *Jove!* from thy superior Throne, ... Il.17.19.288.
Or while thou may'st, avoid the threaten'd Fate; ..... Il.17.35.289.
While yet thou may'st, avoid the threaten'd Fate; ..... Il.17.35A.289.
Thou dar'st not meet the Terrors of his Eye; ..... Il.17.185.294.
And lo! already, thou prepar'st to fly. ..... Il.17.186.294.
And thou be Witness, if I fear to Day; ..... Il.17.202.295.
Thou stand'st, and Armies tremble at thy Sight ..... Il.17.234.297.
Thou from the mighty Dead those Arms hast torn ..... Il.17.237.297.
A Blaze of Glory, e'er thou fad'st away. ..... Il.17.240.297.
Dost thou at length to *Menelaus* yield? ..... Il.17.660.313.
Sad Tydings, Son of *Peleus!* thou must hear; ..... Il.18.21.324.
Oh had'st thou still, a Sister of the Main, ... Il.18.109.328.
When *Hector* falls, thou dy'st.—Let *Hector* die, ... Il.18.125.328.
But can'st thou, naked, issue to the Plains? ..... Il.18.167.330.
Rise, and prevent (if yet thou think of Fame) ..... Il.18.217.332.
Thou com'st in vain, he cries (with Fury warm'd) ..... Il.18.225.332.
Dar'st thou dispirit whom the Gods incite? ..... Il.18.345.338.
And thou the Mother of that martial Line? ..... Il.18.422.341.
But thou, in Pity, by my Pray'r be won; ..... Il.18.527.347.
But thou! appeas'd, propitious to our Pray'r, ... Il.19.141.377.
Tho' god-like Thou art by no Toils oppress, ... Il.19.155.378.
Witness thou First! thou greatest Pow'r above! ..... Il.19.267.383.
Witness thou First! thou greatest Pow'r above! ..... Il.19.267.383.
Thou too, *Patroclus!* (thus his Heart he vents) ..... Il.19.335.386.
And dost thou thus desert the Great in War? ..... Il.19.365.387.
From heav'nly *Venus* thou deriv'st thy Strain, ... Il.20.136.399.
Go; while thou may'st, avoid the threaten'd Fate; ..... Il.20.238.403.
If yet thou farther seek to learn my Birth ..... Il.20.252.404.
To all those Insults thou hast offer'd here, ... Il.20.306.407.
Wretch! Thou hast scap'd again. Once more thy Flight ..... Il.20.519.416.
But long thou shalt not thy just Fate withstand, ... Il.20.521.416.
"And thou, dost thou, bewail Mortality?" ..... Il.21.118.426.
"And thou, dost thou, bewail Mortality?" ..... Il.21.118.426.
See'st thou not me, whom Nature's Gifts adorn, ... Il.21.119.426.
What art thou, boldest of the Race of Man? ..... Il.21.166.428.
Sprung from a River didst thou boast thy Line, ... Il.21.203.429.
How durst thou vaunt thy wat'ry Progeny? ..... Il.21.205.430.

THOU (CONTINUED)

But thou, the Counsel Heav'n suggests, attend! Il.21.338.435.
Submissive I desist, if thou command, Il.21.436.438.
Thou drov'st a Mortal to insult a God; Il.21.461.440.
Hast thou not yet, insatiate Fury! known, Il.21.478.441.
Juno, whom thou rebellious dar'st withstand, Il.21.480.441.
Rash as thou art to prop the *Trojan* Throne, Il.21.514.443.
Hast thou forgot, how at the Monarch's Pray'r, Il.21.517.443.
Dost thou, for this, afford proud *Ilion* Grace, Il.21.531.443.
Great as thou art, ev'n thou may'st stain with Gore Il.21.697.450.
Great as thou art, ev'n thou may'st stain with Gore Il.21.697.450.
Thou robb'st me of a Glory justly mine, Il.22.27.453.
Implacable *Achilles!* might'st thou be Il.22.55.455.
Against his Rage if singly thou proceed, Il.22.120.458.
Should'st thou (but Heav'n avert it!) should'st thou bleed, Il.22.121.458.
Should'st thou (but Heav'n avert it!) should'st thou bleed, Il.22.121.458.
Detested as thou art, and ought to be, Il.22.335.470.
To thee (presumptuous as thou art) unknown, Il.22.359.470.
But first, try thou my Arm; and may this Dart Il.22.367.471.
Die thou the first! When *Jove* and Heav'n ordain, Il.22.461.474.
Would I had never been!—O thou, the Ghost Il.22.616.481.
Thou to the dismal Realms for ever gone! Il.22.618.481.
But thou my *Hector* ly'st expos'd in Air, Il.22.654.483.
Ev'n great and god-like Thou art doom'd to fall. Il.23.102.491.
And is it thou (he answers) to my Sight Il.23.109.492.
Once more return'st thou from the Realms of Night? Il.23.110.492.
Lest thro' Incaution failing, thou may'st be Il.23.415.506.
So shalt thou pass the Goal, secure of Mind, Il.23.417.506.
Rise if thou dar'st, before thy Chariot stand, Il.23.661.515.
Superior as thou art, forgive th' Offence, Il.23.669.516.
Thou know'st the Errors of unripen'd Age, Il.23.671.516.
The Prize I quit, if thou thy Wrath resign; Il.23.673.516.
The Mare, or ought thou ask'st, be freely thine, Il.23.674.516.
Accept thou this, O sacred Sire! (he said) Il.23.707.517.
Take thou this Token of a grateful Heart, Il.23.711.518.
Go thou, my Son! by gen'rous Friendship led, Il.23.743.519.
Those due distinctions thou so well can'st pay, Il.23.749.520.
'Twas thou, *Euryalus!* who durst aspire Il.23.783.521.
Or let me lift thee, Chief, or lift thou me: Il.23.840.523.
No firstling Lambs, unheedful! didst thou vow, Il.23.1022.529.
Thou com'st fair *Thetis,* but with Grief o'ercast, Il.24.137.540.
No longer then (his Fury if thou dread) Il.24.171.543.
Nor shalt thou Death, nor shalt thou Danger dread; Il.24.217.546.
Nor shalt thou Death, nor shalt thou Danger dread; Il.24.217.546.
Then thus to *Hermes.* Thou whose constant Cares Il.24.411.552.
Is seal'd in Sleep, thou wander'st thro' the Night? Il.24.448.555.
What couldst thou hope, should these thy Treasures view, Il.24.451.555.
For what Defence alas! couldst thou provide? Il.24.453.555.
But say, convey'st thou thro' the lonely Plains Il.24.467.556.
Or fly'st thou now? What Hopes can *Troy* retain? Il.24.471.556.
The King alarm'd. Say what, and whence thou art, Il.24.473.556.
If then thou art of stern *Pelides'* Train, Il.24.495.557.
But thou, oh gen'rous Youth! this Goblet take, Il.24.525.558.
Thou ow'st thy Guidance to no mortal Hand: Il.24.564.559.
Ah think, thou favour'd of the Pow'rs Divine! Il.24.598.561.
Think from some pow'rful Foe thou see'st him fly, Il.24.606.562.
Alas! what Weight of Anguish hast thou known? Il.24.653.564.
Thou too, Old Man, hast happier Days beheld; Il.24.683.565.
Thou can'st not call him from the *Stygian* Shore, Il.24.694.566.
But thou alas! may'st live, to suffer more! Il.24.695.566.
Thou, as thou may'st, these boundless Stores enjoy; Il.24.701.566.
Thou, as thou may'st, these boundless Stores enjoy; Il.24.701.566.
Safe may'st thou sail, and turn thy Wrath from *Troy;* Il.24.702.566.
Nor com'st thou but by Heav'n; nor com'st alone, Il.24.711.567.
I show thee, King! thou tread'st on hostile Land; Il.24.717.567.
Nor thou O Father! thus consum'd with Woe, Il.24.755.568.
And sleep'st thou Father! (thus the Vision said) Il.24.851.572.
Now dost thou sleep, when *Hector* is restor'd? Il.24.852.572.
Thou to the dismal Realms for ever gone! Il.24.910.574.
Thou too my Son! to barb'rous Climes shalt goe, Il.24.922.574.
Why gav'st thou not to me thy dying Hand? Il.24.934.575.
Some Word thou would'st have spoke, which sadly dear, Il.24.936.575.
Oh thou, the best, the dearest to my Heart! Il.24.943.575.
Of all my Race thou most by Heav'n approv'd, Il.24.944.575.
Yet glow'st thou fresh with ev'ry living Grace, Il.24.954.576.
Sad *Helen* has no Friend now thou art gone! Il.24.978.576.
O thou! from whom the whole creation springs, Od.1.57.33.
Stranger! whoe'er thou art, securely rest Od.1.161.40.
Now first to me this visit dost thou daign, Od.1.223.43.
Hast thou not heard how young *Orestes* fir'd Od.1.387.51.
Thou, heedful of advice, secure proceed; Od.1.397.51.
Assist him, *Jove!* thou regent of the skies! Od.2.42.62.
But you oh Peers! and thou oh Prince! give ear: Od.2.127.67.
Here thou art sage in vain—I better read the skies. Od.2.210.72.
Ulysses lies: oh wert thou lay'd as low! Od.2.214.72.
And but augment the wrongs thou would'st redress. Od.2.222.72.
"Guard thou his age, and his behests obey.] Od.2.258.74.
Would'st thou to rise in arms the *Greeks* advise? Od.2.277.74.
Thou to the court ascend; and to the shores Od.2.327.77.
To whom the Prince. O thou whose guardian care Od.2.394.80.
The watry way, ill-fated if thou try, Od.2.412.80.
Whoe'er thou art, whom fortune brings to keep Od.3.55.89.
Oh thou! whose arms this ample globe embrace, Od.3.69.89.
Enquir'st thou, father! from what coast we came? Od.3.94.90.
O friend! what sorrows dost thou bring to mind? Od.3.126.92.
Back to thy native Islands might'st thou sail, Od.3.143.92.
Art thou the son of that illustrious sire? Od.3.151.93.
So fell *Ægysthus;* and may'st thou, my friend, Od.3.242.97.
The prudent youth reply'd. Oh thou, the grace Od.3.246.97.
Attend (tho' partly thou hast guest) the truth. Od.3.317.102.
And thou return, with disappointed toil, Od.3.403.106.
Or if by land thou chuse thy course to bend, Od.3.415.106.
Well hast thou spoke (the blue-ey'd maid replies) Od.3.455.109.
View'st thou un-mov'd, O ever-honour'd most! Od.4.83.123.
And *thou, to whom 'tis giv'n to gild the sphere! Od.4.458.142.
Whoe'er thou art, (the azure Goddess cries,) Od.4.501.144.

THOU (CONTINUED)

I thus: O thou, whose certain eye foresees Od.4.627.149.
An exile thou, nor cheering face of friend, Od.4.640.149.
A Goddess thou, hast commerce with the Gods; Od.4.1086.168.
What cannot Wisdom do? Thou may'st restore Od.5.34.172.
Hermes, thou chosen messenger of heav'n! Od.5.39.172.
Arriv'st thou here, an unexpected guest? Od.5.112.177.
Lov'd as thou art, thy free injunctions lay; Od.5.113.177.
Swear then, thou mean'st not what my soul forebodes; Od.5.231.182.
And thou oh *Styx!* whose formidable floods Od.5.239.183.
Thus wilt thou leave me, are we thus to part? Od.5.260.184.
Farewel! and ever joyful may'st thou be, Od.5.261.184.
But ah *Ulysses!* wert thou giv'n to know Od.5.263.184.
Lov'd and ador'd, oh Goddess, as thou art, Od.5.275.184.
Then thus address'd him. Thou, whom heav'n decrees Od.5.430.193.
Whoe'er thou art, I shall not blindly join Od.5.454.194.
Whoe'er thou art, before whose stream unknown Od.5.568.199.
And sleep'st thou, careless of the bridal day? Od.6.30.205.
Five sons thou hast; three wait the bridal day, Od.6.75.208.
Thou visit earth, a daughter of the skies, Od.6.178.218.
But since thou tread'st our hospitable shore, Od.6.233.221.
But would'st thou soon review thy native plain? Od.6.347.228.
Attend, and speedy thou shalt pass the main: Od.6.348.229.
Seek thou the Queen along the rooms of state; Od.6.366.229.
So shalt thou view with joy thy natal shore, Od.6.375.230.
High-thron'd, and feasting, there thou shalt behold Od.7.65.237.
If in that form thou com'st a guest divine: Od.7.267.248.
Cam'st thou not hither, wond'rous stranger! say, Od.7.318.251.
Tell then whence art thou? whence that Princely air? Od.7.320.251.
Such as thou art, thy thought and mine were one, Od.7.399.256.
Nor thou unwilling to be call'd my son. Od.7.400.256.
In such alliance could'st thou wish to join, Od.7.401.256.
Do thou make perfect! sacred be his words! Od.7.424.258.
Well hast thou spoke, (*Euryalus* replies) Od.8.153.271.
Thine is the guest, invite him thou to rise. Od.8.154.271.
To glory give the space thou hast to stay; Od.8.164.271.
Well hast thou spoke, and well thy gen'rous tongue Od.8.269.277.
Wou'dst thou enchain'd like *Mars,* oh *Hermes,* lye, Od.8.375.284.
Say wilt thou bear the Mulct? He instant cries, Od.8.389.285.
And thou, *Euryalus,* redeem thy wrong: Od.8.431.287.
And blest be thou my friend, *Ulysses* cries, Od.8.447.287.
And never, never may'st thou want this sword! Od.8.450.287.
To me thou ow'st, to me, the vital air. Od.8.502.289.
If faithful thou record the tale of fame, Od.8.543.291.
So shalt thou instant reach the realm assign'd, Od.8.603.294.
But say thro' what waste regions hast thou stray'd, Od.8.625.296.
Then thus *Ulysses.* Thou, whom first in sway Od.9.1.298.
If home thou send us, and vouchsafe to spare. Od.9.413.323.
And never shalt thou taste this Nectar more. Od.9.416.323.
Whoe'er thou art that bear'st celestial wine! Od.9.420.323.
First thou wert wont to crop the flow'ry mead, Od.9.527.328.
Thou mov'st, as conscious of thy master's woe! Od.9.532.328.
Seest thou these lids that now unfold in vain? Od.9.533.328.
Oh! didst thou feel for thy afflicted Lord, Od.9.535.328.
Soon might'st thou tell me, where in secret here Od.9.537.328.
Thou meditat'st thy meal in yonder cave; Od.9.560.329.
Hear me, oh *Neptune!* thou whose arms are hurl'd Od.9.617.332.
If thine I am nor thou my birth disown, Od.9.619.332.
Ulysses here! what Dæmon cou'dst thou meet Od.10.71.342.
Wast thou not furnish'd by our choicest care Od.10.73.342.
Never, alas! thou never shalt return, Od.10.317.359.
Ah whither roam'st thou? much-enduring man! Od.10.334.360.
Think'st thou by wit to model their escape? Od.10.339.360.
Sooner shalt thou, a stranger to thy shape, Od.10.340.360.
What art thou? say! from whence, from whom you came? Od.10.387.363.
Not mortal thou, nor mortal is thy brain. Od.10.390.363.
Or art thou he? the man to come (foretold Od.10.391.363.
O thou of fraudful heart! shall I be led Od.10.403.364.
Celestial as thou art, yet stand deny'd: Od.10.407.364.
Me wou'dst thou please? for them thy cares imploy, Od.10.455.365.
Soon shalt thou reach old Ocean's utmost ends, Od.10.602.372.
Why, mortal, wandrest thou from chearful day, Od.11.116.386.
If heav'n thou please; and how to please attend! Od.11.133.387.
So peaceful shalt thou end thy blissful days, Od.11.164.389.
Com'st thou, my son, alive, to realms beneath, Od.11.190.391.
Com'st thou alive from pure, ætherial day? Od.11.192.391.
Com'st thou a wand'rer from the *Phrygian* shores? Od.11.197.391.
Hast thou thy *Ithaca,* thy bride, beheld? Od.11.199.391.
The court is joyless, for thou art not there! Od.11.227.393.
Thou, thou my son wert my disease and death; Od.11.245.393.
Thou, thou my son wert my disease and death; Od.11.245.393.
Fly'st thou, lov'd shade, while I thus fondly mourn? Od.11.253.394.
For know, thou *Neptune* view'st! and at my nod Od.11.305.397.
If thou the circling year my stay controul, Od.11.444.406.
O King! for such thou art, and sure thy blood Od.11.450.406.
Saw'st thou the Worthies of the *Grecian* Host? Od.11.461.407.
Death thou hast seen in all her ghastly forms; Od.11.516.409.
By woman here thou tread'st this mournful strand, Od.11.543.410.
Com'st thou alive to view the *Stygian* bounds, Od.11.583.412.
And dead, thou rul'st a King in these abodes. Od.11.594.412.
If mad with transport, freedom thou demand, Od.12.65.433.
If but to seize thy arms thou make delay, Od.12.153.439.
And thou whose guiding hand directs our way, Od.12.258.445.
O cruel thou! some fury sure has steel'd Od.12.333.448.
And cruel, enviest thou a short repose? Od.12.336.448.
Vengeance, ye Pow'rs, (he cries) and thou whose hand Od.12.445.452.
O thou, the first in merit and command! Od.13.47.3.
Thou art, that wander'st in this desart place! Od.13.276.19.
Arriv'st thou here a stranger to our name? Od.13.284.19.
Thou seest an Island, not to those unknown Od.13.285.19.
Secure thou seest thy native shore at last? Od.13.337.23.
Know'st thou not me? who made thy life my care, Od.13.342.24.
And tell what more thou must from fate expect. Od.13.348.24.
But thou be silent, nor reveal thy state; Od.13.351.24.
If thou but equal to thy self be found, Od.13.449.27.
Why would'st not thou, oh all-enlighten'd mind! Od.13.484.29.

THOU (CONTINUED)

Then tell me whence thou art? and what the share ....Od.14.55.38.
Of woes and wand'rings thou wert born to bear? ....Od.14.56.38.
Such thou may'st be. But he whose name you crave ....Od.14.154.43.
(Distrustful as thou art) nor doubt the Gods. ....Od.14.174.44.
Thou first be witness, hospitable *Jove!* ....Od.14.182.44.
O thou! whom Age has taught to understand, ...Od.14.425.56.
Oh be thou dear (*Ulysses* cry'd) to *Jove,* ....Od.14.490.59.
As well thou claim'st a grateful stranger's love! ....Od.14.491.59.
Well hast thou spoke (rejoin'd th' attentive swain) ....Od.14.576.64.
Nor garment shalt thou want, nor ought beside, ...Od.14.578.64.
Too long in vain, too widely hast thou stray'd. ....Od.15.12.70.
But seek thou first the Master of the swine, ...Od.15.45.72.
That thou safe sailing from the *Pylian* strand ....Od.15.49.72.
Mean-time may'st thou with happiest speed regain ....Od.15.142.75.
Brooks no repulse, nor cou'dst thou soon depart: ....Od.15.237.79.
Himself will seek thee here, nor wilt thou find ....Od.15.238.79.
O thou! that dost thy happy course prepare ....Od.15.282.82.
If on that god-less race thou wouldst attend, ...Od.15.346.86.
And, oh *Eumæus!* thou (he cries) hast felt ....Od.15.409.89.
Then to *Peiræus—Thou* whom time has prov'd ....Od.15.581.98.
And is it thou? my ever dear delight! ....Od.16.23.103.
O art thou come to bless my longing sight! ....Od.16.24.103.
For should'st thou suffer, pow'rless to relieve ....Od.16.87.106.
But tell me, dost thou Prince, dost thou behold ....Od.16.97.107.
But tell me, dost thou Prince, dost thou behold ....Od.16.97.107.
How art thou chang'd! (he cry'd) a God appears! ....Od.16.197.113.
Thou art not—no, thou can'st not be my sire. ....Od.16.215.114.
Thou art not—no, thou can'st not be my sire. ....Od.16.215.114.
Other *Ulysses* shalt thou never see, ...Od.16.224.114.
So *Pallas* wills—but thou my son, explain ....Od.16.258.117.
But thou, when morn salutes th' aerial plain, ...Od.16.290.119.
Their lawless insults, tho' thou strive in vain: ....Od.16.299.120.
Jove grants henceforth, if thou hast spoke from *Jove?* ....Od.16.343.122.
Hast thou forgot, (ingrateful as thou art) ....Od.16.442.128.
Hast thou forgot, (ingrateful as thou art) ....Od.16.442.128.
And wou'dst thou evil for his good repay? ....Od.16.448.128.
But thou attentive, what we order heed; ....Od.17.10.133.
So snatch'd from all our cares!—Tell, hast thou known ....Od.17.54.135.
Say wilt thou not (ere yet the Suitor-crew ....Od.17.120.137.
Say wilt thou not the least account afford? ....Od.17.122.137.
And thou whose lustre gilds the rowling sphere! ....Od.17.149.139.
With truth I answer; thou the truth attend. ....Od.17.159.139.
Dearly, full dearly shalt thou buy thy bread, ...Od.17.270.145.
Bring'st thou these vagrants to infest the land? ....Od.17.451.155.
Bestow, my friend! thou dost not seem the worst ....Od.17.497.156.
Unless at distance, wretch! thou keep behind, ...Od.17.530.158.
Another *Ægypt,* shalt thou quickly find. ....Od.17.532.158.
From all thou beg'st, a bold audacious slave; ....Od.17.533.158.
Nor all can give so much as thou canst crave. ....Od.17.534.158.
Take that, ere yet thou quit this princely throng: ....Od.17.545.159.
If true, if faithful thou, her grateful mind ....Od.17.638.163.
Lest dragg'd in vengeance, thou repent thy stay; ....Od.18.15.167.
And canst thou envy, when the great relieve? ....Od.18.25.168.
Proud as thou art, henceforth no more be proud, ...Od.18.28.168.
How wouldst thou fly, nor ev'n in thought return? ....Od.18.31.168.
Instant thou sail'st, to *Echetus* resign'd, ...Od.18.96.171.
Nor from the sire art thou the son declin'd; ....Od.18.155.173.
O may'st thou, favour'd by some guardian pow'r, ...Od.18.175.175.
Beneath thy roof, and cou'dst thou tamely stand? ....Od.18.264.179.
If thou the stranger's righteous cause decline, ...Od.18.265.179.
Now, Grief, thou all art mine! the Gods o'ercast ....Od.18.299.181.
Thou bold intruder on a princely train? ....Od.18.376.185.
Fierce in the van: Then wou'dst thou, wou'dst thou, say, ...Od.18.420.189.
Fierce in the van: Then wou'dst thou, wou'dst thou, say, ...Od.18.420.189.
'Tis thou injurious art, not I am base. ....Od.18.423.189.
But know, thou art not valorous, but vain. ....Od.18.425.189.
Art thou from wine, or innate folly, bold? ....Od.18.433.189.
Seek thou repose; whilst here I sole remain, ...Od.19.54.195.
But thou on whom my palace-cares depend, ...Od.19.117.198.
O thou, she cry'd, whom first inclement fate ....Od.19.288.209.
Art thou foredoom'd my pest? the Heroe cry'd: ....Od.19.561.224.
Oh thou, of mortals most inur'd to woes! ....Od.20.41.234.
Be such my lot! Or thou *Diana* speed ....Od.20.94.237.
Say thou, to whom my youth its nurture owes, ...Od.20.161.241.
Before thou quit the dome (nor long delay) ....Od.20.289.247.
Those arms are dreadful which thou canst not bear. ....Od.21.178.268.
But thou *Eumæus,* as 'tis born away, ...Od.21.250.272.
Better than that, if thou approve our chear, ...Od.21.331.276.
Hold, lawless rustic! whither wilt thou go? ....Od.21.391.279.
To whom, insensate, dost thou bear the bow? ....Od.21.392.279.
To thy own dogs a prey thou shalt be made; ....Od.21.395.279.
Aim'st thou at Princes? (all amaz'd they said) ....Od.22.31.288.
Thy last of games unhappy hast thou play'd; ....Od.22.32.288.
Ulysses lives, and thou the mighty man, ...Od.22.58.289.
Great are thy wrongs, and much hast thou sustain'd ....Od.22.59.289.
First may'st thou see the springing dawn of light; ....Od.22.214.297.
What hop'st thou here? Thee first the sword shall slay, ...Od.22.239.298.
Thus, and thus only, shalt thou join thy friend. ....Od.22.243.298.
Art thou *Ulysses?* where then shall we find ....Od.22.246.298.
Priest as thou art! for that detested band ....Od.22.357.304.
Thou, with the heav'n-taught bard, in peace resort ....Od.22.415.308.
Woman, experienc'd as thou art, controul ....Od.22.448.309.
But thou sincere! Oh *Euryclea,* say, ...Od.22.456.310.
Nor shalt thou in the day of danger find ....Od.23.127.326.
Canst thou, *Penelope,* when heav'n restores ....Od.23.167.328.
Canst thou, oh cruel, unconcern'd survey ....Od.23.169.328.
When thou must learn what I must speak with tears? ....Od.23.282.337.
And full of days, thou gently yield thy breath; ....Od.23.306.337.
Triumph, thou happy victor of thy woes! ....Od.23.308.338.
Thou, for thy Lord; while me th' immortal pow'rs ....Od.23.379.343.
Thou with thy Maids within the Palace stay, ...Od.23.391.343.
Com'st thou the first, to view this dreary state? ....Od.24.39.349.
Oh! better hadst thou sunk in *Trojan* ground, ...Od.24.43.350.
Thrice happy thou! to press the martial plain ....Od.24.53.350.
The shades thou seest, from yon' fair realms above. ....Od.24.213.358.

THOU (CONTINUED)

But thou! whom years have taught to understand, ...Od.24.310.364.
What years have circled since thou saw'st that guest? ....Od.24.335.365.
But tell me, who thou art? and what thy race? ....Od.24.348.365.
Or com'st thou single, or attend thy train? ....Od.24.352.365.
"(If such thou art) to manifest thee mine." ....Od.24.383.367.
Say, hast thou doom'd to this divided state ....Od.24.544.374.

THOUGH (OMITTED)

6

THOUGHT

What oft was *Thought,* but ne'er so well *Exprest,* ....1.EOC.298.273.
What oft was *Thought,* but ne'er before *Exprest,* ....1.EOC.298A.273.
Expression is the *Dress* of *Thought,* and still ....1.EOC.318.274.
With some *unmeaning* Thing they call a *Thought,* ....1.EOC.355.279.
And each *exalted* Stanza *teems* with *Thought!* ....1.EOC.423.288.
In yon clear lake, and thought it handsome too: ....1.TrPA.97.369.
Thought a short Life well lost for endless Fame. ....1.TrSt.717.440.
Let him not dare to vent his dang'rous Thought; ....2.ChJM.164.23.
And thought no Mortal cou'd dispute his Choice: ....2.ChJM.251.26.
And thought no Mortal cou'd dispute this choice: ....2.ChJM.251A.26.
But first thought fit th' Assistance to receive, ...2.ChJM.375.32.
Nor if she thought her self in Heav'n or Hell. ....2.ChJM.423.35.
I thought your Patience had been better try'd: ....2.ChJM.759.51.
By Heav'n, I swore but what I *thought* I saw. ....2.ChJM.794.53.
And saw but one, 'tis thought, in all his Days; ....2.ChWB.10.57.
But oh good Gods! whene'er a Thought I cast ....2.ChWB.221.67.
He kept, 'twas thought, a private Miss or two: ....2.ChWB.230.68.
If e'er one Vision touch'd thy infant Thought, ...2.RL1.29.147.
If e'er one Vision touch thy infant Thought, ...2.RL1.29A.147.
He said; when *Shock,* who thought she slept too long, ...2.RL1.115.154.
The close Recesses of the Virgin's Thought; ....2.RL3.140.178.
Some thought it mounted to the Lunar Sphere, ...2.RL5.113.208.
Sate fix'd in Thought the mighty *Stagyrite;* ....2.TemF.233.274.
Ev'n thought meets thought ere from the lips it part, ...2.ElAb.95.327.
Ev'n thought meets thought ere from the lips it part, ...2.ElAb.95.327.
One thought of thee puts all the pomp to flight, ...2.ElAb.273.342.
Devotion's self shall steal a thought from heav'n, ...2.ElAb.357.348.
What thin partitions Sense from Thought divide: ....3.EOM1.226.43.
Chaos of Thought and Passion, all confus'd; ....3.EOM2.13.55.
Too rash for Thought, for Action too refin'd: ....3.Ep1.201A.32.
(Tho' past the recollection of the thought) ....3.Ep1.47.18.
Too quick for Thought, for Action too refin'd: ....3.Ep1.201.32.
Her Head's untouch'd, that noble Seat of Thought: ....3.Ep2.74.56.
With too much Thinking to have common Thought: ....3.Ep2.98.58.
To kill those foes to Fair ones, Time and Thought. ....3.Ep2.112.59.
No Thought advances, but her Eddy Brain ....3.Ep2.121.60.
But never, never, reach'd one gen'rous Thought. ....3.Ep2.162.64.
No thought of Peace or Happiness at home. ....3.Ep2.224.68.
To raise the Thought and touch the Heart, be thine! ....3.Ep2.250.70.
And well (he thought) advis'd him, "Live like me." ....3.Ep3.316.119.
Some scruple rose, but thus he eas'd his thought, ...3.Ep3.365.123.
As brings all Brobdignag before your thought. ....3.Ep4.104.147.
The Soul stood forth, nor kept a Thought within; ....4.HS1.54.9.
As deep in *Debt,* without a thought to pay, ...4.JD4.21.27.
There sober Thought pursu'd th'amusing theme ....4.JD4.188.41.
Here still Reflection led on sober Thought, ...4.JD4.188A.41.
Thus Bethel spoke, who always speaks his thought, ...4.HS2.129.65.
And thought a Lye in Verse or Prose the same: ....4.Arbu.339.120.
That harmless Mother thought no Wife a Whore,— ....4.Arbu.384.126.
Explore the Thought, explain the asking Eye, ...4.Arbu.412.127.
So *Luther* thought the *Pater noster* long, ...4.JD2A.111.142.
So Luther thought the Paternoster long, ...4.JD2.105.143.
And certain Laws, by Suff'rers thought unjust, ...4.2HE2.60.169.
A Hackney-Coach my chance to spoil a Thought, ...4.2HE2.101.171.
Teach ev'ry Thought within its bounds to roll, ...4.2HE2.204.179.
Or lengthen'd Thought that gleams thro' many a page, ...4.2HE1.113.205.
My Liege! why Writers little claim your thought, ...4.2HE1.356.225.
"I thought the Dean had been too proud, ...4.HS6.53.253.
But makes a diff'rence in his thought ....4.1HE7.37.271.
And where's the Glory? 'twill be only thought ....4.EpS1.25.299.
Whose names once up, they thought it was not wrong ....4.1740.21.333.
Sinking from thought to thought, a vast profound! ....5.DunA1.112.77.
Sinking from thought to thought, a vast profound! ....5.DunA1.112.77.
Mears, Warner, Wilkins run: Delusive thought! ....5.DunA2.117.111.
Joy fills his soul, joy innocent of thought: ....5.DunA3.245.178.
Silent the monarch gaz'd; yet ask'd in thought ....5.DunA3.245A.178.
Sinking from thought to thought, a vast profound! ....5.DunB1.118.278.
Sinking from thought to thought, a vast profound! ....5.DunB1.118.278.
Mears, Warner, Wilkins run: delusive thought! ....5.DunB2.125.301.
Joy fills his soul, joy innocent of thought; ....5.DunB3.249.332.
Confine the thought, to exercise the breath; ....5.DunB4.159.357.
Wrapt up in Self, a God without a Thought, ...5.DunB4.485.389.
Thought fit to drown him in her tears: ....6.5.16.12.
E'er fruitful *Thought* conceiv'd Creation's Birth, ...6.8.5.17.
And thought *Herself* just risen from the Waves. ....6.9vi.2.21.
Luxurious Nature's Wealth in Thought surveys, ...6.17iii.20.58.
While he, serene in thought, shall calm survey ....6.21.19.69.
Were silent, which kind Fate thought worthy ....6.30.10A.86.
Cost our high thought more care and time ....6.30.58A.88.
What *Plato* thought, and godlike *Cato* was: ....6.32.18.96.
In pensive thought recall the fancy'd scene, ...6.45.33.125.
Thought wond'rous honest, tho' of mean Degree, ...6.49i.19.138.
Rome's pompous glories rising to our thought! ....6.52.24.156.
Now as he scratch'd to fetch up Thought, ...6.58.29.172.
The Great Ones are thought mad, the Small Ones Fools: ....6.60.2.178.
Nor raise a Thought, nor draw an Eye; ....6.64.8.189.
First struck out this, and then that Thought; ....6.77.2.214.
For why? he thought no Man his Mate, ...6.79.27A.218.
Calm ev'ry thought, inspirit ev'ry Grace, ...6.86.13.245.
Calm ev'ry thought, and spirit ev'ry Grace, ...6.86.13A.245.
A Woman, long thought barren, ...6.94.10.259.
All thought him just what thought King *Achiz.* ....6.101.18.290.
All thought him just what thought King *Achiz.* ....6.101.18.290.
If *France* excel him in one free-born thought, ...6.107.25.311.

THOUGHT (CONTINUED)

Whose Art was Nature, and whose Pictures thought; ....6.108.2.312.
Just of thy word, in ev'ry thought sincere, ...6.109.5.314.
Go, just of word, in ev'ry thought sincere, ...6.109.5A.314.
Just of thy word, and in each thought sincere, ...6.109.5B.314.
Explore my *Thought,* and watch my asking *Eye?* ....6.117.12.333.
Thought by all Heav'n a burning Shame; ....6.119.10.337.
Here lies a round Woman, who thought *mighty odd* ....6.124i.1.346.
But never, never, reach'd one gen'rous Thought. ....6.139.6.377.
Where, nobly-pensive, ST. JOHN sate and thought; ....6.142.10.383.
There, nobly-pensive, ST. JOHN sate and thought; ....6.142.10A.383.
Here, nobly-pensive, ST. JOHN sate and thought; ....6.142.10B.383.
No Thought advances, but her eddy Brain ....6.154.7.403.
She, in soft Sorrows, and in pensive Thought, ...Il.1.451.109.
Elate in Thought, he sacks untaken *Troy:* ....Il.2.46.129.
While to his Neighbour each express'd his Thought; ....Il.2.332.143.
Rush to her Thought, and force a tender Tear. ....Il.3.186.200.
But when *Ulysses* rose, in Thought profound, ...Il.3.279.207.
And thought the Steeds (your large Supplies unknown) ....Il.5.254.279.
Struck with the Thought, should *Helen's* Lord be slain, ...Il.5.695.301.
Some God, they thought, who rul'd the Fate of Wars, ...Il.6.133.330.
Brave *Glaucus* then each narrow Thought resign'd, ...Il.6.290.340.
In Words like these his prudent Thought exprest. ....Il.7.391.383.
Swifter than Thought the Wheels instinctive fly, ...Il.8.544.422.
A Thought unfinish'd in that gen'rous Mind; ....Il.9.84.436.
Hear then a Thought, not now conceiv'd in hast, ...Il.9.139.438.
I thought (but some kind God that Thought suppress) ....Il.9.588.463.
I thought (but some kind God that Thought suppress) ....Il.9.588.463.
The Gods (I thought) revers'd their hard Decree, ...Il.9.614.464.
Whatever Counsels can inspire our Thought, ...Il.10.165.9.
Hector (he thought) had sent, and check'd his hast, ...Il.10.424.22.
When brave *Tydides* stopp'd; a gen'rous Thought ....Il.10.435.23.
None stoop'd a Thought to base inglorious Flight; ....Il.11.95.39.
To speak his Thought, is ev'ry Freeman's Right, ...Il.12.249.90.
Greece sunk they thought, and this their fatal Hour; ....Il.13.123.110.
Small Thought retrieves the Spirits of the Brave. ....Il.13.156.112.
Compos'd his Thought, determin'd is his Eye, ...Il.13.368.123.
Forthwith *Æneas* rises to his Thought; ....Il.13.576.133.
Above the Thought of Man, supremely wise! ....Il.13.790.142.
But in cool Thought and Counsel to excel; ....Il.13.911.148.
Fluctuates, in doubtful Thought, the *Pylian* Sage; ....Il.14.28.158.
On speedy Measures then employ your Thought; ....Il.14.67.160.
To think such Meanness, or the Thought declares? ....Il.14.103.162.
In Thought, a Length of Lands he trod before, ...Il.15.87.200.
If Thought of Man can match the Speed of Gods. ....Il.15.91.200.
Thou wouldst have thought, so furious was their Fire, ...Il.15.844.229.
My Wrongs, my Wrongs, my constant Thought engage, ...Il.16.72.238.
Troy saw, and thought the dread *Achilles* nigh, ...Il.16.336.255.
Thus while he thought, beside him *Phœbus* stood, ...Il.16.873.277.
In thought they view'd him still, with martial Joy, ...Il.17.442.304.
A Chief, once thought no Terror of the Field; ....Il.17.661.313.
What Force of Thought and Reason can supply; ....Il.18.322.337.
Just as responsive to his Thought, the Frame ....Il.18.447.342.
Ev'n then, these Arts employ'd my infant Thought; ....Il.18.467.344.
Int'rest, or Thought, has room to harbour there; ....Il.19.212.381.
I thought alone with Mortals to contend, ...Il.20.397.411.
No stop, no stay; no thought to ask, or tell, ...Il.21.719.451.
Neglect that Thought, thy dearer Glory save. ....Il.22.79.456.
Honour and Shame th' ungen'rous Thought recall: ....Il.22.139.459.
But why this Thought? Unarm'd if I should go, ...Il.22.164.460.
No Thought but Rage, and never-ceasing Strife, ...Il.22.341.470.
Till Death extinguish Rage, and Thought, and Life. ....Il.22.342.470.
Then his fell Soul a Thought of Vengeance bred, ...Il.22.495.476.
Wrapt round in Mists he lies, and lost to Thought: ....Il.23.812.521.
Assist O Goddess! (thus in Thought he pray'd) ....Il.23.901.525.
And present at his Thought, descends the Maid. ....Il.23.902.525.
Thought follows Thought, and Tear succeeds to Tear. ....Il.24.16.535.
Thought follows Thought, and Tear succeeds to Tear. ....Il.24.16.535.
Some Thought there must be, in a Soul so brave, ...Il.24.193.544.
Some Thought there must be, in a Soul so brave, ...Il.24.223.546.
Tell me thy Thought: My Heart impells to go ....Il.24.239.546.
And what he greatly thought, he nobly dar'd. ....Od.2.312.76.
Leave thought to Age, and drain the flowing bowl. ....Od.2.344.77.
In publick sentence, or in private thought; ....Od.3.156.93.
Mentor, no more—the mournful thought forbear; ....Od.3.298.100.
Too long, mis-judging, have I thought thee wise: ....Od.4.38.122.
Just is thy thought, the King assenting cries, ...Od.4.197.129.
For martial deeds, and depth of thought renown'd; ....Od.4.368.137.
Then speeding back, involv'd in various thought, ...Od.4.779.155.
The Prince in rural bow'r they fondly thought, ...Od.4.864.159.
In the young soul illustrious thought to raise, ...Od.4.914.161.
In his young breast the daring thought inspir'd: ....Od.4.946.162.
Telemachus in thought already slain! ....Od.4.1100.169.
And learn'd in all the wiles of human thought. ....Od.5.236.182.
Nor break the transport with one thought of me. ....Od.5.262.184.
While thus he thought, a monst'rous wave up-bore ....Od.5.542.198.
Mean-time in dubious thought the King awaits, ...Od.6.169.216.
No bird so light, no thought so swift as they. ....Od.7.48.235.
In pleasing thought he ran the prospect o'er, ...Od.7.180.244.
Let no such thought (with modest grace rejoin'd ....Od.7.281.249.
Such as thou art, thy thought and mine were one, ...Od.7.399.256.
This man with energy of thought controuls, ...Od.8.189.272.
Hither some fav'ring God, beyond our thought, ...Od.9.165.312.
I thought, devis'd, and *Pallas* heard my prayer. ....Od.9.377.321.
Each scheme I turn'd, and sharpen'd ev'ry thought; ....Od.9.502.326.
Whilst to his neighbour each express'd his thought, ...Od.10.41.341.
Was first my thought: but speeding back to shore ....Od.10.178.349.
While full of thought, revolving fates to come, ...Od.10.369.362.
For swift as thought, the Goddess had been there, ...Od.10.687.376.
Now turn thy thought, and joys within our pow'r. ....Od.14.193.45.
I then explor'd my thought, what course to prove? ....Od.14.301.50.
(And sure the thought was dictated by *Jove,* ....Od.14.302.50.
He thought, and answer'd: hardly waking yet, ...Od.14.551.63.
How sprung a thought so monstrous in thy mind? ....Od.15.345.86.
O friends forbear! and be the thought withstood: ....Od.16.416.126.
If this raise anger in the stranger's thought, ...Od.17.16.133.

THOUGHT (CONTINUED)

The bold *Melanthius* to their thought replies. ....Od.17.445.155.
Telemachus absorpt in thought severe, ...Od.17.582.160.
His ev'ry step and ev'ry thought is wise. ....Od.17.665.164.
While fix'd in thought the pensive Heroe sate, ...Od.18.1.166.
How wouldst thou fly, nor ev'n in thought return? ....Od.18.31.168.
To whom with thought mature the King replies: ....Od.18.151.173.
Absorpt in thought, on vengeance fix'd he stood. ....Od.18.394.186.
Suggest, that *Jove* the peaceful thought inspir'd, ...Od.19.13.193.
The same you think, have all beholders thought. ....Od.19.449.216.
And from the present bliss abstracts her thought. ....Od.19.559.223.
A visionary thought I'll now relate, ...Od.19.625.226.
For many a dreary thought, and many a doleful dream! ....Od.19.682.229.
Your future thought let sable Fate employ; ....Od.20.308.247.
This bow shall ease us of that idle thought, ...Od.21.168.267.
All else have cast him from their very thought, ...Od.21.217.270.
Enough—on other cares your thought imploy, ...Od.21.242.271.
Who wrongs his Princess with a thought so mean. ....Od.21.344.276.
Or (as my thought misgives) by *Dolius'* son. ....Od.22.175.295.
And human thought, with unresisted sway, ...Od.23.15.319.
Cautious to act what thought mature inspires. ....Od.23.118.326.
And thus with thought mature the Monarch said. ....Od.23.376.343.
Is not thy thought my own? (the God replies ....Od.24.547.374.

THOUGHT'S

—What are you thinking? *Fr.* Faith, the thought's no Sin, ...4.EpS2.122.320.
And in thy Bosom lurks in *Thought's* Disguise; ....6.8.20.18.

THOUGHTED

Divine oblivion of low-thoughted care! ....2.ElAb.298.343.

THOUGHTFUL

Or wandring thoughtful in the silent Wood, ...1.W-F.249.172.
War, horrid war, your thoughtful walks invades, ...6.51i.7.151.
Then deeply thoughtful, pausing e'er he spoke, ...Il.2.346.143.
And now *Ulysses'* thoughtful Temples press'd. ....Il.10.318.17.
To this his steps the thoughtful Prince inclin'd; ....Od.1.538.57.
And gen'rous wine, which thoughtful sorrow flies. ....Od.2.330.77.
Silent and thoughtful while the board he ey'd, ...Od.14.134.42.
Thus thoughtful answer'd: Those we shall not move, ...Od.17.88.136.
The thoughtful Son beheld, and call'd his swain: ....Od.17.417.152.
But shook his thoughtful head, nor more complain'd, ...Od.17.550.159.
Mean-time revolving in his thoughtful mind ....Od.19.454.216.
With dire revenge his thoughtful bosom glows, ...Od.20.7.230.
That rite compleat, up-rose the thoughtful man, ...Od.21.290.274.

THOUGHTLESS

Some thoughtless Town, with Ease and Plenty blest, ...1.W-F.107.161.
Oh thoughtless Mortals! ever blind to Fate, ...2.RL3.101.175.
Just as a blockhead rubs his thoughtless skull, ...6.41.7.113.
Thoughtless of ill, accepts the fraudful feast. ....Od.4.716.152.
While thoughtless we, indulge the genial rite, ...Od.9.649.333.
To warn the thoughtless self-confiding train, ...Od.13.174.14.
The best our Lords consume; those thoughtless Peers, ...Od.14.99.40.
Thoughtless and gay, *Eurymachus* began. ....Od.18.398.187.
Are seemlier hid; my thoughtless youth they blame, ...Od.19.21.193.
Which thoughtless we in games would waste away: ....Od.21.275.273.
I thoughtless err'd in) well secure that door: ....Od.22.173.295.

THOUGHTS

The Thoughts of Gods let *Granville's* Verse recite, ...1.W-F.425.193.
I know there are, to whose presumptuous Thoughts ....1.EOC.169.259.
And glitt'ring Thoughts struck out at ev'ry Line; ....1.EOC.290.271.
See *Dionysius Homer's* Thoughts refine, ...1.EOC.665.314.
Returning Thoughts in endless Circles roll, ...1.TrSt.75.413.
While future Realms his wandring Thoughts delight, ...1.TrSt.445.428.
These Thoughts he fortify'd with Reasons still, ...2.ChJM.19.16.
For when thy Charms my sober Thoughts engage, ...2.ChJM.569.42.
For when thy Beauty does my Thoughts engage, ...2.ChJM.569A.42.
As one whose Thoughts were on his Spouse intent; ....2.ChJM.751.51.
All but the *Sylph—With* careful Thoughts opprest, ...2.RL2.53.163.
Why rove my thoughts beyond this last retreat? ....2.ElAb.5.319.
Why words so flowing, thoughts so free, ...4.HOde1.39.153.
Thoughts, which at Hyde-Park-Corner I forgot, ...4.2HE2.208.179.
How random Thoughts now meaning chance to find, ...5.DunA1.229.90.
How random thoughts now meaning chance to find, ...5.DunB1.275.290.
In these gay Thoughts the Loves and Graces shine, ...6.19.1.62.
While thousand grateful thoughts arise; ....6.51ii.30.153.
And finds a thousand grateful thoughts arise; ....6.51ii.30A.153.
Such thoughts, as prompt the brave to lie, ...6.141.6.380.
Distracting Thoughts by turns his Bosom rul'd, ...Il.1.253.98.
In his black Thoughts Revenge and Slaughter roll, ...Il.1.638.118.
But thou, nor they, shall search the Thoughs that roll ....Il.1.710.121.
Allur'd the Fair with moving Thoughts of Joy, ...Il.5.513.292.
These claim thy Thoughts by Day, thy Watch by Night: ....Il.5.598.297.
The Thoughts of Glory past, and present Shame, ...Il.6.588.355.
All but the King; with various Thoughts oppress, ...Il.10.3.1.
If ought of use thy waking Thoughts suggest, ...Il.10.106.7.
Their loyal Thoughts and pious Loves conspire ....Il.10.192.10.
With deathful Thoughts they trace the dreary way, ...Il.10.354.18.
Such Thoughts revolving in his careful Breast, ...Il.11.521.57.
"Yet cooler Thoughts thy elder Years attend; ....Il.11.918.76.
Conquest, not Safety, fill the Thoughts of all; ....Il.12.325.93.
Then, what for common Good my Thoughts inspire, ...Il.14.143.164.
What Thoughts, regardless Chief! thy Breast employ? ....Il.16.659.270.
Since Battel is renounc'd, thy Thoughts employ ....Il.17.159.293.
Far be the Omen which my Thoughts suggest! ....Il.22.584.480.
No more our Thoughts to those we lov'd make known, ...Il.23.97.491.
The thoughts which rowl within my ravish'd breast, ...Od.1.259.45.
Heroic thoughts infus'd his heart dilate, ...Od.1.417.52.
And manly thoughts inspir'd by manly age, ...Od.2.354.78.
Search, for some thoughts, thy own suggesting mind; ....Od.3.34.87.
He said: new thoughts my beating heart employ, ...Od.4.741.153.
If from your thoughts *Ulysses* you remove, ...Od.5.18.171.
While thus his thoughts an anxious council hold, ...Od.5.464.195.
Her thoughts intentive on the bridal day: ....Od.6.80.208.

THOUGHTS (CONTINUED)
To you, the thoughts of no inhuman heart. ....Od.7.247.248.
To gloomy care my thoughts alone are free; ....Od.8.169.271.
'Till all the coward thoughts of death gave way. ....Od.10.57.342.
Strait to my anxious thoughts the sound convey'd ....Od.12.320.447.
The various thoughts and talents of mankind, ...Od.14.265.49.
(For still to thee his loyal thoughts incline) ....Od.15.46.72.
What grateful thoughts still in this bosom glow, ...Od.15.169.76.
No, thy ill-judging thoughts the brave disgrace; ....Od.18.422.189.
Wav'ring his thoughts in dubious balance hung; ....Od.20.14.231.
Then, happier thoughts return the nodding scale, ...Od.20.279.246.
These boding thoughts, and what he is, to prove! ....Od.23.112.325.

THOUSAND
And ere he starts, a thousand Steps are lost. ....1.W-F.154.164.
In the bright *Muse* tho' thousand *Charms* conspire, ...1.EOC.339.277.
When *Patriarch-Wits* surviv'd a *thousand Years;* ....1.EOC.479.293.
To gain her Sight, a thousand Forms he wears, ...1.TrVP.29.378.
A thousand court you, tho' they court in vain, ...1.TrVP.74.380.
A thousand Sylvans, Demigods, and Gods, ...1.TrVP.75.380.
A thousand tender Words, I hear and speak; ....1.TrSP.151.400.
A thousand melting Kisses, give, and take: ....1.TrSP.152.400.
And thousand Furies haunt his guilty Soul. ....1.TrSt.76.413.
When by a thousand Darts the *Python* slain ....1.TrSt.664.438.
And now a thousand Lives together fled, ...1.TrSt.744.441.
A thousand Authors have this Truth made out, ...2.ChJM.629.45.
Of thousand bright Inhabitants of Air! ....2.RL1.28.147.
Swift to the Lock a thousand Sprights repair, ...2.RL3.135.178.
A thousand Wings, by turns, blow back the Hair, ...2.RL3.136.178.
The gather'd Winter of a thousand Years. ....2.TemF.60.256.
These and a Thousand more of doubtful Fame, ...2.TemF.129.264.
Rais'd on a thousand Pillars, wreath'd around ....2.TemF.139.264.
A Thousand busy Tongues the Goddess bears, ...2.TemF.268.276.
And Thousand open Eyes, and Thousand list'ning Ears. ....2.TemF.269.276.
And Thousand open Eyes, and Thousand list'ning Ears. ....2.TemF.269.276.
Thro thousand Vents, impatient forth they flow, ...2.TemF.481.286.
Around, a thousand winged Wonders fly, ...2.TemF.487.287.
A thousand movements scarce one purpose gain; ....3.EOM1.54.20.
As who began a thousand years ago. ....3.EOM1.76.23.
26.As who began ten thousand years ago. ....3.EOM1.76A.23.
"For me, the mine a thousand treasures brings; ....3.EOM1.137.32.
"For me, health gushes from a thousand springs; ....3.EOM1.138.32.
A thousand ways, is there no black or white? ....3.EOM2.214.81.
Because he wants a thousand pounds a year. ....3.EOM4.192.145.
Thy boasted Blood, a thousand years or so, ...3.EOM4.207A.146.
Contracts, inverts, and gives ten thousand dyes. ....3.Ep1.28.17.
His Life, to forfeit it a thousand ways; ....3.Ep1.197.32.
But cares not if a thousand are undone. ....3.Ep2.176.64.
"Sir, Spain has sent a thousand jars of oil; ....3.Ep3.44.89.
When Hopkins dies, a thousand lights attend ....3.Ep3.291.116.
The vast Parterres a thousand hands shall make, ...3.Ep4.73.144.
Lord *Fanny* spins a thousand such a Day. ....4.HS1.6.5.
Not so, who of Ten Thousand gull'd her Knight, ...4.HAdv.7.75.
Then ask'd Ten Thousand for a second Night: ....4.HAdv.8.75.
Great *Homer* dy'd three thousand years ago. ....4.Arbu.124.104.
Three thousand Suns went down on *Welsted's* Lye: ....4.Arbu.375.123.
He, with a thousand Arts refin'd, ...4.HOde1.15A.151.
That turn'd ten thousand Verses, now stands still. ....4.2HE2.79.171.
In the dry Desert of a thousand lines, ...4.2HE1.112.205.
'Tis He, who gives my breast a thousand pains, ...4.1HE1.342.225.
On the broad base of fifty thousand rise, ...4.1HE6.74.241.
"I have a thousand thanks to give— ....4.HS6.210.263.
"Pray then what wants he?" fourscore thousand pounds, ...4.1HE1.86.285.
"Lord *Fanny* spun a thousand lines a day? ....4.EpS1.8A.297.
Are what ten thousand envy and adore. ....4.EpS1.166.309.
Now thousand tongues are heard in one loud din: ....5.DunA2.227.128.
Scream, like the winding of ten thousand Jacks: ....5.DunA3.154.164.
Lo thousand thousand, ev'ry nameless name, ...5.DunA3.151A.164.
Lo thousand thousand, ev'ry nameless name, ...5.DunA3.151A.164.
Now thousand tongues are heard in one loud din: ....5.DunB2.235.307.
Scream like the winding of ten thousand jacks: ....5.DunB3.160.328.
In twice ten thousand rhyming nights and days, ...5.DunB4.172.358.
Turn'd to the Sun, she casts a thousand dyes, ...5.DunB4.539.395.
To View a thousand real Blessings rise; ....6.17iii.9.58.
And twice ten thousand bite the ground in death; ....6.21.18.69.
With *Two* or *Three* thousand Pound lost at their Houses, ...6.36.6.104.
When thousand Worlds are round. ....6.50.24.147.
While thousand grateful thoughts arise; ....6.51ii.30.153.
And finds a thousand grateful thoughts arise; ....6.51ii.30A.153.
Blooms in thy colours for a thousand years. ....6.52.58.157.
For Six-pence, I'd have giv'n a thousand Pound. ....6.96iv.80.278.
But cares not if a thousand are undone. ....6.139.20.377.
Here lies wrapt up in forty thousand towels ....6.147ii.1.390.
A thousand Schemes the Monarch's Mind employ; ....Il.2.45.129.
Still unreveng'd a thousand Heroes bleed? ....Il.2.214.138.
To count them all, demands a thousand Tongues, ...Il.2.580.155.
Roar thro' a thousand Chanels to the Main; ....Il.4.519.246.
A thousand Griefs shall waken at the Name! ....Il.6.589.355.
A thousand Measures to the Royal Tent. ....Il.7.563.392.
A thousand Piles the dusky Horrors gild, ...Il.8.703.428.
(That spreads her Conquest o'er a thousand States, ...Il.9.502.458.
From thousand *Trojan* Fires the mounting Blaze; ....Il.10.14.2.
A thousand Cares his lab'ring Breast revolves; ....Il.10.23.3.
No Pass thro' those, without a thousand Wounds, ...Il.12.73.84.
When twice ten thousand shake the lab'ring Field; ....Il.14.174.165.
Him thro' a thousand Forms of Death I bore, ...Il.15.33.195.
The flamy Cuirass, of a thousand Dyes; ....Il.16.165.244.
We boldly camp'd beside a thousand Sail. ....Il.18.306.336.
Or fetch a thousand Circles round the Plain, ...Il.18.329.337.
Three thousand Mares his spacious Pastures bred, ...Il.20.262.405.
Three thousand Foals beside their Mothers fed. ....Il.20.263.405.
A thousand Woes, a thousand Toils remain. ....Il.21.694.450.
A thousand Woes, a thousand Toils remain. ....Il.21.694.450.
On thousand Ships, and wither'd half a Host: ....Il.24.482.556.
On thousand Ships, and wither'd half an Host: ....Il.24.482A.556.
These, and a thousand more swarm'd o'er the ground, ...Od.11.53.383.

THOUSAND (CONTINUED)
Around ten thousand thousand spectres stand ....Od.11.699.419.
Around ten thousand thousand spectres stand ....Od.11.699.419.
O friends, a thousand ways frail mortals lead ....Od.12.403.450.
The name of him awakes a thousand woes. ....Od.14.195.45.
With thousand kisses wander'd o'er his face, ...Od.24.374.367.

THOUSANDS
And thousands more in equal Mirth maintains. ....2.RL4.66.189.
Pregnant with thousands flits the Scrap unseen, ...3.Ep3.77.93.
But thousands die, without or this or that, ...3.Ep3.97.97.
And fame; this lord of useless thousands ends. ....3.Ep3.314.119.
The Lord of thousands, than if now *Excis'd;* ....4.HS2.134.65.
The Lord of thousands, than ev'n now *Excis'd;* ....4.HS2.134A.65.
He bought at thousands, what with better wit ....4.2HE2.236.181.
Thousands on ev'ry side shall yield their breath; ....6.21.17.69.
Yes, Thousands. But in Pity to their Kind, ...6.96iii.13.274.
How did I tremble, when by thousands bound, ...6.96iv.67.278.
Pour'd forth by Thousands, darkens all the Coast. ....Il.2.110.132.
Collects his Flock from Thousands on the Plain. ....Il.2.563.154.
Shall fall by thousands at the Hero's Feet. ....Il.15.68.199.
The Toil of thousands in a Moment falls. ....Il.15.421.213.
The Great, the Bold, by Thousands daily fall, ...Il.19.225.382.
And giving thousands, offer thousands more; ....Il.22.440.473.
And giving thousands, offer thousands more; ....Il.22.440.473.
And the fiends haunt him with a thousands stings. ....Od.11.340.398.

THOUSANDTH
Tenth or ten thousandth, breaks the chain alike. ....3.EOM1.246.45.

THRACE
Thus fell two Heroes; one the Pride of *Thrace,* ....Il.4.624.250.
So stalks in Arms the grizly God of *Thrace,* ....Il.7.252.376.
And nurs'd in *Thrace* where snowy Flocks are fed. ....Il.11.286.48.
From *Thrace* they fly, call'd to the dire Alarms ....Il.13.390.124.
(The Pledge of Treaties once with friendly *Thrace)*<:> ....Il.24.288.548.
They burst; and *Mars* to *Thrace* indignant flies: ....Od.8.394.285.

THRACIA
Then turn'd to *Thracia* from the Field of Fight ....Il.13.5.103.
Rhigmus, whose Race from fruitful *Thracia* came, ...Il.20.561.417.

THRACIA'S
In dread Array, from *Thracia's* wintry Coasts; ....Il.2.1023.171.
Swells o'er the Sea, from *Thracia's* frozen Shore, ...Il.9.7.431.

THRACIAN
High on the Stern the *Thracian* rais'd his Strain, ...6.11.39.31.
The *Thracian* rais'd his Strain, ...6.11.39A.31.
(Who from cold *Ænus* led the *Thracian* Crew) ....Il.4.600.250.
The *Thracian* Bands against the Victor prest; ....Il.4.620.250.
In Form like *Acamas,* the *Thracian* Guide, ...Il.5.563.295.
The *Thracian Acamas* his Faulchion found, ...Il.6.9.323.
With *Thracian* Wines recruit thy honour'd Guests, ...Il.9.99.437.
And let the *Thracian* Steeds reward our Toil: ....Il.10.533.27.
Arriving where the *Thracian* Squadrons lay, ...Il.10.542.27.
Till twelve lay breathless of the *Thracian* Band. ....Il.10.569.28.
Of *Thracian* Lineage are the Steeds ye view, ...Il.10.656.31.
King *Helenus* wav'd high the *Thracian* Blade, ...Il.13.728.139.
Across the *Thracian* Seas their Course they bore; ....Il.23.286.501.
(A *Thracian* Blade, distinct with Studs of Gold) ....Il.23.952.527.

THRACIANS
The *Thracians* utmost, and a-part from all. ....Il.10.503.26.
The yet-warm *Thracians* panting on the Coast; ....Il.10.612.29.
And hardy *Thracians* tame the savage Horse; ....Il.13.8.104.

THRASIMED
But godlike *Thrasimed* prevents his Rage, ...Il.16.383.258.
But godly *Thrasimed* prevents his Rage, ...Il.16.383A.258*.

THRASIMEDES'
He said: and seizing *Thrasimedes'* Shield, ...Il.14.13.157.

THRASIUS
Thrasius, Astypylus, and *Mnesus* slew; ....Il.21.226.430.

THRASYMED
And pass'd the Groin of valiant *Thrasymed,* ....1.TrES.264.459.
The gen'rous *Thrasymed,* in Arms renown'd: ....Il.9.112.437.
A two-edg'd Faulchion *Thrasymed* the brave, ...Il.10.301.16.
And pass'd the Groin of valiant *Thrasymed,* ....Il.16.569.266.
Where *Nestor* sate with youthful *Thrasymed.* ....Od.3.50.89.
Then *Perseus, Aretus,* and *Thrasymed;* ....Od.3.527.113.
The axe was held by warlike *Thrasymed,* ....Od.3.561.115.
Strong *Thrasymed* discharg'd the speeding blow ....Od.3.570.115.

THRASYMEDE
But bids bold *Thrasymede* those troops sustain; ....Il.17.791.319.

THREAD
Death with his Scythe cut off the fatal Thread, ...1.TrSt.745.441.
Feels at each thread, and lives along the line: ....3.EOM1.218.42.
He spins the slight, self-pleasing thread anew: ....4.Arbu.90.102.
Still spin the slight, self-pleasing thread anew; ....4.Arbu.90A.102.
My Mind resumes the thread it dropt before; ....4.2HE2.207.179.
Suck the thread in, then yield it out again: ....5.DunA3.50.155.
Or quite unravel all the reas'ning thread, ...5.DunB1.179.283.
Suck the thread in, then yield it out again: ....5.DunB3.58.323.
She furl'd her Sampler, and hawl'd in her Thread, ...6.96ii.5.270.
As closely following as the running Thread ....Il.23.890.524.
The spacious loom, and mix'd the various thread: ....Od.2.104.66.
For Fate has wove the thread of life with pain, ...Od.7.263.248.
For heav'n has wove his thread of life with pain. ....Od.16.64.105.
A spacious loom, and mix'd the various thread; ....Od.24.153.355.

THREADS
With crimson threads, while busy damsels cull ....Od.6.63.208.
Part twist the threads, and part the wool dispose, ...Od.6.369.229.
The flying shuttle thro' the threads to guide: ....Od.7.139.242.
Thin, as the filmy threads the spider weaves. ....Od.8.324.281.
The fleecy threads her ivory fingers drew. ....Od.17.113.137.

THREAT
This Day, black Omens threat the brightest Fair ....2.RL2.101.166.
The Champions in distorted Postures threat, ...2.TemF.220.272.
And dar'st thou threat to snatch my Prize away, ...Il.1.213.97.
Go, threat thy Earth-born *Myrmidons;* but here ....Il.1.239.98.
Durst threat with Chains th' Omnipotence of Heav'n. ....Il.1.521.113.
A dreadful Front! they shake the Brands, and threat ....Il.8.264.410.
Pant for the Fight, and threat the Fleet with Fire: ....Il.12.102.85.
Such was his Threat, ah now too soon made good, ...Il.14.53.160.
(For *Fate* preserves them) from the Hunter's Threat ....Il.15.311A.209.
His Threat, and guard inviolate the Slain: ....Il.23.227.498.
Thus He. The Coursers at their Master's Threat ....Il.23.495.510.
With ardent eyes the rival train they threat, ...Od.2.177.70.
And both the Prince and Augur threat in vain: ....Od.2.228.72.
Threat on, oh Prince! elude the bridal day, ...Od.2.231.72.
Threat on, till all thy stores in waste decay. ....Od.2.232.72.
Our force successful shall our threat make good, ...Od.22.237.298.
In vain we threat; *Telemachus* commands: ....Od.24.200.358.

THREAT'NING
Threat'ning the Fort, and black'ning in the Field; ....1.TrES.58.451.
All pale with Rage, and shake the threat'ning Lance. ....Il.3.426.212.
Already met the threat'ning Heroes stand; ....Il.5.697.301.
And threat'ning, thus his adverse Chief addrest. ....Il.7.272.377.
Their threat'ning Tents already shade our Wall, ...Il.9.306.449.
Threat'ning the Fort, and black'ning in the Field; ....Il.12.402.96.
Threat'ning he said: The hostile Chiefs advance; ....Il.21.179.429.
So spake he, threat'ning: But the Gods made vain ....Il.23.226.498.
Threat'ning to answer from the dark recess. ....Od.4.384.139.
Ulysses? oh! thy threat'ning fury cease, ...Od.10.395.363.

THREATEN
And ten-horn'd fiends and Giants threaten war. ....5.DunA3.232A.177.
But threaten more destructive flames. ....6.5.10A.12.
'Tis mine to threaten, Prince, and thine to fear. ....Il.1.240.98.

THREATEN'D
The Reader's threaten'd (not in vain) with *Sleep.* .... 1.EOC.353.279.
Well might, alas! that threaten'd vessel fail, ...6.3.3.7.
That heav'n, the threaten'd world to spare, ...6.5.15.12.
Incens'd he threaten'd, and his Threats perform'd: ....Il.1.503.112.
Haste, Warrior, haste! preserve thy threaten'd State; ....Il.5.593.296.
Or while thou may'st, avoid the threaten'd Fate; ....Il.17.35.289.
While yet thou may'st, avoid the threaten'd Fate; ....Il.17.35A.289.
Go; while thou may'st, avoid the threaten'd Fate; ....Il.20.238.403.
Mad as he was, he threaten'd servile Bands, ...Il.21.527.443.
A two-edg'd faulchion threaten'd by his side, ...Od.2.6.60.

THREATENS
While that Prince Threatens, and while this Commands. ....1.TrSt.272.421.
He flies indeed, but threatens as he flies, ...Il.17.119.292.
When a lov'd mother threatens to depart, ...Od.21.107.264.

THREATNED
Torn from the rock, which threatned as it flew; ....1.TrPA.145.372.
Greece yet may live, her threatned Fleet maintain, ...Il.13.85.109.
Such stern Decrees, such threatned Woes to come, ...Il.15.105.200.

THREATNING
See! the bold Youth strain up the threatning Steep, ...1.W-F.155.164.
And *stares, Tremendous!* with a *threatning Eye,* ....1.EOC.586.306.
Gods! how his Eyes with threatning Ardour glow! ....1.TrSt.256.421.
Those threatning Heroes, bear them both away; ....Il.5.319.281.
And fearless dar'd the threatning God of Day; ....Il.5.526.294.
Peasants in vain with threatning cries pursue, ...Od.15.182.77.
And first loud-threatning, *Agelaus* cry'd. ....Od.22.234.298.

THREATS
That threats a Fight, and spurns the rising Sand. ....1.PSp.48.65.
A *Sylph* too warn'd me of the Threats of Fate, ...2.RL4.165.197.
The distant Threats of Vengeance on his head, ...4.Arbu.348.120.
Famine threats; ....6.96i.42.269.
Thy Aid we need not, and thy Threats defy. ....Il.1.226.97.
Incens'd he threaten'd, and his Threats perform'd: ....Il.1.503.112.
Which now, alas! too nearly threats my Son. ....Il.1.549.114.
And threats aloud: The *Greeks* with longing Eyes ....Il.5.367.284.
Where are thy Threats, and where thy glorious Boast, ...Il.5.576.296.
In vain our Threats, in vain our Pow'r we use; ....Il.5.1102.319.
And threats his Followers with retorted Eye. ....Il.11.695.66.
Threats urge the fearful, and the valiant, Praise. ....Il.12.316.93.
Hector! come on, thy empty Threats forbear: ....Il.13.1022.153.
Lo still he vaunts, and threats the Fleet with Fires, ...Il.14.425.184.
Not but his Threats with Justice I disclaim, ...Il.15.234.206.
Exhort their Men, with Praises, Threats, Commands; ....Il.15.424.213.
As furious, *Hector* thunder'd Threats aloud, ...Il.15.832.229.
Think with what Threats you dar'd the *Trojan* Throng, ...Il.16.240.248.
Now plies the Lash, and sooths and threats in vain; ....Il.17.489.307.
High on pois'd Pinions, threats their callow Young. ....Il.17.848.321.
In distant Threats he brav'd the Goddess-born. ....Il.20.116.398.
(Ye Gods avert it) threats the *Trojan* State. ....Il.22.583.480.
His Threats *Deiphobus* and *Dius* hear, ...Il.24.313.549.
He fear'd my threats, and follow'd with the rest. ....Od.10.530.369.
Nor threats, thy bold intrusion will reclaim. ....Od.20.228.244.
The threats of vain imperious youth despise: ....Od.20.337.249.
Fierce for his son, he breathes his threats in air; ....Od.24.538.373.

THREDDED
Sung on direct, and thredded ev'ry ring. ....Od.21.462.282.

THREE
Where the three Roads the *Phocian* Fields divide: ....1.TrSt.92.414.
Three were just tolerable, two were bad. ....2.ChWB.57.59.
The three were Old, but rich and fond beside, ...2.ChWB.58.59.
These three right Ancient Venerable Sires. ....2.ChWB.149.63.
Thus with my first three Lords I past my Life; ....2.ChWB.205.66.
On which three Wives successively had twin'd ....2.ChWB.395.76.
Provok'd to Vengeance, three large Leaves I tore, ...2.ChWB.415.77.
There lay three Garters, half a Pair of Gloves; ....2.RL2.39.161.
And breathes three am'rous Sighs to raise the Fire. ....2.RL2.42.162.
Here Thou, Great *Anna!* whom three Realms obey, ...2.RL3.7.169.
Strait the three Bands prepare in Arms to join, ...2.RL3.29.171.
In three *Seal-Rings;* which after, melted down, ...2.RL5.91.207.
Lie in three words, Health, Peace, and Competence. ....3.EOM4.80.136.
To just three millions stinted modest Gage. ....3.Ep3.130.103.
Whose Place is *quarter'd out,* three Parts in four, ...4.JD4.136.37.
That's all three Lovers have for their Estate! ....4.HAdv.12.75.
Three things another's modest wishes bound, ...4.Arbu.47.99.
Great *Homer* dy'd three thousand years ago. ....4.Arbu.124.104.
Three thousand Suns went down on *Welsted's* Lye: ....4.Arbu.375.123.
Or if three Ladies like a luckless Play, ...4.1HE6.87.243.
"That makes three Members, this can chuse a May'r." ....4.1HE6.106.245.
'Tis (let me see) three years and more, ...4.HS6.83.255.
And when three Sov'reigns dy'd, could scarce be vext, ...4.EpS1.107.306.
Three wicked imps of her own Grubstreet Choir ....5.DunA2.115.110.
Room for my Lord! three Jockeys in his train; ....5.DunA2.184.124.
Improve we these. Three cat-calls be the bribe ....5.DunA2.223.128.
From dreams of millions, and three groats to pay! ....5.DunA2.242.129.
Three Cambridge Sophs and three pert Templars came, ...5.DunA2.347.143.
Three Cambridge Sophs and three pert Templars came, ...5.DunA2.347.143.
(His only suit) for twice three years before: ....5.DunA3.30.154.
And Pope's, translating three whole years with Broome. ....5.DunA3.328.191.
Three wicked imps, of her own Grubstreet choir, ...5.DunB2.123.301.
Room for my Lord! three jockeys in his train; ....5.DunB2.192.305.
Improve we these. Three Cat-calls be the bribe ....5.DunB2.231.307.
From dreams of millions, and three groats to pay. ....5.DunB2.252.307.
Then sighing, thus, "And am I now three-score? ....5.DunB2.285.309.
Three College Sophs, and three pert Templars came, ...5.DunB2.379.315.
Three College Sophs, and three pert Templars came, ...5.DunB2.379.315.
(His only suit) for twice three years before: ....5.DunB3.38.322.
On whom three hundred gold-capt youths await, ...5.DunB4.117.353.
To three essential Partriges in one? ....5.DunB4.562.397.
Tyrant supreme! shall three Estates command, ...5.DunB4.603.403.
Snuff just three Times, and read again.) ....6.10.66.26.
Two or *Three* Visits, and *Two* or *Three* Bows, ...6.36.1.104.
Two or *Three* Visits, and *Two* or *Three* Bows, ...6.36.1.104.
Two or *Three* civil Things, *Two* or *Three* Vows, ...6.36.2.104.
Two or *Three* civil Things, *Two* or *Three* Vows, ...6.36.2.104.
Two or *Three* Kisses, with *Two* or *Three* Sighs, ...6.36.3.104.
Two or *Three* Kisses, with *Two* or *Three* Sighs, ...6.36.3.104.
Two or *Three* Jesus's—and let me dyes— ....6.36.4.104.
Two or *Three* Squeezes, and *Two* or *Three* Towses, ...6.36.5.104.
Two or *Three* Squeezes, and *Two* or *Three* Towses, ...6.36.5.104.
With *Two* or *Three* thousand Pound lost at their Houses, ...6.36.6.104.
Can never fail Cuckolding *Two* or *Three* Spouses. ....6.36.7.104.
Two or *Three* Visits, with *Two* or *Three* Bows. ....6.36.1A.105.
Two or *Three* Visits, with *Two* or *Three* Bows. ....6.36.1A.105.
Two or *Three* Visits, *Two* or *Three* Bows, ...6.36.1B.105.
Two or *Three* Visits, *Two* or *Three* Bows, ...6.36.1B.105.
Two or *Three* Kisses, and *Two* or *Three* Sighs, ...6.36.3A.105.
Two or *Three* Kisses, and *Two* or *Three* Sighs, ...6.36.3A.105.
Two or *Three* Kisses, *Two* or *Three* Sighs, ...6.36.3B.105.
Two or *Three* Kisses, *Two* or *Three* Sighs, ...6.36.3B.105.
Two or *Three* Squeezes, *Two* or *Three* Towses, ...6.36.5A.105.
Two or *Three* Squeezes, *Two* or *Three* Towses, ...6.36.5A.105.
With *Two* or *Three* hundred Pounds lost at their Houses, ...6.36.6A.105.
The *Polygott—three Parts,—my Text,* ....6.39.13.110.
Three Parts—the Polyglott,—my *Text,* .... 6.39.13A.110.
To morning walks, and pray'rs three hours a day; ....6.45.14.125.
Save Three-pence, and his Soul. ....6.47.12.128.
Of Courtiers from you Three, ...6.61.30.182.
There may you meet us, three to three, ...6.61.40.182.
There may you meet us, three to three, ...6.61.40.182.
Of Courtiers 'twixt you Three, ...6.61.30A.182.
You have the *Nine* in your *Wit,* and *Three* in your *Faces.* ....6.62i.2.185.
You've the *Nine* in your *Wit,* and the *Three* in your *Face* ..... 6.62i.2A.185.
They may tell of three Goddesses in *Ida* Vales, ...6.62ii.1A.185.
And Mistress *Biddel* sure is Fifty three. ....6.96iv.24.276.
Three Shillings cost the first, the last sev'n Groats; ....6.96iv.53.277.
Next in three Books, sunk human *Nature,* .... 6.101.10.290.
For three whole days you here may rest ....6.114.9.321.
Has lopp'd three Trees, the Value of three Farthings: ....6.143.2.385.
Has lopp'd three Trees, the Value of three Farthings: ....6.143.2.385.
Has cut three Trees, the Value of three Farthings: ....6.143.2A.385.
Has cut three Trees, the Value of three Farthings: ....6.143.2A.385.
There in three Tribes divides his native Band, ...Il.2.809.163.
Three Ships with *Nireus* sought the *Trojan* Shore, ...Il.2.815.163.
Three Towns are *Juno's* on the *Grecian* Plains, ...Il.4.75.224.
Yet more—three Daughters in my Court are bred, ...Il.9.187.441.
Heaps in a Brazen Vase three Chines entire: ....Il.9.272.447.
Yet more—three Daughters in his Court are bred, ...Il.9.374.451.
Rang'd in three Lines they view the prostrate Band; ....Il.10.544.27.
Three glitt'ring Dragons to the Gorget rise, ...Il.11.33.36.
(*Jove's* wond'rous Bow, of three celestial Dyes, ...Il.11.37.36.
Till in three Heads th' embroider'd Monster ends. ....Il.11.52.36.
My Sire three hundred chosen Sheep obtain'd. ....Il.11.835.73.
Three Days were past, when *Elis* rose to War, ...Il.11.842.73.
From Realm to Realm three ample Strides he took, ...Il.13.32.106.
See! on one *Greek* three *Trojan* Ghosts attend, ...Il.13.560.133.
With three bold Sons was gen'rous *Prothous* blest, ...Il.14.130.164.
Three Brother Deities from *Saturn* came, ...Il.15.210.204.
And thrice three Heroes at each Onset slew. ....Il.16.949.280.
My three brave Brothers in one mournful Day ....Il.19.311.385.
Three thousand Mares his spacious Pastures bred, ...Il.20.262.405.
Three thousand Foals beside their Mothers fed. ....Il.20.263.405.
Three Sons renown'd adorn'd his nuptial Bed, ...Il.20.276.406.

THREE (CONTINUED)
Thus three times round the *Trojan* Wall they fly; .... Il.22.217.464.
Now three times turn'd in prospect of the Goal, ... Il.23.899.525.
Scarce three strong *Greeks* could lift its mighty Weight, ... Il.24.559.559.
Three sons remain'd: To climb with haughty fires .... Od.2.27.61.
For three long years the royal fraud behold? .... Od.2.102.66.
Unheard, unseen, three years her arts prevail; .... Od.2.121.67.
Of men decay, and thro' three Ages shin'd, ... Od.3.304.101.
Three chosen chiefs of dauntless soul command: .... Od.4.552.146.
With three associates of undaunted mind. .... Od.4.590.147.
Three sprightly coursers, and a polish'd car: .... Od.4.806.156.
Where three at least might winter's cold defy, ... Od.5.626.201.
Five sons thou hast; three wait the bridal day, ... Od.6.75.208.
And three brave sons, from great *Alcinous* sprung. .... Od.8.124.269.
Three men were sent, deputed from the crew, ... Od.9.99.307.
The three we sent, from off th' inchanting ground .... Od.9.111.308.
Strait in three squadrons all our crew we part, ... Od.9.182.313.
These, three and three, with osier bands we ty'd, ... Od.9.507.326.
These, three and three, with osier bands we ty'd, ... Od.9.507.326.
Three gallant sons the joyful Monarch told, ... Od.11.347.399.
And drag'd the three-mouth'd dog to upper day; .... Od.11.770.424.
Her jaws grin dreadful with three rows of teeth; .... Od.12.113.437.
Three chosen maids attend him to the main; .... Od.13.83.5.
Three years thy house their lawless rule has seen, ... Od.13.431.27.
Three now were absent on the rural care; .... Od.14.28.36.
Three golden goblets in the porch she found, ... Od.15.503.94.
Three days have spent their beams, three nights have run .... Od.17.606.161.
Three days have spent their beams, three nights have run .... Od.17.606.161.
Three vases heap'd with copious fires display .... Od.18.355.184.
Three years successful in my art conceal'd, ... Od.19.174.200.
So *Pandarus,* thy hopes, three orphan fair .... Od.20.78.236.
Three porkers for the feast, all brawny chin'd, ... Od.20.204.243.
Three hundred sheep, and all the shepherd swains; .... Od.21.22.260.
Three times, with beating heart, he made essay; .... Od.21.131.264.
Three times, unequal to the task, gave way: .... Od.21.132.264.
Unheard, unseen, three years her arts prevail; .... Od.24.168.356.

THREE-MOUTH'D
And drag'd the three-mouth'd dog to upper day; .... Od.11.770.424.

THREE-PENCE
Save Three-pence, and his Soul. .... 6.47.12.128.

THREE-SCORE
Then sighing, thus, "And am I now three-score? .... 5.DunB2.285.309.

THREEFOLD
Its utmost Verge a threefold Circle bound; .... Il.18.553.348.
A threefold off'ring to his Altar bring, ... Od.11.160.389.

THREESCORE
And bare Threescore is all ev'n That can boast: .... 1.EOC.481.293.
Beneath the Weight of threescore Years I bend, ... 2.ChJM.87.19.
Then sighing, thus. "And I am now threescore? .... 5.DunA2.273.135.

THRESH
For DUCK can *thresh,* you know, as well as *write.* .... 6.116vi.6.327.

THRESHOLD
And treads the brazen Threshold of the Gods. .... Il.18.184.331.
The marble threshold of the *Delphic* God, ... Od.8.76.266.
Now on the threshold of the dome they stood, ... Od.10.252.354.
Before the threshold of his rustic gate; .... Od.14.8.35.
Then like a Lion o'er the threshold bounds; .... Od.17.37.134.
Then, resting on the threshold of the gate, ... Od.17.414.152.
He fill'd his scrip, and to the threshold sped; .... Od.17.495.156.
When fierce the Heroe o'er the threshold strode; .... Od.22.1.284.
But from the threshold shall his darts be sped, ... Od.22.85.290.
Thus laden, o'er the threshold as he stept, ... Od.22.201.297.
With deaden'd sound, one on the threshold falls, ... Od.22.284.300.
Some, turn'd by *Pallas,* on the threshold fall, ... Od.22.302.301.
Fierce on the threshold then in arms he stood; .... Od.24.203.358.

THREW
The Cyclops follow'd, and a stone he threw, ... 1.TrPA.144.372.
Two sounding Darts the *Lycian* Leader threw, ... 1.TrES.267.459.
How many Pisspots on the Sage she threw; .... 2.ChWB.390.76.
A Charge of *Snuff* the wily Virgin threw; .... 2.RL5.82.206.
But 'twas my Guest at whom they threw the dirt? .... 4.EpS2.145.321.
Between their Horns the salted Barley threw, ... Il.1.600.116.
Around him next the Regal Mantle threw, ... Il.2.54.129.
O'er her fair Face a snowy Veil she threw, ... Il.3.187.200.
And in the Dust their bleeding Bodies threw, ... Il.3.365.210.
The *Trojan* first his shining Jav'lin threw; .... Il.3.427.212.
The Casque, enrag'd, amidst the *Greeks* he threw; .... Il.3.463.214.
At *Ajax, Antiphus* his Jav'lin threw; .... Il.4.562.248.
A broken Rock the Force of *Pirus* threw, ... Il.4.599.250.
Then threw the Force of *Tydeus'* warlike Son; .... Il.5.1048.316.
Till in the sev'nth it fix'd. Then *Ajax* threw, ... Il.7.299.379.
Amidst the greedy Flames *Patroclus* threw; .... Il.9.288.448.
O'er his broad Back his moony Shield he threw, ... Il.11.672.65.
Around his Waste his pious Arms he threw, ... Il.13.676.137.
His eager Arms around the Goddess threw. .... Il.14.394.181.
His Lance bold *Meges* at the Victor threw; .... Il.15.616.220.
Beyond the foremost Ranks; his Lance he threw, ... Il.15.688.222.
The Mist of Darkness *Jove* around them threw, ... Il.15.808.227.
Two sounding Darts the *Lycian* Leader threw; .... Il.16.572.266.
His Spear *Æneas* at the Victor threw, ... Il.16.739.272.
And sent his Soul with ev'ry Lance he threw. .... Il.17.647.313.
On the hard Soil his groaning Breast he threw, ... Il.18.31.325.
Last o'er the Dead the milkwhite Veil they threw; .... Il.18.415.340.
Last o'er the Dead the milkwhite Linen threw; .... Il.18.415A.340.
Last o'er the Dead the milkwhite Mantle threw; .... Il.18.415B.340.
There stuck the Lance. Then rising e'er he threw, ... Il.20.321.407.
And at its Master's Feet the Weapon threw. .... Il.20.372.410.
Before the Bier the bleeding *Hector* threw, ... Il.23.34.488.

THREW (CONTINUED)
Each stood in order: First *Epæus* threw; .... Il.23.995.529.
And skilful *Teucer:* In the Helm they threw .... Il.23.1018.529.
Around his Neck her milk-white Arms she threw, ... Il.24.907.574.
O'er his fair limbs a flow'ry vest he threw, ... Od.3.596.117.
Th' imperial mantle o'er his vest he threw; .... Od.4.414.140.
And glowing violets threw odors round. .... Od.5.94.176.
Forth from her snowy hand *Nausicaa* threw .... Od.6.133.213.
Already, when the dreadful rock he threw, ... Od.9.581.330.
With weighty steps, 'till at the ship I threw .... Od.10.198.350.
One o'er the couches painted carpets threw, ... Od.10.417.364.
A vest and tunick o'er me next she threw, ... Od.10.429.365.
All hasty on the hissing coals he threw; .... Od.14.89.40.
Some in the flames, bestrow'd with flour, they threw; .... Od.14.478.59.
The splendid mantle round him first he threw, ... Od.15.68.72.
Then o'er their limbs refulgent robes they threw, ... Od.17.102.136.
Before his feet the well-fill'd scrip he threw, ... Od.17.553.159.
He said, and with full force a footstool threw: .... Od.18.436.189.
Before his feet the ratling show'r he threw, ... Od.22.5.286.
And down reluctant on the pavement threw. .... Od.22.204.297.
Then all at once their mingled lances threw, ... Od.22.280.300.

THRICE
Thrice the wrought Slipper knock'd against the Ground, ... 2.RL1.17A.145.
Thrice rung the Bell, the Slipper knock'd the Ground, ... 2.RL1.17.146.
And thrice they twitch'd the Diamond in her Ear, ... 2.RL3.137.178.
Thrice she look'd back, and thrice the Foe drew near. .... 2.RL3.138.178.
Thrice she look'd back, and thrice the Foe drew near. .... 2.RL3.138.178.
Thrice from my trembling hand the *Patch-box* fell; .... 2.RL4.162.197.
B. Thrice happy man! enabled to pursue .... 3.Ep3.275A.116.
"Thrice happy man! enabled to pursue .... 3.Ep3.275.116.
The Fool whose Wife elopes some thrice a quarter, ... 4.1HE1.150.291.
With that, he lifted thrice the sparkling brand, ... 5.DunA1.203.87.
And thrice he dropt it from his quiv'ring hand: .... 5.DunA1.204.87.
Thrice Budgel aim'd to speak, but thrice suppress .... 5.DunA2.365.144.
Thrice Budgel aim'd to speak, but thrice suppress .... 5.DunA2.365.144.
And thrice he lifted high the Birth-day brand, ... 5.DunB1.245.288.
And thrice he dropt it from his quiv'ring hand; .... 5.DunB1.246.288.
Thrice Budgel aim'd to speak, but thrice suppress .... 5.DunB2.397.316.
Thrice Budgel aim'd to speak, but thrice suppress .... 5.DunB2.397.316.
Thrice as long as you preach. .... 6.91.26.254.
WELCOME, thrice welcome to thy native Place! .... 6.96iv.1.276.
Thrice rushing furious, at the Chief he strook; .... Il.5.529.294.
His blazing Buckler thrice *Apollo* shook: .... Il.5.530.294.
Thrice our bold Foes the fierce Attack have giv'n, ... Il.6.556.354.
Thrice turn'd the Chief, and thrice imperial *Jove* .... Il.8.206.407.
Thrice turn'd the Chief, and thrice imperial *Jove* .... Il.8.206.407.
Thrice to its pitch his lofty Voice he rears; .... Il.11.580.60.
The well-known Voice thrice *Menelaus* hears: .... Il.11.581.60.
And thrice the Number of unrival'd Steeds, ... Il.11.824.73.
Thrice happy Race! that, innocent of Blood, ... Il.13.11.104.
Thrice at the Battlements *Patroclus* strook, ... Il.16.859.276.
His blazing *Ægis* thrice *Apollo* shook: .... Il.16.860.276.
Thrice on the Press like *Mars* himself he flew, ... Il.16.948.280.
And thrice three Heroes at each Onset slew. .... Il.16.949.280.
Thrice the slain Hero by the Foot he drew; .... Il.18.193.331.
Thrice to the Skies the *Trojan* Clamours flew. .... Il.18.194.331.
Thrice from the Trench his dreadful Voice he rais'd; .... Il.18.269.335.
And thrice they fled, confounded and amaz'd. .... Il.18.270.335.
Thrice struck *Pelides* with indignant Heart, ... Il.20.515.416.
Thrice in impassive Air he plung'd the Dart: .... Il.20.516.416.
The Foe thrice tugg'd, and shook the rooted Wood; .... Il.21.191.429.
Her Walls thrice circled, and her Chief pursu'd. .... Il.22.318.469.
The Troops obey'd; and thrice in order led .... Il.23.15.486.
And thrice their Sorrows and Laments renew; .... Il.23.17.487.
But thrice they clos'd, and thrice the Charge renew'd. .... Il.23.964.527.
But thrice they clos'd, and thrice the Charge renew'd. .... Il.23.964.527.
And thrice *Patroclus!* round thy Monument .... Il.24.25.536.
While thrice the sun his annual journey made, ... Od.2.119.67.
(Who thrice has seen the perishable kind .... Od.3.303.101.
Slow-pacing thrice around th' insidious pile; .... Od.4.378.139.
Each noted leader's name you thrice invoke, ... Od.4.379.139.
So when the covert of the thrice-ear'd field .... Od.5.159.179.
Happy! thrice happy! who in battle slain .... Od.5.393.191.
Add thrice the chains, and thrice more firmly bind; .... Od.8.378.284.
Add thrice the chains, and thrice more firmly bind; .... Od.8.378.284.
And thrice we call'd on each unhappy Shade. .... Od.9.74.305.
Thrice drain'd, and pour'd the deluge on his soul. .... Od.9.428.323.
Thrice in my arms I strove her shade to bind, ... Od.11.248.393.
Thrice thro' my arms she slipt like empty wind, ... Od.11.249.393.
Thrice in her gulphs the boiling seas subside, ... Od.12.131.438.
Thrice in dire thunders she refunds the tyde. .... Od.12.132.438.
And thrice he hop'd, and thrice again he fear'd. .... Od.21.134.264.
And thrice he hop'd, and thrice again he fear'd. .... Od.21.134.264.
Thrice happy thou! to press the martial plain .... Od.24.53.350.
And, Blest! thrice blest this happy day! he cries, ... Od.24.594.376.

THRICE-EAR'D
So when the covert of the thrice-ear'd field .... Od.5.159.179.

THRID
Some thrid the mazy Ringlets of her Hair, ... 2.RL2.139.168.
How many Dutchmen she vouchsaf'd to thrid? .... 5.DunA3.43.154.
How many Dutchmen she vouchsaf'd to thrid? .... 5.DunB3.51.323.
Thrid ev'ry science, run thro' ev'ry school? .... 5.DunB4.256.369.

THRIFT
But vain with Youth, and yet to Thrift inclin'd, ... Il.5.252.279.

THRILL'D
And *Greece* around sate thrill'd with sacred Awe. .... Il.19.266.383.

THRILLING
The thrilling Steel transpierc'd the brawny Part, ... Il.11.327.49.
Thro' his fair Neck the thrilling Arrow flies; .... Il.15.528.217.
Forth thro' the Navel burst the thrilling Steel; .... Il.20.481.414.

THRILLING (CONTINUED)
My bold companions thrilling fear confounds, ...Od.9.304.319.

THRILLS
The blessing thrills thro' all the lab'ring throng, ...4.2HE1.239.215.
That thrills my Arm and shoots thro ev'ry Vein, ...Il.16.638.269.
And tender sorrow thrills in ev'ry vein; ......Od.11.676.417.

THRIV'D
Sprung the rank Weed, and thriv'd with large Increase; ......1.EOC.535.297.

THRIVE
And says our *Wars thrive ill,* because *delay'd;* ......4.JD4.163.39.
All you, who think the *City* ne'er can thrive, ...4.HAdv.47.79.
But (thanks to *Homer)* since I live and thrive, ...4.2HE2.68.169.
We thrive at *Westminster* on Fools like you, ...6.145.11.388.
The Gods still love them, and they always thrive. ......Il.23.926.526.
And starve by strolling, not by work to thrive. ......Od.18.409.188.

THRIVES
And feeds and thrives on Publick Miseries. ......1.TrSt.713.440.
Fufidia thrives in Money, Land, and Stocks: ......4.HAdv.18.77.
Than these in him; by these he lives and thrives ......4.JD2A.89.140.
Farewel the stage! if just as thrives the Play, ...4.2HE1.302.221.

THRIVING
The thriving plants ignoble broomsticks made, ...3.Ep4.97.146.
Tall thriving trees confess'd the fruitful mold; ......6.35.5.103.
Tall thriving trees confess'd the fruitful mold; ......Od.7.146.243.

THRO
And scornful Hisses run thro all the Croud. ......2.TemF.405.283.
And scornful Hisses ran thro all the Croud. ......2.TemF.405A.283.
Thro undulating Air the Sounds are sent, ...2.TemF.446.285.
Thro thousand Vents, impatient forth they flow, ...2.TemF.481.286.
Born by the Trumpet's Blast, and scatter'd thro the Sky. ......2.TemF.488.287.
Which first should issue thro the narrow Vent: ......2.TemF.492.287.
And pond'rous slugs cut swiftly thro the sky; ......5.DunB1.182.283.
Thro the thick Files he darts his searching Eyes, ...Il.4.235.232.
Thro Haste, or Danger, had not drawn the Dart) ......Il.5.827.305.
Pass'd thro the Hosts, and reach'd the Royal Tent. ......Il.9.787.472.
But pierc'd not thro: Unfaithful to his Hand, ...Il.13.217.116.
That thrills my Arm and shoots thro ev'ry Vein, ...Il.16.638.269.
Æneas thro the Form assum'd descries ......Il.17.388.302.
Shouts of Applause run rattling thro the Skies. ......Il.23.847.523.
And thro surrounding Friends the Chariot rolls. ......Il.24.402.552.

THRO'
Let Vernal Airs thro' trembling Osiers play, ...1.PSp.5.60.
Thro' verdant Forests, and thro' flow'ry Meads. ......1.PSu.4A.71.
Thro' verdant Forests, and thro' flow'ry Meads. ......1.PSu.4A.71.
Thro' Rocks and Caves the Name of *Delia* sounds, ...1.PAu.49.83.
Thro' Rocks and Caves the Name of Thyrsis sounds, ...1.PAu.49A.83.
Nor Rivers winding thro' the Vales below, ...1.PWi.3.88.
The hollow Winds thro' naked Temples roar; ......1.W-F.68.156.
Rush thro' the Thickets, down the Vallies sweep, ...1.W-F.156.164.
When thro' the Clouds he drives the trembling Doves; ......1.W-F.188.167.
Thro' the fair Scene rowl slow the lingring Streams, ...1.W-F.217.169.
While thro' the Skies his shining Current strays, ...1.W-F.228A.170.
I seem thro' consecrated Walks to rove, ...1.W-F.267.173.
Stretch his long Triumphs down thro' ev'ry Age, ...1.W-F.304.177.
Which, without passing thro' the *Judgment,* gains ......1.EOC.156.258.
In the next Line, it *whispers thro' the Trees;* ......1.EOC.351.279.
As things seem *large* which we thro' *Mists* descry, ...1.EOC.392.285.
Are Mortals urg'd thro' *Sacred Lust of Praise!* ......1.EOC.521.296.
The rock asunder cleav'd, and thro' the chink ......1.TrPA.155.372.
As when thro' Clouds th'emerging Sun appears, ...1.TrVP.115.381.
Thus thro' the trembling boughs in sighs complains. ......1.TrFD.68.389.
Yet latent life thro' her new branches reign'd, ...1.TrFD.102.390.
I burn, I burn, as when thro' ripn'd Corn ......1.TrSP.9.393.
Thro' lonely Plains, and thro' the silent Grove, ...1.TrSP.160.400.
Thro' lonely Plains, and thro' the silent Grove, ...1.TrSP.160.400.
Thro' dreary Coasts which I, tho' Blind, behold: ......1.TrSt.84.413.
Thro' Crouds of Airy Shades she wing'd her Flight, ...1.TrSt.130.415.
And thro' th' *Achaian* Cities send the Sound. ......1.TrSt.164.417.
Thro' violated Nature force his way, ...1.TrSt.332.424.
For her, thro' *Ægypt's* fruitful Clime renown'd, ...1.TrSt.375.425.
His wandring Stream, and thro' the briny Tydes, ...1.TrSt.384.426.
Haste then, *Cyllenius,* thro' the liquid Air, ...1.TrSt.415.427.
Thus, thro' the parting Clouds the Son of *May* ......1.TrSt.437.428.
(His *Thebes* abandon'd) thro' th' *Aonian* Groves, ...1.TrSt.444.428.
And brings, descending thro' the silent Air, ...1.TrSt.480.430.
Rush thro' the Mounds, and bear the Dams away: ......1.TrSt.505.431.
Thro' the brown Horrors of the Night he fled, ...1.TrSt.516.432.
Thro' thickest Woods, and rouz'd the Beasts of Prey. ......1.TrSt.529.432.
Thro' the thick Desarts headlong urg'd his Flight: ......1.TrSt.558.433.
Or thro' what Veins our ancient Blood has roll'd? ......1.TrSt.800.443.
When direful Meteors spread thro' glowing Air ......1.TrSt.843.445.
Rings to the Skies, and ecchoes thro' the Fields, ...1.TrES.64.452.
And thro' his Buckler drove the trembling Wood; ......1.TrES.138.454.
Then thundring thro' the Planks, with forceful Sway, ...1.TrES.195.456.
Then pouring after, thro' the gaping Space ......1.TrES.205.457.
Deep Groans and hollow Roars rebellow thro' the Wood. ......1.TrES.299.460.
Urg'd by fierce Drivers thro' the dusty Space, ...1.TrUl.8.465.
Yet had his Mind, thro' tedious Absence, lost ......1.TrUl.56.467.
Thro' ten Years Wand'ring, and thro' ten Years War; ......1.TrUl.176.471.
Thro' ten Years Wand'ring, and thro' ten Years War; ......1.TrUl.176.471.
And Airy Musick warbled thro' the Shade. ......2.ChJM.464.37.
They found the Art of Kissing thro' a Wall. ......2.ChJM.519.40.
His Heav'nly Progress thro' the *Twins* had run; ......2.ChJM.610.44.
Thro' Hatred one, and one thro' too much Love; ......2.ChWB.402.76.
Thro' Hatred one, and one thro' too much Love; ......2.ChWB.402.76.
As thro' the Moon-light shade they nightly stray, ...2.RL*A*2.177.137.
Sol thro' white Curtains shot a tim'rous Ray, ...2.RL1.13.145.
Sol thro' white Curtains did his Beams display, ...2.RL1.13A.145.
The *Sylphs* thro' mystick Mazes guide their Way, ...2.RL1.92.152.

THRO' (CONTINUED)
Thro' all the giddy Circle they pursue, ...2.RL1.93.152.
Or roll the Planets thro' the boundless Sky. ......2.RL2.80.165.
And see thro' all things with his half-shut Eyes) ......2.RL3.118.176.
Safe past the *Gnome* thro' this fantastick Band, ...2.RL4.55.188.
Expos'd thro' Crystal to the gazing Eyes, ...2.RL4.114.193.
While thro' the Press enrag'd *Thalestris* flies, ...2.RL5.57.203.
A sudden Star, it shot thro' liquid Air, ...2.RL5.127.210.
And pleas'd pursue its Progress thro' the Skies. ......2.RL5.132.211.
When next he looks thro' *Galilæo's* Eyes; ......2.RL5.138.211.
Within, stood Heroes who thro' loud Alarms ......2.TemF.149.265.
Superior Worlds, and look all Nature thro'. ......2.TemF.237.274.
And last Eternal thro' the Length of Days. ......2.TemF.275.276.
Thro' the big Dome the doubling Thunder bounds: ......2.TemF.333.280.
The dire Report thro' ev'ry Region flies: ......2.TemF.335.280.
And swam to Empire thro' the purple Flood. ......2.TemF.347.280.
Led thro' a sad variety of woe: ......2.ElAb.36.321.
Back thro' the paths of pleasing sense I ran, ...2.ElAb.69.324.
Thro' dreary wastes, and weep each other's woe; ......2.ElAb.242.339.
Thro' worlds unnumber'd tho' the God be known, ...3.EOM1.21.15.
He, who thro' vast immensity can pierce, ...3.EOM1.23.15.
Thro' worlds unbounded tho' the God be known, ...3.EOM1.21A.15.
Look'd thro'? or can a part contain the whole? ......3.EOM1.32.17.
Or quick effluvia darting thro' the brain, ...3.EOM1.199.40.
Or quick effluvia darting thro' his brain, ...3.EOM1.199B.40.
Or keen effluvia darting thro' the brain, ...3.EOM1.199A.40.
Thro' gen'ral Life, behold the Scale arise ......3.EOM1.207A.41.
To that which warbles thro' the vernal wood: ......3.EOM1.216.42.
See, thro' this air, this ocean, and this earth, ...3.EOM1.233.44.
Planets and Suns run lawless thro' the sky, ...3.EOM1.252.46.
Planets and Suns rush lawless thro' the sky, ...3.EOM1.252A.46.
That, chang'd thro' all, and yet in all the same, ...3.EOM1.269.47.
Lives thro' all life, extends thro' all extent, ...3.EOM1.273.48.
Lives thro' all life, extends thro' all extent, ...3.EOM1.273.48.
Or, meteor-like, flame lawless thro' the void, ...3.EOM2.65.63.
Thro' life 'tis followed, ev'n at life's expence; ......3.EOM2.171.75.
Lust, thro' some certain strainers well refin'd, ...3.EOM2.189.77.
Hope travels thro', nor quits us when we die. ......3.EOM2.274.88.
Or breathes thro' air, or shoots beneath the deeps, ...3.EOM3.116.104.
Grew by like means, and join'd, thro' love or fear. ......3.EOM3.202.113.
So drives Self-love, thro' just and thro' unjust, ...3.EOM3.269.120.
So drives Self-love, thro' just and thro' unjust, ...3.EOM3.269.120.
Heav'n breaths thro' ev'ry member of the whole ......3.EOM4.61.134.
Has crept thro' scoundrels ever since the flood, ...3.EOM4.212.147.
But looks thro' Nature, up to Nature's God; ......3.EOM4.332.160.
Ask you why *Clodio* broke thro' ev'ry rule? ......3.Ep1.206A.33.
Crawl thro' the Street, shov'd on, or rudely press'd ......3.Ep1.230A.35.
Or come discolour'd thro' our Passions shown. ......3.Ep1.26.17.
Like following life thro' creatures you dissect, ...3.Ep1.39.18.
Faithless thro' Piety, and dup'd thro' Wit? ......3.Ep1.151.28.
Faithless thro' Piety, and dup'd thro' Wit? ......3.Ep1.151.28.
Ask you why Wharton broke thro' ev'ry rule? ......3.Ep1.206.33.
She sins with Poets thro' pure Love of Wit. ......3.Ep2.76.56.
Sick of herself thro' very selfishness! ......3.Ep2.146.62.
Thro' reconcil'd extremes of drought and rain, ...3.Ep3.168.107.
The next a Fountain, spouting thro' his Heir, ...3.Ep3.176.107.
Pleas'd Vaga echoes thro' her winding bounds, ...3.Ep3.251.114.
But clear and artless, pouring thro' the plain ......3.Ep3.257.114.
Or call the winds thro' long Arcades to roar, ...3.Ep4.35.140.
Or cut wide views thro' Mountains to the Plain, ...3.Ep4.75.144.
Thro' his young Woods how pleas'd Sabinus stray'd, ...3.Ep4.89.146.
Here Amphitrite sails thro' myrtle bow'rs; ......3.Ep4.123.149.
First thro' the length of yon hot Terrace sweat, ...3.Ep4.130.150.
And roll obedient Rivers thro' the Land; ......3.Ep4.202.156.
Shall call the winds thro' long Arcades to roar, ...3.Ep4.35A.140.
My Head and Heart thus flowing thro' my Quill, ...4.HS1.63.11.
When the tir'd Glutton labours thro' a Treat, ...4.HS2.31.57.
And yours my friends? thro' whose free-opening gate ......4.HS2.157.67.
They pierce my Thickets, thro' my Grot they glide, ...4.Arbu.8.96.
Friend thro' my Life, (which did'st not thou prolong, ...4.Arbu.27A.98.
Lull'd by soft Zephyrs thro' the broken Pane, ...4.Arbu.42.99.
Who shames a Scribler? break one cobweb thro', ...4.Arbu.89.102.
Scriblers like Spiders, break one cobweb thro', ...4.Arbu.89A.102.
To help me thro' this long Disease, my Life, ...4.Arbu.132.105.
Nor like a Puppy daggled thro' the Town, ...4.Arbu.225.112.
The good Man walk'd innoxious thro' his Age. ......4.Arbu.395.126.
Sense, past thro' him, no longer is the same, ...4.JD2.33.135.
For you, he walks the streets thro' rain or dust, ...4.JD2.73.139.
Absent I follow thro' th'extended Dream, ...4.HOde1.42.153.
Lord! how we strut thro' *Merlin's* Cave, to see ......4.2HE2.139.175.
Bright thro' the rubbish of some hundred years; ......4.2HE2.166.177.
Could she behold us tumbling thro' a hoop. ......4.2HE1.48.199.
Or lengthen'd Thought that gleams thro' many a page, ...4.2HE1.113.205.
To pant, or tremble thro' an Eunuch's throat. ......4.2HE1.154.209.
The blessing thrills thro' all the lab'ring throng, ...4.2HE1.239.215.
Triumphant Malice rag'd thro' private life. ......4.2HE1.254.217.
And snatch me, o'er the earth, or thro' the air, ...4.2HE1.346.225.
Look thro', and trust the Ruler with his Skies, ...4.1HE6.8.237.
Thro' Taverns, Stews, and Bagnio's take our round, ...4.1HE6.119.245.
Away they come, thro' thick and thin, ...4.HS6.185.261.
In at a Corn-loft thro' a Chink; ......4.1HE7.52.271.
Proud Fortune, and look shallow Greatness thro': ......4.1HE1.108.287.
Be grac'd thro' Life, and flatter'd in his Grave. ......4.EpS1.86.305.
Hear her black Trumpet thro' the Land proclaim, ...4.EpS1.159.309.
If one, thro' Nature's Bounty or his Lord's, ...4.EpS2.173.323.
Thro' Clouds of Passion P[ulteney]'s views are clear, ...4.1740.9.332.
Keen, hollow winds howl thro' the bleak recess, ...5.DunA1.29.63.
Beholds thro' fogs that magnify the scene: ......5.DunA1.78.68.
And pond'rous slugs cut swiftly thro' the sky; ......5.DunA1.178.84.
As when a dab-chick waddles thro' the copse, ...5.DunA2.59.105.
And Bernard! Bernard! rings thro' all the Strand. ......5.DunA2.70.106.
And Lintot! Lintot! rings thro' all the Strand. ......5.DunA2.70B.10(
Thro' half the heav'ns he pours th' exalted urn; 5.DunA2.175.122
Chetwood, thro' perfect modesty o'ercome, ...5.DunA2.181.124
Chapman thro' perfect modesty o'ercome. 5.DunA2.181B.12
Osborn thro' perfect modesty o'ercome. 5.DunA2.181C.1

THRO' (CONTINUED)

There wander'd *Menelaus* thro' foreign shores, ... Od.3.384.105.
And soars an Eagle thro' the liquid skies. ... Od.3.475.110.
'Twas then that issuing thro' the palace gate ... Od.4.27.121.
Thro' regions fatten'd with the flows of *Nile*. ... Od.4.100.124.
'Till haply piercing thro' the dark disguise ... Od.4.340.136.
Loud grief resounded thro' the tow'rs of *Troy*, ... Od.4.355.136.
Then thro' th' illumin'd dome, to balmy rest ... Od.4.407.140.
When thro' the Zone of heav'n the mounted sun ... Od.4.539.146.
Thro' each vain passive form constrain his flight. ... Od.4.568.147.
Swift thro' the valves the visionary fair ... Od.4.1093.169.
That high thro' fields of air his flight sustain ... Od.5.58.174.
And thro' the loom the golden shuttle guides. ... Od.5.79.176.
With purple clusters blushing thro' the green. ... Od.5.89.176.
With storms pursu'd them thro' the liquid world. ... Od.5.138.178.
Glide thro' the shades, and bind th' attesting Gods! ... Od.5.240.183.
(Thick strown by tempest thro' the bow'ry shade) ... Od.5.625.201.
Thro' seas retreating from the sound of war, ... Od.6.10.203.
To his high palace thro' the fields of air ... Od.6.19.204.
Thro' the thick gloom the shining portals blaze; ... Od.6.23.204.
Glides thro' the valves, and hovers round her head; ... Od.6.26.205.
Thro' heav'n's eternal gates that blaz'd with day. ... Od.6.56.208.
Where thro' the vales the mazy waters stray? ... Od.6.72.208.
That breath'd a fragrance thro' the balmy sky. ... Od.6.256.222.
Full thro' the narrow mouths descend the tides: ... Od.6.314.226.
Climb the steep surge, and thro' the tempest fly; ... Od.6.326.227.
Shot thro' the western clouds a dewy ray; ... Od.6.382.230.
Thro' the proud street she moves, the publick gaze; ... Od.7.3.232.
Thro' many woes and wand'rings, lo! I come ... Od.7.31.235.
When thro' the street she gracious deigns to move, ... Od.7.90.238.
The flying shuttle thro' the threads to guide: ... Od.7.139.242.
This thro' the gardens leads its streams around, ... Od.7.170.244.
Unseen he glided thro' the joyous crowd, ... Od.7.186.245.
Shoots from the starry vault thro' fields of air; ... Od.8.8.261.
Tost by rude tempest thro' a war of waves: ... Od.8.28.263.
Sonorous thro' the shaded air it sings; ... Od.8.214.274.
Or thro' cærulean billows plow the way: ... Od.8.284.278.
Stung to the soul, indignant thro' the skies ... Od.8.313.281.
Restore me safe thro' weary wand'rings tost, ... Od.8.507.289.
Frantic thro' clashing swords she runs, she flies, ... Od.8.573.293.
Fearless thro' darkness and thro' clouds they fly: ... Od.8.610.295.
Fearless thro' darkness and thro' clouds they fly: ... Od.8.610.295.
But say thro' what waste regions hast thou stray'd, ... Od.8.625.296.
With heavy hearts we labour thro' the tyde, ... Od.9.117.308.
Where savage goats thro' pathless thickets rove: ... Od.9.136.311.
Or wretched hunters thro' the wintry cold ... Od.9.138.311.
Thro' all-surrounding shade our navy brought; ... Od.9.166.312.
Now driv'n before him, thro' the arching rock, ... Od.9.280.318.
Thus far ye wander thro' the wat'ry way? ... Od.9.300.318.
Pyrates perhaps, who seek thro' seas unknown ... Od.9.301.318.
His voice like thunder thro' the cavern sounds: ... Od.9.303.318.
Thro' various seas by various perils tost, ... Od.9.309.319.
Thro' all their inmost-winding caves resound. ... Od.9.470.325.
The Giant spoke, and thro' the hollow rock ... Od.9.543.328.
No sooner freed, and thro' th' enclosure past, ... Od.9.545.328.
Be it thro' toils and suff'rings, long and late; ... Od.9.624.332.
And joy and music thro' the Isle resound: ... Od.10.10.340.
Thro' the wide wound the vital spirit flies. ... Od.10.190.349.
To glide with ghosts thro' *Pluto's* gloomy gate. ... Od.10.201.350.
And heard a voice resounding thro' the wood: ... Od.10.253.354.
Thro' the lone thicket, and the desart land. ... Od.10.296.358.
The plant I give thro' all the direful bow'r ... Od.10.343.360.
And sobs of joy re-eccho'd thro' the bow'r: ... Od.10.472.366.
And a cold fear ran shivering thro' my blood; ... Od.11.56.383.
There, wand'ring thro' the gloom I first survey'd, ... Od.11.65.383.
My feet thro' wine unfaithful to their weight, ... Od.11.77.385.
For thee thro' hell's eternal dungeons stray: ... Od.11.241.393.
Thrice thro' my arms she slipt like empty wind, ... Od.11.249.393.
And here thro' sev'n wide portals rush'd the war. ... Od.11.324.398.
Thro' all his woes the Hero shines confest; ... Od.11.419.405.
Thro' veins (he cry'd) of royal fathers flow'd; ... Od.11.451.406.
Steal thro' the ear, and win upon the soul; ... Od.11.457.407.
Thro' the fond bosom where she reign'd ador'd! ... Od.11.534.409.
Nor glides a Phantom thro' the realms of night. ... Od.11.568.411.
Thro' the thick gloom his friend *Achilles* knew, ... Od.11.581.412.
How, lost thro' love, *Eurypylus* was slain, ... Od.11.635.415.
And shook astonish'd thro' her hundred states; ... Od.11.684.418.
And breath'd his manly spirit thro' the wound. ... Od.11.686.418.
Touch'd at his sour retreat, thro' deepest night, ... Od.11.693.419.
Thro' hell's black bounds I had pursu'd his flight, ... Od.11.694.419.
Thro' the wide dome of *Dis*, a trembling band. ... Od.11.700.419.
Swift thro' the gloom a Giant-hunter flies; ... Od.11.704.420.
Ev'n hell I conquer'd, thro' the friendly aid ... Od.11.771.424.
Sing thro' the shrouds, and stretch the swelling sails. ... Od.11.794.426.
Thro' heav'n's bright portals pours the beamy day. ... Od.12.6.430.
Alive to pass thro' hell's eternal gates! ... Od.12.30.431.
And guard thy various passage thro' the tyde. ... Od.12.70.433.
Thro' the vast waves the dreadful wonders move, ... Od.12.73.434.
And guard thee thro' the tumult of the floods. ... Od.12.159.439.
Thro' tedious toils to view thy native coast. ... Od.12.177.440.
Now thro' the rocks, appal'd with deep dismay, ... Od.12.278.445.
Thro' every breast, and spread from man to man, ... Od.12.331.447.
Low thro' the grove, or range the flow'ry plain: ... Od.12.390.450.
When thro' the ports of heav'n I pour the day, ... Od.12.448.452.
Still may thy beams thro' heav'n's bright portals rise, ... Od.12.454.453.
Thro' tumbling billows, and a war of wind. ... Od.12.502.456.
Urg'd by fierce drivers thro' the dusty space, ... Od.13.99.6.
Yet had his mind thro' tedious absence lost ... Od.13.223.16.
Thro' ten years wand'ring, and thro' ten years war; ... Od.13.343.24.
Thro' ten years wand'ring, and thro' ten years war; ... Od.13.343.24.
Thro' the wild ocean plow the dang'rous way, ... Od.13.482.29.
Thro' mazy thickets of the woodland shade, ... Od.14.2.32.
Or torn by birds are scatter'd thro' the sky. ... Od.14.157.43.
Thro' the mid seas the nimble pinnace sails, ... Od.14.329.51.
Thro' both, *Eurymachus* pursues the dame, ... Od.15.21.70.
Thro' spacious *Argos*, and the Realms of *Greece*, ... Od.15.92.73.

THRO' (CONTINUED)

And now, when thro' the royal dome they pass'd, ... Od.15.146.75.
Thro' the long dangers of the ten-years war. ... Od.15.171.76.
And wander'd thro' the wide ethereal way ... Od.15.196.78.
Thro' all the dangers of the boundless main, ... Od.15.199.78.
Whose fate enquiring, thro' the world we rove; ... Od.15.294.83.
Then cautious thro' the rocky reaches wind, ... Od.15.320.85.
Thro' the wide fields of air, and cleaves the skies; ... Od.16.169.111.
And I shall praise thee thro' the boundless earth. ... Od.17.500.157.
Scourge thro' the publick street, and cast thee there, ... Od.17.570.160.
Constrain'd, his nostril eccho'd thro' the crowd. ... Od.17.625.163.
Should *Greece* thro' all her hundred states survey ... Od.18.287.180.
With dreadful inroad thro' the walks of war. ... Od.18.308.181.
Ends in a stream, and murmurs thro' the vales: ... Od.19.241.206.
Thus half discover'd thro' the dark disguise, ... Od.19.446.216.
Sure thro' six circlets flew the whizzing dart. ... Od.19.673.229.
Who thro' the rings directs the feather'd reed. ... Od.19.677.229.
Tost thro' the void, illimitable space: ... Od.20.75.236.
Were doom'd to wander thro' the devious air; ... Od.20.79.236.
Dim thro' th' eclipse of fate, the rays divine ... Od.20.243.244.
The well-aim'd arrow thro' the distant ring, ... Od.21.4.258.
She moves majestic thro' the wealthy room, ... Od.21.53.261.
And thro' twelve ringlets the fleet arrow send, ... Od.21.76.262.
To speed the flying shaft thro' ev'ry ring, ... Od.21.102.263.
The feather'd arrow thro' the destin'd ring, ... Od.21.118.264.
Now thro' the press the bow *Eumæus* bore, ... Od.21.389.279.
A gen'ral horror ran thro' all the race, ... Od.21.450.282.
Thro' ev'ry ringlet levelling his view; ... Od.21.459.282.
Pierc'd thro' and thro', the solid gate resounds. ... Od.21.464.282.
Pierc'd thro' and thro', the solid gate resounds. ... Od.21.464.282.
Full thro' his throat *Ulysses'* weapon past, ... Od.22.19.287.
Full thro' his liver past the mortal wound, ... Od.22.101.291.
The brazen weapon driving thro' his back, ... Od.22.108.291.
Thence thro' his breast its bloody passage tore; ... Od.22.109.292.
What-e'er thro' life's whole series I have done ... Od.22.228.297.
Pierc'd thro' the breast the rude *Ctesippus* bled, ... Od.22.316.301.
Thro' all his bowels: down he tumbles prone, ... Od.22.328.302.
Confus'd, distracted, thro' the rooms they fling, ... Od.22.334.302.
Full thro' his neck the weighty faulchion sped: ... Od.22.365.305.
Then gliding thro' the marble valves in state, ... Od.23.91.323.
Whose flaming steeds, emerging thro' the night, ... Od.23.263.336.
For, to *Tiresias* thro' th' eternal gates ... Od.23.269.336.
How struggling thro' the surge, he reach'd the shores ... Od.23.359.342.
Minerva rushes thro' th' aereal way, ... Od.23.372.343.
My Queen, my consort! thro' a length of years, ... Od.23.377.343.
They move, and murmurs run thro' all the rock: ... Od.24.12.347.
And solemn sadness thro' the gloom of hell, ... Od.24.33.348.
A voice of loud lament thro' all the main ... Od.24.67.350.
But *Agamemnon*, thro' the gloomy shade, ... Od.24.127.354.
Thro' ev'ry ring the victor arrow went. ... Od.24.202.358.
Thro' rows of shade with various fruitage crown'd, ... Od.24.255.361.
Or screaming vulturs scatter thro' the air: ... Od.24.343.365.
Ulysses parting thro' the sable flood; ... Od.24.362.366.
Quick thro' the father's heart these accents ran; ... Od.24.367.366.
If, while the news thro' ev'ry city flies, ... Od.24.413.369.
Thro' all the city, of the Suitors dead. ... Od.24.475.371.

THROAT

Is it for thee the linnet pours his throat? ... 3.EOM3.33.95.
Oldfield, with more than Harpy throat endu'd, ... 4.HS2.25.55.
And Lands and Tenements go down her Throat. ... 4.HAdv.14.75.
See wretched *Monsieur* flies to save his Throat, ... 4.HAdv.53.79.
To pant, or tremble thro' an Eunuch's throat. ... 4.2HE1.154.209.
Cramm'd to the throat with Ortolans: ... 4.1HE7.62.273.
She ceas'd. Then swells the Chapel-royal throat: ... 5.DunB1.319.293.
Down his own throat he risqu'd the Grecian gold; ... 5.DunB4.382.380.
A Throat of Brass, and Adamantine Lungs. ... Il.2.581.155.
Fix'd in his Throat, the Javelin drank his Blood. ... Il.5.708.301.
Transfix'd his Throat, and drank the vital Blood; ... Il.5.817.305.
Whose Throat surpass'd the Force of fifty Tongues. ... Il.5.979.313.
Her gaping Throat emits infernal Fire. ... Il.6.224.337.
Or bids the brazen Throat of War to roar; ... Il.10.8.2.
He stung the Bird, whose Throat receiv'd the Wound: ... Il.12.236.90.
Him *Teucer* pierc'd between the Throat and Ear; ... Il.13.239.116.
Full on his Throat discharg'd the forceful Spear: ... Il.13.490.130.
He pierc'd his Throat; the bending Head deprest ... Il.13.686.137.
Full on his Breast and Throat with Force descends; ... Il.14.477.187.
Plung'd in his Throat the smoaking Weapon lies; ... Il.16.398.258.
It pierc'd his Throat, and bent him to the Plain; ... Il.17.50.289.
Plung'd in his Throat, the Weapon drank his Blood, ... Il.17.358.301.
Where 'twixt the Neck and Throat the jointed Plate ... Il.22.408.472.
He heard, he took, and pouring down his throat ... Od.9.417.323.
And turn my gen'rous vintage down their throat. ... Od.17.621.162.
A tongue so flippant, with a throat so wide! ... Od.18.33.168.
Full thro' his throat *Ulysses'* weapon past, ... Od.22.19.287.

THROATS

While all its throats the Gallery extends, ... 4.2HE1.326.223.
Has drench'd their wide, insatiate Throats with Blood) ... Il.16.197.247.
And cram'd their filthy throats with human food. ... Od.10.144.347.

THROB

No Cheek is known to blush, no Heart to throb, ... 4.EpS1.103.305.

THROBS

In Fulvia's buckle ease the throbs below, ... 3.Ep3.90.96.

THROES

Why have I born thee with a Mother's Throes, ... Il.1.542.114.
(The Pow'rs that cause the teeming Matron's Throes, ... Il.11.349.50.
Fruit of her Throes, and First-born of her Loves, ... Il.17.6.288.

THRON'D

Thron'd in the Centre of his thin designs; ... 4.Arbu.93.102.
Thron'd in the Centre of their thin designs; ... 4.Arbu.93A.102.
Thron'd on sev'n hills, the Antichrist of Wit. ... 5.DunA2.12.97.

THRON'D (CONTINUED)

Thron'd on sev'n hills, the Antichrist of wit. ....5.DunB2.16.297.
Then thron'd in glass, and nam'd it CAROLINE: ....5.DunB4.409.382.
Th' Eternal Thunderer, state thron'd in Gold. ....Il.8.551.422.
High-thron'd amidst the great *Olympian* Hall, ...Il.13.661.137.
High-thron'd in Gold, beheld the Fields below; ....Il.14.180.168.
Say, Muses, thron'd above the starry Frame, ...Il.16.140.243.
Oh thou Supreme! high-thron'd, all Height above! ....Il.16.284.250.
Thron'd next the King, a fair attendant brings ....Od.4.63.122.
Thron'd in omnipotence, supremest *Jove* ....Od.4.325.134.
High-thron'd, and feasting, there thou shalt behold ....Od.7.65.237.

THRONE

Around his Throne the Sea-born Brothers stood, ...1.W-F.337.182.
To part his Throne and share his Heav'n with thee; ....1.TrSt.42.411.
A fatal Throne to two contending Kings, ...1.TrSt.52.412.
That scorns the dull Reversion of a Throne; ....1.TrSt.181.418.
And singly fill a fear'd and envy'd Throne! ....1.TrSt.223.419.
Patient of Right, familiar in the Throne? ....1.TrSt.261.421.
Full in the midst, and on a Starry Throne, ...1.TrSt.280.422.
And from his Throne return'd this stern Reply. ....1.TrSt.403.426.
And swells on an imaginary Throne. ....1.TrSt.450.428.
But two fair Daughters heir'd his State and Throne. ....1.TrSt.544.433.
Stretch'd on rich Carpets, on his Iv'ry Throne; ....1.TrSt.614.436.
Spoke from his Throne the Cloud-compelling *Jove:* ....1.TrES.323.461.
And guard with Arms Divine the *British Throne.* ....2.RL2.90.165.
Two Handmaids wait the Throne: Alike in Place, ...2.RL4.25.185.
High on a Throne with Trophies charg'd, I view'd ....2.TemF.151.265.
Eternal Adamant compos'd his Throne; ....2.TemF.183.270.
Troy flam'd in burning Gold, and o'er the Throne ....2.TemF.208.272.
Troy flam'd in burnish'd Gold, and o'er the Throne ....2.TemF.208A.272.
The *Roman Rostra* deck'd the Consul's Throne: ....2.TemF.239.274.
And all on fire appear'd the glowing Throne; ....2.TemF.255.275.
We here appeal to thy superior Throne: ....2.TemF.303.278.
Enslave their Country, or usurp a Throne; ....2.TemF.407.283.
Of these a gloomy Tribe surround the Throne, ...2.TemF.412.283.
Strait chang'd the Scene, and snatch'd me from the Throne. ....2.TemF.419.283.
Himself, his throne, his world, I'd scorn 'em all: ....2.ElAb.86.326.
And Nature tremble to the throne of God: ....3.EOM1.256.46.
The throne a Bigot keep, a Genius quit, ...3.Ep1.150.28.
Bear, like the *Turk*, no brother near the throne, ...4.Arbu.198.110.
If on a Pillory, or near a Throne, ...4.Arbu.366.122.
And better got than *Bestia's* from the Throne. ....4.Arbu.391.126.
And better got than Clodio's from the Throne. ....4.Arbu.391A.126.
And better got than *Bestia's* from a Throne. ....4.Arbu.391B.126.
With Terrors round can Reason hold her throne, ...4.2HE2.310.187.
And Asia's Tyrants tremble at your Throne— ....4.2HE1.403.229.
Or WYNDHAM, just to Freedom and the Throne, ...4.EpS2.88.318.
Or WYNDHAM, arm'd for Freedom and the Throne, ...4.EpS2.88A.318.
Safe from the Bar, the Pulpit, and the Throne, ...4.EpS2.210.325.
And free at once the Senate and the Throne; ....4.1740.90.337.
Four guardian Virtues, round, support her Throne; ....5.DunA1.44.65.
Where rebel to thy throne if Science rise, ...5.DunA1.157.82.
Where 'gainst thy throne if rebel Science rise, ...5.DunA1.157A.82.
'Till Albion, as Hibernia, bless my throne! ....5.DunA1.254.93.
A Nursing-mother, born to rock the throne! ....5.DunA1.251Z4.93.
Henley's gilt Tub, or Fleckno's Irish Throne, ...5.DunA2.2.96.
Against her throne, from Hyperborean skies, ...5.DunA3.77A.156.
"Thou too, great Woolston! here exalt thy throne, ...5.DunA3.209.175.
Close to those walls where Folly holds her throne, ...5.DunB1.29.271.
Four guardina Virtues, round, support her throne: ....5.DunB1.46.274.
And I, a Nursing-mother, rock the throne, ...5.DunB1.312.293.
Henley's gilt tub, or Fleckno's Irish throne, ...5.DunB2.2.296.
She mounts the Throne: her head a Cloud conceal'd, ...5.DunB4.17.341.
And all the Nations summon'd to the Throne. ....5.DunB4.72.348.
To stick the Doctor's Chair into the Throne, ...5.DunB4.177.359.
"Mistress! dismiss that rabble from your throne: ....5.DunB4.209.363.
Prop thine, O Empress! like each neighbour Throne, ...5.DunB4.333.376.
And aspect ardent to the Throne appeal. ....5.DunB4.402.381.
Bland and familiar to the throne he came, ...5.DunB4.497.391.
Guard my Prerogative, assert my Throne: ....5.DunB4.583.400.
She comes! she comes! the sable Throne behold ....5.DunB4.629.407.
The Gloom rolls on, the sable Throne behold ....5.DunB4.629A.407.
Who, like her Mistresse on Britannia's Throne, ...6.43.7.120.
How safe must be the King upon this Throne, ...6.48ii.5.134.
Bear, like the Turk, no Brother near the Throne; ....6.49iii.12.143.
Bear, like the Turk, no Brother on the Throne; ....6.49iii.12A.143.
Bear, like the Turk, no Brother to the Throne; ....6.49iii.12B.143.
And ill can bear a Brother on the Throne. ....6.82ix(a).2.234.
And ill can bear no living near the Throne. ....6.82ix(a).2A.234.
Bear, like the *Turk,* no Brother near the Throne; ....6.98.48.284.
The Monarch started from his shining Throne; ....Il.1.128.93.
With Giant-Pride at *Jove's* high Throne he stands, ...Il.1.526.113.
Trembling they stand, while *Jove* assumes the Throne, ...Il.1.694.120.
Thus with injurious Taunts attack'd the Throne. ....Il.2.274.140.
Sedition silence, and assert the Throne. ....Il.2.339.143.
Who in the Heav'n of Heav'ns hast fix'd thy Throne, ...Il.2.490.150.
Who in the Heav'n of Heav'ns has fix'd thy Throne, ...Il.2.490A.150.
Say, Virgins, seated round the Throne Divine, ...Il.2.572.155.
In ancient Time, when *Otreus'* fill'd the Throne, ...Il.3.246.204.
Dauntless he enters, and demands the Throne. ....Il.4.439.241.
Braces of Gold suspend the moving Throne: ....Il.5.897.308.
Where far apart the Thund'rer fills his Throne, ...Il.5.938.311.
Thus pour'd his Plaints before th' immortal Throne. ....Il.5.1067.317.
Fast by the Throne of Heav'ns superior Lord. ....Il.5.1119.321.
Let me be foremost to defend the Throne, ...Il.6.568.354.
O Thou! whose Glory fills th' Ætherial Throne, ...Il.6.604.356.
Who in the highest Heav'n hast fix'd thy Throne, ...Il.7.243.376.
High on the Throne he shines: His Coursers fly, ...Il.8.55.398.
She shook her Throne that shook the starry Pole: ....Il.8.241.409.
Strength and Omnipotence invest thy Throne; ....Il.8.576.424.
Around her Throne the vivid Planets roll, ...Il.8.691.428.
For him they mediate to the Throne above: ....Il.9.632.465.
Th' eternal Monarch, on his awful Throne, ...Il.11.108.39.
And proud *Atrides* tremble on his Throne. ....Il.11.747.68.
With *Priam's* Sons, a Guardian of the Throne, ...Il.13.237.116.

THRONE (CONTINUED)

Shook the fix'd Splendours of the Throne of *Jove.* ....Il.13.1061.155.
A splendid Footstool, and a Throne, that shine ....Il.14.272.175.
Starts from her azure Throne to calm the God. ....Il.15.141.202.
This Menace fix'd the Warrior to his Throne; ....Il.15.160.202.
Spoke from this Throne the Cloud-compelling *Jove.* ....Il.16.810.274.
Laugh'st thou not, *Jove!* from thy superior Throne, ...Il.17.19.288.
The Mother Goddess from her crystal Throne ....Il.18.43.325.
High on a Throne, with Stars of silver grac'd ....Il.18.457.343.
He reach'd the Throne where pensive *Thetis* sate; ....Il.18.492.345.
When thus, not rising from his lofty Throne, ...Il.19.79.375.
Assum'd his Throne amid the bright Abodes, ...Il.20.21.393.
Leap'd from his Throne, lest *Neptunes* Arm should lay ....Il.20.85.397.
And prove his Merits to the Throne of *Troy?* ....Il.20.217.403.
Rash as thou art to prop the *Trojan* Throne, ...Il.21.514.443.
Consign'd his Daughter with *Lelegia's* Throne) ....Il.22.69.455.
Where the sad Sons beside their Father's Throne ....Il.24.197.545.
Jove heard his Pray'r, and from the Throne on high ....Il.24.387.552.
From the high Throne divine *Achilles* rose; ....Il.24.648.563.
Two Urns by *Jove's* high Throne have ever stood, ...Il.24.663.564.
To manly years shou'd re-assert the throne. ....Od.1.52.33.
Fast by the Throne obsequious *Fame* resides, ...Od.1.497.56.
Refer the choice to fill the vacant Throne. ....Od.1.510.56.
His Father's throne he fill'd: while distant stood ....Od.2.17.61.
Where antient *Neleus* sate, a rustic throne; ....Od.3.521.113.
And the chaste partner of his bed and throne, ...Od.4.147.127.
The youth wou'd vindicate the vacant throne. ....Od.4.224.130.
Then soon th' invaders of his bed and throne, ...Od.4.465.142.
Now graceful seated on her shining throne, ...Od.5.109.177.
He fill'd the throne where *Mercury* had sate. ....Od.5.250.183.
I bend, a suppliant at thy wat'ry throne, ...Od.5.569.199.
To great *Alcinous* on his royal throne. ....Od.6.360.229.
High on a throne, amid the *Scherian* pow'rs, ...Od.6.371.229.
This Queen he graces, and divides the throne; ....Od.7.87.238.
Direct to great *Alcinous'* throne he came, ...Od.7.188.245.
Remain'd: Beside him, on a splendid throne, ...Od.7.312.251.
Then from his glitt'ring throne *Alcinous* rose; ....Od.8.25.263.
High on a radiant throne sublime in state, ...Od.8.61.265.
With silver shone the throne; his Lyre well strung ....Od.8.63.265.
Fast by *Alcinous* on a throne of state. ....Od.8.512.290.
No council held, no Monarch fills the throne, ...Od.9.128.310.
The morn conspicuous on her golden throne. ....Od.10.646.375.
A pompous wretch! accurs'd upon a throne. ....Od.11.336.398.
Almighty *Jove* had trembled on his throne. ....Od.11.390.403.
Great in his *Pthia,* and his throne maintains; ....Od.11.606.413.
High on a throne, tremendous to behold, ...Od.11.697.419.
And the bright partner of thy royal throne. ....Od.12.536.459.
Before the throne of mighty *Jove* he stood; ....Od.13.146.12.
The Morn, conspicuous on her golden throne. ....Od.14.569.64.
High on a throne the King each stranger plac'd. ....Od.15.147.75.
And bids the rural throne with osiers rise. ....Od.16.48.104.
To mark the damsels that attend the throne: ....Od.16.341.122.
Eumæus sage approach'd th' imperial throne, ...Od.16.356.123.
'Till from his throne *Amphinomus* ascends, ...Od.16.409.126.
Then soon th' invaders of his bed, and throne, ...Od.17.156.139.
To joyn the Peers, resumes his throne, and mourns. ....Od.18.186.175.
'Till on her eastern throne *Aurora* glows. ....Od.19.61.195.
Thus, whilst *Aurora* mounts her purple throne, ...Od.20.110.238.
Heir of my Father's strength, as well as throne. ....Od.21.122.264.
All, all the treasures that enrich'd our throne ....Od.22.73.290.
Between the laver and the silver throne; ....Od.22.376.306.
These (ev'ry table cleans'd, and ev'ry throne, ...Od.22.476.312.
And joys and happiness attend thy throne! ....Od.24.464.370.

THRONES

The coming God, and from their Thrones of State ....Il.1.691.120.
Th' Immortals slumber'd on their Thrones above; ....Il.2.3.126.
The Gods, with *Jove,* assume their Thrones of Gold: ....Il.4.2.220.
Shakes all the Thrones of Heav'n, and bends the Poles. ....Il.15.119.201.
Else had my Wrath, Heav'ns Thrones all shaking round, ...Il.15.252.206.
On Marble Thrones with lucid Columns crown'd, ...Il.20.17.393.
And take their Thrones around th' Æthereal Sire. ....Il.21.604.447.
By him, and all th' immortal thrones above, ...Od.1.484.55.
There then arriv'd, on thrones around him plac'd, ...Od.3.500.112.
See! from their thrones thy kindred monarchs sigh! ....Od.6.40.206.
But on immortal thrones the blest repose: ....Od.6.53.208.
Fair thrones within from space to space were rais'd, ...Od.7.124.240.
And fill the shining thrones along the bay. ....Od.8.6.261.
Then to the radiant thrones they move in state: ....Od.8.457.288.
On thrones around, with downy coverings grac'd, ...Od.10.268.355.
Kings on their thrones for lovely *Pero* burn, ...Od.11.351.399.
And heav'n and heav'n's immortal thrones adore, ...Od.12.398.450.
Snatch'd for his beauty to the thrones above: ....Od.15.273.82.
Recumbent on the shining thrones of state. ....Od.16.425.127.
Jove, and etherial thrones! with heav'n to friend ....Od.20.120.239.

THRONG

And yet my Numbers please the rural Throng, ...1.PSu.49.75.
So vast a Throng the Stage can ne'er contain. ....1.EOC.283.271.
The Stage can ne'er so vast a Throng contain. ....1.EOC.283A.271.
So much they scorn the Crowd, that if the Throng ....1.EOC.426.288.
The lofty Ramparts, through the Warlike Throng, ...1.TrES.78.452.
The lofty Ramparts, through the martial Throng, ...1.TrES.78A.452.
Ye Bards! renown'd among the tuneful Throng ....2.ChJM.335.30.
A *Beau* and *Witling* perish'd in the Throng, ...2.RL5.59.204.
Thicker than arguments, temptations throng, ...3.EOM2.75.64.
There, every Grace and Muse shall throng, ...4.HOde1.27.153.
To Theatres, and to Rehearsals throng, ...4.2HE1.173.209.
To Op'ra's, Theatres, Rehearsals throng, ...4.2HE1.173A.209.
The blessing thrills thro' all the lab'ring throng, ...4.2HE1.239.215.
Involves a vast involuntary throng, ...5.DunB4.82.349.
Not to draw Envy from the baser throng. ....6.38.11Z6.108.
Hither we sail'd, a voluntary Throng, ...Il.1.207.96.
Thersites only clamour'd in the Throng, ...Il.2.255.139.
Two valiant Brothers rule th' undaunted Throng, ...Il.2.612.156.
And next the wisest of the Rev'rend Throng, ...Il.3.196.200.

THRONG (CONTINUED)

They said, while *Pallas* thro' the *Trojan* Throng Il.4.115.226.
To *Crete's* brave Monarch and his martial Throng; Il.4.287.234.
So to the Fight the thick *Battalions* throng, Il.4.484.243.
Him, the bold * Leader of th' *Abantian* Throng Il.4.530.246.
Born from the Conflict by his *Lycian* Throng, Il.5.824.305.
Thence, to relieve the fainting *Argive* Throng, Il.5.970.312.
He said; and hasty, o'er the gasping Throng Il.8.190.406.
Scarce had he pass'd the Steeds and *Trojan* Throng Il.10.401.21.
Thence the black Fury thro' the *Grecian* Throng Il.11.13.35.
His sever'd Head was toss'd among the Throng, Il.11.189.43.
And Pain augmented, thus exhorts the Throng. Il.11.354.50.
Fierce *Ajax* thus o'erwhelms the yielding Throng, Il.11.618.61.
Before great *Ajax*, see the mingled Throng Il.11.646.62.
O'er heapy Shields, and o'er the prostrate Throng, Il.11.886.75.
He, like a Whirlwind, toss'd the scatt'ring Throng, Il.12.45.83.
The lofty Ramparts, through the martial Throng; Il.12.422.97.
Th' impatient *Trojans*, in a gloomy Throng, Il.13.61.107.
Spears lean on Spears, on Targets Targets throng, Il.13.181.114.
Thus his bright Armour o'er the dazled Throng Il.13.323.120.
The Helm fell off, and roll'd amid the Throng: Il.13.730.139.
Far on the Left amid the Throng he found Il.13.961.151.
Thus Rank on Rank the thick Battalions throng, Il.13.1006.153.
They join, they throng, they thicken at his Call, Il.15.676.222.
The Coward-Counsels of a tim'rous Throng Il.15.874.230.
To the black Fount they rush a hideous Throng, Il.16.198.247.
Think with what Threats you dar'd the *Trojan* Throng, Il.16.240.248.
So Helm to Helm, and Crest to Crest they throng, Il.16.260.249.
Fierce to the Charge great *Hector* led the Throng; Il.17.308.299.
Confusion, Tumult, Horror, o'er the Throng Il.17.823.320.
They join, they throng, they thicken to the War. Il.20.430.412.
Set wide your Portals to the flying Throng. Il.21.622.448.
Giv'n to the Rage of an insulting Throng! Il.22.509.477.
Here, where but one could pass, to shun the Throng, Il.23.501.510.
Whose Arms support him, reeling thro' the Throng, Il.23.808.521.
Stern *Polypœtes* stept before the Throng, Il.23.991.529.
At length compos'd, he join'd the suitor-throng, Od.1.419.52.
And ere the sacrificing throng he join'd, Od.3.17.87.
Then to the palace move: A gath'ring throng, Od.8.49.264.
Now swarms the populace; a countless throng, Od.8.111.268.
Mean-while the Gods the dome of *Vulcan* throng, Od.8.361.283.
The Bard an herald guides: the gazing throng Od.8.515.290.
The lowing herds return; around them throng Od.10.487.367.
Take that, ere yet thou quit this princely throng: Od.17.545.159.
'Twas riot all amid the Suitor-throng, Od.17.685.165.
He, only he of all the Suitor-throng, Od.21.155.266.
A gazing throng, a torch in ev'ry hand. Od.22.534.314.
To throng my empty'd folds, with gifts or spoils. Od.23.384.343.
When from the Palace to the wond'ring throng Od.24.504.372.

THRONG'D

See thy bright Altars throng'd with prostrate Kings, 1.Mes.93.121.
Where are those Troops of Poor that throng'd before 4.JD2A.119.142.
Where are those Troops of poor, that throng'd of yore 4.JD2.113.143.
So throng'd, so close, the *Grecian* Squadrons stood Il.2.558.154.
Throng'd in bright Arms, a pressing Fight maintain; Il.13.898.148.
Vision divine! The throng'd spectators gaze Od.3.476.110.
Ghost throng'd on ghost (a dire assembly) stood! Od.11.276.395.
Throng'd with pale ghosts, familiar with the dead? Od.11.586.412.
The throng'd assembly, and the feast of joy: Od.17.321.147.
The female train who round him throng'd to gaze, Od.19.271.208.

THRONGING

See thronging Millions to the Pagod run, 4.EpS1.157.309.
Back to th' Assembly roll the thronging Train, Il.2.247.139.
The thronging Troops obscure the dusky Fields, Il.7.69.366.
The thronging *Greeks* behold with wond'ring Eyes Il.22.465.474.
Of thronging *Grecians* round *Achilles* stood; Il.23.291.501.
In thronging Crowds they issue to the Plains, Il.24.882.573.
When thronging thick to bask in open air, Od.4.603.148.
Of thronging multitudes the shore rebounds; Od.8.16.262.

THRONGS

With Throngs promiscuous strow the level Green. 2.RL3.80.173.
Unnumber'd Throngs on ev'ry side are seen 2.RL4.47.187.
In various Garbs promiscuous Throngs appear'd; 2.TemF.281.277.
Soon as the Throngs in Order mov'd appear, Il.2.125.133.
In Throngs around his native Bands repair, Il.2.990.170.
And proud *Miletus*; came the *Carian* Throngs, Il.2.1058.172.
In mingled Throngs, the *Greek* and *Trojan* Train Il.7.502.389.
In friendly throngs they gather, to embrace Od.3.45.88.
Fat sheep and goats in throngs we drove before, Od.9.547.328.
Back started the pale throngs, and trembling stood. Od.11.62.383.
Uprose the throngs tumultuous round the hall; Od.22.28.287.
In throngs they rise, and to the palace crowd; Od.24.476.371.

THRONUS

Which *Bessa*, *Thronus*, and rich *Cynos* send: Il.2.635.157.

THROUGH

As *Bodies* perish through Excess of *Blood*. 1.EOC.304.274.
The *Vulgar* thus through *Imitation* err; 1.EOC.424.288.
And stung with anguish bellow through the groves. 1.TrPA.135.371.
Now smoothly steers through Air his equal Flight, 1.TrSt.439.428.
And a glad Horror shoots through ev'ry Vein: 1.TrSt.580.434.
The lofty Ramparts, through the Warlike Throng, 1.TrES.78.452.
The lofty Ramparts, through the martial Throng, 1.TrES.78A.452.
And sweetly flow through all the Royal Line. 4.HS1.32.7.
Burn through the Tropic, freeze beneath the Pole! 4.1HE1.72.283.
Shine through the soul, and drive its clouds away! 6.23.14.73.
He turn'd up through the Gore; 6.79.130.222.
Or sway'd by Envy, or through Pride of Mind, 6.96iii.14.275.
Through the long Instant of Eternity. 6.109.16Z2.314.
Where lingering Drops through Mineral Roofs distill, 6.142.3A.382.
Stalked through a mead of daffodillies 6.157.2.406.
Guideless, alone, through Night's dark Shade to go, Il.10.47.4.

THROUGH (CONTINUED)

The lofty Ramparts, through the martial Throng; Il.12.422.97.
And bears the blazing Present through the Skies. Il.18.712.357.
Safe through the level seas we sweep our way; Od.14.286.49.

THROUGHOUT

But blest with her, 'tis Spring throughout the Year. 1.PSp.84.69.

THROW

When *Ajax* strives, some Rock's vast Weight to throw, 1.EOC.370.282.
"Haste *Sapho*, haste, from high *Leucadia* throw 1.TrSP.197.402.
Now here, now there, the reeling Vessel throw: 1.TrSt.268.421.
A pondrous Stone bold *Hector* heav'd to throw, 1.TrES.183.456.
For half to heap, and half to throw away. 3.Ep3.6A.83.
For some to heap, and some to throw away. 3.Ep3.6.83.
Presume Thy Bolts to throw, 6.50.26.147.
What? throw away a *Fool in Red*: 6.64.20.190.
Each aking Nerve refuse the Lance to throw, Il.2.464.149.
In empty Air their sportive Jav'lins throw, Il.2.940.168.
In Act to throw, but first prefers his Pray'rs. Il.3.432.212.
In Act to throw; but cautious, look'd around. Il.4.570.248.
He swung it round; and gath'ring Strength to throw, Il.5.373.285.
Till scarce at distance of a Javelin's throw, Il.10.425.22.
A pond'rous Stone bold *Hector* heav'd to throw, Il.12.537.101.
That shook the pond'rous Lance, in Act to throw, Il.13.735.139.
These wield the Mace, and those the Javelin throw. Il.15.449.214.
Far as an able Hand a Lance can throw, Il.16.717.272.
Then graceful as he stood, in act to throw Il.21.689.450.
O'er all the Corse their scatter'd Locks they throw. Il.23.166.495.
Wide o'er the Pyle the sable Wine they throw, Il.23.311.502.
Thy signal throw transcends the utmost bound Od.8.223.274.
Arise to throw: the strongest throws in vain. Od.8.226.274.
If with this throw the strongest Caster vye, Od.8.231.275.
In fighting fields as far the spear I throw, Od.8.261.276.
Then in the brazen helm the lotts we throw, Od.10.236.352.
Gloomy as night he stands, in act to throw Od.11.749.423.
Poising his lifted lance in act to throw: Od.19.522.221.
'Tis now (brave friends) our turn, at once to throw Od.22.288.300.

THROWN

A Robe obscene was o'er her Shoulders thrown, 1.TrSt.154.416.
But Fortune now (the Lots of Empire thrown) 1.TrSt.218.419.
But Cost on Graves is meerly thrown away. 2.ChWB.250.69.
Where all cry out, "What sums are thrown away!" 3.Ep4.100.147.
At am'rous Flavio is the Stocking thrown? 4.1HE1.148.291.
And must no Egg in *Japhet's* Face be thrown, 4.EpS2.189.324.
And thus upon the Stage 'tis fairly *thrown*, 6.60.37.179.
A broken Rock by *Nestor's* Son was thrown, Il.5.711.301.
Yet not in vain, *Tlepolemus*, was thrown Il.5.820.305.
Else, sing'd with Light'ning, had'st thou heen thrown, Il.5.1106.320.
Then in the Gen'rals Helm the Fates are thrown. Il.7.212.374.
Or far, oh far from steep *Olympus* thrown, Il.8.15.395.
Not till the Flames, by *Hector's* Fury thrown, Il.9.767.472.
Thro' the strong Brass the ringing Javelin thrown, Il.11.547.58.
To whom the King. On *Greece* no blame be thrown, Il.13.291.119.
First the sharp Lance was by *Atrides* thrown; Il.13.757.141.
Not vainly yet the forceful Lance was thrown; Il.15.500.216.
For *Jove* his Splendour round the Chief had thrown, Il.15.734.224.
The brazen-pointed Spear, with Vigour thrown, Il.16.368.257.
Large as a Rock, was by his Fury thrown. Il.16.501.262.
Oh gen'rous *Greek!* when with full Vigour thrown Il.16.713.271.
When thus (his Eyes on Heav'ns Expansion thrown) Il.21.311.433.
Pour forth their Lives, and on the Pyre are thrown. Il.23.211.498.
Have thrown the Horse and Horseman to the Ground? Il.23.624.514.
O'er which the panther's various hide was thrown. Od.19.71.196.
Support him, round the lov'd *Ulysses* thrown; Od.24.404.368.

THROWS

Black Melancholy sits, and round her throws 2.ElAb.165.333.
And to the skies its incense throws. 6.4iv.18.11.
On *Arimè* when he the Thunder throws, Il.2.952.169.
About her much-lov'd Son her Arms she throws, Il.5.389.285.
Her *Ægis*, *Pallas* o'er his Shoulders throws; Il.18.242.334.
The God pursues, a huger Billow throws, Il.21.278.432.
(Roll'd in his Helmet, these *Achilles* throws.) Il.23.428.507.
He flies more fast, and throws up all the Rein. Il.23.510.510.
Far, as a Swain his whirling Sheephook throws, Il.23.1001.529.
The hair collected in the fire he throws. Od.3.567.115.
Arise to throw: the strongest throws in vain. Od.8.226.274.
Around, a spacious arch of waves he throws, Od.11.291.396.
At distance far the feather'd shaft he throws, Od.21.173.268.

THRUSH

The Thrush may chant to the forsaken Groves, 1.PSp.14.61.

THRUSHES

The doves or thrushes flap their wings in air. Od.22.506.313.

THRUST

How should I thrust my self between? 4.HS6.50.253.
Compos'd he stood, bold Benson thrust him by: 5.DunB4.110.352.
Thrust some Mechanic Cause into his place; 5.DunB4.475.387.
Forth thrust a white Neck, and red Crest. 6.14i.20.42.
Each forward Bird must thrust his head in, 6.93.13.257.
Each forward Bird will thrust his head in, 6.93.13A.257.
Then slyly thrust it up *that same*, 6.94.43.260.
Fierce from his Knees the hapless Chief he thrust; Il.6.79.327.
Chersidamas, beneath the Navel thrust, Il.11.533.57.
The driving Javelin thro' his Shoulder thrust, Il.14.527.189.

THRUSTS

I puke, I nauseate,—yet he thrusts in more; 4.JD4.153.37.
And thrusts his person full into your face. 5.DunA3.132.161.
And thrusts his person full into your face. 5.DunB3.140.326.
Thrusts your poor Vowell from his Notch: 6.30.22.86.

THRYOËSSA
High on a Rock fair *Thryoëssa* stands, Il.11.846.74.

THRYON'S
And *Thryon's* Walls *Alphëus'* Streams inclose: Il.2.720.160.

THULÈ
Then snatch'd a sheet of Thulè from her bed; 5.DunA1.214.89.
Then snatch'd a sheet of Thulè from her bed, 5.DunB1.258.289.

THUMB
She with one Finger and a Thumb subdu'd: 2.RL5.80.206.

THUND'RER
Honour and Fame at least the Thund'rer ow'd, Il.1.464.110.
The Thund'rer sate, where old *Olympus* shrouds Il.1.648.118.
To this the Thund'rer: Seek not thou to find Il.1.704.121.
The Thund'rer spoke, nor durst the Queen reply; Il.1.736.122.
If you submit, the Thund'rer stands appeas'd; Il.1.750.123.
Then on the Thund'rer fix'd them, and replies. Il.4.74.224.
Where far apart the Thund'rer fills his Throne, Il.5.938.311.
To whom assenting, thus the Thund'rer said: Il.5.952.312.
Th' Almighty Thund'rer with a Frown replies, Il.7.542.391.
To drag, by this, the Thund'rer down to Earth: Il.8.28.397.
In vain the gloomy Thund'rer might repine: Il.8.249.409.
At *Thetis'* Suit the partial Thund'rer nods. Il.8.450.418.
And now the Thund'rer meditates his Flight Il.8.542.422.
Incessant Cataracts the Thund'rer pours, Il.12.27.82.
When now the Thund'rer, on the Sea-beat Coast, Il.13.1.103.
Observ'd the Thund'rer, nor observ'd in vain. Il.13.18.104.
The panting Thund'rer nods, and sinks to Rest. Il.14.406.183.
The Thund'rer spoke: Imperial *Juno* mourn'd, Il.15.39.195.
Well-pleas'd the Thund'rer saw their earnest care, Il.15.176.203.
See, and be strong! the Thund'rer sends thee Aid. Il.15.289.208.
Sudden, the Thund'rer, with a flashing Ray, Il.16.356.257.
The Thund'rer, unsuspicious of the Fraud, Il.19.111.376.
Grief seiz'd the Thund'rer, by his Oath engag'd; Il.19.123.377.
Then thus the Thund'rer checks th' imperial Dame: Il.24.84.539.
(Reply'd the Thund'rer to the Martial Maid) Od.1.85.35.
Sudden the Thund'rer blackens all the skies, Od.3.367.104.
Who blest th' Almighty Thund'rer in her arms; Od.11.318.397.
When lo! a murky cloud the Thund'rer forms Od.12.475.454.

THUND'RER'S
E'er Pallas issued from the Thund'rer's head, 5.DunA1.8.61.
E'er Pallas issu'd from the Thund'rer's head, 5.DunB1.10.269.
Shall not the Thund'rer's dread Command restrain, Il.15.148.202.
Go wait the Thund'rer's Will (*Saturnia* cry'd) Il.15.164.202.

THUND'RERS
Not ev'n the Thund'rers Favour brings Relief. Il.18.100.328.

THUND'RING
Of arts, but thund'ring against Heathen lore; 5.DunA3.94.158.
Of arts, but thund'ring against heathen lore; 5.DunB3.102.324.
Hark! how the thund'ring Giant roars. 6.78ii.8.216.
With thund'ring Offspring all around, 6.135.46.368.
With thund'ring Infants all around, 6.135.46A.368.
And sue for Vengeance to the Thund'ring God. Il.1.513.112.
And thund'ring Footsteps shake the sounding Shore: Il.2.549.153.
And styl'd the Consort of the thund'ring *Jove.* Il.4.86.224.
The Race of those which once the thund'ring God Il.5.328.282.
Or fierce *Bellona* thund'ring at the Wall, Il.5.411.286.
Thro' such a Space of Air, with thund'ring Sound, Il.5.962.312.
When shouting Millions shake the thund'ring Field. Il.5.1055.317.
Nor aught the Warrior's thund'ring Mace avail'd. Il.7.176.372.
The huge Stone thund'ring thro' his Buckler broke; Il.7.323.379.
When dreadful *Hector,* thund'ring thro' the War, Il.8.111.403.
While *Meleager's* thund'ring Arm prevail'd: Il.9.666.467.
Full on the *Lycian's* Helmet thund'ring down, Il.12.459.98.
Down sinks the Warrior with a thund'ring Sound, Il.12.481.99.
Then thund'ring thro' the Planks, with forceful Sway, Il.12.549.101.
'Tis not thy Arm, 'tis thund'ring *Jove* we fear: Il.13.1023.153.
Such was the Voice, and such the thund'ring Sound Il.14.175.165.
We saw him, late, by thund'ring *Ajax* kill'd; Il.15.326.209.
Thund'ring he falls, and drops th' extinguish'd Fires. Il.15.491.216.
And issu'd at his Breast. With thund'ring Sound Il.15.640.221.
Thund'ring he falls; his falling Arms resound, Il.15.694.222.
And still hear *Hector* thund'ring at their Gates. Il.17.720.315.
Heav'ns Queen, and Consort of the thund'ring *Jove,* Il.18.428.341.
(To meet the thund'ring Lance) his dreadful Shield, Il.20.311.407.
Prone from his Car the thund'ring Chief descends, Il.20.564.418.
The thund'ring Voice of *Jove* abhors to hear, Il.21.215.430.
Now bursting on his Head with thund'ring Sound, Il.21.263.431.
Thund'ring he falls; a Mass of monstrous Size, Il.21.472.441.
No sooner had he spoke, but thund'ring near Il.23.579.513.
Then hurl'd the Hero, thund'ring on the Ground Il.23.973.528.
By righteous *Themis* and by thund'ring *Jove,* Od.2.74.64.
And near the ship came thund'ring on the flood. Od.9.568.329.
Who bore *Alcides* to the thund'ring God; Od.11.326.398.
The boiling billows thund'ring roll below; Od.12.72.434.
The rock rebellows with a thund'ring sound; Od.12.290.446.
And offer hecatombs to thund'ring *Jove?* Od.12.408.450.
To whom the thund'ring Pow'r: O source of day! Od.12.452.453.
And dire *Charybdis* rolls her thund'ring waves. Od.12.506.457.
Since fix'd are thy resolves, may thund'ring *Jove* Od.15.126.75.
Oh! if this promis'd bliss by thund'ring *Jove,* Od.15.202.78.
By mighty *Pallas,* and by thund'ring *Jove.* Od.16.283.118.
With many a footstool thund'ring at thy head. Od.17.271.145.
Flat falls he thund'ring on the marble floor, Od.22.110.292.

THUND'ROUS
Nor winter's boreal blast, nor thund'rous show'r, Od.19.513.221.
And howling *Scylla* whirls her thund'rous waves, Od.23.354.341.

THUNDER
Got by fierce Whirlwinds, and in Thunder born! 1.PAu.92.87.
Strait a short Thunder breaks the frozen Sky. 1.W-F.130.162.
Bear *Britain's* Thunder, and her Cross display, 1.W-F.387.189.
Here point your Thunder, and exhaust your Rage! 1.EOC.555.304.
And sleeps thy Thunder in the Realms above? 1.TrSt.110.414.
And unregarded Thunder rolls in vain: 1.TrSt.305.423.
Thy own *Arcadians* there the Thunder claim, 1.TrSt.386.426.
From Pole to Pole the Thunder roars aloud, 1.TrSt.496.431.
While Thunder roars, and Lightning round him flies. 1.TrSt.525.432.
Rain follows Thunder, that was all he said. 2.ChWB.392.76.
And falls like Thunder on the prostrate *Ace.* 2.RL3.98.174.
Jove's Thunder roars, Heav'n trembles all around; 2.RL5.49.203.
Not all at once, as Thunder breaks the Cloud; 2.TemF.310.279.
Thro' the big Dome the doubling Thunder bounds: 2.TemF.333.280.
Forget to thunder, and recall her fires? 3.EOM4.124.139.
With Gun, Drum, Trumpet, Blunderbuss & Thunder? 4.HS1.26.7.
And all the Thunder of the Pit ascends! 4.2HE1.327.223.
And hurls the Thunder of the Laws on *Gin.* 4.EpS1.130.307.
ARGYLE, the State's whole Thunder born to wield, 4.EpS2.86.318.
Loud thunder to its bottom shook the bog, 5.DunA1.259.95.
Hoarse thunder to its bottom shook the bog, 5.DunA1.259A.95.
With thunder rumbling from the mustard-bowl, 5.DunA2.218.127.
Sudden, a burst of thunder shook the flood. 5.DunA2.301.139.
Wings the red lightning, and the thunder rolls. 5.DunA3.252.178.
Rolls the loud thunder, and the light'ning wings! 5.DunA3.252A.178.
This Box my Thunder, this right hand my God? 5.DunB1.202.284.
Loud thunder to its bottom shook the bog, 5.DunB1.329.294.
With Thunder rumbling from the mustard bowl, 5.DunB2.226.307.
When lo! a burst of thunder shook the flood. 5.DunB2.325.313.
Wings the red lightning, and the thunder rolls. 5.DunB3.256.332.
When thunder roars, and lightning blasts the plain, 6.21.8.69.
Thunder breaks! 6.96i.40.269.
In Peals of Thunder now she roars, and now 6.96ii.9.270.
Like Peals of Thunder now she roars, and now 6.96ii.9A.270.
Who rolls the Thunder o'er the vaulted Skies. Il.1.671.119.
And Thunder rolling shook the Firmament. Il.2.419.147.
And foam and thunder on the stony Shore. Il.2.473.149.
Oh Thou! whose Thunder rends the clouded Air, Il.2.489.150.
And break the Ranks, and thunder thro' the War. Il.2.933.167.
On *Arimè* when he the Thunder throws, Il.2.952.169.
His fiery Coursers thunder o'er the Plains. Il.2.1017.171.
The Sire whose Thunder shakes the cloudy Skies, Il.4.45.223.
Bare his red Arm, and bid the Thunder roll; Il.4.201.230.
Foam o'er the Rocks, and thunder to the Skies. Il.4.483.243.
His triple Thunder, and his Bolts of Fire. Il.5.560.295.
Flame in the Front, and thunder at their Head: Il.5.727.302.
Tho *Mars* and *Hector* thunder in their Face; Il.5.861.307.
Can *Mars* rebel, and does no Thunder roll? Il.5.943.311.
And bids the Thunder of the Battel rise. Il.6.128.330.
Implore the God whose Thunder rends the Skies. Il.7.240.376.
Be witness, *Jove!* whose Thunder rolls on high. Il.7.488.388.
While the deep Thunder shook th' Aerial Hall. Il.7.575.393.
Thick Light'nings flash; the mutt'ring Thunder rolls; Il.8.95.401.
Roll'd the big Thunder o'er the vast Profound: Il.8.162.405.
Now swift pursue, now thunder uncontroll'd; Il.8.234.408.
My self will arm, and thunder at thy side. Il.8.456.418.
The Wounds impress'd by burning Thunder deep. Il.8.497.420.
The Wounds impress'd by burning Thunder deep. Il.8.517.421.
Theirs are his Omens, and his Thunder theirs. Il.9.310.449.
Whose Thunder shakes the dark aerial Hall. Il.10.390.21.
The Coursers ply, and thunder tow'rds the Fleet. Il.10.623.29.
The Care of him who bids the Thunder roar, Il.10.652.30.
Ev'n *Jove,* whose Thunder spoke his Wrath, distill'd Il.11.69.37.
And the thick Thunder beats the lab'ring Ground. Il.11.198.44.
Shake the dry Field, and thunder tow'rd the Fleet. Il.11.641.62.
Redoubling Clamours thunder in the Skies. Il.12.298.92.
Rapt from the less'ning Thunder of the War; Il.13.679.137.
And all the Thunder of the Battel rag'd) Il.13.858.146.
And bids anew the martial Thunder rise. Il.13.950.151.
That bears *Jove's* Thunder on its dreadful Wings, Il.13.1000.152.
Shall *Hector* thunder at your Ships again? Il.14.424.184.
But *Jove* shall thunder thro' th' Ethereal Dome, Il.15.104.200.
Dares, tho' the Thunder bursting o'er my Head Il.15.132.201.
And *Troy* and *Hector* thunder in the Rear. Il.15.371.211.
The Horses thunder, Earth and Ocean roar! Il.15.405.212.
And Peals of Thunder shook the Firmament. Il.15.437.214.
While thus the Thunder of the Battel rag'd, Il.15.450.215.
But now in Peals of Thunder calls to Arms; Il.15.877.230.
Tho' *Jove* in Thunder should command the War, Il.16.114.240.
And sends his Voice in Thunder to the Skies: Il.17.96.291.
And hear the Thunder of the sounding Steeds. Il.17.196.295.
The God, whose Thunder rends the troubled Air, Il.17.226.296.
Involv'd the Mount; the Thunder roar'd aloud; Il.17.671.314.
And level'd Thunder strike my guilty Head! Il.19.276.383.
And grasps the Thunder in his awful Hands, Il.20.24.393.
Above, the Sire of Gods his Thunder rolls, Il.20.75.397.
But shrinks and shudders, when the Thunder flies. Il.20.422.412.
Heav'n in loud Thunder bids the Trumpet sound; Il.21.452.439.
Which bears *Jove's* Thunder on its dreadful Field; Il.21.465.440.
Then rustling, crackling, crashing, thunder down. Il.23.149.495.
And up the Champain thunder from the Shore: Il.23.440.507.
From the pleas'd Crowd new Peals of Thunder rise, Il.23.1042.530.
Daughter of *Jove!* whose arms in thunder wield Od.6.385.230.
Mean-while the God whose hand the thunder forms, Od.9.75.306.
His voice like thunder thro' the cavern sounds: Od.9.303.318.
And *Jove's* scorn'd thunder serves to drench our fields) Od.9.424.323.
With voice like thunder, and a direful yell. Od.9.474.325.
But the great God, whose thunder rends the skies, Od.9.645.333.
And the hoarse din like distant thunder dies; Od.12.313.447.
Recoiling, mutter'd thunder in his breast. Od.20.22.232.
Loud from a saphire sky his thunder sounds: Od.20.128.239.
By him at whose behest the thunder flies! Od.20.404.252.
Their fall in thunder ecchoes round the walls. Od.22.297.300.
Then, when the surge in thunder mounts the sky, Od.23.251.335.
Who rolls the thunder o'er the vaulted skies) Od.24.548.374.

THUNDER (CONTINUED)
But *Jove's* red arm the burning thunder aims; ....Od.24.622.377.

THUNDER'D
If nature thunder'd in his op'ning ears, ...3.EOM1.201.40.
On *Ida's* Summits thunder'd from above. ....Il.8.207.407.
She took, and thunder'd thro' the Seas and Land. ....Il.11.10.35.
War thunder'd at the Gates, and Blood distain'd the Tow'rs. ...Il.12.40.83.
As furious, *Hector* thunder'd Threats aloud, ...Il.15.832.229.
A Rock's large Fragment thunder'd on his Head; ....Il.16.706.271.
Pour'd on the Rear, and thunder'd close behind; ....Il.18.190.331.
Burst o'er the float, and thunder'd on his head. ....Od.5.467.195.
It thunder'd as it fell. We trembled then, ...Od.9.278.318.
When war has thunder'd with its loudest storms, ...Od.11.515.409.
This arm that thunder'd o'er the *Phrygian* plain, ...Od.11.611.414.
Thunder'd the deeps, the smoking billows roll'd! ....Od.12.241.443.
Jove thunder'd on their side. Our guilty head ....Od.14.298.50.
Jove thunder'd on their side: our guilty head ....Od.17.519.157.
In lightning burst; *Jove* thunder'd from on high. ....Od.21.453.282.

THUNDER'S
She, 'midst the light'ning's blaze, and thunder's sound, ...3.EOM3.249.117.

THUNDERBOLT
And *Hicetaon,* Thunderbolt of War. ....Il.20.287.406.

THUNDERBOLTS
Nor each stern *Ajax,* Thunderbolts of War: ....Il.8.100.402.
Once Sons of *Mars,* and Thunderbolts of War! ....Il.15.891.231.
Thoas and *Merion,* Thunderbolts of War, ...Il.19.246.383.

THUNDERER
And sets th'avenging Thunderer in Arms. ....1.TrSt.339.424.
(That dreadful Oath which binds the Thunderer) ....1.TrSt.412.427.
Th' Eternal Thunderer, state thron'd in Gold. ....Il.8.551.422.
Shall see th' Almighty Thunderer in Arms. ....Il.8.587.424.

THUNDERING
No further speech the thundering rock affords, ...1.TrPA.146.372.

THUNDERS
Heav'n trembles, roar the Mountains, thunders all the Ground. .1.TrES.66A.452.
Like broken Thunders that at distance roar, ...2.TemF.23.255.
With Heav'n's own thunders shook the world below, ...3.EOM3.267.119.
No furious Husband thunders at the Door; ....4.HAdv.167.89.
And Jove's own Thunders follow Mars's Drums. ....5.DunB4.68.348.
And shook the Stage with Thunders all his own! ....6.128.16.356.
And shouts and thunders in the Fields below. ....Il.4.596.250.
Rapt thro' the Ranks he thunders o'er the Plain, ...Il.5.113.272.
Fame calls, *Mars* thunders, and the Fields in Flames. ....Il.5.634.298.
The Lord of Thunders view'd, and stern bespoke. ....Il.5.1093.318.
His pond'rous Buckler thunders on the Ground. ....Il.8.314.412.
War shakes her Walls, and thunders at her Gates. ....Il.9.688.468.
In happy Thunders promis'd *Greece* their Aid; ....Il.11.58.37.
And happy Thunders of the fav'ring God, ...Il.12.276.91.
Heav'n trembles, roar the Mountains, thunders all the Ground. .Il.12.410.96.
Impetuous *Hector* thunders at the Wall; ....Il.13.167.112.
Whirls, leaps, and thunders down, impetuous to the Plain: ....Il.13.198.115.
And his broad Buckler thunders on the Ground. ....Il.13.252.117.
With answ'ring Thunders fill'd the echoing Plain; ....Il.13.1059.155.
Not he that thunders from th' aerial Bow'r, ...Il.14.61.160.
And lull the Lord of Thunders in her Arms. ....Il.14.190.168.
Both Armies join: Earth thunders, Ocean roars. ....Il.14.456.185.
The Lord of Thunders from his lofty Height ....Il.15.246.206.
Had heard the Thunders to the Deeps of Hell. ....Il.15.255.207.
The Chief so thunders, and so shakes the Fleet. ....Il.15.759.225.
And thunders after *Hector; Hector* flies, ...Il.16.462.260.
He falls, Earth thunders, and his Arms resound. ....Il.16.990.281.
And lo! it bursts, it thunders on our Heads! ....Il.17.289.299.
The Lord of Thunders sent the blue-ey'd Maid. ....Il.17.615.312.
And thunders to his Steeds these dread Commands. ....Il.19.439.389.
And now she thunders from the *Grecian* Walls. ....Il.20.68.396.
As he that thunders to the Stream that flows. ....Il.21.208.430.
To him whose Thunders blacken Heav'n with Night? ....Il.21.582.446.
Tears up the Shore, and thunders tow'rd the Main. ....Il.23.454.508.
Before the God who thunders from on high, ...Od.5.6.171.
When he who thunders rent his bark in twain, ...Od.5.167.180.
Thunders impetuous down, and smoaks along the ground. ....Od.11.738.422.
Ev'n I who from the Lord of thunders rose, ...Od.11.765.424.
Thrice in dire thunders she refunds the tyde. ....Od.12.132.438.
Air thunders, rolls the ocean, groans the ground. ....Od.12.374.449.
Lo! my red arm I bare, my thunders guide, ...Od.12.456.453.
Then *Jove* in anger bids his thunders roll, ...Od.12.485.456.
Broad burst the lightnings, deep the thunders roll; ....Od.14.338.51.
Father of Gods and men! whose thunders rowl ....Od.20.141.240.
And the mixt clamour thunders in the skies. ....Od.24.90.352.
He falls, earth thunders, and his arms resound. ....Od.24.607.376.

THUNDRING
Bursts out, resistless, with a thundring Tyde! ....1.EOC.630.310.
Full on the *Lycian's* Helmet thundring down, ...1.TrES.105.453.
Down sinks the Warrior, with a thundring Sound, ...1.TrES.127.454.
Then thundring thro' the Planks, with forceful Sway, ...1.TrES.195.456.
While mighty WILLIAM's thundring Arm prevail'd. ....4.2HE2.63.169.
Down sinks the Warrior with a thundring Sound, ...Il.5.73.269.
From trampling Steeds, and thundring Charioteers, ...Il.5.618.297.
His thundring Arm a deadly Stroke imprest ....Il.6.11.323.
Forth burst the stormy Band with thundring Roar, ...Il.23.264.500.

THUS (OMITTED)
1286

THWART
All must be false that thwart this One great End, ...3.EOM3.309.125.
Or thwart the synod of the gods in vain. ....Od.1.101.36.
To thwart thy passage, and repel thy fleet? ....Od.10.72.342.

THWARTS
Alike he thwarts the hospitable end, ...Od.15.81.73.

THY
Fair *Thames* flow gently from thy sacred Spring, ...1.PSp.3.59.
While on thy Banks *Sicilian* Muses sing, ...1.PSp.4.60.
Thy Victim, Love, shall be the Shepherd's Heart, ...1.PSp.52.66.
And give the Conquest to thy *Sylvia's* Eyes. ....1.PSp.88.69.
That adds this Wreath of Ivy to thy Bays; ....1.PSu.10.72.
While in thy Heart Eternal Winter reigns. ....1.PSu.22.73.
But since those Graces please thy Eyes no more, ...1.PSu.29.74.
Ah wretched Shepherd, what avails thy Art, ...1.PSu.33.74.
To cure thy Lambs, but not to heal thy Heart! ....1.PSu.34.74.
To cure thy Lambs, but not to heal thy Heart! ....1.PSu.34.74.
But since those Graces please thy Sight no more, ...1.PSu.29A.74.
The Captive Bird that sings within thy Bow'r! ....1.PSu.46.75.
Then might my Voice thy list'ning Ears employ, ...1.PSu.47.75.
Are half so charming as thy Sight to me. ....1.PAu.46.83.
The Shepherds cry, "Thy Flocks are left a Prey—" ....1.PAu.78.85.
And swell the future Harvest of thy Field! ....1.PWi.16A.89.
How all things listen, while thy Muse complains! ....1.PWi.77.94.
Thy Name, thy Honour, and thy Praise shall live! ....1.PWi.84.94.
Thy Name, thy Honour, and thy Praise shall live! ....1.PWi.84.94.
Thy Name, thy Honour, and thy Praise shall live! ....1.PWi.84.94.
Exalt thy Tow'ry Head, and lift thy Eyes! ....1.Mes.86.120.
Exalt thy Tow'ry Head, and lift thy Eyes! ....1.Mes.86.120.
See, a long Race thy spatious Courts adorn; ....1.Mes.87.121.
See barb'rous Nations at thy Gates attend, ...1.Mes.91.121.
Walk in thy Light, and in thy Temple bend. ....1.Mes.92.121.
Walk in thy Light, and in thy Temple bend. ....1.Mes.92.121.
See thy bright Altars throng'd with prostrate Kings, ...1.Mes.93.121.
But lost, dissolv'd in thy superior Rays; ....1.Mes.101.122.
O'erflow thy Courts: The LIGHT HIMSELF shall shine ....1.Mes.103.122.
Thy *Realm* for ever lasts! thy own *Messiah* reigns! ....1.Mes.108.122.
Thy *Realm* for ever lasts! thy own *Messiah* reigns! ....1.Mes.108.122.
Thy Forests, *Windsor!* and thy green Retreats, ...1.W-F.1.148.
Thy Forests, *Windsor!* and thy green Retreats, ...1.W-F.1.148.
Nor envy *Windsor!* since thy Shades have seen ....1.W-F.161.164.
Thy Offspring, *Thames!* the fair *Lodona* nam'd, ...1.W-F.172.165.
"Ah *Cynthia!* ah—tho' banish'd from thy Train, ...1.W-F.200.168.
And future Navies on thy Shores appear. ....1.W-F.222.170.
Like the bright Beauties on thy Banks below; ....1.W-F.232.170.
And future Navies on thy Banks appear. ....1.W-F.222A.170.
Than the fair Nymphs that gild thy Shore below; ....1.W-F.232A.170.
Than the fair Nymphs that grace thy side below; ....1.W-F.232B.170.
Still in thy Song shou'd vanquish'd *France* appear, ...1.W-F.309.178.
Thy Trees, fair *Windsor!* now shall leave their Woods, ...1.W-F.385.189.
And half thy Forests rush into my Floods, ...1.W-F.386.189.
Oh stretch thy Reign, fair *Peace!* from Shore to Shore, ...1.W-F.407.192.
Here cease thy Flight, nor with unhallow'd Lays ....1.W-F.423.193.
Yet let not each gay *Turn* thy Rapture move, ...1.EOC.390.284.
Cremona now shall ever boast thy Name, ...1.EOC.707.322.
Great queen of love! how boundless is thy sway; ....1.TrPA.13.366.
Thy force the barb'rous Polyphemus try'd, ...1.TrPA.15.366.
Nor thy contempt cou'd cause me thus to mourn, ...1.TrPA.118.370.
But Acis, Acis is thy dear delight; ....1.TrPA.120.370.
Or cast his limbs into thy guilty flood, ...1.TrPA.128.371.
And mix thy waters with his reeking blood! ....1.TrPA.129.371.
And stood the helpless witness of thy fate; ....1.TrFD.54.388.
Embrac'd thy boughs, the rising bark delay'd, ...1.TrFD.55.388.
Thy branches hung with humid pearls appear, ...1.TrFD.65.388.
Embrac'd thy boughs, thy rising bark delay'd, ...1.TrFD.55A.388.
Embrac'd thy boughs, thy rising bark delay'd, ...1.TrFD.55A.388.
My son, thy mother's parting kiss receive, ...1.TrFD.94.390.
While yet thy mother has a kiss to give. ....1.TrFD.95.390.
To thy Remembrance lost, as to thy Love! ....1.TrSP.4.393.
To thy Remembrance lost, as to thy Love! ....1.TrSP.4.393.
If to no Charms thou wilt thy Heart resign, ...1.TrSP.45.395.
Yet once thy *Sapho* cou'd thy Cares employ, ...1.TrSP.49.395.
Yet once thy *Sapho* cou'd thy Cares employ, ...1.TrSP.49.395.
The fair *Sicilians* now thy Soul inflame; ....1.TrSP.63.396.
Pride of thy Age, and Glory of thy Race, ...1.TrSP.105.398.
Pride of thy Age, and Glory of thy Race, ...1.TrSP.105.398.
No Gift on thee thy *Sapho* cou'd confer, ...1.TrSP.117A.398.
And *why this Grief? thy Daughter lives;* he cries. ....1.TrSP.138.399.
My Woes, thy Crimes, I to the World proclaim; ....1.TrSP.141.399.
And Birds defer their Songs till thy Return: ....1.TrSP.174.401.
"Thy wretched Weight, nor dread the Deeps below!" ....1.TrSP.198.402.
Spread thy soft Wings, and waft me o'er the Main, ...1.TrSP.210.403.
Thy Charms than those may far more pow'rful be, ...1.TrSP.220.403.
Dash'd on these Rocks, than to thy Bosom prest? ....1.TrSP.225.403.
Dash'd on sharp Rocks, than to thy Bosom prest? ....1.TrSP.225A.403.
Dash'd on those Rocks, than to thy Bosom prest? ....1.TrSP.225B.403.
To these fond Eyes restore thy welcome Sails? ....1.TrSP.247.404.
O launch thy Bark, nor fear the watry Plain, ...1.TrSP.250.404.
O launch thy Bark, secure of prosp'rous Gales, ...1.TrSP.252.404.
And fix, O Muse! the Barrier of thy Song, ...1.TrSt.20.410.
Nor yet attempt to stretch thy bolder Wing, ...1.TrSt.23.410.
And Thou, great Heir of all thy Father's Fame, ...1.TrSt.31.411.
Oh bless thy *Rome* with an Eternal Reign, ...1.TrSt.33.411.
Tho' all the Skies, ambitious of thy Sway, ...1.TrSt.37.411.
And in thy Glories more serenely shine; ....1.TrSt.40.411.
Then to fierce *Capaneus* thy Verse extend, ...1.TrSt.67.413.
Assist, if *Oedipus* deserve thy Care! ....1.TrSt.86.413.
Taught by thy self to win the promis'd Reign: ....1.TrSt.94.414.
And sleeps thy Thunder in the Realms above? ....1.TrSt.110.414.
Their ready Guilt preventing thy Commands: ....1.TrSt.121.415.
What Joys, oh Tyrant! swell'd thy Soul that Day, ...1.TrSt.220.419.
Pleas'd to behold unbounded Pow'r thy own, ...1.TrSt.222.419.
On thy own Offspring hast thou fix'd this Fate, ...1.TrSt.245.420.
Thy Curse, oh *Oedipus,* just Heav'n alarms, ...1.TrSt.338.424.
I from the Root thy guilty Race will tear, ...1.TrSt.340.424.
Yet since thou wilt thy Sister-Queen controul, ...1.TrSt.366.425.
Since still the Lust of Discord fires thy Soul, ...1.TrSt.367.425.
Derive Incitements to renew thy Rage; ....1.TrSt.380.425.
Thy own *Arcadians* there the Thunder claim, ...1.TrSt.386.426.

THY (CONTINUED)
These in thy dangers timely aid shall bring, ... 6.21.25.69.
And fix thy foot upon the Lion's crest. .... 6.21.32.70.
At length, my soul! thy fruitless hopes give o'er, ... 6.22.1.71.
Who fix't thy self amidst the rowling frame, ... 6.23.7.73.
The source of good; thy splendor to descry, ... 6.23.11.73.
And on thy self, undazled, fix her eye. .... 6.23.12.73.
And on thy self, fix her undazzl'd Eye! .... 6.23.12A.73.
A thorny crown transpierc'd thy sacred brow, ... 6.25.7.77.
For me in tortures thou resign'd'st thy breath, ... 6.25.9.77.
Embrac'd me on the cross, and sav'd me by thy death. .... 6.25.10.77.
Such as then was, and is, thy love to me, ... 6.25.13.77.
Fly Pegasæan *Steed, thy Rider bear,* .... 6.26ii.1.79.
Thy Name De Urfey or D'Urfey. .... 6.30.6A.85.
Cease, fond Nature, cease thy strife, ... 6.31ii.5.94.
O Grave! where is thy Victory? .... 6.31ii.17.94.
O Death! where is thy Sting? .... 6.31ii.18.94.
Where mighty Death! Oh where's thy Sting? .... 6.31ii.6Z6.94.
Parson, these Things in thy possessing .... 6.39.1.110.
For which thy Patron's weekly thank'd: .... 6.39.8.110.
A *Chrysostom* to smooth thy Band in: .... 6.39.12.110.
Howe're, the *Coxcomb's* thy own Merit, ... 6.44.29.123.
Thy Fools no more I'll teize: .... 6.47.2.128.
Lintot, farewell! thy Bard must go; .... 6.47.17.129.
Heaven gives thee for thy Loss of *Rowe,* .... 6.47.19.129.
Ingenious Writer, lest thy Barrel split, ... 6.48i.5.133*.
Unbarrel thy just Sense, and broach thy Wit. .... 6.48i.6.133*.
Unbarrel thy just Sense, and broach thy Wit. .... 6.48i.6.133*.
Then shall thy Barrel be of gen'ral Use. .... 6.48i.9.133*.
Thy Pestle braining all the Sons of *Rome.* .... 6.48ii.8.134.
Before thy Pen vanish the Nation's Ills, ... 6.48ii.9.134.
As all Diseases fly before thy Pills. .... 6.48ii.10.134.
But thou too gently hast laid on thy Satyr; .... 6.48iii.7.134.
O *Button!* summon all thy Sons of Wit! .... 6.48iii.12.135.
But ev'n as Coughs thy *Spanish* Liquorish heals, ... 6.48iv.3.135.
So thy deep Knowledge Dark Designs reveals. .... 6.48iv.4.135.
Thy Works in *Spanish* shou'd have been translated, ... 6.48iv.6.136.
Thy Politicks should ope the Eyes of *Spain,* .... 6.48iv.7.136.
Go on, Great Wit, contemn thy Foe's Bravado, ... 6.48iv.9.136.
In thy defence I'll draw *Toledo's* Spado. .... 6.48iv.10.136.
What Blessings thy free Bounty gives, ... 6.50.17.146.
What pleasures thy free Bounty gives, ... 6.50.17A.146.
Thy Goodness let me bound; .... 6.50.22.147.
Presume Thy Bolts to throw, ... 6.50.26.147.
On each I judge thy Foe. .... 6.50.28.147.
If I am wrong, Thy Grace impart .... 6.50.31.147.
If I am right, thy grace impart .... 6.50.29B.147.
Of those that seek thy Face; .... 6.50.30A.147.
At ought thy Wisdom has deny'd, ... 6.50.35.148.
Or ought thy Goodness lent. .... 6.50.36.148.
Since quicken'd by thy Breath, ... 6.50.42.148.
And let Thy Will be done. .... 6.50.48.148.
And arts but soften us to feel thy flame. .... 6.51ii.4.152.
Whether thy hand strike out some free design, ... 6.52.3.156.
So just thy skill, so regular my rage. .... 6.52.12.156.
Here thy well-study'd Marbles fix our eye; .... 6.52.33.157.
Match *Raphael's* grace, with thy lov'd *Guido's* air, ... 6.52.36.157.
Muse! at that name thy sacred sorrows shed, ... 6.52.47.157.
Blooms in thy colours for a thousand years. .... 6.52.58.157.
Free as thy stroke, yet faultless as thy line! .... 6.52.64.158.
Free as thy stroke, yet faultless as thy line! .... 6.52.64.158.
New graces yearly, like thy works, display; .... 6.52.65.158.
Yet should the Graces all thy figures place, ... 6.52.71.158.
With *Zeuxis' Helen* thy *Bridgewater* vie, ... 6.52.75.158.
Ah *Moore!* thy Skill were well employ'd, ... 6.53.29.162.
Vain is thy Art, thy Powder vain, ... 6.53.35.162.
Vain is thy Art, thy Powder vain, ... 6.53.35.162.
Now, *Tonson,* list thy Forces all, ... 6.58.69.174.
Muse, 'tis enough: at length thy labour ends, ... 6.63.1.188.
Wide o'er th' aerial Vault extends thy sway, ... 6.65.3.192.
On thy third Reign look down; disclose our Fate, ... 6.65.5.192.
When shall we nest thy hallow'd Altars raise, ... 6.65.7.192.
And Quires of Virgins celebrate thy praise? .... 6.65.8.192.
Wide o'er th' Æthereal Walks extends thy sway, ... 6.65.3A.192.
On thy third Realm *look down;* unfold our Fate, ... 6.65.5A.192.
Where shall we next thy lasting Temples raise, ... 6.65.7A.192.
Touch'd by thy hand, again Rome's glories shine, ... 6.71.46.204.
Nor blush, these studies thy regard engage; .... 6.71.49.204.
Then shall thy CRAGS (and let me call him mine) .... 6.71.63.204.
Thy reliques, *Rowe,* to this fair urn we trust, ... 6.72.1.208.
To which thy tomb shall guide inquiring eyes. .... 6.72.4.208.
Peace to thy gentle shade, and endless Rest! .... 6.72.5.208.
Blest in thy genius, in thy love too blest! .... 6.72.6.208.
Blest in thy genius, in thy love too blest! .... 6.72.6.208.
One grateful woman to thy fame supplies .... 6.72.7.208.
Thy reliques, *Rowe,* to this fair shrine we trust, ... 6.72.1B.208.
Thy reliques, *Rowe,* to this fair tomb we trust, ... 6.72.1C.208.
To which thy urn shall guide inquiring eyes. .... 6.72.4B.208.
One Grateful woman to thy fame supply'd .... 6.72.7A.208.
Lord! Lord! how rattl'd then thy Stones, ... 6.79.55.219.
Right did thy Gossip call thee: .... 6.79.66.220.
Thy Mouth yet durst not ope, ... 6.79.74.220.
"Know'st thou not me, nor yet thy self? .... 6.79.83.220.
"Tho' laid thus low beneath thy breech,) .... 6.79.91.221.
Such were the Notes, thy once-lov'd Poet sung, ... 6.84.1.238.
Recall those Nights that clos'd thy toilsom Days, ... 6.84.15.239.
Still hear thy *Parnell* in his living Lays: .... 6.84.16.239.
Beholds thee glorious only in thy Fall. .... 6.84.20.239.
In vain to Desarts thy Retreat is made; .... 6.84.27.239.
The Muse attends thee to thy silent Shade: .... 6.84.28A.239.
My Muse attending strews thy path with Bays, ... 6.84.31Z7.239.
Ev'n now she shades thy Evening Walk with Bays, ... 6.84.35.240.
Eyes the calm Sun-set of thy Various Day, ... 6.84.38.240.
She still with pleasure eyes thy Evening Ray, ... 6.84.31Z9.240.
The calmer Sunsett of thy Various Day; .... 6.84.31Z10.240.
Oh let thy once-lov'd Friend inscribe thy Stone, ... 6.85.7.242.

THY (CONTINUED)
Oh let thy once-lov'd Friend inscribe thy Stone, ... 6.85.7.242.
Let then thy once-lov'd Friend inscribe thy Stone, ... 6.85.7A.242.
Let then thy once-lov'd Friend inscribe thy Stone, ... 6.85.7A.242.
Yet let thy once-lov'd Friend inscribe thy Stone, ... 6.85.7B.242.
Yet let thy once-lov'd Friend inscribe thy Stone, ... 6.85.7B.242.
Glow in thy heart, and smile upon thy face. .... 6.86.14.245.
Glow in thy heart, and smile upon thy face. .... 6.86.14.245.
Glow in thy heart, and sparkle in thy face. .... 6.86.14A.245.
Glow in thy heart, and sparkle in thy face. .... 6.86.14A.245.
In some soft Dream may thy mild Soul remove, ... 6.86.19A.246.
Or let thy soul in some soft dream remove, ... 6.86.19B.246.
And be thy latest Gasp a Sigh of Love. .... 6.86.20A.246.
So Ireland change thy tone, ... 6.90.12.251.
Reach thy Size? .... 6.96i.4.268.
All thy Fire! .... 6.96i.10.268.
Nigh thy Ear, ... 6.96i.45.269.
On thy Hand .... 6.96i.47.269.
"Within thy Reach I set the Vinegar? .... 6.96ii.18.270.
"While Pepper-Water-Worms thy Bait supply'd; .... 6.96ii.20.270.
"Where twin'd the Silver Eel around thy Hook, ... 6.96ii.21.270.
"Vain is thy Courage, *Grilly,* vain thy Boast; .... 6.96ii.25.271.
"Vain is thy Courage, *Grilly,* vain thy Boast; .... 6.96ii.25.271.
"How then thy fairy Footsteps can I find? .... 6.96ii.40.272.
Thy Pigmy Island and thy tiny Spouse .... 6.96ii.30Z33.272.
Thy Pigmy Island and thy tiny Spouse .... 6.96ii.30Z33.272.
And the babes play-things that adorn thy house. .... 6.96ii.30Z34.272.
Or at the Glow-worm warm thy frozen legs? .... 6.96ii.30Z50.272.
Or chase the mite that bore thy cheese away, ... 6.96ii.30Z51.272.
"Within the King-Cup if thy Limbs are spread, ... 6.96ii.47.273.
"But ah! I fear thy little Fancy roves .... 6.96ii.51.273.
"Thy Pigmy Children, and thy tiny Spouse, ... 6.96ii.53.273.
"Thy Pigmy Children, and thy tiny Spouse, ... 6.96ii.53.273.
"The Baby Play-things that adorn thy House, ... 6.96ii.54.273.
"Thy Bark a Bean-shell, and a Straw thy Oar? .... 6.96ii.58.273.
"Thy Bark a Bean-shell, and a Straw thy Oar? .... 6.96ii.58.273.
"Or in thy Box, now bounding on the Main? .... 6.96ii.59.273.
"Shall I ne'er bear thy self and House again? .... 6.96ii.60.273.
"A Dish of Tea like Milk-Pail on thy Head? .... 6.96ii.68.273.
"How chase the Mite that bore thy Cheese away, ... 6.96ii.69.273.
O squander not thy Grief, those Tears command .... 6.96ii.75.273.
And *Europe* taste thy Sorrows in a Dish. .... 6.96ii.78.274.
And let each grateful *Houyhnhnm* neigh thy Praise. .... 6.96iii.4.274.
By thy sweet Sojourn in those virtuous Climes, ... 6.96iii.6.274.
Where reign our Sires! There, to thy Countrey's Shame, ... 6.96iii.7.274.
Our Labours here must touch thy gen'rous Heart, ... 6.96iii.23.275.
And *Europe* taste thy Sorrows in her Dish. .... 6.96ii.78A.274.
WELCOME, thrice welcome to thy native Place! .... 6.96iv.1.276.
Have I for this thy tedious Absence born, ... 6.96iv.3.276.
And wak'd and wish'd whole Nights for thy Return? .... 6.96iv.4.276.
'Tis said, that thou shouldst cleave unto thy Wife; .... 6.96iv.9.276.
Hear and relent! hark, how thy Children moan; .... 6.96iv.11.276.
Be kind at least to these, they are thy own: .... 6.96iv.12.276.
Thy Christian Seed, our mutual Flesh and Bone: .... 6.96iv.17.276.
Be kind at least to these, they are thy own. .... 6.96iv.18.276.
At least thy Consort's cleaner than thy *Groom.* .... 6.96iv.28.277.
At least thy Consort's cleaner than thy *Groom.* .... 6.96iv.28.277.
Why then that dirty Stable-boy thy Care? .... 6.96iv.29.277.
(Studious in ev'ry Thing to please thy Taste) .... 6.96iv.50.277.
'Tis all my Pleasure thy past Toil to know, ... 6.96iv.63.278.
At ev'ry Danger pants thy Consort's Breast, ... 6.96iv.65.278.
But when thy Torrent quench'd the dreadful Blaze, ... 6.96iv.71.278.
For when he sign'd thy Death, he sentenc'd me. .... 6.96iv.78.278.
And all thy Dangers I weep o'er again! .... 6.96iv.86.278.
Teach me to wooe thee by thy best-lov'd Name! .... 6.96iv.96.279.
Or *Glumglum's* humbler Title sooth thy Ear: .... 6.96iv.104.279.
Thy Children's Noses all should twang the same. .... 6.96iv.108.279.
But send him, honest *Job,* thy *Wife.* .... 6.101.34.291.
'Tis generous, *Tibald!* in thee and thy brothers, ... 6.105v.1.302.
For who will help us e'er to read thy own? .... 6.105v.4.302.
Thro' thy blest Shades (La Source) I seem to rove .... 6.106ii.2.307.
I see thy fountains fall, thy waters roll .... 6.106ii.3.307.
I see thy fountains fall, thy waters roll .... 6.106ii.3.307.
And breath the Zephyrs that refresh thy Grove .... 6.106ii.4.307.
Or thy grieved country's copper chains unbind; .... 6.106iv.6.307.
From thy Bœotia, lo! the fog retires, ... 6.106iv.9.307.
And worthy of thy *prince's ear.* .... 6.106v.3A.308.
Thy silent whisper is the sacred test.] .... 6.107.32.311.
Just of thy word, in ev'ry thought sincere, ... 6.109.5.314.
Go, and exalt thy Moral to Divine. .... 6.109.10.314.
Just of thy word, and in each thought sincere, ... 6.109.5B.314.
Thy Country's friend, but more of Human kind. .... 6.113.2.320.
Thy martial spirit, or thy Social love! .... 6.113.8.320.
Thy martial spirit, or thy Social love! .... 6.113.8.320.
Thy prudence, MOORE, is like that Irish Wit, ... 6.116i.3.325.
But, gentle COLLEY, should thy verse prevail, ... 6.116vi.3.327.
Wherefore thy claim resign, allow his right; .... 6.116vi.5.327.
Did MILTON'S Prose, O CHARLES, thy Death defend .... 6.116viii.1.328.
The murd'rous Critic has aveng'd thy Murder. .... 6.116viii.6.328.
May Heav'n, dear Father! now, have *all* thy Heart. .... 6.123.2.343.
Unblam'd thro' Life, lamented in thy End. .... 6.125.8.350.
These are Thy Honours! not that here thy Bust .... 6.125.9.350.
These are Thy Honours! not that here thy Bust .... 6.125.9.350.
Is mix'd with Heroes, or with Kings thy dust; .... 6.125.10.350.
Belov'd thro' Life, lamented in thy End .... 6.125.8B.350.
Those are Thy Honours! not that here thy Bust .... 6.125.9A.350.
Those are Thy Honours! not that here thy Bust .... 6.125.9A.350.
Go then indulge thy age in Wealth and ease .... 6.130.11.358.
Alas what *ease* those furies of thy life .... 6.130.15.358.
But in thy Poet wretched as a King! .... 6.131i.2.360.
Thy Realm disarm'd of each offensive Tool, ... 6.131i.3.360.
Thy happy Reign all other Discord quells; .... 6.131i.5.360.
Apollo's genuine Sons thy fame shall raise .... 6.131i.7.360.
And all Mankind, but Cibber, sing thy praise. .... 6.131i.8.360.
Cibber! write all thy Verses upon Glasses, ... 6.131ii.1.360.
This weeping marble had not ask'd thy Tear, ... 6.132.5.362.

THY (CONTINUED)

Who last, beneath thy Vengeance, press'd the Plain; ... Il.16.848.276.
When Heav'n itself thy fatal Fury led, ... Il.16.849.276.
Defies thy Lance; not fated yet to fall; ... Il.16.864.277.
Thy Friend, thy greater far, it shall withstand, ... Il.16.865.277.
Thy Friend, thy greater far, it shall withstand, ... Il.16.865.277.
(Thy Brother, *Hecuba!* from *Dymas* spring; ... Il.16.875.277.
And in *Patroclus'* Blood efface thy Shame. ... Il.16.882.277.
Perhaps *Apollo* shall thy Arms succeed, ... Il.16.883.277.
And Heav'n ordains him by thy Lance to bleed. ... Il.16.884.277.
There ends thy Glory! there the Fates untwine ... Il.16.950.280.
Apollo dreadful stops thy middle way; ... Il.16.952.280.
Thy Pride once promis'd, of subverting *Troy;* ... Il.16.1004.282.
And thy soft Pleasures serv'd with captive Dames! ... Il.16.1006.282.
Thy own *Achilles* cannot lend thee Aid; ... Il.16.1010.282.
Had twenty Mortals, each thy Match in Might, ... Il.16.1022.282.
Euphorbus next; the third mean Part thy own. ... Il.16.1025.282.
The Gods inspire it, and it sounds thy Death. ... Il.16.1027.283.
Black Fate hangs o'er thee, and thy Hour draws nigh; ... Il.16.1029.283.
Laugh'st thou not, *Jove!* from thy superior Throne, ... Il.17.19.288.
Presumptous Youth! like his shall be thy Doom, ... Il.17.33.289.
Go, wait thy Brother to the *Stygian* Gloom; ... Il.17.34.289.
Come, for my Brother's Blood repay thy own. ... Il.17.38.289.
His weeping Father claims thy destin'd Head, ... Il.17.39.289.
On these thy conquer'd Spoils I shall bestow, ... Il.17.41.289.
To wait thy Brother to the *Stygian* Gloom; ... Il.17.34A.289.
Since Battel is renounc'd, thy Thoughts employ ... Il.17.159.293.
What other Methods may preserve thy *Troy?* ... Il.17.160.293.
What from thy thankless Arms can we expect? ... Il.17.165.294.
Thy Friend *Sarpedon* proves thy base Neglect: ... Il.17.166.294.
Thy Friend *Sarpedon* proves thy base Neglect: ... Il.17.166.294.
I deem'd thee once the wisest of thy Kind, ... Il.17.191.294.
Ah wretched Man! unmindful of thy End! ... Il.17.231.296.
Thou stand'st, and Armies tremble at thy Sight ... Il.17.234.297.
As at *Achilles* self! Beneath thy Dart ... Il.17.235.297.
From thy tir'd Limbs unbrace *Pelides'* Arms! ... Il.17.244.297.
Alas! thy Friend is slain, and *Hector* wields ... Il.17.538.309.
Unite thy Force, my Friend, and we prevail. ... Il.17.557.310.
Poor as it is, some Off'ring to thy Shade. ... Il.17.607.312.
What *Grecian* now shall tremble at thy Name? ... Il.17.659.313.
If *Greece* must perish, we thy Will obey, ... Il.17.731.316.
Now, now, *Atrides!* cast around thy Sight, ... Il.17.737.317.
For sadder Tydings never touch'd thy Ear; ... Il.17.772.318.
Thy Eyes have witness'd what a fatal Turn! ... Il.17.773.318.
'Tis well (said *Ajax)* be it then thy Care ... Il.17.801.319.
Why mourns my Son? thy late-preferr'd Request ... Il.18.95.327.
Why mourns my Son? thy Anguish let me share, ... Il.18.97.327.
Thy Charms submitted to a mortal Love: ... Il.18.108.328.
E'er the sad Fruit of thy unhappy Womb ... Il.18.113.328.
The Host to succour, and thy Friends to save, ... Il.18.165.330.
Thy radiant Arms the *Trojan* Foe detains, ... Il.18.168.330.
Yet, yet awhile, thy gen'rous Ardor stay; ... Il.18.171.330.
Thy Friend's Disgrace, thy own eternal Shame! ... Il.18.218.332.
Thy Friend's Disgrace, thy own eternal Shame! ... Il.18.218.332.
Thy want of Arms (said *Iris)* well we know, ... Il.18.235.333.
E'er thy dear Relicks in the Grave are laid, ... Il.18.391.340.
Shall *Hector's* Head be offer'd to thy Shade; ... Il.18.392.340.
That, with his Arms, shall hang before thy Shrine, ... Il.18.393.340.
Their Lives effus'd around thy flaming Pyre. ... Il.18.396.340.
Bathe thy cold Face, and sob upon thy Breast! ... Il.18.398.340.
Bathe thy cold Face, and sob upon thy Breast! ... Il.18.398.340.
While *Trojan* Captives here thy Mourners stay, ... Il.18.399.340.
At last thy Will prevails: Great *Peleus'* Son ... Il.18.419.341.
Rises in Arms: Such Grace thy *Greeks* have won. ... Il.18.420.341.
To her the Artist-God. Thy Griefs resign, ... Il.18.531.347.
And claims thy Promise to be King of Kings. ... Il.19.122.377.
My martial Troops , my Treasures , are thy own: ... Il.19.138.377.
Whate'er *Ulysses* promis'd at thy Tent: ... Il.19.140.377.
Resume thy Arms, and shine again in War. ... Il.19.142.377.
To keep, or send the Presents, be thy Care; ... Il.19.145.377.
Stretch not henceforth, O Prince! thy sov'reign Might, ... Il.19.179.379.
To him the Monarch. Just is thy Decree, ... Il.19.183.379.
Thy Words give Joy, and Wisdom breathes in thee. ... Il.19.184.379.
These to select, *Ulysses,* be thy Care: ... Il.19.192.379.
Thy Praise it is in dreadful Camps to shine, ... Il.19.217.381.
Thy friendly Hand uprear'd me from the Plain, ... Il.19.313.385.
Thy sweet Society, thy winning Care, ... Il.19.337.386.
Thy sweet Society, thy winning Care, ... Il.19.337.386.
Is then *Achilles* now no more thy Care, ... Il.19.364.387.
Thy rage in safety thro' the Files of War: ... Il.19.453.391.
Nor ours the Fault, but God decrees thy Doom. ... Il.19.455.391.
Fell thy *Patroclus,* but by heav'nly Force. ... Il.19.457.391.
All were in vain—The Fates thy Death demand, ... Il.19.462.391.
From heav'nly *Venus* thou deriv'st thy Strain, ... Il.20.136.399.
Then lift thy Weapon for a noble Blow, ... Il.20.140.400.
Grant that beneath thy Lance *Achilles* dies, ... Il.20.218.403.
Sons he has many, those thy Pride may quell; ... Il.20.220.403.
Or, in reward of thy victorious Hand, ... Il.20.222.403.
Ev'n this, perhaps, will hardly prove thy Lot: ... Il.20.226.403.
The *Dardan* Prince, O *Neptune,* be thy Care; ... Il.20.360.410.
Henceforth beware, nor antedate thy Doom, ... Il.20.383.411.
Defrauding Fate of all thy Fame to come. ... Il.20.384.411.
Secure, no *Grecian* Force transcends thy own. ... Il.20.388.411.
Receives thee dead, tho' *Gygæ* boast thy Birth; ... Il.20.450.413.
Come, and receive thy Fate!, He spake no more. ... Il.20.498.415.
I know thy Force to mine superior far; ... Il.20.503.415.
Wretch! Thou hast scap'd again. Once more thy Flight ... Il.20.519.416.
But long thou shalt not thy just Fate withstand, ... Il.20.521.416.
Fly then inglorious! But thy Flight this Day ... Il.20.523.416.
To spare a Form, an Age so like thy own! ... Il.20.540.417.
Thy Life *Echeclus!* next the Sword bereaves, ... Il.20.549.417.
Thy well-known Captive, great *Achilles!* see, ... Il.21.84.425.
Once more *Lycaon* trembles at thy Knee; ... Il.21.85.425.
Who shar'd the Gifts of *Ceres* at thy Board, ... Il.21.87.425.
Whom late thy conqu'ring Arm to *Lemnos* bore, ... Il.21.88.425.
Now Sums immense thy Mercy shall repay. ... Il.21.91.425.

THY (CONTINUED)

Lo! *Jove* again submits me to thy Hands, ... Il.21.94.425.
Once more *Lycaon* trembling at thy Knee; ... Il.21.85A.425.
If ever yet soft Pity touch'd thy mind, ... Il.21.105.426.
Not the same Mother gave thy Suppliant Breath, ... Il.21.107.426.
With his, who wrought thy lov'd *Patroclus'* Death. ... Il.21.108.426.
He, far thy Better, was fore-doom'd to die, ... Il.21.117.426.
Thy bloated Corse, and suck thy goary Wound: ... Il.21.136.427.
Thy bloated Corse, and suck thy goary Wound: ... Il.21.136.427.
There no sad Mother shall thy Fun'rals weep, ... Il.21.137.427.
Now lift thy Arm, and try that Hero's Son! ... Il.21.178.429.
So ends thy Glory! Such the Fate they prove ... Il.21.201.429.
Sprung from a River didst thou boast thy Line, ... Il.21.203.429.
How durst thou vaunt thy wat'ry Progeny? ... Il.21.205.430.
'Tis not on me thy Rage should heap the Dead. ... Il.21.234.430.
Content, thy Slaughters could amaze a God. ... Il.21.238.430.
O sacred Stream! thy Word we shall obey; ... Il.21.241.431.
The Pow'r of Ocean first. Forbear thy Fear, ... Il.21.332.435.
O Son of *Peleus!* Lo thy Gods appear! ... Il.21.333.435.
Behold! from *Jove* descending to thy Aid, ... Il.21.334.435.
'Tis not thy Fate to glut his angry Wave. ... Il.21.337.435.
Nor breathe from Combate, nor thy Sword suspend, ... Il.21.339.435.
And *Hector's* Blood shall smoke upon thy Lance. ... Il.21.343.435.
Call then thy subject Streams, and bid them roar, ... Il.21.362.435.
From all thy Fountains swell thy wat'ry Store, ... Il.21.363.435.
From all thy Fountains swell thy wat'ry Store, ... Il.21.363.435.
Thy wasteful Arm: Assemble all thy Fires! ... Il.21.387.436.
Thy wasteful Arm: Assemble all thy Fires! ... Il.21.387.436.
Go, mighty in thy Rage! display thy Pow'r, ... Il.21.394.436.
Go, mighty in thy Rage! display thy Pow'r, ... Il.21.394.436.
O *Vulcan,* oh! what Pow'r resists thy Might? ... Il.21.418.437.
Ah—bend no more thy fiery Arms on me! ... Il.21.421.437.
Ah why, *Saturnia!* must thy Son engage ... Il.21.432.438.
What mov'd thy Madness, thus to disunite ... Il.21.458.440.
What wonder this, when in thy frantick Mood ... Il.21.460.440.
Thy impious Hand *Tydides'* Jav'lin bore, ... Il.21.462.440.
How far *Minerva's* Force transcends thy own? ... Il.21.479.441.
Corrects thy Folly thus by *Pallas'* Hand; ... Il.21.481.441.
Thus meets thy broken Faith with just Disgrace, ... Il.21.482.441.
Come, prove thy Arm! for first the War to wage, ... Il.21.512.443.
(Forgetful of my Wrongs, and of thy own) ... Il.21.515.443.
Thy Task it was, to feed the bellowing Droves ... Il.21.521.443.
Thy Force can match the great Earth-shaking Pow'r. ... Il.21.552.444.
Thy Pride to face the Majesty of Heav'n? ... Il.21.556.445.
The wretched Matron feels thy piercing Dart; ... Il.21.559.445.
Thy Sexe's Tyrant, with a Tyger's Heart? ... Il.21.560.445.
Thy certain Arrows pierce the savage Race? ... Il.21.562.445.
How dares thy Rashness on the Pow'rs divine ... Il.21.563.445.
Employ those Arms, or match thy Force with mine? ... Il.21.564.445.
Vain thy past Labour, and thy present vain: ... Il.22.20.453.
Vain thy past Labour, and thy present vain: ... Il.22.20.453.
While here thy frantick Rage attacks a God. ... Il.22.22.453.
And bloody Dogs grow fiercer from thy Gore. ... Il.22.58.455.
Valiant in vain! by thy curst Arm destroy'd: ... Il.22.60.455.
And spare thy self, thy Father, spare us all! ... Il.22.77.456.
And spare thy self, thy Father, spare us all! ... Il.22.77.456.
Save thy dear Life; or if a Soul so brave ... Il.22.78.456.
Neglect that Thought, thy dearer Glory save. ... Il.22.79.456.
While yet thy Father feels the Woes he bears, ... Il.22.81.456.
Or still'd thy infant Clamours at this Breast; ... Il.22.117.457.
Nor must thy Corps lye honour'd on the Bier, ... Il.22.122.458.
Exert thy Will: I give the Fates their Way. ... Il.22.240.465.
Falls by thy Hand, and mine! Nor Force, nor Flight ... Il.22.283.468.
Of this Distress, and sorrow'd in thy Flight: ... Il.22.296.468.
Jove by these Hands shall shed thy noble Life; ... Il.22.328.469.
No vile Dishonour shall thy Corse pursue; ... Il.22.329.470.
Now plight thy mutual Oath, I ask no more. ... Il.22.332.470.
Rouze then thy Forces this important Hour; ... Il.22.343.470.
Collect thy Soul, and call forth all thy Pow'r. ... Il.22.344.470.
Collect thy Soul, and call forth all thy Pow'r. ... Il.22.344.470.
Now hovers round, and calls thee to thy Death. ... Il.22.348.470.
Or what must prove my Fortune or thy own. ... Il.22.360.470.
End all my Country's Woes, deep buried in thy Heart! ... Il.22.368.471.
A God deceiv'd me; *Pallas,* 'twas thy Deed. ... Il.22.381.471.
Then low in Dust thy Strength and Glory lay'd. ... Il.22.420.472.
By thy own Soul! by those who gave thee Breath! ... Il.22.426.473.
Thy Rage, Implacable! too well I knew: ... Il.22.446.474.
Thee, *Hector!* last: Thy Loss (divinely brave) ... Il.22.542.478.
Oh had thy gentle Spirit past in Peace, ... Il.22.544.479.
While both thy Parents wept thy fatal Hour, ... Il.22.546.479.
While both thy Parents wept thy fatal Hour, ... Il.22.546.479.
Patient of Horrors, to behold thy Death? ... Il.22.555.479.
O *Hector,* late thy Parents Pride and Joy, ... Il.22.556.479.
Shall cry, "Begone! Thy Father feasts not here": ... Il.22.640.483.
Far from thy Parents' and thy Consort's Care, ... Il.22.655.483.
Far from thy Parents' and thy Consort's Care, ... Il.22.655.483.
All hail *Patroclus!* let thy honour'd Ghost ... Il.23.25.488.
The bloody *Hector* stretch'd before thy Feet. ... Il.23.28.488.
Their Lives effus'd around thy fun'ral Pyre. ... Il.23.32.488.
The grassy Mound, and clip thy sacred Hair. ... Il.23.56.489.
(O King of Men!) it claims thy royal Care, ... Il.23.61.489.
Now give thy Hand; for to the farther Shore ... Il.23.93.491.
That golden Urn thy Goddess Mother gave ... Il.23.107.491.
Where to the Day thy silver Fountains rise, ... Il.23.183.497.
Thy Altars stand, perfum'd with native Flow'rs! ... Il.23.185.497.
All hail, *Patroclus!* let thy vengeful Ghost ... Il.23.220.498.
Twelve *Trojan* Heroes offer'd to thy Shade; ... Il.23.223.498.
My Son! tho' youthful Ardor fire thy Breast, ... Il.23.375.505.
To guide thy Conduct, little Precept needs; ... Il.23.379.505.
Fear not thy Rivals, tho' for Swiftness known, ... Il.23.381.505.
Compare those Rivals Judgment, and thy own: ... Il.23.382.505.
While thy strict Hand his Fellows Head restrains, ... Il.23.410.506.
Tho' thy fierce Rival drove the matchless Steed ... Il.23.419.506.
Thy Lot, *Meriones,* the fourth was cast; ... Il.23.431.507.
So far *Antilochus!* thy Chariot flew ... Il.23.513.510.
Thy Tongue too hastily confers the Prize. ... Il.23.557.511.

THY (CONTINUED)

Just is thy thought, the King assenting cries, ... Od.4.197.129.
Thy voice, O King! with pleas'd attention heard, ... Od.4.213.129.
Thy cheeks, *Pisistratus*, the tears bedew, ... Od.4.253.131.
While pictur'd to thy mind appear'd in view ... Od.4.254.131.
Thy martial *Brother; on the *Phrygian* plain ... Od.4.255.131.
And charm attention, with thy copious praise: ... Od.4.260.131.
To crown thy various gifts, the sage assign'd ... Od.4.261.131.
Such, happy *Nestor!* was thy glorious doom; ... Od.4.289.132.
Around thee full of years, thy offspring bloom, ... Od.4.290.132.
The gifts of heav'n to guard thy hoary state. ... Od.4.292.132.
To move thy suit, *Telemachus*, delay, ... Od.4.295.133.
The storied labours of thy father's friend: ... Od.4.468.142.
Thy conduct ill deserves the praise of wise: ... Od.4.502.144.
Is death thy choice, or misery thy boast, ... Od.4.503.144.
Is death thy choice, or misery thy boast, ... Od.4.503.144.
Thy brave associates droop, a meagre train ... Od.4.505.144.
With famine pale, and ask thy care in vain? ... Od.4.506.144.
Whate'er thy title in thy native sky, ... Od.4.508.144.
Whate'er thy title in thy native sky, ... Od.4.508.144.
O Goddess! on thy aid my hopes rely: ... Od.4.532.146.
With me repair; and from thy warrior band ... Od.4.551.146.
Thy guilt absolv'd, a prosp'rous voyage gain. ... Od.4.638.149.
To the firm sanction of thy fate attend! ... Od.4.639.149.
Must view his billows white beneath thy oar, ... Od.4.645.150.
To thy long vows a safe return accord. ... Od.4.648.150.
To know, what known will violate thy peace: ... Od.4.662.150.
Thy breast will heave, and tears eternal flow. ... Od.4.664.150.
Whose arms with conquest in thy cause were crown'd, ... Od.4.668.150.
But lives a victim for thy vengeful sword; ... Od.4.736.153.
Thy patient ear hath heard me long relate ... Od.4.799.156.
Thus thy alternate; while with artful care ... Od.4.839.158.
If e'er *Ulysses* to thy fane prefer'd ... Od.4.1007.164.
And on the suitors let thy wrath descend. ... Od.4.1012.164.
Thy son, the Gods propitious will restore, ... Od.4.1063.167.
Is not already in thy soul decreed, ... Od.5.32.172.
Lov'd as thou art, thy free injunctions lay; ... Od.5.113.177.
And prosp'rous gales to waft thee on thy way. ... Od.5.216.182.
In peace shall land thee at thy native home. ... Od.5.220.182.
Some other motive, Goddess! sways thy mind, ... Od.5.223.182.
Dark as I am, unconscious of thy will. ... Od.5.230.182.
Lurks in the counsel of thy faithful friend; ... Od.5.242.183.
Is then thy home the passion of thy heart? ... Od.5.259.184.
Is then thy home the passion of thy heart? ... Od.5.259.184.
Thy heart might settle in this scene of ease, ... Od.5.265.184.
Might banish from thy mind an absent wife. ... Od.5.268.184.
Against *Ulysses* shall thy anger rise? ... Od.5.274.184.
Tho' well I see thy graces far above ... Od.5.277.184.
Thy loom, *Calypso!* for the future sails ... Od.5.329.187.
What I suggest thy wisdom will perform; ... Od.5.434.193.
Forsake thy float, and leave it to the storm: ... Od.5.435.193.
Strip off thy garments; *Neptune's* fury brave ... Od.5.436.193.
To reach *Phæacia* all thy nerves extend, ... Od.5.438.193.
There Fate decrees thy miseries shall end. ... Od.5.439.193.
This heav'nly Scarf beneath thy bosom bind, ... Od.5.440.193.
And live; give all thy terrors to the wind. ... Od.5.441.194.
Soon as thy arms the happy shore shall gain, ... Od.5.442.194.
Cast it far off, and turn thy eyes away. ... Od.5.445.194.
Thy pleaded reason, but consult with mine: ... Od.5.455.194.
Thy voice foretells me shall conclude my toil. ... Od.5.457.194.
Whate'er thy Fate, the ills our wrath could raise ... Od.5.484.195.
Shall last remember'd in thy best of days. ... Od.5.485.195.
I bend, a suppliant at thy wat'ry throne, ... Od.5.569.199.
Let then thy waters give the weary rest, ... Od.5.574.200.
Oh indolent! to waste thy hours away! ... Od.6.29.205.
Thy spousal ornament neglected lies; ... Od.6.31.205.
Haste, to the limpid stream direct thy way, ... Od.6.35.206.
Haste to the stream! companion of thy care ... Od.6.37.206.
Lo I thy steps attend, thy labours share. ... Od.6.38.206.
Lo I thy steps attend, thy labours share. ... Od.6.38.206.
See! from their thrones thy kindred monarchs sigh! ... Od.6.40.206.
Say, with thy garments shall I bend my way ... Od.6.71.208.
(Imperial Virgin) boast thy glorious birth, ... Od.6.176.217.
So breathes an air divine! But if thy race ... Od.6.181.218.
Be mortal, and this earth thy native place, ... Od.6.182.218.
Blest are the brethren who thy blood divide, ... Od.6.185.218.
Oh let soft pity touch thy gen'rous mind! ... Od.6.212.220.
Crown the chaste wishes of thy virtuous soul, ... Od.6.218.220.
On thy soft hours their choicest blessings shed, ... Od.6.219.220.
Blest with a husband be thy bridal bed, ... Od.6.220.220.
Blest be thy husband with a blooming race, ... Od.6.221.220.
To whom the Nymph: O stranger cease thy care, ... Od.6.227.220.
Wise is thy soul, but man is born to bear: ... Od.6.228.220.
Who breathes, must mourn: thy woes are from above. ... Od.6.232.221.
To cloath the naked, and thy way to guide— ... Od.6.235.221.
Lo, to the Palace I direct thy way: ... Od.6.304.225.
But hear, tho' wisdom in thy soul presides, ... Od.6.307.225.
Speaks from thy tongue and ev'ry action guides; ... Od.6.308.225.
But would'st thou soon review thy native plain? ... Od.6.347.228.
And to the lofty palace bend thy way: ... Od.6.362.229.
But to the Queen thy mournful tale disclose, ... Od.6.373.229.
So shalt thou view with joy thy natal shore, ... Od.6.375.230.
Forsook by thee, in vain I sought thy aid ... Od.6.387.230.
Go then secure, thy humble suit prefer, ... Od.7.97.238.
And owe thy country and thy friends to her. ... Od.7.98.238.
And owe thy country and thy friends to her. ... Od.7.98.238.
To thee, thy consort, and this royal train, ... Od.7.196.245.
But wait thy word, the gentle guest to grace ... Od.7.218.247.
Alas! a mortal, like thy self, am I; ... Od.7.283.249.
Lest rash suspicion might alarm thy mind: ... Od.7.393.256.
Such as thou art, thy thought and mine were one, ... Od.7.399.256.
But if reluctant, who shall force thy stay? ... Od.7.403.256.
'Till then, let slumber close thy careful eyes; ... Od.7.406.256.
Where thy soul rests, and labour is no more. ... Od.7.410.257.
Far as *Eubæa* tho' thy country lay, ... Od.7.411.257.
Dumb be thy voice, and mute th' harmonious string; ... Od.8.94.267.

THY (CONTINUED)

Father, arise! for thee thy port proclaims ... Od.8.159.271.
Wide wanders, *Laodame*, thy erring tongue, ... Od.8.175.271.
O forward to proclaim thy soul unwise! ... Od.8.184.272.
Thy signal throw transcends the utmost bound ... Od.8.223.274.
Well hast thou spoke, and well thy gen'rous tongue ... Od.8.269.277.
Warm are thy words, but warm without offence; ... Od.8.271.278.
Thy worth is known. Then hear our country's claim, ... Od.8.273.278.
When blest with ease thy woes and wand'rings end, ... Od.8.277.278.
Teach them thy consort, bid thy sons attend; ... Od.8.278.278.
Teach them thy consort, bid thy sons attend; ... Od.8.278.278.
Thy absent spouse neglectful of thy charms ... Od.8.335.281.
Thy absent spouse neglectful of thy charms ... Od.8.335.281.
Prefers his barb'rous *Sintians* to thy arms! ... Od.8.336.281.
Thy captives; I ensure the penal claim. ... Od.8.384.284.
Thy praise was just; their skill transcends thy praise. ... Od.8.420.286.
Thy praise was just; their skill transcends thy praise. ... Od.8.420.286.
And thou, *Euryalus*, redeem thy wrong: ... Od.8.431.287.
And if, he cry'd, my words affect thy mind, ... Od.8.442.287.
Far from thy mind those words, ye whirlwinds bear, ... Od.8.443.287.
To thy calm hours continu'd peace afford, ... Od.8.449.287.
O sole belov'd! command thy menial train ... Od.8.460.288.
Insolvable these gifts, thy care demands: ... Od.8.480.288.
Lest, in thy slumbers on the watry main, ... Od.8.481.288.
To thy fond wish thy long-expected shores, ... Od.8.500.289.
To thy fond wish thy long-expected shores, ... Od.8.500.289.
Whose worth the splendors of thy race adorns, ... Od.8.504.289.
My life, thy gift I boast! He said, and sate ... Od.8.511.290.
O more than man! thy soul the Muse inspires, ... Od.8.531.291.
The God himself inspires thy breast with flame: ... Od.8.544.291.
In ev'ry land, thy monument of praise. ... Od.8.546.292.
How to thy dome, *Deiphobus!* ascends ... Od.8.565.293.
Dumb be thy voice, and mute the tuneful string: ... Od.8.586.294.
Thy Lay too deeply moves: then cease the lay, ... Od.8.589.294.
Say what thy birth, and what the name you bore, ... Od.8.597.294.
Say why the fate the *Troy* awak'd thy cares, ... Od.8.629.297.
Why heav'd thy bosom, and why flow'd thy tears? ... Od.8.630.297.
Why heav'd thy bosom, and why flow'd thy tears? ... Od.8.630.297.
As first in virtue, these thy realms obey! ... Od.9.2.298.
Amid these joys, why seeks thy mind to know ... Od.9.11.301.
Low at thy knee thy succour we implore; ... Od.9.317.319.
Low at thy knee thy succour we implore; ... Od.9.317.319.
Cyclop! since human flesh has been thy feast, ... Od.9.408.322.
We to thy shore the precious freight shall bear, ... Od.9.412.323.
The sons of men shall ne'er approach thy shore, ... Od.9.415.323.
Declare thy name; not mortal is this juice, ... Od.9.421.323.
Thy promis'd boon, O *Cyclop!* now I claim, ... Od.9.431.323.
When all thy wretched crew have felt my pow'r, ... Od.9.437.324.
Or thieves insidious thy fair flock surprize? ... Od.9.483.325.
"To *Jove* or to thy father *Neptune* pray." ... Od.9.489.326.
Thy fleecy fellows usher to their bow'r. ... Od.9.530.328.
Thou mov'st, as conscious of thy master's woe! ... Od.9.532.328.
Oh! didst thou feel for thy afflicted Lord, ... Od.9.535.328.
Thou meditat'st thy meal in yonder cave; ... Od.9.560.329.
Thy barb'rous breach of hospitable bands, ... Od.9.563.329.
Thy sounding voice directs his aim again; ... Od.9.583.330.
Cyclop! if any, pitying thy disgrace, ... Od.9.587.330.
From that vast bulk dislodge thy bloody mind, ... Od.9.612.332.
And if th' unhappy *Cyclop* be thy Son; ... Od.9.620.332.
To thwart thy passage, and repel thy fleet? ... Od.10.72.342.
To thwart thy passage, and repel thy fleet? ... Od.10.72.342.
For *Greece*, for home, and all thy soul held dear? ... Od.10.74.343.
Thy fleet accurs'd to leave our hallow'd land. ... Od.10.84.343.
We went, *Ulysses!* (such was thy command) ... Od.10.295.357.
O King belov'd of *Jove!* thy servant spare, ... Od.10.315.359.
And ah, thy self the rash attempt forbear! ... Od.10.316.359.
Here feast and loiter, and desert thy train. ... Od.10.322.360.
O blind to fate! what led thy steps to rove ... Od.10.335.360.
Sooner shalt thou, a stranger to thy shape, ... Od.10.340.360.
Fall prone their equal: First thy danger know, ... Od.10.341.360.
Now hear her wicked arts. Before thy eyes ... Od.10.345.360.
Draw forth and brandish thy refulgent sword, ... Od.10.350.361.
Nor shun the blessing proffer'd to thy arms, ... Od.10.353.361.
So shall thy tedious toils a respite find, ... Od.10.355.361.
And thy lost friends return to humankind. ... Od.10.356.361.
Hence, to thy fellows! (dreadful she began) ... Od.10.381.363.
O more than human! tell thy race, thy name. ... Od.10.388.363.
O more than human! tell thy race, thy name. ... Od.10.388.363.
Not mortal thou, nor mortal is thy brain. ... Od.10.390.363.
Ulysses? oh! thy threat'ning fury cease, ... Od.10.395.363.
Sheath thy bright sword, and join our hands in peace; ... Od.10.396.363.
Beneath thy charms when my companions groan, ... Od.10.401.363.
To share thy feast-rites, or ascend thy bed; ... Od.10.404.364.
To share thy feast-rites, or ascend thy bed; ... Od.10.404.364.
That, all unarm'd, thy vengeance may have vent, ... Od.10.405.364.
Swear, in thy soul no latent frauds remain, ... Od.10.409.364.
To quaff thy bowls, or riot in thy feasts. ... Od.10.454.365.
To quaff thy bowls, or riot in thy feasts. ... Od.10.454.365.
Me wou'dst thou please? for them thy cares imploy, ... Od.10.455.365.
Haste to thy vessel on the sea-beat shore, ... Od.10.477.366.
Unload thy treasures, and thy gally moor; ... Od.10.478.366.
Unload thy treasures, and thy gally moor; ... Od.10.478.366.
Then bring thy friends, secure from future harms, ... Od.10.479.366.
And in our grotto's stow thy spoils and arms. ... Od.10.480.366.
What other joy can equal thy return? ... Od.10.497.367.
Be mindful, Goddess, of thy promise made; ... Od.10.570.370.
If but a moment parted from thy eyes, ... Od.10.574.370.
Ah hope not yet to breathe thy native air! ... Od.10.578.370.
Far other journey first demands thy care; ... Od.10.579.370.
Thy fated road (the magic Pow'r reply'd) ... Od.10.598.372.
The northern winds shall wing thee on thy way. ... Od.10.601.372.
There fix thy vessel in the lonely bay, ... Od.10.606.373.
First draw thy faulchion, and on ev'ry side ... Od.10.614.374.
With promis'd off'rings on thy native shore; ... Od.10.621.374.
A sable ram, the pride of all thy breed. ... Od.10.625.374.
Be next thy care the sable sheep to place ... Od.10.628.374.

THY (CONTINUED)

The presence of thy guest shall best reward ..... Od.15.587.98.
(If long thy stay) the absence of my Lord. ..... Od.15.588.98.
Hard task, he cries, thy virtue gives thy friend, ... Od.16.69.105.
Hard task, he cries, thy virtue gives thy friend, ... Od.16.69.105.
'Till then, thy guest amid the rural train ..... Od.16.81.106.
At once to pity and resent thy wrong. ..... Od.16.94.107.
Say, do thy subjects in bold faction rise, ... Od.16.99.107.
Or are thy brothers, who should aid thy pow'r, ... Od.16.101.107.
Or are thy brothers, who should aid thy pow'r, ... Od.16.101.107.
Why to thy god-like son this long disguise? ..... Od.16.181.112.
Stand forth reveal'd: with him thy cares employ ..... Od.16.182.112.
Against thy foes; be valiant, and destroy! ..... Od.16.183.112.
To combat by thy side, thy guardian pow'r. ..... Od.16.185.112.
To combat by thy side, thy guardian pow'r. ..... Od.16.185.112.
Far other vests thy limbs majestic grace, ... Od.16.198.113.
Far other glories lighten from thy face! ..... Od.16.199.113.
If heav'n be thy abode, with pious care ..... Od.16.200.113.
Lo! gifts of labour'd gold adorn thy shrine, ... Od.16.202.113.
To win thy grace: O save us, pow'r divine! ..... Od.16.203.113.
I am thy father. O my son! my son! ..... Od.16.206.114.
That father, for whose sake thy days have run ..... Od.16.207.114.
Give to thy father but a father's claim: ..... Od.16.223.114.
O'er earth (returns the Prince) resounds thy name, ... Od.16.262.117.
Thy well-try'd wisdom, and thy martial fame, ... Od.16.263.117.
Thy well-try'd wisdom, and thy martial fame, ... Od.16.263.117.
Yet at thy words I start, in wonder lost; ..... Od.16.264.117.
Bear it my son! repress thy rising rage: ..... Od.16.295.119.
Bear it my son! howe'er thy heart rebel. ..... Od.16.297.120.
But by my blood that in thy bosom glows, ... Od.16.322.121.
The secret that thy father lives, retain ..... Od.16.324.121.
Lock'd in thy bosom from the houshold train; ..... Od.16.325.121.
Thy wealth in riot, the delay enjoy. ..... Od.16.339.122.
And cries aloud, Thy son, oh Queen returns: ..... Od.16.355.123.
Mistaking fame proclaims thy generous mind; ..... Od.16.436.128.
Thy deeds denote thee of the basest kind. ..... Od.16.437.128.
Who sav'd thy father with a friendly part? ..... Od.16.443.128.
O prudent Princess! bid thy soul confide. ..... Od.16.453.129.
Thy mandate born, my soul disdain'd to stay. ..... Od.16.489.130.
Thy father's fate, and tell me all thy own. ..... Od.17.55.135.
Thy father's fate, and tell me all thy own. ..... Od.17.55.135.
From death and treason to thy arms restor'd. ..... Od.17.59.135.
With all thy handmaids thank th' immortal Pow'rs; ..... Od.17.61.135.
Just thy advice, (the prudent Chief rejoin'd) ..... Od.17.216.142.
Or we perhaps might take him off thy hands. ..... Od.17.261.144.
Yet hear me! if thy impudence but dare ..... Od.17.268.145.
Approach yon walls, I prophecy thy fare: ..... Od.17.269.145.
Dearly, full dearly shalt thou buy thy bread, ... Od.17.270.145.
With many a footstool thund'ring at thy head. ..... Od.17.271.145.
Some rude insult thy rev'rend age may bear; ..... Od.17.330.147.
Just is, oh friend, thy caution, and addrest ..... Od.17.332.147.
And is this present, swineherd! of thy hand? ..... Od.17.450.155.
Thy passion, Prince, belies thy knowing mind. ..... Od.17.459.155.
Thy passion, Prince, belies thy knowing mind. ..... Od.17.459.155.
To love *Ulysses* is to raise thy hate. ..... Od.17.473.156.
Thanks to thy care! whose absolute command ..... Od.17.480.156.
To give another's is thy hand so slow? ..... Od.17.486.156.
And dumb for ever be thy sland'rous tongue! ..... Od.17.546.159.
Peace wretch! and eat thy bread without offence, ... Od.17.568.160.
Unblest thy hand! if in this low disguise ..... Od.17.576.160.
A private audience if thy grace impart, ... Od.17.602.161.
Thy other wants her subjects shall supply. ..... Od.17.641.163.
These sons of murder thirst thy life to take; ..... Od.17.674.165.
O guard it, guard it, for thy servant's sake! ..... Od.17.675.165.
Hence dotard, hence! and timely speed thy way, ... Od.18.14.167.
Lest dragg'd in vengeance, thou repent thy stay; ..... Od.18.15.167.
Lest I imprint my vengeance in thy blood; ..... Od.18.29.168.
Gird well thy loins, approach, and feel my might: ..... Od.18.37.168.
Who casts thy mangled ears and nose a prey ..... Od.18.98.171.
With ev'ry blessing crown thy happy hours! ..... Od.18.138.173.
Our freedom to thy prowess'd arm we owe ..... Od.18.139.173.
From bold intrusion of thy coward foe; ..... Od.18.140.173.
A beam of glory o'er thy future day! ..... Od.18.148.173.
Such was thy father! an imperial state, ... Od.18.153.173.
Then hear my words, and grave them in thy mind! ..... Od.18.156.173.
Thy soul, *Penelope,* from heav'n inspires; ..... Od.18.188.175.
Thy husband's wonder, and thy son's to raise, ... Od.18.191.175.
Thy husband's wonder, and thy son's to raise, ... Od.18.191.175.
Go warn thy son, nor be the warning vain, ... Od.18.201.176.
That warmth of soul that urg'd thy younger years? ..... Od.18.256.179.
Thy riper days no growing worth impart, ... Od.18.257.179.
Thy well-knit frame unprofitably strong, ... Od.18.259.179.
Beneath thy roof, and cou'dst thou tamely stand? ..... Od.18.264.179.
Thy finish'd charms, all *Greece* would own thy sway, ... Od.18.288.180.
Thy finish'd charms, all *Greece* would own thy sway, ... Od.18.288.180.
Dispeopling realms to gaze upon thy eyes: ..... Od.18.290.180.
Thy arms, (he cry'd) perhaps to find a grave: ..... Od.18.304.181.
Resign, and happy be thy bridal day! ..... Od.18.314.182.
Yet never, never from thy dome we move, ... Od.18.333.184.
Oh whither wanders thy distemper'd brain, ... Od.18.375.185.
Is it that vanquish'd *Irus* swells thy mind? ..... Od.18.381.186.
Who shortning with a storm of blows thy stay, ... Od.18.383.186.
Thy Lord shall curb that insolence of tongue; ..... Od.18.386.186.
But idly thus thy soul prefers to live, ... Od.18.408.188.
Beneath my labours how thy wond'ring eyes ..... Od.18.416.189.
No, thy ill-judging thoughts the brave disgrace; ..... Od.18.422.189.
But oft revolve the vision in thy heart: ..... Od.19.51.195.
Nor think thy self exempt: that rosy prime ..... Od.19.100.197.
And her lov'd Lord unplume thy tow'ring pride. ..... Od.19.104.197.
Yet him, my guest, thy venom'd rage hath stung; ..... Od.19.115.198.
Thy head shall pay the forfeit of thy tongue! ..... Od.19.116.198.
Thy head shall pay the forfeit of thy tongue! ..... Od.19.116.198.
Thy name, thy lineage, and thy natal land. ..... Od.19.126.198.
Thy name, thy lineage, and thy natal land. ..... Od.19.126.198.
Thy name, thy lineage, and thy natal land. ..... Od.19.126.198.
In wavy gold thy summer vales are dress'd; ..... Od.19.131.199.

THY (CONTINUED)

Thy autumns bend with copious fruit oppress'd: ..... Od.19.132.199.
And fish of ev'ry fin thy seas afford: ..... Od.19.134.199.
But, stranger! as thy days seem full of fate, ... Od.19.184.200.
Divide discourse, in turn thy birth relate: ..... Od.19.185.200.
Thy Port asserts thee of distinguish'd race; ..... Od.19.186.200.
Stranger! that e'er thy hospitable roof ..... Od.19.253.207.
With all thy wants the name of poor shall end; ..... Od.19.290.209.
Envy shall sicken at thy vast reward. ..... Od.19.357.211.
Conscious of worth revil'd, thy gen'rous mind ..... Od.19.438.216.
In thy whole form *Ulysses* seems exprest: ..... Od.19.443.216.
Thy milky founts my infant lips have drain'd; ..... Od.19.562.224.
And have the Fates thy babling age ordain'd ..... Od.19.563.224.
To violate the life thy youth sustain'd? ..... Od.19.564.224.
At length return'd, some God inspires thy breast ..... Od.19.567.224.
To know thy King, and here I stand confest. ..... Od.19.568.224.
Reserve, the treasure of thy inmost mind: ..... Od.19.570.224.
With their lewd mates, thy undistinguish'd age ..... Od.19.573.224.
What words, my son, have pass'd thy lips severe? ..... Od.19.576.224.
When heav'n, auspicious to thy right avow'd, ... Od.19.579.224.
Shall prostrate to thy sword the Suitor-crowd; ..... Od.19.580.224.
Thy aid avails me not, the Chief reply'd; ..... Od.19.583.224.
Suffice it thee thy Monarch to conceal. ..... Od.19.586.224.
View in this plumy form thy victor Lord; ..... Od.19.643.227.
In all thy speech what pleasing force I find! ..... Od.19.688.229.
O'er my suspended woe thy words prevail, ... Od.19.689.229.
Of wounded honour, and thy rage restrain. ..... Od.20.24.233.
Not fiercer woes thy fortitude cou'd foil, ... Od.20.25.233.
When the brave partners of thy ten years toil ..... Od.20.26.233.
Beneath thy palace-roof forget thy care; ..... Od.20.43.234.
Beneath thy palace-roof forget thy care; ..... Od.20.43.234.
Blest in thy Queen! blest in thy blooming heir! ..... Od.20.44.234.
Blest in thy Queen! blest in thy blooming heir! ..... Od.20.44.234.
Just is thy kind reproach (the chief rejoin'd) ..... Od.20.47.234.
Or if by *Jove's,* and thy auxiliar aid, ... Od.20.51.234.
Inspires thy counsels, and thy toils attends. ..... Od.20.58.235.
Inspires thy counsels, and thy toils attends. ..... Od.20.58.235.
In me affianc'd, fortify thy breast, ... Od.20.59.235.
Tho' myriads leagu'd thy rightful claim contest; ..... Od.20.60.235.
And edge thy sword to reap the glorious field. ..... Od.20.62.235.
Diana! speed thy deathful ebon dart, ... Od.20.72.235.
So *Pandarus,* thy hopes, three orphan fair ..... Od.20.78.236.
Thy self untimely and thy consort dy'd, ... Od.20.80.236.
Thy self untimely and thy consort dy'd, ... Od.20.80.236.
Thy shaft, and send me joyful to the dead: ..... Od.20.95.237.
Nor threats, thy bold intrusion will reclaim. ..... Od.20.228.244.
And spin thy future with a whiter clue! ..... Od.20.250.245.
Unpiteous of the race thy will began, ... Od.20.253.245.
The fool of fate, thy manufacture, man, ... Od.20.254.245.
Upbraids thy pow'r, thy wisdom, or thy will: ..... Od.20.258.245.
Upbraids thy pow'r, thy wisdom, or thy will: ..... Od.20.258.245.
Upbraids thy pow'r, thy wisdom, or thy will: ..... Od.20.258.245.
To whom the Chief: In thy capacious mind ..... Od.20.283.247.
Thy wish produc'd in act, with pleas'd survey, ... Od.20.290.247.
Thy wond'ring eyes shall view: his rightful reign ..... Od.20.291.247.
No vulgar roof protects thy honour'd age; ..... Od.20.329.249.
This dome a refuge to thy wrongs shall be, ... Od.20.330.249.
Had not th' inglorious wound thy malice aim'd ..... Od.20.373.251.
Nor shou'd thy Sire a Queen his daughter boast, ... Od.20.376.251.
Thy charity we praise, but not thy choice; ..... Od.20.450.255.
Thy charity we praise, but not thy choice; ..... Od.20.450.255.
What words ill-omen'd from thy lips have fled? ..... Od.21.176.268.
Thy coward function ever is in fear; ..... Od.21.177.268.
Philætius thus. Oh were thy word not vain? ..... Od.21.205.269.
Thy master's weapon to his hand convey. ..... Od.21.251.272.
To thy strict charge, *Philætius!* we consign ..... Od.21.256.272.
Is common sense quite banish'd from thy breast? ..... Od.21.310.274.
And much thy betters wine can overthrow: ..... Od.21.316.274.
Retire oh Queen! thy houshold task resume, ... Od.21.377.277.
Tend, with thy maids, the labors of the loom; ..... Od.21.378.278.
To thy own dogs a prey thou shalt be made; ..... Od.21.395.279.
Young as I am, thy Prince's vengeful hand ..... Od.21.401.279.
And bears thy fate, *Antinous,* on its wings: ..... Od.22.12.287.
Thy last of games unhappy hast thou play'd; ..... Od.22.32.288.
Thy erring shaft has made our bravest bleed, ... Od.22.33.288.
And death, unlucky guest, attends thy deed. ..... Od.22.34.288.
If, as thy words import, (he thus began) ..... Od.22.57.289.
Great are thy wrongs, and much hast thou sustain'd ..... Od.22.59.289.
In thy spoil'd Palace, and exhausted land; ..... Od.22.60.289.
Lo! at thy feet unjust *Antinous* bleeds. ..... Od.22.62.289.
To slay thy son, thy kingdoms to divide, ... Od.22.64.289.
To slay thy son, thy kingdoms to divide, ... Od.22.64.289.
Thy suppliant people, and receive their pray'r! ..... Od.22.67.290.
'Till then thy wrath is just— *Ulysses* burn'd ..... Od.22.71.290.
Thy spear, *Telemachus!* prevents th' attack, ... Od.22.107.291.
From thy own hand, of this detested deed? ..... Od.22.183.296.
There pass thy pleasing night, oh gentle swain! ..... Od.22.212.297.
To drive thy victims to the Suitors feast. ..... Od.22.216.297.
Come, ever welcome, and thy succour lend; ..... Od.22.225.297.
Thy frantic arm to lend *Ulysses* aid; ..... Od.22.236.298.
And with the sire's and son's commix thy blood. ..... Od.22.238.298.
Then lop thy whole posterity away; ..... Od.22.240.298.
Far hence thy banish'd consort shall we send; ..... Od.22.241.298.
With his, thy forfeit lands and treasures blend; ..... Od.22.242.298.
Thus, and thus only, shalt thou join thy friend. ..... Od.22.243.298.
What for thy country now, thy Queen, thy son? ..... Od.22.253.299.
What for thy country now, thy Queen, thy son? ..... Od.22.253.299.
What for thy country now, thy Queen, thy son? ..... Od.22.253.299.
Thy hand, *Telemachus,* it lightly raz'd; ..... Od.22.307.301.
Thy death, ennobled by *Ulysses'* spear. ..... Od.22.313.301.
There end thy pompous vaunts, and high disdain; ..... Od.22.318.301.
O gracious hear, nor let thy suppliant bleed; ..... Od.22.349.304.
Thy house, for me, remains; by me repress'd ..... Od.22.351.304.
Thy lying prophecies deceiv'd the land: ..... Od.22.358.304.
Against *Ulysses* have thy vows been made; ..... Od.22.359.304.
For them, thy daily orisons were paid: ..... Od.22.360.304.

THY (CONTINUED)

Yet more, ev'n to our bed thy pride aspires:	Od.22.361.304.
O King! to mercy be thy soul inclin'd,	Od.22.379.306.
A deed like this thy future fame would wrong,	Od.22.381.306.
Save then the Poet, and thy self reward;	Od.22.387.307.
And let thy son attest, nor sordid pay	Od.22.391.307.
If yet he breathes, permit thy son to give	Od.22.399.307.
O Prince! O Friend! lo here thy *Medon* stands;	Od.22.407.307.
Indecent joy, and feast thy secret soul.	Od.22.449.309.
Then she. In these thy kingly walls remain	Od.22.458.310.
Permit me first thy royal robes to bring:	Od.22.525.314.
Ah! whither wanders thy distemper'd mind?	Od.23.12.319.
Truth, by their high decree, thy voice forsakes,	Od.23.17.319.
Why must I wake to grieve, and curse thy shore?	Od.23.23.320.
But age is sacred, and we spare thy age.	Od.23.26.320.
Ulysses lives, his own *Ulysses* reigns:	Od.23.28.320.
He, he is thine! thy son, his latent guest	Od.23.31.320.
When Death had seiz'd her prey, thy son attends,	Od.23.45.321.
Thy heart had leap'd the Heroe to survey,	Od.23.49.321.
Haste, daughter haste, thy own *Ulysses* calls!	Od.23.54.321.
Thy every wish the bounteous Gods bestow,	Od.23.55.321.
He lives to thy *Telemachus* and thee!	Od.23.58.321.
Excess of joy disturbs thy wand'ring mind;	Od.23.60.321.
Flow from this tongue, then let thy servant die!	Od.23.80.322.
Wise is thy soul, but errors seize the wise;	Od.23.82.322.
Be that thy care, *Telemachus* replies,	Od.23.123.326.
Thy coward son degen'rate lag behind.	Od.23.128.326.
Thy lost *Ulysses* to his native shores,	Od.23.168.328.
Thy lost *Ulysses,* on this signal day?	Od.23.170.328.
If fears remain, or doubts distract thy heart?	Od.23.210.333.
Let not against thy spouse thine anger rise!	Od.23.216.333.
Pour out my soul, and dye within thy arms!	Od.23.226.333.
Since what no eye has seen thy tongue reveal'd,	Od.23.245.335.
To whom the Queen. Thy word we shall obey,	Od.23.273.336.
Why in this hour of transport wound thy ears,	Od.23.281.337.
Heav'n, by the *Theban* ghost, thy spouse decrees	Od.23.283.337.
Torn from thy arms, to sail a length of seas;	Od.23.284.337.
And full of days, thou gently yield thy breath;	Od.23.306.337.
Triumph, thou happy victor of thy woes!	Od.23.308.338.
Thou, for thy Lord; while me th' immortal pow'rs	Od.23.379.343.
Thou with thy Maids within the Palace stay,	Od.23.391.343.
With all thy full-blown honours cover'd round!	Od.24.44.350.
Historic marbles to record thy praise:	Od.24.46.350.
Thy praise eternal on the faithful load	Od.24.47.350.
Had with transmissive glories grac'd thy son.	Od.24.48.350.
Midst heaps of heroes in thy quarrel slain:	Od.24.54.350.
Then to the fleet we bore thy honour'd load,	Od.24.60.350.
Struck at the news, thy azure mother came;	Od.24.65.350.
And like a God adorn'd, thy earthly part expires.	Od.24.86.352.
Sunk what was mortal of thy mighty name,	Od.24.92.352.
We then collect thy snowy bones, and place	Od.24.93.352.
There we thy relicks, great *Achilles!* blend	Od.24.97.352.
Thy next-belov'd, *Antilochus'* remains.	Od.24.100.353.
Thy destin'd tomb, and cast a mighty mound;	Od.24.102.353.
And such thy honours, oh belov'd of heaven!	Od.24.116.353.
Dear to mankind thy fame survives, nor fades	Od.24.117.353.
Inform thy guest; for such I was of yore	Od.24.140.354.
His sudden rapture) in thy Consort blest!	Od.24.219.358.
Not more his wisdom, than her virtue, shin'd;	Od.24.220.358.
Not more his patience, than her constant mind.	Od.24.221.358.
Not such, oh *Tyndarus!* thy daughter's deed,	Od.24.226.358.
Great is thy skill, oh father! great thy toil,	Od.24.287.363.
Great is thy skill, oh father! great thy toil,	Od.24.287.363.
Thy careful hand is stamp'd on all the soil,	Od.24.288.363.
Thy squadron'd vineyards well thy art declare,	Od.24.289.363.
Thy squadron'd vineyards well thy art declare,	Od.24.289.363.
And not one empty spot escapes thy care.	Od.24.291.363.
On ev'ry plant and tree thy cares are shown,	Od.24.292.364.
Nothing neglected, but thy self alone.	Od.24.293.364.
Not for thy sloth, I deem thy Lord unkind;	Od.24.296.364.
Not for thy sloth, I deem thy Lord unkind;	Od.24.296.364.
Nor speaks thy form a mean or servile mind:	Od.24.297.364.
The same thy aspect, if the same thy care;	Od.24.299.364.
The same thy aspect, if the same thy care;	Od.24.299.364.
Who then thy master, say? and whose the land	Od.24.302.364.
So dress'd and manag'd by thy skilful hand?	Od.24.303.364.
This is the land; but ah! thy gifts are lost,	Od.24.326.365.
Thy ancient friend, oh stranger, is no more!	Od.24.329.365.
Full recompence thy bounty else had born;	Od.24.330.365.
But tell me, who thou art? and what thy race?	Od.24.348.365.
Thy town, thy parents, and thy native place?	Od.24.349.365.
Thy town, thy parents, and thy native place?	Od.24.349.365.
Thy town, thy parents, and thy native place?	Od.24.349.365.
What port receiv'd thy vessel from the main?	Od.24.351.365.
Or com'st thou single, or attend thy train?	Od.24.352.365.
Thy son, with twenty winters now grown old;	Od.24.376.367.
Thy son, so long desir'd, so long detain'd;	Od.24.377.367.
When by thy self and by *Anticlia* sent,	Od.24.386.367.
Yet by another sign thy offspring know;	Od.24.388.368.
And trod thy footsteps with unequal pace.	Od.24.391.368.
Be all the rest; and set thy soul at ease.	Od.24.416.369.
There wait thy faithful band of rural friends,	Od.24.419.369.
Could work this wonder: welcome to thy own!	Od.24.463.370.
And joys and happiness attend thy throne!	Od.24.464.370.
Who knows thy blest, thy wish'd return? oh say,	Od.24.465.371.
Who knows thy blest, thy wish'd return? oh say,	Od.24.465.371.
May I presume to search thy secret soul?	Od.24.542.374.
Declare thy purpose; for thy will is Fate.	Od.24.546.374.
Declare thy purpose; for thy will is Fate.	Od.24.546.374.
Is not thy thought my own? (the God replies	Od.24.547.374.
Had not long since thy knowing soul decreed,	Od.24.549.374.
'Tis done, and at thy will the Fates succeed.	Od.24.551.374.
Regard thy self, the living, and the dead.	Od.24.589.376.
Thy eyes, great father! on this battle cast,	Od.24.590.376.
Then whirling high, discharge thy lance in air.	Od.24.601.376.

THYESTES

To rich *Thyestes* next the Prize descends;	Il.2.134.134.
Where late in regal pomp *Thyestes* reign'd;	Od.4.690.151.

THYMAETES

The King the first; *Thymætes* at his side;	Il.3.193.200.

THYMBRAEUS

And from his Car the proud *Thymbræus* fell:	Il.11.416.53.

THYMBRAS'

And *Phrygia's* Horse, by *Thymbras'* ancient Wall;	Il.10.502.26.

THYMOETES
See THYMAETES.

THYRSIS

To *Thyrsis* Ear the tender Notes convey!	1.PAu.18A.82.
Thus, far from Thyrsis, to the Winds I mourn,	1.PAu.21A.82.
What have I said?—where-e'er my Thyrsis flies,	1.PAu.35A.82.
Come, Thyrsis, come; ah why this long Delay?	1.PAu.48A.83.
Thro' Rocks and Caves the Name of Thyrsis sounds,	1.PAu.49A.83.
Thyrsis, each Cave and ecchoing Rock rebounds,	1.PAu.50A.83.
Thyrsis, the Musick of that murm'ring Spring	1.PWi.1.88.

THYRSIS'

Curs'd be the Fields that cause my Thyrsis' Stay:	1.PAu.32A.82.

THYSELF

Know then thyself, presume not God to scan;	3.EOM2.1.53.
Then drop into thyself, and be a fool!	3.EOM2.30.59.
'Tis in thyself, and not in God's good Thing:	4.HAdv.103.83.
Spite of thyself a glorious minister!	4.1740.44.334.
And scream thyself as none e'er scream'd before!	5.DunB3.306.335.
What but thyself can now deserve my love?	6.25.12.77.

TIAR

A Tiar wreath'd her head with many a fold;	Od.10.651.375.

TIARA'S

His Feet on Sceptres and *Tiara's* trod,	2.TemF.153.266.

TIBALD

'Tis generous, *Tibald!* in thee and thy brothers,	6.105v.1.302.

TIBALDS

From slashing *Bentley* down to pidling *Tibalds.*	4.Arbu.164.108.
From daring Bentley down to pidling *Tibalds.*	4.Arbu.164B.108.

TIBBALD

Call *Tibbald Shakespear,* and he'll swear the Nine	4.2HE2.137.175.
"God save King Tibbald!" Grubstreet alleys roar.	5.DunA1.256.94.
Great Tibbald sate: The proud Parnassian sneer,	5.DunA2.5.97.
Great Tibbald nods: The proud Parnassian sneer,	5.DunA2.5A.97.
There hapless Shakespear, yet of Tibbald sore,	5.DunB1.133.279.
Can make a Cibber, Tibbald, or Ozell.	5.DunB1.286.290.
This suit dear TIBBALD kindly hatch;	6.116ii.6.326.
As fopling CIBBER, or Attorney T[IBBAL]D	6.116v.2.327.

TIBBALD'S

So humble, he has knock'd at *Tibbald's* door,	4.Arbu.372.123.
But chief, in Tibbald's monster-breeding breast;	5.DunA1.106.75.

TIBBALDS

From slashing *B[entle]y* down to pidling *T[ibbald]s:*	6.98.14.283.
From sanguine *Sew[ell]* down to pidling *T[ibbald]s:*	6.98.14A.283.

TIBERIUS

To raise *Tiberius Gracchus* Ghost;	6.10.72.26.

TIBULLUS

"My dear *Tibullus!*" if that will not do,	4.2HE2.143.175.

TICKELL

E'en sits him down, and writes to honest *T[ickell]*	6.49ii.14.140.
Tickell and *Addison* combine,	6.58.59.173.

TICKETS

Despise all loss of Tickets, or Codille;	3.Ep2.266A.71.
Disdains all loss of Tickets, or Codille;	3.Ep2.266.71.

TICKL'D

Touch'd to the Quick, and tickl'd at the Soul.	2.ChJM.277.27.

TICKLE

"He wins this Patron who can tickle best."	5.DunA2.188.124.
"He wins this Patron, who can tickle best."	5.DunB2.196.305.

TICKLED

Pleas'd with a rattle, tickled with a straw:	3.EOM2.276.88.

TICKLEST

The more thou ticklest, gripes his fist the faster.	5.DunA2.202.126.
The more thou ticklest, gripes his fist the faster.	5.DunB2.210.306.

TICKLETH

The Ducke sore tickleth his Erse Roote:	6.14i.18.42.

TICKLISH

It had been civil in these ticklish Times,	6.60.19.178.

TIDE
See TYDE.

A Tide of *Trojans* flows, and fills the Place;	1.TrES.206.457.
It so befel, in that fair Morning-tide,	2.ChJM.617.45.
There (so the Dev'l ordain'd) one Christmas-tide	3.Ep3.383.124.

TIDE (CONTINUED)
Pour the full Tide of Eloquence along, ... 4.2HE2.171.177.
"And fill'd the Cruet with the Acid Tide, ... 6.96ii.19.270.
And like a Mist she rose above the Tide; .... Il.1.471.110.
These rang'd in Order on the floating Tide, ... Il.2.628.157.
In forty Vessels cut the yielding Tide. .... Il.2.640.157.
Each leads ten Vessels thro' the yielding Tide. .... Il.2.754.161.
When thy tall Ships triumphant stem'd the Tide, ... Il.3.66.192.
The Shaft infix'd, and saw the gushing Tide: .... Il.4.179.230.
And slaughter'd Heroes swell the dreadful Tide. .... Il.4.515.246.
The Soul comes floating in a Tide of Gore. .... Il.4.537.247.
War with a fiercer Tide once more returns, ... Il.7.83.367.
Where *Celadon* rolls down his rapid Tide. .... Il.7.166.372.
And slaughter'd Heroes swell the dreadful Tide. .... Il.8.82.399.
Forth rush a Tide of *Greeks*, the Passage freed; .... Il.8.315.412.
And all the Gates sustain'd an equal Tide; .... Il.12.202.88.
Full in the Mouth is stopp'd the rushing Tide, ... Il.17.312.299.
That all shall know, *Achilles* swells the Tide. .... Il.18.162.330.
His loaded Shield bends to the rushing Tide; .... Il.21.265.431.
And winds his Course before the following Tide; .... Il.21.286.432.
High o'er the surging Tide, by Leaps and Bounds, ... Il.21.352.435.
Slow rolls the Chariot thro' the following Tide; .... Il.24.897.573.
Above restraint the tide of sorrow rose: .... Od.4.206.129.
Fast streams a tide from beauteous *Helen's* eyes; .... Od.4.250.131.
The nymphs withdrawn, at once into the tide .... Od.6.265.223.
Contract its mouth, and break the rushing tide. .... Od.10.104.345.
And in soft mazes rouls a silver Tide: .... Od.11.286.396.
Decree to plunge us in the whelming tide, ... Od.12.414.451.
Eumæus pours on high the purple tide; .... Od.14.135.42.
The fifth fair morn we stem th' *Egyptian* tide, ... Od.14.288.49.
My naked breast, and shot along the tide. .... Od.14.386.53.
To some new channel soon, the changeful tide .... Od.19.102.197.
By sage *Eumæus* born: the purple tide .... Od.20.318.248.

TIDES
Go, measure earth, weigh air, and state the tides; .... 3.EOM2.20.56.
Prescient, the tides or tempests to withstand, ... 3.EOM3.101.102.
Roll all their tides, then back their circles bring; .... 5.DunB3.56.323.
Roll all their tides, then back their circles bring. .... 6.9iii.2.21.
And into *Peneus* rolls his easy Tides; .... Il.2.911.167.
Pamper'd and proud, he seeks the wonted Tides, ... Il.6.654.359.
What Tides of Blood have drench'd *Scamander's* Shore? .... Il.7.394.383.
The Blood in brisker Tides began to roll, ... Il.17.251.297.
And breaks its Force, and turns the winding Tides. .... Il.17.842.321.
Attend her Way. Wide-opening part the Tides, ... Il.18.87.327.
And plenteous *Hermus* swells with Tides of Gold, ... Il.20.452.413.
Tire'd by the Tides, his Knees relax with Toil; .... Il.21.309.433.
And now the mingled Tides together flow: .... Il.24.639.563.
And *Wealth* incessant rolls her golden tides. .... Od.1.498.56.
The best I chuse, to waft thee o'er the tides. .... Od.2.334.77.
The bark, to waft thee o'er the swelling tides. .... Od.2.346.77.
And to the stern retreating roll the tides. .... Od.2.469.83.
Laertes' son: girt with circumfluous tides, ... Od.4.753.154.
Full thro' the narrow mouths descend the tides: .... Od.6.314.226.
Like man intelligent, they plow the tides, ... Od.8.606.295.
Safe as they pass, and safe repass the tides, ... Od.8.614.295.
She dreins the ocean with the refluent tides: .... Od.12.289.446.
And in the roaring whirlpools rush the tides. .... Od.12.510.457.
So they aloud: and tears in tides had run, ... Od.16.242.116.
The tides of life regain'd their azure course. .... Od.19.537.222.
The tides of lust that swell their boiling veins: .... Od.20.214.243.

TIDINGS
The heavy Tidings griev'd the Godlike Man; .... Il.4.242.232.
Let doleful Tidings greet his Mother's Ear, ... Il.14.591.191.
Or come sad Tidings from our native Land? .... Il.16.18.235.
The least glad tidings of my absent Lord? .... Od.17.123.137.

TIE
See TYE.
The common int'rest, or endear the tie: .... 3.EOM2.254.86.
But swear her first by those dread oaths that tie .... Od.10.357.361.

TIES
And Sacred Thirst of Sway; and all the Ties .... 1.TrSt.178.417.
Love, free as air, at sight of human ties, ... 2.ElAb.75.325.
But of this frame the bearings, and the ties, ... 3.EOM1.29.16.
Of this vast frame the bearings, and the ties, ... 3.EOM1.29A.16.
Reflection, Reason, still the ties improve, ... 3.EOM3.133.106.
This binds in Ties more easie, yet more strong, ... 6.19.67.64.
Urge all the Ties to former Service ow'd, ... Il.1.512.112.
The Ties of Faith, the sworn Alliance broke, ... Il.7.424.385.
Molus receiv'd, the Pledge of social Ties; .... Il.10.316.17.
Now Heav'n averse, our Hands from Battel ties, ... Il.14.79.161.
Once more their Minds in mutual Ties engage, ... Il.14.241.172.
For *Juno's* Love, and *Somnus'* pleasing Ties, ... Il.14.415.183.
By ev'ry Oath that Pow'rs immortal ties, ... Il.15.41.195.
Dear as he was, by ties of kindred bound, ... Od.10.519.368.
And these my *friends shall guard the sacred ties .... Od.18.72.170.

TIGHT
Or, when a tight, neat Girl, will serve the Turn, ... 4.HAdv.151.87.

TIL
'Til great *Sarpedon* tow'r'd amid the Field; .... 1.TrES.4A.449.

TILL
'Till in your Native Shades You tune the Lyre: .... 1.PSp.12.61.
Thus sung the Shepherds till th'Approach of Night, ... 1.PAu.97.87.
Till hov'ring o'er 'em sweeps the swelling Net. .... 1.W-F.104.160.
Till Conquest cease, and Slav'ry be no more: .... 1.W-F.408.192.
Till the freed *Indians* in their native Groves .... 1.W-F.409.192.
His Praise is lost, who stays till *All* commend; .... 1.EOC.475.292.
And found the springs that ne'er till then deny'd .... 1.TrFD.51.388.
Till all dissolving in the Trance we lay, ... 1.TrSP.61.396.
And Birds defer their Songs till thy Return: .... 1.TrSP.174.401.

TILL (CONTINUED)
Till he beheld, where from *Larissa's* Height .... 1.TrSt.530.432.
And waits 'till pleasing Slumbers seal his Eyes. .... 1.TrSt.538.433.
Till led by Fate, the *Theban's* Steps he treads, ... 1.TrSt.561.433.
Till Nature quicken'd by th'Inspiring Ray, ... 1.TrSt.586.434.
'Till bold *Sarpedon* rush'd into the Field; .... 1.TrES.4.449.
'Till by this Arm the Foe shall be repell'd; .... 1.TrES.86.453.
'Till poiz'd aloft, the resting Beam suspends 1.TrES.169.455
So stood the War, till *Hector's* matchless Might 1.TrES.171Z1.4
'Till *Hector* came, to whose Superior Might 1.TrES.173.456
Nods, groans, and reels, 'till with a crackling Sound 1.TrES.290.460
Nods to the Axe, till with a groaning Sound 1.TrES.290A.46
Till the proud Suitors, for their Crimes, afford .... 1.TrUl.62.468.
Till I beheld thy radiant Form once more, ... 1.TrUl.199.472.
'Till, what with Proofs, Objections, and Replies, ... 2.ChJM.143.21.
There let him lye, 'till his relenting Dame .... 2.ChJM.365.32.
There let him lye, 'till the relenting Dame 2.ChJM.365A.3
'Tis sung, he labour'd 'till the dawning Day, ... 2.ChJM.384.33.
'Till Coughs awak'd him near the Morning Light. .... 2.ChJM.421.35.
'Till the Bell toll'd, and All arose to Pray. .... 2.ChJM.425.35.
'Till both were conscious what each other meant. .... 2.ChJM.499.39.
'Till their wise Husbands, gull'd by Arts like these, ... 2.ChJM.667.47.
But 'till your Sight's establish'd, for a while, ... 2.ChJM.797.53.
Then preach till Midnight in your easie Chair; .... 2.ChWB.83.60.
Then, nor 'till then, the Veil's remov'd away, ... 2.ChWB.104.61
And Chiefs contend 'till all the Prize is lost! .... 2.RL5.108.208.
Till the bright Mountains prop th' incumbent Sky: .... 2.TemF.58.256.
Till to the Roof her tow'ring Front she rais'd. 2.TemF.261.27
Till to the Clouds their curling Heads aspire, ... 2.TemF.477.28
And wait, till 'tis no sin to mix with thine. 2.ElAb.176.334
Till ev'ry motion, pulse, and breath, be o'er; 2.ElAb.333.346
Till he's exalted to what state he wou'd? 3.EOM1.108Z2
'Till one Man's weakness grows the strength of all. 3.EOM2.252.85
'Till tir'd he sleeps, and Life's poor play is o'er! 3.EOM2.282.88
'Till then, Opinion gilds with varying rays .... 3.EOM2.283A.
And, 'till he ends the being, makes it blest; .... 3.EOM3.66.98.
Stays 'till we call, and then not often near; 3.EOM3.87.10
Each sex desires alike, 'till two are one. 3.EOM3.122.1
'Till common int'rest plac'd the sway in one. 3.EOM3.210.1
'Till then by Nature crown'd, each Patriarch sate, ... 3.EOM3.215.1
'Till drooping, sick'ning, dying, they began 3.EOM3.223.1
'Till Superstition taught the tyrant awe, ... 3.EOM3.246.1
'Till jarring int'rests of themselves create 3.EOM3.293.1
Short and but rare, 'till Man improv'd it all. 3.EOM4.116.1
'Till lengthen'd on to Faith, and unconfin'd, ... 3.EOM4.343.1
That ne'er shall answer till a Husband cool, ... 3.Ep2.261A.71.
That never answers till a Husband cools .... 3.Ep2.261B.71.
Who never answers till a Husband cools .... 3.Ep2.261C.71.
She, who ne'er answers till a Husband cools, ... 3.Ep2.261.71.
And men and dogs shall drink him 'till they burst. .... 3.Ep3.178.108.
'Till all the Dæmon makes his full descent, ... 3.Ep3.371.123.
Till Kings call forth th' Idea's of your mind, ... 3.Ep4.195.155.
Till Kings call forth th' Idea's of thy mind, ... 3.Ep4.195A.15
Ridotta sips and dances, till she see .... 4.HS1.47.9.
Till I cry'd out, "You prove yourself so able, ... 4.JD4.82.33.
Till Fancy colour'd it, and form'd a Dream. .... 4.JD4.189.43.
Oh blast it, South-winds! till a stench exhale, ... 4.HS2.27.55.
The *Robin-red-breast* till of late had rest, ... 4.HS2.37.57.
Till *Becca-ficos* sold so dev'lish dear .... 4.HS2.39.57.
More pleas'd to keep it till their friends could come, ... 4.HS2.95.61.
Better to keep it till their friends could come, ... 4.HS2.95A.61.
More pleas'd to keep it till their friends should come, ... 4.HS2.95B.61.
Till ev'ry Cuckold-maker's flea'd alive; .... 4.HAdv.48.79.
Till grown more frugal in his riper days, ... 4.Arbu.241.113.
Till like the Sea, they compass all the land, ... 4.JD2.85.141.
Those Suns of Glory please not till they set. .... 4.2HE1.22.195.
Nor dare to practise till they've learn'd to dance. 4.2HE1.184.21
Till friend with friend, and families at strife, ... 4.2HE1.253.21
Till Earth's extremes your mediation own, ... 4.2HE1.402.22
All this is mine but till I die; .... 4.HS6.10.251.
And kept you up so oft till one; .... 4.1HE7.48.271.
Grave, righteous S[andys] joggs on till, past belief, ... 4.1740.13.332*.
Till having done whate'er was fit or fine, ... 4.1740.37.334.
'Till genial Jacob, or a warm Third-day .... 5.DunA1.55.66.
For thee explain a thing till all men doubt it, ... 5.DunA1.169.8
And labours, 'till it clouds itself all o'er. 5.DunA1.172.8
Impatient waits, till ** grace the quire. 5.DunA1.250Z
'Till each fam'd Theatre my empire own, ... 5.DunA1.253.9
'Till Albion, as Hibernia, bless my throne! 5.DunA1.254.9
'Till *Albion*, as *Hibernia*, bless my sway. 5.DunA1.251Z6
'Till all tun'd equal, send a gen'ral hum. 5.DunA2.354.1
Till Peter's Keys some christen'd Jove adorn, ... 5.DunA3.101.1
Till one wide Conflagration swallows all. 5.DunA3.236.1
Till rais'd from Booths to Theatre, to Court, ... 5.DunA3.301.1
"Proceed great days! till Learning fly the shore, ... 5.DunA3.329.1
Till Birch shall blush with noble blood no more, ... 5.DunA3.330.1
Till Thames see Eton's sons for ever play, ... 5.DunA3.331.1
Till Westminster's whole year be holiday; 5.DunA3.332.1
Till Isis' Elders reel, their Pupils' sport; 5.DunA3.333.1
'Till genial Jacob, or a warm Third day, ... 5.DunB1.57.274
Impatient waits 'till H[erv]y grace the quire. .... 5.DunB1.298A.
'Till Senates nod to Lullabies divine, ... 5.DunB1.317.29
'Till show'rs of Sermons, Characters, Essays, ... 5.DunB2.361.31
'Till all tun'd equal, send a gen'ral hum. 5.DunB2.386.31
'Till Peter's keys some christ'ned Jove adorn, ... 5.DunB3.109.32
'Till one wide conflagration swallows all. 5.DunB3.240.33
'Till rais'd from booths, to Theatre, to Court, ... 5.DunB3.299.33
"Proceed, great days! 'till Learning fly the shore, ... 5.DunB3.333.33
'Till Birch shall blush with noble blood no more, ... 5.DunB3.334.33
'Till Thames see Eaton's sons for ever play, ... 5.DunB3.335.33
'Till Westminster's whole year be holiday, ... 5.DunB3.336.33
'Till Isis' Elders reel, their pupils' sport, ... 5.DunB3.337.33
And keep them in the pale of Words till death. 5.DunB4.160.35
For thee explain a thing till all men doubt it, ... 5.DunB4.251.36
And labours till it clouds itself all o'er. 5.DunB4.254.36
Blest in one Niger, till he knows of two." 5.DunB4.370.37

TILL (CONTINUED)

And reason downward, till we doubt of God: ....5.DunB4.472.387.
'*till* drown'd was Sense, and Shame, and Right, and Wrong— .5.DunB4.625.406.
Of thee they drank, till blushing fruit ....6.6ii.21.15.
Till mischief learn'd to mix with wine. ....6.6ii.24.15.
'Till wrangling *Science* taught it Noise and Show, ...6.8.11.18.
Till the Roofs all around ....6.11.8.30.
Till, by degrees, remote and small, ...6.11.18.30.
'Till having drown'd their Reason, they think f ....6.17iv.9.59.
'Till rallying all, the Feast became the Text; ....6.17iv.16.59.
'Till Fate scarce felt his gentle Breath suppress, ...6.19.13.62.
'Till Death scarce felt did o'er his Pleasures creep, ...6.19.13A.62.
'Till death scarce felt his gentle Breath suppress, ...6.19.13B.62.
'Till the last Trumpet rend the Ground; ....6.31ii.6Z11.95.
Till the Trumpet rends the Ground; ....6.31ii.6Z11A.95.
But shines himselfe till they are seen no more. ....6.43.12.120.
And shines himselfe till they are seen no more. ....6.43.12A.121.
Till the third watchman toll; ....6.47.10.128.
'Till some new Tyrant lifts his purple hand, ...6.51i.23.152.
And these be sung 'till *Granville's Myra* die; ....6.52.76.158.
'Till Death untimely stop'd his tuneful Tongue. ....6.84.2.238.
Till Death unfelt that tender frame destroy, ...6.86.17.245.
Till all true *Englishmen* cry'd, hang her! ....6.101.4.290.
And till we share your joys, forgive our grief; ....6.109.18.314.
Till you are Dust like me. ' *he.* Dear Shade! I will: ....6.123.4.343.
Yet ne'er a friend forgetting, till forgot. ....6.147vii.2.391.
'Till Time shall rifle ev'ry youthful Grace, ...Il.1.41.87.
'Till, safe at distance, to his God he prays, ...Il.1.51.88.
'Till the great King, without a Ransom paid, ...Il.1.123.93.
The *Pæans* lengthen'd 'till the Sun descends: ....Il.1.619.117.
'Till rosie Morn had purpled o'er the Sky: ....Il.1.623.117.
'Till now the *Grecian* Camp appear'd in view. ....Il.1.629.117.
'Till the proud King, and all th' *Achaian* Race ....Il.1.660.118.
Nor 'till the Sun descended, touch'd the Ground: ....Il.1.763.123.
'Till *Troy's* proud Structures shou'd in Ashes lie. ....Il.2.353.144.
'Till ev'ry Soldier grasp a *Phrygian* Wife, ...Il.2.421.147.
'Till *Helen's* Woes at full reveng'd appear, ...Il.2.422.147.
No Rest, no Respite, 'till the Shades descend; ....Il.2.459.149.
'Till Darkness, or 'till Death shall cover all: ....Il.2.460.149.
'Till Darkness, or 'till Death shall cover all: ....Il.2.460.149.
'Till bath'd in Sweat be ev'ry manly Breast, ...Il.2.462.149.
'Till vain of Mortal's empty Praise, he strove ....Il.2.723.160.
'Till great *Alcides* made the Realms obey: ....Il.2.826.164.
But ne'er 'till now such Numbers charg'd a Field. ....Il.2.969.169.
Who fair *Zeleia's* wealthy Vallies till, ...Il.2.998.170.
For this I mourn, 'till Grief or dire Disease ....Il.3.233.203.
'Till vast Destruction glut the Queen of Heav'n! ....Il.4.58.223.
'Till the barb'd Point approach the circling Bow; ....Il.4.155.228.
'Till yon' tall Vessels blaze with *Trojan* Fire? ....Il.4.283.234.
'Till black as Night the swelling Tempest shows, ...Il.4.318.235.
Till, with the growing Storm, the Deeps arise, ...Il.4.482.243.
'Till from the dying Chief, approaching near, ...Il.4.614.250.
'Till the bright Point look'd out beneath the Chin. ....Il.5.356.283.
'Till the Mass scatters as the Winds arise, ...Il.5.647.299.
'Till pierc'd at distance from their native Den, ...Il.5.685.300.
'Till trampled flat beneath the Courser's Feet, ...Il.5.719.301.
'Till in the Steely Circle straiten'd round, ...Il.5.774.303.
Our Eyes, till now, that Aspect ne'er beheld, ...Il.6.153.333.
The fatal Tablets, till that Instant seal'd, ...Il.6.217.336.
Stay, till I bring the Cup with *Bacchus* crown'd, ...Il.6.322.342.
Till Heaps of Dead alone defend her Wall; ....Il.6.411.347.
Till Fate condemns me to the silent Tomb. ....Il.6.627.358.
Till *Greece*, provok'd, from all her Numbers show ....Il.7.45.365.
Till *Ilion* falls, or till yon' Navy burns. ....Il.7.84.367.
Till *Ilion* falls, or till yon' Navy burns. ....Il.7.84.367.
Till I, the youngest of the Host, appear'd, ...Il.7.185.373.
Till Godlike *Ajax* finds the Lot his own; ....Il.7.224.375.
Till in the sev'nth it fix'd. Then *Ajax* threw, ...Il.7.299.379.
Till the new Sun restores the chearful Light: ....Il.7.447.386.
Till to supply his Place and rule the Car, ...Il.8.157.405.
Till their proud Navy wrapt in Smoak and Fires, ...Il.8.222.407.
Till ev'ry Shaft in *Phrygian* Blood be dy'd. ....Il.8.358.414.
Till great *Alastor*, and *Mecistheus*, bore ....Il.8.399.416.
Till with a snowy Veil he screen'd the Blaze. ....Il.8.549.422.
Ev'n till the Day, when certain Fates ordain ....Il.8.592.424.
Till the bright Morn her purple Beam displays: ....Il.8.634.426.
A pensive Scene! 'till *Tydeus'* warlike Son ....Il.9.41.433.
My self will stay, till *Troy* or I expire; ....Il.9.66.434.
In Silence waiting till he ceas'd the Song. ....Il.9.254.445.
Till Rage at length inflam'd his lofty Breast, ...Il.9.667.467.
Nor stay, till yonder Fleets ascend in Fire: ....Il.9.710.469.
Rest undetermin'd till the dawning Day. ....Il.9.732.470.
Not till amidst yon' sinking Navy slain, ...Il.9.765.472.
Not till the Flames, by *Hector's* Fury thrown, ...Il.9.767.472.
There, till the sacred Morn restor'd the Day, ...Il.9.777.472.
Till Sleep descending o'er the Tents, bestows ....Il.9.836.474.
Till scarce at distance of a Javelin's throw, ...Il.10.425.22.
In cruel Chains; till your Return reveal ....Il.10.514.26.
Till twelve lay breathless of the *Thracian* Band. ....Il.10.569.28.
But sure till now no Coursers struck my Sight ....Il.10.648.30.
Till in three Heads th' embroider'd Monster ends. ....Il.11.52.36.
Bear down the Furrows, till their Labours meet; ....Il.11.91.38.
But not till half the prostrate Forests lay ....Il.11.123.41.
Then, nor till then, the *Greeks* impulsive Might ....Il.11.125.41.
Till to the Main the burning Sun descend, ...Il.11.251.46.
Till to the Main the burning Sun descend, ...Il.11.267.47.
Till grasp'd with Force, he wrench'd it from his Hands. ....Il.11.306.48.
Till *Hector's* Arm involve the Ships in Flame? ....Il.11.408.53.
Till Life's warm Vapour issuing thro' the Wound, ...Il.11.598.60.
Ev'n till the Flames consume our Fleet, he stays, ...Il.11.810.72.
Till *Pallas* stopp'd us where *Alisium* flows. ....Il.11.890.75.
Till some wide Wound lets out their mighty Soul. ....Il.12.168.87.
Till great *Sarpedon* tow'r'd amid the Field; ....Il.12.348.94.
Till by this Arm the Foe shall be repell'd; ....Il.12.440.97.
Till pois'd aloft, the resting Beam suspends ....Il.12.525.101.
So stood the War, till *Hector's* matchless Might ....Il.12.527.101.

TILL (CONTINUED)

Unseen, unthought, till this amazing Day! ....Il.13.138.111.
Till *Jove* himself descends, his Bolts to shed, ...Il.13.408.125.
Till sad *Mecistheus* and *Alastor* bore ....Il.13.531.131.
Till faint with Labour, and by Foes repell'd, ...Il.13.652.136.
Till Death for Death be paid, and Blow for Blow. ....Il.13.988.152.
Leave these at Anchor till the coming Night: ....Il.14.83.161.
Then, nor till then, shall great *Achilles* rise: ....Il.15.74.199.
Not till that Day shall *Jove* relax his Rage, ...Il.15.78.199.
Let *Ilion* conquer, till th' *Achaian* Train ....Il.15.262.207.
Till sad *Polydamas* the Steeds restrain'd, ...Il.15.532.217.
Till *Greece* at once, and all her Glory end; ....Il.15.660.221.
Then, nor till then, the Scale of War shall turn, ...Il.15.720.223.
Loud roars the Deluge till it meets the Main; ....Il.16.474.261.
Nods to the Axe, till with a groaning Sound ....Il.16.595.267.
Till *Glaucus'* turning, all the rest inspir'd. ....Il.16.720.272.
The Sun shall see her conquer, till his Fall ....Il.17.522.308.
Till late, reluctant, at the Dawn of Day ....Il.17.747.317.
Till on the Left the Chief he sought, he found; ....Il.17.769.318.
Till *Thetis'* Sorrows thus began to flow. ....Il.18.68.326.
On these Conditions will I breathe: Till then, ...Il.18.121.328.
Till *Thetis* bring me at the dawn of Day ....Il.18.228.332.
Till his spent Coursers seek the Fleet again: ....Il.18.330.337.
Thus let me lie till then! thus, closely prest, ...Il.18.397.340.
Till now a Stranger, in a happy Hour ....Il.18.455.343.
For this he griev'd; and till the *Greeks* opprest ....Il.18.519.346.
To shine with Glory, till he shines no more! ....Il.18.530.347.
Till from the Fleet our Presents be convey'd, ...Il.19.189.379.
Till my insatiate Rage be cloy'd with Blood: ....Il.19.208.381.
Till yonder Sun descend, ah let me pay ....Il.19.327.386.
But till the News of my sad Fate invades ....Il.19.358.387.
Till at the length, by some brave Youth defy'd, ...Il.20.203.402.
Nor, till he reach'd *Lyrnessus*, turn'd his Head. ....Il.20.231.403.
Was not. The Natives were content to till ....Il.20.258.404.
Till her last Flame be quench'd with her last Gore, ...Il.20.365.410.
Till at the Battel's utmost Verge they light, ...Il.20.377.410.
That drowns his Bosom, till he pants no more. ....Il.20.546.417.
Thus, till the *Grecian* Vengeance is compleat; ....Il.21.148.427.
Till roll'd between the Banks, it lies the Food ....Il.21.221.430.
But not till *Troy* the destin'd Vengeance pay, ...Il.21.242.431.
Not till within her Tow'rs the perjur'd Train ....Il.21.243.431.
Not till proud *Hector*, Guardian of her Wall, ...Il.21.245.431.
And make her conquer, till *Hyperion's* Fall ....Il.21.253.431.
Till *Troy* receive her flying Sons , till all ....Il.21.340.435.
Till *Troy* receive her flying Sons , till all ....Il.21.340.435.
Scorch all the Banks! and (till our Voice reclaim) ....Il.21.396.436.
Till *Greece* shall gird her with destructive Flame, ...Il.21.440.438.
Till Death extinguish Rage, and Thought, and Life. ....Il.22.342.470.
Till on the Pyre I place thee; till I rear ....Il.23.55.489.
Till on the Pyre I place thee; till I rear ....Il.23.55.489.
Till then, the Spirit finds no resting place, ...Il.23.89.490.
Till on the Pyle the gather'd Tempest falls. ....Il.23.269.500.
So watch'd the Flames, till now they flam'd no more. ....Il.23.279.501.
Till I shall follow to th' Infernal Shade. ....Il.23.305.501.
So watch'd the Flames, till now they flame no more. ....Il.23.279A.501*.
And turns him short; till, doubling as they roll, ...Il.23.411.506.
O'er both their Marks it flew; till fiercely flung ....Il.23.999.529.
Till thus at last the Kingly Suppliant spoke, ...Il.24.597.561.
Till now, encourag'd by the Grace you give, ...Il.24.810.571.
Till then, our Arms suspend the Fall of *Troy*. ....Il.24.839.572.
(Strong Guards and Spies, till all the Rites were done, ...Il.24.1009.577.
'Till the fleet hours restore the circling year. ....Od.1.375.50.
'Till *Pallas*, piteous of her plaintive cries, ...Od.1.463.54.
"Cease, 'till to great *Laertes* I bequeath ....Od.2.109.66.
'Till righteous heav'n reclaim her stubborn breast. ....Od.2.142.68.
For 'till she leaves thy court, it is decreed, ...Od.2.145.68.
'Till big with knowledge of approaching woes ....Od.2.185.71.
'Till she retires, determin'd we remain, ...Od.2.227.72.
Threat on, till all thy stores in waste decay. ....Od.2.232.72.
'Till the fleet hours restore the circling year; ....Od.2.248.73.
Untouch'd they stood, 'till his long labours o'er ....Od.2.388.80.
'Till great *Ulysses* views his native land. ....Od.2.397.80.
'Till twice six times descends the lamp of day: ....Od.2.421.81.
Still lab'ring on, 'till scarce at last we found ....Od.3.147.92.
'Till in loud tumult all the *Greeks* arose: ....Od.3.180.94.
Fields after fields fly back, till close of day: ....Od.3.617.117.
'Till pitying *Jove* my native realm restor'd— ....Od.4.44.122.
'Till heav'n's revolving lamp restores the day. ....Od.4.296.133.
'Till haply piercing thro' the dark disguise ....Od.4.340.136.
'Till he the lines and *Argive* fleet regain'd ....Od.4.348.136.
'Till on his tongue the flutt'ring murmurs dy'd: ....Od.4.392.139.
'Till night with grateful shade involv'd the skies, ...Od.4.582.147.
Thus 'till the sun had travel'd half the skies, ...Od.4.601.148.
'Till coasting nigh the Cape, where *Malea* shrowds ....Od.4.685.151.
'Till the twelfth moon had wheel'd her pale career; ....Od.4.704.152.
'Till night with silent shade invests the pole; ....Od.4.782.156.
'Till *Grecian* cliffs appear'd, a blissful view! ....Od.4.798.156.
'Till from his eastern goal, the joyous sun ....Od.4.803.156.
'Till the twelfth dawn the light of heav'n reveal'd. ....Od.4.987.163.
Then take repast, 'till *Hesperus* display'd ....Od.4.1035.166.
'Till now the distant Island rose in view: ....Od.5.69.175.
'Till dimm'd with rising grief, they stream'd again. ....Od.5.108.177.
'Till now a stranger, in a happy hour ....Od.5.115.177.
'Till in *Ortygia*, *Dian's* winged dart ....Od.5.157.179.
'Till dimm'd with rising grief, they stream'd again. ....Od.5.204.181.
'Till heav'n by miracle his life restore) ....Od.5.510.197.
'Till the huge surge roll'd off. Then backward sweep ....Od.5.548.198.
'Till *Pallas* pour'd soft slumbers on his eyes; ....Od.5.635.202.
'Till the *Cyclopean* race in arms arose, ...Od.6.7.203.
Never, I never view'd 'till this blest hour ....Od.6.191.218.
'Till our consenting sires a spouse provide ....Od.6.345.228.
'Till great *Ulysses* hail'd his native land. ....Od.6.394.230.
Nor 'till oblique he slop'd his evening ray, ...Od.7.372.254.
'Till then, let slumber close thy careful eyes; ....Od.7.406.256.
'Till great *Alcinous* mildly thus began. ....Od.8.268.277.
'Till *Jove* refunds his shameless daughter's dow'r. ....Od.8.358.282.

TILL (CONTINUED)

'Till the glad mariners incline to sail, ...Od.9.159.312.
'Till safe we anchor'd in the shelter'd bay: ....Od.9.171.312.
Here, till the setting sun rowl'd down the light, ...Od.9.188.313.
The grain deep-piercing till it scoops it out: ....Od.9.460.325.
'Till one resolve my varying counsel ends. ....Od.9.504.326.
'Till evening *Phœbus* roll'd away the light: ....Od.9.651.333.
'Till ruddy morning purpled o'er the east. ....Od.9.653.333.
'Till all the coward thoughts of death gave way. ....Od.10.57.342.
With weighty steps, 'till at the ship I threw ....Od.10.198.350.
There, 'till the setting sun rowl'd down the light, ...Od.10.208.350.
'Till now approaching nigh the magic bow'r, ...Od.10.327.360.
'Till all the form in full proportion rise, ...Od.10.467.366.
'Till the full circle of the year came round. ....Od.10.555.369.
Melting I heard; yet 'till the sun's decline ....Od.10.564.369.
'Till awful from the shades arise the *Seer.* ....Od.10.641.374.
'Till awful, from the shades *Tiresias* rose. ....Od.11.64.383.
'Till rising up, *Aretè* silence broke, ...Od.11.416.404.
'Till the sun flames along th' etherial plain; ....Od.11.437.405.
'Till in the vault of heav'n the stars decay, ...Od.11.468.407.
'Till side by side along the dreary coast ....Od.11.575.411.
'Till from the waves th' *Ææan* hills arise. ....Od.12.2.427.
'Till *Phœbus,* downward plung'd his burning ray; ....Od.12.40.431.
'Till dying off, the distant sounds decay: ....Od.12.237.443.
'Till the fell fiend arise to seize her prey. ....Od.12.273.445.
'Till wrathful thus *Eurylochus* began. ....Od.12.332.447.
Nor cease the tears, 'till each in slumber shares ....Od.12.365.449.
'Till now from sea or flood no succour found, ...Od.12.393.450.
The flames ascend: 'Till evening they prolong ....Od.13.31.2.
'Till age and death shall gently call thee hence, ...Od.13.76.5.
'Till great *Alcinous* rising own'd the sign. ....Od.13.195.15.
Till the proud suitors for their crimes afford ....Od.13.229.17.
'Till I beheld thy radiant form once more, ...Od.13.366.25.
'Till his return, no title shall I plead, ...Od.14.178.44.
'Till the whole circle of the year goes round; ....Od.14.226.46.
'Till the swift sun his annual circle made. ....Od.14.324.50.
And safe I slept, till brightly-dawning shone ....Od.14.568.64.
'Till heav'n decrees to bless thee in a bride. ....Od.15.30.71.
Here wait we rather, till approaching day ....Od.15.59.72.
'Till night descending intercepts the way. ....Od.15.209.78.
'Till urg'd by wrongs a foreign realm he chose, ...Od.15.254.80.
'Till good *Telemachus* accepts his guest ....Od.15.357.86.
'Till radiant rose the messenger of day. ....Od.15.534.95.
'Till we returning shall our guest demand, ...Od.15.583.98.
'Till then, thy guest amid the rural train ....Od.16.81.106.
All night we watch'd, 'till with her orient wheels ....Od.16.380.124.
Wait ye, till he to arms in council draws ....Od.16.390.124.
'Till from his throne *Amphinomus* ascends, ...Od.16.409.126.
Nor ceas'd, 'till *Pallas* bid her sorrows fly, ...Od.16.468.130.
'Till the keen rage of craving hunger fled: ....Od.16.499.131.
Nor fits my age to till the labour'd lands, ...Od.17.24.133.
Much ask'd the Seniors; till *Piræus* came. ....Od.17.83.136.
'Till then, retain the gifts.—The Heroe said, ...Od.17.96.136.
'Till now the rage of thirst and hunger ceast. ....Od.17.115.137.
'Till then in ev'ry sylvan chace renown'd, ...Od.17.352.148.
Nor claim my story 'till the sun descend; ....Od.17.651.164.
'Till now declining tow'rd the close of day, ...Od.17.687.165.
Till propp'd reclining on the palace walls; ....Od.18.123.172.
For thee I mourn till death dissolves my frame. ....Od.18.244.178.
'Till silence thus th' imperial matron broke; ....Od.18.254.179.
'Till *Hymen* lights the torch of spousal love. ....Od.18.334.184.
'Till *Hesperus* leads forth the starry train; ....Od.18.352.184.
Ev'n till the morning lamp adorns the sky; ....Od.18.364.185.
Ev'n till the morning, with unwearied care, ...Od.18.365.185.
'Till mutual thus the Peers indignant cry; ....Od.18.445.190.
'Till thus *Amphinomus* the silence broke. ....Od.18.459.190.
'Till on her eastern throne *Aurora* glows. ....Od.19.61.195.
"Till this funereal web my labours end: ....Od.19.165.200.
"Cease, till to good *Laertes* I bequeath ....Od.19.166.200.
'Till thus the Queen the tender theme renews. ....Od.19.252.207.
And rode the storm; 'till by the billows tost, ...Od.19.319.209.
'Till copious wealth might guard his regal state. ....Od.19.328.210.
'Till *Phœbus* wheeling to the western goal ....Od.19.495.220.
'Till soft oblivious shade *Minerva* spread, ...Od.19.703.229.
I'll grieve, 'till sorrow sink me to the grave! ....Od.20.266.246.
'Till the next dawn this ill-tim'd strife forgoe, ...Od.21.276.273.
But since 'till then, this tryal you delay, ...Od.21.300.274.
Boundless the *Centaur* rag'd; 'till one and all ....Od.21.319.275.
'Till gentle *Pallas,* piteous of her cries, ...Od.21.387.279.
Nor wait 'till ev'ning for the genial joy. ....Od.21.472.283.
'Till then thy wrath is just— *Ulysses* burn'd ....Od.22.71.290.
'Till pale as yonder wretch each Suitor lies. ....Od.22.78.290.
(Who-e'er he be) 'till ev'ry Prince lie dead. ....Od.22.86.290.
To keep inclos'd his masters till they fall. ....Od.22.187.296.
'Till the warm sun exhales their soul away. ....Od.22.431.309.
The Suitors death unknown, 'till we remove ....Od.23.137.327.
Nor had they ended till the morning ray: ....Od.23.259.335.
'Till *Jove* in wrath the ratling Tempest guides, ...Od.23.357.342.
Cluster'd they hang, till at some sudden shock, ...Od.24.11.347.
What man is happy, till he knows his end? ....Od.24.50.350.
Nor ceas'd the strife, 'till *Jove* himself oppos'd, ...Od.24.58.350.
'Till sev'nteen nights and sev'nteen days return'd, ...Od.24.81.352.
'Till this funereal web my labours end: ....Od.24.157.355.
Cease, till to good *Laertes* I bequeath ....Od.24.158.355.

TILL'D

Or till'd their Fields along the Coast oppos'd; ....Il.2.768.162.
And till'd the Banks where silver *Satnio* flow'd. ....Il.6.42.325.
There rich in Fortune's Gifts, his Acres till'd, ...Il.14.138.164.
And from his half-till'd Field the Lab'rer flies. ....Il.17.621.312.

TILLS

The knave deserves it, when he tills the soil, ...3.EOM4.152.142.

TILT

To run a Muck, and tilt at all I meet; ....4.HS1.70.11.

TILTING

The fleet swift tilting o'er the surges flew, ...Od.4.797.156.
And tilting o'er the bay the vessels ride: ....Od.14.289.49.
For nine long days the billows tilting o'er, ...Od.14.349.51.
Arriving then, where tilting on the tydes ....Od.15.507.94.

TIM'D

But Wisdom's Triumph is well-tim'd Retreat, ...3.Ep2.225.68.
A well-tim'd Counsel with a willing Ear? ....Il.4.124.226.
Unruly Murmurs, or ill-tim'd Applause, ...Il.19.85.375.
When justly tim'd with equal sweep they row, ...Od.7.419.258.
The ill-tim'd efforts of officious love; ....Od.15.78.72.
Why with this ill-tim'd gladness leaps my heart? ....Od.21.108.264.
'Till the next dawn this ill-tim'd strife forgoe, ...Od.21.276.273.

TIM'ROUS

Sol thro' white Curtains shot a tim'rous Ray, ...2.RL1.13.145.
Tim'rous by Nature, of the Rich in awe, ...4.HS1.7.5.
A tim'rous foe, and a suspicious friend, ...4.Arbu.206.110.
A tim'rous Foe and a suspicious Friend: ....6.49iii.20.143.
A tim'rous Foe, and a suspicious Friend, ...6.98.56.285.
Once from the Walls your tim'rous Foes engag'd, ...Il.5.982.314.
Once from their Walls your tim'rous Foes engag'd, ...Il.5.982A.314.
Like tim'rous Flocks the *Trojans* in their Wall ....Il.8.160.405.
Fall from that trembling Tongue, and tim'rous Heart? ....Il.14.91.162.
The Coward-Counsels of a tim'rous Throng ....Il.15.874.230.
The mourning Matron dries her tim'rous Tears. ....Il.24.396.552.
But modest awe hath chain'd his tim'rous tongue. ....Od.4.212.129.
A tim'rous hind the lion's court invades, ...Od.4.450.141.
A tim'rous hind the lion's court invades, ...Od.17.141.138.
To this poor, tim'rous, toil-detesting drone? ....Od.20.452.255.
Me other work requires—With tim'rous awe ....Od.22.417.308.
And tim'rous pass'd, and awfully withdrew. ....Od.24.126.354.

TIMBER

On lofty Beams of solid Timber hung. ....1.TrES.194.456.
On lofty Beams of solid Timber hung. ....Il.12.548.101.
Th' enormous Timber lumbring down the Hill. ....Il.17.836.321.
To load the Timber and the Pile to rear, ...Il.23.136.493.
Go, fell the timber of yon' lofty grove, ...Od.5.210.181.

TIMBREL

Let weeping *Nilus* hear the Timbrel sound. ....1.TrSt.376.425.

TIME

Time conquers All, and We must Time obey. ....1.PWi.88.95.
Time conquers All, and We must Time obey. ....1.PWi.88.95.
The Time shall come, when free as Seas or Wind ....1.W-F.397.190.
Nor Time nor Moths e'er spoil'd so much as they: ....1.EOC.113.252.
Once on a time, *La Mancha's* Knight, they say, ...1.EOC.267.270.
When mellowing Time does full Perfection give, ...1.EOC.490A.294
Yet he shall find, wou'd time th'occasion shew, ...1.TrPA.124.370.
No Time the dear Remembrance can remove, ...1.TrSP.51.396.
O useful Time for Lovers to employ! ....1.TrSP.104.398.
The Time will come, when a diviner Flame ....1.TrSt.47.411.
Mean time the banish'd *Polynices* roves ....1.TrSt.443.428.
'Twas now the Time when *Phœbus* yields to Night, ...1.TrSt.474.430.
But in due Time, when Sixty Years were o'er, ...2.ChJM.9.15.
Think not I dote; 'tis Time to take a Wife, ...2.ChJM.123.20.
Think not my Virtue lost, tho' Time has shed ....2.ChJM.131.21.
The Time approach'd, to Church the Parties went, ...2.ChJM.309.29.
Mean time the vig'rous Dancers beat the Ground, ...2.ChJM.353.31.
Then rose the Guests; and as the time requir'd, ...2.ChJM.371.32.
Yet hoping Time th'Occasion might betray, ...2.ChJM.396.34.
It so befell, in Holy Time of *Lent,* ....2.ChWB.277.70.
I still have shifts against a Time of Need: ....2.ChWB.297.71.
Long time I heard, and swell'd, and blush'd, and frown'd, ...2.ChWB.411.77.
What Time wou'd spare, from Steel receives its date, ...2.RL3.171.182.
(What Time the Morn mysterious Visions brings, ...2.TemF.7.253.
The greater Part by hostile Time subdu'd; ....2.TemF.32.255.
From Time's first Birth, with Time it self shall last; ....2.TemF.50.256.
Grav'd o'er their Seats the Form of *Time* was found, ...2.TemF.147.265.
His time a moment, and a point his space. ....3.EOM1.72.22.
Correct old Time, and regulate the Sun; ....3.EOM2.22.57.
Correct old Time, and teach the Sun his way; ....3.EOM2.22A.57.
'Tis to mistake them, costs the time and pain. ....3.EOM2.216.81.
They love themselves, a third time, in their race. ....3.EOM3.124.105.
All love themselves, a third time, in their race. 3.EOM3.124A.10
Oh! while along the stream of Time thy name ....3.EOM4.383.165.
Time, that on all things lays his lenient hand, ...3.Ep1.224.34.
The wisest Fool that Time has ever made. ....3.Ep2.124A.60.
To kill those foes to Fair ones, Time and Thought. ....3.Ep2.112.59.
The wisest Fool much Time has ever made. ....3.Ep2.124.60.
Bids seed-time, harvest, equal course maintain, ...3.Ep3.167.107.
The Tempter saw his time; the work he ply'd; ....3.Ep3.369.123.
Nature shall join you, Time shall make it grow ....3.Ep4.69.143.
Who-e'er offends, at some unlucky Time ....4.HS1.77.13.
Well, if it be my time to quit the Stage, ...4.JD4.1.27.
So Time, that changes all things, had ordain'd! ....4.JD4.43.29.
In time to come, may pass for *Holy Writ.* ....4.JD4.287.49.
Not but we may exceed, some Holy time, ...4.HS2.85.61.
Happy! to catch me, just at Dinner-time. ....4.Arbu.14.97.
Time, Praise, or Money, is the least they crave, ...4.Arbu.114Z1.104
Time, that at last matures a Clap to Pox, ...4.JD2.47.137.
Whom ripening Time, that Turns a Clap to Pox ....4.JD2A.53.136.
Nor yet shall Waller yield to time, ...4.HOde9.7.159.
Nay worse, to ask for Verse at such a time! ....4.2HE2.31.167.
This subtle Thief of Life, this paltry Time, ...4.2HE2.76.171.
There is a time when Poets will grow dull: ....4.2HE2.200.179.
If Time improve our Wit as well as Wine, ...4.2HE1.49.199.
Time was, a sober Englishman wou'd knock ....4.2HE1.161.209.
The Zeal of Fools offends at any time, ...4.2HE1.406.229.
Yet Time ennobles, or degrades each Line; ....4.1HE6.44.239.

IME (CONTINUED)

Once on a time (so runs the Fable) 4.HS6.157.259.
F. Why so? if Satire know its Time and Place, 4.EpS1.87.305.
Which not at present having time to do— 4.EpS2.156.322.
In eldest time, e'er mortals writ or read, 5.DunA1.7.61.
How Time himself stands still at her command, 5.DunA1.69.68.
In eldest time, e'er mortals writ or read, 5.DunB1.9.269.
How Time himself stands still at her command, 5.DunB1.71.275.
To whom Time bears me on his rapid wing, 5.DunB4.6.339.
He may indeed (if sober all this time) 5.DunB4.259.369.
Thou fly'st, like time, with eager haste; 6.6ii.5.14.
His Time, the Muse, the Witty, and the Fair. 6.19.10.62.
Tho' not too strictly bound to Time and Place: 6.19.28.63.
No matter for the Rules of Time and Place: 6.19.28A.63.
Lest kinder time shou'd hide our miseries, 6.20.24.66.
Who wert, e're time his rapid race begun, 6.23.5.73.
Cost studious *Cabalists* more Time. 6.30.58.88.
Cost our high thought more care and time 6.30.58A.88.
Cost studious Providence more Time. 6.30.58B.88.
Tho' Plays for Honour in old Time he made, 6.34.17.101.
With Gay, who Petition'd you once on a time, 6.42i.3.116.
Tis rumour'd, *Budgell* on a time 6.44.1.123.
To pass her time 'twixt reading and Bohea, 6.45.15.125.
So when your slave, at some dear, idle time, 6.45.41.125.
Tho' many a Wit from time to time has rose 6.48iii.1.134.
Tho' many a Wit from time to time has rose 6.48iii.1.134.
Rack your Inventions some, and some *in time* translate. 6.48iii.14.135.
Says *Addison* to *Steele,* 'Tis Time to go. 6.49ii.11.140.
At length my Friend (while Time, with still career, 6.55.1.166.
Perhaps in time you'll leave High Diet, 6.61.33.182.
Time, health, and fortune, are not lost in vain. 6.63.6.188.
"Mean Time on every Pissing-Post 6.79.141.223.
With silver sounds, and sweetly tune out time. 6.82xii.2.237.
'Tis the first time I dare to say, 6.121.3.340.
Yes, 'tis the time! I cry'd, impose the chain! 6.146.1.389.
The wisest Fool much Time has ever made: 6.154.10.403.
Daughter of Memory! from elder Time 6.155.4.404.
Daughter of Memory! from Time 6.155.4B.404.
'Till Time shall rifle ev'ry youthful Grace, Il.1.41.87.
'Tis time to save the few Remains of War. Il.1.82.90.
But this when Time requires—It now remains Il.1.181.96.
Mean time *Atrides* launch'd with num'rous Oars Il.1.404.107.
Mean time, secure within thy Ships from far Il.1.552.114.
Expect the Time to *Troy's* Destruction giv'n, Il.2.364.144.
Cease to consult, the Time for Action calls, Il.2.966.169.
But Wise thro' Time, and Narrative with Age, Il.3.200.200.
In ancient Time, when *Otreus'* fill'd the Throne, Il.3.246.204.
No Strength or Skill, but just in Time, be try'd: Il.4.349.237.
In ancient Time the happy Walls possest, Il.6.192.335.
Thy Hate to *Troy,* is this the Time to show? Il.6.406.346.
The Chief reply'd: This Time forbids to rest: Il.6.450.348.
Thou, in thy Time, more sound Advice hast giv'n; Il.7.434.386.
Regard in time, O Prince divinely brave! Il.9.326.450.
There was a time ('twas when for *Greece* I fought) Il.9.464.455.
No Time shall part us, an no Fate divide. Il.9.573.462.
Hence, let us go—why waste we Time in vain? Il.9.737.470.
But now (what time in some sequester'd Vale Il.11.119.39.
Then with his Spear, unseen, his Time he took, Il.11.325.49.
The Time is come, when yon' despairing Host Il.11.744.68.
Mean time *Patroclus,* by *Achilles* sent, Il.11.788.71.
Now the slow Course of all-impairing Time Il.11.814.72.
For lo! the fated Time, th' appointed Shore; Il.13.165.112.
His Time observ'd; for clos'd by Foes around, Il.13.698.138.
The time shall come, when chas'd along the Plain, Il.13.1032.153.
And all-confirming Time has Fate fulfill'd. Il.14.60.160.
What-time old *Saturn,* from *Olympus* cast, Il.14.234.172.
What-time, deserting *Ilion's* wasted Plain, Il.14.285.176.
'Tis now no time for Wisdom or Debates; Il.15.602.220.
'Tis time our Fury should relent at last: Il.16.83.238.
The Time allow'd: *Troy* thicken'd on the Shore, Il.17.114.292.
'Tis time to try if *Ilion's* State can stand Il.17.161.293.
In happy time (the Charioteer replies) Il.17.540.309.
Our Swords kept time, and conquer'd side by side. Il.18.402.340.
The third time labour'd by the sweating Hind; Il.18.628.354.
But come it will, the fatal Time must come, Il.19.454.391.
What-time, a vengeful Monster of the Main Il.20.178.401.
The Spear a fourth time bury'd in the Cloud, Il.20.517.416.
But this no time our Vigour to display, Il.23.347.503.
With matchless Strength; that time *Ulysses* found Il.23.843.523.
What time young *Paris,* simple Shepherd Boy, Il.24.39.537.
What time the Herald and the hoary King Il.24.429.554.
Remains unask'd; what Time the Rites require Il.24.825.571.
Mean time *Telemachus,* the blooming heir Od.1.110.36.
What time this dome rever'd her prudent Lord; Od.1.298.47.
Mean time the Lyre rejoins the sprightly lay; Od.1.531.57.
But come it will, the time when manhood grants Od.2.67.64.
Is this (returns the Prince) for mirth a time? Od.2.347.78.
Mean time, o'er all the dome, they quaff, they feast, Od.2.363.78.
And grief destroy what time a while would spare. Od.2.423.81.
Long time with thee before proud *Ilion's* wall Od.3.104.91.
Far as thy mind thro' backward time can see, Od.3.122.91.
Nor lost in time, nor circumscrib'd by place. Od.3.288.100.
Mean time from flaming *Troy* we cut the way, Od.3.350.103.
What time the *Greeks* combin'd their social arms, Od.4.195.129.
What-time, with hunger pin'd, my absent mates Od.4.497.144.
While she with work and song the time divides, Od.5.78.176.
Mean time (the care and fav'rite of the skies) Od.6.129.213.
Destroys perhaps the strength that time wou'd spare: Od.8.150.271.
Short is the time, and lo! ev'n now the gales Od.8.165.271.
To seize the time, and with a sudden wound Od.9.356.321.
The hand of Time had silver'd o'er with snow, Od.11.429.405.
Time for discourse, and time for soft repose, Od.11.473.407.
Time for discourse, and time for soft repose, Od.11.473.407.
But sure the eye of Time beholds no name Od.11.591.412.
The time would fail should I in order tell Od.11.633.415.
Sweet time of slumber! be the night obey'd! Od.12.348.448.

TIME (CONTINUED)

What-time the Judge forsakes the noisy bar Od.12.519.457.
'Tis sweet to play the fool in time and place, Od.14.519.62.
But when the softly-stealing pace of time Od.15.390.88.
What-time it chanc'd the palace entertain'd Od.15.458.92.
Then to *Peiræus—Thou* whom time has prov'd Od.15.581.98.
What length of time must we consume in vain, Od.16.336.122.
Pale grief destroy what time a while forbears. Od.16.353.123.
Time steals away with unregarded wing, Od.17.612.161.
The time, my Lord, invites me to repair Od.17.672.165.
Yet taught by time, my heart has learn'd to glow Od.18.269.179.
Must share the general doom of with'ring time: Od.19.101.197.
When time shall prove the storied blessing true: Od.19.355.211.
What time the sun, from ocean's peaceful stream, Od.19.505.221.
Lest time or worms had done the weapon wrong, Od.21.429.281.
Time shall the truth to sure remembrance bring: Od.23.115.325.
Now chang'd with time, with absence, and with woe? Od.24.252.361.
Time was (my fortunes then were at the best) Od.24.314.364.

TIME'S

From Time's first Birth, with Time it self shall last; 2.TemF.50.256.
With Time's first Birth began the Heav'nly Lays, 2.TemF.274.276.
Now in the time's full process forth she brings Od.11.309.397.

TIMELESS

Timeless, indecent, but retire to rest. Od.3.430.107.

TIMELY

While others timely, to the neighbouring Fleet 5.DunA2.395.149.
All others timely, to the neighbouring Fleet 5.DunA2.395A.149.
While others, timely, to the neighb'ring Fleet 5.DunB2.427.318.
These in thy dangers timely aid shall bring, 6.21.25.69.
And blest, that timely from our Scene remov'd 6.152.9.400.
His wounded Brother claims thy timely Care; Il.4.239.232.
And timely join me, e're I leave the Walls. Il.6.455.348.
The *Trojan* Warrior, touch'd with timely Fear, Il.13.219.116.
Fellows in Arms! your timely Aid unite; Il.13.608.135.
Struck for th' immortal Race with timely Fear, Il.15.142.202.
If he refuse, then let him timely weigh Il.15.184.203.
This if refus'd, he bids thee timely weigh Il.15.200.204.
Timely he flies the yet-untasted Food, Il.15.706.223.
Which, timely follow'd but the former Night, Il.22.142.459.
To save the state; and timely to restrain Od.1.114.37.
(A long procession) timely marching home Od.3.498.112.
You timely will return a welcome guest, Od.4.739.153.
May timely intercept their ruffian rage, Od.4.977.163.
Prais'd be thy counsel, and thy timely aid: Od.13.438.27.
Hence dotard, hence! and timely speed thy way, Od.18.14.167.
So timely rise, when morning streaks the east, Od.22.215.297.

TIMES

Rapt into future Times, the Bard begun; 1.Mes.7.113.
The World's great Oracle in Times to come; 1.W-F.382.188.
Nor fear a Dearth in these Flagitious Times. 1.EOC.529.297.
From the dire Nation in its early Times, 1.TrSt.6.409.
But if thou must reform the stubborn Times, 1.TrSt.377.425.
The rest, succeeding Times shall ripen into Fate. 1.TrSt.428.427.
And Criticks learn'd explain to Modern Times. 2.ChJM.380.33.
The wiser Wits of later Times declare 2.ChJM.671.47.
Five times in lawful Wedlock she was join'd; 2.ChWB.15.57.
Happy! ah ten times happy, had I been, 2.RL4.149.196.
At all times Just, but when he sign'd the Shell. 2.TemF.173.269.
Which serv'd the past, and must the times to come! 3.EOM2.52.62.
Ah! how unlike the man of times to come! 3.EOM3.161.109.
Tenets with Books, and Principles with Times. 3.Ep1.167.29.
It stands on record, that in *Richard's* Times 4.HS1.145.19.
It stands on record, that in ancient Times 4.HS1.145A.19.
Why had not I in those good times my birth, 4.HS2.97.61.
And buy a Rope, that future times may tell 4.HS2.109.63.
Alas! 'tis ten times worse when they *repent.* 4.Arbu.108.103.
Trust me, 'tis ten times worse when they *repent.* 4.Arbu.108A.103.
I, who at some times spend, at others spare, 4.2HE2.290.185.
Had ancient Times conspir'd to dis-allow 4.2HE1.135.207.
Now Times are chang'd, and one Poetick Itch 4.2HE1.169.209.
But Times corrupt, and Nature, ill-inclin'd, 4.2HE1.251.217.
Let me for once presume t'instruct the times, 4.2HE1.340.225.
Charles, to late times to be transmitted fair, 4.2HE1.380.227.
Old scenes of glory, times long cast behind, 5.DunA3.55.155.
Th' Augustus born to bring Saturnian times: 5.DunA3.318.186.
Old scenes of glory, times long cast behind 5.DunB3.63.323.
Th' Augustus born to bring Saturnian times. 5.DunB3.320.335.
[But (happy for him as the times went then) 5.DunB4.115.352.
Snuff just three Times, and read again.) 6.10.66.26.
Ten times more like him, I profess, 6.10.103.27.
With *Styx* nine times round her, 6.11.91.33.
Let future times of *Cleopatra* tell, 6.20.15.66.
And, lost in ancient times, the golden fleece 6.38.9.107.
But would your charms to distant times extend, 6.38.27.108.
It had been civil in these ticklish Times, 6.60.19.178.
Fair Mirrour of foul Times! whose fragile Sheene 6.137.1.373.
Let this Example future Times reclaim, Il.3.437.213.
A great Example drawn from Times of old; Il.9.650.467.
From eldest Times: emboss'd with Studs of Gold, Il.11.774.69.
But this the Gods in later Times perform; Il.12.37.83.
What Shame to *Greece* for future times to tell, Il.17.628.312.
In elder Times to guard *Alcides* made, Il.20.176.401.
There fix'd from eldest times; black, craggy, vast: Il.21.470.441.
Thus three times round the *Trojan* Wall they fly; Il.22.217.464.
Circling around the Place, where Times to come Il.23.156.495.
Now three times turn'd in prospect of the Goal, Il.23.899.525.
'Till twice six times descends the lamp of day: Od.2.421.81.
Make future times thy equal act adore, Od.3.244.97.
In elder times the soft *Phæacian* train Od.6.5.203.
Lo! when nine times the moon renews her horn, Od.11.299.396.
Nine times Commander, or by land or main, Od.14.267.49.
Three times, with beating heart, he made essay; Od.21.131.264.

TIMES (CONTINUED)

Three times, unequal to the task, gave way: ....Od.21.132.264.

TIMID

He stood the furious Foe, the timid Friend, ...4.Arbu.343.120.
Let others creep by timid steps, and slow, ...5.DunB4.465.386.
Timid and therefore treacherous to the last ....6.130.20.358.

TIMOLEON

Timoleon, glorious in his Brother's Blood; ....2.TemF.162.267.

TIMON

Greatness, with Timon, dwells in such a draught ....3.Ep4.103.147.
Greatness, with Timon, dwells with such a draught ....3.Ep4.103A.147.
F. A hundred smart in *Timon* and in *Balaam:* ....4.HS1.42.9.
His Wealth brave Timon gloriously confounds; ....4.1HE6.85.243.

TIMON'S

At Timon's Villa let us pass a day, ...3.Ep4.99.146.

TIMOTHEUS

And what *Timotheus* was, is *Dryden* now. ....1.EOC.383.284.

TIMOTHEUS'

Hear how *Timotheus'* vary'd Lays surprize, ...1.EOC.374.283.
Hear how *Timotheus'* various Lays surprize, ...1.EOC.374A.283.

TIN

Twice ten of Tin, the twelve of ductile Gold; ....Il.11.32.36.
And stubborn Brass, and Tin, and solid Gold: ....Il.18.546.348.
And Pales of glitt'ring Tin th' Enclosure grace. ....Il.18.656.355.
The Greaves of ductile Tin, the Helm imprest ....Il.18.707.357.
Of Tin each inward, and the middle Gold: ....Il.20.320.407.
Bright with the mingled Blaze of Tin and Gold, ...Il.23.584.513.

TINCLING

See TINKLING.
And on the tincling Verge more faintly rung. ....Il.13.518.131.

TINCTUR'D

That tinctur'd as it runs, with Lethe's streams, ...5.DunA2.315.140.
That tinctur'd as it runs with Lethe's streams, ...5.DunB2.339.314.

TINCTURE

Dipt in the richest Tincture of the Skies, ...2.RL2.65.163.
All Manners take a tincture from our own, ...3.Ep1.25.17.

TINDAL

One, who believes as Tindal leads the way, ...4.1HE6.64.241.
Toland and Tindal, prompt at Priests to jeer, ...5.DunA2.367.144.
Toland and Tindal, prompt at priests to jeer, ...5.DunB2.399.316.
Where Tindal dictates, and Silenus snores." ....5.DunB4.492.390.

TINDAL'S

In Toland's, Tindal's, and in Woolston's days. ....5.DunA3.208.175.
In Toland's, Tindal's, and in Woolston's days. ....5.DunB3.212.330.

TINDER

But burnt so long, may soon turn Tinder, ...6.10.55.26.

TING'D

New-ting'd with *Tyrian* Dye: In Dust below, ...Il.15.634.220.
This ting'd with Sulphur, sacred first to Flame, ...Il.16.278.249.
Has *Hector* ting'd with Blood of Victims slain? ....Il.24.45.537.
Had ting'd the mountains with her earliest red, ...Od.15.215.78.
A mantle purple-ting'd, and radiant vest, ...Od.19.275.208.

TINGLING

The pale Boy-Senator yet tingling stands, ...5.DunB4.147.355.

TINKLING

See TINCLING.
The grots that eccho to the tinkling rills, ...2.ElAb.158.332.

TINSEL

Ye tinsel Insects! whom a Court maintains, ...4.EpS2.220.325.

TINSEL'D

She, tinsel'd o'er in robes of varying hues, ...5.DunA1.79.69.
She, tinsel'd o'er in robes of varying hues, ...5.DunB1.81.275.

TINTS

Or blend in beauteous tints the colour'd mass, ...6.52.5.156.

TINY

Thy Pigmy Island and thy tiny Spouse ....6.96ii.30Z33.272.
"Thy Pigmy Children, and thy tiny Spouse, ...6.96ii.53.273.

TIP

Sudden, she storms! she raves! You tip the wink, ...3.Ep2.33.52.
The Nose of Hautgout, and the Tip of Taste, ...3.Ep2.80.57.
They'l praise her *Elbow, Heel,* or *Tip o' th' Ear.* ....4.HAdv.123.85.
If neither Gems adorn, nor Silver tip ....4.HAdv.147.87.
Chanc'd, with a Touch of just the Tip, ...6.135.5.366.
Did, with a Touch of just the Tip, ...6.135.5A.366.
And tip with Silver ev'ry Mountain's Head; ....Il.8.694.428.

TIPS

And tips with silver all the walls: ....4.HS6.192.261.
And last, a little Ajax tips the spire. ....5.DunA1.142.81.

TIPT

Not sulphur-tipt, emblaze an Ale-house fire; ....5.DunB1.235.287.
Bright with the gilded button tipt its head, ...5.DunB4.408.382.
And tipt the Mountains with a purple Ray. ....Il.7.501.389.

TIPTOE

On Tiptoe then the Squire he stood, ...6.94.57.261.

TIR'D

'Till tir'd he sleeps, and Life's poor play is o'er! ....3.EOM2.282.8.
For ever exercis'd, yet never tir'd; ....3.EOM4.322.1.
Tir'd, not determin'd, to the last we yield, ...3.Ep1.43.18.
So when the Sun's broad beam has tir'd the sight, ...3.Ep2.253.70.
But you are tir'd—I'll tell a tale.—B. A greed. ....3.Ep3.338B.12.
But you are tir'd—I'll tell a tale. Agreed. ....3.Ep3.338.120.
Tir'd of the scene Parterres and Fountains yield, ...3.Ep4.87.166.
Treated, caress'd, and tir'd, I take my leave, ...3.Ep4.165.153.
When the tir'd Glutton labours thro' a Treat, ...4.HS2.31.57.
Or tir'd in search of Truth, or search of Rhyme. ....4.HS2.86.61.
Tir'd with a tedious March, one luckless night, ...4.2HE2.35.167.
When the tir'd nation breath'd from civil war. ....4.2HE1.273.21.
Tir'd with vain hopes, and with complaints as vain, ...6.56.1.168.
So when the sun's broad beam has tir'd the sight, ...6.106i.4A.306.
Eyes the rough Waves, and tir'd returns at last. ....Il.5.739.302.
Now tir'd with Toils, thy fainting Limbs recline, ...Il.6.444.348.
Tir'd with the Toils of Day, and Watch of Night: ....Il.10.111.7.
And tir'd with Toils, neglect the Watch of Night? ....Il.10.470.24.
When his tir'd Arms refuse the Axe to rear, ...Il.11.121.41.
Who breathless, pale, with length of Labours tir'd, ...Il.13.118.110.
His tir'd, slow Steps, he drags from off the Field. ....Il.13.653.136.
Tir'd with th' incessant Slaughters of the Fight. ....Il.13.888.147.
Pale, trembling, tir'd, the Sailors freeze with Fears; ....Il.15.756.225.
On his tir'd Arm the weighty Buckler hung; ....Il.16.132.242.
From thy tir'd Limbs unbrace *Pelides'* Arms! ....Il.17.244.297.
So may his Rage be tir'd, and labour'd down; ....Il.18.331.337.
Now tir'd with Slaughter, from the *Trojan* Band ....Il.21.34.422.
From my tir'd Body wash the Dirt and Blood, ...Il.21.660.449.
From my tir'd Body wash the Dust and Blood, ...Il.21.660A.449.
Apollo now to tir'd *Achilles* turns; ....Il.22.13.453.
Tir'd with his Chase around the *Trojan* Wall, ...Il.23.75.489.
While the long Strife ev'n tir'd the Lookers-on, ...Il.23.838.522.
From their tir'd Bodies wipe the Dust away, ...Il.23.861.523.
Tir'd with long toil, we willing sunk to rest. ....Od.10.553.369.

TIRE

To tire our *Patience,* than mis-lead our *Sense:* ....1.EOC.4.239.
Or *one vain Wit's,* that might a hundred tire. ....1.EOC.45.244.
Or *one vain Wit's,* that wou'd a hundred tire. ....1.EOC.45A.244.
Tho' oft the Ear the *open Vowels* tire, ...1.EOC.345.278.
A Hiss from all the Snaky Tire went round; ....1.TrSt.162.417.
A Place to tire the rambling Wits of *France* ....2.ChJM.452.36.
Riches that vex, and Vanities that tire. ....6.86.4.245.
Ev'n the sweet Charms of sacred Numbers tire. ....Il.13.798.143.
No Force could tame them, and no Toil could tire; ....Il.15.845.229.

TIRE'D

Tire'd by the Tides, his Knees relax with Toil; ....Il.21.309.433.

TIRES

Th' *increasing* Prospect tires our wandring Eyes, ...1.EOC.231.265
With Limbs and Soul untam'd, he tires a War. ....Il.19.168.378.

TIRESIAS

Black as these regions, to *Tiresias* bleed. ....Od.11.42.381.
'Till awful, from the shades *Tiresias* rose. ....Od.11.64.383.
To seek *Tiresias* in the nether sky, ...Od.11.201.391.
For, to *Tiresias* thro' th' eternal gates ....Od.23.269.336.
To seek *Tiresias* in the vales of death; ....Od.23.348.341.

TIRESIAS'

To seek *Tiresias'* awful shade below, ...Od.10.677.376.

TIS

But blest with her, 'tis Spring throughout the Year. ....1.PSp.84.69.
'Tis done, and Nature's various Charms decay; ....1.PWi.29.91.
'Tis he th'obstructed Paths of Sound shall clear, ...1.Mes.41.116.
Here too, 'tis sung, of old *Diana* stray'd, ...1.W-F.165.165.
'Tis yours, my Lord, to bless our soft Retreats, ...1.W-F.283.174.
'Tis hard to say, if greater Want of Skill ....1.EOC.1.239.
'Tis with our *Judgments* as our *Watches,* none ....1.EOC.9.239.
Authors are partial to their *Wit,* 'tis true, ...1.EOC.17.241.
'Tis more to *guide* than *spur* the Muse's Steed; ....1.EOC.84.248.
'Tis not a *Lip,* or *Eye,* we Beauty call, ...1.EOC.245.267.
'Tis not enough no Harshness gives Offence, ...1.EOC.364.281.
And 'tis but just to let 'em live *betimes.* ....1.EOC.477.292.
'Tis what the *Vicious fear,* the *Virtuous shun;* ....1.EOC.506.295.
By *Fools* 'tis *hated,* and by *Knaves undone!* ....1.EOC.507.295.
'Tis most our *Trouble* when 'tis most *admir'd;* ....1.EOC.502B.29?
'Tis most our *Trouble* when 'tis most *admir'd;* ....1.EOC.502B.29?
For 'tis but *half* a *Judge's Task,* to *Know.* ....1.EOC.561.304.
'Tis not enough, Taste, Judgment, Learning, join; ....1.EOC.562.305.
'Tis not enough your Counsel still be *true,* ....1.EOC.572.305.
'Tis not enough, Wit, Art, and Learning join; 1.EOC.562A.305
'Tis best sometimes your Censure to restrain, ...1.EOC.596.308.
Such shameless *Bards* we have; and yet 'tis true, ...1.EOC.610.309.
(A pleasing *Off'ring* when 'tis made by you;) ....1.TrVP.97.381.
Think, 'tis *Vertumnus* begs you to be kind! ....1.TrVP.107.381.
'Tis thou art all my Care and my Delight, ...1.TrSP.143.399.
'Tis fix'd; th'irrevocable Doom of *Jove;* ....1.TrSt.413.427.
And 'tis a Deed too glorious to disown. ....1.TrSt.762.442.
Be this thy Comfort, that 'tis thine t'efface ....1.TrSt.822.443.
'Tis thine the Seeds of future War to know, ...1.TrSt.841.444.
'Tis ours, the Dignity They give, to grace; ....1.TrES.37.451.
His Fame ('tis all the Dead can have!) shall live. ....1.TrES.253.459.
'Tis his alone, t'avenge the Wrongs I bear; ....1.TrUl.90.469.
'Tis what concerns my Soul's Eternal Bliss; ....2.ChJM.114.20.
Think not I dote; 'tis Time to take a Wife, ...2.ChJM.123.20.
'Tis true, Perfection none must hope to find ....2.ChJM.190.24.
'Tis well, 'tis wondrous well, the Knight replies, ...2.ChJM.216.25.
'Tis well, 'tis wondrous well, the Knight replies, ...2.ChJM.216.25.
That 'tis too much for Human Race to know ....2.ChJM.270.27.

TIS (CONTINUED)

If not, 'tis I must be asham'd of You. 6.73.17.210.
I'm told (but 'tis not true I hope) 6.74.3.211.
'Tis *Pope* must be asham'd of *Craggs.* 6.74.8.211.
So would I draw (but oh, 'tis vain to try 6.75.3.211.
Ah friend, 'tis true— this truth you lovers know— 6.81.1.225.
Can touch Immortals, 'tis a Soul like thine: 6.84.22.239.
'Tis hers, the brave Man's latest Steps to trace, 6.84.29.239.
'Tis theirs, the brave Man's latest Steps to trace, 6.84.29A.239.
Ah, no! 'tis vain to strive—It will not be. 6.85.9Z1.242.
Is that a Birth-day? 'tis alas! too clear, 6.86.9.245.
'Tis but the Fun'ral of the former year. 6.86.10.245.
Is this a Birth-day? 'tis alas! too clear, 6.86.9C.245.
Is that a Birth-day? ah! tis sadly clear, 6.86.9B.245.
Why, Zounds! and Blood! 'tis true! 6.94.16.259.
Cry'd sagely, 'Tis not safe, I hold, 6.94.23.259.
'Tis pity that two Squires so Gent— 6.94.39.260.
'Tis so unsav'ry a-Bit.) 6.94.48.260.
For 'tis a Pleasure to support a Friend. 6.96iii.36.275.
'Tis said, that thou shouldst cleave unto thy Wife; 6.96iv.9.276.
'Tis not for that I grieve; no, 'tis to see 6.96iv.59.278.
'Tis not for that I grieve; no, 'tis to see' 6.96iv.59.278.
'Tis all my Pleasure thy past Toil to know, 6.96iv.63.278.
'Tis not for that I grieve; O, 'tis to see 6.96iv.59A.278.
'Tis not for that I grieve; O, 'tis to see 6.96iv.59A.278.
'Tis sure some Virtue to conceal its Shame. 6.96v.20.280.
'Tis Hunger, and not Malice, makes them print, 6.98.5.283.
Each Man's true Merit 'tis not hard to find; 6.98.25.284.
Wesley, if Wesley 'tis they mean, 6.102.1.294.
'Tis ten to one he'll ne'er come back. 6.103.4.295.
'Tis generous, *Tibald!* in thee and thy brothers, 6.105v.1.302.
Tis granted Sir; the Busto's a damn'd head, 6.105vi.1A.302.
When freedom is the cause, 'tis hers to fight; 6.107.11.310.
'Tis to his *British* heart he trusts for fame. 6.107.24.311.
'Tis all a Father, all a Friend can give! 6.109.20.314.
—Tis not the *sober Satyrist* you should dread, 6.120.11.339.
'Tis the first time I dare to say, 6.121.3.340.
'Tis the first coin I'm bold to say, 6.121.3A.340.
'Tis known all the Dives's ever went there. 6.122.12.341.
O! sure to King George 'tis a dismal disaster, 6.122.17.342.
'Tis good to have a Friend at Court. 6.124iv.4.348.
Then *Bounce* ('tis all that *Bounce* can crave) 6.135.81.369.
'Tis true, but something in her was *forgot.* 6.139.2.377.
"'Tis Venus, Venus gives these arms; 6.140.27.379.
Yes, 'tis the time! I cry'd, impose the chain! 6.146.1.389.
And 'tis a wise design on pitying heav'n, 6.146.6.389.
Tis half their business, Blows to ward, or give, 6.147iv.2.391.
'Tis true, Great Bard, thou on my shelf shall lye 6.147ix.3.392.
And 'tis certain, dear Cibber, that you may *speak last;* 6.149.2A.397.
'Tis where God sent some that adore him, 6.151.7.399.
'Tis time to save the few Remains of War. Il.1.82.90.
'Tis sure, the Mighty will revenge at last. Il.1.106.92.
'Tis mine to threaten, Prince, and thine to fear. Il.1.240.98.
'Tis just, O Goddess! I thy Dictates hear. Il.1.288.100.
'Tis ours, the Chance of fighting Fields to try, Il.1.301.101.
So much 'tis safer thro' the Camp to go, Il.1.303.101.
But 'tis for *Greece* I fear: For late was seen Il.1.718.122.
Declare, ev'n now 'tis giv'n him to destroy Il.2.13.128.
Monarch awake! 'tis *Jove's* Command I bear, Il.2.31.128.
Ev'n now, O King! 'tis giv'n thee to destroy Il.2.35.129.
Monarch awake! 'tis *Jove's* Command I bear, Il.2.81.130.
Ev'n now, O King! 'tis giv'n thee to destroy Il.2.85.130.
'Tis Nature's Voice, and Nature we obey. Il.2.168.136.
'Tis thine whate'er the Warrior's Breast inflames, Il.2.277.141.
'Tis just, my Brother, what your Anger speaks: Il.3.86.193.
'Tis not in me the Vengeance to remove; Il.4.79.224.
'Tis not for us, but guilty *Troy* to dread, Il.4.270.234.
'Tis ours, to labour in the glorious Fight. Il.4.473.242.
If 'tis a God, he wears that Chief's Disguise; Il.5.234.278.
Know, 'tis not honest in my Soul to fear, Il.5.312.281.
'Tis not with *Troy,* but with the Gods ye fight. Il.5.749.302.
'Tis hers t'offend; and ev'n offending share Il.5.1078.318.
Brother, 'tis just (reply'd the beauteous Youth) Il.6.418.347.
'Tis now enough: now Glory spreads her Charms, Il.6.424.347.
'Tis Man's to fight, but Heav'n's to give Success. Il.6.427.347.
'Tis *Hector* speaks, and calls the Gods to hear: Il.7.86.367.
'Tis Man's bold Task the gen'rous Strife to try, Il.7.117.369.
'Tis Heav'n the Counsel of my Breast inspires, Il.7.420.385.
'Tis not in Man his fix'd Decree to move: Il.8.175.406.
'Tis thine to punish; ours to grieve alone. Il.8.577.424.
And if we fly, 'tis what our King commands. Il.9.60.434.
'Tis he that offers, and I scorn them all. Il.9.509.458.
Do this, my *Phœnix,* 'tis a gen'rous Part, Il.9.729.470.
'Tis just Resentment, and becomes the brave; Il.9.761.472.
'Tis well, my Sons, your nightly Cares employ, Il.10.225.12.
Oh, turn to Arms; 'tis *Ajax* claims your Aid. Il.11.715.67.
'Tis now no Season for these kind Delays; Il.11.792.71.
If 'tis his Will our haughty Foes to tame, Il.12.77.84.
'Tis ours, the Dignity they give, to grace; Il.12.381.95.
'Tis yours, O Warriors, all our Hopes to raise; Il.13.73.108.
'Tis yours to save us, if you cease to fear; Il.13.75.108.
'Tis not your Cause, *Achilles'* injur'd Fame: Il.13.151.111.
'Tis Heav'n, alas! and *Jove's* all-pow'rful Doom, Il.13.295.119.
'Tis but the Wish to strike before the rest. Il.13.371.123.
But 'tis not ours, with Forces not our own Il.13.989.152.
'Tis not thy Arm, 'tis thund'ring *Jove* we fear: Il.13.1023.153.
'Tis not thy Arm, 'tis thund'ring *Jove* we fear: Il.13.1023.153.
But know, 'tis Madness to contest with *Jove:* Il.15.115.201.
Shall find its Match—No more: 'Tis ours to fight. Il.15.563.218.
And, for our Country, 'tis a Bliss to die. Il.15.583.219.
'Tis now no time for Wisdom or Debates; Il.15.602.220.
'Tis hostile Ground you tread; your native Lands Il.15.900.232.
'Tis time our Fury should relent at last: Il.16.83.238.
His Fame ('tis all the Dead can have!) shall live. Il.16.558.266.
'Tis half the Glory to maintain our Prize. Il.16.686.270.
Strong as you are, 'tis mortal Force you trust, Il.16.751.273.

TIS (CONTINUED)

'Tis not to *Hector,* but to Heav'n I yield. Il.17.108.291.
'Tis time to try if *Ilion's* State can stand Il.17.161.293.
'Tis mine to prove the rash Assertion vain; Il.17.194.295.
'Tis not this Corpse alone we guard in vain, Il.17.284.298.
For yet 'tis giv'n to *Troy,* to ravage o'er Il.17.520.308.
'Tis *Hector* comes; and when he seeks the Prize, Il.17.572.311.
'Tis in our Hands alone our Hopes remain, Il.17.797.319.
'Tis our own Vigour must the Dead regain; Il.17.798.319.
'Tis well (said *Ajax)* be it then thy Care Il.17.801.319.
'Tis not in Fate th' Alternate now to give; Il.18.117.328.
'Tis past—I quell it; I resign to Fate. Il.18.144.329.
'Tis better gen'rously bestow'd on those, Il.18.351.338.
Vulcan draw near, 'tis *Thetis* asks your Aid. Il.18.460.343.
'Tis thine, fair *Thetis,* the Command to lay, Il.18.497.345.
To us, 'tis equal: All we ask is War. Il.19.146.377.
'Tis the chief Praise that e'er to Kings belong'd, Il.19.181.379.
Whate'er we feel, 'tis *Jove* inflicts the Woe: Il.19.282.384.
'Tis true (the Cloud-compelling Pow'r replies) Il.20.29.394.
And 'tis his Fault to love those Sons too well. Il.20.221.403.
'Tis true, the great *Æneas* fled too fast. Il.20.235.403.
'Tis not in Words the glorious strife can end. Il.20.251.404.
Such is our Race: 'Tis Fortune gives us Birth, Il.20.290.406.
Receive this Answer: 'Tis my flying Spear. Il.20.307.407.
'Tis not in me, tho' favour'd by the Sky, Il.20.405.412.
Some Dæmon urges! 'tis my Doom to die! Il.21.104.426.
'Tis not on me thy Rage should heap the Dead. Il.21.234.430.
'Tis not thy Fate to glut his angry Wave. Il.21.337.435.
Such is his Swiftness, 'tis in vain to fly, Il.21.667.449.
Howe'er, 'tis better, fighting for the State, Il.21.669.449.
Consult, ye Pow'rs! ('tis worthy your Debate) Il.22.229.465.
'Tis *Pallas, Pallas* gives thee to my Lance. Il.22.346.470.
'Tis so—Heav'n wills it, and my Hour is nigh! Il.22.378.471.
Death, and black Fate approach! 'Tis I must bleed. Il.22.382.471.
'Tis true I perish, yet I perish great: Il.22.386.471.
Invades my Ear? 'Tis sure my Mother's Voice. Il.22.579.480.
'Tis true, 'tis certain; Man, tho' dead, retains Il.23.122.492.
'Tis true, 'tis certain; Man, tho' dead, retains Il.23.122.492.
'Tis more by Art, than Force of num'rous Strokes, Il.23.385.505.
And 'tis the Artist wins the glorious Course, Il.23.389.506.
Mark then the Goal, 'tis easy to be found; Il.23.399.506.
'Tis now *Atrides'* turn to yield to thee. Il.23.686.517.
Not but (my Friend) 'tis still the wiser way Il.23.689.517.
Tho' 'tis not thine to hurl the distant Dart, Il.23.712.518.
Others 'tis own'd, in Fields of Battle shine, Il.23.773.520.
'Tis *Jove* that calls. And why (the Dame replies) Il.24.117.540.
'Tis Heav'n commands me, and you urge in vain. Il.24.270.547.
'Tis just (said *Priam)* to the Sire above Il.24.369.551.
Sentenc'd, 'tis true, by his inhuman Doom, Il.24.950.575.
'Tis mine, to form his green, unpractis'd years, Od.1.112.37.
But if, to honour lost, 'tis still decreed Od.1.481.55.
But if, to honour lost, 'tis still decreed Od.2.165.70.
'Tis sacred truth I ask, and ask of thee. Od.3.124.91.
And *thou, to whom 'tis giv'n to gild the sphere! Od.4.458.142.
'Tis not, reply'd the Sage, to *Medon* giv'n Od.4.944.162.
'Tis impious to surmize, the pow'rs divine Od.4.995.164.
'Tis *Jove's* decree *Ulysses* shall return: Od.5.41.172.
'Tis mine, with joy and duty to obey. Od.5.114.177.
'Tis past—and *Jove* decrees he shall remove; Od.5.175.180.
'Tis mine to master with a constant mind; Od.5.285.185.
'Tis *Jove* himself the swelling tempest rears; Od.5.391.191.
'Tis mine to bid the wretched grieve no more, Od.6.234.221.
'Tis death with hostile step these shores to tread; Od.6.242.221.
'Tis ours this son of sorrow to relieve, Od.6.245.222.
'Tis what the happy to th' unhappy owe. Od.7.199.245.
A pledge of love! 'tis all a wretch can give. Od.8.522.290.
'Tis what the happy to th' unhappy owe: Od.9.320.319.
'Tis what the Gods require: Those Gods revere, Od.9.321.319.
'Tis what my parents call me, and my peers. Od.9.434.324.
Rise, rise my mates! 'tis *Circe* gives command; Od.10.655.375.
'Tis not the Queen of Hell who thee deceives: Od.11.261.394.
Tread you my steps: 'Tis mine to lead the race, Od.11.440.406.
Be stop'd against the song! 'tis death to hear! Od.12.62.433.
'Tis better six to lose, than all to die. Od.12.138.438.
'Tis thine alone (thy friends and navy lost) Od.12.176.440.
'Tis his alone t'avenge the wrongs I bear; Od.13.257.18.
'Tis *Jove* that sends the stranger and the poor. Od.14.68.39.
'Tis sweet to play the fool in time and place, Od.14.519.62.
'Tis true, the fervor of his gen'rous heart Od.15.236.79.
With what success, 'tis *Jove's* alone to know, Od.15.563.97.
'Tis mine with food the hungry to supply, Od.16.83.106.
'Tis giv'n at length to view my native coast. Od.16.227.114.
'Tis mine to judge if better to employ Od.16.260.117.
Vengeance resolv'd 'tis dang'rous to deferr. Od.16.335.122.
'Tis horrible to shed imperial blood! Od.16.417.126.
Destroy his heir?—but cease, 'tis I command. Od.16.451.129.
The day shall come; nay, 'tis already near, Od.17.296.146.
Howe'er 'tis well! that Sleep a-while can free Od.18.237.178.
My sentence is gone forth, and 'tis decreed Od.18.309.181.
'Tis right; 'tis man's prerogative to give, Od.18.331.183.
'Tis right; 'tis man's prerogative to give, Od.18.331.183.
'Tis thou injurious art, not I am base. Od.18.423.189.
'Tis *Jove's* high will, and be his will obey'd! Od.19.99.197.
Or were he dead, 'tis wisdom to beware: Od.19.105.197.
'Tis hard, he cries, to bring to sudden sight Od.19.257.207.
'Tis ours, with good the scanty round to grace. Od.19.378.212.
But thou *Eumæus,* as 'tis born away, Od.21.250.272.
'Tis impious, Prince! to harm the stranger-guest, Od.21.334.276.
'Tis you that offer, and I scorn them all: Od.22.76.290.
Falshood is folly, and 'tis just to own Od.22.168.295.
'Tis now (brave friends) our turn, at once to throw Od.22.288.300.
'Tis thine to merit, mine is to record. Od.22.388.307.
'Tis thine, oh Queen, to say: And now impart, Od.23.209.333.
'Twas his to suffer, and 'tis mine to mourn! Od.24.339.365.
'Tis so—the Suitors for their wrongs have paid— Od.24.411.369.
'Tis done, and at thy will the Fates succeed. Od.24.551.374.

TISIPHONE
Tisiphone! that oft hast heard my Pray'r, ...1.TrSt.85.413.

TISN'T
'Tis, (no 'tisn't) like Miss *Meadows*. ....6.70.5.201.

TISSUE
That under Cloth of Gold or Tissue, ...6.135.31.367.

TITAN
Whether the Style of *Titan* please thee more, ...1.TrSt.857.445.
To bless, whom Titan touch'd with purer Fire, ...6.49iii.8.142.
Then call'd by thee: the Monster *Titan* came, ...II.1.522.113.
Where *Titan* hides his hoary Head in Snow, ...II.2.894.166.

TITANIAN
There arm once more the bold *Titanian* Band; ....II.8.603.425.
Whom Mortals name the dread *Titanian* Gods. ....II.14.316.178.

TITANS
Encourag'd thus, Witt's *Titans* brav'd the Skies, ...1.EOC.552.304.
Where chain'd on burning Rocks the *Titans* groan. ......II.5.1107.320.
Call the black Titans that with *Chronos* dwell, ...II.14.309.177.

TITARESIUS
Or where the pleasing *Titaresius* glides, ...II.2.910.167.

TITHONUS
From him *Tithonus*, now in Cares grown old, ...II.20.284.406.

TITHONUS'
Now rose refulgent from *Tithonus'* Bed; ....II.11.2.34.
Now rose refulgent from *Tithonus'* bed; ....Od.5.2.170.

TITIAN'S
Paulo's free stroke, and *Titian's* warmth divine. ....6.52.38.157.

TITILLATING
The pungent Grains of titillating Dust. ....2.RL5.84.207.

TITLE
Then to Confirm his Title by the Laws, ...4.JD2A.96.140.
Great without Title, without Fortune bless'd, ...4.1HE1.181.293.
His public virtue makes his title good. ....4.1740.96.337.
O thou! whatever Title please thine ear, ...5.DunA1.17.62.
O Thou! whatever title please thine ear, ...5.DunB1.19.270.
"Who gain'd no title, and who lost no friend, ...6.71.70.204.
Or *Glumglum's* humbler Title sooth thy Ear: ....6.96iv.104.279.
Who gain'd no Title, and who lost no Friend, ...6.97.4.282.
Attend whatever title please thine ear, ...6.106iv.7.307.
Britain, by juster title, makes her own. ....6.107.10.310.
She claims some Title to transgress our Will. ....II.8.501.420.
She claims some Title to transgress his Will. ....II.8.521.421.
To your pretence their title wou'd precede. ....Od.1.506.56.
May boast a title to the loudest fame: ....Od.4.370.137.
Whate'er thy title in thy native sky, ...Od.4.508.144.
And plead my title: *Noman* is my name. ....Od.9.432.323.
'Till his return, no title shall I plead, ...Od.14.178.44.
And urg'd, for title to a consort Queen, ...Od.20.355.244.

TITLED
Or for a Titled Punk, or Foreign Flame, ...4.1HE6.124.245.

TITLES
What once had beauty, titles, wealth, and fame. ....2.Elegy.70.368.
Stuck o'er with titles and hung round with strings, ...3.EOM4.205.146.
Things change their titles, as our manners turn: ....3.Ep3.379.123.
Displays his Titles, lays forth all his Parts, ...4.JD2A.61.138.
In Noble's Titles; Pride and Simony, ...4.JD2A.87.140.
On Poets' Tombs see Benson's titles writ! ....5.DunB3.325.336.
The Queen confers her *Titles* and *Degrees*. ....5.DunB4.566.398.
Still gain new Titles with new Forms; ....6.14v(b).22.50.
Nor let false Shows, or empty Titles please: ....6.19.47.63.
Unenvy'd Titles grace our mighty Names, ...6.48iv.13.136.
Whose Private Name all Titles recommend, ...6.134.3.364.
Not Titles here, but Works, must prove our Worth. ....II.10.77.6.

TITT'RING
Comes titt'ring on, and shoves you from the stage: ....4.2HE2.325.187.
And titt'ring push'd the Pedants off the place: ....5.DunB4.276.371.

TITTLE
There he stopt short, nor since has writ a tittle, ...6.49i.9.137.

TITUS
And Nero reigns a Titus, if he will. ....3.EOM2.198.79.
Was made for Caesar—but for Titus too: ....3.EOM4.146.142.
And give to Titus old Vespasian's due. ....6.71.18.203.

TITYUS
There *Tityus* large and long, in fetters bound, ...Od.11.709.420.

TITYUS'
Thy Shafts aveng'd lewd *Tityus'* guilty Flame, ...1.TrSt.847.445.

TLEPOLEMUS
Tlepolemus, the Son of *Hercules*, : ....II.2.793.162.
While thus they strive, *Tlepolemus* the great ....II.5.776.303.
Yet not in vain, *Tlepolemus*, was thrown ....II.5.820.305.
The *Greeks* with slain *Tlepolemus* retir'd; ....II.5.828.305.
And last, *Tlepolemus* and *Pyres* bleed. ....II.16.509.262.

TMOLUS
Or whom the Vales in Shade of *Tmolus* hide, ...II.2.1053.172.
Beneath the Shades of *Tmolus*, crown'd with Snow, ...II.20.443.413.

TO (OMITTED)
9900

TO-DAY
The lamb thy riot dooms to bleed to-day, ...3.EOM1.81.23.
Or, "Have you nothing new to-day ....4.HS6.93.255.
To-day with pow'r elate, in strength he blooms; ....Od.18.159.174.
Yet still to-morrow falser than to-day. ....Od.21.166.267.
Trust it one moment to my hands to-day: ....Od.21.301.274.
One vent'rous game this hand has won to-day, ...Od.22.7.286.

TO-MORROW
I'd scorn your Prentice, shou'd you die to-morrow. ....2.ChWB.123.62.
P. Not yet, my Friend! to-morrow 'faith it may; ....4.EpS2.2.313.
To-morrow with thee will I fight ....6.79.101.221.
"No not to-morrow, but to night ....6.79.103.221.
To-morrow for my self I must provide, ...Od.15.328.85.
Yet still to-morrow falser than to-day. ....Od.21.166.267.
To-morrow let your arms dispute the prize, ...Od.21.298.274.

TO-MORROW'S
Make your own Terms; and ere to-morrow's Sun .....2.ChJM.563.42.
"Not one survives to breath<e> to-morrow's air." .....Od.17.589.161.

TOAD
Or at the Ear of *Eve*, familiar Toad, ...4.Arbu.319.118.
A Nest, a Toad, a Fungus, or a Flow'r. ....5.DunB4.400.381.
A baneful *Hunch-back'd Toad*, with look Maligne, ...6.26i.10.79.

TOADS
Turns Hares to Larks, and Pigeons into Toads. ....5.DunB4.554.397.

TOADSTOOL'S
Or tumbl'd from the Toadstool's slippery round ....6.96ii.30Z9.271.
"Or tumbled from the Toadstool's slipp'ry Round, ...6.96ii.43.272.

TOAST
Already see you a degraded Toast, ...2.RL4.109.192.
The wise Man's Passion, and the vain Man's Toast? ..2.RL5.10.199.
To Toast our wants and wishes, is her way; ....3.Ep2.88.57.
Toast Church and Queen, explain the News, ...6.39.21.111.
Whose game is Whisk, whose treat a toast in sack, ...6.45.24.125.

TOASTS
Toasts live a scorn, and Queens may die a jest. ....3.Ep2.282.73.
By names of Toasts retails each batter'd jade; ....5.DunA2.126.112.
By names of Toasts retails each batter'd jade; ....5.DunB2.134.301.
But from this Pell-mell-Pack of Toasts, ...6.59.7.177.

TOBACCO
A Brandy and Tobacco Shop is near, ...6.14ii.12.43.

TODAY
The blest today is as completely so, ...3.EOM1.75.23.

TOES
Come near, they trod upon your Toes; ....6.79.19.218.
He tweak'd his Nose, trod on his Toes, ...6.79.59.219.

TOGETHER
Not *Chaos*-like *together crush'd and bruis'd*, ...1.W-F.13.149.
And now a thousand Lives together fled, ...1.TrSt.744.441.
At last agreed, together out they fly, ...2.TemF.493.287.
Together let us beat this ample field, ...3.EOM1.9.13.
Shakes all together, and produces—You. ....3.Ep2.280.73.
"Always together, *tête à tête*, ...4.HS6.106.257.
Me and the Butterflies together. ....4.1HE7.20.269.
Together mix'd; sweet recreation, ...6.1.14.3.
Oh! may all *gentle* Bards together place ye, ...6.40.7.112.
Freedom and Arts together fall; ....6.51i.26.152.
Together o'er the *Alps* methinks we fly, ...6.52.25.157.
Together let us battel on the Plain; ....II.13.309.119.
Thus by Despair, Hope, Rage, together driv'n, ...II.13.428.126.
Thick, undistinguish'd Plumes, together join'd, ...II.16.262.249.
On Earth together lay the Lovers spread. ....II.21.499.442.
Together have we liv'd, together bred, ...II.23.105.491.
Together have we liv'd, together bred, ...II.23.105.491.
And now the mingled Tides together flow: ....II.24.639.563.
Down rush'd the night. East, west, together roar, ...Od.5.379.190.
Together clung, it rolls around the field; ....Od.5.419.192.
The sable ewe and ram, together bound. ....Od.10.686.376.
To bloom together, fade away, and dye. ....Od.23.222.333.

TOIL
See TOYL.
While lab'ring Oxen, spent with Toil and Heat, ...1.PAu.61.84.
And reap'd an Iron Harvest of his Toil; ....1.TrSt.10.409.
On the cold Marble spent with Toil he lies, ...1.TrSt.537.432.
From each she nicely culls with curious Toil, ...2.RL1.131.156.
For when Success a Lover's Toil attends, ...2.RL2.33.161.
There great *Alcides* stooping with his Toil, ...2.TemF.81.258.
Or hand to toil, aspir'd to be the head? ....3.EOM1.260.46.
The merchant's toil, the sage's indolence. ....3.EOM2.172.75.
Where grows?—where grows it not?—If vain our toil, ..3.EOM4.13.129.
Heav'n still with laughter the vain toil surveys, ...3.EOM4.75.135.
That, Vice may merit; 'tis the price of toil; ....3.EOM4.151.142.
In vain th' observer eyes the builder's toil, ...3.Ep1.220.34.
Another's Toil, why not another's Wife? ....3.Ep3.28.88.
Behold Villario's ten-years toil compleat; ....3.Ep4.79.145.
Whose chearful Tenants bless their yearly toil, ...3.Ep4.183.154.
Ease of their toil and part'ners of their care: ....4.2HE1.246.215.
The toil, the danger of the Seas; ....4.HS6.37.253.
Turn what they will to Verse, their toil is vain, ...5.DunB4.213.363.
Make Life a Scene of Pain, and constant Toil, ...6.17iii.6.57.
How finish'd with illustrious toil appears ....6.52.39.157.
Nor Sleep to Toil so easing ....6.78i.7.215.

TOIL (CONTINUED)

Not Sleep to Toil so easing ... 6.78i.7A.215.
No Sleep to Toil so easing ... 6.78i.7B.215.
'Tis all my Pleasure thy past Toil to know, ... 6.96iv.63.278.
We share with Justice, as with Toil we gain: ... Il.1.160.95.
They toil, they sweat, thick Clouds of Dust arise, ... Il.2.187.137.
That caus'd the Contest, shall reward the Toil. ... Il.3.130.196.
'Twas form'd of Horn, and smooth'd with artful Toil; ... Il.4.137.227.
Fix'd to thy Side, in ev'ry Toil I share, ... Il.4.304.235.
Too early expert in the martial Toil, ... Il.5.677.300.
O'erspent with Toil, reposing on the Ground; ... Il.5.989.314.
First gain the Conquest, then reward the Toil. ... Il.6.88.327.
There Heifers graze, and lab'ring Oxen toil; ... Il.9.203.442.
There Heifers graze, and lab'ring Oxen toil; ... Il.9.390.452.
With Toil protected from the prowling Train; ... Il.10.212.11.
And spent with Toil neglect the Watch of Night? ... Il.10.366.19.
And let the *Thracian* Steeds reward our Toil: ... Il.10.533.27.
Then in the polish'd Bath, refresh'd from Toil, ... Il.10.675.32.
Hot with his Toil, and bath'd in hostile Blood. ... Il.11.222.45.
No martial Toil I shun, no Danger fear; ... Il.11.411.53.
Her Force encreasing, as her Toil renews. ... Il.11.959.78.
To toil and struggle thro' the well-fought Day. ... Il.13.4.103.
So when two lordly Bulls, with equal Toil, ... Il.13.879.147.
The Toil of thousands in a Moment falls. ... Il.15.421.213.
Asks Toil, and Sweat, and Blood: Their utmost Might ... Il.15.562.218.
No Force could tame them, and no Toil could tire; ... Il.15.845.229.
Haste, bring the Flames! the Toil of ten long Years ... Il.15.870.230.
And Toil to Toil, and Woe succeeds to Woe. ... Il.16.139.243.
And Toil to Toil, and Woe succeeds to Woe. ... Il.16.139.243.
The Body then they bathe with pious Toil, ... Il.18.411.340.
The hearty Draught rewards, renews their Toil; ... Il.18.633.354.
Tire'd by the Tides, his Knees relax with Toil; ... Il.21.309.433.
Then call the Handmaids with assistant Toil ... Il.24.730.568.
Condemn'd to toil for some inhuman Lord. ... Il.24.925.575.
Assembled there, from pious Toil they rest, ... Il.24.1013.577.
To naval arts inur'd, and stormy toil. ... Od.1.232.43.
Propitious to the search. Direct your toil ... Od.1.368.50.
Your widow'd hours, apart, with female toil ... Od.1.455.54.
If to the right to urge the pilot's toil, ... Od.3.205.95.
To steer the bounding bark with steddy toil, ... Od.3.356.103.
And thou return, with disappointed toil, ... Od.3.403.106.
Sweet *Polycaste,* took the pleasing toil ... Od.3.594.116.
(*Sidon* the Capital) I stretch'd my toil ... Od.4.99.124.
With teeming plenty to reward their toil. ... Od.4.240.130.
For perilous th' assay, unheard the toil, ... Od.4.535.146.
Let their auxiliar force befriend the toil, ... Od.4.553.146.
Hard toil! the prophet's piercing eye to shun; ... Od.4.596.148.
After long woes, and various toil endur'd, ... Od.4.629.149.
There fondly thinks the Gods conclude his toil! ... Od.4.695.151.
Thy voice foretells me shall conclude my toil. ... Od.5.457.194.
Where Fate has destin'd he shall toil no more. ... Od.5.495.196.
Tho' fenc'd from cold, and tho' my toil be past, ... Od.5.608.201.
Then with a short repast relieve their toil, ... Od.6.109.211.
For sailing arts and all the naval toil, ... Od.7.137.242.
What histories of toil could I declare? ... Od.7.293.250.
He bathes: the damsels with officious toil, ... Od.8.491.289.
Unlearn'd in all th' industrious arts of toil. ... Od.9.150.311.
A floating Isle! High-rais'd by toil divine, ... Od.10.3.335.
And take the painful sense of toil away. ... Od.10.428.365.
Tir'd with long toil, we willing sunk to rest. ... Od.10.553.369.
Again the restless orb his toil renews, ... Od.11.739.422.
That stubborn soul, by toil untaught to yield! ... Od.12.334.448.
As weary plowman spent with stubborn toil, ... Od.13.39.3.
(In absence of his Lord, with honest toil ... Od.14.11.35.
Obedient handmaids with assistant toil ... Od.17.100.136.
And with her golden lamp his toil befriends: ... Od.19.39.194.
To diff'rent tasks their toil the Nymphs addres'd: ... Od.19.73.196.
Of matchless deed: untrain'd to martial toil ... Od.19.212.203.
His sinews shrunk with age, and stiff with toil, ... Od.19.366.212.
Of strength superior to the toil assign'd.— ... Od.19.413.214.
The bath renew'd, she ends the pleasing toil ... Od.19.589.225.
Repose to night, and toil to day decreed: ... Od.19.692.229.
When the brave partners of thy ten years toil ... Od.20.26.233.
Thus urging to their toil the menial train. ... Od.20.185.242.
To this poor, tim'rous, toil-detesting drone? ... Od.20.452.255.
Nor prov'd the toil too hard; nor have I lost ... Od.21.467.282.
(The swains unite their toil) the walls, the floor ... Od.22.489.313.
Urge the fleet courser's or the racer's toil; ... Od.24.88.352.
Just as she finish'd her illustrious toil, ... Od.24.175.356.
Great is thy skill, oh father! great thy toil, ... Od.24.287.363.

TOIL-DETESTING

To this poor, tim'rous, toil-detesting drone? ... Od.20.452.255.

TOIL'D

And toil'd most piteously to please their Bride: ... 2.ChWB.59.59.
Where mix'd with Slaves the groaning Martyr toil'd; ... 6.71.6.202.
Thus toil'd the Chiefs in diff'ring Parts engag'd, ... Il.5.110.272.
Thus toil'd the Chiefs in diff'rent Parts engag'd, ... Il.5.110A.272.
So toil'd the *Greeks:* Meanwhile the Gods above ... Il.7.526.390.
Toil'd thro' the Tents, and all his Army fir'd, ... Il.8.267.410.
For whom o'er-toil'd I grind the golden grain: ... Od.20.148.240.

TOILET

And now, unveil'd, the *Toilet* stands display'd, ... 2.RL1.121.155.
Fop at the Toilet, Flatt'rer at the Board, ... 4.Arbu.328.119.

TOILET'S

Or Sappho at her toilet's greazy task, ... 3.Ep2.25.52.

TOILETTE

And the long Labours of the *Toilette* cease— ... 2.RL3.24.171.

TOILS

The Woods and Fields their pleasing Toils deny. ... 1.W-F.120.161.
The wild Desires of Men, and Toils of Day, ... 1.TrSt.479.430.

TOILS (CONTINUED)

Thus still his Courage, with his Toils, encreas'd; ... 1.TrSt.527.432.
Such once employ'd *Alcides'* youthful Toils, ... 1.TrSt.569.434.
From all the Dangers and the Toils of War; ... 1.TrES.234.458.
Much Danger long, and mighty Toils he bore, ... 1.TrUl.17.466.
Due to the Toils of many a bloody Day.) ... 1.TrUl.147.470.
But with their Toils their People's Safety bought: ... 2.TemF.160.267.
Their flow'ry Toils, and sip the fragrant Dew, ... 2.TemF.283.277.
Then see them broke with toils, or sunk in ease, ... 3.EOM4.297.156.
Then see them broke with toils, or lost in ease, ... 3.EOM4.297A.15
And shall not Britain now reward his toils, ... 3.Ep3.215.110.
Ploughs, burns, manures, and toils from Sun to Sun; ... 4.2HE2.271.185.
After a Life of gen'rous Toils endur'd, ... 4.2HE1.9.195.
Why all your Toils? your Sons have learn'd to sing. ... 5.DunB4.546.396
Chang'd as he was, with age, and toils, and cares, ... 6.15.5.51.
Lo *I,* his *God!* in all his toils am near: ... 6.21.33.70.
The husband toils the Adulterer sweats in vain: ... 6.130.30.359.
May *Jove* restore you, when your Toils are o'er, ... Il.1.25.86.
Is this the Pay our Blood and Toils deserve, ... Il.1.211.97.
With these of old to Toils of Battel bred, ... Il.1.351.105.
Whose just Division crown'd the Soldier's Toils; ... Il.1.481.111.
What mighty Toils to either Host remain, ... Il.2.49.129.
A safe Return was promis'd to our Toils, ... Il.2.143.135.
So many Years the Toils of *Greece* remain; ... Il.2.395.145.
Prepar'd new Toils and doubled Woes on Woes. ... Il.2.501.150.
The Warrior's Toils, and combate by his side. ... Il.2.997.170.
Thus with a lasting League your Toils may cease, ... Il.3.105.194.
A World engages in the Toils of Fight. ... Il.3.136.197.
Perhaps the Chiefs, from warlike Toils at ease, ... Il.3.307.208.
Thus with a lasting League our Toils may cease, ... Il.3.326.208.
The Queen of Pleasures shares the Toils of Fight, ... Il.4.14.221.
What glorious Toils, what Wonders they recite, ... Il.4.428.240.
Let him the *Greeks* to hardy Toils excite, ... Il.4.472.242.
The Sons to Toils of glorious Battel bred; ... Il.5.18.266.
Let the brave Chiefs their glorious Toils divide; ... Il.5.41.268.
From Troop to Troop he toils thro' all the Plain. ... Il.5.650.299.
Then mix in Combate and their Toils renew. ... Il.5.704.301.
Foremost he press'd, in glorious Toils to share, ... Il.5.1000.314.
And the brave Prince in num'rous Toils engag'd. ... Il.6.200.336.
Nor ended here his Toils: His *Lycian* Foes ... Il.6.231.337.
Our Troops to hearten, and our Toils to share? ... Il.6.415.347.
Now tir'd with Toils, thy fainting Limbs recline, ... Il.6.444.348.
With Toils, sustain'd for *Paris'* sake and mine: ... Il.6.445.348.
So when triumphant from successful Toils, ... Il.6.610.357.
O'erwhelms the Nations with new Toils and Woes; ... Il.7.82.367.
Ajax, in all the Toils of Battel bred? ... Il.7.236.376.
Awake thy Squadrons to new Toils of Fight. ... Il.7.397.383.
Then late refresh'd with Sleep from Toils of Fight, ... Il.7.578.393.
Shall recompence the Warrior's Toils with Love. ... Il.8.354.414.
Greece with her Ships, and crown our Toils with Fame: ... Il.8.624.425.
A safe Return was promis'd to our toils, ... Il.9.27.433.
Long Toils, long Perils in their Cause I bore, ... Il.9.416.453.
His tedious Toils, and hoary Hairs demand ... Il.9.552.460.
Tir'd with the Toils of Day, and Watch of Night: ... Il.10.111.7.
What Toils attend thee, and what Woes remain? ... Il.10.120.7.
For strong *Necessity* our Toils demands, ... Il.10.134.8.
Ill fits thy Age these Toils to undertake. ... Il.10.189.10.
These Toils, my Subjects and my Sons might bear, ... Il.10.191.10.
Who, all my Motions, all my Toils survey! ... Il.10.330.17.
And tir'd with Toils, neglect the Watch of Night? ... Il.10.470.24.
As with the Light and Warriors Toils begun. ... Il.11.68.37.
Than worn to Toils, and active in the Fight! ... Il.11.542.58.
Toils unforeseen, and fiercer, are decreed; ... Il.12.263.91.
Nor vain (said *Merion)* are our martial Toils; ... Il.13.347.122.
The Toils, the Sorrows, and the Wounds of War. ... Il.14.564.190.
Then *Greece* shall breathe from Toils—The Godhead said; ... Il.15.264.207.
Due to the Toils of many a well-fought Day; ... Il.16.77.238.
From all the Dangers and the Toils of War; ... Il.16.537.265.
And mix'd with Mortals in the Toils of Fight: ... Il.17.88.291.
Full oft' the God his Son's hard Toils bemoan'd, ... Il.19.133.377.
Tho' god-like Thou art by no Toils oppress'd, ... Il.19.155.378.
Shrunk with dry Famine, and with Toils declin'd, ... Il.19.165.378.
And Toils, and Terrors, fill'd the dreadful Day. ... Il.21.612.447.
A thousand Woes, a thousand Toils remain. ... Il.21.694.450.
To shameful Bondage and unworthy Toils. ... Il.22.62.455.
A stately Mule, as yet by Toils unbroke, ... Il.23.755.520.
What Toils they shar'd, what martial Works they wrought, ... Il.24.13.535.
These Toils continue nine succeeding Days, ... Il.24.993.577.
On stormy seas unnumber'd toils he bore, ... Od.1.7.28.
Vain toils! their impious folly dar'd to prey ... Od.1.9.28.
So bright a genius with the toils of state! ... Od.1.494.56.
Those toils (*Telemachus* serene replies) ... Od.1.495.56.
Then urg'd, she perfects her illustrious toils; ... Od.2.125.67.
What toils by sea! where dark in quest of prey ... Od.3.129.92.
What toils by land! where mixt in fatal fight ... Od.3.131.92.
What stratagems we form'd, what toils we bore? ... Od.3.146.92.
How fav'ring heav'n repaid my glorious toils ... Od.4.121.126.
Son of my friend, by glorious toils approv'd, ... Od.4.227.130.
If *Phrygian* camps the friendly toils attest, ... Od.4.443.141.
The partners of his fame and toils at *Troy,* ... Od.4.721.152.
In toils of state the miseries of age: ... Od.4.994.164.
Of wise *Ulysses,* and his toils relates; ... Od.5.9.171.
To toils like these, her husband, and her friend. ... Od.5.180.180.
Now toils the Heroe; trees on trees o'erthrown ... Od.5.311.186.
To end his toils. Is then our anger vain? ... Od.5.373.190.
This life of toils, and what my destin'd end? ... Od.5.384.190.
The wand'ring Chief, with toils on toils oppress'd, ... Od.5.424.192.
The wand'ring Chief, with toils on toils oppress'd, ... Od.5.424.192.
Down rush'd the toils, enwrapping as they lay ... Od.8.339.282.
Be it thro' toils and suff'rings, long and late; ... Od.9.624.332.
Then first my eyes, by watchful toils oppress'd, ... Od.10.34.341.
Whilst we, the wretched part'ners of his toils, ... Od.10.45.341.
The sailors spent with toils their folly mourn, ... Od.10.89.343.
His double toils may claim a double pay, ... Od.10.99.345.
So shall thy tedious toils a respite find, ... Od.10.355.361.
Already, friends! ye think your toils are o'er, ... Od.10.671.375.

TOILS (CONTINUED)

Alas! I hop'd, the toils of war o'ercome, ...Od.11.535.409.
A slave to some poor hind that toils for bread; ....Od.11.599.412.
Greece to reward her soldier's gallant toils ....Od.11.653.416.
Bore toils and dangers, and a weight of woes; ....Od.11.766.424.
Then she: O worn by toils, oh broke in fight, ...Od.12.143.439.
Still are new toils and war thy dire delight? ....Od.12.144.439.
Thro' tedious toils to view thy native coast. ....Od.12.177.440.
Whatever toils the great *Ulysses* past, ...Od.13.5.1.
Much danger<,> long and mighty toils he bore, ...Od.13.108.6.
Due to the toils of many a bloody day) ....Od.13.314.21.
How wou'd the Gods my righteous toils succeed, ...Od.14.447.57.
In toils his equal, and in years the same. ....Od.15.223.79.
(The female train retir'd) your toils to guide? ....Od.19.28.193.
The series of my toils, to sooth her woe, ...Od.19.57.195.
Inspires thy counsels, and thy toils attends. ....Od.20.58.235.
With varied toils the rest adorn the dome. ....Od.20.198.243.
By farther toils decreed the brave to try, ...Od.22.259.299.
And scarce the meshy toils the copious draught contain, ...Od.22.427.308.
Soon as soft slumber eas'd the toils of day, ...Od.23.371.343.
Be it my care, by loans, or martial toils, ...Od.23.383.343.
Successful toils, and battles bravely won? ....Od.24.120.353.
Each following night revers'd the toils of day. ....Od.24.167.356.

TOILSOM

Recall those Nights that clos'd thy toilsom Days, ...6.84.15.239.
This toilsom voyage o'er the surgy main? ....Od.4.424.140.

TOILSOME

Still think on those gay Nights of toilsome Days, ...6.84.15A.239.
Returning sad, when toilsome day declines. ....Od.1.250.45.
Measur'd a length of seas, a toilsome length, in vain. ....Od.1.339.48.
Still turn'd the toilsome mill with anxious mind; ....Od.20.139.240.

TOKEN

The silver Token, and the circled Green, ...2.RL1.32.148.
No grace of Heav'n or token of th' Elect; ....3.Ep3.18.84.
He bears no token of the sabler streams, ...5.DunA2.285.137.
He bears no token of the sabler streams, ...5.DunB2.297.310.
My *only* Token was a Cup like Horn, ...6.96iv.57.278.
Some lasting Token of the *Phrygian* Foe, ...Il.8.640.426.
Take thou this Token of a grateful Heart, ...Il.23.711.518.
Which noted token of the woodland war ....Od.19.545.223.
Let each a token of esteem bestow: ....Od.20.361.250.

TOKENS

The Tokens on my Ribs, in Black and Blue: ....2.ChWB.256.69.

TOLAND

Toland and Tindal, prompt at Priests to jeer, ...5.DunA2.367.144.
C[ollin]s and Toland prompt at Priests to jeer, ...5.DunA2.367B.144.
Toland and Tindal, prompt at priests to jeer, ...5.DunB2.399.316.

TOLAND'S

In Toland's, Tindal's, and in Woolston's days. ....5.DunA3.208.175.
In Toland's, Tindal's, and in Woolston's days. ....5.DunB3.212.330.

TOLD

And told in Sighs to all the trembling Trees; ....1.PWi.62.93.
His ready Tale th'inventive Hero told. ....1.TrUl.139.470.
One Caution yet is needful to be told, ...2.ChJM.99.19.
And told them all, their Pains were at an End. ....2.ChJM.253.26.
I told'em, *Thus you say,* and *thus you do*— ....2.ChWB.150.63.
And told'em false, but *Jenkin* swore 'twas true. ....2.ChWB.151.63.
To her I told whatever cou'd befal; ....2.ChWB.269.70.
That e'er he told a Secret to his Dame. ....2.ChWB.276.70.
To her I told whatever did befal. ....2.ChWB.269A.70.
Such was her Form, as antient Bards have told, ...2.TemF.266.276.
Scarce any Tale was sooner heard than told; ....2.TemF.469.286.
And all who told it, added something new, ...2.TemF.470.286.
Cæsar perhaps had told you he was beat. ....3.Ep1.82A.21.
And gingling down the back-stairs, told the crew, ...3.Ep3.67.93.
A wizard told him in these words our fate: ....3.Ep3.136.104.
There are (I scarce can think it, but am told) ....4.HS1.1.5.
The truth once told, (and wherefore shou'd we lie?) ....4.Arbu.81.101.
I told you when I went, I could not write; ....4.2HE2.28.167.
Our Friend Dan *Prior* told, (you know) ....4.HS6.153.259.
I'm told, you think to take a Step some ....6.10.49.26.
And from those pretty Things you speak have told, ...6.37.9.106.
I'm told (but 'tis not true I hope) ....6.74.3.211.
The rest is told you in a Line or two. ....6.82vi.10.232.
No Grief, that can be told, is felt for 'thee. ....6.85.9Z2.242.
But *M[o]l[y]n[eu]x,* who heard this told, ...6.94.21.259.
Of him told, ...6.96i.12.268.
Bethel, I'm told, will soon be here: ....6.114.2.321.
Or sadly told, how many Hopes lie here! ....6.132.6.362.
Rich Heaps of Brass shall in thy Tent be told; ....Il.6.61.326.
With Tablets seal'd, that told his dire Intent. ....Il.6.210.336.
Thus told the Dictates of his sacred Breast. ....Il.7.50.365.
(Five Girls beside the rev'rend Herald told) ....Il.10.373.19.
Vast Heaps of Brass shall in your Ships be told, ...Il.10.451.23.
But gen'ral Murmurs told their Griefs above, ...Il.11.105.39.
Large Heaps of Brass in Ransome shall be told, ...Il.11.175.43.
Oft' had the Father told his early Doom, ...Il.13.837.145.
Haste, to his Father let the Tale be told: ....Il.14.588.190.
Has Fame not told, how, while my trusty Sword ....Il.15.282.207.
As yet no Messenger had told his Fate, ...Il.22.564.479.
The Morning Planet told th' approach of Light; ....Il.23.281.501.
As many Vests, as many Mantles told, ...Il.24.283.548.
What ancient bards in hall and bow'r have told, ...Od.1.434.53.
Has told the glories of his noble name, ...Od.3.101.91.
And bounteous, from the royal treasure told ....Od.4.175.128.
(In order told, we make the sum compleat.) ....Od.4.608.148.
To bribe whose vigilance, *Ægisthus* told ....Od.4.701.152.
Full oft I told: at length for parting mov'd; ....Od.10.17.340.
Each others face, and each his story told: ....Od.10.536.369.

TOLD (CONTINUED)

Three gallant sons the joyful Monarch told, ...Od.11.347.399.
The wond'rous youths had scarce nine winters told, ...Od.11.381.401.
And what so tedious as a twice-told tale? ....Od.12.538.459.
His ready tale th' inventive hero told. ....Od.13.306.21.
The cautious Chief his ready story told. ....Od.14.219.46.
She told her name, her race, and all she knew. ....Od.15.465.93.
Some God has told them, or themselves survey ....Od.16.372.124.
My cause of coming told, he thus rejoin'd; ....Od.17.136.138.
This told *Atrides,* and he told no more. ....Od.17.168.139.
This told *Atrides,* and he told no more. ....Od.17.168.139.
To thee the purpose of my soul I told, ...Od.19.111.198.
So, melted with the pleasing tale he told, ...Od.19.242.206.
In all he told she recognis'd her Lord: ....Od.19.285.208.
An exile have I told, with weeping eyes, ...Od.19.565.224.
While thus the Chief his woes indignant told, ...Od.20.217.243.
To him sev'n talents of pure ore I told, ...Od.24.320.365.
Well-pleas'd you told its nature, and its name, ...Od.24.393.368.

TOLEDO'S

In thy defence I'll draw *Toledo's* Spado. ....6.48iv.10.136.

TOLERABLE

Three were just tolerable, two were bad. ....2.ChWB.57.59.

TOLERABLY

Narcissa's nature, tolerably mild, ...3.Ep2.53.54.
Extremely clean, and tolerably fair, ...4.HAdv.162.89.

TOLL

But some excising Courtier will have Toll. ....4.JD4.147.37.
Till the third watchman toll; ....6.47.10.128.

TOLL'D

'Till the Bell toll'd, and All arose to Pray. ....2.ChJM.425.35.

TOLLING

Now sink in sorrows with a tolling Bell. ....5.DunA2.220.128.
Now sinks in sorrows with a tolling bell; ....5.DunB2.228.307.

TOLLO

Shall *Arthur* use him like King *Tollo,* ....6.101.26.290.

TOM

See T.
Tom struts a Soldier, open, bold, and brave; ....3.Ep1.105.22.
Rank'd in the Name of *Tom D'Urfy.* ....6.30.6.85.
Of fam'd *Tom Durfy,* or *De Urfe.* ....6.30.6B.85.
To the sweet Name of *Tom D'Urfy.* ....6.30.12.86.
In the great Name of *Tom D'Urfy.* ....6.30.18.86.
Than be no Part in *Tom D'Urfy.* ....6.30.26.86.
To form the Name of Tom: D'Urfey ....6.30.12A.86.
Than be no Part of *Tom* D'Urfey. ....6.30.26A.86.
For only one in *Tom Durfeius.* ....6.30.33.87.
In the great Name of *Tom Durfy.* ....6.30.47.87.
T—Tom—a—as—De—Dur—fe—fy. ....6.30.54.88.
Unless i' th' Name of *Tom D'Urfy.* ....6.30.63.88.
To have a Place in *Tom D'Urfy.* ....6.30.74.88.
Except ith' Name of *Tom D'Urfy.* ....6.30.63A.88.
To the great Name of *Tom Durfy.* ....6.30.83.89.
Tho' *Tom* the Poet writ with Ease and Pleasure, ...6.34.23.101.
The Comick *Tom* abounds in other Treasure. ....6.34.24.101.
Tom B[ur]n[e]t or *Tom D' Urfy* may, ...6.58.51.173.
Tom B[ur]n[e]t or *Tom D' Urfy* may, ...6.58.51.173.
T[o]m W[oo]d of *Ch[i]sw[i]c[k],* deep divine, ...6.121.1.340.
May *Tom,* whom heav'n sent down to raise ....6.150.15.399.

TOM'S

This day *Tom's* fair account has run ....6.150.3.398.

TOMB

Sing, while beside the shaded Tomb I mourn, ...1.PWi.19.90.
Make sacred *Charles's* Tomb for ever known, ...1.W-F.319.180.
Presumptuous *Crete,* that boasts the Tomb of *Jove?* ....1.TrSt.393.426.
A Marble Tomb and Pyramid shall raise, ...1.TrES.251.459.
His Friends a Tomb and Pyramid shall rear; ....1.TrES.333.461.
A Tomb, indeed, with fewer Sculptures grac'd, ...2.ChWB.247.69.
Propt on some tomb, a neighbour of the dead! ....2.ElAb.304.344.
Propt in some tomb, a neighbour of the dead! ....2.ElAb.304A.344.
Nor hallow'd dirge be mutter'd o'er thy tomb? ....2.Elegy.62.367.
Of half that live the butcher and the tomb; ....3.EOM3.162.109.
A Tomb of boil'd, and roast, and flesh, and fish, ...4.HS2.70.59.
Neglected die! and tell it on his Tomb; ....4.Arbu.258.114.
Who praises now? his Chaplain on his Tomb. ....5.DunB4.514.393.
Call round her tomb each object of desire, ...6.52.49.157.
To which thy tomb shall guide inquiring eyes. ....6.72.4.208.
Thy reliques, *Rowe,* to this fair tomb we trust, ...6.72.1C.208.
Peaceful sleep out the Sabbath of the Tomb, ...6.86.19.246.
One day I mean to Fill Sir Godfry's tomb, ...6.88.1.249.
Pensive hast follow'd to the silent tomb, ...6.109.12.314.
Blest Maid; hast follow'd to the silent tomb, ...6.109.12A.314.
The shaded Tomb of old *Æpytus* stood; ....Il.2.732.161.
Who from *Æsetes'* Tomb observ'd the Foes; ....Il.2.961.169.
(This for *Myrinnè's* Tomb th' Immortals know, ...Il.2.984.170.
Wrapt in the cold Embraces of the Tomb; ....Il.3.312.208.
All I can ask of Heav'n, an early Tomb! ....Il.6.519.351.
The Mountain Nymphs the rural Tomb adorn'd, ...Il.6.531.353.
Till Fate condemns me to the silent Tomb. ....Il.6.627.358.
High o'er them all a gen'ral Tomb be rais'd. ....Il.7.405.384.
And round the Pile a gen'ral Tomb they rear'd. ....Il.7.519.389.
Near *Ilus'* Tomb, in Order rang'd around, ...Il.11.73.37.
Now past the Tomb where ancient *Ilus* lay, ...Il.11.217.45.
With solemn Fun'rals and a lasting Tomb. ....Il.11.573.59.
A marble Tomb and Pyramid shall raise, ...Il.16.556.266.
His Friends a Tomb and Pyramid shall rear; ....Il.16.820.275.
Still as a Tomb-stone, never to be mov'd, ...Il.17.492.307.

TOMB (CONTINUED)
These his cold Rites, and this his wat'ry Tomb. .... Il.21.377.436.
Has that curst Hand sent headlong to the Tomb? .... Il.22.541.478.
Shall view *Patroclus'* and *Achilles'* Tomb. .... Il.23.157.495.
Meantime erect the Tomb with pious Hands, ... Il.23.306.501.
(Some Tomb perhaps of old, the Dead to grace; .... Il.23.405.506.
Round his Friend's Tomb *Achilles* drags the Dead; .... Il.24.508.557.
Thy noble Corse was dragg'd around the Tomb, ... Il.24.951.576.
(The Tomb of him thy warlike Arm had slain) .... Il.24.952.576.
And rais'd the Tomb, Memorial of the Dead. .... Il.24.1008.577.
Whose bones, defrauded of a regal tomb .... Od.1.208.42.
Cold in the tomb, or in the deeps below .... Od.2.213.72.
His good old Sire with sorrow to the tomb .... Od.4.144.127.
A tomb along the wat'ry margin raise, ... Od.11.93.385.
The tomb with manly arms and trophies grace, ... Od.11.94.385.
And bow his age with sorrow to the tomb! .... Od.11.239.393.
Imperial Phantom, bow'd thee to the tomb? .... Od.11.494.408.
A rising tomb, the silent dead to grace, ... Od.12.19.430.
The rising tomb a lofty column bore, ... Od.12.21.430.
To the cold tomb, and dreadful all to tread; .... Od.12.404.450.
Thy destin'd tomb, and cast a mighty mound: .... Od.24.102.353.
May point *Achilles'* tomb, and hail the mighty ghost. .... Od.24.106.353.

TOMB-STONE
Still as a Tomb-stone, never to be mov'd, ... Il.17.492.307.

TOMBS
The Fox obscene to gaping Tombs retires, ... 1.W-F.71.156.
Pale Spectres, gaping Tombs, and Purple Fires: .... 2.RL4.44.187.
"Then happy Man who shows the Tombs!" said I, ... 4.JD4.102.33.
On Poets' Tombs see Benson's titles writ! .... 5.DunB3.325.336.
Ev'n in those tombs where their proud names survive, ... 6.22.16.72.
The very Tombs now vanish'd like their dead! .... 6.71.4.202.

TOMES
Dry'd Butterflies, and Tomes of Casuistry. .... 2.RL5.122.209.

TOMORROW
"Tomorrow my Appeal comes on, ... 4.HS6.71.255.

TOMPION
A *Bubble-boy* and *Tompion* at her Side, ... 6.9vii.2.22.

TONE
(Mild were his Looks, and pleasing was his Tone) .... 2.ChJM.148.21.
Then mount the clerks; and in one lazy tone, ... 5.DunA2.355.143.
Then mount the Clerks, and in one lazy tone .... 5.DunB2.387.316.
So Ireland change thy tone, ... 6.90.12.251.
Sharp was his Voice; which in the shrillest Tone, ... Il.2.273.140.

TONGS
His left with Tongs turns the vex'd Metal round; .... Il.18.549.348.
And the strong tongs to turn the metal round. .... Od.3.551.114.

TONGU'D
For whom thus rudely pleads my loud-tongu'd Gate, ... 6.100i.1.288.
A smooth-tongu'd sailor won her to his mind; .... Od.15.462.93.

TONGUE
And make my Tongue victorious as her Eyes; .... 1.PSp.50.66.
And with their forky Tongue shall innocently play. .... 1.Mes.84.120.
And with their forky Tongue, and pointless Sting shall play. ... 1.Mes.84A.120.
There the last Numbers flow'd from *Cowley's* Tongue. .... 1.W-F.272.173.
With his own Tongue still edifies his Ears, ... 1.EOC.614.309.
You stop'd with Kisses my inchanting Tongue, ... 1.TrSP.55.396.
And suck'd new Poisons with his triple Tongue) .... 1.TrSt.667.438.
Your Tongue with constant Flatt'ries feed my Ear, ... 2.ChWB.108.61.
And Empire o'er his Tongue, and o'er his Hand. .... 2.ChWB.433.78.
Leapt up, and wak'd his Mistress with his Tongue. .... 2.RL1.116.154.
And gath'ring Scandals grew on ev'ry Tongue. .... 2.TemF.337.280.
In ev'ry Ear it spread, on ev'ry Tongue it grew. .... 2.TemF.472.286.
Full grown, and fit to grace a mortal Tongue, ... 2.TemF.480.286.
And truths divine came mended from that tongue. .... 2.ElAb.66.324.
Deaf the prais'd ear, and mute the tuneful tongue. .... 2.Elegy.76.368.
Their law his eye, their oracle his tongue. .... 3.EOM3.218.114.
His angel Tongue, no mortal can persuade; .... 3.Ep1.199A.32.
His angel Tongue, no mortal could persuade; .... 3.Ep1.199B.32.
An angel Tongue, which no man can persuade; .... 3.Ep1.199.32.
Just brought out this, when scarce his tongue could stir, ... 3.Ep1.254.37.
Her Tongue bewitch'd as odly as her Eyes, ... 3.Ep2.47.54.
With Eyes that pry not, Tongue that ne'er repeats, ... 4.HS1.135.19.
He forms one Tongue exotic and refin'd. .... 4.JD4.49.29.
Whose Tongue can complement you to the Devil. .... 4.JD4.57.31.
A Tongue that can cheat Widows, cancel Scores, ... 4.JD4.58.31.
'Tis to small purpose that you hold your tongue, ... 4.2HE2.155.175.
Rich with the Treasures of each foreign Tongue; .... 4.2HE2.173.177.
What better teach a Foreigner the tongue? .... 4.2HE1.206.213.
The Honey dropping from *Favonio's* tongue, ... 4.EpS1.67.302.
The Honey dropping from *Ty[rconne]l's* tongue, ... 4.EpS1.67A.302.
Or those foul copies of thy face and tongue, ... 4.1740.53.334.
Full, and eternal privilege of tongue." .... 5.DunA2.346.142.
Blest with his father's front, and mother's tongue, ... 5.DunA2.384.148.
Ev'n *N[orto]n*, gifted with his mother's tongue, ... 5.DunA2.383A.148.
How fluent nonsense trickles from his tongue! .... 5.DunA3.197.174.
How honey'd nonsense trickles from his tongue! .... 5.DunA3.197A.174.
"Full and eternal privilege of tongue." .... 5.DunB2.378.315.
Bless'd with his father's front, and mother's tongue, ... 5.DunB2.416.318.
How fluent nonsense trickles from his tongue! .... 5.DunB3.201.330.
And since my Tongue is in thy praises slow, ... 6.2.4.5.
The tongue mov'd gently first, and Speech was low, ... 6.8.10.18.
Thy very want of Tongue makes thee a kind of Fame. .... 6.8.27.18.
Eurydice still trembled on his Tongue, ... 6.11.114.34.
That plies the Tongue, and wags the Tail, ... 6.14v(a).23.49.
Which, in our Tongue, as I translate, is, ... 6.24iii(a).2.75.
His tongue (with Eye that markd his cunning) .... 6.67.3.195.
'Till Death untimely stop'd his tuneful Tongue. .... 6.84.2.238.

TONGUE (CONTINUED)
When Death untimely stop'd his tuneful Tongue. .... 6.84.2A.238.
Her Tongue still run, on credit from her Eyes, ... 6.99.5.286.
Still must that Tongue some wounding Message bring, ... Il.1.133.93.
Loquacious, loud, and turbulent of Tongue: .... Il.2.256.140.
Curb that impetuous Tongue, nor rashly vain .... Il.2.308.142.
To curb the factious Tongue of Insolence. .... Il.2.337.143.
To hear the Wisdom of his heav'nly Tongue. .... Il.2.345.143.
And the cold Tongue and grinning Teeth divides. .... Il.5.98.271.
Crash'd all his Jaws, and cleft the Tongue within, ... Il.5.355.283.
(How my Heart trembles while my Tongue relates!) .... Il.6.571.354.
The Laws of Council bid my Tongue be bold. .... Il.9.46.434.
My Tongue shall utter, and my Deeds make good. .... Il.9.409.452.
What *Dolon* knows, his faithful Tongue shall own. .... Il.10.485.25.
Are these the faithful Counsels of thy Tongue? .... Il.12.269.91.
Thy warm Impatience makes thy Tongue offend. .... Il.13.976.152.
Fall from that trembling Tongue, and tim'rous Heart? .... Il.14.91.162.
If Truth inspires thy Tongue, proclaim our Will .... Il.15.57.196.
With Paunch distended, and with lolling Tongue, ... Il.16.199.247.
The Teeth it shatter'd, and the Tongue it rent. .... Il.17.698.314.
So voluble a Weapon is the Tongue; .... Il.20.297.406.
Thy Tongue too hastily confers the Prize. .... Il.23.557.511.
Rage gnaw'd the lip, and wonder chain'd the tongue. .... Od.1.488.55.
O insolence of youth! whose tongue affords .... Od.2.95.65.
Deeds then undone my faithful tongue foretold; .... Od.2.201.71.
From him some bribe thy venal tongue requires, ... Od.2.217.72.
Dumb ye all stand, and not one tongue affords .... Od.2.273.74.
My wars, the copious theme of ev'ry tongue, ... Od.4.119.125.
But modest awe hath chain'd his tim'rous tongue. .... Od.4.212.129.
'Till on his tongue the flutt'ring murmurs dy'd: .... Od.4.392.139.
But truth severe shall dictate to my tongue: .... Od.4.470.142.
And on her tongue imperfect accents dye. .... Od.4.937.162.
The windy satisfaction of the tongue. .... Od.4.1092.169.
Speaks from thy tongue and ev'ry action guides; .... Od.6.308.225.
Wide wanders, *Laodame,* thy erring tongue, ... Od.8.175.271.
Ill bear the brave a rude ungovern'd tongue, ... Od.8.199.273.
Well hast thou spoke, and well thy gen'rous tongue .... Od.8.269.277.
A gen'rous heart repairs a sland'rous tongue. .... Od.8.432.287.
In vain essay'd, nor would his tongue obey, ... Od.10.289.357.
But sheath thy ponyard, while my tongue relates .... Od.11.120.386.
Celestial music warbles from their tongue, ... Od.12.220.442.
Mean-time from man to man my tongue exclaims, ... Od.12.460.453.
And all you ask his faithful tongue shall tell. .... Od.13.474.29.
And want too oft betrays the tongue to lye. .... Od.14.149.42.
Or from the fluent tongue produce the tale, ... Od.14.221.46.
Since audience mild is deign'd, permit my tongue .... Od.16.93.107.
And dumb for ever be thy sland'rous tongue! .... Od.17.546.159.
A tongue so flippant, with a throat so wide! .... Od.18.33.168.
The tongue speaks wisely, when the soul is wise; .... Od.18.152.173.
Who smooth of tongue, in purpose insincere, ... Od.18.199.176.
Thy Lord shall curb that insolence of tongue; .... Od.18.386.186.
Should I not punish that opprobrious tongue; .... Od.18.431.189.
Thy head shall pay the forfeit of thy tongue! .... Od.19.116.198.
Rage gnaw'd the lip, amazement chain'd the tongue. .... Od.20.335.249.
Fit for the praise of ev'ry tongue but mine. .... Od.21.114.264.
Mentor beware, nor let that tongue perswade .... Od.22.235.298.
And Folly, with the tongue of Wisdom speaks. .... Od.23.18.319.
O *Troy—may* never tongue pronounce thee more! .... Od.23.24.320.
Flow from this tongue, then let thy servant die! .... Od.23.80.322.
Since what no eye has seen thy tongue reveal'd, ... Od.23.245.335.

TONGUES
To tell 'em, wou'd a *hundred Tongues* require, ... 1.EOC.44.244.
Hear, in *all Tongues* consenting Pæans ring! .... 1.EOC.186.262.
Hear, in *all Tongues* Triumphant *Pæans* ring! .... 1.EOC.186A.262.
But what so pure, which envious Tongues will spare? .... 2.ChJM.43.17.
Sighs, Sobs, and Passions, and the War of Tongues. .... 2.RL4.84.190.
A Thousand busy Tongues the Goddess bears, ... 2.TemF.268.276.
Of various Tongues the mingled Sounds were heard; .... 2.TemF.280.277.
The Doctor's Wormwood Style, the Hash of Tongues, ... 4.JD4.52.29.
Had once a pretty Gift of Tongues enough. .... 4.JD4.77.31.
Now thousand tongues are heard in one loud din: .... 5.DunA2.227.128.
"Sense, speech, and measure, living tongues and dead, ... 5.DunA3.161.165.
Now thousand tongues are heard in one loud din: .... 5.DunB2.235.307.
"Sense, speech, and measure, living tongues and dead, ... 5.DunB3.167.328.
But could'st thou seize some Tongues that now are free, ... 6.8.28.18.
There learn'd she Speech from Tongues that never cease. .... 6.14ii.32.44.
And the sharp arrows of censorious tongues. .... 6.21.6.69.
Those printed unknown Tongues, 'tis said, ... 6.29.7Z1.83.
Then smile Belinda at reproachful tongues, ... 6.38.25.108.
To count them all, demands a thousand Tongues, ... Il.2.580.155.
With mingled Clamors, and with barb'rous Tongues. .... Il.2.1059.172.
Whose Throat surpass'd the Force of fifty Tongues. .... Il.5.979.313.
While *Phœbus* shines, or Men have tongues to praise? .... Il.10.252.13.
Now immolate the Tongues, and mix the wine, ... Od.3.425.107.
The tongues they cast upon the fragrant flame, ... Od.3.437.108.
The care to shun the blast of sland'rous tongues; .... Od.6.328.227.
The tongues of all with transport sound her praise, ... Od.7.92.238.
And the rude insults of ungovern'd tongues. .... Od.16.86.106.
Thus in a wordy war their tongues display .... Od.18.40.169.
To rouze *Ulysses,* points the Suitors' tongues: .... Od.18.396.187.
In various tongues avow their various claims: .... Od.19.199.202.
And distant tongues extoll the patron-name. .... Od.19.386.212.
And the rude licence of ungovern'd tongues, ... Od.23.30.320.

TONSON
So seize them Flames, or take them *Tonson.* .... 6.10.36.25.
Farewell, unhappy *Tonson!* .... 6.47.18.129.
Now, *Tonson,* list thy Forces all, ... 6.58.69.174.

TONSON'S
I hear the Beat of *Tonson's* Drums, ... 6.58.41A.172.

TOO (OMITTED)
418

TOOK
If leaving *Polybus,* I took my Way ... 1.TrSt.89.413.
With eager Speed the well-known Journey took, ... 1.TrSt.142.416.
But when the Fury took her Stand on high, ... 1.TrSt.160.416.
Nor Silver Vases took the forming Mold, ... 1.TrSt.207.419.
Which o'er the Warrior's Shoulder took its Course, ... 1.TrES.283.460.
In a *Phænician* Vessel took my Flight; ... 1.TrUl.149.470.
The Maker saw, took pity, and bestow'd ... 2.ChJM.63.17.
She took th'Impressions of the Love-sick Squire, ... 2.ChJM.432A.35.
She took the Wards in Wax before the Fire, ... 2.ChJM.510.40.
Secret, and undescry'd, he took his Way, ... 2.ChJM.537.41.
When Un-endow'd, I took thee for my own, ... 2.ChJM.550.41.
And climbing, in the Summit took his Place: ... 2.ChJM.606.44.
Sure to be lov'd, I took no Pains to please, ... 2.ChWB.62.59.
And swore the Rambles that I took by Night, ... 2.ChWB.156.64.
In pure good Will I took this jovial Spark, ... 2.ChWB.263.69.
Who took it patiently, and wip'd his Head; ... 2.ChWB.391.76.
I took him such a Box as turn'd him blue, ... 2.ChWB.423.77.
I took to Heart the Merits of the Cause, ... 2.ChWB.429.77.
Was it for this you took such constant Care ... 2.RL4.97.191.
If, after this, you took the graceless Lad, ... 4.2HE2.21.165.
Tore down a Standard, took the Fort and all. ... 4.2HE2.41.167.
Who felt the wrong, or fear'd it, took th' alarm, ... 4.2HE1.255.217.
To see a Footman kick'd that took his pay: ... 4.EpS2.151.322.
Whose Speech you took, and gave it to a Friend? ... 4.EpS2.167.323.
And last, his own cold Æschylus took fire. ... 5.DunA1.210.88.
Amid that Area wide she took her stand, ... 5.DunA2.23.99.
In that wide space the Goddess took her stand, ... 5.DunA2.23A.99.
Amid that area wide they took their stand, ... 5.DunB2.27.297.
Walker with rev'rence took, and lay'd aside. ... 5.DunB4.206.363.
And by his Hand obscene the Porter took, ... 6.14ii.44.44.
A Copy of young *Venus* might have took: ... 6.37.8.106.
First from a Worm they took their Rise, ... 6.53.19A.162.
Whence deathless *Kit*-Cat took its Name, ... 6.59.1.177.
In five long Years I took no second Spouse; ... 6.96iv.5.276.
Then took his Muse at once, and dipt her ... 6.101.13.290.
Took the same course to the same quiet shore, ... 6.109.13A.314.
Achilles with *Patroclus* took his Way, ... Il.1.402.107.
High Heav'n with trembling the dread Signal took, ... Il.1.686.120.
But from the teeming Furrow took his Birth, ... Il.2.659.158.
Antenor took the Word, and thus began: ... Il.3.265.205.
Which o'er the Warrior's Shoulder took its Course, ... Il.5.23.266.
So took my Bow and pointed Darts in hand, ... Il.5.256.279.
Him *Phœbus* took: He casts a Cloud around ... Il.5.429.289.
Then call'd his Coursers, and his Chariot took; ... Il.8.49.398.
Dreadful he shouts: from Earth a Stone he took, ... Il.8.387.416.
Then from the Royal Tent they took their way; ... Il.9.232A.444.
A Child I took thee, but a Hero gave. ... Il.9.607.464.
Th' *Ætolians,* long disdain'd, now took their turn, ... Il.9.707.469.
He heard, return'd, and took his painted Shield: ... Il.10.168.9.
Next him *Ulysses* took a shining Sword, ... Il.10.307.16.
She took, and thunder'd thro' the Seas and Land. ... Il.11.10.35.
This took the charge to combat, that to guide: ... Il.11.140.41.
Th' unkindled Light'ning in his Hand he took, ... Il.11.239.46.
Thence took the long, laborious March by Land. ... Il.11.296.48.
Then with his Spear, unseen, his Time he took, ... Il.11.325.49.
And took their Seats beneath the shady Tent. ... Il.11.763.69.
From Realm to Realm three ample Strides he took, ... Il.13.32.106.
Supported on their Spears, they took their way, ... Il.14.45.160.
Prest in his own, the Gen'ral's Hand he took, ... Il.14.157.165.
With Smiles she took the Charm; and smiling prest ... Il.14.255.173.
And took the Joint, and cut the Nerves in twain: ... Il.14.545.189.
The Goddess said, and sullen took her Place; ... Il.15.108.200.
But *Crœsmus'* Bosom took the flying Spear; ... Il.15.619.220.
From thence he took a Bowl, of antique Frame, ... Il.16.273.249.
Which o'er the Warrior's Shoulder took its course, ... Il.16.588.267.
So spoke th' inspiring God; then took his flight, ... Il.16.885.277.
Alternate, each th' attesting Scepter took, ... Il.18.587.351.
First silver-shafted *Phœbus* took the Plain ... Il.20.91.398.
Nor pierc'd the Windpipe yet, nor took the Pow'r ... Il.22.411.472.
He said: Experienc'd *Merion* took the Word; ... Il.23.1017.529.
Then took the golden Cup his Queen had fill'd, ... Il.24.374.551.
He said, then took the Chariot at a Bound, ... Il.24.541.558.
He said, and entring, took his Seat of State, ... Il.24.746.568.
We saw, as unperceiv'd we took our stand, ... Od.2.123.67.
Indulgent to his pray'r, the Goddess took ... Od.2.305.76.
Thus he, and *Nestor* took the word: My son, ... Od.3.258.98.
But chief the rev'rend Sage admir'd; he took ... Od.3.478.110.
Sweet *Polycaste,* took the pleasing toil ... Od.3.594.116.
The Monarch took the word, and grave reply'd. ... Od.4.91.123.
Nor took a kind adieu, nor sought consent!— ... Od.4.964.163.
He took the path that winded to the cave. ... Od.5.71.175.
At the cool cave arriv'd, they took their state; ... Od.5.249.183.
At length he took the passage to the Wood, ... Od.5.613.201.
A fav'rite virgin's blooming from she took, ... Od.6.27.205.
To town *Ulysses* took the winding way. ... Od.7.18.234.
And humbled in the ashes took his place. ... Od.7.207.246.
Then took the shelter of the neighb'ring wood. ... Od.7.367.254.
Took down our masts, and row'd our ships to shore. ... Od.9.82.306.
Then took a goatskin fill'd with precious wine, ... Od.9.229.316.
He heard, he took, and pouring down his throat ... Od.9.417.323.
I took, and quaff'd it, confident in heav'n: ... Od.10.379.363.
In a *Phænician* vessel took my flight, ... Od.13.316.22.
And took the spreading shelter of the wood. ... Od.14.388.53.
Thus speaking, with dispatchful hand he took ... Od.14.463.58.
Beneath *Troy* walls by night we took our way: ... Od.14.531.63.
The Prince the variegated present took. ... Od.15.145.75.
Thus spoke the dame, and homeward took the road. ... Od.15.491.94.
He took th' occasion as they stood intent, ... Od.15.499.94.
Th' observing Augur took the Prince aside, ... Od.15.571.98.
To seek thee, friend, I hither took my way. ... Od.16.32.103.
Took in the ocean with a broad survey: ... Od.16.383.124.
He took his place, and Plenty heap'd the board. ... Od.17.309.146.
Obscene with reptiles, took his sordid bed. ... Od.17.359.149.
Eumæus took, and plac'd it near his Lord. ... Od.17.407.152.
Unhappy me a *Cyprian* took a-board, ... Od.17.524.158.

TOOK (CONTINUED)
Thus she, and good *Eumæus* took the word. ... Od.17.601.161.
Then, with a manly pace, he took his stand; ... Od.21.129.264.
Thus speaking, from the ground the sword he took ... Od.22.363.304.
And show'd, as unperceiv'd we took our stand, ... Od.24.170.356.
Took their laborious rest, and homely fare; ... Od.24.241.360.

TOOL
Not Lucre's Madman, nor Ambition's Tool, ... 4.Arbu.335.120.
Nor Lucre's Madman, nor Ambition's Tool, ... 4.Arbu.335A.120.
Thy Realm disarm'd of each offensive Tool, ... 6.131i.3.360.

TOOLS
Of Honour bind me, not to maul his Tools; ... 4.EpS2.147.321.
The dextrous smith the tools already drew: ... Od.3.549.114.

TOOTH
And sweet Adonis—you have lost a Tooth. ... 6.129.8.357.

TOOTHLESS
His Saws are toothless, and his Hatchets Lead. ... 4.EpS2.149.321.
Nor had the toothless Satyr caus'd complaining, ... 6.12.8.37.

TOOTING
Would drink and doze at *Tooting* or *Earl's-Court.* ... 4.2HE2.113.173.

TOP
And on its Top descends the Mystic Dove. ... 1.Mes.12.113.
And *Carmel's* flow'ry Top perfumes the Skies! ... 1.Mes.28.115.
And *Cynthus'* Top forsook for *Windsor* Shade; ... 1.W-F.166.165.
High on *Parnassus'* Top her Sons she show'd, ... 1.EOC.94.250.
Where vast *Cythæron's* Top salutes the Sky, ... 1.TrSt.161.416.
Scarce to the Top I stretch'd my aking Sight, ... 2.TemF.246.275.
Top-gallant he, and she in all her Trim, ... 4.JD4.230.45.
As to soft gales top-heavy pines bow low ... 5.DunA2.359.143.
As to soft gales top-heavy pines bow low ... 5.DunB2.391.316.
For Shrubs, when nothing else at top is, ... 6.67.9.195.
Or on the House-top by the *Monkey* cramm'd; ... 6.96iv.84.278.
And (what's the Top of all your Tricks) ... 6.135.11.366.
Beneath, beside me, and a top, ... 6.135.47.368.
Beneath, beside her, and a top, ... 6.135.47A.368.
Then *Jove* from *Ida's* Top his Horrors spreads; ... Il.8.93.401.
But *Jove* incens'd from *Ida's* Top survey'd, ... Il.8.486.420.
From *Ida's* Top her golden Wings display'd; ... Il.8.503.420.
To *Ida's* Top successful *Juno* flies: ... Il.14.331.179.
On *Ida's* Top he waits with longing Eyes, ... Il.15.718.223.
From *Pelion's* cloudy Top an Ash entire ... Il.19.422.389.
Far on *Olyumpus'* Top in secret State ... Il.20.33.394.
(As on a Fig-tree Top, his sounding Steel ... Il.21.44A.423.
High on the Top the manly Corse they lay, ... Il.23.204.498.
To the tall Top a milk-white Dove they tye, ... Il.23.1012.529.
This shorten'd of its top, I gave my train ... Od.9.384.321.
On *Parnass'* top I chac'd the tusky boar. ... Od.21.229.270.
Near the high top he strain'd it strongly round, ... Od.22.501.313.

TOP-GALLANT
Top-gallant he, and she in all her Trim, ... 4.JD4.230.45.

TOP-HEAVY
As to soft gales top-heavy pines bow low ... 5.DunA2.359.143.
As to soft gales top-heavy pines bow low ... 5.DunB2.391.316.

TOPHAM
He buys for Topham, Drawings and Designs, ... 3.Ep4.7.134.

TOPMOST
The topmost Branch a Mother-Bird possest; ... Il.2.376.145.
With offer'd Vows, in *Ilion's* topmost Tow'r. ... Il.6.112.329.
Soon as to *Ilion's* topmost Tow'r they come, ... Il.6.370.344.
But when to *Ida's* topmost Height he came, ... Il.8.57.398.
That Hour, *Achilles* from the topmost Height ... Il.11.730.67.
With Voice divine from *Ilion's* topmost Tow'rs, ... Il.20.72.397.

TOPS
While curling Smokes from Village-Tops are seen, ... 1.PAu.63.84.
And *lash'd* so long, like *Tops,* are lash'd *asleep.* ... 1.EOC.601.308.
Here the prest Herbs with bending Tops betray ... 1.TrSP.169.401.
Trims *Europe's* Balance, tops the Statesman's part, ... 4.JD4.154.39.
Stands our Digamma, and o'er-tops them all. ... 5.DunB4.218.364.
And from *Olympus'* lofty Tops descends. ... Il.1.62.89.
Where high *Olympus'* cloudy Tops arise. ... Il.8.4.395.
Whose taper tops refulgent Gold adorns. ... Il.10.350.18.
On *Ida's* Tops, their Father's fleecy Sheep. ... Il.11.142.42.
And first the Mountain Tops are cover'd o'er, ... Il.12.337.93.
Where *Ida's* misty Tops confus'dly rise; ... Il.13.22.105.
Their Tops connected, but at wider space ... Il.23.828.522.
And from *Olympus'* snowy Tops descends. ... Il.24.156.542.
Soon as *Malæa's* misty tops arise, ... Od.3.366.104.
And spiry tops, the tufted trees above, ... Od.10.175.349.

TOPT
Behind the cloud-topt hill, an humbler heav'n; ... 3.EOM1.104.27.
And seems a moving Mountain topt with Snow. ... Il.13.948.150.

TORCH
Shook high her flaming Torch, in open Sight, ... 2.ChJM.329.30.
The torch of *Venus* burns not for the dead; ... 2.ElAb.258.340.
The Torch of Discord blazing in her Hand, ... Il.11.6.35.
The lighted torch the sage *Euryclea* bears. ... Od.1.540.57.
To light his torch, and give me up to cares; ... Od.18.316.182.
'Till *Hymen* lights the torch of spousal love. ... Od.18.334.184.
From space to space the torch wide-beaming burns, ... Od.18.357.184.
His royal hands; Each torch refulgent burns ... Od.18.392.186.
It aids our torch-light, and reflects the ray. ... Od.18.402.187.
A gazing throng, a torch in ev'ry hand. ... Od.22.534.314.
Instant they bid the blazing torch display ... Od.23.311.338.

TORCH (CONTINUED)
A torch she bears to light with guiding fires ... Od.23.315.338.

TORCH-LIGHT
It aids our torch-light, and reflects the ray. ... Od.18.402.187.

TORCHES
With Torches flaming, to the nuptial Bed; ... Il.18.572.350.
Which boys of gold with flaming torches crown'd; ... Od.7.129.241.
With torches blazing in their hands they past, ... Od.7.431.258.
Be it my task the torches to supply ... Od.18.363.185.

TORE
Those empty Orbs, from whence he tore his Eyes, ... 1.TrSt.78.413.
Tore from these Orbs the bleeding Balls of Sight. ... 1.TrSt.100A.414.
Which these dire Hands from my slain Father tore; ... 1.TrSt.114.415.
Devouring Dogs the helpless Infant tore, ... 1.TrSt.695.439.
Then from the yawning Wound with Fury tore ... 1.TrES.125.454.
He cry'd, he roar'd, he storm'd, he tore his Hair; ... 2.ChJM.756.51.
He cry'd, he roar'd, he rag'd, he tore his Hair: ... 2.ChJM.756A.51.
I tore my Gown, I soil'd my Locks with Dust, ... 2.ChWB.309.71.
Provok'd to Vengeance, three large Leaves I tore, ... 2.ChWB.415.77.
Unconquer'd *Cato* shews the Wound he tore, ... 2.TemF.176.269.
Tore down a Standard, took the Fort and all. ... 4.2HE2.41.167.
Good M[arch]m[on]t's fate tore P[olwar]th from thy side, ... 4.1740.79.336.
And proud *Philosophy* with breeches tore, ... 5.DunA3.191z3.172.
She wept, she blubber'd, and she tore her Hair. ... 6.96ii.2.270.
Devouring Dogs and hungry Vultures tore. ... Il.1.6.85.
And from their Hills the shaggy *Centaurs* tore. ... Il.1.357.105.
The Folds it pierc'd, the plaited Linen tore, ... Il.4.168.229.
Whose forky Point the hollow Breastplate tore, ... Il.5.130.273.
Pierc'd the deep Ranks; their strongest Battel tore; ... Il.8.307.412.
Thy Breast, brave *Archeptolemus!* it tore, ... Il.8.379.416.
That levell'd Harvests, and whole Forests tore: ... Il.9.660.467.
Whose visionary Steel his Bosom tore: ... Il.10.580.28.
Then, from the yawning Wound with Fury tore ... Il.12.479.99.
Whom in the Chance of War a Javelin tore, ... Il.13.281.119.
From his broad Shoulders tore the Spoils away; ... Il.13.697.138.
Tore off his Arms, and loud-exulting said. ... Il.13.778.141.
A Shout, that tore Heav'ns Concave, and above ... Il.13.1060.155.
Tore all the Brawn, and rent the Nerves away: ... Il.16.374.257.
Beneath the Brain the Point a Passage tore, ... Il.16.416.259.
His breathless Bosom, tore the Lance away; ... Il.16.1043.283.
While the fierce *Spartan* tore his Arms away. ... Il.17.66.290.
With headlong Force the foremost Ranks he tore; ... Il.17.330.300.
Now here, now there, the Carcasses they tore: ... Il.18.623.352.
They tore his Flesh, and drank the sable Blood. ... Il.18.674.356.
Beat her sad Breast, and tore her golden Hair; ... Il.19.300.384.
(Confest we saw him) tore his Arms away. ... Il.19.459.391.
The rolling Wheels of *Greece* the Body tore, ... Il.20.455.413.
The spiky Wheels thro' Heaps of Carnage tore; ... Il.20.585.418.
He said; then from the Bank his Jav'lin tore, ... Il.21.217.430.
But (hapless youth) the hideous *Cyclops* tore ... Od.2.25.61.
The splitting Raft the furious tempest tore; ... Od.7.358.254.
He tore, and dash'd on earth the goary brand: ... Od.9.472.325.
Frantic they tore their manly growth of hair; ... Od.10.680.376.
His deathful pounces tore a trembling dove; ... Od.15.567.97.
The mournful hour that tore his son away ... Od.16.148.109.
That sadly tore my royal Lord away: ... Od.18.302.181.
With glancing rage the tusky savage tore. ... Od.19.463.218.
Aslope they glanc'd, the sinewy fibres tore, ... Od.19.526.221.
Thence thro' his breast its bloody passage tore; ... Od.22.109.292.
The Prince's jav'lin tore its bloody way ... Od.22.327.302.
How dash'd like dogs, his friends the *Cyclops* tore, ... Od.23.337.340.

TORIES
While Tories call me Whig, and Whigs a Tory. ... 4.HS1.68.11.
Said, "Tories call'd him Whig, and Whigs a Tory;" ... 4.EpS1.8.297.
And save the state by cackling to the Tories? ... 5.DunA1.192.86.
And cackling save the Monarchy of Tories? ... 5.DunB1.212.285.
Censor of Tories, President of Satyr, ... 6.48ii.2.134.

TORMENT
No fiends torment, no Christians thirst for gold! ... 3.EOM1.108.28.
No fiends torment, nor Christians thirst for gold! ... 3.EOM1.108A.28.
Poor Avarice one torment more would find; ... 3.Ep3.47.90.
The pointed torment on his visual ball. ... Od.9.454.324.

TORMENTING
O sight tormenting to an husband's eyes! ... Od.8.354.282.

TORMENTOR
A Self-Tormentor, worse than (in the Play) ... 4.HAdv.25.77.

TORMENTORS
Find sure tormentors in the guilty breast; ... Od.14.108.41.

TORMENTS
Serene in Torments, unconcern'd in Death; ... 2.ChJM.674.47.
He roar'd, and torments gave his soul to hell— ... Od.22.514.314.

TORN
Thou wert from *Ætna's* burning Entrails torn, ... 1.PAu.91.86.
Torn from the rock, which threatned as it flew; ... 1.TrPA.145.372.
All torn my Garments, and my Bosom bare, ... 1.TrSP.140.399.
Old Limbs of Trees from crackling Forests torn, ... 1.TrSt.506.431.
While from torn Rocks the massy Fragments roll'd; ... 1.TrSt.511A.431.
'Twas torn to Fragments, and condemn'd to Flames. ... 2.ChWB.435.78.
Appear more glorious as more hack'd and torn, ... 5.DunB4.124.354.
A Morning's Pleasure, and at Evening torn: ... 6.19.66.64.
Our Cordage torn, decay'd our Vessels lie, ... Il.2.163.136.
Since fair *Briseïs* from his Arms was torn, ... Il.2.841.164.
So from their Seats the Brother-Chiefs are torn, ... Il.5.210.277.
And Pines and Oaks, from their Foundations torn, ... Il.11.616.61.
From his torn Liver the red Current flow'd, ... Il.11.706.66.
As from some Mountain's craggy Forehead torn, ... Il.13.191.114.

TORN (CONTINUED)
From his torn Arm the *Grecian* rent away ... Il.13.673.137.
Has torn the Shepherd's Dog, or Shepherd Swain; ... Il.15.703.223.
And the torn Boar resigns his Thirst and Life. ... Il.16.998.281.
Torn from his Friend, by right of Conquest mine. ... Il.17.210.295.
Thou from the mighty Dead those Arms hast torn ... Il.17.237.297.
'Twas where by Force of wintry Torrents torn, ... Il.23.499.510.
E'er I become (from thy dear Friendship torn) ... Il.23.675.516.
Torn from her breast, that hour, *Ulysses* dies. ... Od.2.284.75.
And dogs had torn him on the naked plains. ... Od.3.323.102.
Now from my fond embrace by tempests torn, ... Od.4.962.163.
Swept from the deck, and from the rudder torn, ... Od.5.405.192.
Torn was his skin, nor had the ribs been whole, ... Od.5.544.198.
Torn with full force, reluctant beats the wave, ... Od.5.551.199.
And all the rattling shrouds in fragments torn. ... Od.9.80.306.
Torn limb from limb, he spreads his horrid feast, ... Od.9.346.320.
Whose oxen long have torn the furrow'd soil, ... Od.13.40.3.
A stag's torn hide is lapt around his reins: ... Od.13.504.30.
Or torn by birds are scatter'd thro' the sky. ... Od.14.157.43.
Torn from his offspring in the eve of life, ... Od.15.378.87.
Torn from th' embraces of his tender wife, ... Od.15.379.87.
Torn from thy country to no hapless end, ... Od.15.526.95.
From the glad walls inglorious lumber torn. ... Od.19.12.193.
Torn from these walls (where long the kinder pow'rs ... Od.19.678.229.
The brass corroded, and the leather torn: ... Od.22.200.297.
Torn from thy arms, to sail a length of seas; ... Od.23.284.337.
His buskins old, in former service torn, ... Od.24.265.361.

TORRENT
The *hoarse, rough Verse* shou'd like the *Torrent* roar. ... 1.EOC.369.282.
Stemm'd the *wild Torrent* of a *barb'rous Age,* ... 1.EOC.695.319.
Or *P[a]ge* pour'd forth the Torrent of his Wit? ... 4.EpS2.159.322.
But when thy Torrent quench'd the dreadful Blaze, ... 6.96iv.71.278.
Down his wan Cheek a briny Torrent flows; ... Il.9.18.431.
As when a Torrent, swell'd with wintry Rains, ... Il.11.614.61.
(Which from the stubborn Stone a Torrent rends) ... Il.13.193.115.
Rush like a fiery Torrent o'er the Field, ... Il.13.421.126.
While Life's red Torrent gush'd from out the Wound. ... Il.13.820.144.
A sanguine Torrent steeps the reeking Ground; ... Il.17.415.303.
The rumbling Torrent thro' the Ruin rolls, ... Il.17.829.321.
And breaks the Torrent of the rushing Bands. ... Il.17.838.321.
Soon shall the sanguine Torrent spread so wide, ... Il.18.161.330.
A rapid Torrent thro' the Rushes roars: ... Il.18.668.356.
This way and that, the spreading Torrent roars; ... Il.20.573.418.
Oft' as he turn'd the Torrent to oppose, ... Il.21.303.433.
Crossing a Ford, the Torrent sweeps away, ... Il.21.328.434.
Pour the red Torrent on the wat'ry Foe, ... Il.21.391.436.
And scarce restrains the Torrent in her Eyes: ... Il.21.574.446.
Grief stops his Voice, a Torrent drowns his Eyes; ... Il.23.477.509.
But *Priam* check'd the Torrent as it rose. ... Il.24.984.576.
This headlong torrent of amazing words? ... Od.1.492.56.
From mouth and nose the briny torrent ran; ... Od.5.584.200.
Then dy'd the sheep; a purple torrent flow'd, ... Od.11.45.381.
But checking the full torrent in its flow, ... Od.16.244.116.
Down her fair cheek the copious torrent roll'd: ... Od.19.243.206.
She veils the torrent of her tearful eyes; ... Od.19.422.214.
And pour at once the torrent of his soul? ... Od.24.278.363.
Down his wan cheek the trickling torrent ran, ... Od.24.487.371.

TORRENTS
Where late was Dust, now rapid Torrents play, ... 1.TrSt.504.431.
Or haste in headlong Torrents to the Main, ... 6.17ii.11.56.
As Torrents roll, increas'd by num'rous Rills, ... Il.4.516.246.
Thus from high Hills the Torrents swift and strong ... Il.5.116.272.
Less Loud the Woods, when Flames in Torrents pour, ... Il.14.461.186.
Th' impetuous Torrents from their Hills obey, ... Il.16.472.261.
So they, while down their Cheeks the Torrents roll; ... Il.22.126.458.
Burst from his Heart, and Torrents from his Eyes: ... Il.23.22.487.
'Twas where by Force of wintry Torrents torn, ... Il.23.499.510.
From the hot Steeds the sweaty Torrents stream; ... Il.23.591.513.
With streaming eyes in briny torrents drown'd, ... Od.5.194.180.
Where *Phlegeton's* loud torrents rushing down, ... Od.10.608.374.

TORT'RING
For this with tort'ring Irons wreath'd around? ... 2.RL4.100.191.

TORTOISE
The Tortoise here and Elephant unite, ... 2.RL1.135.156.

TORTUR'D
Their tortur'd Minds repining Envy tears, ... 1.TrSt.176.417.
And Cries of tortur'd Ghosts. ... 6.11.62.32.
And see! the tortur'd Ghosts respire, ... 6.11.64.32.
This said, they left him, tortur'd as he lay, ... Od.22.217.297.

TORTURE
The Wound to torture, and the Blood to flow. ... Il.11.985.79.
Of other wretches care the torture ends: ... Od.20.100.237.

TORTURES
Pleasures above, for Tortures felt below: ... 2.ChWB.437.78.
The Poet's Hell, its Tortures, Fiends and Flames, ... 4.JD4.7.27.
Chromatic tortures soon shall drive them hence, ... 5.DunB4.55.347.
My Racks and tortures soon shall drive them hence, ... 5.DunB4.55A.34
For me in tortures thou resign'd'st thy breath, ... 6.25.9.77.
Heav'n, as its purest Gold, by Tortures try'd; ... 6.115.9.323.
Then grinding Tortures his strong Bosom rend, ... Il.11.347.50.
So study'd tortures his vile days shall end. ... Od.22.192.296.

TORY
While Tories call me Whig, and Whigs a Tory. ... 4.HS1.68.11.
Now Whig, now Tory, what we lov'd we hate; ... 4.2HE1.157.209.
Said, "Tories call'd him Whig, and Whigs a Tory;" ... 4.EpS1.8.297.
Who know how like Whig-Ministers to Tory, ... 4.EpS1.106.306.
Point she to Priest or Elder, Whig or Tory, ... 4.EpS2.96.318.
The Goddess smiles on Whig and Tory race, ... 5.DunA3.284.18

TORY (CONTINUED)
Our Goddess smiles on Whig and Tory race, 5.DunA3.284A.183.
Still with dry Eyes the Tory *Celia* sate, 6.33.2.99.
Let not the whigs our tory club rebuke; 6.42v.1.119.
Extract from *Tory* Barrels all *French* Juice, 6.48i.7.133*.
And tho' no Doctors, Whig or Tory ones, 6.135.83.369.

TOSS
Haste to the Fleet, and toss the blazing Brands! 1.TrES.178.456.
Toss their high Heads, and scour along the Plain; 1.TrUl.9.465.
Each Man an *Ascapart,* of Strength to toss 4.JD4.276.49.
In single Fight to toss the beamy Lance; Il.3.180.199.
In measur'd Lists to toss the weighty Lance; Il.3.323.208.
Fight each with Flames, and toss the blazing Brand; Il.8.221.407.
Hast to the Fleet, and toss the blazing Brands! Il.12.532.101.
Their Fellows routed, toss the distant Spear, Il.17.437.304.
The Quoit to toss, the pond'rous Mace to wield, Il.23.713.518.
Hath plac'd beneath the storms which toss the great! Od.1.280.46.
Toss it on high, and whirl it to the skies. Od.11.732.421.
They toss, they foam, a wild confusion raise, Od.12.284.446.
And toss with rising storms the wat'ry way, Od.12.344.448.
Toss their high heads, and scour along the plain; Od.13.100.6.

TOSS'D
Thus in a sea of folly toss'd, 4.HS6.125.257.
This Mess, toss'd up of Hockley-hole and White's; 5.DunB1.222.286.
His sever'd Head was toss'd among the Throng, Il.11.189.43.
He, like a Whirlwind, toss'd the scatt'ring Throng, Il.12.45.83.
He poiz'd, and swung it round; then toss'd on high, Il.12.457.98.
The snowy Fleece, he toss'd, and shook in Air: Il.12.542.101.
Toss'd like a Ball, and whirl'd in Air away, Il.13.271.117.
Toss'd round and round, the missive Marble flings; Il.14.475.187.
Dreadful he spoke, then toss'd the Head on high; Il.14.595.191.
And the toss'd Navies beat the heaving Main. Il.20.82.397.
So shall thy god-like father, toss'd in vain Od.15.198.78.

TOSSES
When the Ship tosses, and the Tempests beat: Il.2.359.144.
His Head now freed, he tosses to the Skies; Il.6.656.359.
Drives the wild Waves, and tosses all the Deeps. Il.11.386.51.
His Head now freed, he tosses to the Skies; Il.15.302.208.
Tosses and drives the scatter'd heaps of corn. Od.5.471.195.

TOSSING
Rough from the tossing surge *Ulysses* moves; Od.6.162.216.
Rein'd the rough storms, and calm'd the tossing floods: Od.12.470.454.

TOST
She tost her meagre Arms; her better Hand 1.TrSt.156.416.
With anxious Hopes his craving Mind is tost, 1.TrSt.455.429.
He poiz'd, and swung it round; then tost on high, 1.TrES.103.453.
The snowy Fleece; he tost, and shook in Air: 1.TrES.188.456.
And first *Sarpedon* tost his weighty Lance, 1.TrES.282.460.
In what new Region is *Ulysses* tost? 1.TrUl.75.468.
For *Pyle* or *Elis* bound; but Tempests tost, 1.TrUl.150.470.
Like varying winds, by other passions tost, 3.EOM2.167.75.
Oft in the Passions' wild rotation tost, 3.Ep1.41.18.
Not to the skies in useless columns tost, 3.Ep3.255.114.
His papers light, fly diverse, tost in air; 5.DunA2.106.109.
His papers light, fly diverse, tost in air; 5.DunB2.114.301.
Long kept by wars, and long by tempests tost, 6.15.2.51.
Tost all the Day in rapid Circles round; Il.1.762.123.
Great *Jove* refus'd, and tost in empty Air: Il.2.499.150.
Prepar'd for Combate, e're the Lance he tost, Il.5.782.303.
This way and that, the boiling Deeps are tost; Il.9.9.431.
When by thy Wiles induc'd, fierce *Boreas* tost Il.15.31.195.
By what wild Passion, Furious! art thou tost? Il.15.146.202.
So whirls a Wheel, in giddy Circle tost, Il.18.695.357.
And round the Banks the ghastly Dead are tost. Il.21.260.431.
And Heaps on Heaps the Clouds are tost before. Il.23.265.500.
I saw him, when like *Jove,* his Flames he tost Il.24.481.556.
But five tall barks the winds and waters tost Od.3.382.105.
For eight slow-circling years by tempests tost, Od.4.97.124.
Fell by disastrous fate; by tempests tost, Od.4.669.150.
Alone, abandon'd, in mid ocean tost, Od.5.169.180.
Ah me! when o'er a length of waters tost, Od.5.524.197.
Tost, and retost, the ball incessant flies. Od.6.114.211.
On what new region is *Ulysses* tost? Od.6.140.214.
Sole on a plank, on boiling surges tost, Od.7.337.253.
Tost by rude tempest thro' a war of waves: Od.8.28.263.
Restore me safe thro' weary wand'rings tost, Od.8.507.289.
Say from what city, from what regions tost, Od.8.601.294.
The tenth we touch'd, by various errors tost, Od.9.95.306.
Thro' various seas by various perils tost, Od.9.309.319.
And my tost limbs now weary'd into rest, Od.10.593.372.
I see! I see, thy bark by *Neptune* tost, Od.11.130.387.
To learn my doom: for tost from woe to woe, Od.11.202.391.
Such, such was I! still tost from care to care, Od.11.763.424.
Tost and retost, it reel'd beneath the blow; Od.12.490.456.
In what new region is *Ulysses* tost? Od.13.242.17.
For *Pyle* or *Elis* bound: but tempest tost Od.13.317.22.
In giddy rounds the whirling ship is tost, Od.14.339.51.
Twice ten sad years o'er earth and ocean tost, Od.16.226.114.
And rode the storm; 'till by the billows tost, Od.19.319.209.
Tempest of wrath his soul no longer tost; Od.20.30.233.
Tost thro' the void, illimitable space: Od.20.75.236.
From vice to vice their appetites are tost, Od.20.215.243.

TOT'NAM
In Tot'nam fields, the brethren with amaze 5.DunA2.249.130.
In Tot'nam fields, the brethren, with amaze, 5.DunB2.261.308.

TOTHER
If you'l but give up one, I'll give up tother. 6.46.4A.127.

TOTT'RING
Thus on each side, alas! our tott'ring State 1.TrSt.269.421.
The tott'ring *China* shook without a Wind, 2.RL4.163.197.
Heav'd on *Olympus* tott'ring *Ossa* stood; Od.11.387.402.

TOTTER
And totter on in bus'ness to the last; 3.Ep1.249.37.
I see the *Savoy* totter to her fall! 5.DunA3.324A.189.
Troy's Turrets totter on the rocking Plain; Il.20.81.397.

TOTTERING
Whose loose head tottering as with wine oppress, Od.18.281.180.

TOTTERS
And *Troy* already totters to her Fall. Il.7.479.388.

TOUCH
Touch the fair Fame of *Albion's* Golden Days. 1.W-F.424.193.
Let soft Compassion touch your gentle Mind; 1.TrVP.106.381.
Nor touch the fatal flow'rs; but, warn'd by me, 1.TrFD.86.389.
No more these Hands shall touch the trembling String: 1.TrSP.235.404.
These touch the vocal Stops, and those the trembling String. 2.ChJM.321.29.
If e'er one Vision touch thy infant Thought, 2.RL1.29A.147.
Hear me, and touch *Belinda* with Chagrin; 2.RL4.77.190.
Or touch, if tremblingly alive all o'er, 3.EOM1.197.39.
His touch, if tremblingly alive all o'er, 3.EOM1.197A.39.
The touch, if tremblingly alive all o'er, 3.EOM1.197B.39.
Or touch, so tremblingly alive all o'er, 3.EOM1.197C.39.
The spider's touch, how exquisitely fine! 3.EOM1.217.42.
Than favour'd Man by touch etherial slain. 3.EOM3.68.98.
The favour'd Man by touch etherial slain, 3.EOM3.68A.98*.
Some wand'ring touch, or some reflected light, 3.Ep2.153.63.
To raise the Thought and touch the Heart, be thine! 3.Ep2.250.70.
P. Alas! few Verses touch their nicer Ear; 4.HS1.33.7.
Ev'n those you touch not, hate you. P. What should ail'em ? 4.HS1.41.9.
But touch me, and no Minister so sore. 4.HS1.76.13.
That touch my Bell, I cannot turn away. 4.HS2.140.67.
"I never touch a Dame of Quality. 4.HAdv.70.81.
Her I transported touch, transported view, 4.HAdv.165.89.
How could Devotion touch the country pews, 4.2HE1.233.215.
Our Courtier scarce could touch a bit, 4.HS6.171.261.
In *Sappho* touch the *Failing of the Sex,* 4.EpS1.15.298.
Rev'rent I touch thee! but with honest zeal; 4.EpS2.216.325.
To touch Achilles' only tender part; 5.DunA2.210.127.
To touch Achilles' only tender part; 5.DunB2.218.306.
Beeves, at his touch, at once to jelly turn, 5.DunB4.551.396.
To touch the Muses future Bard: 6.82vii.4.233.
Can touch Immortals, 'tis a Soul like thine: 6.84.22.239.
Lofty Poet! touch the Sky. 6.96i.50.269.
Our Labours here must touch thy gen'rous Heart, 6.96iii.23.275.
—What, touch me not? what, shun a Wife's Embrace? 6.96iv.2.276.
Not touch me! never Neighbour call'd me Slut! 6.96iv.25.277.
Not to his patient touch, or happy flame, 6.107.23.311.
Chanc'd, with a Touch of just the Tip, 6.135.5.366.
Did, with a Touch of just the Tip, 6.135.5A.366.
The King of Kings, shall touch that sacred Head. Il.1.116.92.
O Sire! can no Resentment touch thy Soul? Il.5.942.311.
To touch the Booty, while a Foe remains. Il.6.86.327.
Its Touch makes Orphans, bathes the cheeks of Sires, Il.11.502.56.
Strength, not their own, the Touch divine imparts, Il.13.89.109.
Thus vanish'd, at thy touch, the Tow'rs and Walls; Il.15.420.213.
Thus vanish, at thy touch, the Tow'rs and Walls; Il.15.420A.213.
Let *Greece* at length with Pity touch thy Breast, Il.16.31.236.
But touch not *Hector, Hector* is my due. Il.16.113.240.
No Drop shall touch me, by almighty *Jove!* Il.23.53.489.
Now seem to touch the Sky, and now the Ground. Il.23.446.508.
His bounding Horses scarcely touch the Fields: Il.23.582.513.
And touch thy Steeds, and swear, thy whole Intent Il.23.663.516.
And touch with momentary Flight the Skies. Il.24.128.540.
His Age, nor touch one venerable Hair, Il.24.192.544.
Thy Age, nor touch one venerable Hair, Il.24.222.546.
From me, no Harm shall touch thy rev'rend Head; Il.24.456.555.
You tempt me, Father, and with Pity touch: Il.24.477.556.
The Deeds of Mortals touch the Ghosts below; Il.24.741.568.
(Ah men unbless'd!) to touch that natal shore. Od.1.12.29.
Can touch my breast; that blessing heav'n denies. Od.3.280.99.
Oh let soft pity touch thy gen'rous mind! Od.6.212.220.
May by his touch alone award the day: Od.8.222.274.
Your hopes already touch your native shore: Od.10.672.375.
His arms he stretch'd; his arms the touch deceive, Od.11.487.408.
Touch the soft lyre, and tune the vocal lay; Od.12.195.441.
Of these fair pastures: If ye touch, ye die. Od.12.382.449.
And publick evil never touch the land! Od.13.61.4.
Unhappy guest! whose sorrows touch my mind! Od.14.395.54.

TOUCH'D
Who touch'd *Isaiah's* hallow'd Lips with Fire! 1.Mes.6.112.
Who touch'd *Isaiah's* hollow'd Lips with Fire! 1.Mes.6A.112.
And secret Transport touch'd the conscious Swain. 1.W-F.90.159.
The *Lines,* tho' touch'd but faintly, are drawn right. 1.EOC.22.241.
Ere warning *Phœbus* touch'd his trembling Ears, 1.EOC.131A.254.
But touch'd with Sorrow for the Dead, too late, 1.TrSt.703.439.
Touch'd with Concern for his unhappy Guest) 1.TrSt.807.443.
Then, touch'd with Grief, the weeping Heav'ns distill'd 1.TrES.256.459.
Touch'd to the Quick, and tickl'd at the Soul. 2.ChJM.277.27.
That scarce they bent the Flow'rs, or touch'd the Ground. 2.ChJM.622.45.
The Knight was touch'd, and in his Looks appear'd 2.ChJM.787.53.
If e'er one Vision touch'd thy infant Thought, 2.RL1.29.147.
And the touch'd Needle trembles to the Pole: 2.TemF.431.284.
For hearts so touch'd, so pierc'd, so lost as mine. 2.ElAb.196.336.
Not touch'd, but rapt; not waken'd, but inspir'd! 2.ElAb.202.336.
As when she touch'd the brink of all we hate. 3.Ep2.52.54.
Yet touch'd and sham'd by *Ridicule* alone. 4.EpS2.211.325.
Touch'd with the Flame that breaks from Virtue's Shrine, 4.EpS2.233.326.
Thou, yet unborn, hast touch'd this sacred shore; 5.DunA3.37.154.
Not touch'd by Nature, and not reach'd by Art." 5.DunA3.228.176.

TOUCH'D (CONTINUED)
Philosophy, that touch'd the Heavens before, 5.DunA3.349.193.
Thou, yet unborn, hast touch'd this sacred shore; 5.DunB3.45.322.
Not touch'd by Nature, and not reach'd by Art." 5.DunB3.230.331.
Touch'd with resentment of ungrateful Man, 6.15.13.51.
To bless, whom Titan touch'd with purer Fire, 6.49iii.8.142.
Touch'd by thy hand, again Rome's glories shine, 6.71.46.204.
Blest Satyrist! who touch'd the Mean so true, 6.118.7.334.
Nor 'till the Sun descended, touch'd the Ground: Il.1.763.123.
The first who boldly touch'd the *Trojan* Shore, Il.2.855.165.
And touch'd with Transport great *Atrides'* Heart. Il.4.361.238.
And touch'd with Grief bespoke the blue-ey'd Maid. Il.5.875.308.
Troy now they reach'd, and touch'd those Banks Divine Il.5.964.312.
He said: Compassion touch'd the Hero's Heart, Il.6.63.326.
(Oh had he perish'd e'er they touch'd our Shore) Il.7.465.387.
Touch'd where the Neck and hollow Chest unite: Il.8.392.416.
A transient Pity touch'd his vengeful Breast. Il.11.735.68.
I, and *Ulysses,* touch'd at *Pthia's* Port, Il.11.904.76.
This touch'd his gen'rous Heart, and from the Tent Il.11.934.77.
Divine Compassion touch'd *Patroclus'* Breast, Il.11.946.77.
He touch'd the Chiefs, and steel'd their manly Souls; Il.13.88.109.
The *Trojan* Warrior, touch'd with timely Fear, Il.13.219.116.
With which a wounded Soldier touch'd his Breast, Il.13.280.119.
But touch'd with Joy the Bosoms of the Brave. Il.13.435.126.
Touch'd ev'ry *Greek,* but *Nestor's* Son the most. Il.13.528.131.
Touch'd with her secret Key, the Doors unfold; Il.14.195.168.
When now they touch'd the Mead's enamel'd Side, Il.14.507.188.
He said, and Sorrow touch'd each *Argive* Breast: Il.14.535.189.
But touch'd the Breast of bold *Peneleus* most: Il.14.570.190.
The first that touch'd th' unhappy *Trojan* Shore: Il.15.857.229.
Then, touch'd with Grief, the weeping Heav'ns distill'd Il.16.561.266.
Soon as his luckless Hand had touch'd the Dead, Il.16.705.271.
Great *Menelaus,* touch'd with gen'rous Woe, Il.17.3.286.
He said, and touch'd his Heart. The raging Pair Il.17.135.293.
For sadder Tydings never touch'd thy Ear; Il.17.772.318.
Approaching now, they touch'd the *Trojan* Land; Il.18.89.327.
If ever yet soft Pity touch'd thy mind, Il.21.105.426.
Fear touch'd the Queen of Heav'n: She saw dismay'd, Il.21.384.436.
His warm Intreaty touch'd *Saturnia's* Ear; Il.21.442.438.
If ever Pity touch'd thee for Mankind. Il.24.414.552.
When *Hermes* greeting, touch'd his royal Hand, Il.24.445.554.
Touch'd with the dear Remembrance of his Sire. Il.24.635.563.
Whose hand reluctant touch'd the warbling wire: Od.1.198.42.
With tender pity touch'd, the Goddess cry'd: Od.1.327.48.
A secret pleasure touch'd *Athena's* soul, Od.3.65.89.
Tydides' vessels touch'd the wish'd-for shore: Od.3.220.96.
How *Agamemnon* touch'd his *Argive* coast, Od.3.234.97.
Apollo touch'd him with his gentle dart; Od.3.359.104.
Her heroe's danger touch'd the pitying Pow'r, Od.5.10.171.
Joy touch'd the Messenger of heav'n: he stay'd Od.5.97.177.
Leucothea saw, and pity touch'd her breast: Od.5.425.193.
That moment, fainting as he touch'd the shore, Od.5.580.200.
Joy touch'd my soul: My soul was joy'd in vain, Od.7.355.253.
Touch'd at the song, *Ulysses* strait resign'd Od.8.79.266.
The tenth we touch'd, by various errors tost, Od.9.95.306.
Joy touch'd my secret soul, and conscious heart, Od.9.491.326.
And touch'd the Youths; but their stern Sire reply'd, Od.10.82.343.
Now touch'd by counter-charms, they change agen, Od.10.463.366.
Shame touch'd *Eurylochus* his alter'd breast, Od.10.529.368.
Touch'd at the sight from tears I scarce refrain, Od.11.675.417.
Touch'd at his sour retreat, thro' deepest night, Od.11.693.419.
She spake, then touch'd him with her pow'rful wand: Od.13.496.29.
Joy touch'd the Hero's tender soul, to find Od.14.61.38.
Before the Græians touch'd the *Trojan* plain, Od.14.266.49.
Touch'd by *Diana's* vengeful arrow, dy'd. Od.15.514.95.
Touch'd at the dreadful story she descends; Od.16.428.128.
Touch'd with the dear remembrance of her Lord; Od.16.467.129.
Soft pity touch'd the mighty master's soul; Od.17.364.149.
With such an image touch'd of human woe; Od.17.441.155.
Then he, with pity touch'd: O Royal Dame! Od.19.298.209.
Touch'd at the dear memorials of his King. Od.21.84.263.
A hope so idle never touch'd his brain: Od.21.341.276.
This hand reluctant touch'd the warbling wire: Od.22.390.307.
Touch'd at her words, the mournful Queen rejoyn'd, Od.23.11.319.
Touch'd at her words, the King with warmth replies, Od.23.184.332.
Touch'd to the soul the King with rapture hears, Od.23.247.335.
When our triumphant navies touch'd your shore; Od.24.141.354.
Spoke when he ceas'd: dumb sorrow touch'd them all. Od.24.503.372.

TOUCHES
With patient Touches of unweary'd Art: 2.TemF.199.271.
Touches some wheel, or verges to some goal; 3.EOM1.59.20.
But touches some above, and some below; 3.EOM4.336.161.
Some wand'ring touches some reflected light, 3.Ep2.153A.63.
Now gentle touches wanton o'er his face, 5.DunA2.193.124.
Now gentle touches wanton o'er his face, 5.DunB2.201.305.
Those useful Touches to impart 6.11.35Z7.31.
This, who but touches, Warriors! is my Foe. Il.23.634.515.
Each vagrant traveller that touches here, Od.14.150.43.

TOUCHING
That touching one must strike the other too; 3.EOM3.292.122.
Such skill in passing all, and touching none. 5.DunB4.258.369.
With *Helen* touching on the *Tyrian* Shore. Il.6.363.344.
Shield touching Shield, a long-refulgent Row; Il.12.311.93.
Shields touching Shields in order blaze above, Il.15.678.222.
And thus, his Hand soft-touching, *Thetis* said. Il.19.10.371.
But kind *Eëtion* touching on the Shore, Il.21.48.424.
The following Car, just touching with his Heel Il.23.601.513.

TOUGH
With Beanstraw, and tough Forage, at the best. 2.ChJM.106.19.
Fans clap, Silks russle, and tough Whalebones crack; 2.RL5.40.202.
Pierce the tough Cors'lets and the brazen Shields. Il.2.652.158.
From the tough Bow directs the feather'd Dart. Il.2.875.165.
Sounds the tough Horn, and twangs the quiv'ring String. Il.4.157.228.

TOUGH (CONTINUED)
Pierc'd the tough Orb, and in his Cuirass hung. Il.5.344.283.
Of tough Bull-hides; of solid Brass the last. Il.7.268.377.
The glitt'ring Javelin pierc'd the tough Bull-hide: Il.13.216.116.
At his full Stretch, as the tough String he drew, Il.15.544.217.
Still the tough bow unmov'd. The lofty man Od.21.262.272.
A ship's tough cable, from a column hung; Od.22.500.313.
Thongs of tough hides, that boast a purple dye; Od.23.204.333.

TOULON
Th' Allies to bomb *Toulon* prepare; 6.10.109.27.

TOUPEE
Sneers at another, in toupee or gown; 5.DunB4.88.349.
Here a bright *Redcoat,* there a smart *Toupee.* 6.9vii.5.22.

TOUR
When in his airy tour, the bird of *Jove* Od.20.302.247.

TOW
There's Danger in assembling Fire and Tow, 2.ChWB.30.58.

TOW'R
Tho' there the Brazen Tow'r was storm'd of old, 1.TrSt.356.425.
Where round some mould'ring tow'r pale ivy creeps, 2.ElAb.243.339.
"I make no question but the *Tow'r* had stood." 4.JD4.85.33.
How shin'd the Soul, unconquer'd in the Tow'r! 4.EpS2.83.317.
This Tow'r it belongs to the Dev'l of Hell; 6.122.2.341.
Now tow'r aloft, and course in airy Rounds; Il.2.544.153.
These, when the *Spartan* Queen approach'd the Tow'r, Il.3.203.201.
So sinks a Tow'r, that long Assaults had stood Il.4.528.246.
Meantime on *Ilion's* Tow'r *Apollo* stood, Il.5.551.295.
With offer'd Vows, in *Ilion's* topmost Tow'r. Il.6.112.329.
With lifted Hands from *Ilion's* lofty Tow'r? Il.6.321.342.
Soon as to *Ilion's* topmost Tow'r they come, Il.6.370.344.
To *Ilion's* steepy Tow'r she bent her way, Il.6.480.350.
Thou, from this Tow'r defend th' important Post; Il.6.552.354.
As from a Brazen Tow'r, o'erlook'd the Field. Il.7.266.377.
But soon as *Ajax* heaves his Tow'r-like Shield, Il.11.606.61.
The bold *Ajaces* fly from Tow'r to Tow'r, Il.12.313.93.
The bold *Ajaces* fly from Tow'r to Tow'r, Il.12.313.93.
Strong as they seem, embattel'd like a Tow'r. Il.13.208.115.
The *Grecian* Phalanx moveless as a Tow'r, Il.15.744.224.
But looks a moving Tow'r above the Bands; Il.15.819.228.
But flaming *Phœbus* kept the sacred Tow'r. Il.16.858.276.
Streams from some lonely Watch-tow'r to the Sky: Il.19.407.389.
Tho' strong in Battel as a brazen Tow'r. Il.20.133.399.
Where the high Watch-tow'r overlooks the Plain; Il.22.192.463.
When tow'r-like *Ajax* and *Ulysses* rose. Il.23.821.522.
Tow'r on the right of yon' æthereal Space. Il.24.364.551.
Tow'r on the right of yon' æthereal Space. Il.24.384.552.

TOW'R-LIKE
But soon as *Ajax* heaves his Tow'r-like Shield, Il.11.606.61.
When tow'r-like *Ajax* and *Ulysses* rose. Il.23.821.522.

TOW'R'D
'Til great *Sarpedon* tow'r'd amid the Field; 1.TrES.4A.449.
Till great *Sarpedon* tow'r'd amid the Field; Il.12.348.94.

TOW'RD
Furious he said, and tow'rd the *Grecian* Crew Il.3.455.213.
Springs from the Mountains tow'rd the guarded Fold: Il.10.214.11.
Shake the dry Field, and thunder tow'rd the Fleet. Il.11.641.62.
As tow'rd the Chief he turn'd his daring Head, Il.13.685.137.
Now man the next, receding tow'rd the Main: Il.15.787.226.
With heavier Strides, that lengthen tow'rd the Town. Il.21.636.448.
Be this the Song, slow-moving tow'rd the Shore, Il.22.493.476.
Tears up the Shore, and thunders tow'rd the Main. Il.23.454.508.
Still edging near, and bears him tow'rd the Steep. Il.23.504.510.
Full tow'rd the east, and mount into the sky. Od.2.182.71.
Tow'rd his lov'd coast he roll'd his eyes in vain, Od.5.107.177.
Host mov'd tow'rd host in terrible array, Od.11.628.414.
'Till now declining tow'rd the close of day, Od.17.687.165.

TOW'RDS
The Coursers ply, and thunder tow'rds the Fleet. Il.10.623.29.
And tow'rds his *Athens* bears the lovely prize; Od.11.402.403.

TOW'RING
Tho' Gods assembled grace his tow'ring Height, 1.W-F.34.151.
Where tow'ring Oaks their growing Honours rear, 1.W-F.221.170.
Where tow'ring Oaks their spreading Honours rear, 1.W-F.221A.170.
There from the Chace *Jove's* tow'ring Eagle bears 1.TrSt.640.437.
Whose tow'ring Summit ambient Clouds conceal'd. 2.TemF.26.255.
Till to the Roof her tow'ring Front she rais'd. 2.TemF.261.276.
While tow'ring o'er your Alphabet, like Saul, 5.DunB4.217.363.
But *Phœbus* now from *Ilion's* tow'ring Height Il.4.585.249.
Tow'ring in Arms, and braves the King of Kings. Il.11.298.48.
Tow'ring they rode in one refulgent Car: Il.11.426.53.
Singly methinks, yon' tow'ring Chief I meet, Il.13.113.110.
Above the rest, two tow'ring Chiefs appear, Il.13.632.136.
High-tow'ring in the Front, the Warrior came. Il.13.756.141.
This said; the tow'ring Chief, prepares to go, Il.13.946.150.
This said; the tow'ring Chief, prepar'd to go, Il.13.946A.150.
The tow'ring *Ajax,* with an ample Stride, Il.13.1020.153.
And tow'ring in the foremost Ranks of War, Il.14.420.183.
(The tow'ring *Ajax* loud-insulting cries) Il.14.550.189.
And *Hector* first came tow'ring to the War. Il.15.347.210.
At one proud Bark, high-tow'ring o'er the Fleet Il.15.482.216.
The tow'ring Chiefs to fiercer Fight advance, Il.16.586.267.
Affrighted *Troy* the tow'ring Victor flies, Il.17.68.290.
Full in the midst, high tow'ring o'er the rest, Il.19.390.388.
With tow'ring Strides *Æneas* first advanc'd; Il.20.194.402.
A tow'ring structure to the palace join'd; Od.1.537.57.
Nine ells aloft they rear'd their tow'ring head, Od.11.383.401.

TOW'RING (CONTINUED)

And tow'ring *Ajax*, an illustrious shade! ..... Od.11.578.412.
A tow'ring spectre of gigantic mold, ... Od.11.742.423.
And her lov'd Lord unplume thy tow'ring pride. ..... Od.19.104.197.
With vollied vengeance blast their tow'ring pride! ..... Od.20.212.243.
The rest ador'd him, tow'ring as he trod; ..... Od.24.26.348.

TOW'RLIKE

But soon as *Ajax* rear'd his tow'rlike Shield, ... Il.17.139.293.

TOW'RS

Must I whose Cares *Phoroneus'* Tow'rs defend, ... 1.TrSt.350.424.
Now springs aloft, and tow'rs th'Ethereal Height, ... 1.TrSt.440.428.
And fam'd *Mycene's* lofty Tow'rs ascend, ... 1.TrSt.459.429.
The Tow'rs, the Fields, and the devoted Ground: ..... 1.TrSt.743.441.
He views the Tow'rs, and meditates their Fall; ..... 1.TrES.23.450.
Let *Telamon* at least our Tow'rs defend, ... 1.TrES.74.452.
At least, let *Telamon* those Tow'rs defend, ... 1.TrES.80Z8.452.
Like some black Tempest gath'ring round the Tow'rs: ..... 1.TrES.92.453.
Nor the bold *Lycians* force the *Grecian* Tow'rs. ..... 1.TrES.156.455.
Against proud *Ilion's* well-defended Tow'rs, ... 1.TrUl.192.472.
But when proud *Ilion's* Tow'rs in Ashes lay, ... 1.TrUl.195A.472.
And strike to Dust th'aspiring Tow'rs of *Troy;* ..... 2.RLA1.138.131.
Where *Thames* with Pride surveys his rising Tow'rs, ... 2.RL3.2.169.
And strike to Dust th' Imperial Tow'rs of *Troy;* ..... 2.RL3.174.182.
Earth shakes her nodding Tow'rs, the Ground gives way; ..... 2.RL5.51.203.
The growing Tow'rs like Exhalations rise, ... 2.TemF.91.259.
And Tow'rs and Temples sink in Floods of Fire. ..... 2.TemF.478.286.
Tenants with sighs the smoakless tow'rs survey, ... 3.Ep3.193.109.
Shall humble to the Dust her lofty Tow'rs. ..... Il.1.166.95.
The lofty Tow'rs of wide-extended *Troy.* ..... Il.2.14.128.
The lofty Tow'rs of wide-extended *Troy.* ..... Il.2.36.129.
The lofty Tow'rs of wide-extended *Troy.* ..... Il.2.86.130.
(The *Greeks* and I) to *Ilion's* hostile Tow'rs, ... Il.2.284.141.
And soon should fall the haughty Tow'rs of *Troy!* ..... Il.2.445.148.
Tow'rs o'er his Armies, and outshines them all: ..... Il.2.565.154.
Where *Dios* from her Tow'rs o'erlooks the Plain, ... Il.2.647.157.
Cleonè, Corinth, with Imperial Tow'rs, ... Il.2.687.159.
Or *Messè's* Tow'rs for silver Doves renown'd, ... Il.2.705.159.
From *Alos, Alopè,* and *Trechin's* Tow'rs; ..... Il.2.830.164.
Th' *Oechalian* Race, in those high Tow'rs contain'd, ... Il.2.884.166.
From rich *Aræsus* and *Adrestia's* Tow'rs, ... Il.2.1004.170.
See! bold *Idomeneus* superior tow'rs ..... Il.3.295.207.
A peaceful Guest, he sought *Mycenæ's* Tow'rs; ..... Il.4.431.241.
His the first Praise were *Ilion's* Tow'rs o'erthrown, ... Il.4.470.242.
Apollo thus from *Ilion's* lofty Tow'rs ..... Il.4.593.249.
So tow'rs his Helmet, and so flames his Shield. ..... Il.5.233.278.
Full o'er your Tow'rs shall fall, and sweep away ..... Il.5.595.297.
Beneath his Arms that *Priam's* Tow'rs should fall; ..... Il.5.880.308.
Raise an embattel'd Wall, with lofty Tow'rs; ..... Il.7.407.385.
They rais'd embattel'd Walls with lofty Tow'rs: ..... Il.7.521.390.
Those on the Fields, and these within their Tow'rs. ..... Il.7.571.392.
To scale our Walls, to wrap our Tow'rs in Flames, ... Il.8.200.407.
Give me to raze *Troy's* long-defended Tow'rs; ..... Il.8.348.414.
And let the Matrons hang with Lights the Tow'rs: ..... Il.8.648.426.
Whose Wrath hung heavy o'er the *Trojan* Tow'rs; ..... Il.8.682.427.
And Tow'rs and Armies humbles to the Dust. ..... Il.9.34.433.
Give to our Arms proud *Ilion's* hostile Tow'rs, ... Il.9.176.441.
Give to our Arms proud *Ilion's* hostile Tow'rs, ... Il.9.363.451.
Of *Greece* he left, and sought the *Theban* Tow'rs, ... Il.10.340.18.
And mark'd the Spot where *Ilion's* Tow'rs arise; ..... Il.11.112.39.
Surveys the Tow'rs, and meditates their Fall. ..... Il.11.236.46.
War thunder'd at the Gates, and Blood distain'd the Tow'rs. ..... Il.12.40.83.
And *Greece* tumultuous from her Tow'rs descend, ... Il.12.160.87.
Maintain'd the Walls and mann'd the lofty Tow'rs: ..... Il.12.172.87.
He views the Tow'rs, and meditates their Fall, ... Il.12.367.94.
Let *Telamon,* at least, our Tow'rs defend, ... Il.12.418.96.
At least, let *Telamon* those Tow'rs defend, ... Il.12.432.97.
Like some black Tempest gath'ring round the Tow'rs; ..... Il.12.446.97.
Nor the bold *Lycians* force the *Grecian* Tow'rs. ..... Il.12.510.100.
But spar'd a while the destin'd *Trojan* Tow'rs: ..... Il.13.441.126.
Thus vanish'd, at thy touch, the Tow'rs and Walls; ..... Il.15.420.213.
Thus vanish, at thy touch, the Tow'rs and Walls; ..... Il.15.420A.213.
Unthinking Man! I fought, those Tow'rs to free, ... Il.16.1007.282.
And the round Bulwarks, and thick Tow'rs reply: ..... Il.18.262.335.
Array'd in Arms, shall line the lofty Tow'rs. ..... Il.18.326.337.
Nine Years imprison'd in those Tow'rs ye lay? ..... Il.18.336.337.
With Voice divine from *Ilion's* topmost Tow'rs, ... Il.20.72.397.
Not till within her Tow'rs the perjur'd Train ..... Il.21.243.431.
Far-stretching in the Shade of *Trojan* Tow'rs. ..... Il.22.8.453.
From *Ida's* Summits, and the Tow'rs of *Troy:* ..... Il.22.226.464.
See, if already their deserted Tow'rs ..... Il.22.478.475.
Jove orders *Iris* to the *Trojan* Tow'rs. ..... Il.24.178.543.
And hurl thee headlong from the Tow'rs of *Troy.* ..... Il.24.929.575.
Then sailing o'er the domes and tow'rs they fly, ... Od.2.181.70.
To shake with war proud *Ilion's* lofty tow'rs, ... Od.2.200.71.
The tow'rs of *Pylos* sink, its views decay, ... Od.3.616.117.
Loud grief resounded thro' the tow'rs of *Troy,* ..... Od.4.355.136.
Th' unwise award to lodge it in the tow'rs, ... Od.8.557.292.
Should bury these proud tow'rs beneath the ground. ..... Od.8.622.296.
The next proud *Lamos'* stately tow'rs appear, ... Od.10.92.343.
Or (since to dust proud *Troy* submits her tow'rs) ..... Od.11.196.391.
Since in the dust proud *Troy* submits her tow'rs. ..... Od.11.205.391.
Here ramparts stood, there tow'rs rose high in air, ... Od.11.323.398.
Against proud *Ilion's* well-defended tow'rs; ..... Od.13.359.24.
Go bathe, and rob'd in white, ascend the tow'rs; ..... Od.17.60.135.

TOW'RY

Exalt thy Tow'ry Head, and lift thy Eyes! ..... 1.Mes.86.120.
There Tow'ry Cities, and the Forests green: ..... 2.TemF.16.254.
Vales, Spires, meandring Streams, and *Windsor's* tow'ry Pride. ..... 6.14ii.54.44.
Pensive she stood on *Ilion's* Tow'ry Height, ... Il.6.468.349.
His Tow'ry Helmet, black with shading Plumes. ..... Il.6.639.358.
Nor shot less swift from *Ilion's* Tow'ry Height: ..... Il.7.26.364.
Or *Ilion* from her tow'ry Height descend, ... Il.15.661.221.
And *Ilion* tumble from her tow'ry Height. ..... Il.21.361.435.

TOW'RY (CONTINUED)

And reach high *Ægæ* and the tow'ry dome. ..... Od.5.487.195.
Thence, where proud *Athens* rears her tow'ry head, ... Od.7.103.239.
Betray'd me tumbling from a tow'ry height, ... Od.11.78.385.

TOWELS

Here lies wrapt up in forty thousand towels ..... 6.147ii.1.390.

TOWER

At home tho' exil'd, free, tho' in the Tower. ..... 4.1HE1.184.293.
Who saw you in Tower, and since ..... 6.68.7.196.
A Tower there is, where six Maidens do dwell; ..... 6.122.1.341.

TOWN

Some thoughtless Town, with Ease and Plenty blest, ... 1.W-F.107.161.
Sudden, before some unsuspecting Town, ... 1.W-F.108A.161.
As several Garbs with Country, Town, and Court. ..... 1.EOC.323.275.
But *catch* the *spreading Notion* of the Town; ..... 1.EOC.409.287.
Nor *Bacchus* less his Native Town defend, ... 1.TrSt.408.427.
Your Fates, your Furies, and your haunted Town. ..... 1.TrSt.819.444.
Far from the Town, a spacious Port appears, ... 1.TrUl.25.466.
He boarded with a Widow in the Town, ... 2.ChWB.265.69.
(My Husband, thank my Stars, was out of Town) ..... 2.ChWB.279.70.
The Judge shall job, the Bishop bite the town, ... 3.Ep3.143A.105.
"And Judges job, and Bishops bite the town, ... 3.Ep3.143.105.
To town he comes, completes the nation's hope, ... 3.Ep3.213.110.
To compass this, his building is a Town, ... 3.Ep4.105.147.
First shade a Country, and then raise a Town. ..... 3.Ep4.190.155.
Can *gratis* see the *Country,* or the *Town?* ..... 4.JD4.145.37.
Shall I, the Terror of this sinful Town, ... 4.JD4.196.43.
And all the Court in Tears, and half the Town, ... 4.HAdv.3.75.
Nor like a Puppy daggled thro' the Town, ... 4.Arbu.225.112.
Why will the Town imagine still I write? ..... 4.Arbu.271A.115.
Let the *Two Curls* of Town and Court, abuse ..... 4.Arbu.380.125.
This Town, I had the Sense to hate it too; ..... 4.JD2A.2.132.
This Town, I had the sense to hate it too: ..... 4.JD2.2.133.
Next pleas'd his Excellence a Town to batter; ..... 4.2HE2.44.167.
And here, while Town, and Court, and City roars, ... 4.2HE2.123.173.
All Worldly's Hens, nay Partridge, sold to town, ... 4.2HE2.234.181.
All He[athco]te's Hens, nay Partridge, sold to town, ... 4.2HE2.234A.181.
Half that the Dev'l o'erlooks from Lincoln Town. ..... 4.2HE2.245.183.
And from the moment we oblige the town, ... 4.2HE1.370.227.
I must by all means come to town, ... 4.HS6.33.253.
"Let my Lord know you've come to town. ..... 4.HS6.44.253.
To Windsor, and again to Town, ... 4.HS6.98.257.
Those Cares that haunt the Court and Town. ..... 4.HS6.132.259.
Name a Town Life, and in a trice, ... 4.HS6.155.259.
Receiv'd a Town Mouse at his Board, ... 4.HS6.159.259.
In town, what Objects could I meet? ..... 4.1HE7.7.269.
And P—x and P* both in town! ..... 4.1HE7.14.269.
And W[ard] and H[enley] both in town! ..... 4.1HE7.14A.269*.
"For Snug's the word: My dear! we'll live in Town." ..... 4.1HE1.147.289.
Blunt *could do Bus'ness,* H[u]ggins *knew the Town,* ..... 4.EpS1.14.298.
And turn this whole illusion on the town. ..... 5.DunA2.124.112.
Escape in Monsters, and amaze the town. ..... 5.DunB1.38.273.
Bays, form'd by nature Stage and Town to bless, ... 5.DunB1.109.277.
At once the Bear and Fiddle of the town. ..... 5.DunB1.224.286.
And turn this whole illusion on the town: ..... 5.DunB2.132.301.
Lo P[op]ple's brow, tremendous to the town, ... 5.DunB3.151.327.
Whate'er of dunce in College or in Town ..... 5.DunB4.87.349.
Stunn'd with his giddy Larum half the town. ..... 5.DunB4.292.373.
The Country Wit, Religion of the Town, ... 6.8.37.19.
Ten Miles from Town, t' a Place call'd *Epsom,* ..... 6.10.50.26.
In ev'ry Town, where *Thamis* rolls his Tyde, ... 6.14ii.1.43.
Such place hath *Deptford,* Navy-building Town, ... 6.14ii.46.44.
The Town in Coach & 6 about ..... 6.14v(b).14A.50.
And thence its current on the town bestows; ..... 6.35.32.104.
Faith, let the modest matrons of the town, ... 6.41.49.114.
Drags from the town to wholsom country air, ... 6.45.2.124.
Vext to be still in town, I knit my brow, ... 6.45.49.126.
Dear, damn'd, distracting Town, farewell! ..... 6.47.1.128.
First sought a Poet's Fortune in the Town: ..... 6.49i.2.137.
Set up with these, he ventur'd on the Town, ... 6.49i.7.137.
Trudges to Town, and first turns Chambermaid; ..... 6.49i.16.138.
In a translated Suit, then tries the Town, ... 6.49i.21.138.
And Pleasure about Town; ..... 6.58.2.170.
In this strange Town a different Course we take, ... 6.82vi.1.232.
Hackney'd in Sin, we beat about the Town, ... 6.82vi.5.232.
Corinna still, and *Fulvia* stay in Town; ..... 6.110.2.316.
Still Cloë, Flavia, Delia, stay in Town: ..... 6.110.2A.316.
Still *Flavia, Chloris, Celia* stay in Town; ..... 6.110.2B.316.
Meantime the Heralds, thro' the crowded Town, ... Il.3.315.208.
Apollo's Altars in his Native Town. ..... Il.4.151.228.
Might fail of Forage in the straiten'd Town: ..... Il.5.255.279.
He left the Town a wide, deserted Plain. ..... Il.5.795.304.
Meanwhile, thou *Hector* to the Town retire, ... Il.6.107.328.
By his Decree I sought the *Trojan* Town, ... Il.6.255.339.
The pompous Structure, and the Town commands, ... Il.6.393.346.
Swift thro' the Town he trod his former way, ... Il.6.489.350.
Swift thro' the Town the Warrior bends his way. ..... Il.6.651.359.
The Town, the Tents, and navigable Seas. ..... Il.8.66.398.
Strait from the Town be Sheep and Oxen sought, ... Il.8.629.426.
Th' insidious Foe the naked Town invade. ..... Il.8.650.426.
Fat Sheep and Oxen from the Town are led, ... Il.8.677.427.
The many-peopled *Orchomenian* Town; ..... Il.9.499.457.
Here, if I stay, before the *Trojan* Town, ... Il.9.534.460.
She paints the Horrors of a conquer'd Town, ... Il.9.703.469.
That Path they take, and speed to reach the Town. ..... Il.11.220.45.
While round the Town the fierce *Epeians* stood. ..... Il.11.869.74.
And whelm in Ruins yon' flagitious Town. ..... Il.13.788.142.
Who held his Seat in *Corinth's* stately Town; ..... Il.13.835.145.
Speed to the Town, and leave the War behind. ..... Il.14.506.188.
And only we destroy th' accursed Town! ..... Il.16.127.242.
Scour o'er the Fields, and stretch to reach the Town. ..... Il.16.453.260.
As when from some beleaguer'd Town arise ..... Il.18.245.334.
The Town, her Gates and Bulwarks shall defend: ..... Il.18.324.337.

TOWN (CONTINUED)

And Dogs shall tear him, e'er he sack the Town. ....Il.18.332.337.
Two mighty Hosts a leaguer'd town embrace, ...Il.18.593.351.
Part to the Town fly diverse o'er the Plain, ...Il.21.4.421.
Apollo enters *Ilion's* sacred Town: ....Il.21.598.446.
With heavier Strides, that lengthen tow'rd the Town. ....Il.21.636.448.
And treat on Terms of Peace to save the Town: ....Il.22.157.459.
Haste, winged Goddess! to the sacred Town, ...Il.24.179.543.
I see the Ruins of your smoking Town! ....Il.24.306.549.
The Fears of *Ilion,* clos'd within her Town, ...Il.24.831.571.
Roll back the gather'd Forests to the Town. ....Il.24.992.577.
The plans of war against the town prepar'd. ....Od.4.350.136.
Hence lies the town as far, as to the ear ....Od.6.357.229.
The lofty palace overlooks the town, ...Od.6.363.229.
To town *Ulysses* took the winding way. ....Od.7.18.234.
And thence its current on the town bestows; ....Od.7.173.244.
(*Artacia's* streams alone supply the town:) ....Od.10.122.346.
The town with walls, and mound inject on mound; ....Od.11.322.398.
Far from the town a spacious port appears, ...Od.13.116.7.
Send to the town thy vessel with thy friends, ...Od.15.44.71.
Swift to the town the well-row'd gally flew: ....Od.15.596.99.
To want like mine, the peopled town can yield ....Od.17.22.133.
My steps *Eumæus* shall to town convey, ...Od.17.29.133.
To town, observant of our Lord's behest, ...Od.17.207.141.
The cavern'd way descending to the town, ...Od.17.231.143.
Holds the chief honours and the town commands, ...Od.17.317.147.
From o'er the porch, appear'd the subject town. ....Od.22.143.294.
The neighbour town? the town shall force the door, ...Od.22.150.294.
The neighbour town? the town shall force the door, ...Od.22.150.294.
While from the town, *Ulysses,* and his band, ...Od.24.234.360.
Thy town, thy parents, and thy native place? ....Od.24.349.365.
Far from the town, an unfrequented bay ....Od.24.359.366.
But what shall guard us, if the town invade? ....Od.24.412.369.

TOWN'S

I never nam'd—the Town's enquiring yet. ....4.EpS2.21.314.

TOWNS

The levell'd Towns with Weeds lie cover'd o'er, ...1.W-F.67.156.
While their weak Heads, like Towns unfortify'd, ...1.EOC.434.288.
Of Towns dispeopled, and the wandring Ghosts ....1.TrSt.55.412.
Towns to one grave, whole nations to the deep? ....3.EOM1.144.33.
Towns to one grave, a Nation to the deep? ....3.EOM1.144A.33.
Towns to one grave, and Nations to the deep? ....3.EOM1.144B.33.
Towns to one grave, or Nations to the deep? ....3.EOM1.144C.33.
"There towns aerial on the waving tree. ....3.EOM3.182.111.
Link Towns to Towns with Avenues of Oak, ...4.2HE2.260.183.
Link Towns to Towns with Avenues of Oak, ...4.2HE2.260.183.
The sons of *Isis* reel! the towns-mens sport; ....5.DunA3.333A.191.
The Business and the Noise of Towns, ...6.1.2A.3.
The rage of courts, and noise of towns; ....6.1.2B.3.
Serve peopled Towns, and stately Cities grace; ....6.17ii.24.56.
And Towns and Armies humbles to the Dust. ....Il.2.150.135.
From *Ripè, Stratie, Tegea's* bord'ring Towns, ...Il.2.733.161.
Where mighty Towns in Ruins spread the Plain, ...Il.2.799.163.
For know, of all the num'rous Towns that rise ....Il.4.65.224.
Three Towns are *Juno's* on the *Grecian* Plains, ...Il.4.75.224.
And Towns and Empires for their Safety bless. ....Il.13.920.148.
On guilty Towns exert the Wrath of Heav'n; ....Il.21.608.447.

TOWNS-MENS

The sons of *Isis* reel! the towns-mens sport; ....5.DunA3.333A.191.

TOWNSEND

Where's such ado with Townsend. ....6.61.16.181.
There's such ado with Townsend. ....6.61.16A.181.

TOWNSHEND'S

All *Townshend's* Turnips, and all *Grovenor's* Mines: ....4.2HE2.273.185.

TOWNSMAN

The Subject of Debate, a Townsman slain: ....Il.18.578.350.

TOWNSMEN

Meantime the Townsmen, arm'd with silent Care, ...Il.18.595.351.

TOWR'D

With high and haughty steps he towr'd along. ....Il.22.32.453.

TOWRING

So pleas'd at first, the towring *Alps* we try, ...1.EOC.225.265.
Then sees *Cythæron* towring o'er the Plain, ...1.TrSt.466.429.
The towring Chiefs to fiercer Fight advance, ...1.TrES.281.460.
The feast, his towring genius marks ....6.150.9.398.

TOWSES

Two or *Three* Squeezes, and *Two* or *Three* Towses, ...6.36.5.104.
Two or *Three* Squeezes, *Two* or *Three* Towses, ...6.36.5A.105.

TOWZE

And that to towze such Things as *flutter,* ....6.135.23.367.

TOWZING

Now *Shock* had giv'n himself the towzing Shake, ...2.RL1.15A.145.

TOY

Sure, if they catch, to spoil the Toy at most, ...3.Ep2.233.69.
Farewell then Verse, and Love, and ev'ry Toy, ...4.1HE1.17.279.
In *Delia's* hand this toy is fatal found, ...6.14iii.7.45.
"To some Lord's Daughter sold the living Toy; ....6.96ii.34.272.
They turn, review, and cheapen every toy. ....Od.15.498.94.

TOYL

See TOIL.
So when the wood-man's toyl her cave surrounds ....Od.4.1041.166.

TOYS

And beads and pray'r-books are the toys of age: ....3.EOM2.280.88.
As toys and empires, for a god-like mind. ....3.EOM4.180.144.
To this were Trifles, Toys, and empty Names. ....4.JD4.8.27.
Not with those Toys the female world admire, ...6.86.3.244.
Not with those Toys the Woman-World admire, ...6.86.3A.244.
Not with those Toys the Female Race admire, ...6.86.3B.244.
Chains, Bracelets, Pendants, all their Toys I wrought. ....Il.18.468.344.
Freighted, it seems, with toys of ev'ry sort ....Od.15.456.92.

TOYSHOP

They shift the moving Toyshop of their Heart; ....2.RL1.100.153.

TRAC'D

Her buskin'd Virgins trac'd the Dewy Lawn. ....1.W-F.170.165.
But as the slightest Sketch, if justly trac'd, ...1.EOC.23.241.
And trac'd the long Records of Lunar Years. ....2.TemF.112.262.
Authors the world and their dull brains have trac'd, ...6.126i.1.353.
Who from *Antenor* trac'd his high Descent. ....Il.4.118.226.
Or trac'd the mazy leveret o'er the lawn. ....Od.17.355.149.
Rare on the mind those images are trac'd, ...Od.19.259.207.
Thus having said, they trac'd the garden o'er, ...Od.24.421.369.

TRACE

And trace the Mazes of the circling Hare. ....1.W-F.122.162.
The shady Empire shall retain no Trace ....1.W-F.371.186.
And trace the Muses *upward* to their *Spring;* ....1.EOC.127.253.
Poets like Painters, thus, unskill'd to trace ....1.EOC.293.272.
At *Oedipus—from* his Disasters trace ....1.TrSt.21.410.
The *Theban* Kings their Line from *Cadmus* trace, ...1.TrSt.317.423.
I look'd again, nor cou'd their Trace be found. ....2.TemF.36.255.
'Tis ours to trace him only in our own. ....3.EOM1.22.15.
Trace Science then, with Modesty thy guide; ....3.EOM2.43.61.
'Tis hers, the brave Man's latest Steps to trace, ...6.84.29.239.
'Tis theirs, the brave Man's latest Steps to trace, ...6.84.29A.239.
But none hath eyes to trace the passing wind, ...6.96ii.30Z29.271.
"But who hath Eyes to trace the passing Wind, ...6.96ii.39.272.
No Trace remain where once the Glory grew. ....Il.7.551.392.
With deathful Thoughts they trace the dreary way, ...Il.10.354.18.
And trace large Furrows with the Shining Share; ....Il.13.882.147.
O Son of *Peleus!* what avails to trace ....Il.21.169.428.
Unskill'd to trace the latent Marks of Heav'n. ....Il.22.18.453.
In me, that Father's rev'rend Image trace, ...Il.24.600.562.
With equal steps the paths of glory trace; ....Od.1.392.51.
By whose commands the raging deeps I trace ....Od.2.299.76.
How trace the tedious series of our fate? ....Od.3.140.92.
With wonder rapt, on yonder cheek I trace ....Od.4.189.129.
New to the plow, unpractis'd in the trace. ....Od.4.861.159.
Who eyes their motion, who shall trace their way? ....Od.10.690.376.
(There curious eyes inscrib'd with wonder trace ....Od.15.440.90.
Who knows their motives, who shall trace their way! ....Od.23.84.322.
While, yet a child, these fields I lov'd to trace, ...Od.24.390.368.

TRACES

In their loose Traces from the Field retreat; ....1.PAu.62.84.
Divides the Traces with his Sword, and freed ....1.TrES.277.460.
Tho' still some traces of our rustic vein ....4.2HE1.270.219.
He fix'd with straiten'd Traces to the Car. ....Il.5.398.286.
Divides the Traces with his Sword, and freed ....Il.16.582.267.
(The silver Traces sweeping at their side) ....Il.19.428.389.
Nine Cubits long the Traces swept the Ground; ....Il.24.337.550.

TRACK

May boldly deviate from the common Track. ....1.EOC.151.257.
Too late returning, snuffs the Track of Men, ...Il.18.374.339.
The Track his flying Wheels had left behind: ....Il.23.586.513.
The track of friendship, not pursuing, sins. ....Od.24.333.365.

TRACKS

"Because I see by all the Tracks about, ...4.1HE1.116.287.
Bright tracks of glory, or a cloud of woes. ....Od.4.530.146.
No tracks of beasts, or signs of men we found, ...Od.10.113.346.

TRACT

Has *Troy* propos'd some spacious Tract of Land? ....Il.20.223.403.
A shelfy tract, and long!) O Seer, I cry, ...Od.4.651.150.
Small tract of fertile lawn, the least to mine. ....Od.4.828.158.
But if, in tract of long experience try'd, ...Od.19.399.213.

TRACTABLE

Grow gentle, tractable, and tame as Geese. ....2.ChJM.668.47.

TRACTS

For much I fear, long Tracts of Land and Sea ....1.TrUl.203.472.
The latent tracts, the giddy heights explore ....3.EOM1.11.13.
The latent tracts, or giddy heights explore ....3.EOM1.11A.13.
Prescient he view'd th' aerial tracts, and drew ....Od.2.187.71.
And measur'd tracts unknown to other ships, ...Od.3.409.106.
Beyond these tracts, and under other skies, ...Od.7.327.252.
And Ocean whitens in long tracts below. ....Od.7.420.258.
For much I fear, long tracts of land and sea ....Od.13.370.25.

TRADE

Set up *themselves,* and drove a *sep'rate* Trade: ....1.EOC.105Z1.251.
Twice-marry'd Dames are Mistresses o' th' Trade: ....2.ChJM.110.20.
How Trade increases, and the World goes well; ....3.Ep1.159.29.
Full sixty years the World has been her Trade, ...3.Ep2.123.60.
B. Trade it may help, Society extend; ....3.Ep3.31A.88.
Trade it may help, Society extend; ....3.Ep3.31.88.
To spoil the nation's last great trade, Quadrille! ....3.Ep3.64.92.
I left no Calling for this idle trade, ...4.Arbu.129.105.
Her Trade supported, and supply'd her Laws; ....4.2HE1.222.213.
All the made trade of Fools and Slaves for Gold? ....4.1HE6.13.237.
You hurt a man that's rising in the Trade. ....4.EpS2.35.314.
As the sage dame, experienc'd in her trade, ...5.DunA2.125.112.
As the sage dame, experienc'd in her trade, ...5.DunB2.133.301.

TRADE (CONTINUED)
Like some free Port of Trade: ......6.14v(b).3.49.
As some free Port of Trade: ......6.14v(b).3A.49.
A *Machiavel* by Trade, ...6.94.6.259.
Full sixty Years the World has been her Trade, ...6.154.9.403.
Arms are her Trade, and War is all her own. ......Il.13.292.119.
The rough *Ciconians* learn'd the Trade of War) ......Il.17.78.291.
Locks in their Chest his Instruments of Trade. ......Il.18.482.345.
For Plowshares, Wheels, and all the rural Trade. ......Il.23.990.529.
Studious of freight, in naval trade well skill'd, ...Od.8.181.272.
Full pails, and vessels of the milking trade. ......Od.9.263.317.
Those hands in work? to tend the rural trade, ...Od.18.405.188.

TRADES
Who trades in Frigates of the second Rate? ......4.HAdv.62.81.

TRADESMAN
The next a Tradesman, meek, and much a lyar; ......3.Ep1.104.22.
And paid a Tradesman once to make him stare, ...3.Ep2.56.55.
Pity mistakes for some poor tradesman craz'd). ......3.Ep3.52.90.
P. If not the Tradesman who set up to day, ...4.EpS2.36.314.

TRADESMEN
Ye Tradesmen vile, in Army, Court, or Hall! ......4.EpS2.17.314.

TRADITION
From no blind Zeal or fond Tradition rise; ......1.TrSt.661.438.
Or plain tradition that this All begun, ...3.EOM3.227.115.

TRADUC'D
Traduc'd your Monarch, and debauch'd your Mother; ......6.116vii.2.328.

TRADUCE
'Those Loving Ladies rudely to traduce. ......6.13.21.39.

TRAFFIC
Or bark of traffic, glides from shore to shore; ......Od.9.146.311.
Your vessel loaded, and your traffic past, ...Od.15.485.93.
A year they traffic, and their vessel load. ......Od.15.492.94.

TRAFFICKS
And Trafficks in the prostituted Laws: ......4.JD2A.73.138.

TRAGEDIES
Dear Rowe, *lets sit and talk of Tragedies:* ......6.49ii.5.140.

TRAGEDY
"A Virgin Tragedy, an Orphan Muse." ......4.Arbu.56.100.
How Tragedy and Comedy embrace; ......5.DunA1.67.68.
How Tragedy and Comedy embrace; ......5.DunB1.69.275.
There to her heart sad Tragedy addrest ......5.DunB4.37.344.
Oft to her heart sad Tragedy addrest ......5.DunB4.37A.344.
In Grecian Buskins *Tragedy shall Mourn,* ......6.26ii.7.79.
—Am I not fit to write a Tragedy? ......6.82ii.6.230.

TRAGIC
One Tragic sentence if I dare deride ......4.2HE1.121.205.
Not but the Tragic spirit was our own, ...4.2HE1.276.219.
For this the Tragic Muse first trod the stage, ...6.32.5.96.
The tragic muse, returning, wept her woes. ......6.107.4.310.
Example dread! and theme of tragic song! ......Od.24.229.358.

TRAIL
Shot the bright Goddess in a Trail of Light. ......Il.4.108.225.
And rolling, drew a bloody Trail along. ......Il.11.190.44.
From Pole to Pole the Trail of Glory flies. ......Il.13.322.120.
And trail those graceful Honours on the Sand! ......Il.23.352.504.

TRAIL'D
Dropt in the Dust are trail'd along the Plains. ......Il.5.714.301.
Trail'd the long Lance that mark'd with Blood the Sand. ......Il.13.748.140.
Trail'd on the Dust beneath the Yoke were spread, ...Il.17.500.308.
His graceful Head was trail'd along the Plain. ......Il.22.500.477.

TRAILING
His length of carcass trailing prints the ground; ......Od.18.121.172.

TRAILS
Long Trails of Light, and shake their blazing Hair. ......1.TrSt.844.445.
That long behind he trails his pompous Robe, ...2.RL3.73.173.
His Flag inverted trails along the ground! ......4.EpS1.154.309.
The Chariot flies, and *Hector* trails behind. ......Il.24.24.535.

TRAIN
Th'Immortal Huntress, and her Virgin Train; ......1.W-F.160.164.
"Ah *Cynthia!* ah—tho' banish'd from thy Train, ...1.W-F.200.168.
Let barb'rous *Ganges* arm a servile Train; ......1.W-F.365.186.
Of all the Virgins of the Sylvan Train, ...1.TrVP.2.377.
Oh wretched we, a vile submissive Train, ...1.TrSt.263.421.
Yon spangled Arch glows with the starry Train, ...1.TrSt.584.434.
His train obey; while all the Courts around ......1.TrSt.605.435.
The Courtly Train, the Strangers, and the rest, ...1.TrSt.652.437.
The Sun descending, the *Phæacian* Train ......1.TrUl.1.465.
Now plac'd in order, the *Phæacian* Train ......1.TrUl.1A.465.
Cou'd swell the Soul to Rage, and fire the Martial Train. ......2.ChJM.325.30.
Damian alone, of all the Menial Train, ...2.ChJM.357.31.
Who pray'd his Spouse, attended by her Train, ...2.ChJM.408.34.
Large was his Train, and gorgeous his Array. ......2.ChJM.447.36.
The Dances ended, all the Fairy Train ......2.ChJM.623.45.
To a long Train of Kindred, Friends, Allies; ......2.ChWB.116.62.
A Train of well-drest Youths around her shone, ...2.RL*A*1.21.127.
While Peers and Dukes, and all their sweeping Train, ...2.RL1.84.152.
That seem'd but *Zephyrs* to the Train beneath. ......2.RL2.58.163.
And Particolour'd Troops, a shining Train, ...2.RL3.43.172.
A Train of Phantoms in wild Order rose, ...2.TemF.9.253.
Fair Virtue's silent Train: Supreme of these ......2.TemF.170.268.

TRAIN (CONTINUED)
Next these the Good and Just, an awful Train, ...2.TemF.318.279.
Next these a youthful Train their Vows exprest, ...2.TemF.378.282.
Love, Hope, and Joy, fair pleasure's smiling train, ...3.EOM2.117.69.
And heads the bold Train-bands, and burns a Pope. ......3.Ep3.214.110.
And close as *Umbra* joins the dirty Train. ......4.JD4.177.41.
One the most meagre of the hungry Train ......4.JD2A.13.132.
Rank'd with their Friends, not number'd with their Train; ......4.EpS2.91.318.
Room for my Lord! three Jockeys in his train; ......5.DunA2.184.124.
Room for my Lord! three jockeys in his train; ......5.DunB2.192.305.
"O *Cara! Cara!* silence all that train: ......5.DunB4.53.346.
Who lead fair Virtue's train along, ...6.51i.11.151.
When Int'rest calls off all her sneaking Train, ...6.84.31.239.
Tho' Int'rest calls off all her sneaking Train, ...6.84.31Z3.239.
Drew after her a Train of Cocks: ......6.93.6.256.
Conven'd to Council all the *Grecian* Train; ......Il.1.75.90.
Wash'd by the briny Wave, the pious Train ......Il.1.412.107.
Defrauds the Votes of all the *Grecian* Train; ......Il.1.508.112.
Conjure him far to drive the *Grecian* Train, ...Il.1.532.113.
The Sire of Gods, and all th' Etherial Train, ...Il.1.554.114.
Bid him in Arms draw forth th' embattel'd Train, ...Il.2.11.127.
In just Array draw forth th' embattel'd Train, ...Il.2.33.128.
In just Array draw forth th' embattel'd Train, ...Il.2.83.130.
So, from the Tents and Ships, a length'ning Train ......Il.2.117.133.
With long-resounding Cries they urge the Train, ...Il.2.185.137.
He runs, he flies, thro' all the Grecian Train, ...Il.2.224.138.
Back to th' Assembly roll the thronging Train, ...Il.2.247.139.
what Heart but melts to leave the tender Train, ...Il.2.356.144.
On that great Day when first the martial Train ......Il.2.416.147.
In Tribes and Nations to divide thy Train: ......Il.2.431.148.
To these succeed *Aspledon's* martial Train, ...Il.2.610.156.
Next move to War the gen'rous *Argive* Train, ...Il.2.675.159.
In sep'rate Squadrons these their Train divide, ...Il.2.753.161.
To *Thoas'* Care now trust the martial Train, ...Il.2.783.162.
A Fleet he built, and with a num'rous Train ......Il.2.805.163.
Such were the Chiefs, and such the *Grecian* Train. ......Il.2.923.167.
The Gates unfolding pour forth all their Train, ...Il.2.978.170.
There, mighty *Chromis* led the *Mysian* Train, ...Il.2.1046.172.
Amphimachus and *Naustes* guide the Train, ...Il.2.1060.172.
So wrapt in gath'ring Dust, the *Grecian* Train ......Il.3.21.189.
How vast thy Empire? Of yon' matchless Train ......Il.3.243.204.
This said, once more he view'd the Warrior-Train: ......Il.3.253.204.
This said, once more he view'd the martial Train: ......Il.3.253A.204.
When *Atreus'* Son harangu'd the list'ning Train, ...Il.3.275.205.
Yet two are wanting of the num'rous Train, ...Il.3.301.207.
Amid the *Grecian* Host and *Trojan* Train ......Il.3.335.209.
Unseen, and silent, from the Train she moves, ...Il.3.523.216.
Wert thou expos'd to all the hostile Train, ...Il.4.188.230.
O Heroes! worthy such a dauntless Train, ...Il.4.326.236.
With strictest Order sets his Train in Arms, ...Il.4.338.236.
But fight, or fall; a firm, embody'd Train. ......Il.4.351.237.
Amid the *Greek,* amid the *Trojan* Train, ...Il.5.112.272.
Stirs all the Ranks, and fires the *Trojan* Train; ......Il.5.562.295.
Produc'd *Æneas* to the shouting Train; ......Il.5.628.298.
Embodied close, the lab'ring *Grecian* Train ......Il.5.637.298.
Nor was the Gen'ral wanting to his Train, ...Il.5.649.299.
With six small Ships, and but a slender Train, ...Il.5.794.304.
Minerva drives him on the *Lycian* Train; ......Il.5.834.305.
The strongest Warrior of th' *Ætolian* Train; ......Il.5.1039.316.
The Sport and Insult of the Hostile Train. ......Il.6.102.328.
Direct the Queen to lead th' assembled Train ......Il.6.109.329.
Nor shall, I trust, the Matron's holy Train ......Il.6.141.331.
He bids the Train in long Procession go, ...Il.6.302.341.
You, with your Matrons, go! a spotless Train, ...Il.6.338.343.
The Train majestically slow proceeds. ......Il.6.369.344.
She, with one Maid of all her Menial Train, ...Il.6.465.349.
Not to the Court (reply'd th' Attendant Train) ......Il.6.478.350.
And there the vengeful *Spartan* fires his Train. ......Il.6.555.354.
Thro' all her Train the soft Infection ran, ...Il.6.645.358.
So welcome these to *Troy's* desiring Train; ......Il.7.9.363.
Then dare the boldest of the hostile Train ......Il.7.55.365.
This seeks the *Grecian,* that the *Phrygian* Train. ......Il.7.371.382.
In mingled Throngs, the *Greek* and *Trojan* Train ......Il.7.502.389.
Thus they in Heav'n: while, o'er the *Grecian* Train, ...Il.7.556.392.
The Gates unfolding pour forth all their Train; ......Il.8.71.399.
Leave thou thy Chariot to our faithful Train: ......Il.8.138.404.
Now hope no more those Honours from thy Train; ......Il.8.198.407.
This Night, refresh and fortify thy Train; ......Il.9.93.437.
Patroclus only of the Royal Train, ...Il.9.251.445.
I only must refund, of all his Train; ......Il.9.440.454.
The best and noblest of the *Grecian* Train; ......Il.9.647.466.
With Toil protected from the prowling Train; ......Il.10.212.11.
Then sleep those Aids among the *Trojan* Train, ...Il.10.494.25.
The Chiefs out-number'd by the *Trojan* Train: ......Il.10.633.30.
Discord alone, of all th' immortal Train, ...Il.11.101.39.
Amidst the Tumult of the routed Train, ...Il.11.161.42.
Dispers'd, disorder'd, fly the *Trojan* Train. ......Il.11.226.45.
But *Jove* with Conquest crowns the *Trojan* Train; ......Il.11.413.53.
Full fifty captive Chariots grac'd my Train: ......Il.11.882.75.
Press'd by fresh Forces her o'er-labour'd Train ......Il.11.932.77.
But should they turn, and here oppress our Train, ...Il.12.81.84.
The Chief's Example follow'd by his Train, ...Il.12.95.84.
So *Jove* once more may drive their routed Train, ...Il.12.327.93.
A Rout undisciplin'd, a straggling Train, ...Il.13.141.111.
So march'd the Leaders of the *Cretan* Train, ...Il.13.394.124.
And breath'd Revenge, and fir'd the *Grecian* Train. ......Il.13.444.126.
These Pow'rs infold the *Greek* and *Trojan* Train ......Il.13.451.127.
These Pow'rs inclose the *Greek* and *Trojan* Train ......Il.13.451A.127.
In order follow all th' embody'd Train; ......Il.13.620.135.
Supine he falls, and to his social Train ......Il.13.694.138.
The bloody Armour, which his Train receiv'd: ......Il.13.802.143.
Him on his Car the *Paphlagonian* Train ......Il.13.821.144.
A Train of Heroes follow'd thro' the Field, ...Il.13.885.147.
Thus in the Van, the *Telamonian* Train ......Il.13.897.148.
Sent from his follo'wing Host: The *Grecian* Train ......Il.13.1058.155.
With helpful Hands themselves assist the Train. ......Il.14.440.184.

TRAIN (CONTINUED)

(*Phorbas* the rich, of all the *Trojan* Train ..... Il.14.575.190.
Laid *Hyrtius,* Leader of the *Mysian* Train. ..... Il.14.606.191.
No Vassal God, nor of his Train am I. ..... Il.15.209.204.
Give him to know, unless the *Grecian* Train ..... Il.15.240.206.
Let *Ilion* conquer, till th' *Achaian* Train ..... Il.15.262.207.
But *Hector's* Voice excites his kindred Train; ..... Il.15.643.221.
Chas'd from the foremost Line, the *Grecian* Train ..... Il.15.786.226.
Press'd by fresh Forces, her o'erlabour'd Train ..... Il.16.62.238.
Due to the Votes of all the *Grecian* Train. ..... Il.16.79.238.
Preserve his Arms, preserve his social Train, ... Il.16.304.254.
Dire *Flight* and *Terror* drove the *Trojan* Train. ..... Il.16.439.259.
The buzzing Flies, a persevering Train, ... Il.16.781.273.
Glad Conquest rested on the *Grecian* Train. ..... Il.16.943.280.
Retires for Succour to his social Train, ... Il.16.985.281.
His Train to *Troy* the radiant Armour bear, ... Il.17.141.293.
I shun great *Ajax?* I desert my Train? ..... Il.17.193.294.
His Train to *Troy* convey'd the massy Load. ..... Il.17.218.296.
Whoe'er shall drag him to the *Trojan* Train, ... Il.17.271.298.
Struck at the Sight, recede the *Trojan* Train: ..... Il.17.368.301.
So flies a Vulture thro' the clam'rous Train ..... Il.17.528.309.
And much admonish'd, much adjur'd his Train. ..... Il.17.752.318.
The Shock of *Hector* and his charging Train: ..... Il.17.804.320.
With hoary *Nereus,* and the watry Train, ... Il.18.42.325.
Mæra, Amphinome, the Train extend, ... Il.18.62.326.
All bath'd in Tears, the melancholy Train ..... Il.18.86.327.
Patroclus, lov'd of all my martial Train, ... Il.18.103.328.
The Goddess thus dismiss'd her azure Train. ..... Il.18.176.331.
Around *Patroclus* mourn'd the *Grecian* Train. ..... Il.18.366.339.
There, in the *Forum* swarm a num'rous Train; ..... Il.18.577.350.
With bended Sickles stand the Reaper-Train: ..... Il.18.638.354.
Where march a Train with Baskets on their Heads, ... Il.18.658.355.
In measur'd Dance behind him move the Train, ... Il.18.663.355.
The Heroes heard, and all the Naval Train ..... Il.19.45.373.
A Train of noble Youth the Charge shall bear; ..... Il.19.191.379.
And the fair Train of Captives close the Rear: ..... Il.19.194.379.
And *Melanippus;* form'd the chosen Train. ..... Il.19.248.383.
First of the Train, the golden Talents bore: ..... Il.19.256.383.
Achilles sought his Tent. His Train before ..... Il.19.291.384.
Now issued from the Ships the warrior Train, ... Il.19.378.387.
Boreas, enamour'd of the sprightly Train, ... Il.20.264.405.
The River here divides the flying Train. ..... Il.21.3.420.
The River here divides the scatt'ring Train. ..... Il.21.3A.420.
In Shoals before him fly the scaly Train, ... Il.21.31.422.
Not till within her Tow'rs the perjur'd Train ..... Il.21.243.431.
But when the circling Seasons in their Train ..... Il.21.523.443.
Thither, all parch'd with Thirst, a heartless Train, ... Il.21.633.448.
When all the starry Train emblaze the Sphere: ..... Il.22.401.472.
(A mourning Princess, and a Train in Tears) ..... Il.22.553.479.
Around, a Train of weeping Sisters stands, ... Il.22.604.481.
Thus humbled in the Dust, the pensive Train ..... Il.23.1.485.
The Chariots first proceed, a shining Train; ..... Il.23.162.495.
With righteous *Æthiops* (uncorrupted Train!) ..... Il.23.256.499.
A Train of Oxen, Mules, and stately Steeds, ... Il.23.324.503.
The Hero, rising, thus addrest the Train. ..... Il.23.340.503.
They stand in order, an impatient Train; ..... Il.23.433.507.
These to the Ships his Train triumphant leads, ... Il.23.595.513.
So let his Friends be nigh, a needful Train ..... Il.23.779.520.
Achilles rising then bespoke the Train: ..... Il.23.878.524.
There plac'd amidst her melancholy Train ..... Il.24.111.539.
Around him furious drives his menial Train: ..... Il.24.292.549.
If then thou art of stern *Pelides'* Train, ... Il.24.495.557.
Or scornful Sister with her sweeping Train, ... Il.24.973.576.
He spoke; and at his Word, the *Trojan* Train ..... Il.24.989.577.
A solemn, silent, melancholy Train. ..... Il.24.1012.577.
Ulysses, sole of all the victor train, ... Od.1.18.30.
The bold intrusion of the Suitor-train; ..... Od.1.115.37.
A menial train the flowing bowl supply: ..... Od.1.145.39.
Far from the Suitor-train, a brutal crowd, ... Od.1.175.41.
Or number'd in my Father's social train? ..... Od.1.224.43.
Where sole of all his train, a Matron sage ..... Od.1.247.44.
Had fall'n surrounded with his warlike train; ..... Od.1.302.47.
By fraud or force the Suitor-train destroy, ... Od.1.385.51.
The genial viands let my train renew; ..... Od.1.404.52.
Their sovereign's step a virgin train attends: ..... Od.1.428.53.
His sage reply, and with her train retires. ..... Od.1.460.54.
Sole o'er my vassals, and domestic train. ..... Od.1.508.56.
The mirthful train dispersing quit the court, ... Od.1.535.57.
Thus she: at once the gen'rous train complies, ... Od.2.115.67.
Bid instant to prepare the bridal train, ... Od.2.131.67.
With ardent eyes the rival train they threat, ... Od.2.177.70.
I see (I cry'd) his woes, a countless train; ..... Od.2.203.71.
True, *Greece* affords a train of lovely dames, ... Od.2.233.72.
But if already wand'ring in the train ..... Od.2.249.73.
But against you, ye *Greeks!* ye coward train, ... Od.2.271.74.
Greece, and the rival train thy voice withstand. ..... Od.2.304.76.
'Twas riot all among the lawless train; ..... Od.2.337.77.
While to the rival train the Prince returns, ... Od.2.428.81.
It rides; and now descends the sailor train. ..... Od.2.441.82.
He bids them bring their stores: th' attending train ..... Od.2.456.83.
Each held five hundred, (a deputed train) ..... Od.3.9.87.
There he, the sweetest of the sacred train, ... Od.3.342.103.
The sober train attended and obey'd. ..... Od.3.432.108.
With steeds, and gilded cars, a gorgeous train ..... Od.4.11.121.
With equal haste a menial train pursue: ..... Od.4.48.122.
Where a bright damsel-train attend the guests ..... Od.4.59.122.
In *Troy* to mingle with the hostile train. ..... Od.4.338.136.
Heav'ns! wou'd a soft, inglorious, dastard train ..... Od.4.447.141.
Thy brave associates droop, a meagre train ..... Od.4.505.144.
Frequent and full; the consecrated train ..... Od.4.545.146.
Part live; the rest, a lamentable train! ..... Od.4.665.150.
A train of coursers, and triumphal cars ..... Od.4.714.152.
Mean-time my train the friendly gifts prepare, ... Od.4.805.156.
The menial train the regal feast prepare: ..... Od.4.840.158.
Attend his voyage, or domestic train? ..... Od.4.869.159.
What will the Suitors? must my servant train ..... Od.4.906.160.

TRAIN (CONTINUED)

Whom to my nuptial train *Icarius* gave, ... Od.4.973.163.
Her pious speed a female train attends: ..... Od.4.1002.164.
Alarm not with discourse the menial train: ..... Od.4.1024.165.
In elder times the soft *Phæacian* train ..... Od.6.5.203.
Arise, prepare the bridal train, arise! ..... Od.6.32.205.
Swift at the royal nod th' attending train ..... Od.6.85.209.
The Queen, assiduous, to her train assigns ..... Od.6.89.209.
The train prepare a cruise of curious mold, ... Od.6.91.209.
A sylvan train the huntress Queen surrounds, ... Od.6.119.212.
And shone transcendent o'er the beauteous train. ..... Od.6.128.212.
And swam the stream: Loud shrieks the virgin train, ... Od.6.135.213.
Then to her maids—Why, why, ye coward train ..... Od.6.239.221.
Your friendly care: retire, ye virgin train! ..... Od.6.258.222.
Slow rowls the car before th' attending train. ..... Od.6.380.230.
But silent march, nor greet the common train ..... Od.7.39.235.
Full fifty handmaids form the household train; ..... Od.7.132.241.
To thee, thy consort, and this royal train, ... Od.7.196.245.
By a sad train of miseries alone ..... Od.7.289.250.
She bade me follow in th' attendant train; ..... Od.7.391.255.
Bids her fair train the purple quilts prepare, ... Od.7.429.258.
Transported with the song, the list'ning train ..... Od.8.87.267.
Securely bid the strongest of the train ..... Od.8.225.274.
But modesty with-held the Goddess-train. ..... Od.8.364.283.
O sole belov'd! command thy menial train ..... Od.8.460.288.
Commands her train a spacious vase to bring, ... Od.8.470.288.
Clos'd with *Circæan* art. A train attends ..... Od.8.485.288.
Then conquest crown'd the fierce *Ciconian* train. ..... Od.9.68.305.
My train obey'd me and the ship unty'd. ..... Od.9.208.314.
Behold the relicks of the *Grecian* train! ..... Od.9.308.319.
Scarce with these few I scap'd; of all my train, ... Od.9.339.320.
This shorten'd of its top, I gave my train ..... Od.9.384.321.
And urge my train the dreadful deed to dare. ..... Od.9.448.324.
(The deed of *Noman* and his wicked train) ..... Od.9.534.328.
He march'd, with twice eleven in his train: ..... Od.10.238.352.
I only wait behind, of all the train; ..... Od.10.305.359.
Here feast and loiter, and desert thy train. ..... Od.10.322.360.
But all at once my interposing train ..... Od.10.521.368.
This with one voice declar'd, the rising train ..... Od.10.527.368.
But when the Seasons, following in their train, ... Od.10.556.369.
Now to the shores we bend, a mournful train, ... Od.11.1.377.
Stalk'd with majestic port, a martial train: ..... Od.11.52.383.
The rest repell'd, a train oblivious fly. ..... Od.11.183.390.
Woes I unfold, of woes a dismal train. ..... Od.11.475.407.
By stern *Ægysthus,* a majestic train, ... Od.11.483.408.
But now the years a num'rous train have ran; ..... Od.11.555.411.
And round him bled his bold *Cetæan* train. ..... Od.11.636.416.
Around we stand, a melancholy train, ... Od.12.15.430.
Swift she descends: A train of nymphs divine ..... Od.12.25.430.
The constant guardians of the woolly train; ..... Od.12.167.440.
Thus to the melancholy train I spoke: ..... Od.12.189.441.
Then bending to the stroke, the active train ..... Od.12.216.442.
To low the ox, to bleat the woolly train. ..... Od.12.319.447.
Thus careful I addrest the list'ning train. ..... Od.12.380.449.
Unhurt the beeves, untouch'd the woolly train ..... Od.12.389.450.
With pray'r they now address th' æthereal train, ... Od.12.423.451.
Sent by *Alcinous:* Of *Arete's* train ..... Od.13.82.5.
Now plac'd in order, the *Phæacian* train ..... Od.13.92.5.
To warn the thoughtless self-confiding train, ... Od.13.174.14.
The suitor-train thy early'st care demand, ... Od.13.429.27.
The fourth drove victims to the suitor-train: ..... Od.14.29.36.
In feast and sacrifice my chosen train ..... Od.14.282.49.
New frauds were plotted by the faithless train, ... Od.14.375.53.
Thous know'st the practice of the female train, ... Od.15.24.71.
Or mingling with the suitors haughty train, ... Od.15.334.85.
A blooming train in rich embroid'ry drest, ... Od.15.351.86.
And Pine and Penury, a meagre train. ..... Od.15.367.87.
So left perhaps to tend the fleecy train, ... Od.15.418.89.
This nymph, where anchor'd the *Phenician* train ..... Od.15.460.93.
'Till then, thy guest amid the rural train ..... Od.16.81.106.
The brave encompass'd by an hostile train, ... Od.16.89.106.
And let some handmaid of her train resort ..... Od.16.164.110.
Wrapt in th' embrace of sleep, the faithful train ..... Od.16.252.117.
The names, and numbers of th' audacious train; ..... Od.16.259.117.
Six are their menial train: twice twelve the boast ..... Od.16.270.118.
The court revisit and the lawless train: ..... Od.16.291.119.
Lock'd in thy bosom from the houshold train; ..... Od.16.325.121.
Too curious to explore the menial train? ..... Od.16.337.122.
Abash'd, the suitor train his voice attends; ..... Od.16.408.126.
He said: The rival train his voice approv'd, ... Od.16.422.127.
Her hasty steps a damsel train attends. ..... Od.16.429.128.
She bath'd; and rob'd in white, with all her train, ... Od.17.69.136.
Heav'ns! would a soft, inglorious, dastard train ..... Od.17.138.138.
The sad survivor of his num'rous train, ... Od.17.163.139.
And I am learn'd in all her train of woes; ..... Od.17.341.148.
Dooms to full vengeance all th' offending train) ..... Od.17.437.154.
See how with nods assent yon princely train! ..... Od.18.16.167.
Thus with loud laughter to the Suitor-train. ..... Od.18.43.169.
A dreaded tyrant o'er the bestial train! ..... Od.18.127.172.
Be dumb when heav'n afflicts! unlike yon' train ..... Od.18.171.175.
(Reply'd the sagest of the royal train) ..... Od.18.202.176.
And to the Queen the damsel train descends: ..... Od.18.234.178.
On either hand a damsel train attends: ..... Od.18.246.178.
The Suitor-train, and raise a thirst to give; ..... Od.18.326.183.
And slow behind her damsel train attends. ..... Od.18.350.184.
'Till *Hesperus* leads forth the starry train; ..... Od.18.352.184.
Thou bold intruder on a princely train? ..... Od.18.376.185.
Proud, to seem brave among a coward train! ..... Od.18.424.189.
The cause demanded by the Suitor-train, ... Od.19.7.193.
(The female train retir'd) your toils to guide? ..... Od.19.28.193.
T' explore the conduct of the female train: ..... Od.19.55.195.
With tapers flaming day his train attends, ... Od.19.58.195.
And to this gay censorious train, appear ..... Od.19.142.199.
The woof unwrought the Suitor-train surprize. ..... Od.19.177.200.
Beeves for his train the *Cnossian* Peers assign, ... Od.19.228.204.
His form, his habit, and his train record. ..... Od.19.256.207.

TRAIN (CONTINUED)

The female train who round him throng'd to gaze, ...Od.19.271.208.
A fav'rite herald in his train I knew ....Od.19.278.208.
His sacrilegious train, who dar'd to prey ....Od.19.313.209.
When the pale Empress of yon' starry train ....Od.19.351.211.
Your other task, ye menial train, forbear; ....Od.19.362.211.
The delicacy of your courtly train ....Od.19.397.213.
And foremost of the train, his cornel spear ....Od.19.509.221.
With joy, and vast surprize, th' applauding train ....Od.19.532.221.
And prostrate to my sword the Suitor-train; ....Od.19.572.224.
And joining to my son's my menial train, ...Od.19.617.226.
A team of twenty geese, (a snow-white train!) ....Od.19.627.226.
Fast by the limpid lake my swan-like train ....Od.19.648.227.
Of winged Lies a light fantastic train: ....Od.19.659.228.
The sov'reign step a beauteous train attends: ....Od.19.700.229.
To seek my Lord among the warrior-train, ...Od.20.96.237.
Instant, O *Jove!* confound the Suitor train, ...Od.20.147.240.
Mean-time the menial train with unctuous wood ....Od.20.153.241.
Thus urging to their toil the menial train. ....Od.20.185.242.
(*Eumæus* in their train) the maids return. ....Od.20.203.243.
Now say sincere, my guest! the Suitor train ....Od.20.208.243.
And to the shades devote the Suitor-train. ....Od.20.293.247.
His menial train attend the stranger guest; ....Od.20.350.249.
From the protected guest, and menial train: ....Od.20.390.251.
Inroll'd, perhaps, in *Pluto's* dreary train.) ....Od.20.408.252.
At distance due a virgin-train attends; ....Od.21.8.258.
Behind, her train the polish'd coffer brings, ...Od.21.63.262.
And artful, thus the Suitor-train address. ....Od.21.138.265.
Of all the train the mightiest and the best. ....Od.21.192.269.
Or if my woes (a long-continu'd train) ....Od.21.305.274.
His sage reply, and with her train retir'd: ....Od.21.382.278.
Now let them comfort their dejected train ....Od.21.470.283.
Alone *Eurymachus* exhorts the train: ....Od.22.83.290.
My self with arms can furnish all the train; ....Od.22.155.294.
So, when by hollow shores the fisher train ....Od.22.425.308.
(My son) full fifty of the handmaid train, ...Od.22.459.310.
He said: The lamentable train appear, ...Od.22.482.312.
And let her with her matron-train descend; ....Od.22.520.314.
The matron-train with all the virgin band ....Od.22.521.314.
The damsel train turn'd pale at every wound, ...Od.23.43.321.
And at his nod the damsel train descends; ....Od.23.46.321.
This spoke the King: Th' observant train obey, ...Od.23.139.327.
And the wild riots of the Suitor-train. ....Od.23.328.340.
Conveys the dead, a lamentable train! ....Od.24.2.345.
The train of those who by *Ægysthus* fell. ....Od.24.34.348.
Was heard, and terror seiz'd the *Grecian* train: ....Od.24.68.350.
"To mourn *Achilles* leads her azure train." ....Od.24.74.351.
The fiction pleas'd: our gen'rous train complies, ...Od.24.164.356.
Then to his train he gives his spear and shield; ....Od.24.253.361.
Or com'st thou single, or attend thy train? ....Od.24.352.365.
The vengeance is compleat; the Suitor-train, ...Od.24.380.367.
And next his sons, a long-succeeding train. ....Od.24.447.370.
With ships he parted and a num'rous train, ...Od.24.491.371.
They meet: *Eupithes* heads the frantic train. ....Od.24.537.373.

TRAIN-BANDS

And heads the bold Train-bands, and burns a Pope. ....3.Ep3.214.110.

TRAIN'D

Who first their Youth in Arts of Virtue train'd, ...1.TrSt.619.436.
And train'd by Him who bears the Silver Bow. ....Il.2.929.167.
Beneath his Cares thy early Youth was train'd, ...Il.13.586.134.

TRAINS

With fleeces sheep, and birds with plumy trains; ....1.TrPA.105.370.
The proud *Ionians* with their sweeping Trains, ...Il.13.860.146.
New trains of dangers, and new scenes of woes: ....Od.11.129.387.
Stern beasts in trains that by his truncheon fell, ...Od.11.707.420.

TRAIPSE

"Lo next two slip-shod Muses traipse along, ...5.DunA3.141.162.
"See next two slip-shod Muses traipse along, ...5.DunA3.141A.162.

TRAITOR

See TRAYTOR.
"Speak'st thou of Syrian Princes? Traitor base! ....5.DunB4.375.379.
Urge the bold traitor to the Regicide? ....Od.1.48.32.
O'er the full bowl, the traitor stab'd his guest; ....Od.11.508.408.

TRAITRESS

By the dire fury of a traitress wife, ...Od.4.115.125.
Nor did my traitress wife these eyelids close, ...Od.11.529.409.

TRAITS

Th' exactest traits of Body or of Mind, ...3.Ep2.191.65.

TRAMP'LING

Methinks the Noise of tramp'ling Steeds I hear ....Il.10.626.30.

TRAMPLED

'Till trampled flat beneath the Courser's Feet, ...Il.5.719.301.
The trampled Center yields a hollow Sound: ....Il.20.189.402.

TRAMPLES

Sweeps the wide Earth, and tramples o'er Mankind, ...Il.9.629.465.

TRAMPLING

The gath'ring Murmur spreads; their trampling Feet ....Il.2.183.137.
From trampling Steeds, and thundering Charioteers, ...Il.5.618.297.
The trampling Steers beat out th' unnumber'd Grain. ....Il.20.580.418.
Contemning laws, and trampling on the right. ....Od.9.251.317.

TRANCE

Starts from her Trance, and trims her wither'd Bays! ....1.EOC.698.319.
Till all dissolving in the Trance we lay, ...1.TrSP.61.396.
In trance extatic may thy pangs be drown'd, ...2.ElAb.339.347.

TRANCE (CONTINUED)

While *Hector* rose, recover'd from the Trance, ...Il.11.462.54.

TRANCES

And *Odin* here in mimick Trances dies. ....2.TemF.124.264.

TRANQUIL

Cannot affect Us in our tranquil State. ....6.17iii.13.58.

TRANQUILITY

Oh Love! be deep Tranquility my Luck! ....4.HAdv.175.89.

TRANSCEND

The Joys are such as far transcend your Rage, ...2.ChJM.339.30.

TRANSCENDENT

And shone transcendent o'er the beauteous train. ....Od.6.128.212.

TRANSCENDING

Behold our Deeds transcending our Commands, ...1.TrES.40.451.
Behold our Deeds transcending our Commands, ...Il.12.384.95.

TRANSCENDS

And say, This Chief transcends his Father's Fame: ....Il.6.613.357.
A Princess rap'd transcends a Navy storm'd: ....Il.13.782.142.
Secure, no *Grecian* Force transcends thy own. ....Il.20.388.411.
How far *Minerva's* Force transcends thy own? ....Il.21.479.441.
Thy signal throw transcends the utmost bound ....Od.8.223.274.
Thy praise was just; their skill transcends thy praise. ....Od.8.420.286.

TRANSFER

But to your *Isis* all my Rites transfer, ...1.TrSt.373.425.
Or back to *Ilion's* Walls transfer the War? ....Il.10.483.25.
To them, to them transfer the love of me: ....Od.18.312.181.

TRANSFERS

Transfers the Glory to the *Trojan* Band; ....Il.17.710.315.

TRANSFIX

Th' Assistants part, transfix, and roast the rest: ....Il.1.611.117.
Th' Assistants part, transfix, and roast the rest; ....Il.2.511.151.
Th' assistants part, transfix, and broil the rest. ....Od.3.591.116.

TRANSFIX'D

(Transfix'd as o'er *Castalia's* Streams he hung, ...1.TrSt.666.438.
Transfix'd his Throat, and drank the vital Blood; ....Il.5.817.305.
Transfix'd the Warrior with his brazen Dart; ....Il.11.336.49.
But falls transfix'd, an unresisting Prey: ....Il.13.504.130.
The Thigh transfix'd, and broke the brittle Bone: ....Il.16.369.257.
All-impotent of Aid, transfix'd with Grief, ...Il.16.627.269.
Transfix'd with deep Regret, they view o'erthrown ....Il.16.673.270.
Transfix'd with deep Regret, they view'd o'erthrown ....Il.16.673A.270.
The Warrior falls, transfix'd from Ear to Ear. ....Il.20.548.417.
Transfix'd the fragments, some prepar'd the food. ....Od.3.44.88.

TRANSFIXES

The Parts transfixes, and with Skill divides. ....Il.9.276.447.

TRANSFIXT

Be stopt in *Vials*, or transfixt with *Pins;* ....2.RL2.126.167.

TRANSFORM

Transform themselves so strangely as the Rich? ....4.1HE1.153.291.

TRANSFORM'D

And Acis was; who now transform'd became ....1.TrPA.163.373.
Transform'd to *Combs,* the speckled and the white. ....2.RL1.136.156.
Return well travell'd, and transform'd to Beasts, ...4.1HE6.123.245.
Transform'd to beasts, with accents not their own. ....Od.10.402.364.
And social joys, the late-transform'd repairs: ....Od.10.532.369.

TRANSFORMED

Transformed, gazes on himself again. ....6.14iv.12.47.

TRANSFORMING

O were I made by some transforming Pow'r, ...1.PSu.45.75.

TRANSFORMS

To hogs transforms 'em, and the Sty receives. ....Od.10.277.356.

TRANSGRESS

Against the *Precept,* ne'er transgress its *End,* ....1.EOC.164.259.
She claims some Title to transgress our Will. ....Il.8.501.420.
She claims some Title to transgress his Will: ....Il.8.521.421.

TRANSGREST

Deaf to Heav'n's voice, the social rite transgrest; ....Od.21.31.260.

TRANSIENT

Think not, when Woman's transient Breath is fled, ...2.RL1.51.149.
While ev'ry Beam new transient Colours flings, ...2.RL2.67.163.
The transient Landscape now in Clouds decays, ...2.TemF.20.254.
See from my cheek the transient roses fly! ....2.ElAb.331.346.
A transient Fit of fond Desire. ....6.51ii.17Z2.153.
What is loose love? a transient gust, ...6.51ii.17.153.
A transient Pity touch'd his vengeful Breast. ....Il.11.735.68.
Steal from corroding care one transient day, ...Od.8.163.271.
Thus with a transient smile the matron cries. ....Od.18.194.176.
Oh were it giv'n to yield this transient breath, ...Od.18.239.178.

TRANSITION

Thence, by a soft Transition, we repair ....2.RL1.49.149.
He came by sure Transition to his own: ....4.JD4.81.31.
He came by soft Transition to his own: ....4.JD4.81A.31.

TRANSITORY

For when my transitory Spouse, unkind, ...2.ChWB.25.58.

TRANSLATE

All these, my modest Satire bad *translate,* ....4.Arbu.189.109.
All these, my modest Satire bid *translate,* ....4.Arbu.189A.109.
And Pope's whole years to comment and translate. ....5.DunA3.328A.191.
And Pope's, ten years to comment and translate. ....5.DunB3.332.336.
Which, in our Tongue, as I translate, is, ...6.24iii(a).2.75.
What then? Gad damn him, he'd Translate, ...6.44.6.123.
Rack your Inventions some, and some *in time* translate. ....6.48iii.14.135.
Read this, e'er you translate one Bit ....6.58.3.170.
Read this ere ye translate one Bit ....6.58.3A.170.
And *P[o]pe* translate with *Jervis.* ....6.58.60.173.
Who dares most impudently—not translate. ....6.60.18.178.
Should modest Satire bid all these *translate,* ....6.98.39.284.
All to the dooming Gods their guilt translate, ...Od.1.43.31.
Haste, from the bridal bow'r the bed translate, ...Od.23.181.329.

TRANSLATED

Thy Works in *Spanish* shou'd have been translated, ...6.48iv.6.136.
In a translated Suit, then tries the Town, ...6.49i.21.138.
Has Cause to wish himself translated. ....6.151.2.399.

TRANSLATING

And Pope's, translating three whole years with Broome. ....5.DunA3.328.191.

TRANSLATION

On *French* translation, and *Italian* song. ....6.32.42.97.
But why shou'd *Hough* desire Translation, ...6.151.3.399.

TRANSLATIONS

Nor suffers *Horace* more in wrong *Translations* ....1.EOC.663.314.

TRANSLATOR

And Butler *with the* Lutrin's *dull Translator,* ....6.17iv.12.59.

TRANSLUCENT

Thou who shalt stop, where *Thames'* translucent Wave ....6.142.1.382.
You who shall stop, where *Thames'* translucent Wave' ....6.142.1A.382.
O Thou who stop'st, where *Thames'* translucent Wave ....6.142.1B.382.
Replenish'd from the cool, translucent springs, ...Od.1.180.41.
And two fair crescents of translucent horn ....Od.4.107.125.
Replenish'd from the cool translucent springs, ...Od.7.231.247.
Replenish'd from the cool, translucent springs; ....Od.10.434.365.
Replenish'd from the pure, translucent springs; ....Od.17.105.137.
A veil translucent o'er her brow display'd, ...Od.18.249.179.

TRANSMIGRATING

Who knows how long, thy transmigrating soul ....5.DunA3.41.154.
Who knows how long thy transmigrating soul ....5.DunB3.49.322.

TRANSMISSIVE

Had with transmissive honour grac'd his Son. ....Od.1.308.47.
From the great sire transmissive to the race, ...Od.4.287.132.
Had with transmissive honours grac'd his son. ....Od.14.406.55.
Had with transmissive glories grac'd thy son. ....Od.24.48.350.

TRANSMITTED

Charles, to late times to be transmitted fair, ...4.2HE1.380.227.

TRANSPARENT

The blue, transparent *Vandalis* appears; ....1.W-F.345.183.
Transparent Forms, too fine for mortal Sight, ...2.RL2.61.163.
Of bright, transparent Beryl were the Walls, ...2.TemF.141.265.
And the transparent Skin with Crimson stain'd. ....Il.5.420.287.
The nymph's fair head a veil transparent grac'd, ...Od.5.295.185.

TRANSPIERC'D

The next transpierc'd *Achilles'* mortal Steed, ...1.TrES.269A.459.
A thorny crown transpierc'd thy sacred brow, ...6.25.7.77.
But now the Monarch's Lance transpierc'd his Shield, ...Il.5.664.300.
The thrilling Steel transpierc'd the brawny Part, ...Il.11.327.49.
Transpierc'd his Back with a dishonest Wound: ....Il.13.691.137.
His Blow prevented, and transpierc'd his Thigh, ...Il.16.373.257.
The next transpierc'd *Achilles'* mortal Steed, ...Il.16.574.266.
Transpierc'd his back, and fix'd him to the ground. ....Od.10.188.349.

TRANSPIERCING

Him, thro' the Hip transpiercing as he fled. ....Il.13.813.144.
And deep transpiercing, thro' the Shoulder stood; ....Il.17.359.301.

TRANSPORT

And secret Transport touch'd the conscious Swain. ....1.W-F.90.159.
With Transport views the airy Rule his own, ...1.TrSt.449.428.
At this, the Chief with Transport was possest, ...1.TrUl.134.470.
A *Vision* Hermits can to Hell transport, ...4.JD4.190.43.
There, where no Passion, Pride, or Shame transport, ...4.EpS1.97.305.
Her seat imperial, Dulness shall transport. ....5.DunA3.302.185.
Dulness with transport eyes the lively Dunce, ...5.DunB1.111.277.
Her seat imperial Dulness shall transport. ....5.DunB3.300.334.
Then wake with Transport at the Sound! ....6.31ii.6Z12.95.
Our shatter'd Barks may yet transport us o'er, ...Il.2.169.136.
Twice twenty Ships transport the warlike Bands, ...Il.2.653.158.
And touch'd with Transport great *Atrides'* Heart. ....Il.4.361.238.
Forgive the Transport of a martial Mind. ....Il.4.415.240.
And two transport *Æneas* o'er the Plain. ....Il.5.335.283.
He spoke, and Transport fill'd *Tydides'* Heart; ....Il.6.261.339.
Then casts before him, and with Transport cries: ....Il.7.226.375.
Thro' ev'ry *Argive* Heart new Transport ran, ...Il.7.259.377.
The *Greeks* beheld, and Transport seiz'd on all: ....Il.8.302.412.
Safe to transport him to his native Plains, ...Il.9.809.473.
And thence my Ships transport me thro' the Main; ....Il.13.569.133.
Then press'd her Hand, and thus with Transport spoke. ....Il.14.338.179.
Shall 'scape with Transport, and with Joy repose. ....Il.19.76.375.
Whence *Tyrian* Sailors did the Prize transport, ...Il.23.869.524.

TRANSPORT (CONTINUED)

He spoke. *Telemachus* with transport glows, ...Od.2.43.62.
Tho' to his breast his spouse with transport flies, ...Od.2.283.75.
And swift transport him to his place of rest. ....Od.5.49.174.
Nor break the transport with one thought of me. ....Od.5.262.184.
And give soft transport to a parent's heart. ....Od.6.34.206.
The tongues of all with transport sound her praise, ...Od.7.92.238.
Safe to transport him to the wish'd-for shore! ....Od.7.255.248.
Our ships with ease transport thee in a day. ....Od.7.412.257.
Big tears of transport stand in ev'ry eye: ....Od.9.551.328.
Some vessel, not his own, transport him o'er; ....Od.9.626.332.
The pleasing transport, and compleats his loves. ....Od.11.294.396.
While yet I spoke, the Shade with transport glow'd, ...Od.11.659.416.
If mad with transport, freedom thou demand, ...Od.12.65.433.
Ev'n when with transport black'ning all the strand, ...Od.13.178.14.
At this, the chief with transport was possest, ...Od.13.301.20.
Not with such transport wou'd my eyes run o'er, ...Od.14.163.43.
And, where my hopes invite me, strait transport ....Od.14.438.57.
He spoke and sate. The Prince with transport flew, ...Od.16.234.114.
Lest to the Queen the swain with transport fly, ...Od.16.480.130.
For farther search, his rapid steeds transport ....Od.17.132.138.
Must be my care; and hence transport thee o'er, ...Od.17.298.146.
Ulysses saw, and thus with transport cry'd. ....Od.22.224.297.
While yet she spoke, the Queen in transport sprung ....Od.23.35.320.
And wild with transport had reveal'd the wound; ....Od.23.77.322.
Stubborn the breast that with no transport glows, ...Od.23.103.324.
Thus in fond kisses, while the transport warms, ...Od.23.225.333.
And plunging forth with transport grasps the land. ....Od.23.256.335.
Why in this hour of transport wound thy ears, ...Od.23.281.337.
With eager transport to disclose the whole, ...Od.24.277.363.

TRANSPORTED

Her I transported touch, transported view, ...4.HAdv.165.89.
Her I transported touch, transported view, ...4.HAdv.165.89.
Transported Demi-Gods stood round, ...6.11.42.31.
Alarm'd, transported, at the well-known Sound, ...Il.19.47.373.
Transported with the song, the list'ning train ....Od.8.87.267.
And sunk transported on the conscious bed. ....Od.8.338.282.
Transported from his seat *Eumæus* sprung, ...Od.16.13.102.
What ship transported thee, O father say, ...Od.16.246.116.
The Peers transported, as outstretch'd he lies, ...Od.18.118.172.

TRANSPORTS

O'er all his Bosom secret Transports reign, ...1.TrSt.579.434.
O'er all his Bosom sacred Transports reign, ...1.TrSt.579A.434.
Attend his Transports, and receive his Vows. ....1.TrUl.243.473.
Such secret Transports warm my melting Heart. ....2.ChJM.572.43.
One instinct seizes, and transports away. ....5.DunB4.74.348.
By the warm Transports and entrancing Languors, ...6.82ii.2.230.
While kindling transports glow'd at our success; ....Od.10.154.347.
To the sweet transports of the genial bed. ....Od.10.412.364.
Attend his transports, and receive his vows! ....Od.13.410.26.
The first fair wind transports him o'er the main; ....Od.21.328.275.
The transports of her faithful heart supply ....Od.23.3.316.

TRAPP

T[raver]s and *T[rapp]* the church and state gave o'er, ...5.DunA2.381A.146.

TRAPPINGS

For well they knew, proud Trappings serve to hide ....4.HAdv.116.85.
As when some stately Trappings are decreed, ...Il.4.170.229.
Rich with immortal Gold their Trappings shine. ....Il.5.887.308.

TRASH

With the same trash mad mortals wish for here? ....3.EOM4.174.144.
Meer *Houshold Trash!* of Birth-Nights, Balls and Shows, ...4.JD4.130.35.
Th' imputed Trash, and Dulness not his own; ....4.Arbu.351.121.
The imputed Trash, the Dulness not his own; ....4.Arbu.351A.121.

TRAV'LER

The trav'ler rising from the banquet gay, ...Od.15.89.73.

TRAV'LERS

Two Trav'lers found an Oyster in their Way; ....6.145.2.388.

TRAVEL

Affirm, 'twas *Travel* made them what they were." ....4.JD4.79.31.
Ev'n Radcliff's Doctors travel first to France, ...4.2HE1.183.211.
As once a week we travel down ....4.HS6.97.257.
By Travel, generous Souls enlarge the Mind, ...6.96v.11.280.

TRAVEL'D

News travel'd with Increase from Mouth to Mouth; ....2.TemF.474.286.
Thus 'till the sun had travel'd half the skies, ...Od.4.601.148.

TRAVELER

And point the wand'ring traveler his way: ....Od.7.36.235.

TRAVELL'D

This Thing has *travell'd,* speaks each Language too, ...4.JD4.46.29.
Return well travell'd, and transform'd to Beasts, ...4.1HE6.123.245.
Thus *Orpheus* travell'd to reform his Kind, ...6.96iii.19.275.
Harpalion had thro' *Asia* travell'd far, ...Il.13.805.143.

TRAVELLER

Whose Seats the weary Traveller repose? ....3.Ep3.260.114.
In Swarms the guiltless Traveller engage, ...Il.16.316.255.
Beholds the Traveller approach the Brake; ....Il.22.131.458.
Oft with some favour'd traveller they stray, ...Od.7.273.249.
Each vagrant traveller that touches here, ...Od.14.150.43.

TRAVELLER'S

Glares on some Traveller's unwary steps, ...6.26i.11.79.

TRAVELLERS

Nay, all that lying Travellers can feign. ....4.JD4.31.29.
Where constant vows by travellers are pay'd, ...Od.17.244.143.

TRAVELS

O'er figur'd Worlds now travels with his Eye. ....1.W-F.246.172.
Of Storms at Sea, and Travels on the Shore, ...2.TemF.451.285.
Hope travels thro', nor quits us when we die. ......3.EOM2.274.88.
Tho' still he travels on no bad pretence, ...4.1740.51.334.
My Travels thence thro' spacious *Greece* extend; ...II.9.598.464.

TRAVERS

T[raver]s and T[rapp] the church and state gave o'er, ...5.DunA2.381A.146.

TRAVERS'D

What seas you travers'd! and what fields you fought! ...4.2HE1.396.229.
The Camp he travers'd thro' the sleeping Crowd, ...II.10.156.8.

TRAVERSE

"To see thee leap the Lines, and traverse o'er .....6.96ii.62.273.
Traverse the Files, and to the Rescue flies; ....II.11.444.54.
The seas to traverse, or the ships to build, ...Od.9.148.311.

TRAVERSES

He traverses the blooming verdant Mead, ...6.17iii.28.58.

TRAYS

As knavish *Pams,* and fawning *Trays;* ....6.135.38.367.

TRAYTOR

See TRAITOR.
Already half turn'd Traytor by surprize. ....4.JD4.169.39.
The Traytor-Gods, by mad Ambition driv'n, ...II.1.520.113.
No—once a Traytor, thou betray'st me more. ....II.10.521.26.
Sev'n years, the traytor rich *Mycenæ* sway'd, ...Od.3.388.105.
And in the traytor friend unmask the foe; ....Od.18.198.176.
Swift as he spoke, he drew his traytor sword, ...Od.22.93.291.

TRAYTOR-GODS

The Traytor-Gods, by mad Ambition driv'n, ...II.1.520.113.

TRAYTORS

And now fierce traytors, studious to destroy ......Od.5.26.172.
Or crush'd by traytors with an iron rod? ....Od.11.213.392.
For traytors wait his way, with dire design ....Od.14.210.45.

TREACH'ROUS

The *treach'rous Colours* the fair Art betray, ...1.EOC.492.294.
The *treach'rous Colours* in few Years decay, ...1.EOC.492A.294.
Where treach'rous *Scylla* cut the Purple Hairs: ..1.TrSt.469.429.
O Fortune, fair, like all thy treach'rous Kind, ...2.ChJM.477.38.
Safe from the treach'rous Friend, the daring Spark, ...2.RL1.73.151.
Safe from the treach'rous Friend, and daring Spark, ...2.RL1.73A.151.
Believe, believe the treach'rous world no more. ...6.22.2.71.
At his Return, a treach'rous Ambush, rose, ...II.6.232.337.
And curs'd the treach'rous Lance that spar'd a Foe; ...II.13.222.116.
Destruction enters in the treach'rous wood, ...Od.8.561.293.
Back from his lip the treach'rous water flies. ....Od.11.724.421.

TREACHEROUS

Timid and therefore treacherous to the last ......6.130.20.358.

TREACHERY

The Treachery you Women use to Man: ....2.ChJM.628.45.

TREAD

Where-e'er you tread, the blushing Flow'rs shall rise, ...1.PSu.75.77.
Mount o'er the Vales, and seem to tread the Sky; ...1.EOC.226.265.
For *Fools* rush in where *Angels* fear to tread. ...1.EOC.625.310.
Nor knows, amaz'd, what doubtful Path to tread, ...1.TrSt.517.432.
And those who tread the burning *Lybian* Lands, ...1.TrSt.814.443.
What if the foot, ordain'd the dust to tread, ...3.EOM1.259.46.
Or tread the mazy round his follow'rs trod, ...3.EOM2.25.58.
The stage how loosely does Astræa tread, ...4.2HE1.290.219.
Or tread the path by vent'rous Heroes trod, ...5.DunB1.201.284.
Nor envies those that on rich Carpets tread. ......6.17iii.29.58.
Thou on the fiery Basilisk shalt tread, ...6.21.29.70.
To tread those dark unwholsome, misty Fens, ...6.26i.13.79.
Others to tread the liquid harvest join, ...6.35.21.103.
For, if I know his Tread, here's Addison. ....6.49ii.10.140.
Ah spare my Slumbers, gently tread the Cave! ......6.87.3.248.
Whoe'er thou art, ah gently tread the Cave! ....6.87.3A.248.
Or laugh to see thee walk with cautious tread, ...6.96ii.30Z45.272.
"How wert thou wont to walk with cautious Tread, ...6.96ii.67.273.
Did never *Yahoo* tread that Ground before? ....6.96iii.12.274.
Let such, such only, tread this sacred Floor, ...6.142.13.383.
Such only such shall tread the sacred Floor, ...6.142.13A.383.
Such only such may tread this sacred Floor, ...6.142.13B.383.
Let such, such only, tread this Poet's Floor, ...6.142.13C.383.
Let such, such only, tread the Poet's Floor, ...6.142.13D.383.
Let such, such only, tread their Poet's Floor, ...6.142.13E.383.
Let such, such only, tread the Poet's Floor, ...6.142.13F.383.
Tho' some of larger Stature tread the Green, ...II.3.223.203.
Of all the Gods who tread the spangled Skies, ...II.5.1096.319.
And trod the Path his Feet must tread no more. ....II.10.400.21.
When, on the hollow way, th' approaching Tread ....II.10.403.21.
And seem to walk on Wings, and tread in Air. ......II.13.106.109.
'Tis hostile Ground you tread; your native Lands ...II.15.900.232.
Tread down whole Ranks, and crush out Hero's Souls. ...II.20.582.418.
To tread the walks of death he stood prepar'd, ...Od.2.311.76.
Condemn'd perhaps some foreign shore to tread; ....Od.3.314.101.
'Tis death with hostile step these shores to tread; ...Od.6.242.221.
Others to tread the liquid harvest join, ...Od.7.162.244.
Unblest! to tread that interdicted shore: ....Od.7.333.253.
What nervous arms he boasts! how firm his tread! ..Od.8.147.270.
To tread th' uncomfortable paths beneath, ...Od.10.580.371.

TREAD (CONTINUED)

How shall I tread (I cry'd) ah *Circe!* say, ...Od.10.594.372.
To tread th' uncomfortable paths beneath, ...Od.10.675.376.
To tread the downward, melancholy way? ....Od.11.117.386.
Tread you my steps: 'Tis mine to lead the race, ...Od.11.440.406.
Nor fear'st the dark and dismal waste to tread, ...Od.11.585.412.
All, soon or late, are doom'd that path to tread; ...Od.12.31.431.
To the cold tomb, and dreadful all to tread; .....Od.12.404.450.
The dogs intelligent confess'd the tread ....Od.16.176.111.
Now strong as youth, magnificent I tread. ....Od.16.231.114.
He, not unconscious of the voice, and tread, ...Od.17.346.148.
Helpless amid the snares of death I tread, ...Od.18.273.179.
That yon' proud Suitors, who licentious tread .....Od.18.279.180.
And nodding helm, I tread th' ensanguin'd field, ...Od.18.419.189.
The righteous pow'rs who tread the starry skies, ...Od.23.13.319.
Since the just Gods who tread the starry plains ...Od.23.275.336.
To tread the downward, melancholy way? ....Od.24.131.354.

TREAD'ST

I show thee, King! thou tread'st on hostile Land; ...II.24.717.567.
But since thou tread'st our hospitable shore, ...Od.6.233.221.
By woman here thou tread'st this mournful strand, ...Od.11.543.410.

TREADING

And not a Cock but would be treading. ....6.93.14.257.

TREADS

Till led by Fate, the *Theban's* Steps he treads, ...1.TrSt.561.433.
When he treads, ...6.96i.21.268.
And treads the brazen Threshold of the Gods. ......II.18.184.331.
Not on the Ground that haughty Fury treads, ...II.19.95.376.
And treads each Footstep e'er the Dust can rise: ...II.23.894.524.
While sad on foreign shores *Ulysses* treads, ...Od.2.151.69.
The neighb'ring main, and sorrowing treads the shores. ...Od.2.294.76.
The footsteps of the Deity he treads. ....Od.2.453.83.
Above the nymphs she treads with stately grace; ...Od.6.124.212.
Then drest in pomp magnificently treads. ....Od.6.270.223.
Not without Care divine the stranger treads ....Od.6.287.224.
"Heav'ns! with what graceful majesty he treads? ...Od.6.332.227.
The footsteps of the Deity he treads, ...Od.7.50.236.
More high he treads, and more enlarg'd he moves: ...Od.8.20.263.
Stern *Vulcan* homeward treads the starry way: ....Od.8.344.282.
And every God that treads the courts above. ....Od.8.468.288.
Age o'er his limbs, that tremble as he treads. ....Od.16.479.130.
Then drest in pomp, magnificent he treads. ....Od.23.152.328.
More high he treads, and issuing forth in state, ...Od.23.163.328.
How high he treads, and how enlarg'd he moves? ....Od.24.432.369.

TREASON

Make *Scots* speak Treason, cozen subtlest Whores, ...4.JD4.59.31.
Within the reach of Treason, or the Law. ....4.JD2.128.145.
The Papist masques his Treason in a Joke; ....6.48iv.2.135.
From death and treason to thy arms restor'd; ......Od.17.59.135.
Us, and our house if treason must o'erthrow, ...Od.17.92.136.

TREASONS

And beg to make th' immortal Treasons known. ......2.TemF.413.283.

TREASUR'D

Since all that Man e'er lost, is treasur'd there. ...2.RLA2.159.136.
Since all things lost on Earth, are treasur'd there. ...2.RL5.114.208.
Where treasur'd Odors breath'd a costly Scent. ....II.6.359.343.
And faithful Guardians of the treasur'd Vow!) .....II.22.326.469.
His treasur'd stores these Cormorants consume, ...Od.1.207.42.
Our task be now thy treasur'd stores to save, ...Od.13.417.26.
Where treasur'd garments cast a rich perfume; .....Od.21.54.261.
Careful he treasur'd in a private room: ....Od.24.194.356.

TREASURE

Where shall this Treasure now in Safety lie? ......1.TrUl.78.468.
And sought no Treasure but thy Heart alone. ....2.ChJM.551.41.
Are not thy Worldly Goods and Treasure mine? ......2.ChWB.125.62.
Another, not to heed to treasure more; ....4.2HE2.293.185.
"Direct my Plow to find a Treasure:" ....4.HS6.20.251.
The Comick *Tom* abounds in other Treasure. ....6.34.24.101.
Purest love's unwasting treasure, ...6.51ii.41.154.
Others bring Goods and Treasure to their Houses, ...6.96iv.55.278.
A Treasure, which, of Royal kind, ...6.135.79.369.
A Treasure worthy Her, and worthy Me. ....II.1.174.96.
With Treasure loaded and triumphant Spoils, ...II.1.480.111.
Our Blood, our Treasure, and our Glory lost. ......II.2.146.135.
His be the Fair, and his the Treasure too. ....II.3.104.194.
His be the Dame, and his the Treasure too. ....II.3.325.208.
With Herds abounding, and with Treasure bless'd; ...II.5.761.303.
The Wife with-held, the Treasure ill detain'd, ...II.22.158.459.
With gifts of price and pond'rous treasure fraught. ...Od.3.397.105.
The sumless treasure of exhausted mines: ....Od.4.86.123.
And bounteous, from the royal treasure told ....Od.4.175.128.
Where shall this treasure now in safety lie? ......Od.13.245.17.
And here his whole collected treasure lay'd; ......Od.14.358.51.
(*Eumæus'* proper treasure bought this slave, ...Od.14.503.60.
With boundless treasure, from *Thesprotia's* shore. ...Od.17.617.162.
Reserve, the treasure of thy inmost mind: ....Od.19.570.224.

TREASURES

His Treasures next, *Alcinous'* Gifts, they laid ...1.TrUl.49.467.
To thee my Treasures and my self commend. ....1.TrUl.11.469.
And now appear, thy Treasures to protect, ...1.TrUl.179.471.
Unnumber'd Treasures ope at once, and here ....2.RL1.129.155.
"For me, the mine a thousand treasures brings; ....3.EOM1.137.32.
Rich with the Treasures of each foreign Tongue; ...4.2HE2.173.177.
Fain would my Muse the flow'ry Treasures sing, ...6.iv.1.47.
The treasures of a land, where, only free, ...6.142.8Z1.383.
The Dame and Treasures let the *Trojan* keep, ...II.3.356.210.
Among my Treasures, still adorns my Board: ....II.6.276.340.
Let *Sparta's* Treasures be this Hour restor'd, ...II.7.422.385.

TREASURES (CONTINUED)
Their Treasures I'll restore, but not the Dame; ....Il.7.437.386.
My Treasures too, for Peace, I will resign; ....Il.7.438.386.
The Spoils and Treasures he to *Ilion* bore, ...Il.7.464.387.
Each, in exchange, proportion'd Treasures gave; ....Il.7.568.392.
Whatever Treasures *Greece* for me design, ...Il.8.349.414.
Not all *Apollo's Pythian* Treasures hold, ...Il.9.525.459.
Lost Herds and Treasures, we by Arms regain, ...Il.9.528.459.
Sunk were her Treasures, and her Stores decay'd; ....Il.18.340.338.
My martial Troops , my Treasures , are thy own: ....Il.19.138.377.
What Heaps of Gold, what Treasures would I give? ....Il.22.67.455.
And where the Treasures of his Empire lay; ....Il.24.231.546.
What couldst thou hope, should these thy Treasures view, ...Il.24.451.555.
May offer all thy Treasures yet contain, ...Il.24.856.572.
To seize his treasures, and divide his state, ...Od.2.377.79.
Where lay the treasures of th' *Ithacian* race: ....Od.2.381.79.
A Palace stor'd with treasures shou'd be thine. ....Od.7.402.256.
Know hence what treasures in our ship we lost, ...Od.9.410.323.
Unload thy treasures, and thy gally moor; ....Od.10.478.366.
And bring our treasures and our arms a-shore: ....Od.10.502.368.
Without new treasures let him not remove, ...Od.13.15.2.
They bore the treasures, and in safety plac'd. ....Od.13.24.2.
His treasures next, *Alcinous'* gifts, they laid ....Od.13.140.11.
To thee my treasures and my self commend. ....Od.13.278.19.
And now appear, thy treasures to protect, ...Od.13.346.24.
Neleus his treasures one long year detains; ....Od.15.256.80.
Then gold and costly treasures will I bring, ...Od.15.487.93.
Enrag'd, his life, his treasures they demand; ....Od.16.446.128.
The gifts and treasures of the *Spartan* King) ....Od.17.87.136.
Where safe repos'd the royal treasures lay; ....Od.21.12.259.
Brass, gold, and treasures shall the spoil defray, ...Od.22.68.290.
All, all the treasures that enrich'd our throne ....Od.22.73.290.
With his, thy forfeit lands and treasures blend; ....Od.22.242.298.

TREAT
On bare *Suspicion* thus to treat your Bride; ....2.ChJM.796.53.
To one Man's Treat, but for another's Ball? ....2.RL1.96.152.
And treat this passion more as friend than foe: ....3.EOM2.164.74.
What care to tend, to lodge, to cram, to treat him, ...3.EOM3.46Z1.96.
But treat the Goddess like a modest fair, ...3.Ep4.51.142.
When the tir'd Glutton labours thro' a Treat, ...4.HS2.31.57.
Think how Posterity will treat thy name; ....4.HS2.108.61.
"Treat on, treat on," is her eternal Note, ...4.HAdv.13.75.
"Treat on, treat on," is her eternal Note, ...4.HAdv.13.75.
They treat themselves with most profound respect; ....4.2HE2.154.175.
Or if your life be one continu'd Treat, ...4.1HE6.110.245.
Or if our life be one continu'd Treat, ...4.1HE6.110A.245.
"Inform us, will the Emp'ror treat? ....4.HS6.114.257.
The Guests withdrawn had left the Treat, ...4.HS6.198.263.
To break my Windows, if I treat a Friend; ....4.EpS2.143.321.
And treat with half the.. ....4.1740.46.334.
To treat those Nymphs like yours of *Drury,* ....6.10.51.26.
And the Fool Treater grew the Treat at last. ....6.17iv.18.59.
Whose game is Whisk, whose treat a toast in sack, ...6.45.24.125.
you did treat him, ...6.68.10.196.
To treat him like her Sister *Scot,* ....6.101.30.291.
Nor thou, *Achilles,* treat our Prince with Pride; ....Il.1.364.105.
And wholsome Garlick crown'd the sav'ry Treat. ....Il.11.771.69.
And treat on Terms of Peace to save the Town: ....Il.22.157.459.
Then bids prepare the hospitable treat: ....Od.4.711.152.
And honey fresh, and *Pramnian* wines the treat: ....Od.10.271.355.
A public treat, with jars of gen'rous wine. ....Od.19.229.204.
Still treat they worth with lordly dull disdain; ....Od.20.209.243.
Dispos'd apart, *Ulysses* shares the treat; ....Od.20.322.248.
And pay the menials for the master's treat. ....Od.20.364.250.

TREATED
Treated, caress'd, where-e'er she's pleas'd to roam— ....2.ChWB.76.60.
And the best Men are treated like the worst, ...2.TemF.321.279.
Treated, caress'd, and tir'd, I take my leave, ...3.Ep4.165.153.

TREATER
And the Fool Treater grew the Treat at last. ....6.17iv.18.59.

TREATETH
He treateth them all, like a Prince of the Air. ....6.122.20A.342.
And treateth them all, like a Prince of the Air. ....6.122.20.342.

TREATIES
Unfinish'd Treaties in each Office slept; ....5.DunB4.616.405.
Nor with new Treaties vex my Peace in vain. ....Il.9.411.452.
(The Pledge of Treaties once with friendly *Thrace)*<:> ....Il.24.288.548.

TREATING
They left their senseless, treating, drunken Host. ....6.17iv.21.59.

TREATISE
A certain Treatise oft at Evening read, ...2.ChWB.356.74.

TREATMENT
Accept such treatment as a swain affords, ...Od.14.71.39.

TREATS
And treats alike his Vassals and his God. ....1.WF.76A.157.
In that cold Season Love but treats his Guest ....2.ChJM.105.19.
And endless Treats, and endless Visits paid, ...2.ChWB.115.62.
While Nymphs take Treats, or Assignations give, ...2.RL3.169.182.

TREBLE
And base, and treble Voices strike the Skies. ....2.RL5.42.202.
Close at my Heel with yelping Treble flies; ....6.14ii.20.43.
Join to the yelping Treble shrilling Cries; ....6.14ii.22.43.

TRECHIN'S
From *Alos, Alopè,* and *Trechin's* Tow'rs; ....Il.2.830.164.

TRECHUS
For manag'd Steeds, and *Trechus* press'd the Ground; ....Il.5.867.307.

TREE
A wondrous *Tree* that Sacred *Monarchs* bears? ....1.PSp.86.69.
But now the Reeds shall hang on yonder Tree, ...1.PSu.43.75.
Yet soon the Reeds shall hang on yonder Tree, ...1.PSu.43A.75.
Fade ev'ry Blossom, wither ev'ry Tree, ...1.PAu.33.82.
The weeping Amber or the balmy Tree, ...1.W-F.30.151.
The chestnut, wilding, plum, and every tree, ...1.TrPA.76.368.
Upon the tree I cast a frightful look; ....1.TrFD.29.387.
The trembling tree with sudden horror shook. ....1.TrFD.30.387.
A springing tree for *Dryope* they find, ...1.TrFD.59.388.
No more a woman, nor yet quite a tree: ....1.TrFD.64.388.
To hail this tree; and say, with weeping eyes, ...1.TrFD.82.389.
Believe a Goddess shrin'd in ev'ry tree. ....1.TrFD.87.389.
And all the nymph was lost within the tree: ....1.TrFD.101.390.
And singled out a Pear-Tree planted nigh: ....2.ChJM.602.44.
As well you view the Leacher in the Tree, ...2.ChJM.643.46.
By easier Steps, to where the Pear-Tree grew: ....2.ChJM.717.49.
Then from your Back I might ascend the Tree; ....2.ChJM.734.50.
She seiz'd a Twig, and up the Tree she went. ....2.ChJM.739.50.
What Feats the Lady in the Tree might do, ...2.ChJM.744.51.
Strait on the Tree his eager Eyes he bent, ...2.ChJM.750.51.
By Strugling with a Man upon a Tree? ....2.ChJM.763.52.
A fatal *Tree* was growing in his Land, ...2.ChWB.394.76.
Give me some Slip of this most blissful Tree, ...2.ChWB.399.76.
"There towns aerial on the waving tree. ....3.EOM3.182.111.
From yon old wallnut-tree a show'r shall fall; ....4.HS2.145.67.
"A most Romantic hollow Tree! ....4.HS6.176.261.
"Give me again my hollow Tree! ....4.HS6.222.263.
Orpheus could charm the trees, but thus a tree ....6.3.9.7.
Where *Daphne,* now a tree as once a maid, ...6.14iv.23.47.
And on each tree the golden apples glow; ....6.20.69.68.
Under the Greenwood Tree; ....6.79.102.221.
Under the Greenwood Tree. ....6.79.136.222.
As long as Moco's happy Tree shall grow, ...6.82i.1.229.
As long as India's happy Tree shall grow, ...6.82i.1A.229.
On the bare Mountains left its Parent Tree; ....Il.1.312.103.
('Twas where the Plane-tree spread its Shades around) ....Il.2.370.145.
Strait to the Tree his sanguine Spires he roll'd, ...Il.2.374.145.
Now near the Beech-tree, and the *Scæan* Gates, ...Il.11.223.45.
(As on a Fig-tree Top, his sounding Steel ....Il.21.44A.423.
A solid Pine-tree barr'd of wond'rous Length; ....Il.24.558.559.
A Tree, and well-dissembled foliage wears. ....Od.4.622.149.
A tree of stateliest growth, and yet undry'd, ...Od.9.381.321.
High in the air the tree its boughs display'd, ...Od.12.515.457.
Swift from the tree, the floating mast to gain, ...Od.12.523.458.
Thus on some tree hung struggling in the snare, ...Od.22.505.313.
Around the tree I rais'd a nuptial bow'r, ...Od.23.195.333.
Beneath a neighb'ring tree, the Chief divine ....Od.24.269.362.
On ev'ry plant and tree thy cares are shown, ...Od.24.292.364.

TREE'S
Just as the Twig is bent, the Tree's inclin'd. ....3.Ep1.102.22.
Beneath the Beech-Tree's consecrated Shades, ...Il.6.298.341.

TREES
Now Leaves the Trees, and Flow'rs adorn the Ground; ....1.PSp.43.65.
And Trees weep Amber on the Banks of *Po;* ....1.PSp.62.67.
Trees, where you sit, shall crowd into a Shade, ...1.PSu.74.77.
Ye Trees that fade when Autumn-Heats remove, ...1.PAu.29.82.
Now hung with Pearls the dropping Trees appear, ...1.PWi.31.91.
And told in Sighs to all the trembling Trees; ....1.PWi.62.93.
The trembling Trees, in ev'ry Plain and Wood, ...1.PWi.63.93.
The Winds and Trees and Floods her Death deplore, ...1.PWi.67.93.
Pants on the Leaves, and dies upon the Trees. ....1.PWi.80.94.
Thin Trees arise that shun each others Shades. ....1.W-F.22.150.
That crown'd with tufted Trees and springing Corn, ...1.W-F.27.150.
And Realms commanded which those Trees adorn. ....1.W-F.32.151.
Where Doves in Flocks the leafless Trees o'ershade, ...1.W-F.127.162.
And absent Trees that tremble in the Floods; ....1.W-F.214.169.
Thy Trees, fair *Windsor!* now shall leave their Woods, ...1.W-F.385.189.
In the next Line, it *whispers thro' the Trees;* ....1.EOC.351.279.
Leaves deck the stately trees; and man is fair, ...1.TrPA.106.370.
None taught the Trees a nobler Race to bear, ...1.TrVP.3.377.
Beheld the Trees with Autumn's Bounty crown'd; ....1.TrVP.58.379.
For thee the fading Trees appear to mourn, ...1.TrSP.173.401.
Old Limbs of Trees from crackling Forests torn, ...1.TrSt.506.431.
The loaded Trees their various Fruits produce, ...1.TrUl.126.470.
Thus Trees are crown'd with Blossoms white as Snow, ...2.ChJM.133.21.
And in soft Murmurs tell the Trees their Pain; ....2.ChJM.528.41.
There Trees, and intermingl'd Temples rise: ....2.TemF.18.254.
Here *Orpheus* sings; Trees moving to the Sound ....2.TemF.83.259.
Than Leaves on Trees, or Sands upon the Shores; ....2.TemF.425.284.
The dying gales that pant upon the trees, ...2.ElAb.159.332.
Glows in the stars, and blossoms in the trees, ...3.EOM1.272.48.
Did here the trees with ruddier burdens bend, ...3.EOM3.203.113.
All bath'd in tears—"Oh odious, odious Trees!" ....3.Ep2.40.53.
Trees cut to Statues, Statues thick as trees, ...3.Ep4.120.149.
Trees cut to Statues, Statues thick as trees, ...3.Ep4.120.149.
And Trees, and Stones, and Farms, and Farmer fall. ....4.2HE2.263.183.
A little House, with Trees a-row, ...4.1HE7.77.273.
Whose trees in summer yield him shade, ...6.1.7.3.
The Trees they water, but thou giv'st the fruit; ....6.2.27.6.
Orpheus could charm the trees, but thus a tree ....6.3.9.7.
While *Argo* saw her kindred Trees ....6.11.40.31.
And *Argo* saw her kindred Trees ....6.11.40A.31.
Here aged trees Cathedral walks compose, ...6.14iv.13.47.
Here *Orange-* trees with blooms and pendants shine, ...6.14iv.17.47.
Tall thriving trees confess'd the fruitful mold; ....6.35.5.103.
Like stunted hide-bound Trees, that just have got ....6.49i.11.137.
Has lopp'd three Trees, the Value of three Farthings: ....6.143.2.385.
Has cut three Trees, the Value of three Farthings: ....6.143.2A.385.
Or Leaves the Trees; or thick as Insects play, ...Il.2.552.153.
Where cold *Dodona* lifts her Holy Trees; ....Il.2.909.167.

TREES (CONTINUED)
As when some Shepherd from the rustling Trees ... Il.3.47.190.
Deluge whole Fields, and sweep the Trees along, ... Il.5.117.273.
Like Leaves on Trees the Race of Man is found, ... Il.6.181.334.
Where yon' wild Fig-Trees join the Wall of *Troy:* ... Il.6.551.354.
O'er the dark Trees a yellower Verdure shed, ... Il.8.693.428.
On ev'ry side the crackling Trees they tear, ... Il.12.165.87.
Leaves, Arms, and Trees aloft in Air are blown, ... Il.16.925.279.
Drink the whole Flood, the crackling Trees devour, ... Il.21.395.436.
The Trees in flaming rows to Ashes turn, ... Il.21.408.437.
Now where the Fig-trees spread their Umbrage broad, ... Il.22.193.463.
Now toils the Heroe; trees on trees o'erthrown ... Od.5.311.186.
Now toils the Heroe; trees on trees o'erthrown ... Od.5.311.186.
The rising forests, and the tufted trees. ... Od.5.513.197.
Tall thriving trees confess'd the fruitful mold; ... Od.7.146.243.
The trees around them all their food produce, ... Od.9.105.307.
And spiry tops, the tufted trees above, ... Od.10.175.349.
The barren trees of *Proserpine's* black woods, ... Od.10.604.373.
Trees of all kinds delicious fruitage spread; ... Od.11.726.421.
The loaded trees their various fruits produce, ... Od.13.293.19.
The sev'ral trees you gave me long ago. ... Od.24.389.368.
Twelve pear-trees bowing with their pendent load, ... Od.24.395.368.

TREMBL'D
Trembl'd, and shook the Heav'ns and Gods he bore. ... 1.TrSt.139.415.
But *Venus* trembl'd for the Prince of Troy: ... Il.3.460.214.

TREMBLE
And absent Trees that tremble in the Floods; ... 1.W-F.214.169.
But *those attain'd,* we tremble to survey ... 1.EOC.229.265.
The *Greeks* behold, they tremble, and they fly, ... 1.TrES.207.457.
And tremble at the Sea that froaths below! ... 2.RL2.136.168.
I tremble too where-e'er my own I find, ... 2.ElAb.33.321.
While Altars blaze, and Angels tremble round. ... 2.ElAb.276.342.
See my lips tremble, and my eye-balls roll, ... 2.ElAb.323.345.
And Nature tremble to the throne of God: ... 3.EOM1.256.46.
A godless Regent tremble at a Star? ... 3.Ep1.149.28.
Hear this, and tremble! you, who 'scape the Laws. ... 4.HS1.118.17.
Tremble before a *noble Serving-Man?* ... 4.JD4.199.43.
Let *Sporus* tremble—"What? that Thing of silk, ... 4.Arbu.305.117.
Let *Paris* tremble—"What? that Thing of silk, ... 4.Arbu.305A.117.
Despise the known, nor tremble at th' unknown? ... 4.2HE2.311.187.
To pant, or tremble thro' an Eunuch's throat. ... 4.2HE1.154.209.
And Asia's Tyrants tremble at your Throne— ... 4.2HE1.403.229.
How did I tremble, when by thousands bound, ... 6.96iv.67.278.
Who dares to tremble on this signal Day, ... Il.2.467.149.
Nor was *Tydides* born to tremble here. ... Il.5.313.281.
The starting Coursers tremble with Affright; ... Il.5.359.283.
And learn to tremble at the Name of Arms. ... Il.5.438.289.
The Spears already tremble in their Hand; ... Il.5.698.301.
To tremble at our Arms, not mix in War? ... Il.5.785.304.
Here rages Force, here tremble Flight and Fear, ... Il.5.915.310.
Submit and tremble at the hand of *Jove.* ... Il.8.257.409.
Your Hearts shall tremble, if our Arms we take, ... Il.8.564.423.
Gleam on the Walls, and tremble on the Spires. ... Il.8.702.428.
Made Nations tremble, and whole Hosts retire, ... Il.9.403.452.
Should start, and tremble at the Heaps of dead. ... Il.10.575.28.
But helpless tremble for themselves, and fly. ... Il.11.152.42.
Whose Sons now tremble at his darted Spear, ... Il.11.489.56.
And proud *Atrides* tremble on his Throne. ... Il.11.747.68.
Proud *Troy* may tremble, and desist from War; ... Il.11.931.77.
But snort and tremble at the Gulph beneath; ... Il.12.58.83.
The *Greeks* behold, they tremble, and they fly; ... Il.12.561.102.
Far-beaming Pendants tremble in her Ear, ... Il.14.211.170.
Pale Mortals tremble, and confess their Fears. ... Il.14.448.185.
The *Trojans* hear, they tremble, and they fly: ... Il.14.596.191.
Proud *Troy* shall tremble, and desert the War: ... Il.16.59.237.
At once they see, they tremble, and they fly, ... Il.16.337.255.
Thou stand'st, and Armies tremble at thy Sight ... Il.17.234.297.
What *Grecian* now shall tremble at thy Name? ... Il.17.659.313.
Who tremble yet, scarce rescu'd from their Fates, ... Il.17.719.315.
All pale they tremble, and forsake the Field. ... Il.17.820.320.
Proud *Troy* shall tremble, and consent to fear; ... Il.18.238.333.
Nor what I tremble but to think, ensue. ... Il.18.320.337.
The Vessels tremble as the Gods alight. ... Il.20.50.396.
Thro' all their Summits tremble *Ida's* Woods, ... Il.20.79.397.
Insult the Brave, who tremble at their Swords: ... Il.20.420.412.
Shall pant, and tremble at our Arms again; ... Il.21.244.431.
Tremble ye not, oh friends! and coward fly, ... Od.2.366.78.
Age o'er his limbs, that tremble as he treads. ... Od.16.479.130.
Drink the cool stream, and tremble to the wind. ... Od.17.241.143.
Amaz'd they see, they tremble, and they fly: ... Od.22.333.302.

TREMBLED
He cry'd, and Ætna trembled with the roar! ... 1.TrPA.139.371.
And the pale Spectres trembled at her View: ... 1.TrSt.133.415.
And startled Nature trembled with the Blast. ... 2.TemF.417.283.
The shrines all trembled, and the lamps grew pale: ... 2.ElAb.112.329.
Once like thy self, I trembled, wept, and pray'd, ... 2.ElAb.311.344.
Eurydice still trembled on his Tongue, ... 6.11.114.34.
They dropt the Fetters, trembled and ador'd. ... Il.1.529.113.
She heard, and trembled for her absent Lord: ... Il.6.483.350.
Grimly he smil'd; Earth trembled as he strode: ... Il.7.256.377.
The Heav'ns attentive trembled as he spoke. ... Il.8.6.395.
And inly trembled for his Brother's sake. ... Il.10.282.14.
Now *Greece* had trembled in her wooden Walls; ... Il.11.404.52.
Th' *Epeians* saw, they trembled, and they fled. ... Il.11.879.75.
The Forests shake! Earth trembled as he trod, ... Il.13.30.105.
Shall these, so late who trembled at your Name, ... Il.13.145.111.
Troy saw and trembled, as this Helmet blaz'd: ... Il.16.96.239.
Olympus trembled, and the Godhead said. ... Il.17.230.296.
And the Spear trembled as his Entrails heav'd. ... Il.17.593.311.
Then trembled *Greece:* The Flight *Peneleus* led; ... Il.17.676.314.
Hosts dropp'd their Arms, and trembled as they heard; ... Il.18.264.335.
Trembled the sparkling Plumes, and the loose Glories shed ... Il.19.415.389.
That trembled as it stuck; nor void of Fear ... Il.20.312.407.

TREMBLED (CONTINUED)
While yet he trembled at his Knees, and cry'd, ... Il.20.543.417.
The Guardian God now trembled for her Wall, ... Il.21.599.447.
It thunder'd as it fell. We trembled then, ... Od.9.278.318.
Almighty *Jove* had trembled on his throne. ... Od.11.390.403.
The Monarch spoke: they trembled and obey'd, ... Od.13.214.16.
And his flesh trembled as aghast he stood: ... Od.18.89.171.
And proud *Nericus* trembled as I storm'd. ... Od.24.438.369.
Then stopt the Goddess, trembled, and retir'd. ... Od.24.625.377.

TREMBLES
The green Reed trembles, and the Bulrush nods. ... 1.Mes.72.119.
Glows while he *reads,* but *trembles* as he *writes)* ... 1.EOC.198.263.
The mouldring Rock that trembles from on high. ... 1.TrSt.854.445.
But dreads the mouldring Rock that trembles from on high. ... 1.TrSt.854A.445.
Heav'n trembles, roar the Mountains, thunders all the Ground. ... 1.TrES.66A.452.
She sees, and trembles at th' approaching Ill, ... 2.RL3.91.174.
Jove's Thunder roars, Heav'n trembles all around; ... 2.RL5.49.203.
And the touch'd Needle trembles to the Pole: ... 2.TemF.431.284.
When the loose mountain trembles from on high, ... 3.EOM4.127.140.
Ev'n *Peter* trembles only for his Ears. ... 4.EpS2.57.315.
He trembles, he glows, ... 6.11.108.34.
The world no longer trembles at their pow'r! ... 6.22.15.71.
The Wretch who trembles in the Field of Fame, ... Il.5.657.299.
(How my Heart trembles while my Tongue relates!) ... Il.6.571.354.
And the Turf trembles, and the Skies resound. ... Il.12.60.83.
Heav'n trembles, roar the Mountains, thunders all the Ground. ... Il.12.410.96.
She sees her *Jove,* and trembles at the Sight. ... Il.14.184.168.
Fair *Ida* trembles underneath the God; ... Il.14.323.178.
Seeks his own Seas, and trembles at our Rage! ... Il.15.251.206.
The Wretch that trembles in the Field of Fame, ... Il.15.672.222.
And *Hector* trembles and recedes with Fear; ... Il.17.184.294.
The River trembles to his utmost Shore, ... Il.17.314.300.
Once more *Lycaon* trembles at thy Knee; ... Il.21.85.425.
Hangs on the Robe, or trembles at the Knee, ... Il.22.633.482.
Fearless herself, yet trembles for her young. ... Od.4.1044.166.
Earth trembles, and the waves confess their God. ... Od.11.306.397.
And the flesh trembles while she churns the blood. ... Od.12.307.447.
She sickens, trembles, falls, and faints away: ... Od.23.212.333.

TREMBLING
Let Vernal Airs thro' trembling Osiers play, ... 1.PSp.5.60.
And told in Sighs to all the trembling Trees; ... 1.PWi.62.93.
The trembling Trees, in ev'ry Plain and Wood, ... 1.PWi.63.93.
And makes his trembling Slaves the Royal Game. ... 1.W-F.64.155.
Intent, his Angle trembling in his Hand; ... 1.W-F.138.163.
Not half so swift the trembling Doves can fly, ... 1.W-F.185.167.
When thro' the Clouds he drives the trembling Doves; ... 1.W-F.188.167.
Ere warning *Phœbus* touch'd his trembling Ears, ... 1.EOC.131A.254.
A Fisher next, his trembling Angle bears. ... 1.TrVP.42.379.
The trembling tree with sudden horror shook. ... 1.TrFD.30.387.
My trembling sister strove to urge her flight, ... 1.TrFD.36.387.
Surpriz'd at this, her trembling hand she heaves ... 1.TrFD.45.387.
Thus thro' the trembling boughs in sighs complains. ... 1.TrFD.68.389.
No more these Hands shall touch the trembling String: ... 1.TrSP.235.404.
And trembling *Ister* check'd his rapid Flood; ... 1.TrSt.26A.410.
When by the Son the trembling Father dy'd, ... 1.TrSt.91.414.
And all the trembling Spheres confess'd the God. ... 1.TrSt.283.422.
And Crimes that grieve the trembling Gods to name? ... 1.TrSt.326.423.
Nor trembling *Cynthia* glimmers on the Deeps; ... 1.TrSt.523.432.
Fed on his trembling Limbs, and lapt the Gore. ... 1.TrSt.696.439.
And thro' his Buckler drove the trembling Wood; ... 1.TrES.138.454.
From side to side the trembling Balance nods, ... 1.TrES.168.455.
The trembling Limbs, and sucks the smoking Blood; ... 1.TrES.298.460.
These touch the vocal Stops, and those the trembling String. ... 2.ChJM.321.29.
What ails my Lord? the trembling Dame reply'd; ... 2.ChJM.758.51.
Trembling, begins the sacred Rites of Pride. ... 2.RL1.128.155.
The Sun-beams trembling on the floating Tydes, ... 2.RL2.48.162.
Anxious, and trembling for the Birth of Fate. ... 2.RL2.142.168.
Trembling, and conscious of the rich Brocade. ... 2.RL3.116.176.
Thrice from my trembling hand the *Patch-box* fell; ... 2.RL4.162.197.
She said: in Air the trembling Musick floats, ... 2.TemF.372.281.
The trembling Surface, by the Motion stir'd, ... 2.TemF.438.284.
Soon as thy letters trembling I unclose, ... 2.ElAb.29.321.
While praying, trembling, in the dust I roll, ... 2.ElAb.279.342.
The hallow'd taper trembling in thy hand, ... 2.ElAb.326.346.
See on these ruby lips the trembling breath, ... 2.Elegy.31.365.
Hope humbly then; with trembling pinions soar; ... 3.EOM1.91.25.
Between each Act the trembling salvers ring, ... 3.Ep4.161.153.
Paint Angels trembling round his *falling Horse?* ... 4.HS1.28.7.
Tell how the Moon-beam trembling falls ... 4.HS6.191.261.
When Truth stands trembling on the edge of Law: ... 4.EpS2.249.327.
And Bacon trembling for his brazen head: ... 5.DunA3.96.158.
And Bacon trembling for his brazen head. ... 5.DunB3.104.325.
In broken Air, trembling, the wild Musick floats; ... 6.11.17.30.
Thou seem'st all trembling, shivr'ing, dying, ... 6.31i.7.93.
Thou seem'st all trembling, fainting, dying, ... 6.31i.7A.93.
Trembling, hoping, ling'ring, flying, ... 6.31ii.3.94.
"Trembling, I've seen thee dare the Kitten's Paw; ... 6.96ii.27.271.
The trembling Priest along the Shore return'd, ... Il.1.47.88.
High Heav'n with trembling the dread Signal took, ... Il.1.686.120.
Trembling they stand, while *Jove* assumes the Throne, ... Il.1.694.120.
Beneath their Footsteps groans the trembling Ground. ... Il.2.120.133.
And heaves huge Surges to the trembling Shores: ... Il.2.250.139.
Trembling he sate, and shrunk in abject Fears, ... Il.2.330.143.
And trembling sought the Pow'rs with Sacrifice, ... Il.2.389.145.
Men, Steeds, and Chariots shake the trembling Ground; ... Il.2.980.170.
Trembling and pale, he starts with wild Affright, ... Il.3.49.191.
Forsook her Cheek; and, trembling, thus she said. ... Il.3.492.215.
Or trembling Sailors on the wintry Main) ... Il.4.104.225.
To save a trembling, heartless, dastard Race? ... Il.4.285.234.
He spoke, and ardent, on the trembling Ground ... Il.4.474.242.
The distant Shepherd trembling hears the Sound: ... Il.4.520.246.
And trembling heard the Jav'lin as it flew. ... Il.4.572.249.
But trembling leaves the scatt'ring Flocks a Prey. ... Il.5.179.275.
Like trembling Hounds before the Lion's Rage. ... Il.5.582.296.

TREMBLING (CONTINUED)

The vig'rous Pow'r the trembling Car ascends, ... Il.5.1030.315.
Both Armies start, and trembling gaze around; ... Il.5.1056.317.
Leap'd from his trembling Chariot to the Ground; ... Il.6.126.330.
And *Thetis'* Arms receiv'd the trembling God. ... Il.6.168.334.
And the big Tear stood trembling in her Eye. ... Il.6.509.351.
I see thee trembling, weeping, Captive led! ... Il.6.579.355.
Breaks from his Stall, and beats the trembling Ground; ... Il.6.653.359.
And trembling met this dreadful Son of War. ... Il.7.132.370.
Gods! should he see our Warriors trembling stand, ... Il.7.155.372.
And trembling all before one hostile Hand; ... Il.7.156.372.
I led my Troops to *Phea's* trembling Wall, ... Il.7.164.372.
Can you stand trembling, and desert the Day? ... Il.7.194.373.
All *Troy* stood trembling at the mighty Man. ... Il.7.260.377.
New to the Field, and trembling at the Fight? ... Il.7.286.378.
And the vast World hangs trembling in my Sight! ... Il.8.32.397.
Trembling they stood before their Sov'reign's Look; ... Il.8.37.397.
Men, Steeds, and Chariots shake the trembling Ground; ... Il.8.73.399.
Before his Wrath the trembling Hosts retire; ... Il.8.97.402.
And *Nestor's* trembling Hand confess'd his Fright. ... Il.8.166.406.
The vig'rous Pow'r the trembling Car ascends; ... Il.8.472.419.
Trembling afar th' offending Pow'rs appear'd, ... Il.8.554.423.
And guards them trembling in their wooden Walls. ... Il.8.626.425.
Scarce can my Knees these trembling Limbs sustain, ... Il.10.100.7.
Or chase thro' Woods obscure the trembling Hinde; ... Il.10.428.23.
Then fix'd in Earth. Against the trembling Wood ... Il.10.443.23.
One Instant snatch'd his trembling Soul to Hell, ... Il.10.526.26.
The Steeds fly trembling from his waving Sword; ... Il.11.207.44.
Springs from his Chariot on the trembling Ground, ... Il.11.270.47.
Vaults from his Chariot on the trembling Ground, ... Il.11.270A.47.
Ulysses hastens with a trembling Heart, ... Il.11.505.56.
Trembling gave way, and turn'd his Back to Flight, ... Il.11.559.58.
And trembling *Greece* for her Physician fear'd. ... Il.11.631.61.
Then, from my Fury fled the trembling Swains, ... Il.11.820.73.
With his huge Trident wounds the trembling Shore, ... Il.12.30.82.
And *Troy* lie trembling in her Walls again. ... Il.12.328.93.
And thro' his Buckler drove the trembling Wood; ... Il.12.492.99.
From side to side the trembling Balance nods, ... Il.12.522.101.
Trembling before th' impending Storm they lie, ... Il.13.121.110.
Stands all aghast his trembling Char<i>oteer, ... Il.13.502.130.
Leap'd from his Chariot on the trembling Ground; ... Il.13.940.149.
Fall from that trembling Tongue, and tim'rous Heart? ... Il.14.91.162.
And at *Prothœnor* shook the trembling Spear; ... Il.14.526.189.
I hung thee trembling, in a golden Chain; ... Il.15.25.195.
And trembling, these submissive Words return'd. ... Il.15.40.195.
The trembling Queen (th' Almighty Order giv'n) ... Il.15.84.199.
The trembling World, and shakes the steady Poles. ... Il.15.173.203.
The trembling, servile, second Race of Heav'n. ... Il.15.223.205.
Go thou my Son! the trembling *Greeks* alarm, ... Il.15.258.207.
While these fly trembling, others pant for Breath, ... Il.15.392.212.
Pale, trembling, tir'd, the Sailors freeze with Fears; ... Il.15.756.225.
The trembling Herdsman far to distance flies: ... Il.15.765.226.
Confessing *Jove,* and trembling at the Sign; ... Il.16.149.243.
And rend the trembling, unresisting Prey. ... Il.16.423.259.
And trembling Man sees all his Labours vain! ... Il.16.475.261.
The trembling Limbs, and sucks the smoking Blood; ... Il.16.603.267.
The only Hope of *Chalcon's* trembling Age: ... Il.16.722.272.
And trembling strook, and rooted in the Field, ... Il.16.742.272.
The village Curs, and trembling Swains retire; ... Il.17.70.290.
(The crystal Drops stood trembling in her Eyes) ... Il.18.500.345.
Of trembling Parents on the Turrets stand. ... Il.18.598.351.
If trembling in the Ships he lags behind. ... Il.19.240.382.
Trembling he stood before the golden Wain, ... Il.19.448.390.
And trembling see another God of War. ... Il.20.62.396.
Now thro' the trembling Shores *Minerva* calls. ... Il.20.67.396.
Now chac'd, and trembling in ignoble flight: ... Il.21.6.421.
As trembling, panting, from the Stream he fled, ... Il.21.60.424.
Once more *Lycaon* trembling at thy Knee; ... Il.21.85A.425.
While all his trembling Frame confest his Fear. ... Il.21.128.426.
(All trembling on the Verge of helpless Age) ... Il.22.83.456.
Shot trembling Rays that glitter'd o'er the Land; ... Il.22.176.461.
Or deep beneath the trembling Thicket shakes; ... Il.22.246.465.
My falt'ring Knees their trembling Frame desert, ... Il.22.580.480.
Atrides, trembling casts his Eye below, ... Il.23.505.510.
But *Greece* now trembling for her Hero's Life, ... Il.23.969.527.
The trembling Mark at which their Arrows fly. ... Il.23.1013.529.
And thus in Whispers greets his trembling Ears. ... Il.24.208.545.
A sudden Trembling shook his aged Frame: ... Il.24.444.554.
His trembling Limbs, his helpless Person, see! ... Il.24.602.562.
The Sire obey'd him, trembling and o'er-aw'd. ... Il.24.720.567.
Wak'd with the Word, the trembling Sire arose, ... Il.24.858.572.
The big round tear hung trembling in his eye: ... Od.2.91.65.
But trembling heard the Fame? and heard, admire ... Od.3.238.97.
Declines his trembling steps; untimely care ... Od.4.145.127.
The monarch-savage rends the trembling prey. ... Od.4.454.141.
The big round tear stands trembling in her eye, ... Od.4.936.162.
The dastard lurks, all trembling with his fear: ... Od.9.538.328.
Struck with unusual fear, she trembling cries, ... Od.10.385.363.
Poplars and willows trembling o'er the floods: ... Od.10.605.373.
Back started the pale throngs, and trembling stood. ... Od.11.62.383.
Thro' the wide dome of *Dis,* a trembling band. ... Od.11.700.419.
All trembling, deafen'd, and aghast we stood! ... Od.12.243.443.
Struck with despair, with trembling hearts we view'd ... Od.12.292.446.
The trembling crowds shall see the sudden shade ... Od.13.182.14.
A rugged staff his trembling hand sustains; ... Od.13.505.30.
His deathful pounces tore a trembling dove; ... Od.15.567.97.
Of pow'r divine, and howling, trembling fled. ... Od.16.177.112.
Propt on a staff, and trembling as he went. ... Od.17.413.152.
In ev'ry joint the trembling *Irus* shook; ... Od.18.101.172.
With triple stars, that cast a trembling light. ... Od.18.346.184.
Sad *Euryclea* rose: with trembling hand ... Od.19.421.214.
Truss'd with his sinewy pounce a trembling dove; ... Od.20.303.247.
Unguided hence my trembling steps I bend, ... Od.20.441.254.
High notes responsive to the trembling string, ... Od.21.441.281.
Trembling they sought their guilty heads to hide, ... Od.22.55.289.
Back by the hair the trembling dastard drew, ... Od.22.203.297.

TREMBLING (CONTINUED)

The lyre, now silent, trembling in his hands; ... Od.22.370.305.
Beneath a table, trembling with dismay, ... Od.22.401.307.
Scarce sure of life, look round, and trembling move ... Od.22.419.308.
(Their life's last scene) they trembling wait their fall. ... Od.22.494.313.
Trembling the Spectres glide, and plaintive vent ... Od.24.7.347.
Trembling with agonies of strong delight ... Od.24.371.367.
Trembling with warmth, the hoary heroes stand, ... Od.24.576.375.

TREMBLINGLY

Or touch, if tremblingly alive all o'er, ... 3.EOM1.197.39.
His touch, if tremblingly alive all o'er, ... 3.EOM1.197A.39.
The touch, if tremblingly alive all o'er, ... 3.EOM1.197B.39.
Or touch, so tremblingly alive all o'er, ... 3.EOM1.197C.39.

TREMBLINGS

By the dear Tremblings of the Bed of Bliss; ... 6.82ii.4.230.
And with unmanly Tremblings shook the Car, ... Il.16.491.262.

TREMENDOUS

And *stares, Tremendous!* with a *threatning Eye,* ... 1.EOC.586.306.
Rend with tremendous Sound your ears asunder, ... 4.HS1.25.7.
Rend with tremendous Sound our ears asunder, ... 4.HS1.25A.7.
Lo *E[usden]* rose, tremendous all in mud! ... 5.DunA2.302A.139.
Lo P[op]ple's brow, tremendous to the town, ... 5.DunB3.151.327.
Goddess of Woods, tremendous in the chace, ... 6.65.1.192.
Have made Tremendous as a Prince ... 6.135.88A.369.
(Tremendous Oath! inviolate to Kings) ... Il.1.316.103.
Dire, black, tremendous! Round the Margin roll'd, ... Il.5.912.309.
Thus march'd the Chief, tremendous as a God; ... Il.7.255.377.
Tremendous Gorgon frown'd upon its Field, ... Il.11.47.36.
The Warrior sinks, tremendous now no more! ... Il.12.216.89.
Tremendous Scene, that gen'ral Horror gave, ... Il.13.434.126.
Swear then (he said) by those tremendous Floods ... Il.14.305.177.
By thy black Waves, tremendous *Styx!* that flow ... Il.15.43.195.
Greece from one Glance of that tremendous Eye ... Il.18.239.333.
What tho' tremendous in the woodland Chase, ... Il.21.561.445.
Low'ring they meet, tremendous to the Sight; ... Il.23.961.527.
Each hand tremendous with a brazen spear, ... Od.1.332.48.
And kills us all in one tremendous draught? ... Od.2.371.78.
Proteus, a name tremendous o'er the main, ... Od.4.521.145.
When *Jove* tremendous in the sable deeps ... Od.7.334.253.
When high in air, tremendous to behold, ... Od.11.382.401.
High on a throne, tremendous to behold, ... Od.11.697.419.
From the pale ghosts, and hell's tremendous shade. ... Od.12.24.430.
Tremendous pest! abhorr'd by man and Gods! ... Od.12.108.436.
Furious and fell, tremendous to behold! ... Od.12.149.439.
Now all at once tremendous scenes unfold; ... Od.12.240.443.
Neptune, tremendous o'er the boundless main! ... Od.13.165.13.
As from a hanging rock's tremendous height, ... Od.14.341.51.

TRENCH

For passing Chariots, and a Trench profound. ... Il.7.409.385.
For passing Chariots; and a Trench profound, ... Il.7.523.390.
High o'er their slighted Trench our Steeds shall bound, ... Il.8.218.407.
Where the deep Trench in Length extended lay, ... Il.8.262.409.
Or in the Trench on Heaps confus'dly fall. ... Il.8.404.416.
When flying they had pass'd the Trench profound, ... Il.8.413.417.
Between the Trench and Wall, let Guards remain: ... Il.9.94.437.
Some line the Trench, and others man the Wall. ... Il.9.120.438.
With Piles, with Ramparts, and a Trench profound? ... Il.9.461.455.
Now let us Jointly to the Trench descend, ... Il.10.109.7.
Assembling there, between the Trench and Gates, ... Il.10.146.8.
Then o'er the Trench the following Chieftains led. ... Il.10.228.12.
Then o'er the Trench the bounding Coursers flew; ... Il.10.664.31.
Close to the Limits of the Trench and Mound, ... Il.11.61.37.
Nor long the Trench or lofty Walls oppose; ... Il.12.5.81.
Wedg'd in the Trench, by our own Troops confus'd, ... Il.12.83.84.
Now in swift Flight they pass the Trench profound, ... Il.15.1.193.
Some seek the Trench, some skulk behind the Wall, ... Il.15.391.212.
Yon' ample Trench had bury'd half her Host. ... Il.16.98.239.
Wedg'd in the Trench, in one vast Carnage bruis'd. ... Il.16.443.260.
Within, without the Trench, and all the way, ... Il.17.851.321.
Let but *Achilles* o'er yon' Trench appear, ... Il.18.237.333.
Thrice from the Trench his dreadful Voice he rais'd; ... Il.18.269.335.
Trench the black earth a cubit long and wide: ... Od.10.615.374.
Round the black trench the gore untasted flows, ... Od.11.63.383.
A trench he open'd; in a line he plac'd ... Od.21.125.264.

TRENCH'D

Of Earth congested, wall'd, and trench'd around; ... Il.20.175.401.

TRENCH'S

Apollo, planted at the Trench's Bound, ... Il.15.406.213.

TRENCHANT

The trenchant Faulchion lopp'd his Hands away; ... Il.11.188.43.

TRENCHES

He leapt the Trenches, scal'd a Castle-Wall, ... 4.2HE2.40.167.
The Trenches past, th' assembl'd Kings around ... Il.10.231.12.
The Walls were rais'd, the Trenches sunk in vain. ... Il.12.8.81.
Exhorts his Armies, and the Trenches shows. ... Il.12.56.83.
Back from the Trenches let your Steeds be led; ... Il.12.88.84.
And o'er the Trenches led the rolling Cars. ... Il.24.550.559.

TRENCHING

And trenching the black earth on ev'ry side, ... Od.11.29.380.

TRENDS

And to the feast magnificently trends. ... Od.8.494.289.

TRENT

Let me but live on this side *Trent:* ... 4.HS6.30.251.
Could I but live on this side *Trent:* ... 4.HS6.30A.251.

TRESSES

His Tresses dropt with Dews, and o'er the Stream	1.W-F.331.182.
The gulphy *Lee* his sedgy Tresses rears:	1.W-F.346.184.
Nor Braids of Gold the vary'd Tresses bind,	1.TrSP.85.397.
I rend my Tresses, and my Breast I wound,	1.TrSP.130.399.
Fair Tresses Man's Imperial Race insnare,	2.RL2.27.161.
Not all the Tresses that fair Head can boast	2.RL5.143.211.
And all those Tresses shall be laid in Dust;	2.RL5.148.212.
With tresses staring from poetic dreams,	5.DunA3.143.162.
Her tresses staring from Poetic dreams,	5.DunB3.17.321.
Thy curling Tresses, and thy silver Lyre,	Il.3.80.193.
And soils its verdant Tresses on the Ground:	Il.13.243.116.
Her artful Hands the radiant Tresses ty'd;	Il.14.204.170.
She rent her Tresses, venerably grey,	Il.22.512.477.

TREUFLES

Thy Treufles, Perigord! thy Hams, Bayonne!	5.DunB4.558.397.

TREZENIAN

Sprung from *Trezenian Ceus,* lov'd by *Jove.*	Il.2.1027.171.

TRIAL

And drew behind a radiant *Trial of Hair.*	2.RL5.128.210.
Attend the trial we propose to make:	5.DunA2.339.142.
"Attend the trial we propose to make:	5.DunB2.371.315.
And dar'd the Trial of the strongest Hands;	Il.7.182.373.

TRIALS

In all these Trials I have born a Part;	2.ChWB.5.57.

TRIBE

The Female Tribe surround him as he lay,	2.ChJM.412.34.
Then came the smallest Tribe I yet had seen,	2.TemF.356.281.
Of these a gloomy Tribe surround the Throne,	2.TemF.412.283.
The Tribe of Templars, Play'rs, Apothecaries,	4.HAdv.1.75.
Seen him, uncumber'd with the Venal tribe,	4.EpS1.31.300.
Glory, and gain, th' industrious tribe provoke;	5.DunA2.29.99.
Of him, whose chatt'ring shames the Monkey tribe;	5.DunA2.224.128.
Glory, and gain, th'industrious tribe provoke;	5.DunB2.33.297.
Of him, whose chatt'ring shames the Monkey tribe:	5.DunB2.232.307.
A tribe, with weeds and shells fantastic crown'd,	5.DunB4.398.381.
Sour with debauch, a reeling tribe, they came.	Od.3.172.94.
(Reply'd *Eumæus*) to the wand'ring tribe.	Od.14.147.42.
The rural tribe in common share the rest,	Od.14.486.59.
Of my own tribe an *Argive* wretch I slew;	Od.15.298.83.
Mean-time instructed is the menial tribe	Od.19.697.229.

TRIBES

His conqu'ring tribes th' Arabian prophet draws,	5.DunA3.89.157.
His conqu'ring tribes th' Arabian prophet draws,	5.DunB3.97.324.
He talks of Senates, and of Courtly Tribes,	6.96v.15.280.
In Tribes and Nations to divide thy Train:	Il.2.431.148.
In Tribes and Nations rank'd on either side.	Il.2.523.151.
And all the Tribes resound the Goddess' Praise.)	Il.2.664.158.
There in three Tribes divides his native Band,	Il.2.809.163.
A Youth there was among the Tribes of *Troy,*	Il.10.371.19.
The wealthy tribes of *Pharian Thebes* obey)	Od.4.170.128.
And portion to his tribes the wide domain.	Od.4.238.130.
Convene the tribes, the murd'rous plot reveal,	Od.4.978.163.
There round his tribes a strength of wall he rais'd,	Od.6.13.204.
Know, the *Phæacian* tribes this land divide;	Od.6.236.221.
The gather'd tribes before the Altars stand,	Od.13.216.16.
The King of Ocean all the tribes implore;	Od.13.218.16.
Two equal tribes this fertile land divide,	Od.15.452.92.
Thesprotian tribes, a duteous race, obey:	Od.19.330.210.
The city-tribes, to pleas'd *Apollo's* grove:	Od.20.343.249.

TRIBUNAL

Mounts the Tribunal, lifts her scarlet head,	4.EpS1.149.309.
Embrace his Knees, at his Tribunal fall;	Il.1.531.113.
The high Tribunal of Immortal *Jove.*	Il.1.561.115.

TRIBUTARY

Who swell with Tributary Urns his Flood.	1.W-F.338.183.
That swell with Tributary Urns his Flood.	1.W-F.338A.183.
And rule the tributary Realms around.	Il.9.206.442.
And rule the tributary Realms around.	Il.9.393.452.

TRIBUTE

A wealthier Tribute, than to thine he gives.	1.W-F.224.170.
Let my good Spouse pay Tribute, do me Right,	2.ChWB.52.59.
Rolls the large tribute of dead dogs to Thames,	5.DunA2.260.133.
Rolls the large tribute of dead dogs to Thames,	5.DunB2.272.309.
My tears eternal tribute shou'd be paid:	6.20.40.67.
Pays the last Tribute of a Saint to Heav'n.	6.132.14.362.
The Tribute of a melancholy Day.	Il.19.230.382.
Nor roll their wonted Tribute to the Deep.	Il.21.236.430.
The constant Tribute of Respect and Love:	Il.24.520.557.
Indulge the tribute of a grateful tear.	Od.4.130.126.
The tribute of a tear is all I crave,	Od.11.89.385.
A gen'ral tribute, which the State shall owe.	Od.13.18.2.
With earth's whole tribute the bright table bends,	Od.15.352.86.

TRICA

Or where her humbler Turrets *Trica* rears,	Il.2.886.166.

TRICE

The Heart resolves this matter in a trice,	4.2HE2.216.179.
Name a Town Life, and in a trice,	4.HS6.155.259.
Or Gods to save them in a trice!	4.HS6.217.263.
All in a Trice he rush'd on *Guise,*	6.79.57.219.
All in a Trice on *Guise* he rush'd,	6.79.57A.219.

TRICK

On one nice *Trick* depends the gen'ral Fate.	2.RL3.94.174.
Dip in the Rainbow, trick her off in Air,	3.Ep2.18.50.

TRICK (CONTINUED)

By any *Trick,* or any *Fault;*	4.HS6.14.251.
Fate plays her old Dog Trick!	6.79.62.220.
Fate shews an old Dog Trick!	6.79.62A.220.
(That Trick of Tyrants) may be born by Slaves.	Il.1.162.95.

TRICK'D

Who trick'd with Gold, and glitt'ring on his Car,	Il.2.1062.172.

TRICKLE

While Tears Celestial trickle from her Eyes)	Il.1.541.114.
And the soft Tears to trickle from her Eyes?	Il.18.158.330.
And Tears shall trickle from cœlestial Eyes:	Il.20.249.404.

TRICKLED

While Tears Celestial trickled from her Eyes)	Il.1.541A.114.

TRICKLES

How fluent nonsense trickles from his tongue!	5.DunA3.197.174.
How honey'd nonsense trickles from his tongue!	5.DunA3.197A.174.
How fluent nonsense trickles from his tongue!	5.DunB3.201.330.

TRICKLING

From ev'ry leaf distills a trickling tear,	1.TrFD.66.388.
And silent Tears fall trickling from my Eyes.	1.TrSP.200.402.
The balm of Dulness trickling in their ear.	5.DunB4.544.395.
In sable Streams soft-trickling Waters shed.	Il.9.20.432.
And the big Tears roll trickling from her Eyes.	Il.11.160.42.
Not faster, trickling to the Plains below,	Il.16.5.234.
And tears ran trickling from her aged eyes.	Od.2.407.80.
Down his wan cheek the trickling torrent ran,	Od.24.487.371.

TRICKS

Or tricks to shew the stretch of human brain,	3.EOM2.47.61.
Of Masquerading Tricks,	6.54.2.164.
Such, Lady *Mary,* are your Tricks;	6.93.27.257.
Such, Lady Mary, are your Tricks,	6.93.27Z1.257.
"Vers'd in Court Tricks, that Money-loving Boy	6.96ii.33.272.
And (what's the Top of all your Tricks)	6.135.11.366.

TRIDENT

Then * He, whose Trident shakes the Earth, began.	Il.7.529.391.
With his huge Trident wounds the trembling Shore,	Il.12.30.82.
Of him, whose Trident rends the solid Ground.	Il.14.176.165.
Ev'n * He whose Trident sways the watry Reign,	Il.20.19.393.
Of *her, whose azure trident awes the main:	Od.4.546.146.
He spoke, and high the forky Trident hurl'd,	Od.5.375.190.

TRIES

Panting with Hope, he tries the furrow'd Grounds,	1.W-F.100.160.
But in low Numbers short Excursions tries:	1.EOC.738.326.
Each Shape he varies, and each Art he tries,	1.TrVP.43.379.
And tries all Forms, that may *Pomona* please.	1.TrVP.93.381.
While the rude Swain his rural Musick tries,	1.TrSt.689.439.
The *Knave* of *Diamonds* tries his wily Arts,	2.RL3.87.174.
Still tries to save the hallow'd taper's end,	3.Ep1.239.36.
The plague is on thee, Britain, and who tries	4.1740.75.336.
Still her old empire to confirm, she tries,	5.DunA1.15.61.
Still her old Empire to restore she tries,	5.DunB1.17.270.
In a translated Suit, then tries the Town,	6.49i.21.138.
He tries our Courage, but resents our Fears.	Il.2.230.138.
Each met in Arms the Fate of Combate tries,	Il.3.181.199.
But vainly here *Diana's* Arts he tries,	Il.5.69.269.
And ev'ry side of wav'ring Combate tries;	Il.5.1025.315.
His arms he poises, and his Motions tries;	Il.19.417.389.
The fourth, he tries to break the Spear in vain;	Il.21.193.429.
In vain he tries the Covert of the Brakes,	Il.22.245.465.
Here each contending Hero's Lot he tries,	Il.22.273.467.
On these the Virtue of his Wand he tries,	Il.24.547.558.
But while the dangers of the deeps he tries,	Od.2.373.78.
Athwart the spacious square each tries his art	Od.17.192.140.

TRIFLE

At ev'ry Trifle scorn to take Offence,	1.EOC.386.284.
Leave such to trifle with more grace and ease,	4.2HE2.326.187.
Learn but to trifle; or, who most observe,	5.DunB4.457.385.
Chearful, he play'd the Trifle, Life, away,	6.19.12.62.
Or o'er cold coffee trifle with the spoon,	6.45.17.125.
Unfold some trifle, but conceal the rest.	Od.11.548.410.

TRIFLER

Let him no trifler from his school,	4.1740.87.337.

TRIFLES

For *not* to know some Trifles, is a Praise.	1.EOC.262.269.
As well as dream such trifles are assign'd,	3.EOM4.179.144.
To this were Trifles, Toys, and empty Names.	4.JD4.8.27.
Trifles themselves are Elegant in him.	6.19.4.62.

TRIFLING

The trifling Head, or the corrupted Heart!	4.Arbu.327.119.
A trifling Head, and a corrupted Heart!	4.Arbu.327A.119.
A trifling head, and a contracted heart.	5.DunB4.504.392.

TRILL

One Trill shall harmonize joy, grief, and rage,	5.DunB4.57.347.

TRIM

To trim his beard, th'unweildy scythe prepares;	1.TrPA.23.366.
The trim of pride, the impudence of wealth,	3.EOM3.4.92.
Gave alms at Easter, in a Christian trim,	3.Ep2.57.55.
Top-gallant he, and she in all her Trim,	4.JD4.230.45.
Sweeter than *Sharon,* in immaculate trim,	4.JD4.252.47.
From no trim Beau's its Name it boasts,	6.59.5.177.
In all her tackle trim, to quit the shore.	Od.4.1032.166.
And sprightly damsels trim the rays by turns.	Od.18.358.184.

TRIMM'D
Morsel for dogs! then trimm'd with brazen sheers ..... Od.22.511.313.

TRIMS
Starts from her Trance, and trims her wither'd Bays! ..... 1.EOC.698.319.
Trims *Europe's* Balance, tops the Statesman's part, ... 4.JD4.154.39.

TRINACRIA'S
Thence to *Trinacria's* shore you bend your way, ... Od.12.160.439.

TRINACRIAN
Where on *Trinacrian* rocks the Ocean roars, ... Od.11.134.387.
To perish in the rough *Trinacrian* sea. ..... Od.19.316.209.

TRIPLE
And suck'd new Poisons with his triple Tongue) ..... 1.TrSt.667.438.
Hemm'd by a triple Circle round, ... 4.HS6.48.253.
At some sick miser's triple-bolted gate, ... 5.DunA2.238.129.
At some sick miser's triple-bolted gate, ... 5.DunB2.248.307.
His triple Thunder, and his Bolts of Fire. ..... Il.5.560.295.
The Triple Dog had never felt his Chain, ... Il.8.447.418.
Each Gemm illumin'd with a triple Star. ..... Il.14.212.170.
Assign'd by Lot, our triple Rule we know; ..... Il.15.212.205.
The teeming Ewes a triple offspring bear; ..... Od.4.106.125.
With triple stars, that cast a trembling light. ..... Od.18.346.184.

TRIPLE-BOLTED
At some sick miser's triple-bolted gate, ... 5.DunA2.238.129.
At some sick miser's triple-bolted gate, ... 5.DunB2.248.307.

TRIPLETS
For routing *Triplets,* and restoring *ed.* ..... 6.98.12Z2.283.

TRIPOD
A Pipkin there like *Homer's Tripod* walks; ..... 2.RL4.51.188.
Some golden Tripod, or distinguish'd Car, ... Il.8.351.414.
(Some golden Tripod, or some lovely Dame) ..... Il.22.214.464.
With kindled Flames the Tripod-Vase surround; ..... Il.23.50.489.
A Goblet or a Tripod let us stake, ... Il.23.569.512.
The Tripod-Vase, and Dame with radiant Eyes: ..... Il.23.594.513.
A massy Tripod for the Victor lies; ..... Il.23.816.521.
That in the tripod o'er the kindled pyle ..... Od.10.423.365.
Each peer a tripod, each a vase bestow, ... Od.13.17.2.
These will the Caldron, these the Tripod give, ... Od.15.97.73.
He said, and high the whirling tripod flung. ..... Od.17.547.159.

TRIPOD-VASE
With kindled Flames the Tripod-Vase surround; ..... Il.23.50.489.
The Tripod-Vase, and Dame with radiant Eyes: ..... Il.23.594.513.

TRIPODS
The Gold, the Vests, the Tripods number'd o'er; ..... 1.TrUl.95.469.
Sev'n sacred Tripods, whose unsully'd Frame ..... Il.9.159.440.
Sev'n sacred Tripods, whose unsully'd Frame ..... Il.9.346.450.
Full twenty Tripods for his Hall he fram'd, ... Il.18.440.341.
A Rowe of six fair Tripods then succeeds; ..... Il.19.251.383.
Vases and Tripods, for the Fun'ral Games, ... Il.23.325.503.
Two Tripods next and twice two Chargers shine, ... Il.24.285.548.
With silver tripods, the kind host assign'd; ..... Od.4.174.128.
The gold, the vests, the tripods, number'd o'er: ..... Od.13.262.18.

TRIPOS
Hail faithful *Tripos!* Hail ye dark Abodes ..... 1.TrSt.596.435.

TRIPP'D
So featly tripp'd the light-foot Ladies round, ... 2.ChJM.620.45.
She tripp'd and laugh'd, too pretty much to stand; ..... 5.DunB4.50.346.

TRIPS
The sprightly *Sylvia* trips along the Green, ... 1.PSp.57.66.
Now trips a Lady, and now struts a Lord. ..... 4.Arbu.329.119.

TRIPTHONGS
Dipthongs, and Tripthongs, swore and stutter'd, ... 6.30.51.88.

TRITONIA
Swift at the Mandate pleas'd *Tritonia* flies, ... Il.22.241.465.

TRITONS
And gaping Tritons spew to wash your face. ..... 3.Ep4.154.152.

TRIUMPH
And a whole Province in his Triumph led. ..... 1.TrSt.746.441.
For, since Fifteen, in Triumph have I led ..... 2.ChWB.7.57.
Let Wreaths of Triumph now my Temples twine, ... 2.RL3.161.180.
He spoke, and speaking, in proud Triumph spread ..... 2.RL4.139.195.
Here dragg'd in Triumph round the *Trojan* Wall. ..... 2.TemF.191.271.
The *Mantuan* there in sober Triumph sate, ... 2.TemF.200.271.
Pursue the triumph, and partake the gale? ..... 3.EOM4.386.165.
But Wisdom's Triumph is well-tim'd Retreat, ... 3.Ep2.225.68.
Turn Arcs of triumph to a Garden-gate; ..... 3.Ep4.30.140.
On Crimes that scape, or triumph o'er the Law: ..... 4.EpS1.168.309.
Exulting in Triumph now swell the bold Notes, ... 6.11.16.30.
She does in Triumph ride ..... 6.14v(b).15A.50.
Shou'd I have liv'd, in *Cæsar's* triumph born, ... 6.20.7.66.
The triumph ceas'd—Tears gush'd from ev'ry eye; ..... 6.32.33.97.
Triumph! All Arts are overthrown, ... 6.119.19A.337.
And his refulgent Arms in Triumph wears; ..... Il.2.698.159.
Where once *Eurytus* in proud Triumph reign'd, ... Il.2.885.166.
Amidst his Triumph to the *Spartan's* Heart? ..... Il.4.126.226.
A Grief to us, a Triumph to the Foe. ..... Il.4.241.232.
And these, the Victor's Prize, in Triumph led. ..... Il.5.295.281.
Our Triumph now, the mighty Warrior lies! ..... Il.5.346.283.
These in proud Triumph to the Fleet convey'd, ... Il.5.401.286.
And bears the Prize in Triumph to the Fleet. ..... Il.5.721.301.
Deck'd in sad Triumph for the mournful Field, ... Il.5.910.309.

TRIUMPH (CONTINUED)
All *Greece* recedes, and 'midst her Triumph fears. ..... Il.6.132.330.
With equal Triumph, sprightly, bold and gay, ... Il.6.660.360.
Their present Triumph, as their late Despair. ..... Il.7.377.382.
Shall see his bloody Spoils in Triumph born, ... Il.8.664.427.
I saw his Coursers in proud Triumph go, ... Il.10.506.26.
The Bulls of *Elis* in glad Triumph led, ... Il.11.818.72.
Loud Shouts of Triumph fill the crowded Plain; ..... Il.14.493.188.
Him, proud in Triumph glitt'ring from afar, ... Il.17.225.296.
The Vanquish'd triumph, and the Victors fly. ..... Il.17.675.314.
If yet this honour'd Corps, in Triumph born, ... Il.17.717.315.
Go matchless Goddess! triumph in the Skies, ... Il.21.583.446.
Some proud in Triumph, some with Rage on fire; ..... Il.21.603.447.
To die or triumph, that, determine Heav'n! ..... Il.22.172.460.
Meanwhile ye Sons of *Greece!* in Triumph bring ..... Il.22.491.476.
The martial Scarf and Robe of Triumph wove. ..... Il.22.657.483.
And great *Patroclus* in short Triumph bore. ..... Il.23.944.526.
Your common Triumph, and your common Woe. ..... Il.24.881.573.
And the gilt roofs with genial triumph ring. ..... Od.4.844.158.
She feels the triumph of a gen'rous breast; ..... Od.7.94.238.
Telemachus in triumph sails the main. ..... Od.16.363.124.
A worthless triumph o'er a worthless foe! ..... Od.18.435.189.
Had made thee buy the brutal triumph dear: ..... Od.20.375.251.
Triumph, thou happy victor of thy woes! ..... Od.23.308.338.

TRIUMPH'D
Her Arts victorious triumph'd o'er our Arms: ..... 4.2HE1.264.217.
Like Cimon triumph'd, both on land and wave: ..... 5.DunA1.84.69.
Like Cimon, triumph'd both on land and wave: ..... 5.DunB1.86.275.
Oft hast thou triumph'd in the glorious Boast, ... Il.1.514.112.
Him, while he triumph'd, *Paris* ey'd from far, ... Il.11.473.55.

TRIUMPH'ST
Thou triumph'st, victor of the high-wrought day, ... 5.DunA2.179.123.
Thou triumph'st, Victor of the high-wrought day, ... 5.DunB2.187.304.

TRIUMPHAL
And hew Triumphal Arches to the Ground. ..... 2.RL3.176.182.
Lo! at the Wheels of her Triumphal Car, ... 4.EpS1.151.309.
To Needham's quick the voice triumphal rode, ... 5.DunB1.323.293.
And while on Fame's triumphal Car they ride, ... 5.DunB4.133.354.
Ev'n when proud *Cæsar* 'midst triumphal cars, ... 6.32.27.96.
A train of coursers, and triumphal cars ..... Od.4.714.152.

TRIUMPHANT
And mounts exulting on triumphant Wings; ..... 1.W-F.112.161.
Hail *Bards Triumphant!* born in *happier Days;* ..... 1.EOC.189.262.
Hear, in *all Tongues* Triumphant *Pæans* ring! ..... 1.EOC.186A.262.
Triumphant o'er th'eluded Rage of *Jove!* ..... 1.TrSt.303.422.
Thou cam'st Triumphant to a Mortal's Arms, ... 1.TrSt.361.425.
And live out all in one triumphant Day. ..... 1.TrSt.452.429.
And to the Shades a Ghost Triumphant send; ..... 1.TrSt.777.442.
Triumphant *Umbriel* on a Sconce's Height ..... 2.RL5.53.203.
And on the Winds triumphant swell the Notes; ..... 2.TemF.373.281.
And up the Winds triumphant swell the Notes; ..... 2.TemF.373A.281.
Triumphant Leaders at an Army's head, ... 3.Ep1.145Z1.27.
Triumphant Malice rag'd thro' private life. ..... 4.2HE1.254.217.
Shall take thro' Grubstreet her triumphant round, ... 5.DunA3.128.160.
Shall take thro' Grub-street her triumphant round; ..... 5.DunB3.136.326.
And while on Fame's triumphant Car they ride, ... 5.DunB4.133A.354
And There Triumphant Sing Thy Soverain's Praise. ..... 6.147ix.6.392.
With Treasure loaded and triumphant Spoils, ... Il.1.480.111.
Renown'd, triumphant, and enrich'd with Spoils. ..... Il.2.144.135.
And *Greece* triumphant held a gen'ral Feast, ... Il.2.156.136.
When thy tall Ships triumphant stem'd the Tide, ... Il.3.66.192.
Let these the brave triumphant Victor grace, ... Il.3.131.196.
And thro' the Ranks of Death triumphant ride. ..... Il.5.251.279.
So when triumphant from successful Toils, ... Il.6.610.357.
Triumphant Shouts and dying Groans arise; ..... Il.8.80.399.
Then pensive thus, to War's triumphant Maid. ..... Il.8.422.417.
Triumphant now, now miserably slain, ... Il.8.530.421.
Return'd triumphant with this Prize of War. ..... Il.10.631.30.
Then back to *Pyle* triumphant take my way. ..... Il.11.893.75.
No more those Coursers with triumphant Joy ..... Il.12.129.86.
That *Troy* triumphant our high Fleet ascends, ... Il.14.72.161.
His radiant Arms triumphant *Meges* bore. ..... Il.15.621.220.
Triumphant *Greece* her rescu'd Decks ascends, ... Il.16.352.256.
Achilles' Arms triumphant in the Fields. ..... Il.17.539.309.
Whom late, triumphant with his Steeds and Car, ... Il.18.279.335.
Oppos'd to *Pallas,* War's triumphant Maid. ..... Il.20.94.398.
Where late their Troops triumphant bore the Fight, ... Il.21.5.421.
These to the Ships his Train triumphant leads, ... Il.23.595.513.
But if *Athena,* War's triumphant maid, ... Od.3.269.99.
Pallas herself, the War-triumphant Maid, ... Od.3.486.111.
And bears triumphant to his native Isle ..... Od.13.160.13.
And back triumphant wing'd his airy way. ..... Od.19.632.227.
Jove's daughter *Pallas,* War's triumphant maid: ..... Od.22.222.297.
When our triumphant navies touch'd your shore; ..... Od.24.141.354.

TRIUMPHANTLY
And Crowds on Crowds triumphantly expir'd. ..... Il.4.637.251.

TRIUMPHING
He sternly views him, and triumphing cries. ..... Il.16.1002.281.
While the proud Victor thus triumphing said, ... Il.21.199.429.
To stern *Pelides,* and triumphing, cries. ..... Il.22.278.467.
While thus triumphing, stern *Achilles* cries. ..... Il.22.414.472.

TRIUMPHS
See TRYUMPHS.
Stretch his long Triumphs down thro' ev'ry Age, ... 1.W-F.304.177.
Inglorious Triumphs, and dishonest Scars. ..... 1.W-F.326.180.
Tho' *Triumphs* were to *Gen'rals* only due, ... 1.EOC.512.296.
Insults my Woes, and triumphs in my Tears, ... 1.TrSP.136.399.
Sad in the midst of Triumphs, sigh'd for Pain; ..... 2.ChJM.358.31.
Great in his Triumphs, in Retirement great. ..... 2.TemF.164.267.

TRIUMPHS (CONTINUED)

Here triumphs He whom *Athens* did expel, ... 2.TemF.172A.269.
T' enroll your triumphs o'er the seas and land; ... 4.2HE1.373.227.
You dream of triumphs in the rural shade; ... 6.45.32.125.
And all her Triumphs shrink into a Coin: ... 6.71.24.203.
And the dire Triumphs of her fatal Eyes. ... Il.3.172.199.
While the proud Foe his frustrate Triumphs mourns, ... Il.6.678.361.
Your hasty Triumphs on the *Lemnian* Shore? ... Il.8.277.410.
Our hasty Triumphs on the *Lemnian* Shore? ... Il.8.277A.410.
And only triumphs to deserve thy Hands. ... Il.9.405.452.
And the pale Matron in our Triumphs mourn. ... Il.14.594.191.
Had grac'd the Triumphs of his *Trojan* Foe; ... Il.17.694.314.
How *Ilion* triumphs, and th' *Achaians* mourn. ... Il.17.774.318.
And oft' the Victor triumphs, but to fall. ... Il.18.360.338.
While his fond soul these fancied triumphs swell'd, ... Od.1.155.40.
That day, ere yet the bloody triumphs cease, ... Od.3.394.105.
Of wars, of triumphs, and disastrous fates; ... Od.23.330.340.

TRIVET

A trivet-table, and ignobler seat, ... Od.20.323.248.

TRIVET-TABLE

A trivet-table, and ignobler seat, ... Od.20.323.248.

TRIVIAL

Applause, in spite of trivial Faults, is due. ... 1.EOC.258.269.
What mighty Contests rise from trivial Things, ... 2.RL1.2.144.
What mighty Quarrels rise from trivial Things, ... 2.RL1.2A.144.
Some trivial Present to my Ships I bear, ... Il.1.219.97.

TROD

And pointed out those arduous Paths they trod, ... 1.EOC.95.250.
The prostrate Prince, and on his Bosom trod; ... 1.TrES.317.461.
His Feet on Sceptres and *Tiara's* trod, ... 2.TemF.153.266.
Or tread the mazy round his follow'rs trod, ... 3.EOM2.25.58.
Nor think, in NATURE'S STATE they blindly trod; ... 3.EOM3.147.107.
To Virtue, in the paths of Pleasure, trod, ... 3.EOM3.233.116.
"Behold yon' Isle, by Palmers, Pilgrims trod, ... 5.DunA3.105.159.
"See'st thou an Isle, by Palmers, Pilgrims trod, ... 5.DunA3.105A.159.
Coach'd, carted, trod upon, now loose, now fast, ... 5.DunA3.293.184.
Or tread the path by vent'rous Heroes trod, ... 5.DunB1.201.284.
"Behold yon' Isle, by Palmers, Pilgrims trod, ... 5.DunB3.113.325.
Coach'd, carted, trod upon, now loose, now fast, ... 5.DunB3.291.334.
For this the Tragic Muse first trod the stage, ... 6.32.5.96.
Come near, they trod upon your Toes; ... 6.79.19.218.
He kicked, and cuff'd, and tweak'd, and trod ... 6.79.23.218.
He tweak'd his Nose, trod on his Toes, ... 6.79.59.219.
Each Step they trod, I felt upon my Heart. ... 6.96iv.70.278.
Swift thro' the Town he trod his former way, ... Il.6.489.350.
And trod the Path his Feet must tread no more. ... Il.10.400.21.
Horse trod by Horse, lay foaming on the Plain. ... Il.11.194.44.
The Forests shake! Earth trembled as he trod, ... Il.13.30.105.
I mark'd his parting, and the Steps he trod, ... Il.13.103.109.
In Thought, a Length of Lands he trod before, ... Il.15.87.200.
The wond'ring Crowds the downward Level trod; ... Il.15.412.213.
One kept the Shore, and one the Vessel trod; ... Il.15.486.216.
The prostrate Prince, and on his Bosom trod; ... Il.16.622.268.
All trod the dark, irremeable Way: ... Il.19.312.385.
Yon' Line of slaughter'd *Trojans* lately trod. ... Il.21.654.449.
Embroider'd sandals glitter'd as he trod, ... Od.2.7.60.
Unwilling, have I trod this pleasing land; ... Od.5.124.178.
He trod her footsteps in the sandy shore. ... Od.5.248.183.
With equal grace *Nausicaa* trod the plain, ... Od.6.127.212.
Late a sad spectacle of woe, he trod ... Od.6.291.224.
For heav'n foretold the contest, when he trod ... Od.8.75.266.
Sudden th' irremeable way he trod, ... Od.8.259.276.
With these gay *Hermes* trod the starry plain; ... Od.8.363.283.
Awful he trod! majestic was his look, ... Od.11.114.386.
There with soft step the fair *Alcmena* trod, ... Od.11.325.398.
There *Ephimedia* trod the gloomy plain, ... Od.11.375.401.
Rose in his majesty, and noblier trod; ... Od.11.660.416.
Down to these worlds I trod the dismal way, ... Od.11.769.424.
Then future means consult—she spoke, and trod ... Od.13.419.26.
He trod so fatally the paths of Fame. ... Od.14.82.40.
The Heroe trod the margin of the main, ... Od.15.597.99.
Late worn with years in weeds obscene you trod, ... Od.16.220.114.
Ere yet he trod these shores! to strife he draws ... Od.18.448.190.
This gift, long since when *Sparta's* shores he trod, ... Od.21.17.259.
Now loftier trod, and dreadful thus began. ... Od.22.287.300.
But learn we instant how the Suitors trod ... Od.23.85.322.
Of hell I trod, to learn my future fates. ... Od.23.270.336.
How sav'd from storms *Phæacia's* coast he trod, ... Od.23.365.342.
The rest ador'd him, tow'ring as he trod; ... Od.24.26.348.
And trod thy footsteps with unequal pace: ... Od.24.391.368.

TROEZENÈ

From high *Trœzenè,* and *Maseta's* Plain, ... Il.2.676.159.

TROILUS

With *Troilus,* dreadful on his rushing Car, ... Il.24.322.550.

TROJAN

The best and bravest of the *Trojan* Force. ... 1.TrES.72.452.
(With Brutal Force he seiz'd my *Trojan* Prey, ... 1.TrUl.146.470.
But when the *Trojan* Piles in Ashes lay, ... 1.TrUl.195.472.
Not half so fixt the *Trojan* cou'd remain, ... 2.RL5.5.199.
Here dragg'd in Triumph round the *Trojan* Wall. ... 2.TemF.191.271.
Like *Trojan* true, to draw for *Hellen:* ... 6.10.84.27.
Jove was alike to Trojan and to *Phrygian,* ... 6.82iii.1A.230.
Why leave we not the fatal *Trojan* Shore, ... Il.1.79.90.
Left by *Achilles* on the *Trojan* Plain, ... Il.1.223.97.
While I, too partial, aid the *Trojan* Arms? ... Il.1.675.119.
Must want a *Trojan* Slave to pour the Wine. ... Il.2.158.136.
Haste then, for ever leave the *Trojan* Wall! ... Il.2.165.136.
Nor let your Flight avert the *Trojan* Fate. ... Il.2.399.145.
If e'er as Friends we join, the *Trojan* Wall ... Il.2.450.149.

TROJAN (CONTINUED)

In radiant Arms, and thirst for *Trojan* Blood. ... Il.2.559.154.
Three Ships with *Nireus* sought the *Trojan* Shore, ... Il.2.815.163.
The first who boldly touch'd the *Trojan* Shore, ... Il.2.855.165.
In *Priam's* Porch the *Trojan* Chiefs she found, ... Il.2.958.169.
Th' Auxiliar Troops and *Trojan* Hosts appear. ... Il.2.987.170.
And fly, the Scandal of thy *Trojan* Host. ... Il.3.60.192.
The *Trojan* Wars she weav'd (herself the Prize) ... Il.3.171.199.
Each hardy *Greek* and valiant *Trojan* Knight, ... Il.3.175.199.
There sate the Seniors of the *Trojan* Race, ... Il.3.191.200.
And from Destruction save the *Trojan* Race. ... Il.3.210.201.
And I, to join them, rais'd the *Trojan* Force: ... Il.3.248.204.
Arise, O Father of the *Trojan* State! ... Il.3.319.208.
Amid the *Grecian* Host and *Trojan* Train ... Il.3.335.209.
The Dame and Treasures let the *Trojan* keep, ... Il.3.356.210.
If by my Brother's Lance the *Trojan* bleed; ... Il.3.358.210.
With Jav'lins fix'd, the *Greek* and *Trojan* Band. ... Il.3.424.212.
The *Trojan* first his shining Jav'lin threw; ... Il.3.427.212.
And lay the *Trojan* gasping in the Dust: ... Il.3.434.212.
The wary *Trojan,* bending from the Blow, ... Il.3.443.213.
To her, beset with *Trojan* Beauties, came ... Il.3.475.214.
Be fix'd for ever to the *Trojan* Shore, ... Il.3.505.215.
They said, while *Pallas* thro' the *Trojan* Throng ... Il.4.115.226.
While some proud *Trojan* thus insulting cries, ... Il.4.212.231.
'Till yon' tall Vessels blaze with *Trojan* Fire? ... Il.4.283.234.
The first who strook a valiant *Trojan* dead: ... Il.4.523.246.
Array'd in Terrors, rowz'd the *Trojan* Pow'rs: ... Il.4.594.249.
Struck with Amaze, and Shame, the *Trojan* Crew ... Il.5.35.267.
Meantime the *Greeks* the *Trojan* Race pursue, ... Il.5.49.268.
Amid the *Greek,* amid the *Trojan* Train, ... Il.5.112.272.
Oh give my Lance to reach the *Trojan* Knight, ... Il.5.150.274.
If e'er with Life I quit the *Trojan* Plain, ... Il.5.268.280.
No longer now a *Trojan* Lord obey'd. ... Il.5.402.286.
Stirs all the Ranks, and fires the *Trojan* Train; ... Il.5.562.295.
Each *Trojan* Bosom with new Warmth he fires. ... Il.5.626.298.
Pours on the *Greeks:* The *Trojan* Troops pursue: ... Il.5.723.302.
Thy Sire, O Prince! o'erturn'd the *Trojan* State, ... Il.5.804.304.
Shall save a *Trojan* from our boundless Rage: ... Il.6.72.327.
One Hour demands me in the *Trojan* Wall, ... Il.6.139.330.
By his Decree I sought the *Trojan* Town, ... Il.6.255.339.
Meantime the Guardian of the *Trojan* State, ... Il.6.296.341.
The *Trojan* Matrons and the *Trojan* Maids ... Il.6.299.341.
The *Trojan* Matrons and the *Trojan* Maids ... Il.6.299.341.
Prone on the Dust before the *Trojan* Wall. ... Il.6.381.345.
The *Trojan* Bands, by hostile Fury prest, ... Il.6.451.348.
This Day, some God who hates our *Trojan* Land ... Il.6.460.349.
Or sought her Sisters in the *Trojan* Court? ... Il.6.477.350.
So spoke the Guardian of the *Trojan* State, ... Il.7.1.363.
Hear all ye *Trojan,* all ye *Grecian* Bands, ... Il.7.79.366.
By *Trojan* Hands and *Trojan* Flames be burn'd. ... Il.7.92.367.
By *Trojan* Hands and *Trojan* Flames be burn'd. ... Il.7.92.367.
(To *Ajax* thus the *Trojan* Prince reply'd) ... Il.7.284.378.
The wary *Trojan* shrinks, and bending low ... Il.7.303.379.
Drove thro' the *Trojan* Targe the knotty Spear; ... Il.7.312.379.
As I shall glad each Chief, and *Trojan* Wife, ... Il.7.360.381.
The *Trojan* Bands returning *Hector* wait, ... Il.7.372.382.
The *Trojan* Peers in nightly Council sate: ... Il.7.415.385.
Cold Counsels, *Trojan,* may become thy Years, ... Il.7.430.386.
Then hear me, Princes of the *Trojan* Name! ... Il.7.436.386.
Of added *Trojan* Wealth to buy the Peace. ... Il.7.467.387.
In mingled Throngs, the *Greek* and *Trojan* Train ... Il.7.502.389.
All Night they feast, the *Greek* and *Trojan* Pow'rs; ... Il.7.570.392.
Low sunk on Earth, the *Trojan* strikes the Skies. ... Il.8.92.401.
Hear ev'ry *Trojan, Lycian, Dardan* Band ... Il.8.210.407.
And ask'd Destruction to the *Trojan* Name. ... Il.8.289.411.
And dy'd his Javelin red with *Trojan* Gore. ... Il.8.308.412.
A *Trojan* Ghost attending ev'ry Dart. ... Il.8.336.413.
What mighty *Trojan* then, on yonder Shore, ... Il.8.461.419.
And warn their Children from a *Trojan* War. ... Il.8.642.426.
For *Trojan* Vulturs a predestin'd Prey. ... Il.8.656.427.
Whose Wrath hung heavy o'er the *Trojan* Tow'rs; ... Il.8.682.427.
How near our Fleet approach the *Trojan* Fires? ... Il.9.104.437.
Besides full twenty Nymphs of *Trojan* Race, ... Il.9.179.441.
In *Trojan* Dust, and this the fatal Day? ... Il.9.319.449.
Besides full twenty Nymphs of *Trojan* Race, ... Il.9.366.451.
And twelve lay smoaking on the *Trojan* Plain: ... Il.9.433.453.
Here, if I stay, before the *Trojan* Town, ... Il.9.534.460.
From thousand *Trojan* Fires the mounting Blaze; ... Il.10.14.2.
To try yon' Camp, and watch the *Trojan* Pow'rs? ... Il.10.44.4.
Scarce had he pass'd the Steeds and *Trojan* Throng, ... Il.10.401.21.
So fast, and with such Fears, the *Trojan* flew; ... Il.10.431.23.
Where lies encamp'd the *Trojan* Chief to Night? ... Il.10.478.24.
Then sleep those Aids among the *Trojan* Train, ... Il.10.494.25.
Swift to the *Trojan* Camp descends the Pow'r, ... Il.10.606.29.
Perhaps some Horses of the *Trojan* Breed ... Il.10.628.30.
The Chiefs out-number'd by the *Trojan* Train: ... Il.10.633.30.
The *Trojan* Lines possess'd the rising Ground. ... Il.11.74.38.
Dispers'd, disorder'd, fly the *Trojan* Train. ... Il.11.226.45.
Now storms the Victor at the *Trojan* Wall; ... Il.11.235.46.
The *Trojan* stoop'd, the Javelin pass'd in Air. ... Il.11.300.48.
His Brother's Corps the pious *Trojan* draws, ... Il.11.331.49.
But *Jove* with Conquest crowns the *Trojan* Train; ... Il.11.413.53.
Had warn'd his Children from the Trojan Field; ... Il.11.428.53.
Without a Wound the *Trojan* Hero stands; ... Il.11.456.54.
Whole Hecatombs of *Trojan* Ghosts shall pay. ... Il.11.472.55.
The laughing *Trojan,* with a joyful Spring ... Il.11.483.55.
This Hour surrounded by the *Trojan* Bands; ... Il.11.969.78.
Oh thou! bold Leader of our *Trojan* Bands, ... Il.12.69.84.
Nor shall a *Trojan* live to tell the Tale. ... Il.12.86.84.
Oh thou! brave Leader of our *Trojan* Bands, ... Il.12.69A.84.
While ev'ry *Trojan* thus, and ev'ry Aid, ... Il.12.123.85.
Mean-time the bravest of the *Trojan* Crew ... Il.12.225.89.
The *Trojan* Warrior, touch'd with timely Fear, ... Il.13.219.116.
And breathes Destruction to the *Trojan* Bands. ... Il.13.276.117.
The rest lies rooted in a *Trojan* Shield. ... Il.13.336.121.
Spears I have store, (and *Trojan* Lances all) ... Il.13.339.121.

TROJAN (CONTINUED)

But spar'd a while the destin'd *Trojan* Tow'rs:	Il.13.441.126.
These Pow'rs infold the *Greek* and *Trojan* Train	Il.13.451.127.
These Pow'rs inclose the *Greek* and *Trojan* Train	Il.13.451A.127.
Not unattended (the proud *Trojan* cries)	Il.13.523.131.
See! on one *Greek* three *Trojan* Ghosts attend,	Il.13.560.133.
The *Trojan* heard; uncertain, or to meet	Il.13.572.133.
Now, *Trojan* Prince, employ thy pious Arms,	Il.13.582.134.
And met the *Trojan* with a low'ring Look.	Il.13.603.135.
(Co-aids and Captains of the *Trojan* Line.)	Il.13.619.135.
The *Trojan* Weapon whizz'd along in Air;	Il.13.636.136.
Disarm'd, he mingled in the *Trojan* Crew;	Il.13.716.138.
Full on his Breast the *Trojan* Arrow fell,	Il.13.737.139.
To yon' tall Ships to bear the *Trojan* Fires;	Il.13.932.149.
Haste the bold Leaders of the *Trojan* Band:	Il.13.952.151.
And lifts the *Trojan* Glory to the Skies.	Il.14.80.161.
And wilt thou thus desert the *Trojan* Plain?	Il.14.98.162.
Soon shalt thou view the scatter'd *Trojan* Bands	Il.14.166.165.
Then back the disappointed *Trojan* drew,	Il.14.469.186.
(*Phorbas* the rich, of all the *Trojan* Train	Il.14.575.190.
Oh! all of *Trojan,* all of *Lycian* Race!	Il.15.494.216.
Thy Fall, great *Trojan!* had renown'd that Day.	Il.15.539.217.
Some God, propitious to the *Trojan* Foe,	Il.15.550.218.
This rouz'd the Soul in ev'ry *Trojan* Breast:	Il.15.590.219.
If once your Vessels catch the *Trojan* Fire?	Il.15.597.219.
Lift the bold Lance, and make some *Trojan* bleed.	Il.15.685.222.
On the fall'n Chief th' invading *Trojan* prest,	Il.15.782.226.
And rush'd enrag'd before the *Trojan* Croud:	Il.15.833.229.
The first that touch'd th' unhappy *Trojan* Shore:	Il.15.857.229.
Whate'er bold *Trojan* arm'd his daring Hands	Il.15.904.232.
That not one *Trojan* might be left alive,	Il.16.124.242.
Great *Jove* with Conquest crown'd the *Trojan* Band.	Il.16.129.242.
How first the Navy blaz'd with *Trojan* Flame?	Il.16.141.243.
Think with what Threats you dar'd the *Trojan* Throng,	Il.16.240.248.
A living Prize not long the *Trojan* stood;	Il.16.396.258.
The *Trojan* Chief, experienc'd in the Field,	Il.16.428.259.
Dire *Flight* and *Terror* drove the *Trojan* Train.	Il.16.439.259.
Sprung on the *Trojan* and the *Lycian* Band;	Il.16.711.271.
Fierce on the *Trojan* and the *Lycian* Crew,	Il.16.839.276.
And pour'd swift Spirits thro' each *Trojan* Breast.	Il.16.890.277.
The *Trojan* thus: The *Spartan* Monarch burn'd	Il.17.17.288.
And doom'd to *Trojan* Dogs th' unhappy Dead;	Il.17.138.293.
Impel one *Trojan* Hand, or *Trojan* Heart;	Il.17.174.294.
Impel one *Trojan* Hand, or *Trojan* Heart;	Il.17.174.294.
The *Trojan* Chief with fixt Resentment ey'd	Il.17.187.294.
Whoe'er shall drag him to the *Trojan* Train,	Il.17.271.298.
Condemn'd to Vulturs on the *Trojan* Plain;	Il.17.285.298.
Struck at the Sight, recede the *Trojan* Train:	Il.17.368.301.
And tells me, *Jove* asserts the *Trojan* Arms.	Il.17.393.302.
Now at *Automedon* the *Trojan* Foe	Il.17.594.311.
A Prey to Dogs beneath the *Trojan* Wall?	Il.17.627.312.
There stood a *Trojan* not unknown to Fame,	Il.17.648.313.
Had grac'd the Triumphs of his *Trojan* Foe;	Il.17.694.314.
And Conquest shifting to the *Trojan* Side,	Il.17.706.315.
Transfers the Glory to the *Trojan* Band;	Il.17.710.315.
Unarm'd, he fights not with the *Trojan* Foe.	Il.17.796.319.
So from the *Trojan* Chiefs the *Grecians* fly,	Il.17.849.321.
(So *Thetis* warn'd) when by a *Trojan* Hand,	Il.18.13.323.
Approaching now, they touch'd the *Trojan* Land;	Il.18.89.327.
No more the *Grecian* Hope, or *Trojan* Dread!	Il.18.152.329.
Thy radiant Arms the *Trojan* Foe detains,	Il.18.168.330.
Thrice to the Skies the *Trojan* Clamours flew.	Il.18.194.331.
Flies any *Trojan?* I shall stop his Flight.	Il.18.346.338.
And twelve, the noblest of the *Trojan* Line,	Il.18.394.340.
While *Trojan* Captives here thy Mourners stay,	Il.18.399.340.
The *Trojan* Ranks, and deal Destruction round,	Il.19.150.377.
Now thro' each *Trojan* Heart he Fury pours	Il.20.71.396.
The sacred *Tros,* of whom the *Trojan* Name.	Il.20.275.405.
Have sworn Destruction to the *Trojan* Kind;	Il.20.362.410.
Lye there *Otryntides!* the *Trojan* Earth	Il.20.449.413.
The panting *Trojan* rivets to the Ground.	Il.20.466.413.
Whole Hecatombs of *Trojan* Ghosts shall pay.	Il.20.524.416.
Now tir'd with Slaughter, from the *Trojan* Band	Il.21.34.422.
And sold to *Lemnos,* stalks on *Trojan* Ground!	Il.21.67.424.
Thus while he spake, the *Trojan* pale with Fears	Il.21.74.424.
In vain a single *Trojan* sues for Grace;	Il.21.113.426.
So perish *Troy,* and all the *Trojan* Line!	Il.21.141.427.
If *Jove* have giv'n thee every *Trojan* Head,	Il.21.233.430.
In glorious Arms before the *Trojan* Wall.	Il.21.320.434.
That blaze so dreadful in each *Trojan* Eye;	Il.21.371.436.
And in one Ruin sink the *Trojan* Name.	Il.21.441.438.
(*Minerva* cries) who guard the *Trojan* Wall!	Il.21.501.442.
Rash as thou art to prop the *Trojan* Throne,	Il.21.514.443.
What if they pass'd me to the *Trojan* Wall,	Il.21.656.449.
Return in safety to my *Trojan* Friends.	Il.21.662.449.
And hopes this day to sink the *Trojan* Name	Il.21.692.450.
The god-like *Trojan* in a Veil of Clouds;	Il.21.706.451.
Far-stretching in the Shade of *Trojan* Tow'rs.	Il.22.8.453.
Where *Trojan* Dames, (e'er yet alarm'd by *Greece,)*	Il.22.203.464.
Thus three times round the *Trojan* Wall they fly;	Il.22.217.464.
Thus step by step, where'er the *Trojan* wheel'd,	Il.22.249.465.
Rest here: My self will lead the *Trojan* on,	Il.22.287.468.
(Ye Gods avert it) threats the *Trojan* State.	Il.22.583.480.
And twelve sad Victims of the *Trojan* Line	Il.23.30.488.
Tir'd with his Chase around the *Trojan* Wall;	Il.23.75.489.
Thee too it waits; before the *Trojan* Wall	Il.23.101.491.
Sad Sacrifice! twelve *Trojan* Captives fell.	Il.23.215.498.
Twelve *Trojan* Heroes offer'd to thy Shade;	Il.23.223.498.
Hector deserves, of all the *Trojan* Race:	Il.24.88.539.
Jove orders *Iris* to the *Trojan* Tow'rs.	Il.24.178.543.
Alone, for so we will: No *Trojan* near;	Il.24.183.544.
Alone, for so he wills: No *Trojan* near,	Il.24.213.546.
(The Gift of *Mysia* to the *Trojan* King.)	Il.24.344.550.
Since *Paris* brought me to the *Trojan* Shore;	Il.24.965.576.
He spoke; and at his Word, the *Trojan* Train	Il.24.989.577.
Atrides, parting for the *Trojan* war,	Od.3.334.102.
Some Dæmon anxious for the *Trojan* doom,	Od.4.375.137.
Prest in *Atrides'* cause the *Trojan* plain:	Od.5.394.191.
To wait my passage from the *Trojan* land.	Od.9.40.303.
Long have his coffers groan'd with *Trojan* spoils;	Od.10.44.341.
(With brutal force he seiz'd my *Trojan* prey,	Od.13.313.21.
But when the *Trojan* piles in ashes lay,	Od.13.362.24.
Before the Græians touch'd the *Trojan* plain,	Od.14.266.49.
Ulysses vengeful from the *Trojan* shore;	Od.22.42.288.
Oh! better hadst thou sunk in *Trojan* ground,	Od.24.43.350.

TROJAN'S

Then gush'd the tears, as from the Trojan's eyes	5.DunA1.211.88.
Say Muse! when *Jove* the *Trojan's* Glory crown'd,	Il.11.387.51.
Full at the *Trojan's* Head he urg'd his Lance,	Il.15.632.220.
Shall he prolong one *Trojan's* forfeit Breath!	Il.22.235.465.

TROJANS

Advance ye *Trojans,* lend your valiant Hands,	1.TrES.177.456.
A Tide of *Trojans* flows, and fills the Place;	1.TrES.206.457.
The distant *Trojans* never injur'd me.	Il.1.200.96.
Let *Greece* be humbled, and the *Trojans* rise;	Il.1.659.118.
With Shouts the *Trojans* rushing from afar	Il.3.3.186.
And plung'd amid the thickest *Trojans* lies.	Il.3.52.191.
The *Greeks* and *Trojans* seat on either Hand;	Il.3.98.194.
Hear, all ye *Trojans,* all ye *Grecian* Bands!	Il.3.123.195.
Prepare ye *Trojans!* while a third we bring	Il.3.143.197.
Ye *Greeks* and *Trojans,* let the Chiefs engage,	Il.3.380.211.
Ye *Trojans, Dardans,* all our gen'rous Foes!	Il.3.568.219.
And the proud *Trojans* first infringe the Peace.	Il.4.94.225.
The Race of *Trojans* in thy Ruin join,	Il.4.190.230.
The *Trojans* rush tumultuous to the War;	Il.4.253.232.
Not so the *Trojans,* from their Host ascends	Il.4.490.243.
Trojans and *Greeks* now gather round the Slain;	Il.4.538.247.
Struck at his Sight the *Trojans* backward drew,	Il.4.571.249.
Trojans be bold, and Force with Force oppose;	Il.4.587.249.
Hither ye *Trojans,* hither drive your Steeds!	Il.5.134.273.
Rowze all thy *Trojans,* urge thy *Aids* to fight;	Il.5.597.297.
Now gives the *Grecians,* now the *Trojans* Aid.	Il.5.1027.315.
With Rage recruited the bold *Trojans* glow,	Il.6.129.330.
Enough of *Trojans* to this Lance shall yield,	Il.6.282.340.
Astyanax the *Trojans* call'd the Boy,	Il.6.502.351.
To guard the *Trojans,* to defend the Crown,	Il.6.607.357.
My Heart weeps Blood at what the *Trojans* say,	Il.6.672.360.
The Squadrons part; th' expecting *Trojans* stand.	Il.7.62.366.
Ye *Trojans, Dardans,* and Auxiliars hear!	Il.7.419.385.
Ye *Trojans, Dardans,* and Auxiliar Bands!	Il.7.444.386.
Strait to their sev'ral Cares the *Trojans* move,	Il.7.494.388.
With these against yon' *Trojans* will we go,	Il.8.139.404.
Like tim'rous Flocks the *Trojans* in their Wall	Il.8.160.405.
The Shouts of *Trojans* thicken in the Wind;	Il.8.192.406.
And see his *Trojans* to the Shades descend.	Il.8.251.409.
The conqu'ring *Trojans* mourn his Beams decay'd;	Il.8.607.425.
Ye valiant *Trojans,* with Attention hear!	Il.8.621.425.
To claim the Tears of *Trojans* yet unborn.	Il.10.334.18.
Where e'er yon' Fires ascend, the *Trojans* wake:	Il.10.489.25.
On Heaps the *Trojans* rush, with wild affright,	Il.10.616.29.
The *Trojans* see the Youths untimely die,	Il.11.151.42.
But thus his *Trojans* and his Aids he fir'd.	Il.11.366.51.
The *Greeks* all fled, the Trojans pouring on:	Il.11.510.56.
With Bands of furious *Trojans* compass'd round.	Il.11.593.60.
Trojans on *Trojans* yonder load the Plain.	Il.11.645.62.
Trojans on *Trojans* yonder load the Plain.	Il.11.645.62.
On *Ajax* thus a Weight of *Trojans* hung,	Il.11.690.66.
Trojans and *Greeks* with clashing Shields engage,	Il.12.3.80.
Advance ye *Trojans!* lend your valiant Hands,	Il.12.531.101.
A Tyde of *Trojans* flows, and fills the Place;	Il.12.560.102.
Th' impatient *Trojans,* in a gloomy Throng,	Il.13.61.107.
Trojans, be firm; this Arm shall make your way	Il.13.205.115.
Thus, *Trojans,* thus, at length be taught to fear;	Il.13.779.141.
How many *Trojans* yield, disperse, or fall?	Il.13.926.149.
By turns the *Greeks,* by turns the *Trojans* bled.	Il.14.524.188.
Trojans! your great *Ilioneus* behold!	Il.14.587.190.
The *Trojans* hear, they tremble, and they fly:	Il.14.596.191.
There saw the *Trojans* fly, the *Greeks* pursue,	Il.15.8.194.
Full on the Front the pressing *Trojans* bear,	Il.15.346.210.
Mount the thick *Trojans* up the *Grecian* Wall;	Il.15.445.214.
Nor could the *Trojans,* thro' that firm Array,	Il.15.472.215.
And stop the *Trojans,* tho' impell'd by *Jove.*	Il.15.679.222.
Now on the Fleet the Tydes of *Trojans* drove,	Il.15.712.223.
The *Trojans* fly, and conquer'd *Ilion* burn.	Il.15.721.223.
There stand the *Trojans,* and here rolls the Deep.	Il.15.899.232.
No Camps, no Bulwarks now the *Trojans* fear,	Il.16.99.239.
Lo there the *Trojans!* bath your Swords in Gore!	Il.16.249.249.
Invade the *Trojans,* and commence the War.	Il.16.313.254.
While far behind, his *Trojans* fall confus'd,	Il.16.442.260.
The Tyde of *Trojans* urge their desp'rate Course,	Il.16.465.260.
So far the *Trojans* from their Lines retir'd;	Il.16.719.272.
With conqu'ring Shouts the *Trojans* shake the Plain,	Il.16.730.272.
Ye *Trojans, Dardans, Lycians,* and Allies!	Il.17.206.295.
Repuls'd, they yield; the *Trojans* seize the slain:	Il.17.325.300.
On Heaps the *Greeks,* on Heaps the *Trojans* bled,	Il.17.416.303.
Thus they. While with one Voice the *Trojans* said,	Il.17.480.306.
No longer *Hector* with his *Trojans* stood,	Il.17.602.311.
Loud shout the *Trojans,* and renew the Fight.	Il.17.810.320.
Thus on retreating *Greece* the *Trojans* pour,	Il.17.817.320.
The frighted *Trojans* (panting from the War,	Il.18.287.335.
(The Work of *Trojans,* with *Minerva's* Aid)	Il.20.177.401.
Trojans to War! Think *Hector* leads you on;	Il.20.417.412.
Swift thro' the foamy Flood the *Trojans* fly,	Il.21.28.422.
Sure I shall see yon' Heaps of *Trojans* kill'd	Il.21.64.424.
Views, from his Arm, the *Trojans* scatter'd Flight,	Il.21.615.448.
On Heaps the *Trojans* crowd to gain the Gate,	Il.21.631.448.
Yon' Line of slaughter'd *Trojans* lately trod.	Il.21.654.449.
Still grudge his Body to the *Trojans* View?	Il.24.47.537.
Perform, ye *Trojans!* what the Rites require,	Il.24.985.576.

TROJANS (CONTINUED)

Various the *Trojans* counsell'd; part consign'd .... Od.8.554.292.
And *Pallas*, by the *Trojans* judg'd the cause. .... Od.11.670.417.
Fame speaks the *Trojans* bold; they boast the skill .... Od.18.305.181.
That courage, once the *Trojans* daily dread, ... Od.22.248.298.

TROOP

A Troop came next, who Crowns and Armour wore, ... 2.TemF.342.280.
Rolls the black troop, and overshades the street, ... 5.DunB2.360.315.
From Troop to Troop he toils thro' all the Plain. .... Il.5.650.299.
From Troop to Troop he toils thro' all the Plain. .... Il.5.650.299.
Sheath'd in bright Arms let ev'ry Troop engage, ... Il.8.659.427.
So fares a Boar, whom all the Troop surrounds .... Il.11.525.57.
Thus urg'd the Chief; a gen'rous Troop appears, ... Il.11.720.67.
A Troop of Wolves th' unguarded Charge survey, ... Il.16.422.259.
Shou'd he return, that troop so blithe and bold, ... Od.1.211.43.
But say, yon' jovial Troop so gaily drest, ... Od.1.289.47.
While this gay friendly troop the King surround, ... Od.4.21.121.
The troop forth issuing from the dark recess, ... Od.4.717.152.
With deep-mouth'd hounds the hunter-troop invades; .... Od.19.504.221.
A troop of matrons, fancy-form'd, condole. .... Od.19.636.227.
Not to this troop, I fear, that phantom soar'd, ... Od.19.664.228.
Say, could one city yield a troop so fair? .... Od.24.132.354.

TROOPS

Thus God-like *Hector* and his Troops contend .... 1.TrES.1A.449.
The Troops pursue their Leaders with Delight, ... 1.TrES.55.451.
Who mows whole Troops, and makes whole Armies fly. .... 1.TrES.216.457.
Who mows whole Troops, and makes an Army fly .... 1.TrES.216A.457.
To lead my Troops, to combate at their Head, ... 1.TrES.304.461.
And Particolour'd Troops, a shining Train, ... 2.RL3.43.172.
Of broken Troops an easie Conquest find. .... 2.RL3.78.173.
Of *Asia's* Troops, and *Africk's* Sable Sons, ... 2.RL3.82.174.
Where are those Troops of Poor that throng'd before .... 4.JD2A.119.142.
Where are those Troops of poor, that throng'd of yore .... 4.JD2.113.143.
"When are the Troops to have their pay? .... 4.HS6.120.257.
Troops take Heed! .... 6.96i.28.269.
To *Pthia's* Realms no hostile Troops they led; .... Il.1.201.96.
To move the Troops to measure back the Main, ... Il.2.97.131.
His Country's Troops to base, inglorious Flight, ... Il.2.425.147.
His sep'rate Troops let ev'ry Leader call, ... Il.2.432.148.
Strait to the Tents the Troops dispersing bend, ... Il.2.474.149.
Now seize th' Occasion, now the Troops survey, ... Il.2.518.151.
With rushing Troops the Plains are cover'd o'er, ... Il.2.548.153.
These head the Troops that Rocky *Aulis* yields, ... Il.2.590.156.
Their Troops in thirty sable Vessels sweep .... Il.2.618.157.
Him, as their Chief, the chosen Troops attend, ... Il.2.634.157.
Phares and *Brysia's* valiant Troops, and those .... Il.2.703.159.
But few his Troops, and small his Strength in Arms. .... Il.2.820.164.
His Troops in forty Ships *Podarces* led, ... Il.2.860.165.
The Troops *Methonè*, or *Thaumacia* yields, ... Il.2.872.165.
Thy Troops, *Argissa*, *Polypœtes* leads, ... Il.2.896.166.
His Troops, neglected on the sandy Shore, ... Il.2.939.168.
The foreign Troops: This Day demands them all. .... Il.2.975.169.
Th' Auxiliar Troops and *Trojan* Hosts appear. .... Il.2.987.170.
From these the congregated Troops obey .... Il.2.1006.170.
Pyrechmes the *Pœonian* Troops attend, ... Il.2.1028.171.
When Godlike *Mygdon* led their Troops of Horse, ... Il.3.247.204.
But seeks in vain along the Troops of *Troy;* .... Il.3.564.219.
And next the Troops of either *Ajax* views: .... Il.4.311.235.
The middle Space suspected Troops supply, ... Il.4.344.237.
Whole Troops before you lab'ring in the Fray? .... Il.4.399.239.
With fewer Troops we storm'd the *Theban* Wall, ... Il.4.460.242.
These singled from their Troops the Fight maintain, ... Il.5.19.266.
Remote they stand, while Alien Troops engage, ... Il.5.581.296.
Pours on the *Greeks:* The *Trojan* Troops pursue: .... Il.5.723.302.
That mows whole Troops, and makes all *Troy* retire. .... Il.6.120.330.
Yet far before the Troops thou dar'st appear, ... Il.6.155.333.
Who mows whole Troops and makes all *Troy* retire. .... Il.6.347.343.
Our Troops to hearten, and our Toils to share? .... Il.6.415.347.
The thronging Troops obscure the dusky Fields, ... Il.7.69.366.
From all your Troops select the boldest Knight, ... Il.7.87.367.
I led my Troops to *Phea's* trembling Wall, ... Il.7.164.372.
He said. The Troops with elevated Eyes, ... Il.7.239.376.
Whole Troops of Heroes, *Greece* has yet to boast, ... Il.7.279.378.
Compacted Troops stand wedg'd in firm Array, ... Il.8.263.410.
Encourag'd by the Sign, the Troops revive, ... Il.8.303.412.
And fir'd the Troops, and call'd the Gods to aid. .... Il.8.416.417.
The Troops exulting sate in order round, ... Il.8.685.428.
To save the Ships, the Troops, the Chiefs from Fire. .... Il.9.547.460.
Plies all the Troops, and orders all the Field. .... Il.11.82.38.
Whole Ranks are broken, and whole Troops o'erthrown. .... Il.11.344.49.
So God-like *Hector* prompts his Troops to dare, ... Il.11.381.51.
Now Troops on Troops the fainting Chief invade, ... Il.11.578.60.
Now Troops on Troops the fainting Chief invade, ... Il.11.578.60.
The Ranks lie scatter'd, and the Troops o'erthrown) .... Il.11.665.63.
In some wide Field by Troops of Boys pursu'd, ... Il.11.683.65.
There, Horse and Foot, the *Pylian* Troops unite, ... Il.11.860.74.
Mingled the Troops, and drove the Field along. .... Il.12.46.83.
Wedg'd in the Trench, by our own Troops confus'd, ... Il.12.83.84.
Ev'n when they saw *Troy's* sable Troops impend, ... Il.12.159.87.
Thus God-like *Hector* and his Troops contend .... Il.12.345.94.
The Troops pursue their Leaders with Delight, ... Il.12.399.96.
No following Troops his brave Associate grace, ... Il.13.889.147.
His Troops unpractis'd in the Fights of Stand .... Il.13.890A.147.
What Troops, out-number'd scarce the War maintain? .... Il.13.927.149.
(Cheering the Troops, and dealing Deaths around) .... Il.13.962.151.
No more the Troops, our hoisted Sails in view, ... Il.14.110.163.
The Troops assent; their martial Arms they change, ... Il.14.437.184.
So *Greece*, that late in conq'ring Troops pursu'd. .... Il.15.314.209.
Ye Troops of *Lycia, Dardanus,* and *Troy!* .... Il.15.571.218.
Him *Hector* singled, as his Troops he led, ... Il.15.652.221.
The Troops of *Troy* recede with sudden Fear, ... Il.15.690.222.
I haste to bring the Troops—The Hero said; .... Il.16.160.244.
This stern Remembrance to his Troops he gave: .... Il.16.238.248.
Meanwhile the Troops beneath *Patroclus'* Care, ... Il.16.312.254.

TROOPS (CONTINUED)

His Troops, that see their Country's Glory slain, ... Il.16.346.256.
And now the Chief (the foremost Troops repell'd) .... Il.16.476.261.
Who mows whole Troops, and makes an Army fly. .... Il.16.519.263.
To lead my Troops, to combate at their Head, ... Il.16.609.268.
First to the Fight his native Troops he warms, ... Il.16.653.270.
Or draw the Troops within the Walls of *Troy.* .... Il.16.872.277.
Or singly, *Hector* and his Troops attend? .... Il.17.104.291.
Fir'd by his Words, the Troops dismiss their Fears, ... Il.17.274.298.
But bids bold *Thrasymede* those troops sustain; .... Il.17.791.319.
With fiercer Shouts his ling'ring Troops he fires, ... Il.18.197.331.
Forth let him bring them, for the Troops to share; .... Il.18.350.338.
My martial Troops , my Treasures , are thy own: .... Il.19.138.377.
Their Troops but lately durst not meet his Eyes; .... Il.20.39.394.
Thro' the thick Troops th' embolden'd Hero prest: .... Il.20.143.400.
To mow whole Troops, and make whole Armies fly: .... Il.20.406.412.
The god-like *Hector* warm'd the Troops of *Troy.* .... Il.20.416.412.
Where late their Troops triumphant bore the Fight, ... Il.21.5.421.
But when within the Walls our Troops take Breath, ... Il.21.625.448.
While all the flying Troops their Speed employ, ... Il.21.717.451.
Safe in their Walls are now her Troops bestow'd, ... Il.22.21.453.
Sign'd to the Troops, to yield his Foe the Way, ... Il.22.269.466.
The Troops obey'd; and thrice in order led .... Il.23.15.486.
The Hero bids his martial Troops appear .... Il.23.158.495.
Enough, *Atrides!* give the Troops Relief: .... Il.23.195.497.
Auxiliar troops combin'd, to conquer *Troy.* .... Od.19.147.199.

TROPE

A T—d instead of Trope. .... 6.79.76.220.

TROPES

And the puff'd Orator bursts out in tropes. .... 5.DunA2.198.125.
And the puff'd orator bursts out in tropes. .... 5.DunB2.206.306.

TROPHEE

The Trophee, dropping yet with *Dolon's* Gore: .... Il.10.621.29.

TROPHIES

And all the Trophies of his former Loves. .... 2.RL2.40.162.
There huge Colosses rose, with Trophies crown'd, ... 2.TemF.121.263.
High on a Throne with Trophies charg'd, I view'd .... 2.TemF.151.265.
Hang their old Trophies o'er the Garden gates, ... 4.1HE1.8.279.
There other *Trophies* deck the truly Brave, ... 4.EpS2.236.326.
Their annual trophies, and their monthly wars. .... 5.DunA3.280.183.
Their annual trophies, and their monthly wars: .... 5.DunB3.282.334.
Let standard-Authors, thus, like trophies born, ... 5.DunB4.123.353.
"Such are the Trophies *Greece* from *Ilion* brings, ... Il.4.214.231.
Heaps fell on Heaps, sad Trophies of his Art, ... Il.8.335.413.
Now call to Mind your ancient Trophies won, ... Il.11.369.51.
And thence these Trophies and these Arms I gain. .... Il.13.344.122.
And whose blest Trophies, will ye raise to Fame? .... Il.14.604.191.
Ah let not *Greece* his conquer'd Trophies boast, ... Il.16.669.270.
This Instant see his short-liv'd Trophies won, ... Il.16.789.274.
And o'er his Seat the bloody Trophies hung. .... Il.17.611.312.
Or to his Arm our bloody Trophies yield. .... Il.22.312.469.
The tomb with manly arms and trophies grace, ... Od.11.94.385.

TROPHY

The *Greeks* with Smiles the polish'd Trophy view. .... Il.3.464.214.
A Trophy destin'd to the blue-ey'd Maid. .... Il.10.672.31.
To stand a Trophy of his Fame in War. .... Il.17.142.293.
In *Theban* Games the noblest Trophy bore, ... Il.23.786.521.

TROPHY'D

The trophy'd arches, story'd halls invade, ... 3.EOM4.303.156.
The trophy'd Arches, story'd Halls invade, ... 6.130.17.358.

TROPIC

Burn through the Tropic, freeze beneath the Pole! .... 4.1HE1.72.283.

TROS

For ravish'd *Ganymede* on *Tros* bestow'd, ... Il.5.329.282.
Observe the Steeds of *Tros,* renown'd in War, ... Il.8.134.404.
The sacred *Tros,* of whom the *Trojan* Name. .... Il.20.275.405.
The Steeds of *Tros* beneath his Yoke compell'd, ... Il.23.360.504.
With those of *Tros,* bold *Diomed* succeeds: .... Il.23.456.508.

TROTH

Nay troth, th' *Apostles,* (tho' perhaps too rough) .... 4.JD4.76.31.

TROUBLE

Then most our *Trouble* still when most *admir'd,* .... 1.EOC.502.295.
The more his *Trouble* as the more *admir'd;* .... 1.EOC.502A.295.
'Tis most our *Trouble* when 'tis most *admir'd;* .... 1.EOC.502B.295.
Still most our trouble when the most admir'd; .... 1.EOC.502C.295.
The most our trouble still when most admir'd; .... 1.EOC.502D.295.
The Youth might save much Trouble and Expence, ... 4.HAdv.67.81.
Without a Pain, a Trouble, or a Fear; .... 6.86.16.245.
Without a Sigh, a Trouble, or a Tear; .... 6.86.16A.245.
Why did you fear to trouble my repose? .... Od.4.969.163.

TROUBLED

A troubled stream; the troubled stream was clear'd; .... 1.TrPA.154.372.
A troubled stream; the troubled stream was clear'd; .... 1.TrPA.154.372.
As the last image of that troubled heap, ... 3.Ep1.45.18.
In troubled waters, but now sleeps in Port. .... 5.DunB4.202.362.
The troubled Pleasure soon chastis'd by Fear, ... Il.6.620.357.
Such various Passions urg'd the troubled Host. .... Il.9.10.431.
The God, whose Thunder rends the troubled Air, ... Il.17.226.296.
(In sign of Tempests from the troubled Air, ... Il.17.618.312.
Thick beats his Heart, the troubled Motions rise, ... Il.21.648.449.
But now let each becalm his troubled breast, ... Od.4.293.133.
Ill the gay sports with troubled hearts agree: .... Od.8.170.271.
Seals ev'ry eye, and calms the troubled breast. .... Od.12.42.431.
'Twas then soft slumber fled my troubled brain: .... Od.12.431.451.
A secret instinct moves her troubled breast .... Od.17.635.163.

TROUBLES
Partake the Troubles of thy Husband's Breast: Il.24.234.546.

TROUBLESOME
"This may be troublesome, is near the Chair; 4.1HE6.105.243.
Who tell us these troublesome stories, 6.42iv.3.118.

TROUTS
Swift Trouts, diversify'd with Crimson Stains, 1.W-F.145.163.

TROWLING
His trowling Wheels they run: 6.79.126A.222.

TROWZES
Ducke in his Trowzes hath he hent, 6.14i.9.41.

TROY
Nor *Troy* cou'd conquer, nor the *Greeks* wou'd yield, 1.TrES.3.449.
Before the Walls of well-defended *Troy,* 1.TrUl.192A.472.
And strike to Dust th'aspiring Tow'rs of *Troy;* 2.RL*A*1.138.131.
And strike to Dust th' Imperial Tow'rs of *Troy;* 2.RL3.174.182.
The Wars of *Troy* were round the Pillar seen: 2.TemF.188.271.
Troy flam'd in burning Gold, and o'er the Throne 2.TemF.208.272.
Troy flam'd in burnish'd Gold, and o'er the Throne 2.TemF.208A.272.
Cou'd Troy be sav'd by any single hand, 5.DunA1.187.85.
Could Troy be sav'd by any single hand, 5.DunB1.197.283.
What else to *Troy* th' assembled Nations draws, Il.1.209.96.
To *Troy's* proud Monarch, and the Friends of *Troy!* Il.1.340.105.
The lofty Tow'rs of wide-extended *Troy.* Il.2.14.128.
The lofty Tow'rs of wide-extended *Troy.* Il.2.36.129.
Elate in Thought, he sacks untaken *Troy:* Il.2.46.129.
The lofty Tow'rs of wide-extended *Troy.* Il.2.86.130.
And *Troy* prevails by Armies not her own. Il.2.160.136.
And dream no more of Heav'n-defended Troy. Il.2.172.136.
And Fate decreed the Fall of *Troy* in vain; Il.2.190.137.
Shall *Troy,* shall *Priam,* and th' Adult'rous Spouse, Il.2.195.137.
And to th' Immortals trust the Fall of *Troy.* Il.2.218.138.
For *Troy* to ransom at a Price too dear? Il.2.286.141.
No wonder *Troy* so long resists our Pow'rs. Il.2.409.147.
And soon should fall the haughty Tow'rs of *Troy!* Il.2.445.148.
In twelve black ships to *Troy* they steer their Course, Il.2.673.158.
And thence to *Troy* his hardy Warriors led. Il.2.764.162.
Assemble all th' united Bands of *Troy;* Il.2.973.169.
Whom *Troy* sent forth, the beauteous *Paris* came: Il.3.26.189.
Troy yet may wake, and one avenging Blow Il.3.83.193.
And *Troy* possess her fertile Fields in Peace; Il.3.106.194.
Then with his Spear restrain'd the Youth of *Troy,* Il.3.110.195.
Two Heralds now dispatch'd to *Troy,* invite Il.3.161.198.
The hostile Gods conspire the Fate of *Troy.* Il.3.218.202.
To *Troy* he came, to plead the *Grecian* Cause; Il.3.268.205.
For distant *Troy* refus'd to sail the Seas: Il.3.308.208.
And *Troy* possess her fertile Fields in Peace; Il.3.327.208.
And drove to *Troy, Antenor* at his Side. Il.3.389.211.
But *Venus* trembl'd for the Prince of Troy: Il.3.460.214.
But seeks in vain along the Troops of *Troy;* Il.3.564.219.
Their careful Eyes on long-contended *Troy.* Il.4.6.221.
And meditate the future Woes of *Troy.* Il.4.30.222.
That *Troy,* and *Troy's* whole Race thou woud'st confound, Il.4.51.223.
When Heav'n no longer hears the Name of *Troy.* Il.4.60.223.
Remember *Troy,* and give the Vengeance way. Il.4.64.224.
None stands so dear to *Jove* as sacred *Troy.* Il.4.68.224.
To make the Breach the faithless Act of *Troy.* Il.4.98.225.
What Gifts from *Troy,* for *Paris* wou'd'st thou gain, Il.4.127.226.
Troy seiz'd of *Helen,* and our Glory lost, Il.4.210.231.
Pierc'd with a winged Shaft (the Deed of *Troy)* Il.4.232.232.
'Tis not for us, but guilty *Troy* to dread, Il.4.270.234.
From fruitful *Tarne* to the Fields of *Troy.* Il.5.60.269.
Drove Armies back, and made all *Troy* retire. Il.5.125.273.
To punish *Troy* for slighted Sacrifice; Il.5.225.278.
When first for *Troy* I sail'd the sacred Seas, Il.5.249.279.
Or safe to *Troy,* if *Jove* assist the Foe. Il.5.283.280.
The War with *Troy* no more the *Grecians* wage; Il.5.469.290.
To quit her Country for some Youth of *Troy;* Il.5.514.293.
And *Greece* and *Troy* with clashing Shields engag'd. Il.5.550.295.
And stretch the Slaughter to the Gates of *Troy?* Il.5.568.295.
'Tis not with *Troy,* but with the Gods ye fight. Il.5.749.302.
Troy felt his Arm, and yon' proud Ramparts stand Il.5.792.304.
Small Aid to *Troy* thy feeble Force can be, Il.5.798.304.
Troy, in whose Cause I fell, shall mourn my Fall. Il.5.847.306.
Oh Sight accurst! Shall faithless *Troy* prevail, Il.5.876.308.
Troy now they reach'd, and touch'd those Banks Divine Il.5.964.312.
For *Troy* they fly, and leave their Lord behind. Il.6.52.326.
And frighted *Troy* within her Walls retir'd; Il.6.90.328.
That mows whole Troops, and makes all *Troy* retire. Il.6.120.330.
Who mows whole Troops and makes all *Troy* retire. Il.6.347.343.
That Pest of *Troy,* that Ruin of our Race! Il.6.353.343.
Troy yet should flourish, and my Sorrows end. Il.6.355.343.
Thy Hate to *Troy,* is this the Time to show? Il.6.406.346.
On Hate of *Troy,* than conscious Shame and Grief: Il.6.421.347.
The young *Astyanax,* the Hope of *Troy.* Il.6.467.349.
Troy fled, she heard, before the *Grecian* Sword; Il.6.482.350.
The young *Astyanax,* the Hope of *Troy.* Il.6.487.350.
From his great Father, the Defence of *Troy.* Il.6.503.351.
Where yon' wild Fig-Trees join the Wall of *Troy:* Il.6.551.354.
But stay my *Hector* here, and guard his *Troy.* Il.6.559.354.
How would the Sons of *Troy,* in Arms renown'd, Il.6.562.354.
The Day when thou, Imperial *Troy!* must bend, Il.6.572.354.
Thus having spoke, th' illustrious Chief of *Troy* Il.6.594.355.
While pleas'd amidst the gen'ral Shouts of *Troy,* Il.6.614.357.
Too much has *Troy* already felt thy Hate, Il.7.33.364.
Then with his Spear restrain'd the Youth of *Troy,* Il.7.60.365.
Be mine the Conquest of this Chief of *Troy.* Il.7.228.376.
All *Troy* stood trembling at the mighty Man. Il.7.260.377.
And sage *Idæus* on the Part of *Troy,* Il.7.334.380.
Exchange some Gift; that *Greece* and *Troy* may say, Il.7.363.382.
Next let a Truce be ask'd, that *Troy* may burn Il.7.450.386.

TROY (CONTINUED)
The Words of *Troy,* and *Troy's* great Monarch hear. Il.7.461.387.
This *Greece* demands, and *Troy* requests in vain. Il.7.469.387.
And *Troy* already totters to her Fall. Il.7.479.388.
To sacred *Troy,* where all her Princes lay Il.7.490.388.
And sadly slow, to sacred *Troy* return'd. Il.7.511.389.
Troy rowz'd as soon; for on this dreadful Day Il.8.69.398.
Of *Greece* and *Troy,* and pois'd the mighty Weight. Il.8.90.401.
Nor *Troy,* yet bleeding in her Heroes lost; Il.8.187.406.
Await on *Troy,* on *Greece* eternal Shame. Il.8.215.407.
And fierce on *Troy* with doubled Fury drive. Il.8.304.412.
This Fury of the Field, this Dog of *Troy,* Il.8.364.414.
Troy yet found Grace before th' *Olympian* Sire, Il.8.401.416.
Soon was your Battel o'er: Proud *Troy* retir'd Il.8.558.423.
Shall crush the *Greeks,* and end the Woes of *Troy.* Il.8.672.427.
Proud *Troy* they hated, and her guilty Race. Il.8.684.427.
Thus joyful *Troy* maintain'd the Watch of Night, Il.9.1.430.
Nor hope the Fall of heav'n-defended *Troy.* Il.9.38.433.
To combate, conquer, and extirpate *Troy.* Il.9.64.434.
My self will stay, till *Troy* or I expire; Il.9.66.434.
To morrow, *Troy* must flame, or *Greece* must fall. Il.9.108.437.
Troy and her aids for ready Vengeance call; Il.9.305.449.
But what's the Quarrel then of *Greece* to *Troy?* Il.9.445.454.
He kept the Verge of *Troy,* nor dar'd to wait Il.9.466.455.
Or *Troy* once held, in Peace and Pride of Sway, Il.9.526.459.
Nor hope the Fall of Heav'n-defended *Troy.* Il.9.541.460.
Nor hope the Fall of Heav'n-protected *Troy;* Il.9.803.473.
And hostile *Troy* was ever full in Sight. Il.10.222.11.
Else must our Host become the Scorn of *Troy.* Il.10.226.12.
Or *Troy* once more must be the Seat of War? Il.10.248.13.
Nor less bold *Hector,* and the Sons of *Troy,* Il.10.357.18.
A Youth there was among the Tribes of *Troy,* Il.10.371.19.
And intercept his hop'd return to *Troy.* Il.10.414.21.
Anxious for *Troy,* the Guard the Natives keep; Il.10.490.25.
These *Troy* but lately to her Succour won, Il.10.504.26.
Nor tempt too far the hostile Gods of *Troy.* Il.10.597.29.
Had watch'd his *Troy,* and mark'd *Minerva's* Flight; Il.10.603.29.
So *Greece* and *Troy* the Field of War divide, Il.11.93.38.
But call'd by Glory to the Wars of *Troy,* Il.11.291.48.
So *Troy* reliev'd from that wide-wasting Hand Il.11.487.56.
And gladden'd *Troy* with Sight of hostile Blood. Il.11.577.60.
Proud *Troy* may tremble, and desist from War; Il.11.931.77.
Ev'n to the Ships victorious *Troy* pursues, Il.11.958.78.
While sacred *Troy* the warring Hosts engag'd; Il.12.12.81.
All *Troy* must perish, if their Arms prevail, Il.12.85.84.
Restore their Master to the Gates of *Troy!* Il.12.130.86.
Troy and her Sons may find a gen'ral Grave, Il.12.289.92.
And *Troy* lie trembling in her Walls again. Il.12.328.93.
Nor *Troy* could conquer, nor the *Greeks* would yield, Il.12.347.94.
Of guilty *Troy,* of Arms, and dying Men: Il.13.14.104.
On other Works tho' *Troy* with Fury fall, Il.13.77.108.
Pant in the Ships; while *Troy* to Conquest calls, Il.13.119.110.
Troy charg'd the first, and *Hector* first of *Troy.* Il.13.190.114.
Troy charg'd the first, and *Hector* first of *Troy.* Il.13.190.114.
E're yet to *Troy* the Sons of *Greece* were led, Il.13.229.116.
Ally'd the Warrior to the House of *Troy.)* Il.13.234.116.
To *Troy,* when Glory call'd his Arms, he came, Il.13.235.116.
To conquer *Troy,* with ours thy Forces join, Il.13.477.130.
The fairest she, of all the Fair of *Troy.* Il.13.544.132.
To *Troy* they drove him, groaning from the Shore, Il.13.680.137.
But *Troy* for ever reaps a dire Delight Il.13.799.143.
Mixt with *Bœotians,* on the Shores of *Troy.* Il.13.876.147.
And here detain the scatter'd Youth of *Troy:* Il.13.943.150.
Imperial *Troy* from her Foundations nods; Il.13.972.151.
Lo! *Greece* is humbled not by *Troy,* but Heav'n. Il.13.1025.153.
They ceas'd; and thus the Chief of *Troy* reply'd. Il.13.1043.154.
That *Troy* triumphant our high Fleet ascends, Il.14.72.161.
Then if impetuous *Troy* forbear the Fight, Il.14.84.161.
What more could *Troy?* what yet their Fate denies Il.14.108.162.
To hide their ignominous Heads in *Troy.* Il.14.170.165.
And set aside the Cause of *Greece* and *Troy?* Il.14.222.172.
Think'st thou that *Troy* has *Jove's* high Favour won, Il.14.299.177.
To check a while the haughty Hopes of *Troy:* Il.14.412.183.
This half-recover'd Day shall *Troy* obtain? Il.14.423.184.
The bleeding Youth: *Troy* sadden'd at the View. Il.14.558.190.
Not *Troy* alone, but haughty *Greece* shall share Il.14.563.190.
Steeps *Troy* in Blood, and ranges round the Plain; Il.15.48.196.
Steeps *Troy* in Blood, and rages round the Plain; Il.15.48A.196.
Greece chas'd by *Troy* ev'n to *Achilles'* Fleet, Il.15.67.197.
Phœbus, propitious still to thee, and *Troy.* Il.15.291.208.
And *Troy* and *Hector* thunder in the Rear. Il.15.371.211.
Troy ends, at last, his Labours and his Life. Il.15.383.211.
Presumptuous *Troy* mistook th' accepting Sign, Il.15.438.214.
Victorious *Troy:* Then, starting from his Seat, Il.15.457.215.
Ye Troops of *Lycia, Dardanus,* and *Troy!* Il.15.571.218.
How *Hector* calls, and *Troy* obeys his Call! Il.15.599.219.
He (e'er to *Troy* the *Grecians* cross'd the Main) Il.15.646.221.
The Troops of *Troy* recede with sudden Fear, Il.15.690.222.
So fears the Youth; all *Troy* with Shouts pursue, Il.15.708.223.
Troy in proud Hopes already view'd the Main Il.15.850.229.
Proud *Troy* shall tremble, and desert the War: Il.16.59.237.
Troy saw and trembled, as this Helmet blaz'd: Il.16.96.239.
Some God, like *Phœbus,* ever kind to *Troy.* Il.16.119.241.
Troy saw, and thought the dread *Achilles* nigh, Il.16.336.255.
And from the half-burn'd Ship proud *Troy* retires: Il.16.349.256.
But *Troy* repuls'd, and scatter'd o'er the Plains, Il.16.362.257.
Troy fled, unmindful of her former Fame. Il.16.425.259.
Bore down half *Troy,* in his resistless way, Il.16.478.261.
Oh too forgetful of the Friends of *Troy!* Il.16.660.270.
Troy, at the Loss, thro' all her Legions shook. Il.16.672.270.
To guard his Body *Troy* in Numbers flies; Il.16.685.270.
Here *Troy* and *Lycia* charge with loud Alarms, Il.16.691.271.
Now sent to *Troy, Achilles'* Arms to aid, Il.16.703.271.
Which sunk him to the dead: when *Troy,* too near Il.16.715.271.
Not empty Boasts the Sons of *Troy* repell, Il.16.759.273.
Now *Troy* had stoop'd beneath his matchless Pow'r, Il.16.857.276.

TROY (CONTINUED)

Troy shall not stoop ev'n to *Achilles'* Hand. ... Il.16.866.277.
Or draw the Troops within the Walls of *Troy*. ... Il.16.872.277.
Thy Pride once promis'd, of subverting *Troy;* ... Il.16.1004.282.
Affrighted *Troy* the tow'ring Victor flies, ... Il.17.68.290.
The Time allow'd: *Troy* thicken'd on the Shore, ... Il.17.114.292.
His Train to *Troy* the radiant Armour bear, ... Il.17.141.293.
What other Methods may preserve thy *Troy?* ... Il.17.160.293.
Ev'n where he dy'd for *Troy,* you left him there, ... Il.17.169.294.
Hence let him march, and give up *Troy* to Fate. ... Il.17.172.294.
And drag yon' Carcase to the Walls of *Troy.* ... Il.17.178.294.
His Train to *Troy* convey'd the massy Load. ... Il.17.218.296.
And glean the Relicks of exhausted *Troy.* ... Il.17.267.298.
And save *Patroclus* from the Dogs of *Troy.* ... Il.17.301.299.
Whole *Troy* embodied, rush'd with Shouts along. ... Il.17.309.299.
And now had *Troy,* by *Greece* compell'd to yield, ... Il.17.370.302.
To save your *Troy,* tho' Heav'n its Fall ordain? ... Il.17.379.302.
And force th' unwilling God to ruin *Troy.* ... Il.17.387.302.
Glorious in Arms, and dealing Deaths to *Troy.* ... Il.17.443.304.
Now to the Ships to force it, now to *Troy.* ... Il.17.457.305.
First perish all, e'er haughty *Troy* shall boast ... Il.17.478.306.
For yet 'tis giv'n to *Troy,* to ravage o'er ... Il.17.520.308.
His Friend descends. The Chief of *Troy* descry'd, ... Il.17.550.309.
Exulting *Troy* with Clamour fills the Fields: ... Il.17.686.314.
Troy pours along, and this way rolls our Fate. ... Il.17.800.319.
What *Troy* can dare, we have already try'd, ... Il.17.806.320.
To *Troy* I sent him; but the Fates ordain ... Il.18.77.326.
To drag him back to *Troy* the Foe contends; ... Il.18.213.332.
Proud *Troy* shall tremble, and consent to fear; ... Il.18.238.333.
Troy starts astonish'd, and the Shores rebound. ... Il.18.258.334.
Far from *Troy* Walls, and on a naked Coast. ... Il.18.302.336.
For *Troy,* for *Troy,* shall henceforth be the Strife, ... Il.18.311.336.
For *Troy,* for *Troy,* shall henceforth be the Strife, ... Il.18.311.336.
If Heav'n permits them then to enter *Troy.* ... Il.18.318.337.
And proud *Mæonia* wasts the Fruits of *Troy.* ... Il.18.342.338.
To *Troy* I sent him! but his native Shore ... Il.18.513.346.
He marches, combates, almost conquers *Troy:* ... Il.18.524.346.
Troy yet shall dare to camp a second Night? ... Il.19.74.375.
And all at once on haughty *Troy* descend. ... Il.19.242.382.
Now perish *Troy!* He said, and rush'd to Fight. ... Il.19.471.391.
Is *Greece* and *Troy* the Subject in debate? ... Il.20.26.393.
To either Host. *Troy* soon must lye o'erthrown, ... Il.20.37.394.
In aid of *Troy, Latona, Phœbus* came, ... Il.20.51.396.
Pale *Troy* beheld, and seem'd already lost; ... Il.20.60.396.
Mars hov'ring o'er his *Troy,* his Terror shrouds ... Il.20.69.396.
Thence on the Gods of *Troy* we swift descend: ... Il.20.168.400.
And prove his Merits to the Throne of *Troy?* ... Il.20.217.403.
Has *Troy* propos'd some spacious Tract of Land? ... Il.20.223.403.
Sure, tho' he wars for *Troy,* he claims our Aid. ... Il.20.348.408.
The god-like *Hector* warm'd the Troops of *Troy.* ... Il.20.416.412.
So perish *Troy,* and all the *Trojan* Line! ... Il.21.141.427.
To check *Achilles,* and to rescue *Troy?* ... Il.21.154.428.
But not till *Troy* the destin'd Vengeance pay, ... Il.21.242.431.
His sacred Arrows in defence of *Troy,* ... Il.21.252.431.
The Man whose Fury is the Fate of *Troy.* ... Il.21.280.432.
Till *Troy* receive her flying Sons , till all ... Il.21.340.435.
For mightier Gods assert the Cause of *Troy.* ... Il.21.435.438.
Then from the lowest Stone shall *Troy* be mov'd— ... Il.21.504.442.
Troy Walls I rais'd (for such were *Jove's* Commands) ... Il.21.519.443.
And from its deep Foundations heave their *Troy?* ... Il.21.534.444.
And *Troy* inglorious to her Walls retir'd; ... Il.21.640.448.
And strong, and many, are the Sons of *Troy.* ... Il.21.696.450.
And pour on Heaps into the Walls of *Troy.* ... Il.21.718.451.
Pale *Troy* against *Achilles* shuts her Gate; ... Il.21.723.451.
The Guardian still of long-defended *Troy.* ... Il.22.12.453.
What boots thee now, that *Troy* forsook the Plain? ... Il.22.19.453.
Less to all *Troy,* if not depriv'd of thee. ... Il.22.75.455.
Which *Troy* shall, sworn, produce; that injur'd *Greece* ... Il.22.162.459.
From *Ida's* Summits, and the Tow'rs of *Troy:* ... Il.22.226.464.
Enough, O Son of *Peleus! Troy* has view'd ... Il.22.317.469.
Now shakes his Lance, and braves the Dread of *Troy.* ... Il.22.356.470.
Shou'd *Troy,* to bribe me, bring forth all her Store, ... Il.22.439.473.
Is not *Troy* fall'n already? Haste, ye Pow'rs! ... Il.22.477.475.
But what is *Troy,* or Glory what to me? ... Il.22.481.475.
The Boast of Nations! the Defence of *Troy!* ... Il.22.557.479.
Since now no more the Father guards his *Troy.* ... Il.22.653.483.
Troy feels the Blast along her shaking Walls, ... Il.23.268.500.
E'er since that Day implacable to *Troy,* ... Il.24.38.537.
Lye pale and breathless round the Fields of *Troy!* ... Il.24.206.545.
For one last Look to buy him back to *Troy!* ... Il.24.290.548.
Gluttons and Flatt'rers, the Contempt of *Troy!* ... Il.24.328.550.
Or fly'st thou now? What Hopes can *Troy* retain? ... Il.24.471.556.
See him, in *Troy,* the pious Care decline ... Il.24.681.565.
Safe may'st thou sail, and turn thy Wrath from *Troy;* ... Il.24.702.566.
Till then, our Arms suspend the Fall of *Troy.* ... Il.24.839.572.
Ye wretched Daughters, and ye Sons of *Troy!* ... Il.24.877.573.
And *Troy* sends forth one universal Groan. ... Il.24.885.573.
And hurl thee headlong from the Tow'rs of *Troy.* ... Il.24.929.575.
In *Troy* deserted, as abhorr'd at Home! ... Il.24.980.576.
All *Troy* then moves to *Priam's* Court again, ... Il.24.1011.577.
Of sacred *Troy,* and raz'd her heav'n-built wall, ... Od.1.4.28.
Ere *Greece* assembled stem'd the tydes to *Troy;* ... Od.1.272.46.
Which voyaging from *Troy* the Victors bore, ... Od.1.423.53.
Mean time from flaming *Troy* we cut the way, ... Od.3.350.103.
Espous'd before the final doom of *Troy:* ... Od.4.10.121.
When *Troy* was ruin'd, had the chief return'd, ... Od.4.230.130.
Will tell *Ulysses'* bold exploit in *Troy:* ... Od.4.332.135.
In *Troy* to mingle with the hostile train. ... Od.4.338.136.
Loud grief resounded thro' the tow'rs of *Troy,* ... Od.4.355.136.
The partners of his fame and toils at *Troy,* ... Od.4.721.152.
From conqu'ring *Troy* around *Achilles* dead) ... Od.5.398.192.
How o'er the feast they doom the fall of *Troy;* ... Od.8.73.266.
Ere yet he loos'd the rage of war on *Troy.* ... Od.8.78.266.
Alone superior in the field of *Troy,* ... Od.8.251.276.
With latent heroes sack'd imperial *Troy.* ... Od.8.542.291.
All *Troy* up-heav'd the steed: of diff'ring mind, ... Od.8.553.292.

TROY (CONTINUED)

Say why the fate the *Troy* awak'd thy cares, ... Od.8.629.297.
Who taught proud *Troy* and all her sons to bow; ... Od.9.315.319.
Before whose arm *Troy* tumbled to the ground. ... Od.9.592.330.
The man from *Troy,* who wander'd Ocean round; ... Od.10.393.363.
Than if return'd to *Ithaca* from *Troy.* ... Od.10.494.367.
A Queen, to *Troy* she saw our legions pass; ... Od.11.106.386.
Or (since to dust proud *Troy* submits her tow'rs) ... Od.11.196.391.
Since in the dust proud *Troy* submits her tow'rs. ... Od.11.205.391.
Fell before *Troy,* and nobly prest the plain? ... Od.11.463.407.
When *Troy* first bled beneath the *Grecian* arms ... Od.11.551.411.
To *Troy* no Hero came of nobler line, ... Od.11.637.416.
'Twas mine on *Troy* to pour th' imprison'd war: ... Od.11.642.416.
To lead their fleets, and carry death to *Troy.* ... Od.14.275.49.
Beneath *Troy* walls by night we took our way: ... Od.14.531.63.
"These glittering weapons, ere he sail'd to *Troy* ... Od.16.308.120.
Then to the King that levell'd haughty *Troy.* ... Od.18.403.187.
Auxiliar troops combin'd, to conquer *Troy.* ... Od.19.147.199.
Had sail'd for *Troy:* but to the genial feast ... Od.19.226.204.
The fall of *Troy* erroneous and forlorn ... Od.19.296.209.
Estrang'd, since dear *Ulysses* sail'd to *Troy!* ... Od.19.696.229.
As when for *Troy* he left my fond embrace: ... Od.20.107.238.
Of *Priam's* race, and lay'd proud *Troy* in dust? ... Od.22.251.299.
Since my dear Lord left *Ithaca* for *Troy:* ... Od.23.22.320.
O *Troy—may* never tongue pronounce thee more! ... Od.23.24.320.
Fix'd in my soul as when he sail'd to *Troy,* ... Od.23.179.329.

TROY'S

Where *Troy's* Majestic Ruins strow the Ground. ... 1.TrUl.133.470.
And *Troy's* proud Walls lie level with the Ground. ... Il.1.24.86.
To *Troy's* proud Monarch, and the Friends of *Troy!* ... Il.1.340.105.
'Till *Troy's* proud Structures shou'd in Ashes lie. ... Il.2.353.144.
Expect the Time to *Troy's* Destruction giv'n, ... Il.2.364.144.
And *Troy's* proud Matrons render Tear for Tear. ... Il.2.423.147.
Or urg'd by Wrongs, to *Troy's* Destruction came? ... Il.2.579.155.
That *Troy,* and *Troy's* whole Race thou woud'st confound, ... Il.4.51.223.
Which *Troy's* proud Glories in the Dust shall lay, ... Il.4.197.230.
And *Troy's* proud Walls lie smoaking on the Ground. ... Il.4.333.236.
To *Troy's* high Fane, and to his Holy Place; ... Il.5.542.294.
Enrag'd, to *Troy's* retiring Chiefs he cry'd. ... Il.5.564.295.
Troy's sacred Walls, nor need a foreign Hand? ... Il.5.578.296.
In *Troy's* Defence *Apollo's* heav'nly Will: ... Il.5.624.297.
While *Troy's* fam'd <*> Streams that bound the deathful
Plain ... Il.6.5.322.
Well hast thou known proud *Troy's* perfidious Land, ... Il.6.69.327.
Of *Troy's* chief Matrons to *Minerva's* Fane; ... Il.6.110.329.
Surpass'd the Nymphs of *Troy's* illustrious Race) ... Il.6.315.341.
Troy's strong Defence, unconquer'd *Pallas,* aid! ... Il.6.379.345.
And *Troy's* proud Dames whose Garments sweep the Ground, . Il.6.563.354.
So welcome these to *Troy's* desiring Train; ... Il.7.9.363.
To *Troy's* high Gates the God-like Man they bear, ... Il.7.376.382.
To *Troy's* high Gates the God-like Chief they bear, ... Il.7.376A.382.
The Words of *Troy,* and *Troy's* great Monarch hear. ... Il.7.461.387.
Give me to raze *Troy's* long-defended Tow'rs; ... Il.8.348.414.
Ev'n when they saw *Troy's* sable Troops impend, ... Il.12.159.87.
What Man could doubt but Troy's victorious Pow'r ... Il.12.187.88.
Fly we at length from *Troy's* oft-conquer'd Bands, ... Il.13.139.111.
For him, in *Troy's* remotest Lines, he sought, ... Il.13.577.133.
Troy's scatt'ring Orders open to the Show'r. ... Il.13.902.148.
Troy's great Defender stands alone unaw'd, ... Il.14.449.185.
Greece sees, in hope, *Troy's* great Defender slain: ... Il.14.494.188.
But lifts to Glory *Troy's* prevailing Bands, ... Il.15.716.223.
In *Troy's* fam'd Fields, and in *Achilles'* Arms ... Il.16.88.238.
Then loudly calls on *Troy's* vindictive Arms; ... Il.16.654.270.
A Chief, who led to *Troy's* beleaguer'd Wall ... Il.16.675.270.
Sunk with *Troy's* heavy Fates, he sees decline ... Il.16.799.274.
And *Troy's* black Sands must drink our Blood alike: ... Il.18.386.339.
Nor *Troy's* glad Fields been fatten'd with our Gore: ... Il.19.64.374.
Troy's black Battalions wait the Shock of Fight. ... Il.20.4.392.
Troy's Turrets totter on the rocking Plain; ... Il.20.81.397.
On *Troy's* whole Force with boundless Fury flies. ... Il.20.438.413.
And partial Aid to *Troy's* perfidious Race. ... Il.21.483.441.
Thro' *Troy's* wide Streets abandon'd shall I roam, ... Il.24.979.576.
Came the stern *Greeks* by *Troy's* assisting hands: ... Od.8.552.292.
From *Troy's* fam'd fields, sad wand'rers o'er the main, ... Od.9.307.319.
When *Troy's* proud bulwarks smok'd upon the ground, ... Od.11.652.416.
Where *Troy's* majestic ruins strow the ground. ... Od.13.300.20.
As when we wrapt *Troy's* heav'n-built walls in fire. ... Od.13.444.27.

TRUANT

There truant WYNDHAM ev'ry Muse gave o'er, ... 5.DunB4.167.357.

TRUCE

Let rev'rend *Priam* in the Truce engage, ... Il.3.145.197.
To seal the Truce and end the dire Debate. ... Il.3.321.208.
The solemn Truce, a fatal Truce to thee! ... Il.4.187.230.
The solemn Truce, a fatal Truce to thee! ... Il.4.187.230.
Next let a Truce be ask'd, that *Troy* may burn ... Il.7.450.386.
Next, O ye Chiefs! we ask a Truce to burn ... Il.7.470.387.
The Peace rejected, but the Truce obtain'd. ... Il.7.493.388.
No truce the warfare of my heart suspends! ... Od.20.101.237.

TRUCKS

Where vile Mundungus trucks for viler rhymes; ... 5.DunB1.234.287.

TRUDGES

Trudges to Town, and first turns Chambermaid; ... 6.49i.16.138.

TRUE

In *Poets* as true *Genius* is but rare, ... 1.EOC.11.240.
True *Taste* as seldom is the *Critick's* Share; ... 1.EOC.12.240.
Authors are partial to their *Wit,* 'tis true, ... 1.EOC.17.241.
Shows most true Mettle when you *check* his Course. ... 1.EOC.87.249.
And *rise* to *Faults* true Criticks *dare not mend;* ... 1.EOC.153.257.
And if the *Means* be just, the *Conduct* true, ... 1.EOC.257.269.
True Wit is *Nature* to Advantage drest, ... 1.EOC.297.272.

TRUE (CONTINUED)
But true *Expression,* like th' unchanging *Sun,* 1.EOC.315.274.
True Ease in Writing comes from Art, not Chance, 1.EOC.362.281.
But blame the *False,* and value still the *True.* 1.EOC.407.287.
But like a Shadow, proves the *Substance* true; 1.EOC.467.292.
Be thou the *first* true Merit to befriend; 1.EOC.474.292.
'Tis not enough your Counsel still be *true,* 1.EOC.572.305.
Such shameless *Bards* we have; and yet 'tis true, 1.EOC.610.309.
Lotis the nymph (if rural tales be true) 1.TrFD.31.387.
Are just to Heav'n, and to their Promise true! 1.TrUl.87.468.
This Blessing lasts, (if those who try, say true) 2.ChJM.57.17.
'Tis true, Perfection none must hope to find 2.ChJM.190.24.
About this Spring (if ancient Fame say true) 2.ChJM.459.37.
The Feats, true Lovers when they list, can do: 2.ChJM.517.40.
While thou art faithful to thy own true Knight, 2.ChJM.553.42.
Whilst thou art faithful to thy own true Knight, 2.ChJM.553A.42.
And all the faithless Sex, for ever to be true. 2.ChJM.655.46.
Jove ne'er spoke Oracle more true than this, 2.ChJM.809.54.
And think, for once, a Woman tells you true. 2.ChWB.4.57.
And told'em false, but *Jenkin* swore 'twas true. 2.ChWB.151.63.
As all true Gamesters by Experience know. 2.ChWB.220.67.
My fourth dear Spouse was not exceeding true; 2.ChWB.229.68.
As true a Rambler as I was before, 2.ChWB.339.73.
'Twas then *Belinda!* if Report say true, 2.RL1.117.154.
In fact, 'tis true, no Nymph we cou'd persuade, 2.TemF.386.282.
All neither wholly false, nor wholly true. 2.TemF.457.285.
'Tis true, said I, not void of Hopes I came, 2.TemF.501.287.
Before true passion all those views remove, 2.ElAb.79.326.
Most souls, 'tis true, but peep out once an age, 2.Elegy.17.363.
In the nice bee, what sense so subtly true 3.EOM1.219.42.
To these we owe true friendship, love sincere, 3.EOM2.255.86.
True faith, true policy, united ran, 3.EOM3.239.116.
True faith, true policy, united ran, 3.EOM3.239.116.
The less, or greater, set so justly true, 3.EOM3.291.122.
The less, and greater, set so justly true, 3.EOM3.291A.122.
"Whatever IS, is RIGHT."—THIS world, 'tis true, 3.EOM4.145.141.
All fame is foreign, but of true desert, 3.EOM4.253.152.
And more true joy Marcellus exil'd feels, 3.EOM4.257.152.
That true SELF-LOVE and SOCIAL are the same; 3.EOM4.396.166.
True, some are open, and to all men known; 3.Ep1.110.23.
'Tis true, but something in her was forgot 3.Ep2.158A.64.
Nothing so true as what you once let fall, 3.Ep2.1.46.
All how unlike each other, all how true! 3.Ep2.6.48.
For true No-meaning puzzles more than Wit. 3.Ep2.114.59.
To draw the Naked is your true delight: 3.Ep2.188.65.
Conscious they act a true Palladian part, 3.Ep4.37.140.
'Tis true, for ten days hence'twill be *King Lear's.* 4.JD4.219.45.
'Tis true, no Turbots dignify my boards, 4.HS2.141.67.
A man's true merit 'tis not hard to find, 4.Arbu.175.109.
True Genius kindles, and fair Fame inspires, 4.Arbu.194.109.
And a true *Pindar* stood without a head) 4.Arbu.236.112.
These as good works, tis true, we all allow, 4.JD2A.127.144.
These, as good works 'tis true we all allow; 4.JD2.121.145.
'Tis true 'tis chang'd from what it was before, 4.JD2.31B.135.
And each true Briton is to Ben so civil, 4.2HE1.41.197.
For Farce the people true delight affords, 4.2HE1.310A.221.
If true, a woful likeness, and if lyes, 4.2HE1.412.229.
Something in Verse as true as Prose; 4.HS6.26.251.
'Tis true, my Lord, I gave my word, 4.1HE7.1.269.
'Tis true, but Winter comes apace: 4.1HE7.16.269.
What right, what true, what fit, we justly call, 4.1HE1.19.279.
Still true to Virtue, and as warm as true: 4.1HE1.30.281.
Still true to Virtue, and as warm as true: 4.1HE1.30.281.
True, conscious Honour is to feel no sin, 4.1HE1.93.285.
A ☉'s true glory his integrity; 4.1740.92.337.
Which as more pond'rous makes their aim more true, 5.DunA1.149.82.
All who true dunces in her cause appear'd, 5.DunA2.21.98.
True to the bottom, see Concanen creep, 5.DunA2.287.137.
True to the bottom, see *R[oome]* and *Wh[atle]y* creep, 5.DunA2.287B.137.
For this, our Queen unfolds to vision true 5.DunA3.53.155.
Nor glad vile Poets with true Criticks' gore. 5.DunA3.172.168.
Which, as more pond'rous, made its aim more true, 5.DunB1.171.282.
All who true Dunces in her cause appear'd, 5.DunB2.25.297.
True to the bottom, see Concanen creep, 5.DunB2.299.310.
For this, our Queen unfolds to vision true 5.DunB3.61.323.
Nor glad vile Poets with true Critic's gore. 5.DunB3.178.329.
See, see, our own true Phœbus wears the bays! 5.DunB3.323.335.
'Tis true, on Words is still our whole debate, 5.DunB4.219.364.
"Ah, think not, Mistress! more true Dulness lies 5.DunB4.239.366.
Lord of an Otho, if I vouch it true; 5.DunB4.369.379.
True, he had wit, to make their value rise; 5.DunB4.377.380.
To prove a dull *Succession* to be true, 6.7.23.16.
Like *Trojan* true, to draw for *Hellen:* 6.10.84.27.
Which, as more pond'rous, makes its Aim more true, 6.17i(a).3.55.
Man the true Worth of his Creation knows. 6.17iii.19.58.
You, 'tis true, have fine black eyes, 6.18.6.61.
You, 'tis true, have fine blew eyes, 6.18.6A.61.
Just to his Prince, and to his Country true: 6.27.6.81.
Durfeius his true *Latin* Name; 6.30.37.87.
D'urfeius the true *Latin* Name; 6.30.37A.87.
Wit's Queen, (if what the Poets sing be true) 6.37.1.106.
There are, 'tis true, who tell another tale, 6.41.15.113.
The man had courage, was a sage, 'tis true, 6.41.39.114.
That all this true is 6.42i.10.116.
And, like true *Sevil* Snuff, awake the Brain. 6.48iv.8.136.
Just to his Prince, yet to his Country true; 6.57.6.169.
and true men, vous-avez; 6.68.14.197.
I'm told (but 'tis not true I hope) 6.74.3.211.
Ah friend, 'tis true— this truth you lovers know— 6.81.1.225.
Most true it is, I dare to say, 6.94.1.259.
Why, Zounds! and Blood! 'tis true! 6.94.16.259.
Each Man's true Merit 'tis not hard to find; 6.98.25.284.
Till all true *Englishmen* cry'd, hang her! 6.101.4.290.
And brings the true Saturnian age of lead. 6.106iv.12.307.
To night, our home-spun author would be true, 6.107.19.311.
The last true Briton lies beneath this stone. 6.113.12.320.

TRUE (CONTINUED)
Blest Satyrist! who touch'd the Mean so true, 6.118.7.334.
Words ever pleasing, yet sincerely true, 6.125.1Z3.349.
If there's a *Briton,* then, true bred and born, 6.128.19.356.
To Reason's equal dictates ever true, 6.134.7.364.
Not one true *Bounce* will be a Thief; 6.135.50.368.
Then might a Royal Youth, and true, 6.135.77.369.
That so a Noble Youth, and true, 6.135.77A.369.
'Tis true, but something in her was *forgot.* 6.139.2.377.
'Tis true, Great Bard, thou on my shelf shall lye 6.147ix.3.392.
True to those Counsels which I judge the best, Il.12.247.90.
Let not my fatal Prophecy be true, Il.18.319.337.
'Tis true (the Cloud-compelling Pow'r replies) Il.20.29.394.
'Tis true, the great *Æneas* fled too fast. Il.20.235.403.
'Tis true I perish, yet I perish great: Il.22.386.471.
'Tis true, 'tis certain; Man, tho' dead, retains Il.23.122.492.
Too true it is, deserted of my Strength, Il.23.721.519.
Are true, my Son! (the godlike Sire rejoin'd) Il.24.460.555.
Nor true are all thy Words, nor erring wide; Il.24.465.556.
Sentenc'd, 'tis true, by his inhuman Doom, Il.24.950.575.
Oh true descendent of a scepter'd line! Od.1.286.46.
True, *Greece* affords a train of lovely dames, Od.2.233.72.
True, while my friend is griev'd, his griefs I share; Od.2.267.74.
True in his deed, and constant to his word; Od.3.121.91.
Is it then true, as distant rumours run, Od.3.259.98.
True to his charge, the Bard preserv'd her long Od.3.336.103.
Are just to heav'n, and to their promise true! Od.13.254.18.
True to his charge, a loyal swain and kind: Od.13.466.28.
Not his true consort can desire him more; Od.14.197.45.
That, true to honour, never lagg'd behind, Od.14.245.48.
True friendship's laws are by this rule exprest, Od.15.83.73.
'Tis true, the fervor of his gen'rous heart Od.15.236.79.
His eye how piercing, and his scent how true, Od.17.384.150.
And if my questions meet a true reply, Od.17.629.163.
If true, if faithful thou, her grateful mind Od.17.638.163.
True are his words, and he whom truth offends Od.18.460.190.
When time shall prove the storied blessing true: Od.19.355.211.

TRUELY
He who discerns thee must be truely wise, Od.13.356.24.

TRUEST
The *truest Notions* in the *easiest way.* 1.EOC.656.314.
The truest Hearts for *Voiture* heav'd with Sighs; 6.19.17.62.
A weighty axe, with truest temper steel'd, Od.5.300.185.

TRULY
He who discerns thee must be truly wise, 1.TrUl.189.472.
Or rather truly, if your Point be Rest, 4.HS1.17.5.
(A Doctrine sage, but truly none of mine) 4.HS2.3.55.
There other *Trophies* deck the truly Brave, 4.EpS1.236.326.
But which, I cannot tell you truly. 6.10.118.28.
Has truly liv'd the space of seventy years, 6.55.1Z2.167.
Thro' Fortune's Cloud One truly Great can see, 6.84.39.240.
One truly Great thro' Fortune's Cloud can see, 6.84.31Z1.240.
May truly say, here lies an honest Man. 6.112.2.318.
O truly great! in whom the Gods have join'd Il.9.73.435.
Ah! check thy Anger, and be truly brave. Il.9.339.450.
Ah tell me truly, where, oh where are laid Il.24.497.557.

TRUMBAL
Thus *Atticus,* and *Trumbal* thus retir'd. 1.W-F.258.172.

TRUMP
Gain'd but one Trump and one *Plebeian* Card. 2.RL3.54.172.
But strait the direful Trump of Slander sounds, 2.TemF.332.280

TRUMPET
The Trumpet sounded, and the Temple shook, 2.TemF.277.276
The Golden Trumpet of eternal Praise: 2.TemF.307.278
The Queen assents, the Trumpet rends the Skies, 2.TemF.392.282
The Trumpet roars, long flaky Flames expire, 2.TemF.414.283
With Gun, Drum, Trumpet, Blunderbuss & Thunder? 4.HS1.26.7.
Hear her black Trumpet thro' the Land proclaim, 4.EpS1.159.309.
And now had Fame's posterior Trumpet blown, 5.DunB4.71.348
Let the loud Trumpet sound, 6.11.7.30.
'Till the last Trumpet rend the Ground; 6.31ii.6Z11.95.
Till the Trumpet rends the Ground; 6.31ii.6Z11A.95
Heav'n in loud Thunder bids the Trumpet sound; Il.21.452.439.

TRUMPET'S
From the black Trumpet's rusty Concave broke 2.TemF.338.280
Born by the Trumpet's Blast, and scatter'd thro the Sky. 2.TemF.488.287
Soft as the Speaking Trumpet's mellow Noise: 6.96ii.72.273.
As the loud Trumpet's brazen Mouth from far Il.18.259.334.

TRUMPETS
The Brazen Trumpets kindle Rage no more: 1.Mes.60.118.
The Trumpets sleep, while chearful Horns are blown, 1.W-F.373.187.
And the shrill Trumpets mix their Silver Sound; 2.ChJM.319.29.
With horns and trumpets now to madness swell, 5.DunA2.219.12
With horns and trumpets now to madness swell, 5.DunB2.227.30

TRUMPS
Let Spades be Trumps! she said, and Trumps they were. 2.RL3.46.172.
Let Spades be Trumps! she said, and Trumps they were. 2.RL3.46.172.
Led off two captive Trumps, and swept the Board. 2.RL3.50.172.

TRUNC
The huge trunc rose, and heav'd into the sky; Od.23.194.333.

TRUNCHEON
Or thy dread truncheon M[arlborough]'s mighty peer? 4.1740.62.335.
Stern beasts in trains that by his truncheon fell, Od.11.707.420.
Let fall th' offensive truncheon from his hand. Od.14.36.37.

TRUNK

Vouchsafe the Trunk between your Arms to take;	2.ChJM.733.50.
With that, his Back against the Trunk he bent;	2.ChJM.738.50.
This said, his Back against the Trunk he bent;	2.ChJM.738A.50.
Which sever'd from the Trunk (as I from thee)	Il.1.311.103.
O'er the fall'n Trunk his ample Shield display'd,	Il.5.365.284.
Rush'd on a *Tamarisk's* strong Trunk, and broke	Il.6.49.325.
Of the thick Foliage. The large Trunk display'd	Il.21.273.432.
Yon' aged Trunk, a Cubit from the Ground;	Il.23.400.506.

TRUNKS

Cloath spice, line trunks, or flutt'ring in a row,	4.2HE1.418.231.

TRUSS

Stoops from the Clouds to truss the quiv'ring Hare.	Il.22.392.471.

TRUSS'D

A Fawn his Talons truss'd (divine Portent)	Il.8.298.412.
His Talons truss'd; alive, and curling round,	Il.12.235.89.
Truss'd with his sinewy pounce a trembling dove;	Od.20.303.247.

TRUST

Secure they trust th'unfaithful Field, beset,	1.W-F.103.160.
Trust not your self; but your Defects to know,	1.EOC.213.264.
With mean Complacence ne'er betray your Trust,	1.EOC.580.306.
An ardent *Judge,* who Zealous in his Trust,	1.EOC.677.316.
An ardent *Judge,* that Zealous in his Trust,	1.EOC.677A.316.
To you I trust the Fortune of the Field,	1.TrES.85.453.
Bids us be certain our Concerns to trust	2.ChJM.180.23.
And trust me, Sir, the chastest you can chuse	2.ChJM.212.24.
And trust in Heav'n I may have many yet.	2.ChWB.24.58.
We trust th'important Charge, the *Petticoat:*	2.RL2.118.167.
And trust me, Dear! good Humour can prevail,	2.RL5.31.201.
But trust the Muse—she saw it upward rise,	2.RL5.123.210.
To trust in ev'ry thing, or doubt of all.	3.EOM4.26.130.
To whom can Riches give Repute, or Trust,	3.EOM4.185.144.
His own Contentment, or another's Trust?	3.EOM4.186A.144.
Trust their *Affections:* soon Affections end;	3.Ep1.161Z1.29.
And laugh at Peers that put their Trust in *Peter.*	4.HS1.40.9.
Who makes a *Trust,* or *Charity,* a Job,	4.JD4.142.37.
Trust me, 'tis ten times worse when they *repent.*	4.Arbu.108A.103.
Beauty that shocks you, Parts that none will trust,	4.Arbu.332.120.
Thus much I've said, I trust without Offence;	4.JD2A.131.144.
For not in Chariots Peter puts his trust;	4.JD2.74.139.
Thus much I've said, I trust without offence;	4.JD2.125.145.
For not in Chariots Coscus puts his trust;	4.JD2.74A.139.
Deny'd all Posts of Profit or of Trust:	4.2HE2.61.169.
Look thro', and trust the Ruler with his Skies,	4.1HE6.8.237.
I trust that sinking Fund, my Life.	4.1HE7.74.273.
"To laugh at Fools who put their trust in *Peter.*"	4.EpS1.10.297.
"Laugh at those Fools who put their trust in *Peter.*"	4.EpS1.10A.297.
No cause, no Trust, no Duty, and no Friend.	5.DunB4.340.376.
"Then trust on Mon, whose yerde can *talke.*"	6.14i.26.42.
Trust not too much your now resistless Charms,	6.19.59.63.
For trust us, friend Mortimer	6.42iv.16.118.
No, trust the Sex's sacred Rule;	6.64.21.190.
Ambition sigh'd; She found it vain to trust	6.71.19.203.
Thy reliques, *Rowe,* to this fair urn we trust,	6.72.1.208.
Thy reliques, *Rowe,* to this fair shrine we trust,	6.72.1B.208.
Thy reliques, *Rowe,* to this fair tomb we trust,	6.72.1C.208.
To trust to *D[avena]nt's* Eyes.	6.94.24.259.
Why did I trust him with that giddy Youth?	6.96ii.30Z19.271.
"Why did I trust thee with that giddy Youth?	6.96ii.31.272.
Thy Reliques, *Rowe!* to this sad Shrine we trust,	6.152.1.400.
Nor trust too far those Ensigns of thy God.	Il.1.38.87.
For I pronounce (and trust a heav'nly Pow'r)	Il.1.281.100.
Reveal the Cause, and trust a Parent's Care.	Il.1.475.110.
And trust the *Vision* that descends from *Jove.*	Il.2.42.129.
He shakes the feeble Props of human Trust,	Il.2.149.135.
And to th' Immortals trust the Fall of *Troy.*	Il.2.218.138.
For our Return we trust the heav'nly Pow'rs;	Il.2.314.142.
Trust in his Omen, and support the War.	Il.2.387.145.
To *Thoas'* Care now trust the martial Train,	Il.2.783.162.
Beauty and Youth, in vain to these you trust,	Il.3.81.193.
Then is it vain in *Jove* himself to trust?	Il.3.451.213.
Jove is with *Greece,* and let us trust in *Jove.*	Il.4.269.234.
Or trust ye, *Jove* a valiant Foe shall chace,	Il.4.284.234.
The good old Warrior bade me trust to these,	Il.5.248.279.
Trust not too much your unavailing Might;	Il.5.748.302.
Nor shall, I trust, the Matron's holy Train	Il.6.141.331.
And if *Apollo,* in whose Aid I trust,	Il.7.93.367.
The Gods, I trust, shall give to *Hector's* Hand,	Il.8.653.426.
Who shakes the feeble Props of human Trust,	Il.9.33.433.
Trust that to Heav'n—but thou, thy Cares engage	Il.9.332.450.
Deceiv'd for once, I trust not Kings again.	Il.9.455.455.
To him thus *Nestor.* Trust the Pow'rs above,	Il.10.114.7.
And trust the War to less important Hands.	Il.11.246.46.
And trust the War to less important Hands.	Il.11.262.47.
Trust thy own Cowardice to 'scape their Fire.	Il.12.288.92.
To you I trust the Fortune of the Field,	Il.12.439.97.
Nor trust the Dart, or aim th' uncertain Spear,	Il.13.342.122.
And that the Rampart, late our surest Trust,	Il.14.73.161.
Strong as you are, 'tis mortal Force you trust,	Il.16.751.273.
The rest dispersing, trust their Fates to Flight.	Il.16.856.276.
Reveal the Cause, and trust a Parent's Care.	Il.18.98.327.
Who trust the Courser, and the flying Car.	Il.23.354.504.
Not those, who trust in Chariots and in Horse.	Il.23.390.506.
Ilus refus'd t'impart the baneful trust:	Od.1.343.49.
Be mild in pow'r, or faithful to his trust!	Od.2.262.74.
But yet, I trust, the boaster means to stay	Od.2.289.75.
But yet I trust, this once ev'n *Mars* would fly	Od.8.355.282.
Will *Neptune* (*Vulcan* then) the faithless trust?	Od.8.385.284.
We sit, and trust the pilot and the wind.	Od.9.88.306.
Let mutual joys our mutual trust combine,	Od.10.397.363.
Say if my spouse maintains her royal trust,	Od.11.214.392.
In you I trust, and in the heav'nly pow'rs,	Od.11.412.404.

TRUST (CONTINUED)

Nor trust the sex that is so rarely wise;	Od.11.546.410.
Think all are false, nor ev'n the faithful trust.	Od.11.564.411.
Nor trust thy virtue to th' enchanting sound.	Od.12.64.433.
A sudden trust from sudden liking grew;	Od.15.464.93.
He shall, I trust; a Heroe scorns despair)	Od.16.106.108.
And trust the presents to his friendly care.	Od.16.349.123.
Our life to heav'n's immortal pow'rs we trust,	Od.17.680.165.
My father, mother, all, I trust to thee;	Od.18.311.181.
The King and Elders trust their common cause.	Od.21.24.260.
To give you firmer faith, now trust your eye:	Od.21.226.270.
Trust it one moment to my hands to-day:	Od.21.301.274.
And die I trust ye shall—He sternly spoke:	Od.22.81.290.

TRUSTED

And trusted Heav'ns informing Prodigies)	Il.6.226.337.
I trusted in the Gods and you, to see	Il.13.133.111.
To your own Hands are trusted all your Fates:	Il.15.603.220.
And trusted to my coat and shield alone!	Od.14.542.63.

TRUSTEES

Curs'd by thy neighbours, thy Trustees, thy self,	4.HS2.106.61.

TRUSTING

When trusting *Jove* and hospitable Laws,	Il.3.267.205.
Vain Archer! trusting to the distant Dart,	Il.11.493.56.

TRUSTS

And trusts her Infant to a Shepherd's Cares.	1.TrSt.683.439.
The Mouse that always trusts to one poor Hole,	2.ChWB.298.71.
The Wretch that trusts them, and the Rogue that cheats.	3.Ep3.238.112.
It is to *History* he trusts for Praise.	4.HS1.36.7.
'Tis to his *British* heart he trusts for fame.	6.107.24.311.
Trusts in God, that as well as he was, he shall be.	6.144.8.386.
At length she trusts her Pow'r; resolv'd to prove	Il.14.187.168.
Who trusts his Fame and Honours in thy Hand,	Il.16.109.240.
This interval, Heav'n trusts him to our care,	Od.7.259.248.

TRUSTY

And gave th'Impression to the trusty Squire.	2.ChJM.511.40.
A trusty Gossip, one dame *Alison.*	2.ChWB.266.69.
Four *Knaves* in Garbs succinct, a trusty Band,	2.RL3.41.171.
Then, well-belov'd and trusty Letters!	6.30.75.89.
The Steeds he left, their trusty Servants hold;	Il.8.145.404.
Has Fame not told, how, while my trusty Sword	Il.15.282.207.
Secret, dispatch'd her trusty Messenger.	Il.18.204.331.
To watch the foe a trusty spy he sent:	Od.24.566.375.

TRUTH

Truth breaks upon us with *resistless Day;*	1.EOC.212.264.
Something, whose Truth convinc'd at Sight we find,	1.EOC.299.273.
In all you speak, let Truth and Candor shine:	1.EOC.563.305.
Without *Good Breeding, Truth* is disapprov'd;	1.EOC.576.306.
Without *Good Breeding, Truth* is not approv'd,	1.EOC.576A.306.
And veiling Truth in plausible Disguise;	1.TrUl.137.470.
As, thank my Stars, in modest Truth I may,	2.ChJM.128.20.
Reflect what Truth was in my Passion shown,	2.ChJM.549.41.
A thousand Authors have this Truth made out,	2.ChJM.629.45.
'Tis Truth I tell, tho' not in Phrase refin'd;	2.ChJM.742.51.
I (to say truth) was twenty more than he:	2.ChWB.318.72.
Oh blind to Truth! the *Sylphs* contrive it all.	2.RL1.104.153.
A Lye and Truth contending for the way;	2.TemF.490.287.
Inseparable now, the Truth and Lye;	2.TemF.494.287.
One truth is clear, "Whatever IS, is RIGHT."	3.EOM1.294.51.
Sole judge of Truth, in endless Error hurl'd:	3.EOM2.17.56.
Let this great truth be present night and day;	3.EOM3.5.92.
Let that great truth be present night and day;	3.EOM3.5A.92.
Oh blind to truth, and God's whole scheme below,	3.EOM4.93.137.
Justice a Conq'ror's sword, or Truth a gown,	3.EOM4.171.143.
Know then this truth (enough for Man to know)	3.EOM4.309.157.
Or in the Cunning, Truth itself's a lye:	3.Ep1.127A.25.
Alas! in truth the man but chang'd his mind,	3.Ep1.79.21.
And in the Cunning, Truth itself's a lye:	3.Ep1.127.25.
With Truth and Goodness, as with Crown and Ball:	3.Ep2.184.65.
Reserve with Frankness, Art with Truth ally'd,	3.Ep2.277.72.
Hear then the truth: "'Tis Heav'n each Passion sends,	3.Ep3.161.106.
A certain truth, which many buy too dear:	3.Ep4.40.140.
"And get by speaking Truth of Monarchs dead,	4.JD4.106.33.
"So much *alone,* (to speak plain Truth between us)	4.JD4.90A.33.
O my fair Mistress, *Truth!* Shall I quit thee,	4.JD4.200.43.
Or tir'd in search of Truth, or search of Rhyme.	4.HS2.86.61.
This Truth, let *L[iddel], J[effer]ys, O[nslo]w* tell.	4.HAdv.178.89.
The truth once told, (and wherefore shou'd we lie?)	4.Arbu.81.101.
But stoop'd to Truth, and moraliz'd his song:	4.Arbu.341.120.
He stoop'd to Truth, and moraliz'd his song:	4.Arbu.341A.120.
He swears but Truth, to give the Divel his due:	4.JD2A.38.134.
Taught on the Wings of Truth, to fly	4.HOde9.3.159.
To hunt for Truth in *Maudlin's* learned Grove.)	4.2HE2.57.169.
Indue a Peer with Honour, Truth, and Grace,	4.2HE2.221.181.
If there be truth in Law, and *Use* can give	4.2HE2.230.181.
Whose Word is Truth, as sacred and rever'd,	4.2HE1.27.197.
And sets the Passions on the side of Truth;	4.2HE1.218.213.
[Plain Truth, dear MURRAY, needs no flow'rs of speech,	4.1HE6.3.237.
BARNARD in spirit, sense, and truth abounds.	4.1HE1.85.285.
Adieu Distinction, Satire, Warmth, and Truth!	4.EpS1.64.302.
While Truth, Worth, Wisdom, daily they decry—	4.EpS1.169.309.
While Truth, Worth, Wisdom, daily we decry—	4.EpS1.169A.309.
When Truth or Virtue an Affront endures,	4.EpS2.199.324.
All, all but Truth, drops dead-born from the Press,	4.EpS2.226.325.
Truth guards the Poet, sanctifies the line,	4.EpS2.246.327.
When Truth stands trembling on the edge of Law:	4.EpS2.249.327.
Where in nice balance, truth with gold she weighs,	5.DunA1.51.66.
Then first (if Poets aught of truth declare)	5.DunA2.73.107.
Fam'd for good-nature, B[urnet] and for truth;	5.DunA3.175.168.
See sculking Truth in her old cavern lye,	5.DunA3.347.193.
Where, in nice balance, truth with gold she weighs,	5.DunB1.53.274.

TRUTH (CONTINUED)

Then first (if Poets aught of truth declare) 5.DunB2.77.299.
See skulking *Truth* to her old Cavern fled, 5.DunB4.641.407.
YE shades, where sacred truth is sought; 6.51i.1.151.
Moral *Truth,* and mystic *Song!* 6.51i.12.151.
A scorn of wrangling, yet a zeal for truth; 6.57.8.169.
In truth by what I can discern, 6.61.29.182.
"Statesman, yet friend to Truth! of soul sincere, 6.71.67.204.
"Statesman, yet friend to Truth! in soul sincere, 6.71.67A.204.
Ah friend, 'tis true— this truth you lovers know— 6.81.1.225.
None from a page can ever learn the truth. 6.96ii.30Z20.271.
"Who from a *Page* can ever learn the Truth? 6.96ii.32.272.
And even a *Yahoo* learn'd the Love of Truth. 6.96iii.10.274.
Statesman, yet Friend to Truth! of Soul sincere, 6.97.1.281.
Statesman, yet Friend to Truth! in Soul sincere, 6.97.1A.281.
Of modest wisdom, and pacifick truth: 6.109.2.313.
Of modest Reason, and pacifick truth: 6.109.2A.313.
When you attack my Morals, Sense, or Truth, 6.129.6.357.
Yet Master *Pope,* whom Truth and Sense 6.135.87.369.
"That dares tell neither Truth nor Lies, 6.140.30.379.
Endu'd with Wisdom, sacred Fear, and Truth. Il.6.204.336.
Thy free Remonstrance proves thy Worth and Truth: Il.6.419.347.
And blame ev'n Kings with Praise, because with Truth. Il.9.80.436.
But say, be faithful, and the Truth recite! Il.10.477.24.
The Truth or Falshood of the News I tell. Il.10.515.26.
Think not to live, tho' all the Truth be shown: Il.10.517.26.
Yet wherefore doubtful? Let this Truth suffice; Il.11.517.57.
If Truth inspires thy Tongue, proclaim our Will Il.15.57.196.
Saturnia ask'd an Oath, to vouch the Truth, Il.19.109.376.
Arm'd or with Truth or Falshood, Right or Wrong, Il.20.296.406.
But shall not we, ourselves, the Truth maintain? Il.23.657.515.
On Female truth assenting faith relies; Od.1.276.46.
Nor uncompell'd the dang'rous truth betray, Od.2.420.81.
Urge him with truth to frame his fair replies; Od.3.25.87.
'Tis sacred truth I ask, and ask of thee. Od.3.124.91.
Attend (tho' partly thou hast guest) the truth. Od.3.317.102.
Urge him with truth to frame his free replies, Od.3.419.107.
Uncertain of the truth, yet uncontroul'd Od.4.187.129.
But truth severe shall dictate to my tongue: Od.4.470.142.
Hear then the truth. By mighty *Jove's* command Od.5.123.178.
By justice, truth, and probity of mind; Od.7.278.249.
This is the truth: And oh ye pow'rs on high! Od.7.382.255.
They, seal'd with truth return the sure reply, Od.11.182.390.
But in thy breast th' important truth conceal, Od.11.303.397.
Truth I revere: For Wisdom never lies. Od.11.572.411.
And veiling truth in plausible disguise, Od.13.304.21.
Thus veil the truth in plausible disguise. Od.16.307.120.
The very truth I undisguis'd declare: Od.17.18.133.
With truth I answer; thou the truth attend. Od.17.159.139.
With truth I answer; thou the truth attend. Od.17.159.139.
Fair truth alone (the patient man reply'd) Od.17.642.163.
True are his words, and he whom truth offends Od.18.460.190.
Not with *Telemachus,* but truth contends; Od.18.461.190.
With fair similitude of truth beguiles Od.19.235.204.
Truth forms my tale; to pleasing truth attend. Od.19.306.209.
Truth forms my tale; to pleasing truth attend. Od.19.306.209.
And bade the Gods this added truth attest, Od.19.331.210.
This heav'n-discover'd truth to thee consign'd, Od.19.569.224.
Deep in my soul the truth shall lodge secur'd, Od.19.577.224.
Where images of truth for passage wait, Od.19.662.228.
Attest, oh *Jove,* the truth I now relate! Od.20.286.247.
This sacred truth attest each genial pow'r, Od.20.287.247.
He knows them all; in all such truth appears, Od.22.537.315.
Truth, by their high decree, thy voice forsakes, Od.23.17.319.
Time shall the truth to sure remembrance bring: Od.23.115.325.
Words seal'd with sacred truth, and truth obey: Od.23.190.332.
Words seal'd with sacred truth, and truth obey: Od.23.190.332.
But tell me, stranger, be the truth confest, Od.24.334.365.

TRUTH'S

O sacred Weapon! left for Truth's defence, 4.EpS2.212.325.

TRUTHS

Blunt Truths more Mischief than *nice Falshoods* do; 1.EOC.573.306.
Leave dang'rous *Truths* to unsuccessful *Satyrs,* 1.EOC.592.307.
Some secret Truths from Learned Pride conceal'd, 2.RL1.37.148.
And truths divine came mended from that tongue. 2.ElAb.66.324.
Truths would you teach, or save a sinking land? 3.EOM4.265.153.
And Truths, invidious to the Great, reveal. Il.1.102.92.
Observe, and in the truths I speak confide: Od.4.518.145.
Unerring truths, oh man, my lips relate; Od.11.170.390.

TRY

First in these Fields I try the Sylvan Strains, 1.PSp.1.59.
Here shall I try the sweet *Alexis'* Strain, 1.PWi.11.89.
So pleas'd at first, the towring *Alps* we try, 1.EOC.225.265.
With equal Rage their airy Quarrel try, 1.TrSt.490.430.
He views his Food, wou'd taste, yet dares not try; 1.TrSt.853A.445.
The Task be mine the Hero's Strength to try, 1.TrES.215.457.
The Task be mine this Hero's Strength to try, 1.TrES.215A.457.
That taught by great Examples, All may try 1.TrES.312.461.
And try the Pleasures of a lawful Bed. 2.ChJM.14.15.
This Blessing lasts, (if those who try, say true) 2.ChJM.57.17.
Wou'd try that Christian Comfort, call'd a Wife: 2.ChJM.80.18.
Pleas'd her best Servant wou'd his Courage try, 2.ChJM.331.30.
Try when you list; and you shall find, my Lord, 2.ChJM.708.49.
Horses (thou say'st) and Asses, Men may try, 2.ChWB.100.61.
Nor fear'd the Chief th'unequal Fight to try, 2.RL5.77.206.
See how the force of others' pray'rs I try, 2.ElAb.149.331.
Try what the open, what the covert yield; 3.EOM1.10.13.
No Courts he saw, no Suits would ever try, 4.Arbu.396.126.
Or gravely try to read the lines 4.HS6.91.255.
So would I draw (but oh, 'tis vain to try 6.75.3.211.
But hold! says *Molly,* first let's try, 6.94.49.260.
'Tis ours, the Chance of fighting Fields to try, Il.1.301.101.
But first with Caution, try what yet they dare, Il.2.95.131.

TRY (CONTINUED)

And try the Faith of *Calchas* and of Heav'n. Il.2.365.144.
'Tis Man's bold Task the gen'rous Strife to try, Il.7.117.369.
Join all, and try th' Omnipotence of *Jove:* Il.8.24.396.
To try yon' Camp, and watch the *Trojan* Pow'rs? Il.10.44.4.
Now, brave *Tydides!* now thy Courage try, Il.10.554.27.
Ah! try the utmost that a Friend can say, Il.11.922.76.
And try the Pass impervious to the Horse. Il.12.66.83.
To save their Fleet, the last Efforts they try, Il.12.173.87.
And try the Prowess of the Seed of *Jove.* Il.13.563.133.
Jove to deceive, what Methods shall she try, Il.14.185.168.
Death is the worst; a Fate which all must try; Il.15.582.218.
The Task be mine this Hero's Strength to try, Il.16.518.263.
That taught by great Examples, all may try Il.16.617.268.
'Tis time to try if *Ilion's* State can stand Il.17.161.293.
Deserted of the God, yet let us try Il.17.715.315.
Whatever be our Fate, yet let us try Il.18.321.337.
Now call the Hosts, and try, if in our Sight, Il.19.73.375.
Great as he is, our Arm he scarce will try, Il.20.399.411.
Lo! he returns! Try then, my flying spear! Il.21.70.424.
Try, if the Grave can hold the Wanderer; Il.21.71.424.
Now lift thy Arm, and try that Hero's Son! Il.21.178.429.
And bravely try if all the Pow'rs were Foes; Il.21.304.433.
Come then, the glorious Conflict let us try, Il.22.309.468.
But now some God within me bids me try Il.22.319.469.
But know, whatever Fate I am to try, Il.22.363.470.
But first, try thou my Arm; and may this Dart Il.22.367.471.
Who bids me try *Achilles'* Mind to move, Il.24.236.546.
The watry way, ill-fated if thou try, Od.2.412.80.
Prepar'd I stand: he was but born to try Od.3.116.91.
Try all those dangers, all those deeps, again. Od.5.178.180.
And yet, ah yet, what fates are we to try? Od.5.600.201.
Be chosen youths prepar'd, expert to try Od.8.33.263.
To try th' illustrious labours of the field: Od.8.144.270.
Ah why th' ill-suiting pastime must I try? Od.8.168.271.
Rise ye *Phæacians,* try your force, he cry'd; Od.8.230.275.
Give me a man that we our might may try! Od.8.246.275.
Go forth, the manners of yon men to try; Od.9.202.314.
And try what social rites a savage lends: Od.9.270.318.
Propos'd, who first the vent'rous deed should try? Od.9.390.322.
But when to try the fortune of the day Od.11.627.414.
Doubt you my oath? yet more my faith to try, Od.14.433.56.
To try his host *Ulysses* thus began. Od.15.325.85.
With such a foe th' unequal fight to try, Od.16.276.118.
And try the bounty of each gracious lord. Od.17.421.152.
Uproots the bearded corn? rise, try the fight, Od.18.36.168.
Yet fearful of disgrace, to try the day Od.18.62.169.
I too may try, and if this arm can wing Od.21.117.264.
By farther toils decreed the brave to try, Od.22.259.299.
Alone, and unattended, let me try Od.24.248.361.

TRY'D

Be not the *first* by whom the *New* are try'd, 1.EOC.335.276.
Thy force the barb'rous Polyphemus try'd, 1.TrPA.15.366.
But vainly boast the Joys they never try'd, 2.ChJM.35.16.
Where, as she try'd his Pulse, he softly drew 2.ChJM.414.35.
I thought your Patience had been better try'd: 2.ChJM.759.51.
More Wives than One by *Solomon* were try'd, 2.ChWB.21.57.
Ward try'd on Puppies, and the Poor, his Drop; 4.2HE1.182.211.
Then * * try'd, but hardly snatch'd from sight, 5.DunA2.283.136
H[ill] try'd the next, but hardly snatch'd from sight, 5.DunA2.283A.1
Try'd all *hors-d'œuvres,* all *liquers* defin'd, 5.DunB4.317.374
A Soul supreme, in each hard Instance try'd, 6.84.23.239.
Heav'n, as its purest Gold, by Tortures try'd; 6.115.9.323.
And, on that Stage of War, the Cause be try'd: Il.3.100.194.
Lampus and *Clytius,* long in Council try'd; Il.3.194.200.
No Strength or Skill, but just in Time, be try'd: Il.4.349.237.
And the sad Father try'd his Arts in vain; Il.5.193.276.
Thy Dart has err'd, and now my Spear be try'd: Il.5.348.283.
As late she try'd with Passion to inflame Il.5.511.292.
He try'd the fourth: When breaking from the Cloud, Il.5.531.294.
And with th' *Arcadian* Spears my Prowess try'd, Il.7.165.372.
That done, once more the Fate of War be try'd, Il.7.452.387.
That done, once more the Fate of War be try'd, Il.7.472.387.
Thus, always thus, thy early Worth be try'd. Il.8.340.413.
What Strength I have, be now in Battel try'd, Il.8.357.414.
He try'd it once, and scarce was sav'd by Fate. Il.9.468.455.
I try'd what Youth could do (at her Desire) Il.9.580.462.
Wise as thou art, be now thy Wisdom try'd: Il.10.163.9.
Like Deeds of Arms thro' all the Forts were try'd, Il.12.201.88.
Brave Deeds of Arms thro' all the Ranks were try'd, Il.15.480.216.
He try'd the fourth; when, bursting from the Cloud, Il.16.861.277.
What *Troy* can dare, we have already try'd, Il.17.806.320.
Have try'd it, and have stood. The Hero said. Il.17.807.320.
Long try'd, long lov'd; much lov'd, but honour'd more! Il.22.302.468.
Thus I with art to move their pity try'd, Od.10.81.343.
O friends! Oh often try'd in adverse storms! Od.12.248.444.
Thy well-try'd wisdom, and thy martial fame, Od.16.263.117.
I try'd, elusive of the bridal hour: Od.19.161.200.
But if, in tract of long experience try'd, Od.19.399.213.
The twanging string, and try'd the stubborn yew: Od.24.198.358.

TRYAL

Haste to the tryal—Lo! I lead the way. Od.21.116.264.
Accept the tryal, and the prize contest. Od.21.144.265.
But since 'till then, this tryal you delay, Od.21.300.274.

TRYUMPHS

See TRIUMPHS.
What wonder tryumphs never turn'd his brain 6.130.7.358.

TUB

Henley's gilt Tub, or Fleckno's Irish Throne, 5.DunA2.2.96.
Henley's gilt tub, or Fleckno's Irish throne, 5.DunB2.2.296.

UBE

He lifts the Tube, and levels with his Eye; ....1.W-F.129.162.
See, in the Tube he pants, and sprawling lies, ...6.96v.7.280.

UFF

But mere tuff-taffety what now remained; ....4.JD4.42.29.

UFF-TAFFETY

But mere tuff-taffety what now remained; ....4.JD4.42.29.

UFTED

That crown'd with tufted Trees and springing Corn, ...1.W-F.27.150.
The rising forests, and the tufted trees. ....Od.5.513.197.
And spiry tops, the tufted trees above, ...Od.10.175.349.

UG

But while he strove to tug th' inserted Dart, ...Il.4.532.246.

UGG

They tugg, they sweat, but neither gain, nor yield, ...1.TrES.159.455.
They tugg, they sweat; but neither gain, nor yield, ...Il.12.513.100.

'UGG'D

And tugg'd their Oars, and measur'd back the Main. ....1.TrUl.52.467.
Th' Ætolian Warrior tugg'd his weighty Spear: ....Il.4.615.250.
And tugg'd the Weapon from the gushing Wound; ....Il.5.143.274.
Forth from the slain he tugg'd the reeking Dart. ....Il.6.82.327.
Strain'd with full Force, and tugg'd from Side to Side, ...Il.17.451.304.
The Foe thrice tugg'd, and shook the rooted Wood; ....Il.21.191.429.

TUGGING

Lo Rufus, tugging at the deadly Dart, ...1.W-F.83.158.
So tugging round the Corps both Armies stood; ....Il.17.454.304.

'UGGS

From the rent Skin the Warrior tuggs again ....Il.5.1052.316.

'UGS

Tugs with full Force, and ev'ry Nerve applies; ....1.TrES.130.454.
Tugs with full force, and ev'ry Nerve applies; ....Il.12.484.99.

'ULIPS

Ladies, like variegated Tulips, show, ...3.Ep2.41.53.
And vary'd Tulips show so dazling gay, ...6.14iv.7.47.

'ULLY

With equal Rays immortal Tully shone, ...2.TemF.238.274.
He'll shine a Tully and a Wilmot too. ....3.Ep1.187.31.
"But Tully has it, Nunquam minus solus:" ....4.JD4.91.33.
Shall be no more than TULLY, or than HYDE! ....4.1HE6.53.241.
Some Athens perishes, some Tully bleeds. ....6.51i.32.152.
Some Athens perishes, or some Tully bleeds. ....6.51i.32A.152.
With thee repose, where Tully once was laid, ...6.52.29.157.

'ULLY'S

The same (my Lord) if Tully's or your own. ....3.EOM4.240.150.

'UMBL'D

Or tumbl'd from the Toadstool's slippery round ....6.96ii.30Z9.271.

'UMBLE

On Heaps they tumble with successless haste; ......Il.11.229.45.
Tho' these proud Bulwarks tumble at our Feet, ...Il.12.262.90.
The clotted Eye-balls tumble on the Shore. ....Il.13.776.141.
And Ilion tumble from her tow'ry Height. ....Il.21.361.435.
And grappling close, thy tumble side by side. ......Il.23.851.523.

TUMBLED

Or rumpled Petticoats, or tumbled Beds, ...2.RL4.72.190.
"Or tumbled from the Toadstool's slipp'ry Round, ...6.96ii.43.272.
With rising Wrath, and tumbled Gods on Gods; ....Il.14.290.176.
The dropping Head first tumbled to the Plain. .....Il.14.546.189.
Full twenty Knights he tumbled from the Car, ...Il.16.976.281.
Then Dryops tumbled to th' ensanguin'd Plain, ...Il.20.526.416.
And, turn'd too short, he tumbled on the Strand, ..Il.23.549.511.
Before whose arm Troy tumbled to the ground. ....Od.9.592.330.

TUMBLER

Never by tumbler thro' the hoops was shown ....5.DunB4.257.369.

TUMBLERS

Two active Tumblers in the Center bound; ....Il.18.698.357.

TUMBLES

Supine he tumbles on the crimson'd Sands, ...Il.4.603.250.
Back from the Car he tumbles to the Ground, ...Il.5.63.269.
Headlong he tumbles: His slack Nerves unbound ...Il.7.21.363.
Subdu'd by Steel, a tall Ash tumbles down, ...Il.13.242.116.
From the high Poop he tumbles on the Sand, ...Il.15.506.216.
Back from the Car he tumbles to the Ground, ...Il.16.412.259.
Pierc'd thro' the dauntless Heart, then tumbles slain; ...Il.16.911.279.
With Nerves relax'd he tumbles to the Ground: ....Il.17.342.300.
Prone from the Seat he tumbles to the Plain; ......Il.17.699.314.
The bleeding Savage tumbles to the Ground: ....Il.19.278.383.
Bent as he stands, he tumbles to the Plain; ....Il.21.194.429.
Thro' all his bowels: down he tumbles prone, ...Od.22.328.302.

TUMBLING

Could she behold us tumbling thro' a hoop. ....4.2HE1.48.199.
Their mighty minions then come tumbling down, ...6.22.22.72.
Wide-rolling, foaming high, and tumbling to the shore. ...Il.13.1005.152.
Then tumbling rolls enormous on the Ground: ....Il.17.591.311.
Came tumbling, heaps on heaps, th' unnumber'd flock: ...Od.9.281.318.
Betray'd me tumbling from a tow'ry height, ...Od.11.78.385.
Where rouls yon smoke, yon tumbling ocean raves; ...Od.12.261.445.
The yawning dungeon, and the tumbling flood; ......Od.12.293.446.

TUMBLING (CONTINUED)

The pilot by the tumbling ruin slain, ...Od.12.483.455.
Thro' tumbling billows, and a war of wind. ....Od.12.502.456.
The tumbling goblet the wide floor o'erflows, ...Od.22.21.287.

TUMOURS

On the round Bunch the bloody Tumours rise; ....Il.2.328.143.
Swell to each Gripe, and bloody Tumours rise. ...Il.23.833.522.

TUMULT

With noisie Care and various Tumult sound. ......1.TrSt.606.435.
The Shore is heap'd with Death, and Tumult rends the Sky. ...1.TrES.208.457.
What means this tumult in a Vestal's veins? ......2.ElAb.4.319.
At length the Tumult sinks, the Noises cease, ...Il.2.253.139.
The Tumult thickens, and the Skies resound. ......Il.2.981.170.
The Tumult silence, and the Fight suspend. ....Il.3.120.195.
The Tumult late begun, they stood intent ....Il.4.386.239.
This swells the Tumult and the Rage of Fight; ....Il.5.728.302.
Scar'd with the Din and Tumult of the Fight, ...Il.6.47.325.
They breathe, and hush the Tumult of the War. ...Il.7.64.366.
The Tumult thickens, and the Skies resound. ......Il.8.74.399.
Pour'd to the Tumult on his whirling Car. ....Il.8.112.403.
The gath'ring Tumult spreads o'er all the Plain; ..Il.10.615.29.
Amidst the Tumult of the routed Train, ...Il.11.161.42.
The Shore is heap'd with Death, and Tumult rends the Sky. ...Il.12.562.102.
To the loud Tumult, and the barb'rous Cry, ...Il.13.63.107.
The Tumult thickens, and the Clamour grows. ......Il.13.226.116.
Attends the Tumult, and expects the War; ....Il.13.597.134.
(Wrapt in the Cloud and Tumult of the Field) ......Il.13.846.146.
Dire Disarray! the Tumult of the Fight, ...Il.14.19.157.
Safe let us stand; and from the Tumult far, ...Il.14.151.165.
Where the War rag'd, and where the Tumult grew. ...Il.16.339.256.
Stopp'd in the Tumult Cleobulus lies, ...Il.16.394.258.
And plung'd amidst the Tumult of the Fight. ......Il.16.886.277.
Then from amidst the Tumult and Alarms, ...Il.16.944.280.
Confusion, Tumult, Horror, o'er the Throng ....Il.17.823.320.
Twelve in the Tumult wedg'd, untimely rush'd .....Il.18.271.335.
There Tumult, there Contention stood confest; .....Il.18.619.352.
Then Tumult rose; fierce Rage and pale Affright ...Il.20.64.396.
'Twas Tumult all, and Violence of Flight; ....Il.21.721.451.
The Tumult wak'd him: From his Eyes he shook ....Il.23.292.501.
'Till in loud tumult all the Greeks arose: ....Od.3.180.94.
The sudden tumult stirr'd him where he lay, ...Od.10.665.375.
And guard thee thro' the tumult of the floods. ....Od.12.159.439.
And horse and foot in mingled tumult rise. ....Od.14.295.50.
And horse and foot in mingled tumult rise. ....Od.17.516.157.
To fill with tumult the dark courts below? ....Od.21.406.279.
Out-lives the tumult of conflicting waves, ...Od.23.254.335.
From all the scene of tumult far away! ....Od.23.392.343.
Their sighs were many, and the tumult loud. ....Od.24.477.371.

TUMULTOUS

Tumultous waves embroil'd the bellowing flood, ...Od.12.242.443.

TUMULTS

Again? new Tumults in my Breast? ....4.HOde1.1.151.
In busie Tumults, and in publick Cares, ...6.17ii.4.56.
Now Shouts and Tumults wake the tardy Sun, ...Il.11.67.37.

TUMULTUOUS

And in tumultuous Raptures dy'd away. ....1.TrSP.62.396.
Tumultuous Clamour mounts, and thickens in the Skies. ...1.TrES.96.453.
If in the Breast tumultuous Joys arise, ...6.11.24.30.
That dash'd on broken Rocks tumultuous roar, ...Il.2.472.149.
The Trojans rush tumultuous to the War; ....Il.4.253.232.
Slow he gave way, the rest tumultuous fled; ....Il.4.583.249.
The brass-hoof'd Steeds tumultuous plunge and bound, ...Il.11.197.44.
And Greece tumultuous from her Tow'rs descend, ..Il.12.160.87.
Tumultuous Clamour mounts, and thickens in the Skies. ...Il.12.450.98.
Th' afflicted Deeps, tumultuous, mix and roar; .....Il.13.1003.152.
Now Steeds, and Men, and Cars, tumultuous pass. ...Il.15.411.213.
In Heaps on Heaps the Foe tumultuous flies, ...Il.16.351.256.
Tumultuous Clamour fills the Fields and Skies; .....Il.16.449.260.
Not with less Noise, with less tumultuous Rage, ...Il.16.929.279.
Swift as the Word, the Winds tumultuous flew; .....Il.23.263.500.
Tumultuous love each beating bosom warms; ....Od.1.466.54.
The boiling bosom of tumultuous Rage; ....Od.4.304.134.
A whirling gust tumultuous from the shore, ...Od.4.687.151.
She spoke, and sudden with tumultuous sounds .....Od.8.15.262.
Youth, and white age, tumultuous pour along; ......Od.8.50.264.
How the Greeks rush'd tumultuous to the main: ....Od.8.548.292.
And his great heart heaves with tumultuous woe; ...Od.8.588.294.
The rough rock roars; tumultuous boil the waves; ...Od.12.283.446.
Arriv'd, with wild tumultuous noise they sate ....Od.16.424.127.
And rushing forth tumultuous reel away. ....Od.18.473.191.
Uprose the throngs tumultuous round the hall; ......Od.22.28.287.

TUN'D

In the same Shades the Cupids tun'd his Lyre, ...1.W-F.295.176.
And tun'd my Heart to Elegies of Woe. ....1.TrSP.8.393.
Not thus Amphion tun'd the warbling Lyre, ...2.ChJM.322.29.
Here happy Horace tun'd th' Ausonian Lyre ....2.TemF.222.273.
'Till all tun'd equal, send a gen'ral hum. ....5.DunA2.354.143.
'Till all tun'd equal, send a gen'ral hum. ....5.DunB2.386.316.
The Musick of a well-tun'd State, ...6.11.35Z5.31.
Apollo tun'd the Lyre; the Muses round ....Il.1.774.124.

TUNBRIDGE

Each Cygnet sweet of Bath and Tunbridge race, ...5.DunB3.155.327.

TUNE

'Till in your Native Shades You tune the Lyre: .....1.PSp.12.61.
But nigh yon' Mountain let me tune my Lays, ...1.PSu.37.75.
But nigh that Mountain let me tune my Lays, ...1.PSu.37A.75.
The Birds shall cease to tune their Ev'ning Song, ...1.PAu.40.83.
Leave such to tune their own dull Rhimes, and know ...1.EOC.358.280.

TUNE (CONTINUED)

For Fame they raise the Voice, and tune the String. ....2.TemF.273.276.
Hum half a tune, tell stories to the squire; ....6.45.20.125.
Look sow'r, and hum a tune—as you may now. ....6.45.50.126.
To Lordings proud I tune my Lay, ...6.79.1.217.
To Lordings proud I tune my Song, ...6.79.1A.217.
With silver sounds, and sweetly tune out time. ....6.82xii.2.237.
Tune soft the Voice, and answer to the Strain. ....Il.18.664.355.
Stood proud to Hymn, and tune his youthful Lyre. ....Il.24.83.538.
Touch the soft lyre, and tune the vocal lay; ....Od.12.195.441.
And thus the sweet deluders tune the song. ....Od.12.221.442.

TUNEFUL

That Flute is mine which *Colin's* tuneful Breath ....1.PSu.39.75.
When tuneful *Hylas* with melodious Moan ....1.PAu.15.81.
While silent Birds forget their tuneful Lays, ...1.PWi.7.89.
Her *Voice* is all these tuneful Fools admire, ...1.EOC.340.277.
Now pour the Wine; and in your tuneful Lays, ...1.TrSt.827.444.
Ye Bards! renown'd among the tuneful Throng ....2.ChJM.335.30.
While tuneful Sprights a merry Consort made, ...2.ChJM.463.37.
Beneath, in Order rang'd, the tuneful Nine ....2.TemF.270.276.
Rise! Muses, rise! add all your tuneful Breath, ...2.TemF.370.281.
Deaf the prais'd ear, and mute the tuneful tongue. ....2.Elegy.76.368.
That urg'd by thee, i turn'd the tuneful art ....3.EOM4.391.166.
Let *Carolina* smooth the tuneful Lay, ...4.HS1.30.7.
And rarely Av'rice taints the tuneful mind. ....4.2HE1.192.211.
Whose tuneful whistling makes the waters pass: ....5.DunB3.156.327.
Fair charmer cease, nor add your tuneful breath ....6.3.1A.7.
Go tuneful bird, forbear to soar, ...6.6i.1.13.
When the full Organ joins the tuneful Quire, ...6.11.126.34.
'Till Death untimely stop'd his tuneful Tongue. ....6.84.2.238.
When Death untimely stop'd his tuneful Tongue. ....6.84.2A.238.
A Hen she had, whose tuneful Clocks ....6.93.5.256.
Superior once of all the tuneful Race, ...Il.2.722.160.
Thus gently checks the minstrel's tuneful hand. ....Od.1.432.53.
Taught by a Master of the tuneful kind: ....Od.3.333.102.
The herald flies the tuneful lyre to bring. ....Od.8.294.278.
Dumb be thy voice, and mute the tuneful string: ....Od.8.586.294.

TUNES

Which *Venus* tunes, and all her Loves inspire. ....1.TrSP.36.395.
Which *Cupid* tunes, and *Venus* does inspire. ....1.TrSP.36A.395.
Joy tunes his voice, joy elevates his wings: ....3.EOM3.32.95.

TUNIC

This does a tunic and white vest convey, ...Od.13.84.5.
Be then my prize a tunic and a vest; ....Od.14.437.56.

TUNICK

A vest and tunick o'er me next she threw, ...Od.10.429.365.
The Goddess with a radiant tunick drest ....Od.10.647.375.

TUNICKS

Twelve cloaks, twelve vests, twelve tunicks stiff with gold, ...Od.24.321.365.

TUNICS

Tunics, and stoles, and robes imperial bears. ....Od.6.88.209.

TUNING

Tuning his voice, and balancing his hands. ....5.DunA3.196.174.
Tuning his voice, and balancing his hands. ....5.DunB3.200.330.

TURBOTS

Yet for *small Turbots* such esteem profess? ....4.HS2.23.55.
'Tis true, no Turbots dignify my boards, ...4.HS2.141.67.

TURBULENCE

So, (fam'd like thee for turbulence and horns,) ....5.DunA2.173.122.
So (fam'd like thee for turbulence and horns) ....5.DunB2.181.304.

TURBULENT

Loquacious, loud, and turbulent of Tongue: ....Il.2.256.140.
And, Why so turbulent of soul? he cries; ....Od.19.87.196.

TURD

See T.

TURENNE

See god-like TURENNE prostrate on the dust! ....3.EOM4.100.137.
It anger'd TURENNE, once upon a day. ....4.EpS2.150.322.

TURF

The Turf with rural Dainties shall be Crown'd, ...1.PSp.99.70.
The Pit fill'd up, with Turf we cover'd o'er, ...2.ChWB.251.69.
And the green turf lie lightly on thy breast: ....2.Elegy.64.367.
Or under this Turf, or e'en what they will; ....6.144.2.386.
Under this Turf, or just what you will; ....6.144.2A.386.
And the Turf trembles, and the Skies resound. ....Il.12.60.83.
And sudden Hyacinths the Turf bestrow, ...Il.14.399.183.
A ready Banquet on the Turf is laid, ...Il.18.647.354.
And common turf, lie naked on the plain, ...Od.1.209.42.
And the dear turf with tears of joy bedews. ....Od.4.698.152.

TURGID

When fed with noxious Herbs his turgid Veins ....Il.22.132.458.

TURK

"Better than lust for Boys, with *Pope* and *Turk,* ....4.HAdv.43.79.
Bear, like the *Turk,* no brother near the throne, ...4.Arbu.198.110.
Verse prays for Peace, or sings down Pope and Turk. ....4.2HE1.236.215.
Bear, like the Turk, no Brother near the Throne; ....6.49iii.12.143.
Bear, like the Turk, no Brother on the Throne; ....6.49iii.12A.143.
Bear, like the Turk, no Brother to the Throne; ....6.49iii.12B.143.
Who think the Turk and Pope a sport ....6.61.3.180.
Who think both Turk and Pope a sport ....6.61.3A.180.
Bear, like the *Turk,* no Brother near the Throne; ....6.98.48.284.

TURKEYS

An hundred Souls of Turkeys in a pye; 5.DunB4.594.4

TURKS

But our Great Turks in wit must reign alone ....6.82ix(a).1.234.

TURN

While yon slow Oxen turn the furrow'd Plain. ....1.PSp.30.63.
And all things flourish where you turn your Eyes. ....1.PSu.76.78.
And then turn Criticks in their own Defence. ....1.EOC.29.242.
Want as much more, to turn it to its use; ....1.EOC.81.248.
Yet let not each gay *Turn* thy Rapture move, ...1.EOC.390.284
What wonder *Modes* in *Wit* shou'd take their Turn? 1.EOC.447.289
Of honest Parents, and may serve my Turn. 2.ChJM.261.27
Weep in her turn, and waste in equal Flame. 2.ChJM.366.32
Paul, knowing One cou'd never serve our Turn, ...2.ChWB.28.58.
That he, and only he, shou'd serve my Turn. 2.ChWB.295.71
Curl'd or uncurl'd, since Locks will turn to grey, ...2.RL5.26.201.
That, in its turn, impels the next above; 2.TemF.445.28
What scenes appear where-e'er I turn my view! 2.ElAb.263.341
And turn their heads to imitate the Sun. ....3.EOM2.28.58.
Or from a judge turn pleader, to persuade 3.EOM2.155.7
Its only thinking thing this turn of mind. ....3.EOM3.78.99.
Each Virtue in each Passion takes its turn; 3.EOM3.136.1
A plain rough Hero turn a crafty Knave? ....3.Ep1.78A.21.
The plain rough Hero turn a crafty Knave? ....3.Ep1.78.21.
Manners with Fortunes, Humours turn with Climes, ...3.Ep1.166.29.
Turn then from Wits; and look on Simo's Mate, ...3.Ep2.101.58.
Her ev'ry turn with Violence pursu'd, ...3.Ep2.131.61.
And turn th' unwilling steeds another way: ....3.Ep3.194.109.
Things change their titles, as our manners turn: ....3.Ep3.379.123.
Turn Arcs of triumph to a Garden-gate; ....3.Ep4.30.140.
First turn plain rash, then vanish quite away. ....4.JD4.45.29.
That touch my Bell, I cannot turn away. ....4.HS2.140.67.
Or, when a tight, neat Girl, will serve the Turn, ...4.HAdv.151.87.
"He'll write a *Journal,* or he'll turn *Divine.*" ....4.Arbu.54.100.
But turn a Wit, and scribble verses too? ....4.JD2.54.137.
Turn, turn to willing Hearts your wanton fires. ....4.HOde1.8.151.
Turn, turn to willing Hearts your wanton fires. ....4.HOde1.8.151.
Turn, turn to willing Hearts your pleasing fires. 4.HOde1.8A.15
Turn, turn to willing Hearts your pleasing fires. 4.HOde1.8A.15
Stop, or turn nonsense at one glance of Thee? 4.HOde1.40.15
Stop, or turn nonsense at one glance from Thee? 4.HOde1.40A.1
Or Virtue, or Religion turn to sport, ...4.2HE1.211.21
Then turn about, and laugh at your own Jest. 4.1HE6.109.24
Turn round to square, and square again to round; 4.1HE1.170.29
Nor *Boileau* turn the Feather to a Star. ....4.EpS2.231.326.
Turn, turn they eyes from wicked men in place, ...4.1740.3.332.
Turn, turn they eyes from wicked men in place, ...4.1740.3.332.
And turn this whole illusion on the town. 5.DunA2.124.1
"Now turn to diff'rent sports (the Goddess cries) 5.DunA2.213.1
In vain! they gaze, turn giddy, rave, and die. 5.DunA3.354.1
See Cibber enters! haste, and turn the Key. ....5.DunB1.300A.
On him, and crowds turn Coxcombs as they gaze. ....5.DunB2.8.296.
And turn this whole illusion on the town: 5.DunB2.132.30
"Now turn to diff'rent sports (the Goddess cries) 5.DunB2.221.3
And turn the Council to a Grammar School! 5.DunB4.180.35
Turn what they will to Verse, their toil is vain, ...5.DunB4.213.36
The vulgar herd turn off to roll with Hogs, ...5.DunB4.525.39
Beeves, at his touch, at once to jelly turn, ...5.DunB4.551.39
In vain! they gaze, turn giddy, rave, and die. 5.DunB4.648.40
And turn a bird of paradise. ....6.6i.4.13.
But burnt so long, may soon turn Tinder, ...6.10.55.26.
I wish you do not turn *Socinian;* ....6.10.80.27.
But if to Solitude we turn our Eyes, ...6.17iii.8.58.
The whistling darts shall turn their points away, ...6.21.15.69.
The monarch dies—one moment's turn destroys ....6.22.10.71.
To turn the Name into good *Latin:* ....6.30.37B.87.
And turn strange Hieroglyphicks there; ....6.30.61.88.
To turn quite backward *D'Urfy's* Name? ....6.30.67.88.
Ev'n *Button's* Wits to Worms shall turn, ...6.53.39.162.
At ev'ry Turn fell to 't; ....6.79.18.218.
"And turn, as now thou dost on me, ...6.79.95.221.
Shall I ne'er see thee turn my watches key 6.96ii.30Z43.272
"No more behold thee turn my Watches Key, ...6.96ii.65.273.
Your Nose you stop, your Eyes you turn away. ....6.96iv.8.276.
Sullen you turn from both, and call for *Oats.* ....6.96iv.54.277.
Quick on its Axle turn.— ....6.100ii.2.288.
Her ev'ry Turn with Violence pursu'd, ...6.154.17.403.
Then to the rest he fill'd; and, in his Turn, ...Il.1.768.124.
With Eyes averted *Hector* hasts to turn ....Il.3.402.211.
The Charge once made, no Warrior turn the Rein, ...Il.4.350.237.
Might Darts be bid to turn their Points away, ...Il.4.632.251.
Practis'd alike to turn, to stop, to chace, ...Il.5.280.280.
They turn, they stand: The *Greeks* their Fury dare, ...Il.5.609.297.
None turn their Backs to mean ignoble Flight, ...Il.5.862.307.
From warring Gods thou bad'st me turn my Spear, ...Il.5.1014.315.
Turn back the Routed, and forbid the Flight; ....Il.6.100.328.
And turn the Tyde of Conflict on the Foe: ....Il.6.130.330.
Turn, charge, and answer ev'ry Call of War, ...Il.7.290.378.
Oh turn and save from *Hector's* direful Rage ....Il.8.121.403.
Practis'd alike to turn, to stop, to chace, ...Il.8.135.404.
For such is Fate, nor can'st thou turn its Course ....Il.8.595.424.
Th' *Ætolians,* long disdain'd, now took their turn, ...Il.9.707.469.
Watch ev'ry Side, and turn to ev'ry Sound. ....Il.10.218.11.
And from the Herd still turn the flying Prey: ....Il.10.430.23.
Oh, turn to Arms; 'tis *Ajax* claims your Aid. ....Il.11.715.67.
But should they turn, and here oppress our Train, ...Il.12.81.84.
Here,.proud *Polydamas,* here turn thy Eyes! ....Il.14.549.189.
Then, nor till then, the Scale of War shall turn, ...Il.15.720.223.
Turn then, ah turn thee to the Field of Fame, ...Il.16.881.277.
Turn then, ah turn thee to the Field of Fame, ...Il.16.881.277.
Turn, and behold the brave *Euphorbus* slain! ....Il.17.84.291.
Still would we turn, still battle on the Plains, ...Il.17.111.292.
With great *Atrides.* Hither turn (he said) ....Il.17.576.311.
Turn, where Distress demands immediate Aid; ....Il.17.577.311.

TURN (CONTINUED)

Thy Eyes have witness'd what a fatal Turn! .... Il.17.773.318.
And turn their Eye-balls from the flashing Ray. .... Il.18.268.335.
And turn their crooked Yokes on ev'ry side. .... Il.18.630.354.
And from the broad Effulgence turn their Eyes. .... Il.19.18.372.
Turn from each other in the Walks of War— .... Il.20.496.415.
Turn then, Impetuous! from our injur'd Flood; .... Il.21.237.430.
Corses and Arms to one bright Ruin turn, ... Il.21.392.436.
The Trees in flaming rows to Ashes turn, ... Il.21.408.437.
Or gasping, turn their Bellies to the Sky. .... Il.21.415.437.
Ev'n now perhaps, e'er yet I turn the Wall, ... Il.21.665.449.
Yet all their Sorrows turn not *Hector's* Heart: .... Il.22.111.457.
The panting Coursers swiftly turn the Goal, ... Il.22.215.464.
Swift round the Goal to turn the flying Wheel. .... Il.23.378.505.
'Tis now *Atrides'* turn to yield to thee. .... Il.23.686.517.
Yet now perhaps, some Turn of human Fate .... Il.24.604.562.
But since the God his Hand has pleas'd to turn, ... Il.24.688.565.
Safe may'st thou sail, and turn thy Wrath from *Troy;* .... Il.24.702.566.
Turn here your steps, and here your eyes employ, ... Il.24.876.573.
And turn th' event, confounding human pride: .... Od.3.162.93.
And the strong tongs to turn the metal round. .... Od.3.551.114.
And is it now my turn, ye mighty pow'rs! .... Od.5.163.179.
(Some close design, or turn of womankind) .... Od.5.224.182.
Cast it far off, and turn thy eyes away. .... Od.5.445.194.
Some turn the mill, or sift the golden grain, ... Od.7.133.241.
Turn and return, and scarce imprint the sand. .... Od.8.414.286.
Untaught to plant, to turn the glebe and sow, ... Od.9.121.310.
Or to what quarter now we turn our eyes, ... Od.10.217.350.
Full o'er the pit, and hell-ward turn their face: .... Od.10.629.374.
Turn to my arms, to my embraces turn! .... Od.11.254.394.
Turn to my arms, to my embraces turn! .... Od.11.254.394.
Turn then, oh peaceful turn, thy wrath controul, ... Od.11.689.418.
Turn then, oh peaceful turn, thy wrath controul, ... Od.11.689.418.
I turn, and view them quivering in the skies; .... Od.12.297.446.
Turn hoar the auburn honours of thy head, ... Od.13.458.28.
From the loath'd object ev'ry sight shall turn, ... Od.13.463.28.
Now turn thy thought, and joys within our pow'r. .... Od.14.193.45.
Me, *Mars* inspir'd to turn the foe to flight, ... Od.14.253.48.
Those Gods, who turn (to various ends design'd) .... Od.14.264.49.
Nor turn the passion into groundless joy .... Od.14.399.55.
To turn the tasteful viand o'er the flame; .... Od.15.340.86.
They turn, review, and cheapen every toy. .... Od.15.498.94.
And the hop'd nuptials turn to joy or woe. .... Od.15.564.97.
And turn my gen'rous vintage down their throat. .... Od.17.621.162.
Proceeds this boldness from a turn of soul, ... Od.18.379.186.
The walls where-e'er my wond'ring sight I turn, ... Od.19.46.195.
Divide discourse, in turn thy birth relate: .... Od.19.185.200.
The wards respondent to the key turn round; .... Od.21.49.261.
'Tis now (brave friends) our turn, at once to throw .... Od.22.288.300.
O vers'd in every turn of human art, ... Od.23.217.333.
This way, and that, we turn, we fly, we fall; .... Od.24.208.358.

TURN'D

The God appear'd; he turn'd his azure Eyes .... 1.W-F.351.184.
Turn'd *Criticks* next, and prov'd plain *Fools* at last; .... 1.EOC.37.243.
Against the Poets *their own Arms* they turn'd, ... 1.EOC.106.251.
And never shock'd, and never turn'd aside, ... 1.EOC.629.310.
When the wide Earth to Heaps of Ashes turn'd, ... 1.TrSt.310.423.
Strait to the Fort great *Ajax* turn'd his Care, ... 1.TrES.81.453.
With Fates prevailing, turn'd the Scale of Fight. .... 1.TrES.171Z2.455.
Or Dotage turn'd his Brain, is hard to find; .... 2.ChJM.12.15.
He spoke with Scorn, and turn'd another way— .... 2.ChJM.220.25.
He spoke; and turn'd, with Scorn, another way— .... 2.ChJM.220A.25.
He turn'd the Key, and made the Gate secure. .... 2.ChJM.542.41.
I took him such a Box as turn'd him blue, ... 2.ChWB.423.77.
And Maids turn'd Bottels, call aloud for Corks. .... 2.RL4.54.188.
With rapid Motion turn'd the Mansion round; .... 2.TemF.422.283.
Now turn'd to heav'n, I weep my past offence, ... 2.ElAb.187.335.
And turn'd on Man a fiercer savage, Man. .... 3.EOM3.168.110.
That urg'd by thee, i turn'd the tuneful art .... 3.EOM4.391.166.
Already half turn'd Traytor by surprize. .... 4.JD4.169.39.
That turn'd ten thousand Verses, now stands still. .... 4.2HE2.79.171.
The prudent Gen'ral turn'd it to a jest, ... 4.EpS2.154.322.
See graceless Venus to a Virgin turn'd, ... 5.DunA3.103.159.
See graceless Venus to a Virgin turn'd, ... 5.DunB3.111.325.
His never-blushing head he turn'd aside, ... 5.DunB3.231.331.
And last turn'd *Air,* the Echo of a Sound! .... 5.DunB4.322.374.
Turn'd to the Sun, she casts a thousand dyes, ... 5.DunB4.539.395.
Would greet the Man who turn'd him to the Wall, ... 6.14ii.43.44.
Liquids grew rough, and *Mutes* turn'd vocal: .... 6.30.8.86.
If you but turn'd your Cheek, a Cuff, ... 6.79.15.218.
He turn'd up through the Gore; .... 6.79.130.222.
They dealt in *Sackcloth,* and turn'd *Cynder-Wenches:* .... 6.95.2.264.
Turn'd aside .... 6.96i.33.269.
Sullen you turn'd from both, and call'd for *Oats.* .... 6.96iv.54A.277.
What wonder tryumphs never turn'd his brain .... 6.130.7.358.
Nor long surviv'd; to Marble turn'd he stands .... Il.2.384.145.
Where, as he view'd her Charms, she turn'd away .... Il.3.531.216.
She turn'd the Shaft, which hissing from above, ... Il.4.166.228.
And, turn'd to *Hector,* these bold Words address'd. .... Il.5.574.296.
These seen, the *Dardan* backward turn'd his Course, ... Il.5.701.301.
The faithful *Mydon* as he turn'd from Fight .... Il.5.709.301.
Broke the thick Ranks, and turn'd the doubtful Day. .... Il.6.8.323.
He said, and turn'd his Brother's vengeful Mind, ... Il.7.139.370.
Thrice turn'd the Chief, and thrice imperial *Jove* .... Il.8.206.407.
(From *Hector Phœbus* turn'd the flying Wound) .... Il.8.377.415.
Thus oft' the *Grecians* turn'd, but still they flew; .... Il.8.411.417.
She spoke, and backward turn'd her Steeds of Light, ... Il.8.534.422.
On Earth he turn'd his all-consid'ring Eyes, ... Il.11.111.39.
Trembling gave way, and turn'd his Back to Flight, ... Il.11.559.58.
So turn'd stern *Ajax,* by whole Hosts repell'd, ... Il.11.680.65.
Menætius, turn'd the Fragments on the Fire. .... Il.11.909.76.
These, turn'd by *Phœbus* from their wonted ways, ... Il.12.23.82.
Strait to the Fort great *Ajax* turn'd his Care, ... Il.12.435.97.
With Fates prevailing, turn'd the Scale of Fight. .... Il.12.528.101.
Then turn'd to *Thracia* from the Field of Fight .... Il.13.5.103.

TURN'D (CONTINUED)

Short as he turn'd, I saw the Pow'r appear: .... Il.13.102.109.
As tow'rd the Chief he turn'd his daring Head, ... Il.13.685.137.
Antilochus, as *Thoon* turn'd him round, ... Il.13.690.137.
As *Areïlycus* had turn'd him round, ... Il.16.366.257.
And turn'd him short, and herded in the Croud. .... Il.16.982.281.
Now enter'd in the *Spartan* Ranks, he turn'd .... Il.17.121.292.
With *Jove* averse, had turn'd the Scale of Fate: .... Il.17.373.302.
For as the brave *Bœotian* turn'd his Head .... Il.17.677.314.
Turn'd by the Hand of *Jove.* Then thus begun, ... Il.17.707.315.
Soon as he bade them blow, the Bellows turn'd .... Il.18.539.348.
He spoke, and from the Warriors turn'd his Face: .... Il.19.329.386.
Hector he sought; in search of *Hector* turn'd .... Il.20.105.398.
Nor, till he reach'd *Lyrnessus,* turn'd his Head. .... Il.20.231.403.
His Back scarce turn'd, the *Pelian* Jav'lin gor'd; .... Il.20.567.418.
Oft' as he turn'd the Torrent to oppose, ... Il.21.303.433.
And turn'd up Bucklers glitter'd as they roll'd. .... Il.21.351.435.
The Goddess spoke, and turn'd her Eyes away .... Il.21.484.441.
And, turn'd too short, he tumbled on the Strand, ... Il.23.549.511.
Pleas'd with the well-turn'd Flattery of a Friend, ... Il.23.636.515.
Now three times turn'd in prospect of the Goal, ... Il.23.899.525.
For this, thy well-aim'd Arrow, turn'd aside, ... Il.23.1024.529.
The Old Man's Cheek he gently turn'd away. .... Il.24.637.563.
(For *Jove* had turn'd the Nation all to Stone:) .... Il.24.770.569.
The Old Man's Fears, and turn'd within the Tent; .... Il.24.841.572.
Observant of her word, he turn'd aside .... Od.5.590.200.
His limbs how turn'd! how broad his shoulders spread! .... Od.8.148.270.
Each scheme I turn'd, and sharpen'd ev'ry thought; .... Od.9.502.326.
I turn'd my eye, and as I turn'd survey'd .... Od.11.733.422.
I turn'd my eye, and as I turn'd survey'd .... Od.11.733.422.
With look serene I turn'd, and thus began. .... Od.12.247.444.
(The *Scherian* states) he turn'd, and thus addrest. .... Od.13.46.3.
We turn'd to flight; the gath'ring vengeance spread .... Od.14.299.50.
And turn'd the deadly weapons from my breast. .... Od.14.312.50.
At length resolv'd, he turn'd his ready hand, ... Od.15.230.79.
Turn'd mean deserters in the needful hour? .... Od.16.102.107.
Turn'd mean deserters in the needful hour. .... Od.16.122.108.
Turn'd his proud step, and left them on their way. .... Od.17.305.146.
Stole unperceiv'd; he turn'd his head, and dry'd .... Od.17.366.149.
We turn'd to flight; the gath'ring vengeance spread .... Od.17.520.157.
By just degrees like well-turn'd columns rise: .... Od.18.77.170.
Still turn'd the toilsome mill with anxious mind; .... Od.20.139.240.
A brazen key she held, the handle turn'd, ... Od.21.9.258.
Turn'd on all sides, and view'd it o'er and o'er; .... Od.21.428.280.
In vain! *Minerva* turn'd them with her breath, ... Od.22.282.300.
Some, turn'd by *Pallas,* on the threshold fall, ... Od.22.302.301.
The damsel train turn'd pale at every wound, ... Od.23.43.321.

TURNER

Alas! 'tis more than Turner finds they give. .... 3.Ep3.84.94.

TURNING

He stay'd, and turning, thus address'd his Bands. .... Il.5.741.302.
Thus, turning, warn'd th' intrepid *Diomed.* .... Il.8.168.406.
A sudden Palsy seiz'd his turning Head; .... Il.10.445.23.
Till *Glaucus'* turning, all the rest inspir'd. .... Il.16.720.272.
Then turning to the martial Hosts, he cries, ... Il.17.205.295.
Then turning to his Friend, with dauntless Mind: .... Il.17.568.310.
But *Ajax* turning, to their Fears they yield, ... Il.17.819.320.
Then turning to the Daughters of the Main, ... Il.18.175.331.
Then back the turning Plow-shares cleave the Soil: .... Il.18.634.354.
Then turning with the word, *Minerva* flies, ... Od.3.474.110.
The turning wheel before the Palace stays. .... Od.7.4.233.
This said, and scornful turning from the shore .... Od.10.325.360.
And turning his grim visage, sternly spoke. .... Od.11.760.424.
But turning stalk'd with giant strides away. .... Od.11.774.424.
And turning sudden, shun the death design'd. .... Od.15.321.85.
Scarce had he spoke, when turning to the strand .... Od.16.366.124.
Then turning to *Antinous,* thus he spoke. .... Od.17.479.156.
Then turning short, disdain'd a further stay, ... Od.18.133.172.

TURNIPS

Had roasted turnips in the Sabin farm. .... 3.Ep1.219.34.
All *Townshend's* Turnips, and all *Grovenor's* Mines: .... 4.2HE2.273.185.

TURNPIKES

Why *Turnpikes* rise, and now no Cit, nor Clown .... 4.JD4.144.37.
Why *Turnpikes* rose, and why no Cit, nor Clown .... 4.JD4.144A.37.
Why *Turnpikes* rose, and now no Cit, nor Clown .... 4.JD4.144B.37.

TURNS

Then sing by turns, by turns the Muses sing, ... 1.PSp.41.64.
Then sing by turns, by turns the Muses sing, ... 1.PSp.41.64.
Persians and *Greeks* like *Turns of Nature* found, ... 1.EOC.380.283.
Each haughty Master's Yoke by turns to bear, ... 1.TrSt.237.420.
Where exil'd Tyrants still by turns command! .... 1.TrSt.242.420.
And win by turns the Kingdom of the Sky: .... 1.TrSt.491.430.
And, ev'n in Gold, turns paler as she dies. .... 1.TrSt.639.437.
By turns on each Celestial Pow'r they call; .... 1.TrSt.650.437.
Each Nymph by turns his wav'ring Mind possest, ... 2.ChJM.230.25.
And to the Knight our Story turns again, ... 2.ChJM.711.49.
Vapours and Pride by turns possess her Brain: .... 2.ChWB.89.61.
The Berries crackle, and the Mill turns round. .... 2.RL3.106.175.
A thousand Wings, by turns, blow back the Hair, ... 2.RL3.136.178.
Of Turns of Fortune, Changes in the State, ... 2.TemF.454.285.
Or turns young Ammon loose to scourge mankind? .... 3.EOM1.160.35.
As Heav'n's blest beam turns vinegar more sowr; .... 3.EOM2.148.72.
Reason the byass turns to good from ill, ... 3.EOM2.197.79.
Tho' each by turns the other's bound invade, ... 3.EOM2.207.80.
(By turns we catch the vital breath, and die) .... 3.EOM3.18.94.
(By turns they catch the vital breath, and die) .... 3.EOM3.18A.94.
Tho' strong the bend, yet quick the turns of mind: .... 3.Ep1.123.25.
What turns him now a stupid silent dunce? .... 3.Ep1.163.29.
Then turns repentant, and his God adores .... 3.Ep1.188.31.
And Atheism and Religion take their turns; .... 3.Ep2.66.55.
Scarce once herself, by turns all Womankind! .... 3.Ep2.116.60.

TURNS (CONTINUED)

To that each Passion turns, or soon or late; ....3.Ep2.133.61.
To all their dated Backs he turns you round, ...3.Ep4.135.150.
At all my Peevishness, and turns his Style. ....4.JD4.123.35.
Turns you from sound Philosophy aside; ....4.HS2.6.55.
She turns her very Sister to a Job, ...4.HAdv.21.77.
Who turns a *Persian* Tale for half a crown, ...4.Arbu.180.109.
Whom ripening Time, that Turns a Clap to Pox ....4.JD2A.53.136.
But turns a Wit, and writes Love Verses too? ....4.JD2A.60.136.
And God the Father turns a School-Divine. ....4.2HE1.102.203.
Now calls in Princes, and now turns away. ....4.2HE1.156.209.
For Merit will by turns forsake them all; ....4.EpS1.89.305.
Quite turns my Stomach— *P.* So does Flatt'ry mine; ....4.EpS2.182.323.
Realms shift their place, and Ocean turns to land. ....5.DunA1.70.68.
The opening clouds disclose each work by turns, ...5.DunA1.207.87.
How Index-learning turns no student pale, ...5.DunA1.233.90.
Spirts in the gard'ner's eyes who turns the cock. ....5.DunA2.170.122.
And one bright blaze turns Learning into air. ....5.DunA3.70.156.
Realms shift their place, and Ocean turns to land. ....5.DunB1.72.275.
The op'ning clouds disclose each work by turns, ...5.DunB1.249.288.
How Index-learning turns no student pale, ...5.DunB1.279.290.
Spirts in the gard'ner's eyes who turns the cock. ....5.DunB2.178.304.
And one bright blaze turns Learning into air. ....5.DunB3.78.324.
The head that turns at super-lunar things, ...5.DunB4.451.384.
And, as she turns, the colours fall or rise. ....5.DunB4.540.395.
Turns Hares to Larks, and Pigeons into Toads. ....5.DunB4.554.397.
Lost in the Maze of Words, he turns again, ...6.8.14.18.
Thus Fire is Water, Water Fire, by turns, ...6.9v.3.21.
But soon, too soon, the Lover turns his Eyes: ....6.11.93.33.
Still turns her beauties from th' invading beam, ...6.14iv.25.47.
At length she turns a Bride: ....6.14v(b).15.50.
The fawning Servant turns a haughty Lord; ....6.19.44.63.
My Friends, by Turns, my Friends confound, ...6.47.29.129.
Trudges to Town, and first turns Chambermaid; ....6.49i.16.138.
Then up comes *Steele;* he turns upon his *Heel,* ....6.49ii.7.140.
What tender passions take their turns, ...6.51ii.33.154.
Dash'd by these Rogues, turns *English* common Draught: ....6.60.14.178.
Who turns a *Persian* Tale for half a Crown, ...6.98.30.284.
Atheism and Superstition rule by Turns; ....6.99.18.287.
Scarce once herself, by Turns all Womankind? ....6.154.2.402.
To that each Passion turns or soon or late, ...6.154.19.403.
Distracting Thoughts by turns his Bosom rul'd, ...Il.1.253.98.
Turns on all hands its deep-discerning Eyes; ....Il.3.150.198.
Let both consent, and both by turns comply: ....Il.4.88.224.
The Nations bleed, where-e'er her Steps she turns, ...Il.4.506.245.
And turns unseen the frustrate Dart away. ....Il.5.237.278.
Revives their Ardor, turns their Steps from Flight, ...Il.5.607.297.
On the bright Axle turns the bidden Wheel, ...Il.5.890.308.
Moves as he moves, and turns the shining Shield. ....Il.8.328.413.
Guards as he turns, and circles as he wheels: ....Il.8.410.417.
Wise *Nestor* turns on each his careful Eye, ...Il.9.233.444.
Above the Coals the smoaking Fragments turns, ...Il.9.281.447.
Revives their Ardour, turns their Steps from flight, ...Il.11.273.47.
Now turns, and backward bears the yielding Bands; ....Il.11.693.66.
And where he turns, the Rout disperse, or die: ....Il.12.52.83.
Nor shuns the Foe, nor turns the Steeds away, ...Il.13.503.130.
And fraught with Vengeance, to the Victor turns; ....Il.13.734.139.
And turns around his apprehensive Eyes. ....Il.13.812.144.
Who bore by turns great *Ajax'* sev'nfold Shield; ....Il.13.886.147.
By turns the *Greeks,* by turns the *Trojans* bled. ....Il.14.524.188.
By turns the *Greeks,* by turns the *Trojans* bled. ....Il.14.524.188.
From that great Hour the War's whole Fortune turns, ...Il.15.76.199.
But enter'd in the *Grecian* Ranks, he turns ....Il.15.710.223.
Waves when he nods, and lightens as he turns: ....Il.15.733.224.
But turns his Javelin to the Work of Death. ....Il.15.903.232.
Yet stops, and turns, and saves his lov'd Allies. ....Il.16.433.259.
And turns the Slaughter on the conqu'ring Bands. ....Il.16.483.262.
Turns, and re-turns her, with a Mother's Care. ....Il.17.8.288.
And now it rises, now it sinks, by turns. ....Il.17.421.303.
Untam'd, untir'd, he turns, attacks, and stings: ....Il.17.645.313.
So turns the Lion from the nightly Fold, ...Il.17.741.317.
But if the Savage turns his glaring Eye, ...Il.17.815.320.
And breaks its Force, and turns the winding Tides. ....Il.17.842.321.
And now it rises, now it sinks by turns. ....Il.18.2.322.
But check'd, he turns; repuls'd, attacks again. ....Il.18.196.331.
His left with Tongs turns the vex'd Metal round; ....Il.18.549.348.
He turns the radiant Gift; and feeds his Mind ....Il.19.23.372.
Great *Jove* but turns it, and the Victor dies! ....Il.19.224.382.
To his bold Spear the Savage turns alone, ...Il.20.204.402.
Now here, now there, he turns on ev'ry side, ...Il.21.285.432.
That turns the glancing Bolt, and forked Fire. ....Il.21.467.440.
Then turns his Face, far-beaming heav'nly Fires, ...Il.21.543.444.
Apollo now to tir'd *Achilles* turns; ....Il.22.13.453.
And with them turns the rais'd Spectator's Soul. ....Il.22.216.464.
So oft' *Achilles* turns him to the Plain: ....Il.22.255.466.
And turns him short; till, doubling as they roll, ...Il.23.411.506.
Now each by turns indulg'd the Gush of Woe; ....Il.24.638.563.
And as he stood, he spoke and wept by turns. ....Od.2.32.61.
Turns the burnt-off'ring with his holy hands, ...Od.3.587.116.
The Monarch turns him to his royal guest; ....Od.3.603.117.
Too well the turns of mortal chance I know, ...Od.5.540.198.
Down rushing, it up-turns a hill of ground. ....Od.8.218.274.
(Vers'd in the turns of various humankind) ....Od.9.336.320.
Who, waiting long, by turns had hop'd and fear'd. ....Od.9.638.333.
The turns of all thy future fate, display, ...Od.10.643.374.
By turns they visit this etherial sky, ...Od.11.371.401.
In silence turns, and sullen stalks away. ....Od.11.692.418.
By turns to question, and by turns to hear. ....Od.17.663.164.
By turns to question, and by turns to hear. ....Od.17.663.164.
For *Pallas* seals his doom: All sad he turns ....Od.18.185.175.
And sprightly damsels trim the rays by turns. ....Od.18.358.184.
Then to the servile task the Monarch turns ....Od.18.391.186.
Incessant turns, impatient for repast: ....Od.20.34.234.
And turns the bow, and chafes it with his hands: ....Od.21.261.272.
While some deriding—How he turns the bow! ....Od.21.431.281.
All he unfolds: His list'ning spouse turns pale ....Od.23.331.340.

TURNUS

The *Latian* Wars, and haughty *Turnus* dead; ....2.TemF.205.272.

TURRET

High on a Turret hoary *Priam* stands, ...Il.21.613.447.
Beneath a Turret, on his Shield reclin'd, ...Il.22.136.458.

TURRET'S

He, hot and careless, on a turret's height ....Od.10.663.375.

TURRETS

And lift her Turrets nearer to the Skies; ....1.W-F.288.175.
Where *Windsor-Domes* and pompous Turrets rise, ...1.W-F.352.184.
These moss-grown domes with spiry turrets crown'd, ...2.ElAb.142.331.
Where *Anemoria's* stately Turrets shine, ...Il.2.625.157.
Or where her humbler Turrets *Trica* rears, ...Il.2.886.166.
Cardamyle with ample Turrets crown'd, ...Il.9.197.442.
Cardamyle with ample Turrets crown'd, ...Il.9.384.451.
And lo! the Turrets nod, the Bulwarks fall. ....Il.15.415.213.
Of trembling Parents on the Turrets stand. ....Il.18.598.351.
Troy's Turrets totter on the rocking Plain; ....Il.20.81.397.
From the high Turrets might oppress the Foe.) ....Il.22.254.466.

TURTLE

As some sad Turtle his lost Love deplores, ...1.PAu.19.82.
The Woods the Turtle-Dove, ...6.78i.2.215.
The Floods the Turtle-Dove, ...6.78i.2A.215.
That drives a Turtle thro' the liquid Skies; ....Il.15.267.207.

TURTLE-DOVE

The Woods the Turtle-Dove, ...6.78i.2.215.
The Floods the Turtle-Dove, ...6.78i.2A.215.

TURTLES

Their early Fruit, and milk-white Turtles bring; ....1.PSu.52.76.
And turtles taken from their airy nest. ....1.TrPA.89.369.
Turtles and Doves of diff'ring Hues, unite, ...1.TrSP.43.395.
In sculptur'd Gold two Turtles seem to drink: ....Il.11.777.69.

TUSKS

Oblique his Tusks, erect his Bristles stood, ...1.TrSt.573.434.
This Beast (when many a Chief his Tusks had slain) ....Il.9.661.467.
He grinds his Iv'ry Tusks; he foams with Ire; ....Il.11.527.57.
They gnash their Tusks, with Fire their Eye-balls roll, ...Il.12.167.87.
His foaming Tusks both Dogs and Men engage, ...Il.13.600.135.
Then arm'd with tusks, and lightning in his eyes, ...Od.4.617.149.
His tusks oblique he aim'd the knee to goar; ....Od.19.525.221.

TUSKY

The brindled Lion, or the tusky Bear. ....Il.11.378.51.
The bear to growl, to foam the tusky boar: ....Od.11.754.423.
As many lodgements for the tusky herd; ....Od.14.124.42.
There, to the tusky herd he bends his way, ...Od.14.600.66.
With glancing rage the tusky savage tore. ....Od.19.463.218.
He brought; the choicest of the tusky kind: ....Od.20.205.243.
On *Parnass'* top I chac'd the tusky boar. ....Od.21.229.270.
The scar indented by the tusky boar. ....Od.24.385.367.

TUTCHIN

And Tutchin flagrant from the scourge, below: ....5.DunA2.140.118.
And T[utchin] flagrant from the lash, below: 5.DunA2.140A.118
And Tutchin flagrant from the lash, below: ....5.DunA2.140B.118.
And Tutchin flagrant from the scourge below. ....5.DunB2.148.302.

TUTELARY

Thy Wife and Sister's Tutelary Care? ....1.TrSt.395.426.
There oft implor'd his tutelary pow'r, ...Od.19.430.215.

TUTOR'D

Were ye not tutor'd with *Ulysses'* praise? ....Od.4.915.161.
Tutor'd by early woes, grow early wise! ....Od.19.24.193.

TUTRESS

Acestis calls, the Tutress of his Race, ...1.TrSt.618A.436.

TWAIN

Fate urg'd the Sheers, and cut the *Sylph* in twain, ...2.RL3.151.179.
And took the Joint, and cut the Nerves in twain: ....Il.14.545.189.
Hurl'd by *Hectorean* Force, it cleft in twain ....Il.16.707.271.
It cleft the Helmets brazen Cheeks in twain; ....Il.17.340.300.
When he who thunders rent his bark in twain, ...Od.5.167.180.
While by the howling tempest rent in twain ....Od.5.407.192.
Rush'd with dire noise, and dash'd the sides in twain; ....Od.12.497.456.
I lopp'd the branchy head; aloft in twain ....Od.23.199.333.

TWANG

Harmonic twang! of leather, horn, and brass. ....5.DunA2.244.129.
Harmonic twang! of leather, horn, and brass; ....5.DunB2.254.307.
Thy Children's Noses all should twang the same. ....6.96iv.108.279.

TWANG'D

The Fleet in View, he twang'd his deadly Bow, ...Il.1.67.89.
He said, and twang'd the String. The Weapon flies ....Il.8.365.414.
The Bow-string twang'd; nor flew the Shaft in vain, ...Il.11.481.55.
And grasp'd the bow, and twang'd it in his hand. ....Od.21.130.264.
Twang'd short and sharp, like the shrill swallow's cry. ....Od.21.449.282.

TWANGING

At once bold *Teucer* draws the twanging Bow, ...1.TrES.135.454.
No Lance he shook, nor bent the twanging Bow, ...Il.7.171.372.
At once bold *Teucer* draws the twanging Bow, ...Il.12.489.99.
He next invites the twanging Bow to bend: ....Il.23.1007.529.
Th' aerial arrow from the twanging bow. ....Od.11.750.423.
Nor the fleet arrow from the twanging bow ....Od.12.101.436.
The twanging string, and try'd the stubborn yew: ....Od.24.198.358.

TWANGS

Sounds the tough Horn, and twangs the quiv'ring String. ....Il.4.157.228.

TWAS

Receiv'd his Laws, and stood convinc'd 'twas fit ....1.EOC.651.313.
Receiv'd his Rules, and stood convinc'd 'twas fit ....1.EOC.651A.313.
'Twas all her Joy the ripening Fruits to tend, ...1.TrVP.7.377.
Sure 'twas not much to bid one kind Adieu, ...1.TrSP.111.398.
'Twas thus I deem'd thy haughty Soul wou'd bear ....1.TrSt.404.427.
'Twas now the Time when *Phœbus* yields to Night, ...1.TrSt.474.430.
For 'twas from *Crete,* my Native Soil, I came; ....1.TrUl.141.470.
Once more 'twas giv'n thee to behold thy Coast: ....1.TrUl.221.473.
Twas by *Rebecca's* Aid that *Jacob* won ....2.ChJM.69.18.
There goes a Saying, and 'twas shrewdly said, ...2.ChJM.101.19.
There goes a Saying, and 'twas wisely said, ...2.ChJM.101A.19.
('Twas *June,* and *Cancer* had receiv'd the Sun) ....2.ChJM.401.34.
For oh, 'twas fix'd, she must possess or die! ....2.ChJM.493.39.
'Twas charg'd with Fruit that made a goodly Show, ...2.ChJM.603.44.
'Twas now the Season when the glorious Sun ....2.ChJM.609.44.
Ah my lov'd Lord! 'twas much unkind (she cry'd) ....2.ChJM.795.53.
'Twas You were jealous, not your Wife unkind: ....2.ChJM.808.54.
Declar'd 'twas better far to Wed, than Burn. ....2.ChWB.29.58.
Hark old Sir *Paul* ('twas thus I us'd to say) ....2.ChWB.74.60.
And told'em false, but *Jenkin* swore 'twas true. ....2.ChWB.151.63.
Then let him—'twas a *Nicety* indeed! ....2.ChWB.169.65.
He kept, 'twas thought, a private Miss or two: ....2.ChWB.230.68.
'Twas when fresh *May* her early Blossoms yields, ...2.ChWB.290.71.
Who drew the *Lion Vanquish'd?* 'Twas a *Man.* .... 2.ChWB.365.75.
'Twas torn to Fragments, and condemn'd to Flames. ....2.ChWB.435.78.
'Twas he had summon'd to her silent Bed ....2.RL1.21.147.
'Twas then *Belinda!* if Report say true, ...2.RL1.117.154.
'Twas this, the Morning *Omens* seem'd to tell; ....2.RL4.161.197.
'Twas this, the Morning *Omens* did fortel; ....2.RL4.161A.197.
And long 'twas doubtful, both so closely pent, ...2.TemF.491.287.
Too soon they taught me 'twas no sin to love. ....2.ElAb.68.324.
All this he knew; but not that 'twas to eat him. ....3.EOM3.46Z2.96.
'Twas VIRTUE ONLY (or in arts or arms, ...3.EOM3.211.114.
'Twas then, the studious head or gen'rous mind, ...3.EOM3.283.121.
'Twas all for fear the Knaves should call him Fool. ....3.Ep1.207.33.
'Twas thus Calypso once our hearts alarm'd, ...3.Ep2.45A.53.
'Twas thus Calypso once each heart alarm'd, ...3.Ep2.45.53.
'Twas no Court-badge, great Scriv'ner! fir'd thy brain, ...3.Ep3.147B.105.
But 'twas thy righteous end, asham'd to see ....3.Ep3.149A.105.
No, 'twas thy righteous end, asham'd to see ....3.Ep3.149.105.
'Twas very want that sold them for two pound. ....3.Ep3.328.120.
Seldom at Church ('twas such a busy life) ....3.Ep3.381.124.
Since 'twas no form'd Design of serving God: ....4.JD4.18.27.
Affirm, 'twas *Travel* made them what they were." ....4.JD4.79.31.
And 'twas their point, I ween, to make it last: ....4.HS2.94.61.
'Twas but to be where CHARLES had been before. ....4.HAdv.82.83.
"Informs you Sir, 'twas when he knew no better. ....4.Arbu.52.100.
'Twas only Suretyship that brought 'em there. ....4.JD2.70.139.
'Twas, "Sir your Law"—and "Sir, your Eloquence"— ....4.2HE2.133.175.
('Twas on the night of a Debate, ...4.HS6.187.261.
('Twas not a Man, it was a Mouse) ....4.1HE7.56.271.
'Twas what I said to Craggs and Child, ...4.1HE7.67.273.
But 'twas my Guest at whom they threw the dirt? ....4.EpS2.145.321.
'Twas here in clouded majesty she shone; ....5.DunA1.43.65.
'Twas on the day, when Thorold, rich and grave, ...5.DunA1.83.69.
'Twas chatt'ring, grinning, mouthing, jabb'ring all, ...5.DunA2.229.128.
'Twas on the day, when * * rich and grave, ...5.DunB1.85.275.
'Twas chatt'ring, grinning, mouthing, jabb'ring all, ...5.DunB2.237.307.
'Twas when the Dog-star's unpropitious ray, ...5.DunB4.9A.340.
At last it fix'd, 'twas on what plant it pleas'd, ...5.DunB4.429.383.
'Twas else th' ambitious *Celia's* aim, ...6.5.17A.12.
'Twas one vast Nothing, All, and All slept fast in thee. ....6.8.3.17.
'Twas *Si Signior,* 'twas *Yaw Mynheer,* .... 6.14v(b).11.49.
'Twas *Si Signior,* 'twas *Yaw Mynheer,* .... 6.14v(b).11.49.
'Twas *S'il vous plaist, Monsieur.* .... 6.14v(b).12.49.
'Twas *Si Signior,* & Yaw *Mynheer,* .... 6.14v(b).11A.49.
('Twas all he cou'd) and fawn'd, and lick'd his feet, ...6.15.16.52.
('Twas all he cou'd) and fawn'd, and kiss'd his feet, ...6.15.16A.52.
And *Q* maintain'd 'twas but his Due ....6.30.15.86.
For tho' without them both, 'twas clear, ...6.30.38.87.
For tho' without their help 'twas clear, ...6.30.38A.87.
For tho' without them ('twas most clear) ....6.30.38B.87.
'Twas all th' Ambition his great Soul could feel, ...6.49i.3.137.
'Twas all th' Ambition his high soul could feel, ...6.49i.3A.137.
Twas Friendship—warm as *Phœbus,* kind as Love, ...6.76.3.212.
Pray Heav'n, 'twas all a wanton Maiden did! ....6.96iv.88.279.
Tho' 'twas by that alone she could be born. ....6.99.8.286.
Who shew'd his breech, to prove 'twas not besh— ....6.116i.4.325.
My Tail indeed 'twas but in play ....6.135.3A.366.
'Twas a fat Oyster——Live in Peace——Adieu. ....6.145.12.388.
If thou hast Strength, 'twas Heav'n that Strength bestow'd, ...Il.1.233.98.
'Twas Night: the Chiefs beside their Vessel lie, ...Il.1.622.117.
'Twas thus the gen'ral Voice the Heroe prais'd, ...Il.2.340.143.
('Twas where the Plane-tree spread its Shades around) ....Il.2.370.145.
'Twas form'd of Horn, and smooth'd with artful Toil; ....Il.4.137.227.
From you 'twas hop'd among the first to dare ....Il.4.394.239.
'Twas in the Son's Defence the Mother bled. ....Il.5.468.290.
'Twas vain to seek Retreat, and vain to fear; ....Il.7.263.377.
'Twas thus the Sage his wholsome Counsel mov'd; ....Il.7.412.385.
'Twas then, the growing Discord to compose, ...Il.7.440.386.
'Twas *Neptune's* Charge his Coursers to unbrace, ...Il.8.546.422.
God bad us fight, and 'twas with God we came. ....Il.9.68.435.
There was a time ('twas when for *Greece* I fought) ....Il.9.464.455.
'Twas then, the Friendship of the Chief to gain, ...Il.11.29.36.
Such as may teach, 'twas still thy brave Delight ....Il.13.376.123.
'Twas thou, bold *Hector!* whose resistless Hand ....Il.15.854.229.
To *Phœbus* then ('twas all he could) he pray'd. ....Il.16.632.269.
Yet 'twas but late, beneath my conqu'ring Steel ....Il.17.27.289.
'Twas not for State we summon'd you so far, ...Il.17.262.298.
'Twas now no Season for prolong'd Debate; ....Il.18.291.336.
'Twas *Jove's* high Will alone, o'eruling all, ...Il.19.285.384.
'Twas Tumult all, and Violence of Flight; ....Il.21.721.451.

TWAS (CONTINUED)

Yet for my Sons I thank ye Gods! 'twas well: ....Il.22.98.456.
A God deceiv'd me; *Pallas,* 'twas thy Deed. ....Il.22.381.471.
'Twas when, emerging thro' the Shades of Night, ...Il.23.280.501.
'Twas where by Force of wintry Torrents torn, ...Il.23.499.510.
'Twas thou, *Euryalus!* who durst aspire ....Il.23.783.521.
'Twas voted, *Hermes* from his god-like Foe ....Il.24.143.541.
'Twas silence all: at last *Ægyptius* spoke; ....Od.2.19.61.
'Twas riot all among the lawless train; ....Od.2.337.77.
'Twas God's high will the victors to divide, ...Od.3.161.93.
'Twas then that issuing thro' the palace gate ....Od.4.27.121.
'Twas night; and cover'd in the foliage deep, ...Od.7.368.254.
'Twas for our lives my lab'ring bosom wrought; ....Od.9.501.326.
'Twas on no coward, no ignoble slave, ...Od.9.559.329.
Say 'twas *Ulysses;* 'twas his deed, declare, ...Od.9.589.330.
Say 'twas *Ulysses;* 'twas his deed, declare, ...Od.9.589.330.
'Twas mine on *Troy* to pour th' imprison'd war: ....Od.11.642.416.
'Twas then soft slumber fled my troubled brain: ....Od.12.431.451.
For 'twas from *Crete* my native soil I came, ...Od.13.308.21.
Once more 'twas giv'n thee to behold thy coast: ....Od.13.388.25.
And joyn'd me with them, ('twas their own command) ....Od.14.529.62.
'Twas but for scraps he ask'd, and ask'd in vain. ....Od.17.259.144.
'Twas riot all amid the Suitor-throng, ...Od.17.685.165.
'Twas then *Melantho* with imperious mien ....Od.19.78.196.
'Twas then to *Crete* the great *Ulysses* came; ....Od.19.215.203.
'Twas caution, oh my Lord! not want of love: ....Od.23.230.334.
'Twas his to suffer, and 'tis mine to mourn! ....Od.24.339.365.
'Twas heav'n that struck, and heav'n was on his side. ....Od.24.515.372.

TWAY

His Aunt, and eke her Daughters tway: ....6.14i.8.41.

TWEAK'D

Look in their Face, they tweak'd your Nose, ...6.79.17.218.
He kicked, and cuff'd, and tweak'd, and trod ....6.79.23.218.
He tweak'd his Nose, trod on his Toes, ...6.79.59.219.

TWEED

Ask where's the North? at York, 'tis on the Tweed; ....3.EOM2.222.82.

TWEEZER

And Beaus' in *Snuff-boxes* and *Tweezer-Cases.* .... 2.RL5.116.209.

TWEEZER-CASES

And Beaus' in *Snuff-boxes* and *Tweezer-Cases.* .... 2.RL5.116.209.

TWELFTH

The twelfth or thirteenth Day of *July,* .... 6.10.117.28.
Returning with the twelfth revolving Light. ....Il.1.559.115.
This the twelfth Evening since he rested there, ...Il.24.505.557.
The twelfth we war, if War be doom'd by Heav'n! ....Il.24.837.571.
'Till the twelfth moon had wheel'd her pale career; ....Od.4.704.152.
His twelfth diurnal race begins to run. ....Od.4.804.156.
'Till the twelfth dawn the light of heav'n reveal'd. ....Od.4.987.163.

TWELVE

Where twelve fair Signs in beauteous Order lye? ....1.PSp.40.64.
Where twelve bright Signs in beauteous Order lye? ....1.PSp.40A.64.
And sleepless Lovers, just at Twelve, awake: ....2.RL1.16.146.
Of twelve vast *French* Romances, neatly gilt. ....2.RL2.38.161.
Before the Lords at Twelve my Cause comes on— ....4.2HE2.96.171.
Of these twelve volumes, twelve of amplest size, ...5.DunA1.135.80.
Of these twelve volumes, twelve of amplest size, ...5.DunA1.135.80.
But such a bulk as no twelve bards could raise, ...5.DunA2.35.100.
Twelve starveling bards of these degen'rate days. ....5.DunA2.36.100.
Twelve starving bards of these degen'rate days. ....5.DunA2.36A.100.
Of these twelve volumes, twelve of amplest size, ...5.DunB1.155.281.
Of these twelve volumes, twelve of amplest size, ...5.DunB1.155.281.
But such a bulk as no twelve bards could raise, ...5.DunB2.39.298.
Twelve starv'ling bards of these degen'rate days. ....5.DunB2.40.298.
Twelve Days the Pow'rs indulge the Genial Rite, ...Il.1.558.115.
Twelve Days were past, and now the dawning Light ....Il.1.640.118.
In twelve black ships to *Troy* they steer their Course, ...Il.2.673.158.
These in twelve Galleys with Vermillion Prores, ...Il.2.773.162.
And twelve young Heifers to her Altars led. ....Il.6.116.329.
Twelve Domes for them and their lov'd Spouses shone, ...Il.6.310.341.
And twelve young Heifers to her Altar led. ....Il.6.343.343.
So twelve young Heifers, guiltless of the Yoke, ...Il.6.382.345.
Twelve Steeds unmatch'd in Fleetness and in Force, ...Il.9.161.440.
Twelve Steeds unmatch'd in Fleetness and in Force, ...Il.9.348.450.
I sack'd twelve ample Cities on the Main, ...Il.9.432.453.
And twelve lay smoaking on the *Trojan* Plain: ....Il.9.433.453.
Till twelve lay breathless of the *Thracian* Band. ....Il.10.569.28.
Now twelve dispatch'd, the Monarch last they found; ....Il.10.576.28.
And twelve beside lay gasping on the Ground. ....Il.10.659.31.
Twice ten of Tin, the twelve of ductile Gold; ....Il.11.32.36.
With twelve black Ships he reach'd *Percope's* Strand, ...Il.11.295.48.
Of twelve bold Brothers, I alone remain! ....Il.11.833.73.
Full twelve, the boldest, in a Moment fell, ...Il.15.908.232.
Twelve in the Tumult wedg'd, untimely rush'd ....Il.18.271.335.
And twelve, the noblest of the *Trojan* Line, ...Il.18.394.340.
Hence sprung twelve others of unrival'd Kind, ...Il.20.268.405.
Twelve chosen Youths he drags alive to Land; ....Il.21.35.422.
And scarce twelve morning Suns have seen me here; ....Il.21.93.425.
And twelve sad Victims of the *Trojan* Line ....Il.23.30.488.
Sad Sacrifice! twelve *Trojan* Captives fell. ....Il.23.215.498.
Twelve *Trojan* Heroes offer'd to thy Shade; ....Il.23.223.498.
Twelve costly Carpets of refulgent Hue, ...Il.24.282.548.
And twelve fair Veils, and Garments stiff with Gold. ....Il.24.284.548.
But two the Goddess, twelve the Queen enjoy'd; ....Il.24.765.569.
Those boasted twelve th' avenging two destroy'd. ....Il.24.766.569.
Twelve Days, nor Foes, nor secret Ambush dread; ....Il.24.987.577.
But by thy care twelve urns of wine be fill'd, ...Od.2.398.80.
T'import twelve mares which there luxurious feed, ...Od.4.859.159.
And twelve young mules, a strong laborious race, ...Od.4.860.159.
Two beeves, twelve fatlings from the flock they bring ....Od.8.53.264.

TWELVE (CONTINUED)

Twelve Princes in our realm dominion share, ...Od.8.425.286.
We thus supply'd, (for twelve were all the fleet.) ....Od.9.187.313.
With only twelve, the boldest and the best, ...Od.9.227.316.
And twelve large vessels of unmingled wine, ...Od.9.238.316.
Twelve moons the foe the captive youth detains ....Od.11.359.400.
Twelve feet deform'd and foul the fiend dispreads; ....Od.12.111.437.
To his high name let twelve black oxen fall. ....Od.13.211.15.
Twelve ample cells, the lodgments of his herd. ....Od.14.18.35.
Twelve herds, twelve flocks, on Ocean's margin feed, ...Od.14.122.41.
Twelve herds, twelve flocks, on Ocean's margin feed, ...Od.14.122.41.
Twelve herds of goats that graze our utmost green; ....Od.14.126.42.
Six are their menial train: twice twelve the boast ....Od.16.270.118.
And twelve our country's pride; to these belong ....Od.16.272.118.
Rich from the artist's hand! twelve clasps of gold ....Od.18.339.184.
Twelve days, while *Boreas* vex'd th' aerial space, ...Od.19.230.204.
Twelve female slaves the gift of *Ceres* grind; ....Od.20.133.240.
And thro' twelve ringlets the fleet arrow send, ...Od.21.76.262.
Twelve shields, twelve lances, and twelve helmets bears: ....Od.22.159.294.
Twelve shields, twelve lances, and twelve helmets bears: ....Od.22.159.294.
Twelve shields, twelve lances, and twelve helmets bears: ....Od.22.159.294.
Twelve cloaks, twelve vests, twelve tunicks stiff with gold, ...Od.24.321.365.
Twelve cloaks, twelve vests, twelve tunicks stiff with gold, ...Od.24.321.365.
Twelve cloaks, twelve vests, twelve tunicks stiff with gold, ...Od.24.321.365.
Twelve pear-trees bowing with their pendent load, ...Od.24.395.368.

TWELVEMONTH

Fr. Not twice a twelvemonth you appear in Print, ...4.EpS1.1.297.
Our walls this twelvemonth should not see the slave. ....Od.17.491.156.

TWENTIETH

And now the twentieth sun descending, laves ....Od.4.487.143.

TWENTY

Who bid me tell this Lye—and twenty more. ....2.ChWB.306.71.
Of twenty Winters' Age he seem'd to be; ....2.ChWB.317.72.
I (to say truth) was twenty more than he: ....2.ChWB.318.72.
The Chanc'ry takes your rents for twenty year: ....4.HS2.172.69.
"Sir, he's your Slave, for twenty pound a year. ....4.2HE2.8.165.
When out of twenty, I can please not two; ....4.2HE2.81.171.
When twenty Fools I never saw ....4.HS6.64.255.
Like twenty River-Gods with all their Urns. ....6.33.6.99.
Twice twenty Ships transport the warlike Bands, ...Il.2.653.158.
In twenty Sail the bold *Perrhebians* came ....Il.2.906.166.
Where twenty Days in Genial Rites he pass'd. ....Il.6.270.340.
Besides full twenty Nymphs of *Trojan* Race, ...Il.9.179.441.
Besides full twenty Nymphs of *Trojan* Race, ...Il.9.366.451.
Full twenty Cubits long, he swings around. ....Il.15.817.228.
Full twenty Knights he tumbled from the Car, ...Il.16.976.281.
Had twenty Mortals, each thy Match in Might, ...Il.16.1022.282.
Full twenty Tripods for his Hall he fram'd, ...Il.18.440.341.
And twenty Forges catch at once the Fires; ....Il.18.542.348.
Of twenty Measures its capacious Size. ....Il.23.332.503.
For twenty beeves by great *Laertes* won; ....Od.1.542.58.
And twenty youths in radiant mail incas'd, ...Od.4.709.152.
With twenty chosen mates a vessel mann'd; ....Od.4.895.160.
And twenty chiefs renown'd for valour chose: ....Od.4.1028.165.
Sudden, full twenty on the plain are strow'd, ...Od.5.313.186.
Scarce twenty measures from the living stream ....Od.9.243.316.
(Scarce twenty four-wheel'd cars, compact and strong, ...Od.9.286.318.
Tho' born by twenty feet, tho' arm'd with twenty hands; ....Od.12.96.436.
Tho' born by twenty feet, tho' arm'd with twenty hands; ....Od.12.96.436.
Twice twenty six, all peers of mighty name, ...Od.16.269.118.
Of *Samos;* twenty from *Zacynthus* coast: ....Od.16.271.118.
His Lord, when twenty tedious years had roll'd, ...Od.17.397.151.
Whose footsteps twenty winters have defac'd: ....Od.19.260.207.
Full twenty annual suns in distant skies: ....Od.19.566.224.
A team of twenty geese, (a snow-white train!) ....Od.19.627.226.
Of twenty virgins to the spring repair: ....Od.20.197.243.
Thy son, with twenty winters now grown old; ....Od.24.376.367.

TWENTY-ONE

The virtues of a saint at twenty-one! ....3.EOM4.184.144.
When the brisk Minor pants for twenty-one; ....4.1HE1.38.281.

TWERE

'Twere well, might Criticks still this Freedom take; ....1.EOC.584.306.
And 'twere a sin to rob them of their Mite. ....4.Arbu.162.108.
'Twere well if she would pare her Nails, ...6.14v(a).5.48.
Grown old in Rhyme 'twere barbarous to discard ....6.34.1.101.
And 'twere a Sin to rob them of their *Mite.* ....6.98.12.283.

TWICE

How twice he tam'd proud *Ister's* rapid Flood, ...1.TrSt.25.410.
Twice taught the *Rhine* beneath his Laws to roll, ...1.TrSt.27.410.
How twice the Mountains ran with *Dacian* Blood, ...1.TrSt.25A.410.
How twice he vanquish'd where the *Rhine* does roll, ...1.TrSt.27A.410.
Who mourn'd her Lord twice ten revolving Years, ...1.TrUl.218.473.
Twice-marry'd Dames are Mistresses o' th' Trade: ......2.ChJM.110.20.
No pious Christian ought to marry twice. ....2.ChWB.12.57.
A Saint in Crape is twice a Saint in Lawn; ....3.Ep1.88.21.
The Crown of Poland, venal twice an age, ...3.Ep3.129.103.
"Where once I went to church, I'll now go twice— ....3.Ep3.367.123.
They scarce can bear their *Laureate* twice a Year: ....4.HS1.34.7.
"I too could write, and I am twice as tall, ...4.Arbu.103.103.
"I too could write, and sure am twice as tall, ...4.Arbu.103A.103.
Shall bless thy name at least some twice a day, ...4.HOde1.30C.153.
Nor cross the Channel twice a year, ...4.HS6.31.253.
Fr. Not twice a twelvemonth you appear in Print, ...4.EpS1.1.297.
The matter's weighty, pray consider twice: ....4.EpS2.43.315.
(His only suit) for twice three years before: ....5.DunA3.30.154.
(His only suit) for twice three years before: ....5.DunB3.38.322.
In twice ten thousand rhyming nights and days, ...5.DunB4.172.358.
And twice ten thousand bite the ground in death; ......6.21.18.69.
She flatters her good Lady twice a Day; ....6.49i.18.138.
For he lives twice, who can at once employ ....6.55.10.167.

TWICE (CONTINUED)

Adam had fallen twice, if for an apple ....6.62iv.1.186.
The sacred rust of twice ten hundred years! ....6.71.38.203.
To fleece their Countrey Clients twice a Year? ....6.96iii.28.275.
Twice sixty Warriors thro' the foaming Seas. ....Il.2.609.156.
Twice twenty Ships transport the warlike Bands, ...Il.2.653.158.
And twice ten Coursers wait their Lord's Command. ....Il.5.247.279.
And twice ten Vases of refulgent Mold; ....Il.9.158.440.
And twice ten Vases of refulgent Mold; ....Il.9.345.450.
For once deceiv'd, was his; but twice, were mine. ....Il.9.491.456.
Twice ten of Tin, the twelve of ductile Gold; ....Il.11.32.36.
And twice ten Bosses the bright Convex crown'd; ....Il.11.46.36.
When twice ten thousand shake the lab'ring Field; ......Il.14.174.165.
Twice ten bright Vases in the midst they laid; ....Il.19.250.383.
And twice the Number of high-bounding Steeds: ....Il.19.252.383.
Of twice six Oxen its reputed Price; ....Il.23.817.521.
And twice ten Axes casts amidst the Round, ...Il.23.1008.529.
Two Tripods next and twice two Chargers shine, ...Il.24.285.548.
Now twice ten Years (unhappy Years) are o'er ....Il.24.964.576.
How twice ten years from shore to shore he roams; .....Od.2.205.71.
Now twice ten years are past, and now he comes! ....Od.2.206.71.
And twice ten measures of the choicest flour ....Od.2.400.80.
'Till twice six times descends the lamp of day: ....Od.2.421.81.
In twice ten days shall fertile *Scheria* find, ...Od.5.44.173.
Twice ten tempestuous nights I roll'd, resign'd ....Od.6.205.220.
We twice as far had furrow'd back the main, ...Od.9.576.330.
He march'd, with twice eleven in his train: ....Od.10.238.352.
More wretched you! twice number'd with the dead! .....Od.12.32.431.
And what so tedious as a twice-told tale? ....Od.12.538.459.
Who mourn'd her Lord twice ten revolving years, ...Od.13.385.25.
Twice ten sad years o'er earth and ocean tost, ...Od.16.226.114.
Twice twenty six, all peers of mighty name, ...Od.16.269.118.
Six are their menial train: twice twelve the boast ......Od.16.270.118.
Your own *Ulysses!* twice ten years detain'd ....Od.21.213.270.
Of these, twice six pursue their wicked way, ...Od.22.462.310.
When twice ten years are past of mighty woes: ....Od.23.104.324.

TWICE-MARRY'D

Twice-marry'd Dames are Mistresses o' th' Trade: ......2.ChJM.110.20.

TWICE-TOLD

And what so tedious as a twice-told tale? ....Od.12.538.459.

TWICK'NAM

And *Twick'nam* such, which fairer Scenes enrich, ...6.14ii.49.44.

TWIG

She seiz'd a Twig, and up the Tree she went. ....2.ChJM.739.50.
Just as the Twig is bent, the Tree's inclin'd. ....3.Ep1.102.22.

TWIGS

Like nets or lime-twigs, for rich Widows hearts? ....4.JD2.58.137.

TWILIGHT

But o'er the twilight groves, and dusky caves, ...2.ElAb.163.332.
Thro' twilight ages hunt th' Athenian fowl, ...5.DunB4.361.378.
Now Twilight veil'd the glaring Face of Day, ...Il.24.427.553.

TWILL

'Twill then be Infamy to seem your Friend! ....2.RL4.112.192.
"Tho' faith, I fear 'twill break his Mother's heart. .....4.2HE2.16.165.
And where's the Glory? 'twill be only thought ....4.EpS1.25.299.

TWIN

Reign the Twin-gods, the fav'rite sons of *Jove.* ....Od.11.374.401.

TWIN-GODS

Reign the Twin-gods, the fav'rite sons of *Jove.* ....Od.11.374.401.

TWIN'D

Round broken Columns clasping Ivy twin'd; ....1.W-F.69.156.
On which three Wives successively had twin'd ....2.ChWB.395.76.
Twin'd with the wreaths Parnassian lawrels yield,. .....3.EOM4.11.129.
"Where twin'd the Silver Eel around thy Hook, ...6.96ii.21.270.
And broke the Nerve my Hands had twin'd with Art, ...Il.15.552.218.
Where silver alders, in high arches twin'd, ...Od.17.240.143.

TWINE

Then round your Neck in wanton Wreaths I twine, ...1.TrSP.149.400.
Let Wreaths of Triumph now my Temples twine, ...2.RL3.161.180.

TWINES

And I this Bowl, where wanton Ivy twines, ...1.PSp.35.63.
Around whose verge a mimic Ivy twines. ....Od.16.54.105.

TWINING

He view'd their twining Branches with Delight, ...1.TrVP.61.379.
He view'd her twining Branches with Delight, ...1.TrVP.61A.379.
(The twining bands the *Cyclop's* bed supply'd) ....Od.9.508.327.
With twining osiers which the bank supply'd. ....Od.10.193.349.

TWINKLING

(Like twinkling Stars the Miscellanies o'er) ....4.2HE1.110.205.
Heav'ns twinkling Sparks draw light, and point their horns. .....5.DunB2.12.296.

TWINS

Two cubs I have, as like as twins can be; ....1.TrPA.90.369.
Then *Sleep* and *Death,* two Twins of winged Race, ...1.TrES.344.462.
His Heav'nly Progress thro' the *Twins* had run; ....2.ChJM.610.44.
Two Twins were near, bold beautiful and young, ...Il.6.27.325.
Then *Sleep* and *Death,* two *Twins* of winged Race, ...Il.16.831.275.
For the fam'd Twins, impatient to survey ....Il.23.735.519.
And twins ev'n from the birth, are misery and man! ....Od.7.264.248.

TWIRL
To plunge the brand, and twirl the pointed wood; ..... Od.9.392.322.
Guide the sharp stake, and twirl it round and round. ..... Od.9.456.324.

TWIRL'D
Or whirligigs, twirl'd round by skilful swain, ... 5.DunA3.49.154.
Or whirligigs, twirl'd round by skilful swain, ... 5.DunB3.57.323.

TWIST
'Tis the same rope at sev'ral ends they twist, ... 5.DunA3.285.184.
'Tis the same rope at different ends they twist; ..... 5.DunB1.207.285.
The snowy fleece, or twist the purpled wool. ..... Od.6.64.208.
Part twist the threads, and part the wool dispose, ... Od.6.369.229.

TWISTED
A twisted Birth-day Ode completes the spire. ..... 5.DunB1.162.282.
The snowie Fleece, and wind the twisted Wool.) ..... Il.3.478.214.
With curling Vines and twisted Ivy bound; ..... Il.6.166.334.
Wide-patch'd, and knotted to a twisted thong. ..... Od.13.507.30.
Wide patch'd, and fasten'd by a twisted thong. ..... Od.17.221.142.
Ill joyn'd, and knotted to a twisted thong. ..... Od.18.132.172.

TWISTING
Her twisting Volumes, and her rowling Eyes, ... 1.TrSt.728.440.
The Eels lie twisting in the Pangs of Death: ..... Il.21.413.437.

TWIT'NAM
All fly to *Twit'nam,* and in humble strain ..... 4.Arbu.21.97.
You please to see, on Twit'nam green, ... 6.114.7.321.

TWITCH'D
And thrice they twitch'd the Diamond in her Ear, ... 2.RL3.137.178.

TWIXT
'Twixt Sense and Nonsense daily change their Side. ..... 1.EOC.435.288.
'Twixt that, and Reason, what a nice barrier; ..... 3.EOM1.223.43.
Where none distinguish twixt your Shame and Pride, ... 3.Ep2.204A.67.
Where none distinguish twixt your Shame or Pride, ... 3.Ep2.204B.67.
There, none distinguish 'twixt your Shame or Pride, ... 3.Ep2.204.67.
Hold out some months 'twixt Sun and Fire, ... 4.1HE7.18.269.
'Twixt Plautus, Fletcher, Congreve, and Corneille, ... 5.DunA1.239.91.
'Twixt Plautus, Fletcher, Shakespear, and Corneille, ... 5.DunB1.285.290.
'Twixt Prince and People close the Curtain draw, ... 5.DunB1.313.293.
To pass her time 'twixt reading and Bohea, ... 6.45.15.125.
Of Courtiers 'twixt you Three, ... 6.61.30A.182.
Shine 'twixt the Hills, or wander o'er the Plain. ..... Il.12.36.83.
And dropp'd the flowing Reins. Him 'twixt the Jaws ..... Il.16.492.262.
Struck 'twixt the Horns, he springs with many a Bound, ... Il.17.590.311.
Where 'twixt the Neck and Throat the jointed Plate ..... Il.22.408.472.

TWO
Two Swains, whom Love kept wakeful, and the Muse, ... 1.PSp.18.62.
I see, I see where two fair Cities bend ..... 1.W-F.379.187.
But, of the two, less dang'rous is th' Offence, ... 1.EOC.3.239.
Two cubs I have, as like as twins can be; ..... 1.TrPA.90.369.
Two little bears, I found them, and did please ..... 1.TrPA.92.369.
A fatal Throne to two contending Kings, ... 1.TrSt.52.412.
As when two Winds with Rival Force contend, ... 1.TrSt.265.421.
Two Races now, ally'd to *Jove,* offend; ..... 1.TrSt.315.423.
But two fair Daughters heir'd his State and Throne. ..... 1.TrSt.544.433.
These, where two Ways in equal Parts divide, ... 1.TrSt.718.440.
Two bleeding Babes depending at her Side; ..... 1.TrSt.720.440.
And while two pointed Jav'lins arm his Hands, ... 1.TrES.11.450.
Two stubborn Swains with Blows dispute their Bounds; ..... 1.TrES.158.455.
As when two Scales are charg'd with doubtful Loads, ... 1.TrES.167.455.
Not two strong Men th'enormous Weight cou'd raise, ... 1.TrES.185.456.
Gloomy as Night, and shakes two shining Spears; ..... 1.TrES.200.456.
As when two Vulturs on the Mountain's Height ..... 1.TrES.219.458.
Two sounding Darts the *Lycian* Leader threw, ... 1.TrES.267.459.
Then *Sleep* and *Death,* two Twins of winged Race, ... 1.TrES.344.462.
Two craggy Rocks, projecting to the Main, ... 1.TrUl.27.466.
Two Marble Doors unfold on either side; ..... 1.TrUl.42.467.
Three were just tolerable, two were bad. ..... 2.ChWB.57.59.
"One of us two must rule, and one obey, ... 2.ChWB.192.65.
He kept, 'twas thought, a private Miss or two: ..... 2.ChWB.230.68.
Then how two Wives their Lord's Destruction prove, ... 2.ChWB.401.76.
And view with scorn *Two Pages* and a *Chair.* ..... 2.RL1.46.149.
Nourish'd two Locks, which graceful hung behind ..... 2.RL2.20.160.
Burns to encounter two adventrous Knights, ... 2.RL3.26.171.
Led off two captive Trumps, and swept the Board. ..... 2.RL3.50.172.
A two-edg'd Weapon from her shining Case; ..... 2.RL3.128.177.
Two Handmaids wait the Throne: Alike in Place, ... 2.RL4.25.185.
These, in two sable Ringlets taught to break, ... 2.RL4.169.197.
This, in two sable Ringlets taught to break, ... 2.RL4.169A.197.
If ever chance two wandring lovers brings ..... 2.ElAb.347.348.
Two Principles in human nature reign; ..... 3.EOM2.53.62.
One in their nature, which are two in ours, ... 3.EOM3.96.101.
Each sex desires alike, 'till two are one. ..... 3.EOM3.122.104.
So two consistent motions act the Soul; ..... 3.EOM3.315.126.
Woman and Fool are two hard things to hit, ... 3.Ep2.113.59.
In Women, two almost divide the kind; ..... 3.Ep2.208.67.
Then in plain prose, were made two sorts of Men, ... 3.Ep3.13A.84.
Then careful Heav'n supply'd two sorts of Men, ... 3.Ep3.13.84.
'Twas very want that sold them for two pound. ..... 3.Ep3.328.120.
And two rich ship-wrecks bless the lucky shore. ..... 3.Ep3.356.122.
And lo! two puddings smoak'd upon the board. ..... 3.Ep3.360.123.
Two Cupids squirt before: a Lake behind ..... 3.Ep4.111.148.
Is what two souls so gen'rous cannot bear; ..... 4.HS2.58.59.
Let the *Two Curls* of Town and Court, abuse ..... 4.Arbu.380.125.
When out of twenty I can please not two; ..... 4.2HE2.81.171.
Two Aldermen dispute it with an Ass? ..... 4.2HE2.105.173.
The *Temple* late two Brother Sergeants saw, ... 4.2HE2.127.173.
Two of a Face, as soon as of a Mind. ..... 4.2HE2.269.183.
Why, of two Brothers, rich and restless one ..... 4.2HE2.270.183.
"We shall not quarrel for a year or two; ..... 4.2HE1.61.199.
About some great Affair, at Two— ..... 4.HS6.74.255.

TWO (CONTINUED)
He had a Story of *two Mice.* ..... 4.HS6.156.259.
So bought an Annual Rent or two. ..... 4.1HE7.71.273.
Here in one bed two shiv'ring sisters lye, ... 5.DunA1.31.63.
There in his seat two spacious Vents appear, ... 5.DunA2.81.108.
Two babes of love close clinging to her waste; ..... 5.DunA2.150.120.
"Ah why, ye Gods! should two and two make four?" ..... 5.DunA2.274.135.
"Ah why, ye Gods! should two and two make four?" ..... 5.DunA2.274.135.
The pond'rous books two gentle readers bring; ..... 5.DunA2.351.143.
"Lo next two slip-shod Muses traipse along, ... 5.DunA3.141.162.
"See next two slip-shod Muses traipse along, ... 5.DunA3.141A.162.
Should wag two serpent tails in Smithfield fair. ..... 5.DunA3.290.184.
Let Bawdry, Bilingsgate, two sisters dear, ... 5.DunB1.307A.292.
There in his seat two spacious vents appear, ... 5.DunB2.85.299.
Two babes of love close clinging to her waist; ..... 5.DunB2.158.303.
"Ah why, ye Gods! should two and two make four?" ..... 5.DunB2.286.309.
"Ah why, ye Gods! should two and two make four?" ..... 5.DunB2.286.309.
The pond'rous books two gentle readers bring; ..... 5.DunB2.383.316.
Courtiers and Patriots in two ranks divide, ... 5.DunB4.107.352.
On two unequal crutches propt he came, ... 5.DunB4.111.352.
Points him two ways, the narrower is the better. ..... 5.DunB4.152.356.
Blest in one Niger, till he knows of two." ..... 5.DunB4.370.379.
But far the foremost, two, with earnest zeal, ... 5.DunB4.401.381.
I but lug out to one or two ..... 6.10.31.25.
And two substantial Meals a day were made. ..... 6.13.7.39.
They ne'er gave *Sixpence* for *two Lines,* ..... 6.29.23.83.
A Scholar, or a Wit or two: ..... 6.29.28.83.
Two plenteous fountains the whole prospect crown'd, ... 6.35.28.103.
Two or *Three* Visits, and *Two* or *Three* Bows, ... 6.36.1.104.
Two or *Three* Visits, and *Two* or *Three* Bows, ... 6.36.1.104.
Two or *Three* civil Things, *Two* or *Three* Vows, ... 6.36.2.104.
Two or *Three* civil Things, *Two* or *Three* Vows, ... 6.36.2.104.
Two or *Three* Kisses, with *Two* or *Three* Sighs, ... 6.36.3.104.
Two or *Three* Kisses, with *Two* or *Three* Sighs, ... 6.36.3.104.
Two or *Three* Jesus's—and let me dyes— ..... 6.36.4.104.
Two or *Three* Squeezes, and *Two* or *Three* Towses, ... 6.36.5.104.
Two or *Three* Squeezes, and *Two* or *Three* Towses, ... 6.36.5.104.
With *Two* or *Three* thousand Pound lost at their Houses, ... 6.36.6.104.
Can never fail Cuckolding *Two* or *Three* Spouses. ..... 6.36.7.104.
Two or *Three* Visits, with *Two* or *Three* Bows. ..... 6.36.1A.105.
Two or *Three* Visits, with *Two* or *Three* Bows. ..... 6.36.1A.105.
Two or *Three* Visits, *Two* or *Three* Bows, ... 6.36.1B.105.
Two or *Three* Visits, *Two* or *Three* Bows, ... 6.36.1B.105.
Two or *Three* Kisses, and *Two* or *Three* Sighs, ... 6.36.3A.105.
Two or *Three* Kisses, and *Two* or *Three* Sighs, ... 6.36.3A.105.
Two or *Three* Kisses, *Two* or *Three* Sighs, ... 6.36.3B.105.
Two or *Three* Kisses, *Two* or *Three* Sighs, ... 6.36.3B.105.
Two or *Three* Squeezes, *Two* or *Three* Towses, ... 6.36.5A.105.
Two or *Three* Squeezes, *Two* or *Three* Towses, ... 6.36.5A.105.
With *Two* or *Three* hundred Pounds lost at their Houses, ... 6.36.6A.105.
Who when two Wits on rival themes contest, ... 6.49iii.23.143.
And two fair Ladies in ..... 6.61.2.180.
For Gay can well make two of me. ..... 6.61.41.182.
For Gay may well make two of me. ..... 6.61.41A.182.
You may meet the *Two Champions* who are no Lord *S[herrar]d* ..... 6.62v.2.186*.
You may meet your *Two Champions* who are no Lord Sherrards. ..... 6.62v.2A.186.
Two hearts like these could e'er expire ..... 6.69ii.2A.199.
Here lye two poor Lovers, who had the mishap ..... 6.69iii.1.201.
The rest is told you in a Line or two. ..... 6.82vi.10.232.
A stone of two foot; ..... 6.90.9.251.
Whom Pope prov'd his Friend in his two chief distresses, ... 6.92.3.255.
We're not two Capons but two Cocks. ..... 6.93.27Z6.257.
We're not two Capons but two Cocks. ..... 6.93.27Z6.257.
'Tis pity that two Squires so Gent— ..... 6.94.39.260.
And now two Legs *St. A-d-re* [*André*] got, ... 6.94.65.261.
And then came two Legs more; ..... 6.94.66.261.
Better two Heads than one; ..... 6.94.86.262.
Which seem'd like two broad Suns in misty Skies: ..... 6.96ii.74.273.
Witness two lovely Girls, two lovely Boys) ..... 6.96iv.40.277.
Witness two lovely Girls, two lovely Boys) ..... 6.96iv.40.277.
Who, if two Wits on rival Themes contest, ... 6.98.59.285.
Now for two ages having snatch'd from fate ..... 6.108.3.312.
When now two Ages, he had snatch'd from Fate ..... 6.108.3A.312.
When now two Ages, he had scratch'd from Fate ..... 6.108.3B.312.
That two, my tallest Sons, might grace ..... 6.135.71.369.
Enjoy at least a Friend—or two: ..... 6.135.78.369.
Might have at least a Friend—or two: ..... 6.135.78A.369.
And now a word or two of Kings ..... 6.135.90A.370.
Two Trav'lers found an Oyster in their Way; ..... 6.145.2.388.
Two Generations now had past away, ... Il.1.333.103.
Two Ages o'er his native Realm he reign'd, ... Il.1.335.104.
To wait his Will two sacred Heralds stood, ... Il.1.420.107.
Two valiant Brothers rule th' undaunted Throng, ... Il.2.612.156.
Two pointed Spears he shook with gallant Grace, ... Il.3.31.189.
Two Lambs, devoted by your Country's Rite, ... Il.3.141.197.
Two Heralds now dispatch'd to *Troy,* invite ..... Il.3.161.198.
Yet two are wanting of the num'rous Train, ... Il.3.301.207.
Two Pow'rs Divine the Son of *Atreus* aid, ... Il.4.9.221.
Assembled Nations, set two Worlds in Arms? ..... Il.4.38.223.
Two Heroes led the secret Squadron on, ... Il.4.446.241.
Thus fell two Heroes; one the Pride of *Thrace,* ..... Il.4.624.250.
And two brave Leaders at an Instant slew; ..... Il.5.183.275.
Two Sons of *Priam* in one Chariot ride, ... Il.5.204.276.
O Friend! two Chiefs of Force immense I see, ... Il.5.302.281.
And two transport *Æneas* o'er the Plain. ..... Il.5.335.283.
Not two strong Men th' enormous Weight could raise, ... Il.5.371.284.
Two shining Spears are brandish'd in his Hands; ..... Il.5.605.297.
So two young Mountain Lions, nurs'd with Blood ..... Il.5.681.300.
And first two Leaders valiant *Hector* slew, ... Il.5.751.302.
Two brazen Rings of Work divine were roll'd. ..... Il.5.895.308.
Two Twins were near, bold beautiful and young, ... Il.6.27.325.
And two fair Infants crown'd his strong Embrace.) ..... Il.6.32.325.
Fierce in the Front he shakes two dazling Spears; ..... Il.6.131.330.
With two brave Sons and one fair Daughter bless'd; ..... Il.6.242.338.

TWO (CONTINUED)
Two hundred Horsemen, and two hundred Cars ..... Il.9.504.458.
Two hundred Horsemen, and two hundred Cars ..... Il.9.504.458.
A two-edg'd Faulchion *Thrasymed* the brave, ... Il.10.301.16.
Now, like two Lions panting for the Prey, ... Il.10.353.18.
As when two Teams of Mules divide the Green, ... Il.10.420.22.
As when two skilful Hounds the Lev'ret winde, ... Il.10.427.22.
Divides the Neck, and cuts the Nerves in two; ..... Il.10.525.26.
And in his Hands two steely Javelins wields, ... Il.11.55.37.
Rang'd in two Bands, their crooked Weapons wield, ... Il.11.90.38.
Two Sons of *Priam* next to Battel move, ... Il.11.137.41.
So two wild Boars outstrip the following Hounds, ... Il.11.421.53.
This Day, two Brothers shall thy Conquest grace, ... Il.11.543.58.
Fix'd as the Bar between two warring Pow'rs, ... Il.11.696.66.
Two Feet support it, and four Handles hold; ..... Il.11.775.69.
In sculptur'd Gold two Turtles seem to drink: ..... Il.11.777.69.
Two Chiefs from each, fell breathless to the Plain. ..... Il.11.883.75.
Of two fam'd Surgeons, *Podalirius* stands ..... Il.11.968.78.
To guard the Gates, two mighty Chiefs attend, ... Il.12.141.86.
As two tall Oaks, before the Wall they rise; ..... Il.12.145.86.
So two wild Boars spring furious from their Den, ... Il.12.163.87.
Gods! shall two Warriors only guard their Gates, ... Il.12.195.88.
And while two pointed Javelins arm his Hands, ... Il.12.355.94.
Two stubborn Swains with Blows dispute their Bounds; ..... Il.12.512.100.
As when two Scales are charg'd with doubtful Loads, ... Il.12.521.100.
Not two strong Men th' enormous Weight could raise, ... Il.12.539.101.
Gloomy as Night! and shakes two shiny Spears: ..... Il.12.554.102.
As two grim Lyons bear across the Lawn ..... Il.13.265.117.
Two, not the worst; nor ev'n this Succour vain. ..... Il.13.310.119.
From thence, two Javelins glitt'ring in his Hand, ... Il.13.315.120.
On his rais'd Arm by two strong Braces stay'd) ..... Il.13.515.131.
Above the rest, two tow'ring Chiefs appear, ... Il.13.632.136.
So when two lordly Bulls, with equal Toil, ... Il.13.879.147.
Of all those Heroes, two alone remain; ..... Il.13.982.152.
And two bold Brothers of *Hippotion's* Line: ..... Il.13.996.152.
When two fell Lyons from the Mountain come, ... Il.15.368.211.
Struck by an Arm unseen, it burst in two; ..... Il.15.545.217.
O'ermatch'd he falls; to two at once a Prey, ... Il.15.656.221.
Two Friends, two Bodies with one Soul inspir'd. ..... Il.16.267.249.
Two Friends, two Bodies with one Soul inspir'd. ..... Il.16.267.249.
In equal Arms two Sons of *Nestor* stand, ... Il.16.376.257.
And two bold Brothers of the *Lycian* Band: ..... Il.16.377.257.
Slain by two Brothers, thus two Brothers bleed, ... Il.16.388.258.
Slain by two Brothers, thus two Brothers bleed, ... Il.16.388.258.
And burst the Helm, and cleft the Head in two: ..... Il.16.503.262.
As when two Vulturs on the Mountain's Height ..... Il.16.522.263.
Two sounding Darts the *Lycian* Leader threw; ..... Il.16.572.266.
Then *Sleep* and *Death,* two *Twins* of winged Race, ... Il.16.831.275.
Two lordly Rulers of the Wood engage; ..... Il.16.916.279.
As when two Mules, along the rugged Road, ... Il.17.832.321.
Then, two by two, ascended up the Strand. ..... Il.18.90.327.
Then, two by two, ascended up the Strand. ..... Il.18.90.327.
The Monarch's Steps two Female Forms uphold, ... Il.18.487.345.
Two Cities radiant on the Shield appear, ... Il.18.567.350.
Two golden Talents lay amidst, in sight, ... Il.18.589.351.
Two mighty Hosts a leaguer'd town embrace, ... Il.18.593.351.
Two Spies at distance lurk, and watchful seem ..... Il.18.605.352.
And Steers slow-moving, and two Shepherd Swains; ..... Il.18.608.352.
Two Lions rushing from the Wood appear'd; ..... Il.18.671.356.
Two active Tumblers in the Center bound; ..... Il.18.698.357.
For when two Heroes, thus deriv'd, contend, ... Il.20.250.404.
The two remaining Sons the Line divide: ..... Il.20.282.406.
Thro' two strong Plates the Point is Passage held, ... Il.20.316.407.
No two of Earth's degen'rate Sons could raise. ..... Il.20.338.407.
Two Sons (alas, unhappy Sons) she bore, ... Il.21.100.426.
And shook two Spears, advancing from the Flood; ..... Il.21.162.428.
Two, while I speak, my Eyes in vain explore, ... Il.22.63.455.
Two from one Mother sprung, my *Polydore,* ..... Il.22.64.455.
Where two fam'd Fountains burst the parted Ground; ..... Il.22.196.463.
Fall two, selected to attend their Lord. ..... Il.23.213.498.
And a large Vase, where two bright Handles rise, ... Il.23.331.503.
Two golden Talents for the fourth were plac'd; ..... Il.23.337.503.
Two Heroes equal to this hardy Fight; ..... Il.23.760.520.
Like two strong Rafters which the Builder forms ..... Il.23.826.522.
These two-edg'd Axes, terrible in War; ..... Il.23.1015.529.
Two Tripods next and twice two Chargers shine, ... Il.24.285.548.
Two Tripods next and twice two Chargers shine, ... Il.24.285.548.
(Two wretched Suppliants) and for Mercy call? ..... Il.24.440.554.
Two Urns by *Jove's* high Throne have ever stood, ... Il.24.663.564.
Two splendid Mantles, and a Carpet spread, ... Il.24.728.568.
But two the Goddess, twelve the Queen enjoy'd; ..... Il.24.765.569.
Those boasted twelve th' avenging two destroy'd. ..... Il.24.766.569.
A two-edg'd faulchion threaten'd by his side, ... Od.2.6.60.
Two Dogs, a faithful guard, attend behind; ..... Od.2.14.60.
With that, two Eagles from a mountain's height ..... Od.2.171.70.
(Leave only two the gally to attend) ..... Od.3.538.113.
Full on his neck, and cut the nerves in two. ..... Od.3.571.115.
Two sprightly youths to form the bounding dance. ..... Od.4.26.121.
Two youths approach, whose semblant features prove ..... Od.4.33.121.
And two fair crescents of translucent horn ..... Od.4.107.125.
Two lavers from the richest ore refin'd, ... Od.4.173.128.
Two, foremost in the roll of *Mars* renown'd, ... Od.4.667.150.
The doom decreed of those disastrous Two ..... Od.4.745.153.
Then fill'd two goat-skins with her hands divine, ... Od.5.337.188.
And now two nights, and now two days were past, ... Od.5.496.196.
And now two nights, and now two days were past, ... Od.5.496.196.
There grew two Olives, closest of the grove, ... Od.5.616.201.
Two nymphs the portals guard, each nymph a Grace. ..... Od.6.24.204.
The jutting land two ample bays divides; ..... Od.6.313.226.
Two rows of stately dogs, on either hand, ... Od.7.118.240.
Two plenteous fountains the whole prospect crown'd; ..... Od.7.169.244.
Two beeves, twelve fatlings from the flock they bring ..... Od.8.53.264.
Two tedious days and two long nights we lay, ... Od.9.83.306.
Two tedious days and two long nights we lay, ... Od.9.83.306.
Snatch'd two, unhappy! of my martial band; ..... Od.9.343.320.
Two more he snatches, murders, and devours. ..... Od.9.369.321.

TWO (CONTINUED)
Next seiz'd two wretches more, and headlong cast, ... Od.9.404.322.
The midmost bore a man; the outward two ..... Od.9.509.327.
That done, two chosen heralds strait attend ..... Od.10.63.342.
Two with our herald thither we command, ... Od.10.115.346.
But two rush'd out, and to the navy flew. ..... Od.10.134.347.
Spent and o'erwatch'd. Two days and nights roll'd on, ... Od.10.167.348.
Two brother heroes shall from thee be born; ..... Od.11.300.396.
Jove's dread vicegerents, in two future Kings; ..... Od.11.310.397.
Two rav'nous vultures furious for their food ..... Od.11.711.421.
High o'er the main two Rocks exalt their brow, ... Od.12.71.433.
Two sister Goddesses possess the plain, ... Od.12.166.440.
Two glitt'ring javelins lighten in my hand; ..... Od.12.271.445.
Two craggy rocks projecting to the main, ... Od.13.118.7.
Two marble doors unfold on either side; ..... Od.13.133.8.
Of two, his cutlace launch'd the spouting blood; ..... Od.14.87.40.
Than when two friends, alone, in peaceful place ..... Od.14.222.46.
Two equal tribes this fertile land divide, ... Od.15.452.92.
Where two fair cities rise with equal pride, ... Od.15.453.92.
Two sew'rs from day to day the revels wait, ... Od.16.274.118.
Two dogs behind, a faithful guard, await: ..... Od.17.73.136.
Two grooms attend him. With an envious look ..... Od.17.248.143.
Two portals firm the various phantoms keep: ..... Od.19.657.228.
Two dogs of chace, a lion-hearted guard, ... Od.20.182.242.
Two grooms assistant bore the victims bound; ..... Od.20.221.244.
A two-edg'd faulchion and a shining spear, ... Od.21.366.277.
Two hundred oxen ev'ry Prince shall pay: ..... Od.22.69.290.
And now his hands two beamy jav'lins wield; ..... Od.22.139.293.
From the dire scene th' exempted two withdraw, ... Od.22.418.308.
Ere the fair Mischief set two worlds in arms, ... Od.23.232.334.

TWO-EDG'D
A two-edg'd Weapon from her shining Case; ..... 2.RL3.128.177.
A two-edg'd Faulchion *Thrasymed* the brave, ... Il.10.301.16.
These two-edg'd Axes, terrible in War; ..... Il.23.1015.529.
A two-edg'd faulchion threaten'd by his side, ... Od.2.6.60.
A two-edg'd faulchion and a shining spear, ... Od.21.366.277.

TWOU'D
'Twou'd burst ev'n *Heraclitus* with the Spleen, ... 4.JD4.236.45.

TWOULD
"Odious! in woollen! 'twould a Saint provoke, ... 3.Ep1.242.36.
I can't but think 'twould sound more clever, ... 4.HS6.11.251.

TWYLIGHT
And twylight gray her evening shade extends. ..... Od.3.422.107.

TY'D
Seiz'd and ty'd down to judge, how wretched I! ..... 4.Arbu.33.98.
Hence Bards, like Proteus long in vain ty'd down, ... 5.DunB1.37.272.
And dropt their Anchors, and the Pinnace ty'd. ..... Il.1.569.115.
Th' embroider'd Sandals on his Feet were ty'd, ... Il.2.55.129.
A radiant Baldric, o'er his Shoulder ty'd, ... Il.3.415.212.
That ty'd his Helmet, dragg'd the Chief along. ..... Il.3.458.214.
There ty'd, they rest in high Celestial Stalls; ..... Il.8.538.422.
A radiant Baldrick, o'er his Shoulder ty'd. ..... Il.11.39.36.
Lay panting. Thus an Oxe, in Fetters ty'd, ... Il.13.721.139.
Her artful Hands the radiant Tresses ty'd; ..... Il.14.204.170.
The fourfold Buckler o'er his Shoulder ty'd; ..... Il.15.565.218.
The brazen Sword a various Baldrick ty'd, ... Il.19.400.388.
Their fiery Mouths resplendent Bridles ty'd, ... Il.19.429.389.
Then ceas'd for ever, by the *Furies* ty'd, ... Il.19.464.391.
Err'd from the Dove, yet cut the Cord that ty'd: ..... Il.23.1025.529.
And close beneath the gather'd Ends were ty'd. ..... Il.24.340.550.
These, three and three, with osier bands we ty'd, ... Od.9.507.326.
The bloody spear, his gather'd feet I ty'd ..... Od.10.192.349.
Or swear that oath by which the Gods are ty'd, ... Od.10.408.364.
His weighty faulchion o'er his shoulder ty'd: ..... Od.14.596.66.
And cast their anchors, and the cables ty'd: ..... Od.15.538.96.
So drawn aloft, athwart the column ty'd, ... Od.22.209.297.

TYBER
Streets pav'd with Heroes, Tyber choak'd with Gods! ..... 5.DunA3.100.158.
Streets pav'd with Heroes, Tyber choak'd with Gods: ..... 5.DunB3.108.325.
Or Tyber, now no longer Roman, rolls, ... 5.DunB4.299.373.

TYBER'S
Tho' *Tyber's* Streams immortal *Rome* behold, ... 1.W-F.357.185.

TYBURN'S
Hence hymning Tyburn's elegiac Lay, ... 5.DunA1.39.O64.
Hence hymning Tyburn's elegiac lines, ... 5.DunB1.41.273.

TYCHIUS
(The Work of *Tychius,* who in *Hylè* dwell'd, ... Il.7.269.377.

TYDCOMB
'Are large and wide; *Tydcomb* and I assure ye. ..... 6.13.25.39.
To *Tydcomb* eke, ... 6.13.27.40.

TYDCOMBE
Tydcombe take Oaths on the Communion; ..... 6.10.46.26.

TYDE
See TIDE.
One Tyde of Glory, one unclouded Blaze, ... 1.Mes.102.122.
Project long Shadows o'er the Chrystal Tyde. ..... 1.W-F.376.187.
Whole Nations enter with each swelling Tyde, ... 1.W-F.399.191.
Then Ships of uncouth Form shall stem the Tyde, ... 1.W-F.403.191.
Bursts out, resistless, with a thundring Tyde! ..... 1.EOC.630.310.
Hippomedon repell'd the hostile Tyde? ..... 1.TrSt.64.413.
While *China's* Earth receives the smoking Tyde. ..... 2.RL3.110.176.
And *China's* Earth receives the smoking Tyde. ..... 2.RL3.110A.176.
And love's warm tyde for ever stopt in thee. ..... 2.ElAb.258Z2.340.
And win my way by yielding to the tyde. ..... 4.1HE1.34.281.

TYDE (CONTINUED)

In ev'ry Town, where *Thamis* rolls his Tyde,	6.14ii.1.43.
Or *China's* Earth receive the sable Tyde;	6.82i.4.229.
Now here, now there, the Tyde of Combate flows;	Il.6.4.322.
And turn the Tyde of Conflict on the Foe:	Il.6.130.330.
Why sunk I not beneath the whelming Tyde,	Il.6.438.348.
The Dart a Tyde of spouting Gore pursu'd,	Il.11.576.60.
Rag'd on the left, and rul'd the Tyde of War:	Il.11.621.61.
A Tyde of *Trojans* flows, and fills the Place;	Il.12.560.102.
Their Force embody'd, in a Tyde they pour;	Il.13.422.126.
Life's purple Tyde, impetuous, gush'd away.	Il.13.557.133.
With such a Tyde superior Virtue sway'd,	Il.13.849.146.
Where gentle *Xanthus* rolls his easy Tyde,	Il.14.508.188.
And ev'ry Ship sustain'd an equal Tyde.	Il.15.481.216.
And slaughter'd Heroes swell the dreadful Tyde.	Il.15.867.230.
The Tyde of *Trojans* urge their desp'rate Course,	Il.16.465.260.
And the warm Purple circled on the Tyde.	Il.21.27.422.
On this, rough *Auster* drove th' impetuous tyde:	Od.3.377.104.
And gushing mouth, effus'd the briny tyde.	Od.5.412.192.
His head, and cast it on the rolling tide.	Od.5.591.201.
To the calm current of the secret tyde;	Od.6.252.222.
Strong was the tyde, which by the northern blast	Od.9.91.306.
With heavy hearts we labour thro' the tyde,	Od.9.117.308.
The strong concussion on the heaving tyde	Od.9.571.330.
While the wing'd vessel flew along the tyde:	Od.11.8.379.
Wild with despair, I shed a copious tyde	Od.11.251.394.
And o'er the pavement floats the dreadful tyde—	Od.11.524.409.
Thus in a tyde of tears our sorrows flow,	Od.11.573.411.
And guard thy various passage thro' the tyde.	Od.12.70.433.
Wing'd her fleet sail, and push'd her o'er the tyde.	Od.12.86.436.
Her bosom terribly o'erlooks the tyde.	Od.12.116.437.
Thrice in dire thunders she refunds the tyde.	Od.12.132.438.
When the tyde rushes from her rumbling caves	Od.12.282.446.
To dash th' offenders in the whelming tyde.	Od.12.457.453.
The tyde of flowing tears a-while suppress;	Od.18.205.177.
Her awful voice detain'd the headlong tyde.	Od.24.613.377.

TYDES

His swelling Waters, and alternate Tydes;	1.W-F.334.182.
Tho' foaming *Hermus* swells with Tydes of Gold,	1.W-F.358.185.
His wandring Stream, and thro' the briny Tydes,	1.TrSt.384.426.
The Sun-beams trembling on the floating Tydes,	2.RL2.48.162.
Roll all their tydes, then back their circles bring;	5.DunA3.48.154.
Not all the golden Tydes of Wealth that crown	Il.9.498.457.
And where low Walls confine the beating Tydes	Il.13.855.146.
Now on the Fleet the Tydes of *Trojans* drove,	Il.15.712.223.
And swift *Dynamene*, now cut the Tydes:	Il.18.57.326.
The floating Tydes the bloody Carcass lave,	Il.21.219.430.
Ere *Greece* assembled stem'd the tydes to *Troy*;	Od.1.272.46.
There, poiz'd a while above the bounding tydes,	Od.5.473.195.
The refluent tydes, and plunge him in the deep.	Od.5.549.198.
Detains the rushing current of his tydes,	Od.5.577.200.
Arriving then, where tilting on the tydes	Od.15.507.94.
And whelms th' offenders in the roaring tydes:	Od.23.358.342.

TYDEUS

The Rage of *Tydeus*, or the Prophet's Fate?	1.TrSt.62.412.
The Rage of *Tydeus*, or the Prophet's Fate?	1.TrSt.63.412.
The raging *Tydeus*, or the Prophet's Fate?	1.TrSt.62A.412.
Lo hapless *Tydeus*, whose ill-fated Hand	1.TrSt.555.433.
The noble *Tydeus* stands confess'd, and known	1.TrSt.792.443.
Oh Son of *Tydeus!* (He, whose Strength could tame	Il.4.422.240.
Such *Tydeus* was, and such his martial Fire;	Il.4.450.241.
O Son of *Tydeus*, cease! be wise and see	Il.5.533.294.
For *Tydeus* left me young, when *Thebè's* Wall	Il.6.277.340.
Rise, Son of *Tydeus!* to the brave and strong	Il.10.180.9.
Great Queen of Arms, whose Favour *Tydeus* won,	Il.10.337.18.
While unresolv'd the Son of *Tydeus* stands,	Il.10.592.28.
And who to *Tydeus* owes his noble Line.	Il.14.38.159.
A Youth, who from the mighty *Tydeus* springs,	Il.14.124.163.
Such *Tydeus* was, the foremost once in Fame!	Il.14.141.164.

TYDEUS'

Next came *Idomeneus* and *Tydeus'* Son,	Il.2.482.149.
Tydeus' and *Atreus'* Sons their Points have found,	Il.5.260.279.
Degen'rate Prince! and not of *Tydeus'* Kind,	Il.5.998.314.
Then threw the Force of *Tydeus'* warlike Son;	Il.5.1048.316.
When daring *Glaucus* and great *Tydeus'* Son	Il.6.148.333.
(Reply'd the Chief) can *Tydeus'* Son enquire?	Il.6.180.334.
From *Tydeus'* Shoulders strip the costly Load,	Il.8.236.409.
A pensive Scene! 'till *Tydeus'* warlike Son	Il.9.41.433.
Saw *Tydeus'* Son with heav'nly Succour blest,	Il.10.604.29.
By *Tydeus'* Lance *Agastrophus* was slain,	Il.11.437.53.
No longer flames the Lance of *Tydeus'* Son;	Il.16.101.239.
Fierce, at the Word, uprose great *Tydeus'* Son,	Il.23.957.527.

TYDIDES

Here fierce *Tydides* wounds the *Cyprian* Queen;	2.TemF.189.271.
But chief *Tydides* bore the Sov'reign Sway;	Il.2.684.159.
He said, and pass'd where great *Tydides* lay,	Il.4.418.240.
To him *Tydides* thus. My Friend forbear,	Il.4.466.242.
Of arm'd *Tydides* rushing to the War.	Il.4.477.242.
But *Pallas* now *Tydides* Soul inspires,	Il.5.1.263.
These from their Steeds, *Tydides* on the Plain.	Il.5.20.266.
Not so, *Tydides*, flew thy Lance in vain,	Il.5.25.266.
In ev'ry Quarter fierce *Tydides* rag'd,	Il.5.111.272.
So rag'd *Tydides*, boundless in his Ire,	Il.5.124.273.
Thus pray'd *Tydides*, and *Minerva* heard,	Il.5.154.274.
Not with less Fury stern *Tydides* flew,	Il.5.182.275.
Who thus, alarm'd, to great *Tydides* cry'd.	Il.5.301.281.
Nor was *Tydides* born to tremble here.	Il.5.313.281.
Then fierce *Tydides* stoops; and from the Fields	Il.5.369.284.
And follow'd where *Tydides* swept the Plain.	Il.5.406.286.
Tydides thus. The Goddess, seiz'd with Dread,	Il.5.439.289.
And shew'd the Wound by fierce *Tydides* giv'n,	Il.5.451.289.
The fierce *Tydides* charg'd his *Dardan* Foe:	Il.5.524.294.

TYDIDES (CONTINUED)

Tydides paus'd amidst his full Carrier;	Il.5.732.302.
Amaz'd no less the great *Tydides* stands;	Il.5.740.302.
(A warlike Circle) round *Tydides* stand.	Il.5.973.313.
While near *Tydides* stood th' *Athenian* Maid:	Il.5.987.314.
Then thus *Minerva*. Brave *Tydides* hear!	Il.5.1020.315.
Stretch'd where he fell, and at *Tydides* flies.	Il.5.1041.316.
To stern *Tydides* now he falls a Prey,	Il.6.21.325.
Near as they drew, *Tydides* thus began.	Il.6.151.333.
That Pass *Tydides*, *Ajax* strive to gain,	Il.6.554.354.
Then bold *Tydides*, great in Arms, appear'd;	Il.7.199.373.
This Task let *Ajax* or *Tydides* prove,	Il.7.217.375.
At length *Tydides* rose, and rising spoke.	Il.7.475.388.
But bold *Tydides* to the Rescue goes,	Il.8.125.404.
Fierce he drove on; *Tydides* whirl'd his Spear.	Il.8.150.405.
O rev'rend Prince! (*Tydides* thus replies)	Il.8.177.406.
Tydides first, of all the *Grecian* Force,	Il.8.305.412.
Then, then shall *Hector* and *Tydides* prove,	Il.8.661.427.
Attend the stern Reply. *Tydides* broke	Il.9.814.473.
Tydides spoke—The Man you seek, is here.	Il.10.260.13.
And ample Buckler, to *Tydides* gave:	Il.10.302.16.
When brave *Tydides* stopp'd; a gen'rous Thought	Il.10.435.23.
To this *Tydides*, with a gloomy Frown:	Il.10.516.26.
Now, brave *Tydides!* now thy Courage try,	Il.10.554.27.
Ulysses stopp'd; to him *Tydides* bore	Il.10.620.29.
The great *Tydides* and *Ulysses* bear,	Il.10.630.30.
Whose hostile King the brave *Tydides* slew;	Il.10.657.31.
But wise *Ulysses* call'd *Tydides* forth,	Il.11.405.52.
The stern *Tydides* strips their shining Arms.	Il.11.432.53.
Tydides follow'd to regain his Lance;	Il.11.461.54.
Tydides mounts, and to the Navy speeds.	Il.11.508.56.
Tydides cut him short, and thus began.	Il.14.120.163.
Eurypylus, *Tydides*, *Artreus'* Son,	Il.16.35.236.
Tydides and *Ulysses* first appear,	Il.19.51.374.
With equal Ardor bold *Tydides* swell'd	Il.23.359.504.
But angry *Phœbus* to *Tydides* flies ,	Il.23.462.508.
Before him far the glad *Tydides* flies;	Il.23.478.509.
Now Victor at the Goal *Tydides* stands,	Il.23.589.513.
(Since great *Tydides* bears the first away)	Il.23.615.514.
Him great *Tydides* urges to contend,	Il.23.789.521.
Yet still the Victor's Due *Tydides* gains,	Il.23.971.527.
With us *Tydides* fear'd, and urg'd his haste:	Od.3.201.95.

TYDIDES'

Tho' now determin'd by *Tydides'* Spear.	Il.5.195.276.
And far avert *Tydides'* wastful Ire,	Il.6.119.330.
He spoke, and Transport fill'd *Tydides'* Heart;	Il.6.261.339.
And far avert *Tydides'* wastful Ire,	Il.6.346.343.
Break thou *Tydides'* Spear, and let him fall	Il.6.380.345.
Full in *Tydides'* Face the Light'ning flew;	Il.8.163.405.
And Voice to Voice resounds *Tydides'* Praise.	Il.9.70.435.
Tydides' Faulchion fix'd him to the Ground.	Il.10.577.28.
Strait to *Tydides'* high Pavilion born,	Il.10.666.31.
If any God assist *Tydides'* Hand.	Il.11.470.55.
Thy impious Hand *Tydides'* Jav'lin bore,	Il.21.462.440.
Not that we hope to match *Tydides'* Horse,	Il.23.484.509.
Tydides' vessels touch'd the wish'd-for shore:	Od.3.220.96.
But most *Tydides'* and my heart alarm'd:	Od.4.382.139.

TYDINGS

For sadder Tydings never touch'd thy Ear;	Il.17.772.318.
Sad Tydings, Son of *Peleus!* thou must hear;	Il.18.21.324.
What tydings, friend? what speaks the voice of fame?	Od.16.483.130.

TYE

See TIE.

Tye up the knocker, say I'm sick, I'm dead,	4.Arbu.2.96.
Oh source of ev'ry social tye,	6.51ii.25.153.
Where Ribbans wave upon the tye,	6.61.38.182.
Indissolubly strong, the fatal Tye	Il.13.453.128.
To the tall Top a milk-white Dove they tye,	Il.23.1012.529.
By the soft tye and sacred name of friend!	Od.11.82.385.

TYES

All Tyes dissolv'd, and ev'ry Sin forgiv'n,	4.EpS1.94.305.
Secures the court, and with a cable tyes	Od.21.422.280.

TYGER

And Boys in flow'ry Bands the Tyger lead;	1.Mes.78.119.

TYGER'S

Thy Sexe's Tyrant, with a Tyger's Heart?	Il.21.560.445.

TYGERS

Wolves gave thee suck, and savage Tygers fed.	1.PAu.90.86.
More fell than Tygers on the *Lybian* Plain;	1.PAu.90A.86.

TYNDAR'S

Leda the fair, the god-like *Tyndar's* bride,	Od.11.366.400.

TYNDARUS

Not such, oh *Tyndarus!* thy daughter's deed,	Od.24.226.358.

TYP'D

With tape-typ'd curtains, never meant to draw,	3.Ep3.302.118.

TYPE

"But, where each Science lifts its modern Type,	5.DunA3.191.172.
Round him, each *Science* by its modern type	5.DunA3.191z1.172.
"But, where each Science lifts its modern type,	5.DunB3.195.329.
A Type of Paradise, the Rural Scene!	6.17iii.39.58.

TYPHOEUS

And fires *Typhœus* with redoubled Blows,	Il.2.953.169.

TYPHON
Where *Typhon*, prest beneath the burning Load, ... Il.2.954.169.

TYRANNICK
Th' Oppressor rul'd Tyrannick where he *durst*, ... 1.W-F.74.157.

TYRANNY
With *Tyranny*, then *Superstitition* join'd, ... 1.EOC.687.317.
Then shar'd the Tyranny, then lent it aid, ... 3.EOM3.247.117.
Then shar'd the Tyranny, and lent it aid, ... 3.EOM3.247A.117.
Oppress'd with Argumental Tyranny, ... 6.8.17.18.
A love to peace, and hate of tyranny; .... 6.57.10.169.
Earth to her Entrails feels not Tyranny. .... 6.142.6Z2.382.
Earth to her entrails feels not Tyranny. .... 6.142.8Z2.383.

TYRANT
And Hell's grim Tyrant feel th'eternal Wound. .... 1.Mes.48.117.
Before him Death, the grisly Tyrant, flies; .... 1.Mes.45Z1.117.
And ev'n the Elements a Tyrant sway'd? .... 1.W-F.52.153.
Like some *fierce Tyrant* in *Old Tapestry!* .... 1.EOC.587.307.
What Joys, oh Tyrant! swell'd thy Soul that Day, ... 1.TrSt.220.419.
How all the Tyrant in his Face appears! .... 1.TrSt.254.421.
And reign'd the short-liv'd Tyrant of his Breast; .... 2.ChJM.231.25.
Had some fierce Tyrant in her stead been found, ... 2.ChJM.436.36.
The *Club's* black Tyrant first her Victim dy'd, ... 2.RL3.69.173.
Be Man the Wit and Tyrant of the whole: .... 3.EOM3.50.97.
Nature that Tyrant checks; he only knows, ... 3.EOM3.51.97.
'Till Superstition taught the tyrant awe, ... 3.EOM3.246.117.
No Bandit fierce, no Tyrant mad with pride, ... 3.EOM4.41.131.
A Tyrant to the wife his heart approves; .... 3.Ep1.202.32.
That buys your sex a Tyrant o'er itself. .... 3.Ep2.288A.73.
Which buys your sex a Tyrant o'er itself. .... 3.Ep2.288.73.
I wish you joy, Sir, of a Tyrant gone; .... 4.2HE2.305.187.
And was, besides, a Tyrant to his Wife. .... 4.EpS2.135.321.
Tyrant supreme! shall three Estates command, ... 5.DunB4.603.403.
Who flies the tyrant to relieve the slave? .... 6.4i.6.9.
But the last Tyrant ever proves the worst. .... 6.19.40.63.
'Till some new Tyrant lifts his purple hand, ... 6.51i.23.152.
Still, when the lust of tyrant pow'r succeeds, ... 6.51i.31.152.
OH tyrant Love! hast thou possest .... 6.51ii.1.152.
Maul the *French* Tyrant, or pull down the Pope! .... 6.128.18.356.
O Tyrant, arm'd with Insolence and Pride! .... Il.1.194.96.
A Prize as small, O Tyrant! match'd with thine, ... Il.1.215.97.
Tyrant, I well deserv'd thy galling Chain, ... Il.1.388.106.
That lawless Tyrant whose Commands you bear; .... Il.1.443.108.
This mighty Tyrant were no Tyrant long. .... Il.2.301.142.
This mighty Tyrant were no Tyrant long. .... Il.2.301.142.
Shall then, O Tyrant of th' Æthereal Reign! .... Il.4.35.222.
The Tyrant feasting with his Chiefs he found, ... Il.4.440.241.
What hast thou said, Oh Tyrant of the Skies! .... Il.8.575.424.
One only valu'd Gift your Tyrant gave, ... Il.9.481.456.
Enough thou know'st the Tyrant of the Skies, ... Il.15.99.200.
Report to yon' mad Tyrant of the Main. .... Il.15.181.203.
What Claim was here the Tyrant of the Sky? .... Il.15.219.205.
I made him Tyrant; gave him Pow'r to wrong .... Il.16.74.238.
Thus having said, the Tyrant of the Sea .... Il.20.172.400.
Thy Sexe's Tyrant, with a Tyger's Heart? .... Il.21.560.445.
Or in their tyrant-Minions vest the pow'r: .... Od.4.919.161.
To *Neptune's* wrath, stern Tyrant of the Seas, ... Od.5.431.193.
The tempest's Lord, and tyrant of the wind; .... Od.10.22.340.
A tyrant, fiercest of the tyrant kind, ... Od.18.97.171.
A tyrant, fiercest of the tyrant kind, ... Od.18.97.171.
A dreaded tyrant o'er the bestial train! .... Od.18.127.172.
Sudden the tyrant of the skies return'd: .... Od.19.638.227.
The tyrant, not the father of the skies! .... Od.20.252.245.

TYRANT-MINIONS
Or in their tyrant-Minions vest the pow'r: .... Od.4.919.161.

TYRANT'S
Before the sleepless Tyrant's guarded Gate; .... 1.TrSt.205.419.
Before the wakeful Tyrant's guarded Gate; .... 1.TrSt.205A.419.
Yet Harbours Vengeance for the Tyrant's Feast. .... 1.TrSt.347.424.
These pleasing Orders to the Tyrant's Ear; .... 1.TrSt.422.427.
The dagger wont to pierce the Tyrant's breast; .... 5.DunB4.38.344.
I hate Alliance with a Tyrant's Race. .... Il.9.515.458.
Well hast thou spoke; but at the Tyrant's Name, ... Il.9.759.471.
The Tyrant's Pride lies rooted in my Breast. .... Il.16.71.238.

TYRANTS
Both doom'd alike for sportive Tyrants bled, ... 1.W-F.59.154.
And Pykes, the Tyrants of the watry Plains. .... 1.W-F.146.163.
And softly curse the Tyrants whom they fear. .... 1.TrSt.229.420.
Where exil'd Tyrants still by turns command! .... 1.TrSt.242.420.
Of Foreign Tyrants, and of Nymphs at home; .... 2.RL3.6.169.
Not Tyrants fierce that unrepenting die, ... 2.RL4.7.183.
There sleep forgot, with mighty Tyrants gone, ... 2.TemF.352.280.
And, form'd like tyrants, tyrants would believe. .... 3.EOM3.260.118.
And, form'd like tyrants, tyrants would believe. .... 3.EOM3.260.118.
Where Madness fights for Tyrants, or for gain. .... 3.EOM4.154A.142.
Where Folly fights for Tyrants, or for gain. .... 3.EOM4.154B.142.
Beauties, like Tyrants, old and friendless grown, ... 3.Ep2.227.68.
Suits Tyrants, Plunderers, but suits not me. .... 4.JD4.195.43.
And Asia's Tyrants tremble at your Throne— .... 4.2HE1.403.229.
Marriage may all those petty Tyrants chace, ... 6.19.37.63.
Tyrants no more their savage nature kept, ... 6.32.7.96.
(That Trick of Tyrants) may be born by Slaves. .... Il.1.162.95.
That worst of Tyrants, an usurping Crowd. .... Il.2.242.139.
And Earth's proud Tyrants low in Ashes laid. .... Il.4.359.238.
Proud Tyrants humbles, and whole Hosts o'erturns. .... Il.5.925.310.
Proud Tyrants humbles, and whole Hosts o'erturns. .... Il.8.475.419.
And lay the Strength of Tyrants on the Ground: .... Il.13.389.124.
Proud Tyrants humbles, and whole hosts o'erturns. .... Od.1.131.38.
Let Tyrants govern with an iron rod, ... Od.2.263.74.

TYRAWLEY
To all defects, *Ty[rawle]y* not so blind: .... 4.HAdv.121.85*.

TYRAWLEY'S
K[innoul]l's lewd Cargo, or Ty[rawle]y's Crew, ... 4.1HE6.121.245.

TYRCONNEL
When did *Ty[rconne]l* hurt you with his Wit? .... 4.EpS2.159A.322.

TYRCONNEL'S
The Honey dropping from *Ty[rconne]l's* tongue, ... 4.EpS1.67A.302.

TYRIAN
The bright-ey'd Perch with Fins of *Tyrian* Dye, ... 1.W-F.142.163.
In glowing colours with the *Tyrian* dye. .... 1.TrFD.24.387.
Be struck with bright Brocade, or Tyrian Dye, ... 4.1HE6.32.239.
The shining Whiteness and the *Tyrian* Dye. .... Il.4.175.229.
That rich with *Tyrian* Dye refulgent glow'd. .... Il.6.274.340.
With *Helen* touching on the *Tyrian* Shore. .... Il.6.363.344.
New-ting'd with *Tyrian* Dye: In Dust below, ... Il.15.634.220.
Whence *Tyrian* Sailors did the Prize transport, ... Il.23.869.524.

TYRINTHÈ'S
Whom strong *Tyrinthè's* lofty Walls surround, ... Il.2.678.159.

TYRO
Tho' *Tyro* nor *Mycene* match her name, ... Od.2.137.67.
Tyro began: whom great *Salmoneus* bred; .... Od.11.281.395.

TYTHE
Tythe-Pig, and mortuary *Guinea:* .... 6.39.6.110.

TYTHE-PIG
Tythe-Pig, and mortuary *Guinea:* .... 6.39.6.110.

U
The *Vowels, U, O, I, E, A,* .... 6.30.2.85.
Still to keep Company with *U;* .... 6.30.16.86.

UCALEGON
Antenor grave, and sage *Ucalegon,* .... Il.3.197.200.

UDDER
And then permits their udder to the lambs. .... Od.9.403.322.

UDDER'D
Big-udder'd ewes, and goats of female kind, ... Od.9.282.318.

UDDERS
How, scarce, my ewes their strutting udders bear; .... 1.TrPA.83.368.
"With cow-like-udders, and with ox-like eyes. .... 5.DunA2.156.120.
"With cow-like udders, and with ox-like eyes. .... 5.DunB2.164.303.
Of half their udders eases first the dams, ... Od.9.290.318.

UGLY
Was just not ugly, and was just not made; .... 3.Ep2.50.54.
'Tis an ugly envious Shrew, ... 6.70.10.201.
Was just not ugly, and was just not mad; .... 6.99.4.286.

ULYSSAEAN
Deaf to the mighty *Ulyssæan* name. .... Od.16.76.106.

ULYSSEAN
The feature of the *Ulyssean* race: .... Od.4.190.129.
But first the *Ulyssean* wealth survey: .... Od.19.336.210.

ULYSSES
Divine *Ulysses* was her Sacred Load, ... 1.TrUl.15.466.
Ulysses sleeping, on his Couch they bore, ... 1.TrUl.47.467.
Mean while *Ulysses* in his Country lay, ... 1.TrUl.53.467.
In what new Region is *Ulysses* tost? .... 1.TrUl.75.468.
O still the same *Ulysses!* she rejoin'd, ... 1.TrUl.166.471.
Ulysses was thy Care, Celestial Maid, ... 1.TrUl.193.472.
Not thus *Ulysses;* he decrees to prove .... 1.TrUl.216.473.
To you once more your own *Ulysses* bows, ... 1.TrUl.242.473.
Like that where once *Ulysses* held the Winds; .... 2.RL4.82.190.
"And (like *Ulysses*) visit Courts, and Men. .... 4.JD4.89A.33.
When wise *Ulysses,* from his native coast .... 6.15.1.51.
Or wise *Ulysses* see perform'd our Will, ... Il.1.188.96.
And sage *Ulysses* with the Conduct grac'd: .... Il.1.407.107.
In *Chrysa's* Port now sage *Ulysses* rode; .... Il.1.566.115.
Ulysses led to *Phœbus* sacred Fane; .... Il.1.573.115.
Ulysses, first in publick Cares, she found, ... Il.2.205.138.
Ulysses heard, nor uninspir'd obey'd. .... Il.2.220.138.
Ulysses or *Achilles* still his Theme; .... Il.2.269.140.
Fierce from his Seat, at this *Ulysses* springs, ... Il.2.302.142.
Ye Gods! what Wonders has *Ulysses* wrought? .... Il.2.333.143.
Then wise *Ulysses* in his Rank was plac'd; .... Il.2.484.150.
Ulysses follow'd thro' the watry Road, ... Il.2.765.162.
Ulysses seated, greater Rev'rence drew. .... Il.3.274.205.
But when *Ulysses* rose, in Thought profound, ... Il.3.279.207.
Slow they proceed: The sage *Ulysses* then .... Il.3.336.209.
Bold *Hector* and *Ulysses* now dispose .... Il.3.390.211.
And next *Ulysses,* with his Subject Bands. .... Il.4.383.239.
And fears *Ulysses,* skill'd in ev'ry Art? .... Il.4.391.239.
Ulysses heard; The Hero's Warmth o'erspread .... Il.4.402.240.
And *Leucus,* lov'd by wise *Ulysses,* slew. .... Il.4.564.248.
This saw *Ulysses,* and with Grief enrag'd .... Il.4.567.248.
And great *Ulysses,* bath'd in hostile Blood. .... Il.5.636.298.
Whose Fall *Ulysses* view'd, with Fury fir'd; .... Il.5.829.305.
And wise *Ulysses* clos'd the daring Band. .... Il.7.204.374.
He rush'd, and on *Ulysses* call'd aloud. .... Il.8.116.403.
Whither, oh whither does *Ulysses* run? .... Il.8.117.403.
Ulysses seeks the Ships, and shelters there. .... Il.8.124.404.
Much he advis'd them all, *Ulysses* most, ... Il.9.235.444.
To his high Tent; the great *Ulysses* leads. .... Il.9.256.445.

ULYSSES (CONTINUED)

Himself, oppos'd t' *Ulysses* full in sight, ... Il.9.285.448.
Not unperceiv'd; *Ulysses* crown'd with Wine ... Il.9.292.448.
Then thus the Goddess-born. *Ulysses*, hear ... Il.9.406.452.
Your King, *Ulysses*, may consult with you. ... Il.9.457.455.
And thus, impatient, to *Ulysses* spoke. ... Il.9.736.470.
The Chiefs return; divine *Ulysses* leads. ... Il.9.774.472.
Ulysses ceas'd: The great *Achaian* Host, ... Il.9.812.473.
Ulysses, Diomed we chiefly need; ... Il.10.123.7.
Ulysses, sudden as the Voice was sent, ... Il.10.158.9.
And great *Ulysses* wish'd, nor wish'd in vain. ... Il.10.274.14.
How can I doubt, while great *Ulysses* stands ... Il.10.285.14.
Next him *Ulysses* took a shining Sword, ... Il.10.307.16.
As from the Right she soar'd, *Ulysses* pray'd, ... Il.10.325.17.
Ulysses mark'd, and thus to *Diomed.* ... Il.10.404.21.
To whom *Ulysses* made this wise Reply; ... Il.10.453.23.
(*Ulysses*, with a scornful Smile, replies) ... Il.10.472.24.
Ulysses thus, and thus *Eumedes'* Son: ... Il.10.484.25.
These great *Ulysses* lifting to the Skies, ... Il.10.530.26.
The welcome Sight *Ulysses* first descries, ... Il.10.550.27.
Ulysses following, as his Part'ner slew, ... Il.10.570.28.
Ulysses now the snowy Steeds detains, ... Il.10.582.28.
Ulysses stopp'd; to him *Tydides* bore ... Il.10.620.29.
The great *Tydides* and *Ulysses* bear, ... Il.10.630.30.
High on the painted Stern *Ulysses* laid, ... Il.10.671.31.
But wise *Ulysses* call'd *Tydides* forth, ... Il.11.405.52.
Hypirochus by great *Ulysses* dies, ... Il.11.433.53.
Ulysses hastens with a trembling Heart, ... Il.11.505.56.
Now on the Field *Ulysses* stands alone, ... Il.11.509.56.
Ulysses reach'd him with the fatal Spear; ... Il.11.536.57.
O great *Ulysses*, much-enduring Man! ... Il.11.540.57.
The Wound not mortal wise *Ulysses* knew, ... Il.11.551.58.
Then thus *Ulysses*, gazing on the Slain. ... Il.11.564.59.
Heav'n owes *Ulysses* yet a longer Date. ... Il.11.567.59.
Ulysses thus, unconquer'd by his Pains, ... Il.11.604.61.
Ulysses, Agamemnon, Diomed<e>, ... Il.11.806.72.
I, and *Ulysses*, touch'd at *Pthia's* Port, ... Il.11.904.76.
Where the tall Fleet of great *Ulysses* lies, ... Il.11.938.77.
The King of Men, *Ulysses* the divine, ... Il.14.37.159.
Thus he. The sage *Ulysses* thus replies, ... Il.14.88.162.
And wise *Ulysses*, at the Navy groan ... Il.16.36.236.
Tydides and *Ulysses* first appear, ... Il.19.51.374.
Whate'er *Ulysses* promis'd at thy Tent: ... Il.19.140.377.
These to select, *Ulysses*, be thy Care: ... Il.19.192.379.
O first of *Greeks* (*Ulysses* thus rejoin'd) ... Il.19.215.381.
And now the Delegates *Ulysses* sent, ... Il.19.243.383.
Nestor, Idomeneus, Ulysses sage, ... Il.19.331.386.
When tow'r-like *Ajax* and *Ulysses* rose. ... Il.23.821.522.
Nor could *Ulysses*, for his Art renown'd, ... Il.23.834.522.
Thus to *Ulysses* spoke great *Telamon.* ... Il.23.839.523.
With matchless Strength; that time *Ulysses* found ... Il.23.843.523.
Ulysses following, on his Bosom lies; ... Il.23.846.523.
Ajax to lift, *Ulysses* next essays, ... Il.23.848.523.
Ulysses next; and he whose Speed surpast ... Il.23.883.524.
The next *Ulysses*, meas'ring Pace with Pace; ... Il.23.888.524.
And *Pallas*, not *Ulysses* won the Day. ... Il.23.920.525.
He to *Ulysses*, still more ag'd and wise; ... Il.23.928.526.
Ulysses, sole of all the victor train, ... Od.1.18.30.
For brave *Ulysses*, still by fate opprest. ... Od.1.62.33.
Whose visual orb *Ulysses* robb'd of light; ... Od.1.90.36.
That wise *Ulysses* to his native land ... Od.1.108.36.
For sure *Ulysses* in your look appears, ... Od.1.269.45.
If yet *Ulysses* views the light, forbear, ... Od.1.374.50.
With your *Ulysses* shar'd an equal doom! ... Od.1.454.54.
Whene'er *Ulysses* roams the realm of Night, ... Od.1.503.56.
By great *Ulysses* taught the path to fame; ... Od.2.24.61.
Since great Ulysses sought the *Phrygian* plains, ... Od.2.33.61.
"Tho' cold in death *Ulysses* breathes no more, ... Od.2.107.66.
While sad on foreign shores *Ulysses* treads, ... Od.2.151.69.
Ulysses comes, and death his steps attends. ... Od.2.192.71.
When great *Ulysses* sought the *Phrygian* shores ... Od.2.199.71.
Ulysses lies: oh wert thou lay'd as low! ... Od.2.214.72.
Should great *Ulysses* stern appear in arms, ... Od.2.281.74.
Torn from her breast, that hour, *Ulysses* dies. ... Od.2.284.75.
Born, the *Ulysses* of thy age to rise! ... Od.2.308.76.
The great *Ulysses* reach'd his native shore. ... Od.2.389.80.
'Till great *Ulysses* views his native land. ... Od.2.397.80.
To seek *Ulysses* thro' the wat'ry way. ... Od.2.405.80.
The great *Ulysses*; fam'd from shore to shore ... Od.3.102.91.
The wise, the good *Ulysses* claim'd thy care; ... Od.3.119.91.
Ulysses first and *Nestor* dis-agreed: ... Od.3.196.95.
When great *Ulysses* shall suppress these harms, ... Od.3.267.98.
Ulysses singly, or all *Greece* in arms. ... Od.3.268.98.
But oh! *Ulysses—deeper* than the rest ... Od.4.131.126.
Who bless'd *Ulysses* with a father's joy, ... Od.4.194.129.
Methinks *Ulysses* strikes my wond'ring eyes: ... Od.4.198.129.
Of cares, which in my cause *Ulysses* bore; ... Od.4.204.129.
Where my *Ulysses* and his race might reign, ... Od.4.237.130.
Ulysses strait with indignation fir'd, ... Od.4.389.139.
If e'er *Ulysses*, to reclaim your right, ... Od.4.441.140.
Ulysses soon shall re-assert his claim. ... Od.4.456.141.
Proclaims you from the sage *Ulysses* sprung. ... Od.4.832.158.
Ulysses let no partial favours fall, ... Od.4.920.161.
If e'er *Ulysses* to thy fane prefer'd ... Od.4.1007.164.
Of wise *Ulysses*, and his toils relates; ... Od.5.9.171.
If from your thoughts *Ulysses* you remove, ... Od.5.18.171.
'Tis *Jove's* decree *Ulysses* shall return: ... Od.5.41.172.
But sad *Ulysses* by himself apart, ... Od.5.103.177.
To seek *Ulysses*, pac'd along the sand. ... Od.5.192.180.
With sighs, *Ulysses* heard the words she spoke, ... Od.5.221.182.
Ulysses! (with a sigh she thus began) ... Od.5.257.184.
But ah *Ulysses!* wert thou giv'n to know ... Od.5.263.184.
Against *Ulysses* shall thy anger rise? ... Od.5.274.184.
Ulysses rob'd him in the cloak and vest. ... Od.5.294.185.
With beating heart *Ulysses* spreads his sails; ... Od.5.344.188.
So joys *Ulysses* at th' appearing shore; ... Od.5.511.197.

ULYSSES (CONTINUED)

To this calm port the glad *Ulysses* prest, ... Od.5.566.199.
Now parting from the stream, *Ulysses* found ... Od.5.594.201.
Beneath this covert, great *Ulysses* crept. ... Od.5.623.201.
Hid in dry foliage thus *Ulysses* lyes, ... Od.5.634.202.
The Goddess shot; *Ulysses* was her care. ... Od.6.20.204.
Wrapt in embow'ring shade, *Ulysses* lies, ... Od.6.130.213.
Wak'd by the shrilling sound, *Ulysses* rose, ... Od.6.137.213.
On what new region is *Ulysses* tost? ... Od.6.140.214.
Rough from the tossing surge *Ulysses* moves; ... Od.6.162.216.
'Till great *Ulysses* hail'd his native land. ... Od.6.394.230.
To town *Ulysses* took the winding way. ... Od.7.18.234.
Mean-while *Ulysses* at the Palace waits, ... Od.7.107.239.
Ulysses in the regal walls alone ... Od.7.311.251.
Heroe and King! (*Ulysses* thus reply'd) ... Od.7.389.255.
Of the high porch, *Ulysses* sleeps profound: ... Od.7.436.258.
That made *Ulysses* and *Achilles* foes: ... Od.8.72.266.
Touch'd at the song, *Ulysses* strait resign'd ... Od.8.79.266.
Again *Ulysses* veil'd his pensive head, ... Od.8.89.267.
To whom with sighs *Ulysses* gave reply: ... Od.8.167.271.
Inces'd *Ulysses* with a frown replies, ... Od.8.183.272.
The friendly voice *Ulysses* hears with joy; ... Od.8.228.274.
Ulysses gaz'd, astonish'd to survey ... Od.8.305.279.
Thus sung the Bard: *Ulysses* hears with joy, ... Od.8.403.285.
Then thus *Ulysses*; Happy King, whose name ... Od.8.417.286.
And blest be thou my friend, *Ulysses* cries, ... Od.8.447.287.
O royal maid, *Ulysses* strait returns, ... Od.8.503.289.
Then from the chine, *Ulysses* carves with art ... Od.8.519.290.
Thus to the Lyrist wise *Ulysses* said. ... Od.8.530.291.
How stern *Ulysses*, furious to destroy, ... Od.8.541.291.
Then thus *Ulysses*. Thou, whom first in sway ... Od.9.1.298.
Behold *Ulysses!* no ignoble name, ... Od.9.19.301.
Say 'twas *Ulysses*; 'twas his deed, declare, ... Od.9.589.330.
Ulysses, far in fighting fields renown'd, ... Od.9.591.330.
And nam'd *Ulysses* as the destin'd hand. ... Od.9.600.331.
Let not *Ulysses* breathe his native air, ... Od.9.621.332.
Ulysses here! what Dæmon cou'dst thou meet ... Od.10.71.342.
We went, *Ulysses!* (such was thy command) ... Od.10.295.357.
Ulysses? oh! thy threat'ning fury cease, ... Od.10.395.363.
Why sits *Ulysses* silent and apart? ... Od.10.445.365.
Of *Circe's* Palace, where *Ulysses* leads. ... Od.10.526.368.
Ulysses, taught by labours to be wise, ... Od.10.540.369.
Is this, *Ulysses*, our inglorious lot? ... Od.10.560.369.
Must sad *Ulysses* ever be delay'd? ... Od.10.571.370.
Divine *Ulysses!* asks no mortal guide. ... Od.10.599.372.
Weary of light, *Ulysses* here explores ... Od.11.126.387.
The direful wreck *Ulysses* scarce survives! ... Od.11.144.387.
Ulysses at his country scarce arrives! ... Od.11.145.387.
And owning her *Ulysses*, thus she speaks. ... Od.11.189.390.
In every land *Ulysses* finds a foe: ... Od.11.203.391.
To land *Ulysses* on his native shores. ... Od.11.413.404.
(*Ulysses* thus replies) a King in mind! ... Od.11.471.407.
O stay, oh pride of *Greece! Ulysses* stay! ... Od.12.222.442.
Yet safe return'd— *Ulysses* led the way. ... Od.12.251.444.
Lo! still the same *Ulysses* is your guide! ... Od.12.253.444.
Whatever toils the great *Ulysses* past, ... Od.13.5.1.
All, but *Ulysses*, heard with fix'd delight: ... Od.13.35.3.
So to *Ulysses* welcome sett the Sun. ... Od.13.44.3.
Ulysses sole with air majestic stands, ... Od.13.72.4.
Divine *Ulysses* was her sacred load, ... Od.13.106.6.
Ulysses sleeping on his couch they bore, ... Od.13.138.9.
Mean-while *Ulysses* in his country lay, ... Od.13.220.16.
In what new region is *Ulysses* tost? ... Od.13.242.17.
O still the same *Ulysses!* she rejoin'd, ... Od.13.333.23.
Ulysses was thy care, celestial maid! ... Od.13.360.24.
Not thus *Ulysses*; he decrees to prove ... Od.13.383.25.
To you once more your own *Ulysses* bows; ... Od.13.409.26.
The gold, the brass, the robes, *Ulysses* brought; ... Od.13.422.26.
To this *Ulysses*. Oh celestial maid! ... Od.13.437.27.
Ulysses found him, busied as he sate ... Od.14.7.35.
Soon as *Ulysses* near th' enclosure drew, ... Od.14.33.36.
The ready meal before *Ulysses* lay'd. ... Od.14.92.40.
That tells, the great *Ulysses* is no more. ... Od.14.112.41.
As lov'd *Ulysses* once more to embrace, ... Od.14.165.43.
Ulysses, friend! shall view his old abodes, ... Od.14.173.43.
His ancient realms *Ulysses* shall survey, ... Od.14.187.45.
Shall lov'd *Ulysses* hail this happy shore, ... Od.14.191.45.
How late *Ulysses* to the country came, ... Od.14.356.51.
That soon *Ulysses* wou'd return, declar'd, ... Od.14.369.53.
He swore, *Ulysses* on the coast of *Crete* ... Od.14.421.56.
If here *Ulysses* from his labours rest, ... Od.14.436.56.
To speed *Ulysses* to his native shore. ... Od.14.471.58.
Oh be thou dear (*Ulysses* cry'd) to *Jove,* ... Od.14.490.59.
Studious of rest and warmth, *Ulysses* lies, ... Od.14.514.62.
Ulysses, Menelas led forth a band, ... Od.14.528.62.
Sudden I jogg'd *Ulysses*, who was laid ... Od.14.545.63.
Not thine, *Ulysses!* Care unseal'd his eyes; ... Od.15.8.70.
And oh! return'd might we *Ulysses* meet! ... Od.15.174.76.
And great *Ulysses* (ever honour'd name!) ... Od.15.291.83.
To try his host *Ulysses* thus began. ... Od.15.325.85.
She too, sad Mother! for *Ulysses* lost ... Od.15.382.88.
Ulysses, and the Monarch of the Swains, ... Od.16.2.100.
His seat *Ulysses* to the Prince resign'd. ... Od.16.42.104.
Thus young *Ulysses* to *Eumæus* said. ... Od.16.56.105.
O that I were from great *Ulysses* sprung, ... Od.16.103.107.
Alone *Ulysses* drew the vital air, ... Od.16.126.108.
This hour shou'd give *Ulysses* to my eyes. ... Od.16.161.110.
Few are my days, *Ulysses* made reply, ... Od.16.204.113.
Other *Ulysses* shalt thou never see, ... Od.16.224.114.
I am *Ulysses*, I (my son) am He. ... Od.16.225.114.
All, all (*Ulysses* instant made reply) ... Od.16.248.117.
Mark well my voice, *Ulysses* strait replies: ... Od.16.280.118.
" *Ulysses* view'd with stern heroic joy; ... Od.16.309.120.
Ulysses sav'd him from th' avenger's hand. ... Od.16.447.128.
Ulysses, when my infant days I led, ... Od.16.458.129.
Ulysses and his son had drest with art ... Od.16.472.130.

ULYSSES (CONTINUED)

UMBRAGEOUS
Then, where the grove with leaves umbrageous bends, ...Od.6.149.214.

UMBRIEL
Umbriel, a dusky melancholy Spright, ...2.RL4.13.183.
But *Umbriel*, hateful *Gnome!* forbears not so; ....2.RL4.141.196.
Triumphant *Umbriel* on a Sconce's Height ....2.RL5.53.203.

UN-ABASH'D
Earless on high, stood un-abash'd Defoe, ...5.DunA2.139.117.

UN-ADMIR'D
Oh had I rather un-admir'd remain'd ....2.RL4.153.196.

UN-AW'D
Persist, by all divine in Man un-aw'd, ...5.DunA3.221.176.

UN-BELIEVING
To please a lewd, or un-believing Court. ....4.2HE1.212.213.

UN-DID
Un-did *Creation* at a Jerk, ...6.101.11.290.

UN-DISTURB'D
Un-fear'd, un-hated, un-disturb'd it lives. ....6.16.6.53.

UN-ELBOW'D
Un-elbow'd by a Gamester, Pimp, or Play'r? ....3.Ep3.242.112.

UN-ENDOW'D
When Un-endow'd, I took thee for my own, ...2.ChJM.550.41.

UN-FATHER'D
No poor un-father'd product of disgrace. ....Od.19.187.200.

UN-FEAR'D
Un-fear'd, un-hated, un-disturb'd it lives. ....6.16.6.53.

UN-HATED
Un-fear'd, un-hated, un-disturb'd it lives. ....6.16.6.53.

UN-HOUS'D
Un-hous'd, neglected, in the publick way; ....Od.17.357.149.

UN-IMPROV'D
And not a Mask went *un-improv'd* away: ....1.EOC.541.299.

UN-INTELLIGIBLE
O'er a learn'd, un-intelligible Place; ....4.JD2A.105.142.

UN-LEARN'D
Un-learn'd, he knew no Schoolman's subtle Art, ...4.Arbu.398.126.

UN-MOV'D
View'st thou un-mov'd, O ever-honour'd most! ....Od.4.83.123.

UN-NERVE
Now years un-nerve him, and his lord is lost! ....Od.17.387.150.

UN-NOTED
Un-wept, un-noted, and for ever dead! ....Od.5.402.192.

UN-OBSERVED
And, un-observed, the glaring sun declines. ....6.106i.7.306.
And, un-observed, the glaring Orb declines. ....6.106i.7A.306.

UN-OFFENDING
Yet why must un-offending *Argos* feel ....1.TrSt.770.442.

UN-PENSION'D
Un-plac'd, un-pension'd, no Man's Heir, or Slave? ....4.HS1.116.17.
Gay dies un-pension'd with a hundred Friends, ...5.DunA3.326.189.

UN-PLAC'D
Un-plac'd, un-pension'd, no Man's Heir, or Slave? ....4.HS1.116.17.

UN-STALL'D
Un-stall'd, unsold; thus glorious mount in fire ....5.DunA1.198.86.

UN-THAW'D
Or fish deny'd, (the River yet un-thaw'd) ....4.HS2.14.55.
Or kept from fish, (the River yet un-thaw'd) ....4.HS2.14A.55.

UN-WATER'D
Un-water'd see the drooping sea-horse mourn, ...3.Ep4.125.149.

UN-WEPT
Un-wept, un-noted, and for ever dead! ....Od.5.402.192.

UNABASH'D
Earless on high, stood unabash'd De Foe, ...5.DunB2.147.302.

UNABATED
With unabated Rage—So let it be! ....Il.19.466.391.

UNABLE
To drop a dear Dispute I was unable, ...2.ChWB.180.65.
I can but grieve, unable to defend. ....Il.1.757.123.
Their headstrong Horse unable to restrain, ...Il.11.167.42.
This *Asius* view'd, unable to contain, ...Il.13.483.130.
His listless Limbs unable for the Course; ....Il.13.650.136.
Whose Bay, the Fleet unable to contain ....Il.14.41.159.
I stand unable to sustain the Spear, ...Il.16.639.269.
But *Anticlus* unable to controul ....Od.4.387.139.
The Sage retir'd: Unable to controul ....Od.4.950.162.
Willing to aid, unable to defend. ....Od.16.70.105.

UNABLE (CONTINUED)
Unable to contain th' unruly joy. ....Od.16.481.130.

UNACTIVE
While useless Words consume th' unactive Hours, ...Il.2.408.147.
Confus'd, unactive, or surpriz'd with Fear; ....Il.4.257.233.
With Hands unactive, and a careless Eye? ....Il.4.425.240.
Him thus unactive, with an ardent Look ....Il.6.404.346.
Let him, unactive on the Sea-beat Shore, ...Il.7.277.378.
Achilles with unactive Fury glows, ...Il.11.898.75.
Expir'd not meanly, in unactive Death: ....Il.24.264.547.

UNAFFECTED
Of softest manners, unaffected mind, ...6.109.7.314.
Of Gentlest manners, unaffected mind, ...6.109.7A.314.
So unaffected, so compos'd a mind, ...6.115.7.323.

UNAIDED
This Hand unaided shall the War sustain: ....1.TrES.214.457.
This Hand, unaided, shall the War sustain: ....Il.16.517.263.
Alone, unaided, in the thickest War? ....Il.17.537.309.
Unaided *Ilion*, and her destin'd State, ...Il.21.439.438.

UNAIDING
With Arms unaiding mourn our *Argives* slain; ....Il.8.44.397.
With Arms unaiding see our *Argives* slain; ....Il.8.581.424.

UNALLAY'D
Pleasures sincere, and unallay'd with Pain, ...6.17iii.10.58.

UNALTERABLE
Nor mov'd great *Jove's* unalterable Mind; ....Il.12.198.88.

UNAMBITIOUS
My humble Muse, in unambitious Strains, ...1.W-F.427.194.
In unambitious silence be my lot, ...6.147vii.1.391.

UNANCHOR'D
Where ships may rest, unanchor'd and unty'd; ....Od.9.158.312.

UNANIMATED
Be what ye seem, unanimated Clay! ....Il.7.115.369.

UNANIMOUS
Arise unanimous; arise and slay! ....Od.12.410.450.

UNAPPARENT
Or glides a ghost with unapparent shades. ....Od.2.152.69.
But unapparent as a viewless shade ....Od.16.173.111.

UNAPPEAS'D
Not unappeas'd, He enters *Pluto's* Gate, ...Il.14.567.190.

UNAPPROACH'D
Can visit unapproach'd by mortal sight. ....Od.19.53.195.

UNARM'D
Thy Breast, unarm'd, receiv'd the *Spartan* Lance. ....Il.16.371.257.
Unarm'd, he fights not with the *Trojan* Foe. ....Il.17.796.319.
Arms I have none, and can I fight unarm'd? ....Il.18.226.332.
But tho unarm'd, yet clad in Terrors, go! ....Il.18.236.333.
Approach unarm'd, and parly with the Foe, ...Il.22.155.459.
But why this Thought? Unarm'd if I should go, ...Il.22.164.460.
That, all unarm'd, thy vengeance may have vent, ...Od.10.405.364.

UNASK'D
Repeat unask'd; lament, the Wit's too fine ....4.2HE1.366.227.
Remains unask'd; what Time the Rites require ....Il.24.825.571.

UNASSISTED
My helpless Corps, an unassisted Prey. ....Il.5.843.305.

UNASSISTING
Nor *Sthenelus*, with unassisting Hands, ...Il.5.395.285.
With unassisting Arms deplor'd the Day. ....Il.12.210.88.
He dropp'd his Arm, an unassisting Weight, ...Il.20.555.417.

UNATTENDED
Not unattended (the proud *Trojan* cries) ....Il.13.523.131.
Nor unattended, see the Shades below. ....Il.16.796.274.
And, unattended by sincere repose, ...Od.19.600.225.
Alone, and unattended, let me try ....Od.24.248.361.

UNATTENDING
The prudent Son with unattending Ears. ....Il.23.374.505.

UNAVAILING
Imploy'd their Wiles and unavailing Care, ...1.TrVP.25.378.
These unavailing Rites he may receive, ...1.TrES.334.462.
Those unavailing Honours we may give! ....1.TrES.335A.462.
Thus pray'd the Chief: His unavailing Pray'r ....Il.2.498.150.
And spreads for Aid his unavailing Hands. ....Il.4.605.250.
And leaves the Father unavailing Tears. ....Il.5.201.276.
In vain they bled: This unavailing Bow ....Il.5.262.279.
Trust not too much your unavailing Might; ....Il.5.748.302.
And unavailing Tears profusely shed, ...Il.13.825.145.
And curs'd the Lance that unavailing flew: ....Il.14.470.186.
Those unavailing Honours we may give! ....Il.16.822.275.
Pours unavailing Sorrows o'er the Dead. ....Il.18.278.335.
That unavailing Care be laid aside, ...Il.19.31.373.
His useless Lance and unavailing Shield) ....Il.21.59.424.
Satiate at length with unavailing Woes, ...Il.24.647.563.
These unavailing Sorrows o'er the Dead; ....Il.24.693.566.
This unavailing impotence of soul. ....Od.4.264.131.
And breath, to waste in unavailing cries. ....Od.4.955.162.

UNAW'D

Unaw'd by Precepts, Human or Divine, ...2.ChJM.31.16.
Persist, by all divine in Man unaw'd, ...5.DunB3.223.331.
Troy's great Defender stands alone unaw'd, ...Il.14.449.185.

UNAWARES

And unawares *Morality* expires. ......5.DunB4.650.409.

UNBALANC'D

Let Earth unbalanc'd from her orbit fly, ...3.EOM1.251.46.
Th' unbalanc'd Mind, and snatch the Man away; ......4.1HE6.25.239.

UNBAR

Where Brown and Mears unbar the gates of Light, ...5.DunA3.20.152.
Where Brown and Mears unbar the gates of Light, ...5.DunB3.28.321.
Unbar the sacred Gates; and seek the Pow'r ......Il.6.111.329.

UNBARR'D

No human Hand the weighty Gates unbarr'd, ...Il.24.713.567.
Unbarr'd the portal of the roseate east ......Od.4.412.140.

UNBARREL

Unbarrel thy just Sense, and broach thy Wit. ......6.48i.6.133*.

UNBARS

As *Pallas'* Priestess, and unbars the Gates. ......Il.6.373.344.

UNBATH'D

Unbath'd he lies, and bleeds along the Shore! ......Il.22.573.480.

UNBELIEVING

Then Unbelieving Priests reform'd the Nation, ...1.EOC.546.300.
And why, oh swain of unbelieving mind! ......Od.14.431.56.

UNBEND

And smile propitious, and unbend thy Bow. ......Il.1.597.116.
Indulge the genial hour, unbend thy soul, ...Od.2.343.77.

UNBENDED

The Wolf's grey Hide, th' unbended Bow and Spear; ......Il.10.529.26.
Th' unbended bow, and arrows wing'd with Fate. ......Od.21.62.262.

UNBENDING

Flies o'er th'unbending Corn, and skims along the Main. ......1.EOC.373.283.

UNBENT

These, with his Bow unbent, he lash'd along; ......Il.10.584.28.
When social mirth unbent his serious soul, ...Od.1.335.48.
Against the wall he set the bow unbent: ......Od.22.137.293.

UNBER'D

Whose unber'd Arms, by fits, thick Flashes send. ......Il.8.706.429.

UNBIASS'D

Unbiass'd, or by *Favour* or by *Spite;* ......1.EOC.633.311.

UNBID

And *Menelaus* came unbid, the last. ......Il.2.485.150.
As yet, unbid they never grac'd our feast, ...Od.7.269.249.

UNBIDDEN

But how, unbidden, shall I dare to steep ......Il.14.281.175.
Unbidden Herbs, and voluntary Flow'rs; ......Il.14.396.182.
Adown his cheek a tear unbidden stole, ...Od.17.365.149.
From his full eyes the tears unbidden spring, ...Od.21.83.263.

UNBIND

Or thy griev'd Country's copper chains unbind; ......5.DunA1.22.62.
Or thy griev'd Country's copper chains unbind; ......5.DunB1.24.271.
Or thy grieved country's copper chains unbind; ......6.106iv.6.307.
With speed the mast they rear, with speed unbind ......Od.2.464.83.
Then from their anchors all our ships unbind, ...Od.9.654.333.
At once the mast we rear, at once unbind ......Od.11.3.377.
The pitying Gods themselves my chains unbind. ......Od.14.384.53.
With speed the mast they rear, with speed unbind ......Od.15.312.84.

UNBLAM'D

Unblam'd thro' Life, lamented in thy End. ......6.125.8.350.
Unblam'd thro' Life, lamented in the End. ......6.125.8C.350.
Unblam'd abundance crown'd the royal board, ...Od.1.297.47.
Venial discourse unblam'd with him to hold. ......Od.19.112.198.

UNBLEMISH'D

Unblemish'd let me live, or die unknown, ...2.TemF.523.289.
Thus *Lucrece* lives unblemish'd in her fame, ...6.38.21.108.

UNBLESS'D

By his own Sons that pass him by unbless'd: ......3.Ep1.231A.35.
By his own son, that passes by unbless'd: ......3.Ep1.231.35.
(Ah men unbless'd!) to touch that natal shore. ......Od.1.12.29.
Unbless'd, abandon'd to the wrath of *Jove?* ......Od.1.83.35.
Unbless'd, abandon'd to the rage of fate! ......Od.20.174.241.

UNBLEST

Alone, and ev'n in Paradise, unblest, ...2.ChJM.60.17.
Ev'n such is Woman's Fame: with this unblest, ...3.Ep2.281A.73.
Be this a Woman's Fame: with this unblest, ...3.Ep2.281.73.
If I, unblest, must see my Son no more, ...Il.5.844.305.
Unblest *Adrastus* next at Mercy lies ......Il.6.45.325.
Unblest *Protesilaus* to *Ilion's* Shore, ...Il.16.341.256.
But flies unblest! Nó grateful Sacrifice, ...Il.23.1021.529.
Unblest he sighs, detain'd by lawless charms, ...Od.5.22.172.
Unblest! to tread that interdicted shore ......Od.7.333.253.
Such as th' unblest *Cyclopean* climes produce, ...Od.9.422.323.
Unblest the man, whom music wins to stay ......Od.12.53.432.
An unblest offspring of a sire unblest! ......Od.16.128.108.

UNBLEST (CONTINUED)

An unblest offspring of a sire unblest! ......Od.16.128.108.
Unblest thy hand! if in this low disguise ......Od.17.576.160.
How to the land of *Lote* unblest he sails; ......Od.23.335.340.

UNBLOODY

Unbrib'd, unbloody, stood the blameless priest: ......3.EOM3.158.109.

UNBODIED

And rest at last, where souls unbodied dwell ......Od.24.19.348.

UNBODY'D

These stop'd the Moon, and call'd th' unbody'd Shades ......2.TemF.101.260.
(Not those which thin, unbody'd Shadows fill, ...6.13.2.39.
But here and there th' unbody'd Spectres chace ......Il.23.90.490.

UNBORN

See future Sons, and Daughters yet unborn ......1.Mes.88.121.
Nations *unborn* your mighty Names shall sound, ...1.EOC.193.263.
And stretch the Ray to Ages yet unborn. ......4.2HE1.228.215.
Thou, yet unborn, hast touch'd this sacred shore; ......5.DunA3.37.154.
Where things destroy'd are swept to things unborn." ......5.DunB1.242.288.
Thou, yet unborn, hast touch'd this sacred shore; ......5.DunB3.45.322.
Wait for my Infants yet unborn. ......6.135.66.368.
Yet such his Acts, as *Greeks* unborn shall tell, ...Il.10.61.5.
To claim the Tears of *Trojans* yet unborn. ......Il.10.334.18.
No—Men unborn, and Ages yet behind, ...Il.16.44.237.

UNBOUGHT

With soups unbought and sallads blest his board. ......3.Ep3.184.109.

UNBOUND

Her Eyes dejected and her Hair unbound. ......2.RL4.90.191.
The glitt'ring Terrors from his Brows unbound, ...Il.6.600.356.
The wanton Courser thus, with Reins unbound, ...Il.6.652.359.
Headlong he tumbles: His slack Nerves unbound, ...Il.7.21.363.
Pallas, meanwhile, her various Veil unbound, ...Il.8.466.419.
The panting Steeds *Eurymedon* unbound. ......Il.11.757.69.
Stop'd his swift Chariot, and his Steeds unbound, ...Il.13.54.107.
As when the pamper'd Steed, with Reins unbound, ...Il.15.298.208.
The stunning Stroke his stubborn Nerves unbound; ......Il.21.474.441.
Unbrac'd their Armour, and the Steeds unbound. ......Il.23.36.488.
With flow'rs of gold: an under robe, unbound, ...Od.5.297.185.
The mindful chief *Leucothea's* scarf unbound; ......Od.5.589.200.
(Their shining veils unbound.) Along the skies ......Od.6.113.211.
Receiv'd the vestures, and the mules unbound. ......Od.7.6.233.
They said: and (oh curs'd fate!) the thongs unbound; ......Od.10.50.341.
The deafen'd ear unlock'd, the chains unbound. ......Od.12.239.443.
Down from the swelling loins, the vest unbound ......Od.18.341.184.
He spoke; then rising, his broad sword unbound, ...Od.21.123.264.

UNBOUNDED

Unbounded *Thames* shall flow for all Mankind, ...1.W-F.398.191.
Pleas'd to behold unbounded Pow'r thy own, ...1.TrSt.222.419.
With boundless Pow'r unbounded Virtue join'd, ...2.TemF.166.268.
All my loose soul unbounded springs to thee. ......2.ElAb.228.338.
Thro' worlds unbounded tho' the God be known, ...3.EOM1.21A.15.
Supreme of Gods! unbounded, and alone! ......Il.2.491.150.
In Rage unbounded, and unmatch'd in Might. ......Il.6.124.330.
Supreme of Gods! unbounded, and alone: ......Il.7.244.376.
For such I reign, unbounded and above; ......Il.8.33.397.
Tho' fierce his Rage, unbounded be his Woe, ...Il.17.795.319.
(A length of Ocean and unbounded sky, ...Od.3.411.106.
From her bright eyes the tears unbounded flow. ......Od.19.237.205.

UNBRAC'D

The Nerves unbrac'd no more his Bulk sustain, ...1.TrES.265.459.
He loos'd, the Corslet from his Breast unbrac'd; ......Il.4.249.232.
The Nerves unbrac'd support his Limbs no more; ......Il.4.536.247.
And from her fragrant Breast the Zone unbrac'd, ...Il.14.245.172.
The Nerves unbrac'd no more his Bulk sustain, ...Il.16.570.266.
There his own Mail unbrac'd, the Field bestrow'd; ......Il.17.217.296.
The Zone unbrac'd, her Bosom she display'd; ......Il.22.112.457.
Unbrac'd their Armour, and the Steeds unbound. ......Il.23.36.488.

UNBRACE

Exhaust thy Spirits, and thy Arms unbrace. ......Il.4.365.238.
His joyful Friends unbrace his Azure Arms. ......Il.7.142.371.
'Twas *Neptune's* Charge his Coursers to unbrace, ...Il.8.546.422.
From thy tir'd Limbs unbrace *Pelides'* Arms! ......Il.17.244.297.

UNBRIB'D

Unbrib'd, unbloody, stood the blameless priest: ......3.EOM3.158.109.

UNBROKE

The second Victor claims a Mare unbroke, ...Il.23.333.503.
A stately Mule, as yet by Toils unbroke, ...Il.23.755.520.
By age unbroke!—but all-consuming care ......Od.8.149.270.

UNBROKEN

Convey'd unbroken faith from sire to son, ...3.EOM3.228.115.
And that unbroken Vow, our Virgin Bed! ......Il.15.46.196.

UNBUCKLING

Next all unbuckling the rich Mail they wore, ...Il.3.157.198.

UNBURIED

On distant shores unwept, unburied lye. ......Od.11.68.383.

UNBURY'D

Of Kings unbury'd, on the wasted Coasts; ......1.TrSt.56.412.
Of Kings unbury'd, in the wasted Coasts; ......1.TrSt.56A.412.
Whose Limbs unbury'd on the naked Shore ......Il.1.5.82.

UNCAG'D
Uncag'd then let the harmless Monster rage, ...6.116vii.7.328.

UNCAUTIOUS
Th' uncautious Herald with impatience burns, ...Od.16.354.123.

UNCEASING
And Gifts unceasing on thine Altars lay. ....Il.8.247.409.

UNCENSUR'D
Whose Right it is, *uncensur'd* to be dull; ....1.EOC.589.307.

UNCERTAIN
Its Site uncertain, if in Earth or Air; ....2.TemF.421.283.
Nor dreads approaching fate's uncertain hour; ....6.55.4.166.
Nor trust the Dart, or aim th' uncertain Spear, ...Il.13.342.122.
The *Trojan* heard; uncertain, he to meet ....Il.13.572.133.
Uncertain of the truth, yet uncontroul'd ....Od.4.187.129.
Heav'ns! how uncertain are the Pow'rs on high? ....Od.5.367.190.
Nine days our fleet th' uncertain tempest bore ....Od.9.93.306.

UNCERTAINTY
By Actions? those Uncertainty divides: ....3.Ep1.170.29.

UNCHANG'D
One *clear, unchang'd,* and *Universal* Light, ...1.EOC.71.247.
Kept fresh by Motion, and unchang'd by Change. ....6.17ii.26.56.
Honour unchang'd; a Principle profest; ....6.27.3.81.
Honour unchang'd, a principle profest, ...6.57.3.169.
Unchang'd his Colour, and unmov'd his Frame; ....Il.13.367.123.
Unchang'd, immortal, and supremely blest! ....Od.4.94.124.

UNCHANGING
But true *Expression,* like th' unchanging *Sun,* ....1.EOC.315.274.

UNCHASTE
Th' unguarded virgin as unchaste I blame, ...Od.6.343.228.
Beauty unchaste is beauty in disgrace. ....Od.8.360.283.

UNCHECK'D
Uncheck'd may rise, and climb from art to art: ....3.EOM2.40.60.

UNCIVIL
Tho the Dean has run from us in manner uncivil; ....6.42i.1.116.
Ah why, good Lord Grantham, were you so uncivil ....6.122.9.341.

UNCIVILIZ'D
And kept *unconquer'd,* and *unciviliz'd,* ....1.EOC.716.323.

UNCLASSIC
Her magic charms o'er all unclassic ground: ....5.DunA3.254.178.
Her magic charms on all unclassic ground: ....5.DunA3.254A.178.
Her magic charms o'er all unclassic ground: ....5.DunB3.258.332.

UNCLE
Alcides' Uncle, old *Lycimnius,* slew; ....Il.2.802.163.
Whose luckless Hand his Royal Uncle slew; ....Il.9.682.468.

UNCLEAN
List'ning delighted to the jest unclean ....5.DunB2.99.300.

UNCLEANLY
But filthy and uncleanly Jades ....6.54.19.165.

UNCLOSE
Soon as thy letters trembling I unclose, ...2.ElAb.29.321.
The Goddess spoke: The rowling Waves unclose; ....Il.1.562.115.
Wak'd at their steps, her flowing eyes unclose; ....Od.18.235.178.

UNCLOUDED
One Tyde of Glory, one unclouded Blaze, ...1.Mes.102.122.
Oh! blest with Temper, whose unclouded ray ....3.Ep2.257.71.
Th' unclouded lustre of her eyes! ....6.4iv.3.10.
Unclouded there, th' Aerial Azure spread, ...Il.17.428.304.

UNCOMFORTABLE
A long, forlorn, uncomfortable Way! ....Il.6.248.338.
In Winter's bleak, uncomfortable Reign, ...Il.12.333.93.
Flits to the lone, uncomfortable Coast; ....Il.16.1034.283.
To tread th' uncomfortable paths beneath, ...Od.10.580.371.
To tread th' uncomfortable paths beneath, ...Od.10.675.376.
The Sun ne'er views th' uncomfortable seats, ...Od.11.17.380.
Points out the long, uncomfortable way. ....Od.24.6.347.

UNCOMMON
I know the thing that's most uncommon; ....6.89.1.250.
I know a thing that's most uncommon; ....6.89.1A.250.
Such bold Exploits uncommon Courage ask, ...Il.10.46.4.
Uncommon are such Favours of the Sky, ...Il.24.568.560.
Red with uncommon wrath, and wrapt in flames: ....Od.12.488.456.

UNCOMPELL'D
Nor uncompell'd the dang'rous truth betray, ...Od.2.420.81.

UNCONCERN'D
Serene in Torments, unconcern'd in Death; ....2.ChJM.674.47.
Thou unconcern'd canst hear the mighty Crack. ....4.Arbu.86.101.
Canst thou, oh cruel, unconcern'd survey ....Od.23.169.328.

UNCONCERN'DLY
Blest! who can unconcern'dly find ....6.1.9.3.

UNCONFIN'D
Blest with a *Taste* exact, yet unconfin'd; ....1.EOC.639.311.
Poets, a *Race* long unconfin'd and free, ...1.EOC.649.313.
'Till lengthen'd on to Faith, and unconfin'd, ...3.EOM4.343.161.

UNCONFIN'D (CONTINUED)
Come on then Satire! gen'ral, unconfin'd, ...4.EpS2.14.314.
Mad *Mathesis* alone was unconfin'd, ...5.DunB4.31.343.
Open she was, and unconfin'd, ...6.14v(b).2.49.
Injustice swift, erect, and unconfin'd, ...Il.9.628.465.

UNCONQUER'D
And kept *unconquer'd,* and *unciviliz'd,* ....1.EOC.716.323.
Unconquer'd *Cato* shews the Wound he tore, ...2.TemF.176.269.
How shin'd the Soul, unconquer'd in the Tow'r! ....4.EpS2.83.317.
But that imperious, that unconquer'd Soul, ...Il.1.378.106.
Say shall we march with our unconquer'd Pow'rs, ...Il.2.283.141.
O Progeny of *Jove!* unconquer'd Maid! ....Il.5.146.274.
Troy's strong Defence, unconquer'd *Pallas,* aid! ....Il.6.379.345.
Unmatch'd our Force, unconquer'd is our Hand: ....Il.8.561.423.
Ye find, *Achilles* is unconquer'd still. ....Il.9.549.460.
Fixt is his Wrath, unconquer'd is his Pride; ....Il.9.795.473.
Daughter of *Jove,* unconquer'd *Pallas!* hear. ....Il.10.336.18.
And questions thus his own unconquer'd Soul. ....Il.11.512.56.
Ulysses thus, unconquer'd by his Pains, ...Il.11.604.61.
While *Greece* unconquer'd kept alive the War, ...Il.12.207.88.
Have prov'd thy Valour and unconquer'd Might; ....Il.13.354.122.
Greece yet unconquer'd, kept alive the War, ...Il.15.848.229.
And thus explor'd his own unconquer'd Mind. ....Il.17.100.291.
And question'd thus his yet-unconquer'd mind. ....Od.5.382.190.
Attend, unconquer'd maid! accord my vows, ...Od.6.389.230.
Pallas, unconquer'd maid, my frame surrounds ....Od.16.228.114.

UNCONQUERABLE
Spadillio first, unconquerable Lord! ....2.RL3.49.172.
The *Smiles* and *Love's* unconquerable Queen! ....Il.21.493.441.

UNCONQUERABLY
Wild, furious herds, unconquerably strong! ....Od.11.356.399.

UNCONSCIOUS
And pin'd, unconscious of his rising fate; ....5.DunA1.110.76.
Th' unconscious flood sleeps o'er thee like a lake. ....5.DunA2.292.138.
Th' unconscious stream sleeps o'er thee like a lake. ....5.DunB2.304.310.
A furious Foe unconscious proves a Friend. ....6.116viii.2.328.
Untam'd, unconscious of the galling Yoke, ...Il.10.348.18.
He, yet unconscious of *Patroclus'* Fall, ...Il.17.464.305.
Pure and unconscious of my manly Loves. ....Il.19.274.383.
Of six years Age, unconscious of the Yoke, ...Il.23.756.520.
(A green old Age unconscious of Decays, ...Il.23.929.526.
Untam'd, unconscious of the galling yoke; ....Od.3.491.111.
Dark as I am, unconscious of thy will. ....Od.5.230.182.
Unconscious of what air I breathe, I stand ....Od.6.213.220.
Rude, and unconscious of a stranger's right; ....Od.9.204.314.
Thus they, unconscious of the deed divine: ....Od.13.194.15.
Dark and unconscious of the will of *Jove:* ....Od.17.89.136.
He, not unconscious of the voice, and tread, ...Od.17.346.148.

UNCONSENTING
Nor unconsenting hear his friend's request; ....Od.15.221.79.

UNCONTROL'D
Yet impotent of mind, and uncontrol'd, ...Od.1.53.33.

UNCONTROLL'D
Now swift pursue, now thunder uncontroll'd; ....Il.8.234.408.
For he, the God, whose Counsels uncontroll'd, ...Il.16.843.276.
But *Jove's* high Will is ever uncontroll'd, ...Il.17.197.295.
Then uncontroll'd in boundless War engage, ...Il.19.37.373.
If uncontroll'd *Achilles* fights alone: ....Il.20.38.394.

UNCONTROUL'D
Rush fearless to the Plains, and uncontroul'd ....Il.5.683.300.
Rage uncontroul'd thro' all the hostile Crew, ...Il.16.112.240.
Uncertain of the truth, yet uncontroul'd ....Od.4.187.129.
And hear their midnight revels uncontroul'd? ....Od.16.98.107.
Mean-time their licence uncontroul'd I bear; ....Od.16.137.109.
Irreverent to the Great, and uncontroul'd, ...Od.18.432.189.

UNCORRUPTED
His hand unstain'd, his uncorrupted heart, ...3.Ep1.141.26.
And uncorrupted, ev'n among the Great; ....6.125.6.350.
Pure Emanation! uncorrupted Flood; ....Il.5.423.288.
The Circles Gold, of uncorrupted Frame, ...Il.5.893.308.
With righteous *Æthiops* (uncorrupted Train!) ....Il.23.256.499.

UNCOUTH
Then Ships of uncouth Form shall stem the Tyde, ...1.W-F.403.191.
The Sister-Lock now sits uncouth, alone, ...2.RL4.171.198.
Prune the luxuriant, the uncouth refine, ...4.2HE2.174.177.
Object uncouth! a man of miseries! ....Od.13.509.30.
Objects uncouth! to check the genial joy. ....Od.17.453.155.

UNCOVER'D
With Head uncover'd, the *Cosmetic* Pow'rs. ....2.RL1.124.155.
Unwept, uncover'd, on the Plain he lay, ...Il.11.319.49.

UNCOWL'D
Men bearded, bald, cowl'd, uncowl'd, shod, unshod, ...5.DunA3.106.159.
Men bearded, bald, cowl'd, uncowl'd, shod, unshod, ...5.DunB3.114.325.

UNCREATING
Light dies before her uncreating word: ....5.DunA3.340.192.
Light dies before thy uncreating word: ....5.DunB4.654.409.

UNCTION
With plenteous unction of ambrosial oil. ....Od.19.590.225.

UNCTUOUS
While those with unctuous fir foment the flame. ....Od.19.77.196.
Mean-time the menial train with unctuous wood ....Od.20.153.241.

UNCUMBER'D
Seen him, uncumber'd with the Venal tribe, ...4.EpS1.31.300.

UNCURL'D
Uncurl'd it hangs, the fatal Sheers demands; ....2.RL4.173.198.
Curl'd or uncurl'd, since Locks will turn to grey, ...2.RL5.26.201.
And Snakes uncurl'd hang list'ning round their Heads. ....6.11.70.32.

UND'R
To call things Woods, for what grows und'r 'em. ....6.67.8.195.

UNDAUNTED
Undaunted Hero! who, divinely brave, ...1.TrSt.753.441.
Th' undaunted Guard of Cloud-compelling *Jove.* ....II.1.517.113.
Two valiant Brothers rule th' undaunted Throng, ...II.2.612.156.
Not so fierce *Capaneus'* undaunted Son, ...II.4.454.241.
The gen'ral Silence, and undaunted spoke. ....II.9.815.473.
Undaunted *Diomed!* what Chief to join ....II.10.277.14.
The Fire which burn'd in that undaunted Breast! ....II.17.86.291.
But swell'd his Bosom with undaunted Might, ...II.20.111.398.
Hector, undaunted, thus. Such Words employ ....II.20.499.415.
To pass thro' Foes, and thus undaunted face ....II.24.655.564.
With three associates of undaunted mind. ....Od.4.590.147.
Once more undaunted on the ruin rode, ...Od.12.525.458.
Hope ye success? undaunted crush the foe. ....Od.16.388.124.

UNDAZLED
And on thy self, undazled, fix her eye. ....6.23.12.73.

UNDAZZL'D
And on thy self, fix her undazzl'd Eye! ....6.23.12A.73.

UNDECAY'D
Yet mine shall sacred last; mine, undecay'd, ...II.22.489.476.

UNDECAYING
Mellifluous, undecaying, and divine! ....Od.9.239.316.

UNDECEIV'D
Their Fears of Danger undeceiv'd in thee! ....II.3.62.192.

UNDECEIVE
I will this Instant undeceive the Knight, ...2.ChJM.651.46.

UNDEFIL'D
Next, your own Honour undefil'd maintain; ....2.ChJM.560.42.
A Place there was, yet undefil'd with Gore, ...II.10.233.12.

UNDER
And bleed for ever under *Britain's* Spear. ....1.W-F.310.179.
Or under Southern Skies exalt their Sails, ...1.W-F.391.189.
When Love approach'd me under Friendship's name; ....2.ElAb.60.324.
List under Reason, and deserve her care; ....3.EOM2.98.66.
Now in the Moon perhaps, now under ground. ....3.Ep1.157.28.
Deep hid the shining mischief under ground: ....3.Ep3.10.84.
To *Berkley,* ev'ry Virtue under Heav'n. ....4.EpS2.73.317.
(As under seas Alphæus' secret sluice ....5.DunA2.317.140.
(As under seas Alphæus' sacred sluice ....5.DunA2.317A.140.
And under his, and under Archer's wing, ...5.DunB1.309.292.
And under his, and under Archer's wing, ...5.DunB1.309.292.
(As under seas Alphæus' secret sluice ....5.DunB2.341.314.
See under Ripley rise a new White-hall, ...5.DunB3.327.336.
First lay this Paper under, then, ...6.10.65.26.
Now under hanging Mountains, ...6.11.97.33.
Under the Greenwood Tree; ....6.79.102.221.
Under the Greenwood Tree. ....6.79.136.222.
Well then, poor *G[ay]* lies under ground! ....6.103.1.295.
That under Cloth of Gold or Tissue, ...6.135.31.367.
Under this Marble, or under this Sill, ...6.144.1.386.
Under this Marble, or under this Sill, ...6.144.1.386.
Or under this Turf, or e'en what they will; ....6.144.2.386.
Under this Turf, or just what you will; ....6.144.2A.386.
Dies under Exigents, or self defence. ....6.147iv.4A.391.
Where under high *Cyllenè* crown'd with Wood, ...II.2.731.161.
In forty Vessels under *Meges* move, ...II.2.761.162.
Last under *Prothous* the *Magnesians* stood, ...II.2.916.167.
And lodg'd in Brazen Dungeons under Ground, ...II.5.476.290.
Heap'd round, and heaving under Loads of slain; ....II.5.1089.318.
Lest under Covert of the Midnight Shade, ...II.8.649.426.
Whelm'd under the huge Mass of Earth and Main. ....II.14.236.172.
Wait under *Ide:* Of thy superior Pow'r ....II.14.351.179.
Deep under Seas, where hoary *Ocean* dwells. ....II.14.354.180.
What Youth he slaughters under *Ilion's* Walls? ....II.15.71.199.
And bleeding Heroes under Axles groan. ....II.16.457.260.
In dust extended under *Ilion's* Wall, ...II.17.465.305.
To whelm some City under Waves of Fire, ...II.17.826.321.
Whelm'd under our dark Gulphs those Arms shall lie ....II.21.370.436.
And anchor under *Mimas'* shaggy brow? ....Od.3.208.96.
With flow'rs of gold: an under robe, unbound, ...Od.5.297.185.
Beyond these tracts, and under other skies, ...Od.7.327.252.

UNDERGO
If *Wit* so much from *Ign'rance* undergo, ...1.EOC.508.295.
Too much does *Wit* from *Ign'rance* undergo, ...1.EOC.508A.295.
What Grief, what Shame must *Glaucus* undergo, ...1.TrES.308.461.
Xantippe made her good Man undergo; ....2.ChWB.388.76.
And me, the Muses help'd to undergo it; ....4.2HE2.66.169.
Which they who love thee not must undergo. ....6.25.4.77.
Which those who love thee not must undergo. ....6.25.4A.77.
What Grief, what Shame must *Glaucus* undergo; ....II.16.613.268.
What fate yet dooms thee, yet, to undergo; ....Od.5.264.184.
But when that Fate which all must undergo ....Od.14.236.48.

UNDERMINE
While these they undermine, and those they rend; ....II.12.306.92.

UNDERMINING
Heaving the Bank, and undermining all; ....II.21.271.432.

UNDERNEATH
And now lies buried underneath a Rood, ...2.ChWB.245.68.
Writ underneath the Country Signs; ....4.HS6.92.255.
Fair *Ida* trembles underneath the God; ....II.14.323.178.

UNDERSTAND
Wou'd all but *stoop* to what they *understand.* ....1.EOC.67.246.
And that's a Text I clearly understand. ....2.ChWB.18.57.
Ye Sov'reign Wives! give Ear, and understand; ....2.ChWB.68.59.
All fear, none aid you, and few understand. ....3.EOM4.266.153.
All Boys may read, and Girls may understand! ....4.EpS1.76.304.
Ev'n *Ra[wlin]son* might understand. ....6.29.16.83.
Even *R[awlinson]* may understand: ....6.29.7Z4.83.
And thus, reveal'd—Hear Prince! and understand ....II.24.563.559.
O thou! whom Age has taught to understand, ...Od.14.425.56.
But thou! whom years have taught to understand, ...Od.24.310.364.

UNDERSTANDING
The solid Pow'r of *Understanding* fails; ....1.EOC.57.245.

UNDERSTANDS
To beg, than work, he better understands; ....Od.17.260.144.

UNDERSTOND
Thilke moral shall ye understond, ...6.14i.3.41.

UNDERSTOOD
Much was *Believ'd,* but little *understood,* ....1.EOC.689.317.
All was *Believ'd,* but nothing *understood,* ....1.EOC.689A.317.
All Discord, Harmony, not understood; ....3.EOM1.291.50.
Pleasure, or wrong or rightly understood, ...3.EOM2.91.65.
No ill could fear in God; and understood, ...3.EOM3.237.116.
God sends not ill; if rightly understood, ...3.EOM4.113.139.
What-ere thou speak'st, let this be understood; ....6.2.35.6.
Thou Great First Cause, least understood! ....6.50.5.146.
O First of Things! least understood! ....6.50.5A.146.
Not look'd in, or, not understood) ....6.64.4.189.
What in my secret Soul is understood, ...II.9.408.452.
Shame is not of his Soul; nor understood, ...II.24.56.538.

UNDERTAKE
Her Answer she shall have, I undertake; ....2.ChJM.706.49.
Ill fits thy Age these Toils to undertake. ....II.10.189.10.

UNDESCRY'D
Secret, and undescry'd, he took his Way, ...2.ChJM.537.41.

UNDESERV'D
"Praise undeserv'd is scandal in disguise:" ....4.2HE1.413.229.

UNDESERVING
Who lose a Length of undeserving Days; ....2.TemF.398.282.
Lose a dull Length of undeserving Days; ....6.17ii.2.56.
Not undeserving, some support obtain. ....Od.15.335.85.

UNDETERMIN'D
Rest undetermin'd till the dawning Day. ....II.9.732.470.
Yet undetermin'd, or to live, or die! ....II.15.595.219.

UNDISCERNING
And undiscerning, scatters Crowns and Chains. ....2.TemF.297.278.

UNDISCHARG'D
For whate'er Work was undischarg'd a-bed, ...2.ChJM.473.38.

UNDISCIPLIN'D
A Rout undisciplin'd, a straggling Train, ...II.13.141.111.

UNDISCOVER'D
To what dark, undiscover'd Shore? ....6.31i.6.93.

UNDISFIGUR'D
Yet undisfigur'd, or in Limb, or Face, ...II.24.509.557.

UNDISGUIS'D
The very truth I undisguis'd declare: ....Od.17.18.133.

UNDISHONOUR'D
Still undishonour'd or by word or deed ....Od.22.350.304.

UNDISMAY'D
Amidst the wrack of nature undismay'd, ...6.21.9.69.
And bar'd the bone: *Ulysses* undismay'd, ...Od.19.527.221.

UNDISSEMBLED
And undissembled Gore pursu'd the Wound. ....II.5.261.279.

UNDISTINGUISH'D
And floated Fields lye undistinguish'd round: ....1.TrSt.499.431.
Falls undistinguish'd by the Victor *Spade!* ....2.RL3.64.172.
Receiv'd of Wits an undistinguish'd race, ...4.Arbu.237.112.
Sons, Sires, and Wives, an undistinguish'd Prey. ....II.5.596.297.
Thick, undistinguish'd Plumes, together join'd, ...II.16.262.249.
Lies undistinguish'd from the vulgar dead. ....II.16.776.273.
His Front, Brows, Eyes, one undistinguish'd Wound, ...II.16.897.278.
And undistinguish'd blend the flying Ring: ....II.18.694.357.
Nose, Mouth and Front, one undistinguish'd Wound: ....II.23.476.509.
With their lewd mates, thy undistinguish'd age ....Od.19.573.224.

UNDIVIDED
Spreads undivided, operates unspent, ...3.EOM1.274.48.

UNDO
And learn of Man each other to undo.) ......1.W-F.124.162.

UNDOES
Scarce hurts the Lawyer, but undoes the Scribe. ......4.EpS2.47.315.

UNDOING
Nature to your undoing arms mankind ......6.38.15.108.

UNDONE
By *Fools'* tis *hated,* and by *Knaves undone!* ......1.EOC.507.295.
A wretch undone: O parents help, and deign ......1.TrPA.142.371.
Who might not—ah! who wou'd not be undone? ......1.TrSP.96.398.
What Reason weaves, by Passion is undone. ......3.EOM2.42.60.
Who first taught souls enslav'd, and realms undone, ...3.EOM3.241.116.
How oft by these at sixty are undone ......3.EOM4.183.144.
And Britain, if not Europe, is undone. ......3.Ep1.161.29.
But cares not if a thousand are undone. ......3.Ep2.176.64.
Where the most lucky are but last undone. ......4.HAdv.52.79.
No wretched Wife cries out, *Undone! Undone!* ......4.HAdv.170.89.
No wretched Wife cries out, *Undone! Undone!* ......4.HAdv.170.89.
Vice is undone, if she forgets her Birth, ...4.EpS1.141.308.
And, if a Borough chuse him, not undone; ......5.DunB4.328.375.
Knight lifts the head, for what are crowds undone ......5.DunB4.561.397.
So Pimps grow rich, while Gallants are undone. ......6.24ii.2.75.
As Pimps grow rich, while Gallants are undone. ......6.34.22.101.
But cares not if a thousand are undone. ......6.139.20.377.
My Hopes are frustrate, and my *Greeks* undone. ......Il.8.452.418.
I fear, I fear, lest *Greece* (not yet undone) ......Il.13.935.149.
The Fight, our glorious Work remains undone. ......Il.19.148.377.
As a poor Father helpless and undone, ...Il.23.274.501.
Shall I, by waste undone, refund the dow'r? ......Od.2.154.69.
Deeds then undone my faithful tongue foretold; ......Od.2.201.71.
To whom with grief—O swift to be undone, ...Od.12.353.448.

UNDOUBTED
This Mule my right? th' undoubted Victor I. ......Il.23.772.520.
Undoubted all your filial claim confess: ......Od.1.512.56.

UNDRESS
The Foe once gone, our Knight prepar'd t'undress, ...2.ChJM.373.32.
The Foe once gone, our Knight wou'd strait undress, ...2.ChJM.373A.32.
The thin Undress of superficial Light, ...6.14iv.6.47.

UNDRESS'D
A Lady's Face is all you see undress'd; ......4.HAdv.124.85.

UNDREST
By this the Sheets were spread, the Bride undrest, ...2.ChJM.381.33.
The shrine with gore unstain'd, with gold undrest, ...3.EOM3.157.109.

UNDROSSY
Of Heav'ns undrossy Gold the God's Array ......Il.8.53.398.

UNDRY'D
And kept the Nerves undry'd, the Flesh entire, ...Il.23.234.499.
A tree of stateliest growth, and yet undry'd, ...Od.9.381.321.

UNDULATING
Thro undulating Air the Sounds are sent, ...2.TemF.446.285.

UNEASILY
On her soft Couch uneasily she lay: ......2.ChJM.419.35.

UNEASY
The soul, uneasy and confin'd from home, ...3.EOM1.97.26.
The soul, uneasy and confin'd at home, ...3.EOM1.97A.26.
But soft recesses of uneasy minds, ...6.81.9.225.
But soft recesses for th' uneasy Mind, ...6.81.9A.225.

UNENVY'D
Unenvy'd Titles grace our mighty Names, ...6.48iv.13.136.
"And prais'd, unenvy'd, by the Muse he lov'd." ......6.71.72.204.
And prais'd unenvy'd, by the Muse he lov'd. ......6.97.6A.282.
And here, unenvy'd, rural dainties taste. ......Od.14.452.57.

UNEQUAL
That mourns in Exile his unequal Fate; ......1.TrSt.195.418.
Prepar'd to labour in th'unequal Fight; ......1.TrES.94.453.
And join'd to them, my own unequal Age; ......2.ChJM.570.42.
And joined to that, my own unequal Age; ......2.ChJM.570A.42.
Nor fear'd the Chief th'unequal Fight to try, ...2.RL5.77.206.
Unequal task! a passion to resign, ...2.ElAb.195.336.
P. But how unequal it bestows, observe, ...3.Ep3.23A.88.
But how unequal it bestows, observe, ...3.Ep3.23.88.
With steps unequal L[into]t urg'd the race, ...5.DunA2.63A.105.
On two unequal crutches propt he came, ...5.DunB4.111.352.
Brave as he was, and shunn'd unequal Force. ......Il.5.702.301.
Great Perils, Father! wait th' unequal Fight; ......Il.8.129.404.
Proud *Hector,* now, th' unequal Fight demands, ...Il.9.404.452.
Prepar'd to labour in th' unequal Fight; ......Il.12.448.97.
Unhelp'd we stand, unequal to engage ......Il.17.580.311.
On these supported, with unequal Gait, ...Il.18.491.345.
I faint, I sink, unequal to the Fight— ......Il.21.419.437.
Learn hence, no more unequal War to wage— ......Il.21.565.445.
Pallas, to these, deplores th' unequal fates ......Od.5.8.171.
(Unequal contest) not his rage and pow'r, ...Od.5.432.193.
With sails outspread we fly th' unequal strife, ...Od.9.71.305.
Unequal to the melancholy tale: ......Od.11.409.404.
Far hence is by unequal Gods remov'd ......Od.14.73.39.
With winds and waves I held unequal strife; ......Od.14.348.51.
With such a foe th' unequal fight to try, ...Od.16.276.118.
Unequal fight! when youth contends with age! ......Od.18.39.169.
One maid, unequal to the task assign'd, ...Od.20.138.240.
Three times, unequal to the task, gave way: ......Od.21.132.264.
How shall this arm, unequal to the bow, ...Od.21.141.265.

UNEQUAL (CONTINUED)
And trod thy footsteps with unequal pace: ......Od.24.391.368.

UNEQUAL'D
The joy unequal'd, if its end it gain, ...3.EOM4.315.158.
The great *Alcides, Jove's* unequal'd Son, ...Il.18.148.329.
Nor paid too dearly for unequal'd charms; ......Od.11.344.399.

UNEQUALL'D
Naubolides with grace unequall'd shone, ...Od.8.121.269.

UNEQUALLY
No single Parts unequally surprize; ......1.EOC.249.268.

UNERRING
Unerring Nature, still divinely bright, ...1.EOC.70.246.
And *Teucer* haste, with his unerring Bow, ...1.TrES.75.452.
And *Teucer* haste, with his unerring Bow, ...1.TrES.80Z9.452.
Say, where full Instinct is th'unerring guide, ...3.EOM3.83.100.
Asks no firm hand, and no unerring line; ......3.Ep2.152.62.
To bend the Bow and aim unerring Darts: ......Il.5.68.269.
Thy winged Arrows and unerring Bow, ...Il.5.219.278.
His Fate was due to these unerring Hands. ......Il.5.241.278.
And *Teucer* haste with his unerring Bow, ...Il.12.419.97.
And *Teucer* haste, with his unerring Bow, ...Il.12.433.97.
From this unerring Hand there flies no Dart ......Il.14.531.189.
The Weapon flew, its Course unerring held, ...Il.22.369.471.
Unerring, but the heav'nly Shield repell'd ......Il.22.370.471.
His Hand unerring steers the steady Horse, ...Il.23.396.506.
Unerring will prescribe your destin'd course. ......Od.4.526.146.
But know—by me unerring Fates disclose ......Od.11.128.387.
Unerring truths, oh man, my lips relate; ......Od.11.170.390.
Elanc'd a-far by his unerring art, ...Od.19.672.228.

UNEVEN
Light quirks of Musick, broken and uneven, ...3.Ep4.143.151.

UNEXHAUSTED
Your preservering, unexhausted Bard: ......6.34.2.101.

UNEXPECTED
Arriv'st thou here, an unexpected guest? ......Od.5.112.177.

UNEXPLOR'D
Oh say what stranger Cause, yet unexplor'd, ...2.RL1.9.145.

UNEXTINGUISH'D
And unextinguish'd Laughter shakes the Skies. ......Il.1.771.124.
And Altars blaze with unextinguish'd Fire. ......Il.4.72.224.
And unextinguish'd laughter shakes the sky. ......Od.8.366.283.

UNFADING
Or from those Meads select unfading Flow'rs, ...1.PWi.74.94.
For her th' unfading rose of *Eden* blooms, ...2.ElAb.217.337.
With Gold unfading, *Somnus,* shall be thine; ......Il.14.273.175.
The fields are florid with unfading prime: ......Od.4.770.155.

UNFAILING
Has, from my Arm unfailing, struck the Bow, ...Il.15.551.218.

UNFAITHFUL
Secure they trust th'unfaithful Field, beset, ...1.W-F.103.160.
The brittle Steel, unfaithful to his Hand, ...Il.3.447.213.
This Bow, unfaithful to my glorious Aims, ...Il.5.270.280.
But pierc'd not thro: Unfaithful to his Hand, ...Il.13.217.116.
My feet thro' wine unfaithful to their weight, ...Od.11.77.385.
Nor err'd this hand unfaithful to its aim; ......Od.21.466.282.

UNFED
Unfed, unhous'd, neglected, on the clay, ...6.15.11.51.

UNFEELING
The broadest mirth unfeeling Folly wears, ...3.EOM4.319.158.
Unlucky Welsted! thy unfeeling master ......5.DunA2.201B.126.
Unlucky Welsted! thy unfeeling master, ...5.DunB2.209.306.

UNFELT
Pale Suns, unfelt, at distance roll away, ...2.TemF.55.256.
The Blow unfelt, the Tear he never shed; ......4.Arbu.349.120.
Till Death unfelt that tender frame destroy, ...6.86.17.245.

UNFILL'D
Unfill'd is yet the measure of my woes. ......Od.5.388.191.

UNFINISH'D
Unfinish'd Things, one knows not what to call, ...1.EOC.42.243.
Retir'd reluctant from th'unfinish'd Fight. ......1.TrES.118.454.
Old James himself unfinish'd left his tale, ...5.DunA2.380.146.
And *** himself unfinish'd left his tale, ...5.DunA2.380A.146.
Motteux himself unfinish'd left his tale, ...5.DunA2.380B.146.
I see th' unfinish'd Dormitory wall, ...5.DunA3.323A.189.
Motteux himself unfinish'd left his tale, ...5.DunB2.412.317.
Unfinish'd Treaties in each Office slept; ......5.DunB4.616.405.
Unfinish'd his proud Palaces remain, ...Il.2.858.165.
A Thought unfinish'd in that gen'rous Mind; ......Il.9.84.436.
Retir'd reluctant from th' unfinish'd Fight. ......Il.12.472.98.
Confounded and appall'd, th' unfinish'd game ......Od.4.884.159.
Their grief unfinish'd with the setting sun: ......Od.16.243.116.
Unfinish'd yet, and yet I thirst to hear! ......Od.17.608.161.
Ulysses will surprize th' unfinish'd game ......Od.19.685.229.

UNFIT
Unfit for publick Rule, or private Care; ......Il.9.89.437.
Tho' now unfit an active War to wage, ...Il.13.648.136.
Unfit to fight, but anxious for the Day. ......Il.14.46.160.

UNFIX'D

Quick as her Eyes, and as unfix'd as those: ....2.RL2.10.160.

UNFLEDG'D

They cry, they scream, their unfledg'd brood a prey ....Od.16.240.116.

UNFOLD

The vivid Green his shining Plumes unfold; ....1.W-F.117.161.
Two Marble Doors unfold on either side; ....1.TrUl.42.467.
Some to the Sun their Insect-Wings unfold, ...2.RL2.59.163.
The Temple shakes, the sounding Gates unfold, ...2.TemF.137.264.
A mortal Man unfold all Nature's law, ...3.EOM2.32.60.
But nobler scenes Maria's dreams unfold, ...3.Ep3.131.104.
On thy third Realm *look down;* unfold our Fate, ...6.65.5A.192.
And now *Olympus'* shining Gates unfold; ....Il.4.1.220.
Could Fates forsee, and mystic Dreams unfold; ....Il.5.191.275.
Close, or unfold, th' Eternal Gates of Day; ....Il.8.482.420.
Let me (my Son) an ancient Fact unfold, ...Il.9.649.466.
Ought, more conducive to our Weal, unfold. ....Il.14.119.163.
Touch'd with her secret Key, the Doors unfold; ....Il.14.195.168.
No story I unfold of public woes, ...Od.2.49.62.
Hear me the bodings of my breast unfold. ....Od.4.188.129.
And o'er soft palls of purple grain unfold ....Od.4.405.139.
Before the Queen *Alcinous'* sons unfold ....Od.8.455.288.
Seest thou these lids that now unfold in vain? ....Od.9.533.328.
And wide unfold the portals of the hall. ....Od.10.263.355.
Woes I unfold, of woes a dismal train. ....Od.11.475.407.
Unfold some trifle, but conceal the rest. ....Od.11.548.410.
There dangling pears exalted scents unfold, ...Od.11.729.421.
Now all at once tremendous scenes unfold; ....Od.12.240.443.
Two marble doors unfold on either side; ....Od.13.133.8.
But hear, tho' wise! This morning shall unfold ....Od.23.389.343.

UNFOLDED

Which still unfolded stand, by Night, by Day, ...2.TemF.426.284.

UNFOLDING

And bid new Musick charm th'unfolding Ear. ....1.Mes.42.116.
Less fragrant Scents th' unfolding Rose exhales; ....2.TemF.316.279.
The Gates unfolding pour forth all their Train, ...Il.2.978.170.
The Gates unfolding pour forth all their Train; ....Il.8.71.399.
Signs from above ensu'd: th' unfolding sky ....Od.21.452.282.

UNFOLDS

For this, our Queen unfolds to vision true ....5.DunA3.53.155.
For this, our Queen unfolds to vision true ....5.DunB3.61.323.
Sloath unfolds her Arms and wakes; ....6.11.32.31.
And the stern purpose of his Mind unfolds. ....Il.23.8.486.
The fourth, her maid unfolds th' amazing tale. ....Od.2.122.67.
For *Jove* unfolds our hospitable door, ...Od.14.67.39.
All he unfolds: His list'ning spouse turns pale ....Od.23.331.340.

UNFOREBODING

Vagrants of air, and unforeboding stray. ....Od.2.212.72. .

UNFORESEEN

Toils unforeseen, and fiercer, are decreed; ....Il.12.263.91.

UNFORGIVING

Shall curse that fierce, that unforgiving Mind. ....Il.16.45.237.

UNFORTIFY'D

While their weak Heads, like Towns unfortify'd, ...1.EOC.434.288.

UNFORTUNATELY

Unfortunately Good! a boding Sigh ....Il.16.66.238.

UNFREED

Shall beauteous *Helen* still remain unfreed, ...Il.2.213.138.

UNFREQUENTED

In the wild Olive's unfrequented Shade; ....1.TrUl.50.467.
In the wild olive's unfrequented shade, ...Od.13.141.11.
Far from the town, an unfrequented bay ....Od.24.359.366.

UNFRIENDED

Unfriended of the gales. All-knowing! say ....Od.4.631.149.
Alone, unfriended, will I tempt my way; ....Od.10.323.360.
Why rowl those eyes unfriended of repose? ....Od.20.42.234.

UNFRIENDLY

His shoulders intercept th' unfriendly rays. ....Od.19.457.217.
The wretch unfriendly to the race of man. ....Od.20.224.244.

UNFRUITFUL

Or were I curst with an unfruitful Bed, ...2.ChJM.119.20.
To light the dead, and warm th' unfruitful urn. ....2.ElAb.262.341.
But now th' unfruitful Glories charm no more. ....Il.9.417.453.

UNFURL

The desp'rate crew ascend, unfurl the sails; ....Od.4.1033.166.
They launch the vessel, and unfurl the sails, ...Od.8.47.264.

UNFURLS

Back from his brows a length of hair unfurls, ...Od.6.273.224.

UNFURNISH'D

When Merlin's Cave is half unfurnish'd yet? ....4.2HE1.355.225.

UNGARDED

Atrides, marking an ungarded Part, ...Il.11.335.49.

UNGEN'ROUS

Honour and Shame th' ungen'rous Thought recall: ....Il.22.139.459.
With Wounds ungen'rous, or with Taunts disgrace. ....Il.22.468.475.
Go, furious Youth! ungen'rous and unwise! ....Il.23.520.510.

UNGEN'ROUS (CONTINUED)

Ungen'rous Insult, impotent and vain! ....Il.24.953.576.
Ungen'rous were the man, and base of heart, ...Od.8.241.275.

UNGENTLE

A Deed ungentle, or a Word unkind: ....Il.24.969.576.
His shoulder-blade receiv'd th' ungentle shock; ....Od.17.548.159.

UNGOVERN'D

And short, or wide, th' ungovern'd Courser drive: ....Il.23.392.506.
Ill bear the brave a rude ungovern'd tongue, ...Od.8.199.273.
And the rude insults of ungovern'd tongues. ....Od.16.86.106.
But if o'erturn'd by rude, ungovern'd hands, ...Od.23.30.320.
...............Od.23.207.333.

UNGRACIOUS

At best, it falls to some ungracious Son ....4.HS2.173.69.
Ungracious Gods! with spite and envy curst! ....Od.5.149.178.
Hear me, oh *Cyclop!* hear ungracious host! ....Od.9.558.329.

UNGRATEFUL

Ah Youth ungrateful to a Flame like mine! ....1.TrSP.20.394.
Yet not ungrateful to the Peasant's Pain, ...1.TrUl.124.470.
Is this your Love, ungrateful and unkind, ...2.ChJM.760.51.
He whom ungrateful *Athens* cou'd expel, ...2.TemF.172.269.
As fruits ungrateful to the planter's care ....3.EOM2.181.76.
Touch'd with resentment of ungrateful Man, ...6.15.13.51.
This, from no venal or ungrateful Muse. ....6.52.52.136.
But thine, Ungrateful, and thy Brother's Cause? ....Il.1.210.97.
Ungrateful Man! deserves not this thy Care, ...Il.6.414.347.
But sound ungrateful in a Warrior's Ears: ....Il.7.431.386.
Ungrateful Prospect to the sullen Pow'r! ....Il.8.253.409.
Ungrateful Off'ring to th' immortal Pow'rs, ...Il.8.681.427.
Who takes the kind, and pays th' ungrateful part; ....Od.8.242.275.
Yet not ungrateful to the peasant's pain, ...Od.13.291.19.
While here, (ungrateful task!) his herds I feed, ...Od.14.47.38.
With din obstrep'rous, and ungrateful cries. ....Od.14.456.57.
My gen'rous soul abhors th' ungrateful part, ...Od.16.460.129.
A steer ungrateful to the bull's embrace, ...Od.20.235.244.

UNGUARDED

He pass'd the Gates which then unguarded lay, ...1.TrSt.535.432.
Men in their loose unguarded hours they take, ...3.EOM4.227.148.
To Heirs unknown descends th' unguarded store ....3.Ep2.149.62.
Thebes' hostile Walls, unguarded and alone, ...Il.4.438.241.
His Flank, unguarded by his ample Shield, ...Il.4.534.247.
Alone, unguarded, once he dar'd to go, ...Il.5.1002.314.
A Troop of Wolves th' unguarded Charge survey, ...Il.16.422.259.
Th' unguarded virgin as unchaste I blame, ...Od.6.343.228.
Does any mortal in th' unguarded hour ....Od.9.481.325.
Whence this unguarded openness of soul, ...Od.18.454.190.
Wing'd *Harpies* snatch'd th' unguarded charge away, ...Od.20.92.237.

UNGUENTS

And roseate Unguents, heav'nly Fragrance! shed: ....Il.23.229.499.
With unguents smooth the lucid marble shone, ...Od.3.520.112.
Then unguents in a vase of gold supply, ...Od.6.255.222.
The Graces unguents shed, ambrosial show'rs, ...Od.8.400.285.
Unguents that charm the Gods! she last assumes ....Od.8.401.285.
Shed sweets shed unguents, in a show'r of oil: ....Od.8.492.289.
With unguents smooth, of polish't marble wrought; ....Od.17.99.136.
Then unguents sweet and tepid streams we shed; ....Od.24.62.350.
With wines and unguents in a golden vase. ....Od.24.94.352.
Nor could his mother fun'ral unguents shed, ...Od.24.344.365.

UNGUIDED

Unguided now, their mighty Master slain. ....Il.16.628.268.
Unguided hence my trembling steps I bend, ...Od.20.441.254.

UNHALLOW'D

Here cease thy Flight, nor with unhallow'd Lays ....1.W-F.423.193.
In impious feasting, and unhallow'd joy; ....Od.12.468.454.

UNHAPPY

Unhappy *Wit,* like most mistaken Things, ...1.EOC.494.294.
I saw, unhappy! what I now relate, ...1.TrFD.53.388.
Behold, *Andræmon* and th'unhappy Sire ....1.TrFD.57.388.
Whose fatal Rage th'unhappy Monarch found; ....1.TrSt.14.410.
My Sons their old, unhappy Sire despise, ...1.TrSt.103.414.
From the first Birth of our unhappy State; ....1.TrSt.246.420.
Unhappy *Cadmus'* Fate who does not know? ....1.TrSt.319.423.
How mean a Fate, unhappy Child! is thine? ....1.TrSt.684.439.
Touch'd with Concern for his unhappy Guest) ....1.TrSt.807.443.
Unhappy Wife, whose Crime was too much Love! ....2.ChJM.765.52.
Yet cry, If Man's unhappy, God's unjust; ....3.EOM1.118.29.
Yet thou unhappy, think 'tis He's unjust; ....3.EOM1.118A.29.
And these be happy call'd, unhappy those; ....3.EOM4.68.135.
And these be call'd unhappy, happy those; ....3.EOM4.68A.135.
If while th'Unhappy hope, the Happy fear ....3.EOM4.70.135.
But fools the Good alone unhappy call, ...3.EOM4.97.137.
Unhappy Wharton, waking, found at last! ....3.Ep3.86.94.
Effects unhappy! from a Noble Cause. ....4.2HE1.160.209.
Unhappy Dryden!—In all Charles's days, ...4.2HE1.213.213.
Far worse unhappy *D[iape]r* succeeds, ...5.DunA2.286Z1.137.
And I, unhappy! left alone. ....6.10.112.27.
Farewell, unhappy *Tonson!* ....6.47.18.129.
Unhappy Son! (fair *Thetis* thus replies, ...Il.1.540.113.
Unhappy Monarch! whom the *Grecian* Race ....Il.2.348.143.
Unhappy *Paris!* but to Women brave, ...Il.3.55.192.
(Seiz'd by the Crest) th' unhappy Warrior drew; ....Il.3.456.213.
(Which oh avert from our unhappy State! ....Il.5.226.278.
But if unhappy, we desert the Fight, ...Il.5.292.281.
Unhappy they, and born of luckless Sires, ...Il.6.157.333.
Althæa's Hate th' unhappy Warrior drew, ...Il.9.681.468.
Th' unhappy Gen'ral of the *Grecian* Bands; ....Il.10.97.7.
Let me, unhappy, to your Fleet be born, ...Il.10.512.26.

UNHAPPY (CONTINUED)

Stretch'd in the Dust th' unhappy Warrior lies, ...Il.11.309.48.
Unhappy Man! whose Death our Hands shall grace! ....Il.11.553.58.
Unhappy Hero! and advis'd in vain! ....Il.12.127.86.
Or bleeds my Friend by some unhappy Wound? ....Il.13.330.121.
Can't thou, unhappy in thy Wiles! withstand ....Il.15.21.194.
It stretch'd in Dust unhappy *Lycophron:* ....Il.15.501.216.
Unhappy Glories! for his Fate was near, ...Il.15.736.224.
Th' unhappy Hero; fled, or shar'd his Fate. ....Il.15.785.226.
The first that touch'd th' unhappy *Trojan* Shore; ....Il.15.857.229.
Unhappy *Glaucus* heard the dying Chief. ....Il.16.628.269.
And doom'd to *Trojan* Dogs th' unhappy Dead; ....Il.17.138.293.
Unhappy Coursers of immortal Strain! ....Il.17.504.308.
E'er the sad Fruit of thy unhappy Womb ....Il.18.113.328.
(Unhappy Change!) now senseless, pale, he found, ...Il.18.281.335.
Sees with Regret unhappy Mortals die. ....Il.20.32.394.
Thus sadly slain, th' unhappy *Polydore;* ....Il.20.486.414.
The valiant Sons of an unhappy Sire; ....Il.20.532.416.
Unhappy Boy! no Pray'r, no moving Art ....Il.20.541.417.
Two Sons (alas, unhappy Sons) she bore, ...Il.21.100.426.
Who, or from whence? Unhappy is the Sire, ...Il.21.167.428.
Of Speech, Unhappy! from the dying Hour. ....Il.22.412.472.
Born with one Fate, to one unhappy Life! ....Il.22.609.481.
Is now that Name no more, unhappy Boy! ....Il.22.652.483.
But grant one last Embrace, unhappy Boy! ....Il.23.113.492.
Prone on the Dust th' unhappy Master fell; ....Il.23.474.509.
Last came, *Admetus!* thy unhappy Son; ....Il.23.609.514.
Unhappy *Ajax* stumbles on the Plain; ....Il.23.906.525.
How long, unhappy! shall thy Sorrows flow, ...Il.24.163.542.
Unhappy Consort of a King distrest! ....Il.24.233.546.
Inglorious Sons of an unhappy Sire! ....Il.24.317.549.
Unhappy, in his Country's Cause he fell! ....Il.24.621.562.
Unhappy Prince! thus guardless and alone ....Il.24.654.564.
Apart from *Priam,* lest th' unhappy Sire ....Il.24.732.568.
Th' unhappy Race the Honours of a Grave. ....Il.24.772.569.
Now twice ten Years (unhappy Years) are o'er ....Il.24.964.576.
Our eyes, unhappy! never greeted more. ....Od.1.274.46.
Ev'n to th' unhappy, that unjustly bleed, ...Od.3.240.97.
Unhappy man! to wasting woes a prey, ...Od.5.207.181.
What shall I do? Unhappy me! who knows ....Od.5.452.194.
Th' unhappy man; ev'n Fate had been in vain: ....Od.5.555.199.
'Tis what the happy to th' unhappy owe. ....Od.7.199.245.
Th' unhappy series of a wand'rer's woe? ....Od.9.12.301.
And thrice we call'd on each unhappy Shade. ....Od.9.74.305.
'Tis what the happy to th' unhappy owe. ....Od.9.320.319.
Snatch'd two, unhappy! of my martial band; ....Od.9.343.320.
And if th' unhappy *Cyclop* be thy Son; ....Od.9.620.332.
With semblance fair th' unhappy men she plac'd. ....Od.10.269.355.
Unhappy race! whom endless night invades, ...Od.11.19.380.
Unhappy stranger! (thus the faithful swain ....Od.14.41.37.
They sought repaste; while to th' unhappy kind, ...Od.14.383.53.
Unhappy guest! whose sorrows touch my mind! ....Od.14.395.54.
Of all the ills unhappy mortals know, ...Od.15.364.87.
A wretch unhappy, meerly for his need? ....Od.17.471.156.
Unhappy me a *Cyprian* took a-board, ...Od.17.524.158.
The bow, bequeath'd by this unhappy hand, ...Od.21.37.261.
Thy last of games unhappy hast thou play'd; ....Od.22.32.288.
Couch'd close to earth, unhappy *Medon* lay, ...Od.22.402.307.

UNHARM'D

Alive, unharm'd, with all his Peers around, ...Il.5.629.298.
Alive, unharm'd, and vig'rous from his Wound. ....Il.7.375.382.
And pass unharm'd the Dangers of the Night; ....Il.10.250.13.
Then how unharm'd he past the *Siren*-coasts, ...Od.23.352.341.

UNHARNESS'D

Their Steeds unharness'd from the weary Car) ....Il.18.288.335.
The mules unharness'd range beside the main, ...Od.6.103.210.

UNHEARD

Alike unheard, unpity'd, and forlorn. ....1.PAu.22.82.
Would die unheard of, as we liv'd unseen. ....2.TemF.361.281.
Thus let me live, unheard, unknown; ....6.1.17.A.4.
Unheard, unknown, ...6.11.102.33.
To sigh unheard in, to the passing winds? ....6.81.10.225.
His fruitless Words are lost unheard in Air; ....Il.8.123.404.
Unheard approach'd, and stood before the Tent. ....Il.11.789.71.
O'er the dead Hero, thus (unheard) replies. ....Il.22.460.474.
Vanish'd at once! unheard of, and unknown! ....Od.1.311.47.
Unheard, unseen, three years her arts prevail; ....Od.2.121.67.
Has *Jove* reserv'd, unheard of, and unknown, ...Od.3.107.91.
For perilous th' assay, unheard the toil, ...Od.4.535.146.
But if unheard, in vain compassion plead, ...Od.11.91.385.
Unheard, unseen, three years her arts prevail; ....Od.24.168.356.

UNHEEDED

The World's great Victor pass'd unheeded by; ....6.32.34.97.
To right, to left, unheeded take your way, ...Il.12.281.91.
And o'er our Heads unheeded Javelins sing. ....Il.13.631.136.
Repast unheeded, while he vents his Woes. ....Il.24.160.542.

UNHEEDFUL

I heard his Counsels with unheedful Mind, ...Il.5.253.279.
Remain'd unheedful of his Lord's Commands: ....Il.5.396.285.
No firstling Lambs, unheedful! didst thou vow, ...Il.23.1022.529.
(Reply'd the Chief) to no unheedful breast; ....Od.17.333.147.

UNHELP'D

Unhelp'd we stand, unequal to engage ....Il.17.580.311.

UNHOLY

Far other raptures, of unholy joy: ....2.ElAb.224.338.

UNHONOUR'D

A sense-less, worth-less, and unhonour'd crowd; ....4.2HE1.306.221.
Unwept, unhonour'd, uninterr'd he lies! ....Il.22.484.476.

UNHONOUR'D (CONTINUED)

While foul in Dust th' unhonour'd Carcase lies, ...Il.24.28.536.
Unmark'd, unhonour'd, at a Monarch's gate; ....Od.1.158.40.

UNHOP'D

These eyes at last behold th' unhop'd-for coast, ...Od.5.525.197.
Light of my eyes! he comes! unhop'd-for joy! ....Od.17.52.135.

UNHOP'D-FOR

These eyes at last behold th' unhop'd-for coast, ...Od.5.525.197.
Light of my eyes! he comes! unhop'd-for joy! ....Od.17.52.135.

UNHOUS'D

Unfed, unhous'd, neglected, on the clay, ...6.15.11.51.

UNHURT

Or quit the Fleet, and pass unhurt away, ...Il.13.933.149.
Unhurt the beeves, untouch'd the woolly train ....Od.12.389.450.

UNIFORM'D

For who by *Phœbus* uniform'd, could know ....Od.8.533.291.

UNINHABITED

But uninhabited, untill'd, unsown ....Od.9.143.311.

UNINJUR'D

Untouch'd she stay'd, uninjur'd she removes, ...Il.9.173.441.
Untouch'd she stay'd, uninjur'd she removes, ...Il.9.360.451.
Whole Years untouch'd, uninjur'd shall remain ....Il.19.33.373.
The rest to *Greece* uninjur'd I'll restore: ....Il.22.331.470.
Of god-like Heroes who uninjur'd stood ....Od.11.477.408.

UNINSCRIB'D

(Obscure the Place, and uninscrib'd the Stone) ....1.W-F.320.180.

UNINSPIR'D

Ulysses heard, nor uninspir'd obey'd. ....Il.2.220.138.

UNINTELLIGIBLE

O'er a learn'd, unintelligible place; ....4.JD2.102.143.

UNINTERR'D

Unwept, unhonour'd, uninterr'd he lies! ....Il.22.484.476.
Nor shall he lye unwept, and uninterr'd; ....Il.24.783.569.

UNION

The Force of pow'rful Union conquers All. ....1.TrES.150.455.
Union the bond of all things, and of Man. ....3.EOM3.150.108.
"Here too all forms of social union find, ...3.EOM3.179.111.
From Order, Union, full Consent of things! ....3.EOM3.296.123.
From Union, Order, full Consent of things! ....3.EOM3.296A.123.
Learns, from this union of the rising Whole, ...3.EOM4.337.161.
Sooner shall *Rowe* lampoon the UNION ....6.10.45.25.
From Sacred Union and consent of Things. ....6.11.35Z10.31.
Nor break the sacred Union of the Sky: ....Il.1.747.123.
A Senate void of Union as of Choice, ...Il.7.416A.385.
The Force of pow'rful Union conquers all. ....Il.12.504.100.
For Strife, I hear, has made the Union cease, ...Il.14.237.172.
For Strife, I hear, has made that Union cease ....Il.14.347.179.
And lasting union crown your blissful days. ....Od.6.222.220.
Firm union on their Favourites below; ....Od.6.224.220.
Man's social days in union, and in joy? ....Od.9.8.301.
And numbers leagu'd in impious union dread: ....Od.18.274.179.

UNISON

While the long solemn Unison went round: ....5.DunB4.612.405.

UNITE

When the ripe Colours *soften* and *unite,* ....1.EOC.488.294.
Turtles and Doves of diff'ring Hues, unite, ...1.TrSP.43.395.
The *Greeks* oppress'd, their utmost Force unite, ...1.TrES.93.453.
Unite, and soon that Hostile Fleet shall fall, ...1.TrES.149.455.
The Tortoise here and Elephant unite, ...2.RL1.135.156.
May one kind grave unite each hapless name, ...2.ElAb.343.347.
More studious to divide than to unite, ...3.EOM2.82.64.
Yet, mix'd and soften'd, in his work unite: ....3.EOM2.112.68.
If white and black blend, soften, and unite ....3.EOM2.213.81.
The Wood supports the Plain, the parts unite, ...3.Ep4.81.145.
Buy *Hymen's* kinder flames unite; ....6.51ii.21.153.
But *Hymen's* flames like stars unite; ....6.51ii.21A.153.
Like friendly colours found them both unite, ...6.52.15.156.
Like friendly colours found our Arts unite, ...6.52.15A.156.
Like friendly colours found our Hearts unite, ...6.52.15B.156.
Let both unite with well-consenting Mind, ...Il.1.370.106.
Unite, and rouze the Sons of *Greece* to Arms. ....Il.2.94.131.
In sixty Sail th' *Arcadian* Bands unite. ....Il.2.740.161.
Phorcys and brave *Ascanius* here unite ....Il.2.1050.172.
Here, at our Gates, your brave Efforts unite, ...Il.6.99.328.
Touch'd where the Neck and hollow Chest unite: ....Il.8.392.416.
There Horse and Foot in mingled Deaths unite, ...Il.11.652.63.
There, Horse and Foot, the *Pylian* Troops unite, ...Il.11.860.74.
Rhesus and *Rhodius* then unite their Rills, ...Il.12.17.82.
The *Greeks,* oppress'd, their utmost Force unite, ...Il.12.447.97.
Unite, and soon that hostile Fleet shall fall; ....Il.12.503.100.
Not vain the weakest, if their Force unite; ....Il.13.311.120.
Fellows in Arms! your timely Aid unite; ....Il.13.608.135.
Unite thy Force, my Friend, and we prevail. ....Il.17.557.310.
Struck where the crossing Belts unite behind, ...Il.20.479.414.
Shall ought avail him, if our Rage unite: ....Il.21.369.436.
(The swains unite their toil) the walls, the floor ....Od.22.489.313.

UNITED

All comes *united* to th' admiring Eyes; ....1.EOC.250.268.
Their Strength, united best may help to bear ....1.TrES.69.452.
Your Strength, united, best may help to bear ....1.TrES.80Z3.452.
True faith, true policy, united ran, ...3.EOM3.239.116.

UNITED (CONTINUED)

If all, united, thy ambition call, ... 3.EOM4.285.155.
And Jones' and Boyle's united labours fall, ... 5.DunA3.324.189.
While Jones' and Boyle's united labours fall: ... 5.DunB3.328.336.
With all th' united labours of the year, ... 6.35.18.103.
United wish, and mutual joy! ... 6.51ii.26.153.
Th' united Strength of all the Gods above ... Il.1.734.122.
Assemble all th' united Bands of *Troy;* ... Il.2.973.169.
While thus their Pray'rs united mount the Sky; ... Il.3.370.211.
And fought united, and united dy'd. ... Il.5.755.303.
And fought united, and united dy'd. ... Il.5.755.303.
Their Strength, united, best may help to bear ... Il.12.413.96.
Your Strength, united, best may help to bear ... Il.12.427.97.
Sprung to their Car; and with united Pains ... Il.23.737.519.
With pow'rs united, obstinately bold ... Od.4.561.147.
With all th' united labours of the year; ... Od.7.159.244.
(So need compells.) Then all united strive ... Od.22.89.290.

UNITES

The Grave unites; where ev'n the Great find Rest, ... 1.W-F.317.179.
(But Airy Substance soon unites again) ...! ... 2.RL3.152.179.
Where to the Hip th' inserted Thigh unites, ... Il.5.375.285.

UNITIES

The *Manners, Passions, Unities,* what not? ... 1.EOC.276.271.

UNIVERSAL

One *clear, unchang'd,* and *Universal* Light, ... 1.EOC.71.247.
Immortal Heirs of *Universal* Praise! ... 1.EOC.190.262.
And sacred Silence reigns, and universal Peace. ... 1.TrSt.291.422.
All partial Evil, universal Good: ... 3.EOM1.292.51.
Here then we rest: "The Universal Cause ... 3.EOM3.1.92.
Learn Dulness, learn! "The Universal Cause ... 3.EOM3.1A.92.
Heav'n's attribute was Universal Care, ... 3.EOM3.159.109.
Remember, Man, "the Universal Cause ... 3.EOM4.35.131.
Or partial Ill is universal Good, ... 3.EOM4.114.139.
When universal homage Umbra pays, ... 3.Ep1.118.24.
To wrap me in the Universal Shade; ... 4.HS1.96.13.
Booth enters—hark! the Universal Peal! ... 4.2HE1.334.223.
And universal Darkness covers all." ... 5.DunA3.356.193.
And universal Dulness cover all." ... 5.DunA3.356A.193.
And universal Darkness buries all." ... 5.DunA3.356B.193.
And Universal Darkness buries All. ... 5.DunB4.656.409.
And Universal Dulness buries All. ... 5.DunB4.656A.409.
One universal, solemn Show'r began; ... Il.24.645.563.
And *Troy* sends forth one universal Groan. ... Il.24.885.573.
But universal night usurps the pole! ... Od.20.430.254.

UNIVERSE

See worlds on worlds compose one universe, ... 3.EOM1.24.16.

UNJUST

Nor be so *Civil* as to prove *Unjust;* ... 1.EOC.581.306.
Unjust Decree! while This enjoys the State, ... 1.TrSt.194.418.
Yet cry, If Man's unhappy, God's unjust; ... 3.EOM1.118.29.
Yet thou unhappy, think 'tis He's unjust; ... 3.EOM1.118A.29.
Gods partial, changeful, passionate, unjust, ... 3.EOM3.257.118.
So drives Self-love, thro' just and thro' unjust, ... 3.EOM3.269.120.
And certain Laws, by Suff'rers thought unjust, ... 4.2HE2.60.169.
When *Athens* sinks by fates unjust, ... 6.51i.17.151.
Should I submit to each unjust Decree: ... Il.1.390.106.
Not all the Gods are partial and unjust. ... Il.4.44.223.
Take back th' unjust Reproach! Behold we stand ... Il.4.404.240.
Thou most unjust, most odious in our Eyes! ... Il.5.1097.319.
See'st thou the *Greeks* by Fates unjust opprest, ... Il.8.244.409.
Must you be Cowards, if your King's unjust? ... Il.13.154.111.
A godless Crew, abandon'd and unjust, ... Il.13.793.142.
Cease then thy Offspring's Death unjust to call; ... Il.15.156.202.
Oh sight (he cry'd) dishonest and unjust! ... Od.7.214.247.
He suffers who gives surety for th' unjust: ... Od.8.386.284.
Whether a race unjust, of barb'rous might, ... Od.9.203.314.
Unjust to me and all that serve the state, ... Od.17.472.156.
Just and unjust recording in their mind, ... Od.17.580.160.
Lo! at thy feet unjust *Antinous* bleeds, ... Od.22.62.289.
T'insult the dead is cruel and unjust; ... Od.22.450.309.
None now the kindred of th' unjust shall own; ... Od.24.554.374.

UNJUSTLY

The fatal Steel unjustly was apply'd, ... 4.HAdv.83.83.
Deem not unjustly by my doom opprest ... Od.1.86.35.
Ev'n to th' unhappy, that unjustly bleed, ... Od.3.240.97.

UNKIND

Have Comfort, Spouse, nor think thy Lord unkind; ... 2.ChJM.567.42.
Is this your Love, ungrateful and unkind, ... 2.ChJM.760.51.
Ah my lov'd Lord! 'twas much unkind (she cry'd) ... 2.ChJM.795.53.
'Twas You were jealous, not your Wife unkind: ... 2.ChJM.808.54.
For when my transitory Spouse, unkind, ... 2.ChWB.25.58.
Nay, *Poll* sate mute, and *Shock* was most Unkind! ... 2.RL4.164.197.
The phantom flies me, as unkind as you. ... 2.ElAb.236.339.
Is Heav'n unkind to Man, and Man alone? ... 3.EOM1.186.37.
Is Heav'n unkind to nothing but to Man? ... 3.EOM1.186A.37.
Nor from a Friend th' unkind Reproach appear'd, ... Il.9.49.434.
A Deed ungentle, or a Word unkind: ... Il.24.969.576.
Unkind confed'rates in his dire intent! ... Od.4.965.163.
Another Isle than *Cyprus* more unkind, ... Od.17.531.158.
Unkind, the fond illusion to impose! ... Od.23.19.319.
A woman like *Penelope* unkind? ... Od.23.100.324.
Not for thy sloth, I deem thy Lord unkind; ... Od.24.296.364.

UNKINDLED

Th' unkindled Light'ning in his Hand he took, ... Il.11.239.46.

UNKINDLY

And punish us unkindly by his death? ... Od.2.375.78.
Unkindly with my love my son conspir'd, ... Od.11.246.393.

UNKINGLY

What shameful Words, (unkingly as thou art) ... Il.14.90.162.

UNKNOWING

These shades, unknowing of the fates, she sought, ... 1.TrFD.17.386.
Those shades, unknowing of the fates, she sought, ... 1.TrFD.17A.386.
Willing I come; unknowing how to fear; ... 1.TrSt.759.442.
And curs'd with hearts unknowing how to yield. ... 2.Elegy.42.366.
And cheats th'unknowing Widow, and the Poor? ... 4.JD4.141.37.
Let not this weak, unknowing hand ... 6.50.25.147.
If ere this weak, unknowing hand ... 6.50.25A.147.
Hector they face; unknowing how to fear, ... Il.8.149.405.
"Oh nurs'd with Gall, unknowing how to yield! ... Il.16.244.249.
Big with a Mule, unknowing of the Yoke: ... Il.23.334.503.
Surveys his charge, unknowing of deceit: ... Od.4.607.148.
Unknowing of the course to *Pyle* design'd, ... Od.4.862.159.
If man on frail unknowing man relies, ... Od.20.56.235.

UNKNOWN

Then gath'ring Flocks on unknown Mountains fed, ... 1.W-F.87.158.
And Things *unknown* propos'd as Things *forgot:* ... 1.EOC.575.306.
This change unknown, astonish'd at the sight ... 1.TrFD.35.387.
Unknown, with Wonder may perplex your Mind. ... 1.TrSt.659.438.
Yet if propitious to a Wretch unknown, ... 1.TrSt.802.443.
And unknown Mountains, crown'd with unknown Woods. ... 1.TrUl.67.468.
And unknown Mountains, crown'd with unknown Woods. ... 1.TrUl.67.468.
Thou seest an Island, not to those unknown, ... 1.TrUl.118.469.
In dead of Night an unknown Port we gain'd, ... 1.TrUl.152.470.
Conscious of Pleasures to the World unknown: ... 2.ChJM.544.41.
Your Statues moulder'd, and your Names unknown. ... 2.TemF.353.280.
Of unknown Dutchesses leud Tales we tell, ... 2.TemF.388.282.
This having heard and seen, some Pow'r unknown ... 2.TemF.418.283.
Unblemish'd let me live, or die unknown, ... 2.TemF.523.289.
Perhaps acts second to some sphere unknown, ... 3.EOM1.58.20.
Perhaps acts second to a sphere unknown ... 3.EOM1.58A.20.
All Nature is but Art, unknown to thee; ... 3.EOM1.289.50.
The chain holds on, and where it ends, unknown. ... 3.EOM3.26.95.
Heav'ns not his own, and worlds unknown before? ... 3.EOM3.106.102.
Thus States were form'd; the name of King unknown, ... 3.EOM3.209.114.
Just what you hear, you have, and what's unknown ... 3.EOM4.239.150.
Hope of known bliss, and Faith in bliss unknown: ... 3.EOM4.346.162.
To Heirs unknown descends th' unnumber'd store ... 3.Ep2.149A.62.
To Heirs unknown descends th' unguarded store ... 3.Ep2.149.62.
Must act on Reasons pow'rful, tho' unknown: ... 3.Ep3.114A.101.
Must act on motives pow'rful, tho' unknown: ... 3.Ep3.114.101.
"His race, his form, his name almost unknown?" ... 3.Ep3.284.116.
And who unknown defame me, let them be ... 4.HS1.139.19.
Why did I write? what sin to me unknown ... 4.Arbu.125.104.
His Life, tho' Long, to sickness past unknown, ... 4.Arbu.402.126.
Despise the known, nor tremble at th' unknown? ... 4.2HE2.311.187.
A youth unknown to Phœbus, in despair, ... 5.DunA2.205.127.
Thence a new world, to Nature's laws unknown, ... 5.DunA3.237.177.
Then a new world, to Nature's laws unknown, ... 5.DunA3.237A.177.
"And are these wonders, Son, to thee unknown? ... 5.DunA3.269.180.
Unknown to thee? These wonders are thy own. ... 5.DunA3.270.180.
A youth unknown to Phœbus, in despair, ... 5.DunB2.213.306.
Thence a new world to Nature's laws unknown, ... 5.DunB3.241.332.
"And are these wonders, Son, to thee unknown? ... 5.DunB3.273.333.
Unknown to thee? These wonders are thy own. ... 5.DunB3.274.333.
Avaunt—is Aristarchus yet unknown? ... 5.DunB4.210.363.
Thus let me live, unseen, unknown; ... 6.1.17.4.
Thus let me live, unheard, unknown; ... 6.1.17A.4.
Unheard, unknown, ... 6.11.102.33.
To all his friends, and ev'n his Queen, unknown, ... 6.15.4.51.
Those printed unknown Tongues, 'tis said, ... 6.29.7Z1.83.
The nymph despis'd, the Rape had been unknown. ... 6.38.4.107.
You, like the *Samian,* visit Lands unknown, ... 6.96iii.17.275.
Passion and Pride were to her soul unknown, ... 6.115.5.322.
To Heirs unknown, descends th' unnumber'd Store, ... 6.154.35.403.
His deep Design unknown, the Hosts approve ... Il.2.173.136.
Unknown alike in Council and in Field! ... Il.2.238.138.
But he, the mystick Will of Heav'n unknown, ... Il.5.83.270.
And thought the Steeds (your large Supplies unknown) ... Il.5.254.279.
Hence great *Anchises* stole a Breed unknown ... Il.5.332.282.
And wide thro' Fens an unknown Journey takes; ... Il.5.735.302.
Each to his Rival yields the Mark unknown, ... Il.7.223.375.
What art thou, speak, that on Designs unknown ... Il.10.90.6.
The rest were vulgar Deaths, unknown to Fame. ... Il.11.394.52.
Tho' then not deedless, nor unknown to Fame; ... Il.13.978.152.
Nor seek, unknown to thee, the sacred Cells ... Il.14.353.179.
There stood a *Trojan* not unknown to Fame, ... Il.17.648.313.
Unknown to him who sits remote on high, ... Il.18.223.332.
Unknown to all the Synod of the Sky. ... Il.18.224.332.
To thee (presumptuous as thou art) unknown, ... Il.22.359.470.
Old like thy self, and not unknown to Fame; ... Il.24.488.556.
And to the dome th' unknown Cælestial leads. ... Od.1.166.40.
Vanish'd at once! unheard of, and unknown! ... Od.1.311.47.
Their unknown guests, and at the banquet place. ... Od.3.46.88.
Where savage Pyrates seek thro' seas unknown ... Od.3.88.90.
Has *Jove* reserv'd, unheard of, and unknown; ... Od.3.107.91.
And measur'd tracts unknown to other ships, ... Od.3.409.106.
Whoe'er thou art, before whose stream unknown ... Od.5.568.199.
A wretched stranger, and of all unknown! ... Od.7.34.235.
Thus having spoke, th' unknown celestial leads: ... Od.7.49.236.
With honours yet to womankind unknown, ... Od.7.86.238.
O'er unknown seas arriv'd from unknown shores. ... Od.8.14.262.
O'er unknown seas arriv'd from unknown shores. ... Od.8.14.262.
To coasts unknown, and oceans yet untry'd. ... Od.9.118.308.
Reveal'd the landscape and the scene unknown, ... Od.9.175.312.
Pyrates perhaps, who seek thro' seas unknown ... Od.9.301.318.
Unknown to pain, in age resign thy breath, ... Od.11.166.389.
Ev'n to thy Queen disguis'd, unknown, return; ... Od.11.562.411.
And unknown mountains, crown'd with unknown woods. ... Od.13.234.17.
And unknown mountains, crown'd with unknown woods. ... Od.13.234.17.
Thou seest an Island, not to those unknown ... Od.13.285.19.
In dead of night an unknown port we gain'd, ... Od.13.319.22.

UNKNOWN (CONTINUED)

And secret walk, unknown to mortal eyes.	Od.13.454.28.
With friendly step precedes his unknown guest,	Od.14.58.38.
Thus he, benevolent; his unknown guest	Od.14.131.42.
The faithful servant joy'd his unknown Lord.	Od.14.489.59.
The skill of weather and of winds unknown,	Od.14.541.63.
Outcasts of earth, to breathe an unknown sky?	Od.16.395.125.
But all unknown, if yet *Ulysses* breathe,	Od.17.130.138.
Spurn'd with his rustic heel the King unknown;	Od.17.273.145.
Tho' all unknown his clime, or noble race.	Od.17.449.155.
With vigorous youth, unknown to cares, engage!	Od.18.61.169.
The Peers with smiles addrest their unknown King:	Od.18.136.173.
And bold *Antinous*, yet untry'd, unknown:	Od.21.190.269.
At length he comes; but comes despis'd, unknown	Od.21.215.270.
A man unknown, a needy wanderer?	Od.21.314.274.
To softness lost, to spousal love unknown,	Od.23.105.324.
The Suitors death unknown, 'till we remove	Od.23.137.327.
The unknown instrument with strange surprize,	Od.23.290.337.
Unknown to pain in age resign my breath,	Od.23.299.337.

UNLAC'D

The radiant helmet from my brows unlac'd,	Od.14.305.50.

UNLADE

They moor the vessel and unlade the stores:	Od.16.375.124.

UNLAMENTED

Thus unlamented pass the proud away,	2.Elegy.43.366.
Thus unlamented let me dye;	6.1.18.4.
And each now wails an unlamented shade.	Od.22.455.310.

UNLEARN'D

Amaze th'unlearn'd, and make the Learned *Smile*.	1.EOC.327.275.
Content, if hence th' Unlearn'd their Wants may view,	1.EOC.739.326.
What you (she cry'd) unlearn'd in Arts to please,	2.TemF.396.282.
Unlearn'd in all th' industrious arts of toil.	Od.9.150.311.

UNLESS

Unless our Desart Cities please thy Sight,	1.TrSt.774.442.
Unless great Acts superior Merit prove,	1.TrES.35.451.
Unless good Sense preserve what Beauty gains:	2.RL5.16.200.
Unless he praise some monster of a King,	4.2HE1.210.213.
Unless the Gods bestow'd a proper Muse?	4.2HE1.234.215.
Unless the Gods bestow'd the proper Muse?	4.2HE1.234A.215.
Unless, good man! he has been fairly in?	4.EpS2.192.324.
Unless the ladies bid them mind their cards.	4.1740.24.333.
Unless i' th' Name of *Tom D'Urfy.*	6.30.63.88.
The jest is lost, unless he prints his Face.	6.105iii.4.301.
The jest is lost, unless you print his Face.	6.105iii.4A.301.
Unless great Acts superior Merit prove,	II.12.379.95.
Give him to know, unless the *Grecian* Train	II.15.240.206.
(Unless ye boast that heav'nly Race in vain)	II.19.441.390.
Unless with filial rage *Orestes* glow,	Od.4.737.153.
Unless at distance, wretch! thou keep behind,	Od.17.530.158.

UNLICENS'D

I poach in Suidas for unlicens'd Greek.	5.DunB4.228.365.
No more unlicens'd thus to brave the main.	Od.13.175.14.
No more unlicens'd brave the deeps, no more	Od.13.208.15.

UNLIKE

Unlike Successes equal Merits found.	2.TemF.295.278.
Ah! how unlike the man of times to come!	3.EOM3.161.109.
All how unlike each other, all how true!	3.Ep2.6.48.
Figures ill-pair'd, and Similes unlike.	5.DunA1.64.67.
Figures ill pair'd, and Similies unlike.	5.DunB1.66.275.
Like, yet unlike these flow'rs am I;	6.4iv.22.11.
Unlike our gross, diseas'd, terrestrial Blood:	II.5.424.288.
How far unlike those Chiefs of Race divine,	II.5.788.304.
In form, ah how unlike their heav'nly kind?	Od.7.285.250.
Among the great, unlike the sons of Fame.	Od.8.178.271.
A form enormous! far unlike the race	Od.9.221.315.
Unlike those vagrants who on falshood live,	Od.11.452.406.
Be dumb when heav'n afflicts! unlike yon' train	Od.18.171.175.

UNLOAD

Some to unload the fertile branches run,	6.35.19.103.
Some to unload the fertile branches run,	Od.7.160.244.
Unload thy treasures, and thy gally moor;	Od.10.478.366.

UNLOADED

Merchants unloaded here their Freight,	6.14v(b).4.49.

UNLOCK

Unlock your Springs, and open all your Shades.	1.W-F.4.148.
Thus the small jett which hasty hands unlock,	5.DunA2.169.122.
Thus the small jett, which hasty hands unlock,	5.DunB2.177.304.

UNLOCK'D

The deafen'd ear unlock'd, the chains unbound.	Od.12.239.443.

UNLOCKS

Of ancient Writ unlocks the learned Store,	1.W-F.247.172.
This Casket *India's* glowing Gems unlocks,	2.RL1.133.156.

UNLOOK'D

She comes unlook'd for, if she comes at all:	2.TemF.514.288.
Oh curst event! and oh unlook'd-for aid!	Od.22.164.295.

UNLOOK'D-FOR

Oh curst event! and oh unlook'd-for aid!	Od.22.164.295.

UNLOOS'D

There *Juno* stop'd, and (her fair Steeds unloos'd)	II.5.966.312.
The *Hours* unloos'd them, panting as they stood,	II.8.536.422.

UNLOOSE

Should *Jove* dire war unloose, with spear and shield	Od.18.418.189.

UNLUCKY

Unlucky, as *Fungoso* in the Play ,	1.EOC.328.275.
The Vengeance due to this unlucky Steel?	1.TrSt.771.442.
Who-e'er offends, at some unlucky Time	4.HS1.77.13.
Here studious I unlucky moderns save,	5.DunA1.161.82.
Unlucky Oldmixon! thy lordly master	5.DunA2.201.126.
Unlucky Welsted! thy unfeeling master	5.DunA2.201B.126.
Unlucky Welsted! thy unfeeling master,	5.DunB2.209.306.
Alas! poor *Æschylus!* unlucky Dog!	6.105i.1.300.
And death, unlucky guest, attends thy deed.	Od.22.34.288.

UNMAN'D

Are left unman'd; or if they yet retain	II.22.479.475.

UNMANGLED

Or yet unmangled rest his cold Remains?	II.24.500.557.

UNMANLY

"Fye, 'tis unmanly thus to sigh and groan;	2.ChWB.197.66.
With base Reproaches and unmanly Pride.	II.5.809.304.
And with unmanly Tears his Life demands.	II.10.448.23.
That flows so fast in these unmanly Tears?	II.16.10.235.
And with unmanly Tremblings shook the Car,	II.16.491.262.
With mean Reproaches, and unmanly Pride:	II.20.243.404.
Unmanly shrieks precede each dying groan,	Od.22.345.304.

UNMANN'D

Again unmann'd a show'r of sorrow shed:	Od.8.90.267.
Some God assisted, and unmann'd us all:	Od.24.209.358.

UNMANS

Their Strength he withers, and unmans their Souls.	II.8.96.402.

UNMARK'D

Some unmark'd fibre, or some varying vein:	3.Ep1.16.17.
Unmark'd, unhonour'd, at a Monarch's gate;	Od.1.158.40.
Where on th' all-bearing earth unmark'd it grew,	Od.10.362.362.

UNMASK

And in the traytor friend unmask the foe;	Od.18.198.176.

UNMATCH'D

A Maid, unmatch'd in Manners as in Face,	II.1.141.93.
In Rage unbounded, and unmatch'd in Might.	II.6.124.330.
Unmatch'd our Force, unconquer'd is our Hand:	II.8.561.423.
Twelve Steeds unmatch'd in Fleetness and in Force,	II.9.161.440.
Skill'd in each Art, unmatch'd in Form divine,	II.9.166.441.
Twelve Steeds unmatch'd in Fleetness and in Force,	II.9.348.450.
Skill'd in each Art, unmatch'd in Form divine,	II.9.353.451.
And sings with unmatch'd force along the skies.	Od.8.138.270.
In dance unmatch'd! a wond'rous ball is brought,	Od.8.407.285.

UNMEANING

With some *unmeaning* Thing they call a *Thought,*	1.EOC.355.279.
Bath'd in unmeaning unrepentant tears	6.130.24.358.

UNMEASUR'D

Since Earth's wide Regions, Heav'n's unmeasur'd Height,	II.2.574.155.
Unmix'd, unmeasur'd are thy Goblets crown'd.	II.4.299.235.
To drink the Dregs of thy unmeasur'd Hate:	II.8.579.424.
And spread a long, unmeasur'd Ruin round.	II.13.1031.153.
And all th' unmeasur'd *Æther* flames with Light.	II.16.361.257.
Not him the Seas unmeasur'd Deeps detain,	II.21.68.424.
And all wide *Hellespont's* unmeasur'd Main.	II.24.687.565.
Will teach you to repass th' unmeasur'd main.	Od.4.576.147.
Such length of ocean and unmeasur'd deep?	Od.5.126.178.
And views wide earth and heav'n's unmeasur'd height.	Od.12.386.449.

UNMILK'D

Unmilk'd, lay bleating in distressful cries.	Od.9.518.327.

UNMINDFUL

Troy fled, unmindful of her former Fame.	II.16.425.259.
Ah wretched Man! unmindful of thy End!	II.17.231.296.
Unmindful of her son, *Anticlea* stands?	Od.11.175.390.

UNMINGLED

And twelve large vessels of unmingled wine,	Od.9.238.316.

UNMINISTERED

Be but a man! unministered, alone,	4.1740.89.337.

UNMIX'D

Unmix'd, to his *Sicilian* River glides.	1.TrSt.385.426.
And this or that unmix'd, no Mortal e'er shall find.	2.TemF.496.287.
The sacred Stream unmix'd with Streams below,	II.2.913.167.
Unmix'd, unmeasur'd are thy Goblets crown'd.	II.4.299.235.
To taste the bad, unmix'd, is curst indeed;	II.24.668.565.
Joys ever-young, unmix'd with pain or fear,	Od.4.767.155.

UNMIXT

They gaze with wonder, not unmixt with fear.	Od.10.251.354.
With wines unmixt, (an honour due to Age,	Od.13.11.2.

UNMOLESTED

Safe on my Shore each unmolested Swain	1.W-F.369.186.
Not unmolested let the Wretches gain	II.8.637.426.

UNMOOR

Unmoor the fleet, and rush into the sea.	Od.4.786.156.

UNMOOR'D

We, with the rising morn our ships unmoor'd, ...Od.3.185.95.

UNMOV'D

With Looks unmov'd, he hopes the Scaly Breed, ...1.W-F.139.163.
Unmov'd remain'd the Ruler of the Sky, ...1.TrSt.402.426.
Unmov'd, th'embody'd *Greeks* their Fury dare, ...1.TrES.153.455.
And bear unmov'd the Wrongs of base Mankind, ...1.TrUl.186.472.
Unmov'd, superior still in every State; ....2.TemF.157.266.
Tho' cold like you, unmov'd, and silent grown, ...2.ElAb.23.320.
So very reasonable, so unmov'd, ...3.Ep2.165.64.
Virtue unmov'd can hear the Call, ...6.69ii.9.199.
So very reasonable, so unmov'd, ...6.139.9.377.
Unmov'd as Death *Achilles* shall remain, ...II.1.444.108.
No—let my *Greeks,* unmov'd by vain Alarms, ...II.2.199.137.
The King, who saw their Squadrons yet unmov'd, ...II.4.388.239.
Unmov'd and silent, the whole War they wait, ...II.5.639.298.
Silent, unmov'd, in dire Dismay they stand, ...II.9.40.433.
Who can, unmov'd, behold the dreadful Light, ...II.9.105.437.
Unmov'd th' embody'd *Greeks* their Fury dare, ...II.12.507.100.
Resistless when he rag'd, and when he stop'd, unmov'd. ....II.13.200.115.
Unchang'd his Colour, and unmov'd his Frame; ....II.13.367.123.
Unmov'd his Mind, and unrestrain'd his Will. ....II.15.101.200.
As long as *Phœbus* bore unmov'd the Shield, ...II.15.360.210.
Unmov'd it hears, above, the Tempest blow, ...II.15.748.224.
Unmov'd, *Euphorbus* thus: That Action known, ...II.17.37.289.
Unmov'd, *Automedon* attends the Fight, ...II.17.566.310.
What more desires my Soul, than here, unmov'd, ...II.17.632.312.
Unmov'd, the Hero kindles at the Show, ...II.19.19.372.
In State unmov'd, the King of Men begun. ....II.19.80.375.
Unmov'd, he heard them, and with Sighs deny'd. ....II.19.324.386.
(Reply'd unmov'd the venerable Man) ....II.24.269.547.
Unmov'd the mind of *Ithacus* remain'd, ...Od.4.385.139.
To whom unmov'd; If this the Gods prepare, ...Od.11.172.390.
And bear unmov'd the wrongs of base mankind, ...Od.13.353.24.
Still the tough bow unmov'd. The lofty man ....Od.21.262.272.

UNNERV'D

Confus'd, unnerv'd in *Hector's* Presence grown, ...II.11.670.65.
His Limbs, unnerv'd, drop useless on the Ground, ...II.13.843.145.
Fear seiz'd the mighty, and unnerv'd the brave; ....Od.12.245.443.
Can these lean shrivel'd limbs unnerv'd with age, ...Od.19.88.196.

UNNERVES

Unnerves the Limbs, and dulls the noble Mind. ....II.6.331.342.
But when a length of years unnerves the strong, ...Od.15.448.92.

UNNOTED

Where the free guest, unnoted, might relate ....Od.1.177.41.

UNNUMBER'D

Know then, unnumber'd Spirits round thee fly, ...2.RL1.41.148.
Unnumber'd Treasures ope at once, and here ....2.RL1.129.155.
Unnumber'd Throngs on ev'ry side are seen ....2.RL4.47.187.
There Names inscrib'd unnumber'd Ages past ....2.TemF.49.256.
Confus'd, unnumber'd Multitudes are found, ...2.TemF.459.285.
Thro' worlds unnumber'd tho' the God be known, ...3.EOM1.21.15.
To Heirs unknown descends th' unnumber'd Store ....3.Ep2.149A.62.
To Heirs unknown, descends th' unnumber'd Store, ...6.154.35.403.
Of Woes unnumber'd, heav'nly Goddess, sing! ....II.1.2.82.
As when the fleecy Flocks unnumber'd stand ....II.4.492.244.
Unnumber'd Woes Mankind from us sustain, ...II.5.473.290.
And Stars unnumber'd gild the glowing Pole, ...II.8.692.428.
The floating Plumes unnumber'd wave above, ...II.13.183.114.
Behind, unnumber'd Multitudes attend, ...II.15.344.210.
Hear all ye Hosts, and hear, unnumber'd Bands ....II.17.260.298.
The trampling Steers beat out th' unnumber'd Grain. ....II.20.580.418.
On stormy seas unnumber'd toils he bore, ...Od.1.7.28.
Unnumber'd Birds glide thro' th' aerial way, ...Od.2.211.72.
Of woes unnumber'd, sent by Heav'n and Fate? ....Od.9.16.301.
Came tumbling, heaps on heaps, th' unnumber'd flock: ....Od.9.281.318.
Rich with unnumber'd gifts the Pyle shall burn; ....Od.11.40.381.
With gifts unnumber'd *Neleus* sought her arms, ...Od.11.343.399.
Heap'd high his navy with unnumber'd spoils. ....Od.11.654.416.
I saw my self the vast unnumber'd store ....Od.14.359.51.
Her various textures of unnumber'd dies, ...Od.15.119.74.
Unnumber'd acres arable and green; ....Od.20.356.249.
Unnumber'd warriors round the burning pyle ....Od.24.87.352.

UNOBSERV'D

And unobserv'd the glaring Orb declines. ....3.Ep2.256.70.
Not unobserv'd they pass'd: the God of Light ....II.10.602.29.
Takes his sad Couch, more unobserv'd to weep, ...II.24.7.535.
Not unobserv'd. *Eumæus* wrathful ey'd, ...Od.22.178.296.
Not unobserv'd: the *Greeks* eluded say ....Od.23.145.328.

UNOP'NING

Curse the sav'd candle, and unop'ning door; ....3.Ep3.196.109.

UNPAID

Thy fate unpity'd, and thy rites unpaid? ....2.Elegy.48.366.
That suit, an unpaid Taylor snatch'd away! ....5.DunA2.110.110.
Nor Vows unpaid, nor slighted Sacrifice, ...II.1.118.92.

UNPARD'NING

Whom *Pallas* with unpard'ning fury fir'd, ...Od.20.351.249.

UNPAWN'D

Where yet unpawn'd, much learned lumber lay, ...5.DunA1.116.77.

UNPAY'D

That suit an unpay'd taylor snatch'd away. ....5.DunB2.118.301.
Nor found the hospitable rites unpay'd. ....Od.15.213.78.

UNPENSION'D

Gay dies unpension'd with a hundred friends, ...5.DunB3.330.336.

UNPEOPLED

Pours forth, and leaves unpeopled half the land; ....5.DunA2.16.98.
Pours forth, and leaves unpeopled half the land. ....5.DunB2.20.297.
Huge Theatres, that now unpeopled Woods, ...6.71.7.202.

UNPERCEIV'D

While summer suns roll unperceiv'd away? ....6.52.18.156.
Not unperceiv'd; *Ulysses* crown'd with Wine ....II.9.292.448.
Beside him sudden, unperceiv'd he stood, ...II.14.409.183.
We saw, as unperceiv'd we took our stand, ...Od.2.123.67.
Fly unperceiv'd, seducing half the flow'r ....Od.4.890.160.
Stole unperceiv'd; he turn'd his head, and dry'd ....Od.17.366.149.
Then unperceiv'd and silent, at the board ....Od.21.425.280.
Behind the felon unperceiv'd they past, ...Od.22.194.296.
And unperceiv'd, enjoys the rising fight. ....Od.22.263.299.
While the soft hours stole unperceiv'd away; ....Od.23.322.339.
And show'd, as unperceiv'd we took our stand, ...Od.24.170.356.

UNPERFORMING

Oh unperforming, false mortality! ....6.22.12.71.
Fame is at best an unperforming Cheat; ....6.34.25.101.
And unperforming friendships of the great; ....6.56.4.168.

UNPERISH'D

Or hardy Fir, unperish'd with the Rains. ....II.23.402.506.

UNPILLAR'D

See, the Cirque falls! th' unpillar'd Temple nods! ....5.DunA3.99.158.
See, the Cirque falls, th' unpillar'd Temple nods, ...5.DunB3.107.325.

UNPITEOUS

Unpiteous of the race thy will began, ...Od.20.253.245.

UNPITY'D

Alike unheard, unpity'd, and forlorn. ....1.PAu.22.82.
To raging Seas unpity'd I'll remove, ...1.TrSP.258.404.
From thee to those, unpity'd, I'll remove, ...1.TrSP.258A.404.
Thy fate unpity'd, and thy rites unpaid? ....2.Elegy.48.366.
Then sunk unpity'd to the dire Abodes, ...II.6.173.334.
Nor less unpity'd young *Alastor* bleeds; ....II.20.537.416.

UNPITYING

I swear by all th'unpitying pow'rs of heav'n, ...1.TrFD.70.389.
The Wretch then lifted to th'unpitying Skies ....1.TrSt.77.413.
Stern, and unpitying! if a Brother bleed, ...II.9.743.471.
O Man unpitying! if of Man thy Race; ....II.16.46.237.
Black Death, and Fate unpitying, seal his Eyes. ....II.16.399.258.
Unpitying Pow'rs! how oft each holy Fane ....II.24.44.537.

UNPLEAS'D

Not fond of flattery , nor unpleas'd with praise. ....Od.8.528.291.

UNPLEASING

Be no unpleasing Melancholy mine: ....4.Arbu.407.127.
Be no unpleasing Melancholy mine. ....6.117.2.333.
I own me conscious of th' unpleasing deed: ....Od.4.983.163.

UNPLUME

And her lov'd Lord unplume thy tow'ring pride. ....Od.19.104.197.

UNPOLISH'D

Unpolish'd Gemms no Ray on Pride bestow, ...6.142.5.382.
Unpolish'd Crystals break the sparkling Rill, ...6.142.4B.382.
A proud, unpolish'd race—To me belongs ....Od.6.327.227.
Unpolish'd men, and boistrous as their seas: ....Od.7.42.235.

UNPRACTIS'D

Hear what from Love unpractis'd Hearts endure, ...1.PSu.11.72.
Nor seek unpractis'd to direct the Car, ...II.4.354.238.
His Troops unpractis'd in the Fights of Stand ....II.13.890A.147.
In close Engagement an unpractis'd Race: ....II.13.890.148.
'Tis mine, to form his green, unpractis'd years, ...Od.1.112.37.
New to the plow, unpractis'd in the trace. ....Od.4.861.159.

UNPROFITABLE

So slow th' unprofitable Moments roll, ...4.1HE1.39.281.

UNPROFITABLY

O great in vain! unprofitably brave! ....II.16.41.237.
Thy well-knit frame unprofitably strong, ...Od.18.259.179.

UNPROPHETIC

Wretch that he was, of unprophetic soul! ....Od.22.13.287.

UNPROPITIOUS

Now flam'd the Dog-star's unpropitious ray, ...5.DunB4.9.340.
'Twas when the Dog-star's unpropitious ray, ...5.DunB4.9A.340.

UNPROSP'ROUS

For nought unprosp'rous shall thy ways attend, ...Od.3.37.88.

UNPUNISH'D

No impious Wretch shall 'scape unpunish'd long, ...2.ChJM.649.46.
And leave unpunish'd this perfidious Race? ....II.2.194.137.
To feast unpunish'd on the Fat of Kings. ....II.21.140.427.
But while your Sons commit th' unpunish'd wrong, ...Od.2.87.65.

UNQUESTION'D

(Restoring *Hector*) Heav'ns unquestion'd Will. ....II.24.743.568.

UNQUIET

A vain, unquiet, glitt'ring, wretched Thing! ....6.19.54.63.
Th' unquiet night strange projects entertain'd; ....Od.3.183.94.

UNRANSOM'D
Unransom'd here receive the spotless Fair; ....Il.1.578.115.

UNRAVEL
Or quite unravel all the reas'ning thread, ...5.DunB1.179.283.

UNRAVELS
This clue once found, unravels all the rest, ...3.Ep1.178.30.

UNRAVISH'D
And all that rests of my unravish'd Prey. ....Il.9.480.456.

UNREAD
Her gray-hair'd Synods damning books unread, ...5.DunA3.95.158.
Her grey-hair'd Synods damning books unread, ...5.DunB3.103.325.

UNRECORDED
Not unrecorded in the rolls of fame: ....Od.4.276.132.

UNREDREST
Requir'd his Arm, he sorrow'd unredrest. ....Il.18.520.346.

UNREGARDED
Jove's harmless lightning unregarded flies; ....1.TrPA.116.370.
And unregarded Thunder rolls in vain: ....1.TrSt.305.423.
Flaunts and goes down, an unregarded thing. ....3.Ep2.252.70.
Nor past the meanest unregarded, one ....5.DunB4.575.399.
An unregarded Carcase to the Sea. ....Il.21.329.434.
Amongst the Happy, unregarded he, ...Il.22.632.482.
And unregarded laughs the rosy wine. ....Od.10.448.365.
Time steals away with unregarded wing, ...Od.17.612.161.

UNREGARDING
Art thou a Father, unregarding Jove! ....1.TrSt.109.414.
Stalks careless on, with unregarding Pride; ....Il.20.202.402.

UNREGUARDED
Guideless I wander, unreguarded mourn, ...1.TrSt.105.414.

UNRELENTING
And Mighty Neptune's unrelenting Rage?— ....1.TrUl.223.473.
Mad, furious Pow'r! whose unrelenting Mind ....Il.5.948.312.
Descends, to punish unrelenting Men. ....Il.9.636.466.
The Gods that unrelenting Breast have steel'd, ...Il.9.749.471.
The Youths address'd to unrelenting Ears: ....Il.11.178.43.
The Youth addrest to unrelenting Ears: ....Il.21.110.426.
Roll'd at the Feet of unrelenting Jove! ....Il.22.286.468.
And th' unrelenting Empress of the Skies: ....Il.24.37.537.
Not unrelenting: Then serene began ....Il.24.651.564.
And mighty Neptune's unrelenting rage? ....Od.13.390.25.
With unrelenting rage, and force from home ....Od.15.300.83.

UNREPENTANT
Bath'd in unmeaning unrepentant tears ....6.130.24.358.

UNREPENTING
Not Tyrants fierce that unrepenting die, ...2.RL4.7.183.

UNREPROV'D
On some good Man, or Woman unreprov'd ....Il.17.493.307.

UNRESIGN'D
Still for one Loss he rages unresign'd, ...Il.24.58.538.

UNRESISTED
Yield to the Force of unresisted Fate, ...1.TrUl.185.471.
The conqu'ring Force of unresisted Steel? ....2.RL3.178.182.
Still unresisted shall the Foe destroy, ...Il.5.567.295.
Urg'd by the Force of unresisted Fate, ...Il.5.777.303.
For now that Chief, whose unresisted Ire, ...Il.9.402.452.
Then sudden wav'd his unresisted Sword; ....Il.12.220.89.
For lo! he comes, with unresisted Sway; ....Il.21.623.448.
Yield to the force of unresisted fate, ...Od.13.352.24.
Ah stop the Heroe's unresisted hands, ...Od.22.408.307.
And human thought, with unresisted sway, ...Od.23.15.319.

UNRESISTING
But falls transfix'd, an unresisting Prey: ....Il.13.504.130.
And rend the trembling, unresisting Prey. ....Il.16.423.259.
She, unresisting, fell; (her Spirits fled) ....Il.21.498.442.
Spurn the hoar Head of unresisting Age, ...Il.22.103.457. .

UNRESOLV'D
While unresolv'd the Son of Tydeus stands, ...Il.10.592.28.

UNRESPECTED
From loveless youth to unrespected age, ...3.Ep2.125.60.
From Loveless Youth to unrespected Age, ...6.154.11.403.

UNRESTRAIN'D
Unmov'd his Mind, and unrestrain'd his Will. ....Il.15.101.200.
Stern God! who rag'd with vengeance unrestrain'd, ...Od.6.393.230.

UNREVEAL'D
Dear fatal name! rest ever unreveal'd, ...2.ElAb.9.319.

UNREVENG'D
Not unreveng'd to bear Sarpedon's Death. ....1.TrES.307.461.
Lie unreveng'd on yon' detested Plain? ....Il.2.198.137.
Still unreveng'd a thousand Heroes bleed? ....Il.2.214.138.
And unreveng'd, his mighty Brother slain." ....Il.4.217.231.
And unreveng'd see Priam's People die? ....Il.5.566.295.
While unreveng'd thy Lycians bite the Ground: ....Il.5.797.304.
Yet unreveng'd permits to press the Field; ....Il.8.156.405.
Nor unreveng'd, lamented Asius lies: ....Il.13.524.131.
And unreveng'd, deplor'd his Offspring dead. ....Il.13.826.145.

UNREVENG'D (CONTINUED)
Not unreveng'd to bear Sarpedon's Death. ....Il.16.612.268.
While unreveng'd the great Sarpedon falls? ....Il.17.168.294.
The Friend of Hector, unreveng'd, is dead: ....Il.17.665.314.
Since unreveng'd, a hundred Ghosts demand ....Il.18.131.329.
Were by false courage unreveng'd to die. ....Od.16.277.118.
(Not unreveng'd) and quaff'd the spouting gore; ....Od.23.338.341.
If unreveng'd your sons and brothers bleed. ....Od.24.499.372.

UNREVEREND
Behold him loaded with unreverend years ....6.130.23.358.

UNREWARDED
Wine lets no Lover unrewarded go, ...2.ChWB.219.67.
Nor unrewarded let your Prince complain, ...Il.1.153.94.

UNRIDDLE
Few Criticks can unriddle; ....6.59.2.177.

UNRIGHTEOUS
Perish'd the nation in unrighteous war, ...Od.7.76.237.
And angry Neptune heard th' unrighteous pray'r. ....Od.9.630.332.

UNRIPEN'D
Thou know'st the Errors of unripen'd Age, ...Il.23.671.516.

UNRIVAL'D
What lofty Looks th'unrival'd Monarch bears! ....1.TrSt.253.421.
Honour forbid! at whose unrival'd Shrine ....2.RL4.105.192.
Whom prostrate Kings beheld unrival'd shine, ...6.20.11.66.
Proud of his Host, unrival'd in his Reign, ...Il.2.699.159.
And his, th' unrival'd Race of Heav'nly Steeds) ....Il.2.937.168.
Thy matchless Skill, thy yet-unrival'd Fame, ...Il.5.220.278.
Not all proud Thebes' unrival'd Walls contain, ...Il.9.500.457.
And Steeds unrival'd on the dusty Plain; ....Il.9.529.459.
And thrice the Number of unrival'd Steeds, ...Il.11.824.73.
Hence sprung twelve others of unrival'd Kind, ...Il.20.268.405.
(A Race unrival'd, which from Ocean's God ....Il.23.345.503.
But Ithacus, unrival'd in his claim, ...Od.4.369.137.
And bore th' unrival'd honours of the day. ....Od.8.132.270.
From all the sons of earth unrival'd praise ....Od.8.253.276.
We in the course unrival'd speed display, ...Od.8.253.278.
She shone unrival'd with a blaze of charms, ...Od.11.552.411.
Grant him unrival'd in these walls to stay, ...Od.18.54.169.

UNRIVALL'D
Still, as at first, unrivall'd lead the Race, ...Il.23.561.511.

UNROLL'D
With Orbs unroll'd lay covering all the Plain, ...1.TrSt.665.438.
With Orbs unroll'd lay stretch'd o'er all the Plain, ...1.TrSt.665A.438.
They, pale with Terror, mark its Spires unroll'd, ...Il.12.241.90.

UNRULY
Unruly Murmurs, or ill-tim'd Applause, ...Il.19.85.375.
To Gods and Goddesses th' unruly Joy ....Il.19.105.376.
Rush to their mothers with unruly joy, ...Od.10.489.367.
Unable to contain th' unruly joy. ....Od.16.481.130.

UNSAFE
Ev'n I unsafe: The Queen in doubt to wed, ...Od.16.73.106.

UNSAID
Thus, (nought unsaid) the much-advising Sage ....Il.23.423.506.

UNSAV'RY
'Tis so unsav'ry a-Bit.) ....6.94.48.260.
Now prone, and groveling on unsav'ry ground. ....Od.10.285.357.

UNSAVOURY
Unsavoury stench of oil, and brackish ooze: ....Od.4.598.148.

UNSEAL'D
Stood shining o'er him, half unseal'd his Sight: ....Il.15.279.207.
Not thine, Ulysses! Care unseal'd his eyes; ....Od.15.8.70.

UNSEALS
Wak'd by the Morning-Cock, unseals his Eyes, ...6.17iii.32.58.
Of secret grief unseals the fruitful source; ....Od.19.190.201.

UNSEEMLY
Unseemly flown with insolence and wine? ....Od.1.292.47.
Which whizzing high, the wall unseemly sign'd. ....Od.20.369.250.

UNSEEN
She runs, but hopes she does not run unseen, ...1.PSp.58.66.
It self unseen, but in th' Effects, remains. ....1.EOC.79.248.
For so the Gods ordain'd, to keep unseen ....1.TrUl.60.468.
Unseen I scap'd; and favour'd by the Night, ...1.TrUl.148.470.
These, tho' unseen, are ever on the Wing, ...2.RL1.43.149.
An Ace of Hearts steps forth: The King unseen ....2.RL3.95.174.
Would die unheard of, as we liv'd unseen. ....2.TemF.361.281.
Useless, unseen, as lamps in sepulchres; ....2.Elegy.20.364.
To Pow'r unseen, and mightier far than they: ....3.EOM3.252.118.
Pregnant with thousands flits the Scrap unseen, ...3.Ep3.77.93.
Safe and unseen the young Æneas past: ....5.DunB4.290.373.
Unseen at Church, at Senate, or at Court, ...5.DunB4.338.376.
Thus let me live, unseen, unknown; ....6.1.17.4.
To sigh unseen into the passing Wind? ....6.81.10A.225.
There, stretch'd unseen in coverts hid from day, ...6.81.13.226.
(Aye watching o'er his Saints with Eye unseen,) ....6.137.3.373.
Unseen she came, and burst the golden Band; ....Il.3.461.214.
Unseen, and silent, from the Train she moves, ...Il.3.523.216.
This, by the Greeks unseen, the Warrior bends, ...Il.4.144.227.
And turns unseen the frustrate Dart away. ....Il.5.237.278.
Hither great Hector pass'd, nor pass'd unseen ....Il.6.312.341.

UNSEEN (CONTINUED)

Unseen the *Grecian* Embassy proceeds ....Il.9.255.445.
The tenth, I forc'd the Gates, unseen of all; ....Il.9.596.464.
Then with his Spear, unseen, his Time he took, ...Il.11.325.49.
Unseen, unthought, till this amazing Day! ....Il.13.138.111.
Thro' Air unseen involv'd in Darkness glide, ...Il.14.319.178.
Struck by an Arm unseen, it burst in two; ....Il.15.545.217.
Unseen of *Hector*, who, elate with Joy, ...Il.22.355.470.
Unseen, thro' all the hostile Camp they went, ...Il.24.551.559.
Unseen by these, the King his Entry made; ....Il.24.584.561.
Unheard, unseen, three years their arts prevail; ....Od.2.121.67.
Unseen of all the rude *Phæacian* race. ....Od.7.52.236.
Unseen he glided thro' the joyous crowd, ...Od.7.186.245.
But all unseen the clouded Island lyes, ...Od.9.169.312.
And all unseen the surge and rowling sea, ...Od.9.170.312.
And unseen armies ambush'd in its womb; ....Od.11.640.416.
Unseen I pass'd by *Scylla's* dire abodes: ....Od.12.527.458.
What hands unseen the rapid bark restrain! ....Od.13.192.15.
For so the Gods ordain'd, to keep unseen ....Od.13.227.17.
Unseen I 'scap'd; and favour'd by the night ....Od.13.315.21.
Seen or unseen, o'er earth at pleasure move) ....Od.16.175.111.
Sad *Philomel*, in bow'ry shades unseen, ...Od.19.605.225.
To see the circle sat, of all unseen. ....Od.20.464.256.
The game as yet unseen, as yet untry'd) ....Od.21.128.264.
Unheard, unseen, three years her arts prevail; ....Od.24.168.356.

UNSEPARATED

Gave to retain th' unseparated soul: ....Od.10.585.372.

UNSHEATH'D

And half unsheath'd the shining Blade; ....6.11.46.32.
While half unsheath'd appear'd the glitt'ring Blade, ...Il.1.260.99.

UNSHOD

Men bearded, bald, cowl'd, uncowl'd, shod, unshod, ...5.DunA3.106.159.
Men bearded, bald, cowl'd, uncowl'd, shod, unshod, ...5.DunB3.114.325.

UNSHOOK

Thou stand'st unshook amidst a bursting World. ....4.Arbu.88.101.

UNSINCERE

To render sleep's soft blessing unsincere? ....Od.4.1060.167.
Not such the sickly beams, which unsincere, ...Od.19.40.194.

UNSKILFUL

And leave unskilful Swiftness far behind. ....Il.23.418.506.

UNSKILFULL

In vain unskilfull to the Goal they strive, ...Il.23.391.506.

UNSKILL'D

Poets like Painters, thus, unskill'd to trace ....1.EOC.293.272.
Unskill'd to judge the Future by the Past, ...Il.1.448.109.
As one unskill'd or dumb, he seem'd to stand, ...Il.3.281.207.
Yet *Helen* bids thee stay, lest thou unskill'd ....Il.3.541.217.
Not void of Soul, and not unskill'd in War: ....Il.7.276.378.
Thy Youth as then in sage Debates unskill'd, ...il.9.568.462.
Unskill'd in Arms to act a manly Part! ....Il.11.494.56.
Unskill'd to trace the latent Marks of Heav'n. ....Il.22.18.453.
Unskill'd in speech, nor yet mature of age? ....Od.3.30.87.
Thus he, unskill'd of what the fates provide! ....Od.4.1021.165.
The rugged race of savages, unskill'd ....Od.9.147.311.

UNSOLD

Un-stall'd, unsold; thus glorious mount in fire ....5.DunA1.198.86.

UNSOUND

When I but call a flagrant Whore unsound, ...6.129.1.357.

UNSOWN

But uninhabited, untill'd, unsown ....Od.9.143.311.

UNSPENT

Spreads undivided, operates unspent, ...3.EOM1.274.48.

UNSPOIL'D

Oh teach us, BATHURST! yet unspoil'd by wealth! ....3.Ep3.226.111.

UNSPOTTED

Liv'd an unspotted Maid in spite of Man: ....2.ChWB.47.58.
Unspotted Names! and memorable long, ...4.Arbu.386.126.
Roscommon only boasts unspotted Bays; ....4.2HE1.214.213.
Unspotted long with human blood. ....6.5Ii.6.151.
Our faith unspotted, and its early date; ....Od.1.244.44.

UNSTAIN'D

The shrine with gore unstain'd, with gold undrest, ...3.EOM3.157.109.
His hand unstain'd, his uncorrupted heart, ...3.Ep1.141.26.
Unstain'd, untouch'd, and yet in maiden sheets; ....5.DunB1.229.287.
Unstain'd, unstitch'd, and yet in maiden sheets; ....5.DunB1.229A.287.
Unstain'd, immortal, and the Gift of Gods. ....Il.2.58.130.
Unstain'd with Blood his cover'd Chariots stand; ....Il.2.942.168.

UNSTITCH'D

Unstain'd, unstitch'd, and yet in maiden sheets; ....5.DunB1.229A.287.

UNSTRINGS

Unstrings my Nerves, and ends my manly Prime; ....Il.11.815.72.

UNSTRUNG

Druids and *Bards* (their once loud Harps unstrung) ....2.TemF.127.264.
His golden lyre *Demodocus* unstrung, ...Od.8.107.268.
Reach'd, in its splendid case, the bow unstrung: ....Od.21.56.262.

UNSUBDU'D

Still breathing Strife, and unsubdu'd of Soul: ....Il.23.853.523.

UNSUCCESSFUL

Leave dang'rous *Truths* to unsuccessful *Satyrs*, ...1.EOC.592.307.
Did the dead Letter unsuccessful prove? ....5.DunB1.193.283.
Worn with nine Years of unsuccessful War? ....Il.2.96.131.
Too daring Bard! whose unsuccessful Pride ....Il.2.725.160.
His unsuccessful Spear he chanc'd to fling ....Il.13.809.143.

UNSUFFERABLE

Approach that hour! unsufferable wrong ....Od.2.69.64.

UNSULLY'D

Such as on HOUGH's unsully'd Mitre shine, ...4.EpS2.240.326.
An hecatomb of pure, unsully'd lays ....5.DunA1.138.81.
An hecatomb of pure, unsully'd lays ....5.DunB1.158.282.
Sev'n sacred Tripods, whose unsully'd Frame ....Il.9.159.440.
Sev'n sacred Tripods, whose unsully'd Frame ....Il.9.346.450.

UNSULLYED

And ample Charger of unsullyed Frame, ...Il.23.1046.531.

UNSUPPORTED

Mere unsupported Man must yield at length; ....Il.19.164.378.

UNSURE

(Unsure the Tenure, but how vast the Fine!) ....2.TemF.508.288.

UNSUSPECTING

Sudden, before some unsuspecting Town, ...1.W-F.108A.161.
All unsuspecting of their freight below. ....Od.9.522.328.

UNSUSPICIOUS

The Thund'rer, unsuspicious of the Fraud, ...Il.19.111.376.

UNSUSTAIN'D

All unsustain'd between the wave and sky, ...Od.12.517.457.

UNTAINTED

Go! fair Example of untainted youth, ...6.109.1.313.
Untouch'd by Worms, untainted by the Air. ....Il.24.506.557.

UNTAKEN

Elate in Thought, he sacks untaken *Troy:* ....Il.2.46.129.

UNTAM'D

Untam'd, unconscious of the galling Yoke, ...Il.10.348.18.
An untam'd Heifer pleas'd the blue-ey'd Maid, ...Il.11.865.74.
His Pow'rs untam'd their bold Assault defy, ...Il.12.51.83.
So rough thy Manners, so untam'd thy Mind. ....Il.16.53.237.
Untam'd, untir'd, he turns, attacks, and stings: ....Il.17.645.313.
With Limbs and Soul untam'd, he tires a War. ....Il.19.168.378.
On their whole War, untam'd the Savage flies; ....Il.21.683.450.
Untam'd, unconscious of the galling yoke; ....Od.3.491.111.

UNTASTED

And with th' untasted Food supplies her Care: ....Il.9.427.453.
He leaves untasted the first Fruits of Joy; ....Il.11.292.48.
Timely he flies the yet-untasted Food, ...Il.15.706.223.
Sow'r he departs, and quits th' untasted Prey. ....Il.17.748.311.
(Untasted joy, since that disastrous hour, ...Od.8.487.289.
Round the black trench the gore untasted flows, ...Od.11.63.383.
Th' untasted viands, and the jovial bowl. ....Od.22.100.291.

UNTAUGHT

The bad must miss; the good, untaught, will find; ....3.EOM4.330.160.
Fear held them mute. Alone untaught to fear, ...5.DunA2.53.103.
Fear held them mute. Alone, untaught to fear, ...5.DunB2.57.298.
Of untaught nature's humble pride, ...6.6ii.18.15.
Eternal breathes on fruits untaught to fail: ....6.35.12.103.
A Face untaught to feign! a judging Eye, ...6.73.5.209.
Fear held them mute: Alone, untaught to fear, ...Il.10.259.13.
Untaught to fear or fly, he hears the Sounds ....Il.21.679.450.
Eternal breathes on fruits untaught to fail: ....Od.7.153.243.
Untaught to plant, to turn the glebe and sow, ...Od.9.121.310.
That stubborn soul, by toil untaught to yield! ....Od.12.334.448.
Untaught to bear, 'gainst heav'n the wretch rebells. ....Od.18.162.174.

UNTHINKING

With earnest Eyes, and round unthinking Face, ...2.RL4.125.194.
To each unthinking being, Heav'n a friend, ...3.EOM3.71.99.
This ready Arm, unthinking, shakes the Dart; ....Il.13.111.110.
Unthinking Man! I fought, those Tow'rs to free, ...Il.16.1007.282.

UNTHOUGHT

Unthought-of Frailties cheat us in the Wise, ...3.Ep1.128.25.
Unseen, unthought, till this amazing Day! ....Il.13.138.111.

UNTHOUGHT-OF

Unthought-of Frailties cheat us in the Wise, ...3.Ep1.128.25.

UNTILL'D

The soil untill'd a ready harvest yields, ...Od.9.123.310.
But uninhabited, untill'd, unsown ....Od.9.143.311.

UNTIMELY

Untimely fell, to be for ever mourn'd? ....1.TrSt.66.413.
Yet well dissembling his untimely Joys, ...1.TrUl.136.470.
'Till Death untimely stop'd his tuneful Tongue. ....6.84.2.238.
When Death untimely stop'd his tuneful Tongue. ....6.84.2A.238.
The Souls of mighty Chiefs untimely slain; ....Il.1.4.82.
Next artful *Phereclus* untimely fell; ....Il.5.75.269.
T' avenge *Atrides*: Now, untimely slain, ...Il.5.679.300.
Beheld the Sons of *Greece* untimely fall.) ....Il.6.278.340.
Why with untimely Sorrows heaves thy Heart? ....Il.6.625.357.

UNTIMELY (CONTINUED)
The *Trojans* see the Youths untimely die, ...Il.11.151.42.
Or yet, with many a Soul's untimely flight, ...Il.16.791.274.
Twelve in the Tumult wedg'd, untimely rush'd ....Il.18.271.335.
Awhile your loud, untimely Joy suspend, ...Il.19.83.375.
All those relentless *Mars* untimely slew, ...Il.24.325.550.
To fall untimely in a foreign Land! ....Il.24.680.565.
But call'd untimely (not the sacred rite ....Od.3.169.94.
Declines his trembling steps; untimely care ....Od.4.145.127.
A blank oblivion, and untimely grave? ....Od.4.943.162.
Yet well dissembling his untimely joys, ...Od.13.303.21.
Old age untimely posting ere his day. ....Od.15.381.88.
For age untimely marks the careful brow. ....Od.19.419.214.
Thy self untimely and thy consort dy'd, ...Od.20.80.236.
For danger waits on all untimely joy. ....Od.21.243.271.
Nor wail'd his father o'er th' untimely dead, ...Od.24.345.365.

UNTIR'D
Still edg'd to wound, and still untir'd with Blows, ...Il.3.90.194.
Untam'd, untir'd, he turns, attacks, and stings: ....Il.17.645.313.

UNTO
'Tis said, that thou shouldst cleave unto thy Wife; ....6.96iv.9.276.

UNTOLD
Let the sad Tale for ever rest untold! ....1.TrSt.801.443.

UNTOUCH'D
Her Head's untouch'd, that noble Seat of Thought: ....3.Ep2.74.56.
Unstain'd, untouch'd, and yet in maiden sheets; ....5.DunB1.229.287.
Untouch'd she stay'd, uninjur'd she removes, ...Il.9.173.441.
Untouch'd she stay'd, uninjur'd she removes, ...Il.9.360.451.
But he impervious and untouch'd remains. ....Il.13.701.138.
He, not untouch'd with Pity, to the Plain ....Il.15.69.199.
Alone, untouch'd, *Pelides'* Javelin stands, ...Il.16.172.244.
Long us'd, untouch'd, in fighting Fields to shine, ...Il.16.962.280.
Whole Years untouch'd, uninjur'd shall remain ....Il.19.33.373.
Untouch'd it rests, and sacred from Decay. ....Il.19.42.373.
And leave untouch'd the Honours of the Day. ....Il.22.270.467.
The third, a Charger yet untouch'd by Flame; ....Il.23.335.503.
Untouch'd by Worms, untainted by the Air. ....Il.24.506.557.
Untouch'd they stood, 'till his long labours o'er ....Od.2.388.80.
Untouch'd and sacred may these vessels stand, ...Od.2.396.80.
Untouch'd before thee stand the cates divine, ...Od.10.447.365.
Unhurt the beeves, untouch'd the woolly train ....Od.12.389.450.

UNTRAIN'D
Of matchless deed: untrain'd to martial toil ....Od.19.212.203.

UNTROD
The Patriot's plain, but untrod path pursue; ....6.73.16.210.

UNTRUTHS
Whom Want itself can force untruths to tell, ...Od.14.180.44.

UNTRY'D
But Wives, a random Choice, untry'd they take; ....2.ChWB.102.61.
To coasts unknown, and oceans yet untry'd. ....Od.9.118.308.
The game as yet unseen, as yet untry'd) ....Od.21.128.264.
And bold *Antinous*, yet untry'd, unknown: ....Od.21.190.269.
Its owner absent, and untry'd so long. ....Od.21.430.281.

UNTUN'D
Untun'd my Lute, and silent is my Lyre, ...1.TrSP.229.403.

UNTUTOR'D
Lo! the poor Indian, whose untutor'd mind ....3.EOM1.99.27.
What God to your untutor'd youth affords ....Od.1.491.55.

UNTWINE
There ends thy Glory! there the Fates untwine ....Il.16.950.280.

UNTY'D
Her Snakes, unty'd, Sulphureous Waters drink; ....1.TrSt.125.415.
Pallas disrobes; Her radiant Veil unty'd, ...Il.5.904.309.
Each from the Yoke the smoaking Steeds unty'd, ...Il.8.675.427.
These in her Left-Hand lock'd, her Right unty'd ....Il.21.567.445.
Where ships may rest, unanchor'd and unty'd; ....Od.9.158.312.
My train obey'd me and the ship unty'd. ....Od.9.208.314.

UNTYE
Approach the Chariot, and the Steeds untye; ....Il.10.555.27.

UNUS'D
(Such as by Youths unus'd to Arms, are worn; ....Il.10.305.16.

UNUSUAL
The Forests wonder'd at th'unusual Grain, ...1.W-F.89.158.
Seiz'd with unusual Fear *Idæus* fled, ...Il.5.27.266.
What, Goddess! this unusual Favour draws? ....Il.18.453.343.
As *Hector* sees, unusual Terrors rise, ...Il.22.179.461.
A Pulse unusual flutters at my Heart. ....Il.22.581.480.
Struck with unusual fear, she trembling cries, ...Od.10.385.363.
And if unusual sounds invade their ear, ...Od.21.415.280.

UNUTTERABLE
Sad Mothers of unutterable Woes!) ....Il.11.350.50.
Who glories in unutterable Pride! ....Il.14.162.165.
His Words infix'd unutterable Care ....Il.17.89.291.
What Anguish I? Unutterable Woe! ....Il.22.73.455.
All wailing with unutterable woes. ....Od.11.664.417.

UNVAILING
These unvailing Rites he may receive, ...1.TrES.334A.462.

UNVARY'D
While they ring round the same *unvary'd Chimes,* ....1.EOC.348.278.
"Mark what unvary'd laws preserve each state, ...3.EOM3.189.112.
"Mark what unvary'd laws preserve their state, ...3.EOM3.189A.112.

UNVEIL'D
And now, unveil'd, the *Toilet* stands display'd, ...2.RL1.121.155.

UNVEILS
When the gay morn unveils her smiling ray: ....Od.6.36.206.
And when the morn unveils her safron ray, ...Od.12.35.431.

UNWARLIKE
To one that fears thee, some unwarlike Boy: ....Il.20.241.404.
To one that dreads thee, some unwarlike Boy: ....Il.20.500.415.

UNWARY
Glares on some Traveller's unwary steps, ...6.26i.11.79.
Th' unwary *Greeks* his Fury may provoke; ....Il.2.231.138.
Along the Path the Spy unwary flew; ....Il.10.417.21.
And wing'd an Arrow at th' unwary Foe; ....Il.11.478.55.
Atrides, watchful of th' unwary Foe, ...Il.13.745.140.
Full on the Cheek of his unwary Foe; ....Il.23.799.521.
Will intercept th' unwary Youth's return. ....Od.4.1078.168.
With joy the Maid th' unwary strangers heard, ...Od.10.125.346.

UNWASH'D
Their Feet unwash'd, their Slumbers on the Ground; ....Il.16.289.253.

UNWASTING
Purest love's unwasting treasure, ...6.51ii.41.154.

UNWATCH'D
And if unwatch'd is sure t' omit Ses Heires: ....4.JD2A.103.140.

UNWEARIED
Ev'n till the morning, with unwearied care, ...Od.18.365.185.

UNWEARY'D
With slaught'ring Guns th'unweary'd Fowler roves, ...1.W-F.125.162.
With patient Touches of unweary'd Art: ....2.TemF.199.271.
If ev'ry Wheel of that unweary'd Mill ....4.2HE2.78.171.
There, thy good Scholiasts with unweary'd pains ....5.DunA1.159.82.
Thy mighty Scholiast, whose unweary'd pains ....5.DunB4.211.363.
Each heav'nly piece unweary'd we compare, ...6.52.35.157.
Th' unweary'd Blaze incessant Streams supplies, ...Il.5.7.266.
Th' unweary'd Watch their list'ning Leaders keep, ...Il.10.209.11.
Dark'ning the Rock, while with unweary'd Wings ....Il.12.191.88.
Now side by side, with like unweary'd Care, ...Il.13.877.147.
Meantime, unweary'd with his heavenly Way, ...Il.18.283.335.
Th' unweary'd Sun, the Moon compleatly round; ....Il.18.559.349.
Exert th' unweary'd Furies of the Flame! ....Il.21.397.436.

UNWEETING
Unweeting Wantons of their wetting Woe! ....6.42vi.2.120.

UNWEIGH'D
Daughter! what words have pass'd thy lips unweigh'd? ....Od.1.84.35.

UNWEILDY
See UNWIELDY.
To trim his beard, th'unweildy scythe prepares; ....1.TrPA.23.366.
Th' unweildy Rock, the Labour of a God. ....Il.12.544.101.

UNWELCOME
Unwelcome Life relenting *Phœbus* gives; ....1.TrSt.781.442.
Th' unwelcome Message to the *Phrygian* King. ....Il.2.965.169.
Unwelcome revellers, whose lawless joy ....Od.1.293.47.
Hither, unwelcome, to the Queen they come; ....Od.2.57.63.
Unwelcome news, or vex the royal ear; ....Od.15.401.88.

UNWEPT
Unwept, uncover'd, on the Plain he lay, ...Il.11.319.49.
Unwept, unhonour'd, uninterr'd he lies! ....Il.22.484.476.
Nor shall he lye unwept, and uninterr'd; ....Il.24.783.569.
On distant shores unwept, unburied lye. ....Od.11.68.383.

UNWHIPP'D
"And then, unwhipp'd, he had the grace to cry: ....4.2HE2.18.165.

UNWHOLSOME
But see, *Orion* sheds unwholsome Dews, ...1.PWi.85.95.
See pale *Orion* sheds unwholsome Dews, ...1.PWi.85A.95.
To tread those dark unwholsome, misty Fens, ...6.26i.13.79.

UNWIELDY
See UNWEILDY.
Cou'd heave th'unwieldy Burthen from the Plain: ....1.TrES.102.453.
Th'unwieldy Rock, the Labour of a God. ....1.TrES.190.456.
His Giant Limbs in State unwieldy spread? ....2.RL3.72.173.
"My wealth unwieldy, and my heap too great." ....4.HS2.114.63.
Could heave th' unwieldy Burthen from the Plain. ....Il.12.456.98.
Drag some vast Beam, or Mast's unwieldy Length; ....Il.17.834.321.
Concludes; then sate, stiff with unwieldy Age. ....Il.23.424.506.
And curse their cumbrous pride's unwieldy weight. ....Od.1.214.43.
Then heaving high the stone's unwieldy weight, ...Od.9.400.322.
Unwieldy, out They rush'd, with gen'ral cry, ...Od.10.461.366.

UNWILLING
And force unwilling Vengeance from the Sky? ....1.TrSt.301.422.
And from the wondring God th'unwilling Youth retir'd. ....1.TrSt.785.443.
And murm'ring from the Corps th'unwilling Soul retires. ....1.TrES.110.453.
There stern religion quench'd th' unwilling flame; ....2.ElAb.39.322.
And turn th' unwilling steeds another way: ....3.Ep3.194.109.
And drop at last, but in unwilling ears, ...4.Arbu.39.98.
Th' unwilling Gratitude of base mankind! ....4.2HE1.14.195.

UNWILLING (CONTINUED)
Think not unwilling I resign'd my breath. ... 6.20.4.66.
From the dear man unwilling she must sever, ... 6.45.5.124.
Th' unwilling Heralds act their Lord's Commands; ... Il.1.426.108.
Patroclus now th'unwilling Beauty brought; ... Il.1.450.109.
Unwilling parts, and oft' reverts her Eye ... Il.6.641.358.
Unwilling he remain'd, for *Paris'* Dart ... Il.8.103.402.
Urg'd me, unwilling, this Attempt to make; ... Il.10.467.24.
The Woes of Men unwilling to survey, ... Il.11.71.37.
Unwilling as I am to lose the Host, ... Il.14.116.163.
Nor pull th' unwilling Vengeance on thy Head, ... Il.15.36.195.
To the dark Shades the Soul unwilling glides, ... Il.16.901.278.
He faints; the Soul unwilling wings her way, ... Il.16.1032.283.
So from the Fold th' unwilling Lion parts, ... Il.17.117.292.
And force th' unwilling God to ruin *Troy.* ... Il.17.387.302.
With weary'd Limbs, but with unwilling Pace: ... Il.17.750.317.
With weary Limbs, but with unwilling Pace: ... Il.17.750A.317*.
And wretched I, th' unwilling Messenger! ... Il.18.22.324.
Unwilling as I am, of force I stay, ... Il.18.227.332.
In Ocean's Waves th' unwilling Light of Day ... Il.18.284.335.
Nor from my Arms, unwilling, force the Dame. ... Il.19.284.384.
With Steps unwilling, to the regal Tent. ... Il.23.48.489.
Unwilling Slumber, and the Chiefs bespoke. ... Il.23.293.501.
And press'd unwilling in *Calypso's* arms. ... Od.5.23.172.
Unwilling, have I trod this pleasing land; ... Od.5.124.178.
Nor thou unwilling to be call'd my son. ... Od.7.400.256.
And forc'd by storms, unwilling, on your coast; ... Od.9.310.319.
And prest unwilling in *Calypso's* arms. ... Od.17.165.139.
They dragg'd th' unwilling *Irus* to the fight; ... Od.18.87.170.
In silent wonder sigh'd unwilling praise. ... Od.19.272.208.

UNWILLINGLY
Howe'er unwillingly it quits its place, ... 4.2HE2.161.177.

UNWISE
Go, furious Youth! ungen'rous and unwise! ... Il.23.520.510.
And be the King the Judge. The most unwise ... Il.23.570.512.
O forward to proclaim thy soul unwise! ... Od.8.184.272.
Th' unwise award to lodge it in the tow'rs, ... Od.8.557.292.
Th' unwise prevail, they lodge it in the walls, ... Od.8.559.292.

UNWISH'D
Whilst heaping unwish'd wealth, I distant roam; ... Od.4.113.125.

UNWONTED
Th'unwonted Weight, or drag the crooked Share, ... 1.TrSt.187.418.
Th' unwonted scene surprize and rapture drew; ... Od.7.179.244.

UNWORTHY
Ah how unworthy those of Race divine? ... 1.TrSt.685.439.
Unworthy He, the voice of Fame to hear, ... 4.HS2.99.61.
That seem'd to fill the Name unworthy ... 6.30.5B.85.
With Fraud, unworthy of a Royal Mind. ... Il.1.196.96.
Are far unworthy, Gods! of your Debate: ... Il.1.743.123.
Nor he unworthy to command the Host; ... Il.2.862.165.
But you, unworthy the high Race you boast, ... Il.5.810.305.
Oh Flight unworthy great *Laertes'* Son! ... Il.8.118.403.
Unworthy Property, unworthy Light, ... Il.9.88.436.
Unworthy Property, unworthy Light, ... Il.9.88.436.
Unworthy the high Race from which we came, ... Il.20.244.404.
Oh how unworthy of the Brave and Great! ... Il.21.326.434.
To shameful Bondage and unworthy Toils. ... Il.22.62.455.
Unworthy Sight! The Man, belov'd of Heav'n, ... Il.22.221.464.
(Unworthy of himself, and of the Dead) ... Il.22.496.476.

UNWOUNDED
Sighs for a Sister with unwounded ear; ... 3.Ep2.260A.71.
Sighs for a Daughter with unwounded ears ... 3.Ep2.260B.71.
Sighs for a Daughter with unwounded ear; ... 3.Ep2.260.71.

UNWROUGHT
The woof unwrought the Suitor-train surprize. ... Od.19.177.200.

UNYOK'D
Like one who late unyok'd the sweating Steers. ... 1.TrVP.36.378.

UNYOKE
These to unyoke the Mules and Horses went, ... Il.24.724.568.

UNYOKES
The Chief himself unyokes the panting Steeds. ... Il.23.596.513.

UP
See! the bold Youth strain up the threatning Steep, ... 1.W-F.155.164.
Set up themselves, and drove a *sep'rate* Trade: ... 1.EOC.105Z1.251.
And fills up all the *mighty Void* of *Sense!* ... 1.EOC.210.264.
For rising Merit will *buoy up* at last. ... 1.EOC.461.291.
Zoilus again would start up from the Dead. ... 1.EOC.465.292.
It draws up Vapours which obscure its Rays; ... 1.EOC.471.292.
The modest Fan was lifted up no more, ... 1.EOC.542.299.
Long reeds sprung up as on a fountain's brink: ... 1.TrPA.156.372.
And give up *Laius* to the Realms of Day, ... 1.TrSt.418.427.
It flew with Force, and labour'd up the Sky; ... 1.TrES.104.453.
Fierce as a Whirlwind, up the Walls he flies, ... 1.TrES.175.456.
Shoots up, and All the rising Host appears. ... 1.TrES.182.456.
To raise up Seed to bless the Pow'rs above, ... 2.ChJM.121.20.
To raise up Seed t'adore the Pow'rs above, ... 2.ChJM.121A.20.
I yield it up; but since I gave my Oath, ... 2.ChJM.701.48.
The longing Dame look'd up, and spy'd her Love ... 2.ChJM.718.49.
She seiz'd a Twig, and up the Tree she went. ... 2.ChJM.739.50.
And give up all his Substance to the Poor; ... 2.ChWB.43.58.
And give up all that's Female to the Devil. ... 2.ChWB.85.60.
The Pit fill'd up, with Turf we cover'd o'er, ... 2.ChWB.251.69.
From House to House we rambled up and down, ... 2.ChWB.280.70.
Mount up, and take a *Salamander's* Name. ... 2.RL1.60.150.
Leapt up, and wak'd his Mistress with his Tongue. ... 2.RL1.116.154.

UP (CONTINUED)
Sent up in Vapours to the *Baron's* Brain ... 2.RL3.119.176.
At length the Wits mount up, the Hairs subside. ... 2.RL5.74.206.
And send up Vows from *Rosamonda's* Lake. ... 2.RL5.136.211.
Then gazing up, a glorious Pile beheld, ... 2.TemF.25.255.
The Domes swell up, the widening Arches bend, ... 2.TemF.90.259.
And up the Winds triumphant swell the Notes; ... 2.TemF.373A.281.
I shriek, start up, the same sad prospect find, ... 2.ElAb.247.339.
Like Aaron's serpent, swallows up the rest. ... 3.EOM2.132.71.
These build up all that knowledge can destroy; ... 3.EOM2.287A.89.
Then, looking up from sire to sire, explor'd ... 3.EOM3.225.115.
But looks thro' Nature, up to Nature's God; ... 3.EOM4.332.160.
It pours the bliss that fills up all the mind. ... 3.EOM4.344.162.
For Wit's false mirror held up Nature's light; ... 3.EOM4.393.166.
And Zeal for his great House which eats thee up. ... 3.Ep3.208A.110.
And Zeal for that great House which eats him up. ... 3.Ep3.208.110.
And when up ten steep slopes you've dragg'd your thighs, ... 3.Ep4.131.150.
Your wine lock'd up, your Butler stroll'd abroad, ... 4.HS2.13.55.
When Luxury has lick'd up all thy pelf, ... 4.HS2.105.61.
Tye up the knocker, say I'm sick, I'm dead, ... 4.Arbu.2.96.
To fetch and carry Sing-song up and down; ... 4.Arbu.226.112.
Now high, now low, now Master up, now Miss, ... 4.Arbu.324.119.
Glean on, and gather up the whole Estate: ... 4.JD2.92.141.
Bred up at home, full early I begun ... 4.2HE2.52.167.
"And you shall rise up *Otway* for your pains." ... 4.2HE2.146.175.
Who, tho' the House was up, delighted sate, ... 4.2HE2.186.177.
How will our Fathers rise up in a rage, ... 4.2HE1.125.205.
His servants up, and rise by five a clock, ... 4.2HE1.162.209.
He serv'd a 'Prenticeship, who sets up shop; ... 4.2HE1.181.211.
The good man heaps up nothing but mere metre, ... 4.2HE1.198.211.
Up, up! cries Gluttony, 'tis break of day, ... 4.1HE6.112.245.
Up, up! cries Gluttony, 'tis break of day, ... 4.1HE6.112.245.
"Send for him up, take no excuse. ... 4.HS6.36.253.
The Moon was up, and Men a-bed, ... 4.HS6.196.263.
The shops shut up in every street, ... 4.1HE7.8.269.
And Fevers raging up and down, ... 4.1HE7.13.269.
"Eat some, and pocket up the rest—" ... 4.1HE7.26.269.
And kept you up so oft till one; ... 4.1HE7.48.271.
To lay this harvest up, and hoard with haste ... 4.1HE1.21.281.
That lock up all the Functions of my soul; ... 4.1HE1.40.281.
From low St. James's up to high St. Paul; ... 4.1HE1.82.285.
Up starts a Palace, lo! th' obedient base ... 4.1HE1.140.289.
I plant, root up, I build, and then confound, ... 4.1HE1.169.291.
All, all look up, with reverential Awe, ... 4.EpS1.167.309.
Some rising Genius sins up to my Song. ... 4.EpS2.9.313.
P. If not the Tradesman who set up to day, ... 4.EpS2.36.314.
Whose names once up, they thought it was not wrong ... 4.1740.21.333.
As for the rest, each winter up they run, ... 4.1740.29.333.
Take up th' Attorney's (once my better) Guide? ... 5.DunA1.190.85.
Her ample presence fills up all the place; ... 5.DunA1.217.89.
Down with the Bible, up with the Pope's Arms." ... 5.DunA2.78.107.
His papers all, the sportive winds up-lift ... 5.DunA2.107A.10
Prick all their ears up, and forget to graze; ... 5.DunA2.250.130.
He buoys up instant, and returns to light; ... 5.DunA2.284A.13
Instand buoys up, and rises into light; ... 5.DunA2.284.137.
He brings up half the bottom on his head, ... 5.DunA2.299.139.
And lick up all their Physick of the Soul. ... 5.DunA3.74.156.
And licks up every blockhead in the way. ... 5.DunA3.298.184.
Take up the Bible, once my better guide? ... 5.DunB1.200.284.
This Mess, toss'd up of Hockley-hole and White's; ... 5.DunB1.222.286.
Not wrap up Oranges, to pelt your sire! ... 5.DunB1.236.287.
Her ample presence fills up all the place; ... 5.DunB1.261.289.
Lift up your gates, ye Princes, see him come! ... 5.DunB1.301.291.
Support his front, and Oaths bring up the rear: ... 5.DunB1.308.292.
Down with the Bible, up with the Pope's Arms. ... 5.DunB2.82.299.
Prick all their ears up, and forget to graze; ... 5.DunB2.262.308.
He buoys up instant, and returns to light: ... 5.DunB2.296.310.
He brings up half the bottom on his head, ... 5.DunB2.321.312.
And lick up all their Physic of the Soul. ... 5.DunB3.82.324.
But lick up ev'ry blockhead in the way. ... 5.DunB3.296.334.
And licks up ev'ry blockhead in the way. ... 5.DunB3.296A.334
With-hold the pension, and set up the head; ... 5.DunB4.96.350.
Or give up Cicero to C or K. ... 5.DunB4.222.364.
Wrapt up in Self, a God without a Thought, ... 5.DunB4.485.389.
Rous'd at his name, up rose the bowzy Sire, ... 5.DunB4.493.390.
Led up the Youth, and call'd the Goddess *Dame.* ... 5.DunB4.498.391.
Up to a *Star,* and like Endymion dies: ... 5.DunB4.520.394.
All up the silver *Thames,* or all a down; ... 6.14ii.52.44.
Own'd his returning Lord, look'd up, and dy'd! ... 6.15.18.52.
But sets up One, a greater, in their Place; ... 6.19.38.63.
And made up half a Pope at least. ... 6.30.30.87.
But gives your feeble sex, made up of fears, ... 6.38.17.108.
Still hoarding up, most scandalously nice, ... 6.41.19.114.
Up to her godly garret after sev'n, ... 6.45.21.125.
If you'l but give up one, I'll give up tother. ... 6.46.4A.127.
If you'l but give up one, I'll give up tother. ... 6.46.4A.127.
May knock up Whores alone. ... 6.47.8.128.
Set up with these, he ventur'd on the Town. ... 6.49i.7.137.
Then up comes *Steele;* he turns upon his *Heel,* ... 6.49ii.7.140.
Now as he scratch'd to fetch up Thought, ... 6.58.29.172.
Beats up for Volunteers. ... 6.58.48.172.
Up leap'd Duke *John,* and knock'd him down, ... 6.79.63.220.
Up didst thou look, oh woeful Duke! ... 6.79.73.220.
And Duke *Nic.* up leap'd he: ... 6.79.98.221.
He turn'd up through the Gore; ... 6.79.130.222.
Lord! what a Brustling up of Feathers! ... 6.93.10.257.
Then slyly thrust it up *that same,* ... 6.94.43.260.
When scaling Armies climb'd up ev'ry Part, ... 6.96iv.69.278.
Got in his Mouth, my Heart was up in mine! ... 6.96iv.82.278.
And hang'd up *Marlborough* in *Arras:* ... 6.101.6.290.
Stood up to dash each vain Pretender's Hope, ... 6.128.17.356.
Can stoop to pick up *Strings* and *Sticks.* ... 6.135.12.366.
Bred up by Hand on Chick and Veal. ... 6.135.56.368.
Bred up by Hand and Chick and Veal. ... 6.135.56A.368.
Here lies wrapt up in forty thousand towels ... 6.147ii.1.390.
Lifts up her Light, and opens Day above. ... Il.2.60.130.

UP 557 UPON

UP (CONTINUED)
Heav'n fill'd up all my Ills, and I accurst ...... Il.6.440.348.
Up-started fierce: But far before the rest ...... Il.7.197.373.
In his strong Hand up-heav'd a flinty Stone, ... Il.7.316.379.
Awakes, starts up, and issues from his Tent. ...... Il.10.159.9.
It flew with Force, and labour'd up the Sky; ...... Il.12.458.98.
Fierce as a Whirlwind up the Walls he flies, ... Il.12.529.101.
Shoots up, and all the rising Host appears. ...... Il.12.536.101.
A pond'rous Stone up-heaving from the Sand, ... Il.14.472.186.
Mount the thick *Trojans* up the *Grecian* Wall; ...... Il.15.445.214.
But when he saw, ascending up the Fleet, ... Il.15.456.215.
He struck his hasty Foot: his Heels up-sprung; ...... Il.15.780.226.
In vain they labour up the steepy Mound; ...... Il.16.446.260.
Shrunk up he sate, with wild and haggard Eye, ... Il.16.488.262.
Hence let him march, and give up *Troy* to Fate. ...... Il.17.172.294.
Then, two by two, ascended up the Strand. ...... Il.18.90.327.
Sheaves heap'd on Sheaves, here thicken up the Ground. ...... Il.18.640.354.
He calls up all his Rage; he grinds his Teeth, ... Il.20.208.402.
Then o'er the Stubble up the Mountain flies, ... Il.20.571.418.
And turn'd up Bucklers glitter'd as they roll'd. ...... Il.21.351.435.
So roll'd up in his Den, the swelling Snake ...... Il.22.130.458.
These fix'd up high behind the rolling Wain, ... Il.22.499.477.
And when still Ev'ning gave him up to Rest, ... Il.22.648.483.
And up the Champain thunder from the Shore: ...... Il.23.440.507.
Tears up the Shore, and thunders tow'rd the Main. ...... Il.23.454.508.
Close up the vent'rous Youth resolves to keep, ... Il.23.503.510.
He flies more fast, and throws up all the Rein. ...... Il.23.510.510.
Uprose great *Ajax;* up *Epæus* rose. ...... Il.23.994.529.
Then starting up, disconsolate he goes ...... Il.24.19.535.
Set up by Jove your Spectacle of Woe? ...... Il.24.300.549.
Mourn at each Step, and give him up to Fate, ... Il.24.404.552.
While thus he thought, a monst'rous wave up-bore ...... Od.5.542.198.
Down rushing, it up-turns a hill of ground. ...... Od.8.218.274.
Up rose nine Seniors, chosen to survey ...... Od.8.295.279.
All *Troy* up-heav'd the steed: of diff'ring mind, ... Od.8.553.292.
Up-bore my load, and prest the sinking sands ...... Od.10.197.350.
Chear up my friends! it is not yet our fate ...... Od.10.200.350.
'Till rising up, *Aretè* silence broke, ... Od.11.416.404.
Up the high hill he heaves a huge round stone; ...... Od.11.736.422.
Up sprung a brisker breeze; with freshning gales ...... Od.12.184.441.
Tears up the deck; then all at once descends: ...... Od.12.482.455.
The skin shrunk up, and wither'd at her hand: ...... Od.13.497.29.
Thus speaking, on the right up-soar'd in air ...... Od.15.565.97.
Bids her cheeks glow, and lights up all her charms, ... Od.18.224.178.
To light his torch, and give me up to cares; ...... Od.18.316.182.
Up-rising early with the purple morn, ... Od.19.365.212.
Up-springing from his couch, with active haste ...... Od.20.116.238.
Up-rose, and thus divin'd the vengeance near. ...... Od.20.422.253.
Now gently winding up the fair ascent, ... Od.21.41.261.
That rite compleat, up-rose the thoughtful man, ... Od.21.290.274.
He said; and mounting up the lofty stairs, ... Od.22.158.294.
Grief seiz'd at once, and wrapt up all the man; ...... Od.24.368.366.

UP-BORE
While thus he thought, a monst'rous wave up-bore ...... Od.5.542.198.
Up-bore my load, and prest the sinking sands ...... Od.10.197.350.

UP-HEAV'D
In his strong Hand up-heav'd a flinty Stone, ... Il.7.316.379.
All *Troy* up-heav'd the steed: of diff'ring mind, ... Od.8.553.292.

UP-HEAVING
A pond'rous Stone up-heaving from the Sand, ... Il.14.472.186.

UP-HELD
By singing Peers up-held on either hand, ... 5.DunB4.49.346.

UP-LIFT
His papers all, the sportive winds up-lift ...... 5.DunA2.107A.109.

UP-RISING
Up-rising early with the purple morn, ... Od.19.365.212.

UP-ROSE
Up-rose, and thus divin'd the vengeance near. ...... Od.20.422.253.
That rite compleat, up-rose the thoughtful man, ... Od.21.290.274.

UP-SOAR'D
Thus speaking, on the right up-soar'd in air ...... Od.15.565.97.

UP-SPRINGING
Up-springing from his couch, with active haste ...... Od.20.116.238.

UP-SPRUNG
He struck his hasty Foot: his Heels up-sprung; ...... Il.15.780.226.

UP-STARTED
Up-started fierce: But far before the rest ...... Il.7.197.373.

UP-TURNS
Down rushing, it up-turns a hill of ground. ...... Od.8.218.274.

UPBORN
His Feet, upborn, scarce the strong Flood divide, ... Il.21.266.431.
Swift as on wings of winds upborn they fly, ... Od.8.127.269.

UPBRAID
Silent, he heard the Queen of Woods upbraid: ...... Il.21.553.444.
And thus posterity upbraid our name. ...... Od.21.356.276.

UPBRAIDED
And its upbraided Godhead thus bespoke. ...... 1.TrSt.756.442.

UPBRAIDING
Rais'd his upbraiding Voice, and angry Eyes: ...... Il.3.450.213.
Him thus upbraiding, with a wrathful Look ...... Il.5.1092.318.

UPBRAIDS
The Man who acts the least, upbraids the most? ...... Il.2.311.142.
He thus upbraids him with a gen'rous Heat. ...... Il.3.54.191.
On *Hector* frowning, thus his Flight upbraids. ...... Il.17.154.293.
Him, thus retreating, *Artemis* upbraids, ... Il.21.545.444.
But thus upbraids his Rival as he flies; ...... Il.23.519.510.
Upbraids thy pow'r, thy wisdom, or thy will: ...... Od.20.258.245.

UPHEAVE
Upheave the Piles that prop the solid Wall; ...... Il.12.307.92.

UPHELD
For *Jove* upheld, and lighten'd of its Load ...... 1.TrES.189.456.
Then, with his suppliant Hands upheld in Air, ... 1.TrUl.238.473.
And drawn supports, upheld by God, or thee? ...... 3.EOM1.34.17.
Let Ireland tell, how Wit upheld her cause, ... 4.2HE1.221.213.
He said, and in his Arms upheld the Chief. ...... Il.11.977.78.
For *Jove* upheld, and lighten'd of its Load ...... Il.12.543.101.
Perform'd their office, or his weight upheld: ...... Od.5.582.200.
Then with his suppliant hands upheld in air, ... Od.13.405.26.

UPHOLD
The Monarch's Steps two Female Forms uphold, ... Il.18.487.345.

UPHOLST'RER
"Your Barber, Cook, Upholst'rer, what you please. ...... 4.2HE2.10.165.

UPLIFT
Songs, sonnets, epigrams the winds uplift, ... 5.DunA2.107.109.
Songs, sonnets, epigrams the winds uplift, ... 5.DunB2.115.301.
Pow'rless to speak, I scarce uplift my eyes, ... Od.23.109.325.

UPLIFTED
Like Steel, uplifted by some strenuous Swain, ... Il.3.91.194.
With Hands uplifted and imploring Eyes, ... Il.6.374.344.
His Hands uplifted to th' attesting Skies, ... Il.19.263.383.
Pensive he muses with uplifted Hands. ...... Il.23.121.492.
With Hands uplifted, eye him as he past, ... Il.24.405.552.
Thus he. The matron with uplifted eyes ...... Od.2.424.81.
With hands uplifted to the starry skies. ...... Od.9.616.332.
With hands uplifted they attest the skies; ...... Od.12.360.448.

UPLIFTS
Uplifts his Eyes, and calls the Pow'r divine. ...... Il.24.376.551.

UPON
Pants on the Leaves, and dies upon the Trees. ...... 1.PWi.80.94.
And break upon thee in a Flood of Day! ...... 1.Mes.98.121.
What Kings first breath'd upon her winding Shore, ... 1.W-F.300.176.
High in the midst, upon his Urn reclin'd, ... 1.W-F.349.184.
And fain *wou'd* be upon the *Laughing Side:* ...... 1.EOC.33.243.
Truth breaks upon us with *resistless Day;* ...... 1.EOC.212.264.
Still make the *Whole* depend upon a *Part,* ...... 1.EOC.264.269.
The *Sense,* they humbly take upon Content. ...... 1.EOC.308.274.
Clears, and *improves* whate'er it shines upon, ... 1.EOC.316.274.
And ready Nature waits upon his Hand; ...... 1.EOC.487.294.
High in the midst, upon this airy steep ...... 1.TrPA.41.367.
And soft as down upon the breast of swans: ...... 1.TrPA.61.367.
Upon the tree I cast a frightful look; ...... 1.TrFD.29.387.
While Discord waits upon divided Pow'r. ...... 1.TrSt.183.418.
And Dust yet white upon each Altar lies, ... 1.TrSt.601.435.
He springs to Fight, and flies upon the Foes. ...... 1.TrES.122.454.
And pleasing Slumbers steal upon his Eyes. ...... 1.TrUl.6.465.
Ye Gods (he cry'd) upon what barren Coast, ... 1.TrUl.74.468.
He fix'd at last upon the youthful *May.* ...... 2.ChJM.243.26.
He wrapt in Silk, and laid upon his Heart. ...... 2.ChJM.399.34.
It happ'd, that once upon a Summer's Day, ... 2.ChJM.521.40.
Seen with both Eyes, and seiz'd upon the Place, ... 2.ChJM.664A.47.
By Strugling with a Man upon a Tree? ...... 2.ChJM.763.52.
And Feasts still kept upon my Wedding-Day: ...... 2.ChWB.113.62.
I levied first a Tax upon his Need, ... 2.ChWB.168.64.
While melting Musick steals upon the Sky, ... 2.RL2.49.162.
Some hang upon the Pendants of her Ear; ...... 2.RL2.140.168.
First *Ariel* perch'd upon a *Matadore,* ...... 2.RL3.33.171.
Eliza stretch'd upon the fun'ral Pyre, ... 2.TemF.206.272.
Fill the wide Earth, and gain upon the Skies. ...... 2.TemF.313.279.
Than Leaves on Trees, or Sands upon the Shores; ...... 2.TemF.425.284.
The dying gales that pant upon the trees, ... 2.ElAb.159.332.
He mounts the storm, and walks upon the wind. ...... 3.EOM2.110.68.
And pours it all upon the peccant part. ...... 3.EOM2.144.72.
And makes her hearty meal upon a Dunce. ...... 3.Ep2.86.57.
Finds all her life one warfare upon earth: ...... 3.Ep2.118.60.
She, while her Lover pants upon her breast, ... 3.Ep2.167.64.
And lo! two puddings smoak'd upon the board. ...... 3.Ep3.360.123.
Make the soul dance upon a Jig to Heaven. ...... 3.Ep4.144.151.
By worthier Footmen pist upon and whipt! ...... 4.HAdv.56.81.
"Who breaks a Butterfly upon a Wheel?" ...... 4.Arbu.308.118.
We Poets are (upon a Poet's word) ...... 4.2HE1.358.225.
To see their Judgments hang upon thy Voice; ...... 4.1HE6.35.239.
Takes the whole House upon the Poet's day. ...... 4.1HE6.88.243.
Upon my word, you must be rich indeed; ...... 4.1HE6.90.243.
A frugal Mouse upon the whole, ... 4.HS6.161.261.
Dwell in a Monk, or light upon a King, ... 4.EpS1.139.308.
It anger'd TURENNE, once upon a day. ...... 4.EpS2.150.322.
And learn to crawl upon poetic feet. ...... 5.DunA1.60.67.
Coach'd, carted, trod upon, now loose, now fast, ... 5.DunA3.293.184.
And learn to crawl upon poetic feet. ...... 5.DunB1.62.274.
Coach'd, carted, trod upon, now loose, now fast, ... 5.DunB3.291.334.
Make Nature still incroach upon his plan; ...... 5.DunB4.473.387.
To dwell at last upon her lover's eyes. ...... 6.4i.4.9.
Which else we durst not gaze upon. ...... 6.5.6.12.
To gaze upon themselves in thee. ...... 6.6ii.12.14.
A *Phœnix* couch'd upon her Fun'ral Nest. ...... 6.9viii.2.22.
Gently steal upon the Ear; ...... 6.11.13.30.
Ixion rests upon his Wheel, ... 6.11.67.32.
The Furies sink upon their Iron Beds, ... 6.11.69.32.

UPON (CONTINUED)

Like a fat Corpse upon a Bed, ...6.14v(a).11.48.
And fix thy foot upon the Lion's crest. ....6.21.32.70.
Streets, chairs, and coxcombs rush upon my sight; ....6.45.48.126.
How safe must be the King upon this Throne, ...6.48ii.5.134.
Then up comes *Steele;* he turns upon his *Heel,* ....6.49ii.7.140.
And in a Moment fastens upon *Steele.* ....6.49ii.8.140.
A while he crawls upon the Earth, ...6.53.7.161.
And thus upon the Stage 'tis fairly *thrown,* ....6.60.37.179.
Where Ribbans wave upon the tye, ...6.61.38.182.
That darts severe upon a rising Lye, ...6.73.6.209.
Come near, they trod upon your Toes; ....6.79.19.218.
Look down upon this Stone; ....6.82viii.2.233.
Glow in thy heart, and smile upon thy face. ....6.86.14.245.
Dost thou for these now Float upon the Main? ....6.96ii.30Z37.272.
To weep upon our Cod in *Newfound-land:* ....6.96ii.76.273.
To weep upon Fresh Cod in *Newfound*-land: ....6.96ii.76A.273.
Each Step they trod, I felt upon my Heart. ....6.96iv.70.278.
Upon something or other, she found better *Fun.* ....6.124i.6.346.
Cibber! write all thy Verses upon Glasses, ...6.131ii.1.360.
She, while her Lover pants upon her breast, ...6.139.11.377.
Finds all her Life one Warfare upon Earth; ....6.154.4.402.
And fainter Murmurs dy'd upon the Ear, ...Il.2.126.133.
Desert the Ships, and pour upon the Plain. ....Il.2.248.139.
And all the War descends upon the Wing. ....Il.3.10.188.
In clanging Arms he leaps upon the Ground ....Il.3.42.190.
Now rest their Spears, or lean upon their Shields; ....Il.3.177.199.
His modest Eyes he fix'd upon the Ground, ...Il.3.280.207.
His gushing Entrails smoak'd upon the Ground, ...Il.4.608.250.
Swift from his Seat he leap'd upon the Ground, ...Il.5.142.274.
Beneath his Helmet, drops upon his Breast. ....Il.8.374.415.
Tremendous Gorgon frown'd upon its Field, ...Il.11.47.36.
He springs to Fight, and flies upon the Foes. ....Il.12.476.99.
Beneath his Helmet, nods upon his Breast; ....Il.13.687.137.
Not *Jove* himself, upon the Past has pow'r. ....Il.14.62.160.
The Victor leaps upon his prostrate Prize; ....Il.15.696.222.
Like Fire from *Jove,* and bursts upon them all: ....Il.15.751.224.
His Eyes on Heaven, his Feet upon the Place ....Il.16.281.250.
The groaning Warrior pants upon the Ground. ....Il.16.345.256.
That breathes or creeps upon the Dust of Earth; ....Il.17.509.308.
Let his last Spirit smoak upon my Dart; ....Il.18.120.328.
Bathe thy cold Face, and sob upon thy Breast! ....Il.18.398.340.
And like a Deluge pour'd upon the Plain. ....Il.19.379.387.
Advanc'd upon the Field there stood a Mound ....Il.20.174.401.
The rushing Entrails pour'd upon the Ground ....Il.20.483.414.
With wild Affright, and dropt upon the Field ....Il.21.58.424.
The reeking Entrails pour upon the Ground. ....Il.21.196.429.
On this his Weight, and rais'd upon his Hand, ...Il.21.275.432.
Beats on his Back, or bursts upon his Head. ....Il.21.306.433.
And *Hector's* Blood shall smoke upon thy Lance. ....Il.21.343.435.
And the pale Crescent fades upon her Brows. ....Il.21.596.446.
And aims his Claws, and shoots upon his Wings: ....Il.22.188.463.
At last is *Hector* stretch'd upon the Plain, ...Il.22.415.472.
No more to smile upon his Sire! no Friend ....Il.22.622.482.
Sunk soft in Down upon the Nurse's Breast, ...Il.22.649.483.
And now the Sun had set upon their Woe; ....Il.23.193.497.
These in fair Order rang'd upon the Plain, ...Il.23.339.503.
Float in their Speed, and dance upon the Wind: ....Il.23.444.508.
Erect with Ardour, pois'd upon the Rein, ...Il.23.449.508.
Quits his bright Car, and springs upon the Sands; ....Il.23.590.513.
The bleeding Hero pants upon the Ground. ....Il.23.805.521.
His glowing Breath upon his Shoulders plays; ....Il.23.895.524.
And gaze upon him as they gaz'd their last. ....Il.24.406.552.
Those, *Cynthia's* Arrows stretch'd upon the Plain. ....Il.24.762.569.
Her breathless Brother stretch'd upon the Bier: ....Il.24.873.573.
Stretch their broad plumes, and float upon the wind. ....Od.2.174.70.
And spread soft hydes upon the yellow sands; ....Od.3.48.88.
The tongues they cast upon the fragrant flame, ...Od.3.437.108.
And sacred wheat upon the victim lay'd, ...Od.3.569.115.
Streams the black blood, and smokes upon the ground. ....Od.3.581.116.
The third fair morn now blaz'd upon the main; ....Od.5.500.196.
Behind him far, upon the purple waves ....Od.5.592.201.
Wav'd high, and frown'd upon the stream below. ....Od.5.615.201.
And rising mountains gain upon our sight. ....Od.10.33.341.
The men, like fish, they stuck upon the flood, ...Od.10.143.347.
Beneath the knife upon your altars fall; ....Od.11.38.381.
A pompous wretch! accurs'd upon a throne. ....Od.11.336.398.
Steal thro' the ear, and win upon the soul; ....Od.11.457.407.
But say, upon the dark and dismal coast, ...Od.11.460.407.
When *Troy's* proud bulwarks smok'd upon the ground, ...Od.11.652.416.
And pleasing slumbers steal upon his eyes. ....Od.13.97.5.
Ye Gods! (he cry'd) upon what barren coast ....Od.13.241.17.
The bounding shafts upon the harness play, ...Od.15.208.78.
O give these eyes to feast upon their lord. ....Od.16.28.103.
His blood in vengeance smokes upon my spear. ....Od.16.457.129.
Dispeopling realms to gaze upon thy eyes: ....Od.18.290.180.
His seat he takes, his eyes upon his Lord. ....Od.21.426.280.
Each sung along, and drop'd upon the ground. ....Od.22.311.301.
And calls a Corn-van: This upon the plain ....Od.23.291.337.

UPPER

Restor'd the groaning God to upper Air. ....Il.5.480.291.
Of upper Heav'n to *Jove* resign'd the Reign, ...Il.14.235.172.
Whom Heaven enamour'd snatch'd to upper Air, ...Il.20.279.406.
Sees, thro' its parting Plates, the upper Air, ...Il.20.329.407.
(The Way fair *Iris* led) to upper Air. ....Il.24.126.540.
And climb the steep ascent to upper day; ....Od.11.270.395.
And drag'd the three-mouth'd dog to upper day; ....Od.11.770.424.
Hence to the upper chambers let me fly, ...Od.22.466.311.

UPRAIS'D

Telemachus uprais'd, and sternly said. ....Od.18.67.170.

UPREAR'D

Thy friendly Hand uprear'd me from the Plain, ...Il.19.313.385.

UPRIGHT

And sipt his Cordial as he sate upright: 2.ChJM.387.33
And supp'd his Cordial as he sate upright: 2.ChJM.387B.3
So upright Quakers please both Man and God. 5.DunB4.208.3
All upright as a Pin, ...6.58.32.172.
A Wood of Spears stood by, that fixt upright, ...Il.10.174.9.
Bristled with upright Spears, that flash'd afar; ....Il.13.431.126.
Pale grew his Face, and upright stood his Hair; ....Il.24.442.554.

UPRISING

Uprising slow, the venerable Sage ....Il.1.95.91.

UPROAR

When loud uproar and lawless riot cease, ...Od.17.654.164.
Then wild uproar and clamour mounts the sky, ...Od.18.444.190.
And all was riot, noise, and wild uproar. ....Od.21.390.279.

UPROOTED

It lies uprooted from its genial Bed, ...Il.17.63.290.
The Plant uprooted to his Weight gave way, ...Il.21.270.432.

UPROOTS

Uproots the bearded corn? rise, try the fight, ...Od.18.36.168.

UPROSE

Fierce, at the Word, uprose great *Tydeus'* Son, ...Il.23.957.527.
Uprose great *Ajax;* up *Epæus* rose. ....Il.23.994.529.
Uprose the virgin with the morning light, ...Od.6.59.208.
To whom the stern *Telemachus* uprose: ....Od.18.452.190.
Uprose the throngs tumultuous round the hall; ....Od.22.28.287.
Uprose *Ulysses* from the genial bed, ...Od.23.375.343.

UPSPRUNG

Then from his eyes upsprung the warrior-maid. ....Od.16.193.112.

UPSTARTED

Upstarted *Thoas* strait, *Andræmon's* son, ...Od.14.564.64.

UPWARD

And trace the Muses *upward* to their *Spring;* 1.EOC.127.253
While all his sad Companions upward gaze, ...1.TrSt.644.437.
But trust the Muse—she saw it upward rise, ...2.RL5.123.210.
Upward the Columns shoot, the Roofs ascend, ...2.TemF.264.27
What would this Man? Now upward will he soar, ...3.EOM1.173.3
The forests dance, the rivers upward rise, ...5.DunA3.241.1
The forests dance, the rivers upward rise, ...5.DunB3.245.3
The crowd gaze upward while it cleaves the skies. ....Od.8.216.274.

UPWARDS

A mournful Glance Sir *Fopling* upwards cast, ...2.RL5.63.205.
And upwards cast the Corps: The reeking Spear ....Il.16.1044.283.

URFE

Of fam'd *Tom Durfy,* or *De Urfe.* ....6.30.6B.85.

URFEY

Thy Name De Urfey or D'Urfey. ....6.30.6A.85.

URFY

Tom B[ur]n[e]t or *Tom D' Urfy* may, ...6.58.51.173.

URG'D

(Beasts, urg'd by us, their Fellow Beasts pursue, ...1.W-F.123.162.
Or as the God, more furious, urg'd the Chace. ....1.W-F.190.167.
And urg'd the rest by equal Steps to rise; ....1.EOC.97.250.
Are Mortals urg'd thro' *Sacred Lust of Praise!* 1.EOC.521.296
Are Mortals urg'd by *Sacred Lust of Praise?* 1.EOC.521A.29
Not she whose Beauty urg'd the *Centaur's* Arms, ...1.TrVP.71.380.
This when the various God had urg'd in vain, ...1.TrVP.112.381
Headlong from thence the Fury urg'd her Flight, ...1.TrSt.169A.41
Thro' the thick Desarts headlong urg'd his Flight: ....1.TrSt.558.433.
His God-like Son, and urg'd him on to Fame. ....1.TrES.6.449.
His matchless Son, and urg'd him on to Fame. ....1.TrES.6A.449.
Urg'd by fierce Drivers thro' the dusty Space, ...1.TrUl.8.465.
The knotty Point was urg'd on either Side; 2.ChJM.140.21
The knotty Point was urg'd on ev'ry Side; 2.ChJM.140A.2
Our rev'rend Knight was urg'd to Am'rous Play: 2.ChJM.522.40
Our noble Knight was urg'd to Am'rous Play: 2.ChJM.522A.4
Fate urg'd the Sheers, and cut the *Sylph* in twain, ...2.RL3.151.179.
That urg'd by thee, i turn'd the tuneful art: 3.EOM4.391.1
Then urg'd by C[artere]t, or by C[artere]t stopt, ...4.1740.31.333.
The wheels above urg'd by the load below; 5.DunA1.180.8
With legs expanded Bernard urg'd the race, ...5.DunA2.63.10
With steps unequal L[into]t urg'd the race, ...5.DunA2.63A.1
The wheels above urg'd by the load below: 5.DunB1.184.2
The Springs above urg'd by the Weight below; ....6.17i(b).2.55.
Still grasp'd his Knees, and urg'd the dear Request. ....Il.1.665.118.
Or urg'd by Wrongs, to *Troy's* Destruction came? ....Il.2.579.155.
Fate urg'd them on! the Sire forwarn'd in vain, ...Il.2.1010.170.
(Great *Menelaus* urg'd the same Request) ....Il.3.269.205.
Fir'd with the Charge, she head-long urg'd her Flight, ...Il.4.99.225.
Shields urg'd on Shields, and Men drove Men along. ....Il.4.485.243.
Or *Phœbus* urg'd me to these Fields in vain. ....Il.5.137.273.
But thou (tho' *Pallas* urg'd thy frantic Deed) ....Il.5.493.291.
And calling *Mars,* thus urg'd the raging God. ....Il.5.552.295.
Mars urg'd him on; yet, ruthless in his Hate, ...Il.5.691.300.
The God but urg'd him to provoke his Fate. ....Il.5.692.301.
Urg'd by the Force of unresisted Fate, ...Il.5.777.303.
The Javelin hiss'd; the Goddess urg'd it on: ....Il.5.1049.316.
(The Sign of Conquest) and thus urg'd the Fight. ....Il.8.209.407.
Such various Passions urg'd the troubled Host. ....Il.9.10.431.
Urg'd me, unwilling, this Attempt to make; ....Il.10.467.24.
Fate urg'd them on; the Father warn'd in vain, ...Il.11.429.53.
Thus urg'd the Chief; a gen'rous Troop appears, ...Il.11.720.67.
Urg'd you to Arms, and found you fierce for Fame. ....Il.11.913.76.
His vaunted Coursers urg'd to meet the War. ....Il.12.126.86.

URG'D (CONTINUED)
His matchless Son, and urg'd him on to Fame. ... Il.12.350.94.
Full of the God that urg'd their burning Breast ... Il.13.115.110.
The close-compacted Legions urg'd their way: ... Il.13.188.114.
Still gath'ring Force, it smoaks; and, urg'd amain, ... Il.13.197.115.
Urg'd with Desire of Fame, beyond the rest, ... Il.13.212.116.
Fierce as the God of Battels, urg'd his Pace. ... Il.13.419.126.
Behold! *Pisander,* urg'd by Fate's Decree, ... Il.13.753.141.
Chief urg'd on Chief, and Man drove Man along: ... Il.13.1007.153.
The first bold Javelin urg'd by *Hector's* Force, ... Il.14.465.186.
Urg'd by the Voice divine, thus *Hector* flew, ... Il.15.306.209.
Full at the *Trojan's* Head he urg'd his Lance, ... Il.15.632.220.
Thro' *Dolops'* Shoulder urg'd his forceful Dart, ... Il.15.638.221.
The God pursu'd her, urg'd, and crown'd his Fire. ... Il.16.221.248.
Shield urg'd on Shield, and Man drove Man along: ... Il.16.261.249.
What Grief thy Heart, what Fury urg'd thy Hand, ... Il.16.712.271.
He urg'd thee on, and urg'd thee on to fall. ... Il.16.846.276.
He urg'd thee on, and urg'd thee on to fall. ... Il.16.846.276.
And urg'd great *Hector* to dispute the Prize, ... Il.17.76.291.
But *Phœbus* urg'd *Æneas* to the Fight; ... Il.17.374.302.
Excessive Spirit, urg'd 'em to the Course; ... Il.17.525.308.
Of Men, Steeds, Chariots, urg'd the Rout along: ... Il.17.824.320.
Me *Agamemnon* urg'd to deadly Hate; ... Il.18.143.329.
With fell *Erynnis,* urg'd my Wrath that Day ... Il.19.89.375.
By *Phœbus* urg'd; but *Phœbus* has bestow'd ... Il.20.343.408.
Urg'd thee to meet *Achilles'* Arm in War? ... Il.20.382.411.
One urg'd by Fury, one by Fear impell'd; ... Il.22.190.463.
They urg'd in vain; the Chief refus'd, and swore. ... Il.23.52.489.
And the fierce Coursers urg'd their rapid Pace ... Il.23.587.513.
Behind, *Atrides* urg'd the Race, more near ... Il.23.599.513.
She urg'd her Fav'rite on the rapid Way, ... Il.23.919.525.
Before th' inspiring God that urg'd them on, ... Il.24.543.558.
Then urg'd, she perfects her illustrious toils; ... Od.2.125.67.
With rapid step the Goddess urg'd her way; ... Od.2.443.82.
Urg'd by the precepts by the Goddess giv'n, ... Od.3.90.90.
(So *Jove,* that urg'd us to our fate, ordain'd.) ... Od.3.184.95.
With us *Tydides* fear'd, and urg'd his haste: ... Od.3.201.95.
Urg'd you with great *Deiphobus* to come, ... Od.4.376.139.
The cause that urg'd the bold attempt declare, ... Od.4.571.147.
Urg'd on by want, and recent from the storms; ... Od.6.163.216.
Or urg'd by *Jove,* or her own changeful heart. ... Od.7.349.253.
Urg'd by some present God, they swift let fall ... Od.9.453.324.
Urg'd on all hands it nimbly spins about, ... Od.9.459.325.
Full oft the Monarch urg'd me to relate ... Od.10.15.340.
Urg'd forth, and drove the bristly herd before; ... Od.10.460.366.
Urg'd by fierce drivers thro' the dusty space, ... Od.13.99.6.
I dread his proffer'd kindness, urg'd in vain. ... Od.15.227.79.
'Till urg'd by wrongs a foreign realm he chose, ... Od.15.254.80.
That warmth of soul that urg'd thy younger years? ... Od.18.256.179.
And urg'd, for title to a consort Queen, ... Od.20.355.249.
But bold *Telemachus* thus urg'd him on. ... Od.21.398.279.
Urg'd the dire task imperious from above. ... Od.22.487.313.

URGE
My trembling sister strove to urge her flight, ... 1.TrFD.36.387.
In fighting Fields, nor urge thy Soul to War. ... 1.TrES.46.451.
And urge the bold *Ajaces* to our Aid; ... 1.TrES.68.452.
Self-love, to urge, and Reason, to restrain; ... 3.EOM2.54.62.
The Senator at Cricket urge the Ball; ... 5.DunB4.592.402.
Well argu'd, Faith! Your Point you urge ... 6.10.91.27.
And while his Guts the keen Emeticks urge, ... 6.82x.5.236.
Urge all the Ties to former Service ow'd, ... Il.1.512.112.
With long-resounding Cries they urge the Train, ... Il.2.185.137.
Urge their swift Steeds to face the coming War) ... Il.4.267.234.
Whose Godlike Virtue we but urge in vain, ... Il.4.327.236.
Your foaming Steeds urge headlong on the Foes! ... Il.4.588.249.
To dare the Shock, or urge the rapid Race: ... Il.5.281.280.
Rowze all thy *Trojans,* urge thy *Aids* to fight; ... Il.5.597.297.
Urge thou thy Knight to march where Glory calls, ... Il.6.454.348.
To dare the Fight, or urge the rapid Race; ... Il.8.136.404.
Retire advis'd, and urge the Chariot hence. ... Il.8.170.406.
Now *Xanthus, Æthon, Lampus!* urge the Chace, ... Il.8.226.408.
Nor urge a Soul already fill'd with fire. ... Il.8.356.414.
Urge by their Father's Fame, their future Praise. ... Il.10.75.6.
Urge thou the Slaughter, while I seize the Steeds. ... Il.10.557.27.
Thro' the mid Field the routed urge their way. ... Il.11.218.45.
Thither, O *Hector,* thither urge thy Steeds; ... Il.11.650.62.
Threats urge the fearful, and the valiant, Praise. ... Il.12.316.93.
Urge those who stand, and those who faint excite; ... Il.12.323.93.
In fighting Fields, nor urge thy Soul to War. ... Il.12.390.96.
And urge the bold *Ajaces* to our Aid; ... Il.12.412.96.
And what thou canst not singly, urge the rest. ... Il.13.300.119.
And urge thy Soul to rival Acts with mine: ... Il.13.308.119.
Swell his bold Heart, and urge his Strength to War: ... Il.15.261.207.
And urge the Gods, with Voices, Eyes, and Hands. ... Il.15.425.213.
I haste to urge him, by his Country's Care, ... Il.15.464.215.
The Tyde of *Trojans* urge their desp'rate Course, ... Il.16.465.260.
Whether to urge their prompt Effect, and call ... Il.16.787.274.
Urge to broad *Hellespont* their headlong Course: ... Il.18.186.331.
Now urge the Course where swift *Scamander* glides: ... Il.21.714.451.
And urge to meet the Fate he cannot shun. ... Il.22.288.468.
But urge the Right, and give him all the Reins; ... Il.23.409.506.
Or urge the Race, or wrestle on the Field. ... Il.23.714.518.
And urge her Monarch to redeem his Son; ... Il.24.180.543.
'Tis Heav'n commands me, and you urge in vain. ... Il.24.270.547.
His Son, his Mother! urge him to bestow ... Il.24.572.560.
Urge the bold traitor to the Regicide? ... Od.1.48.32.
"Cease yet a while to urge the bridal hour; ... Od.2.108.66.
If this displease, why urge ye here your stay? ... Od.2.161.70.
Urge him with truth to frame his fair replies; ... Od.3.25.87.
If to the right to urge the pilot's toil, ... Od.3.205.95.
Urge him with truth to frame his free replies, ... Od.3.419.107.
He learn'd what best might urge the *Dardan* fate: ... Od.4.352.136.
To whom appeas'd: No more I urge delay; ... Od.8.391.285.
Or from the bounding courser urge the war. ... Od.9.58.304.
And urge my train the dreadful deed to dare. ... Od.9.448.324.

URGE (CONTINUED)
And urge their chief with animating cries. ... Od.10.559.369.
New chains they add, and rapid urge the way, ... Od.12.236.443.
Why urge we not to blows? Well-pleas'd they spring ... Od.18.48.169.
Shall urge—and wav'd it hissing in her hand. ... Od.19.85.196.
Urge not this breast to heave, these eyes to weep; ... Od.19.139.199.
My anxious parents urge a speedy choice, ... Od.19.180.200.
I for *Dulichium* urge the wat'ry way, ... Od.19.335.210.
Mean-time the Suitors urge the Prince's fate, ... Od.20.300.247.
And to the youthful Prince to urge the laws, ... Od.21.23.260.
Urge the fleet courser's or the racer's toil; ... Od.24.88.352.

URGENT
Or strong Necessity, or urgent Fear: ... Il.9.262.445.
Their Pray'rs were urgent, and their Proffers great: ... Il.9.692.468.

URGES
Heir urges Heir, like Wave impelling Wave: ... 4.2HE2.253.183.
The Combate urges, and my Soul's on fire. ... Il.6.453.348.
Claims all our Hearts, and urges all our Hands. ... Il.10.135.8.
And urges to desert the hopeless War; ... Il.17.702.315.
Some Dæmon urges! 'tis my Doom to die! ... Il.21.104.426.
Him great *Tydides* urges to contend, ... Il.23.789.521.
Part, the storm urges on the coast of *Creet,* ... Od.3.371.104.

URGING
But urging Vengeance and severer Fight; ... 1.TrES.142.454.
But urging Vengeance, and severer Fight; ... Il.12.496.99.
Thus urging to their toil the menial train. ... Od.20.185.242.

URIAH
Shall *David* as *Uriah* slay him, ... 6.101.27.291.

URN
And Palms Eternal flourish round his Urn. ... 1.W-F.312.179.
Grav'd on his Urn appear'd the Moon, that guides ... 1.W-F.333.182.
High in the midst, upon his Urn reclin'd, ... 1.W-F.349.184.
While These exalt their Scepters o'er my Urn; ... 1.TrSt.106.414.
If e'er I laid my Husband in his Urn, ... 2.ChWB.294.71.
To light the dead, and warm th' unfruitful urn. ... 2.ElAb.262.341.
And swallows roost in Nilus' dusty Urn. ... 3.Ep4.126.149.
My Verse, and QUEENSB'RY weeping o'er thy Urn! ... 4.Arbu.260.114.
Hang the sad Verse on CAROLINA's Urn, ... 4.EpS1.80.304.
Thro' half the heav'ns he pours th' exalted urn; ... 5.DunA2.175.122.
Thro' half the heav'ns he pours th' exalted urn; ... 5.DunB2.183.304.
And the huge Boar is shrunk into an Urn: ... 5.DunB4.552.396.
In *Hallifax's* Urn; ... 6.47.26.129.
Or wait inspiring dreams at *Maro's* Urn: ... 6.52.28.157.
Thy reliques, *Rowe,* to this fair urn we trust, ... 6.72.1.208.
To which thy urn shall guide inquiring eyes. ... 6.72.4B.208.
Each to his Lips apply'd the nectar'd Urn. ... Il.1.769.124.
Pour the full Urn; Then draws the *Grecian* Lord ... Il.3.340.209.
Pour the full Urn; Then drew the *Grecian* Lord ... Il.3.340A.209.
From the same Urn they drink the mingled Wine, ... Il.3.368.210.
The Lots of Fight, and shakes the brazen Urn. ... Il.3.403.211.
Her slaughter'd Heroes, and their Bones in-urn. ... Il.7.451.386.
Our slaughter'd Heroes, and their Bones in-urn. ... Il.7.471.387.
Let their large Gifts procure an Urn at least, ... Il.22.431.473.
Her fair-hair'd Handmaids heat the brazen Urn, ... Il.22.570.480.
That golden Urn thy Goddess Mother gave ... Il.23.107.491.
And pour in Tears, e'er yet they close the Urn. ... Il.23.277.501.
The Urn a Veil of Linen cover'd o'er. ... Il.23.316.502.
A silver Urn; that full six Measures held, ... Il.23.865.524.
And left the Urn *Ulysses'* rich Reward. ... Il.23.914.525.
And fill thy Measure from his bitter Urn, ... Il.24.689.566.
Last o'er the Urn the sacred Earth they spread, ... Il.24.1007.577.
An urn shall recompence your prudent choice: ... Od.4.834.158.
A polish'd Urn the seeming Virgin bore, ... Od.7.26.235.
And death release me from the silent urn! ... Od.11.610.413.
Soon from the fount, with each a brimming urn, ... Od.20.202.243.
In the same urn a sep'rate space contains ... Od.24.99.353.

URNS
Who swell with Tributary Urns his Flood. ... 1.W-F.338.183.
That swell with Tributary Urns his Flood. ... 1.W-F.338A.183.
Those from whose Urns the rowling Rivers flow, ... 1.TrSt.288.422.
Where Bowls and Urns were form'd of living Stone, ... 1.TrUl.35.467.
So from the Sun's broad beam, in shallow urns ... 5.DunB2.11.296.
Grots, Statues, Urns, and *Jo—n's Dog* and *Bitch:* ... 6.14ii.50.44.
Like twenty River-Gods with all their Urns. ... 6.33.6.99.
So decent Urns their snowy Bones may keep, ... Il.7.402.384.
And sprinkles sacred Salt from lifted Urns; ... Il.9.282.447.
Two Urns by *Jove's* high Throne have ever stood, ... Il.24.663.564.
But by thy care twelve urns of wine be fill'd, ... Od.2.398.80.
Next these in worth, and firm those urns be seal'd; ... Od.2.399.80.
Pour'd the full urns; the youths the goblets crown'd: ... Od.3.434.108.
For fair *Enipeus,* as from fruitful urns ... Od.11.283.396.
Water, instead of wine, is brought in urns, ... Od.12.427.451.
Where bowls and urns were form'd of living stone, ... Od.13.126.8.
In marble urns receiv'd it from above, ... Od.17.238.143.

US (OMITTED)
256

US'D
A Muse by these is like a Mistress us'd, ... 1.EOC.432.288.
Those tempting Words were all to *Sapho* us'd. ... 1.TrSP.68.396.
Which *Danaus* us'd in sacred Rites of old, ... 1.TrSt.635.436.
He us'd from Noise and Business to retreat; ... 2.ChJM.470.38.
You ne'er had us'd these killing Words to me. ... 2.ChJM.775.52.
Hark old Sir *Paul* ('twas thus I us'd to say) ... 2.ChWB.74.60.
As Poison heals, in just proportion us'd: ... 3.Ep3.234.111.
And I'm not us'd to Panegyric strains: ... 4.2HE1.405.229.
Because they see me us'd so well. ... 4.HS6.102.257.
So us'd to sighs, so long inur'd to tears, ... 6.4i.11.9.
Rather to starve, as they are us'd to do, ... 6.17iv.25.60.

US'D (CONTINUED)

He'd ne'er be us'd so like a Beast; ....6.30.28A.86.
Which *Chiron* gave, and *Æsculapius* us'd. ....II.4.251.232.
Those Chiefs, that us'd her utmost Rage to meet, ...II.11.960.78.
Long us'd to ward the Death in fighting Fields: ....II.13.552.132.
"Stern Son of *Peleus* (thus ye us'd to say, ...II.16.242.248.
Long us'd, untouch'd, in fighting Fields to shine, ...II.16.962.280.
Those slaught'ring Arms, so us'd to bathe in Blood, ...II.18.368.339.
(Such as the good man ever us'd to give.) ....Od.10.249.354.
And us'd that pow'r to justify my wrongs. ....Od.18.168.175.
As on the listed field he us'd to place ....Od.19.670.228.
Ill-us'd by all! to ev'ry wrong resign'd, ...Od.24.189.356.

USAL

Nor Kitchen shine with more than usal Fire ....4.JD2A.118.142.

USE

Want as much more, to turn it to its use; ....1.EOC.81.248.
Make use of ev'ry *Friend*—and ev'ry *Foe*. ....1.EOC.214.264.
Still fit for Use, and ready at Command. ....1.EOC.674.316.
For whom should *Sapho* use such Arts as these? ....1.TrSP.87.397.
Whose Use old Bards describe in luscious Rhymes, ...2.ChJM.379.33.
The Treachery you Women use to Man: ....2.ChJM.628.45.
And use the copious Talent it has giv'n; ....2.ChWB.51.59.
And use that Weapon which they have, their Pen; ....2.ChWB.372.75.
Or who would learn one earthly Thing of Use? ....2.RL5.22.200.
What then remains, but well our Pow'r to use, ...2.RL5.29.201.
Yet serves to second too some other use. ....3.EOM1.56.20.
His actions', passions', being's, use and end; ....3.EOM1.66.21.
Earth for whose use? Pride answers, 'Tis for mine: ....3.EOM1.132.31.
Made for his use all creatures if he call, ...3.EOM1.177.36.
Say what their use, had he the pow'rs of all? ....3.EOM1.178.36.
Say what the use, were finer optics giv'n, ...3.EOM1.195.39.
Reason still use, to Reason still attend: ....3.EOM2.78.64.
In Man they join to some mysterious use; ....3.EOM2.206.80.
While Man exclaims, "See all things for my use!" ....3.EOM3.45.96.
Taught Pow'r's due use to People and to Kings, ...3.EOM3.289.121.
"Extremes in Man concur to gen'ral use." ....3.Ep3.164.107.
What tho' (the use of barb'rous spits forgot) ....3.Ep3.181.109.
And pompous buildings once were things of Use. ....3.Ep4.24.139.
'Tis Use alone that sanctifies Expence, ...3.Ep4.179.154.
Advice; and (as you use) without a Fee. ....4.HS1.10.5.
Well, if the Use be mine, can it concern one ....4.HS2.165.69.
Yea, tho' the Blessing's more than he can use, ...4.HAdv.100.83.
Well let Them pass and so may those that use ....4.JD2A.41.136.
(For Use will father what's begot by Sense) ....4.2HE2.170.177.
If there be truth in Law, and *Use* can give ....4.2HE2.230.181.
Of little use the Man you may suppose, ...4.2HE1.201.211.
"Lewis, the Dean will be of use, ...4.HS6.35.253.
We only furnish what he cannot use, ...5.DunB4.261.369.
His Numbers such, as Sanger's self might use. ....6.12.3.37.
Or waste, for others Use, their restless Years ....6.17ii.3.56.
At once their Motion, Sweetness, and their Use; ....6.17ii.10.56.
Lintot's for gen'ral Use are fit; ....6.29.23.83.
To various use their various streams they bring, ...6.35.33.104.
Then shall thy Barrel be of gen'ral Use. ....6.48i.9.133*.
They use white Powder, and wear Holland-Smocks. ....6.95.4.264.
Shall *Arthur* use him like King *Tollo* ....6.101.26.290.
Jove frown'd, and "Use (he cry'd) those Eyes ....6.119.5.336.
Use, use (quoth Jove) those piercing eyes, ...6.119.5A.336.
Use, use (quoth Jove) those piercing eyes, ...6.119.5A.336.
Use, use (cry'd Jove) those skilful Eyes, ...6.119.5B.336.
Use, use (cry'd Jove) those skilfull Eyes, ...6.119.5B.336.
In vain our Threats, in vain our Pow'r we use; ....II.5.1102.319.
To sprinkle to the Gods, its better Use. ....II.6.333.342.
Obey the Night, and use her peaceful Hours ....II.8.627.425.
If ought of use thy waking Thoughts suggest, ...II.10.106.7.
This done, whate'er a Warrior's Use requires ....II.18.705.357.
Presents th' occasion, could we use it right. ....II.23.494.510.
But, set apart for sacred Use, commands ....II.23.1062.533.
Temper'd with drugs of sov'reign use, t'assuage ....Od.4.303.134.
To various use their various streams they bring, ...Od.7.174.244.
And the soul saddens by the use of pain. ....Od.10.551.369.
Establish'd use enjoins; to rest and joy ....Od.19.695.229.
Those arguments I'll use: nor conscious shame, ...Od.20.227.244.
To rush between, and use the shorten'd sword. ....Od.22.115.292.

USEFUL

Hear how learn'd *Greece* her useful Rules indites, ...1.EOC.92.250.
From great *Examples useful Rules* were giv'n; ....1.EOC.98A.250.
Thus *useful Arms* in Magazines we place, ...1.EOC.671.315.
Licence repress'd, and *useful Laws* ordain'd; ....1.EOC.682.316.
O useful Time for Lovers to employ! ....1.TrSP.104.398.
In useful Craft successfully refin'd; ....1.TrUl.167.471.
And have observ'd this useful Maxim still, ...2.ChJM.158.22.
Who taught that useful Science, to be *good*. ....2.TemF.108.261.
Useful, we grant, it serves what life requires, ...3.Ep3.29A.88.
Useful, I grant, it serves what life requires, ...3.Ep3.29.88.
And (tho' no Soldier) useful to the State. ....4.2HE1.204.211.
Those useful Touches to impart ....6.11.35Z7.31.
Their Books are useful but to few, ...6.29.27.83.
Eye the blue Vault, and bless the useful Light. ....II.8.698.428.
More useful to preserve, than I to kill) ....II.18.136.329.
In useful craft successfully refin'd! ....Od.13.334.23.
An useful work! adorn'd by ancient Kings. ....Od.17.235.143.
With useful buildings round the lowly court: ....Od.24.239.360.

USELESS

And with your Golden.Darts, now useless grown, ...1.PWi.25.90.
But useless Lances into Scythes shall bend, ...1.Mes.61.118.
Useless, unseen, as lamps in sepulchres; ....2.Elegy.20.364.
Gives not the useless knowledge of its end: ....3.EOM3.72.99.
Not to the skies in useless columns tost, ...3.Ep3.255.114.
And vile Attornies, now an useless race. ....3.Ep3.274.116.
And fame; this lord of useless thousands ends. ....3.Ep3.314.119.
Thus *either Men in private useless Ease* ....6.17ii.1.56.

USELESS (CONTINUED)

Wits starve as useless to a Common weal ....6.82ix(d).1.235.
Blind to himself, and useless to his Host, ...II.1.447.109.
While useless Words consume th' unactive Hours, ...II.2.408.147.
His Brother-Chief, whose useless Arms lay round, ...II.6.399.346.
Drop the cold useless Members on the Ground. ....II.7.22.363.
And his numb'd Hand dismiss'd his useless Bow. ....II.8.396.416.
His Limbs, unnerv'd, drop useless on the Ground, ...II.13.843.145.
His painful Arm, yet useless with the Smart ....II.16.629.269.
His useless Lance and unavailing Shield) ....II.21.59.424.
Useless to thee, from this accursed Day! ....II.22.659.484.

USES

Like Puppy tame that uses ....6.58.18.171.
Court Puppy tame that uses ....6.58.18A.171.

USHER

Thy fleecy fellows usher to their bow'r. ....Od.9.530.328.
One rogue is usher to another still. ....Od.17.251.143.

USHER'D

Still breath'd in sighs, still usher'd with a tear. ....2.ElAb.32.321.
The good *Eumæus* usher'd to your court. ....Od.17.447.155.

USHERS

One ushers Friends to *Bathurst's* Door; ....6.135.63.368.

USUAL

With more than usual Lightning in her Eyes; ....2.RL5.76.206.
And stretch'd on bulks, as usual, Poets lay. ....5.DunA2.388.1◄
And stretch'd on bulks, as usual, Poets lay. 5.DunB2.420.31

USURE

Out-usure Jews, or Irishmen out-swear; ....4.JD2.38.135.
T' out doe Italians, and out usure Jews; ....4.JD2A.42.136.

USURP

Wou'd you usurp the Lover's dear-bought Praise? ....2.TemF.399.282.
Enslave their Country, or usurp a Throne; ....2.TemF.407.283.
His stores ye ravage and usurp his state. ....Od.4.923.161.
T'usurp the honours due to silver hairs ....Od.16.45.104.

USURPERS

My King returns; the proud Usurpers dye. ....Od.20.282.247.

USURPING

That worst of Tyrants, an usurping Crowd. ....II.2.242.139.
Our sovereign seat a lewd usurping race. ....Od.4.429.140.
No profit springs beneath usurping pow'rs; ....Od.15.404.89.

USURPS

But universal night usurps the pole! ....Od.20.430.254.

UTMOST

The *Greeks* oppress'd, their utmost Force unite, ...1.TrES.93.453.
Nor those, that plac'd beneath his utmost Reign, ...1.TrUl.120.470.
Our utmost bound, and our eternal stay! ....6.23.20.73.
To give their utmost date to all your hairs; ....6.38.12.107.
Perhaps ev'n *Britain's* utmost shore ....6.51i.19.151.
And *Anthedon*, *Bæotia's* utmost Bound. ....II.2.607.156.
A City stands on *Argos'* utmost Bound. ....II.6.189.335.
Where on her utmost Verge the Seas resound; ....II.8.598.424.
The *Thracians* utmost, and a-part from all. ....II.10.503.26.
Here stand his utmost Force—The Warrior said; ....II.11.451.54.
Our utmost Frontier on the *Pylian* Lands; ....II.11.847.74.
Ah! try the utmost that a Friend can say, ...II.11.922.76.
Those Chiefs, that us'd her utmost Rage to meet, ...II.11.960.78.
The *Greeks*, oppress'd, their utmost Force unite, ...II.12.447.97.
Asks Toil, and Sweat, and Blood: Their utmost Might ....II.15.562.218.
Exhorts, adjures, to guard these utmost Shores; ....II.15.794.226.
What Aids expect you in this utmost Strait? ....II.15.894.232.
The River trembles to his utmost Shore, ...II.17.314.300.
Its utmost Verge a threefold Circle bound; ....II.18.553.348.
Till at the Battel's utmost Verge they light, ...II.20.377.410.
This hard Adventure claims thy utmost Care: ....II.24.436.554.
Next, *Æthiopia's* utmost bound explore, ...Od.4.101.124.
Of utmost earth, where *Rhadamanthus* reigns. ....Od.4.766.155.
For *Elis* I shou'd sail with utmost speed, ...Od.4.858.159.
On the lone Island's utmost verge there stood ....Od.5.305.185.
Thy signal throw transcends the utmost bound ....Od.8.223.274.
Soon shalt thou reach old Ocean's utmost ends, ...Od.10.602.372.
When lo! we reach'd old Ocean's utmost bounds, ...Od.11.13.379.
Stun my scar'd ears, and pierce hell's utmost bounds. ....Od.11.782.425.
Nor those that plac'd beneath his utmost reign ....Od.13.287.19.
Twelve herds of goats that graze our utmost green; ....Od.14.126.42.
Nor will that hand to utmost need afford ....Od.17.539.158.
The utmost gate. (The cable strongly wrought ....Od.21.423.280.
And *Leucas'* rock, and *Ocean's* utmost streams, ...Od.24.17.347.

UTOPIANS

My Lord, forsake your Politick Utopians, ...6.42ii.1.117.

UTTER

My Tongue shall utter, and my Deeds make good. ....II.9.409.452.
My Soul might keep, or utter with a Tear; ....II.24.937.575.

UTTER'D

Utter'd a speech, and ask'd their friends to dine; ....4.1740.38.334.

UTTERS

Then, mix'd with pray'rs, he utters these commands. ....Od.15.167.76.

UXORIO

Shall then Uxorio, if the stakes he sweep, ...3.Ep3.59.91.

VACANT
Then gay Ideas crowd the vacant Brain; .... 2.RL1.83.151.
Plant the fair Column o'er the vacant grave, ... Od.1.380.51.
Refer the choice to fill the vacant Throne. .... Od.1.510.56.
The youth wou'd vindicate the vacant throne. .... Od.4.224.130.
The cave we found, but vacant all within, ... Od.9.252.317.

VACUITY
And each vacuity of sense by Pride: .... 3.EOM2.286.89.

VADIUS
Poor Vadius, long with learned spleen devour'd, ... 6.71.41.204.

VAGA
Pleas'd Vaga echoes thro' her winding bounds, ... 3.Ep3.251.114.

VAGABOND
A vagabond! for him the great destroy .... Od.18.450.190.

VAGRANT
Sent with a Pass, and vagrant thro' the land; .... 5.DunB1.232.287.
The vagrant Dead around the dark Abode, ... Il.23.91.490.
Each vagrant traveller that touches here, ... Od.14.150.43.
Or chuse ye vagrant from their rage to fly .... Od.16.394.125.
A surly vagrant of the giant kind, ... Od.18.3.166.
Vagrant begone! before this blazing brand .... Od.19.84.196.
The wordy vagrant to the dole aspires, ... Od.20.167.241.
Here, vagrant still! offensive to my Lords! .... Od.20.225.244.

VAGRANT'S
Hence, to the vagrant's rendezvous repair; .... Od.18.377.185.

VAGRANTS
That sturdy Vagrants, Rogues in Rags, ... 6.135.21.366.
Ye Vagrants of the Sky! your Wings extend, ... Il.12.279.91.
Vagrants of air, and unforeboding stray. .... Od.2.212.72.
Unlike those vagrants who on falshood live, ... Od.11.452.406.
Bring'st thou these vagrants to infest the land? .... Od.17.451.155.
I cheer no lazy vagrants with repast; .... Od.19.31.194.

VAIL'D
His Hat, which never vail'd to human pride, ... 5.DunB4.205.362.

VAIN
Each am'rous Nymph prefers her Gifts in vain, ... 1.PSu.53.76.
In vain kind Seasons swell'd the teeming Grain, ... 1.W-F.53.154.
Soft Show'rs distill'd, and Suns grew warm in vain; .... 1.W-F.54.154.
In vain on Father *Thames* she calls for Aid, ... 1.W-F.197.168.
Faint, breathless, thus she pray'd, nor pray'd in vain; .... 1.W-F.199.168.
In vain on Father *Thames* she call'd for Aid, ... 1.W-F.197A.168.
And gasping Furies thirst for Blood in vain. .... 1.W-F.422.193.
Or *one vain Wit's*, that might a hundred tire. .... 1.EOC.45.244.
Or *one vain Wit's*, that wou'd a hundred tire. .... 1.EOC.45A.244.
By vain Ambition still to make them more: .... 1.EOC.65.246.
By vain Ambition still t'extend them more: .... 1.EOC.65A.246.
To teach vain Wits a Science *little known*, ... 1.EOC.199.263.
To teach vain Wits that Science *little known*, ... 1.EOC.199A.263.
The Reader's threaten'd (not in vain) with *Sleep*. .... 1.EOC.353.279.
And *charitably* let the Dull be *vain:* .... 1.EOC.597.308.
And *charitably* let dull Fools be *vain:* .... 1.EOC.597A.308.
Not *free* from Faults, nor yet too vain to *mend*. .... 1.EOC.744.326.
Thus scorning prophecy, and warn'd in vain, ... 1.TrPA.35.366.
A thousand court you, tho' they court in vain, ... 1.TrVP.74.380.
This when the various God had urg'd in vain, ... 1.TrVP.112.381.
In vain to free her fasten'd feet she strove, ... 1.TrFD.41.387.
She stood and cry'd, "O you that love in vain! .... 1.TrSP.187.401.
"In vain he lov'd, relentless *Pyrrha* scorn'd; .... 1.TrSP.194.402.
"Deucalion scorn'd, and *Pyrrha* lov'd in vain. .... 1.TrSP.196.402.
This Breast which once, in vain! you lik'd so well; .... 1.TrSP.226.403.
Nor let desiring Worlds intreat in vain! .... 1.TrSt.34.411.
In vain the Chiefs contriv'd a specious way, ... 1.TrSt.192.418.
For lost *Europa* search'd the World in vain, ... 1.TrSt.248.420.
And unregarded Thunder rolls in vain: .... 1.TrSt.305.423.
But Flames consum'd, and Billows rag'd in vain. .... 1.TrSt.314.423.
The Father's Care and Prophet's Art were vain, ... 1.TrSt.553.433.
Thus *Hector*, great in Arms, contends in vain .... 1.TrES.1.449.
In vain loud Mastives bay him from afar, ... 1.TrES.17.450.
In vain he calls, the Din of Helms and Shields .... 1.TrES.63.452.
The Breach lyes open, but your Chief in vain .... 1.TrES.147.455.
And sought around his Native Realm in vain; .... 1.TrUl.71.468.
Vain Fortune's Favours, never at a Stay, ... 2.ChJM.53.17.
And sigh'd full oft, but sigh'd and wept in vain; .... 2.ChJM.491.39.
And sigh'd for Woe, but sigh'd and wept in vain; .... 2.ChJM.491A.39.
If highly born, intolerably vain; .... 2.ChWB.88.61.
And half the Night was thus consum'd in vain; .... 2.ChWB.414.77.
While clog'd he beats his silken Wings in vain; .... 2.RL2.130.168.
(*Sir Plume*, of *Amber Snuff-box* justly vain, ... 2.RL4.123.194.
Who speaks so well shou'd ever speak in vain. .... 2.RL4.132.194.
In vain *Thalestris* with Reproach assails, ... 2.RL5.3.199.
While *Anna* begg'd and *Dido* rag'd in vain. .... 2.RL5.6.199.
The wise Man's Passion, and the vain Man's Toast? .... 2.RL5.10.199.
How vain are all these Glories, all our Pains, ... 2.RL5.15.200.
Beauties in vain their pretty Eyes may roll; .... 2.RL5.33.201.
In ev'ry place is sought, but sought in vain: .... 2.RL5.110.208.
To just Contempt, ye vain Pretenders, fall, ... 2.TemF.400.282.
How vain that second Life in others' Breath, ... 2.TemF.505.288.
In vain lost *Eloisa* weeps and prays, ... 2.ElAb.15.320.
Nor tears, for ages, taught to flow in vain. .... 2.ElAb.28.321.
Heav'n claims me all in vain, while he has part, ... 2.ElAb.25A.321.
Ah wretch! believ'd the spouse of God in vain, ... 2.ElAb.177.334.
And not a vanity is giv'n in vain; .... 3.EOM2.290.89.
All feed on one vain Patron, and enjoy .... 3.EOM3.61.98.
Which heavier Reason labours at in vain. .... 3.EOM3.92.101.

VAIN (CONTINUED)
"In vain thy Reason finer webs shall draw, ... 3.EOM3.191.112.
Where grows?—where grows it not?—If vain our toil, ... 3.EOM4.13.129.
Some swell'd to Gods, confess ev'n Virtue vain; .... 3.EOM4.24.130.
One doubts of All, one owns ev'n Virtue vain. .... 3.EOM4.28Z2.130.
Heav'n still with laughter the vain toil surveys, ... 3.EOM4.75.135.
Are giv'n in vain, but what they seek they find) .... 3.EOM4.348.162.
In vain the grave, with retrospective eye, ... 3.Ep1.51A.19.
In vain sedate reflections we would make, ... 3.Ep1.33.18.
In vain the Sage, with retrospective eye, ... 3.Ep1.51.19.
In vain th' observer eyes the builder's toil, ... 3.Ep1.220.34.
Ah Friend! to dazzle let the Vain design, ... 3.Ep2.249.70.
Bankrupt, at Court in vain he pleads his cause, ... 3.Ep3.217A.111.
Giv'n to the Fool, the Mad, the Vain, the Evil, ... 3.Ep3.19.85.
In vain may Heroes fight, and Patriots rave; .... 3.Ep3.37.88.
In vain at Court the Bankrupt pleads his cause, ... 3.Ep3.217.111.
Load some vain Church with old Theatric state, ... 3.Ep4.29.140.
For Locke or Milton 'tis in vain to look, ... 3.Ep4.139.150.
Nor the vain Itch *t'admire*, or *be admir'd;* .... 4.JD4.10.27.
As *vain*, as *idle*, and as *false*, as they .... 4.JD4.22.27.
'Tis yet in vain, I own, to keep a pother .... 4.HS2.45.57.
Apply to me, to keep them mad or vain. .... 4.Arbu.22.97.
Destroy his Fib, or Sophistry; in vain, ... 4.Arbu.91.102.
'Tis all in vain, deny it as I will. .... 4.Arbu.277.115.
Curs'd be the Wretch! so venal and so vain; .... 4.JD2.63.139.
Vain of this State, what does my Coxcomb do .... 4.JD2A.59.136.
Vain was the chief's and sage's pride .... 4.HOde9.13.159.
In vain they schem'd, in vain they bled .... 4.HOde9.15.159.
In vain they schem'd, in vain they bled .... 4.HOde9.15.159.
In vain, bad Rhimers all mankind reject, ... 4.2HE2.153.175.
And feels that grace his pray'r besought in vain, ... 4.2HE1.238.215.
Invention strives to be before in vain; .... 4.EpS2.7.313.
Names, which I long have lov'd, nor lov'd in vain, ... 4.EpS2.90.318.
And what young AMMON wish'd, but wish'd in vain. .... 4.EpS2.117.320.
A Monarch's sword when mad Vain-glory draws, ... 4.EpS2.229.325.
Say from what cause, in vain decry'd and curst, ... 5.DunA1.5.61.
But senseless, lifeless! Idol void and vain! .... 5.DunA2.42.100.
All vain petitions, mounting to the sky, ... 5.DunA2.85.108.
Whose vain petitions, mounting to the sky, ... 5.DunA2.85A.108.
All vain petitions, sent by winds on high, ... 5.DunA2.85B.108.
Heav'n rings with laughter: Of the laughter vain, ... 5.DunA2.113.110.
Smedley in vain resounds thro' all the coast. .... 5.DunA2.282.136.
E[usden] in vain resounds thro' all the coast. .... 5.DunA2.282A.136.
While K[ennet], B[ramston], W[arren], preach in vain. .... 5.DunA3.200.174*.
While Kennet, Hare, and Gibson preach in vain. .... 5.DunA3.200B.174.
In vain! they gaze, turn giddy, rave, and die. .... 5.DunA3.354.193.
To their first Chaos Wit's vain works shall fall, ... 5.DunA3.355A.193.
You by whose care, in vain decry'd and curst, ... 5.DunB1.5.269.
Hence Bards, like Proteus long in vain ty'd down, ... 5.DunB1.37.272.
But senseless, lifeless! idol void and vain! .... 5.DunB2.46.298.
All vain petitions, mounting to the sky, ... 5.DunB2.89.300.
Heav'n rings with laughter: Of the laughter vain, ... 5.DunB2.121.301.
Smedley in vain resounds thro' all the coast. .... 5.DunB2.294.310.
While Sherlock, Hare, and Gibson preach in vain. .... 5.DunB3.204.330.
While Kennett, Hare, and Gibson preach in vain. .... 5.DunB3.204A.330.
Turn what they will to Verse, their toil is vain, ... 5.DunB4.213.363.
Vain of Italian Arts, Italian Souls: .... 5.DunB4.300.373.
But here, vain Icarus! thy flight confine, ... 5.DunB4.601A.403.
In vain, in vain,—the all-composing Hour .... 5.DunB4.627.407.
In vain, in vain,—the all-composing Hour .... 5.DunB4.627.407.
Wit shoots in vain its momentary fires, ... 5.DunB4.633.407.
In vain! they gaze, turn giddy, rave, and die. .... 5.DunB4.648.409.
From us that serv'd so long in vain, ... 6.4iii.3.10.
While wretched lovers sing in vain. .... 6.6i.16.14.
But Rebel Wit deserts thee oft in vain; .... 6.8.13.18.
In vain he strains to reach your Ear, ... 6.10.23.25.
In vain you think to 'scape Rhyme-free, ... 6.10.38.25.
And pale *Narcissus* on the bank, in vain .... 6.14iv.11.47.
Nor seeks in vain for succour to the Stream. .... 6.14iv.26.47.
A vain, unquiet, glitt'ring, wretched Thing! .... 6.19.54.63.
Vex'd with vain rage, and impotently great, ... 6.20.20.66.
Let not a suppliant Queen entreat in vain, ... 6.20.50.67.
In vain, for all that empty greatness brings, ... 6.22.7.71.
Look on this marble, and be vain no more! .... 6.27.17.81.
Ignobly vain and impotently great, ... 6.32.29.96.
In vain you boast Poetick Dames of yore, ... 6.43.1.120.
To write their Praise you but in vain essay, ... 6.43.9.120.
In vain you boast Poetick Names of yore, ... 6.43.1A.121.
How e're be not too vain, Friend *Budgell!* .... 6.44.13.123.
Fool! 'tis in vain from Wit to Wit to roam; .... 6.49ii.15.140.
In vain your guiltless laurels stood, ... 6.51i.5.151.
Wisdom and wit in vain reclaim, ... 6.51ii.3.152.
Then view this marble, and be vain no more! .... 6.52.54.157.
Vile Reptile, weak, and vain! .... 6.53.6.161.
Proud Reptile, Vile, and vain .... 6.53.6A.161.
Vile reptile, Proud, and vain .... 6.53.6B.161.
Vain is thy Art, thy Powder vain, ... 6.53.35.162.
Vain is thy Art, thy Powder vain, ... 6.53.35.162.
Tir'd with vain hopes, and with complaints as vain, ... 6.56.1.168.
Tir'd with vain hopes, and with complaints as vain, ... 6.56.1.168.
And teach dull *Harlequins* to grin in vain. .... 6.60.16.178.
Time, health, and fortune, are not lost in vain. .... 6.63.6.188.
And love the brightest eyes, but love in vain! .... 6.66.8.194.
Ambition sigh'd; She found it vain to trust .... 6.71.19.203.
So would I draw (but oh, 'tis vain to try .... 6.75.3.211.
Learning not vain, and wisdom not severe .... 6.75.7.212.
In vain my structures rise, my gardens grow, ... 6.81.2.225.
In vain fair Thames reflects the double scenes .... 6.81.3.225.
Dear to the Muse, to HARLEY dear—in vain! .... 6.84.6.238.
In vain to Desarts thy Retreat is made; .... 6.84.27.239.
Tho' next the Servile drop thee next the Vain, ... 6.84.31Z4.239.
And all th' Oblig'd desert, and all the Vain; .... 6.84.32.240.
When all th'Oblig'd desert, and all the Vain; .... 6.84.32A.240.
How vain is Reason, Eloquence how weak, ... 6.85.5.242.
Ah, no! 'tis vain to strive—It will not be. .... 6.85.9Z1.242.
Some joy still lost, as each vain year runs o'er, ... 6.86.7.245.

VALDE
Hiatus mî valde deflendus! 6.30.23.86.
Hiatus mihi *valde Deflendus!* 6.30.23A.86.

VALE
Pour'd o'er the whitening Vale their fleecy Care, 1.PSp.19.62.
In life's low vale, the soil the virtues like, 3.Ep1.95.22.
Whose Cause-way parts the vale with shady rows? 3.Ep3.259.114.
Or scoops in circling theatres the Vale, 3.Ep4.60.142.
There, in a dusky vale where Lethe rolls, 5.DunA3.15.151.
Here, in a dusky vale where Lethe rolls, 5.DunB3.23.321.
Content with Sciênce in the Vale of Peace. 6.112.6.318.
And o'er the Vale descends the living Cloud. Il.2.116.133.
Amidst the dreadful Vale the Chiefs advance, Il.3.425.212.
Those fifty slaughter'd in the gloomy Vale, Il.4.448.241.
But now (what time in some sequester'd Vale Il.11.119.39.
As thro' the shrilling Vale, or Mountain Ground, Il.16.767.273.
As thro' the Forest, o'er the Vale and Lawn, Il.22.243.465.
The Palace in a woody vale they found, Od.10.240.352.
A Palace in a woody vale we found Od.10.297.358.

VALERIUS
Valerius, whole; and of St. *Jerome,* Part; 2.ChWB.359.74.

VALES
In flow'ry *Vales* they fed their fleecy Care; 1.PSp.17z4.62.
Begin, the Vales shall ev'ry Note rebound. 1.PSp.44.65.
Begin, the Vales shall Echo to the Sound. 1.PSp.44A.65.
Or else where *Cam* his winding Vales divides? 1.PSu.26.74.
Lose the low Vales, and steal into the Skies. 1.PAu.60.84.
Nor Rivers winding thro' the Vales below, 1.PWi.3.88.
Adieu ye *Vales,* ye *Mountains, Streams* and *Groves,* 1.PWi.89.95.
Here Hills and Vales, the Woodland and the Plain, 1.W-F.11.149.
Hills, Vales, and Floods appear already crost, 1.W-F.153.164.
Mount o'er the Vales, and seem to tread the Sky; 1.EOC.226.265.
To isles of fragrance, lilly-silver'd vales, 5.DunB4.303.374.
While the fair Vales beneath so humbly lie, 6.9xi.3.23.
Vales, Spires, meandring Streams, and *Windsor's* tow'ry Pride. 6.14ii.54.44.
Not always glide thro' gloomy Vales, and rove 6.17ii.21.56.
They may talk of the *Goddesses* in *Ida* Vales, 6.62ii.1.185.
They may tell of three Goddesses in *Ida* Vales, 6.62ii.1A.185.
Safe in her Vales my warlike Coursers fed: Il.1.202.96.
From *Pthia's* spacious Vales, and *Hella,* blest Il.2.831.164.
Or whom the Vales in Shade of *Tmolus* hide, Il.2.1053.172.
The hollow Vales incessant Bleating fills, Il.4.494.244.
Rush to the Vales, and pour'd along the Plain, Il.4.518.246.
Then shine the Vales, the Rocks in Prospect rise, Il.8.695.428.
Where o'er the Vales th' *Olenian* Rocks arose; Il.11.889.75.
And Streams, and Vales, and Forests strike the Eyes, Il.16.359.257.
They shout incessant, and the Vales resound. Il.17.74.291.
From rich *Pæonia's* Vales the Warrior came, Il.17.402.303.
And o'er the Vales, and o'er the Forrest bounds; Il.18.375.339.
Along fair *Ida's* Vales, and pendent Groves. Il.21.522.443.
Where thro' the vales the mazy waters stray? Od.6.72.208.
In wavy gold thy summer vales are dress'd; Od.19.131.199.
Ends in a stream, and murmurs thro' the vales: Od.19.241.206.
And images the rills, and flowry vales: Od.23.336.340.
To seek *Tiresias* in the vales of death; Od.23.348.341.

VALETUDINAIRE
The gayest Valetudinaire, 6.47.39.129.

VALIANT
Ye valiant Leaders of our warlike Bands! 1.TrES.80Z1.452.
Now valiant *Lycomede,* exert your Might, 1.TrES.83.453.
Advance ye *Trojans,* lend your valiant Hands, 1.TrES.177.456.
When now the Chief his valiant Friends beheld 1.TrES.209.457.
And pass'd the Groin of valiant *Thrasymed,* 1.TrES.264.459.
The Poor, the Rich, the Valiant, and the Sage, 2.TemF.290.277.
Next goes his Wool—to clothe our valiant bands, 3.Ep3.211.110.
But what concerns the valiant and the fair, 6.38.5.107.
Rode forth the valiant *Guise;* 6.79.108.221.
Thine to look on, and bid the Valiant dye. Il.1.302.101.
Now, valiant Chiefs! since Heav'n itself alarms, Il.2.93.131.
Say would'st thou seize some valiant Leader's Prize? Il.2.288.141.
Two valiant Brothers rule th' undaunted Throng, Il.2.612.156.
Ajax the less, *Oïleus'* valiant Son; Il.2.631.157.
Phares and *Brysia's* valiant Troops, and those Il.2.703.159.
Thoas came next, *Andræmon's* valiant Son, Il.2.775.162.
The valiant Victor seiz'd the golden Prize. Il.2.1067.172.
Each hardy *Greek* and valiant *Trojan* Knight, Il.3.175.199.
All valiant Chiefs, and Men of mighty Fame. Il.3.300.207.
Or trust ye, *Jove* a valiant Foe shall chace, Il.4.284.234.
The first who strook a valiant *Trojan* dead: Il.4.523.246.
O Prince (*Lycaon's* valiant Son reply'd) Il.5.288.281.
He thus advancing, *Nestor's* valiant Son Il.5.693.301.
And first two Leaders valiant *Hector* slew, Il.5.751.302.
Thus shall he say: "A valiant *Greek* lies there, Il.7.101.368.
Ye valiant *Trojans,* with Attention hear! Il.8.621.425.
He seems remiss, but bears a valiant Mind; Il.10.139.8.
Bold *Merion* strove, and *Nestor's* valiant Heir; Il.10.272.14.
Glory of *Greece,* old *Neleus'* valiant Son! Il.11.633.61.
Threats urge the fearful, and the valiant, Praise. Il.12.316.93.
Ye valiant Leaders of our warlike Bands! Il.12.425.97.
Now valiant *Lycomede!* exert your Might, Il.12.437.97.
Advance ye *Trojans!* lend your valiant Hands, Il.12.531.101.
In *Thoas'* Voice, *Andræmon's* valiant Son, Il.13.286.119.
Valiant as *Mars, Meriones* drew near, Il.13.668.137.
(His valiant Offspring) hasten'd to the Field; Il.14.14.157.
His strongest Spear each valiant *Grecian* wield, Il.14.431.184.
Each valiant *Grecian* seize his broadest Shield; Il.14.432.184.
The strong and cumb'rous Arms the valiant wield, Il.14.441.184.
The valiant Leader of the *Cretan* Band, Il.15.341.210.
Laerces' valiant Offspring led the last. Il.16.235.248.
Which pierc'd below the Shield his valiant Heart. Il.16.485.262.
And pass'd the Groin of valiant *Thrasymed,* Il.16.569.266.

VALIANT (CONTINUED)
In Action valiant, and in Council wise, Il.16.664.270.
Oh valiant Leader of the *Dardan* Host! Il.16.749.273.
To crown *Achilles'* valiant Friend with Praise Il.16.793.274.
A valiant Warrior, haughty, bold, and young.) Il.16.876.277.
Ye came to fight; a valiant Foe to chase, Il.17.264.298.
In vain belov'd by valiant *Lycomede;* Il.17.397.302.
Was't not enough, ye valiant Warriors say, Il.18.335.337.
The Sons of *Nestor, Phyleus'* valiant Heir, Il.19.245.383.
The valiant Sons of an unhappy Sire; Il.20.532.416.
Not less resolv'd, *Antenor's* valiant Heir Il.21.685.450.
How many valiant Sons I late enjoy'd, Il.22.59.455.
Valiant in vain! by thy curst Arm destroy'd: Il.22.60.455.
How many valiant Sons, in early Bloom, Il.22.540.478.
Behold the Prizes, valiant *Greeks!* decreed Il.23.341.503.
The valiant few o'ermatch an host of foes. Od.2.280.74.
Shall speed aboard, a valiant chosen band. Od.2.332.77.
Against thy foes; be valiant, and destroy! Od.16.183.112.
The valiant with the valiant must contend: Od.24.586.376.
The valiant with the valiant must contend: Od.24.586.376.

VALLEY
As when a Flame the winding Valley fills, Il.20.569.418.
Loud as a bull makes hill and valley ring, Od.21.51.261.

VALLIES
Sink down ye Mountains, and ye Vallies rise: 1.Mes.34.116.
Waste sandy Vallies, once perplex'd with Thorn, 1.Mes.73.119.
Rush thro' the Thickets, down the Vallies sweep, 1.W-F.156.164.
Range in the woods, and in the vallies roam: 1.TrPA.79.368.
There painted vallies of eternal green, 5.DunA1.74.68.
Fast by, fair vallies of eternal green, 5.DunA1.74A.6
There painted vallies of eternal green, 5.DunB1.76.275
With *gentle Philips* shall the Vallies ring. 6.40.2.112.
Vallies wide: 6.96i.18.268.
And bounded there, where o'er the Vallies rose Il.2.749.161.
Who fair *Zeleia's* wealthy Vallies till, Il.2.998.170.
From rich *Pæonia's* Vallies I command Il.21.171.428.
And her rich vallies wave with golden corn. Od.15.445.92.

VALLY
My haughty step, I stalk'd the vally o'er. Od.10.326.360.

VALOR
Say, Chief, is all thy ancient Valor lost, Il.5.575.296.

VALOR'S
On Valor's side the Odds of Combate lie, Il.5.655.299.

VALOROUS
But know, thou art not valorous, but vain. Od.18.425.189.

VALOUR
Or long before, with early Valour strove 1.TrSt.29.411.
The first in Valour, as the first in Place: 1.TrES.38.451.
With equal Valour, and with equal Rage. 1.TrES.224.458.
For know, vain Man! thy Valour is from God. Il.1.234.98.
Your ancient Valour on the Foes approve; Il.4.268.234.
Our Valour equal, tho' our Fury less. Il.4.459.242.
In vain his Valour, and illustrious Line. Il.4.598.250.
Lov'd for that Valour which preserves Mankind. Il.6.196.335.
Who honour Worth, and prize thy Valour most. Il.9.756.471.
So prov'd my Valour for my Country's Good. Il.11.897.75.
The first in Valour, as the first in Place. Il.12.382.95.
Have prov'd thy Valour and unconquer'd Might; Il.13.354.122.
The Fear of each, or Valour, stands confest. Il.13.358.123.
Himself supreme in Valour, as in Sway. Il.16.209.247.
By Valour, Numbers, and by Arts of War, Il.17.381.302.
In Valour matchless, and in Force divine! Il.21.232.430.
And such his Valour, that who stands must die. Il.21.668.449.
For valour much, for hardy suff'ring more. Od.3.103.91.
And twenty chiefs renown'd for valour chose: Od.4.1028.165.
Fierce in his look his ardent valour glow'd, Od.11.645.416.
My valour was my plea, a gallant mind Od.14.244.48.
But strength of youth, or valour of the brave Od.24.113.353.

VALOUR'S
And of my Valour's Prize defrauds my Arms, Il.1.507.112.
On Valour's side the odds of Combate lie, Il.15.670.221.

VALU'D
No Fool to laugh at, which he valu'd more. 3.Ep3.312.119.
So dearly valu'd, and so justly mine. Il.1.150.94.
One only valu'd Gift your Tyrant gave, Il.9.481.456.
(His valu'd Coursers, to his Squire consign'd, Il.13.485.130.
(That valu'd Life, O *Phœbus!* was thy Care) Il.15.618.220.
A female Captive, valu'd but at four. Il.23.819.522.
Enchas'd with gold, this valu'd gift be thine; Od.15.129.75.

VALUE
And value *Books,* as Women *Men,* for *Dress:* 1.EOC.306.274.
But blame the *False,* and value still the *True.* 1.EOC.407.287.
The Sense to value Riches, with the Art 3.Ep3.219.111.
It is the rust we value, not the gold. 4.2HE1.36.197.
True, he had wit, to make their value rise; 5.DunB4.377.380
Th' inscription value, but the rust adore; 6.71.36.203.
Has lopp'd three Trees, the Value of three Farthings: 6.143.2.385.
Has cut three Trees, the Value of three Farthings: 6.143.2A.385.
Shall learn the Value of the Man they lost: Il.11.745.68.
So rich the value of a store so vast Od.19.337.210.

VALUES
He values these; but yet (alas) complains, 1.TrVP.98.381.

VALUING 565 VAPOURS

VALUING
Some valuing those of their own *Side*, or *Mind*, ... 1.EOC.452.290.

VALVE
The spacious valve, with art inwrought, conjoins; .... Od.23.197.333.

VALVES
Self-clos'd behind her shut the Valves of Gold. .... Il.14.196.168.
Secur'd the valves. There, wrap'd in silent shade, ... Od.1.555.58.
The bolted Valves are pervious to her flight. .... Od.4.1056.167.
Swift thro' the valves the visionary fair .... Od.4.1093.169.
Glides thro' the valves, and hovers round her head; .... Od.6.26.205.
Full where the dome its shining valves expands, ... Od.8.495.289.
Full where the dome its shining valves expands, ... Od.16.430.128.
Full where the dome its shining valves expands, ... Od.18.247.178.
The gate oppos'd pellucid valves adorn, ... Od.19.660.228.
The bars fall back; the flying valves resound; .... Od.21.50.261.
A double strength of valves secur'd the place, ... Od.22.144.294.
Then gliding thro' the marble valves in state, ... Od.23.91.323.

VAMP'D
A past, vamp'd, future, old, reviv'd, new piece, ... 5.DunA1.238.91.
A past, vamp'd, future, old, reviv'd, new piece, ... 5.DunB1.284.290.

VAN
If vile Van-muck lov'd Sixpence, more than he. .... 4.2HE2.229.181.
How Van wants grace, who never wanted wit! .... 4.2HE1.289.219.
When, to the Van, before the Sons of Fame .... Il.3.25.189.
Plung'd in the Rear, or blazing in the Van; .... Il.11.86.38.
I seiz'd his Car, the Van of Battel led; .... Il.11.878.75.
Great *Hector* glorious in the Van of these, ... Il.12.103.85.
Great *Hector* glories in the Van of these, ... Il.12.103A.85.
I fight conspicuous in the Van of War. .... Il.13.350.122.
Thus in the Van, the *Telamonian* Train .... Il.13.897.148.
Full in the blazing Van great *Hector* shin'd, ... Il.13.1010.153.
Fierce to the Van of Flight *Patroclus* came; .... Il.16.709.271.
And names a *Van:* there fix it on the plain, ... Od.11.158.389.
Before the van, impatient for the fight, ... Od.11.629.414.
Fierce in the van: Then wou'dst thou, wou'dst thou, say, ... Od.18.420.189.
And calls a Corn-van: This upon the plain .... Od.23.291.337.

VAN-MUCK
If vile Van-muck lov'd Sixpence, more than he. .... 4.2HE2.229.181.

VANDAL
Had brav'd the *Goth*, and many a *Vandal* slain, ... 6.128.2.355.

VANDALIS
The blue, transparent *Vandalis* appears; .... 1.W-F.345.183.

VANDALS
And drove those *Holy Vandals* off the Stage. .... 1.EOC.696.319.
Embody's dark, what clouds of Vandals rise! .... 5.DunA3.78.156.
In dulness strong, th' avenging Vandals rise; .... 5.DunA3.78A.156.
Embody'd thick, what clouds of Vandals rise! .... 5.DunA3.78B.156.
Embody'd dark, what clouds of Vandals rise! .... 5.DunB3.86.324.

VANE
(I promis'd I never would mention Miss Vane.) .... 6.122.14.342.

VANISH
First turn plain rash, then vanish quite away. .... 4.JD4.45.29.
Or, in a jointure, vanish from the Heir, ... 4.HS2.170.69.
Thus vanish sceptres, coronets, and balls, ... 6.45.39.125.
Gay pats my shoulder, and you vanish quite; .... 6.45.47.126.
Before thy Pen vanish the Nation's Ills, ... 6.48ii.9.134.
Whole Squadrons vanish, and proud Heads lie low. .... Il.11.206.44.
Thus vanish, at thy touch, the Tow'rs and Walls; .... Il.15.420A.213.
Start from the goal, and vanish o'er the strand: .... Od.8.126.269.

VANISH'D
The Groves of *Eden*, vanish'd now so long, ... 1.W-F.7.148.
She spoke, and vanish'd with the Voice—I rise, ... 1.TrSP.199.402.
But all the Vision vanish'd from thy Head. .... 2.RL1.120.155.
Then [Aaron] essay'd: scarce vanish'd out of sight .... 5.DunA2.283B.136.
Then * essay'd; scarce vanish'd out of sight, ... 5.DunB2.295.310.
While fancy brings the vanish'd piles to view, ... 6.52.31.157.
The very Tombs now vanish'd like their dead! .... 6.71.4.202.
The *Phantome* said; then, vanish'd from his sight, ... Il.2.43.129.
Now vanish'd like their Smoke: The Faith of Men! .... Il.2.407.147.
The Ruin vanish'd, and the Name no more .... Il.7.555.392.
She said, and vanish'd: *Hector*, with a Bound, ... Il.11.269.47.
Thus vanish'd, at thy touch, the Tow'rs and Walls; .... Il.15.420.213.
That fell this instant, vanish'd from my Sword! .... Il.20.396.411.
Swift as the Word, she vanish'd from their View; .... Il.23.262.500.
She spoke, and vanish'd. *Priam* bids prepare .... Il.24.225.546.
Thus having said, he vanish'd from his Eyes, ... Il.24.574.560.
Vanish'd at once! unheard of, and unknown! .... Od.1.311.47.
Vanish'd are all the visionary joys: .... Od.4.246.131.
And in a moment vanish'd from her eye. .... Od.5.190.180.
The rest are vanish'd, none repass'd the gate; .... Od.10.307.359.
The heroine shades; they vanish'd at her call. .... Od.11.481.408.
His substance vanish'd, and his strength decay'd, ... Od.11.489.408.
Instant, the racer vanish'd off the ground; .... Od.14.566.64.
Pin'd out her bloom, and vanish'd to a ghost. .... Od.15.383.88.
The Suitor now had vanish'd in a ghost: .... Od.20.377.251.
The whizzing arrow vanish'd from the string, ... Od.21.461.282.

VANITIES
That all her Vanities at once are dead: .... 2.RL1.52.149.
Succeeding Vanities she still regards, ... 2.RL1.53.149.
With varying Vanities, from ev'ry Part, ... 2.RL1.99.152.
In search of Vanities from Nature strays: .... 4.HAdv.99.83.
Riches that vex, and Vanities that tire. .... 6.86.4.245.

VANITY
These Sparks with aukward Vanity display .... 1.EOC.329.275.
But soon the Short-liv'd Vanity is lost! .... 1.EOC.497.294.
Deduct what is but Vanity, or Dress, ... 3.EOM2.45.61.
That Virtue's ends from Vanity can raise, ... 3.EOM2.245.85.
And not a vanity is giv'n in vain; .... 3.EOM2.290.89.
His charitable Vanity supplies. .... 3.Ep4.172.153.
Thy charitable Vanity supplies. .... 3.Ep4.172A.153.
Who has the Vanity to call you Friend, ... 4.Arbu.295.117.
And sell his Soul for Vanity, ... 6.58.23.171.
Theirs is the Vanity, the Learning thine: .... 6.71.45.204.
And yet in this no Vanity is shown; .... 6.105ii.3.300.
But sure in this no Vanity is shown; .... 6.105ii.3A.300.

VANITY'S
O you! whom Vanity's light bark conveys .... 4.2HE1.296.221.

VANQUISH
Like thee to vanquish, or like me to die. .... 1.TrES.313.461.
We yet may vanquish in a happier Hour: .... Il.3.546.217.
May vanquish *Hector* by a *Grecian* Hand. .... Il.6.461.349.
Forget to vanquish, and consent to fear. .... Il.15.317.209.
Like thee to vanquish, or like me to die. .... Il.16.618.268.

VANQUISH'D
And vanquish'd Nature seems to charm no more. .... 1.PSp.76.68.
Still in thy Song shou'd vanquish'd *France* appear, ... 1.W-F.309.178.
How twice he vanquish'd where the *Rhine* does roll, ... 1.TrSt.27A.410.
Who drew the *Lion Vanquish'd?* 'Twas a *Man*. .... 2.ChWB.365.75.
But still in Fancy vanquish'd ev'ry Maid; .... 2.TemF.387.282.
The vanquish'd roses lose their pride, ... 6.4iv.5.10.
And vanquish'd realms supply recording gold? .... 6.71.56.204.
But vanquish'd! baffled! oh eternal Shame! .... Il.2.363.144.
Victors and Vanquish'd join promiscuous Cries, ... Il.4.512.246.
In Dust the Vanquish'd, and the Victor lies. .... Il.4.627.250.
There brav'd, and vanquish'd, many a hardy Knight; .... Il.5.1004.314.
Vanquish'd I fled: Ev'n I, the God of Fight, ... Il.5.1086.318.
As Pity pleaded for his vanquish'd Prize, ... Il.6.65.327.
The Stone shall tell your vanquish'd Hero's Name, ... Il.7.103.368.
Had giv'n the Vanquish'd, now the Victor bore. .... Il.7.178.372.
Victors and Vanquish'd join promiscuous Cries, ... Il.8.79.399.
The Warrior heard, he vanquish'd, and he sav'd. .... Il.9.706.469.
Of all the Plunder of the vanquish'd Host; .... Il.10.368.19.
Vanquish'd at last by *Hector's* Lance he lies. .... Il.15.73.199.
The Vanquish'd triumph, and the Victors fly. .... Il.17.675.314.
Your Swiftness? Vanquish'd by a female Foe? .... Il.23.488.509.
The Vanquish'd bear the massy Bowl away. .... Il.23.766.520.
And singly vanquish'd the *Cadmæan* Race. .... Il.23.788.521.
And sooth the vanquish'd with a victor's pray'r. .... Od.4.572.147.
What foes were vanquish'd, and what numbers fell; .... Od.11.634.415.
Then (*Neleus* vanquish'd, and consign'd the Fair .... Od.15.262.80.
Is it that vanquish'd *Irus* swells thy mind? .... Od.18.381.186.
Ulysses lives his vanquish'd foes to see; .... Od.23.57.321.

VAP'RISH
Pallas grew vap'rish once and odd, ... 6.119.1.336.

VAPOR
The pois'nous Vapor blots the purple Skies, ... 2.TemF.340.280.
Of Air condens'd a Vapor circumfus'd: .... Il.5.967.312.
Imbrown'd with vapor of the smould'ring flame. .... Od.19.22.193.
Gild the gross vapor of this nether sphere! .... Od.19.41.194.

VAPORS
And dusky Vapors rise, and intercept the Day: .... 2.ChJM.801.53.
Parents of Vapors and of Female Wit, ... 2.RL4.59.189.
Him close she curtain'd round with vapors blue, ... 5.DunA3.3.150.
A Night of Vapors round the Mountain-Heads, ... Il.3.16.188.
The low-hung Vapors motionless and still, ... Il.5.645.299.
As Vapors blown by *Auster's* sultry Breath, ... Il.5.1058.317.
Black from the Tents the sav'ry Vapors flew. .... Il.7.559.392.
Or chilly vapors breathing from the flood .... Od.5.604.201.

VAPOUR
And in a Vapour reach'd the dismal Dome. .... 2.RL4.18.184.
A constant *Vapour* o'er the Palace flies; .... 2.RL4.39.186.
The Vapour mild o'er each Committee crept; .... 5.DunB4.615.405.
A vapour fed from wild desire, ... 6.51ii.19.153.
Than all his Books can vapour; .... 6.58.74.174.
Till Life's warm Vapour issuing thro' the Wound, ... Il.11.598.60.
Dark o'er the Fields th' ascending Vapour flies, ... Il.16.436.259.
No Vapour rested on the Mountain's Head, ... Il.17.429.304.
Sure of the Vapour in the tainted Dews, ... Il.22.247.465.
Lur'd with the vapour of the fragrant feast, ... Od.1.189.42.
To winde the vapour in the tainted dew? .... Od.17.385.150.
A winy vapour melting in a tear. .... Od.19.143.199.

VAPOURS
Where cooling Vapours breathe along the Mead, ... 1.W-F.136.163.
It draws up Vapours which obscure its Rays; .... 1.EOC.471.292.
From the damp Earth impervious Vapours rise, ... 1.TrSt.486.430.
Vapours and Pride by turns possess her Brain: .... 2.ChWB.89.61.
Sent up in Vapours to the *Baron's* Brain .... 2.RL3.119.176.
Spleen, Vapours, or Small-pox, above them all, ... 3.Ep2.267.72.
A Fit of Vapours clouds this Demi-god. .... 4.1HE1.188.293.
And wafting vapours from the Land of Dreams, ... 5.DunA2.316.140.
And wafting Vapours from the Land of dreams, ... 5.DunB2.340.314.
Here brisker vapours o'er the Temple creep, ... 5.DunB2.345.314.
Him close she curtains round with Vapours blue, ... 5.DunB3.3.320.
Him close she curtain'd round with Vapours blue, ... 5.DunB3.3A.320.
Slow from the Main the heavy Vapours rise, ... Il.4.316.235.
The Winds to Heav'n the curling Vapours bore. .... Il.8.680.427.
O'er his dim Sight the misty Vapours rise, ... Il.11.459.54.
While *Jove* yet rests, while yet my Vapours shed .... Il.14.413.183.
Who 'midst surrounding Frosts, and Vapours chill, ... Il.16.286.252.
Gath'ring like Vapours of a noxious kind .... Il.18.141.329.

VAPOURS (CONTINUED)
And choak'd with Vapours, feels his Bottom glow. ....Il.21.429.438.
And the red Vapours purple all the Sky. ....Il.21.610.447.
And woody mountains, half in vapours lost; ....Od.5.358.189.
No rains descend, no snowy vapours rise; ....Od.6.52.207.
And woody mountains half in vapours lost. ....Od.7.354.253.

VARIANCE
How much at variance are her Feet and Eyes! ....1.PSp.60.66.
Is there a variance? enter but his door, ...3.Ep3.271.115.

VARIED
Whilst warbling to the varied strain, advance ....Od.4.25.121.
To vernal airs attunes her varied strains; ....Od.19.606.226.
With varied toils the rest adorn the dome. ....Od.20.198.243.

VARIEGATED
Ladies, like variegated Tulips, show, ...3.Ep2.41.53.
The Prince the variegated present took. ....Od.15.145.75.

VARIES
Each Shape he varies, and each Art he tries, ...1.TrVP.43.379.
Add, that he varies ev'ry Shape with ease, ...1.TrVP.92.381.
How Instinct varies in the grov'ling swine, ...3.EOM1.221.43.
How *Instinct* varies! what a Hog may want, ...3.EOM1.221A.43.
Next, that he varies from himself no less: ....3.Ep1.20.17.
Surprizes, varies, and conceals the Bounds. ....3.Ep4.56.142.
Joins willing woods, and varies shades from shades, ...3.Ep4.62.142.

VARIETY
Where Order in Variety we see, ...1.W-F.15.149.
Led thro' a sad variety of woe: ....2.ElAb.36.321.
By their Encrease, and their Variety; .... 6.17iii.2.57.
A sad variety of woes I mourn! ....Od.19.612.226.

VARIOUS
The various Seasons of the rowling Year; ....1.PSp.38.64.
'Tis done, and Nature's various Charms decay; ....1.PWi.29.91.
Our plenteous Streams a various Race supply; ....1.W-F.141.163.
Hear how *Timotheus'* various Lays surprize, ...1.EOC.374A.283.
In various Shapes of *Parsons, Criticks, Beaus;* .... 1.EOC.459.291.
This when the various God had urg'd in vain, ...1.TrVP.112.381.
With noisie Care and various Tumult sound. ....1.TrSt.606.435.
And silent Hours to various Talk invite. ....1.TrSt.795.443.
The loaded Trees their various Fruits produce, ...1.TrUl.126.470.
In various Talk the chearful hours they past, ...2.RL*A*1.75.129.
The various Off'rings of the World appear; ....2.RL1.130.155.
Ye know the Spheres and various Tasks assign'd, ...2.RL2.75.164.
In various Talk th' instructive hours they past, ...2.RL3.11.169.
Of various Habit and of various Dye, ...2.RL3.84.174.
Of various Habit and of various Dye, ...2.RL3.84.174.
In various Habits and of various Dye, ...2.RL3.84A.174.
In various Habits and of various Dye, ...2.RL3.84A.174.
Of Bodies chang'd to various Forms by *Spleen.* .... 2.RL4.48.187.
On various Tempers act by various ways, ...2.RL4.61.189.
On various Tempers act by various ways, ...2.RL4.61.189.
Inscriptions here of various Names I view'd, ...2.TemF.31.255.
Of various Structure, but of equal Grace: ....2.TemF.66.257.
Which o'er each Object casting various Dies, ...2.TemF.133.264.
And various Animals his Sides surround; ....2.TemF.235.274.
With various-colour'd Light the Pavement shone, ...2.TemF.254.275.
Of various Tongues the mingled Sounds were heard; ....2.TemF.280.277.
In various Garbs promiscuous Throngs appear'd; ....2.TemF.281.277.
All various Sounds from Earth, and Seas, and Skies, ...2.TemF.433.284.
There various News I heard, of Love and Strife, ...2.TemF.448.285.
"Acts to one end, but acts by various laws." ....3.EOM3.2.92.
See Matter next, with various life endu'd, ...3.EOM3.13.93.
Behold it next, with various life endu'd, ...3.EOM3.13A.93.
And mourn our various portions as we please, ...3.EOM4.33.131.
Teach me, like thee, in various nature wise, ...3.EOM4.377.165.
Shall parts so various aim at nothing new? ....3.Ep1.186.31.
In Men, we various Ruling Passions find, ...3.Ep2.207.67.
Various of Temper, as of Face or Frame, ...4.2HE2.282.185.
And hears the various Vows of fond mankind, ...5.DunA2.83.108.
There hears the various Vows of fond mankind, ...5.DunA2.83A.108.
And hears the various vows of fond mankind; ....5.DunB2.87.300.
Then various Elements against thee join'd, ...6.8.7.17.
In one more various Animal combin'd, ...6.8.8.17.
From various Discords to create ....6.11.35Z4.31.
Now all her various States worn out ....6.14v(b).13A.50.
Beds of all various herbs, for ever green, ...6.35.26.103.
To various use their various streams they bring, ...6.35.33.104.
To various use their various streams they bring, ...6.35.33.104.
What various joys on one attend, ...6.51ii.27.153.
Eyes the calm Sun-set of thy Various Day, ...6.84.38.240.
The calmer Sunsett of thy Various Day; ....6.84.31Z10.240.
Thessalians all, tho' various in their Name, ...Il.2.835.164.
But various *Iris, Jove's* Commands to bear, ...Il.2.956.169.
We know him by the various Plume he wears. ....Il.3.118.195.
The various Goddess of the Rain-bow flies: ....Il.3.166.199.
Then all dispersing, various Tasks attend; ....Il.3.527.216.
With equal Lustre various Colours vie, ...Il.4.174.229.
Such Clamours rose from various Nations round, ...Il.4.496.244.
The various Textures and the various Dies, ...Il.6.365.344.
The various Textures and the various Dies, ...Il.6.365.344.
Pallas, meanwhile, her various Veil unbound, ...Il.8.466.419.
Swift as the Wind, the various-colour'd Maid ....Il.8.502.420.
Such various Passions urg'd the troubled Host. ....Il.9.10.431.
All but the King; with various Thoughts opprest, ...Il.10.3.1.
The various-colour'd Scarf, the Shield he rears, ...Il.10.84.6.
Reflected various Light, and arching bow'd, ...Il.11.35.36.
On Wings of Winds descends the various Maid. ....Il.11.254.46.
Survey'd the various Fortune of the War. ....Il.11.643.62.
With various Skill and high Embroid'ry grac'd. ....Il.14.246.173.
Our high Decree let various *Iris* know, ...Il.15.59.196.
And various *Iris* wing their airy way. ....Il.15.169.203.

VARIOUS (CONTINUED)
There lay on Heaps his various Garments roll'd, ...Il.16.270.249.
The various Goddess of the show'ry Bow, ...Il.18.205.331.
The various Goddess of the painted Bow, ...Il.18.205A.331.
And various Artifice, the Queen she plac'd; ....Il.18.458.343.
Rich, various Artifice emblaz'd the Field; ....Il.18.552.348.
With various Sculpture, and the golden Crest. ....Il.18.708.357.
The brazen Sword a various Baldrick ty'd, ...Il.19.400.388.
E'er yet the Gods their various Aid employ, ...Il.20.55.396.
While thus the Gods in various League engage, ...Il.20.103.398.
Five Plates of various Metal, various Mold, ...Il.20.318.407.
Five Plates of various Metal, various Mold, ...Il.20.318.407.
The certain Hound his various Maze pursues. ....Il.22.248.465.
The Various Goddess to partake the Rites. ....Il.23.251.499.
With solemn Pace thro' various Rooms he went, ...Il.24.578.560.
The Man, for Wisdom's various arts renown'd, ...Od.1.1.25.
Viands of various kinds allure the taste, ...Od.1.185.41.
And various labours of the loom, beguile; ....Od.1.456.54.
The spacious loom, and mix'd the various thread: ....Od.2.104.66.
Wise as he was, by various Counsels sway'd, ...Od.3.197.95.
From various precedents, and various laws. ....Od.3.307.101.
From various precedents, and various laws. ....Od.3.307.101.
To crown thy various gifts, the sage assign'd ....Od.4.261.131.
With various simples cloaths the fat'ned soil. ....Od.4.318.134.
Heroes in various climes my self have found, ...Od.4.367.137.
There fast in chains constrain the various God: ....Od.4.524.145.
His various arts he soon resumes in aid: ....Od.4.614.148.
After long woes, and various toil endur'd, ...Od.4.629.149.
Then speeding back, involv'd in various thought, ...Od.4.779.155.
Without the grot, a various sylvan scene ....Od.5.80.176.
The various ball; the ball erroneous flew, ...Od.6.134.213.
Where various carpets with embroidry blaz'd, ...Od.7.125.240.
Beds of all various herbs, for ever green, ...Od.7.167.244.
To various use their various streams they bring, ...Od.7.174.244.
To various use their various streams they bring, ...Od.7.174.244.
Viands of various kinds invite the taste, ...Od.7.236.247.
Various the *Trojans* counsell'd; part consign'd ....Od.8.554.292.
The tenth we touch'd, by various errors tost, ...Od.9.95.306.
Thro' various seas by various perils tost, ...Od.9.309.319.
Thro' various seas by various perils tost, ...Od.9.309.319.
(Vers'd in the turns of various humankind) ....Od.9.336.320.
The man, for Wisdom's various arts renown'd. ....Od.10.394.363.
Viands of various kinds allure the taste, ...Od.10.439.365.
To me are known the various woes ye bore, ...Od.10.542.369.
And, heap'd with various wealth, a blazing pyle: ....Od.10.623.374.
And guard thy various passage thro' the tyde. ....Od.12.70.433.
A various casket that, of rich inlay, ...Od.13.85.5.
The loaded trees their various fruits produce, ...Od.13.293.19.
Those Gods, who turn (to various ends design'd) ....Od.14.264.49.
The various thoughts and talents of mankind, ...Od.14.265.49.
Restless he griev'd, with various fears opprest, ...Od.15.9.70.
Her various textures of unnumber'd dies, ...Od.15.119.74.
Viands of various kinds allure the taste ....Od.15.154.76.
Hermes to me his various gifts imparts, ...Od.15.336.85.
O'er which the panther's various hide was thrown. ....Od.19.71.196.
In various tongues avow their various claims: ....Od.19.199.202.
In various tongues avow their various claims: ....Od.19.199.202.
Two portals firm the various phantoms keep: ....Od.19.657.228.
Deeds full of fate distract my various mind, ...Od.20.48.234.
With pomp of various architrave o'erlay'd. ....Od.21.46.261.
(With rich inlay the various floor was grac'd) ....Od.21.172.267.
A spacious loom, and mix'd the various thread; ....Od.24.153.355.
Thro' rows of shade with various fruitage crown'd, ...Od.24.255.361.
Of various vines that then began to blow, ...Od.24.398.368.

VARIOUS-COLOUR'D
With various-colour'd Light the Pavement shone, ...2.TemF.254.275.
Swift as the Wind, the various-colour'd Maid ....Il.8.502.420.
The various-colour'd Scarf, the Shield he rears, ...Il.10.84.6.

VARIOUSLY
Fortune her gifts may variously dispose, ...3.EOM4.67.134.
The very best will variously incline, ...3.EOM4.143.141.

VARIUS
Varius with blushes owns he loves, ...6.51ii.7A.152.

VARLET
Obscene with filth the varlet lies bewray'd, ...5.DunA2.71A.106.

VARLETS
Breval, Besaleel, Bond, the Varlets caught. ....5.DunA2.118.111.
Breval, Bond, Besaleel, the varlets caught. ....5.DunB2.126.301.

VARNISH
Art shall be theirs to varnish an Offence, ...2.ChJM.661.46.
None shall want Arts to varnish an Offence, ...2.ChJM.661A.46.
This the blue varnish, that the green endears, ...6.71.37.203.

VARNISH'D
Which Heav'n has varnish'd out, and made a *Queen:* .... 3.Ep2.182.64.
Such painted Puppets, such a varnish'd Race ....4.JD4.208.43.

VARNISHER
Thou Varnisher of *Fools,* and Cheat of all the *Wise.* .... 6.8.21.18.

VARY
You laugh, if Coat and Breeches strangely vary, ...4.1HE1.163.291.
Still vary Shapes and Dyes; ....6.14v(b).21.50.
My Numbers too for ever will I vary, ...6.40.3.112.

VARY'D
Hear how *Timotheus'* vary'd Lays surprize, ...1.EOC.374.283.
Nor Braids of Gold the vary'd Tresses bind, ...1.TrSP.85.397.
What vary'd being peoples ev'ry star, ...3.EOM1.27.16.
Such vary'd light in one promiscuous blaze? ....5.DunB4.412.382.

VARY'D (CONTINUED)
And vary'd *Tulips* show so dazling gay, ... 6.14iv.7.47.
My vary'd Belt repell'd the flying Wound. .... Il.4.225.232.
Vary'd each Face; then Discord sounds Alarms, ... Il.20.65.396.
Thy Sire and I were one; nor vary'd aught .... Od.3.155.93.
In *Areas* vary'd with mosaic art, ... Od.4.847.158.

VARYING
Ah! what avail his glossie, varying Dyes, ... 1.W-F.115.161.
With varying Vanities, from ev'ry Part, ... 2.RL1.99.152.
Like varying winds, by other passions tost, ... 3.EOM2.167.75.
Mean-while Opinion gilds with varying rays .... 3.EOM2.283.89.
'Till then, Opinion gilds with varying rays .... 3.EOM2.283A.89.
Smit with her varying plumage, spare the dove? .... 3.EOM3.54.97.
Some unmark'd fibre, or some varying vein: .... 3.Ep1.16.17.
The varying verse, the full resounding line, ... 4.2HE1.268.217.
She, tinsel'd o'er in robes of varying hues, ... 5.DunA1.79.69.
She, tinsel'd o'er in robes of varying hues, ... 5.DunB1.81.275.
And all its varying Rain-bows die away. .... 5.DunB4.632.407.
And all her varying Rain-bows die away. .... 5.DunB4.632A.407.
And varying still in State Æ form .... 6.14v(b).22A.50.
Your accent varying as their spouses spoke: .... Od.4.380.139.
Matter is chang'd, and varying forms decay; .... Od.4.764.155.
'Till one resolve my varying counsel ends. .... Od.9.504.326.
The varying hues in gay confusion rise .... Od.18.338.184.

VASE
Each Silver Vase in mystic Order laid. .... 2.RL1.122.155.
Heaps in a Brazen Vase three Chines entire: .... Il.9.272.447.
The Brazen Vase *Automedon* sustains, ... Il.9.273.447.
Beneath the Vase, and climbs around the Sides: .... Il.18.408.340.
With kindled Flames the Tripod-Vase surround; .... Il.23.50.489.
And in the golden Vase dispose with Care; .... Il.23.303.501.
With Tears collected, in the golden Vase. .... Il.23.314.502.
And a large Vase, where two bright Handles rise, ... Il.23.331.503.
The Tripod-Vase, and Dame with radiant Eyes: .... Il.23.594.513.
(With Tears collected) in a golden Vase; .... Il.24.1004.577.
The golden Vase in purple Palls they roll'd, ... Il.24.1005.577.
With copious water the bright vase supplies .... Od.1.181.41.
The vase extending to receive the blood. .... Od.3.563.115.
High on a massy vase of silver mold, ... Od.4.65.122.
To *Sparta's* Queen of old the radiant vase .... Od.4.167.128.
And that rich vase, with living sculpture wrought, ... Od.4.179.128.
I take the present of the promis'd Vase; .... Od.4.820.157.
Then unguents in a vase of gold supply, ... Od.6.255.222.
Whose polish'd vase with copious streams supplies .... Od.7.232.247.
Commands her train a spacious vase to bring, ... Od.8.470.288.
The spacious vase with ample streams suffice, ... Od.8.471.288.
Of this an ample vase we heav'd a-board, ... Od.9.246.317.
An ample vase receives the smoking wave, ... Od.10.425.365.
With copious water the bright vase supplies .... Od.10.435.365.
Each peer a tripod, each a vase bestow, ... Od.13.17.2.
The silver vase with living sculpture wrought. .... Od.15.135.75.
With copious streams the shining vase supplies .... Od.15.150.76.
In the deep vase, that shone like burnish'd gold, ... Od.19.452.216.
The mingled fluids from the vase redound; .... Od.19.549.223.
The vase reclining floats the floor around! .... Od.19.549.223.
She to the fount conveys th' exhausted vase: .... Od.19.588.224.
In each discolour'd vase the viands lay: .... Od.20.418.253.
With wines and unguents in a golden vase. .... Od.24.94.352.
(The vase to *Thetis Bacchus* gave of old, ... Od.24.95.352.

VASE'S
Let some refresh the vase's sullied mold; .... Od.20.190.242.

VASES
Nor Silver Vases took the forming Mold, ... 1.TrSt.207.419.
There Heroes' Wits are kept in pondrous Vases, ... 2.RL5.115.208.
Fair Coursers, Vases, and alluring Dames. .... 3.Ep3.58.91.
Gold, Silver, Iv'ry, Vases sculptur'd high, ... 4.2HE2.264.183.
And twice ten Vases of refulgent Mold; .... Il.9.158.440.
And twice ten Vases of refulgent Mold; .... Il.9.345.450.
Twice ten bright Vases in the midst they laid; .... Il.19.250.383.
Vases and Tripods, for the Fun'ral Games, ... Il.23.325.503.
The King himself the vases rang'd with care; .... Od.13.25.2.
Three vases heap'd with copious fires display .... Od.18.355.184.

VASSAL
Slave to a Wife or Vassal to a Punk, ... 4.1HE1.62.283.
First slave to Words, then vassal to a Name, ... 5.DunB4.501.391.
Your Vassal Godheads grudgingly obey; .... Il.15.117.201.
No Vassal God, nor of his Train am I. .... Il.15.209.204.

VASSALS
And serv'd alike his Vassals and his God. .... 1.W-F.76.157.
And treats alike his Vassals and his God. .... 1.WF.76A.157.
Command thy Vassals, but command not Me. .... Il.1.391.106.
Sole o'er my vassals, and domestic train. .... Od.1.508.56.
To them my vassals had resign'd a soil, ... Od.4.239.130.

VAST
So *vast* is Art, so *narrow* Human Wit: .... 1.EOC.61.246.
So vast a Throng the Stage can ne'er contain. .... 1.EOC.283.271.
The Stage can ne'er so vast a Throng contain. .... 1.EOC.283A.271.
When *Ajax* strives, some Rock's vast Weight to throw, ... 1.EOC.370.282.
For oh! how vast a Memory has Love? .... 1.TrSP.52.396.
Where vast *Cythæron's* Top salutes the Sky, ... 1.TrSt.161.416.
Th' *Inachians* view the Slain with vast Surprize, ... 1.TrSt.727.440.
Some with vast Beams the squallid Corps engage, ... 1.TrSt.733.440.
Th' *Inachians* view'd the Slain with vast Surprize, ... 1.TrSt.727A.440.
Still as his Mind revolv'd with vast Delight .... 2.ChJM.349.31.
For, like a Prince, he bore the vast Expence .... 2.ChJM.444.36.
Of twelve vast *French* Romances, neatly gilt. .... 2.RL2.38.161.
Pleas'd with the strange Success, vast Numbers prest .... 2.TemF.394.282.
(Unsure the Tenure, but how vast the Fine!) .... 2.TemF.508.288.
He, who thro' vast immensity can pierce, ... 3.EOM1.23.15.

VAST (CONTINUED)
Of this vast frame the bearings, and the ties, ... 3.EOM1.29A.16.
Vast Range of Sense! from Man's imperial race .... 3.EOM1.209A.41.
Vast chain of being, which from God began, ... 3.EOM1.237.44.
On life's vast ocean diversely we sail, ... 3.EOM2.107.67.
The vast Parterres a thousand hands shall make, ... 3.Ep4.73.144.
Proud of a vast Extent of flimzy lines. .... 4.Arbu.94.102.
So vast our best Divines, we must confess, ... 4.JD2A.100.140.
In the vast reach of our huge Statute Law .... 4.JD2A.134.144.
So vast, our new Divines, we must confess, ... 4.JD2.97.141.
And gathers by Degrees, a vast Estate. .... 4.JD2A.95.140.
All vast Possessions (just the same the case .... 4.2HE2.254.183.
To make poor Pinky eat with vast applause! .... 4.2HE1.293.221.
Sinking from thought to thought, a vast profound! .... 5.DunA1.112.77.
Lo! one vast Egg produces human race. .... 5.DunA3.244.177.
Sinking from thought to thought, a vast profound! .... 5.DunB1.118.278.
Lo! one vast Egg produces human race. .... 5.DunB3.248.332.
Involves a vast involuntary throng, ... 5.DunB4.82.349.
'Twas one vast Nothing, All, and All slept fast in thee. .... 6.8.3.17.
Into the vast Abyss of future Life; .... 6.17ii.6.56.
Go now, learn all vast Science can impart; .... 6.27.12.81.
But *Lintot* is at vast Expence, ... 6.29.25.83.
Convinc'd, she now contracts her vast design, ... 6.71.23.203.
"O'er his vast heaps in drunkenness of pride .... 6.130.33.359.
Round the vast Orb an hundred Serpents roll'd, ... Il.2.528.151.
How vast thy Empire? Of yon' matchless Train .... Il.3.243.204.
'Till vast Destruction glut the Queen of Heav'n! .... Il.4.58.223.
And Fate now labours with some vast Event: .... Il.4.112.225.
Vast was his Wealth, and these the only Heirs .... Il.5.198.276.
Heav'd with vast Force, a Rocky Fragment wields. .... Il.5.370.284.
How vast the Diff'rence of the Gods and Thee; .... Il.5.534.294.
Or one vast Burst of all-involving Fate .... Il.5.594.296.
How vast the Diff'rence of their Deeds and thine? .... Il.5.789.304.
So vast, the broad Circumference contains .... Il.5.920.310.
From vast *Olympus* to the gleaming Plain .... Il.7.24.364.
Black, craggy, vast: To this his Force he bends; .... Il.7.317.379.
Vast Drifts of Sand shall change the former Shore; .... Il.7.554.392.
And the vast World hangs trembling in my Sight! .... Il.8.32.397.
Roll'd the big Thunder o'er the vast Profound: .... Il.8.162.405.
Flame thro' the Vast of Air, and reach the Sky. .... Il.8.545.422.
My self will give the Dow'r; so vast a Store, ... Il.9.193.442.
Himself will give the Dow'r; so vast a Store, ... Il.9.380.451.
Vast Heaps of Brass shall in your Ships be told, ... Il.10.451.23.
Words now forgot, tho' now of vast Import. .... Il.11.921.76.
Vast Stones and Piles from their Foundation heaves, ... Il.12.31.82.
Vast was the Leap, and headlong hung the Steep; .... Il.12.62.83.
From the vast Concave of the spangled Sky, ... Il.15.24.195.
And one vast Ruin whelm th' *Olympian* State. .... Il.15.155.202.
Wraps the vast Mountains, and involves the Poles. .... Il.15.729.224.
High on the Decks, with vast gigantic Stride, ... Il.15.820.228.
Might only we the vast Destruction shun, ... Il.16.126.242.
Wedg'd in the Trench, in one vast Carnage bruis'd. .... Il.16.443.260.
Drag some vast Beam, or Mast's unwieldy Length; .... Il.17.834.321.
Where vast *Olympus* starry Summits shine: .... Il.18.180.331.
Tho' vast the Heaps that strow the crimson Plain, ... Il.19.221.382.
Girds the vast Globe; the Maid in Arms renown'd; .... Il.20.46.396.
The World's vast Concave, when the Gods contend. .... Il.20.90.397.
There fix'd from eldest times; black, craggy, vast: .... Il.21.470.441.
If e'er ye rush'd in Crowds, with vast Delight .... Il.24.878.573.
Pond'rous and vast; which when her fury burns .... Od.1.130.38.
Who eye the dazling roofs with vast delight; .... Od.4.54.122.
And view'd his filial love with vast surprize; .... Od.4.154.127.
With vast munificence th' imperial guest: .... Od.4.172.128.
When the vast fabric of the Steed we rear'd! .... Od.4.374.137.
Of four vast *Phocæ* takes, to veil her wiles; .... Od.4.594.148.
By *Juno's* guardian aid, the wat'ry Vast .... Od.4.683.151.
He ceas'd, and plunging in the vast profound, ... Od.4.777.155.
Aside, sequester'd from the vast resort, ... Od.4.849.158.
With vast applause the sentence all approve; .... Od.4.900.160.
Huge, horrid, vast! where scarce in safety sails .... Od.5.227.182.
That lay before him, indistinct and vast, ... Od.5.359.189.
As pious children joy with vast delight .... Od.5.506.196.
The vast profound, and bid the vessel fly: .... Od.8.34.263.
Green from the wood; of height and bulk so vast, ... Od.9.382.321.
From that vast bulk dislodge thy bloody mind, ... Od.9.612.332.
Thro' the vast waves the dreadful wonders move, ... Od.12.73.434.
Fierce to *Phæacia* crost the vast profound. .... Od.13.185.15.
I saw my self the vast unnumber'd store .... Od.14.359.51.
So rich the value of a store so vast .... Od.19.337.210.
Envy shall sicken at thy vast reward. .... Od.19.357.211.
With joy, and vast surprize, th' applauding train .... Od.19.532.221.
With vast increase beneath my care it spreads, ... Od.20.269.246.
And bade *Melanthius* a vast pyle prepare; .... Od.21.182.268.
Vast as some mighty column's bulk on high .... Od.23.193.332.

VATICAN
A Gothic Vatican! of Greece and Rome .... 5.DunA1.125.78.

VATICIDE
The caitiff Vaticide conceiv'd a prayer. .... 5.DunA2.74.107.
The caitiff Vaticide conceiv'd a pray'r. .... 5.DunB2.78.299.

VAULT
Then sacred seem'd th'etherial vault no more; .... 3.EOM3.263.119.
This Vault of Air, this congregated Ball, ... 4.1HE6.5.237.
Wide o'er th' aerial Vault extends thy sway, ... 6.65.3.192.
Shot down avenging, from the Vault of Stars. .... Il.6.134.330.
Eye the blue Vault, and bless the useful Light. .... Il.8.698.428.
His fervid Orb thro' half the Vault of Heav'n; .... Il.16.939.280.
End in the starry vault, and prop the sphears.) .... Od.1.70.34.
Shoots from the starry vault thro' fields of air; .... Od.8.8.261.
'Till in the vault of heav'n the stars decay, ... Od.11.468.407.
My echoing griefs the starry vault invade. .... Od.19.603.225.
O'er the *Cerulean* Vault, and shake the Pole; .... Od.20.142.240.

VAULTED
With *Phœbus'* Name resounds the vaulted Hall. 1.TrSt.651.437.
The vaulted Roofs with ecchoing Musick ring, 2.ChJM.320.29.
With louder Clamours rend the vaulted Skie: 2.ChJM.755.51.
With such loud Clamours rend the vaulted Skie: 2.ChJM.755A.51.
Restore the Lock! the vaulted Roofs rebound. 2.RL5.104.208.
Who rolls the Thunder o'er the vaulted Skies. Il.1.671.119.
Then with a Voice that shook the vaulted Skies, Il.5.431.289.
Whose Shrieks and Clamours fill the vaulted Dome; Il.24.204.545.
The shrilling airs the vaulted roof rebounds, Od.1.425.53.
And loud applauses rend the vaulted sky. Od.8.404.285.
The vaulted roofs and solid pavement rung. Od.10.255.355.
And with their sobs the vaulted roofs resound. Od.10.538.369.
Swift from the float I vaulted with a bound, Od.12.511.457.
With bursts of laughter rend the vaulted skies: Od.18.119.172.
With quav'ring cries the vaulted roofs resound: Od.20.222.244.
Ascends the roof; the vaulted roof rebounds; Od.23.144.328.
Who rolls the thunder o'er the vaulted skies) Od.24.548.374.

VAULTS
In weeping Vaults her hallow'd Earth contains! 1.W-F.302.177.
Wide Vaults appear, and Roofs of fretted Gold: 2.TemF.138.264.
Vaults from his Chariot on the trembling Ground, Il.11.270A.47.
He shifts his Seat, and vaults from one to one; Il.15.827.228.
Snatches the Reins, and vaults into the Seat. Il.17.549.309.
And thick, strong Strokes, the doubling Vaults rebound. Il.18.550.348.

VAUNT
And the proud Vaunt in just Derision ends. Il.5.580.296.
Hector may vaunt, but who shall heed the Boast? Il.8.185.406.
Where's now th' imperious Vaunt, the daring Boast Il.13.289.119.
Behold, *Deiphobus!* nor vaunt in vain. Il.13.559.133.
Enormous Boaster! doom'd to vaunt in vain. Il.13.1045.155.
To vaunt his Swiftness, wheels around the Plain, Il.20.477.414.
How durst thou vaunt thy wat'ry Progeny? Il.21.205.430.

VAUNTED
His vaunted Coursers urg'd to meet the War. Il.12.126.86.
From the proud Archer strike his vaunted Bow. Il.15.575.218.
He show'd, and vaunted of his matchless Boy: Il.19.106.376.

VAUNTER
Mistaken Vaunter! *Diomed* reply'd; Il.5.347.283.

VAUNTING
Nor fear the vaunting of a mortal Foe. Il.20.141.400.
Not so *Saturnia* bore the vaunting Maid; Il.21.554.444.

VAUNTS
"The race by vigor, not by vaunts is won; 5.DunA2.55.105.
"The race by vigour, not by vaunts is won; 5.DunB2.59.298.
That vaunts these Eyes shall view the Light no more. Il.5.153.274.
Drown *Hector's* Vaunts in loud Exhorts of Fight; Il.12.324.93.
Vaunts of his Gods, and calls high *Jove* his Sire. Il.13.82.108.
The King consented, by his Vaunts abus'd; Il.13.463.128.
Lo still he vaunts, and threats the Fleet with Fires, Il.14.425.184.
Vain are thy Vaunts, Success is still from Heav'n; Il.16.754.273.
Man only vaunts his Force, and vaunts in vain. Il.17.24.288.
Man only vaunts his Force, and vaunts in vain. Il.17.24.288.
Nor dread the Vaunts of *Peleus'* haughty Son; Il.20.418.412.
But vaunts not long, with all his Swiftness slain. Il.20.478.414.
Presumptuous are the vaunts, and vain the pride Od.4.92.124.
These empty vaunts will make the voyage vain; Od.4.1023.165.
There end thy pompous vaunts, and high disdain; Od.22.318.301.

VEAL
Take a knuckle of Veal 6.91.1.253.
Veal-Cutlets in their Place. 6.94.80.261.
Bred up by Hand on Chick and Veal. 6.135.56.368.
Bred up by Hand and Chick and Veal. 6.135.56A.368.

VEAL-CUTLETS
Veal-Cutlets in their Place. 6.94.80.261.

VEGETABLE
Or more improv'd the Vegetable Care. 1.TrVP.4.377.
The Fields their Vegetable Life renew, Il.23.681.516.
Of vegetable venom, taints the plain; Od.4.320.134.

VEGETABLES
See dying vegetables life sustain, 3.EOM3.15.93.

VEGETATE
See life dissolving vegetate again: 3.EOM3.16.93.

VEHICLES
From earthly Vehicles to these of Air. 2.RL1.50.149.

VEIL
Its bright Pavilions in a Veil of Clouds. 1.TrSt.172.417.
Diffus'd around a Veil of thicken'd Air: 1.TrUl.59.468.
As with cold lips I kiss'd the sacred veil, 2.ElAb.111.329.
First, Silks and Diamonds veil no finer Shape, 4.HAdv.106.85.
A veil of fogs dilates her awful face; 5.DunA1.218.89.
A veil of fogs dilates her awful face: 5.DunB1.262.289.
As half to shew, half veil the deep Intent. 5.DunB4.4.339.
Wraps in her Veil, and frees from sense of Shame. 5.DunB4.336.376.
Before the Night her gloomy Veil extends, Il.2.493.150.
O'er her fair Face a snowy Veil she threw, Il.3.187.200.
(For Gods can all things) in a Veil of Clouds. Il.3.468.214.
Screen'd from the Foe behind her shining Veil, Il.5.391.285.
Thro' her bright Veil the daring Weapon drove Il.5.417.287.
Th' Ambrosial Veil which all the Graces wove; Il.5.418.287.
Pallas disrobes; Her radiant Veil unty'd, Il.5.904.309.
(The labour'd Veil her heav'nly Fingers wove) Il.5.906.309.
She chose a Veil that shone superior far, Il.6.366.344.

VEIL (CONTINUED)
The Priestess then the shining Veil displays, Il.6.376.344.
Pallas, meanwhile, her various Veil unbound, Il.8.466.419.
Till with a snowy Veil he screen'd the Blaze. Il.8.549.422.
And drew behind the cloudy Veil of Night: Il.8.606.425.
The youthful Heroes in a Veil of Clouds. Il.11.885.75.
Then o'er her Head she casts a Veil more white Il.14.213.170.
Supine, and Shades eternal veil his Eyes. Il.14.522.188.
A Veil of Clouds involv'd his radiant Head: Il.15.349.210.
Last o'er the Dead the milkwhite Veil they threw; Il.18.415.340.
With Clouds encompass'd, and a Veil of Air: Il.20.181.401.
The favour'd Hero in a Veil of Clouds. Il.20.514.416.
As soon as Night her dusky Veil extends, Il.21.661.449.
The god-like *Trojan* in a Veil of Clouds; Il.21.706.451.
The Veil and Diadem, flew far away; Il.22.602.481.
He pour'd around a Veil of gather'd Air, Il.23.233.499.
The Urn a Veil of Linen cover'd o'er. Il.23.316.502.
A veil of richest texture wrought, she wears, Od.1.429.53.
Studious to veil the grief, in vain represt, Od.4.151.127.
Of four vast *Phocæ* takes, to veil her wiles; Od.4.594.148.
Vain shews of love to veil his felon hate! Od.4.712.152.
The nymph's fair head a veil transparent grac'd, Od.5.295.185.
With that, her hand the sacred veil bestows, Od.5.446.194.
Around him spread a veil of thicken'd air; Od.7.20.234.
Then from around him drop'd the veil of night; Od.7.190.245.
Tho' clouds and darkness veil th' encumber'd sky, Od.8.609.295.
And clouds and double darkness veil the skies; Od.12.370.449.
Diffus'd around a veil of thicken'd air: Od.13.226.17.
The shining veil, and thus endearing said. Od.15.137.75.
She said, and gave the veil; with grateful look, Od.15.144.75.
Thus veil the truth in plausible disguise. Od.16.307.120.
A veil translucent o'er her brow display'd, Od.18.249.179.
Whilst night extends her soft oblivious veil, Od.20.99.237.
And with her veil conceals the coming tears: Od.21.66.262.
The latent warriors in a veil of clouds. Od.23.399.344.

VEIL'D
I find the Shades that veil'd our Joys before, 1.TrSP.167.400.
Veil'd her fair Glories in the Shades of Night. 1.TrSt.137.415.
And veil'd the Starry Glories of his Head: 1.TrSt.432.428.
Veil'd in a Cloud, to silver *Simois* Shore: 1.TrES.339.462.
And veil'd her Blushes in a silken Shade; Il.3.522.216.
There veil'd in spacious Coverlets they stand; Il.5.246.279.
Veil'd in a Mist of Fragrance him they found, Il.15.174.203.
Veil'd in a Cloud, to silver *Simois'* Shore: Il.16.826.275.
She spake, and veil'd her Head in sable Shade, Il.24.122.540.
Now Twilight veil'd the glaring Face of Day, Il.24.427.553.
His purple garment veil'd the falling tear. Od.4.208.129.
Again *Ulysses* veil'd his pensive head, Od.8.89.267.

VEIL'S
Then, nor 'till then, the Veil's remov'd away, 2.ChWB.104.61.

VEILING
And veiling Truth in plausible Disguise; 1.TrUl.137.470.
And veiling truth in plausible disguise, Od.13.304.21.
And veiling decent with a modest shade Od.16.432.128.

VEILS
Religion blushing veils her sacred fires, 5.DunB4.649.409
Veils his fair glories, while he spies 6.4iv.2.10.
As when a gen'ral Darkness veils the Main, Il.7.71.366.
And cast, far off, the regal Veils away. Il.22.513.477.
And twelve fair Veils, and Garments stiff with Gold. Il.24.284.548.
(Their shining veils unbound.) Along the skies Od.6.113.211.
Veils the dire monster, and confounds the sight. Od.12.277.445.
She veils the torrent of her tearful eyes; Od.19.422.214.

VEIN
Th'impatient Courser pants in ev'ry Vein, 1.W-F.151.164.
Still *run on* Poets in a raging Vein, 1.EOC.606.308.
Still *run on* Poets in a frantick Vein, 1.EOC.606A.308.
And a glad Horror shoots through ev'ry Vein: 1.TrSt.580.434.
Some unmark'd fibre, or some varying vein: 3.Ep1.16.17.
Tho' still some traces of our rustic vein 4.2HE1.270.219.
And all that voluntary Vein, 4.1HE7.49.271.
And quick sensations skip from vein to vein, 5.DunA2.204.126
And quick sensations skip from vein to vein, 5.DunA2.204.126
And quick sensations skip from vein to vein; 5.DunB2.212.306.
And quick sensations skip from vein to vein; 5.DunB2.212.306.
O'er ev'ry vein a shudd'ring horror runs; 5.DunB4.143.355.
Tho' prostrate *Greece* should bleed at ev'ry Vein: Il.1.445.108.
From the clear Vein a Stream immortal flow'd, Il.5.421.287.
The hollow Vein that to the Neck extends Il.13.692.138.
That thrills my Arm and shoots thro ev'ry Vein, Il.16.638.269.
Then tho' pale death froze cold in ev'ry vein, Od.11.527.409.
And tender sorrow thrills in ev'ry vein; Od.11.676.417.
Antinous hears, and in a jovial vein, Od.18.42.169.

VEINS
Or thro' what Veins our ancient Blood has roll'd? 1.TrSt.800.443.
And warm the swelling Veins to Feats of Love: 2.ChWB.216.67.
What means this tumult in a Vestal's veins? 2.ElAb.4.319.
That the Blood, circling, flows in human Veins; 6.96v.6.280.
Nor Wine's inflaming Juice supplies their Veins.) Il.5.426.289.
No Drop of all thy Father warms thy Veins. Il.5.1009.315.
Thy Veins no more with ancient Vigour glow, Il.8.131.404.
As now my Veins receive the pleasing Fire. Il.14.372.180.
Thro' all his Veins a sudden Vigour flew, Il.17.250.297.
When fed with noxious Herbs his turgid Veins Il.22.132.458.
His virgin sword Ægysthus' veins imbru'd; Od.1.389.51.
But since thy veins paternal virtue fires, Od.2.317.76.
Nor bounds the blood along the purple veins; Od.11.264.394.
Thro' veins (he cry'd) of royal fathers flow'd; Od.11.451.406.
Glows in our veins, and opens ev'ry soul, Od.11.522.409.
And my cold blood hangs shiv'ring in my veins; Od.11.784.425.

VEINS (CONTINUED)
The tides of lust that swell their boiling veins: ....Od.20.214.243.

VELLOM
Lo some are Vellom, and the rest as good ....3.Ep4.137.150.

VELVET
Draw forth to Combat on the Velvet Plain. ....2.RL3.44.172.
Was velvet in the youth of good Queen Bess, ...4.JD4.41.29.
"That's Velvet for a King!" the Flattr'er swears; ....4.JD4.218.45.
And cram'd it in the Velvet Bag ....6.94.75.261.
"Or in the golden Cowslip's Velvet Head; ....6.96ii.48.273.

VEN'SON
A Rogue with Ven'son to a Saint without. ....3.Ep1.139.26.
To live on Ven'son when it sold so dear. ....3.Ep3.120.101.
Our Fathers prais'd rank Ven'son. You suppose ....4.HS2.91.61.
His Ven'son too, a Guinea makes your own: ....4.2HE2.235.181.

VENAL
The Crown of Poland, venal twice an age, ...3.Ep3.129.103.
Yet then did Gildon draw his venal quill; ....4.Arbu.151.107.
Curs'd be the Wretch! so venal and so vain; ....4.JD2.63.139.
Than ev'n in Brothels venal Strumpets are. ....4.JD2A.75.138.
Seen him, uncumber'd with the Venal tribe, ...4.EpS1.31.300.
He thinks one Poet of no venal kind. ....4.EpS1.34A.300.
Of dull and venal a new World to mold, ...5.DunB4.15.341.
The Venal quiet, and intrance the Dull; ....5.DunB4.624.406.
If meagre Gildon draws his venal quill, ...6.49iii.1.142.
If meaner Gildon draws his venal quill, ...6.49iii.1A.142.
This, from no venal or ungrateful Muse. ....6.52.2.156.
If meagre Gildon draws his venal Quill, ...6.98.1.283.
In vain his consort bribes for venal song ....6.130.28.358.
From him some bribe thy venal tongue requires, ...Od.2.217.72.

VENERABLE
By God-like Poets Venerable made: ....1.W-F.270.173.
And first to Light expos'd the Venerable Shade. ....1.TrSt.509A.431.
This rich, this am'rous, venerable Knight, ...2.ChJM.481.38.
These three right Ancient Venerable Sires. ....2.ChWB.149.63.
The Walls in venerable Order grace: ....2.TemF.72.258.
And mount the Hill in venerable rows: ....6.14iv.14.47.
Suppliant the Venerable Father stands, ...Il.1.17.86.
Uprising slow, the venerable Sage ....Il.1.95.91.
All view'd with Awe the Venerable Man; ....Il.1.337.104.
Who thus the venerable King addrest. ....Il.3.318.208.
With that, the venerable Warrior rose; ....Il.10.150.8.
Not Calchas this, the venerable Seer; ....Il.13.101.109.
And thus the venerable Hero spoke. ....Il.14.158.165.
And thus the venerable Warrior spoke. ....Il.14.158A.165.
Ev'n Jove rever'd the Venerable Dame. ....Il.14.296.176.
With Joy, the venerable King reply'd. ....Il.23.718.518.
His Age, nor touch one venerable Hair, ...Il.24.192.544.
Thy Age, nor touch one venerable Hair, ...Il.24.222.546.
(Reply'd unmov'd the venerable Man) ....Il.24.269.547.
Sudden, (a venerable Sight!) appears; ....Il.24.586.561.
Those silver Hairs, that venerable Face; ....Il.24.601.562.
Before old Neleus' venerable walls. ....Od.3.6.86.
On themes remote the venerable Sage: ....Od.3.302.101.
Echeneus sage, a venerable man! ....Od.7.209.246.
And now, my venerable guest! declare ....Od.14.214.45.
The Queen invites thee, venerable guest! ....Od.17.634.163.
(His venerable eyes bedimm'd with tears) ....Od.24.325.365.
Dolius the first, the venerable man, ...Od.24.446.370.

VENERABLY
Cool Age advances venerably wise, ...Il.3.149.198.
She rent her Tresses, venerably grey, ...Il.22.512.477.

VENETIAN
Proud to catch cold at a Venetian door; ....3.Ep4.36.140.
Palladian walls, Venetian doors, ...4.HS6.193.263.

VENGEANCE
There purple Vengeance bath'd in Gore retires, ...1.W-F.417.193.
No wilful crime this heavy vengeance bred, ...1.TrFD.71.389.
Oh hear, and aid the Vengeance I require; ....1.TrSt.101.414.
And force unwilling Vengeance from the Sky? ....1.TrSt.301.422.
Yet Harbours Vengeance for the Tyrant's Feast. ....1.TrSt.347.424.
Curs'd Thebes the Vengeance it deserves, may prove,— ....1.TrSt.364.425.
To date his Vengeance; to what Bounds confin'd? ....1.TrSt.382.425.
The Vengeance due to this unlucky Steel? ....1.TrSt.771.442.
Be mine the Vengeance, as the Crime my own. ....1.TrSt.779.442.
But urging Vengeance and severer Fight; ....1.TrES.142.454.
An ample Vengeance to her injur'd Lord. ....1.TrUl.63.468.
An ample Vengeance to their injur'd Lord. ....1.TrUl.63A.469.
'Tis Strugling with a Vengeance, (quoth the Knight:) ....2.ChJM.767.52.
Provok'd to Vengeance, three large Leaves I tore, ...2.ChWB.415.77.
Shall feel sharp Vengeance soon o'ertake his Sins, ...2.RL2.125.167.
He springs to Vengeance with an eager pace, ...2.RL3.97.174.
Fancy restores what vengeance snatch'd away, ...2.ElAb.226.338.
On all the line a sudden vengeance waits, ...2.Elegy.37.365.
The distant Threats of Vengeance on his head, ...4.Arbu.348.120.
The Tales of Vengeance; Lyes so oft o'erthrown; ....4.Arbu.350A.121.
And promis'd Vengeance on a barb'rous age. ....5.DunB4.40.345.
(Infus'd in Vengeance of insulted Fame) ....6.82x.2.236.
Or learn the wastful Vengeance to remove, ...Il.1.85.90.
Apollo's Vengeance for his injur'd Priest. ....Il.1.120.93.
This whispers soft his Vengeance to controul, ...Il.1.257.99.
The daring Crime, behold the Vengeance too. ....Il.1.272.100.
Hard as it is, my Vengeance I suppress: ....Il.1.289.100.
Shall stream in Vengeance on my reeking Blade. ....Il.1.399.107.
T'avert the Vengeance of the Pow'r Divine. ....Il.1.501.112.
And sue for Vengeance to the Thund'ring God. ....Il.1.513.112.
If, fir'd to Vengeance at thy Priests request, ...Il.1.594.116.
And glut his Vengeance with my People slain. ....Il.1.725.122.

VENGEANCE (CONTINUED)
In gen'rous Vengeance of the King of Kings. ....Il.2.303.142.
Must shake, and heavy will the Vengeance fall! ....Il.2.451.149.
His Brother follows, and to Vengeance warms ....Il.2.701.159.
And shun the Vengeance of th' Herculean Race, ...Il.2.804.163.
Thus fond of Vengeance, with a furious Bound, ...Il.3.41.190.
In Thirst of Vengeance, at his Rival's Heart, ...Il.3.466.214.
At length, ripe Vengeance o'er their Heads impends, ...Il.4.41.223.
To boundless Vengeance the wide Realm be giv'n, ...Il.4.57.223.
Remember Troy, and give the Vengeance way. ....Il.4.64.224.
'Tis not in me the Vengeance to remove; ....Il.4.79.224.
With Thirst of Vengeance, and assaults the Foes. ....Il.5.757.303.
Or pour his Vengeance on the Lycian Crew. ....Il.5.831.305.
Stern Agamemnon swift to Vengeance flies, ...Il.6.66.327.
Shall rise in Vengeance, and lay waste the Plain. ....Il.8.594.424.
All this I give, his Vengeance to controul, ...Il.9.207.442.
Troy and her aids for ready Vengeance call; ....Il.9.305.449.
What calls for Vengeance but a Woman's Cause? ....Il.9.447.454.
In Vengeance of neglected Sacrifice; ....Il.9.658.467.
But urging Vengeance, and severer Fight; ....Il.12.496.99.
To Vengeance rising with a sudden Spring, ...Il.13.487.130.
And fraught with Vengeance, to the Victor turns; ....Il.13.734.139.
And wing'd the feather'd Vengeance at the Foe. ....Il.13.832.145.
And one devouring Vengeance swallow all. ....Il.13.974.152.
A worthy Vengeance for Prothœnor slain? ....Il.14.552.189.
Nor seem'd the Vengeance worthy such a Son; ....Il.15.30.195.
Nor pull th' unwilling Vengeance on thy Head, ...Il.15.36.195.
Forgive me Gods, and yield my Vengeance way: ....Il.15.129.201.
Then grim in Arms, with hasty Vengeance flies, ...Il.15.136.202.
Well was the Crime, and well the Vengeance spar'd; ....Il.15.256.207.
Press'd by the Vengeance of an angry Wife; ....Il.15.382.211.
Then, fir'd to Vengeance, rush'd amidst the Foe; ....Il.15.534.217.
So Mars, when human Crimes for Vengeance call, ...Il.15.726.223.
And with superior Vengeance, greatly glows. ....Il.16.678.270.
He pays due Vengeance to his Kinsman's Shade. ....Il.16.704.271.
The Vengeance due, and meditates the Fates; ....Il.16.786.274.
Who last, beneath thy Vengeance, press'd the Plain; ....Il.16.848.276.
Vent his mad Vengeance on our rocky Walls, ...Il.18.328.337.
Sacred to Vengeance, by this Hand expire; ....Il.18.395.340.
Not wreak my Vengeance on one guilty Land? ....Il.18.430.341.
If this be false, Heav'n all its Vengeance shed, ...Il.19.275.383.
Resolv'd on Vengeance, or resolv'd on Death. ....Il.20.209.402.
Thus, till the Grecian Vengeance is compleat; ....Il.21.148.427.
But not till Troy the destin'd Vengeance pay, ...Il.21.242.431.
And destin'd Vengeance on the perjur'd King. ....Il.21.530.443.
Then Pallas thus: Shall he whose Vengeance forms ....Il.22.233.465.
Who fear'd no Vengeance for Patroclus slain? ....Il.22.416.472.
Then his fell Soul a Thought of Vengeance bred, ...Il.22.495.476.
Sacred to Vengeance, instant shall expire, ...Il.23.31.488.
Vent his mad Vengeance on the sacred Dead: ....Il.24.150.541.
Nor vent on senseless Earth thy Vengeance vain, ...Il.24.173.543.
In Hector's Blood his Vengeance shall enjoy, ...Il.24.928.575.
Soon may your Sire discharge the vengeance due, ...Od.1.329.48.
Be future vengeance to the pow'rs divine. ....Od.1.351.49.
Cries to the Gods, and vengeance sleeps too long. ....Od.2.70.64.
How from my father should I vengeance dread? ....Od.2.155.69.
Vengeance I vow, and for your wrongs ye die. ....Od.2.170.70.
Vengeance deserv'd thy malice shall repress, ...Od.2.221.72.
Just was the vengeance, and to latest days ....Od.3.248.97.
An hour of vengeance for th' afflicted state; ....Od.3.266.98.
Hence on the guilty race her vengeance hurl'd ....Od.5.137.178.
Stern God! who rag'd with vengeance unrestrain'd, ...Od.6.393.230.
Swift vengeance waits: and Art subdues the strong! ....Od.8.368.283.
So may dread Jove (whose arm in vengeance forms ....Od.8.505.289.
But one, the vengeance fated from above ....Od.9.561.329.
That, all unarm'd, thy vengeance may have vent, ...Od.10.405.364.
But vengeance hastes amain! These eyes behold ....Od.11.150.388.
Is the foul fiend from human vengeance freed? ....Od.12.141.439.
Vengeance is on the wing, and heav'n in arms! ....Od.12.442.452.
Vengeance, ye Pow'rs, (he cries) and thou whose hand ....Od.12.445.452.
Vengeance, ye Gods! or I the skies forego, ...Od.12.450.452.
The vengeance vow'd for eyeless Polypheme. ....Od.13.145.12.
And menac'd vengeance, ere he reach'd his shore; ....Od.13.153.13.
(Weak, daring creatures!) is not vengeance thine? ....Od.13.169.13.
A mark of vengeance on the sable deep: ....Od.13.173.14.
An ample vengeance to their injur'd Lord. ....Od.13.230.17.
Vouchsafe the means of vengeance to debate, ...Od.13.441.27.
When Jove in vengeance gives a land away; ....Od.14.106.41.
While schemes of vengeance ripen in his breast. ....Od.14.133.42.
We turn'd to flight; the gath'ring vengeance spread ....Od.14.299.50.
Then doom'd high Jove due vengeance to prepare. ....Od.14.334.51.
And pull descending vengeance from on high. ....Od.15.349.86.
And vengeance strikes whom heav'n has doom'd to fall. ....Od.16.301.120.
The thinking mind, my soul to vengeance fires; ....Od.16.303.120.
And noting, ere we rise in vengeance prove ....Od.16.330.121.
Vengeance resolv'd 'tis dang'rous to deferr. ....Od.16.335.122.
His blood in vengeance smokes upon my spear. ....Od.16.457.129.
And call Jove's vengeance on their guilty deed. ....Od.17.63.135.
And call'd Jove's vengeance on the guilty deed. ....Od.17.71.136.
If death to these, and vengeance heav'n decree, ...Od.17.94.136.
Secret revolves; and plans the vengeance due. ....Od.17.183.140.
Dooms to full vengeance all th' offending train) ....Od.17.437.154.
We turn'd to flight; the gath'ring vengeance spread ....Od.17.520.157.
Lest dragg'd in vengeance, thou repent thy stay; ....Od.18.15.167.
Lest I imprint my vengeance in thy blood; ....Od.18.29.168.
Lest heav'n in vengeance send some mightier woe. ....Od.18.129.172.
But Vengeance and Ulysses wing their way. ....Od.18.174.175.
Absorpt in thought, on vengeance fix'd he stood. ....Od.18.394.186.
With vollied vengeance blast their tow'ring pride! ....Od.20.212.243.
Up-rose, and thus divin'd the vengeance near. ....Od.20.422.253.
The hour of vengeance, wretches, now is come, ...Od.22.51.289.
The arm of vengeance o'er their guilty heads; ....Od.22.331.302.
Phemius alone the hand of vengeance spar'd, ...Od.22.367.305.
And burst at once in vengeance on the foes. ....Od.23.34.320.
The will of Jove, he gave the vengeance way; ....Od.24.192.356.
The vengeance is compleat; the Suitor-train, ...Od.24.380.367.

VENGEANCE 570 VENUS'

VENGEANCE (CONTINUED)
Prove that we live, by vengeance on his head, ...Od.24.500.372.

VENGEFUL
For not the vengeful Pow'r, that glow'd with Rage, ...1.TrSt.782.442.
The sinners fall, and bless the vengeful day! ....6.21.20.69.
And last, the vengeful Arrows fix'd in Man. ....Il.1.70.89.
Rais'd on the Ruins of his vengeful Hand: ....Il.5.793.304.
Atrides o'er him shakes the vengeful Steel; ....Il.6.54.326.
Thy close Resentment, and their vengeful Ire. ....Il.6.409.347.
And there the vengeful *Spartan* fires his Train. ....Il.6.555.354.
Since vengeful Goddesses confed'rate join ....Il.7.37.364.
He said, and turn'd his Brother's vengeful Mind, ...Il.7.139.370.
And point at ev'ry Ship their vengeful Flame! ....Il.9.308.449.
Infernal *Jove*, the vengeful Fiends below, ...Il.9.584.463.
His Sisters follow'd; ev'n the vengeful Dame, ...Il.9.696.468.
When Night descending, from his vengeful Hand ....Il.10.235.12.
Nor stopp'd the Fury of his vengeful Hand, ...Il.10.568.28.
And vengeful Anger fill'd his sacred Breast. ....Il.10.605.29.
The vengeful Monarch gave this stern Reply; ....Il.11.179.43.
The vengeful Victor rages round the Fields ....Il.11.341.49.
He sigh'd; but sighing, rais'd his vengeful Steel, ...Il.11.415.53.
From *Paris'* Bow a vengeful Arrow fled. ....Il.11.709.66.
A transient Pity touch'd his vengeful Breast. ....Il.11.735.68.
(Young as they were) the vengeful Squadrons led. ....Il.11.845.74.
And made, with force, the vengeful Weapon fly: ....Il.13.510.131.
Doom'd by great *Ajax'* vengeful Lance to bleed; ....Il.17.339.300.
So burns the vengeful Hornet (Soul all o'er) ....Il.17.642.313.
Not by my self, but vengeful *Ate* driv'n; ....Il.19.92.375.
What-time, a vengeful Monster of the Main ....Il.20.178.401.
And brave that vengeful Heart, that dreadful Hand. ....Il.20.426.412.
Then fell on *Polydore* his vengeful Rage, ...Il.20.471.414.
What hope of Mercy from this vengeful Foe? ....Il.22.165.460.
All hail, *Patroclus!* let thy vengeful Ghost ....Il.23.220.498.
The proud Oppressors fly the vengeful sword. ....Od.1.154.40.
And while in wrath to vengeful Fiends she cries, ...Od.2.157.69.
How from their hell would vengeful Fiends arise? ....Od.2.158.69.
But lives a victim for thy vengeful sword; ....Od.4.736.153.
And vengeful slaughter, fierce for human blood. ....Od.8.562.293.
Then forth the vengeful instrument I bring; ....Od.9.451.324.
And vengeful murther red with human blood. ....Od.11.756.423.
Restrain'd the rage the vengeful foe exprest, ...Od.14.311.50.
Yet 'scap'd he death; and vengeful of his wrong ....Od.15.260.80.
Touch'd by *Diana's* vengeful arrow, dy'd. ....Od.15.514.95.
"Lest when the bowl inflames, in vengeful mood ....Od.16.314.121.
To fell the Giant at one vengeful blow, ...Od.18.105.172.
Ulysses, cautious of the vengeful foe, ...Od.18.438.189.
Else if the Gods my vengeful arm sustain, ...Od.19.571.224.
But vengeful *Pallas* with preventing speed ....Od.20.467.256.
Young as I am, thy Prince's vengeful hand ....Od.21.401.279.
Ulysses vengeful from the *Trojan* shore; ....Od.22.42.288.
Ulysses brandish'd high his vengeful steel, ...Od.22.324.301.

VENI'S
When pamper'd *Cupids*, bestly *Veni's*, ... 6.135.39.367.

VENIAL
Those venial sins, an Atom, or a Straw: ....4.JD4.243.47.
To *W[alpole]* guilty of some venial Sin, ...4.EpS2.162.322 .
With venial freedom let me now demand ....Od.1.219.43.
Venial discourse unblam'd with him to hold. ....Od.19.112.198.

VENICE
From dirt and sea-weed as proud Venice rose; ....3.EOM4.292.155.
From dirt and sea-weed as proud Venice rose; .... 6.130.2.358.

VENOM
Half Froth, half Venom, spits himself abroad, ...4.Arbu.320.119.
Rage strait Collects his Venom all at once, ...6.26i.14.79.
Or by some Flea with mortal venom stung? ....6.96ii.30Z6.271.
Of vegetable venom, taints the plain; ....Od.4.320.134.

VENOM'D
The World's great Ruler, felt her venom'd Dart; ....Il.19.101.376.
But venom'd was the bread, and mix'd the bowl, ...Od.10.272.355.
Yet him, my guest, thy venom'd rage hath stung; ....Od.19.115.198.

VENT
Their growing Fears in secret Murmurs vent, ...1.TrSt.225.420.
Let him not dare to vent his dang'rous Thought; ....2.ChJM.164.23.
And all the Furies issued at the Vent. ....2.RL4.92.191.
Which first should issue thro the narrow Vent: ....2.TemF.492.287.
And all your Courtly Civet-Cats can vent, ...4.EpS2.183.324.
The gushing Waters find a Vent below: ....6.33.4.99.
The gushing Waters found a Vent below: ....6.33.4A.99.
Or if the Purpose of thy Heart thou vent, ...Il.12.271.91.
The Soul came issuing at the narrow Vent: ....Il.13.842.145.
But dare not murmur, dare not vent a Sigh; ....Il.15.123.201.
The Soul, exhaling, issu'd at the vent. ....Il.16.738.272.
These Sons of *Panthus* vent their haughty Mind. ....Il.17.26.288.
Vent his mad Vengeance on our rocky Walls, ...Il.18.328.337.
And vent their Anger, impotent and loud. ....Il.20.303.407.
Wide on the lonely Beach to vent his Woes. ....Il.24.20.535.
Vent his mad Vengeance on the sacred Dead: ....Il.24.150.541.
Nor vent on senseless Earth thy Vengeance vain, ...Il.24.173.543.
Nine Days to vent our Sorrows I request, ...Il.24.834.571.
That, all unarm'd, thy vengeance may have vent, ...Od.10.405.364.
Trembling the Spectres glide, and plaintive vent ....Od.24.7.347.

VENT'ROUS
Or tread the path by vent'rous Heroes trod, ...5.DunB1.201.284.
Alone, with vent'rous Arms, the King of *Crete;* .... Il.13.573.133.
Long since too vent'rous, at thy bold Command, ...Il.14.283.176.
His vent'rous Spear first drew the Hero's Gore; ....Il.16.978.281.
His vent'rous Act the white-arm'd Queen survey'd, ...Il.20.144.400.
Close up the vent'rous Youth resolves to keep, ...Il.23.503.510.

VENT'ROUS (CONTINUED)
The lives of others, vent'rous of their own. ....Od.3.89.90.
Propos'd, who first the vent'rous deed should try? ....Od.9.390.322.
One vent'rous game this hand has won to-day, ...Od.22.7.286.

VENTS
Thro thousand Vents, impatient forth they flow, ...2.TemF.481.286.
There in his seat two spacious Vents appear, ...5.DunA2.81.108.
There in his seat two spacious Vents appear, ...5.DunB2.85.299.
The daring *Rhodian* vents his haughty Boast. ....Il.5.783.303.
And vents his Soul effus'd with gushing Gore. ....Il.16.387.258.
So grieves *Achilles;* and impetuous vents ....Il.18.377.339.
Thou too, *Patroclus!* (thus his Heart he vents) ....Il.19.335.386.
He vents his Fury, and inflames the Crowd. ....Il.20.402.412.
He vents his Fury on the flying Crew, ...Il.21.225.430.
Repast unheeded, while he vents his Woes. ....Il.24.160.542.
And *Nestor's* Youngest stops the vents of breath. ....Od.3.579.116.
Each vents a groan, and drops a tender tear; ....Od.22.483.312.

VENTUR'D
Set up with these, he ventur'd on the Town. ....6.49i.7.137.
"Hast thou for these now ventur'd from the Shore, ...6.96ii.57.273.

VENTURE
But, at these Years, to venture on the Fair! ....2.ChJM.208.24.
(Should Ripley venture, all the World would smile) ....4.2HE1.186.211.
Will venture it now—you have ....6.68.11.196.
Or in a Bean-shell venture from the shore ....6.96ii.30Z13.271.
Dares greatly venture for a rich Reward? ....Il.10.362.19.

VENTURE'S
The Venture's greater, I'll presume to say, ...2.ChJM.182.23.

VENTURES
Who ventures Sacred Marriage to defame. ....2.ChJM.223A.25.

VENUS
Celestial *Venus* haunts *Idalia's* Groves, ...1.PSp.65.67.
In Woods bright *Venus* with *Adonis* stray'd. ....1.PSu.61.76.
Averse from *Venus* and the Nuptial Joy; ....1.TrVP.18.377.
Which *Venus* tunes, and all her Loves inspire. ....1.TrSP.36.395.
Which *Cupid* tunes, and *Venus* does inspire. ....1.TrSP.36A.395.
Have pity, *Venus*, on your Poet's Pains! ....1.TrSP.70.396.
And gave to *Venus* all my Life to come; ....1.TrSP.92.397.
Venus for those had rapt thee to the Skies, ...1.TrSP.101.398.
Venus for thee shall smooth her native Main. ....1.TrSP.251.404.
And lovely *Venus*, Goddess of Delight, ...2.ChJM.328.30.
Fair *Venus* gave me Fire and sprightly Grace, ...2.ChWB.325.72.
And *Venus* sets ere *Mercury* can rise: ....2.ChWB.370.75.
And *Venus* sets when *Mercury* does rise: ....2.ChWB.370A.75.
This, the blest Lover shall for *Venus* take, ...2.RL5.135.211.
The torch of *Venus* burns not for the dead; ....2.ElAb.258.340.
Ah spare me, Venus! let me, let me rest! ....4.HOde1.2.151.
O spare me, Venus! let me, let me rest ....4.HOde1.2A.151.
O long a stranger, Venus! let me rest ....4.HOde1.2B.151.
Venus shall give him Form, and Anstis Birth. ....4.1HE6.82.243.
As taught by Venus, Paris learnt the art ....5.DunA2.209.127.
See graceless Venus to a Virgin turn'd, ...5.DunA3.103.159.
As taught by Venus, Paris learnt the art ....5.DunB2.217.306.
See graceless Venus to a Virgin turn'd, ...5.DunB3.111.325.
But chief her shrine where naked Venus keeps, ...5.DunB4.307.374.
This glorious Youth, and add one Venus more. ....5.DunB4.330.375.
Venus beheld her, 'midst her Crowd of Slaves, ...6.9vi.1.21.
Venus and *Pallas* both had Children been. ....6.37.6.106.
A Copy of young *Venus* might have took: ....6.37.8.106.
"'Tis Venus, Venus gives these arms; ....6.140.27.379.
"'Tis Venus, Venus gives these arms; ....6.140.27.379.
With which a Lover golden *Venus* arms; ....Il.3.94.194.
But *Venus* trembl'd for the Prince of Troy: ....Il.3.460.214.
My Absence ill, let *Venus* ease his Care. ....Il.3.502.215.
Should *Venus* leave thee, ev'ry Charm must fly, ...Il.3.515.216.
Not thus fair *Venus* helps her favour'd Knight, ...Il.4.13.221.
If *Venus* mingle in the martial Band, ...Il.5.168.275.
But Heav'nly *Venus*, mindful of the Love ....Il.5.385.285.
The raging Chief in chace of *Venus* flies: ....Il.5.408.286.
And, calling *Venus*, thus addrest his Child. ....Il.5.518.293.
First rosie *Venus* felt his brutal Rage; ....Il.5.557.295.
Venus, and *Phœbus* with the dreadful Bow, ...Il.5.946.311.
And *Venus* only found Resistance here. ....Il.5.1015.315.
The heav'nly *Venus* first his Fury found, ...Il.5.1084.318.
Like golden *Venus* tho' she charm'd the Heart, ...Il.9.512.458.
How long (To *Venus* thus apart she cry'd) ....Il.14.219.172.
Ah yet, will *Venus* aid *Saturnia's* Joy, ...Il.14.221.172.
Then *Venus* to the Courts of *Jove* withdrew; ....Il.14.257.173.
The Son of *Venus* to the Counsel yields; ....Il.17.558.310.
From heav'nly *Venus* thou deriv'st thy Strain, ...Il.20.136.399.
So dread, so fierce, as *Venus* is to me; ....Il.21.503.442.
(The Gift of *Venus* on her bridal Day) ....Il.22.603.481.
Celestial *Venus* hover'd o'er his Head, ...Il.23.228.498.
Resembling *Venus* in attractive state. ....Od.4.20.121.
(Her beauteous cheeks the blush of *Venus* wear, ...Od.17.46.134.
Such *Venus* shines, when with a measur'd bound ....Od.18.229.178.
Her cheeks the warmer blush of *Venus* wear, ...Od.19.66.196.
Venus in tender delicacy rears ....Od.20.82.236.

VENUS'
But *Mars* on thee might look with *Venus'* Eyes. ....1.TrSP.102.398.
Yet led astray by *Venus'* soft Delights, ...2.ChJM.5.15.
Anchises' Son, by *Venus'* stol'n Embrace, ...Il.2.993.170.
Fair *Venus'* Neck, her Eyes that sparkled Fire, ...Il.3.489.215.
To whom the Chief of *Venus'* Race begun. ....Il.5.217.278.
This said, she wip'd from *Venus'* wounded Palm ....Il.5.505.292.
Then *Phœbus* bore the Chief of *Venus'* Race ....Il.5.541.294.
The Seed of *Thetis* thus to *Venus'* Son. ....Il.20.213.402.
Thetis' this Day, or *Venus'* Offspring dies, ...Il.20.248.404.

VERSE (CONTINUED)
But, gentle Colley, should thy verse prevail, ...6.116vi.3.327.
On Milton's Verse does B[en]tl[e]y comment— Know ....6.116viii.3.328.
Against the *Gothick* Sons of frozen Verse; ....6.128.14.356.
Quoth *Cibber* to *Pope,* tho' in Verse you foreclose, ...6.149.1.397.
In ever-consecrating verse, complain. ....Od.24.78.352.

VERSE-MAN
Verse-man or Prose-man, term me which you will, ...4.HS1.64.11.

VERSES
P. Alas! few Verses touch their nicer Ear; ....4.HS1.33.7.
Had no *new Verses,* or *new Suit* to show; ....4.JD4.13.27.
But turn a Wit, and scribble verses too? ....4.JD2.54.137.
One wou'd move Love; by Rhymes; but Verses charms ....4.JD2A.23.134.
But turns a Wit, and writes Love Verses too? ....4.JD2A.60.136.
That turn'd ten thousand Verses, now stands still. ....4.2HE2.79.171.
I'll e'en leave Verses to the Boys at school: ....4.2HE2.201.179.
But were his Verses vile, his Whisper base, ...4.EpS1.49.301.
Nor think your Verses Sterling, ...6.58.6.171.
He'll lose his Pains and Verses too; ....6.77.6.214.
Purge all your verses from the sin of wit ....6.82ix(f).2.235.
Cibber! write all thy Verses upon Glasses, ...6.131ii.1.360.

VERTÙ
Impale a Glow-worm, or Vertù profess, ...5.DunB4.569.398.

VERTUE
By Vertue of this pow'rful Constellation, ...2.ChWB.327.72.

VERTUE'S
For Vertue's self may too much Zeal be had; ....4.1HE6.26.239.

VERTUMNUS
But most *Vertumnus* did his Love profess, ...1.TrVP.27A.378.
Like these, *Vertumnus* own'd his faithful Flame, ...1.TrVP.27.378.
A Female Form at last *Vertumnus* wears, ...1.TrVP.45.379.
Fix on *Vertumnus,* and reject the rest. ....1.TrVP.82.380.
To distant Lands *Vertumnus* never roves; ....1.TrVP.85.380.
Think, 'tis *Vertumnus* begs you to be kind! ....1.TrVP.107.381.

VERY
And, in the very Act, restore his Sight: ....2.ChJM.652.46.
A very Woman, and a very Wife! ....2.ChWB.206.66.
A very Woman, and a very Wife! ....2.ChWB.206.66.
And view'd a Friend, with Eyes so very kind, ...2.ChWB.234.68.
From pride, from pride, our very reas'ning springs; ....3.EOM1.161.35.
So, cast and mingled with his very frame, ...3.EOM2.137.71.
Ev'n those who dwell beneath its very zone, ...3.EOM2.227.83.
Ev'n those who dwell beneath her very zone, ...3.EOM2.227A.83.
That very life his learned hunger craves, ...3.EOM3.63.98.
The very best will variously incline, ...3.EOM4.143.141.
Less pleasing far than Virtue's very tears. ....3.EOM4.320.159.
Others so very close, they're hid from none; ....3.Ep1.111.23.
A Rebel to the very king he loves; ....3.Ep1.203.32.
That very Cæsar, born in Scipio's days, ...3.Ep1.216.33.
A very Heathen in the carnal part, ...3.Ep2.67.55.
Sick of herself thro' very selfishness! ....3.Ep2.146.62.
So very reasonable, so unmov'd, ...3.Ep2.165.64.
For very want; he could not build a wall. ....3.Ep3.324.120.
For very want; he could not pay a dow'r. ....3.Ep3.326.120.
'Twas very want that sold them for two pound. ....3.Ep3.328.120.
A Man was hang'd for very honest Rhymes. ....4.HS1.146.19.
Whose Air cries Arm! whose very Look's an Oath: ....4.JD4.261.47.
And always thinks the very thing he ought: ....4.HS2.130.65.
She turns her very Sister to a Job, ...4.HAdv.21.77.
His very Minister who spy'd them first, ...4.Arbu.71.100.
God knows, may hurt the very ablest Head. ....4.2HE2.103.173.
Late, very late, correctness grew our care, ...4.2HE1.272.219.
So take it in the very words of *Creech.]* ....4.1HE6.4.237.
And even the very Dogs at ease! ....4.HS6.140.259.
And what, the very best of all? ....4.HS6.152.259.
And like its Master, very low, ...4.1HE7.78.273.
That very night he longs to lye alone. ....4.1HE1.149.291.
But 'faith your very Friends will soon be sore; ....4.EpS1.23.299.
And for that very cause I print to day. ....4.EpS2.3.313.
The very worsted still look'd black and blue: ....5.DunA2.142.118.
And see! thy very Gazetteers give o'er, ...5.DunB1.215.285.
Now, see thy very Gazetteers give o'er, ...5.DunB1.215A.285.
The very worsted still look'd black and blue. ....5.DunB2.150.302.
And what the last? a very Poet still. ....5.DunB4.164.357.
Thy very want of Tongue makes thee a kind of Fame. ....6.8.27.18.
Was very learn'd, but not polite— ....6.10.96.27.
Th' impartial worms that very *dust* devour. ....6.22.18.72.
Tis plain, tis very plain, was *Cary.* ....6.44.28.123.
Man is a very Worm by Birth, ...6.53.5.161.
Tho very chaste people, to die of a Clap. ....6.69iii.2.201.
The very Tombs now vanish'd like their dead! ....6.71.4.202.
For I am very large, and very wide. ....6.88.4.249.
For I am very large, and very wide. ....6.88.4.249.
"Do something very fine, and wise—" ....6.119.7A.336.
So very much is said, ...6.133.2A.363.
So very reasonable, so unmov'd, ...6.139.9.377.
Sick of herself thro' very Selfishness. ....6.154.32.403.
Struck at the word, my very heart was dead: ....Od.10.588.372.
But lives a very Brother in my heart. ....Od.14.170.43.
The very truth I undisguis'd declare: ....Od.17.18.133.
All else have cast him from their very thought, ...Od.21.217.270.

VESPASIAN'S
And give to Titus old Vespasian's due. ....6.71.18.203.

VESSEL
Now here, now there, the reeling Vessel throw: ....1.TrSt.268.421.
So mounts the bounding Vessel o'er the Main: ....1.TrUl.10.465.
In a *Phænician* Vessel took my Flight; ....1.TrUl.149.470.
But now secure the painted Vessel glides, ...2.RL2.47.162.
So weak a Vessel, and so rich a Prize! ....4.JD4.229.45.
If our intemp'rate Youth the Vessel drains? ....4.HS2.90.61.
Whether my Vessel be first-rate or not? ....4.2HE2.297.185.
Well might, alas! that threaten'd vessel fail, ...6.3.3.7.
So when the first bold Vessel dar'd the Seas, ...6.11.38.31.
When the first Vessel dar'd the Seas, ...6.11.38A.31.
'Twas Night: the Chiefs beside their Vessel lie, ...Il.1.622.117.
Sev'n were his Ships; each Vessel fifty row, ...Il.2.876.165.
The Gales blow grateful, and the Vessel flies: ....Il.7.8.363.
He climb'd his Vessel, prodigal of Breath, ...Il.13.839.145.
One kept the Shore, and one the Vessel trod; ....Il.15.486.216.
The shining Charger to his Vessel sent. ....Il.23.702.517.
To arm the vessel, *Mentor!* by thy care, ...Od.2.286.75.
The winged vessel studious I prepare, ...Od.2.325.77.
Wide o'er the bay, by vessel vessel rides; ....Od.2.333.77.
Wide o'er the bay, by vessel vessel rides; ....Od.2.333.77.
The Goddess shov'd the vessel from the shores, ...Od.2.438.82.
Lo! on the seas prepar'd the vessel stands; ....Od.2.450.83.
The ready vessel rides, the sailors ready stand. ....Od.2.455.83.
Now on the coast of *Pyle* the vessel falls, ...Od.3.5.86.
There in the vessel shall I pass the night; ....Od.3.466.109.
Across the deep his lab'ring vessel bore. ....Od.4.688.151.
His vessel sunk, and dear companions lost, ...Od.4.759.155.
Or was the vessel seiz'd by fraud or force? ....Od.4.871.159.
(*Noëmon* cry'd) the vessel was resign'd. ....Od.4.873.159.
With twenty chosen mates a vessel mann'd; ....Od.4.895.160.
With wine and viands I the vessel stor'd: ....Od.4.985.163.
Where anchor'd in the bay the vessel rides; ....Od.4.1030.166.
To store the vessel let the care be mine, ...Od.5.213.181.
Then o'er the vessel rais'd the taper mast, ...Od.5.324.187.
To shield the vessel from the rowling sea; ....Od.5.519.197.
But the tall mast above the vessel rear, ...Od.6.323.226.
The vast profound, and bid the vessel fly: ....Od.8.34.263.
They launch the vessel, and unfurl the sails, ...Od.8.47.264.
For there no vessel with vermilion prore, ...Od.9.145.311.
And nine fat goats each vessel bears away: ....Od.9.185.313.
I left my vessel at the point of land, ...Od.9.225.316.
Fast by your shore the gallant vessel broke. ....Od.9.338.320.
And reach our vessel on the winding shore. ....Od.9.548.328.
Roll'd back the vessel to the Island's side: ....Od.9.572.330.
Some vessel, not his own, transport him o'er; ....Od.9.626.332.
Clear of the rocks th' impatient vessel flies; ....Od.10.151.347.
Haste to thy vessel on the sea-beat shore, ...Od.10.477.366.
Left the black vessel by the murm'ring main. ....Od.10.528.368.
There fix thy vessel in the lonely bay, ...Od.10.606.373.
While the wing'd vessel flew along the tyde: ....Od.11.8.379.
Or saw gay vessel stem the wat'ry plain, ...Od.11.154.389.
Thus o'er the rolling surge the vessel flies, ...Od.12.1.427.
Oh if thy vessel plow the direful waves ....Od.12.133.438.
The vessel light along the level glides. ....Od.12.187.441.
While to the shore the rapid vessel flies, ...Od.12.218.442.
No more the vessel plow'd the dreadful wave, ...Od.12.244.443.
Strain ev'ry nerve, and bid the vessel fly. ....Od.12.255.444.
Now from the rocks the rapid vessel flies, ...Od.12.312.447.
Thus I: and while to shore the vessel flies, ...Od.12.359.448.
So mounts the bounding vessel o'er the main. ....Od.13.101.6.
In a *Phænician* vessel took my flight, ...Od.13.316.22.
(Stripp'd of my own) and to the vessel bound. ....Od.14.380.53.
To launch thy vessel for thy natal shore: ....Od.15.18.70.
Send to the town thy vessel with thy friends, ...Od.15.44.71.
No farther from our vessel, I implore, ...Od.15.224.79.
Your vessel loaded, and your traffic past, ...Od.15.485.93.
A year they traffic, and their vessel load. ....Od.15.492.94.
Gave her the sign, and to his vessel went. ....Od.15.500.94.
Prepar'd to launch the freighted vessel rides; ....Od.15.508.94.
Between the Heroe and the Vessel pour ....Od.15.569.98.
What vessel bore him o'er the wat'ry way? ....Od.16.58.105.
With speed they guide the vessel to the shores; ....Od.16.346.123.
See to the port secure the vessel fly! ....Od.16.371.124.
They moor the vessel and unlade the stores: ....Od.16.375.124.
When first our vessel anchor'd in your road. ....Od.17.185.140.
Nor saw gay vessel stem the surgy plain, ...Od.23.287.337.
What port receiv'd thy vessel from the main? ....Od.24.351.365.
Reliev'd our weary'd vessel from the sea. ....Od.24.360.366.

VESSEL'S
His Armour buckling at his Vessel's side. ....Il.10.40.4.
This said, I climb'd my vessel's lofty side; ....Od.9.207.314.

VESSELS
And ring suspected Vessels ere they buy, ...2.ChWB.101.61.
And sound suspected Vessels ere they buy, ...2.ChWB.101A.61.
Or when rich *China* Vessels, fal'n from high, ...2.RL3.159.180.
Haste, launch thy Vessels, fly with Speed away, ...Il.1.235.98.
Where near his Tents his hollow Vessels lay. ....Il.1.403.107.
Far, far from *Ilion* should thy Vessels sail, ...Il.1.547.114.
Our Cordage torn, decay'd our Vessels lie, ...Il.2.163.136.
Nor drew his sable Vessels to the Flood. ....Il.2.208.138.
Their Troops in thirty sable Vessels sweep ....Il.2.618.157.
In forty Vessels cut the yielding Tide. ....Il.2.640.157.
A hundred Vessels in long Order stand, ...Il.2.695.159.
Each leads ten Vessels thro' the yielding Tide. ....Il.2.754.161.
In forty Vessels under *Meges* move, ...Il.2.761.162.
His forty Vessels follow thro' the Main. ....Il.2.784.162.
Led nine swift Vessels thro' the foamy Seas; ....Il.2.794.163.
Lo his proud Vessels scatter'd o'er the Main, ...Il.4.216.231.
'Till yon' tall Vessels blaze with *Trojan* Fire? ....Il.4.283.234.
(The hollow Vessels to his Voice reply'd) ....Il.8.275.410.
The *Myrmidonian* Tents and Vessels lay; ....Il.9.244.444.
Then shall you see our parting Vessels crown'd, ...Il.9.471.455.
Consume your Vessels, and approach my own; ....Il.9.768.472.

VESSELS (CONTINUED)

Then to their Vessels, thro' the gloomy Shades, ...Il.9.773.472.
All Night the Chiefs before their Vessels lay, ...Il.10.1.1.
If once your Vessels catch the *Trojan* Fire? ....Il.15.597.219.
While the black Vessels smoak'd with human Gore. ....Il.16.2.233.
Arm, e'er our Vessels catch the spreading Flame; ....Il.16.158.244.
Full fifty Vessels, mann'd with fifty Oars: ....Il.16.207.247.
To their black Vessels all the *Greeks* return'd. ....Il.19.290.384.
Greece sheath'd in Arms, beside her Vessels stood; ....Il.20.2.392.
The Vessels tremble as the Gods alight. ....Il.20.50.396.
Deny your vessels; ye deny in vain; ....Od.2.357.78.
Untouch'd and sacred may these vessels stand, ...Od.2.396.80.
He join'd our vessels in the *Lesbian* bay, ...Od.3.203.95.
Before the whistling winds the vessels fly, ...Od.3.214.96.
Tydides' vessels touch'd the wish'd-for shore: ....Od.3.220.96.
With shatter'd vessels, and disabled oars: ....Od.3.381.105.
One seek the harbour where the vessels moor, ...Od.3.536.113.
There anchor'd vessels safe in harbour lye, ...Od.4.485.143.
Nor friends are there, nor vessels to convey, ...Od.5.24.172.
His vessels loaded with a plenteous store ....Od.5.50.174.
There all his vessels sunk beneath the wave! ....Od.5.139.178.
Beneath cold *Ismarus,* our vessels bore. ....Od.9.42.304.
Impell'd, our vessels on *Cythera* cast. ....Od.9.92.306.
And twelve large vessels of unmingled wine, ...Od.9.238.316.
Full pails, and vessels of the milking trade. ....Od.9.263.317.
And gain'd the Island where our vessels lay. ....Od.9.636.332.
And all my vessels, all my people, lost! ....Od.9.648.333.
What rare device those vessels might enclose? ....Od.10.39.341.
Mean-while our vessels plough the liquid plain, ...Od.10.58.342.
The crackling vessels burst; hoarse groans arise, ...Od.10.141.347.
Before the *Boreal* blast the vessels fly; ....Od.14.285.49.
And tilting o'er the bay the vessels ride: ....Od.14.289.49.
No sailors there, no vessels to convey, ...Od.17.166.139.
His vessels moor'd, (an incommodious port!) ....Od.19.220.204.
That anchor'd in his port the vessels stand, ...Od.19.333.210.

VEST

His Manly Members in th'Immortal Vest, ...1.TrES.341.462.
around her Shoulders flew the waving Vest. ....1.TrUl.105.469.
Gave him the cassock, surcingle, and vest; ....5.DunA2.326.141.
All as the vest, appear'd the wearer's frame, ...5.DunA3.31.154.
Gave him the cassock, surcingle, and vest. ....5.DunB2.350.314.
All as the vest, appear'd the wearer's frame, ...5.DunB3.39.322.
Or vest dull Flatt'ry in the sacred Gown; ....5.DunB4.97.350.
First on his Limbs a slender Vest he drew, ...Il.2.53.129.
The Goddess softly shook her silken Vest ....Il.3.479.214.
The purple Current wand'ring o'er his Vest. ....Il.5.145.274.
His mighty Limbs in an immortal Vest. ....Il.5.1117.321.
His manly Members in th' immortal Vest; ....Il.16.828.275.
The Youths all graceful in the glossy Vest; ....Il.18.686.356.
Weeping she grasp'd his Knees: Th' Ambrosial Vest ....Il.21.591.446.
The duteous dame receiv'd the purple vest: ....Od.1.550.58.
The purple vest with decent care dispos'd, ...Od.1.551.58.
O'er his fair limbs a flow'ry vest he threw, ...Od.3.596.117.
His face he shrowded with his purple vest: ....Od.4.152.127.
Th' imperial mantle o'er his vest he threw; ....Od.4.414.140.
Or in their tyrant-Minions vest the pow'r: ....Od.4.919.161.
Ulysses rob'd him in the cloak and vest. ....Od.5.294.185.
Clogg'd by the cumbrous vest *Calypso* gave: ....Od.5.410.192.
His limbs dis-cumbers of the clinging vest, ...Od.5.474.195.
Propitious to my wants, a Vest supply ....Od.6.215.220.
A vest and robe, with rich embroid'ry gay: ....Od.6.254.222.
Ordains the fleecy couch, and cov'ring vest; ....Od.7.428.258.
Before his eyes the purple vest he drew, ...Od.8.81.267.
A vest, a robe, and imitate your King: ....Od.8.428.287.
A vest and tunick o'er me next she threw, ...Od.10.429.365.
My limbs, and o'er me cast a silken vest. ....Od.10.648.375.
Tho' labour'd gold and many a dazling vest ....Od.13.13.2.
This does a tunic and white vest convey, ...Od.13.84.5.
Around her shoulders flew the waving vest, ...Od.13.272.19.
His vest succinct then girding round his waste, ...Od.14.83.40.
Be then my prize a tunic and a vest; ....Od.14.437.56.
There all but I, well fenc'd with cloak and vest, ...Od.14.538.63.
A cloak and vest—but I am nothing now! ....Od.14.575.64.
For here one vest suffices ev'ry swain; ....Od.14.581.65.
Close to the less'ning waist the vest infold; ....Od.18.340.184.
Down from the swelling loins, the vest unbound ....Od.18.341.184.
A vest, that dazzl'd like a cloudless sun: ....Od.19.270.208.
A mantle purple-ting'd, and radiant vest, ...Od.19.275.208.
The vest much envy'd on your native coast, ...Od.19.292.209.
Adjusting to his limbs the tatter'd vest, ...Od.19.591.225.
His ragged vest then drawn aside disclos'd ....Od.21.230.270.
Embroider'd sandals, a rich cloak and vest, ...Od.21.367.277.

VESTAL

Demure and chast as any Vestal Nun, ...2.ChJM.202.24.
No Kitchens emulate the Vestal Fire. ....4.JD2.112.143.

VESTAL'S

What means this tumult in a Vestal's veins? ....2.ElAb.4.319.
How happy is the blameless Vestal's lot! ....2.ElAb.207.336.

VESTMENTS

Ah no—in sacred vestments may'st thou stand, ...2.ElAb.325.346.

VESTS

The Gold, the Vests, the Tripods number'd o'er; ....1.TrUl.95.469.
As many Vests, as many Mantles told, ...Il.24.283.548.
With liquid odors, and embroider'd vests. ....Od.4.60.122.
Where their fair vests *Phæacian* virgins lave. ....Od.6.44.207.
The vests, the robes, and heaps of shining gold; ....Od.8.456.288.
The robes the vests are rang'd, and heaps of gold: ....Od.8.476.288.
The gold, the vests, the tripods, number'd o'er: ....Od.13.262.18.
Far other vests thy limbs majestic grace, ...Od.16.198.113.
In squalid vests with many a gaping rent, ...Od.17.412.152.
Dis-roab'd, their vests apart in order lay, ...Od.20.312.248.

VESTS (CONTINUED)

Roab thee in heav'nly vests, and round thee weep. ....Od.24.76.351.
Twelve cloaks, twelve vests, twelve tunicks stiff with gold, ...Od.24.321.365.

VESTURE

If so, a cloak and vesture be my meed; ....Od.14.177.44.
Safe in thy mother's care the vesture lay, ...Od.15.140.75.

VESTURES

There lay the Vestures, of no vulgar Art, ...Il.6.360.343.
There polish'd chests embroider'd vestures grac'd; ....Od.2.383.79.
Of brass, of vestures, and resplendent Ore; ....Od.5.51.174.
And plunge the vestures in the cleansing wave: ....Od.6.106.211.
(The vestures cleans'd o'erspread the shelly sand, ...Od.6.107.211.
Receiv'd the vestures, and the mules unbound. ....Od.7.6.233.
Embroider'd vestures, gold, and brass are laid ....Od.16.254.117.
At once his vestures change; at once she sheds ....Od.16.478.130.

VET'RAN

For thee the hardy Vet'ran drops a tear, ...6.113.5.320.

VET'RANS

Dead, by regardless Vet'rans born on high ....6.130.25.358.

VETERANS

See how the World its Veterans rewards! ....3.Ep2.243.69.

VEX

Sure *some* to *vex,* but never *all* to *please;* ....1.EOC.505.295.
Come down, and vex your tender Heart no more: ....2.ChJM.790.53.
How can ye, Mothers, vex your Children so? ....6.14ii.7.43.
Riches that vex, and Vanities that tire. ....6.86.4.245.
Peace, factious Monster, born to vex the State, ...Il.2.306.142.
So when inclement Winters vex the Plain ....Il.3.5.188.
Nor with new Treaties vex my Peace in vain. ....Il.9.411.452.
Unwelcome news, or vex the royal ear; ....Od.15.401.88.

VEX'D

Nor less Impatience vex'd her Am'rous Squire, ...2.ChJM.494.39.
Vex'd with vain rage, and impotently great, ...6.20.20.66.
His left with Tongs turns the vex'd Metal round; ....Il.18.549.348.
White curl the waves, and the vex'd ocean roars. ....Od.4.788.156.
Twelve days, while *Boreas* vex'd th' aerial space, ...Od.19.230.204.

VEXING

And vexing ev'ry Wight, tears Cloaths and all to Tatters. ....6.14ii.36.44.
This vexing him who gave her Birth, ...6.119.9.337.
This vexing him that gave her Birth, ...6.119.9B.337.

VEXT

And when three Sov'reigns dy'd, could scarce be vext, ...4.EpS1.107.306.
Vext to be still in town, I knit my brow, ...6.45.49.126.
Vext when he spoke, yet still they heard him speak. ....Il.2.272.140.
Long gall'd by Herdsmen, and long vext by Hounds, ...Il.17.743.317.

VI'LET

Here the bright Crocus and blue Vi'let glow; ....1.PSp.31.63.

VI'LETS

Here on green Banks the blushing Vi'lets glow; ....1.PSp.31A.63.
Thick new-born Vi'lets a soft Carpet spread, ...Il.14.397.182.

VIAL

A Vial next she fills with fainting Fears, ...2.RL4.85.190.
He breaks the Vial whence the Sorrows flow. ....2.RL4.142.196.

VIALS

Be stopt in *Vials,* or transfixt with *Pins;* ....2.RL2.126.167.

VIAND

The maids the viand, and the bowl supply'd: ....Od.6.296.225.
To turn the tasteful viand o'er the flame; ....Od.15.340.86.

VIANDS

Viands of various kinds allure the taste, ...Od.1.185.41.
The genial viands let my train renew; ....Od.1.404.52.
The bowl, and tasteful viands tempt in vain, ...Od.4.134.126.
And with keen gust the sav'ry viands share. ....Od.4.300.133.
With wine and viands I the vessel stor'd: ....Od.4.985.163.
And the full decks with copious viands stor'd. ....Od.5.340.188.
The sumptuous viands, and the flav'rous wines. ....Od.6.90.209.
But haste, the viands and the bowl provide— ....Od.6.295.225.
Viands of various kinds invite the taste, ...Od.7.236.247.
Viands of various kinds allure the taste, ...Od.10.439.365.
Bear the rich viands and the generous wine: ....Od.12.26.430.
And smoaking back the tasteful viands drew, ...Od.14.90.40.
Some choice domestic viands to prepare; ....Od.15.88.73.
Viands of various kinds allure the taste ....Od.15.154.76.
Thick o'er the board the plenteous viands lay, ...Od.16.51.104.
Is pil'd with viands and the strength of bread. ....Od.17.109.137.
These viands, and this bread, *Eumæus!* bear, ...Od.17.418.152.
The limbs; then all the tasteful viands share. ....Od.19.493.220.
In each discolour'd vase the viands lay: ....Od.20.418.253.
Th' untasted viands, and the jovial bowl. ....Od.22.100.291.

VIBRATES

Perhaps, yet vibrates on his Sovereign's Ear— ....4.Arbu.357.122.
The long Lance shakes, and vibrates in the Wound: ....Il.13.555.132.

VIBRATIONS

In long Vibrations spent its Fury there. ....Il.17.599.311.

VICE

Is *Pride,* the *never-failing Vice of Fools.* ....1.EOC.204.264.
And Vice *admir'd* to find a *Flatt'rer there!* ....1.EOC.551.304.
Will needs *mistake* an Author *into Vice;* ....1.EOC.557.304.

VICE (CONTINUED)

Pure let them be, and free from Taint of Vice;   2.ChWB.38.58.
As soothing Folly, or exalting Vice: 2.TemF.516.289.
The virtue nearest to our vice ally'd;   3.EOM2.196.79.
Where ends the Virtue, or begins the Vice.   3.EOM2.210.81.
That Vice or Virtue there is none at all.   3.EOM2.212.81.
Vice is a monster of so frightful mien,   3.EOM2.217.81.
But where th'Extreme of Vice, was ne'er agreed: 3.EOM2.221.82.
But where the *Point* of Vice, was ne'er agreed: 3.EOM2.221A.82.
For, Vice or Virtue, Self directs it still;   3.EOM2.236.84.
That disappoints th'effect of ev'ry vice: 3.EOM2.240.84.
Of Vice or Virtue, whether blest or curst,   3.EOM4.87.136.
Count all th'advantage prosp'rous Vice attains,   3.EOM4.89.136.
Who fancy Bliss to Vice, to Virtue Woe!   3.EOM4.94.137.
"But sometimes Virtue starves, while Vice is fed."   3.EOM4.149.142.
That, Vice may merit; 'tis the price of toil;   3.EOM4.151.142.
All see 'tis Vice, and itch of vulgar praise.   3.Ep1.119.24.
Grown all to all, from no one vice exempt,   3.Ep1.194.31.
Were means, not ends; Ambition was the vice.   3.Ep1.215.33.
Each is a sort of *Virtue*, and of *Vice*.   3.Ep2.206A.67.
That each may seem a Virtue, or a Vice,   3.Ep2.206.67.
"And am so clear too of all other vice."   3.Ep3.368.123.
Is Vice too high, reserve it for the next: 4.HS1.60.11.
But grave *Epistles*, bringing Vice to light,   4.HS1.151.21.
"And tho' the Court show *Vice* exceeding clear,   4.JD4.96.33.
About one Vice, and fall into the other: 4.HS2.46.57.
One Giant-Vice, so excellently ill,   4.JD2.4.133.
"Men only feel the Smart, but not the Vice."   4.2HE2.217.179.
Proud Vice to brand, or injur'd Worth adorn,   4.2HE1.227.215.
Proud Vice to lash, or injur'd Worth adorn,   4.2HE1.227A.215.
Preserv'd the freedom, and forbore the vice.   4.2HE1.260.217.
Go dine with Chartres, in each Vice out-do   4.1HE6.120.245.
Bubo observes, he lash'd no sort of *Vice*:   4.EpS1.12.298.
To Vice and Folly to confine the jest,   4.EpS1.57.302.
But shall the Dignity of *Vice* be lost?   4.EpS1.114.306.
Vice thus abus'd, demands a Nation's care;   4.EpS1.128.307.
Vice is undone, if she forgets her Birth,   4.EpS1.141.308.
Vice with such Giant-strides comes on amain,   4.EpS2.6.313.
Spare then the Person, and expose the Vice.   4.EpS2.12.314.
But Sir, I beg you, for the Love of Vice!   4.EpS2.42.315.
Sole Dread of Folly, Vice, and Insolence!   4.EpS2.213.325.
And gather'd ev'ry Vice on Christian ground;   5.DunB4.312.374.
Your Pleasure is a Vice, but not your Pride;   6.19.34.63.
Amidst their virtues, a reserve of vice.   6.41.20.114.
As show'd, Vice had his Hate and Pity too.   6.118.8.334.
"And if a Vice dares keep the field,   6.140.7.378.
Fools! will ye perish for your Leader's Vice?   Il.13.149.111.
Great without vice, that oft attends the great: Od.18.154.173.
From vice to vice their appetites are tost,   Od.20.215.243.
From vice to vice their appetites are tost,   Od.20.215.243.
Of vice, who teem'd with many a dead-born jest;   Od.20.354.249.

VICEGERENTS

Jove's dread vicegerents, in two future Kings;   Od.11.310.397.

VICES

With due Regret I view my Vices past,   2.ChJM.92.19.
Of all, our Vices have created Arts: 3.EOM2.50.61.
'Tis the first Virtue, Vices to abhor;   4.1HE1.65.283.
Some Vices were too high but none too low   6.130.10.358.
And Courtly Vices, Beastly Venyes,   6.135.39Z2.367.
With guiltless Blood, for Vices not his own?   Il.20.346.408.

VICIOUS

'Tis what the *Vicious fear,* the *Virtuous shun;*   1.EOC.506.295.
He vow'd to lead this Vicious Life no more.   2.ChJM.10.15.
He vow'd to lead that Vicious Life no more.   2.ChJM.10A.15.
Virtuous and vicious ev'ry Man must be,   3.EOM2.231.83.

VICISSITUDE

Or who in sweet vicissitude appears   3.Ep2.109.58.
(Painful vicissitude!) his bosom tear.   Od.1.151.40.
Grateful vicissitude! Yet me withdrawn,   Od.19.693.229.

VICISSITUDES

And long vicissitudes of human things)   Od.24.72.351.

VICTIM

Thy Victim, Love, shall be the Shepherd's Heart,   1.PSp.52.66.
Th'Immortal Victim of thy Mother's Fame;   1.TrSt.848.445.
What tender Maid but must a Victim fall   2.RL1.95.152.
Proves the just Victim of his Royal Rage.   2.RL3.60.172.
The *Club's* black Tyrant first her Victim dy'd,   2.RL3.69.173.
Love's victim then, tho' now a sainted maid: 2.ElAb.312.344.
Is now a victim, and now Ægypt's God: 3.EOM1.64.21.
Are destin'd *Hymen's* willing Victim too,   6.19.58.63.
The Barley sprinkled, and the Victim slew.   Il.2.503.150.
While the fat Victim feeds the sacred Fire.   Il.2.509.151.
Then, the sad Victim of the Publick Rage.   Il.3.520.216.
Falls as he flies, a Victim to his Fear.   Il.4.281.234.
She fell a Victim to *Diana's* Bow.   Il.6.543.353.
The Victim falls, they strip the smoaking Hide,   Il.7.382.382.
No God consulted, and no Victim slain!   Il.7.535.391.
With ev'ry Shaft some hostile Victim slew,   Il.8.323.413.
Their Pow'rs neglected and no Victim slain,   Il.12.7.81.
This, my third Victim, to the Shades I send.   Il.13.561.133.
A Victim ow'd to my brave Brother's Death.   Il.14.566.190.
And fell the Victim of his coward Fear,   Il.16.487.262.
And sunk the Victim of all-conqu'ring Death.   Il.18.150.329.
The Victim-Ox the sturdy Youth prepare;   Il.18.649.355.
Talthybius shall the Victim Boar convey ,   Il.19.195.379.
The sacred Herald rolls the Victim slain   Il.19.279.384.
An instant Victim to *Achilles* Hands: Il.20.342.408.
The Victim Bull; the Rocks rebellow round,   Il.20.469.414.
Again, her Victim cruel Fate demands!   Il.21.95.425.
No vulgar Victim must reward the Day,   Il.22.208.464.

VICTIM (CONTINUED)

His Friends prepare the Victim, and dispose   Il.24.159.542.
He said, and rising, chose the Victim Ewe   Il.24.786.569.
Stratius and *Echephron* the victim led;   Od.3.560.115.
And sacred wheat upon the victim lay'd,   Od.3.569.115.
No vows had we prefer'd, nor victim slain!   Od.4.475.142.
But lives a victim for thy vengeful sword;   Od.4.736.153.
Slay the due Victim in the genial hour: Od.11.163.389.
And pour'd prophanely as the victim burns.   Od.12.428.451.
A victim Oxe beneath the sacred hand   Od.13.27.2.
Forth on the sands the victim oxen led: Od.13.215.16.
Expert the destin'd victim to dis-part   Od.14.482.59.
And from the field the victim flocks they drive: Od.17.195.141.
Hither a victim to the Gods convey.   Od.17.679.165.
Shall bleed a victim to vindictive rage.   Od.19.574.224.
The victim portion'd and the goblet crown'd.   Od.24.424.369.

VICTIM-OX

The Victim-Ox the sturdy Youth prepare;   Il.18.649.355.

VICTIM'S

The stubborn Bristles from the Victim's Brow   Il.19.261.383.
The victim's horn with circumfusile gold.   Od.3.541.114.
The victim's heel is answer'd with this spear.   Od.22.323.301.

VICTIMS

No Lambs or Sheep for Victims I'll impart,   1.PSp.51.66.
The wanton Victims of his *Sport* remain.   1.W-F.78.157.
Nor Victims sink beneath the Sacred Stroke,   1.TrSt.372.425.
And there, in Flames the slaughter'd Victims fry.   1.TrSt.612.436.
And there, in Flames the slaughter'd Victims fly.   1.TrSt.612A.436.
When victims at yon' altar's foot we lay?   2.ElAb.108.328.
Sent his own lightning, and the Victims seiz'd.   6.69i.6.198.
Victims so pure Heav'n saw well pleas'd   6.69ii.3.199.
Beneath the Deck the destin'd Victims stow'd: Il.1.567.115.
And with their Heads to Heav'n the Victims slew: Il.1.601.117.
And burns the Victims with his holy Hands,   Il.1.607A.117.
Our verdant Altars, and the Victims blaz'd;   Il.2.369.145.
Vow'd with Libations and with Victims then,   Il.2.406.147.
Bring the rich Wine and destin'd Victims down.   Il.3.316.208.
From the sign'd Victims crops the curling Hair,   Il.3.342.209.
With that, the Chief the tender Victims slew,   Il.3.364.210.
But on his Car the slaughter'd Victims laid,   Il.3.387.211.
To bid our Altars flame, and Victims fall: Il.6.140.330.
What Altar smoak'd not with our Victims Gore?   Il.8.287.411.
The just Partition, and due Victims pay'd.   Il.11.841.73.
What Victims perish round the mighty Dead?   Il.17.279.298.
Sad Victims! destin'd to *Patroclus'* Shade.   Il.21.39.423.
And twelve sad Victims of the *Trojan* Line   Il.23.30.488.
The bristly Victims hissing o'er the Fire;   Il.23.40.488.
And the pil'd Victims round the Body spread.   Il.23.207.498.
And Victims promis'd, and Libations cast,   Il.23.240.499.
Where late the slaughter'd Victims fed the Fire)   Il.23.910.525.
Has *Hector* ting'd with Blood of Victims slain?   Il.24.45.537.
Suppliant he pray'd. And now the victims drest   Od.3.78.90.
There land, and pay due victims to the pow'rs: Od.3.192.95.
Let the flea'd victims in the flames be cast,   Od.10.635.374.
The ready victims at our bark we found,   Od.10.685.376.
The victims, vow'd to each *Tartarean* pow'r,   Od.11.25.380.
Strait the flea'd victims to the flames are cast,   Od.11.58.383.
What human victims stain the feast-ful floor!   Od.13.451.27.
The fourth drove victims to the suitor-train: Od.14.29.36.
Their garments, and succinct the victims slay.   Od.17.200.141.
Our rural victims mount in blazing flames!   Od.17.285.146.
In festival devour'd, and victims vow'd.)   Od.20.4.230.
Two grooms assistant bore the victims bound;   Od.20.221.244.
Then all with speed succinct the victims slay: Od.20.313.248.
For whom my victims bleed, my vintage flows;   Od.21.70.262.
To drive thy victims to the Suitors feast.   Od.22.216.297.
And oft *Ulysses* smoking victims laid.   Od.22.374.306.
Of victims vow'd, a ram, a bull, a boar: Od.23.294.337.
Due victims slay to all th' æthereal pow'rs.   Od.23.296.337.

VICTOR

And the *World's Victor* stood subdu'd by *Sound!*   1.EOC.381.284.
To *Argos'* Realms the Victor God resorts,   1.TrSt.668.438.
The Victor God did to these Realms resort,   1.TrSt.668A.438.
Swift to the Battlement the Victor flies,   1.TrES.129.454.
Th'insulting Victor with Disdain bestrode   1.TrES.316.461.
And march'd a Victor from the verdant Field.   2.RL3.52.172.
Falls undistinguish'd by the Victor *Spade!*   2.RL3.64.172.
There, Victor of his health, of fortune, friends,   3.Ep3.313.119.
And now the Victor stretch'd his eager hand   5.DunA2.101.109.
Thou triumph'st, victor of the high-wrought day,   5.DunA2.179.123.
And hail him victor in both gifts of Song,   5.DunA2.255.131.
And now the victor stretch'd his eager hand   5.DunB2.109.300.
Thou triumph'st, Victor of the high-wrought day,   5.DunB2.187.304.
All hail him victor in both gifts of song,   5.DunB2.267.308.
Th' eluded victor, envious of my fate,   6.20.19.66.
The World's great Victor pass'd unheeded by;   6.32.34.97.
The valiant Victor seiz'd the golden Prize.   Il.2.1067.172.
Let these the brave triumphant Victor grace,   Il.3.131.196.
Left to *Atrides*, (Victor in the Strife)   Il.3.499.215.
To spoil his Arms the Victor strove in vain;   Il.4.619.250.
The *Thracian* Bands against the Victor prest;   Il.4.620.250.
In Dust the Vanquish'd, and the Victor lies.   Il.4.627.250.
Lifts his bright Lance, ,and at the Victor flies;   Il.5.690.300.
The youthful Victor mounts his empty Seat,   Il.5.720.301.
The ruthless Victor stripp'd their shining Arms.   Il.6.34.325.
His Fate Compassion in the Victor bred;   Il.6.526.352.
Had giv'n the Vanquish'd, now the Victor bore.   Il.7.178.372.
Swift to the Spoil the hasty Victor falls,   Il.11.149.42.
Then, where the thickest fought, the Victor flew;   Il.11.191.44.
Now storms the Victor at the *Trojan* Wall;   Il.11.235.46.
While the proud Victor bore his Arms away.   Il.11.320.49.
The vengeful Victor rages round the Fields   Il.11.341.49.

VICTOR (CONTINUED)
The Victor rushing to despoil the Dead, Il.11.708.66.
The Victor Eagle, whose sinister Flight Il.12.257.90.
Swift to the Battlement the Victor flies, Il.12.483.99.
To seize his beamy Helm the Victor flies, Il.13.253.117.
Repuls'd he yields; the Victor *Greeks* obtain Il.13.259.117.
The Victor from his Breast the Weapon tears; Il.13.646.136.
Th' exulting Victor leaping where he lay, Il.13.696.138.
And fraught with Vengeance, to the Victor turns; Il.13.734.139.
Lo thus (the Victor cries) we rule the Field, Il.14.529.189.
The Victor seiz'd; and as aloft he shook Il.14.585.190.
His Lance bold *Meges* at the Victor threw; Il.15.616.220.
The Victor stooping, from the Death withdrew: Il.15.617.220.
The Victor leaps upon his prostrate Prize; Il.15.696.222.
Th' insulting Victor with Disdain bestrode Il.16.621.268.
His Spear *Æneas* at the Victor threw, Il.16.739.272.
While the proud Victor thus his Fall derides, Il.16.902.278.
Affrighted *Troy* the tow'ring Victor flies, Il.17.68.290.
And oft' the Victor triumphs, but to fall. Il.18.360.338.
Great *Jove* but turns it, and the Victor dies! Il.19.224.382.
The Victor to the Stream the Carcass gave, Il.21.133.427.
While the proud Victor thus triumphing said, Il.21.199.429.
So the proud Courser, victor of the prize, Il.22.33.453.
To them I swear; if Victor in the Strife Il.22.327.469.
Proud on his Car th' insulting Victor stood, Il.22.501.477.
The glorious Victor to the King of Kings. Il.23.46.488.
The second Victor claims a Mare unbroke, Il.23.333.503.
And crowns him Victor of the labour'd Race. Il.23.480.509.
Now Victor at the Goal *Tydides* stands, Il.23.589.513.
This Mule my right? th' undoubted Victor I. Il.23.772.520.
To rear his fallen Foe, the Victor lends Il.23.806.521.
A massy Tripod for the Victor lies; Il.23.816.521.
Since Victor of thy Fears, and slighting mine, Il.24.357.551.
Ulysses, sole of all the victor train, Od.1.18.30.
Arriv'd the last of all the victor host. Od.1.373.50.
And loud-acclaiming *Greeks* the victor bless'd: Od.4.464.142.
And loud-acclaiming *Greeks* the victor blest: Od.17.155.139.
Then to his hand a staff the victor gave, Od.18.124.172.
Then thus the hoary Chief. "My victor arms Od.19.477.220.
View in this plumy form thy victor Lord; Od.19.643.227.
L<e>iodes first before the victor falls: Od.22.347.304.
Triumph, thou happy victor of thy woes! Od.23.308.338.
Thro' ev'ry ring the victor arrow went. Od.24.202.358.

VICTOR'S
Were all those Realms the guilty Victor's Prize! 1.TrSt.217.419.
His Captive Daughter from the Victor's Chain. Il.1.16.86.
His beauteous Daughter from the Victor's Chain; Il.1.485.111.
And these, the Victor's Prize, in Triumph led. Il.5.295.281.
The Victor's Knees, and thus his Pray'r addressed. Il.6.56.326.
My Mother liv'd to bear the Victor's Bands, Il.6.538.353.
To bear the Victor's hard Commands, or bring Il.6.582.355.
And distant Ages learn the Victor's Fame. Il.7.104.368.
Mean while the Victor's Shouts ascend the Skies; Il.9.699.468.
The Victor's Rage, the dying, and the dead. Il.11.114.39.
Loud o'er the Rout was heard the Victor's Cry, Il.16.454.260.
And in the Victor's Hands the shining Prey. Il.17.94.291.
Strikes the fresh Garland from the Victor's Brow! Il.17.200.295.
Yet still the Victor's Due *Tydides* gains, Il.23.971.527.
Driv'n hence a Slave before the Victor's Sword; Il.24.924.575.
And sooth the vanquish'd with a victor's pray'r. Od.4.572.147.
To grace the victor's welcome from the wars, Od.4.713.152.

VICTORIOUS
And make my Tongue victorious as her Eyes; 1.PSp.50.66.
Matchless his Pen, victorious was his Lance; 1.W-F.293.175.
Here to the Clouds victorious *Perseus* flies; 1.TrSt.637.437.
And curs'd for ever this Victorious Day. 2.RL3.104.175.
Her Arts victorious triumph'd o'er our Arms: 4.2HE1.264.217.
Yet Musick and Love were Victorious. 6.11.92.33.
Then leaps victorious o'er the lofty Mound. Il.5.181.275.
That both shall fall by one victorious Hand; Il.5.323.282.
And pass victorious o'er the levell'd Mound. Il.8.219.407.
And still victorious in the dusty Course: Il.9.162.440.
And still victorious in the dusty Course: Il.9.349.450.
Victorious *Ajax* plies the routed Crew; Il.11.610.61.
Detain'd his Chariot and victorious Horse.) Il.11.839.73.
Ev'n to the Ships victorious *Troy* pursues, Il.11.958.78.
What Man could doubt but Troy's victorious Pow'r Il.12.187.88.
And swarms victorious o'er their yielding Walls: Il.13.120.110.
Brave *Greece* victorious, and her Navy free: Il.13.134.111.
Of *Greece* victorious, and proud *Ilion* lost? Il.13.290.119.
When we, victorious, shall to *Greece* return, Il.14.593.191.
Victorious *Troy:* Then, starting from his Seat, Il.15.457.215.
He bears victorious, while our Army flies. Il.17.663.313.
Or, in reward of thy victorious Hand, Il.20.222.403.
And scoffing, thus, to War's victorious Maid. Il.21.491.441.
On these the Rage of Fire victorious preys, Il.23.216.498.
And hear his Shouts victorious o'er the Plain. Il.23.563.512.
Victorious then in ev'ry solemn Game Il.23.725.519.
The gloves of death, victorious in the fray. Od.8.140.270.
O why was I victorious in the strife! Od.11.671.417.

VICTORS
Victors and Vanquish'd join promiscuous Cries, Il.4.512.246.
Victors and Vanquish'd join promiscuous Cries, Il.8.79.399.
The Victors keep the Field; and *Hector* calls Il.8.609.425.
Stretch'd on one Heap, the Victors spoil the slain. Il.15.389.212.
The Vanquish'd triumph, and the Victors fly. Il.17.675.314.
The *Greeks,* late Victors, now to quit the Plains? Il.18.10.323.
Which voyaging from *Troy* the Victors bore, Od.1.423.53.
'Twas God's high will the victors to divide, Od.3.161.93.
Victors of late, but humble suppliants now! Od.9.316.319.
The rest retreat: the victors now advance, Od.22.298.300.

VICTORY
(The Victory cry'd) the glorious Prize is mine! 2.RL3.162.180.
And swifter than *His* Arms, give *Victory:* 6.17iv.6.59.
O Grave! where is thy Victory? 6.31ii.17.94.
But mark, how 'midst of Victory, 6.79.61.220.
But in the Hands of God is Victory. Il.7.118.369.
These if we gain, then Victory, ye Pow'rs! Il.8.238.409.
And level pois'd the wings of Victory: Od.22.260.299.

VIDA
A *Raphael* painted, and a *Vida* sung! 1.EOC.704.320.
Immortal *Vida!* on whose honour'd Brow 1.EOC.705.320.

VIE
Adorn'd with blossoms, promis'd fruits that vie 1.TrFD.23.386.
With Royal Favourites in Flatt'ry vie, 4.JD4.60.31.
A Fav'rite's *Porter* with his Master vie, 4.EpS1.117.306.
And all th' ambitious Vowels vie, 6.30.72.88.
With *Zeuxis' Helen* thy *Bridgewater* vie, 6.52.75.158.
With equal Lustre various Colours vie, Il.4.174.229.
For this, he bids those nervous Artists vie, Il.23.981.528.
At Chess they vie, to captivate the Queen, Od.1.143.39.

VIES
Whose shining scene with rich *Hesperia* vies. 6.20.71.68.

VIEW
As in the Crystal Spring I view my Face, 1.PSu.27.74.
Thus when we view some well-proportion'd Dome, 1.EOC.247.268.
Content, if hence th' Unlearn'd their Wants may view, 1.EOC.739.326.
I'm not so monst'rous; I my face did view 1.TrPA.96.369.
And view the Boughs with happy Burthens bend. 1.TrVP.8A.377.
I view the *Grotto,* once the Scene of Love, 1.TrSP.163.400.
And the pale Spectres trembled at her View: 1.TrSt.133.415.
His Sons with Scorn their Eyeless Father view, 1.TrSt.336.424.
Th' *Inachians* view the Slain with vast Surprize, 1.TrSt.727.440.
Who view the *Western* Sea's extreamest Bounds, 1.TrSt.816.443.
Around the Walls he gaz'd, to view from far 1.TrES.59.451.
With pleasing Smiles to view the God-like Man; 1.TrUl.161.471.
With due Regret I view my Vices past, 2.ChJM.92.19.
A speaking Sigh, and cast a mournful View; 2.ChJM.415.35.
A heaving Sigh, and cast a mournful View; 2.ChJM.415A.35.
The Knight and Lady walk'd beneath in View, 2.ChJM.607.44.
As well you view the Leacher in the Tree, 2.ChJM.643.46.
And set the Strumpet here in open View, 2.ChJM.653.46.
Yet view the lovely Fruit before my Eye? 2.ChJM.731.50.
This, ev'n *Belinda* may vouchsafe to view: 2.RL1.4.144.
And view with scorn *Two Pages* and a *Chair.* 2.RL1.46.149.
Clapt his glad Wings, and sate to view the Fight: 2.RL5.54.203.
To *Proculus* alone confess'd in view.) 2.RL5.126.210.
This *Partridge* soon shall view in cloudless Skies, 2.RL5.137.211.
High on his Car *Sesostris* struck my View, 2.TemF.113.262.
His piercing Eyes, erect, appear to view 2.TemF.236.274.
And ampler *Vista's* open'd to my View, 2.TemF.263.276.
Before my View appear'd a Structure fair, 2.TemF.420.283.
Full in my view set all the bright abode, 2.ElAb.127.330.
I view my crime, but kindle at the view, 2.ElAb.185.335.
I view my crime, but kindle at the view, 2.ElAb.185.335.
I hear thee, view thee, gaze o'er all thy charms, 2.ElAb.233.339.
I wake—no more I hear, no more I view, 2.ElAb.235.339.
What scenes appear where-e'er I turn my view! 2.ElAb.263.341.
Fair eyes, and tempting looks (which yet I view!) 2.ElAb.295.343.
But HEAV'N's great view is One, and that the Whole: 3.EOM2.238.84.
View thy own World; behold the chain of Love 3.EOM3.7A.92.
To Man imparts it; but with such a view 3.EOM3.73.99.
Painful preheminence! yourself to view 3.EOM4.267.153.
Something as dim to our internal view, 3.Ep1.49.18.
Our bolder Talents in full view display'd, 3.Ep2.201A.67.
How many pictures of one Nymph we view, 3.Ep2.5.48.
Still out of reach, yet never out of view, 3.Ep2.232.68.
Her I transported touch, transported view, 4.HAdv.165.89.
View him with scornful, yet with jealous eyes, 4.Arbu.199.110.
And view this dreadful All without a fear. 4.1HE6.10.237.
Or he, who bids thee face with steddy view 4.1HE1.107.287.
The Scene, the Master, opening to my view, 4.EpS2.68.316.
Obliquely wadling to the mark in view. 5.DunA1.150.82.
There Ridpath, Roper, cudgell'd might ye view; 5.DunA2.141.118.
There kick'd and cudgel'd R— might ye view; 5.DunA2.141A.118.
Thy mental eye, for thou hast much to view: 5.DunA3.54.155.
Now stretch thy view, and open all thy mind. 5.DunA3.201Z2.175.
Obliquely wadling to the mark in view: 5.DunB1.172.282.
There Ridpath, Roper, cudgell'd might ye view, 5.DunB2.149.302.
Thy mental eye, for thou hast much to view: 5.DunB3.62.323.
So from one cloud soft show'rs we view, 6.5.9.12.
And thus thro' mists we view the sun, 6.5.5A.12.
We view a milder firmament, 6.6ii.15.15.
And guides it surer to the Mark in view; 6.17i(a).4.55.
To View a thousand real Blessings rise; 6.17iii.9.58.
Pleas'd while with Smiles his happy Lines you view, 6.19.75.64.
Still out of reach, tho' ever in their view. 6.22.6.71.
And view familiar, in its native skies, 6.23.10.73.
And view familiar, in her native skies, 6.23.10A.73.
Pleas'd in these lines, *Belinda,* you may view 6.38.1.107.
View him with scornful, yet with jealous eyes, 6.49iii.13.143.
View him with Jealous, yet with Scornful eyes, 6.49iii.13A.143.
While fancy brings the vanish'd piles to view, 6.52.31.157.
Then view this marble, and be vain no more! 6.52.54.157.
In one short view subjected to your eye 6.71.33.203.
In one short view subjected to our eye 6.71.33A.203.
Her Gods, and god-like Heroes rise to view, 6.71.47.204.
What, do ye doubt my View? 6.94.14.259.
Full in my View how all my Husband came, 6.96iv.73.278.
Here view him stretch'd. The Microscope explains, 6.96v.5.280.
View him with scornful, yet with fearful eyes, 6.98.49.284.
And view the Mine without a Wish for Gold. 6.142.8A.382.
The Fleet in View, he twang'd his deadly Bow, Il.1.67.89.

VIEW (CONTINUED)

That sacred Seer whose comprehensive View Il.1.93.91.
From *Atreus'* Son? Then let those Eyes that view Il.1.271.100.
Such, as no more these aged Eyes shall view! Il.1.346.105.
So short a Space the Light of Heav'n to view! Il.1.544.114.
'Till now the *Grecian* Camp appear'd in view. Il.1.629.117.
And view, with Envy, our successful Wars. Il.2.415.147.
But those who view fair *Elis* o'er the Seas Il.2.759.162.
Shot forth to View, a scaly Serpent sees; Il.3.48.191.
Approach, and view the wond'rous Scene below! Il.3.174.199.
Erect, the *Spartan* most engag'd our View, Il.3.273.205.
From East to West, and view from Pole to Pole! Il.3.349.209.
Nor view the Danger of so dear a Son. Il.3.383.211.
The *Greeks* with Smiles the polish'd Trophy view. Il.3.464.214.
Who dares to act whate'er thou dar'st to view. Il.4.409.240.
Or slain, or fled, the Sons of *Dares* view: Il.5.36.267.
That vaunts these Eyes shall view the Light no more. Il.5.153.274.
And set to View the warring Deities. Il.5.165.275.
Great *Hector* saw, and raging at the View Il.5.722.302.
But yon' proud Work no future Age shall view, Il.7.550.392.
Those radiant Eyes shall view, and view in vain. Il.8.589.424.
Those radiant Eyes shall view, and view in vain. Il.8.589.424.
These radiant Eyes shall view, and view in vain. Il.8.589A.424.
These radiant Eyes shall view, and view in vain. Il.8.589A.424.
Your Eyes shall view, when Morning paints the Sky Il.9.800.473.
This, tho' surrounding Shades obscur'd their View, Il.10.323.17.
Rang'd in three Lines they view the prostrate Band; Il.10.544.27.
And wond'ring view the Slaughters of the Night. Il.10.617.29.
Of *Thracian* Lineage are the Steeds ye view, Il.10.656.31.
Th' Event of Things the Gods alone can view. Il.11.973.78.
Around the Walls he gaz'd, to view from far Il.12.403.96.
The wide Horizon shut him from their View. Il.13.96.109.
As *Pallas'* self might view with fixt Delight; Il.13.174.113.
And Death's dim Shadows swam before his View. Il.13.726.139.
As thus he spoke, behold in open View, Il.13.1038.154.
Soon as the Prospect open'd to his View, Il.14.17.157.
No more the Troops, our hoisted Sails in view, Il.14.110.163.
Soon shalt thou view the scatter'd *Trojan* Bands Il.14.166.165.
Gazing he spoke, and kindling at the view, Il.14.393.181.
The bleeding Youth: *Troy* sadden'd at the View. Il.14.558.190.
Round the wide Fields he cast a careful view, Il.15.7.194.
And round the black Battalions cast his View. Il.15.689.222.
To view the Navy blazing to the Skies; Il.15.719.223.
She clear'd, restoring all the War to view; Il.15.809.227.
Such their dread Strength, and such their deathful View. Il.16.203.247.
Transfix'd with deep Regret, they view o'erthrown Il.16.673.270.
O'er all the black Battalions sent his View, Il.17.123.292.
And round on all sides sent his piercing View. Il.17.760.318.
So short a space the Light of Heav'n to view, Il.18.79.327.
The rest in publick View the Chiefs dispose, Il.19.257.383.
Suffice, from yonder Mount to view the Scene; Il.20.164.400.
Ye mighty Gods! what Wonders strike my View: Il.21.62.424.
Mark with what Insolence, in open view, Il.21.494.442.
Here, and in publick view, to meet my Fate. Il.21.670.450.
Safe from Pursuit, and shut from mortal View, Il.21.707.451.
And what (he cries) has *Peleus'* Son in view, Il.22.15.453.
And mounts the Walls, and sends around her View: Il.22.595.480.
Gloomy he said, and (horrible to view) Il.23.33.488.
Shall view *Patroclus'* and *Achilles'* Tomb. Il.23.157.495.
Swift as the Word, she vanish'd from their View; Il.23.262.500.
The Hero's Bones with careful view select: Il.23.297.501.
Of those who view the Course, not sharpest ey'd, Il.23.558.511.
Some Gift must grace *Eumelus;* view thy Store Il.23.629.514.
Still grudge his Body to the *Trojans* View? Il.24.47.537.
To view that deathful Eye, and wander o'er Il.24.249.547.
What couldst thou hope, should these thy Treasures view, Il.24.451.555.
The winged Deity forsook their View, Il.24.864.572.
And issu'd, like a God to mortal view. Od.3.597.117.
From room to room their eager view they bend; Od.4.57.122.
View my friend's son? (the King exulting cries) Od.4.226.130.
While pictur'd to thy mind appear'd in view Od.4.254.131.
The man entranc'd wou'd view the deathful scene. Od.4.314.134.
The Monarch rose: magnificent to view, Od.4.413.140.
(For what's sequester'd from celestial view?) Od.4.514.144.
Must view his billows white beneath thy oar, Od.4.645.150.
To view the sun, or breathe the vital air. Od.4.728.153.
'Till *Grecian* cliffs appear'd, a blissful view! Od.4.798.156.
A small but verdant Isle appear'd in view, Od.4.1103.169.
The patient man shall view his old abodes, Od.5.42.172.
'Till now the distant Island rose in view: Od.5.69.175.
For pow'rs celestial to each other's view Od.5.100.177.
(Already dry'd.) These pointing out to view, Od.5.309.186.
Once more I view the face of humankind: Od.6.211.220.
What scenes have I survey'd of dreadful view? Od.6.262.222.
So shalt thou view with joy thy natal shore, Od.6.375.230.
The beauteous city opening to his view, Od.7.24.235.
Then set the genial banquet in his view, Od.7.222.247.
That view vouchsaf'd, let instant death surprise Od.7.305.250.
The Queen, on nearer view, the guest survey'd Od.7.314.251.
Thither of old, Earth's * Giant-son to view, Od.7.413.257.
Perhaps from realms that view the rising day, Od.8.29.263.
(An herald one) the dubious coast to view, Od.9.100.307.
With wonder seiz'd, we view the pleasing ground, Od.9.176.312.
Fast by the sea a lonely cave we view, Od.9.212.314.
But round the grott we gaze, and all we view Od.9.254.317.
Curious to view the man of monstrous kind, Od.9.269.318.
With joy the sailors view their friends return'd, Od.9.549.328.
From the high point I mark'd, in distant view, Od.10.173.349.
And send out spies the dubious coast to view. Od.10.180.349.
Whose purple lustre glow'd against the view: Od.10.418.364.
And view the realms of darkness and of death. Od.10.581.371.
Com'st thou alive to view the *Stygian* bounds, Od.11.583.412.
Curious to view the Kings of ancient days, Od.11.775.424.
No more that wretch shall view the joys of life, Od.12.55.432.
Thro' tedious toils to view thy native coast. Od.12.177.440.
I turn, and view them quivering in the skies; Od.12.297.446.

VIEW (CONTINUED)

And now the glitt'ring mountains rise to view. Od.12.315.447.
In vain! I view perform'd the direful deed, Od.12.462.453.
With pleasing smiles to view the god-like man. Od.13.328.23.
Ulysses, friend! shall view his old abodes, Od.14.173.43.
They part; while less'ning from the Hero's view, Od.15.595.99.
Nigh to the lodge, and now appear'd in view. Od.16.12.102.
Never, I never hop'd to view this day, Od.16.25.103.
'Tis giv'n at length to view my native coast. Od.16.227.114.
But from th' *Hermæan* height I cast a view, Od.16.490.130.
Lowly she sate, and with dejected view Od.17.112.137.
Their guilty deeds, in hearing, and in view Od.17.182.140.
His son, who gave me first to view the day! Od.19.209.203.
Delineate to my view my warlike Lord, Od.19.255.207.
When my lov'd *Crete* receiv'd my final view, Od.19.389.213.
"To view his mother's soil, my *Delphic* dome Od.19.482.220.
To view their death thus imag'd in a dream: Od.19.634.227.
View in this plumy form thy victor Lord; Od.19.643.227.
And hov'ring o'er his head in view confess'd, Od.20.39.234.
Thy wond'ring eyes shall view: his rightful reign Od.20.291.247.
Thro' ev'ry ringlet levelling his view; Od.21.459.282.
No more they view the golden light of day; Od.23.9.319.
For never must *Ulysses* view this shore; Od.23.69.322.
Com'st thou the first, to view this dreary state? Od.24.39.349.
On each majestic form they cast a view, Od.24.125.354.
(Rev'rend and wise, whose comprehensive view Od.24.518.373.

VIEW'D

He view'd their twining Branches with Delight, 1.TrVP.61.379.
He view'd her twining Branches with Delight, 1.TrVP.61A.379.
Th' *Inachians* view'd the Slain with vast Surprize, 1.TrSt.727A.440.
But view'd the Shrine with a superior Look, 1.TrSt.755.441.
Jove view'd the Combate, whose Event foreseen, 1.TrES.225.458.
So seldom view'd, and ever in Disguise. 1.TrUl.190.472.
And view'd a Friend, with Eyes so very kind, 2.ChWB.234.68.
Sudden he view'd, in spite of all her Art, 2.RL3.143.178.
Inscriptions here of various Names I view'd, 2.TemF.31.255.
High on a Throne with Trophies charg'd, I view'd 2.TemF.151.265.
With honest scorn the first fam'd *Cato* view'd 6.32.39.97.
All view'd with Awe the Venerable Man; Il.1.337.104.
Late had she view'd the Silver-footed Dame, Il.1.696.120.
With Wonder *Priam* view'd the Godlike Man. Il.3.239.203.
This said, once more he view'd the Warrior-Train: Il.3.253.204.
This said, once more he view'd the martial Train: Il.3.253A.204.
The King then ask'd (as yet the Camp he view'd) Il.3.289.207.
Where, as he view'd her Charms, she turn'd away Il.3.531.216.
Who view'd him lab'ring thro' the Ranks of Fight! Il.4.429.240.
With deep Concern divine *Æneas* view'd Il.5.212.277.
Whose Fall *Ulysses* view'd, with Fury fir'd; Il.5.829.305.
With Joy *Sarpedon* view'd the wish'd Relief, Il.5.840.305.
The Lord of Thunders view'd, and stern bespoke. Il.5.1093.318.
Not long *Lycurgus* view'd the Golden Light, Il.6.161.333.
The soften'd Chief with kind Compassion view'd, Il.6.622.357.
While pierc'd with Grief the much-lov'd Youth he view'd, Il.11.323.49.
Eager they view'd the Prospect dark and deep, Il.12.61.83.
This *Asius* view'd, unable to contain, Il.13.483.130.
Great *Hector* view'd him with a sad Survey, Il.15.492.216.
Troy in proud Hopes already view'd the Main Il.15.850.229.
Divine *Achilles* view'd the rising Flames, Il.16.154.243.
Jove view'd the Combate, whose Event foreseen, Il.16.528.264.
Transfix'd with deep Regret, they view'd o'erthrown Il.16.673A.270.
Jove view'd the Combate with a stern Survey, Il.16.783.274.
Meanwhile *Apollo* view'd with envious Eyes, Il.17.75.291.
He darts his anxious Eye; and instant, view'd Il.17.91.291.
Who view'd his Fall, and grieving at the Chance, Il.17.398.302.
In thought they view'd him still, with martial Joy, Il.17.442.304.
When *Hector* view'd, all ghastly in his Gore Il.20.485.414.
Enough, O Son of *Peleus! Troy* has view'd Il.22.317.469.
Oft have these Eyes that godlike *Hector* view'd Il.24.479.556.
Prescient he view'd th' aerial tracts, and drew Od.2.187.71.
She view'd her honours, and enjoy'd the sight. Od.3.553.114.
And view'd his filial love with vast surprize; Od.4.154.127.
Eludes my search: but when his form I view'd Od.4.343.136.
I view'd th' effects of that disastrous flame, Od.4.358.137.
Him in *Calypso's* cave of late I view'd, Od.4.755.154.
There view'd the *Pleiads,* and the northern Team, Od.5.347.188.
Never, I never view'd 'till this blest hour Od.6.191.218.
At length the kingly palace gates he view'd: Od.7.61.236.
I view'd the coast, a region flat and low; Od.10.222.351.
But never have thy eyes astonish'd view'd Od.11.519.409.
Struck with despair, with trembling hearts we view'd Od.12.292.446.
So seldom view'd, and ever in disguise! Od.13.357.24.
" *Ulysses* view'd with stern heroic joy; Od.16.309.120.
Ulysses view'd an image of his own. Od.19.283.208.
View'd his enormous bulk extended on the plain. Od.19.533.221.
In lodgments first secure his care he view'd, Od.20.206.243.
Eager they view'd; with joy they stood amaz'd; Od.21.232.271.
Turn'd on all sides, and view'd it o'er and o'er; Od.21.428.280.
When, moving slow, the regal form they view'd Od.24.31.348.
For so reported the first man I view'd, Od.24.306.364.

VIEW'ST

Who view'st these eyes for ever fixt in death, 6.20.3.66.
View'st thou un-mov'd, O ever-honour'd most! Od.4.83.123.
For know, thou *Neptune* view'st! and at my nod Od.11.305.397.

VIEWING

Who viewing first his Foes with scornful Eyes, Il.20.200.402.
Whom *Hermes* viewing, thus declines the War. Il.21.580.446.

VIEWLESS

Repass'd, and viewless mix'd with common air. Od.4.1094.169.
Light as the viewless air, the warrior Maid Od.6.25.205.
Their feet half-viewless quiver in the skies: Od.8.304.279.
And thence had glided, viewless as the air: Od.10.688.376.
But unapparent as a viewless shade Od.16.173.111.

VIEWLESS (CONTINUED)

Minerva viewless on her charge attends, Od.19.38.194.

VIEWS

Short Views we take, nor see the *Lengths behind,* 1.EOC.222.265.
He views and practises a milder look. 1.TrPA.26.366.
The sun all objects views beneath the sky, 1.TrPA.110.370.
In frightful Views, and makes it Day within; 1.TrSt.74.413.
Not All bright *Phœbus* views in early Morn, 1.TrSt.212.419.
With Transport views the airy Rule his own, 1.TrSt.449.428.
And views astonish'd from the Hills afar 1.TrSt.512.431.
And views their Arms and Habit with Surprize. 1.TrSt.566.434.
He views his Food, but dreads, with lifted Eye, 1.TrSt.853.445.
He views his Food, wou'd taste, yet dares not try; 1.TrSt.853A.445.
He views the Tow'rs, and meditates their Fall; 1.TrES.23.450.
Nor bound thy narrow Views to Things below. 2.RL1.36.148.
Before true passion all those views remove, 2.ElAb.79.326.
The starving chemist in his golden views 3.EOM2.269.87.
But future views of better, or of worse. 3.EOM4.72.135.
Or cut wide views thro' Mountains to the Plain, 3.Ep4.75.144.
One boundless Green, or flourish'd Carpet views, 3.Ep4.95.146.
To stop thy foolish views, thy long desires, 4.1HE1.75.283.
Thro' Clouds of Passion P[ulteney]'s views are clear, 4.1740.9.332.
With self-applause her wild creation views, 5.DunA1.80.69.
Millions and millions on these banks he views, 5.DunA3.23.152.
With self-applause her wild creation views; 5.DunB1.82.275.
The King descending, views th' Elysian Shade. 5.DunB3.14.320.
Millions and millions on these banks he views, 5.DunB3.31.322.
She views the story with attentive eyes, 6.14iii.13.46.
Or views his smiling progeny; 6.51ii.32.153.
He views the Wretch, and sternly thus replies. Il.2.305.142.
And fair *Lilæa* views the rising Flood. Il.2.627.157.
And high *Cerinthus* views the neighb'ring Main. Il.2.648.157.
The beauteous Champion views with Marks of Fear, Il.3.44.190.
And next the Troops of either *Ajax* views: Il.4.311.235.
His Danger views with Anguish and Despair, Il.5.387.285.
Great *Menelaus* views with pitying Eyes, Il.5.689.300.
Great *Agamemnon* views with joyful Eye Il.8.337.413.
How ill agree the Views of vain Mankind, Il.10.116.7.
He views the Tow'rs, and meditates their Fall, Il.12.367.94.
By fits he breathes, half views the fleeting Skies, Il.14.513.188.
With Anguish *Ajax* views the piercing Sight, Il.15.508.216.
Stern *Hector,* as the bleeding Chief he views, Il.16.987.281.
He sternly views him, and triumphing cries. Il.16.1002.281.
The long, long Views of poor, designing Man! Il.18.384.339.
And views contending Gods with careless Eyes. Il.21.455.440.
The scornful Dame her Conquest views with Smiles, Il.21.476.441.
Views, from his Arm, the *Trojans* scatter'd Flight, Il.21.615.448.
If yet *Ulysses* views the light, forbear, Od.1.374.50.
'Till great *Ulysses* views his native land. Od.2.397.80.
And views *Gortyna* on the western side; Od.3.376.104.
The tow'rs of *Pylos* sink, its views decay, Od.3.616.117.
Views the broad heav'ns disclos'd the lawless joy. Od.8.312.281.
As some fond matron views in mortal fight Od.8.571.293.
The Sun ne'er views th' uncomfortable seats, Od.11.17.380.
Or say in *Pyle?* for yet he views the light, Od.11.567.411.
And views wide earth and heav'n's unmeasur'd height. Od.12.386.449.
And views that object which she wants the most! Od.19.245.206.
Some wretch reluctant views aerial light, Od.19.401.214.
Minerva fix'd her mind on views remote, Od.19.558.223.
To whom the Queen. If Fame ingage your views, Od.21.357.276.
All pale, with ooze deform'd, he views the strand, Od.23.255.335.

VIG'ROUS

Ye vig'rous Swains! while Youth ferments your Blood, 1.W-F.93.159.
When vig'rous Blood forbids a chaster Life: 2.ChJM.124.20.
Wou'd busie the most Vig'rous of us all. 2.ChJM.211.24.
Mean time the vig'rous Dancers beat the Ground, 2.ChJM.353.31.
But vig'rous still, a lively buxom Dame, 2.ChWB.319.72.
"Did I demand, in my most vig'rous hour, 4.HAdv.89.83.
Vig'rous he rises; from th' effluvia strong 5.DunA2.97.109.
Vig'rous he rises; from th' effluvia strong 5.DunB2.105.300.
Erect he stood, and vig'rous from his Wound: Il.5.630.298.
The vig'rous Pow'r the trembling Car ascends, Il.5.1030.315.
Thus, Heroes! thus the vig'rous Combate wage! Il.6.84.327.
Alive, unharm'd, and vig'rous from his Wound. Il.7.375.382.
The vig'rous Offspring of a stol'n Embrace, Il.8.344.414.
The vig'rous Pow'r the trembling Car ascends; Il.8.472.419.
To Chiefs of vig'rous Youth, and manly Race! Il.13.132.111.
Ev'n then, the Spear the vig'rous Arm confest. Il.13.519.131.
The whirling Lance with vig'rous Force addrest, Il.17.400.303.
Where high Rewards the vig'rous Youth inflame, Il.22.213.464.
(Vig'rous no more, as when his young Embrace Il.22.538.478.
Be swift, be vig'rous, and regain the Prize! Il.23.524.510.
Scarce did the Chief the vig'rous Strife propose, Il.23.820.522.
Oh had you seen him, vig'rous, bold and young, Od.17.380.150.

VIGILANCE

To bribe whose vigilance, *Ægisthus* told Od.4.701.152.

VIGILIUS

And ev'n th' Antipodes Vigilius mourn. 5.DunA3.98.158.
And ev'n th' Antipodes Vigilius mourn. 5.DunB3.106.325.

VIGILS

The Stations duly, and the Vigils kept; 2.ChWB.285.70.
With Studies pale, with Midnight Vigils blind; 2.TemF.301.278.
Shrines! where their vigils pale-ey'd virgins keep, 2.ElAb.21.320.
While pensive Poets painful vigils keep, 5.DunA1.91.70.
But pensive Poets painful vigils keep, 5.DunA1.91A.70.
While pensive Poets painful vigils keep, 5.DunB1.93.276.

VIGOR

And praise the *Easie Vigor* of a Line, 1.EOC.360.280.
Wakes to new Vigor with the rising Day. 1.TrSt.587.434.
Wild Nature's vigor working at the root. 3.EOM2.184.77.

VIGOR (CONTINUED)

"The race by vigor, not by vaunts is won; 5.DunA2.55.105.
That on his vigor and superior size. 5.DunA2.162.121.
He feels each Limb with wonted Vigor light; Il.5.156.274.
With Vigor arm'd him, and with Glory crown'd. Il.5.544.294.
Who dies in Youth, and Vigor, dies the best, Il.22.100.456.
Behold his Vigor in this active Race! Il.23.931.526.
These aged nerves with new-born vigor strung, Od.20.296.247.
These aged sinews with new vigor strung Od.21.207.269.
Oh! could the vigor of this arm as well Od.21.403.279.
That ancient vigor, once my pride and boast. Od.21.468.283.

VIGOROUS

With vigorous youth, unknown to cares, engage! Od.18.61.169.
(Exclaims *Antinous)* can a vigorous foe Od.18.92.171.

VIGOUR

With Spirits feeds, with Vigour fills the whole, 1.EOC.77.248.
Joy to my Soul, and Vigour to my Song: 1.TrSP.239.404.
And a new Vigour springs in ev'ry Part. 2.ChJM.130.21.
Indulge the Vigour of your mounting Blood, 2.ChJM.172.23.
See the same man, in vigour, in the gout; 3.Ep1.130.25.
As Fits give vigour, just when they destroy. 3.Ep1.223.34.
To Chartres, Vigour; Japhet, Nose and Ears? 3.Ep3.88.95.
"The race by vigour, not by vaunts is won; 5.DunB2.59.298.
One on his vigour and superior size. 5.DunB2.170.304.
But Warriors, you, that youthful Vigour boast, Il.7.191.373.
Thy Veins no more with ancient Vigour glow, Il.8.131.404.
As if new Vigour from new Fights they won, Il.15.846.229.
The brazen-pointed Spear, with Vigour thrown, Il.16.368.257.
Oh gen'rous *Greek!* when with full Vigour thrown Il.16.713.271.
Had fix'd thy active Vigour to the Ground. Il.16.748.273.
Were thine my Vigour, this successful Spear Il.16.879.277.
Vain was his Vigour, and as vain his Pride. Il.17.30.289.
Thro' all his Veins a sudden Vigour flew, Il.17.250.297.
She breathes new Vigour in her Hero's Breast, Il.17.639.312.
'Tis our own Vigour must the Dead regain; Il.17.798.319.
But this no time our Vigour to display, Il.23.347.503.
But slow, and past their Vigour, are my Steeds. Il.23.380.505.
And fills his Steeds with Vigour. At a Stroke, Il.23.469.509.
Thy present Vigour Age has overthrown, Il.23.715.518.
Your noble Vigour, oh my Friends restrain; Il.23.856.523.
That youthful Vigour, and that manly Mind, Il.24.12.535.
Withers the blooming vigour of his heir; Od.4.146.127.
His drooping vigour, and exhausted stores. Od.4.492.143.
Such was my boast, while vigour crown'd my days, Od.8.203.273.
Observe what vigour Gratitude can lend, Od.22.255.299.

VILE

A vile Conceit in pompous Words exprest, 1.EOC.320.275.
A vile Conceit in pompous Style exprest, 1.EOC.320A.275.
No Pardon vile *Obscenity* should find, 1.EOC.530.297.
But the vile Vulgar, ever discontent, 1.TrSt.224.419.
Oh wretched we, a vile submissive Train, 1.TrSt.263.421.
But vile Suspicions had aspers'd her Fame; 2.ChJM.239.26.
But when no End of these vile Tales I found, 2.ChWB.412.77.
Vile worm!—oh Madness, Pride, Impiety! 3.EOM1.258.46.
As full, as perfect, in vile Man that mourns, 3.EOM1.277.48.
And vile Attornies, now an useless race. 3.Ep3.274.116.
Should'ring God's altar a vile image stands, 3.Ep3.293.117.
And he himself one vile Antithesis. 4.Arbu.325.119.
Did ever Smock-face act so vile a Part? 4.Arbu.326A.119.
Seeks from the Stage his vile Support to gain: 4.JD2A.14.132.
Vile tho' they be, by far the vilest yet 4.JD2A.33.134.
If vile D[evonshire] lov'd Sixpence, more than he. 4.2HE2.229A.181.
If vile Van-muck lov'd Sixpence, more than he. 4.2HE2.229.181.
A vile Encomium doubly ridicules; 4.2HE1.410.229.
But were his Verses vile, his Whisper base, 4.EpS1.49.301.
Ye Tradesmen vile, in Army, Court, or Hall! 4.EpS2.17.314.
Nor glad vile Poets with true Criticks' gore. 5.DunA3.172.168.
Like the vile straw that's blown about the streets 5.DunA3.291.184.
Where vile Mundungus trucks for viler rhymes; 5.DunB1.234.287.
Of link-boys vile, and watermen obscene; 5.DunB2.100.300.
Nor glad vile Poets with true Critic's gore. 5.DunB3.178.329.
Like the vile straw that's blown about the streets, 5.DunB3.289.334.
And lo the wretch! whose vile, whose insect lust 5.DunB4.415.382.
'Allyes and Lanes are Terms too vile and base, 6.13.22.39.
Vile Reptile, weak, and vain! 6.53.6.161.
Proud Reptile, Vile, and vain 6.53.6A.161.
Vile reptile, Proud, and vain 6.53.6B.161.
"Lye there, thou Caitiff vile! quoth *Guise,* 6.79.77.220.
But if a clam'rous vile *Plebeian* rose, Il.2.235.138.
From his vile Visage wip'd the scalding Tears. Il.2.331.143.
With Shame deserting, heap with vile Disgrace. Il.2.349.143.
Pierc'd in the Back, a vile, dishonest Wound? Il.8.120.403.
A Day more black, a Fate more vile, ensues. Il.13.162.112.
(Like some vile Worm extended on the Ground) Il.13.819.144.
Like some vile Swain, whom, on a rainy Day, Il.21.327.434.
No vile Dishonour shall thy Corse pursue; Il.22.329.470.
To vile Reproach what Answer can we make? Il.23.568.512.
The vile assassin, and adult'rous dame. Od.3.393.105.
In the vile habit of a village slave, Od.4.336.136.
Thus with vile censure taint my spotless name. Od.6.330.227.
While such a monster as vile *Noman* lives. Od.9.542.328.
Vile wretch, begone! this instant I command Od.10.83.343.
So vile a deed, so dire a scene of blood. Od.11.520.409.
Vers'd in vile arts, and foe to humankind, Od.14.320.50.
Like some vile swine's, that greedy of his prey Od.18.35.168.
In vile ignoble jars, the feast of joy. Od.18.451.190.
And with my life such vile dishonours end. Od.20.386.251.
So study'd tortures his vile days shall end. Od.22.192.296.

VILER

Where vile Mundungus trucks for viler rhymes; 5.DunB1.234.287.

VILEST
Vile tho' they be, by far the vilest yet ....4.JD2A.33.134.
Disgrac'd, dishonour'd, like the vilest Slave! ....Il.9.762.472.

VILLA
At Timon's Villa let us pass a day, ...3.Ep4.99.146.
Whether you call them Villa, Park, or Chace) ....4.2HE2.255.183.

VILLA'S
Behold! th'ascending *Villa's* on my Side ....1.W-F.375.187.

VILLAGE
While curling Smokes from Village-Tops are seen, ...1.PAu.63.84.
Ne Village is without, on either side, ...6.14ii.51.44.
The village Curs, and trembling Swains retire; ....Il.17.70.290.
In the vile habit of a village slave, ...Od.4.336.136.

VILLAGE-TOPS
While curling Smokes from Village-Tops are seen, ...1.PAu.63.84.

VILLAIN
'Tis phrase absurd to call a Villain Great: ....3.EOM4.230.148.
The poor and friendless Villain, than the Great? ....4.EpS2.45.315.
And hence the villain has supply'd their war. ....Od.22.171.295.
Fierce on the villain from each side they leapt, ...Od.22.202.297.

VILLAIN'S
Fame but from death a villain's name can save, ...3.EOM4.249.151.

VILLAINS
Calm, thinking Villains, whom no Faith cou'd fix, ...2.TemF.410.283.
Calm, thinking Villains, whom no Faith can fix, ...2.TemF.410B.283.

VILLAINY
Still, as of old, incumber'd Villainy! ....3.Ep3.36.88.

VILLANY
Blind as I am, some glorious Villany! ....1.TrSt.119.415.
"Nothing is Sacred now but Villany." ....4.EpS1.170.309.
"Wretch! this is villany, and this is sin." ....Od.14.110.41.

VILLARIO
Enjoy them, you! Villario can no more; ....3.Ep4.86.146.

VILLARIO'S
Behold Villario's ten-years toil compleat; ....3.Ep4.79.145.

VILLERS
Great Villers lies—alas! how chang'd from him, ...3.Ep3.305.118.

VILLETE'S
Villete's soft Voice and St John's silver Lyre ....6.106ii.6.307.

VIN'YARDS
Half Pasture green, and half with Vin'yards crown'd.) ....Il.9.694.468.

VINDICATE
And Vindicate the bounteous Pow'rs above: ....1.TrES.36.451.
But vindicate the ways of God to Man. ....3.EOM1.16.14.
The birds of heav'n shall vindicate their grain: ....3.EOM3.38.96.
Dispatch yon' *Greek,* and vindicate the Gods. ....Il.5.556.295.
And vindicate the bount'ous Pow'rs above. ....Il.12.380.95.
And vindicate by Oath th' ill-gotten Prize. ....Il.23.660.515.
The youth wou'd vindicate the vacant throne. ....Od.4.224.130.
Should vindicate my injur'd Father's fame, ...Od.11.613.414.

VINDICATES
Re-passes Lintot, vindicates the race, ...5.DunA2.99.109.
Re-passes Lintot, vindicates the race, ...5.DunB2.107.300.
Still from *Apollo* vindicates her shade, ...6.14iv.24.47.
The Lordly Savage vindicates his Prey. ....Il.11.603.61.
Again the fury vindicates her prey, ...Od.12.154.439.

VINDICTIVE
Then loudly calls on *Troy's* vindictive Arms; ....Il.16.654.270.
The God vindictive doom'd them never more ....Od.1.11.29.
While storms vindictive intercept the shore. ....Od.1.424.53.
And storms vindictive intercept the shore. ....Od.7.359.254.
To his black forge vindictive *Vulcan* flies: ....Od.8.314.281.
Shall bleed a victim to vindictive rage. ....Od.19.574.224.

VINE
And grapes in clusters from the vine depend; ....1.TrPA.71.368.
The curling Vine her swelling Clusters spread; ....1.TrVP.60.379.
Yet this tall Elm, but for his Vine (he said) ....1.TrVP.63.380.
And this fair Vine, but that her Arms surround ....1.TrVP.65.380.
Man, like the gen'rous vine, supported lives; ....3.EOM3.311.125.
Bring, bring the madding Bay, the drunken Vine; ....5.DunB1.303.291.
Explains the *Seve* and *Verdeur* of the Vine. ....5.DunB4.556.397.
Explains the *Seve* and Verdure of each Vlne. ....5.DunB4.556A.397.
Was ravisht from the tender vine; ....6.6ii.22.15.
Vine, bay, or cabbage fit to wear, ...6.106v.2.308.
Vine, Laurel, cabbage fit to wear, ...6.106v.2A.308.
For Flocks *Erythræ, Glissa* for the Vine; ....Il.2.602.156.
(Tho' sure our vine the largest cluster yields, ...Od.9.423.323.
He drest the vine, and bad the garden blow, ...Od.16.151.109.
Wild springs the vine, no more the garden blows. ....Od.16.155.110.

VINEGAR
As Heav'n's blest beam turns vinegar more sowr; ....3.EOM2.148.72.
And is at once their vinegar and wine. ....4.HS2.54.59.
At such a feast old vinegar to spare, ...4.HS2.57.59.
"Within thy Reach I set the Vinegar? ....6.96ii.18.270.
"Within the reach I set the Vinegar? ....6.96ii.18A.270.

VINES
And swelling Clusters bend the curling Vines: ....1.PSp.36.64.
Their Vines a Shadow to their Race shall yield; ....1.Mes.65.118.
Sometimes his Pruning-hook corrects the Vines, ...1.TrVP.37.378.
And Hills where Vines their Purple Harvest yield? ....1.TrES.30.450.
Now, forms my Quincunx, and now ranks my Vines, ...4.HS1.130.17.
To happy Convents, bosom'd deep in vines, ...5.DunB4.301.373.
Here order'd vines in equal ranks appear ....6.35.17.103.
Here are the flow'r descry'd, ...6.35.23.103.
Th' *Isteian* Fields for gen'rous Vines renown'd, ...Il.2.645.157.
With curling Vines and twisted Ivy bound; ....Il.6.166.334.
And sacred *Pedasus,* for Vines renown'd; ....Il.9.198.442.
And sacred *Pedasus,* for Vines renown'd; ....Il.9.385.451.
And Hills where Vines their purple Harvest yield, ...Il.12.374.95.
Beheld his Vines their liquid Harvest yield, ...Il.14.139.164.
Bent with the pond'rous Harvest of its Vines; ....Il.18.652.355.
Of Hills for Vines, and Arable for Grain? ....Il.20.225.403.
With feeble steps from marshalling his Vines ....Od.1.249.45.
Depending vines the shelving cavern screen, ...Od.5.88.176.
Here order'd vines in equal ranks appear, ...Od.7.158.244.
Here are the vines in early flow'r descry'd, ...Od.7.164.244.
And vines that flourish in eternal green, ...Od.9.154.312.
Her sloping hills the mantling vines adorn, ...Od.15.444.92.
Of various vines that then began to blow, ...Od.24.398.368.

VINEYARD
Next, rip in yellow Gold, a Vineyard shines, ...Il.18.651.355.
Here a rich juice the royal vineyard pours; ....Od.6.355.229.

VINEYARDS
And flatted Vineyards, one sad Waste appear; ....Il.5.121.273.
With Woods, with Vineyards, and with Harvests crown'd. ....Il.6.240.338.
Thy squadron'd vineyards well thy art declare, ...Od.24.289.363.

VINTAGE
In solid gold the purple vintage flows, ...Od.4.67.122.
And with the generous vintage thirst asswag'd. ....Od.6.298.225.
Bleeds a whole hecatomb, a vintage flows. ....Od.14.116.41.
And turn my gen'rous vintage down their throat. ....Od.17.621.162.
For whom my victims bleed, my vintage flows; ....Od.21.70.262.
A future vintage! when the *Hours* produce ....Od.24.399.368.

VINY
And *Epidaure* with Viny Harvests crown'd: ....Il.2.679.159.

VIOLATE
To know, what known will violate thy peace: ....Od.4.662.150.
He dar'd not violate your royal ear. ....Od.4.989.163.
My woes awak'd will violate your ear; ....Od.19.141.199.
To violate the life thy youth sustain'd? ....Od.19.564.224.
And violate all hospitable laws! ....Od.23.66.321.

VIOLATED
The violated blossoms drop with blood; ....1.TrFD.28.387.
Thro' violated Nature force his way, ...1.TrSt.332.424.
The violated Rites, the ravish'd Dame, ...Il.13.785.142.
With Fury swells the violated Flood. ....Il.21.152.427.
Lest arms avenge the violated peace. ....Od.20.333.249.

VIOLATES
He violates the Laws of Man and God. ....Il.24.69.538.

VIOLENCE
Her ev'ry turn with Violence pursu'd, ...3.Ep2.131.61.
And Heav'n is won by violence of Song. ....4.2HE1.240.215.
Her ev'ry Turn with Violence pursu'd, ...6.154.17.403.
Still breathing Rapine, Violence, and Lust! ....Il.13.794.142.
'Twas Tumult all, and Violence of Flight; ....Il.21.721.451.
Forbear (he cry'd) this Violence of Woes, ...Il.24.893.573.
No mark of Pain, or Violence of Face; ....Il.24.955.576.
You make the Arm of Violence too strong. ....Od.2.88.65.
He shall this violence of death decreed, ...Od.4.975.163.
And steals with modest violence our souls, ...Od.8.190.272.
Relentless mocks her violence of woe, ...Od.8.578.293.
Than see the hand of violence invade ....Od.16.113.108.
This is the house of violence and wrong: ....Od.17.329.147.
I stand: the hand of violence is here: ....Od.17.647.164.
Let not the hand of violence invade ....Od.18.462.190.
Dishonest wounds, or violence of soul, ...Od.19.15.193.
Your violence and scorn, ye Suitors cease, ...Od.20.332.249.

VIOLENT
Scourge of thy People, violent and base! ....Il.1.305.101.
The Gust continu'd, violent, and strong, ...Il.11.397.52.

VIOLETS
And glowing violets threw odors round. ....Od.5.94.176.

VIOLS
Sound, sound ye Viols, be the Cat-call dumb! ....5.DunB1.302.291.

VIPER
This harmless Grove no lurking Viper hides, ...1.PSu.67.77.

VIRAGO
To Arms, to Arms! the fierce Virago cries, ...2.RL5.37.201.
Now meet thy Fate, th'incens'd Virago cry'd, ...2.RL5.87A.207.

VIRGIL
To *Cato, Virgil* pay'd one honest line; ....4.EpS2.120.320.
For me, what Virgil, Pliny may deny, ...5.DunB4.225.365.
Virgil, when call'd *Pasiphae Virgo* ....6.10.89.27.
To *Homer,* Virgil, or to any; ....6.29.22.83.
A Virgil there, and here an Addison. ....6.71.62.204.
Let Horace blush, and Virgil too. ....6.138.4.376.
"In Dryden's Virgil see the print. ....6.140.28.379.

VIRGIN
A *Virgin* shall conceive, a *Virgin* bear a Son! 1.Mes.8.113.
A *Virgin* shall conceive, a *Virgin* bear a Son! 1.Mes.8.113.
Th'Immortal Huntress, and her Virgin Train; 1.W-F.160.164.
The silver Stream her Virgin Coldness keeps, 1.W-F.205.168.
Still bears the Name the hapless Virgin bore, 1.W-F.207.168.
These Cares alone her Virgin Breast imploy, 1.TrVP.17.377.
Before my Sight a Watry Virgin stood, 1.TrSP.186.401.
Where Filial Love with Virgin Sweetness join'd. 1.TrSt.673.438.
Like a fair Virgin in her Beauty's Bloom, 1.TrUl.164.471.
All hail! Ye Virgin Daughters of the Main; 1.TrUl.240.473.
Of a stale Virgin with a Winter Face; 2.ChJM.104.19.
If you, my Friends, this Virgin can procure, 2.ChJM.266.27.
When *Florio* speaks, what Virgin could withstand, 2.RL1.97.152.
As Thou, sad Virgin! for thy ravish'd Hair. 2.RL4.10.183.
A Charge of *Snuff* the wily Virgin threw; 2.RL5.82.206.
(Her Virgin Handmaids) still attend the Shrine: 2.TemF.271.276.
Shame to the virgin, to the matron pride, 3.EOM2.242.84.
Serene in Virgin Modesty she shines, 3.Ep2.255.70.
"A Virgin Tragedy, an Orphan Muse." 4.Arbu.56.100.
Or from the soft-ey'd Virgin steal a tear! 4.Arbu.286.116.
See graceless Venus to a Virgin turn'd, 5.DunA3.103.159.
See graceless Venus to a Virgin turn'd, 5.DunB3.111.325.
Nor ever did askance like modest Virgin look. 6.14ii.45.44.
Where *Lillies* smile in virgin robes of white, 6.14iv.5.47.
The stream at once preserves her virgin leaves, 6.14iv.27.48.
Absolves the virgin when by force constrain'd. 6.38.20.108.
As some fond virgin, whom her mother's care 6.45.1.124.
Chaste as cold *Cynthia's* virgin light, 6.51ii.23.153.
'Tis a Virgin hard of Feature, 6.70.6.201.
(A Virgin Muse, not prostitute to praise). 6.84.31Z8.240.
Serene, in virgin majesty, she shines; 6.106i.6.306.
Serene, in virgin Modesty, she shines; 6.106i.6A.306.
High in the midst the blue-ey'd Virgin flies; Il.2.524.151.
Whose Virgin-Charms subdu'd the God of War: Il.2.615.157.
With that, the blue-ey'd Virgin wing'd her Flight; Il.5.170.275.
At once a Virgin, and at once a Bride! Il.11.314.49.
And that unbroken Vow, our Virgin Bed! Il.15.46.196.
The Virgin Captives, with disorder'd Charms, Il.18.33.325.
The first lov'd Consort of my virgin Bed Il.19.309.385.
My birth I boast (the blue-ey'd Virgin cries) Od.1.227.43.
His virgin sword Ægysthus' veins imbru'd; Od.1.389.51.
Their sovereign's step a virgin train attends: Od.1.428.53.
The virgin-choir *Alector's* daughter led. Od.4.14.121.
Allur'd *Eumelus* to her virgin-arms; Od.4.1050.167.
Virgin awake! the marriage hour is nigh, Od.6.39.206.
Uprose the virgin with the morning light, Od.6.59.208.
The blooming virgin with dispatchful cares Od.6.87.209.
Exults *Latona* as the virgin moves. Od.6.126.212.
And swam the stream: Loud shrieks the virgin train, Od.6.135.213.
(Imperial Virgin) boast thy glorious birth, Od.6.176.217.
Your friendly care: retire, ye virgin train! Od.6.258.222.
Th' unguarded virgin as unchaste I blame, Od.6.343.228.
With skill the virgin guides th' embroider'd rein, Od.6.379.230.
His step a Virgin met, and stood before: Od.7.25.235.
A polish'd Urn the seeming Virgin bore, Od.7.26.235.
The winds to *Marathon* the Virgin bore; Od.7.102.239.
He pours his wat'ry store, the Virgin burns; Od.11.284.396.
Like a fair virgin in her beauty's bloom, Od.13.331.23.
All hail! Ye virgin daughters of the main! Od.13.407.26.
In form, a virgin in soft beauty's bloom, Od.16.170.111.
For such a Lord! who crown'd your virgin-love Od.19.302.209.
Shall I my virgin nuptial vow revere; Od.19.616.226.
Impatient strait to flesh his virgin-sword, Od.20.461.255.
At distance due a virgin-train attends; Od.21.8.258.
On either side awaits a virgin fair; Od.21.67.262.
Again made frustrate by the virgin pow'r. Od.22.301.301.
The matron-train with all the virgin band Od.22.521.314.
But from on high the blue-ey'd Virgin cry'd; Od.24.612.377.
The King obey'd. The Virgin-seed of *Jove* Od.24.629.377.

VIRGIN-ARMS
Allur'd *Eumelus* to her virgin-arms; Od.4.1050.167.

VIRGIN-CHARMS
Whose Virgin-Charms subdu'd the God of War: Il.2.615.157.

VIRGIN-CHOIR
The virgin-choir *Alector's* daughter led. Od.4.14.121.

VIRGIN-LOVE
For such a Lord! who crown'd your virgin-love Od.19.302.209.

VIRGIN-SEED
The King obey'd. The Virgin-seed of *Jove* Od.24.629.377.

VIRGIN-SWORD
Impatient strait to flesh his virgin-sword, Od.20.461.255.

VIRGIN-TRAIN
At distance due a virgin-train attends; Od.21.8.258.

VIRGIN'S
The Pest a Virgin's Face and Bosom bears; 1.TrSt.707.439.
At this, the Blood the Virgin's Cheek forsook, 2.RL3.89.174.
The close Recesses of the Virgin's Thought; 2.RL3.140.178.
The virgin's wish without her fears impart, 2.ElAb.55.323.
The hero's glory, or the virgin's love; 6.32.10.96.
A fav'rite virgin's blooming from she took, Od.6.27.205.

VIRGINIA
October, store, and best *Virginia*, 6.39.5.110.
October, store, the best *Virginia*, 6.39.5A.110.

VIRGINITY
No Precept for Virginity he found: 2.ChWB.33.58.

VIRGINS
Her buskin'd Virgins trac'd the Dewy Lawn. 1.W-F.170.165.
And Virgins *smil'd* at what they *blush'd* before— 1.EOC.543.299.
Of all the Virgins of the Sylvan Train, 1.TrVP.2.377.
Ye *Lesbian* Virgins, and ye *Lesbian* Dames, 1.TrSP.232.404.
But young and tender Virgins, rul'd with Ease, 2.ChJM.111.20.
Or Virgins visited by Angel-Pow'rs, 2.RL1.33.148.
Not scornful Virgins who their Charms survive, 2.RL4.4.183.
Shrines! where their vigils pale-ey'd virgins keep, 2.ElAb.21.320.
For her white virgins *Hymenæals* sing; 2.ElAb.220.338.
The tender Labyrinth of a Virgins Ear: 4.JD2A.66.138.
There, Youths and Virgins ever gay, 4.HOde1.29A.153.
For Virgins, to keep chaste, must go 6.61.47.182.
And Quires of Virgins celebrate thy praise? 6.65.8.192.
Say, Virgins, seated round the Throne Divine, Il.2.572.155.
Beside him, *Helen* with her Virgins stands, Il.6.402.346.
Nor *Grecian* virgins shriek'd his obsequies, Od.3.321.102.
Where their fair vests *Phæacian* virgins lave. Od.6.44.207.
O'er the green mead the sporting virgins play: Od.6.112.211.
To rocks, to caves, the frighted virgins fly; Od.6.166.216.
Attends his steps: th' astonish'd virgins gaze. Od.6.282.224.
While thus his mother to her virgins spoke. Od.17.585.161.
Of twenty virgins to the spring repair: Od.20.197.243.
Bid the gay youth and sprightly virgins rise, Od.23.130.326.

VIRGO
Virgil, when call'd *Pasiphae Virgo* 6.10.89.27.

VIRRO
For what has Virro painted, built, and planted? 3.Ep4.13.137.

VIRTUE
Who first their Youth in Arts of Virtue train'd, 1.TrSt.619.436.
Chorœbus, fam'd for Virtue as for Arms; 1.TrSt.715.440.
And conscious Virtue, still its own Reward, 1.TrSt.758.442.
With such amazing Virtue durst engage. 1.TrSt.783.442.
Your former Fame, and ancient Virtue lost? 1.TrES.146.455.
Think not my Virtue lost, tho' Time has shed 2.ChJM.131.21.
That was with Sense, but not with Virtue blest; 2.ChJM.240.26.
With well-dissembl'd Virtue in her Face: 2.ChJM.812.54.
Ease, Pleasure, Virtue, All, our Sex resign. 2.RL4.106.192.
Behold the first in Virtue, as in Face! 2.RL5.18.200.
With boundless Pow'r unbounded Virtue join'd, 2.TemF.166.268.
Since living Virtue is with Envy curst, 2.TemF.320.279.
What Virtue seem'd, was done for thee alone. 2.TemF.349.280.
And all that Virtue seem'd, was done for thee alone. 2.TemF.349A.280.
To follow Virtue ev'n for Virtue's sake. 2.TemF.365.281.
O grace serene! oh virtue heav'nly fair! 2.ElAb.297.343.
Nor left one virtue to redeem her Race. 2.Elegy.28.365.
Were there all harmony, all virtue here; 3.EOM1.166.35.
And Grace and Virtue, Sense and Reason split, 3.EOM2.83.64.
Their Virtue fix'd; 'tis fix'd as in a frost, 3.EOM2.102.67.
Strong grows the Virtue with his nature mix'd; 3.EOM2.178.76.
Nor Virtue, male or female, can we name, 3.EOM2.193.78.
The virtue nearest to our vice ally'd; 3.EOM2.196.79.
Where ends the Virtue, or begins the Vice. 3.EOM2.210.81.
That Vice or Virtue there is none at all. 3.EOM2.212.81.
For, Vice or Virtue, Self directs it still; 3.EOM2.236.84.
Each Virtue in each Passion takes its turn; 3.EOM3.136.106.
'Twas VIRTUE ONLY (or in arts or arms, 3.EOM3.211.114.
Then VIRTUE ONLY (or in arts or arms, 3.EOM3.211A.114.
To Virtue, in the paths of Pleasure, trod, 3.EOM3.233.116.
Forc'd into virtue thus by Self-defence, 3.EOM3.279.121.
Some swell'd to Gods, confess ev'n Virtue vain; 3.EOM4.24.130.
One doubts of All, one owns ev'n Virtue vain. 3.EOM4.28Z2.130.
And Peace, oh Virtue! Peace is all thy own. 3.EOM4.82.136.
Of Vice or Virtue, whether blest or curst, 3.EOM4.87.136.
'Tis but what Virtue flies from and disdains: 3.EOM4.90.136.
And Peace, fair Virtue! Peace is all thy own. 3.EOM4.82A.136.
And Peace, O Virtue! Peace is all thy own. 3.EOM4.82B.136.
Who fancy Bliss to Vice, to Virtue Woe! 3.EOM4.94.137.
Was this their Virtue, or Contempt of Life? 3.EOM4.102.138.
Say, was it Virtue, more tho' Heav'n ne'er gave, 3.EOM4.103.138.
Tell me, if Virtue made the Son expire, 3.EOM4.105.138.
And what rewards your Virtue, punish mine. 3.EOM4.144.141.
Or he whose Virtue sigh'd to lose a day? 3.EOM4.148.142.
"But sometimes Virtue starves, while Vice is fed." 3.EOM4.149.142.
What then? Is the reward of Virtue bread? 3.EOM4.150.142.
Rewards, that either would to Virtue bring 3.EOM4.181.144.
"Virtue alone is Happiness below." 3.EOM4.310.157.
Since but to wish more Virtue, is to gain. 3.EOM4.326.160.
His greatest Virtue with his greatest Bliss, 3.EOM4.350.162.
That VIRTUE only makes our Bliss below; 3.EOM4.397.166.
All know 'tis Virtue, for he thinks them knaves: 3.Ep1.117.24.
Each is a sort of *Virtue*, and of *Vice*. 3.Ep2.206A.67.
Aw'd without Virtue, without Beauty charm'd; 3.Ep2.46.54.
Virtue she finds too painful an endeavour, 3.Ep2.163.64.
That each may seem a Virtue, or a Vice. 3.Ep2.206.67.
T'enjoy them, and the Virtue to impart, 3.Ep3.220.111.
Enough, that Virtue fill'd the space between; 3.Ep3.289.116.
"Virtue! and Wealth! what are ye but a name!" 3.Ep3.334.120.
P. What? arm'd for *Virtue* when I point the Pen, 4.HS1.105.15.
To VIRTUE ONLY and HER friends, A FRIEND, 4.HS1.121.17.
"None shou'd, by my Advice, learn *Virtue* there." 4.JD4.97.33.
What, and how great, the Virtue and the Art 4.HS2.1.55.
Give Virtue scandal, Innocence a fear, 4.Arbu.285.116.
Welcome for thee, fair Virtue! all the past: 4.Arbu.358.122.
For thee, fair Virtue! welcome ev'n the *last!* 4.Arbu.359.122.
If there be Force in Virtue, or in Song. 4.Arbu.387.126.
In Pow'r, Wit, Figure, Virtue, Fortune, plac'd 4.2HE2.302.187.
All human Virtue to its latest breath 4.2HE1.15.195.
In ev'ry publick Virtue we excell, 4.2HE1.45.197.
Or Virtue, or Religion turn to sport, 4.2HE1.211.213.
And pours each human Virtue in the heart. 4.2HE1.220.213.

VIRTUE (CONTINUED)

Who Virtue and a Church alike disowns, 4.1HE6.65.241.
Still true to Virtue, and as warm as true: 4.1HE1.30.281.
'Tis the first Virtue, Vices to abhor; 4.1HE1.65.283.
Here, Wisdom calls: "Seek Virtue first! be bold! 4.1HE1.77.285.
"As Gold to Silver, Virtue is to Gold." 4.1HE1.78.285.
"And then let Virtue follow, if she will." 4.1HE1.80.285.
"Virtue, brave boys! 'tis Virtue makes a King." 4.1HE1.92.285.
"Virtue, brave boys! 'tis Virtue makes a King." 4.1HE1.92.285.
Adieu to Virtue if you're once a Slave: 4.1HE1.118.287.
And wear their strange old Virtue as they will. 4.EpS1.44.301.
At Sense and Virtue, balance all agen. 4.EpS1.60.302.
Virtue, I grant you, is an empty boast; 4.EpS1.113.306.
Virtue may chuse the high or low Degree, 4.EpS1.137.308.
'Tis just alike to Virtue, and to me; 4.EpS1.138.308.
And sees pale Virtue carted in her stead! 4.EpS1.150.309.
Else might he take to Virtue some years hence— 4.EpS2.60.315.
To *Berkley,* ev'ry Virtue under Heav'n. 4.EpS2.73.317.
I follow *Virtue,* where she shines, I praise, 4.EpS2.95.318.
Find you the Virtue, and I'll find the Verse. 4.EpS2.105.319.
No Pow'r, when Virtue claims it, can withstand: 4.EpS2.119.320.
When Truth or Virtue an Affront endures, 4.EpS2.199.324.
His public virtue makes his title good. 4.1740.96.337.
That beams on earth, each Virtue he inspires, 5.DunA3.218.176.
That beams on earth, each Virtue he inspires, 5.DunB3.220.331.
Held forth the Virtue of the dreadful wand; 5.DunB4.140.355.
Find Virtue local, all Relation scorn, 5.DunB4.479.389.
And boundless pow'r with boundless virtue join'd; 6.20.47.67.
To make mankind, in conscious virtue bold, 6.32.3.96.
And foes to virtue wonder'd how they wept. 6.32.8.96.
Virtue confess'd in human shape he draws, 6.32.17.96.
And show, you have the virtue to be mov'd. 6.32.38.97.
No guard but virtue, no redress but tears. 6.38.18.108.
Your virtue equal, tho' your loss be less. 6.38.24.108.
Why, virtue, does thou blame desire, 6.51ii.9.153.
Here pitying heav'n that virtue mutual found, 6.69i.3.197.
When God calls Virtue to the grave, 6.69ii.6.199.
Virtue unmov'd can hear the Call, 6.69ii.9.199.
Or Virtue's Virtue scarce would last a Day. 6.82vi.8.232.
Reason, you found, and Virtue were the same. 6.96iii.8.274.
You went, you saw, you heard: With Virtue fraught, 6.96iii.21.275.
'Tis sure some Virtue to conceal its Shame. 6.96v.20.280.
Humility's the Virtue of the Great. 6.96v.34.281.
Convinc'd, that Virtue only is our own. 6.115.6.322.
Tho' he talk'd much of Virtue, her Head always run 6.124i.5.346.
And ev'ry opening Virtue blooming round, 6.132.2.362.
The living Virtue now had shone approv'd, 6.132.7.362.
Whose Publick Virtue knew no Party rage: 6.134.2.364.
In Death, by Friendship, Honour, Virtue; mourn'd. 6.134.10.364.
Virtue she finds too painful an endeavour, 6.139.7.377.
The good their Virtue might effect, or sense, 6.147iv.3.391.
The good their Virtue would effect, or sense, 6.147iv.3A.391.
Whose Godlike Virtue we but urge in vain, Il.4.327.236.
Wake each Paternal Virtue in thy Soul: Il.5.161.274.
Warm'd with some Virtue, some Regard of Fame! Il.6.443.348.
Whose Virtue charm'd him as her Beauty fir'd, Il.6.473.350.
Your former Fame, and ancient Virtue lost! Il.12.500.99.
For Riches much, and more for Virtue fam'd, Il.13.834.145.
With such a Tyde superior Virtue sway'd, Il.13.849.146.
If Heav'n have lodg'd this Virtue in my Breast, Il.13.921.148.
In ev'ry Virtue, or of Peace or War: Il.15.777.226.
Thee first in Virtue, as in Pow'r supreme, Il.23.1054.533.
And Heav'n, that ev'ry Virtue bears in mind, Il.24.523.558.
On these the Virtue of his Wand he tries, Il.24.547.558.
The suffering virtue of the wise and brave? Od.1.79.35.
Beneath our roof with Virtue cou'd reside; Od.1.296.47.
For wealth and beauty less than virtue please. Od.2.236.73.
But since thy veins paternal virtue fires, Od.2.317.76.
In whom stern courage with soft virtue join'd, Od.3.137.92.
Then Virtue was no more (her guard away) Od.3.344.103.
Great as he is, such virtue shall devour. Od.5.433.193.
In virtue rich; in blessing others, blest. Od.7.96.238.
Who bears the virtue of the sleepy rod. Od.7.185.244.
Like thee in beauty, nor in virtue less. Od.7.377.254.
As first in virtue, these thy realms obey! Od.9.2.298.
She bore the virtue of the magic wand. Od.10.458.366.
O Monarch great in virtue as in sway! Od.11.443.406.
Nor trust thy virtue to th' enchanting sound. Od.12.64.433.
Sure fixt on Virtue may your nation stand, Od.13.60.4.
To other regions is his virtue known. Od.13.489.29.
Hard task, he cries, thy virtue gives thy friend, Od.16.69.105.
Ill suits it, female virtue to be seen Od.18.217.177.
Know Friend! that Virtue is the path to praise. Od.21.360.277.
Then ceas'd; the filial virtue made reply. Od.22.167.295.
Not more thy wisdom, than her virtue, shin'd; Od.24.220.358.
Strive for fair Virtue, and contest for Fame! Od.24.597.376.

VIRTUE'S

Fair Virtue's silent Train: Supreme of these 2.TemF.170.268.
To follow Virtue ev'n for Virtue's sake. 2.TemF.365.281.
Exalt their kind, and take some Virtue's name. 3.EOM2.100.67.
That Virtue's ends from Vanity can raise, 3.EOM2.245.85.
Is Virtue's prize: A better would you fix? 3.EOM4.169.143.
Less pleasing far than Virtue's very tears. 3.EOM4.320.159.
That not for Fame, but Virtue's better end, 4.Arbu.342.120.
To Virtue's Work provoke the tardy Hall, 4.EpS2.218.325.
Touch'd with the Flame that breaks from Virtue's Shrine, 4.EpS2.233.326.
Who lead fair Virtue's train along, 6.51i.11.151.
Where every grace with every Virtue's join'd 6.75.6.212.
Were Virtue's self in Silks,—faith keep away! 6.82vi.7.232.
Or Virtue's Virtue scarce would last a Day. 6.82vi.8.232.
And thou must fall, thy Virtue's Sacrifice. Il.6.515.351.
Nor fraud mistrusts in virtue's fair disguise. Od.2.116.67.
For Virtue's image yet possest her mind, Od.3.332.102.
Nor fraud mistrusts in virtue's fair disguise. Od.24.165.356.

VIRTUES

The growing Virtues of my youthful Son, 1.TrUl.245.474.
But if her Virtues prove the larger Share, 2.ChJM.192.24.
To blaze those Virtues which the Good would hide. 2.TemF.369.281.
The surest Virtues thus from Passions shoot, 3.EOM2.183.77.
The virtues of a saint at twenty-one! 3.EOM4.184.144.
Court-virtues bear, like Gems, the highest rate, 3.Ep1.93.22.
In life's low vale, the soil the virtues like, 3.Ep1.95.22.
Poets heap Virtues, Painters Gems at will, 3.Ep2.185.65.
Your Virtues open fairest in the shade. 3.Ep2.202.67.
With all a Woman's Virtues but the P—x, 4.HAdv.17.75.
"Take him with all his Virtues, on my word; 4.2HE2.13.165.
They had, and greater Virtues, I'll agree. 4.2HE1.96.203.
To teach their frugal Virtues to his Heir; 4.2HE1.166.209.
Yet think great Sir! (so many Virtues shown) 4.2HE1.376.227.
Four guardian Virtues, round, support her Throne; 5.DunA1.44.65.
With all thy Father's virtues blest, be born! 5.DunA3.133.161.
Four guardina Virtues, round, support her throne: 5.DunB1.46.274.
With all thy Father's virtues blest, be born! 5.DunB3.141.326.
The Sire saw, one by one, his Virtues wake: 5.DunB4.285.372.
The Sire saw, smiling, his own Virtues wake: 5.DunB4.285A.372.
Amidst their virtues, a reserve of vice. 6.41.20.114.
Nor wish to lose a Foe these Virtues raise; 6.73.11.210.
Endu'd with all the *Virtues* of a *Horse.* 6.96iv.110.279.
Made *William's* Virtues wipe the bare A—— 6.101.5.290.
Still leave some ancient virtues to our age: 6.113.10.320.
The Virtues of Humanity be thine— Il.9.337.450.
Thy growing Virtues justify'd my Cares, Il.9.616.464.
Your great Forefathers Virtues, and your own. Il.11.370.51.
(She that all Simples' healing Virtues knew, Il.11.876.75.
Your great Forefathers Virtues, and your own. Il.15.893.231.
And blame those Virtues which they cannot share. Il.22.149.459.
(On whom the virtues of thy sire descend) Od.3.243.97.
The growing virtues of my youthful son, Od.13.412.26.
Of all the virtues of thy generous mind. Od.15.173.76.
My virtues last: my brightest charm is love. Od.18.298.181.

VIRTUOUS

'Tis what the *Vicious fear,* the *Virtuous shun;* 1.EOC.506.295.
With Virtuous Acts thy Ancestor's Disgrace, 1.TrSt.823.444.
And charm'd with virtuous Joys, and sober Life, 2.ChJM.79.18.
The solid Comforts of a virtuous Life. 2.ChJM.558.42.
How constant, chast, and virtuous, Women are. 2.ChJM.672.47.
How virtuous chast and constant, Women are. 2.ChJM.672A.47.
"I know thee for a virtuous, faithful Wife." 2.ChWB.133.62.
Kind, virtuous drops just gath'ring in my eye, 2.ElAb.278.342.
Virtuous and vicious ev'ry Man must be, 3.EOM2.231.83.
See FALKLAND dies, the virtuous and the just! 3.EOM4.99.137.
See FALKLAND falls, the virtuous and the just! 3.EOM4.99A.137.
As that the virtuous son is ill at ease, 3.EOM4.119.139.
Self-love but serves the virtuous mind to wake, 3.EOM4.363.163.
And virtuous Alfred, a more sacred Name, 4.2HE1.8.195.
Be Virtuous, and be happy for your pains. 4.1HE6.62.241.
For the dull Glory of a virtuous Wife! 6.19.46.63.
The Wise, the Learn'd, the Virtuous, and the Brave; 6.27.8.81.
That virtuous ladies envy while they rail; 6.41.16.113.
The prudent, learn'd, and virtuous breast? 6.51ii.2.152.
By thy sweet Sojourn in those virtuous Climes, 6.96iii.6.274.
With native Humour temp'ring virtuous Rage, 6.125.3.350.
Fir'd with the Thirst which Virtuous Envy breeds, Il.1.353.105.
They gave thee not—a brave and virtuous Soul. Il.9.56.434.
Thy Country's Friend; and virtuous, tho' in vain! Il.11.312.49.
There have been Heroes, who by virtuous Care, Il.17.380.302.
Rise then ye Peers! with virtuous anger rise! Od.2.71.64.
Charm'd with that virtuous draught, th' exalted mind Od.4.307.134.
Crown the chaste wishes of thy virtuous soul, Od.6.218.220.
Lest malice, prone the virtuous to defame, Od.6.329.227.
And should Posterity one virtuous find, Od.11.539.409.
Fly, whilst thy Mother virtuous yet withstands Od.15.19.70.
Scornful of age, to taunt the virtuous man, Od.18.397.187.
The lewd to death devote, the virtuous spare. Od.19.582.224.
Pleas'd with her virtuous fears, the King replies, Od.23.113.325.

VIRUMQUE

Of Arma Virumque 6.42iv.5.118.

VISAGE

A hundred Snakes her gloomy Visage shade, 1.TrSt.144.416.
With visage from his shelves with dust besprent? 5.DunA3.182A.170.
Blank'd his bold visage, and a thin Third day: 5.DunB1.114.278.
From his vile Visage wip'd the scalding Tears. Il.2.331.143.
But first, to hide her Heav'nly Visage, spread Il.5.1036.316.
At *Hector's* Feet the goary Visage lay. Il.13.272.117.
The goary Visage, thus insulting spoke, Il.14.586.190.
The parted Visage falls on equal Sides: Il.20.446.413.
And glares on the pale Visage of the Dead. Il.23.133.493.
Deep are his sighs, his visage pale, his dress Od.11.232.393.
And turning his grim visage, sternly spoke. Od.11.760.424.
With bloodless visage, and with hideous yell, Od.11.780.425.
From his blank visage fled the coward blood, Od.18.88.170.
His visage solemn sad, of sable hue: Od.19.279.208.

VISCOUNT'S

His daughter flaunts a Viscount's tawdry wife; 3.Ep3.391.124.

VISIBLE

Of darkness visible so much be lent, 5.DunB4.3.339.

VISIGOTHS

See, the fierce Visigoths on Spain and Gaul. 5.DunA3.86.157.
See the fierce Visigoths on Spain and Gaul! 5.DunB3.94.324.

VISION

His daily Vision, and his Dream by Night; 1.TrSt.446.428.
If e'er one Vision touch'd thy infant Thought, 2.RL1.29.147.
If e'er one Vision touch thy infant Thought, 2.RL1.29A.147.

VISION (CONTINUED)

But all the Vision vanish'd from thy Head.	2.RL1.120.155.
which Fancy colour'd, and a Vision wrought	4.JD4.189A.43.
A *Vision* Hermits can to Hell transport,	4.JD4.190.43.
And Poet's vision of eternal fame.	5.DunA3.12.150.
For this, our Queen unfolds to vision true	5.DunA3.53.155.
He wak'd, and all the Vision mix'd with air.	5.DunA3.358A.193.
And thro' the Ivory Gate the Vision flies.	5.DunA3.358.155.
And Poet's vision of eternal Fame.	5.DunB3.12.320.
For this, our Queen unfolds to vision true	5.DunB3.61.323.
And thro' the Iv'ry Gate the Vision flies.	5.DunB3.340.336.
Which Theocles in raptur'd vision saw,	5.DunB4.488.389.
Then give one flirt, and all the vision flies.	6.45.38.125.
And thus commands the *Vision* of the Night.	II.2.8.127.
And trust the *Vision* that descends from *Jove.*	II.2.42.129.
The Vision spoke, and past in Air away.	II.2.92.131.
Nor doubt the Vision of the Pow'rs Divine;	II.2.102.131.
The golden Vision round his sacred Head;	II.14.414.183.
The fainting Hero, as the Vision bright	II.15.278.207.
And sleep'st thou Father! (thus the Vision said)	II.24.851.572.
And in his raptured soul The Vision glows.	Od.1.558.58.
Vision divine! The throng'd spectators gaze	Od.3.476.110.
Close to her head the pleasing vision stands,	Od.4.1057.167.
The vision, manifest of future fate,	Od.4.1097.169.
From *Dymas* sprung, and thus the vision spoke:	Od.6.28.205.
Obedient to the vision of the night.	Od.6.60.208.
Then manifest of heav'n the vision stood,	Od.7.271.249.
A mournful vision! the *Sisyphan* shade;	Od.11.734.422.
Ev'n now a Vision stood before my eye,	Od.14.560.64.
And sure the warning Vision was from high:	Od.14.561.64.
But oft revolve the vision in thy heart:	Od.19.51.195.
O Queen! no vulgar vision of the sky	Od.19.641.227.
The vision self-explain'd (the Chief replies.)	Od.19.650.227.
I deem it sure a vision of the skies.	Od.20.109.238.
In vision rap'd <rapt>; the * *Hyperesian* Seer	Od.20.421.253.
And still to last, the vision of my night!	Od.21.80.262.

VISIONARY

And drest in all its visionary Charms,	1.TrSP.147.400.
Made visionary Fabricks round them rise,	2.TemF.103.261.
Or lull to rest the visionary maid:	2.ElAb.162.332.
Why dimly gleams the visionary sword?	2.Elegy.4.362.
Where Thames reflects the visionary Scene.	4.HOde1.24.153.
Whilst Thames reflects the visionary Scene.	4.HOde1.24A.153.
Whose Visionary Form like *Nestor* came,	II.2.73.130.
Whose visionary Steel his Bosom tore;	II.10.580.28.
In vain to grasp the visionary Shade;	II.23.116.492.
Vanish'd are all the visionary joys:	Od.4.246.131.
Swift thro' the valves the visionary fair	Od.4.1093.169.
Thin airy shoals, and visionary shades.	Od.10.633.374.
Thin, airy shoals of visionary ghosts:	Od.11.48.383.
A visionary thought I'll now relate,	Od.19.625.226.
His care dissolves in visionary joys:	Od.20.66.235.

VISIONS

Whose Raptures fire me, and whose Visions bless,	1.W-F.260.173.
Or bright as Visions of expiring Maids.	2.RL4.42.187.
In mystic Visions, now believ'd too late!	2.RL4.166.197.
(What Time the Morn mysterious Visions brings,	2.TemF.7.253.
And melts in visions of eternal day.	2.ElAb.222.338.
Alas! 'tis more than (all his Visions past)	3.Ep3.85.94.
Like forms in clouds, or visions of the night!	5.DunA2.104.109.
Like forms in clouds, or visions of the night.	5.DunB2.112.300.
Where heav'nly visions *Plato* fir'd,	6.51i.3.151.
There as the wond'rous visions I survey'd,	Od.11.104.385.
But wond'rous visions drew my curious eye.	Od.11.696.419.
The wond'rous visions, and the laws of Hell.	Od.12.46.431.
With visions manifest of future fate.	Od.19.663.228.

VISIT

Oh deign to visit our forsaken Seats,	1.PSu.71.77.
To visit *Damian,* and divert his Pain.	2.ChJM.409.34.
Who gave the *Ball,* or paid the *Visit* last:	2.RL3.12.170.
Who gave a *Ball,* or paid the *Visit* last;	2.RL3.12A.170.
"And (like *Ulysses*) visit Courts, and Men.	4.JD4.89A.33.
And visit alehouse where ye first did grow."	5.DunA1.202.87.
And visit alehouse where ye first begun."	5.DunA1.202A.87.
Did slumbring visit, and convey to stews?	5.DunA2.390.148.
Thus visit not thy own! on this blest age	5.DunA3.113.160.
Did slumb'ring visit, and convey to stews;	5.DunB2.422.318.
Thus visit not thy own! on this blest age	5.DunB3.121.325.
You'd at present do nothing but give us a Visit.	6.42i.8.116.
We'll not be slow to visit Dr. Swift.	6.42vi.6.120.
You, like the *Samian,* visit Lands unknown,	6.96iii.17.275.
And if he'll visit me, I'll wave my Right.	6.143.4.385.
I visit these, to whose indulgent Cares	II.14.345.179.
And give the *Greeks* to visit *Greece* again.	II.16.107.240.
Now first to me this visit dost thou daign,	Od.1.223.43.
Why this first visit to reprove my fear?	Od.4.1068.167.
Thou visit earth, a daughter of the skies,	Od.6.178.218.
To visit *Paphos* and her blooming groves,	Od.8.396.285.
I deem'd it best to visit first my crew,	Od.10.179.349.
By turns they visit this etherial sky,	Od.11.371.401.
My swains to visit, and the works survey.	Od.15.544.96.
Can visit unapproach'd by mortal sight.	Od.19.53.195.

VISITANT

Griev'd that a Visitant so long shou'd wait	Od.1.157.40.
Some visitant of pure etherial race,	Od.19.48.195.

VISITED

Or Virgins visited by Angel-Pow'rs,	2.RL1.33.148.

VISITS

As thine, which visits *Windsor's* fam'd Abodes,	1.W-F.229.170.
Than thine, which visits *Windsor's* fam'd Abodes,	1.W-F.229A.170.

VISITS (CONTINUED)

And endless Treats, and endless Visits paid,	2.ChWB.115.62.
Visits to ev'ry Church we daily paid,	2.ChWB.283.70.
While *Visits* shall be paid on solemn Days,	2.RL3.167.181.
Who cause the Proud their Visits to delay,	2.RL4.63.189.
To pay due Visits, and address the Fair:	2.TemF.385.282.
Heav'n visits with a Taste the wealthy fool,	3.Ep4.17.137.
Visits each plant, and waters all the ground:	6.35.30.103.
Two or *Three* Visits, and *Two* or *Three* Bows,	6.36.1.104.
Two or *Three* Visits, with *Two* or *Three* Bows.	6.36.1A.105.
Two or *Three* Visits, *Two* or *Three* Bows,	6.36.1B.105.
Who visits with a gun, presents you birds,	6.45.25.125.
What mean those Visits to the *Sorrel Mare?*	6.96iv.30.277.
Visits each plant, and waters all the ground:	Od.7.171.244.

VISTA

His Son's fine Taste an op'ner Vista loves,	3.Ep4.93.146.

VISTA'S

And ampler *Vista's* open'd to my View,	2.TemF.263.276.

VISTO

Some Dæmon whisper'd, "Visto! have a Taste."	3.Ep4.16.137.

VISTO'S

What brought Sir Visto's ill got wealth to waste?	3.Ep4.15.137.

VISUAL

He from thick Films shall purge the visual Ray,	1.Mes.39.116.
Whose visual orb *Ulysses* robb'd of light;	Od.1.90.36.
With clouds of darkness quench'd his visual ray,	Od.8.59.265.
Ev'n he who sightless wants his visual ray,	Od.8.221.274.
The pointed torment on his visual ball.	Od.9.454.324.

VITAL

The Sun's mild Lustre warms the vital Air;	1.PSp.74.68.
So may kind Rains their vital Moisture yield,	1.PWi.15.89.
The Vital Sap then rising from below:	2.ChJM.134.21.
That while my Nostrils draw the vital Air,	2.RL4.137.195.
Each vital humour which should feed the whole,	3.EOM2.139.71.
(By turns we catch the vital breath, and die)	3.EOM3.18.94.
(By turns they catch the vital breath, and die)	3.EOM3.18A.94.
The vital flame, and swells the genial seeds.	3.EOM3.118.104.
As man's mæanders to the vital spring	5.DunA3.47.154.
As man's Mæanders to the vital spring	5.DunB3.55.323.
As man's meanders to the vital spring	6.9iii.1.21.
Vital spark of heav'nly flame!	6.31ii.1.94.
Long as *Achilles* breathes this vital Air,	II.1.112.92.
The vital Spirit issu'd at the Wound,	II.3.366.210.
Which driv'n by *Pallas,* pierc'd a vital Part;	II.5.352.283.
Transfix'd his Throat, and drank the vital Blood;	II.5.817.305.
But from our Lips the vital Spirit fled,	II.9.530.459.
Their Breasts no more the vital Spirit warms;	II.11.431.53.
Thy good *Menœtius* breathes the vital Air,	II.16.20.236.
For *Peleus* breaths no more the vital Air;	II.19.356.387.
Long as the vital Spirit moves my Heart?	II.22.486.476.
He lives, he breathes this heav'nly vital air,	Od.1.256.45.
To view the sun, or breathe the vital air.	Od.4.728.153.
The vital streams a chilling horror froze:	Od.4.935.162.
To me thou ow'st, to me, the vital air.	Od.8.502.289.
Thro' the wide wound the vital spirit flies.	Od.10.190.349.
A weight of woes, and breath the vital air,	Od.11.598.412.
While in your world I drew the vital air;	Od.11.764.424.
A chilly fear congeal'd my vital blood,	Od.12.435.452.
Alone *Ulysses* drew the vital air,	Od.16.126.108.
Ev'n now they envy me the vital air:	Od.16.138.109.
Wide as the sun displays his vital fire.	Od.17.469.156.
Breathes in no distant clime the vital air:	Od.19.308.209.

VITALS

Whose panting Vitals, warm with Life, she draws,	1.TrSt.721.440.
Their Bones he cracks, their reeking Vitals draws,	II.11.155.42.

VITRUVIUS

And be whate'er Vitruvius was before:	3.Ep4.194.155.

VIVE

And Swift cry wisely, "Vive la Bagatelle!"	4.1HE6.128.246.

VIVID

The vivid Green his shining Plumes unfold;	1.W-F.117.161.
The vivid Em'ralds there revive the Eye;	2.TemF.250.275.
Around her Throne the vivid Planets roll,	II.8.691.428.
Where bloomy meads with vivid greens were crown'd,	Od.5.93.176.

VIXEN

My vixen Mistress squalls;	6.47.22.129.
No Vixen Civet-Cat so sweet,	6.79.31.218.
No Vixen Civet-Cat more sweet,	6.79.31A.218.

VIZOR

Pierc'd thro' his Helmet's brazen Vizor, fell;	II.12.214.88.
(The Helm and Vizor he had cast aside	II.21.57.424.

VOCAL

But tell the Reeds, and tell the vocal Shore,	1.PWi.59.93.
A God, a God! the vocal Hills reply,	1.Mes.31.116.
Reveres *Apollo's* vocal Caves, and owns	1.TrSt.577.434.
These touch the vocal Stops, and those the trembling String.	2.ChJM.321.29.
And only vocal with the Maker's praise.	2.ElAb.140.331.
All vocal beings hymn'd their equal God:	3.EOM3.156.108.
High sounds, attempred to the vocal nose.	5.DunA2.246.129.
High Sound, attemp'red to the vocal nose;	5.DunB2.256.308.
High Notes, attemp'red to the vocal nose;	5.DunB2.256A.308.
This vocal wood had drawn the poet too.	6.3.12.7.
Liquids grew rough, and *Mutes* turn'd vocal:	6.30.8.86.

VOICE (CONTINUED)

An omen'd Voice invades his ravish'd ear. ....Od.20.131.240.
Cries one, with scornful leer and mimic voice, ...Od.20.449.255.
Deaf to Heav'n's voice, the social rite transgrest; ....Od.21.31.260.
We dread the all-arraigning voice of Fame; ....Od.21.348.276.
Thus will the common voice our deed defame, ...Od.21.355.276.
Then to the lute's soft voice prolong the night, ...Od.21.473.283.
Or Fame's eternal voice in future days: ....Od.22.50.289.
And thus with grateful voice address'd his ears: ....Od.22.406.307.
A scream of joy her feeble voice essay'd: ....Od.22.446.309.
Truth, by their high decree, thy voice forsakes, ...Od.23.17.319.
The voice, attun'd to instrumental sounds, ...Od.23.143.328.
A voice of loud lament thro' all the main ....Od.24.67.350.
Her awful voice detain'd the headlong tyde. ....Od.24.613.377.
Fear shook the nations. At the voice divine ....Od.24.616.377.

VOICE'S

Fair charmer cease, nor make your voice's prize ....6.3.1.7.

VOICES

And base, and treble Voices strike the Skies. ....2.RL5.42.202.
And marks distinct the Voices of the Foe. ....Il.10.16.2.
And urge the Gods, with Voices, Eyes, and Hands. ....Il.15.425.213.
So like your voices, and your words so wise, ...Od.3.153.93.
Then female voices from the shore I heard: ....Od.7.374.254.

VOID

And fills up all the *mighty Void* of Sense! ....1.EOC.210.264.
Old as he was, and void of Eye-sight too, ...2.ChJM.728.49.
Yet graceful Ease, and Sweetness void of Pride, ...2.RL2.15.160.
Nor void of Emblem was the mystic Wall, ...2.TemF.135.264.
'Tis true, said I, not void of Hopes I came, ...2.TemF.501.287.
No craving Void left aking in the breast: ....2.ElAb.94.327.
Or in the full creation leave a void, ...3.EOM1.243.45.
Or, meteor-like, flame lawless thro' the void, ...3.EOM2.65.63.
Who feeds yon Alms-house, neat, but void of state, ...3.Ep3.265A.115.
He feeds yon Alms-house, neat, but void of state, ...3.Ep3.265B.115.
Yet was not Cotta void of wit or worth: ....3.Ep3.180.109.
Behold yon Alms-house, neat, but void of state, ...3.Ep3.265.115.
"Lest stiff, and stately, void of fire, or force, ...4.1HE1.15.279.
"Lest stiff, and stately, void of fire, and force, ...4.1HE1.15A.279.
But senseless, lifeless! Idol void and vain! ....5.DunA2.42.100.
But senseless, lifeless! idol void and vain! ....5.DunB2.46.298.
There Nature reigns, and Passion void of Art, ...6.33.9.99.
Here Nature reigns, and Passion void of Art, ...6.33.9A.99.
If thou could'st make the Courtier void ....6.53.31.162.
And o'er th' infernal Regions void of day, ...6.65.4.192.
And o'er th' infernal Mansions void of day, ...6.65.4A.192.
Old, and void of all good-nature; ....6.70.7.201.
A soul as full of Worth, as void of Pride, ...6.73.1.209.
So full of Fibs, so void of Wit? ....6.127.2.355.
Not void of Soul, and not unskill'd in War: ....Il.7.276.378.
A Senate void of Order as of Choice, ...Il.7.416.385.
Old Man, if void of Fallacy or Art, ...Il.7.432.386.
A Senate void of Union as of Choice, ...Il.7.416A.385.
Curs'd is the Man, and void of Law and Right, ...Il.9.87.436.
Surpriz'd the Monarch feels, yet void of Fear ....Il.11.329.49.
Already have I met, nor void of Fear ....Il.20.119.399.
That trembled as it stuck; nor void of Fear ....Il.20.312.407.
And enter there the kingdoms void of day: ....Od.10.607.373.
Our woods not void of hospitality. ....Od.14.54.38.
And void of pain, the silent arrows kill. ....Od.15.451.92.
O void of faith! of all bad men the worst! ....Od.16.434.128.
Tost thro' the void, illimitable space: ....Od.20.75.236.

VOITURE

The truest Hearts for *Voiture* heav'd with Sighs; ....6.19.17.62.
Voiture was wept by all the brightest Eyes; ....6.19.18.62.

VOITURE'S

Ev'n Rival Wits did *Voiture's* Death deplore, ...6.19.15.62.
The *Smiles* and *Loves* had dy'd in *Voiture's* Death, ...6.19.19.62.
Ev'n Rival Wits did *Voiture's* Fate deplore, ...6.19.15A.62.
Let mine, like *Voiture's*, a gay Farce appear, ...6.19.25A.62.
Thus *Voiture's* early Care still shone the same, ...6.19.69.64.

VOLE

Shortly no Lad shall *chuck*, or Lady *vole*, ...4.JD4.146.37.

VOLGA'S

Let *Volga's* Banks with Iron Squadrons shine, ...1.W-F.363.186.

VOLLIED

With vollied vengeance blast their tow'ring pride! ....Od.20.212.243.

VOLLIES

But *ratling Nonsense* in full *Vollies* breaks; ....1.EOC.628.310.

VOLUBLE

So voluble a Weapon is the Tongue; ....Il.20.297.406.
Oh sharp in scandal, voluble and vain! ....Od.22.319.301.

VOLUME

For all their Lies) were in one Volume bound. ....2.ChWB.358.74.
As for the Volume that revil'd the Dames, ...ChWB.434.78.
Swift to whose hand a winged volume flies: ....5.DunA3.230.176.
Swift to whose hand a winged volume flies: ....5.DunB3.234.331.
His stretch'd-out arm display'd a Volume fair; ....5.DunB4.106.351.
To lug the pond'rous volume off in state.] ....5.DunB4.118.353.

VOLUMES

The silver Eel, in shining Volumes roll'd, ...1.W-F.143.163.
Her twisting Volumes, and her rowling Eyes, ...1.TrSt.728.440.
Volumes, whose size the space exactly fill'd; ....5.DunA1.117.77.
Of these twelve volumes, twelve of amplest size, ...5.DunA1.135.80.
Of these twelve volumes, twelve of amplest size, ...5.DunB1.155.281.

VOLUMES (CONTINUED)

Mount in dark volumes, and descend in snow. ....5.DunB2.364.315.
And roll in smoaking Volumes to the Skies. ....Il.5.620.297.
The gloomy Volumes, pierc'd with Light, divide. ....Il.5.935.311.
O'er the high Stern the curling Volumes rise, ...Il.16.152.243.
On spiry volumes there a Dragon rides; ....Od.4.619.149.
But smoaky volumes rolling from the ground. ....Od.10.114.346.

VOLUNTARY

Repentant sighs, and voluntary pains: ....2.ElAb.18.320.
And all that voluntary Vein, ...4.1HE7.49.271.
Hither we sail'd, a voluntary Throng, ...Il.1.207.96.
Unbidden Herbs, and voluntary Flow'rs; ....Il.14.396.182.
She fell, to lust a voluntary prey. ....Od.3.345.103.
The eighth, she voluntary moves to part, ...Od.7.348.253.

VOLUNTEER

But honest Instinct comes a volunteer; ....3.EOM3.88.100.

VOLUNTEERS

Beats up for Volunteers. ....6.58.48.172.

VOMIT

And the fresh vomit run for ever green!" ....5.DunA2.148.119.
And the fresh Vomit run for ever green!" ....5.DunB2.156.303.
Smiles on the Vomit, and enjoys the Purge. ....6.82x.6.236.

VORACIOUS

The Haunt of the voracious *Stork* or *Bittern*, ...6.26i.4.79.
Grim as voracious Wolves that seek the Springs ....Il.16.194.246.
Voracious Hounds, that many a Length before ....Il.17.813.320.
In rush'd the Suitors with voracious haste: ....Od.1.190.42.

VORTEX

Roll in her Vortex, and her pow'r confess. ....5.DunB4.84.349.

VOT'RESS

His Sister sends, her vot'ress, from above. ....5.DunA2.208.127.
His sister sends, her vot'ress, from above. ....5.DunB2.216.306.

VOT'RY'S

Forth from the heap she pick'd her Vot'ry's pray'r. ....5.DunA2.91.108.
Forth from the heap she pick'd her Vot'ry's pray'r, ...5.DunB2.95.300.

VOTARIES

Bacchus, and *Bacchus'* Votaries he drove ....Il.6.163.334.

VOTARY

Succeed my wish; your votary restore: ....Od.17.288.146.

VOTE

Have bled and purg'd me to a simple *Vote*. ....4.2HE2.197.179.
By Vote selected, to the Gen'ral's Bed. ....Il.1.483.111.
You join your suffrage to the public vote; ....Od.19.448.216.

VOTED

Or H[ardwic]k[e]'s quibbles voted into law? ....4.1740.64.335.
And voted *Helen's* Stay, for *Paris'* Gold. ....Il.11.164.42.
'Twas voted, *Hermes* from his god-like Foe ....Il.24.143.541.
The master Ram was voted mine by all: ....Od.9.642.333.

VOTES

Bows and votes on, in Court and Parliament; ....4.2HE2.275.185.
Fall, by the Votes of their degen'rate Line! ....4.EpS2.253.327.
Defrauds the Votes of all the *Grecian* Train; ....Il.1.508.112.
Due to the Votes of all the *Grecian* Train. ....Il.16.79.238.

VOUCH

Lord of an Otho, if I vouch it true; ....5.DunB4.369.379.
Saturnia ask'd an Oath, to vouch the Truth, ...Il.19.109.376.

VOUCHING

Nor disputant, in vouching Texts, leave out ....4.JD2A.106.142.

VOUCHSAF'D

How many Dutchmen she vouchsaf'd to thrid? ....5.DunA3.43.154.
How many Dutchmen she vouchsaf'd to thrid? ....5.DunB3.51.323.
Nor *Jove* vouchsaf'd his hapless Offspring Aid. ....Il.16.642.269.
Vouchsaf'd thy presence to my wond'ring eyes, ...Od.2.298.76.
The pow'r defrauding who vouchsaf'd to save. ....Od.4.676.151.
That view vouchsaf'd, let instant death surprise ....Od.7.305.250.
Without reply vouchsaf'd, *Antinous* ceas'd: ....Od.20.340.249.
Nor farther conference vouchsaf'd to stay; ....Od.24.308.364.

VOUCHSAFE

Yet stay, great *Cæsar!* and vouchsafe to reign ....1.TrSt.43.411.
Vouchsafe the Trunk between your Arms to take; ....2.ChJM.733.50.
Vouchsafe the Bole between your Arms to take; ....2.ChJM.733A.50.
"Wou'd I vouchsafe to sell what Nature gave, ...2.ChWB.201.66.
This, ev'n *Belinda* may vouchsafe to view: ....2.RL1.4.144.
As thus, "Vouchsafe, oh gracious Maker! ....4.HS6.17.251.
Vouchsafe, O *Thetis!* at our Board to share ....Il.18.475.344.
O, piteous of my fate, vouchsafe to shew, ...Od.4.513.144.
If home thou send us, and vouchsafe to spare. ....Od.9.413.323.
Vouchsafe the means of vengeance to debate, ...Od.13.441.27.
Vouchsafe the sanction of a sign above. ....Od.20.125.239.

VOUCHSAFES

When-e'er his influence *Jove* vouchsafes to show'r ....Od.4.285.132.
Vouchsafes the rev'rend stranger to display ....Od.8.157.271.

VOUS

'Twas *S'il vous plaist, Monsieur.* ....6.14v(b).12.49.
& *S'il vous plaist, Monsieur.* ....6.14v(b).12A.49.
and true men, vous-avez; ....6.68.14.197.

VOUS-AVEZ
and true men, vous-avez; ... 6.68.14.197.

VOW
Fair *Geraldine,* bright Object of his Vow, ... 1.W-F.297.176.
I pawn'd my Honour and ingag'd my Vow, ... 2.ChWB.293.71.
That not one Woman keeps her Marriage Vow. ... 2.ChWB.375.75.
And cry'd, "I vow you're mighty neat. ... 4.HS6.174.261.
A Vow to God He then did make ... 6.94.25.260.
But witness, Heralds, and proclaim my Vow, ... Il.1.440.108.
Not such at *Argos* was their gen'rous Vow, ... Il.2.350.144.
For whom must *Helen* break her second Vow? ... Il.3.497.215.
But first, to speed the Shaft, address thy Vow ... Il.4.131.226.
Now hear a Monarchs Vow: If Heav'ns high Pow'rs ... Il.8.347.414.
Hear all ye *Greeks,* and witness what I vow. ... Il.9.156.439.
And ruthless *Proserpine,* confirm'd his Vow. ... Il.9.585.463.
Accords their Vow, succeeds their Enterprize. ... Il.10.352.18.
They vow Destruction to the *Grecian* Name, ... Il.13.65.107.
Fond Love, the gentle Vow, the gay Desire, ... Il.14.249.173.
And that unbroken Vow, our Virgin Bed! ... Il.15.46.196.
He crops, and off'ring meditates his Vow. ... Il.19.262.383.
And faithful Guardians of the treasur'd Vow!) ... Il.22.326.469.
No firstling Lambs, unheedful! didst thou vow, ... Il.23.1022.529.
Vengeance I vow, and for your wrongs ye die. ... Od.2.170.70.
His holy vow: the fav'ring Goddess heard. ... Od.3.495.111.
Swear, by the Vow which never can be vain. ... Od.10.410.364.
To ev'ry God vow hecatombs to bleed, ... Od.17.62.135.
By precious gifts the vow sincere display: ... Od.18.323.182.
Shall I my virgin nuptial vow revere; ... Od.19.616.226.
They name the standard of their dearest vow. ... Od.20.46.234.

VOW'D
He vow'd to lead this Vicious Life no more. ... 2.ChJM.10.15.
He vow'd to lead that Vicious Life no more. ... 2.ChJM.10A.15.
I vow'd, I scarce cou'd sleep since first I knew him, ... 2.ChWB.300.71.
C vow'd, he'd frankly have releas'd ... 6.30.31.87.
Vow'd with Libations and with Victims then, ... Il.2.406.147.
So vow'd the Matrons, but they vow'd in vain. ... Il.6.387.345.
So vow'd the Matrons, but they vow'd in vain. ... Il.6.387.345.
I vow'd his much-lov'd Offspring to restore, ... Il.18.381.339.
And burst like Light'ning thro' the Ranks, and vow'd ... Il.20.107.398.
Those curling Locks which from his Youth he vow'd, ... Il.23.174.496.
The curling Locks which from his Youth he vow'd, ... Il.23.174A.496.
To whom we vainly vow'd, at our return, ... Il.23.180.497.
So vow'd my Father, but he vow'd in vain. ... Il.23.186.497.
So vow'd my Father, but he vow'd in vain; ... Il.23.186.497.
The victims, vow'd to each *Tartarean* pow'r, ... Od.11.25.380.
The vengeance vow'd for eyeless *Polypheme.* ... Od.13.145.12.
To ev'ry God vow'd hecatombs to bleed, ... Od.17.70.136.
Here with his goats, (not vow'd to sacred flame, ... Od.17.246.143.
In festival devour'd, and victims vow'd.) ... Od.20.4.230.
Of victims vow'd, a ram, a bull, a boar: ... Od.23.294.337.

VOWEL
I, Consonant and Vowel too, ... 6.30.34.87.

VOWELL
Thrusts your poor Vowell from his Notch: ... 6.30.22.86.

VOWELS
Tho' oft the Ear the *open Vowels* tire, ... 1.EOC.345.278.
The *Vowels, U, O, I, E, A,* ... 6.30.2.85.
And all th' ambitious Vowels vie, ... 6.30.72.88.
Cons'nants! and Vowels, (much their betters,) ... 6.30.76.89.
Cons'nants! and Vowels, too (their Betters) ... 6.30.76A.89.

VOWS
Oft on the Rind I carv'd her Am'rous Vows, ... 1.PAu.67.85.
The Garlands fade, the Vows are worn away; ... 1.PAu.69.85.
The Vows you never will return, receive; ... 1.TrSP.107.398.
And pays in hollow Rocks his awful Vows, ... 1.TrSt.862.446.
Attend his Transports, and receive his Vows. ... 1.TrUl.243.473.
With secret Vows, to favour his Design. ... 2.ChJM.417.35.
Both, pleas'd and blest, renew'd their mutual Vows, ... 2.ChJM.815.54.
There broken Vows, and Death-bed Alms are found, ... 2.RL5.117.209.
And send up Vows from *Rosamonda's* Lake. ... 2.RL5.136.211.
Next these a youthful Train their Vows exprest, ... 2.TemF.378.282.
And Saints with wonder heard the vows I made. ... 2.ElAb.114.329.
And hears the various Vows of fond mankind, ... 5.DunA2.83.108.
There hears the various Vows of fond mankind, ... 5.DunA2.83A.108.
What force have pious vows! the Queen of Love ... 5.DunA2.207.127.
And hears the various vows of fond mankind; ... 5.DunB2.87.300.
What force have pious vows! The Queen of Love ... 5.DunB2.215.306.
While vows and service nothing gain'd, ... 6.4iii.9.10.
To Heav'n familiar his bold vows shall send, ... 6.21.3.69.
Two or *Three* civil Things, *Two* or *Three* Vows, ... 6.36.2.104.
In days of old they pardon'd breach of vows, ... 6.41.29.114.
What *Redriff* Wife so long hath kept her Vows? ... 6.96iv.6.276.
Ye Kings and Warriors! may your Vows be crown'd, ... Il.1.23.86.
If broken Vows this heavy Curse have laid, ... Il.1.87.91.
To whom thy Hands the Vows of *Greece* convey, ... Il.1.110.92.
Nor Vows unpaid, nor slighted Sacrifice, ... Il.1.118.92.
This seals thy Suit, and this fulfills thy Vows— ... Il.1.682.119.
In Peace enjoy the Fruits of broken Vows? ... Il.2.196.137.
Then offers Vows with Hecatombs to crown ... Il.4.150.228.
Not thus our Vows, confirm'd with Wine and Gore, ... Il.4.192.230.
With offer'd Vows, in *Ilion's* topmost Tow'r. ... Il.6.112.329.
And pay due Vows to all the Gods around. ... Il.6.324.342.
And Vows like these ascend from all the Bands. ... Il.7.214.375.
To *Saturn's* Son be all your Vows addrest: ... Il.7.230.376.
Said I in secret? No, your Vows declare, ... Il.7.233.376.
Who wearies Heav'n with Vows for *Hector's* Life. ... Il.7.361.381.
To thee my Vows were breath'd from ev'ry Shore; ... Il.8.286.411.
His Vows, in Bitterness of Soul preferr'd; ... Il.8.294.411.
Who paid their Vows to *Panomphæan Jove;* ... Il.8.300.412.
They pour forth Vows their Embassy to bless, ... Il.9.241.444.

VOWS (CONTINUED)
Are mov'd by Off'rings, Vows, and Sacrifice; ... Il.9.621.465.
For *Jove,* averse, our humble Vows denies, ... Il.10.53A.4.
To all the Gods his constant Vows were paid; ... Il.20.347.408.
And Vows omitted forfeited the Prize. ... Il.23.626.514.
With Vows of firstling Lambs, and grateful Sacrifice. ... Il.23.1033.530.
She seems attentive to their pleaded vows, ... Od.1.321.48.
But angry *Jove* dispers'd our vows in air, ... Od.3.194.95.
With impious thanks and mockery of vows, ... Od.3.347.103.
Soon as due vows on ev'ry part were pay'd, ... Od.3.568.115.
With double vows invoking *Hymen's* pow'r, ... Od.4.5.119.
No vows had we prefer'd, nor victim slain! ... Od.4.475.142.
What guilt provokes him, and what vows appease? ... Od.4.516.145.
What vows repentant will the Pow'r appease, ... Od.4.633.149.
To thy long vows a safe return accord. ... Od.4.648.150.
Attend, unconquer'd maid! accord my vows, ... Od.6.389.230.
To thee, my Goddess, I address my vows, ... Od.8.510.290.
These solemn vows and holy off'rings paid ... Od.10.626.374.
And sacred vows, and mystic song, apply'd ... Od.10.636.374.
Thus solemn rites and holy vows we paid ... Od.11.43.381.
And mutter'd vows, and mystic song apply'd ... Od.11.59.383.
Attend his transports, and receive his vows! ... Od.13.410.26.
They slight the pledges of their former vows; ... Od.15.26.71.
His ardent vows, the stranger thus addrest. ... Od.15.281.82.
By that dread pow'r to whom thy vows are paid; ... Od.15.284.82.
Where constant vows by travellers are pay'd, ... Od.17.244.143.
O destin'd head! The pious vows are lost; ... Od.19.434.215.
E're second vows my bridal faith profane. ... Od.20.97.237.
(Of granted vows a certain signal sent) ... Od.20.144.240.
With equal vows *Eumæus* too implor'd ... Od.21.209.270.
Those vows the Gods accord: Behold the man! ... Od.21.212.270.
Against *Ulysses* have thy vows been made; ... Od.22.359.304.
Where oft *Laertes* holy vows had paid, ... Od.22.373.306.
Each faithful youth, and breathes out ardent vows: ... Od.24.471.371.

VOYAG'D
I voyag'd, leader of a warrior host, ... Od.6.196.219.
Mean-time he voyag'd to explore the will ... Od.14.363.52.
Thence safe I voyag'd to my native shore. ... Od.17.169.139.

VOYAGE
On Fame's mad voyage by the wind of Praise; ... 4.2HE1.297.221.
Let these return: Our Voyage, or our Stay, ... Il.9.731.470.
I steer my voyage to the *Brutian* strand; ... Od.1.234.43.
Thence speed your voyage to the *Spartan* strand, ... Od.1.371.50.
To keep my voyage from the royal ear, ... Od.2.419.81.
And end their voyage with the morning ray. ... Od.2.475.84.
And crown our voyage with desir'd success. ... Od.3.75.90.
Then warp my voyage on the southern gales, ... Od.4.103.124.
This toilsom voyage o'er the surgy main? ... Od.4.424.140.
To speed a prosp'rous voyage o'er the seas? ... Od.4.634.149.
Thy guilt absolv'd, a prosp'rous voyage gain. ... Od.4.638.149.
Attend his voyage, or domestic train? ... Od.4.869.159.
From me the purpos'd voyage to conceal: ... Od.4.967.163.
These empty vaunts will make the voyage vain; ... Od.4.1023.165.
O fatal voyage, source of all my woes!) ... Od.6.198.219.
A speedy voyage to his native shores. ... Od.8.174.271.
A prosp'rous voyage to his native shores; ... Od.11.127.387.
Attend thy voyage, and impel thy sails: ... Od.11.141.387.
To mark distinct thy voyage o'er the main: ... Od.12.68.433.
Attend thy voyage, and impell thy sails; ... Od.12.173.440.
To *Sol's* bright Isle our voyage we pursue, ... Od.12.314.447.
Intent to voyage to th' *Egyptian* shores; ... Od.14.281.49.
His instant voyage challeng'd all her care. ... Od.15.4.69.
He wing'd his voyage to the *Phrygian* shore. ... Od.19.233.204.
To speed his voyage to the *Grecian* strand. ... Od.19.324.210.

VOYAGER
A private voyager I pass the main. ... Od.2.358.78.
And ask'd each voyager each Hero's fate; ... Od.3.226.96.

VOYAGING
For voyaging to learn the direful art ... Od.1.340.48.
Which voyaging from *Troy* the Victors bore, ... Od.1.423.53.
But him, thus voyaging the deeps below, ... Od.5.361.189.

VULCAN
From shelves to shelves see greedy Vulcan roll, ... 5.DunA3.73.156.
From shelves to shelves see greedy Vulcan roll, ... 5.DunB3.81.324.
The Feast disturb'd with Sorrow *Vulcan* saw, ... Il.1.738.122.
Thus *Vulcan* spoke; and rising with a Bound, ... Il.1.752.123.
Vulcan with awkward Grace his Office plies, ... Il.1.770.124.
By *Vulcan* form'd, from *Jove* to *Hermes* came: ... Il.2.130.133.
And had not *Vulcan* lent Celestial Aid, ... Il.5.29.267.
With Skill divine had *Vulcan* form'd the Bow'r, ... Il.14.193.168.
The Work of *Vulcan;* to indulge thy Ease, ... Il.14.274.175.
With Skill divine has *Vulcan* form'd thy Bow'r, ... Il.14.383.181.
Vulcan to *Jove* th' immortal Gift consign'd, ... Il.15.352.210.
Fierce as a Flood of Flame by *Vulcan* sent, ... Il.17.97.291.
Vulcan draw near, 'tis *Thetis* asks your Aid. ... Il.18.460.343.
Oh *Vulcan!* say, was ever Breast divine ... Il.18.501.345.
Secure, what *Vulcan* can, is ever thine. ... Il.18.532.347.
Next this, the Eye the Art of *Vulcan* leads ... Il.18.677.356.
Behold what Arms by *Vulcan* are bestow'd, ... Il.19.13.372.
(The Work of *Vulcan)* sate the Pow'rs around. ... Il.20.18.393.
(The Work of *Vulcan)* sate the Gods around. ... Il.20.18A.393.
And *Vulcan,* the black Sov'reign of the Fire: ... Il.20.48.396.
With fiery *Vulcan* last in Battle stands ... Il.20.99.398.
While *Vulcan* breath'd the fiery Blast around. ... Il.21.405.437.
O *Vulcan,* oh! what Pow'r resists thy Might? ... Il.21.418.437.
As by some artist to whom *Vulcan* gives ... Od.6.275.224.
These *Vulcan* form'd with art divine, to wait ... Od.7.120.240.
To his black forge vindictive *Vulcan* flies: ... Od.8.314.281.
Stern *Vulcan* homeward treads the starry way: ... Od.8.344.282.
Mean-while the Gods the dome of *Vulcan* throng, ... Od.8.361.283.
More swift than *Mars,* and more than *Vulcan* slow? ... Od.8.370.283.

VULCAN (CONTINUED)
Yet *Vulcan* conquers, and the God of arms ....Od.8.371.283.
And free, he cries, oh *Vulcan!* free from shame ....Od.8.383.284.
Will *Neptune* (*Vulcan* then) the faithless trust? .....Od.8.385.284.
As by some artist to whom *Vulcan* gives ....Od.23.157.328.

VULCAN'S
The shining Monuments of *Vulcan's* Art: ....Il.1.779.124.
In *Vulcan's* Fane the Father's Days were led, ...Il.5.17.266.
And *Vulcan's* Joy, and Duty, to obey, ...Il.18.498.345.
She call'd aloud, and summon'd *Vulcan's* Aid. ....Il.21.385.436.
By *Vulcan's* art, the verge with gold enchas'd: ....Od.4.836.158.
And *Vulcan's* art enrich'd the sculptur'd gold). ....Od.24.96.352.

VULCANIAN
Vulcanian Arms, the Labour of a God: ....Il.8.237.409.
Vulcanian Arms, the Labour of a God. ....Il.18.174.331.
Vulcanian Arms: What other can I wield? ....Il.18.229.332.
Vulcanian Arms: What other should I wield? ....Il.18.229A.332.
Reach'd the *Vulcanian* Dome, Eternal Frame! ....Il.18.432.341.
One struck, but pierc'd not the *Vulcanian* Shield; ...Il.21.182.429.
Nodding at ev'ry Step: (*Vulcanian* Frame!) ....Il.22.397.472.
To me this present, of *Vulcanian* frame, ...Od.15.130.75.
I gave, enamel'd with Vulcanian art: ....Od.19.274.208.
Heap'd high the genial hearth, *Vulcanian* food: ....Od.20.154.241.

VULGAR
From *vulgar Bounds* with *brave Disorder* part, ...1.EOC.154.257.
The *Vulgar* thus through *Imitation* err; ....1.EOC.424.288.
But the vile Vulgar, ever discontent, ...1.TrSt.224.419.
(Whom Envy to the Great, and vulgar Spight ....1.TrSt.232.420.
Above the vulgar flight of low desire? ....2.Elegy.12.363.
'Tis Education forms the vulgar mind, ...3.Ep1.101A.22.
All see 'tis Vice, and itch of vulgar praise. ....3.Ep1.101.24.
Above the reach of vulgar Song; ....4.HOde9.4.159.
The Vulgar boil, the Learned roast an Egg; ....4.2HE2.85.171.
For vulgar eyes, and point out ev'ry line. ....4.2HE1.367.227.
The heroes sit; the vulgar form a ring. ....5.DunA2.352.143.
One Cell there is, conceal'd from vulgar eye, ...5.DunB1.33.271.
The heroes sit, the vulgar form a ring. ....5.DunB2.384.316.
The vulgar herd turn off to roll with Hogs, ...5.DunB4.525.394.
Our author shuns by vulgar springs to move, ...6.32.9.96.
Roll'd down *Scamander* with the Vulgar Dead. ....Il.2.1049.172.
For which nine Oxen paid (a vulgar Price) ....Il.6.293.341.
There lay the Vestures, of no vulgar Art, ...Il.6.360.343.
Mix'd with the Vulgar shall thy Fate be found, ...Il.8.119.403.
And dipp'd its Feathers in no vulgar Gore. ....Il.8.380.416.
With more than vulgar Grief he stood opprest; ....Il.9.21.432.
The same I chose for more than vulgar Charms, ...Il.9.167.441.
The same he chose for more than vulgar Charms, ...Il.9.354.451.
No vulgar Counsels our Affairs demand; ....Il.10.50.4.
And scorn the Guidance of a vulgar Hand; ....Il.10.474.24.
The rest were vulgar Deaths, unknown to Fame. ....Il.11.394.52.
Nor for the Deed expect a vulgar Prize. ....Il.14.302.177.
Nor speak him vulgar, nor of vulgar Race; ....Il.14.554.190.
Nor speak him vulgar, nor of vulgar Race. ....Il.14.554.190.
Lies undistinguish'd from the vulgar dead. ....Il.16.776.273.
Lies pierc'd with Wounds among the vulgar Dead. ...Il.17.2.286.
And dash'd their Axles with no vulgar Gore. ....Il.20.456.413.
Swift was the Course; No vulgar Prize they play, ...Il.22.207.464.
No vulgar Victim must reward the Day, ...Il.22.208.464.
No vulgar Gift) *Eumelus,* shall be thine. ....Il.23.642.515.
Speak him descended of no vulgar race: ....Od.1.518.57.
No vulgar manhood, no ignoble age. ....Od.3.483.111.
For vulgar parents cannot strip their race ....Od.4.75.123.
The leader, mingling with the vulgar host, ...Od.4.397.139.
To shun th' encounter of the vulgar crowd, ...Od.7.21.235.
The youngest of our band, a vulgar soul ....Od.10.661.375.
Hail happy nymph! no vulgar births are ow'd ....Od.11.297.396.
And mark the ruins of no vulgar man. ....Od.14.250.48.
And chose the largest; with no vulgar art ....Od.15.120.74.
His bulk and beauty speak no vulgar praise; ....Od.17.370.150.
The vulgar of my sex I most exceed ....Od.19.372.212.
O Queen! no vulgar vision of the sky ....Od.19.641.227.
On this high feast the meanest vulgar boast ....Od.20.229.244.
No vulgar roof protects thy honour'd age; ....Od.20.329.249.
No vulgar task! Ill suits this courtly crew ....Od.21.94.263.
Speak him descended from no vulgar race. ....Od.21.362.277.
Not vulgar born, from *Aphidas* the King ....Od.24.355.366.

VULTUR
Swift as a Vultur leaping on his Prey, ...Il.13.672.137.

VULTURE
So flies a Vulture thro' the clam'rous Train ....Il.17.528.309.
Or parent vulture, mourns her ravish'd young; ....Od.16.239.116.

VULTURES
Devouring Dogs and hungry Vultures tore. ....Il.1.6.85.
Thee, Vultures wild should scatter round the Shore, ...Il.22.57.455.
Must feast the Vultures on the naked Plains. ....Il.22.125.458.
Nor rob the Vultures of one Limb of thee. ....Il.22.444.474.
To Dogs, to Vultures, and to *Peleus'* Son! ....Il.24.260.547.
Nor Dogs nor Vultures have thy *Hector* rent, ...Il.24.503.557.
Two rav'nous vultures furious for their food ....Od.11.711.421.

VULTURS
As when two Vulturs on the Mountain's Height ....1.TrES.219.458.
In Form like Vulturs, on the Beeche's Height ....Il.7.67.366.
In Form of Vulturs, on the Beeche's Height ....Il.7.67A.366.
For *Trojan* Vulturs a predestin'd Prey. ....Il.8.656.427.
More grateful, now, to Vulturs than their Wives! .....Il.11.212.44.
And hov'ring Vulturs scream around their Prey. ....Il.11.571.59.
But feed the Vulturs on this hateful Strand, ...Il.13.304.119.
As when two Vulturs on the Mountain's Height ....Il.16.522.263.
But thou a Prey to Vulturs shalt be made! ....Il.16.1009.282.

VULTURS (CONTINUED)
Condemn'd to Vulturs on the *Trojan* Plain; ....Il.17.285.298.
Vulturs shall tear thee—Thus incens'd they spoke, ...Od.22.35.288.
Not half so keen, fierce vulturs of the chace ....Od.22.337.303.
Or screaming vulturs scatter thro' the air: ....Od.24.343.365.

VY'D
His kitchen vy'd in coolness with his grot? ....3.Ep3.182.109.
Vy'd for his love in jetty bow'rs below; ....5.DunA2.311.139.
Vy'd for his love in jetty bow'rs below, ...5.DunB2.335.314.
And vy'd with *Pallas* in the Works of Art. ....Il.9.513.458.
Saturn's great Sons in fierce Contention vy'd, ...Il.13.436.126.

VYE
(Where *Kent* and Nature vye for PELHAM's LOVE) ....4.EpS2.67.316.
As Berecynthia, while her offspring vye ....5.DunA3.123.160.
As Berecynthia, while her offspring vye ....5.DunB3.131.326.
If with this throw the strongest Caster vye, ...Od.8.231.275.

W
B and *L* swore Bl—and W—s ....6.30.42.87.
And *W* would not lose, not he, ...6.30.45.87.
And *W* wou'd lose, not he, ...6.30.45A.87.

WA<I>VE
Yet thus by woes impair'd, no more I wa<i>ve ....Od.8.207.273.

WADDLES
As when a dab-chick waddles thro' the copse, ...5.DunA2.59.105.
As when a dab-chick waddles thro' the copse ....5.DunB2.63.298.

WADES
On feet and wings, and flies, and wades, and hops; ....5.DunA2.60.105.
On legs and wings, and flies and wades, and hops; ....5.DunA2.60A.105.
On feet and wings, and flies, and wades, and hops; ....5.DunB2.64.299.
He wades, and mounts; the parted Wave resounds. ....Il.21.353.435.

WADLING
Obliquely wadling to the mark in view. ....5.DunA1.150.82.
Obliquely wadling to the mark in view: ....5.DunB1.172.282.

WAFT
And Winds shall waft it to the Pow'rs above. ....1.PSu.80.78.
Spread thy soft Wings, and waft me o'er the Main, ...1.TrSP.210.403.
Waft on the Breeze, or sink in Clouds of Gold. ....2.RL2.60.193.
And waft a sigh from *Indus* to the *Pole.* ....2.ElAb.58.323.
Tears that delight, and sighs that waft to heav'n. ......2.ElAb.214.337.
"Seas roll to waft me, suns to light me rise; ....3.EOM1.139.32.
A single leaf may waft an Army o'er, ...3.Ep3.73A.93.
A single leaf can waft an Army o'er, ...3.Ep3.73B.93.
A single leaf shall waft an Army o'er, ...3.Ep3.73.93.
Th' *Arabian* coast, and waft us on our way. ....6.4v.8.11.
Raise in their arms, and waft thee on their wing, ...6.21.26.69.
And waft the Sacrifice to *Chrysa's* Shores, ...Il.1.183.96.
My Fleet shall waft me to *Thessalia's* Shore. ....Il.1.222.97.
My Bark shall waft her to her native Land; ....Il.1.242.98.
And waft their grateful Odours to the Skies. ....Il.1.417.107.
Now hostile Fleets must waft those Infants o'er, ...Il.24.920.574.
A bark to waft me o'er the rolling main; ....Od.2.242.73.
The best I chuse, to waft thee o'er the tides. ....Od.2.334.77.
The bark, to waft thee o'er the swelling tides. ....Od.2.346.77.
Propitious winds, to waft us o'er the main: ....Od.4.490.143.
And prosp'rous gales to waft thee on thy way. ....Od.5.216.182.
The waters waft it, and the nymph receives. ....Od.5.593.201.
And gave the gales to waft me on the way. ....Od.7.352.253.
Then gently waft thee to the pleasing shore, ...Od.7.409.257.
What bark to waft me, and what wind to blow? ....Od.10.597.372.
To speed our course, and waft us o'er the floods, ...Od.11.36.381.
A few revolving months shou'd waft him o'er, ...Od.14.423.56.
He now but waits the wind, to waft him o'er ....Od.17.616.162.
To waft the Heroe to his natal land. ....Od.19.334.210.

WAFTED
Heav'd by the surge and wafted by the breeze. ....Od.12.530.458.
The rest in ships are wafted o'er the main. ....Od.24.480.371.

WAFTING
Or wafting ginger, round the streets to go, ...5.DunA1.201.87.
Or wafting ginger, round the streets to run, ...5.DunA1.201A.87.
And wafting vapours from the Land of Dreams, ...5.DunA2.316.140.
And wafting Vapours from the Land of dreams, ...5.DunB2.340.314.
By the soft Fannings of the wafting Sheets, ...6.82ii.3.230.
Incumbent on the wings of wafting gales: ....Od.6.48.207.

WAFTS
Thames wafts it thence to Rufus' roaring hall, ...5.DunA2.253.130.
Thames wafts it thence to Rufus' roaring hall, ...5.DunB2.265.308.
Wafts the smooth Eunuch and enamour'd swain. ....5.DunB4.310.374.
Wafts on his gentle wing his eightieth year) ....6.55.2.166.
The watchful Mother wafts th' envenom'd Fly. ....Il.4.163.228.
Far from *Achilles* wafts the winged Death: ....Il.20.508.415.
The tenth soft wafts me to *Thesprotia's* shore. ......Od.14.350.51.

WAG
Those Monkey-Tails that wag behind their Head! .....4.JD4.247.47.
Some Wag observes me thus perplext, ...4.HS6.51.253.
Should wag two serpent tails in Smithfield fair. ......5.DunA3.290.184.
Should'st wag a serpent-tail in Smithfield fair! ......5.DunB3.288.334.
Shall wag her Tail within the Grave. ....6.135.82.369.
And wag their tails, and fawning lick their feet. ......Od.10.245.354.

WAG'D
I wag'd no war with *Bedlam* or the *Mint.* ....4.Arbu.156.107.
Around the Spectre bloody Wars are wag'd, ...Il.5.549.295.

WAGD
Those Monkey-Tails that wagd behind their Head! ....4.JD4.247B.47.

WAGE
And earth, and heav'n, and hell her battles wage. ....5.DunA1.108.76.
Intestine War no more our *Passions* wage, ...6.11.34.31.
And who'l wage War with Bedlam or the Mint? ....6.49iii.6.142.
And who'd wage War with Bedlam or the Mint ....6.49iii.6A.142.
And who'll wage War with *Bedlam* or the *Mint?* .... 6.98.6.283.
What Shame to *Greece* a fruitless War to wage, ...Il.2.151.135.
Whose Cause we follow, and whose War we wage; ....Il.4.469.242.
At distance wound, or wage a flying War ....Il.5.315A.281.
The War with *Troy* no more the *Grecians* wage; ....Il.5.469.290.
Thus, Heroes! thus the vig'rous Combate wage! ....Il.6.84.327.
Against his Country's Foes the War to wage, ...Il.6.608.357.
Against the Highest who shall wage the War? ....Il.8.489.420.
Divide his Heart, and wage a doubtful War. ....Il.10.22.3.
And this the last brave Battel he shall wage: ....Il.11.717.67.
Tho' now unfit an active War to wage, ...Il.13.648.136.
Advent'rous Combats and bold Wars to wage, ...Il.14.96.162.
Desists at length his Rebel-war to wage, ...Il.15.250.206.
Come on—a distant War no longer wage, ...Il.15.658.221.
Of all neglectful, wage a hateful War.) ....Il.19.348.386.
Such War th' Immortals wage: Such Horrors rend ....Il.20.89.397.
Come, prove thy Arm! for first the War to wage, ...Il.21.512.443.
Learn hence, no more unequal War to wage— ....Il.21.565.445.

WAGGISH
And own, the *Spaniard* did a *waggish thing,* .... 4.EpS1.17.298.

WAGGONS
With Mules and Waggons sends a chosen Band; ....Il.23.135.493.

WAGS
The Monkey-Tail that wags behind his Head ....4.JD4.247A.47.
That plies the Tongue, and wags the Tail, ...6.14v(a).23.49.

WAIL
To wail his Fate in Death's eternal Gloom. ....Il.13.536.132.
Now doom'd a wakeful bird to wail the beauteous boy. ....Od.19.610.226.

WAIL'D
The drooping Mother wail'd her Children gone. ....Il.2.381.145.
Thus wail'd the Father, grov'ling on the Ground, ...Il.22.550.479.
Nor wail'd his father o'er th' untimely dead, ...Od.24.345.365.

WAILD'
Thus sow'rly waild' he, sputt'ring Dirt and Gore; ....Il.23.921.525.

WAILING
Thus wildly wailing, at the Gates they lay; ....Il.24.890.573.
And to the deaf woods wailing, breath'd his woes. ....Od.6.138.214.
All wailing with unutterable woes. ....Od.11.664.417.
Thus wailing, slow and sadly she descends, ...Od.18.245.178.

WAILS
All comfortless he sits, and wails his Friend: ....Il.19.367.387.
Or if no more her absent Lord she wails, ...Od.11.216.392.
And each now wails an unlamented shade. ....Od.22.455.310.

WAIN
When Clouds conceal *Boötes'* golden Wain, ...1.TrSt.521.432.
Trembling he stood before the golden Wain, ...Il.19.448.390.
These fix'd up high behind the rolling Wain, ...Il.22.499.477.
The sad Attendants load the groaning Wain: ....Il.24.342.550.
The Mules preceding draw the loaded Wain, ...Il.24.399.552.
At *Scæa's* Gates they meet the mourning Wain, ...Il.24.886.573.
Their Mules and Oxen harness to the Wain, ...Il.24.990.577.

WAIST
At last a youth above the waist arose, ...1.TrPA.159.372.
Two babes of love close clinging to her waist; ....5.DunB2.158.303.
Close to the less'ning waist the vest infold; ....Od.18.340.184.

WAIT
No nightly Bands in glitt'ring Armour wait ....1.TrSt.204.419.
Nor nightly Bands in glitt'ring Armour wait ....1.TrSt.204A.419.
No nightly Bands in glitt'ring Arms did wait ....1.TrSt.204B.419.
Around, at awful Distance, wait the rest. ....1.TrSt.616.436.
Where endless Honours wait the Sacred Shade. ....1.TrES.349.462.
With beating Hearts the dire Event they wait, ...2.RL2.141.168.
Two Handmaids wait the Throne: Alike in Place, ...2.RL4.25.185.
The sage Historians in white Garments wait; ....2.TemF.146.265.
Let wealth, let honour, wait the wedded dame, ...2.ElAb.77.326.
And wait, till 'tis no sin to mix with thine. ....2.ElAb.176.334.
Wait the great teacher Death, and God adore! ....3.EOM1.92.25.
Wait but for wings, and in their season, fly. ....3.Ep3.172.107.
Than not to wait too long, nor pay too dear. ....4.HAdv.160.89.
She bids him wait her to the sacred Dome; ....5.DunA1.221.89.
With ready quills the dedicators wait; ....5.DunA2.190.124.
As when the long-ear'd milky mothers wait ....5.DunA2.237.129.
She bids him wait her to her sacred Dome: ....5.DunB1.265.289.
With ready quills the Dedicators wait; ....5.DunB2.198.305.
As when the long-ear'd milky mothers wait ....5.DunB2.247.307.
Or wait inspiring dreams at *Maro's* Urn: ....6.52.28.157.
Wait, to the Scaffold, or the silent Cell, ...6.84.31Z1.239.
Let's rather wait one year for better luck; ....6.116v.3.327.
Wait for my Infants yet unborn. ....6.135.66.368.
To wait his Will two sacred Heralds stood, ...Il.1.420.107.
The shining Synod of th' Immortals wait ....Il.1.690.120.
But wait the Tenth, for *Ilion's* Fall decreed: ....Il.2.396.145.
Obey, ye *Grecians!* with Submission wait, ...Il.2.398.145.
And crowded Nations wait his dread Command. ....Il.2.696.159.
Eager of Fight, and only wait Command: ....Il.3.24.189.
Her Handmaids *Clymenè* and *Æthra* wait ....Il.3.189.200.
The Nations call, thy joyful People wait, ...Il.3.320.208.

WAIT (CONTINUED)
A Hand-maid Goddess at his Side to wait, ...Il.3.503.215.
The Maids officious round their Mistress wait, ...Il.3.526.216.
Such mighty Woes on perjur'd Princes wait; ....Il.4.204.231.
Still must ye wait the Foes, and still retire, ...Il.4.282.234.
Alastor, Chromius, Hæmon round him wait, ...Il.4.340.237.
In wealthy Folds, and wait the Milker's Hand, ...Il.4.493.244.
And twice ten Coursers wait their Lord's Command. ....Il.5.247.279.
Condense their Pow'rs, and wait the growing War. ....Il.5.610.297.
Unmov'd and silent, the whole War they wait, ...Il.5.639.298.
They sit conceal'd, and wait the future Fight. ....Il.7.68.366.
The *Trojan* Bands returning *Hector* wait, ...Il.7.372.382.
To wait th' Event, the Herald bent his way. ....Il.7.491.388.
Great Perils, Father! wait th' unequal Fight; ....Il.8.129.404.
And ardent Warriors wait the rising Morn. ....Il.8.708.429.
He kept the Verge of *Troy,* nor dar'd to wait ....Il.9.466.455.
The *Greeks* expect them, and our Heroes wait. ....Il.9.740.471.
Condense their Pow'rs, and wait the coming War. ....Il.11.276.47.
Let *Hector* come; I wait his Fury here. ....Il.11.412.53.
Descending *Hector* and his Battel wait; ....Il.13.178.113.
And thou, Imperious! if thy Madness wait ....Il.13.1052.155.
Wait under *Ide:* Of thy superior Pow'r ....Il.14.351.179.
Go wait the Thund'rer's Will (*Saturnia* cry'd) ....Il.15.164.202.
Yet where the Oars are plac'd, he stands to wait ....Il.15.884.231.
Where endless Honours wait the sacred Shade. ....Il.16.836.276.
Go, wait thy Brother to the *Stygian* Gloom; ....Il.17.34.289.
To wait thy Brother to the *Stygian* Gloom; ....Il.17.34A.289.
On my Command if any *Lycian* wait, ...Il.17.171.294.
Troy's black Battalions wait the Shock of Fight. ....Il.20.4.392.
Safe in the Crowd he ever scorn'd to wait, ...Il.22.588.480.
On his slow Wheels the following People wait, ...Il.24.403.552.
Ev'n to the Palace the sad Pomp they wait: ....Il.24.898.573.
(Those Wives must wait'em) to a foreign Shore! ....Il.24.921.574.
Where yet new labours his arrival wait; ....Od.1.26.30.
Griev'd that a Visitant so long shou'd wait ....Od.1.157.40.
Nor let a race of Princes wait in vain. ....Od.2.132.67.
With due observance wait the chief's command; ....Od.2.463.83.
On whom a radiant pomp of Graces wait, ...Od.4.19.121.
Refresh'd, they wait them to the bow'r of state, ...Od.4.61.122.
Dubious to press the tender theme, or wait ....Od.4.155.127.
He ceas'd; the menial fair that round her wait, ...Od.4.401.139.
Ambush'd we lie, and wait the bold emprise: ....Od.4.602.148.
Makes her with hope her son's arrival wait. ....Od.4.1098.169.
And in close ambush wait the murd'rous deed. ....Od.4.1108.169.
Five sons thou hast; three wait the bridal day, ...Od.6.75.208.
There wait embowr'd, while I ascend alone ....Od.6.359.229.
These *Vulcan* form'd with art divine, to wait ....Od.7.120.240.
But wait thy word, the gentle guest to grace ....Od.7.218.247.
And ships shall wait thee with the morning ray. ....Od.7.405.256.
To wait my passage from the *Trojan* land. ....Od.9.40.303.
My self the fifth. We stand, and wait the hour. ....Od.9.395.322.
I only wait behind, of all the train; ....Od.10.305.359.
The circling year I wait, with ampler stores ....Od.11.446.406.
For traytors wait his way, with dire design ....Od.14.210.45.
On sev'n bright years successive blessings wait; ....Od.14.317.50.
And wait the woes heav'n dooms me yet to bear. ....Od.14.394.54.
Here wait we rather, till approaching day ....Od.15.59.72.
With due observance wait the chief's command: ....Od.15.311.84.
On all their weary ways wait Care and Pain, ...Od.15.366.87.
Two sew'rs from day to day the revels wait, ...Od.16.274.118.
Wait ye, till he to arms in council draws ....Od.16.390.124.
Wait for a space without, but wait not long; ....Od.17.328.147.
Wait for a space without, but wait not long; ....Od.17.328.147.
Attendant Nymphs in beauteous order wait ....Od.19.64.195.
Where images of truth for passage wait, ...Od.19.662.228.
Since due regard must wait the Prince's friend, ...Od.20.360.249.
At ev'ry portal let some matron wait, ...Od.21.252.272.
At ev'ry portal let some matron wait, ...Od.21.413.280.
Nor wait 'till ev'ning for the genial joy. ....Od.21.472.283.
(Their life's last scene) they trembling wait their fall. ....Od.22.494.313.
There wait thy faithful band of rural friends, ...Od.24.419.369.

WAITED
The Fate fore-doom'd that waited from my Birth: ....Il.23.100.491.
I waited long, and ey'd the doors in vain: ....Od.10.306.359.
The sea-green sisters waited on the dame. ....Od.24.66.350.
"The rites have waited long." The chief commands ....Od.24.456.370.

WAITING
In Silence waiting till he ceas'd the Song. ....Il.9.254.445.
Who, waiting long, by turns had hop'd and fear'd. ....Od.9.638.333.
The sailors waiting, and the ships prepar'd. ....Od.14.370.53.

WAITS
Such Silence waits on *Philomela's* Strains, ...1.PWi.78.94.
And ready Nature waits upon his Hand; ....1.EOC.487.294.
And Love, the God that ever waits on thee, ...1.TrSP.122.399.
While Discord waits upon divided Pow'r. ....1.TrSt.183.418.
And waits 'till pleasing Slumbers seal his Eyes. ....1.TrSt.538.433.
Patroclus lights, and sternly waits the War. ....1.TrES.218.457.
Behind, *Rome's Genius* waits with *Civic* Crowns, ...2.TemF.242.274.
On all the line a sudden vengeance waits, ...2.Elegy.37.365.
Impatient waits, till ** grace the quire. ....5.DunA1.250Z2.92.
Impatient waits 'till H[erv]y grace the quire. ....5.DunB1.298A.291.
She waits, or to the Scaffold, or the Cell, ...6.84.33.240.
My second (Child of Fortune!) waits ....6.135.59.368.
And nodding *Ilion* waits th' impending Fall. ....Il.2.18.128.
And nodding *Ilion* waits th' impending Fall. ....Il.2.40.129.
And nodding *Ilion* waits th' impending Fall. ....Il.2.90.130.
He lies, and waits thee on the well-known Bed: ....Il.3.484.215.
Then say ye Pow'rs! what signal Issue waits ....Il.4.19.222.
See ready *Pallas* waits thy high Commands, ...Il.4.91.224.
Bright *Hebè* waits; by *Hebè,* ever young, ...Il.5.888.308.
Antenor's Consort, fair *Theano,* waits ....Il.6.372.344.
He waits but for the Morn, to sink in Flame ....Il.9.314.449.
In vain *Ætolia* her Deliv'rer waits, ...Il.9.687.468.

WAITS (CONTINUED)
Near the Night-Guards, our chosen Council waits. ....Il.10.147.8.
The Hero haults, and his Associates waits. ....Il.11.224.45.
And waits the rising of the fatal Blaze. ....Il.11.811.72.
On *Ida's* Top he waits with longing Eyes, ...Il.15.718.223.
And waits the Combate with impatient Eyes. ....Il.16.311.254.
Patroclus lights, and sternly waits the War. ....Il.16.521.263.
Who waits for that, the dire Effect shall find, ...Il.19.239.382.
Achilles waits ye, and expects the Fight. ....Il.19.288.384.
Thee too it waits; before the *Trojan* Wall ....Il.23.101.491.
The son's destruction waits the mother's fame: ....Od.2.144.68.
Fast by the door the wise *Euryclea* waits; ....Od.2.391.80.
Mean-while *Ulysses* at the Palace waits, ...Od.7.107.239.
The King in council your attendance waits: ....Od.8.12.262.
Swift vengeance waits: and Art subdues the strong! ....Od.8.368.283.
With fraudful care he waits the finny prize, ...Od.12.302.447.
But lo! an ambush waits his passage o'er; ....Od.13.492.29.
And witness ev'ry houshold pow'r that waits ....Od.14.184.44.
He now but waits the wind, to waft him o'er ....Od.17.616.162.
Bestow'd the stranger guest? Or waits he griev'd, ...Od.20.163.241.
From the wise Chief he waits the deathful word. ....Od.20.462.255.
For danger waits on all untimely joy. ....Od.21.243.271.
Her prompt obedience on his order waits; ....Od.21.419.280.

WAK'D
Leapt up, and wak'd his Mistress with his Tongue. ....2.RL1.116.154.
He wak'd, and all the Vision mix'd with air. ....5.DunA3.358A.193.
Wak'd by the Morning-Cock, unseals his Eyes, ...6.17iii.32.58.
And wak'd and wish'd whole Nights for thy Return? ....6.96iv.4.276.
Thus wak'd the Fury of his partial Queen. ....Il.4.8.221.
Soon as the rosy Morn had wak'd the Day, ...Il.7.456.387.
Already wak'd, *Atrides* he descry'd, ...Il.10.39.4.
The Tumult wak'd him: From his Eyes he shook ....Il.23.292.501.
Wak'd with the Word, the trembling Sire arose, ...Il.24.858.572.
The whistling winds already wak'd the sky; ....Od.3.213.96.
Wak'd by the shrilling sound, *Ulysses* rose, ...Od.6.137.213.
And snapt the spinal joint, and wak'd in hell. ....Od.10.668.375.
Wak'd at their steps, her flowing eyes unclose; ....Od.18.235.178.
By grief relax'd, she wak'd again to weep: ....Od.20.69.235.

WAKE
With joyous Musick wake the dawning Day! ....1.PSp.24.62.
And all things wake to Life and Joy, but I, ...1.TrSP.156.400.
And all the Furies wake within their Breast. ....1.TrSt.175.417.
And all their Furies wake within their Breast. ....1.TrSt.175A.417.
And bids renew the Feasts, and wake the Fires. ....1.TrSt.604.435.
And bids renew the Feasts, and wake the sleeping Fires. ....1.TrSt.604A.435.
They dream in Courtship, but in Wedlock wake. ....2.ChWB.103.61.
Call forth the Greens, and wake the rising Flowers; ....2.TemF.2.253.
'Obedient slumbers that can wake and weep'; ....2.ElAb.212.337.
I wake—no more I hear, no more I view, ...2.ElAb.235.339.
And wake to all the griefs I left behind. ....2.ElAb.248.339.
Self-love but serves the virtuous mind to wake, ...3.EOM4.363.163.
I nod in Company, I wake at Night, ...4.HS1.13.5.
Command old words that long have slept, to wake, ...4.2HE2.167.177.
We wake next morning in a raging Fit, ...4.2HE1.179.209.
If there be man who o'er such works can wake, ...5.DunA2.340.142.
"If there be man, who o'er such works can wake, ...5.DunB2.372.315.
Wake the dull Church, and lull the ranting Stage; ....5.DunB4.58.347.
The Sire saw, one by one, his Virtues wake: ....5.DunB4.285.372.
The Sire saw, smiling, his own Virtues wake: ....5.DunB4.285A.372.
Think for her love what crowds of wretches wake. ....6.4i.10.9.
Wake into Voice each silent String, ...6.11.3.29.
Then wake with Transport at the Sound! ....6.31ii.6Z12.95.
Then wake with pleasure at the Sound! ....6.31ii.6Z12A.95.
To wake the soul by tender strokes of art, ...6.32.1.96.
And wake to Raptures in a Life to come. ....6.86.20.246.
I wake, I rise, and shiv'ring with the Frost, ...6.96iv.43.277.
Troy yet may wake, and one avenging Blow ....Il.3.83.193.
Wake each Paternal Virtue in thy Soul: ....Il.5.161.274.
Returns no more to wake the silent dead. ....Il.9.531.459.
To wake *Atrides* in the Royal Tent. ....Il.10.38.4.
Let younger *Greeks* our sleeping Warriors wake; ....Il.10.188.10.
Where e'er yon' Fires ascend, the *Trojans* wake: ....Il.10.489.25.
Now Shouts and Tumults wake the tardy Sun, ...Il.11.67.37.
To rise afresh, and once more wake the War, ...Il.15.64.197.
There wake her with the news—The matron cry'd; ....Od.22.468.311.
Why must I wake to grieve, and curse thy shore? ....Od.23.23.320.
To wake his son; and bid his friends arise. ....Od.23.394.343.

WAKEFUL
Two Swains, whom Love kept wakeful, and the Muse, ...1.PSp.18.62.
Before the wakeful Tyrant's guarded Gate; ....1.TrSt.205A.419.
Or in soft Slumbers seals the wakeful Eye; ....1.TrSt.434.428.
All, but the ever-wakeful Eyes of *Jove*. ....Il.2.4.127.
A wakeful Squadron, each in Arms prepar'd: ....Il.10.208.11.
Nestor with Joy the Wakeful Band survey'd, ...Il.10.223.11.
On high Designs the wakeful Hours employ; ....Il.10.358.19.
Or in soft Slumbers seals the wakeful Eye; ....Il.24.422.553.
Or in soft slumber seals the wakeful eye: ....Od.5.61.174.
The wakeful mariners shall watch the skies, ...Od.7.407.256.
The night assists my ever-wakeful woes: ....Od.19.601.225.
Now doom'd a wakeful bird to wail the beauteous boy. ....Od.19.610.226.
Wakeful to weep and watch the tardy dawn ....Od.19.694.229.
Scenes of lewd loves his wakeful eyes survey, ...Od.20.10.230.
The sounds assault *Ulysses'* wakeful ear; ....Od.20.112.238.
Or in soft slumber seals the wakeful eye, ...Od.24.4.347.

WAKEN
The dull may waken to a Humming-bird; ....5.DunB4.446.384.
Perhaps may waken to a Humming-bird; ....5.DunB4.446A.384.
A thousand Griefs shall waken at the Name! ....Il.6.589.355.

WAKEN'D
Not touch'd, but rapt; not waken'd, but inspir'd! ....2.ElAb.202.336.

WAKENS
Thus wakens *Hector* from the Sleep of Death? ....Il.15.281.207.

WAKES
Wakes to new Vigor with the rising Day. ....1.TrSt.587.434.
"For me kind Nature wakes her genial pow'r, ...3.EOM1.133.32.
Rymes e'er he wakes, and prints before *Term* ends, ...4.Arbu.43.99.
Sloath unfolds her Arms and wakes; ....6.11.32.31.
Her Husband's Love, and wakes her former Fires; ....Il.3.184.200.
And wakes anew the dying Flames of Fight. ....Il.5.608.297.
And wakes *Hippocoon* in the Morning-Hour, ...Il.10.607.29.
And wakes anew the dying Flames of Fight. ....Il.11.274.47.
Wakes all our Force, and seconds all our Fires. ....Il.15.879.230.
Confus'd he wakes; Amazement breaks the Bands ....Il.23.119.492.
He wakes, he lights the fire, he milks the dams, ...Od.9.366.321.

WAKING
Unhappy Wharton, waking, found at last! ....3.Ep3.86.94.
Thence beauty, waking all her forms, supplies ....6.52.45.157.
Awake, but waking this Advice approve, ...Il.2.41.129.
If ought of use thy waking Thoughts suggest, ...Il.10.106.7.
The soul scarce waking, in the arms of death. ....Od.5.587.200.
He thought, and answer'd: hardly waking yet, ...Od.14.551.63.
And catch the glances of the waking morn. ....Od.19.396.213.
When woes the waking sense alone assail, ...Od.20.98.237.

WALES
There liv'd in Wales a goodly Yeoman, ...6.93.1A.256.

WALK
Where-e'er you walk, cool Gales shall fan the Glade, ...1.PSu.73.77.
Walk in thy Light, and in thy Temple bend. ....1.Mes.92.121.
Here let us walk, he said, observ'd by none, ...2.ChJM.543.41.
Far as the solar walk, or milky way; ....3.EOM1.102.27.
Shall walk the World, in credit, to his grave. ....4.HS1.120.17.
Shall walk in peace and credit to the grave. ....4.HS1.120A.17.
Shall walk the World in quiet to his grave. ....4.HS1.120B.17.
Shall walk in peace, and credit, to his grave. ....4.HS1.120C.17.
"He, ev'ry Day, from *King* to *King* can walk, ...4.JD4.104.33.
To sigh each Bill, about he now must walk; ....4.JD2A.76.138.
Walk with respect behind, while we at ease ....4.2HE2.141.175.
And much too wise to walk into a Well: ....4.2HE2.191.179.
Walk sober off; before a sprightlier Age ....4.2HE2.324.187.
A Terras-walk, and half a Rood ....4.HS6.5.251.
And men must walk at least before they dance. ....4.1HE1.54.283.
While all your smutty sisters walk the streets. ....5.DunB1.230.287.
Walk round and round, now prying here, now there; ....5.DunB4.353.377.
But none but you can give us Strength to walk; ....6.2.29.6.
Ev'n now she shades thy Evening Walk with Bays, ...6.84.35.240.
Or laugh to see thee walk with cautious tread, ...6.96ii.30Z45.272.
"How wert thou wont to walk with cautious Tread, ...6.96ii.67.273.
Here, here's the place, where these bright angels walk. ....6.126i.4.353.
Walk to his grave without reproach, ...6.150.19.399.
Pensive they walk along the barren Sands: ....Il.1.427.108.
And the red Fiends that walk the nightly Round. ....Il.9.686.468.
And seem to walk on Wings, and tread in Air. ....Il.13.106.109.
I blush to walk among the Race of Men. ....Il.18.122.328.
Like Youths and Maidens in an Evening Walk: ....Il.22.170.460.
And walk delighted, and expatiate round. ....Od.9.177.312.
Where the wan Spectres walk eternal rounds; ....Od.11.584.412.
And secret walk, unknown to mortal eyes. ....Od.13.454.28.
Returns he? Ambush'd we'll his walk invade, ...Od.16.398.125.
To dress the walk, and form th' embow'ring shade. ....Od.18.406.188.

WALK'D
The Knight and Lady walk'd beneath in View, ...2.ChJM.607.44.
Man walk'd with beast, joint tenant of the shade; ....3.EOM3.152.108.
The good Man walk'd innoxious thro' his Age. ....4.Arbu.395.126.
The old man early rose, walk'd forth, and sate ....Od.3.518.112.
And near them walk'd, with solemn pace and slow, ...Od.11.397.403.

WALKER
Walker with rev'rence took, and lay'd aside. ....5.DunB4.206.363.
Walker! our hat"—nor more he deign'd to say, ...5.DunB4.273.371.

WALKER'S
Some talk'd of *W[a]lk[e]r's* Merit, ...6.94.18.259*.

WALKING
This Clerk and I were walking in the Fields. ....2.ChWB.291.71.
The Clerk and I were walking in the Fields. ....2.ChWB.291A.71.
Each walking with Majestick Pace ....6.135.72A.369.

WALKS
Swarm o'er the Lawns, the Forest Walks surround, ...1.W-F.149.164.
I seem thro' consecrated Walks to rove, ...1.W-F.267.173.
Sweating he walks, while Loads of golden Grain ....1.TrVP.31.378.
About the Realm she walks her dreadful Round, ...1.TrSt.710.440.
A Pipkin there like *Homer's Tripod* walks; ....2.RL4.51.188.
A mighty maze! of walks without a plan; ....3.EOM1.6A.11.
Eye Nature's walks, shoot Folly as it flies, ...3.EOM1.13.14.
He mounts the storm, and walks upon the wind. ....3.EOM2.110.68.
Then from the *Mint* walks forth the Man of Ryme, ...4.Arbu.13.96.
For you, he walks the streets thro' rain or dust, ...4.JD2.73.139.
He walks, an Object new beneath the Sun! ....4.2HE2.119.173.
Our Courtier walks from dish to dish, ...4.HS6.200.263.
Crown'd with the Jordan, walks contented home. ....5.DunA2.182.124.
Crown'd with the Jordan, walks contented home. ....5.DunB2.190.304.
Here aged trees Cathedral walks compose, ...6.14iv.13.47.
To morning walks, and pray'rs three hours a day; ....6.45.14.125.
War, horrid war, your thoughtful walks invades, ...6.51i.7.151.
Wide o'er th' Æthereal Walks extends thy sway, ...6.65.3A.192.
Some morning-walks along the Mall, ...6.114.3.321.
(Happiest of Dogs!) in *Cobham's* Walks: ....6.135.62.368.
Thro' Streets of Palaces and Walks of State; ....Il.6.490.350.
All dreadful in the crimson Walks of War? ....Il.8.460.419.

WALKS (CONTINUED)

The sacred Eagle, from his Walks above ..... Il.17.763.318.
Turn from each other in the Walks of War— ..... Il.20.496.415.
To tread the walks of death he stood prepar'd, ... Od.2.311.76.
Shut from the walks of men, to pleasure lost, ... Od.16.156.110.
Alone, indecent, in the walks of men. ..... Od.18.218.177.
With dreadful inroad thro' the walks of war. ..... Od.18.308.181.

WALL

And leave inanimate the naked Wall; ..... 1.W-F.308.178.
And level with the Dust the *Spartan* Wall: ..... 1.TrSt.369.425.
To sure Destruction dooms the *Grecian* Wall; ..... 1.TrES.24.450.
To sure Destruction dooms th' aspiring Wall; ..... 1.TrES.24A.450.
Nor these can keep, nor those can win the Wall: ..... 1.TrES.162.455.
Raise scaling Engines, and ascend the Wall: ..... 1.TrES.180.456.
They found the Art of Kissing thro' a Wall. ..... 2.ChJM.519.40.
Had but my Husband Pist against a Wall, ... 2.ChWB.270.70.
And half the Mountain rolls into a Wall: ..... 2.TemF.88.259.
And half the Mountain roll'd into a Wall: ..... 2.TemF.88A.259.
The Wall in Lustre and Effect like Glass, ... 2.TemF.132.264.
Nor void of Emblem was the mystic Wall, ... 2.TemF.135.264.
Here dragg'd in Triumph round the *Trojan* Wall. ..... 2.TemF.191.271.
For Chartres' head reserve the hanging wall? ..... 3.EOM4.130.140.
Shov'd from the wall perhaps, or rudely press'd ..... 3.Ep1.230.35.
Silence without, and Fasts within the wall; ..... 3.Ep3.190.109.
For very want; he could not build a wall. ..... 3.Ep3.324.120.
On some patch'd dog-hole ek'd with ends of wall, ... 3.Ep4.32.140.
On ev'ry side you look, behold the Wall! ..... 3.Ep4.114.148.
Or whiten'd Wall provoke the Skew'r to write, ... 4.HS1.98.13.
What Lady's Face is not a whited Wall? ..... 4.JD4.151.37.
For hung with *Deadly Sins* I see the Wall, ... 4.JD4.274.49.
And grapes, long-lingering on my only wall, ... 4.HS2.146.67.
He leapt the Trenches, scal'd a Castle-Wall, ... 4.2HE2.40.167.
Be this thy Screen, and this thy Wall of Brass; ..... 4.1HE1.95.285.
He, whose long Wall the wand'ring Tartar bounds. ..... 5.DunA3.68.156.
While naked mourns the Dormitory wall, ... 5.DunA3.323.189.
I see th' unfinish'd Dormitory wall, ... 5.DunA3.323A.189.
From her black grottos near the Temple-wall, ... 5.DunB2.98.300.
He, whose long wall the wand'ring Tartar bounds; ..... 5.DunB3.76.324.
Pity! the charm works only in our wall, ... 5.DunB4.165.357.
Some play, some eat, some cack against the Wall, ... 6.14ii.8.43.
Would greet the Man who turn'd him to the Wall, ... 6.14ii.43.44.
Destruction hangs o'er yon' devoted Wall, ... Il.2.17.128.
Destruction hangs o'er yon' devoted Wall, ... Il.2.39.129.
Destruction hangs o'er yon' devoted Wall, ... Il.2.89.130.
Haste then, for ever leave the *Trojan* Wall! ..... Il.2.165.136.
If e'er as Friends we join, the *Trojan* Wall ..... Il.2.450.149.
Or proud *Iölcus* lifts her Airy Wall: ..... Il.2.867.165.
Mycenæ, Argos, and the *Spartan* Wall; ..... Il.4.77.224.
With fewer Troops we storm'd the *Theban* Wall, ... Il.4.460.242.
Who bathe in Blood, and shake the lofty Wall! ..... Il.5.40.267.
Who bath'st in Blood, and shak'st the lofty Wall! ..... Il.5.40A.267.
Or fierce *Bellona* thund'ring at the Wall, ... Il.5.411.286.
Who bathe in Blood, and shake th' embattel'd Wall! ..... Il.5.554.295.
Yet let me die in *Ilion's* sacred Wall; ..... Il.5.846.306.
If warring Gods for ever guard the Wall? ..... Il.5.881.308.
One Hour demands me in the *Trojan* Wall, ... Il.6.139.330.
For *Tydeus* left me young, when *Thebè's* Wall ..... Il.6.277.340.
Prone on the Dust before the *Trojan* Wall. ..... Il.6.381.345.
Till Heaps of Dead alone defend her Wall; ..... Il.6.411.347.
Where yon' wild Fig-Trees join the Wall of *Troy:* ..... Il.6.551.354.
Forth issues *Paris* from the Palace Wall. ..... Il.6.649.358.
I led my Troops to *Phea's* trembling Wall, ... Il.7.164.372.
Raise an embattel'd Wall, with lofty Tow'rs; ..... Il.7.407.385.
Let Conquest make them ours: Fate shakes their Wall, ... Il.7.478.388.
And whelm'd beneath thy Waves, drop the huge Wall: ..... Il.7.553.392.
Like tim'rous Flocks the *Trojans* in their Wall ..... Il.8.160.405.
In vain they skulk behind their boasted Wall, ... Il.8.216.407.
Since rallying from our Wall we forc'd the Foe, ... Il.8.359.414.
The *Greeks*, repuls'd, retreat behind their Wall, ... Il.8.403.416.
Now thro' the Circuit of our *Ilian* Wall, ... Il.8.643.426.
Between the Trench and Wall, let Guards remain: ..... Il.9.94.437.
Some line the Trench, and others man the Wall. ..... Il.9.120.438.
Their threat'ning Tents already shade our Wall, ... Il.9.306.449.
And favour'd by the Night, o'er leap'd the Wall. ..... Il.9.597.464.
Prepare to meet us near the Navy-wall; ..... Il.10.145.8.
And *Phrygia's* Horse, by *Thymbras'* ancient Wall; ..... Il.10.502.26.
Now storms the Victor at the *Trojan* Wall; ..... Il.11.235.46.
The Weight of Waters saps the yielding Wall, ... Il.12.25.82.
Black Death attends behind the *Grecian* Wall, ... Il.12.131.86.
Swift thro' the Wall their Horse and Chariots past, ... Il.12.135.86.
As two tall Oaks, before the Wall they rise; ..... Il.12.145.86.
To guard their Navies, and defend the Wall. ..... Il.12.158.87.
And wrap in rowling Flames the Fleet and Wall. ..... Il.12.228.89.
Furious he spoke, and rushing to the Wall, ... Il.12.295.92.
Upheave the Piles that prop the solid Wall; ..... Il.12.307.92.
Seek not your Fleet, but sally from the Wall; ..... Il.12.326.93.
To sure Destruction dooms th' aspiring Wall; ..... Il.12.368.94.
Nor these can keep, nor those can win the Wall. ..... Il.12.516.100.
Raise scaling Engines, and ascend the Wall: ..... Il.12.534.101.
And pour her Armies o'er our batter'd Wall; ..... Il.13.78.108.
Impetuous *Hector* thunders at the Wall; ..... Il.13.167.112.
That shed a Lustre round th' illumin'd Wall. ..... Il.13.340.122.
Behold! distress'd within yon' hostile Wall, ... Il.13.925.149.
High on the Wall some breath'd their Souls away. ..... Il.13.960.151.
Your boasted City and your god-built Wall ..... Il.13.1029.153.
The Wall in Ruins, and the *Greeks* in Flight. ..... Il.14.20.157.
The Wall, our late inviolable Bound, ... Il.14.63.160.
Lies whelm'd in Ruins of the *Theban* Wall, ... Il.14.128.163.
Rose in huge Ranks, and form'd a watry Wall ..... Il.14.454.185.
Aghast they gaze, around the Fleet and Wall, ... Il.14.597.191.
Some seek the Trench, some skulk behind the Wall, ... Il.15.391.212.
Then with his Hand he shook the mighty Wall; ..... Il.15.414.213.
Mount the thick *Trojans* up the *Grecian* Wall; ..... Il.15.445.214.
And flank the Navy with a brazen Wall; ..... Il.15.677.222.
As when a circling Wall the Builder forms, ... Il.16.256.249.

WALL (CONTINUED)

A Chief, who led to *Troy's* beleaguer'd Wall ..... Il.16.675.270.
Around, in heaps on heaps, a dreadful Wall ..... Il.16.803.274.
Patroclus! cease: This Heav'n-defended Wall ..... Il.16.863.277.
In dust extended under *Ilion's* Wall, ... Il.17.465.305.
A Prey to Dogs beneath the *Trojan* Wall? ..... Il.17.627.312.
Assist them Gods! or *Ilion's* sacred Wall ..... Il.20.41.394.
Not till proud *Hector,* Guardian of her Wall, ... Il.21.245.431.
In glorious Arms before the *Trojan* Wall. ..... Il.21.320.434.
Her routed Squadrons pant behind their Wall: ..... Il.21.341.435.
(*Minerva* cries) who guard the *Trojan* Wall! ..... Il.21.501.442.
The Guardian God now trembled for her Wall, ... Il.21.599.447.
What if they pass'd me to the *Trojan* Wall, ... Il.21.656.449.
Ev'n now perhaps, e'er yet I turn the Wall, ... Il.21.665.449.
Yet shun *Achilles!* enter yet the Wall; ..... Il.22.76.455.
Where lyes my Way? To enter in the Wall? ..... Il.22.138.458.
In Field at least, and fighting for her Wall. ..... Il.22.153.459.
Thus three times round the *Trojan* Wall they fly; ..... Il.22.217.464.
But he secure lyes guarded in the Wall. ..... Il.22.380.471.
Tir'd with his Chase around the *Trojan* Wall; ..... Il.23.75.489.
Thee too it waits; before the *Trojan* Wall ..... Il.23.101.491.
Of sacred *Troy,* and raz'd her heav'n-built wall, ... Od.1.4.28.
Long time with thee before proud *Ilion's* wall ..... Od.3.104.91.
Oh! had I dy'd before that well-fought wall, ... Od.5.395.191.
There round his tribes a strength of wall he rais'd, ... Od.6.13.204.
A strength of wall the guarded city bounds: ..... Od.6.312.226.
The wall was stone from neighbouring quarries born, ... Od.14.13.35.
"Then, beaming o'er th' illumin'd wall they shone: ..... Od.16.310.120.
He props his spear against the pillar'd wall; ..... Od.17.36.134.
This house holds sacred in her ample wall! ..... Od.17.179.140.
Which whizzing high, the wall unseemly sign'd. ..... Od.20.369.250.
Against the wall he set the bow unbent: ..... Od.22.137.293.
Within the stricture of this palace wall ..... Od.22.186.296.
Some wound the gate, some ring against the wall; ..... Od.22.303.301.
Drive to yon' court, without the Palace wall, ... Od.22.478.312.
There compass'd close between the dome and wall, ... Od.22.493.313.
Thus speaking, on the circling wall he strung ..... Od.22.499.313.
Or well-defending some beleaguer'd wall, ... Od.24.138.354.

WALL'D

Her private Orchards wall'd on ev'ry side, ... 1.TrVP.19.377.
Wall'd round with Sterns, a gloomy, desp'rate Band. ..... Il.15.789.226.
Of Earth congested, wall'd, and trench'd around; ..... Il.20.175.401.

WALLER

Nor yet shall Waller yield to time, ... 4.HOde9.7.159.
Waller was smooth; but Dryden taught to join ..... 4.2HE1.267.217.

WALLER'S

With *Waller's* Strains, or *Granville's* moving Lays! ..... 1.PSp.46.65.
Where *Denham's* Strength, and *Waller's* Sweetness join. ..... 1.EOC.361.280.
Not *Waller's* Wreath can hide the Nation's Scar, ... 4.EpS2.230.325.

WALLNUT

From yon old wallnut-tree a show'r shall fall; ..... 4.HS2.145.67.

WALLNUT-TREE

From yon old wallnut-tree a show'r shall fall; ..... 4.HS2.145.67.

WALLOW

"Go wallow Harpyes and your prey divide" ..... 6.130.34.359.

WALLOWING

There wallowing warm, th' enormous herd exhales ..... Od.4.547.146.

WALLS

First rais'd our Walls on that ill-omen'd Plain ..... 1.TrSt.251.421.
The shelving Walls reflect a glancing Light; ..... 1.TrSt.531.432.
Around the Walls he gaz'd, to view from far ..... 1.TrES.59.451.
The brazen Hinges fly, the Walls resound, ... 1.TrES.65A.452.
High on the Walls appear'd the *Lycian* Pow'rs, ... 1.TrES.91.453.
Rent from the Walls, a Rocky Fragment lay; ..... 1.TrES.100.453.
A mighty Breach appears, the Walls lye bare, ... 1.TrES.133.454.
Fierce as a Whirlwind, up the Walls he flies, ... 1.TrES.175.456.
Before the Walls of well-defended *Troy,* ..... 1.TrUl.192A.472.
Was compass'd round with Walls of solid Stone; ..... 2.ChJM.449.36.
The Walls, the Woods, and long Canals reply. ..... 2.RL3.100.174.
The Walls in venerable Order grace: ..... 2.TemF.72.258.
The fourfold Walls in breathing Statues grace: ..... 2.TemF.72A.258.
And the Learn'd Walls with Hieroglyphics grac'd. ..... 2.TemF.118.263.
Of bright, transparent Beryl were the Walls, ... 2.TemF.141.265.
With ceaseless Noise the ringing Walls resound: ..... 2.TemF.423.283.
Relentless walls! whose darksom round contains ..... 2.ElAb.17.320.
You rais'd these hallow'd walls; the desert smil'd, ... 2.ElAb.133.330.
In these lone walls (their day's eternal bound) ..... 2.ElAb.141.331.
And more than Echoes talk along the walls. ..... 2.ElAb.306.344.
To *Paraclete's* white walls, and silver springs, ... 2.ElAb.348.348.
The floors of plaister, and the walls of dung, ... 3.Ep3.300.118.
And Nero's Terraces desert their walls: ..... 3.Ep4.72.144.
What Walls can guard me, or what Shades can hide? ..... 4.Arbu.7.96.
With desp'rate Charcoal round his darken'd walls? ..... 4.Arbu.20.97.
What tho' my Name stood rubric on the walls? ..... 4.Arbu.215.111.
That both Extremes were banish'd from their walls, ... 4.JD2.117.143.
"Go on, my Friend (he cry'd) see yonder Walls! ..... 4.2HE2.46.167.
Enclose whole Downs in Walls, 'tis all a joke! ..... 4.2HE2.261.183.
And tips with silver all the walls: ..... 4.HS6.192.261.
Palladian walls, Venetian doors, ... 4.HS6.193.263.
Sepulchral lyes our holy walls to grace, ... 5.DunA1.41.65.
What City-Swans once sung within the walls; ..... 5.DunA1.94.70.
Walls, steeples, skies, bray back to him again: ..... 5.DunA2.248.130.
In Lud's old walls, tho' long I rul'd renown'd, ... 5.DunA3.275.183.
Close to those walls where Folly holds her throne, ... 5.DunB1.29.271.
Sepulchral Lyes, our holy walls to grace, ... 5.DunB1.43.273.
What City Swans once sung within the walls; ..... 5.DunB1.96.276.
Walls, steeples, skies, bray back to him again. ..... 5.DunB2.260.308.
In Lud's old walls tho' long I rul'd, renown'd ..... 5.DunB3.277.333.

WALLS (CONTINUED)

And leave you in lone woods, or empty walls. ....6.45.40.125.
And *Troy's* proud Walls lie level with the Ground. ....Il.1.24.86.
And Walls of Rocks, secure my native Reign, ...Il.1.204.96.
And they whom *Thebè's* well-built Walls inclose, ...Il.2.604.156.
From *Chalcis'* Walls, and strong *Eretria;* ....Il.2.644.157.
Whom strong *Tyrinthè's* lofty Walls surround, ...Il.2.678.159.
And those whom *Œtylos'* low Walls contain, ...Il.2.707.159.
And *Thryon's* Walls *Alphëus'* Streams inclose: ....Il.2.720.160.
From *Pleuron's* Walls and chalky *Calydon,* ....Il.2.776.162.
From *Ephyr's* Walls, and *Sellè's* winding Shore, ...Il.2.798.163.
Then, when the Chief the *Theban* Walls o'erthrew, ...Il.2.843.164.
War, horrid War, approaches to your Walls! ....Il.2.967.169.
From great *Arisba's* Walls and *Selle's* Coast, ...Il.2.1014.171.
Lean'd on the Walls, and bask'd before the Sun. ....Il.3.198.200.
Ah! had I dy'd, e're to these Walls I fled, ...Il.3.229.203.
In yonder Walls that Object let me shun, ...Il.3.382.211.
The matchless *Helen* o'er the Walls reclin'd: ....Il.3.474.214.
Safe from the Fight, in yonder lofty Walls, ...Il.3.482.215.
Still *Priam's* Walls in peaceful Honours grow, ...Il.4.25.222.
Burst all her Gates, and wrap her Walls in Fire! ....Il.4.54.223.
And *Troy's* proud Walls lie smoaking on the Ground. ....Il.4.333.236.
Thebes' hostile Walls, unguarded and alone, ...Il.4.438.241.
Of Force and Fire; its Walls besmear'd with Blood. ....Il.4.529.246.
Troy's sacred Walls, nor need a foreign Hand? ....Il.5.578.296.
Once from the Walls your tim'rous Foes engag'd, ...Il.5.982.314.
Once from their Walls your tim'rous Foes engag'd, ...Il.5.982A.314.
In fair *Arisba's* Walls (his native Place) ....Il.6.17.325.
And frighted *Troy* within her Walls retir'd; ....Il.6.90.328.
In ancient Time the happy Walls possest, ...Il.6.192.335.
My Son from Fight, when *Greece* surrounds our Walls? ....Il.6.319.341.
And timely join me, e're I leave the Walls. ....Il.6.455.348.
The fierce *Achilles* wrapt our Walls in Fire, ...Il.6.524.352.
To raze her Walls, tho' built by Hands Divine. ....Il.7.38.364.
Guard well the Walls, relieve the Watch of Night, ...Il.7.446.386.
They rais'd embattel'd Walls with lofty Tow'rs: ....Il.7.521.390.
See the long Walls extending to the Main, ...Il.7.534.391.
To scale our Walls, to wrap our Tow'rs in Flames, ...Il.8.200.407.
The Chariot propt against the Crystal Walls. ....Il.8.539.422.
A martial Council near the Navy-Walls: ....Il.8.610.425.
And guards them trembling in their wooden Walls. ....Il.8.626.425.
Gleam on the Walls, and tremble on the Spires. ....Il.8.702.428.
Has he not Walls no human Force can shake? ....Il.9.459.455.
Not all proud *Thebes'* unrival'd Walls contain, ...Il.9.500.457.
War shakes her Walls, and thunders at her Gates. ....Il.9.688.468.
The Walls are scal'd; the rolling Flames arise; ....Il.9.700.468.
Hangs o'er the Fleet, and shades our Walls below? ....Il.10.183.10.
And mingles with the Guards that watch the Walls; ....Il.10.434.23.
Or back to *Ilion's* Walls transfer the War? ....Il.10.483.25.
Now *Greece* had trembled in her wooden Walls; ....Il.11.404.52.
Shall seek their Walls, and *Greece* respire again. ....Il.11.933.77.
Nor long the Trench or lofty Walls oppose; ....Il.12.5.81.
The Walls were rais'd, the Trenches sunk in vain. ....Il.12.8.81.
The Stakes beneath, the *Grecian* Walls behind? ....Il.12.72.84.
Maintain'd the Walls and mann'd the lofty Tow'rs: ....Il.12.172.87.
Thro' the long Walls the stony Show'rs were heard, ...Il.12.203.88.
And *Troy* lie trembling in her Walls again. ....Il.12.328.93.
Around the Walls he gaz'd, to view from far ....Il.12.403.96.
The brazen Hinges fly, the Walls resound, ...Il.12.409.96.
High on the Walls appear'd the *Lycian* Pow'rs, ...Il.12.445.97.
Rent from the Walls a rocky Fragment lay; ....Il.12.454.98.
A mighty Breach appears; the Walls lie bare; ....Il.12.487.99.
Fierce as a Whirlwind up the Walls he flies, ...Il.12.529.101.
And swarms victorious o'er their yielding Walls: ....Il.13.120.110.
From high *Cabesus'* distant Walls he came; ....Il.13.460.128.
And where low Walls confine the beating Tydes ....Il.13.855.146.
And the gall'd *Ilians* to their Walls retir'd; ....Il.13.904.148.
Who *Pleuron's* Walls and *Calydon* possest: ....Il.14.131.164.
What Youth he slaughters under *Ilion's* Walls? ....Il.15.71.199.
Thus vanish'd, at thy touch, the Tow'rs and Walls; ....Il.15.420.213.
Thus vanish, at thy touch, the Tow'rs and Walls; ....Il.15.420A.213.
Nor lead to *Ilion's* Walls the *Grecian* Race; ....Il.16.117.241.
The Chief who taught our lofty Walls to yield, ...Il.16.683.270.
Agacleus' Son, from *Budium's* lofty Walls: ....Il.16.700.271.
Or draw the Troops within the Walls of *Troy.* ....Il.16.872.277.
Say, shall our slaughter'd Bodies guard your Walls ....Il.17.167.294.
And drag yon' Carcase to the Walls of *Troy.* ....Il.17.178.294.
Struck from the Walls, the Echoes float on high, ...Il.18.261.335.
Far from *Troy* Walls, and on a naked Coast. ....Il.18.302.336.
Vent his mad Vengeance on our rocky Walls, ...Il.18.328.337.
What, coop whole Armies in our Walls again? ....Il.18.334.337.
But while inglorious in her Walls we stay'd, ...Il.18.339.338.
And shuts the *Grecians* in their wooden Walls: ....Il.18.344.338.
(So long a Stranger) to these honour'd Walls? ....Il.18.496.345.
And now she thunders from the *Grecian* Walls. ....Il.20.68.396.
Her lofty Walls not long our Progress stay'd; ....Il.20.232.403.
Dardania's Walls he rais'd; for *Ilion,* then, ...Il.20.256.404.
From *Hyde's* Walls, he rul'd the Lands below. ....Il.20.444.413.
Troy Walls I rais'd (for such were *Jove's* Commands) ....Il.21.519.443.
Fast as he could, he sighing quits the Walls; ....Il.21.619.448.
But when within the Walls our Troops take Breath, ...Il.21.625.448.
And *Troy* inglorious to her Walls retir'd; ....Il.21.640.448.
And pour on Heaps into the Walls of *Troy.* ....Il.21.718.451.
Close to the Walls advancing o'er the Fields, ...Il.22.5.453.
Safe in their Walls are now her Troops bestow'd, ...Il.22.21.453.
But by our Walls secur'd, repel the Foe. ....Il.22.119.458.
May share our Wealth, and leave our Walls in Peace. ....Il.22.163.459.
He leaves the Gates, he leaves the Walls behind; ....Il.22.181.462.
Now circling round the Walls their Course maintain, ...Il.22.191.463.
Her Walls thrice circled, and her Chief pursu'd. ....Il.22.318.469.
I, only I, will issue from your Walls, ...Il.22.531.478.
Now from the Walls the Clamours reach her Ear, ...Il.22.574.480.
Shut from our Walls! I fear, I fear him slain! ....Il.22.587.480.
And mounts the Walls, and sends around her View: ....Il.22.595.480.
Astyanax, from her well-guarded Walls, ...Il.22.651.483.
Troy feels the Blast along her shaking Walls, ...Il.23.268.500.

WALLS (CONTINUED)

For *Hector's* sake these Walls he bids thee leave, ...Il.24.211.545.
For with the Morn the *Greeks* attack your Walls; ....Il.24.492.556.
And now they reach'd the naval Walls, and found ....Il.24.545.558.
War, and the Blood of Men, surround thy Walls! ....Il.24.691.566.
And at what distance from our Walls aspire ....Il.24.832.571.
Nor Man, nor Woman, in the Walls remains. ....Il.24.883.573.
Within these walls inglorious silence reigns. ....Od.2.34.62.
While yet he spoke, she fill'd the walls with cries, ...Od.2.406.80.
Before old *Neleus'* venerable walls. ....Od.3.6.86.
Thus from my walls the much-lov'd son to send ....Od.3.445.108.
Sparta, whose walls a range of hills surrounds: ....Od.4.2.119.
When near the fam'd *Phæacian* walls he drew, ...Od.7.23.235.
And deep intrenchments, and high walls of stone, ...Od.7.59.236.
The walls were massy brass: the cornice high ....Od.7.112.240.
Refulgent pedestals the walls surround, ...Od.7.128.241.
Ulysses in the regal walls alone ....Od.7.311.251.
How ev'n in *Ilion's* walls, in deathful bands, ...Od.8.551.292.
Th' unwise prevail, they lodge it in the walls, ...Od.8.559.292.
Strong walls of brass the rocky coast confine. ....Od.10.4.339.
The town with walls, and mound inject on mound; ....Od.11.322.398.
But hear me, Princes! whom these walls inclose, ...Od.13.9.2.
Shou'd hide our walls, or whelm beneath the ground. ....Od.13.205.15.
Else had I seen my native walls in vain, ...Od.13.439.27.
As when we wrapt *Troy's* heav'n-built walls in fire. ....Od.13.444.27.
Beneath *Troy* walls by night we took our way: ....Od.14.531.63.
The last I purpose in your walls to rest: ....Od.15.327.85.
Return, and riot shakes our walls a-new) ....Od.17.121.137.
Approach yon walls, I prophecy thy fare: ....Od.17.269.145.
High walls and battlements the courts inclose, ...Od.17.318.147.
Our walls this twelvemonth should not see the slave. ....Od.17.491.156.
Grant him unrival'd in these walls to stay, ...Od.18.54.169.
Till propp'd reclining on the palace walls; ....Od.18.123.172.
From the glad walls inglorious lumber torn. ....Od.19.12.193.
The walls where-e'er my wond'ring sight I turn, ...Od.19.46.195.
Torn from these walls (where long the kinder pow'rs ....Od.19.678.229.
With sanguine drops the walls are rubied round: ....Od.20.426.254.
Say you, whom these forbidden walls inclose, ...Od.21.69.262.
Some may betray, and yonder walls may hear. ....Od.21.245.271.
Nor shall these walls such insolence contain; ....Od.21.327.275.
Th' oppressive Suitors from my walls expell! ....Od.21.404.279.
One strikes the gate, one rings against the walls; ....Od.22.285.300.
Their fall in thunder ecchoes round the walls. ....Od.22.297.300.
Then she. In these thy kingly walls remain ....Od.22.458.310.
(The swains unite their toil) the walls, the floor ....Od.22.489.313.
He purg'd the walls and blood-polluted rooms. ....Od.22.530.314.
Heap'd lie the dead without the Palace walls,— ....Od.23.53.321.

WALPOLE

To *W[alpole]* guilty of some venial Sin, ...4.EpS2.162.322 .
Rise, rise great W[alpole] fated to appear, ...4.1740.43.334.

WALSH

Such late was *Walsh,—the* Muse's Judge and Friend, ...1.EOC.729.325.
And knowing *Walsh,* would tell me I could write; ....4.Arbu.136.105.

WALTER

From you to me, from me to Peter Walter, ...4.HS2.168.69.
Whom (saving W[alter]) every S. *harper bites,* ....4.1740.26.333*.

WALTERS

So drink with Walters, or with *Chartres* eat, ...4.HS1.89B.13.

WAN

Down his wan Cheek a briny Torrent flows; ....Il.9.18.431.
Then the wan shades and feeble ghosts implore, ...Od.10.620.374.
Now the wan shades we hail, th' infernal Gods, ...Od.11.35.381.
Or pale and wan beholds these nether skies? ....Od.11.571.411.
Where the wan Spectres walk eternal rounds; ....Od.11.584.412.
With tears your wan distorted cheeks are drown'd; ....Od.20.425.253.
Down his wan cheek the trickling torrent ran, ...Od.24.487.371.

WAND

Peace o'er the World her Olive-Wand extend, ...1.Mes.19.114.
He seiz'd the Wand that causes Sleep to fly, ...1.TrSt.433.428.
He seiz'd his Wand that causes Sleep to fly, ...1.TrSt.433A.428.
He rais'd his Azure Wand, and thus begun. ....2.RL2.72.164.
Grave *Zoroaster* waves the circling Wand: ....2.TemF.98.260.
Sancho's dread Doctor and his Wand were there. ....3.Ep4.160.153.
Ah! still o'er Britain stretch that peaceful wand, ...5.DunA1.155.82.
As Argus' eyes, by Hermes' wand opprest, ...5.DunA3.343.192.
Held forth the Virtue of the dreadful wand; ....5.DunB4.140.355.
But Annius, crafty Seer, with ebon wand, ...5.DunB4.347.377.
As Argus' eyes by Hermes' wand opprest, ...5.DunB4.637.407.
Did wave his Wand so white, ...6.79.118.222.
Then grasps the Wand that causes Sleep to fly, ...Il.24.421.553.
On these the Virtue of his Wand he tries, ...Il.24.547.558.
He grasps the wand that causes sleep to fly, ...Od.5.60.174.
God of the golden wand! on what behest ....Od.5.111.177.
Instant her circling wand the Goddess waves, ...Od.10.276.356.
Soon as she strikes her wand, and gives the word, ...Od.10.349.361.
Then wav'd the wand, and then the word was giv'n. ....Od.10.380.363.
By *Hermes* pow'rful with the wand of gold) ....Od.10.392.363.
She bore the virtue of the magic wand. ....Od.10.458.366.
She spake, then touch'd him with her pow'rful wand: ....Od.13.496.29.
She said, and o'er him waves her wand of gold; ....Od.16.186.112.
She waves her golden wand, and reassumes ....Od.16.476.130.
The golden wand, that causes sleep to fly, ...Od.24.3.345.

WAND'RER

Before the wand'rer smooths the wat'ry way, ...Od.5.578.200.
While thus the weary Wand'rer sunk to rest, ...Od.6.1.203.
To *Jove,* who guides the wand'rer on his way; ....Od.7.221.247.
To *Jove,* who guides the wand'rer on his way. ....Od.7.241.248.
Com'st thou a wand'rer from the *Phrygian* shores? ....Od.11.197.391.
To this the Queen. The wand'rer let me hear, ...Od.17.618.162.

WAND'RER (CONTINUED)
To wash a wretched wand'rer wou'd disdain; Od.19.398.213.
Ulysses from his state a wand'rer still, Od.20.257.245.

WAND'RER'S
And foam impervious cross the Wand'rer's way, Il.5.737.302.
Th' unhappy series of a wand'rer's woe? Od.9.12.301.

WAND'RERS
From *Troy's* fam'd fields, sad wand'rers o'er the main, Od.9.307.319.
Exiles and wand'rers now, where-e're ye go, Od.10.548.369.

WAND'RING
Explores the lost, the wand'ring Sheep directs, 1.Mes.51.117.
Or back to Life compells the wand'ring Ghosts. 1.TrSt.436A.428.
Thro' ten Years Wand'ring, and thro' ten Years War; 1.TrUl.176.471.
Here sailing Ships delight the wand'ring Eyes; 2.TemF.17.254.
Shew by what Laws the wand'ring Planets stray 3.EOM2.21A.56.
Some wand'ring touches some reflected light, 3.Ep2.153A.63.
Some wand'ring touch, or some reflected light, 3.Ep2.153.63.
In Fancy's Maze that wand'ring not too long, 4.Arbu.340A.120.
He, whose long Wall the wand'ring Tartar bounds. 5.DunA3.68.156.
He, whose long wall the wand'ring Tartar bounds; 5.DunB3.76.324.
But more diffusive in its wand'ring Race; 6.17ii.23.56.
Ah fleeting Spirit! wand'ring Fire, 6.31i.1.93.
What is loose Love? A wand'ring Fire, 6.51ii.17Z1.153.
What flatt'ring scenes our wand'ring fancy wrought, 6.52.23.156.
And wand'ring o'er the Camp, requir'd their Lord. Il.2.945.168.
The purple Current wand'ring o'er his Vest. Il.5.145.274.
By wand'ring Birds, that flit with ev'ry Wind? Il.12.278.91.
A naked, wand'ring, melancholy Ghost! Il.16.1035.283.
So to Night-wand'ring Sailors, pale with Fears, Il.19.404.389.
Sad Dreams of Care yet wand'ring in their Breast. Il.24.845.572.
Wand'ring from clime to clime, observant stray'd, Od.1.5.28.
Now make the wand'ring *Greek* their public care, Od.1.104.36.
What *Greeks,* now wand'ring in the *Stygian* gloom, Od.1.453.54.
But if already wand'ring in the train Od.2.249.73.
He, wand'ring long, a wider circle made, Od.3.407.106.
Here shall the wand'ring stranger find his home, Od.3.453.109.
In mazy windings wand'ring down the hill: Od.5.92.176.
The wand'ring Chief, with toils on toils opprest, Od.5.424.192.
And point the wand'ring traveler his way: Od.7.36.235.
A wand'ring merchant he frequents the main, Od.8.179.272.
And sees me wand'ring still from coast to coast; Od.9.647.333.
This happy port affords our wand'ring fleet Od.10.13.340.
There, wand'ring thro' the gloom I first survey'd, Od.11.65.383.
Thro' ten years wand'ring, and thro' ten years war; Od.13.343.24.
(Reply'd *Eumæus)* to the wand'ring tribe. Od.14.147.42.
Meet, for the wand'ring suppliant to provide. Od.14.579.64.
Him, child-like wand'ring forth, I'll lead away, Od.15.489.94.
At rest, or wand'ring in his country's shade, Od.17.181.140.
Have learn'd the fortunes of my wand'ring Lord? Od.17.600.161.
The storied labours of my wand'ring Lord, Od.19.113.198.
Search'd the wide country for his wand'ring mares, Od.21.26.260.
Accept a wand'ring stranger for my Lord? Od.21.340.276.
Excess of joy disturbs thy wand'ring mind; Od.23.60.321.

WAND'RINGS
And shine in mazy Wand'rings o'er the Plains. Il.21.298.433.
Which in my wand'rings oft reliev'd my woe: Od.4.42.122.
Thro' many woes and wand'rings, lo! I come Od.7.31.235.
When blest with ease thy woes and wand'rings end, Od.8.277.278.
Restore me safe thro' weary wand'rings tost, Od.8.507.289.
So may I find, when all my wand'rings cease, Od.13.54.4.
Of wand'rings and of woes a wretched share? Od.13.481.29.
Of woes and wand'rings thou wert born to bear? Od.14.56.38.
Ulysses' wand'rings to his royal mate; Od.15.333.85.
A life of wand'rings is the greatest woe: Od.15.365.87.
While I, so many wand'rings past and woes, Od.15.530.95.
By woes and wand'rings from this hapless land: Od.21.214.270.

WANDER
And ships, in safety, wander to and fro. 1.TrPA.28.366.
Guideless I wander, unreguarded mourn, 1.TrSt.105.414.
The young dismiss'd to wander earth or air, 3.EOM3.127.105.
Or who shall wander where the Muses sing? 4.2HE1.352.225.
May wander in a wilderness of Moss; 5.DunB4.450.384.
But tho' from Flame to Flame you wander, 6.10.53.26.
Dost thou bewilder'd wander all alone 6.96ii.30Z7.271.
"Dost thou bewilder'd wander all alone, 6.96ii.41.272.
Confus'd, and sad, I wander thus alone, Il.10.103.7.
Shine 'twixt the Hills, or wander o'er the Plain. Il.12.36.83.
All pale they wander on the *Stygian* Coast; Il.22.71.455.
But now forgot, I wander in the Air: Il.23.86.490.
To view that deathful Eye, and wander o'er Il.24.249.547.
Thus far ye wander thro' the watry way? Od.3.85.90.
Fated to wander from his natal coast! Od.4.248.131.
A God might gaze, and wander with delight! Od.5.96.177.
Go, wander helpless on the wat'ry way: Od.5.481.195.
What savage beasts may wander in the waste? Od.5.609.201.
Thus far ye wander thro' the wat'ry way? Od.9.300.318.
To glide in shades, and wander with the dead? Od.11.72.383.
To wander with the wind in empty air, Od.11.266.394.
Far on the swelling seas to wander hence? Od.14.207.45.
Long doom'd to wander o'er the land and main, Od.16.63.105.
Wander, perhaps, some inmate of the skies; Od.17.577.160.
Were doom'd to wander thro' the devious air; Od.20.79.236.
That she should wander, and that *Greece* should bleed: Od.23.236.334.

WANDER'D
And wander'd in the solitary Shade: 2.ChJM.62.17.
And each bright Image wander'd o'er his Heart. 2.ChJM.233.25.
And each bright Image wander'd in his Heart. 2.ChJM.233A.25.
That not in Fancy's Maze he wander'd long, 4.Arbu.340.120.
Silent he wander'd by the sounding Main: Il.1.50.88.
Of willing Exiles wander'd o'er the Main; Il.2.806.163.

WANDER'D (CONTINUED)
Chearless he breath'd, and wander'd in the Gloom, Il.6.172.334.
There wander'd *Menelaus* thro' foreign shores, Od.3.384.105.
Since wide he wander'd on the wat'ry waste; Od.5.497.196.
The man from *Troy,* who wander'd Ocean round; Od.10.393.363.
Have wander'd many a sea, and many a land. Od.14.145.42.
And wander'd thro' the wide ethereal way Od.15.196.78.
With thousand kisses wander'd o'er his face, Od.24.374.367.

WANDER'ST
Thou art, that wander'st in this desart Place, 1.TrUl.109.469.
Is seal'd in Sleep, thou wander'st thro' the Night? Il.24.448.555.
Thou art, that wander'st in this desart place! Od.13.276.19.

WANDERER
(For Taste, eternal wanderer, now flies 4.2HE1.312.221.
(Taste, that eternal wanderer, which flies 4.2HE1.312A.221.
Try, if the Grave can hold the Wanderer; Il.21.71.424.
A man unknown, a needy wanderer? Od.21.314.274.

WANDERERS
Benighted wanderers, the forest o'er, 3.Ep3.195.109.

WANDERS
Disconsolate he wanders on the Coast: 1.TrUl.97.469.
There deviates Nature, and here wanders Will. 3.EOM4.112.138.
Or wanders, Heav'n-directed, to the Poor. 3.Ep2.150.62.
Or wanders wild in Academic Groves; 5.DunB4.490.390.
Or where *Hebrus* wanders, 6.11.99.33.
Or wanders, Heaven directed, to the Poor. 6.154.36.403.
As some way-faring Man, who wanders o'er Il.15.86.199.
Ah! whither wanders thy distemper'd Mind, Il.24.243.546.
He wanders, Outcast both of Earth and Heav'n. Il.24.670.565.
Whether he wanders on some firendless coast, Od.4.141.127.
Wide wanders, *Laodame,* thy erring tongue, Od.8.175.271.
He wanders with them, and he feels their wrongs. Od.9.324.319.
Disconsolate he wanders on the coast, Od.13.264.18.
Pensive and pale he wanders half a ghost. Od.16.157.110.
Oh whither wanders thy distemper'd brain, Od.18.375.185.
Ah! whither wanders thy distemper'd mind? Od.23.12.319.

WANDREST
Why, mortal, wandrest thou from chearful day, Od.11.116.386.

WANDRING
Or wandring thoughtful in the silent Wood, 1.W-F.249.172.
Th' *increasing* Prospect *tires* our wandring Eyes, 1.EOC.231.265.
That wandring Heart which I so lately lost; 1.TrSP.66.396.
Of Towns dispeopled, and the wandring Ghosts 1.TrSt.55.412.
When banish'd *Cadmus* wandring o'er the Main, 1.TrSt.247.420.
And those that give the wandring Winds to blow, 1.TrSt.289.422.
And Heav'n it self the wandring Chariot burn'd. 1.TrSt.311.423.
His wandring Stream, and thro' the briny Tydes, 1.TrSt.384.426.
While future Realms his wandring Thoughts delight, 1.TrSt.445.428.
Some guide the Course of wandring Orbs on high, 2.RL2.79.164.
The wandring streams that shine between the hills, 2.ElAb.157.332.
Alas no more!—methinks we wandring go 2.ElAb.241.339.
If ever chance two wandring lovers brings 2.ElAb.347.348.
Wandring in the Myrtle Grove, 6.11.80.33.
A wandring, self-consuming fire. 6.51ii.20.153.
Those Ghosts of Beauty wandring here reside, 6.110.3A.316.
The wandring Nation of a Summer's Day, Il.2.553.154.
Thus leads you wandring in the silent Night? Il.10.161.9.
His Senses wandring to the Verge of Death. Il.15.14.194.
A naked, wandring, melancholy Ghost! Il.22.458.474.
Our wandring course, and drove us on your shore: Od.24.358.366.

WANE
Or wane and wax alternate like the Moon. 2.TemF.486.287.
In the next month renews her faded wane, Od.19.352.211.

WANT
'Tis hard to say, if greater Want of Skill 1.EOC.1.239.
Want as much more, to turn it to its use; 1.EOC.81.248.
Yet want as much again to manage it; 1.EOC.81A.248.
And hide with *Ornaments* their *Want of Art.* 1.EOC.296.272.
(For none want Reasons to confirm their Will) 2.ChJM.20.16.
She shall not want an Answer at her Need. 2.ChJM.658.46.
None shall want Arts to varnish an Offence, 2.ChJM.661A.46.
And what we want in Pleasure, grant in Fame. 2.TemF.391.282.
Shall shortly want the gen'rous tear he pays; 2.Elegy.78.368.
To want the strength of bulls, the fur of bears. 3.EOM1.176.36.
Each seeming want compensated of course, 3.EOM1.181.37.
How *Instinct* varies! what a Hog may want, 3.EOM1.221A.43.
Each want of happiness by Hope supply'd, 3.EOM2.285.89.
One they must want, which is, to pass for good. 3.EOM4.92.137.
"No—shall the good want Health, the good want Pow'r?" 3.EOM4.158.143.
"No—shall the good want Health, the good want Pow'r?" 3.EOM4.158.143.
Worth makes the man, and want of it, the fellow; 3.EOM4.203.146.
Behold a rev'rend sire, whom want of grace 3.Ep1.228.34.
"Say, what can Cloe want?"—she wants a Heart. 3.Ep2.160.64.
And show their zeal, and hide their want of skill. 3.Ep2.186.65.
B. To Want or Worth well-weigh'd, be Bounty giv'n, 3.Ep3.229A.111.
That "every man in want is knave or fool:" 3.Ep3.104.99.
To Want or Worth well-weigh'd, be Bounty giv'n, 3.Ep3.229.111.
Where Age and Want sit smiling at the gate: 3.Ep3.266.115.
"What all so wish, but want the pow'r to do! 3.Ep3.276.116.
Want with a full, or with an empty purse? 3.Ep3.320.120.
For very want; he could not build a wall. 3.Ep3.324.120.
For very want; he could not pay a dow'r. 3.Ep3.326.120.
'Twas very want that sold them for two pound. 3.Ep3.328.120.
What but a want, which you perhaps think mad, 3.Ep3.331.120.
Yet numbers feel, the want of what he had. 3.Ep3.332.120.
To help who want, to forward who excel; 4.HS1.137.19.
Are no rewards for Want, and Infamy! 4.HS2.104.61.
To laugh, were want of Goodness and of Grace, 4.Arbu.35.98.

WANT (CONTINUED)

"I want a Patron; ask him for a Place." ... 4.Arbu.50.100.
If want provok'd, or madness made them print, ... 4.Arbu.155.107.
And all they want is spirit, taste, and sense. ... 4.Arbu.160.108.
Sure I should want the Care of ten *Monroes,* ... 4.2HE2.70.169.
But grant I may relapse, for want of Grace, ... 4.2HE2.88.171.
The more you want, why not with equal ease ... 4.2HE2.214.179.
You purchase as you want, and bit by bit; ... 4.2HE2.237.181.
My Heir may sigh, and think it want of Grace ... 4.2HE2.286.185.
And pleas'd, if sordid Want be far away. ... 4.2HE2.295.185.
But Kings in Wit may want discerning spirit. ... 4.2HE1.385.227.
The fear to want them is as weak a thing: ... 4.1HE6.19.237.
What ev'ry day will want, and most, the last. ... 4.1HE1.22.281.
As want of figure, and a small Estate. ... 4.1HE1.68.283.
Of hisses, blows, or want, or loss of ears: ... 5.DunA1.46.65.
Of hisses, blows, or want, or loss of ears: ... 5.DunB1.48.274.
None want a place, for all their Centre found, ... 5.DunB4.77.349.
All-seeing in thy mists, we want no guide, ... 5.DunB4.469.386.
Thy very want of Tongue makes thee a kind of Fame. ... 6.8.27.18.
That is to say, the Want of Coin. ... 6.10.70.26.
(Tho' Dinners oft they want and Suppers too) ... 6.17iv.24.60.
My tears the want of off'rings had supply'd; ... 6.20.41.67.
Want your assistance now to clear 'em. ... 6.42v.4.119.
(Not plagu'd with headachs, or the want of rhime) ... 6.45.42.125.
For Want of you, we spend our random Wit on ... 6.82vi.3.232.
O! may'st thou never want an easy Pad! ... 6.96iii.38.275.
And all they want is Spirit, Taste, and Sense. ... 6.98.10.283.
Want nothing else, except your wife. ... 6.114.12.321.
Secure in dullness, madness, want, and age. ... 6.116vii.8.328.
When prest by Want and Weakness, *Dennis* lies; ... 6.128.10.356.
"Say what can Cloë want?"—She wants a *Heart:* ... 6.139.4.377.
There want not Chiefs in such a Cause to fight, ... Il.1.227.98.
Must want a *Trojan* Slave to pour the Wine. ... Il.2.158.136.
There want not Gods to favour us above; ... Il.3.547.217.
Not *Hector's* self should want an equal Foe. ... Il.7.190.373.
Nor shall great *Hector* want an equal Foe; ... Il.8.140.404.
Confiding in our want of Worth, he stands, ... Il.9.59.434.
From Danger guards them, and from Want defends; ... Il.9.425.453.
Thy want of Arms (said *Iris*) well we know, ... Il.18.235.333.
E'er Thirst and Want his Forces have opprest, ... Il.19.368.387.
"Shall want in death a shroud to grace his shade." ... Od.2.114.67.
All born to want; a miserable race! ... Od.3.63.89.
Nor want of herbage makes the dairy fail, ... Od.4.111.125.
Urg'd on by want, and recent from the storms; ... Od.6.163.216.
Forbid that want shou'd sink me to a lye. ... Od.7.383.255.
The nobler portion want, a knowing mind. ... Od.8.196.273.
And never, never may'st thou want this sword! ... Od.8.450.287.
Reproach'd by want, our fruitless labours mourn, ... Od.10.46.341.
But speaking tears the want of words supply, ... Od.10.291.357.
Famine and meager want besieg'd us round. ... Od.12.394.450.
And want too oft betrays the tongue to lye. ... Od.14.149.42.
Whom Want itself can force untruths to tell, ... Od.14.180.44.
And these indulge their want, and those their woe, ... Od.14.415.56.
Nor garment shalt thou want, nor ought beside, ... Od.14.578.64.
Want feeds not there, where Luxury devours, ... Od.15.405.89.
No want, no famine the glad natives know, ... Od.15.446.92.
To want like mine, the peopled town can yield ... Od.17.22.133.
What cannot *Want?* the best she will expose, ... Od.17.340.148.
How ill, alas! do want and shame agree? ... Od.17.423.152.
It is not so with Want! how few that feed ... Od.17.470.156.
Yet starving Want amidst the riot weeps. ... Od.17.542.158.
But for meer want, how hard to suffer wrong? ... Od.17.562.159.
Want brings enough of other ills along! ... Od.17.563.160.
"Want the last duties of a daughter's hand." ... Od.19.171.200.
'Twas caution, oh my Lord! not want of love: ... Od.23.230.334.
Want the last duties of a daughter's hand. ... Od.24.163.356.

WANTED

Where *wanted,* scorn'd, and envy'd where acquir'd; ... 1.EOC.503A.295.
And one had Grace, that wanted all the rest. ... 2.ChJM.241.26.
And one had Grace, yet wanted all the rest. ... 2.ChJM.241A.26.
He wanted Art to hide, and Means to tell. ... 2.ChJM.395.34.
Only to show, how many Tastes he wanted. ... 3.Ep4.14.137.
The World had wanted many an idle Song) ... 4.Arbu.28.98.
Ev'n copious Dryden, wanted, or forgot, ... 4.2HE1.280.219.
How Van wants grace, who never wanted wit! ... 4.2HE1.289.219.
What RICHELIEU wanted, LOUIS scarce could gain, ... 4.EpS2.116.319.
We may be wanted on some busie Day, ... Il.2.296.142.
Now, now thy Country calls her wanted Friends, ... Il.5.579.296.
Nor wanted heav'nly Aid: *Apollo's* Might ... Il.7.327.380.
The wanted Weapons; those my Tent can give. ... Il.13.338.121.
Or to the Left our wanted Succour lend? ... Il.13.398.125.

WANTING

And wanting nothing but an honest heart; ... 3.Ep1.193.31.
Can there be wanting to defend Her Cause, ... 4.HS1.109.15.
He, who still wanting tho' he lives on theft, ... 4.Arbu.183.109.
Nor wert thou, Isis! wanting to the day, ... 5.DunB4.193.361.
A Page is blotted, or Leaf wanting: ... 6.29.18.83.
In Sense still wanting, tho' he lives on Theft, ... 6.98.33.284.
Yet two are wanting of the num'rous Train, ... Il.3.301.207.
Nor was the Gen'ral wanting to his Train, ... Il.5.649.299.
Nor wines were wanting; those from ample jars ... Od.9.190.313.

WANTON

And I this Bowl, where wanton Ivy twines, ... 1.PSp.35.63.
The wanton Victims of his *Sport* remain. ... 1.W-F.78.157.
Wanton as kids; and more delicious far, ... 1.TrPA.58.367.
How oft the *Satyrs* and the wanton *Fawns,* ... 1.TrVP.21.378.
That fly disorder'd with the wanton Wind: ... 1.TrSP.86.397.
Then round your Neck in wanton Wreaths I twine, ... 1.TrSP.149.400.
He kiss'd his balmy Spouse, with wanton Play, ... 2.ChJM.388.33.
Sport with her Tail, and wanton in the Sun; ... 2.ChWB.145.63.
Wanton and wild, and chatter'd like a Pye. ... 2.ChWB.210.66.
Stain all my soul, and wanton in my eyes! ... 2.ElAb.266.341.
Who for thy table feeds the wanton fawn, ... 3.EOM3.29.95.

WANTON (CONTINUED)

The bow'r of wanton Shrewsbury and love; ... 3.Ep3.308.119.
"And 'tis for that the wanton Boy has Wings." ... 4.HAdv.140.87.
Turn, turn to willing Hearts your wanton fires. ... 4.HOde1.8.151.
Now gentle touches wanton o'er his face, ... 5.DunA2.193.124.
Now gentle touches wanton o'er his face, ... 5.DunB2.201.305.
Nor lends to Wanton Songs an Ear, ... 6.54.3.164.
That Bag—which *Jenny,* wanton Slut , ... 6.94.77.261.
Pray Heav'n, 'twas all a wanton Maiden did! ... 6.96iv.88.279.
Tho, once my Tail in wanton play, ... 6.135.3.366.
The wanton Courser thus, with Reins unbound, ... Il.6.652.359.
The sportive Wanton, pleas'd with some new Play, ... Il.15.418.213.
And slightly on her Breast the Wanton strook: ... Il.21.497.442.
Whose Days the Feast and wanton Dance employ, ... Il.24.327.550.
The wanton youth inglorious peace enjoy'd; ... Od.3.325.102.
The wanton lovers, as entwin'd they lay, ... Od.8.318.281.
The careless lovers in their wanton play: ... Od.8.340.282.
Why was I born? see how the wanton lies! ... Od.8.353.282.
Smooth flows the gentle stream with wanton pride, ... Od.11.285.396.
That speak disdain, the wanton thus replies. ... Od.18.374.185.
Perhaps, like thee, poor guest! in wanton pride ... Od.19.436.216.
With wanton glee, the prostituted fair. ... Od.20.12.230.
Like me had *Helen* fear'd, with wanton charms ... Od.23.231.334.

WANTON'D

Hung at her knee, or wanton'd at her breast; ... Od.11.554.411.

WANTONNESS

As flow'ry Bands in Wantonness are worn; ... 6.19.65.64.

WANTONS

Unweeting Wantons of their wetting Woe! ... 6.42vi.2.120.

WANTS

What wants in *Blood* and *Spirits,* swell'd with *Wind;* ... 1.EOC.208.264.
Content, if hence th' Unlearn'd their Wants may view, ... 1.EOC.739.326.
And build on wants, and on defects of mind, ... 3.EOM2.247.85.
Wants, frailties, passions, closer still ally ... 3.EOM2.253.85.
The scale to measure others wants by thine. ... 3.EOM2.292.90.
And helps, another creature's wants and woes. ... 3.EOM3.52.97.
And feels, another creature's wants and woes. ... 3.EOM3.52A.97.
On mutual Wants built mutual Happiness: ... 3.EOM3.112.103.
But mutual wants this Happiness increase, ... 3.EOM4.55.133.
Because he wants a thousand pounds a year. ... 3.EOM4.192.145.
And where no wants, no wishes can remain, ... 3.EOM4.325.159.
To Toast our wants and wishes, is her way; ... 3.Ep2.88.57.
Childless with all her Children, wants an Heir. ... 3.Ep2.148.62.
"Say, what can Cloe want?"—she wants a Heart. ... 3.Ep2.160.64.
B. What Nature wants, commodious Gold bestows, ... 3.Ep3.21A.85.
What Nature wants, commodious Gold bestows, ... 3.Ep3.21.85.
What Nature wants (a phrase I much distrust) ... 3.Ep3.25.88.
Why Shylock wants a meal, the cause is found, ... 3.Ep3.117.101.
Wants reach all States; they beg but better drest, ... 4.JD4.224.45.
So, when a Statesman wants a Day's defence, ... 4.Arbu.251.114.
Yet wants the Honour injur'd to defend; ... 4.Arbu.296.117.
That wants or Force, or Light, or Weight, or Care, ... 4.2HE2.160.177.
Suppose he wants a year, will you compound? ... 4.2HE1.57.199.
How Van wants grace, who never wanted wit! ... 4.2HE1.289.219.
And a thin Court that wants your Face, ... 4.1HE7.12.269.
Which done, the poorest can no wants endure, ... 4.1HE1.45.281.
"Pray then what wants he?" fourscore thousand pounds, ... 4.1HE1.86.285.
Such wholsome Foods as Nature's Wants supply, ... 6.17iii.26.58.
Or other's wants with Scorn deride ... 6.50.35B.148.
In Wants, in Sickness, shall a *Friend* be nigh, ... 6.117.11.333.
Yet wants the honour, injur'd to defend: ... 6.120.4.339.
My master wants no Key of State, ... 6.135.35.367.
"Say what can Cloë want?"—She wants a *Heart:* ... 6.139.4.377.
Childless with all her Children, wants an Heir: ... 6.154.34.403.
Now wants that Succour which so oft' he lent. ... Il.11.971.78.
The Kindest but his present Wants allay, ... Il.22.636.482.
The wants of nature with repast suffice, ... Od.4.581.147.
Studious to save what human wants require, ... Od.5.632.202.
Propitious to my wants, a Vest supply ... Od.6.215.220.
But still long-weary'd nature wants repair; ... Od.7.294.250.
My wants, and lent these robes that strike your eyes. ... Od.7.381.255.
Ev'n he who sightless wants his visual ray, ... Od.8.221.274.
Add all the wants and the decays of life, ... Od.13.461.28.
To early wants! a man of miseries! ... Od.15.413.89.
The poor, distinguish'd by their wants alone? ... Od.17.461.155.
A gift in season which his wants require. ... Od.17.631.163.
Thy other wants her subjects shall supply. ... Od.17.641.163.
And views that object which she wants the most! ... Od.19.245.206.
With all thy wants the name of poor shall end; ... Od.19.290.209.
His age not honour'd, nor his wants reliev'd? ... Od.20.164.241.
And wants and insults, make me less than man? ... Od.21.306.274.

WAPPING

Tho' born at *Wapping,* and from *Daniel* sprung, ... 5.DunA2.384A.148.
Woolwich and *Wapping,* smelling strong of Pitch; ... 6.14ii.47.44.

WAR

When *Albion* sends her eager Sons to War, ... 1.W-F.106.161.
The Youth rush eager to the Sylvan War; ... 1.W-F.148.164.
Of War or Blood, but in the Sylvan Chace, ... 1.W-F.372.187.
Destructive *War,* and all-involving *Age.* ... 1.EOC.184.262.
Destructive *War,* and all-devouring *Age.* ... 1.EOC.184A.262.
Seldom at *Council,* never in a *War:* ... 1.EOC.537.298.
Their kindred Souls to mutual Hate and War. ... 1.TrSt.117.415.
Whom Fury drove precipitate to War. ... 1.TrSt.191.418.
And give the Nations to the Waste of War. ... 1.TrSt.341.424.
Hence Strife shall rise, and mortal War succeed; ... 1.TrSt.344.424.
Nor doom to War a Race deriv'd from thee; ... 1.TrSt.397.426.
The Floods descending and the watry War, ... 1.TrSt.513.431.
'Tis thine the Seeds of future War to know, ... 1.TrSt.841.444.
Thou dost the Seeds of future War foreknow, ... 1.TrSt.841A.444.
And Shepherds gaul him with an Iron War; ... 1.TrES.18.450.

WAR (CONTINUED)

In fighting Fields, nor urge thy Soul to War. ... 1.TrES.46.451.
What Aid appear'd t'avert th'approaching War, ... 1.TrES.60.451.
The bloody Labours of the doubtful War: ... 1.TrES.70.452.
The bloody Labours of the doubtful War: ... 1.TrES.80Z4.452.
And thus bespoke his Brothers of the War: ... 1.TrES.82.453.
The War begins; mix'd Shouts and Groans arise; ... 1.TrES.95.453.
The War renews, mix'd Shouts and Groans arise; ... 1.TrES.95A.453.
And like a Deluge rushes in the War. ... 1.TrES.134.454.
And fix'd support the Weight of all the War: ... 1.TrES.154.455.
So stood the War, till *Hector's* matchless Might ... 1.TrES.171Z1.455.
This Hand unaided shall the War sustain: ... 1.TrES.214.457.
Patroclus lights, and sternly waits the War. ... 1.TrES.218.457.
From all the Dangers and the Toils of War; ... 1.TrES.234.458.
The glorious Dangers of destructive War, ... 1.TrES.303.461.
Thence, from the War, the breathless Hero bore, ... 1.TrES.338.462.
Thro' ten Years Wand'ring, and thro' ten Years War; ... 1.TrUl.176.471.
Now move to War her Sable *Matadores,* ... 2.RL3.47.172.
Sad Chance of War! now, destitute of Aid, ... 2.RL3.63.172.
Sighs, Sobs, and Passions, and the War of Tongues. ... 2.RL4.84.190.
Of Peace and War, Health, Sickness, Death, and Life; ... 2.TemF.449.285.
Wits, just like fools, at war about a Name, ... 3.EOM2.85.65.
What War could ravish, Commerce could bestow, ... 3.EOM3.205.113.
Some War, some Plague, some Famine they foresee, ... 3.Ep3.115A.101.
Some War, some Plague, or Famine they foresee, ... 3.Ep3.115.101.
Chiefs, out of War, and Statesmen, out of Place. ... 4.HS1.126.17.
The whole Artill'ry of the Terms of War, ... 4.JD4.54.29.
And all the Man is one intestine war) ... 4.HS2.72.59.
In Peace provides fit arms against a War? ... 4.HS2.128.65.
A War-horse never for the Service chose, ... 4.HAdv.114.85.
I wag'd no war with *Bedlam* or the *Mint.* ... 4.Arbu.156.107.
Or Envy holds a whole Week's war with Sense, ... 4.Arbu.252.114.
When the tir'd nation breath'd from civil war. ... 4.2HE1.273.219.
How keen the war, if Dulness draw the sword! ... 5.DunA3.112.160.
How keen the war, if Dulness whet the sword! ... 5.DunA3.112A.160.
But fool with fool is barb'rous civil war. ... 5.DunA3.170.167.
And ten-horn'd fiends and Giants rush to war. ... 5.DunA3.232.177.
And ten-horn'd fiends and Giants threaten war. ... 5.DunA3.232A.177.
How keen the war, if Dulness draw the sword! ... 5.DunB3.120.325.
But fool with fool is barb'rous civil war. ... 5.DunB3.176.329.
And ten-horn'd fiends and Giants rush to war. ... 5.DunB3.236.332.
Give law to Words, or war with Words alone, ... 5.DunB4.178.359.
To talk of War, and live in Peace; ... 6.10.42.25.
Intestine War no more our *Passions* wage, ... 6.11.34.31.
And Gods of war, lye lost within the grave! ... 6.22.21.72.
And who'l wage War with Bedlam or the Mint? ... 6.49iii.6.142.
And who'd wage War with Bedlam or the Mint ... 6.49iii.6A.142.
War, horrid war, your thoughtful walks invades, ... 6.51i.7.151.
War, horrid war, your thoughtful walks invades, ... 6.51i.7.151.
But Fool 'gainst Fool, is barb'rous Civil War. ... 6.60.6.178.
And who'll wage War with *Bedlam* or the *Mint?* ... 6.98.6.283.
He sent him War, or Plague, or Famine sore. ... 6.137.10.373.
'Tis time to save the few Remains of War. ... Il.1.82.90.
What Cause have I to war at thy Decree? ... Il.1.199.96.
Or barren Praises pay the Wounds of War. ... Il.1.220.97.
Or nobly face the horrid Front of War? ... Il.1.300.101.
Thee, the first Honours of the War adorn, ... Il.1.366.105.
My Prize of War, yet tamely see resumed; ... Il.1.393.106.
Behold the Field, nor mingle in the War. ... Il.1.553.114.
And plunge the *Greeks* in all the Woes of War: ... Il.2.6.127.
Directs in Council, and in War presides, ... Il.2.28.128.
Directs in Council and in War presides, ... Il.2.78.130.
Worn with nine Years of unsuccessful War? ... Il.2.96.131.
Heroes of *Greece,* and Brothers of the War! ... Il.2.140.135.
What Shame to *Greece* a fruitless War to wage, ... Il.2.151.135.
Since first the Labours of this War begun: ... Il.2.162.136.
Swept to the War, the Lumber of a Land. ... Il.2.240.139.
Trust in his Omen, and support the War. ... Il.2.387.145.
We march to War if thou direct the Way. ... Il.2.411.147.
When thus distinct they war, shall soon be known, ... Il.2.436.148.
Let all excite the fiery Steeds of War, ... Il.2.456.149.
Let the War bleed, and let the Mighty fall! ... Il.2.461.149.
And lead to War, when Heav'n directs the Way. ... Il.2.519.151.
Whose Virgin-Charms subdu'd the God of War: ... Il.2.615.157.
Epistrophus and *Schedius* head the War. ... Il.2.621.157.
Next move to War the gen'rous *Argive* Train, ... Il.2.675.159.
And *Merion,* dreadful as the God of War. ... Il.2.792.162.
They hear the brazen Voice of War no more; ... Il.2.838.164.
But soon to rise in Slaughter, Blood, and War. ... Il.2.846.164.
And break the Ranks, and thunder thro' the War. ... Il.2.933.167.
War, horrid War, approaches to your Walls! ... Il.2.967.169.
War, horrid War, approaches to your Walls! ... Il.2.967.169.
They rush'd to War, and perish'd on the Plain. ... Il.2.1011.170.
The fierce *Pelasgi* next, in War renown'd, ... Il.2.1018.171.
Rode like a Woman to the Field of War. ... Il.2.1063.172.
Proclaim their Motions, and provoke the War: ... Il.3.4.188.
And all the War descends upon the Wing. ... Il.3.10.188.
And, on that Stage of War, the Cause be try'd: ... Il.3.100.194.
What *Paris,* Author of the War, demands. ... Il.3.124.196.
Me *Paris* injur'd; all the War be mine. ... Il.3.138.197.
Ceas'd is the War, and silent all the Fields. ... Il.3.178.199.
Great in the War, and great in Arts of Sway. ... Il.3.236.203.
Oh give that Author of the War to Fate, ... Il.3.399.211.
The tame Spectators of his Deeds of War. ... Il.4.12.221.
Or rowze the Furies and awake the War? ... Il.4.22.222.
And Queen of War, in close Consult engag'd. ... Il.4.28.222.
To spread the War, I flew from Shore to Shore; ... Il.4.39.223.
The *Trojans* rush tumultuous to the War; ... Il.4.253.232.
Urge their swift Steeds to face the coming War) ... Il.4.267.234.
Thy firm Associate in the Day of War. ... Il.4.305.235.
The Foot (the Strength of War) he rang'd behind; ... Il.4.343.237.
Content with Jav'lins to provoke the War. ... Il.4.355.238.
The Peace infring'd, nor heard the Sounds of War; ... Il.4.385.239.
The Shock of Armies, and commence the War. ... Il.4.395.239.
Forewarn'd the Horrors of the *Theban* War. ... Il.4.435.241.
Whose Cause we follow, and whose War we wage; ... Il.4.469.242.

WAR (CONTINUED)

Of arm'd *Tydides* rushing to the War. ... Il.4.477.242.
The War renews, the Warriors bleed again; ... Il.4.539.247.
Stern Pow'r of War! by whom the Mighty fall, ... Il.5.39.267.
War be thy Province, thy Protection mine; ... Il.5.159.274.
Skill'd in the Bow, on Foot I sought the War, ... Il.5.242.278.
Observe my Father's Steeds, renown'd in War. ... Il.5.279A.280.
The bounding Coursers rush amidst the War. ... Il.5.299.281.
And save a Life, the Bulwark of our War. ... Il.5.307.281.
At distance wound, or wage a flying War ... Il.5.315A.281.
With hostile Blood shall glut the God of War. ... Il.5.350.283.
His panting Steeds, remov'd from out the War, ... Il.5.397.286.
The War with *Troy* no more the *Grecians* wage; ... Il.5.469.290.
Condense their Pow'rs, and wait the growing War. ... Il.5.610.297.
Unmov'd and silent, the whole War they wait, ... Il.5.639.298.
In ev'ry Art of glorious War renown'd) ... Il.5.753.303.
To tremble at our Arms, not mix in War? ... Il.5.785.304.
False he detain'd, the just Reward of War: ... Il.5.807.304.
She spoke: *Minerva* burns to meet the War: ... Il.5.884.308.
The Coursers joins, and breathes Revenge and War. ... Il.5.903.309.
Here all the Terrors of grim War appear, ... Il.5.914.310.
While fierce in War divine *Achilles* rag'd; ... Il.5.983.314.
And scarce refrain'd when I forbad the War. ... Il.5.1001.314.
Thy Hands I arm'd, and sent thee forth to War: ... Il.5.1007.315.
The daring *Greek;* the dreadful God of War! ... Il.5.1043.316.
And you whom distant Nations send to War! ... Il.6.136.330.
Observ'd each other, and had mark'd for War. ... Il.6.150.333.
For Husbands, Brothers, Sons, engag'd in War. ... Il.6.301.341.
I go to rowze soft *Paris* to the War; ... Il.6.349.343.
And wastful War in all its Fury burns. ... Il.6.413.347.
Beheld the War, and sicken'd at the Sight; ... Il.6.469.350.
Nor that alone, but all the Works of War. ... Il.6.561.354.
Against his Country's Foes the War to wage, ... Il.6.608.357.
Where Heroes war, the foremost Place I claim, ... Il.6.636.358.
Thy Pow'r in War with Justice none contest; ... Il.6.668.360.
For much they suffer, for thy sake, in War. ... Il.6.675.360.
The Bands are chear'd, the War awakes again. ... Il.7.10.363.
War soon shall kindle, and great *Ilion* bend; ... Il.7.36.364.
What Art shall calm the furious Sons of War? ... Il.7.42.364.
They breathe, and hush the Tumult of the War. ... Il.7.64.366.
War with a fiercer Tide once more returns, ... Il.7.83.367.
By *Hector* slain, the mighty Man of War[."] ... Il.7.102.368.
And trembling met this dreadful Son of War. ... Il.7.132.370.
Of ev'ry Chief who sought this glorious War, ... Il.7.152.372.
When fierce in War, where *Jardan's* Waters fall, ... Il.7.163.372.
And *Merion,* dreadful as the God of War: ... Il.7.202.374.
Not void of Soul, and not unskill'd in War: ... Il.7.276.378.
Turn, charge, and answer ev'ry Call of War, ... Il.7.290.378.
Each sounds your Praise, and War is all your own. ... Il.7.340.381.
Hereafter we shall meet in glorious War, ... Il.7.353.381.
Some Space at least permit the War to breathe, ... Il.7.398.383.
That done, once more the Fate of War be try'd, ... Il.7.452.387.
What *Paris,* Author of the War, declares. ... Il.7.463.387.
That done, once more the Fate of War be try'd, ... Il.7.472.387.
With Heroes Corps: I war not with the Dead: ... Il.7.485.388.
Commutual Death the Fate of War confounds, ... Il.8.85.399.
Nor each stern *Ajax,* Thunderbolts of War: ... Il.8.100.402.
When dreadful *Hector,* thund'ring thro' the War, ... Il.8.111.403.
Observe the Steeds of *Tros,* renown'd in War, ... Il.8.134.404.
Thus said the Chief; and *Nestor,* skill'd in War, ... Il.8.143.404.
Rose *Archeptolemus,* the fierce in War. ... Il.8.158.405.
All fam'd in War, and dreadful hand to hand. ... Il.8.211.407.
I war not with the Highest. All above ... Il.8.256.409.
With Coursers dreadful in the Ranks of War; ... Il.8.352.414.
All dreadful in the crimson Walks of War? ... Il.8.460.419.
Against the Highest who shall wage the War? ... Il.8.489.420.
And warn their Children from a *Trojan* War. ... Il.8.642.426.
Fellows in Arms, and Princes of the War! ... Il.9.24.432.
That Wretch, that Monster, who delights in War: ... Il.9.90.437.
Heav'n fights his War, and humbles all our Bands. ... Il.9.152.439.
Thither the Spoils of this long War shall pass, ... Il.9.477.456.
He bade me teach thee all the ways of War. ... Il.9.570.462.
And matchless *Idas,* more than Man in War; ... Il.9.672.467.
War shakes her Walls, and thunders at her Gates. ... Il.9.688.468.
Inspires her War, and bids her Glory shine. ... Il.9.805.473.
Or bids the brazen Throat of War to roar; ... Il.10.8.2.
Divide his Heart, and wage a doubtful War. ... Il.10.22.3.
Or *Troy* once more must be the Seat of War? ... Il.10.248.13.
So fam'd, so dreadful, in the Works of War? ... Il.10.288.14.
That bear *Pelides* thro' the Ranks of War. ... Il.10.382.20.
And those swift Steeds that sweep the Ranks of War, ... Il.10.466.24.
Or back to *Ilion's* Walls transfer the War? ... Il.10.483.25.
Discharge their Souls of half the Fears of War. ... Il.10.493.25.
Return'd triumphant with this Prize of War. ... Il.10.631.30.
And leaning from the Clouds, except the War. ... Il.11.60.37.
So *Greece* and *Troy* the Field of War divide, ... Il.11.93.38.
Commutual Death the Fate of War confounds, ... Il.11.117.39.
And claim a Respite from the Sylvan War; ... Il.11.122.41.
And trust the War to less important Hands: ... Il.11.246.46.
The Chief she found amidst the Ranks of War, ... Il.11.255.46.
And trust the War to less important Hands. ... Il.11.262.47.
Condense their Pow'rs, and wait the coming War. ... Il.11.276.47.
Nor prompts alone, but leads himself the War. ... Il.11.382.51.
The Sons of *Merops* shone amidst the War; ... Il.11.425.53.
And thus bespoke his Brother of the War. ... Il.11.448.54.
(The Spouse of *Helen,* the fair Cause of War) ... Il.11.474.55.
Great *Ajax,* like the God of War, attends. ... Il.11.591.60.
Rag'd on the left, and rul'd the Tyde of War: ... Il.11.621.61.
Survey'd the various Fortune of the War. ... Il.11.643.62.
When the proud *Elians* first commenc'd the War. ... Il.11.831.73.
Three Days were past, when *Elis* rose to War, ... Il.11.842.73.
Bright Scenes of Arms, and Works of War appear; ... Il.11.872.74.
Proud *Troy* may tremble, and desist from War; ... Il.11.931.77.
War thunder'd at the Gates, and Blood distain'd the Tow'rs. ... Il.12.40.83.
His vaunted Coursers urg'd to meet the War. ... Il.12.126.86.
And that *Leonteus,* like the God of War. ... Il.12.144.86.

WAR (CONTINUED)

Oppos'd their Breasts, and stood themselves the War. ....Il.12.162.87.
While *Greece* unconquer'd kept alive the War, ...Il.12.207.88.
In Peace and War, in Council, and in Fight; ....Il.12.250.90.
And Shepherds gaul him with an Iron War; ....Il.12.362.94.
In fighting Fields, nor urge thy Soul to War. ....Il.12.390.96.
What Aid appear'd t' avert th' approaching War, ...Il.12.404.96.
The bloody Labours of the doubtful War: ....Il.12.414.96.
The bloody Labours of the doubtful War: ....Il.12.428.97.
And thus bespoke his Brothers of the War. ....Il.12.436.97.
The War renews, mix'd Shouts and Groans arise; ....Il.12.449.98.
And, like a Deluge, rushes in the War. ....Il.12.488.99.
And fix'd support the Weight of all the War: ....Il.12.508.100.
So stood the War, till *Hector's* matchless Might ....Il.12.527.101.
Or had the God of War inclin'd his Eyes, ...Il.13.175.113.
The God of War had own'd a just Surprize. ....Il.13.176.113.
On him the War is bent, the Darts are shed, ...Il.13.201.115.
Whom in the Chance of War a Javelin tore, ...Il.13.281.119.
Arms are her Trade, and War is all her own. ....Il.13.292.119.
Leads forth th' embattel'd Sons of *Crete* to War; ....Il.13.334.121.
Tho' I, disdainful of the distant War, ...Il.13.341.122.
I fight conspicuous in the Van of War. ....Il.13.350.122.
And ev'ry Art of dang'rous War thy own. ....Il.13.373.123.
And breathing Slaughter, follow'd to the War. ....Il.13.383.123.
All dreadful glar'd the Iron Face of War, ...Il.13.430.126.
In War and Discord's adamantine Chain; ....Il.13.452.127.
Call'd by the Voice of War to martial Fame, ...Il.13.459.128.
Attends the Tumult, and expects the War; ....Il.13.597.134.
The youthful Offspring of the God of War, ...Il.13.605.135.
Like Gods of War, dispensing Fate, they stood, ...Il.13.634.136.
Tho' now unfit an active War to wage, ...Il.13.648.136.
Detain'd from bloody War by *Jove* and *Fate*. ....Il.13.663.137.
Rapt from the less'ning Thunder of the War; ....Il.13.679.137.
O Race perfidious, who delight in War! ....Il.13.780.142.
Following his martial Father to War; ....Il.13.806.143.
Each *Ajax* labour'd thro' the Field of War. ....Il.13.878.147.
And ev'ry Art of glorious War thy own; ....Il.13.910.148.
To some the Pow'rs of bloody War belong, ...Il.13.915.148.
What Troops, out-number'd scarce the War maintain? ....Il.13.927.149.
The former Day; the next, engag'd in War.) ....Il.13.998.152.
The Skill of War to us not idly giv'n, ...Il.13.1024.153.
While War hangs doubtful, while his Soldiers fight? ....Il.14.107.162.
Tho' not Partaker, Witness of the War. ....Il.14.148.164.
Inspire the Ranks, and rule the distant War. ....Il.14.152.165.
And grizly War appears a pleasing Sight. ....Il.14.178.165.
And tow'ring in the foremost Ranks of War, ...Il.14.420.183.
Speed to the Town, and leave the War behind. ....Il.14.506.188.
The Toils, the Sorrows, and the Wounds of War. ....Il.14.564.190.
And, 'midst the War, the Monarch of the Main. ....Il.15.10.194.
To rise afresh, and once more wake the War, ...Il.15.64.197.
Desists at length his Rebel-war to wage, ...Il.15.250.206.
Swell his bold Heart, and urge his Strength to War: ....Il.15.261.207.
What grief, what wound, withholds him from the War? ....Il.15.277.207.
And *Hector* first came tow'ring to the War. ....Il.15.347.210.
To rise in Arms, and shine again in War. ....Il.15.465.215.
Sprung from the Tent, and left the War behind. ....Il.15.469.215.
Preserv'd their Line, and equal kept the War. ....Il.15.479.216.
In Peace, in War, for ever at his side, ...Il.15.504.216.
Return'd to *Ilion*, and excell'd in War: ....Il.15.649.221.
Come on—a distant War no longer wage, ...Il.15.658.221.
Then, nor till then, the Scale of War shall turn, ...Il.15.720.223.
In ev'ry Virtue, or of Peace or War: ....Il.15.777.226.
She clear'd, restoring all the War to view; ....Il.15.809.227.
Greece yet unconquer'd, kept alive the War, ...Il.15.848.229.
And each contends, as his were all the War. ....Il.15.853.229.
Once Sons of *Mars*, and Thunderbolts of War! ....Il.15.891.231.
Proud *Troy* shall tremble, and desert the War: ....Il.16.59.237.
Tho' *Jove* in Thunder should command the War, ...Il.16.114.240.
In Peace his Friend, and Part'ner of the War) ....Il.16.180.245.
Directs their Order, and the War commands. ....Il.16.205.247.
Had call'd the Chiefs, and order'd all the War, ...Il.16.237.248.
Confirm his Heart, and string his Arm to War: ....Il.16.299.254.
Invade the *Trojans*, and commence the War. ....Il.16.313.254.
The War stood still, and all around them gaz'd, ...Il.16.334.255.
Where the War rag'd, and where the Tumult grew. ....Il.16.339.256.
Where the War bleeds, and where the thickest die. ....Il.16.455.260.
Smoaks thro' the Ranks, o'ertakes the flying War, ...Il.16.461.260.
Patroclus mark'd him as he shunn'd the War, ...Il.16.490.262.
This Hand, unaided, shall the War sustain: ....Il.16.517.263.
Patroclus lights, and sternly waits the War. ....Il.16.521.263.
From all the Dangers and the Toils of War; ....Il.16.537.265.
The glorious Dangers of destructive War, ...Il.16.608.268.
And sigh, at distance from the glorious War. ....Il.16.640.269.
Breathe their brave Souls out, in another's War. ....Il.16.662.270.
In glorious Action, is the Task of War. ....Il.16.762.273.
Thence from the War the breathless Hero bore, ...Il.16.825.275.
The Lash resounds; the Coursers rush to War. ....Il.16.888.277.
Defends the Body, and provokes the War. ....Il.16.914.279.
While yet he learn'd his Rudiments of War; ....Il.16.977.281.
The rough *Ciconians* learn'd the Trade of War) ....Il.17.78.291.
Deep in great *Hector's* Soul: Thro' all the War ....Il.17.90.291.
Pierce the thick Battel, and provoke the War. ....Il.17.136.293.
To stand a Trophy of his Fame in War. ....Il.17.142.293.
To boast our Numbers, and the Pomp of War; ....Il.17.263.298.
To die, or conquer, are the Terms of War. ....Il.17.269.298.
And thus bespoke his Brother of the War. ....Il.17.281.298.
All, whom I see not thro' this Cloud of War, ...Il.17.299.299.
Hippothous, dragg'd the Carcase thro' the War; ....Il.17.335.300.
By Valour, Numbers, and by Arts of War, ...Il.17.381.302.
And in an Orb, contracts the crowded War, ...Il.17.411.303.
Fixt on the Spot they war; and wounded, wound; ....Il.17.414.303.
There burn'd the War, and there the Mighty bled. ....Il.17.435.304.
Safe to the Navy thro' the Storm of War. ....Il.17.519.308.
The kindling Chariot thro' the parted War: ....Il.17.527.308.
Alone, unaided, in the thickest War? ....Il.17.537.309.
War knows no mean: he wins it, or he dies. ....Il.17.573.311.
Descends impetuous, and renews the War; ....Il.17.613.312.
Or from the Rage of Man, destructive War) ....Il.17.619.312.
This weary'd Arm, and ward the Storm of War! ....Il.17.635.312.
And urges to desert the hopeless War; ....Il.17.702.315.
Behind them rages all the Storm of War; ....Il.17.822.320.
When Men distrest hang out the Sign of War) ....Il.18.248.334.
With shrilling Clangor sounds th' Alarm of War; ....Il.18.260.335.
He sent refulgent to the Field of War, ...Il.18.280.335.
The frighted *Trojans* (panting from the War, ...Il.18.287.335.
The Image one of Peace, and one of War. ....Il.18.568.350.
Glow'd with refulgent Arms, and horrid War. ....Il.18.592.351.
They rise, take Horse, approach, and meet the War; ....Il.18.616.352.
And the whole War came out, and met the Eye; ....Il.18.625.352.
Then uncontroll'd in boundless War engage, ...Il.19.37.373.
Here then my Anger ends: Let War succeed, ...Il.19.71.374.
Resume thy Arms, and shine again in War. ....Il.19.142.377.
To us, 'tis equal: All we ask is War. ....Il.19.146.377.
What boastful Son of War, without that Stay, ...Il.19.161.378.
With Limbs and Soul untam'd, he tires a War. ....Il.19.168.378.
When the stern Fury of the War is o'er, ...Il.19.199.381.
Those call to War! and might my Voice incite, ...Il.19.203.381.
Expect a second Summons to the War; ....Il.19.238.382.
Thoas and *Merion*, Thunderbolts of War, ...Il.19.246.383.
Once stay'd *Achilles*, rushing to the War. ....Il.19.338.386.
Of all neglectful, wage a hateful War.) ....Il.19.348.386.
Oft' stay'd *Achilles* rushing to the War. ....Il.19.338A.386.
And dost thou thus desert the Great in War? ....Il.19.365.387.
Shakes down Diseases, Pestilence and War; ....Il.19.413.389.
Thy rage in safety thro' the Files of War: ....Il.19.453.391.
Thus round *Pelides* breathing War and Blood, ...Il.20.1.392.
And Death stands ardent on the Edge of War. ....Il.20.28.393.
And trembling see another God of War. ....Il.20.62.396.
Such War th' Immortals wage: Such Horrors rend ....Il.20.89.397.
Lo great *Æneas* rushing to the War; ....Il.20.147.400.
And leave to War the Fates of mortal Men. ....Il.20.165.400.
Seeks he to meet *Achilles'* Arm in War, ...Il.20.215.403.
And *Hicetaon*, Thunderbolt of War. ....Il.20.287.406.
Perhaps excel us in this wordy War; ....Il.20.301.406.
Urg'd thee to meet *Achilles'* Arm in War? ....Il.20.382.411.
The Scene of War came rushing on his Sight. ....Il.20.392.411.
Trojans to War! Think *Hector* leads you on; ....Il.20.417.412.
They join, they throng, they thicken to the War. ....Il.20.430.412.
Turn from each other in the Walks of War— ....Il.20.496.415.
But Heav'n alone confers Success in War: ....Il.20.504.415.
The great *Asteropeus* to mortal War; ....Il.21.156.428.
Rise to the War! th' insulting Flood requires ....Il.21.386.436.
And first assaults the radiant Queen of War ....Il.21.457.440.
Come, prove thy Arm! for first the War to wage, ...Il.21.512.443.
Learn hence, no more unequal War to wage— ....Il.21.565.445.
Whom *Hermes* viewing, thus declines the War. ....Il.21.580.446.
Dishonour'd Relicks of *Diana's* War. ....Il.21.588.446.
Wild with Revenge, insatiable of War. ....Il.21.638.448.
On their whole War, untam'd the Savage flies; ....Il.21.683.450.
Confronts *Achilles*, and awaits the War, ...Il.21.686.450.
Full at the *Scæan* Gates expects the War; ....Il.22.48.454.
On my rash Courage charge the Chance of War, ...Il.22.148.459.
(Cause of the War, and Grievance of the Land) ....Il.22.159.459.
War is our Business; but to whom is giv'n ....Il.22.171.460.
Drunk with Renown, insatiable of War, ...Il.22.282.467.
Not yet (my brave Companions of the War) ....Il.23.9.486.
High on their Cars, in all the Pomp of War; ....Il.23.159.495.
The great *Ætolian* Chief, renown'd in War. ....Il.23.555.511.
These two-edg'd Axes, terrible in War; ....Il.23.1015.529.
This beamy Jav'lin in thy Brother's War. ....Il.23.1059.533.
Mestor the brave, renown'd in Ranks of War, ...Il.24.321.549.
War, and the Blood of Men, surround thy Walls! ....Il.24.691.566.
The twelfth we war, if War be doom'd by Heav'n! ....Il.24.837.571.
The twelfth we war, if War be doom'd by Heav'n! ....Il.24.837.571.
Who saves her Infants from the Rage of War? ....Il.24.919.574.
Intemp'rate rage a wordy war began; ....Od.1.467.55.
Such railing eloquence, and war of words. ....Od.2.96.65.
To shake with war proud *Ilion's* lofty tow'rs, ...Od.2.200.71.
[When fierce in arms he sought the scenes of war, ...Od.2.255.74.
Oh then, if ever thro' the ten years war ....Od.3.118.91.
In ev'ry danger and in ev'ry war: ....Od.3.272.99.
Atrides, parting for the *Trojan* war, ...Od.3.334.102.
Pallas herself, the War-triumphant Maid, ...Od.3.486.111.
Speak you, (who saw) his wonders in the war. ....Od.4.334.135.
The plans of war against the town prepar'd. ....Od.4.350.136.
A furious onset with the sound of war. ....Od.4.612.148.
In the black ocean, or the wat'ry war, ...Od.5.284.185.
Thro' seas retreating from the sound of war, ...Od.6.10.203.
Perish'd the nation in unrighteous war, ...Od.7.76.237.
Tost by rude tempest thro' a war of waves: ....Od.8.28.263.
Ere yet he loos'd the rage of war on *Troy*. ....Od.8.78.266.
In scenes of death, by tempest and by war. ....Od.8.206.273.
Or from the bounding courser urge the war. ....Od.9.58.304.
Promiscuous death the form of war confounds, ...Od.9.65.305.
For arms and weapons of the sylvan war; ....Od.9.181.313.
Pleas'd with the din of war, and noble shout of foes. ....Od.11.316.397.
And here thro' sev'n wide portals rush'd the war. ....Od.11.324.398.
Amidst a war of spears in foreign lands, ...Od.11.478.408.
Of war and slaughter, and the clash of arms? ....Od.11.498.408.
Of war and slaughter, and the clash of arms. ....Od.11.504.408.
When war has thunder'd with its loudest storms, ...Od.11.515.409.
Alas! I hop'd, the toils of war o'ercome, ...Od.11.535.409.
War was his joy, and pleas'd with loud alarms, ...Od.11.579.412.
'Twas mine on *Troy* to pour th' imprison'd war: ....Od.11.642.416.
Pants for the battle, and the war demands; ....Od.11.648.416.
Thus great in glory from the din of war ....Od.11.655.416.
With him the strength of war, the soldiers pride, ...Od.11.673.417.
There war and havoc the destruction stood, ...Od.11.755.423.
Still are new toils and war thy dire delight? ....Od.12.144.439.
If from yon justling rocks and wavy war ....Od.12.256.444.
Thro' tumbling billows, and a war of wind. ....Od.12.502.456.

WAR (CONTINUED)
To take repast, and stills the wordy war; Od.12.520.457.
Mild I obey'd, for who shall war with thee? Od.13.155.13.
Thro' ten years wand'ring, and thro' ten years war; Od.13.343.24.
Great in the praise, rich in the spoils of war: Od.14.269.49.
But when great *Jove* that direful war decreed, Od.14.272.49.
Thro' the long dangers of the ten-years war. Od.15.171.76.
Sunk the fair City by the rage of war, Od.15.415.89.
If they forbid, I war not with the skies. Od.16.421.127.
Thus in a wordy war their tongues display Od.18.40.169.
With dreadful inroad thro' the walks of war. Od.18.308.181.
Should *Jove* dire war unloose, with spear and shield Od.18.418.189.
Instant convey those steely stores of war Od.19.5.193.
The *Dorians,* plum'd amid the files of war, Od.19.202.202.
For, elemental war, and wintry *Jove,* Od.19.216.204.
Ulysses wav'd, to rouze the savage war. Od.19.510.221.
Which noted token of the woodland war Od.19.545.223.
Hence with long war the double race was curst, Od.21.323.275.
And hence the villain has supply'd their war. Od.22.171.295.
The guilty war; *Eurynomus* succeeds; Od.22.265.299.
A Boar fierce-rushing in the sylvan war Od.23.75.322.
To move the great *Ulysses* to the war. Od.24.143.355.
The opening gates at once their war display: Od.24.578.375.

WAR-HORSE
A War-horse never for the Service chose, 4.HAdv.114.85.

WAR-TRIUMPHANT
Pallas herself, the War-triumphant Maid, Od.3.486.111.

WAR'S
While War's fierce Goddess fires the *Grecian* Foe, Il.4.595.250.
The War's whole Art with Wonder had he seen, Il.4.634.251.
Taught by this Stroke, renounce the War's Alarms, Il.5.437.289.
Then pensive thus, to War's triumphant Maid. Il.8.422.417.
But why should'st thou suspect the War's Success? Il.12.285.92.
The youth had dwelt; remote from War's alarms, Il.13.231.116.
From that great Hour the War's whole Fortune turns, Il.15.76.199.
Oppos'd to *Pallas,* War's triumphant Maid. Il.20.94.398.
And scoffing, thus, to War's victorious Maid. Il.21.491.441.
Back to *Olympus,* from the War's Alarms, Il.21.601.447.
But if *Athena,* War's triumphant maid, Od.3.269.99.
Jove's daughter *Pallas,* War's triumphant maid: Od.22.222.297.

WARB'LING
Teach thou the warb'ling Polypheme to roar, 5.DunB3.305.334.

WARBLE
So sweetly warble, or so smoothly flow. 1.PWi.4.89.
Others the Syren Sisters warble round, 5.DunB4.541.395.

WARBLED
And Airy Musick warbled thro' the Shade. 2.ChJM.464.37.
Hush'd in attention to the warbled song. Od.1.420.52.
Thus the sweet charmers warbled o'er the main; Od.12.232.443.

WARBLES
To that which warbles thro' the vernal wood: 3.EOM1.216.42.
Celestial music warbles from their tongue, Od.12.220.442.

WARBLING
When warbling *Philomel* salutes the Spring? 1.PSp.26.63.
Not thus *Amphion* tun'd the warbling Lyre, 2.ChJM.322.29.
When you, like *Orpheus,* strike the warbling Lyre, 6.7.9.15.
Let the warbling Lute complain: 6.11.6.30.
To these a Youth awakes the warbling Strings, Il.18.661.355.
Whose hand reluctant touch'd the warbling wire: Od.1.198.42.
Warbling the *Grecian* woes with harp and voice: Od.1.446.54.
Whilst warbling to the varied strain, advance Od.4.25.121.
And warbling sweet, makes earth and heav'n rejoice. Od.6.116.211.
And *Itylus* sounds warbling o'er the plains; Od.19.607.226.
This hand reluctant touch'd the warbling wire: Od.22.390.307.

WARD
To Ward, to Waters, Chartres, and the Devil. 3.Ep3.20.85.
Ward try'd on Puppies, and the Poor, his Drop; 4.2HE1.182.211.
To cheat a Friend, or Ward, he leaves to Peter; 4.2HE1.197.211.
See Ward by batter'd Beaus invited over, 4.1HE6.56.241.
Rather than so, see Ward invited over, 4.1HE6.56A.241.
And W[ard] and H[enley] both in town! 4.1HE7.14A.269*.
Shall *Ward* draw Contracts with a Statesman's skill? 4.EpS1.119.306.
Is it for *W[a]rd* or *Peter* (paltry Things!) 4.EpS1.121A.307.
Or shipp'd with Ward to ape and monkey lands, 5.DunA1.200.86.
As thick as eggs at Ward in Pillory. 5.DunA3.26.152.
Another Durfey, Ward! shall sing in thee. 5.DunA3.138.161.
Not sail, with Ward, to Ape-and-monkey climes, 5.DunB1.233.287.
Where wretched Withers, Ward, and Gildon rest, 5.DunB1.296.291.
As thick as eggs at Ward in Pillory. 5.DunB3.34.322.
Another Durfey, Ward! shall sing in thee. 5.DunB3.146.326.
Tis half their business, Blows to ward, or give, 6.147iv.2.391.
Long us'd to ward the Death in fighting Fields: Il.13.552.132.
This weary'd Arm, and ward the Storm of War! Il.17.635.312.
The rock rush'd sea-ward, with impetuous roar Od.4.681.151.
(The sea-ward prow invites the tardy gales) Od.4.1034.166.

WARDENS
Talk with Church-Wardens about Pews, 6.39.22.111.

WARDROBE
The *Phrygian* Queen to her rich Wardrobe went, Il.6.358.343.
Where the rich wardrobe breath'd a costly scent. Od.15.115.74.

WARDROBES
And but esteem'd as antient Wardrobes are, 4.JD2A.129.144.
Like rich old Wardrobes, things extremely rare, 4.JD2.123.145.
The largest Mantle her rich Wardrobes hold, Il.6.113.329.

WARDROBES (CONTINUED)
The largest Mantle your full Wardrobes hold, Il.6.340.343.

WARDS
She took the Wards in Wax before the Fire, 2.ChJM.510.40.
Each Danger wards, and constant in her Care Il.4.15.221.
The fainting Chief, and wards the mortal Wound. Il.5.430.289.
Fierce in his Front: but *Neptune* wards the Blow, Il.13.712.138.
The wards respondent to the key turn round; Od.21.49.261.

WARE
Is she who shows what Ware she has to sell; 4.HAdv.109.85.

WARFARE
Finds all her life one warfare upon earth: 3.Ep2.118.60.
Finds all her Life one Warfare upon Earth; 6.154.4.402.
Great *Jove* averse our Warfare to compose, Il.7.81.367.
No truce the warfare of my heart suspends! Od.20.101.237.

WARILY
Bear close to this, and warily proceed, Il.23.407.506.

WARLIKE
The lofty Ramparts, through the Warlike Throng, 1.TrES.78.452.
Ye valiant Leaders of our warlike Bands! 1.TrES.80Z1.452.
Might stop the Progress of his warlike Host, 1.TrES.116.454.
His warlike *Amazon* her Host invades, 2.RL3.67.173.
Safe in her Vales my warlike Coursers fed: Il.1.202.96.
The Warlike Maid, and Monarch of the Main, Il.1.519.113.
The Voice Divine confess'd the Warlike Maid, Il.2.219.138.
Twice twenty Ships transport the warlike Bands, Il.2.653.158.
The warlike Bands that distant *Lycia* yields, Il.2.1070.172.
And * both her warlike Lords outshin'd in *Helen's* Eyes? Il.3.72.193.
Perhaps the Chiefs, from warlike Toils at ease, Il.3.307.208.
The warlike *Pandarus,* for strength renown'd; Il.4.120.226.
No longer with his warlike Steeds he stay'd, Il.4.260.233.
(The warlike *Sthenelus* attends his side) Il.4.420.240.
And stern *Lycaon's* warlike Race begun. Il.5.339.283.
(A warlike Circle) round *Tydides* stand: Il.5.973.313.
Then threw the Force of *Tydeus'* warlike Son; Il.5.1048.316.
(*Argos* the fair for warlike Steeds renown'd) Il.6.190.335.
He said, nor answer'd *Priam's* warlike Son; Il.6.430.347.
Lay'd *Thebè* waste, and slew my warlike Sire! Il.6.525.352.
From warlike *Salamis* I drew my Birth, Il.7.237.376.
A pensive Scene! 'till *Tydeus'* warlike Son Il.9.41.433.
His warlike Hand a pointed Javelin held. Il.10.30.3.
A warlike Form appear'd before his Tent, Il.10.579.28.
Who from the *Lapiths* warlike Race descend; Il.12.142.86.
Ye valiant Leaders of our warlike Bands! Il.12.425.97.
Might stop the Progress of his warlike Host, Il.12.470.98.
By *Teucer's* Arm the warlike *Imbrius* bleeds, Il.13.227.116.
He, like the warlike Eagle speeds his Pace, Il.21.281.432.
(The Tomb of him thy warlike Arm had slain) Il.24.952.576.
Had fall'n surrounded with his warlike train; Od.1.302.47.
Beneath *Achilles'* warlike son's command. Od.3.229.96.
The axe was held by warlike *Thrasymed,* Od.3.561.115.
Whose pious rule a warlike race obey! Od.19.130.199.
Delineate to my view my warlike Lord, Od.19.255.207.
Each warlike *Greek* the moving music hears, Od.24.79.352.
Now all the sons of warlike *Greece* surround Od.24.101.353.

WARM
As some coy Nymph her Lover's warm Address 1.W-F.19.150.
Soft Show'rs distill'd, and Suns grew warm in vain; 1.W-F.54.154.
And *Phœbus* warm the ripening Ore to Gold. 1.W-F.396.190.
Where Beams of warm *Imagination* play, 1.EOC.58.245.
Enlights the *present,* and shall warm the *last:* 1.EOC.403.286.
And the warm Maid confess'd a mutual Love. 1.TrVP.123.382.
And print warm kisses on the panting rind, 1.TrFD.60.388.
Shall warm my Breast to sing of *Cæsar's* Fame: 1.TrSt.48.411.
Whose panting Vitals, warm with Life, she draws, 1.TrSt.721.440.
Such secret Transports warm my melting Heart. 2.ChJM.572.43.
And warm the swelling Veins to Feats of Love: 2.ChWB.216.67.
When kind Occasion prompts their warm Desires, 2.RL1.75.151.
But felt th'Approaches of too warm a Sun; 2.TemF.42.256.
Now warm in love, now with'ring in thy bloom, 2.ElAb.37.322.
Now warm in love, now with'ring in my bloom, 2.ElAb.37A.322.
Warm from the soul, and faithful to its fires, 2.ElAb.54.323.
And each warm wish springs mutual from the heart. 2.ElAb.96.327.
When, warm in youth, I bade the world farewell? 2.ElAb.110.329.
And love's warm tyde for ever stopt in thee. 2.ElAb.258Z2.340.
To light the dead, and warm th' unfruitful urn. 2.ElAb.262.341.
Then Marble soften'd into life grew warm, 4.2HE1.147.207.
And you shall see, the first warm Weather, 4.1HE7.19.269.
Still true to Virtue, and as warm as true: 4.1HE1.30.281.
'Till genial Jacob, or a warm Third-day 5.DunA1.55.66.
Glad chains, warm furs, broad banners, and broad faces) 5.DunA1.86.69.
Gold chains, warm furs, broad banners, and broad faces) 5.DunA1.86A.69.
'Till genial Jacob, or a warm Third day, 5.DunB1.57.274.
Glad chains, warm furs, broad banners, and broad faces) 5.DunB1.88.275.
Their Wit still sparkling and their Flames still warm. 6.19.72.64.
Still warm our hearts, and still inspire our songs. 6.38.26.108.
Her modest cheek shall warm a future age. 6.52.56.157.
Twas Friendship—warm as *Phœbus,* kind as Love, 6.76.3.212.
By the warm Transports and entrancing Languors, 6.82ii.2.230.
Wit is like faith by such warm Fools profest 6.82ix(b).1.234.
Or at the Glow-worm warm thy frozen legs? 6.96ii.30Z50.272.
On the warm Limits of the farthest Main, Il.1.555.115.
And the warm Life came issuing from the Wound. Il.4.609.250.
Beneath one Foot the yet-warm Corps he prest, Il.5.768.303.
His warm Reproofs the list'ning Kings inflame, Il.7.195.373.
With copious Love shall crown his warm Embrace; Il.9.180.441.
With copious Love shall crown thy warm Embrace; Il.9.367.451.
While Life's warm Spirit beats within my Breast. Il.9.720.470.
Achilles slept; and in his warm Embrace Il.9.780.472.
Warm with the softest Wool, and doubly lin'd. Il.10.153.8.

WARM (CONTINUED)

The yet-warm *Thracians* panting on the Coast;	Il.10.612.29.
And early Honour warm his gen'rous Breast,	Il.11.288.48.
This, while yet warm, distill'd the purple Flood;	Il.11.345.50.
Till Life's warm Vapour issuing thro' the Wound,	Il.11.598.60.
A Day to fire the brave, and warm the cold,	Il.12.321.93.
Thy warm Impatience makes thy Tongue offend.	Il.13.976.152.
To win the wisest, and the coldest warm:	Il.14.248.173.
But let the few whom brisker Spirits warm,	Il.15.334.210.
Let their warm Heads with Scenes of Battle glow,	Il.19.235.382.
And the warm Purple circled on the Tyde.	Il.21.27.422.
Oh! had I dy'd in Fields of Battel warm,	Il.21.321.434.
His warm Intreaty touch'd *Saturnia's* Ear;	Il.21.442.438.
And pour to Dogs the Life-blood scarcely warm;	Il.22.105.457.
Warm with the Hopes of Conquest for his Friend,	Il.23.790.521.
There, warm with filial love, the cause enquire	Od.1.120.38.
O'er the warm *Libyan* wave to spread my sails:	Od.4.104.124.
Mean-time with genial joy to warm the soul,	Od.4.301.133.
There wallowing warm, th' enormous herd exhales	Od.4.547.146.
Damps the warm wishes of my raptur'd mind:	Od.4.812.157.
To curl old Ocean, and to warm the skies.	Od.5.342.188.
Soon as warm life its wonted office found,	Od.5.588.200.
Warm are thy words, but warm without offence;	Od.8.271.278.
Warm are thy words, but warm without offence;	Od.8.271.278.
Th' aereal region now grew warm with day,	Od.12.210.442.
To cheer the grave, and warm the Poet's rage)	Od.13.12.2.
In the warm bath foment with fragrant oil.	Od.19.367.212.
The warm pavilion of a dreadful boar.	Od.19.516.221.
Now press the sovereign dame with warm desire	Od.20.397.251.
Thus he; but pleasing hopes his bosom warm	Od.22.231.298.
'Till the warm sun exhales their soul away.	Od.22.431.309.
Springs to his master with a warm embrace,	Od.24.458.370.

WARM'D

Both warm'd by Love, and by the Muse inspir'd;	1.PSp.17z2.62.
One *Daphne* warm'd, and the *Cretan* Dame;	1.TrSP.28.394.
And warm'd the Womb of Earth with Genial Beams.	2.ChJM.616.44.
Cold is that breast which warm'd the world before,	2.Elegy.33.365.
The fur that warms a monarch, warm'd a bear.	3.EOM3.44.96.
That long hast warm'd my tender Breast,	6.31i.2.93.
Be justly warm'd with your own native rage.	6.32.44.97.
Warm'd in the Brain the brazen Weapon lies,	Il.4.526.246.
(*Jove* warm'd his Bosom and enlarg'd his Mind)	Il.6.291.340.
Warm'd with some Virtue, some Regard of Fame!	Il.6.443.348.
Warm'd in his Liver, to the Ground it bore	Il.13.521.131.
Thou com'st in vain, he cries (with Fury warm'd)	Il.18.225.332.
The god-like *Hector* warm'd the Troops of *Troy*.	Il.20.416.412.
Warm'd in the Brain the smoaking Weapon lies,	Il.20.551.417.
The pleasing sounds each latent warrior warm'd,	Od.4.381.139.
But when the rosy morning warm'd the east,	Od.10.212.350.
Vain hope! ten suns had warm'd the western strand,	Od.19.224.204.

WARMER

Then kiss'd the Fair; (his Kisses warmer grow	1.TrVP.55.379.
To warmer Seas the Cranes embody'd fly,	Il.3.7.188.
A warmer Couch with num'rous Carpets spread.	Il.9.734.470.
And fast behind, *Aurora's* warmer Ray	Il.23.282.501.
Her cheeks the warmer blush of *Venus* wear,	Od.19.66.196.

WARMLY

His habit coarse, but warmly wrapt around;	Od.24.262.361.

WARMS

The Sun's mild Lustre warms the vital Air;	1.PSp.74.68.
Whose Judgment sways us, and whose Spirit warms!	1.PAu.10.81.
Whose Judgment sways us, and whose Rapture warms!	1.PAu.10A.81.
Feeds from his Hand, and in his Bosom warms:	1.Mes.54.117.
Where *Nature moves*, and *Rapture warms* the Mind;	1.EOC.236.266.
But gen'rous Rage the bold *Chorœbus* warms,	1.TrSt.714.440.
His fainting Squadrons to new Fury warms.	1.TrES.144.454.
With this Reproach his flying Host he warms,	1.TrES.211.457.
Or Men, whose Bosom tender Pity warms?	1.TrUl.77.468.
Still warms me to the Bottom of my Heart.	2.ChWB.224.67.
Warms in the sun, refreshes in the breeze,	3.EOM1.271.48.
Whatever warms the heart, or fills the head,	3.EOM2.141.71.
The fur that warms a monarch, warm'd a bear.	3.EOM3.44.96.
And him and his if more devotion warms,	5.DunA2.77.107.
And him and his, if more devotion warms,	5.DunB2.81.299.
How martial Musick every Bosom warms!	6.11.37.31.
With this, each *Grecian's* manly Breast she warms,	Il.2.530.151.
His Brother follows, and to Vengeance warms;	Il.2.701.159.
The Chiefs advises, and the Soldiers warms.	Il.4.339.236.
Fills with her Force, and warms with all her Fires,	Il.5.2.263.
No Drop of all thy Father warms thy Veins.	Il.5.1009.315.
Pallas (this said) her Hero's Bosom warms,	Il.10.558.27.
His fainting Host, and ev'ry Bosom warms.	Il.11.376.51.
Their Breasts no more the vital Spirit warms;	Il.11.431.53.
His fainting Squadrons to new Fury warms.	Il.12.498.99.
For He that *Juno's* heav'nly Bosom warms,	Il.13.209.115.
Yet, as he moves, the Fight his Bosom warms;	Il.14.31.158.
That Pow'r, which Mortals and Immortals warms,	Il.14.226.172.
Oh yet, if Glory any Bosom warms,	Il.14.429.184.
Warms the bold Son of *Nestor* in his Cause.	Il.15.681.222.
Not more the Mother's Soul that Infant warms,	Il.16.13.235.
Achilles speeds from Tent to Tent, and warms	Il.16.190.246.
With this Reproach his flying Host he warms,	Il.16.514.263.
First to the Fight his native Troops he warms,	Il.16.653.270.
A God (nor is he less) my Bosom warms,	Il.17.392.302.
Not *Pallas'* self, her Breast when Fury warms,	Il.17.458.305.
Soon as the Morn the purple Orient warms	Il.18.353.338.
Soon as the Morn the rosie *Welkin* Warms	Il.18.353A.338.
Soon as the Morn the rosie Orient warms	Il.18.353B.338.
When next the morning warms the purple east,	Od.1.354.49.
Tumultuous love each beating bosom warms;	Od.1.466.54.
While the bowl circles, and the banquet warms;	Od.2.282.75.
Or men, whose bosom tender pity warms?	Od.6.142.214.

WARMS (CONTINUED)

Or men, whose bosom tender pity warms?	Od.8.628.296.
Or Men, whose bosom tender pity warms?	Od.13.244.17.
With riper beams when *Phœbus* warms the day.	Od.17.30.133.
Thus in fond kisses, while the transport warms,	Od.23.225.333.

WARMTH

With *Warmth* gives Sentence, yet is always *Just;*	1.EOC.678.316.
With equal Warmth, and rouze the Warrior's Fire;	1.TrES.54.451.
By Spirit robb'd of Pow'r, by Warmth of Friends,	3.Ep2.144.62.
Adieu Distinction, Satire, Warmth, and Truth!	4.EpS1.64.302.
Paulo's free stroke, and *Titian's* warmth divine.	6.52.38.157.
And boasts a Warmth that from no Passion flows;	6.73.4.209.
By Spirit, robb'd of Power; by Warmth, of Friends;	6.154.30.403.
Let not thy Words the Warmth of *Greece* abate;	Il.4.222.231.
Ulysses heard; The Hero's Warmth o'erspread	Il.4.402.240.
Each *Trojan* Bosom with new Warmth he fires.	Il.5.626.298.
The Monarch spoke: the Words with Warmth addrest	Il.6.77.327.
With equal Warmth, and rouze the Warrior's Fire;	Il.12.398.96.
The Heroes thus their mutual Warmth express'd.	Il.13.116.110.
Let mutual Reverence mutual Warmth inspire,	Il.15.668.221.
Studious of rest and warmth, *Ulysses* lies,	Od.14.514.62.
With warmth replies the man of mighty woes.	Od.16.92.106.
That warmth of soul that urg'd thy younger years?	Od.18.256.179.
Whilst with pathetic warmth his hand he press'd;	Od.20.248.245.
To whom with warmth: My soul a lie disdains;	Od.23.27.320.
Touch'd at her words, the King with warmth replies,	Od.23.184.332.
Trembling with warmth, the hoary heroes stand,	Od.24.576.375.

WARN

To warn the Nations, and to curb the Great!	Il.6.76.327.
And warn their Children from a *Trojan* War.	Il.8.642.426.
And warn the *Greeks* the wiser Choice to make:	Il.9.539.460.
For sure to warn us *Jove* his Omen sent,	Il.12.255.90.
To warn the wretch, that young *Orestes* grown	Od.1.51.33.
To warn the thoughtless self-confiding train,	Od.13.174.14.
Go warn thy son, nor be the warning vain,	Od.18.201.176.

WARN'D

Thus scorning prophecy, and warn'd in vain,	1.TrPA.35.366.
Nor touch the fatal flow'rs; but, warn'd by me,	1.TrFD.86.389.
Warn'd by thy *Sylph*, oh Pious Maid beware!	2.RL1.112.154.
Warn'd by the *Sylph*, oh Pious Maid beware!	2.RL1.112A.154.
A *Sylph* too warn'd me of the Threats of Fate,	2.RL4.165.197.
Loth I gave way, and warn'd our *Argive* Bands:	Il.5.1017.315.
Thus, turning, warn'd th' intrepid *Diomed*.	Il.8.168.406.
Had warn'd his Children from the Trojan Field;	Il.11.428.53.
Fate urg'd them on; the Father warn'd in vain,	Il.11.429.53.
Warn'd by the Words, to pow'rful *Jove* I yield,	Il.15.232.206.
Warn'd, he retreats. Then swift from all sides pour	Il.16.150.243.
(So *Thetis* warn'd) when by a *Trojan* Hand,	Il.18.13.323.
And warn'd to shun *Hectorean* Force in vain!	Il.18.18.324.
Warn'd of the coming fury of the Gods.	Od.3.200.95.
Hence warn'd, my son beware! nor idly stand	Od.3.398.106.
Warn'd by the God who sheds the golden day,	Od.8.343.282.
Warn'd by my ills beware, the Shade replies,	Od.11.545.410.
Warn'd by their awful voice these shores to shun,	Od.12.322.447.
Warn'd by the high command of heav'n, be aw'd;	Od.12.383.449.
By many such have I been warn'd; but chief	Od.14.417.56.
Yet warn'd in vain, with laughter loud elate	Od.20.431.254.
(Oft warn'd by *Mentor* and my self in vain)	Od.24.523.373.

WARNER

Mears, Warner, Wilkins run: Delusive thought!	5.DunA2.117.111.
Mears, Warner, Wilkins run: delusive thought!	5.DunB2.125.301.

WARNING

Ere warning *Phœbus* touch'd his trembling Ears,	1.EOC.131A.254.
Ah gentle Sir, take Warning of a Friend,	2.ChJM.194.24.
A Warning to these Ladies, and to You,	2.ChJM.654.46.
Forbid it Heav'n! this Warning should be lost!	Il.2.104.132.
And sure the warning Vision was from high:	Od.14.561.64.
Go warn thy son, nor be the warning vain,	Od.18.201.176.

WARNINGS •

Observe the warnings of a pow'r divine:	Od.15.32.71.

WARNS

Or warns me not to doe,	6.50.14.146.
But *Phœbus* warns him from high Heav'n, to shun	Il.20.431.412.
Nor idly warns the hoary Sire, nor hears	Il.23.373.505.
And *Circe* warns! O be their voice obey'd:	Od.12.327.447.

WARP

Then warp my voyage on the southern gales,	Od.4.103.124.

WARP'D

Most warp'd to Flatt'ry's side; but some, more nice,	4.2HE1.259.217.
Not warp'd by Passion, aw'd by Rumour,	6.89.5.250.

WARR'D

Dennis, who long had warr'd with modern *Huns*,	6.128.11.356.
Warr'd on the King of Heav'n with stern Disdain,	Il.13.443.126.
So warr'd both Armies on th' ensanguin'd Shore,	Il.16.1.233.
Nine years we warr'd; the tenth saw *Ilion* fall;	Od.14.276.49.
While love and duty warr'd within his breast.	Od.15.229.79.

WARRANT

"To get my Warrant quickly sign'd:	4.HS6.76.255.

WARREN

While K[ennet], B[ramston], W[arren], preach in vain.	5.DunA3.200.174*.
You'd take her for a Warren.	6.94.12.259.

WARRING

When the bold *Argives* led their warring Pow'rs ... 1.TrUl.191.472.
And set to View the warring Deities. ... Il.5.165.275.
Wrapt in a Mist above the warring Crew. ... Il.5.442.289.
If warring Gods for ever guard the Wall? ... Il.5.881.308.
From warring Gods thou bad'st me turn my Spear, ... Il.5.1014.315.
The warring Nations to suspend their Rage; ... Il.7.54.365.
Fix'd as the Bar between two warring Pow'rs, ... Il.11.696.66.
While sacred *Troy* the warring Hosts engag'd; ... Il.12.12.81.
Of warring *Phlegyans*, and *Ephyrian* Arms; ... Il.13.391.124.
As warring Winds, in *Sirius'* sultry Reign, ... Il.13.424.126.
Before his Chariot warring on the Plain; ... Il.13.484.130.
Then sudden mix'd among the warring Crew, ... Il.13.803.143.
How widely differs this from warring well? ... Il.13.912.148.
He spoke, then rush'd amid the warring Crew; ... Il.14.171A.165.
No less the Wonder of the warring Crew. ... Il.15.831.229.
The warring Nations meet, the Battel roars, ... Il.15.842.229.
For this in Arms the warring Nations stood, ... Il.15.858.229.
And round his Son confounds the warring Hosts, ... Il.16.697.271.
And stuck with Darts by warring Heroes shed; ... Il.16.775.273.
And calls th' *Ajaces* from the warring Croud, ... Il.17.575.311.
On adverse Parts the warring Gods engage. ... Il.20.44.395.
Of warring Heroes, and of bounding Steeds. ... Il.20.376.410.
And boldly bids the warring Gods be Foes! ... Il.21.367.436.
The warring Gods in fierce Contention join: ... Il.21.449.439.
To roaring billows, and the warring wind; ... Od.6.206.220.
When the bold *Argives* led their warring pow'rs, ... Od.13.358.24.

WARRIOR

Down sinks the Warrior, with a thundring Sound, ... 1.TrES.127.454.
Then as a Friend, and as a Warrior, fight; ... 1.TrES.310.461.
Otho a warrior, Cromwell a buffoon? ... 3.Ep1.147.27.
The boldest Warrior of the *Grecian* Race. ... Il.1.539.113.
There whelm'd with Waves the gawdy Warrior lies; ... Il.2.1066.172.
So from the King the shining Warrior flies, ... Il.3.51.191.
This said, once more he view'd the Warrior-Train: ... Il.3.253.204.
The beauteous Warrior now arrays for Fight, ... Il.3.409.212.
The raging Warrior to the spacious Skies ... Il.3.449.213.
(Seiz'd by the Crest) th' unhappy Warrior drew; ... Il.3.456.213.
Not like a Warrior parted from the Foe, ... Il.3.485.215.
The recreant Warrior, hateful as the Grave. ... Il.3.566.219.
This, by the *Greeks* unseen, the Warrior bends, ... Il.4.144.227.
And clasp'd the Warrior to his armed Breast. ... Il.4.291.234.
The Charge once made, no Warrior turn the Rein, ... Il.4.350.237.
Then give thy Warrior-Chief a Warrior's Due, ... Il.4.408.240.
Th' *Ætolian* Warrior tugg'd his weighty Spear: ... Il.4.615.250.
Down sinks the Warrior with a thundring Sound, ... Il.5.73.269.
The good old Warrior bade me trust to these, ... Il.5.248.279.
Our Triumph now, the mighty Warrior lies! ... Il.5.346.283.
Lost in a dizzy Mist the Warrior lies; ... Il.5.381.285.
Haste, Warrior, haste! preserve thy threaten'd State; ... Il.5.593.296.
The strongest Warrior of th' *Ætolian* Train; ... Il.5.1039.316.
From the rent Skin the Warrior tuggs again ... Il.5.1052.316.
(Fiercest of Men) and those the Warrior slew. ... Il.6.228.337.
In Earth the gen'rous Warrior fix'd his Dart, ... Il.6.262.339.
The recreant Warrior hear the Voice of Fame. ... Il.6.351.343.
Silent the Warrior smil'd, and pleas'd resign'd ... Il.6.504.351.
Swift thro' the Town the Warrior bends his way. ... Il.6.651.359.
A Warrior worthy to be *Hector's* Foe. ... Il.7.46.365.
He said: The Warrior heard the Word with Joy. ... Il.7.59.365.
The mightiest Warrior of th' *Achaian* Name ... Il.7.135.370.
Sheath'd in bright Steel the Giant-Warrior shone: ... Il.7.250.376.
A single Warrior 'midst a Host of Foes; ... Il.8.126.404.
Pleas'd *Hector* braves the Warrior as he flies. ... Il.8.195.407.
The double Offspring of the Warrior-God. ... Il.9.114.437.
Althæa's Hate th' unhappy Warrior drew, ... Il.9.681.468.
The Warrior heard, he vanquish'd, and he sav'd. ... Il.9.706.469.
With that, the venerable Warrior rose; ... Il.10.150.8.
The Warrior saw the hoary Chief, and said. ... Il.10.185.10.
The Warrior rouz'd, and to th' Entrenchments led. ... Il.10.206.10.
But let some other chosen Warrior join, ... Il.10.263.13.
The Horses yok'd beside each Warrior stand. ... Il.10.545.27.
Back by the Foot each slaughter'd Warrior drew; ... Il.10.571.28.
Each Bosom boils, each Warrior starts to Arms. ... Il.11.16.35.
That round the Warrior cast a dreadful Shade; ... Il.11.44.36.
Stretch'd in the Dust th' unhappy Warrior lies, ... Il.11.309.48.
Transfix'd the Warrior with his brazen Dart; ... Il.11.336.49.
The Warrior thus, and thus the Friend reply'd. ... Il.11.410.53.
Here stand his utmost Force—The Warrior said; ... Il.11.451.54.
Thou Woman-Warrior with the curling Hair; ... Il.11.492.56.
These, in the Warrior, their own Fate inclose; ... Il.11.523.57.
Near as he drew, the Warrior thus began. ... Il.11.539.57.
A single Warrior, half an Host sustains: ... Il.11.605.61.
The Warrior rescue, and your Country save. ... Il.11.719.67.
What wounded Warrior late his Chariot brought? ... Il.11.749.68.
The Foe dispers'd, their bravest Warrior kill'd, ... Il.11.880.75.
The Warrior sinks, tremendous now no more! ... Il.12.216.89.
Down sinks the Warrior with a thund'ring Sound, ... Il.12.481.99.
The *Trojan* Warrior, touch'd with timely Fear, ... Il.13.219.116.
Ally'd the Warrior to the House of *Troy.)* ... Il.13.234.116.
To these the Warrior sent his Voice around. ... Il.13.607.135.
His Shield revers'd o'er the fall'n Warrior lies; ... Il.13.688.137.
High-tow'ring in the Front, the Warrior came. ... Il.13.756.141.
Or fell the distant Warrior to the Ground. ... Il.13.896.148.
Appears a Warrior furrow'd o'er with Age; ... Il.14.156.165.
He spoke, then rush'd amid the Warrior Crew; ... Il.14.171.165.
And thus the venerable Warrior spoke. ... Il.14.158A.165.
The weaker Warrior takes a lighter Shield. ... Il.14.442.184.
The pious Warrior of *Anchises'* Line, ... Il.14.500.188.
Struck thro' the Belly's Rim, the Warrior lies ... Il.14.521.188.
As by his side the groaning Warrior fell, ... Il.14.537.189.
Eternal Darkness wrapt the Warrior round, ... Il.14.613.192.
This Menace fix'd the Warrior to his Throne; ... Il.15.160.202.
The Warrior spoke, the list'ning *Greeks* obey, ... Il.15.338.210.
The Warrior wields; and his great Brother joins, ... Il.15.569.218.
The Warrior falls, extended on the Ground. ... Il.15.641.221.

WARRIOR (CONTINUED)

The luckless Warrior at his Stern lay dead: ... Il.15.907.232.
His pointless Spear the Warrior shakes in vain; ... Il.16.146.243.
The groaning Warrior pants upon the Ground. ... Il.16.345.256.
In Darkness, and in Death, the Warrior lay. ... Il.16.375.257.
Prone to the Ground the breathless Warrior fell, ... Il.16.504.262.
Then as a Friend, and as a Warrior, fight; ... Il.16.615.268.
A valiant Warrior, haughty, bold, and young.) ... Il.16.876.277.
Warrior! desist, nor tempt an equal Blow: ... Il.17.14.288.
Prone sinks the Warrior, and his Arms resound. ... Il.17.52.289.
Where lab'ring on the left the Warrior stood, ... Il.17.125.292.
From such a Warrior such a Speech shou'd hear? ... Il.17.190.294.
The Warrior rais'd his Voice, and wide around ... Il.17.292.299.
The boldest Warrior, and the noblest Mind: ... Il.17.355.301.
From rich *Pæonia's* Vales the Warrior came, ... Il.17.402.303.
The youthful Warrior heard with silent Woe, ... Il.17.781.319.
Fal'n is the Warrior, and *Patroclus* he! ... Il.18.16.323.
And mourns the Warrior with a Warrior's Heart; ... Il.18.38.325.
A lofty Bier the breathless Warrior bears; ... Il.18.275.335.
One Fate the Warrior and the Friend shall strike, ... Il.18.385.339.
The best and bravest of the Warrior-Kind! ... Il.19.216.381.
Now issued from the Ships the warrior Train, ... Il.19.378.387.
The Warrior falls, transfix'd from Ear to Ear. ... Il.20.548.417.
(Reply'd the Warrior) our illustrious Race? ... Il.21.170.428.
And left the breathless Warrior in his Gore. ... Il.21.218.430.
The Warrior-Shield, the Helm, and Lance lay down, ... Il.22.156.459.
Prone on the Field the bleeding Warrior lies, ... Il.22.413.472.
For such a Warrior *Thetis* aids their Woe, ... Il.23.19.487.
From his dead Friend the pensive Warrior went, ... Il.23.47.488.
Hear from thy heav'ns above, oh warrior-maid! ... Od.2.301.76.
Big with revenge, the mighty warrior flies: ... Od.2.369.78.
The pleasing sounds each latent warrior warm'd, ... Od.4.381.139.
Such to our wish the warrior soon restore, ... Od.4.461.142.
With me repair; and from thy warrior band ... Od.4.551.146.
Light as the viewless air, the warrior Maid ... Od.6.25.205.
I voyag'd, leader of a warrior host, ... Od.6.196.219.
The warrior Goddess gives his frame to shine ... Od.6.271.223.
Of warrior Kings, and joyn'd th' illustrious shades. ... Od.11.662.416.
Whoever was the warrior, he must be ... Od.14.142.42.
His purpose when the gen'rous warrior heard, ... Od.15.108.74.
Then from his eyes upsprung the warrior-maid. ... Od.16.193.112.
Such to our wish the warrior soon restore, ... Od.17.152.139.
A sabre, when the warrior press'd to part, ... Od.19.273.208.
To seek my Lord among the warrior-train, ... Od.20.96.237.
The adverse host the phantom warrior ey'd, ... Od.22.233.298.
Who thus the warrior to revenge inspires. ... Od.22.245.298.
The Warrior-Goddess gives his frame to shine ... Od.23.153.328.
Son of *Arcesius*, rev'rend warrior, hear! ... Od.24.599.376.

WARRIOR-CHIEF

Then give thy Warrior-Chief a Warrior's Due, ... Il.4.408.240.

WARRIOR-GOD

The double Offspring of the Warrior-God. ... Il.9.114.437.

WARRIOR-GODDESS

The Warrior-Goddess gives his frame to shine ... Od.23.153.328.

WARRIOR-KIND

The best and bravest of the Warrior-Kind! ... Il.19.216.381.

WARRIOR-MAID

Hear from thy heav'ns above, oh warrior-maid! ... Od.2.301.76.
Then from his eyes upsprung the warrior-maid. ... Od.16.193.112.

WARRIOR-SHIELD

The Warrior-Shield, the Helm, and Lance lay down, ... Il.22.156.459.

WARRIOR-TRAIN

This said, once more he view'd the Warrior-Train: ... Il.3.253.204.
To seek my Lord among the warrior-train, ... Od.20.96.237.

WARRIOR'S

With equal Warmth, and rouze the Warrior's Fire; ... 1.TrES.54.451.
Sarpedon's Friend; Across the Warrior's Way, ... 1.TrES.99.453.
Which o'er the Warrior's Shoulder took its Course, ... 1.TrES.283.460.
'Tis thine whate'er the Warrior's Breast inflames, ... Il.2.277.141.
The Warrior's Toils, and combate by his side. ... Il.2.997.170.
Restore our Blood, and raise the Warrior's Souls, ... Il.4.297.235.
Can *Peteus'* Son forget a Warrior's Part, ... Il.4.390.239.
Then give thy Warrior-Chief a Warrior's Due, ... Il.4.408.240.
Which o'er the Warrior's Shoulder took its Course, ... Il.5.23.266.
Her Words allay th' impetuous Warrior's Heat, ... Il.5.45.268.
Without a Warrior's Arms, the Spear and Shield! ... Il.5.267.280.
The Warrior's Fury let this Arm sustain; ... Il.5.285.280.
Haste all, and take the gen'rous Warrior's Part. ... Il.5.571.296.
Old *Nestor* saw, and rowz'd the Warrior's Rage; ... Il.6.83.327.
Nor aught the Warrior's thund'ring Mace avail'd. ... Il.7.176.372.
But sound ungrateful in a Warrior's Ears: ... Il.7.431.386.
O'erwhelm me Earth! and hide a Warrior's Shame. ... Il.8.182.406.
Shall recompence the Warrior's Toils with Love. ... Il.8.354.414.
The dreadful Weapons of the Warrior's Rage, ... Il.10.86.6.
The Warrior's Fury, there the Battel glows; ... Il.11.625.61.
Salubrious Draughts the Warrior's Thirst allay, ... Il.11.786.70.
With equal Warmth, and rouze the Warrior's Fire; ... Il.12.398.96.
Sarpedon's Friend; A-cross the Warrior's way, ... Il.12.453.98.
Come, and the Warrior's lov'd Remains defend. ... Il.13.585.134.
Shalt run, forgetful of a Warrior's Fame, ... Il.13.1036.153.
(Where Heaps<,> lay'd loose beneath the Warrior's Feet, ... Il.14.473.186.
Which o'er the Warrior's Shoulder took its course, ... Il.16.588.267.
Stern *Hector* fastens on the Warrior's Head, ... Il.16.919.279.
And mourns the Warrior with a Warrior's Heart; ... Il.18.38.325.
This done, whate'er a Warrior's Use requires ... Il.18.705.357.
Apollo wedg'd him in the Warrior's Way, ... Il.20.110.398.
Securely cas'd the Warrior's Body o'er. ... Il.22.406.472.
That *Greece* the Warrior's fun'ral Pile prepare, ... Il.23.62.489.

WARRIOR'S (CONTINUED)

I'll pay my brother's ghost a warrior's due, ...Od.4.274.132.

WARRIORS

Nor ardent Warriors meet with hateful Eyes, ...1.Mes.58.118.
Or ardent Warriors meet with hateful Eyes, ...1.Mes.58A.118.
Or raise old Warriors whose ador'd Remains ....1.W-F.301.177.
The Warriors thus oppos'd in Arms engage, ...1.TrES.223.458.
Warriors she fires with animated Sounds; ....6.11.28.30.
Warriors she fires by sprightly Sounds; ....6.11.28A.30.
There warriors frowning in historic brass: ....6.71.58.204.
Ye Kings and Warriors! may your Vows be crown'd, ...Il.1.23.86.
The Spoils of Cities raz'd, and Warriors slain; ....Il.1.159.95.
Do you, young Warriors, hear my Age advise. ....Il.1.361.105.
Warriors like you, with Strength and Wisdom blest, ...Il.2.227.138.
Ye *Grecian* Warriors! lay your Fears aside. ....Il.2.391.145.
But now, ye Warriors, take a short Repast; ....Il.2.452.149.
The hardy Warriors whom *Bœtia* bred, ...Il.2.586.155.
Twice sixty Warriors thro' the foaming Seas. ....Il.2.609.156.
Thro' roaring Seas the wond'ring Warriors bear; ....Il.2.744.161.
And thence to *Troy* his hardy Warriors led. ....Il.2.764.162.
He led the Warriors from th' *Ætolian* Shore, ...Il.2.779.162.
And saw their blooming Warriors early slain. ....Il.2.800.163.
Girtonè's Warriors; and where *Orthè* lies, ...Il.2.898.166.
The Council breaks, the Warriors rush to Arms. ....Il.2.977.169.
Forbear ye Warriors! lay the Darts aside: ....Il.3.116.195.
Me too ye Warriors hear, whose fatal Right ....Il.3.135.196.
And her dead Warriors strow the mournful Plains. ....Il.4.273.234.
To bar his Passage fifty Warriors lay; ....Il.4.445.241.
The War renews, the Warriors bleed again; ....Il.4.539.247.
Retire then Warriors, but sedate and slow; ....Il.5.746.302.
And see thy Warriors fall, thy Glories end. ....Il.6.573.355.
And now the Warriors passing on the way, ...Il.6.664.360.
Gods! should he see our Warriors trembling stand, ...Il.7.155.372.
But Warriors, you, that youthful Vigour boast, ...Il.7.191.373.
Warriors! I claim the Lot, and arm with Joy; ....Il.7.227.375.
The Monarch spoke: the Warriors snatch'd with haste ....Il.7.454.387.
And ardent Warriors wait the rising Morn. ....Il.8.708.429.
Of all the Warriors yonder Host can send, ...Il.9.269.446.
The Day may come, when all our Warriors slain, ...Il.9.324.450.
Let younger *Greeks* our sleeping Warriors wake; ....Il.10.188.10.
Thou first of Warriors, and thou best of Friends, ...Il.10.276.14.
The panting Warriors seize him as He stands, ...Il.10.447.23.
As with the Light and Warriors Toils begun. ....Il.11.68.37.
The Brother-Warriors of *Antenor's* Line; ....Il.11.78.38.
In the same Car the Brother-Warriors ride, ...Il.11.139.41.
While his keen Faulchion drinks the Warriors Lives; ....Il.11.211.44.
The Warriors standing on the breezy Shore, ...Il.11.758.69.
Hear then ye Warriors! and obey with speed; ....Il.12.87.84.
Gods! shall two Warriors only guard their Gates, ...Il.12.195.88.
'Tis yours, O Warriors, all our Hopes to raise; ....Il.13.73.108.
The Pride of haughty Warriors to confound, ...Il.13.388.124.
Inspire thy Warriors then with manly Force, ...Il.15.292.208.
These drink the Life of gen'rous Warriors slain; ....Il.15.358.210.
Behold, ye Warriors, and exert your Pow'rs. ....Il.15.581.218.
How long, ye Warriors of the *Argive* Race, ...Il.15.592.219.
He spoke—The Warriors, at his fierce Command, ...Il.15.880.230.
Such were your words—Now Warriors grieve no more, ...Il.16.248.249.
Oh Warriors, Part'ners of *Achilles'* Praise! ....Il.16.324.255.
The Warriors thus oppos'd in Arms, engage ....Il.16.526.264.
Shields, Helmets rattle, as the Warriors close; ....Il.16.765.273.
So fell the Warriors, and so rung their Arms. ....Il.16.772.273.
But hope not, Warriors! for *Achilles'* Aid. ....Il.17.794.319.
High from the Ground the Warriors heave the Dead; ....Il.17.808.320.
Was't not enough, ye valiant Warriors say, ...Il.18.335.337.
He spoke, and from the Warriors turn'd his Face: ....Il.19.329.386.
Swift interpos'd between the Warriors flies, ...Il.20.369.410.
The flouncing Steeds and shrieking Warriors drown'd. ....Il.21.13.421.
This, who but touches, Warriors! is my Foe. ....Il.23.634.515.
To those brave warriors, who, with glory fir'd, ...Od.4.125.126.
Embracing left? Must I the warriors weep, ...Od.4.657.150.
Ghastly with wounds the forms of warriors slain ....Od.11.51.383.
Greece gave her latent warriors to my care, ...Od.11.641.416.
Fraught with bold warriors and a boundless store. ....Od.14.424.56.
The latent warriors in a veil of clouds. ....Od.23.399.344.
Unnumber'd warriors round the burning pyle ....Od.24.87.352.

WARRIORS'

Conceals the Warriors' shining Helms in Night: ....Il.17.319.300.

WARRIOUR

To this the King: Fly, mighty Warriour! fly, ...Il.1.225.97.

WARS

A dreadful Series of Intestine Wars, ...1.W-F.325.180.
When first young *Maro* sung of Kings and *Wars,* ....1.EOC.130A.254.
In *Theban* Wars an humbler Theme may chuse: ....1.TrSt.50.411.
Must I, of *Jove!* in bloody Wars contend? ....1.TrSt.351.424.
The Wars of *Troy* were round the Pillar seen: ....2.TemF.188.271.
The *Latian* Wars, and haughty *Turnus* dead; ....2.TemF.205.272.
And says our *Wars thrive ill,* because delay'd; ....4.JD4.163.39.
In *Anna's* Wars, a Soldier poor and old, ...4.2HE2.33.167.
Their annual trophies, and their monthly wars. ....5.DunA3.280.183.
Their annual trophies, and their monthly wars: ....5.DunB3.282.334.
Long kept by wars, and long by tempests tost, ...6.15.2.51.
The spoils of nations, and the pomp of wars, ...6.32.28.96.
In living medals see her wars enroll'd, ...6.71.55.204.
And Wars and Horrors are thy savage Joy. ....Il.1.232.98.
So small their Number, that if Wars were ceas'd, ...Il.2.155.135.
With all the Wealth our Wars and Blood to bestow, ...Il.2.279.141.
And view, with Envy, our successful Wars. ....Il.2.415.147.
And sends the brave *Abantes* to the Wars; ....Il.2.642.157.
The *Trojan* Wars she weav'd (herself the Prize) ....Il.3.171.199.
Silent they slept, and heard of Wars no more. ....Il.3.314.208.
Or carry Wars to some soft *Asian* Plain? ....Il.3.496.215.
Jove, the great Arbiter of Peace and Wars! ....Il.4.114.226.

WARS (CONTINUED)

Thee milder Arts befit, and softer Wars, ...Il.5.520.293.
Around the Spectre bloody Wars are wag'd, ...Il.5.549.295.
Some God, they thought, who rul'd the Fate of Wars, ...Il.6.133.330.
And gives whole Nations to the Waste of Wars. ....Il.7.254.376.
Thy high Commands must spirit all our Wars. ....Il.9.98.437.
Yet hear me farther: When our Wars are o'er, ...Il.9.183.441.
Yet hear me farther: When our Wars are o'er, ...Il.9.370.451.
From each wide Portal issuing to the Wars) ....Il.9.505.458.
But call'd by Glory to the Wars of *Troy,* ....Il.11.291.48.
And this the Period of our Wars and Fame? ....Il.11.955.78.
Or terrifies th' offending World with Wars: ....Il.13.320.120.
And Wars whole Fury burns around thy Head. ....Il.13.924.149.
Advent'rous Combats and bold Wars to wage, ...Il.14.96.162.
He bids thee from forbidden Wars repair ....Il.15.198.204.
To fight our Wars, he left his native Air. ....Il.15.513.216.
And all our Wars and Glories at an end! ....Il.17.283.298.
His partial Favour, and assists your Wars, ...Il.17.385.302.
Sure, tho' he wars for *Troy,* he claims our Aid. ....Il.20.348.408.
But *Jove* he dreads, nor wars against his Son. ....Il.21.210.430.
To 'scape the Wars, to *Agamemnon* gave, ...Il.23.366.504.
All who the Wars of ten long years surviv'd, ...Od.1.16.30.
My wars, the copious theme of ev'ry tongue, ...Od.4.119.125.
To grace the victor's welcome from the wars, ...Od.4.713.152.
By seas, by wars, so many dangers run, ...Od.5.287.185.
We drain'd, the prize of our *Ciconian* wars. ....Od.9.191.313.
The wars and wisdom of thy gallant son: ....Od.11.618.414.
Was ever Chief for wars like these renown'd? ....Od.17.574.160.
With shields indented deep in glorious wars. ....Od.19.37.194.
Of wars, of triumphs, and disastrous fates; ....Od.23.330.340.

WARWICK

Earl *Warwick* make your Moan, ...6.47.6.128.

WARWICK'S

Let *W[a]rw[ic]k's* Muse with *Ash[urs]t* join, ...6.58.57.173.

WARY

(Right wary He and wise) ....6.94.22.259.
The wary *Trojan,* bending from the Blow, ...Il.3.443.213.
The wary *Trojan* shrinks, and bending low ....Il.7.303.379.
Yet should the Fears that wary Mind suggests ....Il.12.291.92.
Before his wary Steps, his ample Shield. ....Il.13.214.116.
The wary *Cretan,* as his Foe drew near, ...Il.13.489.130.
Dispatch a wary messenger with haste: ....Od.15.486.93.
The wary Chief the rushing foe represt, ...Od.22.95.291.

WAS (OMITTED)

871

WAS'T

Was't not enough, ye valiant Warriors say, ...Il.18.335.337.

WASH

A brighter Wash; to curl their waving Hairs, ...2.RL2.97.165.
Already written—wash it out, my tears! ....2.ElAb.14.320.
To make a wash, would hardly stew a child, ...3.Ep2.54.55.
And gaping Tritons spew to wash your face. ....3.Ep4.154.152.
'Tis mine to wash a few slight Stains; but theirs ....4.JD4.284.49.
Wash Bladen white, and expiate Hay's stain. ....5.DunB4.560.397.
To dry their Sweat, and wash away the Gore, ...Il.11.759.69.
With lukewarm Water wash the Gore away, ...Il.11.964.78.
Deriv'd from thee whose Waters wash the Earth, ...Il.16.211.247.
Cleanse the pale Corse, and wash each honour'd Wound. ....Il.18.404.340.
From my tir'd Body wash the Dirt and Blood, ...Il.21.660.449.
From my tir'd Body wash the Dust and Blood, ...Il.21.660A.449.
To wash the Body, and anoint with Oil; ....Il.24.731.568.
They wash. The tables in fair order spread, ...Od.1.183.41.
Wash, and partake serene the friendly feast. ....Od.4.294.133.
Wash their fair garments in the limpid streams; ....Od.6.100.210.
Then wash their hands, and hasten to the feast. ....Od.10.207.350.
They wash. The tables in fair order spread, ...Od.15.152.76.
To wash her robes descending to the main, ...Od.15.461.93.
They wash: the table, in fair order spread, ...Od.17.108.137.
Some whey, to wash his bowels, he might earn. ....Od.17.265.145.
Now wash the stranger, and the bed prepare; ....Od.19.363.211.
To wash a wretched wand'rer wou'd disdain; ....Od.19.398.213.
To wash, to scent, and purify the room. ....Od.22.475.312.
They wash, and to *Ulysses* take their way, ...Od.22.515.314.

WASH'D

And now, by rolling Waters wash'd away. ....4.HOde1.48B.153.
The wild *Mæander* wash'd the Artist's face: ....5.DunA2.168A.122.
And never wash'd, but in Castalia's streams. ....5.DunA3.144.162.
The wild Meander wash'd the Artist's face: ....5.DunB2.176.304.
And never wash'd, but in Castalia's streams. ....5.DunB3.18.321.
Wash'd by the briny Wave, the pious Train ....Il.1.412.107.
He eas'd; and wash'd the clotted Gore away. ....Il.5.995.314.
Wash'd by broad *Hellespont's* resounding Seas, ...Il.7.100.368.
The Wounds they wash'd, their pious Tears they shed, ...Il.7.506.389.
The Wound he wash'd, the Styptick Juice infus'd. ....Il.11.983.79.
He purg'd; and wash'd it in the running Stream. ....Il.16.279.249.
Wash'd from beneath him, slides the slimy Soil; ....Il.21.310.433.
Wash'd their fair Garments in the Days of Peace. ....Il.22.204.464.
I wash'd. The table in fair order spread, ...Od.10.437.365.
Wash'd with th' effusive wave, are purg'd of gore. ....Od.22.490.313.
Perfum'd and wash'd, and gorgeously array'd. ....Od.24.426.369.

WASHES

Or plung'd in Lakes of bitter *Washes* lie, ...2.RL2.127.168.

WASPISH

This jealous, waspish, wrong-head, rhiming Race; ....4.2HE2.148.175.

WASPS 598 WATCH

WASPS
But look how Wasps from hollow Crannies drive, ...Il.12.189.88.
As Wasps, provok'd by Children in their Play, ...Il.16.314.254.

WASSE
Are things which Kuster, Burman, Wasse shall see, ...5.DunB4.237.366.

WAST
Wast thou not furnish'd by our choicest care ....Od.10.73.342.

WASTE
Waste sandy Vallies, once perplex'd with Thorn, ...1.Mes.73.119.
The Seas shall waste; the Skies in Smoke decay; ....1.Mes.105.122.
Like verdant Isles the sable Waste adorn. ....1.W-F.28.150.
A dreary Desart and a gloomy Waste, ...1.W-F.44.153.
Cities laid waste, they storm'd the Dens and Caves, ...1.W-F.49.153.
A Waste for Beasts, himself deny'd a Grave! ....1.W-F.80.157.
A Belt her Waste, a Fillet binds her Hair, ...1.W-F.178.166.
And give the Nations to the Waste of War. ....1.TrSt.341.424.
The Prince with Wonder did the Waste behold, ...1.TrSt.510A.431.
Weep in her turn, and waste in equal Flame. ....2.ChJM.366.32.
I waste the Matin lamp in sighs for thee, ...2.ElAb.267.341.
Some happier island in the watry waste, ...3.EOM1.106.28.
Is it less strange, the Prodigal should waste ....3.Ep4.3.134.
What brought Sir Visto's ill got wealth to waste? ....3.Ep4.15.137.
What brought Sir *Shylock's* ill got wealth to waste? ....3.Ep4.15A.137.
Two babes of love close clinging to her waste; ....5.DunA2.150.120.
The freezing Tanais thro' a waste of Snows, ...5.DunA3.80.156.
The freezing Tanais thro' a waste of snows, ...5.DunB3.88.324.
But wherefore waste I words? I see advance ....5.DunB4.271.370.
Or waste, for others Use, their restless Years ....6.17ii.3.56.
Quoth *Sandys: To Waste-Paper.* ....6.58.76.174.
Quoth Sand's *To Waste-Paper.* ....6.58.76A.174.
Quoth *Sandys: Into Waste*-Paper. ....6.58.76B.174.
See the wild Waste of all-devouring years! ....6.71.1.202.
To waste long Nights in indolent Repose? ....Il.2.30.128.
To waste long Nights in indolent Repose. ....Il.2.80.130.
Hence let us fly, and let him waste his Store ....Il.2.294.141.
Shall waste the Form whose Crime it was to please! ....Il.3.234.203.
And flatted Vineyards, one sad Waste appear; ....Il.5.121.273.
Saw the wide Waste of his destructive Hand: ....Il.5.127.273.
Depopulate the Stalls and waste the Fold; ....Il.5.684.300.
The Waste of Slaughter, and the Rage of Fight, ...Il.5.1099.319.
Lay'd *Thebè* waste, and slew my warlike Sire! ....Il.6.525.352.
And gives whole Nations to the Waste of Wars. ....Il.7.254.376.
Shall rise in Vengeance, and lay waste the Plain. ....Il.8.594.424.
Hence, let us go—why waste we Time in vain? ....Il.9.737.470.
Crops the tall Harvest, and lays waste the Plain; ....Il.11.685.65.
And one bright Waste hides all the Works of Men: ....Il.12.340.93.
I waste no Anger, for they feel no Shame: ....Il.13.158.112.
Around his Waste his pious Arms he threw, ...Il.13.676.137.
Cease we at length to waste our Blood in vain, ...Il.14.81.161.
Wide o'er the wat'ry Waste, a Light appears, ...Il.19.405.389.
And marks the Waste of his destructive Hands; ....Il.21.614.448.
And roll'd his Eyes around the wat'ry Waste. ....Il.23.177.497.
And thy Heart waste with life-consuming Woe? ....Il.24.164.542.
To distant *Sparta* and the spacious waste ....Od.1.118.37.
Waste in wild riot what your land allows, ...Od.1.479.55.
Shall I, by waste undone, refund the dow'r? ....Od.2.154.69.
Waste in wild riot what your land allows, ...Od.2.163.70.
Threat on, till all thy stores in waste decay. ....Od.2.232.72.
The waste of nature let the feast repair, ...Od.4.71.122.
But now let sleep the painful waste repair ....Od.4.399.139.
And breath, to waste in unavailing cries. ....Od.4.955.162.
Like a broad shield amid the watry waste. ....Od.5.360.189.
Since wide he wander'd on the wat'ry waste; ....Od.5.497.196.
What savage beasts may wander in the waste? ....Od.5.609.201.
Oh indolent! to waste thy hours away! ....Od.6.29.205.
And there the garden yields a waste of flow'rs. ....Od.6.356.229.
But say thro' what waste regions hast thou stray'd, ...Od.8.625.296.
Wide o'er the waste the rage of *Boreas* sweeps, ...Od.9.77.306.
Her waste was circled with a zone of gold. ....Od.10.652.375.
Nor fear'st the dark and dismal waste to tread, ...Od.11.585.412.
The Goddess spoke; in feasts we waste the day, ...Od.12.39.431.
And flow'ry meads they waste the joyous hours. ....Od.12.171.440.
His vest succinct then girding round his waste, ...Od.14.83.40.
Than see the wealth of Kings consum'd in waste, ...Od.16.115.108.
While in debate they waste the hours away, ...Od.16.344.122.
Why must I waste a tedious life in tears, ...Od.18.241.178.
Demands the pomp of centuries to waste! ....Od.19.338.210.
Which thoughtless we in games would waste away: ....Od.21.275.273.
The waste of years refunded in a day. ....Od.22.70.290.

WASTE-PAPER
Quoth *Sandys: To Waste-Paper.* ....6.58.76.174.

WASTED
Of Kings unbury'd, on the wasted Coasts; ....1.TrSt.56.412.
Of Kings unbury'd, in the wasted Coasts; ....1.TrSt.56A.412.
And wasted in the soft, infectious Fire. ....2.ChJM.433.35.
With falling Woods to strow the wasted Plain. ....Il.3.92.194.
Woes heap'd on Woes consum'd his wasted Heart; ....Il.6.249.339.
Woes heap'd on Woes oppress'd his wasted Heart; ....Il.6.249A.339.
What-time, deserting *Ilion's* wasted Plain, ...Il.14.285.176.
So sweeps the Hero thro' the wasted Shores; ....Il.20.574.418.
There worn and wasted, lose our cares in sleep ....Od.12.9.430.
When now was wasted more than half the night, ...Od.14.543.63.

WASTEFUL
Thy wasteful Arm: Assemble all thy Fires! ....Il.21.387.436.
The smallest portion of a wasteful board, ...Od.17.540.158.
These wasteful love-debates, a mourning bride?— ....Od.19.624.226.

WASTES
Here was she seen o'er Airy Wastes to rove, ...1.W-F.167.165.
And wastes the Days in Grief, the Nights in Tears. ....1.TrUl.219.473.

WASTES (CONTINUED)
Here naked Rocks, and empty Wastes were seen, ...2.TemF.15.254.
Thro' dreary wastes, and weep each other's woe; ....2.ElAb.242.339.
While *Agamemnon* wastes the Ranks around, ...Il.11.243.46.
While *Agamemnon* wastes the Ranks around, ...Il.11.259.47.
Raging he spoke; nor farther wastes his Breath, ...Il.15.902.232.
(Ev'n while he lives, he wastes with secret Woe) ....Il.18.515.346.
And wastes the wise frugality of Kings. ....Od.2.62.63.
Wastes all her widow'd hours in tender moan. ....Od.4.148.127.
And bowls flow round, and riot wastes the day. ....Od.9.50.304.
Pale hunger wastes the manly strength away. ....Od.12.406.450.
And wastes the days in grief, the nights in tears. ....Od.13.386.25.
And inly bleeds, and silent wastes away: ....Od.13.434.27.
Sole, and all comfortless he wastes away, ...Od.15.380.87.
But lost to every joy, she wastes the day ....Od.16.37.104.

WASTFUL
Or learn the wastful Vengeance to remove, ...Il.1.85.90.
Once more attend! avert the wastful Woe, ...Il.1.596.116.
And far avert *Tydides'* wastful Ire, ...Il.6.119.330.
And far avert *Tydides'* wastful Ire, ...Il.6.346.343.
And wastful War in all its Fury burns. ....Il.6.413.347.
Doom'd to supply the Suitors wastful feast, ...Od.14.21.35.
All to the suitors wastful board preferr'd. ....Od.14.130.42.

WASTFULL
Me, only me, with all his wastfull Rage? ....Il.21.433.438.

WASTING
The wasting Moth ne'er spoil'd my best Array; ....2.ChWB.288.71.
There hid in Shades, and wasting Day by Day, ...6.81.13A.226.
But wasting Cares lay heavy on his Mind: ....Il.1.637.118.
But wasting Years that wither human Race, ...Il.4.364.238.
So *Troy* reliev'd from that wide-wasting Hand ....Il.11.487.56.
Spoils of my Arms, and thine; when, wasting wide, ...Il.18.401.340.
Unhappy man! to wasting woes a prey, ...Od.5.207.181.
Now wasting years my former strength confound, ...Od.14.247.48.
The good old man, to wasting woes a prey, ...Od.23.387.343.

WASTS
And proud *Mæonia* wasts the Fruits of *Troy.* ....Il.18.342.338.

WAT'RY
Fill all the wat'ry Plain, and to the Margin dance. ....2.TemF.441.284.
So Jove's bright bow displays its wat'ry round, ...5.DunB2.173.304
Where aged *Ocean* holds his wat'ry Reign, ...Il.1.469.110.
Jove first ascending from the Wat'ry Bow'rs, ...Il.1.642.118.
(Soft *Zephyr* curling the wide wat'ry Plain) ....Il.7.72.366.
Who plow'd, with Fates averse, the wat'ry way; ....Il.8.655.427.
To the blue Monarch of the wat'ry Main. ....Il.11.867.74.
Then *Ida's* Summits pour'd their wat'ry Store; ....Il.12.16.82.
Thalia, Glauce, (ev'ry wat'ry Name) ....Il.18.47.325.
Pursu'd the Pleasures of the wat'ry Reign; ....Il.18.110.328.
And smiling, thus the wat'ry Queen address'd. ....Il.18.452.343.
I, only I, of all the wat'ry Race, ...Il.18.505.346.
Wide o'er the wat'ry Waste, a Light appears, ...Il.19.405.389.
Whose ev'ry Wave some wat'ry Monster brings, ...Il.21.139.427.
How durst thou vaunt thy wat'ry Progeny? ....Il.21.205.430.
(A wat'ry Bulwark) screen the Band who fly. ....Il.21.262.431.
So oft' the Surge, in wat'ry Mountains spread, ...Il.21.305.433.
From all thy Fountains swell thy wat'ry Store, ...Il.21.363.435.
These his cold Rites, and this his wat'ry Tomb. ....Il.21.377.436.
Pour the red Torrent on the wat'ry Foe, ...Il.21.391.436.
The wat'ry Willows hiss before the Fire. ....Il.21.411.437.
And roll'd his Eyes around the wat'ry Waste. ....Il.23.177.497.
The heaving Deeps in wat'ry Mountains rise: ....Il.23.267.500.
The wat'ry Fairies dance in mazy Rings, ...Il.24.776.569.
To seek *Ulysses* thro' the wat'ry way. ....Od.2.405.80.
What godhead interdicts the wat'ry way? ....Od.4.574.147.
What Godhead interdicts the wat'ry way? ....Od.4.632.149.
By *Juno's* guardian aid, the wat'ry Vast ....Od.4.683.151.
Mean-time the Suitors plow the wat'ry plain, ...Od.4.1099.169.
So wat'ry fowl, that seek their fishy food, ...Od.5.64.174.
In the black ocean, or the wat'ry war, ...Od.5.284.185.
Rolls clouds on clouds, and stirs the wat'ry world, ...Od.5.376.190.
The raging God a wat'ry mountain roll'd; ....Od.5.465.195.
Go, wander helpless on the wat'ry way: ....Od.5.481.195.
Since wide he wander'd on the wat'ry waste; ....Od.5.497.196.
And a dead silence still'd the wat'ry world. ....Od.5.503.196.
I bend, a suppliant at thy wat'ry throne, ...Od.5.569.199.
Before the wand'rer smooths the wat'ry way, ...Od.5.578.200.
On canvas wings to cut the wat'ry way; ....Od.7.47.235.
Ogygia nam'd, in *Ocean's* wat'ry arms: ....Od.7.328.252.
Thus far ye wander thro' the wat'ry way? ....Od.9.300.318.
A tomb along the wat'ry margin raise, ...Od.11.93.385.
Or saw gay vessel stem the wat'ry plain, ...Od.11.154.389.
To calm the God that holds the wat'ry reign; ....Od.11.159.389.
He pours his wat'ry store, the Virgin burns; ....Od.11.284.396.
And all the monsters of the wat'ry way; ....Od.12.120.437.
And toss with rising storms the wat'ry way, ...Od.12.344.448.
Or fowl that screaming haunt the wat'ry way. ....Od.12.392.450.
And bound for *Greece* we plow'd the wat'ry way; ....Od.13.363.24.
The driving storm the wat'ry west-wind pours, ...Od.14.512.62.
Swift let us measure back the wat'ry way, ...Od.15.73.72.
What vessel bore him o'er the wat'ry way? ....Od.16.58.105.
That you to *Pylos* plow'd the wat'ry way, ...Od.16.153.110.
Our murd'rous ambush on the wat'ry way. ....Od.16.393.125.
Th' eluded Suitors stem the wat'ry way. ....Od.16.495.131.
I for *Dulichium* urge the wat'ry way, ...Od.19.335.210.
Sudden his eyes releas'd their wat'ry store; ....Od.24.273.363.

WATCH
She saw him watch the Motions of her Eye, ...2.ChJM.601.44.
And the press'd Watch return'd a silver Sound. ....2.RL1.18.146.
Watch all their Ways, and all their Actions guide: ....2.RL2.88.165.
And, *Momentilla,* let the Watch be thine; ....2.RL2.114.166.

WATCH (CONTINUED)

Bright clouds descend, and Angels watch thee round, 2.ElAb.340.347.
The Watch would hardly let him pass at noon, 4.JD4.32.29.
Nor sly Informer watch my Words to draw 4.JD2A.133.144.
No sly Informer watch these words to draw 4.JD2.127.145.
Baskets of Fish at *Billingsgate* did watch, 6.14ii.30.44.
A Gold watch found on Cinder Whore, 6.116iii.1.326.
Explore my *Thought,* and watch my asking *Eye?* 6.117.12.333.
To watch the Motion, dubious of th' Event. Il.4.387.239.
These claim thy Thoughts by Day, thy Watch by Night: Il.5.598.297.
Commission'd in alternate Watch they stand, Il.5.930.311.
Commission'd in alternate Watch to stand, Il.5.930A.311.
Guard well the Walls, relieve the Watch of Night, Il.7.446.386.
Commission'd in alternate Watch they stand, Il.8.480.419.
Commission'd in alternate Watch to stand, Il.8.480A.419.
Thus joyful *Troy* maintain'd the Watch of Night, Il.9.1.430.
To try yon' Camp, and watch the *Trojan* Pow'rs? Il.10.44.4.
Whose Son, with *Merion,* o'er the Watch presides.) Il.10.68.5.
Tir'd with the Toils of Day, and Watch of Night: Il.10.111.7.
Th' unweary'd Watch their list'ning Leaders keep, Il.10.209.11.
Watch ev'ry Side, and turn to ev'ry Sound. Il.10.218.11.
Watch thus, and *Greece* shall live—The Hero said; Il.10.227.12.
What Watch they keep, and what Resolves they take: Il.10.364.19.
And spent with Toil neglect the Watch of Night? Il.10.366.19.
And mingles with the Guards that watch the Walls; Il.10.434.23.
And tir'd with Toils, neglect the Watch of Night? Il.10.470.24.
Their other Princes? tell what Watch they keep? Il.10.480.25.
No certain Guards the nightly Watch partake; Il.10.488.25.
Take due Refreshment, and the Watch attend. Il.18.348.338.
Streams from some lonely Watch-tow'r to the Sky: Il.19.407.389.
Where the high Watch-tow'r overlooks the Plain; Il.22.192.463.
To watch this Quarter my Adventure falls, Il.24.491.556.
To pass the Ramparts, and the Watch to blind. Il.24.849.572.
Watch with insidious care his known abode; Od.4.523.145.
The wakeful mariners shall watch the skies, Od.7.407.256.
In dreadful watch around the magic bow'r? Od.10.514.368.
Sleepless I watch; for I have learn'd to bear. Od.18.366.185.
Wakeful to weep and watch the tardy dawn Od.19.694.229.
To watch the foe a trusty spy he sent: Od.24.566.375.

WATCH-TOW'R

Streams from some lonely Watch-tow'r to the Sky: Il.19.407.389.
Where the high Watch-tow'r overlooks the Plain; Il.22.192.463.

WATCH'D

Watch'd by the Sylvan *Genius* of the Place. 1.TrSP.184.401.
Was Captive kept; he watch'd her Night and Day, 2.ChJM.488.39.
Watch'd as she was, yet cou'd He not refrain 2.ChJM.496.39.
Watch'd as she was, yet cou'd not He refrain 2.ChJM.496A.39.
Tho' watch'd, and captive, yet in spight of all, 2.ChJM.518.40.
He watch'd th' Ideas rising in her Mind, 2.RL3.142.178.
And careful watch'd the Planetary Hour. 2.TemF.106.261.
Here, as I watch'd the dying lamps around, 2.ElAb.307.344.
Ascendant Phœbus watch'd that hour with care, 3.Ep2.285.73.
Watch'd both by Envy's and by Flatt'ry's eye: 5.DunB4.36.343.
Strong Guards they plac'd, and watch'd nine Nights entire; Il.9.594.464.
Thus watch'd the *Grecians,* cautious of Surprize, Il.10.219.11.
Had watch'd his *Troy,* and mark'd *Minerva's* Flight; Il.10.603.29.
Minerva watch'd it falling on the Land, Il.22.353.470.
She watch'd him all the Night, and all the Day, Il.23.230.499.
So watch'd the Flames, till now they flam'd no more. Il.23.279.501.
So watch'd the Flames, till now they flame no more. Il.23.279A.501*.
For *Phœbus* watch'd it with superior Care, Il.24.30.536.
Watch'd from the rising to the setting Sun) Il.24.1010.577.
And watch'd all night, all day; a faithful guard. Od.2.393.80.
There watch'd this guardian of his guilty fear, Od.4.703.152.
Jove's daughter *Pallas* watch'd the fav'ring hour. Od.5.489.195.
All night we watch'd, 'till with her orient wheels Od.16.380.124.

WATCHES

'Tis with our *Judgments* as our *Watches,* none 1.EOC.9.239.
And striking Watches the tenth Hour resound. 2.RL1.18A.145.
And Death-watches Physicians. 6.53.24.162.
Shall I ne'er see thee turn my watches key 6.96ii.30Z43.272.
"No more behold thee turn my Watches Key, 6.96ii.65.273.

WATCHFUL

A watchful Sprite, and *Ariel* is my Name. 2.RL1.106.153.
That e'er deserv'd a watchful Spirit's Care; 2.RL2.102.166.
At best more watchful this, but that more strong. 3.EOM2.76.64.
"(So long by watchful Ministers withstood) 3.Ep3.138.104.
So watchful Bruin forms with plastic care 5.DunA1.99.71.
So watchful Bruin forms, with plastic care, 5.DunB1.101.276.
The watchful Mother wafts th' envenom'd Fly. Il.4.163.228.
Watchful he wheels, protects it ev'ry way, Il.5.363.284.
But *Ajax* watchful as his Foe drew near, Il.7.311.379.
Then leaning on his Hand his watchful Head, Il.10.88.6.
Beset with watchful Dogs, and shouting Swains, Il.11.675.65.
Atrides, watchful of th' unwary Foe, Il.13.745.140.
Could charm the Cares of *Nestor's* watchful Soul: Il.14.2.156.
So watchful Shepherds strive to force, in vain, Il.18.199.331.
Their Wives, their Children, and the watchful Band, Il.18.597.351.
Two Spies at distance lurk, and watchful seem Il.18.605.352.
The watchful Caution of his artful Foe. Il.23.837.522.
And pours deep Slumber on their watchful Eyes: Il.24.548.559.
Nor clos'd in sleep his ever-watchful eyes. Od.5.346.188.
Then first my eyes, by watchful toils oppress'd, Od.10.34.341.
Calls, to succeed his cares, the watchful swain; Od.10.95.345.
Here watchful o'er the flocks, in shady bow'rs Od.12.170.440.
Four savage dogs, a watchful guard, attend. Od.14.24.35.
No pow'rful hands are there, no watchful eyes: Od.15.103.73.
(For watchful Age is ready to surmize) Od.15.482.93.
These with their watchful dogs (a constant guard) Od.17.224.142.

WATCHING

(Aye watching o'er his Saints with Eye unseen,) 6.137.3.373.

WATCHINGS

I pass my Watchings o'er thy helpless Years, Il.9.612.464.

WATCHMAN

A drowzy Watchman, that just gives a knock, 5.DunB4.443.384.
A drowzy Watchman in the land of Nod. 5.DunB4.444A.384.
Till the third watchman toll; 6.47.10.128.

WATCHMEN

To rowze the Watchmen of the Publick Weal, 4.EpS2.217.325.

WATER

New Falls of Water murm'ring in his Ear: 1.Mes.70.119.
Here Earth and Water seem to strive again, 1.W-F.12.149.
Around whose rocky sides the water flows: 1.TrPA.40.367.
On this side *Lerna's* pois'nous Water lies, 1.TrSt.533.432.
Soft yielding Minds to Water glide away, 2.RL1.61.150.
Or water all the Quorum ten miles round? 3.Ep3.42.89.
By land, by water, they renew the charge, 4.Arbu.9.96.
The Trees they water, but thou giv'st the fruit; 6.2.27.6.
To her 'tis Water, but to us 'tis Flame: 6.9v.2.21.
Thus Fire is Water, Water Fire, by turns, 6.9v.3.21.
Thus Fire is Water, Water Fire, by turns, 6.9v.3.21.
Put no water at all; 6.91.17.253.
"While Pepper-Water-Worms thy Bait supply'd; 6.96ii.20.270.
With Water purify their Hands, and take Il.1.586.116.
The cleansing Water from the living Spring. Il.9.228.444.
With lukewarm Water wash the Gore away, Il.11.964.78.
The boiling Water bubbles to the Brim: Il.18.410.340.
Soft Rills of Water from the bubbling Springs, Il.21.290.433.
The purest Water of the living Spring; Il.24.372.551.
With copious water the bright vase supplies Od.1.181.41.
With water from the rock, and rosie wine, Od.5.214.181.
With water one, and one with sable wine; Od.5.338.188.
And water her ambrosial couch with tears. Od.7.347.253.
The fuming water bubble o'er the blaze. Od.8.474.288.
We climb'd the beach, and springs of water found, Od.9.97.307.
The water pours; the bubling waters boil: Od.10.424.365.
With copious water the bright vase supplies Od.10.435.365.
And living water from the chrystal spring. Od.10.619.374.
When to the water he his lip applies, Od.11.723.421.
Back from his lip the treach'rous water flies. Od.11.724.421.
Water, instead of wine, is brought in urns, Od.12.427.451.
Where *Arethusa's* sable water glides; Od.13.470.28.
The sable water and the copious mast Od.13.471.29.
Replete with water from the chrystal springs; Od.15.149.75.

WATER'D

Amidst the Plain of some wide-water'd Fen, Il.15.761.225.
And instant, blows the water'd Gardens dry: Il.21.403.437.
(Fair *Ida,* water'd with descending Floods) Il.23.145.495.
The couch, for ever water'd with my tears) Od.17.119.137.

WATERMEN

Of link-boys vile, and watermen obscene; 5.DunB2.100.300.

WATERS

Where dancing Sun-beams on the Waters play'd, 1.PSu.3.71.
Where gentle *Thames* his winding Waters leads 1.PSu.3A.71.
His swelling Waters, and alternate Tydes; 1.W-F.334.182.
Tempt Icy Seas, where scarce the Waters roll, 1.W-F.389.189.
And smooth as shells that gliding waters wear; 1.TrPA.55.367.
And mix thy waters with his reeking blood! 1.TrPA.129.371.
Insulting waters yield a murmuring sound: 1.TrPA.158.372.
A Spring there is, whose Silver Waters show, 1.TrSP.179.401.
Her Snakes, unty'd, Sulphureous Waters drink; 1.TrSt.125.415.
Perpetual Waters o'er the Pavement glide; 1.TrUl.41.467.
And soften'd Sounds along the Waters die. 2.RL2.50.162.
Like Citron-Waters Matrons' Cheeks inflame, 2.RL4.69.189.
O'er dusky Fields and shaded Waters fly, 2.TemF.285.277.
Or moving spirit bade the waters flow; 2.ElAb.254.340.
To Ward, to Waters, Chartres, and the Devil. 3.Ep3.20.85.
From the dry rock who bade the waters flow? 3.Ep3.254.114.
That tells the Waters or to rise, or fall, 3.Ep4.58.142.
So drink with *Waters,* or with *Chartres* eat, 4.HS1.89.13.
From wicked Waters ev'n to godly— 4.JD2.80.141.
And now, on rolling Waters snatch'd away. 4.HOde1.48.153.
And now, by rolling Waters snatch'd away. 4.HOde1.48A.153.
And now, by rolling Waters wash'd away. 4.HOde1.48B.153.
His rapid waters in their passage burn. 5.DunA2.176.123.
His rapid waters in their passage burn. 5.DunB2.184.304.
Whose tuneful whistling makes the waters pass: 5.DunB3.156.327.
In troubled waters, but now sleeps in Port. 5.DunB4.202.362.
Thus from the waters first did rise. 6.5.4A.12.
So Waters putrifie with Rest, and lose 6.17ii.9.56.
The gushing Waters find a Vent below: 6.33.4.99.
The gushing Waters found a Vent below: 6.33.4A.99.
Visits each plant, and waters all the ground: 6.35.30.103.
And to the Murmur of these Waters sleep; 6.87.2.248.
I see thy fountains fall, thy waters roll 6.106ii.3.307.
Where *Pheræ* hears the neighb'ring Waters fall, Il.2.866.165.
And 'midst the Roarings of the Waters dy'd? Il.6.439.348.
The Weight of Waters from *Hyperia's* Spring. Il.6.583.355.
When fierce in War, where *Jardan's* Waters fall, Il.7.163.372.
In sable Streams soft-trickling Waters shed. Il.9.20.432.
Soft *Minyas* rolls his Waters to the Main. Il.11.859.74.
The Weight of Waters saps the yielding Wall, Il.12.25.82.
The wond'ring Waters leave his Axle dry. Il.13.49.107.
The Mass of Waters will no Wind obey; Il.14.25.158.
From the tall Rock the sable Waters flow. Il.16.6.234.
Deriv'd from thee whose Waters wash the Earth, Il.16.211.247.
Spreads his broad Waters o'er the level Plains, Il.17.840.321.
Meanwhile, where *Hellespont's* broad Waters flow Il.18.3.322.

WATERS (CONTINUED)
Deep groan'd the Waters with the dying Sound; ....Il.21.25.422.
Deep groan the Waters with the dying Sound; ....Il.21.25A.422.
With all his refluent Waters circled round) ....Il.21.160.428.
T'avenge his Waters choak'd with Heaps of Dead. ....Il.21.164.428.
Loud flash the Waters to the rushing Fall ....Il.21.272.432.
O'er all th' expanded Plain the Waters spread; ....Il.21.348.435.
And the shrunk Waters in their Chanel boil: ....Il.21.401.436.
The bubbling Waters yield a hissing Sound. ....Il.21.423.437.
The Waters foam, the heavy Smoak aspires: ....Il.21.427.438.
(So, e're a Storm, the Waters heave and roll) ....Il.21.649.449.
As a large Fish, when Winds and Waters roar, ...Il.23.802.521.
Then thro' the World of Waters, they repair ....Il.24.125.540.
There, as the waters o'er his hands he shed, ...Od.2.295.76.
The sacred Sun, above the waters rais'd, ...Od.3.1.85.
(For God had smooth'd the waters of the deep) ....Od.3.190.95.
But five tall barks the winds and waters tost ....Od.3.382.105.
And limpid waters from the living spring. ....Od.3.545.114.
Thus o'er the world of waters *Hermes* flew, ...Od.5.68.175.
A world of waters! far from all the ways ....Od.5.127.178.
What raging winds? what roaring waters round? ....Od.5.390.191.
Ah me! when o'er a length of waters tost, ...Od.5.524.197.
A falling stream with gentler waters glide; ....Od.5.563.199.
Let then thy waters give the weary rest, ...Od.5.574.200.
The waters waft it, and the nymph receives. ....Od.5.593.201.
Where thro' the vales the mazy waters stray? ....Od.6.72.208.
But o'er the world of waters wing'd her way: ....Od.7.100.239.
Visits each plant, and waters all the ground: ....Od.7.171.244.
And healing waters for the bath prepare: ....Od.8.462.288.
The water pours; the bubling waters boil: ....Od.10.424.365.
Cocytus' lamentable waters spread; ....Od.10.611.374.
Then living waters from the chrystal spring; ....Od.11.32.381.
Lash'd by the stroke the frothy waters fly. ....Od.12.207.441.
Like waters bubbling o'er the fiery blaze; ....Od.12.285.446.
Then where a fountain's gurgling waters play, ...Od.12.361.448.
Perpetual waters o'er the pavement glide; ....Od.13.132.8.
And copious waters pure for bathing bear: ....Od.20.193.242.
The cleansing waters from the limpid spring: ....Od.21.287.273.

WATRY
The *Naiads* wept in ev'ry Watry Bow'r, ...1.PSu.7.72.
Fresh rising Blushes paint the watry Glass, ...1.PSu.28.74.
And lonely Woodcocks haunt the watry Glade. ....1.W-F.128.162.
And Pykes, the Tyrants of the watry Plains. ....1.W-F.146.163.
The watry Landskip of the pendant Woods, ...1.W-F.213.169.
T'admit your offspring in your watry reign! ....1.TrPA.143.371.
Not distant far a watry *Lotos* grows; ....1.TrFD.21.386.
Before my Sight a Watry Virgin stood, ...1.TrSP.186.401.
O launch thy Bark, nor fear the watry Plain, ...1.TrSP.250.404.
O'er the wide Earth, and o'er the watry Main, ...1.TrSt.44.411.
For this, my Brother of the watry Reign ....1.TrSt.312.423.
The Floods descending and the watry War, ...1.TrSt.513.431.
And, bound for *Greece*, we plow'd the Watry way; ....1.TrUl.196.472.
Some happier island in the watry waste, ...3.EOM1.106.28.
So Jove's bright bow displays its watry round, ...5.DunA2.165.121.
Shines a broad Mirrour thro' the watry Cave; ....6.142.2B.382.
We launch a Bark to plow the watry Plains, ...Il.1.182.96.
Or milk-white Swans in *Asius'* watry Plains, ...Il.2.541.152.
And *Eteon's* Hills, and *Hyrie's* watry Fields, ...Il.2.591.156.
In fourscore Barks they plow the watry Way. ....Il.2.685.159.
Ulysses follow'd thro' the watry Road, ...Il.2.765.162.
And *Antron's* watry Dens and cavern'd Ground. ....Il.2.852.164.
And *Greece* returning plow the watry Deep. ....Il.3.357.210.
So falls a Poplar, that in watry Ground ....Il.4.552.247.
Where Lakes surround low *Hylè's* watry Plain; ....Il.5.872.308.
Meantime the * Monarch of the watry Main ....Il.13.17.104.
Gambol around him, on the watry way; ....Il.13.44.107.
Rose in huge Ranks, and form'd a watry Wall ....Il.14.454.185.
With watry Drops the Chief they sprinkle round, ...Il.14.509.188.
Command the Sea-God to his watry Reign: ....Il.15.62.197.
The roaring Deeps in watry Mountains rise, ...Il.15.441.214.
And sees the watry Mountains break below. ....Il.15.749.224.
So when a Horseman from the watry Mead ....Il.15.822.228.
With hoary *Nereus*, and the watry Train, ...Il.18.42.325.
Ev'n * He whose Trident sways the watry Reign, ...Il.20.19.393.
Safe in the court, nor tempt the watry way. ....Od.2.290.75.
And lo, with speed we plow the watry way; ....Od.2.323.76.
The watry way, ill-fated if thou try, ...Od.2.412.80.
Thus far ye wander thro' the watry way? ....Od.3.85.90.
While yet we doubted of our watry way; ....Od.3.204.95.
Go then; to *Sparta* take the watry way, ...Od.3.413.106.
The delegate of *Neptune's* watry reign. ....Od.4.522.145.
Like a broad shield amid the watry waste. ....Od.5.360.189.
Lest, in thy slumbers on the watry main, ...Od.8.481.288.
Great *Neptune's* blessing on the watry way: ....Od.9.606.331.
That forc'd *Ulysses* o'er the watry way, ...Od.23.74.322.

WATTS
Well-purg'd, and worthy *W[esle]y, W[att]s*, and *Bl[ome]* ....5.DunA1.126A.78.
Well-purg'd, *W[att]s, Q[uarle]s*, and *Bl[ome]*. ....5.DunA1.126B.78.
W[att]s, B[ake]r, M[ilbour]n, all the poring kind, ...5.DunA3.188A.172.

WAV'D
Then grave *Clarissa* graceful wav'd her Fan; ....2.RL5.7.199.
His Silver Beard wav'd gently o'er his Breast; ....2.TemF.185.270.
But fierce *Atrides* wav'd his Sword and strook ....Il.3.445.213.
Then sudden wav'd his flaming Faulchion round, ...Il.4.616.250.
Then sudden wav'd his unresisted Sword; ....Il.12.220.89.
King *Helenus* wav'd high the *Thracian* Blade, ...Il.13.728.139.
Shorn from the Crest. *Atrides* wav'd his Steel: ....Il.13.771.141.
Part o'er her Shoulders wav'd like melted Gold. ....Il.14.206.170.
Stern *Hector* wav'd his Sword; and standing near ....Il.16.142.243.
Circled their arching Necks, and wav'd in State, ...Il.17.499.307.
Circled their arched Necks, and wav'd in State, ...Il.17.499A.307*.
Wav'd o'er their Backs, and to the Chariot join'd. ....Il.19.431.389.
A glitt'ring spear wav'd awful in her hand. ....Od.1.137.39.

WAV'D (CONTINUED)
Wav'd high, and frown'd upon the stream below. ....Od.5.615.201.
Then wav'd the wand, and then the word was giv'n. ....Od.10.380.363.
Wide o'er the pool thy faulchion wav'd around ....Od.10.638.374.
Now swift I wav'd my faulchion o'er the blood; ....Od.11.61.383.
Shall urge—and wav'd it hissing in her hand. ....Od.19.85.196.
Ulysses wav'd, to rouze the savage war. ....Od.19.510.221.
With manly grasp he wav'd a martial spear, ...Od.20.156.241.

WAV'RING
This way and that, the wav'ring Sails they bend, ...1.TrSt.266.421.
Each Nymph by turns his wav'ring Mind possest, ...2.ChJM.230.25.
But faithless still, and wav'ring as the Wind! ....2.ChJM.478.38.
Loose on the point of ev'ry wav'ring Hour; 4.2HE2.249.183
And clips, like thine, his wav'ring wings. ....6.6i.12.14.
And Youth itself an empty wav'ring State: ....Il.3.148.198.
And ev'ry side of wav'ring Combate tries; ....Il.5.1025.315.
These shall I slight? and guide my wav'ring Mind ....Il.12.277.91.
While wav'ring Counsels thus his Mind engage, ...Il.14.27.158.
Yet suffers least, and sways the wav'ring Fight; ....Il.17.419.303.
The Scale of Conquest ever wav'ring lies , ...Il.19.223.382.
Now, wav'ring doubt succeeds to long despair; ....Od.19.615.226.
Wav'ring his thoughts in dubious balance hung; ....Od.20.14.231.

WAVE
And chalky *Wey*, that rolls a milky Wave: ....1.W-F.344.183.
But wave whate'er to *Cadmus* may belong, ...1.TrSt.19.410.
Colours that change whene'er they wave their Wings. ....2.RL2.68.164.
Wave high, and murmur to the hollow wind, ...2.ElAb.156.332.
Build on the wave, or arch beneath the sand? 3.EOM3.102.102
Heir urges Heir, like Wave impelling Wave: ....4.2HE2.253.183.
Heir urges Heir, like Wave impelling Wave: ....4.2HE2.253.183.
Where wave the tatter'd ensigns of Rag-Fair, ...5.DunA1.27.63.
Like Cimon triumph'd, both on land and wave: ....5.DunA1.84.69.
Of the mixt wave, and all who drink grow dull. 5.DunA2.320.14
Like Cimon, triumph'd both on land and wave: ....5.DunB1.86.275.
Pours into Thames: and hence the mingled wave 5.DunB2.343.314
Where Ribbans wave upon the tye, ...6.61.38.182.
And little Eagles wave their wings in gold. ....6.71.30.203.
Did wave his Wand so white, ...6.79.118.222.
Did wave his Hand so white, ...6.79.118A.222.
Thou who shalt stop, where *Thames'* translucent Wave ....6.142.1.382.
You who shall stop, where *Thames'* translucent Wave ....6.142.1A.382.
O Thou who stop'st, where *Thames'* translucent Wave ....6.142.1B.382.
And if he'll visit me, I'll wave my Right. ....6.143.4.385.
Wash'd by the briny Wave, the pious Train ....Il.1.412.107.
The Wave behind rolls on the Wave before; ....Il.4.481.243.
The Wave behind rolls on the Wave before; ....Il.4.481.243.
Thro' ruin'd Moles the rushing Wave resounds, ...Il.5.118.273.
The Swords wave harmless, and the Javelins fail: ....Il.5.392.285.
And rocky *Imbrus* breaks the rolling Wave: ....Il.13.52.107.
The floating Plumes unnumber'd wave above, ...Il.13.183.114.
And all their Faulchions wave around his Head. ....Il.13.202.115.
Bursts as a Wave, that from the Clouds impends, ...Il.15.752.224.
And instant Death on ev'ry Wave appears. ....Il.15.757.225.
Float in one Sea, and wave before the Wind. ....Il.16.263.249.
Wave their thick Falchions, and their Jav'lins show'r: ....Il.17.818.320.
Iæra now the verdant Wave divides; ....Il.18.58.326.
While the long Pomp the silver Wave divides. ....Il.18.88.327.
The Sea-green Sisters plunge beneath the Wave: ....Il.18.182.331.
The Forests wave, the Mountains nod around; ....Il.20.78.397.
And thus insults him, floating on the Wave ....Il.21.134.427.
Whose ev'ry Wave some wat'ry Monster brings, ...Il.21.139.427.
And beat against it, Wave succeeding Wave; ....Il.21.220.430.
And beat against it, Wave succeeding Wave; ....Il.21.220.430.
'Tis not thy Fate to glut his angry Wave. ....Il.21.337.435.
He wades, and mounts; the parted Wave resounds. ....Il.21.353.435.
To wave Contention with superior Sway; ....Il.23.690.517.
So past the Goddess thro' the closing Wave, ...Il.24.109.539.
O'er the warm *Libyan* wave to spread my sails: ....Od.4.104.124.
His oozy limbs. Emerging from the wave, ...Od.4.543.146.
When to his realm I plow'd the orient wave. ....Od.4.838.158.
Alone, and floating to the wave and wind. ....Od.5.45.173.
Then swift ascending from the azure wave, ...Od.5.70.175.
There all his vessels sunk beneath the wave! ....Od.5.139.178.
A man, an outcast to the storm and wave, ...Od.5.165.179.
A mighty wave rush'd o'er him as he spoke, ...Od.5.403.192.
Long press'd he heav'd beneath the weighty wave, ...Od.5.409.192.
With naked strength, and plunge into the wave. ....Od.5.437.193.
When lifted on a ridgy wave, he spies ....Od.5.504.196.
While thus he thought, a monst'rous wave up-bore ....Od.5.542.198.
Torn with full force, reluctant beats the wave, ...Od.5.551.199.
For rough the way, and distant rolls the wave ....Od.6.43.207.
The lucid wave a spacious bason fills. ....Od.6.102.210.
And plunge the vestures in the cleansing wave: ....Od.6.106.211.
The foul pollution of the briny wave: ....Od.6.260.222.
O'er all his limbs his hands the wave diffuse, ...Od.6.267.223.
Full nine days floating to the wave and wind. ....Od.7.339.253.
With naked force, and shoot along the wave, ...Od.7.361.254.
To plunge it headlong in the whelming wave; ....Od.8.556.292.
With wheat and barley wave the golden fields, ...Od.9.124.310.
Luxuriant on the wave-worn bank he lay, ...Od.10.185.349.
An ample vase receives the smoking wave, ...Od.10.425.365.
No more the vessel plow'd the dreadful wave, ...Od.12.244.443.
There o'er my hands the living wave I pour; ....Od.12.397.450.
All unsustain'd between the wave and sky, ...Od.12.517.457.
Moulders in earth, or welters on the wave, ...Od.14.155.43.
Soon as remote from shore they plow the wave, ...Od.14.377.53.
Then pour'd of offer'd wine the sable wave: ....Od.14.499.60.
And her rich vallies wave with golden corn. ....Od.15.445.92.
Thence born to *Ithaca* by wave and wind; ....Od.15.519.95.
Supply the limpid wave, and fragrant oil: ....Od.17.101.136.
Me with his whelming wave let Ocean shroud! ....Od.20.77.236.
Wash'd with th' effusive wave, are purg'd of gore. ....Od.22.490.313.

WAVE-WORN
Luxuriant on the wave-worn bank he lay, ...Od.10.185.349.

WAVER
The empty corse to waver with the wind. ....Od.22.508.313.

WAVER'D
A sliding Noose, and waver'd in the Wind. ....2.ChWB.396.76.

WAVES
And with Celestial Tears augments the Waves. ....1.W-F.210.169.
And floating Forests paint the Waves with Green. ....1.W-F.216.169.
The figur'd Streams in Waves of Silver roll'd, ...1.W-F.335.182.
And the hush'd Waves glide softly to the Shore. ....1.W-F.354.184.
And softly lay me on the Waves below! ....1.TrSP.208.403.
Within, the Waves in softer Murmurs glide, ...1.TrUl.29.466.
Smooth flow the Waves, the Zephyrs gently play, ...2.RL2.51.162.
Grave *Zoroaster* waves the circling Wand: ....2.TemF.98.260.
Clouds interpose, waves roar, and winds arise. ....2.ElAb.246.339.
Where winds can carry, or where waves can roll, ...4.1HE6.70.241.
Love-whisp'ring woods, and lute-resounding waves. ....5.DunB4.306.374.
Waves to the tepid Zephyrs of the spring, ...5.DunB4.422.383.
Int'rest, that waves on Party-colour'd wings: ....5.DunB4.538.395.
And thought *Herself* just risen from the Waves. ....6.9vi.2.21.
The Waves run frighted to the Shores. ....6.78ii.7.216.
The Goddess-Mother heard. The Waves divide; ....Il.1.470.110.
The Goddess spoke: The rowling Waves unclose; ....Il.1.562.115.
In thirty Sail the sparkling Waves divide, ...Il.2.888.166.
There whelm'd with Waves the gawdy Warrior lies; ....Il.2.1066.172.
Eyes the rough Waves, and tir'd returns at last. ....Il.5.739.302.
The Waves scarce heave, the Face of Ocean sleeps, ...Il.7.73.366.
And whelm'd beneath thy Waves, drop the huge Wall: ....Il.7.553.392.
Floats in rich Waves, and spreads the Court of *Jove*. ....Il.8.469.419.
Heaps Waves on Waves, and bids th' *Ægean* roar; ....Il.9.8.431.
Heaps Waves on Waves, and bids th' *Ægean* roar; ....Il.9.8.431.
His azure Length in easy Waves extends, ...Il.11.51.36.
Drives the wild Waves, and tosses all the Deeps. ....Il.11.386.51.
And whelms the smoaky Ruin in the Waves. ....Il.12.32.82.
The parting Waves before his Coursers fly; ....Il.13.48.107.
The Waves behind impel the Waves before, ...Il.13.1004.152.
The Waves behind impel the Waves before, ...Il.13.1004.152.
The Waves just heaving on the purple Deeps; ....Il.14.22.158.
And his hush'd Waves lie silent on the Main. ....Il.14.280.175.
By thy black Waves, tremendous *Styx!* that flow ....Il.15.43.195.
My Court beneath the hoary Waves I keep, ...Il.15.216.205.
Waves when he nods, and lightens as he turns: ....Il.15.733.224.
Where some swoln River disembogues his Waves, ...Il.17.311.299.
To whelm some City under Waves of Fire, ...Il.17.826.321.
In Ocean's Waves th' unwilling Light of Day ....Il.18.284.335.
In living Silver seem'd the Waves to roll, ...Il.18.703.357.
Above the Waves that blush'd with early Red, ...Il.19.2.371.
Those beauteous Fields where *Hyllus'* Waves are roll'd, ...Il.20.451.413.
Arm'd with his Sword, high-brandish'd o'er the Waves; ....Il.21.23.422.
Or pant and heave beneath the floating Waves. ....Il.21.33.422.
Then blacken'd the wild Waves; the Murmur rose; ....Il.21.277.432.
The Waves flow after, wheresoe'er he wheels, ...Il.21.287.432.
And still indignant bounds above the Waves. ....Il.21.308.433.
And a Foam whitens on the purple Waves. ....Il.21.381.436.
Now glow the Waves, the Fishes pant for Breath, ...Il.21.412.437.
In his right Hand he waves the Weapon round, ...Il.22.403.472.
Sperchius! whose Waves in mazy Errors lost ....Il.23.178.497.
The ruddy Morning rises o'er the Waves; ....Il.24.22.535.
Down plung'd the Maid; (the parted Waves resound) ....Il.24.105.539.
The Waves of People at his Word divide, ...Il.24.896.573.
Whose bounds the deep circumfluent waves embrace. ....Od.1.230.43.
O'er the wide waves success thy ways attends: ....Od.2.310.76.
High o'er the roaring waves the spreading sails ....Od.2.466.83.
His glowing axle in the western waves; ....Od.4.488.143.
Round the descending nymph the waves redounding roar. ....Od.4.578.147.
White curl the waves, and the vex'd ocean roars. ....Od.4.788.156.
Ride the wild waves, and quit the safer shore? ....Od.4.941.162.
The winds and waves he tempts in early bloom, ...Od.4.948.162.
To break the rowling waves, and ruffling storm: ....Od.4.1106.169.
In snowy waves flow'd glitt'ring on the ground. ....Od.5.298.185.
Of surging waves, and steer the steady course) ....Od.5.328.187.
The wild waves fury, here I fix'd remain: ....Od.5.459.195.
And bear him soft on broken waves away; ....Od.5.493.195.
Roar the wild waves; beneath, is sea profound! ....Od.5.529.198.
Behind him far, upon the purple waves ....Od.5.592.201.
Active he bounds; the flashing waves divide: ....Od.6.266.223.
Where o'er the furrows waves the golden grain: ....Od.6.310.225.
Floats a strong shout along the waves of air. ....Od.6.358.229.
Tost by rude tempest thro' a war of waves. ....Od.8.28.263.
Ev'n the stern God that o'er the waves presides, ...Od.8.613.295.
Where high *Neritus* waves his woods in air: ....Od.9.22.302.
Instant her circling wand the Goddess waves, ...Od.10.276.356.
Where rocks controul his waves with ever-during mounds. ....Od.11.14.379.
But if his herds ye seize, beneath the waves ....Od.11.142.387.
Here lakes profound, there floods oppose their waves, ...Od.11.194.391.
Around, a spacious arch of waves he throws, ...Od.11.291.396.
Earth trembles, and the waves confess their God. ....Od.11.306.397.
Here in the court, or yonder on the waves; ....Od.11.411.404.
Has fate oppress'd thee in the roaring waves, ...Od.11.496.408.
Has Fate oppress'd me on the roaring waves! ....Od.11.502.408.
Stern *Minos* waves a mace of burnish'd gold; ....Od.11.698.419.
And pines with thirst amidst a sea of waves: ....Od.11.722.421.
Swift o'er the waves we fly; the fresh'ning gales ....Od.11.793.426.
'Till from the waves th' *Ææan* hills arise. ....Od.12.2.427.
Thro' the vast waves the dreadful wonders move, ...Od.12.73.434.
And the waves flashing seem to burn with fires. ....Od.12.82.435.
Breaks the wild waves, and forms a dang'rous streight; ....Od.12.126.437.
Oh if thy vessel plow the direful waves ....Od.12.133.438.
And waves below, at once forgot to move! ....Od.12.203.441.
Hush'd the loud winds, and charm'd the waves to sleep. ....Od.12.205.441.
Tumultous waves embroil'd the bellowing flood, ...Od.12.242.443.
Bear wide thy course, nor plow those angry waves ....Od.12.260.445.

WAVES (CONTINUED)
The rough rock roars; tumultuous boil the waves; ....Od.12.283.446.
And dire *Charybdis* rolls her thund'ring waves. ....Od.12.506.457.
The mast refunded on her refluent waves. ....Od.12.522.458.
Within, the waves in softer murmurs glide, ...Od.13.120.7.
With winds and waves I held unequal strife; ....Od.14.348.51.
When o'er the waves you plow'd the desp'rate way. ....Od.16.26.103.
The Goddess beck'ning waves her deathless hands; ....Od.16.178.112.
She said, and o'er him waves her wand of gold; ....Od.16.186.112.
She waves her golden wand, and reassumes ....Od.16.476.130.
Floats in bright waves redundant o'er the ground. ....Od.18.342.184.
Crete awes the circling waves, a fruitful soil! ....Od.19.196.201.
Out-lives the tumult of conflicting waves, ...Od.23.254.335.
And howling *Scylla* whirls her thund'rous waves, ...Od.23.354.341.

WAVING
The Winds to breathe, the waving Woods to move, ...1.PAu.41.83.
Here waving Groves a checquer'd Scene display, ...1.W-F.17.150.
Here *Ceres'* Gifts in waving Prospect stand, ...1.W-F.39.152.
Wind the shrill Horn, or spread the waving Net. ....1.W-F.96.159.
(His Sea-green Mantle waving with the Wind) ....1.W-F.350.184.
No more my Robes in waving Purple flow, ...1.TrSP.81.397.
In waving Circles whirl'd a Fun'ral Brand; ....1.TrSt.157.416.
around her Shoulders flew the waving Vest. ....1.TrUl.105.469.
And shakes the waving Forests on his Sides! ....1.TrUl.233.473.
A brighter Wash; to curl their waving Hairs, ...2.RL2.97.165.
"There towns aerial on the waving tree. ....3.EOM3.182.111.
A waving Glow his bloomy beds display, ...3.Ep4.83.145.
His bloomy Beds a waving Glow display, ...3.Ep4.83A.145.
A waving Glow the bloomy beds display, ...3.Ep4.83B.145.
With scarlet hats, wide waving, circles round, ...5.DunA2.10.97.
With scarlet hats wide-waving circled round, ...5.DunB2.14.297.
Hide the deceitful Ground, whose waving Heads ....6.26i.2.79.
With nodding Plumes and Groves of waving Spears. ....Il.2.182.137.
Where high *Neritos* shakes his waving Woods, ...Il.2.770.162.
The waving Horse-hair nodded on his Head. ....Il.3.418.212.
The Steeds fly trembling from his waving Sword; ....Il.11.207.44.
The crowded Bulwarks blaze with waving Arms, ...Il.12.310.93.
Whose waving Woods o'erhung the Deeps below, ...Il.13.20.105.
The waving Silver seem'd to blush with Blood. ....Il.18.618.352.
Another Field rose high with waving Grain; ....Il.18.637.354.
And shook his Jav'lin like a waving Flame. ....Il.20.490.415.
Where waving groves on airy *Neion* grow, ...Od.1.239.44.
Along the waving fields their way they hold, ...Od.3.627.118.
On whose high branches, waving with the storm, ...Od.5.84.176.
Where waving shades obscure the mazy streams. ....Od.6.250.222.
She added not, but waving as she wheel'd ....Od.6.377.230.
Fields waving high with heavy crops are seen, ...Od.9.153.312.
Then sudden whirling like a waving flame ....Od.10.383.363.
But as my waving sword the blood surrounds, ...Od.11.102.385.
Around her shoulders flew the waving vest, ...Od.13.272.19.
And shakes the waving forests on his sides. ....Od.13.400.26.

WAVY
Such wavy ringlets o'er his shoulders flow! ....Od.4.202.129.
His hyacinthine locks descend in wavy curls. ....Od.6.274.224.
If from yon justling rocks and wavy war ....Od.12.256.444.
In wavy gold thy summer vales are dress'd; ....Od.19.131.199.
Back from his brows in wavy ringlets fly ....Od.23.155.328.
The gay *Aurora* in the wavy main: ....Od.23.262.336.

WAX
We form like Wax, and mold them as we please. ....2.ChJM.112.20.
She took the Wards in Wax before the Fire, ...2.ChJM.510.40.
When numerous Wax-lights in bright Order blaze, ...2.RL3.168.182.
Or wane and wax alternate like the Moon. ....2.TemF.486.287.
Now pox on those who shew a *Court in Wax!* ....4.JD4.206.43.
"Mere Wax as yet, you fashion him with ease, ...4.2HE2.9.165.
The ductile wax with busy hands I mold, ...Od.12.208.441.
The wax dissolv'd beneath the burning ray; ....Od.12.211.442.

WAX-LIGHTS
When numerous Wax-lights in bright Order blaze, ...2.RL3.168.182.

WAXEN
Their Waxen Works, or from the Roof depend. ....1.TrUl.40.467.
Such waxen Noses, stately, staring things, ...4.JD4.210.43.
Assert their waxen Domes, and buzzing Progeny. ....Il.16.319.255.
Their waxen works, or from the roof depend. ....Od.13.131.8.

WAY
Prepare the Way! a God, a God appears. ....1.Mes.30.116.
Be smooth ye Rocks, ye rapid Floods give way! ....1.Mes.36.116.
Thus *Pegasus*, a nearer way to take, ...1.EOC.150.257.
The growing Labours of the lengthen'd Way, ...1.EOC.230.265.
A certain *Bard* encountring on the Way, ...1.EOC.268.270.
But ev'n those Clouds at last adorn its Way, ...1.EOC.472.292.
The *truest Notions* in the *easiest way*. ....1.EOC.656.314.
But when its way th'impetuous Passion found, ...1.TrSP.129.399.
If leaving *Polybus*, I took my Way ....1.TrSt.89.413.
But rend the Reins, and bound a diff'rent way, ...1.TrSt.188.418.
In vain the Chiefs contriv'd a specious way, ...1.TrSt.192.418.
This way and that, the wav'ring Sails they bend, ...1.TrSt.266.421.
Thro' violated Nature force his way, ...1.TrSt.332.424.
Wings on the whistling Winds his rapid way, ...1.TrSt.438.428.
With his broad Shield oppos'd, he forc'd his way ....1.TrSt.528.432.
And to the Regal Palace bent his way; ....1.TrSt.536.432.
Scorns not to take our *Argos* in her Way. ....1.TrSt.811.443.
Regardless, furious he pursues his way; ....1.TrES.19.450.
Sarpedon's Friend; Across the Warrior's Way, ...1.TrES.99.453.
Drives the sharp Rock; the solid Beams give way, ...1.TrES.196.456.
And, bound for *Greece*, we plow'd the Watry way; ....1.TrUl.196.472.
He spoke with Scorn, and turn'd another way— ....2.ChJM.220.25.
Each, in his own Opinion, went his Way; ....2.ChJM.225.25.
He spoke; and turn'd, with Scorn, another way— ....2.ChJM.220A.25.
But prove the Scourge to lash you on your Way: ....2.ChJM.288.28.

WAY (CONTINUED)

His Task perform'd, he sadly went his Way, 2.ChJM.363.31.
Secret, and undescry'd, he took his Way, 2.ChJM.537.41.
Pray Heav'n, this Magick work the proper Way: 2.ChJM.773.52.
"Let that frail Thing, weak Woman, have her way. 2.ChWB.194.65.
Not with my Body, in a filthy way— 2.ChWB.232.68.
(This by the Way, but to my Purpose now.) 2.ChWB.376.75.
The *Sylphs* thro' mystick Mazes guide their Way, 2.RL1.92.152.
Resolv'd to win, he meditates the way, 2.RL2.31.161.
Where the gilt *Chariot* never marks the Way, 2.RL4.155.196.
Where the gilt *Chariot* never mark'd the Way, 2.RL4.155A.196.
Earth shakes her nodding Tow'rs, the Ground gives way; 2.RL5.51.203.
Steep its Ascent, and slipp'ry was the Way; 2.TemF.28.255.
Pervious to Winds, and open ev'ry way. 2.TemF.427.284.
A Lye and Truth contending for the way; 2.TemF.490.287.
And follow still where Fortune leads the way; 2.TemF.518.289.
(While the long fun'rals blacken all the way) 2.Elegy.40.366.
Far as the solar walk, or milky way; 3.EOM1.102.27.
Correct old Time, and teach the Sun his way; 3.EOM2.22A.57.
Who forms the phalanx, and who points the way? 3.EOM3.108.103.
Ask of the Learn'd the way, the Learn'd are blind, 3.EOM4.19.129.
But some way leans and hearkens to the kind. 3.EOM4.40.131.
It hurries all too fast to mark their way. 3.Ep1.32.18.
To Toast our wants and wishes, is her way; 3.Ep2.88.57.
Lets Fops or Fortune fly which way they will; 3.Ep2.265.71.
And turn th' unwilling steeds another way: 3.Ep3.194.109.
Whose Cause-way parts the vale with shady rows? 3.Ep3.259.114.
Who *live* at *Court,* for going once that Way! 4.JD4.23.27.
"No Lessons now are taught the *Spartan* way: 4.JD4.93.33.
A dire Dilemma! either way I'm sped, 4.Arbu.31.98.
As shallow streams run dimpling all the way. 4.Arbu.316.118.
To catch and then to starve by way of Cure: 4.JD2A.10.132.
And punish'd him that put it in his way. 4.2HE2.26.167.
And Peers give way, exalted as they are, 4.2HE2.106.173.
One, who believes as Tindal leads the way, 4.1HE6.64.241.
Yet to his Guest tho' no way sparing, 4.HS6.169.261.
And win my way by yielding to the tyde. 4.1HE1.34.281.
The way they take is strangely round about. 4.EpS2.125.320.
Full in the middle way there stood a lake, 5.DunA2.65.105.
"And see! my son, the hour is on its way, 5.DunA3.115.160.
Let all give way—and Durgen may be read. 5.DunA3.162.165.
Let all give way—and Morris may be read. 5.DunA3.162A.165.
And licks up every blockhead in the way. 5.DunA3.298.184.
Already, Opera prepares the way, 5.DunA3.303.185.
Full in the middle way there stood a lake, 5.DunB2.69.299.
"And see, my son! the hour is on its way, 5.DunB3.123.325.
Let all give way—and Morris may be read. 5.DunB3.168.328.
But lick up ev'ry blockhead in the way. 5.DunB3.296.334.
Already Opera prepares the way, 5.DunB3.301.334.
And licks up ev'ry blockhead in the way. 5.DunB3.296A.334.
Thou, only thou, directing all our way! 5.DunB4.296.373.
They to Salvation shew the arduous way, 6.2.28.6.
Th' *Arabian* coast, and waft us on our way. 6.4v.8.11.
And yet is ever on the way. 6.6ii.8.14.
Right then, there passen by the Way, 6.14i.7.41.
At once our means, our end, our guide, our way, 6.23.19.73.
At once our Strength, our Aid, our guide, our way, 6.23.19A.73.
Fate rules us: then to Fate give way! 6.24iii(a).3.75.
Like eyes a-squint, look every way but straight. 6.38.11Z8.108.
There starve and pray, for that's the way to heav'n. 6.45.22.125.
To find that better Way. 6.50.32.147.
To know the better Way. 6.50.32B.147*.
See there! you're always in my Way! 6.64.10.189.
Sore mutt'ring all the way, 6.79.138.222.
Was there no other Way to set him free? 6.96iv.93.279.
Has but one way to teaze—by *Law.* 6.116ii.5.326.
The only way to save 'em from our A[sse]s. 6.131ii.2.360.
Now frisking this, and then that way, 6.135.4.366.
Now flurting this and now that way, 6.135.4A.366.
Two Trav'lers found an Oyster in their Way; 6.145.2.388.
To take the only way to be forgiven. 6.146.8.389.
Achilles with *Patroclus* took his Way, Il.1.402.107.
Which held to *Juno* in a chearful way, Il.1.754.123.
While to the Fleet *Atrides* bends his way. Il.2.64.130.
We march to War if thou direct the Way. Il.2.411.147.
And lead to War, when Heav'n directs the Way. Il.2.519.151.
Breathing Revenge, in Arms they take their Way Il.2.643.157.
In fourscore Barks they plow the watry Way. Il.2.685.159.
Remember *Troy,* and give the Vengeance way. Il.4.64.224.
And Heav'n shall act as we direct the way. Il.4.90.224.
Stung with the Shame, within the winding Way, Il.4.444.241.
Slow he gave way, the rest tumultuous fled; Il.4.583.249.
His Arms resound, the Spirit wings its way. Il.5.56.269.
Watchful he wheels, protects it ev'ry way, Il.5.363.284.
To *Mars,* who sate remote, they bent their way; Il.5.445.289.
Flush'd with Celestial Blood pursu'd his way, Il.5.525.294.
Thro' his broad Belt the Weapon forc'd its way; Il.5.666.300.
And foam impervious cross the Wand'rer's way, Il.5.737.302.
Forc'd he gives way, and sternly quits the Ground. Il.5.775.303.
Lash'd her white Steeds along th' Aerial Way. Il.5.957.312.
Loth I gave way, and warn'd our *Argive* Bands: Il.5.1017.315.
Great *Ajax* first to Conquest led the way, Il.6.7.322.
A long, forlorn, uncomfortable Way! Il.6.248.338.
Stood in the Gates, and ask'd what way she bent Il.6.474.350.
To *Ilion's* steepy Tow'r she bent her way, Il.6.480.350.
Swift thro' the Town he trod his former way, Il.6.489.350.
Swift thro' the Town the Warrior bends his way. Il.6.651.359.
And now the Warriors passing on the way, Il.6.664.360.
Once more impetuous dost thou bend thy way, Il.7.31.364.
Deep in a winding Way his Breast assail'd, Il.7.175.372.
And cease the Strife when *Hector* shows the way. Il.7.348.381.
To the black Ships *Idæus* bent his way: Il.7.457.387.
To wait th' Event, the Herald bent his way. Il.7.491.388.
The Spear with erring Haste mistook its way, Il.8.151.405.
Who plow'd, with Fates averse, the wat'ry way; Il.8.655.427.
This way and that, the boiling Deeps are tost; Il.9.9.431.

WAY (CONTINUED)

Swift thro' the Gates the Guards direct their way. Il.9.110.437.
Then from the Royal Tent they take their way; Il.9.232.444.
Then from the Royal Tent they took their way; Il.9.232A.444.
Content to follow when we lead the way. Il.10.141.8.
Thro' yon' black Camps to bend my dang'rous way, Il.10.261.13.
0 thou! for ever present in my way, Il.10.329.17.
With deathful Thoughts they trace the dreary way, Il.10.354.18.
Ev'n to the Royal Tent pursue my way, Il.10.385.21.
When, on the hollow way, th' approaching Tread Il.10.403.21.
Moving this way, or hast'ning to the Fleet; Il.10.406.21.
Now lost, now seen, they intercept his way, Il.10.429.23.
On Sheep or Goats, resistless in his way, Il.10.566.27.
Safe to the Ships, he wisely clear'd the way, Il.10.573.28.
Thick'ning this way, and gath'ring on my Ear; Il.10.627.30.
But swift thro' rustling Thickets bursts her way; Il.11.158.42.
Thro' the mid Field the routed urge their way. Il.11.218.45.
Bid him give way; but issue forth Commands, Il.11.245.46.
Mark how this way yon' bending Squadrons yield! Il.11.449.54.
Trembling gave way, and turn'd his Back to Flight, Il.11.559.58.
Then back to *Pyle* triumphant take my way. Il.11.893.75.
Proceed on Foot, and *Hector* lead the way. Il.12.90.84.
The moving Legions speed their headlong way: Il.12.120.85.
In airy Circles wings his painful way, Il.12.238.90.
To right, to left, unheeded take your way, Il.12.281.91.
Regardless, furious, he pursues his way; Il.12.363.94.
Sarpedon's Friend; A-cross the Warrior's way, Il.12.453.98.
Drives the sharp Rock; the solid Beams give way, Il.12.550.101.
Gambol around him, on the watry way; Il.13.44.107.
The Father of the Floods pursues his way; Il.13.58.107.
The close-compacted Legions urg'd their way: Il.13.188.114.
Trojans, be firm; this Arm shall make your way Il.13.205.115.
The crashing Bones before its Force gave way; Il.13.773.141.
Where yonder Heroes faint, I bend my way, Il.13.944.150.
Supported on their Spears, they took their way, Il.14.45.160.
Slow moving on; *Atrides* leads the way. Il.14.154.165.
Thro' Heav'n, thro' Earth, and all th' aerial Way; Il.14.200.169.
They wing their way, and *Imbrus'* Sea-beat Soil, Il.14.318.178.
O'er Earth and Seas, and thro' th' aerial way, Il.14.350.179.
My self, ye *Greeks!* my self will lead the way. Il.14.436.184.
The Legions march, and *Neptune* leads the way: Il.14.444.185.
Nor dare to act, but when we point the way. Il.15.56.196.
As some way-faring Man, who wanders o'er Il.15.86.199.
And thou great *Mars,* begin and shew the way. Il.15.121.201.
Forgive me Gods, and yield my Vengeance way: Il.15.129.201.
And various *Iris* wing their airy way. Il.15.169.203.
Ev'n I will make thy fiery Coursers way, Il.15.294.208.
When lo! a Lyon shoots across the way: Il.15.312.209.
A sudden Road! a long and ample way. Il.15.409.213.
Force, to the Fleet and Tents, th' impervious way. Il.15.473.215.
And had the Weapon found the destin'd way, Il.15.538.217.
To some great City thro' the publick way; Il.15.825.228.
Pour from their Mansions by the broad High-way, Il.16.315.255.
Bore down half *Troy,* in his resistless way, Il.16.478.261.
Now *Greece* gives way, and great *Epigeus* falls; Il.16.699.271.
This way and that, the ratt'ling Thicket bends, Il.16.927.279.
Apollo dreadful stops thy middle way; Il.16.952.280.
He faints; the Soul unwilling wings her way, Il.16.1032.283.
Come, thro' yon' Squadrons let us hew the Way, Il.17.201.295.
Pass'd this, and that way, thro' the Ranks of Fight: Il.17.768.318.
What Sorrow dictates, but no Word found way. Il.17.784.319.
Troy pours along, and this way rolls our Fate. Il.17.800.319.
Within, without the Trench, and all the way, Il.17.851.321.
Attend her Way. Wide-opening part the Tides, Il.18.87.327.
Meantime, unweary'd with his heavenly Way, Il.18.283.335.
Then swift pursue thee on the darksome way. Il.18.390.340.
She, as a Falcon cuts th' Aerial way, Il.18.710.357.
All trod the dark, irremeable Way: Il.19.312.385.
Not brighter, *Phœbus* in th' Æthereal Way, Il.19.436.389.
Apollo wedg'd him in the Warrior's Way, Il.20.110.398.
But lest some adverse God now cross his Way, Il.20.156.400.
Cœrulean *Neptune,* rose, and led the Way. Il.20.173.400.
Forc'd thro' his brazen Helm its furious Way, Il.20.460.413.
This way and that, the spreading Torrent roars; Il.20.573.418.
Ploughs thro' the boiling Surge his desp'rate Way. Il.21.256.431.
The Plant uprooted to his Weight gave way, Il.21.270.432.
So, when the Falcon wings her way above, Il.21.575.446.
He comes, and Desolation marks his way! Il.21.624.448.
To check my Conquests in the middle way: Il.22.24.453.
Where lyes my Way? To enter in the Wall? Il.22.138.458.
Obliquely wheeling thro' th' aerial Way; Il.22.186.463.
Exert thy Will: I give the Fates their Way. Il.22.240.465.
Sign'd to the Troops, to yield his Foe the Way, Il.22.269.466.
To the dark Realm the Spirit wings its Way, Il.22.455.474.
No more their Way the startled Horses held; Il.23.471.509.
Since great *Minerva* wings their rapid Way, Il.23.485.509.
Observes the Compass of the hollow way. Il.23.498.510.
This narrow way? Take larger Field (he cry'd) Il.23.508.510.
Already at their Heels they wing their Way, Il.23.528.511.
He well observ'd the Chief who led the way, Il.23.535.511.
And other Steeds, than lately led the Way? Il.23.543.511.
With frantick Fury from the destin'd Way. Il.23.551.511.
Not but (my Friend) 'tis still the wiser way Il.23.689.517.
The brave *Epeians* gave my Glory way, Il.23.727.519.
She urg'd her Fav'rite on the rapid Way, Il.23.919.525.
(The Way fair *Iris* led) to upper Air. Il.24.126.540.
Guard of his Life, and Partner of his Way. Il.24.190.544.
Guard of thy Life, and Partner of thy Way. Il.24.220.546.
And lead thy way with heav'nly Augury: Il.24.362.551.
Now forward fares the Father on his way, Il.24.407.552.
Thus arm'd, swift *Hermes* steers his airy way, Il.24.423.553.
My Steps, and send thee, Guardian of my way. Il.24.462.556.
Safe to *Pelides'* Tent conduct my way. Il.24.528.558.
Guard of thy Life, and Partner of thy Way. Il.24.538.558.
For him, thro' hostile Camps I bent my way, Il.24.622.562.
Forth, by the flaming Lights, they bend their way, Il.24.814.571.

WAY (CONTINUED)

Be humbled all, and lead ye Great! the way. ..... Od.2.196.71.
Unnumber'd Birds glide thro' th' aerial way, ... Od.2.211.72.
Safe in the court, nor tempt the watry way. ..... Od.2.290.75.
And lo, with speed we plow the watry way; ..... Od.2.323.76.
To seek *Ulysses* thro' the wat'ry way. ..... Od.2.405.80.
The watry way, ill-fated if thou try, ... Od.2.412.80.
With rapid step the Goddess urg'd her way; ..... Od.2.443.82.
Thus all the night they stem the liquid way, ... Od.2.474.84.
She spoke, and led the way with swiftest speed: ..... Od.3.39.88.
As swift, the youth pursu'd the way she led; ..... Od.3.40.88.
Thus far ye wander thro' the watry way? ..... Od.3.85.90.
Dauntless we rov'd; *Achilles* led the way: ..... Od.3.130.92.
While yet we doubted of our watry way; ..... Od.3.204.95.
With rapid swiftness cut the liquid way, ... Od.3.215.96.
Mean time from flaming *Troy* we cut the way, ... Od.3.350.103.
Go then; to *Sparta* take the watry way, ... Od.3.413.106.
Guides of thy road, companions of thy way. ..... Od.3.418.107.
And be thy son companion of his way. ..... Od.3.473.110.
Then sunk the Sun, and darken'd all the way. ..... Od.3.618.117.
Along the waving fields their way they hold, ... Od.3.627.118.
What godhead interdicts the wat'ry way? ..... Od.4.574.147.
What Godhead interdicts the wat'ry way? ..... Od.4.632.149.
But now to *Pyle* permit my destin'd way, ... Od.4.817.157.
Nor oars to cut th' immeasurable way. ..... Od.5.25.172.
With fraud defeated measure back their way. ..... Od.5.37.172.
What oars to cut the long laborious way? ..... Od.5.182.180.
And prosp'rous gales to waft thee on thy way. ..... Od.5.216.182.
Nor my return the end, nor this the way, ... Od.5.225.182.
Then to the neighb'ring forest led the way. ..... Od.5.304.185.
Full sev'nteen nights he cut the foamy way; ..... Od.5.355.189.
Go, wander helpless on the wat'ry way: ..... Od.5.481.195.
Before the wand'rer smooths the wat'ry way, ... Od.5.578.200.
To prowling bears, or lions in their way. ..... Od.5.611.201.
Haste, to the limpid stream direct thy way, ... Od.6.35.206.
For rough the way, and distant rolls the wave ..... Od.6.43.207.
Hither the Goddess wing'd th' aereal way, ... Od.6.55.208.
Say, with thy garments shall I bend my way ..... Od.6.71.208.
With conscious strength elate, he bends his way ..... Od.6.157.216.
To cloath the naked, and thy way to guide— ..... Od.6.235.221.
Lo, to the Palace I direct thy way: ..... Od.6.304.225.
We bend our way: a bubling fount distills ..... Od.6.351.229.
And to the lofty palace bend thy way: ..... Od.6.362.229.
A child may point the way. With earnest gait ..... Od.6.365.229.
To town *Ulysses* took the winding way. ..... Od.7.18.234.
And point the wand'ring traveler his way: ..... Od.7.36.235.
On canvas wings to cut the wat'ry way; ..... Od.7.47.235.
But o'er the world of waters wing'd her way: ..... Od.7.100.239.
To *Jove,* who guides the wand'rer on his way; ..... Od.7.221.247.
To *Jove,* who guides the wand'rer on his way. ..... Od.7.241.248.
And shine before him all the desart way: ..... Od.7.274.249.
And gave the gales to waft me on the way. ..... Od.7.352.253.
Why not her self did she conduct the way, ... Od.7.387.255.
Jove bids to set the stranger on his way, ... Od.7.404.256.
Then to the Council seat they bend their way, ... Od.8.5.261.
In state they move; *Alcinous* leads the way: ..... Od.8.44.264.
Or swifter in the race devour the way: ..... Od.8.102.268.
In state they move, *Alcinous* leads the way: ..... Od.8.106.268.
Clytonius sprung: he wing'd the rapid way, ... Od.8.131.270.
Sudden th' irremeable way he trod, ... Od.8.259.276.
Or thro' cærulean billows plow the way: ..... Od.8.284.278.
Stern *Vulcan* homeward treads the starry way: ..... Od.8.344.282.
Thus far ye wander thro' the wat'ry way? ..... Od.9.300.318.
This way and that, I cast to save my friends, ... Od.9.503.326.
Great *Neptune's* blessing on the watry way: ..... Od.9.606.331.
'Till all the coward thoughts of death gave way. ..... Od.10.57.342.
Thus fierce he said: we sighing went our way, ... Od.10.87.343.
So near the pastures, and so short the way, ... Od.10.98.345.
Who blindly follow where she leads the way. ..... Od.10.265.355.
His swelling heart deny'd the words their way: ..... Od.10.290.357.
They blindly follow where she leads the way. ..... Od.10.304.359.
And bade him guide the way, resolv'd to go. ..... Od.10.312.359.
Alone, unfriended, will I tempt my way; ..... Od.10.323.360.
Then rise and follow where I lead the way. ..... Od.10.504.368.
The dark descent, and who shall guide the way? ..... Od.10.595.372.
The northern winds shall wing thee on thy way. ..... Od.10.601.372.
Let him, Oraculous, the end, the way ..... Od.10.642.374.
And down he hasten'd, but forgot the way; ..... Od.10.666.375.
Who eyes their motion, who shall trace their way? ..... Od.10.690.376.
To tread the downward, melancholy way? ..... Od.11.117.386.
Dire is the region, dismal is the way! ..... Od.11.193.391.
But from the dark dominions speed thy way, ... Od.11.269.394.
But let our King direct the glorious way ..... Od.11.432.405.
Down to these worlds I trod the dismal way, ... Od.11.769.424.
Here *Phœbus* rising in th' etherial way, ... Od.12.5.430.
Spread your broad sails, and plow the liquid way: ..... Od.12.36.431.
Plows o'er that roaring surge its desp'rate way; ..... Od.12.80.435.
And all the monsters of the wat'ry way; ..... Od.12.120.437.
Thence to *Trinacria's* shore you bend your way, ... Od.12.160.439.
Swift to her dome the Goddess held her way. ..... Od.12.179.440.
New chains they add, and rapid urge the way, ... Od.12.236.443.
Yet safe return'd— *Ulysses* led the way. ..... Od.12.251.444.
And thou whose guiding hand directs our way, ... Od.12.258.445.
We bend our course, and stem the desp'rate way; ..... Od.12.279.445.
And toss with rising storms the wat'ry way, ... Od.12.344.448.
Sheds her bright beam, pursue the destin'd way. ..... Od.12.350.448.
Or fowl that screaming haunt the wat'ry way. ..... Od.12.392.450.
Mean-time *Lampetiè* mounts th' aereal way, ... Od.12.443.452.
Whose radiant lamp adorns the azure way, ... Od.12.453.453.
The mast gives way, and crackling as it bends, ... Od.12.481.455.
Fast by the rocks beheld the desp'rate way: ..... Od.12.508.457.
When home, with feeble knees, he bends his way ..... Od.13.42.3.
Swift as a swallow sweeps the liquid way, ... Od.13.186.15.
And bound for *Greece* we plow'd the wat'ry way; ..... Od.13.363.24.
Thro' the wild ocean plow the dang'rous way, ... Od.13.482.29.
For traytors wait his way, with dire design ..... Od.14.210.45.

WAY (CONTINUED)

Safe through the level seas we sweep our way; ..... Od.14.286.49.
To *Lybia* then he meditates the way; ..... Od.14.325.50.
Beneath *Troy* walls by night we took our way: ..... Od.14.531.63.
There, to the tusky herd he bends his way, ... Od.14.600.66.
Shall prompt our speed, and point the ready way. ..... Od.15.60.72.
Swift let us measure back the wat'ry way, ... Od.15.73.72.
Eludes the labours of the tedious way. ..... Od.15.90.73.
And wander'd thro' the wide ethereal way ..... Od.15.196.78.
'Till night descending intercepts the way. ..... Od.15.209.78.
Some well-known friend (*Eumæus)* bends this way; ..... Od.16.9.102.
When o'er the waves you plow'd the desp'rate way. ..... Od.16.26.103.
To seek thee, friend, I hither took my way. ..... Od.16.32.103.
What vessel bore him o'er the wat'ry way? ..... Od.16.58.105.
That you to *Pylos* plow'd the wat'ry way, ... Od.16.153.110.
And what blest hands have oar'd thee on the way? ..... Od.16.247.116.
And plan the scene of death, I bend my way: ..... Od.16.257.117.
Then measur'd back the way—The suitor band ..... Od.16.358.123.
The bark escap'd; and measure back their way. ..... Od.16.373.124.
Our murd'rous ambush on the wat'ry way. ..... Od.16.393.125.
Th' eluded Suitors stem the wat'ry way. ..... Od.16.495.131.
And scarce those few, for tears, could force their way. ..... Od.17.51.135.
Nor oars to cut th' immeasurable way— ..... Od.17.167.139.
My feeble step, since rugged is the way. ..... Od.17.219.142.
A staff *Eumæus* gave. Along the way ..... Od.17.222.142.
The cavern'd way descending to the town, ... Od.17.231.143.
Turn'd his proud step, and left them on their way. ..... Od.17.305.146.
Or I first ent'ring introduce the way? ..... Od.17.327.147.
Un-hous'd, neglected, in the publick way; ..... Od.17.357.149.
Hence dotard, hence! and timely speed thy way, ... Od.18.14.167.
But to the palace measur'd back the way. ..... Od.18.134.172.
But Vengeance and *Ulysses* wing their way. ..... Od.18.174.175.
The gifts of love; with speed they take the way. ..... Od.18.336.184.
I for *Dulichium* urge the wat'ry way, ... Od.19.335.210.
And back triumphant wing'd his airy way. ..... Od.19.632.227.
Swift to the inmost room she bent her way, ... Od.21.11.259.
Haste to the tryal—Lo! I lead the way. ..... Od.21.116.264.
Three times, unequal to the task, gave way: ..... Od.21.132.264.
Some moments you, and let me lead the way. ..... Od.21.247.271.
The miscreant we suspected takes that way; ..... Od.22.180.296.
The Prince's jav'lin tore its bloody way ..... Od.22.327.302.
No help, no flight; but wounded ev'ry way, ... Od.22.341.304.
The matron moves, the Prince directs the way. ..... Od.22.437.309.
Of these, twice six pursue their wicked way, ... Od.22.462.310.
To the base court the females take their way; ..... Od.22.492.313.
They wash, and to *Ulysses* take their way, ... Od.22.515.314.
The Nurse with eager rapture speeds her way; ..... Od.23.2.316.
That forc'd *Ulysses* o'er the watry way, ... Od.23.74.322.
Who knows their motives, who shall trace their way! ..... Od.23.84.322.
And dauntless follow where you lead the way; ..... Od.23.126.326.
Minerva rushes thro' th' aereal way, ... Od.23.372.343.
And pass the City-gate; *Ulysses* leads the way. ..... Od.23.397.343.
Points out the long, uncomfortable way. ..... Od.24.6.347.
And deluges of blood flow'd round you ev'ry way. ..... Od.24.57.350.
To tread the downward, melancholy way? ..... Od.24.131.354.
The will of *Jove,* he gave the vengeance way; ..... Od.24.192.356.
This way, and that, we turn, we fly, we fall; ..... Od.24.208.358.
Not so: his judgment takes the winding way ..... Od.24.279.363.
Heedless he whistled, and pursu'd his way. ..... Od.24.309.364.
They commun'd thus; while homeward bent their way ..... Od.24.444.370.
Fought as he fought, and mark'd his way with blood: ..... Od.24.513.372.
Stood in the way, and at a glance beheld ..... Od.24.568.375.
Fierce they rush forth: *Ulysses* leads the way. ..... Od.24.579.376.

WAY-FARING

As some way-faring Man, who wanders o'er ..... Il.15.86.199.

WAYS

To what base Ends, and by what abject Ways, ... 1.EOC.520.296.
These, where two Ways in equal Parts divide, ... 1.TrSt.718.440.
And long-continu'd Ways, and winding Floods, ... 1.TrUl.66.468.
And study'd Men, their Manners, and their Ways; ..... 2.ChJM.157.22.
Heav'n calls us different Ways, on these bestows ..... 2.ChWB.40.58.
Watch all their Ways, and all their Actions guide: ..... 2.RL2.88.165.
On various Tempers act by various ways, ... 2.RL4.61.189.
But vindicate the ways of God to Man. ..... 3.EOM1.16.14.
A thousand ways, is there no black or white? ..... 3.EOM2.214.81.
His Life, to forfeit it a thousand ways; ..... 3.Ep1.197.32.
Bid Harbors open, public Ways extend, ... 3.Ep4.197.156.
But Man corrupt, perverse in all his ways, ... 4.HAdv.98.83.
That, if he pleas'd, he pleas'd by manly ways; ..... 4.Arbu.337.120.
Of all these ways, if each pursues his own, ... 4.1HE1.134.289.
In circling fleeces whiten all the ways: ..... 5.DunB2.362.315.
Points him two ways, the narrower is the better. ..... 5.DunB4.152.356.
Then scorn to gain a Friend by servile ways, ... 6.73.10.210.
He bade me teach thee all the ways of War. ..... Il.9.570.462.
Oh speed our Labours, and direct our ways! ..... Il.10.535.27.
These, turn'd by *Phœbus* from their wonted ways, ... Il.12.23.82.
With well-taught Feet: Now shape, in oblique ways, ... Il.18.691.357.
To stern *Achilles* now direct my ways, ... Il.24.379.551.
O'er the wide waves success thy ways attends: ..... Od.2.310.76.
For nought unprosp'rous shall thy ways attend, ... Od.3.37.88.
Wise are thy words, and just are all thy ways. ..... Od.3.424.107.
A world of waters! far from all the ways ..... Od.5.127.178.
Just are the ways of heav'n: From heav'n proceed ..... Od.8.631.297.
O friends, a thousand ways frail mortals lead ..... Od.12.403.450.
And long-continu'd ways, and winding floods, ... Od.13.233.17.
And cavern'd ways, the shaggy coast along, ... Od.14.3.32.
Far from gay cities, and the ways of men, ... Od.14.410.55.
On all their weary ways wait Care and Pain, ... Od.15.366.87.
Those to whose eyes the Gods their ways reveal, ... Od.17.464.155.

WAYWARD

Then thus addrest the Pow'r—Hail wayward Queen! ..... 2.RL4.57.188.

WE (OMITTED)
856

WE'D
Sooner we'd quit our Part in thee, ... 6.30.25A.86.
We'd be the best, good-natur'd things alive. .... 6.41.14.113.

WE'LL
"For Snug's the word: My dear! we'll live in Town." .... 4.1HE1.147.289.
We'll not be slow to visit Dr. Swift. .... 6.42vi.6.120.
Returns he? Ambush'd we'll his walk invade, ... Od.16.398.125.

WE'RE
We're not two Capons but two Cocks. .... 6.93.27Z6.257.
But now we're so frugal, I'd have you to know it, ... 6.105vii.3.302.

WEAK
The Sick and Weak the healing Plant shall aid; .... 1.Mes.15.114.
(That on weak Wings, from far, pursues your Flights; .... 1.EOC.197.263.
What the weak Head with strongest Byass rules, ... 1.EOC.203.263.
(That with weak Wings, from far, pursues your Flights; .... 1.EOC.197A.263.
While their weak Heads, like Towns unfortify'd, ... 1.EOC.434.288.
Weak, sinful Laymen were but Flesh and Blood. .... 2.ChJM.8.15.
Weak was her Voice, as while she spoke she cry'd. .... 2.ChJM.576.43.
When their weak Legs scarce dragg'd 'em out of Doors; .... 2.ChWB.155.64.
"Let that frail Thing, weak Woman, have her way. .... 2.ChWB.194.65.
Why form'd so weak, so little, and so blind! .... 3.EOM1.36.18.
Why made so weak, so little, and so blind! .... 3.EOM1.36A.18.
As strong or weak, the organs of the frame; .... 3.EOM2.130.70.
In this weak queen, some fav'rite still obey. .... 3.EOM2.150.73.
She but removes weak passions for the strong: .... 3.EOM2.158.74.
Grant that the pow'rful still the weak controul, ... 3.EOM3.49.97.
"Still for the strong too weak, the weak too strong. .... 3.EOM3.194.113.
"Still for the strong too weak, the weak too strong. .... 3.EOM3.194.113.
She taught the weak to bend, the proud to pray, ... 3.EOM3.251.118.
Fear made her Devils, and weak Hope her Gods; .... 3.EOM3.256.118.
Where small and great, where weak and mighty, made .... 3.EOM3.297.123.
Think we, like some weak Prince, th'Eternal Cause, ... 3.EOM4.121.139.
The good man may be weak, be indolent, ... 3.EOM4.155.142.
Weak, foolish man! will Heav'n reward us there .... 3.EOM4.173.144.
Not that themselves are wise, but others weak. .... 3.EOM4.228.148.
Nor that themselves are wise, but others weak. .... 3.EOM4.228A.148.
As weak, as earnest, and as gravely out, ... 3.Ep1.250.37.
The Frail one's advocate, and weak one's friend: .... 3.Ep2.30A.52.
The Frail one's advocate, the Weak one's friend: .... 3.Ep2.30.52.
Fine by defect, and delicately weak. .... 3.Ep2.44.53.
The Lines are weak, another's pleas'd to say, ... 4.HS1.5.5.
So weak a Vessel, and so rich a Prize! .... 4.JD4.229.45.
Courts are too much for Wits so weak as mine; .... 4.JD4.280.49.
Courts are no match for Wits so weak as mine; .... 4.JD4.280A.49.
But most, when straining with too weak a wing, ... 4.2HE1.368.227.
If weak the pleasure that from these can spring, ... 4.1HE6.18.237.
The fear to want them is as weak a thing: .... 4.1HE6.19.237.
Weak tho' I am of limb, and short of sight, ... 4.1HE1.49.283.
But who, weak rebels, more advance her cause. .... 5.DunB4.86.349.
Let not this weak, unknowing hand .... 6.50.25.147.
If ere this weak, unknowing hand .... 6.50.25A.147.
Vile Reptile, weak, and vain! .... 6.53.6.161.
How vain is Reason, Eloquence how weak, ... 6.85.5.242.
A weak officious Friend becomes a Foe. .... 6.116viii.4.328.
And dropt her Offspring from her weak Embrace. .... Il.5.428.289.
His Shield too weak the furious Dart to stay, ... Il.5.665.300.
Weak is thy Servant, and thy Coursers slow. .... Il.8.132.404.
Weak Bulwarks! destin'd by this Arm to fall. .... Il.8.217.407.
With Accent weak these tender Words return'd. .... Il.9.561.461.
Weak was his Pace, but dauntless was his Heart. .... Il.11.945.77.
Let, to the weak, the lighter Arms belong, ... Il.14.433.184.
Than Man more weak, calamitous, and blind? .... Il.17.511.308.
Scarce their weak Drivers guide them thro' the Fight: .... Il.17.555.309.
Whether the Weak or Strong discharge the Dart, ... Il.17.711.315.
Weak are its Counsels, headlong is its Rage. .... Il.23.672.516.
Thy self not young, a weak old Man thy Guide. .... Il.24.454.555.
Of his weak Age, to live the Curse of thine! .... Il.24.682.565.
A weak old Man to see the Light and live! .... Il.24.704.566.
Not this weak pigmy-wretch, of mean design, ... Od.9.603.331.
Or weak and old, my youthful arm demands, ... Od.11.607.413.
She mocks the weak attempts of human might; .... Od.12.151.439.
(Weak, daring creatures!) is not vengeance thine? .... Od.13.169.13.
Mov'd by no weak surmize, but sense of shame, ... Od.21.347.276.
And foes how weak, oppos'd against a friend! .... Od.22.256.299.
Some weak, or pond'rous with the brazen head, ... Od.22.304.301.
How weak is mortal pride! To heav'n alone .... Od.22.320.301.
The weak enlighten and confound the wise; .... Od.23.14.319.
It mocks the weak attempts of human hands; .... Od.23.187.332.
More gentle methods on weak age employs, ... Od.24.281.363.

WEAKEN'D
Pallas assists, and (weaken'd in its Force) .... Il.4.160.228.

WEAKER
Why form'd no weaker, blinder, and no less! .... 3.EOM1.38:18.
Why made no weaker, blinder, and no less! .... 3.EOM1.38A.18.
A weaker may surprise, a stronger take? .... 3.EOM3.276.120.
The weaker Warrior takes a lighter Shield. .... Il.14.442.184.

WEAKEST
The weakest Woman sometimes may .... 6.94.3.259.
Not vain the weakest, if their Force unite; .... Il.13.311.120.
The weakest Atheist-Wretch all Heav'n defies, ... Il.20.421.412.
The weakest woman: all can wrong the brave. .... Od.21.350.276.

WEAKNESS
Of blindness, weakness, Heav'n bestows on thee. .... 3.EOM1.284.49.
With too much weakness for the Stoic's pride, ... 3.EOM2.6.53.
With too much weakness for a Stoic's pride, ... 3.EOM2.6A.53.
'Till one Man's weakness grows the strength of all. .... 3.EOM2.252.85.

WEAKNESS (CONTINUED)
Above life's weakness, and its comforts too. .... 3.EOM4.268.153.
Weakness or Delicacy; all so nice, ... 3.Ep2.205.67.
In pitying love we but our weakness show, ... 6.32.11.96.
Soft without weakness, without glaring gay; .... 6.52.66.158.
When prest by Want and Weakness, *Dennis* lies; .... 6.128.10.356.
Good without Show, and without weakness kind: .... 6.134.6.364.
But spare the Weakness of my feeble Age: .... Il.3.381.211.
Forgive the weakness of a human heart. .... Od.5.276.184.
(For heav'n forbid, such weakness should endure) .... Od.21.140.265.
Our weakness scorn? *Antinous* thus reply'd. .... Od.21.271.272.
Forgive the weakness of a woman's heart! .... Od.23.218.333.

WEAL
An hour, and not defraud the Publick Weal? .... 4.2HE1.6.195.
To rowze the Watchmen of the Publick Weal, ... 4.EpS2.217.325.
O'er head and ears plunge for the plublick weal. .... 5.DunA1.196.86.
Wits starve as useless to a Common weal .... 6.82ix(d).1.235.
Our Cares are only for the Publick Weal: .... Il.1.146.94.
Is more than Armies to the publick Weal. .... Il.11.637.62.
Ought, more conducive to our Weal, unfold. .... Il.14.119.163.

WEALTH
In the fat Age of Pleasure, Wealth, and Ease, ... 1.EOC.534.297.
My Brother next, neglecting Wealth and Fame, ... 1.TrSP.75.397.
All Wealth, all Honours, the supreme Degree .... 2.ChJM.633.45.
But since their Wealth (the best they had) was mine, ... 2.ChWB.60.59.
If foul, her Wealth the lusty Lover lures, ... 2.ChWB.94.61.
Oh thou hast slain me for my Wealth (I cry'd) .... 2.ChWB.420.77.
Let wealth, let honour, wait the wedded dame, ... 2.ElAb.77.326.
Fame, wealth, and honour! what are you to Love? .... 2.ElAb.80.326.
What once had beauty, titles, wealth, and fame. .... 2.Elegy.70.368.
The trim of pride, the impudence of wealth, ... 3.EOM3.4.92.
"How those in common all their wealth bestow, ... 3.EOM3.185.112
Oh wealth ill-fated! which no act of fame 3.EOM4.299.156
By Wealth of Follow'rs! without one distress .... 3.Ep2.145.62.
Had Colepepper's whole wealth been hops and hogs, ... 3.Ep3.53.90.
Oh teach us, BATHURST! yet unspoil'd by wealth! .... 3.Ep3.226.111.
Wealth in the gross is death, but life diffus'd, ... 3.Ep3.233.111.
Behold what blessings Wealth to life can lend! .... 3.Ep3.297.117.
"Virtue! and Wealth! what are ye but a name!" .... 3.Ep3.334.120.
His wealth, yet dearer, forfeit to the Crown: .... 3.Ep3.400.124.
His wealth, to purchase what he ne'er can taste? .... 3.Ep4.4.134.
What brought Sir Visto's ill got wealth to waste? .... 3.Ep4.15.137.
What brought Sir *Shylock's* ill got wealth to waste? .... 3.Ep4.15A.137.
"My wealth unwieldy, and my heap too great." .... 4.HS2.114.63.
Oh Impudence of wealth! with all thy store, ... 4.HS2.117.63.
Whom Crimes gave wealth, and wealth gave impudence: .... 4.JD2.46.137.
Whom Crimes gave wealth, and wealth gave impudence: .... 4.JD2.46.137.
Then strongly fencing ill-got wealth by law, ... 4.JD2.93.141.
Indeed, could Wealth bestow or Wit or Merit, ... 4.2HE2.226.181.
Is Wealth thy passion? Hence! from Pole to Pole, ... 4.1HE6.69.241.
A Man of wealth is dubb'd a Man of worth, ... 4.1HE6.81.243.
His Wealth brave Timon gloriously confounds; .... 4.1HE6.85.243.
If Wealth alone then make and keep us blest, ... 4.1HE6.95.243.
"Get Place and Wealth, if possible, with Grace; .... 4.1HE1.103.287.
"If not, by any means get Wealth and Place." .... 4.1HE1.104.287.
Their Country's wealth our mightier Misers drain, ... 4.1HE1.126.289.
Honour *and Wealth, the Joys we seek,*deny .... 6.17iii.1.57.
Luxurious Nature's Wealth in Thought surveys, ... 6.17iii.20.58.
Go then indulge thy age in Wealth and ease .... 6.130.11.358.
Alas what *wealth,* which no one act of fame .... 6.130.13.358.
Thou see'st that Island's Wealth, where only free, ... 6.142.6Z1.382.
You see that Island's Wealth, where only free, ... 6.142.6Z1A.382.
By Wealth, of Followers; without one Distress, ... 6.154.31.403.
With all the Wealth our Wars and Blood to bestow, ... Il.2.279.141.
But grant the Host with Wealth the Gen'ral load, ... Il.2.316.142.
And Show'rs of Wealth descending from the Skies. .... Il.2.814.163.
For beauteous *Helen* and the Wealth she brought; .... Il.3.102.194.
Be his the Wealth and beauteous Dame decreed: .... Il.3.359.210.
Be therefore now the *Spartan* Wealth restor'd, ... Il.3.571.219.
Vast was his Wealth, and these the only Heirs .... Il.5.198.276.
With ample Wealth (the Wish of Mortals) blest, ... Il.5.585.296.
Of added *Trojan* Wealth to buy the Peace. .... Il.7.467.387.
Their proffer'd Wealth, nor ev'n the *Spartan* Dame. .... Il.7.477.388.
Our Wealth, our People, and our Glory lost. .... Il.9.30.433.
The Wealth I gather'd, and the Spoils I made. .... Il.9.435.454.
The Wealth he left for this detested Shore: .... Il.9.476.456.
Not all the golden Tydes of Wealth that crown .... Il.9.498.457.
For this, our Wealth, our Products you enjoy, ... Il.17.266.298.
(Their Grandsire's Wealth, by right of Birth their own, ... Il.22.68.455.
May share our Wealth, and leave our Walls in Peace. .... Il.22.163.459.
Base Wealth preferring to eternal Praise. .... Il.23.368.505.
Who more than *Peleus* shone in Wealth and Pow'r? .... Il.24.673.565.
And *Wealth* incessant rolls her golden tides. .... Od.1.498.56.
Of wealth and fame a youthful bosom fire: .... Od.1.500.56.
Be You the spoilers, and our wealth consume. .... Od.2.84.64.
In wealth and beauty worthy of our flames: .... Od.2.234.72.
For wealth and beauty less than virtue please. .... Od.2.236.73.
The wealth of Kings, and made my youth a prey. .... Od.2.352.78.
Lest heedless absence wear thy wealth away, ... Od.3.400.106.
Whilst heaping unwish'd wealth, I distant roam; .... Od.4.113.125.
And, heap'd with various wealth, a blazing pyle: .... Od.10.623.374.
For since kind heav'n with wealth our realm has blest, ... Od.11.426.405.
None match'd this hero's wealth, of all who reign .... Od.14.117.41.
A willing widow's copious wealth supply'd. .... Od.14.243.48.
Than see the wealth of Kings consum'd in waste, ... Od.16.115.108.
Thy wealth in riot, the delay enjoy. .... Od.16.339.122.
Nor be the wealth of Kings consum'd in vain. .... Od.16.405.125.
Wealth, servants, friends, were mine in better days; .... Od.17.503.157.
Who make their Queen and all her wealth a prey: .... Od.18.173.175.
Your patrimonial wealth, a prudent heir. .... Od.19.26.193.
A Palace, wealth, and slaves, I late possess'd, ... Od.19.94.197.
'Till copious wealth might guard his regal state. .... Od.19.328.210.
But first the *Ulyssean* wealth survey: .... Od.19.336.210.
To wed, as wealth or worth her choice inspire: .... Od.20.398.251.

WEALTH (CONTINUED)
Our house, our wealth, our helpless handmaids lay: .... Od.22.44.288.
An absent Heroe's wealth they made their spoil: .... Od.24.525.373.
Each future day increase of wealth shall bring, ... Od.24.556.375.

WEALTHIER
A wealthier Tribute, than to thine he gives. .... 1.W-F.224.170.

WEALTHY
And Feather'd People crowd my wealthy Side, ... 1.W-F.404.191.
Then on the Sands he rang'd his wealthy Store, ... 1.TrUl.94.469.
Heav'n visits with a Taste the wealthy fool, ... 3.Ep4.17.137.
St. John has ever been a wealthy Fool— .... 4.EpS2.132.320.
Thine in each Conquest is the wealthy Prey, ... Il.1.217.97.
Him *Pallas* plac'd amidst her wealthy Fane, ... Il.2.661.158.
Who fair *Zeleia's* wealthy Vallies till, ... Il.2.998.170.
In wealthy Folds, and wait the Milker's Hand, ... Il.4.493.244.
A wealthy Priest, but rich without a Fault; .... Il.5.16.266.
Whose Sire *Diöcleus,* wealthy, brave and great, ... Il.5.671.300.
In fat *Bœotia* held his wealthy Sway, ... Il.5.871.308.
Oblig'd the Wealthy, and reliev'd the Poor. .... Il.6.20.325.
His blameless Wife, *Aëtion's* wealthy Heir: .... Il.6.493.351.
As sweating Reapers in some wealthy Field, ... Il.11.89.38.
(*Asius* the Great, who held his wealthy Reign .... Il.17.656.313.
The richest, once, of *Asia's* wealthy Kings; .... Il.20.261.404.
With wealthy dow'r, and bridal gifts of price. .... Od.1.363.50.
With wealthy dow'r, and bridal gifts of price. .... Od.2.226.72.
The wealthy tribes of *Pharian Thebes* obey) .... Od.4.170.128.
Aboard in haste they heave the wealthy sheep, ... Od.9.553.328.
For wealthy Kings are loyally obey'd! .... Od.11.449.406.
Then on the sands he rang'd his wealthy store, ... Od.13.261.18.
My father *Arybas,* of wealthy fame; .... Od.15.467.93.
She moves majestic thro' the wealthy room, ... Od.21.53.261.
For him forsake this lov'd, this wealthy dome, ... Od.21.78.262.

WEANLING
Whose shrine with weanling lambs he wont to load.) .... Od.19.469.219.

WEAPON
Fix'd in his Belt the feather'd Weapon stood, ... 1.TrES.137.454.
Then drew the Weapon from his panting Heart, ... 1.TrES.318.461.
And use that Weapon which they have, their Pen; .... 2.ChWB.372.75.
A two-edg'd Weapon from her shining Case; .... 2.RL3.128.177.
Satire's my Weapon, but I'm too discreet .... 4.HS1.69.11.
O sacred Weapon! left for Truth's defence, ... 4.EpS2.212.325.
His gray-goose-weapon must have made her stand. .... 5.DunA1.188.85.
That gray-goose-weapon must have made her stand. .... 5.DunA1.188A.85.
This grey-goose weapon must have made her stand. .... 5.DunB1.198.283.
Ah! leave not this, this Weapon to a Fool. .... 6.131i.4.360.
"What *well?* what *weapon?* (Flavia cries) .... 6.140.13.378.
Thro' *Paris'* Shield the forceful Weapon went, ... Il.3.440.213.
Th' impatient Weapon whizzes on the Wing, ... Il.4.156.228.
Diverts the Weapon from its destin'd Course. .... Il.4.161.228.
Diverts the Weapon from the destin'd Course. .... Il.4.161A.228.
Warm'd in the Brain the brazen Weapon lies, ... Il.4.526.246.
The Weapon enter'd close above his Ear, ... Il.4.575.249.
From *Menelaus'* Arm the Weapon sent, ... Il.5.71.269.
Swift thro' his crackling Jaws the Weapon glides, ... Il.5.97.271.
And tugg'd the Weapon from the gushing Wound; .... Il.5.143.274.
On his broad Shield the sounding Weapon rung, ... Il.5.343.283.
Thro' her bright Veil the daring Weapon drove .... Il.5.417.287.
Thro' his broad Belt the Weapon forc'd its way; .... Il.5.666.300.
Full in the Boaster's Neck the Weapon stood, ... Il.5.816.305.
From *Mars* his Arm th' enormous Weapon fled: .... Il.5.1045.316.
Fix'd in his Front the brazen Weapon lies, ... Il.6.13.323.
Thro' six Bull-hides the furious Weapon drove, ... Il.7.298.379.
He said, and twang'd the String. The Weapon flies .... Il.8.365.414.
He said, and high in Air the Weapon cast, ... Il.10.441.23.
With ev'ry Weapon, Art or Fury yields: .... Il.11.342.49.
A Coward's Weapon never hurts the Brave. .... Il.11.498.56.
In his broad Buckler many a Weapon stood, ... Il.11.698.66.
Fix'd in his nervous Thigh the Weapon stood, ... Il.11.710.66.
The Weapon drank the mingled Brains and Gore; .... Il.12.215.89.
Fix'd in his Belt the feather'd Weapon stood, ... Il.12.491.99.
Full on the Shield's round Boss the Weapon rung; .... Il.13.256.117.
And made, with force, the vengeful Weapon fly: .... Il.13.510.131.
The *Trojan* Weapon whizz'd along in Air; .... Il.13.636.136.
The Victor from his Breast the Weapon tears; .... Il.13.646.136.
In the broad Buckler half the Weapon stood; .... Il.13.714.138.
Full in his Eye the Weapon chanc'd to fall, ... Il.14.577.190.
And had the Weapon found the destin'd way, ... Il.15.538.217.
So well the Chief his Naval Weapon sped, ... Il.15.906.232.
Whose Son's great Arm alone the Weapon wields, ... Il.16.176.245.
Plung'd in his Throat the smoaking Weapon lies; .... Il.16.398.258.
Then drew the Weapon from his panting Heart, ... Il.16.623.268.
The well-aim'd Weapon on the Buckler rings, ... Il.17.46.289.
Plung'd in his Throat, the Weapon drank his Blood, ... Il.17.358.301.
Between his Cheek and Ear the Weapon went, ... Il.17.697.314.
With that, his Weapon deep inflicts the Wound; .... Il.19.277.383.
Then lift thy Weapon for a noble Blow, ... Il.20.140.400.
So voluble a Weapon is the Tongue; .... Il.20.297.406.
Thro' the thin Verge the *Pelian* Weapon glides, ... Il.20.325.407.
And at its Master's Feet the Weapon threw. .... Il.20.372.410.
Warm'd in the Brain the smoaking Weapon lies, ... Il.20.551.417.
Spun forth, in Earth the fasten'd Weapon stood. .... Il.21.184.429.
Repulsive of his Might the Weapon stood: .... Il.21.192.429.
The Weapon flew, its Course unerring held, ... Il.22.369.471.
In his right Hand he waves the Weapon round, ... Il.22.403.472.
Whose Weapon strikes yon' flutt'ring Bird, shall bear .... Il.23.1014.529.
With melted lard they soak the weapon o'er, ... Od.21.185.268.
Thy master's weapon to his hand convey. .... Od.21.251.272.
Thus they. Aghast he laid the weapon down, ... Od.21.397.279.
Lest time or worms had done the weapon wrong, ... Od.21.429.281.
Full thro' his throat *Ulysses'* weapon past, ... Od.22.19.287.
The brazen weapon driving thro' his back, ... Od.22.108.291.

WEAPONS
Her Weapons blunted, and extinct her Fires: .... 1.W-F.418.193.
No common Weapons in their Hands are found, ... 2.RL5.43.202.
"Secure the radiant weapons wield; .... 6.140.5.378.
Receiv'd the weapons of the sky; .... 6.140.10.378.
Your Weapons enter, and your Strokes they feel. .... Il.4.590.249.
The dreadful Weapons of the Warrior's Rage, ... Il.10.86.6.
Thro' the brown Shade the fulgid Weapons shin'd. .... Il.10.547.27.
Rang'd in two Bands, their crooked Weapons wield, ... Il.11.90.38.
The wanted Weapons; those my Tent can give. .... Il.13.338.121.
For arms and weapons of the sylvan war; .... Od.9.181.313.
And turn'd the deadly weapons from my breast. .... Od.14.312.50.
"These glittering weapons, ere he sail'd to *Troy* .... Od.16.308.120.
All scatter'd round their glitt'ring weapons lie; .... Od.24.618.377.

WEAR
All Nature laughs, the Groves fresh Honours wear, ... 1.PSp.73A.68.
To sing those Honours you deserve to wear, ... 1.W-F.289.175.
And smooth as shells that gliding waters wear; .... 1.TrPA.55.367.
This Hand, which won it, shall for ever wear. .... 2.RL4.138.195.
I only wear it in a Land of Hectors, ... 4.HS1.71.11.
Which tho they're rich, are Things that none will wear .... 4.JD2A.130.144.
Extremely fine, but what no man will wear. .... 4.JD2.124.145.
Sons, Sires, and Grandsires, all will wear the Bays, ... 4.2HE1.171.209.
And wear their strange old Virtue as they will. .... 4.EpS1.44.301.
Far other *Stars* than *and** wear, ... 4.EpS2.238.326.
Beneath his reign, shall Eusden wear the bays, ... 5.DunA3.319.186.
And wear a cleaner Smock. .... 6.14v(a).6.48.
A Papist wear the Lawrel! is it fit? .... 6.48iii.11.135.
To wear red Stockings, and to dine with *St[eel]* .... 6.49i.4.137.
How oft' in pleasing tasks we wear the day, ... 6.52.17.156.
To keep this Cap, for such as will, to wear; .... 6.60.34.179.
Let him that takes it, wear it as his own. .... 6.60.38.179.
They use white Powder, and wear Holland-Smocks. .... 6.95.4.264.
Vine, bay, or cabbage fit to wear, ... 6.106v.2.308.
Vine, Laurel, cabbage fit to wear, ... 6.106v.2A.308.
May wear a Pick-lock at his Side; .... 6.135.34.367.
To strip those Arms thou ill deserv'st to wear, ... Il.2.323.142.
Which ev'n the Graces might be proud to wear, ... Il.17.54.289.
Lest heedless absence wear thy wealth away, ... Od.3.400.106.
Here by the stream if I the night out-wear, ... Od.5.601.201.
But he that scorns the chains of sleep to wear .... Od.10.96.345.
It fits thee now to wear a dark disguise, ... Od.13.453.28.
(Her beauteous cheeks the blush of *Venus* wear, ... Od.17.46.134.
Her cheeks the warmer blush of *Venus* wear, ... Od.19.66.196.
In crowds we wear the badge of hungry Fate, ... Od.19.90.196.

WEARER'S
All as the vest, appear'd the wearer's frame, ... 5.DunA3.31.154.
All as the vest, appear'd the wearer's frame, ... 5.DunB3.39.322.
Adds graceful terror to the wearer's side. .... Od.8.440.287.

WEARIED
And wearied heav'n with wishes for his Lord. .... Od.14.32.36.

WEARIES
Who wearies Heav'n with Vows for *Hector's* Life. .... Il.7.361.381.

WEARING
"Your only wearing is your *Padua-soy.*" .... 4.JD4.113.35.

WEARS
To gain her Sight, a thousand Forms he wears, ... 1.TrVP.29.378.
A Female Form at last *Vertumnus* wears, ... 1.TrVP.45.379.
A Lyon's yellow Skin the *Theban* wears, ... 1.TrSt.567.434.
Which long she wore, and now *Belinda* wears.) .... 2.RL5.96.207.
But now no face divine contentment wears, ... 2.ElAb.147.331.
Now wears a Garland, an Ægyptian God .... 3.EOM1.64A.21.
The broadest mirth unfeeling Folly wears, ... 3.EOM4.319.158.
See, see, our own true Phœbus wears the bays! .... 5.DunB3.323.335.
His beaver'd brow a birchen garland wears, ... 5.DunB4.141.355.
She wears no Colours (sign of Grace) .... 6.14v(a).13.49.
And his refulgent Arms in Triumph wears; .... Il.2.698.159.
We know him by the various Plume he wears. .... Il.3.118.195.
If 'tis a God, he wears that Chief's Disguise; .... Il.5.234.278.
Now wears a mortal Form; like *Calchas* seen, ... Il.13.69.108.
His Father's Arms not long *Achilles* wears, ... Il.17.223.296.
And the whole City wears one Face of Woe. .... Il.22.517.478.
A veil of richest texture wrought, she wears, ... Od.1.429.53.
Instant he wears, elusive of the rape, ... Od.4.563.147.
A Tree, and well-dissembled foliage wears. .... Od.4.622.149.

WEARY
When weary Reapers quit the sultry Field, ... 1.PSu.65.77.
Then weary grown, to shady grotts retires, ... 1.TrPA.37.366.
And weary all the wild Efforts of Rage. .... 1.TrSt.734.441.
The weary Sun, as Learned Poets write, ... 2.ChJM.367.32.
Then on the Couch his weary Limbs he cast; .... 2.ChJM.390.33.
Worn out in public, weary ev'ry eye, ... 3.Ep2.229.68.
Whose Seats the weary Traveller repose? .... 3.Ep3.260.114.
In Days of Ease, when now the weary Sword .... 4.2HE1.139.207.
But shall a *Printer,* weary of his life, ... 4.EpS1.125.307.
(Now, if you're weary of my Style, ... 6.10.63.26.
The last kind Refuge weary Wit can find, ... 6.16.2.53.
Then, wet and weary, home he far'd, ... 6.79.137.222.
That long had heav'd the weary Oar in vain, ... Il.7.6.363.
The weary Wood-man spreads his sparing Meal, ... Il.11.120.41.
Confus'd, and weary all the Pow'rs with Pray'r; .... Il.15.423.213.
Glut all your Hearts! and weary all your Hands! .... Il.16.251.249.
With weary Limbs, but with unwilling Pace: Il.17.750A.317*
Their Steeds unharness'd from the weary Car) .... Il.18.288.335.
And copious Banquets, glad your weary Souls. .... Il.19.206.381.
Nor weary out your gen'rous Strength in vain. .... Il.23.857.523.
Restless he roll'd around his weary Bed, ... Il.24.9.535.
Sooths weary Life, and softens human Pain. .... Il.24.166.542.
(Of *Alpheus'* race) the weary youths retreat. .... Od.3.620.117.

WEARY (CONTINUED)

For who, self-mov'd, with weary wing wou'd sweep ....Od.5.125.178.
Let then thy waters give the weary rest, ...Od.5.574.200.
While thus the weary Wand'rer sunk to rest, ...Od.6.1.203.
Stiff are my weary joints; and I resign ....Od.8.264.277.
Restore me safe thro' weary wand'rings tost, ...Od.8.507.289.
Weary of light, *Ulysses* here explores ....Od.11.126.387.
With many a weary step, and many a groan, ...Od.11.735.422.
Weary and wet th' *Ogygian* shores I gain, ...Od.12.531.458.
As weary plowman spent with stubborn toil, ...Od.13.39.3.
And strong with pales, by many a weary stroke ....Od.14.15.35.
On all their weary ways wait Care and Pain, ...Od.15.366.87.
My weary nature craves the balm of rest: ....Od.23.173.329.

WEARY'D

This weary'd Arm can scarce the Bolt sustain, ...1.TrSt.304.423.
This weary'd Arm, and ward the Storm of War! ....Il.17.635.312.
With weary'd Limbs, but with unwilling Pace: ....Il.17.750.317.
When round and round with never-weary'd Pain, ...Il.20.579.418.
Retire, while from my weary'd limbs I lave ....Od.6.259.222.
But still long-weary'd nature wants repair; ....Od.7.294.250.
And my tost limbs now weary'd into rest, ...Od.10.593.372.
Mean-while the weary'd King the bath ascends; ....Od.23.149.328.
Reliev'd our weary'd vessel from the sea. ....Od.24.360.366.

WEASEL

A Weasel once made shift to slink ....4.1HE7.51.271.

WEATHER

And you shall see, the first warm Weather, ...4.1HE7.19.269.
The skill of weather and of winds unknown, ...Od.14.541.63.

WEAV'D

The *Trojan* Wars she weav'd (herself the Prize) ....Il.3.171.199.
An ell in length the pliant wisp I weav'd, ...Od.10.194.350.

WEAVE

"Learn of the mole to plow, the worm to weave; ....3.EOM3.176.111.
Weave Laurel Crowns, and take what Names we please. ....4.2HE2.142.175.
Taught by my care to cull the fleece, or weave, ...Od.22.460.310.

WEAVES

What Reason weaves, by Passion is undone. ....3.EOM2.42.60.
Thin, as the filmy threads the spider weaves. ....Od.8.324.281.

WEB

Art thou in Spider's web, entangled hung? ....6.96ii.30Z5.271.
The golden Web her own sad Story crown'd, ...Il.3.170.199.
O'er the fair web the rising figures shine, ...Od.10.256.355.
"Till this funereal web my labours end: ....Od.19.165.200.
Fine as a filmy web beneath it shon ....Od.19.269.208.
'Till this funereal web my labours end: ....Od.24.157.355.
The mingled web, whose gold and silver ray ....Od.24.173.356.

WEBS

Their Webs Divine of Purple mix'd with Gold. ....1.TrUl.38.467.
"In vain thy Reason finer webs shall draw, ...3.EOM3.191.112.
Their webs divine of purple mix'd with gold. ....Od.13.129.8.

WEBSTER

There Webster! peal'd thy voice, and Whitfield! thine. ....5.DunB2.258.308.

WED

But his high Courage prick'd him forth to wed, ...2.ChJM.13.15.
Those are too wise for Batchelors to wed; ....2.ChJM.108.19.
The righteous End were lost for which I wed, ...2.ChJM.120.20.
Who dare to wed in your declining Days. ....2.ChJM.171.23.
Heav'n that (said he) inspir'd me first to wed, ...2.ChJM.254.26.
Her will I wed, if gracious Heav'n so please; ....2.ChJM.262.27.
Heav'n put it past your Doubt whene'er you wed, ...2.ChJM.279.27.
Declar'd 'twas better far to Wed, than Burn. ....2.ChWB.29.58.
The mighty *Czar* what mov'd to wed a Punk? ....3.Ep1.83A.21.
Or wed to what he must divorce, a Muse: ....5.DunB4.262.369.
Her shalt thou wed whom most thy Eyes approve, ...Il.9.378.451.
If she must wed, from other hands require ....Od.2.59.63.
These sons their sisters wed, and all remain ....Od.10.7.339.
Ev'n I unsafe: The Queen in doubt to wed, ...Od.16.73.106.
Then wed whom choice approves: the Queen be giv'n ....Od.16.406.125.
To wed, as wealth or worth her choice inspire: ....Od.20.398.251.

WEDDED

When tender Youth has wedded stooping Age. ....2.ChJM.340.30.
Let wealth, let honour, wait the wedded dame, ...2.ElAb.77.326.
Papillia, wedded to her am'rous spark ....2.Ep.37A.53.
Papillia, wedded to her doating spark, ...3.Ep.37.53.
To *Samos'* Isle she sent the wedded fair; ....Od.15.392.88.

WEDDING

Will be your father by your wedding me. ....1.TrPA.113.370.
Christ saw a Wedding once, the Scripture says, ...2.ChWB.9.57.
And Feasts still kept upon my Wedding-Day: ....2.ChWB.113.62.

WEDDING-DAY

And Feasts still kept upon my Wedding-Day: ....2.ChWB.113.62.

WEDG'D

Or wedg'd whole Ages in a *Bodkin's* Eye: ....2.RL2.128.168.
His Steeds and Chariots wedg'd in firm Array, ...Il.4.419.240.
Compacted Troops stand wedg'd in firm Array, ...Il.8.263.410.
Wedg'd in the Trench, by our own Troops confus'd, ...Il.12.83.84.
Then all alighting, wedg'd in firm Array, ...Il.12.89.84.
Wedg'd in one Body at the Tents they stand, ...Il.15.788.226.
Ranks wedg'd in Ranks; of Arms a steely Ring ....Il.16.254.249.
Wedg'd in the Trench, in one vast Carnage bruis'd. ....Il.16.443.260.
Wedg'd in one Body like a Flight of Cranes, ...Il.17.846.321.
Twelve in the Tumult wedg'd, untimely rush'd ....Il.18.271.335.

WEDG'D (CONTINUED)

Apollo wedg'd him in the Warrior's Way, ...Il.20.110.398.

WEDGE

And next, a wedge to drive with sweepy sway: ....Od.5.303.185.

WEDLOCK

That honest Wedlock is a glorious Thing: ....2.ChJM.22.16.
And since I speak of Wedlock, let me say, ...2.ChJM.127.20.
The Charms of Wedlock all his Soul imploy: ....2.ChJM.229.25.
No less in Wedlock than in Liberty. ....2.ChJM.332.30.
Five times in lawful Wedlock she was join'd; ....2.ChWB.15.57.
They dream in Courtship, but in Wedlock wake. ....2.ChWB.103.61.

WEDLOCK'S

To slander Wives, and Wedlock's holy Name. ....2.ChJM.223.25.
And join'd my Heart, in Wedlock's sacred Band: ....2.ChJM.582.43.

WEDS

Who wisely weds in his maturer Years. ....2.ChJM.24.16.
Weds the rich Dulness of some Son of earth? ....4.1HE6.43.239.
For him she weeps, and him she weds agen. ....4.EpS2.109.319.
Perhaps she weds regardless of her fame, ...Od.16.75.106.
Lo! the Queen weds! we hear the spousal lay! ....Od.23.136.327.
Lo! the Queen weds! we hear the spousal lay! ....Od.23.146.328.
Thus they—but nobly chaste she weds no more. ....Od.23.148.328.

WEE

And cite those Sapphoes wee admire no more; ....6.43.2.120.

WEED

And od'rous Myrtle to the noisome Weed. ....1.Mes.76.119.
Sprung the rank Weed, and thriv'd with large Increase; ....1.EOC.535.297.
From dirt and sea-weed as proud Venice rose; ....3.EOM4.292.155.
If I but ask, if any weed can grow? ....4.2HE1.120.205.
From dirt and sea-weed as proud Venice rose; ....6.130.2.358.

WEEDS

The levell'd Towns with Weeds lie cover'd o'er, ...1.W-F.67.156.
What tho' no friends in sable weeds appear, ...2.Elegy.55.367.
A Wild, where weeds and flow'rs promiscuous shoot, ...3.EOM1.7.13.
Or Wild, where weeds and flow'rs promiscuous shoot, ...3.EOM1.7A.13.
Taller or stronger than the weeds they shade? ....3.EOM1.40.18.
He search'd for coral but he gather'd weeds. ....5.DunA2.286Z2.137.
A tribe, with weeds and shells fantastic crown'd, ...5.DunB4.398.381.
Late worn with years in weeds obscene you trod, ...Od.16.220.114.
An aged mendicant in tatter'd weeds. ....Od.16.293.119.
These tatter'd weeds (my decent robe resign'd.) ....Od.19.391.213.

WEEDY

And from his locks compress the weedy ooze; ....Od.6.268.223.

WEEK

One solid dish his week-day meal affords, ...3.Ep3.345.122.
As once a week we travel down ....4.HS6.97.257.
And crucify poor Shakespear once a week. ....5.DunA1.164.83.
Is, I've been well a Week, or so. ....6.10.106.27.
I need but once a Week. ....6.47.36.129.

WEEK-DAY

One solid dish his week-day meal affords, ...3.Ep3.345.122.

WEEK'S

Not so: a Buck was then a week's repast, ...4.HS2.93.61.
Or Envy holds a whole Week's war with Sense, ...4.Arbu.252.114.

WEEKLY

The MAN of Ross divides the weekly bread: ....3.Ep3.264.115.
They change their weekly Barber, weekly News, ...4.1HE1.155.291.
They change their weekly Barber, weekly News, ...4.1HE1.155.291.
Hence springs each weekly Muse, the living boast ....5.DunA1.37.O64.
"The stream, be his the Weekly Journals, bound. ....5.DunA2.268.134.
Hence Miscellanies spring, the weekly boast ....5.DunB1.39.273.
"The stream, be his the Weekly Journals bound, ...5.DunB2.280.309.
For which thy Patron's weekly thank'd: ....6.39.8.110.

WEEN

And 'twas their point, I ween, to make it last: ....4.HS2.94.61.
Scolds answer foul-mouth'd Scolds; bad Neighbourhood I
     ween. ....6.14ii.18.43.
(A Milliner's I ween) ....6.61.39.182.
O! happy would it be, I ween, ...6.94.81.262.

WEEP

And Trees weep Amber on the Banks of *Po*; ....1.PSp.62.67.
Taught Rocks to weep, and made the *Mountains* groan. ....1.PAu.16.82.
"My native Shades—there weep, and murmur there." ....1.W-F.202.168.
I rave, then weep, I curse, and then complain, ...1.TrSP.131.399.
Weep in her turn, and waste in equal Flame. ....2.ChJM.366.32.
To spin, to weep, and cully Human Race. ....2.ChWB.161.64.
And pitying saints, whose statues learn to weep! ....2.ElAb.22.320.
To read and weep is all they now can do. ....2.ElAb.48.323.
Now turn'd to heav'n, I weep my past offence, ...2.ElAb.187.335.
Thro' dreary wastes, and weep each other's woe; ....2.ElAb.242.339.
Here grief forgets to groan, and love to weep, ...2.ElAb.314.344.
Bear home six Whores, and make his Lady weep? ....3.Ep3.60.91.
To cry "You weep the Favours of her GRACE? ....4.HAdv.95.83.
Who would not weep, if *Atticus* were he! ....4.Arbu.214.111.
Here *Argus* soon might weep himself quite blind, ...6.9x.2.22.
Then as a lover give me leave to weep; ....6.20.62.67.
Who would not weep, if A[ddiso]n were He? ....6.49iii.30.143.
To weep upon our Cod in *Newfound-land:* ....6.96iii.76.273.
To weep upon Fresh Cod in *Newfound-*land. ....6.96ii.76A.273.
And all thy Dangers I weep o'er again! ....6.96iv.86.278.
Who would not weep, if A[ddiso]n were he'? ....6.98.66.285.
Or weep the Wounds her bleeding Country bore. ....Il.6.471.350.

WEEP (CONTINUED)

Shall neither hear thee sigh, nor see thee weep. ..... Il.6.593.355.
And pious Children o'er their Ashes weep. ..... Il.7.403.384.
Condemn'd for ten revolving Years to weep ..... Il.8.496.420.
Your selves condemn'd ten rolling Years to weep ..... Il.8.516.421.
The circling *Nereids* with their Mistress weep, ... Il.18.45.325.
Weep all the Night, and murmur all the Day: ..... Il.18.400.340.
And endless were the Grief, to weep for all. ..... Il.19.226.382.
There no sad Mother shall thy Fun'rals weep, ... Il.21.137.427.
Then parting from the Pyle he ceas'd to weep, ... Il.23.288.501.
Takes his sad Couch, more unobserv'd to weep, ... Il.24.7.535.
None by to weep them, to inhume them none; ..... Il.24.769.569.
They weep, and place him on the Bed of State. ..... Il.24.899.573.
You weep not for a perish'd Lord, alone. ..... Od.1.452.54.
Embracing left? Must I the warriors weep, ... Od.4.657.150.
All on the lonely shore he sate to weep, ... Od.5.105.177.
Too great a bliss to weep within her arms? ..... Od.11.256.394.
Their wonted grace, but only serve to weep. ..... Od.18.296.180.
Urge not this breast to heave, these eyes to weep; ..... Od.19.139.199.
I long must weep! nor will *Ulysses* come, ... Od.19.360.211.
Wakeful to weep and watch the tardy dawn ..... Od.19.694.229.
By grief relax'd, she wak'd again to weep: ..... Od.20.69.235.
To weep abroad, and leave to us the bow: ..... Od.21.93.263.
Roab thee in heav'nly vests, and round thee weep. ..... Od.24.76.351.

WEEP'

'Obedient slumbers that can wake and weep'; ..... 2.ElAb.212.337.

WEEPING

Ye weeping *Loves,* the Stream with Myrtles hide, ... 1.PWi.23.90.
The weeping Amber or the balmy Tree, ... 1.W-F.30.151.
In weeping Vaults her hallow'd Earth contains! ..... 1.W-F.302.177.
To hail this tree; and say, with weeping eyes, ... 1.TrFD.82.389.
Let weeping *Nilus* hear the Timbrel sound. ..... 1.TrSt.376.425.
Then, touch'd with Grief, the weeping Heav'ns distill'd ..... 1.TrES.256.459.
The Corps amidst his weeping Friends they laid, ... 1.TrES.348.462.
And *Ariel* weeping from *Belinda* flew, ... 2.RL4.12.183.
No weeping orphan saw his father's stores ..... 2.ElAb.135.330.
What tho' no weeping Loves thy ashes grace, ... 2.Elegy.59.367.
My Verse, and QUEENSB'RY weeping o'er thy Urn! ..... 4.Arbu.260.114.
This weeping marble had not ask'd thy Tear, ... 6.132.5.362.
Far from her native Soil, and weeping Sire. ..... Il.1.46.88.
Our weeping Wives, our tender Children call: ..... Il.2.166.136.
Behold them weeping for their native Shore! ..... Il.2.354.144.
I see thee trembling, weeping, Captive led! ..... Il.6.579.355.
(His sad Associates round with weeping Eyes) ..... Il.15.12.194.
No weeping Sister his cold Eye shall close, ... Il.15.398.212.
Then, touch'd with Grief, the weeping Heav'ns distill'd ..... Il.16.561.266.
The Corpse amidst his weeping Friends they laid, ... Il.16.835.275.
His weeping Father claims thy destin'd Head, ... Il.17.39.289.
Weeping she grasp'd his Knees: Th' Ambrosial Vest ..... Il.21.591.446.
Should *Dardan Priam,* and his weeping Dame ..... Il.22.441.473.
Should *Dardan Priam,* and the weeping Dame ..... Il.22.441A.473.
Around, a Train of weeping Sisters stands, ... Il.22.604.481.
Thro' Desarts wild now pours a weeping Rill; ..... Il.24.774.569.
Soft Sleep a Stranger to my weeping Eyes, ... Il.24.808.570.
First to the Corse the weeping Consort flew; ..... Il.24.906.574.
Thus to her weeping Maids she makes her Moan; ..... Il.24.940.575.
Her weeping Handmaids echo Groan for Groan. ..... Il.24.941.575.
With grief renew'd the weeping fair descends; ..... Od.1.427.53.
The weeping Monarch swells the mighty woe: ..... Od.4.252.131.
My knees, and weeping thus his suit address'd. ..... Od.10.314.359.
She faints, she falls; she lifts her weeping eyes. ..... Od.10.386.363.
The weeping sailors; nor less fierce their joy ..... Od.10.493.367.
But rarely seen, or seen with weeping eyes. ..... Od.15.558.96.
With'ring at heart to see the weeping Fair, ... Od.19.246.206.
And from my weeping eyes her cliffs withdrew; ..... Od.19.390.213.
An exile have I told, with weeping eyes, ... Od.19.565.224.
Weeping they bear the mangled heaps of slain, ... Od.24.478.371.

WEEPS

For ever murmurs, and for ever weeps; ..... 1.W-F.206.168.
Here o'er the Martyr-King the Marble weeps, ... 1.W-F.313.179.
In vain lost *Eloisa* weeps and prays, ... 2.ElAb.15.320.
She kneels, she weeps, and worse! resigns her Dow'r. ..... 4.HAdv.172.89.
For him she weeps, and him she weds agen. ..... 4.EpS2.109.319.
Beneath her Palm here sad Judæa weeps, ... 6.71.26.203.
My Heart weeps Blood at what the *Trojans* say, ... Il.6.672.360.
My Heart weeps blood to see your Glory lost! ..... Il.13.160.112.
And weeps his Country with a Father's Eyes. ..... Il.15.472.213.
From her lov'd Breast, with fonder Passion weeps; ..... Il.16.12.235.
There *Eriphylè* weeps, who loosely sold ..... Od.11.406.404.
In tedious cares, and weeps the night away. ..... Od.16.38.104.
My heart weeps blood, to see a soul so brave ..... Od.16.95.107.
But old *Laertes* weeps his life away, ... Od.16.145.109.
Yet starving Want amidst the riot weeps. ..... Od.17.542.158.
The King too weeps, the King too grasps their hands, ... Od.21.238.271.
Weeps a sad life in solitude away. ..... Od.23.388.343.

WEIGH

Weigh thy Opinion against Providence; ..... 3.EOM1.114.29.
Go, measure earth, weigh air, and state the tides; ..... 3.EOM2.20.56.
Weigh well the Cause from whence these Evils spring, ... 4.HAdv.102.83.
I weigh what author's heaviness prevails, ... 5.DunA2.336.142.
"I weigh what author's heaviness prevails; ..... 5.DunB2.368.315.
As Seamen at a Capstain Anchors weigh? ..... 6.96ii.30Z44.272.
"As Seamen at a Capstern Anchors weigh? ..... 6.96ii.66.273.
Convok'd to Council, weigh the Sum of things. ..... Il.13.930.149.
If he refuse, then let him timely weigh ..... Il.15.184.203.
This if refus'd, he bids thee timely weigh ..... Il.15.200.204.
Or weigh the great Occasion, and be more. ..... Il.16.682.270.
With sails we wing the masts, our anchors weigh, ... Od.4.785.156.
Of courts, presume to weigh their private cares? ..... Od.4.875.159.
And with consummate woe to weigh me down, ... Od.4.1073.167.
Nor weigh the labour, but relieve the woe) ..... Od.7.257.248.
My sword our cables cut, I call'd to weigh; ..... Od.10.146.347.

WEIGH (CONTINUED)

Their stores compleat, and ready now to weigh, ... Od.15.493.94.
With that, their anchors he commands to weigh, ... Od.15.589.98.
Weigh then my counsels in an equal scale, ... Od.24.528.373.

WEIGH'D

Is weigh'd with Judgment, and befits a Lord: ..... 2.ChJM.167.23.
But grant the worst; shall Women then be weigh'd ..... 2.ChJM.682.48.
His comprehensive head! all Int'rests weigh'd, ... 3.Ep1.142.26.
B. To Want or Worth well-weigh'd, be Bounty giv'n, ... 3.Ep3.229A.111.
To Want or Worth well-weigh'd, be Bounty giv'n, ... 3.Ep3.229.111.
Long weigh'd the Signal, and to *Hector* spoke. ..... Il.12.244.90.
Pensive, the rules the Goddess gave, he weigh'd; ..... Od.1.556.58.
With all my affluence when my woes are weigh'd, ... Od.4.95.124.
His words well-weigh'd, the gen'ral voice approv'd ..... Od.13.62.4.

WEIGHING

Dame *Justice,* weighing long the doubtful Right, ... 6.145.7.388.

WEIGHS

With nice Exactness weighs her woolly Store) ..... 1.TrES.168Z2.455.
Weighs the Men's Wits against the Lady's Hair; ..... 2.RL5.72.206.
One self-approving hour whole years out-weighs ..... 3.EOM4.255.152.
Where in nice balance, truth with gold she weighs, ... 5.DunA1.51.66.
Where, in nice balance, truth with gold she weighs, ... 5.DunB1.53.274.
With nice Exactness weighs her woolly Store) ..... Il.12.524.101.
Weighs down the Cloud, and blackens in the Sky, ... Il.14.24.158.
Orion's Dog (the Year when Autumn weighs) ..... Il.22.39.454.
And weighs, with equal Hand, their Destinies. ..... Il.22.274.467.
Jove weighs affairs of earth in dubious scales, ... Od.6.229.220.

WEIGHT

When *Ajax* strives, some Rock's vast Weight to throw, ... 1.EOC.370.282.
"Thy wretched Weight, nor dread the Deeps below!" ..... 1.TrSP.198.402.
And Fancy sinks beneath a Weight of Woe. ..... 1.TrSP.231.403.
Th'unwonted Weight, or drag the crooked Share, ... 1.TrSt.187.418.
Each sacred Accent bears eternal Weight, ... 1.TrSt.298.422.
And fix'd support the Weight of all the War: ..... 1.TrES.154.455.
Each equal Weight, nor this, nor that descends. ..... 1.TrES.170.455.
Not two strong Men th'enormous Weight cou'd raise, ... 1.TrES.185.456.
Beneath the Weight of threescore Years I bend, ... 2.ChJM.87.19.
To ease the Soul of one oppressive weight, ... 3.Ep1.57.19.
That Casting-weight Pride adds to Emptiness, ... 4.Arbu.177.109.
That wants or Force, or Light, or Weight, or Care, ... 4.2HE2.160.177.
Yet let me show, a Poet's of some weight, ... 4.2HE1.203.211.
Drag out with all its dirt and all its weight, ... 4.1740.71.336.
As clocks to weight their nimble motion owe, ... 5.DunA1.179.84.
Not so bold Arnall, with a weight of scull, ... 5.DunA2.293A.138.
As clocks to weight their nimble motion owe, ... 5.DunB1.183.283.
Not so bold Arnall; with a weight of skull, ... 5.DunB2.315.312.
Deserv'd of Gold an equal Weight? ..... 6.10.78.26.
The Springs above urg'd by the Weight below; ..... 6.17i(b).2.55.
Arriv'd Express, with News of Weight, ... 6.94.7.259.
That casting Weight, Pride adds to Emptiness; ..... 6.98.27.284.
Not two strong Men th' enormous Weight could raise, ... Il.5.371.284.
Great *Juno's* self has born her Weight of Pain, ... Il.5.481.291.
The Weight of Waters from *Hyperia's* Spring. ..... Il.6.583.355.
Of *Greece* and *Troy,* and pois'd the mighty Weight. ..... Il.8.90.401.
On *Ajax* thus a Weight of *Trojans* hung, ... Il.11.690.66.
A massy Weight: yet heav'd with ease by him, ... Il.11.778.69.
The Weight of Waters saps the yielding Wall, ... Il.12.25.82.
Bent with the Weight the nodding Woods are seen, ... Il.12.339.93.
And fix'd support the Weight of all the War: ..... Il.12.508.100.
Each equal Weight; nor this, nor that, descends. ..... Il.12.526.101.
Not two strong Men th' enormous Weight could raise, ... Il.12.539.101.
He drops the Weight, disabled with the Pain, ... Il.13.670.137.
Lays its eternal Weight; or fix'd as stands ..... Il.17.494.307.
Ordain'd, to sink me with the Weight of Woe? ..... Il.18.12.323.
For *Thetis* only such a Weight of Care? ..... Il.18.504.346.
He dropp'd his Arm, an unassisting Weight, ... Il.20.555.417.
The Plant uprooted to his Weight gave way, ... Il.21.270.432.
On this his Weight, and rais'd upon his Hand, ... Il.21.275.432.
Heavy with Death it sinks, and Hell receives the Weight. ..... Il.22.276.467.
By none in Weight or Workmanship excell'd: ..... Il.23.866.524.
Whose Weight and Size the circling *Greeks* admire, ... Il.23.975.528.
From the bent Angle sinks the loaden Weight; ..... Il.24.108.539.
Scarce three strong *Greeks* could lift its mighty Weight, ... Il.24.559.559.
Alas! what Weight of Anguish hast thou known? ..... Il.24.653.564.
And curse their cumbrous pride's unwieldy weight. ..... Od.1.214.43.
Have charms, with all their weight, t'allure the wise. ..... Od.1.496.56.
Perform'd their office, or his weight upheld: ..... Od.5.582.200.
Whom Fate has loaded with a weight of woes; ..... Od.7.288.250.
Then, heav'd on high, a rock's enormous weight ..... Od.9.284.318.
Then heaving high the stone's unwieldy weight, ... Od.9.400.322.
Prest with the weight of sleep that tames the strong: ..... Od.9.442.324.
Shake at the weight, and refluent beat the shore. ..... Od.9.634.332.
My feet thro' wine unfaithful to their weight, ... Od.11.77.385.
The earth o'erburthen'd groan'd beneath their weight, ... Od.11.379.401.
A weight of woes, and breath the vital air, ... Od.11.598.412.
Bore toils and dangers, and a weight of woes; ..... Od.11.766.424.
Against a cypress pillar lean'd his weight; ..... Od.17.415.152.
Full on the shoulder the rude weight descends: ..... Od.18.109.172.
Their feeble weight no more; his arms alone ..... Od.24.403.368.

WEIGHTY

And first *Sarpedon* tost his weighty Lance, ... 1.TrES.282.460.
And first *Sarpedon* whirl'd his weighty Lance, ... 1.TrES.282A.460.
These weighty Motives *January* the Sage ..... 2.ChJM.77.18.
As weighty Bodies to the Center tend, ... 2.TemF.429.284.
Fit to bestow the Laureat's weighty place. ..... 4.2HE1.379.227.
The matter's weighty, pray consider twice: ..... 4.EpS2.43.315.
(Tho' ne'er so weighty) reach a wondrous height; ..... 6.7.16.16.
The branch here bends beneath the weighty pear, ... 6.35.9.103.
The weighty Sceptre on his Back descends: ..... Il.2.327.143.
In measur'd Lists to toss the weighty Lance; ..... Il.3.323.208.
Ordain'd the first to whirl the weighty Lance. ..... Il.3.405.212.

WEIGHTY (CONTINUED)

Th' *Ætolian* Warrior tugg'd his weighty Spear: Il.4.615.250.
Full on his Neck, from *Hector's* weighty Hand; Il.7.17.363.
Great is thy Sway, and weighty are thy Cares; Il.9.97.437.
Wise, weighty Counsels aid a State distrest, Il.9.101.437.
Ten weighty Talents of the purest Gold, Il.9.157.440.
Ten weighty Talents of the purest Gold, Il.9.344.450.
Foretells the ratling Hail, or weighty Show'r, Il.10.6.2.
At once, his weighty Sword discharg'd a Wound Il.11.307.48.
Deep thro' his Front the weighty Faulchion fell. Il.13.772.141.
On his tir'd Arm the weighty Buckler hung; Il.16.132.242.
And first *Sarpedon* whirl'd his weighty Lance, Il.16.587.267.
At *Stenelaus* flew the weighty Stone, Il.16.714.271.
The weighty Shock his Neck and Shoulders feel; Il.16.956.280.
The Fields resounded with his weighty Fall. Il.17.361.301.
With *Merion's* Aid, the weighty Corse to rear; Il.17.802.319.
Fierce, at the Word, his weighty Sword he drew, Il.22.389.471.
At length *Epæus* dealt a weighty Blow Il.23.798.521.
With Force conjoin'd heave off the weighty Prize. Il.23.1005.529.
No human Hand the weighty Gates unbarr'd, Il.24.713.567.
Ye young, ye old, the weighty cause disclose: Od.2.37.62.
Sudden she sunk beneath the weighty woes; Od.4.934.162.
A weighty axe, with truest temper steel'd, Od.5.300.185.
Long press'd he heav'd beneath the weighty wave, Od.5.409.192.
The branch here bends beneath the weighty pear, Od.7.150.243.
Fit words attended on his weighty sense, Od.7.212.247.
Spontaneous wines from weighty clusters pour, Od.9.125.310.
With weighty steps, 'till at the ship I threw Od.10.198.350.
The belt in which my weighty faulchion hung; Od.10.310.359.
A weighty ax, and cleft the solid oak; Od.14.464.58.
His weighty faulchion o'er his shoulder ty'd: Od.14.596.66.
Peer against Peer; and what the weighty cause? Od.18.449.190.
The long incumbrance of the weighty spear Od.22.113.292.
Full thro' his neck the weighty faulchion sped: Od.22.365.305.

WELCOM'D

The good old *Priam* welcom'd her, and cry'd, Il.3.211.201.
Welcom'd with gifts of price, a sumless store! Od.19.312.209.

WELCOME

To these fond Eyes restore thy welcome Sails? 1.TrSP.247.404.
When opening Buds salute the welcome Day, 2.TemF.3.253.
To welcome death, and calmly pass away. 3.EOM2.260.86.
Welcome the coming, speed the going guest.) 4.HS2.160.67.
Welcome for thee, fair Virtue! all the past: 4.Arbu.358.122.
For thee, fair Virtue! welcome ev'n the *last!* 4.Arbu.359.122.
At Senate, and at Bar, how welcome would'st thou be! 6.8.30.18.
WELCOME, thrice welcome to thy native Place! 6.96iv.1.276.
WELCOME, thrice welcome to thy native Place! 6.96iv.1.276.
Welcome, my brave Hereditary Guest! Il.6.264.339.
So welcome these to *Troy's* desiring Train; Il.7.9.363.
Welcome, tho' *Greeks!* for not as Foes ye came; Il.9.263.445.
The welcome Sight *Ulysses* first descries, Il.10.550.27.
With joyful Tears to welcome *Hector* home; Il.17.242.297.
All hail, and welcome! whatsoe'er the Cause: Il.18.454.343.
Thee, welcome Goddess! what Occasion calls, Il.18.495.345.
Propitious once, and kind! Then welcome Fate! Il.22.385.471.
Of social welcome, mix'd the racy wine, Od.3.503.112.
Accept this welcome to the *Spartan* court; Od.4.70.122.
To grace the victor's welcome from the wars, Od.4.713.152.
You timely will return a welcome guest, Od.4.739.153.
The tenth presents our welcome native shore: Od.10.31.340.
The welcome burden, and bespoke my crew. Od.10.199.350.
So to *Ulysses* welcome sett the Sun. Od.13.44.3.
Take with free welcome what our hands prepare, Od.14.97.40.
Welcome the coming, speed the parting guest. Od.15.84.73.
Nor other hands than ours the welcome give. Od.15.554.96.
Riches are welcome then, not else, to me. Od.17.95.136.
Made welcome to my hospitable gate; Od.19.289.209.
His honour'd host, a welcome inmate there. Od.20.446.254.
Come, ever welcome, and thy succour lend; Od.22.225.297.
Soon as her eyes the welcome object met, Od.22.444.309.
Could work this wonder: welcome to thy own! Od.24.463.370.

WELKIN

Sound forth, my Brayers, and the welkin rend." 5.DunA2.236.129.
Sound forth my Brayers, and the welkin rend." 5.DunB2.246.307.
Soon as the Morn the rosie *Welkin* Warms Il.18.353A.338.

WELL

Blest Nymphs, whose Swains those Graces sing so well! 1.PSp.96.70.
To Plains with well-breath'd Beagles we repair, 1.W-F.121.161.
To Plains with well-bred Beagles we repair, 1.W-F.121A.161.
These *born* to Judge, as well as those to Write. 1.EOC.14.240.
And *censure freely* who have *written well.* 1.EOC.16.241.
Each might his *sev'ral Province* well command, 1.EOC.66.246.
Know well each ANCIENT'S proper *Character,* 1.EOC.119.252.
For there's a *Happiness* as well as *Care.* 1.EOC.142.255.
Thus when we view some well-proportion'd Dome, 1.EOC.247.268.
What oft was *Thought,* but ne'er so well *Exprest,* 1.EOC.298.273.
And such were *Prais'd* who but *endeavour'd well:* 1.EOC.511.295.
And such were *Prais'd* as but *endeavour'd well:* 1.EOC.511A.295.
'Twere well, might Criticks still this Freedom take; 1.EOC.584.306.
Tho' Learn'd, well-bred; and tho' well-bred, sincere; 1.EOC.635.311.
Tho' Learn'd, well-bred; and tho' well-bred, sincere; 1.EOC.635.311.
Nature's chief Master-piece is writing well. 1.EOC.724.323.
Well, he may please himself, and you may share 1.TrPA.122.370.
Is well by Wit's more lasting Flames supply'd. 1.TrSP.38.395.
Is well by Wit's more lasting Charms supply'd. 1.TrSP.38A.395.
Not Him, who made me love those Shades so well, 1.TrSP.168A.400.
This Breast which once, in vain! you lik'd so well; 1.TrSP.226.403.
Does with glad Speed the well-known Journey go, 1.TrSt.142A.415.
With eager Speed the well-known Journey took, 1.TrSt.142.416.
Thought a short Life well lost for endless Fame. 1.TrSt.717.440.
His wretched Father, known too well by Fame? 1.TrSt.809.443.
Yet well dissembling his untimely Joys, 1.TrUl.136.470.

WELL (CONTINUED)

In Arts of Counsel, and Dissembling well: 1.TrUl.172.471.
Against proud *Ilion's* well-defended Tow'rs, 1.TrUl.192.472.
Before the Walls of well-defended *Troy,* 1.TrUl.192A.472.
Full well they merit all they feel, and more: 2.ChJM.30.16.
But fix'd before, and well resolv'd was he, 2.ChJM.83.18.
How I have liv'd, alas you know too well, 2.ChJM.89.19.
(Who, tho' not *Faith,* had *Sense* as well as We) 2.ChJM.179.23.
Who knows too well the State you thus commend 2.ChJM.195.24.
'Tis well, 'tis wondrous well, the Knight replies, 2.ChJM.216.25.
'Tis well, 'tis wondrous well, the Knight replies, 2.ChJM.216.25.
Well sung sweet *Ovid,* in the Days of yore, 2.ChJM.514.40.
I have a Soul to save as well as You; 2.ChJM.578.43.
Sow'd in a Sack, and plung'd into a Well: 2.ChJM.588.43.
Of Earthly Bliss, was well bestow'd on thee! 2.ChJM.634.45.
As well you view the Leacher in the Tree, 2.ChJM.643.46.
And well this Honourable Knight you see: 2.ChJM.644.46.
Well, I'm a Woman, and as such must speak; 2.ChJM.694.48.
As surely seize thee, as I saw too well. 2.ChJM.771.52.
With well-dissembl'd Virtue in her Face: 2.ChJM.812.54.
To be so well deluded by their Wives. 2.ChJM.820.54.
Freakish when well, and fretful when she's Sick. 2.ChWB.91.61.
I, like a Dog, cou'd bite as well as whine; 2.ChWB.152.64.
Well, I may make my Will in Peace, and die, 2.ChWB.178.65.
"Well shou'd you practise, who so well can teach. 2.ChWB.187.65.
"Well shou'd you practise, who so well can teach. 2.ChWB.187.65.
Full well the Secrets of my Soul she knew, 2.ChWB.267.69.
And knew full well to raise my Voice on high; 2.ChWB.338.73.
A Train of well-drest Youths around her shone, 2.RL*A*1.21.127.
A well-bred *Lord* t'assault a gentle *Belle?* 2.RL1.8.145.
Fair Nymphs, and well-drest Youths around her shone, 2.RL2.5.159.
In equal Curls, and well conspir'd to deck 2.RL2.21.160.
Who speaks so well shou'd ever speak in vain. 2.RL4.132.194.
What then remains, but well our Pow'r to use, 2.RL5.29.201.
And wise *Aurelius,* in whose well-taught Mind 2.TemF.165.268.
The constant Tenour of whose well-spent Days 2.TemF.330.280.
Yet would the World believe us, all were well. 2.TemF.389.282.
That well-known name awakens all my woes. 2.ElAb.30.321.
Sad proof how well a lover can obey! 2.ElAb.172.334.
Such if there be, who loves so long, so well; 2.ElAb.363.348.
The well-sung woes will sooth my pensive ghost; 2.ElAb.365.348.
The well-sung woes shall sooth my pensive ghost; 2.ElAb.365A.348.
Is it, in heav'n, a crime to love too well? 2.Elegy.6.362.
The lights and shades, whose well accorded strife 3.EOM2.121.70.
Ah! if she lend not arms, as well as rules, 3.EOM2.151.73.
Lust, thro' some certain strainers well refin'd, 3.EOM2.189.77.
As, in some well-wrought picture, light and shade, 3.EOM2.208.81.
For, what one likes if others like as well, 3.EOM3.273.120.
Th'according music of a well-mix'd State. 3.EOM3.294.122.
There needs but thinking right, and meaning well; 3.EOM4.32.131.
As well as dream such trifles are assign'd, 3.EOM4.179.144.
Act well your part, there all the honour lies. 3.EOM4.194.145.
Nature well known, no Miracles remain, 3.Ep1.208A.33.
Men may be read, as well as Books too much. 3.Ep1.10.16.
How Trade increases, and the World goes well; 3.Ep1.159.29.
Nature well known, no prodigies remain, 3.Ep1.208.33.
But he's a bolder man who dares be well: 3.Ep2.130.61.
'Tis well—but, Artists! who can paint or write, 3.Ep2.187.65.
But Wisdom's Triumph is well-tim'd Retreat, 3.Ep2.225.68.
And yet, believe me, good as well as ill, 3.Ep2.269.72.
Well then, since with the world we stand or fall 3.Ep3.79A.94.
B. To Want or Worth well-weigh'd, be Bounty giv'n, 3.Ep3.229A.111.
To Want or Worth well-weigh'd, be Bounty giv'n, 3.Ep3.229.111.
But well-dispers'd, is Incense to the Skies. 3.Ep3.236.111.
And well (he thought) advis'd him, "Live like me." 3.Ep3.316.119.
As well his Grace reply'd, "Like you, Sir John? 3.Ep3.317.119.
The well-bred cuckolds in St. James's air: 3.Ep3.388.124.
The rich Buffet well-colour'd Serpents grace, 3.Ep4.153.152.
The doubling Lustres dance as well as she; 4.HS1.48A.9.
What-e'er my Fate, or well or ill at Court, 4.HS1.92.13.
Well, if it be my time to quit the Stage, 4.JD4.1.27.
Well met (he cries) and happy sure for each, 4.JD4.66A.31.
"Oh! Sir, politely well! nay, let me dye, 4.JD4.112A.35.
For these are Actors too, as well as those: 4.JD4.223.45.
Thou hast at least bestow'd one penny well. 4.HS2.110.63.
Well, if the Use be mine, can it concern one 4.HS2.165.69.
Weigh well the Cause from whence these Evils spring, 4.HAdv.102.83.
For well they knew, proud Trappings serve to hide 4.HAdv.116.85.
Well-natur'd *Garth* inflam'd with early praise, 4.Arbu.137.105.
Well might they rage; I gave them but their due. 4.Arbu.174.109.
Curst be the Verse, how well soe'er it flow, 4.Arbu.283.116.
So well-bred Spaniels civilly delight 4.Arbu.313.118.
Well, I cou'd wish that still in Richmens Homes 4.JD2A.121.142.
Well, I could wish, that still in lordly domes 4.JD2.115.143.
Well let Them pass and so may those that use 4.JD2A.41.136.
"Prodigious well!" his great Commander cry'd, 4.2HE2.42.167.
But knottier Points we knew not half so well, 4.2HE2.58.169.
Not quite so well however as one ought; 4.2HE2.100.171.
And much too wise to walk into a Well: 4.2HE2.191.179.
Well, on the whole, *plain* Prose must be my fate: 4.2HE2.198.179.
Confess as well your Folly, as Disease? 4.2HE2.215.179.
Well, on the whole, then Prose must be my fate: 4.2HE2.198A.179.
The Laws of God, as well as of the Land, 4.2HE2.246.183.
A part I will enjoy, as well as keep. 4.2HE2.285.185.
Learn to live well, or fairly make your Will; 4.2HE2.322.187.
We build, we paint, we sing, we dance as well, 4.2HE1.46.197.
If Time improve our Wit as well as Wine, 4.2HE1.49.199.
Or well-mouth'd Booth with emphasis proclaims, 4.2HE1.123.205.
So well in paint and stone they judg'd of merit: 4.2HE1.384.227.
Well may he blush, who gives it, or receives; 4.2HE1.414.231.
If to live well means nothing but to eat; 4.1HE6.111.245.
Return well travell'd, and transform'd to Beasts, 4.1HE6.123.245.
The Man that loves and laughs, must sure do well. 4.1HE6.129.246.
Well, now I have all this and more, 4.HS6.7.251.
Because they see me us'd so well: 4.HS6.102.257.
My lord, your Favours well I know; 4.1HE7.21.269.

WELL (CONTINUED)

Can I retrench? Yes, mighty well, 4.1HE7.75.273.
Shou'd chance to make the well-drest Rabble stare; 4.1HE1.111.287.
Well, if a King's a Lion, at the least 4.1HE1.120.287.
"Well, but the Poor"—the Poor have the same itch: 4.1HE1.154.291.
But well may put some Statesmen in a fury. 4.EpS1.52.302.
And all the well-whipt Cream of Courtly Sense, 4.EpS1.70.303.
Ten Metropolitans in preaching well; 4.EpS1.132.307.
And C[hesterfiel]d who speaks so well and writes, 4.1740.25.333.
Well-purg'd, and worthy Withers, Quarles, and Blome. 5.DunA1.126.78.
Well-purg'd, and worthy *W[esle]y, W[att]s,* and *Bl[ome]* 5.DunA1.126A.78.
Well-purg'd, *W[att]s, Q[uarle]s,* and *Bl[ome].* 5.DunA1.126B.78.
Well-pleas'd he enter'd, and confess'd his Home: 5.DunA1.222.90.
She form'd this image of well-bodied air, 5.DunA2.38.100.
With pert flat eyes she window'd well its head, 5.DunA2.39.100.
But that this well-disputed game may end, 5.DunA2.235.129.
"Or dark dexterity of groping well. 5.DunA2.266.134.
Right well mine eyes arede the myster wight, 5.DunA3.183.170.
Right well mine eyes arede that myster wight, 5.DunA3.183A.170.
Well purg'd, and worthy Settle, Banks, and Broome. 5.DunB1.146.280.
Well pleas'd he enter'd, and confess'd his home. 5.DunB1.266.289.
She form'd this image of well-body'd air; 5.DunB2.42.298.
With pert flat eyes she window'd well its head; 5.DunB2.43.298.
But that this well-disputed game may end, 5.DunB2.245.307.
"Or dark dexterity of groping well. 5.DunB2.278.309.
Thro' Lud's fam'd gates, along the well-known Fleet 5.DunB2.359.315.
"Right well mine eyes arede the myster wight, 5.DunB3.187.329.
See now, half-cur'd, and perfectly well-bred, 5.DunB4.323.375.
And well dissembled em'rald on his hand, 5.DunB4.348.377.
Bid me with Pollio sup, as well as dine: 5.DunB4.392.380.
Well might, alas! that threaten'd vessel fail, 6.3.3.7.
(You see how well I can contrive a 6.10.19.25.
And for a Butcher's well-fed Daughter 6.10.61.26.
Well argu'd, Faith! Your Point you urge 6.10.91.27.
But lov'd her full as well it may be, 6.10.99.27.
Is, I've been well a Week, or so. 6.10.106.27.
The Musick of a well-tun'd State, 6.11.35Z5.31.
'But the well-worn Paths of the Nymphs of Drury 6.13.24.39.
'Twere well if she would pare her Nails, 6.14v(a).5.48.
With Wit well-natur'd, and with Books well-bred; 6.19.8.62.
With Wit well-natur'd, and with Books well-bred; 6.19.8.62.
Well might you wish for Change, by those accurst, 6.19.39.63.
Howe're she liv'd none ever dy'd so well. 6.20.16.66.
So hop'd to stand as well as he 6.30.17A.86.
Then, well-belov'd and trusty Letters! 6.30.75.89.
And wild ambition well deserves its woe. 6.32.12.96.
Well, if our author in the Wife offends, 6.41.25.114.
Well spread with Sense, shall be the Nation's Plaister. 6.48ii.12.134.
Whatever Conscience thinks not well 6.50.13A.146*.
Here thy well-study'd Marbles fix our eye; 6.52.33.157.
This small, well-polish'd gem, the work of years! 6.52.40.157.
Ah *Moore!* thy Skill were well employ'd, 6.53.29.162.
Ev'n so all Things shall prosper well, 6.54.11.164.
The present well, and ev'n the past enjoy. 6.55.11.167.
Nor Standish well japan'd, avails 6.58.11.171.
Since you have Brains as well as Men, 6.58.67.173.
For Gay can well make two of me. 6.61.41.182.
For Gay may well make two of me. 6.61.41A.182.
Might e'en as well be termd the Sea; 6.67.18.195.
Hearts so sincere th' Almighty saw well pleas'd, 6.69i.5.198.
Victims so pure Heav'n saw well pleas'd 6.69ii.3.199.
Live well and fear no sudden fate; 6.69ii.5.199.
For you well know, that Wit's of no Religion. 6.82iii.2.230.
And the gay Conscience of a life well spent, 6.86.12.245.
And the glad Conscience of a life well spent, 6.86.12A.245.
And saw her Cocks well serve her Hens. 6.93.4.256.
His Rump well pluck'd with Nettles stings, 6.93.21.257.
Well may they rage; I give them *but* their Due. 6.98.24.284.
Well may they rage; I gave them *but* their Due. 6.98.24A.284.
Well then, poor *G[ay]* lies under ground! 6.103.1.295.
Well, Sir, suppose, the *Busto's* a damn'd head, 6.105vi.1.302.
Well-pleas'd to give our neighbours due applause, 6.107.21.311.
The man, as well as poet, is in fault. 6.107.26.311.
Few words are best; I wish you well: 6.114.1.321.
Great G[eorge ii]! such servants since thou well can'st lack, 6.116v.5.327.
For DUCK can *thresh,* you know, as well as *write.* 6.116vi.6.327.
And dipt them in the sable Well, 6.140.11.378.
"What *well?* what *weapon?* (Flavia cries) 6.140.13.378.
Trusts in God, that as well as he was, he shall be. 6.144.8.386.
The Cause of Strife remov'd so rarely well, 6.145.9.388.
But he's a bolder Man who dares be well; 6.154.16.403.
The due Reward of many a well-fought Field? Il.1.158.95.
Let both unite with well-consenting Mind, Il.1.370.106.
Tyrant, I well deserv'd thy galling Chain, Il.1.388.106.
A well-rigg'd Ship for *Chrysa's* sacred Shores: Il.1.405.107.
Is but to mention what too well you know. Il.1.477.110.
Then well may this long Stay provoke their Tears, Il.2.360.144.
In Arts of Council, and in speaking well! Il.2.441.148.
And, well refresh'd, to bloody Conflict haste. Il.2.453.149.
And they whom *Thebè's* well-built Walls inclose, Il.2.604.156.
And shuns the Fate he well deserv'd to find. Il.3.46.190.
She seem'd an ancient Maid, well-skill'd to cull Il.3.477.214.
Grœa, her Fav'rite Maid, well-skill'd to cull Il.3.477A.214.
He lies, and waits thee on the well-known Bed: Il.3.484.215.
A well-tim'd Counsel with a willing Ear? Il.4.124.226.
Fits the sharp Arrow to the well-strung Bow. Il.4.147.227.
Born to the Fate ye well deserve to find! Il.4.277.234.
Well might I wish, could Mortal Wish renew Il.4.370.238.
His high Concern may well excuse this Rage, Il.4.468.242.
In well-built *Pheræ* held his lofty Seat: Il.5.672.300.
Whose perjur'd Monarch well deserv'd his Fate; Il.5.805.304.
Well may we deem the wond'rous Birth thy own. Il.5.1081.318.
And Steel well-temper'd, and persuasive Gold. Il.6.62.326.
Well hast thou known proud *Troy's* perfidious Land, Il.6.69.327.
And well her Natives merit at thy Hand! Il.6.70.327.
The well-arm'd *Greeks* to *Agamemnon* lead. Il.7.379.382.

WELL (CONTINUED)

Guard well the Walls, relieve the Watch of Night, Il.7.446.386.
And well the plenteous Freight supply'd the Host: Il.7.567.392.
And all your Masters well-spent Care repay. Il.8.229.408.
Still first to act what you advise so well. Il.9.76.436.
And each well worthy of a Royal Bed; Il.9.188.441.
(The well-wrought Harp from conquer'd *Thebæ* came, Il.9.247.445.
And each well worthy of a Royal Bed; Il.9.375.451.
Well hast thou spoke; but at the Tyrant's Name, Il.9.759.471.
'Tis well, my Sons, your nightly Cares employ, Il.10.225.12.
A well-prov'd Casque with Leather Braces bound Il.10.309.16.
And his the Glory to have serv'd so well. Il.10.370.19.
And Steel well temper'd, and refulgent Gold. Il.10.452.23.
And steel well-temper'd, and persuasive Gold. Il.11.176.43.
Well be Apollo are thy Pray'rs repaid, Il.11.467.54.
The well-known Voice thrice *Menelaus* hears: Il.11.581.60.
I know him well, distinguish'd o'er the Field Il.11.648.62.
For Words well meant, and Sentiments sincere? Il.12.246.90.
To toil and struggle thro' the well-fought Day. Il.13.4.103.
With well-rang'd Squadrons strongly circled round: Il.13.172.113.
Her hardy Heroes from the well-fought Plains Il.13.293.119.
To the cool Fountains, thro' the well-known Meads. Il.13.625.135.
As on some ample Barn's well-harden'd Floor, Il.13.739.139.
How widely differs this from warring well? Il.13.912.148.
Better from Evils, well foreseen, to run, Il.14.86.162.
Mark well his Port! his Figure and his Face Il.14.553.189.
He spake, and smil'd severe, for well he knew Il.14.557.190.
Thy soft Deceits, and well-dissembled Love. Il.15.38.195.
Well-pleas'd the Thund'rer saw their earnest care, Il.15.176.203.
Well was the Crime, and well the Vengeance spar'd; Il.15.256.207.
Well was the Crime, and well the Vengeance spar'd; Il.15.256.207.
He snuffs the Females in the well known Plain, Il.15.304.208.
The well-stor'd Quiver on his Shoulders hung: Il.15.520.217.
And fam'd for Prowess in a well-fought Field; Il.15.624.220.
(Well known in Fight on *Selles'* winding Shore, Il.15.627.220.
Thus on a Roe the well-breath'd Beagle flies, Il.15.697.222.
In Wisdom great, in Arms well known to Fame: Il.15.771.226.
So well the Chief his Naval Weapon sped, Il.15.906.232.
A Soul well-suiting that tempestuous Kind, Il.16.52.237.
Due to the Toils of many a well-fought Day; Il.16.77.238.
A *Dardan* Youth there was, well-known to Fame, Il.16.972.281.
Why not as well *Achilles'* Fate be giv'n Il.16.1040.283.
The well-aim'd Weapon on the Buckler rings, Il.17.46.289.
All, whom this well-known Voice shall reach from far, Il.17.298.299.
Tho' well he knew, to make proud *Ilion* bend, Il.17.468.305.
Who dares desert this well-disputed Day! Il.17.475.306.
And in his well-known Voice to *Sparta* calls. Il.17.625.312.
'Tis well (said *Ajax)* be it then thy Care Il.17.801.319.
Thy want of Arms (said *Iris)* well we know, Il.18.235.333.
When Morning dawns, our well-appointed Pow'rs Il.18.325.337.
O could I hide him from the Fates as well, Il.18.533.347.
With well-taught Feet: Now shape, in oblique ways, Il.18.691.357.
Alarm'd, transported, at the well-known Sound, Il.19.47.373.
And 'tis his Fault to love those Sons too well. Il.20.221.403.
His well-known Face when great *Achilles* ey'd, Il.21.56.424.
Thy well-known Captive, great *Achilles!* see, Il.21.84.425.
Beneath one Roof of well-compacted Shields Il.22.6.453.
Yet for my Sons I thank ye Gods! 'twas well: Il.22.98.456.
Well have they perish'd, for in Fight they fell. Il.22.99.456.
The well-breath'd Beagle drives the flying Fawn; Il.22.244.465.
Furious he drove the well-directed Dart: Il.22.410.472.
Thy Rage, Implacable! too well I knew: Il.22.446.474.
Astyanax, from her well-guarded Walls, Il.22.651.483.
Now from the well-fed Swine black Smokes aspire, Il.23.39.488.
And well-fed Sheep, and sable Oxen slay: Il.23.205.498.
He well observ'd the Chief who led the way, Il.23.535.511.
I well discern him, as he shakes the Rein, Il.23.562.511.
The well-ply'd Whip is hung athwart the Beam; Il.23.592.513.
Pleas'd with the well-turn'd Flattery of a Friend, Il.23.636.515.
Wisely and well, my Son, thy Words have prov'd Il.23.719.518.
Those due distinctions thou so well can'st pay, Il.23.749.520.
Now prove that Prowess you have prov'd so well. Il.23.859.523.
A well-fed Ox was for the second plac'd; Il.23.876.524.
The well-fed Bull (the second Prize) he shar'd, Il.23.913.525.
For this, thy well-aim'd Arrow, turn'd aside, Il.23.1024.529.
(Well-pleas'd to share the Feast,) amid the Quire Il.24.82.538.
And last a large well-labour'd Bowl had place, Il.24.287.548.
Last to the Yoke the well-match'd Mules they bring, Il.24.343.550.
And know so well how god-like *Hector* dy'd? Il.24.475.556.
Large was the Door, whose well-compacted Strength Il.24.557.559.
Admonish'd thus his well-attending mind. Od.3.18.87.
How well the son appeas'd his slaughter'd sire! Od.3.239.97.
Well hast thou spoke (the blue-ey'd maid replies) Od.3.455.109.
A well-fed bullock from the grassy mead; Od.3.535.113.
Right well, reply'd the King, your speech displays Od.4.365.137.
A Tree, and well-dissembled foliage wears. Od.4.622.149.
Tho' well I see thy graces far above Od.5.277.184.
Of youth eternal well the diff'rence know Od.5.279.185.
Too well alas! the island Goddess knew, Od.5.385.190.
Oh! had I dy'd before that well-fought wall, Od.5.395.191.
Too well the turns of mortal chance I know, Od.5.540.198.
Well known to me the palace you enquire, Od.7.37.235.
She past, delighted with the well-known seats; Od.7.105.239.
Whose well-taught mind the present age surpast, Od.7.210.247.
With silver shone the throne; his Lyre well strung Od.8.63.265.
O friends, he cries, the stranger seems well-skill'd Od.8.143.270.
Well hast thou spoke, (*Euryalus* replies) Od.8.153.271.
Studious of freight, in naval trade well skill'd, Od.8.181.272.
But heav'n denies the praise of thinking well. Od.8.198.273.
My well-aim'd shaft with death prevents the foe: Od.8.250.276.
As flies an arrow from the well-drawn bow. Od.8.262.276.
By storms and hunger worn: Age well may fail, Od.8.265.277.
Well hast thou spoke, and well thy gen'rous tongue Od.8.269.277.
Well hast thou spoke, and well thy gen'rous tongue Od.8.269.277.
The woe of *Greece,* and sing so well the woe? Od.8.534.291.
The well-fill'd palace, the perpetual feast, Od.9.5.301.

WELL (CONTINUED)
All haste assembled, at his well-known roar, ...Od.9.477.325.
Well fed, and largest of the fleecy care. ....Od.9.506.326.
But soon his sons their well-known guest descry'd, ...Od.10.69.342.
For well I know that soon the heav'nly pow'rs ....Od.11.85.385.
Well to deserve, be all my cares employ'd: ....Od.11.435.405.
His words well-weigh'd, the gen'ral voice approv'd ....Od.13.62.4.
Yet well dissembling his untimely joys, ...Od.13.303.21.
In arts of counsel, and dissembling well. ....Od.13.339.24.
Against proud *Ilion's* well-defended tow'rs; ....Od.13.359.24.
To form strong buskins of well-season'd hyde. ....Od.14.26.36.
Oh! had he perisht on some well-fought day, ...Od.14.401.55.
As well thou claim'st a grateful stranger's love! ....Od.14.491.59.
There all but I, well fenc'd with cloak and vest, ...Od.14.538.63.
Well hast thou spoke (rejoin'd th' attentive swain) ....Od.14.576.64.
Well arm'd, and fenc'd against nocturnal air; ....Od.14.595.66.
From those the well-pair'd mules we shall receive, ...Od.15.98.73.
Well pleas'd, and pleasing, in our cottage rest, ...Od.15.356.86.
Well pleas'd the hospitable rites to pay. ....Od.15.586.98.
Swift to the town the well-row'd gally flew: ....Od.15.596.99.
Some well-known friend (*Eumæus)* bends this way; ....Od.16.9.102.
Thy well-try'd wisdom, and thy martial fame, ...Od.16.263.117.
Mark well my voice, *Ulysses* strait replies: ....Od.16.280.118.
The Prince well pleas'd to disappoint their wiles, ...Od.16.496.131.
Well may this Palace admiration claim, ...Od.17.314.147.
Full well I mark'd the features of his face, ...Od.17.448.155.
Before his feet the well-fill'd scrip he threw, ...Od.17.553.159.
Gird well thy loins, approach, and feel my might: ....Od.18.37.168.
Why urge we not to blows? Well-pleas'd they spring ....Od.18.48.169.
A kid's well-fatted entrails (tasteful food!) ....Od.18.51.169.
And fears well-feign'd, disguis'd his dauntless heart: ....Od.18.57.169.
By just degrees like well-turn'd columns rise: ....Od.18.77.170.
Swell o'er his well-strung limbs, and brace his frame! ....Od.18.85.170.
A kid's well fatted entrails, rich with blood: ....Od.18.144.173.
Howe'er 'tis well! that Sleep a-while can free ....Od.18.237.178.
Thy well-knit frame unprofitably strong, ...Od.18.259.179.
Well-pleas'd *Ulysses* hears his Queen deceive ....Od.18.325.182.
The well-horn'd foot indissolubly join'd; ....Od.20.368.250.
The well-aim'd arrow thro' the distant ring, ...Od.21.4.258.
Across her knees she lay'd the well-known bow, ...Od.21.57.262.
I well remember (for I gaz'd him o'er ....Od.21.96.263.
Heir of my Father's strength, as well as throne. ....Od.21.122.264.
And each lock fast the well-compacted gate: ....Od.21.253.272.
They heard well pleas'd: the ready heralds bring ....Od.21.286.273.
Oh! could the vigor of this arm as well ....Od.21.403.279.
And each lock fast the well-compacted gate; ....Od.21.414.280.
And now his well-known bow the Master bore, ...Od.21.427.280.
I thoughtless err'd in) well secure that door: ....Od.22.173.295.
Averse they heard me when I counsell'd well, ...Od.22.353.304.
With well-concerted art to end his woes, ...Od.23.33.320.
Or well-defending some beleaguer'd wall, ...Od.24.138.354.
But well repair'd; and gloves against the thorn. ....Od.24.266.361.
Thy squadron'd vineyards well thy art declare, ...Od.24.289.363.
Well hop'd we then to meet on this fair shore, ...Od.24.365.366.
Well-pleas'd you told its nature, and its name, ...Od.24.393.368.

WELL-AIM'D
The well-aim'd Weapon on the Buckler rings, ...Il.17.46.289.
For this, thy well-aim'd Arrow, turn'd aside, ...Il.23.1024.529.
My well-aim'd shaft with death prevents the foe: ....Od.8.250.276.
The well-aim'd arrow thro' the distant ring, ...Od.21.4.258.

WELL-APPOINTED
When Morning dawns, our well-appointed Pow'rs ....Il.18.325.337.

WELL-ARM'D
The well-arm'd *Greeks* to *Agamemnon* lead. ....Il.7.379.382.

WELL-ATTENDING
Admonish'd thus his well-attending mind. ....Od.3.18.87.

WELL-BELOV'D
Then, well-belov'd and trusty Letters! ....6.30.75.89.

WELL-BODIED
She form'd this image of well-bodied air, ...5.DunA2.38.100.

WELL-BODY'D
She form'd this image of well-body'd air; ....5.DunB2.42.298.

WELL-BREATH'D
To Plains with well-breath'd Beagles we repair, ...1.W-F.121.161.
Thus on a Roe the well-breath'd Beagle flies, ...Il.15.697.222.
The well-breath'd Beagle drives the flying Fawn; ....Il.22.244.465.

WELL-BRED
To Plains with well-bred Beagles we repair, ...1.W-F.121A.161.
Tho' Learn'd, well-bred; and tho' well-bred, sincere; ....1.EOC.635.311.
Tho' Learn'd, well-bred; and tho' well-bred, sincere; ....1.EOC.635.311.
A well-bred *Lord* t'assault a gentle *Belle?* .... 2.RL1.8.145.
The well-bred cuckolds in St. James's air: ....3.Ep3.388.124.
So well-bred Spaniels civilly delight ....4.Arbu.313.118.
See now, half-cur'd, and perfectly well-bred, ...5.DunB4.323.375.
With Wit well-natur'd, and with Books well-bred; ....6.19.8.62.

WELL-BUILT
And they whom *Thebè's* well-built Walls inclose, ...Il.2.604.156.
In well-built *Pheræ* held his lofty Seat: ....Il.5.672.300.

WELL-COLOUR'D
The rich Buffet well-colour'd Serpents grace, ...3.Ep4.153.152.

WELL-COMPACTED
Beneath one Roof of well-compacted Shields ....Il.22.6.453.
Large was the Door, whose well-compacted Strength ....Il.24.557.559.
And each lock fast the well-compacted gate: ....Od.21.253.272.

WELL-COMPACTED (CONTINUED)
And each lock fast the well-compacted gate; ....Od.21.414.280.

WELL-CONCERTED
With well-concerted art to end his woes, ...Od.23.33.320.

WELL-CONSENTING
Let both unite with well-consenting Mind, ...Il.1.370.106.

WELL-DEFENDED
Against proud *Ilion's* well-defended Tow'rs, ...1.TrUl.192.472.
Before the Walls of well-defended *Troy,* .... 1.TrUl.192A.472.
Against proud *Ilion's* well-defended tow'rs; ....Od.13.359.24.

WELL-DEFENDING
Or well-defending some beleaguer'd wall, ...Od.24.138.354.

WELL-DIRECTED
Furious he drove the well-directed Dart: ....Il.22.410.472.

WELL-DISPERS'D
But well-dispers'd, is Incense to the Skies. ....3.Ep3.236.111.

WELL-DISPUTED
But that this well-disputed game may end, ...5.DunA2.235.129.
But that this well-disputed game may end, ...5.DunB2.245.307.
Who dares desert this well-disputed Day! ....Il.17.475.306.

WELL-DISSEMBL'D
With well-dissembl'd Virtue in her Face: ....2.ChJM.812.54.

WELL-DISSEMBLED
Thy soft Deceits, and well-dissembled Love. ....Il.15.38.195.
A Tree, and well-dissembled foliage wears. ....Od.4.622.149.

WELL-DRAWN
As flies an arrow from the well-drawn bow. ....Od.8.262.276.

WELL-DREST
A Train of well-drest Youths around her shone, ...2.RL*A*1.21.127.
Fair Nymphs, and well-drest Youths around her shone, ...2.RL2.5.159.
Shou'd chance to make the well-drest Rabble stare; ....4.1HE1.111.287.

WELL-FATTED
A kid's well-fatted entrails (tasteful food!) ....Od.18.51.169.

WELL-FED
And for a Butcher's well-fed Daughter ....6.10.61.26.
Now from the well-fed Swine black Smokes aspire, ...Il.23.39.488.
And well-fed Sheep, and sable Oxen slay: ....Il.23.205.498.
A well-fed Ox was for the second plac'd; ....Il.23.876.524.
The well-fed Bull (the second Prize) he shar'd, ...Il.23.913.525.
A well-fed bullock from the grassy mead; ....Od.3.535.113.

WELL-FEIGN'D
And fears well-feign'd, disguis'd his dauntless heart: ....Od.18.57.169.

WELL-FILL'D
The well-fill'd palace, the perpetual feast, ...Od.9.5.301.
Before his feet the well-fill'd scrip he threw, ...Od.17.553.159.

WELL-FOUGHT
The due Reward of many a well-fought Field? ....Il.1.158.95.
To toil and struggle thro' the well-fought Day. ....Il.13.4.103.
Her hardy Heroes from the well-fought Plains ....Il.13.293.119.
And fam'd for Prowess in a well-fought Field; ....Il.15.624.220.
Due to the Toils of many a well-fought Day; ....Il.16.77.238.
Oh! had I dy'd before that well-fought wall, ...Od.5.395.191.
Oh! had he perisht on some well-fought day, ...Od.14.401.55.

WELL-GUARDED
Astyanax, from her well-guarded Walls, ...Il.22.651.483.

WELL-HARDEN'D
As on some ample Barn's well-harden'd Floor, ...Il.13.739.139.

WELL-HORN'D
The well-horn'd foot indissolubly join'd; ....Od.20.368.250.

WELL-KNIT
Thy well-knit frame unprofitably strong, ...Od.18.259.179.

WELL-KNOWN
Does with glad Speed the well-known Journey go, ...1.TrSt.142A.415.
With eager Speed the well-known Journey took, ...1.TrSt.142.416.
That well-known name awakens all my woes. ....2.ElAb.30.321.
Thro' Lud's fam'd gates, along the well-known Fleet ....5.DunB2.359.315.
He lies, and waits thee on the well-known Bed: ....Il.3.484.215.
The well-known Voice thrice *Menelaus* hears: ....Il.11.581.60.
To the cool Fountains, thro' the well-known Meads. ....Il.13.625.135.
A *Dardan* Youth there was, well-known to Fame, ...Il.16.972.281.
All, whom this well-known Voice shall reach from far, ...Il.17.298.299.
And in his well-known Voice to *Sparta* calls. ....Il.17.625.312.
Alarm'd, transported, at the well-known Sound, ...Il.19.47.373.
His well-known Face when great *Achilles* ey'd, ...Il.21.56.424.
Thy well-known Captive, great *Achilles!* see, ...Il.21.84.425.
She past, delighted with the well-known seats; ....Od.7.105.239.
All haste assembled, at his well-known roar, ...Od.9.477.325.
But soon his sons their well-known guest descry'd, ...Od.10.69.342.
Some well-known friend (*Eumæus)* bends this way; ....Od.16.9.102.
Across her knees she lay'd the well-known bow, ...Od.21.57.262.
And now his well-known bow the Master bore, ...Od.21.427.280.

WELL-LABOUR'D
And last a large well-labour'd Bowl had place, ...Il.24.287.548.

WELL-MATCH'D
Last to the Yoke the well-match'd Mules they bring, ...Il.24.343.550.

WELL-MIX'D
Th'according music of a well-mix'd State. ....3.EOM3.294.122.

WELL-MOUTH'D
Or well-mouth'd Booth with emphasis proclaims, ...4.2HE1.123.205.

WELL-NATUR'D
Well-natur'd *Garth* inflam'd with early praise, ...4.Arbu.137.105.
With Wit well-natur'd, and with Books well-bred; ....6.19.8.62.

WELL-PAIR'D
From those the well-pair'd mules we shall receive, ...Od.15.98.73.

WELL-PLEAS'D
Well-pleas'd he enter'd, and confess'd his Home: ....5.DunA1.222.90.
Well-pleas'd to give our neighbours due applause, ...6.107.21.311.
Well-pleas'd the Thund'rer saw their earnest care, ...Il.15.176.203.
(Well-pleas'd to share the Feast,) amid the Quire ....Il.24.82.538.
Why urge we not to blows? Well-pleas'd they spring ....Od.18.48.169.
Well-pleas'd *Ulysses* hears his Queen deceive ....Od.18.325.182.
Well-pleas'd you told its nature, and its name, ...Od.24.393.368.

WELL-PLY'D
The well-ply'd Whip is hung athwart the Beam; ....Il.23.592.513.

WELL-POLISH'D
This small, well-polish'd gem, the work of years! ....6.52.40.157.

WELL-PROPORTION'D
Thus when we view some well-proportion'd Dome, ...1.EOC.247.268.

WELL-PROV'D
A well-prov'd Casque with Leather Braces bound ....Il.10.309.16.

WELL-PURG'D
Well-purg'd, and worthy Withers, Quarles, and Blome. ....5.DunA1.126.78.
Well-purg'd, and worthy W[esle]y, W[att]s, and B[lome] ....5.DunA1.126A.78.
Well-purg'd, W[att]s, Q[uarle]s, and B[lome]. ....5.DunA1.126B.78.

WELL-RANG'D
With well-rang'd Squadrons strongly circled round: ....Il.13.172.113.

WELL-RIGG'D
A well-rigg'd Ship for *Chrysa's* sacred Shores: ....Il.1.405.107.

WELL-ROW'D
Swift to the town the well-row'd gally flew: ....Od.15.596.99.

WELL-SEASON'D
To form strong buskins of well-season'd hyde. ....Od.14.26.36.

WELL-SKILL'D
She seem'd an ancient Maid, well-skill'd to cull ....Il.3.477.214.
Grœa, her Fav'rite Maid, well-skill'd to cull ....Il.3.477A.214.
O friends, he cries, the stranger seems well-skill'd ....Od.8.143.270.

WELL-SPENT
The constant Tenour of whose well-spent Days ....2.TemF.330.280.
And all your Masters well-spent Care repay. ....Il.8.229.408.

WELL-STOR'D
The well-stor'd Quiver on his Shoulders hung: ....Il.15.520.217.

WELL-STRUNG
Fits the sharp Arrow to the well-strung Bow. ....Il.4.147.227.
Swell o'er his well-strung limbs, and brace his frame! ....Od.18.85.170.

WELL-STUDY'D
Here thy well-study'd Marbles fix our eye; ....6.52.33.157.

WELL-SUITING
A Soul well-suiting that tempestuous Kind, ...Il.16.52.237.

WELL-SUNG
The well-sung woes will sooth my pensive ghost; ....2.ElAb.365.348.
The well-sung woes shall sooth my pensive ghost; ....2.ElAb.365A.348.

WELL-TAUGHT
And wise *Aurelius*, in whose well-taught Mind ....2.TemF.165.268.
With well-taught Feet: Now shape, in oblique ways, ...Il.18.691.357.
Whose well-taught mind the present age surpast, ...Od.7.210.247.

WELL-TEMPER'D
And Steel well-temper'd, and persuasive Gold. ....Il.6.62.326.
And steel well-temper'd, and persuasive Gold. ....Il.11.176.43.

WELL-TIM'D
But Wisdom's Triumph is well-tim'd Retreat, ...3.Ep2.225.68.
A well-tim'd Counsel with a willing Ear? ....Il.4.124.226.

WELL-TRY'D
Thy well-try'd wisdom, and thy martial fame, ...Od.16.263.117.

WELL-TUN'D
The Musick of a well-tun'd State, ...6.11.35Z5.31.

WELL-TURN'D
Pleas'd with the well-turn'd Flattery of a Friend, ...Il.23.636.515.
By just degrees like well-turn'd columns rise: ....Od.18.77.170.

WELL-WEIGH'D
B. To Want or Worth well-weigh'd, be Bounty giv'n, ...3.Ep3.229A.111.
To Want or Worth well-weigh'd, be Bounty giv'n, ...3.Ep3.229.111.

WELL-WEIGH'D (CONTINUED)
His words well-weigh'd, the gen'ral voice approv'd ....Od.13.62.4.

WELL-WHIPT
And all the well-whipt Cream of Courtly Sense, ...4.EpS1.70.303.

WELL-WORN
'But the well-worn Paths of the Nymphs of Drury ....6.13.24.39.

WELL-WROUGHT
As, in some well-wrought picture, light and shade, ...3.EOM2.208.81.
(The well-wrought Harp from conquer'd *Thebæ* came, ...Il.9.247.445.

WELLING
(Forth welling from the Wound, as prone he lay) ....Il.17.93.291.

WELSTED
Welsted his mouth with Classic flatt'ry opes, ...5.DunA2.197.124.
But Welsted most the Poet's healing balm ....5.DunA2.199B.125.
Unlucky Welsted! thy unfeeling master ....5.DunA2.201B.126.
Not Welsted so: drawn endlong by his scull, ...5.DunA2.293.138.
But nimbler W[elste]d reaches at the ground, ...5.DunA2.293B.138.
"Flow Welsted, flow! like thine inspirer, Beer, ...5.DunA3.163.166.
But Welsted most the Poet's healing balm ....5.DunB2.207.306.
Unlucky Welsted! thy unfeeling master, ...5.DunB2.209.306.
"Flow Welsted, flow! like thine inspirer, Beer, ...5.DunB3.169.328.

WELSTED'S
Three thousand Suns went down on *Welsted's* Lye: ....4.Arbu.375.123.
And furious D[enni]s foam in W[elsted]'s rage. ....5.DunA1.104B.72*.

WELTER
Or doom'd to welter in the whelming main. ....Od.1.210.42.

WELTERS
Moulders in earth, or welters on the wave, ...Od.14.155.43.

WENCH
Still to his wench he creeps on knocking knees, ...3.Ep1.232A.35.
Still to his wench he crawls on knocking knees, ...3.Ep1.232.35.
But here's his point; A Wench (he cries) for me! ....4.HAdv.69.81.
Call himself Barrister to ev'ry wench, ...4.JD2.59.139.
Calls himself Barrister to ev'ry Wench, ...4.JD2A.63.138.
(Wench, I'd have said did Rhyme not hinder) ....6.10.57.26.
So some coarse Country Wench, almost decay'd, ...6.49i.15.138.

WENCHES
They dealt in *Sackcloth*, and turn'd *Cynder-Wenches*: ....6.95.2.264.

WENCHING
I tax'd them oft with Wenching and Amours, ...2.ChWB.154.64.

WENT
And not a Mask went *un-improv'd* away: ....1.EOC.541.299.
A Hiss from all the Snaky Tire went round; ....1.TrSt.162.417.
Each, in his own Opinion, went his Way; ....2.ChJM.225.25.
The Time approach'd, to Church the Parties went, ...2.ChJM.309.29.
And Songs were sung, and flowing Bowls went round; ....2.ChJM.354.31.
His Task perform'd, he sadly went his Way, ...2.ChJM.363.31.
And Songs were sung, and Healths went nimbly round; ....2.ChJM.354A.31.
They left the Hall, and to his Lodging went; ....2.ChJM.411.34.
Thus singing as he went, at last he drew ....2.ChJM.716.49.
She seiz'd a Twig, and up the Tree she went. ....2.ChJM.739.50.
That oft a Day I to this Gossip went; ....2.ChWB.278.70.
"Where once I went to church, I'll now go twice— ....3.Ep3.367.123.
Yet went to COURT!—the Dev'l wou'd have it so. ....4.JD4.14.27.
Horace and he went hand in hand in song. ....4.Arbu.234.112.
Three thousand Suns went down on *Welsted's* Lye: ....4.Arbu.375.123.
I told you when I went, I could not write; ....4.2HE2.28.167.
[But (happy for him as the times went then) ....5.DunB4.115.352.
So back to Pollio, hand in hand, they went. ....5.DunB4.396.381.
While the long solemn Unison went round: ....5.DunB4.612.405.
No chains I felt, but went a glorious ghost, ...6.20.17.66.
She sigh'd not that They stay'd, but that She went. ....6.45.10.125.
She went, to plain-work, and to purling brooks, ...6.45.11.125.
She went from Op'ra, park, assembly, play, ...6.45.13.125.
You went, you saw, you heard: With Virtue fraught, ...6.96iii.21.275.
'Tis known all the Dives's ever went there. ....6.122.12.341.
And whither *Enoch* went before him. ....6.151.8.399.
Thro' *Paris'* Shield the forceful Weapon went, ...Il.3.440.213.
Deep in his Breast above the Pap it went, ...Il.4.611.250.
Thro' his broad Back and heaving Bosom went: ....Il.5.72.269.
Thro' *Amphius'* Belt and heaving Belly went: ....Il.5.759.303.
The *Phrygian* Queen to her rich Wardrobe went, ...Il.6.358.343.
Her parting Step? If to the Fane she went, ...Il.6.475.350.
When to grim *Pluto's* gloomy Gates he went; ....Il.8.446.418.
Thus (with a Javelin in his Hand) he went, ...Il.10.37.4.
He went a Legat, but return'd a Foe: ....Il.10.342.18.
Then to consult on farther Methods went, ...Il.11.762.69.
Along the Shore with hasty Strides he went; ....Il.11.935.77.
Then to the Ships with surly Speed he went, ...Il.13.223.116.
Beneath his Ear the pointed Arrow went; ....Il.13.841.145.
But mindful of the Gods, *Achilles* went ....Il.16.268.249.
Between the Jaw and Ear the Javelin went; ....Il.16.737.272.
It flew, and fir'd the Nations as it went. ....Il.17.98.291.
Between his Cheek and Ear the Weapon went, ...Il.17.697.314.
Achilles to the Strand obedient went; ....Il.19.43.373.
From his dead Friend the pensive Warrior went, ...Il.23.47.488.
Sunk was his Heart; his Colour went and came; ....Il.24.443.554.
Unseen, thro' all the hostile Camp they went, ...Il.24.551.559.
With solemn Pace thro' various Rooms he went, ...Il.24.578.560.
These to unyoke the Mules and Horses went, ...Il.24.724.568.
This felt no Chains, but went a glorious Ghost ....Il.24.948.575.
They went, and found a hospitable race: ....Od.9.102.307.
Thus fierce he said: we sighing went our way, ...Od.10.87.343.
They went, and kept the wheel's smooth-beaten road ....Od.10.117.346.

WENT (CONTINUED)

They went; but as they ent'ring saw the Queen ....Od.10.127.347.
We went, *Ulysses!* (such was thy command) ....Od.10.295.357.
Mean-time the King, his Son, and *Helen,* went ....Od.15.114.74.
Gave her the sign, and to his vessel went. ....Od.15.500.94.
Propt on a staff, and trembling as he went. ....Od.17.413.152.
By many an easy step, the matron went; ....Od.21.42.261.
Thro' ev'ry ring the victor arrow went. ....Od.24.202.358.
To old *Autolycus's* realms I went. ....Od.24.387.367.
A son of *Dolius* on the message went, ...Od.24.567.375.

WEPT

The *Naiads* wept in ev'ry Watry Bow'r, ...1.PSu.7.72.
And sigh'd full oft, but sigh'd and wept in vain; ....2.ChJM.491.39.
And sigh'd for Woe, but sigh'd and wept in vain; ....2.ChJM.491A.39.
He wept, kind Soul! and stoop'd to kiss my Face; ....2.ChWB.422.77.
Once like thy self, I trembled, wept, and pray'd, ...2.ElAb.311.344.
"Why,—if I must—(then wept) I give it Paul." ....3.Ep1.259.37.
Thou wept'st, and with thee wept each gentle Muse. ....5.DunB4.44.345.
He ceas'd, and wept. With innocence of mien, ...5.DunB4.419.382.
Voiture was wept by all the brightest Eyes, ...6.19.18.62.
Here lies the Friend most wept, the Son most dear: ....6.85.2D.242.
She wept, she blubber'd, and she tore her Hair. ....6.96ii.2.270.
Prais'd, wept, and honour'd, by the Muse he lov'd. ....6.97.6.282.
The tragic muse, returning, wept her woes. ....6.107.4.310.
Wept by each Friend, forgiv'n by ev'ry Foe: ....6.128.4.355.
For each he wept, but for his *Rhesus* most: ....Il.10.613.29.
They wept, and shar'd in human Miseries. ....Il.17.487.307.
So flam'd his fiery Mail. Then wept the Sage; ....Il.22.43.454.
While both thy Parents wept thy fatal Hour, ...Il.22.546.479.
And wept her god-like Son's approaching Doom: ....Il.24.114.539.
And as he stood, he spoke and wept by turns. ....Od.2.32.61.
Around their sov'reign wept the menial fair, ...Od.4.956.162.
Conceal'd he wept: the King observ'd alone ....Od.8.91.267.
Ev'n *Circe* wept, her adamantine heart ....Od.10.473.366.
For thee, my son, I wept my life away; ....Od.11.240.393.
With thee we fell; *Greece* wept thy hapless fates, ...Od.11.683.418.
They wept abundant, and they wept aloud. ....Od.16.237.114.
They wept abundant, and they wept aloud. ....Od.16.237.114.
She saw, she wept, she ran with eager pace, ...Od.17.41.134.
Those winged deaths that many a matron wept. ....Od.21.16.259.
Thus had their joy wept down the setting sun, ...Od.21.240.271.

WEPT'ST

Thou wept'st, and with thee wept each gentle Muse. ....5.DunB4.44.345.

WERE (OMITTED)
389

WERT

Thou wert from *Ætna's* burning Entrails torn, ...1.PAu.91.86.
Thou wert my guide, philosopher, and friend? ....3.EOM4.390.166.
Nor wert thou, Isis! wanting to the day, ...5.DunB4.193.361.
Thou wert e'er Nature's self began to be, ...6.8.2.17.
Thou wert e'er Nature first began to be, ...6.8.2A.17.
Who wert, e're time his rapid race begun, ...6.23.5.73.
All this thou wert; and being this before, ...6.73.8.210.
"How wert thou wont to walk with cautious Tread, ...6.96ii.67.273.
When wert thou known in ambush'd Fights to dare, ...Il.1.299.101.
Wert thou expos'd to all the hostile Train, ...Il.4.188.230.
What once thou wert, oh ever might'st thou be. ....Il.4.366.238.
But wert thou greater, thou must yield to me. ....Il.5.799.304.
Ulysses lies: oh wert thou lay'd as low! ....Od.2.214.72.
But ah *Ulysses!* wert thou giv'n to know ....Od.5.263.184.
First thou wert wont to crop the flow'ry mead, ...Od.9.527.328.
Thou, thou my son wert my disease and death; ....Od.11.245.393.
Of woes and wand'rings thou wert born to bear? ....Od.14.56.38.

WESLEY

Well-purg'd, and worthy *W[esle]y, W[att]s,* and *Bl[ome]* ....5.DunA1.126A.78.
Wesley, if Wesley 'tis they mean, ...6.102.1.294.
Wesley, if Wesley 'tis they mean, ...6.102.1.294.

WESLEY'S

And furious D[enni]s foam in W[esley]'s rage. ....5.DunA1.104E.72*.

WEST

Or when his Evening Beams the West adorn, ...1.TrSt.213.419.
Thus flying East and West, and North and South, ...2.TemF.473.286.
From East to West, and view from Pole to Pole! ....Il.3.349.209.
The Cloud condensing as the West-Wind blows: ....Il.4.319.236.
A double Tempest of the West and North ....Il.9.6.431.
Full from the west she bids fresh breezes blow; ....Od.2.460.83.
Down rush'd the night. East, west, together roar, ...Od.5.379.190.
And now the west-wind whirls it o'er the sea. ....Od.5.423.192.
Wide to the west the horid gulph extends, ...Od.12.103.436.
Oh should the fierce south-west his rage display, ...Od.12.343.448.
The gloomy West, and whistles in the skies. ....Od.12.478.455.
Now sunk the West, and now a southern breeze ....Od.12.503.457.
The driving storm the wat'ry west-wind pours, ...Od.14.512.62.

WEST-WIND

The Cloud condensing as the West-Wind blows: ....Il.4.319.236.
And now the west-wind whirls it o'er the sea. ....Od.5.423.192.
The driving storm the wat'ry west-wind pours, ...Od.14.512.62.

WESTERN

Here Western Winds on breathing Roses blow. ....1.PSp.32.63.
Where-e'er you find *the cooling Western Breeze,* ....1.EOC.350.279.
The Sun wou'd sink into the Western Main, ...1.TrSt.328.424.
Who view the *Western* Sea's extreamest Bounds, ...1.TrSt.816.443.
Behold him sinking in the Western Main. ....1.TrUl.121.470.
Some beg an eastern, some a western wind: ....5.DunA2.84.108.
Some for an eastern, some a western wind: ....5.DunA2.84A.108.
And all the Western World believe and sleep. ....5.DunA3.92.157.

WESTERN (CONTINUED)

Some beg an eastern, some a western wind: ....5.DunB2.88.300.
And all the western world believe and sleep. ....5.DunB3.100.324.
The balmy spirit of the western gale. ....6.35.11.103.
Fair, o'er the western world, renew'd his light, ...6.107.2.310.
And as on Corn when Western Gusts descend, ...Il.2.179.137.
As when a western Whirlwind, charg'd with Storms, ...Il.11.395.52.
Or beat the Pinions of the Western Gale, ...Il.19.461.391.
Rush the swift Eastern and the Western Wind: ....Il.21.389.436.
The *Western Spirit,* and the *North* to rise; ....Il.23.259.499.
Down sunk the Sun behind the western hills. ....Od.2.437.82.
And views *Gortyna* on the western side; ....Od.3.376.104.
His glowing axle in the western waves; ....Od.4.488.143.
The fragrant murmurs of the western gale. ....Od.4.774.155.
His golden circlet in the western shade. ....Od.4.1036.166.
Shot thro' the western clouds a dewy ray; ....Od.6.382.230.
The balmy spirit of the western gale ....Od.7.152.243.
Or nations subject to the western ray. ....Od.8.30.263.
Behold him sinking in the western main. ....Od.13.288.19.
Vain hope! ten suns had warm'd the western strand, ...Od.19.224.204.
'Till *Phœbus* wheeling to the western goal ....Od.19.495.220.

WESTMINSTER

To him who notches Sticks at Westminster. ....4.1HE1.84.285.
We thrive at *Westminster* on Fools like you, ...6.145.11.388.

WESTMINSTER'S

Till Westminster's whole year be holiday; ....5.DunA3.332.191.
'Till Westminster's whole year be holiday, ...5.DunB3.336.336.
All Flesh is humbled, Westminster's bold race ....5.DunB4.145.355.

WESTPHALY

As Hog to Hog in Huts of *Westphaly;* ....4.EpS2.172.323.

WESTWARD

Westward, a sumptuous Frontispiece appear'd, ...2.TemF.75.258.

WET

The flowing Bowl, will you not wet your Lip? ....4.HAdv.148.87.
Then, wet and weary, home he far'd, ...6.79.137.222.
Beat by rude blasts, and wet with wintry show'rs, ...Od.6.154.216.
Weary and wet th' *Ogygian* shores I gain, ...Od.12.531.458.

WETT

Yet Dew or Rain may wett us to the Shift, ...6.42vi.5.120.

WETTING

Unweeting Wantons of their wetting Woe! ....6.42vi.2.120.

WEY

And chalky *Wey,* that rolls a milky Wave: ....1.W-F.344.183.

WHALE

Tho' stiff with Hoops, and arm'd with Ribs of Whale. ....2.RL2.120.167.
Or some enormous whale the God may send, ...Od.5.538.198.

WHALEBONES

Fans clap, Silks russle, and tough Whalebones crack; ....2.RL5.40.202.

WHALES

Whales sport in woods, and dolphins in the skies, ...5.DunA3.242.177.
Whales sport in woods, and dolphins in the skies; ....5.DunB3.246.332.
And heavy Whales in aukward Measures play: ....Il.13.45.107.

WHARTON

If Parts allure thee, think how Wh[arton] shin'd, ...3.EOM4.281A.154.
Wh[arton], the Shame and Scandal of mankind: ....3.EOM4.282A.154.
The prospect clears, and Wharton stands confest. ....3.Ep1.179.30.
Wharton, the scorn and wonder of our days, ...3.Ep1.180.30.
Ask you why Wharton broke thro' ev'ry rule? ....3.Ep1.206.33.
Comets are regular, and Wharton plain. ....3.Ep1.209.33.
Unhappy Wharton, waking, found at last! ....3.Ep3.86.94.
Poor W[harton] nipt in Folly's broadest bloom, ...5.DunB4.513.392*.

WHARTON'S

And furious D[enni]s foam in W[harton]'s rage. ....5.DunA1.104C.72*.

WHAT (OMITTED)
1428

WHAT-E'ER

What-e'er my Fate, or well or ill at Court, ...4.HS1.92.13.
What-e'er he gives, are giv'n for You to hate. ....5.DunA3.220.176.
What-e'er thro' life's whole series I have done ....Od.22.228.297.

WHAT-ERE

What-ere thou speak'st, let this be understood; ....6.2.35.6.

WHAT-TIME

What-time old *Saturn,* from *Olympus* cast, ...Il.14.234.172.
What-time, deserting *Ilion's* wasted Plain, ...Il.14.285.176.
What-time, a vengeful Monster of the Main ....Il.20.178.401.
What-time, with hunger pin'd, my absent mates ....Od.4.497.144.
What-time the Judge forsakes the noisy bar ....Od.12.519.457.
What-time it chanc'd the palace entertain'd ....Od.15.458.92.

WHAT'ER

And oh! what'er heav'n destin'd to betide ....Od.3.114.91.
Should he return, what'er my beauties prove, ...Od.18.297.181.

WHAT'S

What's *roundly smooth,* or *languishingly slow;* ....1.EOC.359.280.
What's Fame? a fancy'd life in others breath, ...3.EOM4.237.149.
What's Fame? that fancy'd life in others breath, ...3.EOM4.237A.149.
Just what you hear, you have, and what's unknown ....3.EOM4.239.150.

WHAT'S (CONTINUED)

And knows what's fit for ev'ry State to do; ....4.JD4.47.29.
Howe'er, what's now *Apocrypha*, my Wit, ...4.JD4.286.49.
And, what's more rare, a Poet shall say *Grace*. ....4.HS2.150.67.
And, what's more rare, the Poet shall say *Grace*. ....4.HS2.150A.67.
What's *Property?* dear Swift! you see it alter ....4.HS2.167.69.
What's wrong is wrong, wherever it be done: ....4.HAdv.78.81.
(For Use will father what's begot by Sense) ....4.2HE2.170.177.
What's long or short, each accent where to place, ...4.2HE1.207.213.
As, "What's o'clock?" And, "How's the Wind?" ....4.HS6.89.255.
Or what's in either of the *Houses:* ....4.HS6.144.259.
Nay half in Heav'n—except (what's mighty odd) ....4.1HE1.187.293.
What's that to you, who ne'er was out nor in? ....4.EpS2.163.322.
And breaks our rest, to tell us what's a clock. ....5.DunB4.444.384.
Plu—Plutarch, what's his name that writes his life? ....6.41.31.114.
And lov'd his country—but what's that to you? ....6.41.40.114.
What's Fame with Men, by Custom of the Nation, ...6.46.1.127.
What's Fame in Men, by Custom of the Nation, ...6.46.1A.127.
Then what's join'd to a place, ...6.91.7.253.
A modest man may like what's not his own. ....6.105ii.4.300.
And (what's the Top of all your Tricks) ....6.135.11.366.
What's He, whose Arms lie scatter'd on the Plain? ....Il.3.254.204.
But what's the Quarrel then of *Greece* to *Troy?* ....Il.9.445.454.
(For what's sequester'd from celestial view?) ....Od.4.514.144.
Shameless they give, who give what's not their own. ....Od.17.536.158.

WHAT'SQUIRE

What'Squire his Lands, what Citizen his Wife? ....4.JD4.149.37.

WHATE'ER

Clears, and *improves* whate'er it shines upon, ...1.EOC.316.274.
But wave whate'er to *Cadmus* may belong, ...1.TrSt.19.410.
For whate'er Work was undischarg'd a-bed, ...2.ChJM.473.38.
And keep good Humour still whate'er we lose? ....2.RL5.30.201.
Whate'er proud *Rome*, or artful *Greece* beheld, ...2.TemF.63.256.
Forget, renounce me, hate whate'er was mine. ....2.ElAb.294.343.
Whate'er the Passion, knowledge, fame, or pelf, ...3.EOM2.261.86.
Whate'er of life all-quick'ning æther keeps, ...3.EOM3.115.103.
Whate'er is best administer'd is best: ....3.EOM3.304.124.
Good, Pleasure, Ease, Content! whate'er thy name: ....3.EOM4.2.128.
Happier as kinder, in whate'er degree, ...3.EOM4.359.163.
Born with whate'er could win it from the Wise, ...3.Ep1.182.30.
Yet is, whate'er she hates or ridicules. ....3.Ep2.120A.60.
Yet is, whate'er she hates and ridicules. ....3.Ep2.120.60.
And be whate'er Vitruvius was before: ....3.Ep4.194.155.
Who tells whate'er you think, whate'er you say, ...4.Arbu.297.117.
Who tells whate'er you think, whate'er you say, ...4.Arbu.297.117.
And write whate'er he pleas'd, except his *Will;* ....4.Arbu.379.125.
At Court, who hates whate'er he read at School. ....4.2HE1.106.203.
Admire whate'er the maddest can admire. ....4.1HE6.68.241.
Till having done whate'er was fit or fine, ...4.1740.37.334.
Whate'er he gives, are giv'n for you to hate. ....5.DunB3.222.331.
Whate'er of dunce in College or in Town ....5.DunB4.87.349.
Whate'er of mungril no one class admits, ...5.DunB4.89.349.
Whate'er the talents, or howe'er design'd, ...5.DunB4.161.357.
Such Sheets as these, whate'er be the Disaster, ...6.48ii.11.134.
Fools grant whate'er ambition craves, ...6.51i.27.152.
Whate'er we think, whate'er we see, ...6.53.3.161.
Whate'er we think, whate'er we see, ...6.53.3.161.
Be not (exalted to whate'er degree) ....6.73.14.210.
Whate'er he draws to please, must all be thine. ....6.107.30.311.
Whate'er was Beauteous, or whate'er was Great, ...6.108.4.312.
Whate'er was Beauteous, or whate'er was Great, ...6.108.4.312.
Whate'er was Beauteous, and whate'er was Great, ...6.108.4A.312.
Whate'er was Beauteous, and whate'er was Great, ...6.108.4A.312.
Yet is whate'er she hates or ridicules. ....6.154.6.403.
But to resume whate'er thy Av'rice craves, ...Il.1.161.95.
'Tis thine whate'er the Warrior's Breast inflames, ...Il.2.277.141.
Whate'er our Master craves, submit we must, ...Il.2.291.141.
Who dares to act whate'er thou dar'st to view. ....Il.4.409.240.
Whate'er thy Will, *Patroclus* shall obey. ....Il.11.741.68.
The Feast, the Dance; whate'er Mankind desire, ...Il.13.797.143.
Whate'er bold *Trojan* arm'd his daring Hands ....Il.15.904.232.
Whate'er the Cause, reveal thy secret Care, ...Il.16.27.236.
To Heav'n is ow'd whate'er your own you call, ...Il.16.1020.282.
This done, whate'er a Warrior's Use requires ....Il.18.705.357.
Whate'er *Ulysses* promis'd at thy Tent: ....Il.19.140.377.
Whate'er we feel, 'tis *Jove* inflicts the Woe: ....Il.19.282.384.
Whate'er of active Force, or acting Fire, ...Il.20.410.412.
Whate'er this Heart can prompt, or Hand obey; ....Il.20.411.412.
Soon as he clears whate'er their passage staid, ...Il.21.293.433.
Whate'er can rest a discontented Shade; ....Il.23.112.492.
Whate'er his Honour asks, or Heart demands. ....Il.24.154.541.
Whate'er thy title in thy native sky, ...Od.4.508.144.
Whate'er the Gods shall destine me to bear ....Od.5.283.185.
Whate'er thy Fate, the ills our wrath could raise ....Od.5.484.195.
That, and whate'er our daughter asks, we give. ....Od.6.84.209.
Whate'er is honest, Stranger, I approve. ....Od.7.397.256.
We know whate'er the Kings of mighty name ....Od.12.228.443.
Whate'er beneath the sun's bright journey lies. ....Od.12.230.443.
To whom whate'er his slave enjoys is ow'd, ...Od.14.75.39.
Whate'er gives man the envy'd name of Great; ....Od.17.502.157.
Close let them keep, whate'er invades their ear; ....Od.21.254.272.
Whate'er my childish fancy ask'd, bestow'd; ....Od.24.394.368.

WHATERE

Whatere it bids me do ....6.50.14A.146*.

WHATEVER

Whatever Nature has in *Worth* deny'd, ...1.EOC.205.264.
Whatever was the Cause, the tender Dame ....2.ChJM.430.35.
To her I told whatever cou'd befal; ....2.ChWB.269.70.
To her I told whatever did befal; ....2.ChWB.269A.70.
Whatever Spirit, careless of his Charge, ...2.RL2.123.167.
Respecting Man, whatever wrong we call, ...3.EOM1.51.19.
From Nature's chain whatever link you strike, ...3.EOM1.245.45.

WHATEVER (CONTINUED)

One truth is clear, "Whatever IS, is RIGHT." ....3.EOM1.294.51.
Whatever warms the heart, or fills the head, ...3.EOM2.141.71.
"Whatever IS, is RIGHT."—THIS world, 'tis true, ...3.EOM4.145.141.
Shew'd erring Pride, WHATEVER IS, IS RIGHT; ....3.EOM4.394.166.
To build, to plant, whatever you intend, ...3.Ep4.47.141.
Her Shape her own, whatever Shape she have, ...4.HAdv.163.89.
Disdain whatever CORNBURY disdains; ....4.1HE6.61.241.
Whatever his religion or his blood, ...4.1740.95.337.
O thou! whatever Title please thine ear, ...5.DunA1.17.62.
O Thou! whatever title please thine ear, ...5.DunB1.19.270.
Whatever Conscience thinks not well ....6.50.13A.146*.
(Whatever was in either Good, ...6.64.3.189.
I hear whatever can delight inspire ....6.106ii.5.307.
Attend whatever title please thine ear, ...6.106iv.7.307.
(Whatever stinking Fops suppose) ....6.135.30.367.
Whatever an Heir, or a Friend in his stead, ...6.144.3.386.
With those I left whatever dear could be; ....Il.5.587.296.
Whatever Treasures *Greece* for me design, ...Il.8.349.414.
Princes all hail! whatever brought ye here, ...Il.9.261A.445.
Princes all hail! whatever brought you here, ...Il.9.261.445.
Whatever means of Safety can be sought, ...Il.10.164.9.
Whatever Counsels can inspire our Thought, ...Il.10.165.9.
Whatever Methods, or to fly, or fight; ....Il.10.166.9.
By chance of Fight whatever Wounds you bore, ...Il.13.374.123.
Whatever Hand shall win *Patroclus* slain, ...Il.17.270.298.
Whatever be our Fate, yet let us try ....Il.18.321.337.
But know, whatever Fate I am to try, ...Il.22.363.470.
Whatever Pity that stern Heart can know. ....Il.24.573.560.
Whatever ill the friendless orphan bears, ...Od.4.219.130.
Forget whatever was in Fortune's pow'r, ...Od.10.544.369.
Whatever toils the great *Ulysses* past, ...Od.13.5.1.
And know, whatever heav'n ordains, is best. ....Od.13.487.29.
Whatever frugal nature needs, is thine, ...Od.15.528.95.
Jove fix'd it certain, that whatever day ....Od.17.392.150.
To him, whatever to a guest is ow'd ....Od.24.318.365.

WHATLEY

True to the bottom, see *R[oome]* and *Wh[atle]y* creep, ...5.DunA2.287B.137.

WHATLEY'S

And furious *D[unto]n* foam in *Wh[atley]'s* rage ....5.DunA1.104A.72*.

WHATSOE'ER

But whatsoe'er the Father's Race, ...6.135.53.368.
All hail, and welcome! whatsoe'er the Cause: ....Il.18.454.343.
But whatsoe'er *Achilles* can inspire, ...Il.20.409.412.
All pow'r is his, and whatsoe'er he wills ....Od.14.496.60.

WHEAT

Let such (a God's Name) with fine Wheat be fed, ...2.ChWB.48.58.
Serv'd with pure Wheat, and by a Princess' Hand; ....Il.8.231.408.
And the full Racks are heap'd with gen'rous Wheat. ....Il.10.669.31.
Honey new-press'd, the sacred Flow'r of Wheat, ...Il.11.770.69.
The strength of wheat, and wines, and ample store. ....Od.2.427.81.
And sacred wheat upon the victim lay'd, ...Od.3.569.115.
With wheat and barley wave the golden fields, ...Od.9.124.310.
Milk newly prest, the sacred flow'r of wheat, ...Od.10.270.355.

WHEATEN

His task it was the wheaten loaves to lay, ...Od.14.506.61.

WHEEDLING

By Murmuring, Wheedling, Stratagem and Force, ...2.ChWB.163.64.

WHEEL

And *Persecution* mourn her broken Wheel: ....1.W-F.420.193.
Touches some wheel, or verges to some goal; ....3.EOM1.59.20.
"Who breaks a Butterfly upon a Wheel?" ....4.Arbu.308.118.
If ev'ry Wheel of that unweary'd Mill ....4.2HE2.78.171.
Ixion rests upon his Wheel, ...6.11.67.32.
To shape the Circle of the bending Wheel) ....Il.4.555.248.
On the bright Axle turns the bidden Wheel, ...Il.5.890.308.
Prone on his Face he sinks beside the Wheel; ....Il.6.53.326.
Still as at either End they wheel around, ...Il.18.631.354.
So whirls a Wheel, in giddy Circle tost, ...Il.18.695.357.
Lopp'd the green Arms to spoke a Chariot Wheel) ....Il.21.45.424.
Swift round the Goal to turn the flying Wheel. ....Il.23.378.505.
Shot headlong from his Seat, beside the Wheel, ...Il.23.473.509.
And brushing with his Tail the whirling Wheel. ....Il.23.602.513.
Above th' assembled Peers they wheel on high, ...Od.2.175.70.
The turning wheel before the Palace stays. ....Od.7.4.233.

WHEEL'D

Thus step by step, where'er the *Trojan* wheel'd, ...Il.22.249.465.
'Till the twelfth moon had wheel'd her pale career; ....Od.4.704.152.
She added not, but waving as she wheel'd ....Od.6.377.230.
(Scarce twenty four-wheel'd cars, compact and strong, ...Od.9.286.318.

WHEEL'S

The Wheel's round Naves appear to brush the Goal. ....Il.23.412.506.
They went, and kept the wheel's smooth-beaten road ....Od.10.117.346.

WHEELING

Then wheeling down the Steep of Heav'n he flies, ...1.TrSt.441.428.
As he to Flight his wheeling Car addrest, ...Il.5.53.269.
Who near him wheeling, drove his Steeds along; ....Il.17.786.319.
Obliquely wheeling thro' th' aerial Way; ....Il.22.186.463.
And round, a Circle for the wheeling Car. ....Il.23.404.506.
'Till *Phœbus* wheeling to the western goal ....Od.19.495.220.

WHEELS

And gives th' eternal wheels to know their rounds. ....3.Ep3.170.107.
Lo! at the Wheels of her Triumphal Car, ...4.EpS1.151.309.
The wheels above urg'd by the load below; ....5.DunA1.180.84.
The wheels above urg'd by the load below: ....5.DunB1.184.283.

WHEELS (CONTINUED)
His rowling Wheels did run: ... 6.79.126.222.
His trowling Wheels they run: ... 6.79.126A.222.
Watchful he wheels, protects it ev'ry way, ... Il.5.363.284.
The whirling Wheels are to the Chariot hung. ... Il.5.889.308.
Guards as he turns, and circles as he wheels: ... Il.8.410.417.
Their Coursers crush'd beneath the Wheels shall lie, ... Il.8.492.420.
Your Horses crush'd beneath the Wheels shall lie ... Il.8.514.421.
Swifter than Thought the Wheels instinctive fly, ... Il.8.544.422.
And mangled Carnage clogs the rapid Wheels. ... Il.11.661.63.
Those Wheels returning ne'er shall mark the Plain; ... Il.12.128.86.
His whirling Wheels the glassy Surface sweep; ... Il.13.42.107.
Of rolling Dust, their winged Wheels employ, ... Il.14.169.165.
But when his Ev'ning Wheels o'erhung the Main, ... Il.16.942.280.
That plac'd on living Wheels of massy Gold, ... Il.18.441.342.
The rolling Wheels of *Greece* the Body tore, ... Il.20.455.413.
To vaunt his Swiftness, wheels around the Plain, ... Il.20.477.414.
The spiky Wheels thro' Heaps of Carnage tore; ... Il.20.585.418.
The Waves flow after, wheresoe'er he wheels, ... Il.21.287.432.
Tempts his Pursuit, and wheels about the Shore. ... Il.21.716.451.
The Track his flying Wheels had left behind: ... Il.23.586.513.
For Plowshares, Wheels, and all the rural Trade. ... Il.23.990.529.
The Dove, in airy Circles as she wheels, ... Il.23.1034.530.
Why teach ye not my rapid Wheels to run, ... Il.24.329.550.
On his slow Wheels the following People wait, ... Il.24.403.552.
Hang on the Wheels, and grovel round the Slain. ... Il.24.887.573.
And now, declining with his sloping wheels, ... Od.2.436.82.
And now proud *Sparta* with their wheels resounds, ... Od.4.1.119.
But when his evening wheels o'erhung the main, ... Od.9.67.305.
All night we watch'd, 'till with her orient wheels ... Od.16.380.124.
The wheels of night retarding, to detain ... Od.23.261.336.
And bids *Aurora* with her golden wheels ... Od.23.373.343.

WHELM
And whelm in Ruins yon' flagitious Town. ... Il.13.788.142.
And one vast Ruin whelm th' *Olympian* State. ... Il.15.155.202.
To whelm some City under Waves of Fire, ... Il.17.826.321.
Shou'd hide our walls, or whelm beneath the ground. ... Od.13.205.15.
Your lives at once, and whelm beneath the deep? ... Od.24.135.354.

WHELM'D
There whelm'd with Waves the gawdy Warrior lies; ... Il.2.1066.172.
And whelm'd beneath thy Waves, drop the huge Wall: ... Il.7.553.392.
Whelm'd in thy Country's Ruins shalt thou fall, ... Il.13.973.152.
Lies whelm'd in Ruins of the *Theban* Wall, ... Il.14.128.163.
Whelm'd under the huge Mass of Earth and Main. ... Il.14.236.172.
Whelm'd under our dark Gulphs those Arms shall lie ... Il.21.370.436.
Whelm'd in the bottom of the monstrous deep? ... Od.4.658.150.
And now had perish'd, whelm'd beneath the main, ... Od.5.554.199.
Whom angry *Neptune* whelm'd beneath the main; ... Od.9.340.320.

WHELMING
Why sunk I not beneath the whelming Tyde, ... Il.6.438.348.
Or doom'd to welter in the whelming main. ... Od.1.210.42.
Like a black sheet the whelming billow spread, ... Od.5.466.195.
To plunge it headlong in the whelming wave; ... Od.8.556.292.
Decree to plunge us in the whelming tide, ... Od.12.414.451.
To dash th' offenders in the whelming tyde. ... Od.12.457.453.
Of whelming mountains overhang their head! ... Od.13.183.15.
Me with his whelming wave let Ocean shroud! ... Od.20.77.236.

WHELMS
Sudden she flies, and whelms it o'er the pyre: ... 5.DunA1.215.89.
Sudden she flies, and whelms it o'er the pyre; ... 5.DunB1.259.289.
And whelms the smoaky Ruin in the Waves. ... Il.12.32.82.
The falling Deluge whelms the Hero round: ... Il.21.264.431.
And whelms th' offenders in the roaring tydes: ... Od.23.358.342.

WHELPS
While your fine Whelps learn all to steal, ... 6.135.55.368.
The whelps of Lions in the midnight hour. ... Od.12.110.437.

WHEN (OMITTED)
1206

WHEN-E'ER
When-e'er his influence *Jove* vouchsafes to show'r ... Od.4.285.132.

WHENCE
Those empty Orbs, from whence he tore his Eyes, ... 1.TrSt.78.413.
Whence, far below, the Gods at once survey ... 1.TrSt.277.421.
From whence he sees his absent Brother fly, ... 1.TrSt.448.428.
Whence some infer, whose Conscience is too nice, ... 2.ChWB.11.57.
Whence is our Neighbour's Wife so rich and gay? ... 2.ChWB.75.60.
He breaks the Vial whence the Sorrows flow. ... 2.RL4.142.196.
Assist me heav'n! but whence arose that pray'r? ... 2.ElAb.179.334.
Weigh well the Cause from whence these Evils spring, ... 4.HAdv.102.83.
(Whence hapless Monsieur much complains at Paris ... 5.DunA2.127.112.
"Far Eastward cast thine eye, from whence the Sun ... 5.DunA3.65.156.
"Far Eastward cast thy eye, from whence the Sun ... 5.DunA3.65A.156.
(Whence hapless Monsieur much complains at Paris ... 5.DunB2.135.301.
"Far eastward cast thine eye, from whence the Sun ... 5.DunB3.73.323.
Surveys its beauties, whence its beauties grow; ... 6.14iv.10.47.
With that pure Stuff from whence we rose, ... 6.53.12Z3.161.
Whence deathless *Kit*-Cat took its Name, ... 6.59.1.177.
Whence Children are bred, ... 6.91.12A.253.
That kindred Deep, from whence his Mother sprung. ... Il.1.457.109.
Then down the Deep she plung'd from whence she rose, ... Il.1.563.115.
From whence this Wrath, or who controuls thy Sway? ... Il.1.715.122.
High on the Mound, from whence in Prospect lay ... Il.2.962.169.
What, or from whence I am, or who my Sire, ... Il.6.179.334.
Go then! resolve to Earth from whence ye grew, ... Il.7.113.369.
Say whence these Coursers? by what Chance bestow'd, ... Il.10.642.30.
Whence hissing Darts, incessant, rain below. ... Il.12.312.93.
But those my Ship contains, whence distant far, ... Il.13.349.122.
From whence this favour to an impious Foe? ... Il.13.792.142.

WHENCE (CONTINUED)
From whence this Menace, this insulting Strain, ... Il.13.1044.155.
Whence rose *Perithous* like the Gods in Fame. ... Il.14.362.180.
Stream into Life, whence *Perseus* brave and bold. ... Il.14.364.180.
Whence godlike *Rhadamanth* and *Minos* sprung. ... Il.14.368.180.
From whence this boding Speech, the stern Decree ... Il.16.1038.283.
Who, or from whence? Unhappy is the Sire, ... Il.21.167.428.
The Monarch sate; from whence with sure survey ... Il.23.534.511.
Whence *Tyrian* Sailors did the Prize transport, ... Il.23.869.524.
The King alarm'd. Say what, and whence thou art, ... Il.24.473.556.
Where round the Bed whence *Acheloüs* springs ... Il.24.775.569.
Sincere, from whence began thy course, recite, ... Od.1.221.43.
What, and from whence? his name and lineage shew. ... Od.1.516.57.
And whence your race? on what adventure, say, ... Od.3.84.90.
Whence with incessant grief my soul annoy'd, ... Od.4.117.125.
Then down the deeps she div'd from whence she rose: ... Od.5.447.194.
Tell then whence art thou? whence that Princely air? ... Od.7.320.251.
Tell then whence art thou? whence that Princely air? ... Od.7.320.251.
This land, from whence their morning course begun, ... Od.7.415.257.
Say whence, ye Gods, contending nations strive ... Od.10.42.341.
What art thou? say! from whence, from whom you came? ... Od.10.387.363.
Then tell me whence thou art? and what the share ... Od.14.55.38.
Sincere from whence begun your course relate, ... Od.14.216.45.
Whence father, from what shore this stranger, say? ... Od.16.57.105.
Whence, great *Telemachus!* this lofty strain? ... Od.17.488.156.
Whence this unguarded openness of soul, ... Od.18.454.190.
Of iv'ry one; whence flit to mock the brain, ... Od.19.658.228.
And to the seat returns from whence he rose. ... Od.21.174.268.
There stood a window near, whence looking down ... Od.22.142.293.
Whence no contending foot could reach the ground. ... Od.22.502.313.
Shame not the line whence glorious you descend, ... Od.24.587.376.

WHENE'ER
Heav'n put it past your Doubt whene'er you wed, ... 2.ChJM.279.27.
And first complain'd, whene'er the Guilt was mine. ... 2.ChWB.153.64.
But oh good Gods! whene'er a Thought I cast ... 2.ChWB.221.67.
Colours that change whene'er they wave their Wings. ... 2.RL2.68.164.
There, all Men may be cur'd, whene'er they please. ... 4.1HE6.59.241.
Whene'er she passed by or Lane or Nook, ... 6.14ii.42A.44.
As Courtiers should, whene'er they strive ... 6.94.35.260.
Our laughter, *R[oom]e,* whene'er he speaks, provokes; ... 6.105iii.1A.301.
Whene'er, by *Jove's* Decree, our conqu'ring Pow'rs ... Il.1.165.95.
These Ills shall cease, whene'er by *Jove's* Decree ... Il.6.676.360.
Whene'er he breath'd, remissive of his Might, ... Il.13.887.147.
Whene'er *Ulysses* roams the realm of Night, ... Od.1.503.56.
Whene'er her choice the royal Dame avows, ... Od.20.409.252.

WHENEVER
M[oo]re always smiles whenever he recites; ... 6.105ii.1.300.
M[oore] always laughs whenever he recites; ... 6.105ii.1A.300.

WHERE (OMITTED)
780

WHERE-E'ER
Where-e'er you walk, cool Gales shall fan the Glade, ... 1.PSu.73.77.
Where-e'er you tread, the blushing Flow'rs shall rise, ... 1.PSu.75.77.
What have I said?—where-e'er my *Delia* flies, ... 1.PAu.35.82.
What have I said?—where-e'er my Thyrsis flies, ... 1.PAu.35A.82.
Where-e'er you find *the cooling Western Breeze,* ... 1.EOC.350.279.
Treated, caress'd, where-e'er she's pleas'd to roam— ... 2.ChWB.76.60.
I tremble too where-e'er my own I find, ... 2.ElAb.33.321.
What scenes appear where-e'er I turn my view! ... 2.ElAb.263.341.
Where-e'er he shines, oh Fortune, gild the scene, ... 3.Ep3.245.113.
The Nations bleed, where-e'er her Steps she turns, ... Il.4.506.245.
Where-e'er the Sun's refulgent Rays are cast, ... Il.7.548.392.
My sire I seek, where-e'er the voice of fame ... Od.3.100.91.
The walls where-e'er my wond'ring sight I turn, ... Od.19.46.195.

WHERE-E'RE
Exiles and wand'rers now, where-e're ye go, ... Od.10.548.369.

WHERE'ER
Where'er he moves, the growing Slaughters spread ... Il.16.510.262.
Still swift *Scamander* rolls where'er he flies: ... Il.21.300.433.
Thus step by step, where'er the *Trojan* wheel'd, ... Il.22.249.465.

WHERE'ERE
Where'ere he mov'd, the Goddess shone before, ... Il.20.127.399.

WHERE'S
But where's the Man, who Counsel *can* bestow, ... 1.EOC.631.310.
Ask where's the North? at York, 'tis on the Tweed; ... 3.EOM2.222.82.
And where's the Glory? 'twill be only thought ... 4.EpS1.25.299.
Fr. Hold Sir! for God's-sake, where's th' Affront to you? ... 4.EpS2.157.322.
Where mighty Death! Oh where's thy Sting? ... 6.31ii.6Z6.94.
Where's such ado with Townsend. ... 6.61.16.181.
The good Priests whisper—Where's the Chevalier? ... 6.82vi.14.232.
Where's now th' imperious Vaunt, the daring Boast ... Il.13.289.119.
For where's an arm, like thine *Ulysses!* strong, ... Od.17.622.162.

WHEREAS
But *you* show your *Wit,* whereas *they* show'd their *Tails.* ... 6.62ii.2.185.

WHEREAT
Whereat the Gentleman began to stare— ... 4.2HE2.194.179.
Whereat he meant to fight. ... 6.79.120A.222.

WHEREFORE
The truth once told, (and wherefore shou'd we lie?) ... 4.Arbu.81.101.
But wherefore all this labour, all this strife? ... 4.1HE6.38.239.
And 'tis but just, I'll tell you wherefore, ... 4.1HE7.33.271.
And 'tis but just, I'll tell ye wherefore, ... 4.1HE7.33A.271.
But wherefore waste I words? I see advance ... 5.DunB4.271.370.
Wherefore thy claim resign, allow his right; ... 6.116vi.5.327.
Yet wherefore doubtful? Let this Truth suffice; ... Il.11.517.57.

WHEREFORE (CONTINUED)
What if?—But wherefore all this vain Debate? .... Il.21.663.449.

WHEREIN
Wherein he meant to fight. .... 6.79.120.222.

WHEREON
For tho' the meat whereon he fed, be known .... 4.JD2A.39.136.

WHERESOE'ER
O lead me wheresoe'er I go, ... 6.50.43.148.
The Waves flow after, wheresoe'er he wheels, ... Il.21.287.432.

WHEREVER
What's wrong is wrong, wherever it be done: .... 4.HAdv.78.81.

WHET
How keen the war, if Dulness whet the sword! .... 5.DunA3.112A.160.
Whet all their Stings, and call forth all their Rage; .... Il.16.317.255.

WHETHER
Oh Father *Phœbus!* whether *Lycia's* Coast .... 1.TrSt.829.444.
Whether to sweet *Castalia* thou repair, ... 1.TrSt.831.444.
Whether the Style of *Titan* please thee more, ... 1.TrSt.857.445.
Whether pure Holiness inspir'd his Mind, ... 2.ChJM.11.15.
Whether she's chast or rampant, proud or civil; .... 2.ChJM.186.23.
Whether an easie, fond, familiar *Fool,* .... 2.ChJM.188.23.
Whether an easie, fond, insipid Fool, ... 2.ChJM.188A.23.
Whether the Nymph shall break *Diana's* Law, ... 2.RL2.105.166.
Or whether Heav'n has doom'd that *Shock* must fall. .... 2.RL2.110.166.
Whether he thinks too little, or too much: .... 3.EOM2.12.55.
Whether with Reason, or with Instinct blest, ... 3.EOM3.79.99.
Of Vice or Virtue, whether blest or curst, ... 3.EOM4.87.136.
Whether the Charmer sinner it, or saint it, ... 3.Ep2.15.49.
Whether old Age, with faint, but chearful Ray, ... 4.HS1.93.13.
Whether the darken'd Room to muse invite, ... 4.HS1.97.13.
And whether to a Bishop, or a Whore? .... 4.JD4.137.37.
Whether the Name belong to Pope or Vernon? .... 4.HS2.166.69.
Whether in florid Impotence he speaks, ... 4.Arbu.317.118.
Whether that Blessing be deny'd, or giv'n, ... 4.Arbu.418.127.
Whether you call them Villa, Park, or Chace) .... 4.2HE2.255.183.
Whether my Vessel be first-rate or not? .... 4.2HE2.297.185.
Whether we dread, or whether we desire, ... 4.1HE6.20.237.
Whether we dread, or whether we desire, ... 4.1HE6.20.237.
Whether we joy or grieve, the same the curse, ... 4.1HE6.22.237.
Whether we ought to chuse our Friends, ... 4.HS6.149.259.
Whether thou chuse Cervantes' serious air, ... 5.DunA1.19.62.
Whether thou chuse Cervantes' serious air, ... 5.DunB1.21.270.
Whether th' *Italian* or the *Dutch,* .... 6.14v(b).8.49.
Whether by Chance, or by Misfortune led .... 6.26i.12.79.
Whether of *England* or of *France;* .... 6.30.4A.85.
Whether his hoary sire he spies, ... 6.51ii.29.153.
Whether thy hand strike out some free design, ... 6.52.3.156.
But whether Man, or He, God knows, ... 6.53.12Z1.161.
Whether the Style of *Grildrig* please thee most, ... 6.96iv.97.279.
Whether thou choose Cervantes' serious air, ... 6.106iv.3.307.
Whether that Blessing be deny'd, or giv'n, ... 6.117.13.333.
But whether he remain, or sail with me, ... Il.9.554.460.
Whether (the Gods succeeding our Desires) .... Il.13.931.149.
All-seeing Monarch! whether *Lycia's* Coast .... Il.16.633.269.
Whether to urge their prompt Effect, and call .... Il.16.787.274.
Whether the Weak or Strong discharge the Dart, ... Il.17.711.315.
Whether to snatch him from impending Fate, ... Il.22.230.465.
Whether in fields by hostile fury slain, ... Od.3.108.91.
Whether he wanders on some friendless coast, ... Od.4.141.127.
Whether a race unjust, of barb'rous might, ... Od.9.203.314.
Whether the night descends, or day prevails, ... Od.11.220.392.
Whether, he cries, they measure back the flood, ... Od.16.486.130.

WHEY
Some whey, to wash his bowels, he might earn. .... Od.17.265.145.

WHICH (OMITTED)
497

WHIG
While Tories call me Whig, and Whigs a Tory. .... 4.HS1.68.11.
Now Whig, now Tory, what we lov'd we hate; .... 4.2HE1.157.209.
Said, "Tories call'd him Whig, and Whigs a Tory;" .... 4.EpS1.8.297.
A Joke on JEKYL, or some odd *Old Whig,* .... 4.EpS1.39.300.
Who know how like Whig-Ministers to Tory, ... 4.EpS1.106.306.
Point she to Priest or Elder, Whig or Tory, ... 4.EpS2.96.318.
The Goddess smiles on Whig and Tory race, ... 5.DunA3.284.183.
Our Goddess smiles on Whig and Tory race, ... 5.DunA3.284A.183.
Whig Maxims, and abjure *Apollo?* .... 6.10.40.25.
And tho' no Doctors, Whig or Tory ones, ... 6.135.83.369.

WHIG-MINISTERS
Who know how like Whig-Ministers to Tory, ... 4.EpS1.106.306.

WHIGS
While Tories call me Whig, and Whigs a Tory. .... 4.HS1.68.11.
Said, "Tories call'd him Whig, and Whigs a Tory;" .... 4.EpS1.8.297.
While maudlin Whigs deplor'd their *Cato's* Fate, ... 6.33.1.99.
Whilst maudlin Whigs deplore their *Cato's* Fate, ... 6.33.1A.99.
While maudlin Whigs deplor'd your *Cato's* Fate, ... 6.33.1B.99*.
Let not the whigs our tory club rebuke; .... 6.42v.1.119.
Let not the *Whigs Geneva's* Stumm infuse, ... 6.48i.8.133*.

WHILE
While on thy Banks *Sicilian* Muses sing; .... 1.PSp.4.60.
But, charm'd to Silence, listens while She sings, ... 1.PSp.15.61.
And while *Aurora* gilds the Mountain's Side, ... 1.PSp.17z5.62.
While yon slow Oxen turn the furrow'd Plain. .... 1.PSp.30.63.
While a kind Glance at her Pursuer flies, ... 1.PSp.59.66.

WHILE (CONTINUED)
While opening Blooms diffuse their Sweets around. .... 1.PSp.100.70.
There while he mourn'd, the Streams forgot to flow, ... 1.PSu.5A.71.
While in thy Heart Eternal Winter reigns. .... 1.PSu.22.73.
While your *Alexis* pines in hopeless Love? .... 1.PSu.24.73.
While one his Mistress mourns, and one his Friend: .... 1.PAu.4A.80.
Next *Ægon* sung, while *Windsor* Groves admir'd; .... 1.PAu.55.84.
While lab'ring Oxen, spent with Toil and Heat, ... 1.PAu.61.84.
While curling Smokes from Village-Tops are seen, ... 1.PAu.63.84.
While She with Garlands hung the bending Boughs: .... 1.PAu.68.85.
While She with Garlands grac'd the bending Boughs: .... 1.PAu.68A.85.
Who lost my Heart while I preserv'd my Sheep. .... 1.PAu.80.86.
While silent Birds forget their tuneful Lays, ... 1.PWi.7.89.
Sing, while beside the shaded Tomb I mourn, ... 1.PWi.19.90.
No more the mounting Larks, while *Daphne* sings, ... 1.PWi.53.92.
There, while You rest in *Amaranthine* Bow'rs, ... 1.PWi.73.94.
How all things listen, while thy Muse complains! .... 1.PWi.77.94.
While Plants their Shade, or Flow'rs their Odours give, ... 1.PWi.83.94.
While by our Oaks the precious Loads are born, ... 1.W-F.31.151.
But while the Subject starv'd, the Beast was fed. .... 1.W-F.60.154.
But Subjects starv'd while Savages were fed. .... 1.W-F.60A.154.
Ye vig'rous Swains! while Youth ferments your Blood, ... 1.W-F.93.159.
While led along the Skies his Current strays, ... 1.W-F.228.170.
While thro' the Skies his shining Current strays, ... 1.W-F.228A.170.
While lasts the Mountain, or while *Thames* shall flow) .... 1.W-F.266.173.
While lasts the Mountain, or while *Thames* shall flow) .... 1.W-F.266.173.
The Trumpets sleep, while chearful Horns are blown, ... 1.W-F.373.187.
While naked Youth and painted Chiefs admire .... 1.W-F.405A.192.
As on the *Land* while *here* the *Ocean* gains, ... 1.EOC.54.245.
Thus in the *Soul* while *Memory* prevails, ... 1.EOC.56.245.
Glows while he *reads,* but *trembles* as he *writes)* .... 1.EOC.198.263.
While from the bounded *Level* of our Mind, ... 1.EOC.221.265.
While *Expletives* their feeble Aid *do* join, ... 1.EOC.346.278.
While they ring round the same *unvary'd Chimes,* .... 1.EOC.348.278.
While, at each Change, the Son of *Lybian Jove* .... 1.EOC.376.283.
While their weak Heads, like Towns unfortify'd, ... 1.EOC.434.288.
And while Self-Love each jealous Writer rules, ... 1.EOC.516.296.
While nice, and anxious in his new disease, ... 1.TrPA.21.366.
Adjusts his shapes; while in the crystal brook .... 1.TrPA.25.366.
While to his reeds he sung his amorous pains, ... 1.TrPA.51.367.
Sweating he walks, while Loads of golden Grain .... 1.TrVP.31.378.
And strait a voice, while yet a voice remains, ... 1.TrFD.67.388.
While yet thy mother has a kiss to give. .... 1.TrFD.95.390.
While I consume with more than *Ætna's* Fires! .... 1.TrSP.12.393.
Or while my Muse in melting Notes complains, ... 1.TrSP.93.397.
See, while I write, my Words are lost in Tears; .... 1.TrSP.109.398.
Yet while I blush, confess how much they please! .... 1.TrSP.154.400.
Poor *Sapho* dies while careless *Phaon* stays. .... 1.TrSP.249.404.
While to his Harp Divine *Amphion* sung? .... 1.TrSt.12.409.
And while her Arms her Second Hope contain, ... 1.TrSt.17.410.
While *Dacian* Mountains stream'd with barb'rous Blood; .... 1.TrSt.26.410.
And while her Arms a second Hope contain, ... 1.TrSt.17A.410.
Mean while permit that my preluding Muse .... 1.TrSt.49.411.
But while he dwells where not a chearful Ray .... 1.TrSt.71.413.
While from his Breast these dreadful Accents broke. .... 1.TrSt.80.413.
While These exalt their Scepters o'er my Urn; .... 1.TrSt.106.414.
The Fury heard, while on *Cocytus'* Brink .... 1.TrSt.124.415.
While Discord waits upon divided Pow'r. .... 1.TrSt.183.418.
Unjust Decree! while This enjoys the State, ... 1.TrSt.194.418.
While freezing *Boreas* and black *Eurus* blow, ... 1.TrSt.267.421.
While that Prince Threatens, and while this Commands. .... 1.TrSt.272.421.
While that Prince Threatens, and while this Commands. .... 1.TrSt.272.421.
The still Creation listen'd while he spoke, ... 1.TrSt.297.422.
While future Realms his wandring Thoughts delight, ... 1.TrSt.445.428.
While from torn Rocks the massy Fragments roll'd; .... 1.TrSt.511A.431.
While Thunder roars, and Lightning round him flies. .... 1.TrSt.525.432.
His train obey; while all the Courts around .... 1.TrSt.605.435.
While all his sad Companions upward gaze, ... 1.TrSt.644.437.
(While with rich Gums the fuming Altars blaze) .... 1.TrSt.654.437.
While the rude Swain his rural Musick tries, ... 1.TrSt.689.439.
Relate your Fortunes, while the friendly Night .... 1.TrSt.794.443.
And while two pointed Jav'lins arm his Hands, ... 1.TrES.11.450.
That while with wondring Eyes our Martial Bands .... 1.TrES.39.451.
While each is bent to conquer or to die. .... 1.TrES.66.452.
While to the Ramparts daring *Glaucus* drew, ... 1.TrES.111.453.
(While some laborious Matron, just and poor, ... 1.TrES.168Z1.455.
While the grim Savage grinds with foamy Jaws .... 1.TrES.297.460.
While on the Deck the Chief in Silence lies, ... 1.TrUl.5.465.
Mean while *Ulysses* in his Country lay, ... 1.TrUl.53.467.
While in th'Embrace of pleasing Sleep I lay, ... 1.TrUl.155.471.
Thus while he spoke, the blue-ey'd Maid began .... 1.TrUl.160.471.
Now lift thy longing Eyes, while I restore .... 1.TrUl.224.473.
While all my Friends applaud my blissful Life, ... 2.ChJM.200.24.
While Fancy pictur'd ev'ry lively Part, ... 2.ChJM.232.25.
While glitt'ring Stars his absent Beams supply, ... 2.ChJM.369.32.
While tuneful Sprights a merry Consort made, ... 2.ChJM.463.37.
While thou art faithful to thy own true Knight, ... 2.ChJM.553.42.
Weak was her Voice, as while she spoke she cry'd. .... 2.ChJM.576.43.
Thus while she spoke, a sidelong Glance she cast, ... 2.ChJM.599.44.
While on a Bank reclin'd of rising Green, ... 2.ChJM.625.45.
Signs of Remorse, while thus his Spouse he chear'd: .... 2.ChJM.788.53.
But 'till your Sight's establish'd, for a while, ... 2.ChJM.797.53.
While yet the Smart was shooting in the Bone. .... 2.ChWB.258.69.
While her rackt Soul Repose and Peace requires, ... 2.RL*A*2.11.132.
While Peers and Dukes, and all their sweeping Train, ... 2.RL1.84.152.
Some fold the Sleeve, while others plait the Gown; .... 2.RL1.147A.158.
While melting Musick steals upon the Sky, ... 2.RL2.49.162.
While ev'ry Beam new transient Colours flings, ... 2.RL2.67.163.
While clog'd he beats his silken Wings in vain; .... 2.RL2.130.168.
Mean while declining from the Noon of Day, ... 2.RL3.19.170.
While *China's* Earth receives the smoking Tyde. .... 2.RL3.110.176.
While frequent Cups prolong the rich Repast. .... 2.RL3.112A.176.
While Fish in Streams, or Birds delight in Air, ... 2.RL3.163.180.
While *Visits* shall be paid on solemn Days, ... 2.RL3.167.181.
While Nymphs take Treats, or Assignations give, ... 2.RL3.169.182.
(While *Hampton's* Ecchos, wretched Maid! reply'd) .... 2.RL4.96.191.

WHILE (CONTINUED)

While the Fops envy, and the Ladies stare! ..... 2.RL4.104.192.
That while my Nostrils draw the vital Air, ... 2.RL4.137.195.
While *Anna* begg'd and *Dido* rag'd in vain. ..... 2.RL5.6.199.
While thro' the Press enrag'd *Thalestris* flies, ... 2.RL5.57.203.
While purer Slumbers spread their golden Wings) ..... 2.TemF.8.253.
While thus I stood, intent to see and hear, ... 2.TemF.497.287.
All is not Heav'n's while *Abelard* has part, ... 2.ElAb.25.321.
Heav'n claims me all in vain, while he has part, ... 2.ElAb.25A.321.
Guiltless I gaz'd; heav'n listen'd while you sung; ..... 2.ElAb.65.324.
While Altars blaze, and Angels tremble round. ..... 2.ElAb.276.342.
While prostrate here in humble grief I lie, ... 2.ElAb.277.342.
While praying, trembling, in the dust I roll, ... 2.ElAb.279.342.
(While the long fun'rals blacken all the way) ..... 2.Elegy.40.366.
While Angels with their silver wings o'ershade ..... 2.Elegy.67.367.
While Man exclaims, "See all things for my use!" ..... 3.EOM3.45.96.
As, while he dreads it, makes him hope it too: ..... 3.EOM3.74.99.
While still too wide or short is human Wit; ..... 3.EOM3.90.101.
While pleasure, gratitude, and hope, combin'd, ... 3.EOM3.145.107.
While those are plac'd in Hope, and these in Fear: ..... 3.EOM4.70.135.
If while th'Unhappy hope, the Happy fear ..... 3.EOM4.70A.135.
"But sometimes Virtue starves, while Vice is fed." ..... 3.EOM4.149.142.
God gives enough, while he has more to give: ..... 3.EOM4.164.143.
Never elated, while one man's oppress'd; ..... 3.EOM4.323.159.
Never dejected, while another's bless'd; ..... 3.EOM4.324.159.
And while the Muse now stoops, or now ascends, ... 3.EOM4.375.164.
Oh! while along the stream of Time thy name ..... 3.EOM4.383.165.
While one there is that charms us with his Spleen. ..... 3.Ep1.121A.24.
While one there is who charms us with his Spleen. ..... 3.Ep1.121.24.
The mighty blessing, "while we live, to live." ..... 3.Ep2.90.57.
Oblige her, and she'll hate you while you live: ..... 3.Ep2.138.62.
She, while her Lover pants upon her breast, ... 3.Ep2.167.64.
That Charm shall grow, while what fatigues the Ring ..... 3.Ep2.251.70.
'Tis thus we riot, while who sow it, starve. ..... 3.Ep3.24.88.
While the gaunt mastiff growling at the gate, ... 3.Ep3.197.109.
While Tories call me Whig, and Whigs a Tory. ..... 4.HS1.68.11.
Yes, while I live, no rich or noble knave ..... 4.HS1.119.17.
Know, while I live, no rich or noble knave ..... 4.HS1.119A.17.
While bashful *Jenny,* ev'n at Morning-Prayer, ... 4.HAdv.33.79.
Attend, while I their Miseries explain, ... 4.HAdv.49.79.
While pure Description held the place of Sense? ..... 4.Arbu.148.106.
While Wits and Templers ev'ry sentence raise, ... 4.Arbu.211.111.
While yet in *Britain* Honour had Applause) ..... 4.Arbu.389.126.
And keep a while one Parent from the Sky! ..... 4.Arbu.413.127.
While mighty WILLIAM's thundring Arm prevail'd. ..... 4.2HE2.63.169.
And here, while Town, and Court, and City roars, ... 4.2HE2.123.173.
Walk with respect behind, while we at ease ..... 4.2HE2.141.175.
While You, great Patron of Mankind, sustain ..... 4.2HE1.1.195.
While you, to measure merits, look in Stowe, ... 4.2HE1.66.199.
While if our Elders break all Reason's laws, ... 4.2HE1.117.205.
And knows no losses while the Muse is kind. ..... 4.2HE1.196.211.
While all its throats the Gallery extends, ... 4.2HE1.326.223.
And Nations wonder'd while they dropp'd the sword! ..... 4.2HE1.399.229.
Sigh, while his Chloë, blind to Wit and Worth, ... 4.1HE6.42.239.
And, while he bids thee, sets th' Example too? ..... 4.1HE1.109.287.
While with the silent growth of ten per Cent, ... 4.1HE1.132.289.
Rich ev'n when plunder'd, honour'd while oppress'd, ... 4.1HE1.182.293.
So *Latin,* yet so *English* all the while, ... 4.EpS1.74.304.
While Truth, Worth, Wisdom, daily they decry— ..... 4.EpS1.169.309.
While Truth, Worth, Wisdom, daily we decry— ..... 4.EpS1.169A.309.
While *Roman* Spirit charms, and *Attic* Wit: ..... 4.EpS2.85.317.
Spirit of *Arnall!* aid me while I lye. ..... 4.EpS2.129.320.
Let Envy howl while Heav'n's whole Chorus sings, ... 4.EpS2.242.326.
While pensive Poets painful vigils keep, ... 5.DunA1.91.70.
While thus each hand promotes the pleasing pain, ... 5.DunA2.203.126.
While Milbourn there, deputed by the rest, ... 5.DunA2.325.141.
While others timely, to the neighbouring Fleet ..... 5.DunA2.395.149.
As Berecynthia, while her offspring vye ..... 5.DunA3.123.160.
"Silence, ye Wolves! while Ralph to Cynthia howls, ... 5.DunA3.159.165.
While happier *Hist'ry* with her comrade *Ale,* ..... 5.DunA3.191z5.172.
While proud Philosophy repines to show ..... 5.DunA3.193.173.
While K[ennet], B[ramston], W[arren], preach in vain. ..... 5.DunA3.200.174*.
While Kennet, Hare, and Gibson preach in vain. ..... 5.DunA3.200B.174.
While opening Hell spouts wild-fire at your head. ..... 5.DunA3.314.186.
While naked mourns the Dormitory wall, ... 5.DunA3.323.189.
While Wren with sorrow to the grave descends, ... 5.DunA3.325.189.
While pensive Poets painful vigils keep, ... 5.DunB1.93.276.
While all your smutty sisters walk the streets. ..... 5.DunB1.230.287.
Yet, yet a while, at Court my H[erv]y stay! ..... 5.DunB1.299A.291.
While thus each hand promotes the pleasing pain, ... 5.DunB2.211.306.
While others, timely, to the neighb'ring Fleet ..... 5.DunB2.427.318.
As Berecynthia, while her offspring vye ..... 5.DunB3.131.326.
"Silence, ye Wolves! while Ralph to Cynthia howls, ... 5.DunB3.165.328.
While proud Philosophy repines to show, ... 5.DunB3.197.330.
While Sherlock, Hare, and Gibson preach in vain. ..... 5.DunB3.204.330.
While Kennett, Hare, and Gibson preach in vain. ..... 5.DunB3.204A.330.
While op'ning Hell spouts wild-fire at your head. ..... 5.DunB3.316.335.
While Jones' and Boyle's united labours fall: ..... 5.DunB3.328.336.
While Wren with sorrow to the grave descends, ... 5.DunB3.329.336.
Suspend a while your Force inertly strong, ... 5.DunB4.7.340.
And while on Fame's triumphal Car they ride, ... 5.DunB4.133.354.
And while on Fame's triumphant Car they ride, ... 5.DunB4.133A.354.
While tow'ring o'er your Alphabet, like Saul, ... 5.DunB4.217.363.
While thro' Poetic scenes the Genius roves, ... 5.DunB4.489.390.
While the long solemn Unison went round: ..... 5.DunB4.612.405.
While the Great Mother bids Britannia sleep, ... 5.DunB4.627Z1.407.
On earth a while with mortals to remain, ... 6.4i.2.9.
And, while we gaze, the gracious form appears ..... 6.4ii.5.9.
While vows and service nothing gain'd, ... 6.4iii.9.10.
Veils his fair glories, while he spies ..... 6.4iv.2.10.
While *Celia's* tears make sorrow bright, ... 6.5.1.12.
While wretched lovers sing in vain. ..... 6.6i.16.14.
While mankind boasts superior sight, ... 6.6ii.9.14.
While the fair Vales beneath so humbly lie, ... 6.9xi.3.23.
—Just while your Coffee stands a Cooling. ..... 6.10.8.24.
While in more lengthen'd Notes and slow, ... 6.11.10.30.

WHILE (CONTINUED)

While *Argo* saw her kindred Trees ..... 6.11.40.31.
While solemn Airs improve the sacred Fire; ..... 6.11.129.34.
While *Procris* panted in the secret shade; ..... 6.14iii.2.45.
While at her feet her swain expiring lies. ..... 6.14iii.4.45.
And pities *Procris,* while her lover dies. ..... 6.14iii.14.46.
Pleas'd while with Smiles his happy Lines you view, ... 6.19.75.64.
And while the Dogstar burns the thirsty field, ... 6.20.64.67.
While he, serene in thought, shall calm survey ..... 6.21.19.69.
So Pimps grow rich, while Gallants are undone. ..... 6.24ii.2.75.
While bloody sweats from ev'ry member flow. ..... 6.25.8.77.
While *Cato* gives his little senate laws, ... 6.32.23.96.
While maudlin Whigs deplor'd their *Cato's* Fate, ... 6.33.1.99.
But while her Pride forbids her Tears to flow, ... 6.33.3.99.
While maudlin Whigs deplor'd your *Cato's* Fate, ... 6.33.1B.99*.
He says, poor Poets lost, while Players won, ... 6.34.21.101.
As Pimps grow rich, while Gallants are undone. ..... 6.34.22.101.
While that in pipes beneath the palace flows, ... 6.35.31.104.
That virtuous ladies envy while they rail; ..... 6.41.16.113.
Ev'n while you write, you take that praise away, ... 6.43.10.120.
While the spread Fan o'ershades your closing eyes; ..... 6.45.37.125.
And while he seems to study, thinks of you: ..... 6.45.44.125.
While Fops and Templars ev'ry Sentence raise, ... 6.49iii.27.143.
While Wits and Templars ev'ry Sentence raise, ... 6.49iii.27B.143.
While thousand grateful thoughts arise; ..... 6.51ii.30.153.
While summer suns roll unperceiv'd away? ..... 6.52.18.156.
While images reflect from art to art? ..... 6.52.20.156.
While fancy brings the vanish'd piles to view, ... 6.52.31.157.
A while he crawls upon the Earth, ... 6.53.7.161.
At length my Friend (while Time, with still career, ... 6.55.1.166.
While as the Light burnt bluely. ..... 6.58.36.172.
Mean while Duke *Guise* did fret and fume, ... 6.79.133.222.
Mean while the *Guise* did fret and fume, ... 6.79.133A.222.
While Berries crackle, or while Mills shall go; ..... 6.82i.2.229.
While Berries crackle, or while Mills shall go; ..... 6.82i.2.229.
While smoking Streams from Silver Spouts shall glide, ... 6.82i.3.229.
While Coffee shall to British Nymphs be dear; ..... 6.82i.5.229.
While fragrant Steams the bended Head shall chear; ..... 6.82i.6.229.
While smoking Streams from Silver Spouts shall flow, ... 6.82i.3A.229.
While yet a Child, I chanc'd to stray, ... 6.82vii.1.233.
While Fools have places purely for their Zeal. ..... 6.82ix(d).2.235.
And while his Guts the keen Emeticks urge, ... 6.82x.5.236.
While the plum'd Beau–monde round her gathers; ..... 6.93.9A.256.
"While Pepper-Water-Worms thy Bait supply'd; ..... 6.96ii.20.270.
While Wits and Templars ev'ry Sentence raise, ... 6.98.63.285.
So while the sun's broad beam yet strikes the sight, ... 6.106i.4.306.
While he but sought his Author's Fame to further, ... 6.116viii.5.328.
While ev'ry Joy, successful Youth! is thine, ... 6.117.1.333.
While you, and every courtly Fop, ... 6.135.25.367.
While your fine Whelps learn all to steal, ... 6.135.55.368.
Shall as it blazeth, break; while Providence ..... 6.137.2.373.
She, while her Lover pants upon her breast, ... 6.139.11.377.
While, Scale in Hand, Dame *Justice* past along. ..... 6.145.4.388.
Oblige her, and she'll hate you while you live. ..... 6.154.24.403.
While half unsheath'd appear'd the glitt'ring Blade, ... Il.1.260.99.
While Tears Celestial trickle from her Eyes) ..... Il.1.541.114.
While Tears Celestial trickled from her Eyes) ..... Il.1.541A.114.
While thus with Arms devoutly rais'd in Air, ... Il.1.588.116.
While I, too partial, aid the *Trojan* Arms? ..... Il.1.675.119.
Trembling they stand, while *Jove* assumes the Throne, ... Il.1.694.120.
While to the Fleet *Atrides* bends his way. ..... Il.2.64.130.
While to his Neighbour each express'd his Thought; ..... Il.2.332.143.
While hov'ring near, with miserable Moan, ... Il.2.380.145.
For while around we gaz'd with wondring Eyes, ... Il.2.388.145.
While useless Words consume th' unactive Hours, ... Il.2.408.147.
The God averse, while yet the Fumes arose, ... Il.2.500.150.
While the fat Victim feeds the sacred Fire. ..... Il.2.509.151.
While vainly fond, in Fancy oft he hears ..... Il.2.713.160.
While stern *Achilles* in his Wrath retir'd: ..... Il.2.935.167.
While scarce the Swains their feeding Flocks survey, ... Il.3.19.188.
While round his dauntless Head the *Grecians* pour ..... Il.3.113.195.
While from the Centre *Hector* rolls his Eyes ..... Il.3.121.195.
Prepare ye *Trojans!* while a third we bring ..... Il.3.143.197.
While thus their Pray'rs united mount the Sky; ..... Il.3.370.211.
Struggling he follow'd, while th' embroider'd Thong ..... Il.3.457.213.
While these to Love's delicious Rapture yield, ... Il.3.559.218.
While the full Bowls flow round, the Pow'rs employ ..... Il.4.5.221.
Thus while he spoke, the Queen of Heav'n enrag'd ..... Il.4.27.222.
They said, while *Pallas* thro' the *Trojan* Throng ..... Il.4.115.226.
And grasp'd his Hand; while all the *Greeks* around ..... Il.4.184.230.
While some proud *Trojan* thus insulting cries, ... Il.4.212.231.
While round the Prince the *Greeks* employ their Care, ... Il.4.252.232.
While dreadful Comets glaring from afar ..... Il.4.434.241.
Our selves to lessen, while our Sires you raise? ..... Il.4.457.242.
While scarce the Skies her horrid Head can bound, ... Il.4.504.245.
But while he strove to tug th' inserted Dart, ... Il.4.532.246.
While War's fierce Goddess fires the *Grecian* Foe, ... Il.4.595.250.
While we from interdicted Fields retire, ... Il.5.43.268.
The hapless Artist, while confus'd he fled, ... Il.5.85.270.
While *Jove* descends in sluicy Sheets of Rain, ... Il.5.122.273.
While the proud Archer thus exulting cry'd. ..... Il.5.133.273.
But while my Nerves are strong, my Force entire, ... Il.5.316.281.
But while my Nerves are strung, my Force entire, ... Il.5.316A.281.
Thus while they spoke, the Foe came furious on, ... Il.5.338.283.
While Flames ascend, and mighty Ruins fall. ..... Il.5.412.286.
Thus they in Heav'n: While on the Plain below ..... Il.5.523.294.
Remote they stand, while Alien Troops engage, ... Il.5.581.296.
While *Hector* idle stands, nor bids the Brave ..... Il.5.591.296.
While thus they strive, *Tlepolemus* the great ..... Il.5.776.303.
While unreveng'd thy *Lycians* bite the Ground: ..... Il.5.797.304.
While the smooth Chariot cuts the liquid Sky. ..... Il.5.927.310.
While fierce in War divine *Achilles* rag'd; ..... Il.5.983.314.
While near *Tydides* stood th' *Athenian* Maid: ..... Il.5.987.314.
While *Troy's* fam'd <*> Streams that bound the deathful Plain ..... Il.6.5.322.
To touch the Booty, while a Foe remains. ..... Il.6.86.327.

WHILE (CONTINUED)

While *Bacchus* headlong sought the briny Flood, Il.6.167.334.
While these appear before the Pow'r with Pray'rs, Il.6.388.345.
But while I arm, contain thy ardent Mind; Il.6.428.347.
While the fat Herds and snowie Flocks they fed, Il.6.536.353.
Yet while my *Hector* still survives, I see Il.6.544.353.
(How my Heart trembles while my Tongue relates!) Il.6.571.354.
There, while you groan beneath the Load of Life, Il.6.584.355.
While pleas'd amidst the gen'ral Shouts of *Troy,* Il.6.614.357.
There, while her Tears deplor'd the Godlike Man, Il.6.644.358.
While the proud Foe his frustrate Triumphs mourns, Il.6.678.361.
Go forth persuasive, and a while engage Il.7.53.365.
Now, while my brightest Arms my Limbs invest, Il.7.229.376.
While we to Flames our slaughter'd Friends bequeathe, Il.7.399.383.
While old *Laömedon's* divine Abodes, Il.7.538.391.
Thus they in Heav'n: while, o'er the *Grecian* Train, Il.7.556.392.
While the deep Thunder shook th' Aerial Hall. Il.7.575.393.
Encourag'd his proud Steeds, while thus he spoke. Il.8.225.408.
While the Feast lasts, and while the Goblet flows; Il.8.279.410.
While the Feast lasts, and while the Goblet flows; Il.8.279.410.
Firm be the Guard, while distant lie our Pow'rs, Il.8.647.426.
While Fear, pale Comrade of inglorious Flight, Il.9.2.430.
Mean while *Patroclus* sweats the Fire to raise; Il.9.277.447.
If not—but hear me, while I number o'er Il.9.342.450.
And while the Fate of suff'ring *Greece* he mourn'd, Il.9.560.461.
While *Pray'rs,* to heal her Wrongs, move slow behind. Il.9.630.465.
While *Meleager's* thund'ring Arm prevail'd: Il.9.666.467.
Mean while the Victor's Shouts ascend the Skies; Il.9.699.468.
While Life's warm Spirit beats within my Breast. Il.9.720.470.
Inly he groans; while Glory and Despair Il.10.21.3.
While others sleep, thus range the Camp alone? Il.10.91.6.
While *Phœbus* shines, or Men have tongues to praise? Il.10.252.13.
How can I doubt, while great *Ulysses* stands Il.10.285.14.
Urge thou the Slaughter, while I seize the Steeds. Il.10.557.27.
While unresolv'd the Son of *Tydeus* stands, Il.10.592.28.
Now while on *Rhesus'* Name he calls in vain, Il.10.614.29.
Mean while the Chiefs, arriving at the Shade Il.10.618.29.
While streamy Sparkles, restless as he flies, Il.11.87.38.
Thus while the Morning-Beams increasing bright Il.11.115.39.
While his keen Faulchion drinks the Warriors Lives; Il.11.211.44.
While *Agamemnon* wastes the Ranks around, Il.11.243.46.
While *Agamemnon* wastes the Ranks around, Il.11.259.47.
While the proud Victor bore his Arms away. Il.11.320.49.
While pierc'd with Grief the much-lov'd Youth he view'd, Il.11.323.49.
This, while yet warm, distill'd the purple Flood; Il.11.345.50.
Stood check'd a while, and *Greece* respir'd again. Il.11.424.53.
While *Hector* rose, recover'd from the Trance, Il.11.462.54.
Him, while he triumph'd, *Paris* ey'd from far, Il.11.473.55.
He spoke, while *Socus* seiz'd with sudden Fright, Il.11.558.58.
Down his cleft Side while fresh the Blood distills, Il.11.596.60.
While here (he cry'd) the flying *Greeks* are slain; Il.11.644.62.
While his swoln Heart at ev'ry Step rebell'd, Il.11.681.65.
While hissing Darts descend in Iron Show'rs: Il.11.697.66.
To guard their wounded Friend: While thus they stand Il.11.722.67.
While *Nestor's* Chariot far from Fight retires: Il.11.727.67.
Here paus'd a moment, while the gentle Gale Il.11.760.69.
While round the Town the fierce *Epeians* stood. Il.11.869.74.
While thus the Hero's pious Cares attend Il.12.1.80.
This stood, while *Hector* and *Achilles* rag'd, Il.12.11.81.
While sacred *Troy* the warring Hosts engag'd; Il.12.12.81.
While ev'ry *Trojan* thus, and ev'ry Aid, Il.12.123.85.
Fierce was the Fight, while yet the *Grecian* Pow'rs Il.12.171.87.
Dark'ning the Rock, while with unweary'd Wings Il.12.191.88.
While *Greece* unconquer'd kept alive the War, Il.12.207.88.
While I the Dictates of high Heav'n obey. Il.12.282.92.
While these they undermine, and those they rend; Il.12.306.92.
And while two pointed Javelins arm his Hands, Il.12.355.94.
While to the Ramparts daring *Glaucus* drew, Il.12.465.98.
(While some laborious Matron, just and poor, Il.12.523.101.
While his high Law suspends the Pow'rs of Heav'n. Il.13.16.104.
Pant in the Ships; while *Troy* to Conquest calls, Il.13.119.110.
While Tears of Rage stand burning in their Eye. Il.13.122.110.
While thus the God the martial Fire awakes. Il.13.130.110.
But spar'd a while the destin'd *Trojan* Tow'rs: Il.13.441.126.
While *Neptune* rising from his azure Main, Il.13.442.126.
(While the Winds sleep) his Breast receiv'd the Stroke. Il.13.550.132.
While Death's strong Pangs distend his lab'ring Side, Il.13.722.139.
While the broad Fan with Force is whirl'd around, Il.13.741.140.
This said, he seiz'd (while yet the Carcass heav'd) Il.13.801.143.
While Life's red Torrent gush'd from out the Wound. Il.13.820.144.
And while beneath his Targe he flash'd along, Il.13.1016.153.
While Clouds of friendly Dust conceal thy Shame. Il.13.1037.154.
While I th' Adventures of the Day explore. Il.14.12.157.
While yet th' expected Tempest hangs on high, Il.14.23.158.
While wav'ring Counsels thus his Mind engage, Il.14.27.158.
While Anger flash'd from his disdainful Eyes. Il.14.89.162.
While War hangs doubtful, while his Soldiers fight? Il.14.107.162.
While War hangs doubtful, while his Soldiers fight? Il.14.107.162.
Fly diverse; while proud Kings, and Chiefs renown'd Il.14.167.165.
Thus while she breath'd of Heav'n, with decent Pride Il.14.203.169.
While sunk in Love's entrancing Joys he lies. Il.14.271.175.
To check a while the haughty Hopes of *Troy:* Il.14.412.183.
While *Jove* yet rests, while yet my Vapours shed Il.14.413.183.
While *Jove* yet rests, while yet my Vapours shed Il.14.413.183.
While stern *Achilles* in his Wrath retires. Il.14.426.184.
While *Phœbus* hastes, great *Hector* to prepare Il.15.63.197.
While on her wrinkled Front, and Eyebrow bent, Il.15.112.200.
Then (while a Smile serenes his awful Brow) Il.15.178.203.
Has Fame not told, how, while my trusty Sword Il.15.282.207.
While these fly trembling, others pant for Breath, Il.15.392.212.
While thus the Thunder of the Battel rag'd, Il.15.450.215.
While the swift Javelin hiss'd along in Air. Il.15.691.222.
While conscious of the Deed, he glares around, Il.15.704.223.
While Stones and Darts in mingled Tempest flew; Il.15.709.223.
Stoops down impetuous, while they light for Food, Il.15.838.229.
While the black Vessels smoak'd with human Gore. Il.16.2.233.
Such Conf'rence held the Chiefs; while on the Strand, Il.16.128.242.
While restless, raging, in your Ships you lay) Il.16.243.248.
Thus while he rowz'd the Fire in ev'ry Breast, Il.16.252.249.
While far behind, his *Trojans* fall confus'd, Il.16.442.260.
Shock; while the madding Steeds break short their Yokes: Il.16.445.260.
While the grim Savage grinds with foamy Jaws Il.16.602.267.
While crackling Forests fall on ev'ry side. Il.16.770.273.
While *Hector* checking at the *Scæan* Gates Il.16.869.277.
Thus while he thought, beside him *Phœbus* stood, Il.16.873.277.
The Charioteer, while yet he held the Rein, Il.16.899.278.
While the proud Victor thus his Fall derides, Il.16.902.278.
While all around, Confusion, Rage, and Fright Il.16.921.279.
While on each Host with equal Tempest fell Il.16.940.280.
While yet he learn'd his Rudiments of War. Il.16.977.281.
Or while thou may'st, avoid the threaten'd Fate; Il.17.35.289.
While yet thou may'st, avoid the threaten'd Fate; Il.17.35A.289.
While the fierce *Spartan* tore his Arms away. Il.17.66.290.
While unreveng'd the great *Sarpedon* falls? Il.17.168.294.
While *Greeks* and *Ilians* equal Strength employ, Il.17.456.305.
Thus they. While with one Voice the *Trojans* said, Il.17.480.306.
While thus relenting to the Steeds he spoke. Il.17.503.308.
Patroclus, while he liv'd, their Rage cou'd tame, Il.17.544.309.
He bears victorious, while our Army flies. Il.17.663.313.
And save our selves, while with impetuous Hate Il.17.799.319.
While thus aloft the Hero's Corse they bear, Il.17.821.320.
While *Greece* a heavy, thick Retreat maintains, Il.17.845.321.
That shriek incessant, while the Faulcon hung Il.17.847.321.
Thus while he thinks, *Antilochus* appears, Il.18.19.324.
While *Nestor's* Son sustains a manlier Part, Il.18.37.325.
While the long Pomp the silver Wave divides. Il.18.88.327.
While his strong Lance around him heaps the Dead: Il.18.232.333.
While shielded from the Darts, the *Greeks* obtain Il.18.273.335.
I deem'd not *Greece* so dreadful, while engag'd Il.18.303.336.
Then, while we hop'd our Armies might prevail, Il.18.305.336.
Haste then to *Ilion,* while the fav'ring Night Il.18.313.336.
But while inglorious in her Walls we stay'd, Il.18.339.338.
While the long Night extends her sable Reign, Il.18.365.339.
While *Trojan* Captives here thy Mourners stay, Il.18.399.340.
While Anger flash'd from her majestick Eyes) Il.18.424.341.
While bath'd in Sweat from Fire to Fire he flew, Il.18.437.341.
While I the Labours of the Forge forego, Il.18.477.344.
While I my Labours of the Forge forego, Il.18.477A.344.
(Ev'n while he lives, he wastes with secret Woe) Il.18.515.346.
Stretch'd o'er *Patroclus'* Corse; while all the rest Il.19.7.371.
While raging *Hector* heap'd our Camps with Dead. Il.19.136.377.
While yet we talk, or but an instant shun Il.19.147.377.
While near impending from a neighb'ring Height, Il.20.3.392.
While great *Achilles,* (Terror of the Plain) Il.20.57.396.
While thus the Gods in various League engage, Il.20.103.398.
Go; while thou may'st, avoid the threaten'd Fate; Il.20.238.403.
While thus *Achilles* glories o'er the Slain. Il.20.448.413.
While yet he trembled at his Knees, and cry'd, Il.20.543.417.
Dash'd from their Hoofs while o'er the Dead they fly, Il.20.583.418.
While fast behind them runs the Blaze of Fire; Il.21.15.422.
Thus while he spake, the *Trojan* pale with Fears Il.21.74.424.
And while above the Spear suspended stood, Il.21.80.424.
While thus these melting Words attempt his Heart. Il.21.83.425.
While all his trembling Frame confest his Fear. Il.21.128.426.
While the proud Victor thus triumphing said, Il.21.199.429.
While all before, the Billows rang'd on high Il.21.261.431.
Floating midst scatter'd Arms; while Casques of Gold Il.21.350.435.
While *Pallas* fills him with immortal Force. Il.21.355.435.
While to their aid, by our Command enjoin'd, Il.21.388.436.
While *Vulcan* breath'd the fiery Blast around. Il.21.405.437.
While these by *Juno's* Will the Strife resign, Il.21.448.439.
And boast my Conquest, while I yield the Prize. Il.21.584.446.
Thus they above: While swiftly gliding down, Il.21.597.446.
While I decline to yonder Path, that leads Il.21.657.449.
While all the flying Troops their Speed employ, Il.21.717.451.
While here thy frantick Rage attacks a God. Il.22.22.453.
While the sad Father on the Rampart stands, Il.22.49.454.
Two, while I speak, my Eyes in vain explore, Il.22.63.455.
Pity, while yet I live, these silver Hairs; Il.22.80.456.
While yet thy Father feels the Woes he bears, Il.22.81.456.
So they, while down their Cheeks the Torrents roll; Il.22.126.458.
To whom, while eager on the Chace they look, Il.22.219.464.
While that but flies, and this pursues, in vain. Il.22.262.466.
While like *Deiphobus* the martial Dame Il.22.291.468.
While Anger flash'd from his disdainful Eyes) Il.22.334.470.
He stoop'd, while o'er his Head the flying Spear Il.22.351.470.
While thus triumphing, stern *Achilles* cries. Il.22.414.472.
While cast to all the Rage of hostile Pow'r, Il.22.423.473.
While some ignobler, the great Dead deface Il.22.467.474.
And thus aloud, while all the Host attends. Il.22.473.475.
While the sad Father answers Groans with Groans, Il.22.515.477.
While strong Affliction gives the Feeble Force: Il.22.525.478.
While both thy Parents wept thy fatal Hour, Il.22.546.479.
While those his Father's former bounty fed, Il.22.634.482.
And sooth my Sorrows, while I bear to live. Il.23.58.489.
Lies inly groaning; while on either Hand Il.23.72.489.
Thus while he spoke, each Eye grew big with Tears: Il.23.130.493.
Thus o'er *Patroclus* while the Hero pray'd, Il.23.190.497.
While those deputed to inter the Slain Il.23.200.497.
While with sure Skill, tho' with inferior Steeds, Il.23.393.506.
While thy strict Hand his Fellows Head restrains, Il.23.410.506.
While hot for Fame, and Conquest all their Care, Il.23.447.508.
While thus young *Nestor* animates his Steeds. Il.23.482.509.
Shot from the Chariot; while his Coursers stray Il.23.550.511.
And lifted his gay Heart, while thus he said. Il.23.684.517.
One lash'd the Coursers, while one rul'd the Reins. Il.23.738.519.
While pleas'd I take the Gift thy Hands present, Il.23.745.519.
While the long Strife ev'n tir'd the Lookers-on, Il.23.838.522.
His Friends (while loud Applauses shake the Skies) Il.23.1004.529.
While foul in Dust th' unhonour'd Carcase lies, Il.24.28.536.
A while they sorrow, then dismiss their Care; Il.24.62.538.

WHILE (CONTINUED)

Repast unheeded, while he vents his Woes. ....Il.24.160.542.
While thus they commun'd, from th' *Olympian* Bow'rs ....Il.24.177.543.
While careful these the gentle Coursers join'd, ...Il.24.349.550.
And while the fav'ring Gods our Steps survey, ...Il.24.527.558.
The Guards repasting, while the Bowls go round; ....Il.24.546.558.
While kindling Anger sparkled in his Eyes) ....Il.24.706.566.
Then, while the Body on the Car they laid, ...Il.24.738.568.
While deeper Sorrows groan from each full Heart, ...Il.24.904.574.
While all my other Sons in barb'rous Bands ....Il.24.946.575.
Fall the round crystal Drops, while thus she cries. ....Il.24.961.576.
And plac'd aloft: while all, with streaming Eyes, ...Il.24.997.577.
Distant he lay: while in the bright abodes ....Od.1.35.31.
Hermes I sent, while yet his soul remain'd ....Od.1.49.32.
While the dear isle in distant prospect lyes, ...Od.1.76.34.
While his fond soul these fancied triumphs swell'd, ...Od.1.155.40.
Mean while, in whispers to his heav'nly guest ....Od.1.201.42.
While storms vindictive intercept the shore. ....Od.1.424.53.
His Father's throne he fill'd: while distant stood ....Od.2.17.61.
But while your Sons commit th' unpunish'd wrong, ...Od.2.87.65.
While thus he spoke, with rage and grief he frown'd, ...Od.2.89.65.
While she, laborious in delusion, spread ....Od.2.103.66.
"Cease yet a while to urge the bridal hour; ....Od.2.108.66.
While thrice the sun his annual journey made, ...Od.2.119.67.
While yet he speaks, *Telemachus* replies. ....Od.2.147.68.
While sad on foreign shores *Ulysses* treads, ...Od.2.151.69.
And while in wrath to vengeful Fiends she cries, ...Od.2.157.69.
He ceas'd; and while abash'd the Peers attend, ...Od.2.253.73.
True, while my friend is griev'd, his griefs I share; ....Od.2.267.74.
While yet he spoke, *Leocritus* rejoyn'd: ....Od.2.275.74.
While the bowl circles, and the banquet warms; ....Od.2.282.75.
The royal dome; while sad the Prince explores ....Od.2.293.75.
But while the dangers of the deeps he tries, ...Od.2.373.78.
While yet he spoke, she fill'd the walls with cries, ...Od.2.406.80.
And grief destroy what time a while would spare. ....Od.2.423.81.
While to the rival train the Prince returns, ...Od.2.428.81.
While yet we doubted of our watry way; ....Od.3.204.95.
Injurious men! who while my soul is sore ....Od.3.252.97.
While us the works of bloody *Mars* employ'd, ...Od.3.324.102.
While yet he exercis'd the steerman's art, ...Od.3.358.103.
While curst *Ægysthus* the detested deed ....Od.3.386.105.
While lawless feasters in thy palace sway; ....Od.3.401.106.
Thus while he speaks, the ruddy sun descends, ...Od.3.421.107.
While to the final sacrifice they rose. ....Od.3.436.108.
While these officious tend the rites divine, ...Od.3.592.116.
While this gay friendly troop the King surround, ...Od.4.21.121.
While thus pathetic to the Prince he spoke, ...Od.4.149.127.
While pictur'd to thy mind appear'd in view ....Od.4.254.131.
While to his regal bow'r the King ascends, ...Od.4.409.140.
The Seer, while Zephyrs curl the swelling deep, ...Od.4.541.146.
While deep attention fix'd my list'ning soul. ....Od.4.816.157.
Thus thy alternate; while with artful care ....Od.4.839.158.
While pensive in the silent slumb'rous shade, ...Od.4.1045.166.
While the fell foes who late in ambush lay, ...Od.5.36.172.
While she with work and song the time divides, ...Od.5.78.176.
Him, while he spoke, with smiles *Calypso* ey'd, ...Od.5.233.182.
Yet ev'ry day, while absent thus I roam, ...Od.5.281.185.
Thus while he spoke, the beamy Sun descends, ...Od.5.289.185.
In one man's favour? while a distant guest ....Od.5.369.190.
While by the howling tempest rent in twain ....Od.5.407.192.
Thus then I judge: while yet the planks sustain ....Od.5.458.194.
While thus his thoughts an anxious council hold, ...Od.5.464.195.
There, poiz'd a while above the bounding tydes, ...Od.5.473.195.
While thus he thought, a monst'rous wave up-bore ....Od.5.542.198.
While thus the weary Wand'rer sunk to rest, ...Od.6.1.203.
With crimson threads, while busy damsels cull ....Od.6.63.208.
And while the robes imbibe the solar ray, ...Od.6.111.211.
And the good suffers, while the bad prevails: ....Od.6.230.221.
Retire, while from my weary'd limbs I lave ....Od.6.259.222.
Advance at distance, while I pass the plain ....Od.6.309.225.
There wait embowr'd, while I ascend alone ....Od.6.359.229.
While with the purple orb the spindle glows. ....Od.6.370.229.
While the slow mules draw on th' imperial maid: ....Od.7.2.232.
While that in pipes beneath the palace flows, ...Od.7.172.244.
Princes and Peers, attend! while we impart ....Od.7.246.248.
Attend, he cry'd, while we our will disclose, ...Od.8.26.263.
While thus the Peerage in the games contends, ...Od.8.141.270.
While others beauteous as th' æthereal kind, ...Od.8.195.273.
Such was my boast, while vigour crown'd my days, ...Od.8.203.273.
The crowd gaze upward while it cleaves the skies. ....Od.8.216.274.
As while the spirit in this bosom glows, ...Od.8.509.290.
While from the shores the winged navy flies: ....Od.8.550.292.
Thus while he sung, *Ulysses'* griefs renew, ...Od.8.569.293.
With fury burns; while careless they convey ....Od.8.615.295.
While, with my single ship, adventurous I ....Od.9.201.314.
While thus my fraudful speech I reassume. ....Od.9.430.323.
Him while he past the monster blind bespoke: ....Od.9.525.328.
While such a monster as vile *Noman* lives. ....Od.9.542.328.
Thus I: while raging he repeats his cries, ...Od.9.615.332.
While thoughtless we; indulge the genial rite, ...Od.9.649.333.
While kindling transports glow'd at our success; ....Od.10.154.347.
Thus while he spoke, the sovereign plant he drew, ...Od.10.361.361.
While full of thought, revolving fates to come, ...Od.10.369.362.
While scenes of woe rose anxious in my breast, ...Od.10.443.365.
While the wing'd vessel flew along the tyde: ....Od.11.8.379.
But sheath thy ponyard, while my tongue relates ....Od.11.120.386.
While yet he spoke, the Prophet I obey'd, ...Od.11.122.387.
Why is she silent, while her Son is nigh? ....Od.11.177.390.
Fly'st thou, lov'd shade, while I thus fondly mourn? ....Od.11.253.394.
While the impassive soul reluctant flies ....Od.11.267.394.
Thus while she spoke, in swarms hell's Empress brings ....Od.11.273.395.
While life informs these limbs, (the King reply'd) ....Od.11.434.405.
Say while the sea, and while the tempest raves, ...Od.11.495.408.
Say while the sea, and while the tempest raves, ...Od.11.495.408.
Nor while the sea, nor while the tempest raves, ...Od.11.501.408.
Nor while the sea, nor while the tempest raves, ...Od.11.501.408.

WHILE (CONTINUED)

While yet I spoke, the Shade with transport glow'd, ...Od.11.659.416.
While yet I speak, the shade disdains to stay, ...Od.11.691.418.
While in your world I drew the vital air; ....Od.11.764.424.
She sate in silence while the tale I tell, ...Od.12.45.431.
O'erwhelm'd it sinks: while round a smoke expires, ...Od.12.81.435.
Attend while I what Heav'n foredooms disclose. ....Od.12.191.441.
While yet I speak the winged gally flies, ...Od.12.200.441.
While to the shore the rapid vessel flies, ...Od.12.218.442.
While yet I speak, at once their oars they seize, ...Od.12.264.445.
And the flesh trembles while she churns the blood. ....Od.12.307.447.
While yet I spoke, a sudden sorrow ran ....Od.12.330.447.
Then while the night displays her awful shade, ...Od.12.347.448.
Thus I: and while to shore the vessel flies, ...Od.12.359.448.
There while the wild winds whistled o'er the main, ...Od.12.379.449.
While thus *Eurylochus* arising said. ....Od.12.402.450.
While on the deck the Chief in silence lies, ...Od.13.96.5.
While in th' embrace of pleasing sleep I lay, ...Od.13.322.23.
Thus while he spoke, the blue-ey'd maid began ....Od.13.327.23.
Now lift thy longing eyes, while I restore ....Od.13.391.25.
While *Pallas,* cleaving the wide fields of air, ...Od.13.510.30.
Sigh'd, while he furnish'd the luxurious board, ...Od.14.31.36.
While here, (ungrateful task!) his herds I feed, ...Od.14.47.38.
While schemes of vengeance ripen in his breast. ....Od.14.133.42.
Silent and thoughtful while the board he ey'd, ...Od.14.134.42.
While here I sojourn'd, oft I heard the fame ....Od.14.355.51.
They sought repaste; while to th' unhappy kind, ...Od.14.383.53.
While pensive in this solitary den, ...Od.14.409.55.
Thus commun'd these; while to their lowly dome ....Od.14.453.57.
While those who from our labours heap their board, ...Od.14.461.57.
These while on sev'ral tables they dispose, ...Od.14.480.59.
On fond pursuits neglectful while you roam, ...Od.15.15.70.
Hence therefore, while thy stores thy own remain; ....Od.15.23.71.
There pass the night; while he his course pursues ....Od.15.47.72.
Then gave the cup; while *Megapenthe* brought ....Od.15.134.75.
While love and duty warr'd within his breast. ....Od.15.229.79.
There, while within the poop with care he stor'd ....Od.15.232.79.
While yet she was , tho' clouded o'er with grief, ...Od.15.386.88.
While I, so many wand'rings past and woes, ...Od.15.530.95.
While in the port of *Ithaca,* the band ....Od.15.535.96.
They part; while less'ning from the Hero's view, ...Od.15.595.99.
While yet he spoke, the Prince advancing drew ....Od.16.11.102.
Kissing his cheek, his hand, while from his eye ....Od.16.15.102.
To whom, while anger in his bosom glows, ...Od.16.91.106.
While yet he spoke, impatient of delay ....Od.16.166.110.
Hung round his neck, while tears his cheek bedew; ....Od.16.235.114.
While the proud foes, industrious to destroy ....Od.16.338.122.
While in debate they waste the hours away, ...Od.16.344.122.
Pale grief destroy what time a while forbears. ....Od.16.353.123.
While in his guest his murd'rer he receives: ....Od.16.439.128.
While I behold the golden light of day? ....Od.16.455.129.
While to th' assembled council I repair; ....Od.17.64.135.
Thus commun'd they: while in the marble court ....Od.17.190.140.
While thus the copious banquet they provide; ....Od.17.203.141.
While the broad beams of *Phœbus* are display'd, ...Od.17.214.142.
Chuse you to mingle, while behind I stay? ....Od.17.326.147.
While thus they gaze and question with their eyes, ...Od.17.444.155.
While thus his mother to her virgins spoke. ....Od.17.585.161.
While yon' luxurious race indulge their cheer, ...Od.17.619.162.
While fix'd in thought the pensive Heroe sate, ...Od.18.1.166.
Swear, to stand neutral while we cope in fight. ....Od.18.65.169.
While with indignant scorn he sternly spoke, ...Od.18.100.172.
While pleas'd he hears, *Antinous* bears the food, ...Od.18.143.173.
Then, while the streaming sorrow dims her eyes, ...Od.18.193.176.
Hides fraud in smiles, while death is ambush'd there. ....Od.18.200.176.
Then while *Eurynomè* the mandate bears, ...Od.18.219.177.
While yet she speaks, the gay *Antinous* cries, ...Od.18.329.183.
Or should we labour while the plowshare wounds ....Od.18.414.189.
While yet he speaks, *Eurymachus* replies, ...Od.18.428.189.
While those with unctuous fir foment the flame. ....Od.19.77.196.
Twelve days, while *Boreas* vex'd th' aerial space, ...Od.19.230.204.
Yet, while I speak, the mighty woe suspend; ....Od.19.305.209.
(While pure libations crown'd the genial feast) ....Od.19.332.210.
While thus the Chief his woes indignant told, ...Od.20.217.243.
While thus the matron, with majestic air. ....Od.21.68.262.
While yet a child) what majesty he bore! ....Od.21.97.263.
While some deriding—How he turns the bow! ....Od.21.431.281.
While each to Chance ascrib'd the wond'rous stroke, ...Od.22.36.288.
While to your lust and spoil a guardless prey, ...Od.22.43.288.
While yet th' auxiliar shafts this hand supply; ....Od.22.123.292.
While yet each shaft flew deathful from his hand: ....Od.22.133.293.
While yet they spoke, in quest of arms again ....Od.22.176.296.
While yet she spoke, the Queen in transport sprung ....Od.23.35.320.
While the sweet Lyrist airs of rapture sings, ...Od.23.133.327.
Then hear sure evidence, while we display ....Od.23.189.332.
While yet he speaks, her pow'rs of life decay, ...Od.23.211.333.
Thus in fond kisses, while the transport warms, ...Od.23.225.333.
If one more happy, while the tempest raves ....Od.23.253.335.
While heav'n a kind release from ills foreshows, ...Od.23.307.337.
While the soft hours stole unperceiv'd away; ....Od.23.322.339.
Thou, for thy Lord; while me th' immortal pow'rs ....Od.23.379.343.
Thus they; while *Hermes* o'er the dreary plain ....Od.24.123.354.
While from the town, *Ulysses,* and his band, ...Od.24.234.360.
Nor ought remits the work, while thus he said. ....Od.24.286.363.
While, yet a child, these fields I lov'd to trace, ...Od.24.390.368.
If, while the news thro' ev'ry city flies, ...Od.24.413.369.
They commun'd thus; while homeward bent their way ....Od.24.444.370.
While thus *Ulysses* to his ancient friend: ....Od.24.454.370.
And strait resum'd his seat) while round him bows ....Od.24.470.371.
This past on earth, while in the realms above ....Od.24.540.373.

WHILST

Whilst thou art faithful to thy own true Knight, ...2.ChJM.553A.42.
Some fold the Sleeve, whilst others plait the Gown; ....2.RL1.147.158.
Whilst Thames reflects the visionary Scene. ....4.HOde1.24A.153.
Whilst maudlin Whigs deplore their *Cato's* Fate, ...6.33.1A.99.

WHILST (CONTINUED)
Whilst Wits and Templars ev'ry Sentence raise, 6.49iii.27A.143.
Whilst pointed Crystals break the sparkling Rill, 6.142.4D.382.
Whilst from *Olympus* pleas'd *Saturnia* flew. Il.14.258.173.
Indulge my rising grief, whilst these (my friend) Od.1.203.42.
Whilst to his couch himself the Prince addrest, Od.1.549.58.
Whilst warbling to the varied strain, advance Od.4.25.121.
Whilst heaping unwish'd wealth, I distant roam; Od.4.113.125.
Whilst limpid springs the failing cask supply. Od.4.486.143.
So, whilst he feeds luxurious in the stall, Od.4.719.152.
Whilst one most jovial thus accosts the board; Od.4.1017.165.
To whom the Queen, (whilst yet her pensive mind Od.4.1065.167.
Whilst to his neighbour each express'd his thought, Od.10.41.341.
Whilst we, the wretched part'ners of his toils, Od.10.45.341.
Whilst thus their fury rages at the bay, Od.10.145.347.
Whilst in the port each wretch encumber'd dies. Od.10.152.347.
Full oft has *Phidon*, whilst he pour'd the wine, Od.14.367.53.
Fly, whilst thy Mother virtuous yet withstands Od.15.19.70.
Whilst *Eteoneus* portions out the shares, Od.15.156.76.
Whilst yet the Monarch paus'd, with doubts oppest, Od.15.190.77.
Seek thou repose; whilst here I sole remain, Od.19.54.195.
Whilst, forming plans of death, *Ulysses* stay'd, Od.19.62.195.
But whilst with grief and rage my bosom burn'd, Od.19.637.227.
Whilst to nocturnal joys impure, repair Od.20.11.230.
But whilst to learn their lots in nuptial love, Od.20.88.237.
Whilst night extends her soft oblivious veil, Od.20.99.237.
Thus, whilst *Aurora* mounts her purple throne, Od.20.110.238.
Whilst lowly thus the Chief adoring bows, Od.20.126.239.
Whilst with pathetic warmth his hand he press'd. Od.20.248.245.
Whilst hope prevail'd to see your Sire restor'd, Od.20.393.251.
Whilst in paternal pomp, with plenty blest, Od.20.401.251.

WHIM
And made a Widow happy, for a whim. 3.Ep2.58.55.
That life of pleasure, and that soul of whim! 3.Ep3.306.118.
And much must flatter, if the Whim should bite 4.2HE2.149.175.
Lo sneering G[oo]de, half malice and half whim, 5.DunA3.147.163.
Lo sneering Goode, half malice and half whim, 5.DunB3.153.327.

WHIMP'RING
The whimp'ring Girl, and hoarser-screaming Boy, 6.14ii.21.43.

WHIMPERS
She gently whimpers like a lowing Cow. 6.96ii.10.270.

WHIMS
Mind not their learned whims and idle talk, 6.126i.3.353.

WHIMSEY
Less mad the wildest whimsey we can frame, 3.Ep3.157.106.

WHIMSIES
Deep Whimsies to contrive; 6.47.38.129.

WHIMZY
Now let some whimzy, or that Dev'l within 4.1HE1.143.289.

WHINE
I, like a Dog, cou'd bite as well as whine; 2.ChWB.152.64.
To cringe, to whine, his idle hands to spread, Od.17.266.145.

WHIP
Came whip and spur, and dash'd thro' thin and thick 5.DunB4.197.361.
Haste, seize the Whip, and snatch the guiding Rein; Il.5.284.280.
The well-ply'd Whip is hung athwart the Beam; Il.23.592.513.

WHIPT
By worthier Footmen pist upon and whipt! 4.HAdv.56.81.
And all the well-whipt Cream of Courtly Sense, 4.EpS1.70.303.

WHIRL
Down, down they larum, with impetuous whirl, 5.DunA3.157.165.
Down, down they larum, with impetuous whirl, 5.DunB3.163.328.
O'er Fields of Death they whirl the rapid Car, Il.2.932.167.
Or whirl the Disk, or bend an idle Bow: Il.2.941.168.
Ordain'd the first to whirl the weighty Lance. Il.3.405.212.
Ordain'd the first to whirl the mighty Lance. Il.3.405A.212.
Such Coursers whirl him o'er the dusty Field, Il.5.232.278.
Or whirl the sounding Pebble from the Sling, Il.13.894.148.
Stunn'd in the Whirl, and breathless with the Fall. Il.15.28.195.
Some whirl the disk, and some the jav'lin dart. Od.4.848.158.
Snatch'd in the whirl, the hurried navy flew, Od.10.52.342.
Toss it on high, and whirl it to the skies. Od.11.732.421.
Prepar'd to whirl the whizzing spear I stay, Od.12.272.445.
With rapid speed to whirl them o'er the sea. Od.15.315.84.
To whirl the disk, or aim the missile dart. Od.17.193.140.

WHIRL'D
In waving Circles whirl'd a Fun'ral Brand; 1.TrSt.157.416.
Are whirl'd in Air, and on the Winds are born; 1.TrSt.507.431.
And first *Sarpedon* whirl'd his weighty Lance, 1.TrES.282A.460.
Whirl'd the long Lance against the sev'nfold Shield. Il.7.296.378.
Fierce he drove on; *Tydides* whirl'd his Spear. Il.8.150.405.
Toss'd like a Ball, and whirl'd in Air away, Il.13.271.117.
While the broad Fan with Force is whirl'd around, Il.13.741.140.
And first *Sarpedon* whirl'd his weighty Lance, Il.16.587.267.
The Son of *Priam* whirl'd the missive Wood; Il.17.688.314.
And whirl'd her headlong down, for ever driv'n Il.19.129.377.
The Charioteer then whirl'd the Lash around, Il.19.432.389.
That whirl'd the Car of proud *Laomedon*. Il.23.422.506.
And snatch'd the Reins, and whirl'd the Lash around: Il.24.542.558.
He whirl'd it round; it sung across the main: Od.9.632.332.
Steer by the higher rock: lest whirl'd around Od.12.262.445.
Then o'er his ample shoulders whirl'd the cloak, Od.15.69.72.
Whirl'd from his arm with erring rage it flew; Od.18.437.189.

WHIRLIGIGS
Or whirligigs, twirl'd round by skilful swain, 5.DunA3.49.154.
Or whirligigs, twirl'd round by skilful swain, 5.DunB3.57.323.

WHIRLING
The giddy Motion of the whirling Mill, 2.RL2.134.168.
Could he, whose rules the whirling Comet bind, 3.EOM2.35B.60.
In Fields, aloft, the whirling Car to guide, Il.5.250.279.
The whirling Wheels are to the Chariot hung. Il.5.889.308.
Pour'd to the Tumult on his whirling Car. Il.8.112.403.
His whirling Wheels the glassy Surface sweep; Il.13.42.107.
But whirling on, with many a fiery round, Il.14.479.187.
High-bounding o'er the Fosse: the whirling Car Il.16.460.260.
The whirling Lance with vig'rous Force addrest, Il.17.400.303.
And here, and there, in Eddies whirling round, Il.21.12.421.
And brushing with his Tail the whirling Wheel. Il.23.602.513.
And from his whirling Arm dismiss in Air: Il.23.978.528.
High o'er the wond'ring Crowds the whirling Circle flew. Il.23.996.529.
Far, as a Swain his whirling Sheephook throws, Il.23.1001.529.
A whirling gust tumultuous from the shore, Od.4.687.151.
Beneath the God the whirling billows bound. Od.4.778.155.
In curious works; the whirling spindle glow'd Od.6.62.208.
Now whirling down the heav'ns, the golden day Od.6.381.230.
Then sudden whirling like a waving flame Od.10.383.363.
Beneath my feet the whirling billows fly. Od.12.518.457.
In giddy rounds the whirling ship is tost, Od.14.339.51.
He said, and high the whirling tripod flung. Od.17.547.159.
Then whirling high, discharge thy lance in air. Od.24.601.376.
And whirling high, dismist the lance in air. Od.24.604.376.

WHIRLPOOLS
Whirlpools and storms his circling arm invest, 5.DunA2.295.139.
Whirlpools and storms his circling arm invest, 5.DunB2.317.312.
'Midst roaring whirlpools, and absorbs the main, Od.12.130.438.
And in the roaring whirlpools rush the tides. Od.12.510.457.

WHIRLS
Quick whirls, and shifting eddies, of our minds? 3.Ep1.30.17.
Whirls it about, and down it goes again. 3.Ep2.122A.60.
Whirls it about, and down it goes again. 6.154.8.403.
He said; the Driver whirls his lengthful Thong; Il.11.359.50.
Whirls, leaps, and thunders down, impetuous to the Plain: Il.13.198.115.
So whirls a Wheel, in giddy Circle tost, Il.18.695.357.
Now down he plunges, now he whirls it round, Il.21.24.422.
And now the west-wind whirls it o'er the sea. Od.5.423.192.
And *Laodame* whirls high, with dreadful sway, Od.8.139.270.
And bending backward whirls it to the sky; Od.8.410.286.
In his broad eye so whirls the fiery wood; Od.9.461.325.
Aloft he whirls, to crush the savage prey; Od.11.706.420.
And whirls him groaning from his native shores: Od.23.342.341.
And howling *Scylla* whirls her thund'rous waves, Od.23.354.341.

WHIRLWIND
Fierce as a Whirlwind, up the Walls he flies, 1.TrES.175.456.
Rides in the whirlwind, and directs the storm. 5.DunA3.260.179.
Rides in the whirlwind, and directs the storm. 5.DunB3.264.333.
Swift as a Whirlwind drives the scatt'ring Foes, Il.5.850.306.
High o'er the dusty Whirlwind scales the Heav'n. Il.5.1063.317.
As when a western Whirlwind, charg'd with Storms, Il.11.395.52.
Fierce as a Whirlwind now I swept the Field: Il.11.881.75.
He, like a Whirlwind, toss'd the scatt'ring Throng, Il.12.45.83.
Jove breath<e>s a Whirlwind from the Hills of *Ide,* Il.12.299.92.
Fierce as a Whirlwind up the Walls he flies, Il.12.529.101.
Swift as a Whirlwind rushing to the Fleet, Il.13.277.117.
As when from gloomy Clouds a Whirlwind springs, Il.13.999.152.
But where the rising Whirlwind clouds the Plains, Il.16.935.279.
When lo! a Whirlwind from high Heav'n invades Il.17.61.290.
Shot in a Whirlwind to the Shore below; Il.18.206.331.
And the lost Courser in the Whirlwind flies; Il.23.442.507.
His Car amidst the dusty Whirlwind roll'd, Il.23.583.513.
Swift as a Whirlwind, on the Message flies, Il.24.100.539.

WHIRLWINDS
Got by fierce Whirlwinds, and in Thunder born! 1.PAu.92.87.
Rouz'd by the Prince of Air, the whirlwinds sweep 3.Ep3.353.122.
Had seen my Death! Why did not Whirlwinds bear Il.6.436.348.
On ev'ry side the dusty Whirlwinds rise, Il.13.426.126.
Far from thy mind those words, ye whirlwinds bear, Od.8.443.287.
When, at the voice of *Jove,* wild whirlwinds rise, Od.12.369.449.
Snatch me, ye whirlwinds! far from humane race, Od.20.74.236.

WHIRRING
See! from the Brake the whirring Pheasant springs, 1.W-F.111.161.

WHISK
And whisk 'em back to Evans, Young, and Swift. 5.DunA2.108.109.
And whisk 'em back to *G[ay],* to *Y[oung],* to *S[wift].* 5.DunA2.108A.109.
And whisk 'em back to Evans, Young, and Swift. 5.DunB2.116.301.
Whose game is Whisk, whose treat a toast in sack, 6.45.24.125.
"This Eve at Whisk ourself will play, 6.79.47.219.

WHISKERS
With hoary Whiskers and a forky Beard; 2.RL3.38.171.
"Pray dip your Whiskers and your Tail in". 4.HS6.205.263.
With Whiskers, Band, and Pantaloon, 6.58.33.172.

WHISKS
Whisks it about, and down it goes again. 3.Ep2.122.60.

WHISP'RING
In some still Ev'ning, when the whisp'ring Breeze 1.PWi.79.94.
And whisp'ring Angels prompt her golden dreams. 2.ElAb.216.337.
The whisp'ring Zephyr, and the purling rill? 3.EOM1.204.40.
Love-whisp'ring woods, and lute-resounding waves. 5.DunB4.306.374.
That shed Perfumes, and whisp'ring thus addrest. Il.3.480.215.
Some voice of God close whisp'ring from within, Od.14.109.41.

WHISP'RING (CONTINUED)
Hush thee, he cry'd, (soft-whisp'ring in my ear) ....Od.14.555.64.
The fleecy pile obeys the whisp'ring gales, ...Od.19.240.205.

WHISPER
The Glance by Day, the Whisper in the Dark; ....2.RL1.74.151.
And all your Honour in a Whisper lost! ....2.RL4.110.192.
Cæsar himself might whisper he was beat. ....3.Ep1.82.21.
He spies me out. I whisper, gracious God! ....4.JD4.62.31.
The Whisper that to Greatness still too near, ...4.Arbu.356.122.
I get a whisper, and withdraw; ....4.HS6.63.255.
But were his Verses vile, his Whisper base, ...4.EpS1.49.301.
Hark! they whisper; Angels say, ...6.31ii.7.94.
The good Priests whisper—Where's the Chevalier? ....6.82vi.14.232.
Thy silent whisper is the sacred test.] ....6.107.32.311.
No Sound, no Whisper, but the Chief's Commands, ...Il.4.487.243.
No Sound, no Whisper, but their Chief's Commands, ...Il.4.487A.243.
To breathe, and whisper to the Fires to rise. ....Il.23.243.499.

WHISPER'D
Her Fate is whisper'd by the gentle Breeze, ...1.PWi.61.93.
Then softly whisper'd in her faithful Ear, ...1.TrSt.621.436.
Or spoke aloud, or whisper'd in the Ear; ....2.TemF.434.284.
One came, methought, and whisper'd in my Ear; ....2.TemF.498.287.
Some Dæmon whisper'd, "Visto! have a Taste." ....3.Ep4.16.137.
Some Dæmon whisper'd, "Knights should have a Taste." ....3.Ep4.16A.137.
Nor Motteux talk'd, nor Naso whisper'd more; ....5.DunA2.382.147.
Nor *** talk'd, nor *S[elkirk]* whisper'd more; ....5.DunA2.382A.147*.
Nor Kelsey talk'd, nor Naso whisper'd more; ....5.DunA2.382B.147.
So he; but pious, whisper'd first his pray'r. ....5.DunB4.354.377.
And catch the Fates, low-whisper'd in the Breeze.) ....Il.16.291.253.

WHISPERING
Suffic'd, soft-whispering thus to *Nestor's* son, ...Od.4.81.123.

WHISPERS
In the next Line, it *whispers thro' the Trees;* .... 1.EOC.351.279.
And thus in Whispers said, or seem'd to say. ....2.RL1.26.147.
Soft o'er the Shrouds Aerial Whispers breathe, ...2.RL2.57.163.
Whispers are heard, with Taunts reviling loud, ...2.TemF.404.283.
Whispers were heard, with Taunts reviling loud, ...2.TemF.404A.283.
At last he whispers "Do, and we go snacks." ....4.Arbu.66.100.
And smiling, whispers to the next, ...4.HS6.52.253.
A Voice there is, that whispers in my ear, ...4.1HE1.11.279.
Who counsels best? who whispers, "Be but Great, ...4.1HE1.101.287.
This whispers soft his Vengeance to controul, ...Il.1.257.99.
But bid in Whispers: These surround their Chief, ...Il.9.15.431.
Speak it in Whispers, lest a *Greek* should hear. ....Il.14.101.162.
And thus in Whispers greets his trembling Ears. ....Il.24.208.545.
Mean while, in whispers to his heav'nly guest ....Od.1.201.42.
In whispers breaths the fondness of his heart. ....Od.17.671.164.

WHISTLE
His whistle (which a hundred reeds compose) ....1.TrPA.45.367.
Her infant Grandame's *Whistle* next it grew, ...2.RL5.93.207.
The *Bells* she gingled, and the *Whistle* blew; ....2.RL5.94.207.
And the winds whistle, and the surges roll ....Od.3.368.104.
The wild winds whistle, and the billows roar; ....Od.7.357.254.

WHISTLED
May Dunce by Dunce be whistled off my hands! ....4.Arbu.254.114.
There while the wild winds whistled o'er the main, ...Od.12.379.449.
Heedless he whistled, and pursu'd his way. ....Od.24.309.364.

WHISTLES
The gloomy West, and whistles in the skies. ....Od.12.478.455.

WHISTLING
Wings on the whistling Winds his rapid way, ...1.TrSt.438.428.
Or ravish'd with the whistling of a Name, ...3.EOM4.283.155.
Whose tuneful whistling makes the waters pass: ....5.DunB3.156.327.
The whistling darts shall turn their points away, ...6.21.15.69.
By the shrill Clang and whistling Wings, they knew. ....Il.10.324.17.
Around their Heads the whistling Javelins sung; ....Il.12.169.87.
Thro' all the whistling Darts his Course he bends, ...Il.20.368.410.
And to their Caves the whistling *Winds* return'd: ....Il.23.285.501.
The whistling winds already wak'd the sky; ....Od.3.213.96.
Before the whistling winds the vessels fly, ...Od.3.214.96.
Then pleas'd and whistling, drives his flock before; ....Od.9.370.321.

WHISTON
Than to the wicked Works of *Whiston;* .... 6.10.22.25.

WHISTON'S
And furious D[enni]s foam in W[histon]'s rage. ....5.DunA1.104D.72*.

WHITE
A Milk-white Bull shall at your Altars stand, ...1.PSp.47.65.
Their early Fruit, and milk-white Turtles bring; ....1.PSu.52.76.
And white-roab'd Innocence from Heav'n descend. ....1.Mes.20.114.
Their ample Bow, a new *White-Hall* ascend! ....1.W-F.380.188.
And glossy Jett is pair'd with shining White. ....1.TrSP.44.395.
And Dust yet white upon each Altar lies, ...1.TrSt.601.435.
Thus Trees are crown'd with Blossoms white as Snow, ...2.ChJM.133.21.
Nay, if my Lord affirm'd that Black was White, ...2.ChJM.160.22.
Sol thro' white Curtains shot a tim'rous Ray, ...2.RL1.13.145.
Sol thro' white Curtains did his Beams display, ...2.RL1.13A.145.
First, rob'd in White, the Nymph intent adores ....2.RL1.123.155.
Transform'd to *Combs,* the speckled and the white. ....2.RL1.136.156.
On her white Breast a sparkling *Cross* she wore, ...2.RL2.7.159.
Her wrinkled Form in *Black* and *White* array'd; ....2.RL4.28.185.
Why round our Coaches crowd the white-glov'd Beaus, ...2.RL5.13.200.
Rise white in Air, and glitter o'er the Coast; ....2.TemF.54.256.
On Doric Pillars of white Marble rear'd, ...2.TemF.76.258.
The sage *Chaldæans* rob'd in White appear'd, ...2.TemF.99.260.
The sage Historians in white Garments wait; ....2.TemF.146.265.

WHITE (CONTINUED)
For her white virgins *Hymenæals* sing; ....2.ElAb.220.338.
To *Paraclete's* white walls, and silver springs, ...2.ElAb.348.348.
If white and black blend, soften, and unite ....3.EOM2.213.81.
A thousand ways, is there no black or white? ....3.EOM2.214.81.
Chameleons who can paint in white and black? ....3.Ep2.156.63.
So first to preach a white-glov'd Chaplain goes, ...4.JD4.250.47.
Make Keys, build Bridges, or repair White-hall: ....4.HS2.120.63.
And others hunt white Aprons in the *Mall.* ....4.HAdv.38.79.
Not Lady-like, displays a milk-white Breast, ...4.HAdv.110.85.
And just that White and Red which Nature gave. ....4.HAdv.164.89.
" *Sporus,* that mere white Curd of Ass's milk? ....4.Arbu.306.117.
"Paris, that mere white Curd of Ass's milk? ....4.Arbu.306A.117.
Let Bear or Elephant be e'er so white, ...4.2HE1.322.223.
The Napkins white, the Carpet red: ....4.HS6.197.263.
White Gloves, and Linnen worthy Lady Mary! ....4.1HE1.164.291.
See under Ripley rise a new White-hall, ...5.DunB3.327.336.
Look'd a white lilly sunk beneath a show'r. ....5.DunB4.104.351.
On some, a Priest succinct in amice white ....5.DunB4.549.396.
Wash Bladen white, and expiate Hay's stain. ....5.DunB4.560.397.
Forth thrust a white Neck, and red Crest. ....6.14i.20.42.
Where *Lillies* smile in virgin robes of white, ...6.14iv.5.47.
All white and black beside: ....6.14v(a).15.49.
So have I seen, in black and white ....6.14v(a).19.49.
Furrow'd his rev'rend face, and white his hairs, ...6.15.6.51.
Lay by your White Staff and gray Habit, ...6.42iv.15.118.
Lay down your White Staff and gray Habit, ...6.42iv.15A.118.
Did wave his Wand so white, ...6.79.118.222.
Did wave his Hand so white, ...6.79.118A.222.
They use white Powder, and wear Holland-Smocks. ....6.95.4.264.
And strip white *Ceres* of her nut-brown Coat. ....6.100vi.3.289.
"Red, Blue, and Green, nay white and black, ...6.140.19.378.
The milk-white Canvas bellying as they blow; ....Il.1.626.117.
Which, with a Smile, the white-arm'd Queen receiv'd. ....Il.1.767.124.
Or milk-white Swans in *Asius'* watry Plains, ...Il.2.541.152.
Or white *Lycastus* glitters to the Skies, ...Il.2.788.162.
Jalyssus, Lindus, and *Camirus* white. ....Il.2.796.163.
To *Earth* a sable, to the *Sun* a white, ...Il.3.142.197.
To join his milk-white Coursers to the Car: ....Il.3.331.209.
So white with Dust the *Grecian* Host appears, ...Il.5.617.297.
Lash'd her white Steeds along th' Aerial Way. ....Il.5.957.312.
(*Laomedon's* white Flocks *Bucolion* fed, ...Il.6.29.325.
(Down his white Beard a Stream of Sorrow flows) ....Il.9.559.460.
A Boar's white Teeth grinn'd horrid o'er his Head. ....Il.10.312.16.
Swift as the Wind, and white as Winter-Snow: ....Il.10.507.26.
And the white Steeds behind his Chariot bound. ....Il.10.549.27.
The milk-white Coursers studious to convey ....Il.10.572.28.
Swift as the Wind, and white as Winter-Snow. ....Il.10.601.29.
Next her white Hand an antique Goblet brings, ...Il.11.772.69.
Fifty white Flocks, full fifty Herds of Swine, ...Il.11.822.73.
And the white Ruin rises o'er the Plain. ....Il.12.344.94.
Who rul'd where *Calydon's* white Rocks arise, ...Il.13.287.119.
Shakes his white Plumes that to the Breezes flow, ...Il.13.947.150.
Then o'er her Head she casts a Veil more white ....Il.14.213.170.
To whom the white-arm'd Goddess thus replies: ....Il.15.98.200.
White are the Decks with Foam; the Winds aloud ....Il.15.754.225.
Beat their white Breasts, and fainted on the Ground: ....Il.18.36.325.
Soon the white Flocks proceeded o'er the Plains, ...Il.18.607.352.
His vent'rous Act the white-arm'd Queen survey'd, ...Il.20.144.400.
He strikes his rev'rend Head now white with Age: ....Il.22.44.454.
Next the white Bones his sad Companions place ....Il.23.313.502.
On whose broad Front a Blaze of shining white, ...Il.23.538.511.
To the tall Top a milk-white Dove they tye, ...Il.23.1012.529.
On his white Beard and Form majestick gaz'd, ...Il.24.650.563.
Around his Neck her milk-white Arms she threw, ...Il.24.907.574.
To feastful mirth be this white hour assign'd, ...Od.4.329.135.
Must view his billows white beneath thy oar, ...Od.4.645.150.
White curl the waves, and the vex'd ocean roars. ....Od.4.788.156.
All rough with rocks, with foamy billows white. ....Od.5.521.197.
Youth, and white age, tumultuous pour along: ....Od.8.50.264.
Half the white stream to hard'ning cheese he prest, ...Od.9.292.318.
Black was the root, but milky white the flow'r; ....Od.10.364.362.
White linnen lay beneath. Another plac'd ....Od.10.419.364.
Long flowing robes of purest white array ....Od.10.649.375.
This does a tunic and white vest convey, ...Od.13.84.5.
Go bathe, and rob'd in white, ascend the tow'rs; ....Od.17.60.135.
She bath'd; and rob'd in white, with all her train, ...Od.17.69.136.
A team of twenty geese, (a snow-white train!) ....Od.19.627.226.

WHITE-ARM'D
Which, with a Smile, the white-arm'd Queen receiv'd. ....Il.1.767.124.
To whom the white-arm'd Goddess thus replies: ....Il.15.98.200.
His vent'rous Act the white-arm'd Queen survey'd, ...Il.20.144.400.

WHITE-GLOV'D
Why round our Coaches crowd the white-glov'd Beaus, ...2.RL5.13.200.
So first to preach a white-glov'd Chaplain goes, ...4.JD4.250.47.

WHITE-HALL
Their ample Bow, a new *White-Hall* ascend! ....1.W-F.380.188.
Make Keys, build Bridges, or repair White-hall: ....4.HS2.120.63.
See under Ripley rise a new White-hall, ...5.DunB3.327.336.

WHITE-ROAB'D
And white-roab'd Innocence from Heav'n descend. ....1.Mes.20.114.

WHITE'S
His Grace will game: to White's a Bull be led, ...3.Ep3.55.91.
To White's be carried, as to ancient games, ...3.Ep3.57.91.
At *Fig's* at *White's,* with *Felons,* or a *Whore,* .... 4.JD4.213.43.
At *Fig's* or *White's,* with *Felons,* or a *Whore,* ....4.JD4.213A.43.
Or when a Duke to Jansen punts at White's, ...4.JD2.88.141.
Or chair'd at White's amidst the Doctors sit, ...5.DunB1.203.284.
This Mess, toss'd up of Hockley-hole and White's; ....5.DunB1.222.286.
Familiar White's , "God save king Colley!" cries; ....5.DunB1.321.293.
Garth at *St James's,* and at *White's,* .... 6.58.47.172.

WHITED

What Lady's Face is not a whited Wall? ....4.JD4.151.37.

WHITEHALL

Friendly at Acton, faithless at Whitehall. ....3.Ep1.135A.25.
Friendly at Hackney, faithless at Whitehall. ....3.Ep1.135.25.

WHITEN

And human Bones yet whiten all the Ground. ....1.TrSt.391.426.
And bask and whiten in the Blaze of Day. ....2.RL2.78.164.
In circling fleeces whiten all the ways: ....5.DunB2.362.315.
Or sends soft Snows to whiten all the Shore, ...Il.10.7.2.
Descend, and whiten all the Fields below. ....Il.12.178.87.
And fleecy Flocks, that whiten all the Scene. ....Il.18.680.356.
Lie human bones, that whiten all the ground; ....Od.12.58.432.

WHITEN'D

When Frosts have whiten'd all the naked Groves; ....1.W-F.126.162.
Or without Wall provoke the Skew'r to write, ...4.HS1.98.13.
And num'rous Flocks, that whiten'd all the Field. ....Il.14.140.164.
The flashing Billows beat the whiten'd Shores: ....Il.21.10.421.
So look'd the Field, so whiten'd was the Ground, ...Il.21.404.437.

WHITENESS

The shining Whiteness and the *Tyrian* Dye. ....Il.4.175.229.
Her Arms whose Whiteness match the falling Snows. ....Il.5.390.285.
Her Arms whose Whiteness match'd the falling Snows. ....Il.5.390A.285.

WHITENING

Pour'd o'er the whitening Vale their fleecy Care, ...1.PSp.19.62.
The whitening Surface of the ruffled Deep. ....Il.2.178.137.
First move the whitening Surface of the Seas, ...Il.4.479.243.
Beneath his Oars the whitening Billows fly. ....Il.9.801.473.
Sharp blew the North; snow whitening all the fields ....Od.14.536.63.

WHITENS

Whose dazling Lustre whitens all the Skies. ....6.82v.4.231.
Drives o'er the Barn, and whitens all the Hinds. ....Il.5.616.297.
Whose dazling Lustre whitens all the Skies. ....Il.19.383.388.
And a Foam whitens on the purple Waves. ....Il.21.381.436.
Their snowy lustre whitens all the strand.) ....Od.6.108.211.
And Ocean whitens in long tracts below. ....Od.7.420.258.
And the sea whitens with the rising gale. ....Od.9.160.312.

WHITER

No whiter page than Addison remains. ....4.2HE1.216.213.
And spin thy future with a whiter clue! ....Od.20.250.245.

WHITFIELD

There Webster! peal'd thy voice, and Whitfield! thine. ....5.DunB2.258.308.

WHITHER

And whither, whither its sad Owner flie? ....1.TrUl.79.468.
And whither, whither its sad Owner flie? ....1.TrUl.79.468.
(They know not whither) in a Chaise and one; ....4.1HE1.158.291.
Whither, ah whither art thou flying! ....6.31i.5.93.
Whither, ah whither art thou flying! ....6.31i.5.93.
And whither *Enoch* went before him. ....6.151.8.399.
Too daring Prince! ah whither dost thou run? ....Il.6.510.351.
Whither, O *Menelaus!* would'st thou run, ...Il.7.127.369.
Whither, oh whither does *Ulysses* run? ....Il.8.117.403.
Whither, oh whither does *Ulysses* run? ....Il.8.117.403.
Ah! whither wanders thy distemper'd Mind, ...Il.24.243.546.
Say whither, Father! when each mortal Sight ....Il.24.447.554.
Oh whither, whither flies my son? she cry'd, ...Od.2.408.80.
Oh whither, whither flies my son? she cry'd, ...Od.2.408.80.
Ah whither roam'st thou? much-enduring man! ....Od.10.334.360.
Whither (he cry'd) ah whither will ye run? ....Od.10.509.368.
Whither (he cry'd) ah whither will ye run? ....Od.10.509.368.
And whither, whither its sad owner fly? ....Od.13.246.18.
And whither, whither its sad owner fly? ....Od.13.246.18.
Oh whither wanders thy distemper'd brain, ...Od.18.375.185.
Hold, lawless rustic! whither wilt thou go? ....Od.21.391.279.
Ah! whither wanders thy distemper'd mind? ....Od.23.12.319.

WHITING

Cod, Whiting, Oyster, Mackrel, Sprat, or Plaice: ....6.14ii.31.44.

WHIZZ'D

The *Trojan* Weapon whizz'd along in Air; ....Il.13.636.136.

WHIZZES

Th' impatient Weapon whizzes on the Wing, ...Il.4.156.228.

WHIZZING

Cold thro' his Temples glides the whizzing Spear; ....Il.4.576.249.
Prepar'd to whirl the whizzing spear I stay, ...Od.12.272.445.
Sure thro' six circlets flew the whizzing dart. ....Od.19.673.229.
Which whizzing high, the wall unseemly sign'd. ....Od.20.369.250.
The whizzing arrow vanish'd from the string, ...Od.21.461.282.

WHO (OMITTED)
1203

WHO-E'ER

Who-e'er offends, at some unlucky Time ....4.HS1.77.13.
Who-e'er neglects to pay distinction due, ...Od.19.370.212.
(Who-e'er he be) 'till ev'ry Prince lie dead. ....Od.22.86.290.

WHO'D

Shou'd it so prove, yet who'd admire? ....6.10.58.26.
Who'd sooner quit our Part in thee, ...6.30.25B.86.
And who'd wage War with Bedlam or the Mint ....6.49iii.6A.142.

WHO'ER

To this sad Shrine, who'er thou art, draw near, ...6.85.1.242.
Who'er this guest (the prudent Queen replies) ....Od.17.664.164.

WHO'L

And who'l wage War with Bedlam or the Mint? ....6.49iii.6.142.

WHO'LL

And who'll wage War with *Bedlam* or the *Mint?* ....6.98.6.283.

WHO'S

"Who's Chariot's that we left behind? ....4.HS6.90.255.
If any ask you, "Who's the Man, so near ....4.EpS1.45.301.
Who's here? cries *Umbra:* "Only *Johnson*"—Oh! ....6.49ii.3.140.
Who's but a *Publisher* himself. ....6.116ii.9.326.

WHOE'ER

To whom the King: Whoe'er of Human Race ....1.TrUl.108.469.
All this avail'd not; for whoe'er he be ....2.ChWB.351.74.
Whoe'er thou art, ah gently tread the Cave! ....6.87.3A.248.
Whoe'er involv'd us in this dire Debate, ...Il.3.398.211.
Know thou, whoe'er with heav'nly Pow'r contends, ...Il.5.228.278.
But know, whoe'er Almighty Pow'r withstand! ....Il.5.495.291.
Then thus aloud: Whoe'er thou art, remain; ....Il.8.560.423.
Whoe'er thou art, be bold, nor fear to die. ....Il.10.439.23.
Glad I submit, whoe'er, or young or old, ...Il.10.454.23.
Whoe'er shall drag him to the *Trojan* Train, ...Il.14.118.163.
Stranger! whoe'er thou art, securely rest ....Il.17.271.298.
Whoe'er thou art, whom fortune brings to keep ....Od.1.161.40.
Whoe'er thou art, (the azure Goddess cries,) ....Od.3.55.89.
Whoe'er thou art, I shall not blindly join ....Od.4.501.144.
Whoe'er thou art, before whose stream unknown ....Od.5.454.194.
Whoe'er thou art that bear'st celestial wine! ....Od.5.568.199.
To whom the King. Whoe'er of humane race ....Od.9.420.323.
Whoe'er from heav'n has gain'd this rare Ostent, ...Od.13.275.19.
Whoe'er from heav'n has gain'd this rare Ostent, ...Od.20.143.240.

WHOE'RE

Whoe're thou art whom this fair statue charms, ...6.20.1.66.

WHOEVER

Whoever thinks a faultless Piece to see, ...1.EOC.253.268.
Know farther yet; Whoever fair and chaste ....2.RL1.67.151.
Whoever borrow'd, could not be to blame, ...4.EpS2.169.323.
Patroclus dead, whoever meets me, dies: ....Il.21.112.426.
Whoever dares deserve so rich a Prize! ....Il.23.946.526.
Whoever was the warrior, he must be ....Od.14.142.42.

WHOLE

Whole Nations enter with each swelling Tyde, ...1.W-F.399.191.
With Spirits feeds, with Vigour fills the whole, ...1.EOC.77.248.
Survey the *Whole,* nor seek slight Faults to find, ...1.EOC.235.266.
The *Whole* at once is *Bold,* and *Regular.* ....1.EOC.252.268.
Still make the *Whole* depend upon a *Part,* ....1.EOC.264.269.
And a whole Province in his Triumph led. ....1.TrSt.746.441.
Who mows whole Troops, and makes whole Armies fly. ....1.TrES.216.457.
Who mows whole Troops, and makes whole Armies fly. ....1.TrES.216.457.
Who mows whole Troops, and makes an Army fly ....1.TrES.216A.457.
My whole Estate shall gratifie your Love: ....2.ChJM.562.42.
Valerius, whole; and of St. *Jerome,* Part; ....2.ChWB.359.74.
He had by Heart the whole Detail of Woe ....2.ChWB.387.76.
Or wedg'd whole Ages in a *Bodkin's* Eye: ....2.RL2.128.168.
The whole Creation open to my Eyes: ....2.TemF.124.254.
Finish'd the whole, and labour'd ev'ry Part, ...2.TemF.198.271.
For thee whole Nations fill'd with Flames and Blood, ...2.TemF.346.280.
Rise *Alps* between us! and whole oceans roll! ....2.ElAb.290.343.
Condemn'd whole years in absence to deplore, ...2.ElAb.361.348.
Look'd thro'? or can a part contain the whole? ....3.EOM1.32.17.
'Tis but a part we see, and not a whole. ....3.EOM1.60.20.
Towns to one grave, whole nations to the deep? ....3.EOM1.144.33.
The gen'ral ORDER, since the whole began, ...3.EOM1.171.36.
Alike essential to th' amazing whole; ....3.EOM1.248.45.
That system only, but the whole must fall. ....3.EOM1.250.46.
Heav'n's whole foundations to its centre nod, ...3.EOM1.255.46.
All are but parts of one stupendous whole, ...3.EOM1.267.47.
Expunge the whole, or lop th'excrescent parts ....3.EOM2.49.61.
Reason's comparing balance rules the whole. ....3.EOM2.60.63.
Parts it may ravage, but preserves the whole. ....3.EOM2.106.67.
The whole employ of body and of mind. ....3.EOM2.126.70.
Each vital humour which should feed the whole, ...3.EOM2.139.71.
But HEAV'N's great view is One, and that the Whole: .....3.EOM2.238.84.
Nothing is foreign: Parts relate to whole; ....3.EOM3.21.94.
Be Man the Wit and Tyrant of the whole: ....3.EOM3.50.97.
But as he fram'd a Whole, the Whole to bless, ...3.EOM3.111.103.
But as he fram'd a Whole, the Whole to bless, ...3.EOM3.111.103.
And one regards Itself, and one the Whole. ....3.EOM3.316.126.
Heav'n breaths thro' ev'ry member of the whole ....3.EOM4.61.134.
Reason's whole pleasure, all the joys of Sense, ...3.EOM4.79.136.
Oh blind to truth, and God's whole scheme below, ...3.EOM4.93.137.
The whole strange purpose of their lives, to find ....3.EOM4.221.148.
One self-approving hour whole years out-weighs ....3.EOM4.255.152.
The whole amount of that enormous fame, ...3.EOM4.307.156.
Learns, from this union of the rising Whole, ...3.EOM4.337.161.
Grasp the whole worlds of Reason, Life, and Sense, ...3.EOM4.357.163.
God loves from Whole to Parts: but human soul ....3.EOM4.361.163.
Must rise from Individual to the Whole. ....3.EOM4.362.163.
Here puzzling Contraries confound the whole, ...3.Ep1.124A.25.
Or puzzling Contraries confound the whole, ...3.Ep1.124.25.
Yet mark the fate of a whole Sex of Queens! ....3.Ep2.219.68.
Whole slaughter'd hecatombs, and floods of wine, ...3.Ep3.203A.110.
Had Colepepper's whole wealth been hops and hogs, ...3.Ep3.53.90.
Drive to St. James's a whole herd of swine? ....3.Ep3.62.92.
Ask you why Phryne the whole Auction buys? ....3.Ep3.121.101.
Sinks deep within him, and possesses whole, ...3.Ep3.373.123.
Parts answ'ring parts shall slide into a whole, ...3.Ep4.66.143.
The whole, a labour'd Quarry above ground. ....3.Ep4.110.148.

WHOLE (CONTINUED)

Sacred to Ridicule! his whole Life long, ... 4.HS1.79.13.
The whole Artill'ry of the Terms of War, ... 4.JD4.54.29.
Cries, "Send me, Gods! a whole Hog *barbecu'd!*" .... 4.HS2.26.55.
He courts the whole *Personæ Dramatis:* .... 4.HAdv.72.81.
There (thank my Stars) my whole Commission ends, ... 4.Arbu.59.100.
To *Bufo* left the whole *Castalian* State. .... 4.Arbu.230.112.
Or Envy holds a whole Week's war with Sense, ... 4.Arbu.252.114.
Some Beasts were kill'd, tho' not whole Hecatombs: .... 4.JD2A.122.142.
Glean on, and gather up the whole Estate: .... 4.JD2.92.141.
Some beasts were kill'd, tho' not whole hecatombs, ... 4.JD2.116.143.
"His whole Ambition was to serve a Lord, ... 4.2HE2.14.165.
Well, on the whole, *plain* Prose must be my fate: .... 4.2HE2.198.179.
Well, on the whole, then Prose must be my fate: .... 4.2HE2.198A.179.
Enclose whole Downs in Walls, 'tis all a joke! .... 4.2HE2.261.183.
Has sanctify'd whole Poems for an age. .... 4.2HE1.114.205.
Takes the whole House upon the Poet's day. .... 4.1HE6.88.243.
A frugal Mouse upon the whole, ... 4.HS6.161.261.
ARGYLE, the State's whole Thunder born to wield, ... 4.EpS2.86.318.
Since the whole House did afterwards the same: .... 4.EpS2.170.323.
Let Envy howl while Heav'n's whole Chorus sings, ... 4.EpS2.242.326.
The Clergy perjur'd, thy whole People sold.' .... 4.1740.82.336.
Founds the whole pyle, of all his works the base; .... 5.DunA1.140.81.
And turn this whole illusion on the town. .... 5.DunA2.124.112.
Heav'ns! what a pyle! whole ages perish there: .... 5.DunA3.69.156.
And last, to give the whole creation grace, ... 5.DunA3.243.177.
And Pope's, translating three whole years with Broome. .... 5.DunA3.328.191.
Till Westminster's whole year be holiday; .... 5.DunA3.332.191.
And Pope's whole years to comment and translate. .... 5.DunA3.328A.191.
Founds the whole pile, of all his works the base: .... 5.DunB1.160.282.
And turn this whole illusion on the town: .... 5.DunB2.132.301.
Heav'ns! what a pile! whole ages perish there, ... 5.DunB3.77.324.
And last, to give the whole creation grace, ... 5.DunB3.247.332.
'Till Westminster's whole year be holiday, ... 5.DunB3.336.336.
'Tis true, on Words is still our whole debate, ... 5.DunB4.219.364.
How parts relate to parts, or they to whole, ... 5.DunB4.235.366.
When Man's whole frame is obvious to a *Flea.* .... 5.DunB4.238.366.
And let the Author of the Whole escape: .... 5.DunB4.456.385.
Whole Years neglected for some Months ador'd, ... 6.19.43.63.
Informs great nature and directs the whole! .... 6.23.4.73.
Two plenteous fountains the whole prospect crown'd, ... 6.35.28.103.
To *sum the whole,—the Close of all.* .... 6.39.16.110.
Whole Systems flaming round .... 6.50.24A.147.
This more than pays whole years of thankless pain; .... 6.63.5.188.
What a whole thankless land to his denies. .... 6.72.8.208.
What a whole thankless land to his deny'd. .... 6.72.8A.208.
And the whole Princesse in my work should shine. .... 6.75.10.212.
And wak'd and wish'd whole Nights for thy Return? .... 6.96iv.4.276.
For three whole days you here may rest .... 6.114.9.321.
The whole amount of that enormous Fame .... 6.130.37.359.
Along the Shore whole Hecatombs were laid, ... Il.1.414.107.
To whom its Safety a whole People owes, ... Il.2.29.128.
To whom its Safety a whole People owes; .... Il.2.79.130.
At whose Command whole Empires rise or fall: .... Il.2.148.135.
All rank'd by Tens; whole Decads when they dine .... Il.2.157.136.
That *Troy,* and *Troy's* whole Race thou woud'st confound, ... Il.4.51.223.
Whole Troops before you lab'ring in the Fray? .... Il.4.399.239.
The War's whole Art with Wonder had he seen, ... Il.4.634.251.
Deluge whole Fields, and sweep the Trees along, ... Il.5.117.273.
That wondrous Force by which whole Armies fall, ... Il.5.223.278.
Unmov'd and silent, the whole War they wait, ... Il.5.639.298.
Proud Tyrants humbles, and whole Hosts o'erturns. .... Il.5.925.310.
Ilion shall perish whole, and bury All; .... Il.6.73.327.
That mows whole Troops, and makes all *Troy* retire. .... Il.6.120.330.
Next the bold *Amazon's* whole Force defy'd; .... Il.6.229.337.
Who mows whole Troops and makes all *Troy* retire. .... Il.6.347.343.
Whole Hosts may hail him with deserv'd Acclaim, ... Il.6.612.357.
And gives whole Nations to the Waste of Wars. .... Il.7.254.376.
Whole Troops of Heroes, *Greece* has yet to boast, ... Il.7.279.378.
Proud Tyrants humbles, and whole Hosts o'erturns. .... Il.8.475.419.
Jove, at whose Nod whole Empires rise or fall, ... Il.9.32.433.
The whole Extent to *Pylos'* sandy Plain .... Il.9.201.442.
The whole Extent to *Pylos'* sandy Plain .... Il.9.388.452.
Made Nations tremble, and whole Hosts retire, ... Il.9.403.452.
That levell'd Harvests, and whole Forests tore: .... Il.9.660.467.
The Matrons ravish'd, the whole Race enslav'd: .... Il.9.705.469.
Fulfill thy Wish, their whole Intention know, ... Il.10.384.21.
Whole Squadrons vanish, and proud Heads lie low. .... Il.11.206.44.
Whole Ranks are broken, and whole Troops o'erthrown. .... Il.11.344.49.
Whole Ranks are broken, and whole Troops o'erthrown. .... Il.11.344.49.
Now the last Ruin the whole Host appalls; .... Il.11.403.52.
Whole Hecatombs of *Trojan* Ghosts shall pay. .... Il.11.472.55.
But stands collected in himself and whole, ... Il.11.511.56.
So turn'd stern *Ajax,* by whole Hosts repell'd, ... Il.11.680.65.
There stops—So *Hector:* Their whole Force he prov'd, ... Il.13.199.115.
There join'd, the whole *Bœotian* Strength remains, ... Il.13.859.146.
And Wars whole Fury burns around thy Head. .... Il.13.924.149.
Whole Nations fear'd: but not an *Argive* shook. .... Il.13.1019.153.
And have whole Streams of Blood been spilt in vain? .... Il.14.99.162.
Roar thro' the Woods, and make whole Forests fall; .... Il.14.460.186.
From that great Hour the War's whole Fortune turns, ... Il.15.76.199.
With equal Hand he guides his whole Design, ... Il.15.476.215.
Shakes his huge Javelin, and whole Armies fall. .... Il.15.727.224.
Whole Fields are drown'd, and Mountains swept away; .... Il.16.473.261.
Who mows whole Troops, and makes an Army fly. .... Il.16.519.263.
And the whole Forest in one Crash descends. .... Il.16.928.279.
Whole *Troy* embodied, rush'd with Shouts along. .... Il.17.309.299.
What, coop whole Armies in our Walls again? .... Il.18.334.337.
Whole Flocks and Herds lye bleeding on the Plains, ... Il.18.613.352.
And the whole War came out, and met the Eye; .... Il.18.625.352.
And beat the Buckler's Verge, and bound the whole. .... Il.18.704.357.
Whole Years untouch'd, uninjur'd shall remain .... Il.19.33.373.
Thus to convene the whole ætherial State? .... Il.20.25.393.
To mow whole Troops, and make whole Armies fly: .... Il.20.406.412.
To mow whole Troops, and make whole Armies fly: .... Il.20.406.412.
On *Troy's* whole Force with boundless Fury flies. .... Il.20.438.413.

WHOLE (CONTINUED)

Whole Hecatombs of *Trojan* Ghosts shall pay. .... Il.20.524.416.
Tread down whole Ranks, and crush out Hero's Souls. .... Il.20.582.418.
Not a whole River stops the Hero's Course, ... Il.21.354.435.
Drink the whole Flood, the crackling Trees devour, ... Il.21.395.436.
On their whole War, untam'd the Savage flies; .... Il.21.683.450.
Hector, whose Zeal whole Hecatombs has slain, ... Il.22.224.464.
Eyes the whole Man, and meditates the Wound; .... Il.22.404.472.
Drain their whole Realm to buy one fun'ral Flame; .... Il.22.442.474.
And the whole City wears one Face of Woe. .... Il.22.517.478.
Scarce the whole People stop his desp'rate Course, ... Il.22.524.478.
And touch thy Steeds, and swear, thy whole Intent .... Il.23.663.516.
Secure, this Hand shall his whole Frame confound, ... Il.23.777.520.
His Hinds and Swains whole years shall be supply'd .... Il.23.988.528.
But whole he lies, neglected in the Tent: .... Il.24.504.557.
O thou! from whom the whole creation springs, ... Od.1.57.33.
Proud Tyrants humbles, and whole hosts o'erturns. .... Od.1.131.38.
Have learnt his fate, the whole dark story clear: .... Od.3.113.91.
Torn was his skin, nor had the ribs been whole, ... Od.5.544.198.
Two plenteous fountains the whole prospect crown'd; .... Od.7.169.244.
Should a whole host at once discharge the bow, ... Od.8.249.276.
The whole sea shook, and refluent beat the shore. .... Od.9.570.330.
Our sight the whole collected navy chear'd, ... Od.9.637.332.
To whom *Persephone,* entire and whole, ... Od.10.584.371.
Bleeds a whole hecatomb, a vintage flows. .... Od.14.116.41.
'Till the whole circle of the year goes round; .... Od.14.226.46.
Not the whole circle of the year wou'd close .... Od.14.227.46.
And here his whole collected treasure lay'd; .... Od.14.358.51.
With earth's whole tribute the bright table bends, ... Od.15.352.86.
Thy whole sad story, from its first, declare: .... Od.15.414.89.
Whose luxury whole patrimonies sweeps, ... Od.17.541.158.
Bid their whole herds and flocks in banquets bleed; .... Od.18.322.182.
In thy whole form *Ulysses* seems exprest: .... Od.19.443.216.
What-e'er thro' life's whole series I have done .... Od.22.228.297.
Then lop thy whole posterity away; .... Od.22.240.298.
Th' important deed our whole attention calls. .... Od.23.122.326.
But the whole earth must move, if heav'n commands. .... Od.23.188.332.
Then polishing the whole, the finish'd mold .... Od.23.205.333.
How his whole flocks and herds exhausted bled, ... Od.23.326.340.
With eager transport to disclose the whole, ... Od.24.277.363.
Oh Pow'r supreme, oh ruler of the whole! .... Od.24.543.374.

WHOLESOM

At length, by wholesom dread of statutes bound, ... 4.2HE1.257.217

WHOLESOME

To wholesome Solitude, the Nurse of Sense: .... 4.JD4.185.41.

WHOLLY

All neither wholly false, nor wholly true. 2.TemF.457.285
All either wholly false, nor wholly true. 2.TemF.457.285
How each for other oft is wholly lost; 3.EOM4.272.15
Nor over-dress, nor leave her wholly bare; .... 3.Ep4.52.142.
Mean tho' I am, not wholly so .... 6.50.41.148.
Mean as I am, not wholly so .... 6.50.41A.148.

WHOLSOM

Drags from the town to wholsom country air, ... 6.45.2.124.
To see no wholsom Motion be withstood, ... Il.9.135.438.

WHOLSOME

And stood content to rule by wholsome Laws; .... 2.ChWB.430.78.
Such wholsome Foods as Nature's Wants supply, ... 6.17iii.26.58.
'Twas thus the Sage his wholsome Counsel mov'd; .... Il.7.412.385.
Those wholsome Counsels which thy Wisdom moves, ... Il.9.77.436.
Those wholsome Counsels which thy Father gave. .... Il.9.327.450.
With him, in wholsome Counsels, to debate .... Il.10.25.3.
And wholsome Garlick crown'd the sav'ry Treat. .... Il.11.771.69.
With wholsome herbage mix'd, the direful bane .... Od.4.319.134.
Their wholsome counsel rashly I declin'd, ... Od.9.268.318.

WHOM (OMITTED)

413

WHOR'D

As with these Eyes I plainy saw thee whor'd; .... 2.ChJM.769.52.
Whor'd by my Slave—Perfidious Wretch! may Hell .... 2.ChJM.770.52.
Intrigu'd with glory, and with spirit whor'd; 5.DunB4.316.37

WHORE

I loath a Whore, and startle at the Name. .... 2.ChJM.592.43.
A *Cheat!* a *Whore!* who starts not at the Name, ... 3.EOM2.220Z1.
That from his cage cries Cuckold, Whore, and Knave, ... 3.Ep1.6.15.
When Cæsar made a noble dame a whore, ... 3.Ep1.213.33.
Than his fine Wife, alas! or finer Whore. .... 3.Ep4.12.136.
Than his fine Wife (my Lord) or finer Whore. .... 3.Ep4.12A.136.
And whether to a Bishop, or a Whore? .... 4.JD4.137.37.
At *Fig's* at *White's,* with *Felons,* or a *Whore,* .... 4.JD4.213.43.
At *Fig's* or *White's,* with *Felons,* or a *Whore,* .... 4.JD4.213A.43.
And makes a Princess whom he found a Whore. .... 4.HAdv.66.81.
What push'd poor *Ellis* on th' Imperial Whore? .... 4.HAdv.81.83.
And has not *Colly* still his Lord, and Whore? .... 4.Arbu.97.102.
That harmless Mother thought no Wife a Whore,— .... 4.Arbu.384.126.
Swear like a Lord? or a *Rich* out-whore a Duke? .... 4.EpS1.116.306.
But 'tis the *Fall* degrades her to a Whore; .... 4.EpS1.143.309.
The Wit of Cheats, the Courage of a Whore, ... 4.EpS1.165.309.
At length to B[ritain] kind, as to thy [whore], ... 4.1740.47.334*.
Whore, Pupil, and lac'd Governor from France. 5.DunB4.272.37
I can't—indeed now—I so hate a whore— .... 6.41.6.113.
A Gold watch found on Cinder Whore, ... 6.116iii.1.326.
When I but call a flagrant Whore unsound, ... 6.129.1.357.

WHORE'S

Silence, the Knave's Repute, the Whore's good Name, ... 6.8.25.18.

WHORES
That thou may'st be by kings, or whores of kings. ... 3.EOM4.206.146.
With the same spirit that he drinks and whores; ... 3.Ep1.189.31.
Bear home six Whores, and make his Lady weep? ... 3.Ep3.60.91.
Who drinks, whores, fights, and in a duel dies: ... 3.Ep3.390.124.
Make *Scots* speak Treason, cozen subtlest Whores, ... 4.JD4.59.31.
As who knows Sapho, smiles at other whores. ... 4.JD2.6.133.
Shameless as carted Whores, that with a Grace, ... 4.JD2A.84.140.
And yet more melancholy Whores: ... 4.1HE7.10.269.
So may the sons of sons of sons of whores, ... 5.DunB4.332.376.
May knock up Whores alone. ... 6.47.8.128.
No wicked Whores shall have such Luck ... 6.54.13.165.

WHOSE (OMITTED)
597

WHOSO
Which whoso tastes, forgets his former friends, ... 5.DunB4.518.394.
(Thence call'd *Lotophagi)* which whoso tastes, ... Od.9.107.308.

WHOSOE'ER
And live he glorious, whosoe'er shall live! ... Il.18.358.338.

WHY (OMITTED)
256

WICKED
Some wicked Wits have libell'd all the Fair: ... 2.ChJM.44.17.
This wicked World was once my dear Delight; ... 2.ChWB.225.67.
More Legends were there here, of wicked Wives, ... 2.ChWB.363.74.
The dull, the proud, the wicked, and the mad; ... 4.Arbu.347.120.
Wicked as Pages, who in early years ... 4.JD2.39.135.
From wicked Waters ev'n to godly— ... 4.JD2.80.141.
Turn, turn they eyes from wicked men in place, ... 4.1740.3.332.
Three wicked imps of her own Grubstreet Choir ... 5.DunA2.115.110.
Blockheads with reason wicked wits abhor, ... 5.DunA3.169.167.
Three wicked imps, of her own Grubstreet choir, ... 5.DunB2.123.301.
Blockheads with reason wicked wits abhor, ... 5.DunB3.175.329.
And wicked *Wit* arose, thy most abusive Foe. ... 6.8.12.18.
Than to the wicked Works of *Whiston;* ... 6.10.22.25.
And did not wicked custom so contrive, ... 6.41.13.113.
No wicked Whores shall have such Luck ... 6.54.13.165.
To sweep the wicked and their Counsels hence; ... 6.137.5.373.
And such as wicked kings may mourn, ... 6.141.11.381.
For never, never, wicked man was wise. ... Od.2.320.76.
(The deed of *Noman* and his wicked train) ... Od.9.534.328.
Now hear her wicked arts. Before thy eyes ... Od.10.345.360.
Such end the wicked found! But *Jove's* intent ... Od.14.345.51.
For wicked ears are deaf to wisdom's call, ... Od.16.300.120.
And shuns (who wou'd not?) wicked men in power; ... Od.17.661.164.
Of these, twice six pursue their wicked way, ... Od.22.462.310.

WICKEDLY
Who wickedly is wise, or madly brave, ... 3.EOM4.231.148.
The Soul subsides; and wickedly inclines ... 4.HS2.79.59.

WICKEDNESS
Thus says the King who knew your Wickedness; ... 2.ChJM.639.46.
Men shou'd stand mark'd with far more Wickedness, ... 2.ChWB.367.75.
Fal'n in the plash his wickedness had lay'd; ... 5.DunA2.72.107.
Fal'n in the plash his wickedness had laid: ... 5.DunB2.76.299.

WICKER
And high in wicker baskets heap'd: the rest ... Od.9.293.318.

WIDE
No Sigh, no Murmur the wide World shall hear, ... 1.Mes.45.117.
See Heav'n its sparkling Portals wide display, ... 1.Mes.97.121.
In *other Parts* it leaves wide sandy Plains; ... 1.EOC.55.245.
And the wide World resounds with *Sapho's* Praise. ... 1.TrSP.32.394.
O'er the wide Fields the furious Mother flew, ... 1.TrSt.16.410.
O'er the wide Earth, and o'er the watry Main, ... 1.TrSt.44.411.
And Fun'ral Flames, that parting wide in Air, ... 1.TrSt.53.412.
When the wide Earth to Heaps of Ashes turn'd, ... 1.TrSt.310.423.
Wide o'er the World in solemn Pomp she drew ... 1.TrSt.476.430.
From the wide Wound gush'd out a Stream of Blood, ... 1.TrES.320.461.
And now the Palace Gates are open'd wide, ... 2.ChJM.315.29.
He first expands the glitt'ring *Forfex* wide ... 2.RL*A*1.115.130.
And guard the wide Circumference around. ... 2.RL2.122.167.
The Peer now spreads the glitt'ring *Forfex* wide, ... 2.RL3.147.179.
O'er the wide Prospect as I gaz'd around, ... 2.TemF.21.254.
Yet wide was spread their Fame in Ages past, ... 2.TemF.33.255.
Wide Vaults appear, and Roofs of fretted Gold: ... 2.TemF.138.264.
Fill the wide Earth, and gain upon the Skies. ... 2.TemF.313.279.
Wide, and more wide, the floating Rings advance, ... 2.TemF.440.284.
Wide, and more wide, the floating Rings advance, ... 2.TemF.440.284.
What modes of sight betwixt each wide extreme, ... 3.EOM1.211.41.
Around, how wide! how deep extend below! ... 3.EOM1.236.44.
While still too wide or short is human Wit; ... 3.EOM3.90.101.
Wide and more wide, th'o'erflowings of the mind ... 3.EOM4.369.164.
Wide and more wide, th'o'erflowings of the mind ... 3.EOM4.369.164.
Or cut wide views thro' Mountains to the Plain, ... 3.Ep4.75.144.
Whose wide Parterres are not asham'd to feed ... 3.Ep4.185A.154.
Had he beheld an Audience gape so wide. ... 4.2HE1.321.223.
Judicious Wits spread wide the Ridicule, ... 4.EpS1.61.302.
With scarlet hats, wide waving, circles round, ... 5.DunA2.10.97.
Amid that Area wide she took her stand, ... 5.DunA2.23.99.
In that wide space the Goddess took her stand, ... 5.DunA2.23A.99.
Wide as a windmill all his figure spread, ... 5.DunA2.62.105.
"Who flings most filth, and wide pollutes around ... 5.DunA2.267.134.
"Who flings most mud, and wide pollutes around ... 5.DunA2.267A.134.
(Earth's wide extreams) her sable flag display'd; ... 5.DunA3.63.155.
Till one wide Conflagration swallows all. ... 5.DunA3.236.177.
With scarlet hats wide-waving circled round, ... 5.DunB2.14.297.
Amid that area wide they took their stand, ... 5.DunB2.27.297.
Wide as a wind-mill all his figures spread, ... 5.DunB2.66.299.

WIDE (CONTINUED)
"Who flings most filth, and wide pollutes around ... 5.DunB2.279.309.
Around him wide a sable Army stand, ... 5.DunB2.355.314.
(Earth's wide extremes) her sable flag display'd, ... 5.DunB3.71.323.
'Till one wide conflagration swallows all. ... 5.DunB3.240.332.
We never suffer it to stand too wide. ... 5.DunB4.154.356.
Wide, and more wide, it spread o'er all the realm; ... 5.DunB4.613.405.
Wide, and more wide, it spread o'er all the realm; ... 5.DunB4.613.405.
'Are large and wide; *Tydcomb* and I assure ye. ... 6.13.25.39.
And the wide *East* ador'd with rites divine! ... 6.20.12.66.
Wide o'er th' aerial Vault extends thy sway, ... 6.65.3.192.
Wide o'er th' Æthereal Walks extends thy sway, ... 6.65.3A.192.
For I am very large, and very wide. ... 6.88.4.249.
Vallies wide: ... 6.96i.18.268.
O'er all his wide Dominion of the Dead, ... Il.1.537.113.
The lofty Tow'rs of wide-extended *Troy.* ... Il.2.14.128.
The lofty Tow'rs of wide-extended *Troy.* ... Il.2.36.129.
The lofty Tow'rs of wide-extended *Troy.* ... Il.2.86.130.
Spreads all the Beach, and wide o'ershades the Plain: ... Il.2.118.133.
Thus num'rous and confus'd, extending wide, ... Il.2.546.153.
Since Earth's wide Regions, Heav'n's unmeasur'd Height, ... Il.2.574.155.
Floats the wide Field, and blazes to the Skies. ... Il.2.949.168.
And wide around the floated Region fills. ... Il.2.1033.171.
To boundless Vengeance the wide Realm be giv'n, ... Il.4.57.223.
Saw the wide Waste of his destructive Hand: ... Il.5.127.273.
Thro' the wide World should make our Glory known. ... Il.5.337.283.
Far distant hence I held my wide Command, ... Il.5.583.296.
Spreads the wide Fan to clear the golden Grain, ... Il.5.612.297.
And wide thro' Fens an unknown Journey takes; ... Il.5.735.302.
He left the Town a wide, deserted Plain. ... Il.5.795.304.
O'er the wide Main extends his boundless Eye, ... Il.5.961.312.
Wide o'er the Field, resistless as the Wind, ... Il.6.51.326.
Wide o'er th' *Aleian* Field he chose to stray, ... Il.6.247.338.
Wide shall it spread, and last thro' Ages long, ... Il.6.448.348.
And *Hippoplacus'* wide-extended Shade) ... Il.6.495.351.
(Soft *Zephyr* curling the wide wat'ry Plain) ... Il.7.72.366.
Thus in thick Orders settling wide around, ... Il.7.75.366.
Wide, as the Morn her golden Beam extends. ... Il.7.537.391.
The skilful Archer wide survey'd the Field, ... Il.8.322.413.
And wide beneath him, all *Olympus* shakes. ... Il.8.553.422.
Wide o'er the Field, high-blazing to the Sky, ... Il.8.631.426.
They gave thee Scepters, and a wide Command, ... Il.9.53.434.
He strows a Bed of glowing Embers wide, ... Il.9.280.447.
From each wide Portal issuing to the Wars) ... Il.9.505.458.
Sweeps the wide Earth, and tramples o'er Mankind, ... Il.9.629.465.
The Paths so many, and the Camp so wide. ... Il.10.73.5.
Wide o'er the Field with guideless Fury rolls, ... Il.11.209.44.
Now breaks the Surge, and wide the bottom bares. ... Il.11.400.52.
So *Troy* reliev'd from that wide-wasting Hand ... Il.11.487.56.
Wide in his Breast appear'd the grizly Wound; ... Il.11.562.59.
In some wide Field by Troops of Boys pursu'd, ... Il.11.683.65.
Thro' wide *Buprasian* Fields we forc'd the Foes, ... Il.11.888.75.
Till some wide Wound lets out their mighty Soul. ... Il.12.168.87.
The wide Horizon shut him from their View. ... Il.13.96.109.
Bold *Merion* aim'd a Stroke (nor aim'd it wide) ... Il.13.215.116.
(The wide Destroyer of the Race of Man) ... Il.13.385.124.
Wide on the Left the Force of *Greece* commands, ... Il.13.847.146.
Wide o'er the blasted Fields the Tempest sweeps, ... Il.13.1001.152.
Wide-rolling, foaming high, and tumbling to the shore. ... Il.13.1005.152.
Round the wide Fields he cast a careful view, ... Il.15.7.194.
O'er the wide Clouds, and o'er the starry Plain, ... Il.15.214.205.
So flies a Herd of Oxen, scatter'd wide, ... Il.15.366.211.
Amidst the Plain of some wide-water'd Fen, ... Il.15.761.225.
The Scene wide-opening to the Blaze of Light. ... Il.15.813.228.
Has drench'd their wide, insatiate Throats with Blood) ... Il.16.197.247.
And round him wide the rising Structure grows. ... Il.16.259.249.
The smiling Scene wide opens to the Sight, ... Il.16.360.257.
From the wide Wound gush'd out a Stream of Blood, ... Il.16.625.268.
Wide o'er the Land was stretch'd his large Domain, ... Il.16.723.272.
Blows following Blows are heard re-echoing wide, ... Il.16.769.273.
Wide thro' the Neck appears the grizly Wound, ... Il.17.51.289.
The Warrior rais'd his Voice, and wide around ... Il.17.292.299.
And skirmish wide: So *Nestor* gave Command, ... Il.17.438.304.
Gape wide, and drink our Blood for Sacrifice! ... Il.17.477.306.
Attend her Way. Wide-opening part the Tides, ... Il.18.87.327.
Soon shall the sanguine Torrent spread so wide, ... Il.18.161.330.
Wide o'er the World was *Ilion* fam'd of old ... Il.18.337.337.
Spoils of my Arms, and thine; when, wasting wide, ... Il.18.401.340.
In its wide Womb they pour the rushing Stream; ... Il.18.409.340.
Wide with distorted Legs, oblique he goes, ... Il.18.480.345.
In those wide Wounds thro' which his Spirit fled, ... Il.19.29.372.
The wide Air floating to her ample Wings. ... Il.19.373.387.
Wide o'er the wat'ry Waste, a Light appears, ... Il.19.405.389.
Swept the wide Shore, and drove him to the Plain. ... Il.20.179.401.
Thro' yon wide Host this Arm shall scatter Fear, ... Il.20.413.412.
Around him wide, immense Destruction pours, ... Il.20.575.418.
And wide around the floated Region fills, ... Il.21.176.428.
Wide o'er the Plain he pours the boundless Blaze; ... Il.21.399.436.
He ceas'd; wide Conflagration blazing round; ... Il.21.422.437.
And wide beneath them groans the rending Ground. ... Il.21.453.439.
Set wide your Portals to the flying Throng. ... Il.21.622.448.
Thus charg'd the rev'rend Monarch: Wide were flung ... Il.21.627.448.
A hundred Foot in length, a hundred wide, ... Il.23.202.497.
To the wide Main then stooping from the Skies, ... Il.23.266.500.
Wide o'er the Pyle the sable Wine they throw, ... Il.23.311.502.
And leads amidst a wide Extent of Plains; ... Il.23.322.503.
And short, or wide, th' ungovern'd Courser drive: ... Il.23.392.506.
Wide on the lonely Beach to vent his Woes. ... Il.24.20.535.
A Lion, not a Man, who slaughters wide ... Il.24.52.537.
Between where *Samos* wide his Forests spreads, ... Il.24.103.539.
Wide as appears some Palace Gate display'd, ... Il.24.391.552.
O'er the wide Earth, and o'er the boundless Main: ... Il.24.420.553.
Nor true are all thy Words, nor erring wide; ... Il.24.465.556.
This *Hermes* (such the Pow'r of Gods) set wide; ... Il.24.561.559.
And all wide *Hellespont's* unmeasur'd Main. ... Il.24.687.565.
Thro' *Troy's* wide Streets abandon'd shall I roam, ... Il.24.979.576.

WIDE (CONTINUED)
O'er earth and ocean wide prepar'd to soar, ... Od.1.128.38.
(A purple carpet spread the pavement wide) ...... Od.1.173.40.
Thro' the wide Ocean first to sandy *Pyle,* ...... Od.1.369.50.
Did not the sun, thro' heav'n's wide azure roll'd, ... Od.2.101.66.
O'er the wide waves success thy ways attends: ...... Od.2.310.76.
Wide o'er the bay, by vessel vessel rides; ...... Od.2.333.77.
And wide o'er earth diffus'd his chearing ray, ... Od.3.3.85.
We past the wide, immeasurable main. ...... Od.3.22.87.
Wide as his will, extends his boundless grace; ...... Od.3.287.100.
His sons and grand-sons the wide circle grac'd. ...... Od.3.501.112.
And portion to his tribes the wide domain. ...... Od.4.238.130.
Fill the wide circle of th' eternal year: ...... Od.4.768.155.
Of *Thessaly* wide stretch'd his ample reign:) ...... Od.4.1052.167.
O'er the wide earth, and o'er the boundless main. ...... Od.5.59.174.
Flam'd on the hearth, and wide perfum'd the Isle; ...... Od.5.77.176.
At length emerging, from his nostrils wide ...... Od.5.411.192.
Stretch'd wide his eager arms, and shot the seas along. ...... Od.5.477.195.
Since wide he wander'd on the wat'ry waste; ...... Od.5.497.196.
Remote from neighbours, in a forest wide, ... Od.5.631.202.
In ease possest the wide *Hyperian* plain; ...... Od.6.6.203.
Or wide *Täygetus'* resounding groves; ...... Od.6.118.212.
Wide o'er the shore with many a piercing cry ...... Od.6.165.216.
Wide o'er the world *Alcinous'* glory shine! ...... Od.7.425.258.
Wide wanders, *Laodame,* thy erring tongue, ... Od.8.175.271.
Wide o'er the waste the rage of *Boreas* sweeps, ... Od.9.77.306.
Far in wide ocean, and from sight of shore: ...... Od.9.94.306.
Spreads his wide arms, and searches round and round: ...... Od.9.494.326.
Thro' the wide wound the vital spirit flies. ...... Od.10.190.349.
And wide unfold the portals of the hall. ...... Od.10.263.355.
Radiant she came; the portals open'd wide: ...... Od.10.302.358.
The lofty gates the Goddess wide display'd: ...... Od.10.372.362.
Then hast'ning to the styes set wide the door, ... Od.10.459.366.
Trench the black earth a cubit long and wide: ...... Od.10.615.374.
Wide o'er the pool thy faulchion wav'd around ...... Od.10.638.374.
A cavern form'd, a cubit long and wide. ...... Od.11.30.380.
There the wide sea with all his billows raves! ...... Od.11.195.391.
And here thro' sev'n wide portals rush'd the war. ...... Od.11.324.398.
Thro' the wide dome of *Dis,* a trembling band. ...... Od.11.700.419.
In verdant meads they sport, and wide around ...... Od.12.57.432.
Wide to the west the horid gulph extends, ... Od.12.103.436.
Bear wide thy course, nor plow those angry waves ...... Od.12.260.445.
In the wide dungeon she devours her food, ... Od.12.306.447.
And views wide earth and heav'n's unmeasur'd height. ...... Od.12.386.449.
How wide the pavements float with guilty gore! ...... Od.13.452.28.
Wide-patch'd, and knotted to a twisted thong. ...... Od.13.507.30.
While *Pallas,* cleaving the wide fields of air, ... Od.13.510.30.
The wide-extended continents obey: ...... Od.14.120.41.
He spreads; and adds a mantle thick and wide; ...... Od.14.589.65.
Thy stately palace, and thy wide domain. ...... Od.15.143.75.
And the wide portal echoes to the sound. ...... Od.15.163.76.
And wander'd thro' the wide ethereal way ...... Od.15.196.78.
Thro' the wide fields of air, and cleaves the skies; ...... Od.16.169.111.
Wide patch'd, and fasten'd by a twisted thong. ...... Od.17.221.142.
Round the wide world are sought those men divine ...... Od.17.462.155.
Wide as the sun displays his vital fire. ...... Od.17.469.156.
A tongue so flippant, with a throat so wide! ...... Od.18.33.168.
From space to space the torch wide-beaming burns, ... Od.18.357.184.
Search'd the wide country for his wand'ring mares, ... Od.21.26.260.
And all wide *Elis'* courser-breeding plain, ... Od.21.374.277.
The tumbling goblet the wide floor o'erflows, ... Od.22.21.287.
Before him wide, in mixt effusion roll ...... Od.22.99.291.
And scatter'd short, or wide, the points of death; ...... Od.22.283.300.
When the wide field extended snares beset, ... Od.22.339.303.
Wide o'er the sands are spread the stiff'ning prey ...... Od.22.430.309.
That wide th' extended *Hellespont* surveys; ...... Od.24.104.353.
Wide o'er the world their martial fame was spread; ...... Od.24.588.376.

WIDE-BEAMING
From space to space the torch wide-beaming burns, ... Od.18.357.184.

WIDE-EXTENDED
The lofty Tow'rs of wide-extended *Troy.* ...... Il.2.14.128.
The lofty Tow'rs of wide-extended *Troy.* ...... Il.2.36.129.
The lofty Tow'rs of wide-extended *Troy.* ...... Il.2.86.130.
And *Hippoplacus'* wide-extended Shade) ...... Il.6.495.351.
The wide-extended continents obey: ...... Od.14.120.41.

WIDE-OPENING
The Scene wide-opening to the Blaze of Light. ...... Il.15.813.228.
Attend her Way. Wide-opening part the Tides, ... Il.18.87.327.

WIDE-PATCH'D
Wide-patch'd, and knotted to a twisted thong. ...... Od.13.507.30.

WIDE-ROLLING
Wide-rolling, foaming high, and tumbling to the shore. ...... Il.13.1005.152.

WIDE-WASTING
So *Troy* reliev'd from that wide-wasting Hand ...... Il.11.487.56.

WIDE-WATER'D
Amidst the Plain of some wide-water'd Fen, ... Il.15.761.225.

WIDE-WAVING
With scarlet hats wide-waving circled round, ... 5.DunB2.14.297.

WIDELY
How widely differs this from warring well? ...... Il.13.912.148.
Too long in vain, too widely hast thou stray'd. ...... Od.15.12.70.

WIDEN
And Arches widen, and long Iles extend. ...... 2.TemF.265.276.

WIDEN'D
The Ocean widen'd, and the shores withdrew. ...... Od.10.53.342.

WIDENING
The Domes swell up, the widening Arches bend, ... 2.TemF.90.259.

WIDER
Which still grew sweeter as they wider spread: 2.TemF.315.279
Affections? they still take a wider range: ...... 3.Ep1.172A.29.
Opinions? they still take a wider range: ...... 3.Ep1.172.29.
(A wider Compass) smoak along the Road. ...... Il.22.194.463.
Their Tops connected, but at wider space ...... Il.23.828.522.
He, wand'ring long, a wider circle made, ... Od.3.407.106.
(A wider circle, but in sight of shore) ...... Od.5.559.199.
Then if a wider course shall rather please ...... Od.15.91.73.

WIDOW
Than that *Mausolus'* Pious Widow plac'd, ... 2.ChWB.248.69
He boarded with a Widow in the Town, ... 2.ChWB.265.69
And made a Widow happy, for a whim. ...... 3.Ep2.58.55.
And cheats th'unknowing Widow, and the Poor? ...... 4.JD4.141.37.
Each Widow asks it for the Best of Men, ... 4.EpS2.108.319
A Widow I, an helpless Orphan He! ...... Il.6.513.351.
And Spouse, a Widow in her bridal Bed. ...... Il.17.40.289.
A widow, and a slave, on foreign shores! ...... Od.8.580.293.

WIDOW'D
The childless Parent and the widow'd Wife ...... 6.152.12.400.
Shall I not force some widow'd Dame to tear ...... Il.18.155.330.
And to his widow'd Mother vainly mourn. ...... Il.22.645.483.
Your widow'd hours, apart, with female toil ...... Od.1.455.54.
Wastes all her widow'd hours in tender moan. ...... Od.4.148.127.

WIDOW'S
Form'd a bast *Buckle* for his Widow's Gown: ...... 2.RL5.92.207.
A willing widow's copious wealth supply'd. ...... Od.14.243.48.

WIDOWS
No crafty Widows shall approach my Bed, ... 2.ChJM.107.19.
And beat my Breasts, as wretched Widows—must. 2.ChWB.310.72
A Tongue that can cheat Widows, cancel Scores, ... 4.JD4.58.31.
Oh! when rank Widows purchase luscious nights, ... 4.JD2.87A.141.
Like nets or lime-twigs, for rich Widows hearts? ...... 4.JD2.58.137.
And when rank Widows purchase luscious nights, ... 4.JD2.87.141.
Some win rich Widows by their Chine and Brawn; 4.1HE1.131.289

WIELD
ARGYLE, the State's whole Thunder born to wield, ... 4.EpS2.86.318.
"Secure the radiant weapons wield; ...... 6.140.5.378.
His sharpen'd Spear let ev'ry *Grecian* wield, ... Il.2.454.149.
Proud, *Areïthous'* dreadful Arms to wield; ...... Il.7.168.372.
To right, to left, the dext'rous Lance I wield, ... Il.7.291.378.
Oh Daughter of that God, whose Arm can wield ...... Il.8.423.417.
O Daughter of that God, whose Arm can wield ...... Il.8.526.421.
O Daughter of that God, whose Arm can wield ...... Il.10.327.17.
The Squires restrain'd: The Foot, with those who wield ...... Il.11.63.37.
Rang'd in two Bands, their crooked Weapons wield, ... Il.11.90.38.
This speaks my Grief; this headless Lance I wield; ...... Il.13.335.121.
The *Locrian* Squadrons nor the Jav'lin wield, ... Il.13.891.148.
For not the Spear the Locrian Squadrons wield ...... Il.13.891A.148.
His strongest Spear each valiant *Grecian* wield, ... Il.14.431.184.
The strong and cumb'rous Arms the valiant wield, ... Il.14.441.184.
And thus their Arms the Race of *Panthus* wield: ...... Il.14.530.189.
These wield the Mace, and those the Javelin throw. ...... Il.15.449.214.
Thy Arms no less suffice the Lance to wield, ... Il.15.556.218.
Vulcanian Arms: What other can I wield? ...... Il.18.229.332.
Vulcanian Arms: What other should I wield? ...... Il.18.229A.332.
(For both his dext'rous Hands the Lance cou'd wield) ...... Il.21.181.429.
The Quoit to toss, the pond'rous Mace to wield, ... Il.23.713.518.
For the bold Champions who the *Cæstus* wield. ...... Il.23.754.520.
Daughter divine of *Jove,* whose arm can wield ...... Od.4.1005.164.
Forth-issuing thus, she gave him first to wield ...... Od.5.299.185.
Daughter of *Jove!* whose arms in thunder wield ...... Od.6.385.230.
None wield the gauntlet with so dire a sway, ... Od.8.101.267.
Stand forth, ye champions, who the gauntlet wield, ... Od.8.233.275.
I wield the gauntlet, and I run the race. ...... Od.8.236.275.
Let other realms the deathful gauntlet wield, ... Od.8.281.278.
My sword I strive to wield, but strive in vain; ...... Od.11.528.409.
Yet leave for each of us a sword to wield, ... Od.16.320.121.
Of summer suns, were both constrain'd to wield ...... Od.18.412.188.
Some wield the sounding ax; the dodder'd oaks ...... Od.20.200.243.
Lo hence I run for other arms to wield, ... Od.22.118.292.
And now his hands two beamy jav'lins wield; ...... Od.22.139.293.
Which old *Laertes* wont in youth to wield, ... Od.22.198.297.

WIELDED
No Dart she wielded, but a Hook did bear, ... 1.TrVP.9A.377.
The pond'rous Targe be wielded by the strong. ...... Il.14.434.184.

WIELDS
Heav'd with vast Force, a Rocky Fragment wields. ...... Il.5.370.284.
And in his Hands two steely Javelins wields, ... Il.11.55.37.
The Warrior wields; and his great Brother joins, ... Il.15.569.218.
Whose Son's great Arm alone the Weapon wields, ... Il.16.176.245.
Alas! thy Friend is slain, and *Hector* wields ...... Il.17.538.309.
A Spear which stern *Achilles* only wields, ... Il.19.424.389.
High o'er his Head the circling Lash he wields; ...... Il.23.581.513.
Hence *Pollux* sprung who wields with furious sway ...... Od.11.367.400.

WIFE
Tho' meant each other's Aid, like *Man* and *Wife.* ...... 1.EOC.83.248.
The *Owner's Wife,* that *other Men* enjoy, ... 1.EOC.501.294.
Thy Wife and Sister's Tutelary Care? ...... 1.TrSt.395.426.
Of a kind Husband, and a loving Wife. ...... 2.ChJM.18.15.
With matchless Impudence they stile a Wife ...... 2.ChJM.45.17.
A Wife is the peculiar Gift of Heav'n: ...... 2.ChJM.52.17.

WILD (CONTINUED)

The wild Meander wash'd the Artist's face: 5.DunB2.176.304.
While op'ning Hell spouts wild-fire at your head. 5.DunB3.316.335.
Or wanders wild in Academic Groves; 5.DunB4.490.390.
In broken Air, trembling, the wild Musick floats; 6.11.17.30.
Amphion thus bade wild Dissention cease. 6.11.35Z1.31.
See, wild as the Winds, o'er the Desart he flies; 6.11.110.34.
And wild ambition well deserves its woe. 6.32.12.96.
When wild *Barbarians* spurn her dust; 6.51i.18.151.
A vapour fed from wild desire, 6.51ii.19.153.
See the wild Waste of all-devouring years! 6.71.1.202.
Rang'd the wild Desarts red with Monsters Gore, Il.1.356.105.
O'er the wild Margin of the Deep he hung, Il.1.456.109.
In wild Resentment for the Fair he lost. Il.1.565.115.
There, from the Fields where wild *Mæander* flows, Il.2.1056.172.
Trembling and pale, he starts with wild Affright, Il.3.49.191.
Too deep my Anguish, and too wild my Woe. Il.3.512.216.
Wild with Delay, and more enrag'd by Pain. Il.5.173.275.
Wild with his Pain, he sought the bright Abodes, Il.5.1064.317.
Pernicious, wild, regardless of the Right. Il.5.1075.318.
Where yon' wild Fig-Trees join the Wall of *Troy:* Il.6.551.354.
On Heaps the *Trojans* rush, with wild affright, Il.10.616.29.
Where the wild Figs th' adjoining Summit crown, Il.11.219.45.
Drives the wild Waves, and tosses all the Deeps. Il.11.386.51.
So two wild Boars outstrip the following Hounds, Il.11.421.53.
Wild Mountain-Wolves the fainting Beast surround; Il.11.599.60.
So two wild Boars spring furious from their Den, Il.12.163.87.
Terror and Death in his wild Eye-balls stare; Il.13.363.123.
Arm'd with wild Terrors, and to Slaughter bred, Il.13.595.134.
By what wild Passion, Furious! art thou tost? Il.15.146.202.
The *Grecians* gaze around with wild Despair, Il.15.422.213.
Shrunk up he sate, with wild and haggard Eye, Il.16.488.262.
So pent by Hills, the wild Winds roar aloud Il.16.923.279.
Such the wild Terror, and the mingled Cry. Il.17.850.321.
With wild Affright, and dropt upon the Field Il.21.58.424.
Then blacken'd the wild Waves; the Murmur rose; Il.21.277.432.
Wild with Revenge, insatiable of War. Il.21.638.448.
Thee, Vultures wild should scatter round the Shore, Il.22.57.455.
Thro' Desarts wild now pours a weeping Rill; Il.24.774.569.
Waste in wild riot what your land allows, Od.1.479.55.
Waste in wild riot what your land allows, Od.2.163.70.
His pride of words, and thy wild dream of fate, Od.2.229.72.
For wild ambition wings their bold desire, Od.4.433.140.
Roam the wild Isle in search of rural cates, Od.4.498.144.
Ride the wild waves, and quit the safer shore? Od.4.941.162.
The wild waves fury, here I fix'd remain: Od.5.459.195.
Roar the wild waves; beneath, is sea profound! Od.5.529.198.
With sister-fruits; one fertile, one was wild. Od.5.619.201.
Possest by wild barbarians fierce in arms, Od.6.141.214.
The wild winds whistle, and the billows roar; Od.7.357.254.
Possest by wild barbarians fierce in arms, Od.8.627.296.
With cries and agonies of wild delight, Od.10.492.367.
Wild with despair, I shed a copious tyde Od.11.251.394.
Wild, furious herds, unconquerably strong! Od.11.356.399.
Breaks the wild waves, and forms a dang'rous streight; Od.12.126.437.
They toss, they foam, a wild confusion raise, Od.12.284.446.
Lash the wild surge, and bluster in the skies; Od.12.342.448.
When, at the voice of *Jove,* wild whirlwinds rise, Od.12.369.449.
There while the wild winds whistled o'er the main, Od.12.379.449.
In the wild olive's unfrequented shade, Od.13.141.11.
Possess'd by wild Barbarians, fierce in arms? Od.13.243.17.
Thro' the wild ocean plow the dang'rous way, Od.13.482.29.
When all was wild expanse of sea and air; Od.14.333.51.
Wild springs the vine, no more the garden blows. Od.16.155.110.
Arriv'd, with wild tumultuous noise they sate Od.16.424.127.
With wild entrancement, and ecstatic tears. Od.17.44.134.
To curb wild riot and to punish wrong? Od.17.623.162.
Then wild uproar and clamour mounts the sky, Od.18.444.190.
Gods! what wild folly from the goblet flows? Od.18.453.190.
And all was riot, noise, and wild uproar. Od.21.390.279.
Not love, but wild ambition was his guide, Od.22.63.289.
And wild with transport had reveal'd the wound; Od.23.77.322.
And the wild riots of the Suitor-train. Od.23.328.340.

WILD-FIRE

While opening Hell spouts wild-fire at your head. 5.DunA3.314.186.
While op'ning Hell spouts wild-fire at your head. 5.DunB3.316.335.

WILDER'D

Long lost and wilder'd in the Maze of Fate! 1.TrSt.589.434.

WILDERNESS

No artful Wilderness to perplex the scene; 3.Ep4.116A.148.
May wander in a wilderness of Moss; 5.DunB4.450.384.

WILDEST

Less mad the wildest whimsey we can frame, 3.Ep3.157.106.

WILDFIRE

So may some Wildfire on your Bodies fall, 2.ChJM.641.46.

WILDGOOSE

In yonder wildgoose, and the larks! 6.150.10.398.

WILDING

The chestnut, wilding, plum, and every tree, 1.TrPA.76.368.

WILDLY

Around in sweet Meanders wildly range, 6.17ii.25.56.
Supine, and wildly gazing on the Skies, Il.16.1016.282.
Thus wildly wailing, at the Gates they lay; Il.24.890.573.
To chains condemn'd as wildly she deplores, Od.8.579.293.

WILDNESS

No artful wildness to perplex the scene; 3.Ep4.116.148.

WILDS

And Starts, amidst the thirsty Wilds, to hear 1.Mes.69.119.
The lonely Lords of empty Wilds and Woods. 1.W-F.48.153.
O'er sandy Wilds were yellow Harvests spread, 1.W-F.88.158.
To Woods and Wilds the pleasing Burden bears, 1.TrSt.682.439.
In *Northern* Wilds, and freeze beneath the Pole; 1.TrSt.813.443.
Late, as I rang'd the Crystal Wilds of Air, 2.RL1.107.153.
By thee to mountains, wilds, and deserts led. 2.ElAb.132.330.
In Woods and Wilds to wound the Savage Race; Il.5.66.269.
The thorny wilds the wood-men fierce assail: Od.19.508.221.

WILES

Imploy'd their Wiles and unavailing Care, 1.TrVP.25.378.
Can'st thou, unhappy in thy Wiles! withstand Il.15.21.194.
When by thy Wiles induc'd, fierce *Boreas* tost Il.15.31.195.
Deceiv'd by *Juno's* Wiles, and female Art. Il.19.102.376.
To tempt the spouseless Queen with am'rous wiles, Od.1.315.47.
A wond'rous monument of female wiles! Od.2.126.67.
Of four vast *Phocæ* takes, to veil her wiles; Od.4.594.148.
And learn'd in all the wiles of human thought. Od.5.236.182.
The Prince well pleas'd to disappoint their wiles, Od.16.496.131.
Thus the fam'd Heroe, perfected in wiles, Od.19.234.204.

WILFUL

No wilful crime this heavy vengeance bred, 1.TrFD.71.389.

WILKINS

Mears, Warner, Wilkins run: Delusive thought! 5.DunA2.117.11
Mears, Warner, Wilkins run: delusive thought! 5.DunB2.125.30

WILKINS'

Poiz'd with a tail, may steer on Wilkins' wings. 5.DunB4.452.38

WILL (MAIN VERB, NOUN)

Their Work, and rev'rence our Superior Will. 1.TrSt.410.427.
(For none want Reasons to confirm their Will) 2.ChJM.20.16.
To let my Betters always have their Will. 2.ChJM.159.22.
Your Will is mine; and is (I will maintain) 2.ChJM.168.23.
Her will I wed, if gracious Heav'n so please; 2.ChJM.262.27.
Take which we like, the Counsel, or our Will. 2.ChWB.35.58.
If you had Wit, you'd say, "Go where you will, 2.ChWB.130.62.
Doubt not, sufficient will be left at Night. 2.ChWB.137.63.
Marry who will, our *Sex* is to be Sold! 2.ChWB.171.65.
Well, I may make my Will in Peace, and die, 2.ChWB.178.65.
He prov'd a Rebel to my Sov'reign Will: 2.ChWB.334.73.
But when to Mischief Mortals bend their Will, 2.RL3.125.177.
Alone made happy, *when* he will, and *where?* 3.EOM1.108Z4.2
The ruling Passion, be it what it will, 3.EOM2.148Z1.7
And Nero reigns a Titus, if he will. 3.EOM2.198.79.
Not one will change his neighbor with himself. 3.EOM2.262.87.
What serves one will, when many wills rebel? 3.EOM3.274.120
There deviates Nature, and here wanders Will. 3.EOM4.112.138
A Gownman, learn'd; a Bishop, what you will; 3.Ep1.90.22.
Will sneaks a Scriv'ner, and exceeding knave: 3.Ep1.106.22.
A Knave this morning, and his Will a Cheat. 3.Ep2.142.62.
Poets heap Virtues, Painters Gems at will, 3.Ep2.185.65.
Lets Fops or Fortune fly which way they will; 3.Ep2.265.71.
"The ruling Passion, be it what it will, 3.Ep3.155.106.
Verse-man or Prose-man, term me which you will, 4.HS1.64.11.
Let Lands and Houses have what Lords they will, 4.HS2.179.69.
The first Lampoon Sir *Will.* or *Bubo* makes. 4.Arbu.280.115.
And write whate'er he pleas'd, except his *Will;* 4.Arbu.379.125.
Call, if you will, bad Rhiming a disease, 4.2HE2.182.177.
Talk what you will of Taste, my Friend, you'll find, 4.2HE2.268.183.
Inclines our Action, not constrains our Will; 4.2HE2.281.185.
Learn to live well, or fairly make your Will; 4.2HE2.322.187.
Style the divine, the matchless, what you will) 4.2HE1.70.199.
To Thebes, to Athens, when he will, and where. 4.2HE1.347.225.
Then hire a Slave, (or if you will, a Lord) 4.1HE6.99.243.
"Or if it be thy Will and Pleasure 4.HS6.19.251.
"And then let Virtue follow, if she will." 4.1HE1.80.285.
And wear their strange old Virtue as they will. 4.EpS1.44.301.
Or *Japhet* pocket, like his Grace, a Will? 4.EpS1.120.306.
Let modest *Foster,* if he will, excell 4.EpS1.131.307.
Let humble *Foster,* if he will, excell 4.EpS1.131A.307.
Turn what they will to Verse, their toil is vain, 5.DunB4.213.363.
Of nought so doubtful as of *Soul* and *Will.* 5.DunB4.482.389.
Who strives to please the Fair *against her Will:* 6.34.6.101.
And fast on Fridays, if he will; 6.39.20.111.
Left free the Human Will. 6.50.12.146.
Left Conscience free, and Will 6.50.12B.146.
And let Thy Will be done. 6.50.48.148.
To keep this Cap, for such as will, to wear; 6.60.34.179.
That which killed King Will, 6.91.9.253.
What? on Compulsion? and against my Will 6.143.5.385.
Or under this Turf, or e'en what they will; 6.144.2.386.
Under this Turf, or just what you will; 6.144.2A.386.
A Knave this Morning, and his Will a Cheat. 6.154.28.403.
Such was the Sov'reign Doom, and such the Will of *Jove.* Il.1.8.85.
Or wise *Ulysses* see perform'd our Will, Il.1.188.96.
To wait his Will two sacred Heralds stood, Il.1.420.107.
The Nod that ratifies the Will Divine, Il.1.680.119.
Thy boundless Will, for me, remains in Force, Il.1.716.122.
Goddess submit, nor dare our Will withstand, Il.1.732.122.
The Monarch's Will, suspend the list'ning Crowd. Il.2.124.133.
The Monarch's Will not yet reveal'd appears; Il.2.229.138.
Such was the Will of *Jove;* and hence we dare Il.2.386.145.
Not Thou, but Heav'ns disposing Will, the Cause; Il.3.216.202.
But he, the mystick Will of Heav'n unknown, Il.5.83.270.
In *Troy's* Defence *Apollo's* heav'nly Will: Il.5.624.297.
She claims some Title to transgress our Will. Il.8.501.420.
She claims some Title to transgress his Will: Il.8.521.421.
And arm in vain: For what I will, shall stand. Il.8.604.425.
His Age be sacred, and his Will be free. Il.9.555.460.
His Pleasure guides me, and his Will confines: Il.9.718.470.

WILL (CONTINUED)

WILL (OMITTED)
313

WILL'D

WILLFUL

WILLIAM

WILLIAM (CONTINUED)

WILLIAM'S

WILLING

WILLOWS

WILLS

WILMOT

WILT

WILY

WIMBLE

WIMBLES
(The wimbles for the work *Calypso* found) .... Od.5.317.186.

WIN
Who cou'd not win the Mistress, woo'd the Maid; .... 1.EOC.105.251.
Taught by thy self to win the promis'd Reign: .... 1.TrSt.94.414.
And win by turns the Kingdom of the Sky: .... 1.TrSt.491.430.
Nor these can keep, nor those can win the Wall: .... 1.TrES.162.455.
Resolv'd to win, he meditates the way, ... 2.RL2.31.161.
Born with whate'er could win it from the Wise, ... 3.Ep1.182.30.
Piecemeal they win this Acre first, then that, ... 4.JD2.91.141.
And win my way by yielding to the tyde. .... 4.1HE1.34.281.
Some win rich Widows by their Chine and Brawn; .... 4.1HE1.131.289.
Smile without Art, and win without a Bribe. .... 4.EpS1.32.300.
"Hold (cry'd the Queen) A Catcall each shall win, ... 5.DunA2.233.129.
"Hold (cry'd the Queen) ye all alike shall win, ... 5.DunA2.233A.129.
"Hold (cry'd the Queen) a Cat-call each shall win; .... 5.DunB2.243.307.
Such plays alone should win a *British* ear, ... 6.32.45A.97.
Explain'd the Matter, and would win the Cause; .... 6.145.6.388.
Now win the Shores, and scarce the Seas remain. .... Il.5.985.314.
By his Instructions learn to win Renown, ... Il.6.256.339.
To win the Damsel, and prevent my Sire. .... Il.9.581.462.
Yet let him pass, and win a little Space; .... Il.10.409.21.
Nor these can keep, nor those can win the Wall. .... Il.12.516.100.
To win the wisest, and the coldest warm: .... Il.14.248.173.
Without thy Person *Greece* shall win the Day, ... Il.16.60.237.
Whatever Hand shall win *Patroclus* slain, ... Il.17.270.298.
Steal thro' the ear, and win upon the soul; .... Od.11.457.407.
To win thy grace: O save us, pow'r divine! .... Od.16.203.113.
Shall end the strife, and win th' imperial dame; .... Od.21.5.258.
And his proud hopes already win the prize. .... Od.21.101.263.

WINCHILSEA
Of Ch[andos] W[inchilsea] who speaks at all, ... 4.1740.19.332*.

WIND
Wind the shrill Horn, or spread the waving Net. .... 1.W-F.96.159.
(His Sea-green Mantle waving with the Wind) .... 1.W-F.350.184.
The Time shall come, when free as Seas or Wind .... 1.W-F.397.190.
What wants in *Blood* and *Spirits,* swell'd with *Wind;* .... 1.EOC.208.264.
Swift as the wind before pursuing love; .... 1.TrPA.65.368.
That fly disorder'd with the wanton Wind: .... 1.TrSP.86.397.
Self-banish'd thence, I sail'd before the Wind, ... 1.TrUl.142.470.
But faithless still, and wav'ring as the Wind! .... 2.ChJM.478.38.
A sliding Noose, and waver'd in the Wind. .... 2.ChWB.396.76.
Loose to the Wind their airy Garments flew, ... 2.RL2.63.163.
The dreadful *East* is all the Wind that blows. .... 2.RL4.20.184.
The tott'ring *China* shook without a Wind, ... 2.RL4.163.197.
Wave high, and murmur to the hollow wind, ... 2.ElAb.156.332.
In each low wind methinks a Spirit calls, ... 2.ElAb.305.344.
Sees God in clouds, or hears him in the wind; .... 3.EOM1.100.27.
That never air or ocean felt the wind; .... 3.EOM1.167.36.
He mounts the storm, and walks upon the wind. .... 3.EOM2.110.68.
Perhaps the Wind just shifted from the east: .... 3.Ep1.64.20.
Improves the keenness of the Northern wind. .... 3.Ep4.112.148.
Where Bile, and wind, and phlegm, and acid jar, ... 4.HS2.71.59.
When Bile, and wind, and Phlegn, and acid jar, ... 4.HS2.71A.59.
On Fame's mad voyage by the wind of Praise; .... 4.2HE1.297.221.
As, "What's o'clock?" And, "How's the Wind?" .... 4.HS6.89.255.
As forc'd from wind-guns, lead itself can fly, ... 5.DunA1.177.84.
He left huge Lintot, and out-stript the wind. .... 5.DunA2.58.105.
Some beg an eastern, some a western wind: .... 5.DunA2.84.108.
Some for an eastern, some a western wind: .... 5.DunA2.84A.108.
On grinning dragons Cibber mounts the wind: .... 5.DunA3.264.179.
As, forc'd from wind-guns, lead itself can fly, ... 5.DunB1.181.283.
He left huge Lintot, and out-strip'd the wind. .... 5.DunB2.62.298.
Wide as a wind-mill all his figures spread, ... 5.DunB2.66.299.
Some beg an eastern, some a western wind: .... 5.DunB2.88.300.
So swells each wind-pipe, Ass intones to Ass, ... 5.DunB2.253.307.
On grinning dragons thou shalt mount the wind. .... 5.DunB3.268.333.
Which some rude wind will always discompose; .... 6.22.4.71.
To sigh unseen into the passing Wind? .... 6.81.10A.225.
But none hath eyes to trace the passing wind, ... 6.96ii.30Z29.271.
"But who hath Eyes to trace the passing Wind, ... 6.96ii.39.272.
Or have a Pimp or Flaterer in the Wind, ... 6.129.2.357.
And high *Enispè* shook by wintry Wind, ... Il.2.738.161.
Which *Jove* refus'd, and mingled with the Wind. .... Il.3.377.211.
The snowie Fleece, and wind the twisted Wool.) .... Il.3.478.214.
The Cloud condensing as the West-Wind blows: .... Il.4.319.236.
There left a Subject to the Wind and Rain .... Il.4.558.248.
Wide o'er the Field, resistless as the Wind, ... Il.6.51.326.
The Shouts of *Trojans* thicken in the Wind; .... Il.8.192.406.
Swift as the Wind, the various-colour'd Maid .... Il.8.502.420.
Then mounting on the Pinions of the Wind, ... Il.8.524.421.
Hears in the passing Wind their Music blow, ... Il.10.15.2.
Swift as the Wind, and white as Winter-Snow: .... Il.10.507.26.
Swift as the Wind, and white as Winter-Snow. .... Il.10.601.29.
Thro' broken Orders, swifter than the Wind, ... Il.11.441.53.
Hector's Approach in ev'ry Wind they hear, ... Il.12.43.83.
These empty Accents mingled with the Wind, ... Il.12.197.88.
By wand'ring Birds, that flit with ev'ry Wind? .... Il.12.278.91.
His winged Lance, resistless as the Wind, ... Il.13.706.138.
The Mass of Waters will no Wind obey; .... Il.14.25.158.
Then swift as Wind, o'er *Lemnos* smoaky Isle, ... Il.14.317.178.
His foaming Coursers, swifter than the Wind, ... Il.14.505.188.
Swift as the Wind, to *Ida's* Hills they came, ... Il.15.170.203.
He spoke; and speaking, swifter than the Wind .... Il.15.468.215.
Sprung from the Wind, and like the Wind in speed; .... Il.16.183.245.
Sprung from the Wind, and like the Wind in speed; .... Il.16.183.245.
Float in one Sea, and wave before the Wind. .... Il.16.263.249.
The sweepy Crest hung floating in the Wind: .... Il.19.411.389.
Swift as their Mother Mares, and Father Wind. .... Il.20.269.405.
My Spear, that parted on the Wings of Wind, ... Il.20.394.411.
Rush the swift Eastern and the Western Wind: .... Il.21.389.436.
Achilles follows like the winged Wind. .... Il.22.182.463.
Float in their Speed, and dance upon the Wind: .... Il.23.444.508.

WIND (CONTINUED)
Close on *Eumelus'* Back they puff the Wind, ... Il.23.457.508.
Stretch their broad plumes, and float upon the wind. .... Od.2.174.70.
The spacious sheet, and stretch it to the wind. .... Od.2.465.83.
All sense of woe delivers to the wind. .... Od.4.308.134.
Heav'n to my fleet refus'd a prosp'rous wind: .... Od.4.474.142.
Alone, and floating to the wave and wind. .... Od.5.45.173.
With crossing sail-yards dancing in the wind; .... Od.5.325.187.
And now the west-wind whirls it o'er the sea. .... Od.5.423.192.
And live; give all thy terrors to the wind. .... Od.5.441.194.
And form'd a bay, impervious to the wind. .... Od.5.565.199.
Nor wind sharp-piercing, nor the rushing show'r; .... Od.5.621.201.
To roaring billows, and the warring wind; .... Od.6.206.220.
Full nine days floating to the wave and wind. .... Od.7.339.253.
A river's mouth, impervious to the wind, ... Od.7.365.254.
We sit, and trust the pilot and the wind. .... Od.9.88.306.
And mount the decks, and call the willing wind. .... Od.9.655.333.
The tempest's Lord, and tyrant of the wind; .... Od.10.22.340.
What bark to waft me, and what wind to blow? .... Od.10.597.372.
The spacious sheet, and stretch it to the wind: .... Od.11.4.379.
Out-fly the nimble sail, and leave the lagging wind? .... Od.11.74.384.
Thrice thro' my arms she slipt like empty wind, ... Od.11.249.393.
To wander with the wind in empty air, ... Od.11.266.394.
Thro' tumbling billows, and a war of wind. .... Od.12.502.456.
Self-banish'd thence. I sail'd before the wind, ... Od.13.309.21.
The driving storm the wat'ry west-wind pours, ... Od.14.512.62.
The spacious sheet, and stretch it to the wind. .... Od.15.313.84.
Then cautious thro' the rocky reaches wind, ... Od.15.320.85.
Thence born to *Ithaca* by wave and wind; .... Od.15.519.95.
Drink the cool stream, and tremble to the wind. .... Od.17.241.143.
He now but waits the wind, to waft him o'er .... Od.17.616.162.
The first fair wind transports him o'er the main; .... Od.21.328.275.
The empty corse to waver with the wind. .... Od.22.508.313.

WIND-GUNS
As forc'd from wind-guns, lead itself can fly, ... 5.DunA1.177.84
As, forc'd from wind-guns, lead itself can fly, ... 5.DunB1.181.28[3]

WIND-MILL
Wide as a wind-mill all his figures spread, ... 5.DunB2.66.299.

WIND-PIPE
So swells each wind-pipe, Ass intones to Ass, ... 5.DunB2.253.307

WIND'S
The roaring wind's tempestuous rage restrain; .... Od.13.119.7.

WINDE
As when two skilful Hounds the Lev'ret winde, ... Il.10.427.22.
To winde the vapour in the tainted dew? .... Od.17.385.150.

WINDED
A cold, long-winded, native of the deep! .... 5.DunA2.288.13[7]
Long-winded both, as natives of the deep! .... 5.DunA2.288A.1[37]
A cold, long-winded, native of the deep: .... 5.DunB2.300.31[0]
He took the path that winded to the cave. .... Od.5.71.175.

WINDHAM'S
Here British sighs from Windham's bosom stole .... 6.142.11G.383.

WINDING
Where gentle *Thames* his winding Waters leads .... 1.PSu.3A.71.
Or else where *Cam* his winding Vales divides? .... 1.PSu.26.74.
Nor Rivers winding thro' the Vales below, ... 1.PWi.3.88.
What Kings first breath'd upon her winding Shore, ... 1.W-F.300.176.
The winding *Isis,* and the fruitful *Tame:* .... 1.W-F.340.183.
And long-continu'd Ways, and winding Floods, ... 1.TrUl.66.468.
Pleas'd Vaga echoes thro' her winding bounds, ... 3.Ep3.251.114.
Scream, like the winding of ten thousand Jacks: 5.DunA3.154.164
Scream like the winding of ten thousand jacks: 5.DunB3.160.328
By all their winding Play; .... 6.53.26.162.
In Silence past along the winding Strand .... Il.1.453A.109.
Then part, where stretch'd along the winding Bay .... Il.1.632.118.
And curl'd around in many a winding Fold. .... Il.2.375.145.
From *Ephyr's* Walls, and *Sellè's* winding Shore, ... Il.2.798.163.
Stung with the Shame, within the winding Way, ... Il.4.444.241.
With levell'd Spears along the winding Shore; .... Il.6.233.337.
Deep in a winding Way his Breast assail'd, ... Il.7.175.372.
In Arms we slept, beside the winding Flood, ... Il.11.868.74.
The Coursers fed on *Selle's* winding Shore. .... Il.12.112.85.
(Well known in Fight on *Selles'* winding Shore, ... Il.15.627.220.
(Who led his Bands from *Axius'* winding Flood) .... Il.16.343.256.
And breaks its Force, and turns the winding Tides. .... Il.17.842.321.
If Sheep or Oxen seek the winding Stream. .... Il.18.606.352.
To this, one Pathway gently winding leads, ... Il.18.657.355.
As when a Flame the winding Valley fills, ... Il.20.569.418.
And close in Rocks or winding Caverns lye. .... Il.21.29.422.
Where winding round the rich *Cydonian* plain, ... Od.3.372.104.
Nor peaceful port was there, nor winding bay, ... Od.5.518.197.
To town *Ulysses* took the winding way. .... Od.7.18.234.
Thro' all their inmost-winding caves resound. .... Od.9.470.325.
And reach our vessel on the winding shore. .... Od.9.548.328.
And long-continu'd ways, and winding floods, ... Od.13.233.17.
Full to the bay within the winding shores .... Od.16.368.124.
Now gently winding up the fair ascent, ... Od.21.41.261.
Not so: his judgment takes the winding way .... Od.24.279.363.

WINDINGS
That o'er the Windings of *Cayster's* Springs, ... Il.2.542.153.
In mazy windings wand'ring down the hill: .... Od.5.92.176.

WINDMILL
Wide as a windmill all his figure spread, ... 5.DunA2.62.105.

WINDOW
There stood a window near, whence looking down ... Od.22.142.293.
To mount yon window, and alarm from thence ... Od.22.149.294.

WINDOW'D
With pert flat eyes she window'd well its head, ... 5.DunA2.39.100.
With pert flat eyes she window'd well its head; ... 5.DunB2.43.298.

WINDOWS
And the dim windows shed a solemn light; ... 2.ElAb.144.331.
To break my Windows, if I treat a Friend; ... 4.EpS2.143.321.
"Doors, Windows, Chimnies, and the spacious Rooms, ... 6.96ii.55.273.
The Windows open; all the Neighbours rise: ... 6.96iv.46.277.

WINDPIPE
So swells each Windpipe; Ass intones to Ass, ... 5.DunA2.243.129.
Nor pierc'd the Windpipe yet, nor took the Pow'r ... Il.22.411.472.

WINDS
Here Western Winds on breathing Roses blow. ... 1.PSp.32.63.
And Winds shall waft it to the Pow'rs above. ... 1.PSu.80.78.
Thus, far from *Delia,* to the Winds I mourn, ... 1.PAu.21.82.
Thus, far from Thyrsis, to the Winds I mourn, ... 1.PAu.21A.82.
The Winds to breathe, the waving Woods to move, ... 1.PAu.41.83.
The Winds and Trees and Floods her Death deplore, ... 1.PWi.67.93.
The hollow Winds thro' naked Temples roar; ... 1.W-F.68.156.
Then bow'd and spoke; the Winds forget to roar, ... 1.W-F.353.184.
Nor Winds, when first your florid Orchard blows, ... 1.TrVP.110.381.
By driving Winds the spreading Flames are born! ... 1.TrSP.10.393.
The Winds my Pray'rs, my Sighs, my Numbers bear, ... 1.TrSP.244.404.
The flying Winds have lost them all in Air! ... 1.TrSP.245.404.
As when two Winds with Rival Force contend, ... 1.TrSt.265.421.
And those that give the wandring Winds to blow, ... 1.TrSt.289.422.
Go mount the Winds, and to the Shades repair; ... 1.TrSt.416.427.
Wings on the whistling Winds his rapid way, ... 1.TrSt.438.428.
At once the rushing Winds with roaring Sound ... 1.TrSt.488.430.
Are whirl'd in Air, and on the Winds are born; ... 1.TrSt.507.431.
The roaring Winds tempestuous Rage restrain; ... 1.TrUl.28.466.
The rest, the Winds dispers'd in empty Air. ... 2.RL2.46.162.
Like that where once *Ulysses* held the Winds; ... 2.RL4.82.190.
From Pole to Pole the Winds diffuse the Sound, ... 2.TemF.308.279.
And on the Winds triumphant swell the Notes; ... 2.TemF.373.281.
And up the Winds triumphant swell the Notes; ... 2.TemF.373A.281.
Pervious to Winds, and open ev'ry way. ... 2.TemF.427.284.
Clouds interpose, waves roar, and winds arise. ... 2.ElAb.246.339.
Still as the sea, ere winds were taught to blow, ... 2.ElAb.253.340.
Like varying winds, by other passions tost, ... 3.EOM2.167.75.
Our fates and fortunes, as the winds shall blow: ... 3.Ep3.76.93.
Or call the winds thro' long Arcades to roar, ... 3.Ep4.35.140.
Shall call the winds thro' long Arcades to roar, ... 3.Ep4.35A.140.
Oh blast it, South-winds! till a stench exhale, ... 4.HS2.27.55.
On Wings of Winds came flying all abroad? ... 4.Arbu.218.111.
Not Winds that round our ruin'd Abbeys roar, ... 4.JD2A.67.138.
Where winds can carry, or where waves can roll, ... 4.1HE6.70.241.
Keen, hollow winds howl thro' the bleak recess, ... 5.DunA1.29.63.
All vain petitions, sent by winds on high, ... 5.DunA2.85B.108.
Songs, sonnets, epigrams the winds uplift, ... 5.DunA2.107.109.
His papers all, the sportive winds up-lift ... 5.DunA2.107A.109.
Keen, hollow winds howl thro' the bleak recess, ... 5.DunB1.35.272.
Songs, sonnets, epigrams the winds uplift, ... 5.DunB2.115.301.
Which winds and lightning both at once assail. ... 6.3.4.7.
Are winds the tempests dreadful to her ears? ... 6.4i.12.9.
By the fragrant Winds that blow ... 6.11.72.33.
See, wild as the Winds, o'er the Desart he flies; ... 6.11.110.34.
To sigh unheard in, to the passing winds? ... 6.81.10.225.
From East and South when Winds begin to roar, ... Il.2.176.137.
The Fires expanding as the Winds arise, ... Il.2.536.152.
Speeds on the Wings of Winds thro' liquid Air; ... Il.2.957.169.
As when the Winds, ascending by degrees, ... Il.4.478.242.
The grey Dust, rising with collected Winds, ... Il.5.615.297.
'Till the Mass scatters as the Winds arise, ... Il.5.647.299.
Thaumantia! mount the Winds, and stop their Car; ... Il.8.488.420.
The Winds to Heav'n the curling Vapours bore. ... Il.8.680.427.
As when the Winds with raging Flames conspire, ... Il.11.201.44.
On Wings of Winds descends the various Maid. ... Il.11.254.46.
Floats on the Winds, and rends the Heav'ns with Cries: ... Il.12.239.90.
He stills the Winds, and bids the Skies to sleep; ... Il.12.335.93.
Fleet as the Winds, and deck'd with golden Manes. ... Il.13.37.106.
As warring Winds, in *Sirius'* sultry Reign, ... Il.13.424.126.
(While the Winds sleep) his Breast receiv'd the Stroke. ... Il.13.550.132.
(The Winds collected at each open Door) ... Il.13.740.140.
The Lance far distant by the Winds was blown. ... Il.13.758.141.
The Winds perfum'd, the balmy Gale Convey ... Il.14.199.169.
When stormy Winds disclose the dark Profound; ... Il.14.458.186.
Less loud the Winds, that from th' *Æolian* Hall ... Il.14.459.186.
By Winds assail'd, by Billows beat in vain, ... Il.15.747.224.
White are the Decks with Foam; the Winds aloud ... Il.15.754.225.
Of Strength defensive against Winds and Storms, ... Il.16.257.249.
His safe Return, the Winds dispers'd in Air. ... Il.16.309.254.
So pent by Hills, the wild Winds roar aloud ... Il.16.923.279.
Less fierce the Winds with rising Flames conspire, ... Il.17.825.320.
No—could our Swiftness o'er the Winds prevail, ... Il.19.460.391.
And winds his Course before the following Tide; ... Il.21.286.432.
Along the Margin winds the running Blaze: ... Il.21.407.437.
Now here, now there, she winds her from the Blow; ... Il.21.570.446.
Swift as the Word, the *Winds* tumultuous flew; ... Il.23.263.500.
And to their Caves the whistling *Winds* return'd: ... Il.23.285.501.
As a large Fish, when Winds and Waters roar, ... Il.23.802.521.
Proof to the wintry Winds and howling Storms, ... Il.23.827.522.
And mounts incumbent on the Wings of Winds, ... Il.24.418.553.
Free breathe the winds, and free the billows flow, ... Od.2.359.78.
Now on the wings of winds our course we keep, ... Od.3.189.95.
The whistling winds already wak'd the sky; ... Od.3.213.96.
Before the whistling winds the vessels fly, ... Od.3.214.96.
And the winds whistle, and the surges roll ... Od.3.368.104.
But five tall barks the winds and waters tost ... Od.3.382.105.

WINDS (CONTINUED)
Propitious winds, to waft us o'er the main: ... Od.4.490.143.
From the bleak pole no winds inclement blow, ... Od.4.771.155.
The winds and waves he tempts in early bloom, ... Od.4.948.162.
He spoke. The God who mounts the winged winds ... Od.5.56.174.
The sport of winds, and driv'n from ev'ry coast, ... Od.5.170.180.
Free as the winds I give thee now to rove— ... Od.5.209.181.
Swells all the winds, and rouzes all the storms ... Od.5.378.190.
What raging winds? what roaring waters round? ... Od.5.390.191.
Back to their caves she bad the winds to fly, ... Od.5.490.195.
The winds were hush'd, the billows scarcely curl'd, ... Od.5.502.196.
There no rude winds presume to shake the skies, ... Od.6.51.207.
The winds to *Marathon* the Virgin bore; ... Od.7.102.239.
The wild winds whistle, and the billows roar; ... Od.7.357.254.
On wings of winds with *Rhadamanth* they flew: ... Od.7.414.257.
Swift as on wings of winds upborn they fly, ... Od.8.127.269.
The winds from *Ilion* to the *Cicons'* shore, ... Od.9.41.303.
But, the cape doubled, adverse winds prevail'd. ... Od.9.90.306.
The scatter'd wreck the winds blew back again. ... Od.9.341.320.
The adverse winds in leathern bags he brac'd, ... Od.10.19.340.
The northern winds shall wing thee on thy way. ... Od.10.601.372.
Sunk were at once the winds; the air above, ... Od.12.202.441.
Hush'd the loud winds, and charm'd the waves to sleep. ... Od.12.205.441.
Oft in the dead of night loud winds arise, ... Od.12.341.448.
There while the wild winds whistled o'er the main, ... Od.12.379.449.
Smooth seas, and gentle winds, invite him home. ... Od.13.8.2.
Who wings the winds, and darkens heav'n with showr's) ... Od.13.30.2.
With winds and waves I held unequal strife; ... Od.14.348.51.
The face of things; the winds began to roar; ... Od.14.511.62.
The skill of weather and of winds unknown, ... Od.14.541.63.

WINDSOR
If *Windsor*-Shades *delight the matchless Maid,* ... 1.PSp.67.67.
Cynthus and *Hybla* yield to *Windsor*-Shade. ... 1.PSp.68.67.
Next *Ægon* sung, while *Windsor* Groves admir'd; ... 1.PAu.55.84.
Thy Forests, *Windsor!* and thy green Retreats, ... 1.W-F.1.148.
Nor envy *Windsor!* since thy Shades have seen ... 1.W-F.161.164.
And *Cynthus'* Top forsook for *Windsor* Shade; ... 1.W-F.166.165.
Make *Windsor* Hills in lofty Numbers rise, ... 1.W-F.287.174.
Oh wou'dst thou sing what Heroes *Windsor* bore, ... 1.W-F.299.176.
Where *Windsor-Domes* and pompous Turrets rise, ... 1.W-F.352.184.
Thy Trees, fair *Windsor!* now shall leave their Woods, ... 1.W-F.385.189.
To Windsor, and again to Town, ... 4.HS6.98.257.
But for thy Windsor, a New Fabric Raise ... 6.147ix.5.392.

WINDSOR-DOMES
Where *Windsor-Domes* and pompous Turrets rise, ... 1.W-F.352.184.

WINDSOR-SHADE
Cynthus and *Hybla* yield to *Windsor*-Shade. ... 1.PSp.68.67.

WINDSOR-SHADES
If *Windsor*-Shades *delight the matchless Maid,* ... 1.PSp.67.67.

WINDSOR'S
Nor blush to sport on *Windsor's* blissful Plains: ... 1.PSp.2.59.
As thine, which visits *Windsor's* fam'd Abodes, ... 1.W-F.229.170.
Than thine, which visits *Windsor's* fam'd Abodes, ... 1.W-F.229A.170.
Vales, Spires, meandring Streams, and *Windsor's* tow'ry Pride. ... 6.14ii.54.44.

WINDY
The windy satisfaction of the tongue. ... Od.4.1092.169.

WINE
And grateful Clusters swell with floods of Wine; ... 1.PAu.74.85.
Blaze on the Brims, and sparkle in the Wine— ... 1.TrSt.209.419.
To fill the Goblet high with sparkling Wine, ... 1.TrSt.634.436.
Now pour the Wine; and in your tuneful Lays, ... 1.TrSt.827.444.
Wine lets no Lover unrewarded go, ... 2.ChWB.219.67.
Critick'd your wine, and analyz'd your meat, ... 3.Ep2.81.57.
Whole slaughter'd hecatombs, and floods of wine, ... 3.Ep3.203A.110.
What slaughter'd hecatombs, what floods of wine, ... 3.Ep3.203.110.
From soup to sweet-wine, and God bless the King. ... 3.Ep4.162.153.
Lettuce and Cowslip Wine; *Probatum est.* ... 4.HS1.18.5.
Your wine lock'd up, your Butler stroll'd abroad, ... 4.HS2.13.55.
And is at once their vinegar and wine. ... 4.HS2.54.59.
The musty wine, foul cloth, or greasy glass. ... 4.HS2.66.59.
If Time improve our Wit as well as Wine, ... 4.2HE1.49.199.
Till mischief learn'd to mix with wine. ... 6.6ii.24.15.
Mixt Wine, mixt Company, and mixt Discourse: ... 6.17iv.27.60.
Since not much Wine, much Company, much Food, ... 6.17iv.28.60.
The groaning presses foam with floods of wine. ... 6.35.22.103.
But Wit, like Wine, from happier Climates brought, ... 6.60.13.178.
He eat the Sops, she sipp'd the Wine: ... 6.93.20.257.
He eat the Sops, she drank the Wine: ... 6.93.20A.257.
Pours the black Wine, and sees the Flames aspire; ... Il.1.608.117.
The Youths with Wine the copious Goblets crown'd, ... Il.1.616.117.
Must want a *Trojan* Slave to pour the Wine. ... Il.2.158.136.
Bring the rich Wine and destin'd Victims down. ... Il.3.316.208.
The Wine they mix, and on each Monarch's Hands ... Il.3.339.209.
From the same Urn they drink the mingled Wine, ... Il.3.368.210.
Shed like this Wine, distain the thirsty Ground; ... Il.3.373.211.
The golden Goblet crowns with Purple Wine: ... Il.4.4.221.
Not thus our Vows, confirm'd with Wine and Gore, ... Il.4.192.230.
Inflaming Wine, pernicious to Mankind, ... Il.6.330.342.
So oft' has steep'd the strength'ning Grain in Wine. ... Il.8.233.408.
And strength'ning Bread, and gen'rous Wine be brought. ... Il.8.630.426.
With gen'rous Wine, and all-sustaining Bread. ... Il.8.678.427.
The Youth with Wine the sacred Goblets crown'd, ... Il.9.229.444.
Mix purer Wine, and open ev'ry Soul. ... Il.9.268.445.
Not unperceiv'd; *Ulysses* crown'd with Wine ... Il.9.292.448.
They daily feast, with Draughts of fragrant Wine. ... Il.9.593.464.
And those are ow'd to gen'rous Wine and Food) ... Il.9.827.474.
And the crown'd Goblet foams with Floods of Wine. ... Il.10.680.32.
Pours a large Potion of the *Pramnian* Wine; ... Il.11.781.70.
When Wine and Feasts thy golden Humours please. ... Il.14.275.175.

WINE (CONTINUED)
Which never Man had stain'd with ruddy Wine, ...Il.16.274.249.
And those augment by gen'rous Wine and Food; ....Il.19.160.378.
With sable Wine; then, (as the Rites direct). ....Il.23.296.501.
Wide o'er the Pyle the sable Wine they throw, ...Il.23.311.502.
A golden Bowl that foam'd with fragrant Wine, ...Il.24.351.550.
On the mid Pavement pours the rosy Wine, ...Il.24.375.551.
And quench with Wine the yet remaining Fire. ....Il.24.1002.577.
With insolence, and wine, elate and loud; ....Od.1.176.41.
Unseemly flown with insolence and wine? ....Od.1.292.47.
Scarce all my wine their midnight hours supplies. ....Od.2.64.63.
And gen'rous wine, which thoughtful sorrow flies. ....Od.2.330.77.
There casks of wine in rows adorn'd the dome. ....Od.2.385.79.
(Pure flav'rous wine, by Gods in bounty giv'n, ...Od.2.386.80.
But by thy care twelve urns of wine be fill'd, ...Od.2.398.80.
And now they ship their oars, and crown with wine ....Od.2.470.83.
Then give thy friend to shed the sacred wine; ....Od.3.59.89.
Gave to *Ulysses'* son the rosie wine. ....Od.3.77.90.
Now immolate the Tongues, and mix the wine, ...Od.3.425.107.
Of social welcome, mix'd the racy wine, ...Od.3.503.112.
And pours the wine, and bids the flames aspire: ....Od.3.588.116.
And in the dazling goblet laughs the wine. ....Od.3.601.117.
Then bread and wine a ready handmaid brings, ...Od.3.608.117.
With wine and viands I the vessel stor'd: ....Od.4.985.163.
With water from the rock, and rosie wine, ...Od.5.214.181.
Ambrosial banquet, and celestial wine. ....Od.5.254.184.
With water one, and one with sable wine; ....Od.5.338.188.
The groaning presses foam with floods of wine. ....Od.7.163.244.
And bad the herald pour the rosy wine. ....Od.7.239.248.
Now each partakes the feast, the wine prepares, ...Od.8.513.290.
And o'er the foaming bowl the laughing wine. ....Od.9.10.301.
Then took a goatskin fill'd with precious wine, ...Od.9.229.316.
And twelve large vessels of unmingled wine, ...Od.9.238.316.
Such was the wine: to quench whose fervent stream, ...Od.9.242.316.
Whoe'er thou art that bear'st celestial wine! ....Od.9.420.323.
He said; then nodding with the fumes of wine ....Od.9.439.324.
There belcht the mingled streams of wine and blood, ...Od.9.443.324.
Who not by strength subdu'd me, but by wine. ....Od.9.604.331.
And unregarded laughs the rosy wine. ....Od.10.448.365.
Prolong'd the feast, and quaff'd the rosy wine: ....Od.10.565.369.
New wine and milk, with honey temper'd, bring, ...Od.10.618.374.
New wine, with honey-temper'd milk, we bring, ...Od.11.31.380.
My feet thro' wine unfaithful to their weight, ...Od.11.77.385.
Bear the rich viands and the generous wine: ....Od.12.26.430.
The barley fail'd, and for libations, wine. ....Od.12.420.451.
Water, instead of wine, is brought in urns, ...Od.12.427.451.
To fill the goblet high with rosy wine: ....Od.13.65.4.
The luscious wine th' obedient herald brought; ....Od.13.68.4.
And bread and wine the third. The chearful mates ....Od.13.86.5.
(With flour imbrown'd) next mingled wine yet new, ...Od.14.93.40.
Full oft has *Phidon,* whilst he pour'd the wine, ...Od.14.367.53.
Then pour'd of offer'd wine the sable wave: ....Od.14.499.60.
And wine can of their wits the wise beguile, ...Od.14.520.62.
The King precedes; a bowl with fragrant wine ....Od.15.164.76.
(The sacred wine yet foaming on the ground) ....Od.15.279.82.
And wine the lengthen'd intervals imploy. ....Od.15.425.89.
(For she needs little) daily bread and wine. ....Od.15.529.95.
In grateful banquet o'er the rosy wine. ....Od.15.540.96.
Nor food nor wine refus'd: but since the day ....Od.16.152.110.
Nor wine nor food he tastes; but sunk in woes, ...Od.16.154.110.
With wine suffic'd me, and with dainties fed: ....Od.16.459.129.
Whose loose head tottering as with wine oppress, ...Od.18.281.180.
Art thou from wine, or innate folly, bold? ....Od.18.433.189.
Retire we hence! but crown with rosy wine ....Od.18.464.190.
Then swill'd with wine, with noise the crowds obey, ...Od.18.472.191.
A public treat, with jars of gen'rous wine. ....Od.19.229.204.
With honey, milk, and wine, their infant years: ....Od.20.83.236.
A bowl of gen'rous wine suffic'd the guest; ....Od.20.171.241.
Wine rosy-bright the brimming goblets crown'd, ...Od.20.317.248.
The goblet high with rosie wine they crown'd, ...Od.21.288.273.
To copious wine this insolence we owe, ...Od.21.315.274.
And much thy betters wine can overthrow: ....Od.21.316.274.
Of floating meats, and wine, and human blood. ....Od.22.26.287.
Soft sleep, fair garments, and the joys of wine, ...Od.24.300.364.

WINE'S
Nor Wine's inflaming Juice supplies their Veins.) ....Il.5.426.289.

WINES
Rich luscious Wines, that youthful Blood improve, ...2.ChWB.215.67.
Of luscious Wines, that youthful Blood improve, ...2.ChWB.215A.67.
With all their brandies or with all their wines? ....3.Ep3.40.89.
The other slights, for Women, Sports, and Wines, ...4.2HE2.272.185.
Where slumber Abbots, purple as their wines: ....5.DunB4.302.373.
Of fragrant Wines the rich *Eunæus* sent ....Il.7.562.392.
With *Thracian* Wines recruit thy honour'd Guests, ...Il.9.99.437.
Delicious wines th' attending herald brought; ....Od.1.187.42.
The luscious wines dishonour'd lose their taste, ...Od.2.349.78.
The strength of wheat, and wines, and ample store. ....Od.2.427.81.
Rich fragrant wines the cheering bowl supply; ....Od.4.842.158.
The sumptuous viands, and the flav'rous wines. ....Od.6.90.209.
And a full goblet foams with gen'rous wines: ....Od.8.66.265.
Spontaneous wines from weighty clusters pour, ...Od.9.125.310.
Nor wines were wanting; those from ample jars ....Od.9.190.313.
And honey fresh, and *Pramnian* wines the treat: ....Od.10.271.355.
With wines unmixt, (an honour due to Age, ...Od.13.11.2.
Confer, and wines and cates the table grace; ....Od.14.223.46.
Then in a bowl he tempers gen'rous wines, ...Od.16.53.105.
Amphinomus; and wines that laugh in gold. ....Od.18.146.173.
The tasteful inwards, and nectareous wines. ....Od.20.325.249.
His generous wines dishonour'd shed in vain, ...Od.23.327.340.
With wines and unguents in a golden vase. ....Od.24.94.352.

WING
And scatters Blessings from her Dove-like Wing. ....1.W-F.430.194.
Prescrib'd her Heights, and prun'd her tender Wing, ...1.EOC.736.325.

WING (CONTINUED)
Nor yet attempt to stretch thy bolder Wing, ...1.TrSt.23.410.
These, tho' unseen, are ever on the Wing, ...2.RL1.43.149.
He asks no Angel's wing, no Seraph's fire; ....3.EOM1.110.28.
He asks no Angel's wing, or Seraph's fire; 3.EOM1.110A.28
He asks no Angel's wing, nor Seraph's fire; 3.EOM1.110B.28
Or wing the sky, or roll along the flood, ...3.EOM3.120.104.
Or Death's black Wing already be display'd ....4.HS1.95.13.
One likes the Pheasant's wing, and one the leg; ....4.2HE2.84.171.
But most, when straining with too weak a wing, ...4.2HE1.368.227.
Oh! could I mount on the Mæonian wing, ...4.2HE1.394.229.
Peace stole her wing, and wrapt the world in sleep; ....4.2HE1.401.229.
These, may some gentle, ministerial Wing ....4.EpS1.95.305.
Spread thy broad wing, and sowze on all the Kind. ....4.EpS2.15.314.
The Muse's wing shall brush you all away: ....4.EpS2.223.325.
And now, on Fancy's easy wing convey'd, ...5.DunA3.13.150.
Instant when dipt, away they wing their flight, ...5.DunA3.19.152.
And under his, and under Archer's wing, ...5.DunB1.309.292.
And now, on Fancy's easy wing convey'd, ...5.DunB3.13.320.
Instant, when dipt, away they wing their flight, ...5.DunB3.27.321.
To whom Time bears me on his rapid wing, ...5.DunB4.6.339.
"Of all th' enamel'd race, whose silv'ry wing ....5.DunB4.421.383.
He who beneath thy shelt'ring wing resides, ...6.21.1.69.
Raise in their arms, and waft thee on their wing, ...6.21.26.69.
The hov'ring Soul is on the Wing; ....6.31ii.6Z5.94.
Wafts on his gentle wing his eightieth year) ....6.55.2.166.
Around his Temples spreads his golden Wing, ...Il.2.23.128.
Seiz'd by the beating Wing, the Monster slew: ....Il.2.383.145.
And all the War descends upon the Wing. ....Il.3.10.188.
Th' impatient Weapon whizzes on the Wing, ...Il.4.156.228.
Shoots on the Wing, and skims along the Sky: ....Il.13.94.109.
But skill'd from far the flying Shaft to wing, ...Il.13.893.148.
Then taking wing from *Athos'* lofty Steep, ...Il.14.263.173.
They wing their way, and *Imbrus'* Sea-beat Soil, ...Il.14.318.178.
And various *Iris* wing their airy way. ....Il.15.169.203.
To wing the Spear, or aim the distant Dart; ....Il.16.231.248.
Of all that wing the mid Aerial Sky, ...Il.17.762.318.
Incens'd, we heav'nward fled with swiftest wing, ...Il.21.529.443.
Already at their Heels they wing their Way, ...Il.23.528.511.
And the free Bird to Heav'n displays her Wing: ....Il.23.1027.530.
Precipitant in fear, wou'd wing their flight, ...Od.1.213.43.
Swift they descend with wing to wing conjoin'd, ...Od.2.173.70.
Swift they descend with wing to wing conjoin'd, ...Od.2.173.70.
A sure presage from ev'ry wing that flew. ....Od.2.188.71.
Brave *Philoctetes,* taught to wing the dart; ....Od.3.231.97.
With sails we wing the masts, our anchors weigh, ...Od.4.785.156.
The birds of broadest wing their mansion form, ...Od.5.85.176.
For who, self-mov'd, with weary wing wou'd sweep ....Od.5.125.178.
And bend the bow, or wing the missile dart; ....Od.9.183.313.
The northern winds shall wing thee on thy way. ....Od.10.601.372.
No bird of air, no dove of swiftest wing, ...Od.12.75.435.
My soul takes wing to meet the heav'nly strain; ....Od.12.233.443.
Vengeance is on the wing, and heav'n in arms! ....Od.12.442.452.
To raise the mast, the missile dart to wing, ...Od.14.261.49.
Time steals away with unregarded wing, ...Od.17.612.161.
Instant the flying sail the slave shall wing ....Od.18.141.173.
But Vengeance and *Ulysses* wing their way. ....Od.18.174.175.
Who now can bend *Ulysses'* bow, and wing ....Od.21.3.257.
Shall end those hopes, and Fate is on the wing! ....Od.21.104.263.
I too may try, and if this arm can wing ....Od.21.117.264.
Then notch'd the shaft, releast, and gave it wing; ....Od.21.460.282.
And o'er the past, *Oblivion* stretch her wing. ....Od.24.557.375.

WING'D
Thro' Crouds of Airy Shades she wing'd her Flight, ...1.TrSt.130.415.
And when th'ascending Soul has wing'd her Flight, ...1.TrES.247.459.
When the wing'd Colonies first tempt the Sky, ...2.TemF.284.277.
For gain, not glory, wing'd his roving flight, ...4.2HE1.71.199.
With that, the blue-ey'd Virgin wing'd her Flight; ....Il.5.170.275.
I wing'd an Arrow, which not idly fell, ...Il.5.238.278.
The fainting Soul stood ready wing'd for Flight, ...Il.5.856.307.
The Feather in his Hand, just wing'd for flight, ...Il.8.391.416.
A long-wing'd Heron great *Minerva* sent; ....Il.10.322.17.
Wing'd with his Fears, on Foot he strove to fly, ...Il.11.439.53.
And wing'd an Arrow at th' unwary Foe; ....Il.11.478.55.
And wing'd the feather'd Vengeance at the Foe. ....Il.13.832.145.
Direct at *Ajax'* Bosom wing'd its Course; ....Il.14.466.186.
Th' Almighty spoke; the Goddess wing'd her Flight ....Il.15.190.203.
Whom the wing'd *Harpye,* swift *Podarge,* bore, ...Il.16.184.245.
And when th' ascending Soul has wing'd her flight, ...Il.16.550.265.
Thus having spoke, *Apollo* wing'd his Flight ....Il.17.87.291.
The swift-wing'd Chaser of the feather'd Game, ...Il.24.389.552.
But if his soul hath wing'd the destin'd flight, ...Od.1.376.50.
With terror wing'd conveys the dread report. ....Od.4.706.152.
Swift to *Phæacia* wing'd her rapid flight. ....Od.6.4.203.
Hither the Goddess wing'd th' aereal way, ...Od.6.55.208.
But o'er the world of waters wing'd her way: ....Od.7.100.239.
Clytonius sprung: he wing'd the rapid way, ...Od.8.131.270.
And learn'd in all wing'd omens of the air) ....Od.9.598.331.
While the wing'd vessel flew along the tyde: ....Od.11.8.379.
Wing'd her fleet sail, and push'd her o'er the tyde. ....Od.12.86.436.
The hawk; *Apollo's* swift-wing'd messenger: ....Od.15.566.97.
He wing'd his voyage to the *Phrygian* shore. ....Od.19.233.204.
Ideas that have wing'd their distant flight: ....Od.19.258.207.
And back triumphant wing'd his airy way. ....Od.19.632.227.
With pomp and joy have wing'd my youthful hours!) ....Od.19.679.229.
Wing'd *Harpies* snatch'd th' unguarded charge away, ...Od.20.92.237.
Th' unbended bow, and arrows wing'd with Fate. ....Od.21.62.262.
And all the wing'd good omens of the skies. ....Od.24.364.366.

WINGED
The winged Courser, like a gen'rous Horse, ...1.EOC.86.249.
From *Teucer's* Hand a winged Arrow flew, ...1.TrES.112.453.
Then *Sleep* and *Death,* two Twins of winged Race, ...1.TrES.344.462.
Thus with spread Sails the winged Gally flies; ....1.TrUl.13.465.
Around, a thousand winged Wonders fly, ...2.TemF.487.287.

WINGED (CONTINUED)

Swift to whose hand a winged volume flies: ....5.DunA3.230.176.
Swift to whose hand a winged volume flies: ....5.DunB3.234.331.
Pierc'd with a winged Shaft (the Deed of *Troy*) ....Il.4.232.232.
Amid the Lungs was fix'd the winged Wood, ...Il.4.612.250.
So spoke he, boastful; but the winged Dart ....Il.5.138.273.
Thy winged Arrows and unerring Bow, ...Il.5.219.278.
To aid her, swift the winged *Iris* flew, ...Il.5.441.289.
Heav'ns golden Gates, kept by the winged Hours; ....Il.5.929.311.
Heav'ns golden Gates, kept by the winged *Hours*, ...Il.8.479.419.
The Prizes purchas'd by their winged Speed) ....Il.9.164.440.
The Prizes purchas'd by their winged Speed) ....Il.9.351.450.
From *Teucer's* Hand a winged Arrow flew; ....Il.12.466.98.
His winged Lance, resistless as the Wind, ...Il.13.706.138.
Of rolling Dust, their winged Wheels employ, ...Il.14.169.165.
The winged *Iris*, and God of Day. ....Il.15.163.202.
The winged Coursers harness'd to the Car. ....Il.16.181.245.
Then *Sleep* and *Death*, two *Twins* of winged Race, ...Il.16.831.275.
Far from *Achilles* wafts the winged Death: ....Il.20.508.415.
Achilles follows like the winged Wind. ....Il.22.182.463.
The winged *Iris* heard the Hero's Call, ...Il.23.244.499.
Haste, winged Goddess! to the sacred Town, ...Il.24.179.543.
Then down her Bow the winged *Iris* drives, ...Il.24.195.544.
His winged Messenger to send from high, ...Il.24.361.551.
The winged Deity forsook their View, ...Il.24.864.572.
Th' aerial space, and mounts the winged gales: ....Od.1.127.38.
To judge the winged Omens of the sky. ....Od.1.262.45.
The winged vessel studious I prepare, ...Od.2.325.77.
He spoke. The God who mounts the winged winds ....Od.5.56.174.
'Till in *Ortygia*, *Dian's* winged dart ....Od.5.157.179.
While from the shores the winged navy flies: ....Od.8.550.292.
While yet I speak the winged gally flies, ...Od.12.200.441.
Thus with spread sails the winged gally flies; ....Od.13.104.6.
The winged Pinnace shot along the sea. ....Od.13.187.15.
Another to the winged son of *May*: ....Od.14.485.59.
Of winged Lies a light fantastic train: ....Od.19.659.228.
Those winged deaths that many a matron wept. ....Od.21.16.259.

WINGS

And all th' Aerial Audience clap their Wings ....1.PSp.16.61.
Shall list'ning in mid Air suspend their Wings, ...1.PWi.54.93.
And mounts exulting on triumphant Wings; ....1.W-F.112.161.
His painted Wings, and Breast that flames with Gold? ....1.W-F.118.161.
(That on weak Wings, from far, pursues your Flights; ....1.EOC.197.263.
(That with weak Wings, from far, pursues your Flights; .....1.EOC.197A.263.
Spread thy soft Wings, and waft me o'er the Main, ...1.TrSP.210.403.
And o'er the *Theban* Palace spreads her Wings, ...1.TrSt.170.417.
Those golden Wings that cut the yielding Skies; ....1.TrSt.430.428.
Wings on the whistling Winds his rapid way, ...1.TrSt.438.428.
Inflames his Heart with Rage, and wings his Feet with Fears. .1.TrSt.519.432.
On golden Wings, the *Phrygian* to the Stars; ....1.TrSt.641.437.
When Night with sable Wings o'erspreads the Ground, ...1.TrSt.711.440.
Levels her Wings, and hov'ring hangs in Air. ....1.TrES.172.455.
Some to the Sun their Insect-Wings unfold, ...2.RL2.59.163.
Colours that change whene'er they wave their Wings. ....2.RL2.68.164.
While clog'd he beats his silken Wings in vain; ....2.RL2.130.168.
A thousand Wings, by turns, blow back the Hair, ...2.RL3.136.178.
Spreads his black Wings, and slowly mounts to Day. ....2.RL4.88.191.
Clapt his glad Wings, and sate to view the Fight; ....2.RL5.54.203.
While purer Slumbers spread their golden Wings) ....2.TemF.8.253.
Wings raise her Arms, and Wings her Feet infold; ....2.TemF.267.276.
Wings raise her Arms, and Wings her Feet infold; ....2.TemF.267.276.
Spreads his light wings, and in a moment flies. ....2.ElAb.76.326.
And wings of Seraphs shed divine perfumes; ....2.ElAb.218.338.
While Angels with their silver wings o'ershade ....2.Elegy.67.367.
Who heaves old Ocean, and who wings the storms, ...3.EOM1.158.35.
Joy tunes his voice, joy elevates his wings: ....3.EOM.3.32.95.
Admires the jay the insect's gilded wings? ....3.EOM.3.55.97.
Shall lend Corruption lighter wings to fly! ....3.Ep3.70A.93.
Now lends Corruption lighter wings to fly! ....3.Ep3.70B.93.
That lends Corruption lighter wings to fly! ....3.Ep3.70.93.
Wait but for wings, and in their season, fly. ....3.Ep3.172.107.
Where Contemplation prunes her ruffled Wings, ...4.JD4.186.41.
Here Contemplation prunes her ruffled Wings, ...4.JD4.186A.41.
There Contemplation prunes her ruffled Wings, ...4.JD4.186B.41.
On morning wings how active springs the Mind, ...4.HS2.81.59.
"And 'tis for that the wanton Boy has Wings." ....4.HAdv.140.87.
On Wings of Winds came flying all abroad? ....4.Arbu.218.111.
Yet let me flap this Bug with gilded wings, ...4.Arbu.309.118.
Taught on the Wings of Truth, to fly ....4.HOde9.3.159.
Estates have wings, and hang in Fortune's pow'r ....4.2HE2.248.183.
Fly then, on all the wings of wild desire! ....4.1HE6.67.241.
Here pleas'd behold her mighty wings out-spread, ...5.DunA1.25.63.
She ceas'd: her owls responsive clap the wings, ...5.DunA1.255A.94.
On feet and wings, and flies, and wades, and hops; ....5.DunA2.60.105.
On legs and wings, and flies and wades, and hops; ....5.DunA2.60A.105.
Dove-like, she gathers to her wings again. ....5.DunA3.118.160.
Wings the red lightning, and the thunder rolls. ....5.DunA3.252.178.
Rolls the loud thunder, and the light'ning wings! ....5.DunA3.252A.178.
Here pleas'd behold her mighty wings out-spread ....5.DunB1.27.271.
On feet and wings, and flies, and wades, and hops; ....5.DunB2.64.299.
Dove-like, she gathers to her wings again. ....5.DunB3.126.325.
Wings the red lightning, and the thunder rolls. ....5.DunB3.256.332.
Poiz'd with a tail, may steer on Wilkins' wings. ....5.DunB4.452.384.
Int'rest, that waves on Party-colour'd wings: ....5.DunB4.538.395.
In those fair beams thy wings display, ...6.6i.5.14.
And clips, like thine, his wav'ring wings. ....6.6i.12.14.
Or Ravenous *Corm'rants* shake their flabby Wings, ...6.26i.6.79.
Lend, lend your wings! I mount! I fly! ....6.31ii.16.94.
Their Souls on Wings of Lightning fly ....6.69ii.4Z1.199.
And little Eagles wave their wings in gold. ....6.71.30.203.
And claps the Brood beneath his Wings. ....6.93.22.257.
"As Children tear the Wings of Flies away; ....6.96ii.16.272.
Which wings the Sun-born Insects of the Air, ...6.96v.2.280.
Here dulness reigns, with mighty wings outspread, ...6.106iv.11.307.
For the fair *Hittite*, when on Seraph's Wings ....6.137.9.373.

WINGS (CONTINUED)

And shining soars and claps her Wings above. ....Il.2.122.133.
Stretch their long Necks, and clap their rustling Wings, ...Il.2.543.153.
Th' extended Wings of Battel to display ....Il.2.667.158.
Speeds on the Wings of Winds thro' liquid Air; ....Il.2.957.169.
Thus from his flaggy Wings when *Notus* sheds ....Il.3.15.188.
His Arms resound, the Spirit wings its way. ....Il.5.56.269.
Thus wings thy Progress from the Realms above? ....Il.7.30.364.
From *Ida's* Top her golden Wings display'd; ....Il.8.503.420.
In Search of Prey she wings the spacious Air, ...Il.9.426.453.
By the shrill Clang and whistling Wings, they knew. ....Il.10.324.17.
The Squadrons spread their sable Wings behind. ....Il.11.66.37.
Iris, with haste thy golden Wings display, ...Il.11.241.46.
On Wings of Winds descends the various Maid. ....Il.11.254.46.
Fate wings its Flight, and Death is on the Steel, ...Il.11.500.56.
The dreary Winter on his frozen Wings; ....Il.12.176.87.
Dark'ning the Rock, while with unweary'd Wings ....Il.12.191.88.
In airy Circles wings his painful way, ...Il.12.238.90.
Ye Vagrants of the Sky! your Wings extend, ...Il.12.279.91.
And seem to walk on Wings, and tread in Air. ....Il.13.106.109.
That bears *Jove's* Thunder on its dreadful Wings, ...Il.13.1000.152.
The Wings of Falcons for thy flying Horse; ....Il.13.1035.153.
On sounding Wings a dexter Eagle flew. ....Il.13.1039.154.
(The Friend of Earth and Heav'n) her Wings display'd; ......Il.14.294.176.
Now to the Navy born on silent Wings, ...Il.14.407.183.
The Wings of Death o'ertook thee on the Dart, ...Il.14.542.189.
And stooping, darkens with his Wings the Flood. ....Il.15.839.229.
He faints; the Soul unwilling wings her way, ...Il.16.1032.283.
(Bold Son of Air and Heat) on angry Wings ....Il.17.644.313.
Lo, where yon' Sails their canvas Wings extend, ...Il.19.366.387.
The wide Air floating to her ample Wings. ....Il.19.373.387.
My Spear, that parted on the Wings of Wind, ...Il.20.394.411.
So, when the Falcon wings her way above, ...Il.21.575.446.
And aims his Claws, and shoots upon his Wings: ....Il.22.188.463.
To the dark Realm the Spirit wings its Way, ...Il.22.455.474.
Since great *Minerva* wings their rapid Way, ...Il.23.485.509.
With flagging Wings alighted on the Mast, ...Il.23.1039.530.
As stooping dexter with resounding Wings ....Il.24.393.552.
And mounts incumbent on the Wings of Winds, ...Il.24.418.553.
And clang their wings, and hovering beat the sky; ....Od.2.176.70.
Now on the wings of winds our course we keep, ...Od.3.189.95.
For wild ambition wings their bold desire, ...Od.4.433.140.
With wings expanded o'er the foaming flood, ...Od.5.65.175.
Incumbent on the wings of wafting gales: ....Od.6.48.207.
To give the feather'd arrow wings to kill, ...Od.6.322.226.
On canvas wings to cut the wat'ry way; ....Od.7.47.235.
On wings of winds with *Rhadamanth* they flew: ....Od.7.414.257.
Swift as on wings of winds upborn they fly, ...Od.8.127.269.
To give the feather'd arrow wings to kill; ....Od.8.248.275.
We rear the masts, we spread the canvas wings; ....Od.9.86.306.
And pendent round it clasps his leathern wings. ....Od.12.514.457.
Who wings the winds, and darkens heav'n with showr's) ......Od.13.30.2.
To give the feather'd arrow wings to kill. ....Od.18.306.181.
And bears thy fate, *Antinous*, on its wings: ....Od.22.12.287.
And level pois'd the wings of Victory: ....Od.22.260.299.
The doves or thrushes flap their wings in air. ....Od.22.506.313.
A sudden youth, and give her wings to fly. ....Od.23.4.318.

WINK

Sudden, she storms! she raves! You tip the wink, ...3.Ep2.33.52.
And for my Soul I cannot sleep a wink. ....4.HS1.12.5.

WINNER

Be ev'ry birth-day more a winner, ...6.150.17.399.

WINNING

Seem'd to her Ear his winning Lips to lay, ...2.RL1.25.147.
What winning Graces! what majestick Mien! ....Il.3.207.201.
Than winning Words and heav'nly Eloquence. ....Il.15.323.209.
Thy sweet Society, thy winning Care, ...Il.19.337.386.
Why thus in silence? why with winning charms ....Od.23.101.324.

WINNINGTON

Veracious W[innington] and frontless Young; ....4.1740.54.334.

WINS

And wins (oh shameful Chance!) the *Queen* of *Hearts*. ....2.RL3.88.174.
Charms strike the Sight, but Merit wins the Soul. ....2.RL5.34.201.
Noble and young, who wins the heart ....4.HOde1.11A.151.
"He wins this Patron who can tickle best." ....5.DunA2.188.124.
"He wins this Patron, who can tickle best." ....5.DunB2.196.305.
Greece, if she conquers, nothing wins from me. ....Il.5.588.296.
Offending Man their high Compassion wins, ...Il.9.622.465.
At length the sov'reign Savage wins the Strife, ...Il.16.997.281.
War knows no mean: he wins it, or he dies. ....Il.17.573.311.
And 'tis the Artist wins the glorious Course, ...Il.23.389.506.
Unblest the man, whom music wins to stay ....Od.12.53.432.

WINTER

While in thy Heart Eternal Winter reigns. ....1.PSu.22.73.
Which summer suns, and winter frosts expel. ....1.TrPA.69.368.
Of a stale Virgin with a Winter Face; ....2.ChJM.104.19.
Like Winter Greens, that flourish all the Year. ....2.ChJM.136.21.
The gather'd Winter of a thousand Years. ....2.TemF.60.256.
As Winter-fruits grow mild e'er they decay? ....4.2HE2.319.187.
'Tis true, but Winter comes apace. ....4.1HE7.16.269.
And write next winter more *Essays on Man*. ....4.EpS2.255.327.
As for the rest, each winter up they run, ...4.1740.29.333.
In winter fire. ....6.1.8.3.
Where *Summer's* beauty midst of *Winter* stays, ...6.14iv.29.48.
But just endur'd the Winter she began, ...6.49i.23.138.
From dusky Clowds the fleecy Winter flyes, ...6.82v.3.231.
Swift as the Wind, and white as Winter-Snow: ....Il.10.507.26.
Swift as the Wind, and white as Winter-Snow. ....Il.10.601.29.
The dreary Winter on his frozen Wings; ....Il.12.176.87.
From dusky Clouds the fleecy Winter flies, ...Il.19.382.388.

WINTER (CONTINUED)

Like Crystal clear, and cold as Winter-Snows.	Il.22.200.463.
Stern winter smiles on that auspicious clime:	Od.4.769.155.
Ev'n when keen winter freezes in the skies,	Od.11.230.393.
The winter pinches, and with cold I die,	Od.14.548.63.

WINTER-FRUITS

As Winter-fruits grow mild e'er they decay?	4.2HE2.319.187.

WINTER-SNOW

Swift as the Wind, and white as Winter-Snow:	Il.10.507.26.
Swift as the Wind, and white as Winter-Snow.	Il.10.601.29.

WINTER-SNOWS

Like Crystal clear, and cold as Winter-Snows.	Il.22.200.463.

WINTER'S

More sweet than winter's sun, or summer's air,	1.TrPA.54.367.
The Winter's past, the Clouds and Tempests fly,	2.ChJM.529.41.
It chanc'd my Husband on a Winter's Night	2.ChWB.377.75.
And Winter's Coolness spite of Summer's rays.	6.14iv.30.48.
In Winter's bleak, uncomfortable Reign,	Il.12.333.93.
Where three at least might winter's cold defy,	Od.5.626.201.
Some friend would fence me from the winter's rage.	Od.14.571.64.
Nor winter's boreal blast, nor thund'rous show'r,	Od.19.513.221.

WINTERS

So when inclement Winters vex the Plain	Il.3.5.188.
The wond'rous youths had scarce nine winters told,	Od.11.381.401.
As some fond sire who ten long winters grieves,	Od.16.17.102.
Whose footsteps twenty winters have defac'd:	Od.19.260.207.
Thy son, with twenty winters now grown old;	Od.24.376.367.

WINTERS'

Of twenty Winters' Age he seem'd to be;	2.ChWB.317.72.

WINTON

Yea, moral Ebor, or religious Winton.	4.1740.58.335.
Eton and Winton shake thro' all their Sons.	5.DunB4.144.355.

WINTRY

Or brew fierce Tempests on the wintry Main,	2.RL2.85.165.
And, one short Month, endure the Wintry Main?	Il.2.357.144.
And high Enispè shook by wintry Wind,	Il.2.738.161.
In dread Array, from Thracia's wintry Coasts;	Il.2.1023.171.
Or trembling Sailors on the wintry Main)	Il.4.104.225.
As when a Torrent, swell'd with wintry Rains,	Il.11.614.61.
'Twas where by Force of wintry Torrents torn,	Il.23.499.510.
Proof to the wintry Winds and howling Storms,	Il.23.827.522.
Beat by rude blasts, and wet with wintry show'rs,	Od.6.154.216.
Or wretched hunters thro' the wintry cold	Od.9.138.311.
For, elemental war, and wintry Jove,	Od.19.216.204.
Forc'd a long month the wintry seas to bear,	Od.24.142.354.

WINY

A winy vapour melting in a tear.	Od.19.143.199.

WIP'D

And as they fell, she wip'd from either Eye	2.ChJM.785.52.
Who took it patiently, and wip'd his Head;	2.ChWB.391.76.
All Tears are wip'd for ever from all Eyes;	4.EpS1.102.305.
She sobb'd a Storm, and wip'd her flowing Eyes,	6.96ii.73.273.
From his vile Visage wip'd the scalding Tears.	Il.2.331.143.
This said, she wip'd from Venus' wounded Palm	Il.5.505.292.

WIPE

To wipe those hundred Eyes—	6.9x.4.22.
Made William's Virtues wipe the bare A——	6.101.5.290.
And hopes, thy Deeds shall wipe the Stain away.	Il.6.673.360.
There safe, they wipe the briny Drops away,	Il.22.3.452.
From their tir'd Bodies wipe the Dust away,	Il.23.861.523.
To wipe the tears from all afflicted eyes,	Od.17.14.133.

WIPES

From ev'ry Face he wipes off ev'ry Tear.	1.Mes.46.117.
He wipes the Tears for ever from our Eyes.	1.Mes.45Z2.117.
The tear she wipes, and thus renews her woes.	Od.18.236.178.

WIRE

Whose hand reluctant touch'd the warbling wire:	Od.1.198.42.
Long as the minstrel swept the sounding wire,	Od.17.430.153.
Or the dumb lute refits with vocal wire,	Od.21.443.281.
This hand reluctant touch'd the warbling wire:	Od.22.390.307.

WISDOM

A Man, in Wisdom equal to a God.	1.TrUl.16.466.
Goddess of Wisdom! (Ithacus replies)	1.TrUl.188.472.
And guard the Wisdom which her self inspires.	1.TrUl.212.472.
And cautious sure; for Wisdom is in Age:	2.ChJM.207.24.
To dear-bought Wisdom give the Credit due,	2.ChWB.3.57.
That Wisdom infinite must form the best,	3.EOM1.44.19.
Go, teach Eternal Wisdom how to rule—	3.EOM2.29.59.
Admir'd such wisdom in an earthly shape,	3.EOM2.33.60.
To written Wisdom, as another's, less:	3.Ep1.13.16.
Old Politicians chew on wisdom past,	3.Ep1.248.37.
Wisdom (curse on it) will come soon or late.	4.2HE2.199.179.
And the first Wisdom, to be Fool no more.	4.1HE1.66.283.
Here, Wisdom calls: "Seek Virtue first! be bold!	4.1HE1.77.285.
That Man divine whom Wisdom calls her own;	4.1HE1.180.293.
While Truth, Worth, Wisdom, daily they decry—	4.EpS1.169.309.
While Truth, Worth, Wisdom, daily we decry—	4.EpS1.169A.309.
The wisdom of the one and other chair,	4.1740.60.335.
And 'tis in thee at last that Wisdom seeks for Rest.	6.8.24.18.
At ought thy Wisdom has deny'd,	6.50.35.148.
Wisdom and wit in vain reclaim,	6.51ii.3.152.
Learning not vain, and wisdom not severe	6.75.7.212.

WISDOM (CONTINUED)

Of modest wisdom, and pacifick truth:	6.109.2.313.
His Anger moral, and his Wisdom gay.	6.118.6.334.
For I must speak what Wisdom would conceal,	Il.1.101.92.
Nor think your Nestor's Years and Wisdom vain.	Il.1.344.105.
Renown'd for Wisdom, and rever'd for Age;	Il.2.22.128.
Warriors like you, with Strength and Wisdom blest,	Il.2.227.138.
To hear the Wisdom of his heav'nly Tongue.	Il.2.345.143.
Such Wisdom soon should Priam's Force destroy,	Il.2.444.148.
A Chief, in Wisdom equal to a God.	Il.2.766.162.
His Fame for Wisdom fills the spacious Earth.	Il.3.264.204.
These Years with Wisdom crowns, with Action those:	Il.4.375.239.
Æolian Sisyphus, with Wisdom blest,	Il.6.191.335.
Endu'd with Wisdom, sacred Fear, and Truth.	Il.6.204.336.
Oh Peleus, old in Arms, in Wisdom old!	Il.7.150.372.
But Wisdom has its Date, assign'd by Heav'n.	Il.7.435.386.
At length his Best-belov'd, the Pow'r of Wisdom, spoke.	Il.8.38.397.
Oh had my Wisdom known this dire Event,	Il.8.445.418.
Those wholsome Counsels which thy Wisdom moves,	Il.9.77.436.
Then Nestor spoke, for Wisdom long approv'd,	Il.9.125.438.
But follow it, and make the Wisdom thine.	Il.9.138.438.
And early Wisdom to thy Soul convey'd:	Il.9.605.464.
But asks high Wisdom, deep Design, and Art.	Il.10.52.4.
Wise as thou art, be now thy Wisdom try'd:	Il.10.163.9.
Wisdom like his might pass thro' Flames of Fire.	Il.10.290.15.
Greece, as the Prize of Nestor's Wisdom, gave)	Il.11.767.69.
Against his Wisdom to oppose her Charms,	Il.14.189.168.
'Tis now no time for Wisdom or Debates;	Il.15.602.220.
In Wisdom great, in Arms well known to Fame:	Il.15.771.226.
Thy Words give Joy, and Wisdom breathes in thee.	Il.19.184.379.
But old Experience and calm Wisdom, mine.	Il.19.218.382.
Ill suits the Wisdom of celestial Mind:	Il.21.536.444.
The Praise of Wisdom, in thy Youth obtain'd,	Il.23.651.515.
The dire restraint his wisdom will defeat,	Od.1.265.45.
The hoary Peers, and Aged Wisdom bow'd.	Od.2.18.61.
And more than woman with deep wisdom crown'd;	Od.2.136.67.
Not first, the Pow'r of Wisdom march'd before,	Od.3.16.87.
And sure he will: For Wisdom never lies.	Od.3.26.87.
But when (by wisdom won) proud Ilion burn'd,	Od.3.159.93.
What cannot Wisdom do? Thou may'st restore	Od.5.34.172.
Oh sprung from Gods! in wisdom more than man.	Od.5.258.184.
What I suggest thy wisdom will perform;	Od.5.434.193.
But fearful to offend, my wisdom sway'd,	Od.6.173.216.
But hear, tho' wisdom in thy soul presides,	Od.6.307.225.
In youth and beauty wisdom is but rare!	Od.7.379.254.
But wisdom the defect of form supplies:	Od.8.188.272.
Earth sounds my wisdom, and high heav'n my fame.	Od.9.20.302.
To draw the sword; but Wisdom held my hand.	Od.9.359.321.
Mature in wisdom rose: Your words, he cries,	Od.11.430.405.
Then from a wretched friend this wisdom learn,	Od.11.561.411.
Truth I revere: For Wisdom never lies.	Od.11.572.411.
The wars and wisdom of thy gallant son:	Od.11.618.414.
The third in wisdom where they all were wise;	Od.11.626.414.
Approach! and learn new wisdom from the wise.	Od.12.227.443.
O stay, and learn new wisdom from the wise!	Od.12.231.443.
Constrain'd I act what wisdom bids me shun.	Od.12.354.448.
A Man, in wisdom equal to a God!	Od.13.107.6.
Goddess of Wisdom! Ithacus replies,	Od.13.355.24.
And guard the wisdom which her self inspires.	Od.13.379.25.
Thy well-try'd wisdom, and thy martial fame,	Od.16.263.117.
Soft were his words; his actions wisdom sway'd;	Od.16.414.126.
Renown'd for wisdom, by th' abuse accurst!	Od.16.435.128.
Or were he dead, 'tis wisdom to beware:	Od.19.105.197.
Firm wisdom interdicts the soft'ning tear.	Od.19.250.206.
Upbraids thy pow'r, thy wisdom, or thy will:	Od.20.258.245.
And Folly, with the tongue of Wisdom speaks.	Od.23.18.319.
For Wisdom all is thine! lo I obey,	Od.23.125.326.
Not more thy wisdom, than her virtue, shin'd;	Od.24.220.358.

WISDOM'S

But Wisdom's Triumph is well-tim'd Retreat,	3.Ep2.225.68.
In Folly's Cap, than Wisdom's grave disguise.	5.DunB4.240.366.
The Man, for Wisdom's various arts renown'd,	Od.1.1.25.
Since Wisdom's sacred guidance he pursues,	Od.8.423.286.
The man, for Wisdom's various arts renown'd.	Od.10.394.363.
For wicked ears are deaf to wisdom's call,	Od.16.300.120.

WISE

You, that too wise for Pride, too Good for Pow'r,	1.PSp.7.61.
Attends the Duties of the Wise and Good,	1.W-F.250.172.
We think our Fathers Fools, so wise we grow;	1.EOC.438.288.
Fear not the Anger of the Wise to raise;	1.EOC.582.306.
Whom Age and long Experience render wise,	1.TrVP.78.380.
When lo! the Guardian Goddess of the Wise,	1.TrUl.100.469.
He who discerns thee must be truly wise,	1.TrUl.189.472.
How prone to Doubt, how cautious are the Wise?	1.TrUl.208.472.
In Days of old, a wise and worthy Knight;	2.ChJM.2.15.
Let not the Wise these slandrous Words regard,	2.ChJM.49.17.
All things wou'd prosper, all the World grow wise.	2.ChJM.68.18.
To the wise Conduct of a prudent Wife:	2.ChJM.72.18.
Those are too wise for Batchelors to wed;	2.ChJM.108.19.
Each wondrous positive, and wondrous wise;	2.ChJM.144.21.
Th'assuming Wit, who deems himself so wise	2.ChJM.162.22.
Most worthy Kinsman, faith, you're mighty wise!	2.ChJM.217.25.
Young, beauteous, artless, innocent and wise;	2.ChJM.259.27.
Argus himself, so cautious and so wise,	2.ChJM.505.39.
'Till their wise Husbands, gull'd by Arts like these,	2.ChJM.667.47.
Let all wise Husbands hence Example take;	2.ChJM.818.54.
'Tis but their Sylph, the wise Celestials know,	2.RL1.77.151.
Coffee, (which makes the Politician wise,	2.RL3.117.176.
The wise Man's Passion, and the vain Man's Toast?	2.RL5.10.199.
And wise Aurelius, in whose well-taught Mind	2.TemF.165.268.
Here too the Wise and Good their Honours claim,	2.TemF.168A.268.
Blame we for this the wise Almighty Cause?	3.EOM1.145A.33.
As Men for ever temp'rate, calm, and wise.	3.EOM1.154.34.
Who finds not Providence all good and wise,	3.EOM1.205.40.

WISE (CONTINUED)

A being darkly wise, and rudely great: 3.EOM2.4.53.
The rogue and fool by fits is fair and wise, 3.EOM2.233.83.
'Tis this, Tho' Man's a fool, yet GOD IS WISE. 3.EOM2.294.90.
"Laws wise as Nature, and as fix'd as Fate. 3.EOM3.190.112.
O'er-look'd, seen double, by the fool, and wise. 3.EOM4.6.128.
More rich, more wise; but who infers from hence 3.EOM4.51.133.
I'll tell you, friend! a Wise man and a Fool. 3.EOM4.200.145.
"Where, but among the Heroes and the Wise?" 3.EOM4.218.147.
No less alike the Politic and Wise, 3.EOM4.225.148.
Not that themselves are wise, but others weak. 3.EOM4.228.148.
Who wickedly is wise, or madly brave, 3.EOM4.231.148.
Nor that themselves are wise, but others weak. 3.EOM4.228A.148.
Tell (for You can) what is it to be wise? 3.EOM4.260.152.
Wise is her present; she connects in this 3.EOM4.349.162.
Wise is the present; she connects in this 3.EOM4.349A.162.
Teach me, like thee, in various nature wise, 3.EOM4.377.165.
Who reasons wisely is not therefore wise, 3.Ep1.69.20.
Wise, if a Minister; but, if a King, 3.Ep1.91.22.
More wise, more learn'd, more just, more ev'rything. 3.Ep1.92.22.
Unthought-of Frailties cheat us in the Wise, 3.Ep1.128.25.
Mad at a Fox-chace, wise at a Debate; 3.Ep1.133.25.
Born with whate'er could win it from the Wise, 3.Ep1.182.30.
Wise Fool! with Pleasures too refin'd to please, 3.Ep2.95A.57.
Wise Wretch! of Pleasures too refin'd to please, 3.Ep2.95B.57.
Less Wit than Mimic, more a Wit than wise: 3.Ep2.48.54.
Wise Wretch! with Pleasures too refin'd to please, 3.Ep2.95.57.
Cloe is prudent—would you too be wise? 3.Ep2.179.64.
They might (were Harpax not too wise to spend) 3.Ep3.93.97.
Wise Peter sees the World's respect for Gold, 3.Ep3.125.102.
Scarce to wise *Peter* complaisant enough, 4.HS1.3.5.
And the wise Justice starting from his chair 4.JD4.36.29.
Than mine, to find a Subject staid and wise, 4.JD4.168.39.
But strong in sense, and wise without the rules. 4.HS2.10.55.
Or whose wise forecast and preventing care 4.HS2.127A.65.
Our ancient Kings (and sure those Kings were wise, 4.HAdv.112.85.
By Nature honest, by Experience wise, 4.Arbu.400.126.
But let the Fit pass o'er, I'm wise enough, 4.2HE2.151.175.
Words, that wise *Bacon*, or brave *Raleigh* spake; 4.2HE2.168.177.
Such as wise *Bacon*, or brave *Raleigh* spake; 4.2HE2.168A.177.
And much too wise to walk into a Well: 4.2HE2.191.179.
A wise man always is or should 4.1HE7.35.271.
The eldest is a fool, the youngest wise; 4.1HE1.44.281.
I study'd SHREWSBURY, the wise and great: 4.EpS2.79.317.
Let him be honest, and he must be wise, 4.1740.86.337.
Oh worthy thou of Ægypt's wise abodes, 5.DunA3.203.175.
Oh worthy thou of Ægypt's wise abodes, 5.DunB3.207.330.
From foolish Greeks to steal them, was as wise; 5.DunB4.378.380.
Thou Varnisher of *Fools*, and Cheat of all the *Wise*. 6.8.21.18.
When wise *Ulysses*, from his native coast 6.15.1.51.
The Wise, the Learn'd, the Virtuous, and the Brave; 6.27.8.81.
In woful wise did sore affright 6.58.15.171.
Lean and fretful; would seem wise; 6.70.8.201.
The sober Follies of the Wise and Great; 6.84.10.238.
(Right wary He and wise) 6.94.22.259.
The World's the native City of the Wise; 6.96v.21.280.
Sylvia my Heart in wond'rous wise alarm'd, 6.99.1.286.
More pert than witty, more a Wit than wise. 6.99.6.286.
"Do something exquisite, and wise—" 6.119.7.336.
"Do something very fine, and wise—" 6.119.7A.336.
Cloë is prudent—would you too be wise? 6.139.23.377.
And 'tis a wise design on pitying heav'n, 6.146.6.389.
Our ancient kings (and sure those kings were wise) 6.147i.1.390.
Calchas the wise, the *Grecian* Priest and Guide, Il.1.92.91.
Bold is the Task, when Subjects grown too wise Il.1.103.92.
Or wise *Ulysses* see perform'd our Will, Il.1.188.96.
Wise by his Rules, and happy by his Sway; Il.1.334.104.
If, in my Youth, ev'n these esteem'd me wise, Il.1.360.105.
Thy Years are awful, and thy Words are wise. Il.1.377.106.
Avenge this Wrong, oh ever just and wise! Il.1.658.118.
Then wise *Ulysses* in his Rank was plac'd; Il.2.484.150.
Cool Age advances venerably wise, Il.3.149.198.
But Wise thro' Time, and Narrative with Age, Il.3.200.200.
Have singled out, is *Ithacus* the Wise: Il.3.262.204.
Oh great in Action, and in Council wise! Il.4.411.240.
And *Leucus*, lov'd by wise *Ulysses*, slew. Il.4.564.248.
Sons of *Eurydamas*, who wise and old, Il.5.190.275.
O Son of *Tydeus*, cease! be wise and see Il.5.533.294.
Wise to consult, and active to defend! Il.6.98.328.
And wise *Ulysses* clos'd the daring Band. Il.7.204.374.
Thy Years are awful, and thy Words are wise. Il.8.178.406.
Wise *Nestor* then his Rev'rend Figure rear'd; Il.9.71.435.
Wise, weighty Counsels aid a State distrest, Il.9.101.437.
Wise *Nestor* turns on each his careful Eye, Il.9.233.444.
Sure ev'ry wise and worthy Man will love. Il.9.451.454.
The Gods (the only great, and only wise) Il.9.620.465.
And the wise Counsels of th' eternal Mind? Il.10.117.7.
Wise as thou art, be now thy Wisdom try'd: Il.10.163.9.
The Wise new Prudence from the Wise acquire, Il.10.267.13.
The Wise new Prudence from the Wise acquire, Il.10.267.13.
To whom *Ulysses* made this wise Reply; Il.10.453.23.
There wise *Polydamas* and *Hector* stood; Il.11.75.38.
But wise *Ulysses* call'd *Tydides* forth, Il.11.405.52.
Socus, the brave, the gen'rous, and the wise: Il.11.538.57.
The Wound not mortal wise *Ulysses* knew, Il.11.551.58.
A wise Physician, skill'd our Wounds to heal, Il.11.636.62.
Th' Advice of wise *Polydamas* obey'd; Il.12.124.85.
And more than Men, or Gods, supremely wise, Il.13.448.127.
Above the Thought of Man, supremely wise! Il.13.790.142.
A wise, extensive, all-consid'ring Mind; Il.13.918.148.
Like Arrows pierce me, for thy Words are wise. Il.14.115.163.
Th' all-wise Disposer of the Fates of Men, Il.15.541.217.
And wise *Ulysses*, at the Navy groan Il.16.36.236.
In Action valiant, and in Council wise, Il.16.664.270.
Fools stay to feel it, and are wise too late. Il.17.36.289.
O full of Days! by long Experience wise! Il.17.631.312.

WISE (CONTINUED)

One wise in Council, one in Action brave.) Il.18.298.336.
The great in Councils, *Ithacus* the Wise. Il.19.154.378.
All good, all-wise, and all-surveying *Jove!* Il.19.268.383.
Fools stay to feel it, and are wise too late. Il.20.239.404.
That wise Advice rejected with Disdain, Il.22.144.459.
And to be swift is less than to be wise: Il.23.384.505.
He to *Ulysses*, still more ag'd and wise; Il.23.928.526.
The suffering virtue of the wise and brave? Od.1.79.35.
That wise *Ulysses* to his native land Od.1.108.36.
From great *Anchialus*, renown'd and wise: Od.1.228.43.
Have charms, with all their weight, t'allure the wise. Od.1.496.56.
With dear esteem: to wise, with jealous strife Od.1.545.58.
The present Synod speaks its author wise; Od.2.41.62.
And wastes the wise frugality of Kings. Od.2.62.63.
Success; and humbles, or confirms the wise) Od.2.76.64.
With thy wise dreams, and fables of the sky. Od.2.208.72.
O Prince, in early youth divinely wise, Od.2.307.76.
Were not wise sons descendent of the wise, Od.2.313.76.
Were not wise sons descendent of the wise, Od.2.313.76.
For never, never, wicked man was wise. Od.2.320.76.
But now the wise instructions of the sage, Od.2.353.78.
Fast by the door the wise *Euryclea* waits; Od.2.391.80.
The Youth, whom *Pallas* destin'd to be wise, Od.3.92.90.
The wise, the good *Ulysses* claim'd thy care; Od.3.119.91.
There wise *Patroclus*, fill an early grave: Od.3.134.92.
So like your voices, and your words so wise, Od.3.153.93.
Wise as he was, by various Counsels sway'd, Od.3.197.95.
And sure he will, for *Menelas* is wise. Od.3.420.107.
Wise are thy words, and just are all thy ways. Od.3.424.107.
Belov'd old man! benevolent as wise. Od.3.456.109.
Too long, mis-judging, have I thought thee wise: Od.4.38.122.
The genuine worth of *Ithacus* the wise! Od.4.210.129.
Wise to resolve, and patient to perform. Od.4.372.137.
Frail is the boasted attribute of wise: Od.4.396.139.
Thy conduct ill deserves the praise of wise: Od.4.502.144.
O early worth! a soul so wise, and young, Od.4.831.158.
Of wise *Ulysses*, and his toils relates; Od.5.9.171.
How prone to doubt, how cautious are the wise? Od.5.237.182.
And wise *Alcinous* held the regal sway. Od.6.18.204.
Wise is thy soul, but man is born to bear: Od.6.228.220.
Thus to the Lyrist wise *Ulysses* said. Od.8.530.291.
His are the gifts of love: The wise and good Od.8.593.294.
Ulysses, taught by labours to be wise, Od.10.540.369.
What heav'n ordains the wise with courage bear. Od.11.173.390.
Demand obedience, for your words are wise. Od.11.431.405.
Wise is thy voice, and noble is thy heart. Od.11.455.407.
Nor trust the sex that is so rarely wise; Od.11.546.410.
The third in wisdom where they all were wise; Od.11.626.414.
These seas o'erpass'd, be wise! but I refrain Od.12.67.433.
To live, or perish! to be safe, be wise! Od.12.193.441.
Approach! and learn new wisdom from the wise. Od.12.227.443.
O stay, and learn new wisdom from the wise! Od.12.231.443.
O friends be wise! nor dare the flocks destroy Od.12.381.449.
When lo! the guardian Goddess of the wise, Od.13.267.18.
He who discerns thee must be truely wise, Od.13.356.24.
How prone to doubt, how cautious are the wise! Od.13.375.25.
They led me to a good man and a wise; Od.14.392.54.
And wine can of their wits the wise beguile, Od.14.520.62.
The people's Saviour, and divinely wise, Od.15.269.81.
The brave and wise, and my great father's fame. Od.16.333.122.
Is he not wise? know this, and strike the blow. Od.16.389.124.
His ev'ry step and ev'ry thought is wise. Od.17.665.164.
Of hospitality, for they are wise. Od.18.73.170.
The tongue speaks wisely, when the soul is wise; Od.18.152.173.
O wise alone in form, and brave in show! Od.18.262.179.
O justly lov'd, and not more fair than wise! Od.18.286.180.
Offspring of Kings, and more than woman wise! Od.18.330.183.
Tutor'd by early woes, grow early wise! Od.19.24.193.
But your wise Lord, (in whose capacious soul Od.19.325.210.
Pleas'd with his wise reply, the Queen rejoin'd: Od.19.403.214.
From the wise Chief he waits the deathful word. Od.20.462.255.
But first the wise-man ceas'd, and thus begun. Od.21.241.271.
The weak enlighten and confound the wise; Od.23.14.319.
Wise is thy soul, but errors seize the wise; Od.23.82.322.
Wise is thy soul, but errors seize the wise; Od.23.82.322.
Indulge, my son, the cautions of the wise; Od.23.114.325.
The world conspires to speak *Ulysses* wise; Od.23.124.326.
But hear, tho' wise! This morning shall unfold Od.23.389.343.
A friend I seek, a wise one and a brave, Od.24.312.364.
(Rev'rend and wise, whose comprehensive view Od.24.518.373.

WISE-MAN

But first the wise-man ceas'd, and thus begun. Od.21.241.271.

WISELY

And wisely curb'd proud Man's pretending Wit: 1.EOC.53.245.
Who wisely weds in his maturer Years. 2.ChJM.24.16.
There goes a Saying, and 'twas wisely said, 2.ChJM.101A.19.
Who, wisely, never thinks the Case his own. 2.ChJM.507.40.
We just as wisely might of Heav'n complain, 3.EOM4.117.139.
Who reasons wisely is not therefore wise, 3.Ep1.69.20.
And Swift cry wisely, "Vive la Bagatelle!" 4.1HE6.128.246.
Then wisely plead, to me they meant no hurt, 4.EpS2.144.321.
With what it wisely, will not hear: 6.10.24.25.
Thus wisely careless, innocently gay, 6.19.11.62.
Safe to the Ships, he wisely clear'd the way, Il.10.573.28.
This saw *Polydamas;* who, wisely brave, Il.12.67.83.
Wisely and well, my Son, thy Words have prov'd Il.23.719.518.
To question wisely men of riper years. Od.3.32.87.
The tongue speaks wisely, when the soul is wise; Od.18.152.173.

WISEMAN'S

But, with the Wiseman's Leave, I must protest, 2.ChJM.153.22.

WISER
(For wiser Brutes were backward to be Slaves.) ... 1.W-F.50.153.
Ask them the Cause; *They're wiser still,* they say; ... 1.EOC.436.288.
And still to Morrow's wiser than to Day. ... 1.EOC.437.288.
Our *wiser Sons,* no doubt, will think *us* so. ... 1.EOC.439.288.
And many Heads are wiser still than one; ... 2.ChJM.96.19.
A wiser Monarch never saw the Sun: ... 2.ChJM.632.45.
The wiser Wits of later Times declare ... 2.ChJM.671.47.
Go, wiser thou! and in thy scale of sense ... 3.EOM1.113.29.
"Thus let the wiser make the rest obey, ... 3.EOM3.196.113.
But Satan now is wiser than of yore, ... 3.Ep3.351.122.
And last (which proves him wiser still than all) ... 4.JD4.150.37.
Why should not we be wiser than our Sires? ... 4.2HE1.44.197.
Which is the happier, or the wiser, ... 4.HS6.147.259.
And by their wiser Morals mend your own. ... 6.96iii.18.275.
And warn the *Greeks* the wiser Choice to make: ... Il.9.539.460.
Not but (my Friend) 'tis still the wiser way ... Il.23.689.517.
Why with our wiser Elders should we strive? ... Il.23.925.526.

WISEST
Or else the Wisest of Mankind's bely'd. ... 2.ChWB.22.57.
The wisest, brightest, meanest of mankind: ... 3.EOM4.282.154.
Yet, in the search, the wisest may mistake, ... 3.Ep1.210A.33.
And just her wisest monarch made a fool? ... 3.Ep1.153.28.
Yet, in this search, the wisest may mistake, ... 3.Ep1.210.33.
The wisest Fool that Time has ever made. ... 3.Ep2.124A.60.
The wisest Fool much Time has ever made. ... 3.Ep2.124.60.
The wisest Man might blush, I must agree, ... 4.2HE2.228.181.
The wisest Man deceive. ... 6.94.4.259.
The wisest Fool much Time has ever made: ... 6.154.10.403.
And next the wisest of the Rev'rend Throng, ... Il.3.196.200.
(For Rage invades the wisest and the best.) ... Il.9.668.467.
To win the wisest, and the coldest warm: ... Il.14.248.173.
I deem'd thee once the wisest of thy Kind, ... Il.17.191.294.
Of humane race the wisest, and the best. ... Od.1.87.35.
(Thus quick reply'd the wisest of mankind) ... Od.14.432.56.
And die asham'd (oh wisest of mankind) ... Od.14.549.63.
But re-consider, since the wisest err, ... Od.16.334.122.
(In woes bewilder'd, oft the wisest errs.) ... Od.20.166.241.
O fair! and wisest of so fair a kind! ... Od.21.345.276.

WISH
Give them to dare, what I might wish to see, ... 1.TrSt.118.415.
As long as Heart can wish—and longer too. ... 2.ChJM.58.17.
Not ev'n in Wish, your Happiness delay, ... 2.ChJM.287.28.
The virgin's wish without her fears impart, ... 2.ElAb.55.323.
And each warm wish springs mutual from the heart. ... 2.ElAb.96.327.
Each pray'r accepted, and each wish resign'd; ... 2.ElAb.210.337.
How would he wish that Heav'n had left him still ... 3.EOM1.203.40.
With the same trash mad mortals wish for here? ... 3.EOM4.174.144.
Since but to wish more Virtue, is to gain. ... 3.EOM4.326.160.
"What all so wish, but want the pow'r to do! ... 3.Ep3,276.116.
You'll wish your hill or shelter'd seat again. ... 3.Ep4.76.144.
You'll wish your Hill, and shelter'd seat again. ... 3.Ep4.76A.144.
My Foes shall wish my Life a longer date, ... 4.HS1.61.11.
But wish you lik'd Retreat a little less; ... 4.JD4.87A.33.
"I wish to God this house had been your own: ... 4.HS2.162.67.
Well, I cou'd wish that still in Richmens Homes ... 4.JD2A.121.142.
What further could I wish the Fop to do, ... 4.JD2.53.137.
Well, I could wish, that still in lordly domes ... 4.JD2.115.143.
I wish you joy, Sir, of a Tyrant gone; ... 4.2HE2.305.187.
Patriots there are, who wish you'd jest no more— ... 4.EpS1.24.299.
The Maid's romantic wish, the Chymist's flame, ... 5.DunA3.11.150.
The Maid's romantic wish, the Chemist's flame, ... 5.DunB3.11.320.
Happy the man, whose wish and care ... 6.1.1.3.
I wish you do not turn *Socinian;* ... 6.10.80.27.
How much I wish you Health and Happiness; ... 6.13.11.39.
Well might you wish for Change, by those accurst, ... 6.19.39.63.
Who hears him groan, and does not wish to bleed? ... 6.32.26.96.
I wish the Man a Dinner, and sit still; ... 6.49iii.2.142.
I wish the Wretch a Dinner, and sit still; ... 6.49iii.2A.142.
I wish the Man a Dinner, and stand still; ... 6.49iii.2B.142.
United wish, and mutual joy! ... 6.51ii.26.153.
And reading wish, like theirs, our fate and fame, ... 6.52.9.156.
Finds not one moment he cou'd wish away, ... 6.55.6.166.
Here learn to live; nor wish, nor fear to die. ... 6.56.6.168.
Nor wish to lose a Foe these Virtues raise; ... 6.73.11.210.
I wish the Man a Dinner, and sit still. ... 6.98.2.283.
Who knew no wish but what the world might hear: ... 6.109.6.314.
Few words are best; I wish you well: ... 6.114.1.321.
Is there on earth one Care, one Wish beside? ... 6.123.7.344.
And eye the Mine without a Wish for Gold. ... 6.142.8.382.
And view the Mine without a Wish for Gold. ... 6.142.8A.382.
I half could wish this people might be sav'd. ... 6.146.4.389.
I half could wish this people should be sav'd. ... 6.146.4A.389.
Has Cause to wish himself translated. ... 6.151.2.399.
Oh might a Parent's careful Wish prevail, ... Il.1.546.114.
Few Leagues remov'd, we wish our peaceful Seat, ... Il.2.358.144.
Whom *Greece* at length shall wish, nor wish in vain. ... Il.2.881.165.
Whom *Greece* at length shall wish, nor wish in vain. ... Il.2.881.165.
No Wish can gain 'em, but the Gods bestow. ... Il.3.96.194.
Well might I wish, could Mortal Wish renew ... Il.4.370.238.
Well might I wish, could Mortal Wish renew ... Il.4.370.238.
With ample Wealth (the Wish of Mortals) blest, ... Il.5.585.296.
Fulfill thy Wish, their whole Intention know, ... Il.10.384.21.
'Tis but the Wish to strike before the rest. ... Il.13.371.123.
Ev'n thou shalt wish, to aid thy desp'rate Course, ... Il.13.1034.153.
Take this, and with it all thy Wish, she said: ... Il.14.254.173.
Fullfil our wish, and let thy glory shine ... Od.3.70.89.
Such to our wish the warrior soon restore, ... Od.4.461.142.
In such alliance could'st thou wish to join, ... Od.7.401.256.
To thy fond wish thy long-expected shores, ... Od.8.500.289.
Not *Circe,* but the Fates your wish deny. ... Od.10.577.370.
Ill, said the King, shou'd I thy wish oppose; ... Od.15.76.72.
Were every wish indulg'd by fav'ring skies, ... Od.16.160.110.
Such to our wish the warrior soon restore, ... Od.17.152.139.

WISH (CONTINUED)
Succeed my wish; your votary restore: ... Od.17.288.146.
Inspire him *Jove!* in ev'ry wish succeed! ... Od.17.427.153.
Thy wish produc'd in act, with pleas'd survey, ... Od.20.290.247.
Thy every wish the bounteous Gods bestow, ... Od.23.55.321.
Beyond our hopes, and to our wish, return'd! ... Od.24.461.370.

WISH'D
There wish'd to grow, and mingle shade with shade. ... 1.TrFD.56.388.
That Rest they wish'd for, grant them in the Grave, ... 2.ChWB.438.78.
He saw, he wish'd, and to the Prize aspir'd: ... 2.RL2.30.161.
Nor wish'd an Angel whom I lov'd a Man. ... 2.ElAb.70.325.
I wish'd the man a dinner, and sate still: ... 4.Arbu.152:107.
I've often wish'd that I had clear ... 4.HS6.1.251.
I often wish'd that I had clear ... 4.HS6.1A.251.
But wish'd it Stilton for his sake; ... 4.HS6.168.261.
And what young Ammon wish'd, but wish'd in vain. ... 4.EpS2.117.320.
And what young Ammon wish'd, but wish'd in vain. ... 4.EpS2.117.320.
Wish'd he had blotted for himself before. ... 5.DunB1.134.279.
And all that were, or wish'd to be, ... 6.30.5.85.
And wak'd and wish'd whole Nights for thy Return? ... 6.96iv.4.276.
With Joy *Sarpedon* view'd the wish'd Relief, ... Il.5.840.305.
The *Spartan* wish'd the second Place to gain, ... Il.10.273.14.
And great *Ulysses* wish'd, nor wish'd in vain. ... Il.10.274.14.
And great *Ulysses* wish'd, nor wish'd in vain. ... Il.10.274.14.
I fix'd its Date; the Day I wish'd appears ... Il.16.84.238.
And for his wish'd Return prepares in vain; ... Il.17.467.305.
He fell, and falling wish'd my Aid in vain. ... Il.18.128.328.
The blameless heroe from his wish'd-for home ... Od.1.65.33.
Let all combine t'atchieve his wish'd return: ... Od.1.99.36.
But of his wish'd return the care resign; ... Od.1.350.49.
Tydides' vessels touch'd the wish'd-for shore: ... Od.3.220.96.
His wish'd return with happy pow'r befriend, ... Od.4.1011.164.
Safe to transport him to the wish'd-for shore: ... Od.7.255.248.
His wish'd recess, and to the Goddess flies; ... Od.8.328.281.
Just as I wish'd, the lots were cast on four; ... Od.9.394.322.
He sate, and ey'd the sun, and wish'd the night; ... Od.13.36.3.
To bring *Penelope* the wish'd-for news, ... Od.15.48.72.
Yet like my self I wish'd thee here preferr'd, ... Od.17.209.141.
Those charms, for whom alone I wish'd to please. ... Od.18.212.177.
Who knows thy blest, thy wish'd return? oh say, ... Od.24.465.371.

WISH'D-FOR
The blameless heroe from his wish'd-for home ... Od.1.65.33.
Tydides' vessels touch'd the wish'd-for shore: ... Od.3.220.96.
Safe to transport him to the wish'd-for shore: ... Od.7.255.248.
To bring *Penelope* the wish'd-for news, ... Od.15.48.72.

WISHES
And all his Joys in length of Wishes lost. ... 1.TrSt.456.429.
Heav'n had not crown his Wishes with a Son, ... 1.TrSt.543.433.
And who but wishes to invert the laws ... 3.EOM1.129.31.
And where no wants, no wishes can remain, ... 3.EOM4.325.159.
To Toast our wants and wishes, is her way; ... 3.Ep2.88.57.
Three things another's modest wishes bound, ... 4.Arbu.47.99.
Be kind, and make him in his Wishes easy, ... 6.34.7.101.
If e'er thou sign'st our Wishes with thy Nod; ... Il.15.432.214.
To him they give their Wishes, Hearts, and Eyes, ... Il.23.897.524.
A Realm, a Goddess, to his Wishes giv'n, ... Il.24.675.565.
Damps the warm wishes of my raptur'd mind: ... Od.4.812.157.
Crown the chaste wishes of thy virtuous soul, ... Od.6.218.220.
And wearied heav'n with wishes for his Lord. ... Od.14.32.36.
Her kindred's wishes, and her Sire's commands; ... Od.15.20.70.
The burden down, and wishes for the day. ... Od.15.377.87.
Each pow'r above, with wishes for his Lord. ... Od.21.210.270.
Ev'n in their wishes, and their pray'rs, forgot! ... Od.21.218.270.

WISHING
And nobly wishing Party-rage to cease, ... 3.Ep3.151.106.
Yet always wishing to retreat, ... 4.HS6.127.257.
The only Honour of the wishing Dame; ... 6.8.26.18.
Wishing to wound, and yet afraid to strike, ... 6.49iii.17B.143.
Wishing to wound, and yet afraid to strike, ... 6.98.53.285.

WISP
An ell in length the pliant wisp I weav'd, ... Od.10.194.350.

WISTFUL
Their wistful eyes in floods of sorrow drown'd. ... Od.10.484.366.

WIT
Thou, whom the Nine with *Plautus'* Wit inspire, ... 1.PAu.7.80.
Authors are partial to their *Wit,* 'tis true, ... 1.EOC.17.241.
In search of *Wit* these lose their *common Sense,* ... 1.EOC.28.242.
And wisely curb'd proud Man's pretending Wit: ... 1.EOC.53.245.
So *vast* is Art, so *narrow* Human Wit: ... 1.EOC.61.246.
Some, to whom Heav'n in Wit has been profuse, ... 1.EOC.80.248.
For *Wit* and *Judgment* often are at strife, ... 1.EOC.82.248.
There are whom Heav'n has blest with store of Wit, ... 1.EOC.80A.248.
For *Wit* and *Judgment* ever are at strife, ... 1.EOC.82A.248.
Pride, where Wit fails, steps in to our Defence, ... 1.EOC.209.264.
A perfect Judge will *read* each Work of Wit ... 1.EOC.233.266.
The *gen'rous Pleasure* to be charm'd with Wit. ... 1.EOC.238.267.
In Wit, as Nature, what affects our Hearts ... 1.EOC.243.267.
As Men of Breeding, sometimes Men of Wit, ... 1.EOC.259.269.
As Men of Breeding, oft the Men of Wit, ... 1.EOC.259A.269
One *glaring Chaos* and *wild Heap* of *Wit:* ... 1.EOC.292.272.
True Wit is *Nature* to Advantage drest, ... 1.EOC.297.272.
So modest Plainness sets off sprightly Wit: ... 1.EOC.302.273.
For *Works* may have more *Wit* than does 'em good, ... 1.EOC.303.274.
(Thus *Wit,* like *Faith,* by each Man is apply'd ... 1.EOC.396.285.
Which not alone the *Southern Wit* sublimes, ... 1.EOC.400.286.
Regard not then if Wit be *Old* or *New,* ... 1.EOC.406.287.
How the *Wit brightens!* How the *Style refines!* ... 1.EOC.421.288.
And are but damn'd for having *too much Wit.* ... 1.EOC.429.288.
What wonder *Modes* in *Wit* shou'd take their Turn? ... 1.EOC.447.289.

WIT (CONTINUED)

The *current Folly* proves the *ready Wit,* ... 1.EOC.449.290.
Parties in *Wit* attend on those of *State,* ... 1.EOC.456.290.
The *current Folly* proves our *ready Wit,* ... 1.EOC.449A.290.
For envy'd Wit, like *Sol* Eclips'd, makes known ... 1.EOC.468.292.
Unhappy *Wit,* like most mistaken Things, ... 1.EOC.494.294.
What is this *Wit* which must our Cares employ? ... 1.EOC.500.294.
What is this *Wit* that does our Cares employ? ... 1.EOC.500A.294.
What is this *Wit* which does our Cares employ? ... 1.EOC.500B.294.
If *Wit* so much from *Ign'rance* undergo, ... 1.EOC.508.295.
Too much does *Wit* from *Ign'rance* undergo, ... 1.EOC.508A.295.
Tho' *Wit* and *Art* conspire to move your Mind; ... 1.EOC.531.297.
Nay *Wits* had *Pensions,* and *young Lords* had *Wit:* ... 1.EOC.539.298.
'Tis not enough, Wit, Art, and Learning join; ... 1.EOC.562A.305.
Such without *Wit* are Poets when they please, ... 1.EOC.590.307.
Who conquer'd *Nature,* shou'd preside o'er *Wit.* ... 1.EOC.652.313.
He, who Supream in Judgment, as in Wit, ... 1.EOC.657.314.
The *Scholar's Learning,* with the *Courtier's* wit. ... 1.EOC.668B.315.
Fierce for the *Liberties of Wit,* and bold, ... 1.EOC.717.323.
To him the Wit of *Greece* and *Rome* was known, ... 1.EOC.727.324.
To me, whose Wit exceeds the Pow'rs Divine, ... 1.TrUl.173.471.
Some prais'd with Wit, and some with Reason blam'd. ... 2.ChJM.142.21.
Th'assuming Wit, who deems himself so wise ... 2.ChJM.162.22.
Or such a *Wit* as no Man e'er can rule? ... 2.ChJM.189.24.
Or else her Wit some Fool-Gallant procures, ... 2.ChWB.95.61.
If you had Wit, you'd say, "Go where you will, ... 2.ChWB.130.62.
For all this Wit is giv'n us from our Birth: ... 2.ChWB.159.64.
And close the Sermon, as beseem'd his Wit, ... 2.ChWB.345.73.
And chose the Sermon, as beseem'd his Wit, ... 2.ChWB.345A.73.
Parents of Vapors and of Female Wit, ... 2.RL4.59.189.
On Wit and Learning the just Prize bestow, ... 2.TemF.304.278.
With all the rash dexterity of Wit: ... 3.EOM2.84.65.
Wit, Spirit, Faculties, but make it worse; ... 3.EOM2.146.72.
What crops of wit and honesty appear ... 3.EOM2.185.77.
Be Man the Wit and Tyrant of the whole: ... 3.EOM3.50.97.
While still too wide or short is human Wit; ... 3.EOM3.90.101.
Ere Wit oblique had broke that steddy light, ... 3.EOM3.231.115.
Faithless thro' Piety, and dup'd thro' Wit? ... 3.Ep1.151.28.
A Fool, with more of Wit than half mankind, ... 3.Ep1.200.32.
That gen'rous God, who Wit and Gold refines, ... 3.Ep2.289A.73.
Less Wit than Mimic, more a Wit than wise: ... 3.Ep2.48.54.
Less Wit than Mimic, more a Wit than wise: ... 3.Ep2.48.54.
She sins with Poets thro' pure Love of Wit. ... 3.Ep2.76.56.
Flavia's a Wit, has too much sense to Pray, ... 3.Ep2.87.57.
For true No-meaning puzzles more than Wit. ... 3.Ep2.114.59.
So much the Fury still out-ran the Wit, ... 3.Ep2.127.61.
The gen'rous God, who Wit and Gold refines, ... 3.Ep2.289.73.
Yet was not Cotta void of wit or worth: ... 3.Ep3.180.109.
Whose table, Wit, or modest Merit share, ... 3.Ep3.241.112.
No Wit to flatter, left of all his store! ... 3.Ep3.311.119.
He pledg'd it to the knight; the knight had wit, ... 3.Ep3.363.123.
What late he call'd a Blessing, now was Wit, ... 3.Ep3.377.123.
And " *sweet Sir Fopling!* you have so much wit!" ... 4.JD4.233.45.
For both the Beauty and the Wit are *bought.* ... 4.JD4.235.45.
Howe'er, what's now *Apocrypha,* my Wit, ... 4.JD4.286.49.
His Wit confirms him but a Slave the more, ... 4.HAdv.65.81.
And curses Wit, and Poetry, and *Pope.* ... 4.Arbu.26.97.
Still to one Bishop *Philips* seem a Wit? ... 4.Arbu.100.102.
Wit makes you foes, learn Prudence of a Friend ... 4.Arbu.102A.103.
A Wit quite angry is quite innocent; ... 4.Arbu.107A.103.
Yet Wit ne'er tastes, and Beauty ne'er enjoys, ... 4.Arbu.312.118.
His Wit all see-saw between *that* and *this,* ... 4.Arbu.323.119.
Wit that can creep, and Pride that licks the dust. ... 4.Arbu.333.120.
The damning Critic, half-approving Wit, ... 4.Arbu.344.120.
Yet soft by Nature, more a Dupe than Wit, ... 4.Arbu.368.123.
Here a lean Bard, whose wit could never give ... 4.JD2.13.133.
Is he who makes his meal on others wit: ... 4.JD2.30.135.
His rank digestion makes it wit no more: ... 4.JD2.32.135.
But turn a Wit, and scribble verses too? ... 4.JD2.54.137.
Is He who makes his Meals of Others Wit; ... 4.JD2A.34.134.
His rank Digestion makes it Wit no more. ... 4.JD2A.36.134.
But turns a Wit, and writes Love Verses too? ... 4.JD2A.60.136.
Make but his riches equal to his Wit. ... 4.HOde1.18.151.
"Oh but a Wit can study in the Streets, ... 4.2HE2.98.171.
And shook his head at *Murray,* as a Wit. ... 4.2HE2.132.175.
Indeed, could Wealth bestow or Wit or Merit, ... 4.2HE2.226.181.
He bought at thousands, what with better wit ... 4.2HE2.236.181.
In Pow'r, Wit, Figure, Virtue, Fortune, plac'd ... 4.2HE2.302.187.
If Time improve our Wit as well as Wine, ... 4.2HE1.49.199.
"I hold that Wit a Classick, good in law. ... 4.2HE1.56.199.
His moral pleases, not his pointed wit; ... 4.2HE1.76.201.
"Of Shakespear's Nature, and of Cowley's Wit; ... 4.2HE1.83.201.
And call for Pen and Ink to show our Wit. ... 4.2HE1.180.211.
Let Ireland tell, how Wit upheld her cause, ... 4.2HE1.221.213.
And heals with Morals what it hurts with Wit. ... 4.2HE1.262.217.
Wit grew polite, and Numbers learn'd to flow. ... 4.2HE1.266.217.
How Van wants grace, who never wanted wit! ... 4.2HE1.289.219.
There still remains to mortify a Wit, ... 4.2HE1.304.221.
How shall we fill a Library with Wit, ... 4.2HE1.354.225.
But Kings in Wit may want discerning spirit. ... 4.2HE1.385.227.
Sigh, while his Chloë, blind to Wit and Worth, ... 4.1HE6.42.239.
Tells me I have more Zeal than Wit, ... 4.HS6.56.253.
But show'd his Breeding, and his Wit, ... 4.HS6.172.261.
The sprightly Wit, the lively Eye, ... 4.1HE7.45.271.
And are, besides, too *Moral* for a Wit. ... 4.EpS1.4.297.
Come *Henley's* Oratory, *Osborn's* Wit! ... 4.EpS1.66.302.
The Wit of Cheats, the Courage of a Whore, ... 4.EpS1.165.309.
While *Roman* Spirit charms, and *Attic* Wit: ... 4.EpS2.85.317.
Or *P[a]ge* pour'd forth the Torrent of his Wit? ... 4.EpS2.159.322.
When did *Ty[rconne]l* hurt you with his Wit? ... 4.EpS2.159A.322.
Whose wit and equally provoke one, ... 4.1740.27.333.
with wit that must ... 4.1740.25Z1.333*.
Then he, "Great Tamer of all Wit and Art! ... 5.DunA1.143A.81.
Thron'd on sev'n hills, the Antichrist of Wit. ... 5.DunA2.12.97.
A Fool, so just a copy of a Wit; ... 5.DunA2.44.101.
A wit it was, and call'd the phantom, More. ... 5.DunA2.46.101.
Oft, as he fish'd her nether realms for wit, ... 5.DunA2.93.108.
No rag, no scrap, of all the beau, or wit, ... 5.DunA2.111.110.
Judge of all present, past, and future wit, ... 5.DunA2.344.142.
Equal in wit, and equally polite, ... 5.DunA3.177.170.
And Namby Pamby be prefer'd for Wit! ... 5.DunA3.322.188.
And *Ambrose Philips* be prefer'd for Wit! ... 5.DunA3.322B.188.
Fruits of dull Heat, and Sooterkins of Wit. ... 5.DunB1.126.278.
Or, if to Wit a coxcomb make pretence, ... 5.DunB1.177.283.
Teach Oaths to Gamesters, and to Nobles Wit? ... 5.DunB1.204.284.
Teach Oaths to Gamesters, and to Nobles—Wit? ... 5.DunB1.204A.284.
This arch Absurd, that wit and fool delights; ... 5.DunB1.221.286.
Thron'd on sev'n hills, the Antichrist of wit. ... 5.DunB2.16.297.
A fool, so just a copy of a wit; ... 5.DunB2.48.298.
A Wit it was, and call'd the phantom More. ... 5.DunB2.50.298.
Where as he fish'd her nether realms for Wit, ... 5.DunB2.101.300.
No rag, no scrap, of all the beau, or wit, ... 5.DunB2.119.301.
"Judge of all present, past, and future wit; ... 5.DunB2.376.315.
Equal in wit, and equally polite, ... 5.DunB3.181.329.
Lo! Ambrose Philips is prefer'd for Wit! ... 5.DunB3.326.336.
And *Wit* dreads Exile, Penalties and Pains. ... 5.DunB4.22.342.
A wit with dunces, and a dunce with wits. ... 5.DunB4.90.349.
And (last and worst) with all the cant of wit, ... 5.DunB4.99.351.
A heavy Lord shall hang at ev'ry Wit, ... 5.DunB4.132.354.
Bind rebel Wit, and double chain on chain, ... 5.DunB4.158.357.
There TALBOT sunk, and was a Wit no more! ... 5.DunB4.168.357.
The critic Eye, that microscope of Wit, ... 5.DunB4.233.365.
As much Estate, and Principle, and Wit, ... 5.DunB4.325.375.
True, he had wit, to make their value rise; ... 5.DunB4.377.380.
Wit shoots in vain its momentary fires, ... 5.DunB4.633.407.
Wit, past thro' thee, no longer is the same, ... 6.7.11.16.
And wicked *Wit* arose, thy most abusive Foe. ... 6.8.12.18.
But Rebel Wit deserts thee oft in vain; ... 6.8.13.18.
The Country Wit, Religion of the Town, ... 6.8.37.19.
If Wit or Critick blame the tender Swain, ... 6.13.16.39.
The last kind Refuge weary Wit can find, ... 6.16.2.53.
So Wit, which most to scorn it does pretend, ... 6.16.11.53.
Railing at Men of Sense, to show their Wit; ... 6.17iv.10.59.
With Wit well-natur'd, and with Books well-bred; ... 6.19.8.62.
Have Humour, Wit, a native Ease and Grace; ... 6.19.27.63.
Criticks in Wit, or Life, are hard to please, ... 6.19.29.63.
Their Wit still sparkling and their Flames still warm. ... 6.19.72.64.
A Scholar, or a Wit or two: ... 6.29.28.83.
And Wit and Humour are no more! ... 6.31i.8.93.
But had they, Miss, your Wit and Beauty seen, ... 6.37.5.106.
But yet if some, with Malice more than Wit, ... 6.38.11Z1.107.
Fate doom'd the fall of ev'ry female Wit, ... 6.43.3.120.
Unbarrel thy just Sense, and broach thy Wit. ... 6.48i.6.133*.
Whose fragrant Wit revives, as one may say, ... 6.48ii.3.134.
Tho' many a Wit from time to time has rose ... 6.48iii.1.134.
O *Button!* summon all thy Sons of Wit! ... 6.48iii.12.135.
Go on, Great Wit, contemn thy Foe's Bravado, ... 6.48iv.9.136.
But has the Wit to make the most of little: ... 6.49i.10.137.
Just Wit enough to make the most of little: ... 6.49i.10A.137.
Fool! 'tis in vain from Wit to Wit to roam; ... 6.49ii.15.140.
Fool! 'tis in vain from Wit to Wit to roam; ... 6.49ii.15.140.
Wisdom and wit in vain reclaim, ... 6.51ii.3.152.
Ye Lords and Commons, Men of Wit ... 6.58.1.170.
A Wit and courtly 'Squire. ... 6.58.16.171.
Since some have writ, and shewn no Wit at all. ... 6.60.8.178.
But Wit, like Wine, from happier Climates brought, ... 6.60.13.178.
Our Author has it now, for ev'ry Wit ... 6.60.35.179.
And Wit and Love no Sin, ... 6.61.4.180.
And Love and Wit no Sin, ... 6.61.4A.180.
Some Wit you have and more may learn, ... 6.61.31.182.
You have the *Nine* in your *Wit,* and *Three* in your *Faces.* ... 6.62i.2.185.
You've the *Nine* in your *Wit,* and the *Three* in your *Face* ... 6.62i.2A.185.
But *you* show your *Wit,* whereas *they* show'd their *Tails.* ... 6.62ii.2.185.
To say that at Court there's a Death of all Wit, ... 6.62iii.3A.185.
To say that at Court there's a Dearth of all Wit, ... 6.62iii.3.185.
They say *A—'s* a Wit, for what? ... 6.62vi.1.186.
You say A[rgyle]'s a wit, for what? ... 6.62vi.1B.186*.
A[rgyle] they say has wit, for what? ... 6.62vi.1C.186*.
Arthur, they say, has wit; for what? ... 6.62vi.1F.186.
Seen with Wit and Beauty seldom. ... 6.70.3.201.
With Greatness easy, and with wit sincere. ... 6.75.8.212.
For Want of you, we spend our random Wit on ... 6.82vi.3.232.
But our Great Turks in wit must reign alone ... 6.82ix(a).1.234.
Wit is like faith by such warm Fools profest ... 6.82ix(b).1.234.
Wit like religion is with spleen profest; ... 6.82ix(b).1A.234.
Wit has its Bigotts, who can bear no jest; ... 6.82ix(b).1B.234.
Wit like religion by such Fools profest. ... 6.82ix(b).1C.234.
Purge all your verses from the sin of wit ... 6.82ix(f).2.235.
And pleas'd to 'scape from Flattery to Wit. ... 6.84.12.239.
Thinks Worth, Wit, Learning, to that Spot confin'd; ... 6.96v.26.280.
More pert than witty, more a Wit than wise. ... 6.99.6.286.
Maul'd human *Wit* in one thick Satyr, ... 6.101.9.290.
When Ambrose Philips was preferr'd for Wit! ... 6.106iii.3.307.
Thy prudence, MOORE, is like that Irish Wit, ... 6.116i.3.325.
The wit & sense of one who bears ... 6.119.15A.337.
You beat your Pate, and fancy Wit will come: ... 6.124iii.1.348.
In Wit, a Man; Simplicity, a Child; ... 6.125.2.349.
A manly wit, a child's simplicity, ... 6.125.1Z1.349.
So full of Fibs, so void of Wit? ... 6.127.2.355.
None but a Peer of Wit and Grace, ... 6.135.67.369.
The mushrooms shew his wit was sudden! ... 6.150.11.398.
So much the Fury still out-ran the Wit, ... 6.154.13.403.
And such Success mere human Wit attend: ... Il.18.426.341.
In wit, in prudence, and in force of mind. ... Od.3.150.93.
The chief I challeng'd; he, whose practis'd wit ... Od.4.341.136.
(Such as his shallow wit, he deem'd was mine) ... Od.9.499.326.
Think'st thou by wit to model their escape? ... Od.10.339.360.
To me, whose wit exceeds the pow'rs divine, ... Od.13.340.24.
Let wit cast off the sullen yoke of sense. ... Od.14.525.62.
Sprung in his mind the momentary wit; ... Od.14.552.63.
(That wit, which or in council, or in fight, ... Od.14.553.64.

WIT (CONTINUED)
And aim to wound the Prince with pointless wit: ... Od.20.448.255.
And sent him sober'd home, with better wit. ... Od.21.322.275.

WIT'S
Or *one vain Wit's,* that might a hundred tire. ... 1.EOC.45.244.
Or *one vain Wit's,* that wou'd a hundred tire. ... 1.EOC.45A.244.
And here *restor'd* Wit's *Fundamental Laws.* ... 1.EOC.722.323.
Is well by Wit's more lasting Flames supply'd. ... 1.TrSP.38.395.
Is well by Wit's more lasting Charms supply'd. ... 1.TrSP.38A.395.
A Wit's a feather, and a Chief a rod; ... 3.EOM4.247.151.
For Wit's false mirror held up Nature's light; ... 3.EOM4.393.166.
Repeat unask'd; lament, the Wit's too fine ... 4.2HE1.366.227.
And, lest we err by Wit's wild, dancing light, ... 5.DunA1.153.82.
To their first Chaos Wit's vain works shall fall, ... 5.DunA3.355A.193.
And lest we err by Wit's wild dancing light, ... 5.DunB1.175.283.
Wit's Queen, (if what the Poets sing be true) ... 6.37.1.106.
For you well know, that Wit's of no Religion. ... 6.82iii.2.230.

WITCH
Did ever Proteus, Merlin, any Witch, ... 4.1HE1.152.291.

WITCHCRAFT
Like those of Witchcraft now can work no harms: ... 4.JD2A.24.134.
You give all royal Witchcraft to the Devil: ... 4.2HE2.219.181.
Say, by what Witchcraft, or what Dæmon led, ... 6.96iv.31.277.

WITCHES
In spight of Witches, Devils, Dreams, and Fire? ... 4.2HE2.313.187.

WITH (OMITTED)
5627

WITH-HELD
Foreseen by me, but ah! with-held from mine. ... 5.DunA3.274.183.
Forseen by me, but ah! with-held from mine. ... 5.DunB3.276.333.
The Wife with-held, the Treasure ill detain'd, ... Il.22.158.459.
Those, tho' the swiftest, by some God with-held, ... Il.23.544.511.
But modesty with-held the Goddess-train. ... Od.8.364.283.
The sire and son's great acts, with-held the day; ... Od.22.258.299.

WITH-HOLD
With-hold the pension, and set up the head; ... 5.DunB4.96.350.
If I oppose thee, Prince! thy Wrath with-hold, ... Il.9.45.434.
If ought from Heav'n with-hold his saving Arm; ... Il.11.927.77.

WITH-HOLDS
Nor Fear with-holds, nor shameful Sloth detains. ... Il.13.294.119.

WITH'RING
And all with Tears the with'ring Herbs bedew. ... 1.TrSP.172.401.
Now warm in love, now with'ring in thy bloom, ... 2.ElAb.37.322.
Now warm in love, now with'ring in my bloom, ... 2.ElAb.37A.322.
Now green in Youth, now with'ring on the Ground, ... Il.6.182.335.
Must share the general doom of with'ring time: ... Od.19.101.197.
With'ring at heart to see the weeping Fair, ... Od.19.246.206.

WITHALL
But then they're so blithe and so buxome withall, ... 6.122.7.341.

WITHDRAW
Blush, Grandeur, blush! proud Courts, withdraw your blaze! ... 3.Ep3.281.116.
I get a whisper, and withdraw; ... 4.HS6.63.255.
But ah! withdraw this all-destroying Hand. ... Il.21.437.438.
But from th' infernal rite thine eye withdraw, ... Od.10.630.374.
From the dire scene th' exempted two withdraw, ... Od.22.418.308.

WITHDRAWING
Then as withdrawing from the starry bow'rs, ... Od.8.325.281.

WITHDRAWN
The Guests withdrawn had left the Treat, ... 4.HS6.198.263.
Now, scarce withdrawn the fierce Earth-shaking pow'r, ... Od.5.488.195.
The nymphs withdrawn, at once into the tide ... Od.6.265.223.
Then to repose withdrawn, apart they lay, ... Od.16.500.131.
Grateful vicissitude! Yet me withdrawn, ... Od.19.693.229.

WITHDRAWS
Yet *Speech,* ev'n there, submissively withdraws ... 6.8.31.18.
Now great *Achilles* from our Aid withdraws, ... Il.2.448.149.
Nor yet from Fight *Idomeneus* withdraws; ... Il.13.533.131.
Infest a God: Th' obedient Flame withdraws: ... Il.21.445.438.

WITHDREW
Swift as she past, the flitting Ghosts withdrew, ... 1.TrSt.132.415.
(Thus *Rome's* great Founder to the Heav'ns withdrew, ... 2.RLa2.170.136.
For, that sad moment, when the *Sylphs* withdrew, ... 2.RL4.11.183.
(So *Rome's* great Founder to the Heav'ns withdrew, ... 2.RL5.125.210.
Withdrew his hand, and clos'd the pompous page. ... 5.DunB4.114.352.
Saw others happy, and with sighs withdrew; ... 6.45.8.124.
The savage Race withdrew, nor dar'd ... 6.82vii.3.233.
And, softly sighing, from the Loom withdrew. ... Il.3.188.200.
At this agreed, the Heav'nly Pow'rs withdrew; ... Il.7.47.365.
Then close beneath the sev'nfold Orb withdrew. ... Il.8.324.413.
Then furious thus, (but first some Steps withdrew.) ... Il.11.552.58.
And glaring round, by tardy Steps withdrew. ... Il.11.673.65.
Then *Venus* to the Courts of *Jove* withdrew; ... Il.14.257.173.
The Victor stooping, from the Death withdrew: ... Il.15.617.220.
Bold as he was, *Antilochus* withdrew: ... Il.15.701.222.
Who stooping forward from the Death withdrew; ... Il.16.740.272.
But swift withdrew the long-protended Wood, ... Il.16.981.281.
Dismiss'd with Fame, the favour'd Youth withdrew. ... Il.21.708.451.
But say, that Stranger-guest who late withdrew, ... Od.1.515.57.
Sternly his head withdrew, and strode away. ... Od.2.362.78.
The Seneshal rebuk'd in haste withdrew; ... Od.4.47.122.
Heart-wounded, to the bed of state withdrew: ... Od.4.1038.166.

WITHDREW (CONTINUED)
The Nymph just show'd him, and with tears withdrew. ... Od.5.310.186.
The Ocean widen'd, and the shores withdrew. ... Od.10.53.342.
The shade withdrew, and mutter'd empty sounds. ... Od.11.103.385.
Swift as it flash'd along the gloom, withdrew; ... Od.11.278.395.
And fresh from bathing, to their seats withdrew. ... Od.17.103.136.
And inly form'd revenge: Then back withdrew, ... Od.17.552.159.
And from my weeping eyes her cliffs withdrew; ... Od.19.390.213.
Now early to repose the rest withdrew; ... Od.20.137.240.
The Masters of the herd and flock withdrew. ... Od.21.194.269.
His eye withdrew, and fix'd it on the ground; ... Od.23.94.323.
And tim'rous pass'd, and awfully withdrew. ... Od.24.126.354.

WITHER
Fade ev'ry Blossom, wither ev'ry Tree, ... 1.PAu.33.82.
But wasting Years that wither human Race, ... Il.4.364.238.
Smile on the Sun; now, wither on the Ground: ... Il.21.540.444.
For this, my hand shall wither ev'ry grace, ... Od.13.455.28.
Wither the strength of man, and awe the Gods. ... Od.16.287.118.

WITHER'D
Their Beauty wither'd, and their Verdure lost. ... 1.PWi.10.89.
Starts from her Trance, and trims her wither'd Bays! ... 1.EOC.698.319.
Smote ev'ry Brain, and wither'd ev'ry Bay; ... 5.DunB4.10.340.
Now nothing's left, but wither'd, pale, and shrunk, ... 6.49i.25.138.
That wither'd all their Host: Like *Mars* he stood, ... Il.8.419.417.
Shot Terrors round, that wither'd ev'n the Strong. ... Il.13.1017.153.
He lifts his wither'd Arms; obtests the Skies; ... Il.22.45.454.
These wither'd Arms and Limbs have fail'd at length. ... Il.23.722.519.
On thousand Ships, and wither'd half a Host: ... Il.24.482.556.
On thousand Ships, and wither'd half an Host: ... Il.24.482A.556.
And wither'd Elders, pale and wrinkled shades: ... Od.11.50.383.
The skin shrunk up, and wither'd at her hand: ... Od.13.497.29.
Or that these wither'd nerves like thine were strung; ... Od.16.104.107.
And give to wither'd age a youthful bloom? ... Od.16.219.114.
With wither'd foliage strew'd, a heapy store! ... Od.19.515.221.
That wither'd all their hearts, *Ulysses* spoke. ... Od.22.40.288.

WITHERS
And withers all before it as it flies. ... 2.TemF.341.280.
Well-purg'd, and worthy Withers, Quarles, and Blome. ... 5.DunA1.126.78.
Where wretched *Withers, Banks,* and *Gildon* rest. ... 5.DunA1.250B.9
Where wretched Withers, Ward, and Gildon rest, ... 5.DunB1.296.291
Here WITHERS rest! thou bravest, gentlest mind, ... 6.113.1.320.
WITHERS adieu! yet not with thee remove ... 6.113.7.320.
And scorch'd by Suns, it withers on the Plain. ... Il.4.559.248.
Their Strength he withers, and unmans their Souls. ... Il.8.96.402.
The tender Plant, and withers all its Shades; ... Il.17.62.290.
The Strong he withers, and confounds the Bold, ... Il.17.198.295.
Withers the blooming vigour of his heir; ... Od.4.146.127.
When clad in wrath he withers hosts of foes: ... Od.8.120.269.
Ev'n with a look she withers all the bold! ... Od.12.150.439.

WITHHOLD
These gaping Wounds withhold us from the Fight. ... Il.14.70.161.

WITHHOLDS
Not Fear, thou know'st, withholds me from the Plains, ... Il.5.1012.315.
What grief, what wound, withholds him from the War? ... Il.15.277.207.

WITHIN
The Captive Bird that sings within thy Bow'r! ... 1.PSu.46.75.
Within her arms, and nourish'd at her breast. ... 1.TrFD.20.386.
Within this plant my hapless parent lies: ... 1.TrFD.83.389.
And all the nymph was lost within the tree: ... 1.TrFD.101.390.
In frightful Views, and makes it Day within; ... 1.TrSt.74.413.
And all the Furies wake within their Breast. ... 1.TrSt.175.417.
And all their Furies wake within their Breast. ... 1.TrSt.175A.417.
Within whose Orb the thick Bull-hides were roll'd, ... 1.TrES.9.450.
Within, the Waves in softer Murmurs glide, ... 1.TrUl.29.466.
Within the Cave, the clustring Bees attend ... 1.TrUl.39.467.
But ev'ry Charm revolv'd within his Mind: ... 2.ChJM.245.26.
The Chimney keeps, and sits content within; ... 2.ChWB.143.63.
Within, stood Heroes who thro' loud Alarms ... 2.TemF.149.265.
Above, below, without, within, around, ... 2.TemF.458.285.
Hide it, my heart, within that close disguise, ... 2.ElAb.11.319.
Confess'd within the slave of love and man. ... 2.ElAb.178.334.
And stir within me ev'ry source of love. ... 2.ElAb.232.339.
What shall divide? The God within the mind. ... 3.EOM2.204.79.
Silence without, and Fasts within the wall; ... 3.Ep3.190.109.
Sinks deep within him, and possesses whole, ... 3.Ep3.373.123.
The Soul stood forth, nor kept a Thought within; ... 4.HS1.54.9.
Within the reach of Treason, or the Law. ... 4.JD2.128.145.
Each prais'd within, is happy all day long. ... 4.2HE2.156.175.
Teach ev'ry Thought within its bounds to roll, ... 4.2HE2.204.179.
That God of Nature, who, within us still, ... 4.2HE2.280.185.
He's arm'd without that's innocent within; ... 4.1HE1.94.285.
Now let some whimzy, or that Dev'l within ... 4.1HE1.143.289.
What City-Swans once sung within the walls; ... 5.DunA1.94.70.
What City Swans once sung within the walls; ... 5.DunB1.96.276.
That lies within a Poet's Head, ... 6.10.76.26.
And Gods of war, lye lost within the grave! ... 6.22.21.72.
Such rage without betrays the fire within; ... 6.41.17.114.
If Charity within this Heart ... 6.50.31A.147.
Their Conscience is a Worm within, ... 6.53.27.162.
Within the same did *Sandys* lurk, ... 6.58.27.171.
If ought within we may descry ... 6.94.51.260.
"Within thy Reach I set the Vinegar? ... 6.96ii.18.270.
"Within the reach I set the Vinegar? ... 6.96ii.18A.270.
Within the Kingcup now his limbs are spread ... 6.96ii.30Z15.271
"Or sunk within the Peach's Down, repose? ... 6.96ii.46.273.
"Within the King-Cup if thy Limbs are spread, ... 6.96ii.47.273.
Shall wag her Tail within the Grave. ... 6.135.82.369.
What they said, or may say of the Mortal within. ... 6.144.6.386.
Mean time, secure within thy Ships from far ... Il.1.552.114.
Your shining Swords within the Sheath restrain, ... Il.3.125.196.

WITHIN (CONTINUED)

Within the Lines they drew their Steeds around, ...Il.3.155.198.
Stung with the Shame, within the winding Way, ...Il.4.444.241.
Crash'd all his Jaws, and cleft the Tongue within, ...Il.5.355.283.
And frighted *Troy* within her Walls retir'd; ......Il.6.90.328.
Those on the Fields, and these within their Tow'rs. ......Il.7.571.392.
Fast by the Brink, within the Steams of Hell; ......Il.8.600.425.
While Life's warm Spirit beats within my Breast. ......Il.9.720.470.
Some God within commands, and I obey. ......Il.10.262.13.
Soft Wool within; without, in order spread, ...Il.10.311.16.
Within its Concave hung a silver Thong, ...Il.11.49.36.
Within whose Orb the thick Bull-Hides were roll'd, ...Il.12.353.94.
Behold! distress'd within yon' hostile Wall, ...Il.13.925.149.
But bathes its Point within a *Grecian* Heart. ......Il.14.532.189.
Or draw the Troops within the Walls of *Troy*. ......Il.16.872.277.
Rank within Rank, on Buckler Buckler spread, ...Il.17.407.303.
Within, without, the Trench, and all the way, ...Il.17.851.321.
On Seats of Stone, within the sacred Place, ...Il.18.585.351.
And plung'd within the Ranks, awaits the Fight. ......Il.20.436.413.
Not till within her Tow'rs the perjur'd Train ......Il.21.243.431.
But when within the Walls our Troops take Breath, ...Il.21.625.448.
Stand I to doubt, within the reach of Fate? ......Il.21.664.449.
But now some God within me bids me try ......Il.22.319.469.
O snatch the Moments yet within thy Pow'r, ...Il.24.167.542.
The Fears of *Ilion*, clos'd within her Town, ...Il.24.831.571.
The Old Man's Fears, and turn'd within the Tent; ......Il.24.841.572.
The thoughts which rowl within my ravish'd breast, ...Od.1.259.45.
Within these walls inglorious silence reigns. ......Od.2.34.62.
And all *Minerva* breathes within her breast, ...Od.2.134.67.
And stow'd within its womb the naval stores. ......Od.2.439.82.
My ship equip'd within the neighb'ring port, ...Od.4.854.159.
Fair thrones within from space to space were rais'd, ...Od.7.124.240.
Within, releas'd from cares *Alcinous* lies; ......Od.7.437.258.
The cave we found, but vacant all within, ...Od.9.252.317.
The monster's club within the cave I spy'd, ...Od.9.380.321.
Within a long recess a bay there lies, ...Od.10.101.345.
And bound within the port their crowded fleet: ......Od.10.106.345.
Plac'd at her loom within, the Goddess sung; ......Od.10.254.354.
Within, irradiate with prophetic light; ......Od.10.583.371.
Too great a bliss to weep within her arms? ......Od.11.256.394.
The stately Oxe, and bleeds within the stalls. ......Od.11.510.408.
When seas retreating roar within her caves, ...Od.12.134.438.
Just when the sea within her gulphs subsides, ...Od.12.509.457.
Within, the waves in softer murmurs glide, ...Od.13.120.7.
Within the cave, the clustring bees attend ......Od.13.130.8.
Frequent and thick. Within the space, were rear'd ......Od.14.17.35.
Some voice of God close whisp'ring from within, ...Od.14.109.41.
Now turn thy thought, and joys within our pow'r. ......Od.14.193.45.
And all thy fortunes roll'd within his breast. ......Od.15.10.70.
While love and duty warr'd within his breast. ......Od.15.229.79.
There, while within the poop with care he stor'd ......Od.15.232.79.
Full to the bay within the winding shores ......Od.16.368.124.
These courts, within these courts like *Irus* bled: ......Od.18.280.180.
Immur'd within the silent bow'r of *Sleep*, ...Od.19.656.227.
Revenge and scorn within his bosom boil: ......Od.20.371.250.
Suffic'd it not within the palace plac'd ......Od.21.311.274.
Within the stricture of this palace wall ......Od.22.186.296.
Pour out my soul, and dye within thy arms! ......Od.23.226.333.
Thou with thy Maids within the Palace stay, ...Od.23.391.343.
His heart within him melts; his knees sustain ......Od.24.402.368.

WITHOUT

Works *without Show*, and *without Pomp* presides: ......1.EOC.75.247.
Works *without Show*, and *without Pomp* presides: ......1.EOC.75.247.
Some dryly plain, without Invention's Aid, ...1.EOC.114.252.
Without all these at once before your Eyes, ...1.EOC.122.252.
Which, without passing thro' the *Judgment*, gains ......1.EOC.156.258.
The Critick else proceeds without Remorse, ...1.EOC.167.259.
All glares *alike*, without *Distinction* gay: ......1.EOC.314.274.
Without *Good Breeding, Truth* is disapprov'd; ......1.EOC.576.306.
Without *Good Breeding, Truth* is not approv'd, ...1.EOC.576A.306.
Such without *Wit* are Poets when they please, ...1.EOC.590.307.
As without *Learning* they can take *Degrees*. ......1.EOC.591.307.
And without Method *talks* us into Sense, ...1.EOC.654.313.
Without their aid, to seal these dying eyes. ......1.TrFD.99.390.
And Ships secure without their Haulsers ride. ......1.TrUl.30.466.
The Deeds of Men appear without Disguise, ...1.TrUl.89.469.
At this, the Council rose, without Delay; ......2.ChJM.224.25.
At this, the Council broke, without Delay; ......2.ChJM.224A.25.
Fair without Spot, whose ev'ry charming Part ......2.ChJM.531.41.
The rest, without much Loss, I cou'd resign. ......2.ChWB.61.59.
The tott'ring *China* shook without a Wind, ...2.RL4.163.197.
Great without Pride, in modest Majesty. ......2.TemF.203.271.
Above, below, without, within, around, ...2.TemF.458.285.
The Great Man's Curse without the Gains endure, ...2.TemF.509.288.
The virgin's wish without her fears impart, ...2.ElAb.55.323.
So peaceful rests, without a stone, a name, ...2.Elegy.69.368.
A mighty maze! but not without a plan, ...3.EOM1.6.11.
A mighty maze! of walks without a plan; ......3.EOM1.6A.11.
Nature to these, without profusion kind, ...3.EOM1.179.37.
Nature to each, without profusion kind, ...3.EOM1.179A.37.
Without this just gradation, could they be ......3.EOM1.229.44.
Sure as De-moivre, without rule or line? ......3.EOM3.104.102.
"And Anarchy without confusion know; ......3.EOM3.186.112.
Without a second, or without a judge: ......3.EOM4.264.153.
Without a second, or without a judge: ......3.EOM4.264.153.
And tastes the good without the fall to ill; ......3.EOM4.312.157.
Without satiety, tho' e'er so blest, ...3.EOM4.317.158.
A Rogue with Ven'son to a Saint without. ......3.Ep1.139.26.
Aw'd without Virtue, without Beauty charm'd; ......3.Ep2.46.54.
Aw'd without Virtue, without Beauty charm'd; ......3.Ep2.46.54.
By Wealth of Follow'rs! without one distress ......3.Ep2.145.62.
"Yet Cloe sure was form'd without a spot—" ......3.Ep2.157.63.
Young without Lovers, old without a Friend, ...3.Ep2.246.70.
Young without Lovers, old without a Friend, ...3.Ep2.246.70.
But thousands die, without or this or that, ...3.Ep3.97.97.

WITHOUT (CONTINUED)

Silence without, and Fasts within the wall; ......3.Ep3.190.109.
Without a Fiddler, Flatt'rer, or Buffoon? ......3.Ep3.240.112.
Without it, proud Versailles! thy glory falls; ......3.Ep4.71.144.
Advice; and (as you use) without a Fee. ......4.HS1.10.5.
As deep in *Debt*, without a thought to pay, ...4.JD4.21.27.
But strong in sense, and wise without the rules. ......4.HS2.10.55.
"Pity! to build, without a son or wife: ......4.HS2.163.67.
And without sneering, teach the rest to sneer; ......4.Arbu.202.110.
And a true *Pindar* stood without a head) ......4.Arbu.236.112.
Can sleep without a Poem in my head, ...4.Arbu.269.115.
And show the Sense of it, without the Love; ......4.Arbu.294.117.
His Death was instant, and without a groan., ...4.Arbu.403.126.
Thus much I've said, I trust without Offence; ......4.JD2A.131.144.
Thus much I've said, I trust without offence; ......4.JD2.125.145.
A man so poor wou'd live without a *Place:* ......4.2HE2.287.185.
And view this dreadful All without a fear. ......4.1HE6.10.237.
"Without your help the Cause is gone— ......4.HS6.72.255.
Near fifty, and without a Wife, ...4.1HE7.73.273.
He's arm'd without that's innocent within; ......4.1HE1.94.285.
Great without Title, without Fortune bless'd, ...4.1HE1.181.293.
Great without Title, without Fortune bless'd, ...4.1HE1.181.293.
Lov'd without youth, and follow'd without power, ...4.1HE1.183.293.
Lov'd without youth, and follow'd without power, ...4.1HE1.183.293.
Smile without Art, and win without a Bribe. ......4.EpS1.32.300.
Smile without Art, and win without a Bribe. ......4.EpS1.32.300.
Then might I sing without the least Offence. ......4.EpS1.77.304.
Ye Gods! shall *Cibber's* Son, without rebuke ......4.EpS1.115.306.
Without a staring Reason on his Brows? ......4.EpS2.194.324.
(Pomps without guilt, of bloodless swords and maces, ...5.DunA1.85.69.
Fair without spot; than greas'd by grocer's hands, ...5.DunA1.199.86.
(Pomps without guilt, of bloodless swords and maces, ...5.DunB1.87.275.
Or impious, preach his Word without a call. ......5.DunB4.94.350.
Without the soul, the Muse's Hypocrit. ......5.DunB4.100.351.
And much Divinity without a *Noûs*. ......5.DunB4.244.367.
I tell the naked fact without disguise, ...5.DunB4.433.383.
Wrapt up in Self, a God without a Thought, ...5.DunB4.485.389.
Rosy and rev'rend, tho' without a Gown. ......5.DunB4.496.391.
Thou without them may'st speak and profit too; ......6.2.23.6.
But without thee, what could the Prophets do? ......6.2.24.6.
What mov'd you, pray, without compelling, ...6.10.83.27.
Ne Village is without, on either side, ...6.14ii.51.44.
Who without Flatt'ry pleas'd the Fair and Great; ......6.19.6.62.
For tho' without them both, 'twas clear, ...6.30.38.87.
For tho' without their help 'twas clear, ...6.30.38A.87.
For tho' without them ('twas most clear) ......6.30.38B.87.
Such rage without betrays the fire within; ......6.41.17.114.
And without sneering, teach the rest to sneer; ......6.49iii.16.143.
Soft without weakness, without glaring gay; ......6.52.66.158.
Soft without weakness, without glaring gay; ......6.52.66.158.
Tho' *Ovid* lay without. ......6.58.28.171.
Nor Nightgown without Sleeves, avails ......6.58.11A.171.
In haste, without his Garter. ......6.58.44.172.
Without a Pain, a Trouble, or a Fear; ......6.86.16.245.
Young without Lovers, old without a Friend; ......6.86.8A.245.
Young without Lovers, old without a Friend; ......6.86.8A.245.
Without a Sigh, a Trouble, or a Tear; ......6.86.16A.245.
And without sneering, teach the rest to sneer; ......6.98.52.284.
Aw'd without Sense, and without Beauty charm'd, ...6.99.2.286.
Aw'd without Sense, and without Beauty charm'd, ...6.99.2.286.
All hail, arch-poet without peer! ......6.106v.1.308.
Good without noise, without pretension great. ......6.109.4.314.
Good without noise, without pretension great. ......6.109.4.314.
Here rests a Woman, good without pretence, ...6.115.1.322.
Dry pomps and Obsequies without a sigh. ......6.130.26.358.
Good without Show, and without weakness kind: ......6.134.6.364.
Good without Show, and without weakness kind: ......6.134.6.364.
Not one without Permission feed, ...6.135.51.368.
Nor one without Permission feed, ...6.135.51A.368.
"Yet Cloë sure was form'd without a Spot—" ......6.139.1.377.
And eye the Mine without a Wish for Gold. ......6.142.8.382.
And view the Mine without a Wish for Gold. ......6.142.8A.382.
(Without a blot) to eighty one. ......6.150.4.398.
Walk to his grave without reproach, ...6.150.19.399.
By Wealth, of Followers; without one Distress ......6.154.31.403.
Speak what thou know'st, and speak without controul. ......Il.1.108.92.
'Till the great King, without a Ransom paid, ...Il.1.123.93.
Thus spoke the Sage: The Kings without Delay ......Il.2.107.132.
His Words succinct, yet full, without a Fault; ......Il.3.277.205.
And only mourn, without my Share of Praise? ......Il.4.207.231.
And can you, Chiefs! without a Blush survey ......Il.4.398.239.
A wealthy Priest, but rich without a Fault; ......Il.5.16.266.
Without a Warrior's Arms, the Spear and Shield! ......Il.5.267.280.
Hector, this heard, return'd without Delay; ......Il.6.488.350.
Else may we miss to meet, without a Guide, ...Il.10.72.5.
Without his Tent, bold *Diomed* they found, ...Il.10.170.9.
Just be thy Choice, without Affection made, ...Il.10.279.14.
Soft Wool within; without, in order spread, ...Il.10.311.16.
Without a Wound the *Trojan* Hero stands; ......Il.11.456.54.
Without the Gods, how short a Period stands ......Il.12.9.81.
No Pass thro' those, without a thousand Wounds, ...Il.12.73.84.
Without a Sign, his Sword the brave Man draws, ...Il.12.283.92.
Without th' Assistance, or the Fear of *Jove*. ......Il.13.784.142.
He lies protected, and without a Wound. ......Il.14.498.188.
He comes not, *Jove!* without thy pow'rful Will; ......Il.15.330.210.
Without thy Person *Greece* shall win the Day, ...Il.16.60.237.
"Without the bloody Arms of *Hector* dead:" ......Il.16.1014.282.
A manly Form, without a manly Mind. ......Il.17.156.293.
How vain, without the Merit is the Name? ......Il.17.158.293.
Within, without, the Trench, and all the way, ...Il.17.851.321.
What boastful Son of War, without that Stay, ...Il.19.161.378.
Smooth-gliding without Step, above the Heads, ...Il.20.375.410.
He spoke in vain—The Chief without Dismay ......Il.21.255.431.
But Woman-like to fall, and fall without a Blow. ......Il.22.166.460.
Go then (return'd the Sire) without delay, ...Il.22.239.465.
Nor ev'n his Stay without the *Scæan* Gate. ......Il.22.565.479.

WITHOUT (CONTINUED)
The Form subsists, without the Body's Aid, ... Il.23.124.492.
Not without Cause incens'd at *Nestor's* Son, ... Il.23.649.515.
Without thy presence vain is thy command; ... Od.2.303.76.
Mean-time the Queen without refection due, ... Od.4.1037.166.
Without the grot, a various sylvan scene ... Od.5.80.176.
Not without Care divine the stranger treads ... Od.6.287.224.
Long worn with griefs, and long without a friend. ... Od.7.201.246.
Not without wonder seen. Then thus began, ... Od.7.316.251.
Warm are thy words, but warm without offence; ... Od.8.271.278.
And fix'd, without, my haulsers to the shore. ... Od.10.110.346.
Without one look the murther'd father dies; ... Od.11.560.411.
Safe he return'd, without one hostile scar; ... Od.11.656.416.
Now without number ghost by ghost arose, ... Od.11.663.417.
Without new treasures let him not remove, ... Od.13.15.2.
And ships secure without their haulsers ride. ... Od.13.121.7.
The deeds of men appear without disguise, ... Od.13.256.18.
A faithful servant, and without a fault. ... Od.14.6.35.
The males without (a smaller race) remain'd; ... Od.14.20.35.
Rich without bounty, guilty without fears! ... Od.14.100.40.
Rich without bounty, guilty without fears! ... Od.14.100.40.
Without some pledge, some monument of love; ... Od.15.96.73.
Rose ominous, nor flies without a God: ... Od.15.574.98.
Wait for a space without, but wait not long; ... Od.17.328.147.
Peace wretch! and eat thy bread without offence, ... Od.17.568.160.
Indecently to rail without offence! ... Od.18.21.167.
What bounty gives, without a rival share, ... Od.18.22.168.
Great without vice, that oft attends the great: ... Od.18.154.173.
And custom bids thee without shame receive; ... Od.18.332.183.
Force I forbear, and without force obey. ... Od.18.457.190.
Without infringing hospitable right, ... Od.19.29.193.
Without retinue, to that friendly shore ... Od.19.311.209.
(The hide, without, imbib'd the morning air.) ... Od.20.118.238.
Behind him sow'rly stalk'd. Without delay ... Od.20.183.242.
Partake my guest, he cry'd, without controul ... Od.20.326.249.
Without reply vouchsaf'd, *Antinous* ceas'd: ... Od.20.340.249.
Drive to yon' court, without the Palace wall, ... Od.22.478.312.
Heap'd lie the dead without the Palace walls,— ... Od.23.53.321.

WITHSTAND
When *Florio* speaks, what Virgin could withstand, ... 2.RL1.97.152.
Prescient, the tides or tempests to withstand, ... 3.EOM3.101.102.
No Pow'r, when Virtue claims it, can withstand: ... 4.EpS2.119.320.
But, Madam, if the Fates withstand, and you ... 6.19.57.63.
Goddess submit, nor dare our Will withstand, ... Il.1.732.122.
But if she dooms, and if no God withstand, ... Il.5.322.282.
But Heav'n and Fate the first Design withstand, ... Il.5.832.305.
But know, whoe'er Almighty Pow'r withstand! ... Il.8.560.423.
Then none (said *Nestor)* shall his Rule withstand, ... Il.10.148.8.
Thou shalt not long the Death deserv'd withstand, ... Il.11.469.55.
Can'st thou, unhappy in thy Wiles! withstand ... Il.15.21.194.
Yet hear my Counsel, and his worst withstand; ... Il.15.332.210.
Thy Friend, thy greater far, it shall withstand, ... Il.16.865.277.
That Fire, that Steel, your *Hector* shou'd withstand, ... Il.20.425.412.
But long thou shalt not thy just Fate withstand, ... Il.20.521.416.
The next, that God whom Men in vain withstand, ... Il.21.52.424.
Juno, whom thou rebellious dar'st withstand, ... Il.21.480.441.
Greece, and the rival train thy voice withstand. ... Od.2.304.76.
Down sate the Sage; and cautious to withstand, ... Od.14.35.36.

WITHSTANDS
And, but some God, some angry God withstands, ... Il.5.240.278.
But He above, the Sire of Heav'n withstands, ... Il.8.437.418.
(Imperial *Jove)* his present Death withstands; ... Il.15.542.217.
Fly, whilst thy Mother virtuous yet withstands ... Od.15.19.70.
Yet Fate withstands! a sudden tempest roars ... Od.23.341.341.

WITHSTOOD
"(So long by watchful Ministers withstood) ... 3.Ep3.138.104.
To see no wholsom Motion be withstood, ... Il.9.135.438.
He roar'd: in vain the Dogs, the Men withstood, ... Il.18.673.356.
O friends forbear! and be the thought withstood: ... Od.16.416.126.
Him no fell Savage on the plain withstood, ... Od.17.382.150.

WITLING
A *Beau* and *Witling* perish'd in the Throng, ... 2.RL5.59.204.

WITLINGS
Those half-learn'd Witlings, num'rous in our Isle, ... 1.EOC.40.243.
I ne'r with Wits or Witlings past my days, ... 4.Arbu.223.112.
I ne'r with Wits and Witlings past my days, ... 4.Arbu.223A.112.
Wits, Witlings, Prigs, and Peers; ... 6.58.46.172.

WITNESS
Believe not me, but come and witness here, ... 1.TrPA.82.368.
And stood the helpless witness of thy fate; ... 1.TrFD.54.388.
Then hear, my Lord, and witness what I swear. ... 2.ChJM.584.43.
Witness the Martyrs, who resign'd their Breath, ... 2.ChJM.673.47.
And witness next what *Roman* Authors tell, ... 2.ChJM.675.47.
And call *your maids* tö Witness how he lies. ... 2.ChWB.73.60.
Takes God to witness he affects your Cause, ... 4.JD2.76.141.
"Witness great Ammon! by whose horns I swore, ... 5.DunB4.387.380.
Witness E. Lewis. ... 6.42i.11.116.
As witness Lady *W[ort]l[e]y.* ... 6.58.68.173.
Witness Ann. prim. of Henry Oct. ... 6.67.14.195.
Witness two lovely Girls, two lovely Boys) ... 6.96iv.40.277.
A heav'nly Witness of the Wrongs I bear ... Il.1.270.100.
But witness, Heralds, and proclaim my Vow, ... Il.1.440.108.
Witness to Gods above, and Men below! ... Il.1.441.108.
Witness the sacred Honours of our Head, ... Il.1.679.119.
What past at *Aulis, Greece* can witness bear, ... Il.2.366.145.
Hear, and be Witness. If, by *Paris* slain, ... Il.3.354.210.
Be witness, *Jove!* whose Thunder rolls on high. ... Il.7.488.388.
The *Greeks* stood witness, all our Army heard. ... Il.9.50.434.
Hear all ye *Greeks,* and witness what I vow. ... Il.9.156.439.
Be witness thou! immortal Lord of all! ... Il.10.389.21.

WITNESS (CONTINUED)
Tho' not Partaker, Witness of the War. ... Il.14.148.164.
To hear, and witness from the Depths of Hell; ... Il.14.310.177.
A mournful Witness of this Scene of Woe: ... Il.15.463.215.
And thou be Witness, if I fear to Day; ... Il.17.202.295.
The Witness is produc'd on either Hand; ... Il.18.581.350.
Witness thou First! thou greatest Pow'r above! ... Il.19.267.383.
(Eternal Witness of all below, ... Il.22.325.469.
I boast a witness of his worth in thee. ... Od.4.280.132.
Sole witness of the deed I now declare; ... Od.4.333.135.
Your eyes shall witness and confirm my tale, ... Od.7.417.258.
Thou first be witness, hospitable *Jove!* ... Od.14.182.44.
And witness ev'ry houshold pow'r that waits ... Od.14.184.44.
And witness every pow'r that rules the sky! ... Od.14.435.56.
Witness the genial rites, and witness all ... Od.17.178.140.
Witness the genial rites, and witness all ... Od.17.178.140.
A witness-judge precludes a long appeal: ... Od.19.585.224.

WITNESS-JUDGE
A witness-judge precludes a long appeal: ... Od.19.585.224.

WITNESS'D
He roll'd his eyes that witness'd huge dismay, ... 5.DunA1.115.77.
What Eye has witness'd, or what Ear believ'd, ... Il.10.55.4.
Thy Eyes have witness'd what a fatal Turn! ... Il.17.773.318.

WITS
But envy *Wits,* as *Eunuchs* envy *Lovers.* ... 1.EOC.31A.242.
Some have at first for *Wits,* then *Poets* past, ... 1.EOC.36.243.
Some neither can for *Wits* nor *Criticks* pass, ... 1.EOC.38.243.
But following Wits from that Intention stray'd; ... 1.EOC.104.251.
Great Wits sometimes may *gloriously offend,* ... 1.EOC.152.257.
To teach vain Wits a Science *little known,* ... 1.EOC.199.263.
To teach vain Wits that Science *little known,* ... 1.EOC.199A.263.
And but so mimick ancient Wits at best, ... 1.EOC.331.276.
When *Patriarch-Wits* surviv'd a *thousand Years;* ... 1.EOC.479.293.
Contending Wits become the *Sport of Fools:* ... 1.EOC.517.296.
Nay *Wits* had *Pensions,* and *young Lords* had *Wit:* ... 1.EOC.539.298.
By *Wits,* then *Criticks* in as wrong *Quotations.* ... 1.EOC.664.314.
Some wicked Wits have libell'd all the Fair: ... 2.ChJM.44.17.
A Place to tire the rambling Wits of *France* ... 2.ChJM.452.36.
The wiser Wits of later Times declare ... 2.ChJM.671.47.
Your idle Wits, and all their Learned Lies. ... 2.ChJM.697.48.
What tho' no Credit doubting Wits may give? ... 2.RL1.39.148.
And Wits take Lodgings in the Sound of *Bow;* ... 2.RL4.118.193.
Weighs the Men's Wits against the Lady's Hair; ... 2.RL5.72.206.
At length the Wits mount up, the Hairs subside. ... 2.RL5.74.206.
There Heroes' Wits are kept in pondrous Vases, ... 2.RL5.115.208.
Some fresh ingrav'd appear'd of Wits renown'd; ... 2.TemF.35.255.
Th' Estate which Wits inherit after Death! ... 2.TemF.506.288.
All luckless Wits their Enemies profest, ... 2.TemF.511.288.
Wits, just like fools, at war about a Name, ... 3.EOM2.85.65.
Turn then from Wits; and look on Simo's Mate, ... 3.Ep2.101.58.
Such Wits and Beauties are not prais'd for nought, ... 4.JD4.234.45.
Courts are too much for Wits so weak as mine; ... 4.JD4.280.49.
Courts are no match for Wits so weak as mine; ... 4.JD4.280A.49.
Pimps, Poets, Wits , Lord *Fanny's,* Lady *Mary's,* ... 4.HAdv.2.75.
While Wits and Templers ev'ry sentence raise, ... 4.Arbu.211.111.
I ne'r with Wits or Witlings past my days, ... 4.Arbu.223.112.
Receiv'd of Wits an undistinguish'd race, ... 4.Arbu.237.112.
I ne'r with Wits and Witlings past my days, ... 4.Arbu.223A.112.
But for the Wits of either Charles's days, ... 4.2HE1.107.203.
And to be kept in my right wits. ... 4.HS6.22.251.
Judicious Wits spread wide the Ridicule, ... 4.EpS1.61.302.
Let Courtly Wits to Wits afford supply, ... 4.EpS2.171.323.
Let Courtly Wits to Wits afford supply, ... 4.EpS2.171.323.
Blockheads with reason wicked wits abhor, ... 5.DunA3.169.167.
Wits, who like Owls see only in the dark, ... 5.DunA3.188.172.
Blockheads with reason wicked wits abhor, ... 5.DunB3.175.329.
Wits, who like owls, see only in the dark, ... 5.DunB3.192.329.
A wit with dunces, and a dunce with wits. ... 5.DunB4.90.349.
When Dulness, smiling—"Thus revive the Wits! ... 5.DunB4.119.353.
Wits have short Memories, and Dunces none) ... 5.DunB4.620.406.
Wits have short Memories, and Dulness none) ... 5.DunB4.620A.406.
By modern Wits call'd *Quixotism.* ... 6.10.82.27.
Of Councils, Classicks, Fathers, Wits; ... 6.14v(a).2.48.
Our Friends the Wits and Poets to advise, ... 6.17iv.23.60.
Ev'n Rival Wits did *Voiture's* Death deplore, ... 6.19.15.62.
Ev'n Rival Wits did *Voiture's* Fate deplore, ... 6.19.15A.62.
He scorn'd to borrow from the Wits of yore; ... 6.34.9.101.
You modern Wits, should each Man bring his Claim, ... 6.34.11.101.
Was rais'd to fame by all the wits of *Greece.* ... 6.38.10.107.
And from all Wits that have a Knack Gad save ye. ... 6.40.10.112.
The Wits in envious Feuds engage; ... 6.47.23.129.
Revenge our Wits and Statesmen on a *Pope.* ... 6.48iii.16.135.
Not of the Wits his Foes, but Fools his Friends. ... 6.49i.14.137.
The constant Index to all *Button's* Wits. ... 6.49ii.2.140.
Who when two Wits on rival themes contest, ... 6.49iii.23.143.
Whilst Wits and Templars ev'ry Sentence raise, ... 6.49iii.27A.143.
While Wits and Templars ev'ry Sentence raise, ... 6.49iii.27B.143.
Ev'n *Button's* Wits to Worms shall turn, ... 6.53.39.162.
Wits, Witlings, Prigs, and Peers; ... 6.58.46.172.
Gray Statesman, or green Wits; ... 6.59.6.177.
For Fools are only laugh'd at, Wits are hated. ... 6.60.4.178.
Wits starve as useless to a Common weal ... 6.82ix(d).1.235.
Now wits gain praise by copying other wits ... 6.82ix(e).1.235.
Now wits gain praise by copying other wits ... 6.82ix(e).1.235.
Who, if two Wits on rival Themes contest, ... 6.98.59.285.
While Wits and Templars ev'ry Sentence raise, ... 6.98.63.285.
And wine can of their wits the wise beguile, ... Od.14.520.62.

WITT
Yet Master P[ope] Whom Witt and Sense ... 6.135.87A.369.

WITT'S

Encourag'd thus, Witt's *Titans* brav'd the Skies, 1.EOC.552.304.

WITTY

Grave Authors say, and witty Poets sing, 2.ChJM.21.16.
Whose Buzz the Witty and the Fair annoys, 4.Arbu.311.118.
Against the Witty, Gallant, Brave and Bold, 4.JD2A.26.134.
His Time, the Muse, the Witty, and the Fair. 6.19.10.62.
Handsome and witty, yet a Friend. 6.89.4.250.
More pert than witty, more a Wit than wise. 6.99.6.286.
With witty Malice, studious to defame, Il.2.259.140.

WIVES

To their Wives Arms, and Childrens dear Embrace. 1.TrUl.215.472.
To slander Wives, and Wedlock's holy Name. 2.ChJM.223.25.
Old Wives there are, of Judgment most acute, 2.ChJM.295.28.
To be so well deluded by their Wives. 2.ChJM.820.54.
And to their dearer Wives for ever cleave. 2.ChWB.20.57.
More Wives than One by *Solomon* were try'd, 2.ChWB.21.57.
And let us honest Wives eat Barley Bread. 2.ChWB.49.58.
Ye Sov'reign Wives! give Ear, and understand; 2.ChWB.68.59.
Cry Wives are false, and ev'ry Woman evil, 2.ChWB.84.60.
But Wives, a random Choice, untry'd they take; 2.ChWB.102.61.
"The Wives of all my Family have rul'd 2.ChWB.195.66.
"The Wives of all my Race have ever rul'd 2.ChWB.195A.66.
More Legends were there here, of wicked Wives, 2.ChWB.363.74.
On which three Wives successively had twin'd 2.ChWB.395.76.
Then how two Wives their Lord's Destruction prove, 2.ChWB.401.76.
Thus shall your wives, and thus your children fall: 2.Elegy.36.365.
He too can say, "With Wives I never sin." 4.HAdv.73.81.
Our Wives read Milton, and our Daughters Plays, 4.2HE1.172.209.
The joy their wives, their sons, and servants share, 4.2HE1.245.215.
Our weeping Wives, our tender Children call: Il.2.166.136.
What cou'd their Wives or helpless Children more? Il.2.355.144.
Their Wives, their Infants, and their Altars save. Il.5.592.296.
Sons, Sires, and Wives, an undistinguish'd Prey. Il.5.596.297.
E're yet their Wives soft Arms the Cowards gain, Il.6.101.328.
Our Wives, our Infants, and our City spare, Il.6.118.330.
Our Wives, our Infants, and our City spare, Il.6.345.343.
The Fate of Fathers, Wives, and Infants lay. Il.8.70.399.
Her Wives, her Infants by my Labours sav'd; Il.9.429.453.
Whose Wives and Infants, from the Danger far, Il.10.492.25.
More grateful, now, to Vulturs than their Wives! Il.11.212.44.
Your Wives, your Infants, and your Parents share: Il.15.799.227.
Their Wives, their Children, and the watchful Band, Il.18.597.351.
Who now protects her Wives with guardian Care? Il.24.918.574.
(Those Wives must wait'em) to a foreign Shore! Il.24.921.574.
Maids, wives, and matrons, mix a shrilling sound. Od.3.573.115.
Their wives made captive, their possessions shar'd, Od.9.45.304.
Daughters and wives of Heroes and of Kings; Od.11.274.395.
Your selves, your wives, your long-descending race, Od.13.58.4.
To their wives arms, and children's dear embrace. Od.13.382.25.
With large possessions and with faithful wives; Od.21.222.270.

WIZARD

And hence th' Egregious Wizard shall foredoom 2.RL5.139.211.
A wizard told him in these words our fate: 3.Ep3.136.104.
With that, a WIZARD OLD his *Cup* extends; 5.DunB4.517.393.

WIZARDS

New wizards rise: here Booth, and Cibber there: 5.DunA3.262.179.
New wizards rise; I see my Cibber there! 5.DunB3.266.333.

WOE

A nearer woe, a sister's stranger fate. 1.TrFD.6.385.
And tun'd my Heart to Elegies of Woe. 1.TrSP.8.393.
Fix'd in a stupid Lethargy of Woe. 1.TrSP.128.399.
And Fancy sinks beneath a Weight of Woe. 1.TrSP.231.403.
And the long Series of succeeding Woe: 1.TrSt.320.423.
The Change of Scepters, and impending Woe; 1.TrSt.842.444.
Then with erected Eyes stood fix'd in Woe, 1.TrUl.72.468.
And sigh'd for Woe, but sigh'd and wept in vain; 2.ChJM.491A.39.
She said; a rising Sigh express'd her Woe, 2.ChJM.783.52.
And he that felt, and I that caus'd the Woe. 2.ChWB.242.68.
Brought her own Spouse and all his Race to Woe; 2.ChWB.380.75.
He had by Heart the whole Detail of Woe 2.ChWB.387.76.
Th'impending Woe sate heavy on his Breast. 2.RL2.54.163.
On the rich Quilt sinks with becoming Woe, 2.RL4.35.186.
Led thro' a sad variety of woe: 2.ElAb.36.321.
Come! with thy looks, thy words, relieve my woe; 2.ElAb.119.329.
Thro' dreary wastes, and weep each other's woe; 2.ElAb.242.339.
For others' good, or melt at others' woe. 2.Elegy.46.366.
And bear about the mockery of woe 2.Elegy.57.367.
Who fancy Bliss to Vice, to Virtue Woe! 3.EOM4.94.137.
Behold a Scene of Misery and Woe! 6.9x.1.22.
Shrieks of Woe, 6.11.59.32.
There oft' are heard the Notes of Infant Woe, 6.14ii.5.43.
That interrupt our Peace, and work our Woe: 6.17iii.5.57.
This breathing stone immortaliz'd my woe: 6.20.26.66.
Still, tho' a rock, can thus relieve her woe, 6.20.58.67.
And wild ambition well deserves its woe. 6.32.12.96.
Unweeting Wantons of their wetting Woe! 6.42vi.2.120.
Teach me to feel another's Woe; 6.50.37.148.
But if I feel another's Woe; 6.50.37B.148.
For pleas'd Remembrance builds Delight on Woe. 6.96iv.64.278.
Lay Fortune-struck, a Spectacle of Woe! 6.128.3.355.
What Shame, what Woe is this to *Greece!* what Joy Il.1.339.104.
He deeply sighing said: To tell my Woe, Il.1.476.110.
Once more attend! avert the wastful Woe, Il.1.596.116.
Crush the dire Author of his Country's Woe. Il.3.84.193.
Too deep my Anguish, and too wild my Woe. Il.3.512.216.
She mounts the Seat oppress'd with silent Woe, Il.5.455.290.
Smile on the Slaughter, and enjoy my Woe. Il.5.947.311.
And seek the Gods, t'avert th' impending Woe. Il.6.303.341.
Our present Woe, and Infamy to come: Il.6.447.348.
When ah! oppress by Life-consuming Woe, Il.6.542.353.

WOE (CONTINUED)

Sought her own Palace, and indulg'd her Woe. Il.6.643.358.
And shun Contention, the sure Source of Woe; Il.9.335.450.
The Father's Grief, the mourning Mother's Woe.) Il.9.678.468.
And when *Jove* gave us Life, he gave us Woe. Il.10.79.6.
This is not half the Story of our Woe. Il.11.803.72.
Let his high Roofs resound with frantic Woe, Il.14.589.190.
A mournful Witness of this Scene of Woe: Il.15.463.215.
And Toil to Toil, and Woe succeeds to Woe. Il.16.139.243.
And Toil to Toil, and Woe succeeds to Woe. Il.16.139.243.
Great *Menelaus,* touch'd with gen'rous Woe, Il.17.3.286.
To sooth a Consort's and a Parent's Woe. Il.17.42.289.
Restive they stood, and obstinate in Woe: Il.17.491.307.
Only alas! to share in mortal Woe? Il.17.507.308.
As when high *Jove,* denouncing future Woe, Il.17.616.312.
This heard, o'er *Hector* spreads a Cloud of Woe, Il.17.666.314.
The youthful Warrior heard with silent Woe, Il.17.781.319.
Tho' fierce his Rage, unbounded be his Woe, Il.17.795.319.
Stood *Nestor's* Son, the Messenger of Woe: Il.18.4.322.
Ordain'd, to sink me with the Weight of Woe? Il.18.12.323.
Hangs on his Arms, amidst his frantic Woe, Il.18.39.325.
Each beat her Iv'ry Breast with silent Woe, Il.18.67.326.
(Ev'n while he lives, he wastes with secret Woe) Il.18.515.346.
Whate'er we feel, 'tis *Jove* inflicts the Woe: Il.19.282.384.
For thee, that ever felt another's Woe! Il.19.320.385.
Seem'd sensible of Woe, and droop'd his Head: Il.19.447.390.
What heav'nly Hand had caus'd his Daughter's Woe? Il.21.594.446.
What Anguish I? Unutterable Woe! Il.22.73.455.
To sooth a Father's and a Mother's Woe; Il.22.430.473.
And the whole City wears one Face of Woe. Il.22.517.478.
In all the raging Impotence of Woe. Il.22.527.478.
For such a Warrior *Thetis* aids their Woe, Il.23.19.487.
Achilles next, oppress with mighty Woe, Il.23.167.496.
And now the Sun had set upon their Woe; Il.23.193.497.
And thy Heart waste with life-consuming Woe? Il.24.164.542.
(Sad Scene of Woe!) His Face his wrapt Attire Il.24.200.545.
Born to his own, and to his Parents Woe! Il.24.258.547.
Set up by Jove your Spectacle of Woe? Il.24.300.549.
Now each by turns indulg'd the Gush of Woe; Il.24.638.563.
Nor thou O Father! thus consum'd with Woe, Il.24.755.568.
She stands her own sad Monument of Woe; Il.24.778.569.
Your common Triumph, and your common Woe. Il.24.881.573.
Th' obedient Tears, melodious in their Woe. Il.24.903.574.
The sad Companion of thy Mother's Woe; Il.24.923.574.
Thence all these Tears, and all this Scene of Woe! Il.24.931.575.
When others curst the Auth'ress of their Woe, Il.24.970.576.
The filial tears, but woe succeeds to woe: Od.1.314.47.
The filial tears, but woe succeeds to woe: Od.1.314.47.
And in the publick woe forget your own; Od.1.451.54.
For my lost Sire, nor add new woe to woe. Od.2.78.64.
For my lost Sire, nor add new woe to woe. Od.2.78.64.
Teach me to seek redress for all my woe, Od.2.355.78.
Which in my wand'rings oft reliev'd my woe: Od.4.42.122.
Still in short intervals of pleasing woe, Od.4.127.126.
The weeping Monarch swells the mighty woe: Od.4.252.131.
Let each deplore his dead: the rites of woe Od.4.269.132.
All sense of woe delivers to the wind. Od.4.308.134.
Too curious of their doom! with friendly woe Od.4.663.150.
But when superior to the rage of woe, Od.4.729.153.
To woe! Did ever sorrows equal mine? Od.4.959.163.
And with consummate woe to weigh me down, Od.4.1073.167.
Immortal life, exempt from age and woe. Od.5.174.180.
Spares only to inflict some mightier woe! Od.6.208.220.
Late a sad spectacle of woe, he trod Od.6.291.224.
A suppliant bends: oh pity human woe! Od.7.198.245.
Nor weigh the labour, but relieve the woe) Od.7.257.248.
Immortal life, exempt from age and woe. Od.7.343.253.
Then grant, what here all sons of woe obtain, Od.8.31.263.
With mighty blessings, mix'd with mighty woe: Od.8.58.265.
The woe of *Greece,* and sing so well the woe? Od.8.534.291.
The woe of *Greece,* and sing so well the woe? Od.8.534.291.
Relentless mocks her violence of woe, Od.8.578.293.
And his great heart heaves with tumultuous woe; Od.8.588.294.
Th' unhappy series of a wand'rer's woe? Od.9.12.301.
Thou mov'st, as conscious of thy master's woe! Od.9.532.328.
Some pow'r divine who pities human woe Od.10.182.349.
Aghast returns; the messenger of woe, Od.10.287.357.
While scenes of woe rose anxious in my breast, Od.10.443.365.
Too faithful memory renews your woe; Od.10.549.369.
Sad at the sight I stand, deep fix'd in woe, Od.11.69.383.
Dæmons accurst, dire ministers of woe! Od.11.76.385.
Struck at the sight I melt with filial woe, Od.11.108.386.
To learn my doom: for tost from woe to woe, Od.11.202.391.
To learn my doom: for tost from woe to woe, Od.11.202.391.
The garb of woe and habit of distress. Od.11.233.393.
O son of woe, the pensive shade rejoyn'd, Od.11.259.394.
Sad *Ariadne,* partner of their woe; Od.11.398.403.
For thee she feels sincerity of woe: Od.11.550.410.
And add new horror to the realms of woe. Od.11.574.411.
O sons of woe! decreed by adverse fates Od.12.29.430.
Aghast I stood, a monument of woe! Od.12.311.447.
Some mighty woe relentless heav'n forbodes: Od.12.328.447.
Then linger life away, and nourish woe! Od.12.416.451.
Then with erected eyes stood fix'd in woe, Od.13.239.17.
Much woe to all, but sure to me the most. Od.14.159.43.
Afresh for thee, my second cause of woe! Od.14.201.45.
And these indulge their want, and those their woe, Od.14.415.56.
A tale from falshood free, not free from woe. Od.15.289.83.
A life of wand'rings is the greatest woe: Od.15.365.87.
And pleas'd remembrance builds delight on woe. Od.15.437.90.
And the hop'd nuptials turn to joy or woe. Od.15.564.97.
Each neighb'ring realm conducive to our woe Od.16.129.109.
Yet busied with his slaves, to ease his woe, Od.16.150.109.
One scene of woe; to endless cares consign'd, Od.16.208.114.
The Prince thus interrupts the solemn woe. Od.16.245.116.
With such an image touch'd of human woe; Od.17.441.155.

WOE (CONTINUED)

Worn as I am with age, decay'd with woe, ... Od.18.58.169.
Meanly decline to combat age and woe? ... Od.18.93.171.
Lest heav'n in vengeance send some mightier woe. ... Od.18.129.172.
For man is changeful as his bliss or woe, ... Od.18.163.174.
His boding mind the future woe forestalls, ... Od.18.183.175.
For others good, and melt at others woe: ... Od.18.270.179.
The series of my toils, to sooth her woe. ... Od.19.57.195.
The Queen's attentive ear: dissolv'd in woe, ... Od.19.236.205.
Yet, while I speak, the mighty woe suspend; ... Od.19.305.209.
On me, confirm'd, and obstinate in woe. ... Od.19.388.212.
O'er my suspended woe thy words prevail, ... Od.19.689.229.
If Monarchs by the Gods are plung'd in woe, ... Od.20.245.244.
O Monarch ever dear!—O man of woe!— ... Od.20.259.245.
And sudden sighs precede approaching woe. ... Od.20.420.253.
The Heroe stands opprest with mighty woe, ... Od.22.162.295.
Enjoy the present good, and former woe; ... Od.23.56.321.
She colour'd all our wretched lives with woe. ... Od.23.238.334.
Immortal life exempt from age and woe: ... Od.23.364.342.
Now chang'd with time, with absence, and with woe? ... Od.24.252.361.

WOEFUL

Up didst thou look, oh woeful Duke! ... 6.79.73.220.

WOES

And still increase the Woes so soon begun? ... 1.TrSP.72.397.
But Thee, the last and greatest of my Woes? ... 1.TrSP.80.397.
And Wrongs and Woes were all you left with her. ... 1.TrSP.118.398.
Insults my Woes, and triumphs in my Tears, ... 1.TrSP.136.399.
My Woes, thy Crimes, I to the World proclaim; ... 1.TrSP.141.399.
What Woes attend this inauspicious Reign? ... 1.TrSt.235.420.
All these the Woes of *Oedipus* have known, ... 1.TrSt.818.444.
Domestick Woes, far heavier to be born, ... 1.TrUl.182.471.
To sooth my Hopes and mitigate my Woes. ... 1.TrUl.206.472.
Let sinful Batchelors their Woes deplore, ... 2.ChJM.29.16.
Behold the Woes of Matrimonial Life, ... 2.ChWB.1.57.
That well-known name awakens all my woes. ... 2.ElAb.30.321.
Then, ages hence, when all my woes are o'er, ... 2.ElAb.345.347.
The well-sung woes will sooth my pensive ghost; ... 2.ElAb.365.348.
The well-sung woes shall sooth my pensive ghost; ... 2.ElAb.365A.348.
And helps, another creature's wants and woes. ... 3.EOM3.52.97.
And feels, another creature's wants and woes. ... 3.EOM3.52A.97.
And woes in Language of the Pleas and Bench ... 4.JD2A.64.138.
If Heav'n, to pity human woes inclin'd, ... 6.20.45.67.
The tragic muse, returning, wept her woes. ... 6.107.4.310.
Of Woes unnumber'd, heav'nly Goddess, sing! ... Il.1.2.82.
Of all the *Grecian* Woes, O Goddess, sing! ... Il.1.2A.82.
And points the Crime, and thence derives the Woes: ... Il.1.499.112.
To Fates averse, and nurs'd for future Woes? ... Il.1.543.114.
And plunge the *Greeks* in all the Woes of War: ... Il.2.6.127.
'Till *Helen's* Woes at full reveng'd appear, ... Il.2.422.147.
Prepar'd new Toils and doubled Woes on Woes. ... Il.2.501.150.
Prepar'd new Toils and doubled Woes on Woes. ... Il.2.501.150.
Who rule the Dead, and horrid Woes prepare ... Il.3.352.209.
And thus express'd a Heart o'ercharg'd with Woes. ... Il.3.379.211.
And meditate the future Woes of *Troy*. ... Il.4.30.222.
Fated to wound, and Cause of future Woes. ... Il.4.149.228.
Such mighty Woes on perjur'd Princes wait; ... Il.4.204.231.
The fatal Cause of all his Country's Woes, ... Il.5.82.270.
Unnumber'd Woes Mankind from us sustain, ... Il.5.473.290.
And Men with Woes afflict the Gods again. ... Il.5.474.290.
And oft' afflicts his Brutal Breast with Woes. ... Il.5.955.312.
Woes heap'd on Woes consum'd his wasted Heart; ... Il.6.249.339.
Woes heap'd on Woes consum'd his wasted Heart; ... Il.6.249.339.
Woes heap'd on Woes oppress'd his wasted Heart; ... Il.6.249A.339.
Woes heap'd on Woes oppress'd his wasted Heart; ... Il.6.249A.339.
That caus'd these Woes, deserves a Sister's Name! ... Il.6.433.348.
And Woes, of which so large a Part was thine! ... Il.6.581.355.
Embitters all thy Woes, by naming me. ... Il.6.587.355.
O'erwhelms the Nations with new Toils and Woes; ... Il.7.82.367.
But feast their Souls on *Ilion's* Woes to come. ... Il.8.571.424.
Shall crush the *Greeks*, and end the Woes of *Troy*. ... Il.8.672.427.
Heav'ns! how my Country's Woes distract my Mind! ... Il.9.316.449.
His Country's Woes he glories to deride, ... Il.9.818.474.
Meanwhile his Brother, prest with equal Woes, ... Il.10.31.4.
And Woes, that only with his Life shall end! ... Il.10.99.7.
What Toils attend thee, and what Woes remain? ... Il.10.120.7.
The Woes of Men unwilling to survey, ... Il.11.71.37.
Sad Mothers of unutterable Woes!) ... Il.11.350.50.
And fix'd the Date of all his Woes to come!) ... Il.11.739.68.
More Woes shall follow, and more Heroes bleed. ... Il.12.264.91.
Such stern Decrees, such threatned Woes to come, ... Il.15.105.200.
With great Revenge, and feeds his inward Woes. ... Il.17.152.293.
Had caus'd such Sorrows past, and Woes to come. ... Il.18.114.328.
New Woes, new Sorrows shall create again: ... Il.18.116.328.
Long, long shall *Greece* the Woes we caus'd, bewail, ... Il.19.65.374.
Long-fest'ring Wounds, inextricable Woes! ... Il.19.98.376.
Who rule the Dead, and horrid Woes prepare ... Il.19.271.383.
What Woes my wretched Race of Life attend? ... Il.19.307.385.
Scarce respited from Woes I yet appear, ... Il.21.92.425.
A thousand Woes, a thousand Toils remain. ... Il.21.694.450.
While yet thy Father feels the Woes he bears, ... Il.22.81.456.
End all my Country's Woes, deep buried in thy Heart! ... Il.22.368.471.
Wide on the lonely Beach to vent his Woes. ... Il.24.20.535.
Repast unheeded, while he vents his Woes. ... Il.24.160.542.
And felt the Woes of miserable Man. ... Il.24.410.552.
Satiate at length with unavailing Woes, ... Il.24.647.563.
A Strength proportion'd to the Woes you feel. ... Il.24.658.564.
Forbear (he cry'd) this Violence of Woes, ... Il.24.893.573.
Long exercis'd in woes, oh Muse! resound. ... Od.1.2.25.
The day predestin'd to reward his woes. ... Od.1.24.30.
Charge all their woes on absolute Decree; ... Od.1.42.31.
Minerva's anger, and the direful woes ... Od.1.422.53.
Warbling the *Grecian* woes with harp and voice: ... Od.1.446.54.
No story I unfold of public woes, ... Od.2.49.62.
'Till big with knowledge of approaching woes ... Od.2.185.71.

WOES (CONTINUED)

For lo! my words no fancy'd woes relate: ... Od.2.197.71.
I see (I cry'd) his woes, a countless train; ... Od.2.203.71.
My num'rous woes, in silence let them dwell. ... Od.2.238.73.
The long historian of my country's woes: ... Od.3.142.92.
And in *Eubea* shun the woes we fear. ... Od.3.212.96.
With all my affluence when my woes are weigh'd, ... Od.4.95.124.
Dismay'd, heart-wounded with paternal woes, ... Od.4.205.129.
Born by his mother to a world of woes! ... Od.4.438.140.
Bright tracks of glory, or a cloud of woes. ... Od.4.530.146.
After long woes, and various toil endur'd, ... Od.4.629.149.
From *Ithaca*, and wond'rous woes survives; ... Od.4.752.154.
He thus; O were the woes you speak the worst! ... Od.4.924.161.
Sudden she sunk beneath the weighty woes; ... Od.4.934.162.
The Queen awakes, deliver'd of her woes; ... Od.4.1095.169.
Unhappy man! to wasting woes a prey, ... Od.5.207.181.
Unfill'd is yet the measure of my woes. ... Od.5.388.191.
But other Gods intend me other woes? ... Od.5.453.194.
Go, learn'd in woes, and other woes essay! ... Od.5.480.195.
Go, learn'd in woes, and other woes essay! ... Od.5.480.195.
Lull'd all his cares, and banish'd all his woes. ... Od.5.637.202.
His woes forgot! But *Pallas* now addrest ... Od.6.131.213.
And to the deaf woods wailing, breath'd his woes. ... Od.6.138.214.
O fatal voyage, source of all my woes!) ... Od.6.198.219.
Who breathes, must mourn: thy woes are from above. ... Od.6.232.221.
With the prevailing eloquence of woes: ... Od.6.374.230.
Bid the Great hear, and pitying heal my woes. ... Od.6.390.230.
Thro' many woes and wand'rings, lo! I come ... Od.7.31.235.
Heav'n's is his life to come, and all the woes behind. ... Od.7.261.248.
Whom Fate has loaded with a weight of woes; ... Od.7.288.250.
And let the morrow's dawn conclude my woes. ... Od.7.302.250.
(Thus sighing spoke the Man of many woes) ... Od.7.323.251.
Yet thus by woes impair'd, no more I wa<i>ve ... Od.8.207.273.
When blest with ease thy woes and wand'rings end, ... Od.8.277.278.
A dreadful story big with future woes, ... Od.8.618.295.
The woes of man; heav'n doom'd the *Greeks* to bleed, ... Od.8.632.297.
Of woes unnumber'd, sent by Heav'n and Fate? ... Od.9.16.301.
Hear then the woes, which mighty *Jove* ordain'd ... Od.9.39.303.
More near and deep, domestic woes succeed! ... Od.9.628.332.
Ye sad companions of *Ulysses'* woes! ... Od.10.215.350.
To me are known the various woes ye bore, ... Od.10.542.369.
New trains of dangers, and new scenes of woes: ... Od.11.129.387.
Yet to thy woes the Gods decree an end, ... Od.11.132.387.
The woes, the horrors, and the laws of Hell. ... Od.11.272.395.
Thro' all his woes the Hero shines confest; ... Od.11.419.405.
Nor better could the Muse record thy woes. ... Od.11.459.407.
Thy woes on earth, the wond'rous scenes in hell, ... Od.11.467.407.
Woes I unfold, of woes a dismal train. ... Od.11.475.407.
Woes I unfold, of woes a dismal train. ... Od.11.475.407.
O injur'd shade, I cry'd, what mighty woes ... Od.11.541.410.
A weight of woes, and breath the vital air, ... Od.11.598.412.
All wailing with unutterable woes. ... Od.11.664.417.
Bore toils and dangers, and a weight of woes; ... Od.11.766.424.
Your woes by land, your dangers on the main. ... Od.12.38.431.
These ills are past; now hear thy future woes. ... Od.12.48.431.
O friends, oh ever partners of my woes, ... Od.12.190.441.
From sleep debarr'd, we sink from woes to woes; ... Od.12.335.448.
From sleep debarr'd, we sink from woes to woes; ... Od.12.335.448.
So will'd some Demon, minister of woes! ... Od.12.352.448.
O fatal slumber, paid with lasting woes! ... Od.12.440.452.
A dreadful story, big with future woes; ... Od.13.199.15.
Domestic woes, far heavier to be born<e>! ... Od.13.349.24.
To sooth my hopes, and mitigate my woes. ... Od.13.373.25.
Of wand'rings and of woes a wretched share? ... Od.13.481.29.
Enough of woes already have I known; ... Od.14.45.38.
Of woes and wand'rings thou wert born to bear? ... Od.14.56.38.
The name of him awakes a thousand woes. ... Od.14.195.45.
My long narration of a life of woes. ... Od.14.228.46.
And added woes have bow'd me to the ground: ... Od.14.248.48.
And wait the woes heav'n dooms me yet to bear. ... Od.14.394.54.
From God's own hand descend our joys and woes; ... Od.14.494.60.
Far from the hateful cause of all his woes. ... Od.15.255.80.
To him the Man of woes. Oh gracious *Jove!* ... Od.15.360.86.
While I, so many wand'rings past and woes, ... Od.15.530.95.
With warmth replies the man of mighty woes. ... Od.16.92.106.
Nor wine nor food he tastes; but sunk in woes, ... Od.16.154.110.
By the false joy to aggravate my woes. ... Od.16.217.114.
And I am learn'd in all her train of woes; ... Od.17.341.148.
Minerva prompts the Man of mighty woes ... Od.17.433.153.
In equal woes, alas! involv'd by heav'n. ... Od.17.645.164.
He strove to drive the man of mighty woes. ... Od.18.13.167.
The Heroe latent in the man of woes, ... Od.18.111.172.
The tear she wipes, and thus renews her woes. ... Od.18.236.178.
My soul with woes, that long, ah long must last! ... Od.18.300.181.
Tutor'd by early woes, grow early wise! ... Od.19.24.193.
My woes awak'd will violate your ear; ... Od.19.141.199.
And sad similitude of woes ally'd, ... Od.19.400.214.
Thus old with woes my fancy paints him now! ... Od.19.418.214.
The night assists my ever-wakeful woes: ... Od.19.601.225.
A sad variety of woes I mourn! ... Od.19.612.226.
Not fiercer woes thy fortitude cou'd foil, ... Od.20.25.233.
Oh thou, of mortals most inur'd to woes! ... Od.20.41.234.
When woes the waking sense alone assail, ... Od.20.98.237.
If the long series of my woes shall end; ... Od.20.121.239.
(In woes bewilder'd, oft the wisest errs.) ... Od.20.166.241.
While thus the Chief his woes indignant told, ... Od.20.217.243.
By great *Ulysses*, and his woes I swear! ... Od.20.406.252.
By woes and wand'rings from this hapless land: ... Od.21.214.270.
Or if my woes (a long-continu'd train) ... Od.21.305.274.
Was it to flatter, or deride my woes? ... Od.23.20.319.
With well-concerted art to end his woes, ... Od.23.33.320.
When twice ten years are past of mighty woes: ... Od.23.104.324.
Decree us to sustain a length of woes, ... Od.23.220.333.
Be deck'd the couch! and peace a-while, my woes! ... Od.23.272.336.
And deck the couch; far hence be woes away! ... Od.23.274.336.
A dreadful story of approaching woes? ... Od.23.280.337.

WOES 641 WOMEN

WOES (CONTINUED)
Triumph, thou happy victor of thy woes! ....Od.23.308.338.
A mournful story of domestic woes, ...Od.23.324.339.
The good old man, to wasting woes a prey, ...Od.23.387.343.
The Archer's strife; the source of future woes, ...Od.24.196.358.
Big was his eye with tears, his heart with woes: ....Od.24.484.371.

WOFUL
What *woful stuff* this Madrigal wou'd be, ...1.EOC.418.287.
Shall die, and leave his woful Wife behind, ...2.ChWB.26.58.
If true, a woful likeness, and if lyes, ...4.2HE1.412.229.
In woful wise did sore affright ....6.58.15.171.
I chose, the livery of a woful mind! ....Od.19.392.213.

WOLF
Or wolf-like howl away the midnight hour ....Od.10.513.368.

WOLF-LIKE
Or wolf-like howl away the midnight hour ....Od.10.513.368.

WOLF'S
A Wolf's grey Hide around his Shoulders hung. ....Il.10.396.21.
The Wolf's grey Hide, th' unbended Bow and Spear; ....Il.10.529.26.

WOLSEY
Sejanus, Wolsey, hurt not honest FLEURY, ...4.EpS1.51.301.
Call *Verres, Wolsey,* any odious name? ....4.EpS2.137.321.
Call *Clodius, Wolsey,* any odious name? ....4.EpS2.137A.321.
Peel'd, patch'd, and pyebald, linsey-wolsey brothers, ...5.DunB3.115.325.

WOLVES
Wolves gave thee suck, and savage Tygers fed. ....1.PAu.90.86.
The Lambs with Wolves shall graze the verdant Mead, ...1.Mes.77.119.
And Wolves with Howling fill the sacred Quires. ....1.W-F.72A.156.
And starving Wolves, ran howling to the Wood. ....1.TrSt.738.441.
With starving Wolves, ran howling to the Wood. ....1.TrSt.738A.441.
Loud as the Wolves on Orcas' stormy steep, ...4.2HE1.328.223.
"Silence, ye Wolves! while Ralph to Cynthia howls, ...5.DunA3.159.165.
"Silence, ye Wolves! while Ralph to Cynthia howls, ...5.DunB3.165.328.
To Mountain-wolves and all the Savage race, ...6.65.2.192.
As o'er their Prey rapacious Wolves engage, ...Il.4.540.247.
Not rabid Wolves more fierce contest their Prey; ....Il.11.97.39.
Wild Mountain-Wolves the fainting Beast surround; ....Il.11.599.60.
The Wolves, tho' hungry, scour dispers'd away; ....Il.11.602.61.
Grim as voracious Wolves that seek the Springs ....Il.16.194.246.
A Troop of Wolves th' unguarded Charge survey, ...Il.16.422.259.
Such Pacts, as Lambs and rabid Wolves combine, ...Il.22.337.470.
Where mountain wolves and bridled lions roam, ...Od.10.242.352.
Of fierce sea-wolves, and monsters of the flood. ....Od.15.517.95.

WOMAN
No more a woman, nor yet quite a tree: ....1.TrFD.64.388.
Woman, the last, the best reserv'd of God. ....2.ChJM.64.17.
Woman, the last, the best Reserve of God. ....2.ChJM.64A.17.
Yet one good Woman is not to be found. ....2.ChJM.638.46.
Yet one good Woman were not to be found. ....2.ChJM.638A.46.
Well, I'm a Woman, and as such must speak; ....2.ChJM.694.48.
And think, for once, a Woman tells you true. ....2.ChWB.4.57.
Cry Wives are false, and ev'ry Woman evil, ...2.ChWB.84.60.
And all the Woman glares in open Day. ....2.ChWB.105.61.
Heav'n gave to woman the peculiar Grace ....2.ChWB.160.64.
"Let that frail Thing, weak Woman, have her way. ....2.ChWB.194.65.
A very Woman, and a very Wife! ....2.ChWB.206.66.
That not one Woman keeps her Marriage Vow. ....2.ChWB.375.75.
Europe a Woman, Child, or Dotard rule, ...3.Ep1.152.28.
Woman and Fool are two hard things to hit, ...3.Ep2.113.59.
But ev'ry Woman is at heart a Rake: ....3.Ep2.216.68.
Which, were you woman, had obtain'd; ....6.4iii.10.10.
Of Gods and heroes, made a Woman stand; ....6.20.30.67.
That Woman is a Worm we find, ...6.53.9.161.
One grateful woman to thy fame supplies ....6.72.7.208.
One Grateful woman to thy fame supply'd ....6.72.7A.208.
Not with those Toys the Woman-World admire, ...6.86.3A.244.
I know a Reasonable Woman, ...6.89.3.250.
Whose Wife, a clean, pains-taking Woman, ...6.93.2.256.
The weakest Woman sometimes may ....6.94.3.259.
A Woman, long thought barren, ...6.94.10.259.
The Woman, thus being brought to Bed, ...6.94.69.261.
Here rests a Woman, good without pretence, ...6.115.1.322.
The Saint sustain'd it, but the Woman dy'd. ....6.115.10.323.
What earthly Good will woman do? ....6.119.18A.337.
What earthly thing will woman do? ....6.119.18B.337.
Here lies a round Woman, who thought *mighty odd* ....6.124i.1.346.
Rode like a Woman to the Field of War. ....Il.2.1063.172.
Me, as a Boy or Woman would'st thou fright, ...Il.7.285.378.
Go, less than Woman in the Form of Man! ....Il.8.199.407.
The Woman, let him (as he may) enjoy; ....Il.9.444.454.
One Woman-Slave was ravish'd from thy Arms: ....Il.9.751.471.
Thou Woman-Warrior with the curling Hair; ....Il.11.492.56.
On some good Man, or Woman unreprov'd ....Il.17.493.307.
But Woman-like to fall, and fall without a Blow. ....Il.22.166.460.
A Woman for the first, in Beauty's Bloom, ...Il.23.329.503.
Nor Man, nor Woman, in the Walls remains. ....Il.24.883.573.
In wond'rous arts than woman more renown'd, ...Od.2.135.67.
And more than woman with deep wisdom crown'd; ....Od.2.136.67.
But the false woman o'er the wife prevails. ....Od.11.217.392.
O Woman, woman, when to ill thy mind ....Od.11.531.409.
O Woman, woman, when to ill thy mind ....Od.11.531.409.
To thy imperial race from woman rose! ....Od.11.542.410.
By woman here thou tread'st this mournful strand, ...Od.11.543.410.
And *Greece* by woman lies a desart land. ....Od.11.544.410.
Skill'd in rich works, a woman of their land. ....Od.15.459.93.
(For Love deceives the best of woman-kind.) ....Od.15.463.93.
Mere woman-glutton! (thus the churl reply'd) ....Od.18.32.168.
O woman, loveliest of the lovely kind, ...Od.18.291.180.
Fall'n ev'n below the rights of woman due! ....Od.18.319.182.

WOMAN (CONTINUED)
Offspring of Kings, and more than woman wise! ....Od.18.330.183.
Into the woman-state asquint to pry; ....Od.19.82.196.
A woman matchless, and almost divine, ...Od.21.113.264.
The weakest woman: all can wrong the brave. ....Od.21.350.276.
Woman, experienc'd as thou art, controul ....Od.22.448.309.
A woman like *Penelope* unkind? ....Od.23.100.324.

WOMAN-GLUTTON
Mere woman-glutton! (thus the churl reply'd) ....Od.18.32.168.

WOMAN-KIND
(For Love deceives the best of woman-kind.) ....Od.15.463.93.

WOMAN-LIKE
But Woman-like to fall, and fall without a Blow. ....Il.22.166.460.

WOMAN-SLAVE
One Woman-Slave was ravish'd from thy Arms: ....Il.9.751.471.

WOMAN-STATE
Into the woman-state asquint to pry; ....Od.19.82.196.

WOMAN-WARRIOR
Thou Woman-Warrior with the curling Hair; ....Il.11.492.56.

WOMAN-WORLD
Not with those Toys the Woman-World admire, ...6.86.3A.244.

WOMAN'S
And once inclos'd in Woman's beauteous Mold; ....2.RL1.48.149.
Think not, when Woman's transient Breath is fled, ...2.RL1.51.149.
Ev'n such is Woman's Fame: with this unblest, ...3.Ep2.281A.73.
A Woman's seen in Private life alone: ....3.Ep2.200.67.
Woman's at best a Contradiction still. ....3.Ep2.270.72.
Be this a Woman's Fame: with this unblest, ...3.Ep2.281.73.
Scarecrow to Boys, the breeding Woman's curse; ....4.JD4.268.47.
With all a Woman's Virtues but the P—x, ...4.HAdv.17.75.
The Woman's deaf, and does not hear. ....6.89.12.250.
But ev'ry Woman's in her Soul a Rake. ....6.99.16.287.
His conqu'ring Sword in any Woman's Cause. ....Il.1.395.107.
And Woman's Frailty always to believe? ....Il.3.494.215.
Or Godlike *Paris* live a Woman's Slave! ....Il.6.671.360.
What calls for Vengeance but a Woman's Cause? ....Il.9.447.454.
Forgive the weakness of a woman's heart! ....Od.23.218.333.
And ev'n the best that bears a Woman's name. ....Od.24.231.358.

WOMANKIND
In all this World, much less in Womankind; ....2.ChJM.191.24.
For much he fear'd the Faith of Womankind. ....2.ChJM.486.39.
Is gentle love, and charms all womankind: ....3.EOM2.190.78.
Scarce once herself, by turns all Womankind! ....3.Ep2.116.60.
Severe to all, but most to Womankind; ....6.19.32.63.
Scarce once herself, by Turns all Womankind? ....6.154.2.402.
Ill-fated *Paris!* Slave to Womankind, ...Il.13.965.151.
Fierce to the feeble Race of Womankind, ...Il.21.558.445.
(Some close design, or turn of womankind) ....Od.5.224.182.
With honours yet to womankind unknown, ...Od.7.86.238.
For since of womankind so few are just, ...Od.11.563.411.
Oh dearest, most rever'd of womankind! ....Od.17.56.135.
Vers'd in all arts of wily womankind. ....Od.24.151.355.

WOMB
If you receiv'd me from *Jocasta's* Womb, ...1.TrSt.87.413.
And stain the sacred Womb where once he lay? ....1.TrSt.333.424.
From whose dark Womb a ratling Tempest pours, ...1.TrSt.494.431.
Her spotted Breast, and gaping Womb imbru'd ....1.TrSt.729.440.
And warm'd the Womb of Earth with Genial Beams. ....2.ChJM.616.44.
Its Womb they deluge, and its Ribs they rend: ....Il.15.443.214.
E'er the sad Fruit of thy unhappy Womb ....Il.18.113.328.
In its wide Womb they pour the rushing Stream; ....Il.18.409.340.
And stow'd within its womb the naval stores. ....Od.2.439.82.
And unseen armies ambush'd in its womb; ....Od.11.640.416.
From her foul womb *Cratæis* gave the air ....Od.12.156.439.

WOMEN
And value *Books,* as Women *Men,* for *Dress:* ....1.EOC.306.274.
Than such as Women on their Sex bestow.) ....1.TrVP.56.379.
The Treachery you Women use to Man: ....2.ChJM.628.45.
Call'd Women Fools, and knew full many a one? ....2.ChJM.670.47.
How constant, chast, and virtuous, Women are. ....2.ChJM.672.47.
How virtuous chast and constant, Women are. ....2.ChJM.672A.47.
But grant the worst; shall Women then be weigh'd ....2.ChJM.682.48.
The Drops, (for Women when they list, can cry.) ....2.ChJM.786.53.
'Tis but a Counsel—and we Women still ....2.ChWB.34.58.
To lye so boldly as we Women can. ....2.ChWB.71.59.
How quaint an Appetite in Women reigns! ....2.ChWB.259.69.
Men, Women, Clergy, Regular and Lay. ....2.ChWB.354.74.
But cou'd we Women write as Scholars can, ...2.ChWB.366.75.
Oft when the World imagine Women stray, ...2.RL1.91.152.
Are, as when Women, wondrous fond of Place. ....2.RL3.36.171.
Priests, Princes, Women, no dissemblers here. ....3.Ep1.177.30.
Women and Fools must like him or he dies; ....3.Ep1.183.30.
"Most Women have no Characters at all". ....3.Ep2.2.46.
In Women, two almost divide the kind; ....3.Ep2.208.67.
"Women and Fools are always in Extreme. ....4.HAdv.28.77.
Spies, Guardians, Guests, old Women, Aunts, and Cozens& ....4.HAdv.129.85.
From gleaming Swords no shrieking Women run; ....4.HAdv.169.89.
The other slights, for Women, Sports, and Wines, ...4.2HE2.272.185.
Women ben full of Ragerie, ...6.14i.1.41.
Women, tho' nat sans Leacherie, ...6.14i.1A.41.
Is call'd in Women only Reputation: ....6.46.2.127.
Oh Women of *Achaia!* Men no more! ....Il.2.293.141.
Unhappy *Paris!* but to Women brave, ...Il.3.55.192.
Women of Greece! Oh Scandal of your Race, ...Il.7.109.369.
Thou hast but done what Boys or Women can; ....Il.11.495.56.

WOMEN (CONTINUED)

Women alone, when in the Streets they jar, ... Il.20.300.406.
The women keep the gen'rous creature bare, ... Od.17.388.150.
Melanthius or the women have betray'd— ... Od.22.165.295.

WOMEN'S

The Reaper's due Repast, the Women's Care. ... Il.18.650.355.
Than works of female skill their women's pride, ... Od.7.138.242.
Mean-time commit we to our women's care ... Od.15.87.73.

WON

By Charms like thine which all my Soul have won, ... 1.TrSP.95.398.
Twas by *Rebecca's* Aid that *Jacob* won ... 2.ChJM.69.18.
Yet, with a Knack, my Heart he cou'd have won, ... 2.ChWB.257.69.
This Hand, which won it, shall for ever wear. ... 2.RL4.138.195.
But when by Man's audacious labour won, ... 3.Ep3.11.84.
And Heav'n is won by violence of Song. ... 4.2HE1.240.215.
"The race by vigor, not by vaunts is won; ... 5.DunA2.55.105.
"The race by vigour, not by vaunts is won; ... 5.DunB2.59.298.
No Game at *Ombre* lost or won. ... 6.10.4.24.
What Authors lose, their Booksellers have won, ... 6.24ii.1.75.
He says, poor Poets lost, while Players won, ... 6.34.21.101.
What fatal Favour has the Goddess won, ... Il.1.722.122.
In secret Woods he won the *Naiad's* Grace, ... Il.6.31.325.
Be mindful of the Wreaths your Arms have won, ... Il.8.212.407.
Autolycus by fraudful Rapine won, ... Il.10.314.17.
Great Queen of Arms, whose Favour *Tydeus* won, ... Il.10.337.18.
These *Troy* but lately to her Succour won, ... Il.10.504.26.
O Friends! O *Greeks!* assert your Honours won; ... Il.11.355.50.
Now call to Mind your ancient Trophies won, ... Il.11.369.51.
These, as my first Essay of Arms, I won; ... Il.11.826.73.
The Sire of Earth and Heav'n, by *Thetis* won ... Il.13.438.126.
He won, and flourish'd where *Adrastus* reign'd: ... Il.14.137.164.
Think'st thou that *Troy* has *Jove's* high Favour won, ... Il.14.299.177.
Which oft, in Cities storm'd, and Battels won, ... Il.15.630.220.
As if new Vigour from new Fights they won, ... Il.15.846.229.
With Gifts of Price he sought and won the Dame; ... Il.16.227.248.
This Instant see his short-liv'd Trophies won, ... Il.16.789.274.
To me the Spoils my Prowess won, resign; ... Il.17.15.288.
(Won by his own, or by *Patroclus'* Arms) ... Il.18.34.325.
Contending Nations won and lost the Day; ... Il.18.310.336.
Rises in Arms: Such Grace thy *Greeks* have won. ... Il.18.420.341.
But thou, in Pity, by my Pray'r be won; ... Il.18.527.347.
Begot my Sire, whose Spear such Glory won: ... Il.21.177.429.
The Sons of *Actor* won the Prize of Horse, ... Il.23.733.519.
But won by Numbers, not by Art or Force: ... Il.23.734.519.
Ye both have won: Let others who excell ... Il.23.858.523.
And *Pallas*, not *Ulysses* won the Day. ... Il.23.920.525.
Won by destructive Lust (Reward obscene) ... Il.24.40.537.
Neptune, by pray'r repentant rarely won, ... Od.1.88.35.
For twenty beeves by great *Laertes* won; ... Od.1.542.58.
But when (by wisdom won) proud *Ilion* burn'd, ... Od.3.159.93.
Hear, Goddess, hear, by those oblations won; ... Od.4.1009.164.
"Won by her pray'r, th' aereal bridegroom flies. ... Od.6.336.227.
Won by prophetic knowledge, to fulfill ... Od.11.363.400.
And won the heart with manly Eloquence! ... Od.11.624.414.
A smooth-tongu'd sailor won her to his mind; ... Od.15.462.93.
For me, suffice the approbation won ... Od.17.474.156.
"And Name the blessing that your pray'rs have won." ... Od.19.476.220.
One vent'rous game this hand has won to-day, ... Od.22.7.286.
Successful toils, and battles bravely won? ... Od.24.120.353.

WOND'RING

He from the wond'ring furrow call'd the food, ... 3.EOM3.219.115.
He from the wond'ring furrow call'd their Food, ... 3.EOM3.219A.115.
Tho' wond'ring Senates hung on all he spoke, ... 3.Ep1.184.31.
Wond'ring he gaz'd: When lo! a Sage appears, ... 5.DunA3.27.153.
Wond'ring he gaz'd: When lo! a Sage appears, ... 5.DunB3.35.322.
Thro' roaring Seas the wond'ring Warriors bear; ... Il.2.744.161.
And Crowds stood wond'ring at the passing Show; ... Il.3.68.192.
Wond'ring we hear, and fix'd in deep Surprize ... Il.3.287.207.
High o'er the wond'ring Hosts he soar'd above, ... Il.8.299.412.
And wond'ring view the Slaughters of the Night. ... Il.10.617.29.
That when with wond'ring Eyes our martial Bands ... Il.12.383.95.
The wond'ring Waters leave his Axle dry. ... Il.13.49.107.
The wond'ring Crowds the downward Level trod; ... Il.15.412.213.
Of wond'ring Ages, and the World's Amaze! ... Il.18.536.347.
The Chief beholds himself with wond'ring eyes; ... Il.19.416.389.
With that, he left him wond'ring as he lay, ... Il.20.389.411.
The thronging *Greeks* behold with wond'ring Eyes ... Il.22.465.474.
High o'er the wond'ring Crowds the whirling Circle flew. ... Il.23.996.529.
The wond'ring Hero eyes his royal Guest; ... Il.24.797.570.
Vouchsaf'd thy presence to my wond'ring eyes, ... Od.2.298.76.
Methinks *Ulysses* strikes my wond'ring eyes; ... Od.4.198.129.
The wond'ring Nymph his glorious port survey'd, ... Od.6.285.224.
With wond'ring eyes the heroe she survey'd, ... Od.8.497.289.
Beneath my labours how thy wond'ring eyes ... Od.18.416.189.
The walls where-e'er my wond'ring sight I turn, ... Od.19.46.195.
Thy wond'ring eyes shall view: his rightful reign ... Od.20.291.247.
(His perfect skill the wond'ring gazers ey'd, ... Od.21.127.264.
When from the Palace to the wond'ring throng ... Od.24.504.372.

WOND'ROUS

And had a wond'rous Gift to quench a Flame. ... 2.ChWB.320.72.
The wond'rous Rock like *Parian* Marble shone, ... 2.TemF.29.255.
Go, wond'rous creature! mount where Science guides, ... 3.EOM2.19.56.
They follow rev'rently each wond'rous wight, ... 4.1740.33.333.
These wond'rous works; so Jove and Fate require) ... 5.DunA1.4.61.
And learn, my sons, the wond'rous pow'r of Noise. ... 5.DunA2.214.127.
And learn, my sons, the wond'rous pow'r of Noise. ... 5.DunB2.222.306.
Each with some wond'rous gift approach'd the Pow'r, ... 5.DunB4.399.381.
Thought wond'rous honest, tho' of mean Degree, ... 6.49i.19.138.
Sylvia my Heart in wond'rous wise alarm'd, ... 6.99.1.286.
Approach, and view the wond'rous Scene below! ... Il.3.174.199.
Well may we deem the wond'rous Birth thy own. ... Il.5.1081.318.
Blest in his Love, this wond'rous Hero stands; ... Il.9.151.439.

WOND'ROUS (CONTINUED)

Such wond'rous Deeds as *Hector's* Hand has done, ... Il.10.57.4.
Wond'rous old Man! whose Soul no Respite knows, ... Il.10.186.10.
(*Jove's* wond'rous Bow, of three celestial Dyes, ... Il.11.37.36.
To few, and wond'rous few, has *Jove* assign'd ... Il.13.917.148.
And lo! the God, and wond'rous Man appear; ... Il.14.451.185.
(Wond'rous to tell) instinct with Spirit roll'd ... Il.18.442.342.
A solid Pine-tree barr'd of wond'rous Length; ... Il.24.558.559.
Where as to life the wond'rous figures rise, ... Od.2.105.66.
A wond'rous monument of female wiles! ... Od.2.126.67.
In wond'rous arts than woman more renown'd, ... Od.2.135.67.
These prodigies of art, and wond'rous cost? ... Od.4.84.123.
What wond'rous conduct in the chief appear'd, ... Od.4.373.137.
From *Ithaca*, and wond'rous woes survives; ... Od.4.752.154.
By *Pallas* taught, he frames the wond'rous mold, ... Od.6.277.224.
Her royal hand a wond'rous work designs, ... Od.6.367.229.
Cam'st thou not hither, wond'rous stranger! say, ... Od.7.318.251.
A wond'rous Net he labours, to betray ... Od.8.317.281.
Her wond'rous robes; and full the Goddess blooms. ... Od.8.402.285.
In dance unmatch'd! a wond'rous ball is brought, ... Od.8.407.285.
A bowl that flames with gold, of wond'rous frame, ... Od.8.465.288.
In wond'rous ships self-mov'd, instinct with mind; ... Od.8.604.294.
And shew'd its nature and its wond'rous pow'r: ... Od.10.363.362.
There as the wond'rous visions I survey'd, ... Od.11.104.385.
To thy chaste bride the wond'rous story tell, ... Od.11.271.395.
The wond'rous youths had scarce nine winters told, ... Od.11.381.401.
What wond'rous man heav'n sends us in our guest! ... Od.11.418.405.
Thy woes on earth, the wond'rous scenes in hell, ... Od.11.467.407.
But wond'rous visions drew my curious eye. ... Od.11.696.419.
Around his breast a wond'rous Zone is row'd, ... Od.11.751.423.
The wond'rous visions, and the laws of Hell. ... Od.12.46.431.
The wond'rous kind a length of age survey, ... Od.12.164.440.
Deep, wond'rous deep, below appears the ground. ... Od.12.291.446.
Who first *Ulysses'* wond'rous bow shall bend, ... Od.21.75.262.
The wond'rous bow, attend another cause. ... Od.21.273.273.
While each to Chance ascrib'd the wond'rous stroke, ... Od.22.36.288.
By *Pallas* taught, he frames the wond'rous mold, ... Od.23.159.328.
Great deeds, oh friends! this wond'rous man has wrought, ... Od.24.489.371.

WONDER

Or hush'd with Wonder, hearken from the Sprays: ... 1.PWi.56.93.
What wonder then, a Beast or Subject slain ... 1.W-F.57.154.
No wonder Savages or Subjects slain ... 1.W-F.57A.154.
(The *World's* just Wonder, and ev'n *thine* O *Rome!*) ... 1.EOC.248.268.
What wonder *Modes* in *Wit* shou'd take their Turn? ... 1.EOC.447.289.
What Wonder then? he was not then Alone. ... 1.TrSt.262.421.
The Prince with Wonder did the Waste behold, ... 1.TrSt.510A.431.
Unknown, with Wonder may perplex your Mind. ... 1.TrSt.659.438.
The Crowd in stupid Wonder fix'd appear, ... 1.TrSt.731.440.
To raise his Wonder, and ingage his Aid? ... 1.TrUl.178.471.
By means of this, some Wonder shall appear, ... 2.ChJM.512.40.
What Wonder then, fair Nymph! thy Hairs shou'd feel ... 2.RL3.177.182.
And Saints with wonder heard the vows I made. ... 2.ElAb.114.329.
Alas what wonder! Man's superior part ... 3.EOM2.39.60.
Clodio, the scorn and wonder of our days, ... 3.Ep1.180A.30.
Wharton, the scorn and wonder of our days, ... 3.Ep1.180.30.
A Work to wonder at—perhaps a Stow. ... 3.Ep4.70.143.
No wonder some Folks bow, and think them *Kings*. ... 4.JD4.211.43.
But wonder how the Devil they got there? ... 4.Arbu.172.108.
But all the wonder is, how they got there? ... 4.Arbu.172A.108.
And wonder with a follish face of praise. ... 4.Arbu.212.111.
Dryden alone (what wonder?) came not nigh, ... 4.Arbu.245.113.
Wonder of Kings! like whom, to mortal eyes ... 4.2HE1.29.197.
No wonder then, when all was Love and Sport, ... 4.2HE1.151.209.
"I wonder what some people mean; ... 4.HS6.104.257.
Have I in silent wonder seen such things ... 4.EpS1.109.306.
To wonder at their Maker, not to serve." ... 5.DunB4.458.385.
And wonder with a foolish Face of Praise: ... 6.49iii.28.143.
Some strangely wonder you're not fond to marry— ... 6.82vi.11.232.
But wonder how the Devil it got there. ... 6.98.22.284.
And wonder with a foolish Face of Praise. ... 6.98.64.285.
You wonder at it—This Sir is the case, ... 6.105iii.3.301.
A softer wonder my pleas'd soul surveys, ... 6.106i.2.306.
You wonder Who this Thing has writ, ... 6.127.1.355.
What wonder tryumphs never turn'd his brain ... 6.130.7.358.
No wonder *Troy* so long resists our Pow'rs. ... Il.2.409.147.
They cry'd, No wonder such Celestial Charms ... Il.3.205.201.
With Wonder *Priam* view'd the Godlike Man, ... Il.3.239.203.
The War's whole Art with Wonder had he seen, ... Il.4.634.251.
No wonder, *Greeks!* that all to *Hector* yield, ... Il.5.742.302.
No Fragment tells where once the Wonder stood; ... Il.12.34.83.
Their martial Fury in their Wonder lost. ... Il.12.232.89.
No less the Wonder of the warring Crew. ... Il.15.831.229.
What wonder this, when in thy frantick Mood ... Il.21.460.440.
All gaze, all wonder: Thus *Achilles* gaz'd: ... Il.24.593.561.
Wonder and joy alternate fire his breast: ... Od.1.416.52.
Rage gnaw'd the lip, and wonder chain'd the tongue. ... Od.1.488.55.
In holy wonder fixt, and still amaze. ... Od.3.477.110.
My wonder dictates is the dome of *Jove*. ... Od.4.90.123.
With wonder rapt, on yonder cheek I trace ... Od.4.189.129.
High rapt in wonder of the future deed, ... Od.4.579.147.
With rev'rence at the lofty wonder gaz'd: ... Od.6.200.219.
The chief with wonder sees th' extended streets, ... Od.7.55.236.
(The publick wonder, and the publick love) ... Od.7.91.238.
Not without wonder seen. Then thus began, ... Od.7.316.251.
With wonder seiz'd, we view the pleasing ground, ... Od.9.176.312.
They gaze with wonder, not unmixt with fear. ... Od.10.251.354.
A painted wonder flying on the main! ... Od.11.155.389.
To raise his wonder, and engage his aid: ... Od.13.345.24.
How will each speech his grateful wonder raise? ... Od.15.176.77.
Fill'd ev'ry breast with wonder and delight. ... Od.15.185.77.
(There curious eyes inscrib'd with wonder trace ... Od.15.440.90.
Yet at thy words I start, in wonder lost; ... Od.16.264.117.
Enquiring all, their wonder they confess, ... Od.17.442.155.
Nor wonder I, at such profusion shown; ... Od.17.535.158.
With wonder gaze, and gazing speak aloud; ... Od.18.81.170.

WONDER (CONTINUED)
Thy husband's wonder, and thy son's to raise, ...Od.18.191.175.
In silent wonder sigh'd unwilling praise. ....Od.19.272.208.
(Whose sage decision I with wonder hear) ....Od.21.295.274.
This hand the wonder fram'd; An olive spread ....Od.23.191.332.
A painted wonder, flying on the main. ....Od.23.288.337.
"Forbear your wonder, and the feast attend; ....Od.24.455.370.
Could work this wonder: welcome to thy own! ....Od.24.463.370.

WONDER'D
The Forests wonder'd at th'unusual Grain, ...1.W-F.89.158.
And Nations wonder'd while they dropp'd the sword! ....4.2HE1.399.229.
And foes to virtue wonder'd how they wept. ....6.32.8.96.
Corneille himself saw, wonder'd, and was fir'd. ....6.107.8.310.

WONDERS
And calls forth all the Wonders of her Face; ....2.RL1.142.157.
Around these Wonders as I cast a Look, ...2.TemF.276.276.
Around, a thousand winged Wonders fly, ...2.TemF.487.287.
They please as Beauties, here as Wonders strike. ....3.Ep1.96.22.
Erect new wonders, and the old repair, ...3.Ep4.192.155.
And no man wonders he's not stung by Pug: ....4.HS1.88.13.
Then thus the wonders of the Deep declares. ....5.DunA2.306.139.
Behold the wonders of th' Oblivious Lake. ....5.DunA3.36.154.
"What pow'r," he cries, "what pow'r these wonders wrought?" .5.DunA3.246.178.
What God or Dæmon all these wonders wrought? ....5.DunA3.246A.178.
"And are these wonders, Son, to thee unknown? ....5.DunA3.269.180.
Unknown to thee? These wonders are thy own. ....5.DunA3.270.180.
Then thus the wonders of the deep declares. ....5.DunB2.330.313.
Behold the wonders of th' oblivious Lake. ....5.DunB3.44.322.
"What pow'r, he cries, what pow'r these wonders wrought' ......5.DunB3.250.332.
"And are these wonders, Son, to thee unknown? ....5.DunB3.273.333.
Unknown to thee? These wonders are thy own. ....5.DunB3.274.333.
You may, with *Addison,* do wonders. ....6.44.20.123.
Imperial wonders rais'd on Nations spoil'd, ...6.71.5.202.
What Wonders there the Man grown old, did! ....6.101.15.290.
Ye Gods! what Wonders has *Ulysses* wrought? ....Il.2.333.143.
What glorious Toils, what Wonders they recite, ...Il.4.428.240.
And will not these (the Wonders he has done) ....Il.9.462.455.
When *Hector's* Prowess no such Wonders wrought; ....Il.9.465.455.
The distanc'd Army wonders at his Deeds. ....Il.11.200.44.
Of Works divine (such Wonders are in Heav'n!) ....Il.18.490.345.
Then thus, amaz'd: What Wonders strike my Mind! ....Il.20.393.411.
Ye mighty Gods! what Wonders strike my View: ....Il.21.62.424.
And wonders at the Rashness of his Foe. ....Il.23.506.510.
The wonders of the Deep expanded lye; ....Od.1.68.34.
Amid the monstrous wonders of the deeps; ....Od.3.410.106.
Speak you, (who saw) his wonders in the war. ....Od.4.334.135.
Thro' the vast waves the dreadful wonders move, ...Od.12.73.434.

WONDRING
The wondring Forests soon shou'd dance again, ...1.PSu.82.79.
But see! where *Daphne* wondring mounts on high, ...1.PWi.69.93.
Or back to Life compells the wondring Ghosts. ....1.TrSt.436.428.
And from the wondring God th'unwilling Youth retir'd. ....1.TrSt.785.443.
That while with wondring Eyes our Martial Bands ....1.TrES.39.451.
That when with wondring Eyes our Martial Bands ....1.TrES.39A.451.
In that nice Moment, lo! the wondring Knight ....2.ChJM.748.51.
Thro' wondring Skies enormous stalk'd along; ....Il.1.524.113.
For while around we gaz'd with wondring Eyes, ...Il.2.388.145.
The wondring Rivals gaze with cares oppress, ...Od.2.183.71.

WONDROUS
A wondrous *Tree* that Sacred *Monarchs* bears? ....1.PSp.86.69.
To him *Apollo* (wondrous to relate! ....1.TrSt.545.433.
Each wondrous positive, and wondrous wise; ....2.ChJM.144.21.
Each wondrous positive, and wondrous wise; ....2.ChJM.144.21.
'Tis well, 'tis wondrous well, the Knight replies, ...2.ChJM.216.25.
Are, as when Women, wondrous fond of Place. ....2.RL3.36.171.
A wondrous Bag with both her Hands she binds, ...2.RL4.81.190.
Or *Sloane,* or *Woodward's* wondrous Shelves contain; ....4.JD4.30.29.
(Tho' ne'er so weighty) reach a wondrous height; ....6.7.16.16.
This wondrous Signal *Jove* himself displays, ...Il.2.392.145.
My self, O King! have seen that wondrous Man; ....Il.3.266.205.
That wondrous Force by which whole Armies fall, ...Il.5.223.278.
A Spear the Hero bore of wondrous Strength, ...Il.6.394.346.
Amaz'd beheld the wondrous Works of Man: ....Il.7.528.391.

WONNES
That wonnes in haulkes and hernes, and *H[erne]* he hight. ......5.DunA3.184A.171.

WONNETH
Of Clerk, that wonneth in *Irelond:* .... 6.14i.4A.41.

WONT
(As Men that ask Advice are wont to be.) ....2.ChJM.84.18.
Procur'd the Key her Knight was wont to bear; ....2.ChJM.509.40.
(Such was her wont, at early dawn to drop ....5.DunA2.67.106.
(Such was her wont, at early dawn to drop ....5.DunB2.71.299.
The dagger wont to pierce the Tyrant's breast; ....5.DunB4.38.344.
Where Bentley late tempestuous wont to sport ....5.DunB4.201.362.
"How wert thou wont to walk with cautious Tread, ...6.96ii.67.273.
Far other Task! than when they wont to keep ....Il.11.141.41.
Lost in *Patroclus* now, that wont to deck ....Il.23.349.503.
This mighty Quoit *Aëtion* wont to rear, ...Il.23.977.528.
Frequent, O King, was *Nestor* wont to raise ....Od.4.259.131.
First thou wert wont to crop the flow'ry mead, ...Od.9.527.328.
His arms deform'd the roof they wont adorn: ....Od.19.11.193.
Whose shrine with weanling lambs he wont to load.) ....Od.19.469.219.
Which old *Laertes* wont in youth to wield, ...Od.22.198.297.

WONTED
Not so *Atrides:* He, with wonted Pride, ...Il.1.492.111.
He feels each Limb with wonted Vigor light; ....Il.5.156.274.
Pamper'd and proud, he seeks the wonted Tides, ...Il.6.654.359.
These, turn'd by *Phœbus* from their wonted ways, ...Il.12.23.82.

WONTED (CONTINUED)
Nor roll their wonted Tribute to the Deep. ....Il.21.236.430.
And soft re-murmur in their wonted Bed. ....Il.21.447.438.
Soon as warm life its wonted office found, ...Od.5.588.200.
Their wonted grace, but only serve to weep. ....Od.18.296.180.
Its wonted lustre let the floor regain; ....Od.20.187.242.

WOO (See WOOE.)
Reap their own Fruits, and woo their Sable Loves, ...1.W-F.410.192.

WOO'D
Who cou'd not win the Mistress, woo'd the Maid; ....1.EOC.105.251.

WOOD
The trembling Trees, in ev'ry Plain and Wood, ...1.PWi.63.93.
Or wandring thoughtful in the silent Wood, ...1.W-F.249.172.
Hairs, like a wood, my head and shoulders grace, ...1.TrPA.102.370.
The Savage Hunter, and the haunted Wood; ....1.TrSt.324.423.
Alive, the Pride and Terror of the Wood. ....1.TrSt.574.434.
And starving Wolves, ran howling to the Wood. ....1.TrSt.738.441.
With starving Wolves, ran howling to the Wood. ....1.TrSt.738A.441.
And thro' his Buckler drove the trembling Wood; ....1.TrES.138.454.
Around the Works a Wood of glitt'ring Spears ....1.TrES.181.456.
Deep Groans and hollow Roars rebellow thro' the Wood. ....1.TrES.299.460.
Fair to be seen, and rear'd of honest Wood. ....2.ChWB.246.68.
To that which warbles thro' the vernal wood: ....3.EOM1.216.42.
Who taught the nations of the field and wood ....3.EOM3.99.101.
Not Man alone, but all that roam the wood, ...3.EOM3.119.104.
In the same temple, the resounding wood, ...3.EOM3.155.108.
The Wood supports the Plain, the parts unite, ...3.Ep4.81.145.
For all his Lordship knows, but they are Wood. ....3.Ep4.138.150.
Buy every stick of Wood that lends them heat, ...4.2HE2.242.183.
Of Land, set out to plant a Wood. ....4.HS6.6.251.
One clasp'd in wood, and one in strong cow-hide. ....5.DunA1.130.80.
One clasp'd in wood, and one in strong cow-hide; ....5.DunB1.150.281.
A poet made the silent wood pursue; ....6.3.11.7.
This vocal wood had drawn the poet too. ....6.3.12.7.
The silent wood, of old, a poet drew ....6.3.11A.7.
A wood? quoth Lewis; and with that, ...6.67.1.195.
If this a Wood you will maintain ....6.67.15.195.
T[o]m W[oo]d of *Ch[i]sw[i]c[k],* deep divine, ...6.121.1.340.
From the cleft Wood the crackling Flames aspire, ...Il.2.508.151.
Where under high *Cyllenè* crown'd with Wood, ...Il.2.731.161.
With Spears erect, a moving Iron Wood; ....Il.4.323.236.
Amid the Lungs was fix'd the winged Wood, ...Il.4.612.250.
Where grazing Heifers range the lonely Wood, ...Il.5.207.276.
In deep Recesses of the gloomy Wood, ...Il.5.682.300.
A Wood of Spears his ample Shield sustain'd; ....Il.5.767.303.
Or foaming Boars, the Terror of the Wood. ....Il.5.975.313.
Or foaming Boars, the Terror of the Wood. ....Il.7.308.379.
Fix'd to the Wood with circling Rings of Gold: ....Il.8.618.425.
A Wood of Spears stood by, that fixt upright, ...Il.10.174.9.
Then fix'd in Earth. Against the trembling Wood ....Il.10.443.23.
The weary Wood-man spreads his sparing Meal, ...Il.11.120.41.
Its Surface bristled with a quiv'ring Wood; ....Il.11.699.66.
Fix'd was the Point, but broken was the Wood. ....Il.11.711.66.
And thro' his Buckler drove the trembling Wood; ....Il.12.492.99.
Around the Works a Wood of glitt'ring Spears ....Il.12.535.101.
A Prey to every Savage of the Wood; ....Il.13.144.111.
At ev'ry Shock the crackling Wood resounds; ....Il.13.196.115.
In their fell Jaws high-lifting thro' the Wood, ...Il.13.267.117.
In their fell Jaws high-lifted thro' the Wood, ...Il.13.267A.117.
Sent from an Arm so strong, the missive Wood ....Il.13.638.136.
Splinter'd on Earth flew half the broken Wood. ....Il.13.715.138.
Smooths the rough Wood, and levels ev'ry Part; ....Il.15.475.215.
And gains the friendly Shelter of the Wood. ....Il.15.707.223.
(When some tall Stag fresh-slaughter'd in the Wood ....Il.16.196.247.
Deep groans, and hollow roars, rebellow thro' the Wood. ....Il.16.604.267.
Two lordly Rulers of the Wood engage; ....Il.16.916.279.
In the deep Bosom of some gloomy Wood; ....Il.16.924.279.
But swift withdrew the long-protended Wood, ...Il.16.981.281.
Thus in the Center of some gloomy Wood, ...Il.17.146.293.
A brazen Bulwark, and an iron Wood. ....Il.17.409.303.
The Son of *Priam* whirl'd the missive Wood; ....Il.17.688.314.
Not fiercer rush along the gloomy Wood, ...Il.17.811.320.
His clam'rous Grief the bellowing Wood resounds. ....Il.18.376.339.
Then heap the lighted Wood; the Flame divides ....Il.18.407.340.
Two Lions rushing from the Wood appear'd; ....Il.18.671.356.
Each fair-hair'd Dryad of the shady Wood, ...Il.20.13.393.
A Wood of Lances rises round his Head, ...Il.20.428.412.
The Foe thrice tugg'd, and shook the rooted Wood; ....Il.21.191.429.
So from some deep grown Wood a Panther starts, ...Il.21.677.450.
The Wood the *Grecians* cleave, prepar'd to burn; ....Il.23.150.495.
The youth of *Pylos,* some on pointed wood ....Od.3.43.88.
The seats to range, the fragrant wood to bring, ...Od.3.544.114.
So when the wood-man's toyl her cave surrounds ....Od.4.1041.166.
Of poplars, pines, and firs, a lofty wood, ...Od.5.306.185.
Now here, now there, impell'd the floating wood. ....Od.5.416.192.
Planks, Beams, dis-parted fly: the scatter'd wood ....Od.5.468.195.
When Morning rises? If I take the wood, ...Od.5.605.201.
At length he took the passage to the Wood, ...Od.5.613.201.
The fair-hair'd *Dryads* of the shady wood, ...Od.6.145.214.
Then took the shelter of the neighb'ring wood. ....Od.7.367.254.
Heap high the wood and bid the flames arise. ....Od.8.472.288.
Destruction enters in the treach'rous wood, ...Od.8.561.293.
Crown'd with rough thickets, and a nodding wood. ....Od.9.224.316.
Amidst *Apollo's* consecrated wood; ....Od.9.233.316.
Green from the wood; of height and bulk so vast, ...Od.9.382.321.
To plunge the brand, and twirl the pointed wood; ....Od.9.392.322.
In his broad eye so whirls the fiery wood; ....Od.9.461.325.
Which to the city drew the mountain wood; ....Od.10.118.346.
Sent a tall stag, descending from the wood, ...Od.10.183.349.
A length of thickets, and entangled wood. ....Od.10.224.351.
And heard a voice resounding thro' the wood: ....Od.10.253.354.
A form divine forth issu'd from the wood, ...Od.10.329.360.
On *Ossa, Pelion* nods with all his wood: ....Od.11.388.403.

WOOD (CONTINUED)

These quarter'd, sing'd, and fix'd on forks of wood, ...Od.14.88.40.
And took the spreading shelter of the wood. ....Od.14.388.53.
None 'scaped him, bosom'd in the gloomy wood; ....Od.17.383.150.
The thorny wilds the wood-men fierce assail: ....Od.19.508.221.
Deep in the rough recesses of the wood, ...Od.19.511.221.
Mean-time the menial train with unctuous wood ....Od.20.153.241.
A blaze of bucklers, and a wood of spears. ....Od.22.161.295.
And clear'd a Plant, encumber'd with its wood. ....Od.24.268.362.

WOOD-MAN

The weary Wood-man spreads his sparing Meal, ...Il.11.120.41.

WOOD-MAN'S

So when the wood-man's toyl her cave surrounds ....Od.4.1041.166.

WOOD-MEN

The thorny wilds the wood-men fierce assail: ....Od.19.508.221.

WOOD'S

Put this pot of Wood's mettle ....6.91.21.254.
Put your pot of Wood's mettle ....6.91.21A.254.

WOODBINE

Now rise, and haste to yonder Woodbine Bow'rs, ...1.PSp.97.70.

WOODCOCKS

And lonely Woodcocks haunt the watry Glade. ....1.W-F.128.162.

WOODEN

The wooden Guardian of our Privacy ....6.100ii.1.288.
Who holds Dragoons and Wooden-Shoes in scorn; ....6.128.20.356.
And guards them trembling in their wooden Walls. ....Il.8.626.425.
Now Greece had trembled in their wooden Walls; ....Il.11.404.52.
Tho' round his Sides a wooden Tempest rain, ...Il.11.684.65.
And shuts the Grecians in their wooden Walls: ....Il.18.344.338.

WOODEN-SHOES

Who holds Dragoons and Wooden-Shoes in scorn; ....6.128.20.356.

WOODLAND

Here Hills and Vales, the Woodland and the Plain, ...1.W-F.11.149.
The Lion rushed thro' the woodland Shade, ...Il.11.601.61.
What tho' tremendous in the woodland Chase, ...Il.21.561.445.
So with her young, amid the woodland shades ....Od.4.449.141.
Rows'd by the woodland nymphs, at early dawn, ...Od.9.178.312.
Shot to Olympus from the woodland shade. ....Od.10.368.362.
Where woodland monsters grin in fretted gold, ...Od.11.752.423.
Thro' mazy thickets of the woodland shade, ...Od.14.2.32.
So with her young, amid the woodland shades, ...Od.17.140.138.
Which noted token of the woodland war ....Od.19.545.223.

WOODMAN

The dext'rous Woodman shapes the stubborn Oaks; ....Il.23.386.505.

WOODMAN'S

The Labours of the Woodman's Axe resound; ....Il.16.768.273.

WOODMEN

The sturdy Woodmen equal Burthens bore ....Il.23.152.495.

WOODS

The Woods shall answer, and their Echo ring. ....1.PSu.16.73.
In Woods bright Venus with Adonis stray'd. ....1.PSu.61.76.
The Winds to breathe, the waving Woods to move, ...1.PAu.41.83.
Farewell ye Woods! adieu the Light of Day! ....1.PAu.94.87.
The lonely Lords of empty Wilds and Woods. ....1.W-F.48.153.
Now range the Hills, the gameful Woods beset, ...1.W-F.95.159.
Now range the Hills, the thickest Woods beset, ...1.W-F.95A.159.
The Woods and Fields their pleasing Toils deny. ....1.W-F.120.161.
The watry Landskip of the pendant Woods, ...1.W-F.213.169.
With joyful Pride survey'st our lofty Woods, ...1.W-F.220.169.
With joyful Pride survey our lofty Woods, ...1.W-F.220A.169.
Thy Trees, fair Windsor! now shall leave their Woods, ...1.W-F.385.189.
Range in the woods, and in the vallies roam: ....1.TrPA.79.368.
That haunt our Mountains and our Alban Woods. ....1.TrVP.76.380.
And when in youth he seeks the shady woods, ...1.TrFD.84.389.
Thro' thickest Woods, and rouz'd the Beasts of Prey. ....1.TrSt.529.432.
To Woods and Wilds the pleasing Burden bears, ...1.TrSt.682.439.
And unknown Mountains, crown'd with unknown Woods. ....1.TrUl.67.468.
Woods crown our Mountains, and in ev'ry Grove ....1.TrUl.128.470.
The Walls, the Woods, and long Canals reply. ....2.RL3.100.174.
And Brachmans deep in desert Woods rever'd. ....2.TemF.100.260.
And breathes a browner horror on the woods, ...2.ElAb.170.333.
Some safer world in depth of woods embrac'd, ...3.EOM1.105.27.
Man cares for all: to birds he gives his woods, ...3.EOM3.57.97.
The woods recede around the naked seat, ...3.Ep3.209.110.
Who hung with woods yon mountain's sultry brow? ....3.Ep3.253.114.
Joins willing woods, and varies shades from shades, ...3.Ep4.62.142.
Thro' his young Woods how pleas'd Sabinus stray'd, ...3.Ep4.89.146.
Those ancient Woods that shaded all the Ground? ....4.JD2A.116.142.
Those ancient Woods, that shaded all the ground? ....4.JD2.110.143.
Slopes at its foot, the woods its sides embrace, ...4.1HE1.141.289.
Whales sport in woods, and dolphins in the skies, ...5.DunA3.242.177.
Whales sport in woods, and dolphins in the skies; ....5.DunB3.246.332.
Love-whisp'ring woods, and lute-resounding waves. ....5.DunB4.306.374.
Eurydice the Woods, ...6.11.115.34.
And leave you in lone woods, or empty walls. ....6.45.40.125.
Goddess of Woods, tremendous in the chace, ...6.65.1.192.
Woods are (not to be too prolix) ....6.67.5.195.
To call things Woods, for what grows und'r 'em. ....6.67.8.195.
Huge Theatres, that now unpeopled Woods, ...6.71.7.202.
The Woods the Turtle-Dove, ...6.78i.2.215.
Over Woods, ...6.96i.19.268.
Where high Neritos shakes his waving Woods, ...Il.2.770.162.
With falling Woods to strow the wasted Plain. ....Il.3.92.194.

WOODS (CONTINUED)

So some fell Lion whom the Woods obey, ...Il.3.561.218.
In Woods and Wilds to wound the Savage Race; ....Il.5.66.269.
In secret Woods he won the Naiad's Grace, ...Il.6.31.325.
With Woods, with Vineyards, and with Harvests crown'd. ....Il.6.240.338.
Thro' breaking Woods her rust'ling Course they hear; ....Il.10.215.11.
Or chase thro' Woods obscure the trembling Hinde; ....Il.10.428.23.
Bent with the Weight the nodding Woods are seen, ...Il.12.339.93.
Whose waving Woods o'erhung the Deeps below, ...Il.13.20.105.
Roar thro' the Woods, and make whole Forests fall; ....Il.14.460.186.
Less Loud the Woods, when Flames in Torrents pour, ...Il.14.461.186.
Thro' all their Summits tremble Ida's Woods, ...Il.20.79.397.
From Ida's Woods he chas'd us to the Field, ...Il.20.121.399.
Fires the high Woods, and blazes to the Skies, ...Il.20.572.418.
Silent, he heard the Queen of Woods upbraid: ....Il.21.553.444.
But when arriv'd at Ida's spreading Woods, ...Il.23.144.495.
Brown with o'er-arching shades and pendent woods, ...Od.3.97.90.
And to the deaf woods wailing, breath'd his woes. ....Od.6.138.214.
Where high Neritus waves his woods in air: ....Od.9.22.302.
Nymphs sprung from fountains, or from shady woods, ...Od.10.415.364.
The barren trees of Proserpine's black wood, ...Od.10.604.373.
And unknown mountains, crown'd with unknown woods. ....Od.13.234.17.
Woods crown our mountains, and in ev'ry grove ....Od.13.295.20.
Our woods not void of hospitality. ....Od.14.54.38.
With Argus, Argus, rung the woods around; ....Od.17.353.149.
To search the woods for sets of flowry thorn, ...Od.24.259.361.

WOODWARD'S

Or Sloane, or Woodward's wondrous Shelves contain; ....4.JD4.30.29.
As one of Woodward's Patients, sick and sore, ...4.JD4.152.37.

WOODY

And woody mountains, half in vapours lost; ....Od.5.358.189.
And woody mountains half in vapours lost. ....Od.7.354.253.
The Palace in a woody vale they found, ...Od.10.240.352.
A Palace in a woody vale we found ....Od.10.297.358.

WOOE (See WOO.)

And wooe in language of the Pleas and Bench? ....4.JD2.60.139.
Teach me to wooe thee by thy best-lov'd Name! ....6.96iv.96.279.
Careless to please, with insolence ye wooe! ....Od.18.320.182.

WOOES

He wooes the Queen with more respectful flame, ...Od.15.561.97.

WOOF

Of softest woof, is bright Alcippe's care. ....Od.4.164.128.
The woof unwrought the Suitor-train surprize. ....Od.19.177.200.
In the rich woof a hound Mosaic drawn ....Od.19.265.208.

WOOL

Next goes his Wool—to clothe our valiant bands, ...3.Ep3.211.110.
With Spanish Wool he dy'd his Cheek, ...6.79.29.218.
The snowie Fleece, and wind the twisted Wool.) ....Il.3.478.214.
Warm with the softest Wool, and doubly lin'd. ....Il.10.153.8.
Soft Wool within; without, in order spread, ...Il.10.311.16.
A Slings soft Wool, snatch'd from a Soldier's side, ...Il.13.751.140.
Which heap'd with wool the beauteous Phylo brought: ....Od.4.180.128.
The snowy fleece, or twist the purpled wool. ....Od.6.64.208.
Part twist the threads, and part the wool dispose, ...Od.6.369.229.
Charg'd with his wool, and with Ulysses' fate. ....Od.9.524.328.
(The partners of her cares) the silver wool; ....Od.18.362.185.

WOOLLEN

"Odious! in woollen! 'twould a Saint provoke, ...3.Ep1.242.36.

WOOLLY

With nice Exactness weighs her woolly Store) ....1.TrES.168Z2.455.
With nice Exactness weighs her woolly Store) ....Il.12.524.101.
First down he sits, to milk the woolly dams, ...Od.9.402.322.
And fast beneath in woolly curls inwove ....Od.9.513.327.
The constant guardians of the woolly train; ....Od.12.167.440.
To low the ox, to bleat the woolly train. ....Od.12.319.447.
Unhurt the beeves, untouch'd the woolly train ....Od.12.389.450.
Short woolly curls o'erfleec'd his bending head, ...Od.19.280.208.

WOOLSEY

Peel'd, patch'd, and pyebald, linsey-woolsey brothers, ...5.DunA3.107.159.

WOOLSTON

W[oolsto]n, the scourge of Scripture, mark with awe, ...5.DunA3.149A.164.
Woolston, the Scourge of Gospel, mark with awe, ...5.DunA3.149B.164.
"Thou too, great Woolston! here exalt thy throne, ...5.DunA3.209.175.

WOOLSTON'S

In Toland's, Tindal's, and in Woolston's days. ....5.DunA3.208.175.
In Toland's, Tindal's, and in Woolston's days. ....5.DunB3.212.330.

WOOLWICH

Woolwich and Wapping, smelling strong of Pitch; ....6.14ii.47.44.

WORD

But fix'd His Word, His saving Pow'r remains: ....1.Mes.107.122.
But Appius reddens at each Word you speak, ...1.EOC.585.306.
Then with each Word, each Glance, each Motion fir'd, ...1.TrSP.59.396.
And each irrevocable Word is Fate. ....1.TrSt.299.422.
Swift as the Word, the Herald speeds along ....1.TrES.77.452.
My Word was this; Your Honour's in the right. ....2.ChJM.161.22.
This Sir affects not you, whose ev'ry Word ....2.ChJM.166.23.
By ev'ry Word that Solomon has said? ....2.ChJM.683.48.
It is not in our Sex to break our Word. ....2.ChJM.709.49.
For not one Word in Man's Arrears am I. ....2.ChWB.179.65.
For not one Word in their Arrears am I. ....2.ChWB.179A.65.
Tho' Honour is the Word with Men below. ....2.RL1.78.151.
At ev'ry Word a Reputation dies. ....2.RL3.16.170.
You hold the word, from Jove to Momus giv'n, ...3.Ep3.3.83.

WORD (CONTINUED)

His word would pass for more than he was worth. 3.Ep3.344.122.
"Live like yourself," was soon my Lady's word; 3.Ep3.359.123.
The World's good word is better than a Song) 4.HS2.102.61.
Whose Word is *If, Perhaps,* and *By-and-By,* 4.HAdv.156.87.
Each Word-catcher that lives on syllables, 4.Arbu.166.108.
The Word-catcher that lives on syllables, 4.Arbu.166A.108.
"Take him with all his Virtues, on my word; 4.2HE2.13.165.
Their own strict Judges, not a word they spare 4.2HE2.159.175.
Whose Word is Truth, as sacred and rever'd, 4.2HE1.27.197.
We Poets are (upon a Poet's word) 4.2HE1.358.225.
How barb'rous rage subsided at your word, 4.2HE1.398.229.
Upon my word, you must be rich indeed; 4.1HE6.90.243.
To do the Honours, and to give the Word; 4.1HE6.100.243.
And, Mr. Dean, one word from you— 4.HS6.82.255.
But let it (in a word) be said, 4.HS6.195.263.
'Tis true, my Lord, I gave my word, 4.1HE7.1.269.
A word, pray, in your Honour's ear. 4.1HE7.42.271.
"For Snug's the word: My dear! we'll live in Town." 4.1HE1.147.289.
Here one poor Word a hundred clenches makes, 5.DunA1.61.67.
Light dies before her uncreating word: 5.DunA3.340.192.
Here one poor word an hundred clenches makes, 5.DunB1.63.274.
And dies, when Dulness gives her Page the word. 5.DunB4.30.343.
Or impious, preach his Word without a call. 5.DunB4.94.350.
Light dies before thy uncreating word: 5.DunB4.654.409.
With such a Gust will I receive thy word. 6.2.12.6.
Thy heav'nly word by Moses to receive, 6.2.14.6.
Or Midwife *Word* gave Aid, and spoke the Infant forth. 6.8.6.17.
Has kept his word, Here's *Teophraste.* 6.44.12.123.
And gave the harmless Fellow a good Word. 6.49i.6.137.
But if you will not take my word, 6.67.11.195.
A Word and Blow was then enough, 6.79.13.218.
A Word-catcher, that lives on Syllables. 6.98.16.283.
Just of thy word, in ev'ry thought sincere, 6.109.5.314.
Go, just of word, in ev'ry thought sincere, 6.109.5A.314.
Just of thy word, and in each thought sincere, 6.109.5B.314.
Every Word she e'er heard in this Church about God. 6.124i.2.346.
Than to bestow a Word on *Kings,* 6.135.90.370.
And now a word or two of Kings 6.135.90A.370.
I'll have the last Word, for by G—d I'll write Prose. 6.149.2.397.
For know, the last Word is the Word that lasts longest. 6.149.4.397.
For know, the last Word is the Word that lasts longest. 6.149.4.397.
You will have the *last word,* after all that is past? 6.149.1A.397*.
First give thy Faith, and plight a Prince's Word Il.1.99.91.
What gen'rous *Greek* obedient to thy Word, Il.1.197.96.
His Word the Law, and He the Lord of all? Il.1.381.106.
Swift as the Word the vain *Illusion* fled, Il.2.19.128.
The gath'ring Hosts the Monarch's Word obey; Il.2.63.130.
Antenor took the Word, and thus began: Il.3.265.205.
How vain the Word to *Menelaus* giv'n Il.5.878.308.
Nor Sloth hath seiz'd me, but thy Word restrains: Il.5.1013.315.
Demands a parting Word, a tender Tear: Il.6.459.348.
He said: The Warrior heard the Word with Joy. Il.7.59.365.
But then by Heralds Voice the Word was giv'n, Il.7.331.380.
This is his Word; and know his Word shall stand. Il.8.511.421.
This is his Word; and know his Word shall stand. Il.8.511.421.
He saw their Soul, and thus his Word imparts. Il.8.556.423.
Yet more to sanctify the Word you send, Il.9.223.444.
Yet hear one word, and lodge it in thy Heart, Il.9.721.470.
Such was his Word; What farther he declar'd, Il.9.806.473.
Contending Leaders at the Word arose; Il.10.269.13.
In haste he mounted, and her Word obey'd; Il.10.599.29.
To God-like *Hector* this our Word convey. Il.11.242.46.
He spoke, and *Iris* at his Word obey'd; Il.11.253.46.
Swift at the Word, his pondrous Javelin fled; Il.11.452.54.
Against the Word, the Will reveal'd of *Jove?* Il.12.274.91.
Swift as the Word, the Herald speeds along Il.12.421.97.
Swift as the Word bold *Merion* snatch'd a Spear, Il.13.382.123.
Such was our Word, and Fate the Word obeys. Il.15.83.199.
Such was our Word, and Fate the Word obeys. Il.15.83.199.
Swift as the Word, the missile Lance he flings, Il.17.45.289.
That seals his Word; the Sanction of the God. Il.17.246.297.
What Sorrow dictates, but no Word found way. Il.17.784.319.
Swift as the Word was giv'n, the Youths obey'd; Il.19.249.383.
The speedy Council at his Word adjourn'd; Il.19.289.384.
He spoke, and sudden as the Word of *Jove* Il.19.370.387.
Die then—He said; and as the Word he spoke Il.21.125.426.
O sacred Stream! thy Word we shall obey; Il.21.241.431.
These from old Ocean at my Word shall blow, Il.21.390.436.
The Pow'r Ignipotent her Word obeys: Il.21.398.436.
Fierce, at the Word, his weighty Sword he drew, Il.22.389.471.
He spoke; they hear him, and the Word obey; Il.23.67.489.
Swift as the Word, she vanish'd from their View; Il.23.262.500.
Swift as the Word, the *Winds* tumultuous flew; Il.23.263.500.
Fir'd at his Word, the Rival Racers rise; Il.23.355.504.
So spoke *Antilochus;* and at the Word Il.23.677.516.
Fierce, at the Word, uprose great *Tydeus'* Son, Il.23.957.527.
He said: Experienc'd *Merion* took the Word; Il.23.1017.529.
His Word the silver-footed Queen attends, Il.24.155.541.
I saw, I heard her, and the Word shall stand. Il.24.274.547.
Wak'd with the Word, the trembling Sire arose, Il.24.858.572.
The Waves of People at his Word divide, Il.24.896.573.
Some Word thou would'st have spoke, which sadly dear, Il.24.936.575.
A Deed ungentle, or a Word unkind: Il.24.969.576.
He spoke; and at his Word, the *Trojan* Train Il.24.989.577.
True in his deed, and constant to his word; Od.3.121.91.
Thus he, and *Nestor* took the word: My son, Od.3.258.98.
Then turning with the word, *Minerva* flies, Od.3.474.110.
Observant of his word. The word scarce spoke, Od.3.606.117.
Observant of his word. The word scarce spoke, Od.3.606.117.
The Monarch took the word, and grave reply'd. Od.4.91.123.
Observant of her word, he turn'd aside Od.5.590.200.
But wait thy word, the gentle guest to grace Od.7.218.247.
Thus he. No word th' experienc'd man replies, Od.7.421.258.
Swift at the word advancing from the croud Od.8.155.271.
Nor can one word be chang'd but for a worse; Od.8.192.272.

WORD (CONTINUED)

Swift at the word, obedient to the King Od.8.293.278.
His word alone the list'ning storms obey, Od.10.23.340.
The sailors catch the word, their oars they seize, Od.10.149.347.
Soon as she strikes her wand, and gives the word, Od.10.349.361.
Then wav'd the wand, and then the word was giv'n. Od.10.380.363.
Struck at the word, my very heart was dead: Od.10.588.372.
And many a long-repented word bring out. Od.14.523.62.
Speak not a word, least any *Greek* may hear— Od.14.556.64.
Thy lips let fall no idle word or vain: Od.14.577.64.
Swift as the word he forms the rising blaze, Od.15.112.74.
Swift as the word his willing mates obey, Od.15.246.80.
Be, nor by signal nor by word betray'd, Od.15.478.93.
Swift at the word descending to the shores, Od.16.374.124.
The matron heard, nor was his word in vain. Od.17.68.136.
He thus: nor insolent of word alone, Od.17.272.145.
Thus she, and good *Eumæus* took the word. Od.17.601.161.
From the wise Chief he waits the deathful word. Od.20.462.255.
Philætius thus. Oh were thy word not vain? Od.21.205.269.
Tears follow'd tears; no word was in their pow'r, Od.21.236.271.
He said: then gave a nod; and at the word Od.21.475.283.
Swift as the word the parting arrow sings, Od.22.11.287.
Still undishonour'd or by word or deed Od.22.350.304.
Swift at the word he cast his skreen aside, Od.22.404.307.
She hears, and at the word obedient flies. Od.22.528.314.
To whom the Queen. Thy word we shall obey, Od.23.273.336.
Sleepless devours each word; and hears, how slain Od.23.333.340.
She said, infusing courage with the word. Od.24.602.376.

WORD-CATCHER

Each Word-catcher that lives on syllables, 4.Arbu.166.108.
The Word-catcher that lives on syllables, 4.Arbu.166A.108.
A Word-catcher, that lives on Syllables. 6.98.16.283.

WORDS

Words are like *Leaves;* and where they most abound, 1.EOC.309.274.
A vile Conceit in pompous Words exprest, 1.EOC.320.275.
Some by *Old Words* to Fame have made Pretence; 1.EOC.324.275.
In *Words,* as *Fashions,* the same Rule will hold; 1.EOC.333.276.
And ten low Words oft creep in one dull Line, 1.EOC.347.278.
The Line too *labours,* and the Words move *slow;* 1.EOC.371.282.
In words like these, which still my mind retains. 1.TrPA.52.367.
O'ertakes the flying boy, and smothers half his words. 1.TrPA.147.372.
Imperfect words, and lisp his mother's name, 1.TrFD.81.389.
And all my Words were Musick to your Ear. 1.TrSP.54.396.
Nor be with all those tempting Words abus'd, 1.TrSP.67.396.
Those tempting Words were all to *Sapho* us'd. 1.TrSP.68.396.
See, while I write, my Words are lost in Tears; 1.TrSP.109.398.
A thousand tender Words, I hear and speak; 1.TrSP.151.400.
He said, his Words the list'ning Chief inspire 1.TrES.53.451.
What Words are these, O Sov'reign of the Skies? 1.TrES.238.458.
Let not the Wise these slandrous Words regard, 2.ChJM.49.17.
Such Prudence, Sir, in all your Words appears, 2.ChJM.149.21.
You ne'er had us'd these killing Words to me. 2.ChJM.775.52.
The Words addrest to the *Samaritan:* 2.ChWB.14.57.
Come! with thy looks, thy words, relieve my woe; 2.ElAb.119.329.
Lie in three words, Health, Peace, and Competence. 3.EOM4.80.136.
(Were the last words that poor Narcissa spoke) 3.Ep1.243.36.
A wizard told him in these words our fate: 3.Ep3.136.104.
Hard Words or Hanging, if your Judge be *Page* 4.HS1.82.13.
"But the best *Words?"*—*"O* Sir, the *Dictionary."* 4.JD4.69.31.
Shrewd words, which woud against him clear the doubt 4.JD2A.107.142.
Nor sly Informer watch my Words to draw 4.JD2A.133.144.
Those words, that would against them clear the doubt. 4.JD2.104.143.
No sly Informer watch these words to draw 4.JD2.127.145.
Why words so flowing, thoughts so free, 4.HOde1.39.153.
Command old words that long have slept, to wake, 4.2HE2.167.177.
Words, that wise *Bacon,* or brave *Raleigh* spake; 4.2HE2.168.177.
So take it in the very words of *Creech.]* 4.1HE6.4.237.
Grac'd as thou art, with all the Pow'r of Words, 4.1HE6.48.239.
Thinks that but words, and this but brick and stones? 4.1HE6.66.241.
Know, there are Words, and Spells, which can controll 4.1HE1.57.283.
With mystic words, the sacred Opium shed; 5.DunA1.242.91.
And empty words she gave, and sounding strain, 5.DunA2.41.100.
Soft, creeping, words on words, the sense compose, 5.DunA2.357.143.
Soft, creeping, words on words, the sense compose, 5.DunA2.357.143.
Who sate the nearest, by the words o'ercome 5.DunA2.369.145.
"Yet oh my sons! a father's words attend: 5.DunA3.211.175.
With mystic words, the sacred Opium shed. 5.DunB1.288.290.
And empty words she gave, and sounding strain, 5.DunB2.45.298.
Soft creeping, words on words, the sense compose, 5.DunB2.389.316.
Soft creeping, words on words, the sense compose, 5.DunB2.389.316.
Who sate the nearest, by the words o'ercome, 5.DunB2.401.316.
"Yet oh, my sons! a father's words attend: 5.DunB3.213.330.
Then thus. "Since Man from beast by Words is known, 5.DunB4.149.356.
Words are Man's province, Words we teach alone. 5.DunB4.150.356.
Words are Man's province, Words we teach alone. 5.DunB4.150.356.
And keep them in the pale of Words till death. 5.DunB4.160.357.
Give law to Words, or war with Words alone, 5.DunB4.178.359.
Give law to Words, or war with Words alone, 5.DunB4.178.359.
'Tis true, on Words is still our whole debate, 5.DunB4.219.364.
But wherefore waste I words? I see advance 5.DunB4.271.370.
First slave to Words, then vassal to a Name, 5.DunB4.501.391.
Speak words of Comfort in my willing Ears; 6.2.3.5.
Speak thou in words, but let me speak in deeds! 6.2.6.5.
Moses indeed may say the words but Thou 6.2.19.6.
Lost in the Maze of Words, he turns again, 6.8.14.18.
Then gives a smacking buss, and cries—No words! 6.45.26.125.
O teach me, Dear, new Words to speak my Flame; 6.96iv.95.279.
Few words are best; I wish you well: 6.114.1.321.
Words ever pleasing, yet sincerely true, 6.125.1Z3.349.
To calm their Passion with the Words of Age, Il.1.329.103.
Words, sweet as Honey, from his Lips distill'd: Il.1.332.103.
Thy Years are awful, and thy Words are wise. Il.1.377.106.
My Words cou'd please thee, or my Actions aid; Il.1.653.118.
Receive my Words, and credit what you hear. Il.2.70.130.

WORDS (CONTINUED)

While useless Words consume th' unactive Hours, Il.2.408.147.
His Words succinct, yet full, without a Fault; Il.3.277.205.
And Words like these are heard thro' all the Bands. Il.3.395.211.
Let not thy Words the Warmth of *Greece* abate; Il.4.222.231.
No Words the Godlike *Diomed* return'd, Il.4.452.241.
Her Words allay th' impetuous Warrior's Heat, Il.5.45.268.
Then heed my Words: My Horses here detain, Il.5.324.282.
And, turn'd to *Hector,* these bold Words address'd. Il.5.574.296.
No Pause of Words admits, no dull Delay; Il.5.632.298.
These Words he seconds with his flying Lance, Il.5.659.299.
The Monarch spoke: the Words with Warmth addrest Il.6.77.327.
Receive my Words; thy Friend and Brother hear! Il.7.52.365.
These Words scarce spoke, with gen'rous Ardour prest, Il.7.119.369.
O Sage! to *Hector* be these Words address'd. Il.7.344.381.
In Words like these his prudent Thought exprest. Il.7.391.383.
The sceptred Kings of *Greece* his Words approv'd. Il.7.413.385.
Thy Words express the Purpose of thy Heart, Il.7.433.386.
He paus'd, and these pacific Words ensue. Il.7.443.386.
The Words of *Troy,* and *Troy's* great Monarch hear. Il.7.461.387.
His fruitless Words are lost unheard in Air; Il.8.123.404.
Thy Years are awful, and thy Words are wise. Il.8.178.406.
Words mixt with Sighs, thus bursting from his Breast. Il.9.22.432.
With Accent weak these tender Words return'd. Il.9.561.461.
Lik'd or not lik'd, his Words we must relate, Il.9.739.471.
The slumb'ring Chief, and in these Words awakes. Il.10.179.9.
The Council opening, in these Words begun. Il.10.240.12.
Hither I came, by *Hector's* Words deceiv'd; Il.10.463.24.
With Words of Friendship and extended Hands Il.10.638.30.
These Words, attended with a Flood of Tears, Il.11.177.43.
With Words like these the fiery Chief alarms Il.11.375.51.
Words now forgot, tho' now of vast Import. Il.11.921.76.
For Words well meant, and Sentiments sincere? Il.12.246.90.
Then hear my Words, nor may my Words be vain: Il.12.253.90.
Then hear my Words, nor may my Words be vain: Il.12.253.90.
He said; his Words the list'ning Chief inspire Il.12.397.96.
Teucer and *Leitus* first his Words excite; Il.13.125.110.
These Words the *Grecians* fainting Hearts inspire, Il.13.169.112.
These Words the Hero's angry Mind asswage: Il.13.991.152.
What shameful Words, (unkingly as thou art) Il.14.90.162.
Like Arrows pierce me, for thy Words are wise. Il.14.115.163.
And thus with gentle Words address'd the God. Il.14.410.183.
And trembling, these submissive Words return'd. Il.15.40.195.
Warn'd by the Words, to pow'rful *Jove* I yield, Il.15.232.206.
Than winning Words and heav'nly Eloquence. Il.15.323.209.
Nor Words from *Jove,* nor *Oracles* he hears; Il.16.69.238.
But heed my Words, and mark a Friend's Command Il.16.108.240.
Such were your words—Now Warriors grieve no more, Il.16.248.249.
What Words are these, O Sov'reign of the Skies? Il.16.541.265.
With Words to combate, ill befits the Brave: Il.16.758.273.
His Words infix'd unutterable Care Il.17.89.291.
But Words are vain—Let *Ajax* once appear, Il.17.183.294.
Fir'd by his Words, the Troops dismiss their Fears, Il.17.274.298.
What Words are these (th' Imperial Dame replies, Il.18.423.341.
Pronounc'd those solemn Words that bind a God. Il.19.112.376.
Thy Words give Joy, and Wisdom breathes in thee. Il.19.184.379.
The solemn Words a deep Attention draw, Il.19.265.383.
The gen'rous *Xanthus,* as the Words he said, Il.19.446.390.
To this *Anchises'* Son. Such Words employ Il.20.240.404.
'Tis not in Words the glorious strife can end. Il.20.251.404.
Long in the Field of Words we may contend, Il.20.294.406.
With Words like these the panting Chief address'd. Il.20.380.411.
Deeds must decide our Fate. Ev'n those with Words Il.20.419.412.
Hector, undaunted, thus. Such Words employ Il.20.499.415.
While thus these melting Words attempt his Heart. Il.21.83.425.
These Words, attended with a Show'r of Tears, Il.21.109.426.
These boastful Words provoke the raging God; Il.21.151.427.
He said, and acting what no Words could say, Il.22.108.457.
The Words of Age; attend a Parent's Pray'r! Il.22.115.457.
Barb'rous of Words! and arrogant of Mind! Il.23.565.512.
Thus spake the Youth, nor did his Words offend; Il.23.635.515.
Wisely and well, my Son, thy Words have prov'd Il.23.719.518.
The Hero's Words the willing Chiefs obey, Il.23.860.523.
With Words of Omen like a Bird of Night. Il.24.268.547.
Thy Words, that speak Benevolence of Mind Il.24.459.555.
Nor true are all thy Words, nor erring wide; Il.24.465.556.
These Words soft Pity in the Chief inspire, Il.24.634.563.
With Words to sooth the miserable Man. Il.24.652.564.
Daughter! what words have pass'd thy lips unweigh'd? Od.1.84.35.
This headlong torrent of amazing words? Od.1.492.56.
Such railing eloquence, and war of words. Od.2.96.65.
For lo! my words no fancy'd woes relate: Od.2.197.71.
Heav'n seal'd my words, and you those deeds behold. Od.2.202.71.
His pride of words, and thy wild dream of fate, Od.2.229.72.
His injur'd Prince the little aid of words. Od.2.274.74.
O pride of words, and arrogance of mind! Od.2.276.74.
The latent Goddess in these words addrest. Od.3.54.89.
So like your voices, and your words so wise, Od.3.153.93.
What words are these, and what imprudence thine? Od.3.283.100.
Wise are thy words, and just are all thy ways. Od.3.424.107.
And let thy words *Telemachus* persuade: Od.3.458.109.
Words to her dumb complaint a pause supplies, Od.4.954.162.
What words are these (reply'd the Pow'r who forms Od.5.30.172.
With sighs, *Ulysses* heard the words she spoke, Od.5.221.182.
Fit words attended on his weighty sense, Od.7.212.247.
Her words addressing to the god-like man. Od.7.317.251.
Do thou make perfect! sacred be his words! Od.7.424.258.
Warm are thy words, but warm without offence; Od.8.271.278.
And if, he cry'd, my words affect thy mind, Od.8.442.287.
Far from thy mind those words, ye whirlwinds bear, Od.8.443.287.
I call'd my fellows, and these words addrest. Od.9.199.314.
Each drooping spirit with bold words repair, Od.9.447.324.
These words the *Cyclops'* burning rage provoke: Od.9.565.329.
At length these words with accent low return'd. Od.10.76.343.
My men I summon'd, and these words addrest. Od.10.213.350.
His swelling heart deny'd the words their way: Od.10.290.357.

WORDS (CONTINUED)

But speaking tears the want of words supply, Od.10.291.357.
The Queen beheld me, and these words addrest. Od.10.444.365.
(These tender words on ev'ry side I hear) Od.10.496.367.
Mature in wisdom rose: Your words, he cries, Od.11.430.405.
Demand obedience, for your words are wise. Od.11.431.405.
Thy words like music every breast controul, Od.11.456.407.
Nor think vain words (he cry'd) can ease my doom; Od.11.596.412.
Attend my words! your oars incessant ply; Od.12.254.444.
The words of *Circe* and the *Theban* Shade; Od.12.321.447.
Enough: In misery, can words avail? Od.12.537.459.
His words well-weigh'd, the gen'ral voice approv'd Od.13.62.4.
And with these words the slumb'ring youth awakes. Od.15.54.72.
To him thy presents show, thy words repeat: Od.15.175.77.
And in these words the *Spartan* chief bespoke. Od.15.187.77.
In words alone, the *Pylian* Monarch kind. Od.15.239.79.
Yet at thy words I start, in wonder lost; Od.16.264.117.
Soft were his words; his actions wisdom sway'd; Od.16.414.126.
Few words she spoke, tho' much she had to say, Od.17.50.135.
And still his words live perfect in my mind. Od.17.137.138.
The stranger's words may ease the royal heart: Od.17.603.161.
My words shall dictate, and my lips shall guide. Od.17.643.163.
Shall her pleas'd ear receive my words in peace. Od.17.655.164.
Thus she. *Eumæus* all her words attends, Od.17.668.164.
Then hear my words, and grave them in thy mind! Od.18.156.173.
Such were his words; and *Hymen* now prepares Od.18.315.182.
True are his words, and he whom truth offends Od.18.460.190.
Her flutt'ring words in melting murmurs dy'd; Od.19.552.223.
What words, my son, have pass'd thy lips severe? Od.19.576.224.
O'er my suspended woe thy words prevail, Od.19.689.229.
Blows have more energy than airy words; Od.20.226.244.
What words ill-omen'd from thy lips have fled? Od.21.176.268.
Revolv'd his words, and plac'd them in her heart. Od.21.384.278.
Proceed false slave, and slight their empty words; Od.21.399.279.
If, as thy words import, (he thus began) Od.22.57.289.
The moving words *Telemachus* attends, Od.22.393.307.
Touch'd at her words, the mournful Queen rejoyn'd, Od.23.11.319.
What words (the matron cries) have reach'd my ears? Od.23.71.322.
Touch'd at her words, the King with warmth replies, Od.23.184.332.
Words seal'd with sacred truth, and truth obey: Od.23.190.332.
As mixing words with sighs, he thus began. Od.24.488.371.
His mod'rate words some better minds persuade: Od.24.530.373.

WORDY

Perhaps excel us in this wordy War; Il.20.301.406.
Intemp'rate rage a wordy war began; Od.1.467.55.
To take repast, and stills the wordy war; Od.12.520.457.
Thus in a wordy war their tongues display Od.18.40.169.
The wordy vagrant to the dole aspires, Od.20.167.241.

WORE

Ah what avail the Beauties Nature wore? 1.PWi.35.91.
What the Fine Gentleman wore *Yesterday!* 1.EOC.330.275.
And painted Sandals on her Feet she wore: 1.TrUl.107.469.
The Cause was this; I wore it ev'ry Day. 2.ChWB.289.71.
On her white Breast a sparkling *Cross* she wore, 2.RL2.7.159.
Her great great Grandsire wore about his Neck 2.RL5.90.207.
Which long she wore, and now *Belinda* wears.) 2.RL5.96.207.
A Troop came next, who Crowns and Armour wore, 2.TemF.342.280.
Known by the band and suit which Settle wore, 5.DunA3.29.153.
Known by the band and suit which Settle wore 5.DunB3.37.322.
Next all unbuckling the rich Mail they wore, Il.3.157.198.
And such in Fight the radiant Arms he wore. Il.5.548.295.
But *Meges, Phyleus'* ample Breastplate wore, Il.15.626.220.
But the rich Mail *Patroclus* lately wore, Il.22.405.472.
In the same Robe he living wore, he came, Il.23.80.490.
In the same Robe the Living wore, he came, Il.23.80A.490.
(The same renown'd *Asteropæus* wore) Il.23.640.515.
Arms, which of late divine *Sarpedon* wore, Il.23.943.526.
A royal robe he wore with graceful pride, Od.2.5.60.
In slumber wore the heavy night away, Od.5.199.181.
In lofty *Thebes* he wore th' imperial crown, Od.11.335.398.
And painted Sandals on her Feet she wore. Od.13.274.19.

WORK

Four Figures rising from the Work appear, 1.PSp.37.64.
A Work t'outlast Immortal *Rome* design'd, 1.EOC.131.254.
And Rules as strict his labour'd Work confine, 1.EOC.137.255.
And did his Work to Rules as strict confine, 1.EOC.137A.255.
A perfect Judge will *read* each Work of Wit 1.EOC.233.266.
In ev'ry Work regard the *Writer's End,* 1.EOC.255.268.
Pleas'd with a Work where nothing's just or fit; 1.EOC.291.272.
In grave *Quintilian's* copious Work we find 1.EOC.669.315.
Their Work, and rev'rence our Superior Will. 1.TrSt.410.427.
To Work by Counsel when Affairs are nice: 2.ChJM.152.22.
So said they rose, nor more the Work delay'd; 2.ChJM.299.28.
For whate'er Work was undischarg'd a-bed, 2.ChJM.473.38.
Pray Heav'n, this Magick work the proper Way: 2.ChJM.773.52.
Nor was the Work impair'd by Storms alone, 2.TemF.41.256.
So *Zembla's* Rocks (the beauteous Work of Frost) 2.TemF.53.256.
Bold was the Work, and prov'd the Master's Fire; 2.TemF.193.271.
A Work outlasting Monumental Brass. 2.TemF.227.273.
But when his own great work is but begun, 3.EOM2.41.60.
Yet, mix'd and soften'd, in his work unite: 3.EOM2.112.68.
The worker from the work distinct was known, 3.EOM3.229.115.
The Workman from the work distinct was known, 3.EOM3.229A.115.
T'invert the world, and counter-work its Cause? 3.EOM3.244.117.
An honest Man's the noblest work of God. 3.EOM4.248.151.
Its last best work, creates this softer Man; 3.Ep2.272A.72.
Its last best work, It forms a softer Man; 3.Ep2.272B.72.
Its last best work, but forms a softer Man; 3.Ep2.272.72.
The Tempter saw his time; the work he ply'd; 3.Ep3.369.123.
Paints as you plant, and, as you work, designs. 3.Ep4.64.143.
A Work to wonder at—perhaps a Stow. 3.Ep4.70.143.
Go work, hunt, exercise! (he thus began) 4.HS2.11.55.
The Creature's at his dirty work again; 4.Arbu.92.102.

WORK (CONTINUED)

Like those of Witchcraft now can work no harms: .... 4.JD2A.24.134.
Verse chears their leisure, Verse assists their work, ... 4.2HE1.235.215.
But fill their purse, our Poet's work is done, ... 4.2HE1.294.221.
Be call'd to Court, to plan some work divine, ... 4.2HE1.374.227.
To Virtue's Work provoke the tardy Hall, ... 4.EpS2.218.325.
The opening clouds disclose each work by turns, ... 5.DunA1.207.87.
Instructive work! whose wry-mouth'd portraiture .... 5.DunA2.137.117.
Call'd to this work by Dulness, Jove, and Fate; .... 5.DunB1.4.269.
The op'ning clouds disclose each work by turns, ... 5.DunB1.249.288.
Instructive work! whose wry-mouth'd portraiture .... 5.DunB2.145.302.
In patch-work flutt'ring, and her head aside .... 5.DunB4.48.346.
Had reach'd the Work, the All that mortal can; .... 5.DunB4.173.358.
Nor could a BARROW work on ev'ry block, ... 5.DunB4.245.367.
That interrupt our Peace, and work our Woe: .... 6.17iii.5.57.
She went, to plain-work, and to purling brooks, ... 6.45.11.125.
This small, well-polish'd gem, the work of years! .... 6.52.40.157.
A Desk he had of curious Work, ... 6.58.25.171.
And the whole Princesse in my work should shine. .... 6.75.10.212.
And so the Work was o'er. .... 6.94.68.261.
And of *Redemption* made damn'd Work. .... 6.101.12.290.
Nor work, nor play, nor paint, nor sing. .... 6.119.4.336.
Not work, nor play nor paint, nor sing. .... 6.119.4A.336.
A rising Mount the Work of human Hands, ... Il.2.983.170.
Stiff with the rich embroider'd Work around, ... Il.4.224.232.
Two brazen Rings of Work divine were roll'd. .... Il.5.895.308.
Oeneus a Belt of matchless Work bestow'd, ... Il.6.273.340.
Bold *Paris* first the Work of Death begun, ... Il.7.11.363.
(The Work of *Tychius,* who in *Hylè* dwell'd, ... Il.7.269.377.
But yon' proud Work no future Age shall view, ... Il.7.550.392.
Beheld the finish'd Work. Their Bulls they slew; .... Il.7.558.392.
Ten Rows of azure Steel the Work infold, ... Il.11.31.36.
With Beauty, Sense, and ev'ry Work of Art: .... Il.13.542.132.
The Work of *Vulcan;* to indulge thy Ease, ... Il.14.274.175.
He raises *Hector* to the Work design'd, ... Il.15.723.223.
But turns his Javelin to the Work of Death. .... Il.15.903.232.
Do her own Work, and leave the rest to Fate. .... Il.16.121.241.
Compacted Stones the thick'ning Work compose, ... Il.16.258.249.
The Work and Present of celestial Hands; .... Il.17.220.296.
And thick and heavy grows the Work of Death: .... Il.17.445.304.
The Work of Death, and still the Battel bleeds. .... Il.17.854.321.
The Fight, our glorious Work remains undone. .... Il.19.148.377.
(The Work of *Vulcan)* sate the Pow'rs around. .... Il.20.18.393.
(The Work of *Vulcan)* sate the Gods around. .... Il.20.18A.393.
Work out our Will. Celestial Pow'rs! descend, ... Il.20.35.394.
(The Work of *Trojans,* with *Minerva's* Aid) .... Il.20.177.401.
A growing Work employ'd her secret Hours, ... Il.22.568.479.
Hereafter *Greece* some nobler Work may raise, ... Il.23.308.502.
(The Work of Soldiers) where the Hero Sate. .... Il.24.556.559.
The work she ply'd; but studious of delay, ... Od.2.117.67.
While she with work and song the time divides, ... Od.5.78.176.
(The wimbles for the work *Calypso* found) .... Od.5.317.186.
Four days were past, and now the work compleat .... Od.5.333.188.
Her royal hand a wond'rous work designs, ... Od.6.367.229.
The work of matrons: These the Princes prest, ... Od.7.126.241.
(The work of *Polybus,* divinely wrought) .... Od.8.408.285.
An useful work! adorn'd by ancient Kings. .... Od.17.235.143.
To beg, than work, he better understands; .... Od.17.260.144.
Those hands in work? to tend the rural trade, ... Od.18.405.188.
And starve by strolling, not by work to thrive. .... Od.18.409.188.
Me other work requires—With tim'rous awe .... Od.22.417.308.
Their bloody work: They lopp'd away the man, ... Od.22.510.313.
The work she ply'd; but studious of delay, ... Od.24.166.356.
Nor ought remits the work, while thus he said. .... Od.24.286.363.
Could work this wonder: welcome to thy own! .... Od.24.463.370.
Who deem this act the work of mortal hand: .... Od.24.509.372.

WORK'D

Has God, thou fool! work'd solely for thy good, ... 3.EOM3.27.95.
Revenge, and doubt, and caution, work'd my breast; .... Od.9.378.321.

WORKER

The worker from the work distinct was known, ... 3.EOM3.229.115.

WORKING

Wild Nature's vigor working at the root. .... 3.EOM2.184.77.
See plastic Nature working to this end, ... 3.EOM3.9.93.
Stretch to the stroke, and brush the working seas. .... Od.12.265.445.

WORKMAN

The Workman from the work distinct was known, ... 3.EOM3.229A.115.
The Workman join'd, and shap'd the bended Horns, ... Il.4.142.227.
Then with a Sponge the sooty Workman drest .... Il.18.483.345.
(Smooth'd by the workman to a polish'd plain) .... Od.17.416.152.

WORKMANSHIP

By none in Weight or Workmanship excell'd: .... Il.23.866.524.

WORKMEN

As when a shipwright stands his workmen o'er, ... Od.9.457.324.

WORKS

And Temples rise, the beauteous Works of Peace. .... 1.W-F.378.187.
Works *without Show,* and *without Pomp* presides: .... 1.EOC.75.247.
Be *Homer's* Works your *Study,* and *Delight,* .... 1.EOC.124.253.
For *Works* may have more *Wit* than does 'em good, ... 1.EOC.303.274.
Some judge of Authors' *Names,* not *Works,* and then .... 1.EOC.412.287.
With *him,* most Authors steal their Works, or buy; .... 1.EOC.618.309.
His *Precepts* teach but what his *Works* inspire. .... 1.EOC.660.314.
Around the Works a Wood of glitt'ring Spears .... 1.TrES.181.456.
Their Waxen Works, or from the Roof depend. .... 1.TrUl.40.467.
Steel cou'd the Works of mortal Pride confound, ... 2.RL3.175.182.
Men prove with Child, as pow'rful Fancy works, ... 2.RL4.53.188.
In human works, tho' labour'd on with pain, ... 3.EOM1.53.19.
Each works its end, to move or govern all: .... 3.EOM2.56.62.
That counter-works each folly and caprice; .... 3.EOM2.239.84.

WORKS (CONTINUED)

"Here subterranean works and cities see; .... 3.EOM3.181.111.
These are Imperial Works, and worthy Kings. .... 3.Ep4.204.156.
What Lines encompass, and what Works defend! .... 4.HAdv.127.85.
Imputes to me and my damn'd works the cause: .... 4.Arbu.24.97.
Sir, let me see your works and you no more. .... 4.Arbu.68.100.
These as good works, tis true, we all allow, ... 4.JD2A.127.144.
But oh, those Works are out of Fashion now: .... 4.JD2A.128.144.
These, as good works 'tis true we all allow; .... 4.JD2.121.145.
But oh! these works are not in fashion now: .... 4.JD2.122.145.
When works are censur'd, not as bad, but new; .... 4.2HE1.116.205.
Long, as to him who works for debt, the Day; .... 4.1HE1.35.281.
These wond'rous works; so Jove and Fate require) .... 5.DunA1.4.61.
Founds the whole pyle, of all his works the base; .... 5.DunA1.140.81.
Had heav'n decreed such works a longer date, ... 5.DunA1.183.85.
Here to her Chosen all her works she shows; .... 5.DunA1.227.90.
Fair as before her works she stands confess'd, ... 5.DunA2.151.120.
If there be man who o'er such works can wake, ... 5.DunA2.340.142.
For works like these let deathless Journals tell, ... 5.DunA3.271.180.
To their first Chaos Wit's vain works shall fall, ... 5.DunA3.355A.193.
Founds the whole pile, of all his works the base: .... 5.DunB1.160.282.
Heav'n had decreed these works a longer date. .... 5.DunB1.196.283.
Heav'n had decreed those works a longer date. .... 5.DunB1.196A.283.
Works damn'd, or to be damn'd! (your father's fault) .... 5.DunB1.226.286.
Here to her Chosen all her works she shews; .... 5.DunB1.273.290.
Fair as before her works she stands confess'd, ... 5.DunB2.159.303.
"If there be man, who o'er such works can wake, ... 5.DunB2.372.315.
Pity! the charm works only in our wall, ... 5.DunB4.165.357.
Than to the wicked Works of *Whiston;* .... 6.10.22.25.
Thy Works in *Spanish* shou'd have been translated, ... 6.48iv.6.136.
How oft' our slowly-growing works impart, ... 6.52.19.156.
New graces yearly, like thy works, display; .... 6.52.65.158.
The Works of all the Muses. .... 6.58.20.171.
They praise no works but what are like their own .... 6.82ix(f).4.235.
To help us thus to read the works of others: .... 6.105v.2.302.
Her works; and dying, fears herself may die. .... 6.108.8.312.
Man and his Works he'll soon renounce, ... 6.135.93.370.
Is room for all Pope's Works—and Pope himself: .... 6.147ix.2.392.
Nor that alone, but all the Works of War. .... Il.6.561.354.
Amaz'd beheld the wondrous Works of Man: .... Il.7.528.391.
What Cause of Fear from mortal Works, cou'd move .... Il.7.546.391.
And vy'd with *Pallas* in the Works of Art. .... Il.9.513.458.
Not Titles here, but Works, must prove our Worth. .... Il.10.77.6.
Else may the sudden Foe our Works invade, ... Il.10.112.7.
So fam'd, so dreadful, in the Works of War? .... Il.10.288.14.
Bright Scenes of Arms, and Works of War appear; .... Il.11.872.74.
With Gods averse th' ill-fated Works arose; .... Il.12.6.81.
Fierce with Impatience on the Works to fall, ... Il.12.227.89.
Close to the Works their rigid Siege they laid. .... Il.12.304.92.
And one bright Waste hides all the Works of Men: .... Il.12.340.93.
Around the Works a Wood of glitt'ring Spears .... Il.12.535.101.
On other Works tho' *Troy* with Fury fall, ... Il.13.77.108.
Sweeps the slight Works and fashion'd Domes away. .... Il.15.419.213.
And lab'ring Armies round the Works engag'd; .... Il.15.451.215.
The boiling Ocean works from Side to Side, ... Il.17.313.299.
High eminent amid the Works divine, ... Il.18.433.341.
Of Works divine (such Wonders are in Heav'n!) .... Il.18.490.345.
What Toils they shar'd, what martial Works they wrought, ... Il.24.13.535.
While us the works of bloody *Mars* employ'd, ... Od.3.324.102.
In curious works; the whirling spindle glow'd .... Od.6.62.208.
Than works of female skill their women's pride, ... Od.7.138.242.
To learn if aught of mortal works appear, ... Od.10.171.349.
Their waxen works, or from the roof depend. .... Od.13.131.8.
But works of peace my soul disdain'd to bear, ... Od.14.259.48.
And fearing *Jove,* whom mercy's works delight. .... Od.14.314.50.
Few can with me in dext'rous works contend, ... Od.15.338.86.
Skill'd in rich works, a woman of their land. .... Od.15.459.93.
My swains to visit, and the works survey. .... Od.15.544.96.
The works of Gods what mortal can survey, ... Od.23.83.322.
And, skill'd in female works, four lovely dames. .... Od.24.323.365.

WORLD

And carrying with you all the World can boast, ... 1.PSp.9.61.
To all the World Illustriously are lost! .... 1.PSp.10.61.
Forsake Mankind, and all the World—but Love! .... 1.PAu.88.86.
Daphne farewell, and all the World adieu! .... 1.PWi.92.95.
Peace o'er the World her Olive-Wand extend, ... 1.Mes.19.114.
No Sigh, no Murmur the wide World shall hear, ... 1.Mes.45.117.
But as the World, harmoniously confus'd: .... 1.W-F.14.149.
She said, the World obey'd, and all was *Peace!* .... 1.W-F.328.181.
And the new World launch forth to seek the Old. .... 1.W-F.402.191.
And taught the World, *with Reason* to *Admire.* .... 1.EOC.101.250.
Where a *new World* leaps out at his command, ... 1.EOC.486.294.
Whom, when they *Praise,* the World believes no more, ... 1.EOC.594.307.
Thence Arts o'er all the *Northern World* advance; .... 1.EOC.711.322.
And the wide World resounds with *Sapho's* Praise. .... 1.TrSP.32.394.
My Woes, thy Crimes, I to the World proclaim; .... 1.TrSP.141.399.
Conspire to court thee from our World away; .... 1.TrSt.38.411.
For lost *Europa* search'd the World in vain, ... 1.TrSt.248.420.
Wide o'er the World in solemn Pomp she drew .... 1.TrSt.476.430.
Fame, that delights around the World to stray, ... 1.TrSt.810.443.
All things wou'd prosper, all the World grow wise. .... 2.ChJM.68.18.
At least, your Courage all the World must praise, ... 2.ChJM.170.23.
In all this World, much less in Womankind; .... 2.ChJM.191.24.
And sigh in Silence, lest the World shou'd hear: .... 2.ChJM.199.24.
Conscious of Pleasures to the World unknown: .... 2.ChJM.544.41.
But shoud'st thou search the spacious World around, ... 2.ChJM.637.45.
Full many a Saint, since first the World began, ... 2.ChWB.46.58.
This wicked World was once my dear Delight; .... 2.ChWB.225.67.
Oft when the World imagine Women stray, ... 2.RL1.91.152.
The various Off'rings of the World appear; .... 2.RL1.130.155.
Belinda smil'd, and all the World was gay. .... 2.RL2.52.162.
That single Act gives half the World the Spleen. .... 2.RL4.78.190.
First at the Shrine the Learned World appear, ... 2.TemF.298.278.
That fills the Circuit of the World around; .... 2.TemF.309.279.
Let fuller Notes th' applauding World amaze, ... 2.TemF.326.279.

WORLD (CONTINUED)
Sweet to the World, and grateful to the Skies. ... 2.TemF.377.281.
Yet would the World believe us, all were well. ... 2.TemF.389.282.
With Sparks, that seem'd to set the World on fire. ... 2.TemF.415.283.
And rush in Millions on the World below. ... 2.TemF.482.286.
Himself, his throne, his world, I'd scorn 'em all: ... 2.ElAb.86.326.
When, warm in youth, I bade the world farewell? ... 2.ElAb.110.329.
From the false world in early youth they fled, ... 2.ElAb.131.330.
The world forgetting, by the world forgot. ... 2.ElAb.208.337.
The world forgetting, by the world forgot. ... 2.ElAb.208.337.
Cold is that breast which warm'd the world before, ... 2.Elegy.33.365.
And now a bubble burst, and now a world. ... 3.EOM1.90.25.
Some safer world in depth of woods embrac'd, ... 3.EOM1.105.27.
Being on being wreck'd, and world on world, ... 3.EOM1.254.46.
Being on being wreck'd, and world on world, ... 3.EOM1.254.46.
The glory, jest, and riddle of the world! ... 3.EOM2.18.56.
Look round our World; behold the chain of Love ... 3.EOM3.7.92.
View thy own World; behold the chain of Love ... 3.EOM3.7A.92.
T'invert the world, and counter-work its Cause? ... 3.EOM3.244.117.
With Heav'n's own thunders shook the world below, ... 3.EOM3.267.119.
In Faith and Hope the world will disagree, ... 3.EOM3.307.125.
But still this world (so fitted for the knave) ... 3.EOM4.131.140.
"Whatever IS, is RIGHT."—THIS world, 'tis true, ... 3.EOM4.145.141.
How Trade increases, and the World goes well; ... 3.Ep1.159.29.
Full sixty years the World has been her Trade, ... 3.Ep2.123.60.
See how the World its Veterans rewards! ... 3.Ep2.243.69.
Kept Dross for Duchesses, the world shall know it, ... 3.Ep2.291.74.
Well then, since with the world we stand or fall ... 3.Ep3.79A.94.
Since then, my Lord, on such a World we fall, ... 3.Ep3.79.94.
Shall walk the World, in credit, to his grave. ... 4.HS1.120.17.
The World beside may murmur, or commend. ... 4.HS1.122.17.
Know, all the distant Din that World can keep ... 4.HS1.123.17.
Shall walk the World in quiet to his grave. ... 4.HS1.120B.17.
Yet, for the World, she would not shew her Leg! ... 4.HAdv.32.77.
The World had wanted many an idle Song) ... 4.Arbu.28.98.
Thou stand'st unshook amidst a bursting World. ... 4.Arbu.88.101.
From these the world will judge of Men and Books, ... 4.Arbu.145.106.
"My only Son, I'd have him see the World: ... 4.2HE2.6.165.
The balanc'd World, and open all the Main; ... 4.2HE1.2.195.
Or Laws establish'd, and the World reform'd; ... 4.2HE1.12.195.
To Thee, the World its present homage pays, ... 4.2HE1.23.195.
(Should Ripley venture, all the World would smile) ... 4.2HE1.186.211.
Peace stole her wing, and wrapt the world in sleep; ... 4.2HE1.401.229.
What I desire the World should know. ... 4.HS6.62.255.
Mix with the World, and battle for the State, ... 4.1HE1.28.281.
But to the world, no bugbear is so great, ... 4.1HE1.67.283.
Sets half the World, God knows, against the rest; ... 4.EpS1.58.302.
In golden Chains the willing World she draws, ... 4.EpS1.147.309.
Sweet to the World, and grateful to the Skies: ... 4.EpS2.245.326.
Rush to the world, impatient for the day. ... 5.DunA3.22.152.
And all the Western World believe and sleep. ... 5.DunA3.92.157.
Thence a new world, to Nature's laws unknown, ... 5.DunA3.237.177.
Then a new world, to Nature's laws unknown, ... 5.DunA3.237A.177.
Rush to the world, impatient for the day. ... 5.DunB3.30.321.
And all the western world believe and sleep. ... 5.DunB3.100.324.
Thence a new world to Nature's laws unknown, ... 5.DunB3.241.332.
Of dull and venal a new World to mold, ... 5.DunB4.15.341.
Steal from the world, and not a stone ... 6.1.19.4.
Jove with a nod may bid the world to rest, ... 6.4i.13.9.
That heav'n, the threaten'd world to spare, ... 6.5.15.12.
Those eyes shou'd set the world on flame. ... 6.5.18A.12.
Fly the forgetful World, and in thy Arms repose. ... 6.8.36.19.
Content at last to leave the World in Peace. ... 6.17iv.8.59.
Still to charm those who charm the World beside. ... 6.19.80.64.
Believe, believe the treach'rous world no more. ... 6.22.2.71.
The world no longer trembles at their pow'r! ... 6.22.15.71.
The world recedes; it disappears! ... 6.31ii.13.94.
The lessening World forsakes my Sight, ... 6.31ii.6Z2.94.
Believe him, he has known the World too long, ... 6.34.19.101.
Believe him, Sirs h'has known the World too long, ... 6.34.19A.101.
Of all examples by the world confest, ... 6.43.5.120.
Thus from the world fair *Zephalinda* flew, ... 6.45.7.124.
The stupid World, like *Assa fetida*. ... 6.48ii.4.134.
T' *inform* the World of what *it better knows,* ... 6.48iii.2.134.
What awes the World is Envy and ill Nature. ... 6.48iii.8.134.
bidst Fortune rule the World below ... 6.50.11A.146*.
For him, thou oft hast bid the World attend, ... 6.84.7.238.
Not with those Toys the female world admire, ... 6.86.3.244.
Not with those Toys the Woman-World admire, ... 6.86.3A.244.
Not as the World its pretty Slaves rewards, ... 6.86.5A.245.
When all the World conspires to praise her, ... 6.89.11.250.
When all the World conspires her praise, ... 6.89.11A.250.
And Mites imagine all the World a Cheese. ... 6.96v.30.281.
Fair, o'er the western world, renew'd his light, ... 6.107.2.310.
Who knew no wish but what the world might hear: ... 6.109.6.314.
In this World, she despis'd every Soul she met here, ... 6.124i.9.347.
Authors the world and their dull brains have trac'd, ... 6.126ii.1.353.
Full sixty Years the World has been her Trade, ... 6.154.9.403.
The God who darts around the World his Rays. ... Il.1.52.88.
Tho' call'd *Bateia* in the World below) ... Il.2.985.170.
A World engages in the Toils of Fight. ... Il.3.136.197.
For nine long Years have set the World in Arms; ... Il.3.206.201.
She stalks on Earth, and shakes the World around; ... Il.4.505.245.
Thro' the wide World should make our Glory known. ... Il.5.337.283.
That clouds the World, and blackens half the Skies. ... Il.7.543.391.
As from that Centre to th' Æthereal World. ... Il.8.20.396.
And the vast World hangs trembling in my Sight! ... Il.8.32.397.
Thence his broad Eye the subject World surveys, ... Il.8.65.398.
He, whose all-conscious Eyes the World behold, ... Il.8.550.422.
The noblest Pow'r that might the World controul ... Il.9.55.434.
And * her, whose Fury bathes the World with Gore. ... Il.10.653.30.
Or terrifies th' offending World with Wars: ... Il.13.320.120.
The trembling World, and shakes the steady Poles. ... Il.15.173.203.
Around the Globe, whose Earthquakes rock the World; ... Il.15.249.206.
Nor He, whose Anger sets the World in Arms, ... Il.17.459.305.
Wide o'er the World was *Ilion* fam'd of old ... Il.18.337.337.

WORLD (CONTINUED)
Thence on the nether World the Fury fell; ... Il.19.131.377.
Yield to our conqu'ring Arms the lower World. ... Il.20.171.400.
Sunk in one Instant to the nether World; ... Il.20.534.416.
Immers'd remain this Terror of the World. ... Il.21.373.436.
Then thro' the World of Waters, they repair ... Il.24.125.540.
Celestial Muse! and to our world relate. ... Od.1.14.29.
Born by his mother to a world of woes! ... Od.4.438.140.
Thus o'er the world of waters *Hermes* flew, ... Od.5.68.175.
A world of waters! far from all the ways ... Od.5.127.178.
With storms pursu'd them thro' the liquid world. ... Od.5.138.178.
Rolls clouds on clouds, and stirs the wat'ry world, ... Od.5.376.190.
And a dead silence still'd the wat'ry world. ... Od.5.503.196.
But o'er the world of waters wing'd her way: ... Od.7.100.239.
Wide o'er the world *Alcinous'* glory shine! ... Od.7.425.258.
From shore to shore, and gird the solid world. ... Od.9.618.332.
While in your world I drew the vital air; ... Od.11.764.424.
Whose fate enquiring, thro' the world we rove; ... Od.15.294.83.
The sea, the land, and shakes the world with arms! ... Od.17.343.148.
Round the wide world are sought those men divine ... Od.17.462.155.
Live, an example for the world to read, ... Od.22.413.307.
The world conspires to speak *Ulysses* wise; ... Od.23.124.326.
Wide o'er the world their martial fame was spread; ... Od.24.588.376.

WORLD'S
The World's great Oracle in Times to come; ... 1.W-F.382.188.
(The *World's* just Wonder, and ev'n *thine* O *Rome!*) ... 1.EOC.248.268.
And the *World's Victor* stood subdu'd by *Sound!* ... 1.EOC.381.284.
Cæsar, the World's great Master, and his own; ... 2.TemF.156.266.
'Should at my feet the world's great master fall, ... 2.ElAb.85.326.
Such is the World's great harmony, that springs ... 3.EOM3.295.122.
Why risk the world's great empire for a Punk? ... 3.Ep1.83.21.
Wise Peter sees the World's respect for Gold, ... 3.Ep3.125.102.
The World's good word is better than a Song) ... 4.HS2.102.61.
The World's great Victor pass'd unheeded by; ... 6.32.34.97.
Spaniard and *French* abuse to the World's End, ... 6.60.21.178.
The World's the native City of the Wise; ... 6.96v.21.280.
The World's Aversion, than their Love before; ... Il.3.518.216.
Their Fame shall fill the World's remotest Ends, ... Il.7.536.391.
The World's great Empress on th' *Ægyptian* Plain, ... Il.9.501.458.
Of wond'ring Ages, and the World's Amaze! ... Il.18.536.347.
The World's great Ruler, felt her venom'd Dart; ... Il.19.101.376.
The World's vast Concave, when the Gods contend. ... Il.20.90.397.
And Heav'n is feasting on the World's green End, ... Il.23.255.499.
There on the world's extreamest verge rever'd, ... Od.1.33.31.

WORLDLY
In worldly Follies, which I blush to tell; ... 2.ChJM.90.19.
How short a Space our Worldly Joys endure? ... 2.ChJM.476.38.
Are not thy Worldly Goods and Treasure mine? ... 2.ChWB.125.62.
And Worldly crying coals from street to street, ... 3.Ep3.50.90.

WORLDLY'S
All Worldly's Hens, nay Partridge, sold to town, ... 4.2HE2.234.181.

WORLDS
O'er figur'd Worlds now travels with his Eye. ... 1.W-F.246.172.
And Worlds applaud that must not yet be *found!* ... 1.EOC.194.263.
Nor let desiring Worlds intreat in vain! ... 1.TrSt.34.411.
Superior Worlds, and look all Nature thro'. ... 2.TemF.237.274.
Thro' worlds unnumber'd tho' the God be known, ... 3.EOM1.21.15.
Thro' worlds unbounded tho' the God be known, ... 3.EOM1.21A.15.
See worlds on worlds compose one universe, ... 3.EOM1.24.16.
See worlds on worlds compose one universe, ... 3.EOM1.24.16.
Heav'ns not his own, and worlds unknown before? ... 3.EOM3.106.102.
Grasp the whole worlds of Reason, Life, and Sense, ... 3.EOM4.357.163.
Hereditary Realms, and worlds of Gold. ... 3.Ep3.132.104.
Say, for such worth are other worlds prepar'd? ... 3.Ep3.335.120.
Survey both Worlds, intrepid and entire, ... 4.2HE2.312.187.
A matchless youth: His nod these worlds controuls, ... 5.DunA3.251.178.
A matchless Youth! his nod these worlds controuls, ... 5.DunB3.255.332.
When thousand Worlds are round. ... 6.50.24.147.
And let it guide the Worlds enquiring Eies ... 6.72.3A.208.
Assembled Nations, set two Worlds in Arms? ... Il.4.38.223.
Down to these worlds I trod the dismal way, ... Od.11.769.424.
Ere the fair Mischief set two worlds in arms, ... Od.23.232.334.

WORM
Vile worm!—oh Madness, Pride, Impiety! ... 3.EOM1.258.46.
"Learn of the mole to plow, the worm to weave; ... 3.EOM3.176.111.
So spins the silk-worm small its slender store, ... 5.DunB4.253.369.
Impale a Glow-worm, or Vertù profess, ... 5.DunB4.569.398.
From the Grub Obscene, & wriggling Worm ... 6.14v(b).23A.50.
Man is a very Worm by Birth, ... 6.53.5.161.
That Woman is a Worm we find, ... 6.53.9.161.
That antient Worm, the Devil. ... 6.53.12.161.
The Blockhead is a Slow-worm; ... 6.53.14.161.
Is aptly term'd a Glow-worm: ... 6.53.16.161.
First from a Worm they take their Rise, ... 6.53.19.162.
And in a Worm decay: ... 6.53.20.162.
That Statesmen have the Worm, is seen ... 6.53.25.162.
Their Conscience is a Worm within, ... 6.53.27.162.
The Worm that never dies! ... 6.53.32.162.
First from a Worm they took their Rise, ... 6.53.19A.162.
Then in a Worm decay: ... 6.53.20A.162.
That Statesmen have a Worm, is seen ... 6.53.25A.162.
Or at the Glow-worm warm thy frozen legs? ... 6.96ii.30Z50.272.
(Like some vile Worm extended on the Ground) ... Il.13.819.144.

WORMIUS
On parchment scraps y-fed, and Wormius hight. ... 5.DunA3.184.171.
On parchment scraps y-fed, and Wormius hight. ... 5.DunB3.188.329.

WORMS
Of hairs, or straws, or dirt, or grubs, or worms; ... 4.Arbu.170.108.
First Grubs obscene, then wriggling Worms, ... 6.14v(b).23.50.

WORMS (CONTINUED)
Th' impartial worms that very *dust* devour. .... 6.22.18.72.
All Humankind are Worms. .... 6.53.4.161.
The Learn'd themselves we Book-Worms name; .... 6.53.13.161.
All Humane Race are Worms. .... 6.53.4A.161.
All Human Race are Worms. .... 6.53.4B.161.
Thus Worms suit all Conditions; .... 6.53.22.162.
Misers are Muckworms, Silk-worms Beaus, ... 6.53.23.162.
Since Worms shall eat ev'n thee. .... 6.53.36.162.
Ev'n *Button's* Wits to Worms shall turn, ... 6.53.39.162.
Some Worms suit all Conditions; .... 6.53.22A.162.
"While Pepper-Water-Worms thy Bait supply'd; .... 6.96ii.20.270.
Of Hairs, or Straws, or Dirt, or Grubs, or Worms: .... 6.98.20.284.
Shall Flies and Worms obscene, pollute the Dead? .... Il.19.30.372.
Untouch'd by Worms, untainted by the Air. .... Il.24.506.557.
Lest time or worms had done the weapon wrong, ... Od.21.429.281.

WORMWOOD
The Doctor's Wormwood Style, the Hash of Tongues, ... 4.JD4.52.29.

WORN
The Garlands fade, the Vows are worn away; .... 1.PAu.69.85.
If *Faith* it self has *diff'rent Dresses* worn, ... 1.EOC.446.289.
A Dress by Fates and Furies worn alone: .... 1.TrSt.155.416.
And worn with Cares, am hastning to my End; .... 2.ChJM.88.19.
Ye rugged rocks! which holy knees have worn; .... 2.ElAb.19.320.
Worn out in public, weary ev'ry eye, ... 3.Ep2.229.68.
'But the well-worn Paths of the Nymphs of Drury .... 6.13.24.39.
Now all her various States worn out .... 6.14v(b).13A.50.
As flow'ry Bands in Wantonness are worn; .... 6.19.65.64.
Worn with nine Years of unsuccessful War? .... Il.2.96.131.
(Such as by Youths unus'd to Arms, are worn; .... Il.10.305.16.
Than worn to Toils, and active in the Fight! .... Il.11.542.58.
Which once the greatest of Mankind had worn. .... Il.17.238.297.
Fast by the Road a Precipice was worn: .... Il.23.500.510.
Of all his kind most worn with misery: .... Od.5.132.178.
Ye Gods! since this worn frame refection knew, ... Od.6.261.222.
Now worn with age, *Eurymedusa* nam'd: .... Od.7.10.233.
Long worn with griefs, and long without a friend. .... Od.7.201.246.
By storms and hunger worn: Age well may fail, ... Od.8.265.277.
Luxuriant on the wave-worn bank he lay, ... Od.10.185.349.
There worn and wasted, lose our cares in sleep .... Od.12.9.430.
Then she: O worn by toils, oh broke in fight, ... Od.12.143.439.
Worn as I am with griefs, with care decay'd; .... Od.12.308.447.
Late worn with years in weeds obscene you trod, ... Od.16.220.114.
Full many a post have those broad shoulders worn, ... Od.17.256.143.
Worn as I am with age, decay'd with woe, ... Od.18.58.169.
Cover'd with dust, with dryness chapt and worn, ... Od.22.199.297.
The ruins of himself! now worn away .... Od.24.271.362.

WORSE
There are, who *judge* still *worse* than he can *write.* .... 1.EOC.35.243.
If rich, she keeps her Priest, or something worse; .... 2.ChWB.87.61.
Wit, Spirit, Faculties, but make it worse; .... 3.EOM2.146.72.
But future views of better, or of worse. .... 3.EOM4.72.135.
But these less taste them, as they worse obtain. .... 3.EOM4.84.136.
But an Inferior not dependant? worse. .... 3.Ep2.136.61.
Resolve me, Reason, which of these is worse, ... 3.Ep3.319.120.
F. You could not do a worse thing for your Life. .... 4.HS1.15.5.
You only make the Matter worse and worse. .... 4.JD4.121.35.
You only make the Matter worse and worse. .... 4.JD4.121.35.
Has yet a strange Ambition to *look worse:* .... 4.JD4.269.47.
A Self-Tormentor, worse than (in the Play) .... 4.HAdv.25.77.
Plunder'd by Thieves, or Lawyers which is worse, ... 4.HAdv.57.81.
She kneels, she weeps, and worse! resigns her Dow'r. .... 4.HAdv.172.89.
Say, is their Anger, or their Friendship worse? .... 4.Arbu.30A.98.
"But Foes like these!"—One Flatt'rer's worse than all; .... 4.Arbu.104.103.
Alas! 'tis ten times worse when they *repent.* .... 4.Arbu.108.103.
"But all these foes!"—One Flatt'rer's worse than all; .... 4.Arbu.104A.103.
Trust me, 'tis ten times worse when they *repent.* .... 4.Arbu.108A.103.
Not to say worse in pamper'd Churchmens Lives .... 4.JD2A.88.140.
Nay worse, to ask for Verse at such a time! .... 4.2HE2.31.167.
Surpriz'd at better, or surpriz'd at worse. .... 4.1HE6.23.237.
(Believe me, many a German Prince is worse, ... 4.1HE6.83.243.
And there I'll die, nor worse nor better. .... 4.1HE7.80.273.
Far worse unhappy *D[iape]r* succeeds, ... 5.DunA2.286Z1.137.
To grow the worse for growing greater; .... 6.74.6.211.
For I assure you, I've read worse. .... 6.147v.2.391.
But an Inferior, not Dependant, worse. .... 6.154.22.403.
Meets Death, and worse than Death, Eternal Shame. .... Il.5.658.299.
Meets Death, and worse than Death, eternal Shame. .... Il.15.673.222.
The worse advice, the better to refuse. .... Il.18.364A.339.
Or, worse than slaughter'd, sold in distant Isles .... Il.22.61.455.
Nor can one word be chang'd but for a worse; .... Od.8.192.272.
Rather than bear dishonour worse than death, ... Od.16.112.108.

WORSHIP
I worship you, and you alone I fear! .... 1.TrPA.115.370.
To worship like his Fathers was his care; .... 4.2HE1.165.209.
Against your worship when had *S[elkir]k* writ? .... 4.EpS2.158.322.
Against your worship what has *S[elkir]k* writ? .... 4.EpS2.158A.322.
worship of one .... 6.155.8Z5.404*.

WORSHIP'D
Like *Pallas* worship'd, like the Sun renown'd; .... Il.8.670.427.
What boots ye now *Scamander's* worship'd Stream, ... Il.21.143.427.

WORSHIPFUL
How pale, each Worshipful and rev'rend Guest .... 4.HS2.75.59.

WORSHIPP'D
Where *Damian* kneeling, worshipp'd as she past. .... 2.ChJM.600.44.

WORSHIPPER
Not Fortune's Worshipper, nor Fashion's Fool, ... 4.Arbu.334.120.

WORSLEY'S
And other Beauties envy *Worsley's* eyes, ... 6.52.60.158.

WORST
Of all this *Servile Herd* the worst is He .... 1.EOC.414.287.
But still the *Worst* with most Regret commend, ... 1.EOC.518.296.
For the *worst Avarice* is that of *Sense:* .... 1.EOC.579.306.
But grant the worst; shall Women then be weigh'd .... 2.ChJM.682.48.
And the best Men are treated like the worst, ... 2.TemF.321.279.
In the worst inn's worst room, with mat half-hung, ... 3.Ep3.299.117.
In the worst inn's worst room, with mat half-hung, ... 3.Ep3.299.117.
Chaucer's worst ribaldry is learn'd by rote, ... 4.2HE1.37.197.
The worst of Madmen is a Saint run mad. .... 4.1HE6.27.239.
Adieu—if this advice appear the worst, ... 4.1HE6.130.246.
For thee supplying, in the worst of days, ... 5.DunA1.167.83.
And (last and worst) with all the cant of wit, ... 5.DunB4.99.351.
But the last Tyrant ever proves the worst. .... 6.19.40.63.
Approves them both, but likes the worst the best: .... 6.49iii.24.143.
Approves of each, but likes the worst the best: .... 6.49iii.24A.143.
Approves of Both, but likes the worst the best: .... 6.49iii.24B.143.
Approves of Both, yet likes the worst the best: .... 6.49iii.24C.143.
Approves of Each, yet likes the worst the best: .... 6.49iii.24D.143.
Approves of each, but likes the worst the best; .... 6.98.60.285.
The worst that Envy, or that Spite .... 6.135.19.366.
That worst of Tyrants, an usurping Crowd. .... Il.2.242.139.
Bore all, and *Paris* of those Ills the worst. .... Il.6.441.348.
And Mortals hate him, as the worst of Gods. .... Il.9.212.443.
Two, not the worst; nor ev'n this Succour vain. .... Il.13.310.119.
Yet hear my Counsel, and his worst withstand; .... Il.15.332.210.
Death is the worst; a Fate which all must try; .... Il.15.582.218.
The worst advice, the better to refuse. .... Il.18.364.339.
This, this is Misery! the last, the worst, ... Il.22.106.457.
Be doom'd the worst of human ills to prove, ... Od.1.82.35.
He thus; O were the woes you speak the worst! .... Od.4.924.161.
Still to your own ætherial race the worst! .... Od.5.150.178.
Enur'd to perils, to the worst resign'd. .... Od.5.286.185.
To my worst foe, if that avenging day .... Od.16.108.108.
O void of faith! of all bad men the worst! .... Od.16.434.128.
Bestow, my friend! thou dost not seem the worst .... Od.17.497.156.
All, ev'n the worst, condemn'd; and some reprov'd. .... Od.17.573.160.
Bear the best humbly, and the worst resign'd; .... Od.18.170.175.
(The worst of mortals, ev'n the worst of Kings) .... Od.21.330.275.
(The worst of mortals, ev'n the worst of Kings) .... Od.21.330.275.

WORSTED
The very worsted still look'd black and blue: .... 5.DunA2.142.118.
The very worsted still look'd black and blue. .... 5.DunB2.150.302.

WORTH
Whatever Nature has in *Worth* deny'd, ... 1.EOC.205.264.
And give each Deed th' exact intrinsic Worth. .... 2.TemF.323.279.
Worth makes the man, and want of it, the fellow; .... 3.EOM4.203.146.
But by your father's worth if yours you rate, ... 3.EOM4.209.147.
B. To Want or Worth well-weigh'd, be Bounty giv'n, ... 3.Ep3.229A.111.
Yet was not Cotta void of wit or worth: .... 3.Ep3.180.109.
To Want or Worth well-weigh'd, be Bounty giv'n, ... 3.Ep3.229.111.
Say, for such worth are other worlds prepar'd? .... 3.Ep3.335.120.
His word would pass for more than he was worth. .... 3.Ep3.344.122.
And tho' no science, fairly worth the sev'n: .... 3.Ep4.44.140.
Insults fal'n Worth, or Beauty in distress, ... 4.Arbu.288.116.
Like that of Papists, now not worth their Hate .... 4.JD2A.12.132.
Poor and disarm'd, and hardly worth your hate. .... 4.JD2.12.133.
Who, if they have not, think not worth their care. .... 4.2HE2.267.183.
Foes to all living worth except your own, ... 4.2HE1.33.197.
Proud Vice to brand, or injur'd Worth adorn, ... 4.2HE1.227.215.
Proud Vice to lash, or injur'd Worth adorn, ... 4.2HE1.227A.215.
Sigh, while his Chloë, blind to Wit and Worth, ... 4.1HE6.42.239.
A Man of wealth is dubb'd a Man of worth, ... 4.1HE6.81.243.
For their own Worth, or our own Ends? .... 4.HS6.150.259.
BARNARD, thou art a *Cit,* with all thy worth; .... 4.1HE1.89.285.
While Truth, Worth, Wisdom, daily they decry— .... 4.EpS1.169.309.
While Truth, Worth, Wisdom, daily we decry— .... 4.EpS1.169A.309.
Patrons, who sneak from living worth to dead, ... 5.DunB4.95.350.
Man the true Worth of his Creation knows. .... 6.17iii.19.58.
Britons attend: Be worth like this approv'd, ... 6.32.37.97.
A soul as full of Worth, as void of Pride, ... 6.73.1.209.
Thinks Worth, Wit, Learning, to that Spot confin'd; .... 6.96v.26.280.
Oh born to Arms! O Worth in Youth approv'd! .... 6.113.3.320.
His Sword and Pen not worth a Straw, ... 6.116ii.2.326.
To Worth like thine? what Praise shall we bestow? .... Il.4.293.235.
To stand the first in Worth as in Command, ... Il.6.257.339.
Thy free Remonstrance proves thy Worth and Truth: .... Il.6.419.347.
To either Host your matchless Worth is known, ... Il.7.339.381.
With Strength of Body, and with Worth of Mind! .... Il.7.351.381.
Thus, always thus, thy early Worth be try'd. .... Il.8.340.413.
Confiding in our want of Worth, he stands, ... Il.9.59.434.
Who honour Worth, and prize thy Valour most. .... Il.9.756.471.
Not Titles here, but Works, must prove our Worth. .... Il.10.77.6.
Let Worth determine here. The Monarch spake, ... Il.10.281.14.
His Soul rekindled, and awak'd his Worth. .... Il.11.406.53.
Oh recollect your ancient Worth and Praise! .... Il.13.74.108.
In such Assays, thy blameless Worth is known, ... Il.13.372.123.
To Gods and Men thy matchless Worth is known, ... Il.13.909.148.
But *Jove* alone endues the Soul with Worth: .... Il.20.291.406.
In ev'ry martial Game thy Worth attest, ... Il.23.1056.533.
If to the son the father's worth descends, ... Od.2.309.76.
Next these in worth, and firm those urns be seal'd; .... Od.2.399.80.
Whose early years for future worth engage, ... Od.3.482.111.
The genuine worth of *Ithacus* the wise! .... Od.4.210.129.
I boast a witness of his worth in thee. .... Od.4.280.132.
O early worth! a soul so wise, and young, ... Od.4.831.158.
With great *Eurymachus,* of worth confest, ... Od.4.851.158.
His manly worth, and share the glorious day? .... Od.8.158.271.
Thy worth is known. Then hear our country's claim, ... Od.8.273.278.
Whose worth the splendors of thy race adorns, ... Od.8.504.289.
To worth in misery a rev'rence pay, ... Od.11.424.405.

WORTH (CONTINUED)
A prize more worth than *Ilion's* noble spoil. ... Od.13.161.13.
Makes man a slave, takes half his worth away. ... Od.17.393.151.
Then as in dignity, be first in worth, ... Od.17.499.157.
Thy riper days no growing worth impart, ... Od.18.257.179.
But he whose in-born worth his acts commend, ... Od.19.383.212.
Conscious of worth revil'd, thy gen'rous mind ... Od.19.438.216.
And modest worth with noble scorn retires. ... Od.20.168.241.
Still treat they worth with lordly dull disdain; ... Od.20.209.243.
For genuine worth, of age mature to know, ... Od.20.380.251.
To wed, as wealth or worth her choice inspire: ... Od.20.398.251.
To Gods alone, and god-like worth, we pay. ... Od.22.386.307.

WORTH-LESS
A sense-less, worth-less, and unhonour'd crowd; ... 4.2HE1.306.221.

WORTHIER
Bid Temples, worthier of the God, ascend; ... 3.Ep4.198.156.
And Temples, worthier of the God, ascend; ... 3.Ep4.198A.156.
By worthier Footmen pist upon and whipt! ... 4.HAdv.56.81.

WORTHIES
Studious thy country's worthies to defame, ... Od.2.97.65.
"All, all the god-like worthies that adorn ... Od.6.339.227.
Thy early care the future worthies claim, ... Od.11.301.397.
Saw'st thou the Worthies of the *Grecian* Host? ... Od.11.461.407.

WORTHLESS
I scarce can think him such a worthless thing, ... 4.2HE1.209.213.
A stately, worthless Animal, ... 6.14v(a).22.49.
But most, her worthless Sons insult my Ear, ... Il.22.147.459.
Down dropt the caitiff corse, a worthless load, ... Od.15.515.95.
To no brave prize aspir'd the worthless swain, ... Od.17.258.144.
Or greet the pavement with his worthless head? ... Od.17.277.145.
For worthless beauty? therefore now despis'd? ... Od.17.373.150.
A worthless triumph o'er a worthless foe! ... Od.18.435.189.
A worthless triumph o'er a worthless foe! ... Od.18.435.189.

WORTHLESSNESS
Justly the price of worthlessness they pay'd, ... Od.22.454.310.

WORTHY
If worthy Thee, and what Thou might'st inspire! ... 1.TrSt.102.414.
In Days of old, a wise and worthy Knight; ... 2.ChJM.2.15.
To bless his Age, and bring a worthy Heir; ... 2.ChJM.26.16.
Most worthy Kinsman, faith, you're mighty wise! ... 2.ChJM.217.25.
Provides a Consort worthy of my Bed; ... 2.ChJM.255.26.
And much his Sickness griev'd his worthy Lord, ... 2.ChJM.407.34.
This aged *January*, this worthy Knight, ... 2.ChJM.481A.38.
She—and my Neice—and one more worthy Wife ... 2.ChWB.272.70.
Oh fool! to think God hates the worthy mind, ... 3.EOM4.189.145.
These are Imperial Works, and worthy Kings. ... 3.Ep4.204.156.
How dar'st thou let one worthy man be poor? ... 4.HS2.118.63.
Sure, worthy Sir, the Diff'rence is not great, ... 4.HAdv.75.81.
That tends to make one worthy Man my foe, ... 4.Arbu.284.116.
A worthy Member, no small Fool, a Lord; ... 4.2HE2.185.177.
Or what remain'd, so worthy to be read ... 4.2HE1.137.207.
White Gloves, and Linnen worthy Lady Mary! ... 4.1HE1.164.291.
The worthy Youth shall ne'er be in a rage: ... 4.EpS1.48.301.
But does the Court a worthy Man remove? ... 4.EpS2.74.317.
Mine, as a Friend to ev'ry worthy mind; ... 4.EpS2.203.324.
Well-purg'd, and worthy Withers, Quarles, and Blome. ... 5.DunA1.126.78.
Well-purg'd, and worthy *W[esle]y*, *W[att]s*, and *Bl[ome]* ... 5.DunA1.126A.78.
A shaggy Tap'stry, worthy to be spread ... 5.DunA2.135.117.
Gives him a cov'ring worthy to be spread ... 5.DunA2.135A.117.
Oh worthy thou of Ægypt's wise abodes, ... 5.DunA3.203.175.
Well purg'd, and worthy Settle, Banks, and Broome. ... 5.DunB1.146.280.
A shaggy Tap'stry, worthy to be spread ... 5.DunB2.143.302.
Oh worthy thou of Ægypt's wise abodes, ... 5.DunB3.207.330.
Worthy to fill Pythagoras's place: ... 5.DunB4.572.399.
Were silent, which kind Fate thought worthy ... 6.30.10A.86.
Worthy thee! ... 6.96i.7.268.
Worthy me! ... 6.96i.8.268.
And worthy of the *prince's ear.* ... 6.106v.3.308.
And worthy of thy *prince's ear.* ... 6.106v.3A.308.
But that the Worthy and the Good shall say, ... 6.125.11.350.
And roar in Numbers worthy *Bounce.* ... 6.135.94.370.
A Treasure worthy Her, and worthy Me. ... Il.1.174.96.
A Treasure worthy Her, and worthy Me. ... Il.1.174.96.
O Heroes! worthy such a dauntless Train, ... Il.4.326.236.
The Gods that make, shall keep the Worthy, Friends. ... Il.4.417.240.
A Warrior worthy to be *Hector's* Foe. ... Il.7.46.365.
A worthy Champion for the *Grecian* State. ... Il.7.216.375.
And each well worthy of a Royal Bed; ... Il.9.188.441.
Gifts worthy thee, his Royal Hand prepares; ... Il.9.341.450.
And each well worthy of a Royal Bed; ... Il.9.375.451.
Sure ev'ry wise and worthy Man will love. ... Il.9.451.454.
Oh worthy better Fate! oh early slain! ... Il.11.311.49.
A worthy Vengeance for *Prothœnor* slain? ... Il.14.552.189.
Nor seem'd the Vengeance worthy such a Son; ... Il.15.30.195.
Is worthy thee; the Duty of the Brave. ... Il.18.166.330.
Arms worthy thee, or fit to grace a God. ... Il.19.14.372.
Consult, ye Pow'rs! ('tis worthy your Debate) ... Il.22.229.465.
The Son of *Nestor,* worthy of his Sire. ... Il.23.940.526.
Worthy the heir of *Ithaca* to give. ... Od.1.406.52.
In wealth and beauty worthy of our flames: ... Od.2.234.72.
And worthy to exalt the feasts of heav'n.) ... Od.2.387.80.
At first with worthy shame and decent pride, ... Od.3.330.102.
Immortal labour! worthy hands divine. ... Od.10.257.355.
O worthy of the pow'r the Gods assign'd, ... Od.11.470.407.
The worthy purchase of a foreign lord. ... Od.15.421.89.

WORTHYS
Or Worthys old, whom Arms or Arts adorn, ... 2.TemF.70.257.

WORTLEY
As witness Lady *W[ort]l[e]y.* ... 6.58.68.173.
And only dwells where WORTLEY casts her eyes. ... 6.81.6.225.

WORTLEY'S
And other Beauties envy *Wortley's* eyes, ... 6.52.60A.158.
Who crost half Europe, led by Wortley's eyes! ... 6.82xi.2.236.

WOT
What is't to me (a Passenger God wot) ... 4.2HE2.296.185.

WOU'D (OMITTED)
105

WOU'D'ST
Yet, wou'd'st thou have the proffer'd Combate stand, ... Il.3.97.194.
What Gifts from *Troy,* for *Paris* wou'd'st thou gain, ... Il.4.127.226.

WOU'DST
Oh wou'dst thou sing what Heroes *Windsor* bore, ... 1.W-F.299.176.
Man? and *for ever?* Wretch! what wou'dst thou have? ... 4.2HE2.252.183.
Belov'd of *Jove, Achilles!* wou'dst thou know ... Il.1.97.91.
Wou'dst thou enchain'd like *Mars,* oh *Hermes,* lye, ... Od.8.375.284.
Me wou'dst thou please? for them thy cares imploy, ... Od.10.455.365.
And wou'dst thou evil for his good repay? ... Od.16.448.128.
Fierce in the van: Then wou'dst thou, wou'dst thou, say, ... Od.18.420.189.
Fierce in the van: Then wou'dst thou, wou'dst thou, say, ... Od.18.420.189.

WOUD
Shrewd words, which woud against him clear the doubt ... 4.JD2A.107.142.
Woud you your writings to some Palates fit ... 6.82ix(f).1.235.

WOUD'ST
That *Troy,* and *Troy's* whole Race thou woud'st confound, ... Il.4.51.223.

WOULD (OMITTED)
178

WOULD'ST
Say, would'st thou be the Man to whom they fall? ... 3.EOM4.276.154.
Yet would'st thou more? In yonder cloud, behold! ... 5.DunA3.249.178.
Yet would'st thou more? In yonder cloud behold, ... 5.DunB3.253.332.
At Senate, and at Bar, how welcome would'st thou be! ... 6.8.30.18.
Woul'st thou the *Greeks* their lawful Prey shou'd yield, ... Il.1.157.95.
Say would'st thou seize some valiant Leader's Prize? ... Il.2.288.141.
Me would'st thou move to base inglorious Flight? ... Il.5.311.281.
Whither, O *Menelaus!* would'st thou run, ... Il.7.127.369.
Me, as a Boy or Woman would'st thou fright, ... Il.7.285.378.
Back to the Skies would'st thou with Shame be driv'n, ... Il.15.150.202.
Some Word thou would'st have spoke, which sadly dear, ... Il.24.936.575.
And but augment the wrongs thou would'st redress. ... Od.2.222.72.
Would'st thou to rise in arms the *Greeks* advise? ... Od.2.277.74.
But would'st thou soon review thy native plain? ... Od.6.347.228.
Why would'st not thou, oh all-enlighten'd mind! ... Od.13.484.29.

WOULDST
Presumptuous Man! the reason wouldst thou find, ... 3.EOM1.35.17.
Ah Bounce! ah gentle Beast! why wouldst thou dye, ... 6.156.1.405.
Or at my Knee, by *Phœnix* wouldst thou stand; ... Il.9.610.464.
Thou wouldst have thought, so furious was their Fire, ... Il.15.844.229.
If on that god-less race thou wouldst attend, ... Od.15.346.86.
How wouldst thou fly, nor ev'n in thought return? ... Od.18.31.168.

WOUND
And Hell's grim Tyrant feel th'eternal Wound. ... 1.Mes.48.117.
Short is his Joy! he feels the fiery Wound, ... 1.W-F.113.161.
I rend my Tresses, and my Breast I wound, ... 1.TrSP.130.399.
And on his naked Arm inflicts a Wound. ... 1.TrES.114.454.
Conceal'd the Wound, and leaping from his Height, ... 1.TrES.117.454.
Then from the yawning Wound with Fury tore ... 1.TrES.125.454.
Their Manly Breasts are pierc'd with many a Wound, ... 1.TrES.163.455.
From the wide Wound gush'd out a Stream of Blood, ... 1.TrES.320.461.
Like Gods they fight, nor dread a mortal Wound. ... 2.RL5.44.202.
Unconquer'd *Cato* shews the Wound he tore, ... 2.TemF.176.269.
This taste the honey, and not wound the flow'r: ... 3.EOM2.90.65.
The fewer still you name, you wound the more; ... 4.HS1.43.9.
Willing to wound, and yet afraid to strike, ... 4.Arbu.203.110.
The Poets learn'd to please, and not to wound: ... 4.2HE1.258.217.
Nor could that fabled dart more surely wound: ... 6.14iii.8.46.
At random wounds, nor knows the wound she gives: ... 6.14iii.12.46.
Nor did that fabled dart more surely wound: ... 6.14iii.8A.46.
Or pleas'd to wound, and yet afraid to strike, ... 6.49iii.17.143.
Willing to wound, and yet afraid to strike, ... 6.49iii.17A.143.
Wishing to wound, and yet afraid to strike, ... 6.49iii.17B.143.
Or pleas'd to wound, but yet afraid to strike, ... 6.49iii.17C.143.
And blasted both, that it might neither wound. ... 6.69i.4.197.
Safe from Wound ... 6.96i.35.269.
Wishing to wound, and yet afraid to strike, ... 6.98.53.285.
Bent was his Bow, the *Grecian* Hearts to wound; ... Il.1.63.89.
Aton'd by Sacrifice, desist to wound. ... Il.1.581.115.
A pois'nous *Hydra* gave the burning Wound, ... Il.2.879.165.
Still edg'd to wound, and still untir'd with Blows, ... Il.3.90.194.
The vital Spirit issu'd at the Wound, ... Il.3.366.210.
Fated to wound, and Cause of future Woes. ... Il.4.149.228.
The shining Barb appear above the Wound. ... Il.4.181.230.
My vary'd Belt repell'd the flying Wound. ... Il.4.225.232.
Arm'd with his Spear, he meditates the Wound, ... Il.4.569.248.
And the warm Life came issuing from the Wound. ... Il.4.609.250.
And gash'd his Belly with a ghastly Wound. ... Il.4.617.250.
In Woods and Wilds to wound the Savage Race; ... Il.5.66.269.
Eurypilus inflicts a deadly Wound; ... Il.5.104.272.
And tugg'd the Weapon from the gushing Wound; ... Il.5.143.274.
Her shalt thou wound: So *Pallas* gives Command. ... Il.5.169.275.
The Savage wound, he rowzes at the Smart, ... Il.5.177.275.
And undissembled Gore pursu'd the Wound. ... Il.5.261.279.
At distance wound, or wage a flying War ... Il.5.315A.281.

WOUND (CONTINUED)

The fainting Chief, and wards the mortal Wound. ..... Il.5.430.289.
Pale was her Cheek, and livid look'd the Wound. ..... Il.5.444.289.
And shew'd the Wound by fierce *Tydides* giv'n, ... Il.5.451.289.
An impious Mortal gave the daring Wound! ..... Il.5.466.290.
Asswag'd the glowing Pangs, and clos'd the Wound. ..... Il.5.490.291.
Raz'd her soft Hand with this lamented Wound. ..... Il.5.516.293.
Latona there and *Phœbe* heal'd the Wound, ... Il.5.543.294.
Lo brave *Æneas* sinks beneath his Wound, ... Il.5.569.295.
Erect he stood, and vig'rous from his Wound: ..... Il.5.630.298.
The grizly Wound dismiss'd his Soul to Hell, ... Il.5.667.300.
Meanwhile his Temples feel a deadly Wound; ..... Il.5.715.301.
To cool his glowing Wound he sate apart, ... Il.5.990.314.
(The Wound inflicted by the *Lycian* Dart) ..... Il.5.991.314.
It pierc'd the God: His Groin receiv'd the Wound. ..... Il.5.1051.316.
Me next encount'ring, me he dar'd to wound; ..... Il.5.1085.318.
And heal'd th' immortal Flesh, and clos'd the Wound. ..... Il.5.1111.320.
The mortal Wound of rich *Elatus* gave, ... Il.6.40.325.
Alive, unharm'd, and vig'rous from his Wound. ..... Il.7.375.382.
Pierc'd in the Back, a vile, dishonest Wound? ..... Il.8.120.403.
(From *Hector Phœbus* turn'd the flying Wound) ..... Il.8.377.415.
Some hostile Wound let ev'ry Dart bestow, ... Il.8.639.426.
But in his Front he felt the fatal Wound, ... Il.11.131.41.
The Point rebated, and repell'd the Wound. ..... Il.11.304.48.
At once, his weighty Sword discharg'd a Wound ..... Il.11.307.48.
But when the Wound grew stiff with clotted Blood, ... Il.11.346.50.
Without a Wound the *Trojan* Hero stands; ..... Il.11.456.54.
Such Hands may wound, but not incense a Man. ..... Il.11.496.56.
The Wound not mortal wise *Ulysses* knew, ... Il.11.551.58.
Wide in his Breast appear'd the grizly Wound; ..... Il.11.562.59.
Till Life's warm Vapour issuing thro' the Wound, ... Il.11.598.60.
On strong *Pandocus* next inflicts a Wound, ... Il.11.612.61.
Had pierc'd *Machaon* with a distant Wound: ..... Il.11.629.61.
An Arrow's Head yet rooted in his Wound, ... Il.11.942.77.
The Wound he wash'd, the Styptick Juice infus'd. ..... Il.11.983.79.
The Wound to torture, and the Blood to flow. ..... Il.11.985.79.
Till some wide Wound lets out their mighty Soul. ..... Il.12.168.87.
He stung the Bird, whose Throat receiv'd the Wound: ..... Il.12.236.90.
And on his naked Arm inflicts a Wound. ..... Il.12.468.98.
Conceal'd the Wound, and leaping from his Height, ... Il.12.471.98.
Then, from the yawning Wound with Fury tore ..... Il.12.479.99.
Their manly Breasts are pierc'd with many a Wound, ... Il.12.517.100.
Or bleeds my Friend by some unhappy Wound? ..... Il.13.330.121.
Him neither Rocks can crush, nor Steel can wound, ... Il.13.412.126.
Vain was his Breastplate to repel the Wound: ..... Il.13.468.128.
Groans to the oft-heav'd Axe, with many a Wound, ... Il.13.495.130.
The long Lance shakes, and vibrates in the Wound: ..... Il.13.555.132.
It ripp'd his Belly with a ghastly Wound, ... Il.13.642.136.
And gnash'd the Dust all bloody with his Wound. ..... Il.13.659.137.
Transpierc'd his Back with a dishonest Wound: ..... Il.13.691.137.
Where sharp the Pang, and mortal is the Wound. ..... Il.13.719.138.
But good *Agenor* gently from the Wound ..... Il.13.749.140.
While Life's red Torrent gush'd from out the Wound. ..... Il.13.820.144.
Dext'rous with these they aim a certain Wound, ... Il.13.895.148.
For these were pierc'd with many a ghastly Wound, ... Il.13.957.151.
Refresh thy Wound, and cleanse the clotted Gore; ..... Il.14.11.157.
He lies protected, and without a Wound. ..... Il.14.498.188.
And the fierce Soul came rushing thro' the Wound. ..... Il.14.614.192.
What grief, what wound, withholds him from the War? ..... Il.15.277.207.
Wounded, they wound; and seek each others Hearts ..... Il.15.862.230.
His Shoulder-blade receives the fatal Wound; ..... Il.16.344.256.
Sharp in his Thigh he felt the piercing Wound; ..... Il.16.367.257.
Kind *Maris,* bleeding in his Brother's Wound, ... Il.16.380.257.
From the wide Wound gush'd out a Stream of Blood, ... Il.16.625.268.
Pierc'd thro' the Bosom with a sudden Wound, ... Il.16.727.272.
His Front, Brows, Eyes, one undistinguish'd Wound, ... Il.16.897.278.
The Lance arrest him with a mortal Wound; ..... Il.16.989.281.
Wide thro' the Neck appears the grizly Wound, ... Il.17.51.289.
(Forth welling from the Wound, as prone he lay) ..... Il.17.93.291.
With Thongs, inserted thro' the double Wound: ..... Il.17.337.300.
The Brain comes gushing thro' the ghastly Wound; ..... Il.17.343.301.
And thro' the Wound the rushing Entrails broke. ..... Il.17.365.301.
Fixt on the Spot they war; and wounded, wound; ..... Il.17.414.303.
Stretch'd forth, and gash'd with many a gaping Wound. ..... Il.18.282.335.
Cleanse the pale Corse, and wash each honour'd Wound. ..... Il.18.404.340.
With that, his Weapon deep inflicts the Wound; ..... Il.19.277.383.
Wounded, we wound; and neither side can fail, ... Il.20.298.406.
The Lance arrests him: an ignoble Wound ..... Il.20.465.413.
Achilles rais'd the Spear, prepar'd to wound; ..... Il.21.78.424.
Thy bloated Corse, and suck thy goary Wound: ..... Il.21.136.427.
His Belly open'd with a ghastly Wound, ... Il.21.195.429.
By no dishonest Wound shall *Hector* die; ..... Il.22.364.470.
Eyes the whole Man, and meditates the Wound; ..... Il.22.404.472.
Then forcing backward from the gaping Wound ..... Il.22.463.474.
With Thongs inserted thro' the double Wound; ..... Il.22.498.477.
Nose, Mouth and Front, one undistinguish'd Wound: ..... Il.23.476.509.
Lies panting: Not less batter'd with his Wound, ... Il.23.804.521.
(Ten double-edg'd, and ten that singly wound.) ..... Il.23.1009.529.
And *Merion* eager meditates the Wound; ..... Il.23.1029.530.
Fate gives the Wound, and Man is born to bear. ..... Il.24.63.538.
O'er all the Corse, and clos'd is ev'ry Wound, ... Il.24.512.557.
(Tho' many a Wound they gave) Some heav'nly Care, ... Il.24.513.557.
But grief and rage alternate wound my breast ..... Od.1.61.33.
And ev'ry piercing note inflicts a wound. ..... Od.1.440.53.
To wound with storied grief the filial ear: ..... Od.4.440.140.
Of human voice the list'ning ear may wound, ... Od.5.515.197.
And bathes with floods of tears the gaping wound; ..... Od.8.576.293.
Wounded they wound, and man expires on man. ..... Od.9.62.304.
To seize the time, and with a sudden wound ..... Od.9.356.321.
Mean-time the *Cyclop* raging with his wound, ... Od.9.493.326.
I lanc'd my spear, and with a sudden wound ..... Od.10.187.349.
Thro' the wide wound the vital spirit flies. ..... Od.10.190.349.
When hand to hand they wound return for wound; ..... Od.11.518.409.
When hand to hand they wound return for wound; ..... Od.11.518.409.
Yet innocent they play'd, and guiltless of a wound. ..... Od.11.658.416.
And breath'd his manly spirit thro' the wound. ..... Od.11.686.418.

WOUND (CONTINUED)

From *Mars* impartial some broad wound we bear; ..... Od.17.560.159.
Ill fits the stranger and the poor to wound. ..... Od.17.575.160.
But fell *Antinous* answer'd with a wound. ..... Od.17.595.161.
Down drop'd he stupid from the stunning wound, ... Od.18.114.172.
Then dragg'd along, all bleeding from the wound, ... Od.18.120.172.
Full on his shoulder it inflicts a wound, ... Od.18.441.190.
The savage renders vain the wound decreed, ... Od.19.523.221.
Soon with redoubl'd force the wound repay'd; ..... Od.19.528.221.
Then chaunting mystic lays, the closing wound ..... Od.19.535.221.
Had not th' inglorious wound thy malice aim'd ..... Od.20.373.251.
And aim to wound the Prince with pointless wit: ..... Od.20.448.255.
Full thro' his liver past the mortal wound, ... Od.22.101.291.
Chief after Chief expir'd at ev'ry wound, ... Od.22.134.293.
Some wound the gate, some ring against the wall; ..... Od.22.303.301.
Not lessen'd of their force (so light the wound) ..... Od.22.310.301.
On all sides thus they double wound on wound, ... Od.22.343.304.
On all sides thus they double wound on wound, ... Od.22.343.304.
The damsel train turn'd pale at every wound, ... Od.23.43.321.
And wild with transport had reveal'd the wound; ..... Od.23.77.322.
Why in this hour of transport wound thy ears, ... Od.23.281.337.
Lo here the wound (he cries) receiv'd of yore, ... Od.24.384.367.
The brass-cheek'd helmet opens to the wound; ..... Od.24.606.376.

WOUNDED

Bleeds in the Forest, like a wounded Hart. ..... 1.W-F.84.158.
That like a wounded Snake, drags its slow length along. ..... 1.EOC.357.280.
The Balls are wounded with the piercing Ray, ... 2.ChJM.800.53.
The Balls seem wounded with the piercing Ray, ... 2.ChJM.800A.53.
These curling aspicks, and these wounded arms, ... 6.20.2.66.
His wounded Brother claims thy timely Care; ..... Il.4.239.232.
The wounded Chief behind his Car retir'd, ... Il.5.140.273.
Such Stream as issues from a wounded God; ..... Il.5.422.287.
This said, she wip'd from *Venus'* wounded Palm ..... Il.5.505.292.
Both strook, both wounded, but *Sarpedon's* slew: ..... Il.5.815.305.
The wounded Hero dragg'd the Lance along. ..... Il.5.825.305.
But when, or wounded by the Spear, or Dart, ... Il.11.247.46.
But when, or wounded by the Spear, or Dart, ... Il.11.263.47.
The wounded Monarch at his Tent they place. ..... Il.11.364.51.
The wounded Offspring of the healing God. ..... Il.11.639.62.
Back to the Lines the wounded *Greek* retir'd, ... Il.11.712.66.
To guard their wounded Friend: While thus they stand ..... Il.11.722.67.
What wounded Warrior late his Chariot brought? ..... Il.11.749.68.
This for the wounded Prince the Dame prepares; ..... Il.11.784.70.
Who asks what Hero, wounded by the Foe, ... Il.11.795.71.
And great *Machaon,* wounded in his Tent, ... Il.11.970.78.
There stretch'd at length the wounded Hero lay, ... Il.11.980.79.
The Cure and Safety of his wounded Friend, ... Il.12.2.80.
With which a wounded Soldier touch'd his Breast, ... Il.13.280.119.
His wounded Brother good *Polites* tends; ..... Il.13.675.137.
And nail'd it to the Eugh<Yew>: The wounded Hand ..... Il.13.747.140.
Then thus impatient, to his wounded Friend. ..... Il.14.4.157.
His wounded Eyes the Scene of Sorrow knew; ..... Il.14.18.157.
Him, in his March, the wounded Princes meet, ... Il.14.35.159.
The Kings, tho' wounded, and oppress'd with Pain, ... Il.14.439.184.
The good *Eurypylus,* his wounded Friend. ..... Il.15.453.215.
Wounded, they wound; and seek each others Hearts ..... Il.15.862.230.
He drew the Dolours from the wounded Part, ... Il.16.649.269.
He strook, he wounded, but he durst no more; ..... Il.16.979.281.
Wounded at once, *Patroclus* yields to fear, ... Il.16.984.281.
Fixt on the Spot they war; and wounded, wound; ..... Il.17.414.303.
By *Hector* wounded, *Leitus* quits the Plain, ... Il.17.680.314.
Their furious Hunters, drive the wounded Boar; ..... Il.17.814.320.
He too sore wounded by *Agenor's* Son. ..... Il.19.55.374.
Wounded, we wound; and neither side can fail, ... Il.20.298.406.
Lent to the wounded God her tender Hand: ..... Il.21.487.441.
Tho' strook, tho' wounded, scarce perceives the Pain, ... Il.21.681.450.
The wounded Bird, e'er yet she breath'd her last, ... Il.23.1038.530.
Dismay'd, heart-wounded with paternal woes, ... Od.4.205.129.
He ceas'd: heart-wounded with afflictive pain, ... Od.4.649.150.
Heart-wounded, to the bed of state withdrew: ..... Od.4.1038.166.
Wounded they wound, and man expires on man. ..... Od.9.62.304.
Of wounded honour, and thy rage restrain. ..... Od.20.24.233.
No help, no flight; but wounded ev'ry way, ... Od.22.341.304.
Stood the great son, heart-wounded with the sight: ..... Od.24.372.367.

WOUNDING

Still must that Tongue some wounding Message bring, ... Il.1.133.93.

WOUNDS

And with her Dart the flying Deer she wounds. ..... 1.W-F.180.166.
Heav'ns! what new Wounds, and how her old have bled? ..... 1.W-F.322.180.
No lightning wounds me but your angry eyes. ..... 1.TrPA.117.370.
Whose Wounds yet fresh, with bloody Hands he strook, ... 1.TrSt.79.413.
Insult his Wounds, and make them bleed anew. ..... 1.TrSt.337.424.
There bath'd his honourable Wounds, and drest ..... 1.TrES.340.462.
My Bosome wounds, and captivates my Heart, ... 2.ChJM.532.41.
Wounds, Charms, and *Ardors,* were no sooner read, ... 2.RL1.119.154.
Here fierce *Tydides* wounds the *Cyprian* Queen; ..... 2.TemF.189.271.
Yet absent, wounds an Author's honest fame; ..... 4.Arbu.292.116.
His Eye-Balls burn, he wounds the smoaking Plain, ... 6.9ix.1.22.
Pours Balm into the bleeding *Lover's* Wounds: ..... 6.11.29.30.
Pours Balm into the *Lover's* Wounds: ..... 6.11.29A.30.
At random wounds, nor knows the wound she gives: ..... 6.14iii.12.46.
Yet *absent,* wounds an author's honest fame: ..... 6.120.2.339.
Or barren Praises pay the Wounds of War. ..... Il.1.220.97.
To Pygmy-Nations Wounds and Death they bring, ... Il.3.9.188.
Nor add Reproaches to the Wounds I bear, ... Il.3.544.217.
Whose Arrow wounds the Chief thou guard'st in Fight; ..... Il.5.151.274.
Or weep the Wounds her bleeding Country bore. ..... Il.6.471.350.
And yet no dire Presage so wounds my Mind, ... Il.6.574.355.
The Wounds they wash'd, their pious Tears they shed, ... Il.7.506.389.
Gash'd with dishonest Wounds, the Scorn of Heav'n: ..... Il.8.14.395.
Each adverse Battel goar'd with equal Wounds. ..... Il.8.86.399.
The Wounds impress'd by burning Thunder deep. ..... Il.8.497.420.
The Wounds impress'd by burning Thunder deep. ..... Il.8.517.421.

WOUNDS (CONTINUED)

Wounds, that long hence may ask their Spouses Care, ...Il.8.641.426.
Each wounds, each bleeds, but none resign the Day. ....Il.11.98.39.
Each adverse Battel goar'd with equal Wounds. ....Il.11.118.39.
Then swift revert, and Wounds return for Wounds. ....Il.11.422.53.
Then swift revert, and Wounds return for Wounds. ....Il.11.422.53.
From the blind Thicket wounds a stately Deer; ....Il.11.595.60.
A wise Physician, skill'd our Wounds to heal, ...Il.11.636.62.
Lie pierc'd with Wounds and bleeding in the Fleet. ....Il.11.961.78.
With his huge Trident wounds the trembling Shore, ...Il.12.30.82.
No Pass thro' those, without a thousand Wounds, ...Il.12.73.84.
By chance of Fight whatever Wounds you bore, ...Il.13.374.123.
Those Wounds were glorious all, and all before; ....Il.13.375.123.
These gaping Wounds withhold us from the Fight. ....Il.14.70.161.
Tho' sore of Battel, tho' with Wounds oppress, ...Il.14.145.164.
But lest new Wounds on Wounds o'erpower us quite, ...Il.14.149.165.
But lest new Wounds on Wounds o'erpower us quite, ...Il.14.149.165.
The Toils, the Sorrows, and the Wounds of War. ....Il.14.564.190.
Lies pierc'd with Wounds, and bleeding in his Tent. ....Il.16.34.236.
More for their Country's Wounds, than for their own. ....Il.16.37.236.
There bath'd his honourable Wounds, and drest ....Il.16.827.275.
Lies pierc'd with Wounds among the vulgar Dead. ....Il.17.2.286.
And Heaps on Heaps by mutual Wounds they bled. ....Il.17.473.306.
Stiff with Fatigue, and fretted sore with Wounds; ....Il.17.744.317.
And fall by mutual Wounds around the Dead. ....Il.18.212.332.
Embalm the Wounds, anoint the Limbs with Oyl; ....Il.18.412.340.
With new-made Wounds; another dragg'd a dead; ....Il.18.622.352.
In those wide Wounds thro' which his Spirit fled, ...Il.19.29.372.
Lame with their Wounds, and leaning on the Spear; ....Il.19.52.374.
Long-fest'ring Wounds, inextricable Woes! ....Il.19.98.376.
All grim with gaping Wounds, our Heroes lye: ....Il.19.202.381.
Pale lyes my Friend, with Wounds disfigur'd o'er, ...Il.19.209.381.
Destruction be my Feast, and mortal Wounds. ....Il.19.213.381.
Where gash'd with cruel Wounds, *Patroclus* lay. ....Il.19.298.384.
Repeated Wounds the red'ning River dy'd, ...Il.21.26.422.
Struck thro' with Wounds, all honest on the Breast. ....Il.22.101.456.
With Wounds ungen'rous, or with Taunts disgrace. ....Il.22.468.475.
Preserv'd from gaping Wounds, and tainting Air; ....Il.24.31.536.
And open all the wounds of *Greece* anew? ....Od.3.128.92.
That sad Idea wounds my anxious breast! ....Od.4.132.126.
Seam'd o'er with wounds, which his own sabre gave, ...Od.4.335.135.
Alas! must open all my wounds anew. ....Od.9.14.301.
Each adverse battel gor'd with equal wounds: ....Od.9.66.305.
Ghastly with wounds the forms of warriors slain ....Od.11.51.383.
Or should we labour while the plowshare wounds ....Od.18.414.189.
Dishonest wounds, or violence of soul, ...Od.19.15.193.
The wounds of Destiny's relentless rage ....Od.19.359.211.
No friend to bathe our wounds! or tears to shed ....Od.24.216.358.

WOVE

Th' Ambrosial Veil which all the Graces wove; ....Il.5.418.287.
(The labour'd Veil her heav'nly Fingers wove) ....Il.5.906.309.
The radiant Robe her sacred Fingers wove, ...Il.8.468.419.
The martial Scarf and Robe of Triumph wove. ....Il.22.657.483.
For Fate has wove the thread of life with pain, ...Od.7.263.248.
Long since, in better days, by *Helen* wove: ....Od.15.139.75.
Array'd in garments her own hands had wove, ...Od.15.394.88.
For heav'n has wove his thread of life with pain. ....Od.16.64.105.

WRACK

Amidst the wrack of nature undismay'd, ...6.21.9.69.

WRANGLE

And all the question (wrangle e'er so long) ....3.EOM1.49.19.

WRANGLING

'Till wrangling *Science* taught it Noise and Show, ...6.8.11.18.
A scorn of wrangling, yet a zeal for truth; ....6.57.8.169.
With wrangling Talents form'd for foul Debate: ....Il.2.307.142.

WRAP

Receive, and wrap me in eternal rest! ....2.ElAb.302.344.
"Wrap my cold limbs, and shade my lifeless face: ....3.Ep1.245.36.
To wrap me in the Universal Shade; ....4.HS1.96.13.
Not wrap up Oranges, to pelt your sire! ....5.DunB1.236.287.
Burst all her Gates, and wrap her Walls in Fire! ....Il.4.54.223.
To scale our Walls, to wrap our Tow'rs in Flames, ...Il.8.200.407.
This Day, we hop'd, would wrap in conq'ring Flame ....Il.8.623.425.
And wrap in rowling Flames the Fleet and Wall. ....Il.12.228.89.

WRAP'D

Secur'd the valves. There, wrap'd in silent shade, ...Od.1.555.58.

WRAPS

Wraps in her Veil, and frees from sense of Shame. ....5.DunB4.336.376.
Wraps the vast Mountains, and involves the Poles. ....Il.15.729.224.
His Hands collect; and Darkness wraps him round. ....Il.20.484.414.
Clouds the dull air, and wraps them round in shades. ....Od.11.20.380.
His destin'd prey, and wraps them all in shades. ....Od.22.38.288.

WRAPT

There wrapt in Clouds the blueish Hills ascend: ....1.W-F.24.150.
Wrapt in a pleasing, deep, and death-like Rest. ....1.TrUl.20.466.
He wrapt in Silk, and laid upon his Heart. ....2.ChJM.399.34.
Wrapt in th' envenom'd Shirt, and set on Fire. ....2.ChWB.382.76.
But what, or where, the Fates have wrapt in Night. ....2.RL2.104.166.
Wrapt in a Gown, for Sickness, and for Show. ....2.RL4.36.186.
Peace stole her wing, and wrapt the world in sleep; ....4.2HE1.401.229.
Wrapt up in Self, a God without a Thought, ...5.DunB4.485.389.
Wrapt round and sanctify'd with *Shakespear's* Name; ....6.98.18.283.
Here lies wrapt up in forty thousand towels ....6.147ii.1.390.
Arising silent, wrapt in Holy Fear, ...Il.1.692.120.
So wrapt in gath'ring Dust, the *Grecian* Train ....Il.3.21.189.
Wrapt in the cold Embraces of the Tomb; ....Il.3.312.208.
Wrapt in a Mist above the warring Crew. ....Il.5.442.289.
The fierce *Achilles* wrapt our Walls in Fire, ...Il.6.524.352.

WRAPT (CONTINUED)

Thy *Hector* wrapt in everlasting Sleep, ...Il.6.592.355.
Till their proud Navy wrapt in Smoak and Fires, ...Il.8.222.407.
In Silence wrapt, in Consternation drown'd, ...Il.9.557.460.
And, wrapt in Tempests, o'er the Fleet descends. ....Il.11.8.35.
Wrapt in the Blaze of boundless Glory sate; ....Il.11.109.39.
(Wrapt in the Cloud and Tumult of the Field) ....Il.13.846.146.
Eternal Darkness wrapt the Warrior round, ...Il.14.613.192.
The fancy'd Scenes, of *Ilion* wrapt in Flames, ...Il.16.1005.282.
And wrapt his Senses in the Cloud of Grief; ....Il.18.26.325.
And wrapt in Clouds, restrain'd the Hand of Fate. ....Il.21.646.449.
These wrapt in double Cauls of Fat, prepare; ....Il.23.302.501.
Wrapt round in Mists he lies, and lost to Thought: ....Il.23.812.521.
(Sad Scene of Woe!) His Face his wrapt Attire ....Il.24.200.545.
Or wrapt in flame, he glows at every limb. ....Od.4.566.147.
Or lies he wrapt in ever-during night? ....Od.4.1088.168.
Wrapt in embow'ring shade, *Ulysses* lies, ...Od.6.130.213.
Red with uncommon wrath, and wrapt in flames: ....Od.12.488.456.
Wrapt in a pleasing, deep, and death-like rest. ....Od.13.111.6.
As when we wrapt *Troy's* heav'n-built walls in fire. ....Od.13.444.27.
Then with these tatter'd rags they wrapt me round, ...Od.14.379.53.
That instant, in his cloak I wrapt me round: ....Od.14.567.64.
Wrapt in th' embrace of sleep, the faithful train ....Od.16.252.117.
Wrapt in a new-slain Oxe's ample hide: ....Od.22.403.307.
His habit coarse, but warmly wrapt around; ....Od.24.262.361.
Grief seiz'd at once, and wrapt up all the man; ....Od.24.368.366.

WRATH

How long shall Man the Wrath of Heav'n defy, ...1.TrSt.300.422.
The Clouds dispers'd, *Apollo's* Wrath expir'd, ...1.TrSt.784.443.
These Honours, still renew'd, his antient Wrath appease. ....1.TrSt.789.443.
Or which must end me, a Fool's Wrath or Love? ....4.Arbu.30.98.
To read in Greek, the Wrath of Peleus' Son. ....4.2HE2.53.169.
The Duke in Wrath call'd for his Steeds, ...6.79.53.219.
Achilles' Wrath, to Greece the direful Spring ....Il.1.1.82.
That Wrath which hurl'd to *Pluto's* gloomy Reign ....Il.1.3.82.
The Wrath of *Peleus'* Son the direful Spring ....Il.1.1A.82.
Now fir'd by Wrath, and now by Reason cool'd: ....Il.1.254.98.
Then rising in his Wrath, the Monarch storm'd; ....Il.1.502.112.
From whence this Wrath, or who controuls thy Sway? ....Il.1.715.122.
Beware! for dreadful is the Wrath of Kings. ....Il.2.234.138.
While stern *Achilles* in his Wrath retir'd: ....Il.2.935.167.
The prudent Goddess yet her Wrath suppress, ...Il.4.32.222.
Struck with his gen'rous Wrath, the King replies; ....Il.4.410.240.
Nor tempt the Wrath of Heav'ns avenging Sire. ....Il.5.44.268.
Rise in thy Wrath! To Hell's abhorr'd Abodes ....Il.5.555.295.
Nor fail'd the Crime th' Immortals Wrath to move, ...Il.6.169.334.
Indulge his Wrath, and aid our Arms no more; ....Il.7.278.378.
But *Jove* averse the Signs of Wrath display'd, ...Il.7.572.392.
Or all must perish in the Wrath of *Jove*. ....Il.8.46.398.
Before his Wrath the trembling Hosts retire; ....Il.8.97.402.
Neptune with Wrath rejects the rash Design: ....Il.8.254.409.
The Wrath appeas'd, by happy Signs declares, ...Il.8.295.411.
What Pow'r Divine shall *Hector's* Wrath asswage? ....Il.8.431.417.
Celestial Minds to tempt the Wrath of *Jove?* ....Il.8.509.420.
Before your Face, and in your Wrath expir'd. ....Il.8.559.423.
The prudent Goddess yet her Wrath represt, ...Il.8.573.424.
Whose Wrath hung heavy o'er the *Trojan* Tow'rs; ....Il.8.682.427.
If I oppose thee, Prince! thy Wrath with-hold, ...Il.9.45.434.
Now seek some means his fatal wrath to end, ...Il.9.145.439.
If Wrath so dreadful fill thy ruthless Mind, ...Il.9.564.461.
Curs'd by *Althæa,* to his Wrath he yields, ...Il.9.669.467.
Fixt is his Wrath, unconquer'd is his Pride; ....Il.9.795.473.
Ev'n *Jove,* whose Thunder spoke his Wrath, distill'd ....Il.11.69.37.
Which to pale Man the Wrath of Heav'n declares, ...Il.13.319.120.
With rising Wrath, and tumbled Gods on Gods; ....Il.14.290.176.
Impow'r'd the Wrath of Gods and Men to tame, ...Il.14.295.176.
While stern *Achilles* in his Wrath retires. ....Il.14.426.184.
Discharg'd his Wrath on half the Host of Heav'n; ....Il.15.139.202.
The Wrath of *Neptune* shall for ever last. ....Il.15.243.206.
Else had my Wrath, Heav'ns Thrones all shaking round, ...Il.15.252.206.
He foames with Wrath; beneath his gloomy Brow ....Il.15.730.224.
Wrath and Revenge from Men and Gods remove: ....Il.18.138.329.
He said: His finish'd Wrath with loud Acclaim ....Il.19.77.375.
With fell *Erynnis,* urg'd my Wrath that Day ....Il.19.89.375.
And Wrath extinguish'd burns my Breast no more. ....Il.19.200.381.
On guilty Towns exert the Wrath of Heav'n; ....Il.21.608.447.
The Prize I quit, if thou thy Wrath resign; ....Il.23.673.516.
By Fate, exceeds; and tempts the Wrath of Heav'n: ....Il.24.65.538.
Let not thy Wrath the Court of Heav'n inflame; ....Il.24.85.539.
Tell him he tempts the Wrath of Heav'n too far: ....Il.24.148.541.
Forbids to tempt the Wrath of Heav'n too far, ...Il.24.170.543.
Large Gifts, proportion'd to thy Wrath, I bear; ....Il.24.624.563.
Safe may'st thou sail, and turn thy Wrath from *Troy;* ....Il.24.702.566.
So was her Pride chastiz'd by Wrath divine, ...Il.24.763.569.
Unbless'd, abandon'd to the wrath of *Jove?* ....Od.1.83.35.
Neptune aton'd, his wrath shall now refrain, ...Od.1.100.36.
On me, on me your kindled wrath asswage, ...Od.2.81.64.
And while in wrath to vengeful Fiends she cries, ...Od.2.157.69.
Why cease we then the wrath of heav'n to stay? ....Od.2.195.71.
And calm *Minerva's* wrath. Oh blind to fate! ....Od.3.177.94.
Their wrath aton'd, to *Agamemnon's* name ....Od.4.793.156.
And on the suitors let thy wrath descend. ....Od.4.1012.164.
For what so dreadful as the wrath of *Jove?* ....Od.5.188.180.
To *Neptune's* wrath, stern Tyrant of the Seas, ...Od.5.431.193.
Whate'er thy Fate, the ills our wrath could raise ....Od.5.484.195.
All wrath ill-grounded, and suspicion base! ....Od.7.396.256.
From that fierce wrath the noble song arose, ...Od.8.71.266.
When clad in wrath he withers hosts of foes: ....Od.8.120.269.
A monument of wrath: how mound on mound ....Od.8.621.296.
Turn then, oh peaceful turn, thy wrath controul, ...Od.11.689.418.
My wrath is kindled, and my soul in flames. ....Od.12.461.453.
Now heav'n gave signs of wrath; along the ground ....Od.12.464.453.
Red with uncommon wrath, and wrapt in flames: ....Od.12.488.456.
How mov'd with wrath that careless we convey ....Od.13.200.15.
(A monument of wrath) and mound on mound ....Od.13.204.15.

WRATH (CONTINUED)
To pour his wrath on yon luxurious prey; ..... Od.15.197.78.
"The hand of wrath, and arm it for the fight." ..... Od.16.317.121.
But much to raise my master's wrath I fear; ..... Od.17.211.141.
The wrath of Princes ever is severe. ..... Od.17.212.142.
And ruminating wrath, he scorns repose. ..... Od.20.8.230.
And bays the stranger groom: so wrath compress ..... Od.20.21.232.
Tempest of wrath his soul no longer tost; ..... Od.20.30.233.
But shook his head, and rising wrath restrain'd. ..... Od.20.232.244.
Nor human right, nor wrath divine revere. ..... Od.20.274.246.
Stretch'd forth in wrath, shall drive thee from the land. ..... Od.21.402.279.
'Till then thy wrath is just— *Ulysses* burn'd ..... Od.22.71.290.
But heav'n, averse to *Greece*, in wrath decreed ..... Od.23.235.334.
'Till *Jove* in wrath the ratling Tempest guides, ... Od.23.357.342.
But when, arising in his wrath t'obey ..... Od.24.191.356.

WRATHFUL
Him thus upbraiding, with a wrathful Look ..... Il.5.1092.318.
The wrathful Chief and angry Gods assuage. ..... Il.9.154.439.
Like Light'ning swift the wrathful Faulchion flew, ... Il.10.524.26.
'Till wrathful thus *Eurylochus* began. ..... Od.12.332.447.
Th' afflictive hand of wrathful *Jove* to bear: ..... Od.18.317.182.
Th' insulted Heroe rouls his wrathful eyes, ... Od.19.86.196.
Not unobserv'd. *Eumæus* wrathful ey'd, ... Od.22.178.296.

WREAK
But should this Arm prepare to wreak our Hate ..... Il.4.61.223.
On her own Son to wreak her Brother's Death: ..... Il.9.684.468.
Not wreak my Vengeance on one guilty Land? ..... Il.18.430.341.
And angry Gods, shall wreak this Wrong on thee; ..... Il.22.450.474.
To wreak his hunger on the destin'd prey; ..... Od.10.132.347.

WREATH
That adds this Wreath of Ivy to thy Bays; ..... 1.PSu.10.72.
Accept the Wreath which You deserve alone, ... 1.PSu.57.76.
Wou'd you with Ivy wreath your flowing Hair, ... 1.TrSP.25.394.
Why rail they then, if but a Wreath of mine ..... 4.EpS2.138.321.
Not *Waller's* Wreath can hide the Nation's Scar, ... 4.EpS2.230.325.
The Net that held them, and the Wreath that crown'd, ... Il.22.601.481.

WREATH'D
For this with tort'ring Irons wreath'd around? ..... 2.RL4.100.191.
Rais'd on a thousand Pillars, wreath'd around ..... 2.TemF.139.264.
A Tiar wreath'd her head with many a fold; ..... Od.10.651.375.

WREATHE
Where Dukes and Butchers join to wreathe my crown, ... 5.DunB1.223.286.

WREATHS
See Nature hasts her earliest Wreaths to bring, ... 1.Mes.23.114.
(On *Cooper's* Hill eternal Wreaths shall grow, ... 1.W-F.265.173.
Whose horned temples reedy wreaths inclose; ..... 1.TrPA.160.373.
And Wreaths of Hay his Sun-burnt Temples shade; ..... 1.TrVP.34.378.
Then round your Neck in wanton Wreaths I twine, ... 1.TrSP.149.400.
With Golden Crowns and Wreaths of heav'nly Flow'rs, ... 2.RL1.34.148.
Let Wreaths of Triumph now my Temples twine, ... 2.RL3.161.180.
Twin'd with the wreaths Parnassian lawrels yield, ... 3.EOM4.11.129.
If e'er with Wreaths I hung thy sacred Fane, ... Il.1.57.88.
Be mindful of the Wreaths your Arms have won, ... Il.8.212.407.
Of those the Locks with flow'ry Wreaths inroll'd, ... Il.18.687.356.

WREATHY
A wreathy foliage, and concealing shades. ..... Od.6.152.215.

WRECK
Heav'n drove my wreck th' *Ogygian* Isle to find, ... Od.7.338.253.
The scatter'd wreck the winds blew back again. ..... Od.9.341.320.
The direful wreck *Ulysses* scarce survives! ..... Od.11.144.387.
A floating fragment of the wreck regain'd, ... Od.19.318.209.

WRECK'D
Being on being wreck'd, and world on world, ... 3.EOM1.254.46.

WRECKS
And two rich ship-wrecks bless the lucky shore. ..... 3.Ep3.356.122.

WREN
While Wren with sorrow to the grave descends, ... 5.DunA3.325.189.
While Wren with sorrow to the grave descends, ... 5.DunB3.329.336.

WRENCH'D
Who wrench'd the Javelin from his sinewy Thigh. ..... Il.5.855.307.
Till grasp'd with Force, he wrench'd it from his Hands. ..... Il.11.306.48.
He wrench'd a rocky fragment from the ground: ..... Od.8.210.273.

WREST
And hopes no captious Fools will wrest my sense ..... 4.JD2A.132.144.
And all his Rapine cou'd from others wrest; ..... Il.9.497.457.

WRESTLE
Or urge the Race, or wrestle on the Field. ..... Il.23.714.518.

WRESTLERS
And calls the Wrestlers to the level Sands: ..... Il.23.815.521.
With fierce embrace the brawny wrestlers joyn; ..... Od.8.133.270.
Stand forth ye wrestlers who these pastimes grace! ..... Od.8.235.275.

WRESTLING
Or firmer, in the wrestling, press the ground. ..... Od.8.104.268.

WRETCH
A wretch undone: O parents help, and deign ..... 1.TrPA.142.371.
(Wretch that I am, to call that *Phaon* mine!) ..... 1.TrSP.237.404.
Wretch that I am, I'd almost call'd him mine! ..... 1.TrSP.237A.404.
The Wretch then lifted to th'unpitying Skies ..... 1.TrSt.77.413.
Yet if propitious to a Wretch unknown, ... 1.TrSt.802.443.

WRETCH (CONTINUED)
O tell a Wretch, in Exile doom'd to stray, ... 1.TrUl.112.469.
No impious Wretch shall 'scape unpunish'd long, ... 2.ChJM.649.46.
Whor'd by my Slave—Perfidious Wretch! may Hell ..... 2.ChJM.770.52.
Wretch that I am, that e'er I was so Kind! ..... 2.ChJM.782.52.
Or as *Ixion* fix'd, the Wretch shall feel ..... 2.RL2.133.168.
Ah wretch! believ'd the spouse of God in vain, ... 2.ElAb.177.334.
Wise Wretch! of Pleasures too refin'd to please, ... 3.Ep2.95B.57.
Wise Wretch! with Pleasures too refin'd to please, ... 3.Ep2.95.57.
"The wretch he starves"—and piously denies: ..... 3.Ep3.106.100.
The Wretch that trusts them, and the Rogue that cheats. ..... 3.Ep3.238.112.
The wretch, who living sav'd a candle's end: ..... 3.Ep3.292.117.
The Wretch, whose Av'rice drove his *Son* away. ..... 4.HAdv.26.77.
And as a Wretch, condemn'd, and judg'd as dead ..... 4.JD2A.15.132.
Curs'd be the Wretch! so venal and so vain; ..... 4.JD2.63.139.
Out drink the Sea and that bold Wretch outswear, ... 4.JD2A.43.136.
Man? and *for ever?* Wretch! what wou'dst thou have? ..... 4.2HE2.252.183.
Satire be kind, and let the wretch alone. ..... 4.1HE1.135.289.
And lo the wretch! whose vile, whose insect lust ..... 5.DunB4.415.382.
The only wretch beneath thy happy reign! ..... 6.20.51.67.
I wish the Wretch a Dinner, and sit still; ..... 6.49iii.2A.142.
The Wretch whom pilfer'd Pastorals renown, ... 6.98.29.284.
Be silent Wretch, and think not here allow'd ..... Il.2.241.139.
He views the Wretch, and sternly thus replies. ..... Il.2.305.142.
That Wretch, too mean to fall by martial Pow'r, ... Il.2.468.149.
And mortal Man! a Wretch of humble Birth, ... Il.5.537.294.
The Wretch would brave high Heav'ns immortal Sire, ... Il.5.559.295.
The Wretch who trembles in the Field of Fame, ... Il.5.657.299.
A Wretch accurst, and hated by the Gods! ..... Il.6.174.334.
Oh would kind Earth the hateful Wretch embrace, ... Il.6.352.343.
(Oh Wretch ill-fated, and thy Country's Foe!) ..... Il.6.407.347.
That Wretch, that Monster, who delights in War: ..... Il.9.90.437.
The Wretch and Hero find their Prize the same; ..... Il.9.419.453.
And learn to scorn the Wretch they basely fear. ..... Il.9.484.456.
The Wretch stood prop'd, and quiver'd as he stood; ..... Il.10.444.23.
Or art some Wretch by hopes of Plunder led, ... Il.10.459.24.
Sternly he spoke, and as the Wretch prepar'd ..... Il.10.522.26.
A Wretch, whose Swiftness was his only Fame, ... Il.10.661.31.
The daring Wretch who once in Council stood ..... Il.11.181.43.
Ah Wretch! no Father shall thy Corps compose, ... Il.11.568.59.
The Wretch relentless, and o'erwhelm with Shame! ..... Il.14.164.165.
To scourge the Wretch insulting them and Heav'n. ..... Il.15.229.205.
The Wretch that trembles in the Field of Fame, ... Il.15.672.222.
The weakest Atheist-Wretch all Heav'n defies, ... Il.20.421.412.
Wretch! Thou hast scap'd again. Once more thy Flight ..... Il.20.519.416.
Yet curst with Sense! a Wretch, whom in his Rage ..... Il.22.82.456.
No, Wretch accurst! Relentless he replies, ... Il.22.433.473.
The Wretch obeys, retiring with a Tear. ..... Il.22.641.483.
Wretch that I am! my bravest Offspring slain, ... Il.24.319.549.
As when a Wretch, (who conscious of his Crime ..... Il.24.590.561.
To most, he mingles both: The Wretch decreed ..... Il.24.667.565.
To warn the wretch, that young *Orestes* grown ..... Od.1.51.33.
Still lives the wretch who wrought the death deplor'd, ... Od.4.735.153.
Behold a wretch whom all the Gods consign ..... Od.4.958.162.
Wretch that I am! what farther Fates attend ..... Od.5.383.190.
A pledge of love! 'tis all a wretch can give. ..... Od.8.522.290.
Know first the man (tho' now a wretch distrest) ..... Od.9.17.301.
Some rustic wretch, who liv'd in heav'n's despight, ... Od.9.250.317.
Not this weak pigmy-wretch, of mean design, ... Od.9.603.331.
Vile wretch, begone! this instant I command ..... Od.10.83.343.
Whilst in the port each wretch encumber'd dies. ..... Od.10.152.347.
A pompous wretch! accurs'd upon a throne. ..... Od.11.336.398.
No more that wretch shall view the joys of life, ... Od.12.55.432.
O tell a wretch in exile doom'd to stray, ... Od.13.279.19.
"Wretch! this is villany, and this is sin." ..... Od.14.110.41.
The Monarch's son a shipwrackt wretch reliev'd, ... Od.14.351.51.
When lo! a wretch ran breathless to the shore, ... Od.15.250.80.
Of my own tribe an *Argive* wretch I slew; ..... Od.15.298.83.
A wretch in safety to her native shore." ..... Od.15.475.93.
The sev'nth, the fraudful wretch (no cause descry'd) ..... Od.15.513.95.
Wretch! to destroy a Prince that friendship gives, ... Od.16.438.128.
But hateful of the wretch, *Eumæus* heav'd ..... Od.17.280.145.
So spoke the wretch; but shunning farther fray, ... Od.17.304.146.
A wretch unhappy, meerly for his need? ..... Od.17.471.156.
Unless at distance, wretch! thou keep behind, ... Od.17.530.158.
Peace wretch! and eat thy bread without offence, ... Od.17.568.160.
But hear me, wretch! if recreant in the fray, ... Od.18.94.171.
Untaught to bear, 'gainst heav'n the wretch rebells. ..... Od.18.162.174.
With soft forgetfulness, a wretch like me; ..... Od.18.238.178.
The coward wretch the privilege to fly. ..... Od.18.284.180.
A wretch, the most compleat that breathes the air! ..... Od.18.318.182.
So pays the wretch, whom fact constrains to roam, ... Od.19.192.201.
Some wretch reluctant views aerial light, ... Od.19.401.214.
Piteous, regard a wretch consum'd with care! ..... Od.20.146.240.
The wretch unfriendly to the race of man. ..... Od.20.224.244.
The lawless wretch, the man of brutal strength, ... Od.21.30.260.
Wretch! is not thine: the arrows of the King ..... Od.21.103.263.
Heav'n to this wretch (another cry'd) be kind! ..... Od.21.435.281.
Wretch that he was, of unprophetic soul! ..... Od.22.13.287.
'Till pale as yonder wretch each Suitor lies. ..... Od.22.78.290.
The wretch, and shorten'd of his nose and ears; ..... Od.22.512.313.
Wretch that he was! and that I am! my son! ..... Od.24.337.365.

WRETCH'S
And calls on Death, the Wretch's last Relief. ..... 2.ChJM.484.38.
Heav'n first taught letters for some wretch's aid, ... 2.ElAb.51.323.

WRETCHE'S
Pow'rful alike to ease the Wretche's Smart; ..... Il.16.635.269.

WRETCHED
Ah wretched Shepherd, what avails thy Art, ... 1.PSu.33.74.
If to the wretched any faith be giv'n; ..... 1.TrFD.69.389.
Must then her Name the wretched Writer prove? ..... 1.TrSP.3.393.
"Thy wretched Weight, nor dread the Deeps below!" ..... 1.TrSP.198.402.
Now wretched *Oedipus*, depriv'd of Sight, ... 1.TrSt.69.413.

WRETCHED (CONTINUED)

If wretched I, by baleful Furies led, ... 1.TrSt.95.414.
Say, wretched Rivals! what provokes your Rage? ... 1.TrSt.210.419.
These now controul a wretched People's Fate, ... 1.TrSt.239.420.
Oh wretched we, a vile submissive Train, ... 1.TrSt.263.421.
His wretched Father, known too well by Fame? ... 1.TrSt.809.443.
And beat my Breasts, as wretched Widows—must. ... 2.ChWB.310.72.
And *Hampton's* Ecchoes, wretched Maid! reply'd) ... 2.RL*A* 2.14.132.
A wretched *Sylph* too fondly interpos'd; ... 2.RL3.150.179.
O wretched Maid! she spread her Hands, and cry'd, ... 2.RL4.95.191.
(While *Hampton's* Ecchos, wretched Maid! reply'd) ... 2.RL4.96.191.
Be envy'd, wretched, and be flatter'd, poor; ... 2.TemF.510.288.
Drive from my Breast that wretched Lust of Praise; ... 2.TemF.522.289.
We, wretched subjects tho' to lawful sway, ... 3.EOM2.149.73.
Mark by what wretched steps their glory grows, ... 3.EOM4.291.155.
Of wretched Shylock, spite of Shylock's Wife: ... 3.Ep3.96.97.
Thy life more wretched, Cutler, was confess'd, ... 3.Ep3.321.120.
See wretched *Monsieur* flies to save his Throat, ... 4.HAdv.53.79.
No wretched Wife cries out, *Undone! Undone!* ... 4.HAdv.170.89.
Seiz'd and ty'd down to judge, how wretched I! ... 4.Arbu.33.98.
Wretched indeed! but far more wretched yet ... 4.JD2.29.135.
Wretched indeed! but far more wretched yet ... 4.JD2.29.135.
With wretched Av'rice, or as wretched Love? ... 4.1HE1.56.283.
With wretched Av'rice, or as wretched Love? ... 4.1HE1.56.283.
But wretched Bug, his *Honour,* and so forth. ... 4.1HE1.90.285.
Arraign no mightier Thief than wretched *Wild,* ... 4.EpS2.39.315.
O Wretched B[ritain], jealous now of all, ... 4.1740.1.332.
Where wretched *Withers, Banks,* and *Gildon* rest. ... 5.DunA1.250B.92.
Where wretched Withers, Ward, and Gildon rest, ... 5.DunB1.296.291.
While wretched lovers sing in vain. ... 6.6i.16.14.
A vain, unquiet, glitt'ring, wretched Thing! ... 6.19.54.63.
If 'ere the Wretched I deny'd ... 6.50.35A.148.
Wretched Lovers, Fate, has past ... 6.78ii.1.216.
Wretched Lovers, quit your Dream, ... 6.78ii.3.216.
Mark by what wretched steps Great * * *grows,* ... 6.130.1.358.
But in thy Poet wretched as a King! ... 6.131i.2.360.
But oh! relieve a wretched Parent's Pain, ... Il.1.27.87.
Is wretched *Thetis* least the Care of *Jove?* ... Il.1.669.119.
The wretched Quarrels of the mortal State ... Il.1.742.123.
And scarce ensure the wretched Pow'r to fly. ... Il.2.164.136.
(We, wretched Mortals! lost in Doubts below, ... Il.2.576.155.
Can wretched Mortals harm the Pow'rs above, ... Il.4.50.223.
And think'st thou not how wretched we shall be, ... Il.6.512.351.
Shall wretched *Greece* no more confess our Care, ... Il.8.426.417.
Lo here the wretched *Agamemnon* stands, ... Il.10.96.6.
Ah wretched Man! unmindful of thy End! ... Il.17.231.296.
What wretched Creature of what wretched kind, ... Il.17.510.308.
What wretched Creature of what wretched kind, ... Il.17.510.308.
And wretched I, th' unwilling Messenger! ... Il.18.22.324.
How wretched, were I mortal, were my Fate! ... Il.18.71.326.
How more than wretched in th' immortal State! ... Il.18.72.326.
For soon alas! that wretched Offspring slain, ... Il.18.115.328.
Me too, a wretched Mother shall deplore, ... Il.18.387.340.
What Woes my wretched Race of Life attend? ... Il.19.307.385.
Or drags a wretched Life of Age and Care, ... Il.19.357.387.
The wretched Matron feels thy piercing Dart; ... Il.21.559.445.
The wretched Monarch of the falling State ... Il.22.522.478.
O wretched Husband of a wretched Wife! ... Il.22.608.481.
O wretched Husband of a wretched Wife! ... Il.22.608.481.
He, wretched Outcast of Mankind! appears ... Il.22.630.482.
To leave him wretched the succeeding Day. ... Il.22.637.482.
Thus wretched, thus retiring all in Tears, ... Il.22.642.483.
To Grief the wretched Days we have to live. ... Il.24.256.547.
Add to the slaughter'd Son the wretched Sire! ... Il.24.278.548.
The Sons their Father's wretched Age revere, ... Il.24.331.550.
(Two wretched Suppliants) and for Mercy call? ... Il.24.440.554.
How oft, alas! has wretched *Priam* bled? ... Il.24.617.562.
Oh hear the Wretched, and the Gods revere! ... Il.24.625.563.
Tho' not so wretched: There he yields to me, ... Il.24.628.563.
Ye wretched Daughters, and ye Sons of *Troy!* ... Il.24.877.573.
The wretched Source of all this Misery! ... Il.24.976.576.
But doom'd a Father's wretched fate to mourn! ... Od.1.284.46.
Nurs'd the most wretched King that breathes the air! ... Od.2.395.80.
To learn what fates thy wretched sire detain, ... Od.3.21.87.
A third lives wretched on a distant coast. ... Od.4.670.150.
In riot to consume a wretched heir. ... Od.4.913.161.
Did he, with all the greatly wretched, crave ... Od.4.942.162.
To guard the wretched from th' inclement sky: ... Od.6.216.220.
'Tis mine to bid the wretched grieve no more, ... Od.6.234.221.
A wretched stranger, and of all unknown! ... Od.7.34.235.
A wretched exile to his country send, ... Od.7.200.245.
Or wretched hunters thro' the wintry cold ... Od.9.138.311.
When all thy wretched crew have felt my pow'r, ... Od.9.437.324.
Whilst we, the wretched part'ners of his toils, ... Od.10.45.341.
Or see the wretched for whose loss we mourn. ... Od.10.318.359.
For fate decreed one wretched man to fall. ... Od.10.658.375.
That wretched I might ev'n my joys lament? ... Od.11.258.394.
Then from a wretched friend this wisdom learn, ... Od.11.561.411.
More wretched you! twice number'd with the dead! ... Od.12.32.431.
Six guilty days my wretched mates employ ... Od.12.467.454.
Of wand'rings and of woes a wretched share? ... Od.13.481.29.
And at his side a wretched scrip was hung, ... Od.13.506.30.
Little alas! was left my wretched share, ... Od.14.240.48.
The last, the wretched proof of filial love. ... Od.15.295.83.
Proud are the lords, and wretched are the swains. ... Od.15.407.89.
Wretched old man! (with tears the Prince returns) ... Od.16.158.110.
The wretched he relieves diffuse his fame, ... Od.19.385.212.
To wash a wretched wand'rer wou'd disdain; ... Od.19.398.213.
What pangs for thee this wretched bosom bears! ... Od.19.425.215.
Of all the wretched harbour'd on our coast, ... Od.19.444.216.
What once I was, whom wretched you despise; ... Od.21.303.274.
The wretched Augur thus for mercy calls. ... Od.22.348.304.
She colour'd all our wretched lives with woe. ... Od.23.238.334.

WRETCHEDNESS

(Dire Pomp of sov'reign Wretchedness!) must fall, ... Il.22.94.456.

WRETCHES

And Wretches hang that Jury-men may Dine; ... 2.RL3.22.170
**, **, and **, the wretches caught. ... 5.DunA2.118
Think for her love what crowds of wretches wake. ... 6.4i.10.9.
To thee, we Wretches of the *Houyhnhnm* Band, ... 6.96iii.1.274.
Destin'd and due to wretches self-enslav'd! ... 6.146.2.389.
Not unmolested let the Wretches gain ... Il.8.637.426.
Next seiz'd two wretches more, and headlong cast, ... Od.9.404.322
So pant the wretches, struggling in the sky, ... Od.12.305.44
Of other wretches care the torture ends: ... Od.20.100.23
"Behold what wretches to the bed pretend ... Od.21.351.27
The hour of vengeance, wretches, now is come, ... Od.22.51.289
In prostrate heaps the wretches beat the ground, ... Od.22.344.30
And heaps on heaps the wretches strow the ground; ... Od.24.207.35

WRIGGLING

First Grubs obscene, then wriggling Worms, ... 6.14v(b).23.5
From the Grub Obscene, & wriggling Worm ... 6.14v(b).23A.

WRINGS

He wrings his Hands, he beats his manly Breast. ... Il.15.459.215.
When scalding Thirst their burning Bowels wrings. ... Il.16.195.247.

WRINKLED

But clear they wrinkled Brown, and quit thy Sorrow, ... 2.ChWB.122.
Her wrinkled Form in *Black* and *White* array'd; ... 2.RL4.28.185
Lame are their Feet, and wrinkled is their Face; ... Il.9.625.465.
While on her wrinkled Front, and Eyebrow bent, ... Il.15.112.200.
To clear the cloudy front of wrinkled Care, ... Od.4.305.134
And wither'd Elders, pale and wrinkled shades: ... Od.11.50.383

WRINKLES

O'er thy smooth skin a bark of wrinkles spread, ... Od.13.457.28
She o'er my limbs old age and wrinkles shed; ... Od.16.230.11

WRIST

Pierc'd thro' the Wrist; and raging with the Pain ... Il.17.681.314.

WRISTS

She said, and seiz'd her Wrists with eager Rage; ... Il.21.566.445.
And to his Wrists the Gloves of Death are bound. ... Il.23.792.521.

WRIT

Of ancient Writ unlocks the learned Store, ... 1.W-F.247.17
With the same Spirit that its Author *writ,* ... 1.EOC.234.26
Jilts rul'd the State, and Statesmen *Farces* writ; ... 1.EOC.538.29
Might boldly censure, as he boldly writ, ... 1.EOC.658.31
Which writ and folded, with the nicest Art, ... 2.ChJM.398.3
Whose Reign Indulgent God, says Holy Writ, ... 2.ChJM.690.4
With some grave Sentence out of Holy Writ. ... 2.ChWB.346.
In time to come, may pass for *Holy Writ.* ... 4.JD4.287.49.
Who neither writes nor pays for what is writ ... 4.JD2A.110.1
"How Beaumont's Judgment check'd what Fletcher writ; ... 4.2HE1.84.20
And ev'ry flow'ry Courtier writ Romance. ... 4.2HE1.146.2
What pert low Dialogue has Farqu'ar writ! ... 4.2HE1.288.2
As Eusden, Philips, Settle, writ of Kings) ... 4.2HE1.417.2
Writ underneath the Country Signs; ... 4.HS6.92.255.
You grow *correct* that once with Rapture writ, ... 4.EpS1.3.297.
Against your worship when had *S[elkir]k* writ? ... 4.EpS2.158.32
Against your worship what has *S[elkir]k* writ? ... 4.EpS2.158A.
Writ not, and *Chartres* scarce could write or read, ... 4.EpS2.186.32
In eldest time, e'er mortals writ or read, ... 5.DunA1.7.61
Then writ, and flounder'd on, in mere despair. ... 5.DunA1.114.
That once so flutter'd, and that once so writ. ... 5.DunA2.112.
In eldest time, e'er mortals writ or read, ... 5.DunB1.9.26
That once so flutter'd, and that once so writ. ... 5.DunB2.120.
On Poets' Tombs see Benson's titles writ! ... 5.DunB3.325.
But ever writ, as none e'er writ before. ... 6.34.10.101.
But ever writ, as none e'er writ before. ... 6.34.10.101.
Tho' *Tom* the Poet writ with Ease and Pleasure, ... 6.34.23.101.
Will needs misconstrue what the Poet writ; ... 6.38.11Z2.108
But doom'd it then when first Ardelia writ. ... 6.43.4.120.
There he stopt short, nor since has writ a tittle, ... 6.49i.9.137.
Since some have writ, and shewn no Wit at all. ... 6.60.8.178.
Of Course resign'd it to the next that writ: ... 6.60.36.179.
And send what *A[rgy]le,* would he *write,* might have writ. ... 6.62iii.4.185.
In [george]'s Reign these fruitless lines were writ, ... 6.106iii.2.307.
Has writ such stuff, as none e'er writ before. ... 6.116i.2.325.
Has writ such stuff, as none e'er writ before. ... 6.116i.2.325.
You wonder Who this Thing has writ, ... 6.127.1.355.
You ask me Who this Thing has writ, ... 6.127.1A.355.
On many a *Grecian* Bosom writ in Blood. ... Il.14.54.160.

WRITE

These *born* to Judge, as well as those to Write. ... 1.EOC.14.240.
Each burns alike, who can, or cannot write, ... 1.EOC.30.242.
Those hate as *Rivals* all that write; and others ... 1.EOC.30A.24
Some hate as *Rivals* all that write; and others ... 1.EOC.30B.24
There are, who *judge* still *worse* than he can *write.* ... 1.EOC.35.243.
Write dull *Receits* how Poems may be made: ... 1.EOC.115.25
For who can *rail* so long as they can *write?* ... 1.EOC.599.30
Garth did not write his own *Dispensary.* ... 1.EOC.619.30
They *judge* with *Fury,* but they *write* with *Fle'me:* ... 1.EOC.662.31
See, while I write, my Words are lost in Tears; ... 1.TrSP.109.39
There liv'd in *Lombardy,* as Authors write, ... 2.ChJM.1.15.
Too long for me to write, or you to read; ... 2.ChJM.306.2
The weary Sun, as Learned Poets write, ... 2.ChJM.367.3
But cou'd we Women write as Scholars can, ... 2.ChWB.366.7
Then down they sit, and in their Dotage write, ... 2.ChWB.374.7
Oh write it not, my hand—The name appears ... 2.ElAb.13.319.
Yet write, oh write me all, that I may join ... 2.ElAb.41.322.
Yet write, oh write me all, that I may join ... 2.ElAb.41.322.
Ah come not, write not, think not once of me, ... 2.ElAb.291.34

RITE (CONTINUED)
'Tis well—but, Artists! who can paint or write, — 3.Ep2.187.65.
F. I'd write no more. *P.* Not write? but then I *think,* — 4.HS1.11.5.
F. I'd write no more. *P.* Not write? but then I *think,* — 4.HS1.11.5.
Fools rush into my Head, and so I write. — 4.HS1.14.5.
Or if you needs must write, write CÆSAR'S Praise: — 4.HS1.21.7.
Or if you needs must write, write CÆSAR'S Praise: — 4.HS1.21.7.
Or whiten'd Wall provoke the Skew'r to write, — 4.HS1.98.13.
Such as a *King* might read, a *Bishop* write, — 4.HS1.152.21.
If Foes, they write, if Friends, they read me dead. — 4.Arbu.32.98.
My Foes will write, my Friends will read me dead — 4.Arbu.32A.98.
"He'll write a *Journal,* or he'll turn *Divine.*" — 4.Arbu.54.100.
"I too could write, and I am twice as tall, — 4.Arbu.103.103.
"I too could write, and sure am twice as tall, — 4.Arbu.103A.103.
Why did I write? what sin to me unknown — 4.Arbu.125.104.
And knowing *Walsh,* would tell me I could write; — 4.Arbu.136.105.
And born to write, converse, and live with ease: — 4.Arbu.196.110.
I sought no homage from the Race that write; — 4.Arbu.219.111.
Heav'ns! was I born for nothing but to write? — 4.Arbu.272.115.
Why will the Town imagine still I write? — 4.Arbu.271A.115.
And write whate'er he pleas'd, except his *Will;* — 4.Arbu.379.125.
These write to Lords, some mean reward to get, — 4.JD2.25.133.
Those write because all write, and so have still — 4.JD2.27.133.
Those write because all write, and so have still — 4.JD2.27.133.
But let them write for You, each Rogue impairs — 4.JD2.99.141.
Some write to Lords in hope reward to get, — 4.JD2A.29.134.
Some write, because all write; and thus have stil — 4.JD2A.31.134.
Some write, because all write; and thus have stil — 4.JD2A.31.134.
I told you when I went, I could not write; — 4.2HE2.28.167.
To court applause by printing what I write: — 4.2HE2.150.175.
The Men, who write such Verse as we can read? — 4.2HE2.158.175.
To seek applause by printing what I write: — 4.2HE2.150A.175.
If such the Plague and pains to write by rule, — 4.2HE2.180.177.
But those who cannot write, and those who can, — 4.2HE1.187.211.
We needs will write Epistles to the King; — 4.2HE1.369.227.
Besides, a fate attends on all I write, — 4.2HE1.408.229.
Writ not, and *Chartres* scarce could write or read, — 4.EpS2.186.324.
But Pens can forge, my Friend, that cannot write. — 4.EpS2.188.324.
And write next winter more *Essays on Man.* — 4.EpS2.255.327.
Amaz'd that one can read, that one can write: — 4.1740.34.333.
And write about it, Goddess, and about it; — 5.DunA1.170.84.
Shall this a Pasquin, that a Grumbler write; — 5.DunA3.178.170.
Shall this a Pasquin, that a Grumbler write; — 5.DunB3.182.329.
And write about it, Goddess, and about it: — 5.DunB4.252.369.
Codrus writes on, and will for ever write; — 6.7.2.15.
I know you dread all those who write, — 6.10.11.24.
The *Granvilles* write their Name plain *Greenfield,* — 6.10.47.26.
He had some Fancy, and cou'd write; — 6.10.95.27.
As 'tis at last the Cause they write no more; — 6.16.10.53.
Few write to those, and none can live to these. — 6.19.30.63.
To write their Praise you but in vain essay, — 6.43.9.120.
Ev'n while you write, you take that praise away, — 6.43.10.120.
He'd write in Prose—To the *Spectator.* — 6.44.4.123.
Was form'd to write, converse, and live, with ease: — 6.49iii.10.142.
And Born to Write, Converse and live at Ease; — 6.49iii.10A.142.
And Born to Write, Converse and Live with Ease; — 6.49iii.10B.142.
And Born to Live, Converse and Write with Ease; — 6.49iii.10C.142.
Ah! why did he write Poetry, — 6.58.21.171.
Write on, nor let me scare ye; — 6.58.38.172.
Write on, nor let me scare you; — 6.58.38A.172.
For tho ye seldome write a book — 6.58.68Z3.173.
And send what *A[rgy]le,* would he *write,* might have writ. — 6.62iii.4.185.
Let *D[enni]s* write, and nameless numbers rail: — 6.63.4.188.
—Am I not fit to write a Tragedy? — 6.82ii.6.230.
And born to write, converse, and live with ease; — 6.98.46.284.
Both were so forward, each would write, — 6.105iv.3.301.
And hers, when freedom is the theme, to write. — 6.107.12.310.
An *Author* that cou'd never *write,* — 6.116iii.3.326.
For DUCK can *thresh,* you know, as well as *write.* — 6.116vi.6.327.
Cibber! write all thy Verses upon Glasses, — 6.131ii.1.360.
"I gave it to you to write again. — 6.140.16.378.
"You'd write as smooth again on glass, — 6.140.21.378.
I'll have the last Word, for by G—d I'll write Prose. — 6.149.2.397.

RITEING
See WRITING.
Excuse for writing and for writeing ill. — 4.JD2A.32.134.

RITER
And while Self-Love each jealous Writer rules, — 1.EOC.516.296.
Must then her Name the wretched Writer prove? — 1.TrSP.3.393.
How great, how just, the Judgment of that Writer! — 6.12.10.37.
How great must be the Judgment of that Writer! — 6.12.10A.37.
Decry'd each past, to raise each present Writer — 6.17iv.13.59.
And all the Writer lives in ev'ry Line; — 6.19.2.62.
Ingenious Writer, lest thy Barrel split, — 6.48i.5.133*.
Comes, as the Writer did too long, — 6.64.5.189.

RITER'S
In ev'ry Work regard the *Writer's End,* — 1.EOC.255.268.

RITERS
Some *foreign* Writers, some our *own* despise; — 1.EOC.394.285.
Some the *French* Writers, some our *own* despise; — 1.EOC.394A.285.
"But Sir, of Writers?"—" *Swift,* for closer Style, — 4.JD4.72.31.
My Liege! why Writers little claim your thought, — 4.2HE1.356.225.
And give to Modern Writers Classic *Law;* — 6.26ii.6.79.

RITES
Ten Censure wrong for one who Writes amiss; — 1.EOC.6.239.
Glows while he *reads,* but *trembles* as he *writes)* — 1.EOC.198.263.
Just writes to make his barrenness appear, — 4.Arbu.181.109.
Who writes a Libel, or who copies out: — 4.Arbu.290.116.
Who neither writes nor pays for what is writ — 4.JD2A.110.142.
But turns a Wit, and writes Love Verses too? — 4.JD2A.60.136.
"His Prince, that writes in Verse, and has his Ear? — 4.EpS1.46.301.

WRITES (CONTINUED)
And C[hesterfiel]d who speaks so well and writes, — 4.1740.25.333.
Ev'n Ralph repents, and Henly writes no more. — 5.DunB1.216.285.
Ev'n Ralph is lost, and Henly writes no more. — 5.DunB1.216A.285.
Codrus writes on, and will for ever write; — 6.7.2.15.
But your damn'd Poet lives and writes agen. — 6.24i.2.75.
But your damn'd Poet lives and writes again. — 6.34.4.101.
Plu—Plutarch, what's his name that writes his life? — 6.41.31.114.
E'en sits him down, and writes to honest *T[ickell]* — 6.49ii.14.140.
If Dennis writes, and rails in furious Pet, — 6.49iii.3B.142.
Just writes to make his Barrenness appear, — 6.98.31.284.
He smiles (you think) approving what he writes; — 6.105ii.2.300.
He reads, and laughs, you think, at what he writes: — 6.105ii.2A.300.
Yet, if he writes, is dull as other folks? — 6.105iii.2.301.
But when he writes, he's dull as other folks? — 6.105iii.2A.301.

WRITHEN
Aims the red bolt, and hurls the writhen brand! — Od.12.446.452.

WRITHES
He writhes his Body, and extracts the Dart. — Il.11.575.60.

WRITING
See WRITEING.
Appear in *Writing* or in *Judging* ill; — 1.EOC.2.239.
True Ease in Writing comes from Art, not Chance, — 1.EOC.362.281.
Nature's chief Master-piece is writing well. — 1.EOC.724.323.
By secret Writing to disclose his Pain, — 2.ChJM.497.39.
Are Fathers of the Church for writing less. — 4.JD2A.101.140.
Excuse for writing, and for writing ill. — 4.JD2.28.133.
Excuse for writing, and for writing ill. — 4.JD2.28.133.
Are Fathers of the Church for writing less. — 4.JD2.98.141.
Excuse for writing and for writeing ill. — 4.JD2A.32.134.
"But Ease in writing flows from Art, not Chance, — 4.2HE2.178.177.
For writing pamphlets, and for burning Popes; — 5.DunA3.282.183.
For writing pamphlets, and for roasting Popes; — 5.DunA3.282A.183.
For writing Pamphlets, and for roasting Popes; — 5.DunB3.284.334.
—And if each writing Author's best pretence, — 6.16.7.53.
Writing a Sonnet, cou'd not rhime; — 6.44.2.123.
To writing of good Sense. — 6.58.12.171.
For writing? no,—for writing not. — 6.62vi.2.186.
For writing? no,—for writing not. — 6.62vi.2.186.

WRITINGS
Nor praise nor blame the *Writings,* but the *Men.* — 1.EOC.413.287.
Nor praise nor damn the *Writings,* but the *Men.* — 1.EOC.413A.287.
The Morals blacken'd when the Writings scape; — 4.Arbu.352.121.
Yet when he sells, the writings he impairs — 4.JD2A.102.140.
Can Popish Writings do the Nations good? — 6.48iii.9.134.
Woud you your writings to some Palates fit — 6.82ix(f).1.235.
In whose Heart, like his Writings, was never found flaw; — 6.92.2.255.

WRITTEN
And *censure freely* who have *written well.* — 1.EOC.16.241.
Already written—wash it out, my tears! — 2.ElAb.14.320.
To written Wisdom, as another's, less: — 3.Ep1.13.16.
So written precepts may successless prove, — 5.DunA1.175A.84.
The written bolt, and blackens heav'n with storms,) — Od.8.506.289.

WRONG
Ten Censure wrong for one who Writes amiss; — 1.EOC.6.239.
And *smooth* or *rough,* with them, is *right* or *wrong;* — 1.EOC.338.277.
And *smooth* or *rough,* with such, is *right,or wrong;* — 1.EOC.338A.277.
By *Chance* go right, they *purposely* go wrong; — 1.EOC.427.288.
Who, if *once wrong,* will needs be *always so;* — 1.EOC.569.305.
That, if *once wrong,* will needs be *always so;* — 1.EOC.569A.305.
Nor suffers *Horace* more in wrong *Translations* — 1.EOC.663.314.
By *Wits,* then *Criticks* in as wrong *Quotations.* — 1.EOC.664.314.
That in my Presence offers such a Wrong. — 2.ChJM.650.46.
None judge so wrong as those who think amiss. — 2.ChJM.810.54.
Is only this, if God has plac'd him wrong? — 3.EOM1.50.19.
Respecting Man, whatever wrong we call, — 3.EOM1.51.19.
Pleasure, or wrong or rightly understood, — 3.EOM2.91.65.
One must go right, the other may go wrong. — 3.EOM3.94.101.
"And right, too rigid, harden into wrong; — 3.EOM3.193.113.
His can't be wrong whose life is in the right: — 3.EOM3.306.124.
Who risk the most, that take wrong means, or right? — 3.EOM4.86.136.
And then mistook reverse of wrong for right. — 3.Ep3.200.110.
For 'faith Lord Fanny! you are in the wrong, — 4.HS2.101.61.
What's wrong is wrong, wherever it be done: — 4.HAdv.78.81.
What's wrong is wrong, wherever it be done: — 4.HAdv.78.81.
Why let him Sing—but when you're in the Wrong, — 4.HAdv.141.87.
If wrong, I smil'd; if right, I kiss'd the rod. — 4.Arbu.158.107.
"To say too much, might do my Honour wrong: — 4.2HE2.12.165.
This jealous, waspish, wrong-head, rhiming Race; — 4.2HE2.148.175.
And, having once been wrong, will be so still. — 4.2HE1.130.207.
Who felt the wrong, or fear'd it, took th' alarm, — 4.2HE1.255.217.
Fr. Strange spleen to *S[elkir]k! P.* Do I wrong the Man? — 4.EpS2.62.316.
Whose names once up, they thought it was not wrong — 4.1740.21.333.
Affect no conquest, but endure no wrong. — 4.1740.94.337.
To cavil, censure, dictate, right or wrong, — 5.DunA2.345.142.
"To cavil, censure, dictate, right or wrong, — 5.DunB2.377.315.
'The RIGHT DIVINE of Kings to govern wrong. ' " — 5.DunB4.188.360.
'*till* drown'd was Sense, and Shame, and Right, and Wrong— — 5.DunB4.625.406.
For fear to wrong them with a Name too low; — 6.9xi.2.23.
Thus *Helens* Rape and *Menelaus'* wrong — 6.38.7.107.
If I am wrong, Thy Grace impart — 6.50.31.147.
If I am wrong, Oh reach my heart — 6.50.31B.147.
To be about you, right or wrong; — 6.64.6.189.
If wrong, I smile; if right, I kiss the Rod. — 6.98.8.283.
T'avenge a private, not a publick Wrong: — Il.1.208.96.
Avenge this Wrong, oh ever just and wise! — Il.1.658.118.
And durst he, as he ought, resent that Wrong, — Il.2.300.142.
And guard from Wrong fair Friendship's holy Name. — Il.3.438.213.
Thy Will is partial, not thy Reason wrong: — Il.12.270.91.
I made him Tyrant; gave him Pow'r to wrong — Il.16.74.238.

WRONG (CONTINUED)
Wrong the best Speaker, and the justest Cause. ....Il.19.86.375.
Arm'd or with Truth or Falshood, Right or Wrong, ...Il.20.296.406.
And angry Gods, shall wreak this Wrong on thee; ....Il.22.450.474.
To you O *Grecians!* be my Wrong declar'd: ....Il.23.654.515.
Hector's dead Earth insensible of Wrong! ....Il.24.67.538.
Approach that hour! unsufferable wrong ....Od.2.69.64.
Or having pow'r to wrong, betray'd the will; ....Od.2.80.64.
But while your Sons commit th' unpunish'd wrong, ...Od.2.87.65.
Match in fierce wrong, the Giant-sons of earth. ....Od.7.280.249.
And, youth, my gen'rous soul resents the wrong: ....Od.8.200.273.
With decent pride refutes a public wrong: ....Od.8.270.278.
Then mutual, thus they spoke: Behold on wrong ....Od.8.367.283.
And thou, *Euryalus,* redeem thy wrong: ....Od.8.431.287.
The herds of *Iphiclus,* detain'd in wrong; ....Od.11.355.399.
How vain thy efforts to avenge the wrong? ....Od.12.147.439.
Yet 'scap'd he death; and vengeful of his wrong ....Od.15.260.80.
At once to pity and resent thy wrong. ....Od.16.94.107.
The cause of suppliants, and revenge of wrong. ....Od.16.441.128.
This is the house of violence and wrong: ....Od.17.329.147.
But for meer want, how hard to suffer wrong? ....Od.17.562.159.
To curb wild riot and to punish wrong? ....Od.17.623.162.
Stranger, if prompted to chastize the wrong ....Od.18.68.170.
But now no crime is theirs: this wrong proceeds ....Od.18.275.179.
To whom with frowns: O impudent in wrong! ....Od.18.385.186.
Slave, I with justice might deserve the wrong, ...Od.18.430.189.
Those who to cruel wrong their state abuse, ...Od.19.379.212.
Their deeds detested, and abjur'd the wrong. ....Od.21.156.266.
The weakest woman: all can wrong the brave. ....Od.21.350.276.
Wrong and oppression no renown can raise; ....Od.21.359.277.
Lest time or worms had done the weapon wrong, ...Od.21.429.281.
A deed like this thy future fame would wrong, ...Od.22.381.306.
Ill-us'd by all! to ev'ry wrong resign'd, ...Od.24.189.356.

WRONG-HEAD
This jealous, waspish, wrong-head, rhiming Race; ....4.2HE2.148.175.

WRONG'D
You wrong'd the Man, by Men and Gods admir'd: ....Il.9.144.439.
Wrong'd in my Love, all Proffers I disdain; ....Il.9.454.454.
To right with Justice, whom with Pow'r they wrong'd. ....Il.19.182.379.
Still must the wrong'd *Telemachus* sustain, ...Od.4.221.130.

WRONGS
And Wrongs and Woes were all you left with her. ....1.TrSP.118.398.
'Tis his alone, t'avenge the Wrongs I bear; ....1.TrUl.90.469.
And bear unmov'd the Wrongs of base Mankind, ...1.TrUl.186.472.
Of wrongs from Duchesses and Lady Mary's) ....5.DunA2.128.112.
Of wrongs from Duchess and Lady Maries;) ....5.DunB2.136.301.
'Tis Thou shalt save him from insidious wrongs, ...6.21.5.69.
A heav'nly Witness of the Wrongs I bear ....Il.1.270.100.
Are tam'd to Wrongs, or this had been thy last. ....Il.1.308.102.
Or urg'd by Wrongs, to *Troy's* Destruction came? ....Il.2.579.155.
Dione then. Thy Wrongs with Patience bear, ...Il.5.471.290.
While *Pray'rs,* to heal her Wrongs, move slow behind. ....Il.9.630.465.
My Wrongs, my Wrongs, my constant Thought engage, ...Il.16.72.238.
My Wrongs, my Wrongs, my constant Thought engage, ...Il.16.72.238.
But bear we this—The Wrongs I grieve, are past; ....Il.16.82.238.
(Forgetful of my Wrongs, and of thy own) ....Il.21.515.443.
What Wrongs attend him, and what Griefs to come? ....Il.22.625.482.
Pursu'd by Wrongs, by meagre Famine driv'n, ...Il.24.669.565.
And all your wrongs the proud oppressors rue! ....Od.1.330.48.
Vengeance I vow, and for your wrongs ye die. ....Od.2.170.70.
And but augment the wrongs thou would'st redress. ....Od.2.222.72.
But heav'n, and all the *Greeks,* have heard my wrongs: ....Od.2.239.73.
He wanders with them, and he feels their wrongs. ....Od.9.324.319.
O taught to bear the wrongs of base mankind! ....Od.11.762.424.
'Tis his alone t'avenge the wrongs I bear; ....Od.13.257.18.
And bear unmov'd the wrongs of base mankind, ...Od.13.353.24.
'Till urg'd by wrongs a foreign realm he chose, ...Od.15.254.80.
Their wrongs and blasphemies ascend the sky, ...Od.15.348.86.
Here dwell in safety from the suitors wrongs, ...Od.16.85.106.
And outrag'd by the wrongs of base mankind. ....Od.16.209.114.
The wrongs and injuries of base mankind ....Od.17.334.147.
Here boundless wrongs the starry skies invade, ...Od.17.648.164.
And us'd that pow'r to justify my wrongs. ....Od.18.168.175.
And now the Martial Maid, by deeper wrongs ....Od.18.395.186.
This dome a refuge to thy wrongs shall be, ...Od.20.330.249.
Or if each other's wrongs ye still support, ...Od.20.382.251.
Who wrongs his Princess with a thought so mean. ....Od.21.344.276.
Great are thy wrongs, and much hast thou sustain'd ....Od.22.59.289.
That stranger, patient of the Suitors wrongs, ...Od.23.29.320.
'Tis so—the Suitors for their wrongs have paid— ....Od.24.411.369.

WROTE
The Mob of Gentlemen who wrote with Ease; ....4.2HE1.108.203.
Yet wrote and flounder'd on, in mere despair. ....5.DunB1.120.278.
Then Dulness was the Cause they wrote before, ...6.16.9.53.
Argyle his Praise, when *Southerne* wrote, ...6.77.1.214.

WROTH
Nay, (quoth the King) dear Madam be not wroth; ....2.ChJM.700.48.

WROUGHT
No Chargers then were wrought in burnish'd Gold, ...1.TrSt.206.419.
Lo thus, my Friends, I wrought to my Desires ....2.ChWB.148.63.
Thrice the wrought Slipper knock'd against the Ground, ...2.RL1.17A.145.
O'er-wrought with Ornaments of barb'rous Pride. ....2.TemF.120.263.
As, in some well-wrought picture, light and shade, ...3.EOM2.208.81.
Becomes the stuff of which our dream is wrought: ....3.Ep1.48.18.
which Fancy colour'd, and a Vision wrought ....4.JD4.189A.43.
Behold the hand that wrought a Nation's cure, ...4.2HE1.225.215.
Thou triumph'st, victor of the high-wrought day, ...5.DunA2.179.123.
"What pow'r," he cries, "what pow'r these wonders wrought?" .5.DunA3.246.178.
What God or Dæmon all these wonders wrought? ....5.DunA3.246A.178.
Thou triumph'st, Victor of the high-wrought day, ...5.DunB2.187.304.

WROUGHT (CONTINUED)
What flatt'ring scenes our wand'ring fancy wrought, ...6.52.23.156.
Ye Gods! what Wonders has *Ulysses* wrought? ....Il.2.333.143.
And ask'd, what God had wrought this guilty Deed? ....Il.5.464.290.
He gave his own, of Gold divinely wrought, ...Il.6.294.341.
(The well-wrought Harp from conquer'd *Thebæ* came, ...Il.9.247.445.
When *Hector's* Prowess no such Wonders wrought; ....Il.9.465.455.
(Inspir'd by *Pallas)* in his Bosom wrought, ...Il.10.436.23.
A Change so shameful, say what Cause has wrought? ....Il.13.147.111.
Chains, Bracelets, Pendants, all their Toys I wrought. ....Il.18.468.344.
With his, who wrought thy lov'd *Patroclus'* Death. ....Il.21.108.426.
With Flow'rs high-wrought, not blacken'd yet by Flame. Il.23.1047.53
What Toils they shar'd, what martial Works they wrought, ...Il.24.13.535.
Who, when his arms had wrought the destin'd fall ....Od.1.3.25.
A veil of richest texture wrought, she wears, ...Od.1.429.53.
By what strange fraud *Ægysthus* wrought, relate, ...Od.3.310.101
So wrought, as *Pallas* might with pride behold. Od.3.556.114
A silver canister divinely wrought, ...Od.4.165.128
And that rich vase, with living sculpture wrought, ...Od.4.179.128
Still lives the wretch who wrought the death deplor'd, ...Od.4.735.153
Wrought of the clouded olive's easy grain; Od.5.302.185
(The work of *Polybus,* divinely wrought) Od.8.408.285
Sev'n golden talents to perfection wrought, ...Od.9.236.316
'Twas for our lives my lab'ring bosom wrought; Od.9.501.326
Inimitably wrought with skill divine. Od.11.758.42
The silver vase with living sculpture wrought. Od.15.135.75
With unguents smooth, of polisht marble wrought; Od.17.99.136
Pisander bears a necklace, wrought with art; Od.18.347.18
By fam'd *Icmalius* wrought, the menials plac'd: Od.19.69.196
The last alone a kind illusion wrought, ...Od.20.104.23
The utmost gate. (The cable strongly wrought Od.21.423.28
Then to the Prince. Nor have I wrought thee shame; Od.21.465.28
Bring first the crew who wrought these guilty deeds. Od.22.470.31
Great deeds, oh friends! this wond'rous man has wrought, ...Od.24.489.37

WROUGHT'
"What pow'r, he cries, what pow'r these wonders wrought' .....5.DunB3.250.

WRUNG
Oft, when his Shoe the most severely wrung, ...2.ChWB.239.

WRY
Instructive work! whose wry-mouth'd portraiture 5.DunA2.137
Instructive work! whose wry-mouth'd portraiture ....5.DunB2.145.

WRY-MOUTH'D
Instructive work! whose wry-mouth'd portraiture 5.DunA2.137
Instructive work! whose wry-mouth'd portraiture ....5.DunB2.145.

WYCHERLEY
Slander'd the Ancients first, then *Wycherley;* .... 6.12.5.37.

WYCHERLY
"How Shadwell hasty, Wycherly was slow; 4.2HE1.85.20
Nay, Mr. *Wycherly* see *Binfield.* .... 6.10.48.26.

WYNDHAM
Or WYNDHAM, just to Freedom and the Throne, ...4.EpS2.88.318
Or WYNDHAM, arm'd for Freedom and the Throne, ...4.EpS2.88A.3
And thy last sigh was heard when W[yndha]m died. 4.1740.80.336
There truant WYNDHAM ev'ry Muse gave o'er, ...5.DunB4.167.
Where *British* Sighs from dying WYNDHAM stole, ...6.142.11.383.
Here Wyndham, thy last Sighs for Liberty 6.142.11C.383
Here Wyndham, this last Sighs for Liberty 6.142.11D.38
Here British groans from dying WYNDHAM stole, ...6.142.11E.383
Here British sighs from dying WYNDHAM stole, ...6.142.11F.383

WYNDHAM'S
Here patriot sighs from Wyndham's bosom stole, ...6.142.11A.38
There partiot sighs from Wyndham's bosom stole 6.142.11B.383
To Wyndham's breast the patriot passion stole 6.142.11H.38

WYNKIN
There Caxton slept, with Wynkin at his side, ...5.DunA1.129.

WYNKYN
There Caxton slept, with Wynkyn at his side, ...5.DunB1.149.

X
X and *Z* cry'd, P—x and Z—s ....6.30.43.87.

XANTHUS
Where gulphy *Xanthus* foams along the Fields. ....Il.2.1071.172.
Remov'd from Fight, on *Xanthus* flow'ry Bounds ....Il.5.47.268.
Young *Xanthus* next and *Thoon* felt his Rage, ...Il.5.196.276.
Where foaming *Xanthus* laves the *Lycian* Land, ...Il.5.584.296.
Now *Xanthus, Æthon, Lampus!* urge the Chace, ...Il.8.226.408.
And lighten glimm'ring *Xanthus* with their Rays. ....Il.8.700.428.
And *Xanthus* foaming from his fruitful Source; ....Il.12.20.82.
Where gentle *Xanthus* rolls his easy Tyde, ...Il.14.508.188.
Xanthus and *Balius,* of immortal Breed, ...Il.16.182.245.
Xanthus and *Balius!* of *Podarges'* Strain, ...Il.19.440.390.
The gen'rous *Xanthus,* as the Words he said, ...Il.19.446.390.
Xanthus whose Streams in golden Currents flow, ...Il.20.53.396.
Xanthus his Name with those of heavenly Birth, ...Il.20.101.398.
Xanthus, Immortal Progeny of *Jove.* .... Il.21.2.420.
Part plunge into the Stream: Old *Xanthus* roars, ...Il.21.9.421.
So plung'd in *Xanthus* by *Achilles'* Force, ...Il.21.18.422.
With equal Rage, indignant *Xanthus* roars, ...Il.21.356.435.
(*Xanthus,* immortal Progeny of *Jove)* .... Il.24.863.572.

XANTHUS'
Where *Xanthus'* Streams enrich the *Lycian* Plain? ....1.TrES.28.450.
The Chief arriv'd at *Xanthus'* silver Flood: ....Il.6.212.336.
Where *Xanthus'* Streams enrich the *Lycian* Plain, ...Il.12.372.95.
And now to *Xanthus'* gliding Stream they drove, ...Il.21.1.420.

NTHUS' (CONTINUED)
When now to *Xanthus'* yellow Stream they drove, ...Il.24.862.572.

NTIPPE
Xantippe made her good Man undergo; ....2.ChWB.388.76.

Cou'd ne'er bring in *Psi* and *Xi;* .... 6.30.69.88.

No less than *Pythagorick Y,* .... 6.30.73.88.

'FED
On parchment scraps y-fed, and Wormius hight. ....5.DunA3.184.171.
On parchment scraps y-fed, and Wormius hight. ....5.DunB3.188.329.

FOND
This in our Tale is plain y-fond, ...6.14i.3A.41.

PENT
"But who is he, in closet close y-pent, ...5.DunA3.181.170.
"But who is he, in closet close y-pent, ...5.DunB3.185.329.

HOO
O happy *Yahoo,* purg'd from human Crimes, ...6.96iii.5.274.
And even a *Yahoo* learn'd the Love of Truth. ....6.96iii.10.274.
Did never *Yahoo* tread that Ground before? ....6.96iii.12.274.

RD
Nor is *Paul's Church* more safe than *Paul's Church-yard:* ....1.EOC.623.310.
In Palace-Yard at Nine you'll find me there— ....4.2HE2.94.171.

RDS
On hoisted Yards extended to the Gales; ....Il.18.6.323.
With crossing sail-yards dancing in the wind; ....Od.5.325.187.
Flew sail and sail-yards ratling o'er the main. ....Od.5.408.192.
Loos'd from the yards invite th' impelling gales. ....Od.12.472.454.

W
'Twas *Si Signior,* 'twas *Yaw Mynheer,* .... 6.14v(b).11.49.
'Twas *Si Signior,* & Yaw *Mynheer,* .... 6.14v(b).11A.49.

WN
Ready to cast, I yawn, I sigh, and sweat: ....4.JD4.157.39.
Ready to cast, I yawn, I sigh, I sweat: ....4.JD4.157A.39.
At ev'ry line, they stretch, they yawn, they doze. ....5.DunA2.358.143.
At ev'ry line they stretch, they yawn, they doze. ....5.DunB2.390.316.
And heard thy everlasting yawn confess ....5.DunB4.343.377.
What Mortal can resist the Yawn of Gods? ....5.DunB4.606.403.
Her six mouths yawn, and six are snatch'd away. ....Od.12.155.439.

WN'D
More she had spoke, but yawn'd—All Nature nods: ....5.DunB4.605.403.
More she had said, but yawn'd—All Nature nods: ....5.DunB4.605A.403.
And Navies yawn'd for Orders on the Main. ....5.DunB4.618.405.

WNING
Strait from the hollow cliff, and yawning ground, ...1.TrPA.157.372.
Sees yawning Rocks in massy Fragments fly, ...1.TrSt.511.431.
Then from the yawning Wound with Fury tore ....1.TrES.125.454.
First may the yawning Earth her Bosome rend, ...2.ChJM.585.43.
A yawning ruin hangs and nods in air; ....5.DunA1.28.63.
And all thy yawning daughters cry, *encore.* .... 5.DunB4.60.347.
Then, from the yawning Wound with Fury tore ....Il.12.479.99.
A yawning cavern casts a dreadful shade: ....Od.12.100.436.
The yawning dungeon, and the tumbling flood; ....Od.12.293.446.

WNS
—but here she stops, she yawns, she nods;— ....5.DunB4.605B.403.

E
Ye shady Beeches, and ye cooling Streams, ...1.PSu.13.72.
Ye shady Beeches, and ye cooling Streams, ...1.PSu.13.72.
Where stray ye Muses, in what Lawn or Grove, ...1.PSu.23.73.
Where are ye Muses, in what Lawn or Grove, ...1.PSu.23A.73.
Ye Gods! and is there no Relief for Love? ....1.PSu.88.79.
Ye *Mantuan* Nymphs, your sacred Succour bring; ....1.PAu.5.80.
Ye Flow'rs that droop, forsaken by the Spring, ...1.PAu.27.82.
Ye Birds, that left by Summer, cease to sing, ...1.PAu.28.82.
Ye Trees that fade when Autumn-Heats remove, ...1.PAu.29.82.
Ye Pow'rs, what pleasing Frensie sooths my Mind! ....1.PAu.51.83.
And cease ye Gales to bear my Sighs away! ....1.PAu.54.84.
Rehearse, ye Muses, what your selves inspir'd. ....1.PAu.56.84.
Resound ye Hills, resound my mournful Strain! ....1.PAu.57.84.
Resound ye Hills, resound my mournful Lay! ....1.PAu.65.85.
Resound ye Hills, resound my mournful Strain! ....1.PAu.71.85.
Resound ye Hills, resound my mournful Lay! ....1.PAu.77.85.
Resound ye Hills, resound my mournful Strains! ....1.PAu.85.86.
Resound ye Hills, resound my mournful Lay! ....1.PAu.93.87.
Farewell ye Woods! adieu the Light of Day! ....1.PAu.94.87.
No more ye Hills, no more resound my Strains! ....1.PAu.96.87.
And said; "Ye Shepherds, sing around my Grave!" ....1.PWi.18.90.
Ye gentle *Muses* leave your Crystal Spring, ...1.PWi.21.90.
Ye weeping *Loves,* the Stream with Myrtles hide, ...1.PWi.23.90.
Adieu ye *Vales,* ye *Mountains, Streams* and *Groves,* .... 1.PWi.89.95.
Adieu ye *Vales,* ye *Mountains, Streams* and *Groves,* .... 1.PWi.89.95.
Adieu ye Shepherd's rural *Lays* and *Loves,* .... 1.PWi.90.95.
Adieu my Flocks, farewell ye *Sylvan* Crew, ...1.PWi.91.95.
Ye Nymphs of *Solyma!* begin the Song: ....1.Mes.1.112.
Ye Heav'ns! from high the dewy Nectar pour, ...1.Mes.13.114.
Sink down ye Mountains, and ye Vallies rise: ....1.Mes.34.116.
Sink down ye Mountains, and ye Vallies rise: ....1.Mes.34.116.
With Heads declin'd, ye Cedars, Homage pay; ....1.Mes.35.116.
Be smooth ye Rocks, ye rapid Floods give way! ....1.Mes.36.116.
Be smooth ye Rocks, ye rapid Floods give way! ....1.Mes.36.116.
Hear him ye Deaf, and all ye Blind behold! ....1.Mes.38.116.

YE (CONTINUED)
Hear him ye Deaf, and all ye Blind behold! ....1.Mes.38.116.
Ye vig'rous Swains! while Youth ferments your Blood, ...1.W-F.93.159.
Ye sacred Nine! that all my Soul possess, ...1.W-F.259.173.
Or where ye Muses sport on *Cooper's* Hill. ....1.W-F.264.173.
Why was I born, ye Gods, a *Lesbian* Dame? ....1.TrSP.64.396.
I go, ye Nymphs! those Rocks and Seas to prove; ....1.TrSP.201.402.
I go, ye Nymphs! where furious Love inspires: ....1.TrSP.203.402.
Ye gentle Gales, beneath my Body blow, ...1.TrSP.207.402.
Ye *Lesbian* Virgins, and ye *Lesbian* Dames, ...1.TrSP.232.404.
Ye *Lesbian* Virgins, and ye *Lesbian* Dames, ...1.TrSP.232.404.
Ye Gods that o'er the gloomy Regions reign ....1.TrSt.81.413.
These Sons, ye Gods! who with flagitious Pride ....1.TrSt.107.414.
Hail faithful *Tripos!* Hail ye dark Abodes ....1.TrSt.596.435.
Ye valiant Leaders of our warlike Bands! ....1.TrES.80Z1.452.
O where, ye *Lycians,* is the Strength you boast, ...1.TrES.145.455.
Advance ye *Trojans,* lend your valiant Hands, ...1.TrES.177.456.
Ye Gods (he cry'd) upon what barren Coast, ...1.TrUl.74.468.
All hail! Ye Virgin Daughters of the Main; ....1.TrUl.240.473.
Ye Streams, beyond my Hopes beheld again! ....1.TrUl.241.473.
Ye Bards! renown'd among the tuneful Throng ....2.ChJM.335.30.
Ye Fair draw near, let *May's* Example move ....2.ChJM.434.35.
Ye Sov'reign Wives! give Ear, and understand; ....2.ChWB.68.59.
Thus shall ye speak, and exercise Command. ....2.ChWB.69.59.
Ye *Sylphs* and *Sylphids,* to your Chief give Ear, ...2.RL2.73.164.
Ye know the Spheres and various Tasks assign'd, ...2.RL2.75.164.
Haste then ye Spirits! to your Charge repair; ....2.RL2.111.166.
To just Contempt, ye vain Pretenders, fall, ...2.TemF.400.282.
Ye rugged rocks! which holy knees have worn; ....2.ElAb.19.320.
Ye grots and caverns shagg'd with horrid thorn! ....2.ElAb.20.320.
Ye soft illusions, dear deceits, arise! ....2.ElAb.240.339.
I come, ye ghosts! prepare your roseate bow'rs, ...2.ElAb.317A.345.
Why bade ye else, ye Pow'rs! her soul aspire ....2.Elegy.11.363.
Why bade ye else, ye Pow'rs! her soul aspire ....2.Elegy.11.363.
Oh sons of earth! attempt ye still to rise, ...3.EOM4.73.135.
Ye little Stars! hide your diminish'd rays. ....3.Ep3.282.116.
"Virtue! and Wealth! what are ye but a name!" ....3.Ep3.334.120.
By what *Criterion* do ye eat, d'ye think, ...4.HS2.29.57.
But why all this? I'll tell ye, 'tis my Theme: ....4.HAdv.27.77.
Think ye to cure the Mischief with a Song? ....4.HAdv.142.87.
Would ye be blest? despise low Joys, low Gains; ....4.1HE6.60.241.
Thus Fools with Compliments besiege ye, ...4.1HE7.29.271.
Contriving never to oblige ye. ....4.1HE7.30.271.
And 'tis but just, I'll tell ye wherefore, ...4.1HE7.33A.271.
To set this matter full before ye, ...4.1HE7.81A.273.
'Tis all from *Horace: Horace* long before ye ....4.EpS1.7.297.
Ye Gods! shall *Cibber's* Son, without rebuke ....4.EpS1.115.306.
Ye Statesmen, Priests, of one Religion all! ....4.EpS2.16.314.
Ye Tradesmen vile, in Army, Court, or Hall! ....4.EpS2.17.314.
Ye Rev'rend Atheists!— *F.* Scandal! name them, Who? ....4.EpS2.18.314.
Ye tinsel Insects! whom a Court maintains, ...4.EpS2.220.325.
And visit alehouse where ye first did grow." ....5.DunA1.202.87.
And visit alehouse where ye first begun." ....5.DunA1.202A.87.
There Ridpath, Roper, cudgell'd might ye view; ....5.DunA2.141.118.
There kick'd and cudgel'd R— might ye view; ....5.DunA2.141A.118.
"Hold (cry'd the Queen) ye all alike shall win, ...5.DunA2.233A.129.
"Ah why, ye Gods! should two and two make four?" ....5.DunA2.274.135.
"Silence, ye Wolves! while Ralph to Cynthia howls, ...5.DunA3.159.165.
And makes Night hideous—Answer him ye Owls! ....5.DunA3.160.165.
(So may the fates preserve the ears ye lend). ....5.DunA3.212A.175.
But learn, ye Dunces! not to scorn your God." ....5.DunA3.222.176.
For new Abortions, all ye pregnant Fair! ....5.DunA3.312.186.
And place it here! here all ye Heroes bow! ....5.DunA3.316.186.
Ye shall not beg, like gratis-given Bland, ...5.DunB1.231.287.
Lift up your gates, ye Princes, see him come! ....5.DunB1.301.291.
Sound, sound ye Viols, be the Cat-call dumb! ....5.DunB1.302.291.
There Ridpath, Roper, cudgell'd might ye view, ...5.DunB2.149.302.
"Ah why, ye Gods! should two and two make four?" ....5.DunB2.286.309.
Ask ye their names? I could as soon disclose ....5.DunB2.309.310.
Ask ye their names? I sooner could disclose ....5.DunB2.309A.310.
"Ye Critics! in whose heads, as equal scales. ....5.DunB2.367.315.
"Silence, ye Wolves! while Ralph to Cynthia howls, ...5.DunB3.165.328.
And makes Night hideous—Answer him, ye Owls! ....5.DunB3.166.328.
But, "Learn, ye Dunces! not to scorn your God" ....5.DunB3.224.331.
For new abortions, all ye pregnant fair! ....5.DunB3.314.335.
And place it here! here all ye Heroes bow! ....5.DunB3.318.335.
Ye Pow'rs! whose Mysteries restor'd I sing, ...5.DunB4.5.339.
Begone ye Criticks, and restrain your Spite, ...6.7.1.15.
Dear Mr. Cromwell, May it please ye! ....6.10.1.24.
With—I protest, and I'll assure ye;— ....6.10.52.26.
Descend ye Nine! descend and sing; ....6.11.1.29.
'Are large and wide; *Tydcomb* and I assure ye. ....6.13.25.39.
Thilke moral shall ye understond, ...6.14i.3.41.
How can ye, Mothers, vex your Children so? ....6.14ii.7.43.
Ye Few, whom better Genius does inspire, ...6.27.10.81.
Et cæt'ra represents ye all: ....6.30.80.89.
Who in your own *Despite* has strove to please ye. ....6.34.8.101.
Oh! may all *gentle* Bards together place ye, ...6.40.7.112.
May *Satire* ne'er befool ye, or beknave ye, ...6.40.9.112.
May *Satire* ne'er befool ye, or beknave ye, ...6.40.9.112.
And from all Wits that have a Knack Gad save ye. ....6.40.10.112.
Those strange examples ne'er were made to fit ye, ...6.41.41.114.
This Year in Peace, ye Critics, dwell, ...6.47.3.128.
Ye Harlots, sleep at Ease! ....6.47.4.128.
Ye shades, where sacred truth is sought; ....6.51i.1.151.
Forsaken, friendless, shall ye fly? ....6.51i.14.151.
Say, will ye bless the bleak *Atlantic* shore? ....6.51i.15.151.
Ye Gods! what justice rules the ball? ....6.51i.25.152.
Ye Lords and Commons, Men of Wit ....6.58.1.170.
Read this ere ye translate one Bit ....6.58.3A.170.
Tho' with a Golden Pen ye scrawl, ...6.58.7A.171.
Write on, nor let me scare ye; ....6.58.38.172.
See, see, ye great New—le comes, ...6.58.43A.172.
Ye *Ladies* too draw forth your Pen, ...6.58.65.173.
Ye Fair ones that are able! ....6.58.68Z2.173.
For tho ye seldome write a book ....6.58.68Z3.173.

(CONTINUED)
Whither (he cry'd) ah whither will ye run? .... Od.10.509.368.
Seek ye to meet those evils ye shou'd shun? .... Od.10.510.368.
Seek ye to meet those evils ye shou'd shun? .... Od.10.510.368.
To me are known the various woes ye bore, ... Od.10.542.369.
Such be your minds as ere ye left your coast, ... Od.10.546.369.
Exiles and wand'rers now, where-e're ye go, ... Od.10.548.369.
Already, friends! ye think your toils are o'er, ... Od.10.671.375.
But if his herds ye seize, beneath the waves .... Od.11.142.387.
Is it, ye pow'rs that smile at human harms! .... Od.11.255.394.
Ye perish all! tho' he who rules the main .... Od.12.135.438.
The Gods, the Gods avenge it, and ye die! .... Od.12.175.440.
Hear heav'n's commands, and rev'rence what ye hear! .... Od.12.325.447.
Haste ye to land! and when the morning ray .... Od.12.349.448.
Of these fair pastures: If ye touch, ye die. .... Od.12.382.449.
Of these fair pastures: If ye touch, ye die. .... Od.12.382.449.
Why cease ye then t' implore the pow'rs above, ... Od.12.407.450.
Why seize ye not yon beeves, and fleecy prey? .... Od.12.409.450.
Oh all ye blissful pow'rs that reign above! .... Od.12.438.452.
Vengeance, ye Pow'rs, (he cries) and thou whose hand .... Od.12.445.452.
Vengeance, ye Gods! or I the skies forego, ... Od.12.450.452.
Ye Gods! (he cry'd) upon what barren coast .... Od.13.241.17.
All hail! Ye virgin daughters of the main! .... Od.13.407.26.
Ye streams, beyond my hopes beheld again! .... Od.13.408.26.
And, oh ye Gods! with all your blessings grace .... Od.14.63.38.
(So dire a fate, ye righteous Gods! avert, ... Od.15.384.88.
"Swear first (she cry'd) ye sailors! to restore .... Od.15.474.93.
"Ye rush to arms, and stain the feast with blood: .... Od.16.315.121.
Hope ye success? undaunted crush the foe. .... Od.16.388.124.
Wait ye, till he to arms in council draws .... Od.16.390.124.
Or chuse ye vagrant from their rage to fly .... Od.16.394.125.
Ye Peers and rivals in this noble love! .... Od.17.556.159.
Careless to please, with insolence ye wooe! .... Od.18.320.182.
You, only you, make her ye love your prey. .... Od.18.324.182.
Alone with men! ye modest maids, away! .... Od.18.360.185.
"Ye Peers, I cry, who press to gain a heart, ... Od.19.162.200.
Your other task, ye menial train, forbear; .... Od.19.362.211.
Snatch me, ye whirlwinds! far from humane race, ... Od.20.74.236.
Your violence and scorn, ye Suitors cease, ... Od.20.332.249.
The sentence I propose, ye Peers, attend: .... Od.20.359.249.
No more ye lewd Compeers, with lawless pow'r .... Od.20.378.251.
Or if each other's wrongs ye still support, ... Od.20.382.251.
A just reproof, ye Peers! Your rage restrain .... Od.20.389.251.
From me, ye Gods! avert such dire disgrace. .... Od.20.412.252.
I share the doom ye Suitors cannot shun. .... Od.20.444.254.
Hence to your fields, ye rusticks! hence away, ... Od.21.87.263.
Come then ye Suitors! and dispute a prize .... Od.21.109.264.
Ye faithful guardians of the herd and flock! .... Od.21.198.269.
Ye peers and rivals in the royal love! .... Od.21.293.274.
Dogs, ye have had your day; ye fear'd no more .... Od.22.41.288.
Dogs, ye have had your day; ye fear'd no more .... Od.22.41.288.
This choice is left ye, to resist or die; .... Od.22.80.290.
And die I trust ye shall—He sternly spoke: .... Od.22.81.290.
Say, for the public did ye greatly fall? .... Od.24.139.354.
Ye Peers (she cry'd) who press to gain my heart .... Od.24.154.355.
Arise (or ye for ever fall) arise! .... Od.24.497.372.
Hear me, ye Peers and Elders of the land, ... Od.24.508.372.
Me too ye fathers hear! from you proceed .... Od.24.520.373.
The ills ye mourn; your own the guilty deed. .... Od.24.521.373.
Ye gave your sons, your lawless sons the rein, ... Od.24.522.373.
"Forbear ye natives! your mad hands forbear .... Od.24.614.377.

EA
Yea, tho' the Blessing's more than he can use, ... 4.HAdv.100.83.
Out-do *Landaffe,* in Doctrine—yea, in Life; .... 4.EpS1.134.308.
Yea, moral Ebor, or religious Winton. .... 4.1740.58.335.
Yea when she passed by or Lane or Nook, ... 6.14ii.42.44.
Yea all to break the Pride of lustful Kings, ... 6.137.6.373.

EAR
And lavish Nature paints the Purple Year? .... 1.PSp.28.63.
The various Seasons of the rowling Year; .... 1.PSp.38.64.
But blest with her, 'tis Spring throughout the Year. .... 1.PSp.84.69.
To lop the Growth of the luxuriant Year. .... 1.TrVP.10.377.
Now gath'ring what the bounteous Year allows, ... 1.TrVP.39.378.
Destroy the Promise of the youthful Year; .... 1.TrVP.109.381.
And the short Monarch of a hasty Year .... 1.TrSt.196.418.
And bids the Year with swifter Motion run. .... 1.TrSt.454.429.
And raging *Sirius* blasts the sickly Year, ... 1.TrSt.748.441.
Like Winter Greens, that flourish all the Year. .... 2.ChJM.136.21.
Grieve for an hour, perhaps, then mourn a year, ... 2.Elegy.56.367.
There the first roses of the year shall blow; .... 2.Elegy.66.367.
Thine the full harvest of the golden year? .... 3.EOM3.39.96.
Because he wants a thousand pounds a year. .... 3.EOM4.192.145.
This Phœbus promis'd (I forget the year) .... 3.Ep2.283.73.
What made Directors cheat in South-sea year? .... 3.Ep3.119.101.
This year a Reservoir, to keep and spare, ... 3.Ep3.175.107.
This man possest—five hundred pounds a year. .... 3.Ep3.280.116.
They scarce can bear their *Laureate* twice a Year: .... 4.HS1.34.7.
On Broccoli and mutton, round the year; .... 4.HS2.138.65.
The Chanc'ry takes your rents for twenty year: .... 4.HS2.172.69.
With rhymes of this *per Cent.* and that *per Year?* .... 4.JD2.56.137.
"Sir, he's your Slave, for twenty pound a year. .... 4.2HE2.8.165.
End all dispute; and fix the year precise .... 4.2HE1.53.199.
Suppose he wants a year, will you compound? .... 4.2HE1.57.199.
"We shall not quarrel for a year or two; .... 4.2HE1.61.199.
I pluck out year by year, as hair by hair, ... 4.2HE1.64.199.
I pluck out year by year, as hair by hair, ... 4.2HE1.64.199.
And estimating Authors by the year, ... 4.2HE1.67.199.
To him commit the hour, the day, the year, ... 4.1HE6.9.237.
For life, six hundred pounds a year, ... 4.HS6.2.251.
Nor cross the Channel twice a year, ... 4.HS6.31.253.
And New-year Odes, and all the Grubstreet race. .... 5.DunA1.42.65.
There sav'd by spice, like mummies, many a year, ... 5.DunA1.131.80.
Till Westminster's whole year be holiday; .... 5.DunA3.332.191.
"Signs following signs lead on the Mighty Year; .... 5.DunA3.335.191.

YEAR (CONTINUED)
Then, when these signs declare the Mighty Year; .... 5.DunA3.335A.191.
And New-year Odes, and all the Grub-street race. .... 5.DunB1.44.274.
There, sav'd by spice, like Mummies, many a year, ... 5.DunB1.151.281.
And ev'ry year be duller than the last. .... 5.DunB3.298.334.
Signs following signs lead on the mighty year! .... 5.DunB3.321.335.
'Till Westminster's whole year be holiday, ... 5.DunB3.336.336.
And verdant olives flourish round the year. .... 6.35.10.103.
With all th' united labours of the year, ... 6.35.18.103.
This Year in Peace, ye Critics, dwell, ... 6.47.3.128.
Wafts on his gentle wing his eightieth year) .... 6.55.2.166.
Some joy still lost, as each vain year runs o'er, ... 6.86.7.245.
'Tis but the Fun'ral of the former year. .... 6.86.10.245.
Let day improve on day, and year on year, ... 6.86.15.245.
Let day improve on day, and year on year, ... 6.86.15.245.
To fleece their Countrey Clients twice a Year? .... 6.96iii.28.275.
And strains, from hard bound Brains, six Lines a Year; .... 6.98.32.284.
Go live! for heav'ns Eternal year is thine, ... 6.109.9.314.
And evening-friends will end the year. .... 6.114.4.321.
Let's rather wait one year for better luck; .... 6.116v.3.327.
One year may make a singing Swan of *Duck.* .... 6.116v.4.327.
The yellow Harvests of the ripen'd Year, ... Il.5.120.273.
The purple Product of th' Autumnal Year. .... Il.18.660.355.
We shar'd the lengthen'd Labours of a Year? .... Il.21.518.443.
Orion's Dog (the Year when Autumn weighs) .... Il.22.39.454.
'Till the fleet hours restore the circling year. .... Od.1.375.50.
'Till the fleet hours restore the circling year; .... Od.2.248.73.
Which scarce the sea-fowl in a year o'erfly) .... Od.3.412.106.
That happy clime! where each revolving year .... Od.4.105.124.
Fill the wide circle of th' eternal year: .... Od.4.768.155.
Lost in delight the circling year wou'd roll, ... Od.4.815.157.
And verdant olives flourish round the year. .... Od.7.151.243.
With all th' united labours of the year; .... Od.7.159.244.
'Till the full circle of the year came round. .... Od.10.555.369.
If thou the circling year my stay controul, ... Od.11.444.406.
The circling year I wait, with ampler stores .... Od.11.446.406.
'Till the whole circle of the year goes round; .... Od.14.226.46.
Not the whole circle of the year wou'd close .... Od.14.227.46.
Neleus his treasures one long year detains; .... Od.15.256.80.
Long nights the now-declining year bestows; .... Od.15.426.89.
A year they traffic, and their vessel load. .... Od.15.492.94.
Divided Right; each ninth revolving year .... Od.19.206.202.

YEAR'S
A standing sermon, at each year's expense, ... 3.Ep4.21.139.
Long as the Year's dull circle seems to run, ... 4.1HE1.37.281.

YEARLING
A yearling bullock to thy name shall smoke, ... Od.3.490.111.
A yearling boar, and gave the Gods their part, ... Od.16.473.130.

YEARLY
But sav'd from Death, our *Argives* yearly pay .... 1.TrSt.662.438.
Whose chearful Tenants bless their yearly toil, ... 3.Ep4.183.154.
Yearly defeated, yearly hopes they give, ... 4.1740.41.334.
Yearly defeated, yearly hopes they give, ... 4.1740.41.334.
New graces yearly, like thy works, display; .... 6.52.65.158.
Like yearly Leaves, that now, with Beauty crown'd, ... Il.21.539.444.
The yearly firstlings of his flock, and herd; .... Od.17.287.146.

YEARS
Swift fly the Years, and rise th'expected Morn! .... 1.Mes.21.114.
Her chearful Head, and leads the golden Years. .... 1.W-F.92.159.
When *Patriarch-Wits* surviv'd a *thousand Years;* .... 1.EOC.479.293.
When mellowing Years their full Perfection give, ... 1.EOC.490.294.
The *treach'rous Colours* in few Years decay, ... 1.EOC.492A.294.
E'er sixteen passing years had overlaid .... 1.TrPA.7.365.
Enur'd to Sorrow from my tender Years, ... 1.TrSP.73.397.
And their ripe Years in modest Grace maintain'd. .... 1.TrSt.620.436.
Thro' ten Years Wand'ring, and thro' ten Years War; .... 1.TrUl.176.471.
Thro' ten Years Wand'ring, and thro' ten Years War; .... 1.TrUl.176.471.
Who mourn'd her Lord twice ten revolving Years, ... 1.TrUl.218.473.
But in due Time, when Sixty Years were o'er, ... 2.ChJM.9.15.
Who wisely weds in his maturer Years. .... 2.ChJM.24.16.
Beneath the Weight of threescore Years I bend, ... 2.ChJM.87.19.
As plainly proves, Experience dwells with Years: .... 2.ChJM.150.21.
But, at these Years, to venture on the Fair! .... 2.ChJM.208.24.
With his broad Sabre next, a Chief in Years, ... 2.RL3.55.172.
The gather'd Winter of a thousand Years. .... 2.TemF.60.256.
And trac'd the long Records of Lunar Years. .... 2.TemF.112.262.
In Years he seem'd, but not impair'd by Years. .... 2.TemF.187.270.
In Years he seem'd, but not impair'd by Years. .... 2.TemF.187.270.
Condemn'd whole years in absence to deplore, ... 2.ElAb.361.348.
Dim lights of life that burn a length of years, ... 2.Elegy.19.364.
As who began a thousand years ago. .... 3.EOM1.76.23.
26.As who began ten thousand years ago. .... 3.EOM1.76A.23.
Thy boasted Blood, a thousand years or so, ... 3.EOM4.207A.146.
One self-approving hour whole years out-weighs .... 3.EOM4.255.152.
The Courtier smooth, who forty years had shin'd .... 3.Ep1.252.37.
Full sixty years the World has been her Trade, ... 3.Ep2.123.60.
Behold Villario's ten-years toil compleat; .... 3.Ep4.79.145.
Swears every *Place entail'd* for Years to come, ... 4.JD4.160.39.
This saving counsel, "Keep your Piece nine years." .... 4.Arbu.40.98.
Nine years! cries he, who high in *Drury-lane* .... 4.Arbu.41.99.
Great *Homer* dy'd three thousand years ago. .... 4.Arbu.124.104.
Full ten years slander'd, did he once reply? .... 4.Arbu.374.123.
Wicked as Pages, who in early years .... 4.JD2.39.135.
Years foll'wing Years, steal something ev'ry day, ... 4.2HE2.72.171.
Years foll'wing Years, steal something ev'ry day, ... 4.2HE2.72.171.
To Books and Study gives sev'n years compleat, ... 4.2HE2.117.173.
Bright thro' the rubbish of some hundred years; .... 4.2HE2.166.177.
Who dy'd, perhaps, an hundred years ago? .... 4.2HE1.52.199.
With growing years the pleasing Licence grew, ... 4.2HE1.249.217.
'Tis (let me see) three years and more, ... 4.HS6.83.255.
P. Strike? why the man was hang'd ten years ago: .... 4.EpS2.55.315.
Else might he take to Virtue some years hence— .... 4.EpS2.60.315.

YEARS (CONTINUED)

(His only suit) for twice three years before: ....5.DunA3.30.154.
And Pope's, translating three whole years with Broome. ....5.DunA3.328.191.
And Pope's whole years to comment and translate. ....5.DunA3.328A.191.
(His only suit) for twice three years before: ....5.DunB3.38.322.
And Pope's, ten years to comment and translate. ....5.DunB3.332.336.
Hours, days, and years slide soft away, ...6.1.10.3.
His years slide silently away, ...6.1.10A.3.
Hours, days, and years slide swift away, ...6.1.10B.3.
Or waste, for others Use, their restless Years ....6.17ii.3.56.
Whole Years neglected for some Months ador'd, ...6.19.43.63.
And bad'st the years in long procession run: ....6.23.6.73.
How *Pallas* talk'd when she was Seven Years old. ....6.37.10.106.
Should you live years forty more ....6.42iv.17.118.
This small, well-polish'd gem, the work of years! ....6.52.40.157.
Blooms in thy colours for a thousand years. ....6.52.58.157.
Some few short Years, no more! ....6.53.38.162.
Has truly liv'd the space of seventy years, ...6.55.1Z2.167.
This more than pays whole years of thankless pain; ....6.63.5.188.
See the wild Waste of all-devouring years! ....6.71.1.202.
The sacred rust of twice ten hundred years! ....6.71.38.203.
With added years if Life bring nothing new, ...6.86.5.245.
With added years if Life give nothing new, ...6.86.5C.245.
In five long Years I took no second Spouse; ....6.96iv.5.276.
Me, when the Cares my better Years have shown ....6.117.7.333.
Behold him loaded with unreverend years ....6.130.23.358.
Full sixty Years the World has been her Trade, ...6.154.9.403.
Nor think your *Nestor's* Years and Wisdom vain. ....Il.1.344.105.
Thy Years are awful, and thy Words are wise. ....Il.1.377.106.
Worn with nine Years of unsuccessful War? ....Il.2.96.131.
Now nine long Years of mighty *Jove* are run, ...Il.2.161.136.
The tedious Length of nine revolving Years. ....Il.2.361.144.
So many Years the Toils of *Greece* remain; ....Il.2.395.145.
To him the King: How much thy Years excell, ...Il.2.440.148.
And *Nestor* first, as most advanc'd in Years. ....Il.2.481.149.
Where as the Years revolve, her Altars blaze, ...Il.2.663.158.
The Hero, when to Manly Years he grew, ...Il.2.801.163.
For nine long Years have set the World in Arms; ....Il.3.206.201.
The Friends and Kindred of thy former Years. ....Il.3.214.202.
But wasting Years that wither human Race, ...Il.4.364.238.
These Years with Wisdom crowns, with Action those: ....Il.4.375.239.
Cold Death o'ertakes them in their blooming Years, ...Il.5.200.276.
Years might again roll back, my Youth renew, ...Il.7.161.372.
Of full five Years, and of the nobler Kind. ....Il.7.381.382.
Cold Counsels, *Trojan,* may become thy Years, ...Il.7.430.386.
Thy Years are awful, and thy Words are wise. ....Il.8.178.406.
Condemn'd for ten revolving Years to weep ....Il.8.496.420.
Your selves condemn'd ten rolling Years to weep ....Il.8.516.421.
And yet those Years that since thy Birth have run, ...Il.9.81.436.
Since more than his my Years, and more my Sway. ....Il.9.214.443.
Blest in kind Love, my Years shall glide away, ...Il.9.520.458.
For Years on Years, and long-extended Days. ....Il.9.537.460.
For Years on Years, and long-extended Days. ....Il.9.537.460.
I pass my Watchings o'er thy helpless Years, ...Il.9.612.464.
Tho' Years and Honours bid thee seek Repose. ....Il.10.187.10.
Yet if my Years thy kind Regard engage, ...Il.10.198.10.
"Yet cooler Thoughts thy elder Years attend; ....Il.11.918.76.
In their kind Arms my tender years were past; ....Il.14.233.172.
I owe the nursing of my tender Years. ....Il.14.346.179.
Haste, bring the Flames! the Toil of ten long Years ....Il.15.870.230.
Forbid by Fate to reach his Father's Years. ....Il.17.224.296.
(The Friend of *Hector,* and of equal Years: ....Il.18.296.336.
Nine Years imprison'd in those Tow'rs ye lay? ....Il.18.336.337.
Nine Years kept secret in the dark Abode, ...Il.18.469.344.
Whole Years untouch'd, uninjur'd shall remain ....Il.19.33.373.
Ah do not thus our helpless Years foregoe, ...Il.22.118.457.
Nor I thy Equal, or in Years, or Sense. ....Il.23.670.516.
Of six years Age, unconscious of the Yoke, ...Il.23.756.520.
His Hinds and Swains whole years shall be supply'd ....Il.23.988.528.
Now twice ten Years (unhappy Years) are o'er ....Il.24.964.576.
Now twice ten Years (unhappy Years) are o'er ....Il.24.964.576.
All who the Wars of ten long years surviv'd, ...Od.1.16.30.
In vain—for now the circling years disclose ....Od.1.23.30.
To manly years shou'd re-assert the throne. ....Od.1.52.33.
'Tis mine, to form his green, unpractis'd years, ...Od.1.112.37.
Who prest with heart-corroding grief and years, ...Od.1.245.44.
The same his features, if the same his years. ....Od.1.270.45.
Mature beyond his years the Queen admires ....Od.1.459.54.
For three long years the royal fraud behold? ....Od.2.102.66.
Unheard, unseen, three years her arts prevail; ....Od.2.121.67.
Who gave me life, and nurs'd my infant years? ....Od.2.150.69.
How twice ten years from shore to shore he roams; ....Od.2.205.71.
Now twice ten years are past, and now he comes! ....Od.2.206.71.
"Years roll'd on years my god-like sire decay, ...Od.2.257.74.
"Years roll'd on years my god-like sire decay, ...Od.2.257.74.
To question wisely men of riper years. ....Od.3.32.87.
Tho' much thy younger, and his years like mine, ...Od.3.60.89.
Oh then, if ever thro' the ten years war ....Od.3.118.91.
Not added years on years my task could close, ...Od.3.141.92.
Not added years on years my task could close, ...Od.3.141.92.
Nine painful years, on that detested shore ....Od.3.145.92.
Sev'n years, the traytor rich *Mycenæ* sway'd, ...Od.3.388.105.
Like years, like tempers, and their Prince's love. ....Od.3.465.109.
Whose early years for future worth engage, ...Od.3.482.111.
By ten long years refin'd, and rosy-bright.) ....Od.3.505.112.
For eight slow-circling years by tempests tost, ...Od.4.97.124.
Bereav'd of parents in his infant years, ...Od.4.220.130.
Around thee full of years, thy offspring bloom, ...Od.4.290.132.
The *Greeks,* (whose arms for nine long years employ'd ....Od.5.133.178.
Nurse of *Nausicaa* from her infant years, ...Od.7.15.234.
And still to live, beyond the pow'r of years. ....Od.7.123.240.
I stay reluctant sev'n continu'd years, ...Od.7.346.253.
But that distinguish'd from my tender years, ...Od.9.433.324.
By lov'd *Telemachus* his blooming years! ....Od.11.84.385.
Regardless of his years, abroad he lies, ...Od.11.236.393.
But now the years a num'rous train have ran; ....Od.11.555.411.

YEARS (CONTINUED)

Thro' ten years wand'ring, and thro' ten years war; Od.13.343.24
Thro' ten years wand'ring, and thro' ten years war; Od.13.343.24
Who mourn'd her Lord twice ten revolving years, ...Od.13.385.25
Three years thy house their lawless rule has seen, ...Od.13.431.27
Now wasting years my former strength confound, ...Od.14.247.48
Nine years we warr'd; the tenth saw *Ilion* fall; Od.14.276.49
On sev'n bright years successive blessings wait; Od.14.317.50
Of five years age, before the pile was led: Od.14.466.58
Thro' the long dangers of the ten-years war. Od.15.171.76
In toils his equal, and in years the same. Od.15.223.79
But when a length of years unnerves the strong, ...Od.15.448.92
Late worn with years in weeds obscene you trod, ...Od.16.220.11
Twice ten sad years o'er earth and ocean tost, ...Od.16.226.11
(The couch deserted now a length of years; Od.17.118.13
Now years un-nerve him, and his lord is lost! Od.17.387.15
His Lord, when twenty tedious years had roll'd, ...Od.17.397.15
That warmth of soul that urg'd thy younger years? Od.18.256.17
Who with the Queen her years an infant led, ...Od.18.369.18
Three years successful in my art conceal'd, ...Od.19.174.20
When the brave partners of thy ten years toil Od.20.26.233
With honey, milk, and wine, their infant years: Od.20.83.236
Your own *Ulysses!* twice ten years detain'd Od.21.213.27
Mature beyond his years, the Queen admir'd Od.21.381.27
The waste of years refunded in a day. Od.22.70.290
Known nine long years, and felt by Heroes dead? Od.22.249.29
When twice ten years are past of mighty woes: Od.23.104.32
My Queen, my consort! thro' a length of years, ...Od.23.377.34
Unheard, unseen, three years her arts prevail; Od.24.168.35
But thou! whom years have taught to understand, ...Od.24.310.36
What years have circled since thou saw'st that guest? Od.24.335.36
Five years have circled since these eyes pursu'd Od.24.361.36

YEARS'

After an hundred and thirty years' nap, ...6.148i.1.395.
A Steer of five Years' Age, large limb'd, and fed, ...Il.2.478.149.

YEILD

See YIELD.
Oh! yeild at last, nor still remain severe; 1.TrPA.114.3

YELKS

Or gulp the yelks of Ants delicious eggs, ...6.96ii.30Z49.

YELL

With voice like thunder, and a direful yell. ....Od.9.474.325.
With bloodless visage, and with hideous yell, ...Od.11.780.42

YELLING

Balk'd of his prey, the yelling monster flies, ...Od.10.135.34

YELLOW

Now blushing Berries paint the yellow Grove; ....1.PAu.75.85.
O'er sandy Wilds were yellow Harvests spread, ...1.W-F.88.158.
The yellow Carp, in Scales bedrop'd with Gold, ...1.W-F.144.16
As all looks yellow to the Jaundic'd Eye. 1.EOC.559.30
"A Yellow Lyon and a bristly Boar." 1.TrSt.548.43
A Lyon's yellow Skin the *Theban* wears, ...1.TrSt.567.434
And bathe in silver Dews thy yellow Hair; 1.TrSt.832.444
(The crooked Keel divides the yellow Sand) ....1.TrUl.46.467.
Is yellow dirt the passion of thy life? ....3.EOM4.279.
Where tawdry yellow strove with dirty red, ...3.Ep3.304.118
In Yellow Meads of *Asphodel,* .... 6.11.75.33.
(The crooked Keel divides the yellow Sand) ....Il.1.631.117.
The yellow Harvests of the ripen'd Year, ...Il.5.120.273.
A Lion's yellow Spoils his Back conceal'd; ....Il.10.29.3.
And whom *Arisba's* yellow Coursers bore, ...Il.12.111.85.
Next, rip in yellow Gold, a Vineyard shines, ...Il.18.651.355.
The yellow Flood began: O Son of *Jove!* .... Il.21.249.431.
And from his Head divides the yellow Hair; ....Il.23.173.496.
When now to *Xanthus'* yellow Stream they drove, ...Il.24.862.572.
And spread soft hydes upon the yellow sands; ....Od.3.48.88.
And yellow apples ripen into gold; Od.11.730.421
(The crooked keel divides the yellow sand) ....Od.13.137.9.

YELLOWER

O'er the dark Trees a yellower Verdure shed, ...Il.8.693.428.

YELPING

Close at my Heel with yelping Treble flies; ....6.14ii.20.43.
Join to the yelping Treble shrilling Cries; ....6.14ii.22.43.

YEOMAN

In *Yorkshire* dwelt a sober Yeoman, ...6.93.1.256.
There liv'd in Wales a goodly Yeoman, ...6.93.1A.256.

YERDE

"Then trust on Mon, whose yerde can *talke.*" .... 6.14i.26.42.

YERNING

Spoke loud the languish of his yerning soul: ....Od.4.388.139.

YES

Yes, or we must renounce the *Stagyrite.* 1.EOC.280.27
Yes, Nature's road must ever be prefer'd; 3.EOM2.161.7
Yes, you despise the man to Books confin'd ....3.Ep1.1.15.
Yes, while I live, no rich or noble knave ....4.HS1.119.17.
"Why yes, 'tis granted, these indeed may pass ....4.JD4.74.31.
And if the Dame says yes, the Dress says no. 4.HAdv.132.87
Yes; thank my stars! as early as I knew ....4.JD2.1.133.
Yes, Sir, how small soever be my heap, ...4.2HE2.284.18
Can I retrench? Yes, mighty well, ...4.1HE7.75.273
F. Why yes: with *Scripture* still you may be free; ....4.EpS1.37.300.
Fr. Yes, strike that *Wild,* I'll justify the blow. ....4.EpS2.54.315.
Yes, I am proud; I must be proud to see 4.EpS2.208.324
Yes, the last Pen for Freedom let me draw, ...4.EpS2.248.327

YES (CONTINUED)
Yes, to my Country I my pen consign, ... 5.DunA1.193.86.
Yes, from this moment, mighty Mist! am thine, ... 5.DunA1.194.86.
Yes she has one, I must aver: .... 6.89.10.250.
Yes, Thousands. But in Pity to their Kind, ... 6.96iii.13.274.
Yes, we are slaves—but yet, by Reason's Force, ... 6.96iii.31.275.
'*she.* Yes, we have liv'd— one pang, and then we part! .... 6.123.1.343.
Yes— *Save my Country, Heav'n,* .... 6.123.8.344.
Yes, I beheld th' Athenian Queen .... 6.140.1.378.
Yes, 'tis the time! I cry'd, impose the chain! .... 6.146.1.389.
Yes—I will meet the Murd'rer of my Friend, ... Il.18.145.329.
Yes, I shall give the Fair those mournful Charms— .... Il.18.159.330.
Achilles! yes! this Day at least we bear .... Il.19.452.391.
Yes, I believe (he cries) almighty *Jove!* .... Od.24.409.368.

YESTER
Of yester dawn disclos'd the tender day, ... Od.4.881.159.

YESTERDAY
What the Fine Gentleman wore *Yesterday!* .... 1.EOC.330.275.
Thou, who since Yesterday, has roll'd o'er all .... 4.JD4.202.43.
That leaves the load of yesterday behind? .... 4.HS2.82.61.

YET (OMITTED)
895

YET-REMAINING
First let us quench the yet-remaining Flame .... Il.23.295.501.

YET-SURVIVING
Her yet-surviving Heroes seem'd to fall. .... Il.16.992.281.

YET-UNCONQUER'D
And question'd thus his yet-unconquer'd mind. .... Od.5.382.190.

YET-UNRIVAL'D
Thy matchless Skill, thy yet-unrival'd Fame, ... Il.5.220.278.

YET-UNTASTED
Timely he flies the yet-untasted Food, ... Il.15.706.223.

YET-WARM
Beneath one Foot the yet-warm Corps he prest, ... Il.5.768.303.
The yet-warm *Thracians* panting on the Coast; .... Il.10.612.29.

YEW
See EUGH (YEW).
The Youth already strain'd the forceful Yew; .... Il.8.389.416.
Cydonians, dreadful with the bended yew, ... Od.19.200.202.
The twanging string, and try'd the stubborn yew: .... Od.24.198.358.

YEWS
With all the mournful family of Yews; .... 3.Ep4.96.146.

YIELD
See YEILD.
Blest *Thames's* Shores the brightest Beauties yield, ... 1.PSp.63.67.
Cynthus and *Hybla* yield to *Windsor*-Shade. .... 1.PSp.68.67.
And crown'd with Corn, their Thanks to *Ceres* yield. .... 1.PSu.66.77.
Just Gods! shall all things yield Returns but Love? .... 1.PAu.76.85.
So may kind Rains their vital Moisture yield, ... 1.PWi.15.89.
Nor fragrant Herbs their native Incense yield. .... 1.PWi.48.92.
Their Vines a Shadow to their Race shall yield; .... 1.Mes.65.118.
Not ice or crystal equal splendor yield, ... 1.TrPA.56.367.
Insulting waters yield a murmuring sound: .... 1.TrPA.158.372.
The Streams and Fountains, no Delights cou'd yield; .... 1.TrVP.6.377.
And crowd their shining Ranks to yield thee place; .... 1.TrSt.36.411.
Nor *Troy* cou'd conquer, nor the *Greeks* wou'd yield, ... 1.TrES.3.449.
And Hills where Vines their Purple Harvest yield? .... 1.TrES.30.450.
It shakes; the pondrous Stones disjoynted yield; .... 1.TrES.131.454.
They tugg, they sweat, but neither gain, nor yield, ... 1.TrES.159.455.
Or to his Doom my bravest Off-spring yield, ... 1.TrES.235.458.
And rising Springs Eternal Verdure yield. .... 1.TrUl.131.470.
Yield to the Force of unresisted Fate, ... 1.TrUl.185.471.
His spacious Garden, made to yield to none, ... 2.ChJM.448.36.
I yield it up; but since I gave my Oath, ... 2.ChJM.701.48.
As many more *Manillio* forc'd to yield, ... 2.RL3.51.172.
Thus far both Armies to *Belinda* yield; .... 2.RL3.65.173.
Or settling, seize the Sweets the Blossoms yield, ... 2.TemF.286.277.
And curs'd with hearts unknowing how to yield. .... 2.Elegy.42.366.
Try what the open, what the covert yield; .... 3.EOM1.10.13.
"Learn from the birds what food the thickets yield; .... 3.EOM3.173.110.
Twin'd with the wreaths Parnassian lawrels yield, ... 3.EOM4.11.129.
Tir'd, not determin'd, to the last we yield, ... 3.Ep1.43.18.
Love, if it makes her yield, must make her hate: .... 3.Ep2.134.61.
Tir'd of the scene Parterres and Fountains yield, ... 3.Ep4.87.146.
Nor yet shall Waller yield to time, ... 4.HOde9.7.159.
May yield, God knows, to strong Temptation. .... 4.HS6.184.261.
Suck the thread in, then yield it out again: .... 5.DunA3.50.155.
Suck the thread in, then yield it out again: .... 5.DunB3.58.323.
Whose trees in summer yield him shade, ... 6.1.7.3.
These to the birds refreshing streams may yield; .... 6.20.65.67.
Thousands on ev'ry side shall yield their breath; .... 6.21.17.69.
Love, if it make her yield, must make her hate. .... 6.154.20.403.
But since for common Good I yield the Fair, ... Il.1.151.94.
Woul'st thou the *Greeks* their lawful Prey shou'd yield, ... Il.1.157.95.
Fierce as thou art, to yield thy captive Fair: .... Il.1.244.98.
To Reason yield the Empire o'er his Mind. .... Il.1.276.100.
Be still thou Slave! and to thy Betters yield; .... Il.2.237.138.
What Fruits his Conduct and his Courage yield? .... Il.2.334.143.
No Chief like thee, *Menestheus! Greece* could yield, ... Il.2.665.158.
This if the *Phrygians* shall refuse to yield, ... Il.3.362.210.
While these to Love's delicious Rapture yield, ... Il.3.559.218.
Now, Goddess, now, thy sacred Succour yield. .... Il.5.149.274.
No wonder, *Greeks!* that all to *Hector* yield, ... Il.5.742.302.
But wert thou greater, thou must yield to me. .... Il.5.799.304.

YIELD (CONTINUED)
Loud, as the Roar encountring Armies yield, ... Il.5.1054.316.
Now Heav'n forsakes the Fight: Th' Immortals yield .... Il.6.1.322.
Enough of *Trojans* to this Lance shall yield, ... Il.6.282.340.
Who yields Assistance, or but wills to yield; .... Il.8.12.395.
Such as himself will chuse, who yield to none, ... Il.9.181.441.
Or yield to *Helen's* heav'nly Charms alone. .... Il.9.182.441.
If thou wilt yield to great *Atrides'* Pray'rs, ... Il.9.340.450.
Such as thy self shall chuse; who yield to none, ... Il.9.368.451.
Or yield to *Helen's* heav'nly Charms alone. .... Il.9.369.451.
And curs'd thee with a Mind that cannot yield. .... Il.9.750.471.
He fought with numbers, and made numbers yield. .... Il.10.344.18.
Old as I am, to Age I scorn to yield, ... Il.10.646.30.
Mark how this way yon' bending Squadrons yield! .... Il.11.449.54.
Tho' deaf to Glory, he may yield to Love. .... Il.11.925.77.
Next *Ormenus* and *Pylon* yield their Breath: .... Il.12.217.89.
Nor *Troy* could conquer, nor the *Greeks* would yield, ... Il.12.347.94.
And Hills where Vines their purple Harvest yield, ... Il.12.374.95.
It shakes; the pond'rous Stones disjointed yield; .... Il.12.485.99.
They tugg, they sweat; but neither gain, nor yield, ... Il.12.513.100.
Nor knew great *Hector* how his Legions yield, ... Il.13.845.146.
How many *Trojans* yield, disperse, or fall? .... Il.13.926.149.
Beheld his Vines their liquid Harvest yield, ... Il.14.139.164.
Loud, as the Shout encountring Armies yield, ... Il.14.173.165.
O say, when *Neptune* made proud *Ilion* yield, ... Il.14.601.191.
Thy Arts have made the godlike *Hector* yield, ... Il.15.19.194.
Forgive me Gods, and yield my Vengeance way: .... Il.15.129.201.
The Skies would yield an ampler Scene of Rage, ... Il.15.153.202.
Warn'd by the Words, to pow'rful *Jove* I yield, ... Il.15.232.206.
But doom'd to *Hector's* stronger Force to yield! .... Il.15.778.226.
"Oh nurs'd with Gall, unknowing how to yield! .... Il.16.244.249.
The best, the dearest of my Friends, I yield: .... Il.16.295.254.
Or to his Doom my bravest Offspring yield, ... Il.16.538.265.
The Chief who taught our lofty Walls to yield, ... Il.16.683.270.
'Tis not to *Hector,* but to Heav'n I yield. .... Il.17.108.291.
We too must yield: The same sad Fate must fall .... Il.17.286.298.
Repuls'd, they yield; the *Trojans* seize the slain: .... Il.17.325.300.
And now had *Troy,* by *Greece* compell'd to yield, ... Il.17.370.302.
To thee I yield the Seat, to thee resign .... Il.17.546.309.
Dost thou at length to *Menelaus* yield? .... Il.17.660.313.
But *Ajax* turning, to their Fears they yield, ... Il.17.819.320.
Mere unsupported Man must yield at length; .... Il.19.164.378.
Then hear my Counsel, and to Reason yield, ... Il.19.219.382.
Yield to our conqu'ring Arms the lower World. .... Il.20.171.400.
Loth as he was to yield his youthful Breath, ... Il.21.76.424.
I yield—Let *Ilion* fall; if Fate decree— .... Il.21.420.437.
The bubbling Waters yield a hissing Sound. .... Il.21.423.437.
Hear then my solemn Oath, to yield to Fate .... Il.21.438.438.
And boast my Conquest, while I yield the Prize. .... Il.21.584.446.
Sign'd to the Troops, to yield his Foe the Way, ... Il.22.269.466.
Or to his Arm our bloody Trophies yield. .... Il.22.312.469.
And curs'd thee with a Heart that cannot yield. .... Il.22.448.474.
And yield the Glory yours—The Steeds obey; .... Il.23.527.511.
'Tis now *Atrides'* turn to yield to thee. .... Il.23.686.517.
I yield; that all may know, my Soul can bend, ... Il.23.697.517.
I yield alas! (to Age who must not yield?) .... Il.23.741.519.
I yield alas! (to Age who must not yield?) .... Il.23.741.519.
Ye see, to *Ajax* I must yield the Prize; .... Il.23.927.526.
But yield to Fate, and hear what *Jove* declares. .... Il.24.140.541.
But yield to Ransom and the Father's Pray'r. .... Il.24.151.541.
But yield to Ransom, and restore the Slain. .... Il.24.174.543.
To yield thy *Hector* I my self intend: .... Il.24.708.567.
And yield his consort to the nuptial bed. .... Od.2.252.73.
Saw stately *Ceres* to her passion yield, ... Od.5.160.179.
To fame arise! for what more fame can yield .... Od.8.161.271.
In such heroic games I yield to none, ... Od.8.237.275.
Or yield to brave *Laodamas* alone: .... Od.8.238.275.
I justly claim; but yield to better days, ... Od.8.254.276.
(When loaded cribs their evening banquet yield) .... Od.10.486.367.
That stubborn soul, by toil untaught to yield! .... Od.12.334.448.
And rising springs eternal verdure yield. .... Od.13.298.20.
Yield to the force of unresisted fate, ... Od.13.352.24.
Might he return, I yield my life a prey .... Od.16.107.108.
I chuse the nobler part, and yield my breath .... Od.16.111.108.
Seems half to yield, yet flies the bridal hour: .... Od.16.136.109.
To want like mine, the peopled town can yield .... Od.17.22.133.
That huge bulk yield this ill-contested day, ... Od.18.95.171.
Oh were it giv'n to yield this transient breath, ... Od.18.239.178.
Where, if they yield their fraight across the main, ... Od.20.457.255.
I yield, I yield! my own *Ulysses* lives! .... Od.23.240.335.
I yield, I yield! my own *Ulysses* lives! .... Od.23.240.335.
Hard and distrustful as I am, I yield. .... Od.23.246.335.
And full of days, thou gently yield thy breath; .... Od.23.306.337.
Say, could one city yield a troop so fair? .... Od.24.132.354.

YIELDED
Ev'n those had yielded to a Foe so brave .... Il.3.565.219.
The first I met, he yielded, or he fell. .... Od.14.258.48.

YIELDING
My yielding Heart keeps Measure to my Strains. .... 1.TrSP.94.398.
His flaming Crest, and lash the yielding Air. .... 1.TrSt.159.416.
His flaming Crest, and lash'd the yielding Air. .... 1.TrSt.159A.416.
Those golden Wings that cut the yielding Skies; .... 1.TrSt.430.428.
Of *Nemea's* Stream the yielding Fair enjoy'd: .... 1.TrSt.677.438.
With loud Complaints she fills the yielding Air, ... 1.TrSt.699.439.
Soft yielding Minds to Water glide away, ... 2.RL1.61.150.
And yielding Metal flow'd to human form: .... 4.2HE1.148.207.
And win my way by yielding to the tyde. .... 4.1HE1.34.281.
The yielding nymph by these confest, ... 6.4v.5.11.
By nature yielding, stubborn but for Fame; .... 6.19.35.63.
In forty Vessels cut the yielding Tide. .... Il.2.640.157.
Each leads ten Vessels thro' the yielding Tide. .... Il.2.754.161.
And pitch your Lances in the yielding Plain. .... Il.3.126.196.
Now with full Force the yielding Horn he bends, ... Il.4.152.228.
Fierce *Ajax* thus o'erwhelms the yielding Throng, ... Il.11.618.61.

YIELDING (CONTINUED)

Now turns, and backward bears the yielding Bands; Il.11.693.66.
The Weight of Waters saps the yielding Wall, Il.12.25.82.
And swarms victorious o'er their yielding Walls: Il.13.120.110.
And in his cave the yielding nymph comprest. Od.1.95.36.
(With yielding osiers fenc'd, to break the force Od.5.327.187.
Neptune's smooth face, and cleave the yielding deep. Od.9.210.314.
(Not yielding to some bulky mountain's height) Od.10.129.347.

YIELDS

The *Thistle* springs, to which the *Lilly* yields? 1.PSp.90.69.
Not proud *Olympus* yields a nobler Sight, 1.W-F.33.151.
The Swain with Tears his frustrate Labour yields, 1.W-F.55.154.
The Swain with Tears to Beasts his Labour yields, 1.W-F.55A.154.
He gathers Health from Herbs the Forest yields, 1.W-F.241.171.
And yields an Off-spring more than Nature gives; 1.TrVP.14.377.
'Twas now the Time when *Phœbus* yields to Night, 1.TrSt.474.430.
And *Jove,* Exalted, his mild Influence yields, 2.ChJM.611.44.
'Twas when fresh *May* her early Blossoms yields, 2.ChWB.290.71.
The silenc'd Preacher yields to potent strain, 4.2HE1.237.215.
These head the Troops that Rocky *Aulis* yields, Il.2.590.156.
And where *Pellenè* yields her fleecy Store, Il.2.691.159.
The Troops *Methonè,* or *Thaumacia* yields, Il.2.872.165.
The warlike Bands that distant *Lycia* yields, Il.2.1070.172.
Sprung from *Alpheus,* plenteous Stream! that yields Il.5.673.300.
Each to his Rival yields the Mark unknown, Il.7.223.375.
Who yields Assistance, or but wills to yield; Il.8.12.395.
Haste to the Joys our native Country yields; Il.9.36.433.
Æpea fair, the Pastures *Hyra* yields, Il.9.199.442.
Æpea fair, the Pastures *Hyra* yields, Il.9.386.451.
Who yields ignobly, or who bravely dies. Il.9.421.453.
Curs'd by *Althæa,* to his Wrath he yields, Il.9.669.467.
With ev'ry Weapon, Art or Fury yields: Il.11.342.49.
Repuls'd he yields; the Victor *Greeks* obtain Il.13.259.117.
Before the pond'rous Stroke his Corselet yields, Il.13.551.132.
Wounded at once, *Patroclus* yields to fear, Il.16.984.281.
The Son of *Venus* to the Counsel yields; Il.17.558.310.
The brittle Point before his Corselet yields; Il.17.685.314.
And reap what Glory Life's short Harvest yields. Il.18.154.330.
Nor yields a Step, nor from his Post retires: Il.18.198.331.
The trampled Center yields a hollow Sound: Il.20.189.402.
And yields to Ocean's hoary Sire, the Prize? Il.21.548.444.
Tho' not so wretched: There he yields to me, Il.24.628.563.
But when their texture to the tempest yields, Od.5.460.195.
And there the garden yields a waste of flow'rs. Od.6.356.229.
Me, aukward me she scorns, and yields her charms Od.8.349.282.
The soil untill'd a ready harvest yields, Od.9.123.310.
(Tho' sure our vine the largest cluster yields, Od.9.423.323.
To him alone the beauteous prize he yields, Od.11.353.399.
The bravely-patient to no fortune yields: Od.17.336.147.
To none it yields but great *Ulysses'* hands; Od.24.199.358.
For ev'ry good man yields a just return: Od.24.331.365.

YOAK

Cages for Gnats, and Chains to Yoak a Flea; 2.RL5.121.209.

YOK'D

The Horses yok'd beside each Warrior stand. Il.10.545.27.

YOKE

And join'd reluctant to the galling Yoke, 1.TrSt.185.418.
Each haughty Master's Yoke by turns to bear, 1.TrSt.237.420.
The marry'd Man may bear his Yoke with Ease, 2.ChJM.37.16.
Silver the Beam, th' extended Yoke was Gold, Il.5.900.309.
The Goddess leaning o'er the bending Yoke, Il.5.996.314.
The shatter'd Chariot from the crooked Yoke: Il.6.50.326.
So twelve young Heifers, guiltless of the Yoke, Il.6.382.345.
Furious he said; then, bending o'er the Yoke, Il.8.224.408.
Each from the Yoke the smoaking Steeds unty'd, Il.8.675.427.
Untam'd, unconscious of the galling Yoke, Il.10.348.18.
Join'd to one Yoke, the stubborn Earth they tear, Il.13.881.147.
Trail'd on the Dust beneath the Yoke were spread, Il.17.500.308.
Big with a Mule, unknowing of the Yoke: Il.23.334.503.
The Steeds of *Tros* beneath his Yoke compell'd, Il.23.360.504.
She breaks his Rivals Chariot from the Yoke; Il.23.470.509.
Of six years Age, unconscious of the Yoke, Il.23.756.520.
Box was the Yoke, embost with costly Pains, Il.24.335.550.
Last to the Yoke the well-match'd Mules they bring, Il.24.343.550.
Untam'd, unconscious of the galling yoke; Od.3.491.111.
The sons obey, and join them to the yoke. Od.3.607.117.
Beneath the bounding yoke alike they held Od.3.614.117.
Let wit cast off the sullen yoke of sense. Od.14.525.62.

YOKES

Shock; while the madding Steeds break short their Yokes: Il.16.445.260.
And turn their crooked Yokes on ev'ry side. Il.18.630.354.

YON

While yon slow Oxen turn the furrow'd Plain. 1.PSp.30.63.
Beneath yon Poplar oft we, past the Day: 1.PAu.66.85.
In yon clear lake, and thought it handsome too: 1.TrPA.97.369.
Yon spangled Arch glows with the starry Train, 1.TrSt.584.434.
Who feeds yon Alms-house, neat, but void of state, 3.Ep3.265A.115.
He feeds yon Alms-house, neat, but void of state, 3.Ep3.265B.115.
Who hung with woods yon mountain's sultry brow? 3.Ep3.253.114.
Behold yon Alms-house, neat, but void of state, 3.Ep3.265.115.
First thro' the length of yon hot Terrace sweat, 3.Ep4.130.150.
From yon old wallnut-tree a show'r shall fall; 4.HS2.145.67.
"His be yon Juno of majestic size, 5.DunA2.155.120.
"Behold yon Pair, in strict embraces join'd; 5.DunA3.173.168.
Yon stars, yon suns, he rears at pleasure higher, 5.DunA3.255.179.
Yon stars, yon suns, he rears at pleasure higher, 5.DunA3.255.179.
"His be yon Juno of majestic size, 5.DunB2.163.303.
"Behold yon Pair, in strict embraces join'd; 5.DunB3.179.329.
Yon stars, yon suns, he rears at pleasure higher, 5.DunB3.259.332.
Yon stars, yon suns, he rears at pleasure higher, 5.DunB3.259.332.

YON (CONTINUED)

Yon Luminary Amputation needs, 6.100v.1.289.
If yon proud Monarch thus thy Son defies, Il.1.466.110.
Haste, launch thy Chariot, thro' yon Ranks to ride; Il.8.455.418.
What Scenes of Slaughter in yon Fields appear! Il.9.301.449.
Thro' yon wide Host this Arm shall scatter Fear, Il.20.413.412.
No glorious native of yon azure sky: Od.7.284.250.
Go forth, the manners of yon men to try; Od.9.202.314.
Each friend you seek in yon enclosure lies, Od.10.337.360.
Those in yon hollow caverns let us lay; Od.10.503.368.
If from yon justling rocks and wavy war Od.12.256.444.
Where rouls yon smoke, yon tumbling ocean raves; Od.12.261.445.
Where rouls yon smoke, yon tumbling ocean raves; Od.12.261.445.
Why seize ye not yon beeves, and fleecy prey? Od.12.409.450.
Against yon destin'd head in vain I swore, Od.13.152.13.
Hurl me from yon dread precipice on high; Od.14.441.57.
To pour his wrath on yon luxurious prey; Od.15.197.78.
But bear, oh bear me o'er yon azure flood; Od.15.302.83.
Yon bird that dexter cuts th' aerial road, Od.15.573.98.
Approach yon walls, I prophecy thy fare: Od.17.269.145.
See how with nods assent yon princely train! Od.18.16.167.
Yon surly mendicants contentious stand; Od.18.47.169.
Yon Archer, comrades, will not shoot in vain; Od.22.84.290.
To mount yon window, and alarm from thence Od.22.149.294.
From blood and carnage to yon open court: Od.22.416.308.

YON'

I'll stake yon' Lamb that near the Fountain plays, 1.PSp.33.63.
But nigh yon' Mountain let me tune my Lays, 1.PSu.37.75.
Not the fair Fruit that on yon' Branches glows 1.TrVP.100.381.
When victims at yon' altar's foot we lay? 2.ElAb.108.328.
The darksom pines that o'er yon' rocks reclin'd 2.ElAb.155.332.
"Behold yon' Isle, by Palmers, Pilgrims trod, 5.DunA3.105.159
"Behold yon' Isle, by Palmers, Pilgrims trod, 5.DunB3.113.325.
Destruction hangs o'er yon' devoted Wall, Il.2.17.128.
Destruction hangs o'er yon' devoted Wall, Il.2.39.129.
Destruction hangs o'er yon' devoted Wall, Il.2.89.130.
Lie unreveng'd on yon' detested Plain? Il.2.198.137.
Low in the Dust be laid yon' hostile Spires, Il.2.494.150.
How vast thy Empire? Of yon' matchless Train Il.3.243.204.
Amidst yon' Circle of his *Cretan* Pow'rs, Il.3.296.207.
And yon' fair Structures level with the Ground? Il.4.52.223.
'Till yon' tall Vessels blaze with *Trojan* Fire? Il.4.283.234.
Against yon' Hero let us bend our Course, Il.5.276.280.
Nor shall yon' Steeds that fierce to Fight convey Il.5.318.281.
Dispatch yon' *Greek,* and vindicate the Gods. Il.5.556.295.
Troy felt his Arm, and yon' proud Ramparts stand Il.5.792.304.
What lawless Rage on yon' forbidden Plain, Il.5.944.311.
Behold yon' glitt'ring Host, your future Spoil! Il.6.87.327.
In the full Harvest of yon' ample Field; Il.6.283.340.
Where yon' wild Fig-Trees join the Wall of *Troy:* Il.6.551.354.
Till *Ilion* falls, or till yon' Navy burns. Il.7.84.367.
But yon' proud Work no future Age shall view, Il.7.550.392.
What God but enters yon' forbidden Field, Il.8.11.395.
With these against yon' *Trojans* will we go, Il.8.139.404.
Soon as before yon' hollow Ships we stand, Il.8.220.407.
Not till amidst yon' sinking Navy slain, Il.9.765.472.
To try yon' Camp, and watch the *Trojan* Pow'rs? Il.10.44.4.
But sleep'st thou now? when from yon' Hill the Foe Il.10.182.9.
Thro' yon' black Camps to bend my dang'rous way, Il.10.261.13.
Where e'er yon' Fires ascend, the *Trojans* wake: Il.10.489.25.
Now on yon' Ranks impell your foaming Steeds; Il.11.373.51.
Mark how this way yon' bending Squadrons yield! Il.11.449.54.
The Time is come, when yon' despairing Host Il.11.744.68.
Nor could I, thro' yon' Cloud, discern his Face, Il.11.752.68.
No Space for Combat in yon' narrow Bounds. Il.12.74.84.
Tho' all our Chiefs amid yon' Ships expire, Il.12.287.92.
Singly methinks, yon' tow'ring Chief I meet, Il.13.113.110.
Thro' yon' square Body, and that black Array: Il.13.206.115.
And whelm in Ruins yon' flagitious Town. Il.13.788.142.
Behold! distress'd within yon' hostile Wall, Il.13.925.149.
To yon' tall Ships to bear the *Trojan* Fires; Il.13.932.149.
But since yon' Ramparts by thy Arms lay low, Il.13.979.152.
To yon' bright Synod on th' *Olympian* Hill; Il.15.58.196.
Descending first to yon' forbidden Plain, Il.15.130.201.
On yon' tall Summit of the fount-ful *Ide:* Il.15.165.203.
Report to yon' mad Tyrant of the Main. Il.15.181.203.
Lay yon' proud Structures level with the Plain, Il.15.241.206.
Bright with Destruction of yon' hostile Fleet. Il.15.873.230.
Perhaps yon' Reliques of the *Grecian* Name, Il.16.24.236.
At the last Edge of yon' deserted Land! Il.16.92.239.
Yon' ample Trench had bury'd half her Host. Il.16.98.239.
Good Heav'ns! what active Feats yon' Artist shows, Il.16.903.278.
And drag yon' Carcase to the Walls of *Troy.* Il.17.178.294.
Come, thro' yon' Squadrons let us hew the Way, Il.17.201.295.
Let but *Achilles* o'er yon' Trench appear, Il.18.237.333.
Fierce on yon' Navy will we pour our Arms. Il.18.354.338.
Sacred to *Jove,* and yon' bright Orb of Day. Il.19.196.379.
Lo, where yon' Sails their canvas Wings extend, Il.19.366.387.
Nor from yon' Boaster shall your Chief retire, Il.20.423.412.
Sure I shall see yon' Heaps of *Trojans* kill'd Il.21.64.424.
And yon' proud Bulwarks grew beneath my Hands: Il.21.520.443.
Now boast no more in yon' celestial Bow'r, Il.21.551.444.
Yon' Line of slaughter'd *Trojans* lately trod. Il.21.654.449.
Behold, inglorious round yon' City driv'n! Il.22.222.464.
Yon' aged Trunk, a Cubit from the Ground; Il.23.400.506.
Haste then; yon' narrow Road before our Sight Il.23.493.510.
Whose Weapon strikes yon' flutt'ring Bird, shall bear Il.23.1014.529.
The Corps of *Hector,* at yon' Navy slain. Il.24.238.546.
If in yon' Camp your Pow'rs have doom'd my Fall, Il.24.276.547.
Tow'r on the right of yon' æthereal Space. Il.24.364.551.
Tow'r on the right of yon' æthereal Space. Il.24.384.552.
But say, yon' jovial Troop so gaily drest, Od.1.289.47.
Soon shou'd yon' boasters cease their haughty strife, Od.1.348.49.
Go, fell the timber of yon' lofty grove, Od.5.210.181.
Amidst yon' revellers a sudden guest Od.17.325.147.

YON' (CONTINUED)
And let yon' mendicant our plenty share: Od.17.419.152.
While yon' luxurious race indulge their cheer, Od.17.619.162.
Be dumb when heav'n afflicts! unlike yon' train Od.18.171.175.
That yon' proud Suitors, who licentious tread Od.18.279.180.
When the pale Empress of yon' starry train Od.19.351.211.
Far hence, before yon' hov'ring deaths descend; Od.20.442.254.
And give yon' impious Revellers to bleed, Od.21.220.270.
The hour is come, when yon' fierce man no more Od.22.272.299.
Drive to yon' court, without the Palace wall, Od.22.478.312.
The shades thou seest, from yon' fair realms above. Od.24.213.358.

YONDER
Now rise, and haste to yonder Woodbine Bow'rs, 1.PSp.97.70.
But now the Reeds shall hang on yonder Tree, 1.PSu.43.75.
Yet soon the Reeds shall hang on yonder Tree, 1.PSu.43A.75.
One Leap from yonder Cliff shall end my Pains. 1.PAu.95.87.
And all *Arabia* breathes from yonder Box. 2.RL1.134.156.
From yonder shrine I heard a hollow sound. 2.ElAb.308.344.
Invites my step, and points to yonder glade? 2.Elegy.2.362.
Or ask of yonder argent fields above, 3.EOM1.41.18.
"Go on, my Friend (he cry'd) see yonder Walls! 4.2HE2.46.167.
Yet would'st thou more? In yonder cloud, behold! 5.DunA3.249.178.
To whom the Sire: In yonder cloud, behold! 5.DunA3.249A.178.
Yet would'st thou more? In yonder cloud behold, 5.DunB3.253.332.
Lost, lost too soon in yonder House or Hall. 5.DunB4.166.357.
In yonder wildgoose, and the larks! 6.150.10.398.
In yonder Walls that Object let me shun, Il.3.382.211.
Safe from the Fight, in yonder lofty Walls, Il.3.482.215.
Else had'st thou seen me sink on yonder Plain, Il.5.1088.318.
Go search your slaughter'd Chiefs on yonder Plain, Il.7.486.388.
What mighty *Trojan* then, on yonder Shore, Il.8.461.419.
Of all the Warriors yonder Host can send, Il.9.269.446.
Nor stay, till yonder Fleets ascend in Fire: Il.9.710.469.
To yonder Camp, or seize some stragling Foe? Il.10.244.13.
Of yonder Fleet a bold Discov'ry make, Il.10.363.19.
Trojans on *Trojans* yonder load the Plain. Il.11.645.62.
On yonder Decks, and yet o'erlooks the Plains! Il.13.938.149.
Where yonder Heroes faint, I bend my way, Il.13.944.150.
The Chiefs you seek on yonder Shore lie slain; Il.13.981.152.
But Heav'n forsakes not thee: O'er yonder Sands Il.14.165.165.
Stretch'd by *Patroclus'* Arm on yonder Plains, Il.16.667.270.
Till yonder Sun descend, ah let me pay Il.19.327.386.
Suffice, from yonder Mount to view the Scene; Il.20.164.400.
While I decline to yonder Path, that leads Il.21.657.449.
Oh if in yonder hostile Camp they live, Il.22.66.455.
Are yonder Horse discern'd by me alone? Il.23.541.511.
If such thy Will, dispatch from yonder Sky Il.24.381.551.
With wonder rapt, on yonder cheek I trace Od.4.189.129.
Thou meditat'st thy meal in yonder cave; Od.9.560.329.
Alas! from yonder Promontory's brow, Od.10.221.351.
But say, why yonder on the lonely strands Od.11.174.390.
Here in the court, or yonder on the waves; Od.11.411.404.
But yonder herds, and yonder flocks forbear; Od.12.355.448.
But yonder herds, and yonder flocks forbear; Od.12.355.448.
Some may betray, and yonder walls may hear. Od.21.245.271.
'Till pale as yonder wretch each Suitor lies. Od.22.78.290.
My haste neglected yonder door to bar, Od.22.170.295.

YONG
The Flow'rs of *Bubo,* and the Flow of *Y[o]ng!* 4.EpS1.68.303.

YORE
Well sung sweet *Ovid,* in the Days of yore, 2.ChJM.514.40.
But Satan now is wiser than of yore, 3.Ep3.351.122.
Where are those Troops of poor, that throng'd of yore 4.JD2.113.143.
He scorn'd to borrow from the Wits of yore; 6.34.9.101.
In vain you boast Poetick Dames of yore, 6.43.1.120.
In vain you boast Poetick Names of yore, 6.43.1A.121.
As erst he scourg'd *Jessides'* Sin of yore 6.137.8.373.
(*Eunæus,* whom *Hypsipyle* of yore Il.7.564.392.
Where now are all your glorious Boasts of yore, Il.8.276.410.
Where now are all our glorious Boasts of yore, Il.8.276A.410.
Oh! had I now that Force I felt of yore, Il.23.723.519.
The great *Mecistheus;* who in Days of yore Il.23.785.521.
The Prince return'd. Renown'd in days of yore Od.15.551.96.
When with *Autolychus's* sons, of yore, Od.21.228.270.
Inform thy guest; for such I was of yore Od.24.140.354.
Lo here the wound (he cries) receiv'd of yore, Od.24.384.367.

YORK
Ask where's the North? at York, 'tis on the Tweed; 3.EOM2.222.82.

YORKSHIRE
In *Yorkshire* dwelt a sober Yeoman, 6.93.1.256.

YOU (OMITTED)
965

YOU'D
If you had Wit, you'd say, "Go where you will, 2.ChWB.130.62.
So quick retires each flying course, you'd swear 3.Ep4.159.153.
"I'm all submission, what you'd have it, make it." 4.Arbu.46.99.
You'd think no Fools disgrac'd the former Reign, 4.2HE1.127.205.
But if you'd have me always near— 4.1HE7.41.271.
Patriots there are, who wish you'd jest no more— 4.EpS1.24.299.
You'd quickly find him in Lord *Fanny's* case. 4.EpS1.50.301.
You'd at present do nothing but give us a Visit. 6.42i.8.116.
You'd take her for a Warren. 6.94.12.259.
"You'd write as smooth again on glass, 6.140.21.378.

YOU'L
Letters, you swear, no more you'l be 6.30.62A.88.
If you'l but give up one, I'll give up tother. 6.46.4A.127.
you'l see in the margin) 6.68.6.196.

YOU'RE
Speak when you're *sure,* yet speak with *Diffidence;* 1.EOC.567A.305.
Most worthy Kinsman, faith, you're mighty wise! 2.ChJM.217.25.
Would Cloe know if you're alive or dead? 3.Ep2.177.64.
My Lords the Judges laugh, and you're dismiss'd. 4.HS1.156.21.
Why let him Sing—but when you're in the Wrong, 4.HAdv.141.87.
And cry'd, "I vow you're mighty neat. 4.HS6.174.261.
Adieu to Virtue if you're once a Slave: 4.1HE1.118.287.
Fr. You're strangely proud. *P.* So proud I am no Slave: 4.EpS2.205.324.
(Now, if you're weary of my Style, 6.10.63.26.
Sir, you're so stiff in your Opinion, 6.10.79.27.
Z—ds, you're as sour as *Cato Censor!* 6.10.102.27.
See there! you're always in my Way! 6.64.10.189.
Some strangely wonder you're not fond to marry— 6.82vi.11.232.
Would Cloë know if you're alive or dead? 6.139.21.377.

YOU'VE
And when up ten steep slopes you've dragg'd your thighs, 3.Ep4.131.150.
You've play'd, and lov'd, and eat, and drank your fill: 4.2HE2.323.187.
"Let my Lord know you've come to town. 4.HS6.44.253.
You've the *Nine* in your *Wit,* and the *Three* in your *Face* 6.62i.2A.185.

YOUNG
The Young, the Old, one Instant makes our Prize, 1.W-F.109A.161.
When first young *Maro* in his boundless Mind 1.EOC.130.254.
When first young *Maro* sung of *Kings* and *Wars,* 1.EOC.130A.254.
Nay *Wits* had *Pensions,* and *young Lords* had *Wit:* 1.EOC.539.298.
Inspir'd young *Perseus* with a gen'rous Flame, 1.TrSP.42.395.
Devours young Babes before their Parents' Eyes, 1.TrSt.712.440.
Then let him chuse a Damsel young and fair, 2.ChJM.25.16.
Old Fish at Table, but young Flesh in Bed. 2.ChJM.102.19.
But young and tender Virgins, rul'd with Ease, 2.ChJM.111.20.
Young, beauteous, artless, innocent and wise; 2.ChJM.259.27.
Procur'd young Husbands in my riper Days. 2.ChWB.208.66.
Instruct the Eyes of young *Coquettes* to roll, 2.RL1.88.152.
Or turns young Ammon loose to scourge mankind? 3.EOM1.160.35.
The young disease, that must subdue at length, 3.EOM2.135.71.
The young dismiss'd to wander earth or air, 3.EOM3.127.105.
Go! and pretend your family is young; 3.EOM4.213.147.
Young without Lovers, old without a Friend, 3.Ep2.246.70.
The young who labour, and the old who rest. 3.Ep3.268.115.
Thro' his young Woods how pleas'd Sabinus stray'd, 3.Ep4.89.146.
F. Alas young Man! your Days can ne'r be long, 4.HS1.101.15.
Perhaps, young men! our Fathers had no nose? 4.HS2.92.61.
No young Divine, new-benefic'd, can be 4.JD2.51.137.
Not Young Divines, new-benefic'd can be 4.JD2A.57.136.
Noble and young, who strikes the heart 4.HOde1.11.151.
Noble and young, who wins the heart 4.HOde1.11A.151.
Shall call the smiling Loves, and young Desires; 4.HOde1.26.153.
Free as young Lyttelton, her cause pursue, 4.1HE1.29.281.
And what young AMMON wish'd, but wish'd in vain. 4.EpS2.117.320.
Veracious W[innington] and frontless Young; 4.1740.54.334.
And whisk 'em back to Evans, Young, and Swift. 5.DunA2.108.109.
And whisk 'em back to *G[ay],* to *Y[oung],* to *S[wift].* 5.DunA2.108A.109.
How young Lutetia, softer than the down, 5.DunA2.309.139.
And whisk 'em back to Evans, Young, and Swift. 5.DunB2.116.301.
How young Lutetia, softer than the down, 5.DunB2.333.313.
The young, the old, who feel her inward sway, 5.DunB4.73.348.
Safe and unseen the young Æneas past: 5.DunB4.290.373.
In *Rome's* proud *Forum* young *Octavius* plac'd, 6.20.28.66.
A Copy of young *Venus* might have took: 6.37.8.106.
A bright example of young *Tarquin's* shame. 6.38.22.108.
Of old *Cats* and young *Kits.* 6.59.8.177.
Young without Lovers, old without a Friend; 6.86.8A.245.
Young as ye are, this youthful Heat restrain, Il.1.343.105.
Do you, young Warriors, hear my Age advise. Il.1.361.105.
Young as you are, this youthful Heat restrain, Il.1.343A.105.
Stretch'd his black Jaws, and crash'd the crying Young; Il.2.379.145.
Young *Amphius* and *Adrastus'* equal Sway; Il.2.1007.170.
The Field of Combate fits the Young and Bold, Il.4.376.239.
Nurs'd the young Stranger with a Mother's Care. Il.5.94.271.
Young *Xanthus* next and *Thoon* felt his Rage, Il.5.196.276.
So two young Mountain Lions, nurs'd with Blood Il.5.681.300.
Bright *Hebè* waits; by *Hebè,* ever young, Il.5.888.308.
Two Twins were near, bold beautiful and young, Il.6.27.325.
And twelve young Heifers to her Altars led. Il.6.116.329.
For *Tydeus* left me young, when *Thebè's* Wall Il.6.277.340.
And twelve young Heifers to her Altar led. Il.6.343.343.
So twelve young Heifers, guiltless of the Yoke, Il.6.382.345.
The young *Astyanax,* the Hope of *Troy.* Il.6.467.349.
The young *Astyanax,* the Hope of *Troy.* Il.6.487.350.
Young *Ageläus* (*Phradmon* was his Sire) Il.8.309.412.
And last young *Teucer* with his bended Bow. Il.8.320.412.
Be that the Duty of the young and bold; Il.9.95.437.
That young and old may in thy Praise combine, Il.9.336.450.
As the bold Bird her helpless Young attends, Il.9.424.453.
The great *Iphidamas,* the bold and young; Il.11.283.47.
(Young as they were) the vengeful Squadrons led. Il.11.845.74.
And pierc'd *Ascalaphus,* the brave and young: Il.13.657.137.
(Young *Ajax* Brother, by a stol'n Embrace; Il.13.871.147.
Glad I submit, whoe'er, or young or old, Il.14.118.163.
Young tho' he be, disdain not to obey: Il.14.123.163.
Not *Phœnix'* Daughter, beautiful and young, Il.14.367.180.
But young *Ilioneus* receiv'd the Spear, Il.14.573.190.
Fierce *Melanippus,* gallant, brave, and young. Il.15.645.221.
Echeclus follows; next young *Megas* bleeds; Il.16.852.276.
A valiant Warrior, haughty, bold, and young.) Il.16.876.277.
Thus round her new fal'n Young, the Heifer moves, Il.17.5.287.
As the young Olive, in some Sylvan Scene, Il.17.57.290.
Thus young, thus beautiful, *Euphorbus* lay Il.17.65.290.
Her tawny Young, beset by Men and Hounds; Il.17.148.293.
Which pass'd the Shield of *Aretus* the young; Il.17.585.311.
High on pois'd Pinions, threats their callow Young. Il.17.848.321.
Roars thro' the Desart, and demands his Young; Il.18.372.339.
Like young *Lycaon,* of the Royal Line, Il.20.113.398.
Nor less unpity'd young *Alastor* bleeds; Il.20.537.416.

YOUNG (CONTINUED)

The young *Lycaon* in his Passage stood; ..... Il.21.41.423.
To young *Agenor* Force divine he gave, ... Il.21.643.449.
(Vig'rous no more, as when his young Embrace ..... Il.22.538.478.
Young *Nestor* leads the Race: *Eumelus* then; ..... Il.23.429.507.
While thus young *Nestor* animates his Steeds. ..... Il.23.482.509.
Young *Nestor* follows (who by Art, not Force, ... Il.23.597.513.
What time young *Paris*, simple Shepherd Boy, ... Il.24.39.537.
Thy self not young, a weak old Man thy Guide. ..... Il.24.454.555.
Whom young *Orestes* to the dreary coast ..... Od.1.39.31.
To warn the wretch, that young *Orestes* grown ..... Od.1.51.33.
Him young *Thoösa* bore, (the bright increase ..... Od.1.92.36.
There young *Telemachus*, his bloomy face ..... Od.1.148.40.
For young *Atrides* to th' *Achaian* coast ..... Od.1.372.50.
Hast thou not heard how young *Orestes* fir'd ..... Od.1.387.51.
Aw'd by the Prince, thus haughty, bold, and young, ... Od.1.487.55.
Ye young, ye old, the weighty cause disclose: ..... Od.2.37.62.
The hand of young *Telemachus*, and spoke. ..... Od.3.479.110.
Young *Aretus* from forth his bridal bow'r ..... Od.3.557.114.
On the bright eminence young *Nestor* shone, ... Od.4.29.121.
His head reclin'd, young *Ithacus* begun. ..... Od.4.82.123.
The brows of all their young increase adorn: ..... Od.4.108.125.
Of young *Telemachus!* the lovely boy, ... Od.4.193.129.
Young and mature! the Monarch thus rejoins, ... Od.4.281.132.
Instant to young *Telemachus* he press'd, ... Od.4.419.140.
So with her young, amid the woodland shades ..... Od.4.449.141.
Joys ever-young, unmix'd with pain or fear, ... Od.4.767.155.
And now, young Prince, indulge my fond request; ..... Od.4.801.156.
My quick return, young *Ithacus* rejoin'd, ... Od.4.811.156.
O early worth! a soul so wise, and young, ... Od.4.831.158.
Whom young *Noëmon* lowly thus addrest. ..... Od.4.853.158.
And twelve young mules, a strong laborious race, ... Od.4.860.159.
In the young soul illustrious thought to raise, ... Od.4.914.161.
In his young breast the daring thought inspir'd: ..... Od.4.946.162.
Fearless herself, yet trembles for her young. ..... Od.4.1044.166.
And spotless robes become the young and gay: ..... Od.6.76.208.
And *Peribæa*, beautiful and young: ..... Od.7.73.237.
The new-fall'n young here bleating for their dams; ..... Od.9.259.317.
More young, more large, more graceful to my eyes. ..... Od.10.468.366.
With leaps and bounds their late-imprison'd young, ... Od.10.488.367.
Lampetie fair, and *Phaethusa* young, ... Od.12.168.440.
Not young *Telemachus*, his blooming heir. ..... Od.14.199.45.
Of young *Telemachus* approach'd the land; ..... Od.15.536.96.
Thus young *Ulysses* to *Eumæus* said. ..... Od.16.56.105.
Or parent vulture, mourns her ravish'd young; ..... Od.16.239.116.
So with her young, amid the woodland shades, ... Od.17.140.138.
Oh had you seen him, vig'rous, bold and young, ... Od.17.380.150.
Scornful they heard: *Melantho*, fair and young, ... Od.18.367.185.
The rich insult him, and the young deride! ..... Od.19.437.216.
The young *Autolyci*, assay the chace. ..... Od.19.502.220.
Young *Ithacus* advanc'd, defies the foe, ... Od.19.521.221.
Young *Itylus*, his parents darling joy! ..... Od.19.608.226.
As o'er her young the mother-mastiff growls, ... Od.20.20.232.
In that blest cause shou'd emulate the young— ..... Od.20.297.247.
Aw'd by the Prince, so haughty, brave, and young, ... Od.20.334.249.
On young *Ulysses Iphitus* bestow'd: ..... Od.21.18.259.
In his blest cause shou'd emulate the young. ..... Od.21.208.270.
And each on young *Telemachus* attend, ... Od.21.224.270.
Young as I am, thy Prince's vengeful hand ..... Od.21.401.279.
(Young as he is) his mother's female band. ..... Od.22.465.311.
Scorn'd by the young, forgotten by the old, ... Od.24.188.356.
And there the young *Telemachus* attends. ..... Od.24.420.369.
The swains and young *Telemachus* they found, ... Od.24.423.369.

YOUNGER

That pleas'd can see a younger charm, or hear ..... 3.Ep2.259A.71.
See yet a younger, by his blushes known, ... 5.DunA3.135A.161.
These younger Champions will oppress thy Might. ..... Il.8.130.404.
Let younger *Greeks* our sleeping Warriors wake; ..... Il.10.188.10.
And awe the younger Brothers of the Pole; ..... Il.15.221.205.
A younger Race, that emulate our Deeds: ..... Il.23.740.519.
Tho' much thy younger, and his years like mine, ... Od.3.60.89.
Who finds thee younger must consult his eyes. ..... Od.3.154.93.
That warmth of soul that urg'd thy younger years? ..... Od.18.256.179.

YOUNGER'S

Poor *Y[ounge]r's* sold for Fifty Pound, ... 6.47.31.129.

YOUNGEST

The eldest is a fool, the youngest wise; ..... 4.1HE1.44.281.
Till I, the youngest of the Host, appear'd, ... Il.7.185.373.
And youngest, met whom all our Army fear'd. ..... Il.7.186.373.
Would hardly stile thee *Nestor's* youngest Son. ..... Il.9.82.436.
The youngest *Grace, Pasithea* the divine. ..... Il.14.304.177.
The youngest *Grace, Pasithea* the divine. ..... Il.14.312.178.
The youngest Hope of *Priam's* stooping Age: ..... Il.20.472.414.
Nor youngest, yet the readiest to decide. ..... Il.23.559.511.
And *Nestor's* Youngest stops the vents of breath. ..... Od.3.579.116.
The youngest of our band, a vulgar soul ..... Od.10.661.375.
A lovely shade, *Amphion's* youngest joy! ..... Od.11.342.398.
With *Ctimene*, her youngest daughter, bred, ... Od.15.388.88.

YOUR (OMITTED)

1062

YOUR-SELVES

Your brave Associates, and Your-selves revere! ..... Il.5.652.299.

YOUR'S

Who copies Yoúr's, or OXFORD's better part, ... 3.Ep3.243.112.

YOURS

'Tis yours, my Lord, to bless our soft Retreats, ... 1.W-F.283.174.
My lips to yours, advance at least to mine. ..... 1.TrFD.93.390.
But by your father's worth if yours you rate, ... 3.EOM4.209.147.
And yours my friends? thro' whose free-opening gate ..... 4.HS2.157.67.

YOURS (CONTINUED)

"Yours *Cowper's* Manner—and yours *Talbot's* Sense." ..... 4.2HE2.134.175.
"Yours *Cowper's* Manner—and yours *Talbot's* Sense." ..... 4.2HE2.134.175.
Yours *Milton's* Genius, and mine *Homer's* Spirit. ..... 4.2HE2.136.175.
A *Property*, that's yours on which you live. ..... 4.2HE2.231.181.
Th' Affront is mine, my Friend, and should be yours. ..... 4.EpS2.200.324.
Let others aim: 'Tis yours to shake the soul 5.DunA2.217.12
'Tis yours, a Bacon, or a Locke to blame, ... 5.DunA3.213.17
Let others aim: 'Tis yours to shake the soul 5.DunB2.225.30
'Tis yours, a Bacon or a Locke to blame, ... 5.DunB3.215.33
To treat those Nymphs like yours of *Drury*, ... 6.10.51.26.
Such praise is yours—and such shall you possess, ... 6.38.23.108.
A common Blessing! now 'tis yours, now mine. ..... 6.60.32.179.
And if poor *Pope* is cl–pt, the Fault is yours. ..... 6.82vi.16.232.
Be mine; and yours the Province to detain. ..... Il.2.98.131.
'Tis yours, O Warriors, all our Hopes to raise; ..... Il.13.73.108.
'Tis yours to save us, if you cease to fear; ..... Il.13.75.108.
Another's is the Crime, but yours the Shame. ..... Il.13.152.111.
All, all *Achilles, Greeks!* is yours to Day. ..... Il.20.412.412.
And yield the Glory yours—The Steeds obey; ..... Il.23.527.511.
May ev'ry joy be yours! nor this the least, ... Od.13.49.3.
Impending Fate is yours, and instant doom. ..... Od.22.52.289.
This arm had aided yours; this hand bestrown ..... Od.24.441.370.

YOURSELF

Painful preheminence! yourself to view 3.EOM4.267.153
And mistress of yourself, tho' China fall. ..... 3.Ep2.268A.72.
"Live like yourself," was soon my Lady's word; ..... 3.Ep3.359.123.
A Light, which in yourself you must perceive; ..... 3.Ep4.45.141.
Till I cry'd out, "You prove yourself so able, ... 4.JD4.82.33.
Yourself for Goose reject Crow Quill, ... 6.10.43.25.
Last to *yourself* my best Respects I pay, ... 6.13.29.40.
Pallas, you give yourself strange Airs; ..... 6.119.13.337.
But you yourself may serve to show it, ... 6.124ii.3.347.

YOURSELVES

Admire new light thro' holes yourselves have made. 5.DunB4.126.354
Rise higher yet: learn ev'n yourselves to know; ..... 6.27.14.81.
Nay, to yourselves alone that knowledge owe. ..... 6.27.15.81.

YOUTH

Ye vig'rous Swains! while Youth ferments your Blood, ... 1.W-F.93.159.
The Youth rush eager to the Sylvan War; ..... 1.W-F.148.164.
See! the bold Youth strain up the threatning Steep, ... 1.W-F.155.164.
While naked Youth and painted Chiefs admire ..... 1.W-F.405A.192.
Whose naked Youth and painted Chiefs admire ..... 1.W-F.405B.192.
In *fearless Youth* we tempt the Heights of Arts, ... 1.EOC.220.265.
In *Youth* alone its empty Praise we boast, ... 1.EOC.496.294.
A lovely youth, and Acis was his name; ..... 1.TrPA.2.365.
At last a youth above the waist arose, ... 1.TrPA.159.372.
With Youth Immortal and with Beauty blest. ..... 1.TrVP.91.381.
And when in youth he seeks the shady woods, ... 1.TrFD.84.389.
Say, lovely Youth, that dost my Heart command, ... 1.TrSP.1.393.
Ah Youth ungrateful to a Flame like mine! ..... 1.TrSP.20.394.
O scarce a Youth, yet scarce a tender Boy! ..... 1.TrSP.103.398.
But why alas, relentless Youth! ah why ..... 1.TrSP.218.403.
Return fair Youth, return, and bring along ..... 1.TrSP.238.404.
Too cruel Youth, that you shou'd fly from me?) ..... 1.TrSP.255.404.
Or how the Youth with ev'ry Grace adorn'd, ... 1.TrSt.65.413.
Who first their Youth in Arts of Virtue train'd, ... 1.TrSt.619.436.
That all the Charms of blooming Youth possest; ..... 1.TrSt.671.438.
The Youth surround her with extended Spears; ..... 1.TrSt.723.440.
And from the wondring God th'unwilling Youth retir'd. ..... 1.TrSt.785.443.
Eternal Charms thy blooming Youth adorn: ..... 1.TrSt.838.444.
When tender Youth has wedded stooping Age. ..... 2.ChJM.340.30.
If I but smil'd, a sudden Youth they found, ... 2.ChWB.66.59.
By pressing Youth attack'd on ev'ry side. ..... 2.ChWB.93.61.
On all the Joys of Youth and Beauty past, ... 2.ChWB.222.67.
Oh had the Youth but been content to seize ..... 2.RL*A*2.19.132.
A Youth more glitt'ring than a *Birth-night Beau*, ... 2.RL1.23.147.
Ah cease rash Youth! desist ere 'tis too late, ... 2.RL3.121.176.
The *Youth* that all things but himself subdu'd; ..... 2.TemF.152.266.
And boasting Youth, and Narrative old Age. ..... 2.TemF.291.277.
Art thou, fond Youth, a Candidate for Praise? ..... 2.TemF.500.287.
When, warm in youth, I bade the world farewell? ..... 2.ElAb.110.329.
From the false world in early youth they fled, ... 2.ElAb.131.330.
Some livelier play-thing gives his youth delight, ... 3.EOM2.277.88.
That pointed back to youth, this on to age; ..... 3.EOM3.144.107.
From loveless youth to unrespected age, ... 3.Ep2.125.60.
In Youth they conquer, with so wild a rage, ... 3.Ep2.221.68.
At last, to follies Youth could scarce defend, ... 3.Ep2.235.69.
A Youth of frolicks, an old Age of Cards, ... 3.Ep2.244.70.
Was velvet in the youth of good Queen *Bess*, ... 4.JD4.41.29.
See! where the *British* Youth, engag'd no more ..... 4.JD4.212.43.
And now the *British* Youth, engag'd no more ..... 4.JD4.212A.43.
If our intemp'rate Youth the Vessel drains? ..... 4.HS2.90.61.
The Youth might save much Trouble and Expence, ... 4.HAdv.67.81.
He, from the taste obscene reclaims our Youth, ... 4.2HE1.217.213.
Lov'd without youth, and follow'd without power, ... 4.1HE1.183.293.
The worthy Youth shall ne'er be in a rage: ..... 4.EpS1.48.301.
P. Dear Sir, forgive the Prejudice of Youth: ..... 4.EpS1.63.302.
Our Youth, all liv'ry'd o'er with foreign Gold, ... 4.EpS1.155.309.
And how did, pray, the Florid Youth offend. ..... 4.EpS2.166.323.
A youth unknown to Phœbus, in despair, ... 5.DunA2.205.127.
"Mark first the youth who takes the foremost place, ... 5.DunA3.131.161.
"Mark first that youth who takes the foremost place, ... 5.DunA3.131A.16
D[uckit] for pious passion to the youth. ..... 5.DunA3.176.169.
D[uckit] for cordial friendship to the youth. 5.DunA3.176B.169
A matchless youth: His nod these worlds controuls, ... 5.DunA3.251.178.
A godlike youth: See *Jove's* own bolt he flings 5.DunA3.251A.178
A youth unknown to Phœbus, in despair, ... 5.DunB2.213.306.
"Mark first that Youth who takes the foremost place, ... 5.DunB3.139.326.
A matchless Youth! his nod these worlds controuls, ... 5.DunB3.255.332.
Plac'd at the door of Learning, youth to guide, ... 5.DunB4.153.356.
This glorious Youth, and add one Venus more. ..... 5.DunB4.330.375.
So shall each youth, assisted by our eyes, ... 5.DunB4.359.378.

YOUTH (CONTINUED)

YOUTH (CONTINUED)

YOUTH'S

YOUTHFUL 666 ZEPHALINDA

YOUTHFUL
And old *Silenus,* youthful in Decay, ...1.TrVP.24.378.
Destroy the Promise of the youthful Year; ....1.TrVP.109.381.
Of charming Features and a youthful Face, ...1.TrVP.121.382.
In youthful Arms t'assert the Cause of *Jove.* ....1.TrSt.30.411.
Such once employ'd *Alcides'* youthful Toils, ...1.TrSt.569.434.
In show a youthful Swain, of Form divine, ...1.TrUl.102.469.
The growing Virtues of my youthful Son, ...1.TrUl.245.474.
He fix'd at last upon the youthful *May.* ....2.ChJM.243.26.
Rich luscious Wines, that youthful Blood improve, ...2.ChWB.215.67.
Of luscious Wines, that youthful Blood improve, ...2.ChWB.215A.67.
Not youthful Kings in Battel seiz'd alive, ...2.RL4.3.183.
What mov'd my Mind with youthful Lords to rome? ....2.RL4.159.197.
Next these a youthful Train their Vows exprest, ...2.TemF.378.282.
For who so fond as youthful Bards of Fame? ....2.TemF.502.288.
And humble glories of the youthful Spring; ....6.14iv.2.47.
Scene of my youthful Loves, and happier hours! ....6.66.2.194.
'Till Time shall rifle ev'ry youthful Grace, ...Il.1.41.87.
Young as ye are, this youthful Heat restrain, ...Il.1.343.105.
Young as you are, this youthful Heat restrain, ...Il.1.343A.105.
His youthful Face a polish'd Helm o'erspread; ....Il.3.417.212.
The youthful Victor mounts his empty Seat, ...Il.5.720.301.
Here dead they lay in all their youthful Charms; ....Il.6.33.325.
Whom from soft *Sidon* youthful *Paris* bore, ...Il.6.362.344.
But Warriors, you, that youthful Vigour boast, ...Il.7.191.373.
When *Greece* of old beheld my youthful Flames, ...Il.9.576.462.
A youthful Steer shall fall beneath the Stroke, ...Il.10.347.18.
With youthful *Acamas,* whose beauteous Face ....Il.11.79.38.
(*Theano's* Sister) to his youthful Arms. ....Il.11.290.48.
The youthful Heroes in a Veil of Clouds. ....Il.11.885.75.
Such then I was, impell'd by youthful Blood; ....Il.11.896.75.
Remain the Prize of *Nestor's* youthful Son. ....Il.13.508.130.
The youthful Offspring of the God of War, ...Il.13.605.135.
The youthful Brothers thus for Fame contend, ...Il.17.440.304.
The youthful Warrior heard with silent Woe, ...Il.17.781.319.
The youthful Dancers in a Circle bound ....Il.18.573.350.
In the first Folly of a youthful Knight, ...Il.20.476.414.
Loth as he was to yield his youthful Breath, ...Il.21.76.424.
And is it thus the youthful *Phœbus* flies, ...Il.21.547.444.
My Son! tho' youthful Ardor fire thy Breast, ...Il.23.375.505.
When youthful Rivals their full Force extend, ...Il.23.512.510.
Your Rivals, destitute of youthful Force, ...Il.23.525.510.
But youthful *Nestor,* jealous of his Fame, ...Il.23.619.514.
Friend of the youthful Chief: Himself content, ...Il.23.701.517.
His youthful Equals, *Nestor's* Son the last. ....Il.23.884.524.
That youthful Vigour, and that manly Mind, ...Il.24.12.535.
Stood proud to Hymn, and tune his youthful Lyre. ....Il.24.83.538.
Six youthful Sons, as many blooming Maids ....Il.24.759.569.
Here, youthful Grace and noble Fire engage, ...Il.24.800.570.
Of wealth and fame a youthful bosom fire: ....Od.1.500.56.
The youthful Hero, with returning light, ...Od.2.3.59.
Proceed my son! this youthful shame expel; ....Od.3.19.87.
Where *Nestor* sate with youthful *Thrasymed.* ....Od.3.50.89.
Consign'd the youthful Consort to his care; ....Od.3.335.102.
The youthful Hero and th' *Athenian* maid ....Od.3.440.108.
And youthful smil'd; but in the low disguise ....Od.7.27.235.
Or weak and old, my youthful arm demands, ...Od.11.607.413.
In show a youthful swain, of form divine, ...Od.13.269.18.
The growing virtues of my youthful son, ...Od.13.412.26.
Slave to the insolence of youthful Lords! ....Od.14.72.39.
With him all night the youthful strangers stay'd, ...Od.15.212.78.
Crept on from childhood into youthful prime, ...Od.15.391.88.
Sincere the youthful Heroe made reply. ....Od.16.118.108.
And give to wither'd age a youthful bloom? ....Od.16.219.114.
Lur'd with the promis'd boon, when youthful prime ....Od.19.484.220.
With pomp and joy have wing'd my youthful hours!) ....Od.19.679.229.
And to the youthful Prince to urge the laws, ...Od.21.23.260.

YOUTHS
And naked Youths and painted Chiefs admire ....1.W-F.405.192.
A Train of well-drest Youths around her shone, ...2.RL*A* 1.21.127.
Fair Nymphs, and well-drest Youths around her shone, ...2.RL2.5.159.
And Youths that dy'd to be by Poets sung. ....2.TemF.128.264.
The Youths hang o'er their Chariots as they run; ....2.TemF.218.272.
There, Youths and Nymphs, in consort gay, ...4.HOde1.29.153.
There, Youths and Virgins ever gay, ...4.HOde1.29A.153.
On whom three hundred gold-capt youths await, ...5.DunB4.117.353.
By the Youths that dy'd for Love, ...6.11.79.33.
The Youths with Wine the copious Goblets crown'd, ...Il.1.616.117.
The Old consulting, and the Youths around. ....Il.2.959.169.
Prest by bold Youths and baying Dogs in vain. ....Il.3.40.190.
In vain the Youths oppose, the Mastives bay ....Il.3.39A.190.
The Youths return'd not from the doubtful Plain, ...Il.5.192.276.
And beardless Youths, our Battlements surround. ....Il.8.646.426.
And beardless Youths, the Battlements surround. ....Il.8.646A.426.
(Such as by Youths unus'd to Arms, are worn; ....Il.10.305.16.
The *Trojans* see the Youths untimely die, ...Il.11.151.42.
The Youths address'd to unrelenting Ears: ....Il.11.178.43.
In vain, brave Youths, with glorious Hopes ye burn, ...Il.17.564.310.
(Fair Maids, and blooming Youths) that smiling bear ....Il.18.659.355.
Of Youths and Maidens, bounding Hand in Hand: ....Il.18.684.356.
The Youths all graceful in the glossy Vest; ....Il.18.686.356.
Swift as the Word was giv'n, the Youths obey'd; ....Il.19.249.383.
Twelve chosen Youths he drags alive to Land; ....Il.21.35.422.
Like Youths and Maidens in an Evening Walk: ....Il.22.170.460.
The Youths contending in the rapid Race. ....Il.23.864.524.
Gay, stripling youths the brimming goblets crown'd. ....Od.1.194.42.
Pour'd the full urns; the youths the goblets crown'd: ....Od.3.434.108.
All Youths the rest, whom to this journey move ....Od.3.464.109.
(Of *Alpheus'* race) the weary youths retreat. ....Od.3.620.117.
Two sprightly youths to form the bounding dance. ....Od.4.26.121.
Two youths approach, whose semblant features prove ....Od.4.33.121.
Conduct the youths to grace the genial feast. ....Od.4.46.122.
And twenty youths in radiant mail incas'd, ...Od.4.709.152.
Be chosen youths prepar'd, expert to try ....Od.8.33.263.
Skill'd in the dance, tall youths, a blooming band, ...Od.8.301.279.

YOUTHS (CONTINUED)
Six blooming youths, in private grandeur bred, ...Od.10.5.339.
And touch'd the Youths; but their stern Sire reply'd, ...Od.10.82.343.
Fair, pensive youths, and soft-enamour'd maids, ...Od.11.49.383.
The wond'rous youths had scarce nine winters told, ...Od.11.381.401.
Such were they Youths! had they to manhood grown, ...Od.11.389.403.
Farewel and prosper, youths! let *Nestor* know ....Od.15.168.76.
The Lyrist strikes the string; gay youths advance, ...Od.23.141.327.
And now the blooming youths and sprightly fair ....Od.23.319.339.

Z
See ZOUNDS.
X and *Z* cry'd, P—x and Z—s ....6.30.43.87.
X and *Z* cry'd, P—x and Z—s ....6.30.43.87.
And ev'ry speech in Z—nds end, ...6.61.18.181.
And ev'ry speech with Z—nds end, ...6.61.18A.181.

ZACINTH
And lofty *Zacinth* crown'd with shady hills. ....Od.16.132.109.

ZACYNTHUS
Crocylia rocky, and *Zacynthus* green. ....Il.2.772.162.
Dulichium, Samè, and *Zacynthus* crown'd ....Od.9.23.302.
Of *Samos;* twenty from *Zacynthus* coast: ....Od.16.271.118.
Zacynthus, green with ever-shady groves, ...Od.19.152.199.

ZACYNTHUS'
Dulichium, and *Zacynthus'* sylvan reign: ....Od.1.318.48.

ZAGS
That slip'd thro' Cracks and Zig-zags of the Head; ....5.DunB1.124.278.

ZAMOLXIS
There sate *Zamolxis* with erected Eyes, ...2.TemF.123.264.

ZANY
Preacher at once, and Zany of thy Age! ....5.DunA3.202.175.
Preacher at once, and Zany of thy age! ....5.DunB3.206.330.

ZEAL
From no blind Zeal or fond Tradition rise; ....1.TrSt.661.438.
Not grace, or zeal, love only was my call, ...2.ElAb.117.329.
See anger, zeal and fortitude supply; ....3.EOM2.187.77.
Zeal then, not charity, became the guide, ...3.EOM3.261.119.
And show their zeal, and hide their want of skill. ....3.Ep2.186.65.
And Zeal for his great House which eats thee up. ....3.Ep3.208A.110.
And Zeal for that great House which eats him up. ....3.Ep3.208.110.
The Zeal of Fools offends at any time, ...4.2HE1.406.229.
But most of all, the Zeal of Fools in ryme. ....4.2HE1.407.229.
For Vertue's self may too much Zeal be had; ....4.1HE6.26.239.
Tells me I have more Zeal than Wit, ...4.HS6.56.253.
Rev'rent I touch thee! but with honest zeal; ....4.EpS2.216.325.
And rival, Curtius! of thy fame and zeal, ...5.DunA1.195.86.
Shall I, like Curtius, desp'rate in my zeal, ...5.DunB1.209.285.
But far the foremost, two, with earnest zeal, ...5.DunB4.401.381.
A scorn of wrangling, yet a zeal for truth; ....6.57.8.169.
Barbarian blindness, Christian zeal conspire, ...6.71.13.203.
While Fools have places purely for their Zeal. ....6.82ix(d).2.235.
In vain a nations zeal a senate's cares ....6.130.31.359.
With hasty Zeal the swift *Talthybius* flies; ....Il.4.234.232.
Neptune, with Zeal encreas'd, renews his Care, ...Il.14.419.183.
Hector, whose Zeal whole Hecatombs has slain, ...Il.22.224.464.
With friendlier zeal my father's soul was fir'd, ...Od.1.344.49.
There with commutual zeal we both had strove, ...Od.4.241.130.
Avow'd his zeal in council or in fight, ...Od.4.442.140.
Ill suits it with your shews of duteous zeal, ...Od.4.966.163.
Since daring zeal with cool debate is join'd; ....Od.20.284.247.

ZEALOTS
And Priests and Party-Zealots, num'rous Bands ....2.TemF.464.286.
For Modes of Faith, let graceless zealots fight; ....3.EOM3.305.124.

ZEALOUS
Once *School-Divines* this zealous Isle o'erspread; ....1.EOC.440.288.
Once *School-Divines* our zealous Isle o'erspread; ....1.EOC.440A.288.
An ardent *Judge,* who Zealous in his Trust, ...1.EOC.677.316.
An ardent *Judge,* that Zealous in his Trust, ...1.EOC.677A.316.
To Failings *mild,* but *zealous* for Desert; ....1.EOC.731.325.
No zealous Pastor blame a failing Spouse, ...4.EpS2.193.324.
Active and pleas'd, the zealous swains fulfil ....Od.22.205.297.

ZELEIA'S
Who fair *Zeleia's* wealthy Vallies till, ...Il.2.998.170.

ZELIA'S
On *Zelia's* Altars, to the God of Day. ....Il.4.134.226.

ZEMBLA
At Greenland, Zembla, or the Lord knows where: ....3.EOM2.224.82.
Or gives to Zembla fruits, to Barca flowers; ....5.DunA1.72.68.
Or gives to Zembla fruits, to Barca flow'rs; ....5.DunB1.74.275.

ZEMBLA'S
So *Zembla's* Rocks (the beauteous Work of Frost) ....2.TemF.53.256.

ZENITH
I shun his Zenith, court his mild Decline; ....4.EpS2.76.317.
Now flaming from the *Zenith, Sol* had driv'n ....Il.16.938.280.

ZENO
And godlike *Zeno* lay inspir'd! ....6.51i.4A.151.

ZEPHALINDA
Thus from the world fair *Zephalinda* flew, ...6.45.7.124.

ZEPHYR

Soft is the Strain when *Zephyr* gently blows, ...1.EOC.366.282.
The whisp'ring Zephyr, and the purling rill? ....3.EOM1.204.40.
(Soft *Zephyr* curling the wide wat'ry Plain) ....Il.7.72.366.
By *Zephyr* pregnant on the breezy Shore. ....Il.16.185.245.
To gentle *Zephyr* and the *Boreal* Blast: ....Il.23.241.499.
Like poplar-leaves when *Zephyr* fans the grove. ....Od.7.135.241.

ZEPHYR'S

Where, in old *Zephyr's* open Courts on high, ...Il.23.246.499.

ZEPHYRETTA'S

The flutt'ring Fan be *Zephyretta's* Care; ....2.RL2.112.166.

ZEPHYRS

The balmy *Zephyrs*, silent since her Death, ...1.PWi.49.92.
Smooth flow the Waves, the Zephyrs gently play, ...2.RL2.51.162.
That seem'd but *Zephyrs* to the Train beneath. ....2.RL2.58.163.
Lull'd by soft Zephyrs thro' the broken Pane, ...4.Arbu.42.99.
Waves to the tepid Zephyrs of the spring, ...5.DunB4.422.383.
And breath the Zephyrs that refresh thy Grove ....6.106ii.4.307.
The Seer, while Zephyrs curl the swelling deep, ...Od.4.541.146.

ZEPHYRUS

But *Zephyrus* exempt, with friendly gales ....Od.10.27.340.

ZETHUS

Hence sprung *Amphion,* hence brave *Zethus* came, ...Od.11.319.397.

ZEUXIS'

With *Zeuxis' Helen* thy *Bridgewater* vie, ...6.52.75.158.

ZIG

That slip'd thro' Cracks and Zig-zags of the Head; ....5.DunB1.124.278.

ZIG-ZAGS

That slip'd thro' Cracks and Zig-zags of the Head; ....5.DunB1.124.278.

ZODIACK

His Sacred Head a radiant Zodiack crown'd, ...2.TemF.234.274.

ZOILUS

Zoilus again would start up from the Dead. ....1.EOC.465.292.

ZON'D

And fair-zon'd damsels form the sprightly dance. ....Od.23.142.328.

ZONE

But by the Crescent and the golden Zone, ...1.W-F.176.166.
Ev'n those who dwell beneath its very zone, ...3.EOM2.227.83.
Ev'n those who dwell beneath her very zone, ...3.EOM2.227A.83.
The clasping Zone, with golden Buckles bound, ...Il.5.515.293.
A golden Zone her swelling Bosom bound. ....Il.14.210.170.
And from her fragrant Breast the Zone unbrac'd, ...Il.14.245.172.
In the rich Belt, as in a starry Zone. ....Il.16.167.244.
The Zone unbrac'd, her Bosom she display'd; ....Il.22.112.457.
The glitt'ring zone athwart his shoulder cast ....Od.4.415.140.
When thro' the Zone of heav'n the mounted sun ....Od.4.539.146.
Her swelling loins a radiant Zone embrac'd ....Od.5.296.185.
That gird the city like a marble zone. ....Od.7.60.236.
Her waste was circled with a zone of gold. ....Od.10.652.375.
Around his breast a wond'rous Zone is row'd, ...Od.11.751.423.
A radiant sabre grac'd his purple zone, ...Od.20.157.241.

ZONES

Ten Zones of Brass its ample Brims surround, ...Il.11.45.36.

ZOROASTER

Grave *Zoroaster* waves the circling Wand: ....2.TemF.98.260.

ZOUNDS

See Z.
Why, Zounds! and Blood! 'tis true! ....6.94.16.259.

The Statistical Summary consists of two parts. The first is the following list of line and word totals, which provides a sense of the scope of the basic poetic text, of the *Concordance* itself, and of Pope's vocabulary. The second is a six-page analytic table showing word-frequency distribution and the ratio between each word and the number of its occurrences (type/token ratio). The table, which begins on the next page, is to be used in conjunction with the Alphabetical List of Word Frequencies (Vol. 1) and Word Frequencies in Rank Order, which appears in Appendix A immediately after the table.

List of Line and Word Totals

Regular lines in Twickenham text of Pope's poetry	53,412
Lines omitted from *Concordance* because of substantial duplication in two versions of *The Rape of the Lock* (see Appendix C)	302
Regular lines in *Concordance*	53,110
Variant lines in Twickenham edition	3,164
Variant lines in *Concordance* (12 additional lines are listed in "Corrections, Additions, and Explanatory Notes")	2,489
Different lines quoted in *Concordance* (lines of regular text plus significant variant lines)	55,599
Context lines appearing in *Concordance* (includes repetitions under separate entries)	269,625
Word forms or separate entries (excluding cross-references)	20,892
Hyphenated compounds listed under each component (usually two) as well as under the compound	1,226
Separate word forms (distinguished as to spelling, number, tense, etc.) in Pope's text excluding hyphenated compounds that are also listed under their components.	19,666

How to Use Table of Type/Token Ratios

The form of the Type/Token table follows the suggestion made by D. R. Tallentire in his essay, "Towards an Archive of Lexical Norms. A Proposal."[1] Used in concert with the word frequency and rank order lists of the concordance, this table can give a complete picture of the frequency distribution of each type (word) and token (separate occurrence of the word) in Pope's vocabulary. For example, a check of the Alphabetical Word Frequency List shows the word "beauty" occurs 75 times. In the Rank Order frequency list one can find the other words occurring with this frequency. Turning next to the table of Type/Token Ratios and looking up frequency 75 in the X column, the reader can follow that line straight across (see illustration at the bottom of this page) to obtain the following information:

There are 8 words with the frequency of 75 (**FX**): these 8 types represent .038292% of the total word types (20,892) in the concordance (%FX). There are 776 types that occur more frequently (SUM FX - FX), and these 8 types, along with the more frequently occurring ones, total 784 (SUM FX) or 3.752503% of the total word types (CUM %FX). The 8 types occurring 75 times represent 600 tokens (FX.X); the total of these 600 tokens plus those tokens of higher frequency is 297,334 (SUM FX) or 69.365538% (CUM %FX.X) of the total tokens (428,647); in other words 3.75% of the types account for 69.36% of the tokens. The 600 tokens are .139975% (%FX.X) of the total number of tokens. The percentages for a single token can be calculated by dividing %FX and %FX.X by FX. The tables for CUM %FX and CUM %FX.X do not add up to 100% because the computer consistently rounds down in its representation of decimals.

[1] *The Computer and Literary Studies,* ed. A. J. Aitken, R. W. Bailey, and N. Hamilton-Smith (Edinburgh: University of Edinburgh Press, 1973), pp. 39-60.

X	FX	%FX	SUM FX	CUM %FX	FX.X	SUM FX.X	%FX.X	CUM %FX.X
75	8	0.038292	784	3.752503	600	297334	0.139975	69.365538

Word-Frequency Distribution and Type/Token Ratios in Pope's Poetry

Definition of Symbols Used in Table

Symbol	Definition	Symbol	Definition
X	Frequency of occurrence	$FX.X = fxX$	Number of tokens accounted for by types of frequency X
$FX = fx$	Number of types of frequency X		
$\%FX$	The ratio of each FX figure over the type total (20,-892) as a percenatge	$SUM\ FX.X = \sum_x fxX$	Sum of tokens due to frequency X and preceding values of X
$SUM\ FX = \sum_x fx$	Sum of types due to frequency X and preceding values of X	$\%FX.X$	The relative per cent frequency of tokens
$CUM\ \%FX = \%\sum_x fx$	Per cent of types due to frequency X and preceding value of X	$CUM\ \%FX.X = \%\sum_x fxX$	Per cent of tokens (total 428,647) due to frequency X and preceding values of X

X	FX	%FX	SUM FX	CUM %FX	FX.X	SUM FX.X	%FX.X	CUM %FX.X
28754	1	0.004786	1	0.004786	28754	28754	6.708083	6.708083
16510	1	0.004786	2	0.009572	16510	45264	3.851654	10.559737
9900	1	0.004786	3	0.014358	9900	55164	2.309592	12.869329
8073	1	0.004786	4	0.019144	8073	63237	1.883367	14.752696
6650	1	0.004786	5	0.023930	6650	69887	1.551393	16.304089
6383	1	0.004786	6	0.028716	6383	76270	1.489104	17.793193
5627	1	0.004786	7	0.033502	5627	81897	1.312735	19.105928
4917	1	0.004786	8	0.038288	4917	86814	1.147097	20.253025
3381	1	0.004786	9	0.043074	3381	90195	0.788760	21.041785
2975	1	0.004786	10	0.047860	2975	93170	0.694044	21.735829
2871	1	0.004786	11	0.052646	2871	96041	0.669781	22.405610
2757	1	0.004786	12	0.057432	2757	98798	0.643186	23.048796
2672	1	0.004786	13	0.062218	2672	101470	0.623356	23.672152
2592	1	0.004786	14	0.067004	2592	104062	0.604693	24.276845
2516	1	0.004786	15	0.071790	2516	106578	0.586963	24.863808
2339	1	0.004786	16	0.076576	2339	108917	0.545670	25.409478
2287	1	0.004786	17	0.081362	2287	111204	0.533539	25.943017
2201	1	0.004786	18	0.086148	2201	113405	0.513476	26.456493
2177	1	0.004786	19	0.090934	2177	115582	0.507877	26.964370
2107	1	0.004786	20	0.095720	2107	117689	0.491546	27.455916
2094	1	0.004786	21	0.100506	2094	119783	0.488513	27.944429
1972	1	0.004786	22	0.105292	1972	121755	0.460052	28.404481
1969	1	0.004786	23	0.110078	1969	123724	0.459352	28.863833
1629	1	0.004786	24	0.114864	1629	125353	0.380032	29.243865
1547	1	0.004786	25	0.119650	1547	126900	0.360903	29.604768
1537	1	0.004786	26	0.124436	1537	128437	0.358570	29.963338
1530	1	0.004786	27	0.129222	1530	129967	0.356937	30.320275
1449	1	0.004786	28	0.134008	1449	131416	0.338040	30.658315
1428	1	0.004786	29	0.138794	1428	132844	0.333141	30.991456
1376	1	0.004786	30	0.143580	1376	134220	0.321010	31.312466
1359	1	0.004786	31	0.148366	1359	135579	0.317044	31.629510
1327	1	0.004786	32	0.153152	1327	136906	0.309578	31.939088
1302	1	0.004786	33	0.157938	1302	138208	0.303746	32.242834
1286	1	0.004786	34	0.162724	1286	139494	0.300013	32.542847
1259	1	0.004786	35	0.167510	1259	140753	0.293714	32.836561
1245	1	0.004786	36	0.172296	1245	141998	0.290448	33.127009
1216	1	0.004786	37	0.177082	1216	143214	0.283683	33.410692

X	FX	%FX	SUM FX	CUM %FX	FX.X	SUM FX.X	%FX.X	CUM %FX.X
1206	1	0.004786	38	0.181868	1206	144420	0.281350	33.692042
1203	1	0.004786	39	0.186654	1203	145623	0.280650	33.972692
1193	1	0.004786	40	0.191440	1193	146816	0.278317	34.251009
1062	1	0.004786	41	0.196226	1062	147878	0.247756	34.498765
1014	1	0.004786	42	0.201012	1014	148892	0.236558	34.735323
987	2	0.009573	44	0.210585	1974	150866	0.460518	35.195841
965	1	0.004786	45	0.215371	965	151831	0.225126	35.420967
937	1	0.004786	46	0.220157	937	152768	0.218594	35.639561
935	1	0.004786	47	0.224943	935	153703	0.218128	35.857689
929	1	0.004786	48	0.229729	929	154632	0.216728	36.074417
901	1	0.004786	49	0.234515	901	155533	0.210196	36.284613
895	1	0.004786	50	0.239301	895	156428	0.208796	36.493409
893	1	0.004786	51	0.244087	893	157321	0.208329	36.701738
871	1	0.004786	52	0.248873	871	158192	0.203197	36.904935
865	1	0.004786	53	0.253659	865	159057	0.201797	37.106732
856	1	0.004786	54	0.258445	856	159913	0.199698	37.306430
844	1	0.004786	55	0.263231	844	160757	0.196898	37.503328
839	1	0.004786	56	0.268017	839	161596	0.195732	37.699060
811	1	0.004786	57	0.272803	811	162407	0.189199	37.888259
800	1	0.004786	58	0.277589	800	163207	0.186633	38.074892
795	1	0.004786	59	0.282375	795	164002	0.185467	38.260359
780	1	0.004786	60	0.287161	780	164782	0.181967	38.442326
765	1	0.004786	61	0.291947	765	165547	0.178468	38.620794
746	1	0.004786	62	0.296733	746	166293	0.174035	38.794829
743	1	0.004786	63	0.301519	743	167036	0.173336	38.968165
740	1	0.004786	64	0.306305	740	167776	0.172636	39.140801
733	1	0.004786	65	0.311091	733	168509	0.171003	39.311804
724	1	0.004786	66	0.315877	724	169233	0.168903	39.480707
689	1	0.004786	67	0.320663	689	169922	0.160738	39.641445
676	1	0.004786	68	0.325449	676	170598	0.157705	39.799150
653	1	0.004786	69	0.330235	653	171251	0.152339	39.951489
641	1	0.004786	70	0.335021	641	171892	0.149540	40.101029
634	1	0.004786	71	0.339807	634	172526	0.147907	40.248936
632	2	0.009573	73	0.349380	1264	173790	0.294881	40.543817
613	1	0.004786	74	0.354166	613	174403	0.143008	40.686825
597	2	0.009573	76	0.363739	1194	175597	0.278550	40.965375
587	1	0.004786	77	0.368525	587	176184	0.136942	41.102317
578	1	0.004786	78	0.373311	578	176762	0.134842	41.237159
577	1	0.004786	79	0.378097	577	177339	0.134609	41.371768
568	1	0.004786	80	0.382883	568	177907	0.132509	41.504277
560	1	0.004786	81	0.387669	560	178467	0.130643	41.634920
557	1	0.004786	82	0.392455	557	179024	0.129943	41.764863
555	1	0.004786	83	0.397241	555	179579	0.129477	41.894340
546	1	0.004786	84	0.402027	546	180125	0.127377	42.021717
544	1	0.004786	85	0.406813	544	180669	0.126910	42.148627
529	1	0.004786	86	0.411599	529	181198	0.123411	42.272038
527	1	0.004786	87	0.416385	527	181725	0.122944	42.394982
517	1	0.004786	88	0.421171	517	182242	0.120612	42.515594
516	1	0.004786	89	0.425957	516	182758	0.120378	42.635972
515	1	0.004786	90	0.430743	515	183273	0.120145	42.756117
512	1	0.004786	91	0.435529	512	183785	0.119445	42.875562
497	1	0.004786	92	0.440315	497	184282	0.115946	42.991508
495	1	0.004786	93	0.445101	495	184777	0.115479	43.106987
492	1	0.004786	94	0.449887	492	185269	0.114779	43.221766
489	1	0.004786	95	0.454673	489	185758	0.114079	43.335845
480	1	0.004786	96	0.459459	480	186238	0.111980	43.447825
459	1	0.004786	97	0.464245	459	186697	0.107081	43.554906
458	1	0.004786	98	0.469031	458	187155	0.106847	43.661753
457	1	0.004786	99	0.473817	457	187612	0.106614	43.768367
450	1	0.004786	100	0.478603	450	188062	0.104981	43.873348
444	1	0.004786	101	0.483389	444	188506	0.103581	43.976929
441	1	0.004786	102	0.488175	441	188947	0.102881	44.079810
434	1	0.004786	103	0.492961	434	189381	0.101248	44.181058
432	1	0.004786	104	0.497747	432	189813	0.100782	44.281840
430	1	0.004786	105	0.502533	430	190243	0.100315	44.382155
418	2	0.009573	107	0.512106	836	191079	0.195032	44.577187
417	1	0.004786	108	0.516892	417	191496	0.097282	44.674469
413	1	0.004786	109	0.521678	413	191909	0.096349	44.770818
412	1	0.004786	110	0.526464	412	192321	0.096116	44.866934
410	1	0.004786	111	0.531250	410	192731	0.095649	44.962583
408	1	0.004786	112	0.536036	408	193139	0.095183	45.057766
402	1	0.004786	113	0.540822	402	193541	0.093783	45.151549
399	2	0.009573	115	0.550395	798	194339	0.186167	45.337716
395	2	0.009573	117	0.559968	790	195129	0.184300	45.522016
390	2	0.009573	119	0.569541	780	195909	0.181967	45.703983

X	FX	%FX	SUM FX	CUM %FX	FX.X	SUM FX.X	%FX.X	CUM %FX.X
389	1	0.004786	120	0.574327	389	196298	0.090750	45.794733
387	1	0.004786	121	0.579113	387	196685	0.090284	45.885017
385	1	0.004786	122	0.583899	385	197070	0.089817	45.974834
383	2	0.009573	124	0.593472	766	197836	0.178701	46.153535
378	1	0.004786	125	0.598258	378	198214	0.088184	46.241719
376	1	0.004786	126	0.603044	376	198590	0.087717	46.329436
374	1	0.004786	127	0.607830	374	198964	0.087251	46.416687
371	1	0.004786	128	0.612616	371	199335	0.086551	46.503238
370	1	0.004786	129	0.617402	370	199705	0.086318	46.589556
368	1	0.004786	130	0.622188	368	200073	0.085851	46.675407
367	1	0.004786	131	0.626974	367	200440	0.085618	46.761025
364	1	0.004786	132	0.631760	364	200804	0.084918	46.845943
351	2	0.009573	134	0.641333	702	201506	0.163771	47.009714
350	1	0.004786	135	0.646119	350	201856	0.081652	47.091366
345	1	0.004786	136	0.650905	345	202201	0.080485	47.171851
342	1	0.004786	137	0.655691	342	202543	0.079785	47.251636
340	2	0.009573	139	0.665264	680	203223	0.158638	47.410274
334	1	0.004786	140	0.670050	334	203557	0.077919	47.488193
332	1	0.004786	141	0.674836	332	203889	0.077453	47.565646
330	1	0.004786	142	0.679622	330	204219	0.076986	47.642632
326	2	0.009573	144	0.689195	652	204871	0.152106	47.794738
325	1	0.004786	145	0.693981	325	205196	0.075819	47.870557
324	3	0.014359	148	0.708340	972	206168	0.226760	48.097317
323	1	0.004786	149	0.713126	323	206491	0.075353	48.172670
322	1	0.004786	150	0.717912	322	206813	0.075120	48.247790
319	1	0.004786	151	0.722698	319	207132	0.074420	48.322210
318	1	0.004786	152	0.727484	318	207450	0.074186	48.396396
313	2	0.009573	154	0.737057	626	208076	0.146040	48.542436
312	2	0.009573	156	0.746630	624	208700	0.145574	48.688010
311	1	0.004786	157	0.751416	311	209011	0.072553	48.760563
310	1	0.004786	158	0.756202	310	209321	0.072320	48.832883
309	1	0.004786	159	0.760988	309	209630	0.072087	48.904970
307	1	0.004786	160	0.765774	307	209937	0.071620	48.976590
306	1	0.004786	161	0.770560	306	210243	0.071387	49.047977
304	1	0.004786	162	0.775346	304	210547	0.070920	49.118897
303	1	0.004786	163	0.780132	303	210850	0.070687	49.189584
301	1	0.004786	164	0.784918	301	211151	0.070220	49.259804
299	2	0.009573	166	0.794491	598	211749	0.139508	49.399312
292	1	0.004786	167	0.799277	292	212041	0.068121	49.467433
291	1	0.004786	168	0.804063	291	212332	0.067888	49.535321
290	1	0.004786	169	0.808849	290	212622	0.067654	49.602975
289	2	0.009573	171	0.818422	578	213200	0.134842	49.737817
287	1	0.004786	172	0.823208	287	213487	0.066954	49.804771
286	1	0.004786	173	0.827994	286	213773	0.066721	49.871492
285	1	0.004786	174	0.832780	285	214058	0.066488	49.937980
283	1	0.004786	175	0.837566	283	214341	0.066021	50.004001
280	3	0.014359	178	0.851925	840	215181	0.195965	50.199966
276	1	0.004786	179	0.856711	276	215457	0.064388	50.264354
274	3	0.014359	182	0.871070	822	216279	0.191766	50.456120
273	1	0.004786	183	0.875856	273	216552	0.063688	50.519808
272	1	0.004786	184	0.880642	272	216824	0.063455	50.583263
269	2	0.009573	186	0.890215	538	217362	0.125511	50.708774
268	1	0.004786	187	0.895001	268	217630	0.062522	50.771296
267	1	0.004786	188	0.899787	267	217897	0.062289	50.833585
266	1	0.004786	189	0.904573	266	218163	0.062055	50.895640
265	1	0.004786	190	0.909359	265	218428	0.061822	50.957462
262	2	0.009573	192	0.918932	524	218952	0.122245	51.079707
258	1	0.004786	193	0.923718	258	219210	0.060189	51.139896
256	5	0.023932	198	0.947650	1280	220490	0.298614	51.438510
255	1	0.004786	199	0.952436	255	220745	0.059489	51.497999
254	1	0.004786	200	0.957222	254	220999	0.059256	51.557255
253	1	0.004786	201	0.962008	253	221252	0.059022	51.616277
252	1	0.004786	202	0.966794	252	221504	0.058789	51.675066
251	2	0.009573	204	0.976367	502	222006	0.117112	51.792178
250	3	0.014359	207	0.990726	750	222756	0.174969	51.967147
249	1	0.004786	208	0.995512	249	223005	0.058089	52.025236
248	1	0.004786	209	1.000298	248	223253	0.057856	52.083092
246	1	0.004786	210	1.005084	246	223499	0.057389	52.140481
243	2	0.009573	212	1.014657	486	223985	0.113380	52.253861
242	1	0.004786	213	1.019443	242	224227	0.056456	52.310317
241	2	0.009573	215	1.029016	482	224709	0.112446	52.422763
240	1	0.004786	216	1.033802	240	224949	0.055990	52.478753
239	1	0.004786	217	1.038588	239	225188	0.055756	52.534509
238	1	0.004786	218	1.043374	238	225426	0.055523	52.590032
237	1	0.004786	219	1.048160	237	225663	0.055290	52.645322

X	FX	%FX	SUM FX	CUM %FX	FX.X	SUM FX.X	%FX.X	CUM %FX.X
235	1	0.004786	220	1.052946	235	225898	0.054823	52.700145
234	2	0.009573	222	1.062519	468	226366	0.109180	52.809325
233	1	0.004786	223	1.067305	233	226599	0.054357	52.863682
232	1	0.004786	224	1.072091	232	226831	0.054123	52.917805
230	2	0.009573	226	1.081664	460	227291	0.107314	53.025119
227	1	0.004786	227	1.086450	227	227518	0.052957	53.078076
226	1	0.004786	228	1.091236	226	227744	0.052724	53.130800
225	3	0.014359	231	1.105595	675	228419	0.157472	53.288272
224	2	0.009573	233	1.115168	448	228867	0.104514	53.392786
222	2	0.009573	235	1.124741	444	229311	0.103581	53.496367
221	1	0.004786	236	1.129527	221	229532	0.051557	53.547924
218	1	0.004786	237	1.134313	218	229750	0.050857	53.598781
217	1	0.004786	238	1.139099	217	229967	0.050624	53.649405
216	1	0.004786	239	1.143885	216	230183	0.050391	53.699796
215	2	0.009573	241	1.153458	430	230613	0.100315	53.800111
214	2	0.009573	243	1.163031	428	231041	0.099849	53.899960
213	3	0.014359	246	1.177390	639	231680	0.149073	54.049033
211	2	0.009573	248	1.186963	422	232102	0.098449	54.147482
210	2	0.009573	250	1.196536	420	232522	0.097982	54.245464
209	3	0.014359	253	1.210895	627	233149	0.146274	54.391738
207	4	0.019146	257	1.230041	828	233977	0.193165	54.584903
206	1	0.004786	258	1.234827	206	234183	0.048058	54.632961
205	2	0.009573	260	1.244400	410	234593	0.095649	54.728610
203	2	0.009573	262	1.253973	406	234999	0.094716	54.823326
202	2	0.009573	264	1.263546	404	235403	0.094250	54.917576
200	3	0.014359	267	1.277905	600	236003	0.139975	55.057551
199	1	0.004786	268	1.282691	199	236202	0.046425	55.103976
197	2	0.009573	270	1.292264	394	236596	0.091917	55.195893
196	4	0.019146	274	1.311410	784	237380	0.182901	55.378794
195	2	0.009573	276	1.320983	390	237770	0.090983	55.469777
193	4	0.019146	280	1.340129	772	238542	0.180101	55.649878
192	1	0.004786	281	1.344915	192	238734	0.044792	55.694670
191	3	0.014359	284	1.359274	573	239307	0.133676	55.828346
190	1	0.004786	285	1.364060	190	239497	0.044325	55.872671
189	1	0.004786	286	1.368846	189	239686	0.044092	55.916763
187	2	0.009573	288	1.378419	374	240060	0.087251	56.004014
186	2	0.009573	290	1.387992	372	240432	0.086784	56.090798
185	1	0.004786	291	1.392778	185	240617	0.043159	56.133957
184	4	0.019146	295	1.411924	736	241353	0.171703	56.305660
182	1	0.004786	296	1.416710	182	241535	0.042459	56.348119
181	6	0.028719	302	1.445429	1086	242621	0.253355	56.601474
180	3	0.014359	305	1.459788	540	243161	0.125977	56.727451
179	2	0.009573	307	1.469361	358	243519	0.083518	56.810969
178	1	0.004786	308	1.474147	178	243697	0.041526	56.852495
177	2	0.009573	310	1.483720	354	244051	0.082585	56.935080
176	2	0.009573	312	1.493293	352	244403	0.082118	57.017198
175	1	0.004786	313	1.498079	175	244578	0.040826	57.058024
174	3	0.014359	316	1.512438	522	245100	0.121778	57.179802
173	2	0.009573	318	1.522011	346	245446	0.080719	57.260521
172	3	0.014359	321	1.536370	516	245962	0.120378	57.380899
171	2	0.009573	323	1.545943	342	246304	0.079785	57.460684
170	4	0.019146	327	1.565089	680	246984	0.158638	57.619322
169	4	0.019146	331	1.584235	676	247660	0.157705	57.777027
168	2	0.009573	333	1.593808	336	247996	0.078386	57.855413
167	5	0.023932	338	1.617740	835	248831	0.194798	58.050211
166	4	0.019146	342	1.636886	664	249495	0.154906	58.205117
165	2	0.009573	344	1.646459	330	249825	0.076986	58.282103
164	4	0.019146	348	1.665605	656	250481	0.153039	58.435142
163	2	0.009573	350	1.675178	326	250807	0.076053	58.511195
162	1	0.004786	351	1.679964	162	250969	0.037793	58.548988
161	4	0.019146	355	1.699110	644	251613	0.150240	58.699228
160	3	0.014359	358	1.713469	480	252093	0.111980	58.811208
159	2	0.009573	360	1.723042	318	252411	0.074186	58.885394
158	3	0.014359	363	1.737401	474	252885	0.110580	58.995974
157	1	0.004786	364	1.742187	157	253042	0.036626	59.032600
156	2	0.009573	366	1.751760	312	253354	0.072787	59.105387
155	3	0.014359	369	1.766119	465	253819	0.108480	59.213867
154	1	0.004786	370	1.770905	154	253973	0.035926	59.249793
153	2	0.009573	372	1.780478	306	254279	0.071387	59.321180
152	4	0.019146	376	1.799624	608	254887	0.141841	59.463021
149	4	0.019146	380	1.818770	596	255483	0.139042	59.602063
148	3	0.014359	383	1.833129	444	255927	0.103581	59.705644
146	3	0.014359	386	1.847488	438	256365	0.102181	59.807825
145	2	0.009573	388	1.857061	290	256655	0.067654	59.875479
144	3	0.014359	391	1.871420	432	257087	0.100782	59.976261
143	8	0.038292	399	1.909712	1144	258231	0.266886	60.243147

X	FX	%FX	SUM FX	CUM %FX	FX.X	SUM FX.X	%FX.X	CUM %FX.X
142	3	0.014359	402	1.924071	426	258657	0.099382	60.342529
141	3	0.014359	405	1.938430	423	259080	0.098682	60.441211
140	2	0.009573	407	1.948003	280	259360	0.065321	60.506532
139	4	0.019146	411	1.967149	556	259916	0.129710	60.636242
138	2	0.009573	413	1.976722	276	260192	0.064388	60.700630
137	6	0.028719	419	2.005441	822	261014	0.191766	60.892396
136	2	0.009573	421	2.015014	272	261286	0.063455	60.955851
135	4	0.019146	425	2.034160	540	261826	0.125977	61.081828
134	3	0.014359	428	2.048519	402	262228	0.093783	61.175611
133	8	0.038292	436	2.086811	1064	263292	0.248222	61.423833
132	3	0.014359	439	2.101170	396	263688	0.092383	61.516216
131	1	0.004786	440	2.105956	131	263819	0.030561	61.546777
130	4	0.019146	444	2.125102	520	264339	0.121311	61.668088
129	2	0.009573	446	2.134675	258	264597	0.060189	61.728277
128	4	0.019146	450	2.153821	512	265109	0.119445	61.847722
127	4	0.019146	454	2.172967	508	265617	0.118512	61.966234
126	1	0.004786	455	2.177753	126	265743	0.029394	61.995628
125	5	0.023932	460	2.201685	625	266368	0.145807	62.141435
124	8	0.038292	468	2.239977	992	267360	0.231425	62.372860
123	2	0.009573	470	2.249550	246	267606	0.057389	62.430249
122	3	0.014359	473	2.263909	366	267972	0.085384	62.515633
121	4	0.019146	477	2.283055	484	268456	0.112913	62.628546
120	6	0.028719	483	2.311774	720	269176	0.167970	62.796516
119	3	0.014359	486	2.326133	357	269533	0.083285	62.879801
118	1	0.004786	487	2.330919	118	269651	0.027528	62.907329
117	2	0.009573	489	2.340492	234	269885	0.054590	62.961919
116	4	0.019146	493	2.359638	464	270349	0.108247	63.070166
115	4	0.019146	497	2.378784	460	270809	0.107314	63.177480
114	6	0.028719	503	2.407503	684	271493	0.159571	63.337051
113	1	0.004786	504	2.412289	113	271606	0.026362	63.363413
112	6	0.028719	510	2.441008	672	272278	0.156772	63.520185
111	4	0.019146	514	2.460154	444	272722	0.103581	63.623766
110	7	0.033505	521	2.493659	770	273492	0.179634	63.803400
109	8	0.038292	529	2.531951	872	274364	0.203430	64.006830
108	4	0.019146	533	2.551097	432	274796	0.100782	64.107612
107	7	0.033505	540	2.584602	749	275545	0.174735	64.282347
106	6	0.028719	546	2.613321	636	276181	0.148373	64.430720
105	6	0.028719	552	2.642040	630	276811	0.146974	64.577694
104	6	0.028719	558	2.670759	624	277435	0.145574	64.723268
103	4	0.019146	562	2.689905	412	277847	0.096116	64.819384
102	4	0.019146	566	2.709051	408	278255	0.095183	64.914567
101	6	0.028719	572	2.737770	606	278861	0.141375	65.055942
100	13	0.062224	585	2.799994	1300	280161	0.303279	65.359221
99	7	0.033505	592	2.833499	693	280854	0.161671	65.520892
98	6	0.028719	598	2.862218	588	281442	0.137175	65.658067
97	9	0.043078	607	2.905296	873	282315	0.203664	65.861731
96	8	0.038292	615	2.943588	768	283083	0.179168	66.040899
95	7	0.033505	622	2.977093	665	283748	0.155139	66.196038
94	7	0.033505	629	3.010598	658	284406	0.153506	66.349544
93	6	0.028719	635	3.039317	558	284964	0.130177	66.479721
92	6	0.028719	641	3.068036	552	285516	0.128777	66.608498
91	4	0.019146	645	3.087182	364	285880	0.084918	66.693416
90	4	0.019146	649	3.106328	360	286240	0.083985	66.777401
89	12	0.057438	661	3.163766	1068	287308	0.249156	67.026557
88	8	0.038292	669	3.202058	704	288012	0.164237	67.190794
87	9	0.043078	678	3.245136	783	288795	0.182667	67.373461
86	10	0.047865	688	3.293001	860	289655	0.200631	67.574092
85	9	0.043078	697	3.336079	765	290420	0.178468	67.752560
84	6	0.028719	703	3.364798	504	290924	0.117579	67.870139
83	10	0.047865	713	3.412663	830	291754	0.193632	68.063771
82	7	0.033505	720	3.446168	574	292328	0.133909	68.197680
81	8	0.038292	728	3.484460	648	292976	0.151173	68.348853
80	10	0.047865	738	3.532325	800	293776	0.186633	68.535486
79	13	0.062224	751	3.594549	1027	294803	0.239591	68.775077
78	12	0.057438	763	3.651987	936	295739	0.218361	68.993438
77	7	0.033505	770	3.685492	539	296278	0.125744	69.119182
76	6	0.028719	776	3.714211	456	296734	0.106381	69.225563
75	8	0.038292	784	3.752503	600	297334	0.139975	69.365538
74	9	0.043078	793	3.795581	666	298000	0.155372	69.520910
73	12	0.057438	805	3.853019	876	298876	0.204363	69.725273
72	14	0.067011	819	3.920030	1008	299884	0.235158	69.960431
71	9	0.043078	828	3.963108	639	300523	0.149073	70.109504
70	8	0.038292	836	4.001400	560	301083	0.130643	70.240147
69	15	0.071797	851	4.073197	1035	302118	0.241457	70.481604

X	FX	%FX	SUM FX	CUM %FX	FX.X	SUM FX.X	%FX.X	CUM %FX.X
68	17	0.081370	868	4.154567	1156	303274	0.269685	70.751289
67	10	0.047865	878	4.202432	670	303944	0.156305	70.907594
66	8	0.038292	886	4.240724	528	304472	0.123178	71.030772
65	20	0.095730	906	4.336454	1300	305772	0.303279	71.334051
64	10	0.047865	916	4.384319	640	306412	0.149307	71.483358
63	14	0.067011	930	4.451330	882	307294	0.205763	71.689121
62	23	0.110089	953	4.561419	1426	308720	0.332674	72.021795
61	20	0.095730	973	4.657149	1220	309940	0.284616	72.306411
60	11	0.052651	984	4.709800	660	310600	0.153972	72.460383
59	12	0.057438	996	4.767238	708	311308	0.165170	72.625553
58	15	0.071797	1011	4.839035	870	312178	0.202964	72.828517
57	13	0.062224	1024	4.901259	741	312919	0.172869	73.001386
56	28	0.134022	1052	5.035281	1568	314487	0.365802	73.367188
55	16	0.076584	1068	5.111865	880	315367	0.205297	73.572485
54	10	0.047865	1078	5.159730	540	315907	0.125977	73.698462
53	21	0.100516	1099	5.260246	1113	317020	0.259654	73.958116
52	27	0.129236	1126	5.389482	1404	318424	0.327542	74.285658
51	20	0.095730	1146	5.485212	1020	319444	0.237958	74.523616
50	25	0.119663	1171	5.604875	1250	320694	0.291615	74.815231
49	25	0.119663	1196	5.724538	1225	321919	0.285782	75.101013
48	23	0.110089	1219	5.834627	1104	323023	0.257554	75.358567
47	25	0.119663	1244	5.954290	1175	324198	0.274118	75.632685
46	31	0.148382	1275	6.102672	1426	325624	0.332674	75.965359
45	33	0.157955	1308	6.260627	1485	327109	0.346438	76.311797
44	31	0.148382	1339	6.409009	1364	328473	0.318210	76.630007
43	31	0.148382	1370	6.557391	1333	329806	0.310978	76.940985
42	33	0.157955	1403	6.715346	1386	331192	0.323342	77.264327
41	28	0.134022	1431	6.849368	1148	332340	0.267819	77.532146
40	34	0.162741	1465	7.012109	1360	333700	0.317277	77.849423
39	33	0.157955	1498	7.170064	1287	334987	0.300247	78.149670
38	33	0.157955	1531	7.328019	1254	336241	0.292548	78.442218
37	25	0.119663	1556	7.447682	925	337166	0.215795	78.658013
36	38	0.181887	1594	7.629569	1368	338534	0.319143	78.977156
35	42	0.201033	1636	7.830602	1470	340004	0.342939	79.320095
34	38	0.181887	1674	8.012489	1292	341296	0.301413	79.621508
33	56	0.268045	1730	8.280534	1848	343144	0.431123	80.052631
32	41	0.196247	1771	8.476781	1312	344456	0.306079	80.358710
31	39	0.186674	1810	8.663455	1209	345665	0.282050	80.640760
30	57	0.272831	1867	8.936286	1710	347375	0.398929	81.039689
29	48	0.229753	1915	9.166039	1392	348767	0.324742	81.364431
28	60	0.287191	1975	9.453230	1680	350447	0.391930	81.756361
27	53	0.253685	2028	9.706915	1431	351878	0.333841	82.090202
26	67	0.320696	2095	10.027611	1742	353620	0.406395	82.496597
25	61	0.291977	2156	10.319588	1525	355145	0.355770	82.852367
24	83	0.397281	2239	10.716869	1992	357137	0.464718	83.317085
23	67	0.320696	2306	11.037565	1541	358678	0.359503	83.676588
22	86	0.411640	2392	11.449205	1892	360570	0.441388	84.117976
21	108	0.516944	2500	11.966149	2268	362838	0.529106	84.647082
20	89	0.426000	2589	12.392149	1780	364618	0.415260	85.062342
19	109	0.521730	2698	12.913879	2071	366689	0.483148	85.545490
18	120	0.574382	2818	13.488261	2160	368849	0.503911	86.049401
17	116	0.555236	2934	14.043497	1972	370821	0.460052	86.509453
16	123	0.588742	3057	14.632239	1968	372789	0.459119	86.968572
15	154	0.737124	3211	15.369363	2310	375099	0.538904	87.507476
14	171	0.818495	3382	16.187858	2394	377493	0.558501	88.065977
13	191	0.914225	3573	17.102083	2483	379976	0.579264	88.645241
12	218	1.043461	3791	18.145544	2616	382592	0.610292	89.255533
11	231	1.105686	4022	19.251230	2541	385133	0.592795	89.848328
10	278	1.330652	4300	20.581882	2780	387913	0.648552	90.496880
9	332	1.589125	4632	22.171007	2988	390901	0.697077	91.193957
8	385	1.842810	5017	24.013817	3080	393981	0.718539	91.912496
7	482	2.307103	5499	26.320920	3374	397355	0.787127	92.699623
6	586	2.804901	6085	29.125821	3516	400871	0.820255	93.519878
5	799	3.824430	6884	32.950251	3995	404866	0.932002	94.451880
4	1100	5.265173	7984	38.215424	4400	409266	1.026485	95.478365
3	1713	8.199310	9697	46.414734	5139	414405	1.198888	96.677253
2	3047	14.584529	12744	60.999263	6094	420499	1.421682	98.098935
1	8148	39.000574	20892	99.999837	8148	428647	1.900864	99.999799

Word Frequencies in Rank Order

(See also "Alphabetical List of Word Frequencies," I, xxxv)

THE (OMITTED)

THE (OMITTED)	28754	GOD	689	FAME	351	SOFT	255
AND (OMITTED)	16510	ARMS	676	LAST	351	KNOW	254
TO (OMITTED)	9900	EYES	653	NAME	350	STOOD	253
OF (OMITTED)	8073	THEE	641	SKIES	345	MIGHTY	252
IN (OMITTED)	6650	MAN	634	ITS (OMITTED)	342	ALONG	251
HIS (OMITTED)	6383	DAY	632	AROUND	340	FOE	251
WITH (OMITTED)	5627	HEAV'N	632	THEM (OMITTED)	340	AGE	250
A (OMITTED)	4917	STILL	613	GROUND	334	LOST	250
HE (OMITTED)	3381	CAN (OMITTED)	597	POW'R	332	NEXT	250
FROM (OMITTED)	2975	WHOSE (OMITTED)	597	SACRED	330	ACHILLES	249
ALL	2871	JOVE	587	AIR	326	GREECE	248
MY (OMITTED)	2757	THOSE (OMITTED)	578	FAR	326	STATE	246
BUT (OMITTED)	2672	SUCH	577	MEN	325	GAVE	243
ON (OMITTED)	2592	FIRST	568	FULL	324	LAND	243
THY	2516	GODS	560	REST	324	SHADE	242
OR (OMITTED)	2339	VAIN	557	TROY	324	SIDE	241
THEIR (OMITTED)	2287	EV'RY	555	RISE	323	SIRE	241
HER (OMITTED)	2201	AN (OMITTED)	546	EVER	322	SONS	240
THAT (OMITTED)	2177	HOW (OMITTED)	544	OLD	319	DOWN	239
AS	2107	HERE (OMITTED)	529	FORCE	318	PRIDE	238
FOR (OMITTED)	2094	LONG	527	ALONE	313	WIT	237
I (OMITTED)	1972	SON	518	WILL (OMITTED)	313	TEARS	235
BY (OMITTED)	1969	HAND	516	BLOOD	312	EYE	234
THIS (OMITTED)	1629	FATE	515	LAY	312	MADE	234
NOT (OMITTED)	1547	HIGH	512	NIGHT	311	TROJAN	233
THEN (OMITTED)	1537	WHICH (OMITTED)	497	FALL	310	GOLD	232
AT (OMITTED)	1530	SOUL	495	JUST	309	MUCH	230
THEY (OMITTED)	1449	FAIR	492	HECTOR	307	SELF	230
WHAT (OMITTED)	1428	MAY (OMITTED)	489	HEAR	306	SPREAD	227
NOW (OMITTED)	1376	SEE	480	FIGHT	304	ONLY	226
NO	1359	OH	459	DEAD	303	BRIGHT	225
OUR (OMITTED)	1327	TIS	458	SAY	301	PLACE	225
IS (OMITTED)	1302	WAR	457	DIVINE	299	STAND	225
THUS (OMITTED)	1286	LOVE	450	EV'N	299	HAS (OMITTED)	224
SHALL (OMITTED)	1259	ONCE	444	TWO	292	PRAISE	224
SO	1245	BEFORE	441	BOLD	291	FRIENDS	222
TH'	1216	ROUND	434	QUEEN	290	TAKE	222
WHEN (OMITTED)	1206	OWN	432	GRACE	289	THOUGHT	221
WHO (OMITTED)	1203	CARE	430	SPOKE	289	SLAIN	218
BE (OMITTED)	1193	KING	418	BENEATH	287	WORDS	217
YOUR (OMITTED)	1062	TOO (OMITTED)	418	MAIN	286	FEAR	216
HIM (OMITTED)	1014	TILL	417	LORD	285	POW'RS	215
MORE	987	WHOM (OMITTED)	413	GOOD	283	VOICE	215
NOR (OMITTED)	987	HEART	412	BEAR	280	FACE	214
YOU (OMITTED)	965	YE	410	GODDESS	280	FIRE	214
IT (OMITTED)	937	FRIEND	408	HAVE (OMITTED)	280	MAKE	213
IF (OMITTED)	935	WAY	402	SWIFT	276	SIGHT	213
SHE (OMITTED)	929	RACE	399	AWAY	274	WISE	213
O'ER	901	THAN	399	EARTH	274	COULD (OMITTED)	211
YET (OMITTED)	895	PLAIN	395	PROUD	274	WIDE	211
ME (OMITTED)	893	WELL	395	GIVE	273	NATIVE	210
WAS (OMITTED)	871	DEATH	390	FIELD	272	SHOULD (OMITTED)	210
THOU	865	TRAIN	390	NEVER	269	NATURE	209
WE (OMITTED)	856	WERE (OMITTED)	389	YOUTH	269	PRINCE	209
SOME	844	HEAD	387	NEW	268	VIEW	209
THESE (OMITTED)	839	RAGE	385	LIGHT	267	AH	207
ONE	811	HAD (OMITTED)	383	BRAVE	266	BLEST	207
ARE (OMITTED)	800	ULYSSES	383	FIERCE	265	LIES	207
GREAT	795	LIFE	378	DEEP	262	SOON	207
WHERE (OMITTED)	780	THO' (OMITTED)	376	JOY	262	DREADFUL	206
LIKE	765	SHORE	374	FLIES	258	KIND	206
LET	746	MUST	371	ABOVE	256	DEAR	205
THRO'	743	MIND	370	FLY	256	ARM	203
EACH	740	SAID	368	HANDS	256	MORTAL	203
WHILE	733	CHIEF	367	US (OMITTED)	256	GO	202
THERE (OMITTED)	724	BREAST	364	WHY (OMITTED)	256	WHOLE	202

Word	#	Word	#	Word	#	Word	#
ART	200	HASTE	154	FOES	121	LABOURS	100
GLORY	200	IMMORTAL	153	LINE	121	PERHAPS	100
GREEKS	200	MAID	153	SAVE	121	SUNK	100
FIELDS	199	GRIEF	152	BROAD	120	SWAY	100
OUT	197	HERO	152	FLEET	120	TOIL	100
SAD	197	STRENGTH	152	OFT	120	WOOD	100
CAME	196	THINK	152	REPLIES	120	DESCENDS	99
EQUAL	196	COAST	149	SHINING	120	FOOL	99
FATHER	196	HUMAN	149	STAY	120	GREEN	99
STRONG	196	NEAR	149	BOSOM	119	LIE	99
CAUSE	195	TURN	149	PLEASE	119	STREAM	99
SENSE	195	BACK	148	SHAME	119	TURN'D	99
BORN	193	TRUE	148	FATHER'S	118	WANT	99
COURT	193	UPON	148	GORE	117	LEARN	98
HALF	193	HONOURS	146	SIR	117	PROVE	98
PART	193	PLEAS'D	146	BRING	116	SHOU'D (OMITTED)	98
BEHOLD	192	WORD	146	FATES	116	SONG	98
SILVER	191	BEHIND	145	SHORT	116	STREAMS	98
WALLS	191	YOUNG	145	WINDS	116	VAST	98
WOES	191	BOUND	144	DUE	115	FEET	97
CRIES	190	CARES	144	GAIN	115	HEAV'NS	97
GOLDEN	189	SLEEP	144	PALE	115	LOW	97
CALL	187	CAR	143	WINE	115	PASS	97
MOST	187	CRY'D	143	BETTER	114	REASON	97
RICH	186	DIE	143	COURSERS	114	ROLL	97
WITHOUT	186	FLIGHT	143	INSTANT	114	SWEET	97
RISING	185	GLORIOUS	143	LOFTY	114	THOUSAND	97
BEST	184	ILL	143	MANKIND	114	TOUCH'D	97
DAYS	184	INTO (OMITTED)	143	PLEASING	114	BEND	96
PAST	184	RAISE	143	BEGAN	113	LIMBS	96
ROYAL	184	DISTANT	142	AMPLE	112	ROLL'D	96
PRIZE	182	HAPPY	142	GIFTS	112	SPRUNG	96
AID	181	WIFE	142	GRAVE	112	TRUST	96
CHARMS	181	AJAX	141	PREY	112	WHITE	96
FORM	181	REIGN	141	SAGE	112	WORK	96
SINCE	181	SHIPS	141	SECRET	112	WRETCH	96
SURE	181	SATE	140	COU'D (OMITTED)	111	FAITHFUL	95
YEARS	181	THREE	140	SEEN	111	HELL	95
FORTH	180	CLOUDS	139	SHINE	111	LIVES	95
SUN	180	E'ER	139	THICK	111	SHOOK	95
TIME	180	NONE	139	BOAST	110	SLOW	95
HEARD	179	SHIELD	139	HEAPS	110	TEN	95
UP	179	SILENT	138	MOTHER	110	URG'D	95
WOULD (OMITTED)	178	VENGEANCE	138	REPLY'D	110	AMIDST	94
COME	177	AGAINST	137	RUN	110	BEARS	94
TREMBLING	177	BLACK	137	TOOK	110	BEAUTEOUS	94
DID (AUXILIARY)	176	EASE	137	WILD	110	HATE	94
END	176	FLAMES	137	DART	109	HELD	94
DUST	175	PALLAS	137	DOME	109	KNEW	94
BORE	174	SOUND	137	FREE	109	SABLE	94
FURY	174	COURSE	136	OTHERS	109	AM (OMITTED)	93
MONARCH	174	SAFE	136	PATROCLUS	109	ATRIDES	93
FEAST	173	BAND	135	PHOEBUS	109	BRAZEN	93
LEFT	173	GIVES	135	TAUGHT	109	DESCEND	93
FOUND	172	LATE	135	WAVES	109	ORDER	93
GRECIAN	172	PEACE	135	FALLS	108	PLEASURE	93
OTHER	172	HEAV'NLY	134	PURPLE	108	FLED	92
AGAIN	171	O	134	SEEK	108	GUIDE	92
SPEAR	171	SEA	134	SHORES	108	HOPES	92
ETERNAL	170	WALL	134	FURIOUS	107	JOYS	92
FIND	170	APPEAR	133	MUSE	107	TROJANS	92
LO	170	CHIEFS	133	PLAC'D	107	WRATH	92
SHADES	170	DIRE	133	REALMS	107	BID	91
HOST	169	SCARCE	133	SCENE	107	BODY	91
MIGHT (OMITTED)	169	SUDDEN	133	THINGS	107	RAIS'D	91
MINE (OMITTED)	169	VARIOUS	133	WRETCHED	107	WRITE	91
WOUND	169	YIELD	133	BANDS	106	LIVING	90
HIMSELF	168	GUEST	132	LITTLE	106	NOBLE	90
LED	168	KNOWN	132	SEAT	106	PRAY'R	90
ATTEND	167	OBEY	132	THUNDER	106	SING	90
BED	167	RETURN	131	TONGUE	106	FAITH	89
BELOW	167	ALAS	130	TROOPS	106	FOOLS	89
SAW	167	FIX'D	130	CALLS	105	HAD	89
THINE	167	MARTIAL	130	CHARIOT	105	LEAST	89
FELL	166	TURNS	130	KEEP	105	PASSION	89
SKY	166	TOILS	129	STRETCH'D	105	PIERC'D	89
STANDS	166	TWAS	129	UNKNOWN	105	PRESENT	89
WOE	166	FLEW	128	WOU'D (OMITTED)	105	SHOW	89
ROSE	165	FLOW	128	APPEARS	104	SOUGHT	89
STERN	165	GENTLE	128	GUARD	104	THENCE	89
LESS	164	LANCE	128	LEAVE	104	UNHAPPY	89
LOV'D	164	BREATH	127	MEET	104	YON'	89
MANY	164	CAST	127	SPEAK	104	BLOW	88
TELL	164	FLAME	127	WITHIN	104	CROWN	88
BOTH	163	SEAS	127	CEASE	103	HONOUR'D	88
GEN'ROUS	163	SWORD	126	COUNTRY	103	HOUSE	88
CROWN'D	162	FIRES	125	DARK	103	OCEAN	88
BOW	161	HENCE	125	PAIN	103	ROCKS	88
HAVE	161	MOVE	125	JOIN	102	SPRING	88
STEEDS	161	POOR	125	PALACE	102	WISDOM	88
WORLD	161	SHARE	125	SPEED	102	BIDS	87
CLOSE	160	ARTS	124	WIND	102	DAUGHTER	87
HEROES	160	DREAD	124	BROTHER	101	HOME	87
LIVE	160	FUTURE	124	LAWS	101	NYMPH	87
COMMAND	159	HOPE	124	LOOK	101	PREPARE	87
EAR	159	SENT	124	MAKES	101	RADIANT	87
HOUR	158	TOWN	124	STRANGER	101	SEND	87
RIGHT	158	TRUTH	124	WAIT	101	STONE	87
SAME	158	WARRIOR	124	ANCIENT	100	TEAR	87
LOUD	157	DAME	123	ARISE	100	HILLS	86
VIRTUE	157	WINGS	123	ART (VERB)	100	NE'ER	86
LENGTH	156	FLOOD	122	GATES	100	PEERS	86
KINGS	155	GAY	122	GIV'N	100	SEES	86
THRONE	155	TENDER	122	HONOUR	100	SEIZ'D	86
WILL	155	DREW	121	JOVE'S	100	SIGHS	86

SILENCE	86	PEOPLE	74	LEARN'D	65	FRESH	58
SORROWS	86	ROAR	74	MARK	65	GALES	58
SPRINGS	86	TWELVE	74	PARTS	65	MOTHER'S	58
WEALTH	86	VICTOR	74	PORT	65	OBEY'D	58
BEHELD	85	COUNTRY'S	73	RAGING	65	RECEIV'D	58
DY'D	85	ENDS	73	RAPID	65	RUSHING	58
EARLY	85	FED	73	RULES	65	SHAKE	58
EMBRACE	85	GATE	73	RUSH	65	SHINES	58
MEAN	85	ILION	73	SAVAGE	65	SOULS	58
MORNING	85	LYE	73	SECOND	65	SPACIOUS	58
NATIONS	85	MAN'S	73	TEACH	65	TWICE	58
T'	85	PITY	73	TOLD	65	VIEWS	58
TOW'RS	85	REV'REND	73	BEGUN	64	DOES (AUXILIARY)	57
BIRTH	84	WITS	73	BURNS	64	HAIL	57
COLD	84	WONDER	73	FEW	64	HARD	57
EMPLOY	84	WOUNDS	73	GUILTY	64	HOLY	57
FATAL	84	ACHILLES'	72	LEST	64	INSPIRE	57
HUNG	84	AWFUL	72	MOVES	64	ISLE	57
KNOWS	84	DARE	72	PREST	64	READY	57
ALIKE	83	FAST	72	RECEIVE	64	SHALT	57
CELESTIAL	83	GRAC'D	72	SHIP	64	SHUN	57
DELIGHT	83	LOVES	72	WHATE'ER	64	THOUGHTS	57
DOOM	83	MARS	72	ADDRESS	63	VENUS	57
LARGE	83	PLAINS	72	APPEAR'D	63	WAT'RY	57
NESTOR	83	RED	72	ATTENDS	63	WHENCE	57
NUMBERS	83	STRIFE	72	BEEN (OMITTED)	63	ABODES	56
READ	83	SWAIN	72	ERE	63	ABSENT	56
WATERS	83	TRY	72	GIFT	63	AMID	56
WORKS	83	VOWS	72	MINERVA	63	BLUE	56
BLAZE	82	WARRIORS	72	MOV'D	63	BREAK	56
BOWL	82	BLESS	71	REVENGE	63	BRED	56
CONQUEST	82	BLOODY	71	SPOILS	63	BRINGS	56
FRAME	82	DIVIDE	71	SPOUSE	63	CALM	56
HECTOR'S	82	FLOCKS	71	STARS	63	CREW	56
ROCK	82	GLORIES	71	THRICE	63	ENVY	56
STRAIT	82	HAS	71	WING	63	FILLS	56
COMMON	81	STEPS	71	BLIND	62	GODLIKE	56
DEED	81	STRAIN	71	BRASS	62	HEIR	56
DIES	81	VERSE	71	COUNSELS	62	HERO'S	56
FLYING	81	WASTE	71	DARKNESS	62	HUGE	56
MOUNTAINS	81	BATTEL	70	EMPTY	62	LAYS	56
RESOUND	81	CEAS'D	70	FIT	62	MILD	56
SPACE	81	DOOM'D	70	GRANT	62	PIOUS	56
TELEMACHUS	81	GLITT'RING	70	GROW	62	POET	56
ANOTHER	80	GREEK	70	HORSE	62	RUSH'D	56
EVERY	80	PURSUE	70	LOAD	62	SEEM	56
FEEL	80	REMAINS	70	MARBLE	62	SMOOTH	56
GLOOMY	80	ANY	69	MORN	62	SUITORS	56
JOIN'D	80	BLEED	69	NEPTUNE	62	TEMPEST	56
MANLY	80	FIR'D	69	POUR	62	TIMES	56
MOURN	80	GOD-LIKE	69	QUIT	62	TOMB	56
PAY	80	HEADS	69	RETURN'D	62	TREAD	56
PENSIVE	80	HIDE	69	SUNG	62	VERY	56
PLAY	80	MOURNFUL	69	TALE	62	ADORN	55
TASTE	80	REMAIN	69	TENT	62	APPROACH	55
CALL'D	79	RENOWN'D	69	URGE	62	BEAT	55
CLAIM	79	ROLLS	69	VALIANT	62	DEBATE	55
DOGS	79	SHONE	69	VIEW'D	62	ENOUGH	55
FEARS	79	TREES	69	WENT	62	FILL	55
FOND	79	VIRGIN	69	CONSTANT	61	FLOODS	55
HUNDRED	79	WISH	69	DEMANDS	61	GROAN	55
IMPERIAL	79	WOODS	69	DONE	61	HOURS	55
LAID	79	BETWEEN	68	DRAWS	61	KNIGHT	55
RULE	79	CHARGE	68	DROVE	61	NYMPHS	55
SCORN	79	COMBATE	68	EY'D	61	PANTING	55
SLAVE	79	COMES	68	FOOD	61	RESTORE	55
WAVE	79	DANCE	68	HEARS	61	SKILL'D	55
ASK	78	FORMS	68	MATCHLESS	61	SNATCH'D	55
COMMANDS	78	HEARTS	68	RUIN	61	VESSELS	55
ENGAGE	78	HONEST	68	SEEM'D	61	ABOUT	54
FORTUNE	78	LABOUR	68	SIGH	61	BOUNDS	54
I'LL	78	MIGHT	68	SORROW	61	CROWD	54
MASTER	78	NINE	68	STORM	61	DOUBT	54
RANKS	78	NOTHING	68	TAKES	61	GROVE	54
RAY	78	POURS	68	TASK	61	GUARDIAN	54
RITES	78	SEIZE	68	THING	61	LOSE	54
SUPERIOR	78	SHAKES	68	ULYSSES'	61	SLAUGHTER	54
VESSEL	78	WEAK	68	WEIGHT	61	THIRST	54
WRONG	78	WORTH	68	WOMAN	61	TREMBLE	54
BESIDE	77	ALREADY	67	DECREED	60	ASCEND	53
DULNESS	77	CLEAR	67	DESCENDING	60	BLISS	53
FELT	77	DULL	67	FOOT	60	CONTENT	53
HOSTILE	77	DYING	67	FRONT	60	COURAGE	53
STEEL	77	FRIENDLY	67	JAVELIN	60	DEEDS	53
SURVEY	77	REPAIR	67	LEAVES	60	EXTENDED	53
YEAR	77	SOUNDING	67	PAID	60	HALL	53
DO	76	STORE	67	RESIGN'D	60	HOLD	53
FOREIGN	76	THRONG	67	SAILS	60	HUNGER	53
GRATEFUL	76	TOUCH	67	SET	60	JUDGE	53
HAST	76	ARMIES	66	TYDIDES	60	MAD	53
LEAD	76	BESTOW	66	BOARD	59	OPEN	53
SECURE	76	HEIGHT	66	CANNOT (OMITTED)	59	PRINCES	53
BEAUTY	75	SOLEMN	66	DESTIN'D	59	REACH	53
CLOUD	75	SPARE	66	EAGER	59	REFULGENT	53
COUNCIL	75	SPREADS	66	GEN'RAL	59	SHOULDERS	53
DRAW	75	WEAPON	66	HOARY	59	SOLID	53
POINT	75	YOUTHFUL	66	HOSTS	59	SOUNDS	53
SHED	75	ACT	65	MORTALS	59	SWEAR	53
SPIRIT	75	DARTS	65	MOUNTAIN	59	TROD	53
WARM	75	EARS	65	STORMS	59	VICE	53
BROKE	74	EITHER	65	USE	59	BANQUET	52
CIRCLE	74	FORM'D	65	WORTHY	59	BOW'R	52
FAM'D	74	GENIAL	65	BROUGHT	58	CHILDREN	52
HAIR	74	HAUGHTY	65	CITY	58	EUMAEUS	52
OFF	74	LEADS	65	DESTROY	58	FLOW'RY	52

Word		Word		Word		Word	
GLOWS	52	MET	48	COUNSEL	44	ITHACA	41
GREW	52	NECK	48	DARING	44	LINES	41
HEAV'N'S	52	PARIS	48	DECLARE	44	NAMES	41
HOLLOW	52	POINTED	48	DROP	44	NATURE'S	41
INFANT	52	PUBLICK	48	FALSE	44	NUM'ROUS	41
MERIT	52	SHOT	48	FOAMING	44	PARENTS	41
MINGLED	52	SPEARS	48	FORESTS	44	PRIAM	41
MOUNT	52	SWELL	48	FORGOT	44	SHOULDER	41
POMP	52	TREE	48	GONE	44	SINKS	41
PRESS'D	52	VENGEFUL	48	HEAV'D	44	STEP	41
PURE	52	ADVANCE	47	HERDS	44	UNDER	41
REALM	52	ALOUD	47	HILL	44	WINGED	41
RESIGN	52	BLOOMING	47	LIFTS	44	ARROW	40
ROLLING	52	CONVEY	47	LIV'D	44	BOUNDLESS	40
SHOUTS	52	DESIRE	47	PHRYGIAN	44	BRIDAL	40
SINK	52	FLAMING	47	PREPAR'D	44	BRIDE	40
SMALL	52	GROVES	47	PROMIS'D	44	CHAINS	40
STRAND	52	IMPATIENT	47	REPLY	44	CHANCE	40
THREW	52	LONGER	47	RETREAT	44	CHARIOTS	40
TRANSPORT	52	MAJESTIC	47	SINGS	44	CHEEK	40
VILE	52	MODEST	47	SLAVES	44	CONTEND	40
VULGAR	52	PERISH	47	SPEAKS	44	CURSE	40
ALARMS	51	PRAY	47	SUSTAIN	44	DREAM	40
AZURE	51	REAR	47	WAITS	44	EASY	40
BARD	51	RING	47	WEIGHTY	44	HELP	40
COURTS	51	SCENES	47	ARM'D	43	IMAGE	40
DARES	51	SLEW	47	BAY	43	IMPIOUS	40
DEFEND	51	SPARTAN	47	BLAZING	43	JUNO	40
DOOR	51	STRUCK	47	BOUNDING	43	LORDS	40
EM	51	SUIT	47	CHILD	43	LOVELY	40
GAZE	51	SURVEY'D	47	CHURCH	43	MONSTER	40
HEAVY	51	THUND'RING	47	DENY'D	43	NOD	40
HUMBLE	51	TRIUMPH	47	DESIGN	43	PASSAGE	40
MOMENT	51	WARMS	47	DISPLAY'D	43	PASSIONS	40
POETS	51	WHETHER	47	EXTENDS	43	PRIAM'S	40
POND'ROUS	51	AGES	46	FIX	43	PRIEST	40
REPOSE	51	BARK	46	GIANT	43	ROOF	40
TALL	51	BREAD	46	INSPIRES	43	SINGLE	40
TORE	51	CERTAIN	46	JAV'LIN	43	SMILE	40
VEIL	51	CRY	46	LOOK'D	43	STAGE	40
WANTS	51	DANGER	46	NIGH	43	SWELLS	40
WARS	51	DISTANCE	46	PROSTRATE	43	TORN	40
BENDS	50	DOUBTFUL	46	PURSU'D	43	TUMULT	40
BILLOWS	50	ELSE	46	RAYS	43	WEEPING	40
BOY	50	FLOW'RS	46	REJOIN'D	43	WIVES	40
BROW	50	GENIUS	46	RESTOR'D	43	WRAPT	40
DECREE	50	ILION'S	46	ROARS	43	ALIVE	39
DESPAIR	50	INGLORIOUS	46	SISTER	43	BEAM	39
FEMALE	50	KEPT	46	SLAUGHTER'D	43	BESTOW'D	39
FIERY	50	MIDST	46	SMILING	43	BLEEDING	39
FORBEAR	50	MIX'D	46	STATELY	43	BLOWS	39
GLOW	50	MUTUAL	46	SUPPLIES	43	CAVE	39
HEADLONG	50	OPPREST	46	TREASURES	43	DISDAIN	39
HOSPITABLE	50	POET'S	46	TRIUMPHANT	43	HELM	39
KNEES	50	REACH'D	46	VICTIM	43	HORRID	39
LAW	50	RURAL	46	WAND'RING	43	HUSBAND	39
MUSES	50	SACRIFICE	46	ADMIRE	42	ILLUSTRIOUS	39
NAKED	50	SCATTER'D	46	AENEAS	42	LIQUID	39
NAVY	50	SENDS	46	AIRY	42	LIST'NING	39
OUGHT	50	STROKE	46	ALMIGHTY	42	MIX	39
PAINS	50	SUPPLIANT	46	AMONG	42	MOVING	39
SHIELDS	50	THEMSELVES	46	BREATHLESS	42	OBEDIENT	39
STRETCH	50	THUNDERS	46	BROTHERS	42	ORB	39
SWELLING	50	VEST	46	BURST	42	PLUNG'D	39
WON	50	VICTIMS	46	CIRCLING	42	POUR'D	39
WOND'ROUS	50	WATRY	46	CUT	42	PRESS	39
WOUNDED	50	ARMOUR	45	DYE	42	PRONE	39
ALTARS	49	BEAMS	45	ENJOY	42	RELATE	39
ALWAYS	49	BLED	45	FORC'D	42	RETIRES	39
BURN	49	BLESSING	45	FRAGRANT	42	SERVE	39
CHANGE	49	BRAIN	45	FRUITFUL	42	SHADY	39
DISPLAY	49	BREATHE	45	GROANS	42	SHOW'R	39
DOUBLE	49	COPIOUS	45	HAPLESS	42	STARRY	39
DROPS	49	DEEPS	45	INSPIR'D	42	SURROUND	39
FILL'D	49	DEMAND	45	LEARNING	42	SYLVAN	39
FIRM	49	DREST	45	LIFTED	42	TRY'D	39
FLOWS	49	DRIVES	45	PEACEFUL	42	WORST	39
GHOST	49	GRACEFUL	45	POLISH'D	42	WRIT	39
LANDS	49	HEROE	45	PRAY'RS	42	WRONGS	39
LYCIAN	49	IMPETUOUS	45	SEEMS	42	ACTS	38
NAY	49	JUSTICE	45	SIGN	42	ANGRY	38
OFFSPRING	49	LAB'RING	45	SINCERE	42	ANGUISH	38
RETURNS	49	MOUNTS	45	SOV'REIGN	42	ANSWER	38
RIVAL	49	PACE	45	SPOIL	42	APPROACHING	38
SAIL	49	PAINTED	45	STRANGE	42	ARRAY	38
SIX	49	POLE	45	WATCH	42	BEYOND	38
SPEECH	49	PRUDENT	45	WHATEVER	42	BIRDS	38
STRIKE	49	REWARD	45	YIELDS	42	BLEEDS	38
SUPPLY	49	ROUGH	45	YON	42	COVER'D	38
TOST	49	SIT	45	AFTER	41	DECAY	38
TROY'S	49	SKILL	45	BAD	41	DECENT	38
TYRANT	49	SOCIAL	45	BEAST	41	DELAY	38
BASE	48	SOIL	45	BIRD	41	DOST	38
BENT	48	TYDE	45	BRAVEST	41	EAT	38
BLAME	48	UNSEEN	45	BREATH'D	41	GENTLY	38
BURNING	48	WEEP	45	CLOS'D	41	GREATER	38
CONSCIOUS	48	WROUGHT	45	CONSORT	41	HORROR	38
DISGRACE	48	YONDER	45	DAWN	41	MAJESTY	38
FOLLOW	48	YOUTHS	45	EXPLORE	41	MUSICK	38
FOUR	48	ANGER	44	FALLING	41	POSSEST	38
GLAD	48	APOLLO	44	FEELS	41	QUITE	38
HERALD	48	BANKS	44	FOLLY	41	RECEIVES	38
LAWLESS	48	BELOV'D	44	GOBLET	41	ROBES	38
LOOKS	48	BENDING	44	GRECIANS	41	SANDS	38
LUST	48	BREATHES	44	IRON	41	SEARCH	38

Word	No.	Word	No.	Word	No.	Word	No.
SEATS	38	SUCCEED	35	CHOSEN	32	NERVES	30
STORES	38	TIDE	35	CHUSE	32	NODDING	30
THIN	38	VIRTUES	35	CONDUCT	32	NOISE	30
THIRD	38	WEARY	35	CONQUER	32	PATIENT	30
VISION	38	WHEELS	35	CRIME	32	PELEUS	30
WAKE	38	WINDING	35	DENNIS	32	PELIDES	30
WITNESS	38	WING'D	35	DO (AUXILIARY)	32	PILE	30
AFFORD	37	ALTERNATE	34	ENTER	32	POW'RFUL	30
BADE	37	AROSE	34	FAITHLESS	32	PROMISE	30
BEAUTIES	37	BREAKS	34	FATHERS	32	REGIONS	30
CHARM	37	CONFEST	34	FIFTY	32	RIOT	30
DENIES	37	DIFF'RENT	34	FLOCK	32	SERVANT	30
DRINK	37	DREAMS	34	FOLLOW'D	32	SEV'N	30
EMPIRE	37	EXPREST	34	FRUITS	32	SHOWN	30
FRIENDSHIP	37	FANCY	34	GHOSTS	32	SPENT	30
HAPPIER	37	LAUGH	34	GROANING	32	STOP	30
HEAP	37	LYRE	34	GUIDES	32	STRAINS	30
HELMET	37	MAST	34	I'M	32	STRING	30
MERION	37	MEAN-TIME	34	INJUR'D	32	STUBBORN	30
PARTIAL	37	NEED	34	JOYFUL	32	SWEAT	30
PRESENTS	37	NOBLER	34	LADY	32	SWEEP	30
RAN	37	OARS	34	LIFT	32	THINKS	30
RETIRE	37	OXEN	34	MONARCH'S	32	TREAT	30
RINGS	37	PARTING	34	NEIGHB'RING	32	TREMBLED	30
SAFETY	37	PASS'D	34	NIGHTS	32	TREMENDOUS	30
SMILES	37	PIERCING	34	OBJECT	32	UNEQUAL	30
SURPRIZE	37	PROSPECT	34	REMOVE	32	VIGOUR	30
URN	37	REINS	34	RISES	32	WEAR	30
VOID	37	RENDS	34	RITE	32	ADVICE	29
WARLIKE	37	REPAST	34	SINKING	32	BALLS	29
WIELD	37	SAND	34	SOLE	32	BROTHER'S	29
ADDRESS'D	36	SAV'D	34	SPORT	32	BULL	29
ANXIOUS	36	SEEKS	34	STAY'D	32	CLAIMS	29
ASCENDS	36	SHAFT	34	TERROR	32	CONFUS'D	29
BLOOM	36	STUDIOUS	34	TONGUES	32	CRITICKS	29
CHOICE	36	TEMPLES	34	UNITE	32	CURIOUS	29
CONFESS	36	THAMES	34	UNMOV'D	32	DECK	29
CONFESS'D	36	TIR'D	34	AERIAL	31	DISGUISE	29
DESTRUCTION	36	UTMOST	34	ASIDE	31	DRESS	29
DIVIDES	36	VASE	34	BALL	31	EXAMPLE	29
DRIV'N	36	VIRTUOUS	34	BALMY	31	FAVOUR	29
DRIVE	36	WARRIOR'S	34	BARB'ROUS	31	FEED	29
ENORMOUS	36	WATER	34	BARDS	31	FINE	29
EVENING	36	WHILST	34	BATH'D	31	FLOW'R	29
EXTEND	36	WORSE	34	BOWS	31	FOUNTAINS	29
FAULT	36	AIM	33	CRIMES	31	GLIDE	29
FOLLOWING	36	ARROWS	33	CROWDS	31	GROWING	29
GROWN	36	ASKS	33	DAUGHTERS	31	GUARDS	29
GROWS	36	AUTHOR	33	DAUNTLESS	31	HIDES	29
HEAP'D	36	BOOKS	33	DEW	31	HOLDS	29
MAIDS	36	BREATHING	33	DIRECTS	31	LASH	29
MELANCHOLY	36	BURN'D	33	DUSKY	31	LUSTRE	29
QUICK	36	CAPTIVE	33	FAULCHION	31	MADNESS	29
REND	36	CHACE	33	FORGET	31	MARCH'D	29
RESTRAIN	36	CHANG'D	33	FOUGHT	31	NUPTIAL	29
RETIR'D	36	CONCEAL'D	33	FUN'RAL	31	OURS	29
SCIENCE	36	DOG	33	HAVING (OMITTED)	31	PATROCLUS'	29
SEX	36	FAT	33	HELPLESS	31	PROFOUND	29
SOBER	36	FLOWING	33	INCESSANT	31	RAG'D	29
SOURCE	36	FRAUD	33	MARK'D	31	REMOTE	29
SPIRITS	36	FURIES	33	MASSY	31	ROAD	29
SQUADRONS	36	HANG	33	MERCY	31	ROCKY	29
SUITOR	36	INDULGE	33	NOTES	31	ROME	29
SURVEYS	36	INVADE	33	OFFENCE	31	SARPEDON	29
THETIS	36	KNAVE	33	PRICE	31	SHRINE	29
TWENTY	36	LABOUR'D	33	PRIVATE	31	SQUIRE	29
UNWILLING	36	LEADER	33	REGAL	31	STAR	29
WAVING	36	LOT	33	SITS	31	STRAY	29
WILLING	36	MANNERS	33	SLUMBERS	31	STRIVE	29
ADD	35	MATRON	33	SOMETHING	31	STUNG	29
ALOFT	35	MEANS	33	SPRIGHTLY	31	SUBJECT	29
ANTINOUS	35	MOTION	33	STEED	31	SUPPLY'D	29
BLUSH	35	NATION	33	TERRORS	31	TEMPLE	29
BROKEN	35	NESTOR'S	33	TOW'RING	31	THROW	29
CONQU'RING	35	NICE	33	VERDANT	31	TORRENT	29
DESERT	35	NODS	33	WEPT	31	WAFT	29
DIRECT	35	PEER	33	AGED	30	APART	28
DWELL	35	PLANT	33	AMBITION	30	ARGOS	28
ENDLESS	35	PLEASURES	33	ARDENT	30	AVENGING	28
FATED	35	POINTS	33	ARDOUR	30	BAYS	28
FEAR'D	35	PYLE	33	BEASTS	30	BLAST	28
FINDS	35	ROAM	33	BOAR	30	BLUE-EY'D	28
FITS	35	ROOM	33	BOW'RS	30	BUCKLER	28
FOREMOST	35	ROSY	33	CAREFUL	30	CATCH	28
FORMER	35	SHOW'RS	33	CIBBER	30	CONFOUND	28
GATH'RING	35	SIDES	33	CONFIN'D	30	CORSE	28
GRAIN	35	SIZE	33	CORPS	30	DASH'D	28
HAIRS	35	STREAMING	33	CURLING	30	DECREES	28
HELEN	35	SWAINS	33	DANGERS	30	DISCLOSE	28
HERMES	35	TALK	33	DEFENCE	30	DISTINGUISH'D	28
IDA'S	35	VALES	33	DESIRES	30	EXPIRE	28
JUDGMENT	35	VITAL	33	FAVOUR'D	30	FAMILIAR	28
JUSTLY	35	VULCAN	33	FLEECY	30	FLOOR	28
LEND	35	WALK	33	GOD'S	30	GOES	28
LION	35	WANTON	33	GRIEVE	30	GRACIOUS	28
MISTRESS	35	WAYS	33	GRIM	30	GRIEFS	28
MOURN'D	35	WELCOME	33	HAPPINESS	30	HERSELF	28
OWE	35	WISH'D	33	HASTY	30	JOURNEY	28
POPE	35	WITHDREW	33	HERD	30	KEEN	28
PROPITIOUS	35	WOMEN	33	HORRORS	30	LASTING	28
SEER	35	WONDERS	33	IMPART	30	LOVERS	28
SHAPE	35	ACTIVE	32	INVADES	30	MAY'ST	28
SHEEP	35	ADOR'D	32	LEARNED	30	MULES	28
SIN	35	ADORN'D	32	LIPS	30	NATAL	28
		AUTHORS	32	NEITHER	30	OPPOS'D	28

RESTLESS	22	PROV'D	21	THIRSTY	20	SOOTH	19
RIVER	22	PUBLIC	21	THRONES	20	SOUTH	19
RUL'D	22	QUIET	21	TREADS	20	SPARKLING	19
SAILORS	22	REAR'D	21	UNCONQUER'D	20	SPED	19
SCEPTRE	22	RELENTLESS	21	UNITED	20	SPOTLESS	19
SERV'D	22	REMAIN'D	21	UNIVERSAL	20	STAIN'D	19
SHOCK	22	REMEMBRANCE	21	VENT	20	STOPP'D	19
SMIL'D	22	RENEWS	21	VIANDS	20	STROKES	19
SPIES	22	RENOWN	21	VOW'D	20	THEBES	19
STRIKES	22	REVERE	21	WARD	20	THEME	19
SUCCESS	22	ROD	21	WAV'D	20	THITHER	19
SUITS	22	SEASON	21	WISEST	20	THROUGH	19
SUPPORT	22	SIGH'D	21	WORLD'S	20	VAINLY	19
SWIFTNESS	22	SMART	21	WORLDS	20	VEIN	19
TEUCER	22	SNOW	21	WORM	20	WEARS	19
TOGETHER	22	SOFTER	21	ABSENCE	19	WEIGH	19
TRIES	22	SPLEEN	21	ADVISE	19	WELL-KNOWN	19
TRIUMPHS	22	STREET	21	AIDS	19	WHOE'ER	19
TY'D	22	SUBJECTS	21	AIM'D	19	WITHSTAND	19
US'D	22	SWAY'D	21	AMAZE	19	ABANDON'D	18
VALOUR	22	SWORE	21	AMBUSH	19	AFFORDS	18
VIG'ROUS	22	TEND	21	ANTILOCHUS	19	ALLOW	18
WAGE	22	THANKS	21	ATTENTION	19	ASSEMBLY	18
WARN'D	22	TIMELY	21	AVENGE	19	BARREN	18
WHITHER	22	TOM	21	AW'D	19	BELINDA	18
WORE	22	TOWNS	21	BANK	19	BOILING	18
YELLOW	22	WANDRING	21	BELT	19	BOLT	18
YOKE	22	WARMTH	21	BESTOWS	19	BOUGHS	18
ADORE	21	WHORE	21	BONE	19	BRANCHES	18
AIRS	21	WINTER	21	BOREAS	19	BREEZE	18
AURORA	21	WRITES	21	BREASTS	19	CENSURE	18
AWAKE	21	AM'ROUS	20	BREED	19	CENTRE	18
BATH	21	BANISH'D	20	BUILD	19	CHARM'D	18
BATTER'D	21	BLAMELESS	20	CAVES	19	CHEAT	18
BEING	21	BOTTOM	20	CLIFFS	19	COACH	18
BLADE	21	BULK	20	COLUMN	19	COMPOSE	18
BLAZ'D	21	CARCASE	20	COMMEND	19	CONQUESTS	18
BOUNTEOUS	21	CHAIR	20	COMPOS'D	19	CONSIGN'D	18
BOWLS	21	CHECK'D	20	CONQUER'D	19	COURTIER	18
BUSINESS	21	COMPLEAT	20	CONSENT	19	DEATHS	18
BUSY	21	CONSPIRE	20	CONVEY'D	19	DESPISE	18
CAESAR	21	CONSULT	20	COURSER	19	DEVOUR	18
CAN'ST	21	DAMES	20	CRACKLING	19	DISMISS	18
CIRCLES	21	DECIDE	20	DEAF	19	DISPOSE	18
CITIES	21	DIM	20	DISCHARG'D	19	DISTRESS	18
CLAMOURS	21	DUKE	20	DOMESTIC	19	DUNCE	18
COMBAT	21	EAGLE	20	DUTY	19	EMBROIDER'D	18
CONDEMN'D	21	EMBRAC'D	20	EAST	19	EMPRESS	18
CONTENDING	21	EVERLASTING	20	EMBATTEL'D	19	ENTER'D	18
COST	21	FIGURE	20	ENGAG'D	19	EVENT	18
CREST	21	FIXT	20	EURYCLEA	19	EXPIRES	18
CRETAN	21	FORSOOK	20	EV'NING	19	FAULTS	18
CRETE	21	FRUIT	20	EVIL	19	FIGHTING	18
CROSS	21	GILDS	20	EXPERIENC'D	19	FISH	18
CROWNS	21	GLAUCUS	20	FAINT	19	FLASH'D	18
DEBT	21	GOATS	20	FLAM'D	19	FOUL	18
DESART	21	HEAVE	20	FOUNTAIN	19	FR	18
DISEASE	21	HEROIC	20	FRAGMENTS	19	FREQUENT	18
DISMAL	21	HORN	20	FRANCE	19	GALE	18
DISPLAYS	21	INSPIRING	20	GARDEN	19	GAPING	18
DROOPING	21	IRE	20	GET	19	GASPING	18
DWELLS	21	JOINS	20	GRASPS	19	GLIDING	18
E'RE	21	JUICE	20	GUSHING	19	GRIEV'D	18
EARTH'S	21	KISS	20	HAUNT	19	GUILT	18
EURYMACHUS	21	KNOWLEDGE	20	HISSING	19	HARDY	18
EXILE	21	LAUGHTER	20	HORSES	19	HATH	18
FIERCER	21	LIBERTY	20	HURT	19	HELL'S	18
FILIAL	21	MASTER'S	20	IDOMENEUS	19	HOARSE	18
FLUNG	21	MEAN-WHILE	20	ITHACUS	19	HORACE	18
FOAM	21	MEANTIME	20	JEALOUS	19	I'D	18
FORBID	21	MELT	20	KINDLY	19	IMPERIOUS	18
FORCEFUL	21	MELTING	20	LATENT	19	INCREASE	18
FORSAKE	21	MONUMENT	20	LIGHT'NING	19	INSULT	18
GAZ'D	21	NEPTUNE'S	20	LIGHTS	19	IRIS	18
GAZING	21	PAGE	20	LIMB	19	JAVELINS	18
GOAL	21	PANT	20	LONELY	19	JUNO'S	18
GUILTLESS	21	PAVEMENT	20	LORD'S	19	KINDRED	18
HATEFUL	21	PEN	20	MARGIN	19	LAMBS	18
HE'S	21	PERISH'D	20	MAY	19	LEGS	18
HUSH'D	21	PLAGUE	20	MINDFUL	19	LOADED	18
ILLS	21	PLAYS	20	MOUNTAIN'S	19	MASS	18
IMPENDING	21	PLUNGE	20	MURM'RING	19	MEADS	18
INDIGNANT	21	POMPOUS	20	NONSENSE	19	MEASUR'D	18
INNOCENT	21	PREVAIL	20	O'ERTHROWN	19	MEAT	18
INT'REST	21	QUOTH	20	OBSERVANT	19	MIRTH	18
ISSUING	21	RAIN	20	OW'D	19	MISERY	18
JAWS	21	RATHER	20	PAINFUL	19	MIST	18
KEEPS	21	RECESS	20	PARTAKE	19	MONSTERS	18
KNEE	21	RENT	20	PARTED	19	MOUND	18
LEAP'D	21	REQUIRES	20	PATRIOT	19	MOUNTING	18
LOVER	21	SAINT	20	PEOPLE'S	19	MURMUR	18
MESSENGER	21	SAYS	20	PIERCE	19	MUSIC	18
MIEN	21	SCANDAL	20	POLYDAMAS	19	NEIGHBOUR	18
MINDS	21	SERENE	20	PROMISCUOUS	19	NOBLY	18
MOON	21	SHOOTS	20	RIDE	19	NURSE	18
OBSCENE	21	SHOUT	20	RILLS	19	OBTAIN	18
OBSERVE	21	SHOW'D	20	ROVE	19	OPEN'D	18
PANTS	21	SINGLY	20	SCAPE	19	PETER	18
PATRON	21	SISTERS	20	SELF-LOVE	19	PORTION	18
PERMIT	21	SLIGHT	20	SHAFTS	19	POSSESS	18
PERSON	21	SPEAKING	20	SHARES	19	PREVENT	18
PINIONS	21	SPLENDID	20	SHEATH'D	19	PRIESTS	18
PLENTEOUS	21	STARTING	20	SHOOT	19	PROLONG	18
PROMPT	21	STONES	20	SON'S	19	PYRE	18
PROPER	21	TEDIOUS	20	SOONER	19	QUITS	18

RAMPARTS	18	PUNISH	17	LENT	16	FLEETS	15
REARS	18	QUESTION	17	LINTOT	16	FOREHEAD	15
REBEL	18	RECLIN'D	17	MEDON	16	FRAIL	15
RECORD	18	REVER'D	17	MELTS	16	FRENCH	15
REGION	18	RINGLETS	17	MEND	16	FROWN'D	15
REVEAL	18	RIVALS	17	MID	16	GOAT	15
SADLY	18	SAIL'D	17	MINISTER	16	GROT	15
SETS	18	SAPHO	17	MISTS	16	HEAVEN	15
SHADED	18	SEALS	17	MIXT	16	HELEN'S	15
SIGNS	18	SERVILE	17	MONSTROUS	16	HUMOUR	15
SIRES	18	SIMPLE	17	MORAL	16	I'VE	15
SORT	18	SINS	17	OBSERV'D	16	IMPELL'D	15
SPHERE	18	SLAY	17	OCEAN'S	16	INCLOSE	15
STRONGEST	18	SPY	17	ORACLES	16	INDUSTRIOUS	15
SUSPEND	18	STERNLY	17	ORIENT	16	INSTINCT	15
SWEPT	18	STOOP	17	P	16	INTERCEPT	15
TAME	18	STREETS	17	PATH	16	LABORIOUS	15
THIGHS	18	STRICT	17	PERFORM'D	16	LADY'S	15
THOUSANDS	18	STRODE	17	PLAY'D	16	LEGIONS	15
TITLE	18	STRUCTURE	17	PLEAD	16	LENGTHEN'D	15
TRIBES	18	STYGIAN	17	PROCEEDS	16	LEWD	15
TROPHIES	18	SUFF'RING	17	PROSP'ROUS	16	LIBATIONS	15
TURNING	18	SUSTAIN'D	17	PROVES	16	LINEAGE	15
UNAVAILING	18	TELLS	17	RAVES	16	LOCK'D	15
UNBOUND	18	THREAT	17	REFUSE	16	MAJESTICK	15
UNERRING	18	TIM'ROUS	17	REMOV'D	16	MALICE	15
UNGRATEFUL	18	UNION	17	REV'RENCE	16	MANSION	15
USEFUL	18	UNRIVAL'D	17	RHYME	16	MEAD	15
USELESS	18	UNTOUCH'D	17	ROWE	16	MEASURES	15
VOCAL	18	URNS	17	RULING	16	MEMORY	15
WHIRLWIND	18	VARYING	17	SERVES	16	METHINKS	15
WOLVES	18	VAULTED	17	SEV'RAL	16	MIDDLE	15
WRITING	18	VEINS	17	SHAGGY	16	MILLIONS	15
XANTHUS	18	VICTOR'S	17	SHAMEFUL	16	MISCHIEF	15
ACHAIAN	17	VIOLENCE	17	SIGHING	16	NAM'D	15
AFAR	17	VIRTUE'S	17	SKILFUL	16	NAVAL	15
ANNUAL	17	WARM'D	17	SKIN	16	NEGLECT	15
ARCH	17	WEEPS	17	STARE	16	NOBLEST	15
BEGIN	17	WERT	17	STOOPING	16	NORTHERN	15
BEWARE	17	WHIRL'D	17	STRANGER'S	16	NOTE	15
BOW'D	17	WILLS	17	STROOK	16	OBLIVION	15
CASTS	17	WILT	17	STUDY	16	OFF'RINGS	15
CIRCLED	17	WISER	17	SUBDU'D	16	OMEN	15
COLLECTED	17	WISHES	17	SUPPREST	16	PAPER	15
COMING	17	WORMS	17	SURFACE	16	PARTNER	15
COURTLY	17	ABROAD	16	TELAMON	16	PATHS	15
CUP	17	AGREE	16	TENTH	16	PHOEBUS'	15
DELUGE	17	ANGEL	16	THO (OMITTED)	16	PLEDGE	15
DEPLOR'D	17	APPROVES	16	TROOP	16	PLENTY	15
DESERVE	17	ATHENS	16	TYDES	16	POSSESS'D	15
DISPERS'D	17	AUTOMEDON	16	UNCONSCIOUS	16	PRESERV'D	15
DOMES	17	BALANCE	16	UNKIND	16	PRESUMPTUOUS	15
DOOMS	17	BATHES	16	UNLESS	16	PRINT	15
DOORS	17	BATTLE	16	UNREVENG'D	16	PROCLAIMS	15
DOVE	17	BEAMING	16	WAKEFUL	16	PROMPTS	15
DRANK	17	BEDS	16	WANDERS	16	PURER	15
EARTHLY	17	BEGINS	16	WASH'D	16	PUREST	15
EASTERN	17	BENDED	16	WASTES	16	RAPT	15
ETHERIAL	17	BITE	16	WED	16	RAPTURE	15
EXCEPT	17	BLESS'D	16	WHEEL	16	RAPTURES	15
EXPERIENCE	17	BOLDLY	16	WITHER'D	16	RASHLY	15
FEARLESS	17	BOYS	16	WOMAN'S	16	REASON'S	15
FEEDS	17	BULWARKS	16	YORE	16	REFUS'D	15
FELLOWS	17	BURSTS	16	AFRAID	15	RELICKS	15
FOAMS	17	CARNAGE	16	ALMOST	15	RELIEF	15
FOLLOWS	17	CHAOS	16	AMBITIOUS	15	RELIQUES	15
FOP	17	CLIME	16	ASS	15	REPAIRS	15
FRANTIC	17	COLOUR'D	16	ASSERT	15	RHYMES	15
GAIN'D	17	COMPELLING	16	ASTONISH'D	15	ROMAN	15
GAINS	17	CREATURE	16	ATTENDANT	15	SAINTS	15
GILDED	17	DESIGNS	16	ATTENDING	15	SCALES	15
GLANCE	17	DISCOURSE	16	ATTENTIVE	15	SCORN'D	15
GLASS	17	DREADS	16	BEAMY	15	SEAL'D	15
GLOW'D	17	DROPPING	16	BECAUSE	15	SEED	15
HARVESTS	17	DUTEOUS	16	BLUSHES	15	SETTING	15
HATED	17	ELOQUENCE	16	BOLDEST	15	SLEEPING	15
HEALING	17	ENJOYS	16	CAN'T	15	SLOWLY	15
HEAVING	17	EXALTED	16	CAPACIOUS	15	SNOWS	15
IGNOBLE	17	EXPIR'D	16	CLIMES	15	SPARTA	15
IMPORTANT	17	EXULTING	16	COELESTIAL	15	SPOT	15
INCENS'D	17	EYE-BALLS	16	COLUMNS	15	STANDING	15
INVITES	17	FAREWELL	16	CONFINE	15	STRINGS	15
ISSUE	17	FIENDS	16	CORN	15	SUBMIT	15
LONGING	17	FLASH	16	COSTLY	15	SUPINE	15
LORDLY	17	FLATT'RY	16	CROWDED	15	SURROUNDING	15
LOWLY	17	FOOTSTEPS	16	CURE	15	SWEEPS	15
MEANT	17	FORTUNE'S	16	CURRENT	15	SWEETS	15
MEDITATES	17	FOURTH	16	DEATHLESS	15	THEIRS	15
MEMBERS	17	FRANTICK	16	DECLARES	15	THRO	15
MIDNIGHT	17	FRAY	16	DECLINE	15	THUNDER'D	15
MISERIES	17	FREEDOM	16	DEEM'D	15	TIES	15
MONARCHS	17	GHASTLY	16	DEPRIV'D	15	TOPS	15
NOBLES	17	GOBLETS	16	DESTROY'D	15	TRIBE	15
NUMBER	17	GOWN	16	DESTRUCTIVE	15	TUNE	15
OLYMPIAN	17	HIT	16	DICTATES	15	TWIXT	15
OWN'D	17	HOP'D	16	DIN	15	TYDEUS	15
PASSING	17	HOUNDS	16	DIRTY	15	UNBLEST	15
PENELOPE	17	HUNGRY	16	DISMAY	15	UNFINISH'D	15
PHANTOM	17	IMPOTENT	16	DOWNWARD	15	UNWORTHY	15
PLUTO'S	17	LAMP	16	EFFECT	15	VALE	15
PORTALS	17	LANCES	16	ENQUIRE	15	VAN	15
PREACH	17	LANE	16	ERECT	15	VAUNTS	15
PRINCE'S	17	LANGUAGE	16	EXALT	15	VINE	15
PROGRESS	17	LASH'D	16	FAMINE	15	VISIONARY	15
PROVIDE	17	LEAPS	16	FAVOURS	15	VISITS	15

Word		Word		Word		Word	
WEAKNESS	15	MERITS	14	CREEP	13	RIVERS	13
WHIRL	15	MINISTERS	14	CYCLOPS	13	ROAR'D	13
WHISPERS	15	MISS	14	CYNTHIA	13	ROB	13
WISELY	15	MOAN	14	DAWNING	13	ROOTED	13
WONT	15	NATION'S	14	DEARER	13	RUDDY	13
WOULD'ST	15	NECTAR	14	DEATH'S	13	SCHOOL	13
ZONE	15	NORTH	14	DEFENDS	13	SEP'RATE	13
ACCENTS	14	O'ERSPREAD	14	DEFORM'D	13	SERIES	13
ACROSS	14	OAK	14	DEGEN'RATE	13	SERVICE	13
ACTIONS	14	OBJECTS	14	DELIA	13	SHE'S	13
ADDISON	14	OBSEQUIOUS	14	DESCRY'D	13	SHEDS	13
AFFRIGHT	14	OLYMPUS'	14	DETAINS	13	SHELVES	13
ALCIDES	14	OVER	14	DETESTED	13	SONGS	13
BECOMES	14	PERJUR'D	14	DID	13	SOVEREIGN	13
BEG	14	PIECE	14	DIRT	13	SPIRES	13
BELONG	14	PLUMES	14	DISHONOUR'D	13	SPOIL'D	13
BISHOP	14	POETIC	14	DISPOS'D	13	STALKS	13
BIT	14	POETRY	14	DISSOLV'D	13	STARTS	13
BITTER	14	PONDROUS	14	DISTREST	13	STOOP'D	13
BOASTED	14	PRETTY	14	DOUBTS	13	STOR'D	13
BOOK	14	PRODUCE	14	DRUNK	13	STRONGER	13
BRIGHTEST	14	PROPHET	14	DRURY	13	STRUNG	13
BRISTLY	14	PUTS	14	DRYDEN	13	SWINE	13
BURSTING	14	RAGS	14	ENJOY'D	13	TEETH	13
CARPETS	14	REFLECT	14	ENVY'D	13	TERRIBLE	13
CAT	14	RESORT	14	EXCELL	13	THEREFORE	13
CATO	14	RESTRAIN'D	14	EXCUSE	13	THIGH	13
CHANC'D	14	ROGUE	14	EXPECTS	13	THOUGHTFUL	13
CHAST	14	ROUZE	14	EXPENCE	13	THRESHOLD	13
CHRISTIAN	14	ROWS	14	FAIRLY	13	THRON'D	13
CLIMB	14	RUGGED	14	FEARFUL	13	THROWS	13
CLOATHS	14	RUSHES	14	FLASHING	13	TOW'RD	13
CLOUDY	14	SANDALS	14	FORTY	13	TRESSES	13
COASTS	14	SANGUINE	14	FRIEND'S	13	TRIBUTE	13
COMPANION	14	SERPENT	14	FRUGAL	13	UNDAUNTED	13
COMPASSION	14	SERVANTS	14	GLANCING	13	UNKNOWING	13
CONFOUNDS	14	SHRIEKS	14	GLARING	13	UNLIKE	13
CONSECRATED	14	SHROUDS	14	GRASP'D	13	UNWEARY'D	13
CONSTRAIN'D	14	SHUT	14	GREATNESS	13	VALLIES	13
COUNT	14	SMOKES	14	GROWTH	13	VERNAL	13
DAZLING	14	SOLDIER	14	HABIT	13	VIGOR	13
DEBATES	14	SPARK	14	HARK	13	VISIONS	13
DEEPER	14	SPEEDY	14	HISS	13	VULTURS	13
DEFY'D	14	SPRINGING	14	HUMANE	13	WANDER'D	13
DEGREES	14	STAFF	14	HUMBLED	13	WAV'RING	13
DELIGHTS	14	STALK'D	14	HUMBLER	13	WEAPONS	13
DEN	14	START	14	IMMENSE	13	WEST	13
DESERV'D	14	STARVE	14	IMPERVIOUS	13	WHENE'ER	13
DESERVES	14	STAYS	14	INCLINE	13	WHERE-E'ER	13
DINE	14	STOPS	14	INFLAME	13	WHISPER	13
DINNER	14	STOPT	14	INLY	13	WIT'S	13
DISDAIN'D	14	STRAW	14	ISSU'D	13	WITHERS	13
DISHONEST	14	STRAY'D	14	JOINT	13	WOMANKIND	13
DISMISS'D	14	STRIP	14	KILL	13	WRETCHES	13
DRINKS	14	STYLE	14	KILL'D	13	ADVANCING	12
DUMB	14	SUCCESSFUL	14	KNOW'ST	13	AMBER	12
EDG'D	14	SUITOR-TRAIN	14	LATEST	13	APPOINTED	12
ELATE	14	SUN'S	14	LEAP	13	ARTIST	12
ELDEST	14	THICKEST	14	LENDS	13	ASHAM'D	12
EMBODY'D	14	THRACIAN	14	LIMITS	13	ASIUS	12
EMBRACES	14	THREAD	14	LOVE'S	13	ASSENT	12
EMPLOY'D	14	TOSS	14	LUCKLESS	13	ASSOCIATES	12
EMULATE	14	TRANSLATE	14	MAINTAINS	13	ATTEMPT	12
ENDURE	14	TROUBLED	14	MANTLE	13	AVAILS	12
EXAMPLES	14	TYDIDES'	14	MATES	13	AXLE	12
EXPLAIN	14	UNHEARD	14	MAZY	13	BABE	12
FAIL'D	14	VENAL	14	MEANER	13	BATTELS	12
FIGURES	14	VISAGE	14	MESSAGE	13	BELLOWING	12
FLEECE	14	WAK'D	14	MISERABLE	13	BETRAY'D	12
FLOAT	14	WANTED	14	MORALS	13	BLOOMS	12
FLOATS	14	WHIRLS	14	MYSTIC	13	BOASTER	12
FORBIDS	14	WONDROUS	14	NURS'D	13	BREEDING	12
FORE	14	YOU'RE	14	OAKS	13	BURY	12
FORFEIT	14	ADMIRES	13	OBSCURE	13	CAPTIVES	12
FRIGHTED	14	ALARM	13	OCCASION	13	CATES	12
GILD	14	ANEW	13	OFFER'D	13	CHARIOTEER	12
GLITTER'D	14	APPLY'D	13	OIL	13	CIRCE	12
GODHEAD	14	ARGIVES	13	OWNS	13	CLAD	12
GREATLY	14	ASCENDING	13	PAY'D	13	CLAY	12
GROAN'D	14	ASPECT	13	PELEUS'	13	CLEAVE	12
GUARDED	14	ATREUS'	13	PELIDES'	13	CLOUD-COMPELLING	12
HANDMAIDS	14	AWAKES	13	PERFORM	13	COLOUR	12
HARMLESS	14	AXE	13	PHAEACIA'S	13	COM'ST	12
HE'LL	14	BALM	13	PHAEACIAN	13	COMMENCE	12
HEED	14	BECOME	13	PHOENIX	13	CONFIRM'D	12
HEIRS	14	BEES	13	PLOW'D	13	CONFUSION	12
HERBS	14	BEEVES	13	POUND	13	CONSUME	12
HOWLING	14	BELONGS	13	PROGENY	13	CONVERSE	12
IMPARTIAL	14	BETWIXT	13	PROPT	13	CREATURES	12
IMPLOR'D	14	BRAND	13	PROWESS	13	CROOKED	12
INFERIOR	14	BRANDISH'D	13	PURCHASE	13	CROUD	12
INSATIATE	14	BRIBE	13	QUARREL	13	DAMSEL	12
INSULTS	14	BRINY	13	QUILL	13	DARLING	12
KEY	14	BULLS	13	READS	13	DEFENDED	12
KISSES	14	CALYPSO	13	REAS'NING	13	DEGREE	12
LAMENTED	14	CANISTERS	13	REDRESS	13	DELIGHTED	12
LAUGHS	14	CARRY	13	REFRESH	13	DEPART	12
LETS	14	CARS	13	RELIGION	13	DEPEND	12
LETTERS	14	CHAMPION	13	RENOUNCE	13	DESIR'D	12
LIBATION	14	CHIEF'S	13	REPULS'D	13	DETAIN'D	12
LION'S	14	CLAP	13	RESERV'D	13	DEVOURS	12
LOADS	14	CLEAN	13	RESOLVES	13	DIANA	12
LOVER'S	14	CLEFT	13	REVIEW	13	DIFF'RENCE	12
LYCIANS	14	CONFLICT	13	REWARDS	13	DISCHARGE	12
MATURE	14	CREDIT	13	RIPE	13	DOCTOR	12

Word	#	Word	#	Word	#	Word	#
DOMAIN	12	REIGN'D	12	DAR'ST	11	RATLING	11
DOWNY	12	REPELL'D	12	DE	11	READING	11
DRAIN	12	REPORT	12	DECAYS	11	RECESSES	11
DROP'D	12	RESTORES	12	DECLAR'D	11	REEDS	11
EASIE	12	RESTRAINS	12	DECLINING	11	REFECTION	11
ELDER	12	RESTS	12	DEIGN	11	REGAIN	11
ELDERS	12	ROBB'D	12	DETERMIN'D	11	REGRET	11
ENDU'D	12	ROOMS	12	DEV'L	11	RELEAS'D	11
ENTERS	12	ROSIE	12	DIGNITY	11	RESENTMENT	11
ESTATE	12	ROUTED	12	DISDAINS	11	REVERSE	11
ETHEREAL	12	ROUZ'D	12	DISTRACTED	11	ROUT	11
EXACT	12	RUSTIC	12	DOVES	11	RULER	11
EXCITE	12	SCATTER	12	DRIVING	11	RULERS	11
EXEMPT	12	SCORNS	12	ECHOING	11	RUNNING	11
EXPRESS'D	12	SCREAM	12	ENAMOUR'D	11	SANCTION	11
FALL'N	12	SELDOM	12	ENVIOUS	11	SATURNIA	11
FOLDS	12	SENATES	12	EXCEL	11	SCAEAN	11
FOLKS	12	SHRUNK	12	EXPECTED	11	SCAR	11
FOOLISH	12	SHUNS	12	EXPOS'D	11	SCATT'RING	11
FOPS	12	SMIT	12	FEMALES	11	SCULPTURE	11
FORBIDDEN	12	STATESMEN	12	FENC'D	11	SECUR'D	11
FORGETS	12	STATUES	12	FETCH	11	SECURELY	11
FRAUDFUL	12	STEALS	12	FLOUR	11	SEDATE	11
FREED	12	STOP'D	12	FLOURISH'D	11	SEEING	11
FROWN	12	STRANGERS	12	FORKY	11	SHELTER	11
GILDON	12	STRIDES	12	FORSAKES	11	SIGN'D	11
GRASP	12	STUCK	12	FOWL	11	SMOKING	11
GRAY	12	SUMMIT	12	FRAGMENT	11	SOLDIERS	11
GREENS	12	SUPPOSE	12	FULFILL	11	SPECTRES	11
GREY	12	SURGES	12	GARDENS	11	SPEEDS	11
GUARDIANS	12	SURROUNDS	12	GEMS	11	STATURE	11
GUISE	12	SUSTAINS	12	GOODS	11	STEELY	11
HARDLY	12	SWIFTLY	12	GRANTED	11	STOOPS	11
HE'D	12	SWORN	12	GREEDY	11	STORM'D	11
HEROE'S	12	SYNOD	12	GREET	11	STORMY	11
HERS	12	TASKS	12	GRUBSTREET	11	STUPID	11
HONEY	12	TEMPER	12	GUESS	11	STYX	11
HUMBLY	12	THETIS'	12	GUIDING	11	SUBLIME	11
HUSBANDS	12	THINKING	12	HARMS	11	SUE	11
ILL-FATED	12	THRONGS	12	HEAVES	11	SUMMER	11
IMAGES	12	TITLES	12	HELMS	11	SUMMITS	11
INCLIN'D	12	TORCH	12	HELP'D	11	SUMMON'D	11
INFAMY	12	TORRENTS	12	HENCEFORTH	11	SUMMONS	11
INFLAM'D	12	TOUGH	12	HIGHER	11	SWARMS	11
INMOST	12	TRULY	12	HONOUR'S	11	SWAYS	11
IRUS	12	TUMBLES	12	HOV'RING	11	SWIFTEST	11
ISLAND	12	TYDEUS'	12	HOWE'ER	11	TALES	11
IV'RY	12	UNBOUNDED	12	HUMANKIND	11	TAPER	11
IVY	12	UNDERSTOOD	12	HURL	11	TEMPER'D	11
JOYOUS	12	UNTAUGHT	12	IDLY	11	TERRIFIC	11
KINDLED	12	VALVES	12	IMPARTS	11	THANK	11
KING'S	12	VANITY	12	INCLEMENT	11	THICKET	11
KNAVES	12	VAPOUR	12	INFOLD	11	THOAS	11
LESBIAN	12	VEIL'D	12	INSTRUCT	11	THOUGHTLESS	11
LIST	12	VENTS	12	INVOLVE	11	THRUST	11
LIVELY	12	VERSES	12	INWARD	11	TORY	11
LODGE	12	VESTS	12	KNOWING	11	TOSS'D	11
LOTS	12	WAND'RINGS	12	LAKES	11	TOW'RY	11
LOUDLY	12	WAR'S	12	LAMENT	11	TRANSPORTS	11
LOVING	12	WINDSOR	12	LANGUISH	11	TREACH'ROUS	11
MANES	12	WINTRY	12	LAP	11	TRIPOD	11
MANGLED	12	YOUNGEST	12	LARGER	11	TRUMPET	11
MATCH'D	12	ADDRESS	11	LEAGUE	11	TUMBLING	11
MATE	12	ADDS	11	LEAN	11	TURRETS	11
MAZE	12	ADORNS	11	LIONS	11	UNABLE	11
MEAL	12	AGHAST	11	LOUDER	11	UNGUARDED	11
METHODS	12	AGO	11	LUSCIOUS	11	UNPERCEIV'D	11
MILKY	12	AIMS	11	LUXURIOUS	11	UNRELENTING	11
MOOR	12	ALARM'D	11	MANDATE	11	UNSKILL'D	11
MUD	12	ALCINOUS'	11	MEAGRE	11	VAULT	11
MURDER	12	ALLOWS	11	MEANING	11	VOLUMES	11
MUSE'S	12	ANSWERS	11	MELANTHIUS	11	VOUCHSAFE	11
NERVE	12	APPLIES	11	MELTED	11	WAKES	11
OFFER	12	ATTEST	11	MENTOR	11	WARBLING	11
OFTEN	12	BELIEV'D	11	MERRY	11	WEDG'D	11
OMENS	12	BELL	11	MILDER	11	WHISPER'D	11
ORE	12	BLACKENS	11	MINGLE	11	WHISTLING	11
OWES	12	BLOSSOMS	11	MODESTY	11	WHORES	11
OX	12	BOUNCE	11	MURD'ROUS	11	WIGHT	11
PANGS	12	BRAINS	11	NAVIES	11	WINS	11
PARTY	12	BRAVELY	11	NODDED	11	WOMB	11
PATIENCE	12	BRIBES	11	NOSTRILS	11	WOOL	11
PERILS	12	BRINK	11	NOUGHT	11	WREATHS	11
PEST	12	CAMPS	11	O'ERCOME	11	ACCENT	10
PHILIPS	12	CAVERN	11	ODIOUS	11	ACCURST	10
PLUME	12	CHAS'D	11	ODOURS	11	ACIS	10
PLUNDER	12	CLAIM'D	11	OFF'RING	11	ACRES	10
PLY	12	CLAMOUR	11	OPENS	11	AEREAL	10
PLY'D	12	CLERK	11	ORBS	11	AFFECTS	10
POSTERITY	12	CLOAK	11	ORESTES	11	AJACES	10
PRECEPTS	12	COMPASS	11	PAINTS	11	ALLY'D	10
PREFERR'D	12	CONSCIENCE	11	PALM	11	AMBUSH'D	10
PRESUME	12	CONSPICUOUS	11	PAUS'D	11	APPLES	10
PRETEND	12	CONSUM'D	11	PHAON	11	ARCHER	10
PREVAILS	12	CONTENDED	11	PHILOSOPHY	11	ARCHES	10
PRINCELY	12	CONTROULS	11	PILES	11	ASSISTANCE	10
PROVIDENCE	12	COPY	11	PLANETS	11	ATHENIAN	10
PURG'D	12	COVER	11	POLITE	11	ATHWART	10
PYLOS	12	CRAVE	11	PORTAL	11	AUXILIAR	10
RAM	12	CREATION	11	PREFER	11	AV'RICE	10
RASHNESS	12	CRUSH	11	PRETENCE	11	BACCHUS	10
RAZ'D	12	CRUSH'D	11	PRINCESS	11	BACON	10
REBOUND	12	DAEMON	11	PRINCIPLE	11	BANQUETS	10
REFLECTS	12	DAMSELS	11	PROFFER'D	11	BAR	10
REGARDLESS	12	DANCING	11	QUIVER	11	BEAU	10

Word		Word		Word		Word	
BEAUTY'S	10	HUNTER	10	SPIGHT	10	CONTAINS	9
BELLOWS	10	IMPROVE	10	SPOUTING	10	CONTINU'D	9
BELLY	10	IMPROVES	10	STAINS	10	CONTRIVE	9
BETTERS	10	INCENSE	10	STALLS	10	CORDIAL	9
BINDS	10	INCLOS'D	10	STATESMAN	10	CORSELET	9
BIRTH-DAY	10	INNOCENCE	10	STEERS	10	COVERT	9
BLOWN	10	INSTRUMENTS	10	STEM	10	CRAGGY	9
BOEOTIAN	10	JAV'LINS	10	STHENELUS	10	CRAVES	9
BOON	10	JOB	10	STRANGER-GUEST	10	CURLS	9
BRANCH	10	JOKE	10	STROW	10	DAINTIES	9
BRAWNY	10	JOVIAL	10	STUPENDOUS	10	DARKEN'D	9
BREACH	10	JUDGES	10	SUBDUE	10	DASH	9
CAUSES	10	KINGLY	10	SULTRY	10	DASTARD	9
CENTER	10	LAME	10	SUMMER'S	10	DAUGHTER'S	9
CHARLES	10	LAUNCH'D	10	SURVIV'D	10	DECAY'D	9
CHARTRES	10	LAUREL	10	SURVIVES	10	DECK'D	9
CHASE	10	LAVE	10	SWEETNESS	10	DEFAME	9
CHEST	10	LAVER	10	TEMPESTUOUS	10	DEIGN'D	9
CLAM'ROUS	10	LAZY	10	THREAT'NING	10	DERIV'D	9
CLOUDED	10	LEADER'S	10	THREATEN'D	10	DESCRIES	9
COMBIN'D	10	LIGHTNINGS	10	THRONG'D	10	DEVOTED	9
COMPELL'D	10	LIKES	10	TRANSFIX'D	10	DEVOURING	9
CONFIRM	10	LIMPID	10	TRANSIENT	10	DIAMONDS	9
CONTENDS	10	MACHAON	10	TRIPLE	10	DIANA'S	9
CONTENTED	10	MADAM	10	TURF	10	DIP	9
CONVEYS	10	MAIL	10	UNBORN	10	DISH	9
COURTIERS	10	MEANEST	10	UNDERGO	10	DISTAIN'D	9
COXCOMB	10	MEDITATED	10	UNDERSTAND	10	DISTINCT	9
CRITICK	10	MEER	10	UNDISTINGUISH'D	10	DOCTORS	9
DANCES	10	MONKEY	10	UNGUENTS	10	DOCTRINE	9
DEARLY	10	MOTIONS	10	UNMEASUR'D	10	DRENCH'D	9
DECEIV'D	10	MOURNING	10	UNRESISTED	10	DRYDEN'S	9
DECEIVE	10	MUTE	10	UNWIELDY	10	DUKES	9
DECKS	10	MYRMIDONS	10	VALUE	10	DWELT	9
DEER	10	NAMELESS	10	VASES	10	EARNEST	9
DEFY	10	NEEDFUL	10	VERDURE	10	EFFORTS	9
DEIPHOBUS	10	NEEDY	10	VICTORS	10	EIGHT	9
DEJECTED	10	NEIGHBOURS	10	VULCANIAN	10	ELUDE	9
DERIDE	10	NOON	10	WASTED	10	EMERGING	9
DESERTED	10	OÏLEUS	10	WEEDS	10	ENRICH	9
DESIRING	10	OBLIG'D	10	WEIGHS	10	ENRICH'D	9
DEWY	10	OBTAIN'D	10	WHIG	10	ENTRANCE	9
DIFFUSE	10	OFFERS	10	WILES	10	ERR	9
DISASTROUS	10	OFFICIOUS	10	WONDRING	10	ERR'D	9
DISPATCH'D	10	OMNIPOTENCE	10	WOODLAND	10	ESCAPE	9
DISTINCTION	10	ONES	10	YOU'D	10	EUROPE	9
DISTRACT	10	PAPERS	10	ABELARD	9	EURYALUS	9
DIVINES	10	PARDON	10	ACCESS	9	EURYLOCHUS	9
DOW'R	10	PARK	10	ACQUIR'D	9	EXCEED	9
DRAG	10	PASTURES	10	ADMIT	9	EXCLAIMS	9
DROPP'D	10	PEAR	10	AEGYSTHUS	9	EXERT	9
DUBIOUS	10	PERFIDIOUS	10	AFFAIRS	9	EXPERT	9
DYES	10	PERSUADE	10	AFFLICTED	9	EXTREME	9
EAS'D	10	PERT	10	AGREED	9	FAINTS	9
ELIS	10	PIETY	10	ALL-SEEING	9	FAIREST	9
ENCOURAG'D	10	PLAGUES	10	ALLAY	9	FAMILY	9
ENDED	10	POIS'D	10	ANCHOR'D	9	FAN	9
ENRAG'D	10	POX	10	ANCHORS	9	FANCY'S	9
ENTIRE	10	PRECIOUS	10	ANTENOR'S	9	FATE'S	9
ERROR	10	PREFER'D	10	ANTIENT	9	FEATURES	9
ERRORS	10	PRINTS	10	ARCHING	9	FLEECES	9
ESTEEM	10	PRIZES	10	ARDOR	9	FLOURISH	9
EURYPYLUS	10	PROPORTION'D	10	ARRAY'D	9	FOAMY	9
EUSDEN	10	PROPOSE	10	ASPIRES	9	FORETOLD	9
EVE	10	PROTECTION	10	ATTACK	9	FRIGHT	9
EXERCISE	10	PROVOKES	10	AUTHOR'S	9	GENUINE	9
EXHAUSTED	10	QUARTER	10	AUTUMN	9	GEORGE	9
EXPANDED	10	RAGES	10	AVAIL	9	GLARE	9
EXPIRING	10	RAPTUR'D	10	BARRIER	9	GRANTS	9
EXPRESS	10	REFRAIN	10	BARS	9	GRATITUDE	9
EXTREMES	10	REJECT	10	BAVIUS	9	GROSS	9
FACT	10	RELATES	10	BEARD	9	HAIR'D	9
FADED	10	REPAY	10	BECAME	9	HANDMAID	9
FAILING	10	REPELL	10	BEDLAM	9	HARE	9
FARCE	10	REPENT	10	BENEVOLENCE	9	HEIFERS	9
FERTILE	10	RESERVE	10	BESIDES	9	HERE'S	9
FIERCELY	10	RESIDE	10	BIER	9	HIDEOUS	9
FLATTER	10	RESIDES	10	BLACK'NING	9	HISS'D	9
FLINGS	10	RESUMES	10	BLASTS	9	HUM	9
FOLLIES	10	RETAIN	10	BLEAK	9	HURTS	9
FOOTED	10	REVEALS	10	BLUSH'D	9	HUSBAND'S	9
FOUNDATIONS	10	RICHEST	10	BRIGHTER	9	HYDE	9
FOUNT	10	RODE	10	BRUTAL	9	IDE	9
FRAGRANCE	10	ROME'S	10	BUILDS	9	IDOMEN	9
FUMES	10	ROW	10	BUS'NESS	9	IMPLORES	9
FURROW'D	10	SARPEDON'S	10	CANVAS	9	IMPLOY	9
GATHER	10	SCAMANDER	10	CARPET	9	IMPOSE	9
GLARES	10	SCAP'D	10	CAUTION	9	IMPOTENCE	9
GLEAM	10	SCYLLA	10	CERES	9	IMPREST	9
GLUT	10	SEEDS	10	CHARACTERS	9	IMPUDENCE	9
GODDESSES	10	SEQUESTER'D	10	CHIN	9	INDIAN	9
GOOSE	10	SEV'NFOLD	10	CLANGING	9	INDULGENT	9
GRAZE	10	SHAKESPEAR	10	CLEAR'D	9	INFLUENCE	9
HALLOW'D	10	SHATTER'D	10	CLIMB'D	9	ISLES	9
HANGING	10	SHEETS	10	CLOSING	9	JACOB	9
HARP	10	SHEPHERDS	10	CLUSTERS	9	KISS'D	9
HATES	10	SHOUTING	10	COLLECTS	9	KNIGHTS	9
HECATOMB	10	SHRILL	10	COMPACTED	9	LAERTES'	9
HIND	10	SICKNESS	10	COMPLAINS	9	LAMENTS	9
HINGES	10	SILKEN	10	CONCLUDE	9	LARGEST	9
HOLE	10	SMOAK	10	CONFER	9	LATELY	9
HOMAGE	10	SOFTLY	10	CONFIDENCE	9	LAWFUL	9
HOMER	10	SOLITARY	10	CONGENIAL	9	LESS'NING	9
HOT	10	SOUL'S	10	CONQUERS	9	LICENCE	9
HOUSES	10	SPAR'D	10	CONSIDER	9	LINEN	9

LISTS	9	SOFTEN'D	9	COMPLY	8	INJURIOUS	8
LIVID	9	SPAN	9	CONCAVE	8	INSIDIOUS	8
LOINS	9	SPONTANEOUS	9	CONFINES	8	INSULTED	8
LONE	9	SPORTS	9	CONFUS'DLY	8	INTREPID	8
LOPP'D	9	SPY'D	9	CONTENTION	8	INVEST	8
MACE	9	SQUIRES	9	CONVINC'D	8	ITCH	8
MAJESTICALLY	9	STALL	9	CORPSE	8	JOURNALS	8
MARBLES	9	STARVES	9	COV'RING	8	KINDLING	8
MARE	9	STEAD	9	CREATE	8	LANGUID	8
MEMORIAL	9	STICKS	9	CRITICS	8	LASTS	8
MENESTHEUS	9	STINGS	9	CURB	8	LATONA	8
MIGHTIER	9	STRIVES	9	CURL'D	8	LAWNS	8
MILK-WHITE	9	STROW'D	9	CUTS	8	LEAF	8
MILTON'S	9	STRUCTURES	9	CYCLOP	8	LEAN'D	8
MINGLING	9	STUDS	9	CYPRIAN	8	LEANING	8
MITE	9	SUBSTANCE	9	DAPHNE	8	LEAPING	8
MONEY	9	SWANS	9	DAPHNE'S	8	LIFTING	8
MONTHS	9	SWEETEST	9	DARKENS	8	LING'RING	8
MOTHERS	9	SWEETLY	9	DAY'S	8	LIP	8
MURD'RER	9	SWIFTER	9	DEIPHOBUS	8	LUMBER	8
MUTTER'D	9	SWIMMING	9	DEAL	8	LUNGS	8
NATIVES	9	SYLPH	9	DECLIN'D	8	LYON	8
NUMBER'D	9	SYLPHS	9	DEFRAUDED	8	MAKER	8
O'ERFLOWS	9	TASTES	9	DELICIOUS	8	MANE	8
O'ERLOOKS	9	TAUNTS	9	DEPTH	8	MARES	8
OATHS	9	TEEMING	9	DESARTS	8	MARRIAGE	8
OBLIGING	9	TERMS	9	DESCRY	8	MAZES	8
OBLIQUELY	9	THEATRES	9	DESERTS	8	MEGES	8
ODD	9	THICKEN	9	DESPIS'D	8	MERIONES	8
OFFENDING	9	THICKETS	9	DEXT'ROUS	8	MINES	8
OLIVE	9	THUNDRING	9	DIFFUS'D	8	MIRROUR	8
ORACLE	9	TIRE	9	DIRECTED	8	MISSILE	8
ORDAINS	9	TOKEN	9	DISTILL'D	8	MOMENTS	8
PALACES	9	TOUCHES	9	DOLON	8	MONTH	8
PALLAS'	9	TRANSLUCENT	9	DOUBLING	8	MOORE	8
PAUL	9	TRANSPORTED	9	DRAGS	8	MOTIVE	8
PAUSE	9	TRIPODS	9	DREADED	8	NAUSICAA	8
PEALS	9	TROUBLE	9	DREGS	8	NE'R	8
PERSUASIVE	9	TRUSTS	9	DRY'D	8	NEARER	8
PICTURES	9	TURK	9	DUCTILE	8	NECKS	8
PILOT	9	UNLUCKY	9	DULICHIUM	8	NEGLECTS	8
PINE	9	UNMATCH'D	9	DUNCES	8	NEIGHBOUR'S	8
PITEOUS	9	VARY'D	9	ECCHO	8	NELEUS	8
PLAN	9	VENT'ROUS	9	ECCHOING	8	NERVOUS	8
PLANTS	9	VENUS'	9	ENCOUNTER	8	NETHER	8
PLUMY	9	VERS'D	9	ENCREASE	8	NEW-BORN	8
POURING	9	WANTING	9	ENGLISH	8	NIC	8
POVERTY	9	WASTING	9	ENLARG'D	8	NILE	8
PRAISES	9	WEARY'D	9	EUMELUS	8	NIMBLE	8
PRAYER	9	WEIGH'D	9	EXALTS	8	NOCTURNAL	8
PRESIDES	9	WELSTED	9	EXCEEDS	8	O'ERCAST	8
PRODUC'D	9	WHELM'D	9	EXIL'D	8	ORDER'D	8
PROPHETIC	9	WHERE'S	9	FA	8	ORNAMENTS	8
PROVOK'D	9	WHITE'S	9	FACES	8	ORPHAN	8
PURSE	9	WHOLSOME	9	FADE	8	OVID	8
PURSUIT	9	WILDS	9	FAWN	8	PALMS	8
PYRATES	9	WILL'D	9	FEATURE	8	PAMPER'D	8
QUIRE	9	WONTED	9	FELLOW	8	PAN	8
RAIL	9	WORTHLESS	9	FERVENT	8	PARADISE	8
RANK'D	9	WYNDHAM	9	FIBRES	8	PARIS'	8
REBUKE	9	YAWNING	9	FIEND	8	PARNASSUS	8
RECALL	9	YOUNGER	9	FIGS	8	PATRIOTS	8
RECITE	9	YOURSELF	9	FLANK	8	PEDASUS	8
RED'NING	9	ABHORR'D	8	FONDLY	8	PERSUASION	8
REGULAR	9	ABHORS	8	FOOTSTOOL	8	PHEMIUS	8
RELEASE	9	ABYSS	8	FOREGO	8	PHRASE	8
RELENTING	9	ACCORD	8	FORGE	8	PINES	8
REMEMBER	9	ADAMANTINE	8	FORGETFUL	8	PIPE	8
REPASTE	9	AFFECT	8	FORGOTTEN	8	PISISTRATUS	8
REPREST	9	AFFRIGHTED	8	FREIGHT	8	PLAINTIVE	8
RESUM'D	9	AGENOR	8	FRENZY	8	PLATES	8
RETREATING	9	ALLOW'D	8	FRET	8	PLEADS	8
RETREATS	9	APPLAUSES	8	FROZEN	8	PLIES	8
RIDES	9	APPLY	8	FRUITLESS	8	POINTING	8
RIGHTS	9	ARGOS'	8	FUNEREAL	8	POISON	8
RILL	9	ARMY'S	8	FURTHER	8	POLES	8
ROSES	9	ASPIRING	8	GALLY	8	POWER	8
ROWZ'D	9	ATTENDED	8	GARLANDS	8	PRECEPT	8
SATIATE	9	ATTIRE	8	GATHERS	8	PREFERS	8
SAVES	9	AUKWARD	8	GENEROUS	8	PRESERVES	8
SAVING	9	AUTUMNĂL	8	GIANTS	8	PRIME	8
SCATTERS	9	AVOW'D	8	GIGANTIC	8	PROFANE	8
SCEPTRED	9	BABES	8	GILT	8	PROOF	8
SCHEME	9	BAFFLED	8	GLEAMS	8	PROPORTION	8
SCREEN'D	9	BEACH	8	GLITTER	8	PROPOS'D	8
SEATED	9	BEARDED	8	GREETS	8	PROTECTS	8
SELECT	9	BEDEW	8	GROUNDS	8	PROTEST	8
SELL	9	BEGOT	8	GUST	8	PULSE	8
SEMBLANCE	9	BEGS	8	HEAL	8	PUNK	8
SHADOWS	9	BENTLEY	8	HEARTY	8	QUIVER'D	8
SHAMELESS	9	BLEATING	8	HEELS	8	RACER	8
SHARPEN'D	9	BLOOMY	8	HELENUS	8	RAFT	8
SHEATH	9	BLUNT	8	HENLEY	8	RAINS	8
SHEWS	9	BODING	8	HISSES	8	RANDOM	8
SHIV'RING	9	BOUNTIES	8	HONOURABLE	8	RANSOM	8
SHRILLING	9	BREEDS	8	HOUND	8	RAPINE	8
SILVER-FOOTED	9	BUG	8	HUNT	8	RECEDES	8
SLAUGHTERS	9	CARCASS	8	IDEAS	8	RECLAIM	8
SLENDER	9	CATO'S	8	ILLUMIN'D	8	REFLECTED	8
SLIDE	9	CELL	8	IMPRISON'D	8	REFLECTION	8
SLIPP'RY	9	CHEAR	8	INCREAS'D	8	REFUGE	8
SMOTE	9	COALS	8	INEXORABLE	8	RELIEV'D	8
SNAKES	9	COMMISSION'D	8	INFLICTS	8	REPEL	8
SNEER	9	COMPAR'D	8	INFUS'D	8	RESPONSIVE	8
SNUFF	9	COMPARE	8	INGAGE	8	RETIRING	8

REVOLV'D	8	VANISH	8	CLASPS	7	GARTH	7
RINGING	8	VAPORS	8	CLEAVES	7	GEESE	7
ROAST	8	VEILS	8	CLOCKS	7	GIRLS	7
ROB'D	8	VESTURES	8	CLOTTED	7	GIVEN	7
ROCK'S	8	VEX	8	COARSE	7	GLADE	7
ROOT	8	VIE	8	COMBINE	7	GLADES	7
ROOTS	8	VINDICATE	8	COMMIT	7	GLEAMING	7
SAILING	8	VOUCHSAF'D	8	CONCERN	7	GLOBE	7
SATYR	8	WAKING	8	CONSTRAINS	7	GOODNESS	7
SCALY	8	WAND'RER	8	CONTEMPT	7	GRAPES	7
SCENT	8	WARY	8	CONTESTED	7	GRIEVES	7
SCEPTER	8	WAX	8	CONTRACTED	7	GRINDS	7
SCHEMES	8	WEEKLY	8	CONVEN'D	7	GRIZLY	7
SEARCH'D	8	WELL-BRED	8	COUCH'D	7	GROAT	7
SELECTED	8	WHARTON	8	COUNCILS	7	GROV'LING	7
SENSELESS	8	WHEAT	8	COY	7	GULLIVER	7
SENSES	8	WHELMING	8	CRAVING	7	GUSH'D	7
SERIOUS	8	WHEREFORE	8	CREEPS	7	HARDEST	7
SETTLE	8	WHISP'RING	8	CREPT	7	HARMONIOUS	7
SHADOW	8	WIDER	8	CRIMSON	7	HARNESS	7
SHAKING	8	WIDOW	8	CURSES	7	HASTES	7
SHAPES	8	WIELDS	8	CUSTOM	7	HEATHEN	7
SHEW'D	8	WINTER'S	8	D'URFY	7	HEAVIER	7
SHORT-LIV'D	8	WOOLLY	8	DAMIAN	7	HEEDLESS	7
SIMOIS	8	WOU'DST	8	DARTING	7	HELMETS	7
SINGING	8	WOVE	8	DEALT	7	HEN	7
SISTER'S	8	WRAP	8	DEITIES	7	HERCULES	7
SLAUGHT'RING	8	WRITER	8	DELIA'S	7	HIGHEST	7
SLEEP'S	8	ABASH'D	7	DELIGHTFUL	7	HOARSE-RESOUNDING	7
SLEEPLESS	8	ABOARD	7	DESCENT	7	HOG	7
SMOAKS	8	ABUSE	7	DESIST	7	HOGS	7
SMOOTH'D	8	ACCLAIM	7	DESPOIL	7	HOMER'S	7
SNARES	8	ACCOSTS	7	DICTATE	7	HOMICIDE	7
SOAR	8	ADMIRING	7	DIDST	7	HOWL	7
SOFTEST	8	ADONIS	7	DIRECTING	7	HUMBLES	7
SOLITUDE	8	ADORES	7	DISAGREE	7	IDEA	7
SPARTA'S	8	ADVANCES	7	DISARM'D	7	IMITATE	7
SPECTRE	8	ADVANTAGE	7	DISCOVER'D	7	IMPASSIVE	7
SPLENDOR	8	AEGIS	7	DISGRAC'D	7	IMPATIENCE	7
SPOUSAL	8	AEGYPTIAN	7	DISPATCH	7	IMPENDS	7
SPOUSES	8	AFFECTION	7	DISTILL	7	INCITE	7
SPOUTS	8	AFFLICTION	7	DISTILLS	7	INDULGENCE	7
STAKE	8	AFFRONT	7	DISTRESS'D	7	INJUSTICE	7
STANDARD	8	AGAMEMNON'S	7	DIVERSE	7	INSECT	7
STEEL'D	8	AGEN	7	DIVIDED	7	INSECTS	7
STIR	8	AMAZING	7	DIVINITY	7	INUR'D	7
STRAIN'D	8	AMBIENT	7	DOES	7	ISIS	7
STRANGELY	8	AMBROSIA	7	DOLIUS	7	ISLANDS	7
STRIPT	8	AMPHION	7	DOMESTICK	7	ISSUES	7
STRUGGLING	8	ANTENOR	7	DOUBLED	7	ITALIAN	7
STUFF	8	APE	7	DRENCH	7	IVORY	7
SUCK	8	ARABIAN	7	DRESS'D	7	JAMES	7
SUES	8	ARGUS	7	DROWN	7	JAMES'S	7
SUGGEST	8	ARRIVES	7	DRURY-LANE	7	JAR	7
SULPHUR	8	ASSAULT	7	DUNGEON	7	JUDG'D	7
SUM	8	ASSISTANT	7	E'EN	7	JUSTER	7
SUPPORTED	8	ATTEMPTS	7	EARTHQUAKES	7	KINDLE	7
SUPPRESS	8	ATTESTING	7	EATS	7	KNOCK'D	7
SUPREMELY	8	ATTONE	7	ECCHOES	7	KNOTTY	7
SURVIVE	8	AUSPICIOUS	7	ECHO	7	LARKS	7
SUSPENDS	8	AWAK'D	7	ECHOES	7	LATIN	7
SWAN	8	AXES	7	EDGE	7	LAUGHING	7
SWEETER	8	BARKS	7	ELEPHANT	7	LEVELL'D	7
TAILS	8	BATTALIONS	7	ELUDED	7	LICK	7
TALENT	8	BEAUS	7	EMBERS	7	LIGHTER	7
TALKS	8	BEGG'D	7	EMBLEM	7	LILLIES	7
TAYLOR	8	BEGGAR	7	EMBROID'RY	7	LOTH	7
TEMPTING	8	BESET	7	EMPTINESS	7	LOYAL	7
TEMPTS	8	BLAZES	7	ENCLOSURE	7	LUCID	7
TEUCER'S	8	BLEW	7	ENSANGUIN'D	7	LUCKY	7
TEXTURE	8	BLINDLY	7	ENSU'D	7	LULL	7
THEY'RE	8	BLOCKHEAD	7	ESCAP'D	7	LYCAON	7
THONG	8	BOIL	7	ESSAY'D	7	LYCIA	7
THRASYMED	8	BOLDER	7	EW'R	7	MANHOOD	7
THRONGING	8	BOND	7	EXCELL'D	7	MANSIONS	7
TIBBALD	8	BORROW'D	7	EXPLOR'D	7	MARINERS	7
TORTURES	8	BOUNDED	7	EXPRESSIVE	7	MAY'RS	7
TOUCHING	8	BRAC'D	7	FAIN	7	MEEK	7
TOYS	8	BRANCHING	7	FAIRER	7	MEETING	7
TRAC'D	8	BRAV'D	7	FAL'N	7	MELANIPPUS	7
TRACTS	8	BRAVES	7	FALLEN	7	MENTOR'S	7
TRANSPIERC'D	8	BREEZES	7	FALSHOOD	7	MISTAKE	7
TREASUR'D	8	BRETHREN	7	FAME'S	7	MOB	7
TRICKLING	8	BRITAIN'S	7	FANS	7	MOMENTARY	7
TRIM	8	BROOD	7	FARE	7	MORSELS	7
TRUCE	8	BUCKLES	7	FAREWEL	7	MOSES	7
TRUNK	8	BULL-HIDES	7	FEATHERS	7	MOUSE	7
TRUSTY	8	BULWARK	7	FETTERS	7	MOUTH'D	7
TRUTHS	8	BURDEN	7	FIERCEST	7	MUCH-LOV'D	7
TUMBLED	8	BURNISH'D	7	FIG	7	MULTITUDES	7
TUN'D	8	BUSIE	7	FIGUR'D	7	MUSING	7
TUSKY	8	BUTTERFLIES	7	FLAT	7	MYRMIDONIAN	7
TWAIN	8	CAESAR'S	7	FLATTERY	7	MYSELF	7
TYRANT'S	8	CALYPSO'S	7	FLIGHTS	7	NATURES	7
TYRIAN	8	CAP	7	FLUTT'RING	7	NEAREST	7
UNBIND	8	CAVERN'D	7	FOLIAGE	7	NEREIDS	7
UNBRAC'D	8	CAVERNS	7	FOOL'S	7	NEST	7
UNREGARDED	8	CHAIN'D	7	FORMIDABLE	7	NORTON	7
UNTAM'D	8	CHEAR'D	7	FRAM'D	7	O'ERFLOW	7
UNWARY	8	CHEARS	7	FRAUGHT	7	O'ERWHELMS	7
UPHELD	8	CHEESE	7	FREEZE	7	OBLIQUE	7
UPLIFTED	8	CHINA	7	FRO	7	OCEANS	7
UPPER	8	CHRYSTAL	7	FROST	7	OFF-SPRING	7
UPWARD	8	CLANG	7	FROWNING	7	OFFENDED	7
VAGRANT	8	CLASHING	7	FRUSTRATE	7	OLIVES	7

Word		Word		Word		Word	
ONE'S	7	STARVING	7	AMAIN	6	DEBTS	6
OP'D	7	STEDFAST	7	AMPHINOMUS	6	DECEIT	6
OPINION	7	STILE	7	AMPLER	6	DECEIVES	6
OTHER'S	7	STIRS	7	ANCHISES'	6	DECLINES	6
OUTWARD	7	STONY	7	ANCIENTS	6	DEFIES	6
OWLS	7	STRIDE	7	ANIMATE	6	DEIGNS	6
PENDENT	7	SUBMISSIVE	7	ANOINTED	6	DEITY	6
PENELEUS	7	SUBSIDES	7	APPEAL	6	DELICACY	6
PERCH'D	7	SUCCESSIVE	7	APPEAS'D	6	DELUSION	6
PERFUME	7	SUCCESSLESS	7	APPEASE	6	DEPLORES	6
PERFUMES	7	SUFF'RINGS	7	APPLAUDING	6	DEPUTED	6
PERSEUS	7	SUFFER'D	7	ARGYLE	6	DESCRIPTION	6
PERSIAN	7	SUFFERS	7	ARIEL	6	DETEST	6
PHILAETIUS	7	SUFFIC'D	7	ARRIVING	6	DEVOTION	6
PIL'D	7	SUFFICIENT	7	ARTHUR	6	DIFFERENT	6
PLANTED	7	SUP	7	ASIUS'	6	DIPT	6
PLUMAGE	7	SUPPLIANT'S	7	ASSAIL	6	DISCLAIM	6
PLUNGING	7	SURELY	7	ASSERTS	6	DISCLOS'D	6
PLUTO	7	SURLY	7	ASSISTS	6	DISCONTENTED	6
POIZ'D	7	SURPAST	7	ASSWAGE	6	DISDAINFUL	6
POLICY	7	SUSPENDED	7	ATON'D	6	DISLIKE	6
POLYBUS	7	SWEARS	7	ATTENDANTS	6	DISMAY'D	6
POPE'S	7	SYLLABLES	7	AUDIENCE	6	DISPATCHFUL	6
POPLAR	7	SYSTEM	7	AUGUR	6	DISPUTED	6
PORCH	7	TABLES	7	AVOID	6	DIVES	6
POTENT	7	TAINT	7	BALAAM	6	DOUBTING	6
PRACTIS'D	7	TALK'D	7	BATTLEMENTS	6	DRAGONS	6
PREDESTIN'D	7	TAM'D	7	BEAUTIFUL	6	DRAIN'D	6
PREGNANT	7	TARDY	7	BENEVOLENT	6	DROWNS	6
PRESIDE	7	TEMPLARS	7	BEQUEATH	6	DROWZY	6
PREVENTING	7	THEMES	7	BERNARD	6	DRUGS	6
PROCESSION	7	THEY'LL	7	BLACKEN	6	DUTCH	6
PRODIGAL	7	THICK'NING	7	BLACKMORE	6	EAGLES	6
PRODUCT	7	THICKENS	7	BLACKMORE'S	6	EFFUS'D	6
PROFEST	7	THIEF	7	BLEND	6	EKE	6
PROFUSION	7	THREATNING	7	BLOCKHEADS	6	ELEMENTS	6
PROSPECTS	7	THYRSIS	7	BOARS	6	ELUDES	6
PROTEUS	7	TIM'D	7	BOLDNESS	6	ELYSIAN	6
PUPPY	7	TIP	7	BOLTED	6	ENDUR'D	6
PURPLED	7	TO-MORROW	7	BOSOME	6	ENDURING	6
PUSH'D	7	TOIL'D	7	BOSOMS	6	ENGLAND	6
QUEENS	7	TRACES	7	BRANDS	6	ESSAY	6
QUENCH'D	7	TRAGEDY	7	BREVAL	6	ET	6
QUICKLY	7	TULLY	7	BRIB'D	6	EUROPE'S	6
RAILS	7	TUSKS	7	BRIGHTEN'D	6	EURYDICE	6
RARELY	7	TWANGING	7	BRISEÏS	6	EVER-HONOUR'D	6
RATE	7	TWELFTH	7	BRITONS	6	EXACTLY	6
RAVE	7	TWINS	7	BROOK	6	EXERCIS'D	6
REBOUNDS	7	TYRANNY	7	BUDGEL	6	EXPLAIN'D	6
RECALL'D	7	UNACTIVE	7	BUDS	6	EXPLORES	6
REDEEM	7	UNARM'D	7	BURTHEN	6	EXPOSE	6
REFLECTING	7	UNCERTAIN	7	BUST	6	EXTENT	6
REJOICE	7	UNCOMFORTABLE	7	BUYS	6	FABLED	6
REMOVES	7	UNCONFIN'D	7	BYASS	6	FACTIONS	6
REPEAT	7	UNFOLDS	7	CALCHAS	6	FADES	6
REQUIR'D	7	UNMANLY	7	CAREER	6	FALCON	6
RESISTS	7	UNTASTED	7	CASTING	6	FANCY'D	6
REVERS'D	7	UNUSUAL	7	CATCH'D	6	FASHION	6
REVIVES	7	UPRIGHT	7	CELLS	6	FAWNS	6
RIPER	7	URGES	7	CENT	6	FEATHER	6
ROMANTIC	7	VALU'D	7	CHAMPIONS	6	FEIGN	6
ROVES	7	VARIES	7	CHANGEFUL	6	FENCE	6
ROWZE	7	VAUNT	7	CHANGES	6	FILTH	6
RUDELY	7	VICTORY	7	CHINE	6	FILTHY	6
RUIN'D	7	VIRGIL	7	CHROMIUS	6	FINER	6
SAFELY	7	VULTURES	7	CIRCE'S	6	FIRMAMENT	6
SAGES	7	WAFTS	7	CLASP	6	FIRST-BORN	6
SALUTE	7	WAIN	7	CLASP'D	6	FLAGRANT	6
SALUTES	7	WAN	7	CLASSIC	6	FLATT'RING	6
SAPPHO	7	WARN	7	CLIFF	6	FOLDED	6
SCAR'D	7	WASTFUL	7	CLOË	6	FOLLY'S	6
SCARLET	7	WEAL	7	CLOSER	6	FONDNESS	6
SCHOOLS	7	WEB	7	CLOTH	6	FORESEES	6
SCOUR	7	WEDS	7	CLUB	6	FORSAKEN	6
SCRIBBLE	7	WELL-FOUGHT	7	CLUNG	6	FRESHNESS	6
SCRIP	7	WELL-PLEAS'D	7	COIN	6	FUME	6
SEA-BEAT	7	WENCH	7	COMELY	6	FUN'RALS	6
SEA-GREEN	7	WHIGS	7	COMPANY	6	G	6
SEAL	7	WHIRLWINDS	7	COMPLAINTS	6	GARLAND	6
SECRETS	7	WHITEN	7	CONCEIV'D	6	GARMENT	6
SEEMING	7	WHITENS	7	CONFERR'D	6	GAUL	6
SEIZES	7	WIDOWS	7	CONFIDE	6	GAV'ST	6
SEVERELY	7	WILY	7	CONFIDING	6	GEN'RAL'S	6
SHEET	7	WITTY	7	CONFOUNDED	6	GENTLER	6
SHEPHERD'S	7	WRATHFUL	7	CONGREVE	6	GENTLEST	6
SHOULD'ST	7	WRITINGS	7	CONSTRAIN	6	GIRT	6
SHRUBS	7	YAWN	7	CONSUMMATE	6	GLEE	6
SICILIAN	7	YEARLY	7	CONTRACTS	6	GLIMM'RING	6
SINEWY	7	ZEALOUS	7	COOK	6	GLOVES	6
SIXTY	7	ZEPHYRS	7	COOLING	6	GLUTTON	6
SKIM	7	ACAMAS	6	CORRUPTION	6	GNOME	6
SLIGHTED	7	ACCOUNT	6	COTTAGE	6	GOARY	6
SLUMB'RING	7	ADMITS	6	COU'DST	6	GORGEOUS	6
SLY	7	ADRASTUS	6	COURTIER'S	6	GRACELESS	6
SMEDLEY	7	AEGYPT'S	6	COW	6	GRASS	6
SMOOTHLY	7	AENEAS'	6	CRACK	6	GRASSY	6
SOOTHS	7	AEOLIAN	6	CRAFTY	6	GROTT	6
SORROWING	7	AETOLIAN	6	CREEPING	6	GUILD	6
SOW'R	7	AFFECTIONS	6	CRITIC	6	GULPHS	6
SPAIN	7	AGELAUS	6	CRITICK'S	6	GULPHY	6
SPEND	7	AJAX'	6	CROPS	6	HAD'ST	6
SPLENDORS	7	ALDERS	6	CROST	6	HANG'D	6
SPORTIVE	7	ALE	6	CROUDS	6	HATCH	6
SPRINKLED	7	ALLURE	6	CUIRASS	6	HEAPY	6
SQUARE	7	ALMS	6	CUPS	6	HEAVINESS	6
				DANC'D	6		

HECUBA	6	OURSELF	6	RUSTLING	6	TWISTED	6
HEEL	6	OZELL	6	RUTHLESS	6	TYE	6
HEIGHTS	6	PANTHUS	6	SAFER	6	UMBRA	6
HELPS	6	PARNASSIAN	6	SAMIAN	6	UNCHANG'D	6
HERBAGE	6	PARTRIDGE	6	SAMOS	6	UNCONTROUL'D	6
HEREDITARY	6	PASTURE	6	SANGUIN	6	UNFAITHFUL	6
HISTORY	6	PATCH'D	6	SATURNIAN	6	UNMIX'D	6
HOMEWARD	6	PEARLS	6	SCAMANDER'S	6	UNPITY'D	6
HOPELESS	6	PENSION	6	SCREEN	6	UNPITYING	6
HORN'D	6	PEOPLED	6	SCRIV'NER	6	UNPRACTIS'D	6
HORRIBLE	6	PER	6	SCULPTUR'D	6	UNSTAIN'D	6
HOVERS	6	PERFECTION	6	SEEST	6	UNTY'D	6
HUNTRESS	6	PERFUM'D	6	SELKIRK	6	UPBRAIDS	6
IDAEAN	6	PERIOD	6	SENIOR	6	UPROSE	6
ILLUSION	6	PERIODS	6	SERMONS	6	VAGRANTS	6
IMAG'D	6	PHALANX	6	SERPENTS	6	VAULTS	6
IMPELLS	6	PHANTOMS	6	SERVING	6	VERTUMNUS	6
IMPOS'D	6	PHARIAN	6	SEVER'D	6	VICES	6
INDULG'D	6	PHORCYS	6	SHADOWY	6	VIEWLESS	6
INFIX'D	6	PISANDER	6	SHAKESPEAR'S	6	VIGILS	6
INFLAMES	6	PITIES	6	SHALLOW	6	VINDICTIVE	6
INNOCENTLY	6	POCKET	6	SHELL	6	VINTAGE	6
INSCRIBE	6	POLISH	6	SHELVING	6	VIRGIN'S	6
INSERTED	6	POLITICKS	6	SHIFT	6	VOLUME	6
INSTRUCTIVE	6	POLYPHEME	6	SHOOTING	6	VOLUNTARY	6
INT'RESTS	6	PORTENTOUS	6	SHORTEN'D	6	VULCAN'S	6
ISLAND'S	6	PORTICO	6	SHRINK	6	WAFTING	6
JARS	6	POSTS	6	SHRINKS	6	WAG	6
JEWS	6	POT	6	SHUN'D	6	WARNING	6
JUSTIFY	6	POUNDS	6	SICK'NING	6	WAVY	6
LAC'D	6	PRACTICE	6	SILK	6	WEDLOCK	6
LAMB	6	PRATE	6	SILKS	6	WELL-FED	6
LAMENTABLE	6	PRECEDE	6	SINFUL	6	WHAT-TIME	6
LAODAMAS	6	PREVAIL'D	6	SINGLED	6	WHEELING	6
LAVISH	6	PREVENTS	6	SIRS	6	WHOEVER	6
LAWRELS	6	PRINCIPLES	6	SLACK	6	WHOLLY	6
LEADEN	6	PRIOR	6	SLANDER	6	WIP'D	6
LEAGU'D	6	PRIZ'D	6	SLANDER'D	6	WIPE	6
LEAGUES	6	PROCURE	6	SLOTH	6	WISDOM'S	6
LEARNT	6	PRODIGIES	6	SMOAKY	6	WITH-HELD	6
LEATHER	6	PRODIGIOUS	6	SNAKE	6	WITH'RING	6
LEAVING	6	PROFESS	6	SOL	6	WOODEN	6
LEER	6	PROFIT	6	SORROW'D	6	WOULDST	6
LEG	6	PROP	6	SPARKLE	6	WREATH	6
LEMNIAN	6	PROSERPINE	6	SPARKLED	6	WRINKLED	6
LICENS'D	6	PROTECT	6	SPELLS	6	ZEPHYR	6
LIGHTEN'D	6	PROUDER	6	SPICY	6	A-WHILE	5
LIK'D	6	PROVINCE	6	SPIRE	6	ABHOR	5
LIN'D	6	PTHIA'S	6	SPIRY	6	ABLE	5
LINK	6	PUFF'D	6	SPOTS	6	ABSURD	5
LISTEN'D	6	PUNS	6	SPURN	6	ABUNDANT	5
LIVER	6	PURCHAS'D	6	SPURN'D	6	ABUS'D	5
LOCKE	6	PURGE	6	STAGG'RING	6	ACCEPTED	5
LORDSHIP	6	PYE	6	STARV'D	6	ACCURS'D	5
LOTOS	6	QUAFF'D	6	STEALTH	6	ACTING	5
LOWING	6	QUEEN'S	6	STOCKS	6	ADAM	5
LULL'D	6	QUENCH	6	STORIED	6	ADVENTURE	5
LUNAR	6	QUESTIONS	6	STREAM'D	6	ADVIS'D	5
LURK	6	RACERS	6	STRETCHES	6	AETHER	5
LUXURIANT	6	REAL	6	STROWS	6	AFFABLE	5
LYCAON'S	6	REAP	6	STUDIES	6	AFFIANC'D	5
MADLY	6	REBELLOW	6	STUNN'D	6	AFFLUENCE	5
MAGICK	6	RECALLS	6	STURDY	6	AKING	5
MAINTAIN'D	6	RECEDE	6	SUCCESSION	6	ALASTOR	5
MANIFEST	6	REDEEM'D	6	SUCCINCT	6	ALBION	5
MANY-COLOUR'D	6	REED	6	SUMPTUOUS	6	ALE-HOUSE	5
MARINER	6	REEL	6	SUMS	6	ALLIES	5
MARKET	6	REEL'D	6	SUNNY	6	ALLOTTED	5
MASTERS	6	REFLUENT	6	SUSPECT	6	ALOOF	5
MEADOWS	6	REFRESH'D	6	SUSPECTED	6	ALPS	5
MEANLY	6	REIN'D	6	SWALLOW	6	AMISS	5
METAL	6	REJECTS	6	SWEEPING	6	AMOROUS	5
MILL	6	RELENT	6	SWIM	6	AMPHIMACHUS	5
MIMIC	6	RELIGIOUS	6	SWIMS	6	AMPHIMEDON	5
MINT	6	REMOTEST	6	SYLVIA	6	ANGEL'S	5
MIRTHFUL	6	REPAIR'D	6	TAINTED	6	ANIMATED	5
MISTAKEN	6	REPEATED	6	TALTHYBIUS	6	ANIMATES	5
MISTY	6	REPENTANT	6	TAMELY	6	ANNE	5
MOOD	6	REPLENISH'D	6	TASTEFUL	6	ANSW'RING	5
MOUTHS	6	REPROACHES	6	TATTER'D	6	ANTIPHUS	5
MR	6	RESCUE	6	TENDS	6	APACE	5
MUCH-ENDURING	6	RESENT	6	TEXT	6	APPLAUD	5
MYRIADS	6	RESOLVE	6	THALESTRIS	6	ARDUOUS	5
NAVEL	6	RESOUNDED	6	THANKLESS	6	ARGUS'	5
NE	6	RESTED	6	THEFT	6	ARISING	5
NET	6	REVEL	6	THICKEN'D	6	ARMOR	5
NEWTON'S	6	REVIVE	6	THORN	6	ARNALL	5
NOISY	6	RHESUS	6	THOUGH (OMITTED)	6	ARRESTS	5
NOMAN	6	RHIME	6	THRACE	6	ASCALAPHUS	5
NOTED	6	RHINE	6	THRIVE	6	ASSEMBLING	5
NUPTIALS	6	RIBS	6	THYSELF	6	ASSENTING	5
O'ERTAKES	6	RID	6	TIN	6	ASSENTS	5
O'ERWHELM'D	6	RIGHTFUL	6	TO-DAY	6	ASTEROPEUS	5
OBLIGE	6	RIGID	6	TOMBS	6	ASTYANAX	5
OBLIVIOUS	6	RIOTS	6	TOPMOST	6	ATONE	5
OBSERVES	6	RIPEN'D	6	TRANSCENDS	6	ATTACKS	5
OBSERVING	6	RIVAL'S	6	TRAYTOR	6	AUDACIOUS	5
OEDIPUS	6	ROGUES	6	TRENCHES	6	AUGHT	5
OFFENDS	6	ROSEATE	6	TRICK	6	AUGMENT	5
OOZE	6	ROWL	6	TRICKS	6	AUGURY	5
OP'NING	6	ROWL'D	6	TRIDENT	6	AUGUST	5
OPPRESS	6	ROWLS	6	TRIFLE	6	AUGUSTUS	5
ORGANS	6	RUFFLED	6	TRIUMPHAL	6	AVARICE	5
ORPHEUS	6	RUMBLING	6	TUGG'D	6	AWAITS	5
ORSILOCHUS	6	RUMOUR	6	TWIN'D	6	AWHILE	5

B	5	CONTENTMENT	5	FASTS	5	ICE	5
BACCHUS'	5	CONTENTS	5	FATTED	5	IDOL	5
BACKS	5	CONTRACT	5	FAULCHIONS	5	IGNOBLY	5
BADGE	5	COOLS	5	FAULTLESS	5	ILUS'	5
BAG	5	CORRECT	5	FAV'RITES	5	IMBROWN'D	5
BARBARIANS	5	CORRUPTED	5	FAWNING	5	IMMUR'D	5
BARLEY	5	COSCUS	5	FEASTFUL	5	IMPELL	5
BARON	5	COVERS	5	FEASTING	5	IMPERFECT	5
BARR'D	5	COWARDS	5	FEATS	5	IMPLORING	5
BASELY	5	CRAWL	5	FELL'D	5	IMPORT	5
BATHURST	5	CREATED	5	FESTIVAL	5	IMPROV'D	5
BEE	5	CRESTED	5	FICTION	5	IMPULSE	5
BEECH	5	CRYSTALS	5	FIFTH	5	INCREASING	5
BEHEST	5	CUBITS	5	FILES	5	INDOLENT	5
BEINGS	5	CULL	5	FINGERS	5	INDULGING	5
BEN	5	CURTAIN	5	FINISH	5	INFECTION	5
BILL	5	CYCLOPEAN	5	FINNY	5	INFORM	5
BLACKEN'D	5	DAMNS	5	FLAGITIOUS	5	INFORMS	5
BLAND	5	DAMS	5	FLATT'RERS	5	INFUSE	5
BLANK	5	DANIEL	5	FLOORS	5	INK	5
BLOODLESS	5	DARDANS	5	FLORID	5	INSCRIPTION	5
BLOT	5	DARK'NING	5	FLUTTER	5	INSOLENT	5
BLUNDERBUSS	5	DEEPEST	5	FLUTTERS	5	INSTRUMENT	5
BLUNDERS	5	DEEPLY	5	FOE'S	5	INTERPOS'D	5
BLUNTED	5	DEFAC'D	5	FOLLOWERS	5	INTERVAL	5
BOASTFUL	5	DEFEATED	5	FORBAD	5	INVENTIVE	5
BOILEAU	5	DEFECTS	5	FORBEARS	5	INVIOLABLE	5
BONDAGE	5	DELAY'D	5	FOREDOOM'D	5	INVITED	5
BONDS	5	DEPENDS	5	FORLORN	5	INVOK'D	5
BOOTH	5	DEPTHS	5	FORT	5	INWROUGHT	5
BOOTS	5	DESCENDENT	5	FORTITUDE	5	ITHACA'S	5
BOW'RY	5	DESCRIBE	5	FOWLS	5	JAPHET	5
BOWELS	5	DESTINY	5	FRAILTIES	5	JEALOUSIE	5
BRAY	5	DEUCALION	5	FREELY	5	JOHNSON	5
BREAKING	5	DEXTER	5	FREEZING	5	JOYN	5
BREATHS	5	DIFF'RING	5	FRETTED	5	JOYN'D	5
BREECHES	5	DIGEST	5	FRIENDLESS	5	JUDGING	5
BREEZY	5	DISABLED	5	FRIENDSHIPS	5	JUPITER	5
BRISTLED	5	DISAPPOINTS	5	FROWNS	5	KEENER	5
BRITANNIA'S	5	DISASTER	5	FULFILL'D	5	KILLING	5
BRITON	5	DISCERN	5	FULL-FED	5	KINDER	5
BROCADE	5	DISCONTENT	5	FURROWS	5	KINDLES	5
BRUTUS	5	DISGUIS'D	5	FURS	5	KINDNESS	5
BUCKLERS	5	DISHONOUR	5	GAINST	5	KINDS	5
BUDGELL	5	DISK	5	GARRETS	5	KINGDOM	5
BURIES	5	DISORDER'D	5	GARTERS	5	KINGDOMS	5
BURNET	5	DISPENSE	5	GASH'D	5	KNOCK	5
CABLES	5	DISPERSE	5	GAUNTLET	5	LA	5
CADMUS	5	DISSEMBLED	5	GILBERT	5	LAD	5
CAET'RA	5	DISSOLVING	5	GIRD	5	LAMPS	5
CALLING	5	DIV'D	5	GLADS	5	LANDED	5
CALYDON	5	DOLEFUL	5	GLEBE	5	LAOMEDON	5
CAPITAL	5	DOMINION	5	GLUTTONS	5	LAUGH'D	5
CARDS	5	DOTH	5	GODLY	5	LAVES	5
CARNAL	5	DOZE	5	GOOD-NATURE	5	LEANS	5
CAS'D	5	DRAGON	5	GOR'D	5	LEONTEUS	5
CASQUE	5	DUPE	5	GORGON	5	LETTER	5
CAUGHT	5	EFFLUVIA	5	GOTHIC	5	LICKS	5
CHALKY	5	EFFULGENCE	5	GOVERN	5	LIDS	5
CHAMBERS	5	EGG	5	GOVERNMENT	5	LIFELESS	5
CHAPLAIN	5	ELIZA	5	GRANDEUR	5	LIGHT'NINGS	5
CHARGER	5	ELM	5	GRANDSIRE	5	LIGHTED	5
CHARIOT'S	5	ELOISA	5	GRANVILLE	5	LIGHTENS	5
CHARYBDIS	5	EMBOSS'D	5	GRATIS	5	LINTOT'S	5
CHATT'RING	5	EMPIRES	5	GRILDRIG	5	LISTEN	5
CHICKS	5	EMPLOYS	5	GRINNING	5	LODG'D	5
CHIEFLY	5	ENAMEL'D	5	GROTTO'S	5	LOP	5
CHOAK'D	5	ENCIRCLED	5	GRUDGE	5	LUTE	5
CHOIR	5	ENCLOSE	5	GUILE	5	LYBIAN	5
CHRUSEÏS	5	ENCOMPASS'D	5	GUINEA	5	MAGNIFICENCE	5
CLARION	5	ENCREAS'D	5	HAIL'D	5	MAGNIFICENT	5
CLASH	5	ENERGY	5	HALLS	5	MAGNIFICENTLY	5
CLASPING	5	ENGINE	5	HANDLE	5	MAGNIFY	5
CLEANS'D	5	ENGROSS	5	HAPLY	5	MARRY	5
CLEANSE	5	ENJOIN'D	5	HARBOUR	5	MAXIMS	5
CLEAVING	5	ENNOBLED	5	HARDEN'D	5	MEDITATE	5
CLIMBS	5	ENT'RING	5	HARM	5	MEDITATING	5
CLINGING	5	ENVIES	5	HARMONY	5	MEN'S	5
CLOATH'D	5	ETERNITY	5	HASTEN	5	MERCURY	5
CLOE	5	EUPHORBUS	5	HASTS	5	METAPHYSIC	5
CLYTIUS	5	EURYNOMÈ	5	HAUNTS	5	MIGHT'ST	5
COCK	5	EVADE	5	HEARTH	5	MIND'S	5
COFFEE	5	EVENTS	5	HEARTLESS	5	MINGLES	5
COINS	5	EVILS"	5	HEIFER	5	MINOS	5
COMBATS	5	EWES	5	HELLESPONT	5	MINSTREL	5
COMMENT	5	EXCESS	5	HELLESPONT'S	5	MIRACLE	5
COMMISSION	5	EXHORTS	5	HENS	5	MISCREANT	5
COMMUN'D	5	EXPANDS	5	HERB	5	MOBS	5
COMPACT	5	EXPECTING	5	HERVEY'S	5	MOMENT'S	5
COMPLETE	5	EXPEL	5	HIGH-BOUNDING	5	MONSIEUR	5
COMPOSING	5	EXPELL'D	5	HINDMOST	5	MOONS	5
CONCEIT	5	EXTENDING	5	HINDS	5	MORROW'S	5
CONCEIVE	5	EXTOLL'D	5	HIPPOTHOUS	5	MOSS	5
CONDEMN	5	EXTREAMEST	5	HIRE	5	MOSSIE	5
CONDITIONS	5	EXTREAMS	5	HIRELING	5	MOTLEY	5
CONFERS	5	EXTREMELY	5	HOOK	5	MOWS	5
CONFLICTING	5	EXULTS	5	HOPS	5	MULE	5
CONNECTS	5	FABLE	5	HORNECK'S	5	MURRAY	5
CONSENTING	5	FACTION	5	HOUSHOLD	5	MUTT'RING	5
CONSIGN	5	FAILS	5	HOVER'D	5	MYRTLES	5
CONSORT'S	5	FAIR-HAIR'D	5	HUES	5	NARRATIVE	5
CONSPIR'D	5	FALCHION	5	HUMAN-KIND	5	NEAT	5
CONTAIN'D	5	FANES	5	HUMMING	5	NECESSITY	5
CONTEMPLATION	5	FAR-BEAMING	5	HUSH	5	NECTAREOUS	5
		FAR-FAM'D	5	HYLAS	5	NIMBLY	5

NOTIONS	5
NOURISH'D	5
NOXIOUS	5
OÏLEUS'	5
O'	5
O'ERLOOK'D	5
OBEDIENCE	5
OBSEQUIES	5
OBSTINATE	5
OBTAINS	5
OD'ROUS	5
ODORS	5
OENEUS	5
OLDMIXON	5
OLIVE'S	5
ONCE-LOV'D	5
OPE	5
OPINIONS	5
OPIUM	5
OSIERS	5
OTHERS'	5
OURSELVES	5
OWNER	5
PAIR'D	5
PALLADIAN	5
PANDARUS	5
PANG	5
PANOPLY	5
PARENTS'	5
PARENT	5
PARNELL	5
PARSON	5
PARTIES	5
PARTNERS	5
PATRON'S	5
PEASANT	5
PEERAGE	5
PERCEIV'D	5
PERCHANCE	5
PETITIONS	5
PHILOMEL	5
PIGMY	5
PILLAR	5
PIN'D	5
PINING	5
PIPES	5
PIT	5
PLANKS	5
PLATE	5
PLATO	5
PLEA	5
PLEADED	5
PLIANT	5
PLUNDER'D	5
POLLUTED	5
PORTENT	5
PORTIONS	5
POSSESSIONS	5
POWDER	5
PRAYS	5
PREROGATIVE	5
PRESCRIB'D	5
PRESSING	5
PREVAILING	5
PRIESTESS	5
PRIVILEGE	5
PRODUCTS	5
PROLONG'D	5
PRONOUNCE	5
PROPERTY	5
PROPHECY	5
PROPHET'S	5
PROPS	5
PROTECTED	5
PROTECTING	5
PROVIDES	5
PUDDING	5
PYRAMID	5
QUALITY	5
QUIRES	5
RAISES	5
RAKE	5
RAPE	5
RATTLING	5
RAVAGE	5
RAVISH	5
REASONABLE	5
REASONS	5
REBELLION	5
REBELLIOUS	5
REGAIN'D	5
REGARDS	5
REJECTED	5
REJOICING	5
REJOYN'D	5
RELIES	5
REMAINING	5
RENDER	5
REPOS'D	5
REPTILE	5
RESIGNS	5
RESPECTFUL	5
RESPLENDENT	5
RESUME	5
RETAINS	5
REVEREND	5
REVIV'D	5
RIDICULE	5
RIDICULES	5
RIND	5
RIPENING	5
RIPENS	5
ROARINGS	5
ROBERT	5
ROSS	5
SABBATH	5
SACK	5
SACK'D	5
SADDENS	5
SADDER	5
SALT	5
SATAN	5
SAV'RY	5
SAVAGES	5
SCARCELY	5
SCEPTER'D	5
SCEPTERS	5
SCORCH'D	5
SCORCHING	5
SCORE	5
SCREAMING	5
SCREAMS	5
SCYTHE	5
SEA-BORN	5
SECT	5
SEE'ST	5
SELLS	5
SERAPH'S	5
SERENELY	5
SERMON	5
SERVANT'S	5
SEVER	5
SHOCKS	5
SHRIEVES	5
SHRINES	5
SHROUD	5
SHUNN'D	5
SIDON	5
SIMILITUDE	5
SKULL	5
SLOATH	5
SLUICE	5
SMELL	5
SMOAK'D	5
SNEERING	5
SNOWIE	5
SOBS	5
SOCIETY	5
SOFTEN	5
SOLACE	5
SOLAR	5
SOLDIER'S	5
SORDID	5
SOT	5
SOUR	5
SOUTHERN	5
SOW'RLY	5
SPARKLES	5
SPARKS	5
SPHERES	5
SPICES	5
SPINDLE	5
SPINS	5
SPORUS	5
SPOUT	5
SQUADRON	5
STAMP	5
STARES	5
STARING	5
STATESMAN'S	5
STEEP'D	5
STEWS	5
STICK	5
STING	5
STINK	5
STINKS	5
STOL'N	5
STOMACH	5
STRAYS	5
STRENGTHEN'D	5
STRENGTHENS	5
STRIKING	5
STRONGLY	5
STRUMPET	5
STRUTS	5
STUDDED	5
STUDY'D	5
SUBMISSION	5
SUBMITS	5
SUBSIDE	5
SUBTLE	5
SUCCEEDED	5
SUCK'D	5
SUITORS'	5
SUMMON	5
SUNSHINE	5
SUPPLIANTS	5
SURER	5
SURPASS'D	5
SURPRIZ'D	5
SURROUNDED	5
SWALLOWS	5
SWEATING	5
SYLVANS	5
SYSTEMS	5
TAINTS	5
TAPHIAN	5
TARGE	5
TAX	5
TELAMONIAN	5
TEMPERANCE	5
TERM	5
THAMES'S	5
THESEUS	5
THIEVES	5
THIRSTS	5
THOON	5
THREADS	5
TIMBER	5
TING'D	5
TIRESIAS	5
TLEPOLEMUS	5
TOAST	5
TONE	5
TORIES	5
TOSSES	5
TOY	5
TRAGIC	5
TRANSFORM'D	5
TRANSPARENT	5
TRAVELLER	5
TRAVELS	5
TREASON	5
TRICE	5
TRIUMPH'D	5
TROS	5
TRUMPETS	5
TUMBLE	5
TWANG'D	5
TWERE	5
TWO-EDG'D	5
UNBLESS'D	5
UNCOMMON	5
UNCONTROLL'D	5
UNCORRUPTED	5
UNCOUTH	5
UNFOLDING	5
UNGEN'ROUS	5
UNGOVERN'D	5
UNINJUR'D	5
UNOBSERV'D	5
UNSPOTTED	5
UNSUCCESSFUL	5
UNSULLY'D	5
UNTRY'D	5
UNUTTERABLE	5
UNWELCOME	5
UNWISE	5
VACANT	5
VANDALS	5
VANITIES	5
VANQUISH	5
VASSALS	5
VELVET	5
VENTURE	5
VEX'D	5
VINDICATES	5
VINEGAR	5
VIOLATE	5
VIOLATED	5
VISUAL	5
VOICES	5
VOITURE'S	5
VOWELS	5
VY'D	5
WALK'D	5
WARDS	5
WARMER	5
WARR'D	5
WATCHES	5
WEDDED	5
WEED	5
WEEK	5
WHELM	5
WHELMS	5
WHIM	5
WHISK	5
WHISTLE	5
WHITEN'D	5
WHITENING	5
WHIZZING	5
WIDE-EXTENDED	5
WIDOW'D	5
WIG	5
WINNING	5
WINTERS	5
WISHING	5
WITHDRAW	5
WITHDRAWN	5
WITHER	5
WITHSTANDS	5
WITHSTOOD	5
WOFUL	5
WORDY	5
WORSHIP	5
WRAPS	5
WREAK	5
WRITERS	5
WRITTEN	5
XANTHUS'	5
YEA	5
AËTION'S	4
A-CROSS	4
ABATE	4
ABLEST	4
ABSOLUTE	4
ABSORPT	4
ABUSIVE	4
ACCEPTS	4
ACCOMPLISH'D	4
ACHAIANS	4
ACTOR	4
ADAMANT	4
ADMIRAL	4
ADOPTED	4
ADULT'ROUS	4
AESCHYLUS	4
AETNA'S	4
AFFLICTIVE	4
AFRESH	4
AGENOR'S	4
AGONIZING	4
ALCATHOUS	4
ALCIDES'	4
ALCOVE	4
ALDERMEN	4
ALEXIS	4
ALL-COMPOSING	4
ALL-SUBDUING	4
ALLIANCE	4
ALPHAEUS'	4
AMAZEMENT	4
AMBROSE	4
AMONGST	4
AMPLEST	4
AMUS'D	4
ANCHISES	4
ANCHOR	4
ANDRÉ	4
ANDROMACHE	4
ANIMAL	4
ANIMATING	4
APPROACHES	4
ARDORS	4
ARETE	4
ARETUS	4
ARGO	4
ARRIVE	4
ARTIFICE	4
ARTISTS	4
ARTLESS	4
ASCENT	4
ASPIR'D	4
ASSAY	4
ASSES	4
ASSIGN	4
ASSIGNS	4
ASSISTANTS	4
ASSISTING	4
ASSOCIATE	4
ASSUM'D	4
ASSUMES	4
ATLAS	4
ATREUS	4
ATTRACTIVE	4
AVENGER	4
AVERTED	4
AVERTING	4
AWAIT	4
AXIUS	4
AXLES	4
BALANC'D	4
BANDED	4
BANEFUL	4
BANISH	4
BASHFUL	4
BASIS	4
BASK	4
BAWL	4
BEASTLY	4
BEEF	4
BEFITS	4
BEFRIEND	4
BEGONE	4
BELIES	4
BELLS	4
BELTS	4
BELY'D	4
BERRIES	4
BESIEG'D	4
BESIEGE	4
BEV'RAGE	4
BEWILDER'D	4
BIBLE	4
BILLOW	4
BISHOPS	4
BITCH	4
BITES	4
BITTERNESS	4
BLACK-EY'D	4
BLANDISHMENT	4

Word		Word		Word		Word	
BLASTED	4	CONFESSORS	4	DUES	4	FROSTS	4
BLINDNESS	4	CONFIRMS	4	DURFY	4	FRY	4
BLITHE	4	CONFLAGRATION	4	DWELL'D	4	FUL	4
BLOCK	4	CONNUBIAL	4	EAR'D	4	FULFIL	4
BLOTS	4	CONSENTED	4	EARL	4	FUMING	4
BLOTTED	4	CONSISTENT	4	EARTH-BORN	4	FUR	4
BOARDS	4	CONSTRAINT	4	ECCHOS	4	FURRY	4
BODKIN	4	CONSUMING	4	ECHO'D	4	GAD	4
BOG	4	CONVULSIVE	4	EDWARD	4	GALL'D	4
BOLTS	4	COOL'D	4	EDWARD'S	4	GALLANTS	4
BOR'D	4	COPIES	4	EEL	4	GALLING	4
BOSOM'D	4	CORD	4	EFFACE	4	GARB	4
BOTTLE	4	CORRODING	4	EFFECTS	4	GEM	4
BOYLE	4	CORSLET	4	EFFORT	4	GENERAL	4
BRANGLING	4	COUCHES	4	EGGS	4	GENTLEMAN	4
BRAVER	4	COURS'D	4	EGYPT	4	GERMANS	4
BRIMMING	4	COURT-BADGE	4	ELBOW	4	GILL	4
BRISEIS	4	COURTEOUS	4	ELF	4	GILL-HOUSE	4
BRISKER	4	COXCOMBS	4	ELIS'	4	GIN	4
BROADEST	4	CRACKS	4	ELUSIVE	4	GIRL	4
BRONZE	4	CRAGGS	4	EMANATION	4	GIVING	4
BROOKS	4	CRASH'D	4	EMBLAZE	4	GLANC'D	4
BRUIS'D	4	CROSSING	4	EMBODIED	4	GLASSY	4
BRUSH	4	CRYING	4	EMBRU'D	4	GLITTERING	4
BRUTES	4	CUCKOLD	4	EMULATION	4	GLORY'S	4
BUBBLE	4	CUFF	4	ENCHANTING	4	GOAT'S	4
BUBO	4	CUNNING	4	ENCUMBER'D	4	GODDESS-MOTHER	4
BULKY	4	CUPID'S	4	ENDEARING	4	GOODLY	4
BULL'S	4	CUPIDS	4	ENDLONG	4	GOUT	4
BUOYS	4	CUR'D	4	ENDURES	4	GRAND	4
BURIED	4	CURL'S	4	ENGINES	4	GRATIFY	4
BURNT	4	CURTAINS	4	ENLARGE	4	GRAVITATION	4
BURY'D	4	CUSTARD	4	ENQUIRING	4	GREAVES	4
BUTCHERS	4	CUTLER	4	ENSLAV'D	4	GRIESLY	4
BUTLER	4	CYNTHIA'S	4	ENSURE	4	GRINS	4
CAELESTIAL	4	CYPRESS	4	ENTANGLED	4	GROTTO	4
CAITIFF	4	D'YE	4	ENTERTAIN'D	4	GRUB	4
CALAMITOUS	4	DAEMONS	4	ENTRANC'D	4	GUARDLESS	4
CAPTAIN	4	DAMNATION	4	EPAEUS	4	GUIDANCE	4
CARESS'D	4	DANGLING	4	EPEIAN	4	GUNS	4
CARTED	4	DAPHNIS	4	EPICLES	4	HALITHERSES	4
CASUISTRY	4	DARDANUS	4	EQUALLY	4	HANDSOME	4
CEASING	4	DARKEN	4	EQUALS	4	HAPPIEST	4
CEAST	4	DEALS	4	ERRONEOUS	4	HARDER	4
CELIA'S	4	DEAR-BOUGHT	4	ESSAYS	4	HASTEN'D	4
CERES'	4	DECEITS	4	ESSENCE	4	HAT	4
CHAC'D	4	DEEDLESS	4	EVEN	4	HAULSERS	4
CHAIRS	4	DEEMS	4	EVER-PLEASING	4	HAVING	4
CHALCIS	4	DEEPENS	4	EXCEEDING	4	HEART-WOUNDED	4
CHALLENG'D	4	DEFENDER	4	EXCELLENCE	4	HEAV'N-DEFENDED	4
CHALLENGE	4	DEFENSIVE	4	EXCHANG'D	4	HEAVENLY	4
CHAMBER	4	DEFER	4	EXCHANGE	4	HEBÈ	4
CHAMPAIN	4	DEFIN'D	4	EXHALES	4	HEEDS	4
CHANC'RY	4	DEFORMS	4	EXPANSE	4	HEIR'D	4
CHANNEL	4	DELUG'D	4	EXPANSION	4	HENLEY'S	4
CHARACTER	4	DELUSIVE	4	EXPATIATE	4	HEROICK	4
CHASTITY	4	DEMODOCUS	4	EXPLAINS	4	HESITATE	4
CHEATS	4	DENS	4	EXPRESSION	4	HEW'D	4
CHECKS	4	DEPARTED	4	EXTINGUISH	4	HIBERNIAN	4
CHEERING	4	DEPARTS	4	EXTINGUISH'D	4	HIGH-THRON'D	4
CHICK	4	DEPENDANT	4	EXTRACT	4	HIGHT	4
CHILDLESS	4	DEPENDING	4	EYEBALLS	4	HINT	4
CHILDREN'S	4	DESERVING	4	F	4	HIP	4
CHINK	4	DESTINIES	4	FACTIOUS	4	HIST'RY	4
CHIRON	4	DESTROYER	4	FADING	4	HISTORIC	4
CHRIST'S	4	DESTROYING	4	FAINTLY	4	HOIST	4
CHRISTIANS	4	DESTROYS	4	FAIRY	4	HOME-FELT	4
CHRYSA'S	4	DETESTS	4	FANNY	4	HOMELY	4
CHRYSES	4	DEVILS	4	FARTHEST	4	HOOFS	4
CHURCHMAN	4	DEVOTE	4	FASTEN'D	4	HOPEFUL	4
CIBBER'S	4	DEVOUR'D	4	FASTENS	4	HORSE-HAIR	4
CICONS	4	DIAMOND	4	FATIGUE	4	HOUYHNHNM	4
CIMMERIAN	4	DIAN	4	FATTEN	4	HOWARD	4
CINCTURE	4	DIGNIFY	4	FEASTED	4	HOWEVER	4
CIT	4	DIMPLED	4	FELON	4	HOWLS	4
CIVET	4	DIN'D	4	FELONS	4	HUE	4
CLAPS	4	DIRECTION	4	FIG'S	4	HUMANITY	4
CLARISSA	4	DIRECTLY	4	FINAL	4	HUNTER'S	4
CLAWS	4	DIRECTORS	4	FINDING	4	HUNTERS	4
CLEANSING	4	DISAPPOINTED	4	FIR	4	HURLS	4
CLEARS	4	DISCOLOUR'D	4	FIRMLY	4	HYMEN	4
CLODIO	4	DISCONSOLATE	4	FIRSTLINGS	4	HYMEN'S	4
CLOSELY	4	DISHEVEL'D	4	FISHER	4	ICARIUS	4
CLOSEST	4	DISHONOURS	4	FLAMY	4	IDA	4
CLOWN	4	DISPERSING	4	FLATT'RER	4	IDAEUS	4
CLUST'RING	4	DISSEMBLING	4	FLATTER'D	4	IGNOMINIOUS	4
COACHES	4	DISTEMPER'D	4	FLAVIA'S	4	ILL-TIM'D	4
COAT	4	DISTINGUISH	4	FLEA	4	ILUS	4
COCKS	4	DISTRACTING	4	FLETCHER	4	IMAGIN'D	4
COLLECT	4	DISTURBS	4	FLUENT	4	IMMEASURABLE	4
COLLEGE	4	DITCH	4	FLUID	4	IMPELLING	4
COLLEY	4	DIVERS	4	FLUSH'D	4	IMPS	4
COMBS	4	DIVERT	4	FOGS	4	IMPUDENTLY	4
COMEDY	4	DOCTOR'S	4	FONDER	4	IMPUTED	4
COMFORTLESS	4	DOE	4	FOPLING	4	INCES'D	4
COMMENDS	4	DOG'S	4	FOREFATHERS	4	INCH	4
COMMERCE	4	DOMINIONS	4	FOREGOE	4	INCUMBENT	4
COMMUTUAL	4	DORIS	4	FORESEEN	4	INCUMBER'D	4
COMPASS'D	4	DOTAGE	4	FORGETFULNESS	4	INDEX	4
COMPREHEND	4	DRAUGHTS	4	FORGIV'N	4	INDIGNATION	4
COMPREST	4	DRAWING	4	FORUM	4	INDISSOLUBLY	4
CONCANEN	4	DRIFTS	4	FOUNDATION	4	INDIVIDUAL	4
CONCEALS	4	DRIVERS	4	FOUNDS	4	INFECTIOUS	4
CONCLUDES	4	DUCK	4	FOX	4	INFEST	4
CONFED'RATE	4	DUCKE	4	FRIGHTFUL	4	INFLICT	4

CHEER	3	CRUMBLING	3	EARLESS	3	FLAMEN	3
CHEQUER'D	3	CUBIT	3	EARLIEST	3	FLATTERERS	3
CHESTERFIELD	3	CUISHES	3	EARTH-SHAKING	3	FLAUNTS	3
CHESTS	3	CUMB'ROUS	3	EASIEST	3	FLAV'ROUS	3
CHETWOOD	3	CUMBROUS	3	EASING	3	FLAVIA	3
CHILDRENS	3	CUPID	3	EASTER	3	FLAW	3
CHILLS	3	CURTIUS	3	EASTWARD	3	FLEA'D	3
CHILLY	3	CUTLACE	3	EBB	3	FLIT	3
CHINA'S	3	CYLLENIUS	3	EBBING	3	FLITTING	3
CHINTZ	3	CYNTHUS	3	ECHETUS	3	FLOATED	3
CHOCOLATE	3	CYTHAERON'S	3	ECLIPSE	3	FLOWERS	3
CHOROEBUS	3	D'URFEY	3	EDDY	3	FLOWN	3
CHORUS	3	DAGGER	3	EELS	3	FLUTTER'D	3
CHRIST	3	DAMNING	3	EGREGIOUS	3	FLY'ST	3
CHRYSA	3	DAMP	3	EIGHTH	3	FOALS	3
CHURL	3	DANGEROUS	3	ELATED	3	FOLDING	3
CIBBERIAN	3	DARKER	3	ELECT	3	FOODFUL	3
CIRCUMFERENCE	3	DAVID	3	ELEMENT	3	FOOT-STOOL	3
CIRCUMFUS'D	3	DAWNS	3	ELEMENTAL	3	FOOTMAN	3
CITRON	3	DAZLED	3	ELOQUENT	3	FORAGE	3
CIVET-CAT	3	DEALING	3	ELPENOR	3	FORBADE	3
CLAMORS	3	DEATH-LIKE	3	ELVES	3	FORBORE	3
CLENCHES	3	DEBAUCH'D	3	EMBATTLED	3	FORE-RUNNER	3
CLEOPATRA	3	DECEMBER	3	EMBLAZ'D	3	FORESEE	3
CLERGY	3	DECENTLY	3	EMBOW'RING	3	FORETELL	3
CLERKS	3	DECRY'D	3	EMBRACING	3	FORG'D	3
CLIPT	3	DEDICATORS	3	EMBRYO	3	FORGETTING	3
CLOATH	3	DEFIANCE	3	EMINENT	3	FORMING	3
CLOCK	3	DEFIL'D	3	EMITS	3	FORSAKING	3
CLOSET	3	DEFRAUD	3	ENCHANTRESS	3	FORTH-ISSUING	3
CLOUDLESS	3	DEFRAUDS	3	ENCHAS'D	3	FORTIFY	3
CLUBS	3	DEIPYRUS	3	ENCOUNTRING	3	FOSTER	3
CLUSTRING	3	DELAYS	3	ENCREASING	3	FOUNDER	3
COBHAM	3	DELEGATE	3	ENDING	3	FOUNTAIN'S	3
COBHAM'S	3	DELEGATES	3	ENLARGING	3	FOURFOLD	3
COBWEB	3	DELPHIC	3	ENNOMUS	3	FRAMES	3
COCYTUS'	3	DELUDED	3	ENSIGN	3	FRATERNAL	3
COD	3	DELUDING	3	ENSIGNS	3	FRAUDS	3
CODILLE	3	DEMANDED	3	ENSUE	3	FREIGHTED	3
CODRUS	3	DEMI	3	ENSUES	3	FRIENDSHIP'S	3
COMBATANTS	3	DEMIGODS	3	ENTERPRIZE	3	FRISKING	3
COMBATES	3	DENOUNC'D	3	ENTERTAIN	3	FRITTER'D	3
COMET	3	DEPREST	3	ENTHRON'D	3	FROLICKS	3
COMETS	3	DERIDES	3	ENTRANCING	3	FROZE	3
COMMANDER	3	DERIVE	3	ENTREAT	3	FULLY	3
COMMANDING	3	DERIVES	3	ENTRING	3	FULNESS	3
COMMENC'D	3	DESCRIB'D	3	EPEIANS	3	FUND	3
COMMODIOUS	3	DESERTERS	3	EPIC	3	FURL'D	3
COMPARING	3	DESIGNING	3	EQUAL'D	3	FURNISH'D	3
COMPELLS	3	DESOLATE	3	ERECTED	3	FURROW	3
COMPLAIN'D	3	DESPAIRING	3	EREUTHALION	3	FYE	3
COMPLEATS	3	DESPIGHT	3	ERST	3	GAILY	3
COMPLIES	3	DETERMINE	3	ESTABLISH'D	3	GALL	3
COMPREHENSIVE	3	DETERMINES	3	ESTATES	3	GAMESTERS	3
COMPRESS'D	3	DEVIATES	3	ESTEEM'D	3	GARBS	3
COMRADE	3	DEVIOUS	3	ETEONEUS	3	GARDEN'S	3
CONCERNS	3	DEXTERITY	3	EUMELUS'	3	GARTER	3
CONDITION	3	DEXTROUS	3	EUNAEUS	3	GASP	3
CONFERENCE	3	DI'MONDS	3	EUNUCHS	3	GAWDY	3
CONGEAL'D	3	DICE	3	EUPITHES	3	GAZES	3
CONQU'ROR	3	DICTATED	3	EURYBATES	3	GAZETTEERS	3
CONSECRATE	3	DIET	3	EURYMEDON	3	GEN'RALS	3
CONSID'RING	3	DILATES	3	EURYNOME	3	GERMAN	3
CONSOLE	3	DISCERNING	3	EURYTUS	3	GIBSON	3
CONSPIRES	3	DISCORDANT	3	EVER-DURING	3	GIRDS	3
CONTEMPTUOUS	3	DISCUS	3	EVIDENCE	3	GLADDEN	3
CONTENTIOUS	3	DISEMBOGUING	3	EWE	3	GLADDEN'D	3
CONTINUAL	3	DISPEL	3	EXACTNESS	3	GLANCES	3
CONTINUE	3	DISPUTES	3	EXECUTE	3	GLEAMY	3
CONTROUL'D	3	DISSOLVES	3	EXERTS	3	GLITTERS	3
COOLNESS	3	DISSONANCE	3	EXHALE	3	GLORYING	3
COPPER	3	DISSUADE	3	EXILES	3	GLOSSY	3
COPSE	3	DISTORTED	3	EXTENSIVE	3	GLUE	3
CORDS	3	DISTRESSFUL	3	EXTINCT	3	GNAW'D	3
CORINNA	3	DISTRUSTFUL	3	EXTRACTS	3	GOAR'D	3
CORNEILLE	3	DISTURB	3	EXULT	3	GODDESS-BORN	3
CORNEL	3	DISTURB'D	3	EYE-BALL	3	GODDESS'	3
CORNER	3	DIVERTS	3	FABLES	3	GODLESS	3
CORRUPT	3	DIVIN'D	3	FABRIC	3	GOE	3
COSTS	3	DIVISION	3	FACULTIES	3	GOING	3
COTTA	3	DO'T	3	FAINTER	3	GOSPEL	3
COUCHING	3	DOLOPS	3	FAIRIES	3	GOSSIP	3
COULD'ST	3	DON'T	3	FALLACIOUS	3	GOTHS	3
COUNTER	3	DOTARD	3	FALLOW	3	GRACE'S	3
COUNTREY'S	3	DOVE-LIKE	3	FAMISH'D	3	GRAINS	3
COURSER'S	3	DOVER	3	FAMOUS	3	GRAMMAR	3
COVET	3	DOWNRIGHT	3	FANNY'S	3	GRANDSIRES	3
COWLEY'S	3	DOWNS	3	FARES	3	GRANDSON	3
COZEN	3	DRAINS	3	FARTHINGS	3	GRANVILLE'S	3
CRACKLE	3	DRAPIER	3	FASHION'D	3	GRAV'D	3
CRADLE	3	DREADING	3	FASTER	3	GRAVER	3
CRAFT	3	DRINKING	3	FATIGU'D	3	GRAVES	3
CRAGS	3	DRUM	3	FAVOURITE	3	GRAZING	3
CRAM	3	DRUMS	3	FEARING	3	GRECIAN'S	3
CRAM'D	3	DRUNKEN	3	FEEBLER	3	GRIEVING	3
CRAMM'D	3	DRYADS	3	FEIGNS	3	GRIN	3
CRANES	3	DRYOPE	3	FELLOW'S	3	GRIPES	3
CRASHING	3	DUEL	3	FEUDS	3	GROATS	3
CREATURE'S	3	DULY	3	FEWER	3	GROIN	3
CRETE'S	3	DUNGEONS	3	FIDDLE	3	GROOM	3
CROAK'D	3	DUNS	3	FILLETS	3	GROTS	3
CROMWELL	3	DURANCE	3	FILMY	3	GRUB-STREET	3
CROP	3	DURING	3	FINGER'D	3	GRUBS	3
CROSS'D	3	DUTCHMAN	3	FISHES	3	GUIDELESS	3
CROUDED	3	DUTIES	3	FLAG	3	GUILD-HALL	3

GULF	3	INDU'D	3	LONG-WINDED	3	MURMURING	3
GULPH	3	INDUSTRY	3	LONGS	3	MURTHER	3
HACK	3	INFINITE	3	LOQUACIOUS	3	MYSIAN	3
HACKNEY	3	INFLAMING	3	LOUIS	3	MYSTER	3
HADST	3	INFLICTED	3	LOW-BORN	3	MYSTERY	3
HAGGARD	3	INFORM'D	3	LUCK	3	NAIL'D	3
HALF-FORM'D	3	INFORMER	3	LUCRE'S	3	NARCISSUS	3
HAM	3	INHABITANT	3	LUCRECE	3	NATUR'D	3
HAM-PYE	3	INHABITANTS	3	LUCRETIA	3	NAVY'S	3
HANDKERCHIEF	3	INHUME	3	LUD'S	3	NEEDLE	3
HANDLES	3	INLAY	3	LULLS	3	NERVELESS	3
HARBOUR'D	3	INROLL'D	3	LURES	3	NETS	3
HARBOURS	3	INSCRIB'D	3	LYCIA'S	3	NEW-MADE	3
HARCOURT	3	INSENSATE	3	LYCOMEDE	3	NEWCASTLE	3
HARDEN	3	INSPECT	3	LYCURGUS	3	NEWTON	3
HARLEY	3	INSTRUCTED	3	LYING	3	NICELY	3
HARNESS'D	3	INSTRUCTIONS	3	LYRA	3	NILUS	3
HARPAX	3	INTEMP'RATE	3	LYRNESSUS	3	NIMBLEST	3
HARPIES	3	INTENDS	3	MACHAÖN	3	NINETY	3
HARPS	3	INTER	3	MADDING	3	NIOBE	3
HARRY	3	INTERCOURSE	3	MADMAN	3	NIREUS	3
HASTENS	3	INTERDICTED	3	MADMEN	3	NOËMON	3
HATRED	3	INTERDICTS	3	MAEANDERS	3	NOBLY-PENSIVE	3
HATS	3	INTEREST	3	MAEONIAN	3	NOOK	3
HAUL'D	3	INTERMINGLED	3	MAGGOTS	3	NOON-DAY	3
HAUNTED	3	INTESTINE	3	MAID'S	3	NOONTIDE	3
HAWK	3	INTRUSION	3	MAIDEN	3	NOSES	3
HAWKERS	3	INVADERS	3	MAKER'S	3	NOTHING'S	3
HAZARD	3	INVITING	3	MAKING	3	NOTION	3
HEADLESS	3	INVOKE	3	MALES	3	NUMEROUS	3
HEADSTRONG	3	INVOKES	3	MANAG'D	3	NURSING	3
HEADY	3	INVOLVES	3	MANGLE	3	OÏLEAN	3
HEALS	3	IRELAND	3	MANNER	3	O'ERHANGS	3
HEARING	3	IRREMEABLE	3	MARCHES	3	O'ERHUNG	3
HEATH	3	ISIS'	3	MARCHING	3	O'ERLABOUR'D	3
HEAV'N-DIRECTED	3	ISSUED	3	MARCHMONT'S	3	O'ERPOW'R'D	3
HEAV'N-TAUGHT	3	JADES	3	MARGINS	3	O'ERSHADES	3
HEAV'NS'	3	JARRING	3	MARRY'D	3	O'ERSPREADS	3
HEBREW	3	JAVELIN'S	3	MARY	3	O'ERTOOK	3
HEEDFUL	3	JEER	3	MASK	3	O'ERWHELM	3
HELLUO	3	JESTS	3	MATER	3	OBSERVANCE	3
HEMM'D	3	JETT	3	MATRON'S	3	OCTOBER	3
HENLY	3	JOHNSON'S	3	MAUL	3	OIL'D	3
HENRY	3	JOINTED	3	MAXIM	3	OLD-AGE	3
HERDSMAN	3	JOURNEY'D	3	MAY'R	3	OLENIAN	3
HEREAFTER	3	JUDICIOUS	3	MECISTHEUS	3	ONSLOW	3
HERMES'	3	JUNCTURE	3	MEDIUM	3	OPERA	3
HERMIT	3	JUSTIN	3	MEED	3	OPERAS	3
HERVEY	3	KEEPERS	3	MEERLY	3	OPPRESSION	3
HEW	3	KEN	3	MELANTHO	3	OPPRESSIVE	3
HIGH-BORN	3	KENNET	3	MELLOWING	3	OPPROBRIOUS	3
HIGH-HEAP'D	3	KEYS	3	MELODIOUS	3	ORANGE	3
HIGH-WROUGHT	3	KINSMAN	3	MEMNON	3	ORATOR	3
HIGHLY	3	KIRKALL	3	MEMORABLE	3	ORCHOMENIAN	3
HINTS	3	KIST	3	MENAC'D	3	ORGAN	3
HISTORIANS	3	KNELLER	3	MENAETIUS'	3	ORNAMENT	3
HO	3	KNIT	3	MENDICANT	3	OSBORN	3
HOAR	3	KNOTS	3	MENELAS	3	OTHO	3
HOCKLEY	3	LAB'RER	3	MENELAUS'	3	OTUS	3
HOCKLEY-HOLE	3	LACE	3	MENIALS	3	OTWAY	3
HOISTED	3	LAGGING	3	MENTION	3	OUTSHIN'D	3
HOLINESS	3	LAMPOON	3	MERIDIAN	3	OUTSPREAD	3
HONESTY	3	LANCH'D	3	MERION'S	3	OVERTHROW	3
HONORARY	3	LANDSCAPE	3	MERLIN'S	3	OVERTHROWN	3
HOOPS	3	LANGUISH'D	3	METEOR	3	OW'ST	3
HOPKINS	3	LAP-DOGS	3	METEORS	3	OYSTER	3
HOSPITALITY	3	LARUM	3	METHOD	3	PADUA	3
HOVER	3	LATIUM	3	METHOUGHT	3	PAINTING	3
HUMID	3	LAUGHTER-LOVING	3	METTLE	3	PALL	3
HUMILITY	3	LAURELS	3	MIDAS	3	PALMERS	3
HUMOURS	3	LAWYER'S	3	MILBOURN	3	PAMPHLETS	3
HUNS	3	LEATHERN	3	MILES	3	PART'NERS	3
HUNTED	3	LEDA	3	MILITARY	3	PARTAKES	3
HUNTSMEN	3	LEMNOS'	3	MILTON	3	PARTERRES	3
HURRIES	3	LENGTHEN	3	MIMICK	3	PARTOOK	3
HYMN	3	LEOCRITUS	3	MINERAL	3	PASSENGERS	3
HYPERBOREAN	3	LESSEN	3	MIRROR	3	PASSIVE	3
ICHOR	3	LESSON	3	MIS-RULE	3	PASTOR	3
IDAEUS'	3	LET'S	3	MISERS	3	PATCH	3
IDEA'S	3	LETHARGY	3	MISTAKES	3	PATHETIC	3
IDIOT	3	LEVEE	3	MITRE	3	PATRIMONIAL	3
IDLENESS	3	LEVELS	3	MIXING	3	PATRIOT'S	3
IDOMENEUS'	3	LEWIS	3	MIXTURE	3	PAVILION	3
IGNORANCE	3	LIBEL	3	MOD'RATE	3	PAW	3
ILIAN	3	LIBELL'D	3	MOLE	3	PAWS	3
ILIANS	3	LIBRARY	3	MOLEST	3	PEARLY	3
ILIONEUS	3	LICENTIOUS	3	MOLLY	3	PEERESS	3
IMAGINARY	3	LILLY	3	MONKEYS	3	PELAGON	3
IMAGINE	3	LIMIT	3	MONKS	3	PELION	3
IMBRU'D	3	LINCOLN'S	3	MONSTER'S	3	PELION'S	3
IMP'D	3	LINCOLN'S-INN	3	MONTAGNE	3	PENITENCE	3
IMPAIR'D	3	LINGERING	3	MONTHLY	3	PENNY	3
IMPEL	3	LINGRING	3	MONY	3	PENS	3
IMPELS	3	LINKS	3	MOONLIGHT	3	PENSION'D	3
IMPENETRABLY	3	LIONESS	3	MOOR'D	3	PENT	3
IMPLACABLE	3	LISTED	3	MORTALITY	3	PERCEIVES	3
IMPRESS'D	3	LISTENS	3	MORTGAGE	3	PERFECTLY	3
IMPULSIVE	3	LOADEN	3	MORTIMER	3	PERITHOUS'	3
INCAS'D	3	LOATH	3	MOSSY	3	PERPLEX	3
INCHANTING	3	LOAVES	3	MOUNTED	3	PERSIST	3
INCLINES	3	LODGING	3	MOURNER	3	PERUSE	3
INCREASES	3	LODGMENTS	3	MOVEMENT	3	PEWS	3
INDECENT	3	LONDON	3	MUCK	3	PHAENICIAN	3
INDENTED	3	LONDON'S	3	MURD'RING	3	PHAERAE	3
INDIA	3	LONG-DESCENDING	3	MURDERS	3	PHEASANT	3

PHERAE	3	RAB'LAIS'	3	SAVIOUR	3	SOV'REIGN'S	3
PHILEMON	3	RABBITS	3	SAVOUR	3	SOW	3
PHILOCTETES	3	RACK	3	SAW'ST	3	SOW'D	3
PHOCIAN	3	RACK'D	3	SAY'ST	3	SPADE	3
PHOEBE	3	RADIANCE	3	SCAFFOLD	3	SPADES	3
PHRENZY	3	RAILING	3	SCALING	3	SPANGLED	3
PHRYGIANS	3	RANCOUR	3	SCARE	3	SPANGLES	3
PHYLACUS	3	RANGING	3	SCENTS	3	SPARES	3
PHYSICK	3	RAT	3	SCHEDIUS	3	SPECIOUS	3
PICK	3	RATIFIES	3	SCHOLAR'S	3	SPECKLED	3
PICKS	3	RATIFY	3	SCHOOLMEN	3	SPEECHLESS	3
PICTUR'D	3	RAZE	3	SCOOPS	3	SPENDS	3
PICTURE	3	RE-APPEAR	3	SCORNING	3	SPERCHIUS	3
PIECES	3	RE-ASSERT	3	SCOTS	3	SPITS	3
PILLARS	3	RE-ECCHOES	3	SCOURS	3	SPLIT	3
PILLORY	3	REACHES	3	SCRAP	3	SPOILERS	3
PILLOW	3	REAP'D	3	SCRAPS	3	SPOKES	3
PINION	3	RECENT	3	SCRATCH	3	SPONGE	3
PINNACE	3	RECEPTION	3	SCRAWL	3	SPRAT	3
PINS	3	RECOGNIZE	3	SCRIBLING	3	SPRINKLE	3
PINT	3	RECOMPENCE	3	SCULL	3	SPRINKLES	3
PIRAEUS	3	RECORDED	3	SCYROS	3	SPRITE	3
PITHOLEON	3	RECORDING	3	SEA-GIRT	3	SPUR	3
PITY'D	3	RECOUNT	3	SEA-GOD	3	SQUINTING	3
PLACEBO	3	RECOVER'D	3	SEA'S	3	STABB'D	3
PLAGU'D	3	REDDEN	3	SEEK'ST	3	STAID	3
PLAINLY	3	REELS	3	SEEM'ST	3	STAIRS	3
PLAISTER	3	REFLECTIONS	3	SELF-MOV'D	3	STAKES	3
PLANN'D	3	REFRESHING	3	SELF-SAME	3	STAMP'D	3
PLASTIC	3	REFRESHMENT	3	SEPULCHRE	3	STANDERS	3
PLAUSIBLE	3	REFUND	3	SERVITUDE	3	STATION	3
PLEAS	3	REGAINS	3	SETT	3	STATUTE	3
PLEIADS	3	REGARDFUL	3	SETTLE'S	3	STATUTES	3
PLEURON'S	3	REHEARSALS	3	SETTLED	3	STEAMING	3
PLIGHT	3	REJOINS	3	SETTLING	3	STEDDY	3
PLOWS	3	REJOYCING	3	SEVERAL	3	STEELE	3
PLUMPS	3	RELIEVES	3	SEXE'S	3	STEEPY	3
PO	3	RELY	3	SHADWELL	3	STEER'D	3
POEM	3	REMARK	3	SHAFTED	3	STEM'D	3
POEMS	3	REMORSE	3	SHAMES	3	STICHIUS	3
POESY	3	REMORSELESS	3	SHAPELESS	3	STILL'D	3
POINTLESS	3	RENDERS	3	SHARPER	3	STORY'D	3
POISES	3	REPAID	3	SHARPEST	3	STOW	3
POIZE	3	REPASS'D	3	SHEAVES	3	STRAINING	3
POLITES	3	REPINES	3	SHEERS	3	STRANDS	3
POLYPHEMUS	3	REPOSING	3	SHEFFIELD	3	STREAMY	3
POMEGRANATE	3	REPRESS'D	3	SHIELD'S	3	STRENGTH'NING	3
POMONA	3	REPROV'D	3	SHIELDED	3	STREPHON	3
PONTIFIC	3	REPROVES	3	SHIFTING	3	STRIPS	3
PONTONOUS	3	REPTILES	3	SHILLINGS	3	STRUT	3
POOP	3	REPULSE	3	SHIPP'D	3	STUBBLE	3
POPES	3	REPUTATION	3	SHIPWRIGHT	3	STYES	3
POSSESSION	3	RESPIRE	3	SHOAR	3	SUBLIMELY	3
POSSIBLE	3	RESTORING	3	SHOPS	3	SUBMITTING	3
POTION	3	RESTRAINT	3	SHOW'RY	3	SUCCESSES	3
POW'RLESS	3	RESULTING	3	SHOWERS	3	SUCKS	3
POYSON	3	RETARD	3	SHOWR'S	3	SUFFICES	3
POYSONS	3	RETARDS	3	SHRIEKING	3	SUITOR-THRONG	3
PREACHER	3	RETENTIVE	3	SHRIN'D	3	SUN-SHINE	3
PRECIPICE	3	RETORTED	3	SHUNNING	3	SUNDAY	3
PRELATE	3	RETRIEVE	3	SHUTTLE	3	SUNDERLAND	3
PRESAGE	3	REV'RENT	3	SIEGE	3	SUPPLICATING	3
PRESAGING	3	REVELLERS	3	SILVER-SHAFTED	3	SUPPORTING	3
PRESSES	3	REVELS	3	SILVER-STREAMING	3	SUPPORTS	3
PREVIOUS	3	REVENG'D	3	SIMOIS'	3	SURGING	3
PRIESTLY	3	REVENGING	3	SIMPLES	3	SURMIZE	3
PRIS'NERS	3	REVERES	3	SING'D	3	SURVIVING	3
PROCRIS	3	REVERSION	3	SINNER	3	SUSPICIOUS	3
PRODUCES	3	REVIEWS	3	SIP	3	SUTTON	3
PROFAN'D	3	REVISIT	3	SIREN	3	SWARTHY	3
PROFUSE	3	RHYM'D	3	SIRIUS	3	SWEEPY	3
PROJECTED	3	RICHMOND'S	3	SITE	3	SWOLN	3
PROJECTING	3	RIFTED	3	SIXPENCE	3	SWORD-KNOT	3
PROJECTS	3	RIGHTLY	3	SKIMMING	3	SYLVIA'S	3
PROLIFIC	3	RIPLEY	3	SKINS	3	TALONS	3
PROMACHUS	3	RISK	3	SKIP	3	TAMER	3
PROMOTES	3	RITUAL	3	SKULK	3	TAMES	3
PRONOUNC'D	3	RIVER'S	3	SLACKEN'D	3	TANTALUS	3
PROPHECIES	3	ROAMS	3	SLASHING	3	TARGETS	3
PROPITIATE	3	ROE	3	SLEEP'ST	3	TASTED	3
PRORES	3	ROMANCE	3	SLIDES	3	TATTERS	3
PROTHOUS	3	ROOME	3	SLIGHTS	3	TAWDRY	3
PRUDE	3	ROSY-FINGER'D	3	SLIMY	3	TAX'D	3
PRUNES	3	ROT	3	SLIP-SHOD	3	TEAM	3
PTHIANS	3	ROUL	3	SLOANE	3	TEMP'RATE	3
PUBLISH	3	ROULS	3	SLOPE	3	TEN-HORN'D	3
PUFF	3	ROW'D	3	SLOW-MOVING	3	TENANTS	3
PULTENEY	3	ROWZES	3	SLUGS	3	TENOUR	3
PURITY	3	RUBRIC	3	SLUMB'ROUS	3	TENTED	3
PURPOS'D	3	RUFF	3	SLUMBER'D	3	TERRIBLY	3
PYLAEMENES	3	RUMOURS	3	SMALL-POX	3	TEST	3
PYLIANS	3	RUSTICKS	3	SMALLEST	3	TEXTURES	3
PYRATE	3	RYMES	3	SMEAR'D	3	THALIA	3
QUAFF	3	SACRIFIC'D	3	SMITE	3	THAMES'	3
QUAINT	3	SACRILEGIOUS	3	SMITH	3	THEANO	3
QUALITIES	3	SADDEN'D	3	SNAP	3	THEATRE	3
QUARRY	3	SADNESS	3	SNAPT	3	THEBÈ	3
QUARTERS	3	SAFEST	3	SNUFFS	3	THEOCLYMENUS	3
QUELL	3	SAGE'S	3	SOCUS	3	THESPROTIA'S	3
QUEST	3	SAGELY	3	SOFT-SMILING	3	THINNER	3
QUESTION'D	3	SALIENT	3	SOIL'D	3	THOMAS	3
QUIBBLES	3	SANCTIFIES	3	SOOTH'D	3	THORNY	3
QUICKEN'D	3	SAP	3	SOPHISTRY	3	THRACIANS	3
QUILLS	3	SAT	3	SORREL	3	THREATEN	3
QUIVERING	3	SATYRS	3	SORTS	3	THREATENS	3

THREATNED	3	VARNISH	3	ACCOMPLISH	2	ANVILS	2
THREESCORE	3	VARY	3	ACCORDING	2	AONIAN	2
THRILLS	3	VAUNTED	3	ACCORDS	2	APARTMENTS	2
THRIVING	3	VEGETABLE	3	ACCUS'D	2	APPALL'D	2
THROATS	3	VEILING	3	ACE	2	APPEARING	2
THROES	3	VENOM'D	3	ACESTIS	2	APPETITE	2
THUNDERBOLTS	3	VEXING	3	ACHING	2	APPLAUDS	2
THWART	3	VICISSITUDE	3	ACORN	2	APT	2
TIME'S	3	VICTIM'S	3	ACQUAINTANCE	2	ARBITERS	2
TIMID	3	VIEW'ST	3	ACQUIRE	2	ARCADES	2
TIPT	3	VILLANY	3	ACTOR'S	2	ARCADIA	2
TITANS	3	VINEYARDS	3	ACTORS	2	ARCADIAN	2
TITUS	3	VIXEN	3	AD	2	ARCESIAN	2
TOAD	3	VOMIT	3	ADDING	2	ARCESIUS	2
TOLAND	3	VOTE	3	ADJOIN'D	2	ARCH'D	2
TONSON	3	VOUS	3	ADJOINING	2	ARCHEPTOLEMUS	2
TOOL	3	VOYAG'D	3	ADJOINS	2	ARCHER'S	2
TOTT'RING	3	VOYAGING	3	ADJOYNING	2	ARCHERS	2
TOTTER	3	W	3	ADJUDG'D	2	ARCHITRAVE	2
TOWER	3	WAIL'D	3	ADJUR'D	2	ARCTURUS	2
TRACKS	3	WAILS	3	ADJURES	2	ARDELIA	2
TRAFFIC	3	WAIST	3	ADMITTED	2	AREÏTHOUS'	2
TRAIN'D	3	WAITING	3	ADO	2	AREA	2
TRAITOR	3	WAKEN	3	ADOWN	2	ARETHUSE	2
TRANSFER	3	WALKING	3	ADVOCATE	2	ARGUMENTS	2
TRANSFIX	3	WALL'D	3	ADVOCATES	2	ARIADNE	2
TRANSGRESS	3	WALLER'S	3	AEACIDES	2	ARIGHT	2
TRANSITION	3	WANDER'ST	3	AEAEAN	2	ARMED	2
TRANSLATED	3	WARBLED	3	AEGERIAN	2	ARMIPOTENT	2
TRAPPINGS	3	WASTEFUL	3	AEGON	2	ARNÈ	2
TRAVERSE	3	WATCHMAN	3	AEGYSTHUS'	2	ARREST	2
TRAYTORS	3	WATTS	3	AEPEA	2	ARRIVE'D	2
TREAD'ST	3	WE'LL	3	AESEPUS	2	ARTACIA'S	2
TREATED	3	WEARER'S	3	AESON	2	ASCRIBE	2
TREATIES	3	WEAVE	3	AETHE	2	ASH	2
TREBLE	3	WEBS	3	AETHIOPIAN	2	ASIAN	2
TRIBUNAL	3	WEDDING	3	AETHON	2	ASKING	2
TRICKLE	3	WELKIN	3	AETNA	2	ASPERS'D	2
TRICKLES	3	WELL-BREATH'D	3	AETOLIANS	2	ASPHODEL	2
TRIFLING	3	WELL-DEFENDED	3	AFFECTATIONS	2	ASS'S	2
TRUEST	3	WELL-DISPUTED	3	AFFIRM'D	2	ASSARACUS	2
TRUMPS	3	WELL-DREST	3	AFFRIGHTS	2	ASSASSIN	2
TRUNCHEON	3	WELL-PURG'D	3	AFRICK'S	2	ASSEMBL'D	2
TRUSS'D	3	WELL-SKILL'D	3	AGGRESSOR	2	ASSEMBLIES	2
TRYAL	3	WELL-TAUGHT	3	AGOG	2	ASSUAGE	2
TUFTED	3	WELL-WEIGH'D	3	AIDING	2	ASSUME	2
TUMULTS	3	WESLEY	3	AIL	2	ASSUMING	2
TUNES	3	WEST-WIND	3	AIMING	2	ASSUR'D	2
TURNPIKES	3	WESTMINSTER'S	3	AIR-BUILT	2	ASSWAG'D	2
TWANG	3	WHALES	3	ALANS	2	ASSYRIAN	2
TWEAK'D	3	WHAT-E'ER	3	ALARIC'S	2	ASTRAY	2
TWILIGHT	3	WHERE'ER	3	ALBION'S	2	ASTYNOUS	2
TWILL	3	WHIP	3	ALCANDRA	2	ATHEISM	2
TYBER	3	WHISKERS	3	ALCESTÈ	2	ATHEIST	2
TYDINGS	3	WHISTLED	3	ALCMENA	2	ATHENIANS	2
UGLY	3	WHITE-ARM'D	3	ALCMENA'S	2	ATHLETIC	2
UMBRIEL	3	WHITE-HALL	3	ALEHOUSE	2	ATLANTIC	2
UNAFFECTED	3	WHITENESS	3	ALFRED	2	ATOM	2
UNASSISTING	3	WHO-E'ER	3	ALISIUM	2	ATTAIN	2
UNAW'D	3	WHO'D	3	ALL-ACCOMPLISH'D	2	ATTAIN'D	2
UNBAR	3	WHOR'D	3	ALL-BEHOLDING	2	ATTAINS	2
UNBENT	3	WIFE'S	3	ALL-BOUNTEOUS	2	ATTEMP'RED	2
UNBODY'D	3	WILLIAM	3	ALL-CONQU'RING	2	ATTEMPER'D	2
UNBROKE	3	WILMOT	3	ALL-CONSCIOUS	2	ATTIC	2
UNBURY'D	3	WIPES	3	ALL-CONSID'RING	2	ATTICUS	2
UNCLASSIC	3	WITCHCRAFT	3	ALL-DEVOURING	2	ATTILA'S	2
UNCLOSE	3	WITH-HOLD	3	ALL-INVOLVING	2	ATTONES	2
UNCONCERN'D	3	WITNESS'D	3	ALL-KNOWING	2	ATTORNEY	2
UNCURL'D	3	WIZARD	3	ALL-WISE	2	ATTUN'D	2
UNDERNEATH	3	WOMEN'S	3	ALLAY'D	2	AUGMENTED	2
UNDESERVING	3	WOOE	3	ALLEN	2	AUGURIES	2
UNDRESS	3	WOOF	3	ALLEYS	2	AULIS	2
UNEQUAL'D	3	WOOLSTON	3	ALPHAEUS	2	AUNTS	2
UNEXTINGUISH'D	3	WORD-CATCHER	3	ALPHEUS'	2	AURELIUS	2
UNFEELING	3	WORKING	3	ALSO	2	AUSTER'S	2
UNFELT	3	WORTHIER	3	ALTAR'S	2	AUTONOUS	2
UNFIT	3	WRANGLING	3	ALTHAEA	2	AVAIL'D	2
UNFREQUENTED	3	WREATH'D	3	ALTHAEA'S	2	AVAUNT	2
UNFRIENDED	3	WRENCH'D	3	ALTHO'	2	AVERR'D	2
UNFRUITFUL	3	WRESTLERS	3	AMARANTHINE	2	AVERSION	2
UNGRACIOUS	3	WYNDHAM'S	3	AMBITION'S	2	AVOWS	2
UNITES	3	YAHOO	3	AMEND	2	AWAKEN'D	2
UNJUSTLY	3	YAWN'D	3	AMOUNT	2	AWAKENS	2
UNLAMENTED	3	YESTERDAY	3	AMPHIALUS	2	AWKWARD	2
UNLICENS'D	3	YEW	3	AMPHISBOENA	2	AX	2
UNLOAD	3	YOU'L	3	AMPHITRITE	2	AXIUS'	2
UNLOCK	3	YOURSELVES	3	AMPHIUS	2	AY	2
UNMARK'D	3	ZEMBLA	3	AMUSE	2	BACCHANALS	2
UNMINDFUL	3	A-BED	2	AMUSEMENTS	2	BAD'ST	2
UNPAID	3	A-BOARD	2	ANCESTOR	2	BAIL	2
UNPEOPLED	3	A-PIECE	2	ANCESTORS	2	BAILIFF	2
UNPERFORMING	3	A-SHORE	2	ANCLES	2	BALANCING	2
UNPLEASING	3	ABIDE	2	ANDRAEMON	2	BALANDINE	2
UNROLL'D	3	ABJECT	2	ANGER'D	2	BALD	2
UNSTRUNG	3	ABORTIONS	2	ANKLE	2	BALDRIC	2
UNVARY'D	3	ABOUND	2	ANNIUS	2	BALEFUL	2
UNWHOLSOME	3	ABOUNDING	2	ANNOY	2	BALIUS	2
UNWOUNDED	3	ABOUNDS	2	ANOINT	2	BALK'D	2
UPLIFT	3	ABRUPT	2	ANON	2	BALLAD	2
UPROAR	3	ABSORBS	2	ANSTIS	2	BANDAGE	2
URGING	3	ABUNDANCE	2	ANTHEIA	2	BANKRUPT	2
USUAL	3	ABYDOS	2	ANTICHRIST	2	BAR'D	2
USURPING	3	ABYSSES	2	ANTINOUS'	2	BARBARIC	2
VARIED	3	ACCEPTING	2	ANTIPODES	2	BARCA	2
VARIOUS-COLOUR'D	3	ACCLAIMING	2	ANTITHESES	2	BARELY	2
				ANTS	2		

BARES	2	BOSS	2	CATTEL	2	COMMISSIONER	2
BARN	2	BOUGH	2	CAULS	2	COMMITS	2
BARNARD	2	BOW'S	2	CAUSELESS	2	COMMITTED	2
BARON'S	2	BOWERS	2	CAUTIONS	2	COMMITTING	2
BARRENNESS	2	BOY'S	2	CAWLS	2	COMMON-PLACE	2
BARRISTER	2	BOYLE'S	2	CAXTON	2	COMMONS	2
BASILISK	2	BRACKISH	2	CEBRION	2	COMPELL	2
BASKS	2	BRAG	2	CECROPS	2	COMPELLER	2
BASON	2	BRAIDS	2	CEDAR	2	COMPETENCE	2
BASTARDY	2	BRAKE	2	CELEBRATE	2	COMPLAINING	2
BATCHELORS	2	BRAN	2	CELESTIALS	2	COMPLAINT	2
BATHING	2	BRANCHY	2	CELSUS	2	COMPLETELY	2
BATTLEMENT	2	BRASIL	2	CENSOR	2	COMPLETES	2
BAWDRY	2	BRASS-HOOF'D	2	CENSORIOUS	2	COMPLEXION	2
BAWLING	2	BRAWN	2	CENTAURS	2	COMPLIMENTS	2
BAYING	2	BRAYERS	2	CENTINEL	2	COMPOUND	2
BEAGLE	2	BRAYING	2	CEPHALENIA	2	COMPULSION	2
BEAGLES	2	BREECH	2	CHANC'RY-LANE	2	COMPUTE	2
BEAKER	2	BRIAREUS	2	CHANDOS	2	COMRADES	2
BEAN	2	BRICK	2	CHANEL	2	CONCURRING	2
BEARDLESS	2	BRIDEWELL	2	CHANT	2	CONDENS'D	2
BEARING	2	BRIDGE	2	CHAPS	2	CONDENSE	2
BEARINGS	2	BRIGHTEN	2	CHARGING	2	CONDUCE	2
BEAU-MONDE	2	BRIGHTENS	2	CHARING	2	CONDUCIVE	2
BEAVER	2	BRIGHTNED	2	CHARING-CROSS	2	CONDUCTS	2
BEAVER'D	2	BRIM	2	CHARITABLE	2	CONE	2
BECALM	2	BRIMS	2	CHASER	2	CONF'RENCE	2
BECK	2	BRINDLED	2	CHASTEN'D	2	CONFED'RATES	2
BECK'NING	2	BRISTLE	2	CHASTIS'D	2	CONFER'D	2
BECOMING	2	BRISTLING	2	CHATTER'D	2	CONFERRING	2
BEDEW'D	2	BRITANNIA	2	CHEAP	2	CONFIRMING	2
BEDFORD	2	BROCADES	2	CHEARING	2	CONFOUNDING	2
BEDLAM'S	2	BROCAS	2	CHECKING	2	CONFRONTS	2
BEECHE'S	2	BROODING	2	CHEERFUL	2	CONGREGATED	2
BEFEL	2	BROOME	2	CHIEFTAINS	2	CONGREVE'S	2
BEFIT	2	BROTHER-WARRIORS	2	CHILDHOOD	2	CONINGSBY	2
BEG'ST	2	BROTHERHOOD	2	CHILL	2	CONJOIN'D	2
BEGGING	2	BROWZING	2	CHILL'D	2	CONJOINS	2
BEGUIL'D	2	BRUIN	2	CHILLING	2	CONJURE	2
BEGUILES	2	BRUSH'D	2	CHIME	2	CONNECTED	2
BEHAVES	2	BUCK	2	CHINES	2	CONQ'RING	2
BEHOLDERS	2	BUCKINGHAM	2	CHINKS	2	CONQU'RORS	2
BEHOLDING	2	BUCOLION	2	CHIRPING	2	CONS'NANTS	2
BEING'S	2	BUDDING	2	CHLOE	2	CONSENTS	2
BELDAM	2	BUFF	2	CHLORIS	2	CONSEQUENCE	2
BELERIUM	2	BUFFET	2	CHOOSE	2	CONSID'RATE	2
BELIEVERS	2	BUFFOON	2	CHRYSOTHEMIS	2	CONSIDER'D	2
BELIEVING	2	BUILDER	2	CHURCHES	2	CONSISTORY	2
BELLONA	2	BUILDER'S	2	CICONIAN	2	CONSISTS	2
BELLOW	2	BULKS	2	CICONIANS	2	CONSOLATION	2
BELLY'S	2	BULLET	2	CILLA	2	CONSONANTS	2
BELONG'D	2	BUOY'D	2	CIMON	2	CONSTANCY	2
BENCH	2	BUPRASIUM	2	CINDER	2	CONSTERNATION	2
BENCHES	2	BURLINGTON'S	2	CIRCAEAN	2	CONSTRUE	2
BENEFIC'D	2	BUSTO'S	2	CIRCLET	2	CONSUL	2
BEQUEATH'D	2	BUSY'D	2	CIRCLETS	2	CONSULTING	2
BEREAV'D	2	BUTT	2	CIRCUIT	2	CONTEMN	2
BERLIN	2	BUTTER	2	CIRCULATE	2	CONTESTS	2
BESALEEL	2	BUTTON	2	CIRCUMFLUENT	2	CONTINENT'S	2
BESEEM'D	2	BUTTON'S	2	CIRCUMSTANCE	2	CONTINENTS	2
BESEEMS	2	BUZZ	2	CIRCUS	2	CONTRARIES	2
BESOUGHT	2	CABBAGE	2	CIRQUE	2	CONTRARY	2
BESPANGLING	2	CACKLING	2	CITIZEN	2	CONTROLL	2
BESPRINKLED	2	CADMUS'	2	CITY'S	2	CONVENE	2
BESTIA	2	CAERULEAN	2	CLAMOR	2	CONVERS'D	2
BESTIA'S	2	CAGE	2	CLANGOR	2	CONVERSING	2
BESTREAK'D	2	CAIUS	2	CLAPT	2	CONVEX	2
BESTRIDES	2	CAKES	2	CLARKE	2	CONVICTED	2
BESTRODE	2	CALF	2	CLASSICKS	2	CONVICTION	2
BESTROW'D	2	CALF'S	2	CLATT'RING	2	CONVINCE	2
BESTROWN	2	CALMER	2	CLAUSE	2	CONVOY	2
BETAKES	2	CALMLY	2	CLEANER	2	CONVULSIONS	2
BEWAIL	2	CALMS	2	CLEARER	2	COON	2
BEWITCH'D	2	CALVIN	2	CLEAREST	2	COOPER'S	2
BIAS	2	CAMPAIGN	2	CLEFTS	2	COPE	2
BIDDEL	2	CANCER	2	CLEVER	2	COPPICE	2
BIDDING	2	CANDOR	2	CLIMATE	2	COQUETTES	2
BIDST	2	CANE	2	CLIMATES	2	CORAL	2
BILE	2	CANKERS	2	CLING	2	CORDAGE	2
BILINGSGATE	2	CANONIST	2	CLOE'S	2	CORINTH'S	2
BILLINGSGATE	2	CANTHARIDES	2	CLOACINA	2	CORK	2
BIRCH	2	CAPITALS	2	CLOE'S	2	CORMORANTS	2
BIRCHEN	2	CAPON	2	CLOGG'D	2	CORNBURY	2
BIRTHRIGHT	2	CAPRICE	2	CLOGS	2	CORONETS	2
BITER	2	CAPS	2	CLONIUS	2	CORRECTS	2
BLANDISHMENTS	2	CAPTIVATE	2	CLOUD-COMPELLER	2	CORRUPTS	2
BLASPHEME	2	CARA	2	CLOWDS	2	CORS'LET	2
BLESSED	2	CARCASSES	2	CLOY'D	2	COSTIVE	2
BLINDER	2	CARDAMYLE	2	CLUE	2	COU'D'ST	2
BLOCKADE	2	CARNATION	2	CLYMENÈ	2	COUGHS	2
BLOOD-POLLUTED	2	CARR	2	CLYTEMNESTRA	2	COULDST	2
BLOOD-STAIN'D	2	CARRIES	2	CNOSSIAN	2	COUNSELL'D	2
BLUST'RING	2	CARRY'D	2	COACH'D	2	COUNTED	2
BOASTER'S	2	CART	2	COAN	2	COUNTESS	2
BOASTERS	2	CARTHUSIAN	2	COBLER	2	COUNTLESS	2
BOASTING	2	CARV'D	2	COBWEBS	2	COUNTRYMEN	2
BOEOTIANS	2	CASH	2	COCKLE	2	COURT'S	2
BOHEA	2	CASHIERS	2	COCKLE-KIND	2	COURTSHIP	2
BOIL'D	2	CASK	2	CODRUS'	2	COUTE	2
BOLE	2	CASSANDRA	2	COERULEAN	2	COW-HIDE	2
BOOTHS	2	CASSOCK	2	COFFER	2	COW'RING	2
BORD'RING	2	CASUISTS	2	COHORTS	2	COWL'D	2
BORDERS	2	CAT-CALL	2	COLE	2	COWLEY	2
BOROUGH	2	CAT-CALLS	2	COLLEGES	2	COWPER	2
BORUS	2	CATS	2	COMFORTS	2	COXCOMB'S	2

FLEET-DITCH	2	GLADSOME	2	HELLEN	2	IN'T	2
FLEETING	2	GLAUCUS'	2	HER'S	2	INACHIANS	2
FLEETNESS	2	GLEAM'D	2	HERDED	2	INANIMATED	2
FLEURY	2	GLEAN	2	HERDSMAN'S	2	INCENCE	2
FLIE	2	GLIDED	2	HERDSMEN	2	INCIRCLED	2
FLING	2	GLIMMER'D	2	HERMIONE	2	INCLEMENCY	2
FLITS	2	GLIMMERS	2	HERMUS	2	INCLOSING	2
FLOCK'D	2	GLOBE'S	2	HEROES'	2	INCONSISTENT	2
FLORA	2	GLORIOUSLY	2	HEROINE	2	INCONSTANT	2
FLOUNCE	2	GLORY'D	2	HERVY	2	INDEX-LEARNING	2
FLOUNCING	2	GLOSSES	2	HESPER	2	INDIA'S	2
FLOUNDER'D	2	GLOV'D	2	HESPERUS	2	INDITE	2
FLOURETS	2	GLOVE	2	HESTER'S	2	INDIVIDUALS	2
FLOWRY	2	GLOW-WORM	2	HEWN	2	INDUC'D	2
FLUIDS	2	GLUMDALCLITCH	2	HEYWOOD'S	2	INDULGES	2
FLUTE	2	GLUTS	2	HIATUS	2	INFANT'S	2
FOAM'D	2	GNOSSUS	2	HIBERNIA	2	INFECTED	2
FOLIO	2	GOAD	2	HICETAON	2	INFER	2
FOLLOW'RS	2	GOATSKIN	2	HIDDEN	2	INFLEXIBLE	2
FOMENT	2	GOD-LESS	2	HIGH-CURLING	2	INFOLDING	2
FOOL'S-CAP	2	GODLIMAN	2	HIGH-DUTCH	2	INFORMING	2
FORD	2	GOODE	2	HIGH-HELD	2	INGAG'D	2
FORE-BUTTOCKS	2	GORGONS	2	HIGH-LIFTED	2	INGENIOUS	2
FORE-DOOM'D	2	GOTTEN	2	HIGH-TOW'RING	2	INGLORIOUSLY	2
FORE-RIGHT	2	GRADATION	2	HILT	2	INGRAV'D	2
FOREDOOM	2	GRAFT	2	HIMSELFE	2	INHABIT	2
FORETELLS	2	GRANDAME'S	2	HIPPASUS	2	INHOSPITABLE	2
FOREWARN'D	2	GRANDSIRE'S	2	HIPPODAMÈ	2	INJUNCTIONS	2
FORFEITED	2	GRAPE	2	HIPPOPLACIA'S	2	INJURIES	2
FORFEX	2	GRASPING	2	HOARD	2	INMATE	2
FORGES	2	GRATIFIE	2	HOISE	2	INNS	2
FORGIVEN	2	GRATIFY'D	2	HOLIDAY	2	INQUIRING	2
FORGIVING	2	GRAVELY	2	HOLLAND	2	INSATIABLE	2
FORKED	2	GRAVITY	2	HOLLOW'D	2	INSHRIN'D	2
FORKS	2	GRAY-GOOSE-WEAPON	2	HONE	2	INSINUATING	2
FORMAL	2	GREEK'S	2	HONORS	2	INSPIRER	2
FORMIDABLY	2	GREENWOOD	2	HOOF'D	2	INSTANCE	2
FORSWEARS	2	GRIEVANCE	2	HOPING	2	INSTINCTIVE	2
FORSWORE	2	GRIFFIN	2	HORIZON	2	INTELLECTUAL	2
FORTHWITH	2	GRILLY'S	2	HORNED	2	INTELLIGENT	2
FORTUN'D	2	GRIMACE	2	HORROUR	2	INTENTION	2
FOSSE	2	GRIMLY	2	HORROURS	2	INTERCEPTS	2
FOULER	2	GRIND	2	HORSEHAIR	2	INTERNAL	2
FOUNT-FUL	2	GRIPE	2	HORSEMAN	2	INTERPOSING	2
FOURSCORE	2	GROOMS	2	HOUSEHOLD	2	INTERRUPTION	2
FRANCIS	2	GROPING	2	HOVERING	2	INTERRUPTS	2
FRANKLY	2	GROUNDLESS	2	HOWE'RE	2	INTERVALS	2
FRAUDULENT	2	GROVEL	2	HUGER	2	INTERWOVE	2
FREAKISH	2	GROVELING	2	HUMMING-BIRD	2	INTONES	2
FREE-MASONS	2	GRUDGINGLY	2	HUNDREDS	2	INTREATY	2
FREE-THINKER	2	GRUMBLER	2	HUNGERFORD	2	INTRUDER	2
FREEZES	2	GRUNTING	2	HURRIED	2	INVASION	2
FRENCHMAN	2	GUIDED	2	HYACINTHINE	2	INVERT	2
FREQUENTS	2	GUILDED	2	HYBLA	2	INVERTED	2
FRESHNING	2	GUILEFUL	2	HYDES	2	INVESTS	2
FRETFUL	2	GULL'D	2	HYLÈ	2	INVIDIOUS	2
FRIGATES	2	GUMS	2	HYMENAEAL	2	INVOLUNTARY	2
FRIGID	2	GUN	2	HYMNING	2	INVOLVING	2
FRINGE	2	GUSH	2	HYMNS	2	INWRAP	2
FRONTIER	2	HABITANTS	2	HYPERENOR	2	IPHIGENIA	2
FRONTLESS	2	HABITS	2	HYPERIA'S	2	IPHITUS	2
FRUGALITY	2	HABITUAL	2	HYPOCRITICK	2	IRELOND	2
FRUITAGE	2	HACK'D	2	HYRA	2	IRRADIATE	2
FULFILLS	2	HACKS	2	IÄLMEN	2	ISAIAH'S	2
FULL-BLOWN	2	HAIRY	2	ICARIAN	2	ISTER'S	2
FULSOM	2	HALF-REAS'NING	2	ICARIUS'	2	ITALY	2
FULSOME	2	HALF-SHUT	2	IGN'RANCE	2	ITCHING	2
FUNCTIONS	2	HALIZONIAN	2	IGNIPOTENT	2	ITHACENSIAN	2
FURL	2	HAMMER	2	IGNOBLER	2	ITSELF'S	2
FURNACE	2	HAMPTON	2	IGNORANT	2	ITYLUS	2
FURNISH	2	HAMPTON'S	2	ILL-GOT	2	IXION	2
FUSILE	2	HAND-MAID	2	ILL-OMEN'D	2	JABB'RING	2
FUSTIAN'S	2	HAPPILY	2	ILL-STARR'D	2	JACK	2
GAIT	2	HARANGU'D	2	ILLUMES	2	JACKS	2
GALATEA	2	HARDNESS	2	ILLUSIONS	2	JACOB'S	2
GALLANTRIES	2	HARLEQUINS	2	ILLUSTRIOUSLY	2	JAKES	2
GALLEY	2	HARLOTS	2	IMAGINATION	2	JANSEN	2
GALLEYS	2	HARMONIC	2	IMBIBES	2	JARDAN	2
GALLIC	2	HARMONIZE	2	IMBRIUS	2	JASON'S	2
GAMEFUL	2	HARPYE	2	IMBROWN	2	JAW-BONE	2
GAMESTER	2	HART	2	IMBRUS	2	JAY	2
GANDER	2	HAST'NING	2	IMITATING	2	JEFFERIES	2
GANGES	2	HASTED	2	IMMEDIATE	2	JENKIN	2
GANYMED	2	HASTENING	2	IMMOLATE	2	JENNY	2
GAPE	2	HASTILY	2	IMMOLATED	2	JESU	2
GARD'NER'S	2	HAWLEY'S	2	IMMORTALITY	2	JETTY	2
GATHERING	2	HAYWOOD	2	IMMORTALIZ'D	2	JIG	2
GAUNT	2	HEADED	2	IMP	2	JINGLING	2
GAZERS	2	HEAL'D	2	IMPAIRS	2	JOCASTA'S	2
GAZETTES	2	HEALTHS	2	IMPALE	2	JOCKEYS	2
GELLIUS	2	HEART-CORRODING	2	IMPASSION'D	2	JOHN'S	2
GENERATIONS	2	HEART-PIERCING	2	IMPEND	2	JOINTLY	2
GENSERIC	2	HEARTED	2	IMPERFECTION	2	JONES	2
GENT	2	HEATS	2	IMPERTINENCE	2	JONES'	2
GENTLEMEN	2	HEAV'N-BORN	2	IMPLICIT	2	JOSEPH	2
GEORGE'S	2	HEAV'N-BRED	2	IMPORTED	2	JOURNEYING	2
GERENIAN	2	HEAV'N-BUILT	2	IMPORTS	2	JOVE-BORN	2
GESTURE	2	HEAV'NWARD	2	IMPOTENTLY	2	JOVES	2
GETS	2	HEAVIEST	2	IMPRECATIONS	2	JOY'D	2
GIN-SHOPS	2	HEBREWS	2	IMPRESSION	2	JUDETH	2
GINGER	2	HECAMEDE	2	IMPRESSIONS	2	JUDGMENTS	2
GIRDING	2	HECTOREAN	2	IMPRINT	2	JUICES	2
GIV'ST	2	HEEDED	2	IMPUDENT	2	JUMBLED	2
GLADIATORS	2	HEIRES	2	IMPURE	2	JUNE	2
GLADLY	2	HELICÈ	2	IN-URN	2	JURY	2

JUSTLE	2	LYCOPHON	2	MODER	2	OBSCUR'D	2
JUSTLING	2	LYCTUS	2	MODERATION	2	OBSCURES	2
JUTTING	2	LYMES	2	MODESTLY	2	OBSERVATION	2
KETTLE	2	LYONS	2	MOHAIR	2	OBSOLETE	2
KEY-HOLE	2	LYTTELTON	2	MOISTURE	2	OBSTINATELY	2
KICK'D	2	MACES	2	MOLES	2	OBSTRUCT	2
KID'S	2	MAEANDER	2	MOLIERE'S	2	OBTESTING	2
KISSING	2	MAERA	2	MOLTEN	2	OBTESTS	2
KITCHEN	2	MAEVIUS	2	MOLYNEUX	2	OBTRUDE	2
KNAVE'S	2	MAGAZINE	2	MONARCHY	2	ODIUS	2
KNAVISH	2	MAGAZINES	2	MONK	2	ODLY	2
KNEELING	2	MAGGOT	2	MONKEY-TAILS	2	ODOUR	2
KNIGHT'S	2	MAIM'D	2	MONST'ROUS	2	OENIDES'	2
KNITS	2	MAJOR	2	MONSTER-BREEDING	2	OENOMAUS	2
KNOCKING	2	MAKETH	2	MOONY	2	OENOPS'	2
KNOCKS	2	MALE	2	MOPE	2	OFFENDER	2
KNUCKLE	2	MALEA'S	2	MORALITY	2	OFFERING	2
LABORS	2	MALIGNANT	2	MORALIZ'D	2	OGYGIA	2
LABYRINTH	2	MANAGER	2	MORGAN	2	OGYGIAN	2
LACK	2	MANKIND'S	2	MORPHEUS	2	OMIT	2
LAIUS	2	MANOR	2	MORRIS	2	ON'T	2
LAMBETH	2	MANTIUS	2	MORSEL	2	OOZY	2
LAMBKIN	2	MANTLES	2	MOSAIC	2	OP'RA'S	2
LAMENTING	2	MANTLING	2	MOTLY	2	OPHELTIUS	2
LANCE'S	2	MANY-HEADED	2	MOULD'RING	2	OPIATE	2
LAND'S	2	MANY-LANGUAG'D	2	MOULDRING	2	OPINE	2
LANGUAG'D	2	MARKD	2	MOUNTAIN-WOLVES	2	OPINION'S	2
LANGUISHING	2	MARKET'S	2	MOUTHING	2	OPPOSITE	2
LAODAME	2	MARKING	2	MOV'ST	2	OPPRESSORS	2
LAODICE	2	MARO'S	2	MOVELESS	2	OPS	2
LAODICE	2	MARS'S	2	MOW	2	OPTICS	2
LAOGONUS	2	MARSHAL'D	2	MUCH-EXPERIENC'D	2	ORACULOUS	2
LAPSE	2	MART	2	MUCH-SUFF'RING	2	ORBIT	2
LAPT	2	MARTIN	2	MUD-NYMPHS	2	ORBITS	2
LARISSA'S	2	MARTYR'D	2	MUGS	2	ORCHARDS	2
LATER	2	MARTYRDOM	2	MULCT	2	ORCHOMENOS	2
LAUREATE	2	MARY'S	2	MULIUS	2	ORDURE'S	2
LAWREL	2	MARYGOLD	2	MULTIPLIES	2	ORESBIUS	2
LAWYER	2	MASQUERADE	2	MUM	2	ORESTES'	2
LEACHER	2	MASSIE	2	MUMMERS	2	ORMENUS	2
LEAD'ST	2	MASTER-PIECE	2	MUMMIES	2	ORPHANS	2
LEAFLESS	2	MASTIFF	2	MUMMIUS	2	ORTYGIA	2
LEARNING'S	2	MATIN	2	MUSE-RID	2	OSSA	2
LEE	2	MATRIMONIAL	2	MUSICK'S	2	OSTROEA	2
LEFT-HAND	2	MATRON-TRAIN	2	MUSTARD	2	OSTROGOTHS	2
LEISTER	2	MATURES	2	MUTTON	2	OTHRYONEUS	2
LEISURE	2	MAW	2	MYCENAE	2	OUT-DO	2
LEISURELY	2	MAWKISH	2	MYDON	2	OUT-NUMBER'D	2
LELEGIA'S	2	MAWL	2	MYNHEER	2	OUT-RAN	2
LENGTH'NING	2	MAY-POLE	2	MYRA	2	OUT-SPREAD	2
LEPELL	2	MEALS	2	MYSTERIOUS	2	OUT-STRETCH'D	2
LESBOS	2	MEATS	2	NAIADS	2	OUTLET	2
LETHE	2	MED'CINE	2	NAMING	2	OUTRAG'D	2
LETHE'S	2	MEDALS	2	NASO	2	OUTRAGE	2
LETTUCE	2	MEDITATION	2	NAT	2	OUTSHONE	2
LEUCADIAN	2	MEGES'	2	NAT'RAL	2	OUTVIE	2
LICK'D	2	MELAMPUS	2	NAUGHTY	2	OVERCOME	2
LIFE-CONSUMING	2	MELEAGER	2	NAUSEATE	2	OVERHANGS	2
LIGHTER'S	2	MEMORIES	2	NAUSITHOUS	2	OVERLOOKS	2
LIKEWISE	2	MENOETIUS	2	NAUSTES	2	OVERSPREAD	2
LILLIPUTIAN	2	MENOETIUS'	2	NAVES	2	OVERTON	2
LIMITATIONS	2	MERCHANTS	2	NECKLACE	2	OVID'S	2
LINCOLN	2	MERCY'S	2	NECTAR'D	2	OWL'S	2
LINEAMENTS	2	MERDAMANTE	2	NEEDHAM	2	OWNING	2
LINSEY	2	MEROPS	2	NEEDHAM'S	2	OX-LIKE	2
LIQUOR	2	MERRIER	2	NEMEA'S	2	OXFORD'S	2
LIQUORS	2	MESS	2	NEPTUNES	2	OYL	2
LISP	2	METAMORPHOSIS	2	NETTLES	2	PAC'D	2
LISTLESS	2	METAPHORS	2	NEW-BENEFIC'D	2	PACIFICK	2
LIVY	2	MEW	2	NEW-BUILT	2	PAEON	2
LOATH'D	2	MICROSCOPE	2	NEW-MARKET'S	2	PAEONIA'S	2
LOBSTER	2	MICROSCOPIC	2	NEW-YEAR	2	PAEONIAN	2
LOCUSTS	2	MID-MOST	2	NICEST	2	PAGAN	2
LOFTIER	2	MID-WAY	2	NICETY	2	PAGEANTS	2
LOLLING	2	MIDMOST	2	NIGHT-GOWN	2	PAGES	2
LONG-ABSENT	2	MIDWIFE	2	NIGRINA	2	PAILS	2
LONG-DEFENDED	2	MILBOURNS	2	NIMBLER	2	PAINTER	2
LONG-EAR'D	2	MILDEST	2	NINTH	2	PAINTERS	2
LONG-EXTENDED	2	MILITIA	2	NISUS'	2	PALACE-CARES	2
LONG-FORGOTTEN	2	MILO	2	NO-THING	2	PALATE	2
LONG-SUCCEEDING	2	MILO-LIKE	2	NOISIE	2	PALE-EY'D	2
LONGINUS	2	MILTONS	2	NOON-TIDE	2	PALES	2
LOOSELY	2	MIMICK'D	2	NOONS	2	PALMY	2
LOPS	2	MIMICKS	2	NOTUS	2	PANDERS	2
LOUD-ACCLAIMING	2	MINDLESS	2	NOURISH	2	PANDION	2
LOUD-RESOUNDING	2	MINIONS	2	NUMB'D	2	PANOPE	2
LOUT	2	MINOR	2	NUN	2	PANTHER	2
LOVE-BORN	2	MINOS'	2	NUNQUAM	2	PANTHER'S	2
LOVE-DARTING	2	MINUS	2	NURSE'S	2	PANTINGS	2
LOVE-SICK	2	MIS-JUDGING	2	NURSING-MOTHER	2	PANURGE	2
LOVELESS	2	MIS-LEAD	2	NURTURE	2	PAPHLAGONIAN	2
LOW-HUNG	2	MISCELLANIES	2	NUTATION	2	PAPHLAGONIANS	2
LOWEST	2	MISER	2	NYMPH'S	2	PAPILLIA	2
LUCKILY	2	MISER'S	2	O'ER-ARCHING	2	PARLIAMENT	2
LUCRE	2	MISERABLY	2	O'ER-LOOK'D	2	PARSON'S	2
LUG	2	MISGUIDE	2	O'ERGROWN	2	PART'NER	2
LUMBERHOUSE	2	MISSING	2	O'ERSHADE	2	PARTITION	2
LUMP	2	MISTAKING	2	O'ERSHADING	2	PARTLY	2
LUR'D	2	MISTRESS'	2	O'ERTAKE	2	PASITHEA	2
LUSTFUL	2	MISTRUSTS	2	O'ERWATCH'D	2	PASQUIN	2
LUSTRES	2	MITRA	2	OAR'D	2	PASSED	2
LUTETIA	2	MIXES	2	OATS	2	PASSENGER	2
LUTHER	2	MOANS	2	OBLOQUY	2	PASSIONS'	2
LYCIAN'S	2	MOCKERY	2	OBSCENER	2	PASTIME	2
LYCON	2	MODEL	2	OBSCENITY	2	PASTIMES	2

PASTORALS	2	PLANETARY	2	PROVERBS	2	RECOILING	2
PATCHES	2	PLANK	2	PROVINCES	2	RECOMMENDS	2
PATE	2	PLANTIN	2	PROVISION	2	RECONCILING	2
PATRIARCH	2	PLASH	2	PROVISIONS	2	RECORDS	2
PATRON-GOD	2	PLAUTUS	2	PROVOKING	2	RECOV'RING	2
PATTERN	2	PLAY-THING	2	PROWLING	2	RECRUITED	2
PAUNCH	2	PLAY'RS	2	PRY	2	RECUMBENT	2
PAUSING	2	PLAYERS	2	PRYN	2	REDOUBL'D	2
PAV'D	2	PLEBEIAN	2	PTELEON	2	REDREST	2
PAVEMENTS	2	PLEDGES	2	PULLS	2	REFER	2
PAVILION'D	2	PLIGHTED	2	PULPIT	2	REFORM	2
PAW'D	2	PLOTS	2	PULSES	2	REFORM'D	2
PAWN'D	2	PLOWMEN	2	PULT'NEY	2	REFUNDED	2
PAXTON	2	PLOWSHARE	2	PUMPINGS	2	REFUNDS	2
PEAR-TREE	2	PLUM	2	PUMPS	2	REGRETS	2
PEARS	2	PLUMBS	2	PUN	2	REHEARSAL	2
PEASANT'S	2	PLUMP	2	PUNISHMENT	2	REHEARSE	2
PEBBLE	2	PLUMS	2	PUPIL	2	REJOIN	2
PECK	2	PLUNGES	2	PUPILS'	2	REJOYN	2
PEDANT	2	PODALIRIUS	2	PUPPETS	2	REKINDLED	2
PEEL'D	2	PODARCES	2	PURGATORY	2	RELATION	2
PEEP	2	PODARGUS	2	PURGINGS	2	RELAX	2
PEEVISHNESS	2	PODES	2	PURIFY	2	RELEAST	2
PEGASUS	2	POKE	2	PURSUING	2	RELENTS	2
PEGASUS'S	2	POLE-AXE	2	PURSUITS	2	RELUCTANCE	2
PEIRAEUS	2	POLISHING	2	PUZZLING	2	REMEMBER'D	2
PELASGI	2	POLITELY	2	PYEBALD	2	REMEMBRING	2
PELASGIC	2	POLITES'	2	PYES	2	REMURMUR	2
PELOPS	2	POLLUTION	2	PYRECHMES	2	REMURMUR'D	2
PEMBROKE	2	POLLUX	2	PYRES	2	RENDING	2
PENALTIES	2	POLWARTH	2	PYRRHA	2	REPASTS	2
PENANCE	2	POLYCTOR	2	PYTHIAN	2	REPAY'D	2
PENDANT	2	POLYPOETES	2	PYTHON	2	REPAYS	2
PENEUS	2	POMATUMS	2	QUACKS	2	REPENTED	2
PENN'D	2	POND	2	QUADRILLE	2	REPINE	2
PENURY	2	POND'RING	2	QUAKER	2	REPLENISH	2
PEPPER	2	PONDER'D	2	QUAKER'S	2	REPLETE	2
PERCEIVE	2	POOREST	2	QUAKING	2	REPRESENTS	2
PERFECTED	2	POPISH	2	QUARREL'D	2	REPROACHFUL	2
PERIL	2	POPULACE	2	QUARRELS	2	REPROOFS	2
PERIPHAS	2	PORCHES	2	QUART	2	REPUTE	2
PERISHES	2	PORING	2	QUARTER'D	2	RESEMBLES	2
PERJURIES	2	PORTEND	2	QUEER	2	RESEMBLING	2
PERJURY	2	PORTENTS	2	QUELL'D	2	RESENTING	2
PERKS	2	PORTER	2	QUELLS	2	RESENTS	2
PERMISSION	2	PORTIA	2	QUERNO	2	RESPECTING	2
PERO	2	PORTRAITURE	2	QUERY	2	RESPONDENT	2
PERSEVERANCE	2	PORTS	2	QUI	2	RESTORER	2
PERTNESS	2	POSSESSING	2	QUICK'NING	2	RESUMING	2
PERVADING	2	POSTURE	2	QUICKEN	2	RETAILS	2
PERVERSE	2	PRAETUS	2	QUICKNESS	2	RETAIN'D	2
PERVIOUS	2	PRAMNIAN	2	QUINCUNX	2	RETINUE	2
PESTILENCE	2	PRATES	2	QUITTING	2	RETORT	2
PET	2	PRATING	2	QUIVERS	2	RETORTS	2
PETER'S	2	PRAYING	2	QUOIT	2	RETOST	2
PETEUS'	2	PRE-EXISTENT	2	QUOTE	2	RETROSPECTIVE	2
PETRONIUS	2	PREACH'D	2	RABBIT	2	REVENGEFUL	2
PETTICOAT	2	PRECARIOUSLY	2	RABBIT'S	2	REVENGES	2
PHAEBUS	2	PRECEDENT	2	RABBLE	2	REVERENTIAL	2
PHALCES	2	PRECEDING	2	RABID	2	REVIL'D	2
PHARMACY	2	PRECIPITANT	2	RACES	2	REVILING	2
PHERECLUS	2	PRECIPITATELY	2	RACINE	2	REVOLVE	2
PHERETIAN	2	PREFACES	2	RACY	2	RHADAMANTH	2
PHIDIAS	2	PREHEMINENCE	2	RAILLERY	2	RHESUS'	2
PHILOMELIDES	2	PREJUDICE	2	RAIN-BOWS	2	RHEXENOR	2
PHOCAE	2	PRELUDING	2	RAINBOW	2	RHIMES	2
PHOEBE'S	2	PRESCRIBES	2	RAINBOWS	2	RHIMING	2
PHOENOPS	2	PRESERVER	2	RALEIGH	2	RHODES	2
PHORCYS'	2	PRESUM'D	2	RALLYING	2	RHODIAN	2
PHRONTES	2	PRETENDERS	2	RAMPIRES	2	RHYMING	2
PHRYGIA'S	2	PREVALENCE	2	RANSOME	2	RIBB'D	2
PHYLEUS	2	PREYS	2	RAP'D	2	RICHARD	2
PHYLEUS'	2	PRIESTHOOD	2	RAPACIOUS	2	RIDGES	2
PHYLO	2	PRIM	2	RAPES	2	RIDICULOUS	2
PHYSICIAN	2	PRIMAEVAL	2	RAPHAEL'S	2	RIDICULOUSLY	2
PHYSICIANS	2	PRINTED	2	RAPP'D	2	RIFLED	2
PICK'D	2	PRINTER	2	RASCAL	2	RIGG'D	2
PICKENBURG	2	PRINTING	2	RAT'LING	2	RIM	2
PICKLE	2	PRISCIAN'S	2	RATIONAL	2	RIPENESS	2
PICQUETTE	2	PRISON	2	RATT'LING	2	RISEN	2
PIECEMEAL	2	PRIVACY	2	RATTLES	2	RIVEN	2
PIERIA	2	PROCLAIM'D	2	RAVENOUS	2	ROASTED	2
PIERIA'S	2	PROCUR'D	2	RAVISHER	2	ROASTING	2
PILGRIMAGE	2	PRODIGY	2	RAWLINSON	2	ROBS	2
PILLS	2	PROFUSELY	2	RAYMENT	2	ROLLI	2
PILOTS	2	PROMONTORY	2	RE-ECHO'D	2	ROMANS	2
PIMPLE	2	PROMONTORY'S	2	RE-JUDGE	2	ROOD	2
PINDAR	2	PROMOTE	2	RE-PASSES	2	ROOF'D	2
PINDARIC	2	PROMPTED	2	RE-SAILING	2	ROPER	2
PINDARS	2	PROOFS	2	RE-SOUNDING	2	ROSAMONDA'S	2
PINDUS	2	PROP'D	2	READER	2	ROSY-BRIGHT	2
PINION'D	2	PROPHAN'D	2	READER'S	2	ROUND-HOUSE	2
PINY	2	PROPHESY'D	2	REAMS	2	ROVERS	2
PIQUE	2	PROPHETICK	2	REAPER	2	ROVING	2
PISA'S	2	PROPOSALS	2	REAPER'S	2	RUBY	2
PISANDER'S	2	PROSPERITY	2	REAPERS	2	RUEFUL	2
PISENOR'S	2	PROSTITUTE	2	REBECCA	2	RUFA	2
PISS	2	PROSTITUTED	2	REBEL-KNAVE	2	RUFUS'	2
PIST	2	PROTECTOR	2	REBELLS	2	RUMP	2
PLAGIARY	2	PROTESILAUS	2	REBELS	2	RUSTY	2
PLAIN-DEALER	2	PROTHOENOR	2	REBUKES	2	RYM'D	2
PLAIST	2	PROTRACT	2	RECEDING	2	S'IL	2
PLAISTER'D	2	PROTRACTED	2	RECITES	2	SABLER	2
PLAIT	2	PROUDLY	2	RECLINES	2	SACKS	2
PLANET	2	PROVERB	2	RECOGNIS'D	2	SADLY-PLEASING	2

TROPHY'D	2	UNSHEATH'D	2	WEEK'S	2	ABBEYS	1
TROUBLESOME	2	UNSHOD	2	WELCOM'D	2	ABBOTS	1
TRUMP	2	UNSINCERE	2	WELL-BUILT	2	ABCHURCH	1
TRUSTING	2	UNSUSPECTING	2	WELL-DISSEMBLED	2	ABCHURCH-LANE	1
TUB	2	UNTAINTED	2	WELL-FILL'D	2	ABDICATED	1
TUBE	2	UNTHOUGHT	2	WELL-NATUR'D	2	ABEL	1
TUGG	2	UNTILL'D	2	WELL-SPENT	2	ABHOR'D	1
TUGGING	2	UNTIR'D	2	WELL-STRUNG	2	ABHORRD	1
TUGS	2	UNTUTOR'D	2	WELL-SUNG	2	ABJUR'D	1
TULIPS	2	UNVEILS	2	WELL-TEMPER'D	2	ABJURE	1
TUMOURS	2	UNWARLIKE	2	WELL-TIM'D	2	ABJURES	1
TUNIC	2	UNWEILDY	2	WELL-TURN'D	2	ABLERUS	1
TUNICK	2	UNWONTED	2	WELL-WROUGHT	2	ABLUTION	1
TUNING	2	UP-BORE	2	WELSTED'S	2	ABLUTIONS	1
TURBOTS	2	UP-HEAV'D	2	WESTMINSTER	2	ABORTION	1
TURBULENCE	2	UP-ROSE	2	WHALE	2	ABRIDG'D	1
TURBULENT	2	UPBORN	2	WHAT'ER	2	ABS-COURT	1
TURENNE	2	UPBRAID	2	WHEEL'S	2	ABSCOND	1
TURNIPS	2	UPBRAIDING	2	WHELPS	2	ABSOLV'D	1
TURRET	2	UPROOTED	2	WHENEVER	2	ABSORBING	1
TURTLE-DOVE	2	UPWARDS	2	WHEREAT	2	ABSTEMIOUS	1
TUTELARY	2	URGENT	2	WHERESOE'ER	2	ABSTERSIVE	1
TUTOR'D	2	USES	2	WHET	2	ABSTRACT	1
TWELVEMONTH	2	USHER	2	WHINE	2	ABSTRACTED	1
TWENTY-ONE	2	USHER'D	2	WHIPT	2	ABSTRACTS	1
TWIG	2	USURE	2	WHIRLIGIGS	2	ABUNDANTLY	1
TWINE	2	UTTER	2	WHITE-GLOV'D	2	ABYDOS'	1
TWINES	2	VALDE	2	WHITEHALL	2	ACADEMIC	1
TWINKLING	2	VALLEY	2	WHITER	2	ACASTUS'	1
TWIRL	2	VALOUR'S	2	WHO'ER	2	ACCESSES	1
TWIRL'D	2	VAMP'D	2	WHOLSOM	2	ACCIDENTS	1
TWISTING	2	VARIANCE	2	WHOSO	2	ACCORDED	1
TWIT'NAM	2	VARIEGATED	2	WICKEDLY	2	ACCOSTED	1
TWOULD	2	VARIOUSLY	2	WIDE-OPENING	2	ACCUSER	1
TYBURN'S	2	VARLETS	2	WIDELY	2	ACCUSES	1
TYDCOMB	2	VARNISH'D	2	WIDOW'S	2	ACCUSTOM'D	1
TYES	2	VATICIDE	2	WIELDED	2	ACHAÏA	1
TYGERS	2	VAUNTING	2	WILD-FIRE	2	ACHAEMENES	1
TYRO	2	VENERABLY	2	WILDERNESS	2	ACHAIA	1
U	2	VENETIAN	2	WILKINS	2	ACHAMAS	1
ULYSSEAN	2	VENICE	2	WILLIAM'S	2	ACHELÖUS	1
UN-OBSERVED	2	VENTUR'D	2	WIND-GUNS	2	ACHELÖUS	1
UN-PENSION'D	2	VERRES	2	WINDE	2	ACHERON	1
UN-THAW'D	2	VESSEL'S	2	WINDINGS	2	ACHIZ	1
UNAIDING	2	VESTAL	2	WINDOW	2	ACQUIT	1
UNAMBITIOUS	2	VESTAL'S	2	WINDOW'D	2	ACQUITS	1
UNAPPARENT	2	VESTURE	2	WINDPIPE	2	ACRED	1
UNASK'D	2	VI'LETS	2	WINK	2	ACRONEUS	1
UNBALANC'D	2	VIAL	2	WINTER-SNOW	2	ACTAEA	1
UNBARR'D	2	VIAND	2	WINTON	2	ACTED	1
UNBELIEVING	2	VIBRATES	2	WITHHOLDS	2	ACTIONS'	1
UNBEND	2	VIDA	2	WIZARDS	2	ACTON	1
UNBENDED	2	VIEWING	2	WOLF'S	2	ACTORIS	1
UNBID	2	VIGILIUS	2	WOOD'S	2	ACTRESS	1
UNBLEMISH'D	2	VIGOROUS	2	WOODWARD'S	2	ACTUATES	1
UNBROKEN	2	VILEST	2	WOOLSTON'S	2	ADAMAS	1
UNCHASTE	2	VILLA	2	WORK'D	2	ADAPTS	1
UNCIVIL	2	VILLAINS	2	WORMIUS	2	ADDER	1
UNCLE	2	VINEYARD	2	WORSHIP'D	2	ADDRES'D	1
UNCONQUERABLE	2	VIOLENT	2	WORSTED	2	ADDRESSED	1
UNCOVER'D	2	VIRAGO	2	WORTLEY	2	ADHERENT	1
UNCOWL'D	2	VIRGINIA	2	WORTLEY'S	2	ADJOURN'D	1
UNCREATING	2	VISIGOTHS	2	WOU'D'ST	2	ADJURATIONS	1
UNCTUOUS	2	VISITANT	2	WOUD	2	ADJURE	1
UNDEFIL'D	2	VITALS	2	WREN	2	ADJUST	1
UNDERTAKE	2	VIZOR	2	WREST	2	ADJUSTING	1
UNDETERMIN'D	2	VOITURE	2	WRETCH'S	2	ADJUSTS	1
UNDISMAY'D	2	VOLUBLE	2	WRIGGLING	2	ADMETUS	1
UNDOUBTED	2	VOT'RESS	2	WRINGS	2	ADMINISTER	1
UNDREST	2	VOT'RY'S	2	WRINKLES	2	ADMINISTER'D	1
UNDRY'D	2	VOUCH	2	WRISTS	2	ADMITTANCE	1
UNFRIENDLY	2	VOUCHSAFES	2	WRY	2	ADOPT	1
UNFURL	2	VOYAGER	2	WRY-MOUTH'D	2	ADORER	1
UNGENTLE	2	VULTURE	2	WYCHERLY	2	ADORING	1
UNGUIDED	2	WADDLES	2	Y-FED	2	ADRASTE	1
UNHALLOW'D	2	WADLING	2	Y-PENT	2	ADRESTIA'S	1
UNHARNESS'D	2	WAFTED	2	YARD	2	ADRESTUS	1
UNHOP'D	2	WAG'D	2	YAW	2	ADRIATIC	1
UNHOP'D-FOR	2	WAGS	2	YEAR'S	2	ADULT'RER	1
UNHURT	2	WAIL	2	YEARLING	2	ADULT'RERS	1
UNINTERR'D	2	WALKER	2	YEARS'	2	ADULTERER	1
UNKINDLY	2	WALLER	2	YELL	2	ADULTERY	1
UNLOCKS	2	WALPOLE	2	YELPING	2	ADULTROUS	1
UNLOOK'D	2	WALSH	2	YEOMAN	2	ADVENTURES	1
UNLOOS'D	2	WALTER	2	YET-WARM	2	ADVENTUROUS	1
UNMANN'D	2	WAND'RER'S	2	YIELDED	2	ADVERSITY	1
UNMEANING	2	WAND'RERS	2	YOKES	2	ADVICES	1
UNMIXT	2	WANE	2	ZANY	2	ADVISES	1
UNMOLESTED	2	WAPPING	2	ZEALOTS	2	ADVISING	1
UNNERVES	2	WARBLE	2	ZENITH	2	AEACUS	1
UNPAY'D	2	WARBLES	2	A-BIT	1	AEAETES	1
UNPILLAR'D	2	WARDROBE	2	A-DOWN	1	AEGEAN	1
UNPROFITABLY	2	WARNER	2	A-FAR	1	AEGEON	1
UNPROPITIOUS	2	WARP'D	2	A-PART	1	AEGIALE	1
UNQUIET	2	WARREN	2	A-ROW	1	AEGILIPA'S	1
UNREAD	2	WARRIOR-MAID	2	A-SQUINT	1	AEGINA	1
UNREGARDING	2	WARRIOR-TRAIN	2	A-TILT	1	AEGION	1
UNRESPECTED	2	WASPS	2	A-YEAR	1	AEGON'S	1
UNRESTRAIN'D	2	WATCH-TOW'R	2	A'TER	1	AEGYALUS	1
UNREWARDED	2	WE'D	2	AARON	1	AEMULOUS	1
UNRIGHTEOUS	2	WE'RE	2	AARON'S	1	AENIANS	1
UNSAV'RY	2	WEATHER	2	AB	1	AENIGMA	1
UNSEAL'D	2	WEAV'D	2	ABANTES	1	AENIUS	1
UNSEALS	2	WEAVES	2	ABANTIAN	1	AENUS	1
UNSEEMLY	2	WEDLOCK'S	2	ABAS	1	AEOLIA'S	1

AEPY	1	ALLEGIANCE	1	ANTIOPE	1	ARTIFICIAL	1
AEPYTUS	1	ALLEY	1	ANTIPATHY	1	ARTIMESIA	1
AESCULAPIUS	1	ALLURING	1	ANTIPHON	1	ARTIST-GOD	1
AESEPUS'	1	ALLY	1	ANTIQUARIES	1	ARTREUS'	1
AESETES'	1	ALLYES	1	ANTITHESIS	1	ARYBAS	1
AESOPUS'	1	ALOM	1	ANTONIUS	1	ASCANIA	1
AESYETES	1	ALOM-STYPTICKS	1	ANTONY	1	ASCANIAN	1
AESYMNUS	1	ALOPÈ	1	ANTRON'S	1	ASCANIUS	1
AETHIOPIA	1	ALOS	1	APAESUS'	1	ASCAPART	1
AETHIOPS	1	ALPHËUS	1	APARTMENT	1	ASCENDANT	1
AETHRA	1	ALPHËUS'	1	APATHY	1	ASCRIB'D	1
AETOLIA	1	ALPHABET	1	APE-AND-MONKEY	1	ASCRIBES	1
AFFAIR	1	ALPHEUS	1	APES	1	ASHEN	1
AFFECTATION	1	ALSOP	1	APHIDAS	1	ASHORE	1
AFFECTED	1	ALTER	1	APISAON	1	ASHURST	1
AFFIRM	1	ALTERNATELY	1	APISAON'S	1	ASHY	1
AFFIX'D	1	ALTERS	1	APOCRYPHA	1	ASIA	1
AFFLUENT	1	ALTES'	1	APOSTLE	1	ASINEN	1
AFFRONTING	1	ALTHOUGH	1	APOSTLES	1	ASK'ST	1
AFFRONTS	1	ALYBAS	1	APOTHECARIES	1	ASKEN	1
AFTERWARDS	1	ALYBEAN	1	APPAL'D	1	ASLOPE	1
AG'D	1	AMARYNCES'	1	APPALL	1	ASOPUS	1
AGACLEUS'	1	AMARYNCEUS'	1	APPALLS	1	ASPERSE	1
AGAMEDE	1	AMASSING	1	APPAREL	1	ASPHALION	1
AGANIPPE'S	1	AMATHEIA	1	APPEAL'D	1	ASPHODILL	1
AGAPENOR	1	AMAZON	1	APPEALING	1	ASPICK'S	1
AGASTROPHUS	1	AMAZON'S	1	APPIUS	1	ASPICKS	1
AGASTROPHUS'S	1	AMAZONS	1	APPLICATION	1	ASPLEDON'S	1
AGATHON	1	AMBASINEUS	1	APPOINTS	1	ASQUINT	1
AGAVE	1	AMBASSADOR	1	APPREHENSIVE	1	ASSA	1
AGELÁUS	1	AMBERGRISE	1	APPRENTIC'D	1	ASSAEUS	1
AGELAUS'	1	AMBIGUOUS	1	APPROBATION	1	ASSAILANTS	1
AGENTS	1	AMBITIOUSLY	1	APRON'D	1	ASSAYS	1
AGGRAVATE	1	AMELIA'S	1	APRONS	1	ASSE	1
AGGRESSOR'S	1	AMICABLE	1	APSEUDES	1	ASSENTED	1
AGIMUR	1	AMICE	1	APTLY	1	ASSERTION	1
AGIS	1	AMID'ST	1	ARABIA	1	ASSIDUOUS	1
AGLAE	1	AMISODARUS	1	ARABY	1	ASSIGNATIONS	1
AGONIZE	1	AMISODARUS'	1	ARACHNE'S	1	ASSISTLESS	1
AGREEABLE	1	AMITY	1	ARAESUS	1	ASSUASIVE	1
AGREES	1	AMMON'S	1	ARBITER	1	ASSURANCE	1
AGRIUS	1	AMNISUS	1	ARBITRATE	1	ASSURANCES	1
AIDED	1	AMOUR	1	ARBOUR	1	ASTERIAN	1
AILS	1	AMOURS	1	ARBUTHNOT	1	ASTERIS	1
AIM'ST	1	AMPHIBIOUS	1	ARBUTHNOT'S	1	ASTONISHT	1
AIR-BRED	1	AMPHICLUS	1	ARCADIA'S	1	ASTRAEA	1
AJACES'	1	AMPHIGENIA'S	1	ARCADIANS	1	ASTRIDE	1
ALACK	1	AMPHINOME	1	ARCESILAS	1	ASTROLOGERS	1
ALARMING	1	AMPHION'S	1	ARCESILAUS	1	ASTRONOMICAL	1
ALBAN	1	AMPHISUS	1	ARCESIUS'	1	ASTURIAN	1
ALBUTIUS	1	AMPHITHEA'S	1	ARCH-POET	1	ASTYALUS	1
ALCAEUS	1	AMPHITHOE	1	ARCHANGEL	1	ASTYNOUS'	1
ALCAEUS'	1	AMPHITRYON'S	1	ARCHED	1	ASTYOCHÈ	1
ALCANDER	1	AMPHIUS'	1	ARCHELOCHUS	1	ASTYPYLUS	1
ALCE	1	AMPHOTERUS	1	ARCHERY	1	AT-HOME	1
ALCIPPE'S	1	AMPHYDAMAS	1	ARCHILOCHUS	1	ATALANTIS	1
ALCMÁON	1	AMPLY	1	ARCHITECTS	1	ATCHIEVE	1
ALCMAON	1	AMPUTATION	1	ARCHITECTURE	1	ATCHIEVEMENT	1
ALCYONE	1	AMUSING	1	ARCS	1	ATCHIEVEMENTS	1
ALDERMAN	1	AMYCLAE	1	AREÏLYCUS	1	ATE	1
ALDGATE	1	AMYDON	1	AREÏTHOUS	1	ATHEIST-WRETCH	1
ALECTOR'S	1	AMYNTOR	1	AREAS	1	ATHEISTS	1
ALEIAN	1	AMYTHAON	1	ARENÈ	1	ATHENA	1
ALEXANDRINE	1	AN'T	1	ARENE'S	1	ATHENA'S	1
ALEXIS'	1	ANALYZ'D	1	ARETÄON	1	ATHOS'	1
ALIA'S	1	ANARCH	1	ARETÈ	1	ATMOSPHERE	1
ALIEN	1	ANARCH'S	1	ARETHUSA'S	1	ATOME	1
ALIEN'S	1	ANCAEUS	1	ARETHYREA	1	ATONEMENT	1
ALIGHTING	1	ANCESTOR'S	1	ARETINE	1	ATOSSA	1
ALISON	1	ANCESTRY	1	ARGENT	1	ATRIDAE	1
ALL-A-ROW	1	ANCIENT'S	1	ARGISSA	1	ATTAINT	1
ALL-ARRAIGNING	1	ANCLE	1	ARGU'D	1	ATTEMP'RING	1
ALL-ASSISTLESS	1	ANCOEUS'	1	ARGUE	1	ATTEMPRED	1
ALL-BEARING	1	ANEMORIA'S	1	ARGUMENTAL	1	ATTENDANCE	1
ALL-BEAUTEOUS	1	ANETOR'S	1	ARGYLE'S	1	ATTENDENCE	1
ALL-BEAUTIFUL	1	ANG'RING	1	ARIMÈ	1	ATTERBURY	1
ALL-COMPELLING	1	ANGEL-LIKE	1	ARISBE	1	ATTERBURY'S	1
ALL-CONFIRMING	1	ANGEL-POW'RS	1	ARISES	1	ATTESTS	1
ALL-CONSUMING	1	ANGELICK	1	ARISTARCH	1	ATTINENT	1
ALL-COV'RING	1	ANGELLS	1	ARISTARCHUS	1	ATTONEMENT	1
ALL-CREATING	1	ANGLER	1	ARISTIPPUS	1	ATTORNEY'S	1
ALL-DESTROYING	1	ANGLES	1	ARISTOPHANES	1	ATTORNIES	1
ALL-DIFFUSIVE	1	ANGUISH'D	1	ARIUS	1	ATTRACTED	1
ALL-ELOQUENT	1	ANIMALS	1	ARK	1	ATTRACTION	1
ALL-EMBRACING	1	ANKLES	1	ARM'RERS	1	ATTRACTS	1
ALL-ENLIGHT'NING	1	ANN	1	ARM'S	1	ATTRIBUTES	1
ALL-ENLIGHTEN'D	1	ANNA'S	1	ARMA	1	ATTUNES	1
ALL-EXTENDING	1	ANNE'S	1	ARMAMENT	1	ATTYS	1
ALL-GOVERNING	1	ANNIHILATED	1	ARMOURY	1	ATYMNIUS	1
ALL-IMPAIRING	1	ANNO	1	ARNAEUS	1	AUBURN	1
ALL-IMPOTENT	1	ANNOY'D	1	AROMATICK	1	AUCTION	1
ALL-INFOLDING	1	ANNOYS	1	ARRAIGN	1	AUDIBLE	1
ALL-POW'RFUL	1	ANODYNE	1	ARRAIGNING	1	AUGIA	1
ALL-PRESERVING	1	ANSWERING	1	ARRANT'ST	1	AUGIA'S	1
ALL-PREVENTING	1	ANT'S	1	ARRAS	1	AUGIAS'	1
ALL-QUICK'NING	1	ANTAEA	1	ARRAYS	1	AUGUR'S	1
ALL-RECORDING	1	ANTEDATES	1	ARREAR	1	AUGURS	1
ALL-REMEMBRING	1	ANTHEDON	1	ARRIA	1	AUGUSTA	1
ALL-REVEALING	1	ANTICKS	1	ARROGANT	1	AUGUSTA'S	1
ALL-RIGHTEOUS	1	ANTICLEA'S	1	ARROW'S	1	AULIS'	1
ALL-SURROUNDING	1	ANTICLIA	1	ARSE	1	AUNT	1
ALL-SURVEYING	1	ANTICLUS	1	ARSINOUS'	1	AUSONIAN	1
ALL-SUSTAINING	1	ANTIDOTE	1	ARTEMIS	1	AUT	1
ALL-TO-BREST	1	ANTILOCHUS'	1	ARTICHOAKS	1	AUTH'RESS	1
				ARTICLES	1	AUTHORITIES	1

AUTHORITY	1	BEACONS	1	BEVY	1	BOW-STRING	1
AUTHORS'	1	BEAD	1	BEWAIL'D	1	BOWING	1
AUTOLYCHUS'S	1	BEAK	1	BEWAILS	1	BOWYER	1
AUTOLYCI	1	BEAKY	1	BIAS'	1	BOWYER'S	1
AUTOLYCUS'S	1	BEAN-SHELL	1	BIBLES	1	BOWZY	1
AUTONOÈ	1	BEANS	1	BICKNELL	1	BOY-SENATOR	1
AUTUMN-HEATS	1	BEANSTRAW	1	BIENOR	1	BOYD'S	1
AUTUMNS	1	BEAR'S	1	BIG-UDDER'D	1	BR	1
AUXILIARS	1	BEAR'ST	1	BIGGER	1	BRACELET	1
AVENGER'S	1	BEAU-KIND	1	BIGOT	1	BRACELETS	1
AVENUES	1	BEAU'S	1	BIGOTS	1	BRACHMANS	1
AVER	1	BEAUMONT'S	1	BIGOTTS	1	BRADY	1
AVEZ	1	BEAUS'	1	BILK'D	1	BRAGGART	1
AVIDIEN	1	BEAUTIFULLY	1	BINDING	1	BRAIDED	1
AVOIDS	1	BEAUTIFY	1	BINFIELD	1	BRAIN'D	1
AVON'S	1	BEAVY	1	BIRTH-NIGHT	1	BRAINING	1
AVOW	1	BECALM'D	1	BIRTH-NIGHTS	1	BRAINLESS	1
AWAKING	1	BECALMS	1	BIRTHS	1	BRAKES	1
AWEFUL	1	BECCA-FICOS	1	BISHOP'S	1	BRAMINS	1
AWFULLY	1	BECKEN	1	BITT	1	BRAMSTON	1
AXIS	1	BECKON	1	BITTERN	1	BRANDIES	1
AXYLUS	1	BECKON'D	1	BITTERS	1	BRANDISH	1
AYE	1	BECKONS	1	BL	1	BRANDISHING	1
B<L>EST	1	BEDEWS	1	BLACK-JOKE	1	BRANDY	1
B***'S	1	BEDFORD-HEAD	1	BLACKER	1	BRASS-CHEEK'D	1
BAAL	1	BEDIGHT	1	BLACKEST	1	BRAVADO	1
BABEL	1	BEDIMM'D	1	BLACKMORES	1	BRAVELY-PATIENT	1
BABO	1	BEDROP'D	1	BLADEN	1	BRAWL'D	1
BABYLON	1	BEE'S	1	BLAM'D	1	BRAZEN-POINTED	1
BACCHANALLS	1	BEECH-TREE	1	BLANK'D	1	BREADTH	1
BACCHANALS'	1	BEECH-TREE'S	1	BLANKETINGS	1	BREATH<E>S	1
BACK-PLATE	1	BEECHEN	1	BLANKETTINGS	1	BREATH<E	1
BACK-STAIRS	1	BEECHES	1	BLASPHEM'D	1	BREDE	1
BACK'D	1	BEET	1	BLASPHEMER	1	BREEDER	1
BACKWARDS	1	BEETLES	1	BLASTING	1	BREEZE'S	1
BAEOTIA	1	BEFALL	1	BLAZETH	1	BREST	1
BAEOTIA'S	1	BEFALLS	1	BLAZON	1	BREW	1
BAEOTIANS	1	BEFOOL	1	BLEAT	1	BRIAREUS'	1
BAGATELLE	1	BEFRIENDED	1	BLEAU	1	BRIBING	1
BAGNIO'S	1	BEFRIENDS	1	BLEMISH	1	BRIDAL-ROOM	1
BALANCES	1	BEFRINGE	1	BLENDED	1	BRIDES	1
BALBUS	1	BEGAT	1	BLESSING'S	1	BRIDG'D	1
BALDNESS	1	BEGET	1	BLINKING	1	BRIDGES	1
BALES	1	BEGETS	1	BLOCKS	1	BRIDGEWATER	1
BALINDINE	1	BEGGED	1	BLOIS	1	BRIDGEWATER'S	1
BALLANC'D	1	BEGIRT	1	BLOODHOUNDS	1	BRIDGMAN	1
BALLANCE	1	BEHAVIOUR	1	BLOODIER	1	BRIDLED	1
BALLAST	1	BEHOV'D	1	BLOOMSB'RY	1	BRIDLES	1
BALMES	1	BEKNAVE	1	BLOOMSB'RY-SQUARE	1	BRIGHT-EY'D	1
BALMS	1	BELCH	1	BLOTCH	1	BRIGHT'NING	1
BANDIT	1	BELCHT	1	BLUBBER'D	1	BRIGHTLY	1
BANISHT	1	BELGIAN	1	BLUBBRING	1	BRIGHTLY-DAWNING	1
BANK-BILL	1	BELISARIUS	1	BLUE-HAIR'D	1	BRIGHTNESS	1
BANQUET'S	1	BELLES	1	BLUEISH	1	BRILLANTE	1
BANSTED	1	BELLIES	1	BLUELY	1	BRING'ST	1
BANSTED-DOWN	1	BELLYING	1	BLUNDER	1	BRINGING	1
BARB	1	BELONGING	1	BLUNTS	1	BRISEÏS'	1
BARBARITIES	1	BELOVED	1	BLUSTER	1	BRISKLY	1
BARBAROUS	1	BEMOAN'D	1	BLUSTRING	1	BRITON'S	1
BARBECU'D	1	BENEFICE	1	BOÄGRIUS	1	BROACH	1
BARBER'S	1	BENEFICENT	1	BOÖTES'	1	BROACHERS	1
BARD'S	1	BENEFIT	1	BOARD'S	1	BROAD-GLITT'RING	1
BAREFAC'D	1	BENEFITS	1	BOARDED	1	BROAD-PATCH'D	1
BARGAIN	1	BENIGN	1	BOARDING	1	BROBDIGNAG	1
BARGE	1	BENIGNER	1	BOAT	1	BROBDINGNAG	1
BARK'S	1	BENLOWES	1	BODES	1	BROBDINGNAG'S	1
BARKING	1	BENUMM'D	1	BODIED	1	BROCAS'S	1
BARN'S	1	BEQUEATHE	1	BODINGS	1	BROCCOLI	1
BARONS	1	BEREAVES.	1	BODKIN'S	1	BROIL	1
BARR	1	BEREFT	1	BODKINS	1	BROILS	1
BARRIERS	1	BERENICE'S	1	BODY'D	1	BROMPTON	1
BARROW	1	BERKELEY	1	BOEBE'S	1	BROOK'D	1
BASE-BORN	1	BERKLEY	1	BOETHOEDES	1	BROOMSTICKS	1
BASER	1	BERKS	1	BOETIA	1	BROTHELS	1
BASEST	1	BERNINI'S	1	BOISTROUS	1	BROTHER-CHIEF	1
BASK'D	1	BERTRAND'S	1	BOLGOLAM'S	1	BROTHER-CHIEFS	1
BASKET	1	BERYL	1	BOLINGBROKE	1	BROTHER-LEADERS	1
BASONS	1	BESEECH	1	BOMB	1	BROTHERIGE	1
BAST	1	BESH	1	BON	1	BROW'D	1
BASTARD	1	BESIEGERS	1	BOOK-WORMS	1	BROWNER	1
BASTARDS	1	BESOT	1	BOOK'S	1	BROWZE	1
BASTO	1	BESPEAKING	1	BOOKFUL	1	BRUNSWICK	1
BAT	1	BESPREAD	1	BOOKSELLERS	1	BRUNSWICK'S	1
BATAVIAN	1	BESPRINKLES	1	BOOMING	1	BRUNT	1
BATEIA	1	BESS	1	BOOT	1	BRUSHING	1
BATH'ST	1	BESSA	1	BOOTY	1	BRUSSELS	1
BATHURST'S	1	BEST-BUILT	1	BORDER	1	BRUSTLING	1
BATHYCLAEUS	1	BEST-LOV'D	1	BOREAS'	1	BRUTE	1
BATS	1	BESTIAL	1	BOREAS'S	1	BRUTIAN	1
BATT'NING	1	BESTLY	1	BORES	1	BRUTISH	1
BATT'RING	1	BESTOR'D	1	BORGIA	1	BRYSIA'S	1
BATTALION	1	BESTREW'D	1	BORN<E	1	BU	1
BATTEL'S	1	BESTRIDE	1	BORROW	1	BUB	1
BATTER	1	BETAKE	1	BOSOME-WIFE	1	BUBBLE-BOY	1
BATTERY*	1	BETHEL'S	1	BOSSES	1	BUCKENBURG	1
BATTL'D	1	BETHOUGHT	1	BOSSIE	1	BUCKHURSTS	1
BAUBLE	1	BETIDE	1	BOSSY	1	BUCKINGHAM'S	1
BAWD	1	BETIDES	1	BOTANISTS	1	BUCKLED	1
BAWL'D	1	BETRAY'ST	1	BOTCH	1	BUCKLING	1
BAYONNE	1	BETT	1	BOTTELS	1	BUCKS	1
BAYS'S	1	BETTE	1	BOTTOMS	1	BUDGELL'S	1
BE-DROPT	1	BETTERTON'S	1	BOUNCES	1	BUDIUM'S	1
BE-MUS'D	1	BETTY	1	BOUNCING	1	BUFFET'S	1
BE-RYM'D	1	BETTY'S	1	BOUNT'OUS	1	BUGBEAR	1
BEACON'S	1	BEVERAGE	1	BOURBON'S	1		

COAGULATES	1	CONFEDERATES	1	COUNSELLORS	1	CUBS	1
COASTING	1	CONFESSES	1	COUNTER-CHARMS	1	CUCKOLD-MAKER'S	1
COATS	1	CONFESSING	1	COUNTER-WORK	1	CUCKOLD'S	1
COBLER-LIKE	1	CONFESSION	1	COUNTER-WORKS	1	CUCKOLDING	1
COCHINE'L	1	CONFESSOR	1	COUNTREY	1	CUCKOLDS	1
COCK-HORSE	1	CONFIDENT	1	COUNTRYS	1	CUCKOW	1
CODES	1	CONFORM'D	1	COUNTS	1	CUDGEL'D	1
COELESTIALS	1	CONFUCIUS	1	COUNTY	1	CUFF'D	1
COERANUS	1	CONFUSIONS	1	COUPLET	1	CULLIES	1
COERCIVE	1	CONFUTED	1	COURIER	1	CULLS	1
COEUR	1	CONGEALS	1	COURSER-BREEDING	1	CULLY	1
COFFERS	1	CONGESTED	1	COURT-SYCOPHANT	1	CULTIVATE	1
COFFIN	1	CONGLOB'D	1	COURT-VIRTUES	1	CULTIVATED	1
COHER'D	1	CONGLOBING	1	COURTED	1	CULTURE	1
COHERENT	1	CONJURER	1	COURTESY	1	CUM	1
COL'NEL	1	CONNECTIONS	1	COURTIN	1	CUMBER	1
COLDER	1	CONNIVANCE	1	COURTINE	1	CUPP'D	1
COLDEST	1	CONQ'ROR'S	1	COUSIN	1	CURBS	1
COLDLY	1	CONQUEROR	1	COV'NANTS	1	CURDS	1
COLDNESS	1	CONQUERORS	1	COV'RINGS	1	CURELESS	1
COLEPEPPER'S	1	CONSECRATES	1	COVERING	1	CURETES	1
COLIN'S	1	CONSECRATING	1	COVERINGS	1	CURETIAN	1
COLINAEUS	1	CONSERVES	1	COVERLETS	1	CURLL	1
COLL	1	CONSIDERING	1	COVERTS	1	CURLL'S	1
COLLECTING	1	CONSIGNS	1	COW-LIKE	1	CURLLS	1
COLLECTIVE	1	CONSIST	1	COW-LIKE-UDDERS	1	CURRENTS	1
COLLEGIATE	1	CONSONANT	1	COWARD-COUNSELS	1	CURRIERS	1
COLLIER'S	1	CONSORTS	1	COWARD'S	1	CURTAIN-LECTURES	1
COLLINS	1	CONSPIRING	1	COWARDICE	1	CUSHION	1
COLLY	1	CONSTELLATION	1	COWL	1	CUSTOM'S	1
COLMAR	1	CONSTITUTE	1	COWLE	1	CUSTOME	1
COLONADE	1	CONSTITUTION	1	COWPER'S	1	CUSTOMS	1
COLONADES	1	CONSTRU'D	1	COWS	1	CUTLETS	1
COLONIES	1	CONSUL'S	1	COWSLIP	1	CYCLOP'S	1
COLONNADE	1	CONSULTED	1	COWSLIP'S	1	CYCLOPS'	1
COLOSSES	1	CONSULTS	1	COXCOMB-PYES	1	CYDONIAN	1
COLOURING	1	CONSUMES	1	COZ	1	CYDONIANS	1
COLUMBUS	1	CONTAGION	1	COZENS	1	CYGNET	1
COLUMBUS-LIKE	1	CONTAGIOUS	1	CRACKLES	1	CYLLENÈ	1
COLUMN'S	1	CONTEMNING	1	CRAGS'S	1	CYMARRS	1
COMB	1	CONTEMNS	1	CRAMS	1	CYMINDIS	1
COMBATING	1	CONTEMPTIBLE	1	CRANAE'S	1	CYMODOCE	1
COMBINING	1	CONTIGUOUS	1	CRANE	1	CYMOTHOE	1
COMELIER	1	CONTINENT	1	CRANE'S	1	CYNDER	1
COMIC	1	CONTINUES	1	CRANNIES	1	CYNDER-WENCHES	1
COMICAL	1	CONTRACTING	1	CRANNY	1	CYNOS	1
COMICK	1	CONTRADICTION	1	CRAPATHUS	1	CYNTHUS'	1
COMMA	1	CONTRIV'D	1	CRASH	1	CYPARISSUS	1
COMMA'S	1	CONTRIVING	1	CRATAEIS	1	CYPHERS	1
COMMANDED	1	CONTROL	1	CRAWFISH	1	CYPHUS	1
COMMANDMENT'S	1	CONUNDRUM	1	CRAWL'D	1	CYPRUS'	1
COMMANDMENTS	1	CONVENES	1	CRAYON	1	CYRRHA'S	1
COMMAS	1	CONVENT	1	CRAZ'D	1	CYTHAERON	1
COMMENCES	1	CONVENT'S	1	CREATES	1	CYTHERA	1
COMMENCING	1	CONVENTS	1	CREECH	1	CYTHERAEA'S	1
COMMENDED	1	CONVERTS	1	CREET	1	CYTHEREA	1
COMMENTAT	1	CONVEY'ST	1	CREIONTIAN	1	CYTORUS	1
COMMENTATOR	1	CONVEYANCE	1	CREMONA	1	D'	1
COMMITTEE	1	CONVICT	1	CREON'S	1	D'URFEIUS	1
COMMIX	1	CONVOCATION	1	CRESCENTS	1	D'URFY'S	1
COMMON-SHOAR	1	CONVOK'D	1	CRESSES	1	DAEDALEAN	1
COMMONWEAL	1	CONVOKE	1	CRESSY	1	DAETOR	1
COMMUNION	1	CONY	1	CRETA'S	1	DAFFODILLIES	1
COMPANION'S	1	COOEVAL	1	CRETAN'S	1	DAGGLED	1
COMPEER	1	COOK-MAID	1	CRETHON	1	DAIGN	1
COMPEERS	1	COOK'D	1	CRIBS	1	DAIRY	1
COMPEL	1	COOKS	1	CRICKET	1	DALILAH	1
COMPENSATED	1	COOLER	1	CRIME'S	1	DAMASTOR'S	1
COMPLACENCE	1	COOP	1	CRIMSON'D	1	DAMASTORIDES	1
COMPLAISANCE	1	COPAE	1	CRIPPLE	1	DAMASUS	1
COMPLAISANT	1	COPREUS	1	CRIPPLED	1	DAMON'S	1
COMPLAISANTLY	1	COPY'D	1	CRIPPLES	1	DAMP'D	1
COMPLEATLY	1	COPYING	1	CRISPISSA	1	DAMSEL-TRAIN	1
COMPLEMENT	1	CORACIAN	1	CRITERION	1	DAN	1
COMPLEXIONS	1	COREGGIO'S	1	CRITIC'S	1	DANAE	1
COMPLIANT	1	CORINTH	1	CRITICISM	1	DANAUS	1
COMPLY'D	1	CORKS	1	CRITICK'D	1	DANAUS'	1
COMPOS'DLY	1	CORM'RANTS	1	CRITICKS'	1	DANCER	1
COMPOSES	1	CORN-LOFT	1	CROAKING	1	DANE	1
COMPOSURE	1	CORN-VAN	1	CROCYLIA	1	DANISH	1
COMPRESS	1	CORNEILLE'S	1	CROESMUS'	1	DANTE	1
COMPRIZ'D	1	CORNELS	1	CROMNA	1	DAPPER	1
COMPTING	1	CORNICE	1	CRONE	1	DAPPERWIT	1
COMPTING-HOUSE	1	CORNISH	1	CRONY'S	1	DAPPL'D	1
COMPTON	1	CORNUS	1	CROP'D	1	DARDAN'S	1
COMTESSE	1	CORNWALL	1	CROPT	1	DARDANIA'S	1
CON	1	CORONE	1	CROUCHEN	1	DARDANIAN	1
CONCEALING	1	CORONATIONS	1	CROUZAZ	1	DARENT	1
CONCEALMENT	1	CORONET	1	CROWING	1	DARIUS	1
CONCEITED	1	CORRECTED	1	CROWN'S	1	DARKLY	1
CONCERTED	1	CORRECTLY	1	CROWS	1	DARTINEUF	1
CONCLUDED	1	CORRECTNESS	1	CRUCIFY	1	DARTY	1
CONCLUDING	1	CORRESPONDENT	1	CRUCIFY'D	1	DASHING	1
CONCLUSION	1	CORRODED	1	CRUELTY	1	DATED	1
CONCLUSIONS	1	CORS'LETS	1	CRUNUS	1	DAULIS	1
CONCLUSIVE	1	CORSES	1	CRUSHING	1	DAUNT	1
CONCORDANCE	1	COS	1	CRUST	1	DAVENANT	1
CONCUR	1	COSINS	1	CRUTCH	1	DAVENANT'S	1
CONCUSSION	1	COSMETIC	1	CRUTCHES	1	DAVID'S	1
CONDEMNS	1	COT	1	CRYD	1	DAVIES	1
CONDENSING	1	COTSWOLD	1	CRYS	1	DAWN'D	1
CONDESCEND	1	COTTS	1	CTESIPPUS'	1	DAY-DEVOURER	1
CONDESCENDED	1	COUGH	1	CTESIUS	1	DAY-DISTRACTING	1
CONDOLE	1	COUNCIL-BOARD	1	CTIMENE	1	DAY-LIGHT	1
CONDUCTED	1	COUNSELLOR	1	CUBIT'S	1	DAZZL'D	1

DAZZLE	1	DERIVING	1	DISARMS	1	DOLESOME	1
DAZZLED	1	DESCANTED	1	DISASTERS	1	DOLOPIANS	1
DAZZLES	1	DESCENDANT	1	DISBURSES	1	DOLOPION'S	1
DEÏPYRUS	1	DESCRIPTIONS	1	DISCARD	1	DOLOPS'	1
DE-MOIVRE	1	DESIRE'S	1	DISCHARGING	1	DOLOURS	1
DEADLIER	1	DESIROUS	1	DISCOMPOSE	1	DOME'S	1
DEAR-LOV'D	1	DESISTS	1	DISCORD'S	1	DONNE	1
DEATH-FUL	1	DESOLATED	1	DISCOUNTENANC'D	1	DOOMING	1
DEATH-WATCHES	1	DESOLATION	1	DISCOURAG'D	1	DORIANS	1
DEATHLIKE	1	DESPERATE	1	DISCOURAGD	1	DORIC	1
DEB'RAH	1	DESPERS'D	1	DISCOURS'D	1	DORIMANT	1
DEBARKING	1	DESPICABLE	1	DISCOV'RIES	1	DORION	1
DEBARR'D	1	DESPISER	1	DISCOV'RY	1	DORSETS	1
DEBAUCHED	1	DESPITE	1	DISCREDIT	1	DORYCLUS	1
DEBENTURES	1	DESPONDING	1	DISCRETION	1	DOSE	1
DEBONAIR	1	DESPOTICK	1	DISCUSS	1	DOTARD'S	1
DEBORAH	1	DESSERT	1	DISEAS'D	1	DOTE	1
DEBTOR	1	DESTINE	1	DISEMBARKING	1	DOTING	1
DECAYING	1	DESTINY'S	1	DISEMBOGUES	1	DOTO	1
DECEAST	1	DETAIL	1	DISFIGURE	1	DOUBLE-CLASPING	1
DECEITFUL	1	DETECT	1	DISGORGES	1	DOUBLE-TAX'D	1
DECENCIES	1	DETERRS	1	DISGRACES	1	DOUBLETS	1
DECIDES	1	DETHRONE	1	DISGRACETH	1	DOUBTLESS	1
DECISION	1	DETRACT	1	DISGUSTS	1	DOUGHTY	1
DECIUS	1	DETRACTION	1	DISHABILLE	1	DOWNCAST	1
DECLAIM	1	DEV'LISH	1	DISJOYN'D	1	DOWRY	1
DECLAIM'D	1	DEV'LL	1	DISJOYNTED	1	DOZ'D	1
DECORATE	1	DEVELLOP	1	DISLODGE	1	DOZENS	1
DECORUM	1	DEVIATE	1	DISMISSION	1	DOZY	1
DECREAST	1	DEVOIR	1	DISMOUNTED	1	DRACIUS	1
DECREPIT	1	DEVOLVE	1	DISOBEY	1	DRAG'D	1
DEDICATE	1	DEVOLVES	1	DISOBEY'D	1	DRAGGING	1
DEDICATION	1	DEVONSHIRE	1	DISOWNS	1	DRAGOONS	1
DEDUCE	1	DEVOTION'S	1	DISPELLS	1	DRAMATIS	1
DEDUCT	1	DEVOTIONS	1	DISPENSARY	1	DRAWING-ROOM	1
DEDUCTIONS	1	DEVOURER	1	DISPEOPLING	1	DREAMING	1
DEEMING	1	DEVOURERS	1	DISPIRIT	1	DREAR	1
DEEP-DISCERNING	1	DEW'D	1	DISPLEASE	1	DREIN	1
DEEP-ECHOING	1	DEX'TROUS	1	DISPLEASES	1	DREIN'D	1
DEEP-FURROW'D	1	DEXAMENE	1	DISPORTS	1	DREINS	1
DEEP-IMAG'D	1	DIADEM	1	DISPOSER	1	DRESSES	1
DEEP-MOUTH'D	1	DIADEM'D	1	DISPOSES	1	DRESUS	1
DEEP-MUSING	1	DIAMOND'S	1	DISPREAD	1	DRIPS	1
DEEP-PIERCING	1	DIAN'S	1	DISPREADS	1	DRIVEN	1
DEEP-PROJECTING	1	DIAPER	1	DISPUTANT	1	DRIVER	1
DEEP-ROOTED	1	DICK	1	DISROBES	1	DRIZLING	1
DEF'RENCE	1	DICTATOR	1	DISSEMBL'D	1	DROLL	1
DEFAULT	1	DICTIONARIES	1	DISSEMBLERS	1	DRONE	1
DEFEND'ST	1	DICTIONARY	1	DISSENTION	1	DRONES	1
DEFERR	1	DIDIUS	1	DISSEVER	1	DROPPINGS	1
DEFERR'D	1	DIDO	1	DISSIMULATION	1	DROV'ST	1
DEFERRING	1	DIED	1	DISSIPATES	1	DROVES	1
DEFINE	1	DIFFERENCE	1	DISTAFF	1	DROWSY	1
DEFRAY	1	DIFFERING	1	DISTANC'D	1	DRUG	1
DEFYING	1	DIFFICULTY	1	DISTANC'T	1	DRUGGERMAN	1
DEGEN'RATES	1	DIGAMMA	1	DISTAST	1	DRUIDS	1
DEGRE	1	DIGGING	1	DISTASTE	1	DRUNKARDS	1
DEICOON'S	1	DIGNIFIES	1	DISTASTES	1	DRUNKENNESS	1
DEIFY'D	1	DIGNIFY'D	1	DISTEMPER	1	DRYAD	1
DEIOCHUS	1	DIGS	1	DISTICH	1	DRYAS	1
DEIOPIS	1	DILATE	1	DISTIL	1	DRYER	1
DEIPYLUS	1	DILATING	1	DISTILLING	1	DRYLY	1
DEJECTS	1	DILEMMA	1	DISTILS	1	DRYNESS	1
DELA	1	DILIGENCE	1	DISTINCTIONS	1	DRYOPS	1
DELIB'RATE	1	DILIGENTLY	1	DISTINCTIVE	1	DU	1
DELICATE	1	DIM'D	1	DISTRACTS	1	DUB	1
DELICATELY	1	DIMENSION'D	1	DISTRESSES	1	DUBS	1
DELIGHTING	1	DIMINISH	1	DISTRIBUTES	1	DUCAL	1
DELINEATE	1	DIMLY	1	DISTRICTS	1	DUCHESS	1
DELIV'RING	1	DIMMS	1	DISTURBANCES	1	DUCK-LANE	1
DELIVERS	1	DIMPLING	1	DISUNITE	1	DUGS	1
DELORAIN	1	DIMS	1	DISUS'D	1	DUILIUS'	1
DELPHI	1	DINES	1	DITTIED	1	DULCET	1
DELUDE	1	DINNER-TIME	1	DIUS	1	DULICHIANS	1
DELUDERS	1	DIOCLES	1	DIVAN	1	DULICHIUM'S	1
DELUDES	1	DIOCLEUS'	1	DIVE	1	DULLEST	1
DELUSIONS	1	DIOMEDÈ	1	DIVEL	1	DULLS	1
DEMANDING	1	DIOMED<E	1	DIVERSELY	1	DULNES	1
DEMEANOUR	1	DIOMED'S	1	DIVERTING	1	DULNESS'	1
DEMI-GODS	1	DIONYSIUS	1	DIVES'S	1	DUM	1
DEMOCOON	1	DIOS	1	DIVESTS	1	DUNKIRK'S	1
DEMOCRITUS	1	DIPP'D	1	DIVINER	1	DUP'D	1
DEMOLEON	1	DIPS	1	DIVINERS'	1	DUR	1
DEMONSTRATION	1	DIRCE'S	1	DIVING	1	DURANTE	1
DEMUCHUS	1	DIRECTIONS	1	DIVINING	1	DURATION	1
DEMURE	1	DIRECTOR	1	DIVISIONS	1	DURER'S	1
DEMURELY	1	DIRGE	1	DIVORCE	1	DURFEI	1
DEMURRS	1	DIS	1	DIVULG'D	1	DURFEY'S	1
DENHAM'S	1	DIS-AGREED	1	DIZZY	1	DURGEN	1
DENIED	1	DIS-ALLOW	1	DMETOR	1	DUTCHESS	1
DENIZENS	1	DIS-ARRAY'D	1	DO'ST	1	DUTCHESSES	1
DENOTE	1	DIS-BARK	1	DOAT	1	DUTCHY	1
DENOUNCE	1	DIS-CUMBERS	1	DOATING	1	DWELLERS	1
DEPARTURE	1	DIS-OBEY'D	1	DOCK'D	1	DY'ST	1
DEPENDENCIES	1	DIS-PART	1	DODDER'D	1	DYD	1
DEPOPULATE	1	DIS-PARTED	1	DODONA	1	DYNAMENE	1
DEPOPULATES	1	DIS-ROAB'D	1	DOG-DAYS	1	EËTION	1
DEPOS'D	1	DIS-ROB'D	1	DOG-HOLE	1	EËTION'S	1
DEPRESS'D	1	DIS-UNITE	1	DOG-STAR	1	E	1
DEPRIVE	1	DIS-UNITED	1	DOGMATIZE	1	E'R	1
DEPRIVES	1	DISABUS'D	1	DOGSTAR	1	E'SHAM	1
DEPTFORD	1	DISAPPOINT	1	DOING	1	EAGLE-SPEED	1
DERISION	1	DISAPPROV'D	1	DOIT	1	EAR-RINGS	1
DERISIVE	1	DISAPPROVES	1	DOL'ROUS	1	EARL'S	1
DERIV'ST	1	DISARM	1	DOLESOM	1		

EARL'S-COURT	1	ENCIRCLE	1	ERINGO'S	1	EXCLAIM	1
EARLE	1	ENCIRCLES	1	ERINNA	1	EXCLUDE	1
EARLS	1	ENCIRCLING	1	ERIPHYLÈ	1	EXCREMENT	1
EARLY'ST	1	ENCOMIUM	1	ERIS	1	EXCREMENT'S	1
EARN'D	1	ENCOMPASS	1	ERMIN	1	EXCRESCENT	1
EARTH-SHAKER	1	ENCOMPAST	1	ERMIN'D	1	EXECUTION	1
EARTH'D	1	ENCORE	1	ERRANT	1	EXEQUIAL	1
EARTHQUAKE	1	ENCOUNT'RING	1	ERRATIC	1	EXERTING	1
EARWIG	1	ENCOUNTERS	1	ERSE	1	EXHALATION	1
EASES	1	ENCOUNTRED	1	ERYALUS	1	EXHALING	1
EATEN	1	ENCOURAGE	1	ERYMANTH	1	EXHORTING	1
EATON'S	1	ENCOURAGES	1	ERYNNIS	1	EXIGENCE	1
EBOR	1	ENCROACHING	1	ERYPHILE	1	EXIGENCIES	1
ECHECLOEUS	1	ENDANGER'D	1	ERYTHINUS'	1	EXIT	1
ECHINADES	1	ENDEAR	1	ERYTHRAE	1	EXOTIC	1
ECLIPS'D	1	ENDEARMENT	1	ESHER'S	1	EXPATIATES	1
ECSTACY	1	ENDEARMENTS	1	ESPALIER	1	EXPECTANTS	1
ECSTASIES	1	ENDEARS	1	ESPALIERS	1	EXPEDITIONS	1
ED	1	ENDIVE	1	ESPECIALLY	1	EXPELLING	1
EDGING	1	ENDOW	1	ESPOUSING	1	EXPENSE	1
EDIFIES	1	ENDOW'D	1	ESPY'D	1	EXPENSIVE	1
EDIFY	1	ENDOWMENTS	1	ESQUIRE	1	EXPERIENCE'D	1
EDITION	1	ENDUES	1	ESSAYING	1	EXPLETIVES	1
EDUCING	1	ENERVATE	1	ESSENC'D	1	EXPLOIT	1
EDWARDI	1	ENFLAM'D	1	ESSENCES	1	EXPLOITS	1
EDWARDS	1	ENFLAME	1	ESTIMATING	1	EXPUNGE	1
EFFAC'D	1	ENGAGEMENT	1	ESTRANG'D	1	EXQUISITELY	1
EFFUSIVE	1	ENGAGEMENTS	1	ESTRANGE	1	EXTACY	1
EFT	1	ENGAGES	1	ETEON'S	1	EXTANT	1
EIDOTHEA	1	ENGENDER'D	1	ETERNALLY	1	EXTERIOR	1
EIES	1	ENGLAND'S	1	ETHEOCLES	1	EXTERNAL	1
EIGHTEEN	1	ENGLISHMAN	1	ETHIOPIANS	1	EXTERNALS	1
EIGHTIETH	1	ENGLISHMEN	1	ETOLIAN	1	EXTIRPATE	1
EIONEUS	1	ENIOPEUS'	1	ETON	1	EXTOLS	1
EIONEUS'	1	ENIPEUS	1	ETON'S	1	EXTREAMLY	1
EJECTING	1	ENIPEUS'	1	EUAEMON'S	1	EYE-BROW	1
EJECTS	1	ENISPÈ	1	EUBEA	1	EYE-BROWN	1
EK'D	1	ENJOIN	1	EUCHENOR	1	EYE-LESS	1
ELABORATE	1	ENJOYNS	1	EUCLID	1	EYE-LIDS	1
ELASUS	1	ENKINDLE	1	EUCLIO	1	EYE-SIGHT	1
ELATREUS'	1	ENLARGEMENTS	1	EUDORUS	1	EYEBROW	1
ELBOWS	1	ENLIGHT'NING	1	EUGENE	1	EYESIGHT	1
ELECTED	1	ENLIGHTEN	1	EUGH<YEW	1	EYRIE	1
ELECTION	1	ENLIGHTEN'D	1	EUPHEMUS	1	FABLING	1
ELECTOR	1	ENLIGHTS	1	EUPHETES	1	FABRICK	1
ELEGIES	1	ENLIVEN	1	EUPHRATES	1	FABRICKS	1
ELEÒN	1	ENMITIES	1	EUPITHES'	1	FACTOR	1
ELEPHANTS	1	ENNOBLE	1	EUPITHEUS'	1	FACTS	1
ELEVATES	1	ENNOBLES	1	EURISTHEUS'	1	FAD'ST	1
ELEVEN	1	ENNOBLING	1	EUROPA'S	1	FAECUNDIFIED	1
ELIAH	1	ENOCH	1	EUROTA'S	1	FAERY	1
ELIANS	1	ENOPS	1	EURUS	1	FAGGOT	1
ELIZ	1	ENOUGH'S	1	EURYADES	1	FAILD	1
ELL	1	ENQUIR'D	1	EURYDICÉ	1	FAIR-ONE'S	1
ELLIS	1	ENQUIR'ST	1	EURYMEDES	1	FAIR-STREAMING	1
ELLS	1	ENQUIRES	1	EURYMEDON'S	1	FAIR-ZON'D	1
ELMS	1	ENQUIRIES	1	EURYMEDUSA	1	FAITHFULLY	1
ELOÏSA'S	1	ENROLL	1	EURYSTHEUS	1	FALCONS	1
ELOCUTION	1	ENROLL'D	1	EURYTION	1	FALLACY	1
ELOISE	1	ENSHRIN'D	1	EURYTUS'	1	FALSER	1
ELOPE	1	ENTAIL	1	EUTRESIS	1	FALSLY	1
ELOPES	1	ENTAIL'D	1	EV'NING-SPY	1	FALT'RING	1
ELPHENOR	1	ENTAILS	1	EV'RYTHING	1	FAMILIES	1
ELSEWHERE	1	ENTANGLE	1	EVAEMON'S	1	FANCIED	1
ELYZIAN	1	ENTANGLING	1	EVANDER'S	1	FANCIES	1
ELZEVIR	1	ENTERPRISE	1	EVANTHEUS'	1	FANCY-FORM'D	1
EM'RALD	1	ENTERTAINING	1	EVASIVE	1	FANCY'ST	1
EM'RALDS	1	ENTERTAINMENTS	1	EVE-REPAST	1	FANGS	1
EMATHIA'S	1	ENTERTAINS	1	EVE'S	1	FANNIA	1
EMATHIAN	1	ENTRANCEMENT	1	EVENING-FRIENDS	1	FANNINGS	1
EMBARK	1	ENTREATIES	1	EVENSONG	1	FANNIUS	1
EMBARK'D	1	ENTREATING	1	EVENUS	1	FANNYS	1
EMBARKING	1	ENTRED	1	EVER-ANXIOUS	1	FAR-DREADED	1
EMBASSADORS	1	ENTRENCHMENTS	1	EVER-BLOOMING	1	FAR-ECHOING	1
EMBITTERS	1	ENTRUST	1	EVER-CONSECRATING	1	FAR-PIERCING	1
EMBODY'S	1	ENUFF	1	EVER-DREADFUL	1	FAR-RESOUNDING	1
EMBODYED	1	ENVIEST	1	EVER-FERTILE	1	FAR-SHOOTING	1
EMBOLDEN'D	1	ENVOY	1	EVER-FLOWING	1	FAR-STRETCHING	1
EMBOSOM'D	1	ENVOYS	1	EVER-FRAGRANT	1	FARCES	1
EMBOWER'D	1	ENWRAPPING	1	EVER-FRUITFUL	1	FARER	1
EMBOWR'D	1	EPALTES	1	EVER-GENTLE	1	FARING	1
EMBROIDRY	1	EPAMINONDAS	1	EVER-INJUR'D	1	FARQU'AR	1
EMBROIL	1	EPEAN	1	EVER-LISTLESS	1	FASHION'S	1
EMBROIL'D	1	EPERITUS	1	EVER-LIVING	1	FASHIONS	1
EMBRUES	1	EPHIMEDIA	1	EVER-MINGLING	1	FAST-FALLING	1
EMERG'D	1	EPHYR'S	1	EVER-OPEN	1	FAST-FLOWING	1
EMERGENCE	1	EPHYRE	1	EVER-SHADY	1	FASTED	1
EMETICKS	1	EPHYRIAN	1	EVER-VERDANT	1	FASTEST	1
EMINENCE	1	EPICURUS	1	EVER-WATCHFUL	1	FASTNED	1
EMOTION	1	EPIDAURE	1	EVER-YOUNG	1	FAT'NED	1
EMOTIONS	1	EPIGEUS	1	EVILLS	1	FATALLY	1
EMP'ROR	1	EPIRUS	1	EVIPPUS	1	FATE-FUL	1
EMP'RORS	1	EPISTOR	1	EW'ER	1	FATHERIGE	1
EMPEROR	1	EPSOM	1	EX	1	FATHERS'	1
EMPHASIS	1	EQUALL	1	EXALTING	1	FATHOM	1
EMPRISE	1	EQUITY	1	EXAMINE	1	FATHOM'S	1
EMPRIZE	1	EQUIVOCAL	1	EXAMINES	1	FATHOMS	1
EMPTIER	1	ERASINUS	1	EXAMPLED	1	FATIGUES	1
EMPTY'D	1	ERATREUS	1	EXCELLENT	1	FATLINGS	1
EMPYREAL	1	ERECTHEUS	1	EXCELLS	1	FATTENS	1
EMULATIONS	1	ERECTHEUS'	1	EXCEPTIONS	1	FAULCON	1
EMULOUS	1	ERECTS	1	EXCESSIVE	1	FAULT'RING	1
ENCAMP	1	ERETMEUS	1	EXCHANGED	1	FAUNUS	1
ENCAMP'D	1	ERETRIA	1	EXCISING	1	FAV'RITE'S	1
ENCAS'D	1	ERGO	1	EXCITES	1	FAVONIO'S	1

FAVOR'D	1	FLOW'R'D	1	FRANK	1	GENERATION'S	1
FAYRE	1	FLOW'RING	1	FRANK'D	1	GENEVA'S	1
FAYS	1	FLOWER	1	FRANKINCENSE	1	GENII	1
FE	1	FLOWR'D	1	FRANKNESS	1	GENITIVE	1
FEAR'ST	1	FLUCTUATES	1	FREE-BORN	1	GENTLENESS	1
FEAST-FUL	1	FLURTING	1	FREE-OPENING	1	GEORGII	1
FEAST-FULL	1	FLUT'RING	1	FREEDOMS	1	GERESTUS	1
FEAT	1	FLUTE'S	1	FREEMAN'S	1	GERRARD	1
FEATLY	1	FLUTTERING	1	FREER	1	GETTING	1
FEEDER	1	FLUX	1	FREES	1	GETTINGS	1
FEELING	1	FLY-BLOW	1	FREEST	1	GEWGAWS	1
FEES	1	FLYES	1	FRENSIE	1	GIANT-BABE	1
FELLOW-CHARIOTEER	1	FOAMES	1	FREQUENTED	1	GIANT-CORSE	1
FELLOW-OPERATOR	1	FOB	1	FRESCO	1	GIANT-GLUTTON	1
FELLS	1	FOG	1	FRESH-BLEEDING	1	GIANT-HUNTER	1
FENCEFUL	1	FOIL	1	FRESH-SLAUGHTER'D	1	GIANT-LOVER	1
FENCELESS	1	FOLDINGS	1	FRESH'NING	1	GIANT-MONSTERS	1
FENNES	1	FOLL'WERS	1	FRESHEST	1	GIANT-PRIDE	1
FERMENTATION	1	FOLL'WING	1	FRESHLY	1	GIANT-SHEPHERD	1
FERMENTS	1	FOLLISH	1	FRESNOY'S	1	GIANT-SON	1
FERRET	1	FOLLO'WING	1	FRIAR	1	GIANT-SONS	1
FERRET'S	1	FOLLOW'R	1	FRIDAYS	1	GIANT-STRIDES	1
FERVID	1	FOLLOWED	1	FRIENDLIER	1	GIANT-VICE	1
FERVOUR	1	FOLLOWER	1	FRINGED	1	GIANT-WARRIOR	1
FEST'RING	1	FOMENTS	1	FRIPPERY	1	GIFTED	1
FETCH'D	1	FOODLESS	1	FRISK	1	GIGANTICK	1
FETIDA	1	FOODS	1	FRISKS	1	GILDER	1
FETLOCKS	1	FOOL-GALLANT	1	FRITTER	1	GILDING	1
FETTER'D	1	FOOL-RENOWN'D	1	FROATHS	1	GINGLE	1
FEV'RISH	1	FOOL'S-COATS	1	FROLIC	1	GINGLED	1
FEVER	1	FOOLING	1	FROLICK	1	GINGLING	1
FIBRE	1	FOOLS-COLOURS	1	FRONT-BOX	1	GIRTONE'S	1
FIBSTER	1	FOOLS'	1	FRONT-BOXES	1	GIVER	1
FICTITIOUS	1	FOOTING	1	FRONTISPIECE	1	GIVERS	1
FIDDLER	1	FOOTMAN'S	1	FRONTS	1	GIVINGS	1
FIDELITY	1	FOOTMEN	1	FROTH	1	GLADDENS	1
FIE	1	FOOTSTEP	1	FROTHY	1	GLADNESS	1
FIERCE-RUSHING	1	FOPLING'S	1	FROWD	1	GLAPHYRA'S	1
FIERCENESS	1	FOR'T	1	FROWDE	1	GLAR'D	1
FIERY-HELM'D	1	FORBEARANCE	1	FRUIT-GROVES	1	GLASSES	1
FIG-TREE	1	FORBIDDING	1	FRY'R	1	GLAUCE	1
FIGTREE	1	FORBODES	1	FRYER	1	GLAZ'D	1
FILCH	1	FORCING	1	FUEL	1	GLENCUS	1
FILE	1	FORE-CAST	1	FUFIDIA	1	GLIB	1
FILLET	1	FORE-DOOM	1	FUGITIVE	1	GLIMMERING	1
FILMS	1	FORE-FATHER	1	FULGID	1	GLIMPSE	1
FIN	1	FORE-FATHERS	1	FULL-DESCENDING	1	GLISSA	1
FIN'D	1	FORE-HAND	1	FULLER	1	GLITTRING	1
FINGER	1	FORE-PIECE	1	FULLEST	1	GLOBES	1
FINGER'S	1	FORE-RUNS	1	FULLFIL	1	GLORIED	1
FINITUS	1	FOREBODED	1	FULVIA	1	GLOSSIE	1
FINNY-PREY	1	FOREBODES	1	FULVIA'S	1	GLOW'ST	1
FINS	1	FOREBODING	1	FUN	1	GLOZETH	1
FIRED	1	FORECAST	1	FUNCTION	1	GLUMGLUM'S	1
FIRENDLESS	1	FORECLOSE	1	FUNDAMENTAL	1	GLUTT	1
FIRMEST	1	FOREDOOMS	1	FUNERAL	1	GLUTTED	1
FIRMNESS	1	FOREFATHER	1	FUNGOSO	1	GLUTTONY	1
FIRR	1	FOREHEADS	1	FUNGUS	1	GNASH	1
FIRST-FRUITS	1	FOREIGNER	1	FURBELO	1	GNASH'D	1
FITTER	1	FOREKNOW	1	FURR	1	GNATS	1
FITZWILLIAMS	1	FORESEEING	1	FURTIVA	1	GNAWS	1
FIX'T	1	FORESHOWS	1	FURY-GODDESS	1	GNOMES	1
FIXED	1	FOREST'S	1	FURY-PASSIONS	1	GNOMES'	1
FLABBY	1	FORESTALLS	1	FUTURITY	1	GOAR	1
FLACCUS	1	FORETEL	1	FY	1	GOAT-NURS'D	1
FLAGGING	1	FORGIVENESS	1	GAGE	1	GOAT-SKINS	1
FLAGGY	1	FORGIVES	1	GAGG'D	1	GOAT'S-MILK	1
FLAIL	1	FORGOE	1	GAIETY	1	GOATHERD'S	1
FLAKE	1	FORMIDINOUS	1	GALANTHIS	1	GOD-BUILT	1
FLANDERS	1	FORNICATIO	1	GALILAEO'S	1	GOD-DESCENDED	1
FLANK'D	1	FORREST	1	GALL'RY	1	GOD-SAKE	1
FLASHES	1	FORSEE	1	GALLANTRY	1	GOD'S-NAME	1
FLASKETS	1	FORSEEN	1	GALLERY	1	GOD'S-SAKE	1
FLATERER	1	FORSHEW	1	GALLO	1	GODDESS-LIKE	1
FLATLY	1	FORSOOTH	1	GALLO-GRECIAN	1	GODDESS-TRAIN	1
FLATT'RIES	1	FORSWEAR	1	GALLOP	1	GODFRY	1
FLATTED	1	FORSWORN	1	GAMBOL	1	GODFRY'S	1
FLATTERER	1	FORTEL	1	GAMBOL'D	1	GODHEADS	1
FLATTERING	1	FORTH-BEAMING	1	GAMBOLLS	1	GOLD-CAPT	1
FLATTERY'S	1	FORTH-SPRINGING	1	GAMBOLS	1	GONOËSSA'S	1
FLATTR'ER	1	FORTIFIES	1	GAMESOME	1	GONSON	1
FLATTRING	1	FORTIFY'D	1	GAMING	1	GONSON'S	1
FLATTRY	1	FORTS	1	GAMMER	1	GOOD-HUMOUR	1
FLAVIO	1	FORTUNE-STRUCK	1	GANTLETS	1	GOOD-NATUR'D	1
FLE'ME	1	FORWARDS	1	GANYMEDE	1	GOOD-SENSE	1
FLEDG'D	1	FORWARN'D	1	GAP'D	1	GOODLIEST	1
FLEETEST	1	FOSTER-FATHER-MOTHER	1	GARD'NER	1	GOODMAN	1
FLEETWOOD	1	FOUL-MOUTH'D	1	GARDEN-GATE	1	GOOSE-PYE	1
FLESHLY	1	FOUNDED	1	GARLICK	1	GOOSE-RUMP'D	1
FLESTRIN	1	FOUNDERS	1	GARRET	1	GORG'D	1
FLETCHER'S	1	FOUNT-FULL	1	GARTER'D	1	GORGEOUSLY	1
FLEURY'S	1	FOUNTAIN-SIDE	1	GASPS	1	GORGET	1
FLIMNAP'S	1	FOUNTS	1	GATH'RERS	1	GORGON'S	1
FLIMZY	1	FOUR-FOLD	1	GATHR'D	1	GORGYTHIO'S	1
FLINTY	1	FOUR-WHEEL'D	1	GAUDY	1	GORMAUND	1
FLIPPANT	1	FOWLE	1	GAULING	1	GORMOGON	1
FLIRT	1	FOWLER	1	GAYEST	1	GORTYNA	1
FLITTS	1	FOWLERS	1	GAYLY	1	GORTYNA'S	1
FLOCK-BED	1	FOX-CHACE	1	GAZER'S	1	GOSSIPS	1
FLOODGATES	1	FOX'S	1	GAZETEER	1	GOTH	1
FLORIO	1	FOXTON	1	GAZETTE	1	GOTHICK	1
FLORISTS	1	FRAGILE	1	GELLY	1	GOUTEZ	1
FLOUND'RING	1	FRAGRANCIES	1	GEMM	1	GOVERN'D	1
FLOUNDERS	1	FRAIGHT	1	GEMMS	1	GOVERNESS	1
FLOURET	1	FRAILTY	1	GEN'ROUSLY	1		

GOVERNING	1	HAEMON	1	HEADACHS	1	HIGHNESS'	1
GOVERNOR	1	HAEMUS	1	HEADSTALLS	1	HILLOCK	1
GOVERNS	1	HAEMUS'	1	HEALTHFUL	1	HILLSBOROUGH'S	1
GOWER	1	HAGS	1	HEALTHY	1	HILLY	1
GOWN'D	1	HAILS	1	HEAPING	1	HIMSELF'S	1
GOWNMAN	1	HAILY	1	HEAR'ST	1	HINCHINBROKE	1
GOWNS	1	HAIR-SHIRT	1	HEARERS	1	HINDE	1
GRACCHUS	1	HAIR'S	1	HEARKEN	1	HINDER	1
GRACCHUS'	1	HALBERDS	1	HEARKENS	1	HINDER'D	1
GRACE-CUP	1	HALE	1	HEARNE	1	HINTED	1
GRADATIONS	1	HALES	1	HEART-EXPANDING	1	HINTON	1
GRAEA	1	HALF-APPROVING	1	HEART-FELT	1	HIPPASIAN	1
GRAECIAN	1	HALF-BREATHLESS	1	HEART'S	1	HIPPEMOLGIAN	1
GRAEIANS	1	HALF-BROTHER	1	HEARTEN	1	HIPPIA	1
GRAFFS	1	HALF-BURN'D	1	HEARTEN'	1	HIPPINA'S	1
GRAFTON	1	HALF-CUR'D	1	HEARTEN'D	1	HIPPOCOON	1
GRAFTS	1	HALF-DROWN'D	1	HEARTILY	1	HIPPODAME'S	1
GRAMMARIANS	1	HALF-EAT	1	HEATHCOTE	1	HIPPODAMAS	1
GRANARIES	1	HALF-EXTINGUISH'D	1	HEATHCOTE'S	1	HIPPODAMUS	1
GRAND-SONS	1	HALF-FORC'D	1	HEATHNISH	1	HIPPOLOCHUS	1
GRANICUS	1	HALF-HEARD	1	HEAV'N-DISCOVER'D	1	HIPPOMACHUS	1
GRANTHAM	1	HALF-HUNG	1	HEAV'N-GATES	1	HIPPOMEDON	1
GRANVILLES	1	HALF-LANGUISHING	1	HEAV'N-ILLUMIN'D	1	HIPPONOUS	1
GRAPPLING	1	HALF-LEARN'D	1	HEAV'N-INSTRUCTED	1	HIPPOPLACUS'	1
GRASHOPPERS	1	HALF-OPEN'D	1	HEAV'N-PROTECTED	1	HIPPOTADES	1
GRASSIE	1	HALF-PERSUADED	1	HEAV'NLY-PENSIVE	1	HIPPOTION	1
GRATIS-GIVEN	1	HALF-PINT	1	HEAVEN'S	1	HIPPOTION'S	1
GRAVEST	1	HALF-RECOVER'D	1	HEAVENS	1	HIRES	1
GRAVING	1	HALF-TILL'D	1	HEBE	1	HISTORIAN	1
GRAY-HAIR'D	1	HALF-VIEWLESS	1	HEBRUS	1	HISTORIES	1
GREAS'D	1	HALIARTUS	1	HECATOMB'S	1	HITCHES	1
GREASY	1	HALIFAX	1	HECTORS	1	HITTITE	1
GREAT-MAN'S	1	HALIUS	1	HEE	1	HIVE	1
GREATLY-DARING	1	HALL'S	1	HEEDING	1	HOADLY	1
GREAZY	1	HALLIFAX	1	HEIDEGGER	1	HOARDING	1
GREENFIELD	1	HALLIFAX'S	1	HEIDEGGRE	1	HOARSER	1
GREENLAND	1	HALTING	1	HEIFER'S	1	HOARSER-SCREAMING	1
GREENSWORD	1	HALTS	1	HEIGHTEN	1	HODIUS	1
GREENWICH	1	HALVES	1	HEIGHTEN'D	1	HOLES	1
GREETED	1	HAMMER'D	1	HEIGHTENS	1	HOLINGSHEDS	1
GREETING	1	HAMOPAON	1	HEINOUS	1	HOLLAND-SMOCKS	1
GREGORIAN	1	HAMPTON-COURT	1	HEINSIUS	1	HOLLOWING	1
GREY-GOOSE	1	HAMS	1	HELENS	1	HOME-BORN	1
GREY-HAIR'D	1	HANDEL	1	HELEON	1	HOME-BRED	1
GRIEV'ST	1	HANG-DOGS	1	HELICE'S	1	HOME-SPUN	1
GRIEVED	1	HANGERS	1	HELL-WARD	1	HOMERS	1
GRILDRIG'S	1	HANMER	1	HELLA	1	HOMES	1
GRILLY	1	HANNONIAE	1	HELLENEANS	1	HOMICIDAL	1
GRINDING	1	HAP	1	HELLESPONTUS	1	HONEY-COMBS	1
GRINN'D	1	HAPP'D	1	HELLWARD	1	HONEY-TEMPER'D	1
GRIPUS	1	HAPPEN	1	HELM'D	1	HONEY'D	1
GRIPUS'	1	HAPPY'R	1	HELMET'S	1	HONEYCOMBS	1
GRISLY	1	HARANGUES	1	HELOS	1	HONOR	1
GROCER'S	1	HARBORS	1	HELPED	1	HONOR'S	1
GROEA	1	HARD-BOUND	1	HELPFUL	1	HONOURING	1
GROEA'S	1	HARD-GOT	1	HELPING	1	HONY	1
GROSSER	1	HARD'NING	1	HELVETIAN	1	HOOD	1
GROSSNESS	1	HARDSHIPS	1	HEMSLEY	1	HOODED	1
GROTESCO	1	HARDWICKE'S	1	HENCE'TWILL	1	HOODS	1
GROTTOS	1	HARES	1	HENETIA	1	HOOP	1
GROTTS	1	HARKNED	1	HENT	1	HOP'ST	1
GROUNDED	1	HARLEQUINI'S	1	HERACLITUS	1	HORID	1
GROVE'S	1	HARLOT	1	HERALD'S	1	HORIZONTAL	1
GROVEL'D	1	HARLOT'S	1	HERBERT	1	HORNET	1
GROVELLING	1	HARMA	1	HERCULEAN	1	HORRIBLY	1
GROVELS	1	HARMONIOUSLY	1	HERETO	1	HORS	1
GROVENOR'S	1	HARP'S	1	HERETOFORE	1	HORS-D'OEUVRES	1
GROWL	1	HARPALION	1	HERMAEAN	1	HORSE-LAUGH	1
GROWLING	1	HARPER	1	HERMION	1	HORSE-TAIL	1
GROWLS	1	HARPY	1	HERMIT'S	1	HORSEMANSHIP	1
GRUBSTREET-STATE	1	HARPYES	1	HERMITAGE	1	HORSEMEN	1
GUARD'ST	1	HARRIDAN	1	HERMITES	1	HOSANNA'S	1
GUARDINA	1	HARRIES	1	HERMITS	1	HOSPITAL	1
GUDGEONS	1	HARSH	1	HERNE	1	HOUGH	1
GUIDE-LESS	1	HARSHNESS	1	HERNES	1	HOUGH'S	1
GUIDO'S	1	HARTS	1	HEROD'S	1	HOUNSLOW	1
GUILD-HALL'S	1	HARTSHORN	1	HEROICKS	1	HOUNSLOW-HEATH	1
GUILDFORD	1	HARVEQUINI'S	1	HEROINS'	1	HOURLY	1
GUILELESS	1	HARVEST-BUG	1	HERON	1	HOUS'D	1
GUISE'S	1	HASH	1	HERRING	1	HOUSE-TOP	1
GULFY	1	HASH'D	1	HERSES	1	HOUYHNHNMS	1
GULP	1	HASTNING	1	HESPERIA	1	HOW'ERE	1
GULPH'D	1	HATCH'D	1	HESPERIAN	1	HOW'S	1
GULPS	1	HATCHETS	1	HEYFERS	1	HOWARDS	1
GUNEUS	1	HAUGHTIEST	1	HEYSHAM	1	HOWBEIT	1
GURGLING	1	HAUL	1	HEYWOOD	1	HOWLINGS	1
GURTON	1	HAULKES	1	HICETAON	1	HUFFING	1
GUSHES	1	HAULTS	1	HIDE-BOUND	1	HUG	1
GUSTS	1	HAUNCH	1	HIDE-PARK	1	HUGG'D	1
GUSTY	1	HAUTGOUT	1	HIEROGLYPHICKS	1	HUGGINS	1
GUTHERIGE	1	HAVEN	1	HIEROGLYPHICS	1	HUM-DRUM	1
GUTHRY	1	HAVOC	1	HIGH-BALANC'D	1	HUM'ROUS	1
GUTS	1	HAWK-NOS'D	1	HIGH-BLAZING	1	HUMANELY	1
GYGAE	1	HAWKER'S	1	HIGH-BRANDISH'D	1	HUMANLY	1
GYGANTIC	1	HAWL'D	1	HIGH-FLAMING	1	HUMBLING	1
GYGES'	1	HAWTHORNS	1	HIGH-FOAMING	1	HUMILITY'S	1
GYPSIES	1	HAY	1	HIGH-HUNG	1	HUMORS	1
GYRAE	1	HAY'S	1	HIGH-LIFTING	1	HUNCH	1
H	1	HAZARDED	1	HIGH-O'ERARCH'D	1	HUNCH-BACK'D	1
H'HAS	1	HAZARDS	1	HIGH-POINTING	1	HUNGERS	1
HABITANT	1	HE'L	1	HIGH-RAIS'D	1	HUNTER-TROOP	1
HACKNEY-COACH	1	HE'LE	1	HIGH-RESENTING	1	HUNTERS'	1
HACKNEY'D	1	HEAD-DRESS	1	HIGH-STRETCH'D	1	HUNTSMAN	1
HACKNY	1	HEAD-LONG	1	HIGH-WAY	1	HURLES	1
HAEC	1	HEAD'S	1	HIGHNESS	1	HURRY	1

HURRY'D	1	IMPERCEPTIBLE	1	INLAYED	1	IRREVERENT	1
HUSBAND-BULL	1	IMPERTINENT	1	INLY-PINING	1	IRRITATE	1
HUSWIFE'S	1	IMPIETY	1	INMOST-WINDING	1	IRROVOCABLE	1
HUTS	1	IMPLICITE	1	INN-KEEPERS	1	IS'T	1
HUZZAS	1	IMPLOY'D	1	INN'S	1	ISLANDER	1
HYACINTH	1	IMPOLLUTE	1	INNATE	1	ISLANDERS	1
HYACINTHS	1	IMPORTANCE	1	INNAVIGABLE	1	ISMARIAN	1
HYADS	1	IMPORTUNATE	1	INNUM'ROUS	1	ISMARUS	1
HYDE-PARK-CORNER	1	IMPOSTHUMATE	1	INOFFENSIVE	1	ISMENOS'	1
HYDE'S	1	IMPOW'R'D	1	INQUIETUDES	1	ISRAEL	1
HYDRA	1	IMPREGNATE	1	INQUIRE	1	ISRAEL'S	1
HYE	1	IMPRINTS	1	INQUISITIVE	1	ISRAELITES	1
HYLÈ'S	1	IMPROPER	1	INRAGE	1	ISSACHAR	1
HYLACIDES	1	IMPRUDENCE	1	INROAD	1	ISTEIAN	1
HYLLUS'	1	IMPURPL'D	1	INSCRIBES	1	ISTER	1
HYMENAEALS	1	IMPUTES	1	INSCRIPTIONS	1	ISTHMUS	1
HYMENAEAN	1	IN-BORN	1	INSEAM'D	1	ISUS	1
HYMN'D	1	INACHIAN	1	INSECT-WINGS	1	IT'S	1
HYPENOR	1	INAMOUR'D	1	INSECT'S	1	ITALIANS	1
HYPENOR'S	1	INANIMATE	1	INSENSIBLE	1	ITH'	1
HYPERESIA	1	INATTENTION	1	INSEPARABLE	1	ITHACENSIANS	1
HYPERESIA'S	1	INAUSPICIOUS	1	INSINCERE	1	ITHACIAN	1
HYPERESIAN	1	INBORN	1	INSIPID	1	ITHOMÈ	1
HYPERIA	1	INBOSOM'D	1	INSNARE	1	ITONA	1
HYPERIAN	1	INCASE	1	INSOLENTLY	1	ITYMONAEUS	1
HYPERION'S	1	INCAUTION	1	INSOLVABLE	1	IV'RY-STUDDED	1
HYPIROCHUS	1	INCESTUOUS	1	INSPECTING	1	IXION'S	1
HYPOCRIT	1	INCIRCLING	1	INSPIRATION	1	J	1
HYPSENOR	1	INCITEMENTS	1	INSPIRIT	1	J'S	1
HYPSENOR'S	1	INCITES	1	INSPIRITING	1	JACKET	1
HYPSIPYLE	1	INCLEMENCIES	1	INSTAND	1	JAGGY	1
HYRIE'S	1	INCLINATION	1	INSTANTLY	1	JAIL	1
HYRMIN	1	INCOHERENT	1	INSTARR'D	1	JALYSSUS	1
HYRTACIDES	1	INCOMMODIOUS	1	INSTILLING	1	JAMMIE	1
HYRTACUS	1	INCONSISTENCIES	1	INSTRUMENTAL	1	JANASSA	1
HYRTIUS	1	INCONSTANCY	1	INSUFFERABLE	1	JANGLE	1
HYSTERIC	1	INCONTINENT	1	INSULT'S	1	JANIRA	1
IÄPETUS	1	INCORRECT	1	INSUPERABLE	1	JAPAN	1
IÄSION	1	INCOURAG'D	1	INTEGRITY	1	JAPAN'D	1
IÄSUS	1	INCREAST	1	INTENDING	1	JAPANNER	1
IÖLCOS	1	INCROACH	1	INTENTIVE	1	JAPHET'S	1
IÖLCUS	1	INCRUST	1	INTENTS	1	JARDAN'S	1
IÜLUS'	1	INCUMBRANCE	1	INTERCEPTED	1	JARGON	1
I'	1	INCURSIONS	1	INTERMINGL'D	1	JASON	1
I'L	1	INDEARS	1	INTERMITTING	1	JAUNDIC'D	1
I'LE	1	INDEAVOUR	1	INTERPOLATIO	1	JAUNSSEN	1
IAERA	1	INDEBTED	1	INTERPOSE	1	JAYLS	1
IAMENUS	1	INDECENTLY	1	INTERPRET	1	JEALOUSIES	1
IBER'S	1	INDELIBLE	1	INTERPRETS	1	JEALOUSY	1
IBERIAN	1	INDENT	1	INTERRUPT	1	JEFFERYS	1
ICARUS	1	INDENTURES	1	INTERRUPTING	1	JEHOVAH	1
ICMALIUS	1	INDEPENDENCY	1	INTERSPERS'D	1	JEKYL	1
ICY	1	INDEX-HAND	1	INTERVENE	1	JEKYLLS	1
IDALIA'S	1	INDIANS	1	INTIMATE	1	JELLY	1
IDAS	1	INDIGESTED	1	INTOLERABLY	1	JELLY'S	1
IDEAL	1	INDISTINCT	1	INTORTED	1	JEMMY	1
IDEOT	1	INDITES	1	INTOXICATE	1	JEREMY	1
IDOL-GODS	1	INDOLENCE	1	INTOXICATES	1	JERK	1
IDOLATER	1	INDOLENTLY	1	INTRANCE	1	JEROME	1
IDOLIZ'D	1	INDOMENEUS	1	INTREAT	1	JERUSALEM	1
IDUME'S	1	INDUE	1	INTREATS	1	JERVAS	1
IGNOMINOUS	1	INDUS	1	INTRENCH'D	1	JERVASE	1
IGNORANTLY	1	INEFFECTUAL	1	INTRENCHMENTS	1	JERVIS	1
ILES	1	INERTLY	1	INTRICACIES	1	JESSE'S	1
ILESION	1	INESTIMABLE	1	INTRIGU'D	1	JESSIDES'	1
ILL-CONTESTED	1	INEVITABLE	1	INTRIGUES	1	JESUIT	1
ILL-EXCHANG'D	1	INEXTRICABLE	1	INTRINSIC	1	JESUITS	1
ILL-GOTTEN	1	INEXTRICABLY	1	INTRODUCE	1	JESUS'S	1
ILL-GROUNDED	1	INFAMOUS	1	INTRUDING	1	JEW	1
ILL-INCLIN'D	1	INFANCY	1	INTWIN'D	1	JIGG	1
ILL-JUDGING	1	INFANT-CHEEKS	1	INUNDATION	1	JIGGS	1
ILL-LOOK'D	1	INFATUATES	1	INUTTERABLE	1	JILTS	1
ILL-MATCH'D	1	INFERS	1	INVADED	1	JO	1
ILL-NATURE	1	INFIDELS	1	INVADER	1	JOAB	1
ILL-PAIR'D	1	INFIX	1	INVENT	1	JOB'S	1
ILL-PERSUADING	1	INFLEXIBLY	1	INVENTION'S	1	JOCASTA	1
ILL-REQUITED	1	INFLICTING	1	INVENTIONS	1	JOCKEY'S	1
ILL-RESTRAIN'D	1	INFRANGIBLE	1	INVERTS	1	JOCUND	1
ILL-SUITING	1	INFRING'D	1	INVINCIBLE	1	JOGG'D	1
ILL-US'D	1	INFRINGE	1	INVISIBLE	1	JOGGS	1
ILLIMITABLE	1	INFRINGING	1	INVITER'S	1	JOHNSTON	1
ILLUMIN	1	INFUSING	1	INWARDS	1	JOHNSTON'S	1
ILLUSTRATE	1	INGENDERS	1	INWOVE	1	JOINING	1
ILYTHIAE	1	INGRATE	1	INWOVEN	1	JOINTURE	1
IMBIB'D	1	INGRATEFUL	1	IONIAN	1	JONATHAN	1
IMBIBE	1	INGRATITUDE	1	IONIANS	1	JORDANS	1
IMBODY'D	1	INGRATITUDE'S	1	IPHEAS	1	JOURNAL	1
IMBRUS'	1	INGREDIENTS	1	IPHICLUS	1	JOURNEY'S	1
IMITATED	1	INGROSS	1	IPHICLUS'	1	JOURNIES	1
IMITATION	1	INGULF'D	1	IPHIDAMAS	1	JOVE-LIKE	1
IMMACULATE	1	INHALE	1	IPHINOUS	1	JOWL	1
IMMATURE	1	INHALING	1	IPHIS	1	JOYLESS	1
IMMENSITY	1	INHANCING	1	IPHTHIMA	1	JOYNING	1
IMMERS'D	1	INHERIT	1	IPHYCLUS	1	JOYNT	1
IMMIX'D	1	INHERITING	1	IPHYCLUS'	1	JUDAEA	1
IMMOD'RATE	1	INHERITS	1	IPHYTION	1	JUDGE'S	1
IMMORTALIZE	1	INIMITABLY	1	IPHYTUS'	1	JUDGED	1
IMMUTABLE	1	INITIATES	1	IRE-FULL	1	JUDGMENT'S	1
IMPAIR	1	INJECT	1	IRISHMEN	1	JULIAN	1
IMPAIRING	1	INJOIN'D	1	IRON-HEART	1	JULY	1
IMPARTED	1	INJUCTION	1	IRON-HEARTED	1	JUMPING	1
IMPEACH	1	INJURES	1	IRON-MACE	1	JUNIA'S	1
IMPEDIMENT	1	INLARG'D	1	IRONS	1	JUNTA	1
IMPENETRABLE	1	INLAY'D	1	IRREGULARLY	1	JURY-MEN	1
IMPENITENTLY	1			IRRESOLUTE	1		

JUSTIFIE	1	LASTLY	1	LIKING	1	LOTE	1
JUSTIFY'D	1	LATE-IMPERVIOUS	1	LILAEA	1	LOTIS	1
JUV'NAL	1	LATE-IMPRISON'D	1	LILIES	1	LOTOPHAGI	1
JUVABIT	1	LATE-PREFERR'D	1	LILLIPUT	1	LOTTS	1
K	1	LATE-RETURNING	1	LILLY-SILVER'D	1	LOUD-EXULTING	1
KEELS	1	LATE-TRANSFORM'D	1	LILY	1	LOUD-INSULTING	1
KEEN-EDG'D	1	LATMOS'	1	LIMB'D	1	LOUD-THREATNING	1
KEENNESS	1	LATTER	1	LIMBO	1	LOUD-TONGU'D	1
KEEP'ST	1	LAUD	1	LIME	1	LOUGH	1
KEEPER	1	LAUGH'ST	1	LIME-TWIGS	1	LOUIS'	1
KELSEY	1	LAUGHD	1	LIMETWIGGS	1	LOVE-DEBATES	1
KENNETT	1	LAUGHT	1	LIMNORIA	1	LOVE-DITTIED	1
KENSINGTON	1	LAUNCE	1	LIMP	1	LOVE-RITES	1
KEW	1	LAUREAT	1	LINDUS	1	LOVE-WHISP'RING	1
KICKED	1	LAUREAT'S	1	LINEAL	1	LOVERS'	1
KID	1	LAUREATES	1	LINGUIST	1	LOW-BENDING	1
KILLED	1	LAURELL'D	1	LINGUISTS	1	LOW-BROW'D	1
KINDEST	1	LAURUS	1	LINK-BOYS	1	LOW-COUCH'D	1
KINDRED'S	1	LAVERS	1	LINNET	1	LOW-DEPENDING	1
KINE	1	LAVISHLY	1	LINNETS	1	LOW-DUTCH	1
KING-CUP	1	LAWFULLY	1	LINSEY-WOLSEY	1	LOW-SINKING	1
KINGCUP	1	LAWREL-FOLIAGE	1	LINSEY-WOOLSEY	1	LOW-THOUGHTED	1
KINNOULL'S	1	LAWREL'D	1	LINTELS	1	LOW-WHISPER'D	1
KINSMAN'S	1	LAYDES	1	LINTOTT	1	LOW'D	1
KIRK	1	LAYMAN	1	LINTOTTUS	1	LOW'RS	1
KIT	1	LAYMEN	1	LINUS	1	LOWE	1
KITCHENS	1	LAYN	1	LION-HEARTED	1	LOWRS	1
KITS	1	LE	1	LIONNESS	1	LOYALLY	1
KITTEN'S	1	LEACHERIE	1	LIQU'RISH	1	LU	1
KNEEL	1	LEADING	1	LIQUERS	1	LUCIFER	1
KNEELS	1	LEAF-LESS	1	LIQUIDS	1	LUCINA'S	1
KNELLER'S	1	LEAGUER	1	LIQUORISH	1	LUCKIER	1
KNIFE	1	LEAGUER'D	1	LISP'D	1	LUCRETIA'S	1
KNIGHTED	1	LEAR'S	1	LISPING	1	LUCRETIUS	1
KNIGHTHOOD	1	LEARND	1	LISTNING	1	LUCULLUS	1
KNIGHTHOODS	1	LEAVERS	1	LITTER	1	LUD	1
KNOCKER	1	LEBANON	1	LITTLENESS	1	LUKEWARM	1
KNOTTIER	1	LECH'ROUS	1	LIV'RY	1	LULLABIES	1
KUSTER	1	LECHER	1	LIV'RY'D	1	LUMB'RING	1
L<E>IODES	1	LECT'RING	1	LIVE-LONG	1	LUMBRING	1
L	1	LECTOS	1	LIVELIER	1	LUMINARY	1
LAÄS	1	LECTURES	1	LIVELONG	1	LUMLEY	1
LAÖDOCUS	1	LEERING	1	LIVERY'D	1	LUMP'D	1
LAÖMEDON'S	1	LEFT-LEGG'D	1	LIVLY	1	LUMPISH	1
LAB'RERS	1	LEGAT	1	LOAF	1	LUNATIC	1
LAB'RINTH	1	LEGENDS	1	LOAN	1	LURE	1
LABORIOUSLY	1	LEGG'D	1	LOANS	1	LURK'D	1
LABOURING	1	LEGION	1	LOATHSOME	1	LUSTRATIONS	1
LABYRINTHS	1	LEGISLATORS	1	LOBSTER-NIGHTS	1	LUTE-RESOUNDING	1
LACEDAEMON'S	1	LEICESTER	1	LOCAL	1	LUTE'S	1
LACHAEA	1	LEIODES	1	LOCKT	1	LUTESTRING	1
LACQUER'D	1	LELEGES	1	LOCRIANS	1	LUTRIN'S	1
LADEN	1	LELIUS	1	LODDON	1	LUX'D	1
LADY-LAP-DOG-SHIP	1	LELY	1	LODGEMENTS	1	LY'D	1
LADY-LIKE	1	LENGTHENS	1	LODGER	1	LY'ST	1
LAELIUS	1	LENGTHFUL	1	LODGINGS	1	LYAR	1
LAERCES'	1	LENGTHS	1	LODONA	1	LYBIA	1
LAERCEUS	1	LENITIVES	1	LODONA'S	1	LYCAÖN'S	1
LAESTRIGONIA'S	1	LEO	1	LOFT	1	LYCASTUS	1
LAESTRIGONIAN	1	LEO'S	1	LOGIC	1	LYCEAN	1
LAGG'D	1	LEOPARD'S	1	LOGICIAN	1	LYCIMNIUS	1
LAGS	1	LERNA	1	LOISELL	1	LYCOMED	1
LAGUERRE	1	LERNA'S	1	LOIT'RERS	1	LYCOMEDES	1
LAIR	1	LESBIA	1	LOIT'RING	1	LYCOPHRON	1
LAIRE	1	LESBOS'	1	LOITER	1	LYNX	1
LAMBENT	1	LESSEN'D	1	LOITRING	1	LYNX'S	1
LAMBKINS	1	LESSENING	1	LOMBARDY	1	LYON'S	1
LAMOS'	1	LESSER	1	LONG-APPLAUDING	1	LYRES	1
LAMPETIÈ	1	LESTRYGONS	1	LONG-DESTROYING	1	LYRIC	1
LAMPETIE	1	LETHARGIC	1	LONG-DISPUTED	1	LYRNESSIAN	1
LAMPOON'D	1	LETHUS	1	LONG-DIVIDED	1	LYSANDER	1
LAMPOONS	1	LETTER'S	1	LONG-FEST'RING	1	LYTTLETON	1
LANC'D	1	LEUCADIA	1	LONG-LAB'RING	1	M	1
LANCASTER	1	LEUCAS'	1	LONG-LINGRING	1	M**O'S	1
LANCE-FAM'D	1	LEUCOTHEA	1	LONG-PREDESTIN'D	1	MACEDONIA'S	1
LANDAFFE	1	LEUCOTHEA'S	1	LONG-PROJECTED	1	MACER	1
LANDING	1	LEUCOTHOË	1	LONG-PROTENDED	1	MACHIAVEL	1
LANDLORD'S	1	LEUCUS	1	LONG-PROTRACTED	1	MACHINES	1
LANDLORDS	1	LEUD	1	LONG-REFULGENT	1	MACHMONT'S	1
LANDSKIP	1	LEV'RET	1	LONG-REPENTED	1	MACKREL	1
LANES	1	LEV'RETS	1	LONG-RESOUNDING	1	MAD-MAN	1
LANESB'ROW	1	LEVEE-DAY	1	LONG-SOUNDING	1	MADAME	1
LANGUISHES	1	LEVELLING	1	LONG-WEARY'D	1	MADDEN	1
LANGUISHINGLY	1	LEVELLS	1	LONG-WING'D	1	MADDEN'D	1
LANGUORS	1	LEVERET	1	LONG'D	1	MADDEST	1
LANQUISH'D	1	LEVIATHAN	1	LONGEN	1	MADRIGAL	1
LAODOCUS	1	LEVIED	1	LONGEST	1	MAEANDER'D	1
LAOMEDON'S	1	LEVITY	1	LONGITUDE	1	MAENETIUS'	1
LAOTHÖE	1	LEY'S	1	LOOK'S	1	MAEONIA	1
LAP-DOG	1	LIAR'S	1	LOOK'ST	1	MAEOTIS	1
LAP'T	1	LIBEL'D	1	LOOKD	1	MAEOTIS'	1
LAPDOGS	1	LIBERTIES	1	LOOKERS	1	MAGDALEN'S	1
LAPELL	1	LIBYAN	1	LOOKERS-ON	1	MAGES	1
LAPITHAE	1	LICENC'D	1	LOOMS	1	MAGI	1
LAPITHS	1	LID	1	LOOSEN'D	1	MAGNESIANS	1
LAPWINGS	1	LIDDEL	1	LOOSENESS	1	MAGPY	1
LARD	1	LIEGE	1	LOOSNED	1	MAGPYE	1
LARDELLA	1	LIFE-BLOOD	1	LOPEZ	1	MAGUS	1
LARE	1	LIFE-LIKE	1	LOPT	1	MAH'MET	1
LARES	1	LIFE-SUSTAINING	1	LORD-CHANCELLOR	1	MAHOMET	1
LARGE-ACRED	1	LIGATURE	1	LORDSHIPS	1	MAHOUND	1
LARISSA	1	LIGHT-ARM'D	1	LOSERS	1	MAIA'S	1
LARK	1	LIGHT-BOUNDING	1	LOSES	1	MAIDEN'S	1
LASHING	1	LIGHT-FOOT	1	LOSING	1	MAIN-MAST	1
LASSITUDE	1	LIGHT'NING'S	1	LOSSES	1	MAJESTICAL	1

MAJOR-GENERAL	1	MEDESICASTE'S	1	MIS-CALL'D	1	MOULDERS	1
MAK'ST	1	MEDIATE	1	MIS-DEEDS	1	MOUNTAIN-BILLOW	1
MALADIES	1	MEDIATES	1	MIS-LED	1	MOUNTAIN-EYRIE	1
MALAEA'S	1	MEDIATION	1	MIS-SHAP'D	1	MOUNTAIN-GOAT	1
MALBRANCHE	1	MEDITAT'ST	1	MIS-SHAPEN	1	MOUNTAIN-GROUND	1
MALEA	1	MEDLEYS	1	MIS-SPENT	1	MOUNTAIN-HEADS	1
MALIGNE	1	MEDUSA	1	MISCALL	1	MOUNTAIN-LIONS	1
MALIGNLY	1	MEEKEST	1	MISCALL'D	1	MOUNTAIN-OAK	1
MALMSEY	1	MEET'ST	1	MISCHANCE	1	MOUNTAIN-SHOULDERS	1
MAMMON	1	MEGAPENTHE	1	MISCONSTRUE	1	MOURNERS	1
MANDEVIL	1	MEGAPENTHES	1	MISGIVES	1	MOURNING-BRIDE	1
MANGERS	1	MEGAPENTHES'	1	MISHAP	1	MOVEMENTS	1
MANGLES	1	MEGARA	1	MISLED	1	MOW'D	1
MANILIUS	1	MEGAS	1	MISMANAGEMENTS	1	MOWERS	1
MANILLIO	1	MEGRIM	1	MISNAME	1	MUCH-ADVISING	1
MANLIER	1	MEIN	1	MISTERIES	1	MUCH-AFFLICTED	1
MANLIKE	1	MELANTHUS	1	MISTRESSE	1	MUCH-INJUR'D	1
MANORS	1	MELAS	1	MISTRESSES	1	MUCKLE	1
MANTEAU'S	1	MELEAGER'S	1	MISTRUST	1	MUCKWORMS	1
MANTINEA'S	1	MELITA	1	MITCHELL'S	1	MUFF	1
MANTL'D	1	MELLIFLUOUS	1	MITES	1	MULIUS'	1
MANTLED	1	MELLOW	1	MITIGATES	1	MULLETS	1
MANTUA	1	MELODIOUSLY	1	MITRED	1	MULTIPLY	1
MANUAL	1	MELODY	1	MIXUTRE	1	MULTITUDE	1
MANUFACTURE	1	MEM'RY	1	MNESTHES	1	MUMBLING	1
MANURE	1	MEMINISSE	1	MNESUS	1	MUNDUNGUS	1
MANURES	1	MEMOIRS	1	MOATS	1	MUNGRIL	1
MANUSCRIPTS	1	MEMORIALS	1	MOB'S	1	MUNIFICENCE	1
MANY-PEOPLED	1	MEMORY'S	1	MOCK	1	MURDER'D	1
MARATHON	1	MENACES	1	MOCK'D	1	MURKY	1
MARCELLUS	1	MENAETIUS	1	MOCO'S	1	MURM'ROUS	1
MARCUS	1	MENANDER'S	1	MODE	1	MURMUR'D	1
MARG'RET	1	MENDED	1	MODELS	1	MURTH'ROUS	1
MARIA'S	1	MENDICANTS	1	MODERATE	1	MURTHER'D	1
MARIES	1	MENDING	1	MOELIBAEA'S	1	MUSCLE	1
MARIS	1	MENDS	1	MOEON	1	MUSCLES	1
MARKET-PLACE	1	MENESTHEUS'	1	MOEONIA'S	1	MUSEFUL	1
MARLB'ROUGH	1	MENESTHIUS	1	MOEOTIS	1	MUSHROOMS	1
MARLBORO'	1	MENON	1	MOHUN	1	MUSIC'S	1
MARLBOROUGH	1	MENS	1	MOIST	1	MUSTARD-BOWL	1
MARLBOROUGH'S	1	MENTES'	1	MOLDERS	1	MUSTER	1
MARLBRO'	1	MENTIONS	1	MOLDS	1	MUSTER-ROLL	1
MARON	1	MERC'RIES	1	MOLE'S	1	MUSTY	1
MARPESSA	1	MERCENARY	1	MOLIERE	1	MUTES	1
MARQUIS	1	MERCHANT'S	1	MOLION	1	MUTTERS	1
MARRIED	1	MERELY	1	MOLL	1	MYCAENA	1
MARRIES	1	MERLIN	1	MOLLY'S	1	MYCALÈ	1
MARROW-BONE	1	MERMER	1	MOLUS	1	MYCALESSIA'S	1
MARRYING	1	MERRILY	1	MOLY	1	MYCENÈ	1
MARS-LIKE	1	MERRY-MEN	1	MOMENTILLA	1	MYCENAE'S	1
MARSEILLE'S	1	MESAULIUS	1	MOMUS	1	MYCENE	1
MARSH	1	MESHY	1	MON	1	MYCENE'S	1
MARSHAL	1	MESSÈ'S	1	MONARCH-SAVAGE	1	MYCENIAN	1
MARSHALLING	1	MESSENA'S	1	MONDE	1	MYCOENÈ	1
MARSHES	1	MESSENGERS	1	MONEY-LOVING	1	MYDÈ	1
MARSHY	1	MESSIAH	1	MONEY'S	1	MYGDON	1
MARTIALS	1	MESTHLES	1	MONK'S	1	MYRINNÈ'S	1
MARTIN'S	1	MESTLES	1	MONKEY-MIMICKS	1	MYRSINUS	1
MARTYR-KING	1	MESTOR	1	MONKEY-MIMICS	1	MYSIA	1
MASCULINE	1	METAPHOR	1	MONKEY-TAIL	1	MYSIANS	1
MASETA'S	1	METAPHYSICS	1	MONKIES	1	MYST'RY	1
MASH	1	METEOR-LIKE	1	MONKISH	1	MYSTERIES	1
MASQUERADES	1	METEOROUS	1	MONMOUTH	1	NÔTRE	1
MASQUERADING	1	METHODIZ'D	1	MONMOUTH-STREET	1	NAÏS	1
MASQUES	1	METHONÈ	1	MONROE	1	NABAL	1
MASSON	1	METROPOLITANS	1	MONROES	1	NAEVIUS	1
MAST'S	1	MEXICO'S	1	MONSTER-GOD	1	NAIAD	1
MASTER-HAND	1	MID-DAY-DEVIL	1	MONTAGUE	1	NAIAD'S	1
MAT	1	MID-NIGHT	1	MONTALTO	1	NAMBY	1
MATADORE	1	MID'ST	1	MONTH'S	1	NAP	1
MATADORES	1	MIDAS'	1	MONTHAUSIER	1	NAPE	1
MATERIAL	1	MIDDLETON	1	MOON-BEAM	1	NAPKINS	1
MATHEMATICKS	1	MIDWIFERY	1	MOON-LIGHT	1	NARCISSA	1
MATHEMATICS	1	MIHI	1	MOON-STRUCK	1	NARCISSA'S	1
MATHESIS	1	MILD-COMMAND	1	MOORS	1	NARDAC	1
MATRON-BROW	1	MILE	1	MORDAUNT	1	NARRATION	1
MATRONS'	1	MILETUS	1	MORDINGTON	1	NARROW'D	1
MATTER'S	1	MILK-PAIL	1	MORNING-BEAMS	1	NARROW'R	1
MATURELY	1	MILKER'S	1	MORNING-COCK	1	NARROWER	1
MATURER	1	MILKING	1	MORNING-DREAM	1	NARSES	1
MAUDLIN'S	1	MILKS	1	MORNING-HOUR	1	NASH	1
MAUL'D	1	MILLINER	1	MORNING-PRAY'R	1	NASO'S	1
MAUSOLUS'	1	MILLINER'S	1	MORNING-PRAYER	1	NASSAU	1
MAY'S	1	MILLS	1	MORNING-TIDE	1	NASTINESS	1
MAYOR	1	MIMAS'	1	MORNING-WALKS	1	NATIVE'S	1
MAYOR'S	1	MIMICS	1	MORNING'S	1	NAUBOLIDES	1
MAZ'D	1	MIN'RAL	1	MORNINGS	1	NAUTES	1
MEÖNIA	1	MINCE	1	MORTALITY'S	1	NAUTILUS	1
MEAD'S	1	MINCING	1	MORTALLY	1	NAVIGABLE	1
MEAGER	1	MINIATURE	1	MORTIFIES	1	NAVY-BUILDING	1
MEAN'ST	1	MINION	1	MORTIFY	1	NAVY-WALL	1
MEANDER	1	MINISTER'D	1	MORTUARY	1	NAVY-WALLS	1
MEANDER'S	1	MINISTER'S	1	MORYS	1	NE'RE	1
MEANDRING	1	MINISTERIAL	1	MOSQUE	1	NEAERA	1
MEANNESS	1	MINISTRANT	1	MOSS-GROWN	1	NEAMAS	1
MEAS'RING	1	MINSTREL-GOD	1	MOTE	1	NEARLY	1
MECHANIC	1	MINSTREL'S	1	MOTH	1	NEATH	1
MECHANICK	1	MINSTRELSIE	1	MOTHER-BIRD	1	NEATLY	1
MECISTES	1	MINUTES	1	MOTHER-LION	1	NEATNESS	1
MEDAEA'S	1	MINYAS	1	MOTHER-MASTIFF	1	NEC	1
MEDAL	1	MIRACULOUS	1	MOTHERIGE	1	NED	1
MEDDLE	1	MIRMYDONS	1	MOTHS	1	NEGLECTING	1
MEDEA	1	MIRTH-INSPIRING	1	MOTIONLESS	1	NEGLIGENCE	1
MEDEA'S	1	MIRTH'S	1	MOULDER	1	NEGLIGENT	1
MEDEON	1	MIS-APPLY	1	MOULDER'D	1	NEGLIGENTLY	1

NEICE	1	NUMB'RING	1	OLIM	1	OUTSTRIP	1
NEIGH'BRING	1	NUMBING	1	OLIVE-WAND	1	OUTSTRIPS	1
NEIGH'D	1	NUMBRED	1	OLOÖSSON'S	1	OUTSWEAR	1
NEIGHBOR	1	NURSES	1	OLYUMPUS'	1	OUTWORKS	1
NEIGHBOURHOOD	1	NURST	1	OLYZÒN'S	1	OVER-DRESS	1
NEIGHING	1	NUTBROWN	1	OMEGA	1	OVER-HUNG	1
NEION	1	NUTRITION	1	OMICRON	1	OVERCAST	1
NEIS	1	NUZZLES	1	OMINOUS	1	OVERCHARG'D	1
NEMERTES	1	NYSSA'S	1	OMITS	1	OVERHANG	1
NEOPTOLEMUS	1	O'CLOCK	1	OMITTED	1	OVERHUNG	1
NEPENTHE	1	O'ER-AW'D	1	OMNIPOTENT	1	OVERLAID	1
NEPHEW	1	O'ER-LABOUR'D	1	ONCE-FAM'D	1	OVERLOOK'D	1
NEREUS	1	O'ER-LEAPING	1	ONCE-FEAR'D	1	OVERSHADES	1
NERICUS	1	O'ER-PAST	1	ONCE-PROUD	1	OVERSIGHT	1
NERITOS	1	O'ER-RUN	1	ONCE-STATELY	1	OVERTAKE	1
NERO	1	O'ER-SHOOT	1	ONCHESTUS	1	OVERTOOK	1
NERO'S	1	O'ER-TOIL'D	1	ONE-EY'D	1	OVERTOPS	1
NESAEA	1	O'ER-TOPS	1	ONEUS	1	OVERTURN	1
NESTOREAN	1	O'ER-WROUGHT	1	OP'NER	1	OVERWATCH'D	1
NETTS	1	O'ERARCH'D	1	OP'RA	1	OWING	1
NEUFGERMAIN	1	O'ERAW'D	1	OPAKE	1	OWLERS	1
NEUTRAL	1	O'ERBURTHEN'D	1	OPE'D	1	OWNER'S	1
NEVER-CEASING	1	O'ERCAME	1	OPE'S	1	OWNERS	1
NEVER-DYING	1	O'ERCASTS	1	OPENINGS	1	OXE'S	1
NEVER-ERRING	1	O'ERCHARG'D	1	OPENNESS	1	OYSTERS	1
NEVER-FAILING	1	O'ERCHARGE	1	OPERA-SONG	1	OZEL'S	1
NEVER-WEARY'D	1	O'ERCOMES	1	OPERATES	1	OZIER	1
NEW-ACCEPTED	1	O'ERFLEEC'D	1	OPERATION	1	OZIER-FRINGED	1
NEW-EAR'D	1	O'ERFLOWING	1	OPERATOR	1	PA-GOD	1
NEW-FALL'N	1	O'ERFLOWINGS	1	OPHELESTES	1	PACES	1
NEW-MARKET-FAME	1	O'ERFLY	1	OPHYR'S	1	PACING	1
NEW-PENSION'D	1	O'ERHEARD	1	OPIATES	1	PACKET	1
NEW-PRESS'D	1	O'ERJOY'D	1	OPITES	1	PACKHORSE	1
NEW-ROB'D	1	O'ERLAY'D	1	OPPONENT	1	PACT	1
NEW-SHORN	1	O'ERLEAPS	1	OPPONENTS	1	PACTOLUS	1
NEW-SLAIN	1	O'ERLOOK	1	OPPOSES	1	PACTS	1
NEW-STREAMING	1	O'ERMATCH	1	OPPOSING	1	PAD	1
NEW-TING'D	1	O'ERMATCH'D	1	OPPRESSES	1	PADLOCK	1
NEWFOUND	1	O'ERPASS'D	1	OPPRESSION'S	1	PADUA-SOY	1
NEWFOUND-LAND	1	O'ERPOW'RING	1	OPUNTIA'S	1	PAEONIANS	1
NEWGATE	1	O'ERPOW'RS	1	OPUS	1	PAEONS	1
NEWLY	1	O'ERPOWER	1	ORAC'LOUS	1	PAGEANT	1
NEXT-BELOV'D	1	O'ERSEES	1	ORANGE-TREES	1	PAGEANTRY	1
NICER	1	O'ERSPENT	1	ORANGES	1	PAGOD	1
NICHES	1	O'ERTAKEN	1	ORATORY	1	PAINS-TAKING	1
NICHOLAS	1	O'ERTHROW	1	ORCADES	1	PAINTER'S	1
NIGER	1	O'ERTHROWS	1	ORCAS'	1	PALACE-ROOF	1
NIGGARD	1	O'ERTURN	1	ORCHARD-BOUNDS	1	PALACE-YARD	1
NIGGARDS	1	O'ERTURNED	1	ORCUS	1	PALAEMON	1
NIGHT-CAP	1	O'ERULING	1	ORCUS'	1	PALANCES	1
NIGHT-DRESS	1	O'ERWROUGHT	1	ORIGINAL	1	PALATES	1
NIGHT-GUARDS	1	OAK'S	1	ORIGINALL	1	PALENESS	1
NIGHT-INVASION	1	OBDURATE	1	ORIGINE	1	PALER	1
NIGHT-REFECTION	1	OBELISKS	1	ORIS	1	PALINURUS	1
NIGHT-WAND'RING	1	OBJECTED	1	ORISONS	1	PALISADES	1
NIGHTGOWN	1	OBJECTIONS	1	ORMENIAN	1	PALLADIO	1
NIGHTINGALE	1	OBLATIONS	1	ORMENUS'	1	PALLID	1
NIGHTINGALES	1	OBLIGINGLY	1	ORNIA'S	1	PALMER'S	1
NIHIL	1	OBSCURER	1	ORPHEUS'	1	PALMUS	1
NIHILO	1	OBSERVATIONS	1	ORRERY	1	PALPABLE	1
NILE'S	1	OBSERVATOR	1	ORTHÈ	1	PALSIE	1
NILUS'	1	OBSERVER	1	ORTHAEUS	1	PALSY	1
NIMROD	1	OBSERVER'S	1	ORTHIAN	1	PAM	1
NINETEEN	1	OBSTACLES	1	ORTOLANS	1	PAMBY	1
NINUS	1	OBSTETRIC	1	ORUS	1	PAMELA	1
NIPPLE	1	OBSTINACY	1	ORYTHIA	1	PAMMON	1
NIPT	1	OBSTREP'ROUS	1	OSBORN'S	1	PAMS	1
NISA	1	OBSTRUCTED	1	OSIER	1	PANDOCUS	1
NISYRUS	1	OBTEND	1	OSTENT	1	PANE	1
NOÚS	1	OBTRUDING	1	OSYRIS	1	PANEGYRIC	1
NOËMON'S	1	OCALEA	1	OTHELLO	1	PANICK	1
NO-MEANING	1	OCCASIONS	1	OTHERWISE	1	PANOMPHAEAN	1
NOAH	1	OCEAN-KING	1	OTREUS'	1	PANOPÉ'S	1
NOBILITY	1	OCT	1	OTRYNTEUS	1	PANOPÈA	1
NOBLE'S	1	OCTAVIUS	1	OTRYNTIDES	1	PANTALOON	1
NOBLIER	1	OCTAVO'S	1	OUT-BID	1	PANTHUS'	1
NOCKS	1	OCTAVOS	1	OUT-CANT	1	PAP	1
NOEMON	1	OCYALUS	1	OUT-CAST	1	PAPAL	1
NOISEFUL	1	ODDLY	1	OUT-DID	1	PAPER-CREDIT	1
NOISES	1	ODIN	1	OUT-DRINK	1	PAPER-DURANCE	1
NOISOME	1	OECHALIA	1	OUT-FLY	1	PAPHIAN	1
NONCENCE	1	OECHALIAN	1	OUT-GO	1	PAPHOS	1
NONJUROR	1	OECONOMY	1	OUT-LIE	1	PARACLETE'S	1
NOON'S	1	OENEUS'	1	OUT-LIVES	1	PARALLEL	1
NOONDAY	1	OENOMÄUS	1	OUT-RIDE	1	PARALLELS	1
NOONTIDE-BELL	1	OENOMAS	1	OUT-SHINE	1	PARAMOUNT	1
NOOSE	1	OETE	1	OUT-SHONE	1	PARCHMENT-FATES	1
NORMAN	1	OETYLOS'	1	OUT-SIDE	1	PARCHT	1
NOS	1	OFFENCES	1	OUT-STERNHOLDED	1	PARD	1
NOS'D	1	OFFERINGS	1	OUT-STRIP'D	1	PARDON'D	1
NOSEGAY	1	OFFICES	1	OUT-STRIPT	1	PARE	1
NOSTER	1	OFFSPRING'S	1	OUT-SWEAR	1	PARENT-GOD	1
NOSTRIL	1	OFSPRING	1	OUT-USURE	1	PARENT-QUEEN	1
NOSTRUM	1	OFT-CONQUER'D	1	OUT-WEAR	1	PARIDEL	1
NOTCH	1	OFT-HEAV'D	1	OUT-WEIGHS	1	PARING	1
NOTCH'D	1	OGLE	1	OUT-WHORE	1	PARISH	1
NOTCHES	1	OGLETHORP	1	OUTCASTS	1	PARKER	1
NOTHINGS	1	OGLING	1	OUTLAST	1	PARLEY	1
NOTICE	1	OICLEUS	1	OUTLASTING	1	PARLY	1
NOTING	1	OILEAN	1	OUTRAGES	1	PARNASS'	1
NOURISHMENT	1	OILY	1	OUTRAGIOUS	1	PARNEL	1
NOVEL	1	OLD-FASHION'D	1	OUTSHINES	1	PARRHASIA	1
NOW-DECLINING	1	OLD-MAN'S	1	OUTSIDE	1	PARROTS	1
NOW-NEGLECTED	1	OLDFIELD'S	1	OUTSTRETCH'D	1	PARSONS	1
NUMA'S	1	OLDMIXONS	1			PARTAKER	1

PARTAKING 1	PERCOTÈ'S 1	PHTHIA'S 1	PLUMY-CRESTED 1
PARTHENIA 1	PERCOTE'S 1	PHYLACÈ 1	PLUNDERERS 1
PARTHENISSA 1	PERFECTS 1	PHYLACE 1	PLUTARCH 1
PARTHENIUS 1	PERFORMS 1	PHYLACIAN 1	PLYE 1
PARTICIPATE 1	PERIBAEA 1	PHYLIDES' 1	POACH 1
PARTICLE 1	PERIBAEA'S 1	PHYSICAL 1	PODARGE 1
PARTICOLOUR'D 1	PERICLIMENUS 1	PICK-LOCK 1	PODARGES' 1
PARTIOT 1	PERIGORD 1	PICK-POCKET 1	POEON'S 1
PARTITIONS 1	PERILOUS 1	PIDDLE 1	POEONIAN 1
PARTRIDGES 1	PERIMEDES 1	PIDYTES 1	POETESS 1
PARTRIGES 1	PERIPHAETES 1	PIECE-MEAL 1	POETRY'S 1
PARTY-COLOUR'D 1	PERIPHES 1	PIERCES 1	POETS' 1
PARTY-RAGE 1	PERISHABLE 1	PIERIAN 1	POINT'S 1
PARTY-ZEALOTS 1	PERISHT 1	PIES 1	POIS'NING 1
PASIPHAE 1	PERITHOUS 1	PIGEON 1	POISING 1
PASSEN 1	PERIWIG 1	PIGEONS 1	POITIERS 1
PASSERAN 1	PERMITTED 1	PIGMY-WRETCH 1	POLAND 1
PASSION'S 1	PEROLLA 1	PIGOT 1	POLAND'S 1
PASSIONATE 1	PERPETUITY 1	PIKES 1	POLEMIC 1
PASTE 1	PERPLEXT 1	PILASTER 1	POLICIES 1
PASTERN 1	PERRHEBIANS 1	PILF'RED 1	POLISHED 1
PASTERN-BONE 1	PERSÈ 1	PILF'RING 1	POLISHT 1
PASTORA 1	PERSECUTE 1	PILFER 1	POLITIC 1
PASTORELLA 1	PERSECUTING 1	PILFER'D 1	POLITICIAN 1
PASTORS 1	PERSECUTION 1	PILGRIM 1	POLITICIANS 1
PASTRY 1	PERSEPHONE 1	PILGRIM'S 1	POLITICK 1
PASTY 1	PERSEVERING 1	PILLAG'D 1	POLITICS 1
PAT 1	PERSIANS 1	PILLAGE 1	POLL 1
PATCH-BOX 1	PERSISTING 1	PILLAGER 1	POLLUTE 1
PATCH-WORK 1	PERSONAE 1	PILLAR'D 1	POLYÏDUS 1
PATENT 1	PERSONAGE 1	PILLORY'D 1	POLYCASTE 1
PATER 1	PERSONS 1	PILOSOPHICK 1	POLYCTOR'S 1
PATERNOSTER 1	PERSU 1	PILOT'S 1	POLYDORUS 1
PATHOS 1	PERSUADED 1	PINCH 1	POLYDUS' 1
PATHWAY 1	PERSUADES 1	PINCHES 1	POLYGLOTT 1
PATIENTLY 1	PERSUADING 1	PINDAR'S 1	POLYGOTT 1
PATIENTS 1	PERSUASIONS 1	PINE-TREE 1	POLYMELE 1
PATRIARCH-WITS 1	PERSUES 1	PINKS 1	POLYMELUS 1
PATRICIAN 1	PERSWADE 1	PINKY 1	POLYNEUS' 1
PATRICIANS 1	PERU 1	PINN'D 1	POLYNICES 1
PATRIMONIES 1	PERUSING 1	PIOUSLY 1	POLYPEMON'S 1
PATRITIO'S 1	PERUVIAN 1	PIPING 1	POLYPHETES 1
PATRON-NAME 1	PERVADE 1	PIPKIN 1	POLYPHIDES 1
PATRONIZ'D 1	PERVERT 1	PIQU'D 1	POLYPOETES' 1
PATRONS 1	PESCENNIUS 1	PIRAEUS' 1	POLYPUS 1
PATS 1	PESTILENTIAL 1	PIREUS 1	POLYXENUS 1
PATTY 1	PESTLE 1	PIRITHOUS 1	POMPOUSLY 1
PAULO'S 1	PETEON 1	PIRITHOUS' 1	PONDER 1
PAUSES 1	PETEUS'S 1	PIRUS 1	PONTEUS 1
PAVILIONS 1	PETITION'D 1	PISSER 1	POOL 1
PAVILLIONS 1	PETRIFY 1	PISSER-BY 1	POOR-BOX 1
PAWING 1	PETT 1	PISSING 1	POOR'S 1
PEA 1	PETTICOATS 1	PISSING-POST 1	POPLAR-LEAVES 1
PEA-CHICKS 1	PETTY 1	PISSPOTS 1	POPP'D 1
PEACEABLY 1	PHAËTON 1	PITCH'D 1	POPPIES 1
PEACH'S 1	PHAEA'S 1	PITCHY 1	POPPLE'S 1
PEAL 1	PHAEBUS' 1	PITEOUSLY 1	POPULARITY 1
PEAL'D 1	PHAEDRA 1	PITYEA'S 1	POPULARLY 1
PEAR-TREES 1	PHAESTAN 1	PLACING 1	POREING 1
PEASANTS 1	PHAESTUS 1	PLAICE 1	PORES 1
PEBBLES 1	PHAETHUSA 1	PLAIN-WORK 1	PORKET 1
PECCANT 1	PHANTOM-SISTER 1	PLAINNESS 1	PORTRAIT 1
PEDAEUS 1	PHANTOME-NATIONS 1	PLAINT 1	POS'D 1
PEDAEUS' 1	PHARAOH 1	PLAINTIFF 1	POSSES'D 1
PEDANTS 1	PHARES 1	PLAINTS 1	POSSESSES 1
PEDESTAL 1	PHEA'S 1	PLAINY 1	POST-BOYS 1
PEDESTALS 1	PHEASANT'S 1	PLAITED 1	POSTERIOR 1
PEDIGREE 1	PHEDON 1	PLANE 1	POSTING 1
PEEP'D 1	PHEGEUS 1	PLANE-TREE 1	POSTPONE 1
PEEPS 1	PHELUS 1	PLANES 1	POSTURES 1
PEERLESS 1	PHENEAN 1	PLANTATIONS 1	POTHECARIES 1
PEEVISH 1	PHENICIAN 1	PLANTER'S 1	POTS 1
PEG 1	PHERES 1	PLATAEA 1	POULT'RERS 1
PEGASAEAN 1	PHERUSA 1	PLATED 1	POULTRY 1
PEICES 1	PHIDAS 1	PLATFORM 1	POUNC'D 1
PELASGIAN 1	PHIDIPPUS 1	PLATO'S 1	POUNCE 1
PELASGUS' 1	PHIDON 1	PLATONIC 1	POUNCES 1
PELHAM 1	PHILETOR'S 1	PLAUTUS' 1	POW'R'S 1
PELHAM'S 1	PHILIP 1	PLAY-HOUSE 1	POWDERS 1
PELIAS 1	PHILIP'S 1	PLAY-THINGS 1	POWERFUL 1
PELIAS' 1	PHILIPS'S 1	PLAY'R 1	POWERS 1
PELL 1	PHILOMED 1	PLAY'S 1	POWR'S 1
PELL-MELL 1	PHILOMEDA'S 1	PLEADER 1	POWRS 1
PELL-MELL-PACK 1	PHILOMELA 1	PLEADING 1	POYS'NOUS 1
PELLENÈ 1	PHILOMELA'S 1	PLEASANTRY 1	POYSON'D 1
PELLUCID 1	PHILOSOPHIC 1	PLEASINGLY 1	PRACTISES 1
PELT 1	PHILTRE 1	PLEASURE'S 1	PRACTIUS' 1
PEN'D 1	PHLEGETON 1	PLEDG'S 1	PRAISD 1
PENAL 1	PHLEGETON'S 1	PLENTIFUL 1	PRAISED 1
PENALTY 1	PHLEGIAS' 1	PLIGHTS 1	PRANCE 1
PENELOPE'S 1	PHLEGM 1	PLINY 1	PRANKS 1
PENETRABLE 1	PHLEGN 1	PLODDING 1	PRAUNC'D 1
PENETRATE 1	PHLEGYANS 1	PLOTTED 1	PRAUNCH'D 1
PENNEL 1	PHOCIANS 1	PLOUGH 1	PRAY'R-BOOKS 1
PENNELL'S 1	PHOCION 1	PLOUGH'D 1	PRE-ORDAIN'D 1
PENSIONER 1	PHOEBÈ'S 1	PLOVERS 1	PREACHES 1
PENSIONS 1	PHOENICIAN 1	PLOW-SHARE 1	PREACHING 1
PENTHEUS' 1	PHOENOMENON 1	PLOW-SHARES 1	PRECARIOUS 1
PENTLOW 1	PHOESTUS 1	PLOWMAN 1	PRECEDENTS 1
PEOPLES 1	PHORBAS 1	PLOWSHARES 1	PRECISE 1
PEPPER-WATER-WORMS 1	PHORONEUS' 1	PLU 1	PRECLUDES 1
PERAULT 1	PHOSPHOR 1	PLUBLICK 1	PREDICTING 1
PERCH 1	PHRADMON 1	PLUCK 1	PREF'RENCE 1
PERCNOS' 1	PHRENSY 1	PLUCK'D 1	PREFACE 1
PERCOPE'S 1	PHRYGIAN'S 1	PLUMPER 1	PREFERR'ST 1

PREFERRING	1	PRUDENTLY	1	RACKT	1	RECTIFY	1
PRELATE'S	1	PRUDERY	1	RADCLIFF'S	1	RECUR	1
PRENTICESHIP	1	PRUDISH	1	RAFTER'D	1	RED-HISSING	1
PREPAR'ST	1	PRUDISHLY	1	RAFTER'S	1	RED-HOT	1
PREPARD	1	PRUN'D	1	RAFTERS	1	REDCOAT	1
PREPARING	1	PRUNE	1	RAG-FAIR	1	REDEEMER	1
PREPOSSESSION	1	PRUNELLA	1	RAGERIE	1	REDEMPTION	1
PREPOSSEST	1	PRUNING	1	RAIL'D	1	REDNING	1
PREPOSSET	1	PRUNING-HOOK	1	RAILER'S	1	REDOUBLES	1
PRESAGES	1	PRYING	1	RAILLY	1	REDOUND	1
PRESBYTERIAN	1	PRYMNEUS	1	RAIN-BOW	1	REDOUNDING	1
PRESCIENCE	1	PRYTANIS	1	RAINY	1	REDRIFF	1
PRESENTED	1	PSALMS	1	RAKES	1	REDUNDANT	1
PRESENTING	1	PSI	1	RALLIES	1	REEDY	1
PRESENTLY	1	PSYRIAN	1	RALLY.	1	REEK'D	1
PRESERVERING	1	PUBLISHER	1	RAMBLED	1	REFIND	1
PRESERVING	1	PUDDEN	1	RAMBLER	1	REFINEMENTS	1
PRESIDENT	1	PUDDINGS	1	RAMBLES	1	REFITS	1
PRESIDING	1	PUFFING	1	RAMBLING	1	REFLECTIVE	1
PRESSD	1	PUFFS	1	RAMBOÜILLET	1	REFORMING	1
PRESUMES	1	PUFT	1	RAMM'D	1	REFRAIN'D	1
PRESUMPTION	1	PUG	1	RAMPANT	1	REFRESHES	1
PRESUMPTOUS	1	PUKE	1	RAMPIRE	1	REFUTE	1
PRETENDER'S	1	PULL'D	1	RANGES	1	REFUTES	1
PRETENDING	1	PULLET	1	RANKER	1	REGARDED	1
PRETENSION	1	PULPITS	1	RANSOM'D	1	REGICIDE	1
PREVENTED	1	PULTENEY'S	1	RANTING	1	REGISTERS	1
PRIAPUS	1	PUNCTUAL	1	RAPHAEL	1	REGRETTED	1
PRIAPUS'	1	PUNGENT	1	RAPINES	1	REGULARLY	1
PRICK'D	1	PUNISHES	1	RAPTURED	1	REGULATE	1
PRICKS	1	PUNTS	1	RAPTUROUS	1	REITHRIAN	1
PRIDE'S	1	PUNY	1	RARITIES	1	REITHRUS	1
PRIEST-CRAFT	1	PUPPET	1	RASE	1	REJOIC'D	1
PRIGS	1	PUPPETTS	1	RATAFIE	1	REJOIND	1
PRIMATE'S	1	PUPPYES	1	RATIFIE	1	REJOINDER	1
PRIMO	1	PURCHASES	1	RATTL'D	1	REJOYCE	1
PRIMUS	1	PURELY	1	RATTLED	1	REKINDL'D	1
PRINCE-LIKE	1	PURGES	1	RAV'NOUS	1	REKINDLES	1
PRINCESS'	1	PURIFY'D	1	RAVAG'D	1	RELAPSE	1
PRINCESSE	1	PURL	1	RAVELL'D	1	RELATED	1
PRINCIPAL	1	PURPLE-TING'D	1	RAVISHT	1	RELATIVE	1
PRIORI	1	PURPOSELY	1	RAW	1	RELAXES	1
PRISCA'S	1	PURSUER	1	RAYMOND	1	RELENTED	1
PRISMATIC	1	PUTRIFIE	1	RAZING	1	RELICK	1
PRITHEE	1	PUZZLES	1	RE-ASCEND	1	RELIGIONS	1
PRIVY	1	PYGMAEAN	1	RE-ASSUME	1	RELISH'D	1
PROBATUM	1	PYGMY	1	RE-CLOS'D	1	RELUCTANTLY	1
PROBITY	1	PYGMY-NATIONS	1	RE-CONSIDER	1	REMAINED	1
PROCEEDED	1	PYKES	1	RE-ECCHO'D	1	REMARKS	1
PROCEEDING	1	PYLADES	1	RE-ECHO	1	REMEMB'RING	1
PROCESS	1	PYLARTES	1	RE-ECHOE	1	REMEMBERS	1
PROCLAIMING	1	PYLENÈ	1	RE-ECHOES	1	REMISS	1
PROCULUS	1	PYLEUS	1	RE-ECHOING	1	REMISSIVE	1
PROCURES	1	PYLON	1	RE-ENTER	1	REMIT	1
PRODUCTIVE	1	PYNE	1	RE-FIT	1	REMITS	1
PROFESS'D	1	PYRAMIDS	1	RE-INSPIRES	1	REMONSTRANCE	1
PROFESSORS	1	PYRAMUS	1	RE-KINDLING	1	REMOUNT	1
PROFFER	1	PYROUS	1	RE-LIGHT	1	REMOUNTS	1
PROFITABLE	1	PYRRHASUS	1	RE-LUM'D	1	REMOVAL	1
PROGRESSIVE	1	PYTHAGORAS'S	1	RE-MURMUR	1	REMOVING	1
PROJECT	1	PYTHAGOREANS	1	RE-MURMUR'D	1	RENDEZVOUS	1
PROJECTORS	1	PYTHAGORICK	1	RE-TURNS	1	RENOUNC'D	1
PROLIX	1	PYTHO	1	RE-VISIT	1	RENT-CHARGE	1
PROLOGUE	1	Q	1	REACHING	1	RENTED	1
PROMACHUS'	1	QUAAKE	1	READIEST	1	RENTS	1
PROMETHEAN	1	QUAE	1	REAPER-TRAIN	1	REPASTING	1
PROMISCUOUSLY	1	QUAEDAM	1	REAPS	1	REPENTENCE	1
PROMISES	1	QUAFFS	1	REASCENDS	1	REPENTS	1
PROMONTORY-SHOULDER	1	QUAIL	1	REASON'D	1	REPIN'D	1
PROMOTING	1	QUAIL-PIPE	1	REASSUME	1	REPINING	1
PROMPTER	1	QUAK'D	1	REASSUMES	1	REPORTED	1
PRONOUS	1	QUAKE	1	REBATE	1	REPOSSESS	1
PROPAGATE	1	QUAKERS	1	REBATED	1	REPRIEV'D	1
PROPERTIES	1	QUARRELLS	1	REBECCA'S	1	REPRIZAL	1
PROPHANE	1	QUARRIES	1	REBEL-WAR	1	REPRIZALS	1
PROPHANELY	1	QUARTO'S	1	REBEL'S	1	REPROACH'D	1
PROPHECY'D	1	QUARTOS	1	REBELL	1	REPROBATE	1
PROPHESY	1	QUAV'RING	1	REBELL'D	1	REPUBLIC	1
PROPHETS	1	QUE	1	REBELLING	1	REPUGNANT	1
PROPOS	1	QUEAN	1	REBELLOWS	1	REPULSIVE	1
PROPOSAL	1	QUEENIES	1	REBOUNDING	1	REPUTED	1
PROPP'D	1	QUEENSB'RY	1	REBUK'D	1	REQUESTED	1
PRORE	1	QUEENSBERRY	1	RECALS	1	REQUESTS	1
PROREUS	1	QUENCH<'D	1	RECEDED	1	REQUITED	1
PROSE-MAN	1	QUIBBLE	1	RECEIT	1	REQUITES	1
PROSECUTE	1	QUICK-GLANCING	1	RECEITS	1	RERE	1
PROSERPINE'S	1	QUICKER	1	RECITATIVO	1	RESEMBLANCE	1
PROSPER'D	1	QUIDNUNC'S	1	RECITING	1	RESENTFUL	1
PROSTITUTES	1	QUIDNUNCS	1	RECK'NING	1	RESERV'DLY	1
PROSYMNA'S	1	QUILT	1	RECKNING	1	RESERVOIR	1
PROTEND	1	QUILTS	1	RECLAIMS	1	RESIGN'D'ST	1
PROTENDS	1	QUIN'S	1	RECLINE	1	RESISTANCE	1
PROTESILAS	1	QUINBUS	1	RECLUSE	1	RESISTED	1
PROTESTANT	1	QUINT	1	RECOLLECT	1	RESOLUTION	1
PROTESTED	1	QUINTILIAN'S	1	RECOLLECTION	1	RESOLVING	1
PROTHOËNOR	1	QUIRKS	1	RECOMPENSE	1	RESORTS	1
PROTHOÖN	1	QUIVER'S	1	RECONCIL'D	1	RESPECTS	1
PROTO	1	QUIXOTISM	1	RECONCILES	1	RESPIR'D	1
PROUDEST	1	QUOITS	1	RECOUNTS	1	RESPITED	1
PROVIDED	1	QUORUM	1	RECOURSE	1	RESTFUL	1
PROVIDENCE'S	1	QUOTATION	1	RECOVERS	1	RESTIVE	1
PROVIDENTIAL	1	QUOTATIONS	1	RECREANT'S	1	RESTRAINED	1
PROVOCATION	1	RABBINS	1	RECREATION	1	RESULT	1
PROW	1	RACER'S	1	RECRUIT	1	RESUMED	1
PROWESS'D	1	RACING	1	RECRUITS	1	RETARDING	1

RETIREMENT	1	ROUGHEN'D	1	SAPHIRE	1	SEA-HORSE	1
RETOUCH	1	ROULING	1	SAPHIRS	1	SEA-MAID'S	1
RETRACING	1	ROUNDELAY	1	SAPP'D	1	SEA-SIDE	1
RETRENCH	1	ROUNDLY	1	SAPPHICK	1	SEA-SURROUNDED	1
RETRIEVES	1	ROUS'D	1	SAPPHOES	1	SEA-WOLVES	1
RETURN'ST	1	ROUSE	1	SARCENET	1	SEAL-RINGS	1
REV'RENC'D	1	ROUTING	1	SARON	1	SEAM	1
REV'RENTLY	1	ROUZES	1	SARSENET	1	SEAM'D	1
REVEALING	1	ROUZING	1	SAT'RIST	1	SEAR'D	1
REVELATION	1	ROV'D	1	SATANS	1	SEARCHES	1
REVERENCE	1	ROWERS	1	SATELLITES	1	SEASON'D	1
REVERING	1	ROWES	1	SATIRE'S	1	SEC	1
REVERT	1	ROWS'D	1	SATISFACTION	1	SECKER	1
REVERTS	1	ROYALL	1	SATISFIE	1	SECONDING	1
REVILE	1	RUB	1	SATNIO'S	1	SECONDLY	1
REVILERS	1	RUBBISH	1	SATNIUS	1	SECRECIE	1
REVILES	1	RUBICON	1	SATURNUS	1	SECRESIE	1
REVISE	1	RUBIED	1	SATYR'S	1	SECRETLY	1
REVIVER	1	RUBIES	1	SATYRION	1	SECUREST	1
REWARDED	1	RUBS	1	SAUCER	1	SECURITY	1
REYNARD	1	RUDDIER	1	SAUL	1	SEDITION	1
RHADAMANTHUS	1	RUDIMENTS	1	SAUNTER'D	1	SEDLEY	1
RHEA	1	RUEFULL	1	SAVD	1	SEDUCEMENTS	1
RHENA	1	RUFA'S	1	SAVIL	1	SEDUCING	1
RHET'RIC	1	RUFFIAN-FORCE	1	SAVIOR	1	SEE-SAW	1
RHETORICK	1	RUFFIAN'S	1	SAVO'RY	1	SEED-TIME	1
RHIGMUS	1	RUFFLING	1	SAVOY	1	SEEMLIER	1
RHIMERS	1	RUFUL	1	SAXON	1	SEEMLY	1
RHODIUS	1	RUFUS	1	SAYINGS	1	SEINE	1
RHODOPE'S	1	RUG	1	SCAFFOLDS	1	SEIS'D	1
RHYME-FREE	1	RUIN'S	1	SCALE'S	1	SEIZING	1
RHYTION'S	1	RUL'ST	1	SCAN	1	SEJANUS	1
RIBALD	1	RUMINATING	1	SCAN'D	1	SELDOME	1
RIBALDRY	1	RUMORS	1	SCANDALS	1	SELECTEST	1
RIBALDS	1	RUMOUR'D	1	SCAPED	1	SELECTS	1
RIBAND	1	RUMP'D	1	SCAPES	1	SELF-APPROVING	1
RIBBALDS	1	RUMPLED	1	SCAPING	1	SELF-BALLANC'D	1
RIBBANDS	1	RUNDEL	1	SCARBOROUGHW	1	SELF-CENTRED	1
RIBBANS	1	RUNIC	1	SCARBROW	1	SELF-CLOS'D	1
RIBBOND	1	RUSHED	1	SCARECROW	1	SELF-CONCEIT	1
RIBBONS	1	RUSSEL	1	SCARES	1	SELF-CONDEMN'D	1
RICHARD'S	1	RUSSET	1	SCARFS	1	SELF-CONFIDING	1
RICHELIEU	1	RUSSIAN	1	SCARLET-CIRCLED	1	SELF-CONFOUNDING	1
RICHLY	1	RUSSLE	1	SCARPHE'S	1	SELF-CONQUER'D	1
RICHMENS	1	RUST'LING	1	SCARR'D	1	SELF-CONSIDERING	1
RICHMOND	1	RUSTED	1	SCARS	1	SELF-CONSUMING	1
RIDDLE	1	RUSTICK	1	SCARSDALE	1	SELF-DEBATE	1
RIDDLER	1	RYMING	1	SCATT'ER	1	SELF-DEFENCE	1
RIDDLES	1	S*Z	1	SCENTED	1	SELF-ENSLAV'D	1
RIDER	1	SABAEAN	1	SCEPTIC	1	SELF-EXPLAIN'D	1
RIDGE	1	SABBATH-DAY	1	SCHEM'D	1	SELF-MURDER'D	1
RIDGY	1	SABBATHS	1	SCHERIANS	1	SELF-SATISFY'D	1
RIDING	1	SABIN	1	SCHISM	1	SELF-TAUGHT	1
RIDOTTA	1	SABINUS	1	SCHOENOS	1	SELF-TORMENTOR	1
RIFE	1	SACKCLOTH	1	SCHOLAR	1	SELFE	1
RIFLE	1	SACRIFICES	1	SCHOLE	1	SELFISHLY	1
RIGHT-HAND	1	SACRIFICING	1	SCHOLE-BOY'S	1	SELLÈ'S	1
RIGHTLIER	1	SADDLE	1	SCHOLIAST	1	SELLES'	1
RIGOROUS	1	SAFE-SEQUESTER'D	1	SCHOOL-BOY'S	1	SELLI	1
RINGLET	1	SAFRON	1	SCHOOL-DIVINE	1	SELY	1
RIOTERS	1	SAGER	1	SCHOOLMAN'S	1	SEMBLANT	1
RIOTOUS	1	SAGEST	1	SCIATICS	1	SEMELE'S	1
RIPÈ	1	SAIL'ST	1	SCIPIO'S	1	SEMELES	1
RIP	1	SAILOR'S	1	SCLAVONIANS	1	SENESHAL	1
RIPN'D	1	SAINTED	1	SCOFFER	1	SENSE-LESS	1
RIPP'D	1	SAINTS'	1	SCOFFS	1	SENTENCES	1
RISQ'D	1	SAINTS'-LIVES	1	SCOLD	1	SEPTIMULEIUS	1
RISQU'D	1	SAINTSHIP	1	SCOLDED	1	SEPTUAGINT	1
RISQUES	1	SAITH	1	SCOLOS	1	SEPULCHRES	1
RIVAL'D	1	SALAMANDER	1	SCONCE'S	1	SEPULCRAL	1
RIVALS'	1	SALAMANDER'S	1	SCOOP'D	1	SEPULTURE	1
RIVELL'D	1	SALAMINIAN	1	SCOPE	1	SERAPH	1
RIVER-GODS	1	SALAMIS	1	SCORCHES	1	SERAPHIM	1
RIVETS	1	SALARY	1	SCORES	1	SERAPHS	1
ROAB	1	SALE	1	SCORND	1	SERENES	1
ROAB'D	1	SALEM	1	SCOTISTS	1	SERENEST	1
ROADS	1	SALESMEN	1	SCOTLAND	1	SERENITY	1
ROAM'ST	1	SALLEE	1	SCOTO	1	SERGEANT	1
ROAMING	1	SALLUST	1	SCOTSMAN	1	SERGEANTS	1
ROBB'ST	1	SALLY	1	SCOUNDRELS	1	SERPENT-LIKE	1
ROBBERS	1	SALLY'D	1	SCOUR'D	1	SERPENT-MAZES	1
ROBE'S	1	SALMON'S	1	SCOUT	1	SERPENT-TAIL	1
ROBERT'S	1	SALMONEUS	1	SCOWR'D	1	SERPENT'S	1
ROBIN	1	SALOMON	1	SCRAPE	1	SERVICES	1
ROBIN-RED-BREAST	1	SALUBRIOUS	1	SCREAM'D	1	SERVING-MAN	1
ROBOAM	1	SALUTARY	1	SCREECHES	1	SESAMUS	1
ROCHESTER	1	SALVERS	1	SCRIBBLER	1	SESOSTRIS	1
ROCK'D	1	SAMÈ	1	SCRIBE	1	SESSION	1
ROCKING	1	SAMARITAN	1	SCRIBLERUM	1	SESTOS	1
RODRIGO	1	SAMOS'	1	SCRIPTUS	1	SET-LOOKS	1
ROES	1	SAMOTHRACIA	1	SCUD	1	SETT'ST	1
ROMAN'S	1	SAMPLE	1	SCUDDING	1	SETTING-SUN	1
ROMANCES	1	SAMPLER	1	SCUDS	1	SETTLEMENT	1
ROMANTICK	1	SAMSON	1	SCULKING	1	SETTLES	1
ROOKS	1	SAMSON'S	1	SCULLER	1	SEVENFOLD	1
ROOST	1	SANCHO'S	1	SCULLS	1	SEVENTY	1
ROOTE	1	SANCTIFIED	1	SCULPTOR'S	1	SEVEREST	1
ROOTING	1	SANCTIFY	1	SCUT	1	SEVERN	1
ROPES	1	SANCTITY	1	SCYRON'S	1	SEVIL	1
ROSALINDA'S	1	SAND'S	1	SCYTHES	1	SEW'RS	1
ROSCOMMON	1	SANDAL	1	SCYTHIAN	1	SEWELL	1
ROSCOMON	1	SANDYS'	1	SDEATH	1	SEX'S	1
ROSTRA	1	SANGER	1	SEA-DOG	1	SEXES	1
ROTATION	1	SANGUINARY	1	SEA-FARER	1	SEXT	1
ROTE	1	SAPERTON'S	1	SEA-FOWL	1	SHADING	1

SHADOW'D	1	SINDG'D	1	SNORT	1	SPILFUL	1
SHADWELL'S	1	SINGE	1	SNORTED	1	SPILL	1
SHADWELLS	1	SINGERS	1	SNOW-WHITE	1	SPILT	1
SHAG	1	SINGING-GIRLS	1	SNUFF-BOXES	1	SPINAGE	1
SHAK'ST	1	SINGLES	1	SNUG	1	SPINSTER'S	1
SHAKESPEARE	1	SINGULAR	1	SNUG'S	1	SPIO	1
SHALLOP	1	SINTHIANS	1	SOAK	1	SPIRIT'S	1
SHARON	1	SINTIANS	1	SOAK'D	1	SPIRITLESS	1
SHARP-PIERCING	1	SIP'D	1	SOARD	1	SPIRITUAL	1
SHARPERS	1	SIPT	1	SOBER'D	1	SPIT	1
SHAVE	1	SIPYLUS	1	SOBERLY	1	SPITTING	1
SHE'D	1	SIRACH	1	SOBERS	1	SPLAY	1
SHE'L	1	SIREN-COASTS	1	SOCIETIES	1	SPLAY-FOOT	1
SHEAR	1	SIRIAN	1	SOCINIAN	1	SPLEENFUL	1
SHEARS	1	SIRIUS'	1	SOCINUS	1	SPLEENWORT	1
SHEATHS	1	SIRREVERENCE	1	SOCK	1	SPLENDOUR	1
SHEDDING	1	SISE-RAH	1	SOFT-CIRCLING	1	SPLINTER'D	1
SHEENE	1	SISERA	1	SOFT-ENAMOUR'D	1	SPLITTING	1
SHEEPHOOK	1	SISERA-HIM	1	SOFT-EXTENDED	1	SPOON	1
SHEEPISHLY	1	SISTER-FRUITS	1	SOFT-EY'D	1	SPORTING	1
SHEER	1	SISTER-LOCK	1	SOFT-TOUCHING	1	SPOUSELESS	1
SHEERING	1	SISTER-QUEEN	1	SOFT-TRICKLING	1	SPRAWL	1
SHELT'RING	1	SISTRUM	1	SOFT-WHISP'RING	1	SPRAWLING	1
SHELTERS	1	SISYPHUS	1	SOFT-WHISPERING	1	SPRAWLS	1
SHELTRED	1	SISYPHYAN	1	SOFT'NING	1	SPRAY	1
SHEPPARD	1	SKELTON	1	SOFTLY-STEALING	1	SPREAD'ST	1
SHERLOCK	1	SKEW'R	1	SOHOE	1	SPRIGHT	1
SHIFTED	1	SKILFULL	1	SOILS	1	SPRIGHTLIER	1
SHILL	1	SKILLFUL	1	SOJOURN	1	SPRIGS	1
SHINY	1	SKIM'D	1	SOJOURN'D	1	SPRINDGES	1
SHIP-WRECKS	1	SKIPS	1	SOLA	1	SPRING'ST	1
SHIP'S	1	SKIRMISH	1	SOLDIERS'	1	SPUNGY	1
SHIPWRACK'D	1	SKREEN	1	SOLE-INVITED	1	SPUR-GALL'D	1
SHIPWRACKT	1	SKULKING	1	SOLELY	1	SPURNING	1
SHIPWRECK'D	1	SKY-DY'D	1	SOLEMNITIES	1	SPUTT'RING	1
SHIPWRIGHT'S	1	SLANDROUS	1	SOLEMNIZ'D	1	SPYES	1
SHIRE	1	SLAV'RY	1	SOLEMNIZE	1	SQUAB	1
SHIVERING	1	SLAVE'S	1	SOLEMNLY	1	SQUADRON'D	1
SHIVERS	1	SLAVER	1	SOLEUM	1	SQUALID	1
SHIVR'ING	1	SLAVISH	1	SOLICITOUS	1	SQUALLID	1
SHOCK'D	1	SLAYING	1	SOLINUS	1	SQUALLS	1
SHOCKING	1	SLEEPER	1	SOLITUDES	1	SQUAR'D	1
SHOCKT	1	SLEEVES	1	SOLLICITES	1	SQUAT	1
SHOE	1	SLEIGHT	1	SOLO	1	SQUAWL	1
SHON	1	SLICES	1	SOLYMÉ'S	1	SQUAWLE	1
SHOOTER'S	1	SLIDD'RING	1	SOLYMA	1	SQUEEZE	1
SHORT-PANTING	1	SLIGHTEST	1	SOMERS	1	SQUEEZINGS	1
SHORTEN	1	SLIGHTING	1	SOMEWHAT	1	SQUIRT	1
SHORTNING	1	SLIGHTLY	1	SOMEWHERE	1	STABLE-BOY	1
SHOUD	1	SLILY	1	SOMMERS	1	STAFFORD	1
SHOUD'ST	1	SLIM	1	SOMNUS'	1	STAG'S	1
SHOULD'RING	1	SLINGS	1	SONGSTER	1	STAGYRITE'S	1
SHOULDER-JOINT	1	SLINK	1	SONNETEER	1	STALKED	1
SHOULDER'S	1	SLIP	1	SOONEST	1	STALKING	1
SHOULDST	1	SLIP'D	1	SOOTE	1	STANCH	1
SHOVES	1	SLIP'RY	1	SOOTERKINS	1	STANDARD-AUTHORS	1
SHOW'R'D	1	SLIPT	1	SOOTHING	1	STANDER	1
SHOWR'D	1	SLIT	1	SOPHONISBA	1	STANDER-BY	1
SHREW	1	SLOATHFUL	1	SOPHY	1	STANDERS-BY	1
SHREWDLY	1	SLOP'D	1	SORER	1	STANHOPE'S	1
SHRILLER	1	SLOTHFUL	1	SORROW-STREAMING	1	STAPLE	1
SHRILLEST	1	SLOVEN	1	SOUNDED	1	STAPLE'S	1
SHRIVEL'D	1	SLOW-CIRCLING	1	SOUNDEST	1	STARERS	1
SHROUDED	1	SLOW-PACING	1	SOUP	1	STARK	1
SHROWD	1	SLOW-WORM	1	SOUPE	1	STARTLING	1
SHROWDED	1	SLOWLY-GROWING	1	SOUPS	1	STARV'LING	1
SHROWDS	1	SLOWLY-RISING	1	SOURCES	1	STARVELING	1
SHUDDERS	1	SLOWNESS	1	SOURNESS	1	STATE-AFFAIRS	1
SHUTZ	1	SLUNK	1	SOUTH-EAST	1	STATE'S	1
SIBYL	1	SLUTS	1	SOUTH-WEST	1	STATED	1
SIBYL'S	1	SLUTTISHNESS	1	SOUTH-WINDS	1	STAUNCH	1
SICANIA	1	SLYLY	1	SOUTHERNE	1	STEAM	1
SICILIA'S	1	SMACKING	1	SOUTHWARD	1	STEARS	1
SICILIANS	1	SMALLER	1	SOV'REIGNS	1	STEEL'S	1
SICKENING	1	SMAR	1	SOVERAIN'S	1	STEELS	1
SICKLES	1	SMELLING	1	SOVEREIGNS	1	STEER-MAN	1
SIDE-BOARD	1	SMINTHEUS	1	SOWR	1	STEERING	1
SIDE-BOX	1	SMITES	1	SOWS	1	STEERMAN'S	1
SIDELONG	1	SMITH'S	1	SOWSE	1	STEMM'D	1
SIDNEY	1	SMOAK'ED	1	SOWSING	1	STENELAUS	1
SIDON'S	1	SMOAKLESS	1	SOWZE	1	STENTOR	1
SIFT	1	SMOCK-FACE	1	SOWZING	1	STENTOR'S	1
SIGH'ST	1	SMOCKS	1	SOY	1	STEPDAME	1
SIGHT'S	1	SMOKY	1	SOYL	1	STERLING	1
SIGILS	1	SMOOTH-BEATEN	1	SPADILLIO	1	STERN-ISSUING	1
SIGN'ST	1	SMOOTH-HAIR'D	1	SPADO	1	STERNER	1
SIGNATURES	1	SMOOTH-TONGU'D	1	SPARAGRASS	1	STERNHOLDED	1
SILENTLY	1	SMOOTHER	1	SPARETH	1	STERNS	1
SILK-WORM	1	SMOTH'RING	1	SPARTANS	1	STEW	1
SILK-WORMS	1	SMOTHER	1	SPATIOUS	1	STEWING	1
SILKWORM	1	SMOTHERS	1	SPATTER'D	1	STICKING	1
SILL	1	SMUT	1	SPECIES	1	STIFFENS	1
SILLIER	1	SMUTTY	1	SPECTACLES	1	STIFFER	1
SILV'RY	1	SNACKS	1	SPECTATOR'S	1	STILL-BELIEVING	1
SILVER-QUIV'RING	1	SNAKY	1	SPEECHES	1	STILL-RENEW'D	1
SILVER-SOUNDING	1	SNAPPISH	1	SPEEDED	1	STILL-REVIVING	1
SIMILES	1	SNEAK	1	SPEEDIEST	1	STILL-SURVIVING	1
SIMILIES	1	SNEAK'D	1	SPENCER	1	STILTON	1
SIMO'S	1	SNEAKS	1	SPENSER	1	STILTS	1
SIMP'RING	1	SNEERS	1	SPEW	1	STINT	1
SIMPLES'	1	SNEEZ'D	1	SPHEARS	1	STINTED	1
SIMPLEX	1	SNOR'D	1	SPHYNXE'S	1	STOB US	1
SIMPLICIUS'	1	SNORE	1	SPIDERS	1	STOBAEUS	1
SINCEREST	1	SNORES	1	SPIED	1	STOCKING	1
SINCERITY	1	SNORING	1	SPIKY	1	STOCKINGS	1

STOICS	1	SUN-BORN	1	TARNE	1	THESSALUS	1
STOLES	1	SUN-BRUNT	1	TARPHE'S	1	THESTOR	1
STOMACHS	1	SUN-BURNT	1	TARQUIN'S	1	THEY'L	1
STONE'S	1	SUN-SET	1	TARTS	1	THEY'VE	1
STOP'ST	1	SUNDAY-MORN	1	TASK'D	1	THICK-DESCENDING'	1
STOPPEN	1	SUNDAYS	1	TASSELS	1	THIGHATIRA'S	1
STOPPING	1	SUNIUM'S	1	TASTFUL	1	THIRD-DAY	1
STOWE	1	SUNSETT	1	TASTLESS	1	THIRSTED	1
STOWS	1	SUPER	1	TASTS	1	THIRSTING	1
STRAFFORD	1	SUPER-LUNAR	1	TATTLE	1	THIRTEEN	1
STRAGGLING	1	SUPERCARGOES	1	TAUNT	1	THIRTEENTH	1
STRAGLERS	1	SUPERFICIAL	1	TAURUS	1	THIRTY-NINE	1
STRAGLING	1	SUPERFLUOUS	1	TAVERNS	1	THISBÈ	1
STRAIGHT	1	SUPERIOR'S	1	TAW	1	THISBE	1
STRAINERS	1	SUPERSTITITION	1	TAWNY	1	THISTLE	1
STRAITEN	1	SUPINELY	1	TAXATIONS	1	THOÖSA	1
STRAITS	1	SUPP'D	1	TEÄTUS'	1	THOA	1
STRANGER-FRIEND	1	SUPPERS	1	TE	1	THOMISTS	1
STRATIE	1	SUPPLICATES	1	TE-HE	1	THONE'S	1
STRAWBERRIES	1	SUPPLYD	1	TEACHER	1	THOROLD	1
STRAWY	1	SUPPLYING	1	TEACHES	1	THOUGHTED	1
STREIGHT	1	SUPREAM	1	TEAMS	1	THOUSANDTH	1
STREIGHTEN'D	1	SUPREMEST	1	TEAPOTS	1	THRASIMEDES'	1
STREIGHTS	1	SURCEASE	1	TEAR-FUL	1	THRASIUS	1
STRENGTH-CONFERRING	1	SURE-FOUNDED	1	TEAR-FULL	1	THRASYMEDE	1
STRENGTHS	1	SURETY	1	TEARING	1	THREDDED	1
STRENUOUS	1	SURETYSHIP	1	TEARLESS	1	THREE-MOUTH'D	1
STRETCH'D-OUT	1	SURFEIT	1	TEAT	1	THREE-PENCE	1
STREW'D	1	SURFIET	1	TEATS	1	THREE-SCORE	1
STRICTEST	1	SURMIS'D	1	TEEM'D	1	THRESH	1
STRICTLY	1	SURMIZES	1	TEEMS	1	THRICE-EAR'D	1
STRICTURE	1	SURVEY'ST	1	TEGEA'S	1	THRIFT	1
STRIDING	1	SURVEYING	1	TELAMON'S	1	THRILL'D	1
STRIFE-FULL	1	SURVIVOR	1	TELESCOPE	1	THRIV'D	1
STRIFES	1	SUSPECTING	1	TEMESÉ	1	THROB	1
STRIKER'S	1	SUSPENDING	1	TEMPÈ	1	THROBS	1
STRIP'D	1	SUSPICIONS	1	TEMP'RANCE	1	THRONUS	1
STROK'D	1	SUSPITIOUS	1	TEMP'RING	1	THROUGHOUT	1
STROLL'D	1	SWALLOW'D	1	TEMPERATES	1	THRUSH	1
STROWN	1	SWALLOW'S	1	TEMPEST'S	1	THRUSHES	1
STRUGGLES	1	SWAN-FOOTED	1	TEMPESTING	1	THRYOËSSA	1
STRUMPETS	1	SWAN-LIKE	1	TEMPLE-BAR	1	THRYON'S	1
STRUTTING	1	SWAN'S	1	TEMPLE-WALL	1	THUMB	1
STUART	1	SWARM'D	1	TEMPLERS	1	THUND'RERS	1
STUDIOUSLY	1	SWARTHS	1	TEMPTATIONS	1	THUNDER'S	1
STUDY-DOOR	1	SWEARING	1	TEN-FOLD	1	THUNDERBOLT	1
STUDYING	1	SWEATY	1	TENACIOUS	1	THUNDERING	1
STUFF'D	1	SWEDE	1	TENANT	1	THWARTS	1
STUMBLES	1	SWEET-WINE	1	TEND'REST	1	THYMAETES	1
STUMBLING	1	SWEETEN'D	1	TENDERLY	1	THYMBRAEUS	1
STUMM	1	SWIFT-GLIDING	1	TENDON	1	THYMBRAS'	1
STUN	1	SWILL	1	TENDONS	1	THYRSIS'	1
STUNTED	1	SWILLS	1	TENFOLD	1	TIAR	1
STUPEFACTION	1	SWINE-HERD	1	TENS	1	TIARA'S	1
STUPIFY'D	1	SWINE'S	1	TENTHREDON'S	1	TIBALD	1
STUTTER'D	1	SWINEHERD	1	TENURE	1	TIBERIUS	1
STUTTERING	1	SWINEHERD'S	1	TEOPHRASTE	1	TIBULLUS	1
STYL'D	1	SWINGING	1	TEREE'S	1	TICKL'D	1
STYMPHELUS	1	SWINGS	1	TEREUS	1	TICKLED	1
STYPTICK	1	SWISS	1	TERGO	1	TICKLETH	1
STYPTICKS	1	SWITCH	1	TERM'D	1	TICKLISH	1
STYRIAN	1	SWITZ	1	TERMAGANTS	1	TIGHT	1
SUËIL	1	SWOL'N	1	TERMD	1	TIL	1
SUBJECT-HERDS	1	SWUM	1	TERRACE	1	TILLS	1
SUBLIMER	1	SYCAMORE	1	TERRACES	1	TILT	1
SUBLIMES	1	SYDNEY'S	1	TERRAS-WALK	1	TIMBREL	1
SUBMISSIONS	1	SYLLABLE	1	TERRESTRIALS	1	TIMELESS	1
SUBMISSIVELY	1	SYLPHIDS	1	TERRIFIES	1	TIMOLEON	1
SUBMITTED	1	SYMAETHIS	1	TERRIFY	1	TIMON'S	1
SUBSIDED	1	SYRENS	1	TERTULLIAN	1	TIMOTHEUS	1
SUBSIDING	1	SYRIA	1	TESTERS	1	TINCLING	1
SUBSISTED	1	SYRTES	1	TESTIFIES	1	TINDER	1
SUBTARTAREAN	1	SYSIPHUS	1	TEUTHRAS	1	TINGLING	1
SUBTERRANEAN	1	TÄYGETUS'	1	TEUTHRAS'	1	TINKLING	1
SUBTILE	1	TABBY	1	THALESTRIS'	1	TINSEL	1
SUBTLEST	1	TABOR	1	THALPIUS	1	TINTS	1
SUBTLY	1	TACKLE	1	THAMAYRIS'	1	TIPTOE	1
SUBVERTING	1	TAENARUS	1	THAME	1	TIRE'D	1
SUCCESSIVELY	1	TAFFETY	1	THAMIS	1	TIRESIAS'	1
SUCKLE	1	TAG	1	THANKFUL	1	TISIPHONE	1
SUCKLED	1	TAINTING	1	THATCH'D	1	TISN'T	1
SUCKLYN	1	TALBOT'S	1	THAUMACIA	1	TISSUE	1
SUDDENLY	1	TALISMANS	1	THAUMANTIA	1	TITARESIUS	1
SUERTYSHIP	1	TALKE	1	THE<E	1	TITHONUS	1
SUFF'RANCE	1	TALKEN	1	THEANO'S	1	TITIAN'S	1
SUFF'RER	1	TALKER	1	THEATRIC	1	TITILLATING	1
SUFF'RERS	1	TALKERS	1	THEATRICALLY	1	TITLED	1
SUFFERING	1	TALL-BOY	1	THEBAE	1	TITTLE	1
SUFFOLK	1	TALLEST	1	THEBAN'S	1	TITYUS	1
SUFFUSE	1	TALTHYBIUS'	1	THEFTS	1	TITYUS'	1
SUGGESTING	1	TAM'RISK	1	THEMIS'	1	TOADS	1
SUIDAS	1	TAM'RISKS	1	THENCEFORTH	1	TOBACCO	1
SUITABLE	1	TAMARISK	1	THEOCLES	1	TODAY	1
SUITOR-CREW	1	TAMARISK'S	1	THEODAMAS	1	TOIL-DETESTING	1
SUITOR-POWRS	1	TAN	1	THEORY	1	TOILET'S	1
SUITOR'S	1	TANTALIZ'D	1	THEREIN	1	TOILETTE	1
SULLIED	1	TANTALUS'S	1	THERSITES	1	TOKENS	1
SULLY'D	1	TAPE	1	THESES	1	TOLEDO'S	1
SULPH'ROUS	1	TAPE-TYP'D	1	THESPIA	1	TOLERABLE	1
SULPHUR-TIPT	1	TAPER'S	1	THESPROT	1	TOLL'D	1
SUMM'D	1	TAPERING	1	THESPROTIA	1	TOLLO	1
SUMMER-DAYS	1	TAPHIANS	1	THESPROTIAN	1	TOM'S	1
SUMMER-HOUSE	1	TAPHOS	1	THESSALIA	1	TOMB-STONE	1
SUMMER-NOON	1	TAPISTRY	1	THESSALIAN	1	TOMES	1
SUMMERS	1	TARDIER	1	THESSALIANS	1	TOMORROW	1

TOMPION	1	TROPHEE	1	UNANIMATED	1	UNLOOSE	1
TONSON'S	1	TROPIC	1	UNANIMOUS	1	UNMAN'D	1
TOOTH	1	TROTH	1	UNAPPEAS'D	1	UNMANGLED	1
TOOTING	1	TROUBLES	1	UNAPPROACH'D	1	UNMANS	1
TOP-GALLANT	1	TROUTS	1	UNASSISTED	1	UNMASK	1
TOPHAM	1	TROWLING	1	UNATTENDING	1	UNMILK'D	1
TORCH-LIGHT	1	TROWZES	1	UNAWARES	1	UNMINGLED	1
TORMENTING	1	TRUANT	1	UNBARREL	1	UNMINISTERED	1
TORMENTOR	1	TRUCKS	1	UNBARS	1	UNMOOR	1
TORMENTORS	1	TRUDGES	1	UNBATH'D	1	UNMOOR'D	1
TORT'RING	1	TRUELY	1	UNBENDING	1	UNNOTED	1
TORTOISE	1	TRUMBAL	1	UNBER'D	1	UNOP'NING	1
TOTHER	1	TRUNC	1	UNBIASS'D	1	UNPARD'NING	1
TOTTERING	1	TRUNKS	1	UNBLOODY	1	UNPAWN'D	1
TOTTERS	1	TRUSS	1	UNBODIED	1	UNPENSION'D	1
TOULON	1	TRUSTEES	1	UNBOUGHT	1	UNPERISH'D	1
TOUR	1	TRUTH'S	1	UNBRIB'D	1	UNPITEOUS	1
TOW	1	TRYUMPHS	1	UNBUCKLING	1	UNPLEAS'D	1
TOW'RLIKE	1	TUFF	1	UNBURIED	1	UNPLUME	1
TOWELS	1	TUFF-TAFFETY	1	UNCAG'D	1	UNPROFITABLE	1
TOWN'S	1	TUG	1	UNCAUTIOUS	1	UNPROPHETIC	1
TOWNS-MENS	1	TUGGS	1	UNCEASING	1	UNPROSP'ROUS	1
TOWNSHEND'S	1	TULLY'S	1	UNCENSUR'D	1	UNQUESTION'D	1
TOWNSMAN	1	TUMBL'D	1	UNCERTAINTY	1	UNRANSOM'D	1
TOWNSMEN	1	TUMBLER	1	UNCHANGING	1	UNRAVEL	1
TOWR'D	1	TUMBLERS	1	UNCHECK'D	1	UNRAVELS	1
TOWZE	1	TUMULTOUS	1	UNCIVILIZ'D	1	UNRAVISH'D	1
TOWZING	1	TUNBRIDGE	1	UNCLEAN	1	UNRECORDED	1
TOYL	1	TUNICKS	1	UNCLEANLY	1	UNREDREST	1
TOYSHOP	1	TUNICS	1	UNCOMPELL'D	1	UNREGUARDED	1
TRACTABLE	1	TURGID	1	UNCONCERN'DLY	1	UNREPENTANT	1
TRADES	1	TURKEYS	1	UNCONQUERABLY	1	UNREPENTING	1
TRADESMEN	1	TURKS	1	UNCONSENTING	1	UNREPROV'D	1
TRADUC'D	1	TURNER	1	UNCONTROL'D	1	UNRESIGN'D	1
TRADUCE	1	TURNUS	1	UNCTION	1	UNRESOLV'D	1
TRAFFICKS	1	TURRET'S	1	UNCUMBER'D	1	UNREVEAL'D	1
TRAGEDIES	1	TUTRESS	1	UND'R	1	UNREVEREND	1
TRAILING	1	TWANGS	1	UNDAZLED	1	UNRIDDLE	1
TRAIN-BANDS	1	TWAY	1	UNDAZZL'D	1	UNRIPEN'D	1
TRAITS	1	TWEED	1	UNDECAY'D	1	UNRIVALL'D	1
TRAMP'LING	1	TWEEZER	1	UNDECAYING	1	UNSAFE	1
TRAMPLES	1	TWEEZER-CASES	1	UNDECEIV'D	1	UNSAID	1
TRANCES	1	TWENTIETH	1	UNDECEIVE	1	UNSAVOURY	1
TRANQUIL	1	TWICE-MARRY'D	1	UNDERMINE	1	UNSEPARATED	1
TRANQUILITY	1	TWICE-TOLD	1	UNDERMINING	1	UNSHOOK	1
TRANSCEND	1	TWICK'NAM	1	UNDERSTANDING	1	UNSKILFUL	1
TRANSCENDENT	1	TWIGS	1	UNDERSTANDS	1	UNSKILFULL	1
TRANSFERS	1	TWIN	1	UNDERSTOND	1	UNSOLD	1
TRANSFIXES	1	TWIN-GODS	1	UNDESCRY'D	1	UNSOUND	1
TRANSFIXT	1	TWITCH'D	1	UNDESERV'D	1	UNSOWN	1
TRANSFORM	1	TWOU'D	1	UNDISCERNING	1	UNSPENT	1
TRANSFORMED	1	TWYLIGHT	1	UNDISCHARG'D	1	UNSPOIL'D	1
TRANSFORMING	1	TYBER'S	1	UNDISCIPLIN'D	1	UNSTITCH'D	1
TRANSFORMS	1	TYCHIUS	1	UNDISCOVER'D	1	UNSTRINGS	1
TRANSGREST	1	TYDCOMBE	1	UNDISFIGUR'D	1	UNSUBDU'D	1
TRANSITORY	1	TYGER	1	UNDISGUIS'D	1	UNSUFFERABLE	1
TRANSLATING	1	TYGER'S	1	UNDISHONOUR'D	1	UNSULLYED	1
TRANSLATIONS	1	TYNDAR'S	1	UNDISSEMBLED	1	UNSUPPORTED	1
TRANSLATOR	1	TYNDARUS	1	UNDIVIDED	1	UNSURE	1
TRANSMITTED	1	TYP'D	1	UNDO	1	UNSUSPICIOUS	1
TRAPP	1	TYPHOEUS	1	UNDOES	1	UNSUSTAIN'D	1
TRAV'LER	1	TYPHON	1	UNDOING	1	UNTAKEN	1
TRAV'LERS	1	TYRANNICK	1	UNDRESS'D	1	UNTHOUGHT-OF	1
TRAVELER	1	TYRANT-MINIONS	1	UNDROSSY	1	UNTO	1
TRAVELLER'S	1	TYRAWLEY	1	UNDULATING	1	UNTOLD	1
TRAVERS	1	TYRAWLEY'S	1	UNEASILY	1	UNTRAIN'D	1
TRAVERSES	1	TYRCONNEL	1	UNEQUALL'D	1	UNTROD	1
TRAYS	1	TYRCONNEL'S	1	UNEQUALLY	1	UNTRUTHS	1
TRAYTOR-GODS	1	TYRINTHÈ'S	1	UNEVEN	1	UNTUN'D	1
TREACHEROUS	1	TYTHE	1	UNEXHAUSTED	1	UNTWINE	1
TREACHERY	1	TYTHE-PIG	1	UNEXPECTED	1	UNTYE	1
TREADING	1	UCALEGON	1	UNEXPLOR'D	1	UNUS'D	1
TREASONS	1	UDDER	1	UNFAILING	1	UNVAILING	1
TREATER	1	UDDER'D	1	UNFED	1	UNVEIL'D	1
TREATING	1	ULYSSAEAN	1	UNFILL'D	1	UNWASH'D	1
TREATISE	1	UMBRAGE	1	UNFIX'D	1	UNWATCH'D	1
TREATMENT	1	UMBRAGEOUS	1	UNFLEDG'D	1	UNWEARIED	1
TRECHIN'S	1	UN-ABASH'D	1	UNFOLDED	1	UNWEETING	1
TRECHUS	1	UN-ADMIR'D	1	UNFOREBODING	1	UNWEIGH'D	1
TRENCH'D	1	UN-AW'D	1	UNFORESEEN	1	UNWHIPP'D	1
TRENCH'S	1	UN-BELIEVING	1	UNFORGIVING	1	UNWILLINGLY	1
TRENCHANT	1	UN-DID	1	UNFORTIFY'D	1	UNWISH'D	1
TRENCHING	1	UN-DISTURB'D	1	UNFORTUNATELY	1	UNWROUGHT	1
TRENDS	1	UN-ELBOW'D	1	UNFREED	1	UNYOK'D	1
TREUFLES	1	UN-ENDOW'D	1	UNFURLS	1	UNYOKE	1
TREZENIAN	1	UN-FATHER'D	1	UNFURNISH'D	1	UNYOKES	1
TRIALS	1	UN-FEAR'D	1	UNGARDED	1	UP-HEAVING	1
TRICA	1	UN-HATED	1	UNHELP'D	1	UP-HELD	1
TRICK'D	1	UN-HOUS'D	1	UNHOLY	1	UP-LIFT	1
TRICKLED	1	UN-IMPROV'D	1	UNHOUS'D	1	UP-RISING	1
TRIFLER	1	UN-INTELLIGIBLE	1	UNIFORM'D	1	UP-SOAR'D	1
TRILL	1	UN-LEARN'D	1	UNINHABITED	1	UP-SPRINGING	1
TRIMM'D	1	UN-MOV'D	1	UNINSCRIB'D	1	UP-SPRUNG	1
TRINACRIA'S	1	UN-NERVE	1	UNINSPIR'D	1	UP-STARTED	1
TRIPLETS	1	UN-NOTED	1	UNINTELLIGIBLE	1	UP-TURNS	1
TRIPOS	1	UN-OFFENDING	1	UNISON	1	UPBRAIDED	1
TRIPTHONGS	1	UN-PLAC'D	1	UNITIES	1	UPHEAVE	1
TRITONIA	1	UN-STALL'D	1	UNIVERSE	1	UPHOLD	1
TRITONS	1	UN-WATER'D	1	UNKINDLED	1	UPHOLST'RER	1
TRIUMPHANTLY	1	UN-WEPT	1	UNKINGLY	1	UPLIFTS	1
TRIVET	1	UNABASH'D	1	UNLAC'D	1	UPRAIS'D	1
TRIVET-TABLE	1	UNABATED	1	UNLADE	1	UPREAR'D	1
TROEZENÈ	1	UNALLAY'D	1	UNLOADED	1	UPRISING	1
TROILUS	1	UNALTERABLE	1	UNLOCK'D	1	UPROOTS	1
TROPE	1	UNANCHOR'D	1	UNLOOK'D-FOR	1		

XANTIPPE	1	YET-REMAINING	1	YOUR-SELVES	1	ZEPHYRETTA'S	1
XI	1	YET-SURVIVING	1	YOUR'S	1	ZEPHYRUS	1
Y	1	YET-UNCONQUER'D	1	ZACINTH	1	ZETHUS	1
Y-FOND	1	YET-UNRIVAL'D	1	ZACYNTHUS'	1	ZEUXIS'	1
YAWNS	1	YET-UNTASTED	1	ZAGS	1	ZIG	1
YEILD	1	YEWS	1	ZAMOLXIS	1	ZIG-ZAGS	1
YELKS	1	YOAK	1	ZELEIA'S	1	ZODIACK	1
YELLING	1	YOK'D	1	ZELIA'S	1	ZOILUS	1
YELLOWER	1	YONG	1	ZEMBLA'S	1	ZON'D	1
YERDE	1	YORK	1	ZENO	1	ZONES	1
YERNING	1	YORKSHIRE	1	ZEPHALINDA	1	ZOROASTER	1
YESTER	1	YOUNGER'S	1	ZEPHYR'S	1	ZOUNDS	1

Appendix B

Hyphenated Compounds

The following reference list is provided, for its stylistic interest, as a convenient index to Pope's use of hyphenated compounds, including Homeric epithets. Quotations using these compounds appear in the *Concordance* both under the compound form and under each of the hyphenated words. The list omits compounds with hyphenated prefixes and suffixes and certain other compounds no longer hyphenated (see "Note to Users," I, ix). The total of compounds listed is 1,226.

Alphabetical List of Hyphenated Compounds

ABCHURCH-LANE

ABCHURCH-LANE	1	BASE-BORN	1	CITY-TRIBES
ABS-COURT	1	BEAN-SHELL	1	CIVET-CAT
AIR-BRED	1	BEAU-KIND	1	CIVET-CATS
AIR-BUILT	2	BEAU-MONDE	2	CLARE-HALL

Word	Count	Word	Count
ABCHURCH-LANE	1	BASE-BORN	1
ABS-COURT	1	BEAN-SHELL	1
AIR-BRED	1	BEAU-KIND	1
AIR-BUILT	2	BEAU-MONDE	2
ALE-HOUSE	5	BEDFORD-HEAD	1
ALL-A-ROW	1	BEECH-TREE	1
ALL-ACCOMPLISH'D	2	BEECH-TREE'S	1
ALL-ARRAIGNING	1	BEST-BELOV'D	3
ALL-ASSISTLESS	1	BEST-BUILT	1
ALL-BEARING	1	BEST-LOV'D	1
ALL-BEAUTEOUS	1	BIG-UDDER'D	1
ALL-BEAUTIFUL	1	BIRTH-NIGHT	1
ALL-BEHOLDING	2	BIRTH-NIGHTS	1
ALL-BOUNTEOUS	2	BLACK-EY'D	4
ALL-COMPELLING	1	BLACK-JOKE	1
ALL-COMPOSING	4	BLOOD-POLLUTED	2
ALL-CONFIRMING	1	BLOOD-STAIN'D	2
ALL-CONQU'RING	2	BLOOMSB'RY-SQUARE	1
ALL-CONSCIOUS	2	BLUE-EY'D	28
ALL-CONSID'RING	2	BLUE-HAIR'D	1
ALL-CONSUMING	1	BOOK-WORMS	1
ALL-COV'RING	1	BOSOME-WIFE	1
ALL-CREATING	1	BOW-STRING	1
ALL-DESTROYING	1	BOY-SENATOR	1
ALL-DEVOURING	2	BRASS-CHEEK'D	1
ALL-DIFFUSIVE	1	BRASS-HOOF'D	2
ALL-ELOQUENT	1	BRAVELY-PATIENT	1
ALL-EMBRACING	1	BRAZEN-POINTED	1
ALL-ENLIGHT'NING	1	BRIDAL-ROOM	1
ALL-ENLIGHTEN'D	1	BRIGHT-EY'D	1
ALL-EXTENDING	1	BRIGHTLY-DAWNING	1
ALL-GOVERNING	1	BROAD-GLITT'RING	1
ALL-IMPAIRING	1	BROAD-PATCH'D	1
ALL-IMPOTENT	1	BROTHER-CHIEF	1
ALL-INFOLDING	1	BROTHER-CHIEFS	1
ALL-INVOLVING	2	BROTHER-KINGS	3
ALL-KNOWING	2	BROTHER-LEADERS	1
ALL-POW'RFUL	1	BROTHER-WARRIORS	2
ALL-PRESERVING	1	BUBBLE-BOY	1
ALL-PREVENTING	1	BULL-DOGS	1
ALL-QUICK'NING	1	BULL-HIDE	1
ALL-RECORDING	1	BULL-HIDES	7
ALL-REMEMBRING	1	BURNT-OFF'RING	1
ALL-REVEALING	1	CAELESTIAL-SWEET	1
ALL-RIGHTEOUS	1	CASTING-WEIGHT	1
ALL-SEEING	9	CASTLE-WALL	1
ALL-SUBDUING	4	CAT-CALL	2
ALL-SURROUNDING	1	CAT-CALLS	2
ALL-SURVEYING	1	CAUSE-WAY	1
ALL-SUSTAINING	1	CEDAR-BEAMS	1
ALL-TO-BREST	1	CELL-BRED	1
ALL-WISE	2	CHANC'RY-LANE	2
ALMS-HOUSE	3	CHAOS-LIKE	1
ALOM-STYPTICKS	1	CHAPEL-ROYAL	1
ANGEL-LIKE	1	CHARING-CROSS	2
ANGEL-POW'RS	1	CHARIOT-SIDE	1
APE-AND-MONKEY	1	CHILD-LIKE	1
ARCH-POET	1	CHINA-JORDAN	1
ARTIST-GOD	1	CHRIST-CHURCH	1
AT-HOME	1	CHRISTMAS-TIDE	1
ATHEIST-WRETCH	1	CHURCH-WARDENS	1
AUTUMN-HEATS	1	CHURCH-YARD	1
BACK-PLATE	1	CITRON-WATERS	1
BACK-STAIRS	1	CITY-BOWL	1
BANK-BILL	1	CITY-GATE	1
BANSTED-DOWN	1	CITY-SWANS	1

Word	Count
CITY-TRIBES	1
CIVET-CAT	3
CIVET-CATS	1
CLARE-HALL	1
CLAY-COLD	1
CLOSE-COMPACTED	1
CLOSE-COMPELL'D	1
CLOSE-EMBODY'D	1
CLOSE-RANG'D	1
CLOUD-COMPELLER	2
CLOUD-COMPELLING	12
CLOUD-TOPT	1
CO-AIDS	1
COBLER-LIKE	1
COCK-HORSE	1
COCKLE-KIND	2
COLUMBUS-LIKE	1
COMMON-PLACE	2
COMMON-SHOAR	1
COMPTING-HOUSE	1
COOK-MAID	1
CORN-LOFT	1
CORN-VAN	1
COUNCIL-BOARD	1
COUNTER-CHARMS	1
COUNTER-WORK	1
COUNTER-WORKS	1
COURSER-BREEDING	1
COURT-BADGE	4
COURT-SYCOPHANT	1
COURT-VIRTUES	1
COW-HIDE	2
COW-LIKE	1
COW-LIKE-UDDERS	1
COWARD-COUNSELS	1
COXCOMB-PYES	1
CUCKOLD-MAKER'S	1
CURTAIN-LECTURES	1
CYNDER-WENCHES	1
DAB-CHICK	2
DAMSEL-TRAIN	1
DAY-DEVOURER	1
DAY-DISTRACTING	1
DAY-LIGHT	1
DEAD-BORN	2
DEAR-BOUGHT	4
DEAR-LOV'D	1
DEATH-BED	2
DEATH-LIKE	3
DEATH-WATCHES	1
DEEP-DISCERNING	1
DEEP-ECHOING	1
DEEP-FURROW'D	1
DEEP-IMAG'D	1
DEEP-MOUTH'D	1
DEEP-MUSING	1
DEEP-PIERCING	1
DEEP-PROJECTING	1
DEEP-ROOTED	1
DEMI-GOD	2
DEMI-GODS	1
DINNER-TIME	1
DOG-DAYS	1
DOG-HOLE	1
DOG-STAR	1
DOG-STAR'S	2

FAST-FALLING

Word	Count
DOUBLE-CLASPING	1
DOUBLE-EDG'D	2
DOUBLE-TAX'D	1
DOVE-LIKE	3
DOWN-RIGHT	2
DRAWING-ROOM	1
DRURY-LANE	7
DRY-NURSE	2
DUCK-LANE	1
DUE-DISTANT	2
EAGLE-SPEED	1
EAR-RINGS	1
EARL'S-COURT	1
EARTH-BORN	4
EARTH-SHAKER	1
EARTH-SHAKING	3
ELDEST-BORN	2
EV'NING-SPY	1
EVE-REPAST	1
EVENING-FRIENDS	1
EVER-ANXIOUS	1
EVER-BLOOMING	1
EVER-CONSECRATING	1
EVER-DREADFUL	1
EVER-DURING	3
EVER-FERTILE	1
EVER-FLOWING	1
EVER-FRAGRANT	1
EVER-FRUITFUL	1
EVER-GENTLE	1
EVER-HONOUR'D	6
EVER-INJUR'D	1
EVER-LISTLESS	1
EVER-LIVING	1
EVER-MINGLING	1
EVER-MUSING	2
EVER-OPEN	1
EVER-PLEASING	4
EVER-SHADY	1
EVER-VERDANT	1
EVER-WAKEFUL	2
EVER-WATCHFUL	1
EVER-YOUNG	1
EYE-BALL	3
EYE-BALLS	16
EYE-BROW	1
EYE-BROWN	1
EYE-LIDS	1
EYE-SIGHT	1
FAIR-HAIR'D	5
FAIR-ONE'S	1
FAIR-ONES	2
FAIR-STREAMING	1
FAIR-ZON'D	1
FANCY-FORM'D	1
FAR-BEAMING	5
FAR-DREADED	1
FAR-ECHOING	1
FAR-FAM'D	5
FAR-PIERCING	1
FAR-RESOUNDING	1
FAR-SEEN	2
FAR-SHOOTING	1
FAR-STREAMING	2
FAR-STRETCHING	1
FAST-FALLING	1

Word	Count	Word	Count	Word	Count	Word	Count
NEVER-ERRING	1	PARENT-GOD	1	SELF-CONQUER'D	1	SULPHUR-TIPT	1
NEVER-FAILING	1	PARENT-QUEEN	1	SELF-CONSIDERING	1	SUMMER-DAYS	1
NEVER-WEARY'D	1	PARTY-COLOUR'D	1	SELF-CONSUMING	1	SUMMER-HOUSE	1
NEW-ACCEPTED	1	PARTY-RAGE	1	SELF-DEBATE	1	SUMMER-NOON	1
NEW-BENEFIC'D	2	PARTY-ZEALOTS	1	SELF-DEFENCE	1	SUN-BEAMS	2
NEW-BORN	8	PASTERN-BONE	1	SELF-ENSLAV'D	1	SUN-BORN	1
NEW-BUILT	2	PATCH-BOX	1	SELF-EXPLAIN'D	1	SUN-BRUNT	1
NEW-EAR'D	1	PATCH-WORK	1	SELF-LOVE	19	SUN-BURNT	1
NEW-FALL'N	1	PATRIARCH-WITS	1	SELF-MOV'D	3	SUN-SET	1
NEW-MADE	3	PATRON-GOD	2	SELF-MURDER'D	1	SUN-SHINE	3
NEW-MARKET-FAME	1	PATRON-NAME	1	SELF-PLEASING	2	SUNDAY-MORN	1
NEW-MARKET'S	2	PEA-CHICKS	1	SELF-SAME	3	SUPER-LUNAR	1
NEW-PENSION'D	1	PEAR-TREE	2	SELF-SATISFY'D	1	SURE-FOUNDED	1
NEW-PRESS'D	1	PEAR-TREES	1	SELF-TAUGHT	1	SWAN-FOOTED	1
NEW-ROB'D	1	PELL-MELL	1	SELF-TORMENTOR	1	SWAN-LIKE	1
NEW-SHORN	1	PELL-MELL-PACK	1	SERPENT-LIKE	1	SWEET-WINE	1
NEW-SLAIN	1	PEPPER-WATER-WORMS	1	SERPENT-MAZES	1	SWIFT-GLIDING	1
NEW-STREAMING	1	PHANTOM-SISTER	1	SERPENT-TAIL	1	SWIFT-WING'D	2
NEW-TING'D	1	PHANTOME-NATIONS	1	SERVING-MAN	1	SWINE-HERD	1
NEW-YEAR	2	PICK-LOCK	1	SET-LOOKS	1	SWORD-KNOT	3
NEWFOUND-LAND	1	PICK-POCKET	1	SETTING-SUN	1	SWORD-KNOTS	2
NEXT-BELOV'D	1	PIECE-MEAL	1	SHARP-PIERCING	1	TALL-BOY	1
NIGHT-CAP	1	PIGMY-WRETCH	1	SHIP-WRECKS	1	TAPE-TYP'D	1
NIGHT-DRESS	1	PINE-TREE	1	SHORT-LIV'D	8	TEAR-FUL	1
NIGHT-GOWN	2	PISSER-BY	1	SHORT-PANTING	1	TEAR-FULL	1
NIGHT-GUARDS	1	PISSING-POST	1	SHOULDER-BLADE	2	TEMPLE-BAR	1
NIGHT-INVASION	1	PLAIN-DEALER	2	SHOULDER-JOINT	1	TEMPLE-WALL	1
NIGHT-REFECTION	1	PLAIN-WORK	1	SIDE-BOARD	1	TEN-FOLD	1
NIGHT-WAND'RING	1	PLANE-TREE	1	SIDE-BOX	1	TEN-HORN'D	3
NO-MEANING	1	PLAY-HOUSE	1	SILK-WORM	1	TEN-YEARS	2
NO-THING	2	PLAY-THING	2	SILK-WORMS	1	TERRAS-WALK	1
NOBLY-PENSIVE	3	PLAY-THINGS	1	SILVER-FOOTED	9	THICK-DESCENDING	1
NOON-DAY	3	PLOW-SHARE	1	SILVER-QUIV'RING	1	THICK-FLAMING	2
NOON-TIDE	2	PLOW-SHARES	1	SILVER-SHAFTED	3	THIRD-DAY	1
NOONTIDE-BELL	1	PLUMY-CRESTED	1	SILVER-SOUNDING	1	THIRTY-NINE	1
NOW-DECLINING	1	POLE-AXE	2	SILVER-STREAMING	3	THIRTY-THOUSANDTH	2
NOW-NEGLECTED	1	POOR-BOX	1	SING-SONG	2	THREE-MOUTH'D	1
NURSING-MOTHER	2	POPLAR-LEAVES	1	SINGING-GIRLS	1	THREE-PENCE	1
NUT-BROWN	4	POST-BOYS	1	SIREN-COASTS	1	THREE-SCORE	1
O'ER-ARCHING	2	PRAY'R-BOOKS	1	SISE-RAH	1	THRICE-EAR'D	1
O'ER-AW'D	1	PRIEST-CRAFT	1	SISERA-HIM	1	TOIL-DETESTING	1
O'ER-LABOUR'D	1	PRINCE-LIKE	1	SISTER-ARTS	2	TOMB-STONE	1
O'ER-LEAPING	1	PROMONTORY-SHOULDER	1	SISTER-FRUITS	1	TOP-GALLANT	1
O'ER-LOOK'D	2	PROSE-MAN	1	SISTER-LOCK	1	TOP-HEAVY	2
O'ER-PAST	1	PRUNING-HOOK	1	SISTER-QUEEN	1	TORCH-LIGHT	1
O'ER-RUN	1	PURPLE-TING'D	1	SIX-PENCE	2	TOW'R-LIKE	2
O'ER-SHOOT	1	PYGMY-NATIONS	1	SKY-DY'D	1	TOWNS-MENS	1
O'ER-TOIL'D	1	QUAIL-PIPE	1	SLIP-SHOD	3	TRAIN-BANDS	1
O'ER-TOPS	1	QUICK-GLANCING	1	SLOW-CIRCLING	1	TRAYTOR-GODS	1
O'ER-WROUGHT	1	RAG-FAIR	1	SLOW-MOVING	3	TRIPLE-BOLTED	2
OCEAN-KING	1	RAIN-BOW	1	SLOW-PACING	1	TRIPOD-VASE	2
OFT-CONQUER'D	1	RAIN-BOWS	2	SLOW-WORM	1	TRIVET-TABLE	1
OFT-HEAV'D	1	REAPER-TRAIN	1	SLOWLY-GROWING	1	TUFF-TAFFETY	1
OLD-AGE	3	REBEL-KNAVE	2	SLOWLY-RISING	1	TURTLE-DOVE	2
OLD-FASHION'D	1	REBEL-WAR	1	SMALL-POX	3	TWEEZER-CASES	1
OLD-MAN'S	1	RED-HISSING	1	SMOCK-FACE	1	TWICE-MARRY'D	1
OLIVE-WAND	1	RED-HOT	1	SMOOTH-BEATEN	1	TWICE-TOLD	1
ONCE-FAM'D	1	RENT-CHARGE	1	SMOOTH-GLIDING	2	TWIN-GODS	1
ONCE-FEAR'D	1	RHYME-FREE	1	SMOOTH-HAIR'D	1	TWO-EDG'D	5
ONCE-LOV'D	5	RIGHT-HAND	1	SMOOTH-TONGU'D	1	TYRANT-MINIONS	1
ONCE-PROUD	1	RIVER-GODS	1	SNIP-SNAP	2	TYTHE-PIG	1
ONCE-STATELY	1	ROBIN-RED-BREAST	1	SNOW-WHITE	1	UNHOP'D-FOR	2
ONE-EY'D	1	ROSY-BRIGHT	2	SNUFF-BOX	2	UNLOOK'D-FOR	1
OPERA-SONG	1	ROSY-FINGER'D	3	SNUFF-BOXES	1	UNTHOUGHT-OF	1
ORANGE-TREES	1	ROUND-HOUSE	2	SOFT-CIRCLING	1	UP-BORE	2
ORCHARD-BOUNDS	1	RUFFIAN-FORCE	1	SOFT-ENAMOUR'D	1	UP-HEAV'D	2
OUT-BID	1	SABBATH-DAY	1	SOFT-EXTENDED	1	UP-HEAVING	1
OUT-CANT	1	SADLY-PLEASING	2	SOFT-EY'D	1	UP-HELD	1
OUT-CAST	1	SAFE-SEQUESTER'D	1	SOFT-SMILING	3	UP-LIFT	1
OUT-DID	1	SAIL-YARDS	2	SOFT-TOUCHING	1	UP-RISING	1
OUT-DO	2	SAINTS'-LIVES	1	SOFT-TRICKLING	1	UP-ROSE	2
OUT-DRINK	1	SCARLET-CIRCLED	1	SOFT-WHISP'RING	1	UP-SOAR'D	1
OUT-FLY	1	SCHOLE-BOY'S	1	SOFT-WHISPERING	1	UP-SPRINGING	1
OUT-GO	1	SCHOOL-BOY'S	1	SOFTLY-STEALING	1	UP-SPRUNG	1
OUT-LIE	1	SCHOOL-DIVINE	1	SOLE-INVITED	1	UP-STARTED	1
OUT-LIVES	1	SCHOOL-DIVINES	2	SORROW-STREAMING	1	UP-TURNS	1
OUT-NUMBER'D	2	SEA-BEAT	7	SOUTH-EAST	1	VAIN-GLORY	1
OUT-RAN	2	SEA-BORN	5	SOUTH-SEA	4	VAN-MUCK	1
OUT-RIDE	1	SEA-DOG	1	SOUTH-WEST	1	VARIOUS-COLOUR'D	3
OUT-SHINE	1	SEA-FARER	1	SOUTH-WINDS	1	VEAL-CUTLETS	1
OUT-SHONE	1	SEA-FOWL	1	SPLAY-FOOT	1	VERSE-MAN	1
OUT-SIDE	1	SEA-GIRT	3	SPUR-GALL'D	1	VICTIM-OX	1
OUT-SPREAD	2	SEA-GOD	3	STABLE-BOY	1	VILLAGE-TOPS	1
OUT-STERNHOLDED	1	SEA-GREEN	7	STANDARD-AUTHORS	1	VIRGIN-ARMS	1
OUT-STRETCH'D	2	SEA-HORSE	1	STANDER-BY	1	VIRGIN-CHARMS	1
OUT-STRIP'D	1	SEA-MAID'S	1	STANDERS-BY	1	VIRGIN-CHOIR	1
OUT-STRIPT	1	SEA-MEW	2	STATE-AFFAIRS	1	VIRGIN-LOVE	1
OUT-SWEAR	1	SEA-SIDE	1	STEER-MAN	1	VIRGIN-SEED	1
OUT-USURE	1	SEA-SURROUNDED	1	STERN-ISSUING	1	VIRGIN-SWORD	1
OUT-WEAR	1	SEA-WARD	2	STILL-BELIEVING	1	VIRGIN-TRAIN	1
OUT-WEIGHS	1	SEA-WEED	2	STILL-RENEW'D	1	VOUS-AVEZ	1
OUT-WHORE	1	SEA-WOLVES	1	STILL-REVIVING	1	WALLNUT-TREE	1
OVER-DRESS	1	SEAL-RINGS	1	STILL-SURVIVING	1	WAR-HORSE	1
OVER-HUNG	1	SEE-SAW	1	STRANGER-FRIEND	1	WAR-TRIUMPHANT	1
OX-LIKE	2	SEED-TIME	1	STRANGER-GUEST	10	WARRIOR-CHIEF	1
OZIER-FRINGED	1	SELF-APPLAUSE	2	STRENGTH-CONFERRING	1	WARRIOR-GOD	1
PADUA-SOY	1	SELF-APPROVING	1	STRETCH'D-OUT	1	WARRIOR-GODDESS	1
PAINS-TAKING	1	SELF-BALLANC'D	1	STRIFE-FULL	1	WARRIOR-KIND	1
PALACE-CARES	2	SELF-BANISH'D	2	STUDY-DOOR	1	WARRIOR-MAID	2
PALACE-ROOF	1	SELF-CENTRED	1	SUBJECT-HERDS	1	WARRIOR-SHIELD	1
PALACE-YARD	1	SELF-CLOS'D	1	SUITOR-CREW	1	WARRIOR-TRAIN	2
PALE-EY'D	2	SELF-CONCEIT	1	SUITOR-CROWD	4	WASTE-PAPER	1
PAPER-CREDIT	1	SELF-CONDEMN'D	1	SUITOR-POWRS	1	WATCH-TOW'R	2
PAPER-DURANCE	1	SELF-CONFIDING	1	SUITOR-THRONG	3	WAVE-WORN	1
PARCHMENT-FATES	1	SELF-CONFOUNDING	1	SUITOR-TRAIN	14	WAX-LIGHTS	1

Hyphenated Compounds in Rank Order

GOD-LIKE

GOD-LIKE	69	WISH'D-FOR	4
BLUE-EY'D	28	ALMS-HOUSE	3
SELF-LOVE	19	BEST-BELOV'D	3
WELL-KNOWN	19	BROTHER-KINGS	3
EYE-BALLS	16	CIVET-CAT	3
SUITOR-TRAIN	14	DEATH-LIKE	3
CLOUD-COMPELLING	12	DOVE-LIKE	3
ILL-FATED	12	EARTH-SHAKING	3
STRANGER-GUEST	10	EVER-DURING	3
ALL-SEEING	9	EYE-BALL	3
MILK-WHITE	9	FOOT-STOOL	3
SILVER-FOOTED	9	FORE-RUNNER	3
NEW-BORN	8	FORTH-ISSUING	3
SHORT-LIV'D	8	GODDESS-BORN	3
WELL-BRED	8	GRUB-STREET	3
BULL-HIDES	7	GUILD-HALL	3
DRURY-LANE	7	HALF-FORM'D	3
HOARSE-RESOUNDING	7	HAM-PYE	3
MUCH-LOV'D	7	HEAV'N-DIRECTED	3
SEA-BEAT	7	HEAV'N-TAUGHT	3
SEA-GREEN	7	HIGH-BORN	3
WELL-FOUGHT	7	HIGH-HEAP'D	3
WELL-PLEAS'D	7	HIGH-WROUGHT	3
EVER-HONOUR'D	6	HOCKLEY-HOLE	3
FIRST-BORN	6	LAP-DOGS	3
MANY-COLOUR'D	6	LAUGHTER-LOVING	3
MUCH-ENDURING	6	LINCOLN'S-INN	3
WELL-FED	6	LONG-DESCENDING	3
WHAT-TIME	6	LONG-WINDED	3
ALE-HOUSE	5	LOW-BORN	3
FAIR-HAIR'D	5	NEW-MADE	3
FAR-BEAMING	5	NOBLY-PENSIVE	3
FAR-FAM'D	5	NOON-DAY	3
FULL-FED	5	OLD-AGE	3
GOOD-NATURE	5	ROSY-FINGER'D	3
HIGH-BOUNDING	5	SEA-GIRT	3
HUMAN-KIND	5	SEA-GOD	3
ONCE-LOV'D	5	SELF-MOV'D	3
SEA-BORN	5	SELF-SAME	3
TWO-EDG'D	5	SILVER-SHAFTED	3
WIDE-EXTENDED	5	SILVER-STREAMING	3
ALL-COMPOSING	4	SLIP-SHOD	3
ALL-SUBDUING	4	SLOW-MOVING	3
BLACK-EY'D	4	SMALL-POX	3
COURT-BADGE	4	SOFT-SMILING	3
DEAR-BOUGHT	4	SUITOR-THRONG	3
EARTH-BORN	4	SUN-SHINE	3
EVER-PLEASING	4	SWORD-KNOT	3
GILL-HOUSE	4	TEN-HORN'D	3
GODDESS-MOTHER	4	VARIOUS-COLOUR'D	3
HEART-WOUNDED	4	WELL-BREATH'D	3
HEAV'N-DEFENDED	4	WELL-DEFENDED	3
HIGH-THRON'D	4	WELL-DISPUTED	3
HOME-FELT	4	WELL-DREST	3
HORSE-HAIR	4	WELL-PURG'D	3
ILL-TIM'D	4	WELL-SKILL'D	3
JOVE-DESCENDED	4	WELL-TAUGHT	3
LONG-CONTENDED	4	WELL-WEIGH'D	3
LONG-CONTINU'D	4	WEST-WIND	3
LONG-EXPECTED	4	WHITE-ARM'D	3
NEVER-BLUSHING	4	WHITE-HALL	3
NUT-BROWN	4	WORD-CATCHER	3
SOUTH-SEA	4	AIR-BUILT	2
SUITOR-CROWD	4	ALL-ACCOMPLISH'D	2
WELL-AIM'D	4	ALL-BEHOLDING	2
WELL-COMPACTED	4	ALL-BOUNTEOUS	2

SCHOOL-DIVINES

ALL-CONQU'RING	2	ILL-GOT	2
ALL-CONSCIOUS	2	ILL-OMEN'D	2
ALL-CONSID'RING	2	ILL-STARR'D	2
ALL-DEVOURING	2	IN-URN	2
ALL-INVOLVING	2	INDEX-LEARNING	2
ALL-KNOWING	2	JAW-BONE	2
ALL-WISE	2	JOVE-BORN	2
BEAU-MONDE	2	KEY-HOLE	2
BLOOD-POLLUTED	2	LEFT-HAND	2
BLOOD-STAIN'D	2	LIFE-CONSUMING	2
BRASS-HOOF'D	2	LONG-ABSENT	2
BROTHER-WARRIORS	2	LONG-DEFENDED	2
CAT-CALL	2	LONG-EAR'D	2
CAT-CALLS	2	LONG-EXTENDED	2
CHANC'RY-LANE	2	LONG-FORGOTTEN	2
CHARING-CROSS	2	LONG-SUCCEEDING	2
CLOUD-COMPELLER	2	LOUD-ACCLAIMING	2
COCKLE-KIND	2	LOUD-RESOUNDING	2
COMMON-PLACE	2	LOVE-BORN	2
COW-HIDE	2	LOVE-DARTING	2
DAB-CHICK	2	LOVE-SICK	2
DEAD-BORN	2	LOW-HUNG	2
DEATH-BED	2	MANY-HEADED	2
DEMI-GOD	2	MANY-LANGUAG'D	2
DOG-STAR'S	2	MASTER-PIECE	2
DOUBLE-EDG'D	2	MATRON-TRAIN	2
DOWN-RIGHT	2	MAY-POLE	2
DRY-NURSE	2	MID-MOST	2
DUE-DISTANT	2	MILO-LIKE	2
ELDEST-BORN	2	MONKEY-TAILS	2
EVER-MUSING	2	MONSTER-BREEDING	2
EVER-WAKEFUL	2	MOUNTAIN-WOLVES	2
FAIR-ONES	2	MUCH-EXPERIENC'D	2
FAR-SEEN	2	MUCH-SUFF'RING	2
FAR-STREAMING	2	MUD-NYMPHS	2
FEAST-RITES	2	MUSE-RID	2
FIG-TREES	2	NEW-BENEFIC'D	2
FIRM-ROOTED	2	NEW-BUILT	2
FIRST-RATE	2	NEW-MARKET'S	2
FLEET-DITCH	2	NEW-YEAR	2
FOOL'S-CAP	2	NIGHT-GOWN	2
FORE-BUTTOCKS	2	NO-THING	2
FORE-DOOM'D	2	NOON-TIDE	2
FORE-RIGHT	2	NURSING-MOTHER	2
FOUNT-FUL	2	O'ER-ARCHING	2
FREE-MASONS	2	O'ER-LOOK'D	2
FREE-THINKER	2	OUT-DO	2
FULL-BLOWN	2	OUT-NUMBER'D	2
GIN-SHOPS	2	OUT-RAN	2
GLOW-WORM	2	OUT-SPREAD	2
GOD-LESS	2	OUT-STRETCH'D	2
GRAY-GOOSE-WEAPON	2	OX-LIKE	2
HALF-REAS'NING	2	PALACE-CARES	2
HALF-SHUT	2	PALE-EY'D	2
HAND-MAID	2	PATRON-GOD	2
HEART-CORRODING	2	PEAR-TREE	2
HEART-PIERCING	2	PLAIN-DEALER	2
HEAV'N-BORN	2	PLAY-THING	2
HEAV'N-BRED	2	POLE-AXE	2
HEAV'N-BUILT	2	RAIN-BOWS	2
HIGH-CURLING	2	REBEL-KNAVE	2
HIGH-DUTCH	2	ROSY-BRIGHT	2
HIGH-HELD	2	ROUND-HOUSE	2
HIGH-LIFTED	2	SADLY-PLEASING	2
HIGH-TOW'RING	2	SAIL-YARDS	2
HUMMING-BIRD	2	SCHOOL-DIVINES	2

SEA-MEW	2	BEST-BUILT	1	EARTH-SHAKER	1	GODDESS-TRAIN	1
SEA-WARD	2	BEST-LOV'D	1	EV'NING-SPY	1	GOLD-CAPT	1
SEA-WEED	2	BIG-UDDER'D	1	EVE-REPAST	1	GOOD-HUMOUR	1
SELF-APPLAUSE	2	BIRTH-NIGHT	1	EVENING-FRIENDS	1	GOOD-NATUR'D	1
SELF-BANISH'D	2	BIRTH-NIGHTS	1	EVER-ANXIOUS	1	GOOD-SENSE	1
SELF-PLEASING	2	BLACK-JOKE	1	EVER-BLOOMING	1	GOOSE-PYE	1
SHOULDER-BLADE	2	BLOOMSB'RY-SQUARE	1	EVER-CONSECRATING	1	GOOSE-RUMP'D	1
SING-SONG	2	BLUE-HAIR'D	1	EVER-DREADFUL	1	GRACE-CUP	1
SISTER-ARTS	2	BOOK-WORMS	1	EVER-FERTILE	1	GRAND-SONS	1
SIX-PENCE	2	BOSOME-WIFE	1	EVER-FLOWING	1	GRATIS-GIVEN	1
SMOOTH-GLIDING	2	BOW-STRING	1	EVER-FRAGRANT	1	GRAY-HAIR'D	1
SNIP-SNAP	2	BOY-SENATOR	1	EVER-FRUITFUL	1	GREAT-MAN'S	1
SNUFF-BOX	2	BRASS-CHEEK'D	1	EVER-GENTLE	1	GREATLY-DARING	1
SUN-BEAMS	2	BRAVELY-PATIENT	1	EVER-INJUR'D	1	GREY-GOOSE	1
SWIFT-WING'D	2	BRAZEN-POINTED	1	EVER-LISTLESS	1	GREY-HAIR'D	1
SWORD-KNOTS	2	BRIDAL-ROOM	1	EVER-LIVING	1	GRUBSTREET-STATE	1
TEN-YEARS	2	BRIGHT-EY'D	1	EVER-MINGLING	1	GUIDE-LESS	1
THICK-FLAMING	2	BRIGHTLY-DAWNING	1	EVER-OPEN	1	GUILD-HALL'S	1
THIRTY-THOUSANDTH	2	BROAD-GLITT'RING	1	EVER-SHADY	1	HACKNEY-COACH	1
TOP-HEAVY	2	BROAD-PATCH'D	1	EVER-VERDANT	1	HAIR-SHIRT	1
TOW'R-LIKE	2	BROTHER-CHIEF	1	EVER-WATCHFUL	1	HALF-APPROVING	1
TRIPLE-BOLTED	2	BROTHER-CHIEFS	1	EVER-YOUNG	1	HALF-BREATHLESS	1
TRIPOD-VASE	2	BROTHER-LEADERS	1	EYE-BROW	1	HALF-BROTHER	1
TURTLE-DOVE	2	BUBBLE-BOY	1	EYE-BROWN	1	HALF-BURN'D	1
UNHOP'D-FOR	2	BULL-DOGS	1	EYE-LIDS	1	HALF-CUR'D	1
UP-BORE	2	BULL-HIDE	1	EYE-SIGHT	1	HALF-DROWN'D	1
UP-HEAV'D	2	BURNT-OFF'RING	1	FAIR-ONE'S	1	HALF-EAT	1
UP-ROSE	2	CAELESTIAL-SWEET	1	FAIR-STREAMING	1	HALF-EXTINGUISH'D	1
WARRIOR-MAID	2	CASTING-WEIGHT	1	FAIR-ZON'D	1	HALF-FORC'D	1
WARRIOR-TRAIN	2	CASTLE-WALL	1	FANCY-FORM'D	1	HALF-HEARD	1
WATCH-TOW'R	2	CAUSE-WAY	1	FAR-DREADED	1	HALF-HUNG	1
WELL-BUILT	2	CEDAR-BEAMS	1	FAR-ECHOING	1	HALF-LANGUISHING	1
WELL-DISSEMBLED	2	CELL-BRED	1	FAR-PIERCING	1	HALF-LEARN'D	1
WELL-FILL'D	2	CHAOS-LIKE	1	FAR-RESOUNDING	1	HALF-OPEN'D	1
WELL-NATUR'D	2	CHAPEL-ROYAL	1	FAR-SHOOTING	1	HALF-PERSUADED	1
WELL-SPENT	2	CHARIOT-SIDE	1	FAR-STRETCHING	1	HALF-PINT	1
WELL-STRUNG	2	CHILD-LIKE	1	FAST-FALLING	1	HALF-RECOVER'D	1
WELL-SUNG	2	CHINA-JORDAN	1	FAST-FLOWING	1	HALF-TILL'D	1
WELL-TEMPER'D	2	CHRIST-CHURCH	1	FATE-FUL	1	HALF-VIEWLESS	1
WELL-TIM'D	2	CHRISTMAS-TIDE	1	FEAST-FUL	1	HAMPTON-COURT	1
WELL-TURN'D	2	CHURCH-WARDENS	1	FEAST-FULL	1	HANG-DOGS	1
WELL-WROUGHT	2	CHURCH-YARD	1	FELLOW-CHARIOTEER	1	HARD-BOUND	1
WHITE-GLOV'D	2	CITRON-WATERS	1	FELLOW-OPERATOR	1	HARD-GOT	1
WIDE-OPENING	2	CITY-BOWL	1	FIERCE-RUSHING	1	HARVEST-BUG	1
WILD-FIRE	2	CITY-GATE	1	FIERY-HELM'D	1	HAWK-NOS'D	1
WIND-GUNS	2	CITY-SWANS	1	FIG-TREE	1	HEAD-DRESS	1
WINTER-SNOW	2	CITY-TRIBES	1	FINNY-PREY	1	HEAD-LONG	1
WRY-MOUTH'D	2	CIVET-CATS	1	FIRST-FRUITS	1	HEART-EXPANDING	1
YET-WARM	2	CLARE-HALL	1	FLOCK-BED	1	HEART-FELT	1
ABCHURCH-LANE	1	CLAY-COLD	1	FLY-BLOW	1	HEAV'N-DISCOVER'D	1
ABS-COURT	1	CLOSE-COMPACTED	1	FOOL-GALLANT	1	HEAV'N-GATES	1
AIR-BRED	1	CLOSE-COMPELL'D	1	FOOL-RENOWN'D	1	HEAV'N-ILLUMIN'D	1
ALL-A-ROW	1	CLOSE-EMBODY'D	1	FOOL'S-COATS	1	HEAV'N-INSTRUCTED	1
ALL-ARRAIGNING	1	CLOSE-RANG'D	1	FOOLS-COLOURS	1	HEAV'N-PROTECTED	1
ALL-ASSISTLESS	1	CLOUD-TOPT	1	FORE-CAST	1	HEAV'NLY-PENSIVE	1
ALL-BEARING	1	CO-AIDS	1	FORE-DOOM	1	HIDE-BOUND	1
ALL-BEAUTEOUS	1	COBLER-LIKE	1	FORE-FATHER	1	HIDE-PARK	1
ALL-BEAUTIFUL	1	COCK-HORSE	1	FORE-FATHERS	1	HIGH-BALANC'D	1
ALL-COMPELLING	1	COLUMBUS-LIKE	1	FORE-HAND	1	HIGH-BLAZING	1
ALL-CONFIRMING	1	COMMON-SHOAR	1	FORE-PIECE	1	HIGH-BRANDISH'D	1
ALL-CONSUMING	1	COMPTING-HOUSE	1	FORE-RUNS	1	HIGH-FLAMING	1
ALL-COV'RING	1	COOK-MAID	1	FORTH-BEAMING	1	HIGH-FOAMING	1
ALL-CREATING	1	CORN-LOFT	1	FORTH-SPRINGING	1	HIGH-HUNG	1
ALL-DESTROYING	1	CORN-VAN	1	FORTUNE-STRUCK	1	HIGH-LIFTING	1
ALL-DIFFUSIVE	1	COUNCIL-BOARD	1	FOSTER-FATHER-MOTHER	1	HIGH-O'ERARCH'D	1
ALL-ELOQUENT	1	COUNTER-CHARMS	1	FOUL-MOUTH'D	1	HIGH-POINTING	1
ALL-EMBRACING	1	COUNTER-WORK	1	FOUNT-FULL	1	HIGH-RAIS'D	1
ALL-ENLIGHT'NING	1	COUNTER-WORKS	1	FOUNTAIN-SIDE	1	HIGH-RESENTING	1
ALL-ENLIGHTEN'D	1	COURSER-BREEDING	1	FOUR-FOLD	1	HIGH-STRETCH'D	1
ALL-EXTENDING	1	COURT-SYCOPHANT	1	FOUR-WHEEL'D	1	HIGH-WAY	1
ALL-GOVERNING	1	COURT-VIRTUES	1	FOX-CHACE	1	HOARSER-SCREAMING	1
ALL-IMPAIRING	1	COW-LIKE	1	FREE-BORN	1	HOLLAND-SMOCKS	1
ALL-IMPOTENT	1	COW-LIKE-UDDERS	1	FREE-OPENING	1	HOME-BORN	1
ALL-INFOLDING	1	COWARD-COUNSELS	1	FRESH-BLEEDING	1	HOME-BRED	1
ALL-POW'RFUL	1	COXCOMB-PYES	1	FRESH-SLAUGHTER'D	1	HOME-SPUN	1
ALL-PRESERVING	1	CUCKOLD-MAKER'S	1	FRONT-BOX	1	HONEY-COMBS	1
ALL-PREVENTING	1	CURTAIN-LECTURES	1	FRONT-BOXES	1	HONEY-TEMPER'D	1
ALL-QUICK'NING	1	CYNDER-WENCHES	1	FRUIT-GROVES	1	HORS-D'OEUVRES	1
ALL-RECORDING	1	DAMSEL-TRAIN	1	FULL-DESCENDING	1	HORSE-LAUGH	1
ALL-REMEMBRING	1	DAY-DEVOURER	1	FURY-GODDESS	1	HORSE-TAIL	1
ALL-REVEALING	1	DAY-DISTRACTING	1	FURY-PASSIONS	1	HOUNSLOW-HEATH	1
ALL-RIGHTEOUS	1	DAY-LIGHT	1	GALLO-GRECIAN	1	HOUSE-TOP	1
ALL-SURROUNDING	1	DEAR-LOV'D	1	GARDEN-GATE	1	HUNCH-BACK'D	1
ALL-SURVEYING	1	DEATH-WATCHES	1	GIANT-BABE	1	HUNTER-TROOP	1
ALL-SUSTAINING	1	DEEP-DISCERNING	1	GIANT-CORSE	1	HUSBAND-BULL	1
ALL-TO-BREST	1	DEEP-ECHOING	1	GIANT-GLUTTON	1	HYDE-PARK-CORNER	1
ALOM-STYPTICKS	1	DEEP-FURROW'D	1	GIANT-HUNTER	1	IDOL-GODS	1
ANGEL-LIKE	1	DEEP-IMAG'D	1	GIANT-LOVER	1	ILL-CONTESTED	1
ANGEL-POW'RS	1	DEEP-MOUTH'D	1	GIANT-MONSTERS	1	ILL-EXCHANG'D	1
APE-AND-MONKEY	1	DEEP-MUSING	1	GIANT-PRIDE	1	ILL-GOTTEN	1
ARCH-POET	1	DEEP-PIERCING	1	GIANT-SHEPHERD	1	ILL-GROUNDED	1
ARTIST-GOD	1	DEEP-PROJECTING	1	GIANT-SON	1	ILL-INCLIN'D	1
AT-HOME	1	DEEP-ROOTED	1	GIANT-SONS	1	ILL-JUDGING	1
ATHEIST-WRETCH	1	DEMI-GODS	1	GIANT-STRIDES	1	ILL-LOOK'D	1
AUTUMN-HEATS	1	DINNER-TIME	1	GIANT-VICE	1	ILL-MATCH'D	1
BACK-PLATE	1	DOG-DAYS	1	GIANT-WARRIOR	1	ILL-NATURE	1
BACK-STAIRS	1	DOG-HOLE	1	GOAT-NURS'D	1	ILL-PAIR'D	1
BANK-BILL	1	DOG-STAR	1	GOAT-SKINS	1	ILL-PERSUADING	1
BANSTED-DOWN	1	DOUBLE-CLASPING	1	GOAT'S-MILK	1	ILL-REQUITED	1
BASE-BORN	1	DOUBLE-TAX'D	1	GOD-BUILT	1	ILL-RESTRAIN'D	1
BEAN-SHELL	1	DRAWING-ROOM	1	GOD-DESCENDED	1	ILL-SUITING	1
BEAU-KIND	1	DUCK-LANE	1	GOD-SAKE	1	ILL-US'D	1
BEDFORD-HEAD	1	EAGLE-SPEED	1	GOD'S-NAME	1	IN-BORN	1
BEECH-TREE	1	EAR-RINGS	1	GOD'S-SAKE	1	INDEX-HAND	1
BEECH-TREE'S	1	EARL'S-COURT	1	GODDESS-LIKE	1	INFANT-CHEEKS	1

INLY-PINING	1	MORNING-COCK	1	PALACE-ROOF	1	SHIP-WRECKS	1
INMOST-WINDING	1	MORNING-DREAM	1	PALACE-YARD	1	SHORT-PANTING	1
INN-KEEPERS	1	MORNING-HOUR	1	PAPER-CREDIT	1	SHOULDER-JOINT	1
INSECT-WINGS	1	MORNING-PRAY'R	1	PAPER-DURANCE	1	SIDE-BOARD	1
IRE-FULL	1	MORNING-PRAYER	1	PARCHMENT-FATES	1	SIDE-BOX	1
IRON-HEART	1	MORNING-TIDE	1	PARENT-GOD	1	SILK-WORM	1
IRON-HEARTED	1	MORNING-WALKS	1	PARENT-QUEEN	1	SILK-WORMS	1
IRON-MACE	1	MOSS-GROWN	1	PARTY-COLOUR'D	1	SILVER-QUIV'RING	1
IV'RY-STUDDED	1	MOTHER-BIRD	1	PARTY-RAGE	1	SILVER-SOUNDING	1
JOVE-LIKE	1	MOTHER-LION	1	PARTY-ZEALOTS	1	SINGING-GIRLS	1
JURY-MEN	1	MOTHER-MASTIFF	1	PASTERN-BONE	1	SIREN-COASTS	1
KEEN-EDG'D	1	MOUNTAIN-BILLOW	1	PATCH-BOX	1	SISE-RAH	1
KING-CUP	1	MOUNTAIN-EYRIE	1	PATCH-WORK	1	SISERA-HIM	1
LADY-LAP-DOG-SHIP	1	MOUNTAIN-GOAT	1	PATRIARCH-WITS	1	SISTER-FRUITS	1
LADY-LIKE	1	MOUNTAIN-GROUND	1	PATRON-NAME	1	SISTER-LOCK	1
LANCE-FAM'D	1	MOUNTAIN-HEADS	1	PEA-CHICKS	1	SISTER-QUEEN	1
LAP-DOG	1	MOUNTAIN-LIONS	1	PEAR-TREES	1	SKY-DY'D	1
LARGE-ACRED	1	MOUNTAIN-OAK	1	PELL-MELL	1	SLOW-CIRCLING	1
LATE-IMPERVIOUS	1	MOUNTAIN-SHOULDERS	1	PELL-MELL-PACK	1	SLOW-PACING	1
LATE-IMPRISON'D	1	MOURNING-BRIDE	1	PEPPER-WATER-WORMS	1	SLOW-WORM	1
LATE-PREFERR'D	1	MUCH-ADVISING	1	PHANTOM-SISTER	1	SLOWLY-GROWING	1
LATE-RETURNING	1	MUCH-AFFLICTED	1	PHANTOME-NATIONS	1	SLOWLY-RISING	1
LATE-TRANSFORM'D	1	MUCH-INJUR'D	1	PICK-LOCK	1	SMOCK-FACE	1
LAWREL-FOLIAGE	1	MUSTARD-BOWL	1	PICK-POCKET	1	SMOOTH-BEATEN	1
LEAF-LESS	1	MUSTER-ROLL	1	PIECE-MEAL	1	SMOOTH-HAIR'D	1
LEFT-LEGG'D	1	NAVY-BUILDING	1	PIGMY-WRETCH	1	SMOOTH-TONGU'D	1
LEVEE-DAY	1	NAVY-WALL	1	PINE-TREE	1	SNOW-WHITE	1
LIFE-BLOOD	1	NAVY-WALLS	1	PISSER-BY	1	SNUFF-BOXES	1
LIFE-LIKE	1	NEVER-CEASING	1	PISSING-POST	1	SOFT-CIRCLING	1
LIFE-SUSTAINING	1	NEVER-DYING	1	PLAIN-WORK	1	SOFT-ENAMOUR'D	1
LIGHT-ARM'D	1	NEVER-ERRING	1	PLANE-TREE	1	SOFT-EXTENDED	1
LIGHT-BOUNDING	1	NEVER-FAILING	1	PLAY-HOUSE	1	SOFT-EY'D	1
LIGHT-FOOT	1	NEVER-WEARY'D	1	PLAY-THINGS	1	SOFT-TOUCHING	1
LILLY-SILVER'D	1	NEW-ACCEPTED	1	PLOW-SHARE	1	SOFT-TRICKLING	1
LIME-TWIGS	1	NEW-EAR'D	1	PLOW-SHARES	1	SOFT-WHISP'RING	1
LINK-BOYS	1	NEW-FALL'N	1	PLUMY-CRESTED	1	SOFT-WHISPERING	1
LINSEY-WOLSEY	1	NEW-MARKET-FAME	1	POOR-BOX	1	SOFTLY-STEALING	1
LINSEY-WOOLSEY	1	NEW-PENSION'D	1	POPLAR-LEAVES	1	SOLE-INVITED	1
LION-HEARTED	1	NEW-PRESS'D	1	POST-BOYS	1	SORROW-STREAMING	1
LIVE-LONG	1	NEW-ROB'D	1	PRAY'R-BOOKS	1	SOUTH-EAST	1
LOBSTER-NIGHTS	1	NEW-SHORN	1	PRIEST-CRAFT	1	SOUTH-WEST	1
LONG-APPLAUDING	1	NEW-SLAIN	1	PRINCE-LIKE	1	SOUTH-WINDS	1
LONG-DESTROYING	1	NEW-STREAMING	1	PROMONTORY-SHOULDER	1	SPLAY-FOOT	1
LONG-DISPUTED	1	NEW-TING'D	1	PROSE-MAN	1	SPUR-GALL'D	1
LONG-DIVIDED	1	NEWFOUND-LAND	1	PRUNING-HOOK	1	STABLE-BOY	1
LONG-FEST'RING	1	NEXT-BELOV'D	1	PURPLE-TING'D	1	STANDARD-AUTHORS	1
LONG-LAB'RING	1	NIGHT-CAP	1	PYGMY-NATIONS	1	STANDER-BY	1
LONG-LINGRING	1	NIGHT-DRESS	1	QUAIL-PIPE	1	STANDERS-BY	1
LONG-PREDESTIN'D	1	NIGHT-GUARDS	1	QUICK-GLANCING	1	STATE-AFFAIRS	1
LONG-PROJECTED	1	NIGHT-INVASION	1	RAG-FAIR	1	STEER-MAN	1
LONG-PROTENDED	1	NIGHT-REFECTION	1	RAIN-BOW	1	STERN-ISSUING	1
LONG-PROTRACTED	1	NIGHT-WAND'RING	1	REAPER-TRAIN	1	STILL-BELIEVING	1
LONG-REFULGENT	1	NO-MEANING	1	REBEL-WAR	1	STILL-RENEW'D	1
LONG-REPENTED	1	NOONTIDE-BELL	1	RED-HISSING	1	STILL-REVIVING	1
LONG-RESOUNDING	1	NOW-DECLINING	1	RED-HOT	1	STILL-SURVIVING	1
LONG-SOUNDING	1	NOW-NEGLECTED	1	RENT-CHARGE	1	STRANGER-FRIEND	1
LONG-WEARY'D	1	O'ER-AW'D	1	RHYME-FREE	1	STRENGTH-CONFERRING	1
LONG-WING'D	1	O'ER-LABOUR'D	1	RIGHT-HAND	1	STRETCH'D-OUT	1
LOOKERS-ON	1	O'ER-LEAPING	1	RIVER-GODS	1	STRIFE-FULL	1
LORD-CHANCELLOR	1	O'ER-PAST	1	ROBIN-RED-BREAST	1	STUDY-DOOR	1
LOUD-EXULTING	1	O'ER-RUN	1	RUFFIAN-FORCE	1	SUBJECT-HERDS	1
LOUD-INSULTING	1	O'ER-SHOOT	1	SABBATH-DAY	1	SUITOR-CREW	1
LOUD-THREATNING	1	O'ER-TOIL'D	1	SAFE-SEQUESTER'D	1	SUITOR-POWRS	1
LOUD-TONGU'D	1	O'ER-TOPS	1	SAINTS'-LIVES	1	SULPHUR-TIPT	1
LOVE-DEBATES	1	O'ER-WROUGHT	1	SCARLET-CIRCLED	1	SUMMER-DAYS	1
LOVE-DITTIED	1	OCEAN-KING	1	SCHOLE-BOY'S	1	SUMMER-HOUSE	1
LOVE-RITES	1	OFT-CONQUER'D	1	SCHOOL-BOY'S	1	SUMMER-NOON	1
LOVE-WHISP'RING	1	OFT-HEAV'D	1	SCHOOL-DIVINE	1	SUN-BORN	1
LOW-BENDING	1	OLD-FASHION'D	1	SEA-DOG	1	SUN-BRUNT	1
LOW-BROW'D	1	OLD-MAN'S	1	SEA-FARER	1	SUN-BURNT	1
LOW-COUCH'D	1	OLIVE-WAND	1	SEA-FOWL	1	SUN-SET	1
LOW-DEPENDING	1	ONCE-FAM'D	1	SEA-HORSE	1	SUNDAY-MORN	1
LOW-DUTCH	1	ONCE-FEAR'D	1	SEA-MAID'S	1	SUPER-LUNAR	1
LOW-SINKING	1	ONCE-PROUD	1	SEA-SIDE	1	SURE-FOUNDED	1
LOW-THOUGHTED	1	ONCE-STATELY	1	SEA-SURROUNDED	1	SWAN-FOOTED	1
LOW-WHISPER'D	1	ONE-EY'D	1	SEA-WOLVES	1	SWAN-LIKE	1
LUTE-RESOUNDING	1	OPERA-SONG	1	SEAL-RINGS	1	SWEET-WINE	1
MAD-MAN	1	ORANGE-TREES	1	SEE-SAW	1	SWIFT-GLIDING	1
MAIN-MAST	1	ORCHARD-BOUNDS	1	SEED-TIME	1	SWINE-HERD	1
MAJOR-GENERAL	1	OUT-BID	1	SELF-APPROVING	1	TALL-BOY	1
MANY-PEOPLED	1	OUT-CANT	1	SELF-BALLANC'D	1	TAPE-TYP'D	1
MARKET-PLACE	1	OUT-CAST	1	SELF-CENTRED	1	TEAR-FUL	1
MARROW-BONE	1	OUT-DID	1	SELF-CLOS'D	1	TEAR-FULL	1
MARS-LIKE	1	OUT-DRINK	1	SELF-CONCEIT	1	TEMPLE-BAR	1
MARTYR-KING	1	OUT-FLY	1	SELF-CONDEMN'D	1	TEMPLE-WALL	1
MASTER-HAND	1	OUT-GO	1	SELF-CONFIDING	1	TEN-FOLD	1
MATRON-BROW	1	OUT-LIE	1	SELF-CONFOUNDING	1	TERRAS-WALK	1
MERRY-MEN	1	OUT-LIVES	1	SELF-CONQUER'D	1	THICK-DESCENDING	1
METEOR-LIKE	1	OUT-RIDE	1	SELF-CONSIDERING	1	THIRD-DAY	1
MID-DAY-DEVIL	1	OUT-SHINE	1	SELF-CONSUMING	1	THIRTY-NINE	1
MILD-COMMAND	1	OUT-SHONE	1	SELF-DEBATE	1	THREE-MOUTH'D	1
MILK-PAIL	1	OUT-SIDE	1	SELF-DEFENCE	1	THREE-PENCE	1
MINSTREL-GOD	1	OUT-STERNHOLDED	1	SELF-ENSLAV'D	1	THREE-SCORE	1
MIRTH-INSPIRING	1	OUT-STRIP'D	1	SELF-EXPLAIN'D	1	THRICE-EAR'D	1
MONARCH-SAVAGE	1	OUT-STRIPT	1	SELF-MURDER'D	1	TOIL-DETESTING	1
MONEY-LOVING	1	OUT-SWEAR	1	SELF-SATISFY'D	1	TOMB-STONE	1
MONKEY-MIMICKS	1	OUT-USURE	1	SELF-TAUGHT	1	TOP-GALLANT	1
MONKEY-MIMICS	1	OUT-WEAR	1	SELF-TORMENTOR	1	TORCH-LIGHT	1
MONKEY-TAIL	1	OUT-WEIGHS	1	SERPENT-LIKE	1	TOWNS-MENS	1
MONMOUTH-STREET	1	OUT-WHORE	1	SERPENT-MAZES	1	TRAIN-BANDS	1
MONSTER-GOD	1	OVER-DRESS	1	SERPENT-TAIL	1	TRAYTOR-GODS	1
MOON-BEAM	1	OVER-HUNG	1	SERVING-MAN	1	TRIVET-TABLE	1
MOON-LIGHT	1	OZIER-FRINGED	1	SET-LOOKS	1	TUFF-TAFFETY	1
MOON-STRUCK	1	PADUA-SOY	1	SETTING-SUN	1	TWEEZER-CASES	1
MORNING-BEAMS	1	PAINS-TAKING	1	SHARP-PIERCING	1	TWICE-MARRY'D	1

TWICE-TOLD	1	WAR-TRIUMPHANT	1	WELL-HORN'D	1	WIDE-WATER'D	1
TWIN-GODS	1	WARRIOR-CHIEF	1	WELL-KNIT	1	WIDE-WAVING	1
TYRANT-MINIONS	1	WARRIOR-GOD	1	WELL-LABOUR'D	1	WIND-MILL	1
TYTHE-PIG	1	WARRIOR-GODDESS	1	WELL-MATCH'D	1	WIND-PIPE	1
UNLOOK'D-FOR	1	WARRIOR-KIND	1	WELL-MIX'D	1	WINDSOR-DOMES	1
UNTHOUGHT-OF	1	WARRIOR-SHIELD	1	WELL-MOUTH'D	1	WINDSOR-SHADE	1
UP-HEAVING	1	WASTE-PAPER	1	WELL-PAIR'D	1	WINDSOR-SHADES	1
UP-HELD	1	WAVE-WORN	1	WELL-PLY'D	1	WINTER-FRUITS	1
UP-LIFT	1	WAX-LIGHTS	1	WELL-POLISH'D	1	WINTER-SNOWS	1
UP-RISING	1	WAY-FARING	1	WELL-PROPORTION'D	1	WISE-MAN	1
UP-SOAR'D	1	WEDDING-DAY	1	WELL-PROV'D	1	WITNESS-JUDGE	1
UP-SPRINGING	1	WEEK-DAY	1	WELL-RANG'D	1	WOLF-LIKE	1
UP-SPRUNG	1	WELL-APPOINTED	1	WELL-RIGG'D	1	WOMAN-GLUTTON	1
UP-STARTED	1	WELL-ARM'D	1	WELL-ROW'D	1	WOMAN-KIND	1
UP-TURNS	1	WELL-ATTENDING	1	WELL-SEASON'D	1	WOMAN-LIKE	1
VAIN-GLORY	1	WELL-BELOV'D	1	WELL-STOR'D	1	WOMAN-SLAVE	1
VAN-MUCK	1	WELL-BODIED	1	WELL-STUDY'D	1	WOMAN-STATE	1
VEAL-CUTLETS	1	WELL-BODY'D	1	WELL-SUITING	1	WOMAN-WARRIOR	1
VERSE-MAN	1	WELL-COLOUR'D	1	WELL-TRY'D	1	WOMAN-WORLD	1
VICTIM-OX	1	WELL-CONCERTED	1	WELL-TUN'D	1	WOOD-MAN	1
VILLAGE-TOPS	1	WELL-CONSENTING	1	WELL-WHIPT	1	WOOD-MAN'S	1
VIRGIN-ARMS	1	WELL-DEFENDING	1	WELL-WORN	1	WOOD-MEN	1
VIRGIN-CHARMS	1	WELL-DIRECTED	1	WHAT-ERE	1	WOODEN-SHOES	1
VIRGIN-CHOIR	1	WELL-DISPERS'D	1	WHEN-E'ER	1	WORTH-LESS	1
VIRGIN-LOVE	1	WELL-DISSEMBL'D	1	WHIG-MINISTERS	1	WRONG-HEAD	1
VIRGIN-SEED	1	WELL-DRAWN	1	WHITE-ROAB'D	1	YET-REMAINING	1
VIRGIN-SWORD	1	WELL-FATTED	1	WIDE-BEAMING	1	YET-SURVIVING	1
VIRGIN-TRAIN	1	WELL-FEIGN'D	1	WIDE-PATCH'D	1	YET-UNCONQUER'D	1
VOUS-AVEZ	1	WELL-GUARDED	1	WIDE-ROLLING	1	YET-UNRIVAL'D	1
WALLNUT-TREE	1	WELL-HARDEN'D	1	WIDE-WASTING	1	YET-UNTASTED	1
WAR-HORSE	1					ZIG-ZAGS	1

Lines with the Same Wording in
Both Versions of The Rape of the Lock

The following table identifies each line in the first 1712—RL*A*) version of *The Rape of the Lock* (consisting of two cantos) that is substantially the same as a line variant in the second (1714—RL) version (consisting five cantos). Lines that are identical are marked with a us (+): all the others in the list are the same in words d word order, differing only in punctuation, spelling .g., "locke," RL*A*; "lock," RL), capitalization, spacing, italicization, except for two instances in which a word rm changes ("Lady" in RL*A*2.6; "Ladies" in RL4.6; pread" in RL*A*2.13; "spreads" in RL4.95). Of the 334

lines in the 1712 poem, 239 lines are identical to lines or variants in the 1714 version; 63 are substantially the same by the foregoing criteria. Of the lines in the 1714 version used in this comparison 27 are variants (identified by a letter following the line number); 22 of the variants are identical to the corresponding 1712 line, and 5 are substantially the same. (The *Concordance* quotes all the lines and significant variants of the 1714 poem and the 32 lines of the 1712 poem that have wording different from the later version.)

1714 Canto	1714 Line	1712 Canto	1712 Line	1714 Canto	1714 Line	1712 Canto	1712 Line	1714 Canto	1714 Line	1712 Canto	1712 Line
I	1	I	1	(II)	15	(I)	31+	(II)	40	(I)	58+
	2A		2+		16		32+		41		59+
	3		3		17		33+		42		60+
	4		4+		19		35+		43		61+
	5		5+		20		36+		44		62+
	6		6		21		37+		45		63+
	7		7+		22A		38+		46		64+
	8		8+		23		39+	III	1	(I)	65+
	9		9+		24		40+		2		66+
	10		10+		25		41+		3		67+
	11A		11		26		42+		4		68+
	12A		12		27		43+		5		69+
	13A		13+		28		44		6		70+
	14A		14+		29		45+		7		71+
	16A		16+		30		46+		8		72+
	17A		17+		31		47+		10		74+
	18A		18+		32		48+		15		79+
II	4	(I)	20		33		49+		16		80+
	7		23+		34		50+		17		81
	8		24+		35		51+		18		82+
	9		25+		36		52+		20		84+
	10		26		37		53+		22		86+
	11		27		38		54+		24		88+
	12		28+		39Z1		55+		106		90
	13		29		39Z2		56+		107		91+
	14		30+		39Z3		57+		108A		92

1714 Canto	1714 Line	1712 Canto	1712 Line	1714 Canto	1714 Line	1712 Canto	1712 Line	1714 Canto	1714 Line	1712 Canto	1712 Line
(III)	109	(I)	93+	(IV)	7	(II)	7+	(IV)	144	(II)	60
	110A		94		8		8+		145		62+
	112A		96+		9		9		146		63+
	117		97+		10		10+		147		64+
	118		98		95		13		148		65+
	119		99+		97		15		149		66+
	120		100		98		17		150		67+
	121		101		100		18+		151		68+
	122		102+		104		22+		152		69
	123		103		105		23+		153		70+
	124		104+		106		24+		154		71+
	127		107+		107		25+		155A		72
	128		108+		108		26+		156		73+
	129		109+		109		27+		157		74+
	130		110+		110		28+		158		75+
	131		111+		111		29+		159		76+
	132		112		112		30+		160		77+
	133		113+		113		31+		161A		78+
	134		114+		114		32		162		79+
	154		118		115		33		163		80+
	156		120		116		34+		164		81
	159		123		117		35+		167A		82+
	160		124+		118		36+		168A		83+
	161		125		119		37+		169A		84+
	162		126+		120		38+		170		85+
	163		127+		121		39+		171		86
	164		128+		122		40+		172		87+
	165		129+		123		41+		173		88
	166		130+		124		42+		174		89+
	167		131+		125		43+		176		20
	168		132		126		44+	V	1	(II)	90+
	169		133+		127		45+		2		91+
	170		134+		128		46+		3		92+
	171		135+		129		47+		4		93+
	172		136+		130		48		5		94+
	173A		137+		131		49+		6		95+
	175		139+		132		50+		37A		96+
	176		140+		133		51		38		97+
	177		141+		134		52+		39		98+
	178		142+		135		53+		40		99+
IV	1	II	1+		136A		54+		41		100
	2		2+		137		55+		42		101+
	3		3+		138		56+		43		102+
	4		4+		139		57		44		103+
	6		6		140		58+		45		104+

1714 Canto	Line	1712 Canto	Line	1714 Canto	Line	1712 Canto	Line	1714 Canto	Line	1712 Canto	Line
7)	46	(II)	105+	(V)	78	(II)	133+	(V)	119	(II)	164
	47		106		79		134+		120		165+
	48		107+		80		135+		121		166+
	49		108+		81		136+		122		167+
	50		109+		82		137+		123		168+
	51		110		85		138+		124		169+
	52		111+		86		139+		126		171+
	57		112+		87A		140+		127		172+
	58		113+		88		141+		128		173+
	59		114+		98		143+		129		174+
	60		115+		99		144+		130A		175+
	61		116+		100		145+		133		176
	62		117+		101		146+		134		178+
	63		118+		103		148+		137		179+
	64		119+		104		149+		138		180+
	65		120+		105		150+		139		181
	66		121		106		151+		140		182+
	67A		122+		107		152		141A		183+
	68		123		108		153+		142		184+
	69		124+		109		154		143		185+
	70		125+		110		155+		144		186
	71		126+		111		156+		145		187+
	72		127		112		157+		146		188+
	73		128+		113		158		147		189+
	74		129+		115		160		148		190+
	75		130+		116		161		149		191+
	76		131+		117		162+		150		192+
	77		132+		118		163				

Selected List of Poem Designations
Order in Twickenham Edition

(For complete list, see I, xxix.)

Vol.	Designation	Title
1	PSp, PSu, PAu, PWi	Pastorals: Spring, Summer, Autumn, Winter
	Mes	Messiah
	W-F	Windsor-Forest
	EOC	Essay on Criticism
		Translations
	TrPA	Polyphemus and Acis
	TrVP	Fable of Vertumnus and Pomona
	TrFD	Fable of Dryope
	TrSP	Sapho to Phaon
	TrSt	First Book of Statius
	TrES	Episode of Sarpedon
	TrUl	Arrival of Ulysses in Ithaca
2	ChJM	Chaucer: January and May
	ChWB	Chaucer: Wife of Bath
	RLA1, RLA2	Rape of the Lock (1712), Cantos 1 and 2
	RL1, RL2, RL3, RL4, RL5	Rape of the Lock (1714), Cantos 1-5
	TemF	Temple of Fame
	ElAb	Eloisa to Abelard
	Elegy	Elegy to the Memory of an Unfortunate Lady
3 (Part 1)	EOM1, EOM2, EOM3, EOM4	Essay on Man, Epistles 1-4
3 (Part 2)		Epistles to Several Persons (Moral Essays)
	Ep1	Epistle 1: To Cobham
	Ep2	Epistle 2: To a Lady
	Ep3	Epistle 3: To Bathurst
	Ep4	Epistle 4: To Burlington
4		Imitations
	HS1	First Satire of the Second Book of Horace
	JD4	Fourth Satire of Dr. John Donne Versified
	HS2	Second Satire of the Second Book of Horace
	Arbu	Epistle to Dr. Arbuthnot
	JD2	Second Satire of Dr. John Donne
	2HE2	Second Epistle of the Second Book of Horace
	2HE1	First Epistle of the Second Book of Horace
	1HE6	Sixth Epistle of the First Book of Horace
	1HE1	First Epistle of First Book of Horace
	EpS1, EpS2	Epilogue to the Satires, Dialogues I and II
5	DunA1, DunA2, DunA3	Dunciad (1729), Books I-III
	DunB1, DunB2, DunB3, DunB4	Dunciad (1743), Books I-IV
6	1-157	Minor Poems (see I, xxx-xxxiv)
7	Il.1-9	Iliad, Books I-IX
8	Il.10-24	Iliad, Books X-XXIV
9	Od.1-12	Odyssey, Books I-XII
10	Od. 13-24	Odyssey, Books XIII-XXIV